ROOT	MEANING	EXAMPLES
clav	key	conclave, clavier, clavicle
lud, clus	close out	recluse, inclusive
coct	cook	concoct, precocious
compl, complet	fill out	complex, complicate, complete
copi	abundant	copious, copy
copul	join	copulate, couple
cor	heart	coronary, cordial
corp, corpor	body	corpulence, corporation
cosmo	universe	cosmology, cosmopolitan
cranio	skull	cranial, cranium
crat	rule, government	democrat, autocrat
cred	believe	incredulous, credible
cret	grown	concrete
cri	judge	criteria, critic, crisis
crypt	hidden	cryptic, cryptogram
cumb, cub	lie down	incubate, succumb, incumbent
cumul	add to	accumulate, cumulus
cur	care	curator, manicure, sinecure
cur, curse	run	concur, current, excursion
da, don	give	donation, data
dear	precious	dearth, darling, endearing
dec	ten	decade, decimal
dem	people	democracy, demagogue
dendr, dendro	tree, plant	rhododendron, dendrite
dent	teeth	indent, dentist
derm	skin	dermatologist, epidermis
dic	say, speak	interdiction, dictate
digit	finger, toe	digital, digitalis
doc	teach	docile, indoctrinate
dog, dox	opinion	dogma, orthodox
dom	home	domain, domestic, kingdom
domin	rule	predominate, domineer
dox	belief	heterodox, orthodox
drom	run, course	hippodrome, syndrome
duc	lead	reduce, deduction
dur	lasting	durable, obdurate
dyna	force, power	dynamic, dynasty
dys	difficult, evil	dyslexia
echino	spiny	echinoderm
eco	home	economy, ecology, ecumenical
ecto	outside	ectoplasm
empt	to buy, to take	exempt, redemption, example
entomo	insect	entomology
epi, eph	on	ephemeral, epicenter
equ	equal	equity, equivocate, equation
ethno	race	ethnic, ethnocentric
eu	good	euphoria, euphemism
ev	an age	primeval, medieval
fac	make, do	facility, manufacture
fall	deceive	fallacious, fallacy
fam	report	infamy, famous
fare	to go	farewell, welfare, thoroughfare
fe	property, cattle	feudalism, fee, fellow
fer	carry	transfer, confer, fertile
fid	faith	fidelity, confident, infidel
fin	end	infinite, final
firm	strong	infirmary, confirm
fissi	split	fissile, fission
fix	fasten	affix, fixture
flagr	burn	conflagration, flagrant
flat	blow	deflate, flatulent
flect, flex	bend	flexible, reflection
flict	strike	conflict, afflict
flu	flow	fluid, confluence
foli	leaf	folio, foliage, portfolio
fric	rub	friction, dentifrice
frig	cold	frigid, refrigerator
fract, fring	break	fraction, fracture, infringe
fug	escape from	fugitive, refuge, centrifuge
fum	smoke	fumigate, perfume
funct	perform	function, defunct, perfunctory
fund, fus	pour	effusive, confuse, refund
gamy	marriage	bigamy, monogamy
ghast	frighten	ghastly, ghost
geo	earth	geology, geometry, perigee
gen	produce, kind	gender, progeny, generation

ROOT	MEANING	EXAMPLES
geo	earth	geology, geometry
gest	carry	gesture, suggestion, digestion
gloss, glot	language	glossary, polyglot
gluc, glyc	sweet	glucose, glycerine
glypto, glyph	carving	hieroglyph
gnomy, gnosis	belief	agnostic, physiognomy
gon	angle	diagonal, polygon
gram	written	telegram, diagram
graph	write	Hagiography, chronograph
gress, grad	step, walk	graduate, retrogress
greg	flock, herd	aggregate, gregarious
gyneco	woman	gynecology
hab	have	habit, exhibit, ability
hedral, hedron	side, sided	tetrahedron, dihedral
helico	spiral	helicopter, helicon
helio	sun	heliocentric, heliograph
hema, hemo	blood	hematology, hemophiliac
her	stick	inherent, coherent, adhesive
hexa	six	hexagon, hexagram
hilar	merry	hilarious, exhilarate
hor	bound	horizon, aphorism
hum	ground	humus, exhume, humiliate
hydro	water	hydraulic, hydrogen
hypno	sleep	hypnotize, hypnotherapy
iasis	disease	psoriasis
iatrics, iatry	medical treatment	pediatrics, podiatry
icon	image	iconoclast, iconography
ideo	idea	ideogram, ideology
idio	own, private	idiosyncrasy, idiom
insul	island	insular, insulate, peninsula
integr	whole	integrate, integrity, integer
iso	equal	isotope, isomorphic
itis	inflammation	bronchitis, tonsillitis
jan	doorway	janitor, January
ject	throw	deject, object
joc	joke	jocular, juggler
journ	day	journal, journey, adjourn
jud	judge	judicial, prejudice
junct	join	junction
jur	swear	jury, adjure, perjury
juv, jun	youth	juvenile, junior, rejuvenate
kine	movement	kinetic, kinesis
la	people	laity, layman
labor	work	laborious, belabor
lacto	milk	lactic, lactose
lam	layer	laminate
lapi	stone	lapidary
lat	carry	translate, ventilate, legislate
lat	wide	dilate, latitude
lav	wash	lavatory
lef	allow, dear	belief, love
leg, lect	read, choose	legend, legible, selective
leg	law	legislative, legal
lepsy	seizure, fit	epilepsy, narcolepsy
lex	word	lexicon
liber	free	liberty, liberal
libr	book	library, libel
lig	bind	ligament, obligation, religion
limin	threshold	eliminate, subliminal
lingu	language	linguistics, bilingual
linqu, lict	leave	relinquish, delinquent, derelict
liter	letter	literature, literal, obliterate
litho	stone	lithograph, monolithic
loft	air	aloft, lift
logo, log	word	logarithm
logue	discourse, talk	epilogue, prologue
logy	study	philology
loqu, locut	speak	eloquent, elocution
luc	light	elucidate, lucent
lud	play	prelude, collusion
lumin	light	luminous, illuminate
lun	moon	lunar, lunette
lys, lyt	to free	analysis, electrolyte
macro	large	macrocosm
magn	large, great	magnanimous, magnitude
man	hand	manicure, manuscript

(Continued on back endpaper)

Webster's New Encyclopedic Dictionary

Webster's
New
Encyclopedic
Dictionary

BD&L
NEW YORK

Copyrights to the Contents:

"Webster's New Dictionary" reprinted from *Merriam-Webster's School Dictionary* Copyright ©1993 by Merriam-Webster Inc. "Guide to Pronunciation" and "English Spelling and Sound Correspondences" reprinted from *Webster's Ninth New Collegiate Dictionary* Copyright ©1991 by Merriam-Webster Inc. "Webster's Thesaurus" reprinted from *Webster's Compact Dictionary of Synonyms* Copyright ©1987 by Merriam-Webster Inc. "Webster's Style Manual" reprinted from *Webster's Compact Writers Guide* Copyright ©1987 by Merriam-Webster Inc. "Forms of Address" reprinted from *The Merriam-Webster Instant Speller* Copyright ©1980 by Merriam-Webster Inc. "Common Abbreviations," "Biographical, Biblical and Mythological Names," and "Geographical Names" reprinted from *Merriam-Webster's School Dictionary* Copyright ©1993 by Merriam-Webster Inc. "Foreign Words and Phrases," "Common English Given Names," and "Signs and Symbols" reprinted from *Merriam-Webster's New Ideal Dictionary, Second Edition* Copyright ©1989 by Merriam-Webster Inc. Illustrations Copyright ©1986 and 1993 by Merriam-Webster Inc.

"Atlas of the World" Copyright ©1993 Swanston Graphics Limited

"Legal Terms," "Computer Terms," "Medical Terms," "Business Terms," and "Scientific Terms" Copyright ©1993 by Helicon

Designed by Martin Lubin

The publisher wishes to thank Michael Harkavy and the staff of Harkavy Publishing Services; Philip Leventhal, Josh Leventhal, Arthur Winer, Ellen Schachter, Diane de Paolis, Laura Livingston, and Rusty Hannon for their editorial contribution and production services.

Copyright ©1993 by BLACK DOG & LEVENTHAL PUBLISHERS INC.

All rights reserved. No part of this book may be reproduced in any form or by any electronic or mechanical means including information storage and retrieval systems without written permission from the copyright holder.

Published by BLACK DOG & LEVENTHAL PUBLISHERS INC., 151 West 19th Street, New York, New York 10011

Distributed by Workman Publishing Company, 708 Broadway, New York, New York 10003

Printed and Bound in the United States of America

Second Printing, 1994

Library of Congress Cataloging in Publication Data

Webster's new encyclopedic dictionary
        p.   cm.
    ISBN: 0-9637056-0-1
    1. Encyclopedias and dictionaries. I. BD&L (Firm)
AG5.W3853 1992
031–dc20   93-6313
                              CIP

Table of Contents

Foreword

This comprehensive reference brings together in one volume material ordinarily available only in many different sources. For students, professionals, and general readers, it will serve as a complete reference library, providing authoritative guidelines for language use in writing and in speech, as well as up-to-date, clear, and accessible information on a wide variety of topics.

Revised in 1993, the definitions of *Webster's New Dictionary* are written in everyday, comprehensible language, making the dictionary appropriate for use by every member of the family. Nearly 1,000 illustrations are included to supplement and clarify written definitions. Following the dictionary itself, the editors have provided several sections on language usage, from such basics as definitions of common prefixes, roots, and suffixes and guides to pronunciation and spelling, to a rhyming dictionary, a manual of style, and a complete thesaurus.

Coverage of other areas of knowledge is equally wide in scope and up-to-date in content. Composed of materials researched from scores of reference works and current periodicals, "History and the World Today" includes a chronology of world history, world population information, and thorough, detailed profiles of nations of the world. For coping with everyday business and personal needs, there are practical glossaries of legal, business, and computer terms. For the general reader interested in learning more about the earth and science, as well as for researchers in search of specific information, *Webster's New Encyclopedic Dictionary* contains more than a dozen sections relating to these areas, including a full current atlas reflecting recent changes in the political, economic, and geographic make-up of the world, a geographic dictionary, glossaries of scientific and medical terms, and easy-to-use charts and tables on astronomy, calendars and time systems, number systems, and common mathematical and scientific formulas.

Created for home, office, and school, the thorough and up-to-date information together with the modern, legible page design of *Webster's New Encyclopedic Dictionary* will assure years of productive use.

Webster's

New

Dictionary

Using The Dictionary

Dictionary Entries

The dictionary is made up of many small paragraphs, each giving information about a particular word or phrase. These paragraphs are known as **dictionary entries,** and the word or phrase being explained is known as the **main entry** or **entry word.** Two features set off the main entry to make it easy to find: it is printed in **boldface type,** and it sticks out into the margin just a little to catch the eye.

The main entry may take any of several forms. It may be a single letter, like *a, b,* or *c,* of a combination of letters, like *TV* or *ESP.* Most main entries are single words, like *run, see, pretzel,* and *eugenics,* but many are combinations of words, like *hitchhike, nitty-gritty,* and *French horn.* There are also main entries that are only parts of words. These include prefixes like *anti-,* suffixes like *-ism,* and combining forms like *bio-* and *-ectomy* that are used only to form other words. It is possible to make any number of new words with prefixes, suffixes, and combining forms.

Order of Entries

Throughout the dictionary, words are alphabetized by first letter, then second letter, and so on, regardless of spaces, hyphens, or of meaning relationships. Thus, you will find the word *basenji* coming after *basement* and before *base on balls* and *houri* between *hourglass* and *hourly.*

Words spelled with a numeral or abbreviation (like *St.* or *Mc*) will be found in the place they would occupy if spelled out (as *Saint* or *Mac*). *A-1* follows *A-OK* and comes before *aorta, 4-H* appears between *four-footed* and *four-hand,* and *McCoy* comes after *Maccabees* and before *mace.*

When main entries are spelled exactly alike but have different functions in the sentence or have different origins, they are called **homographs.** Each homograph is entered at its own place and distinguished from other homographs by a small raised numeral at the very beginning.

¹**American** . . . *n* . . .

²**American** *adj* . . .

The order of homographs is historical. That is, the oldest word is entered first, and related homographs (all those having the same origin) are grouped together. Thus, ²*bow* ("a bending of the head or body in respect, submission, agreement, or greeting"), which is related to ¹*bow* ("to bend the head, body, or knee in greeting, reverence, respect, or submission"), comes before ³*bow* ("RAINBOW"). And ⁴*bow* ("to bend into a curve") follows the related ³*bow* and is ahead of ⁵*bow* ("the forward part of a ship").

Main entries that are spelled with all of the same letters but differ in the appearance of a space or hyphen or in capitalization are *not* homographs. They are alphabetized according to the following rules.

● Full words are entered before word parts, and beginning word elements come ahead of final word elements.

ad . . . *n* . . .

ad- . . . *prefix* . . .

-ad . . . *adv suffix* . . .

● Entries printed in small letters come before capitalized ones.

¹**box•er** . . . *n* . . .

²**boxer** *n* . . .

Box•er . . . *n* . . .

● Compounds that are written as one word are entered before hyphenated compounds, and hyphenated compounds are entered ahead of those made up of separate words.

lay•off . . . *n* . . .

lay off . . . *vb* . . .

lay–up . . . *n* . . .

lay up . . . *vt* . . .

low•down . . . *n* . . .

low–down . . . *adj* . . .

Guide Words

To aid you in finding the right word quickly, *Webster's New Encyclopedic Dictionary* has a pair of **guide words** at the top of every page. The guide words are usually the alphabetically first and last boldface entries on the page. Any boldface term—a main entry, a variant spelling, an inflected form, a word run on undefined at the end of an entry, a phrase run on and defined at the end of an entry, or even a word in a list of undefined words—can be a guide word as long as it is alphabetically the first or last word on the page. The first word of the pair is normally the first main entry on the page and the second is usually the last main entry.

The guide words themselves are always in alphabetical order. When the alphabetically last word on one page would follow the first guide word on the next page, it is not picked as a guide word.

Variant Entries

A number of main entries have a second or sometimes a third spelling shown in boldface type. These alternate spellings are called **variants.**

Variants separated by the word *or* are equal variants. That means each is current in standard English usage and either spelling is correct for you to use. When equal variants are used with about the same frequency, we list them in alphabetical order.

bobby socks *or* **bobby sox** . . .

But when the evidence indicates that one spelling is somewhat more common than another, the variants are listed in the order of relative frequency of use.

bo•gey *or* **bo•gy** *or* **bo•gie** . . .

skep•tic *or* **scep•tic** . . .

When the word *also* separates variants, it means that the following variant is considerably less common in standard English. Nevertheless, the *also* variant is a part of standard English usage and you may freely use it without being wrong, although many people prefer the more common spelling.

mor•tise *also* **mor•tice** . . .

Occasionally we use both *or* and *also* in separating a number of variants at a single entry.

ce•sar•e•an *or* **ce•sar•i•an** *also* **cae•sar•e•an** . . .

tick•tack•toe *also* **tic-tac-toe** . . . *or* **tit-tat-toe** . . .

In the first instance, the first two spellings are roughly equal in frequency and the last is of a secondary nature. In the second example, the last two variants are of relatively equal frequency with respect to each other, but they both are much less common than the first. Whenever one variant form is more common with one meaning than with others, it is listed before the particular definition with some indication of how common or prominent it is.

¹**clew** *or* **clue** . . . **2** *usually* **clue** . . .

¹**nick•el** . . . **2 a** *also* **nick•le** . . .

¹**la•bor** . . . **5** *usually* **La•bour** . . .

If the variant is shown in boldface at the beginning of the entry, it is shown in italic before the definition (as in the first example). When it is not shown at the beginning of the entry, it is given in boldface before the definition.

Centered Dots and Hyphenation

Printers, typists, and writers often have to divide a word at the end of a line if it is too long to fit on one line. The **centered dots** in the boldface entry words show you acceptable places to put a hyphen when the word is broken at the end of a line. For example, *mor•al•is•tic* may be divided at any of three places.

mor- *or* moral- *or* moralis-
alistic istic tic

We use centered dots in all boldface entries except as follows.

● Only the first of two or more homographs is divided if the pronunciation and division are the same for each.

¹**mas•ter** . . . *n* . . .

²**master** *vt* . . .

³**master** *adj* . . .

● A word in a compound made up of two or more separate words is divided only if it is not entered as an individual entry. For example, we show no division for the entry *gamma radiation* because there are entries for *gam•ma* and *ra•di•a•tion*. The first word in the entry *Mo•lo•tov cocktail* is divided but the second is not, because there is no separate entry for *Mo•lo•tov* but there is for *cock•tail*. There are no entries for the individual elements of *pri•ma don•na,* thus both elements of the compound are divided.

It is customary to avoid breaking a word so as to leave a single letter at the end of one line or at the beginning of the next, so we do not show any division for single letters at the beginning or end of words, as in *idea* or *flighty*.

It is important to understand that the centered dots in the entry words *do not* necessarily separate the syllables of a word. Syllables are indicated *only* by the use of hyphens in the pronunciation, and the placement and number of centered dots is not always the same as the placement and number of hyphens in the pronunciation.

eter•ni•ty \i-'tər-nət-ē\

When a boldface entry word is broken at the end of a line, a hyphen replaces the centered dots at that point. *Webster's New Encyclopedic Dictionary* also uses a special **double hyphen** at the end of a line any time the word that is divided is normally spelled with a hyphen. When you see the double hyphen, you will know to keep the hyphen even when you write the word all on one line.

self–mastery \'self-'mas-tə-rē, -trē\ *n* : SELF-COMMAND, SELF-CONTROL

The double hyphen here indicates that *self-command* is always spelled with a hyphen.

The Function of Words

Words are used in many different ways in a sentence. A word may serve as the name of something being talked about or to indicate an action. It may be used to tell something about the thing or person being talked about or to describe the way something happens. The many different functions of words are known as **parts of speech.** *Webster's New Encyclopedic Dictionary* identifies the function of most entry words with one of eight traditional part-of-speech labels, abbreviated and placed immediately after the boldface entry or after the pronunciation, when one is shown.

gui•tar . . . *n* (noun) **you** . . . *pron* (pronoun)

de•ploy . . . *vb* (verb) **for** . . . *prep* (preposition)

snide . . . *adj* (adjective) **and** . . . *conj* (conjunction)

hap•pi•ly . . . *adv* (adverb) **ouch** . . . *interj* (interjection)

When the main entry is a noun that is always used in the plural, the label *n pl* is used.

bin•oc•u•lars . . . *n pl* . . .

An entry word may be spelled as a plural and be considered a plural in some uses—such as being used with a plural verb—and yet be considered singular in other uses—such as being used with a singular verb.

ac•ro•bat•ics . . . *n sing or pl* . . .

(The word *acrobatics* may be singular in such uses as "acrobatics is a strenuous activity" or plural in "you make these acrobatics look easy.")

Some entries that are singular in most uses may have one or more specific plural uses.

fix•ing . . . *n* . . . **2** *pl* : TRIMMINGS

(In this sense the usage might be "a turkey dinner with all the fixings.")

Other entries will have one or more senses that are always spelled as plural but when used as the subject of a sentence will take a singular verb.

lanc•er . . . **2** *pl but sing in construction* . . .

(An example of this use might be "the lancers is an interesting dance.")

Pronouns, too, can sometimes be singular in form but take a plural or singular verb.

³all *pron, pl in construction* . . .

²any *pron, sing or pl in construction* . . .

(A typical use in the first example might be "all of us are going," where the word *all* occurs only with a plural verb. In the second example, *any* may be used with a singular verb, as in "I want some pie. Is there any left?" or with a plural verb in "are any of you tired?")

When variant plural forms are shown for an entry but only one is used with a particular meaning, that plural is shown at the definition *following* the abbreviation *pl.*

²die . . . *n, pl* **dice** . . . *or* **dies**
 1 *pl* **dice** : . . . **2** *pl* **dies** : . . .

(The plural form for the first meaning of *die,* the little cube with dots on it, is *dice* : "roll the dice." That for meaning 2, a tool to stamp an impression, is *dies* : "it takes two dies to stamp both sides of a coin.")

When a particular meaning is only plural and only one variant plural form is used for that meaning, the form is shown *ahead* of the abbreviation *pl.*

¹folk . . . *n, pl* **folk** *or* **folks** . . .
 3 *folks pl* : . . .

(In this meaning, the word is always plural and only the form *folks* is used: "I'm going home to see my folks.")

Webster's New Encyclopedic Dictionary makes no distinction at verb entries between transitive verbs (those that take a direct object) and intransitive verbs. The label *vb* is used for verb entries that have both transitive and intransitive uses. Verb entries that are used only as transitive verbs or only as intransitive verbs are given a specific *vt* (transitive verb) or *vi* (intransitive verb) label.

an•nul . . . *vt* . . .   **be•long** . . . *vi* . . .

In addition to the traditional part-of-speech labels, there are a number of other function labels that we use in this dictionary. *Prefix, suffix,* and *combining form* are relatively common and have already been introduced. The following identifying labels appear much less frequently.

may . . . *auxiliary verb*	**the** . . . *definite article*
me•thinks . . . *vb impersonal*	**Fris•bee** . . . *trademark*
gid•dap . . . *imperative verb*	**Air Express** *service mark*
an . . . *indefinite article*	**Realtor** . . . *collective mark*
-rd *symbol*	

Prefixes, suffixes, and combining forms are sometimes shown with a part-of-speech label when all compounds formed are of one part of speech.

-al•gia . . . *n combining form* . . .

-ana . . . *n pl suffix* . . .

In these examples, the compounds formed by either of these elements are always nouns, and in the second example the compounds are always plural nouns.

Sometimes an entry has more than one function label.

ago . . . *adj or adv* . . .

betwixt . . . *adv or prep* . . .

The *or* in these two examples indicates that the entry may at one time function as one part of speech and at another time as another part of speech without any significant difference in meaning.

We do not show part-of-speech labels or other function labels for idiomatic phrases defined at the end of a main entry or for main entry phrases that consist of two nouns joined by a preposition, like *act of God* and *man in the street.*

The Forms of Words

The plurals of nouns (and a few pronouns and adjectives), the past tense, past participle, and present participle forms of verbs, and the comparative and superlative forms of adjectives and adverbs are known as **inflected forms.** For most entries, these inflected forms are regular (that is, they are formed by the addition of -*s* or -*es* to nouns, -*ed* and -*ing* to verbs, and -*er* and -*est* to adjectives and adverbs), and these regular forms, since they normally present no problems in spelling, are not shown in *Webster's New Encyclopedic Dictionary.*

We do show irregular inflected forms, such as those that involve a change in the spelling of the base word or a doubling of a final letter, and any that we feel you might have reasonable doubts about.

Plurals are shown in this book when there is no change made in the base word,

deer . . . *n, pl* **deer** . . .

when a final -*y* changes to -*i*- before the addition of -*es,*

ba•by . . . *n, pl* **babies** . . .

when the plural involves a change in the spelling of the base word,

ax•is . . . *n, pl* **ax•es** . . .

¹that . . . *pron, pl* **those** . . .

and when the word has kept a foreign plural.

se•ta . . . *n, pl* **se•tae** . . .

Plurals are also shown for all nouns that end in -*o* or -*ey,*

ego . . . *n, pl* **egos** . . .

don•key . . . *n, pl* **donkeys** . . .

for those that are pluralized in a way you may not expect,

³dry *n, pl* **drys** . . .

goose•foot . . . *n, pl* **goosefoots** . . .

and for any others we think you might have questions about.

¹pi . . . *n, pl* **pis** . . .

ninth . . . *n, pl* **ninths** . . .

Most compounds pluralize the final element. These are considered regular plurals, and they are not shown when the final element is a recognizable word entered at its own place in the dictionary, such as *charwoman* or *thimbleberry*. We do show plurals for compounds that pluralize any element but the last,

    moth•er–in–law . . . *n, pl* **moth•ers–in–law** . . .

    postmaster general *n, pl* **postmasters general**

and for all entries that have variant plural forms.

    bis•cuit . . . *n, pl* **biscuits** *also* **biscuit** . . .

    ¹fish . . . *n, pl* **fish** *or* **fish•es** . . .

Plurals are not shown for nouns that do not regularly have a plural use, like *paleontology.*

Principal parts are usually not shown for regular verbs—those that simply add *-ed* and *-ing,* either directly to the base word or after dropping a final *-e* —but they are shown for verbs that inflect in other ways. In such cases the past tense and present participle forms are always shown. The past participle is shown only when it differs from the past tense, and when it is shown it comes between the past tense and the present participle.

Inflections are shown when one or more principal parts change the spelling of the base word,

    ¹know . . . *vb* **knew** . . .; **known** . . .; **know•ing** . . .

when a final consonant is doubled before the addition of *-ed* or *-ing,*

    ²crib *vb* **cribbed; crib•bing** . . .

and when a final *-y* becomes *-i-* before *-ed.*

    ¹hur•ry . . . *vb* **hur•ried; hur•ry•ing** . . .

Inflections are also shown for verbs when the final *-c* is changed to *-ck* before *-ed* and *-ing,*

    ²picnic *vi* **pic•nicked; pic•nick•ing**

when the base word ends in *-ee* or *-ey,*

    agree . . . *vb* **agreed; agree•ing** . . .

    ¹sur•vey . . . *vt* **sur•veyed; sur•vey•ing** . . .

when there are variant forms of the inflections,

    ³bias *vt* **bi•ased** *or* **bi•assed; bi•as•ing** *or* **bi•as•sing** . . .

and when we feel you might have reasonable doubts about the forms.

    ²visa *vt* **vi•saed** . . .; **vi•sa•ing**

In order to save space in showing inflections, we show only the last part of the inflected forms for long words—those of more than two syllables. The form is usually cut back to the point that corresponds to the last indicated end-of-line division in the main entry.

    the•o•ry . . . *n, pl* **-ries** . . .

    lot•tery . . . *n, pl* **-ter•ies**

    lep•to•ceph•a•lus . . . *n, pl* **-li** . . .

    mod•i•fy . . . *vb* **-fied; -fy•ing** . . .

The cutback form is also used for verbs that end in *-l* when there are space-consuming variant forms,

    ³tinsel *vt* **-seled** *or* **-selled** ; **-sel•ing** *or* **sel•ling** . . .

and for verb compounds when the second element is a recognizable verb with irregular inflections.

    ¹re•take . . . *vt* **-took** . . .; **-tak•en** . . .; **-tak•ing** . . .

Most adjectives and adverbs form their comparatives and superlatives with *more* or *most* or with the addition of *-er* and *-est,* either directly to the base word or

after dropping a final *-e.* These are considered regular formations and are not shown in *Webster's New Encyclopedic Dictionary.* We do show all irregularly formed inflections of adjectives and adverbs, and many of these are cut back in the superlative to just *-est.*

Comparative and superlative forms are shown for entries that change the base word,

    ¹good . . . *adj* **bet•ter** . . .; **best** . . .

    ³well *adv* **bet•ter** . . .; **best** . . .

for those that double the final consonant before *-er* or *-est,*

    ¹flat . . . *adj* **flat•ter; flat•test** . . .

for those that change the final *-y* to an *-i* before the suffixes,

    handy . . . *adj* **hand•i•er; -est** . . .

for any adjectives or adverbs ending in *-ey,*

    ca•gey . . . *adj* **ca•gi•er; -est** . . .

and for those with variant forms.

    sly . . . *adj* **sli•er** *also* **sly•er** . . .; **sli•est** . . . *also* **sly•est** . . .

Whenever one inflected form but not another is in current use, we show only the current form in full with an appropriate label.

    ²mere *adj, superlative* **mer•est** . . .

Sometimes we write out in full regular inflections or inflections that might normally be cut back in order to show the pronunciation of one or more forms.

    daz•zle . . . *vt* **daz•zled; daz•zling** \'daz-ling, -ə-ling \ . . .

    ²model *vb* **mod•eled** *or* **mod•elled; mod•el•ing** *or* **mod•el•ling** \'mäd-ling, -l-ing\ . . .

    ¹long . . . *adj* **long•er** \'lȯng-gər\; **long•est** \'lȯng-gəst\ . . .

The Meaning of Words

The **definition** is the core of the dictionary. It gives the meaning of the entry word. Every definition in *Webster's New Encyclopedic Dictionary* is set off by a boldface colon whether or not there is a number before it.

    blue jeans *n pl* **:** pants usually made of blue denim

    blue law *n* **1** **:** one of many strict laws regulating morals and conduct in colonial New England

Often an entry or numbered meaning has more than one definition set off by a colon.

    ¹glad . . . **1 a :** experiencing pleasure, joy, or delight **:** made happy

    ²glint . . . **1 :** a small bright flash of light **:** SPARKLE

These different definitions, known as **substitutes,** are so close in meaning that either one can be substituted for the entry word in context without any change in meaning. Often the only difference between substitutes is in the point of view from which they are written.

When a main entry has a number of different **meanings** or **senses,** the meanings are arranged in historical order, with the oldest recorded meaning coming first, then the next oldest, and so on. The most recent meanings will normally be given last. With this method of ordering senses, you can follow the development of a word as the meanings have changed over the years. Here is an example that illustrates this historical development.

> **⁴dock** *n* **I** : an artificial basin to receive ships that has gates to keep the water in or out **2** : a slip or waterway usually between two piers to receive ships **3** : a wharf or platform for the loading or unloading of materials. . . **4** : a place or scaffolding for the inspection and repair of aircraft

From the order of senses in this entry, the development of the various senses of *dock* can be seen at a glance. From the oldest meaning, that of a basin or surrounding structure for ships—often the dock was used for building and repairing ships—the word acquired a broader, though still nautical, meaning: an area partly surrounded by a structure at which a ship could tie up. The use gradually expanded to include the pier or platform itself to which the ship tied up for loading and eventually to include any loading platform—even for trucks. Finally, in the most recent use, the word has come to refer to a docking place for repairing aircraft—a meaning that recalls the original sense as it applied to ships.

The historical ordering of senses should not be taken to mean, however, that each sense necessarily developed directly from the earlier one. In many instances, each of the various successive senses may all have derived independently from the original meaning.

In addition to the division of definitions into numbered senses, some entries have the meanings further broken down into **subsenses.** These subsenses, marked by letters (**a, b, c,** etc.) are used when related meanings are grouped together. The order of subsenses is historical insofar as the dates can be established, but subsenses may not be in strict historical order with respect to the broader numbered senses.

> **¹bag** . . . *n* **I a** : a flexible usually closed container for holding, storing, or carrying something **b** : PURSE; *esp* : HANDBAG **c** : TRAVELING BAG, SUITCASE **2** : something resembling a bag: as **a** : a pouched or pendulous bodily part or organ; *esp* : UDDER **b** : a puffed-out sag or bulge in cloth **c** : a square white canvas container to mark a base in baseball **3** : the amount contained in a bag **4** : a quantity of game taken or permitted to be taken **5** : a slovenly unattractive woman

In this example, the numbered senses of *bag* are all in historical order and the subsenses within a numbered sense grouping are also offered by date of first occurrence. But sense **Ic,** meaning "a suitcase," properly belongs with the other senses that refer to a container—yet it actually came into use much later than sense number **4.** And the baseball sense, **2c,** also developed after sense **4,** but it is grouped with the other senses at **2** because it is related in the idea of "something resembling a bag."

When further subdivision of a sense is needed, we indicate it by numerals in parentheses.

> **food** . . . **I a** : . . . **b** (1) : inorganic substances absorbed by plants. . . (2) : organic material produced by green plants. . .

Sometimes senses are divided by one of two italic labels: We use the sense divider *esp* (especially) to introduce the most common meaning covered by the more general definition immediately before it (as in senses 1b and 2a of *bag*). We use *also* to introduce a closely related use obviously derived from the basic sense.

base•ball . . . *n* : a game played with a bat and ball between two teams of nine players each on a field with four bases that mark the course a runner must take to score; *also* : the ball used in this game.

Cross-references

Words printed in small capitals are **cross-references.** A cross-reference in a definition is called a **synonymous cross-reference.** It is another word that means the same thing as the main entry word, or a *synonym* of the word.

You may see a synonym appearing as a second substitute, as at the first sense of *glint* which appears on page xiv, or standing in place of a definition.

> **³flip** *adj* : FLIPPANT

This tells you that the meaning of this homograph of *flip* and the meaning of *flippant* are the same and that the definition given at *flippant* also defines this use of *flip*.

Sometimes a synonymous cross-reference includes a sense number, meaning that only one sense of the synonym is the same as the entry word.

> **rile** . . . **I** : ROIL 1
>
> **roil** . . . **I** : to make cloudy or muddy by stirring up sediment

When we use a cross-reference, it is always to a word that is of the same part of speech as the entry word. For example, a cross-reference at a noun entry word is always to another noun. When the synonym has two homographs that are the same part of speech, we use a homograph number with the cross-reference.

> **fly ball** *n* : ²FLY 5
>
> **²fly** *n, pl* **flies** . . . **5** : a baseball hit high into the air

When a synonymous cross-reference is to a word with more than one sense and the cross-reference does not indicate a specific sense, you know that the words are synonymous in all senses.

> **cow•punch•er** . . . *n* : COWBOY
>
> **cow•boy** . . . *n* **I** : one who tends or drives cattle; *esp* : a usually mounted cattle ranch hand **2** : a participant in rodeos

Many entries or senses are defined only by two synonymous cross-references separated by a comma. You might think of these paired synonyms as two substitutes at a sense. When the first cross-reference is to an entry that has several senses, it usually includes a sense number,

> **²charge** . . . *n* . . . **3a** : OBLIGATION 2, REQUIREMENT

unless both synonyms are common words that together help define the entry word and leave no doubt as to the intended meaning.

> . . . **4** : INSTRUCTION, COMMAND

In addition to the synonymous cross-references in the definitions, there are three other types of cross-references used in *Webster's New Encyclopedic Dictionary.* Cross-references that follow a dash and the words *see* or *compare* (usually at the end of a definition) are called **directional cross-references.** They direct the reader to look at another entry for an explanation or related information.

> **digital computer** *n* : a computer that operates numbers in the form of digits — compare ANA-LOG COMPUTER

li•ter *or* **li•tre** \\'lēt-ər\\ *n* : a metric unit of capacity equal to one cubic decimeter — see METRIC SYSTEM table

The "see" directional cross-reference may also be used in place of a definition.

Genesis — see BIBLE table

Two other kinds of cross-references appear only in place of definitions. These are like the directional cross-references in that they direct the reader to other entries for information. The **cognate cross-reference** is used when a variant form of a word is entered at its own alphabetical place in the dictionary and the reader is directed to see the entry at the more common variant.

des•patch \\dis-'patch\\ *variant of* DISPATCH

li•quo•rice *chiefly British variant of* LICORICE

An **inflectional cross-reference** is used when an inflected form of an entry is entered at its own alphabetical place. It tells you to go to the base word.

¹**done** \\'dən\\ *past participle of* DO

was *past 1st & 3d sing of* BE

The Usage of Words

New or unusual words, even when they have been defined, may sometimes seem like nothing more than abstractions to you until you understand how the words are actually used in writing or speaking. And there are times when an example of how a word is used can do more than a definition to convey meaning and proper usage. Sometimes too the meanings of individual senses are similar, but the way the senses are normally used in sentences is quite different. *Webster's New Encyclopedic Dictionary* gives brief examples of the words in everyday language as illustrations of idiomatic usage for many of the entries and senses. These **verbal illustrations** follow the definitions and are enclosed in angle brackets, and the entry word, or an inflection of it, is printed in italics.

¹**ar•rest** \\ə-'rest\\ *vt* **1** : to stop the progress or movement of : CHECK, SLOW ⟨*arrest* a disease⟩ **2** : to take or keep in custody by authority of law ⟨*arrested* on suspicion of robbery⟩ **3** : to attract and hold the attention of ⟨colors that *arrest* the eye⟩

short•ly \\'shȯrt-lē\\ *adv* **1 a** : in a few words : BRIEFLY **b** : in an abrupt manner : CURTLY **2 a** : in a short time : SOON ⟨will arrive *shortly*⟩ **b** : at a short interval ⟨*shortly* after⟩

The dictionary also gives information about word usage in two other ways. The first is by means of italic labels immediately following the part-of-speech or function label or, when the information applies only to one sense, just after the sense number or letter. These labels indicate limited areas of use in the English-speaking world or special subject matter with which a word or sense is used. They also indicate when a word's use is restricted with respect to a standard usage and when you should capitalize the word.

A word or sense current chiefly in Great Britain or the Commonwealth countries is labeled *British,* and there are labels for particular areas within the Commonwealth.

an•o•rak . . . *n, chiefly British* : PARKA

foot•ball . . . **1** . . . **a** *British* : SOCCER

laird . . . *n, Scottish* : a landed proprietor

Many words or senses have use limited to a particular region of the United States.

pone . . . *n, Southern & Midland* : CORN PONE

And some words may be encountered only in dialect, but the use is over so wide an area that no specific regional label applies.

lar•rup . . . *vt, dialect* : WHIP 2a, 4

Italic labels are also used to indicate that various entries or individual senses are not current in English usage. We enter a few words in this dictionary because of their historical importance in literature, but the words have not been an active part of the language for many years. The label *obsolete* tells you a word or sense has not been used in more than 200 years.

¹**tide** . . . **1a** *obsolete* : a space of time : PERIOD

Old words and meanings that have been used only occasionally or not at all during the 20th century or that may occur only in special uses (for example, in church liturgies) we label *archaic.*

for•fend . . . **1a** *archaic* : FORBID 1

Some of the entries in the dictionary, although commonly used, are still not a part of what is considered standard usage. To help the student recognize these words and meanings, most of which are not appropriate for formal writing, three additional labels are used: *substandard,* for words that have some currency in all areas of the United States but which are not normally used by educated writers and speakers; *nonstandard,* for words that are sometimes used by well-educated people but which nevertheless are not always considered appropriate for good usage; and *slang,* words and senses that convey a flavor of extreme informality, consist of colorful and sometimes unconventional coinages and figures of speech, and are used chiefly by a particular cultural group.

learn . . . **2** *substandard* : to cause to learn : TEACH

thoro . . . *nonstandard variant of* THOROUGH

³**flick** *n, slang* : MOVIE

Entry words are spelled without an initial capital letter if they usually occur in print without a capital or if most senses are not capitalized. The label *cap* shows that an entry may be capitalized in some uses and not in others,

an•gli•cize . . . *vt, often cap* . . .

ky•rie elei•son . . . *n, often cap K&E*

or in some senses and not in others.

am•a•zon . . . *n* **1** *cap* : a member of a race of women warriors . . . **2** : a very tall strong woman

na•tion•al•ist . . . *n* **1** : an advocate of nationalism **2** *cap* : a member of a political party . . .

Occasionally a word that is entered with an initial capital will have a particular sense used without a capital.

Gyp•sy . . . *n* . . . **1** : one of a . . .people coming originally from India. . . **3** *not cap* : one that resembles a Gypsy

The italic labels that appear before the definitions are one way we give information on how words are used. Another way is through **usage notes** that follow the definitions. A usage note is set off from the definition by a dash. These notes are normally used to give information on usage that is not a proper part of the definitions and that cannot be given adequately by labels.

> **bi-** *prefix*. . . **2 b** . . .— often disapproved in this sense because of the likelihood of confusion with sense 1b;. . .

Usage notes usually show a limited range of application of the word

> **²bias** . . . — used chiefly of fabrics and their cut
>
> **le•ga•to** . . . *adv or adj* . . . — used as a direction in music
>
> **dick•ens** . . . — used chiefly as a mild oath. . .

or give information about context.

> **³zero** . . . **3** . . . — usually used with *in*
>
> **¹dint** . . . — used chiefly in the phrase *by dint of*

Sometimes when usage for a sense is mostly plural—but not enough to permit a *pl* label before the definition—we give you that information in a usage note.

> **²narrow** . . . — usually used in pl.

There are times when we use usage notes in place of definitions if the word has a special use that cannot be easily explained in the definition.

> **²please** *adv* **1** — used as a function word to express politeness. . .
>
> **Ms.** . . . *n* — used instead of *Miss* or *Mrs.* as a courtesy title for a woman whose marital status is unknown or irrelevant

The History of Words

This dictionary shows when and how the various main-entry words originated and developed in the **etymology,** which is in square brackets following the definition.

The etymology traces the word as far back in English as possible, sometimes all the way to Old English, the earliest language of the English people —from about A.D. 600 to about 1100. In the etymology, the entry word's ancestors are given in italics and their meanings in quotation marks.

> **³bit** *n* **1** : a small piece or amount. . . ⟨a little *bit* of luck⟩ . . . [Old English *bita* "piece bitten off"]

When the etymology gives a language from which the main-entry word derived but does not show the word form in that language, it means the form of the word in the earlier language was the same as that of the main entry. When there is no meaning given in the etymology, the meaning of the older word was the same as the *first* sense of the main entry.

> **¹arm** . . . **1 a** : a human upper limb;. . . [Old English *earm*]
>
> **¹blind** . . . **1 a** : SIGHTLESS . . . [Old English]

In the first example, the etymology shows that the modern English word *arm* can be traced back to the Old English word *earm* which had the same meaning as the first sense of *arm*. The second example tells us that the Old English word *blind,* meaning "without sight," was the ancestor of our modern English word *blind.*

When the etymology shows that an entry word has been traced back only into Middle English (from about 1100 to about 1500), it indicates that there is no evidence of it from Old English manuscripts and no indication that it was borrowed from another language.

> **¹bur•row** . . . [Middle English *borow*]

The etymologies in *Webster's New Encyclopedic Dictionary* trace the development of words in reverse order, giving the most recent ancestors first and moving backward to the oldest. Whenever a word form or a meaning is not shown at a particular stage in the etymology, it is the same as the form or meaning given before, or if none has been given before in the etymology, the same as that of the main entry.

> **pope** . . . *n, often cap* : the head of the Roman Catholic Church [Old English *pāpa*, from Late Latin *papa*, from Greek *pappas*, title of bishops, literally, "papa"]
>
> **¹fi•nance** . . . **1** *pl* : liquid resources (as money). . . [Middle English, "payment, ransom", from Middle French, from *finer* "to end, pay", from *fin* "end", from Latin *finis*]

In the first example the modern English word *pope* is derived from Old English *pāpa*, meaning "pope," which in turn came from the Late Latin word *papa*, also meaning "pope." The Latin word came from the Greek *pappas*, which meant literally "papa" and had been used as a title of bishops. In the second example, the modern English word *finance* meaning "money resources" came from the Middle English word *finance*, which meant "payment" or "ransom." This Middle English word was derived from a Middle French word that had the same spelling and the same meaning as the Middle English word *finance*. This Middle French word came from an earlier Middle French word *finer*, which meant "to end" or "to pay," which was itself derived from the early Middle French word *fin,* which meant "end." And the early Middle French word *fin* was derived from the still earlier Latin word *finis*, which also meant "end."

Words borrowed directly into modern English show first the language from which the word was borrowed.

> **ro•deo** . . . **1** : ROUNDUP 1 . . . [Spanish, from *rodear* "to surround", from *rueda* "wheel", from Latin *rota* "wheel"]
>
> **te•pee** . . . [of American Indian origin]
>
> **caf•tan** *or* **kaf•tan** . . . [Russian *kaftan,* from Turkish, from Persian *qaftān*]
>
> **gin•seng** . . . [Chinese (Pekingese dialect) *jen²-shen¹*]

The small numbers that appear at the end of words in languages—like Chinese—that distinguish similar sounds by voice tones are indications of the *tones* for the particular language and have nothing to do with meaning or homographs of English words.

Words that are formed in modern English from other English words do not normally have etymologies, since the origin is usually obvious. Thus, the entry *likable* does not have an etymology because the word is derived from English *like* by addition of an ordinary English suffix *-able*. However, etymologies are given for words that are made up of parts of other words.

> **aero•sol** . . . [*aer-* + *³sol*]
>
> **brunch** . . . [*br*eakfast + l*unch*]
>
> **¹GI** . . . [*g*alvanized *i*ron; from abbreviation used in listing such articles as garbage cans, but taken as an abbreviation for *government issue*]
>
> **ra•dar** . . . [*ra*dio *d*etecting *a*nd *r*anging]

When a word comes from a person's name, we show that in the etymology,

der·by . . . l : any of several horse races. . . [Edward Stanley, died 1834, 12th earl of *Derby*]

but we do not show the name of a person who first used a word—unless the word was coined, that is, created as an original word that did not exist before in English or any other language.

blurb . . . [coined by Gelett Burgess, died 1951, American humorist]

For a number of entries whose origins are particularly interesting, we give additional information in an **origin paragraph** beyond what is found in the etymology. In some cases the paragraph also contains information on how the meaning of the word has changed in English over the centuries.

Ori·ent \ˈȯr-ē-ənt, ˈȯr-, -ē-ˌoement \ *n* : EAST 2; *esp* : the countries of eastern Asia [Middle French, from Latin *oriens,* from *oriri* "to rise"]
□ ORIGIN The noun *orient* is derived from the Latin adjective *oriens,* which comes from the present participle of the verb *oriri,* "to rise or come forth". The earliest English sense of *orient* is "the place on the horizon where the sun rises when it is near one of the equinoxes", that is, the east. *Orient* has come to be used today to refer to the Asian countries to the east of Europe. With the spread of Christianity into Europe it became customary to build churches with their longitudinal axes pointing eastward toward Jerusalem. This practice gave rise to the use of *orient* as a verb meaning "to cause to face or point to the east". This sense became generalized to yield the sense "to set or arrange in any determinate position, especially in relation to the points of the compass".

Run-on Entries

At the end of many entries are additional boldface words and sometimes boldface phrases. These are known as **run-on entries.** These words and compounds are derived from the main-entry word in different ways. They may come about through a shift in function (as the verb *research* comes from the noun *research*) or they may be formed by the addition of suffixes (as the adverb *closely* and the noun *closeness* come from the adjective *close*). These derived words are run on without definitions when their meaning is obvious. But if the meaning of a derivative word is not obvious from the meaning of the base word and the meaning of any added suffix, we always enter it as a main entry with a definition.

Boldface phrases that are common idioms whose meanings are more than the sum of the meanings of the individual words, are run on with definitions as the last element of many entries. These phrases are generally entered under the first major element (for example, a noun or verb or sometimes an adjective or adverb, rather than a preposition or article).

For example, the phrases *on board, in any case,* and *to date* will appear at the entries *board, case,* and *date* respectively. *Break camp, cast lots, pull one's leg,* and *now and then* appear respectively under *break, cast, pull,* and *now.*

All run-ons, whether derivative words or idiomatic phrases, are introduced with a dash. Run-on derivatives always have a part-of-speech label, usually have centered dots to indicate end-of-line division, and often have a pronunciation. Run-on phrases have none of these.

Synonym Paragraphs

The synonyms that appear in small capitals in definitions are words that have essentially the same meaning as the main entry and can usually be substituted in most contexts. *Webster's New Encyclopedic Dictionary* also treats a number of synonyms in individual synonym articles set off as separate paragraphs at the end of entries. These synonym paragraphs help the reader discriminate among a number of similar and often confused words. At the entry for every word that is discussed in a synonym paragraph, there is a cross-reference, indicated by " SYN see. . .," to the entry where the paragraph is located.

de·mol·ish . . . SYN see DESTROY

de·stroy . . .
□ SYN DEMOLISH, ANNIHILATE: DESTROY implies any force that wrecks, kills, annihilates, or tears down or apart ⟨*destroy* a friendship by deceit⟩ DEMOLISH implies a pulling or smashing to pieces or a tearing down to the point of ruin ⟨*demolish* a building⟩ ANNIHILATE suggests destruction so complete as to make any restoration impossible ⟨*annihilate* a city by nuclear attack⟩

Lists of Undefined Words

Lists of words without definitions appear at the following prefix entries:

anti-	mini-	over-	sub-
co-	mis-	post-	super-
counter-	multi-	pre-	trans-
hyper-	non-	quasi-	ultra-
inter-	out-	re-	un-
mal-			

The meanings of the compounds formed with these prefixes are readily understandable from the meaning of the prefix and the meaning of the base word, and these words are entered here to indicate to the reader that they are relatively common words and to show spelling. Compounds that are not readily understandable from the sum of the elements are given own-place entry with definitions.

ABBREVIATIONS USED IN THE DICTIONARY

ab	about
abbr	abbreviation
abl	ablative
acc	accusative
AD, A.D.	anno Domini
adj	adjective
adv	adverb
AF	Anglo-French
alter	alteration
Am	American
am, a.m.	ante meridiem
AmerF	American French
AmerInd	American Indian
AmerSp	American Spanish
Ar	Arabic
Aram	Aramaic
BC, B.C.	before Christ
BCE, B.C.E.	before the Common Era
Brit	British
C	Celsius, centigrade
Calif	California
CanF	Canadian French
cap	capital, capitalized
CE, C.E.	Common Era
Celt	Celtic
cent	century
Chin	Chinese
CIS, C.I.S.	Commonwealth of Independent States
comb	combining
compar	comparative
conj	conjunction
Dan	Danish
dat	dative
deriv	derivative
dial	dialect
dim	diminutive
E	east, eastern, English
Egypt	Egyptian
ENE	east-northeast
Eng	English
ESE	east-southeast
Esk	Eskimo
esp	especially
F	Fahrenheit, French
fem	feminine
Flem	Flemish
fr	from
G	German
Gael	Gaelic
Gk	Greek
Gmc	Germanic
Heb	Hebrew
Hung	Hungarian
Icel	Icelandic
imit	imitative
imper	imperative
interj	interjection
Ir	Irish
IrGael	Irish Gaelic
irreg	irregular
It, Ital	Italian
Jp	Japanese
K	Kelvin
L	Latin
LaF	Louisiana French
LG	Low German
LGk	Late Greek
LHeb	Late Hebrew
lit	literally
LL	Late Latin
masc	masculine
ME	Middle English
MexSp	Mexican Spanish
MF	Middle French
MGk	Middle Greek
ML	Medieval Latin
modif	modification
MS	manuscript
n	noun
n pl	noun plural
N, No	north, northern
NE	northeast, northeastern
neut	neuter
NGk	New Greek
NHeb	New Hebrew
NL	New Latin
NNE	north-northeast
NNW	north-northwest
Norw	Norwegian
NW	northwest, northwestern
obs	obsolete
OE	Old English
OF	Old French
OIt	Old Italian
ON	Old Norse
OPer	Old Persian
OProv	Old Provençal
orig	originally
OW	Old Welsh
part	participle
Per	Persian
perh	perhaps
Pg	Portuguese
pl	plural
pm, p.m.	post meridiem
Pol	Polish
pp	past participle
prep	preposition
pres	present
prob	probably
pron	pronoun, pronunciation
prp	present participle
Russ	Russian
S, So	south, southern
Sc	Scotch, Scots
Scand	Scandinavian
ScGaelic	Scottish Gaelic
Scot	Scottish
SE	southeast, southeastern
Serb	Serbian
sing	singular
Skt	Sanskrit
Slav	Slavic
Sp	Spanish
SSE	south-southeast
SSW	south-southwest
St	Saint
superl	superlative
SW	southwest, southwestern
Sw	Swedish
syn	synonym
trans	translation
Turk	Turkish
US, U.S.	United States
USSR, U.S.S.R.	Union of Soviet Socialist Republics
usu	usually
var	variant
vb	verb
vi	verb intransitive
VL	Vulgar Latin
vt	verb transitive
W	Welsh, west, western
WNW	west-northwest
WSW	west-southwest

Aa

¹a \ˈā\ *n, pl* **a's** *or* **as** \ˈāz\ *often cap* **1** : the 1st letter of the English alphabet **2** : the musical tone A **3** : a grade rating a student's work as superior

²a \ə, ā, ˈā\ *indefinite article* **1** : some one unspecified ⟨*a* person overboard⟩ ⟨*a* dozen⟩ **2** : the same : ONE ⟨two of *a* kind⟩ ⟨birds of *a* feather⟩ **3** : ANY ⟨*a* person who is sick can't work⟩ — used in all senses before words beginning with a consonant sound; compare ¹AN [Middle English *an, a,* from Old English *ān* "one"]

³a \ə\ *prep* **1** *chiefly dialect* : ON, IN, AT **2** : in, to, or for each — used before words with an initial consonant sound ⟨twice *a* week⟩ ⟨dime *a* dozen⟩ [Old English *an, on, a-*]

¹a- \ə\ *prefix* **1** : on : in : at ⟨*a*bed⟩ **2** : in (such) a state or condition ⟨*a*fire⟩ ⟨*a*sleep⟩ **3** : in (such) a manner ⟨*a*loud⟩ **4** : in the act or process of ⟨gone *a*-hunting⟩ [Old English]

²a- \ā, ˈā *also* a, ˈa, ä, ˈä\ *or* **an-** \an, ˈan\ *prefix* : not : without ⟨*a*sexual⟩ — *a-* before consonants other than *h* and sometimes even before *h, an-* before vowels and usually before *h* ⟨*an*astigmatic⟩ ⟨*an*hydrous⟩ [Greek]

aard·vark \ˈärd-ˌvärk\ *n* : a large burrowing African mammal with a long sticky tongue which it uses to feed on ants and termites [Afrikaans, literally, "earth pig"]

Aa·ron·ic \a-ˈrän-ik, e-\ *adj* : of or relating to the lower order of the Mormon priesthood [*Aaron,* brother of Moses]

ab- *prefix* : from : away : off ⟨*ab*normal⟩ [Latin *ab-, abs-, a-*]

ab·a·ca \ˌab-ə-ˈkä\ *n* : MANILA HEMP [Spanish *abacá,* from Tagalog *abaká*]

aback \ə-ˈbak\ *adv* **1** *archaic* : BACK, BACKWARD **2** : by surprise : UNAWARES ⟨taken *aback* by the turn of events⟩

aba·cus \ˈab-ə-kəs, ə-ˈbak-əs\ *n, pl* **aba·ci** \ˈab-ə-ˌsī, -ˌkē; ə-ˈbak-ˌī\ *or* **aba·cus·es** **1** : a slab that forms the uppermost part of the capital of a column **2** : an instrument for making calculations by sliding counters along rods or in grooves [Latin, from Greek *abax* "board, slab"]

¹abaft \ə-ˈbaft\ *adv* : toward or at the stern : AFT [¹*a-* + obsolete *baft* "behind"]

²abaft *prep* : to the rear of; *esp* : toward the stern from

ab·a·lo·ne \ˌab-ə-ˈlō-nē, ˈab-ə-ˌ\ *n* : any of several mollusks with flattened slightly spiral shells perforated along the edge and lined with mother-of-pearl [American Spanish *abulón*]

¹aban·don \ə-ˈban-dən\ *vt* **1** : to give up completely ⟨*abandon* a difficult task⟩ **2** : to withdraw from often in the face of danger ⟨*abandon* ship⟩ **3** : to withdraw protection, support, or help from **4** : to give (oneself) over to an emotion without restraint [Middle French *abandoner,* from *a bandon* "in one's power"] — **aban·don·er** *n* — **aban·don·ment** \-dən-mənt\ *n* □

SYN ABANDON, DESERT, FORSAKE mean to leave or go away from. ABANDON may stress withdrawing protection or care from ⟨*abandon* a property⟩ DESERT implies leaving in violation of a duty or promise ⟨*desert* a sen-

try post⟩ FORSAKE implies breaking ties with something familiar or cherished.

²abandon *n* **1** : a complete yielding to natural impulses **2** : carefree enthusiasm : EXUBERANCE

aban·doned \ə-ˈban-dənd\ *adj* **1** : that has been deserted : FORSAKEN ⟨an *abandoned* house⟩ **2** : wholly given up to wickedness or vice ⟨an *abandoned* criminal⟩

abase \ə-ˈbās\ *vt* : to lower in rank or position : HUMBLE, DEGRADE [Middle French *abaisser*] — **abase·ment** \-mənt\ *n*

abash \ə-ˈbash\ *vt* : to destroy the self-possession or self-confidence of : DISCONCERT [Middle French *esbaiss-,* stem of *esbair* "to be astonished", from *ex-* + *baer* "to yawn"] SYN SEE EMBARRASS — **abash·ment** \-mənt\ *n*

abate \ə-ˈbāt\ *vb* : to reduce or decrease in degree, amount, or intensity [Old French *abattre* "to beat down"] — **abat·er** *n*

abate·ment \ə-ˈbāt-mənt\ *n* **1** : the act or process of abating : the state of being abated **2** : an amount abated; *esp* : a deduction from the full amount of a tax

ab·at·toir \ˈab-ə-ˌtwär\ *n* : SLAUGHTERHOUSE [French, from *abattre* "to beat down"]

ab·ba·cy \ˈab-ə-sē\ *n, pl* **-cies** : the office, term of office, position, or jurisdiction of an abbot

ab·ba·tial \ə-ˈbā-shəl, a-\ *adj* : of or relating to an abbot, abbess, or abbey

ab·bé \a-ˈbā, ˈab-ˌā\ *n* : a French cleric not in a religious order — used as a title [French, from Late Latin *abbas* "abbot"]

ab·bess \ˈab-əs\ *n* : the superior of a convent of nuns

ab·bey \ˈab-ē\ *n, pl* **abbeys** **1 a** : a monastery governed by an abbot **b** : a convent governed by an abbess **2** : a church that once belonged to an abbey ⟨Westminster *Abbey*⟩ [Old French *abaïe,* from Late Latin *abbatia,* from *abbas* "abbot"]

ab·bot \ˈab-ət\ *n* : the superior of a monastery [Old English *abbod,* from Late Latin *abbas,* from Late Greek, from Aramaic *abbā* "father"]

ab·bre·vi·ate \ə-ˈbrē-vē-ˌāt\ *vt* : to make briefer; *esp* : to reduce (as a word) to a shorter form intended to stand for the whole [Late Latin *abbreviare,* from Latin *ad-* + *brevis* "short, brief"] SYN SEE SHORTEN — **ab·bre·vi·a·tor** \-ˌāt-ər\ *n*

ab·bre·vi·a·tion \ə-ˌbrē-vē-ˈā-shən\ *n* **1** : the act or result of abbreviating : ABRIDGMENT **2** : a shortened form of a written word or phrase used in place of the whole

ABC \ˌā-ˌbē-ˈsē\ *n, pl* **ABC's** *or* **ABCs** \-ˈsēz\ **1** : ALPHABET — usually used in pl. **2 a** : the rudiments of reading, writing, and spelling — usually used in pl. **b** : the rudiments of a subject

Ab·di·as \ab-ˈdī-əs\ *n* — see BIBLE table

ab·di·cate \ˈab-di-ˌkāt\ *vb* : to give up sovereign power, office, or responsibility usually formally : RENOUNCE [Latin *abdicare,* from *ab-* + *dicare* "to proclaim"] — **ab·di·ca·tion** \ˌab-di-ˈkā-shən\ *n* — **ab·di·ca·tor** \ˈab-di-ˌkāt-ər\ *n*

ab·do·men \ˈab-də-mən, ab-ˈdō-mən\ *n* **1** : the part of the body between the chest and the pelvis; *also* : the

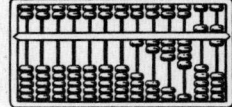

abacus 2

abdomen
abdomen 2

\ə\ abut		\ng\ sing
\ər\ further		\ō\ bone
\a\ mat		\ȯ\ saw
\ā\ take		\ȯi\ coin
\ä\ cot, cart		\th\ thin
\aȯ\ out		\th\ this
\ch\ chin		\ü\ food
\e\ pet		\u̇\ foot
\ē\ easy		\y\ yet
\g\ go		\yü\ few
\i\ tip		\yu̇\ cure
\ī\ life		\zh\ vision
\j\ job		

body cavity containing the chief digestive organs **2** : the hind portion of the body behind the thorax or cephalothorax in an arthropod [Latin] — **ab·dom·i·nal** \ab-'däm-ən-l\ *adj* — **ab·dom·i·nal·ly** \-l-ē\ *adv*

ab·du·cens \ab-'dü-ˌsenz, -'dyü-\ *n* : either of the 6th pair of cranial nerves supplying muscles of the eyes — called also *abducens nerve* [Latin, "leading away"]

ab·duct \ab-'dəkt\ *vt* **1** : to carry (a person) off by force **2** : to draw (a part of the body) away from the median axis of the body; *also* : to move (similar parts) apart ⟨*abduct* adjoining fingers⟩ [Latin *abducere*, literally, "to lead away", from *ab-* + *ducere* "to lead"] — **ab·duc·tion** \-'dək-shən\ *n*

ab·duc·tor \-'dək-tər\ *n* : one that abducts; *esp* : a muscle that draws a body part away from the median axis — compare ADDUCTOR

abeam \ə-'bēm\ *adv or adj* : on a line at right angles to a ship's keel

abed \ə-'bed\ *adv or adj* : in bed

Ab·er·deen An·gus \ˌab-ər-ˌdēn-'ang-gəs\ *n* : any of a breed of black hornless beef cattle originating in Scotland — called also *Angus* [*Aberdeen* and *Angus*, counties in Scotland]

ab·er·rant \a-'ber-ənt\ *adj* **1** : straying from the right or normal way **2** : deviating from the usual or natural type : ATYPICAL [Latin *aberrare* "to go astray", from *ab-* + *errare* "to wander, err"] — **ab·er·rance** \-əns\ *n* — **ab·er·ran·cy** \-ən-sē\ *n* — **ab·er·rant·ly** *adv*

ab·er·ra·tion \ˌab-ə-'rā-shən\ *n* **1** : the act of deviating especially from a moral standard or normal state **2** : failure of a mirror or lens to produce exact correspondence between an object and its image **3** : unsoundness or disorder of the mind **4** : a small periodic change of apparent position in heavenly bodies due to the combined effect of the motion of light and the motion of the observer **5** : an aberrant organ or individual : SPORT 5 — **ab·er·ra·tion·al** \-shnəl, -shən-l\ *adj*

abet \ə-'bet\ *vb* **abet·ted; abet·ting** : to encourage or aid especially in doing wrong [Middle French *abeter*, from *a-* "ad-" + *beter* "to bait"] SYN see INCITE — **abet·ment** \-mənt\ *n* — **abet·tor** \-'bet-ər\ *n*

abey·ance \ə-'bā-əns\ *n* : a temporary suspension of activity ⟨plans held in *abeyance*⟩ [Middle French *abeance* "expectation", from *abaer* "to desire", from *a-* "ad-" + *baer* "to yawn, gape"] — **abey·ant** \-ənt\ *adj*

ab·hor \ab-'hȯr, əb-\ *vt* **ab·horred; ab·hor·ring** **1** : to feel extreme aversion for : LOATHE **2** : to turn aside or keep away from in scorn or disgust : REJECT [Latin *abhorrēre*, from *ab-* + *horrēre* "to shudder"] SYN see HATE — **ab·hor·rence** \-'hȯr-əns, -'här-\ *n* — **ab·hor·rer** \-'hȯr-ər\ *n*

ab·hor·rent \-'hȯr-ənt, -'här-\ *adj* **1** : feeling or showing abhorrence **2** : not agreeable ⟨a notion *abhorrent* to their beliefs⟩ **3** : DETESTABLE SYN see REPUGNANT — **ab·hor·rent·ly** *adv*

abid·ance \ə-'bīd-ns\ *n* **1** : the act or state of abiding **2** : COMPLIANCE ⟨*abidance* by the rules⟩

abide \ə-'bīd\ *vb* **abode** \-'bōd\ *or* **abid·ed; abid·ing** **1** *archaic* : to wait for : AWAIT **2 a** : to endure without yielding : WITHSTAND **b** : to bear patiently : TOLERATE **3** : to accept without objection ⟨*abide* the court's decision⟩ **4** : to remain stable or fixed in a state **5** : to reside or continue in a place : DWELL [Old English *ābīdan*, from *ā-*, prefix denoting completion + *bīdan* "to bide"] SYN see STAY — **abid·er** *n* — **abide by** : to accept the terms of : be obedient to ⟨*abide by* the rules⟩

abid·ing *adj* : LASTING, CONTINUING ⟨an *abiding* interest in nature⟩ — **abid·ing·ly** \-ing-lē\ *adv*

abil·i·ty \ə-'bil-ət-ē\ *n, pl* **-ties** **1 a** : the quality or state of being able; *esp* : physical, mental, or legal power to do something **b** : competence in doing : SKILL **2** : natural talent or acquired proficiency : APTITUDE

-abil·i·ty *also* **-ibil·i·ty** \ə-'bil-ət-ē\ *n suffix, pl* **-ties** : capacity, fitness, or tendency to act or be acted on in a (specified) way ⟨melt*ability*⟩ ⟨read*ability*⟩

abio·gen·e·sis \ˌā-ˌbī-ō-'jen-ə-səs\ *n, pl* **-e·ses** \-ˌsēz\ : SPONTANEOUS GENERATION

abi·ot·ic \ˌā-bī-'ät-ik\ *adj* : not living or composed of living things ⟨soil acidity is an *abiotic* environmental factor⟩

ab·ject \'ab-ˌjekt\ *adj* **1** : sunk to a low condition **2 a** : having no pride or spirit ⟨made *abject* by suffering⟩ **b** : showing utter resignation : HOPELESS ⟨*abject* surrender⟩ **3** : expressing or offered in a humble often ingratiating spirit ⟨an *abject* apology⟩ [Latin *abjectus*, from *abicere* "to cast off", from *ab-* + *jacere* "to throw"] — **ab·ject·ly** \'ab-ˌjekt-lē, ab-'\ *adv* — **ab·ject·ness** \-ˌjekt-nəs, -'jekt-\ *n*

ab·jure \ab-'jùr\ *vt* **1 a** : to renounce upon oath ⟨*abjure* allegiance⟩ **b** : to reject solemnly : REPUDIATE ⟨*abjure* one's old beliefs⟩ **2** : to abstain from : AVOID ⟨*abjure* extravagance⟩ [Latin *abjurare*, from *ab-* + *jurare* "to swear"] — **ab·ju·ra·tion** \ˌab-jə-'rā-shən\ *n* — **ab·jur·er** *n*

ab·late \a-'blāt\ *vb* **1** : to remove by cutting, melting, evaporation, or vaporization **2** : to undergo ablation

ab·la·tion \a-'blā-shən\ *n* : the process of ablating: as **a** : surgical removal **b** : removal of a part (as the outside of a nose cone) by melting or vaporization

ab·la·tive \'ab-lət-iv\ *adj* : of, relating to, or constituting a grammatical case expressing typically the relations of separation and source and also frequently such relations as cause or instrument [Latin *ablat-*, stem of *auferre* "to carry away, remove", from *au-* "ab-" + *ferre* "to carry"] — **ablative** *n*

ablative absolute *n* : a construction in Latin that consists of a noun or pronoun and its modifier both in the ablative case and together forming an adverbial phrase expressing generally the time, cause, or an attendant circumstance of an action

ablaze \ə-'blāz\ *adj* **1** : being on fire **2** : radiant with light or bright color

able \'ā-bəl\ *adj* **abler** \-bə-lər, -blər\; **ablest** \-bə-ləst, -bləst\ **1 a** : having enough power, skill, or resources to do something ⟨*able* to swim⟩ **b** : free from restrictions preventing an action ⟨*able* to vote⟩ **2** : marked by intelligence, knowledge, skill, or competence ⟨an *able* news editor⟩ [Middle French, from Latin *habilis* "handy, apt", from *habēre* "to have, hold"] — **ably** \'ā-blē\ *adv* □ SYN ABLE, CAPABLE, COMPETENT mean having power to do or accomplish. ABLE may further imply skill that is above average and proved by performance ⟨an *able* trial lawyer⟩ CAPABLE stresses having necessary qualities or skill for a specified function or action ⟨a *capable* nurse⟩ COMPETENT suggests having necessary training, experience, or special knowledge ⟨a *competent* judge of figure skating⟩

-able *also* **-ible** \ə-bəl\ *adj suffix* **1** : capable of, fit for, or worthy of (being so acted upon or toward) — chiefly in adjectives derived from verbs ⟨eat*able*⟩ ⟨resist*ible*⟩ **2** : tending, given, or liable to ⟨knowledge*able*⟩ ⟨perish*able*⟩ [Latin *-abilis*, *-ibilis*]

able–bod·ied \ˌā-bəl-'bäd-ēd\ *adj* : having a sound strong body : physically fit

able seaman *n* : an experienced deckhand qualified to perform routine duties at sea — called also *able-bodied seaman*

abloom \ə-'blüm\ *adj* : being in bloom

ab·lu·tion \a-'blü-shən, ə-'blü-\ *n* : the washing of oneself especially as a religious rite [Latin *abluere* "to wash away", from *ab-* + *lavere* "to wash"]

ABM \ˌā-ˌbē-'em\ *n, pl* **ABM's** *or* **ABMs** : ANTIBALLISTIC MISSILE

ab·ne·gate \'ab-ni-ˌgāt\ *vt* **1** : to give up or surrender (as a right or privilege) : RELINQUISH **2** : to deny to or reject for oneself : RENOUNCE ⟨*abnegate* outworn beliefs) — **ab·ne·ga·tion** \ˌab-ni-'gā-shən\ n — **ab·ne·ga·tor** \'ab-ni-ˌgāt-ər\ n

ab·nor·mal \ab-'nȯr-məl, 'ab-'\ adj : differing from the normal or average; esp : markedly irregular — **ab·nor·mal·ly** \-mə-lē\ adv

ab·nor·mal·i·ty \ˌab-nər-'mal-ət-ē, -nȯr-\ n, pl **-ties** 1 : the quality or state of being abnormal 2 : something abnormal

¹**aboard** \ə-'bōrd, -'bȯrd\ adv 1 : on, onto, or within a car, ship, or airplane 2 : ALONGSIDE

²**aboard** prep : on or into especially for passage ⟨go aboard ship⟩

abode \ə-'bōd\ n : a dwelling place : RESIDENCE [Middle English abod, from abiden "to abide"]

abol·ish \ə-'bäl-ish\ vt : to do away with wholly : put an end to [Middle French aboliss-, stem of abolir, from Latin abolēre] — **abol·ish·able** \-ə-bəl\ adj — **abol·ish·er** n — **abol·ish·ment** \-mənt\ n

ab·o·li·tion \ˌab-ə-'lish-ən\ n : the act of abolishing : the state of being abolished; esp : the abolishing of slavery — **ab·o·li·tion·ary** \-'lish-ə-ˌner-ē\ adj

ab·o·li·tion·ist \-'lish-nəst, -ə-nəst\ n : a person who is in favor of abolition especially of Negro slavery — **ab·o·li·tion·ism** \-'lish-ə-ˌniz-əm\ n

ab·oma·sum \ˌab-ō-'mā-səm\ n, pl **-sa** \-sə\ : the fourth or true digestive stomach of a ruminant (as a cow) [Latin ab- + omasum "tripe of a bullock"] — **ab·oma·sal** \-səl\ adj

A–bomb \'ā-ˌbäm\ n : ATOM BOMB — **A–bomb** vb

abom·i·na·ble \ə-'bäm-nə-bəl, -ə-nə-\ adj 1 : deserving or causing loathing or hatred : DETESTABLE ⟨abominable behavior⟩ 2 : quite disagreeable ⟨abominable weather⟩ — **abom·i·na·bly** \-blē\ adv

abominable snow·man \-'snō-mán, -ˌman\ n, often cap A&S : a creature thought to exist in the Himalayas and usually held to be a bear

abom·i·nate \ə-'bäm-ə-ˌnāt\ vt : to hate or loathe intensely [Latin abominari, literally, "to deprecate as an ill omen", from ab- + omen "omen"] — **abom·i·na·tor** \-ˌnāt-ər\ n

abom·i·na·tion \ə-ˌbäm-ə-'nā-shən\ n 1 : something abominable 2 : extreme disgust and hatred : LOATHING

ab·o·rig·i·nal \ˌab-ə-'rij-nəl, -ən-l\ adj 1 a : INDIGENOUS, ORIGINAL b : PRIMITIVE 3a, b 2 : of or relating to aborigines SYN see NATIVE — **ab·o·rig·i·nal·ly** \-ē\ adv

ab·o·rig·i·ne \ˌab-ə-'rij-ə-ˌnē\ n : an indigenous inhabitant especially as contrasted with an invading or colonizing people [Latin aborigines, pl., from ab origine "from the beginning"]

aborn·ing \ə-'bȯr-niŋ\ adv : while being born or produced

abort \ə-'bȯrt\ vb 1 : to bring forth or cause to bring forth premature offspring 2 : to become checked in development ⟨pollen grains that aborted⟩ 3 : to terminate prematurely ⟨abort a project⟩ [Latin abortus, past participle of aboriri "to miscarry", from ab- + oriri "to rise, be born"]

abor·tion \ə-'bȯr-shən\ n 1 : a premature birth whether natural or induced artificially that occurs before the fetus can survive — compare MISCARRIAGE 2 : failure of a project or action to reach full development; also : a result of such failure

abor·tion·ist \-shə-nəst, -shnəst\ n : a person who induces abortions especially illegally

abor·tive \ə-'bȯrt-iv\ adj 1 : failing to achieve the desired end : UNSUCCESSFUL ⟨an abortive attempt⟩ 2 : imperfectly formed or developed : RUDIMENTARY — **abor·tive·ly** adv — **abor·tive·ness** n

abound \ə-'baùnd\ vi 1 : to be present in large numbers or in great quantity ⟨wildlife abounds⟩ 2 : to be filled or abundantly supplied ⟨a stream abounding in fish⟩ [Middle French abonder, from Latin abundare, from ab- + unda "a wave"]

¹**about** \ə-'baùt\ adv 1 : on all sides : AROUND ⟨had neighbors living all about⟩ 2 a : APPROXIMATELY ⟨about three years⟩ b : ALMOST ⟨about starved⟩ 3 : here and there ⟨pace about⟩ 4 : in the vicinity : NEAR ⟨people standing about⟩ 5 : in succession : ALTERNATELY ⟨turn about is fair play⟩ 6 : in the opposite direction ⟨face about⟩ [Old English abūtan, from ¹a- + būtan "outside", from be "by" + ūtan "outside", from ūt "out"]

²**about** prep 1 : on every side of : AROUND 2 a : in the immediate neighborhood of : NEAR ⟨fish are abundant about the reef⟩ b : on or near the person of ⟨carried a knife about him⟩ c : in the makeup of ⟨something strange about them⟩ d : at the command of ⟨keep your wits about you⟩ 3 a : engaged in ⟨do it thoroughly while you're about it⟩ b : on the verge of ⟨about to join the army⟩ 4 : with regard to : CONCERNING ⟨told me about it⟩ 5 : over, through, or in different parts of ⟨traveled about the country⟩

about–face \ə-'baùt-ˌfās\ n 1 : a reversal of direction 2 : a reversal of attitude or point of view — **about–face** vi

¹**above** \ə-'bəv\ adv 1 : in or to a higher place : OVERHEAD 2 : higher on the same page or on a preceding page 3 : in or to a higher rank or number [Old English abufan, from ¹a- + bufan "above", from be "by" + ufan "above, over"]

²**above** prep 1 : in or to a higher place than : OVER 2 a : superior to (as in rank, quality, or degree) ⟨a captain is above a lieutenant⟩ b : out of reach of ⟨above criticism⟩ c : too proud or honorable to stoop to ⟨above such petty tricks⟩ 3 : exceeding in number, quantity, or size ⟨above the average⟩ 4 : as distinct from and in addition to ⟨heard the whistle above the roar of the crowd⟩

³**above** n : something that is above

⁴**above** adj : located or written higher on the same page or on a preceding page ⟨the above diagram⟩

above all adv : before every other consideration : ESPECIALLY

¹**above–board** \ə-'bəv-ˌbōrd, -ˌbȯrd\ adv : in a straightforward manner : OPENLY

²**aboveboard** adj : free from concealment or deceit : STRAIGHTFORWARD

ab·ra·ca·dab·ra \ˌab-rə-kə-'dab-rə\ n 1 : a magical charm or incantation against calamity 2 : unintelligible language : JARGON [Late Latin]

abrade \ə-'brād\ vb 1 : to rub or wear away especially by friction : ERODE 2 : to irritate or roughen by rubbing [Latin abradere "to scrape off", from ab- + radere "to scrape"] — **abrad·er** n

abra·sion \ə-'brā-zhən\ n 1 : a rubbing or wearing away ⟨protect the surface from abrasion⟩ 2 : a place where the surface has been rubbed or scraped off ⟨had an abrasion on my knee⟩ [Medieval Latin abrasio, from Latin abradere "to abrade"]

¹**abra·sive** \ə-'brā-siv, -ziv\ adj 1 : having the effect of abrading 2 : causing annoyance ⟨an abrasive manner⟩

²**abrasive** n : a substance (as emery, pumice, fine sand) used for grinding, smoothing, or polishing

abreast \ə-'brest\ adv or adj 1 : side by side with bodies in line ⟨soldiers standing five abreast⟩ 2 : up to a standard or level especially of knowledge ⟨keep abreast of the times⟩

abridge \ə-'brij\ vt 1 a archaic : DEPRIVE b : to reduce in scope : DIMINISH ⟨forbidden to abridge the rights of citizens⟩ 2 : to shorten in duration or extent ⟨modern transportation that abridges distance⟩ 3 : to shorten by omitting words without sacrificing the sense : CONDENSE [Middle French abregier, from Late Latin abbreviare "to abbreviate"] — **abridg·er** n

abridg·ment or **abridge·ment** \ə-'brij-mənt\ n 1 : the action of abridging : the state of being abridged 2 : a shortened form of a work retaining the general sense and unity of the original

\ə\ abut	\ng\ sing
\ər\ further	\ō\ bone
\a\ mat	\ȯ\ saw
\ā\ take	\ȯi\ coin
\ä\ cot, cart	\th\ thin
\aù\ out	\th\ this
\ch\ chin	\ü\ food
\e\ pet	\ù\ foot
\ē\ easy	\y\ yet
\g\ go	\yü\ few
\i\ tip	\yù\ cure
\ī\ life	\zh\ vision
\j\ job	

abroad \ə-'brȯd\ *adv or adj* **1** : over a wide area : WIDELY **2** : away from one's home ⟨walk *abroad* after lunch⟩ **3** : in or to foreign countries ⟨travel *abroad*⟩ **4** : in wide circulation ⟨disturbing rumors were *abroad*⟩

ab·ro·gate \'ab-rə-ˌgāt\ *vt* **1** : to annul or repeal by authoritative action ⟨*abrogate* a law⟩ **2** : to do away with [Latin *abrogare*, from *ab-* + *rogare* "to ask, propose"] — **ab·ro·ga·tion** \ˌab-rə-'gā-shən\ *n*

abrupt \ə-'brəpt\ *adj* **1** : broken off **2 a** : SUDDEN ⟨*abrupt* change in the weather⟩ **b** : impolitely curt ⟨*abrupt* manner⟩ **c** : marked by sudden changes in topic : DISCONNECTED ⟨an *abrupt* style of speaking⟩ **3** : rising or dropping sharply : STEEP ⟨a high *abrupt* bank bounded the stream⟩ [Latin *abruptus*, from *abrumpere* "to break off", from *ab-* + *rumpere* "to break"] — **abrupt·ly** *adv* — **abrupt·ness** \ə-'brəpt-nəs, -'brəp-\ *n*

ab·scess \'ab-ˌses\ *n* : a localized collection of pus surrounded by inflamed tissue [Latin *abscessus*, literally, "departure", from *abscedere* "to go away", from *ab-*, *abs-* + *cedere* "to go"] — **ab·scessed** \-ˌsest\ *adj*

ab·scis·sa \ab-'sis-ə\ *n, pl* **-scis·sas** *also* **-scis·sae** \-'sis-ē\ : the horizontal coordinate of a point in a plane Cartesian coordinate system obtained by measuring parallel to the x-axis — called also *x-coordinate*; compare ORDINATE [New Latin; from Latin *abscindere* "to cut off", from *ab-* + *scindere* "to cut"]

ab·scis·sion \ab-'sizh-ən\ *n* : the natural separation of flowers, fruit, or leaves from plants at a special separation layer

ab·scond \ab-'skänd\ *vi* : to depart secretly and hide oneself [Latin *abscondere* "to hide away", from *ab-*, *abs-* + *condere* "to store up, conceal", from *com-* + *-dere* "to put"] — **ab·scond·er** *n*

ab·sence \'ab-səns\ *n* **1** : the state of being absent **2** : the time that one is absent **3** : WANT, LACK ⟨an *absence* of detail⟩ **4** : inattention to things present ⟨*absence* of mind⟩

¹ab·sent \'ab-sənt\ *adj* **1** : not present or attending : MISSING **2** : not existing : LACKING **3** : INATTENTIVE ⟨an *absent* mood⟩ [Latin *absens*, from *abesse* "to be away", from *ab-* + *esse* "to be"] — **ab·sent·ly** *adv*

²ab·sent \ab-'sent\ *vt* : to keep (oneself) away

ab·sen·tee \ˌab-sən-'tē\ *n* **1** : one that is absent **2** : a proprietor that lives elsewhere — **absentee** *adj*

absentee ballot *n* : a ballot submitted (as by mail) before an election by a voter who cannot be present at the polls

ab·sen·tee·ism \ˌab-sən-'tē-ˌiz-əm\ *n* **1** : protracted absence of an owner from his property **2** : chronic absence from duty

ab·sent·mind·ed \ˌab-sənt-'mīn-dəd\ *adj* : lost in thought and unaware of one's surroundings or actions — **ab·sent·mind·ed·ly** *adv* — **ab·sent·mind·ed·ness** *n*

ab·sinthe *or* **ab·sinth** \'ab-ˌsinth\ *n* : a green liqueur flavored with aromatics (as wormwood and anise) [French *absinthe*, from Latin *absinthium* "wormwood", from Greek *apsinthion*]

ab·so·lute \'ab-sə-ˌlüt, ˌab-sə-'\ *adj* **1 a** : free from imperfection : PERFECT **b** : free or relatively free from mixture : PURE ⟨*absolute* alcohol⟩ **c** : OUTRIGHT ⟨an *absolute* lie⟩ **2** : completely free from constitutional or other restraint or limitation ⟨an *absolute* monarch⟩ **3 a** : lacking grammatical connection with any other word in a sentence ⟨the *absolute* construction *this being the case* in "this being the case, let us go"⟩ **b** : standing alone without a modified substantive ⟨the *absolute* adjective *blind* in "help the blind"⟩ ⟨the *absolute* possessive pronoun *ours* in "your work and ours"⟩ **c** : having no object in a particular construction though normally transitive ⟨*kill* in "if looks could kill" is an *absolute* verb⟩ **4** : having no restriction, exception, or qualification ⟨*absolute* freedom⟩ **5** : free from doubt : CERTAIN, UNQUESTIONABLE ⟨*absolute*

proof⟩ **6 a** : independent of standards of measurement : ACTUAL ⟨*absolute* brightness of a star⟩ ⟨*absolute* motion⟩ **b** : relating to or derived from the fundamental units of length, mass, and time ⟨*absolute* electric units⟩ **c** : relating to the absolute-temperature scale ⟨10° *absolute*⟩ **7** : perfectly embodying the nature of a thing ⟨*absolute* justice⟩ [Latin *absolutus*, from *absolvere* "to set free, absolve"] — **absolute** *n* — **ab·so·lute·ly** \'ab-sə-ˌlüt-lē, ˌab-sə-'\ *adv* — **ab·so·lute·ness** \-ˌlüt-nəs, -'lüt-\ *n*

absolute pitch *n* **1** : the position of a tone in a standard scale independently determined by its rate of vibration **2** : the ability to sing a note asked for or name a note heard

absolute temperature *n* : temperature measured on a scale that has absolute zero as the zero point

absolute value *n* **1** : the numerical value of a real number without regard to its sign **2** : the positive square root of the sum of the squares of the real and imaginary parts of a complex number — called also *modulus*

absolute zero *n* : a hypothetical temperature characterized by complete absence of heat and equivalent to approximately −273.15°C or −459.67°F

ab·so·lu·tion \ˌab-sə-'lü-shən\ *n* : the act of absolving; *esp* : a forgiving of sins by a confessor in the sacrament of penance

ab·so·lut·ism \'ab-sə-ˌlüt-ˌiz-əm\ *n* **1 a** : a political theory that absolute power should be vested in one or more rulers **b** : government by an absolute ruler or authority **2** : advocacy of absolute standards or principles — **ab·so·lut·ist** \-ˌlüt-əst\ *n or adj* — **ab·so·lu·tis·tic** \ˌab-sə-ˌlü-'tis-tik\ *adj*

ab·solve \əb-'zälv, -'sälv, -'zȯlv, -'sȯlv\ *vt* **1** : to set free from an obligation or from the consequences of guilt **2** : to forgive (a sin) by absolution [Latin *absolvere*, from *ab-* + *solvere* "to loosen"] — **ab·solv·er** *n*

ab·sorb \əb-'sȯrb, -'zȯrb\ *vt* **1** : to take in or swallow up : INCORPORATE ⟨the corporation *absorbed* three small companies⟩ **2** : to suck or take up or in ⟨a sponge *absorbs* water⟩ **3** : to engage or hold the interest of : ENGROSS ⟨*absorbed* in thought⟩ **4** : to receive without recoil or echo ⟨a sound-*absorbing* surface⟩ [Latin *absorbēre*, from *ab-* + *sorbēre* "to suck up"] — **ab·sorb·abil·i·ty** \əb-ˌsȯr-bə-'bil-ət-ē, -ˌzȯr-\ *n* — **ab·sorb·able** \əb-'sȯr-bə-bəl, -'zȯr-\ *adj* — **ab·sorb·er** *n* □ SYN ABSORB, ASSIMILATE mean to take in. ABSORB may imply that matter or energy enters a body and is retained without essential change to itself or to the receiving body ⟨plant roots *absorb* moisture⟩ ASSIMILATE may apply to an active process of incorporating substance into the substance of the receiving body ⟨the body *assimilates* nourishment from milk⟩

ab·sorbed \-'sȯrbd, -'zȯrbd\ *adj* : wholly occupied or interested in a thought or activity : ENGROSSED — **ab·sorb·ed·ly** \-'sȯr-bəd-lē, -'zȯr-\ *adv*

ab·sor·ben·cy \əb-'sȯr-bən-sē, -'zȯr-\ *n, pl* **-cies** : the quality or state of being absorbent

ab·sor·bent \-bənt\ *adj* : able to absorb ⟨*absorbent* cotton⟩ — **absorbent** *n*

ab·sorb·ing *adj* : fully taking one's attention : ENGROSSING — **ab·sorb·ing·ly** \-bing-lē\ *adv*

ab·sorp·tion \əb-'sȯrp-shən, -'zȯrp-\ *n* **1** : the process of absorbing or being absorbed: as **a** : the passing of digested food through the intestinal wall into the blood or lymph **b** : interception especially of light or sound waves **2** : complete occupation of the mind — **ab·sorp·tive** \-'sȯrp-tiv, -'zȯrp-\ *adj*

ab·stain \əb-'stān\ *vi* : to refrain voluntarily especially from an action ⟨*abstain* from voting⟩ [Middle French *abstenir*, from Latin *abstinēre*, from *ab-*, *abs-* + *tenēre* "to hold"] SYN see REFRAIN — **ab·stain·er** *n*

ab·ste·mi·ous \ab-'stē-mē-əs\ *adj* : sparing especially in eating and drinking [Latin *abstemius*, from *ab-*, *abs-* + *temetum* "mead"] — **ab·ste·mi·ous·ly** *adv*

ab·sten·tion \əb-'sten-chən\ *n* : the act or practice of abstaining; *esp* : a usually formal refusal to vote ⟨3 ayes, 5 nays, and 2 *abstentions*⟩ [Late Latin *abstentio*, from Latin *abstinēre* "to abstain"] — **ab·sten·tious** \-chəs\ *adj*

ab·sti·nence \'ab-stə-nəns\ *n* **1** : an abstaining especially from indulgence of appetite or from eating certain foods **2** : habitual abstaining from alcoholic liquors [Latin *abstinēre* "to abstain"] — **ab·sti·nent** \-nənt\ *adj* — **ab·sti·nent·ly** *adv*

¹ab·stract \ab-'strakt, 'ab-\ *adj* **1 a** : considered apart from a particular instance or object ⟨whiteness is an *abstract* quality⟩ ⟨*abstract* concept⟩ **b** : difficult to understand ⟨*abstract* problems⟩ **c** : IDEAL ⟨*abstract* justice⟩ **d** : insufficiently factual : purely formal ⟨possessed only an *abstract* right⟩ **2** : expressing a quality considered apart from an object (the word *poem* is concrete; the word *poetry* is *abstract*) **3 a** : dealing with a subject in purely abstract terms : THEORETICAL ⟨*abstract* algebra⟩ **b** : IMPERSONAL ⟨the *abstract* compassion of a surgeon⟩ **4** : having only generalized form with little or no attempt at precise representation ⟨*abstract* painting⟩ [Medieval Latin *abstractus*, from Latin *abstrahere* "to draw away", from *ab-, abs-* + *trahere* "to draw"] — **ab·stract·ly** \ab-'strak-tlē, -lē, 'ab-,\ *adv* — **ab·stract·ness** \ab-'strakt-nəs, -'strak-, 'ab-,\ *n*

²ab·stract \'ab-,strakt, *in sense 2 also* ab-'\ *n* **1** : a brief statement of the main points or facts : SYNOPSIS ⟨an *abstract* of a book⟩ **2** : an abstract thing or state **3** : ABSTRACTION 4

³ab·stract \ab-'strakt, 'ab-,, *in sense 3 usually* 'ab-,\ *vt* **1** : REMOVE, SEPARATE ⟨add or *abstract* baser metal during minting⟩ **2** : to consider apart from application to a particular instance ⟨*abstract* the idea of roundness from a ball⟩ **3** : to make an abstract of : CONDENSE **4** : to draw away the attention of **5** : to take away secretly or dishonestly : STEAL — **ab·strac·tor** *or* **ab·stract·er** *n*

ab·stract·ed \ab-'strak-təd, 'ab-,\ *adj* : PREOCCUPIED, ABSENTMINDED — **ab·stract·ed·ly** *adv* — **ab·stract·ed·ness** *n*

ab·strac·tion \ab-'strak-shən\ *n* **1 a** : the act or process of abstracting : the state of being abstracted **b** : an abstract idea or term ⟨a mind full of *abstractions*⟩ **2** : inattention to one's surroundings : ABSENTMINDEDNESS **3** : abstract quality or character **4** : an artistic composition or creation characterized by designs that do not precisely represent actual objects or figures — **ab·strac·tive** \-'strak-tiv\ *adj*

ab·strac·tion·ism \ab-'strak-shə-,niz-əm\ *n* **1** : the creation of abstractions in art **2** : the principles or ideals of abstract art — **ab·strac·tion·ist** \-shə-nəst, -shnəst\ *adj or n*

ab·struse \ab-'strüs, əb-\ *adj* : hard to understand [Latin *abstrusus*, from *abstrudere* "to conceal", from *ab-, abs-* + *trudere* "to push"] — **ab·struse·ly** *adv* — **ab·struse·ness** *n*

ab·surd \əb-'sərd, -'zərd\ *adj* : ridiculously unreasonable, unsound, or incongruous [Middle French *absurde*, from Latin *absurdus*, from *ab-* + *surdus* "deaf, stupid"] — **ab·surd·ly** *adv* — **ab·surd·ness** *n*

ab·sur·di·ty \əb-'sərd-ət-ē, -'zərd-\ *n, pl* **-ties** **1** : the state of being absurd **2** : something that is absurd

abun·dance \ə-'bən-dəns\ *n* **1** : an ample or overflowing quantity : PROFUSION **2** : AFFLUENCE, WEALTH ⟨a life of *abundance*⟩ **3** : relative quantity or amount : degree of plentifulness ⟨the *abundance* of various species⟩

abun·dant \-dənt\ *adj* : existing in or having abundance : ABOUNDING [Latin *abundare* "to abound"] SYN see PLENTIFUL — **abun·dant·ly** *adv*

¹abuse \ə-'byüz\ *vt* **1** : to attack in words : REVILE **2** : to put to a wrong or improper use : MISUSE ⟨*abuse* a privilege⟩ **3** : to use so as to injure or damage : MALTREAT ⟨*abused* the car⟩ ⟨*abused* the dog⟩ [Middle French *abuser*, from Latin *abuti* "to misuse", from *ab-* + *uti* "to use"] — **abus·er** *n*

²abuse \ə-'byüs\ *n* **1** : a corrupt practice or custom ⟨election *abuses*⟩ **2** : improper use or treatment : MISUSE ⟨drug *abuse*⟩ **3** : abusive language **4** : physical maltreatment ⟨child *abuse*⟩ □ SYN ABUSE, INVECTIVE, VITUPERATION mean vigorous condemnation. ABUSE stresses the offensive character of the language used; INVECTIVE may add additional suggestion of logical effectiveness and serious purpose in directing abuse; VITUPERATION suggests an unrestrained torrent of abuse.

abu·sive \ə-'byü-siv, -ziv\ *adj* **1** : expressive of or characterized by disrespect or contempt ⟨an *abusive* manner⟩; *esp* : containing or using harsh insulting language **2** : physically injurious — **abu·sive·ly** *adv* — **abu·sive·ness** *n*

abut \ə-'bət\ *vb* **abut·ted; abut·ting** **1** : to touch along a border or with a projecting part : BORDER ⟨the farm *abuts* on the road⟩ ⟨stores *abut* the sidewalk⟩ **2 a** : to terminate at a point of contact **b** : to lean for support [Old French *abouter*, from *a* "to" + *bout* "end"] — **abut·ter** *n*

abut·ment \ə-'bət-mənt\ *n* **1** : the action or place of abutting **2** : something against which another thing rests its weight or pushes with force ⟨*abutments* that support a bridge⟩

abut·tals \ə-'bət-lz\ *n pl* : the boundaries of lands with respect to adjacent lands

abysm \ə-'biz-əm\ *n* : ABYSS [Old French *abisme*, from Late Latin *abyssus*]

abys·mal \ə-'biz-məl\ *adj* **1** : resembling an abyss : immeasurably deep **2** : ABYSSAL — **abys·mal·ly** \-mə-lē\ *adv* □ SYN ABYSMAL, ABYSSAL mean unfathomable by ordinary means. ABYSMAL applies chiefly to figurative depths that seem to be without a lower limit ⟨*abysmal* ignorance⟩ ⟨*abysmal* poverty⟩ ABYSSAL refers to the ocean bottom at great depths ⟨fauna of the *abyssal* zone⟩ ⟨*abyssal* sediments⟩

abyss \ə-'bis\ *n* **1** : the bottomless gulf, pit, or chaos in old accounts of the origins of the universe **2** : an immeasurably deep gulf or great space [Late Latin *abyssus*, from Greek *abyssos*, from *abyssos* "bottomless", from *a-* + *byssos* "depth"]

abys·sal \ə-'bis-əl\ *adj* **1** : UNFATHOMABLE **2** : of or relating to the bottom waters of the ocean depths SYN see ABYSMAL

Ab·ys·sin·i·an cat \,ab-ə-'sin-ē-ən-, -'sin-yən-\ *n* : any of a breed of small slender cats of African origin with short brownish hair ticked with darker color

ac- — see AD-

-ac \,ak, *in a few words* ik *or* ək\ *n suffix* : one affected with ⟨insomni*ac*⟩ [Greek *-akos* "of or relating to"]

aca·cia \ə-'kā-shə\ *n* **1** : GUM ARABIC **2** : any of numerous woody plants of the legume family with ball-shaped white or yellow flower clusters and often pinnate leaves [Latin]

ac·a·deme \'ak-ə-,dēm\ *n* **1 a** : a place of instruction : SCHOOL **b** : the academic environment **2** : PEDANT 2

ac·a·dem·ic \,ak-ə-'dem-ik\ *adj* **1** : of or relating to school or college ⟨*academic* costume⟩ **2** : literary or general rather than technical or vocational ⟨an *academic* course⟩ **3** : conforming to the traditions or rules of a school (as of literature or art) or an official academy : CONVENTIONAL ⟨*academic* verse⟩ **4** : having no practical significance : THEORETICAL ⟨an *academic* question⟩ — **ac·a·dem·i·cal·ly** \-'dem-i-kə-lē, -klē\ *adv*

academic freedom *n* : freedom to teach or to learn without interference (as by government officials)

ac·a·de·mi·cian \,ak-əd-ə-'mish-ən, ə-,kad-ə-\ *n* : a member of an academy for promoting science, art, or literature

ac·a·dem·i·cism \,ak-ə-'dem-ə-,siz-əm\ *also* **acad·e·mism** \ə-'kad-ə-,miz-əm\ *n* : academic manner, style, or content : FORMALISM

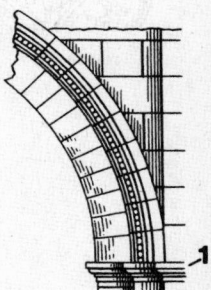

1 abutment of an arch

\ə\	abut	\ng\	sing
\ər\	further	\ō\	bone
\a\	mat	\ȯ\	saw
\ā\	take	\ȯi\	coin
\ä\	cot, cart	\th\	thin
\au̇\	out	\th\	this
\ch\	chin	\ü\	food
\e\	pet	\u̇\	foot
\ē\	easy	\y\	yet
\g\	go	\yü\	few
\i\	tip	\yu̇\	cure
\ī\	life	\zh\	vision
\j\	job		

acad·e·my \ə-'kad-ə-mē\ *n, pl* **-mies** **1** *cap* : the school of philosophy founded by Plato **2 a** : a school usually above the elementary level; *esp* : a private high school **b** : an institution for training in special subjects or skills **3** : a society of learned persons united to advance art, science, or literature [Greek *Akadēmeia,* gymnasium in the suburbs of Athens where Plato established his school]

Aca·di·an \ə-'kād-ē-ən\ *n* **1** : a native or inhabitant of Acadia **2 a** : a Louisianian descended from French-speaking immigrants from Acadia **b** : a dialect of French spoken by Acadians

acan·thus \ə-'kan-thəs, -'kant-\ *n, pl* **acan·thus·es** *also* **acan·thi** \-'kan-,thī\ **1** : any of a genus of prickly herbs of the Mediterranean region **2** : an ornamentation representing the leaves of the acanthus [Greek *akanthos,* a kind of acanthus]

acanthus 2

a cap·pel·la *also* **a ca·pel·la** \,äk-ə-'pel-ə\ *adv or adj* : without instrumental accompaniment [Italian *a cappella* "in chapel style"]

ac·cede \ak-'sēd\ *vi* **1 a** : to become a party (as to an agreement) (were invited to *accede* to the treaty) **b** : to give consent : AGREE (*accede* to a proposed plan) **2** : to enter upon an office or dignity (*acceded* to the throne in 1838) [Latin *accedere* "to go to", from *ad-* + *cedere* "to go"] SYN see ASSENT

ac·ce·le·ran·do \ä-,chel-ə-'rän-dō\ *adv or adj* : gradually faster — used as a direction in music [Italian]

ac·cel·er·ate \ik-'sel-ə-,rāt, ak-\ *vb* **1** : to bring about at an earlier time (*accelerated* their departure) **2 a** : to hasten the ordinary progress or development of **b** : to speed up (a course of study) **3 a** : to add to the speed of **b** : to cause to undergo acceleration; *esp* : to increase the velocity of **4** : to move or progress faster [Latin *accelerare,* from *ad-* + *celer* "swift"] — **ac·cel·er·a·tive** \-,rāt-iv\ *adj*

ac·cel·er·a·tion \ik-,sel-ə-'rā-shən, ak-\ *n* **1** : the act or process of accelerating : the state of being accelerated **2** : change of velocity or the time rate of such change

acceleration of gravity : the acceleration of a freely falling body under the influence of gravity expressed as the rate of increase of velocity per unit of time with the value being about 980.616 centimeters per second per second

ac·cel·er·a·tor \ik-'sel-ə-,rāt-ər, ak-\ *n* : one that accelerates: as **a** : a pedal in a motor vehicle used for varying the supply of fuel-air mixture to the combustion chamber and so controlling the speed of the motor **b** : an apparatus for imparting high velocities to charged particles (as electrons and protons)

accelerator nerve *n* : a nerve which functions to increase the rate of the heartbeat

ac·cel·er·om·e·ter \ik-,sel-ə-'räm-ət-ər, ak-\ *n* : an instrument for measuring acceleration or vibrations

accent mark 2

¹ac·cent \'ak-,sent\ *n* **1** : a peculiar or characteristic manner of speech (foreign *accent*) **2** : special prominence given to one syllable of a word only by increase of stress or change of pitch group of words in speaking especially by increase of stress or change of pitch (*before* has the *accent* on the last syllable) **3** : rhythmically significant stress on the syllables of a verse usually at regular intervals **4** *archaic* : UTTERANCE **5 a** : a mark (as ´, `, ˆ) used chiefly to indicate a specific sound value, stress, or pitch — compare ACUTE, CIRCUMFLEX, GRAVE **b** : a mark (as ' or ‚) identifying a syllable that is accented in speaking **6 a** : greater stress given to one musical tone than to its neighbors; *also* : a mark indicating this **b** : the principle of regularly recurring stresses which serve to distribute a succession of pulses into measures **7 a** : EMPHASIS 2 **b** : a small detail in sharp contrast with its surroundings **8** : a mark (as a prime or double prime) placed to the right of a letter or number and usually slightly above it [Middle French, from Latin *accentus,* from *ad-* + *cantus* "song, chant"]

²accent \ak-'sent, 'ak-,\ *vt* **1 a** : to utter with accent : STRESS (*accent* the first syllable of *after*) **b** : to mark with a written or printed accent **2** : to give prominence to or increase the prominence of

accent mark *n* **1** : ACCENT 5 **2** : one of several symbols used to indicate musical accent

ac·cen·tu·al \ak-'sench-wəl, -ə-wəl\ *adj* : of, relating to, or characterized by accent — **ac·cen·tu·al·ly** \-ē\ *adv*

ac·cen·tu·ate \ak-'sen-chə-,wāt\ *vt* **1** : to pronounce or mark with an accent **2** : EMPHASIZE (dark clouds *accentuated* an atmosphere of mystery) — **ac·cen·tu·a·tion** \,ak-,sen-chə-'wā-shən\ *n*

ac·cept \ik-'sept, ak-\ *vb* **1 a** : to receive with consent or approval (*accept* a gift) (was *accepted* as a member) **b** : to be able or designed to take or hold (something applied or added) (a computer program ready to *accept* commands) **2 a** : to receive as true **b** : to regard as proper, normal, or inevitable **c** : to take without protest : TOLERATE **3 a** : to make an affirmative or favorable response to (*accept* an offer) **b** : to undertake the responsibility of **4** : to assume an obligation to pay (*accept* a bill of exchange) **5** : to receive officially (the Senate *accepted* the report) [Middle French *accepter,* from Latin *acceptare,* from *accipere* "to receive", from *ad-* + *capere* "to take"] SYN see RECEIVE — **ac·cept·er** *or* **ac·cep·tor** \-'sep-tər\ *n*

ac·cept·able \ik-'sep-tə-bəl, ak-\ *adj* **1** : capable or worthy of being accepted : SATISFACTORY (an *acceptable* excuse) **2** : barely adequate (plays an *acceptable* game) **3** : capable of being endured : TOLERABLE (*acceptable* losses) — **ac·cept·abil·i·ty** \-,sep-tə-'bil-ət-ē\ *n* — **ac·cept·able·ness** \-'sep-tə-bəl-nəs\ *n* — **ac·cept·ably** \-blē\ *adv*

ac·cept·ance \ik-'sep-təns, ak-\ *n* **1 a** : the act of accepting **b** : favorable reception : APPROVAL **2** : the quality or state of being accepted or acceptable

ac·cep·ta·tion \,ak-,sep-'tā-shən\ *n* **1** : ACCEPTANCE; *esp* : favorable reception **2** : the generally accepted meaning of a word or expression

¹ac·cess \'ak-,ses\ *n* **1** : a sudden outburst of intense feeling **2 a** : permission, liberty, or ability to enter, approach, communicate with, pass to and from, or make use of (*access* to the president) **b** : a way or means of approach (a nation's *access* to the sea) **3** : an increase by addition (a sudden *access* of wealth) [Latin *accessus* "approach", from *accedere* "to go to", from *ad-* + *cedere* "to go"]

²access *vt* : to get at : gain access to

ac·ces·si·ble \ak-'ses-ə-bəl, ik-\ *adj* **1** : easy to reach (*accessible* by train or car) **2** : open to influence (a mind *accessible* to reason) **3** : OBTAINABLE (*accessible* information) — **ac·ces·si·bil·i·ty** \,ak-,ses-ə-'bil-ət-ē, ik-\ *n* — **ac·ces·si·ble·ness** \ak-'ses-ə-bəl-nəs, ik-\ *n* — **ac·ces·si·bly** \-blē\ *adv*

ac·ces·sion \ak-'sesh-ən, ik-\ *n* **1** : something added : ACQUISITION (new *accessions* to the museum) **2** : ADHERENCE (*accession* to a treaty) **3 a** : increase by something added **b** : acquisition of additional property (as by growth or increase) **4** : the act of assenting or agreeing (*accession* to a proposal) **5** : the act of coming to high office or a position of honor or power (the *accession* of a king) **6** : ACCESS 1 — **ac·ces·sion·al** \-'sesh-nəl, -ən-l\ *adj*

¹ac·ces·so·ry *also* **ac·ces·sa·ry** \ak-'ses-rē, ik-, -ə-rē\ *n, pl* **-ries** **1 a** : a thing of secondary or subordinate importance : ADJUNCT **b** : an object or device not essential in itself but adding to the beauty, convenience, or effectiveness of something else (automobile *accessories*) **2** : a person who aids or encourages another in the commission of a crime or an attempt to escape justice

²accessory *adj* : aiding or contributing in a secondary way

accessory fruit *n* : a fruit (as the apple or the strawberry) of which a conspicuous part consists of tissue other than that of the ripened ovary

access time *n* : the time lag between the time stored information (as in a computer) is requested and the time it is delivered

ac·ci·dence \'ak-səd-əns, -sə-,dens\ *n* : the part of grammar that deals with inflections

ac·ci·dent \'ak-səd-ənt, -sə-,dent\ *n* **I a** : an event occurring by chance or from unknown causes **b** : lack of intention or necessity : CHANCE (we met by *accident*) **2** : an unintended and usually sudden and unexpected happening and especially one resulting in loss or injury (an automobile *accident*) **3 a** : a nonessential property : ATTRIBUTE **b** : a chance circumstance (the *accident* of noble birth) [Middle French, from Latin *accidens* "nonessential quality, chance", from *accidere* "to happen, befall", from *ad-* + *cadere* "to fall"]

¹ac·ci·den·tal \,ak-sə-'dent-l\ *adj* **I** : arising from secondary causes : NONESSENTIAL **2 a** : occurring unexpectedly or by chance (an *accidental* discovery of oil) **b** : happening without intent or from carelessness often with unfortunate results (an *accidental* shooting) — **ac·ci·den·tal·ly** \-'dent-lē, -'dent-l-ē\ *adv* — **ac·ci·den·tal·ness** \-'dent-l-nəs\ *n* □ SYN ACCIDENTAL, CASUAL, FORTUITOUS mean happening by chance. ACCIDENTAL implies an absence of immediate intention (an *accidental* discovery) or reasonably foreseeable probability (*accidental* death) CASUAL stresses absence of prearrangement or premeditation (*casual* encounters with friends) FORTUITOUS stresses chance so strongly that it often connotes entire absence of cause (*fortuitous* presence of a witness)

²accidental *n* : a note whose pitch is altered (as by a sharp or flat) from that indicated by the key signature

ac·cip·i·ter \ak-'sip-ət-ər\ *n* : any of various hawks with short wings and long legs that dart in and out among trees [Latin, "hawk"]

¹ac·claim \ə-'klām\ *vb* **I** : to welcome with applause or great praise (a novel *acclaimed* by the critics) **2** : to declare or proclaim by or as if by acclamation (was *acclaimed* a hero) [Latin *acclamare*, from *ad-* + *clamare* "to shout"] — **ac·claim·er** *n*

²acclaim *n* **I** : the act of acclaiming **2** : APPLAUSE, PRAISE (the symphony received worldwide *acclaim*)

ac·cla·ma·tion \,ak-lə-'mā-shən\ *n* **I** : a loud eager expression of approval, praise, or assent **2** : an overwhelming affirmative vote by voice rather than by ballot

ac·cli·mate \ə-'klī-mət, 'ak-lə-,māt\ *vt* : ACCLIMATIZE — **ac·cli·ma·tion** \,ak-,lī-'mā-shən, -lə-\ *n*

ac·cli·ma·tize \ə-'klī-mə-,tīz\ *vb* : to adapt to a new temperature, altitude, climate, environment, or situation — **ac·cli·ma·ti·za·tion** \ə-,klī-mət-ə-'zā-shən\ *n*

ac·cliv·i·ty \ə-'kliv-ət-ē, a-\ *n, pl* **-ties** : a slope that ascends [Latin *acclivitas*, from *ad-* + *clivus* "slope"]

ac·co·lade \'ak-ə-,lād\ *n* **I** : a ceremonial embrace **2** : a formal salute (as a tap on the shoulder with the blade of a sword) that marks the conferring of knighthood **3 a** : a mark of recognition of merit : COMMENDATION **b** : AWARD 1 [French, from *accoler* "to embrace", derived from Latin *ad-* + *collum* "neck"]

ac·com·mo·date \ə-'käm-ə-,dāt\ *vb* **I a** : to make fit or suitable : ADAPT **b** : to adapt oneself; *esp* : to undergo accommodation **2** : to furnish with something desired: as **a** : to provide with lodgings **b** : to have or make room for [Latin *accommodare*, from *ad-* + *commodus* "convenient, suitable"] SYN SEE ADAPT, CONTAIN — **ac·com·mo·da·tive** \-,dāt-iv\ *adj* — **ac·com·mo·da·tive·ness** *n*

ac·com·mo·dat·ing *adj* : inclined to be helpful or obliging — **ac·com·mo·dat·ing·ly** \-,dāt-ing-lē\ *adv*

ac·com·mo·da·tion \ə-,käm-ə-'dā-shən\ *n* **I** : something supplied for convenience or to satisfy a need **b** *pl* : lodging, food, and services or seat, berth, or other space occupied together with services available (overnight *accommodations*) **2** : the act of accommodating : the state of being accommodated: as **a** : the provision of what is needed or desired for convenience (tables for the *accommodation* of picnickers) **b** : an adjustment of differences : SETTLEMENT **c** : the automatic adjustment of the eye for seeing at different distances

ac·com·pa·ni·ment \ə-'kəmp-nē-mənt, -ə-nē-\ *n* **I** : music to support or complement a principal voice or instrument **2** : an accompanying object, situation, or event

ac·com·pa·nist \ə-'kəmp-nəst, -ə-nəst\ *n* : one (as a pianist) that plays an accompaniment

ac·com·pa·ny \ə-'kəmp-nē, -ə-nē\ *vb* **-nied; -ny·ing** **I** : to go with or attend as an associate or companion **2** : to perform an accompaniment to or for **3** : to occur at the same time as or along with (a thunderstorm *accompanied* by high winds)

ac·com·plice \ə-'käm-pləs, -'kəm-\ *n* : one associated with another in wrongdoing [archaic *complice* (in the phrase *a complice*), derived from Latin *com-* + *plicare* "to fold"]

ac·com·plish \ə-'käm-plish, -'kəm-\ *vt* : to bring to a successful finish : PERFORM [Middle French *acompliss-*, stem of *acomplir*, from Latin *ad-* + *complēre* "to fill up, complete"] — **ac·com·plish·able** \-ə-bəl\ *adj*

ac·com·plished *adj* **I** : ESTABLISHED (an *accomplished* fact) **2 a** : complete in skills or acquirements as the result of practice or training : EXPERT (an *accomplished* pianist) **b** : proficient in social graces : POLISHED (an *accomplished* hostess)

ac·com·plish·ment \ə-'käm-plish-mənt, -'kəm-\ *n* **I** : the act of accomplishing : COMPLETION **2** : something accomplished : ACHIEVEMENT **3** : an ability, a social quality, or a special skill acquired by training or practice

¹ac·cord \ə-'kord\ *vb* **I** : to grant as suitable or proper (*accords* the right of appeal) **2** : to be in harmony : AGREE (the decision *accords* with our sense of justice) [Old French *acorder*, from Latin *ad-* + *cord-, cor* "heart"]

²accord *n* **I a** : AGREEMENT, HARMONY (were in *accord* with the company's policy) **b** : an agreement between parties (the disputants reached an *accord*) **2** : voluntary or spontaneous impulse to act

ac·cor·dance \ə-'kord-ns\ *n* **I** : AGREEMENT, CONFORMITY (in *accordance* with a rule) **2** : the act of according

ac·cor·dant \-'kord-nt\ *adj* **I** : CONSONANT 1, AGREEING **2** : HARMONIOUS (*accordant* tones) — **ac·cor·dant·ly** *adv*

ac·cord·ing as *conj* **I** : in accord with the way in which **2 a** : depending on how **b** : depending on whether : IF

ac·cord·ing·ly \ə-'kord-ing-lē\ *adv* **I** : in accordance : CORRESPONDINGLY (believed they had won, and acted *accordingly*) **2** : CONSEQUENTLY, so (unable to find jobs, many graduates *accordingly* returned to school)

according to *prep* **I** : in agreement or conformity with (lined up *according to* height) **2** : as stated by (*according to* our teacher) **3** : depending on (will succeed or fail *according to* circumstances)

¹ac·cor·di·on \ə-'kord-ē-ən\ *n* : a portable keyboard wind instrument in which the wind is forced past metallic reeds by means of a hand-operated bellows [German *akkordion*] — **ac·cor·di·on·ist** \-ē-ə-nəst\ *n*

²accordion *adj* : folding or creased or hinged to fold like an accordion (*accordion* doors)

ac·cost \ə-'kost\ *vt* : to approach and speak first to often in a challenging or aggressive way [Middle French *accoster*, derived from Latin *ad-* + *costa* "rib, side"]

¹ac·count \ə-'kaunt\ *n* **I** : a chronological record of debits and credits covering transactions involving a particular item, person, or concern **2** : a collection of items to be balanced **3** : an explanation of one's conduct **4 a** : a list of charged purchases and credits pre-

accipiter

¹accordion

\ə\ abut	\ng\ sing
\ər\ further	\ō\ bone
\a\ mat	\o\ saw
\ā\ take	\oi\ coin
\ä\ cot, cart	\th\ thin
\aú\ out	\th\ this
\ch\ chin	\ü\ food
\e\ pet	\ú\ foot
\ē\ easy	\y\ yet
\g\ go	\yü\ few
\i\ tip	\yú\ cure
\ī\ life	\zh\ vision
\j\ job	

sented periodically **b** : the transactions between a business and an individual customer **5 a** : VALUE, IMPORTANCE ⟨a person of little *account*⟩ **b** : ESTEEM ⟨held in high *account*⟩ **6** : PROFIT, ADVANTAGE ⟨used our knowledge to good *account*⟩ **7 a** : a statement of reasons, causes, or motives **b** : a reason giving rise to an action or other result ⟨on that *account* we refused the offer⟩ **c** : careful thought : CONSIDERATION ⟨take *account* of the unexpected⟩ **8** : a statement of facts or events ⟨newspaper *accounts* of the trial⟩ **9** : HEARSAY, REPORT — usually used in pl. ⟨by all *accounts* a dedicated artist⟩ **10** : a sum of money deposited in a bank and subject to withdrawal by the depositor — **on account** : on credit — **on account of** : for the sake of : by reason of : because of — **on no account** : under no circumstances — **on one's account** : for one's benefit or sake ⟨don't do it just *on my account*⟩

²account *vb* **1** : to think of as ⟨*account* oneself lucky⟩ **2** : to furnish a detailed analysis or a justifying explanation ⟨*account* for your expenditures⟩ **3 a** : to be the reason ⟨poor diet *accounts* for many illnesses⟩ **b** : to bring about the capture or destruction of something ⟨*accounted* for two rabbits⟩ [Middle French *acompter*, from *a-* "ad-" + *compter* "to count"]

ac·count·able \ə-ˈkau̇nt-ə-bəl\ *adj* **1** : responsible for giving an account (as of one's acts) : ANSWERABLE ⟨*accountable* to one's superiors⟩ **2** : capable of being accounted for : EXPLAINABLE — **ac·count·abil·i·ty** \-ˌkau̇nt-ə-ˈbil-ət-ē\ *n* — **ac·count·able·ness** \-ˈkau̇nt-ə-bəl-nəs\ *n* — **ac·count·ably** \-blē\ *adv*

ac·coun·tan·cy \ə-ˈkau̇nt-n-sē\ *n* : the profession or practice of accounting

ac·coun·tant \ə-ˈkau̇nt-nt\ *n* : a person professionally trained in the practice of accounting SYN see BOOKKEEPER

ac·count·ing \ə-ˈkau̇nt-ing\ *n* **1** : the system or practice of recording and analyzing money transactions of a person or business **2** : the action of giving an account ⟨management is required to make an *accounting* to the stockholders⟩

ac·cou·tre *or* **ac·cou·ter** \ə-ˈküt-ər\ *vt* **-cou·tred** *or* **-coutered**; **-cou·tring** *or* **-cou·ter·ing** \-ˈküt-ə-ring, -ˈkü-tring\ : to provide with equipment or furnishings : OUTFIT [French *accoutrer*]

ac·cou·tre·ment *or* **ac·cou·ter·ment** \ə-ˈkü-trə-mənt, -ˈküt-ər-mənt\ *n* **1** : the act of accoutring : the state of being accoutred **2** : an accessory item of clothing or equipment — usually used in pl. **3** : an identifying often superficial characteristic — usually used in pl. ⟨*accoutrements* of power⟩

ac·cred·it \ə-ˈkred-ət\ *vt* **1 a** : to send with credentials and authority to act as an official representative ⟨*accredit* an ambassador to France⟩ **b** : to vouch for as in conformity with a standard **c** : to recognize (an educational institution) as maintaining standards that qualify the graduates for admission to higher or more specialized institutions or for professional practice **2** : CREDIT 3 — **ac·cred·i·ta·tion** \ə-ˌkred-ə-ˈtā-shən\ *n*

ac·cre·tion \ə-ˈkrē-shən\ *n* **1** : the process of growth or enlargement; *esp* : increase by external addition or accumulation **2** : a product or result of accretion [Latin *accretio*, from *accrescere* "to increase", from *ad-* + *crescere* "to grow"] — **ac·cre·tion·ary** \-shə-ˌner-ē\ *adj*

ac·cru·al \ə-ˈkrü-əl\ *n* **1** : the action or process of accruing **2** : something that accrues or has accrued

ac·crue \ə-ˈkrü\ *vb* **1** : to come by way of increase or addition ⟨benefits *accrue* to society from education⟩ **2** : to accumulate over a period of time ⟨*accrued* interest⟩ [Middle French *acreue* "increase", from *acreistre* "to increase", from Latin *accrescere*] — **ac·crue·ment** \-mənt\ *n*

ac·cul·tur·a·tion \ə-ˌkəl-chə-ˈrā-shən\ *n* : modification of the culture of one or more peoples or of an individ-

ual through continuous and prolonged contact with an alien people — **ac·cul·tur·ate** \-ˈkəl-chə-ˌrāt\ *vb*

ac·cu·mu·late \ə-ˈkyü-myə-ˌlāt\ *vb* **1** : to pile up : AMASS ⟨*accumulated* old newspapers⟩ **2** : COLLECT, GATHER ⟨*accumulates* friends easily⟩ **3** : to increase in quantity, number, or amount ⟨rubbish *accumulates* quickly⟩ [Latin *accumulare*, derived from *ad-* + *cumulus* "heap, pile"] □ SYN ACCUMULATE, AMASS mean to collect so as to form a large quantity. ACCUMULATE implies building up by successive small increases ⟨knickknacks *accumulate* dust⟩ AMASS suggests a more vigorous action during a limited time and applies especially to a putting together of something valuable ⟨*amass* a fortune⟩

ac·cu·mu·la·tion \ə-ˌkyü-myə-ˈlā-shən\ *n* **1** : a collecting together : AMASSING **2** : increase or growth by addition especially when continuous or repeated ⟨*accumulation* of interest⟩ **3** : something that has accumulated or has been accumulated

ac·cu·mu·la·tive \ə-ˈkyü-myə-ˌlāt-iv, -lət-\ *adj* : CUMULATIVE — **ac·cu·mu·la·tive·ly** *adv* — **ac·cu·mu·la·tive·ness** *n*

ac·cu·mu·la·tor \ə-ˈkyü-myə-ˌlāt-ər\ *n* : one that accumulates; *esp* : a part (as in a computer) where numbers are totaled or stored

ac·cu·ra·cy \ˈak-yə-rə-sē\ *n, pl* **-cies** **1** : freedom from mistake or error : CORRECTNESS **2 a** : conformity to a standard : EXACTNESS **b** : degree of conformity of a measure to a standard or a true value

ac·cu·rate \ˈak-yə-rət\ *adj* **1** : free from mistakes especially as the result of care **2** : conforming exactly to truth or to a standard : EXACT ⟨*accurate* instruments⟩ [Latin *accuratus*, from *accurare* "to take care of", from *ad-* + *cura* "care"] SYN see CORRECT — **ac·cu·rate·ly** \-yə-rət-lē, -yərt-\ *adv* — **ac·cu·rate·ness** \-nəs\ *n*

ac·cursed \ə-ˈkərst, -ˈkər-səd\ *or* **ac·curst** \ə-ˈkərst\ *adj* **1** : being under a curse **2** : DETESTABLE, DAMNABLE — **ac·curs·ed·ly** \-ˈkər-səd-lē\ *adv* — **ac·curs·ed·ness** \-ˈkər-səd-nəs\ *n*

ac·cus·al \ə-ˈkyü-zəl\ *n* : ACCUSATION

ac·cu·sa·tion \ˌak-yə-ˈzā-shən\ *n* **1** : the act of accusing : the state or fact of being accused **2** : a charge of wrongdoing

ac·cu·sa·tive \ə-ˈkyü-zət-iv\ *adj* **1** : of, relating to, or constituting the grammatical case that marks the direct object of a verb or the object of any of several prepositions — compare OBJECTIVE **2** : ACCUSATORY — **accusative** *n*

ac·cu·sa·to·ry \ə-ˈkyü-zə-ˌtōr-ē, -ˌtȯr-\ *adj* : expressing accusation

ac·cuse \ə-ˈkyüz\ *vb* : to charge with a fault or especially with a criminal offense [Old French *acuser*, from Latin *accusare* "to call to account", from *ad-* + *causa* "lawsuit, cause"] — **ac·cus·er** *n* — **ac·cus·ing·ly** \-ˈkyü-zing-lē\ *adv*

ac·cused \ə-ˈkyüzd\ *n, pl* **accused** : one charged with an offense; *esp* : the defendant in a criminal case

ac·cus·tom \ə-ˈkəs-təm\ *vt* : to make familiar through use or experience : HABITUATE

ac·cus·tomed \-təmd\ *adj* **1** : familiar through use or long experience **2** : being in the habit or custom ⟨*accustomed* to making decisions⟩ SYN see USUAL

¹ace \ˈās\ *n* **1 a** : a die face or domino end marked with one spot **b** : a playing card bearing in its center one large pip **2** : a very small amount or degree ⟨came within an *ace* of winning⟩ **3** : a point scored on a stroke (as in tennis) that an opponent fails to touch **4** : a golf hole made in one stroke **5** : a combat pilot who has brought down at least five enemy airplanes **6** : one that excels at something [Old French *as*, from Latin, "unit, a copper coin"]

²ace *vt* **1** : to score an ace against (as a tennis opponent) **2** : to earn a grade of A on (an examination)

³ace *adj* : of first or high rank or quality ⟨an *ace* reporter⟩

acel·lu·lar \'ā-'sel-yə-lər\ *adj* : not made up of cells

-a·ceous \'ā-shəs\ *adj suffix* **1** : characterized by : consisting of : having the nature or form of ⟨carbon*aceous*⟩ ⟨sapon*aceous*⟩ **2** : of or relating to a group of animals characterized by (such) a form or (such) a feature ⟨cet*aceous*⟩ ⟨test*aceous*⟩ [Latin *-aceus*]

acerb \ə-'sərb, a-\ *adj* : ACERBIC [Latin *acerbus*, from *acer* "sharp"]

acer·bic \ə-'sər-bik\ *adj* : sharp or biting in temper, mood, or tone — **acer·bi·cal·ly** \-bi-kə-lē, -klē\ *adv*

acer·bi·ty \ə-'sər-bət-ē\ *n, pl* **-ties** : sharpness of temper, manner, or tone

acet- *or* **aceto-** *combining form* : acetic acid : acetic ⟨*acetyl*⟩ [Latin *acetum* "vinegar"]

ac·e·tab·u·lum \,as-ə-'tab-yə-ləm\ *n, pl* **-lums** *or* **-la** \-lə\ : a cup-shaped socket (as in the hipbone) [Latin, literally, "vinegar cup"]

ac·et·al·de·hyde \,as-ə-'tal-də-,hīd\ *n* : a colorless volatile water-soluble liquid compound C_2H_4O used chiefly in making organic chemicals

ac·et·amin·o·phen \,as-ət-ə-'min-ə-fən\ *n* : a crystalline compound $C_8H_9NO_2$ used in chemical synthesis and in medicine to relieve pain and fever

ac·et·an·i·lide *or* **ac·et·an·i·lid** \,as-ə-'tan-l-,īd, -l-əd\ *n* : a white crystalline compound C_8H_9NO made from aniline and acetic acid and used especially to check pain or fever

ac·e·tate \'as-ə-,tāt\ *n* **1** : a salt or ester of acetic acid **2** : cellulose acetate or one of its products **3** : a phonograph record made of an acetate or coated with cellulose acetate

ace·tic \ə-'sēt-ik\ *adj* : of, relating to, or producing acetic acid or vinegar [Latin *acetum* "vinegar", from *acēre* "to be sour"]

acetic acid *n* : a colorless pungent liquid acid $C_2H_4O_2$ that is the chief acid of vinegar and that is used especially in synthesis (as of plastics)

ac·e·tone \'as-ə-,tōn\ *n* : a volatile fragrant colorless flammable liquid compound C_3H_6O used chiefly as a solvent and in organic synthesis

ace·tyl \ə-'sēt-l\ *n* : the radical CH_3CO of acetic acid

ace·tyl·cho·line \ə-,sēt-l-'kō-,lēn\ *n* : a compound $C_7H_{17}NO_3$ released at autonomic nerve endings that functions in the transmission of nerve impulses

ace·tyl·cho·lin·es·ter·ase \-,kō-lə-'nes-tə-,rās, -,rāz\ *n* : an enzyme that promotes the hydrolysis of acetylcholine

ace·tyl–coA \ə-,sēt-l-,kō-'ā\ *n* : ACETYL COENZYME A

acetyl coenzyme A *n* : a compound $C_{25}H_{38}N_7O_{17}P_3S$ formed as an intermediate in metabolism and active as a coenzyme in biological reactions involving addition of an acetyl radical

acet·y·lene \ə-'set-l-ən, -l-,ēn\ *n* : a colorless gaseous hydrocarbon C_2H_2 made especially by the action of water on calcium carbide and used chiefly as a fuel in welding and soldering and in organic synthesis

ace·tyl·sal·i·cyl·ic acid \ə-,sēt-l-,sal-ə-,sil-ik-\ *n* : ASPIRIN 1

¹Achae·an \ə-'kē-ən, -'kā-\ *adj* : of or relating to a group of city-states in the southern part of ancient Greece forming a political confederation about 280 B.C.

²Achaean *n* **1** : one of a Greek people dominant on the Greek mainland from 1600 to 1100 B.C. **2** : a Greek of the Homeric period

¹ache \'āk\ *vi* **1** : to suffer a usually dull persistent pain **2** : to long earnestly : YEARN [Old English *acan*]

²ache *n* : a usually dull persistent pain — **achy** \'ā-kē\ *adj*

achene \ə-'kēn\ *n* : a small dry one-seeded fruit (as of the buttercup) that ripens without bursting its sheath [²a- + Greek *chainein* "to yawn"]

achieve \ə-'chēv\ *vb* **1** : to carry out successfully : ACCOMPLISH ⟨*achieved* our purpose⟩ **2** : to get by effort ⟨*achieve* greatness⟩ [Middle French *achever*, from *a-* "ad-" + *chief* "head"] — **achiev·able** \-'chē-və-bəl\ *adj* — **achiev·er** \-ər\ *n*

achieve·ment \-mənt\ *n* **1** : the act of achieving **2** : something achieved especially by great effort or persistence ⟨heroic *achievements* of the early settlers⟩ SYN see FEAT

Achil·les' heel \ə-'kil-ēz-\ *n* : a vulnerable point [from the legend that Achilles was vulnerable only in the heel]

Achilles tendon *n* : the strong tendon joining the muscles in the calf of the leg to the bone of the heel

achon·dro·pla·sia \,ā-,kän-drə-'plā-zhē-ə, -zhə\ *n* : failure of normal development of cartilage resulting in dwarfism [²a- + Greek *chondros* "grain, cartilage"] — **achon·dro·plas·tic** \-'plas-tik\ *adj*

ach·ro·mat·ic \,ak-rə-'mat-ik\ *adj* **1** : giving an image practically free from colors not in the object ⟨*achromatic* lens⟩ **2** : being black, gray, or white : COLORLESS

¹ac·id \'as-əd\ *adj* **1** : sour, sharp, or biting to the taste : resembling vinegar in taste **2** : sour in temper : CROSS ⟨*acid* remarks⟩ **3** : of, relating to, or having the characteristics of an acid [Latin *acidus*, from *acēre* "to be sour"] SYN see SOUR — **ac·id·ly** *adv* — **ac·id·ness** *n*

²acid *n* **1** : a sour substance **2** : any of various typically water-soluble and sour compounds that are capable of reacting with a base to form a salt, that redden litmus, that are hydrogen-containing molecules or ions able to give up a proton to a base, or that are substances able to accept an unshared pair of electrons from a base **3** : LSD

ac·id–fast \'as-əd-,fast\ *adj* : not easily decolorized by acids

acid·ic \ə-'sid-ik\ *adj* **1** : acid-forming **2** : ACID

acid·i·fy \ə-'sid-ə-,fī\ *vb* **-fied; -fy·ing** **1** : to make or become acid **2** : to change into an acid — **acid·i·fi·ca·tion** \ə-,sid-ə-fə-'kā-shən\ *n*

acid·i·ty \ə-'sid-ət-ē\ *n, pl* **-ties** **1** : the quality, state, or degree of being acid : TARTNESS **2** : the quality or state of being abnormally or excessively acid : HYPERACIDITY

ac·i·do·sis \,as-ə-'dō-səs\ *n* : an abnormal state of reduced alkalinity of the blood and of the body tissues — **ac·i·dot·ic** \-'dät-ik\ *adj*

acid rain *n* : rain with increased acidity that is caused by environmental factors (as atmospheric pollutants)

acid test *n* : a severe or crucial test

acid·u·late \ə-'sij-ə-,lāt\ *vt* : to make acid or slightly acid — **acid·u·la·tion** \ə-,sij-ə-'lā-shən\ *n*

acid·u·lous \ə-'sij-ə-ləs\ *adj* : acid in taste or manner : HARSH ⟨an *acidulous* remark⟩

ack–ack \'ak-,ak\ *n* : an antiaircraft gun; *also* : antiaircraft fire [British signalmen's pronunciation of *AA*, abbreviation of *antiaircraft*]

ac·knowl·edge \ik-'näl-ij, ak-\ *vt* **1** : to admit the truth or existence of ⟨*acknowledged* our mistake⟩ **2** : to recognize the rights, authority, or status of **3** : to make known that something has been received or noticed ⟨*acknowledge* a letter⟩ [ac- (as in *accord*) + knowledge] □ SYN ACKNOWLEDGE, ADMIT, CONFESS mean to disclose against one's will or inclination. ACKNOWLEDGE implies disclosing what has been or might be denied or concealed; ADMIT implies some degree of reluctance in disclosing or conceding; CONFESS implies admitting a weakness, failure, or guilt usually under compulsion.

ac·knowl·edged \-ijd\ *adj* : generally recognized or accepted ⟨the *acknowledged* leader of the group⟩ — **ac·knowl·edged·ly** \-ijd-lē, -ij-əd-\ *adv*

ac·knowl·edg·ment *or* **ac·knowl·edge·ment** \ik-'näl-ij-mənt, ak-\ *n* **1 a** : the act of acknowledging **b** : recognition or favorable notice of an act or achievement **2** : a thing done or given in recognition of something received

\ə\	abut	\ng\	sing
\ər\	further	\ō\	bone
\a\	mat	\ȯ\	saw
\ā\	take	\ȯi\	coin
\ä\	cot, cart	\th\	thin
\au̇\	out	\th\	this
\ch\	chin	\ü\	food
\e\	pet	\u̇\	foot
\ē\	easy	\y\	yet
\g\	go	\yü\	few
\i\	tip	\yu̇\	cure
\ī\	life	\zh\	vision
\j\	job		

ac·me \'ak-mē\ *n* : the highest point : PEAK ⟨the *acme* of a scientist's ambition⟩ [Greek *akmē*]

ac·ne \'ak-nē\ *n* : a skin disorder caused by inflammation of skin glands and hair follicles and characterized by pimples especially on the face [Greek *aknē* "eruption on the face", from *akmē*, literally, "point"]

ac·o·lyte \'ak-ə-,līt\ *n* 1 : a person who assists the clergyman in a service 2 : one that attends or assists : FOLLOWER [Medieval Latin *acoluthus*, from Greek *akolouthos* "following", from *a-, ba-* "same" + *keleuthos* "path"]

ac·o·nite \'ak-ə-,nīt\ *n* 1 : any of a genus of poisonous usually blue-flowered or purple-flowered plants related to the buttercups — compare MONKSHOOD 2 : a drug obtained from the common Old World monkshood [Greek *akoniton*]

acorn \'ā-,kȯrn, -kərn\ *n* : the nut of an oak tree [Old English *æcern*]

acorn squash *n* : an acorn-shaped dark green winter squash with a ridged surface and sweet yellow to orange flesh

acorn worm *n* : any of a group of burrowing marine animals resembling worms that have an acorn-shaped proboscis and are usually classed with the chordates

acorn: *top* white oak, *middle* black oak, *bottom* red oak

acous·tic \ə-'kü-stik\ *adj* 1 : of or relating to the sense or organs of hearing, to sound, or to the science of sounds: as **a** : deadening or absorbing sound ⟨*acoustic* tile⟩ **b** : operated by or utilizing sound waves 2 : of, relating to, or being a musical instrument whose sound is not electronically modified ⟨an *acoustic* guitar⟩ [Greek *akoustikos* "of hearing", from *akouein* "to hear"] — **acous·ti·cal** \-sti-kəl\ *adj* — **acous·ti·cal·ly** \-sti-kə-lē, -klē\ *adv*

ac·ous·ti·cian \,ak-,ü-'stish-ən, ə-,kü-\ *n* : a specialist in acoustics

acous·tics \ə-'kü-stiks\ *n sing or pl* 1 : the science dealing with sound 2 *also* **acous·tic** \-stik\ : the qualities in a room or hall that make it easy or hard for a person in it to hear distinctly

ac·quaint \ə-'kwānt\ *vt* 1 : to cause to know socially ⟨became *acquainted* through mutual friends⟩ 2 : to make familiar ⟨*acquainted* us with our duties⟩ [Old French *acointier*, derived from Late Latin *accognoscere* "to know perfectly", from Latin *ad-* + *cognoscere* "to know"]

ac·quain·tance \ə-'kwānt-ns\ *n* 1 : knowledge gained by personal observation, contact, or experience ⟨had some *acquaintance* with the subject⟩ 2 : a person one knows but not intimately — **ac·quain·tance·ship** \-,ship\ *n*

ac·qui·esce \,ak-wē-'es\ *vi* : to accept, agree, or comply silently or passively [French *acquiescer*, from Latin *acquiescere*, from *ad-* + *quiescere* "to be quiet"] — **ac·qui·es·cence** \-'es-ns\ *n*

ac·qui·es·cent \-'es-nt\ *adj* : acquiescing or disposed to acquiesce — **ac·qui·es·cent·ly** *adv*

ac·quire \ə-'kwīr\ *vt* 1 : to come into possession of especially by one's own efforts : GAIN ⟨*acquired* great wealth⟩ 2 **a** : to come to have as a characteristic, trait, or ability often by sustained effort ⟨*acquired* good study skills⟩ **b** : to develop after birth usually as a result of environmental forces ⟨an *acquired* disease⟩ 3 : to locate and hold (a desired object) in a detector ⟨*acquire* a target by radar⟩ [Middle French *aquerre*, from Latin *acquirere*, from *ad-* + *quaerere* "to seek"] — **ac·quir·able** \-'kwī-rə-bəl\ *adj*

ac·quire·ment \-'kwīr-mənt\ *n* 1 : the act of acquiring 2 : an attainment of mind or body usually resulting from continued effort ⟨the *acquirements* expected of a high-school graduate⟩

ac·qui·si·tion \,ak-wə-'zish-ən\ *n* 1 : the act of acquiring ⟨the *acquisition* of property⟩ 2 : something acquired or gained ⟨the book was a recent *acquisition*⟩ [Latin *acquisitio*, from *acquirere* "to acquire"]

ac·quis·i·tive \ə-'kwiz-ət-iv\ *adj* : strongly desirous of acquiring — **ac·quis·i·tive·ly** *adv* — **ac·quis·i·tive·ness** *n*

ac·quit \ə-'kwit\ *vt* **ac·quit·ted; ac·quit·ting** 1 : to set free or discharge completely (as from an obligation or accusation) ⟨the court *acquitted* the prisoner⟩ 2 : to conduct (oneself) usually satisfactorily ⟨*acquitted* themselves well⟩ [Old French *aquiter*, from *a-* "ad-" + *quite* "free, quit"] — **ac·quit·ter** *n*

ac·quit·tal \ə-'kwit-l\ *n* : the setting free of a person from the charge of an offense by verdict, sentence, or other legal process

ac·quit·tance \-ns\ *n* : a document (as a receipt) showing a release from an obligation

acr- *or* **acro-** *combining form* 1 : beginning : end ⟨*acro*nym⟩ 2 **a** : peak : height ⟨*acro*phobia⟩ **b** : extremity of the body ⟨*acro*megaly⟩ [Greek *akros* "topmost, extreme"]

acre \'ā-kər\ *n* 1 *pl* : LANDS, ESTATE 2 : a unit of area equal to 43,560 square feet (about 4047 square meters) — see MEASURE table 3 : a broad expanse or great quantity [Old English *æcer*]

acre·age \'ā-kə-rij, -krij\ *n* : area in acres : ACRES

acre-foot \'ā-kər-'fu̇t\ *n* : the volume (as of irrigation water) that would cover one acre to a depth of one foot and that is equal to 43,560 cubic feet (about 1233 cubic meters)

ac·rid \'ak-rəd\ *adj* 1 : biting or bitter in taste or odor 2 : bitterly irritating to the feelings ⟨an *acrid* remark⟩ [Latin *acr-, acer* "sharp"] — **acrid·i·ty** \a-'krid-ət-ē, ə-\ *n* — **ac·rid·ly** \'ak-rəd-lē\ *adv* — **ac·rid·ness** *n*

ac·ri·mo·ni·ous \,ak-rə-'mō-nē-əs\ *adj* : marked by acrimony : BITTER, RANCOROUS ⟨an *acrimonious* dispute⟩ — **ac·ri·mo·ni·ous·ly** *adv* — **ac·ri·mo·ni·ous·ness** *n*

ac·ri·mo·ny \'ak-rə-,mō-nē\ *n, pl* -**nies** : harsh or biting sharpness especially of words, manner, or disposition [Latin *acrimonia*, from *acr-, acer* "sharp"]

ac·ro·bat \'ak-rə-,bat\ *n* 1 : one that performs feats requiring agility and balance 2 : one adept at swiftly changing position or viewpoint [Greek *akrobatēs*, from *akros* "topmost" + *bainein* "to step, go"] — **ac·ro·bat·ic** \,ak-rə-'bat-ik\ *adj* — **ac·ro·bat·i·cal·ly** \-'bat-i-kə-lē, -klē\ *adv*

ac·ro·bat·ics \,ak-rə-'bat-iks\ *n sing or pl* 1 : the art or performance of an acrobat 2 : a striking performance involving great agility or maneuverability ⟨the soprano's vocal *acrobatics*⟩

ac·ro·meg·a·ly \,ak-rō-'meg-ə-lē\ *n* : a disorder caused by excessive secretion of the pituitary gland and marked by progressive enlargement of hands, feet, and face [*acr-* + Greek *megal-, megas* "large"] — **ac·ro·me·gal·ic** \-mə-'gal-ik\ *adj*

ac·ro·nym \'ak-rə-,nim\ *n* : a word (as *radar*) formed from the initial letter or letters of each of the successive parts or major parts of a compound term [*acr-* + -*onym* (as in *homonym*)]

ac·ro·pho·bia \,ak-rə-'fō-bē-ə\ *n* : abnormal dread of being at a great height

acrop·o·lis \ə-'kräp-ə-ləs\ *n* : the upper fortified part of an ancient Greek city [Greek *akropolis*, from *akros* "topmost" + *polis* "city"]

¹across \ə-'krȯs\ *adv* 1 : so as to reach or pass from one side to the other ⟨boards sawed directly *across*⟩ 2 : to or on the opposite side ⟨got *across* in a boat⟩ 3 : so as to be understandable, acceptable, or successful ⟨put a point *across*⟩ [Anglo-French *an crois-*, from *an* "in" + *crois* "cross", from Latin *crux*]

²across *prep* 1 : to or on the opposite side of ⟨*across* the street⟩ 2 : so as to intersect or pass at an angle ⟨lay one stick *across* another⟩ 3 : into an accidental meeting or contact with ⟨ran *across* an old friend⟩

across-the-board *adj* 1 : placed in combination to win, place, or show ⟨an *across-the-board* bet⟩ 2 : including or affecting all classes or categories ⟨an *across-the-board* wage increase⟩

acros·tic \ə-'kros-tik, -'kras-\ *n* : a composition usually in verse in which sets of letters (as the initial or final letters of the lines) taken in order form a word or phrase or a regular sequence of letters of the alphabet [Greek *akrostichis,* from *akros* "extreme" + *stichos* "line"] — **acrostic** *adj* — **acros·ti·cal·ly** \-ti-kə-lē, -klē\ *adv*

¹**acryl·ic** \ə-'kril-ik\ *adj* : of or relating to acrylic acid or its derivatives ⟨*acrylic* polymers⟩ [derived from Latin *acr-, acer* "sharp"]

²**acrylic** *n* **1 a** : ACRYLIC RESIN **b** : a paint in which the vehicle is acrylic resin **2** : ACRYLIC FIBER

acrylic acid *n* : an unsaturated liquid acid $C_3H_4O_2$ that polymerizes readily to form useful products (as a constituent of paint)

acrylic fiber *n* : a quick-drying synthetic textile fiber made by the polymerization of acrylonitrile

acrylic resin *n* : a glassy synthetic organic plastic used for cast and molded parts or as coatings and adhesives

ac·ry·lo·ni·trile \,ak-rə-lō-'nī-trəl, -,trēl\ *n* : a colorless flammable liquid C_3H_3N used chiefly in polymerization

¹**act** \'akt\ *n* **1** : something that is done : DEED ⟨an *act* of kindness⟩ **2** : the doing of something ⟨caught in the *act* of murder⟩ **3** : a law made by a governing body (as a legislature) ⟨an *act* of Congress⟩ **4 a** : one of the main divisions of a play or opera **b** : one of the successive parts of a variety show or circus **5** : a display of insincere behavior : PRETENSE [Latin *actus* "action" and *actum* "thing done", both derived from *agere* "to do"]

²**act** *vb* **1** : to represent or perform especially on the stage **2** : to play the part of ⟨*act* the villain⟩ **3 a** : to behave in a manner suitable to ⟨*act* your age⟩ **b** : to conduct oneself ⟨*act* like a fool⟩ **4** : PRETEND 2 **5** : to take action : MOVE ⟨think before you *act*⟩ **6 a** : to perform a specified function : SERVE ⟨trees *acting* as a windbreak⟩ **b** : to produce an effect : WORK ⟨wait for a medicine to *act*⟩ **7** : to make a decision ⟨*act* on a proposal⟩ — **act·abil·i·ty** \,ak-tə-'bil-ət-ē\ *n* — **act·able** \'ak-tə-bəl\ *adj*

ACTH \,ā-,sē-,tē-'āch\ *n* : a protein hormone of the anterior lobe of the pituitary gland that stimulates the cortex of the adrenal gland [*a*dreno*c*ortico*t*rophic *h*ormone]

ac·tin \'ak-tən\ *n* : a protein of muscle that is active in muscular contraction [Latin *actus* "action"]

¹**act·ing** \'ak-ting\ *adj* : serving temporarily or in place of another ⟨*acting* president⟩

²**acting** *n* **1** : the art or practice of representing a character on a stage or before cameras **2** : affected behavior

ac·ti·nide \'ak-tə-,nīd\ *n* : a heavy radioactive metallic element in the series of increasing atomic numbers beginning with actinium or thorium and ending with lawrencium

ac·ti·nism \'ak-tə-,niz-əm\ *n* : the property of radiant energy by which chemical changes are produced — **ac·tin·ic** \ak-'tin-ik\ *adj*

ac·tin·i·um \ak-'tin-ē-əm\ *n* : a radioactive metallic element found especially in pitchblende [Greek *aktin-, aktis* "ray"] — see ELEMENT table

ac·ti·no·my·cete \,ak-tə-nō-'mī-,sēt, -mī-'sēt\ *n* : any of an order (Actinomycetales) of filamentous or rod-shaped bacteria including soil saprophytes and disease producers [Greek *aktis* "ray" + *mykēs* "fungus"]

ac·ti·no·my·co·sis \,ak-tə-nō-mī-'kō-səs\ *n* : infection with or disease caused by actinomycetes — **ac·ti·no·my·cot·ic** \-'kät-ik\ *adj*

ac·tion \'ak-shən\ *n* **1** : a proceeding in a court of justice by which one demands or enforces one's right or the redress or punishment of a wrong **2** : the working of one thing on another so as to produce a change ⟨the *action* of acids on metals⟩ **3** : the doing of something usually in stages or with the possibility of continuation ⟨the *action* of singing⟩ **4 a** : a thing done : DEED **b**

pl : BEHAVIOR, CONDUCT **c** : readiness to engage in daring activity : INITIATIVE ⟨a person of *action*⟩ **5** : combat in war **6** : the unfolding of the events of a drama or work of fiction : PLOT **7** : an operating mechanism ⟨the *action* of a firearm⟩ **8** : an area or state of vigorous activity ⟨where the *action* is⟩

ac·tion·able \'ak-shə-nə-bəl, -shnə-\ *adj* : subject to or giving ground for a legal action or lawsuit ⟨*actionable* negligence⟩ — **ac·tion·ably** \-blē\ *adv*

ac·ti·vate \'ak-tə-,vāt\ *vt* : to make active or more active: as **a** : to make (as molecules) reactive **b** : to make (a substance) radioactive **c** : to treat (as carbon or alumina) so as to improve adsorptive properties **d** : to aerate (sewage) so as to favor the growth of organisms that cause decomposition **e** : to place on active duty ⟨*activate* the reserves⟩ — **ac·ti·va·tion** \,ak-tə-'vā-shən\ *n* — **ac·ti·va·tor** \'ak-tə-,vāt-ər\ *n*

ac·tive \'ak-tiv\ *adj* **1** : characterized by action rather than contemplation **2** : producing, requiring, or involving action or movement ⟨an *active* sport⟩ **3** : of, relating to, or constituting a verb form or voice indicating that the person or thing represented by the grammatical subject performs the action represented by the verb ⟨*hit* in "they hit the ball" is *active*⟩ **4** : quick in physical movement : LIVELY **5 a** : disposed to action : ENERGETIC ⟨*active* interest⟩ **b** : engaged in an action or activity : PARTICIPATING ⟨an *active* club member⟩ **c** : marked by vigorous activity : BUSY ⟨an *active* mind⟩ **6** : involving full-time service especially in the armed forces ⟨*active* duty⟩ **7** : marked by present action, operation, movement, or use ⟨an *active* account⟩ ⟨a student's *active* vocabulary⟩ **8 a** : capable of acting or reacting **b** : tending to progress or increase ⟨*active* tuberculosis⟩ — **ac·tive·ly** *adv* — **ac·tive·ness** *n*

active immunity *n* : immunity produced by the individual when exposed to an antigen — compare PASSIVE IMMUNITY

active transport *n* : movement of a substance by expenditure of energy through a gradient (as across a cell membrane) in concentration or electrical potential opposite to the direction of normal diffusion

ac·tiv·ism \'ak-ti-,viz-əm\ *n* : a doctrine or practice that emphasizes vigorous action (as a mass demonstration) for political ends — **ac·tiv·ist** \-vəst\ *n or adj*

ac·tiv·i·ty \ak-'tiv-ət-ē\ *n, pl* -**ties 1** : the quality or state of being active **2** : vigorous or energetic action : LIVELINESS **3 a** : natural or normal function **b** (1) : a process that an organism carries on or participates in by virtue of being alive (2) : a similar process actually or potentially involving mental function **4 a** : PURSUIT 2 **b** : a form of organized, supervised, often extracurricular recreation

act of God : an extraordinary interruption of the usual course of events by a natural cause (as a flood or earthquake) that could not reasonably have been foreseen or prevented

ac·to·my·o·sin \,ak-tə-'mī-ə-sən\ *n* : a contractile complex of actin and myosin that functions together with ATP in muscular contraction

ac·tor \'ak-tər\ *n* **1 a** : one that acts : DOER **b** : one that acts a part; *esp* : a theatrical performer **2** : PARTICIPANT

ac·tress \'ak-trəs\ *n* : a woman who is an actor

Acts \'aks, 'akts\ *or* **Acts of the Apostles** *n* — see BIBLE table

ac·tu·al \'ak-chə-wəl, -chəl; 'aksh-wəl\ *adj* **1 a** : existing in fact : EXISTENT ⟨our *actual* intentions⟩ **b** : really acted on or carried out ⟨in *actual* life⟩ ⟨the *actual* conditions⟩ **2** : not false : GENUINE **3** : present or active at the time [Middle French *actuel,* derived from Latin *actus* "act"] SYN see REAL

ac·tu·al·i·ty \,ak-chə-'wal-ət-ē\ *n, pl* -**ties 1** : the quality or state of being actual **2** : something that is actual ⟨face the *actualities* of the situation⟩

ac·tu·al·ize \'ak-chə-wə-,līz, -chə-,līz, 'aksh-wə-\ *vb* : to make or become actual — **ac·tu·al·iza·tion** \,ak-chə-wə-lə-'zā-shən, -chə-lə-, ,aksh-wə-\ *n*

ac·tu·al·ly \'ak-chə-wə-lē, -chə-lē, 'aksh-wə-, 'aksh-lē\ *adv* : in fact : in truth : REALLY ⟨can *actually* read Latin⟩ ⟨*actually,* I haven't done it yet⟩

ac·tu·ary \'ak-chə-,wer-ē\ *n, pl* **-ar·ies** : one that calculates insurance and annuity premiums, reserves, and dividends [Latin *actuarius* "one who keeps accounts", from *actum* "thing done, record"] — **ac·tu·ar·i·al** \,ak-chə-'wer-ē-əl\ *adj* — **ac·tu·ar·i·al·ly** \-ē-ə-lē\ *adv*

ac·tu·ate \'ak-chə-,wāt\ *vt* **1** : to put into action ⟨the windmill *actuates* the pump⟩ **2** : to move to action : arouse to activity ⟨the students were *actuated* by the hope of winning prizes⟩ [Medieval Latin *actuare,* from Latin *actus* "act"] SYN see MOVE — **ac·tu·a·tion** \,ak-chə-'wā-shən\ *n*

act up *vi* : to act or function in an unruly, abnormal, or annoying way

acu·ity \ə-'kyü-ət-ē\ *n* : keenness of perception : SHARPNESS ⟨visual *acuity*⟩ [Middle French *acuité,* derived from Latin *acutus* "sharp"]

acu·men \ə-'kyü-mən\ *n* : keenness of insight especially in practical matters : SHREWDNESS [Latin, literally, "point", from *acuere* "to make sharp"]

acu·punc·ture \'ak-yù-,pəng-chər, -,pəngk-\ *n* : an originally Chinese practice of puncturing the body (as with needles) to cure disease or relieve pain [Latin *acus* "needle" + English *puncture*]

acute \ə-'kyüt\ *adj* **1 a** : measuring less than a right angle ⟨*acute* angle⟩ **b** : composed of acute angles ⟨*acute* triangle⟩ **2 a** : marked by keen discernment or intellectual perception especially of subtle distinctions : PENETRATING **b** : responsive to slight impressions or influences ⟨*acute* observer⟩ **3** : marked by sharpness or severity ⟨an *acute* pain⟩ **4** : HIGH, SHRILL ⟨an *acute* sound⟩ **5 a** : having a sudden onset and short duration ⟨*acute* disease⟩ **b** : being at or near a turning point : URGENT, CRITICAL ⟨an *acute* situation that may lead to war⟩ **6** : of, marked by, or being an accent mark having the form ´ [Latin *acutus* "sharp", from *acuere* "to sharpen", from *acus* "needle"] SYN see SHARP — **acute·ly** *adv* — **acute·ness** *n*

ad \'ad\ *n* : ADVERTISEMENT 2

ad- *or* **ac-** *or* **af-** *or* **ag-** *or* **al-** *or* **ap-** *or* **as-** *or* **at-** *prefix* **1** : to : toward — usually **ac-** before *c, k,* or *q* ⟨*ac*culturation⟩ and **af-** before *f* and **ag-** before *g* and **al-** before *l* ⟨*al*literation⟩ and **ap-** before *p* and **as-** before *s* and **at-** before *t* ⟨*at*tune⟩ and **ad-** before other sounds but sometimes **ad-** even before one of the listed consonants ⟨*ad*sorb⟩ **2** : near : adjacent to — in this sense always **ad-** ⟨*ad*renal⟩ [Latin, from *ad* "to"]

-ad \,ad, əd\ *adv suffix* : in the direction of : toward ⟨caud*ad*⟩ [Latin *ad* "to"]

ad·age \'ad-ij\ *n* : a saying often in metaphorical form that embodies a common observation [Middle French, from Latin *adagium*]

¹**ada·gio** \ə-'däj-ō, -'däj-ē-,ō, -'däzh-\ *adv or adj* : in an easy graceful manner : SLOWLY — used chiefly as a direction in music [Italian, from *ad* "to" + *agio* "ease"]

²**adagio** *n, pl* **-gi·os** **1** : a musical composition or movement in adagio tempo **2** : a ballet duet by a man and woman or a trio of dancers displaying difficult feats of balance, lifting, or spinning

Adam *adj* : of or relating to an 18th century style of furniture characterized by straight lines, surface decoration, and conventional designs (as festooned garlands and medallions) [Robert *Adam,* died 1792, and James *Adam,* died 1794, Scottish designers]

¹**ad·a·mant** \'ad-ə-mənt *also* -,mant\ *n* **1** : a stone believed to be of impenetrable hardness **2** : an extremely hard substance [Old French, from Latin *adamas* "hardest metal, diamond", from Greek]

²**adamant** *adj* : unshakable or immovable especially in opposition : UNYIELDING — **ad·a·man·cy** \-mən-sē\ *n* — **ad·a·mant·ly** *adv*

addax

ad·a·man·tine \,ad-ə-'man-,tēn, -,tīn\ *adj* **1** : made of or having the quality of adamant **2** : rigidly firm : UNYIELDING **3** : resembling the diamond in hardness or luster

Ad·am's apple \'ad-əmz-\ *n* : the projection in the front of the neck formed by the largest cartilage of the larynx

adapt \ə-'dapt\ *vb* : to make or become suitable; *esp* : to change so as to fit a new or specific use or situation ⟨*adapt* to life in a new school⟩ ⟨*adapt* the novel for children⟩ [Latin *adaptare,* derived from *ad-* + *aptus* "apt, fit"] — **adapt·abil·i·ty** \-,dap-tə-'bil-ət-ē\ *n* — **adapt·able** \-'dap-tə-bəl\ *adj* □ SYN ADAPT, ADJUST, ACCOMMODATE, CONFORM mean to bring one into correspondence with another. ADAPT implies suiting or fitting by modification and may suggest pliability or readiness; ADJUST implies bringing into close or exact correspondence; ACCOMMODATE implies adapting or adjusting to by yielding or compromising; CONFORM implies bringing or coming into accord with a pattern or principle.

ad·ap·ta·tion \,ad-,ap-'tā-shən, -əp-\ *n* **1** : the act or process of adapting : the state of being adapted **2** : adjustment to environmental conditions: as **a** : adjustment of a sense organ to the intensity or quality of stimulation **b** : inherited modification of an organism that increases its chances for survival in its environment; *also* : a change or structure resulting from such modification **3** : something that is adapted; *esp* : a composition rewritten into a new form ⟨the movie is an *adaptation* of the book⟩ — **ad·ap·ta·tion·al** \-shnəl, -shən-l\ *adj* — **ad·ap·ta·tion·al·ly** \-ē\ *adv*

adapt·ed \ə-'dap-təd\ *adj* : SUITABLE 1

adapt·er *also* **adap·tor** \ə-'dap-tər\ *n* **1** : one that adapts **2 a** : a device for connecting two parts (as of different diameters) of an apparatus **b** : an attachment for adapting apparatus for uses not originally intended

adap·tive \ə-'dap-tiv\ *adj* : showing or having a capacity for or tendency toward adaptation — **adap·tive·ly** *adv*

ad·ax·i·al \'a-'dak-sē-əl\ *adj* : situated on the same side as or facing the axis especially of a plant

add \'ad\ *vb* **1** : to join or unite to a thing so as to enlarge or improve it ⟨*add* a wing to the house⟩ **2** : to introduce as an addition ⟨*add* sugar to tea⟩ ⟨let me *add* a word⟩ **3** : to combine numbers into a single sum [Latin *addere,* from *ad-* + *-dere* "to put"] — **add·able** *or* **add·ible** \'ad-ə-bəl\ *adj*

ad·dax \'ad-,aks\ *n, pl* **ad·dax·es** : a large light-colored antelope of North Africa, Arabia, and Syria [Latin]

ad·dend \'ad-,end, ə-'dend\ *n* : a number that is to be added to another number [short for *addendum*]

ad·den·dum \ə-'den-dəm\ *n, pl* **-den·da** \-'den-də\ : a thing added : ADDITION [Latin, from *addere* "to add"]

¹**ad·der** \'ad-ər\ *n* **1** : a poisonous European viper; *also* : any of several related snakes **2** : any of several harmless North American snakes (as a hognose snake) [Middle English *nadder* (the phrase *a nadder* being understood as *an adder*), from Old English *nædre*]

²**add·er** \'ad-ər\ *n* : one that adds

ad·der's-tongue \'ad-ərz-,təng\ *n* **1** : a fern whose fruiting spike resembles a snake's tongue **2** : DOGTOOTH VIOLET

¹**ad·dict** \ə-'dikt\ *vt* **1** : to devote or surrender (oneself) to something habitually or obsessively ⟨*addicted* to gambling⟩ **2** : to cause (a person) to become physically dependent upon a drug [Latin *addicere* "to favor", from *ad-* + *dicere* "to say"]

²**ad·dict** \'ad-ikt, -,ikt\ *n* **1** : one who is addicted (as to a drug) **2** : DEVOTEE 2 ⟨a detective novel *addict*⟩

ad·dic·tion \ə-'dik-shən\ *n* **1** : the quality or state of being addicted ⟨*addiction* to reading⟩ **2** : compulsive physical need for a habit-forming drug (as heroin)

ad·dic·tive \ə-'dik-tiv\ *adj* : causing or characterized by addiction ⟨an *addictive* drug⟩

Ad·di·son's disease \'ad-ə-sənz-\ *n* : a destructive disease marked by deficient secretion of the adrenal cortical hormone [Thomas *Addison,* died 1860, English physician]

ad·di·tion \ə-'dish-ən\ *n* **1** : the result of adding : INCREASE **2** : the act or process of adding **3** : the operation of adding numbers to obtain their sum **4** : a part added (as to a building) **5** : direct chemical combination of substances into a single product — **in addition** : ²BESIDES — **in addition to** : over and above

ad·di·tion·al \-'dish-nəl, -'dish-ən-l\ *adj* : being an addition : ADDED ⟨an *additional* charge⟩ — **ad·di·tion·al·ly** \-ē\ *adv*

¹ad·di·tive \'ad-ət-iv\ *adj* : relating to, characterized by, or produced by addition — **ad·di·tive·ly** *adv*

²additive *n* : a substance added to another in relatively small amounts to add or improve desirable properties or suppress undesirable properties ⟨food *additives*⟩

additive identity *n* : an element (as zero in the set of real numbers) of a mathematical set that leaves every element of the set unchanged when added to it

additive inverse *n* : a number that when added to a given number gives zero — compare OPPOSITE 2

ad·dle \'ad-l\ *vb* **ad·dled; ad·dling** \'ad-ling, -l-ing\ **1** : to make or become confused **2** : to become rotten : SPOIL ⟨*addled* eggs⟩ [from earlier *addle* "rotten, empty", from Old English *adela*]

¹ad·dress \ə-'dres\ *vt* **1 a** : to direct the attention of (oneself) ⟨*addressed* myself to my work⟩ **b** : to deal with : TREAT ⟨failed to *address* the issues⟩ **2 a** : to communicate directly to a person or group ⟨*address* a petition to the governor⟩ **b** : to deliver a formal speech to ⟨*address* the convention⟩ **3** : to mark directions for delivery on ⟨*address* a letter⟩ **4** : to greet by a prescribed form **5** : to identify (as a peripheral or a piece of information) by an address [Middle French *adresser,* from *a-* "ad-" + *dresser* "to arrange, dress"] — **ad·dress·er** *n*

²ad·dress \ə-'dres, *for* 4, 5, & 7 *also* 'ad-,res\ *n* **1** : dutiful attention especially in courtship — usually used in pl. **2** : readiness and capability for dealing (as with a person or problem) skillfully **3 a** : BEARING, DEPORTMENT ⟨a person of rude *address*⟩ **b** : the manner of speaking or singing : DELIVERY **4** : a formal communication; *esp* : a prepared speech **5 a** : a place where a person or organization may be communicated with **b** : directions for delivery on the outside of an object (as a letter or package) **c** : the designation of place of delivery above the salutation on a business letter **6** : a location (as in the memory of a computer) where particular information is stored; *also* : the digits that identify it

ad·dress·able \ə-'dres-ə-bəl\ *adj* : accessible through an address ⟨*addressable* registers in a computer⟩

ad·dress·ee \,ad-,res-'ē, ə-,dres-'ē\ *n* : one to whom something is addressed

ad·duce \ə-'düs, -'dyüs\ *vt* : to offer as example, reason, or proof in discussion or analysis [Latin *adducere,* literally, "to lead to", from *ad-* + *ducere* "to lead"] — **ad·duc·er** *n*

ad·duct \ə-'dəkt\ *vt* : to draw (a part of the body) toward or past the median axis of the body; *also* : to bring (similar parts) together [Latin *adductus,* past participle of *adducere* "to lead to, adduce"] — **ad·duc·tive** \-'dək-tiv\ *adj*

ad·duc·tion \ə-'dək-shən\ *n* **1** : the action of adducting : the state of being adducted **2** : the act or action of adducing or bringing forward

ad·duc·tor \ə-'dək-tər\ *n* : a muscle that draws a body part toward the median axis — compare ABDUCTOR

-ade \'ād\ *n suffix* **1** : act : action ⟨blockade⟩ **2** : sweet drink ⟨limeade⟩ [derived from Latin *-ata,* feminine of *-atus* "-ate"]

ad·e·nine \'ad-n-,ēn\ *n* : a purine base $C_5H_5N_5$ that is a constituent of ATP and that codes hereditary information in the polynucleotide chain of DNA and RNA — compare CYTOSINE, GUANINE, THYMINE, URACIL [Greek *adēn* "gland"; from its presence in glandular tissue]

¹ad·e·noid \'ad-n-,oid, 'ad-,noid\ *or* **ad·e·noi·dal** \,ad-n-'oid-l\ *adj* **1** : of, relating to, or resembling glands or glandular or lymphoid tissue **2** : of or relating to adenoids or adenoid disorder [Greek *adenoeidēs* "glandular", from *adēn* "gland"]

²adenoid *n* : an enlarged mass of lymphoid tissue at the back of the pharynx characteristically obstructing breathing — usually used in pl.

aden·o·sine \ə-'den-ə-,sēn\ *n* : a compound $C_{10}H_{13}N_5O_4$ that is a constituent of RNA and ATP and that is composed of adenine and ribose [blend of *adenine* and *ribose*]

adenosine di·phos·phate \-dī-'fäs-,fāt\ *n* : ADP

adenosine mo·no·phos·phate \-,män-ə-'fäs-,fāt, -,mō-nə-\ *n* : AMP

adenosine tri·phos·phate \-trī-'fäs-,fāt\ *n* : ATP

¹ad·ept \'ad-,ept\ *n* : a highly skilled or well-trained individual : EXPERT [New Latin *adeptus* "alchemist who has attained the knowledge of how to change base metals to gold", from Latin *adipisci* "to attain", from *ad-* + *apisci* "to reach"]

²adept \ə-'dept\ *adj* : thoroughly proficient : EXPERT SYN see PROFICIENT — **adept·ly** *adv* — **adept·ness** \-'dep-nəs, -'dept-\ *n*

ad·e·quate \'ad-i-kwət\ *adj* **1** : suitable or fully sufficient for a specific requirement **2** : barely sufficient or satisfactory ⟨their performance was *adequate* but not really good⟩ [Latin *adaequare* "to make equal", from *ad-* + *aequus* "equal"] SYN see SUFFICIENT — **ad·e·qua·cy** \-kwə-sē\ *n* — **ad·e·quate·ly** \-kwət-lē\ *adv* — **ad·e·quate·ness** *n*

ad·here \ad-'hiər, əd-\ *vi* **1** : to give support or maintain loyalty (as to a cause) **2** : to hold fast or stick by or as if by gluing **3** : to agree to observe ⟨*adhere* to a treaty⟩ [Latin *adhaerēre* "to stick to", from *ad-* + *haerēre* "to stick"] SYN see STICK

ad·her·ence \-'hir-əns\ *n* **1** : the action or quality of adhering **2** : steady or faithful attachment : FIDELITY ⟨*adherence* to a cause⟩

¹ad·her·ent \-'hir-ənt\ *adj* **1** : able or tending to adhere **2** : connected or associated with something ⟨nations *adherent* to the world organization⟩ — **ad·her·ent·ly** *adv*

²adherent *n* : one that adheres: as **a** : a follower of a leader or party **b** : a believer in or advocate of something (as an idea or church)

ad·he·sion \ad-'hē-zhən, əd-\ *n* **1** : steady or firm attachment : ADHERENCE **2** : the action or state of adhering **3** : the abnormal union of tissues by fibrous tissue following inflammation (as after surgery) **4** : the molecular attraction exerted between the surfaces of bodies in contact [Latin *adhaesio,* from *adhaerēre* "to adhere"] — **ad·he·sion·al** \-'hēzh-nəl, -'hē-zhən-l\ *adj*

¹ad·he·sive \ad-'hē-siv, əd-, -ziv\ *adj* **1** : tending to remain in association or memory **2** : tending to adhere **3** : prepared for adhering : STICKY — **ad·he·sive·ly** *adv* — **ad·he·sive·ness** *n*

²adhesive *n* : an adhesive substance (as glue or cement)

adhesive tape *n* : tape coated on one side with an adhesive and used especially for fixing bandages or supporting injuries

ad hoc \ad-'häk, 'ad-, -'hōk\ *adv or adj* : for the particular purpose or case at hand ⟨a decision made *ad hoc*⟩ ⟨an *ad hoc* committee⟩ [Latin, "for this"]

ad ho·mi·nem \ad-'häm-ə-,nem, 'ad-\ *adj* : appealing to feelings or prejudices rather than intellect especially through attack on an opponent's character rather than response to the opponent's arguments ⟨an *ad hominem* argument⟩ [New Latin, literally, "to the man"]

adi·a·bat·ic \,ad-ē-ə-'bat-ik, ,ā-,dī-ə-\ *adj* : occurring without loss or gain of heat ⟨*adiabatic* expansion of a body of air⟩ [Greek *adiabatos* "impassable", from *a-*

\ə\	abut	\ng\	sing
\ər\	further	\ō\	bone
\a\	mat	\o˙\	saw
\ā\	take	\oi˙\	coin
\ä\	cot, cart	\th\	thin
\au˙\	out	\th\	this
\ch\	chin	\ü\	food
\e\	pet	\u˙\	foot
\ē\	easy	\y\	yet
\g\	go	\yü\	few
\i\	tip	\yu˙\	cure
\ī\	life	\zh\	vision
\j\	job		

+ dia- + bainein "to go"] — **adi·a·bat·i·cal·ly** \-'bat-i-kə-lē, -klē\ adv

adieu \ə-'dü, -'dyü\ n, pl **adieus** or **adieux** \-'düz, -'dyüz\ : FAREWELL 1 — often used interjectionally [Middle French, from a "to" + Dieu "God"]

ad in·fi·ni·tum \,ad-,in-fə-'nīt-əm\ adv or adj : without end or limit [Latin]

ad in·ter·im \ad-'in-tə-rəm, 'ad-, -,rim\ adv or adj : for the intervening time ⟨serving ad interim⟩ ⟨an ad interim appointment⟩ [Latin]

ad·i·pose \'ad-ə-,pōs\ adj : of or relating to animal fat : FATTY [Latin adip-, adeps "fat"] — **ad·i·pos·i·ty** \,ad-ə-'päs-ət-ē\ n

adipose tissue n : tissue in which fat is stored and which has the cells swollen by droplets of fat

ad·ja·cent \ə-'jās-nt\ adj 1 a : not distant ⟨the city and adjacent suburbs⟩ b : having a common border ⟨a field adjacent to the road⟩ 2 : having a vertex or a vertex and side in common ⟨adjacent angles⟩ ⟨adjacent sides of a rectangle⟩ [Latin adjacēre "to lie near", from ad- + jacēre "to lie"] — **ad·ja·cen·cy** \-n-sē\ n — **ad·ja·cent·ly** adv

ad·jec·ti·val \,aj-ik-'tī-vəl\ adj : ADJECTIVE — **ad·jec·ti·val·ly** \-və-lē\ adv

¹**ad·jec·tive** \'aj-ik-tiv\ adj : of, relating to, or functioning as an adjective ⟨adjective clause⟩ [Late Latin adjectivus, from Latin adjicere "to throw to, add to", from ad- + jacere "to throw"] — **ad·jec·tive·ly** adv

²**adjective** n : a word typically serving as a modifier of a noun to denote a quality of the thing named, to indicate its quantity or extent, or to specify a thing as distinct from something else

ad·join \ə-'join\ vt 1 : to add or attach by joining 2 : to lie next to or in contact with

ad·join·ing adj : touching or bounding at a point or line ⟨adjoining lots⟩

ad·journ \ə-'jərn\ vb 1 : to suspend further proceedings or business for an indefinite or stated period of time ⟨Congress adjourned⟩ ⟨adjourn a meeting⟩ 2 : to move to another place ⟨adjourn to the study after dinner⟩ [Middle French ajourner, from a- "ad-" + jour "day"] — **ad·journ·ment** \-mənt\ n

ad·judge \ə-'jəj\ vt 1 : to decide or rule upon as a judge : ADJUDICATE 2 : to hold or pronounce to be : DEEM ⟨adjudged the book to be a success⟩

ad·ju·di·cate \ə-'jüd-i-,kāt\ vt : to settle judicially ⟨adjudicate a claim⟩ [Latin adjudicare, from ad- + judicare "to judge"] — **ad·ju·di·ca·tive** \-,kāt-iv\ adj — **ad·ju·di·ca·tor** \-,kāt-ər\ n

ad·ju·di·ca·tion \-,jüd-i-'kā-shən\ n 1 : the act or process of adjudicating 2 : a judicial decision — **ad·ju·di·ca·to·ry** \-'jüd-i-kə-,tōr-ē, -,tȯr-\ adj

¹**ad·junct** \'aj-,əngt, -,əngkt\ n 1 : something joined or added to another thing but not an essential part of it 2 : a word or word group that qualifies or completes the meaning of another word or other words and is not a major structural element in its sentence ⟨in the sentence "most children eat heartily", most is an adjunct to the subject children and heartily is an adjunct to the verb eat⟩ 3 : a person associated with or assisting another [Latin adjunctum, from adjungere "to adjoin", from ad- + jungere "to join"] — **ad·junc·tive** \ə-'jəng-tiv, -'jəngk-\ adj

²**adjunct** adj 1 : added or joined as an accompanying object or circumstance 2 : attached in a subordinate or temporary capacity to a staff ⟨an adjunct psychiatrist⟩

ad·jure \ə-'jür\ vt 1 : to charge or command solemnly under or as if under oath 2 : to entreat or advise earnestly [Latin adjurare, from ad- + jurare "to swear"] — **ad·ju·ra·tion** \,aj-ə-'rā-shən\ n — **ad·jur·a·to·ry** \ə-'jür-ə-,tōr-ē, -,tȯr-\ adj

ad·just \ə-'jəst\ vb 1 : to bring to a more satisfactory state: a : SETTLE, RESOLVE ⟨adjust conflicts⟩ b : RECTIFY ⟨adjust an error⟩ c : to make correspondent or con-

formable : ADAPT 2 : to move the parts of an instrument or a piece of machinery until they fit together in the best working order ⟨adjust a watch⟩ ⟨adjust the brakes on a car⟩ 3 : to determine the amount of an insurance claim 4 : to adapt oneself to external conditions ⟨had to adjust to city living⟩ [French ajuster, from a- "ad-" + juste "exact, just"] SYN see ADAPT — **ad·just·able** \-'jəs-tə-bəl\ adj — **ad·just·er** also **ad·jus·tor** \-'jəs-tər\ n

ad·just·ment \ə-'jəst-mənt, -'jəs-\ n 1 : the act or process of adjusting 2 : a settlement of a claim or debt 3 : the state of being adjusted 4 : a means of adjusting one part (as in a machine) to another ⟨an adjustment for focusing a microscope⟩ 5 : a correction or modification to reflect actual conditions — **ad·just·ment·al** \ə-,jəst-'ment-l, -,jəs-\ adj

ad·ju·tan·cy \'aj-ət-ən-sē\ n : the office or rank of an adjutant

ad·ju·tant \'aj-ət-ənt\ n 1 : a staff officer (as in the army) assisting the commanding officer and responsible especially for correspondence 2 : one who helps : ASSISTANT [Latin adjutare "to aid"]

adjutant general n, pl **adjutants general** : the chief administrative officer of an army or of one of its major units (as a division or corps)

ad·ju·vant \'aj-ə-vənt\ n : something (as a drug or procedure) that enhances the effectiveness of medical treatment [Latin adjuvare "to aid"]

¹**ad–lib** \ad-'lib, 'ad-\ adj : spoken, composed, or performed without preparation

²**ad–lib** vb **ad–libbed; ad–lib·bing** 1 : to deliver spontaneously 2 : to improvise lines or a speech

ad lib adv : without restraint or limit [New Latin ad libitum "in accordance with desire"]

ad li·bi·tum \ad-'lib-ət-əm, 'ad-\ adj : omissible according to a performer's wishes — used as a direction in music [New Latin]

ad·man \'ad-,man\ n : one who writes, solicits, or places advertisements

ad·min·is·ter \əd-'min-ə-stər\ vb **ad·min·is·tered; ad·min·is·ter·ing** \-stə-ring, -string\ 1 : to manage or supervise the execution, use, or conduct of ⟨administer a trust fund⟩ 2 a : to mete out : DISPENSE ⟨administer justice⟩ b : to give ritually ⟨administer last rites⟩ c : to give as a remedy ⟨administer a drug⟩ 3 : to furnish aid or relief ⟨administer to an ailing friend⟩ — **ad·min·is·tra·ble** \-strə-bəl\ adj — **ad·min·is·trant** \-strənt\ n

ad·min·is·tra·tion \əd-,min-ə-'strā-shən, ,ad-\ n 1 : the act or process of administering 2 : performance of executive duties : MANAGEMENT 3 : the execution of public affairs as distinguished from policy making 4 a : a body of persons who administer b cap : the people who make up the political executive in a presidential government c : a governmental agency or board 5 : the term of office of an administrative officer or body

ad·min·is·tra·tive \əd-'min-ə-,strāt-iv, -strət-\ adj : of or relating to administration ⟨an administrative position⟩ — **ad·min·is·tra·tive·ly** adv

ad·min·is·tra·tor \əd-'min-ə-,strāt-ər\ n 1 : one that is legally appointed to administer an estate 2 a : one that administers especially business, school, or governmental affairs b : a priest appointed to administer temporarily a diocese or parish

ad·min·is·tra·trix \-,min-ə-'strā-triks\ n, pl **-is·tra·tri·ces** \-'strā-trə-,sēz\ : a woman who administers an estate

ad·mi·ra·ble \'ad-mə-rə-bəl, -mrə-bəl\ adj : deserving the highest esteem : EXCELLENT — **ad·mi·ra·ble·ness** n — **ad·mi·ra·bly** \-blē\ adv

ad·mi·ral \'ad-mə-rəl, -mrəl\ n 1 a : a naval officer of flag rank b : an officer rank in the Navy and Coast Guard above vice admiral 2 : any of several brightly colored butterflies [Medieval Latin admirallus, from Arabic amīr-al-baḥr "commander of the sea"] □ ORIGIN Admiral, in spite of its appearance, is not related to admire. It is a descendant of Arabic *amīr-al-baḥr* "commander of the sea". (*Amīr* means "commander"; *baḥr* means "sea"; *al* is the definite article.) When *amīr-al-* was borrowed into Latin in the Middle Ages, the insertion of a *d* into the word was probably influenced by the similar Latin word *admirari* "to admire". The two words are not otherwise connected. A relative of *admiral* is *emir,* also derived from Arabic *amīr.*

¹ad·mi·ral·ty \'ad-mə-rəl-tē, -mrəl-\ *n* **1** *cap* : a body of officials formerly having general authority over the British navy **2** : a court having jurisdiction of maritime questions

²admiralty *adj* : of, relating to, or having jurisdiction over maritime affairs ⟨*admiralty* law⟩

ad·mi·ra·tion \,ad-mə-'rā-shən\ *n* **1** : an object of admiring esteem **2** : a feeling of delighted approval

ad·mire \əd-'mīr\ *vt* **1** *archaic* : to marvel at **2** : to look at with a feeling of pleasure ⟨*admire* the view⟩ **3** : to think highly of ⟨*admired* their capacity for work⟩ [Middle French *admirer,* from Latin *admirari,* from *ad-* + *mirari* "to wonder"] SYN see REGARD — **ad·mir·er** \-'mīr-ər\ *n*

ad·mis·si·ble \əd-'mis-ə-bəl\ *adj* : that can be or is worthy to be admitted or allowed : ALLOWABLE ⟨*admissible* evidence⟩ — **ad·mis·si·bil·i·ty** \-,mis-ə-'bil-ət-ē\ *n*

ad·mis·sion \əd-'mish-ən\ *n* **1** : a granting of something that has not been fully proved ⟨an *admission* of guilt⟩ **2** : the act of admitting **3** : the right or permission to enter ⟨standards of *admission* to a school⟩ **4** : the price of entrance to a place [Latin *admissus,* past participle of *admittere* "to admit"] SYN see ADMITTANCE — **ad·mis·sive** \-'mis-iv\ *adj*

ad·mit \əd-'mit\ *vb* **ad·mit·ted; ad·mit·ting 1** : to allow scope : PERMIT ⟨a question that *admits* of two answers⟩ **2** : to allow entry : let in ⟨*admit* a state to the Union⟩ **3** : to concede as true or valid ⟨reluctantly *admitted* failure⟩ [Latin *admittere* "to allow entry, permit", from *ad-* + *mittere* "to send, let go"] SYN see ACKNOWLEDGE — **ad·mit·ted·ly** \-'mit-əd-lē\ *adv*

ad·mit·tance \əd-'mit-ns\ *n* : permission to enter a place : ENTRANCE □ SYN ADMITTANCE, ADMISSION mean permitted entrance. ADMITTANCE applies usually to mere physical entrance into a building or locality; ADMISSION implies formal acceptance that carries with it rights, privileges, or membership.

ad·mix \ad-'miks\ *vt* : MINGLE, MIX ⟨*admix* soil and gravel⟩ [back-formation from obsolete *admixt* "mingled (with)", from Latin *admixtus*]

ad·mix·ture \ad-'miks-chər\ *n* **1 a** : the act of mixing ⟨made by *admixture* of chemicals⟩ **b** : the fact of being mixed **2 a** : something added by mixing **b** : a product of mixing : MIXTURE

ad·mon·ish \ad-'män-ish\ *vt* **1** : to reprove gently but seriously : warn of a fault **2** : to give friendly advice or encouragement to [Middle French *admonester,* from Latin *admonēre* "to warn", from *ad-* + *monēre* "to warn, remind"] — **ad·mon·ish·er** *n* — **ad·mon·ish·ing·ly** \-'män-i-shing-lē\ *adv* — **ad·mon·ish·ment** \-'män-ish-mənt\ *n*

ad·mo·ni·tion \,ad-mə-'nish-ən\ *n* : a gentle or friendly reproof or warning [Middle French, from Latin *admonitio,* from *admonēre* "to admonish"]

ad·mon·i·to·ry \ad-'män-ə-,tōr-ē, -,tȯr-\ *adj* : expressing admonition : WARNING

ad nau·se·am \ad-'nȯ-zē-əm\ *adv* : to a sickening degree [Latin]

ado \ə-'dü\ *n* : FUSS, TROUBLE ⟨much *ado* about nothing⟩

ado·be \ə-'dō-bē\ *n* **1** : a brick made of clayey mud dried in the sun **2** : a building made of adobe bricks [Spanish, from Arabic *aṭ-ṭub* "the brick"]

ad·o·les·cence \,ad-l-'es-ns\ *n* : the state or process of growing up; *also* : the period of life from puberty to maturity

¹ad·o·les·cent \-nt\ *n* : one that is in the state of adolescence : a person not fully mature [Latin *adolescere* "to grow up"]

²adolescent *adj* : of, relating to, or being in adolescence

adopt \ə-'däpt\ *vt* **1** : to take legally as one's own child ⟨*adopt* an orphan⟩ **2** : to take up and practice as one's own **3** : to accept formally and put into effect ⟨the assembly *adopted* a constitution⟩ **4** : to choose (a textbook) for required study in a course [Middle French *adopter,* from Latin *adoptare,* from *ad-* + *optare* "to choose"] — **adopt·abil·i·ty** \ə-,däp-tə-'bil-ət-ē\ *n* — **adopt·able** \ə-'däp-tə-bəl\ *adj* — **adopt·er** *n* — **adop·tion** \ə-'däp-shən\ *n*

adop·tive \ə-'däp-tiv\ *adj* : made by or associated with adoption ⟨*adoptive* parents⟩ — **adop·tive·ly** *adv*

ador·able \ə-'dōr-ə-bəl, -'dȯr-\ *adj* **1** : deserving to be adored **2** : extremely charming ⟨an *adorable* child⟩ — **ador·abil·i·ty** \ə-,dōr-ə-'bil-ət-ē, -,dȯr-\ *n* — **ador·able·ness** *n* — **ador·ably** \ə-'dōr-ə-blē, -'dȯr-\ *adv*

adore \ə-'dōr, -'dȯr\ *vt* **1** : WORSHIP ⟨*adore* God⟩ **2** : to be extremely fond of [Middle French *adorer,* from Latin *adorare,* from *ad-* + *orare* "to speak, pray"] — **ad·o·ra·tion** \,ad-ə-'rā-shən\ *n* — **ador·er** \ə-'dōr-ər, -'dȯr-\ *n*

adorn \ə-'dȯrn\ *vt* : to decorate with ornaments : BEAUTIFY [Middle French *adorner,* from Latin *adornare,* from *ad-* + *ornare* "to furnish, ornament"] □ SYN DECORATE, EMBELLISH: ADORN implies enhancing appearance by adding something beautiful in itself ⟨*adorned* with jewels⟩ DECORATE suggests relieving plainness or monotony by adding color or design ⟨*decorate* a birthday cake with colored icing⟩ EMBELLISH often stresses the adding of superfluous ornament ⟨*embellish* a page with floral borders⟩

adorn·ment \-mənt\ *n* **1** : the action of adorning : the state of being adorned **2** : something that adorns

ADP \,ā-,dē-'pē\ *n* : a derivative of adenosine that is formed in living cells and is reversibly converted to ATP by the addition of a phosphate group [*a*denosine *d*i*p*hosphate]

¹ad·re·nal \ə-'drēn-l\ *adj* **1** : adjacent to the kidneys **2** : of, relating to, or derived from adrenal glands or secretion

²adrenal *n* : ADRENAL GLAND

adrenal cor·ti·co·tro·phic hormone \-,kȯrt-i-kō-'trō-fik-\ *n* : ACTH

adrenal gland *n* : either of a pair of complex endocrine organs occurring one near each kidney and consisting of an outer cortex that produces steroid hormones and an inner medulla that produces adrenaline

Adren·a·lin \ə-'dren-l-ən\ *trademark* — used for a preparation of adrenaline

adren·a·line \-l-ən\ *n* : EPINEPHRINE

ad·ren·er·gic \,ad-rə-'nər-jik\ *adj* : liberating or activated by adrenaline or a substance like adrenaline ⟨an *adrenergic* nerve⟩ [Greek *ergon* "work"]

adre·nin \ə-'drēn-ən, -'dren-\ *n* : ADRENALINE

ad·re·no·cor·ti·cal \ə-,drē-nō-'kȯrt-i-kəl\ *adj* : of, relating to, or derived from the cortex of the adrenal glands

ad·re·no·cor·ti·co·tro·phic hormone \ə-,drē-nō-,kȯrt-i-kō-'trō-fik-\ *or* **ad·re·no·cor·ti·co·trop·ic hormone** \-'träp-ik-\ *n* : ACTH

adrift \ə-'drift\ *adv or adj* **1** : without motive power, anchor, or mooring ⟨a damaged ship *adrift* in the storm⟩ **2** : without guidance or purpose

adroit \ə-'drȯit\ *adj* **1** : skillful in the use of the hands **2** : showing shrewdness or resourcefulness in coping with difficulty [French, from *à droit* "properly", from *à* "to, at" + *droit* "right"] SYN see DEXTEROUS — **adroit·ly** *adv* — **adroit·ness** *n*

ad·sorb \ad-'sȯrb, -'zȯrb\ *vt* : to take up and hold by adsorption [*ad-* + *-sorb* (as in *absorb*)] — **ad·sor·bent** \-'sȯr-bənt, -'zȯr-\ *adj or n*

adobe 2

ad·sorp·tion \-'sȯrp-shən, -'zȯrp-\ *n* : the adhesion in an extremely thin layer of molecules (as of gases, solutes, or liquids) to the surfaces of solid bodies or liquids with which they are in contact — compare AB-SORPTION — **ad·sorp·tive** \-'sȯrp-tiv, -'zȯrp-\ *adj*

ad·u·late \'aj-ə-,lāt\ *vt* : to flatter or admire excessively or slavishly [derived from Latin *adulari* "to flatter"] — **ad·u·la·tion** \,aj-ə-'lā-shən\ *n* — **ad·u·la·tor** \'aj-ə-,lāt-ər\ *n* — **ad·u·la·to·ry** \'aj-ə-lə-,tōr-ē, -,tȯr-\ *adj*

¹adult \ə-'dəlt, 'ad-,əlt\ *adj* **1** : fully developed and mature : GROWN-UP **2** : of, relating to, or characteristic of adults [Latin *adultus*, past participle of *adolescere* "to grow up"] — **adult·hood** \ə-'dəlt-,hùd\ *n* — **adult·ness** \ə-'dəlt-nəs, 'ad-,əlt-\ *n*

²adult *n* **1** : a fully grown person, animal, or plant **2** : a person having attained legal majority

adul·ter·ant \ə-'dəl-tə-rənt\ *n* : something used to adulterate another thing

adul·ter·ate \ə-'dəl-tə-,rāt\ *vt* : to weaken or make impure by adding a foreign or inferior substance; *esp* : to prepare for sale by replacing more valuable with less valuable ingredients [Latin *adulterare*, from *ad-* + *alter* "other"] — **adul·ter·a·tion** \ə-,dəl-tə-'rā-shən\ *n* — **adul·ter·a·tor** \ə-'dəl-tə-,rāt-ər\ *n*

adul·tery \ə-'dəl-tə-rē, -trē\ *n, pl* **-ter·ies** : voluntary sexual intercourse by a married person with anyone other than his or her spouse — compare FORNICATION [Latin *adulterium*, from *adulterare* "to adulterate"] — **adul·ter·er** \-tər-ər\ *n* — **adul·ter·ess** \-tə-rəs, -trəs\ *n* — **adul·ter·ous** \-tə-rəs, -trəs\ *adj* — **adul·ter·ous·ly** *adv*

ad·um·brate \'ad-əm-,brāt, ə-'dəm-\ *vt* **1** : to foreshadow vaguely : INTIMATE **2** : to suggest or disclose partially [Latin *adumbrare*, from *ad-* + *umbra* "shadow"] — **ad·um·bra·tion** \,ad-,əm-'brā-shən\ *n* — **ad·um·bra·tive** \ə-'dəm-brət-iv\ *adj* — **ad·um·bra·tive·ly** *adv*

ad va·lo·rem \,ad-və-'lōr-əm, -'lȯr-\ *adj* : based on a percentage of the monetary value of the goods ⟨an *ad valorem* tariff⟩ [Latin, "according to the value"]

¹ad·vance \əd-'vans\ *vb* **1** : to move forward ⟨*advance* a few yards⟩ **2** : to further the progress of ⟨*advance* the cause of freedom⟩ **3** : to raise to a higher rank : PROMOTE ⟨was *advanced* from clerk to assistant manager⟩ **4** : to supply in expectation of repayment ⟨*advance* a loan⟩ **5** : to bring forward : PROPOSE ⟨*advance* a new plan⟩ **6** : to raise or rise in rate or price ⟨gasoline *advanced* another two cents⟩ [Old French *avancier*, from Latin *abante* "before", from *ab* "from" + *ante* "before"] — **ad·vanc·er** *n*

²advance *n* **1** : a forward movement **2** : progress in development : IMPROVEMENT **3** : a rise in price, value, or amount **4** : a first approach : OFFER **5 a** : a provision of something (as money or goods) before a return is received ⟨never ask for an *advance* on your salary⟩ **b** : the money or goods supplied — **in advance** : BEFORE, BEFOREHAND ⟨knew of the change two weeks *in advance*⟩ — **in advance of** : ahead of

³advance *adj* **1** : made, sent, or furnished ahead of time ⟨an *advance* payment⟩ **2** : going or situated before

ad·vanced \əd-'vanst\ *adj* **1** : far on in time or course ⟨an *advanced* case of tuberculosis⟩ **2 a** : being beyond the elementary or introductory ⟨*advanced* mathematics⟩ **b** : being far along in progress or development ⟨an *advanced* civilization⟩

ad·vance·ment \əd-'vans-mənt\ *n* : the action of advancing : the state of being advanced: **a** : promotion to a higher rank **b** : progression to a higher stage of development

ad·van·tage \əd-'vant-ij\ *n* **1** : superiority of position or condition ⟨high ground gave the enemy the *advantage*⟩ **2** : BENEFIT, GAIN; *esp* : benefit resulting from a course of action ⟨changing jobs will be of *advantage* to you⟩ **3** : something that benefits its possessor ⟨speed is an *advantage* in sports⟩ **4** : the 1st point won in

tennis after deuce [Middle French *avantage*, from *avant* "before", from Latin *abante*] — **to advantage** : so as to produce a favorable impression or effect

ad·van·ta·geous \,ad-,van-'tā-jəs, -vən-\ *adj* : giving an advantage : HELPFUL, FAVORABLE SYN see BENEFICIAL — **ad·van·ta·geous·ly** *adv* — **ad·van·ta·geous·ness** *n*

ad·vec·tion \ad-'vek-shən\ *n* : the horizontal movement of a mass of air causing weather changes (as a drop in temperature) [Latin *advectio* "act of bringing", from *advehere* "to carry to", from *ad-* + *vehere* "to carry"] — **ad·vec·tive** \-'vek-tiv\ *adj*

Ad·vent \'ad-,vent\ *n* **1** : a penitential season beginning four Sundays before Christmas **2** : the coming of Christ at the Incarnation or as judge on the last day **3** *not cap* : first or new appearance ⟨the *advent* of spring⟩ [Medieval Latin *adventus*, from Latin, "arrival", from *advenire* "to arrive, happen", from *ad-* + *venire* "to come"]

Ad·vent·ist \ad-'vent-əst, ad-', 'ad-,\ *n* **1** : one who believes Christ's second coming near at hand **2** : SEVENTH DAY ADVENTIST — **Ad·vent·ism** \'ad-,vent-,iz-əm\ *n* — **Adventist** *adj*

ad·ven·ti·tious \,ad-(,)ven-'tish-əs, -vən-\ *adj* **1** : not inherent or fundamental ⟨*adventitious* additions to a plan⟩ **2** : appearing out of the usual or normal place ⟨*adventitious* buds⟩ [Latin *adventicius* "coming from outside", from *advenire* "to arrive"] — **ad·ven·ti·tious·ly** *adv* — **ad·ven·ti·tious·ness** *n*

Advent Sunday *n* : the first Sunday in Advent

¹ad·ven·ture \əd-'ven-chər\ *n* **1** : an undertaking involving unknown dangers and risks **2** : the encountering of risks **3** : an unusual experience [Old French *aventure*, from Latin *advenire* "to arrive, happen", from *ad-* + *venire* "to come"]

²adventure *vb* **-ven·tured; -ven·tur·ing** \-'vench-ring, -ə-ring\ **1** : RISK 1, VENTURE ⟨*adventure* their capital in foreign trade⟩ **2** : to proceed despite danger or risk

ad·ven·tur·er \-'vench-rər, -ə-rər\ *n* **1** : one that adventures: as **a** : SOLDIER OF FORTUNE **b** : one that engages in risky commercial enterprises for profit **2** : a person who lives by his wits

ad·ven·ture·some \-'ven-chər-səm\ *adj* : inclined to take risks

ad·ven·tur·ess \-'vench-rəs, -ə-rəs\ *n* : a woman adventurer; *esp* : one who lives by her wits

ad·ven·tur·ous \əd-'vench-rəs, -ə-rəs\ *adj* **1** : ready to seek adventure or to cope with the new and unknown **2** : characterized by unknown dangers and risks — **ad·ven·tur·ous·ly** *adv* — **ad·ven·tur·ous·ness** *n* □ SYN VENTURESOME, DARING: ADVENTUROUS stresses a willingness to try the unknown regardless of possible or probable danger; VENTURESOME may stress the tendency to take chances; DARING heightens the implication of fearlessness in accepting risks that could be avoided.

ad·verb \'ad-,vərb\ *n* : a word used to modify a verb, an adjective, another adverb, a preposition, a phrase, a clause, or a sentence and often used to show degree, manner, place, or time [Middle French *adverbe*, from Latin *adverbium*, from *ad-* + *verbum* "word, verb"] — **adverb** *adj*

ad·ver·bi·al \ad-'vər-bē-əl\ *adj* : of, relating to, or having the function of an adverb ⟨*adverbial* phrase⟩ — **adverbial** *n* — **ad·ver·bi·al·ly** \-bē-ə-lē\ *adv*

¹ad·ver·sary \'ad-vər-,ser-ē, -və-\ *n, pl* **-sar·ies** : one that contends with, opposes, or resists SYN see OPPONENT

²adversary *adj* : having or involving opposing parties or interests

ad·ver·sa·tive \əd-'vər-sət-iv\ *adj* : expressing opposition or adverse circumstance ⟨the *adversative* conjunction *but*⟩ — **ad·ver·sa·tive·ly** *adv*

ad·verse \ad-'vərs, 'ad-,\ *adj* **1** : acting in a contrary direction ⟨*adverse* winds⟩ **2** : opposed to one's interests ⟨*adverse* testimony⟩; *esp* : UNFAVORABLE ⟨*adverse* criticism⟩ **3** : causing harm : HARMFUL ⟨*adverse* effects of a drug⟩ ⟨an *adverse* impact on the environment⟩ [Middle French *advers,* from Latin *adversus,* from *advertere* "to turn toward", from *ad-* + *vertere* "to turn"] — **ad·verse·ly** *adv* — **ad·verse·ness** *n*

ad·ver·si·ty \ad-'vǝr-sǝt-ē\ *n, pl* **-ties** : a condition or experience of serious or continued misfortune

ad·vert \ad-'vǝrt\ *vb* : to direct attention : REFER ⟨*advert* to a previous remark⟩ [Middle French *advertir*]

ad·ver·tise \'ad-vǝr-ˌtīz\ *vb* **1** : to announce publicly especially by a printed notice or a broadcast ⟨*advertise* a sale⟩ **2** : to call public attention to especially by emphasizing desirable qualities so as to arouse a desire to buy or patronize ⟨*advertise* a new book⟩ **3** : to issue or sponsor advertising ⟨*advertise* for a secretary⟩ [Middle French *advertiss-,* stem of *advertir* "to inform", from Latin *advertere* "to turn toward"] — **ad·ver·tis·er** *n*

ad·ver·tise·ment \ˌad-vǝr-'tīz-mǝnt, ǝd-'vǝrt-ǝz-\ *n* **1** : the act or process of advertising **2** : a public notice; *esp* : one published or broadcast

ad·ver·tis·ing \'ad-vǝr-ˌtī-zing\ *n* **1** : the action of calling something to the attention of the public especially by paid announcements **2** : ADVERTISEMENTS **3** : the business of preparing advertisements for publication or broadcast

ad·vice \ǝd-'vīs\ *n* **1** : recommendation regarding a decision or course of conduct : COUNSEL **2** : information or notice given : NEWS — usually used in pl. [Old French *avis* "opinion"]

ad·vis·able \ǝd-'vī-zǝ-bǝl\ *adj* : reasonable or proper under the circumstances : WISE, PRUDENT ⟨it is *advisable* to stay fit⟩ SYN see EXPEDIENT — **ad·vis·abil·i·ty** \ǝd-ˌvī-zǝ-'bil-ǝt-ē\ *n* — **ad·vis·ably** \ǝd-'vī-zǝ-blē\ *adv*

ad·vise \ǝd-'vīz\ *vb* **1 a** : to give advice to : COUNSEL **b** : RECOMMEND ⟨they *advised* caution⟩ **2** : to give information or notice to : INFORM **3** : to take counsel : CONSULT ⟨they *advised* with their lawyer⟩ — **ad·vis·er** *or* **ad·vi·sor** \-'vī-zǝr\ *n*

ad·vis·ed·ly \-'vī-zǝd-lē\ *adv* : with or after consideration : DELIBERATELY

ad·vise·ment \ǝd-'vīz-mǝnt\ *n* : careful consideration ⟨take a matter under *advisement*⟩

ad·vi·so·ry \ǝd-'vīz-rē, -ǝ-rē\ *adj* **1** : having the power or right to advise ⟨an *advisory* committee⟩ **2** : giving or containing advice ⟨an *advisory* opinion⟩ — **advisory** *n*

ad·vo·ca·cy \'ad-vǝ-kǝ-sē\ *n* : the act of advocating : public support ⟨*advocacy* of a proposal⟩

¹ad·vo·cate \'ad-vǝ-kǝt, -ˌkāt\ *n* **1** : one that pleads the cause of another especially before a court **2** : one that argues for, recommends, or supports a cause or policy [Middle French *advocat,* from Latin *advocatus,* from *advocare* "to summon", from *ad-* + *vocare* "to call"]

²ad·vo·cate \-ˌkāt\ *vt* : to support or recommend openly ⟨*advocate* a new plan⟩

adz *or* **adze** \'adz\ *n* : a cutting tool that has a thin arched blade set at right angles to the handle and is used for shaping wood [Old English *adesa*]

ae \'ā\ *adj, chiefly Scottish* : ONE [Middle English *a*]

ae·cio·spore \'ē-sē-ǝ-ˌspōr, -ˌspór\ *n* : a spore formed in an aecium

ae·ci·um \'ē-shē-ǝm, -sē-\ *n, pl* **-cia** \-shē-ǝ, -sē-ǝ\ : a fruiting body of a rust fungus in which the first binucleate spores are formed [Greek *aikia* "assault"] — **ae·cial** \'ē-shē-ǝl, -shǝl, -sē-ǝl\ *adj*

aë·des \ā-'ēd-ēz\ *n, pl* **aëdes** : any of a genus of mosquitoes including carriers of disease (as yellow fever) [Greek *aēdēs* "unpleasant", from *a-* + *ēdos* "pleasure"]

ae·dile \'ē-ˌdīl\ *n* : an official in ancient Rome in charge of public works and games, police, and the grain supply [Latin *aedilis,* from *aedes* "temple"]

ae·gis \'ē-jǝs\ *n* **1** : PROTECTION 1, DEFENSE **2** : PATRON-AGE 1, SPONSORSHIP [Greek *aigis* "shield made of goat-skin"]

-aemia — see -EMIA

ae·o·lian \ē-'ō-lē-ǝn, -'ōl-yǝn\ *variant of* EOLIAN

Aeolian *n* : one of a group of ancient Greeks colonizing Lesbos and the adjacent coast of Asia Minor

aeolian harp *n* : a box-shaped musical instrument that produces musical sounds when air currents pass over stretched strings

ae·on *or* **eon** \'ē-ǝn, 'ē-ˌän\ *n* **1** : an immeasurably or indefinitely long period of time : AGE **2** : a unit of geologic time equal to one billion years [Latin, from Greek *aiōn*]

aer- *or* **aero-** *combining form* **1** : air : atmosphere ⟨*aer*ate⟩ **2** : gas ⟨*aero*sol⟩ **3** : aviation ⟨*aero*drome⟩ [Greek *aēr*]

aer·ate \'ar-ˌāt, 'er-\ *vt* **1** : to supply (blood) with oxygen by respiration **2** : to supply or impregnate with air **3** : to combine or charge with gas — **aer·a·tion** \ˌar-'ā-shǝn, ˌer-\ *n* — **aer·a·tor** \'ar-ˌāt-ǝr, 'er-\ *n*

¹ae·ri·al \'ar-ē-ǝl, 'er-; ā-'ir-ē-ǝl\ *adj* **1 a** : of, relating to, or occurring in the air or atmosphere **b** : living or growing in the air rather than on the ground or in water **c** : operating or operated overhead on elevated cables or rails **2 a** : lacking substance : THIN **b** : IMAGINARY, IDEAL **3 a** : of or relating to aircraft **b** : designed for use in, taken from, or operating from or against aircraft — **ae·ri·al·ly** \-ē-ǝ-lē\ *adv*

²ae·ri·al \'ar-ē-ǝl, 'er-\ *n* **1** : ANTENNA 2 **2** : FORWARD PASS

ae·ri·al·ist \'ar-ē-ǝ-lǝst, 'er-, ā-'ir-\ *n* : a performer of feats above the ground especially on a flying trapeze

aerial root *n* : a root (as for clinging to a wall) that does not enter the soil and usually arises adventitiously

ae·rie \'aǝr-ē, 'eǝr-, 'iǝr-\ *or* **ey·rie** \'īǝr-ē, *or like* AERIE\ *n* **1** : the nest of a bird on a cliff or a mountaintop **2** : a dwelling or room placed high up [Medieval Latin *aerea,* from Old French *aire*]

aer·o·bat·ics \ˌar-ǝ-'bat-iks, ˌer-\ *n sing or pl* : spectacular flying feats and maneuvers [*aer-* + *-batics* (as in *acrobatics*)]

aer·o·bic \ˌa-'rō-bik, ˌe-\ *adj* **1** : living or active only in the presence of oxygen **2** : of, relating to, or caused by aerobic organisms — **aer·obe** \'ar-ˌōb, 'er-\ *n* — **aer·o·bi·cal·ly** \ˌa-'rō-bi-kǝ-lē, ˌe-, -klē\ *adv*

aer·o·bics \-biks\ *n sing or pl* : a system of exercises intended to develop the body's ability to take in and use oxygen

aero·drome \'ar-ǝ-ˌdrōm, 'er-\ *n, British* : AIRFIELD, AIRPORT

aero·dy·nam·ics \ˌar-ō-dī-'nam-iks, ˌer-\ *n* : a branch of dynamics that deals with the motion of gaseous fluids (as air) and with the forces acting on bodies in motion relative to such fluids — **aero·dy·nam·ic** \-ik\ *adj* — **aero·dy·nam·i·cal·ly** \-i-kǝ-lē, -klē\ *adv*

aero·naut \'ar-ǝ-ˌnót, 'er-, -ˌnät\ *n* : one that operates or travels in an airship or balloon [French *aéronaute,* from *aér-* "aer-" + Greek *nautēs* "sailor"]

aero·nau·tics \ˌar-ǝ-'nót-iks, ˌer-\ *n* **1** : a science dealing with the construction and operation of aircraft **2** : the art or science of flight — **aero·nau·tic** \-'nót-ik\ *adj* — **aero·nau·ti·cal** \-'nót-i-kǝl\ *adj* — **aero·nau·ti·cal·ly** \-i-kǝ-lē, -klē\ *adv*

aero·pause \'ar-ō-ˌpóz, 'er-\ *n* : the level above the earth's surface where the atmosphere becomes ineffective for human and aircraft functions

aero·plane \'ar-ǝ-ˌplān, 'er-\ *chiefly British variant of* AIRPLANE

aero·sol \-ˌsäl, -ˌsól\ *n* **1** : a suspension of fine solid or liquid particles (as smoke or fog) in gas **2** : a substance (as an insecticide) dispensed from a pressurized container; *also* : the container itself [*aer-* + *³sol*]

¹aero·space \'ar-ō-ˌspās, 'er-\ *n* **1** : the earth's atmosphere and the space beyond **2** : a physical science dealing with aerospace

²aerospace *adj* : of or relating to aerospace, to the manufacture or use of vehicles used in aerospace, or to travel in aerospace

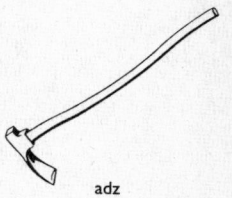
adz

\ǝ\ abut	\ng\ sing
\ǝr\ further	\ō\ bone
\a\ mat	\ó\ saw
\ā\ take	\ói\ coin
\ä\ cot, cart	\th\ thin
\au̇\ out	\th\ this
\ch\ chin	\ü\ food
\e\ pet	\u̇\ foot
\ē\ easy	\y\ yet
\g\ go	\yü\ few
\i\ tip	\yu̇\ cure
\ī\ life	\zh\ vision
\j\ job	

aery \'aər-ē, 'eər-\ *adj* **aer·i·er; -est** : having an aerial quality : ETHEREAL

Ae·so·pi·an \ē-'sō-pē-ən\ *adj* : conveying an innocent meaning to an outsider but a concealed meaning to an informed member of a conspiracy or underground movement ⟨*Aesopian* language⟩

aes·thete *also* **es·thete** \'es-ˌthēt\ *n* : one having or pretending sensitivity to the beautiful especially in art

aes·thet·ic *or* **es·thet·ic** \es-'thet-ik, is-\ *adj* **1** : having to do with beauty or with what is beautiful especially as distinguished from what is useful ⟨a work of *aesthetic* value⟩ **2** : appreciative of or responsive to what is beautiful ⟨an *aesthetic* person⟩ [derived from Greek *aisthanesthai* "to perceive"] SYN see ARTISTIC — **aes·thet·i·cal·ly** \-'thet-i-kə-lē, -klē\ *adv*

aes·thet·i·cism \es-'thet-ə-ˌsiz-əm, is-\ *n* : devotion to or emphasis on beauty or the cultivation of the arts

aes·thet·ics *also* **es·thet·ics** \es-'thet-iks, is-\ *n sing or pl* **1** : a branch of philosophy that studies and explains the principles and forms of beauty especially in art and literature **2** : description and explanation of artistic effects and aesthetic experience by means of other sciences (as psychology)

aes·ti·vate *or* **es·ti·vate** \'es-tə-ˌvāt\ *vi* : to pass the summer in a state of torpor [Latin *aestivare* "to spend the summer", from *aestivus* "of summer", from *aestas* "summer"] — **aes·ti·va·tion** \ˌes-tə-'vā-shən\ *n*

af- — see AD-

afar \ə-'fär\ *adv* : from, to, or at a great distance

afeard *or* **afeared** \ə-'fiərd\ *adj, dialect* : AFRAID

af·fa·ble \'af-ə-bəl\ *adj* **1** : being pleasant and at ease in talking to others **2** : characterized by ease and friendliness ⟨an *affable* manner⟩ [Middle French, from Latin *affabilis*, from *affari* "to speak to", from *ad-* + *fari* "to speak"] — **af·fa·bil·i·ty** \ˌaf-ə-'bil-ət-ē\ *n* — **af·fa·bly** \'af-ə-blē\ *adv*

af·fair \ə-'faər, -'feər\ *n* **1 a** *pl* : personal, commercial, professional, or public business ⟨government *affairs*⟩ **b** : MATTER, CONCERN ⟨not your *affair* at all⟩ **2 a** : EVENT, ACTIVITY ⟨attended a social *affair*⟩ **b** : PRODUCT, THING ⟨the house was a 2-story *affair*⟩ **3 a** *also* **af·faire** : a typically brief romantic or passionate relationship **b** : a matter causing public anxiety, controversy, or scandal [Middle French *affaire*, from *a faire* "to do"]

¹af·fect \ə-'fekt, a-\ *vt* **1** : to be given to : FANCY ⟨*affect* flashy clothes⟩ **2** : to make a display of liking or using ⟨*affect* a worldly manner⟩ **3** : to put on a pretense of : FEIGN ⟨*affect* indifference⟩ [Middle French *affecter*, from Latin *affectare* "to aim at", from *afficere* "to act on, influence"]

²affect *vt* : to produce an effect upon: as **a** : to produce a usually harmful physical effect upon or change in ⟨lungs *affected* by cancer⟩ **b** : to produce a material change in **c** : to act upon so as to bring about a response ⟨criticism *affected* their efforts⟩ □ SYN AFFECT, EFFECT are often confused because both verbs take the same word *effect* as the corresponding noun. AFFECT applies to the action of an agency in causing a change in or alteration of something ⟨moisture *affects* steel⟩ ⟨the climate *affected* their health⟩ EFFECT applies to the producing of a result by an intelligent agent ⟨asked how the prisoner *effected* the escape⟩ SYN see in addition INFLUENCE

af·fec·ta·tion \ˌaf-ˌek-'tā-shən\ *n* **1** : an assuming or displaying of an attitude or kind of behavior not natural or not genuine **2** : artificial quality in speech or behavior □ SYN MANNERISM, POSE: AFFECTATION applies to a specific trick of speech or behavior that impresses others as being deliberately assumed and insincere; MANNERISM designates a peculiarity or eccentricity in behavior that is not deliberately assumed but results from unconscious, accidentally acquired habit; POSE implies an attitude deliberately assumed in order to impress others.

af·fect·ed *adj* : not natural or genuine ⟨an *affected* interest in music⟩ — **af·fect·ed·ly** *adv* — **af·fect·ed·ness** *n*

af·fect·ing *adj* : arousing pity, sympathy, or sorrow ⟨an *affecting* story⟩ — **af·fect·ing·ly** \ə-'fek-ting-lē, a-\ *adv*

¹af·fec·tion \ə-'fek-shən\ *n* **1** : a tender feeling of attachment : FONDNESS **2** : PROPENSITY, BENT

²affection *n* : DISEASE, DISORDER ⟨an *affection* of the brain⟩

af·fec·tion·ate \ə-'fek-shə-nət, -shnət\ *adj* : feeling or showing a great liking for a person or thing : TENDER — **af·fec·tion·ate·ly** *adv*

af·fec·tive \a-'fek-tiv\ *adj* : relating to, arising from, or influencing feelings or emotions : EMOTIONAL

af·fer·ent \'af-ə-rənt, 'af-ˌer-ənt\ *adj* : bearing or conducting inward; *esp* : conveying impulses toward a nerve center — compare EFFERENT [Latin *afferre* "to bring to", from *ad-* + *ferre* "to carry"]

af·fi·ance \ə-'fī-əns\ *vt* : to solemnly promise (oneself or another) in marriage : BETROTH ⟨the *affianced* couple⟩

af·fi·da·vit \ˌaf-ə-'dā-vət\ *n* : a sworn written statement; *esp* : one made under oath before an authorized official [Medieval Latin, "he has made an oath", from *affidare* "to give surety", derived from Latin *ad-* + *fides* "faith"]

¹af·fil·i·ate \ə-'fil-ē-ˌāt\ *vb* : to connect closely often as a member, branch, or associate ⟨*affiliated* themselves with a political party⟩ ⟨a school *affiliated* with the university⟩ [Medieval Latin *affiliare* "to adopt as a son", from Latin *ad-* + *filius* "son"] — **af·fil·i·a·tion** \ə-ˌfil-ē-'ā-shən\ *n*

²af·fil·i·ate \ə-'fil-ē-ət\ *n* : an affiliated person or organization

af·fin·i·ty \ə-'fin-ət-ē\ *n, pl* **-ties** **1** : relationship by marriage **2 a** : sympathy marked by community of interest : KINSHIP ⟨they felt a strange *affinity* with each other⟩ **b** : an attraction to or liking for ⟨developed an *affinity* for politics⟩ **c** : an attractive force between substances or particles that causes them to enter into and remain in chemical combination **3** : a relation between biological groups indicating community of origin [Latin *affinitas*, from *affinis* "bordering on, related by marriage", from *ad-* + *finis* "end, border"]

af·firm \ə-'fərm\ *vb* **1 a** : CONFIRM, RATIFY ⟨*affirm* a contract⟩ **b** : to state positively or with confidence : declare to be true **2** : to make a solemn and formal declaration or assertion in place of an oath [Middle French *afermer*, from Latin *affirmare*, from *ad-* + *firmus* "firm"]

af·fir·ma·tion \ˌaf-ər-'mā-shən\ *n* **1** : the act of affirming **2** : something affirmed

¹af·fir·ma·tive \ə-'fər-mət-iv\ *adj* **1** : asserting that the fact is so **2** : capable of being applied in a constructive way ⟨an *affirmative* approach to the problem⟩ **3** : favoring or supporting a proposition or motion — **af·firm·a·tive·ly** *adv*

²affirmative *n* **1** : an expression (as the word *yes*) of affirmation or agreement **2** : the affirmative side in a debate or vote

affirmative action *n* : the establishment of policies and practices intended to discourage discrimination (as in employment) on the basis of race or sex

¹af·fix \ə-'fiks\ *vt* **1** : to attach physically : FASTEN ⟨*affix* a stamp to a letter⟩ **2** : to attach in any way : ADD ⟨*affix* one's signature to a letter⟩ — **af·fix·a·tion** \ˌaf-ik-'sā-shən\ *n*

²af·fix \'af-ˌiks\ *n* : one or more sounds or letters attached to the beginning or end of a word and serving to produce a derivative word or an inflectional form — **af·fix·al** \-ˌik-səl\ *or* **af·fix·i·al** \a-'fik-sē-əl\ *adj*

af·fla·tus \ə-'flāt-əs\ *n* : a divine imparting of knowledge or power : INSPIRATION [Latin, "act of blowing or breathing on", from *afflare* "to blow on"]

af·flict \ə-'flikt\ *vt* **1** : to distress so severely as to cause continued suffering ⟨people *afflicted* by famine⟩ **2** : to have a harmful effect on ⟨political theories *afflicted* with confused thinking⟩ [Latin *affligere* "to cast down", from *ad-* + *fligere* "to strike"] □ **SYN TORMENT, TORTURE, RACK: AFFLICT** is general and applies to the causing of pain, annoyance, or distress; **TORMENT** suggests persecution or the repeated inflicting of suffering or annoyance; **TORTURE** adds the implication of causing to writhe with unbearable pain; **RACK** stresses straining or wrenching.

af·flic·tion \ə-'flik-shən\ *n* **1** : the state of being afflicted **2** : a cause of continued pain or distress

af·flic·tive \ə-'flik-tiv\ *adj* : causing affliction : DISTRESSING — **af·flic·tive·ly** *adv*

af·flu·ence \'af-,lü-əns *also* a-'flü- *or* ə-'flü-\ *n* **1** : an abundant flow or supply **2** : abundance of wealth or property

¹af·flu·ent \-ənt\ *adj* **1** : flowing in abundance : COPIOUS **2** : having an abundance of material possessions : WEALTHY, RICH [Middle French, from Latin *affluere* "to flow to", from *ad-* + *fluere* "to flow"] — **af·flu·ent·ly** *adv*

²affluent *n* : a tributary stream

af·ford \ə-'fōrd, -'ford\ *vt* **1** : to manage to do, give, or bear without serious harm ⟨you can't *afford* to waste your strength⟩ **2** : to manage to pay for ⟨unable to *afford* a new car⟩ **3** : PROVIDE **4** : FURNISH ⟨playing tennis *affords* healthful exercise⟩ [Old English *geforthian* "to carry out"] — **af·ford·able** \-ə-bəl\ *adj*

af·for·es·ta·tion \,a-,fōr-ə-'stā-shən, -,fär-\ *n* : the act or process of establishing a forest especially on land not previously forested

af·fray \ə-'frā\ *n* : a noisy quarrel or fight : BRAWL [Middle French, from *affreer* "to startle"]

af·fri·cate \'af-ri-kət\ *n* : a stop immediately followed by a related fricative (as the \d\ and \zh\ that make up the \j\ sounds of *judge*)

¹af·fright \ə-'frīt\ *vt* : FRIGHTEN 1, ALARM

²affright *n* : sudden and great fear : TERROR

¹af·front \ə-'frənt\ *vt* **1** : to insult especially to the face by language or behavior : OFFEND **2** : to face in defiance : CONFRONT [Middle French *afronter* "to defy", derived from Latin *ad-* + *frons* "forehead"] **SYN** see OFFEND

²affront *n* : a deliberately offensive act or utterance □ **SYN INSULT, INDIGNITY: AFFRONT** implies an open, deliberate act of disrespect; **INSULT** implies an attack intended to humiliate and degrade; **INDIGNITY** suggests an outrageous offense to one's personal dignity.

Af·ghan \'af-,gan *also* -gən\ *n* **1** : a native or inhabitant of Afghanistan **2** : PASHTO **3** *not cap* : a blanket or shawl of colored wool knitted or crocheted in strips or squares — **Afghan** *adj*

Afghan hound *n* : a tall slim swift hunting dog native to the Near East with a coat of silky thick hair and a long silky topknot

afi·cio·na·do \ə-,fish-ē-ə-'näd-ō, -,fis-ē-\ *n, pl* **-dos** : DEVOTEE 2, FAN [Spanish]

afield \ə-'fēld\ *adv* **1** : to, in, or on the field **2** : away from home **3** : out of a regular, planned, or proper course : ASTRAY

afire \ə-'fīr\ *adj or adv* : on fire : BLAZING

aflame \ə-'flām\ *adj or adv* : AFIRE

afloat \ə-'flōt\ *adv or adj* **1 a** : borne on or as if on the water **b** : at sea **2** : free of difficulties : SELF-SUFFICIENT ⟨enough money to keep the business *afloat*⟩ **3** : circulating about : RUMORED **4** : flooded with or submerged under water : AWASH

aflut·ter \ə-'flət-ər\ *adj* **1** : moving with brisk irregularity **2** : nervously excited

afoot \ə-'fut\ *adv or adj* **1** : on foot ⟨they traveled *afoot*⟩ **2** : in the process of development : under way ⟨a plan was *afoot* to seize power⟩

afore \ə-'fōr, -'for\ *adv or conj or prep, chiefly dialect* : BEFORE

afore·men·tioned \-,men-chənd\ *adj* : mentioned previously

afore·said \-,sed\ *adj* : said or named previously

afore·thought \-,thot\ *adj* : previously in mind : DELIBERATE ⟨with malice *aforethought*⟩

a for·ti·o·ri \,ä-,fōrt-ē-'ōr-ē, ,ä-,fort-ē-'ōr-,ī, -,'or-\ *adv* : with greater reason or more convincing force — used in drawing a conclusion that is inferred to be even more certain than another [New Latin, literally, "from the stronger (argument)"]

afoul of \ə-'faul-əv\ *prep* **1** : in or into collision or entanglement with ⟨one ship ran *afoul of* the other⟩ **2** : in or into conflict with ⟨they fell *afoul of* the law⟩

Afr- *or* **Afro-** *combining form* **1** : African ⟨*Afro-American*⟩ **2** : African and ⟨*Afro-Asiatic*⟩

afraid \ə-'frād, *South also* -'freəd *or* -'fred\ *adj* **1** : filled with fear or apprehension ⟨*afraid* of snakes⟩ **2** : filled with concern or regret over a possibly unfavorable occurrence ⟨*afraid* that they might be late⟩ **3** : UNWILLING, AVERSE ⟨*afraid* to work hard⟩ [Middle English *affraied*, from past participle of *affraien* "to frighten"]

afresh \ə-'fresh\ *adv* : from a new start : AGAIN

Af·ri·can \'af-ri-kən\ *n* **1** : a native or inhabitant of Africa **2** : a person of African and especially black ancestry — **African** *adj*

African sleeping sickness *n* : SLEEPING SICKNESS 1

African violet *n* : a tropical African plant related to the gloxinias and widely grown as a house plant for its velvety fleshy leaves and showy purple, pink, or white flowers

Af·ri·kaans \,af-ri-'käns, -'känz\ *n* : a language developed from 17th century Dutch that is one of the official languages of the Republic of South Africa [Afrikaans, from *afrikaans* "African"]

Af·ri·ka·ner \-'kän-ər\ *n* : a native South African of European descent; *esp* : an Afrikaans-speaking descendant of the 17th century Dutch settlers [Afrikaans]

¹Af·ro \'af-,rō\ *adj* : having the hair shaped into a round bushy mass [probably from *Afro-American*]

²Afro *n, pl* **Afros** : an Afro hairstyle

Af·ro–Amer·i·can \,af-rō-ə-'mer-ə-kən\ *adj* : of or relating to Americans of African and especially of black ancestry ⟨*Afro-American* history⟩ — **Afro–American** *n*

Af·ro–Asi·at·ic languages \,af-rō-,ā-zhē-'at-ik-, -zē-\ *n pl* : a family of languages widely distributed over southwestern Asia and northern Africa comprising the Semitic, Egyptian, Berber, Cushitic, and Chad subfamilies

aft \'aft\ *adv* : near, toward, or in the stern of a ship or the tail of an aircraft [Old English *æftan* "from behind, behind"]

¹af·ter \'af-tər\ *adv* : following in time or place : AFTERWARD, BEHIND ⟨returned 20 years *after*⟩ [Old English *æfter*]

²after *prep* **1 a** : behind in place ⟨following *after* them⟩ **b** : following in time or order ⟨*after* dinner⟩ **c** : subsequent to and in view of ⟨*after* all our advice⟩ **2** — used as a function word to indicate an object or goal ⟨go *after* gold⟩ ⟨ask *after* a friend⟩ **3 a** : in accordance with ⟨*after* an old custom⟩ **b** : with the name of or a name derived from that of ⟨named Pennsylvania *after* William Penn⟩ **c** : in imitation or resemblance of ⟨patterned *after* a Gothic cathedral⟩

³after *conj* : later than the time when

⁴after *adj* **1** : later in time : SUBSEQUENT ⟨in *after* years⟩ **2** : located toward the stern of a ship or tail of an aircraft

after all *adv* : NEVERTHELESS ⟨decided to go *after all*⟩

af·ter·birth \'af-tər-,bərth\ *n* : the placenta and fetal membranes that are expelled from the uterus after delivery

Afghan hound

\ə\ abut	\ng\ sing
\ər\ further	\ō\ bone
\a\ mat	\o\ saw
\ā\ take	\oi\ coin
\ä\ cot, cart	\th\ thin
\au\ out	\th\ this
\ch\ chin	\ü\ food
\e\ pet	\u\ foot
\ē\ easy	\y\ yet
\g\ go	\yü\ few
\i\ tip	\yu\ cure
\ī\ life	\zh\ vision
\j\ job	

af·ter·burn·er \-ˌbər-nər\ *n* **1** : an auxiliary burner attached to the tail pipe of a turbojet engine for injecting fuel into the hot exhaust gases and burning it to provide extra thrust **2** : a device for removing unburned carbon compounds from exhaust gases (as of a car)

af·ter·care \-ˌkeər, -ˌkaər\ *n* : the care, nursing, or treatment of a convalescent patient

af·ter·deck \-ˌdek\ *n* : the rear half of the deck of a ship

af·ter·ef·fect \-ə-ˌfekt\ *n* : an effect that follows its cause after some time has passed or after a first effect has subsided ⟨the *aftereffects* of surgery⟩

af·ter·glow \-ˌglō\ *n* **1** : a glow remaining (as in the sky after sunset) where a light has disappeared **2** : a reflection of past splendor, success, or emotion

af·ter·im·age \-ˌim-ij\ *n* : a usually visual sensation continuing after the stimulus causing it has ended

af·ter·life \-ˌlīf\ *n* **1** : an existence after death **2** : a later period in one's life

af·ter·math \'af-tər-ˌmath\ *n* **1** : a second-growth crop especially of hay **2** : EFFECT 1, RESULT ⟨felt guilty as an *aftermath* of the accident⟩ **3** : the period immediately following a usually ruinous event ⟨in the *aftermath* of the war⟩ [Old English *mæth* "mowing", from *māwan* "to mow"]

af·ter·noon \ˌaf-tər-ˈnün\ *n* : the part of day between noon and sunset — **afternoon** *adj*

af·ter·noons \-ˈnünz\ *adv* : in the afternoon repeatedly ⟨*afternoons* we take a nap⟩

af·ter·taste \'af-tər-ˌtāst\ *n* : a sensation (as of flavor) continuing after the stimulus causing it has ended

af·ter·thought \-ˌthȯt\ *n* **1** : an idea occurring later **2** : a part, feature, or device added to an earlier whole ⟨the porch was added as an *afterthought*⟩

af·ter·ward \'af-tər-wərd, -tə-\ *or* **af·ter·wards** \-wərdz\ *adv* : at a later time

af·ter·world \'af-tər-ˌwərld\ *n* : a future world : a world after death

ag- — see AD-

again \ə-ˈgen, -ˈgin, -ˈgān\ *adv* **1** : in return ⟨give them the message and bring us word *again*⟩ **2** : another time : ANEW ⟨come see us *again*⟩ **3** : in addition ⟨half as much *again*⟩ **4** : on the other hand ⟨we may, and *again* we may not⟩ **5** : FURTHER, MOREOVER ⟨*again*, there is another matter to consider⟩ [Middle English, "opposite, again", from Old English *ongēan* "opposite, back", from *on* + *gēan* "still, again"]

against \ə-ˈgenst, -ˈginst, -ˈgānst\ *prep* **1** : directly opposite : FACING ⟨over *against* the park⟩ **2 a** : in opposition or hostility to ⟨campaign *against* the enemy⟩ **b** : as a protection from ⟨a shield *against* aggression⟩ **3** : in preparation for ⟨storing food *against* the winter⟩ **4 a** : in the direction of and into contact with ⟨ran *against* a tree⟩ **b** : in contact with ⟨leaning *against* the wall⟩ **5** : in a direction opposite to ⟨walk *against* the wind⟩ **6** : before the background of ⟨green trees *against* the blue sky⟩ **7** : as a basis for disapproval of ⟨I have nothing *against* them⟩ **8** : in exchange for ⟨lend money *against* a promissory note⟩ [Middle English, from *again*]

¹agape \ə-ˈgāp *also* ə-ˈgap\ *adj* : having the mouth open (as in wonder or surprise)

²aga·pe \ä-ˈgä-ˌpā, 'äg-ə-ˌpā\ *n* **1** : LOVE 3a **2** : LOVE FEAST 1 [Greek *agapē*, literally, "love"]

agar \ˈäg-ər\ *or* **agar–agar** \ˌäg-ər-ˈäg-ər\ *n* **1** : a jelly-like extract of a red alga used especially in culture media or as a stabilizing agent in foods **2** : a culture medium containing agar [Malay *agar-agar*]

aga·ric \ˈag-ə-rik, ə-ˈgar-ik\ *n* **1** : any of several corky fungi used especially in the preparation of punk **2** : any of a family of gill fungi including the common brown-spored edible meadow mushroom [Greek *agarikon*, a kind of fungus]

ag·ate \'ag-ət\ *n* **1** : a fine-grained variegated quartz having its colors arranged in stripes, blended in clouds, or showing mosslike forms **2** : a child's playing marble of agate or of glass resembling agate **3** : a small size of type approximately 5½ point [Middle French, from Latin *achates*, from Greek *achatēs*]

ag·ate·ware \-ˌwaər, -ˌweər\ *n* : pottery veined and mottled to resemble agate

aga·ve \ə-ˈgäv-ē\ *n* : any of a genus of plants of the amaryllis family which have spiny-edged leaves and flowers in tall branched clusters and some of which are cultivated for fiber or for ornament [Greek *Agauē*, a daughter of Cadmus]

¹age \'āj\ *n* **1 a** : the time from birth to a specified date ⟨a child six years of *age*⟩ **b** (1) : the time of life when a person attains some right or capacity ⟨voting *age*⟩ (2) : MAJORITY **c** : the later part of life **d** : normal lifetime **2** : a period of time in history or in the development of human beings or in the history of the earth; *esp* : one characterized by some distinguishing feature ⟨machine *age*⟩ ⟨*Age* of Discovery⟩ ⟨*Age* of Reptiles⟩ **3** : a long period of time ⟨it happened *ages* ago⟩ [Old French *aage*, from Latin *aetas*] SYN see PERIOD — **of age** : having reached a time of maturity and especially of legal majority

²age *vb* **aged; ag·ing** *or* **age·ing** **1** : to become old : show the effects of increasing age **2** : to become or cause to become mellow or mature : RIPEN **3** : to cause to seem old especially prematurely (as by strain or suffering)

-age \ij\ *n suffix* **1** : aggregate : collection ⟨track*age*⟩ **2 a** : action : process ⟨haul*age*⟩ **b** : cumulative result of ⟨break*age*⟩ **c** : rate of ⟨dos*age*⟩ **3** : house or place of ⟨orphan*age*⟩ **4** : state : rank ⟨vassal*age*⟩ **5** : fee : charge ⟨post*age*⟩ [Old French, from Latin *-aticum*]

aged \'ā-jəd, *in senses 1b and 2b* 'ājd\ *adj* **1** : grown old: as **a** : of an advanced age **b** : having reached a specified age ⟨a person *aged* 40 years⟩ **2 a** : typical of old age **b** : having gained a desirable quality with age ⟨*aged* whiskey⟩ — **aged·ness** *n*

age·ism *also* **ag·ism** \'ā-ˌjiz-əm\ *n* : prejudice or discrimination against people of a particular age and especially against the elderly — **age·ist** \-jist\ *adj*

age·less \'āj-ləs\ *adj* **1** : not growing old or showing the effects of age **2** : TIMELESS, ETERNAL ⟨an *ageless* story⟩ — **age·less·ly** *adv* — **age·less·ness** *n*

age·long \'āj-ˌlȯng\ *adj* : lasting for a long time : EVERLASTING

agen·cy \'ā-jən-sē\ *n, pl* **-cies** **1** : the capacity, condition, or state of acting or of exerting power : OPERATION **2** : a person or thing through which power is exerted or an end is achieved ⟨registered my complaint through the *agency* of my lawyer⟩ **3 a** : the office or function of an agent **b** : the relationship between a principal and his or her agent **4** : an establishment engaged in doing business for another ⟨advertising *agency*⟩ **5** : an administrative division (as of a government) ⟨Central Intelligence *Agency*⟩

agen·da \ə-ˈjen-də\ *n* : a list of things to be considered (as at a meeting) or done [Latin, "things to be done", from *agere* "to do"]

agent \'ā-jənt\ *n* **1 a** : something that produces or is capable of producing an effect ⟨a cleansing *agent*⟩ **b** : a chemically, physically, or biologically active principle **2** : one that acts or exerts power **3** : one who acts for or in the place of another and by the other's authority ⟨government *agents*⟩ ⟨a real estate *agent*⟩ [Medieval Latin *agens*, from Latin *agere* "to drive, lead, act, do"]

agent pro·vo·ca·teur \ˌäzh-ˌäⁿ-prō-ˌväk-ə-ˈtər, 'ā-jənt-\ *n, pl* **agents provocateurs** \ˌäzh-ˌäⁿ-prō-ˌväk-ə-ˈtər, 'ājənts-prō-\ : a person paid to associate with members of a suspected group and to pretend sympathy with their aims so as to incite them to a legally punishable act [French, literally, "provoking agent"]

Age of Fishes : DEVONIAN 1
Age of Mammals : CENOZOIC 1
Age of Reptiles : MESOZOIC 1

age-old \'āj-'ōld\ *adj* : having existed for ages : ANCIENT

ag·er·a·tum \,aj-ə-'rāt-əm\ *n* : any of a large genus of tropical American composite herbs often cultivated for their small showy heads of blue, white, or pink flowers [Greek *agēratos* "ageless", from *a-* + *gēras* "old age"]

Ag·ge·us \a-'gē-əs\ *n* — see BIBLE table

ag·gie \'ag-ē\ *n* : an agate playing marble

¹ag·glom·er·ate \ə-'gläm-ə-,rāt\ *vb* : to gather into a ball, mass, or cluster [Latin *agglomerare* "to heap up", from *ad-* + *glomus* "ball"]

²ag·glom·er·ate \-rət\ *n* 1 : a jumbled mass or collection 2 : a rock composed of volcanic fragments of various sizes

ag·glom·er·a·tion \ə-,gläm-ə-'rā-shən\ *n* 1 : the action or process of collecting in a mass 2 : a heap or cluster of dissimilar elements — **ag·glom·er·a·tive** \ə-'gläm-ə-,rāt-iv\ *adj*

ag·glu·ti·nate \ə-'glüt-n-,āt\ *vb* 1 : to cause to adhere : FASTEN 2 : to cause to clump 3 : to unite into a group or gather into a mass 4 : to form words by agglutination [Latin *agglutinare*, from *ad-* + *gluten* "glue"]

ag·glu·ti·na·tion \ə-,glüt-n-'ā-shən\ *n* 1 : the action or process of agglutinating 2 : a mass or group formed by the union of separate elements 3 : the formation of derivative or compound words by putting together constituents of which each expresses a single definite meaning 4 : a reaction in which particles (as red blood cells or bacteria) suspended in a liquid collect into clumps usually as a response to a specific antibody — **ag·glu·ti·na·tive** \ə-'glüt-n-,āt-iv\ *adj*

ag·glu·ti·nin \ə-'glüt-n-ən\ *n* : an antibody causing agglutination

ag·glu·tin·o·gen \,ag-lü-'tin-ə-jən\ *n* : an antigen whose presence results in the formation of an agglutinin

ag·gran·dize \ə-'gran-,dīz, 'ag-rən-\ *vt* : to make great or greater (as in power or resources) [French *agrandiss-*, stem of *agrandir*, from *a-* "ad-" + *grandir* "to increase"] — **ag·gran·dize·ment** \ə-'gran-dəz-mənt, -,dīz-; ,ag-rən-'dīz-mənt\ *n* — **ag·gran·diz·er** *n*

ag·gra·vate \'ag-rə-,vāt\ *vt* 1 : to make worse, more serious, or more severe (problems *aggravated* by neglect) 2 : to rouse to displeasure or anger by usually persistent often petty goading [Latin *aggravare* "to make heavier", from *ad-* + *gravis* "heavy, grave"] SYN see INTENSIFY, IRRITATE

ag·gra·va·tion \,ag-rə-'vā-shən\ *n* 1 : the act of making something worse or more severe : an increase in severity (the treatment caused an *aggravation* of the pain) 2 : something that aggravates (the cold winter was an *aggravation* of their misery) 3 : the act of irritating or annoying

¹ag·gre·gate \'ag-ri-gət\ *adj* 1 : formed by the collection of units or particles into a whole (*aggregate* expenses) 2 : clustered in a dense mass or head (an *aggregate* flower) [Latin *aggregare* "to add to", from *ad-* + *greg-, grex* "flock"] — **ag·gre·gate·ly** *adv* — **ag·gre·gate·ness** *n*

²ag·gre·gate \-,gāt\ *vt* 1 : to collect or gather into a mass or whole 2 : to amount to altogether : TOTAL 2

³ag·gre·gate \-gət\ *n* 1 : a collection or sum of units or parts somewhat loosely associated 2 : the whole sum or amount : SUM TOTAL 3 a : any of several hard inert materials used for mixing with a cementing material to form concrete, mortar, or plaster b : a clustered mass of individual soil particles considered the basic structural unit of soil SYN see SUM

aggregate fruit *n* : a compound fruit (as a raspberry) made up of the several separate ripened ovaries of a single flower

ag·gre·ga·tion \,ag-ri-'gā-shən\ *n* 1 : the collecting of units or parts into a mass or whole 2 : a group, body, or mass composed of many distinct parts : ASSEMBLAGE

ag·gres·sion \ə-'gresh-ən\ *n* 1 : a forceful action or procedure; *esp* : an unprovoked attack 2 : the practice of making attacks or encroachments; *esp* : unprovoked violation by one country of the territorial integrity of another 3 : hostile, injurious, or destructive behavior or outlook especially when caused by frustration [Latin *aggressus*, past participle of *aggredi* "to attack", from *ad-* + *gradi* "to step, go"]

ag·gres·sive \ə-'gres-iv\ *adj* 1 a : tending toward or practicing aggression (an *aggressive* nation) b : showing readiness to fight or attack (an *aggressive* dog) 2 a : marked by initiative and vigor (an *aggressive* fund-raising campaign) b : obtrusively self-assertive (annoyed by an *aggressive* salesperson) — **ag·gres·sive·ly** *adv* — **ag·gres·sive·ness** *n*

ag·gres·sor \ə-'gres-ər\ *n* : one that commits or practices aggression

ag·grieved \ə-'grēvd\ *adj* 1 : troubled or distressed in spirit 2 : having a grievance; *esp* : suffering from injury or loss

aghast \ə-'gast\ *adj* : struck with terror, amazement, or horror : SHOCKED [Middle English *agast*, from *agasten* "to frighten", from *gast, gost* "ghost"]

ag·ile \'aj-əl, -,īl\ *adj* 1 : able to move quickly and easily : NIMBLE 2 : mentally quick [Middle French, from Latin *agilis*, from *agere* "to act, do"] — **ag·ile·ly** \-əl-lē, -ə-lē\ *adv*

agil·i·ty \ə-'jil-ət-ē\ *n, pl* **-ties** : the quality or state of being agile (the grace and *agility* of a gymnast)

aging *present participle of* AGE

agism, agist *variant of* AGEISM, AGEIST

ag·i·tate \'aj-ə-,tāt\ *vb* 1 : to shake jerkily : set in violent irregular motion (water *agitated* by wind) 2 : to stir up : EXCITE, DISTURB (*agitated* by bad news) 3 : to attempt to arouse or influence public interest in something especially by discussion or appeals (*agitate* for better schools) [Latin *agitare*, from *agere* "to drive, act, do"] SYN see SHAKE — **ag·i·tat·ed·ly** \-,tāt-əd-lē\ *adv* — **ag·i·ta·tion** \,aj-ə-'tā-shən\ *n*

agi·ta·to \,aj-ə-'tät-ō\ *adv or adj* : in a restless and agitated manner — used as a direction in music [Italian]

ag·i·ta·tor \'aj-ə-,tāt-ər\ *n* : one that agitates: as a : one who stirs up public feeling on controversial issues b : a device for stirring or shaking

agleam \ə-'glēm\ *adj* : BRIGHT, SHINING (eyes *agleam* with tears)

agley \ə-'glā, -'glē, -'glī\ *adv, chiefly Scottish* : AWRY 2, WRONG [Scots, from ¹*a-* + *gley* "to squint"]

aglit·ter \ə-'glit-ər\ *adj* : GLITTERY, SPARKLING

aglow \ə-'glō\ *adj* : radiating (as heat, light, or emotion) strongly

ag·nos·tic \ag-'näs-tik, əg-\ *n* : a person who holds that whether God exists is not known and probably cannot be known [Greek *agnōstos* "unknown, unknowable", from *a-* + *gnōstos* "known", from *gignōskein* "to know"] SYN see ATHEIST — **agnostic** *adj* — **ag·nos·ti·cism** \-'näs-tə-,siz-əm\ *n*

Ag·nus Dei \,äg-,nùs-'dā-,ē, ,än-,yüs-, -'dā; ,ag-nəs-'dē-,ī\ *n* 1 : a liturgical prayer said or sung to Christ as Savior 2 : an image of a lamb often with a halo and a banner and cross as a symbol of Christ [Late Latin, "lamb of God"; from its opening words]

ago \ə-'gō\ *adj or adv* : earlier than the present time (a week *ago*) [Middle English *agon, ago*, from *agon* "to pass away", from Old English *āgān*, from *ā-*, prefix denoting completion + *gān* "to go"]

agog \ə-'gäg\ *adj* : full of intense interest or excitement : EAGER [Middle French *en gogues* "in mirth"]

a-go-go \ä-'gō-,gō\ *n* : a usually small nightclub for dancing to live music [*Whisky à Gogo*, cafe and nightclub in Paris, France, from French *à gogo* "galore"]

\ə\ abut		\ng\ sing	
\ər\ further		\ō\ bone	
\a\ mat		\o̊\ saw	
\ā\ take		\o̊i\ coin	
\ä\ cot, cart		\th\ thin	
\au̇\ out		\th\ this	
\ch\ chin		\ü\ food	
\e\ pet		\u̇\ foot	
\ē\ easy		\y\ yet	
\g\ go		\yü\ few	
\i\ tip		\yu̇\ cure	
\ī\ life		\zh\ vision	
\j\ job			

ag·o·nal \'ag-ən-l\ *adj* : of, relating to, or associated with agony and especially the death agony

ag·o·nize \'ag-ə-ˌnīz\ *vb* 1 : to suffer or cause to suffer extreme physical or mental pain or anguish 2 : to strive desperately : STRUGGLE — **ag·o·niz·ing·ly** \-ˌnī-zing-lē\ *adv*

ag·o·ny \'ag-ə-nē\ *n, pl* **-nies** 1 a : intense physical or mental pain : ANGUISH, TORTURE b : the throes of death 2 : a strong sudden display of emotion ⟨an *agony* of delight⟩ [Greek *agōnia* "struggle, anguish", from *agōn* "gathering, contest for a prize"] SYN see DISTRESS □ ORIGIN In ancient Greece *agōn* was a public assembly or gathering, especially one for games and athletic contests. *Agōnia* was the struggle for the prize in such contests. From the meaning "a struggle for victory in the games", *agōnia* came to be used first for any physical struggle, then for any activity involving difficulty or pain, and finally for mental anguish as well. Our English word *agony* is a descendant of this Greek *agōnia*.

ag·o·ra \'ag-ə-rə\ *n, pl* **-ras** *or* **-rae** \-ˌrē, -ˌrī\ : the marketplace or place of assembly in an ancient Greek city [Greek]

ag·o·ra·pho·bia \ˌag-ə-rə-'fō-bē-ə\ *n* : abnormal fear of crossing or of being in open spaces — **ag·o·ra·pho·bic** \-'fō-bik, -'fäb-ik\ *adj*

agou·ti \ə-'güt-ē\ *n* 1 : a tropical American rodent about the size of a rabbit 2 : a grizzled color of fur resulting from the barring of each hair in several alternate dark and light bands [French, from Spanish *aguti*, of American Indian origin]

agouti 1

¹**agrar·i·an** \ə-'grer-ē-ən, -'grar-\ *adj* 1 : of or relating to the land or its ownership ⟨*agrarian* reforms⟩ 2 : of, relating to, or concerned with farmers or farming interests ⟨an *agrarian* political party⟩ 3 : AGRICULTURAL 2 ⟨an *agrarian* country⟩ [Latin *agr-, ager* "field"]

²**agrarian** *n* : a member of an agrarian party or movement

agrar·i·an·ism \-ē-ə-ˌniz-əm\ *n* : a social or political movement designed chiefly to improve the economic status of the farmer

agree \ə-'grē\ *vb* **agreed; agree·ing** 1 : to give one's approval : CONSENT ⟨*agree* to a plan⟩ 2 : ADMIT, CONCEDE ⟨*agreed* it was a good idea⟩ 3 : to be alike : CORRESPOND ⟨both copies *agree*⟩ 4 : to get on well together 5 : to come to terms ⟨*agree* on a price⟩ 6 : to be fitting or healthful : SUIT ⟨the climate *agrees* with them⟩ 7 : to correspond grammatically in gender, number, case, or person [Middle French *agreer*, from *a-* "ad-" + *gre* "pleasure", from Latin *gratus* "pleasant, agreeable"]

agree·able \ə-'grē-ə-bəl\ *adj* 1 : pleasing to the mind or senses ⟨an *agreeable* climate⟩ ⟨an *agreeable* fragrance⟩ 2 : ready or willing to agree 3 : being in harmony : CONSONANT — **agree·able·ness** *n* — **agree·ably** \-blē\ *adv*

agreed \ə-'grēd\ *adj* : settled by agreement ⟨a previously *agreed* price⟩

agree·ment \ə-'grē-mənt\ *n* 1 a : the act of agreeing b : harmony of opinion, action, or character : CONCORD 2 : a mutual arrangement or understanding as to a course of action; *also* : a written record of such an agreement 3 : the fact of agreeing grammatically

ag·ri·cul·tur·al \ˌag-ri-'kəlch-rəl, -ə-rəl\ *adj* 1 : of, relating to, or used in agriculture 2 : engaged in or concerned with agriculture ⟨an *agricultural* society⟩ — **ag·ri·cul·tur·al·ly** \-ē\ *adv*

ag·ri·cul·ture \'ag-ri-ˌkəl-chər\ *n* : the science, art, or occupation of cultivating the soil, producing crops, and raising livestock : FARMING [French, from Latin *agricultura*, from *ager* "field" + *cultura* "cultivation"] — **ag·ri·cul·tur·ist** \ˌag-ri-'kəlch-rəst, -ə-rəst\ *n*

ag·ri·mo·ny \'ag-rə-ˌmō-nē\ *n, pl* **-nies** : a common yellow-flowered herb of the rose family having toothed leaves and fruits like burs [Latin *agrimonia*]

agron·o·my \ə-'grän-ə-mē\ *n* : a branch of agriculture that deals with the raising of crops and the care of the soil [Greek *agros* "field" + *nomos* "law"] — **ag·ro·nom·ic** \ˌag-rə-'näm-ik\ *adj* — **ag·ro·nom·i·cal·ly** \-'näm-i-kə-lē, -klē\ *adv* — **agron·o·mist** \ə-'grän-ə-məst\ *n*

aground \ə-'graund\ *adv or adj* 1 : on or onto the shore or the bottom of a body of water ⟨a ship run *aground*⟩ 2 : on the ground ⟨planes aloft and *aground*⟩

ague \'ā-gyü\ *n* 1 : a fever (as malaria) marked by outbreaks of chills, fever, and sweating that recur at regular intervals 2 : a fit of shivering : CHILL [Middle French *aguë*, from Medieval Latin *febris acuta*, literally, "sharp fever"] — **agu·ish** \'ā-ˌgyü-ish\ *adj* — **agu·ish·ly** *adv*

ah \'ä\ *interj* — used to express delight, relief, regret, or contempt [Middle English]

aha \ä-'hä\ *interj* — used to express surprise, triumph, or derision [Middle English]

ahead \ə-'hed\ *adv or adj* 1 a : in a forward direction or position : FORWARD ⟨go *ahead*⟩ b : in front ⟨the car *ahead*⟩ 2 : in, into, or for the future ⟨think *ahead*⟩ 3 : in or toward a more advantageous position ⟨trying to get *ahead*⟩ 4 : in advance ⟨make payments *ahead*⟩

ahead of *prep* 1 : in front or advance of 2 : in excess of : ABOVE

ahem *a throat-clearing sound; often read as* ə-'hem\ *interj* — used especially to attract attention [imitative]

A–ho·ri·zon \'ā-hə-ˌrīz-n\ *n* : the outermost dark-colored layer of a soil profile consisting of topsoil containing partly disintegrated organic debris

ahoy \ə-'hoi\ *interj* — used in hailing ⟨ship *ahoy*⟩ [*a-* (as in *aha*) + Middle English *hoy*, interjection]

¹**aid** \'ād\ *vb* 1 : to provide with what is useful or necessary in achieving an end 2 : to give assistance [Middle French *aider*, from Latin *adjutare*, from *adjuvare*, from *ad-* + *juvare* "to help"]

²**aid** *n* 1 a : the act of helping b : help given : ASSISTANCE 2 a : an assisting person or group b : something (as a device) by which assistance is given ⟨a visual *aid*⟩

aide \'ād\ *n* : one that acts as an assistant; *esp* : a military officer acting as assistant to a superior [short for *aide-de-camp*]

aide–de–camp \ˌād-di-'kamp, -'kän\ *n, pl* **aides–de–camp** \ˌādz-di-\ : a military aide [French *aide de camp*, literally, "camp assistant"]

AIDS \'ādz\ *n* : a disease of the human immune system that is characterized by greatly reduced numbers of helper T cells due to infection with HIV, that renders the subject highly vulnerable to life-threatening infections, and that is commonly transmitted in blood, blood products, and bodily secretions (as semen) [*a*cquired *i*mmuno*d*eficiency *s*yndrome]

AIDS–related complex *n* : a group of symptoms (as fever, weight loss, and enlarged lymph nodes) that is associated with the presence of antibodies to HIV and that may be followed by the development of AIDS

AIDS virus *n* : HIV

ai·grette \ā-'gret, 'ā-\ *n* : a plume or decorative tuft for the head [French]

ai·ki·do \ˌī-ki-'dō\ *n* : a Japanese art of self-defense that consists of not actively resisting an attack but moving in such a way that the attacker's own momentum works against him [Japanese *aikidō*, from *ai-* "together" + *ki* "spirit" + *dō* "art"]

ail \'āl\ *vb* 1 : to be the matter with : TROUBLE ⟨what *ails* you?⟩ 2 : to have something the matter; *esp* : to suffer ill health [Old English *eglan*]

ai·lan·thus \ā-'lan-thəs, -'lant-\ *n* : a widely grown quick-growing Asian tree with pinnate leaves and terminal clusters of ill-scented greenish flowers — called also *tree of heaven* [Amboinese (the language of Ambon, an Indonesian island) *ai lanto,* literally, "tree of heaven"]

ai·le·ron \'ā-lə-ˌrän\ *n* : a movable portion of an airplane wing or a movable airfoil external to the wing for imparting a rolling motion [French, from *aile* "wing", from Latin *ala*]

ail·ment \'āl-mənt\ *n* : a bodily disorder : SICKNESS

¹aim \'ām\ *vb* **1 a** : to direct a course ⟨a goal to *aim* for⟩ **b** : to point a weapon at an object **2** : to direct one's efforts : ASPIRE ⟨*aim* high⟩ **3** : to have as a purpose : INTEND ⟨*aims* to win⟩ **4** : POINT **5a** ⟨telescopes *aimed* toward Mars⟩ [Middle French *aesmer* "to aim, estimate", from Latin *aestimare* "to estimate"]

²aim *n* **1 a** : the pointing of a weapon or a missile at a mark **b** : the ability to hit a target ⟨your *aim* is deadly⟩ **2** : GOAL 2, PURPOSE SYN see INTENTION

aim·less \'ām-ləs\ *adj* : lacking aim or purpose ⟨*aimless* wandering⟩ — **aim·less·ly** *adv* — **aim·less·ness** *n*

ain't \'ānt\ **1 a** : are not **b** : is not **c** : am not — though disapproved by many and more common in less educated speech, used orally in most parts of the United States by many educated speakers especially in a few set phrases ⟨you *ain't* seen nothing yet⟩ **2** *substandard* **a** : have not **b** : has not [probably contraction of *are not*]

Ai·nu \'ī-nü\ *n* **1** : a member of an indigenous Caucasoid people of Japan living chiefly in the northern islands **2** : the language of the Ainu people [Ainu, *aynu* "person"]

¹air \'aər, 'eər\ *n* **1 a** : the invisible mixture of odorless tasteless gases (as nitrogen and oxygen) that surrounds the earth **b** : a light breeze **2** : COMPRESSED AIR ⟨*air* sprayer⟩ **3 a** : a field of operation for aircraft ⟨transport by *air*⟩ **b** : AIRCRAFT ⟨*air* attack⟩ ⟨*air* mechanic⟩ ⟨*air* patrol⟩ **c** : AVIATION ⟨*air* safety⟩ ⟨*air* rights⟩ **d** : AIR FORCE ⟨*air* headquarters⟩ **e** (1) : the medium of transmission of radio waves (2) : RADIO, TELEVISION ⟨went on the *air*⟩ **4 a** : outward appearance : apparent nature ⟨an *air* of dignity⟩ **b** *pl* : an artificial or affected manner : HAUGHTINESS ⟨put on *airs*⟩ **c** : a surrounding or pervading influence : ATMOSPHERE ⟨an *air* of mystery⟩ **5** : TUNE 1, MELODY [Old French, from Latin *aer,* from Greek *aēr*]

²air *vt* **1** : to place in the air for cooling, refreshing, or cleansing ⟨*air* blankets⟩ **2** : to make known in public ⟨*air* one's complaints⟩

air bag *n* : an automobile safety device that is a bag designed to inflate automatically in front of an occupant in case of an accident

air bladder *n* : a sac in a fish containing gas and especially air and serving as a float regulating buoyancy or assisting respiration — called also *swim bladder*

air·borne \-ˌbōrn, -ˌbȯrn\ *adj* : supported or transported by air

air brake *n* **1** : a brake operated by a piston driven by compressed air **2** : a surface that may be projected into the air for lowering the speed of an airplane

air·brush \-ˌbrəsh\ *n* : an atomizer for applying by compressed air a fine spray (as of paint) — **airbrush** *vt*

air-con·di·tion \ˌaər-kən-'dish-ən, ˌeər-\ *vt* : to equip with an apparatus for cleaning air and controlling its humidity and temperature — **air con·di·tion·er** \-'dish-nər, -ə-nər\ *n*

air-cool \'aər-ˌkül, 'eər-\ *vt* : to cool the cylinders of (an internal-combustion engine) solely by the use of air

air·craft \'aər-ˌkraft, 'eər-\ *n, pl* **aircraft** : a machine (as an airplane, blimp, or helicopter) for navigation of the air that is supported either by its own buoyancy or by the action of the air against its surfaces

aircraft carrier *n* : a warship with a deck on which airplanes can be launched and landed

air-crew \'aər-ˌkrü, 'eər-\ *n* : the crew manning an airplane

air·drome \-ˌdrōm\ *n* : AIRPORT

air·drop \-ˌdräp\ *n* : delivery of cargo or personnel by parachute from an airplane in flight — **air-drop** \-ˌdräp\ *vt*

Aire·dale \'aər-ˌdāl, 'eər-\ *n* : any of a breed of large terriers with a hard wiry coat that is dark on the back and sides and tan elsewhere [*Airedale,* valley of the Aire river, England]

Air Express *service mark* — used for package transport by air

air·field \'aər-ˌfēld, 'eər-\ *n* **1** : the landing field of an airport **2** : AIRPORT

air·foil \-ˌfȯil\ *n* : an airplane surface (as a wing or rudder) designed to produce reaction (as lift or drag) from the air through which it moves

air force *n* : the military organization of a nation for air warfare

air·frame \-ˌfrām\ *n* : the structure of an airplane or rocket without the power plant

air gun *n* : any of various hand tools that work by compressed air; *esp* : AIRBRUSH

air hole *n* **1** : a hole to admit or discharge air **2** : AIR POCKET

air lane *n* : an airway that is customarily followed by airplanes

air letter *n* **1** : a letter sent by airmail **2** : a sheet of airmail stationery that can be folded and sealed with the message inside and the address outside

air·lift \'aər-ˌlift, 'eər-\ *n* : a supply line operated by aircraft — **airlift** *vt*

air·line \-ˌlīn\ *n* : an air transportation system including equipment, routes, and personnel

air line *n* : BEELINE

air·lin·er \-ˌlī-nər\ *n* : an airplane operated by an airline

air lock *n* : an air space with two airtight doors for permitting movement between two spaces with different pressures or different atmospheres

air·mail \'aər-ˌmāl, 'eər-\ *n* : the system of transporting mail by airplanes; *also* : the mail transported — **air-mail** *vt*

air·man \-mən\ *n* **1** : an enlisted rank in the Air Force above airman basic and below airman first class **2** : a civilian or military pilot or aviator

airman basic *n* : the lowest enlisted rank in the Air Force

airman first class *n* : an enlisted rank in the Air Force above airman and below sergeant

air mass *n* : a body of air extending hundreds or thousands of miles horizontally and sometimes as high as the stratosphere and maintaining as it travels nearly uniform conditions of temperature and humidity at any given level

air mattress *n* : MATTRESS 2

air-mind·ed \'aər-'mīn-dəd, 'eər-\ *adj* : interested in aviation or in air travel — **air-mind·ed·ness** *n*

air piracy *n* : the hijacking of a flying airplane

air·plane \-ˌplān\ *n* : a fixed-wing aircraft heavier than air that is driven by a propeller or by a rearward jet and supported by the reaction of the air against its wings [alteration of *aeroplane,* from Greek *aēr* "air" + *planos* "wandering", from *planasthai* "to wander"]

air plant *n* **1** : EPIPHYTE **2** : BRYOPHYLLUM

air pocket *n* : a condition of the atmosphere (as a down current) that causes an airplane to drop suddenly

air police *n* : the military police of an air force

air·port \'aər-ˌpōrt, 'eər-, -ˌpȯrt\ *n* : a tract of land or water that is maintained for the landing and takeoff of airplanes and for receiving and discharging passengers and cargo and that usually has facilities for the shelter, supply, and repair of planes

air pump *n* : a pump for exhausting air from a closed space or for compressing air or forcing it through other apparatus

airbrush

airplane

\ə\ abut	\ng\ sing	
\ər\ further	\ō\ bone	
\a\ mat	\ȯ\ saw	
\ā\ take	\ȯi\ coin	
\ä\ cot, cart	\th\ thin	
\au̇\ out	\th\ this	
\ch\ chin	\ü\ food	
\e\ pet	\u̇\ foot	
\ē\ easy	\y\ yet	
\g\ go	\yü\ few	
\i\ tip	\yu̇\ cure	
\ī\ life	\zh\ vision	
\j\ job		

air raid *n* : an attack by armed aircraft on a surface target

air rifle *n* : a rifle that shoots BBs or pellets by compressed air

air sac *n* **1** : one of the air-filled spaces connected with the lungs of a bird **2** : one of the thin-walled microscopic pouches in which gases are exchanged in the lungs — called also *alveolus*

air·ship \'aər-,ship, 'eər-\ *n* : a lighter-than-air aircraft having propulsion and steering systems

air·sick \-,sik\ *adj* : affected with motion sickness associated with flying — **air·sick·ness** *n*

air·space \-,spās\ *n* : the space lying above a nation and coming under its jurisdiction

air·speed \-,spēd\ *n* : the speed of an airplane relative to the air as opposed to its speed relative to the earth

air·strip \-,strip\ *n* : a runway without normal airport facilities

air·tight \-'tīt\ *adj* **1** : so tightly sealed that no air can get in or out **2** : leaving no opening for attack ⟨*airtight* defenses⟩ ⟨an *airtight* argument⟩ — **air·tight·ness** *n*

air·wave \-,wāv\ *n* : the medium of radio and television transmission — usually used in pl.

air·way \-,wā\ *n* **1** : a passage for a current of air **2** : a regular route for airplanes from airport to airport; *esp* : such a route equipped with navigational aids **3** : AIRLINE

air·wor·thy \-,wər-ˌthē\ *adj* : fit or safe for operation in the air ⟨a very *airworthy* plane⟩ — **air·wor·thi·ness** *n*

airy \'aər-ē, 'eər-\ *adj* **air·i·er; -est 1 a** : of or relating to air : ATMOSPHERIC **b** : high in the air : LOFTY ⟨*airy* perches⟩ **2** : consisting of air **3** : performed in the air : AERIAL ⟨*airy* leaps⟩ **4** : lacking a sound or solid basis ⟨*airy* romance⟩ **5** : resembling air in lightness : ETHEREAL **6** : open to the air : BREEZY ⟨an *airy* room⟩ — **air·i·ly** \'ar-ə-lē, 'er-\ *adv* — **air·i·ness** \'ar-ē-nəs, 'er-\ *n*

aisle \'īl\ *n* **1** : the side of a church separated by piers from the nave **2 a** : a passage (as in a theater) between sections of seats **b** : a passage (as in a store) for inside traffic [Middle French *aile* "wing", from Latin *ala*]

ajar \ə-'jär\ *adj or adv* : slightly open ⟨a door *ajar*⟩ [earlier *on char*, from *on* + *char* "turn", from Old English *cierr*]

akim·bo \ə-'kim-bō\ *adj or adv* **1** : having the hand on the hip and the elbow turned outward **2** : set in a bent position ⟨legs *akimbo*⟩ [Middle English *in kenebowe*]

akin \ə-'kin\ *adj* **1** : related by blood : descended from a common ancestor or prototype **2** : essentially similar or related : ALIKE

Ak·ka·di·an \ə-'kād-ē-ən\ *n* **1** : one of a Semitic people invading and settling central Mesopotamia north of the Sumerians (3000–1900 B.C.) **2** : an ancient Semitic language of Mesopotamia used from about the 28th to the 1st century B.C. — **Akkadian** *adj*

al- — see AD-

¹-al \əl, ᵊl\ *adj suffix* : of, relating to, or characterized by ⟨direction*al*⟩ ⟨fiction*al*⟩ [Latin *-alis*]

²-al *n suffix* : action : process ⟨rehears*al*⟩ [Old French *-aille*, from Latin *-alia*, neuter plural of *-alis*]

ala \'ā-lə\ *n, pl* **alae** \-,lē\ : a wing-shaped anatomic process or part : WING [Latin] — **alar** \'ā-lər\ *adj* — **ala·ry** \-lə-rē\ *adj*

a la *or* **à la** \,ä-,lä, ,ä-lə, ,a-lə\ *prep* : in the manner of [French *à la*]

al·a·bas·ter \'al-ə-,bas-tər\ *n* **1** : a compact fine-textured usually white and translucent gypsum that is carved into objects (as vases) **2** : a hard compact calcite that is translucent and sometimes banded [Latin *alabaster* "vase of alabaster", from Greek *alabastros*]

a la carte \,ä-lə-'kärt, ,a-\ *adj or adv* : according to a menu that prices each item separately [French *à la carte* "by the bill of fare"]

alack \ə-'lak\ *interj, archaic* — used to express sorrow, regret, or reproach [Middle English]

albatross

alac·ri·ty \ə-'lak-rət-ē\ *n* : promptness in response : a cheerful readiness to do something [Latin *alacritas*, from *alacer* "lively, eager"] SYN see CELERITY — **alac·ri·tous** \-rət-əs\ *adj*

a la mode \,ä-lə-'mōd, ,al-\ *adj* **1** : FASHIONABLE, STYLISH **2** : topped with ice cream [French *à la mode* "according to the fashion"]

al·a·nine \'al-ə-,nēn\ *n* : amino acid $C_3H_7NO_2$ formed especially by the hydrolysis of proteins [German *alanin*, derived from *aldehyd* "aldehyde"]

¹alarm \ə-'lärm\ *also* **alar·um** \ə-'lär-əm, -'lar-\ *n* **1** *usually* **alarum,** *archaic* : a call to arms **2 a** : a signal (as a loud noise or flashing light) that warns or alerts **b** : a device that warns or signals **3** : fear caused by a sudden sense of danger [Middle French *alarme*, from Italian *all'arme* "to arms"]

²alarm *also* **alarum** *vt* **1** : to notify of danger : put on the alert **2** : to strike with fear : FRIGHTEN — **alarm·ing·ly** \-'lär-ming-lē\ *adv*

alarm clock *n* : a clock that can be set to sound an alarm at a desired time

alarm·ist \ə-'lär-məst\ *n* : one inclined to alarm others especially needlessly — **alarm·ism** \-,miz-əm\ *n*

alas \ə-'las\ *interj* — used to express unhappiness, pity, or concern [Old French, from *a* "ah" + *las* "weary", from Latin *lassus*]

Alas·kan malamute \ə-'las-kən-\ *n* : any of a breed of powerful heavy-coated deep-chested dogs of Alaskan origin with erect ears, heavily cushioned feet, and plumy tail

Alas·ka time \ə-'las-kə-\ *n* : the time of the 9th time zone west of Greenwich that includes most of Alaska

alate \'ā-,lāt\ *adj* : having wings or a winglike part [Latin *alatus*, from *ala* "wing"]

alb \'alb\ *n* : a full-length white linen vestment with long sleeves worn by a priest at Mass [Medieval Latin *alba*, from Latin *albus* "white"]

al·ba·core \'al-bə-,kōr, -,kȯr\ *n, pl* **-core** *or* **-cores** : a large pelagic tuna with long pectoral fins that is the source of most canned tuna; *also* : any of several tunas [Portuguese *albacor*, from Arabic *al-bakūrah* "the albacore"]

Al·ba·nian \al-'bā-nē-ən, -nyən\ *n* **1** : a native or inhabitant of Albania **2** : the Indo-European language of the Albanian people — **Albanian** *adj*

al·ba·tross \'al-bə-,trȯs, -,träs\ *n, pl* **-tross** *or* **-tross·es** : any of various large web-footed seabirds that are related to the petrels and include the birds of the sea with the greatest wingspread [probably alteration of *alcatras* "water bird", from Portuguese or Spanish *alcatraz* "pelican"]

al·be·do \al-'bēd-ō\ *n* : the fraction of incident radiant energy reflected from a surface (as of the earth) [Late Latin, "whiteness", from Latin *albus* "white"]

al·be·it \ȯl-'bē-ət, al-\ *conj* : even though : ALTHOUGH [Middle English, literally, "all though it be"]

al·bi·no \al-'bī-nō\ *n, pl* **-nos** : an organism deficient in coloring matter; *esp* : a human being or lower animal that is congenitally deficient in pigment and usually has a milky or translucent skin, white or colorless hair, and eyes with pink or blue iris and deep red pupil [Portuguese, from Spanish, from *albo* "white", from Latin *albus*] — **al·bi·nism** \'al-bə-,niz-əm, al-'bī-\ *n* — **al·bi·nis·tic** \,al-bə-'nis-tik\ *adj* — **albino** *adj* — **al·bi·not·ic** \,al-bə-'nät-ik, -,bī-\ *adj*

al·bite \'al-,bīt\ *n* : a usually white feldspar containing sodium [Swedish *albit*, from Latin *albus* "white"]

al·bum \'al-bəm\ *n* **1 a** : a book with blank pages used for a collection (as of photographs) **b** : a container for a phonograph record **c** : one or more phonograph records or tape recordings produced as a single unit **2** : a collection usually in book form of literary selections, musical compositions, or pictures : ANTHOLOGY [Latin, "white tablet", from *albus* "white"]

al·bu·men \al-'byü-mən\ *n* **1** : the white of an egg **2** : ALBUMIN [Latin, from *albus* "white"]

al·bu·min \al-'byü-mən\ *n* : any of numerous heat-co-agulable water-soluble proteins found especially in blood, the whites of eggs, and various animal and plant tissues [Latin *albumen* "white of an egg"]

al·bu·min·ous \al-'byü-mə-nəs\ *adj* : relating to, containing, or having the properties of albumen or albumin

al·ca·zar \al-'käz-ər, -kaz-\ *n* : a Spanish fortress or palace [Spanish *alcázar,* from Arabic *al-qasr* "the castle"]

al·che·my \'al-kə-mē\ *n* **1** : a medieval chemical science and philosophy aiming to achieve the conversion of base metals into gold, the discovery of a universal cure for disease, and the discovery of a means of indefinitely prolonging life **2** : a power or process of transforming something common into something precious [Medieval Latin *alchymia,* from Arabic *al-kimiyā'* "the alchemy", from Late Greek *chēmeia* "alchemy"] — **al·chem·i·cal** \al-'kem-i-kəl\ *adj* — **al·chem·i·cal·ly** \-kə-lē, -klē\ *adv* — **al·che·mist** \'al-kə-məst\ *n*

al·co·hol \'al-kə-,hol\ *n* **1 a** : a colorless volatile flammable liquid C_2H_5OH that is the intoxicating agent in fermented and distilled liquors (as beer, wine, whiskey) — called also *ethyl alcohol* **b** : any of various carbon compounds that are similar to ethyl alcohol in having at least one hydroxyl group **2** : a beverage (as beer, wine, or whiskey) containing alcohol; *also* : LIQUORS [Medieval Latin, "powdered antimony", from Spanish, from Arabic *al-kuhul* "the powdered antimony"]

¹al·co·hol·ic \,al-kə-'hol-ik, -'häl-\ *adj* **1** : of, relating to, caused by, or containing alcohol **2** : affected with alcoholism — **al·co·hol·i·cal·ly** \-i-kə-lē, -klē\ *adv*

²alcoholic *n* : one affected with alcoholism

al·co·hol·ism \'al-kə-,hȯ-,liz-əm\ *n* : continued excessive and usually uncontrollable use of alcoholic drinks; *also* : the abnormal state associated with such use

al·cove \'al-,kōv\ *n* **1** : a small recessed section of a room : NOOK **2** : an arched opening (as in a wall) [French *alcôve,* from Spanish *alcoba,* from Arabic *al-qubbah* "the arch"]

Al·deb·a·ran \al-'deb-ə-rən\ *n* : a red star that is seen in the eye of Taurus and is the brightest star in the Hyades [Arabic *al-dabarān,* literally, "the follower"]

al·de·hyde \'al-də-,hīd\ *n* **1** : ACETALDEHYDE **2** : any of various highly reactive organic compounds typified by acetaldehyde and characterized by the group —CHO [German *aldehyd,* from New Latin *al. dehyd.,* abbreviation of *alcohol dehydrogenatum* "dehydrogenated alcohol"]

al·der \'ȯl-dər\ *n* : any of a genus of toothed-leaved trees or shrubs related to the birches and found especially in moist ground [Old English *alor*]

al·der·fly \-,flī\ *n* : any of several winged insects closely related to the dobsonflies

al·der·man \'ȯl-dər-mən\ *n* **1** : a high Anglo-Saxon government official **2** : a member of a governing or legislative body of some counties, cities, towns, or boroughs [Old English *ealdorman,* from *ealdor* "elder, parent"] — **al·der·man·ic** \,ȯl-dər-'man-ik\ *adj*

al·der·wom·an \-,wu̇m-ən\ *n* : a woman with the rank and office of an alderman

al·dol·ase \'al-də-,lās, -,lāz\ *n* : an enzyme of living systems that catalyzes reversibly the cleavage of a fructose ester into sugars with three carbon atoms [*ald*ehyde + *-ol* + *-ase*]

al·do·ste·rone \al-'däs-tə-,rōn, ,al-dō-stə-'rōn\ *n* : a steroid hormone of the adrenal cortex that functions in the regulation of the salt and water balance of the body [derived from *ald*ehyde + *sterol*]

al·drin \'ȯl-drən, 'al-\ *n* : a long-acting insecticide that is a chlorinated derivative of naphthalene [Kurt *Alder,* died 1958, German chemist]

ale \'āl\ *n* **1** : an alcoholic beverage brewed from malt and hops that is usually heavier bodied and more bitter than beer **2** : an English country festival at which ale is the chief beverage [Old English *ealu*]

alee \ə-'lē\ *adv* : on or toward the lee

ale·house \'āl-,hau̇s\ *n* : a place where ale is sold to be drunk on the premises

alem·bic \ə-'lem-bik\ *n* : an apparatus formerly used in distillation [Medieval Latin *alembicum,* from Arabic *al-anbīq* "the still", derived from Greek *ambix* "cap of a still"]

aleph–null \'äl-,ef-'nəl, -əf-\ *n* : a number that is the smallest infinite cardinal number and that is equal to the number of elements in any set that can be put into a one-to-one correspondence with the positive integers [from *aleph,* the first letter of the Hebrew alphabet]

¹alert \ə-'lərt\ *adj* **1 a** : watchful and prompt to meet danger **b** : quick to perceive and act **2** : briskly active : LIVELY ⟨an *alert* movement⟩ [Italian *all'erta,* literally, "on the ascent"] SYN see CLEVER, WATCHFUL — **alert·ly** *adv* — **alert·ness** *n*

²alert *n* **1** : a signal of danger **2 a** : the state of readiness of those warned by an alert **b** : the period during which an alert is in effect — **on the alert** : on the lookout for danger

³alert *vt* : to call to a state of readiness : WARN

al·eu·rone \'al-yə-,rōn\ *n* : granular protein matter in the endosperm of a seed [Greek *aleuron* "flour"]

Aleut \ə-'lüt\ *n* **1** : a member of a people of the Aleutian and Shumagin islands and the western part of Alaska peninsula **2** : the language of the Aleuts [Russian]

ale·wife \'āl-,wīf\ *n* : an anadromous food fish of the herring family abundant along the Atlantic coast

Al·ex·an·dri·an \,al-ig-'zan-drē-ən, ,el-\ *adj* : HELLENISTIC [from the prominence of Alexandria, Egypt, in the intellectual and cultural life of the Hellenistic period]

al·ex·an·drine \-'zan-drən\ *n, often cap* : a line of poetry consisting of six iambic feet [Middle French *vers alexandrin,* literally, "verse of Alexander"; from its use in a poem on Alexander the Great]

al·fal·fa \al-'fal-fə\ *n* : a deep-rooted European leguminous plant with purple flowers and leaves like clover that is widely grown for hay and forage [Spanish, from Arabic dialect *al-fasfasah* "the alfalfa"]

al·fres·co \al-'fres-kō\ *adv or adj* : in the open air ⟨an *alfresco* lunch⟩ [Italian]

al·ga \'al-gə\ *n, pl* **al·gae** \'al-jē\ : any plant of a group (Algae) that forms the lowest division of the plant kingdom and includes seaweeds and related forms mostly growing in water, lacking a vascular system, and having chlorophyll often masked by brown or red coloring matter [Latin, "seaweed"] — **al·gal** \'al-gəl\ *adj*

al·ge·bra \'al-jə-brə\ *n* : a branch of mathematics in which symbols (as letters and numerals) representing various entities (as numbers or functions) are combined according to special rules of operation [Medieval Latin, from Arabic *al-jabr,* literally, "the reduction"] — **al·ge·bra·ist** \-,brā-əst\ *n*

al·ge·bra·ic \,al-jə-'brā-ik\ *adj* **1** : of or relating to algebra ⟨*algebraic* expression⟩ **2** : involving only a finite number of repetitions of addition, subtraction, multiplication, division, extraction of roots, and raising to powers — **al·ge·bra·i·cal·ly** \-'brā-ə-kə-lē, -klē\ *adv*

-al·gia \'al-jē-ə, -jə\ *n combining form* : pain ⟨neural-*gia*⟩ [Greek *algos*]

al·gin \'al-jən\ *n* : any of various colloidal substances from brown algae including some used especially as stabilizers or emulsifiers

Al·gol \'al-,gäl, -,gȯl\ *n* : a binary star in the constellation Perseus whose larger component revolves about and eclipses the smaller brighter star causing periodic variation in brightness [Arabic *al-ghūl,* literally, "the ghoul"]

alga: *top* laminaria, *middle* ulva, *bottom* kelp

\ə\ abut	\ng\ sing
\ər\ further	\ō\ bone
\a\ mat	\ȯ\ saw
\ā\ take	\ȯi\ coin
\ä\ cot, cart	\th\ thin
\au̇\ out	\th\ this
\ch\ chin	\ü\ food
\e\ pet	\u̇\ foot
\ē\ easy	\y\ yet
\g\ go	\yü\ few
\i\ tip	\yu̇\ cure
\ī\ life	\zh\ vision
\j\ job	

AL·GOL \\'al-ˌgäl, -ˌgȯl\ *n* : a language for programming a computer especially to work scientific problems [*algo*rithmic *l*anguage]

Al·gon·qui·an \al-'gän-kwē-ən, -'gäng-\ *n* **1** : an Indian people of the Ottawa river valley **2** : a stock of Indian languages spoken from Labrador to the Carolinas and westward to the Great Plains **3** : a member of the Indian peoples speaking Algonquian languages — **Algonquian** *adj*

al·go·rithm \\'al-gə-ˌrith-əm\ *n* : a rule of procedure for solving a mathematical problem (as finding the greatest common divisor of two numbers) in a finite number of steps that frequently involves repetition of an operation [Medieval Latin *algorismus,* from Arabic *al-khuwārizmi,* from *al-Khuwarizmi,* flourished 825 A.D., Arab mathematician] — **al·go·rith·mic** \ˌal-gə-'rith-mik\ *adj*

¹alias \\'ā-lē-əs, 'āl-yəs\ *adv* : otherwise called : otherwise known as [Latin, "otherwise", from *alius* "other"]

²alias *n* : an assumed name

¹al·i·bi \\'al-ə-ˌbī\ *n* **1** : a plea made by an accused person that he was elsewhere when the incident occurred; *also* : the fact or state of having been elsewhere at the time **2** : a plausible excuse (as for failure) [Latin, "elsewhere", from *alius* "other"]

²alibi *vb* **-bied; -bi·ing 1** : to offer an excuse **2** : to make an excuse for

¹alien \\'ā-lē-ən, 'āl-yən\ *adj* **1** : belonging or relating to another person or place : STRANGE **2** : relating, belonging, or owing allegiance to another country : FOREIGN (*alien* residents) **3** : wholly different in nature or character (an effect *alien* from the one intended) **4** : not properly belonging to something (a detail *alien* to the argument) **5** : repugnant in nature (an *alien* idea) [Old French, from Latin *alienus,* from *alius* "other"]

²alien *n* **1** : a person of another family, race, or nation **2** : a foreign-born resident who has not been naturalized and is still a subject or citizen of a foreign country

alien·able \\'āl-yə-nə-bəl, 'ā-lē-ə-nə-\ *adj* : transferable to the ownership of another (*alienable* property) — **alien·abil·i·ty** \ˌāl-yə-nə-'bil-ət-ē, ˌā-lē-ə-nə-\ *n*

alien·ate \\'ā-lē-ə-ˌnāt, 'āl-yə-ˌnāt\ *vt* **1** : to transfer (as a title, property, or right) to another **2** : to cause to lose feelings of love, loyalty, or attachment (*alienated* by their constant complaints) **3** : to cause to be withdrawn or diverted (*alienate* funds from a project) — **alien·ation** \ˌā-lē-ə-'nā-shən, ˌāl-yə-'nā-\ *n* — **alien·ator** \\'ā-lē-ə-ˌnāt-ər, 'āl-yə-ˌnāt-\ *n*

alien·ist \\'ā-lē-ə-nəst, 'āl-yə-nəst\ *n* : PSYCHIATRIST; *esp* : one who testifies in a legal proceeding

¹alight \ə-'līt\ *vi* **alight·ed** \-'līt-əd\ *also* **alit** \ə-'lit\; **alight·ing 1** : to come down from something : DISMOUNT **2** : to descend from the air and settle : LAND

²alight *adj* : lighted up : ILLUMINATED

align *also* **aline** \ə-'līn\ *vb* **1** : to bring or come into line or alignment **2** : to cause to support or be in disapprove something (as a cause or party) [French *aligner,* from Old French, from *ligne* "line", from Latin *linea*] — **align·er** *n*

align·ment *also* **aline·ment** \ə-'līn-mənt\ *n* **1 a** : the act of aligning : the state of being aligned **b** : the proper positioning or state of adjustment of parts (as of a mechanical or electronic device) in relation to each other **2** : an arrangement of groups or forces (a new political *alignment*)

¹alike \ə-'līk\ *adj* : LIKE 1a — **alike·ness** *n*

²alike *adv* : in the same manner, form, or degree

al·i·ment \\'al-ə-mənt\ *n* : NUTRIMENT; *also* : food for the mind or spirit [Latin *alimentum,* from *alere* "to nourish"] — **al·i·men·tal** \ˌal-ə-'ment-l\ *adj* — **al·i·men·tal·ly** \-l-ē\ *adv*

al·i·men·ta·ry \ˌal-ə-'ment-ə-rē, -'men-trē\ *adj* : of or relating to nourishment or nutrition

alimentary canal *n* : the tube that extends from mouth to anus and functions in digestion and absorption of food and in elimination of residual waste

al·i·mo·ny \\'al-ə-ˌmō-nē\ *n, pl* **-nies** : an allowance of money made to one spouse by the other for support pending or after legal separation or divorce [Latin *alimonia* "support", from *alere* "to nourish"]

al·i·phat·ic \ˌal-ə-'fat-ik\ *adj* : belonging to a group of organic compounds whose structure is in the form of a chain whose ends are not joined [Greek *aleiphar* "oil"]

al·i·quot \\'al-ə-ˌkwät, -kwət\ *adj* : contained an exact number of times in another (5 is an *aliquot* part of 15) [Medieval Latin *aliquotus,* from Latin *aliquot* "some, several"]

alive \ə-'līv\ *adj* **1** : having life : LIVING (the proudest person *alive*) **2** : still in existence, force, or operation : ACTIVE (keep hope *alive*) **3** : knowingly aware or conscious : SENSITIVE (*alive* to the danger) **4** : marked by much life, animation, or activity : SWARMING (blossoms *alive* with bees) — **alive·ness** *n*

aliz·a·rin \ə-'liz-ə-rən\ *n* : an orange or red crystalline compound $C_{14}H_8O_4$ made synthetically and used as a red dye and in making red pigments [probably from French *alizarine*]

al·ka·li \\'al-kə-ˌlī\ *n, pl* **-lies** *or* **-lis 1** : a substance (as a hydroxide or carbonate of an alkali metal) having marked basic properties **2** : ALKALI METAL **3** : a soluble salt or a mixture of soluble salts present in some soils of arid regions [Medieval Latin, from Arabic *al-qili* "the soda ash"]

alkali metal *n* : any of the univalent mostly basic metals of the group lithium, sodium, potassium, rubidium, cesium, and francium

al·ka·line \\'al-kə-ˌlīn, -lən\ *adj* : of, relating to, or having the properties of an alkali; *esp* : having a pH of more than 7 — **al·ka·lin·i·ty** \ˌal-kə-'lin-ət-ē\ *n*

alkaline earth *n* **1** : an oxide of any of several strongly basic metals comprising calcium, strontium, and barium and sometimes also magnesium, radium, or less often beryllium **2** : ALKALINE-EARTH METAL

alkaline–earth metal *n* : any of the metals whose oxides are the alkaline earths

al·ka·loid \\'al-kə-ˌlȯid\ *n* : any of numerous usually colorless, complex, and bitter organic bases (as morphine or codeine) that contain nitrogen and usually oxygen and occur especially in seed plants — **al·ka·loi·dal** \ˌal-kə-'lȯid-l\ *adj*

al·kyd \\'al-kəd\ *n* : any of numerous thermoplastic synthetic resins made by heating alcohols with acids or their anhydrides and used especially for protective coatings [probably derived from German *alkohol* "alcohol"]

¹all \\'ȯl\ *adj* **1 a** : the whole of (sat up *all* night) **b** : the greatest possible (told in *all* seriousness) **2** : every member or individual part of (*all* students will go) **3** : the whole number or sum of (*all* the angles of a triangle are equal to two right angles) **4** : EVERY (*all* manner of hardship) **5** : any whatever (beyond *all* doubt) **6 a** : completely taken up with or absorbed by (became *all* attention) **b** : having or seeming to have a prominent physical feature (*all* thumbs) **c** : paying full attention with (*all* ears) **7** : being more than one person or thing (who *all* was there) [Old English *eall*]

²all *adv* **1** : WHOLLY, ALTOGETHER (sat *all* alone) (*all* across the country) **2** *obsolete* : ONLY 1b, SOLELY **3** *archaic* : quite as indicated : JUST **4** : so much (*all* the better for it) **5** : for each side : APIECE (the score is two *all*)

³all *pron, pl in construction* **1** : the whole number, quantity, or amount (*all* that I have) (*all* of us) **2** : EVERYBODY, EVERYTHING (sacrificed *all* for love) (known to *all*) — **all in all** : on the whole (*all in all,* it could be worse) — **at all** : in any way (no good *at all*)

all- *or* **allo-** *combining form* : other : different : atypical ⟨*allo*tropy⟩ [Greek *allos* "other"]

¹**al·la breve** \,al-ə-'brev, ,äl-ə-'brev-,ā\ *adv or adj* : in duple or quadruple time with the beat represented by the half note [Italian, literally, "according to the breve"]

²**alla breve** *n* : the sign ¢ marking a piece or passage to be played alla breve; *also* : a passage so marked

Al·lah \'äl-ə, 'al-ə, 'äl-,ä, ä-'lä\ *n* : the Supreme Being of Islam [Arabic *Allāh*]

all along *adv* : all the time ⟨knew the truth *all along*⟩

all-Amer·i·can \,òl-ə-'mer-ə-kən\ *adj* **1** : representative of American ideals ⟨an *all-American* city⟩ **2** : selected as the best in the United States ⟨the *all-American* team⟩ — **all-American** *n*

al·lan·to·is \ə-'lant-ə-wəs\ *n, pl* **al·lan·to·ides** \,al-ən-'tō-ə-,dēz\ : a fetal membrane of higher vertebrates that is covered with blood vessels and is associated with the chorion in formation of the placenta in mammals [New Latin, derived from Greek *allas* "sausage"] — **al·lan·to·ic** \,al-ən-'tō-ik\ *adj*

al·lar·gan·do \,äl-,är-'gän-dō\ *adv or adj* : gradually slower with the same or greater volume — used as a direction in music [Italian, literally, "widening"]

all-around \,ò-lə-'raùnd\ *adj* : competent in many fields

al·lay \ə-'lā\ *vt* **-layed; -lay·ing 1** : to make less severe : RELIEVE ⟨*allay* pain⟩ **2** : to make quiet : CALM ⟨*allay* anxiety⟩ [Old English *ālecgan*, from *ā-*, prefix denoting completion + *lecgan* "to lay"]

all but *adv* : very nearly : ALMOST ⟨would be *all but* impossible⟩

all clear *n* : a signal that a danger has passed

al·le·ga·tion \,al-i-'gā-shən\ *n* **1** : the act of alleging **2** : something alleged; *esp* : an assertion unsupported by proof or evidence

al·lege \ə-'lej\ *vt* **1** : to state positively but without offering proof ⟨the newspaper *alleged* the mayor's guilt⟩ **2** : to offer as a reason or an excuse ⟨*allege* illness to avoid work⟩ [Old French *alleguer*, from Latin *allegare* "to dispatch, cite", from *ad-* + *legare* "to depute"]

al·leged \ə-'lejd, -'lej-əd\ *adj* : asserted or believed to be so without proof ⟨the *alleged* criminal⟩ — **al·leg·ed·ly** \ə-'lej-əd-lē\ *adv*

al·le·giance \ə-'lē-jəns\ *n* **1** : loyalty and obedience owed to one's country or government **2** : devotion or loyalty to a person, group, or cause [Middle English *allegeaunce*, from Old French *ligeance*, from *lige* "liege"] SYN see FIDELITY

al·le·go·rize \'al-ə-,gòr-,īz, -,gór-, -gər-\ *vt* **1** : to make into allegory **2** : to treat or explain as allegory — **al·le·go·ri·za·tion** \,al-ə-,gòr-ə-'zā-shən, -,gór-\ *n* — **al·le·go·riz·er** *n*

al·le·go·ry \'al-ə-,gòr-ē, -,gór-\ *n, pl* **-ries** : a story in which the characters and events are symbols expressing truths about human life [Latin *allegoria*, from Greek *allēgoria*, from *allēgorein* "to speak figuratively", from *allos* "other" + *-agorein* "to speak", from *agora* "public assembly"] — **al·le·gor·i·cal** \,al-ə-'gòr-i-kəl, -'gär-\ *adj* — **al·le·gor·i·cal·ly** \-k(ə)-lē\ *adv*

al·le·gret·to \,al-ə-'gret-ō, ,äl-\ *adv or adj* : faster than andante but not so fast as allegro — used as a direction in music [Italian, from *allegro*]

¹**al·le·gro** \ə-'leg-rō, -'lā-grō\ *adv or adj* : in a brisk lively manner — used as a direction in music [Italian, literally, "merry", derived from Latin *alacer* "lively"]

²**allegro** *n, pl* **-gros** : a piece or movement in allegro tempo

al·lele \ə-'lēl\ *n* : any of the group of genes from which a pair of genes occupying identical places on homologous chromosomes can be drawn [German *allel*, short for *allelomorph*, from Greek *allēlōn* "of one another" + *morphē* "form"] — **al·le·lic** \-'lē-lik, -'lel-ik\ *adj*

al·le·lu·ia \,al-ə-'lü-yə\ *interj* : HALLELUJAH

al·ler·gen \'al-ər-jən\ *n* : a substance that induces allergy — **al·ler·gen·ic** \,al-ər-'jen-ik\ *adj*

al·ler·gic \ə-'lər-jik\ *adj* **1** : of, relating to, inducing, or affected by allergy ⟨an *allergic* reaction⟩ ⟨*allergic* to cat fur⟩ **2** : having a dislike for ⟨*allergic* to hard work⟩

al·ler·gist \'al-ər-jəst\ *n* : a specialist in allergy

al·ler·gy \'al-ər-jē\ *n, pl* **-gies 1** : exaggerated or abnormal reaction (as by sneezing, itching, or rashes) to substances, situations, or physical states that do not have such a strong effect on most people **2** : a feeling of dislike [German *allergie*, from Greek *allos* "other" + *ergon* "work"]

al·le·vi·ate \ə-'lē-vē-,āt\ *vt* **1** : to make more bearable : RELIEVE ⟨*alleviate* pain⟩ **2** : to remove or correct in part ⟨*alleviate* a labor shortage⟩ [Late Latin *alleviare*, from *ad-* + *levis* "light"] SYN see RELIEVE — **al·le·vi·a·tion** \ə-,lē-vē-'ā-shən\ *n* — **al·le·vi·a·tive** \ə-'lē-vē-,āt-iv\ *adj*

¹**al·ley** \'al-ē\ *n, pl* **al·leys 1** : a garden or park walk bordered by trees or bushes **2** : a place for bowling or skittles; *esp* : a hardwood lane for bowling **3** : a narrow street or passageway between buildings; *esp* : one giving access to the rear of buildings [Old French *alee*, from *aler* "to go"]

²**alley** *n, pl* **alleys** : a superior playing marble [from *alabaster*]

al·ley·way \'al-ē-,wā\ *n* **1** : a narrow passageway **2** : ALLEY 3

All Fools' Day *n* : APRIL FOOLS' DAY

all fours *n pl* : all four legs of a four-legged animal or the two legs and two arms of a person

all get-out \,òl-'get-,aùt; -get-'aùt, -git-\ *n* : the highest degree ⟨talented as *all get-out*⟩

all hail *interj* — used to express greeting, welcome, or acclamation

All·hal·lows \,òl-'hal-ōz, -əz\ *n* : ALL SAINTS' DAY

al·li·ance \ə-'lī-əns\ *n* **1 a** : the state of being allied **b** : a bond or connection between families, parties, or individuals **2 a** : an association (as by treaty) of two or more nations to further their common interests **b** : a treaty of alliance

al·lied \ə-'līd, 'al-,īd\ *adj* **1** : joined together ⟨two families *allied* by marriage⟩ **2 a** : joined in alliance especially by treaty ⟨*allied* nations⟩ **b** *cap* : of or relating to the nations united against Germany and its allies in World War I or World War II **3** : related especially by common properties, characteristics, or ancestry ⟨chemistry and *allied* subjects⟩

al·li·ga·tor \'al-ə-,gāt-ər\ *n* **1** : either of two large short-legged reptiles resembling crocodiles but having a shorter and broader snout **2** : leather made from alligator's hide [Spanish *el lagarto* "the lizard"]

alligator pear *n* : AVOCADO

all-im·por·tant \,ó-lim-'pòrt-nt, -ənt\ *adj* : of very great importance

al·lit·er·ate \ə-'lit-ə-,rāt\ *vb* **1** : to form an alliteration **2** : to arrange so as to make alliteration

al·lit·er·a·tion \ə-,lit-ə-'rā-shən\ *n* : the repetition of a sound at the beginning of two or more neighboring words (as in *wild and woolly* or *a babbling brook*) [*ad-* + Latin *littera* "letter"] — **al·lit·er·a·tive** \ə-'lit-ə-,rāt-iv, -rət-\ *adj* — **al·lit·er·a·tive·ly** *adv*

allo- — see ALL-

al·lo·cate \'al-ə-,kāt\ *vt* **1** : to divide and distribute for a specific purpose or among particular persons or things ⟨*allocate* funds among charities⟩ **2** : to set aside for a particular purpose ⟨*allocate* materials for a project⟩ SYN see ALLOT — **al·lo·ca·tion** \,al-ə-'kā-shən\ *n*

al·lo·phone \'al-ə-,fōn\ *n* : one of two or more variants of the same phoneme ⟨the \t\ of *tip* and the \t\ of *pit* are *allophones* of the phoneme \t\⟩ — **al·lo·phon·ic** \,al-ə-'fän-ik\ *adj*

all-or-none \,ó-lər-'nən\ *adj* : marked either by entire or complete operation or effect or by none at all

alligator 1

al·lot \ə-'lät\ *vt* **al·lot·ted; al·lot·ting** : to assign as a share or portion : ALLOCATE ⟨*allot* 10 minutes for each speech⟩ [Middle French *aloter,* from *a-* "ad-" + *lot* "lot", of Germanic origin] □ SYN APPORTION, ASSIGN, ALLOCATE: ALLOT may imply haphazard or arbitrary distribution; ASSIGN may stress an authoritative and fixed allotting without implying an even division; APPORTION implies a dividing according to some regular principle; ALLOCATE implies a fixed appropriation for a particular use.

al·lot·ment \ə-'lät-mənt\ *n* **1** : the act of allotting **2** : something that is allotted

al·lot·ro·py \ə-'lä-trə-pē\ *n* : the existence of a chemical element in two or more different forms in the same phase that show different chemical or physical properties ⟨diamond and graphite show the *allotropy* of carbon⟩ [Greek *tropos* "turn, manner"] — **al·lo·trope** \'al-ə-,trōp\ *n* — **al·lo·trop·ic** \,al-ə-'träp-ik\ *adj*

all–out \'ò-'laùt\ *adj* : made with maximum effort ⟨an *all-out* effort to win⟩

all out *adv* : with maximum effort ⟨go *all out*⟩

all–over \'ò-,lō-vər\ *adj* : covering the whole extent or surface

all over *adv* **1** : over the whole extent **2** : EVERYWHERE **3** : in every respect : THOROUGHLY

al·low \ə-'laù\ *vb* **1 a** : to assign as a share or suitable amount (as of time or money) **b** : to allot as a deduction or an addition ⟨*allow* a gallon for leakage⟩ **2** : ADMIT **3**, CONCEDE ⟨*allowed* that the situation was serious⟩ **3 a** : PERMIT ⟨gaps *allow* passage⟩ ⟨refused to *allow* smoking⟩ **b** : to fail to restrain or prevent : LET ⟨*allow* the roast to burn⟩ **4** : to make allowance ⟨*allow* for growth⟩ [Middle French *alouer* "to assign, allocate" (from Medieval Latin *allocare*) and *allouer* "to approve", from Latin *allaudare,* from *ad-* + *laudare* "to praise"] SYN see LET — **al·low·able** \-ə-bəl\ *adj*

al·low·ance \ə-'laù-əns\ *n* **1 a** : a share or portion allotted or granted **b** : a sum granted ⟨a weekly *allowance*⟩ ⟨*allowance* for expenses⟩ **c** : a reduction from a list price or stated price ⟨a trade-in *allowance*⟩ **2** : an allowed dimensional difference between mating parts of a machine **3** : the act of allowing : PERMISSION **4** : the taking into account of things that may partly excuse an offense or mistake ⟨make *allowances* for inexperience⟩

¹al·loy \'al-,òi, ə-'lòi\ *n* : a substance composed of two or more metals or of a metal and a nonmetal united usually by being melted together [Middle French *aloi,* from *aloier* "to ally, combine", from Latin *alligare* "to bind"]

²al·loy \ə-'lòi, 'al-,òi\ *vt* **1** : to reduce the purity of by mixing with a less valuable metal **2** : to mix so as to form an alloy **3** : to debase by admixture

all–pur·pose \'òl-'pər-pəs\ *adj* : suitable for many uses ⟨*all-purpose* flour⟩

¹all right *adv* **1** : reasonably well ⟨does *all right* in school⟩ **2** : very well : YES ⟨*all right,* I'll be there⟩ **3** : beyond doubt : CERTAINLY ⟨that's fast, *all right*⟩

²all right *adj* **1** : SATISFACTORY, CORRECT **2** : SAFE, WELL

all–round \'òl-'raùnd\ *adj* : ALL-AROUND

All Saints' Day *n* : November 1 observed as a church festival in honor of the saints

All Souls' Day *n* : November 2 observed in some churches as a day of prayer for the souls of the faithful departed

all·spice \'òl-,spīs\ *n* : the berry of a West Indian tree of the myrtle family; *also* : a mildly pungent and aromatic spice prepared from it

all–star \,òl-,stär\ *adj* : made up chiefly or entirely of stars ⟨an *all-star* cast⟩ ⟨an *all-star* team⟩ — **all–star** \'òl-,stär\ *n*

all told *adv* : with everything counted : in all

al·lude \ə-'lüd\ *vi* : to make indirect reference ⟨*alluding* to a recent scandal⟩ [Latin *alludere,* literally, "to play with", from *ad-* + *ludere* "to play"] SYN see REFER

¹al·lure \ə-'lùr\ *vt* : to attract by something tempting or fascinating — **al·lure·ment** \-mənt\ *n*

²allure *n* : power of attraction : CHARM

al·lu·sion \ə-'lü-zhən\ *n* **1** : the act of alluding or hinting **2** : an implied or indirect reference [Latin *allusus,* past participle of *alludere* "to play with"] — **al·lu·sive** \ə-'lü-siv, -ziv\ *adj* — **al·lu·sive·ly** *adv* — **al·lu·sive·ness** *n*

al·lu·vi·al \ə-'lü-vē-əl\ *adj* : relating to, composed of, or found in alluvium

al·lu·vi·um \-vē-əm\ *n, pl* **-vi·ums** *or* **-via** \-vē-ə\ : soil material (as clay, silt, sand, or gravel) deposited by running water [Late Latin, from Latin *alluere* "to wash against", from *ad-* + *lavere* "to wash"]

¹al·ly \ə-'lī, 'al-,ī\ *vb* **al·lied; al·ly·ing 1** : to form (as by marriage or treaty) a connection between : join in an alliance : UNITE **2** : to form (as by likeness or compatibility) a relation between [Old French *alier,* from Latin *alligare* "to bind to", from *ad-* + *ligare* "to bind"]

²al·ly \'al-,ī, ə-'lī\ *n, pl* **al·lies 1** : a plant or animal linked to another by genetic or evolutionary relationship ⟨ferns and their *allies*⟩ **2 a** : one associated or united with another for a common purpose **b** *pl, cap* : the Allied nations in World War I or World War II

-al·ly \ə-lē, lē\ *adv suffix* : **²-LY** ⟨terrific*ally*⟩ — in adverbs formed from adjectives in *-ic* with no alternative form in *-ical* [**¹-al** + *-ly*]

al·ma ma·ter \,al-mə-'mät-ər\ *n* : a school, college, or university that one has attended [Latin, "fostering mother"]

al·ma·nac \'òl-mə-,nak, 'al-\ *n* **1** : a publication containing astronomical and meteorological data arranged according to the days, weeks, and months of the year and often including various other information **2** : an annual publication containing statistical and general information [Medieval Latin *almanach,* probably from Arabic *al-manākh* "the almanac"]

al·man·dine \'al-mən-,dēn\ *n* : ALMANDITE

al·man·dite \-,dīt\ *n* : a deep red garnet containing iron and aluminum [derived from Medieval Latin *alabandina,* from *Alabanda,* ancient city in Asia Minor]

al·mighty \òl-'mīt-ē\ *adj, often cap* : having absolute power over all ⟨*Almighty* God⟩

Almighty *n* : GOD 1 — used with *the*

al·mond \'äm-ənd, 'am-; 'al-mənd, 'äl-\ *n* : a small tree of the rose family having flowers like those of a peach tree; *also* : the edible kernel of its fruit used as a nut [Old French *almande,* from Late Latin *amandula,* from Latin *amygdala,* from Greek *amygdalē*]

almond eye *n* : a somewhat triangular obliquely set eye — **al·mond–eyed** \-'īd\ *adj*

al·mo·ner \'al-mə-nər, 'äm-ə-\ *n* : a person who distributes alms [Old French *almosnier,* from *almosne* "alms", from Late Latin *eleemosyna*]

al·most \'òl-,mōst, òl-'\ *adv* : only a little less than : NEARLY

alms \'ämz, 'älmz\ *n, pl* **alms** : something (as money) given to help the poor [Old English *ælmesse,* from Late Latin *eleemosyna,* from Greek *eleēmosynē* "pity, alms"] — **alms·giv·er** \-,giv-ər\ *n* — **alms·giv·ing** \-,giv-ing\ *n*

alms·house \-,haùs\ *n* : POORHOUSE

al·ni·co \'al-ni-,kō\ *n* : a powerful permanent-magnet alloy containing iron, nickel, aluminum, and one or more of the elements cobalt, copper, and titanium [*al*uminum + *ni*ckel + *co*balt]

al·oe \'al-ō\ *n* **1** : any of a large genus of succulent chiefly southern African plants of the lily family with spikes of often showy flowers **2** *usually pl* : the dried bitter juice of the leaves of an aloe used as a purgative and tonic [Late Latin, from Latin, "dried juice of aloe leaves", from Greek *aloē*]

aloft \ə-'lòft\ *adv or adj* **1** : at or to a great height **2** : in the air; *esp* : in flight **3** : at, on, or to the masthead or the higher rigging of a ship [Old Norse *ā lopt,* from *ā* "in" + *lopt* "air"]

alo·ha \ə-'lō-ə, ä-, -,hä\ *interj* — used to express greeting or farewell [Hawaiian *aloha* "love"]

¹alone \ə-'lōn\ *adj* **1** : separated from others : ISOLATED ⟨*alone* in my room⟩ **2** : exclusive of anyone or anything else ⟨I *alone* know the secret⟩ [Middle English, from *al* "all" + *one* "one"] □ SYN LONELY, LONESOME: ALONE stresses the objective fact of being entirely by oneself; LONELY adds the suggestion of longing for companionship; LONESOME may add an impression of being deserted or desolate.

²alone *adv* **1** : without any other : SOLELY, EXCLUSIVELY ⟨the proof rests on that statement *alone*⟩ **2** : without company, aid, or support ⟨I'd rather do it *alone*⟩

¹along \ə-'lȯng\ *prep* **1** : lengthwise of : parallel with the length or direction of ⟨walk *along* the beach⟩ **2** : in accordance with ⟨research *along* several lines⟩ [Old English *andlang,* from *and-* "against" + *lang* "long"]

²along *adv* **1** : progressively onward ⟨hurry *along* toward home⟩ **2** : as a companion or associate ⟨brought the child *along*⟩ ⟨work *along* with colleagues⟩ **3** : at or to an advanced point ⟨plans are far *along*⟩ **4** : at or on hand ⟨had their guns *along*⟩

along·shore \-,shōr, -,shȯr\ *adv or adj* : along the shore or coast

¹along·side \-,sīd\ *adv* : along or close at the side : in parallel position

²alongside *prep* : side by side with; *esp* : parallel to

¹aloof \ə-'lüf\ *adv* : at a distance : out of involvement ⟨stood *aloof* from their quarrels⟩ [obsolete *aloof* "to windward"]

²aloof *adj* : removed or distant in interest or feeling : RESERVED ⟨a shy, *aloof* manner⟩ — **aloof·ly** *adv* — **aloof·ness** *n*

aloud \ə-'laud\ *adv* **1** *archaic* : LOUDLY **2** : so as to be clearly heard

alp \'alp\ *n* **1** : a high rugged mountain **2** : a mountain pasture [from *Alps,* mountain system of Europe]

al·paca \al-'pak-ə\ *n* **1** : a mammal with fine long woolly hair domesticated in Peru and related to the llama **2** : wool of the alpaca or a thin cloth made of it; *also* : a rayon or cotton imitation of this cloth [Spanish, of American Indian origin]

al·pha \'al-fə\ *n* **1** : the 1st letter of the Greek alphabet — A or α **2** : something that is first : BEGINNING **3** : the chief or brightest star of a constellation

al·pha·bet \'al-fə-,bet, -bət\ *n* **1** : the characters (as letters) of a written language arranged in their customary order **2** : a system of signs or signals that serve as equivalents for letters [Greek *alphabētos,* from *alpha* + *bēta* "beta"]

al·pha·bet·i·cal \,al-fə-'bet-i-kəl\ *or* **al·pha·bet·ic** \-'bet-ik\ *adj* **1** : of, relating to, or employing an alphabet **2** : arranged in the order of the letters of the alphabet — **al·pha·bet·i·cal·ly** \-i-k(ə-)lē\ *adv*

al·pha·bet·ize \'al-fə-bə-,tīz\ *vt* : to arrange in alphabetical order — **al·pha·bet·i·za·tion** \,al-fə-,bet-ə-'zā-shən\ *n* — **al·pha·bet·iz·er** \'al-fə-bə-,tī-zər\ *n*

alpha helix *n* : the coiled structural arrangement of many proteins consisting of a single amino-acid chain that is stabilized by hydrogen bonds

al·pha·nu·mer·ic \,al-fə-nù-'mer-ik, -nyù-\ *adj* : consisting of both letters and numbers

alpha particle *n* : a positively charged particle that is identical with the nucleus of a helium atom, consists of 2 protons and 2 neutrons, and is ejected at high speed in various radioactive transformations

alpha ray *n* **1** : an alpha particle moving at high speed **2** : a stream of alpha particles — called also *alpha radiation*

alpha rhythm *or* **alpha wave** *n* : electrical activity of the brain that can be recorded by an electroencephalograph and is often associated with a state of wakeful relaxation

al·pine \'al-,pīn\ *n* : a plant native to alpine or boreal regions

Alpine *adj* **1** *often not cap* **a** : relating to or resembling the Alps or any mountains **b** : of, relating to, or growing on upland slopes above timberline **2** : of or relating to a central and southeastern European human Caucasoid stock marked by broad heads, stocky build, medium height, and brown hair and eyes

al·ready \ȯl-'red-ē\ *adv* **1** : before a stated or implied time : PREVIOUSLY ⟨we had *already* been there⟩ **2** : so soon ⟨surprised to find it done *already*⟩

al·right \ȯl-'rīt, 'ȯl-; 'ȯl-,\ *adv or adj* : all right

Al·sa·tian \al-'sā-shən\ *n* : GERMAN SHEPHERD [*Alsace*]

al·sike clover \'al-,sak-, -,sīk-\ *n* : a European perennial clover widely grown as a forage plant [*Alsike,* Sweden]

al·so \'ȯl-sō\ *adv* **1** : LIKEWISE 1 **2** : in addition : TOO

al·so–ran \-,ran\ *n* **1** : a horse or dog that finishes out of the money in a race **2** : a contestant that does not win

Al·ta·ic \al-'tā-ik\ *n* : a language family including the Turkic, Tungusic, and Mongolic subfamilies [*Altai* mountains, Asia] — **Altaic** *adj*

Al·tair \al-'tīr, -'taər, -'teər\ *n* : the first-magnitude star in Aquila [Arabic *al-ṭā'ir,* literally, "the flier"]

al·tar \'ȯl-tər\ *n* **1** : a usually raised structure or place on which sacrifices are offered or incense is burned in worship **2** : a table used in consecrating the eucharistic elements or as a center of worship or ritual [Old English, from Latin *altare*]

altar boy *n* : ACOLYTE 1

altar call *n* : an appeal by an evangelist to worshipers to come forward and commit their lives to Christ

al·tar·piece \'ȯl-tər-,pēs\ *n* : a work of art to decorate the space above and behind the altar

al·ter \'ȯl-tər\ *vb* **1** : to change partly but usually not completely ⟨*alter* a dress⟩ ⟨my opinion has never *altered*⟩ **2** : CASTRATE, SPAY [Middle French *alterer,* from Medieval Latin *alterare,* from *alter* "other (of two)"] SYN see CHANGE — **al·ter·abil·i·ty** \,ȯl-tə-rə-'bil-ət-ē, -trə-'\ *n* — **al·ter·able** \'ȯl-tə-rə-bəl, -trə-bəl\ *adj* — **al·ter·ably** \-blē\ *adv*

al·ter·ation \,ȯl-tə-'rā-shən\ *n* **1** : the act or process of altering **2** : the result of altering : MODIFICATION

al·ter·ca·tion \,ȯl-tər-'kā-shən\ *n* : a noisy or angry dispute : WRANGLE [Latin *altercari* "to wrangle", from *alter* "other"]

al·ter ego \,ȯl-tər-'ē-gō *also* -'eg-ō\ *n* **1** : a trusted friend or personal representative **2** : oneself in a changed form [Latin, literally, "second I"]

¹al·ter·nate \'ȯl-tər-,nāt *also* 'al-\ *vb* **1** : to do, occur, or act by turns **2** : to cause to alternate

²al·ter·nate \-nət\ *adj* **1** : occurring or succeeding by turns ⟨a day of *alternate* sunshine and rain⟩ **2 a** : occurring first on one side and then on the other at different levels along an axis ⟨leaves *alternate*⟩ — compare OPPOSITE **b** : arranged one above or alongside another ⟨*alternate* layers of cake and filling⟩ **3** : every other : every second ⟨works on *alternate* days⟩ **4** : being an alternative ⟨took the *alternate* route⟩ [Latin *alternare* "to alternate", from *alternus* "alternate", from *alter* "other"] — **al·ter·nate·ly** *adv*

³al·ter·nate \-nət\ *n* **1** : ALTERNATIVE **2** : a person named to take the place of another whenever necessary

alternate angle *n* : either of a pair of angles that are on opposite sides of a transversal at its intersection with two other lines: **a** : one of a pair of angles inside the two intersected lines — called also *alternate interior angle* **b** : one of a pair of angles outside the two intersected lines — called also *alternate exterior angle*

alternating current *n* : an electric current that reverses its direction at regular intervals — abbreviation *AC*

al·ter·na·tion \,ȯl-tər-'nā-shən *also* ,al-\ *n* **1** : the act or process of alternating **2** : alternate position or occurrence : SUCCESSION

alpaca 1

alternate angles: a, a¹; b, b¹; c, c¹; d, d¹

\ə\ abut		\ng\ sing	
\ər\ further		\ō\ bone	
\a\ mat		\ȯ\ saw	
\ā\ take		\ȯi\ coin	
\ä\ cot, cart		\th\ thin	
\au\ out		\th\ this	
\ch\ chin		\ü\ food	
\e\ pet		\u\ foot	
\ē\ easy		\y\ yet	
\g\ go		\yü\ few	
\i\ tip		\yu\ cure	
\ī\ life		\zh\ vision	
\j\ job			

alternation of generations : the successive occurrence of two or more different forms in the life cycle of a plant or animal; *esp* : the alternation of a sexual generation with an asexual one

¹al·ter·na·tive \òl-'tər-nət-iv *also* al-\ *adj* : offering or expressing a choice ⟨*alternative* sources of energy⟩ — **al·ter·na·tive·ly** *adv* — **al·ter·na·tive·ness** *n*

²alternative *n* **1** : a chance to choose between two things ⟨the *alternative* of going by train or by air⟩ **2** : one of two or more things among which a choice is to be made **SYN** see **CHOICE**

al·ter·na·tor \'òl-tər-,nāt-ər *also* 'al-\ *n* : an electric generator for producing alternating current

alt·horn \'alt-,hòrn\ *n* : the alto member of the saxhorn family used chiefly in bands where it often replaces the French horn [German, from *alt* "alto" + *horn* "horn"]

al·though *also* **al·tho** \òl-'thō\ *conj* : in spite of the fact that : **THOUGH**

al·tim·e·ter \al-'tim-ət-ər, 'al-tə-,mēt-ər\ *n* : an instrument for measuring altitude; *esp* : an aneroid barometer that registers changes in atmospheric pressure accompanying changes in altitude

al·ti·tude \'al-tə-,tüd, -,tyüd\ *n* **1 a** : the angular height of a celestial object above the horizon **b** : the vertical distance of an object above sea level **c** : a perpendicular line segment from a vertex of a geometric figure (as a triangle or a pyramid) to the opposite side or the opposite side extended or from a side or face to a parallel side or face or the side or face extended **d** : the length of an altitude **2 a** : vertical distance or extent **b** : position at a height **c** : an elevated region — usually used in pl. [Latin *altitudo* "height, depth", from *altus* "high, deep"] **SYN** see **HEIGHT** — **al·ti·tu·di·nal** \,al-tə-'tüd-nəl, -'tyüd-n-əl\ *adj*

al·to \'al-tō\ *n, pl* **altos** **1 a** : **COUNTERTENOR** **b** : **CONTRALTO** **c** : the second highest voice part in a 4-part chorus — compare **BASS, SOPRANO, TENOR** **2** : the second highest member of a family of musical instruments; *esp* : **ALTHORN** [Italian, literally, "high", from Latin *altus*]

al·to·cu·mu·lus \,al-tō-'kyü-myə-ləs\ *n* : a fleecy cloud formation consisting of large whitish globular cloudlets with shaded portions

¹al·to·geth·er \,òl-tə-'geth-ər\ *adv* **1** : **WHOLLY, THOROUGHLY** ⟨the tool was *altogether* useless⟩ **2** : in all : all told ⟨the bill comes to $14 *altogether*⟩ **3** : on the whole ⟨*altogether* it compares favorably⟩

²altogether *n* : **NUDE 2** ⟨posed in the *altogether*⟩

al·to·stra·tus \,al-tō-'strāt-əs, -'strat-\ *n* : a cloud formation similar to cirrostratus but darker and at a lower level

al·tri·cial \al-'trish-əl\ *adj* : having the young hatched in a very immature and helpless condition so as to require care for some time — compare **PRECOCIAL** [Latin *altrix* "nurse", from *alere* "to nourish"]

al·tru·ism \'al-trù-,iz-əm\ *n* : unselfish interest in or care for the welfare of others [French *altruisme*, from *autrui* "other people", derived from Latin *alter* "other"] — **al·tru·ist** \-trù-əst\ *n* — **al·tru·is·tic** \,al-trù-'is-tik\ *adj* — **al·tru·is·ti·cal·ly** \-'is-ti-kə-lē, -klē\ *adv*

al·um \'al-əm\ *n* **1** : either of two colorless crystalline compounds containing aluminum $KAl(SO_4)_2 \cdot 12H_2O$ or $NH_4Al(SO_4)_2 \cdot 12H_2O$ that have a sweetish-sourish taste and a puckering effect on the mouth and are used in medicine (as to check local sweating or to stop bleeding) **2** : an aluminum compound $Al_2(SO_4)_3$ made from bauxite and used in paper manufacture, dyeing, and sewage treatment [Middle French, from Latin *alumen*]

alu·mi·na \ə-'lü-mə-nə\ *n* : the oxide of aluminum Al_2O_3 that occurs native as corundum and in bauxite and is used as a source of aluminum, as an abrasive, and as an absorbent

al·u·min·i·um \,al-yə-'min-ē-əm\ *n, chiefly British* : **ALUMINUM**

alu·mi·nize \ə-'lü-mə-,nīz\ *vt* : to treat or coat with aluminum

alu·mi·num \ə-'lü-mə-nəm\ *n* : a silver-white malleable ductile light metallic element with good electrical and thermal conductivity and resistance to oxidation that is the most abundant metal in the earth's crust — see **ELEMENT** table [Latin *alumen* "alum"]

aluminum oxide *n* : **ALUMINA**

alum·na \ə-'ləm-nə\ *n, pl* **-nae** \-,nē\ : a girl or woman who has attended or has graduated from a particular school, college, or university [Latin, feminine of *alumnus*]

alum·nus \ə-'ləm-nəs\ *n, pl* **-ni** \-,nī\ : one and especially a man or boy that has attended or graduated from a particular school, college, or university [Latin, "foster son, pupil", from *alere* "to nourish"]

al·ve·o·lar \al-'vē-ə-lər\ *adj* **1** : of, relating to, resembling, or having alveoli **2** : pronounced with the tip of the tongue touching or near the teethridge — **al·ve·o·lar·ly** *adv*

al·ve·o·lus \al-'vē-ə-ləs\ *n, pl* **-li** \-,lī, -,lē\ **1** : a small cavity or pit: as **a** : a socket for a tooth **b** : **AIR SAC 2** **2** : **TEETHRIDGE** [Latin, from *alveus* "cavity, hollow", from *alvus* "belly"]

al·way \'òl-,wā\ *adv, archaic* : **ALWAYS**

al·ways \'òl-wēz, -wəz, -,wāz\ *adv* **1** : at all times : **INVARIABLY** ⟨you're *always* right⟩ **2** : through all time : **FOREVER** ⟨remember me *always*⟩

alys·sum \ə-'lis-əm\ *n* **1** : any of a genus of Old World herbs of the mustard family with small usually yellow flowers **2** : **SWEET ALYSSUM** [Greek *alysson*, a plant believed to cure rabies, from *a-* + *lyssa* "rabies"]

Alz·hei·mer's disease \'älts-,hī-mərz-, 'alts-\ *n* : a degenerative disease of the central nervous system characterized especially by premature senile mental deterioration — called also *Alzheimer's* [Alois *Alzheimer*, died 1915, German physician]

am *present 1st sing of* **BE** [Old English *eom*]

AM \'ā-,em\ *n* : a system of broadcasting using amplitude modulation; *also* : a receiver of radio waves broadcast by such a system — **AM** *adj*

amah \'äm-ə, 'äm-,ä\ *n* : an Oriental woman employed as a servant; *esp* : a Chinese nurse [Portuguese *ama* "wet nurse", from Medieval Latin *amma*]

amain \ə-'mān\ *adv* **1** : with all one's might **2 a** : at full speed **b** : in great haste

amal·gam \ə-'mal-gəm\ *n* **1** : an alloy of mercury with some other metal or metals that is used for tooth filling **2** : a combination or mixture of different ingredients [Middle French *amalgame*, from Medieval Latin *amalgama*]

amal·gam·ate \ə-'mal-gə-,māt\ *vb* **1** : to unite in an amalgam **2** : to combine into a single body — **amal·gam·ator** \-,māt-ər\ *n*

amal·gam·ation \ə-,mal-gə-'mā-shən\ *n* **1 a** : the act or process of amalgamating ⟨the *amalgamation* of mercury with silver⟩ **b** : the state of being amalgamated **2** : the result of amalgamating — **amal·gam·ative** \-'mal-gə-,māt-iv\ *adj*

am·a·ni·ta \,am-ə-'nīt-ə, -'nēt-\ *n* : any of various mostly poisonous white-spored fungi with a bulbous sac about the base of the stem [Greek *amanitai*, a kind of fungus]

aman·u·en·sis \ə-,man-yə-'wen-səs\ *n, pl* **-en·ses** \-,sēz\ : a person employed to write from dictation or to copy manuscript [Latin, from *servus a manu* "slave with secretarial duties"]

am·a·ranth \'am-ə-,ranth\ *n* **1** : an imaginary flower that never fades **2** : any of a large genus of coarse herbs including pigweeds and various forms cultivated for their showy flowers or for color [Latin *amarantus*, a kind of flower, from Greek *amaranton*, from *a-* + *marainein* "to wither, fade"]

am·a·ran·thine \\,am-ə-'ran-thən, -'ran-,thīn\\ *adj* : relating to or resembling an amaranth : UNFADING, UNDYING

am·a·ryl·lis \\,am-ə-'ril-əs\\ *n* : any of various plants of a family related to the lily family; *esp* : any of several African bulbous herbs grown for their umbels of large showy flowers [probably from the name of a shepherdess in Vergil's *Eclogues*]

amass \\ə-'mas\\ *vt* **1** : to collect for oneself : ACCUMULATE ⟨*amass* a fortune⟩ **2** : to pile up into a mass : GATHER ⟨*amass* statistics from many sources⟩ SYN see ACCUMULATE — **amass·er** *n*

am·a·teur \\'am-ə-,tər, -ət-ər, -ə-,tür, -ə-,tyür, -ə-,chür\\ *n* **1** : a person who takes part in an activity (as a study or sport) for pleasure and not for pay **2** : a person who engages in something without experience or competence [French, literally, "lover", from Latin *amator*, from *amare* "to love"] — **amateur** *adj* — **am·a·teur·ish** \\,am-ə-'tər-ish, -'tür-, -'tyür-, -'chür-\\ *adj* — **am·a·teur·ish·ly** *adv* — **am·a·teur·ish·ness** *n* — **am·a·teur·ism** \\'am-ə-,tər-,iz-əm, -ət-ər-, -ə-,tür-, -ə-,tyür-, -ə-,chür-\\ *n*

am·a·to·ry \\'am-ə-,tōr-ē, -,tòr-\\ *adj* : of, relating to, or expressing sexual love

amaze \\ə-'māz\\ *vt* : to surprise or astonish greatly : fill with wonder : ASTOUND [Old English *āmasian*]

amaze·ment \\ə-'māz-mənt\\ *n* : great surprise or astonishment

amaz·ing *adj* : causing amazement or wonder — **amaz·ing·ly** \\-'mā-zing-lē\\ *adv*

am·a·zon \\'am-ə-,zän, -ə-zən\\ *n* **1** *cap* : a member of a race of women warriors repeatedly warring with the Greeks in classical mythology **2** : a tall very strong woman

Am·a·zo·nian \\,am-ə-'zō-nē-ən, -'zō-nyən\\ *adj* **1** : of, relating to, or resembling an Amazon **2** : of or relating to the Amazon river or its valley

am·bas·sa·dor \\am-'bas-əd-ər, əm-, -'bas-ə-,dòr\\ *n* **1** : an official envoy; *esp* : a diplomatic agent of the highest rank who is the resident representative of his or her own government or appointed for a special temporary assignment **2** : an authorized representative or messenger [Middle French *ambassadeur*, of Germanic origin] — **am·bas·sa·do·ri·al** \\am-,bas-ə-'dōr-ē-əl, -'dòr-\\ *adj* — **am·bas·sa·dor·ship** \\am-'bas-əd-ər-,ship\\ *n*

am·ber \\'am-bər\\ *n* **1** : a hard yellowish to brownish translucent fossil resin that takes a fine polish and is used mostly for jewelry **2** : a dark orange yellow [Middle French *ambre*, from Medieval Latin *ambra*, from Arabic *'anbar* "ambergris"] — **amber** *adj*

am·ber·gris \\'am-bər-,gris, -,grēs\\ *n* : a waxy substance from the sperm whale that is used in the manufacture of perfumes [Middle French *ambre gris*, literally, "gray amber"]

ambi- *prefix* : both ⟨*ambi*valent⟩ [Latin, "both, around"]

am·bi·dex·trous \\,am-bi-'dek-strəs\\ *adj* : using both hands with equal ease [Latin *ambi-* + *dextera* "right hand"] — **am·bi·dex·trous·ly** *adv*

am·bi·ence *or* **am·bi·ance** \\'am-bē-əns, äⁿ-byäⁿs\\ *n* : a feeling or mood associated with a particular place, person, or thing : ATMOSPHERE [French *ambiance*, from *ambiant* "ambient"]

am·bi·ent \\'am-bē-ənt\\ *adj* : surrounding on all sides : ENCOMPASSING [Latin *ambiens*, present participle of *ambire* "to go around"]

am·bi·gu·i·ty \\,am-bə-'gyü-ət-ē\\ *n, pl* **-ties** **1** : the quality or state of being ambiguous in meaning **2** : an ambiguous word or passage

am·big·u·ous \\am-'big-yə-wəs\\ *adj* **1** : doubtful or uncertain especially from being obscure or indistinct ⟨an *ambiguous* color⟩ **2** : not clear in meaning because of being able to be understood in more than one way [Latin *ambiguus*, from *ambigere* "to wander about",

from *ambi-* "around" + *agere* "to lead, drive"] — **am·big·u·ous·ly** *adv* — **am·big·u·ous·ness** *n*

am·bi·tion \\am-'bish-ən\\ *n* **1 a** : a strong desire for status, fame, or power **b** : desire to achieve a particular end : ASPIRATION **2** : the object of ambition ⟨attain your life's *ambition*⟩ **3** : desire to work or be active ⟨I have no *ambition* today⟩ [Latin *ambitio* "canvass for votes", literally, "going around", from *ambire* "to go around", from *ambi-* "around" + *ire* "to go"] □ ORIGIN The literal meaning of Latin *ambitio*, a derivative of *ambire* "to go around", was "going around". The word also meant "soliciting of votes", because candidates for public office in ancient Rome were in the habit of going about the city for that purpose. From this political sense *ambitio* was extended a bit further, to mean "desire for honor or power". This is the meaning of English *ambition*, derived from Latin *ambitio*. □ SYN ASPIRATION: AMBITION implies a strong desire for personal advancement and may apply either to a praiseworthy or an inordinate and ruthless desire; ASPIRATION implies a striving after something higher than oneself which may be admirable and ennobling or merely presumptuous.

am·bi·tious \\am-'bish-əs\\ *adj* **1 a** : having or driven by ambition ⟨an *ambitious* politician⟩ **b** : having a particular ambition ⟨*ambitious* to be captain of the team⟩ **2** : showing ambition ⟨an *ambitious* plan⟩ — **am·bi·tious·ly** *adv*

am·biv·a·lence \\am-'biv-ə-ləns\\ *n* : simultaneous attraction toward and repulsion from something or someone — **am·biv·a·lent** \\-lənt\\ *adj* — **am·biv·a·lent·ly** *adv*

am·bi·vert \\'am-bi-,vərt\\ *n* : a person having characteristics of both extravert and introvert — **am·bi·ver·sion** \\,am-bi-'vər-zhən\\ *n*

¹am·ble \\'am-bəl\\ *vi* **am·bled; am·bling** \\-bə-ling, -bling\\ : to go at an amble [Middle French *ambler*, from Latin *ambulare* "to walk"] — **am·bler** \\-bə-lər, -blər\\ *n*

²amble *n* **1** : an easy gait of a horse in which the legs on the same side of the body move together **2** : a gentle easy pace

am·bly·opia \\,am-blē-'ō-pē-ə\\ *n* : dimness of sight without apparent change in the eye structures that is associated especially with toxic effects or dietary deficiencies [Greek *amblyōpia*, from *amblys* "dull" + -*ōpia* "vision"]

am·bro·sia \\am-'brō-zhē-ə, -zhə\\ *n* **1** : the food of the Greek and Roman gods **2** : something extremely pleasing to taste or smell [Latin, from Greek, literally, "immortality", from *ambrotos* "immortal"] — **am·bro·sial** \\-zhē-əl, -zhəl\\ *adj* — **am·bro·sial·ly** \\-ē\\ *adv*

am·bu·lance \\'am-byə-ləns\\ *n* : a vehicle equipped for transporting the injured or the sick [French, "field hospital", from *ambulant* "itinerant", from Latin *ambulare* "to walk"]

am·bu·lant \\'am-byə-lənt\\ *adj* : moving about; *esp* : AMBULATORY

am·bu·late \\-,lāt\\ *vi* : to move or walk from place to place

¹am·bu·la·to·ry \\'am-byə-lə-,tōr-ē, -,tòr-\\ *adj* **1** : of, relating to, or adapted to walking **2** : able to walk about ⟨*ambulatory* patients in a hospital⟩ [Latin *ambulare* "to walk"]

²ambulatory *n, pl* **-ries** : a sheltered place (as in a cloister) for walking

am·bus·cade \\'am-bə-,skad\\ *n* : AMBUSH [Middle French *embuscade*] — **ambuscade** *vb* — **am·bus·cad·er** *n*

¹am·bush \\'am-,bush\\ *vt* **1** : to station (as troops) in ambush **2** : to attack from an ambush : WAYLAY [Old French *embuschier*, from *en* "in" + *busche* "firewood"]

²ambush *n* : a trap in which concealed persons lie in wait to attack by surprise; *also* : the persons so concealed or their position

\\ə\\ abut		\\ng\\ sing	
\\ər\\ further		\\ō\\ bone	
\\a\\ mat		\\ò\\ saw	
\\ā\\ take		\\òi\\ coin	
\\ä\\ cot, cart		\\th\\ thin	
\\aù\\ out		\\th\\ this	
\\ch\\ chin		\\ü\\ food	
\\e\\ pet		\\ù\\ foot	
\\ē\\ easy		\\y\\ yet	
\\g\\ go		\\yü\\ few	
\\i\\ tip		\\yù\\ cure	
\\ī\\ life		\\zh\\ vision	
\\j\\ job			

am·bys·to·ma \am-'bis-tə-mə\ *n* : TIGER SALAMANDER [derived from Greek *amblys* "dull, blunt" + *stoma* "mouth"]

ame·ba, ame·ban, ame·bic, ame·boid *variant of* AMOEBA, AMOEBAN, AMOEBIC, AMOEBOID

am·e·bi·a·sis \,am-i-'bī-ə-səs\ *n, pl* **-a·ses** \-ə-,sēz\ : infection with or disease caused by amoebas

amebic dysentery *n* : acute intestinal amebiasis of humans marked by dysentery, griping pain, and injury to the intestinal wall

ame·lio·rate \ə-'mēl-yə-,rāt\ *vb* : to make or grow better or more tolerable : IMPROVE [alteration of *meliorate*] — **ame·lio·ra·tion** \-,mēl-yə-'rā-shən\ *n* — **ame·lio·ra·tive** \-'mēl-yə-,rāt-iv\ *adj* — **ame·lio·ra·tor** \-,rāt-ər\ *n* — **ame·lio·ra·to·ry** \-rə-,tōr-ē, -,tȯr-\ *adj*

amen \'ä-'men, 'ā-; 'ä- *when sung*\ *interj* — used to express solemn agreement or hearty approval [Hebrew *āmēn*]

ame·na·ble \ə-'mē-nə-bəl, -'men-ə-\ *adj* 1 : liable to be called to account ⟨*amenable* to the law⟩ 2 : easily influenced or managed : RESPONSIVE ⟨*amenable* to discipline⟩ [Middle French *amener* "to lead to", from *a-* "ad-" + *mener* "to lead", from Latin *minare* "to drive"] — **ame·na·bil·i·ty** \-,mē-nə-'bil-ət-ē, -,men-ə-\ *n* — **ame·na·bly** \-'mē-nə-blē, -'men-ə-\ *adv*

amend \ə-'mend\ *vb* 1 : to change for the better : IMPROVE 2 : ALTER 1; *esp* : to alter formally by modification, deletion, or addition ⟨*amend* the constitution⟩ [Old French *amender*, from Latin *emendare* "to emend"] SYN *see* CORRECT — **amend·able** \-'men-də-bəl\ *adj* — **amen·da·to·ry** \-'men-də-,tōr-ē, -,tȯr-\ *adj* — **amend·er** *n*

amend·ment \ə-'mend-mənt, -'men-\ *n* 1 : the act or process of amending especially for the better 2 : a modification, addition, or deletion (as to a law, bill, or motion) made or proposed

amends \ə-'menz\ *n sing or pl* : something done or given to make up for a loss or injury one has caused ⟨make *amends*⟩

ame·ni·ty \ə-'men-ət-ē, -'mē-nət-\ *n, pl* **-ties** 1 : the quality of being pleasant or agreeable 2 : something that makes life easier or more pleasant — usually used in pl. [Latin *amoenitas*, from *amoenus* "pleasant"]

ament \'am-ənt, 'ā-mənt\ *n* : a flower cluster in which flowers all of one sex and without petals grow in close circular rows on a slender stalk (as in the alder, willow, birch, and poplar) : CATKIN [Latin *amentum* "thong, strap"]

¹Amer·i·can \ə-'mer-ə-kən\ *n* : a native or inhabitant of North America or South America; *esp* : a citizen of the United States

²American *adj* 1 : of or relating to America or its inhabitants ⟨the *American* coastline⟩ 2 : of or relating to the United States or its inhabitants

Amer·i·ca·na \ə-,mer-ə-'kan-ə, -'kän-ə, -'kā-nə\ *n pl* : materials about America, its civilization, or its culture; *also* : a collection of such materials

American bison *or* **American buffalo** *n* : BUFFALO 2a

American chameleon *n* : a long-tailed lizard of the southeastern United States that can change its color

American cheese *n* : a mild process cheese made from American cheddar cheese

American egret *n* : a large North American heron with a yellow bill, snow white plumage, and black legs and feet

American Indian *n* : a member of any of the aboriginal peoples of the western hemisphere except usually the Eskimos; *esp* : an American Indian of North America and especially the United States

Amer·i·can·ism \ə-'mer-ə-kə-,niz-əm\ *n* 1 : a characteristic feature of English as used in the United States 2 : attachment or loyalty to the traditions, interests, or ideals of the United States 3 : a custom or trait peculiar to the United States or to Americans

amer·i·can·ize \-kə-,nīz\ *vb, often cap* : to make or become American — **amer·i·can·iza·tion** \ə-,mer-ə-kə-nə-'zā-shən\ *n, often cap*

American lobster *n* : the common lobster of the northeastern coast of North America

American plan *n* : a hotel plan whereby the daily rate covers the cost of both room and meals — compare EUROPEAN PLAN

American robin *n* : ROBIN 2

American Sign Language *n* : a sign language for the deaf

am·er·i·ci·um \,am-ə-'rish-ē-əm, -'ris-\ *n* : a radioactive metallic chemical element produced by bombardment of plutonium with high-energy neutrons — see ELEMENT table [New Latin, from *America*]

Am·er·in·di·an \,am-ə-'rin-dē-ən\ *n* : AMERICAN INDIAN — **Am·er·ind** \'am-ə-,rind\ *n* — **Amerindian** *adj* — **Am·er·in·dic** \,am-ə-'rin-dik\ *adj*

am·e·thyst \'am-ə-thəst\ *n* 1 : a clear purple or bluish violet variety of crystallized quartz used as a gem 2 : a moderate purple [Greek *amethystos*, from *a-* + *methyein* "to be drunk"; from its supposed usefulness as a remedy for drunkenness] □ ORIGIN Gemstones were once believed to have magical and medicinal properties. An amethyst, for example, was supposed to have the power to prevent or cure drunkenness in its wearer. For this reason the Greeks gave it a name, *amethystos,* derived from the prefix *a-,* meaning "not", and *methyein* "to be drunk", from *methy* "wine".

ami·a·ble \'ā-mē-ə-bəl\ *adj* : generally agreeable; *esp* : having a friendly and sociable disposition [Middle French, from Late Latin *amicabilis* "friendly", from Latin *amicus* "friend"] — **ami·a·bil·i·ty** \,ā-mē-ə-'bil-ət-ē\ *n* — **ami·a·ble·ness** \'ā-mē-ə-bəl-nəs\ *n* — **ami·a·bly** \-blē\ *adv*

am·i·ca·ble \'am-i-kə-bəl\ *adj* : characterized by friendly good-will : PEACEABLE ⟨an *amicable* settlement of differences⟩ — **am·i·ca·bil·i·ty** \,am-i-kə-'bil-ət-ē\ *n* — **am·i·ca·ble·ness** *n* — **am·i·ca·bly** \'am-i-kə-blē\ *adv*

am·ice \'am-əs\ *n* : a white linen cloth worn about the neck and shoulders under other vestments by a priest at Mass [probably derived from Latin *amictus* "cloak"]

amid \ə-'mid\ *or* **amidst** \-'midst, -'mitst\ *prep* : in or into the middle of : AMONG

am·ide \'am-,īd, -əd\ *n* : a compound resulting from replacement of an atom of hydrogen in ammonia by a metal or radical or of one or more atoms of hydrogen in ammonia by univalent acid radicals [*am*monia + *-ide*]

amid·ships \ə-'mid-,ships\ *adv* : in or near the middle of a ship

amine \ə-'mēn, 'am-,ēn\ *n* : any of various compounds derived from ammonia by replacement of hydrogen by one or more univalent hydrocarbon radicals

ami·no \ə-'mē-nō\ *adj* : relating to or containing the group NH_2 united to a radical

amino acid *n* : any of numerous organic acids that contain the amino group NH_2 and include some which can combine in chains to form proteins and are synthesized by living cells or are obtained as essential components of the diet

amir \ə-'miər, ä-\ *variant of* EMIR

Amish \'äm-ish, 'am-, 'ām-\ *adj* : of or relating to a strict Mennonite sect that settled in America [Jacob *Amman* or *Amen,* flourished 1693, Swiss Mennonite bishop] — **Amish** *n* — **Amish·man** \-ish-mən\ *n*

¹amiss \ə-'mis\ *adv* 1 : in a mistaken way : WRONGLY 2 : off the right path

²amiss *adj* : not satisfactory : WRONG, FAULTY ⟨something is *amiss* here⟩

ami·to·sis \,ā-mī-'tō-səs\ *n, pl* **-to·ses** \-'tō-,sēz\ : cell division in which simple cleavage of the nucleus is followed by the division of the cytoplasm without the appearance of chromosomes or a spindle [*²a-* + *mitosis*] — **ami·tot·ic** \-'tät-ik\ *adj*

am·i·ty \'am-ət-ē\ *n, pl* **-ties** : friendly relations especially between nations [Middle French *amité,* from Medieval Latin *amicitas,* from Latin *amicus* "friend"]

am·me·ter \'am-ˌēt-ər\ *n* : an instrument for measuring electric current in amperes

am·mo \'am-ō\ *n, pl* **ammos** : AMMUNITION

am·mo·nia \ə-'mō-nyə\ *n* **1** : a colorless gas NH₃ that is a compound of nitrogen and hydrogen, has a sharp smell and taste, is very soluble in water, can be easily liquefied by cold and pressure, is used in the manufacture of fertilizers and explosives, and is the chief nitrogenous waste product of many aquatic organisms **2** : a solution of ammonia in water — called also *ammonia water* [Latin *sal ammoniacus* "sal ammoniac", literally, "salt of Ammon"; from its discovery near a temple of the Egyptian god Ammon (Amon)] — **am·mo·ni·a·cal** \ˌam-ə-'nī-ə-kəl\ *adj*

am·mo·ni·fi·ca·tion \ə-ˌmän-ə-fə-'kā-shən, -ˌmō-nə-\ *n* : decomposition with production of ammonia or ammonium compounds especially by the action of bacteria on nitrogenous organic matter — **am·mo·ni·fy** \-ˌfī\ *vb*

am·mo·nite \'am-ə-ˌnīt\ *n* : any of numerous flat spiral fossil shells of mollusks especially abundant in the Mesozoic [Latin *cornu Ammonis,* literally, "horn of Ammon (Amon)"]

Am·mon·ite \'am-ə-ˌnīt\ *n* : a member of a Semitic people living in Old Testament times east of the Jordan river [*Ammon,* son of Lot] — **Ammonite** *adj*

am·mo·ni·um \ə-'mō-nē-əm\ *n* : an ion NH₄⁺ or radical NH₄ derived from ammonia by combination with a hydrogen ion or atom and known in compounds (as ammonium chloride)

ammonium chloride *n* : a white crystalline volatile salt NH₄Cl used in dry cells and as an expectorant — called also *sal ammoniac*

ammonium hydroxide *n* : a compound NH₅O that is formed when ammonia dissolves in water and that exists only in solution

ammonium nitrate *n* : a colorless crystalline salt N₂H₄O₃ used in explosives and fertilizers

ammonium sulfate *n* : a colorless crystalline salt N₂H₈SO₄ used chiefly as a fertilizer

am·mu·ni·tion \ˌam-yə-'nish-ən\ *n* **1** : something that can be hurled at a target; *esp* : something (as a bullet, shell, grenade, or bomb) propelled by or containing explosives **2** : material that may be used (as in a controversy) in attack or defense [obsolete French *amunition,* alteration of *munition*]

am·ne·sia \am-'nē-zhə\ *n* : loss of memory due usually to brain injury, shock, fatigue, repression, or illness [Greek *amnēsia* "forgetfulness"] — **am·ne·si·ac** \-zhē-ˌak, -zē-\ *or* **am·ne·sic** \-zik, -sik\ *adj or n*

am·nes·ty \'am-nə-stē\ *n, pl* **-ties** : a general pardon granted by a ruler or government to a large group of persons guilty of a political offense (as treason or rebellion) [Greek *amnēstia* "forgetfulness", from *a-* + *mnasthai* "to remember"]

am·nio·cen·te·sis \ˌam-nē-ō-ˌsen-'tē-səs\ *n, pl* **-te·ses** \-'tē-ˌsēz\ : the surgical insertion of a hollow needle through the abdominal wall and uterus of a pregnant female into the amnion especially to obtain amniotic fluid for the determination of sex or of chromosomal abnormality in the fetus [*amnion* + Greek *kentesis* "puncture", from *kentein* "to prick"]

am·ni·on \'am-nē-ˌän, -ən\ *n, pl* **-nions** *or* **-nia** \-nē-ə\ : a thin membrane forming a closed sac about the embryo of a reptile, bird, or mammal and containing a serous fluid in which the embryo is immersed [Greek, "caul"] — **am·ni·ot·ic** \ˌam-nē-'ät-ik\ *adj*

amoe·ba *also* **ame·ba** \ə-'mē-bə\ *n, pl* **-bas** *or* **-bae** \-ˌbē\ : any of numerous naked protozoans (group Rhizopoda) that have lobed and separate pseudopodia and no permanent cell organs or supporting structures and are widespread in fresh and salt water and in moist soils [Greek *amoibē* "change"] — **amoe·bic** \-bik\ *also* **amoe·ban** \-bən\ *adj*

amoe·boid *also* **ame·boid** \-ˌbȯid\ *adj* : resembling an amoeba especially in moving or changing in shape by means of protoplasmic flow

amok \ə-'mək, -'mäk\ *or* **amuck** \-'mək\ *adv* : in a violently frenzied state ⟨run *amok*⟩ [Malay]

among \ə-'məng\ *also* **amongst** \-'məngst, -'məngkst\ *prep* **1** : in or through the midst of ⟨*among* the crowd⟩ **2** : in company with ⟨living *among* artists⟩ **3** : through all or most of ⟨discontent *among* the poor⟩ **4** : in the number or class of ⟨wittiest *among* poets⟩ **5** : in shares to each of ⟨divided *among* the heirs⟩ **6** : through the joint action of ⟨made a fortune *among* themselves⟩ [Old English *on gemonge* "in the crowd"] SYN see BETWEEN

amon·til·la·do \ə-ˌmän-tə-'läd-ō\ *n, pl* **-dos** : a pale dry sherry [Spanish, from *a* "to" + *montilla,* a wine from Montilla, Spain]

amor·al \ā-'mȯr-əl, a-, 'ā-, 'a-, -'mär-\ *adj* : neither moral nor immoral; *esp* : outside the sphere to which moral judgments apply — **amor·al·ly** \-ə-lē\ *adv*

Am·o·rite \'am-ə-ˌrīt\ *n* : a member of one of various Semitic peoples living in Mesopotamia, Syria, and Palestine during the 3d and 2d millenniums B.C.; *esp* : one of the group founding the first Babylonian empire [Hebrew *Ěmōrī*] — **Amorite** *adj*

am·o·rous \'am-rəs, -ə-rəs\ *adj* **1** : inclined to love : easily falling in love ⟨an *amorous* nature⟩ **2** : of, relating to, or caused by love ⟨an *amorous* glance⟩ [Middle French, from Latin *amor* "love", from *amare* "to love"] — **am·o·rous·ly** *adv* — **am·o·rous·ness** *n*

amor·phous \ə-'mȯr-fəs\ *adj* **1** : having no determinate form : SHAPELESS **2** : having no crystalline form [Greek *amorphos,* from *a-* + *morphē* "form"] — **amor·phous·ly** *adv* — **amor·phous·ness** *n*

am·or·tize \'am-ər-ˌtīz *also* ə-'mȯr-ˌtīz\ *vt* : to pay off (an obligation) gradually usually by periodic payments on the principal [Middle French *amortir* "to deaden", from Latin *ad-* + *mors* "death"] — **am·or·ti·za·tion** \ˌam-ərt-ə-'zā-shən *also* ə-ˌmȯrt-ə-\ *n*

Amos \'ā-məs\ *n* — see BIBLE table

¹amount \ə-'maunt\ *vi* **1** : to add up ⟨the bill *amounted* to 10 dollars⟩ **2** : to be equivalent ⟨acts that *amount* to treason⟩ [Old French *amonter,* from *amont* "upward", from *a-* "ad-" + *mont* "mountain"]

²amount *n* **1** : the total number or quantity : AGGREGATE **2** : the whole effect, significance, or import **3** : a principal sum and the interest on it SYN see SUM

amour \ə-'mur, a-, ä-\ *n* : a love affair; *esp* : a secret love affair [Old French, "love", derived from Latin *amor*]

amour pro·pre \ˌam-ˌur-'prōpr, ˌäm-\ *n* : SELF-ESTEEM [French *amour-propre,* literally, "love of oneself"]

AMP \ˌā-ˌem-'pē\ *n* : a compound of adenine that is reversibly convertible to ADP and ATP in metabolic reactions [*a*denosine *m*ono*p*hosphate]

am·per·age \'am-pə-rij, -prij, -ˌpiər-ij\ *n* : the strength of a current of electricity expressed in amperes

am·pere \'am-ˌpiər, -ˌpeər\ *n* : a unit of electric current equal to a constant current which when maintained in two straight parallel conductors of infinite length and negligible cross section one meter apart in a vacuum produces between the conductors a force equal to 2 × 10⁻⁷ newton per meter of length [André M. *Ampère,* died 1836, French physicist]

am·per·sand \'am-pər-ˌsand\ *n* : a character & standing for the word *and* [*and* (&) *per se and,* literally, "(the character) & by itself (is the word) *and*"]

am·phet·amine \am-'fet-ə-ˌmēn, -mən\ *n* : a compound C₉H₁₃N or one of its derivatives used especially as a stimulant of the central nervous system and formerly for relief of nasal congestion [*a*lpha + *m*ethyl + *ph*en- + *et*hyl + *amine*]

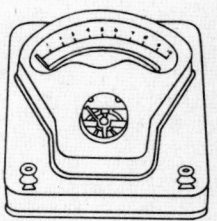

ammeter

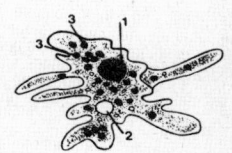

amoeba: *1* nucleus, *2* contractile vacuole, *3* food vacuoles

\ə\ abut	\ng\ si**ng**
\ər\ fur**ther**	\ō\ b**o**ne
\a\ m**a**t	\ȯ\ s**aw**
\ā\ t**a**ke	\ȯi\ c**oi**n
\ä\ c**o**t, c**a**rt	\th\ **th**in
\au\ **ou**t	\th\ **th**is
\ch\ **ch**in	\ü\ f**oo**d
\e\ p**e**t	\u̇\ f**oo**t
\ē\ **ea**sy	\y\ **y**et
\g\ **g**o	\yü\ f**ew**
\i\ t**i**p	\yu̇\ c**u**re
\ī\ l**i**fe	\zh\ vi**s**ion
\j\ **j**ob	

amphi- *or* **amph-** *prefix* : on both sides : of both kinds : both ⟨*amphi*oxus⟩ [Greek *amphi* "around, on both sides"]

am·phib·ia \am-'fib-ē-ə\ *n pl* : AMPHIBIANS

am·phib·i·an \-ē-ən\ *n* **1** : an amphibious organism; *esp* : any of a class (Amphibia) of cold-blooded vertebrate animals (as frogs and newts) that are intermediate in many respects between fishes and reptiles and have gilled aquatic larvae and air-breathing adults **2** : an airplane designed to take off from and land on either land or water **3** : a flat-bottomed vehicle that moves on tracks having finlike extensions by means of which it is propelled on land or water — **amphibian** *adj*

am·phib·i·ous \-ē-əs\ *adj* **1** : able to live both on land and in water ⟨*amphibious* plants⟩ **2 a** : relating to or adapted for both land and water ⟨*amphibious* vehicles⟩ **b** : trained or organized for invasion from the sea; *also* : executed by amphibious forces ⟨an *amphibious* assault⟩ [Greek *amphi* + *bios* "life, mode of life"] — **am·phib·i·ous·ly** *adv* — **am·phib·i·ous·ness** *n*

am·phi·bole \'am-fə-ˌbōl, 'amp-\ *n* : any of a group of white, gray, green, or black rock-forming minerals that are complex hydrous silicates and contain calcium, magnesium, iron, aluminum, and sodium [French, from Late Latin *amphibolus*, from Greek *amphibolos* "ambiguous"]

am·phi·ox·us \ˌam-fē-'äk-səs, ˌamp-\ *n, pl* **-oxi** \-'äk-ˌsī\ *or* **-oxus·es** : any of various small translucent marine animals related to the vertebrates — called also *lancelet* [*amphi-* + Greek *oxys* "sharp"]

am·phi·pod \'am-fi-ˌpäd, 'amp-\ *n* : any of a large group (Amphipoda) of crustaceans comprising the beach fleas and related forms — **amphipod** *adj*

am·phi·the·ater \'am-fə-ˌthē-ət-ər, 'amp-\ *n* **1** : a round or oval building with seats rising in curved rows around an open space on which games and plays take place **2** : something resembling an amphitheater (as a piece of level ground surrounded by hills) [derived from Greek *amphitheatron*, from *amphi* "around" + *theatron* "theater"]

am·pho·ra \'am-fə-rə, 'amp-\ *n, pl* **-pho·rae** \-ˌrē, -ˌrī\ *or* **-pho·ras** : an ancient Greek or Roman jar with two handles that rise almost to the level of the mouth [Latin, from Greek *amphoreus*, from *amphi* + *pherein* "to carry"]

amphora

am·pho·ter·ic \ˌam-fə-'ter-ik, ˌamp-\ *adj* : capable of reacting chemically either as an acid or as a base [Greek *amphoteros* "each of two", from *amphō* "both"]

am·pi·cil·lin \ˌam-pə-'sil-ən\ *n* : an antibiotic of the penicillin group that is effective against many bacteria [*am*ine + *penicillin*]

am·ple \'am-pəl\ *adj* **am·pler** \-pə-lər, -plər\; **am·plest** \-pə-ləst, -pləst\ **1** : generous in size, scope, or capacity : COPIOUS **2** : enough to satisfy : ABUNDANT [Middle French, from Latin *amplus*] SYN SEE PLENTIFUL — **am·ple·ness** *n* — **am·ply** \-plē\ *adv*

am·pli·fi·ca·tion \ˌam-plə-fə-'kā-shən\ *n* **1** : an act, example, or product of amplifying **2 a** : matter by which a statement is expanded **b** : an expanded statement

am·pli·fi·er \'am-plə-ˌfīr\ *n* : one that amplifies; *esp* : an electronic device used to obtain amplification of voltage, current, or power

am·pli·fy \'am-plə-ˌfī\ *vt* **-fied**; **-fy·ing** **1** : to make larger; *esp* : to expand with clarifying details or illustration ⟨*amplify* a statement⟩ **2** : to increase (voltage, current, or power) in magnitude or strength **3** : to make louder ⟨*amplify* the voice by using a megaphone⟩

am·pli·tude \'am-plə-ˌtüd, -ˌtyüd\ *n* **1** : the quality or state of being ample **2** : the extent or range of something: as **a** : the extent of a vibratory movement (as of a pendulum) measured from the mean position to an extreme **b** : the height or depth of a periodic wave (as

an alternating current) compared to its average value **3** : the angle that determines the final position of the radius vector in polar coordinates

amplitude modulation *n* : modulation of the amplitude of a radio carrier wave in accordance with the strength of the audio or other signal; *also* : a broadcasting system using such modulation

am·pul *or* **am·pule** *or* **am·poule** \'am-ˌpyül, -ˌpül\ *n* : a small sealed bulbous glass vessel used to hold a solution for hypodermic injection [derived from Latin *ampulla* "flask"]

am·pul·la \am-'pùl-ə, -'pəl-\ *n, pl* **-lae** \-ˌē, -ˌī\ **1** : a glass or earthenware flask with a globular body and two handles **2** : an anatomic sac or pouch [Latin] — **am·pul·lar** \-ər\ *adj*

am·pu·tate \'am-pyə-ˌtāt\ *vt* : to cut or lop off; *esp* : to cut (as a limb) from the body [Latin *amputare*, from *am-*, *amb-* "around" + *putare* "to cut, prune"] — **am·pu·ta·tion** \ˌam-pyə-'tā-shən\ *n* — **am·pu·ta·tor** \'am-pyə-ˌtāt-ər\ *n*

am·pu·tee \ˌam-pyə-'tē\ *n* : one that has had a limb amputated

amuck *variant of* AMOK

am·u·let \'am-yə-lət\ *n* : a small object worn as a charm against evil [Latin *amuletum*]

amuse \ə-'myüz\ *vt* **1** : to entertain or occupy with something pleasant ⟨*amuse* a child with a toy⟩ **2** : to appeal to the sense of humor of ⟨the story *amused* everyone⟩ [Middle French *amuser*, from *a-* "ad-" + *muser* "to muse"] — **amus·ing·ly** \-'myü-zing-lē\ *adv* □ SYN ENTERTAIN, DIVERT: AMUSE implies engaging the attention so as to keep one interested usually lightly or frivolously; ENTERTAIN suggests supplying amusement by specially prepared activity or performance; DIVERT stresses distracting the attention from worry or routine concern especially with something causing laughter or gaiety.

amuse·ment \ə-'myüz-mənt\ *n* **1** : the condition of being amused **2** : pleasant diversion **3** : something that amuses

amusement park *n* : a commercially operated park with various devices (as a merry-go-round or roller coaster) for entertainment

am·yl \'am-əl\ *n* : a univalent hydrocarbon radical C_5H_{11} occurring in various isomeric forms [derived from Greek *amylon* "starch"]

amyl alcohol *n* : any of eight isomeric alcohols $C_5H_{12}O$ used especially as solvents

am·y·lase \'am-ə-ˌlās, -ˌlāz\ *n* : an enzyme that accelerates the hydrolysis of starch or glycogen

am·y·lop·sin \ˌam-ə-'läp-sən\ *n* : the amylase of the pancreatic juice

¹an \ən, an, 'an\ *indefinite article* : ²A — used (1) usually in speech and writing before words beginning with a vowel sound ⟨*an* oak⟩ ⟨*an* hour⟩ ⟨*an* X ray⟩; (2) usually in speech and less often in writing before *h*-initial words with an unstressed first syllable in which \h\ is often lost after *an* ⟨*an* historian⟩; (3) sometimes especially in England before words whose initial letter is a vowel and whose initial sound is a consonant ⟨*an* unique occurrence⟩ ⟨such *an* one⟩; compare ²A [Old English *ān* "one"]

²an \ən, an\ *prep* : ³A **2** — used before words with an initial vowel sound ⟨once *an* afternoon⟩ ⟨fifty cents *an* hour⟩ [Old English *an, on, a-* "on, in"]

³an *or* **an'** *conj* **1** *see* AND\ : AND **2** \'an\ *archaic* : IF **1**

an- — see A-

¹-an *or* **-ian** *also* **-ean** *n suffix* **1** : one that belongs to ⟨Americ*an*⟩ ⟨Boston*ian*⟩ ⟨crustac*ean*⟩ **2** : one skilled in or specializing in ⟨phonetic*ian*⟩ [Latin *-anus*, *-ianus*, adjective and noun suffix]

²-an *or* **-ian** *also* **-ean** *adj suffix* **1** : of or belonging to ⟨Americ*an*⟩ ⟨Florid*ian*⟩ **2** : characteristic of : resembling ⟨Mozart*ean*⟩

³-an *n suffix* **1** : unsaturated carbon compound **2** : anhydride of a carbohydrate [alteration of *-ane*]

ana- *or* **an-** *prefix* : up : upward ⟨*ana*bolism⟩ [Greek, "up, back, again"]

-ana \'an-ə, 'än-ə, 'ā-nə\ *or* **-i·ana** \ē-'\ *n pl suffix* : collected items of information especially anecdotal or bibliographical concerning ⟨American*a*⟩ ⟨Johnson*iana*⟩ [Latin, neuter plural of *-anus, -ianus* "-an"]

an·a·bae·na \,an-ə-'bē-nə\ *n* : a common filamentous freshwater blue-green alga [Greek *anabainein* "to go up, shoot up"]

Ana·bap·tist \,an-ə-'bap-təst\ *n* : a Protestant of one of several 16th century sects rejecting infant baptism [Late Greek *anabaptizein* "to rebaptize"] — **Anabaptist** *adj*

anab·o·lism \ə-'nab-ə-,liz-əm\ *n* : metabolism concerned with building up the substance of plants and animals — compare CATABOLISM [*ana-* + *-bolism* (as in metabolism)] — **an·a·bol·ic** \,an-ə-'bäl-ik\ *adj*

anach·ro·nism \ə-'nak-rə-,niz-əm\ *n* **1** : the placing of persons, events, objects, or customs in times to which they do not belong **2** : a person or thing especially from a former age that is out of place in the present [Late Greek *anachronizein* "to be late", from Greek *ana-* + *chronos* "time"] — **anach·ro·nis·tic** \ə-,nak-rə-'nis-tik\ *adj* — **anach·ro·nis·ti·cal·ly** \-ti-kə-lē, -klē\ *adv*

an·a·co·lu·thon \,an-ə-kə-'lü-,thän\ *n, pl* **-tha** \-thə\ *or* **-thons** : lack of connection between the parts of one continuous stretch of speech or writing especially as the result of a shift from one construction to another in the middle of a sentence (as in "you really ought — well, do it your own way") [Greek *a-* + *akolouthos* "following"]

an·a·con·da \,an-ə-'kän-də\ *n* : a large South American snake of the boa family that kills or quiets its prey by squeezing in its coils [probably from Sinhalese *henakandayā*, a kind of snake]

an·a·dem \'an-ə-,dem\ *n, archaic* : a wreath for the head [Latin *anadema*, from Greek *anadēma*, from *anadein* "to wreathe"]

anad·ro·mous \ə-'nad-rə-məs\ *adj* : ascending rivers from the sea for breeding ⟨shad and some salmon are *anadromous*⟩ — compare CATADROMOUS [Greek *anadromos* "running upward"]

anae·mia *variant of* ANEMIA

an·aer·obe \'an-ə-,rōb; an-'ar-,ōb, -'er-\ *n* : an anaerobic organism

an·aer·o·bic \,an-ə-'rō-bik; ,an-,a-'rō-, -,e-'rō-\ *adj* : living, active, or occurring in the absence of free oxygen — **an·aer·o·bi·cal·ly** *adv*

anaerobic respiration *n* : FERMENTATION 1

an·aes·the·sia, an·aes·thet·ic, anaes·the·tist, anaes·the·tize *variant of* ANESTHESIA, ANESTHETIC, ANESTHETIST, ANESTHETIZE

ana·gram \'an-ə-,gram\ *n* : a word or phrase made out of another by changing the order of the letters ⟨*rebate* is an *anagram* of *beater*⟩ [derived from Greek *anagrammatizein* "to transpose letters", from *ana-* + *gramma* "letter"]

anal \'ān-l\ *adj* : of, relating to, or situated near the anus — **anal·ly** \-l-ē\ *adv*

anal fin *n* : an unpaired median fin located behind the vent of a fish

an·al·ge·sia \,an-l-'jē-zhə, -zhē-ə, -zē-ə\ *n* : insensibility to pain without loss of consciousness [Greek *analgēsia*, from *a-* + *algos* "pain"] — **an·al·ge·sic** \-'jē-zik, -sik\ *adj or n* — **an·al·get·ic** \-'jet-ik\ *adj or n*

analog computer *n* : a computer that operates with numbers represented by directly measurable physical quantities — compare DIGITAL COMPUTER

an·a·log·i·cal \,an-l-'äj-i-kəl\ *adj* **1** : of, relating to, or based on analogy **2** : expressing or implying analogy — **an·a·log·i·cal·ly** \-kə-lē, -klē\ *adv*

anal·o·gous \ə-'nal-ə-gəs\ *adj* **1** : showing an analogy or a likeness permitting one to draw an analogy **2** : similar in biological function but different in structure and origin ⟨the wing of a bird is *analogous* to the wing of a butterfly⟩ [Latin *analogus*, from Greek *analogos*, literally, "proportionate", from *ana* "up, in accordance with" + *logos* "reason, ratio"] SYN see SIMILAR — **anal·o·gous·ly** *adv* — **anal·o·gous·ness** *n*

an·a·logue *or* **an·a·log** \'an-l-,óg, -,äg\ *n* : something that is analogous or similar to something else

anal·o·gy \ə-'nal-ə-jē\ *n, pl* **-gies** **1** : an inference that if two or more things agree with one another in some respects they will probably agree in others **2** : resemblance in some particulars between things otherwise unlike : SIMILARITY **3** : correspondence in function between anatomical parts of different structure and origin — compare HOMOLOGY

ana·lyse *chiefly British variant of* ANALYZE

anal·y·sis \ə-'nal-ə-səs\ *n, pl* **anal·y·ses** \-'nal-ə-,sēz\ **1** : separation of a whole into its parts **2 a** : an examination of a whole to discover its elements and their relations **b** : a statement of such an analysis **c** : an examination and interpretation of the nature and significance of something (as a news event) **3** : the identification or separation of ingredients of a substance **4** : proof of a proposition by assuming the result and deducing a valid statement by a series of reversible steps **5** : PSYCHOANALYSIS [Greek, from *analyein* "to break up", from *ana-* + *lyein* "to loosen"]

an·a·lyst \'an-l-əst\ *n* **1** : a person who analyzes or who is skilled in analysis ⟨a news *analyst*⟩ **2** : a specialist in psychoanalysis : PSYCHOANALYST

an·a·lyt·ic \,an-l-'it-ik\ *adj* **1 a** : of or relating to analysis; *esp* : separating something into its parts or elements **b** : skilled in or using analysis **2** : involving or applying the methods of algebra and calculus rather than geometry ⟨*analytic* trigonometry⟩ — **an·a·lyti·cal** \-i-kəl\ *adj* — **an·a·lyt·i·cal·ly** \-kə-lē, -klē\ *adv*

analytic geometry *n* : the study of geometric properties by means of algebraic symbols representing parts or relations of figures in a coordinate system — called also *coordinate geometry*

an·a·lyze \'an-l-,īz\ *vt* : to make an analysis of; *esp* : to study or determine the nature and relationship of the parts of by analysis ⟨*analyze* a traffic pattern⟩ — **an·a·lyz·a·ble** \-,ī-zə-bəl\ *adj* — **an·a·lyz·er** \-,ī-zər\ *n*

an·a·pest \'an-ə-,pest\ *n* : a metrical foot consisting of two unaccented syllables followed by one accented syllable (as in *the accused*) [Latin *anapaestus* "foot of two short syllables followed by one long", from Greek *anapaistos*, literally, "struck back", from *ana-* + *paiein* "to strike"; from its being a dactyl reversed] — **an·a·pes·tic** \,an-ə-'pes-tik\ *adj*

ana·phase \'an-ə-,fāz\ *n* : the stage of mitosis and meiosis in which the chromosomes move toward the opposite poles of the spindle

ana·phy·lax·is \,an-ə-fə-'lak-səs\ *n* : hypersensitivity (as to a drug) resulting from sensitization during an earlier exposure to the causative agent [*ana-* + *-phylaxis* (as in *prophylaxis*)] — **ana·phy·lac·tic** \-'lak-tik\ *adj*

an·ar·chic \a-'när-kik, ə-\ *adj* : of, relating to, or tending toward anarchy : LAWLESS — **an·ar·chi·cal** \-ki-kəl\ *adj* — **an·ar·chi·cal·ly** \-ki-kə-lē, -klē\ *adv*

an·ar·chism \'an-ər-,kiz-əm, -,är-\ *n* **1** : a political theory that holds all governmental authority to be unnecessary and undesirable and advocates a society based on the voluntary cooperation of individuals and groups **2** : the support or practice of anarchistic principles

an·ar·chist \'an-ər-kəst, -,är-\ *n* **1** : one who rebels against any authority, established order, or ruling power **2** : one who believes in, supports, or promotes anarchism; *esp* : one who uses violent means to overthrow the established order — **anarchist** *or* **an·ar·chis·tic** \,an-ər-'kis-tik, -,är-\ *adj*

anaconda

\ə\ abut	\ng\ sing
\ər\ further	\ō\ bone
\a\ mat	\ó\ saw
\ā\ take	\ói\ coin
\ä\ cot, cart	\th\ thin
\aú\ out	\th\ this
\ch\ chin	\ü\ food
\e\ pet	\ú\ foot
\ē\ easy	\y\ yet
\g\ go	\yü\ few
\i\ tip	\yú\ cure
\ī\ life	\zh\ vision
\j\ job	

an·ar·chy \'an-ər-kē, -ˌär-\ *n* **1** : the condition of a society without a government **2** : a state of lawlessness, confusion, or disorder **3** : an ideal society made up of individuals who have no government and enjoy complete freedom [Greek *anarchia,* from *a-* + *archein* "to rule"] □ SYN ANARCHY, CHAOS mean absence, suspension, or breakdown of government, law, and order. ANARCHY stresses the absence of government; CHAOS implies the utter absence of order.

an·astig·mat·ic \ˌan-ə-stig-'mat-ik, ˌan-ˌas-tig-\ *adj* : not astigmatic — used especially of lenses that are able to form approximately point images of object points — **an·as·tig·mat** \a-'nas-tig-ˌmat, ˌan-ə-'stig-\ *n*

anas·to·mose \ə-'nas-tə-ˌmōz, -ˌmōs\ *vb* : to connect or communicate by anastomosis

anas·to·mo·sis \ə-ˌnas-tə-'mō-səs\ *n, pl* **-mo·ses** \-ˌsēz\ : the union of parts or branches (as of streams or blood vessels) so as to intercommunicate; *also* : NETWORK, MESH [Greek *anastomōsis,* from *ana-* + *stoma* "mouth, opening"]

anath·e·ma \ə-'nath-ə-mə\ *n* **1 a** : a curse solemnly pronounced by church authority and accompanied by excommunication **b** : a vigorous denunciation : CURSE **2** : one that is cursed or intensely disliked [Greek]

anath·e·ma·tize \-ˌtīz\ *vt* : to pronounce an anathema upon : DAMN

anat·o·mist \ə-'nat-ə-məst\ *n* : a specialist in anatomy

anat·o·mize \-ˌmīz\ *vt* **1** : to dissect so as to show or to examine the structure and use of the parts **2** : ANALYZE

anat·o·my \ə-'nat-ə-mē\ *n, pl* **-mies 1** : a branch of knowledge that deals with the structure of organisms; *also* : a writing on bodily structure **2** : structural makeup especially of an organism or any of its parts **3** : separation into parts for examination : ANALYSIS [derived from Greek *anatemnein* "to dissect", from *ana-* + *temnein* "to cut"] — **an·a·tom·ic** \ˌan-ə-'täm-ik\ *or* **an·a·tom·i·cal** \-'täm-i-kəl\ *adj* — **an·a·tom·i·cal·ly** \-kə-lē, -klē\ *adv*

-ance \əns, ᵊns\ *n suffix* **1** : action or process ⟨further*ance*⟩ : instance of an action or process ⟨perform*ance*⟩ **2** : quality or state : instance of a quality or state ⟨protuber*ance*⟩ **3** : amount or degree ⟨conduct*ance*⟩ [Latin *-antia,* from *-ans* "-ant"]

an·ces·tor \'an-ˌses-tər\ *n* **1** : one from whom an individual, group, or species is descended **2** : FORERUNNER 2, PROTOTYPE [Old French *ancestre,* from Latin *antecessor* "one that goes before", from *antecedere* "to go before"]

an·ces·tral \an-'ses-trəl\ *adj* : of, relating to, or derived from an ancestor — **an·ces·tral·ly** \-trə-lē\ *adv*

an·ces·tress \'an-ˌses-trəs\ *n* : a female ancestor

an·ces·try \'an-ˌses-trē\ *n* **1** : line of descent : LINEAGE **2** : individuals making up a line of descent : ANCESTORS

¹an·chor \'ang-kər\ *n* **1** : a heavy iron or steel device attached to a boat or ship by a cable and so made that when thrown overboard it digs into the bottom and holds the boat or ship in place **2** : something that secures or steadies or that gives a feeling of stability **3 a** : ANCHORMAN 1 **b** : ANCHORPERSON [Latin *anchora,* from Greek *ankyra*]

²anchor *vb* **an·chored; an·chor·ing** \-kə-ring, -kring\ **1** : to hold in place by means of an anchor ⟨*anchor* a ship⟩ **2** : to secure firmly ⟨*anchor* the cables of a bridge⟩ **3** : to drop anchor : become anchored ⟨the boat *anchored* in the harbor⟩ **4** : to act as an anchorperson

an·chor·age \'ang-kə-rij, -krij\ *n* **1** : a place where boats may be anchored **2** : a secure hold to resist a strong pull **3** : a means of security : REFUGE

an·cho·rite \'ang-kə-ˌrīt\ *n* : a person who gives up worldly things and lives in solitude usually for religious reasons [Medieval Latin *anchorita,* from Late Greek *anachōrētēs,* from Greek *anachorein* "to withdraw"]

an·chor·man \'ang-kər-ˌman\ *n* **1** : one who competes or is placed last ⟨the *anchorman* on a relay team⟩ **2** : ANCHORPERSON

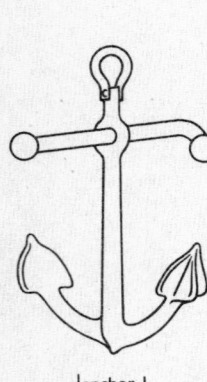

¹anchor 1

an·chor·per·son \-ˌpərs-n\ *n* : a news broadcaster who coordinates the activities of other broadcasters

an·chor·wom·an \-ˌwum-ən\ *n* : a woman who anchors a broadcast

an·cho·vy \'an-ˌchō-vē, an-'\ *n, pl* **-vies** *or* **-vy** : any of numerous small fishes resembling herrings; *esp* : a common Mediterranean fish used especially for sauces and relishes [Spanish *anchova*]

an·cien ré·gime \ˌäⁿs-'yäⁿ-rā-'zhēm\ *n* **1** : the political and social system of France before the Revolution of 1789 against the monarchy and aristocracy **2** : a system or mode no longer prevailing [French, literally, "old regime"]

¹an·cient \'ān-shənt, -chənt; 'āng-shənt, 'āngk-\ *adj* **1** : having existed for many years : very old ⟨*ancient* customs⟩ **2** : of or relating to a period of time long past or to those living in such a period; *esp* : of or relating to the historical period from the earliest civilizations to the fall of the western Roman Empire A.D. 476 **3** : having the qualities of age or long existence [Middle French *ancien,* from Latin *ante* "before"] SYN see OLD — **an·cient·ness** *n*

²ancient *n* **1** : an aged person **2** *pl* : the civilized peoples of ancient times and especially of Greece and Rome

an·cient·ly \-lē\ *adv* : in ancient times

an·cil·lary \'an-sə-ˌler-ē, an-'sil-ə-rē\ *adj* **1** : SUBSIDIARY 1b **2** : serving to aid or assist : SUPPLEMENTARY [Latin *ancilla* "female servant"]

-an·cy \ən-sē, ᵊn-sē\ *n suffix, pl* **-ancies** : quality or state ⟨piqu*ancy*⟩ [Latin *-antia* "-ance"]

and \ənd, ən, and, an, 'and, *usually* ᵊnd *or* ᵊn *after* t, d, s, z, *often* ᵊm *after* p *or* b, *sometimes* ᵊng *after* k *or* g\ *conj* **1** : added to ⟨2 *and* 2 make 4⟩ **2** : as well as ⟨you *and* I⟩ — used as a function word to join words or word groups of the same grammatical rank or function (as two nouns that are subjects of the same verb) [Old English]

¹an·dan·te \än-'dän-ˌtā, an-'dant-ē\ *adv or adj* : moderately slow — used as a direction in music [Italian, literally, "going"]

²andante *n* : a musical piece or movement in andante tempo

an·dan·ti·no \ˌän-ˌdän-'tē-nō\ *adv or adj* : somewhat quicker in tempo than andante — used as a direction in music [Italian, from *andante*]

an·des·ite \'an-di-ˌzīt\ *n* : an extrusive usually dark grayish rock consisting essentially of feldspar [*Andes* mountains] — **an·des·it·ic** \ˌan-di-'zit-ik\ *adj*

and·iron \'an-ˌdīrn, -ˌdī-ərn\ *n* : either of a pair of metal supports for firewood in a fireplace [Old French *andier*]

and/or \'and-'or\ *conj* — used as a function word to indicate that either *and* or *or* may apply ⟨cats *and/or* dogs means cats *and* dogs or cats *or* dogs⟩

an·dra·dite \an-'drad-ˌīt, 'an-drə-ˌdīt\ *n* : a garnet ranging from yellow and green to brown and black and containing calcium and iron [José B. de *Andrada* e Silva, died 1838, Brazilian geologist]

an·dro·gen \'an-drə-jən\ *n* : a male sex hormone [Greek *andr-, anēr* "male"] — **an·dro·gen·ic** \ˌan-drə-'jen-ik\ *adj*

an·drog·y·nous \an-'dräj-ə-nəs\ *adj* **1** : having both male and female characteristics **2** : bearing both staminate and pistillate flowers in the same cluster [Greek *andr-, anēr* "man, male" + *gynē* "woman"]

An·drom·e·da \an-'dräm-əd-ə\ *n* : a northern constellation directly south of Cassiopeia between Pegasus and Perseus

-ane \ˌān\ *n suffix* : saturated or completely hydrogenated carbon compound (as a hydrocarbon) ⟨meth*ane*⟩ [alteration of *-ene, -ine*]

an·ec·dote \'an-ik-ˌdōt\ *n* : a short narrative of an interesting, amusing, or biographical incident [French, derived from Greek *anekdotos* "unpublished", from *a-*

+ *ekdidonai* "to publish", from *ex-* "out" + *didonai* "to give"] — **an·ec·dot·al** \,an-ik-'dōt-l\ *adj* — **an·ec·dot·al·ly** \-l-ē\ *adv*

ane·mia *also* **anae·mia** \ə-'nē-mē-ə\ *n* 1 : a condition in which the blood is deficient in red blood cells, in hemoglobin, or in total volume and which is usually marked by pale skin, shortness of breath, and irregular heart action 2 : lack of vitality [Greek *anaimia* "bloodlessness", from *a-* + *haima* "blood"] — **ane·mic** \-mik\ *adj* — **ane·mi·cal·ly** \-mi-kə-lē, -klē\ *adv*

an·e·mom·e·ter \,an-ə-'mäm-ət-ər\ *n* : an instrument for measuring the speed of the wind [Greek *anemos* "wind"]

anem·o·ne \ə-'nem-ə-nē\ *n* 1 : any of a large genus of herbs related to the buttercups that have showy flowers without petals but with conspicuous often colored sepals — called also *windflower* 2 : SEA ANEMONE [Latin, from Greek *anemōnē*]

anent \ə-'nent\ *prep* : ABOUT 4, CONCERNING [Old English *on efen* "together, alongside", from *on* + *efen* "even"]

an·er·oid barometer \'an-ə-,ròid-\ *n* : a barometer in which a change in atmospheric pressure is made to move a pointer [French *anéroïde* "without liquid", from *a-* + Late Greek *nēron* "water"]

an·es·the·sia *also* **an·aes·the·sia** \,an-əs-'thē-zhə\ *n* : loss of bodily sensation with or without loss of consciousness [Greek *anaisthēsia* "insensibility", from *a-* + *aisthanesthai* "to perceive"]

an·es·the·si·ol·o·gist \-,thē-zē-'äl-ə-jəst\ *n* : ANESTHETIST; *esp* : a physician specializing in anesthesia and the administration of anesthetics — **an·es·the·si·ol·o·gy** \-jē\ *n*

¹**an·es·thet·ic** *also* **an·aes·thet·ic** \,an-əs-'thet-ik\ *adj* : of, relating to, or capable of producing anesthesia — **an·es·thet·i·cal·ly** \-'thet-i-kə-lē, -klē\ *adv*

²**anesthetic** *also* **anaesthetic** *n* : a substance that produces either local or general anesthesia

anes·the·tist *also* **anaes·the·tist** \ə-'nes-thət-əst\ *n* : a person who administers anesthetics

anes·the·tize *also* **anaes·the·tize** \ə-'nes-thə-,tīz\ *vt* : to make insensible to pain especially by the use of an anesthetic

an·eu·rysm *also* **an·eu·rism** \'an-yə-,riz-əm\ *n* : a permanent abnormal expansion of a blood vessel containing fluid or clotted blood and resulting from disease of the vessel wall [Greek *aneurysma*, from *aneurynein* "to dilate", from *ana-* + *eurys* "wide"]

anew \ə-'nü, -'nyü\ *adv* : over again : AFRESH (begin *anew*)

an·gel \'ān-jəl\ *n* 1 a : a spiritual being serving God especially as a messenger or as a guardian of people b : a robed winged figure of human form in fine art 2 : an attendant spirit or guardian 3 : a person felt to resemble an angel (as in virtue or beauty) 4 : a financial backer (as of a theatrical venture) [Old French *angele*, from Late Latin *angelus*, from Greek *angelos*, literally, "messenger"] — **an·gel·ic** \an-'jel-ik\ *or* **an·gel·i·cal** \-i-kəl\ *adj* — **an·gel·i·cal·ly** \-i-kə-lē, -klē\ *adv*

an·gel·fish \'ān-jəl-,fish\ *n* 1 : any of several compressed bright-colored bony fishes of warm seas 2 : SCALARE

an·gel·i·ca \an-'jel-i-kə\ *n* : a biennial herb of the carrot family whose roots and fruits furnish a flavoring oil

An·ge·lus \'an-jə-ləs\ *n* 1 : a Roman Catholic devotion that commemorates the Incarnation and is said morning, noon, and evening 2 : a bell announcing the time for the Angelus [Medieval Latin, "angel"; from the first word of the opening versicle]

¹**an·ger** \'ang-gər\ *n* : a strong feeling of displeasure and usually of antagonism (easily aroused to *anger*) [Middle English, "affliction, anger", from Old Norse *angr* "grief"] □ SYN RAGE, WRATH, FURY: ANGER is the general term for an emotional reaction of displeasure in any degree of intensity; RAGE implies loss of self-

control from violence of emotion; WRATH implies usually righteous rage with a desire to avenge or punish; FURY suggests a violence of emotion amounting to temporary madness.

²**anger** *vt* **an·gered; an·ger·ing** \-gə-ring, -gring\ : to make angry

An·ge·vin \'an-jə-vən\ *adj* : of, relating to, or characteristic of Anjou or the Plantagenets [French, derived from Medieval Latin *Andegavia* "Anjou"] — **Angevin** *n*

an·gi·na \an-'jī-nə, 'an-jə-\ *n* : a disorder marked by spasmodic attacks of intense pain: as a : a severe inflammatory condition of the mouth or throat b : ANGINA PECTORIS [Latin, "quinsy", from *angere* "to choke"] — **an·gi·nal** \an-'jīn-l, 'an-jən-\ *adj*

angina pec·to·ris \-'pek-tə-rəs, -trəs\ *n* : a heart disorder marked by brief recurrent attacks of intense chest pain caused by insufficient supply of oxygen to the heart muscles by the blood [New Latin, literally, "angina of the chest"]

an·gio·sperm \'an-jē-ə-,spərm\ *n* : FLOWERING PLANT [Greek *angeion* "vessel" + *sperma* "seed"] — **an·gio·sper·mous** \,an-jē-ə-'spər-məs\ *adj*

¹**an·gle** \'ang-gəl\ *n* 1 : the figure formed by two lines extending from the same point or by two plane surfaces diverging from the same line 2 : a measure of the amount of turning that would be required to cause one line of an angle to coincide with the other at all points 3 : a sharp projecting corner 4 a : POINT OF VIEW, ASPECT (consider the problem from a new *angle*) b : a special approach or technique for accomplishing an objective 5 : an abruptly diverging course or direction [Latin *angulus* "corner, angle"] — **an·gled** \-gəld\ *adj*

²**angle** *vb* **an·gled; an·gling** \-gə-ling, -gling\ 1 : to turn, move, or direct at an angle 2 : to present (as a news story) from a particular often biased point of view : SLANT

³**angle** *vi* **an·gled; an·gling** \-gə-ling, -gling\ 1 : to fish with hook and line 2 : to use sly means to get what one wants [Middle English *angelen*, from angel "fishhook", from Old English, from *anga* "hook"]

An·gle \'ang-gəl\ *n* : a member of a Germanic people conquering England with the Saxons and Jutes in the 5th century A.D. and merging with them to form the Anglo-Saxon people [Latin *Angli* "Angles", of Germanic origin]

angle bracket *n* : BRACKET 3b

angle of depression : an angle formed by the horizontal plane at the level of the eye and the line of sight to an object below this plane

angle of elevation : an angle formed by the horizontal plane at the level of the eye and the line of sight to an object above this plane

angle of incidence : the angle that a line (as a ray of light) falling on a surface makes with a perpendicular to the surface at the point of incidence

angle of reflection : the angle between a reflected ray and the perpendicular to a reflecting surface drawn at the point of incidence

an·gler \'ang-glər\ *n* 1 : FISHERMAN; *esp* : a person who fishes for sport 2 : a sea fish having a large flat head with projections that attract other fish within reach of its broad mouth

an·gler·fish \-,fish\ *n* : ANGLER 2

an·gle·worm \'ang-gəl-,wərm\ *n* : EARTHWORM [³angle]

An·gli·can \'ang-gli-kən\ *n* : a member of the established Church of England or of one of the related churches in communion with it [Medieval Latin *anglicus* "English", from Latin *Angli* "Angles"] — **Anglican** *adj* — **An·gli·can·ism** \-kə-,niz-əm\ *n*

an·gli·cism \'ang-glə-,siz-əm\ *n*, *often cap* 1 : a characteristic feature of English occurring in another language 2 : adherence or attachment to English customs or ideas

anemometer

an·gli·cize \'ang-glə-,sīz\ *vt, often cap* **1** : to make English (as in habits, speech, character, or outlook) **2** : to borrow (a foreign word or phrase) into English without changing form or spelling and sometimes without changing pronunciation — **an·gli·ci·za·tion** \,ang-glə-sə-'zā-shən\ *n, often cap*

an·gling \'ang-gling\ *n* : the act or sport of fishing with hook and line

An·glo- *combining form* **1** \'ang-,glō, -glə\ : English ⟨*Anglo*-Norman⟩ **2** \-,glō\ : English and ⟨*Anglo*-Japanese⟩ [Late Latin *Angli* "English people", from Latin, "Angles"]

An·glo-French \,ang-glō-'french\ *n* : the French language used in medieval England

An·glo–Nor·man \-'nȯr-mən\ *n* **1** : one of the Normans living in England after the Norman conquest **2** : the form of Anglo-French used by Anglo-Normans

an·glo·phile \'ang-glə-,fīl\ *n, often cap* : a person who greatly admires England and English things

an·glo·phobe \-,fōb\ *n, often cap* : a person who strongly dislikes England and English things

An·glo–Sax·on \,ang-glō-'sak-sən\ *n* **1** : a member of the Germanic people conquering England in the 5th century A.D. and forming the ruling class until the Norman conquest — compare ANGLE, JUTE, SAXON **2** : a native or inhabitant of England **3** : a person of English ancestry **4 a** : OLD ENGLISH 1 **b** : direct plain English — **Anglo–Saxon** *adj*

an·go·ra \ang-'gōr-ə, an-, -'gȯr-\ *n* **1** : yarn or cloth made from the hair of the Angora goat or the Angora rabbit **2** *cap* **a** : ANGORA CAT **b** : ANGORA GOAT **c** : ANGORA RABBIT

Angora cat *n* : a long-haired domestic cat [*Angora* (Ankara), Turkey]

Angora goat

Angora goat *n* : any of a breed or variety of the domestic goat raised for its long silky hair which is the true mohair

Angora rabbit *n* : a usually white rabbit raised for its long fine soft hair

an·gry \'ang-grē\ *adj* **an·gri·er; -est 1 a** : stirred by anger : ENRAGED ⟨became *angry* at the insult⟩ **b** : showing or arising from anger ⟨*angry* words⟩ **c** : threatening as if in anger ⟨an *angry* sky⟩ **2** : painfully inflamed ⟨an *angry* rash⟩ — **an·gri·ly** \-grə-lē\ *adv* — **an·gri·ness** \-grē-nəs\ *n*

angst \'ängst, 'angst\ *n* : a feeling of anxiety : DREAD [German]

ang·strom \'ang-strəm\ *n* : a unit of length used especially of wavelengths (as of light) and equal to one ten-billionth of a meter — abbreviation *A* [Anders J. *Ångström*, died 1874, Swedish physicist]

an·guish \'ang-gwish\ *n* : extreme pain or distress of body or mind [Old French *angoisse*, from Latin *angustiae* "straits, distress", from *angustus* "narrow"] SYN see SORROW

an·guished \'ang-gwisht\ *adj* : full of anguish : TORMENTED ⟨an *anguished* call for help⟩

an·gu·lar \'ang-gyə-lər\ *adj* **1 a** : having one or more angles **b** : forming an angle : sharp-cornered : POINTED ⟨an *angular* mountain peak⟩ **2** : measured by an angle ⟨*angular* distance⟩ **3** : being lean and bony ⟨an *angular* figure⟩ — **an·gu·lar·i·ty** \,ang-gyə-'lar-ət-ē\ *n* — **an·gu·lar·ly** *adv*

angular velocity *n* : the time rate of change of angular position

An·gus \'ang-gəs\ *n* : ABERDEEN ANGUS

an·hy·dride \an-'hī-,drīd, 'an-\ *n* : a compound derived from another (as an acid) by removing a molecule of water

an·hy·drite \-'hī-,drīt\ *n* : a mineral $CaSO_4$ consisting of an anhydrous calcium sulfate

an·hy·drous \-'hī-drəs\ *adj* : free from water and especially water of crystallization

an·i·line \'an-l-ən\ *n* : an oily liquid poisonous amine C_6H_7N made especially from nitrobenzene and used chiefly in organic synthesis (as of dyes) [German *anilin*, from *anil* "indigo", derived from Arabic *an-nīl* "the indigo plant", from Sanskrit *nīlī*, from *nīla* "dark blue"]

an·i·mad·ver·sion \,an-ə-,mad-'vər-zhən, -məd-, -shən\ *n* **1** : a critical remark or comment **2** : unfriendly criticism

an·i·mad·vert \-'vərt\ *vi* : to make a critical remark : comment unfavorably ⟨*animadvert* on a display of bad manners⟩ [Latin *animadvertere* "to pay attention to, censure", from *animum advertere* "to turn the mind to"]

¹an·i·mal \'an-ə-məl\ *n* **1** : any of a kingdom (Animalia) of living beings typically differing from plants in capacity for active movement, in rapid response to stimulation, and in lack of cellulose cell walls **2 a** : one of the lower animals as distinguished from humans **b** : MAMMAL [Latin, from *animalis* "animate", from *anima* "breath, soul"]

²animal *adj* **1** : of, relating to, or derived from animals **2** : of or relating to the physical nature of a person as contrasted with the intellectual; *esp* : SENSUOUS ⟨the *animal* appetites that plague humanity⟩

an·i·mal·cule \,an-ə-'mal-kyül\ *n* : a very small animal that is invisible or nearly invisible to the naked eye [New Latin *animalculum*, from Latin *animal*]

animal heat *n* : heat produced in the body of a living animal by its chemical and physical activity

animal husbandry *n* : a branch of agriculture concerned with the production and care of domestic animals

an·i·mal·ism \'an-ə-mə-,liz-əm\ *n* **1** : qualities typical of animals **2** : total concern with the satisfaction of physical needs or wants — **an·i·mal·ist** \-mə-ləst\ *n* — **an·i·mal·is·tic** \,an-ə-mə-'lis-tik\ *adj*

animal kingdom *n* : the basic group of natural objects that includes all living and extinct animals — compare MINERAL KINGDOM, PLANT KINGDOM

animal starch *n* : GLYCOGEN

¹an·i·mate \'an-ə-mət\ *adj* **1** : having life : ALIVE **2** : ANIMATED 1b, c, LIVELY [Latin *animare* "to give life to", from *anima* "breath, soul"] — **an·i·mate·ly** *adv* — **an·i·mate·ness** *n*

²an·i·mate \'an-ə-,māt\ *vt* **1** : to give life to : make alive ⟨belief that the soul *animates* the body⟩ **2** : to give spirit and vigor to : ENLIVEN **3** : to make appear to move ⟨*animate* a cartoon⟩

an·i·mat·ed \-,māt-əd\ *adj* **1 a** : ALIVE 1, LIVING **b** : full of movement and activity **c** : full of vigor and spirit : VIVACIOUS **2** : having the appearance or movement of something alive SYN see LIVELY — **an·i·mat·ed·ly** *adv*

animated cartoon *n* : a motion picture made from a series of drawings simulating motion by means of slight progressive changes

an·i·ma·tion \,an-ə-'mā-shən\ *n* **1** : SPIRIT 4, LIVELINESS ⟨discussed their plans with *animation*⟩ **2 a** : ANIMATED CARTOON **b** : the preparation of animated cartoons

an·i·ma·to \,an-ə-'mät-ō\ *adv or adj* : with animation — used as a direction in music [Italian]

an·i·ma·tor \'an-ə-,māt-ər\ *n* : one that contributes to the making of an animated cartoon

an·i·mism \'an-ə-,miz-əm\ *n* : attribution of conscious life to nature as a whole or to inanimate objects — **an·i·mist** \-məst\ *n* — **an·i·mis·tic** \,an-ə-'mis-tik\ *adj*

an·i·mos·i·ty \,an-ə-'mäs-ət-ē\ *n, pl* **-ties** : ill will or resentment tending toward active hostility [Late Latin *animositas*, derived from Latin *animus* "spirit, mind, courage, anger"] SYN see ENMITY

an·i·mus \'an-ə-məs\ *n* **1** : basic attitude : INTENTION **2** : deep-seated hostility : ANTAGONISM [Latin, "mind, spirit, anger"]

an·ion \'an-,ī-ən\ *n* : a negatively charged ion [Greek, from *anienai* "to go up", from *ana-* + *ienai* "to go"] — **an·ion·ic** \,an-ī-'än-ik\ *adj*

an·ise \'an-əs\ *n* : an herb of the carrot family with aromatic seeds; *also* : ANISEED [derived from Greek *anison*]

ankh

ani·seed \'a n-ə-ˌsēd, -əs-\ *n* : the seed of anise often used as a flavoring in cordials and in cooking

an·isog·a·mous \ˌan-ī-'säg-ə-məs\ *adj* : involving un-like gametes ⟨*anisogamous* reproduction⟩ — **an·isog-a·my** \-ī-'säg-ə-mē\ *n*

ankh \'ängk\ *n* : a cross having a loop for its upper vertical arm and serving especially in ancient Egypt as an emblem of life [Egyptian *'nḫ*]

an·kle \'ang-kəl\ *n* : the joint between the foot and the leg; *also* : the region of this joint [Old English *anclēow*]

an·kle·bone \-'bōn, -ˌbōn\ *n* : TALUS 1

an·klet \'ang-klət\ *n* **1** : something (as an ornament) worn around the ankle **2** : a short sock reaching slight-ly above the ankle

an·ky·lo·saur \'ang-kə-lō-ˌsòr\ *n* : any of several plant-eating dinosaurs having a thickset body with bony plates covering the back [Greek *ankylos* "crooked" + *sauros* "lizard"]

an·ky·lo·sis \ˌang-ki-'lō-səs\ *n, pl* **-lo·ses** \-ˌsēz\ : a growing together of parts (as bones) into a rigid whole; *also* : stiffness of a joint resulting from such growth [derived from Greek *ankylos* "crooked"] — **an·ky·lose** \'ang-ki-ˌlōs, -ˌlōz\ *vb*

an·na \'än-ə\ *n* **1** : a former monetary unit of Burma, India, and Pakistan equal to 1/16 rupee **2** : a coin repre-senting one anna [Hindi *ānā*]

an·nal·ist \'an-l-əst\ *n* : a writer of annals : HISTORIAN — **an·nal·is·tic** \ˌan-l-'is-tik\ *adj*

an·nals \'an-lz\ *n pl* **1** : a record of events arranged in yearly sequence **2** : historical records : CHRONICLES **3** : records of the activities of an organization [Latin *annales*, from *annalis* "yearly", from *annus* "year"]

An·nam·ese \ˌan-ə-'mēz, -'mēs\ *n, pl* **Annamese 1 a** : a Mongolian people of Vietnam **b** *or* **An·nam·ite** \'an-ə-ˌmīt\ : a member of this people **2** : the language of the Annamese people : VIETNAMESE [*Annam*, region of Vi-etnam] — **Annamese** *adj*

an·neal \ə-'nēl\ *vt* **1** : to heat and then cool (as steel or glass) for softening and making less brittle **2** : STRENGTHEN, TOUGHEN ⟨*annealed* by hardship⟩ [Old En-glish *onǣlan* "to set on fire", from *on* + *ǣlan* "to burn"]

an·ne·lid \'an-l-əd\ *n* : any of a phylum (Annelida) of long segmented invertebrate animals (as an earthworm or a leech) having a body cavity [Latin *annellus* "little ring", from *annulus* "ring"] — **annelid** *adj*

¹an·nex \ə-'neks, 'an-ˌeks\ *vt* **1** : to add as an additional part : APPEND ⟨a protocol *annexed* to the treaty⟩ **2** : to incorporate (a territory) within one's own domain ⟨the United States *annexed* Texas in 1845⟩ [Middle French *annexer*, from Latin *annectere* "to bind to", from *ad-* + *nectere* "to bind"] — **an·nex·a·tion** \ˌan-ˌek-'sā-shən\ *n* — **an·nex·a·tion·al** \-shnəl, -shən-l\ *adj* — **an·nex·a·tion·ist** \-shə-nəst, -shnəst\ *n*

²an·nex \'an-ˌeks, -iks\ *n* : something annexed or ap-pended; *esp* : a part (as a wing) added to a building

an·ni·hi·late \ə-'nī-ə-ˌlāt\ *vt* : to destroy completely ⟨*annihilate* an entire army⟩ [Latin *annihilare* "to re-duce to nothing", from *ad-* + *nihil* "nothing"] SYN see DESTROY — **an·ni·hi·la·tion** \-ˌnī-ə-'lā-shən\ *n* — **an·ni-hi·la·tor** \-'nī-ə-ˌlāt-ər\ *n*

an·ni·ver·sa·ry \ˌan-ə-'vərs-rē, -ə-rē\ *n, pl* **-ries 1** : the annual recurrence of a date marking a notable event **2** : the celebration of an anniversary [Latin *anniversar-ius* "returning annually", from *annus* "year" + *vert-ere* "to turn"]

an·no Do·mi·ni \ˌan-ō-'däm-ə-nē, -'dō-mə-, -ˌnī\ *adv, of-ten cap A* — used to indicate that a time division falls within the Christian era; abbreviation A.D. [Medieval Latin, "in the year of the Lord"]

an·no·tate \'an-ə-ˌtāt\ *vb* : to make or furnish with crit-ical or explanatory notes or comment — **an·no·ta·tor** \-ˌtāt-ər\ *n*

an·no·ta·tion \ˌan-ə-'tā-shən\ *n* **1** : the act of annotat-ing **2** : a note of comment or explanation

an·nounce \ə-'naùns\ *vb* **1** : to make known publicly : PROCLAIM **2 a** : to give notice of the arrival, presence, or readiness of **b** : to indicate beforehand : FORETELL **3** : to serve as an announcer [Middle French *annoncer*, from Latin *annuntiare*, from *ad-* + *nuntiare* "to re-port", from *nuntius* "messenger"] SYN see DECLARE

an·nounce·ment \ə-'naùns-mənt\ *n* **1** : the act of an-nouncing **2** : a public notice announcing something

an·nounc·er \ə-'naùn-sər\ *n* : one that announces; *esp* : a person who introduces television or radio programs, makes announcements, and gives the news and station identification

an·noy \ə-'nòi\ *vb* : to disturb or irritate especially by repeated disagreeable acts : VEX [Old French *enuier*, from Late Latin *inodiare* "to make hateful", from Lat-in *in* "in" + *odium* "hatred"] — **an·noy·er** *n* — **an-noy·ing·ly** \-ing-lē\ *adv* □ SYN ANNOY, WORRY, HA-RASS mean to disturb or irritate by persistent acts. AN-NOY implies disturbing one's composure or peace of mind by intrusion, interference, or petty attacks; WOR-RY suggests incessant attacks intending to drive one to desperation or defeat; HARASS implies petty persecu-tions or burdensome demands that exhaust one's nerv-ous or mental power.

an·noy·ance \ə-'nòi-əns\ *n* **1 a** : the act of annoying or of being annoyed **b** : the state or feeling of being an-noyed : VEXATION **2** : a source of irritation : NUISANCE

¹an·nu·al \'an-yə-wəl, 'an-yəl\ *adj* **1** : covering the pe-riod of a year **2** : occurring or performed once a year : YEARLY **3** : completing the life cycle in one growing season [Late Latin *annualis*, from Latin *annus* "year"] — **an·nu·al·ly** \-ē\ *adv*

²annual *n* **1** : a publication appearing yearly **2** : an event that occurs yearly **3** : an annual plant

annual ring *n* : the layer of wood produced by a single year's growth of a woody plant

an·nu·itant \ə-'nü-ət-ənt, -'nyü-\ *n* : a beneficiary of an annuity

an·nu·ity \ə-'nü-ət-ē, -'nyü-\ *n, pl* **-ties 1** : a sum of money paid at regular intervals (as every year) **2** : a contract providing for the payment of an annuity [Mid-dle French *annuité*, derived from Latin *annuus* "yearly", from *annus* "year"]

an·nul \ə-'nəl\ *vt* **an·nulled; an·nul·ling 1** : to make in-effective or inoperative ⟨*annul* a drug's effect⟩ **2** : to declare or make legally void ⟨*annul* a marriage⟩ [Mid-dle French *annuller*, derived from Latin *ad-* + *nullus* "not any"] SYN see NULLIFY

an·nu·lar \'an-yə-lər\ *adj* : of, relating to, or forming a ring [Latin *annulus* "ring"]

annular eclipse *n* : an eclipse in which a thin outer ring of the sun's disk is not covered by the apparently smal-ler dark disk of the moon

an·nu·late \'an-yə-lət, -ˌlāt\ *adj* : furnished with or composed of rings : RINGED

an·nul·ment \ə-'nəl-mənt\ *n* : the act of annulling or state of being annulled; *esp* : a legal declaration that a marriage is invalid

an·nu·lus \'an-yə-ləs\ *n, pl* **-li** \-ˌlī, -ˌlē\ *also* **-lus·es** : RING; *esp* : a part, structure, or marking resembling a ring ⟨*annuli* of the earthworm⟩ [Latin]

an·nun·ci·ate \ə-'nən-sē-ˌāt\ *vt* : ANNOUNCE — **an·nun-ci·a·tor** \-ˌāt-ər\ *n* — **an·nun·ci·a·to·ry** \-sē-ə-ˌtōr-ē, -ˌtòr-\ *adj*

an·nun·ci·a·tion \ə-ˌnən-sē-'ā-shən\ *n* : the act of an-nouncing : ANNOUNCEMENT

Annunciation *n* : March 25 observed as a church festival in commemoration of the announcement of the Incar-nation to the Virgin Mary

an·ode \'an-ˌōd\ *n* **1** : the positive electrode of an elec-trolytic cell to which the negative ions are attracted — compare CATHODE **2** : the negative terminal of a primary cell or of a storage battery that is delivering

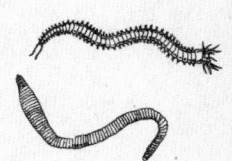

annelid: *top* clam worm, *bottom* earthworm

\ə\ abut	\ng\ sing
\ər\ further	\ō\ bone
\a\ mat	\ò\ saw
\ā\ take	\òi\ coin
\ä\ cot, cart	\th\ thin
\aù\ out	\ṯh\ this
\ch\ chin	\ü\ food
\e\ pet	\ù\ foot
\ē\ easy	\y\ yet
\g\ go	\yü\ few
\i\ tip	\yù\ cure
\ī\ life	\zh\ vision
\j\ job	

current **3** : the electron-collecting electrode of an electron tube [Greek *anodos* "way up", from *ana-* + *hodos* "way"] — **an·od·ic** \a-'näd-ik\ *adj*

an·od·ize \'an-ə-ˌdīz\ *vt* : to subject (a metal) to electrolytic action as the anode of a cell in order to coat with a protective or decorative film

¹**an·o·dyne** \'an-ə-ˌdīn\ *adj* : serving to relieve pain : SOOTHING [Greek *anōdynos*, from *a-* + *odynē* "pain"]

²**anodyne** *n* : an anodyne drug or agent

anoint \ə-'nȯint\ *vt* **1** : to rub over with oil or an oily substance **2 a** : to apply oil to as a sacred rite **b** : to consecrate with or as if with oil [Middle French *enoindre*, from Latin *inunguere*, from *in-* + *unguere* "to smear"] — **anoint·er** *n* — **anoint·ment** \-mənt\ *n*

anointing of the sick : a sacrament that consists of anointing a usually critically ill person and praying for his or her recovery and salvation

anom·a·lous \ə-'näm-ə-ləs\ *adj* **1** : deviating from a general rule or method or from accepted notions of fitness or order **2** : being not what would naturally be expected [Late Latin *anomalus*, from Greek *anōmalos*, literally, "uneven", from *a-* + *homalos* "even", from *homos* "same"] — **anom·a·lous·ly** *adv* — **anom·a·lous·ness** *n*

anom·a·ly \ə-'näm-ə-lē\ *n, pl* **-lies 1** : deviation from what is usual or expected **2** : something anomalous

anon \ə-'nän\ *adv* **1** *obsolete* : at once : IMMEDIATELY **2** *archaic* : SHORTLY 2a, SOON **3** : after a while : LATER [Old English on *ān*, from *on* "in" + *ān* "one"]

anon·y·mi·ty \ˌan-ə-'nim-ət-ē\ *n, pl* **-ties 1** : the quality or state of being anonymous **2** : one that is anonymous

anon·y·mous \ə-'nän-ə-məs\ *adj* **1** : having or giving no name ⟨an *anonymous* author⟩ **2** : of unknown or unnamed source or origin ⟨*anonymous* gifts⟩ ⟨an *anonymous* letter⟩ **3** : lacking individuality or personality [Late Latin *anonymus*, from Greek *anōnymos*, from *a-* + *onyma* "name"] — **anon·y·mous·ly** *adv* — **anon·y·mous·ness** *n*

anoph·e·les \ə-'näf-ə-ˌlēz\ *n* : any of a genus of mosquitoes that includes all mosquitoes which transmit malaria to humans [Greek *anōphelēs* "useless"] — **anoph·e·line** \-ˌlīn\ *adj or n*

an·o·rak \'an-ə-ˌrak\ *n, chiefly British* : PARKA [Greenland Eskimo *annoraaq*]

an·orex·ia \ˌa-nə-'rek-sē-ə, -'rek-shə\ *n* : ANOREXIA NERVOSA [Greek, "loss of appetite," from *a-* + *orexis* "appetite"]

anorexia ner·vo·sa \-nər-'vō-sə, -zə\ *n* : a serious eating disorder primarily of young women in their teens that is characterized especially by an abnormal fear of weight gain leading to faulty eating patterns and usually excessive weight loss [New Latin, literally, "nervous loss of appetite"]

an·orex·ic \ˌan-ə-'rek-sik\ *adj* : affected with anorexia nervosa

an·or·thite \ə-'nȯr-ˌthīt\ *n* : a white, grayish, or reddish calcium-containing feldspar [French, from Greek *a-* + *orthos* "straight"]

an·or·tho·site \ə-'nȯr-thə-ˌsīt\ *n* : a granular plutonic igneous rock composed chiefly of a plagioclase feldspar (as labradorite) [French *anorthose*, from Greek *a-* + *orthos* "straight"]

¹**an·oth·er** \ə-'nəth-ər\ *adj* **1** : different or distinct from the one considered ⟨from *another* angle⟩ **2** : some other : LATER ⟨at *another* time⟩ **3** : being one more in addition ⟨bring *another* cup⟩

²**another** *pron* **1** : an additional one **2** : one that is different from the first or present one **3** : one of an indefinite or unspecified group ⟨for one reason or *another*⟩

an·ox·ia \a-'näk-sē-ə\ *n* : a condition (as at high altitudes) in which insufficient oxygen reaches the tissues — **an·ox·ic** \-sik\ *adj*

¹**an·swer** \'an-sər\ *n* **1 a** : something spoken or written in reply especially to a question **b** : a correct response

2 : a reply to a charge or accusation : DEFENSE **3** : an act done in response **4** : a solution to a problem [Old English *andswaru*]

²**answer** *vb* **an·swered; an·swer·ing** \'ans-ring, -ə-ring\ **1** : to speak or write in reply or in reply to **2 a** : to be or make oneself responsible or accountable ⟨*answered* for the children's safety⟩ **b** : to make amends : ATONE ⟨must *answer* for their negligence⟩ **3** : CONFORM, CORRESPOND ⟨*answered* to the description⟩ **4** : to act in response ⟨the ship *answers* to the helm⟩ **5** : to be adequate : SERVE ⟨*answer* the purpose⟩ **6** : to offer or find a solution for — **an·swer·er** \'an-sər-ər\ *n*

an·swer·able \'ans-rə-bəl, -ə-rə-\ *adj* **1** : subject to be called to account : RESPONSIBLE ⟨*answerable* for a debt⟩ **2** : capable of being answered ⟨an *answerable* argument⟩

ant \'ant\ *n* : any of a family of colonial insects that are related to the wasps and bees and have a complex social organization with various castes performing special duties [Middle English *ante, emete*, from Old English *æmette*]

ant- see ANTI-

¹**-ant** \ənt, ᵊnt\ *n suffix* **1 a** : one that performs (a specified action) ⟨cool*ant*⟩ **b** : one that promotes (a specified action or process) ⟨expector*ant*⟩ **2** : one that is acted upon (in a specified manner) ⟨inhal*ant*⟩ [Latin *-ant-, -ans*, present participle suffix of some verbs]

²**-ant** *adj suffix* **1** : performing (a specified action) or being (in a specified condition) ⟨somnambul*ant*⟩ **2** : promoting (a specified action or process) ⟨expector*ant*⟩

ant·ac·id \ant-'as-əd, 'ant-\ *n* : a remedy for stomach acidity — **antacid** *adj*

an·tag·o·nism \an-'tag-ə-ˌniz-əm\ *n* **1 a** : active opposition or hostility **b** : opposition between two conflicting forces, tendencies, or principles **2** : opposition in physiological action (as of two drugs or muscles) SYN see ENMITY

an·tag·o·nist \-nəst\ *n* **1** : one that opposes another especially in combat : ADVERSARY **2** : an agent of physiological antagonism; *esp* : a drug that opposes the action of another SYN see OPPONENT

an·tag·o·nis·tic \an-ˌtag-ə-'nis-tik\ *adj* : characterized by or resulting from antagonism — **an·tag·o·nis·ti·cal·ly** \-ti-kə-lē, -klē\ *adv*

an·tag·o·nize \an-'tag-ə-ˌnīz\ *vt* **1** : to act in opposition to : COUNTERACT **2** : to incur or provoke the hostility of [Greek *antagōnizesthai*, from *anti-* + *agōn* "contest"]

ant·arc·tic \ant-'ärk-tik, 'ant-, -'ärt-ik\ *adj, often cap* : of or relating to the south pole or to the region near it [Latin *antarcticus*, from Greek *antarktikos*, from *anti-* + *arktikos* "arctic"]

antarctic circle *n, often cap A&C* : the parallel of latitude that is approximately 66½ degrees south of the equator

An·tar·es \an-'taər-ˌēz, -'teər-\ *n* : a giant red star of very low density that is the brightest star in Scorpio [Greek *Antarēs*]

ant bear *n* : a large South American anteater with shaggy gray fur, a black band across the breast, and a white shoulder stripe

ant cow *n* : an aphid from which ants obtain honeydew

¹**an·te** \'ant-ē\ *n* : a poker stake usually put up before the deal to build the pot [*ante-*]

²**ante** *vt* **an·ted; an·te·ing** : to put up (an ante); *also* : PAY 1 — often used with *up*

ante- *prefix* **1** : prior to : earlier ⟨*ante*date⟩ **2** : anterior : in front of ⟨*ante*room⟩ [Latin *ante* "before, in front of"]

ant·eat·er \'ant-ˌēt-ər\ *n* : any of several mammals (as an echidna or aardvark) that feed largely or entirely on ants; *esp* : an edentate with a long narrow snout and very long extensible tongue

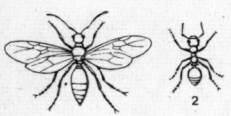

ant: *1* winged male, *2* worker

ant bear

an·te·bel·lum \,ant-i-'bel-əm\ *adj* : existing before a war; *esp* : existing before the Civil War [Latin *ante bellum* "before the war"]

¹an·te·ce·dent \,ant-ə-'sēd-nt\ *n* **1** : a noun, pronoun, phrase, or clause referred to by a personal or relative pronoun ⟨in "the house that Jack built", *house* is the *antecedent* of *that*⟩ **2** : the first term of a mathematical ratio **3** : a preceding event, condition, or cause **4 a** : a predecessor in a series; *esp* : a model or stimulus for later developments **b** *pl* : ANCESTORS, PARENTS [Latin *antecedens* "one that goes before", from *antecedere* "to go before", from *ante-* + *cedere* "to go"]

²antecedent *adj* : coming earlier in time or order SYN see PRECEDING — **an·te·ce·dent·ly** *adv*

an·te·cham·ber \'ant-i-,chām-bər\ *n* : ANTEROOM

an·te·date \'ant-i-,dāt\ *vt* **1** : to date (as a check) with a date prior to that of actual writing **2** : to precede in time ⟨automobiles *antedate* airplanes⟩

an·te·di·lu·vi·an \,ant-i-də-'lü-vē-ən, -dī-\ *adj* **1** : of or relating to the period before the Flood described in the Bible **2** : very old or old-fashioned : ANTIQUATED [*ante-* + Latin *diluvium* "flood"] — **antediluvian** *n*

an·te·lope \'ant-l-,ōp\ *n, pl* **-lope** *or* **-lopes 1 a** : any of various Old World ruminant mammals that are related to the goats and oxen but differ from the true oxen especially in lighter racier build and horns directed upward and backward **b** : PRONGHORN **2** : leather from antelope hide [Middle English, a fabulous heraldic beast, probably from Middle French *antelop*, a savage animal with sawlike horns, derived from Late Greek *antholops*]

an·te me·ri·di·em \,ant-i-mə-'rid-ē-əm, -ē-,em\ *adj* : being before noon — abbreviation *a.m.* [Latin]

an·ten·na \an-'ten-ə\ *n, pl* **-ten·nae** \-'ten-,ē\ *or* **-ten·nas 1** : any of one or two pairs of long slender segmented sensory organs on the head of an arthropod (as an insect or a crab) **2** *pl usually* **antennas** : a usually metallic device (as a rod or wire) for sending or receiving radio waves [Latin, "sail yard"] ◻ ORIGIN Latin *antenna* meant "sail yard" — a sail yard is a long spar that supports and spreads the sail on a sailing vessel. The Greek word for a sail yard was *keraia*, but "sail yard" was only the secondary meaning of this word. The primary meaning was "horn". The philosopher Aristotle used *keraiai* for the feelers of insects, probably because of their resemblance to the horns of some larger animals. In a Latin translation of Aristotle's work made during the Renaissance, the word *antennae* was used for Greek *keraiai*. In English we still use *antennae* for insects' feelers. And now we also use *antenna* with a regular English plural ending *-s* for the metal rods which pick up radio waves and seem to feel the air like the antennae of an insect.

an·ten·nule \an-'ten-yül\ *n* : a small antenna (as of a crayfish)

an·te·pen·di·um \,ant-i-'pen-dē-əm\ *n, pl* **-di·ums** *or* **-dia** \-dē-ə\ : a hanging for the front of an altar, pulpit, or lectern [Medieval Latin, from Latin *ante-* + *pendēre* "to hang"]

an·te·pe·nult \,ant-i-'pē-,nəlt\ *n* : the 3d syllable of a word counting from the end ⟨*-cu-* is the *antepenult* in *accumulate*⟩ — **an·te·pen·ul·ti·mate** \-pi-'nəl-tə-mət\ *adj or n*

an·te·ri·or \an-'tir-ē-ər\ *adj* **1 a** : situated before or toward the front **b** : situated near or toward the head or the part most nearly corresponding to a head **2** : coming before in time : ANTECEDENT [Latin, comparative of *ante* "before"] — **an·te·ri·or·ly** *adv*

an·te·room \'ant-i-,rüm, -,rum\ *n* : a room used as an entrance to another room or as a waiting room

anth- — see ANTI-

an·them \'an-thəm, 'ant-\ *n* **1** : a sacred vocal composition with words usually from the Scriptures **2** : a song or hymn of praise or gladness [Old English *antefn* "antiphon", from Late Latin *antiphona*]

an·ther \'an-thər, 'ant-\ *n* : the part of a stamen that produces and contains pollen and is usually borne on a stalk [Latin *anthera* "medicine made of flowers", from Greek *anthēra*, from *anthos* "flower"] — **an·ther·al** \-thə-rəl\ *adj*

an·ther·id·i·um \,an-thə-'rid-ē-əm, ,ant-\ *n, pl* **-ia** \-ē-ə\ : the male reproductive organ of a cryptogamic plant (as a moss or club moss) — **an·ther·id·i·al** \-ē-əl\ *adj*

ant·hill \'ant-,hil\ *n* : a mound thrown up by ants or termites in digging their nest

an·tho·cy·a·nin \,an-thə-'sī-ə-nən, ,ant-\ *n* : any of various soluble pigments producing blue to red coloring in flowers and plants [Greek *anthos* "flower" + *kyanos* "dark blue"]

an·thol·o·gize \an-'thäl-ə-,jīz\ *vt* : to compile or publish in an anthology ⟨the story has often been *anthologized*⟩ — **an·thol·o·gist** \-jəst\ *n*

an·thol·o·gy \an-'thäl-ə-jē\ *n, pl* **-gies 1** : a collection of selected literary pieces or passages **2** : a collection of selected pieces in any art form (as songs, recordings, or paintings) [Greek *anthologia* "gathering of flowers", from *anthos* "flower" + *legein* "to gather"]

an·tho·zo·an \,an-thə-'zō-ən, ,ant-\ *n* : any of a class (Anthozoa) of marine coelenterates (as the corals and sea anemones) having polyps with radial partitions [Greek *anthos* "flower" + *zōion* "animal"] — **anthozoan** *adj*

an·thra·cene \'an-thrə-,sēn, 'ant-\ *n* : a crystalline hydrocarbon $C_{14}H_{10}$ obtained from coal-tar distillation

an·thra·cite \'an-thrə-,sīt, 'ant-\ *n* : a hard glossy coal that burns without much smoke or flame [Greek *anthrakitis*, from *anthrax* "coal, carbuncle"] — **an·thra·cit·ic** \,an-thrə-'sit-ik, ,ant-\ *adj*

an·thrax \'an-,thraks\ *n* : an infectious and usually fatal bacterial disease of warm-blooded animals (as cattle and sheep) that is transmissible to humans [Latin *anthrax* "carbuncle", from Greek, "coal, carbuncle"]

anthrop- *or* **anthropo-** *combining form* : human being ⟨*anthropo*centric⟩ [Greek *anthrōpos*]

an·thro·po·cen·tric \,an-thrə-pə-'sen-trik, ,ant-\ *adj* : interpreting or regarding the world in terms of human values and experiences

¹an·thro·poid \'an-thrə-,pöid, 'ant-\ *adj* **1** : resembling a human being **2** : resembling an ape ⟨*anthropoid* mobsters⟩

²anthropoid *n* : any of a family of large tailless upright apes including the gibbons, chimpanzee, orangutan, and gorilla

an·thro·pol·o·gy \,an-thrə-'päl-ə-jē, ,ant-\ *n* : a science that deals with human beings and especially with their physical characteristics, origin and distribution into races, environmental and social relations, and culture — **an·thro·po·log·i·cal** \-pə-'läj-i-kəl\ *adj* — **an·thro·po·log·i·cal·ly** \-'läj-i-kə-lē, -klē\ *adv* — **an·thro·pol·o·gist** \-'päl-ə-jəst\ *n*

an·thro·pom·e·try \,an-thrə-'päm-ə-trē, ,ant-\ *n* : the study of human body measurements — **an·thro·po·met·ric** \-pə-'metrik\ *adj*

an·thro·po·mor·phic \,an-thrə-pə-'mor-fik, ,ant-\ *adj* **1** : described or thought of as having a human form or human attributes ⟨*anthropomorphic* deities⟩ **2** : ascribing human characteristics to nonhuman things ⟨*anthropomorphic* interpretations of animal behavior⟩ — **an·thro·po·mor·phi·cal·ly** \-fi-kə-lē, -klē\ *adv* — **an·thro·po·mor·phism** \-,fiz-əm\ *n*

an·thro·po·mor·phize \-'mor-,fīz\ *vt* : to attribute human form or personality to

an·thro·poph·a·gous \,an-thrə-'päf-ə-gəs, ,ant-\ *adj* : feeding on human flesh — **an·thro·poph·a·gy** \-'päf-ə-jē\ *n*

¹an·ti \'an-,tī, 'ant-ē\ *n* : one that is opposed [*anti-*]

²anti *prep* : opposed to : AGAINST

anti- *or* **ant-** *or* **anth-** *prefix* **1** : opposite in kind, position, or action ⟨*anti*climax⟩ ⟨*anti*clockwise⟩ ⟨*anti*mat-

antelope 1a: *top* hartebeest, *bottom* kudu

\ə\ abut		\ng\ sing
\ər\ further		\ō\ bone
\a\ mat		\o\ saw
\ā\ take		\oi\ coin
\ä\ cot, cart		\th\ thin
\aů\ out		\th\ this
\ch\ chin		\ü\ food
\e\ pet		\ů\ foot
\ē\ easy		\y\ yet
\g\ go		\yü\ few
\i\ tip		\yů\ cure
\ī\ life		\zh\ vision
\j\ job		

ter) **2 a** : hostile toward ⟨*anti*clerical⟩ ⟨*anti*-Semite⟩ **b** : opposing in effect or activity : counteracting ⟨*ant*acid⟩ ⟨*anti*coagulant⟩ **3** : serving to prevent or cure ⟨*anti*malarial⟩ **4** : combating or defending against ⟨*anti*aircraft⟩ ⟨*anti*ballistic missile⟩ [Greek *anti* "against"]

See *anti-* and 2d element

antiabortion	antiepilepsy	antiobscenity
antiabortionist	antiepileptic	antiorganization
antiacademic	antierotic	antipapal
antiadministration	antiestablishment	antipesticide
antiaggression	antievolution	antiplague
antiaging	antievolutionary	antipleasure
antialien	antievolutionism	antipolice
anti-American	antievolutionist	antipolio
anti-Americanism	anti-fascism	antipornographic
antiapartheid	anti-fascist	antipornography
anti-Arab	antifatigue	antipoverty
antiaristocrat	antifemale	antiprofiteering
antiaristocratic	antifeminine	antiprogressive
antiart	antifeminism	antiprostitution
antiarthritic	antifeminist	antirabies
antiarthritis	antiflu	antiracketeering
antiasthma	antiforeclosure	antiradical
antiatheism	antiforeign	antirape
antiauthoritarian	antiforeigner	antirealism
antiauthoritarianism	antifraud	antirecession
antibias	anti-French	antireform
antibillboard	antigambling	antirejection
antiblack	anti-German	antireligious
anti-Bolshevik	antiglare	antirevolutionary
antibourgeois	antigovernment	antirheumatic
antiboycott	antiguerrilla	antiriot
anti-British	antigun	antiromantic
antibureaucratic	antihijack	antiromanticism
antiburglar	antihomosexual	anti-Russian
antiburglary	antihuman	antirust
antibusiness	antihumanism	antisecrecy
anticapitalism	antihumanistic	antisegregation
anticapitalist	antihunting	antisentimental
anticarcinogen	antihysteric	antisex
anticarcinogenic	anti-icing	antisexist
anticaries	anti-imperialism	antisexual
anti-Catholic	anti-imperialist	antisexuality
anticensorship	anti-infective	antishock
anticholesterol	anti-inflammatory	antishoplifting
anti-Christian	anti-inflation	antislavery
anti-Christianity	anti-inflationary	antisleep
antichurch	anti-institutional	antislip
anticigarette	anti-integration	antismoking
anticlassical	anti-intellectual	antismuggling
anticlotting	anti-intellectualism	antismut
anticollision	anti-Italian	anti-Soviet
anticolonial	antijamming	antispeculative
anticolonialism	anti-Japanese	antispending
anticolonialist	anti-Jewish	antistatic
anticommercialism	antilabor	antistrike
anticommunism	antileprosy	antistudent
anticommunist	antileukemic	antisubmarine
anticonservation	antiliberal	antisubversion
anticonservationist	antiliberalism	antisubversive
anticonsumer	antilitter	antisuicide
anticonventional	antilittering	antisyphilitic
anticorrosion	antilynching	anti-tarnish
anticorrosive	antimalaria	antitax
anticorruption	antimale	antitechnological
anticrime	antimanagement	antitechnology
anticruelty	antimaterialism	antiterrorism
anticultural	antimaterialist	antiterrorist
antidandruff	antimilitarism	antitheft
anti-Darwinian	antimilitarist	antitheoretical
anti-Darwinism	antimilitary	antitobacco
antidemocratic	antimiscegenation	antitotalitarian
antidiabetic	antimonarchist	antitraditional
antidiarrheal	antimonopolist	antitubercular
antidiscrimination	antimonopoly	antituberculosis
antidogmatic	antimosquito	antitumor
antidumping	antinausea	antityphoid
antieconomic	antinepotism	antiulcer
antiemetic	antinoise	anti-
anti-English	antiobesity	unemployment

antiunion	antivivisection	anti-Western
antiuniversity	antivivisectionist	antiwhite
antiurban	antiwar	antiwoman
antiviolence	antiwear	antiwrinkle
antiviral	anti-West	

an·ti·air·craft \,ant-ē-'aər-,kraft, -'eər-\ *adj* : designed or used for defense against aircraft — **antiaircraft** *n*

an·ti·bac·te·ri·al \,ant-i-bak-'tir-ē-əl, ,an-,tī-\ *adj* : directed or effective against bacteria

an·ti·bal·lis·tic missile \,ant-i-bə-,lis-tik-, ,an-,tī-\ *n* : a missile for intercepting and destroying ballistic missiles

an·ti·bi·o·sis \-bī-'ō-səs, -bē-\ *n* : antagonistic association between organisms to the detriment of one of them or between one organism and a metabolic product of another

an·ti·bi·ot·ic \-bī-ät-ik, -bē-\ *n* : a substance produced by a microorganism (as a fungus or bacterium) that in dilute solution inhibits or kills another microorganism — **antibiotic** *adj* — **an·ti·bi·ot·i·cal·ly** \-'ät-i-kə-lē, -klē\ *adv*

an·ti·body \'ant-i-,bäd-ē\ *n* : any of several globulins in the blood that react with specific antigens (as a toxin), bacteria, or cells to render them harmless to the organism

an·ti·bus·ing \,ant-i-'bəs-ing, ,an-,tī-\ *adj* : opposed to the busing of children as a means of racially balancing pupil population in the schools

¹an·tic \'ant-ik\ *n* **1** : a silly, playful, or ludicrous act or action : CAPER ⟨carnival *antics*⟩ **2** *archaic* : CLOWN, BUFFOON [Italian *antico*, adj., "ancient", from Latin *antiquus*] □ ORIGIN In the ruins of ancient Roman buildings Renaissance Italians found fantastic mural paintings. In Renaissance England any similarly fantastic painting of more modern date that showed strange combinations of human, animal, and floral forms was called *antike* or *anticke*, from the Italian word for "ancient", *antico*. And any odd gesture or strange behavior reminiscent of the ancient Roman paintings became in English an *antic*.

²antic *adj* **1** *archaic* : GROTESQUE, BIZARRE **2** : whimsically grotesque or extravagant ⟨an *antic* comedy⟩

an·ti·can·cer \,ant-i-'kan-sər, ,an-,tī-\ *also* **an·ti·can·cer·ous** \-'kans-rəs, -ə-rəs\ *adj* : used or effective against cancer ⟨*anticancer* drugs⟩

An·ti·christ \'ant-i-,krīst\ *n* **1** : one who denies or opposes Christ; *esp* : a great antagonist expected to fill the world with wickedness but to be conquered forever by Christ at the second coming **2** : a false Christ

an·tic·i·pate \an-'tis-ə-,pāt\ *vb* **1 a** : to take into consideration in advance ⟨*anticipate* the result of an action⟩ ⟨*anticipate* a plan⟩ **b** : to deal with before the expected or proper time ⟨*anticipate* a bill⟩ **2 a** : to deal with before another can act or interfere ⟨an idea *anticipated* by an earlier inventor⟩ **b** : to act before (another) often so as to check or counter **3** : to use in advance of actual possession ⟨*anticipate* one's income⟩ **4** : to look forward to : EXPECT ⟨*anticipate* a holiday⟩ [Latin *anticipare*, from *ante-* + *capere* "to take"] SYN SEE FORESEE — **an·tic·i·pa·tor** \-,pāt-ər\ *n*

an·tic·i·pa·tion \,an-,tis-ə-'pā-shən\ *n* **1 a** : a prior action that takes into account or forestalls a later action **b** : the act of looking forward; *esp* : pleasurable expectation **2** : a picturing beforehand of a future event or state — **an·tic·i·pa·to·ry** \an-'tis-ə-pə-,tōr-ē, -,tòr-\ *adj*

an·ti·cler·i·cal \,ant-i-'kler-i-kəl, ,an-,tī-\ *adj* : opposed to the influence of the clergy in secular affairs — **anticlerical** *n* — **an·ti·cler·i·cal·ism** \-'kler-i-kə-,liz-əm\ *n*

an·ti·cli·max \,ant-i-'klī-,maks\ *n* **1** : the usually sudden change in writing or speaking from a significant idea to a trivial or ludicrous idea; *also* : an instance of such change **2** : an event especially closing a series that is strikingly less important than what has preceded it — **an·ti·cli·mac·tic** \-klī-'mak-tik\ *adj* — **an·ti-cli·mac·ti·cal·ly** \-ti-kə-lē, -klē\ *adv*

an·ti·cline \'ant-i-ˌklīn\ *n* : an arch of stratified rock in which the layers bend downward in opposite directions from the crest — compare SYNCLINE [Greek *klinein* "to lean"]

an·ti·clock·wise \ˌant-i-'kläk-ˌwīz, ˌan-ˌtī-\ *adj or adv* : COUNTERCLOCKWISE

an·ti·co·ag·u·lant \-kō-'ag-yə-lənt\ *n* : a substance that hinders clotting of blood — **anticoagulant** *adj*

an·ti·com·pet·i·tive \-kəm-'pet-ət-iv\ *adj* : tending to restrict free competition

an·ti·cy·clone \ˌant-i-'sī-ˌklōn\ *n* : a system of winds that rotates about a center of high atmospheric pressure clockwise in the northern hemisphere and counterclockwise in the southern, that usually advances at 30 to 40 kilometers per hour, and that usually has a diameter of 2500 to 4000 kilometers — **an·ti·cy·clon·ic** \-sī-'klän-ik\ *adj*

an·ti·de·pres·sant \ˌant-i-di-'pres-nt, ˌan-ˌtī-\ *or* **an·ti-de·pres·sive** \-di-'pres-iv\ *adj* : used or tending to relieve psychic depression — **antidepressant** *n*

an·ti·dote \'ant-i-ˌdōt\ *n* **1** : a remedy to counteract the effects of poison **2** : something that relieves, prevents, or counteracts [Latin *antidotum,* from Greek *antidotos,* derived from *anti-* + *didonai* "to give"]

an·ti·drug \'an-ˌtī-ˌdrəg, ˌan-tī-'\ *adj* : acting against or opposing illegal drugs

an·ti·elec·tron \ˌant-ē-ə-'lek-ˌträn, ˌan-ˌtī-\ *n* : POSITRON

an·ti·fed·er·al·ist \ˌant-i-'fed-rə-ləst, ˌan-ˌtī-, -ə-rə-\ *n, often cap A&F* : a member of the group that opposed in 1787–88 the adoption of the United States Constitution

an·ti·fer·til·i·ty \-fər-'til-ət-ē\ *adj* : intended to control excess or unwanted fertility : CONTRACEPTIVE

an·ti·freeze \'ant-i-ˌfrēz\ *n* : a substance (as ethylene glycol) added to a liquid (as the water in an automobile radiator) to prevent its freezing

an·ti·gen \'ant-i-jən\ *n* : a substance (as a toxin or enzyme) that when introduced into the body stimulates the production of an antibody — **an·ti·gen·ic** \ˌant-i-'jen-ik\ *adj* — **an·ti·gen·i·cal·ly** \-'jen-i-kə-lē, -klē\ *adv* — **an·ti·ge·nic·i·ty** \-jə-'nis-ət-ē\ *n*

an·ti·he·mo·phil·ic \ˌant-i-ˌhē-mə-'fil-ik, ˌan-ˌtī-\ *adj* : counteracting the bleeding tendency in hemophilia

an·ti·hero \'ant-i-ˌhē-ˌrō, 'an-ˌtī-, -ˌhiər-ˌō\ *n* : a principal character (as in a story or play) completely lacking in heroic qualities — **an·ti·he·ro·ic** \ˌant-i-hi-'rō-ik, ˌan-ˌtī-\ *adj*

an·ti·his·ta·mine \ˌant-i-'his-tə-ˌmēn, ˌan-ˌtī-, -mən\ *n* : any of various drugs that counteract histamine in the body and are used for treating allergic reactions and cold symptoms

an·ti·knock \ˌant-i-'näk\ *n* : a substance that when added to the fuel of an internal-combustion engine helps to prevent knocking

an·ti·lock \'an-ˌtī-ˌläk, 'ant-i-\ *adj* : being a braking system for a motor vehicle designed to keep the wheels from locking and skidding

an·ti·log·a·rithm \ˌant-i-'lȯg-ə-ˌrith-əm, ˌan-ˌtī-, -'läg-\ *n* : the number corresponding to a given logarithm

an·ti·ma·cas·sar \ˌant-i-mə-'kas-ər\ *n* : a covering to protect the back or arms of furniture [*anti-* + *Macassar* oil, a hair dressing]

an·ti·ma·lar·i·al \ˌant-i-mə-'ler-ē-əl, ˌan-ˌtī-\ *adj* : serving to prevent, check, or cure malaria — **antimalarial** *n*

an·ti·mat·ter \'ant-i-ˌmat-ər\ *n* : matter composed of antiparticles

an·ti·mi·cro·bi·al \ˌant-i-mī-'krō-bē-əl\ *adj* : inhibiting or destructive to microbes — **antimicrobial** *n*

an·ti·mo·ny \'ant-ə-ˌmō-nē\ *n* : a metallic silvery white crystalline and brittle element that is used especially as a constituent of alloys and in medicine — see ELE-

MENT table [Medieval Latin *antimonium*] — **an·ti·mo·ni·al** \ˌant-ə-'mō-nē-əl\ *adj*

an·ti·neu·tri·no \ˌant-i-nü-'trē-ˌnō, ˌan-ˌtī-, -nyü-\ *n* : the antiparticle of the neutrino

an·ti·neu·tron \-'nü-ˌträn, -'nyü-\ *n* : the antiparticle of the neutron

an·ti·ox·i·dant \ˌant-ē-'äk-səd-ənt, ˌan-ˌtī-\ *n* : a substance that opposes oxidation or inhibits reactions promoted by oxygen — **antioxidant** *adj*

an·ti·par·ti·cle \'ant-i-ˌpärt-i-kəl, 'an-ˌtī-\ *n* : an elementary particle identical to another in mass but opposite to it in electric or magnetic properties that when brought together with its counterpart produces mutual annihilation

an·ti·pas·to \ˌant-i-'pas-tō, ˌänt-i-'päs-\ *n, pl* **-pas·ti** \-tē\ : any of various typically Italian hors d'oeuvres; *also* : a number of these served especially as the first course of a meal [Italian, from *anti-* "before" (from Latin *ante-*) + *pasto* "food", from Latin *pastus*]

an·tip·a·thy \an-'tip-ə-thē\ *n, pl* **-thies** **1** : strong feeling against someone or something : AVERSION **2** : a person or thing that arouses strong dislike — **an·ti·pa·thet·ic** \ˌant-i-pə-'thet-ik\ *adj* — **an·ti·pa·thet·i·cal·ly** \-i-kə-lē, -klē\ *adv*

an·ti·per·son·nel \ˌant-i-ˌpərs-n-'el, ˌan-ˌtī-\ *adj* : designed for use against military personnel

an·ti·per·spi·rant \-'pər-spə-rənt, -sprənt\ *n* : a cosmetic preparation used to check excessive perspiration

an·ti·phon \'ant-ə-fən, -ˌfän\ *n* **1** : a psalm, anthem, or verse sung alternately by divisions of a choir or congregation **2** : a verse usually from Scripture said or sung before and after a canticle, psalm, or psalm verse [Late Latin *antiphona,* from Late Greek *antiphōna,* from Greek *antiphōnos* "responsive", from *anti-* + *phōnē* "sound"]

an·tiph·o·nal \an-'tif-ən-l\ *adj* : performed by two alternating groups ⟨*antiphonal* singing⟩ — **an·tiph·o·nal·ly** \-l-ē\ *adv*

an·tip·o·dal \an-'tip-əd-l\ *adj* **1** : of or relating to the antipodes; *esp* : situated at the opposite side of the earth **2** : diametrically opposite **3** : differing greatly

an·ti·pode \'ant-ə-ˌpōd\ *n, pl* **an·tip·o·des** \an-'tip-ə-ˌdēz\ **1** : the parts of the earth diametrically opposite — usually used in pl. **2** : the exact opposite or contrary [Latin *antipodes* "persons living at opposite points on the globe", from Greek, from *antipous* "with feet opposite", from *anti-* + *pous* "foot"] — **an·tip·o·de·an** \ˌan-ˌtip-ə-'dē-ən\ *adj*

an·ti·pol·lu·tion \ˌant-i-pə-'lü-shən, ˌan-ˌtī-\ *adj* : intended to prevent, reduce, or eliminate pollution ⟨*antipollution* devices on automobiles⟩

an·ti·pope \'ant-i-ˌpōp\ *n* : one elected or claiming to be pope in opposition to the pope canonically chosen

an·ti·pro·ton \ˌant-i-'prō-ˌtän, ˌan-ˌtī-\ *n* : the antiparticle of the proton

an·ti·py·ret·ic \-pī-'ret-ik\ *n* : an agent that reduces fever [Greek *pyretos* "fever", from *pyr* "fire"] — **antipyretic** *adj*

¹an·ti·quar·i·an \ˌant-ə-'kwer-ē-ən\ *n* : ANTIQUARY

²antiquarian *adj* : of or relating to antiquaries or antiquities

an·ti·quary \'ant-ə-ˌkwer-ē\ *n, pl* **-quar·ies** : a person who collects or studies antiquities

an·ti·quate \'ant-ə-ˌkwāt\ *vt* : to make old or obsolete

an·ti·quat·ed *adj* **1** : OLD-FASHIONED, OUTMODED **2** : of long standing or great age ⟨*antiquated* prejudices⟩

¹an·tique \an-'tēk\ *adj* **1** : belonging to antiquity **2** : belonging to an earlier period ⟨*antique* furniture⟩ **3** : belonging to or resembling a former style or fashion : OLD-FASHIONED ⟨silver of an *antique* design⟩ [Middle French, from Latin *antiquus,* from *ante* "before"] SYN see OLD — **an·tique·ly** *adv* — **an·tique·ness** *n*

²antique *n* : an object of an earlier period; *esp* : a work of art, piece of furniture, or decorative object made at an earlier period

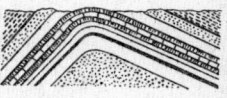

anticline

\ə\ abut	\ng\ sing
\ər\ further	\ō\ bone
\a\ mat	\ȯ\ saw
\ā\ take	\ȯi\ coin
\ä\ cot, cart	\th\ thin
\au̇\ out	\th\ this
\ch\ chin	\ü\ food
\e\ pet	\u̇\ foot
\ē\ easy	\y\ yet
\g\ go	\yü\ few
\i\ tip	\yu̇\ cure
\ī\ life	\zh\ vision
\j\ job	

an·tiq·ui·ty \an-'tik-wət-ē\ *n, pl* **-ties** **1** : ancient times; *esp* : those before the Middle Ages **2** : the quality of being ancient **3** *pl* **a** : relics or monuments of ancient times **b** : matters relating to the life or culture of ancient times

an·ti·scor·bu·tic \,ant-i-skòr-'byüt-ik, ,an-,tī-\ *adj* : tending to prevent or relieve scurvy

an·ti-Sem·ite \-'sem-,īt\ *n* : a person who is hostile to or discriminates against Jews — **anti-Se·mit·ic** \-sə-'mit-ik\ *adj* — **an·ti-Sem·i·tism** \-'sem-ə-,tiz-əm\ *n*

an·ti·sep·sis \,ant-ə-'sep-səs\ *n* : the inhibiting of the growth and multiplication of microorganisms by antiseptic means

an·ti·sep·tic \,ant-ə-'sep-tik\ *adj* **1** : preventing or stopping the growth of germs that cause disease or decay ⟨*antiseptic* agents⟩ **2** : relating to or characterized by the use of antiseptics ⟨*antiseptic* treatments⟩ **3 a** : protecting or protected from what is undesirable ⟨lives in *antiseptic* seclusion⟩ **b** : extremely neat or orderly; *esp* : neat to the point of being bare or uninteresting **c** : free from living microorganisms : ASEPTIC ⟨*antiseptic* wounds⟩ **d** : coldly impersonal ⟨an *antiseptic* greeting⟩ [*anti-* + Greek *sēptikos* "putrefying, septic"] — **antiseptic** *n* — **an·ti·sep·ti·cal·ly** \-ti-kə-lē, -klē\ *adv*

an·ti·se·rum \'ant-i-,sir-əm, 'an-,tī-, -,ser-\ *n* : a serum containing antibodies

an·ti·so·cial \,ant-i-'sō-shəl, ,an-,tī-\ *adj* **1** : contrary or hostile to the well-being of society ⟨crime is *antisocial*⟩ **2** : disliking or avoiding the company of others : UNSOCIABLE

an·ti·tank \-'tangk\ *adj* : designed to destroy or check tanks

an·tith·e·sis \an-'tith-ə-səs\ *n, pl* **-e·ses** \-ə-,sēz\ **1** : the rhetorical contrast of ideas by means of parallel arrangements of words, clauses, or sentences **2 a** : a direct or striking contrast **b** : the second of two contrasted things **3** : the direct opposite ⟨dictatorship is the *antithesis* of democracy⟩ [Late Latin, from Greek, literally, "opposition", from *antitithenai* "to place opposite, oppose", from *anti-* + *tithenai* "to put"] — **an·ti·thet·ic** \,ant-ə-'thet-ik\ *adj* — **an·ti·thet·i·cal** \-'thet-i-kəl\ *adj* — **an·ti·thet·i·cal·ly** \-i-kə-lē, -klē\ *adv*

an·ti·tox·in \,ant-i-'täk-sən\ *n* : an antibody that is capable of neutralizing a particular toxin, is formed in response to the introduction of toxin into the body, and is produced commercially in lower animals for use in treating human diseases (as diphtheria) in which such a toxin is present; *also* : a serum containing antitoxins — **an·ti·tox·ic** \-sik\ *adj*

an·ti·trust \,ant-i-'trəst, ,an-,tī-\ *adj* : opposing or designed to restrict the power of trusts and similar business combinations ⟨*antitrust* laws⟩

an·ti·ven·in \,ant-i-'ven-ən, ,an-,tī-\ *n* : a serum containing an antitoxin to a venom (as of a snake)

ant·ler \'ant-lər\ *n* : the solid deciduous horn of an animal of the deer family or a branch of such horn [Middle French *antoillier*, derived from Latin *ante-* + *oculus* "eye"] — **ant·lered** \-lərd\ *adj*

ant lion *n* : any of various 4-winged insects (order Neuroptera) with a long-jawed larva that digs a conical pit in which it lies in wait to catch insects (as ants) on which it feeds

an·to·nym \'ant-ə-,nim\ *n* : a word of opposite meaning ⟨*hot* and *cold* are *antonyms*⟩ [*anti-* + Greek *onyma, onoma* "name"] — **an·ton·y·mous** \an-'tän-ə-məs\ *adj*

an·uran \ə-'nùr-ən, a-, -'nyùr-\ *adj or n* : SALIENTIAN [²*a-* + Greek *oura* "tail"]

anus \'ā-nəs\ *n* : the posterior opening of the alimentary canal [Latin]

an·vil \'an-vəl\ *n* **1** : a heavy usually steel-faced iron block on which metal is shaped **2** : INCUS [Old English *anfilt*]

aoudad

anx·i·ety \ang-'zī-ət-ē\ *n, pl* **-eties** **1 a** : painful or fearful uneasiness of mind usually over an impending or anticipated event **b** : a cause of such uneasiness **2** : a strong concern or desire mixed with doubt and fear ⟨*anxiety* to succeed⟩ [Latin *anxietas,* from *anxius* "anxious"]

anx·ious \'ang-shəs, 'angk-\ *adj* **1** : fearful of what may happen : WORRIED ⟨*anxious* about their son's health⟩ **2** : desiring earnestly ⟨*anxious* to make good⟩ [Latin *anxius*] SYN see EAGER — **anx·ious·ly** *adv* — **anx·ious·ness** *n*

¹any \'en-ē\ *adj* **1 a** : one taken at random ⟨*any* person you meet⟩ **b** : EVERY — used to indicate one selected without restriction ⟨*any* child would know that⟩ **2** : one, some, or all indiscriminately of whatever quantity ⟨have you *any* money⟩ ⟨need *any* help they can get⟩ **3** : unmeasured or unlimited in amount, number, or extent ⟨*any* quantity you desire⟩ [Old English *ǣnig*]

²any *pron, sing or pl in construction* **1** : any person or persons **2 a** : any thing or things **b** : any part, quantity, or number

³any *adv* : to any extent or degree : at all ⟨can't go *any* farther⟩ ⟨you're not helping *any*⟩

any·body \'en-ē-,bäd-ē, -,bəd-\ *pron* : ANYONE

any·how \-,haù\ *adv* **1** : in any way, manner, or order **2** : at any rate : in any case

any·more \,en-ē-'mòr, -'mór\ *adv* : at the present time : NOWADAYS ⟨we never see them *anymore*⟩

any·one \'en-ē-,wən, -wən\ *pron* : any person at all

any·place \-,plās\ *adv* : in any place : ANYWHERE

any·thing \-,thing\ *pron* : any thing at all

any·way \'en-ē-,wā\ *adv* : ANYHOW

any·ways \-,wāz\ *adv, chiefly dialect* : in any case

any·where \-,hweər, -,hwaər, -,weər, -,waər\ *adv* : in, at, or to any place

any·wise \-,wīz\ *adv* : in any way whatever : at all

A–OK \,ā-,ō-'kā\ *adj* : working or going well : FINE

A1 \'ā-'wən\ *adj* : of the finest quality : FIRST-RATE

aor·ta \ā-'órt-ə\ *n, pl* **aortas** *or* **aor·tae** \-'órt-ē\ : the main artery of the circulatory system that carries blood from the heart to be distributed by branch arteries through the body [Greek *aortē,* from *aeirein* "to lift"] — **aor·tic** \-'órt-ik\ *adj*

aou·dad \'aù-,dad, 'ä-ủ-\ *n* : a wild sheep of North Africa [French, from Berber *audad*]

¹ap- — see AD-

²ap- *or* **apo-** *prefix* : away from : off ⟨*aphelion*⟩ [Greek *apo* "away, off"]

apace \ə-'pās\ *adv* : at a quick pace : SWIFTLY

apache \ə-'pach-ē, in sense 2 ə-'pash\ *n, pl* **apache** *or* **apaches** \-'pach-ēz, -'pash-əz\ **1** *cap* : a member of an Indian people of the American Southwest **2 a** : a member of a gang of criminals especially in Paris **b** : RUFFIAN [sense 1 from Spanish; sense 2 from French, from *Apache* "Apache Indian"]

¹apart \ə-'pärt\ *adv* **1** : at a distance in space or time ⟨two towns five miles *apart*⟩ **2** : as a separate unit : INDEPENDENTLY ⟨considered *apart* from other points⟩ **3** : ASIDE ⟨joking *apart*, that's probably true⟩ **4** : into pieces ⟨tear a book *apart*⟩

²apart *adj* **1** : different or separated from others ⟨a breed *apart*⟩ **2** : holding different opinions : DIVIDED — **apartness** *n*

apart from *prep* : other than : BESIDES

apart·heid \ə-'pär-,tāt, -,tīt\ *n* : a policy of racial segregation practiced in the Republic of South Africa [Afrikaans, literally, "separateness"]

apart·ment \ə-'pärt-mənt\ *n* **1** : a room or set of rooms used as a dwelling **2** : ROOM 2a **3** : APARTMENT BUILDING

apartment building *n* : a building divided into individual dwelling units — called also *apartment house*

ap·a·thet·ic \,ap-ə-'thet-ik\ *adj* **1** : having or showing little or no feeling or emotion : SPIRITLESS **2** : having little or no interest or concern : INDIFFERENT SYN see

IMPASSIVE — **ap·a·thet·i·cal·ly** \-'thet-i-kə-lē, -klē\ *adv*

ap·a·thy \'ap-ə-thē\ *n* **1** : lack of feeling or emotion **2** : lack of interest or concern : **INDIFFERENCE**

ap·a·tite \'ap-ə-ˌtīt\ *n* : any of a group of minerals of variable color that are phosphates of calcium usually with some fluorine and that are used as a source of phosphorus and its compounds [German *apatit,* from Greek *apatē* "deceit"]

apat·o·sau·rus \ə-ˌpat-ə-'sȯr-əs\ *n* : **BRONTOSAURUS** [Greek *apatē* "deceit" + *sauros* "lizard"]

¹ape \'āp\ *n* **1 a** : **MONKEY**; *esp* : one of the larger tailless or short-tailed forms **b** : any of a family of large semierect primates (as the chimpanzee or gorilla) **2 a** : **MIMIC** **b** : a large uncouth person [Old English *apa*] — **ape·like** \'ā-ˌplīk\ *adj*

²ape *vt* : to follow as a pattern or model **SYN** see **IMITATE** — **ap·er** *n*

ape–man \'āp-ˌman, -ˌman\ *n* : a primate (as pithecanthropus) intermediate in character between true humans and the higher apes

ape·ri·ent \ə-'pir-ē-ənt\ *n* : **LAXATIVE** [Latin *aperire* "to open"] — **aperient** *adj*

aper·i·tif \ˌäp-ˌer-ə-'tēf, ə-'per-ə-\ *n* : an alcoholic drink taken (as a cocktail) before a meal as an appetizer [French *apéritif,* derived from Latin *aperire* "to open"]

ap·er·ture \'ap-ər-ˌchu̇r, 'ap-ə-, -chər\ *n* **1** : an opening or open space : **HOLE** **2** : the opening in a lens that admits light; *also* : the diameter of this opening [Latin *apertura,* from *aperire* "to open"]

apex \'ā-ˌpeks\ *n, pl* **apex·es** *or* **api·ces** \'ā-pə-ˌsēz, 'ap-ə-\ **1 a** : the uppermost point : **TOP** **b** : the narrowed or pointed end : **TIP** ⟨*apex* of a leaf⟩ **2** : the highest or culminating point ⟨*apex* of a career⟩ [Latin] **SYN** see **SUMMIT**

apha·sia \ə-'fā-zhē-ə, -zhə\ *n* : loss or impairment of the power to use and understand words [Greek, from *a-* + *phasia* "speech", from *phanai* "to say"] — **apha·sic** \-zik\ *n or adj*

aph·elion \a-'fēl-yən\ *n, pl* **aph·elia** \-yə\ : the point of a planet's or comet's orbit most distant from the sun — compare **PERIHELION** [*apo-* + Greek *hēlios* "sun"]

aphid \'ā-fəd, 'af-əd\ *n* : any of numerous small sluggish insects that suck the juices of plants

aphis \'ā-fəs, 'af-əs\ *n, pl* **aphi·des** \'ā-fə-ˌdēz, 'af-ə-\ : **APHID** [New Latin *Aphid-, Aphis,* genus name]

aph·o·rism \'af-ə-ˌriz-əm\ *n* : a short sentence stating a general truth or practical observation [Middle French *aphorisme,* derived from Greek *aphorizein* "to define", from *apo-* + *horizein* "to bound"] — **aph·o·rist** \-rəst\ *n* — **aph·o·ris·tic** \ˌaf-ə-'ris-tik\ *adj* — **aph·o·ris·ti·cal·ly** \-ti-kə-lē, -klē\ *adv*

aph·ro·dis·i·ac \ˌaf-rə-'dē-zē-ˌak, -'diz-ē-\ *adj* : exciting sexual desire [Greek *aphrodisiakos* "sexual", derived from *Aphroditē* "Aphrodite"] — **aphrodisiac** *n* — **aph·ro·di·si·a·cal** \ˌaf-rəd-ə-'zī-ə-kəl, -'sī-\ *adj*

api·ary \'ā-pē-ˌer-ē\ *n, pl* **-ar·ies** : a place where bees are kept; *esp* : a collection of hives of bees [Latin *apiarium,* from *apis* "bee"]

ap·i·cal \'ā-pi-kəl *also* 'ap-i-\ *adj* : of, relating to, or situated at an apex [Latin *apic-, apex* "apex"] — **ap·i·cal·ly** \-kə-lē, -klē\ *adv*

apiece \ə-'pēs\ *adv* : for each one : **INDIVIDUALLY** ⟨selling for ten cents *apiece*⟩

ap·ish \'ā-pish\ *adj* **1** : given to slavish imitation **2** : extremely silly or affected — **ap·ish·ly** *adv* — **ap·ish·ness** *n*

aplomb \ə-'pläm, -'pləm\ *n* : complete composure or self-assurance : **POISE** [French, literally, "perpendicularity", from *à plomb* "according to the plumb bob"]

apo- — see **²AP-**

apoc·a·lypse \ə-'päk-ə-ˌlips\ *n* **1 a** : a Jewish or early Christian symbolic writing about a final cataclysm destroying the powers of evil and ushering in the king-dom of God **b** *cap* : the biblical book of Revelation **2** : a prophetic revelation [Late Latin *apocalypsis,* from Greek *apokalypsis,* literally, "uncovering", from *apo-* + *kalyptein* "to cover"] — **apoc·a·lyp·tic** \ə-ˌpäk-ə-'lip-tik\ *adj* — **apoc·a·lyp·ti·cal·ly** \-'lip-ti-kə-lē, -klē\ *adv*

apoc·o·pe \ə-'päk-ə-ˌpē\ *n* : the loss of one or more sounds or letters at the end of a word (as in *sing* from Old English *singan*) [Late Latin, from Greek *apokopē,* literally, "cutting off"]

apoc·ry·pha \ə-'päk-rə-fə\ *n sing or pl* **1** : writings or statements of dubious authenticity **2** *cap* **a** : books included in the Septuagint and Vulgate but excluded from the Jewish and Protestant canons of the Old Testament — see **BIBLE** table **b** : early Christian writings not included in the New Testament [Medieval Latin, from Late Latin *apocryphus* "not canonical", from Greek *apokryphos* "obscure", from *apokryptein* "to hide away", from *apo-* + *kryptein* "to hide"]

apoc·ry·phal \-fəl\ *adj* **1** *often cap* : of or resembling the Apocrypha **2** : of doubtful authenticity : **SPURIOUS** — **apoc·ry·phal·ly** \-fə-lē\ *adv* — **apoc·ry·phal·ness** *n*

apo·gee \'ap-ə-ˌjē\ *n* **1** : the point farthest from the center of a celestial body (as the earth or moon) reached by an object (as a satellite) orbiting it — compare **PERIGEE** **2** : the farthest or highest point : **CULMINATION** [French *apogée,* derived from Greek *apo-* + *gē* "earth"]

apol·o·get·ic \ə-ˌpäl-ə-'jet-ik\ *adj* **1** : offered in defense or by way of excuse or apology **2** : expressing or seeming to express apology ⟨an *apologetic* face⟩ — **apol·o·get·i·cal·ly** \-'jet-i-kə-lē, -klē\ *adv*

apol·o·get·ics \-'jet-iks\ *n* : systematic argument in defense especially of the divine origin and authority of Christianity; *also* : a branch of theology devoted to the defense of a religious faith

apo·lo·gia \ˌap-ə-'lō-jē-ə, -jə\ *n* : a defense especially of one's opinions, actions, or position [Late Latin]

apol·o·gist \ə-'päl-ə-jəst\ *n* : one who speaks or writes in defense of a faith, a cause, a person, or an institution

apol·o·gize \ə-'päl-ə-ˌjīz\ *vi* : to make an apology : express regret for something one has done — **apol·o·giz·er** *n*

apol·o·gy \-jē\ *n, pl* **-gies** **1** : a formal justification or defense **2** : an admission of error or discourtesy accompanied by an expression of regret **3** : a poor substitute [Middle French *apologie,* from Late Latin *apologia,* from Greek, from *apo-* + *logos* "speech"] ☐ **SYN** **EXCUSE**: **APOLOGY** implies that one has been actually or apparently in the wrong; it may offer an explanation or it may simply acknowledge error and express regret; **EXCUSE** implies an intent to remove blame or censure for a wrong, mistake, or failure.

apo·mix·is \ˌap-ə-'mik-səs\ *n, pl* **-mix·es** \-ˌsēz\ : reproduction (as parthenogenesis) involving specialized generative tissues but not dependent on fertilization [*apo-* + Greek *mixis* "act of mixing"]

ap·o·plec·tic \ˌap-ə-'plek-tik\ *adj* **1** : of, relating to, or caused by apoplexy ⟨*apoplectic* symptoms⟩ **2 a** : affected with or inclined to apoplexy ⟨*apoplectic* patients⟩ **b** : highly excited or excitable — **ap·o·plec·ti·cal·ly** \-ti-kə-lē, -klē\ *adv*

ap·o·plexy \'ap-ə-ˌplek-sē\ *n, pl* **-plex·ies** : **STROKE** 5 [Late Latin *apoplexia,* from Greek *apoplēxia,* from *apoplēssein* "to cripple by a stroke", from *apo-* + *plēssein* "to strike"]

apos·ta·sy \ə-'päs-tə-sē\ *n, pl* **-sies** **1** : renunciation of a religious faith **2** : abandonment of a previous loyalty : **DEFECTION** [Late Latin *apostasia,* from Greek, literally, "revolt", from *aphistasthai* "to revolt", from *apo-* + *histasthai* "to stand"]

apos·tate \ə-'päs-ˌtāt, -tət\ *n* : one who commits apostasy — **apostate** *adj*

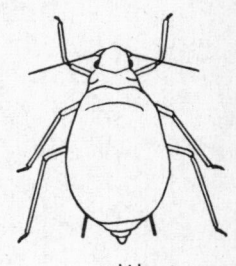
aphid

apogee 1

\ə\ abut	\ng\ sing
\ər\ further	\ō\ bone
\a\ mat	\ȯ\ saw
\ā\ take	\ȯi\ coin
\ä\ cot, cart	\th\ thin
\au̇\ out	\t̶h̶\ this
\ch\ chin	\ü\ food
\e\ pet	\u̇\ foot
\ē\ easy	\y\ yet
\g\ go	\yü\ few
\i\ tip	\yu̇\ cure
\ī\ life	\zh\ vision
\j\ job	

apos·ta·tize \ə-'päs-tə-ˌtīz\ *vi* : to commit apostasy

a pos·te·ri·o·ri \ˌä-pä-ˌstir-ē-'ōr-ē, -pō-, -ˌster-, -'ȯr-\ *adj* : relating to or derived by reasoning from known or observed facts to a conclusion [Latin, literally, "from the latter"] — **a posteriori** *adv*

apos·tle \ə-'päs-əl\ *n* **1** : one sent on a religious mission: as **a** *often cap* : one of an authoritative New Testament group made up especially of Christ's twelve original disciples and Paul **b** : the first Christian missionary to a region **2 a** : one that first advocates a cause or movement **b** : an ardent advocate or supporter [Late Latin *apostolus,* from Greek *apostolos,* literally, "one sent forth", from *apo-* + *stellein* "to send"] — **apos·tle·ship** \-əl-ˌship\ *n*

Apostles' Creed *n* : a Christian creed ascribed to the Twelve Apostles that begins "I believe in God the Father Almighty"

apos·to·late \ə-'päs-tə-ˌlāt, -lət\ *n* **1** : the office or mission of an apostle **2** : a group dedicated to the spreading of a religion or a doctrine

ap·os·tol·ic \ˌap-ə-'stäl-ik\ *adj* **1 a** : of or relating to an apostle **b** : of or relating to the New Testament apostles or their times or teachings **2 a** : of or forming a succession of spiritual authority from the apostles held in Catholic tradition to be perpetuated by successive ordinations of bishops and to be necessary for the validity of sacraments and orders **b** : PAPAL — **apos·to·lic·i·ty** \ə-ˌpäs-tə-'lis-ət-ē\ *n*

apostolic delegate *n* : a representative of the Holy See in a country with which it has no formal diplomatic relations

¹apos·tro·phe \ə-'päs-trə-fē\ *n* : the rhetorical addressing of an absent person as if present or of an abstract idea or inanimate object as if capable of understanding (as in "O grave, where is thy victory?") [Latin, from Greek *apostrophē,* literally, "act of turning away", from *apo-* + *strephein* "to turn"]

²apostrophe *n* : a mark ' or ' used to show the omission of letters or figures (as in *can't* for *cannot* or *'76* for *1776*), the possessive case (as in *Chicago's*), or the plural of letters or figures (as in *cross your t's, six 7's*)

apos·tro·phize \ə-'päs-trə-ˌfīz\ *vb* **1** : to address by or in apostrophe **2** : to make use of apostrophe

apothecaries' weight *n* : a system of weights used chiefly by pharmacists — see MEASURE table

apoth·e·cary \ə-'päth-ə-ˌker-ē\ *n, pl* **-car·ies 1** : DRUGGIST, PHARMACIST **2** : PHARMACY 2 [Late Latin *apothecarius* "shopkeeper", from Latin *apotheca* "storehouse", from Greek *apothēkē,* from *apotithenai* "to put away"]

apo·thegm \'ap-ə-ˌthem\ *n* : a concise instructive saying or formulation : APHORISM [Greek *apophthegma,* from *apo-* + *phthengesthai* "to utter"]

apo·them \'ap-ə-ˌthem\ *n* : the perpendicular from the center to one of the sides of a regular polygon [*apo-* + Greek *thema* "something laid down, theme"]

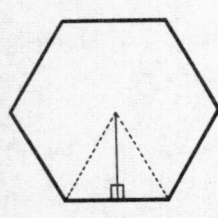

apothem

apo·the·o·sis \ə-ˌpäth-ē-'ō-səs, ˌap-ə-'thē-ə-səs\ *n, pl* **-o·ses** \-'ō-ˌsēz, -ə-ˌsēz\ **1** : elevation to divine status : DEIFICATION **2** : a perfect example [Late Latin, from Greek *apotheōsis,* from *apotheoun* "to deify", from *apo-* + *theos* "god"] — **ap·o·the·o·size** \ˌap-ə-'thē-ə-ˌsīz, ə-'päth-ē-ə-\ *vt*

ap·pall \ə-'pȯl\ *vt* : to overcome with fear or dread : HORRIFY, SHOCK [Middle French *apalir* "to make pale", from *a-* "ad-" + *palir* "to grow pale"]

ap·pall·ing *adj* : inspiring horror or dismay : SHOCKING (living under *appalling* conditions) — **ap·pall·ing·ly** \-'pȯ-ling-lē\ *adv*

Ap·pa·loo·sa \ˌap-ə-'lü-sə\ *n* : a rugged American saddle horse that has a mottled skin and a dark-blotched patch of white hair over the rump and loins [probably from *Palouse,* an Indian people of Washington and Idaho]

Appaloosa

ap·pa·nage \'ap-ə-nij\ *n* **1** : a grant (as of land or revenue) made by a sovereign or a legislative body to a member of the royal family or a person of noble rank **2** : a customary or rightful possession or privilege [French *apanage,* from Provençal *apanar* "to support", derived from Latin *ad-* + *panis* "bread"]

ap·pa·rat \'ap-ə-ˌrat, ˌäp-ə-'rät\ *n* : APPARATUS 2 [Russian]

ap·pa·ra·tchik \ˌäp-ə-'räch-ik\ *n, pl* **-ratchiks** or **-ratchi·ki** \-'räch-ə-ˌkē\ : a member of a Communist apparatus [Russian, from *apparat*]

ap·pa·ra·tus \ˌap-ə-'rat-əs, -'rät-\ *n, pl* **-tus·es** or **-tus 1 a** : the equipment used to do a particular kind of work **b** : an instrument or appliance for a specific operation **2** : the system of persons and agencies through which an organization functions; *esp* : the administrative machinery of a Communist party [Latin, from *apparare* "to prepare", from *ad-* + *parare* "to prepare"]

¹ap·par·el \ə-'par-əl\ *vt* **-eled** or **-elled; -el·ing** or **-el·ling 1** : CLOTHE, DRESS **2** : ADORN, EMBELLISH [Old French *apareillier* "to prepare", derived from Latin *apparare*]

²apparel *n* : personal attire : CLOTHING

ap·par·ent \ə-'par-ənt, -'per-\ *adj* **1** : open to view : VISIBLE (the flaw in the material was *apparent*) **2** : clear to the understanding (it was *apparent* that the road was little used) **3** : seemingly real or true (an *apparent* contradiction) [Old French *aparent,* from Latin *apparēre* "to appear"] — **ap·par·ent·ly** *adv* — **ap·par·ent·ness** *n* □ SYN APPARENT, EVIDENT mean readily perceived or grasped. APPARENT implies having outward signs that may prove on deeper analysis to be misleading (the *apparent* cause of the accident) EVIDENT suggests an appearance unmistakably corresponding with reality (our *evident* delight at your gift)

ap·pa·ri·tion \ˌap-ə-'rish-ən\ *n* **1** : an unusual or unexpected sight : PHENOMENON **2** : GHOST 2 [Late Latin *apparitio* "appearance", from Latin *apparēre* "to appear"] — **ap·pa·ri·tion·al** \-'rish-nəl, -ən-l\ *adj*

¹ap·peal \ə-'pēl\ *n* **1 a** : a legal proceeding by which a case is brought from a lower to a higher court for a reexamination **b** : a request for such a proceeding **2 a** : a request made to an authority for a confirmation or decision (an *appeal* to the referee) **b** : an earnest request : PLEA (an *appeal* for financial support) **3** : the power of arousing a sympathetic response : ATTRACTION

²appeal *vb* **1** : to take action to have a case or decision reviewed by a higher court or authority (*appeal* to the supreme court) **2** : to call upon another for corroboration or vindication **3** : to make an earnest request **4** : to arouse a sympathetic response [Middle French *apeler* "to accuse, appeal", from Latin *appellare*] — **ap·peal·able** \ə-'pē-lə-bəl\ *adj*

ap·peal·ing *adj* : having appeal : ATTRACTIVE — **ap·peal·ing·ly** \-'pē-ling-lē\ *adv*

ap·pear \ə-'piər\ *vi* **1** : to come into sight : become evident : SHOW (stars *appeared* in the sky) **2** : to come formally before an authoritative body (*appear* in court) **3** : to have an outward aspect : SEEM (things are not always as they *appear*) (*appear* to be tired) **4 a** : to come out in printed form (a book scheduled to *appear* next month) **b** : to come before the public on stage or screen (*appears* on television) [Old French *aparoir,* from Latin *apparēre,* from *ad-* + *parēre* "to show oneself"]

ap·pear·ance \ə-'pir-əns\ *n* **1** : the act, action, or process of appearing **2 a** : outward aspect : LOOK **b** : external show : SEMBLANCE **c** *pl* : outward indications or show (guilty to all *appearances*) (keep up *appearances*) **3 a** : something that appears : PHENOMENON **b** : an instance of appearing (a personal *appearance*)

ap·pease \ə-'pēz\ *vt* **1** : to make calm or quiet : ALLAY **2** : to make concessions to (a potential aggressor) usually at the sacrifice of principles : CONCILIATE [Old French *apaisier,* from *a-* "ad-" + *pais* "peace"] SYN see PACIFY — **ap·pease·ment** \-mənt\ *n* — **ap·peas·er** *n*

ap·pel·lant \ə-'pel-ənt\ *n* : one that appeals; *esp* : one that appeals from a judicial decision or decree

ap·pel·late \ə-'pel-ət\ *adj* : of or relating to appeals ⟨*appellate* jurisdiction⟩; *esp* : having the power to review the decisions of a lower court ⟨an *appellate* court⟩

ap·pel·la·tion \,ap-ə-'lā-shən\ *n* : an identifying or descriptive name or title : DESIGNATION

ap·pel·lee \,ap-ə-'lē\ *n* : one against whom an appeal is taken

ap·pend \ə-'pend\ *vt* : to add as a supplement ⟨*append* a postscript to a letter⟩ [French *appendre,* from Latin *appendere* "to weigh", from *ad-* + *pendere* "to weigh"]

ap·pend·age \ə-'pen-dij\ *n* **1** : something attached to a larger or more important thing **2** : a subordinate or derivative body part; *esp* : a limb or an analogous part

ap·pen·dec·to·my \,ap-ən-'dek-tə-mē\ *n, pl* **-mies** : surgical removal of the human appendix

ap·pen·di·ci·tis \ə-,pen-də-'sīt-əs\ *n* : inflammation of the appendix

ap·pen·dic·u·lar \,ap-ən-'dik-yə-lər\ *adj* : of or relating to an appendage and especially a limb ⟨the *appendicular* skeleton⟩

ap·pen·dix \ə-'pen-diks\ *n, pl* **-dix·es** *or* **-di·ces** \-də-,sēz\ **1** : supplementary material usually attached at the end of a piece of writing **2 a** : a small tubular outgrowth from the cecum of the intestine — called also *vermiform appendix* **b** : a bodily outgrowth or process other than the appendix of the intestine [Latin, "addition", from *appendere* "to append"]

ap·per·ceive \,ap-ər-'sēv\ *vt* : to understand (something perceived) in terms of previous experience

ap·per·cep·tion \,ap-ər-'sep-shən\ *n* : the process of apperceiving — **ap·per·cep·tive** \-'sep-tiv\ *adj*

ap·per·tain \,ap-ər-'tān\ *vi* : to belong or be connected as a possession, part, or right : PERTAIN ⟨duties that *appertain* to the office of governor⟩ [Middle French *apartenir,* derived from Latin *ad-* + *pertinēre* "to belong"]

ap·pe·tite \'ap-ə-,tīt\ *n* **1** : one of the instinctive desires necessary to keep up organic life; *esp* : the desire to eat **2 a** : an inherent craving **b** : TASTE 5, PREFERENCE [Middle French *apetit,* from Latin *appetitus,* from *appetere* "to strive after", from *ad-* + *petere* "to go to"]

ap·pe·tiz·er \-,tī-zər\ *n* : a food or drink that stimulates the appetite and is usually served before a meal

ap·pe·tiz·ing \-,tī-zing\ *adj* : appealing to the appetite — **ap·pe·tiz·ing·ly** \-zing-lē\ *adv*

ap·plaud \ə-'plòd\ *vb* **1** : PRAISE, APPROVE ⟨*applaud* their efforts⟩ **2** : to show approval especially by clapping the hands [Latin *applaudere,* from *ad-* + *plaudere* "to clap"] — **ap·plaud·able** \-ə-bəl\ *adj* — **ap·plaud·ably** \-blē\ *adv* — **ap·plaud·er** *n*

ap·plause \ə-'plòz\ *n* : approval publicly expressed (as by clapping the hands) : ACCLAIM [Medieval Latin *applausus,* from Latin *applaudere* "to applaud"]

ap·ple \'ap-əl\ *n* : a rounded fruit with a red, yellow, or green skin, firm white flesh, a seedy core, and usually a tart taste; *also* : the tree of the rose family that bears this fruit [Old English *æppel*]

ap·ple·cart \-,kärt\ *n* : PLAN, SCHEME ⟨upset the *applecart*⟩

ap·ple·jack \-,jak\ *n* : brandy distilled from cider

apple–pie \'ap-əl-,pī\ *adj* **1** : EXCELLENT, PERFECT ⟨in *apple-pie* order⟩ **2** : of or relating to traditional American values ⟨*apple-pie* wholesomeness⟩

ap·pli·ance \ə-'plī-əns\ *n* **1** : a piece of equipment for adapting a tool or machine to a special purpose : ATTACHMENT **2** : an instrument or device designed for a

particular use; *esp* : a piece of household equipment that is operated by gas or electricity

ap·pli·ca·ble \'ap-li-kə-bəl, ə-'plik-ə-\ *adj* : capable of being or suitable to be applied : APPROPRIATE — **ap·pli·ca·bil·i·ty** \,ap-li-kə-'bil-ət-ē, ə-,plik-ə-\ *n*

ap·pli·cant \'ap-li-kənt\ *n* : a person who applies for something ⟨an *applicant* for work⟩ ⟨*applicants* for admission⟩

ap·pli·ca·tion \,ap-lə-'kā-shən\ *n* **1** : the act or an instance of applying ⟨*application* of paint to a house⟩ **2** : something put or spread on a surface ⟨hot *applications* on a sprained ankle⟩ **3** : ability to fix one's attention on a task **4 a** : PETITION ⟨an *application* for aid⟩ **b** : a request made personally or in writing ⟨an *application* for a job⟩; *also* : a form used in making such a request **5** : capacity for practical use

ap·pli·ca·tor \'ap-lə-,kāt-ər\ *n* : one that applies; *esp* : a device for applying a substance (as medicine or polish)

ap·plied \ə-'plīd\ *adj* : put to practical use; *esp* : applying general principles to solve definite problems ⟨*applied* sciences⟩

¹**ap·pli·qué** \,ap-lə-'kā\ *n* : a cutout decoration fastened to a larger piece of material [French, past participle of *appliquer* "to put on", from Latin *applicare*]

²**appliqué** *vt* **-quéd; -qué·ing** : to apply (an appliqué) to a larger surface

ap·ply \ə-'plī\ *vb* **ap·plied; ap·ply·ing** **1 a** : to put to use especially for some practical or specific purpose ⟨*apply* knowledge⟩ **b** : to bring into action ⟨*apply* the brakes⟩ **c** : to lay or spread on ⟨*apply* paint with a brush⟩ **d** : to place in contact ⟨*apply* heat⟩ **e** : to put into operation or effect ⟨*apply* a law⟩ **2** : to employ diligently or with close attention ⟨*apply* yourself to your work⟩ **3** : to have relevance ⟨this law *applies* to everyone⟩ **4** : to make an appeal or request especially in the form of a written application ⟨*apply* for a job⟩ [Middle French *aplier,* from Latin *applicare,* from *ad-* + *plicare* "to fold"] — **ap·pli·er** \-'plī-ər\ *n*

ap·pog·gia·tu·ra \ə-,päj-ə-'tùr-ə\ *n* : an embellishing note or tone preceding an essential melodic note or tone and usually written as a note of smaller size [Italian, literally, "support"]

ap·point \ə-'pòint\ *vt* **1** : to fix or set officially ⟨*appoint* a day for a meeting⟩ **2** : to name officially especially to an office or position ⟨the president *appoints* the members of the cabinet⟩ [Middle French *apointier,* from *a-* "ad-" + *point* "point"]

ap·point·ed *adj* : FURNISHED, EQUIPPED ⟨a well-*appointed* house⟩

ap·poin·tee \ə-,pòin-'tē, ,a-,pòin-\ *n* : a person appointed to a position or an office

ap·point·ive \ə-'pòint-iv\ *adj* : of, relating to, or filled by appointment ⟨an *appointive* office⟩

ap·point·ment \ə-'pòint-mənt\ *n* **1** : the act or an instance of appointing : DESIGNATION ⟨holds office by *appointment*⟩ **2** : a position or office to which a person is named but not elected ⟨received an *appointment* from the president⟩ **3** : an agreement to meet at a fixed time ⟨an *appointment* with the dentist⟩ **4** : EQUIPMENT, FURNISHINGS — usually used in pl. ⟨a house with modern *appointments*⟩

ap·por·tion \ə-'pōr-shən, -'pòr-\ *vt* **-tioned; -tion·ing** \-shə-ning, -shning\ : to divide and distribute proportionately ⟨time carefully *apportioned* among various projects⟩ SYN see ALLOT

ap·por·tion·ment \-shən-mənt\ *n* : the act or result of apportioning; *esp* : the apportioning of representatives or taxes among states or districts according to population

ap·pose \a-'pōz\ *vt* : to place near or in close relationship [Middle French *aposer,* from *a-* "ad-" + *poser* "to place, pose"]

ap·po·site \'ap-ə-zət\ *adj* : highly pertinent or appropriate : APT [Latin *appositus,* from *apponere* "to place

appoggiatura

near'', from *ad-* + *ponere* ''to put''] — **ap·po·site·ly** *adv* — **ap·po·site·ness** *n*

ap·po·si·tion \,ap-ə-'zish-ən\ *n* **1 a** : a grammatical construction in which a noun or noun equivalent is followed by another that explains it (as *the poet* and *Burns* in ''a biography of the poet Burns'') **b** : the relation of one of such a pair of nouns or noun equivalents to the other **2 a** : the deposition of new layers (as in cell walls) upon those already present **b** : the state of being in close relationship — **ap·po·si·tion·al** \-'zish-nəl, -ən-l\ *adj*

¹ap·pos·i·tive \ə-'päz-ət-iv\ *adj* : of, relating to, or standing in grammatical apposition — **ap·pos·i·tive·ly** *adv*

²appositive *n* : the second of a pair of nouns or noun equivalents in apposition

ap·prais·al \ə-'prā-zəl\ *n* **1** : an act or instance of appraising **2** : a determination of the value of property by an appraiser; *also* : the value so determined

ap·praise \ə-'prāz\ *vt* **1** : to set a value on; *esp* : to give an expert judgment of the money value of ⟨a house *appraised* at $39,000⟩ **2** : to estimate the significance or status of ⟨*appraise* the situation⟩ [Middle French *aprisier*, from *a-* ''ad-'' + *prisier* ''to value, prize''] **SYN** see ESTIMATE — **ap·praise·ment** \-mənt\ *n*

ap·prais·er \ə-'prā-zər\ *n* : one that appraises; *esp* : an official who appraises real estate and personal property for purposes of taxation

ap·pre·cia·ble \ə-'prē-shə-bəl *also* -'prish-ə-\ *adj* : large enough to be recognized and measured or to be felt ⟨an *appreciable* difference in temperature⟩ — **ap·pre·cia·bly** \-blē\ *adv*

ap·pre·ci·ate \ə-'prē-shē-,āt *also* -'prish-ē-,āt\ *vb* **1 a** : to grasp with full knowledge and understanding ⟨*appreciate* the difference between right and wrong⟩ **b** : to admire greatly **c** : to appraise perceptively : be fully aware of ⟨had to see it to *appreciate* it⟩ **d** : to recognize with gratitude ⟨I *appreciate* your help⟩ **2** : to increase in number or value [Late Latin *appretiare*, from Latin *ad-* + *pretium* ''price''] — **ap·pre·ci·a·tor** \-,āt-ər\ *n*

ap·pre·ci·a·tion \ə-,prē-shē-'ā-shən *also* -,prē-sē- *or* -,prish-ē-\ *n* **1** : the action or an instance of appreciating **2 a** : awareness or grasp of worth or value **b** : expression of appreciation ⟨this commendation in *appreciation* of your work⟩ **3** : a gain in value

ap·pre·cia·tive \ə-'prē-shət-iv, -shē-,āt-iv *also* -'prish-ət-, -'prish-ē-\ *adj* : having or showing appreciation ⟨an *appreciative* audience⟩ — **ap·pre·cia·tive·ly** *adv* — **ap·pre·cia·tive·ness** *n*

ap·pre·hend \,ap-ri-'hend\ *vb* **1** : ARREST, SEIZE ⟨*apprehend* a suspect⟩ **2 a** : to become aware of : PERCEIVE **b** : to anticipate especially with anxiety, dread, or fear **3** : to grasp with the understanding : UNDERSTAND [Latin *apprehendere*, literally, ''to seize'', from *ad-* + *prehendere* ''to seize, grasp''] — **ap·pre·hen·si·ble** \-'hen-sə-bəl\ *adj* — **ap·pre·hen·si·bly** \-blē\ *adv*

ap·pre·hen·sion \,ap-ri-'hen-chən\ *n* **1** : CAPTURE, ARREST ⟨*apprehension* of a burglar⟩ **2** : COMPREHENSION 2, UNDERSTANDING **3** : fear of what may be coming : dread of the future [Late Latin *apprehensio*, from Latin *apprehendere* ''to seize'']

ap·pre·hen·sive \,ap-ri-'hen-siv\ *adj* : feeling apprehension : fearful of what may be coming — **ap·pre·hen·sive·ly** *adv*

¹ap·pren·tice \ə-'prent-əs\ *n* **1** : a person legally bound to serve a master for a specified period to receive instruction in an art or trade **2** : one who is learning a trade, art, or calling by practical experience under skilled workers [Middle French *aprentis*, from *aprendre* ''to learn'', from Latin *apprehendere* ''to apprehend''] — **ap·pren·tice·ship** \-ə-,ship, -əsh-,ship, -əs-,ship\ *n*

²apprentice *vt* : to bind or set at work as an apprentice

ap·prise \ə-'prīz\ *vt* : to give notice to : INFORM [French *appris*, past participle of *apprendre* ''to learn, teach'', from Latin *apprehendere* ''to apprehend'']

¹ap·proach \ə-'prōch\ *vb* **1 a** : to draw close : come near or nearer **b** : APPROXIMATE 2 **2** : to take preliminary steps toward [Old French *aprochier*, from Late Latin *appropiare*, from Latin *ad-* + *prope* ''near'']

²approach *n* **1 a** : an act or instance of approaching ⟨the *approach* of winter⟩ **b** : APPROXIMATION **2 a** : a preliminary step toward an end **b** : way of dealing with something (as a problem) ⟨try a new *approach*⟩ **3 a** : a means of access : AVENUE **b** : the descent of an aircraft as it prepares to land

ap·proach·able \ə-'prō-chə-bəl\ *adj* **1** : capable of being approached : ACCESSIBLE **2** : easy to meet or deal with ⟨a very *approachable* person⟩ — **ap·proach·abil·i·ty** \-,prō-chə-'bil-ət-ē\ *n*

ap·pro·ba·tion \,ap-rə-'bā-shən\ *n* **1** : the act of approving formally or officially **2** : COMMENDATION, PRAISE [Latin *approbare* ''to approve'']

¹ap·pro·pri·ate \ə-'prō-prē-,āt\ *vt* **1** : to take exclusive possession of **2** : to set apart for a particular purpose or use ⟨Congress *appropriated* funds for naval research⟩ **3** : to take without permission : STEAL [Late Latin *appropriare*, from Latin *ad-* + *proprius* ''one's own''] — **ap·pro·pri·a·tor** \-,āt-ər\ *n*

²ap·pro·pri·ate \-prē-ət\ *adj* : especially suitable or fitting : PROPER SYN see FIT — **ap·pro·pri·ate·ly** *adv* — **ap·pro·pri·ate·ness** *n*

ap·pro·pri·a·tion \ə-,prō-prē-'ā-shən\ *n* **1** : an act or instance of appropriating **2** : something that has been appropriated; *esp* : a sum of money formally set aside for a specific use

ap·prov·al \ə-'prü-vəl\ *n* **1** : an act or instance of approving : APPROBATION **2** *pl* : postage stamps for collectors sent on approval to prospective purchasers — **on approval** : subject to a prospective buyer's acceptance or refusal ⟨goods sent *on approval*⟩

ap·prove \ə-'prüv\ *vb* **1** : to have or express a favorable judgment : take a favorable view **2 a** : to accept as satisfactory **b** : to give formal or official sanction to ⟨the council *approved* the plans for the new school⟩ [Old French *aprover*, from Latin *approbare*, from *ad-* + *probare* ''to prove''] — **ap·prov·ing·ly** \-'prü-ving-lē\ *adv* □ **SYN** APPROVE, ENDORSE, SANCTION mean to have or express a favorable opinion of. APPROVE may imply no more than this or it may suggest some degree of admiration; ENDORSE adds the implication of backing with an explicit statement; SANCTION implies both approving and authorizing.

¹ap·prox·i·mate \ə-'präk-sə-mət\ *adj* : nearly correct or exact ⟨the *approximate* cost⟩ [Late Latin *approximare* ''to come near'', from Latin *ad-* + *proximus* ''nearest, next''] — **ap·prox·i·mate·ly** *adv*

²ap·prox·i·mate \-,māt\ *vb* **1** : to bring or come close together ⟨*approximate* two boards⟩ **2** : to find the approximate value of ⟨*approximate* a cost⟩

ap·prox·i·ma·tion \ə-,präk-sə-'mā-shən\ *n* **1** : the act or process of approximating **2** : the quality or state of being close especially in value **3** : something that is approximate; *esp* : a nearly exact estimate of a value or cost

ap·pur·te·nance \ə-'pərt-nəns, -n-əns\ *n* **1** : a secondary right (as a right-of-way) attached to a principal property right **2** : a subordinate part **3** *pl* : accessory objects ⟨sold the house, its furniture, and all other *appurtenances*⟩ [Anglo-French *apurtenance*, from Old French *apartenir* ''to appertain''] — **ap·pur·te·nant** \-'pərt-nənt, -n-ənt\ *adj*

ap·ri·cot \'ap-rə-,kät, 'ā-prə-\ *n* : an oval orange-colored fruit resembling the related peach and plum in flavor; *also* : a tree that bears apricots [derived from Arabic *al-birqūq* ''the apricot'']

April \'ā-prəl\ *n* : the 4th month of the year [Latin *Aprilis*]

April fool *n* : a person who is tricked on April Fools' Day

April Fools' Day *n* : April 1 characteristically marked by the playing of practical jokes

a pri·o·ri \,ä-prē-'ōr-ē, -'òr-\ *adj* **1** : of or relating to reasoning from self-evident propositions **2** : estimated from available facts without close examination : PRE-SUMPTIVE [Latin, "from the former"] — **a priori** *adv*

apron \'ā-prən, -pərn\ *n* **1** : a garment worn on the front of the body to protect the clothing **2** : the part of the stage in front of the proscenium arch **3** : a shield (as of concrete, planking, or brushwood) along the bank of a river to prevent erosion **4** : the extensive paved part of an airport immediately adjacent to the terminal area or hangars [Middle English *napron* (the phrase *a napron* being understood as *an apron*), from Middle French *naperon*, from *nape* "cloth", from Latin *mappa* "napkin"]

¹ap·ro·pos \,ap-rə-'pō, 'ap-rə-,\ *adv* **1** : at the right time : SEASONABLY **2** : by the way : INCIDENTALLY [French *à propos*, literally, "to the purpose"]

²apropos *adj* : being to the point : PERTINENT

apropos of *prep* : with regard to : CONCERNING

apse \'aps\ *n* : a usually semicircular projection on the end of a building (as a church) [Medieval Latin *apsis*, from Latin, "arch, orbit", from Greek *hapsis*, from *haptein* "to fasten"] — **ap·si·dal** \'ap-səd-l\ *adj*

apt \'apt\ *adj* **1** : FITTING, SUITABLE (an *apt* quotation) **2 a** : having a tendency : LIKELY **b** : ordinarily disposed (*apt* to worry) **3** : keenly alert : quick to learn (an *apt* pupil) [Latin *aptus*, literally, "fastened", from *apere* "to fasten, fit"] — **apt·ly** *adv* — **apt·ness** \'ap-nəs, 'apt-\ □ SYN LIKELY, LIABLE: APT implies an inherent or habitual tendency and may apply to the past or present as well as the future (children are *apt* to imitate their parents) LIKELY stresses probability and is used in predictions (it is *likely* to rain tomorrow) LIA-BLE implies exposure to a risk or danger and suggests chance rather than probability (cars are *liable* to skid on wet roads)

ap·ti·tude \'ap-tə-,tüd, -,tyüd\ *n* **1** : capacity for learning **2** : a natural inclination or ability : TALENT (an *aptitude* for math)

aqua·cade \'ak-wə-,kād, 'äk-\ *n* : an elaborate water spectacle consisting of exhibitions of swimming, diving, and acrobatics accompanied by music [*Aquacade*, a water spectacle originally at Cleveland, Ohio (1937), from Latin *aqua* "water" + English *-cade* (as in *cavalcade*)]

aqua·cul·ture *also* **aqui·cul·ture** \'ak-wə-,kəl-chər, 'äk-\ *n* : the cultivation of the natural produce of water; *esp* : the raising of fish in enclosed ponds [Latin *aqua* "water" + English *-culture* (as in *agriculture*)] — **aqua·cul·tur·al** \,kəlch-rəl, -ə-rəl\ *adj*

aqua·for·tis \,ak-wə-'fòrt-əs, ,äk-\ *n* : NITRIC ACID [New Latin *aqua fortis*, literally, "strong water"]

aqua·ma·rine \,ak-wə-mə-'rēn, ,äk-\ *n* **1** : a transparent semiprecious bluish or greenish stone that is a variety of beryl **2** : a pale blue to light greenish blue [Latin *aqua marina* "sea water"]

aqua·naut \'ak-wə-,nòt, 'äk-, -,nät\ *n* : one that lives for an extended period in an underwater shelter which serves as a base for research [Latin *aqua* + English *-naut* (as in *aeronaut*)]

aqua·plane \'ak-wə-,plān, 'äk-\ *n* : a board towed behind a speeding motorboat and ridden by a person standing on it — **aquaplane** *vi* — **aqua·plan·er** *n*

aqua re·gia \,ak-wə-'rē-jē-ə, ,äk-, -jə\ *n* : a mixture of nitric and hydrochloric acids that dissolves gold or platinum [New Latin, literally, "royal water"]

aquar·ist \ə-'kwar-əst, -'kwer-\ *n* : one who keeps an aquarium

aquar·i·um \ə-'kwar-ē-əm, -'kwer-\ *n, pl* **-i·ums** *or* **-ia** \-ē-ə\ : a container (as a glass tank) in which living water animals or plants are kept; *also* : an establish-ment where such aquatic collections are kept and shown [Latin, "watering place for cattle", from *aqua* "water"]

Aquar·i·us \ə-'kwar-ē-əs, -'kwer-\ *n* **1** : a zodiacal constellation south of Pegasus **2** : the 11th sign of the zodiac; *also* : one born under this sign [Latin, literally, "water carrier"]

¹aquat·ic \ə-'kwät-ik, -'kwat-\ *adj* **1** : growing or living in or frequenting water **2** : performed in or on water (*aquatic* sports) — **aquat·i·cal·ly** \-i-kə-lē, -klē\ *adv*

²aquatic *n* **1** : an aquatic animal or plant **2** *pl* : water sports

aq·ua·tint \'ak-wə-,tint, 'äk-\ *n* : an etching in which the printing plate is treated to produce an effect resembling a drawing in watercolors or india ink — **aquatint** *vt*

aq·ue·duct \'ak-wə-,dəkt\ *n* **1** : an artificial channel for carrying flowing water **2** : a structure that carries the water of a canal over a river or hollow [Latin *aquae-ductus*, from *aqua* "water" + *ductus* "act of leading"]

aqueduct 2

aque·ous \'ā-kwē-əs, 'ak-wē-\ *adj* **1** : of, relating to, or resembling water **2** : made of, by, or with water (an *aqueous* solution)

aqueous humor *n* : a clear fluid between the lens and the cornea of the eye

aq·ui·fer \'ak-wə-fər, 'äk-\ *n* : a water-bearing stratum of permeable rock, sand, or gravel — **aquif·er·ous** \a-'kwif-ə-rəs, ä-\ *adj*

Aq·ui·la \'ak-wə-lə\ *n* : a northern constellation in the Milky Way south of Lyra and Cygnus [Latin, literally, "eagle"]

aq·ui·le·gia \,ak-wə-'lē-jē-ə, -jə\ *n* : COLUMBINE [New Latin, genus name]

aq·ui·line \'ak-wə-,līn, -lən\ *adj* **1** : of, relating to, or resembling an eagle **2** : curving like an eagle's beak (an *aquiline* nose) [Latin *aquilinus*, from *aquila* "eagle"]

-ar \ər *also* ,är\ *adj suffix* : of or relating to : being : resembling (molecul*ar*) (oracul*ar*) (spectacul*ar*) [Latin *-aris*, alteration of *-alis* "-al"]

Ar·ab \'ar-əb\ *n* **1 a** : a member of the Semitic people of the Arabian peninsula **b** : a member of an Arabic-speaking people **2** : ARABIAN HORSE — **Arab** *adj*

ar·a·besque \,ar-ə-'besk\ *n* : an ornament or a style of decoration consisting of interlacing lines and figures usually of flowers, foliage, or fruit [French, from Italian *arabesco* "Arabian in style"] — **arabesque** *adj*

¹Ara·bi·an \ə-'rā-bē-ən\ *adj* : of or relating to Arabia or the Arabs

²Arabian *n* : a native or inhabitant of Arabia : ARAB

Arabian horse *n* : a horse of the stock used by the natives of Arabia and adjacent regions; *esp* : one of a breed noted for graceful build, speed, intelligence, and spirit

¹Ar·a·bic \'ar-ə-bik\ *adj* **1** : ARABIAN, ARAB **2** : expressed in or utilizing Arabic numerals (21 is an *Arabic* number) (*Arabic* notation)

²Arabic *n* : a Semitic language of Arabia spoken also in Jordan, Lebanon, Syria, Iraq, Egypt, and parts of northern Africa

Arabic numeral *n* : one of the number symbols 1, 2, 3, 4, 5, 6, 7, 8, 9, and 0 — see NUMBER table

ar·a·ble \'ar-ə-bəl\ *adj* : fit for or cultivated by plowing or tillage : suitable for producing crops [Latin *ara-bilis*, from *arare* "to plow"] — **ar·a·bil·i·ty** \,ar-ə-'bil-ət-ē\ *n* — **arable** *n*

arach·nid \ə-'rak-nəd, -,nid\ *n* : any of a class (Arachni-da) of arthropods including the spiders, scorpions, mites, and ticks and having a segmented body divided into two regions of which the front part bears four pairs of legs but no antennae [derived from Greek *ar-achnē* "spider"] — **arachnid** *adj*

arach·noid \-,nòid\ *n* : a thin membrane of the brain and spinal cord that lies between the dura mater and

\ə\ abut		\ng\ sing	
\ər\ further		\ō\ bone	
\a\ mat		\ò\ saw	
\ā\ take		\òi\ coin	
\ä\ cot, cart		\th\ thin	
\aù\ out		\th\ this	
\ch\ chin		\ü\ food	
\e\ pet		\ù\ foot	
\ē\ easy		\y\ yet	
\g\ go		\yü\ few	
\i\ tip		\yù\ cure	
\ī\ life		\zh\ vision	
\j\ job			

the pia mater [derived from Greek *arachnē* "spider, spider web"] — **arachnoid** *adj*

ara·go·nite \ə-'rag-ə-,nīt, 'ar-ə-gə-\ *n* : a mineral that is chemically the same as calcite but is denser and has different crystalline form [German *aragonit,* from *Aragon,* Spain]

Ar·a·mae·an \,ar-ə-'mē-ən\ *n* **1** : a member of a Semitic people of the 2d millennium B.C. in Syria and Upper Mesopotamia **2** : ARAMAIC [Latin *Aramaeus,* derived from Hebrew *'Arām,* ancient name for Syria] — **Aramaean** *adj*

Ar·a·ma·ic \,ar-ə-'mā-ik\ *n* : a Semitic language of the Aramaeans later used extensively in southwest Asia (as by the Jews after the Babylonian exile) — **Aramaic** *adj*

ar·a·mid \'ar-ə-məd, -,mid\ *n* : any of a group of light but very strong heat-resistant synthetic materials used especially in textiles and plastics [*ar*omatic poly*amide,* name of a group of chemical compounds]

Arap·a·ho *or* **Arap·a·hoe** \ə-'rap-ə-,hō\ *n, pl* **-ho** *or* **-hos** *or* **-hoe** *or* **-hoes** : a member of an Algonquian people of the central western plains

Arau·ca·ni·an \ə-,raù-'kän-ē-ən\ *n* : a member of a group of Indian peoples of Chile and Argentina [Spanish *araucano,* from *Arauco,* province in Chile] — **Araucanian** *adj*

Ar·a·wak \'ar-ə-,wäk\ *n, pl* **-wak** *or* **-waks** : a member of an Indian people chiefly of Guyana

ar·bi·ter \'är-bət-ər\ *n* **1** : ARBITRATOR, UMPIRE **2** : a person having absolute authority to judge and decide what is right or proper ⟨an *arbiter* of taste⟩ [Latin]

ar·bit·ra·ment \är-'bi-trə-mənt\ *n* **1** : ARBITRATION **2** : a decision or award made by an arbiter

ar·bi·trary \'är-bə-,trer-ē\ *adj* **1** : depending on choice or discretion rather than defined by law ⟨an *arbitrary* settlement of a dispute⟩ **2** : based on opinion, preference, or whim ⟨made an *arbitrary* choice⟩ **3** : not controlled or restrained by law : DESPOTIC ⟨*arbitrary* use of power by government officials⟩ — **ar·bi·trar·i·ly** \,är-bə-'trer-ə-lē\ *adv* — **ar·bi·trar·i·ness** \'är-bə-,trer-ē-nəs\ *n*

ar·bi·trate \'är-bə-,trāt\ *vb* **1** : to settle a dispute after hearing and considering the arguments of both sides : hear and decide as an arbiter ⟨a committee appointed to *arbitrate* between the company and the union⟩ **2** : to submit to arbitration ⟨agreed to *arbitrate* their differences⟩ [Latin *arbitrari* "to render judgment", from *arbiter* "judge"] — **ar·bi·tra·ble** \-bə-trə-bəl\ *adj* — **ar·bi·tra·tive** \-,trāt-iv\ *adj*

ar·bi·tra·tion \,är-bə-'trā-shən\ *n* : the act of arbitrating; *esp* : the settling of a dispute in which both parties agree beforehand to abide by the decision of an arbitrator or body of arbitrators — **ar·bi·tra·tion·al** \-shnəl, -shən-l\ *adj*

ar·bi·tra·tor \'är-bə-,trāt-ər\ *n* : a person chosen to settle the differences between two parties in controversy

¹ar·bor \'är-bər\ *n* : a bower of vines or branches or of latticework covered with climbing shrubs or vines [Old French *berbier* "plot of grass", from *herbe* "herb, grass"]

²arbor *n* : a shaft on which a revolving cutting tool is mounted or on which work is mounted for turning [Latin, "tree, shaft"]

Arbor Day *n* : a day set aside for planting trees

ar·bo·re·al \är-'bōr-ē-əl, -'bòr-\ *adj* **1** : of, relating to, or resembling a tree **2** : living in or frequenting trees [Latin *arboreus,* from *arbor* "tree"] — **ar·bo·re·al·ly** \-ē-ə-lē\ *adv*

ar·bo·res·cent \,är-bə-'res-nt\ *adj* : resembling a tree in growth, structure, or appearance; *esp* : branching repeatedly like a tree — **ar·bo·res·cence** \-ns\ *n* — **ar·bo·res·cent·ly** *adv*

ar·bo·re·tum \,är-bə-'rēt-əm\ *n, pl* **-re·tums** *or* **-re·ta** \-'rēt-ə\ : a place where trees, shrubs, and herbaceous plants are grown for scientific and educational pur-

¹arch 1: *1* round, 2 lancet, 3 trefoil, 4 ogee

poses [Latin, "place grown with trees", from *arbor* "tree"]

ar·bor·ist \'är-bə-rəst\ *n* : a specialist in the care and maintenance of trees

ar·bor·vi·tae \,är-bər-'vīt-ē\ *n* : any of various evergreen trees of the pine family that have leaves closely overlapping like scales and are often grown for ornament and in hedges [New Latin *arbor vitae,* literally, "tree of life"]

ar·bu·tus \är-'byüt-əs\ *n* **1** : any of a genus of shrubs and trees of the heath family with white or pink flowers and scarlet berries **2** : a trailing plant of the heath family that has fragrant pinkish flowers borne in early spring and is found in eastern North America [Latin, a kind of tree of the heath family]

¹arc \'ärk\ *n* **1** : something arched or curved; *esp* : a sustained luminous discharge of electricity across a gap in a circuit or between electrodes **2** : a continuous portion (as part of the circumference of a circle) of a curved line [Middle French, "bow", from Latin *arcus* "bow, arch, arc"]

²arc *vi* **arced** \'ärkt\; **arc·ing** **1** : to form an electric arc **2** : to follow an arc-shaped course

ar·cade \är-'kād\ *n* **1** : a row of arches with the columns that support them **2** : an arched or covered passageway; *esp* : one lined with shops [French, from Italian *arcata,* from *arco* "arch"] — **ar·cad·ed** \-'kād-əd\ *adj*

ar·ca·dia \är-'kād-ē-ə\ *n, often cap* : a region or scene of simple pleasure and quiet [*Arcadia,* region of ancient Greece often chosen as a setting for pastoral poetry] — **ar·ca·di·an** \-ē-ən\ *adj or n, often cap*

ar·cane \är-'kān\ *adj* : SECRET 1a, MYSTERIOUS [Latin *arcanus,* from *arca* "chest for valuables"]

ar·ca·num \är-'kā-nəm\ *n, pl* **-na** \-nə\ : mysterious knowledge known only to the initiate [Latin, from *arcanus* "secret"]

¹arch \'ärch\ *n* **1** : a usually curved structural member spanning an opening and serving as a support (as for the wall above the opening) **2** : something resembling an arch in form or function; *esp* : either of two vaulted portions of the bony structure of the foot that impart elasticity to it and cushion it against shock (as in running and walking) **3** : ARCHWAY [Old French *arche,* from Latin *arcus* "bow, arch"]

²arch *vb* **1** : to cover or provide with an arch **2** : to form or bend into an arch **3** : to move in an arch : ARC

³arch *adj* **1** : PRINCIPAL, CHIEF ⟨their *arch* foe⟩ **2** : playfully saucy : ROGUISH, MISCHIEVOUS ⟨an *arch* smile⟩ [*arch-*] — **arch·ly** *adv* — **arch·ness** *n*

arch- *prefix* **1** : chief : principal **2** : extreme [Greek *arch-, archi-,* from *archein* "to begin, rule"]

archae- *or* **archaeo-** *also* **archeo-** *combining form* : ancient : primitive ⟨*Archeo*zoic⟩ [Greek *archaios* "ancient", from *archē* "beginning"]

ar·chae·ol·o·gy *or* **ar·che·ol·o·gy** \,är-kē-'äl-ə-jē\ *n* : the science that deals with past human life and activities as shown by fossil relics and by the monuments and artifacts left by ancient peoples — **ar·chae·o·log·i·cal** \-kē-ə-'läj-i-kəl\ *adj* — **ar·chae·ol·o·gist** \-kē-'äl-ə-jəst\ *n*

ar·chae·op·ter·yx \,är-kē-'äp-tə-riks\ *n* : a primitive extinct Mesozoic European bird with reptilian characteristics as well as wings and feathers [Greek *pteryx* "wing"]

ar·cha·ic \är-'kā-ik\ *adj* **1** : of, relating to, or characteristic of an earlier or more primitive time : ANTIQUATED **2** : having the characteristics of the language of the past and surviving chiefly in specialized uses ⟨the *archaic* words *methinks* and *saith*⟩ **3** : surviving from an earlier period ⟨an *archaic* plant⟩ [Greek *archaïkos,* from *archē* "beginning"] SYN see OLD

ar·cha·ism \'är-kē-,iz-əm, -kā-\ *n* **1** : the use of archaic words **2** : an archaic word or expression

arch·an·gel \'ärk-ˌān-jəl\ *n* : an angel of high rank — **arch·an·gel·ic** \ˌärk-ˌan-'jel-ik\ *adj*

arch·bish·op \'ärch-'bish-əp\ *n* : the bishop of highest rank in a group of dioceses — **arch·bish·op·ric** \-'bish-ə-ˌprik\ *n*

arch·dea·con \'ärch-'dē-kən\ *n* : a clergyman having the duty of assisting a bishop — **arch·dea·con·ate** \-kə-nət\ *n* — **arch·dea·con·ry** \-kən-rē\ *n*

arch·di·o·cese \'ärch-'dī-ə-səs, -ˌsēz, -ˌsēs\ *n* : the diocese of an archbishop — **arch·di·oc·e·san** \ˌärch-dī-'äs-ə-sən\ *adj*

arch·du·cal \'ärch-'dü-kəl, -'dyü-\ *adj* : of or relating to an archduke or archduchy

arch·duch·ess \'ärch-'dəch-əs\ *n* **1** : the wife or widow of an archduke **2** : a woman having in her own right the rank of archduke

arch·duchy \-'dəch-ē\ *n* : the territory of an archduke or archduchess

arch·duke \-'dük, -'dyük\ *n* : a sovereign prince; *esp* : a prince of the imperial family of Austria — **arch·duke·dom** \-dəm\ *n*

Ar·che·an *or* **Ar·chae·an** \ är-'kē-ən\ *adj* **1** : of, relating to, or being the earliest eon of geological history or the corresponding system of rocks — see GEOLOGIC TIME table **2** : PRECAMBRIAN [Greek *archaios* "ancient"] — **Archean** *n*

ar·che·go·ni·um \ˌär-ki-'gō-nē-əm\ *n, pl* **-nia** \-nē-ə\ : a flask-shaped female sex organ found especially in mosses and ferns [Greek *archegonos* "originator", from *archein* "to begin" + *gonos* "procreation"] — **ar·che·go·ni·al** \-nē-əl\ *adj*

arch·en·e·my \'ärch-'en-ə-mē\ *n* : a principal enemy

arch·en·ter·on \ är-'kent-ə-ˌrän, -rən\ *n* : the cavity of the gastrula of an embryo

Ar·cheo·zo·ic \ˌär-kē-ə-'zō-ik\ *n* : ARCHEAN 1 — **Archeozoic** *adj*

ar·cher \'är-chər\ *n* : a person who uses a bow and arrow [Old French, derived from Latin *arcus* "bow"]

ar·chery \'ärch-rē, -ə-rē\ *n* **1** : the art, practice, or skill of shooting with bow and arrow **2** : a body of archers

ar·che·type \'är-ki-ˌtīp\ *n* : the original pattern or model of a work or the model from which others are copied : PROTOTYPE [Latin *archetypum*, from Greek *archetypon*, from *archein* "to begin" + *typos* "type"] — **ar·che·typ·al** \ˌär-ki-'tī-pəl\ *or* **ar·che·typ·i·cal** \-'tip-i-kəl\ *adj*

arch·fiend \'ärch-'fēnd\ *n* : a chief fiend; *esp* : DEVIL 1

ar·chi·epis·co·pal \ˌär-kē-ə-'pis-kə-pəl\ *adj* : of or relating to an archbishop [Late Latin *archiepiscopus* "archbishop", from Late Greek *archiepiskopos*, from *archi-* "arch-" + *episkopos* "bishop"]

ar·chi·pel·a·go \ˌär-kə-'pel-ə-ˌgō, ˌär-chə-\ *n, pl* **-goes** *or* **-gos** **1** : an expanse of water with many scattered islands **2** : a group of islands [*Archipelago* "Aegean sea", from Italian *Arcipelago*, literally, "chief sea", from *arci-* "arch-" + Greek *pelagos* "sea"] — **ar·chi·pe·lag·ic** \-pə-'laj-ik\ *adj*

ar·chi·tect \'är-kə-ˌtekt\ *n* : a person who designs buildings and oversees their construction [derived from Greek *architektōn* "master builder", from *archi-* "arch-" + *tektōn* "builder, carpenter"]

ar·chi·tec·ton·ic \ˌär-kə-ˌtek-'tän-ik\ *adj* : of, relating to, or according with the principles of architecture : ARCHITECTURAL — **ar·chi·tec·ton·i·cal·ly** \-'tän-i-kə-lē, -klē\ *adv*

ar·chi·tec·ton·ics \-'tän-iks\ *n sing or pl* : structural design : STRUCTURE, ORDER, PLAN

ar·chi·tec·tur·al \ˌär-kə-'tek-chə-rəl, -'tek-shrəl\ *adj* : of, relating to, or conforming to the rules of architecture — **ar·chi·tec·tur·al·ly** \-ē-ē\ *adv*

ar·chi·tec·ture \'är-kə-ˌtek-chər\ *n* **1** : the art or science of designing and building habitable structures **2** : architectural work : BUILDINGS **3** : a method or style of building ⟨a church of modern *architecture*⟩

ar·chi·trave \'är-kə-ˌtrāv\ *n* : the lowest division of an entablature resting immediately on the capital of the column in an ancient Greek or Roman building [Middle French, from Italian, from *archi-* "arch-" + *trave* "beam", from Latin *trabs*]

ar·chive \'är-ˌkīv\ *n* : a place in which public records or historical documents are preserved; *also* : the material preserved — usually used in pl. [Latin *archivum*, from Greek *archeia* "government documents", from *archē* "beginning, rule, government"] — **ar·chi·val** \är-'kī-vəl\ *adj*

ar·chi·vist \'är-kə-vəst, -ˌkī-\ *n* : a person in charge of archives

ar·chon \'är-ˌkän, -kən\ *n* : one of the chief magistrates in ancient Athens [Latin, from Greek *archōn*, from *archein* "to rule"]

ar·cho·saur \'är-kə-ˌsȯr\ *n* : any of a subclass of reptiles comprising the dinosaurs, pterosaurs, and crocodilians [Greek *archos* "chief" + *sauros* "lizard"]

arch·way \'ärch-ˌwā\ *n* : a way or passage under an arch; *also* : an arch over a passage

-archy \ˌär-kē, *in a few words also* ər-kē\ *n combining form, pl* **-archies** : rule : government ⟨squire*archy*⟩ [Greek *-archia*, from *archein* "to rule"]

arc lamp *n* : a lamp whose light is produced when an electric current passes between two hot electrodes surrounded by gas — called also *arc light*

¹arc·tic \'ärk-tik, 'ärt-ik\ *adj* **1** *often cap* : of or relating to the north pole or the region around it **2** : very cold : FRIGID [Latin *arcticus*, from Greek *arktikos*, from *arktos* "bear, Ursa Major, north"]

²arc·tic \'ärt-ik, 'ärk-tik\ *n* : a rubber overshoe reaching to the ankle or above

arctic circle *n, often cap A&C* : the parallel of latitude that is approximately 66½ degrees north of the equator

arctic fox *n* : a small fox of arctic regions that is blue-gray or brownish in summer and white in winter

Arc·tu·rus \ärk-'tu̇r-əs, -'tyu̇r-\ *n* : a large bright fixed star in Boötes [Latin, from Greek *Arktouros*, literally, "bear watcher"]

-ard \-ərd\ *also* **-art** \ərt\ *n suffix* : one that is characterized by performing some action, possessing some quality, or being associated with some thing especially conspicuously or excessively ⟨bragg*art*⟩ ⟨dull*ard*⟩ [Old French, of Germanic origin]

ar·dent \'ärd-nt\ *adj* **1 a** : characterized by warmth of feeling : PASSIONATE ⟨an *ardent* admirer⟩ **b** : ZEALOUS, DEVOTED ⟨an *ardent* champion of justice⟩ **2** : extremely hot : FIERY ⟨the *ardent* sun⟩ [Middle French, from Latin *ardēre* "to burn"] — **ar·den·cy** \-n-sē\ *n* — **ar·dent·ly** *adv*

ar·dor \'ärd-ər\ *n* **1** : a warmth of feeling or sentiment **2** : ZEAL, EAGERNESS [Latin, from *ardēre* "to burn"] SYN SEE PASSION

ar·du·ous \'ärj-wəs, -ə-wəs\ *adj* : extremely difficult : LABORIOUS, STRENUOUS ⟨an *arduous* climb⟩ [Latin *arduus* "steep, high, difficult"] — **ar·du·ous·ly** *adv* — **ar·du·ous·ness** *n*

¹are *present 2d sing or present pl of* BE [Old English *earun*, present plural]

²are \'aər, 'eər, 'är\ *n* — see METRIC SYSTEM table [French, from Latin *area* "level space"]

ar·ea \'ar-ē-ə, 'er-\ *n* **1** : a particular piece of ground often set aside for special use ⟨a picnic *area*⟩ **2** : the amount of surface included within a closed figure; *also* : the number of unit squares equal in measure to the surface **3 a** : REGION ⟨a farming *area*⟩ **b** : a field of activity ⟨*area* of knowledge⟩ **4** : a part of the cerebral cortex having a particular function [Latin, "piece of level ground, threshing floor", from *arēre* "to be dry, burn"] — **ar·e·al** \-ē-əl\ *adj* — **ar·e·al·ly** \-ē-ə-lē\ *adv*

area code *n* : a 3-digit number that identifies a particular telephone service area in the United States or Canada

arctic fox

\ə\ abut	\ng\ sing
\ər\ further	\ō\ bone
\a\ mat	\ȯ\ saw
\ā\ take	\ȯi\ coin
\ä\ cot, cart	\th\ thin
\au̇\ out	\th\ this
\ch\ chin	\ü\ food
\e\ pet	\u̇\ foot
\ē\ easy	\y\ yet
\g\ go	\yü\ few
\i\ tip	\yu̇\ cure
\ī\ life	\zh\ vision
\j\ job	

area·way \-ē-ə-ˌwā\ *n* : a sunken space affording access, air, and light to a basement

are·na \ə-'rē-nə\ *n* **1** : an area in a Roman amphitheater for gladiatorial combats **2 a** : an enclosed area used for public entertainment **b** : a building containing an arena **3** : a sphere of interest or activity [Latin, "sand, sandy place"]

arena theater *n* : a theater having the stage in the center of the auditorium with the audience seated on all sides

aren't \ärnt, 'ärnt, 'är-ənt\ : are not

are·o·la \ə-'rē-ə-lə\ *n, pl* **-lae** \-ˌlē\ *or* **-las** : a colored ring (as about the nipple) [Latin, "small open space", from *area*] — **are·o·lar** \-lər\ *adj*

arête \ə-'rāt\ *n* : a sharp-crested ridge in rugged mountains [French, literally, "fish bone", from Latin *arista* "beard of grain"]

¹ar·gent \'är-jənt\ *n* : the heraldic color silver or white [Latin *argentum* "silver"]

²argent *adj* : resembling silver : SILVERY, SHINING

ar·gen·tite \'är-jən-ˌtīt\ *n* : a dark gray mineral Ag₂S that is a silver sulfide and constitutes an ore of silver

ar·gil·la·ceous \ˌär-jə-'lā-shəs\ *adj* : of, relating to, or containing clay or the minerals of clay [Latin *argilla* "clay"]

ar·gi·nine \'är-jə-ˌnēn\ *n* : an amino acid $C_6H_{14}O_2N_4$ found in various proteins and essential to the diet of rats [German *arginin*]

Ar·give \'är-ˌjīv, -ˌgīv\ *adj* : of or relating to the Greeks or Greece and especially to the Achaean city of Argos or the surrounding territory of Argolis — **Argive** *n*

ar·gon \'är-ˌgän\ *n* : a colorless odorless inert gaseous chemical element found in the air and in volcanic gases and used especially as a filler for electric bulbs — see ELEMENT table [Greek, neuter of *argos* "idle, lazy", from *a-* + *ergon* "work"]

ar·go·naut \'är-gə-ˌnot, -ˌnät\ *n* **1** *cap* : one of a band of heroes sailing with Jason in quest of the Golden Fleece **2** : PAPER NAUTILUS [Greek *Argonautēs*, from *Argō*, name of Jason's ship + *nautēs* "sailor"]

ar·go·sy \'är-gə-sē\ *n, pl* **-sies** : a large ship; *esp* : a large merchant ship [Italian *ragusea* "vessel of Ragusa", from *Ragusa*, Dalmatia (now Dubrovnik, Croatia)]

ar·got \'är-gət, -ˌgō\ *n* : a more or less secret vocabulary used by a particular class or group — compare DIALECT [French]

ar·gu·able \'är-gyə-wə-bəl\ *adj* : open to argument, dispute, or question — **ar·gu·ably** \-blē\ *adv*

ar·gue \'är-gyü\ *vb* **1** : to give reasons for or against ⟨*argue* in favor of lowering taxes⟩ **2** : to debate or discuss some matter : DISPUTE ⟨*argue* about politics⟩ **3** : to persuade by giving reasons ⟨tried to *argue* their parents into getting a new car⟩ **4** : INDICATE ⟨your manner *argues* your guilt⟩ [Latin *arguere* "to make clear, accuse" and Middle French *arguer* "to accuse, reason"] SYN see DISCUSS — **ar·gu·er** *n*

ar·gu·ment \'är-gyə-mənt\ *n* **1 a** : a reason for or against something **b** : a discussion in which arguments are presented : DISPUTE, DEBATE **2** : a heated dispute : QUARREL

ar·gu·men·ta·tion \ˌär-gyə-mən-'tā-shən, -ˌmen-\ *n* **1** : the act or process of forming reasons and of drawing conclusions and applying them to a case under discussion **2** : DEBATE, DISCUSSION

ar·gu·men·ta·tive \ˌär-gyə-'ment-ət-iv\ *adj* : marked by or given to argument : DISPUTATIOUS — **ar·gu·men·ta·tive·ly** *adv*

Ar·gus–eyed \ˌär-gə-'sīd\ *adj* : vigilantly observant

ar·gyle \'är-ˌgīl, är-'\ *n* : a geometric knitting pattern of variously colored diamonds on a single background color; *also* : a sock knit in this pattern [*Argyle,* branch of the Scottish clan of Campbell, from whose tartan the design was adapted]

Ar·gy·rol \'är-jə-ˌrol, -ˌrōl\ *trademark* — used for a silver-protein compound whose aqueous solution is used as an antiseptic

aria \'är-ē-ə\ *n* : MELODY, TUNE; *esp* : an accompanied elaborate melody sung (as in an opera) by a single voice [Italian, literally, "atmospheric air", from Latin *aer,* from Greek *aēr*]

-ar·i·an \'er-ē-ən, 'ar-\ *n suffix* **1** : believer ⟨Unit*arian*⟩ : advocate ⟨disciplin*arian*⟩ **2** : producer ⟨disciplin*arian*⟩ [Latin *-arius* "-ary" + English *-an*]

ar·id \'ar-əd\ *adj* **1** : very dry; *esp* : having too little rainfall to support agriculture **2** : lacking in interest : DULL [Latin *aridus*] — **arid·i·ty** \ə-'rid-ət-ē, a-\ *n*

Ar·ies \'er-ˌēz, 'er-ē-ˌēz, 'ar-\ **1** : a zodiacal constellation between Pisces and Taurus **2** : the 1st sign of the zodiac; *also* : one born under this sign [Latin, literally, "ram"]

aright \ə-'rīt\ *adv* : RIGHTLY, CORRECTLY

ar·il \'ar-əl\ *n* : an outer covering or appendage of some seeds that develops after fertilization [probably from Medieval Latin *arillus* "raisin, grape seed"]

arise \ə-'rīz\ *vi* **arose** \-'rōz\; **aris·en** \-'riz-n\; **aris·ing** \-'rī-zing\ **1** : to move upward : ASCEND **2** : to get up from sleep or after lying down **3** : to come into existence : spring up ⟨a dispute *arose* between the leaders⟩ [Old English *ārisan,* from *ā-,* prefix denoting completion + *rīsan* "to rise"]

ar·is·toc·ra·cy \ˌar-ə-'stäk-rə-sē\ *n, pl* **-cies** **1** : government by the best individuals or by a small privileged class **2 a** : a government in which power is exercised by a minority especially of those felt to be best qualified **b** : a state with such a government **3 a** : a governing body or upper class usually made up of an hereditary nobility **b** : a group felt to be superior in birth, wealth, culture, or intelligence [derived from Greek *aristokratia,* from *aristos* "best" + *-kratia* "-cracy"]

aris·to·crat \ə-'ris-tə-ˌkrat, a-; 'ar-ə-stə-\ *n* **1** : a member of an aristocracy; *esp* : NOBLE **2** : one with habits and viewpoints typical of the aristocracy — **aris·to·crat·ic** \ə-ˌris-tə-'krat-ik, a-ˌris-tə-, ˌar-ə-stə-\ *adj* — **aris·to·crat·i·cal·ly** \-i-kə-lē, -i-klē\ *adv*

Ar·is·to·te·lian *or* **Ar·is·to·te·lean** \ˌar-ə-stə-'tēl-yən\ *adj* : of, relating to, or characteristic of Aristotle or his philosophy — **Ar·is·to·te·lian·ism** \-yə-ˌniz-əm\ *n*

arith·me·tic \ə-'rith-mə-ˌtik\ *n* **1** : a branch of mathematics that deals with real numbers and computations with them **2** : an act or method of computing : CALCULATION ⟨a mistake in *arithmetic*⟩ [Old French *arismetique,* from Latin *arithmetica,* from Greek *arithmētikē,* from *arithmein* "to count", from *arithmos* "number"] — **ar·ith·met·ic** \ˌar-ith-'met-ik\ *or* **ar·ith·met·i·cal** \-'met-i-kəl\ *adj* — **ar·ith·met·i·cal·ly** \-kə-lē, -klē\ *adv*

arith·me·ti·cian \ə-ˌrith-mə-'tish-ən\ *n* : a person skilled in arithmetic

arithmetic mean \ˌar-ith-'met-ik-\ *n* **1** : a value computed by dividing the sum of a set of terms by the number of terms ⟨the *arithmetic mean* of 6, 5, and 4 is 5⟩ **2** : one of the terms in an arithmetic progression between two given terms ⟨in 3, 5, 7, and 9, the terms 5 and 7 are *arithmetic means* between 3 and 9⟩

arithmetic progression \ˌar-ith-'met-ik-\ *n* : a sequence of numbers (as 3, 5, 7, 9, . . .) in which the difference between any two successive terms is the same

-ar·i·um \'ar-ē-əm, 'er-\ *n suffix, pl* **-ar·i·ums** *or* **-ar·ia** \-ē-ə\ : thing or place relating to ⟨planet*arium*⟩ [Latin, from neuter of *-arius* "-ary"]

ark \'ärk\ *n* **1 a** : the ship in which Noah and his family were preserved from the Flood **b** : a clumsy boat or ship **2 a** : a sacred chest in which the ancient Hebrews kept the two tablets of the Law **b** : a place of deposit in or against the wall of a synagogue for the scrolls of the Torah [Old English *arc,* from Latin *arca* "chest"]

¹arm \'ärm\ *n* **1 a** : a human upper limb; *esp* : the part between the shoulder and wrist **b** : a corresponding limb of a lower vertebrate **2** : something resembling an arm: as **a** : a lateral branch of a tree **b** : an inlet of water (as from the sea) **c** : a slender usually functional projecting part (as of a machine) **3** : POWER, MIGHT ⟨the *arm* of the law⟩ **4** : a support (as on a chair) for the elbow and forearm **5** : SLEEVE 1 **6** : a division of an organization [Old English *earm*] — **armed** \'ärmd\ *adj* — **arm·less** \'ärm-ləs\ *adj*

²**arm** *vb* **1** : to provide with weapons ⟨*arm* a new regiment⟩ **2** : to provide with a means of defense ⟨*arm* oneself with facts⟩ **3** : to provide oneself with arms and armament ⟨the country *armed* for war⟩ **4** : to equip or ready for action or operation ⟨*arm* a bomb⟩ [Old French *armer*, from Latin *armare*, from *arma* "weapons, tools"]

³**arm** *n* **1 a** : a means of offense or defense : WEAPON; *esp* : FIREARM **b** : a branch of an army (as the infantry or artillery) that actually fights **c** : a branch of the military forces (as the navy) **2** *pl* : the heraldic devices of a family or a government **3 a** *pl* : active hostilities : WARFARE **b** *pl* : military service — **armed** \'ärmd\ *adj*

ar·ma·da \är-'mäd-ə, -'mad-, -'mäd-\ *n* **1** : a large fleet of warships **2** *cap* : the fleet sent by Spain against England in 1588 **3** : a large number of moving objects (as vehicles) [Spanish, from Medieval Latin *armata* "army, fleet", from Latin *armare* "to arm"]

ar·ma·dil·lo \,är-mə-'dil-ō\ *n*, *pl* **-los** : any of several small burrowing chiefly nocturnal mammals of warm parts of the Americas having body and head encased in small bony plates [Spanish, from *armado* "armed one", from Latin *armare* "to arm"]

Ar·ma·ged·don \,är-mə-'ged-n\ *n* **1 a** : a final and conclusive battle between the forces of good and evil **b** : the site or time of Armageddon **2** : a vast decisive conflict [Greek *Armageddōn*, scene of the battle foretold in Revelation 16:14–16]

ar·ma·ment \'är-mə-mənt\ *n* **1** : the whole military strength and equipment of a nation **2** : the total supply of war materials (as of a military unit or system of defense) **3** : means of protection or defense : ARMOR **4** : the process of preparing for war

ar·ma·ture \'är-mə-chər, -,chùr\ *n* **1** : a protective or defensive mechanism or covering (as the spines of a cactus) **2** : the part of an electric generator that consists of coils of wire around an iron core and that induces an electric current when it is rotated in a magnetic field **3** : the part of an electric motor that consists of coils of wire around an iron core and that is caused to rotate in a magnetic field when an electric current is passed through the coils **4** : the movable part of an electromagnetic device (as an electric bell) **5** : a framework used by a sculptor to support a figure being modeled (as in clay) [Latin *armatura* "armor, equipment", from *armare* "to arm"]

¹**arm·chair** \'ärm-,cheər, -,chaər, 'ärm-'-\ *n* : a chair with arms

²**armchair** *adj* **1** : remote from direct dealing with problems ⟨*armchair* strategist⟩ **2** : sharing vicariously in another's experiences ⟨*armchair* traveler⟩

armed forces *n pl* : the combined military, naval, and air forces of a nation

Ar·me·ni·an \är-'mē-nē-ən, -nyən\ *n* **1** : a member of a people dwelling chiefly in Armenia **2** : the Indo-European language of the Armenians — **Armenian** *adj*

arm·ful \'ärm-,fùl\ *n*, *pl* **arm·fuls** \-,fùlz\ *or* **arms·ful** \'ärmz-,fùl\ : as much as a person's arm can hold ⟨carrying an *armful* of books⟩

arm·hole \'ärm-,hōl\ *n* : an opening for the arm in a garment

ar·mi·stice \'är-mə-stəs\ *n* : a pause in fighting brought about by agreement between the two sides : TRUCE [New Latin *armistitium*, from Latin *arma* "arms" + *-stitium* (as in *solstitium* "solstice")]

Armistice Day *n* : VETERANS DAY [from the *armistice* which ended World War I on November 11, 1918]

arm·let \'ärm-lət\ *n* : a bracelet or band for the upper arm

ar·mor \'är-mər\ *n* **1** : defensive covering for the body; *esp* : covering (as of metal) used in combat **2** : something that affords protection ⟨safe in the *armor* of wealth⟩ **3** : a protective covering (as the steel plates of a battleship or a sheathing for wire) **4** : armored forces and vehicles (as tanks) [Old French *armure*, from Latin *armatura*, from *armare* "to arm"]

ar·mored \-mərd\ *adj* **1** : protected by armor ⟨an *armored* car⟩ ⟨*armored* reptiles⟩ **2** : supplied with armored equipment ⟨an *armored* force⟩

ar·mor·er \'är-mər-ər\ *n* **1** : one that makes armor or arms **2** : one that repairs, assembles, and tests firearms or that services and loads aircraft armament including bombs

ar·mo·ri·al \är-'mōr-ē-əl, -'mòr-\ *adj* : of, relating to, or bearing heraldic arms

ar·mo·ry \'ärm-rē, -ə-rē\ *n*, *pl* **-ries** **1** : a supply of arms **2** : a place where arms are stored; *esp* : one used for training military reserve personnel **3** : a place where arms are manufactured

ar·mour \'är-mər\ *chiefly British variant of* ARMOR

arm·pit \'ärm-,pit\ *n* : the hollow beneath the junction of the arm and shoulder

arm·rest \-,rest\ *n* : a support for the arm

arm wrestling *n* : a contest of strength in which individuals face each other and place usually their right elbows on a surface, grasp hands, and seek to force the other person's arm down

ar·my \'är-mē\ *n*, *pl* **ar·mies** **1 a** : a large body of persons organized and armed for land warfare **b** : a military unit capable of independent action and consisting usually of a headquarters, two or more corps, and auxiliary troops **c** *often cap* : the complete military organization of a nation for land warfare **2** : a great multitude ⟨an *army* of insects⟩ **3** : a body of persons organized to advance a cause [Middle French *armee*, from Medieval Latin *armata* "army, fleet", from Latin *armare* "to arm"]

army ant *n* : any of various nomadic social ants

ar·my·worm \-,wərm\ *n* : any of numerous moth larvae that are often abundant and destructive on crops (as grasses or grain); *also* : any other stage of this insect

ar·ni·ca \'är-ni-kə\ *n* : dried flower heads of a mountain herb related to the daisies that are used especially in the form of a tincture as a liniment; *also* : this tincture [New Latin, genus name]

aro·ma \ə-'rō-mə\ *n* **1** : a distinctive and usually pleasing smell ⟨the *aroma* of fresh coffee⟩ — compare FRAGRANCE **2** : a distinctive quality or atmosphere : FLAVOR ⟨the *aroma* of suspense⟩ [Old French *aromat* "spice", from Latin *aroma*, from Greek *arōma*] SYN see SMELL

ar·o·mat·ic \,ar-ə-'mat-ik\ *adj* **1** : of, relating to, or having aroma **2** : of, relating to, or characterized by the presence of at least one benzene ring — used of hydrocarbons and their derivatives — **aromatic** *n*

arose *past of* ARISE

¹**around** \ə-'raùnd\ *adv* **1 a** : in circumference ⟨a tree five feet *around*⟩ **b** : in, along, or through a curving or roundabout course ⟨the road goes *around* by the lake⟩ **2 a** : on all or various sides ⟨papers lying *around*⟩ **b** : NEARBY ⟨stick *around*⟩ **3 a** : here and there in various places ⟨traveled *around* from state to state⟩ **b** : to a particular place ⟨come *around* for dinner⟩ **4 a** : in rotation or succession ⟨pass the candy *around*⟩ **b** : from beginning to end ⟨mild the year *around*⟩ **c** : to a customary or improved condition ⟨the medicine brought the patient *around*⟩ **5** : in or to an opposite direction or position ⟨turned *around* and waved goodbye⟩ **6** : APPROXIMATELY ⟨a price of *around* $20⟩

armadillo

armor 1

\ə\ abut		\ng\ sing	
\ər\ further		\ō\ bone	
\a\ mat		\ò\ saw	
\ā\ take		\òi\ coin	
\ä\ cot, cart		\th\ thin	
\aù\ out		\th\ this	
\ch\ chin		\ü\ food	
\e\ pet		\ù\ foot	
\ē\ easy		\y\ yet	
\g\ go		\yü\ few	
\i\ tip		\yù\ cure	
\ī\ life		\zh\ vision	
\j\ job			

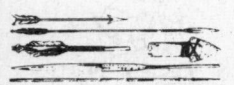

arrow 1

²**around** *prep* **1 a :** on all or various sides of ⟨yard with a fence *around* it⟩ ⟨fields *around* the village⟩ **b :** so as to encircle or enclose ⟨seated *around* the table⟩ **c :** on or to another side of ⟨voyage *around* Cape Horn⟩ **d :** in the neighborhood of : NEAR ⟨somewhere *around* here⟩ **2 :** here and there in or throughout ⟨traveling *around* the country⟩

arous·al \ə-'rau̇-zəl\ *n* : the act of arousing or the state of being aroused

arouse \ə-'rau̇z\ *vb* **1 :** to awaken from sleep **2 :** to rouse to action : EXCITE [*a-* (as in *arise*) + *rouse*]

ar·peg·gio \är-'pej-ō, -'pej-ē-,ō\ *n, pl* **-gi·os :** production of the tones of a chord in succession and not simultaneously; *also* : a chord so played [Italian, from *arpeggiare* "to play on the harp", from *arpa* "harp", of Germanic origin]

ar·que·bus \'är-kwi-bəs, -,bəs\ *variant of* HARQUEBUS

ar·raign \ə-'rān\ *vt* **1 :** to call before a court to answer to an indictment : CHARGE **2 :** to accuse of wrong, inadequacy, or imperfection [Middle French *araisnier* "to speak to, arraign", from *a-* "ad-" + *raisnier* "to speak", from Latin *ratio* "reason"] — **ar·raign·ment** \-mənt\ *n*

ar·range \ə-'rānj\ *vb* **1 :** to put in order; *esp* : to put in a particular order ⟨*arrange* books on shelves⟩ **2 :** to make plans for ⟨*arrange* a meeting⟩ **3 :** ADJUST, SETTLE ⟨*arrange* one's affairs to have the weekend free⟩ **4 :** to make a musical arrangement of [Middle French *arangier*, from Old French *a-* "ad-" + *reng* "row, rank"] — **ar·rang·er** *n*

ar·range·ment \ə-'rānj-mənt\ *n* **1 :** a putting in order : the order in which things are put ⟨the *arrangement* of furniture in a room⟩ **2 :** a preliminary measure : PREPARATION ⟨travel *arrangements*⟩ **3 :** something made by arranging ⟨a flower *arrangement*⟩ **4 :** an adaptation of a musical composition to voices or instruments other than those originally intended

ar·rant \'ar-ənt\ *adj* : being utterly or notoriously such ⟨*arrant* knaves⟩ [alteration of *errant*] — **ar·rant·ly** *adv*

¹**ar·ray** \ə-'rā\ *vt* **1 :** to set in order : draw up : MARSHAL **2 :** to dress or decorate especially splendidly or impressively [Old French *arayer*, of Germanic origin] — **ar·ray·er** *n*

²**array** *n* **1 :** regular order or arrangement; *also* : military order ⟨troops in *array*⟩ **2 :** rich or beautiful apparel : FINERY **3 :** an imposing group : large number ⟨an *array* of problems⟩ **4 :** a group of mathematical elements (as numbers or letters) arranged in rows and columns

ar·rears \ə-'riərz\ *n pl* **1 :** the state of being behind in paying debts owed ⟨two months in *arrears* on their rent⟩ **2 :** an unpaid and overdue debt [Middle French *arrere* "behind, backward", from Latin *ad* "to" + *retro* "backward"]

¹**ar·rest** \ə-'rest\ *vt* **1 :** to stop the progress or movement of : CHECK, SLOW ⟨*arrest* a disease⟩ **2 :** to take or keep in custody by authority of law ⟨*arrested* on suspicion of robbery⟩ **3 :** to attract and hold the attention of ⟨colors that *arrest* the eye⟩ [Middle French *arester* "to rest, arrest", from Latin *ad-* + *restare* "to remain, rest"]

²**arrest** *n* **1 a :** the act of stopping : CHECK **b :** the state of being stopped **2 :** the act of taking or holding in custody by authority of law

ar·rest·ing *adj* : catching the attention : STRIKING

ar·riv·al \ə-'rī-vəl\ *n* **1 :** the act of arriving ⟨await the *arrival* of guests⟩ **2 :** a person or thing that has arrived ⟨late *arrivals*⟩

ar·rive \ə-'rīv\ *vi* **1 :** to reach a destination ⟨*arrive* home at six o'clock⟩ **2 :** to gain an end or object ⟨*arrive* at a decision⟩ **3 :** COME 4a ⟨the moment has *arrived*⟩ **4 :** to be successful [Old French *ariver*, from Latin *ad* "to" + *ripa* "shore"]

ar·ro·gance \'ar-ə-gəns\ *n* : a sense of one's own superiority that shows itself in an offensively proud manner : HAUGHTINESS

ar·ro·gant \-gənt\ *adj* **1 :** exaggerating one's own worth or importance in an overbearing manner **2 :** marked by arrogance ⟨*arrogant* remarks⟩ [Latin *arrogare* "to claim", from *ad-* + *rogare* "to ask"] — **ar·ro·gant·ly** *adv*

ar·ro·gate \'ar-ə-,gāt\ *vt* **1 :** to take or claim for one's own without justification ⟨the dictator *arrogated* the powers of parliament⟩ **2 :** to attribute to another especially without good reason — **ar·ro·ga·tion** \,ar-ə-'gā-shən\ *n*

ar·ron·disse·ment \ə-'rän-dəs-mənt, 'ar-,ōⁿ-dē-'smäⁿ\ *n* **1 :** the largest division of a French governmental department **2 :** an administrative district of some large French cities [French]

ar·row \'ar-ō\ *n* **1 :** a missile that is intended to be shot from a bow and that usually has a slender shaft, a pointed head, and feathers at the butt **2 :** a mark (as on a map or signboard) to indicate direction [Old English *arwe*]

ar·row·head \-,hed\ *n* **1 :** the usually wedge-shaped piercing tip fixed to the front of an arrow **2 :** something (as a wedge-shaped mark) resembling an arrowhead **3 :** any of a genus of aquatic plants with leaves shaped like arrowheads

ar·row·root \-,rüt, -,ruṫ\ *n* : any of several tropical American plants with starchy tuberous roots; *also* : an edible starch from these roots

ar·row·worm \-,wərm\ *n* : any of a small phylum (Chaetognatha) of marine worms with movable bristles on either side of the mouth

ar·royo \ə-'roi-ə, -'roi-ō\ *n, pl* **-roy·os 1 :** a watercourse (as a creek or stream) in a dry region **2 :** an often dry gully or channel carved by water [Spanish]

ar·se·nal \'ärs-nəl, -n-əl\ *n* **1 a :** a place where arms are manufactured or stored **b :** a collection of weapons **2 :** STORE 2, SUPPLY [Italian *arsenale*, from Arabic *dār ṣinā'ah* "house of manufacture"]

ar·sen·ate \'ärs-nət, -n-ət, -n-,āt\ *n* : a salt or ester of arsenic acid

ar·se·nic \'ärs-nik, -n-ik\ *n* **1 :** a solid poisonous chemical element commonly metallic steel-gray, crystalline, and brittle — see ELEMENT table **2 :** a white poisonous trioxide As_2O_3 or As_4O_6 of arsenic used especially as an insecticide or weed killer — called also *arsenic trioxide* [Latin *arsenicum*, from Greek *arsenikon* "yellow orpiment"]

ar·sen·ic acid \är-'sen-ik-\ *n* : a white crystalline poisonous compound $H_3AsO_4 \cdot \frac{1}{2}H_2O$

ar·sen·i·cal \är-'sen-i-kəl\ *adj* : of, relating to, or containing arsenic ⟨an *arsenical* drug⟩ — **arsenical** *n*

ar·se·no·py·rite \,ärs-n-ō-'pī-,rīt\ *n* : a hard tin-white mineral FeAsS consisting of iron, arsenic, and sulfur

ar·sine \är-'sēn, 'är-,\ *n* : a colorless flammable extremely poisonous gas AsH_3 with an odor like garlic

ar·son \'ärs-n\ *n* : the malicious burning of property (as a building) [Old French, derived from Latin *ardēre* "to burn"] — **ar·son·ist** \'ärs-nəst, -n-əst\ *n*

ars·phen·a·mine \ärs-'fen-ə-,mēn, -mən\ *n* : an arsenic-containing substance formerly used in the treatment of spirochetal diseases [*arsenic* + *phen-* + *amine*]

¹**art** \ärt, 'ärt, ərt\ *archaic present 2d sing of* BE [Old English *eart*]

²**art** \'ärt\ *n* **1 :** skill in performance acquired by experience, study, or observation : KNACK ⟨the *art* of making friends⟩ **2 :** an occupation that requires a natural skill in addition to training and practice ⟨the *art* of cooking⟩ **3 :** the rules or ideas that a person must know in order to follow a profession or craft ⟨the *art* of medicine⟩ ⟨the theater *arts*⟩ **4 :** a branch of learning; *esp* : one of the nonscientific branches of learning (as history or literature) — usually used in pl. ⟨College of *Arts* and Sciences⟩ **5 :** the study of drawing,

painting, and sculpture **6** : the works produced by artists [Old French, from Latin *ars*] □ **SYN SKILL, CRAFT**: **ART** may be distinct from the other two in implying personal, unanalyzable creative or imaginative power and resource; **SKILL** stresses technical knowledge and proficiency gained through practice and experience; **CRAFT** implies expertness in workmanship.

-art — see **-ARD**

art de·co \ˌär-dā-ˈkō, ˌärt-; ˌär-ˈdā-, ˌärt-\ *n, often cap A&D* : a decorative style of the 1920s and 1930s characterized by bold outlines, streamlined forms, and the use of new materials (as plastic) [French *Art Déco*, from *Exposition Internationale des Arts Décoratifs*, an exposition of decorative arts held in Paris, France in 1925]

artefact *variant of* **ARTIFACT**

arteri- *or* **arterio-** *combining form* : artery : arterial and ⟨*arterio*venous⟩

¹ar·te·ri·al \är-ˈtir-ē-əl\ *adj* **1 a** : of or relating to an artery **b** : being the bright red oxygen-rich blood present in most arteries **2** : of, relating to, or being routes for through traffic ⟨*arterial* roads⟩ — **ar·te·ri·al·ly** \-ē-ə-lē\ *adv*

²arterial *n* : a through street or highway

ar·te·ri·ole \är-ˈtir-ē-ˌōl\ *n* : a very small artery connecting a larger artery with capillaries — **ar·te·ri·o·lar** \-ˌtir-ē-ˈō-ˌlär, -lər\ *adj*

ar·te·rio·scle·ro·sis \är-ˌtir-ē-ō-sklə-ˈrō-səs\ *n* : a chronic disease in which the arterial walls are abnormally thickened and hardened — **ar·te·rio·scle·rot·ic** \-ˈrät-ik\ *adj or n*

ar·te·rio·ve·nous \är-ˌtir-ē-ō-ˈvē-nəs\ *adj* : of, relating to, or connecting the arteries and veins

ar·tery \ˈärt-ə-rē\ *n, pl* **-ter·ies** **1** : one of the tubular branching muscular-walled and elastic-walled vessels that carry blood from the heart through the body **2** : a channel (as a river or highway) of transportation or communication [Latin *arteria*, from Greek *artēria*]

ar·te·sian well \är-ˈtē-zhən-\ *n* **1** : a bored well from which water flows up like a fountain **2** : a deep-bored well [French *artésien*, literally, "of Artois", from *Artois*, region of France where such wells were common]

art·ful \ˈärt-fəl\ *adj* **1** : performed with or showing art or skill ⟨an *artful* violin performance⟩ **2** : produced by art : **ARTIFICIAL** **3 a** : using or characterized by art and skill : **DEXTEROUS** ⟨an *artful* writing style⟩ **b** : skillful or ingenious in gaining an end : **WILY** ⟨an *artful* cross-examiner⟩ **SYN** see **SLY** — **art·ful·ly** \-fə-lē\ *adv* — **art·ful·ness** *n*

ar·thri·tis \är-ˈthrīt-əs\ *n* : inflammation of the joints [Latin, from Greek, from *arthron* "joint"] — **ar·thrit·ic** \-ˈthrit-ik\ *adj or n* — **ar·thrit·i·cal·ly** \-ˈthrit-i-kə-lē, -klē\ *adv*

ar·thro·pod \ˈär-thrə-ˌpäd\ *n* : any of a phylum (Arthropoda) of invertebrate animals (as insects, arachnids, and crustaceans) with body and limbs segmented [Greek *arthron* "joint" + *pod-, pous* "foot"] — **ar·thropod** *adj* — **ar·throp·o·dan** \är-ˈthräp-əd-ən\ *adj*

ar·ti·choke \ˈärt-ə-ˌchōk\ *n* : a tall herb resembling the thistle; *also* : its edible flower head which is cooked as a vegetable [Italian dialect *articiocco*, from Arabic *al-khurshūf* "the artichoke"]

¹ar·ti·cle \ˈärt-i-kəl\ *n* **1** : a distinct part of a document (as a contract or treaty) dealing with a single subject **2** : a nonfictional prose composition forming an independent part of a publication and usually dealing with a single topic ⟨an *article* on winter sports⟩ **3** : a word (as *a, an,* or *the*) used with nouns to limit or give definiteness to their application **4** : a member of a class of things; *esp* : **COMMODITY** b ⟨*articles* of value⟩ [Old French, from Latin *articulus* "joint, division", from *artus* "joint"]

²article *vt* **-cled; -cling** \-kə-ling, -kling\ : to bind by the articles of a contract ⟨an *articled* apprentice⟩

ar·tic·u·lar \är-ˈtik-yə-lər\ *adj* : of or relating to a joint

¹ar·tic·u·late \är-ˈtik-yə-lət\ *adj* **1 a** : divided clearly into words and syllables : **INTELLIGIBLE** **b** : able to speak; *esp* : able to express oneself clearly or effectively **2** : consisting of segments united by joints : **JOINTED** ⟨*articulate* animals⟩ [Latin *articulus* "joint"] — **ar·tic·u·late·ly** *adv* — **ar·tic·u·late·ness** *n*

²ar·tic·u·late \-ˌlāt\ *vb* **1 a** : to speak in distinct syllables or words **b** : to express clearly and distinctly ⟨*articulate* every shade of meaning⟩ **2** : to unite or become united or connected by or as if by a joint

ar·tic·u·la·tion \är-ˌtik-yə-ˈlā-shən\ *n* **1** : the action or manner of articulating : the state of being articulated **2** : the making of articulate sounds (as in pronunciation) **3 a** : a joint between rigid parts of an animal; *esp* : one between bones or cartilages **b** : a joint between plant parts; *also* : a node or internode of a stem — **ar·tic·u·la·to·ry** \är-ˈtik-yə-lə-ˌtōr-ē, -ˌtôr-\ *adj*

ar·tic·u·la·tor \är-ˈtik-yə-ˌlāt-ər\ *n* : a movable vocal organ (as a lip or the tongue)

ar·ti·fact *or* **ar·te·fact** \ˈärt-ə-ˌfakt\ *n* : a usually simple object (as a tool or ornament) showing human work or alteration [Latin *arte factum* "made by art"] — **ar·ti·fac·tu·al** \ˌärt-ə-ˈfak-chə-wəl, -chəl\ *adj*

ar·ti·fice \ˈärt-ə-fəs\ *n* **1 a** : a wily or artful stratagem : **TRICK** **b** : false or insincere behavior ⟨social *artifices*⟩ **2** : clever or artful skill : **INGENUITY** [Middle French, from Latin *artificium*, from *artifex* "artificer", from *art-, ars* "art" + *facere* "to make"]

ar·tif·i·cer \är-ˈtif-ə-sər, ˈärt-ə-fə-sər\ *n* : a skilled or artistic worker

ar·ti·fi·cial \ˌärt-ə-ˈfish-əl\ *adj* **1** : built or produced by humans ⟨an *artificial* lake⟩ **2** : lacking in natural quality : **AFFECTED** ⟨an *artificial* smile⟩ **3** : made or changed to resemble something natural : **IMITATION** ⟨*artificial* flowers⟩ — **ar·ti·fi·ci·al·i·ty** \-ˌfish-ē-ˈal-ət-ē\ *n* — **ar·ti·fi·cial·ly** \-ˈfish-lē, -ə-lē\ *adv* — **ar·ti·fi·cial·ness** \-ˈfish-əl-nəs\ *n* □ **SYN SYNTHETIC, ERSATZ**: **ARTIFICIAL** may apply to anything that is not the result of natural process or conditions ⟨the state is an *artificial* society⟩ but especially to something that has a natural counterpart ⟨*artificial* teeth⟩ **SYNTHETIC** applies especially to a manufactured substance or to a natural substance that is treated to resemble and substitute for another; **ERSATZ** often implies the use of an inferior substitute for a natural product.

artificial insemination *n* : introduction of semen into the uterus or oviduct by artificial means

artificial intelligence *n* : the power of a machine to imitate intelligent human behavior

artificial respiration *n* : the rhythmic forcing of air into and out of the lungs of one whose breathing has stopped

artificial selection *n* : the process of modifying organisms by selection in breeding controlled by the breeder

ar·til·lery \är-ˈtil-rē, -ə-rē\ *n* **1** : large-caliber crew-operated mounted firearms (as guns, howitzers, or rockets) **2** : a branch of an army armed with artillery [Middle French *artillerie*]

ar·tio·dac·tyl \ˌärt-ē-ō-ˈdak-tl\ *n* : any of an order (Artiodactyla) of hoofed mammals (as the camel or ox) with an even number of functional toes on each foot [Greek *artios* "fitting, even-numbered" + *daktylos* "finger, toe"]

ar·ti·san \ˈärt-ə-zən\ *n* : a person (as a carpenter) who works at a trade requiring skill with the hands [Middle French, from Italian *artigiano*, from *arte* "art", from Latin *ars*]

art·ist \ˈärt-əst\ *n* **1** : a person skilled in one of the arts (as painting, sculpture, music, or writing); *esp* : **PAINTER** **2** : a person showing unusual ability in an occupation requiring skill ⟨a makeup *artist*⟩

ar·tiste \är-ˈtēst\ *n* : a skilled adept performer; *esp* : a musical or theatrical entertainer [French]

artichoke

\ə\ abut	\ng\ sing
\ər\ further	\ō\ bone
\a\ mat	\ȯ\ saw
\ā\ take	\ȯi\ coin
\ä\ cot, cart	\th\ thin
\aů\ out	\th\ this
\ch\ chin	\ü\ food
\e\ pet	\ů\ foot
\ē\ easy	\y\ yet
\g\ go	\yü\ few
\i\ tip	\yů\ cure
\ī\ life	\zh\ vision
\j\ job	

art·is·tic \är-'tis-tik\ *adj* **1** : relating to or characteristic of art or artists **2** : showing imaginative skill in arrangement or execution — **ar·tis·ti·cal·ly** \-'tis-ti-kə-lē, -klē\ *adv* □ SYN AESTHETIC: ARTISTIC implies the point of view of one who produces art and thinks in terms of creating beautiful forms; AESTHETIC stresses the point of view of one who analyzes and reflects upon the effect a work of art has; either term may suggest a contrast with the practical, the functional, or the moral aspects of anything.

art·ist·ry \'ärt-ə-strē\ *n* **1** : artistic quality of effect or workmanship **2** : artistic ability

art·less \'ärt-ləs\ *adj* **1** : lacking art, knowledge, or skill : UNCULTURED **2 a** : made without skill : CRUDE **b** : being simple and natural ⟨*artless* grace⟩ **3** : free from guile or deceit — **art·less·ly** *adv* — **art·less·ness** *n*

art nou·veau \,är-nü-'vō, ,ärt-\ *n, often cap A&N* : a decorative style of late 19th century origin characterized by curving lines and leaflike forms [French, literally, "new art"]

arty \'ärt-ē\ *adj* **art·i·er; -est** : showily or pretentiously artistic — **art·i·ly** \'ärt-l-ē\ *adv* — **art·i·ness** \'ärt-ē-nəs\ *n*

ar·um \'ar-əm, 'er-\ *n* : any of a family of plants (as the jack-in-the-pulpit or the skunk cabbage) having heart-shaped or sword-shaped leaves and flowers in a fleshy spike enclosed in a leafy sheath [Latin, from Greek *aron*]

¹-ary \ *usually* ,er-ē *after an unstressed syllable,* ə-rē *or* rē *after a stressed syllable, in Britain usually* ə-rē *or* rē *in all cases* \ *n suffix, pl* **-aries** : thing or person belonging to or connected with ⟨syllab*ary*⟩ ⟨functionary⟩ [Latin *-arius, -aria, -arium,* from *-arius,* adjective suffix]

²-ary *adj suffix* : of, relating to, or connected with ⟨budget*ary*⟩ [Latin *-arius*]

¹Ary·an \'ar-ē-ən, 'er-, 'är-yən\ *adj* **1** : INDO-EUROPEAN **2** : of or relating to the Aryans **3** : of or relating to a hypothetical ethnic type represented by early speakers of Indo-European languages

²Aryan *n* **1** : a member of the Indo-European-speaking people occupying the Iranian plateau and later entering India and conquering the non-Indo-European inhabitants **2 a** : a member of the people speaking the language from which the Indo-European languages are derived **b** : a member of any of the peoples speaking an Indo-European language **c** : NORDIC 2 **d** : GENTILE 1 [Sanskrit *ārya* "noble, Aryan"]

¹as \əz, az, ,az\ *adv* **1** : to the same degree or extent ⟨*as* light as a feather⟩ **2** : for instance ⟨various trees, *as* oak or pine⟩ [Old English *eallswā* "likewise, just a", from *eall* "all" + *swā* "so"]

²as *conj* **1** : as if ⟨felt *as* I were dead⟩ **2** : in or to the same degree that ⟨bright *as* day⟩ **3** : in the way or manner that ⟨do *as* I do⟩ **4** : WHILE, WHEN ⟨spilled the milk *as* I got up⟩ **5** : regardless of the degree to which : THOUGH ⟨strange *as* it seems, it's true⟩ **6** : for the reason that ⟨stayed home *as* they had no car⟩ **7** : that the result is — used after *so* or *such* ⟨so clearly guilty *as* to leave no doubt⟩ — **as is** : in its present condition

³as *pron* **1** : THAT, WHO, WHICH — used after *same* or *such* ⟨the same school *as* the mayor attended⟩ **2** : a fact that ⟨is a foreigner, *as* is evident from the accent⟩

⁴as *prep* **1** : LIKE 2 ⟨all rose *as* one person⟩ **2** : in the character or position of ⟨working *as* an editor⟩

⁵as \'as\ *n, pl* **as·ses** \'as-,ēz, 'as-əz\ **1** : an ancient Roman unit of value **2** : a bronze coin representing one as [Latin]

as- — see AD-

as·a·fet·i·da *or* **as·a·foe·ti·da** \,as-ə-'fit-əd-ē, -'fet-əd-ə\ *n* : a gum resin that comes from several oriental plants of the carrot family, has an unpleasant smell and taste, and was formerly used in medicine [Medieval Latin *asafoetida,* from Persian *azā* "mastic" + Latin *foetidus* "fetid"]

⁵as 2

ascot

as·bes·tos \as-'bes-təs, az-\ *n* : a mineral (as chrysotile) that readily separates into long flexible fibers suitable for use as a fireproof, nonconducting, and chemically resistant material [Latin, from Greek *asbestos* "quicklime", from *asbestos* "inextinguishable"]

as·ca·rid \'as-kə-rəd\ *n* : any of a family of roundworms that includes the common large roundworm parasitic in the human intestine [derived from Greek *askaris* "intestinal worm"]

as·ca·ris \'as-kə-rəs\ *n, pl* **as·car·i·des** \a-'skar-ə-,dēz\ : ASCARID

as·cend \ə-'send\ *vb* **1** : to go up or upward : CLIMB, RISE ⟨*ascend* a hill⟩ ⟨smoke *ascends*⟩ **2** : to succeed to : OCCUPY ⟨*ascended* the throne in 1918⟩ [Latin *ascendere,* from *ad-* + *scandere* "to climb"] — **as·cend·able** \-'sen-də-bəl\ *adj* □ SYN ASCEND, MOUNT, CLIMB, SCALE mean to move upward or toward the top. ASCEND implies no more than this; MOUNT implies reaching the top ⟨*mount* a ladder⟩ CLIMB suggests effort and often the use of hands and feet; SCALE implies the use of a ladder or rope in climbing vertically.

as·cen·dan·cy \ə-'sen-dən-sē\ *n* : governing or controlling influence : DOMINATION SYN see SUPREMACY

¹as·cen·dant \ə-'sen-dənt\ *n* **1** : the sign of the zodiac on the eastern horizon **2** : a state or position of dominant power or importance

²ascendant *adj* **1** : moving or directed upward : RISING **2** : increasingly superior in position or power

as·cen·sion \ə-'sen-chən\ *n* : the act or process of ascending

Ascension Day *n* : the Thursday 40 days after Easter observed in commemoration of Christ's ascension into heaven

as·cent \ə-'sent\ *n* **1** : the act of rising or moving upward : CLIMB **2** : an upward slope : RISE

as·cer·tain \,as-ər-'tān\ *vt* : to learn with certainty : find out ⟨*ascertain* the date of the concert⟩ [Middle French *acertainer,* from *a-* "ad-" + *certain*] — **as·cer·tain·able** \-'tā-nə-bəl\ *adj* — **as·cer·tain·ment** \-'tān-mənt\ *n*

as·cet·ic \ə-'set-ik\ *adj* **1** : practicing strict self-denial especially for religious discipline ⟨*ascetic* in their way of life⟩ **2** : harshly simple or restrained : AUSTERE ⟨*ascetic* surroundings⟩ [Greek *askētikos,* literally, "laborious", from *askein* "to work, exercise"] — **ascetic** *n* — **as·cet·i·cism** \ə-'set-ə-,siz-əm\ *n*

as·cid·i·an \ə-'sid-ē-ən\ *n* : any of various simple or compound tunicates [derived from Greek *askidion* "little wineskin", from *askos* "wineskin, bladder"]

ASCII \'as-kē, -,kē\ *n* : a computer code for expressing numerals, letters, and other symbols [*A*merican *S*tandard *C*ode for *I*nformation *I*nterchange]

as·co·carp \'as-kə-,kärp\ *n* : the fruiting body of an ascomycetous fungus

as·co·my·cete \,as-kō-'mī-,sēt, -mī-'sēt\ *n* : any of a class (Ascomycetes) of higher fungi (as yeasts, molds) with septate hyphae and spores formed in asci [Greek *askos* "wineskin, bladder" + *mykēs* "fungus"] — **as·co·my·ce·tous** \-,mī-'sēt-əs\ *adj*

ascor·bic acid \ə-'skȯr-bik-\ *n* : VITAMIN C [²*a-* + New Latin *scorbutus* "scurvy"]

as·co·spore \'as-kə-,spȯr, -,spȯr\ *n* : a spore produced in an ascus

as·cot \'as-kət, -,kät\ *n* : a broad scarf with one end passed over the other under the chin and often pinned [*Ascot* Heath, English racetrack]

as·cribe \ə-'skrīb\ *vt* : to refer to a supposed cause, source, or author : ATTRIBUTE [Middle French *ascrivre,* from Latin *ascribere,* from *ad-* + *scribere* "to write"] — **as·crib·able** \-'skrī-bə-bəl\ *adj* □ SYN ASCRIBE, ATTRIBUTE, IMPUTE, CREDIT mean to lay something to the account of a person or thing. ASCRIBE suggests inferring or conjecturing the cause, source, or author of something; ATTRIBUTE implies more definiteness or stronger evidence for ascribing; IMPUTE suggests ascribing something that brings discredit by way of accusation or blame; **CREDIT** implies ascribing a thing to a person or other thing as its agent, source, or explanation.

as·crip·tion \ə-'skrip-shən\ *n* : the act of ascribing

as·cus \'as-kəs\ *n, pl* **as·ci** \'as-,ī, -,kī, -,kē\ : a membranous oval or tubular spore sac of an ascomycete usually bearing eight spores [Greek *askos* "wineskin, bladder"]

-ase \,ās, ,āz\ *n suffix* : enzyme ⟨malt*ase*⟩ [French, from *diastase* "diastase, enzyme"]

asep·sis \ā-'sep-səs, ə-\ *n* : the condition of being aseptic; *also* : the methods of making or keeping aseptic

asep·tic \-'sep-tik\ *adj* **1** : preventing infection; *also* : free or freed from disease-causing microorganisms **2** **a** : lacking life, emotion, or warmth ⟨*aseptic* essays⟩ **b** : being emotionally detached : **OBJECTIVE** ⟨an *aseptic* view of life⟩ — **asep·ti·cal·ly** \-ti-kə-lē, -klē\ *adv*

asex·u·al \ā-'sek-shə-wəl, 'ā-, -shəl\ *adj* **1** : lacking sex ⟨*asexual* organisms⟩ **2** : occurring or formed without sexual action ⟨*asexual* reproduction⟩ — **asex·u·al·ly** \-ē\ *adv*

as for *prep* : with regard to : **CONCERNING** ⟨*as for* me⟩

¹ash \'ash\ *n* **1** : any of a genus of trees of the olive family with thin furrowed bark and winged seeds **2** : the tough elastic wood of an ash [Old English *æsc*]

²ash *n* **1** **a** : the solid residue left when material is thoroughly burned or is oxidized by chemical means **b** : fine particles of mineral matter from a volcanic vent **2** *pl* **a** : a collection of ash left after something has been burned **b** : the last traces of something : **RUINS** **c** : the remains of a dead human body especially after cremation **3** *pl* : something that symbolizes grief, repentance, or humiliation **4** *pl* : deathly pallor [Old English *asce*]

ashamed \ə-'shāmd\ *adj* **1** : feeling shame, guilt, or disgrace ⟨*ashamed* of your behavior⟩ **2** : kept back by pride ⟨*ashamed* to beg⟩ — **asham·ed·ly** \-'shā-məd-lē\ *adv*

Ashan·ti \ə-'shant-ē, -'shänt-\ *n, pl* **Ashanti** *or* **Ashantis** : a member of a people of southern Ghana

¹ash·en \'ash-ən\ *adj* : of, relating to, or made from the wood of the ash tree

²ashen *adj* **1** : of the color of ashes **2** : deadly pale : **BLANCHED** ⟨*ashen* with fear⟩

Ash·ke·nazi \,ash-kə-'naz-ē\ *n, pl* **-naz·im** \-'naz-əm\ : a member of one of the two great divisions of Jews comprising the eastern European Yiddish-speaking Jews — compare **SEPHARDI** [Hebrew *Ashkĕnāzī*] — **Ash·ke·naz·ic** \-'naz-ik\ *adj*

ash·lar \'ash-lər\ *n* **1** : dressed or squared stone; *also* : masonry of such stone **2** : a thin squared and dressed stone used for facing [Middle French *aisselier* "traverse beam", derived from Latin *assis* "board"]

ashore \ə-'shōr, -'shȯr\ *adv* : on or to the shore

ash·tray \'ash-,trā\ *n* : a container for tobacco ashes and cigarette and cigar butts

Ash Wednesday *n* : the first day of Lent

ashy \'ash-ē\ *adj* **ash·i·er; -est** **1** : of, relating to, or resembling ashes **2** : ²**ASHEN** 2

Asian \'ā-zhən, 'ā-shən\ *n* **1** : a native or inhabitant of Asia **2** : a person of Asian descent — **Asian** *adj*

Asian influenza *or* **Asian flu** *n* : influenza caused by a mutant strain of the influenza virus discovered in China in 1957

Asi·at·ic cholera \'ā-zhē-,at-ik-, -zē-\ *n* : a destructive bacterial disease of humans especially in Asia marked by violent vomiting and purging

¹aside \ə-'sīd\ *adv* **1** : to or toward the side ⟨stepped *aside*⟩ **2** : out of the way : **AWAY** ⟨took them *aside*⟩ **3** : out of one's thoughts ⟨*all* kidding aside⟩

²aside *n* **1** : words meant to be inaudible to someone; *esp* : an actor's words supposedly not heard by others on the stage **2** : a straying from the theme : **DIGRESSION**

aside from *prep* **1** : in addition to : **BESIDES** **2** : except for

as if *conj* **1** : as it would be if ⟨it was *as if* you had lost your last friend⟩ **2** : as one would do if ⟨they ran *as if* ghosts were chasing them⟩ **3** : **THAT** ⟨it seemed *as if* the day would never end⟩

as·i·nine \'as-n-,īn\ *adj* **1** : **OBSTINATE** 1 **2** : marked by inexcusable failure to use intelligence or good judgment ⟨an *asinine* statement⟩ [Latin *asininus,* from *asinus* "ass"] — **as·i·nine·ly** *adv* — **as·i·nin·i·ty** \,as-n-'in-ət-ē\ *n*

ask \'ask\ *vb* **1** : to seek information : **INQUIRE** **2** : to make a request ⟨*ask* for help⟩ **3** : to set as a price ⟨*ask* $20 for a bicycle⟩ **4** : **INVITE** ⟨*ask* friends to a party⟩ **5** : to seek or look for punishment or retaliation ⟨*asking* for trouble⟩ [Old English *āscian*] — **ask·er** *n* □ **SYN** **ASK, REQUEST** mean to try to obtain by making known one's wants. **ASK** implies simply the statement of the desire; **REQUEST** suggests some formality or courtesy in asking and implies an expectation of an affirmative response.

askance \ə-'skans\ *adv* **1** : with a side glance : **OBLIQUELY** **2** : with disapproval or distrust [origin unknown]

askew \ə-'skyü\ *adv or adj* : out of line : **AWRY** ⟨the picture hung *askew*⟩ **SYN** see **CROOKED**

¹aslant \ə-'slant\ *adv or adj* : in a slanting direction : **OBLIQUELY**

²aslant *prep* : over or across in a slanting direction

¹asleep \ə-'slēp\ *adj* **1** : being in a state of sleep **2** : lacking sensation : **NUMB** ⟨my *arm* is asleep⟩ **3** : not alert : **SLUGGISH**

²asleep *adv* : into a state of sleep

as long as *conj* **1** : provided that ⟨the team can get away with murder *as long as* they win⟩ **2** : inasmuch as : **SINCE** ⟨*as long as* you're going, I'll go too⟩

aso·cial \ā-'sō-shəl\ *adj* **1** : inconsiderate of others : **SELFISH** **2** : withdrawn from social activity — compare **ANTISOCIAL** 2

as of *prep* : **ON, AT, FROM** ⟨takes effect *as of* July 1⟩

asp \'asp\ *n* : a small venomous snake of Egypt [Latin *aspis,* from Greek]

as·par·a·gine \ə-'spar-ə-,jēn\ *n* : an amino acid $C_4H_8N_2O_3$ that is found in many plants [French, from Latin *asparagus*]

as·par·a·gus \ə-'spar-ə-gəs\ *n* : a tall branching perennial herb of the lily family widely grown for its thick edible young shoots [Latin, from Greek *asparagos*]

as·par·tic acid \ə-'spärt-ik-\ *n* : a crystalline amino acid $C_4H_7NO_4$ found especially in plants [derived from Latin *asparagus*]

as·pect \'as-,pekt\ *n* **1** **a** : the position of planets or stars with respect to one another held by astrologers to influence human affairs **b** : a position facing a particular direction : **EXPOSURE** ⟨the house has a southern *aspect*⟩ **2** : a particular way in which something appears or may be regarded ⟨studied every *aspect* of the question⟩ [Latin *aspectus,* from *aspicere* "to look at", from *ad-* + *specere* "to look"] — **as·pec·tu·al** \a-'spek-chə-wəl, -chəl\ *adj*

as·pen \'as-pən\ *n* : any of several poplars with leaves that flutter in the lightest breeze [Old English *æspe*]

as·per·i·ty \a-'sper-ət-ē, ə-'sper-\ *n, pl* **-ties** **1** : **RIGOR** 3, **SEVERITY** ⟨the *asperities* of winter weather⟩ **2** : roughness of surface (as of a leaf) : **UNEVENNESS** **3** : harshness of temper, manner, or tone ⟨argued with asperity⟩ [Old French *aspretê,* from *aspre* "rough", from Latin *asper*]

as·perse \ə-'spərs, a-\ *vt* : to make aspersions against : **SLANDER** ⟨*asperse* someone's character⟩ [Latin *aspergere,* literally, "to sprinkle", from *ad-* + *spargere* "to scatter"]

as·per·sion \ə-'spər-zhən\ *n* : an injurious or offensive charge or implication ⟨cast *aspersions* on a person⟩

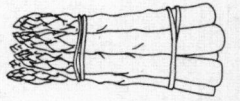

asparagus

\ə\	abut	\ng\	sing
\ər\	further	\ō\	bone
\a\	mat	\ȯ\	saw
\ā\	take	\ȯi\	coin
\ä\	cot, cart	\th\	thin
\aů\	out	\th\	this
\ch\	chin	\ü\	food
\e\	pet	\ů\	foot
\ē\	easy	\y\	yet
\g\	go	\yü\	few
\i\	tip	\yů\	cure
\ī\	life	\zh\	vision
\j\	job		

¹as·phalt \'as-ˌfȯlt\ *or* **as·phal·tum** \as-'fȯl-təm\ *n* **1** : a brown to black substance that is found in natural beds or obtained as a residue in petroleum refining and that consists chiefly of hydrocarbons **2** : any of various compositions of asphalt having diverse uses (as for pavement or for waterproof cement or paint) [Late Latin *aspaltus,* from Greek *asphaltos*] — **as·phal·tic** \as-'fȯl-tik\ *adj*

²asphalt *vt* : to cover with asphalt

as·pho·del \'as-fə-ˌdel\ *n* : any of several herbs of the lily family with white or yellow flowers in long erect spikes [Latin *asphodelus,* from Greek *asphodelos*]

as·phyx·ia \as-'fik-sē-ə\ *n* : a lack of oxygen or excess of carbon dioxide in the body that is usually caused by interruption of breathing and results in unconsciousness [Greek, "stopping of the pulse", from *a-* + *sphyzein* "to throb"]

as·phyx·i·ate \as-'fik-sē-ˌāt\ *vt* : to cause asphyxia in; *also* : to kill or make unconscious by interference with the normal oxygen intake — **as·phyx·i·a·tion** \ˌas-ˌfik-sē-'ā-shən\ *n* — **as·phyx·i·a·tor** \as-'fik-sē-ˌāt-ər\ *n*

as·pic \'as-pik\ *n* : a jelly (as of fish or meat stock) used cold especially to mold meat, fish, or vegetables [French, literally, "asp"]

as·pi·dis·tra \ˌas-pə-'dis-trə\ *n* : an Asian plant of the lily family with large basal leaves that is often grown as a houseplant [derived from Greek *aspis* "shield"]

as·pi·rant \'as-pə-rənt, -prənt, ə-'spī-rənt\ *n* : one that aspires

¹as·pi·rate \'as-pə-ˌrāt\ *vt* **1** : to pronounce with an initial \h\-sound ⟨we do not *aspirate* the word hour⟩ **2** : to draw or remove by suction ⟨blood *aspirated* from a vein by a syringe⟩ [Latin *aspirare* "to breathe on, aspire"]

²as·pi·rate \'as-pə-rət, -prət\ *n* **1** : an independent sound \h\ or a character (as the letter *h*) representing it **2** : a consonant having as its final element an \h\-like sound in the same syllable ⟨\t\ in English *toe* is an *aspirate*⟩

as·pi·ra·tion \ˌas-pə-'rā-shən\ *n* **1 a** (1) : pronunciation with an aspirate ⟨*aspiration* of the word *herb*⟩ (2) : pronunciation as an aspirate ⟨occasional *aspiration* of the final \t\ in *hot*⟩ **b** : an independent sound \h\ or its symbol **2** : a drawing of something in, out, up, or through by or as if by suction **3 a** : a strong desire to achieve something high or great **b** : an object of such desire SYN see AMBITION

as·pi·ra·tor \'as-pə-ˌrāt-ər\ *n* : an apparatus for producing suction or moving or collecting materials by suction

as·pire \ə-'spīr\ *vb* : to seek to attain something high or great ⟨*aspired* to the presidency⟩ [Latin *aspirare* "to breathe on, favor, aspire", from *ad-* + *spirare* "to breathe"] — **as·pir·er** *n*

as·pi·rin \'as-pə-rən, -prən\ *n* **1** : a white crystalline drug $C_9H_8O_4$ used as a remedy for pain and fever **2** : a tablet of aspirin [*a*cetyl + *spir*aeic acid (former name of salicylic acid), from New Latin *Spiraea*, genus of shrubs]

as regards *or* **as respects** *prep* : in regard to : with respect to

ass \'as\ *n* **1** : an animal resembling but smaller than the related horse and having a shorter mane, shorter hair on the tail, and longer ears : DONKEY **2** : a dull stupid person [Old English *assa*]

as·sail \ə-'sāl\ *vt* : to attack violently with blows or words [Old French *asaillir,* from Latin *assilire* "to leap upon", from *ad-* + *salire* "to leap"] SYN see ATTACK — **as·sail·able** \-'sā-lə-bəl\ *adj* — **as·sail·ant** \-'sā-lənt\ *n*

as·sas·sin \ə-'sas-n\ *n* : a person who kills another by surprise attack; *esp* : a murderer of a prominent person either for hire or from fanatical motives [Medieval Latin *assassinus,* from Arabic *ḥashshāshīn,* plural of

ḥashshāsh "one who chews or smokes hashish"]

□ **ORIGIN** During the time of the Crusades the members of a certain secret Muslim sect terrorized their enemies by performing murders as a religious duty. Because these acts were carried out under the influence of hashish, the killers became known as *ḥashshāshīn,* "eaters or smokers of hashish". This Arabic term was brought back to the West by the Crusaders, passing into Medieval Latin and thence into other European languages. English *assassin* was eventually extended to mean any murderer, though it is used especially for one who murders a politically important person.

as·sas·si·nate \ə-'sas-n-ˌāt\ *vt* **1** : to murder by a surprise attack especially for pay **2** : to injure or destroy unexpectedly and treacherously ⟨*assassinate* a person's character⟩ SYN see KILL — **as·sas·si·na·tion** \ə-ˌsas-n-'ā-shən\ *n*

¹as·sault \ə-'sȯlt\ *n* **1** : a violent physical or verbal attack : ONSLAUGHT **2** : an apparent attempt or a threat to do harm to another — compare BATTERY 1b [Old French *assaut,* from Latin *ad-* + *saltus* "leap", from *salire* "to leap"]

²assault *vt* : to make an assault upon SYN see ATTACK

assault rifle *n* : any of various automatic or semiautomatic rifles designed for military use

¹as·say \'as-ˌā, a-'sā\ *n* **1** *archaic* : TRIAL, ATTEMPT **2** : analysis (as of an ore, a metal, or a drug) to determine the presence, absence, or quantity of one or more substances [Old French *essai, assai* "test, essay, effort"]

²as·say \a-'sā, 'as-ˌā\ *vb* **1** : TRY, ATTEMPT **2 a** : to analyze (as an ore) for one or more valuable substances **b** : to judge the worth of : ESTIMATE — **as·say·er** *n*

as·se·gai *or* **as·sa·gai** \'as-i-ˌgī\ *n* : a slender hardwood usually iron-tipped spear used in southern Africa [derived from Arabic *az-zaghāya* "the assegai"]

as·sem·blage \ə-'sem-blij\ *n* **1** : a collection of persons or things : GATHERING **2** : the act of assembling : the state of being assembled

as·sem·ble \ə-'sem-bəl\ *vb* **-bled; -bling** \-bə-ling, -bling\ **1** : to collect into one place or group ⟨*assembled* the crew⟩ **2** : to fit together the parts of ⟨*assemble* a bicycle⟩ **3** : to meet together ⟨the right to *assemble* peacefully⟩ [Old French *assembler,* from Latin *ad-* + *simul* "together"] SYN see GATHER

as·sem·bler \ə-'sem-blər, -bə-lər\ *n* **1** : one that assembles **2 a** : a computer program that automatically converts instructions written in an assembly language into the equivalent machine language **b** : ASSEMBLY LANGUAGE

as·sem·bly \ə-'sem-blē\ *n, pl* **-blies 1** : a body of persons gathered together (as for deliberation, worship, or entertainment) **2** *cap* : a legislative body; *esp* : the lower house of a legislature **3** : the act or state of coming together : ASSEMBLAGE **4** : a signal for troops to assemble **5** : a collection of parts that go to make up a complete unit **6** : the translation of assembly language to machine language by an assembler

assembly language *n* : a code for programming a computer that is a close approximation of machine language but is more easily understood by humans

assembly line *n* : an arrangement of machines, equipment, and workers in which work passes from operation to operation in direct line until the product is assembled

as·sem·bly·man \ə-'sem-blē-mən\ *n* : a member of a legislative assembly

as·sem·bly·wom·an \-ˌwùm-ən\ *n* : a woman who is a member of a legislative assembly

¹as·sent \ə-'sent\ *vi* : to agree to something especially after thoughtful consideration : CONCUR [Old French *assenter,* from Latin *assentire,* from *ad-* + *sentire* "to feel"] □ SYN ASSENT, CONSENT, ACCEDE mean to agree with what has been proposed. ASSENT implies the action of the understanding or judgment toward propositions or opinions; CONSENT involves the will or the feelings and indicates acceptance or approval of or compliance with what is desired or requested; ACCEDE suggests a yielding, often under pressure, of assent or consent.

²**assent** *n* : an act of assenting : ACQUIESCENCE, AGREEMENT

as·sert \ə-'sərt\ *vt* **1** : to state clearly and strongly : declare positively ⟨*assert* an opinion⟩ **2** : to defend forcefully ⟨*assert* your rights⟩ [Latin *asserere*, from *ad-* + *serere* "to join"] □ SYN DECLARE, AFFIRM, AVOW: ASSERT implies stating confidently without need for proof or evidence; DECLARE often adds to ASSERT an implication of open or public statement; AFFIRM implies conviction of truth and willingness to stand by one's statement; AVOW implies open and emphatic declaration and personal responsibility for a statement. SYN see in addition MAINTAIN — **assert oneself** : to insist that others recognize one's rights

as·ser·tion \ə-'sər-shən\ *n* : the act of asserting; *also* : something asserted : DECLARATION

as·sert·ive \ə-'sərt-iv\ *adj* : characterized by self-confidence and boldness in expressing opinions — **as·sert·ive·ly** *adv* — **as·sert·ive·ness** *n*

asses *pl of* AS *or of* ASS

as·sess \ə-'ses\ *vt* **1** : to fix the rate or amount of ⟨*assessed* damages of $5000⟩ **2** : to set a value on (as property) for tax purposes ⟨a house *assessed* at $40,000⟩ **3** : to lay a tax or charge on ⟨the city *assessed* all car owners $5.00⟩ **4** : to determine the importance, size, or value of ⟨*assess* your chances of winning⟩ [probably from Medieval Latin *assessus*, past participle of *assidēre* "to assess", from Latin, "to sit beside, assist in giving judgment", from *ad-* + *sedēre* "to sit"] SYN see ESTIMATE — **as·sess·able** \ə-'ses-ə-bəl\ *adj*

as·sess·ment \ə-'ses-mənt\ *n* **1** : the act of assessing : APPRAISAL **2** : the amount or value assessed

as·ses·sor \ə-'ses-ər\ *n* : an official who assesses property for taxation

as·set \'as-ˌet\ *n* **1** *pl* : all the property (as cash, securities, real estate, or goods) of a person, corporation, or estate that may be used in payment of debts **2** : ADVANTAGE, RESOURCE [back-formation from obsolete *assets*, singular, "sufficient property to pay debts and legacies", from Old French *assez* "enough", from Latin *ad* "to" + *satis* "enough"]

as·sev·er·ate \ə-'sev-ə-ˌrāt\ *vt* : to state firmly or earnestly : AVER [Latin *asseverare*, from *ad-* + *severus* "severe"] — **as·sev·er·a·tion** \ə-ˌsev-ə-'rā-shən\ *n*

as·si·du·i·ty \ˌas-ə-'dü-ət-ē, -'dyü-\ *n* : the quality or state of being assiduous : DILIGENCE

as·sid·u·ous \ə-'sij-wəs, -ə-wəs\ *adj* : steadily attentive : DILIGENT [Latin *assiduus*, from *assidēre* "to sit beside", from *ad-* + *sedēre* "to sit"] — **as·sid·u·ous·ly** *adv* — **as·sid·u·ous·ness** *n*

as·sign \ə-'sīn\ *vt* **1** : to transfer to another ⟨*assign* a patent to the heirs⟩ **2 a** : to appoint to a post or duty **b** : PRESCRIBE ⟨*assign* the lesson⟩ **3** : to fix authoritatively ⟨*assign* a limit⟩ **4** : to attribute as a motive or reason ⟨ill health was *assigned* as the cause of the suicide⟩ [Old French *assigner*, from Latin *assignare*, from *ad-* + *signare* "to mark", from *signum* "mark, sign"] SYN see ALLOT — **as·sign·able** \ə-'sī-nə-bəl\ *adj* — **as·sign·er** \ə-'sī-nər\ *n*

as·sig·na·tion \ˌas-ig-'nā-shən\ *n* **1** : ASSIGNMENT 2 : TRYST 1

as·sign·ee \ə-ˌsī-'nē, ˌas-ˌī-; ˌas-ə-'nē\ *n* : a person to whom something is assigned

as·sign·ment \ə-'sīn-mənt\ *n* **1** : the act of assigning ⟨*assignment* of seats⟩ **2** : something assigned : an assigned task ⟨an *assignment* in arithmetic⟩ SYN see TASK

as·sim·i·late \ə-'sim-ə-ˌlāt\ *vb* **1 a** : to take something in and make it part of and like the thing it has joined ⟨*assimilate* nutrients into the body⟩ ⟨the nation assi-

milated millions of immigrants⟩ **b** : to comprehend thoroughly : ABSORB **2 a** : to make similar **b** : to alter by assimilation [Medieval Latin *assimilare*, from Latin *assimulare* "to make similar", from *ad-* + *simulare* "to make similar, simulate"] SYN see ABSORB — **as·sim·i·la·bil·i·ty** \-ˌsim-ə-lə-'bil-ət-ē\ *n* — **as·sim·i·la·ble** \-'sim-ə-lə-bəl\ *adj* — **as·sim·i·la·tor** \-'sim-ə-ˌlāt-ər\ *n*

as·sim·i·la·tion \ə-ˌsim-ə-'lā-shən\ *n* **1** : the act or process of assimilating; *esp* : the conversion of nutrients (as digested food) into protoplasm **2** : change of a sound in speech so that it becomes identical with or similar to a neighboring sound (in the word *impractical* the \n\ of the prefix *in-* has undergone *assimilation*) — **as·sim·i·la·tive** \-'sim-ə-ˌlāt-iv, -lət-\ *adj*

¹**as·sist** \ə-'sist\ *vb* : to give support or aid : HELP [Latin *assistere* "to help, stand by", from *ad-* + *sistere* "to stand"]

²**assist** *n* **1** : an act of assistance : AID **2** : the action of a player who by passing a ball or puck enables a teammate to make a putout or score a goal

as·sis·tance \ə-'sis-təns\ *n* : the act of assisting or the aid supplied : SUPPORT

as·sis·tant \ə-'sis-tənt\ *n* : one that assists : HELPER; *also* : one that serves in a subordinate capacity — **assistant** *adj*

as·size \ə-'sīz\ *n* : a session of an English superior court formerly held periodically for the trial of civil and criminal cases in most counties by judges traveling on circuit — usually used in pl. [Old French *assise* "session, settlement", from *asseoir* "to seat", from Latin *assidēre* "to sit beside"]

¹**as·so·ci·ate** \ə-'sō-shē-ˌāt, -sē-ˌāt\ *vb* **1** : to join or come together as partners, friends, or companions **2** : to connect or bring (as ideas) together or into a relationship **3** : to combine or join with other parts : UNITE [Latin *associare* "to unite", from *ad-* + *sociare* "to join", from *socius* "companion"]

²**as·so·ci·ate** \ə-'sō-shət; ə-'sō-shē-ət, -'sō-sē-, -ˌāt\ *n* **1** : a fellow worker : COLLEAGUE **2** : COMPANION 1, COMRADE **3** *often cap* : a degree conferred especially by a junior college ⟨*associate* in arts⟩ — **associate** *adj*

as·so·ci·a·tion \ə-ˌsō-sē-'ā-shən, -ˌsō-shē-\ *n* **1** : the act of associating : the state of being associated **2** : an organization of persons having a common interest : SOCIETY **3** : a feeling, memory, or thought connected with a person, place, or thing ⟨pleasant *associations* with the beach⟩ **4** : the formation of polymers by linkage through hydrogen bonds **5** : a major ecological unit characterized by essential uniformity — **as·so·ci·a·tion·al** \-shnəl, -shən-l\ *adj*

association football *n* : SOCCER

as·so·ci·a·tive \ə-'sō-shē-ˌāt-iv, -'sō-sē-, -'sō-shət-iv\ *adj* **1** : of, relating to, or involved in association and especially mental association ⟨*associative* powers of the mind⟩ **2** : dependent on or acquired by association or learning **3** : combining or concerning the combination of mathematical elements in such a manner that when the order remains the same the result is independent of the grouping — **as·so·ci·a·tive·ly** *adv* — **as·so·cia·tiv·i·ty** \ə-ˌsō-shē-ə-'tiv-ət-ē, -ˌsō-sē-ə-, -ˌsō-shə-'tiv-\ *n*

associative neuron *n* : a neuron that transmits impulses along the path from a sensory neuron to a motor neuron

as·so·nance \'as-ə-nəns\ *n* **1** : resemblance of sound in words or syllables **2** : repetition of vowels without repetition of consonants (as in *story* and *holy*) used as an alternative to rhyme in verse [French, from Latin *assonare* "to answer with the same sound", from *ad-* + *sonare* "to sound"] — **as·so·nant** \-nənt\ *adj or n*

as soon as *conj* : immediately at or just after the time that ⟨left *as soon as* the meeting was over⟩

as·sort \ə-'sȯrt\ *vb* **1** : to distribute into groups of a like kind : CLASSIFY **2** : to agree in kind : HARMONIZE

\ə\	abut	\ng\	sing
\ər\	further	\ō\	bone
\a\	mat	\ȯ\	saw
\ā\	take	\ȯi\	coin
\ä\	cot, cart	\th\	thin
\au̇\	out	\th\	this
\ch\	chin	\ü\	food
\e\	pet	\u̇\	foot
\ē\	easy	\y\	yet
\g\	go	\yü\	few
\i\	tip	\yu̇\	cure
\ī\	life	\zh\	vision
\j\	job		

[Middle French *assortir,* from *a-* "ad-" + *sorte* "sort"] — **as·sort·a·tive** \ə-'sȯrt-ət-iv\ *adj* — **as·sort·er** *n*

as·sort·ed \ə-'sȯrt-əd\ *adj* **1** : consisting of various kinds **2** : suited by nature, character, or design ⟨an ill-*assorted* pair⟩

as·sort·ment \ə-'sȯrt-mənt\ *n* **1 a** : arrangement in classes **b** : VARIETY **2** : a collection of assorted things or persons

as·suage \ə-'swāj\ *vt* **1** : to lessen the intensity of (as pain) : EASE **2** : SLAKE 2, QUENCH ⟨*assuage* thirst with cool water⟩ [Old French *assouagier,* from Latin *ad-* + *suavis* "sweet, pleasant"] — **as·suage·ment** \-mənt\ *n*

as·sume \ə-'süm\ *vb* **1** : to take up or in or on : RECEIVE ⟨what values may x *assume*⟩ **2 a** : to take to or upon oneself ⟨*assume* a responsibility⟩ **b** : to put on (clothing) : DON **3** : to take as one's right or possession : SEIZE **4** : to put on in appearance only : FEIGN **5** : to take for granted : SUPPOSE [Latin *assumere,* from *ad-* + *sumere* "to take up, take", from *sub-* "up" + *emere* "to take, buy"] ☐ SYN ASSUME, PRESUME mean to suppose to be true or real. ASSUME may imply either reasonable grounds for supposing or a deliberate purpose in taking as definite something not actually settled or determined; PRESUME implies greater confidence in supposing without proof or justification.

as·sumed \ə-'sümd\ *adj* **1 a** : PRETENDED ⟨an *assumed* role⟩ **b** : FALSE ⟨an *assumed* name⟩ **2** : taken for granted ⟨the *assumed* reason for absence⟩

as·sum·ing *adj* : ARROGANT 1, PRESUMPTUOUS

as·sump·tion \ə-'səm-shən, -'səmp-\ **1** *cap* : August 15 observed as a church festival in commemoration of the taking up of the Virgin Mary into heaven **2** : a taking to or upon oneself **3** : the act of laying claim to or taking possession of **4 a** : the supposition that something is true **b** : a fact or statement taken for granted [Latin *assumptio* "taking up", from *assumere* "to take up, assume"]

as·sur·ance \ə-'shùr-əns\ *n* **1** : the act of assuring : PLEDGE **2** : the state of being sure or certain **3** : SAFETY 1 **4** *chiefly British* : INSURANCE 2 **5** : SELF-RELIANCE **6** : extreme self-confidence : PRESUMPTION

as·sure \ə-'shùr\ *vt* **1** : INSURE 1 **2** : REASSURE 2 ⟨tried to *assure* the worried neighbors⟩ **3** : to make sure or certain **4** : to inform positively ⟨can *assure* you of their dependability⟩ [Middle French *assurer,* from Medieval Latin *assecurare,* from Latin *ad-* + *securus* "secure"]

¹as·sured \ə-'shùrd\ *adj* **1** : characterized by certainty or security : GUARANTEED ⟨an *assured* market⟩ **2 a** : SELF-CONFIDENT ⟨an *assured* dancer⟩ **b** : SELF-SATISFIED **3** : satisfied as to the certainty or truth of a matter : CONVINCED — **as·sur·ed·ly** \-'shùr-əd-lē\ *adv* — **as·sur·ed·ness** \-əd-nəs\ *n*

²assured *n* : a person whose life or property is insured

As·syr·i·an \ə-'sir-ē-ən\ *n* **1** : a member of an ancient Semitic race forming the Assyrian nation **2** : the Semitic language of the Assyrians — **Assyrian** *adj*

as·ta·tine \'as-tə-,tēn\ *n* : a radioactive chemical element discovered by bombarding bismuth with helium nuclei — see ELEMENT table [Greek *astatos* "unsteady", from *a-* + *statos* "standing", from *histanai* "to cause to stand"]

as·ter \'as-tər\ *n* **1** : any of various mostly fall-blooming leafy-stemmed composite herbs usually with showy white, pink, purple, or yellow flower heads **2** : a system of radiating fibers about a centrosome of a cell occurring especially during mitosis and meiosis [Latin, from Greek *astēr,* literally, "star"]

as·ter·isk \'as-tə-,risk\ *n* : a character * used as a reference mark or to show the omission of letters or words [Late Latin *asteriscus,* from Greek *asteriskos,* literally, "little star", from *astēr* "star"] — **asterisk** *vt*

as·ter·ism \'as-tə-,riz-əm\ *n* : a star-shaped figure of light exhibited by some crystals and caused by reflection from internal imperfections

astern \ə-'stərn\ *adv* **1** : behind a ship or airplane : in the rear **2** : at or toward the stern of a ship or aircraft **3** : BACKWARD

as·ter·oid \'as-tə-,rȯid\ *n* : one of thousands of small planets chiefly between Mars and Jupiter with diameters from a fraction of a kilometer to nearly 800 kilometers [Greek *asteroeidēs* "starlike", from *astēr* "star"]

asteroid belt *n* : the region of interplanetary space between the orbits of Mars and Jupiter in which asteroids are formed

as·the·nia \as-'thē-nē-ə\ *n* : lack or loss of strength : DEBILITY [Greek *asthenia,* from *asthenēs* "weak", from *a-* + *sthenos* "strength"]

as·then·ic \-'then-ik\ *adj* **1** : of, relating to, or exhibiting asthenia : WEAK **2** : characterized by slender build and slight muscular development : ECTOMORPHIC

as·theno·sphere \as-'then-ə-,sfiər\ *n* : a zone of the earth which lies beneath the lithosphere and within which material yields readily to persistent stresses [Greek *asthenēs* "weak" + English *sphere*]

asth·ma \'az-mə\ *n* : a condition often of allergic origin that is marked by labored breathing with wheezing, a feeling of tightness in the chest, and coughing [Medieval Latin *asma,* from Greek *asthma*] — **asth·mat·ic** \az-'mat-ik\ *adj or n* — **asth·mat·i·cal·ly** \-'mat-i-kə-lē, -klē\ *adv*

as though *conj* : as if

astig·ma·tism \ə-'stig-mə-,tiz-əm\ *n* : a defect of an optical system (as of the eye) that prevents light from focusing accurately and results in a blurred image or indistinct vision [²*a-* + Greek *stigma* "mark"] — **as·tig·mat·ic** \,as-tig-'mat-ik\ *adj* — **as·tig·mat·i·cal·ly** \-'mat-i-kə-lē, -klē\ *adj*

astir \ə-'stər\ *adj* **1** : being in a state of activity **2** : being out of bed : UP

as to *prep* **1** : with regard or reference to : as for : ABOUT ⟨at a loss *as to* how to explain the mistake⟩ **2** : according to : BY ⟨graded *as to* size and color⟩

as·ton·ish \ə-'stän-ish\ *vt* : to strike with sudden wonder : surprise greatly : AMAZE [probably from earlier *astony,* from Old French *estoner,* from Latin *ex-* + *tonare* "to thunder"] SYN see SURPRISE

as·ton·ish·ing *adj* : causing astonishment : AMAZING — **as·ton·ish·ing·ly** \-'stän-i-shing-lē\ *adv*

as·ton·ish·ment \ə-'stän-ish-mənt\ *n* **1** : the state of being astonished **2** : a cause of amazement or wonder

as·tound \ə-'staùnd\ *vb* : to fill with bewilderment and wonder [Middle English *astoned,* past participle of *astonen* "to astonish", from Old French *estoner*] SYN see SURPRISE

astrad·dle \ə-'strad-l\ *adv or prep* : ASTRIDE

as·trag·a·lus \ə-'strag-ə-ləs\ *n, pl* -**li** \-,lī, -,lē\ : a proximal bone of the tarsus [New Latin, from Greek *astragalos*]

as·tra·khan *or* **as·tra·chan** \'as-trə-kən, -,kan\ *n, often cap* **1** : karakul of Russian origin **2** : a cloth with a usually wool, curled, and looped pile resembling karakul [*Astrakhan,* Russia]

as·tral \'as-trəl\ *adj* **1** : of or relating to the stars : STARRY **2** : of or relating to a cell aster **3 a** : VISIONARY **b** : elevated in station or position [Latin *astrum* "star", from Greek *astron*] — **as·tral·ly** *adv*

astray \ə-'strā\ *adv or adj* **1** : off the right path or route : STRAYING **2** : into error : MISTAKEN

¹astride \ə-'strīd\ *adv* : with one leg on each side

²astride *prep* : on or above and with one leg on each side of

¹as·trin·gent \ə-'strin-jənt\ *adj* **1** : able or tending to shrink body tissues ⟨*astringent* lotions⟩ ⟨an *astringent* fruit⟩ **2** : AUSTERE 1a ⟨an *astringent* manner⟩ [Latin *astringere* "to bind fast, contract", from *ad-* + *stringere* "to bind tight"] — **as·trin·gen·cy** \-jən-sē\ *n* — **as·trin·gent·ly** *adv*

²astringent *n* : an astringent agent or substance

astro- *combining form* : star : heavens : astronomical 〈*astro*physics〉 [Greek *astron* "star"]

as·tro·labe \'as-trə-ˌlāb\ *n* : a compact instrument used to observe the positions of celestial bodies before the invention of the sextant [Medieval Latin *astrolabium*, derived from Greek *astrolabos*, from *astron* "star" + *lambanein* "to take"]

as·trol·o·ger \ə-'sträl-ə-jər\ *n* : one who practices astrology

as·trol·o·gy \-jē\ *n* : study of or divination based on the effect that the stars and their aspects and positions are held to have on human affairs — **as·tro·log·i·cal** \ˌas-trə-'läj-i-kəl\ *adj* — **as·tro·log·i·cal·ly** \-'läj-i-kə-lē, -klē\ *adv*

as·tro·naut \'as-trə-ˌnȯt, -ˌnät\ *n* : a traveler in a spacecraft; *also* : a trainee for spaceflight [*astro-* + *-naut* (as in *aeronaut*)] — **as·tro·nau·ti·cal** \ˌas-trə-'nȯt-i-kəl\ *adj* — **as·tro·nau·ti·cal·ly** \-i-kə-lē, -klē\ *adv*

as·tro·nau·tics \-'nȯt-iks\ *n* : the science of the construction and operation of spacecraft

as·tron·o·mer \ə-'strän-ə-mər\ *n* : one who is skilled in astronomy or who observes celestial phenomena

as·tro·nom·i·cal \ˌas-trə-'näm-i-kəl\ *or* **as·tro·nom·ic** \-'näm-ik\ *adj* **1** : of or relating to astronomy **2** : extremely or unimaginably large 〈an *astronomical* amount of money〉 — **as·tro·nom·i·cal·ly** \-'näm-i-kə-lē, -klē\ *adv*

astronomical unit *n* : a unit of length used in astronomy equal to the mean distance of the earth from the sun or about 150 million kilometers

as·tron·o·my \ə-'strän-ə-mē\ *n* : the science of the celestial bodies and of their physical characteristics, relative motions, composition, and history [Old French *astronomie*, from Latin *astronomia*, from Greek, from *astron* "star" + *nomos* "law"]

as·tro·phys·ics \ˌas-trə-'fiz-iks\ *n* : a branch of astronomy dealing with the physical and chemical makeup of the celestial bodies — **as·tro·phys·i·cal** \-'fiz-i-kəl\ *adj* — **as·tro·phys·i·cist** \-'fiz-ə-səst\ *n*

as·tute \ə-'stüt, a-, -'styüt\ *adj* : CLEVER 〈an *astute* business person〉; *also* : SLY 1 [Latin *astutus*, from *astus* "craft"] SYN see SHREWD — **as·tute·ly** *adv* — **as·tute·ness** *n*

asun·der \ə-'sən-dər\ *adv or adj* **1** : into parts 〈torn *asunder*〉 **2** : apart from each other 〈as in position or nature〉

¹as well as *conj* : and in addition 〈brave *as well as* loyal〉 〈fish for food *as well as* for sport〉

²as well as *prep* : in addition to : BESIDES 〈*as well as* being a poet, she is an exciting story teller〉

as yet *adv* : up to the present time : YET

asy·lum \ə-'sī-ləm\ *n* **1** : a place of refuge and protection giving shelter to criminals and debtors **2** : a place of retreat and security : SHELTER **3** : protection afforded by or as if by an asylum : REFUGE 〈a political refugee given *asylum* in the embassy〉 **4** : an institution for the relief or care of the destitute or afflicted and especially the insane [Latin, from Greek *asylon*, from *asylos* "inviolable", from *a-* + *sylon* "right of seizure"]

asym·met·ric \ˌā-sə-'me-trik\ *adj* : not symmetrical — **asym·met·ri·cal** \-tri-kəl\ *adj* — **asym·met·ri·cal·ly** \-tri-kə-lē, -klē\ *adv* — **asym·me·try** \'ā-'sim-ə-trē\ *n*

as·ymp·tote \'as-əm-ˌtōt, -əmp-\ *n* : a straight line that is approached more and more closely by a curve that never coincides with it no matter how far the curve is extended [Greek *asymptōtos* "not meeting", from *a-* + *sympiptein* "to meet", from *syn-* + *piptein* "to fall"] — **as·ymp·tot·ic** \ˌas-əm-'tät-ik, -əmp-\ *adj*

asyn·de·ton \ə-'sin-də-ˌtän\ *n, pl* **-detons** *or* **-de·ta** \-dət-ə\ : omission of the connectives ordinarily expected 〈as in I came, I saw, I conquered〉 [Late Latin, from Greek, from *asyndetos* "unconnected", from *a-* + *syndein* "to bind together", from *syn-* + *dein* "to bind"] — **as·yn·det·ic** \ˌas-n-'det-ik\ *adj* — **as·yn·det·i·cal·ly** \-'det-i-kə-lē, -klē\ *adv*

at \ət, at, 'at\ *prep* — used as a function word to indicate (1) location in space or time 〈staying *at* a hotel〉 〈be here *at* six〉 〈sick *at* heart〉, (2) a goal 〈aim *at* a target〉 〈laugh *at* them〉, (3) a condition 〈*at* work〉 〈*at* liberty〉 〈*at* ease〉, (4) a means, cause, or source 〈sold *at* auction〉 〈angry *at* this answer〉 〈suffered *at* their hands〉, or (5) a rate, degree, or position in a scale or series 〈drove *at* 40 kilometers an hour〉 〈retire *at* 65〉 [Old English *æt*]

at- — see AD-

at all \ət-'ȯl, ə-'tȯl, at-'ȯl\ *adv* : in any way or respect : to the least extent or degree : under any circumstances 〈not *at all* likely〉 〈doesn't smoke *at all*〉

at·a·rac·tic \ˌat-ə-'rak-tik\ *or* **at·a·rax·ic** \-'rak-sik\ *n* : a tranquilizer drug [Greek *ataraktos* "calm", from *a-* + *tarassein* "to disturb"] — **ataractic** *adj*

at·a·vism \'at-ə-ˌviz-əm\ *n* **1** : recurrence in an organism of a character typical of ancestors more remote than the parents usually due to recombination of ancestral genes **2** : an individual or character manifesting atavism [French *atavisme*, from Latin *atavus* "ancestor"] — **at·a·vis·tic** \ˌat-ə-'vis-tik\ *adj*

atax·ia \ə-'tak-sē-ə, ā-\ *n* : inability to coordinate voluntary muscular movements [Greek, "confusion", from *a-* + *tassein* "to put in order"] — **atax·ic** \-sik\ *adj*

ate *past of* EAT

¹-ate \ət, ˌāt\ *n suffix* **1** : one acted upon (in a specified way) 〈distill*ate*〉 **2** : chemical compound derived from a (specified) compound or element; *esp* : salt or ester of an acid with a name ending in *-ic* 〈borate〉 [Latin *-atus, -atum,* masculine and neuter of *-atus,* past participle ending]

²-ate *n suffix* **1** : office : function : rank : group of persons holding a (specified) office or rank 〈professor*ate*〉 **2** : state : dominion : jurisdiction 〈emir*ate*〉 〈khan*ate*〉 [Latin *-atus*]

³-ate *adj suffix* : marked by having 〈chord*ate*〉 [Latin *-atus,* past participle ending]

⁴-ate \ˌāt\ *vb suffix* **1** : cause to be modified or affected by 〈camphor*ate*〉 **2** : cause to become 〈activ*ate*〉 **3** : furnish with 〈aer*ate*〉 [Middle English *-aten,* from Latin *-atus,* past participle ending]

ate·lier \ˌat-l-'yā\ *n* **1** : an artist's or designer's studio **2** : WORKSHOP [French]

a tem·po \ä-'tem-pō\ *adv or adj* : in time — used as a direction in music to return to the original rate of speed [Italian]

Ath·a·na·sian Creed \ˌath-ə-'nā-zhən-, -ˌnā-shən-\ *n* : a Christian creed originating in Europe about A.D. 400 and relating especially to the Trinity and Incarnation [*Athanasius,* died 373, bishop of Alexandria]

athe·ism \'ā-thē-ˌiz-əm\ *n* : the belief that there is no God : denial of the existence of a supreme being [Middle French *athéisme,* from Greek *atheos* "godless", from *a-* + *theos* "god"]

athe·ist \-thē-əst\ *n* : a person who believes there is no God — **athe·is·tic** \ˌā-thē-'is-tik\ *adj* — **athe·is·ti·cal·ly** \-'is-ti-kə-lē, -klē\ *adv* □ SYN ATHEIST, AGNOSTIC, FREETHINKER mean one who does not take an orthodox religious position. An ATHEIST denies the existence of God and rejects all religious faith and practice; an AGNOSTIC withholds belief because of unwillingness to accept the evidence of revelation and spiritual experience; a FREETHINKER is one who has lost or rejected traditional faith and believes only in what is rational and credible.

ath·el·ing \'ath-ə-ling, 'ath-\ *n* : an Anglo-Saxon prince or nobleman [Old English *ætheling,* from *æthelu* "nobility"]

ath·e·nae·um *or* **ath·e·ne·um** \ˌath-ə-'nē-əm\ *n* **1** : a literary or scientific association **2** : LIBRARY 1 [Latin *Athenaeum,* a school in ancient Rome for the study of arts, from Greek *Athēnaion,* a temple of Athena, from *Athēnē* "Athena"]

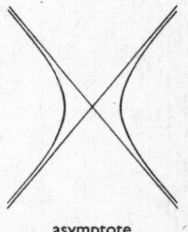

asymptote

\ə\ abut   \ng\ si**ng**
\ər\ fu**r**the**r**   \ō\ b**o**ne
\a\ m**a**t   \ȯ\ s**a**w
\ā\ t**a**ke   \ȯi\ c**oi**n
\ä\ c**o**t, c**a**rt   \th\ **th**in
\aú\ **ou**t   \th\ **th**is
\ch\ **ch**in   \ü\ f**oo**d
\e\ p**e**t   \ú\ f**oo**t
\ē\ **e**asy   \y\ **y**et
\g\ **g**o   \yü\ f**ew**
\i\ t**i**p   \yú\ c**u**re
\ī\ l**i**fe   \zh\ vi**s**ion
\j\ **j**ob

ath·ero·scle·ro·sis \,ath-ə-rō-sklə-'rō-səs\ *n* : an arteriosclerosis in which fatty substances are deposited in
the inner layer of the arteries [Latin *atheroma* "tumor
containing matter resembling gruel", from Greek
athērōma, from *athēra* "gruel"] — **ath·ero·scle·rot·ic**
\-sklə-'rät-ik\ *adj*

athirst \ə-'thərst\ *adj* **l** *archaic* : THIRSTY **2** : having a
strong desire : EAGER [Old English *ofthyrst,* past participle of *ofthyrstan* "to suffer from thirst", from *of*
"off, from" + *thyrstan* "to thirst"]

ath·lete \'ath-,lēt\ *n* : a person who is trained in or
good at games and exercises that require physical
skill, endurance, and strength [Latin *athleta,* from
Greek *athlētēs,* from *athlein* "to contend for a prize",
from *athlon* "prize, contest"]

athlete's foot *n* : ringworm of the feet

ath·let·ic \ath-'let-ik\ *adj* **l** : of, relating to, or characteristic of athletes or athletics **2** : VIGOROUS 1, ACTIVE
3 : characterized by heavy frame, large chest, and powerful muscular development **4** : used by athletes —
ath·let·i·cal·ly \-'let-i-kə-lē, -klē\ *adv*

ath·let·ics \ath-'let-iks\ *n sing or pl* : games, sports,
and exercises requiring strength and skill

athletic supporter *n* : a supporter for the genitals worn
by men participating in sports or other strenuous activities

-athon \ə-,thän\ *n combining form* : contest of endurance [*marathon*]

¹athwart \ə-'thwȯrt, *nautical often* -'thȯrt\ *adv* :
across especially in an oblique direction

²athwart *prep* **l** : ACROSS **2** : in opposition to

atilt \ə-'tilt\ *adj or adv* : in a tilted position

-a·tion \'ā-shən\ *n suffix* : action or process : something connected with an action or process
⟨discolor*ation*⟩ ⟨flirt*ation*⟩ [Latin *-ation-, -atio*]

-a·tive \,āt-iv, ət-\ *adj suffix* **l** : of, relating to, or connected with ⟨authorit*ative*⟩ **2** : tending to ⟨talk*ative*⟩
[Latin *-ativus,* from *-atus* "-ate" + *-ivus* "-ive"]

At·lan·tic salmon \ət-'lant-ik-\ *n* : SALMON 1a

Atlantic time *n* : the time of the 4th time zone west of
Greenwich that includes the Canadian Maritime provinces

at·las \'at-ləs\ *n* **l a** : a book of maps often including
descriptive text **b** : a book of tables, charts, or illustrations ⟨an *atlas* of anatomy⟩ **2** : the first vertebra of the
neck [*Atlas,* a Titan of Greek mythology] □ ORIGIN Atlas was one of the Titans or giants of Greek mythology,
whose rule of the world in an early age was overthrown by Zeus in a mighty battle. Atlas was believed
to be responsible for holding up the sky, a task which
he tried unsuccessfully to have Hercules assume. In
his published collection of maps, the 16th century
Flemish cartographer Gerhardus Mercator included on
the title page a picture of Atlas supporting the heavens, and he gave the book the title *Atlas.* Other early
collections of maps subsequently included similar pictures of Atlas, and such books came to be called *at-
lases.*

at·mo·sphere \'at-mə-,sfiər\ *n* **l a** : the whole mass of
air surrounding the earth **b** : a gaseous mass surrounding a celestial body (as a planet) **2** : the air in a particular place ⟨the stuffy *atmosphere* of this room⟩ **3** : a
surrounding influence or environment ⟨the home *atmosphere*⟩ **4** : a unit of pressure equal to the pressure
of the air at sea level or about 14.7 pounds per square
inch (about 10 newtons per square centimeter)
[Greek *atmos* "vapor" + Latin *sphaera* "sphere"] —
at·mo·spher·ic \,at-mə-'sfiər-ik, -'sfer-\ *adj* — **at·mo·
spher·i·cal·ly** \-i-kə-lē, -klē\ *adv*

at·mo·spher·ics \,at-mə-'sfiər-iks, -'sfer-\ *n pl* : static
produced by atmospheric electrical phenomena (as
lightning); *also* : the electrical phenomena causing
such disturbances

atoll \'a-,tȯl, -,täl, -,tōl, 'ā-\ *n* : a ring-shaped coral island
or string of islands consisting of a coral reef surround-

ing a lagoon [*atolu,* from a language of the Maldive
islands]

at·om \'at-əm\ *n* **l** : a tiny particle : BIT **2 a** : the smallest particle of an element that can exist either alone
or in combination ⟨an *atom* of hydrogen⟩ **b** : ATOMIC
ENERGY [Latin *atomus* "indivisible particle", from
Greek *atomos,* from *atomos* "indivisible", from *a-* +
temnein "to cut"] □ ORIGIN Some ancient philosophers believed that matter is infinitely divisible, that
any particle, no matter how small, can always be divided into smaller particles. Others believed that there
must be a limit, that everything in the universe must
be made up of tiny indivisible particles. Such a hypothetical particle was called in Greek *atomos,* which
means "indivisible". According to modern atomic theory, all matter is made up of tiny particles called *atoms* after the ancient Greek *atomos,* and the atoms of
any one chemical element are identical. Although the
atom is the smallest particle of an element that has the
characteristics of that element, it has turned out that
atoms are not indivisible after all. Indeed, the splitting
of atoms has been used, as in the explosion of atom
bombs, to produce vast amounts of energy.

atom bomb *n* : a bomb whose violent explosive power
is due to the sudden release of atomic energy; *esp* : a
bomb whose energy results from the splitting of nuclei of a heavy chemical element (as plutonium or uranium) by neutrons in a very rapid chain reaction — **at·
om–bomb** \,at-əm-'bäm\ *vt*

atom·ic \ə-'täm-ik\ *adj* **l** : of, relating to, or concerned
with atoms, atomic energy, or atom bombs **2** : extremely small : MINUTE **3** : existing in the state of separate atoms ⟨*atomic* hydrogen⟩ — **atom·i·cal·ly** \-i-kə-
lē, -klē\ *adv*

atomic age *n* : the period of history characterized by
the use of atomic energy

atomic bomb *n* : ATOM BOMB

atomic clock *n* : a precision clock that depends for its
operation on an electrical oscillator regulated by the
natural vibration frequencies of an atomic system (as a
cesium atom)

atomic energy *n* : energy that can be liberated by
changes in the nucleus of an atom (as by fission of a
heavy nucleus or fusion of light nuclei into heavier
ones with accompanying loss of mass)

atomic mass *n* : the mass of any species of atom usually
expressed in atomic mass units

atomic mass unit *n* : a unit of mass for expressing
masses of atoms, molecules, or nuclear particles equal
to ¹/₁₂ of the atomic mass of the most abundant isotope
of carbon

atomic number *n* : a number that is characteristic of a
chemical element and represents the number of protons in the nucleus

atomic pile *n* : REACTOR 2b

atom·ics \ə-'täm-iks\ *n pl* : the science of atoms especially when involving atomic energy

atomic theory *n* **l** : a theory of the nature of matter: all
material substances are composed of minute particles
or atoms of a comparatively small number of kinds and
all the atoms of the same kind are uniform in size,
weight, and other properties **2** : any of several theories of the structure of the atom; *esp* : one holding that
the atom is composed essentially of a small positively
charged comparatively heavy nucleus surrounded by a
comparatively large arrangement of electrons

atomic weight *n* : the average atomic mass of an element compared to ¹/₁₂ the mass of the most abundant
isotope of carbon

at·om·ize \'at-ə-,mīz\ *vt* **l** : to reduce to minute particles or to a fine spray **2** : to treat as made up of many
discrete units **3** : to subject to atom-bombing — **at·
om·iza·tion** \,at-ə-mə-'zā-shən\ *n*

at·om·iz·er \'at-ə-,mī-zər\ *n* : a device for atomizing a
liquid (as a perfume or disinfectant)

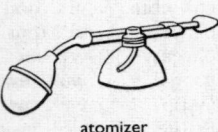

atomizer

atom smasher *n* : ACCELERATOR b

aton·al \'ā-tōn-l, 'a-\ *adj* : characterized by avoidance of traditional musical tonality — **ato·nal·i·ty** \,ā-tō-'nal-ət-ē\ *n* — **atonal·ly** \'ā-tōn-l-ē, 'a-\ *adv*

atone \ə-'tōn\ *vb* : to do something to make up for a wrong done : make amends [Middle English *atonen* "to become reconciled", from *at on* "in harmony", from *at* + *on* "one"]

atone·ment \-mənt\ *n* **1** : the reconciliation of God and humanity held by Christians to have come through the death of Jesus Christ **2** : reparation for an offense or injury : SATISFACTION

¹atop \ə-'täp\ *prep* : on top of

²atop *adv* : on, to, or at the top

ATP \,ā-,tē-'pē, ā-'tē-,pē\ *n* : a nucleotide that is a derivative of adenosine and supplies energy for many processes of living cells by undergoing conversion to ADP and surrendering a phosphate group [*a*denosine *trip*hosphate]

atri·al \'ā-trē-əl\ *adj* : of or relating to an atrium

atrio·ven·tric·u·lar \,ā-trē-ō-ven-'trik-yə-lər, -vən-\ *adj* : of, relating to, or located between an atrium and ventricle of the heart

atri·um \'ā-trē-əm\ *n, pl* **atria** \-trē-ə\ *also* **atri·ums** **1** : the central hall of a Roman house **2** : an anatomical cavity or passage; *esp* : the chamber or either of the chambers of the heart that receives blood from the veins [Latin]

atro·cious \ə-'trō-shəs\ *adj* **1** : extremely wicked, brutal, or cruel **2** : APPALLING ⟨the *atrocious* weapons of modern war⟩ **3 a** : utterly revolting ⟨*atrocious* working conditions⟩ **b** : of very bad quality ⟨*atrocious* handwriting⟩ [Latin *atroc-, atrox* "gloomy, atrocious", from *ater* "black"] SYN see OUTRAGEOUS — **atro·cious·ly** *adv* — **atro·cious·ness** *n*

atroc·i·ty \ə-'träs-ət-ē\ *n, pl* **-ties** **1** : the quality or state of being atrocious **2** : an atrocious act, object, or situation

¹at·ro·phy \'a-trə-fē\ *n, pl* **-phies** : decrease in size or wasting away of a body part or tissue [Late Latin *atrophia*, from Greek, from *atrophos* "ill fed", from *a-* + *trephein* "to nourish"] — **atroph·ic** \ā-'trō-fik, 'ā-'\ *adj*

²at·ro·phy \'a-trə-fē, -,fī\ *vi* **-phied; -phy·ing** : to undergo atrophy

at·ro·pine \'a-trə-,pēn\ *n* : a poisonous white crystalline compound $C_{17}H_{23}NO_3$ from belladonna and related plants used especially to relieve spasms and to dilate the pupil of the eye [New Latin *Atropa*, genus name of belladonna, from Greek *Atropos*, one of the Fates]

at·tach \ə-'tach\ *vb* **1** : to take money or property by legal authority especially to secure payment of a debt ⟨*attach* one's salary⟩ **2** : to tie or bind by feelings of affection ⟨they were *attached* to their dog⟩ **3** : to fasten to something (as by tying or gluing) ⟨*attach* a label to a package⟩ **4** : to think of as belonging to something : ATTRIBUTE ⟨*attach* no importance to a remark⟩ **5** : to be associated or connected ⟨the interest that naturally *attaches* to a statement by the president⟩ [Middle French *attacher*, from Old French *estachier*, from *estache* "stake", of Germanic origin] — **at·tach·able** \-ə-bəl\ *adj*

at·ta·ché \,at-ə-'shā, ,a-,ta-, ə-,ta-\ *n* **1** : a technical expert on the diplomatic staff of a country at a foreign capital ⟨a military *attaché*⟩ **2** : ATTACHÉ CASE [French, past participle of *attacher*]

at·ta·ché case \,at-ə-'shā-,, ,a-,ta-; ə-'tash-,ā-,\ *n* : a small thin suitcase used especially for carrying papers and documents

at·tach·ment \ə-'tach-mənt\ *n* **1** : a seizure by legal process or the writ commanding such seizure **2** : the state of being personally attached : FIDELITY, FONDNESS **3** : a device that can be attached to a machine or implement ⟨*attachments* for a vacuum cleaner⟩ **4** : the

physical connection by which one thing is attached to another **5** : the process of physically attaching

¹at·tack \ə-'tak\ *vb* **1** : to set upon forcefully **2** : to threaten (a piece in chess) with immediate capture **3** : to use unfriendly or bitter words against **4** : to begin to affect or to act upon injuriously ⟨*attacked* by fever⟩ **5** : to set to work on ⟨*attack* a problem⟩ [Middle French *attaquer*, from Italian *attaccare* "to attach, attack", of Germanic origin] — **at·tack·er** *n* □ SYN ASSAIL, ASSAULT, STORM: ATTACK implies taking the initiative in a struggle; ASSAIL implies trying to break down resistance by repeated blows or shots; ASSAULT suggests a direct attempt to overpower by suddenness and violence; STORM implies trying to overrun or capture a defended position by the irresistible weight of rapidly advancing numbers.

²attack *n* **1** : the act of attacking : ASSAULT **2** : the beginning of destructive action (as by a chemical agent) **3** : a setting to work : START **4** : a fit of sickness; *esp* : an active episode of a chronic or recurrent disease **5 a** : an offensive or scoring action in a game **b** : offensive players on a team

at·tain \ə-'tān\ *vb* **1** : GAIN 1, ACHIEVE **2** : to come into possession of : OBTAIN **3** : to arrive or arrive at ⟨*attain* the top of the mountain⟩ ⟨*attain* to maturity⟩ [Old French *ataindre*, from Latin *attingere*, from *ad-* + *tangere* "to touch"] — **at·tain·abil·i·ty** \ə-,tā-nə-'bil-ət-ē\ *n* — **at·tain·able** \-'tā-nə-bəl\ *adj* — **at·tain·able·ness** *n*

at·tain·der \ə-'tān-dər\ *n* : the taking away of a person's civil rights when the person has been declared an outlaw or sentenced to death [Middle French *ataindre* "to attain, accuse"]

at·tain·ment \ə-'tān-mənt\ *n* **1** : the act of attaining : the state of being attained **2** : something attained : ACCOMPLISHMENT

at·tar \'at-ər, 'a-,tär\ *n* : a fragrant essential oil (as from rose petals) [Persian *'atir* "perfumed", from Arabic, from *'itr* "perfume"]

¹at·tempt \ə-'tempt\ *vt* : to make an effort to do, accomplish, or solve ⟨*attempt* to swim the river⟩ [Latin *attemptare*, from *ad-* + *temptare* "to touch, try"] SYN see TRY

²attempt *n* : the act or an instance of attempting; *esp* : an unsuccessful effort

at·tend \ə-'tend\ *vb* **1** : to look after : take charge of ⟨*attend* to your own work⟩ **2** : to go or stay with as a servant, nurse, or companion **3** : to be present at ⟨*attend* a party⟩ **4** : to be present with : ACCOMPANY ⟨illness *attended* by fever⟩ **5** : to pay attention : HEED [Old French *atendre*, from Latin *attendere*, from *ad-* + *tendere* "to stretch"]

at·ten·dance \ə-'ten-dəns\ *n* **1** : the act of attending ⟨a doctor in *attendance*⟩ **2 a** : the persons or number of persons attending **b** : the number of times a person attends

¹at·ten·dant \ə-'ten-dənt\ *adj* : accompanying or following as a consequence

²attendant *n* : one that attends another to perform a service; *esp* : an employee who waits on customers ⟨a parking-lot *attendant*⟩

at·ten·tion \ə-'ten-chən\ *n* **1** : the act or the power of fixing one's mind upon something : careful listening or watching **2** : careful consideration of something with a view to taking action on it ⟨a matter requiring *attention*⟩ **3** : an act of kindness, care, or courtesy **4** : a position taken by a soldier with heels together, body erect, arms at the side, and eyes to the front — often used as a command [Latin *attentio*, from *attendere* "to attend"] — **at·ten·tion·al** \ə-'tench-nəl, -'ten-chən-l\ *adj*

at·ten·tive \ə-'tent-iv\ *adj* **1** : paying attention : OBSERVANT **2** : heedful of the comfort of others : COURTEOUS — **at·ten·tive·ly** *adv* — **at·ten·tive·ness** *n*

\ə\ abut		\ng\ sing	
\ər\ further		\ō\ bone	
\a\ mat		\ȯ\ saw	
\ā\ take		\ȯi\ coin	
\ä\ cot, cart		\th\ thin	
\au̇\ out		\t̲h\ this	
\ch\ chin		\ü\ food	
\e\ pet		\u̇\ foot	
\ē\ easy		\y\ yet	
\g\ go		\yü\ few	
\i\ tip		\yu̇\ cure	
\ī\ life		\zh\ vision	
\j\ job			

at·ten·u·ate \ə-'ten-yə-ˌwāt\ *vb* : to make or become thin or less (as in density, force, value, or vitality) ⟨*attenuate* a virus⟩ ⟨*attenuate* oil by heating⟩ ⟨sorrows *attenuate* with time⟩ [Latin *attenuare,* from *ad-* + *tenuis* "thin"] — **at·ten·u·a·tion** \ə-ˌten-yə-'wā-shən\ *n*

at·test \ə-'test\ *vb* **1** : to indicate to be true or genuine especially by signing as a witness ⟨*attest* a will⟩ **2** : to be proof of : SHOW ⟨my conduct *attests* my innocence⟩ **3** : TESTIFY ⟨*attest* to the truth of the statement⟩ [Middle French *attester,* from Latin *attestari,* from *ad-* + *testis* "witness"] — **at·tes·ta·tion** \ˌa-ˌtes-'tā-shən\ *n* — **at·test·er** \ə-'tes-tər\ *n*

at·tic \'at-ik\ *n* **1** : a low story or wall at the top of a classical facade **2** : a room or a space immediately below the roof of a building [French *attique,* from *attique* "of Attica", from Latin *Atticus*] □ ORIGIN The ancient Greek city-state of Athens included the whole of the Attic peninsula, the region called Attica. Typical of the Athenian or Attic style of architecture is the use of rectangular columns projecting from, but attached to, the wall. These take the place of the free-standing and usually rounded pillars common in other architectural styles. Occasionally the large columns at the front of a building are topped by a similar but smaller decorative structure, usually in the Attic style. The French named this structure *attique.* The English borrowed the name, respelling it according to a common pattern. From its originally specialized sense, *attic* was extended to cover the top story, just under the roof, of any building.

At·tic \'at-ik\ *adj* **1** : of or relating to Athens **2** : marked by simplicity, purity, and refinement [Latin *Atticus* "of Attica, Athenian", from Greek *Attikos,* from *Attikē* "Attica, Greece"]

¹at·tire \ə-'tīr\ *vt* : to put garments on : DRESS; *esp* : to clothe in rich garments [Old French *atirier,* from *a-* "ad-" + *tire* "order, rank", of Germanic origin]

²attire *n* : DRESS, CLOTHES; *esp* : fine clothing

at·ti·tude \'at-ə-ˌtüd, -tyüd\ *n* **1** : the arrangement of the body or figure : POSTURE **2** : a mental position or feeling regarding a fact or state **3** : the position of something (as an aircraft or spacecraft) in relation to a reference point (as the horizon or a star) [French, from Italian *attitudine,* literally, "aptitude", from Late Latin *aptitudo*]

at·ti·tu·di·nize \ˌat-ə-'tüd-n-ˌīz, -'tyüd-\ *vi* : to assume an affected mental attitude : POSE

at·to- \'at-ō\ *combining form* : one quintillionth (10⁻¹⁸) part of [Danish or Norwegian *atten* "eighteen"]

at·tor·ney \ə-'tər-nē\ *n, pl* **-neys** : one who is legally appointed by another to transact business for him; *esp* : LAWYER [Middle French *atorné,* past participle of *atorner* "to transfer homage or service", from *a-* "ad-" + *torner* "to turn"]

attorney general *n, pl* **attorneys general** *or* **attorney generals** : the chief law officer of a nation or state who represents the government in legal matters and serves as its principal legal advisor

at·tract \ə-'trakt\ *vb* : to cause to approach or adhere: as **a** : to pull to or toward oneself or itself ⟨a magnet *attracts* iron⟩ **b** : to draw by appealing to interest or feeling ⟨*attract* attention⟩ [Latin *attrahere,* from *ad-* + *trahere* "to draw"]

at·trac·tant \ə-'trak-tənt\ *n* : something that attracts; *esp* : a substance (as a pheromone) that attracts animals (as insects)

at·trac·tion \ə-'trak-shən\ *n* **1 a** : the act, process, or power of attracting **b** : a feature that attracts; *esp* : personal charm or beauty **2** : a force acting mutually between particles of matter, tending to draw them together, and resisting their separation

at·trac·tive \ə-'trak-tiv\ *adj* : having the power or quality of attracting; *esp* : CHARMING, PLEASING ⟨an *attrac-*

tive smile⟩ — **at·trac·tive·ly** *adv* — **at·trac·tive·ness** *n*

¹at·tri·bute \'a-trə-ˌbyüt\ *n* **1** : an inherent characteristic or quality **2** : an object closely associated with a specific person, thing, or office ⟨crown and scepter are *attributes* of royalty⟩ **3** : a word ascribing a quality; *esp* : ADJECTIVE [Latin *attributus,* past participle of *attribuere* "to attribute", from *ad-* + *tribuere* "to bestow"] SYN see QUALITY

²at·trib·ute \ə-'trib-yət\ *vt* **1** : to explain by way of cause ⟨*attribute* their success to hard work⟩ **2 a** : to regard as characteristic of a person or thing ⟨*attributed* the worst motives to them⟩ **b** : to consider to have originated in an indicated fashion SYN see ASCRIBE — **at·trib·ut·able** \-yət-ə-bəl\ *adj* — **at·trib·ut·er** *n*

at·tri·bu·tion \ˌa-trə-'byü-shən\ *n* : the act of attributing; *also* : an ascribed quality, character, or right

at·trib·u·tive \ə-'trib-yət-iv\ *adj* : relating to or of the nature of an attribute; *esp* : joined directly to a modified noun without a linking verb ⟨red in *red hair* is an *attributive* adjective⟩ — compare PREDICATE — **attributive** *n* — **at·trib·u·tive·ly** *adv*

at·tri·tion \ə-'trish-ən\ *n* **1** : the act of wearing or grinding down by friction **2** : the act of weakening or exhausting by constant harassment or abuse **3** : gradual reduction of personnel as a result of resignation, retirement, or death [Latin *attritio,* from *atterere* "to rub against", from *ad-* + *terere* "to rub"] — **at·tri·tion·al** \-'trish-nəl, -ən-l\ *adj*

at·tune \ə-'tün, -'tyün\ *vt* : to bring into harmony : TUNE — **at·tune·ment** \-mənt\ *n*

atyp·i·cal \ā-'tip-i-kəl, 'ā-'\ *adj* : not typical : IRREGULAR — **atyp·i·cal·ly** \-kə-lē, -klē\ *adv*

au·burn \'ó-bərn\ *adj* : of a reddish brown color ⟨*auburn* hair⟩ [Middle French *auborne* "blond", from Medieval Latin *alburnus* "whitish", from Latin *albus* "white"]

¹auc·tion \'ók-shən\ *n* : a public sale of property to the highest bidder [Latin *auctio,* literally, "increase", from *augēre* "to increase"]

²auction *vt* **auc·tioned; auc·tion·ing** \-shə-ning, -shning\ : to sell at auction

auction bridge *n* : a bridge game differing from contract bridge only in the scoring

auc·tion·eer \ˌók-shə-'niər\ *n* : a person who conducts an auction — **auctioneer** *vt*

auc·to·ri·al \ók-'tōr-ē-əl, -'tór-\ *adj* : of or relating to an author

au·da·cious \ó-'dā-shəs\ *adj* **1 a** : FEARLESS, DARING **b** : recklessly bold : RASH **2** : INSOLENT, IMPUDENT [Latin *audac-, audax* "bold", from *audēre* "to dare", from *avidus* "eager, avid"] — **au·da·cious·ly** *adv* — **au·da·cious·ness** *n*

au·dac·i·ty \ó-'das-ət-ē\ *n, pl* **-ties** **1** : DARING, BOLDNESS **2** : a disrespectful or insolent attitude SYN see TEMERITY

au·di·ble \'ód-ə-bəl\ *adj* : loud enough to be heard [Latin *audire* "to hear"] — **au·di·bil·i·ty** \ˌód-ə-'bil-ət-ē\ *n* — **au·di·bly** \'ód-ə-blē\ *adv*

au·di·ence \'ód-ē-əns\ *n* **1** : an assembled group that listens or watches (as at a play) **2** : an opportunity of being heard; *esp* : a formal interview with a person of high rank **3** : those of the general public who give attention to something said, done, or written ⟨the radio *audience*⟩ ⟨the *audience* for a new novel⟩ [Middle French, from Latin *audientia,* from *audire* "to hear"]

¹au·dio \'ód-ē-ō\ *adj* **1** : of or relating to electrical or other vibrational frequencies corresponding to normally audible sound waves which are of frequencies approximately from 15 to 20,000 hertz **2 a** : of or relating to sound or its reproduction and especially high-fidelity reproduction **b** : relating to or used in the transmission or reception of sound — compare VIDEO

²audio *n* **1** : the transmission, reception, or reproduction of sound **2** : the section of television equipment that deals with sound

audio- *combining form* **1** : hearing ⟨*audio*meter⟩ **2** : sound ⟨*audio*phile⟩ **3** : auditory and ⟨*audio*visual⟩ [Latin *audire* "to hear"]

au·di·om·e·ter \ˌȯd-ē-'äm-ət-ər\ *n* : an instrument used in measuring acuteness of hearing — **au·dio·met·ric** \ˌȯd-ē-ə-'me-trik\ *adj* — **au·di·om·e·try** \ˌȯd-ē-'äm-ə-trē\ *n*

au·dio·phile \'ȯd-ē-ō-ˌfīl\ *n* : one who is enthusiastic about high-fidelity sound reproduction

au·dio·vi·su·al \ˌȯd-ē-ō-'vizh-wəl, -'vizh-ə-wəl, -'vizh-əl\ *adj* : of, relating to, or making use of both hearing and sight ⟨*audiovisual* teaching aids⟩

au·dio·vi·su·als \-wəlz, -əlz\ *n pl* : audiovisual instructional materials

¹aud·it \'ȯd-ət\ *n* : a thorough examination and verification of accounts and account books especially of a business or society; *also* : the final report of such an examination [Latin *auditus* "act of hearing", from *audire* "to hear"]

²audit *vt* : to make an audit of ⟨*audit* accounts⟩

¹au·di·tion \ȯ-'dish-ən\ *n* **1** : the power or sense of hearing **2** : a critical hearing; *esp* : a trial performance to appraise an entertainer's merits

²audition *vb* **-di·tioned; -di·tion·ing** \-'dish-ning, -ə-ning\ **1** : to test in an audition ⟨*audition* a new trumpeter⟩ **2** : to give a trial performance ⟨the singers *auditioned* for the choir⟩

au·di·tor \'ȯd-ət-ər\ *n* **1** : one that hears or listens **2** : a person authorized to audit accounts

au·di·to·ri·um \ˌȯd-ə-'tōr-ē-əm, -'tȯr-\ *n* **1** : the part of a public building where an audience sits **2** : a room, hall, or building used for public gatherings

au·di·to·ry \'ȯd-ə-ˌtōr-ē, -ˌtȯr-\ *adj* : of or relating to hearing or to the sense or organs of hearing ⟨*auditory* canal⟩ ⟨*auditory* sensation⟩

auditory nerve *n* : either of the 8th pair of cranial nerves that connect the inner ear with the brain and transmit impulses concerned with hearing and balance

Au·ge·an \ȯ-'jē-ən\ *adj* : extremely difficult and sometimes distasteful [from *Augeas,* king of Elis; from the legend that his stable, left neglected for 30 years, was finally cleaned by Hercules]

Augean stable *n* : a condition or place marked by great accumulation of filth or corruption — usually used in pl.

au·ger \'ȯ-gər\ *n* **1** : a tool for boring holes in wood **2** : any of various instruments made like an auger and used for boring (as in soil) [Middle English *nauger* (the phrase *a nauger* being understood as *an auger*), from Old English *nafogār,* from *nafu* "nave" + *gār* "spear"; from its use for boring holes in the naves of wheels] □ **ORIGIN** Old English *nafela,* "navel", is closely related to Old English *nafu,* "nave". The nave is the central part of a wheel. From it the spokes radiate, and through it a hole is pierced for the axle. (This is not the same word as the *nave* of a church.) The navel is the depression more or less in the center of a person's abdomen. In Old English a compound was formed from *nafu* and *gār,* "spear". *Nafogār* was the "nave spear", the tool used to pierce the hole in the nave of a wheel. The form of the word became *nauger* in Middle English, and in the 15th century *a nauger* began to be divided as *an auger.* Thus we have the modern name of a tool used for boring holes.

¹aught \'ȯt, 'ät\ *pron* **1** *archaic* : ANYTHING **2** : ALL ⟨for *aught* I care, you can stay home⟩ [Old English *āwiht,* from *ā* "ever" + *wiht* "creature, thing"]

²aught *n* : ZERO 1, CIPHER [*naught,* the phrase *a naught* being understood as *an aught*]

au·gite \'ȯ-ˌjīt\ *n* : a black to dark green variety of pyroxene [Latin *augites,* a kind of precious stone, from Greek *augitēs*]

aug·ment \ȯg-'ment\ *vb* : to enlarge or increase especially in size, amount, or degree [Middle French *augmenter,* from Late Latin *augmentare,* from *augmentum* "increase", from Latin *augēre* "to increase"] — **aug·ment·able** \-ə-bəl\ *adj* — **aug·ment·er** *n*

aug·men·ta·tion \ˌȯg-mən-'tā-shən, -ˌmen-\ *n* **1** : the act of augmenting **2** : something that augments : INCREASE, ENLARGEMENT

aug·men·ta·tive \ȯg-'ment-ət-iv\ *adj* : capable of augmenting or serving to augment

au gra·tin \ō-'grät-n, ȯ-, -'grat-\ *adj* : covered with bread crumbs, butter, and cheese and browned [French]

¹au·gur \'ȯ-gər\ *n* : SOOTHSAYER, DIVINER [Latin]

²augur *vb* **1** : to predict especially from signs or omens **2** : to serve as a sign : INDICATE ⟨the report *augurs* well for our success⟩

au·gu·ry \'ȯ-gyə-rē, -gə-\ *n, pl* **-ries** **1** : divination from omens or portents or from chance events (as the fall of lots) **2** : an indication of the future : OMEN

au·gust \ȯ-'gəst\ *adj* : marked by majestic dignity or grandeur [Latin *augustus*] — **au·gust·ly** *adv* — **au·gust·ness** *n*

Au·gust \'ȯ-gəst\ *n* : the 8th month of the year [Latin *Augustus,* from Augustus Caesar]

Au·gus·tan \ȯ-'gəs-tən\ *adj* : of, relating to, or characteristic of Augustus Caesar or his time — **Augustan** *n*

¹Au·gus·tin·i·an \ˌȯ-gə-'stin-ē-ən\ *adj* **1** : of or relating to Saint Augustine or his doctrines **2** : of or relating to any of several religious orders under a rule ascribed to Saint Augustine — **Au·gus·tin·i·an·ism** \-ē-ə-ˌniz-əm\ *n*

²Augustinian *n* **1** : a follower of Saint Augustine **2** : a member of an Augustinian order; *esp* : a friar of the Hermits of Saint Augustine founded in 1256 and devoted to educational, missionary, and parish work

auk \'ȯk\ *n* : any of several thickset black-and-white short-necked diving seabirds that breed in colder parts of the northern hemisphere [Old Norse *ālka*]

auld \'ȯl, 'ȯld, 'äl, 'äld\ *adj, chiefly Scottish* : OLD

auld lang syne \ˌȯl-ˌang-'zīn, -ˌdang-, -ˌlang-, -ˌdlang-, ˌȯl-\ *n* : the good old times [Scottish, literally, "old long ago"]

aunt \'ant, 'änt\ *n* **1** : the sister of one's father or mother **2** : the wife of one's uncle [Old French *ante,* from Latin *amita*]

au·ra \'ȯr-ə\ *n* **1** : a distinctive atmosphere or impression surrounding a person or thing ⟨an *aura* of respectability⟩ **2** : a luminous radiation : NIMBUS [Latin, "air, breeze", from Greek]

au·ral \'ȯr-əl\ *adj* : of or relating to the ear or sense of hearing [Latin *auris* "ear"] — **au·ral·ly** \-ə-lē\ *adv*

au·re·ate \'ȯr-ē-ət\ *adj* **1** : of a golden color or brilliance **2** : GRANDILOQUENT, ORNATE ⟨*aureate* rhetoric⟩ [Medieval Latin *aureatus* "adorned with gold", from Latin *aureus* "golden", from *aurum* "gold"]

au·re·lia \ȯ-'rēl-yə\ *n* : any of a genus of large jellyfishes [probably from Latin *aurum* "gold"]

au·re·ole \'ȯr-ē-ˌōl\ *or* **au·re·o·la** \ȯ-'rē-ə-lə\ *n* **1** : a radiant light around the head or body of a representation of a sacred person **2** : a bright area surrounding a bright light (as the sun) when seen through thin cloud or mist [Medieval Latin *aureola,* from Latin *aureolus* "golden", from *aurum* "gold"]

au·ric \'ȯr-ik\ *adj* : of, relating to, or derived from gold especially when trivalent [Latin *aurum* "gold"]

au·ri·cle \'ȯr-i-kəl\ *n* **1** : PINNA 2 **2** : an atrium of a heart [Latin *auricula,* from *auris* "ear"]

au·ric·u·lar \ȯ-'rik-yə-lər\ *adj* **1** : of or relating to the ear or the sense of hearing **2** : told privately ⟨an *auricular* confession⟩ **3** : known by the sense of hearing **4** : of or relating to an auricle [Latin *auricula* "little ear", from *auris* "ear"]

au·ric·u·lo·ven·tric·u·lar \ȯ-ˌrik-yə-ˌlō-ven-'trik-yə-lər\ *adj* : ATRIOVENTRICULAR

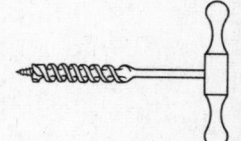

auger 1

auk

\ə\ abut	\ng\ sing
\ər\ further	\ō\ bone
\a\ mat	\ȯ\ saw
\ā\ take	\òi\ coin
\ä\ cot, cart	\th\ thin
\aú\ out	\th\ this
\ch\ chin	\ü\ food
\e\ pet	\ú\ foot
\ē\ easy	\y\ yet
\g\ go	\yü\ few
\i\ tip	\yú\ cure
\ī\ life	\zh\ vision
\j\ job	

au·rif·er·ous \ȯ-'rif-rəs, -ə-rəs\ *adj* : gold-bearing [Latin *aurum* "gold"]

Au·ri·ga \ȯ-'rī-gə\ *n* : a constellation between Perseus and Gemini [Latin, literally, "charioteer"]

Au·ri·gna·cian \,ȯr-ēn-'yā-shən\ *adj* : of or relating to an Upper Paleolithic culture with finely made stone and bone tools, paintings, and engravings [*Aurignac*, France]

au·rochs \'aùr-,äks, 'ȯr-\ *n, pl* **aurochs** *also* **au·rochs·es** **1** : URUS **2** : WISENT [German]

au·ro·ra \ə-'rōr-ə, ȯ-'rōr-, -'rȯr-\ *n, pl* **auroras** *or* **au·ro·rae** \-,ē\ **1** : DAWN **1** **2** : AURORA BOREALIS **3** : AURORA AUSTRALIS [Latin] — **au·ro·ral** \-əl\ *adj*

aurora aus·tra·lis \-ȯ-'strā-ləs, -ä-'strä-\ *n* : a display of light in the southern hemisphere corresponding to the aurora borealis [New Latin, literally, "southern aurora"]

aurora bo·re·al·is \-,bōr-ē-'al-əs, -,bȯr-\ *n* : streamers or arches of light in the sky at night of geomagnetic and electrical origin that appear to best advantage in the arctic regions [New Latin, literally, "northern aurora"]

au·rous \'ȯr-əs\ *adj* : of, relating to, or containing gold especially when univalent [Latin *aurum* "gold"]

aus·cul·ta·tion \,ȯ-skəl-'tā-shən\ *n* : the act of listening to sounds arising within organs (as the lungs) as an aid to diagnosis and treatment [Latin *auscultatio* "act of listening", from *auscultare* "to listen"] — **aus·cul·tate** \'ȯ-skəl-,tāt\ *vt*

aus·pice \'ȯ-spəs\ *n, pl* **aus·pic·es** \-spə-səz, -,sēz\ **1** : observation especially of the flight and feeding of birds to discover omens **2** : OMEN; *esp* : a favorable omen **3** *pl* : kindly patronage and guidance : PROTECTION (a concert given under the *auspices* of the school) [Latin *auspicium*, from *auspex* "diviner by birds", from *avis* "bird" + *specere* "to look at"]

aus·pi·cious \ȯ-'spish-əs\ *adj* **1** : promising success : FAVORABLE (an *auspicious* beginning) **2** : blessed with good auspices : HAPPY, FORTUNATE (on this *auspicious* occasion) — **aus·pi·cious·ly** *adv* — **aus·pi·cious·ness** *n*

aus·tere \ȯ-'stiər\ *adj* **1 a** : stern and cold in appearance or manner (*austere* Puritans) **b** : SOMBER, GRAVE (an *austere* critic) **2** : morally strict : ASCETIC **3** : plainly simple and unadorned (an *austere* office) (an *austere* style of writing) (wore *austere* black) **4** : giving little or no scope for pleasure (an *austere* budget) (*austere* diets) [Middle French, from Latin *austerus*, from Greek *austēros* "harsh, severe"] SYN see SEVERE — **aus·tere·ly** *adv* — **aus·tere·ness** *n*

aus·ter·i·ty \ȯ-'ster-ət-ē\ *n, pl* -**ties** **1** : the quality or state of being austere **2** : something that is austere **3** : enforced or extreme economy

¹Austr- *or* **Austro-** *combining form* **1** : south : southern **2** : Australian and (*Austro*-Malayan) [Latin *Austr-, Auster* "south wind"]

²Austr- *or* **Austro-** *combining form* : Austrian and (*Austro*-Hungarian)

aus·tral \'ȯs-trəl, 'äs-\ *adj* : SOUTHERN

Aus·tra·lian ballot \ȯ-'strāl-yən-, ä-\ *n* : an official ballot printed at public expense containing the names of all candidates and all proposals, distributed only at the polling place, and marked in secret

Aus·tra·loid \'ȯs-trə-,lȯid, 'äs-\ *adj* : of or relating to an ethnic group including the Australian aborigines and related peoples — **Australoid** *n*

aus·tra·lo·pith·e·cine \ȯ-,strä-lō-'pith-ə-,sīn, ä-,strä-\ *adj* : of or relating to a group of extinct southern African apes with near-human dentition [Latin *australis* "southern" + Greek *pithēkos* "ape"] — **australopithecine** *n*

aut- *or* **auto-** *combining form* **1** : self : same one (*auto*biography) **2** : automatic : self-acting : self-regulating [Greek *autos* "same, self"]

aut·ecol·o·gy \,ȯt-i-'käl-ə-jē\ *n* : ecology dealing with individual organisms or individual kinds of organisms

au·then·tic \ə-'thent-ik, ȯ-\ *adj* **1** : being really what it seems to be : GENUINE (an *authentic* signature of George Washington) **2** : true to life or to the facts (an *authentic* copy of an antique table) [Middle French *autentique*, derived from Greek *authentikos*, from *authentēs* "perpetrator, author"] — **au·then·ti·cal·ly** \-'thent-i-kə-lē, -klē\ *adv* — **au·then·tic·i·ty** \,ȯ-,then-'tis-ət-ē, -thən-\ *n* ☐ SYN GENUINE, BONA FIDE: AUTHENTIC implies being fully trustworthy as according with fact or actuality (an *authentic* record of the campaign) GENUINE implies accordance with an original or an accepted type without counterfeiting, admixture, or adulteration (*genuine* maple syrup) BONA FIDE often applies when good faith or sincerity is in question (a *bona fide* proposal)

au·then·ti·cate \ȯ-'thent-i-,kāt, ə-\ *vt* : to prove, establish, or attest to be authentic SYN see CONFIRM — **au·then·ti·ca·tion** \ə-,thent-i-'kā-shən, ȯ-\ *n* — **au·then·ti·ca·tor** \ə-'thent-i-,kāt-ər, ȯ-\ *n*

au·thor \'ȯ-thər\ *n* **1** : a person who writes or composes a literary work (as a book) **2** : one that originates or makes : CREATOR [Old North French *auctour*, from Latin *auctor* "promoter, originator, author", from *augēre* "to increase"] — **au·thor** *vt* — **au·tho·ri·al** \ȯ-'thōr-ē-əl, -'thȯr-\ *adj*

au·thor·ess \'ȯ-thə-rəs, -thrəs\ *n* : a woman who is an author

au·thor·i·tar·i·an \ə-,thȯr-ə-'ter-ē-ən, ȯ-, -,thär-\ *adj* : relating to or demanding total submission to authority especially as concentrated in a powerful leader (an *authoritarian* government) — **authoritarian** *n* — **au·thor·i·tar·i·an·ism** \-ē-ə-,niz-əm\ *n*

au·thor·i·ta·tive \ə-'thȯr-ə-,tāt-iv, ȯ-, -'thär-\ *adj* **1** : having authority : coming from or based on authority (*authoritative* teachings) **2** : entitled to obedience or acceptance (an *authoritative* order) **3** : having an air of authority : POSITIVE (an *authoritative* manner) (*authoritative* tones) — **au·thor·i·ta·tive·ly** *adv* — **au·thor·i·ta·tive·ness** *n*

au·thor·i·ty \ə-'thȯr-ət-ē, ȯ-, -'thär-\ *n, pl* -**ties** **1 a** : a person, text, or prior decision used to support a position **b** : a person appealed to as an expert **2** : the right to give commands or to carry out or enforce others' commands **3** : a person or persons having powers of government (local *authorities*) [Old French *auctorité*, from Latin *auctoritas* "opinion, decision, power", from *auctor* "author"]

au·tho·rize \'ȯ-thə-,rīz\ *vt* **1** : to give authority to : EMPOWER **2** : to give legal or official approval to (*authorize* a loan) (an *authorized* abridgment) **3** : to establish by or as if by authority : SANCTION (customs *authorized* by time) — **au·tho·ri·za·tion** \,ȯ-thə-rə-'zā-shən, -thrə-'zā-\ *n* — **au·tho·riz·er** \'ȯ-thə-,rī-zər\ *n*

au·thor·ship \'ȯ-thər-,ship\ *n* **1** : the profession of writing **2** : the origin of a literary work (a novel of unknown *authorship*)

au·tism \'ȯ-,tiz-əm\ *n* : absorption in self-centered mental activity (as daydreams, fantasies, delusions, and hallucinations) especially when accompanied by marked withdrawal from reality — **au·tis·tic** \ȯ-'tis-tik\ *adj*

au·to \'ȯt-ō, 'ät-\ *n, pl* **autos** : AUTOMOBILE

au·to·bi·og·ra·phy \,ȯt-ə-bī-'äg-rə-fē, -bē-\ *n* : one's own biography told by oneself — **au·to·bi·og·ra·pher** \-rə-fər\ *n* — **au·to·bio·graph·ic** \-,bī-ə-'graf-ik\ *or* **au·to·bio·graph·i·cal** \-'graf-i-kəl\ *adj* — **au·to·bio·graph·i·cal·ly** \-i-kə-lē, -klē\ *adv*

au·toch·tho·nous \ȯ-'täk-thə-nəs\ *adj* : INDIGENOUS, NATIVE (*autochthonous* malaria) [Greek *autochthōn*, from *autos* "same, self" + *chthōn* "earth"]

au·to·clave \'ȯt-ō-,klāv\ *n* : an apparatus (as for sterilizing) using steam under pressure [French, from *aut-* + Latin *clavis* "key"] — **autoclave** *vt*

au·toc·ra·cy \ȯ-'täk-rə-sē\ *n, pl* **-cies** **1** : government in which one person possesses unlimited power **2** : a community or state governed by autocracy

au·to·crat \'ȯt-ə-ˌkrat\ *n* : a person having or acting as if having unlimited power

au·to·crat·ic \ˌȯt-ə-'krat-ik\ *adj* : of, relating to, characteristic of, or resembling autocracy or an autocrat 〈*autocratic* rule〉 — **au·to·crat·i·cal·ly** \-'krat-i-kə-lē, -klē\ *adv*

au·to·cross \'ȯt-ō-ˌkrȯs, 'ät-\ *n* : an automobile contest that tests driving skill

au·to·erot·i·cism \ˌȯt-ō-i-'rät-ə-ˌsiz-əm\ *n* : sexual gratification without the participation of someone else — **au·to·erot·ic** \-'rät-ik\ *adj* — **au·to·erot·i·cal·ly** \-'rät-i-kə-lē, -klē\ *adv*

au·tog·e·nous \ȯ-'täj-ə-nəs\ *or* **au·to·gen·ic** \ˌȯt-ə-'jen-ik\ *adj* : originating within or derived from the same individual 〈an *autogenous* graft〉 — **au·tog·e·nous·ly** *adv*

¹au·to·graph \'ȯt-ə-ˌgraf\ *n* : something written with one's own hand; *esp* : a person's handwritten signature

²autograph *vt* : to write one's signature in or on

au·to·im·mune \ˌȯt-ō-im-'yün\ *adj* : of, relating to, or caused by antibodies produced by an organism against constituents of its own tissues 〈*autoimmune* diseases〉

au·to·in·tox·i·ca·tion \ˌȯt-ō-in-ˌtäk-sə-'kā-shən\ *n* : a state of being poisoned by substances produced within the body

Au·to·mat \'ȯt-ə-ˌmat\ *service mark* — used for a cafeteria in which food is obtained especially from coin-operated compartments

au·to·mate \'ȯt-ə-ˌmāt\ *vt* **1** : to operate by automation **2** : to convert to automatic operation

¹au·to·mat·ic \ˌȯt-ə-'mat-ik\ *adj* **1 a** : largely or wholly involuntary; *esp* : REFLEX **2 b** : acting or done spontaneously or unconsciously **c** : resembling an automaton : MECHANICAL **2** : having a self-acting or self-regulating mechanism 〈*automatic* washer〉 [Greek *automatos* "self-acting"] SYN see SPONTANEOUS — **au·to·mat·i·cal·ly** \-'mat-i-kə-lē, -klē\ *adv*

²automatic *n* : an automatic machine or apparatus; *esp* : an automatic firearm

au·to·ma·tion \ˌȯt-ə-'mā-shən\ *n* **1** : the method of making an apparatus, a process, or a system operate automatically **2** : the state of being operated automatically **3** : automatic operation of an apparatus, process, or system by mechanical or electronic devices that take the place of human operators

au·tom·a·tize \ȯ-'täm-ə-ˌtīz\ *vt* : to make automatic — **au·tom·a·ti·za·tion** \ȯ-ˌtäm-ət-ə-'zā-shən\ *n*

au·tom·a·ton \ȯ-'täm-ət-ən, -'täm-ə-ˌtän\ *n, pl* **-atons** *or* **-a·ta** \-ət-ə\ **1** : a mechanism that is relatively self-acting; *esp* : ROBOT **2** : a person who acts in a mechanical fashion

¹au·to·mo·bile \'ȯt-ə-mō-ˌbēl, ˌȯt-ə-mō-'bēl, ˌȯt-ə-'mō-ˌbēl\ *adj* : AUTOMOTIVE

²automobile *n* : a usually four-wheeled motor vehicle designed for passenger transportation on streets and roadways and commonly propelled by an internal-combustion engine — **automobile** *vi* — **au·to·mo·bil·ist** \-mō-'bē-ləst\ *n*

au·to·mo·tive \ˌȯt-ə-'mōt-iv\ *adj* **1** : SELF-PROPELLED **2** : of, relating to, or concerned with automotive vehicles and especially automobiles and motorcycles

au·to·nom·ic \ˌȯt-ə-'näm-ik\ *adj* : of, relating to, controlled by, or being the autonomic nervous system — **au·to·nom·i·cal·ly** \-'näm-i-kə-lē, -klē\ *adv*

autonomic nervous system *n* : a part of the vertebrate nervous system that regulates activity (as of glands, cardiac muscle, or smooth muscle) not under voluntary control and that consists of two parts — compare PARASYMPATHETIC NERVOUS SYSTEM, SYMPATHETIC NERVOUS SYSTEM

au·ton·o·mous \ȯ-'tän-ə-məs\ *adj* **1** : possessing autonomy : SELF-GOVERNING **2** : existing, responding, react-ing, or developing independently of the whole 〈an *autonomous* growth〉 [Greek *autonomos* "independent", from *autos* "self" + *nomos* "law"] — **au·ton·o·mous·ly** *adv*

au·ton·o·my \-mē\ *n, pl* **-mies** : the power or right of self-government

au·top·sy \'ȯ-ˌtäp-sē, 'ȯt-əp-\ *n, pl* **-sies** : POSTMORTEM EXAMINATION [Greek *autopsia* "act of seeing with one's own eyes", from *autos* "self" + *opsis* "sight"] — **autopsy** *vt*

au·to·ra·dio·graph \ˌȯt-ō-'rād-ē-ə-ˌgraf\ *or* **au·to·ra·dio·gram** \-ˌgram\ *n* : an image produced on a photographic film or plate by the radiations from a radioactive substance in an object — **au·to·ra·dio·graph·ic** \-ˌrād-ē-ə-'graf-ik\ *adj* — **au·to·ra·di·og·ra·phy** \-ˌrād-ē-'äg-rə-fē\ *n*

au·to·some \'ȯt-ə-ˌsōm\ *n* : a chromosome other than a sex chromosome — **au·to·so·mal** \ˌȯt-ə-'sō-məl\ *adj*

au·to·sug·ges·tion \ˌȯt-ō-səg-'jes-chən, -sə-'jes-, -'jesh-\ *n* : an influencing of one's own attitudes, behavior, or physical condition by mental processes other than conscious thought

au·tot·o·my \ȯ-'tät-ə-mē\ *n, pl* **-mies** : reflex separation of a part from the body : division of the body into two or more pieces

au·to·troph \'ȯt-ə-ˌtrōf, -ˌträf\ *n* : an organism that is able to live and grow on carbon from carbon dioxide or carbonates and on nitrogen from a simple inorganic compound [German, from Greek *autotrophos* "supplying one's own food", from *autos* "self" + *trephein* "to nourish"] — **au·to·tro·phic** \ˌȯt-ə-'trōf-ik\ *adj* — **au·to·tro·phi·cal·ly** \ˌȯt-ə-'träf-i-kə-lē, -klē\ *adv* — **au·tot·ro·phy** \ȯ-'tä-trə-fē\ *n*

au·tumn \'ȯt-əm\ *n* **1** : the season between summer and winter comprising in the northern hemisphere usually the months of September, October, and November or, as determined astronomically, extending from the September equinox to the December solstice — called also *fall* **2** : a time of full maturity or beginning decline 〈in the *autumn* of our lives〉 [Latin *autumnus*] — **au·tum·nal** \ȯ-'təm-nəl\ *adj*

autumn crocus *n* : MEADOW SAFFRON

¹aux·il·ia·ry \ȯg-'zil-yə-rē; -'zil-rē, -ə-rē\ *adj* **1** : offering or providing help : SUPPLEMENTARY 〈an *auxiliary* engine〉 **2** : being a verb that accompanies another verb and typically expresses such things as person, number, mood, or tense [Latin *auxiliaris*, from *auxilium* "help"]

²auxiliary *n, pl* **-ries** **1** : an auxiliary person, group, or device **2** : an auxiliary verb

aux·in \'ȯk-sən\ *n* : a plant hormone (as indoleacetic acid) that stimulates shoot elongation and plays a role in water metabolism in the plant; *also* : PLANT HORMONE [Greek *auxein* "to increase"]

¹avail \ə-'vāl\ *vb* : to be of use or advantage : HELP 〈all our effort *availed* nothing〉 [Middle English *vailen*, *availen*, from Old French *valoir* "to be of worth", from Latin *valēre* "to be strong"] — **avail oneself of** : to make use of : take advantage of 〈we must *avail ourselves of* the facilities we now have〉

²avail *n* : help or benefit toward reaching a goal : USE 〈the effort was of little *avail*〉

avail·able \ə-'vā-lə-bəl\ *adj* **1** : present or ready for use : at hand 〈will use any *available* excuse to stay home〉 **2** : ACCESSIBLE, OBTAINABLE 〈the book is *available* at your library〉 — **avail·abil·i·ty** \ə-ˌvā-lə-'bil-ət-ē\ *n* — **avail·able·ness** \ə-'vā-lə-bəl-nəs\ *n* — **avail·ably** \-blē\ *adv*

av·a·lanche \'av-ə-ˌlanch\ *n* **1** : a large mass of snow, ice, earth, or rock sliding down a mountainside or over a steep cliff **2** : a sudden overwhelming rush of something seeming to come down like an avalanche 〈an *avalanche* of words〉 [French]

avant–garde \ˌäv-ˌän-'gärd, ˌäv-ˌänt-, ˌav-, ˌav-; ə-'vänt-\ *n* : people (as artists) who create or use new or exper-

\ə\ abut		\ng\ sing	
\ər\ further		\ō\ bone	
\a\ mat		\ȯ\ saw	
\ā\ take		\ȯi\ coin	
\ä\ cot, cart		\th\ thin	
\au̇\ out		\t͟h\ this	
\ch\ chin		\ü\ food	
\e\ pet		\u̇\ foot	
\ē\ easy		\y\ yet	
\g\ go		\yü\ few	
\i\ tip		\yu̇\ cure	
\ī\ life		\zh\ vision	
\j\ job			

imental ideas [French, "vanguard"] — **avant–garde**
adj

av·a·rice \'av-rəs, -ə-rəs\ *n* : too strong a desire for
wealth or gain : GREED [Old French, from Latin *avari-
tia,* from *avarus* "greedy", from *avēre* "to covet"]

av·a·ri·cious \,av-ə-'rish-əs\ *adj* : greedy especially for
money SYN see COVETOUS — **av·a·ri·cious·ly** *adv* — **av-
a·ri·cious·ness** *n*

avast \ə-'vast\ *imperative verb* — used as a nautical
command to stop or cease [perhaps from Dutch *houd
vast* "hold fast"]

av·a·tar \'av-ə-,tär\ *n* : an embodiment (as of a concept, philosophy, or tradition) usually in human form
[Sanskrit *avatāra* "descent, incarnation of a deity"]

avaunt \ə-'vònt, ə-'vänt\ *adv, archaic* : AWAY, HENCE
— used as an interjection [Middle French *avant,* from
Latin *abante* "forward, before", from *ab* "from" +
ante "before"]

Ave Ma·ria \,äv-,ä-mə-'rē-ə\ *n* : HAIL MARY [Medieval
Latin, "hail, Mary"]

avenge \ə-'venj\ *vt* : to take vengeance for or on behalf
of ⟨*avenge* an insult⟩ [Middle English *vengen, aven-
gen,* from Old French *vengier,* from Latin *vindicare*]
— **aveng·er** *n* □ SYN REVENGE: AVENGE implies inflicting deserved punishment especially on one who has
injured someone other than oneself; REVENGE implies
getting even or paying back in kind or degree.

av·e·nue \'av-ə-,nü, -,nyü\ *n* 1 : a way or passage by
which a place may be approached or left 2 : a way or
means to an end 3 : a street especially when broad and
attractive [Middle French, from *avenir* "to come to",
from Latin *advenire,* from *ad-* + *venire* "to come"]

aver \ə-'vər\ *vt* **averred; aver·ring** : to declare positively : ASSERT [Middle French *averer* "to verify", derived
from Latin *ad-* + *verus* "true"]

¹**av·er·age** \'av-rij, -ə-rij\ *n* 1 : a single value representative of a set of other values; *esp* : ARITHMETIC MEAN
2 : something typical of a group, class, or series ⟨their
work is above the *average*⟩ 3 : a ratio of successful
tries to total tries ⟨batting *average*⟩ [earlier *average*
"distribution of costs of damage to ship or cargo",
from Middle French *avarie* "damage to ship or
cargo", from Italian *avaria,* from Arabic *'awārīyah*
"damaged merchandise"] □ ORIGIN *Average* came into English from Middle French *avarie,* a derivative (by
way of Italian) of Arabic *'awārīyah,* "damaged merchandise". French *avarie* originally meant damage
sustained by a ship or its cargo. It came, by transference, to mean the expenses of such damage and later
included other maritime expenses. When the English
borrowed the French word, they altered it to conform
to the pattern of such English words as *pilotage* and
towage. When a ship or its cargo was damaged at sea,
the owners or insurers of both ship and cargo had to
share the expense or average. An average-adjuster determined a fair division of costs among those held accountable. An *average* then became any equal distribution or division, like the determination of an arithmetic mean. Soon the arithmetic mean itself was
called an *average.* Now the word may be applied to
any mean or middle value or level. □ SYN AVERAGE,
MEAN, MEDIAN apply to a value that represents in some
way a middle point between extremes. AVERAGE is the
result obtained by dividing the sum total of a set of
figures by the number of figures; MEAN may be the average or it may be the value midway between two extremes ⟨a high of 70° and a low of 50° give a *mean* of
60°⟩ MEDIAN applies to the value that represents the
point at which there are as many instances above as
there are below ⟨the *average* of a group of persons
earning 3, 4, 5, 8, and 10 dollars an hour is 6 dollars
an hour, but the *median* is 5 dollars⟩

²**average** *adj* 1 : equaling or approximating an arithmetic mean 2 a : being about midway between extremes b : being not out of the ordinary : COMMON ⟨the

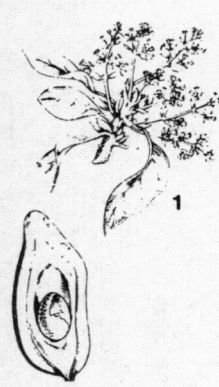

avocado: 1 flowering
branch, 2 fruit

average person⟩ — **av·er·age·ly** *adv* — **av·er·age-
ness** *n*

³**average** *vb* 1 : to do, get, or have on the average ⟨we
average six calls a day⟩ 2 : to amount to on the average : be usually ⟨those children *average* four feet in
height⟩ 3 : to find the average of 4 : to divide among a
number proportionally

averse \ə-'vərs\ *adj* : having an active feeling of repugnance or distaste ⟨*averse* to strenuous exercise⟩ [Latin
aversus, past participle of *avertere* "to turn away,
avert"] — **averse·ly** *adv* — **averse·ness** *n*

aver·sion \ə-'vər-zhən\ *n* 1 : a strong feeling of dislike
⟨an *aversion* to spiders⟩ 2 : something disliked ⟨carrots
are my *aversion*⟩

avert \ə-'vərt\ *vt* 1 : to turn away ⟨*avert* one's eyes⟩ 2 :
to prevent from happening ⟨narrowly *averted* an acci-
dent⟩ [Middle French *avertir,* from Latin *avertere,*
from *ab-* + *vertere* "to turn"] SYN see PREVENT

avi·an \'ā-vē-ən\ *adj* : of, relating to, or derived from
birds [Latin *avis* "bird"]

avi·ary \'ā-vē-,er-ē\ *n, pl* **-ar·ies** : a place (as a large
cage or a building) where many live birds are kept
usually for exhibition — **avi·a·rist** \-vē-ə-rəst\ *n*

avi·a·tion \,ā-vē-'ā-shən, ,av-ē-\ *n* 1 : the operation of
heavier-than-air aircraft 2 : military aircraft 3 : aircraft
manufacture, development, and design [French, from
Latin *avis* "bird"] — **aviation** *adj*

aviation cadet *n* : a student officer in the air force

avi·a·tor \'ā-vē-,āt-ər, 'av-ē-\ *n* : the pilot of a heavier-
than-air aircraft — **avi·a·tress** \-,ā-trəs\ *n* — **avi·a-
trix** \,ā-vē-'ā-triks, ,av-ē-\ *n*

av·id \'av-əd\ *adj* 1 : desirous to the point of being
greedy : craving very much ⟨*avid* for praise⟩ 2 :
marked by eagerness and enthusiasm ⟨*avid* readers⟩
[Latin *avidus,* from *avēre* "to covet"] — **avid·i·ty** \ə-
'vid-ət-ē, a-\ *n* — **av·id·ly** \'av-əd-lē\ *adv* — **av·id-
ness** *n*

avi·on·ics \,ā-vē-'än-iks, ,av-ē-\ *n* : the development and
production of electrical and electronic devices for use
in aviation, missilery, and astronautics [*aviation* elec-
tronics] — **avi·on·ic** \-ik\ *adj*

avi·ta·min·osis \,ā-,vīt-ə-mə-'nō-səs\ *n, pl* **-min·oses**
\-'nō-,sēz\ : disease resulting from a deficiency of one
or more vitamins — **avi·ta·min·ot·ic** \-mə-'nät-ik\ *adj*

av·o·ca·do \,av-ə-'käd-ō, ,äv-\ *n, pl* **-dos** : the usually
green pulpy pear-shaped or egg-shaped oily edible
fruit of a tropical American tree; *also* : the tree that
bears this fruit — called also *alligator pear* [Spanish
aguacate, from Nahuatl *āhuacatl*]

av·o·ca·tion \,av-ə-'kā-shən, 'av-ə-,\ *n* : an occupation
or interest pursued especially for enjoyment : HOBBY
[Latin *avocatio,* from *avocare* "to call away", from
ab- + *vocare* "to call"] SYN see VOCATION — **av·o·ca-
tion·al** \-shnəl, -shən-l\ *adj*

av·o·cet \'av-ə-,set\ *n* : any of several rather large long-
legged shorebirds with webbed feet and a slender upward-curving bill [French *avocette,* from Italian *avo-
cetta*]

avoid \ə-'vóid\ *vt* 1 : to make legally void : ANNUL
⟨*avoid* a contract⟩ 2 a : to keep away from : SHUN
⟨*avoid* quarrelsome neighbors⟩ b : to keep from happening ⟨*avoid* accidents⟩ [Middle English *avoiden* "to
empty out", from Old French *esvuidier,* from *es-*
"ex-" + *vuide* "empty, void"] — **avoid·able** \-ə-bəl\
adj — **avoid·ably** \-blē\ *adv*

avoid·ance \ə-'vóid-ns\ *n* 1 : the act of annulling 2 :
the act of keeping away from or clear of

av·oir·du·pois \,av-ərd-ə-'póiz\ *n* 1 : AVOIRDUPOIS
WEIGHT 2 : HEAVINESS, WEIGHT [Middle English *avoir
de pois* "goods sold by weight", from Old French, literally, "goods of weight"]

avoirdupois weight *n* : the series of units of weight
based on the pound of 16 ounces and the ounce of 16
drams — see MEASURE table

avouch \ə-'vauch\ *vt* **1** : to declare positively : AFFIRM **2** : to vouch for : GUARANTEE [Middle English *avouchen* "to cite as authority", from Middle French *avochier* "to summon", from Latin *advocare,* from *ad-* + *vocare* "to call"] — **avouch·ment** \-mənt\ *n*

avow \ə-'vau\ *vt* : to declare or acknowledge openly and frankly [Old French *avouer* "to appeal to", from Latin *advocare* "to summon", from *ad-* + *vocare* "to call"] SYN see ASSERT

avow·al \ə-'vau-əl, -'vaul\ *n* : an open declaration or acknowledgment

avowed \ə-'vaud\ *adj* : openly acknowledged or declared : ADMITTED — **avowed·ly** \-'vau-əd-lē, -'vaud-lē\ *adv*

avun·cu·lar \ə-'vəng-kyə-lər\ *adj* : of, relating to, or characteristic of an uncle [Latin *avunculus* "maternal uncle"]

aw \'o\ *interj* — used to express mild sympathy, entreaty, disbelief, or disgust

await \ə-'wāt\ *vb* **1** : to wait for : stay for : EXPECT ⟨*await* a train⟩ **2** : to be ready or waiting for ⟨a reward *awaits* them⟩

¹awake \ə-'wāk\ *vb* **awoke** \-'wōk\ *also* **awaked** \-'wākt\; **awaked** *or* **awo·ken** \-'wō-kən\ *also* **awoke**; **awak·ing** **1** : to cease sleeping **2** : to become aware of something ⟨*awoke* to their danger⟩ **3** : AROUSE 1 **4** : to make or become active : STIR ⟨*awoke* old memories⟩

²awake *adj* : roused from sleep : ALERT

awak·en \ə-'wā-kən\ *vb* **awak·ened; awak·en·ing** \-'wāk-ning, -ə-ning\ : AWAKE — **awak·en·er** \-'wāk-nər, -ə-nər\ *n*

¹award \ə-'word\ *vt* **1** : to give by judicial decision (as after a lawsuit) ⟨*award* damages⟩ **2** : to give or grant as a reward ⟨*award* a prize⟩ [Old North French *eswarder* "to examine, decide", from *es-* "ex-" + *warder* "to watch, guard", of Germanic origin] — **award·able** \-ə-bəl\ *adj* — **award·er** *n*

²award *n* : something that is conferred or bestowed : PRIZE

aware \ə-'waər, -'weər\ *adj* : having or showing realization, perception, or knowledge : CONSCIOUS [Old English *gewær,* from *wær* "wary"] — **aware·ness** *n*

awash \ə-'wosh, -'wäsh\ *adj* **1** : washed by waves or tide **2** : floating in water : AFLOAT **3** : overflowed by water

¹away \ə-'wā\ *adv* **1** : on the way : ALONG ⟨get *away* early⟩ **2** : from this or that place : HENCE, THENCE ⟨go *away*⟩ **3 a** : in another place ⟨stayed *away*⟩ **b** : in another direction ⟨turn *away*⟩ **4** : out of existence : to an end ⟨echoes dying *away*⟩ **5** : from one's possession ⟨gave *away* a fortune⟩ **6 a** : without stopping : CONTINUOUSLY ⟨clocks ticking *away*⟩ **b** : without hesitation or delay ⟨talk *away*⟩ **7** : by a long distance or interval : FAR ⟨*away* back in 1910⟩

²away *adj* **1** : absent from a place : GONE ⟨be *away* from home⟩ **2** : DISTANT ⟨a lake 10 kilometers *away*⟩

¹awe \'o\ *n* **1** : a profoundly humble and reverential attitude in the presence of deity or something sacred or sublime **2** : abashed fear inspired by authority or power [Middle English, "terror, awe", from Old Norse *agi* "terror"]

²awe *vt* : to inspire with awe

aweigh \ə-'wā\ *adj* : raised just clear of the bottom — used of an anchor

awe·some \'o-səm\ *adj* **1** : expressive of awe ⟨an *awesome* silence⟩ **2** : inspiring awe ⟨an *awesome* responsibility⟩ — **awe·some·ly** *adv* — **awe·some·ness** *n*

awe·strick·en \'o-,strik-ən\ *or* **awe·struck** \-,strək\ *adj* : filled with awe

¹aw·ful \'o-fəl\ *adj* **1** : inspiring awe **2** : very disagreeable or objectionable **3** : very great ⟨took an *awful* chance⟩ — **aw·ful·ness** *n*

²awful *adv* : VERY 1, EXTREMELY

aw·ful·ly *usually* 'o-fə-lē *in sense 1,* 'o-flē *in senses 2 & 3*\ *adv* **1** : in a manner to inspire awe **2** : in a dis-

agreeable or objectionable manner **3** : VERY 1 ⟨an *awfully* cold day⟩

awhile \ə-'hwīl, -'wīl\ *adv* : for a while : for a short time

awhirl \ə-'hwərl, -'wərl\ *adv or adj* : in a whirl

awk·ward \'o-kwərd\ *adj* **1** : lacking dexterity or skill especially in the use of the hands or of instruments : CLUMSY **2 a** : lacking ease or grace of movement or expression **b** : large and badly proportioned **3** : causing embarrassment **4** : poorly adapted for use or handling [Middle English *awke* "turned the wrong way", from Old Norse *öfugr*] — **awk·ward·ly** *adv* — **awk·ward·ness** *n* □ SYN CLUMSY, GAUCHE, INEPT: AWKWARD is widely applicable and may suggest unhandiness or inconvenience of things, lack of muscular coordination or grace of movement, lack of tact, or embarrassment of circumstances or situation; CLUMSY implies stiffness and heaviness and so connotes unwieldiness or lack of ordinary skill; GAUCHE implies the effects of shyness or inexperience; INEPT is likely to imply a general inadequacy.

awl \'ol\ *n* : a pointed tool for marking surfaces or making small holes (as in leather or wood) [Old Norse *alr*]

awn \'on\ *n* : one of the slender bristles that terminate the glumes in some cereal and other grasses [Old Norse *ögn*] — **awned** \'ond\ *adj* — **awn·less** \'on-ləs\ *adj*

aw·ning \'on-ing, 'än-\ *n* : a rooflike cover over or in front of something to provide shade or shelter [origin unknown]

awoke *past of* AWAKE

AWOL \'ā-,wol, ,ā-,dəb-əl-yu-,ō-'el\ *n* : a person (as a soldier or sailor) who is absent without permission [*a*bsent *w*ith*o*ut *l*eave] — **AWOL** *adv or adj*

awry \ə-'rī\ *adv or adj* **1** : turned or twisted toward one side : ASKEW **2** : out of the right course : AMISS SYN see CROOKED

ax *or* **axe** \'aks\ *n* **1** : a cutting tool that consists of a heavy edged head fixed to a handle and is used for chopping and splitting wood **2** : abrupt discharge or removal (as from a job or a budget) ⟨get the *ax*⟩ [Old English *æcx*] — **ax** *or* **axe** *vt* — **ax to grind** : a usually selfish reason for wanting something done

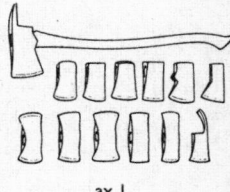

ax 1

ax·i·al \'ak-sē-əl\ *or* **ax·al** \-səl\ *adj* **1** : of, relating to, or functioning as an axis **2** : situated around, in the direction of, on, or along an axis — **ax·i·al·ly** \-sē-ə-lē\ *adv*

axial skeleton *n* : the skeleton of the trunk and head

ax·il \'ak-səl, -,sil\ *n* : the angle between a branch or leaf and the stem from which it arises [Latin *axilla* "armpit"]

ax·il·la \ag-'zil-ə, ak-'sil-\ *n, pl* **-lae** \-ē, -,ī\ *or* **-las** : ARMPIT [Latin]

ax·il·lary \'ak-sə-,ler-ē\ *adj* **1** : of, relating to, or located near the axilla **2** : situated in or growing from an axil — **axillary** *n*

ax·i·om \'ak-sē-əm\ *n* **1** : a maxim widely accepted as obvious **2 a** : a proposition regarded as a self-evident truth **b** : POSTULATE 1 [Latin *axioma,* from Greek *axiōma,* literally, "honor", from *axioun* "to think worthy", from *axios* "worthy"]

ax·i·om·at·ic \,ak-sē-ə-'mat-ik\ *adj* : of, relating to, or having the nature of an axiom — **ax·i·om·at·i·cal·ly** \-'mat-i-kə-lē, -klē\ *adv*

ax·is \'ak-səs\ *n, pl* **ax·es** \'ak-,sēz\ **1 a** : a straight line about which a body or a geometric figure rotates or may be supposed to rotate **b** : AXIS OF SYMMETRY **c** : one of the reference lines of a coordinate system **2 a** : the second vertebra of the neck on which the head turns as on a pivot **b** : an anatomical structure that is an axis of symmetry ⟨the cerebrospinal *axis*⟩; *esp* : the main stem of a plant from which leaves and branches arise **3** : a main line of direction, motion, growth, or extension **4** : ALLIANCE 2a [Latin, "axis, axle"]

Axis *adj* : of or relating to the three powers Germany, Italy, and Japan engaged against the Allies in World War II

axis of symmetry : a straight line with respect to which a body, figure, or curve is symmetrical ⟨a circle has an infinite number of *axes of symmetry* but a parabola only one⟩

ax·le \'ak-səl\ *n* **1** : a pin or shaft on or with which a wheel or pair of wheels revolves **2** : AXLETREE [from Old Norse *ǫxull* "axle"]

axle·tree \-,trē\ *n* : a fixed bar with bearings at its ends on which wheels (as of a cart) revolve

ax·o·lotl \'ak-sə-,lät-l\ *n* : any of several salamanders of mountain lakes of Mexico and the western United States that ordinarily live and breed without metamorphosing [Nahuatl *āxōlōtl]*

ax·on \'ak-,sän\ *also* **ax·one** \-,sōn\ *n* : a usually long and single nerve-cell process that as a rule conducts impulses away from the cell body [Greek *axōn*]

ayah \'ī-ə; 'ä-yə, -,yä\ *n* : a native nurse or maid in India [Hindi *āyā,* from Portuguese *aia,* from Latin *avia* "grandmother"]

¹aye *also* **ay** \'ā\ *adv* : FOREVER 1, ALWAYS [Old Norse *ei*]

²aye *also* **ay** \'ī\ *adv* : YES [perhaps from Middle English *ye*]

³aye *also* **ay** \'ī\ *n, pl* **ayes** : an affirmative vote or voter

aye–aye \'ī-,ī\ *n* : a nocturnal lemur of Madagascar [French, from Malagasy *aiay*]

Ayr·shire \'aər-,shiər, 'eər-, -shər\ *n* : any of a breed of hardy dairy cattle that vary in color from white to red or brown

aza·lea \ə-'zāl-yə\ *n* : any of numerous shrubs with funnel-shaped flowers that are related to the true rhododendrons but usually have deciduous leaves [Greek *azaleos* "dry"]

az·i·do·thy·mi·dine \ə-,zid-ō-thī-mə-dēn\ *n* : an antiviral drug used to treat AIDS — called also *AZT*

az·i·muth \'az-məth, -ə-məth\ *n* : an arc of the horizon measured between a fixed point (as true north) and the vertical circle passing through the center of an object [Arabic *as-sumūt* "the azimuth", plural of *assamt* "the way"]

azo \'az-ō\ *adj* : relating to or containing the group of nitrogen atoms —N=N— united at both ends to carbon ⟨an *azo* dye⟩ [French *azote* "nitrogen", from Greek *a-* + *zōē* "life"]

azon·al \'ā-,zōn-l\ *adj* : of, relating to, or being a soil or a major soil group lacking well-developed horizons — compare INTRAZONAL

Az·tec \'az-,tek\ *n* **1** : a member of a Nahuatl people that founded the Mexican empire and were conquered by Cortes in 1519 **2** : the language of the Aztec people [Spanish *azteca,* from Nahuatl, plural of *aztecatl*] — **Az·tec·an** \-ən\ *adj*

azure \'azh-ər\ *n* : the blue color of the clear sky [Old French *azur,* derived from Arabic *lāzaward*] — **azure** *adj*

azur·ite \'azh-ə-,rīt\ *n* : a blue mineral $Cu_3(OH)_2(CO_3)_2$ consisting of carbonate of copper, occurring in crystals, in mass, and in earthy form, and constituting an ore of copper

Bb

b \'bē\ *n, pl* **b's** *or* **bs** \'bēz\ *often cap* **1** : the 2d letter of the English alphabet **2** : the musical tone B **3** : a grade rating a student's work as good

baa *or* **ba** \'ba, 'bä\ *n* : the bleat of a sheep [imitative] — **baa** *vi*

Baal \'bāl, 'bā-əl\ *n, pl* **Baals** *or* **Baa·lim** \'bā-ləm, -ə-ləm\ : one of the local fertility gods of ancient Canaan [Hebrew *ba'al* "lord"]

Bab·bitt \'bab-ət\ *n* : a business or professional person who accepts without thought prevailing middle-class standards [George F. *Babbitt,* character in the novel *Babbitt* (1922) by Sinclair Lewis] — **Bab·bitt·ry** \'bab-ə-trē\ *n*

babbitt metal *n* : an alloy used for bearings; *esp* : one containing tin, copper, and antimony [Isaac *Babbitt,* died 1862, American inventor]

bab·ble \'bab-əl\ *vb* **bab·bled; bab·ling** \'bab-ling, -ə-ling\ **1 a** : to make meaningless sounds **b** : to talk foolishly or excessively : CHATTER **2** : to sound as though babbling ⟨a *babbling* brook⟩ **3** : to reveal by too free talk ⟨*babble* a secret⟩ [Middle English *babelen*] — **babble** *n* — **bab·bler** \'bab-lər, -ə-lər\ *n*

babe \'bāb\ *n* : INFANT, BABY

ba·bel \'bā-bəl, 'bab-əl\ *n, often cap* **1** : a confusion of sounds or voices **2** : a scene of noise or confusion [Hebrew *Bābhel,* a city where the building of a tower is said in the Book of Genesis to have been interrupted by the confusion of tongues]

ba·boon \ba-'bün\ *n* : any of several large African and Asian apes having a doglike muzzle and usually a short tail [Middle French *babouin,* from *baboue* "grimace"] — **ba·boon·ish** \-'bü-nish\ *adj*

ba·bush·ka \bə-'büsh-kə, -'bush-\ *n* : a kerchief for the head usually folded triangularly [Russian, "grandmother"]

¹ba·by \'bā-bē\ *n, pl* **babies** **1 a** : a very young child or animal **b** : the youngest of a group **2** : a childish person [Middle English] — **ba·by·hood** \-,hud\ *n* — **ba·by·ish** \-ish\ *adj*

²baby *vt* **ba·bied; ba·by·ing** **1** : to treat as a baby : FONDLE, PET **2** : to treat or operate with care

baby boom *n* : a marked rise in birthrate (as in the United States immediately following World War II) — **baby boom·er** \-'bü-mər\ *n*

Bab·y·lon \'bab-ə-lən, -,län\ *n* : a city noted for its wealth, luxury, and vice [*Babylon,* ancient capital of Babylonia]

baby's breath *n* : a tall much-branched perennial gypsophila having clusters of small white or pink flowers

ba·by-sit \'bā-bē-,sit\ *vi* **-sat** \-,sat\; **-sit·ting** : to care for children usually during a short absence of the parents [back-formation from *baby-sitter*] — **ba·by-sitter** *n*

bac·ca·lau·re·ate \,bak-ə-'lòr-ē-ət, -'lär-\ *n* **1** : the degree of bachelor conferred by universities and colleges **2** : a sermon to a graduating class or the service at which such a sermon is delivered [Medieval Latin *baccalaureatus*, from *baccalaureus* "bachelor"]

bac·ca·rat \,bäk-ə-'rä, ,bak-\ *n* : a card game played in casinos [French *baccara*]

¹**bac·cha·nal** \'bak-ən-l\ *adj* : BACCHANALIAN

²**bac·cha·nal** \'bak-ən-l; ,bak-ə-'nal, -'näl\ *n* **1 a** : a devotee of Bacchus; *esp* : one who celebrates the Bacchanalia **b** : CAROUSER **2** : BACCHANALIA

bac·cha·na·lia \,bak-ə-'näl-yə\ *n, pl* **bacchanalia 1** *pl, cap* : a Roman festival of Bacchus celebrated with dancing, song, and revelry **2** : a drunken feast : ORGY [Latin] — **bac·cha·na·lian** \-'näl-yən\ *adj or n*

bac·chant \bə-'kant, -'känt; 'bak-ənt\ *n, pl* **bacchants** *or* **bacchantes** \bə-'kants, -'känts, -'kant-ēz, -'känt-ēz\ : BACCHANAL 1 — **bacchant** *adj* — **bac·chan·tic** \bə-'kant-ik, -'känt-\ *adj*

bac·chante \bə-'kant, -'känt, -'kant-ē, -'känt-ē\ *n* : a priestess or woman follower of Bacchus

bac·chic \'bak-ik\ *adj* **1** : of or relating to Bacchus **2** : BACCHANALIAN

bach·e·lor \'bach-lər, -ə-lər\ *n* **1** : a young knight who fights under the banner of another **2** : a person who has received what is usually the lowest degree conferred by a four-year college, university, or professional school ⟨*bachelor* of arts⟩ **3 a** : an unmarried man **b** : an unmated male animal [Old French *bacheler*, from Medieval Latin *baccalarius, baccalaureus* "tenant farmer, advanced student", of Celtic origin] — **bach·e·lor·hood** \-,hu̇d\ *n*

bachelor's button *n* : a European plant of the aster family that has blue, pink, or white flower heads and is often cultivated in North America — called also *cornflower*

bac·il·la·ry \'bas-ə-,ler-ē, bə-'sil-ə-rē\ *or* **ba·cil·lar** \bə-'sil-ər, 'bas-ə-lər\ *adj* **1** : shaped like a rod; *also* : consisting of small rods **2** : of, relating to, or produced by bacilli

ba·cil·lus \bə-'sil-əs\ *n, pl* **-cil·li** \-'sil-,ī, *also* -ē\ : any of numerous straight aerobic rod-shaped bacteria usually producing endospores; *also* : a disease-producing bacterium [Medieval Latin, "small staff, rod", from Latin *baculus* "staff, rod"]

¹**back** \'bak\ *n* **1 a** (1) : the rear part of the human body especially from the neck to the end of the spine (2) : the corresponding part of a quadruped or other lower animal **b** (1) : SPINAL COLUMN ⟨break one's *back*⟩ (2) : the muscles and ligaments near the spinal column ⟨strain one's *back*⟩ **2 a** : the hinder part : REAR; *also* : the farther or reverse side **b** : something at or on the back for support ⟨the *back* of a chair⟩ **3** : a position in some games behind the front line of players; *also* : a player in this position [Old English *bæc*] — **backed** \'bakt\ *adj* — **back·less** \'bak-ləs\ *adj*

²**back** *adv* **1 a** : to, toward, or at the rear **b** : in or into the past : AGO **c** : in or into a reclining position **d** : under restraint ⟨held *back*⟩ **2 a** : to, toward, or in a former place, state, or time ⟨go *back*⟩ **b** : in return or reply ⟨write *back*⟩

³**back** *adj* **1 a** : being at or in the back ⟨*back* door⟩ **b** : distant from a central or main area or route : REMOTE ⟨*back* roads⟩ **c** : pronounced with closure or narrowing at or toward the back of the oral passage ⟨the *back* vowels \ä\ and \u̇\⟩ **2** : being in arrears : OVERDUE ⟨*back* rent⟩ **3** : moving or operating backward **4** : not current ⟨*back* numbers of a magazine⟩

⁴**back** *vb* **1 a** : to give aid or support to : ASSIST ⟨*backed* the new enterprise by investing in it⟩ **b** : SUBSTANTIATE **1 2** : to move or cause to move back, backward, or in reverse ⟨*back* a car⟩ **3 a** : to furnish with a back **b** : to be at the back of **c** : to form a back for — **back·er** *n*

back·ache \'bak-,āk\ *n* : pain in the back; *esp* : dull persistent pain in the lower back

back–bench·er \-'ben-chər\ *n* : a rank-and-file member of a British legislature

back·bite \-,bīt\ *vb* **-bit** \-,bit\; **-bit·ten** \-,bit-n\; **-bit·ing** \-,bīt-ing\ : to say mean or spiteful things about someone who is absent : SLANDER — **back·bit·er** *n*

back·board \-,bōrd, -,bȯrd\ *n* : a board or construction placed at the back or serving as a back; *esp* : one behind the basket on a basketball court

back·bone \-,bōn, -,bȯn\ *n* **1** : SPINAL COLUMN **2** : the foundation or sturdiest part of something **3** : firm and resolute character — **back·boned** \-,bōnd, -,bȯnd\ *adj*

back·break·ing \-,brāk-ing\ *adj* : demanding all one's strength or endurance ⟨*backbreaking* labor⟩

back·cross \'bak-,krȯs\ *vt* : to cross (a first-generation hybrid) with one parent or parent strain — **backcross** *n*

back·drop \'bak-,dräp\ *n* : an often scenic cloth hung across the back of a stage

back·field \-,fēld\ *n* : the football players who line up behind the line of scrimmage

¹**back·fire** \-,fīr\ *n* **1** : a fire started to check an advancing fire by clearing an area **2** : a loud noise caused by the improperly timed explosion of fuel in the cylinder of an internal-combustion engine

²**backfire** *vi* **1** : to make or undergo a backfire **2** : to have an effect opposite to the one desired or expected

back–formation *n* **1** : a word formed by dropping a real or supposed affix from an already existing longer word (as *pea* from *pease*) **2** : the creation of a back-formation

back·gam·mon \'bak-,gam-ən, bak-'\ *n* : a game played by two persons on a double board with 12 spaces on each side in which each player has 15 pieces whose movements are determined by throwing dice [perhaps from *back* + Middle English *gamen, game* "game"]

back·ground \'bak-,grȧund\ *n* **1** : the scenery, ground, or surface behind an object seen or represented (as in a painting) **2** : an inconspicuous position ⟨keeps in the *background*⟩ **3 a** : the setting within which something takes place **b** (1) : the circumstances or events leading up to a situation or development (2) : information essential to understanding a problem or situation **c** : the total of a person's experience, knowledge, and education **4** : sound that interferes with received or recorded electronic signals **5** : a somewhat steady level of radiation in the natural environment (as from cosmic rays or radioactivity)

¹**back·hand** \'bak-,hand\ *n* **1 a** : a stroke made with the back of the hand turned in the direction of movement **b** : a catch made with the arm across the body and the palm turned away from the body **2** : handwriting whose strokes slant downward from left to right

²**backhand** *adj* : using or made with a backhand

³**backhand** *vt* : to do, hit, or catch with a backhand

⁴**backhand** *or* **back·hand·ed** \-,han-dəd\ *adv* : with a backhand

back·hand·ed \-,han-dəd\ *adj* **1** : BACKHAND **2 a** : not direct or straightforward **b** : SARCASTIC ⟨a *backhanded* compliment⟩ **3** : written in backhand

back·hoe \-,hō\ *n* : an excavating machine having a bucket that is attached to a rigid bar hinged to a boom and that is drawn toward the machine in operation

back·ing \-ing\ *n* **1** : something forming a back **2 a** : SUPPORT, AID **b** : APPROVAL 1, ENDORSEMENT **3** : those who support a person or enterprise ⟨a candidate with a wide *backing*⟩

back·lash \'bak-,lash\ *n* **1** : a sudden violent backward movement or reaction **2** : a strong adverse reaction (as to a recent social or political development)

back·log \-,lȯg, -,läg\ *n* **1** : a large log at the back of a hearth fire **2** : a reserve especially of unfilled orders **3** : an accumulation of work not done

back of *prep* : BEHIND

¹**back·pack** \-,pak\ *n* : a camping pack worn on the back

²**backpack** *vb* **1** : to carry (supplies) in a backpack **2** : to hike with a backpack — **back·pack·er** *n*

¹backhand 1a

back·rest \'bak-,rest\ *n* : something to support the back

back·side \-,sīd\ *n* : BUTTOCK 2

back·slap \-,slap\ *vb* : to be excessively cordial — **back·slap·per** *n* — **back·slap·ping** *n*

back·slide \-,slīd\ *vi* **-slid** \-,slid\; **-slid** *or* **-slid·den** \-,slid-n\; **-slid·ing** \-,slīd-ing\ : to slip back into bad moral or religious practices — **back·slid·er** \-,slīd-ər\ *n*

back·spin \-,spin\ *n* : a backward rotary motion (as of a ball)

¹back·stage \'bak-'stāj\ *adv* **1** : in or to a backstage area **2** : in secret or private ⟨worked *backstage* to gain support⟩

²backstage *adj* **1** : of, relating to, or occurring in the backstage **2** : SECRET, HIDDEN, COVERT ⟨*backstage* negotiations⟩

³backstage *n* : the part of a theater behind the curtain and especially behind the stage

back·stay \-,stā\ *n* **1** : a stay extending from the mast-heads to the side of a ship and slanting aft **2** : a strengthening or supporting device at the back

¹back·stop \-,stäp\ *n* : something serving as a stop behind something else; *esp* : a screen or fence used in baseball or other games to keep a ball from leaving the field of play

²backstop *vt* : to back up : SUPPORT ⟨found funds to *backstop* the program⟩ — **back·stop·per** *n*

back·stretch \-,strech, -'strech\ *n* : the side opposite the homestretch on a racecourse

back·stroke \-,strōk\ *n* : a swimming stroke executed by a swimmer lying on his back

back·swept \-,swept\ *adj* : swept or slanting backward

back swimmer *n* : a water bug that swims on its back

back talk *n* : an insolent or argumentative reply

back·track \'bak-,trak\ *vi* **1** : to retrace one's course **2** : to reverse a position or stand

¹back·ward \-wərd\ *or* **back·wards** \-wərdz\ *adv* **1 a** : toward the back **b** : with the back foremost ⟨ride *backward*⟩ **2 a** : in a reverse or opposite direction or way ⟨count *backward*⟩ **b** : toward the past **c** : toward a worse state

²backward *adj* **1 a** : directed or turned backward ⟨a *backward* glance⟩ **b** : done or executed backward **2** : DIFFIDENT, SHY **3** : relatively undeveloped ⟨*backward* nations⟩ — **back·ward·ly** *adv* — **back·ward·ness** *n*

back·wash \-,wòsh, -,wäsh\ *n* **1** : backward movement (as of water or air) produced by a propelling force (as the motion of oars) **2** : a consequence or by-product of an event

back·wa·ter \'bak-,wòt-ər, -,wät-\ *n* **1** : a body of relatively stagnant water formed by the back flow or overflow of a river or sea **2** : a backward stagnant place or condition

back·woods \-'wùdz, -,wùdz\ *n pl* **1** : wooded or partly cleared areas on a frontier **2** : a remote and culturally backward area — **back·woods·man** \-mən\ *n*

back·yard \-'yärd\ *n* **1** : an often enclosed area behind a dwelling **2** : an accessible place or situation ⟨we must clean up our own *backyard* before criticizing others⟩

ba·con \'bā-kən\ *n* : salted and smoked meat from the sides and sometimes the back of a pig [Middle French, of Germanic origin]

Ba·co·ni·an \bā-'kō-nē-ən\ *adj* : of, relating to, or characteristic of Francis Bacon or his doctrines

bacteria *pl of* BACTERIUM

bac·te·ri·cid·al \bak-,tir-ə-ə-'sīd-l\ *adj* : destroying bacteria — **bac·te·ri·cide** \-'tir-ə-,sīd\ *n*

bac·te·rio·chlo·ro·phyll \bak-,tir-ē-ō-'klōr-ə-,fil, -'klòr-\ *n* : a substance in photosynthetic bacteria related to the chlorophyll of higher plants

bac·te·ri·ol·o·gy \bak-,tir-ē-'äl-ə-jē\ *n* **1** : a science that deals with bacteria and their relations to medicine, industry, and agriculture **2** : bacterial life and

¹badger

phenomena — **bac·te·ri·o·log·ic** \-ē-ə-'läj-ik\ *or* **bac·te·ri·o·log·i·cal** \-'läj-i-kəl\ *adj* — **bac·te·ri·o·log·i·cal·ly** \-'läj-i-kə-lē, -klē\ *adv* — **bac·te·ri·ol·o·gist** \-ē-'äl-ə-jəst\ *n*

bac·te·rio·phage \bak-'tir-ē-ə-,fāj, -,fāzh\ *n* : any of various viruses that attack bacteria

bac·te·rio·stat·ic \bak-,tir-ē-ō-'stat-ik\ *adj* : tending to inhibit growth of bacteria without causing their destruction

bac·te·ri·um \bak-'tir-ē-əm\ *n, pl* **-ria** \-ē-ə\ : any of a class of microscopic plants that live in soil, water, organic matter, or the bodies of plants and animals and are important to man because of their chemical effects and as causers of disease [New Latin, from Greek *baktērion* "small staff"] — **bac·te·ri·al** \-ē-əl\ *adj*

Bac·tri·an camel \'bak-trē-ən-\ *n* : CAMEL 1b

¹bad \'bad\ *adj* **worse** \'wərs\; **worst** \'wərst\ **1 a** : below standard : POOR ⟨in *bad* repair⟩ **b** : UNFAVORABLE ⟨made a *bad* impression⟩ **c** : ROTTEN 1 **2 a** : morally evil **b** : NAUGHTY, DISOBEDIENT **3** : INADEQUATE ⟨*bad* lighting⟩ **4** : of a kind to pain or distress ⟨*bad* news⟩ **5 a** : INJURIOUS, HARMFUL **b** : SEVERE ⟨had a *bad* cold⟩ **6** : INCORRECT, FAULTY ⟨*bad* spelling⟩ **7** : ILL, SICK ⟨feel *bad*⟩ **8** : REGRETFUL, SORRY ⟨felt *bad* about the fire⟩ **9** : INVALID, VOID ⟨a *bad* check⟩ [Middle English] — **bad·ness** *n*

²bad *n* **1** : something that is bad **2** : an evil or unhappy state

³bad *adv* : BADLY

bad blood *n* : ill feeling : BITTERNESS

bade *past of* BID

badge \'baj\ *n* **1** : something (as an emblem or device) worn to show that a person belongs to a certain group, class, or rank ⟨a police officer's *badge*⟩ **2** : an outward sign **3** : an emblem awarded for some achievement ⟨a scout's merit *badge*⟩ [Middle English *bage, bagge*]

¹bad·ger \'baj-ər\ *n* : any of several sturdy burrowing mammals widely distributed in the northern hemisphere; *also* : the pelt or fur of a badger [probably from *badge*; from the white mark on its forehead]

²badger *vt* **bad·gered; bad·ger·ing** \'baj-ring, -ə-ring\ : to harass persistently [from the practice of baiting badgers]

bad·i·nage \,bad-n-'äzh\ *n* : playful talk back and forth : BANTER [French]

bad·land \'bad-,land\ *n* : a region where erosion has formed the soft rocks into sharp and intricate shapes and where plant life is scarce — often used in pl.

bad·ly \'bad-lē\ *adv* **1** : in a bad manner ⟨played *badly*⟩ **2** : to a great or intense degree ⟨want something *badly*⟩

bad·min·ton \'bad-,mint-n\ *n* : a court game played with a light racket and a shuttlecock volleyed over a net [*Badminton,* residence of the Duke of Beaufort, England]

bad–mouth \'bad-,maùth, -,maùth\ *vt* : to criticize severely

¹baf·fle \'baf-əl\ *vt* **baf·fled; baf·fling** \'baf-ling, -ə-ling\ **1** : to defeat or check by confusing **2 a** : to check or turn the flow of by or as if by a baffle **b** : to prevent (sound waves) from interfering with each other (as by a baffle) [probably from Middle English *bawchillen* "to discredit publicly"] SYN *see* FRUSTRATE — **baf·fle·ment** \-əl-mənt\ *n* — **baf·fler** \'baf-lər, -ə-lər\ *n*

²baffle *n* : a device (as a plate, wall, or screen) to deflect, check, or regulate flow (as of a fluid or of light or sound)

¹bag \'bag\ *n* **1 a** : a flexible usually closed container for holding, storing, or carrying something **b** : PURSE; *esp* : HANDBAG **c** : TRAVELING BAG, SUITCASE **2** : something resembling a bag: as **a** : a pouched or pendulous bodily part or organ; *esp* : UDDER **b** : a puffed-out sag or bulge in cloth **c** : a square white canvas container to mark a base in baseball **3** : the amount contained in a bag **4** : a quantity of game taken or permitted to be taken **5** : a slovenly unattractive woman [Old Norse *baggi*] — **bag·like** \-,līk\ *adj* — **in the bag** : SURE, CERTAIN

²**bag** *vb* **bagged; bag·ging** **1 a** : to swell out : BULGE **b** : to hang loosely **2** : to put into a bag **3 a** : to take (animals) as game **b** : CAPTURE, SEIZE; *also* : to shoot down : DESTROY ⟨*bag* an enemy plane⟩

ba·gasse \bə-'gas\ *n* : plant residue (as of sugarcane) left after a product (as juice) has been extracted [French]

bag·a·telle \,bag-ə-'tel\ *n* **1** : TRIFLE 1 **2** : a game played with a cue and balls on an oblong table having cups or cups and arches at one end [French, from Italian *bagattella*]

ba·gel \'bā-gəl\ *n* : a hard glazed doughnut-shaped roll [Yiddish *beygl*]

bag·gage \'bag-ij\ *n* **1** : the traveling bags and personal belongings of a traveler : LUGGAGE **2** : the equipment carried with a military force **3** : unnecessary or unwanted things or circumstances or ideas **4** : a worthless saucy woman or girl [Middle French *bagage*, from *bague* "bundle"]

bag·ging \'bag-ing\ *n* : material (as cloth) for bags

bag·gy \'bag-ē\ *adj* **bag·gi·er; -est** : loose, puffed out, or hanging like a bag ⟨*baggy* pants⟩ — **bag·gi·ly** \'bag-ə-lē\ *adv* — **bag·gi·ness** \'bag-ē-nəs\ *n*

ba·gnio \'ban-yō\ *n, pl* **bagnios** : BROTHEL [obsolete English *bagnio* "prison", from Italian *bagno* "public bath, prison"]

bag·pipe \'bag-,pīp\ *n* : a wind instrument consisting of a leather bag, a valve-stopped tube, and three or four pipes — often used in pl. — **bag·pip·er** \-,pī-pər\ *n*

ba·guette \ba-'get\ *n* : a gem having the shape of a long narrow rectangle [French, literally, "rod"]

bag·worm \'bag-,wərm\ *n* : a moth whose larva lives in a silk case covered with plant debris and is often destructive to the foliage of trees and shrubs

bah \'bä, 'ba\ *interj* — used to express disdain or contempt

¹**bail** \'bāl\ *n* **1** : security that guarantees the appearance of a prisoner in court when legally required and that is given in order to obtain his or her release from prison until that time **2** : the temporary release of a prisoner upon security **3** : one who provides bail [Middle French, "custody", from *baillier* "to have in charge", from Latin *bajulare* "to carry a burden", from *bajulus* "porter"]

²**bail** *vt* **1** : to entrust (personal property) to another for a specific purpose and a limited time **2 a** : to release under bail **b** : to gain the release of by giving bail — **bail·able** \'bā-lə-bəl\ *adj*

³**bail** *n* : a container used to remove water from a boat [Middle French *baille* "bucket", from Medieval Latin *bajula* "water vessel", from Latin *bajulus* "porter"]

⁴**bail** *vt* : to remove (water) from a boat by dipping and throwing over the side; *also* : to clear (a boat) of water in this way

⁵**bail** *n* **1 a** : a supporting half hoop **b** : a hinged bar for holding paper against the platen of a typewriter **2** : the arched handle of a kettle or pail [Middle English *beil, baile*]

bail·ee \bā-'lē\ *n* : the person to whom property is bailed

bai·ley \'bā-lē\ *n* : an outer wall of a castle or the space within it [Old French *baille, balie*]

bai·liff \'bā-ləf\ *n* **1 a** : an official employed by a British sheriff to serve writs and processes and make arrests **b** : a minor officer of some United States courts usually serving as a messenger or doorkeeper **2** *chiefly British* : one who manages an estate or farm [Old French *baillif*, from *bail* "custody"] — **bai·liff·ship** \-,ship\ *n*

bai·li·wick \'bā-li-,wik\ *n* **1** : the office or jurisdiction of a bailiff **2** : one's area of special interest or competence [Middle English *bailliff* "bailiff" + *wik* "dwelling place, village"]

bail·or \bā-'lór, 'bā-lər\ *or* **bail·er** \'bā-lər\ *n* : one that entrusts personal property to another

bail out *vb* **1** : to jump with a parachute from an airplane in flight **2** : to escape or help to escape a difficult situation — **bail-out** \'bāl-,aut\ *n*

bails·man \'bālz-mən\ *n* : one who gives bail for another

bairn \'baərn, 'beərn\ *n, chiefly Scottish* : CHILD [Middle English *bern, barn*, from Old English *bearn* and Old Norse *barn*]

¹**bait** \'bāt\ *vb* **1 a** : to torment by repeated and usually unfair verbal attacks **b** : to nag at : GOAD **2 a** : to abuse (an animal) by setting on dogs **b** : to attack by biting and tearing **3 a** : to furnish (as a hook) with bait **b** : ENTICE, LURE **4** : to give food and drink to (an animal) especially on the road [Old Norse *be-ita*] — **bait·er** *n*

²**bait** *n* **1** : something used in luring especially to a hook or trap; *also* : a poisonous material distributed in food to kill pests **2** : an often treacherous lure

baize \'bāz\ *n* : a coarse woolen or cotton fabric finished to imitate felt [Middle French *baies*, from *bai* "bay-colored"]

¹**bake** \'bāk\ *vb* **1** : to cook or be cooked in a dry heat especially in an oven **2** : to dry or harden by heat ⟨*bake* bricks⟩ **3** : to prepare baked foods [Old English *bacan*] — **bak·er** *n*

²**bake** *n* **1** : the act or process of baking **2** : baked food

Ba·ke·lite \'bā-kə-,līt, -,klīt\ *trademark* — used for any of various synthetic resins and plastics

baker's dozen *n* : THIRTEEN

baker's yeast *n* : a yeast used or suitable for use as leaven — compare BREWER'S YEAST

bak·ery \'bā-kə-rē, -krē\ *n, pl* **-er·ies** : a place where bread, cakes, and pastry are made or sold

bake·shop \'bāk-,shäp\ *n* : BAKERY

baking powder *n* : a powder that consists of a carbonate, an acid, and a starch and that makes the dough (as of cake) rise and become light

baking soda *n* : SODIUM BICARBONATE

bak·sheesh \'bak-,shēsh, bak-'\ *n, pl* **baksheesh** : money paid for service especially in the Near East [Persian *bakhshīsh*]

bal·a·lai·ka \,bal-ə-'lī-kə\ *n* : a triangular wooden instrument of Russian origin that is related to the guitar [Russian *balalaĭka*]

¹**bal·ance** \'bal-əns\ *n* **1** : an instrument for measuring mass or weight (as a beam that is supported freely in the center and has two pans of equal weight suspended from its ends) **2** : a counterbalancing weight, force, or influence **3** : a vibrating wheel operating with a hairspring to regulate the movement of a timepiece **4 a** : equilibrium between contrasting or interacting elements ⟨a sane *balance* between right and need⟩ ⟨the *balance* of nature⟩ **b** : equality between the totals of the two sides of an account **5** : an aesthetically pleasing integration of elements : HARMONY **6** : something left over : REMAINDER; *esp* : the amount by which one side of an account is greater than the other ⟨a *balance* of $10 on the credit side⟩ **7** : mental and emotional steadiness [Old French, derived from Latin *bi-* "two" + *lanx* "plate"] □ SYN BALANCE, REMAINDER, REST mean that which is left after subtraction or removal of a part. BALANCE strictly involves a comparison of two amounts, where one falls short of the other and must be equalized ⟨a bank *balance* is the amount left in an account after withdrawals and other deductions⟩ REMAINDER refers to what remains after a major or significant part of a group or mass has been taken away or accounted for ⟨a few went ahead, but the *remainder* of the party turned back⟩ REST and REMAINDER are interchangeable although REST often suggests a less precisely measured REMAINDER ⟨the United States and the *rest* of the free world⟩

²**balance** *vb* **1 a** (1) : to compute the difference between the debits and credits of an account (2) : to pay

bagpipe

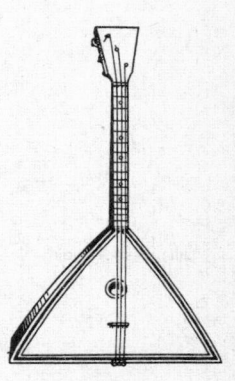

balalaika

\ə\ abut		\ng\ sing	
\ər\ further		\ō\ bone	
\a\ mat		\ó\ saw	
\ā\ take		\th\ thin	
\ä\ cot, cart		\th\ this	
\aú\ out		\ü\ food	
\ch\ chin		\ú\ foot	
\e\ pet		\y\ yet	
\ē\ easy		\yü\ few	
\g\ go		\yú\ cure	
\i\ tip		\zh\ vision	
\ī\ life			
\j\ job			

the amount due on : **SETTLE** **b** : to make two parts exactly equal ⟨*balance* equations⟩ **c** : to complete (a chemical equation) so that the same number of atoms and electric charges of each kind appears on each side **2 a** : to make up for : **OFFSET** **b** : to equal or equalize in weight, number, or proportion **3** : to compare the weight of in or as if in a balance **4 a** : to bring or come to a state or position of equilibrium **b** : to poise in or as if in balance **c** : to bring into harmony or proportion; *also* : to so plan and prepare that all needed elements will be present ⟨*balance* a diet⟩ ⟨a *balanced* aquarium⟩ **5** : to move with a swaying or swinging motion **SYN** see **COMPENSATE** — **bal·anc·er** *n*

balance beam *n* : a narrow wooden beam supported in a horizontal position above the floor and used for balancing feats in gymnastics

balance of power : an equilibrium of power sufficient to discourage or prevent one nation or party from imposing its will on another

balance of trade : the difference in value over a period of time between a country's imports and exports

balance sheet *n* : a statement of the financial condition of an enterprise at a given date

balance wheel *n* : a wheel that regulates or stabilizes the motion of a mechanism (as in a timepiece or a sewing machine)

ba·la·ta \bə-ˈlät-ə\ *n* : a substance like gutta-percha that is the dried juice of tropical American trees related to the sapodilla and is used especially in belting and golf balls; *also* : a tree yielding balata [Spanish, of American Indian origin]

bal·boa \bal-ˈbō-ə\ *n* **I** : the basic monetary unit of Panama **2** : a coin representing one balboa [Spanish, from Vasco Núñez de *Balboa,* died 1517, Spanish explorer]

bal·brig·gan \bal-ˈbrig-ən\ *n* : a knitted cotton fabric used especially for underwear or hosiery [*Balbriggan,* Ireland]

bal·co·ny \ˈbal-kə-nē\ *n, pl* **-nies** **I** : a platform enclosed by a low wall or a railing and built out from the side of a building **2** : a gallery inside a building (as a theater or auditorium) [Italian *balcone,* of Germanic origin]

bald \ˈbȯld\ *adj* **I** : lacking a natural or usual covering (as of hair) **2** : **UNADORNED, PLAIN** ⟨the *bald* truth⟩ [Middle English *balled*] — **bald·ly** *adv* — **bald·ness** \ˈbȯld-nəs, ˈbȯl-\ *n*

bal·da·chin \ˈbȯl-də-kən, ˈbal-\ *or* **bal·da·chi·no** \ˌbal-də-ˈkē-nō, ˌbäl-\ *n, pl* **-chins** *or* **-chi·nos** : an ornamental canopy fixed or carried over a dignitary or scared object as a mark of honor [Italian *baldacchino,* from *Baldacco* "Baghdad"]

bald cypress *n* : either of two large swamp trees of the southern United States; *also* : the hard red wood of bald cypress

bald eagle *n* : an eagle of North America that is wholly dark when young but has white feathers covering the head and neck when mature

bal·der·dash \ˈbȯl-dər-ˌdash\ *n* : **NONSENSE 1** [origin unknown]

bald·pate \ˈbȯld-ˌpāt, ˈbȯl-\ *n* **I** : a bald-headed person **2** : a white-crowned North American widgeon

bal·dric \ˈbȯl-drik\ *n* : an often ornamented belt worn over one shoulder to support a sword or bugle [Middle English *baudrik*]

¹bale \ˈbāl\ *n* **I** : great evil **2** : mental suffering : **WOE** [Old English *bealu*]

²bale *n* : a large bundle of goods; *esp* : one closely pressed, bound together, and often wrapped ⟨a *bale* of hay⟩ [Old French, of Germanic origin]

³bale *vt* : to make up into a bale — **bal·er** *n*

ba·leen \bə-ˈlēn, ˈba-ˌlēn\ *n* : **WHALEBONE** [Latin *ballaena* "whale", from Greek *phallaina*]

baleen whale *n* : **WHALEBONE WHALE**

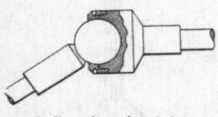

ball-and-socket joint

bale·ful \ˈbāl-fəl\ *adj* **I** : deadly or harmful in influence **2** : portending evil — **bale·ful·ly** \-fə-lē\ *adv* — **bale·ful·ness** *n*

¹balk \ˈbȯk\ *n* **I** : a ridge of land left unplowed or missed in plowing **2** : **BEAM, RAFTER** **3** : something that hinders **4** : failure of a player to complete a motion begun; *esp* : an illegal motion of a baseball pitcher while in position [Old English *balca*]

²balk *vb* **I** *archaic* : to pass over : fail to grasp **2** : to check or stop by or as if by an obstacle : **BLOCK** **3** : to stop short and refuse to continue or act ⟨they *balked* at the extra work⟩ **4** : to commit a balk in sports — **balk·er** *n*

bal·kan·ize \ˈbȯl-kə-ˌnīz\ *vt, often cap* : to break up (as a region) into smaller and often hostile units [*Balkan* peninsula] — **bal·kan·iza·tion** \ˌbȯl-kə-nə-ˈzā-shən\ *n, often cap*

balky \ˈbȯ-kē\ *adj* **balk·i·er; -est** : likely to balk — **balk·i·ness** *n*

¹ball \ˈbȯl\ *n* **I** : a round or roundish body or mass: as **a** : a usually spherical body used in a game or sport **b** : **EARTH, GLOBE** **c** : a usually round solid shot for a firearm **d** (1) : the rounded bulge at the base of the thumb (2) : the rounded broad part of the sole of the human foot between the toes and the arch **2** : a game in which a ball is thrown, kicked, or struck; *esp* : **BASEBALL** **3** : a pitched baseball not struck at by the batter that fails to pass through the strike zone [Old Norse *bôllr*]

²ball *vb* : to form or gather into a ball

³ball *n* : a large formal gathering for social dancing [French *bal,* ultimately from Late Latin *ballare* "to dance", from Greek *ballizein*]

bal·lad \ˈbal-əd\ *n* **I** : a simple song : **AIR** **2** : a narrative poem usually in stanzas of two or four lines and suitable for singing; *esp* : one of unknown authorship handed down orally from generation to generation **3** : a popular song; *esp* : a slow romantic or sentimental dance song [Middle French *balade,* from Provençal *balada* "dance, dancing song", from Late Latin *ballare* "to dance"] — **bal·lad·ry** \-ə-drē\ *n*

ball-and-socket joint *n* : a joint (as in the hip) in which a rounded part moves within a socket so as to allow movements in many directions

¹bal·last \ˈbal-əst\ *n* **I** : heavy material used to improve the stability and control the draft of a ship or the ascent of a balloon **2** : gravel, cinders, or crushed stone used in making a roadbed (as of a railroad) or in making concrete [probably from Low German, of Scandinavian origin]

²ballast *vt* : to provide with ballast

ball bearing *n* **I** : a bearing in which the revolving part turns on steel balls that roll easily in a groove **2** : one of the balls in a ball bearing

ball boy *n* : a boy who retrieves balls for the players in a tennis tournament

ball·car·ri·er \ˈbȯl-ˌkar-ē-ər\ *n* : the football player carrying the ball in an offensive play

bal·le·ri·na \ˌbal-ə-ˈrē-nə\ *n* : a woman ballet dancer [Italian]

bal·let \ˈba-ˌlā, ba-ˈ\ *n* **I a** : dancing in which conventional poses and steps are combined with light flowing figures and movements **b** : a theatrical art form using ballet dancing to convey a story, theme, or atmosphere **2** : music for a ballet **3** : a group that performs ballets [French, from Italian *balletto,* derived from Late Latin *ballare* "to dance"]

bal·let·o·mane \ba-ˈlet-ə-ˌmān\ *n* : a person who loves ballet [*ballet* + *-o-* + *-mane,* from *mania*]

ball girl *n* : a girl who retrieves balls for the players in a tennis tournament

bal·lis·ta \bə-ˈlis-tə\ *n* : an ancient military weapon used for hurling large missiles [Latin, derived from Greek *ballein* "to throw"]

bal·lis·tic \bə-'lis-tik\ *adj* : of or relating to ballistics or to a body in motion according to the laws of ballistics

ballistic missile *n* : a self-propelled missile guided in the ascent of a high-arch path and freely falling in the descent

bal·lis·tics \bə-'lis-tiks\ *n sing or pl* **1 a** : the science of the motion of projectiles in flight **b** : the flight characteristics of a projectile **2 a** : the firing characteristics of a firearm or cartridge

ball lightning *n* : a rare form of lightning consisting of a luminous ball that may move along solid objects or float in the air

¹bal·loon \bə-'lün\ *n* **1** : a nonporous bag filled with heated air or with a gas lighter than air so as to rise and float above the ground **2** : a toy consisting of a rubber bag that can be inflated with air or gas [French *ballon*, from Italian dialect *ballone*, from *balla* "ball", of Germanic origin] — **bal·loon·ist** \-'lü-nəst\ *n*

²balloon *vb* **1** : to ascend or travel in a balloon **2** : to swell or puff out **3** : to increase rapidly ⟨costs *ballooned*⟩

¹bal·lot \'bal-ət\ *n* **1 a** : a small ball used in secret voting **b** : a sheet of paper used to cast a vote **2 a** : the action or a system of secret voting **b** : the right to vote **3** : the number of votes cast [Italian *ballotta*, from *balla* "ball"]

²ballot *vi* : to vote or decide by ballot — **bal·lot·er** *n*

ball park *n* : a park in which ball and especially baseball is played — **in the ball park** : reasonably accurate or acceptable

ball·point \'bȯl-,pȯint\ *n* : a pen having as the writing point a small rotating steel ball that inks itself by contact with an inner ink supply

ball·room \'bȯl-,rüm, -,rum\ *n* : a large room for dances

bal·ly·hoo \'bal-ē-,hü\ *n, pl* **-hoos 1** : a noisy attention-getting demonstration or talk **2** : sensational or exaggerated advertising or propaganda [origin unknown] — **ballyhoo** *vt*

balm \'bäm, 'bälm\ *n* **1** : a resin from small tropical evergreen trees **2** : a fragrant healing or soothing preparation (as an ointment) **3** : something that comforts or refreshes ⟨sleep is *balm* to a tired body⟩ **4** : any of several spicy fragrant herbs (as lemon balm) **5** : a spicy aromatic odor [Old French *baume*, from Latin *balsamum* "balsam"]

balm of Gil·e·ad \-'gil-ē-əd\ **1 a** : a small African and Asian tree with aromatic evergreen leaves; *also* : its fragrant oleoresin **b** : any of several aromatic plants (as a balsam fir) **2** : an agency that soothes, relieves, or heals [*Gilead*, region of ancient Palestine known for its balm]

balmy \'bäm-ē, 'bäl-mē\ *adj* **balm·i·er; -est 1 a** : having the qualities of balm : SOOTHING **b** : MILD ⟨*balmy* weather⟩ **2** : lacking good sense : INSANE — **balm·i·ly** \'bäm-ə-lē, 'bäl-mə-\ *adv* — **balm·i·ness** \'bäm-ē-nəs, 'bäl-mē-\ *n*

ba·lo·ney \bə-'lō-nē\ *n* : silly or absurd talk : NONSENSE [alteration of *bologna*]

bal·sa \'bȯl-sə\ *n* **1** : a tropical American tree with extremely light strong wood used especially for floats; *also* : its wood **2** : a raft made of bundles of grass or reeds lashed together **3** : a life raft made of two cylinders of metal or wood joined by a framework and often used for reaching the shore through surf [Spanish]

bal·sam \'bȯl-səm\ *n* **1 a** : an aromatic and usually oily and resinous substance flowing from various plants **b** : a preparation containing or smelling like balsam **2 a** : a tree that yields balsam **b** : IMPATIENS; *esp* : one grown as an ornamental **3** : BALM 2 [Latin *balsamum*, from Greek *balsamon*] — **bal·sam·ic** \bȯl-'sam-ik\ *adj*

balsam fir *n* : a resinous American evergreen tree of the pine family widely used for pulpwood and as a Christmas tree

balsam of Pe·ru \-pə-'rü\ : a balsam from a tropical American leguminous tree used in perfumery and medicine

balsam poplar *n* : a North American poplar with resin-coated buds that is often cultivated as a shade tree — called also *hackmatack, tacamahac*

Bal·tic \'bȯl-tik\ *adj* **1** : of or relating to the Baltic sea or to the states of Lithuania, Latvia, and Estonia **2** : of or relating to a branch of the Indo-European languages containing Latvian and Lithuanian

Bal·ti·more oriole \'bȯl-tə-,mōr-, -,mȯr-, -mər-\ *n* : a common American oriole of which the male is brightly colored with orange, black, and white and the female is largely brown and greenish yellow [George Calvert, Lord *Baltimore*]

bal·us·ter \'bal-ə-stər\ *n* : an upright rounded, square, or vase-shaped support of a rail (as in the railing of a staircase or balcony) [French *balustre*, from Italian *balaustro*, from *balaustra* "pomegranate flower"]

bal·us·trade \'bal-ə-,strād\ *n* : a row of balusters topped by a rail; *also* : a low parapet or barrier

bam·bi·no \bam-'bē-nō\ *n, pl* **bambinos** or **bam·bi·ni** \-'bē-nē\ **1** : CHILD 2a; *esp* : BABY 1 **2** *pl usually* **bambini** : a representation of the infant Christ [Italian]

bam·boo \bam-'bü\ *n, pl* **bamboos 1** : any of various chiefly tropical tall woody grasses including some with strong hollow stems used for building, furniture, or utensils **2** : the tough woody stem or tissue of a bamboo [Malay *bambu*] — **bamboo** *adj*

bamboo curtain *n* : an iron curtain isolating areas under Chinese Communist control

bam·boo·zle \bam-'bü-zəl\ *vt* **-boo·zled; -boo·zling** \-'büz-ling, -ə-ling\ : to deceive by trickery : HOODWINK [origin unknown] — **bam·boo·zle·ment** \-'bü-zəl-mənt\ *n*

¹ban \'ban\ *vb* **banned; ban·ning 1** *archaic* : CURSE 1 **2** : to prohibit especially by legal means or social pressure [Old English *bannan* "to summon"] SYN see FORBID

²ban *n* **1** : ANATHEMA 1a **2** : MALEDICTION, CURSE **3** : an official prohibition **4** : censure or condemnation especially through public opinion

ba·nal \bə-'nal, ba-, -'näl; bā-'nal; 'bān-l\ *adj* : lacking originality, freshness, or novelty : TRITE, COMMONPLACE [French, from Middle French, "of feudal service, commonplace", from *ban* "summons to feudal service", of Germanic origin] SYN see INSIPID — **ba·nal·i·ty** \bā-'nal-ət-ē, bə-\ *n* — **ba·nal·ly** \bə-'nal-lē, -'näl-; bān-l-lē, -ē\ *adv*

ba·nana \bə-'nan-ə\ *n* : a treelike tropical plant with large leaves and with flower clusters that develop into a bunch of finger-shaped fruit which are yellow or red when ripe; *also* : its fruit [of African origin]

banana oil *n* : a colorless liquid acetate that has a pleasant fruity odor and is used as a solvent

¹band \'band\ *n* **1** *archaic* : something (as a fetter or shackle) that confines or constricts **2** : something that binds or restrains legally, morally, or spiritually ⟨we must break the *bands* of prejudice⟩ **3** : a strip serving to join or hold things together **4** : a thin encircling strip that confines, supports, or protects ⟨protect the baby's navel with a soft *band*⟩ **5 a** : a strip with a distinctive characteristic (as color, texture, or composition) ⟨a *band* of nerve fibers⟩ **b** : a range of wavelengths or frequencies between two specified limits **c** : a narrow strip serving chiefly as decoration **d** *pl* : a pair of strips hanging at the front of the neck as part of a clerical, legal, or academic dress **e** : a strip of grooves on a phonographic record containing a single piece or a section of a long piece [partly from Old Norse, "something that constricts" and partly from Middle French *bende, bande* "strip", of Germanic origin] — **band·ed** \'ban-dəd\ *adj*

²band *vb* **1** : to put a band on or fasten with a band **2** : to finish with a band **3 a** : to attach (oneself) to a

bamboo 1

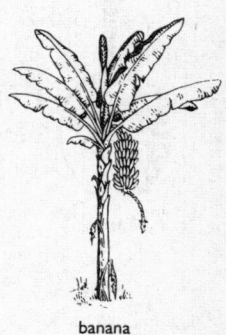

banana

\ə\ abut	\ng\ sing
\ər\ **further**	\ō\ bone
\a\ mat	\ȯ\ saw
\ā\ take	\ȯi\ coin
\ä\ cot, cart	\th\ thin
\au\ out	\th\ this
\ch\ chin	\ü\ food
\e\ pet	\u̇\ foot
\ē\ easy	\y\ yet
\g\ go	\yü\ few
\i\ tip	\yu̇\ cure
\ī\ life	\zh\ vision
\j\ job	

group **b** : to gather together or summon for a purpose **c** : to unite in a company or confederacy or for a common purpose — **band·er** *n*

³**band** *n* : a group of persons, animals, or things; *esp* : a group of musicians organized for playing together [Middle French *bande* "troop"]

ban·dage \'ban-dij\ *n* : a strip of fabric used especially to dress and bind up wounds — **bandage** *vt*

Band–Aid \'ban-'dād\ *trademark* — used for a small adhesive strip with a gauze pad for covering minor wounds

ban·dan·na *or* **ban·dana** \ban-'dan-ə\ *n* : a large figured handkerchief with usually a red or blue background [Hindi *bā̃dhnū*, cloth dyed by knotting portions so as to leave them undyed, derived from Sanskrit *badhnāti* "he ties"]

band·box \'band-,bäks, 'ban-\ *n* : a usually cylindrical box for holding light articles of clothing

ban·deau \ban-'dō\ *n, pl* **ban·deaux** \-'dōz\ **1** : a band especially for the hair **2** : BRASSIERE [French]

ban·de·role *or* **ban·de·rol** \'ban-də-,rōl\ *n* : a long narrow forked flag or streamer [French *banderole*, from Italian *banderuola*, from *bandiera* "banner", of Germanic origin]

ban·di·coot \'ban-di-,küt\ *n* : any of various small insect-eating and plant-eating marsupial mammals especially of Australia [Telugu (a Dravidian language of India) *pandikokku*]

bandicoot

ban·dit \'ban-dət\ *n, pl* **ban·dits 1** *pl also* **ban·dit·ti** \ban-'dit-ē\ : BRIGAND **2** : an unethical or criminal person (as a profiteer or gangster) [Italian *bandito*, from *bandire* "to banish", of Germanic origin] — **ban·dit·ry** \'ban-də-trē\ *n*

band·mas·ter \'band-,mas-ter, 'ban-\ *n* : a conductor of a musical band

ban·dog \'ban-,dȯg\ *n* : a fierce dog formerly kept tied as a watchdog [Middle English *band + dogge* "dog"]

ban·do·lier *or* **ban·do·leer** \,ban-də-'liər\ *n* : a belt worn over the shoulder and across the breast to carry something (as cartridges) or as part of an official or ceremonial dress [Middle French *bandouliere*, derived from Spanish *bando* band]

band saw *n* : a saw in the form of an endless steel belt running over pulleys

band shell *n* : a bandstand backed by a sounding board shaped like a huge concave seashell

bands·man \'banz-mən, 'bandz-\ *n* : a member of a musical band

band·stand \'ban-,stand, 'band-\ *n* : a usually roofed outdoor platform on which a band or orchestra performs

band·wag·on \-,wag-ən\ *n* **1** : a wagon carrying musicians in a parade **2** : a candidate, side, or movement that attracts increasing support or approval because it seems to be winning or gaining popularity — used in phrases like *climb on the bandwagon*

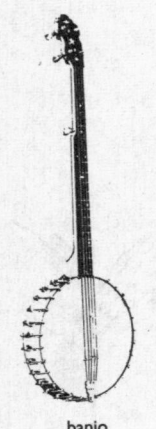

banjo

¹**ban·dy** \'ban-dē\ *vb* **ban·died; ban·dy·ing 1** : to treat in a careless or high-handed manner **2 a** : EXCHANGE; *esp* : to exchange in argument ⟨*bandy* sharp words⟩ **b** : to discuss lightly or glibly or as a subject of gossip **3** *archaic* : to band together [probably from Middle French *bander* "to bat a tennis ball back and forth"]

²**bandy** *adj* : curved especially outward : BOWED ⟨*bandy* legs⟩ [probably from *bandy* "hockey stick"]

ban·dy–legged \,ban-dē-'legd, -'leg-əd\ *adj* : having bandy legs : BOWLEGGED

bane \'bān\ *n* **1** : something that destroys life; *esp* : deadly poison **2** : a source of injury, harm, ruin, or woe : a destructive influence [Old English *bana* "murderer"]

bane·ful \'bān-fəl\ *adj* **1** *archaic* : having poisonous qualities : NOXIOUS **2** : causing destruction or woe : RUINOUS — **bane·ful·ly** \-fə-lē\ *adv*

¹**bang** \'bang\ *vb* **1** : to strike against : BUMP **2** : to strike with a sharp noise **3** : to produce a sharp often explosive noise or series of noises [probably of Scandinavian origin]

²**bang** *n* **1** : a resounding blow **2** : a sudden loud noise **3 a** : a sudden striking effect **b** : a quick burst of energy **c** : an emotional thrill

³**bang** *adv* : EXACTLY, DIRECTLY ⟨*bang* in the middle⟩

⁴**bang** *n* : a fringe of banged hair — usually used in pl. [probably from *bangtail* "short tail"]

⁵**bang** *vt* : to cut (as front hair) short and squarely across

ban·gle \'bang-gəl\ *n* **1** : an ornamental circlet worn as a bracelet or anklet **2** : a small ornament hanging (as from a bracelet) loosely [Hindi *baṅglī*]

bang·tail \'bang-,tāl\ *n* **1** : RACEHORSE **2** : a wild horse

bang–up \'bang-,əp\ *adj* : of the best quality : FIRST-RATE ⟨had a *bang-up* time⟩

ban·ish \'ban-ish\ *vt* **1** : to compel by authority to leave a country ⟨the king *banished* the traitors⟩ **2** : to drive out from or as if from a home : EXPEL ⟨*banish* fears⟩ [Middle French *baniss-*, stem of *banir*, of Germanic origin] — **ban·ish·er** *n* — **ban·ish·ment** \-ish-mənt\ *n*

ban·is·ter *also* **ban·nis·ter** \'ban-ə-stər\ *n* **1** : one of the upright supports of a handrail alongside a staircase **2** : a handrail with its supporting posts **3** : HANDRAIL [alteration of *baluster*]

ban·jo \'ban-,jō\ *n, pl* **banjos** *also* **banjoes** : a musical instrument related to the guitar with a long narrow fretted neck and small drum-shaped body [probably of African origin] — **ban·jo·ist** \-,jō-əst\ *n*

¹**bank** \'bangk\ *n* **1** : a mound, pile, or ridge (as of earth) **2** : a piled up mass of cloud or fog **3** : an undersea elevation rising especially from the continental shelf : SHOAL **4** : rising ground bordering a lake, river, or sea or forming the edge of a hollow (as a cut) **5** : a steep slope (as of a hill) **6** : the inward tilt of a surface along a curve or of a vehicle (as an airplane) when taking a curve [probably of Scandinavian origin]

²**bank** *vb* **1** : to raise a bank about **2** : to heap or pile in a bank **3** : to rise in or form a bank **4** : to cover (a fire) with fresh fuel so as to reduce the speed of burning **5** : to build (a curve) with the roadbed or track inclined laterally upward from the inside edge **6** : to incline an airplane laterally when turning **7** : to form or group in a tier

³**bank** *n* **1** : a bench for the rowers of a galley **2** : a group or series of objects (as oars or typewriter keys) arranged close together in a row or a tier [Old French *banc* "bench", of Germanic origin]

⁴**bank** *n* **1** : a place of business that receives, lends, issues, exchanges, and takes care of money, extends credit, and provides ways of sending funds quickly from place to place **2** : a small container in which coins or bills are saved **3 a** : a supply of something held in reserve **b** (1) : the fund of the banker or dealer in a card or board game (2) : a fund of pieces belonging to a game (as dominoes) from which the players draw **4** : a storage place for a reserve supply ⟨eye *bank*⟩ [Italian *banca*, literally, "bench", of Germanic origin] □ ORIGIN The literal meaning of Italian *banca* was "bench", but the word was also used for the benchlike counter at which an early money changer transacted business and later for the money changer's shop itself, the bank. When the banking trade spread from Italy to France, and so to England, the Italian word went with it and became our English *bank*.

Although they come from different languages, the English homographs of *bank* are all related and are related to the English word *bench* as well. The original meaning of the words in this group was probably something like "shelf".

⁵**bank** *vb* **1** : to act as a banker **2** : to have an account in a bank **3** : to deposit in a bank ⟨*banks* $10 every week⟩ — **bank on** *or* **bank upon** : to depend upon

bank·book \'bangk-ˌbùk\ *n* : a depositor's book in which a bank records each deposit and withdrawal — called also *passbook*

bank card *n* : a credit card issued by a bank

bank·er \'bang-kər\ *n* **1** : one that engages in the business of banking **2** : the player who keeps the bank in a card or board game

bank holiday *n, British* : LEGAL HOLIDAY

bank·ing *n* : the business of a bank or a banker

bank note *n* : a promissory note issued by a bank, payable to bearer on demand without interest, and acceptable as money

bank·roll \'bangk-ˌrōl\ *n* : supply of money : FUNDS

¹bank·rupt \'bang-ˌkrəpt\ *n* **1** : a person who becomes unable to pay his debts; *esp* : one whose property is turned over by court order to a trustee to be administered for the benefit of his creditors **2** : one that lacks completely a specified quality or thing ⟨a moral *bankrupt*⟩ [Italian *bancarotta* "bankruptcy", literally, "broken bank"]

²bankrupt *vt* : to make bankrupt

³bankrupt *adj* **1 a** : fallen into a state of financial ruin : IMPOVERISHED **b** : legally declared a bankrupt **2** : DEPLETED, DESTITUTE 1 — used with *of* or *in*

bank·rupt·cy \'bang-ˌkrəp-sē, -krəp-\ *n, pl* **-cies** : the condition of being bankrupt

¹ban·ner \'ban-ər\ *n* **1 a** : a piece of cloth attached by one edge to a staff and used as a standard **b** : ⁴FLAG 1 **c** : an ensign displaying a distinctive or symbolic device or inscription **2** : a headline in large type running across a newspaper page **3** : a strip of cloth on which a sign is painted **4** : a name, slogan, or goal associated with a particular group or point of view ⟨crusading under the *banner* of progress⟩ [Old French *banere*, of Germanic origin]

²banner *adj* : unusually good ⟨a *banner* year for apple growers⟩

ban·nock \'ban-ək\ *n* : an often unleavened bread of oat or barley flour baked in flat loaves [Middle English *bannok*]

banns \'banz\ *n pl* : public announcement especially in church of a proposed marriage [Middle English *bane, ban* "proclamation, ban"]

¹ban·quet \'bang-kwət, 'ban-, -ˌkwet\ *n* : an elaborate often ceremonious meal for many people frequently in celebration of a special occasion [Middle French, from Italian *banchetto*, from *banca* "bench, bank"]

²banquet *vb* **1** : to entertain with a banquet : FEAST **2** : to partake of a banquet — **ban·quet·er** *n*

ban·quette \bang-'ket, ban-\ *n* : a long upholstered seat especially along a wall

ban·shee \'ban-ˌshē, ban-'\ *n* : a female spirit in Gaelic folklore whose appearance or wailing warns of approaching death [Scottish Gaelic *bean sith*]

¹ban·tam \'bant-əm\ *n* **1** : any of numerous small domestic fowls that are often miniatures of members of the standard breeds **2** : a small and often quarrelsome person [*Bantam*, former territorial unit in Java]

²bantam *adj* **1** : SMALL 1, DIMINUTIVE **2** : pertly quarrelsome : SAUCY

ban·tam·weight \-ˌwāt\ *n* : a boxer in a weight division having the approximate range of 51 to 54 kilograms

¹ban·ter \'bant-ər\ *vb* **1** : to speak to in a witty and teasing manner : RALLY **2** : to talk or act playfully or wittily [origin unknown] — **ban·ter·er** \-ər-ər\ *n* — **ban·ter·ing·ly** \'bant-ə-ring-lē\ *adv*

²banter *n* : good-natured and witty teasing or joking

bant·ling \'bant-ling\ *n* : a very young child [perhaps from German *bänkling* "bastard"]

Ban·tu \'ban-ˌtü, 'bän-\ *n* **1** : a member of a family of negroid peoples occupying equatorial and southern Africa **2** : a group of African languages spoken generally south of a line from Cameroon to Kenya — **Bantu** *adj*

Ban·tu·stan \ˌban-tù-'stan, ˌbän-tù-'stän\ *n* : an all-black unit of territory in the Republic of South Africa with a limited degree of self-government [*Bantu* + *-stan* "land" (as in *Hindustan*)]

ban·yan \'ban-yən\ *n* : a large East Indian tree related to the fig from whose branches aerial roots grow downward into the ground and form new supporting trunks [*banyan* "Hindu merchant", from Hindi *baniyā*; from a merchant's pagoda built under such a tree in Iran]

ban·zai \bän-'zī, 'bän-\ *n* : a Japanese cheer or cry of triumph — usually used interjectionally [Japanese]

bao·bab \'baù-ˌbab, 'bā-ə-ˌbab\ *n* : an Old World tropical tree with a broad trunk, an edible acid fruit resembling a gourd, and bark used in making paper, cloth, and rope [New Latin *bahobab*]

bap·tism \'bap-ˌtiz-əm\ *n* **1** : a Christian sacrament signifying spiritual rebirth and admitting the recipient to the Christian community through the ritual use of water **2** : a non-Christian ceremony using water for ritual purification **3** : an act, experience, or ordeal by which one is named, purified, or initiated into a new life ⟨a soldier's *baptism* of fire⟩ — **bap·tis·mal** \bap-'tiz-məl\ *adj* — **bap·tis·mal·ly** \-mə-lē\ *adv*

Bap·tist \'bap-təst\ *n* : a Protestant of an evangelical denomination practicing congregational government and baptism by immersion for believers — **Baptist** *adj*

bap·tis·tery *or* **bap·tis·try** \'bap-tə-strē\ *n, pl* **-ter·ies** *or* **-tries** : a part of a church or formerly a separate building used for baptism

bap·tize \bap-'tīz, 'bap-ˌ\ *vt* **1** : to administer baptism to **2 a** : to purify spiritually especially by a cleansing experience or ordeal **b** : INITIATE 1 **3** : to give a name to (as at baptism) : CHRISTEN [Greek *baptizein* "to dip, baptize"] — **bap·tiz·er** *n*

¹bar \'bär\ *n* **1 a** : a rigid piece (as of wood or metal) that is longer than it is wide and has various uses (as for a lever, barrier, or fastening) **b** : a usually rectangular solid piece or block of material longer than it is wide ⟨*bar* of soap⟩ ⟨candy *bar*⟩ **2** : something that obstructs or prevents passage, progress, or action : IMPEDIMENT: as **a** : any intangible or nonphysical impediment **b** : a submerged or partly submerged bank along a shore or in a river **3 a** : the railing in a courtroom that encloses the place where the business of the court is transacted **b** : a court or system of courts **c** : an authority or tribunal that renders judgment (before the *bar* of public opinion) **d** : the body of lawyers qualified to practice in a jurisdiction (the New York *bar*); *also* : the profession of lawyer **4** : a straight stripe, band, or line much longer than it is wide **5 a** : a counter for serving food or especially alcoholic beverages **b** : BARROOM **6 a** : a vertical line across the musical staff before the initial measure accent **b** : MEASURE 4c [Old French *barre*]

²bar *vt* **barred; bar·ring** **1 a** : to fasten with a bar **b** : to place bars across to prevent passage **2** : to mark with bars : STRIPE **3** : to block off : OBSTRUCT ⟨*bar* the road to traffic⟩ **4 a** : to keep out : EXCLUDE ⟨*bar* reporters from the meeting⟩ **b** : PREVENT, FORBID ⟨the order *bars* discrimination in hiring⟩

³bar *prep* : with the exception of ⟨*bar* none⟩

¹barb \'bärb\ *n* **1 a** : a sharp projection extending backward (as from the point of an arrow or fishhook) and preventing easy removal **b** : any of various natural objects (as a hooked plant hair or a lateral filament of a feather) resembling a barb **2** : a biting or pointedly critical remark or comment [Middle French *barbe*, literally, "beard", from Latin *barba*]

²barb *vt* : to furnish with a barb

³barb *n* : a horse of a breed related to the Arab and introduced into Spain by the Moors [French *barbe*, from Italian *barbero*, from *barbero* "of Barbary"]

bar·bar·i·an \bär-'ber-ē-ən, bär-'bar-\ *adj* **1** : of, relating to, or being a land, culture, or people alien to and

¹bar 6a

\ə\ abut	\ng\ sing
\ər\ further	\ō\ bone
\a\ mat	\ò\ saw
\ā\ take	\òi\ coin
\ä\ cot, cart	\th\ thin
\aù\ out	\th\ this
\ch\ chin	\ü\ food
\e\ pet	\ù\ foot
\ē\ easy	\y\ yet
\g\ go	\yü\ few
\i\ tip	\yù\ cure
\ī\ life	\zh\ vision
\j\ job	

usually felt to be inferior to one's own **2** : lacking refinement, learning, or artistic or literary culture [Latin *barbarus,* from Greek *barbaros* "foreign, ignorant"] — **barbarian** *n* — **bar·bar·i·an·ism** \-ē-ə-,niz-əm\ *n*

☐ SYN BARBARIAN, BARBAROUS, BARBARIC, SAVAGE mean characteristic of an uncivilized person. BARBARIAN often implies a state somewhere between tribal savagery and full civilization; BARBAROUS tends to stress the harsher or more brutal side of uncivilized life; BARBARIC suggests crudeness of taste and fondness for gorgeous and unrestrained display; SAVAGE suggests more primitive culture than BARBARIAN and greater harshness or fierceness than BARBAROUS.

bar·bar·ic \bär-'bar-ik\ *adj* **1** : of, relating to, or characteristic of barbarians **2 a** : marked by a lack of restraint **b** : having a bizarre, primitive, or unsophisticated quality ⟨*barbaric* splendor⟩ SYN see BARBARIAN

bar·ba·rism \'bär-bə-,riz-əm\ *n* **1** : an idea, act, word, or expression that offends against contemporary standards of good taste or acceptability **2 a** : a barbarian state of social or intellectual development **b** : the practice or display of barbarian acts, attitudes, or ideas

bar·bar·i·ty \bär-'bar-ət-ē\ *n, pl* **-ties 1** : BARBARISM **2 a** : barbarous cruelty **b** : an act or instance of barbarous cruelty

bar·ba·rize \'bär-bə-,rīz\ *vb* : to make or become barbarian or barbarous — **bar·ba·ri·za·tion** \,bär-bə-rə-'zā-shən, -brə-\ *n*

bar·ba·rous \'bär-bə-rəs, -brəs\ *adj* **1** : characterized by the use of barbarisms in speech or writing **2 a** : of or relating to a backward land or people **b** : lacking culture or refinement **3** : mercilessly harsh or cruel SYN see BARBARIAN — **bar·ba·rous·ly** *adv* — **bar·ba·rous·ness** *n*

Bar·ba·ry ape \'bär-bə-rē-, -brē-\ *n* : a tailless monkey of North Africa and Gibraltar

¹bar·be·cue \'bär-bi-,kyü\ *n* **1** : an often portable fireplace over which meat and fish are roasted or broiled **2** : a large animal (as a hog or steer) roasted or broiled whole or split over an open fire or bed of hot coals **3** : a social gathering especially outdoors at which barbecued food is eaten [American Spanish *barbacoa*]

²barbecue *vt* **1** : to roast or broil on a rack over hot coals or on a revolving spit before or over a source of heat **2** : to cook in a highly seasoned vinegar sauce

barbed \'bärbd\ *adj* **1** : having a barb **2** : bitingly critical ⟨a *barbed* comment⟩

barbed wire \'bärb-'dwīr, 'bäb-, -'wīr\ *n* : twisted wires armed with sharp points — called also *barbwire*

bar·bel \'bär-bəl\ *n* **1** : a European freshwater fish of the carp family with four barbels on its upper jaw **2** : a slender tactile process on the lips of a fish [Middle French, derived from Latin *barba* "beard"]

bar·bell \'bär-,bel\ *n* : a bar with adjustable weighted disks attached to each end that is used for exercise and in weight lifting

¹bar·ber \'bär-bər\ *n* : one whose business is cutting and dressing hair, shaving and trimming beards, and performing related services [Middle French *barbeor,* from *barbe* "beard", from Latin *barba*]

²barber *vb* **bar·bered; bar·ber·ing** \-bə-ring, -bring\ : to perform the services of a barber

bar·ber·ry \'bär-,ber-ē\ *n* : any of a genus of spiny yellow-flowered shrubs with bright red oblong berries often grown for hedges or ornament [Arabic *barbārīs*]

¹bar·ber·shop \'bär-bər-,shäp\ *n* : a barber's place of business

²barbershop *adj* : having a style of unaccompanied vocal harmonizing of popular songs especially by a quartet

barber's itch *n* : ringworm of the face and neck

bar·bette \bär-'bet\ *n* : a cylinder of armor protecting a gun turret on a warship

bar·bi·can \'bär-bi-kən\ *n* : an outer defensive work; *esp* : a tower at a gate or bridge [Medieval Latin *barbacana*]

bar·bi·tal \'bär-bə-,tol\ *n* : a white habit-forming drug used especially to induce sleep

bar·bi·tu·rate \bär-'bich-ə-rət, -,rāt\ *n* : any of various derivatives of barbituric acid used especially as sedatives or hypnotics

bar·bi·tu·ric acid \,bär-bə-'tyür-ik-, -'tur-\ *n* : a crystalline acid $C_4H_4N_2O_3$ used in making plastics and drugs [German *barbitursäure,* from the name *Barbara* + New Latin *urea* + German *säure* "acid"]

bar·bule \'bär-,byül\ *n* : a minute barb; *esp* : one of the processes that fringe the barbs of a feather

bar·ca·role *or* **bar·ca·rolle** \'bär-kə-,rōl\ *n* **1** : a Venetian boat song characterized by a beat suggesting a rowing rhythm **2** : a piece of music imitating a barcarole [French *barcarolle,* from Italian *barcarola,* from *barca* "bark"]

bar chart *n* : BAR GRAPH

bar code *n* : a code made up of variously spaced bars and sometimes numerals that is designed to be scanned and read into computer memory as identification of the object it labels

bard \'bärd\ *n* **1** : a tribal poet-singer gifted in composing and reciting verses on heroes and their deeds **2** : POET [Irish and Scottish Gaelic] — **bard·ic** \'bärd-ik\ *adj*

¹bare \'baər, 'beər\ *adj* **1 a** : lacking a natural, usual, or appropriate covering ⟨trees *bare* of leaves⟩ **b** : lacking clothing **2** : open to view : EXPOSED ⟨their guilt was laid *bare*⟩ **3 a** : completely unfurnished or only scantily supplied **b** : DESTITUTE ⟨*bare* of all safeguards⟩ **4 a** : having nothing left over or added : MERE ⟨a *bare* majority⟩ **b** : not adorned or expanded : PLAIN ⟨the *bare* facts⟩ [Old English *bær*] — **bare·ness** *n*

²bare *vt* : to make or lay bare : UNCOVER, REVEAL

³bare *archaic past of* BEAR

bare·back \-,bak\ *or* **bare·backed** \-'bakt\ *adv or adj* : on the bare back of a horse : without a saddle ⟨learned to ride *bareback*⟩ ⟨a *bareback* rider in the circus⟩

bare·faced \-'fāst\ *adj* **1** : having the face uncovered **2** : SHAMELESS, BOLD ⟨a *barefaced* lie⟩ — **bare·faced·ly** \-'fā-səd-lē, -'fāst-lē\ *adv* — **bare·faced·ness** \-'fā-səd-nəs; -'fāst-nəs\ *n*

bare·foot \-,fut\ *or* **bare·foot·ed** \-'fut-əd\ *adv or adj* : with the feet bare : UNSHOD ⟨went *barefoot* in summer⟩

bare·hand·ed \-'han-dəd\ *adv or adj* **1** : with the hands bare : without gloves or mittens **2** : without tools or weapons

bare·head·ed \-'hed-əd\ *adv or adj* : with the head bare : without a hat

bare·ly *adv* **1** : SCARCELY, HARDLY ⟨*barely* enough money to live on⟩ **2** : in a scanty manner ⟨a *barely* furnished room⟩

barf \'bärf\ *vi* : VOMIT 1 [origin unknown]

¹bar·gain \'bär-gən\ *n* **1** : an agreement between parties settling what each is to give or receive in a transaction **2** : something gained by or as if by bargaining; *esp* : an advantageous purchase ⟨at 35 percent off, the suit was a real *bargain*⟩ **3** : a situation or event with important good or bad results ⟨got the worst of a bad *bargain*⟩ [Middle French *bargaigne,* from *bargaigner* "to bargain", of Germanic origin]

²bargain *vb* **1** : to talk over the terms of a purchase, agreement, or contract; *esp* : to try to win advantageous terms from the other party to a proposed bargain **2** : to sell or dispose of by bargaining — **bar·gain·er** *n* — **bargain for** : to count on in advance : EXPECT ⟨more trouble than we *bargained for*⟩

¹barge \'bärj\ *n* **1** : a broad flat-bottomed boat used chiefly for the transport of goods on inland waterways **2** : a ship's boat for the use of a naval officer ranking above a captain [Old French, "boat, small ship", from Late Latin *barca*]

²barge *vb* **1** : to carry by barge **2** : to move or thrust oneself clumsily or rudely ⟨they *barged* right in without being invited⟩

barge·man \-mən\ *n* : the master or a deckhand of a barge

bar graph *n* : a graphic means of comparing numbers by rectangles whose lengths are proportional to the numbers represented — called also *bar chart*

bar·ite \'baər-ˌīt, 'beər-\ *n* : barium sulfate $BaSO_4$ occurring as a mineral

¹bari·tone *also* **bary·tone** \'bar-ə-ˌtōn\ *n* **1 a** : a male singing voice of medium range between bass and tenor **b** : a man having such a voice **2** : the saxhorn intermediate in size between althorn and tuba — called also *baritone horn* [derived from Greek *barys* "heavy" + *tonos* "tone"] — **bari·tonal** \ˌbar-ə-'tōn-l\ *adj*

²baritone *also* **barytone** *adj* : relating to or having the range or part of a baritone

bar·i·um \'bar-ē-əm, 'ber-\ *n* : a silver-white malleable toxic bivalent metallic chemical element that occurs only in combination — see ELEMENT table [New Latin, from Greek *barys* "heavy"]

barium sulfate *n* : a colorless crystalline insoluble compound $BaSO_4$ that is used as a pigment, as a filler, and as a substance opaque to X rays in medical photography of the alimentary canal

¹bark \'bärk\ *vb* **1** : to utter a bark or similar sound **2** : to speak or utter in a curt loud usually angry tone ⟨*bark* out an order⟩ **3** : to advertise by persistent outcry ⟨vendors *barked* their wares⟩ [Old English *beorcan*] — **bark up the wrong tree** : to speak or act on the basis of a misunderstanding

²bark *n* : the characteristic short loud cry of a dog

³bark *n* : the tough largely corky exterior covering of a woody root or stem [Old Norse *bǫrkr*]

⁴bark *vt* **1** : to strip the bark from **2** : to rub off or abrade the skin of

⁵bark *or* **barque** *n* **1 a** : a small sailing ship **b** : a 3-masted sailing vessel with foremast and mainmast square-rigged and mizzenmast fore-and-aft rigged **2** : a craft propelled by sails or oars [Middle French *barque*, from Provençal *barca*, from Late Latin]

bar·keep·er \'bär-ˌkē-pər\ *or* **bar·keep** \-ˌkēp\ *n* : a person who owns, operates, or tends a bar

bar·ken·tine *also* **bar·quen·tine** \'bär-kən-ˌtēn\ *n* : a 3-masted sailing vessel having the foremast square-rigged and the mainmast and mizzenmast fore-and-aft rigged [⁵*bark* + -*entine*, alteration of -*antine* (as in *brigantine*)]

bark·er \'bär-kər\ *n* : a person who stands at the entrance to a show and tries to attract customers to it with loud fluent talk

barky \'bär-kē\ *adj* **bark·i·er; -est** : covered with or resembling bark

bar·ley \'bär-lē\ *n* : a cereal grass with flowers in dense spikes with three spikelets at each joint; *also* : its seed used in malt beverages and as food or stock feed [Old English *bærlic* "of barley"]

bar·ley·corn \-ˌkȯrn\ *n* : a grain of barley

barm \'bärm\ *n* : yeast formed on fermenting malt liquors [Old English *beorma*]

bar·maid \'bär-ˌmād\ *n* : a woman who works as a bartender

bar·man \-mən\ *n* : a man who works as a bartender

Bar·me·cid·al \ˌbär-mə-'sīd-l\ *or* **Bar·me·cide** \'bär-mə-ˌsīd\ *adj* : providing only an apparent abundance ⟨a *Barmecidal* feast⟩ [*Barmecide*, a wealthy Persian, who, in a tale of *The Arabian Nights*, invited a beggar to a feast of imaginary food]

¹bar mitz·vah \bär-'mits-və\ *n, often cap B&M* **1** : a Jewish boy who reaches his 13th birthday and attains the age of religious duty and responsibility **2** : the ceremony recognizing a boy as a bar mitzvah [Hebrew *bar miṣwāh*, literally, "son of the law"]

²bar mitzvah *vt* **bar mitz·vahed; bar mitz·vahing** : to administer the ceremony of bar mitzvah to

barn \'bärn\ *n* : a building used chiefly for storing grain and hay and for housing farm animals (as cows and horses) [Old English *bereærn*, from *bere* "barley" + *ærn* "place"]

bar·na·cle \'bär-ni-kəl\ *n* : any of numerous marine crustaceans (order Cirripedia) that are free-swimming as larvae but fixed (as to rocks or pilings) as adults [Middle English *bernake*, a goose once believed to grow from barnacles, of Celtic origin] — **bar·na·cled** \-kəld\ *adj*

barn dance *n* : an American social dance originally held in a barn and featuring square dances, round dances, and traditional music and calls

barn·storm \'bärn-ˌstȯrm\ *vi* **1** : to tour through rural districts staging theatrical performances usually in one-night stands **2** : to travel from place to place making brief stops (as in political campaigning) **3** : to pilot an airplane in sight-seeing flights with passengers or in exhibition stunts in an unscheduled course especially in rural districts — **barn·storm·er** *n*

barn swallow *n* : a common swallow of both the Old World and the New World that usually attaches its nest to beams and rafters of barns

barn·yard \-ˌyärd\ *n* : a usually fenced area adjoining a barn

baro- *combining form* : weight : pressure ⟨*baro*meter⟩ [Greek *baros* "weight"]

baro·graph \'bar-ə-ˌgraf\ *n* : a barometer that records atmospheric pressure changes on a graph

ba·rom·e·ter \bə-'räm-ət-ər\ *n* **1** : an instrument for determining the pressure of the atmosphere that is used to forecast weather and to determine altitude **2** : something that registers changes (as in public opinion) — **bar·o·met·ric** \ˌbar-ə-'me-trik\ *adj*

bar·on \'bar-ən\ *n* **1 a** : a tenant holding rights and title usually by military service directly from a feudal superior (as a king) **b** : a member of the nobility : PEER **2** : a member of the lowest grade of the British peerage **3** : a person of great or excessive power or influence in some field ⟨cattle *baron*⟩ [Old French, of Germanic origin]

bar·on·age \-ə-nij\ *n* : the whole body of barons or peers

bar·on·ess \-ə-nəs\ *n* **1** : the wife or widow of a baron **2** : a woman who holds a baronial title in her own right

bar·on·et \'bar-ə-nət\ *n* : a person holding a rank of honor below a baron but above a knight

ba·ro·ni·al \bə-'rō-nē-əl\ *adj* : of, relating to, or suitable for a baron or the baronage ⟨lives in *baronial* splendor⟩

bar·ony \'bar-ə-nē\ *n, pl* **bar·on·ies** : the domain, rank, or dignity of a baron

ba·roque \bə-'rōk, ba-, -'räk\ *adj* : of or relating to a style of artistic expression especially of the 17th century marked by elaborate and sometimes grotesque ornamentation and the use of curved and exaggerated figures in art and architecture, by improvisation, contrast, and tension in music, and by complex form and bizarre, ingenious, and often ambiguous imagery in literature [French, from Italian *barocco*] — **baroque** *n*

ba·rouche \bə-'rüsh\ *n* : a four-wheeled carriage with a driver's seat high in front, two double seats inside facing each other, and a folding top [German *barutsche*, from Italian *biroccio*, derived from Latin *bi-* "two" + *rota* "wheel"]

barque \'bärk\ *variant of* BARK

barquentine *variant of* BARKENTINE

bar·rack \'bar-ək, -ik\ *n* **1** : a building or group of buildings in which soldiers are quartered — usually used in pl. **2** : a plain large building — usually used in pl. [French *baraque* "hut", from Catalan *barraca*]

bar·ra·cu·da \ˌbar-ə-'küd-ə\ *n, pl* **-da** *or* **-das** : any of several large predatory marine fishes of warm seas related to the gray mullets [American Spanish]

¹bar·rage \'bär-ij\ *n* : an artificial dam placed in a watercourse to increase the depth of water or to divert it

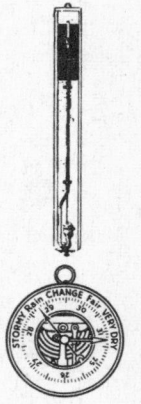

barometer 1: *top* mercury, *bottom* aneroid

\ə\ abut	\ng\ sing
\ər\ further	\ō\ bone
\a\ mat	\ȯ\ saw
\ā\ take	\ȯi\ coin
\ä\ cot, cart	\th\ thin
\au̇\ out	\th̲\ this
\ch\ chin	\ü\ food
\e\ pet	\u̇\ foot
\ē\ easy	\y\ yet
\g\ go	\yü\ few
\i\ tip	\yu̇\ cure
\ī\ life	\zh\ vision
\j\ job	

into a channel for navigation or irrigation [French, from *barrer* "to bar"]

²bar·rage \bə-'räzh, -'räj\ *n* **1** : a barrier of continuous artillery or machine-gun fire directed upon a narrow strip of ground close to friendly troops to screen and protect them **2** : a rapid or concentrated delivery or outpouring (as of speech or writing) — **barrage** *vt*

bar·ra·try \'bar-ə-trē\ *n, pl* **-tries** **1** : the purchase or sale of offices of honor or profit in church or state **2** : a fraudulent breach of duty by the master or crew of a ship intended to harm the owner or cargo **3** : the practice of inciting lawsuits or quarrels [Middle French *baraterie* "deception", from *barater* "to deceive, exchange"]

barred \'bärd\ *adj* : having alternate bands of different color

¹bar·rel \'bar-əl\ *n* **1** : a round bulging container that is longer than it is wide and has flat ends **2 a** : the amount held by a barrel; *esp* : the amount (as 159 liters of petroleum) fixed for a product and used as a unit of measure **b** : a great quantity ⟨a *barrel* of fun⟩ **3** : a cylindrical or tubular part ⟨gun *barrel*⟩ **4** : the body proper of a four-footed animal [Middle French *baril*] — **bar·reled** \-əld\ *adj*

²barrel *vb* **-reled** *or* **-relled; -rel·ing** *or* **-rel·ling** **1** : to put or pack in a barrel **2** : to travel at a high speed

bar·rel·ful \'bar-əl-ˌfül\ *n, pl* **bar·rel·fuls** \-əl-ˌfülz\ *or* **bar·rels·ful** \-əlz-ˌfül\ : as much or as many as a barrel will hold

barrel organ *n* : a musical instrument consisting of a revolving cylinder studded with pegs that open a series of valves to admit air from a bellows to a set of pipes

¹bar·ren \'bar-ən\ *adj* **1 a** : incapable of producing offspring **b** : habitually failing to bear fruit ⟨*barren* apple trees⟩ **2 a** : producing little or no vegetation : DESOLATE ⟨*barren* deserts⟩ **b** : producing inferior crops ⟨*barren* soil⟩ **c** : unproductive of results or gain : FRUITLESS ⟨a *barren* scheme⟩ **3** : lacking interest, information, or charm [Old French *barain*] — **bar·ren·ly** *adv* — **bar·ren·ness** \-ən-nəs\ *n*

²barren *n* **1** : a tract of barren land **2** *pl* : a wide usually level tract with stunted or scrub trees or little vegetation

bar·rette \bä-'ret, bə-\ *n* : a clip or bar for holding the hair in place [French]

¹bar·ri·cade \'bar-ə-ˌkād, ˌbar-ə-'\ *vt* **1** : to block off or stop up with a barricade **2** : to prevent access to by means of a barricade

²barricade *n* : a hastily made barrier for protecting against attack or for blocking the way [French, derived from Middle French *barrique* "barrel"]

bar·ri·er \'bar-ē-ər\ *n* **1** : a material object or set of objects that separates or marks off or serves as a barricade **2** : something immaterial that separates ⟨language *barriers* between peoples⟩ **3** : a factor (as a canyon or lack of food) that keeps organisms from interbreeding or spreading into new territory [Middle French *barriere,* from *barre* "bar"]

barrier reef *n* : a coral reef roughly parallel to a shore and separated from it by a lagoon

bar·ring \'bär-ing\ *prep* **1** : with the exception of ⟨*barring* none⟩ **2** : apart from the possibility of ⟨we will be there on time, *barring* accidents⟩

bar·rio \'bär-ē-ˌō, 'bar-\ *n, pl* **-ri·os** **1** : a district of a city or town in Spanish-speaking countries **2** : a Spanish-speaking section of a city or town in the United States [Spanish, from Arabic *barrī* "of the open country"]

bar·ris·ter \'bar-ə-stər\ *n* : a British lawyer who is permitted to plead cases in court — compare SOLICITOR [from ¹*bar*]

bar·room \'bär-ˌrüm, -ˌrüm\ *n* : a room or establishment whose main feature is a bar for the sale of liquor

¹bar·row \'bar-ō\ *n* : a large burial mound of earth or stones [Old English *beorg* "mountain, mound"]

²barrow *n* : a male hog castrated before sexual maturity [Old English *bearg*]

³barrow *n* **1 a** : HANDBARROW **b** : WHEELBARROW **2** : a cart with a shallow box body, two wheels, and shafts for pushing it : PUSHCART [Old English *bearwe*]

bar·tend·er \'bär-ˌten-dər\ *n* : one that serves alcoholic beverages at a bar

¹bar·ter \'bärt-ər\ *vb* : to trade one commodity directly for another without the use of money ⟨*bartered* for furs with tobacco and rum⟩ [Middle French *barater*] — **bar·ter·er** \'bärt-ər-ər\ *n*

²barter *n* : the exchange of goods without the use of money; *also* : something given in such an exchange

Bar·tho·lin's gland \'bärt-l-ənz-, 'bär-thə-lənz-\ *n* : either of two oval racemose glands lying one to each side of the lower part of the vagina and secreting a lubricating mucus [Kaspar *Bartholin,* died 1738, Danish physician]

bar·ti·zan \'bärt-ə-zən\ *n* : a small overhanging or projecting structure (as a turret) for lookout or defense [Middle English *bretasing*]

Ba·ruch \bə-'rük, 'bär-ˌük\ *n* — see BIBLE table

bary·on \'bar-ē-ˌän\ *n* : any of a group of elementary particles that have a mass equal to or greater than that of the proton [Greek *barys* "heavy"]

bary·tone \'bar-ə-ˌtōn\ *variant of* BARITONE

bas·al \'bā-səl, -zəl\ *adj* **1** : relating to, situated at, or forming the base **2** : of, relating to, or forming a foundation or basis : FUNDAMENTAL — **bas·al·ly** \-ē\ *adv*

basal body *n* : a minute distinctively staining cell organelle found at the base of a flagellum or cilium and resembling a centriole in structure

basal metabolic rate *n* : the rate at which heat is given off by an organism at complete rest

basal metabolism *n* : the metabolic activities of a fasting and resting organism in which energy is being used solely to maintain vital cellular activity, respiration, and circulation

ba·salt \bə-'sólt, 'bā-,\ *n* : a dark fine-grained igneous rock [Latin *basaltes*] — **ba·sal·tic** \bə-'sól-tik\ *adj*

bas·cule \'bas-ˌkyül\ *n* : an apparatus or structure (as a bridge) in which one end is counterbalanced by the other on the principle of the seesaw or by weights [French, "seesaw"]

¹base \'bās\ *n, pl* **bas·es** \'bā-səz\ **1 a** : the bottom of something that serves as its support : FOUNDATION **b** : a side or face of a geometrical figure usually from which an altitude can be constructed; *esp* : one on which the figure stands **c** : the length of a base **2 a** : a main ingredient **b** : an inert ingredient that carries the main ingredient (as of a medicine) **3** : the fundamental part of something : GROUNDWORK **4 a** : the point or line from which a start is made in an action or undertaking **b** : the locality or installations from which a military force operates **c** : a number (as 5 in $5^{6.44}$ or 5^7) that is raised to a power; *esp* : the number that when raised to a power equal to the logarithm of a number yields the number itself ⟨the logarithm of 100 to the *base* 10 is 2 since $10^2 = 100$⟩ **d** : a number equal to the number of units in a given digit's place that for a given system of writing numbers is required to give the numeral 1 in the next higher place ⟨the decimal system uses a *base* of 10⟩; *also* : such a system of writing numbers using an indicated base ⟨convert from *base* 10 to *base* 2⟩ **e** : ROOT 5 **5 a** : the starting place or goal in various games **b** : any of the four stations a runner in baseball must touch in order to score **6** : any of various compounds that are capable of reacting with an acid to form a salt, that when dissolved in water have a strong somewhat bitter taste, turn litmus blue, and yield hydroxyl ions, that have a molecule or ion which can take up a proton from an acid, or that are substances able to give up to an acid an unshared pair of electrons [Latin *basis*, from Greek, from *bainein* "to go"] — **based** \'bāst\ *adj* — **off base** **1** : seriously or absurdly mistaken **2** : by surprise : UNAWARES

²**base** *vt* **1** : to make, form, or serve as a base for **2** : to use as a base or basis for : ESTABLISH **3** : STATION

³**base** *adj* : constituting or serving as a base

⁴**base** *adj* **1** *archaic* : of humble birth : LOWLY **2 a** : being of comparatively low value and having inferior properties (as resistance to corrosion) ⟨a *base* metal such as iron⟩ **b** : made of or alloyed with a base metal **3** : morally low : MEAN, CONTEMPTIBLE ⟨*base* conduct⟩ [Middle French *bas* "low", from Medieval Latin *bassus*] — **base·ly** *adv* — **base·ness** *n*

base angle *n* : either of the angles of a triangle that have one side in common with the base

base·ball \'bās-,ból\ *n* : a game played with a bat and ball between two teams of nine players each on a field with four bases that mark the course a runner must take to score; *also* : the ball used in this game

base·board \-,bōrd, -,bórd\ *n* : a line of boards or molding covering the joint of a wall and a floor

base·born \-'bórn\ *adj* **1** : of humble birth : LOWLY **2** : of illegitimate birth : BASTARD

base exchange *n* : a post exchange at a naval or air force base

base hit *n* : a hit in baseball enabling the batter to reach base safely with no error made and no base runner forced out

base·less \'bās-ləs\ *adj* : having no cause or reason

base line *n* **1** : a line that forms or represents a base **2** : the area within which a baseball player must keep when running between bases

base·ment \'bās-mənt\ *n* **1** : the part of a building that is wholly or partly below ground level **2** : BASE 1a

ba·sen·ji \bə-'sen-jē, -'zen-\ *n* : any of an African breed of small compact curly-tailed dogs that have a chestnut-brown coat and that rarely bark [of Bantu origin]

base on balls : an advance to first base given to a baseball player who receives four balls during a turn at bat

base path *n* : the area between the bases of a baseball field used by a base runner

base runner *n* : a baseball player of the team at bat who is on base or is attempting to reach a base — **base·run·ning** \'bās-,rən-ing\ *n*

¹**bash** \'bash\ *vb* **1** : to strike violently : BEAT **2** : to smash by a blow **3** : CRASH 1a [origin unknown]

²**bash** *n* **1** : a forceful blow **2** : a festive social gathering : PARTY

bash·ful \'bash-fəl\ *adj* **1** : inclined to shrink from public attention : SHY, DIFFIDENT **2** : characterized by or resulting from extreme sensitiveness or self-consciousness [Middle English *basshen* "to be abashed"] SYN see SHY — **bash·ful·ly** \-fə-lē\ *adv* — **bash·ful·ness** *n*

¹**ba·sic** \'bā-sik, -zik\ *adj* **1** : of, relating to, or forming the base or foundation : FUNDAMENTAL ⟨*basic* industries⟩ ⟨the *basic* facts⟩ **2** : constituting or serving as a basis or starting point ⟨*basic* course in French⟩ **3 a** : of, relating to, containing, or having the character of a base **b** : having an alkaline reaction **4** : containing relatively little silica ⟨*basic* rocks⟩ — **ba·si·cal·ly** \-si-klē, -kə-lē\ *adv* — **ba·sic·i·ty** \bā-'sis-ət-ē\ *n*

²**basic** *n* : something that is basic : FUNDAMENTAL

BA·SIC \'bā-sik, -zik\ *n* : a relatively easy language for programming and interacting with a computer [*B*eginner's *A*ll-purpose *S*ymbolic *I*nstruction *C*ode]

ba·sid·io·my·cete \bə-,sid-ē-ō-'mī-,sēt, -,mī-'sēt\ *n* : any of a large class (Basidiomycetes) of fungi (as rusts, smuts, or puffballs) having septate hyphae and spores borne on a basidium [*basidium* + Greek *mykēt-, mykēs* "fungus"] — **ba·sid·io·my·ce·tous** \-ō-mī-'sēt-əs\ *adj*

ba·sid·io·spore \bə-'sid-ē-ə-,spōr, -,spór\ *n* : a spore produced by a basidium

ba·sid·i·um \bə-'sid-ē-əm\ *n, pl* **-ia** \-ē-ə\ : a specialized cell of a basidiomycete bearing usually four basidiospores [New Latin, from Latin *basis*]

bas·il \'baz-əl, 'bāz-, 'bas-, 'bās-\ *n* : any of several plants of the mint family; *esp* : either of two plants with aromatic leaves used in cookery [Greek *basilikon*, from *basilikos* "royal"]

bas·i·lar \'baz-ə-lər, 'bas-\ *adj* : of, relating to, or situated at a base

ba·sil·i·ca \bə-'sil-i-kə, -'zil-\ *n* **1** : an oblong public building of ancient Rome ending in an apse **2** : an early Christian church building consisting of nave and aisles with clerestory and apse **3** : a Roman Catholic church with certain ceremonial privileges [Latin, from Greek *basilikē*, literally, "royal (hall)", from *basileus* "king"] — **ba·sil·i·can** \-kən\ *adj*

bas·i·lisk \'bas-ə-,lisk, 'baz-\ *n* **1** : a legendary reptile with fatal breath and glance **2** : any of several crested tropical American lizards related to the iguanas

ba·sin \'bās-n\ *n* **1 a** : a wide shallow usually round dish or bowl with sloping or curving sides for holding liquid **b** : the amount that a basin holds **2 a** : a dock built in a tidal river or harbor **b** : an enclosed or partly enclosed water area **3 a** : a large or small depression in the surface of the land or in the ocean floor **b** : the land drained by a river and its branches **c** : a great depression in the surface of the lithosphere occupied by an ocean **4** : a broad area of the earth beneath which the strata dip from the sides toward the center [Old French *bacin*, from Late Latin *bacchinon*]

ba·sis \'bā-səs\ *n, pl* **ba·ses** \'bā-,sēz\ **1** : the base, foundation, or chief supporting part **2** : the principal component of something **3** : something on which something else is constructed or established **4** : the basic principle [Latin]

bask \'bask\ *vi* : to lie in or expose oneself to a pleasant warmth or atmosphere ⟨*basked* in the sun⟩ ⟨*basking* in their recent fame⟩ [Old Norse *bathask* "to bathe oneself"]

bas·ket \'bas-kət\ *n* **1 a** : a woven container (as of cane or strips of wood) **b** : the contents of a basket **2** : something that resembles a basket in shape or use **3 a** : a net open at the bottom and suspended from a metal ring that forms the goal in basketball **b** : a field goal in basketball [Middle English] — **bas·ket·work** \-,wərk\ *n*

bas·ket·ball \-,ból\ *n* : a court game in which each of two teams of five players each tries to toss an inflated ball through a raised goal; *also* : the ball used in this game

basket–of–gold *n* : a European perennial herb widely cultivated for its grayish foliage and yellow flowers

basket case *n* **1** : a person who has had all four limbs amputated **2** : one that is totally disabled or inoperative

bas·ket·ry \'bas-kə-trē\ *n* **1** : the art or craft of making baskets or objects woven like baskets **2** : objects produced by basketry

basket weave *n* : a textile weave resembling the checkered pattern of a plaited basket

bas mitz·vah \bäs-'mits-və\ *n, often cap B&M* **1** : a Jewish girl who at about 13 years of age assumes religious responsibilities **2** : the ceremony recognizing a girl as a bas mitzvah [Hebrew *bath miṣwāh*, literally, "daughter of the law"]

ba·so·phil \'bā-sə-,fil, -zə-\ *or* **ba·so·phile** \-,fīl\ *n* : a basophilic substance or structure; *esp* : a white blood cell with basophilic granules

ba·so·phil·ic \,bā-sə-'fil-ik, -zə-\ *adj* : staining readily with basic dyes

Basque \'bask\ *n* **1** : a member of a people inhabiting a region bordering on the Bay of Biscay in northern Spain and southwestern France **2** : the language of the Basque people [French, from Latin *Vasco*] — **Basque** *adj*

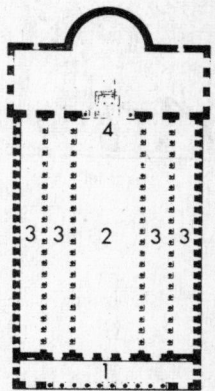

basilica 2: *1* narthex, *2* nave, *3* aisle, *4* altar

\ə\ abut	\ng\ sing
\ər\ further	\ō\ bone
\a\ mat	\ó\ saw
\ā\ take	\ói\ coin
\ä\ cot, cart	\th\ thin
\aú\ out	\th\ this
\ch\ chin	\ü\ food
\e\ pet	\ú\ foot
\ē\ easy	\y\ yet
\g\ go	\yü\ few
\i\ tip	\yú\ cure
\ī\ life	\zh\ vision
\j\ job	

bas-relief

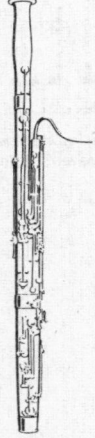
bassoon

bas·re·lief \,bä-ri-'lēf\ *n* : a sculpture in relief in which the design is raised very slightly from the background [French, from *bas* "low" + *relief* "raised work"]

¹**bass** \'bas\ *n, pl* **bass** *or* **bass·es** : any of several spiny-finned freshwater or marine sport and food fishes [Old English *bærs*]

²**bass** \'bās\ *n* **1** : a deep or low-pitched tone : a low-pitched sound **2 a** (1) : the lowest voice part in a 4-part chorus — compare ALTO, SOPRANO, TENOR (2) : the lower half of the instrumental tonal range — compare TREBLE **b** (1) : the lowest male singing voice (2) : a singer having such a voice **c** : the lowest member in range of a family of instruments; *esp* : DOUBLE BASS [Middle French *bas* "low, base"] — **bass** *adj*

bass clef *n* **1** : a clef placing the F below middle C on the 4th line of the staff **2** : the bass staff

bass drum *n* : a large drum having two heads and giving a low booming sound

bas·set hound \'bas-ət-\ *n* : any of an old French breed of short-legged slow-moving hunting dogs with very long ears and crooked front legs — called also *basset* [French *basset*, derived from Middle French *bas* "low"]

bass horn *n* : TUBA

bas·si·net \,bas-ə-'net\ *n* : an infant's bed often with a hood over one end [probably from French *barcelonnette*, from *berceau* "cradle"]

bas·so \'bas-ō, 'bäs-\ *n, pl* **bassos** : a bass singer; *esp* : an operatic bass [Italian, from Medieval Latin *bassus* "low"]

bas·soon \bə-'sün, ba-\ *n* : a tenor or bass woodwind instrument having a long doubled conical wooden body connected to the mouthpiece by a thin metal tube [French *basson*, from Italian *bassone*, from *basso*] — **bas·soon·ist** \-'sü-nəst\ *n*

bass viol *n* : DOUBLE BASS

bass·wood \'bas-,wùd\ *n* **1** : any of several linden trees of North America **2** : the pale straight-grained wood of a basswood [*bass* "bast", alteration of *bast*]

bast \'bast\ *n* **1** : PHLOEM **2** : a strong woody fiber obtained chiefly from the phloem of plants and used especially in cordage and matting [Old English *bæst*]

¹**bas·tard** \'bas-tərd\ *n* **1** : an illegitimate child **2** : something that is spurious, irregular, inferior, or of questionable origin [Old French] — **bas·tard·ly** *adj*

²**bastard** *adj* **1** : ILLEGITIMATE **2** : of an inferior or irregular kind, stock, or form **3** : not genuine or authoritative — **bas·tardy** \-ē\ *n*

¹**baste** \'bāst\ *vt* : to sew with long loose temporary stitches [Middle French *bastir*, of Germanic origin] — **bast·er** *n*

²**baste** \'bāst\ *vt* : to moisten (as roasting meat) with a sauce or fat [origin unknown] — **bast·er** *n*

Bastille Day *n* : July 14 observed in France as a national holiday in commemoration of the fall of the Bastille in 1789

bas·ti·na·do \,bas-tə-'nād-ō, -'näd-\ *n, pl* **-does** : a punishment consisting of beating the soles of the feet with a stick [Spanish *bastonada*, from *bastón* "stick", from Late Latin *bastum*] — **bastinado** *vt*

bast·ing \'bā-stiŋ\ *n* : the thread used in loose stitching or the stitching made by this thread

bas·tion \'bas-chən\ *n* **1** : a projecting part of a fortification **2** : a fortified area or position **3** : a firmly established place or position [Middle French, from *bastille* "fort", from Provençal *bastida*, from *bastir* "to build", of Germanic origin]

¹**bat** \'bat\ *n* **1** : a stout solid stick : CLUB **2** : a sharp blow **3 a** : a wooden implement used for hitting the ball in various games **b** : a paddle used in various games (as table tennis) **4** : a turn at batting **5** *or* **batt** : BATTING **2** — usually used in pl. **6** : BINGE [Old English *batt*] — **at bat** : serving as the batter in baseball — **off the bat** : IMMEDIATELY

³bat

²**bat** *vb* **bat·ted; bat·ting** **1** : to strike or hit with or as if with a bat **2 a** : to advance (a base runner) by batting **b** : to have a batting average of **3** : to take one's turn at bat in baseball

³**bat** *n* : any of an order (Chiroptera) of nocturnal flying mammals with the forelimbs modified to function as wings [alteration of Middle English *bakke*]

⁴**bat** *vt* **bat·ted; bat·ting** : to wink especially in surprise or emotion ⟨never *batted* an eye⟩

bat·boy \'bat-,bòi\ *n* : a boy who looks after the equipment (as bats) for a baseball team

batch \'bach\ *n* **1** : a quantity baked at one time ⟨the first *batch* of cookies⟩ **2 a** : a quantity of any material for use at one time or produced at one operation ⟨a *batch* of cement⟩ **b** : a group of jobs to be run on a computer at one time with the same program **3** : a group of persons or things : LOT ⟨a *batch* of letters⟩ [Middle English *bache*]

bate \'bāt\ *vt* **1** : to reduce the force or intensity of ⟨listen with *bated* breath⟩ **2** : to take away : DEDUCT [Middle English *baten*, from *abaten* "to abate"]

ba·teau *also* **bat·teau** \ba-'tō\ *n, pl* **ba·teaux** \-'tō, -'tōz\ : any of various small craft; *esp* : a flat-bottomed boat with slanted bow and stern and flaring sides [French *bateau*, from Old English *bāt* "boat"]

bath \'bath, 'bàth\ *n, pl* **baths** \'bathz, 'baths, 'bàthz, 'bàths\ **1** : a washing or soaking (as in water) of all or part of the body **2 a** : water used for bathing ⟨drew a *bath*⟩ **b** : a liquid in which objects are placed so that it can act upon them ⟨a dyeing *bath*⟩; *also* : the container holding such a liquid **c** : a contained medium for regulating the temperature of something ⟨a hot water *bath*⟩ **3 a** : BATHROOM ⟨a house with two *baths*⟩ **b** : a building containing rooms designed for bathing **c** : SPA — usually used in pl. [Old English *bæth*]

bathe \'bāth\ *vb* **1** : to take a bath **2** : to go swimming **3 a** : to wash in a liquid (as water) **b** : MOISTEN, WET **4** : to apply water or a liquid medicament to **5** : to flow along the edge of : LAVE **6** : to surround or cover as a liquid does ⟨trees *bathed* in moonlight⟩ — **bath·er** \'bā-thər\ *n* — **bath·ing** \-thiŋ\ *n*

ba·thet·ic \bə-'thet-ik\ *adj* : characterized by bathos — **ba·thet·i·cal·ly** \-i-kə-lē, -klē\ *adv*

bath·house \'bath-,haùs, 'bàth-\ *n* **1** : a building equipped for bathing **2** : a building containing dressing rooms for bathers

bathing suit *n* : SWIMSUIT

batho·lith \'bath-ə-,lith\ *n* : a great mass of intrusive plutonic rock of unknown depth [Greek *bathos* "depth"]

ba·thos \'bā-,thäs\ *n* **1 a** : the sudden appearance of the commonplace in otherwise elevated matter or style **b** : ANTICLIMAX **2** : FLATNESS, TRITENESS **3** : insincere or overdone pathos [Greek, literally, "depth"]

bath·robe \'bath-,rōb, 'bàth-\ *n* : a loose usually absorbent robe worn before and after bathing or as a dressing gown

bath·room \'bath-,rüm, 'bàth-, -,rùm\ *n* : a room containing a bathtub or shower and usually a washbowl and toilet

bath·tub \'bath-,təb, 'bàth-\ *n* : a usually fixed tub for bathing

bathy·al \'bath-ē-əl\ *adj* : DEEP-SEA

bathy·scaphe \'bath-i-,skaf, -,skāf\ *also* **bathy·scaph** \-,skaf\ *n* : a navigable submersible ship for deep-sea exploration having a spherical watertight cabin attached to its underside [Greek *bathys* "deep" + *skaphē* "light boat"]

bathy·sphere \'bath-i-,sfiər\ *n* : a strongly built sphere-shaped diving apparatus for deep-sea observation

ba·tik \bə-'tēk, 'bat-ik\ *n* **1 a** : an Indonesian method of hand-printing textiles by coating the parts not to be dyed with wax **b** : a design so executed **2** : a fabric printed by batik [Malay]

ba·tiste \bə-'tēst, ba-\ *n* : a fine soft sheer fabric of plain weave [French]

bat·man \'bat-mən\ *n* : an orderly of a British military officer [French *bât* "packsaddle"]

ba·ton \bə-'tän, ba-, -'tōⁿ\ *n* **1** : a staff borne as a symbol of office **2** : a stick or wand with which a leader directs a band or orchestra **3** : a hollow cylinder carried by each member of a relay team and passed to the succeeding runner **4** : a smooth staff with a ball usually at one end carried by a drum major or baton twirler [French *bâton* "stick", derived from Late Latin *bastum*]

ba·tra·chi·an \bə-'trā-kē-ən\ *n* : FROG 1a, TOAD, SALIENTIAN [Greek *batrachos* "frog"] — **batrachian** *adj*

bats·man \'bat-smən\ *n* : a batter especially in cricket

batt *variant of* BAT

bat·tal·ion \bə-'tal-yən\ *n* **1** : a large organized body of troops : ARMY **2** : a military unit made up of a headquarters and two or more companies, batteries, or subunits **3** : a large body of persons organized to act together ⟨labor *battalions*⟩ [derived from Late Latin *battalia* "combat"]

¹bat·ten \'bat-n\ *vb* **bat·tened; bat·ten·ing** \'bat-ning, -n-ing\ **1 a** : to grow or make fat : FATTEN **b** : to feed gluttonously **2** : to grow prosperous : THRIVE [probably from Old Norse *batna* "to improve"]

²batten *n* **1** : a thin narrow strip of lumber used especially to seal or reinforce a joint **2** : a strip, bar, or support like or used like a batten [French *bâton* "stick"]

³batten *vt* : to furnish or fasten with battens ⟨*batten* down the hatches⟩

¹bat·ter \'bat-ər\ *vb* **1** : to beat with successive violent, heavy, or shattering blows ⟨*batter* down the door⟩ **2** : to wear or damage by blows or hard usage ⟨a hat *battered* by long use⟩ [Middle English *bateren*, probably from *batten* "to bat"]

²batter *n* : a mixture that consists chiefly of flour and liquid and is thin enough to pour or drop from a spoon

³batter *n* : one that bats; *esp* : the baseball player who is batting

battering ram *n* **1** : a military siege engine used in ancient times to beat down the walls of a besieged place **2** : a heavy metal bar with handles used to batter down doors and walls

bat·tery \'bat-ə-rē, 'ba-trē\ *n, pl* **-ter·ies** **1 a** : the act of battering or beating **b** : the unlawful beating or use of force upon a person — compare ASSAULT 2 **2 a** : a tactical grouping of artillery pieces **b** : the guns of a warship **3** : an artillery unit in the army equivalent to a company **4** : a group of two or more electric cells connected together for furnishing electric current; *also* : a single electric cell ⟨a flashlight *battery*⟩ **5 a** : a number of machines or devices grouped together or forming a unit ⟨a *battery* of lights or of cameras⟩ **b** : a group of persons working together **6** : the pitcher and catcher of a baseball team

battery jar *n* : a glass container with straight sides used especially in biology and chemistry laboratories

bat·ting \'bat-ing\ *n* **1 a** : the action of one who bats **b** : use of or ability with a bat **2** : layers or sheets of raw cotton or wool used for lining quilts or for stuffing or packaging

batting average *n* : a ratio of base hits to official times at bat for a baseball player or team

¹bat·tle \'bat-l\ *n* **1** : a general encounter between armies, ships of war, or airplanes **2** : a combat between two persons **3** : an extended contest, struggle, or controversy ⟨a *battle* of wits⟩ [Old French *bataille*, from Late Latin *battalia* "combat", derived from Latin *battuere* "to beat"]

²battle *vb* **bat·tled; bat·tling** \'bat-ling, -l-ing\ **1** : to engage in battle : FIGHT ⟨armies *battling* for a city⟩ **2** : to struggle using all possible resources (as strength or

craft) ⟨*battle* for a cause⟩ **3** : to fight against ⟨*battle* a fire⟩ — **bat·tler** \-l-ər, -l-ər\ *n*

bat·tle-ax *or* **bat·tle-axe** \'bat-l-,aks\ *n* : a broadax formerly used as a weapon of war

battle cruiser *n* : a large heavily armed warship that is lighter, faster, and more maneuverable than a battleship

battle cry *n* : WAR CRY

bat·tle·field \-,fēld\ *n* : a place where a battle is fought — called also **battleground**

battle group *n* : a military unit normally made up of five companies

bat·tle·ment \'bat-l-mənt\ *n* : a parapet placed at the top of a wall for ornament or defense — **bat·tle·ment·ed** \-,ment-əd\ *adj*

battle royal *n, pl* **battles royal** *or* **battle royals** **1 a** : a fight involving more than two combatants; *esp* : such a contest in which the last one in the ring or standing is declared the winner **b** : a violent struggle **2** : a heated dispute

bat·tle·ship \'bat-l-,ship\ *n* : a warship of the largest and most heavily armed and armored class [short for *line-of-battle ship*]

bat·tle·wag·on \-,wag-ən\ *n* : BATTLESHIP

bat·ty \'bat-ē\ *adj* **bat·ti·er; -est** : mentally unstable : CRAZY [³*bat*]

bau·ble \'bȯ-bəl, 'bäb-əl\ *n* **1** : TRINKET 1 **2** : a jester's scepter **3** : TRIFLE 1 [Middle French *babel*]

baud \'bȯd, 'bōd\ *n* : a unit of speed (as one bit per second) at which data is sent in communications [after J.M.E. *Baudot*, died 1903, French inventor]

baux·ite \'bȯk-,sīt, 'bäk-\ *n* : an impure mixture of earthy hydrous aluminum oxides and hydroxides that is the principal ore of aluminum [French, from Les *Baux*, near Arles, France]

baw·bee *or* **bau·bee** \'bȯ-bē, -,bē\ *n* **1** : HALFPENNY **2** : TRIFLE 1 [probably from Alexander Orrok, laird of Sille*bawbe*, flourished 1538, Scottish master of the mint]

bawd \'bȯd\ *n* : one that keeps a house of prostitution; *also* : PROSTITUTE [Middle English *bawde*]

bawd·ry \'bȯ-drē\ *n, pl* **bawdries** : offensively suggestive or dirty language : BAWDINESS

bawdy \'bȯd-ē\ *adj* **bawd·i·er; -est** : OBSCENE 2, LEWD — **bawd·i·ly** \'bȯd-l-ē\ *adv* — **bawd·i·ness** \'bȯd-ē-nəs\ *n*

¹bawl \'bȯl\ *vb* **1** : to cry out loudly and without restraint : YELL **2** : WEEP 1, WAIL [Middle English *baulen*] — **bawl·er** *n*

²bawl *n* : a loud prolonged cry : OUTCRY

bawl out *vb* : to scold severely

¹bay \'bā\ *adj* : of the color bay [Middle French *bai*, from Latin *badius*]

²bay *n* **1** : a horse with a bay-colored body and black mane, tail, and points — compare CHESTNUT 3 **2** : a reddish brown

³bay *n* **1 a** : LAUREL 1 **b** : any of several shrubs or trees resembling the laurel **2** : a wreath especially of laurel given as a token of honor for victory or excellence — usually used in pl. [Middle French *baie* "berry", from Latin *baca*]

⁴bay *n* **1** : a section of a building set off from other parts (as by pillars or beams) **2** : a compartment in a barn for storing fodder (as hay) **3** : BAY WINDOW 1 **4 a** : the forward part of a ship on each side between decks that is often used as a ship's hospital **b** : any of several compartments in the fuselage of an airplane **5** : a vertical support for electronic equipment [Old French *baee* "opening", from *baer* "to gape"]

⁵bay *vb* **1** : to utter a bay or similar sound **2 a** : to bark at ⟨wolves *baying* the moon⟩ **b** : to utter in long deep tones **3** : to bring (as an animal) to bay [Old French *abaüer*]

⁶bay *n* **1** : the position of one unable to retreat and forced to face danger ⟨the stag at *bay* turned on its

battlement

pursuers) **2** : the position of one checked ⟨police kept the rioters at *bay*⟩ **3** : a baying of dogs

⁷bay *n* : an indentation into the land formed by a body of water and usually larger than an inlet and smaller than a gulf [Middle French *baie*] SYN see GULF

bay·ber·ry \'bā-,ber-ē\ *n* **1** : a West Indian tree of the myrtle family yielding a yellow aromatic oil **2 a** : a hardy shrub of coastal eastern North America related to the wax myrtles and bearing dense clusters of small globular nuts covered with grayish white wax **b** : the fruit of a bayberry

bay leaf *n* : the dried leaf of the European laurel used in cooking

¹bay·o·net \'bā-ə-nət, -,net, ,bā-ə-'net\ *n* : a steel blade made to be attached at the muzzle end of a rifle and used in hand-to-hand combat [French *baionette,* from *Bayonne,* France]

²bayonet *vt* **-net·ed** *also* **-net·ted; -net·ing** *also* **-net·ting** : to stab with a bayonet

bay·ou \'bī-ü, 'bī-ō\ *n* : a usually marshy or sluggish body of water (as a stream on a delta or an offshoot of a river) [Louisiana French, from Choctaw *bayuk*]

bay rum *n* : a fragrant cosmetic and medicinal liquid

bay window *n* **1** : a window or a set of windows projecting outward from the wall of a building **2** : POTBELLY 1

ba·zaar \bə-'zär\ *n* **1** : an Oriental market that consists of rows of shops or stalls selling miscellaneous goods **2 a** : a place for the sale of goods **b** : DEPARTMENT STORE **3** : a fair for the sale of articles especially for charitable purposes [Persian *bāzār*]

ba·zoo·ka \bə-'zü-kə\ *n* : a light portable shoulder weapon that consists of a tube open at both ends and shoots an explosive rocket able to pierce armor [*bazooka,* a crude musical instrument made of pipes and a funnel]

BB \'bē-,bē\ *n* : a small round shot pellet

BCD \,bē-,sē-'dē\ *n* : a computer code for representing alphanumeric information [*b*inary-*c*oded *d*ecimal]

B cell \'bē-,sel\ *n* [*b*one-marrow-derived *cell*] : any of the lymphocytes that are concerned primarily with antibody formation and do not undergo a stage of development in the thymus — called also *B lymphocyte*; compare T CELL

B complex *n* : VITAMIN B COMPLEX

be \bē, 'bē\ *vb, past 1st and 3d sing* **was** \wəz, 'wəz, 'wäz\; *2d sing* **were** \wər, 'wər\; *pl* **were;** *past subjunctive* **were;** *past participle* **been** \bin, 'bin, *chiefly British* bēn or 'bēn\; *present participle* **be·ing** \'bē-ing\; *present 1st sing* **am** \əm, m, am, 'am\; *2d sing* **are** \ər, är, 'är\; *3d sing* **is** \iz, 'iz, əz, z\; *pl* **are;** *present subjunctive* **be 1 a** : to have the same meaning as : serve as a sign for ⟨January *is* the first month⟩ ⟨let x *be* 10⟩ **b** : to have identity with ⟨the first person I met *was* my best friend⟩ **c** : to constitute the same class as **d** : to have the quality or character of ⟨the leaves *are* green⟩ **e** : to belong to the class of ⟨the fish *is* a trout⟩ ⟨apes *are* mammals⟩ **2 a** : to have reality : EXIST, LIVE ⟨I think, therefore I *am*⟩ ⟨once there *was* a knight⟩ **b** : to have, keep, or occupy a place, situation, or position ⟨the book *is* on the table⟩ **c** : to remain unmolested, undisturbed, or uninterrupted — used only in infinitive form ⟨let it *be*⟩ **d** : to take place : OCCUR ⟨the concert *was* last night⟩ **3** — used with the past participle of transitive verbs as a passive-voice auxiliary ⟨the money *was* found⟩ ⟨the house has *been* built⟩ **4** — used as the auxiliary of the present participle in progressive tenses expressing continuous action ⟨I have *been* sleeping⟩ **5** — used with the past participle of some intransitive verbs as an auxiliary forming archaic perfect tenses **6** — used with the infinitive with *to* to express futurity, arrangement in advance, or obligation ⟨I *am* to interview them today⟩ ⟨they *were* to become famous⟩ [Old English *bēon*]

be- *prefix* **1** : on : around : over ⟨*be*daub⟩ ⟨*be*smear⟩ **2** : to a great or greater degree : thoroughly ⟨*be*fuddle⟩ ⟨*be*rate⟩ **3** : excessively : ostentatiously ⟨*be*deck⟩ **4** : about : to : upon ⟨*be*speak⟩ ⟨*be*stride⟩ **5** : make : cause to be ⟨*be*fool⟩ ⟨*be*little⟩ **6** : affect, provide, or cover with especially excessively ⟨*be*fog⟩ [Old English *bi-, be-*]

¹beach \'bēch\ *n* : a shore of an ocean, sea, or lake or the bank of a river covered by sand, gravel, or larger rock fragments : STRAND [origin unknown]

²beach *vt* : to run or drive ashore ⟨*beach* a boat⟩

beach·comb·er \'bēch-,kō-mər\ *n* **1** : a drifter, loafer, or casual worker along the seacoast **2** : one that searches along a shore for useful or salable debris and refuse

beach flea *n* : any of numerous small leaping crustaceans common on ocean beaches

beach·head \'bēch-,hed\ *n* **1** : an area of an enemy-held shore occupied by an advance attacking force to protect the later landing of troops or supplies **2** : FOOTHOLD 2

beach plum *n* : a shrubby plum with showy white flowers that grows along the Atlantic shores of the northern United States and Canada; *also* : its dark purple fruit often used in preserves

beach wagon *n* : STATION WAGON

¹bea·con \'bē-kən\ *n* **1** : a signal fire commonly on a hill, tower, or pole **2 a** : a signal (as a lighthouse) for guidance **b** : a radio transmitter sending out signals for guidance of aircraft [Old English *bēacen* "sign"]

²beacon *vb* **1** : to furnish or light up with a beacon **2** : to shine as a beacon

¹bead \'bēd\ *n* **1** *pl* : a series of prayers said with a rosary **2** : a small piece of material pierced for threading on a string or wire **3** : a small ball-shaped body: as **a** : a drop of sweat or blood **b** : a bubble formed in or on a beverage **c** : a small metal knob on a firearm used as a front sight **4** : a projecting rim, band, or molding [Middle English *bede* "prayer, prayer bead", from Old English *bed* "prayer"] □ ORIGIN Middle English *bede* originally meant "a prayer". The word is related to modern English *bid*. The number and order of a series of prayers are often kept track of with the aid of a string of small round balls. Because each of these balls stands for a prayer, the word *bede,* now *bead* in modern English, was transferred to the balls themselves. Today *bead* is used to refer to any small piece of material pierced for threading on a string or wire. The sense is also extended to refer to any small, round object, such as a drop of sweat.

²bead *vb* **1** : to adorn or cover with beads or beading **2** : to string together like beads **3** : to form into a bead

bead·ing \'bēd-ing\ *n* **1** : material or a part or piece consisting of beads **2** : an openwork trimming **3** : BEADWORK

bea·dle \'bēd-l\ *n* : a minor parish official whose duties include ushering and keeping order in church and sometimes at civic functions [Old English *bydel*]

bead·roll \'bēd-,rōl\ *n* **1** : a list of names : CATALOG **2** : ROSARY [from the reading in church of a list of names of persons for whom prayers are to be said]

beads·man \'bēdz-mən\ *n, archaic* : a person who prays for another

bead·work \'bēd-,wərk\ *n* : ornamental work of or with beads

beady \'bēd-ē\ *adj* **bead·i·er; -est** : resembling beads; *esp* : small, round, and shiny with interest or greed ⟨*beady* eyes⟩

bea·gle \'bē-gəl\ *n* : a small short-legged smooth-coated hound [Middle English *begle*]

beak \'bēk\ *n* **1 a** : the bill of a bird; *esp* : the bill of a bird of prey adapted for striking and tearing **b** : any of various rigid projecting mouth structures (as of a turtle); *also* : the long sucking mouth of some insects **c** : the human nose **2** : a pointed structure or formation : **a** : a pointed beam projecting from the bow of an ancient galley for piercing an enemy ship **b** : the spout of a vessel [Old French *bec,* from Latin *beccus,* of Gaulish origin] SYN see BILL — **beaked** \'bēkt\ *adj*

bea·ker \'bē·kər\ *n* **1** : a large widemouthed drinking cup **2** : a deep widemouthed vessel that often has a projecting lip and is used especially by chemists and pharmacists [Old Norse *bikarr*]

¹beam \'bēm\ *n* **1 a** : a long heavy piece of timber or metal used especially as a main horizontal support of a building or a ship **b** : a wood or metal cylinder in a loom on which the warp is wound **2** : the bar of a balance from which the scales hang **3** : the width of a ship at its widest part **4 a** : a ray or shaft of light **b** : a collection of nearly parallel rays (as X rays) or particles (as electrons) **5** : a constant directional radio signal sent out for the guidance of pilots along a particular course; *also* : the course indicated by this signal [Old English *bēam* "tree, beam"] — **off the beam 1** : on a wrong course **2** : INCORRECT, MISTAKEN — **on the beam 1** : on a true course **2** : exactly correct

²beam *vb* **1** : to send out in beams or as a beam **2 a** : to aim (a broadcast) by directional antennas **b** : to direct to a particular audience **3** : to send out beams of light **4** : to smile with joy

bean \'bēn\ *n* **1 a** : BROAD BEAN **b** : the seed or pod of any of various erect or climbing leguminous plants **c** : a plant bearing beans **2 a** : a valueless item **b** *pl* : the slightest amount ⟨doesn't know *beans* about it⟩ **3** : a seed or fruit like a bean ⟨coffee *beans*⟩ **4** : HEAD, BRAIN [Old English *bēan*]

bean·bag \'bēn-,bag\ *n* **1** : a small cloth bag partly filled with beans and used (as for tossing or passing) in many games **2** : a game played with one or more beanbags

bean counter *n* : a person involved in corporate financial decisions and especially one reluctant to spend money

bean·ie \'bē-nē\ *n* : a small round tight-fitting skullcap

¹bear \'baər, 'beər\ *n, pl* **bears 1** *or pl* **bear** : any of a family (order Carnivora) of large heavy mammals having long shaggy hair and rudimentary tail, walking on the soles of its feet, and feeding largely on fruit and insects as well as on flesh **2** : a surly, uncouth, or clumsy person **3** : one who sells securities or commodities in expectation of a price decline — compare ¹BULL 2 [Old English *bera*] — **bear·able** \'bar-ə-bəl, 'ber-\ *adj*

²bear *vb* **bore** \'bōr, 'bȯr\; **borne** \'bōrn, 'bȯrn\ *also* **born** \'bȯrn\; **bear·ing 1 a** : to move while holding up : CARRY ⟨arrived *bearing* gifts⟩ **b** : to be equipped with ⟨entitled to *bear* arms⟩ **c** : to have as a feature or characteristic ⟨*bears* a good reputation⟩ ⟨*bore* a resemblance to a cousin⟩ **d** : to hold in the mind : HARBOR ⟨has *borne* a grudge for years⟩ **e** : to pass on to others ⟨constantly *bearing* tales⟩ **f** : to bring foward in testifying ⟨*bear* false witness⟩ **g** : BEHAVE 1, CONDUCT ⟨*bore* themselves proudly⟩ **2 a** : to give birth to ⟨has *borne* many children⟩ **b** : PRODUCE 2, YIELD **3 a** : to support the weight of : hold up : SUSTAIN ⟨a colonnade *bore* the roof⟩ **b** : to support a burden or strain ⟨*bears* up well in times of grief⟩ **c** : ENDURE 2 **d** : ASSUME 2a, ACCEPT ⟨*bore* all the costs⟩ ⟨had to *bear* the blame⟩ **e** : to be able to withstand : ALLOW ⟨can hardly *bear* scrutiny⟩ **4** : THRUST 1, PRESS ⟨*borne* along by the crowd⟩ **5 a** : to move, extend, or incline in an indicated direction ⟨*bear* right at the next fork⟩ **b** : to become directed or aimed ⟨brought the guns to *bear* on the target⟩ **6 a** : APPLY 3, PERTAIN ⟨facts *bearing* on the question⟩ **b** : to exert influence or force ⟨brings pressure to *bear* to win votes⟩ [Old English *beran*]

bear·ber·ry \'baər,ber-ē, 'beər-\ *n* : a trailing evergreen plant of the heath family with glossy red berries; *also* : any of several related plants (as a cranberry)

beaker 2

¹beard \'biərd\ *n* **1** : the hair that grows on a man's face and neck; *also* : a growth of beard in a particular style often not including a mustache **2** : a hairy or bristly growth or tuft (as on the chin of a goat or on a head of rye) [Old English] — **beard·ed** \-əd\ *adj* — **beard·less** \-ləs\ *adj*

²beard *vt* : to confront and oppose daringly : DEFY

bear down *vb* **1** : OVERWHELM, OVERCOME **2** : to press or weigh down **3** : to make an all-out effort — **bear down on 1** : EMPHASIZE **2** : to weigh heavily on : BURDEN

bear·er \'bar-ər, 'ber-\ *n* : one that bears: as **a** : PORTER **b** : a plant yielding fruit **c** : a person holding a check, draft, or order for payment **d** : PALLBEARER

bear hug *n* : a vigorous tight embrace

bear·ing \'baər-ing, 'beər-\ *n* **1** : the manner in which one bears or comports oneself : CARRIAGE, BEHAVIOR **2 a** : the act, power, or time of bringing forth offspring or fruit **b** : a product of bearing : CROP **3 a** : PRESSURE 2, THRUST **b** : ENDURANCE 2 **4 a** : an object, surface, or point that supports something **b** : a machine part in which one part (as a journal or pin) turns or slides **5** : a figure in a coat of arms ⟨armorial *bearings*⟩ **6 a** : the position or direction of one point with respect to another or to the compass **b** : a determination of position ⟨to take a *bearing*⟩ **c** *pl* : comprehension of one's position, environment, or situation ⟨lose one's *bearings*⟩ **d** : CONNECTION **2** ⟨the cost had no *bearing* at all on the decision⟩

bear·ish \-ish\ *adj* **1** : resembling a bear in roughness, gruffness, or surliness **2** : marked by or expecting a decline in stock prices — **bear·ish·ly** *adv* — **bear·ish·ness** *n*

bear out *vt* : to attest to the truth of : CONFIRM ⟨research *bore out* the theory⟩

bear·skin \'baər-,skin, 'beər-\ *n* **1** : the skin of a bear **2** : an article (as a rug or military hat) made of the skin of a bear

beast \'bēst\ *n* **1 a** : ANIMAL 1; *esp* : a lower mammal as distinguished on the one hand from humans and on the other from lower vertebrate and invertebrate animals **b** : a domesticated mammal; *esp* : a draft animal **2** : a vicious or brutal person [Old French *beste,* from Latin *bestia*]

¹beast·ly \'bēst-lē\ *adj* **beast·li·er; -est 1** : of, relating to, or resembling a beast : BESTIAL **2** : ABOMINABLE 2, NASTY ⟨*beastly* weather⟩ — **beast·li·ness** *n*

²beastly *adv* : VERY ⟨a *beastly* cold day⟩

beast of burden : an animal (as a mule or an ox) used for carrying or pulling heavy loads

¹beat \'bēt\ *vb* **beat; beat·en** \'bēt-n\ *or* **beat; beat·ing 1** : to strike repeatedly : **a** : to hit repeatedly so as to inflict pain **b** : to dash against ⟨rain *beating* on the roof⟩ **c** : to range over to stir up or drive out game **d** : to mix by stirring : WHIP **e** : to strike repeatedly to produce music or a signal ⟨*beat* a drum⟩ **2 a** : to drive or force by blows ⟨*beat* off the intruder⟩ **b** : to make by repeated treading or driving over ⟨a *beaten* path⟩ **c** : to shape by repeated blows ⟨*beat* swords into plowshares⟩; *esp* : to flatten thin by blows **d** : to sound or express especially by a drumbeat **3** : to cause to strike or flap repeatedly **4 a** : OVERCOME 1, DEFEAT; *also* : SURPASS 1 **b** : to prevail despite ⟨*beat* the odds⟩ **c** : BEWILDER 2, BAFFLE **d** : EXHAUST 2b, DISPIRIT **e** : CHEAT **5 a** (1) : to act ahead of usually so as to forestall (2) : to report a news item in advance of **b** : to come or arrive before **c** : to evade or offset the effects of : CIRCUMVENT ⟨*beat* the system⟩ **6** : to indicate by beats ⟨*beat* the tempo⟩ **7 a** : DASH 1 **b** : to glare or strike with oppressive intensity **8 a** : PULSATE **b** : TICK 1 **c** : to sound upon being struck **9 a** : to sail with much tacking **b** : to progress with difficulty [Old English *bēatan*] — **beat about the bush** *or* **beat around the bush** : to approach a matter in a roundabout manner — **beat it** : to leave immediately : SCRAM — **beat the bushes** : to search thoroughly through all possible areas

¹beaver 1

²**beat** n **1 a** : a single stroke or blow especially in a series; *also* : PULSATION, TICK **b** : a sound produced by or as if by beating ⟨the *beat* of waves against the rock⟩ **c** : a driving impact or force **2** : each of the pulsations of amplitude produced by the union of sound or radio waves or electric currents having different frequencies **3 a** : a metrical or rhythmic stress in poetry or music or the rhythmic effect or pattern produced by such stresses **b** : musical tempo as indicated by the conductor's baton or hand **4** : a regularly traversed round ⟨a police officer's *beat*⟩ **5 a** : something that excels **b** : the reporting of a news story ahead of competitors **6** : DEADBEAT

³**beat** *adj* **1** : very tired **2** : sapped of resolution or morale

beat·er \'bēt-ər\ n **1** : one that beats **2** : a person who flushes game for hunters

be·a·tif·ic \,bē-ə-'tif-ik\ *adj* : giving or expressing great joy or blessedness : BLISSFUL ⟨a *beatific* experience⟩ ⟨a *beatific* smile⟩ — **be·a·tif·i·cal·ly** \-'tif-i-kə-lē, -klē\ *adv*

beatific vision n : the direct knowledge of God held to be enjoyed by the blessed in heaven

be·at·i·fy \bē-'at-ə-,fī\ *vt* -**fied**; -**fy·ing** **1** : to make supremely happy **2** : to declare to have attained the blessedness of heaven and authorize the title "Blessed" and limited public religious honor for [Late Latin *beatificare,* from Latin *beatus* "blessed, happy"] — **be·at·i·fi·ca·tion** \-,at-ə-fə-'kā-shən\ n

be·at·i·tude \bē-'at-ə-,tüd, -,tyüd\ n **1** : supreme bliss **2** : a declaration made in the Sermon on the Mount (Matthew 5:3–12) beginning "Blessed are"

beat·nik \'bēt-nik\ n : a person who expresses dissatisfaction with established values and mores by withdrawing from society and dressing and behaving unconventionally

beau \'bō\ n, *pl* **beaux** \'bōz\ *or* **beaus** \'bōz\ **1 a** : a man who dresses very carefully in the latest fashion : DANDY **2 a** : a man who is courting : LOVER, ADMIRER **b** : ESCORT 1b [French, from *beau* "beautiful", from Latin *bellus* "pretty"]

Beau Brum·mell \bō-'brəm-əl\ n : BEAU 1 [nickname of George B. *Brummell,* died 1840, English dandy]

Beau·fort scale \'bō-fərt-\ n : a scale in which the force of the wind is indicated by numbers from 0 for velocities less than 1.6 kilometers per hour to 12 for velocities greater than 117.5 kilometers per hour [Sir Francis *Beaufort,* died 1857, British admiral]

beau geste \bō-'zhest\ n, *pl* **beaux gestes** *or* **beau gestes** \bō-'zhest\ : a gracious or generous act; *esp* : one made to please or impress someone else [French, "beautiful gesture"]

beau ide·al \,bō-,ī-'dē-əl, -'dēl\ n, *pl* **beau ideals** : the perfect type or model [French *beau idéal* "ideal beauty"]

beau monde \bō-'mänd\ n, *pl* **beau mondes** *or* **beaux mondes** \bō-'mänz\ : the world of high society and fashion [French, literally, "beautiful world"]

beau·te·ous \'byüt-ē-əs\ *adj* : BEAUTIFUL 1 — **beau·te·ous·ly** *adv* — **beau·te·ous·ness** n

beau·ti·cian \byü-'tish-ən\ n : COSMETOLOGIST

beau·ti·ful \'byüt-i-fəl\ *adj* **1** : having beauty : pleasing to the mind, spirit, or senses ⟨a *beautiful* picture⟩ **2** : generally agreeable : FINE ⟨*beautiful* weather⟩ ⟨a *beautiful* dinner⟩ — **beau·ti·ful·ly** \-fə-lē, -flē\ *adv* — **beau·ti·ful·ness** \-fəl-nəs\ n □ SYN LOVELY, FAIR, PRETTY: BEAUTIFUL applies to whatever excites the keenest pleasure in the mind and senses and stirs emotion by its suggestion of perfection or the ideal ⟨a *beautiful* scene⟩ LOVELY is close to BEAUTIFUL but applies to a narrower range of emotional excitation in suggesting the graceful, delicate, or exquisite ⟨a *lovely* melody⟩ FAIR suggests beauty because of purity, flawlessness, or freshness ⟨a *fair* face⟩ PRETTY often implies

an immediate but superficial or insubstantial impression of attractiveness.

beau·ti·fy \'byüt-ə-,fī\ *vt* -**fied**; -**fy·ing** : to make beautiful or more beautiful — **beau·ti·fi·ca·tion** \,byüt-ə-fə-'kā-shən\ n — **beau·ti·fi·er** \'byüt-ə-,fīr\ n

beau·ty \'byüt-ē\ n, *pl* **beauties** **1** : the qualities of a person or a thing that give pleasure to the senses : LOVELINESS **2** : a lovely person or thing **3** : someone or something outstanding ⟨that's a *beauty* of a black eye⟩ [Old French *biauté,* from *biau, bel* "beautiful", from Latin *bellus* "pretty"]

beauty shop n : an establishment or department where hairdressing, facials, and manicures are done — called also *beauty parlor, beauty salon*

beaux arts \bō-'zär\ n pl : FINE ARTS [French]

¹**bea·ver** \'bē-vər\ n, *pl* **beaver** *or* **beavers** **1** : a large fur-bearing mammal with webbed hind feet and a broad flat tail that builds dams and underwater houses of mud and branches; *also* : its fur **2** : a hat made of beaver fur or of a fabric imitating it [Old English *beofor*]

²**beaver** n **1** : a piece of armor protecting the lower part of the face **2** : a helmet visor [Middle French *baviere*]

be·calm \bi-'käm, -'kälm\ *vt* **1** : to bring to a stop or keep motionless by lack of wind **2** : to make calm : SOOTHE

be·cause \bi-'kòz, -'kəz, -kəz\ *conj* : for the reason that

because of *prep* : by reason of : on account of

be·chance \bi-'chans\ *vb, archaic* : BEFALL

bêche-de-mer \,bāsh-də-'meər\ n, *pl* **bêche-de-mer** *or* **bêches-de-mer** \,bāsh-də-, ,bāsh-əz-də-\ : TREPANG [French]

beck \'bek\ n **1** : a beckoning gesture **2** : SUMMONS **3**, COMMAND ⟨servants at their *beck* and call⟩

beck·et \'bek-ət\ n : a device for holding something in place; *esp* : a loop of rope with a knot at one end [origin unknown]

beck·on \'bek-ən\ *vb* **beck·oned**; **beck·on·ing** \'bek-ning, -ə-ning\ **1** : to summon or signal to a person with a gesture (as a wave or nod) **2** : to appear inviting : ATTRACT [Old English *bīecnan,* from *bēacen* "sign"]

be·cloud \bi-'klaůd\ *vt* : to obscure with or as if with a cloud

be·come \bi-'kəm\ *vb* -**came** \-'kām\; -**come**; -**com·ing** **1** : to grow to be ⟨a tadpole *becomes* a frog⟩ ⟨the days *become* shorter as summer ends⟩ **2** : to look well on : be suitable to : SUIT — **become of** : to happen to : be the state of ⟨whatever *became of* them⟩

be·com·ing \bi-'kəm-ing\ *adj* : SUITABLE; *esp* : attractively suitable ⟨a *becoming* outfit⟩ — **be·com·ing·ly** \-ing-lē\ *adv*

¹**bed** \'bed\ n **1 a** : a piece of furniture on or in which one may lie and sleep **b** : a place or time for sleeping **2** : a flat or level surface: as **a** : a plot of ground prepared for plants **b** : the bottom of a body of water **3** : a supporting surface or structure : FOUNDATION **4** : LAYER 2, STRATUM [Old English *bedd*]

²**bed** *vb* **bed·ded**; **bed·ding** **1 a** : to furnish with a bed or bedding **b** : to put or go to bed ⟨*bedded* down for the night⟩ **2 a** : to fix in a foundation : EMBED ⟨*bedded* on rock⟩ **b** : to plant or arrange in beds **3** : to lay flat or in a layer ⟨*bed* bricks in mortar⟩ **4** : to form a layer

be·daub \bi-'dòb, -'däb\ *vt* : to daub over with something dirty or sticky

be·daz·zle \bi-'daz-əl\ *vt* : DAZZLE — **be·daz·zle·ment** \-əl-mənt\ n

bed·bug \'bed-,bəg\ n : a wingless bloodsucking bug sometimes infesting houses and especially beds

bed·clothes \'bed-,klōz, -,klōthz\ n pl : the covering (as sheets and blankets) used on a bed

bed·ding \'bed-ing\ n **1** : BEDCLOTHES **2** : a bottom layer : FOUNDATION **3** : material to provide a bed for livestock **4** : the arrangement of rock in layers

be·deck \bi-'dek\ *vt* : to adorn with showy things ⟨*be-decked* with furs and jewels⟩

be·dev·il \bi-'dev-əl\ *vt* : to drive frantic : HARASS, TORMENT — **be·dev·il·ment** \-mənt\ *n*

be·dew \bi-'dyü, -'dü\ *vt* : to wet with or as if with dew

bed·fast \'bed-,fast\ *adj* : BEDRIDDEN

bed·fel·low \'bed-,fel-ō\ *n* **1** : one who shares a bed with another **2** : a close associate : ALLY ⟨politics makes strange *bedfellows*⟩

be·dight \bi-'dīt\ *adj, archaic* : ADORNED, DECORATED [Middle English *dighten* "to adorn", from Old English *dihtan* "to arrange, compose", derived from Latin *dictare* "to dictate, compose"]

be·dim \bi-'dim\ *vt* : to make dim or obscure

be·di·zen \bi-'dīz-n, -'diz-\ *vt* : to dress or adorn in a gaudy way [*disen* "to dress a distaff with flax", from Dutch] — **be·di·zen·ment** \-mənt\ *n*

bed·lam \'bed-ləm\ *n* : a place or scene of uproar and confusion [*Bedlam,* popular name for the Hospital of Saint Mary of Bethlehem, London, an insane asylum, from Middle English *Bedlem* "Bethlehem"]

bed·lam·ite \'bed-lə-,mīt\ *n* : a crazy person

Bed·ling·ton terrier \'bed-ling-tən-\ *n* : a swift rough=coated terrier of light build usually groomed to resemble a lamb [*Bedlington,* England]

bed·ou·in \'bed-wən, -ə-wən\ *n, pl* **bedouin** *or* **bedouins** *often cap* : a nomadic Arab of the Arabian, Syrian, or North African deserts [French *bédouin,* from Arabic *bidwān,* pl. of *badawi* "desert dweller"]

bed·pan \'bed-,pan\ *n* : a shallow pan for use as a toilet by a person confined to bed

bed·post \-,pōst\ *n* : a usually turned or carved post of a bed

be·drag·gled \bi-'drag-əld\ *adj* **1** : limp, soggy, or dirty from or as if from rain or mud ⟨a wet and *bedraggled* cat⟩ **2** : showing the effect of much use or lack of care : SHABBY, DILAPIDATED ⟨*bedraggled* buildings⟩

bed·rid·den \'bed-,rid-n\ *adj* : confined to bed by illness or weakness [Old English *bedreda* "one confined to bed", literally, "bed rider"]

bed·rock \'bed-'räk, -,räk\ *n* **1** : the solid rock underlying surface materials (as soil) **2** : a solid foundation

bed·roll \'bed-,rōl\ *n* : bedding rolled up for carrying

bed·room \-,rüm, -,rum\ *n* : a room used for sleeping

bed·side \'bed-,sīd\ *n* : the side of a bed or the place beside a bed especially of a sick or dying person

bedside manner *n* : the often solicitous and sympathetic manner that a physician assumes toward a patient

bed·sore \'bed-,sōr, -,sȯr\ *n* : a sore caused by constant pressure against a bed (as in a long illness)

bed·spread \-,spred\ *n* : a decorative cloth cover for a bed

bed·spring \-,spring\ *n* : a spring supporting a mattress

bed·stead \-,sted\ *n* : the framework of a bed usually including head, foot, and side rails

bed·straw \-,strȯ\ *n* : an herb of the madder family with angled stems, opposite or whorled leaves, and small flowers [from its former use for mattresses]

bed·time \'bed-,tīm\ *n* : time to go to bed

bedtime story *n* : a simple story for children at bedtime

bee \'bē\ *n* **1** : a social colonial 4-winged insect often kept in hives for the honey that it produces; *also* : any of numerous related insects that differ from the wasps especially in the heavier hairier body and in having sucking as well as chewing mouthparts **2** : an eccentric notion : FANCY ⟨a *bee* in one's bonnet⟩ **3** : a gathering of people for a specific purpose ⟨quilting *bee*⟩ [Old English *bēo*]

bee balm *n* : any of several plants (as Oswego tea) of the mint family attractive to bees

bee·bread \'bē-,bred\ *n* : a bitter yellowish brown pollen mixture stored in honeycomb cells and used with honey by bees as food

beech \'bēch\ *n, pl* **beech·es** *or* **beech** : any of a genus of hardwood trees with smooth gray bark and small edible nuts; *also* : the wood of a beech [Old English *bēce*] — **beech·en** \'bē-chən\ *adj*

beech·nut \'bēch-,nət\ *n* : the edible nut of a beech

¹beef \'bēf\ *n, pl* **beefs** \'bēfs\ *or* **beeves** \'bēvz\ **1** : the flesh of a steer, cow, or bull; *also* : the dressed carcass of a beef animal **2** : a steer, cow, or bull especially when fattened for food **3** : muscular flesh : BRAWN **4** *pl* **beefs** : COMPLAINT [Old French *buef* "ox, beef", from Latin *bov-, bos* "head of cattle"]

²beef *vb* **1** : to add weight, strength, or power to — usually used with *up* ⟨*beef* up the staff⟩ **2** : COMPLAIN ⟨*beefing* about work⟩

beef cattle *n pl* : cattle developed primarily for the efficient production of meat and marked by capacity for rapid growth, heavy well-fleshed body, and stocky build

beef·eat·er \'bē-,fēt-ər\ *n* : a yeoman of the guard of an English king or queen

beef·steak \'bēf-,stāk\ *n* : a slice of beef suitable for broiling or frying

beefy \'bē-fē\ *adj* **beef·i·er; -est** : THICKSET, BRAWNY ⟨a *beefy* bodyguard⟩

¹bee·hive \'bē-,hīv\ *n* **1** : a hive for bees **2** : something resembling a hive for bees; *esp* : a scene of crowded activity

²beehive *adj* : resembling a dome-shaped or conical beehive

bee·keep·er \-,kē-pər\ *n* : one that raises bees — **bee·keep·ing** *n*

bee·line \'bē-,līn\ *n* : a straight direct course [from the belief that nectar-laden bees return to their hives in a direct line]

been *past part of* BE

beep·er \'bē-pər\ *n* : a portable electronic device used to page the person carrying it that beeps when it receives a special radio signal

beer \'biər\ *n* **1** : an alcoholic drink made from malt and flavored with hops **2** : a nonalcoholic drink made from roots or other parts of plants ⟨ginger *beer*⟩ [Old English *bēor*] — **beery** \'biər-ē\ *adj*

bees·wax \'bēz-,waks\ *n* : WAX 1

beet \'bēt\ *n* : a biennial garden plant of the goosefoot family with thick long-stalked edible leaves and a swollen root used as a vegetable, as a source of sugar, or for forage; *also* : this root [Old English *bēte,* from Latin *beta*]

¹bee·tle \'bēt-l\ *n* **1** : any of an order (Coleoptera) of insects having four wings of which the outer pair are modified into stiff cases that protect the inner membranous pair when at rest **2** : any of various insects resembling a beetle [Old English *bitula,* from *bītan* "to bite"]

²beetle *n* : a heavy tool usually with a wooden head for hammering [Old English *bīetel*]

³beetle *adj* : being prominent and overhanging ⟨*beetle* brows⟩ [Middle English *bitel-browed* "having overhanging brows"]

⁴beetle *vi* **bee·tled; bee·tling** \'bēt-ling, -l-ing\ : to jut out : OVERHANG

be·fall \bi-'fȯl\ *vb* **fell** \-'fel\; **-fall·en** \-'fȯ-lən\; **-fall·ing** **1** : to come to pass : HAPPEN **2** : to happen to

be·fit \bi-'fit\ *vt* : to be suitable to or proper for ⟨words that *befit* the occasion⟩

be·fit·ting \bi-'fit-ing\ *adj* : SUITABLE 1, 2 — **be·fit·ting·ly** *adv*

be·fog \bi-'fȯg, -'fäg\ *vt* **1** : to make foggy : OBSCURE **2** : CONFUSE 2a

be·fool \bi-'fül\ *vt* : DECEIVE 1

¹be·fore \bi-'fōr, -'fȯr\ *adv* **1** : in advance : AHEAD ⟨go on *before*⟩ **2** : at an earlier time : PREVIOUSLY ⟨has been here *before*⟩ [Old English *beforan,* from *be-* + *foran* "before"]

²before *prep* **1 a** (1) : in front of ⟨sat *before* the fire⟩ (2) : in the presence of ⟨speaking *before* the whole class⟩ **b** : under the consideration of ⟨the case *before*

¹beetle 1

\ə\ abut			\ng\ sing	
\ər\ further			\ō\ bone	
\a\ mat			\ȯ\ saw	
\ā\ take			\ȯi\ coin	
\ä\ cot, cart			\th\ thin	
\aú\ out			\th\ this	
\ch\ chin			\ü\ food	
\e\ pet			\u̇\ foot	
\ē\ easy			\y\ yet	
\g\ go			\yü\ few	
\i\ tip			\yu̇\ cure	
\ī\ life			\zh\ vision	
\j\ job				

the court) **c** : in store for ⟨many years of life still *before* them⟩ **2** : earlier than : previously to ⟨come *before* six o'clock⟩ **3** : in a higher or more important position than ⟨put quantity *before* quality⟩

³before *conj* **1** : earlier than the time when ⟨think *before* you speak⟩ **2** : more willingly than ⟨I will starve *before* I will steal⟩

be·fore·hand \-,hand\ *adv* : in advance : ahead of time ⟨think out *beforehand* what you are going to say⟩

be·foul \bi-'faůl\ *vt* : to make dirty : SOIL

be·friend \bi-'frend\ *vt* : to act as a friend to

be·fud·dle \bi-'fəd-l\ *vt* **1** : to dull the senses of : STUPEFY ⟨the drugs had *befuddled* them⟩ **2** : to confuse the understanding of : PERPLEX ⟨a problem that has *befuddled* the experts⟩ — **be·fud·dle·ment** \-l-mənt\ *n*

beg \'beg\ *vb* **begged; beg·ging 1** : to ask for money, food, or help as a charity ⟨*beg* in the streets⟩ **2** : to ask earnestly or politely ⟨*beg* a favor⟩ [Middle English *beggen*] □ SYN BEG, BESEECH, IMPLORE, ENTREAT mean to ask urgently : BEG suggests earnestness or insistence especially in asking for a favor; BESEECH implies great eagerness or anxiety; IMPLORE adds a suggestion of greater urgency or anguished appeal; ENTREAT implies an attempt to persuade or to overcome resistance. — **beg the question 1** : to assume as true or take for granted the thing that is the subject of the argument **2** : to dodge the issue

be·gat \bi-'gat\ *past of* BEGET

be·get \bi-'get\ *vt* **-got** \-'gät\; **-got·ten** \-'gät-n\ *or* **-got; -get·ting 1** : to become the father of : SIRE **2** : CAUSE 1 — **be·get·ter** *n*

¹beg·gar \'beg-ər\ *n* **1** : one that begs; *esp* : one that lives by asking for gifts **2** : PAUPER **3** : FELLOW 4b

²beggar *vt* **1** : to reduce to beggary **2** : to exceed the resources or capacity of ⟨the lavish costumes *beggar* description⟩

beg·gar·ly \'beg-ər-lē\ *adj* **1** : befitting or resembling a beggar **2** : contemptibly small, poor, or mean — **beg·gar·li·ness** *n*

beg·gar's–lice \'beg-ərz-,līs\ *or* **beg·gar–lice** \-ər-,līs\ *n sing or pl* : any of several plants with prickly or adhesive fruits; *also* : one of these fruits

beg·gar–ticks *or* **beg·gar's–ticks** \-,tiks\ *n sing or pl* **1** : BUR MARIGOLD; *also* : its prickly fruits **2** : BEGGARS-LICE

beg·gary \'beg-ə-rē\ *n* : extreme poverty

be·gin \bi-'gin\ *vb* **be·gan** \-'gan\; **be·gun** \-'gən\; **be·gin·ning 1 a** : to do the first part of an action ⟨please *begin*⟩ **b** : to undertake or undergo initial steps : COMMENCE ⟨*began* the program with a song⟩ **2 a** : to come into existence : ARISE ⟨how the Civil War *began*⟩ **b** : to have a starting point ⟨the road *begins* there⟩ **3** : to do or succeed in the least degree ⟨does not *begin* to fill our needs⟩ **4** : to bring into existence : FOUND ⟨*begin* a dynasty⟩ **5** : to come first in ⟨the letter *A begins* the alphabet⟩ [Old English *beginnan*]

be·gin·ner \bi-'gin-ər\ *n* : one that is beginning something or doing something for the first time

be·gin·ning \bi-'gin-ing\ *n* **1** : the point at which something begins **2** : the first part **3** : primary source or cause : ORIGIN **4** : a first stage or early period

be·gone \bi-'gȯn, -'gän\ *vi* : to go away : DEPART — usually used in the imperative ⟨*begone* from my sight!⟩

be·go·nia \bi-'gō-nyə\ *n* : any of a large genus of tropical herbs often grown for their shining leaves and bright waxy flowers [Michel *Bégon,* died 1710, French governor of Santo Domingo]

be·grime \bi-'grīm\ *vt* : to make dirty with grime

be·grudge \bi-'grəj\ *vt* **1** : to give, do, or allow reluctantly ⟨*begrudge* a person a favor⟩ **2** : to envy a person's possession or enjoyment of ⟨I don't *begrudge* them their success⟩ — **be·grudg·ing·ly** \-ing-lē\ *adv*

be·guile \bi-'gīl\ *vt* **1** : to deceive by cunning means ⟨was *beguiled* by vague promises⟩ **2** : to draw notice or interest by wiles or charm ⟨the view *beguiled* them⟩

3 : to cause (as time) to pass pleasantly ⟨*beguile* the wait by telling stories⟩ SYN see DECEIVE — **be·guile·ment** \-mənt\ *n* — **be·guil·er** *n*

be·guine \bi-'gēn\ *n* : a vigorous popular dance of the islands of Saint Lucia and Martinique [American French *béguine,* from French *béguin* "flirtation"]

be·gum \'bē-gəm\ *n* : a Muslim woman of high rank [Hindi *begam*]

be·half \bi-'haf, -'häf\ *n* : useful aid : HELP, SUPPORT ⟨spoke in my *behalf*⟩ [Middle English, from *by* + *half* "half, side"] — **in behalf of** *or* **on behalf of 1** : in the interest of : for the benefit of ⟨worked *in behalf of* the government⟩ **2** : as a representative of ⟨accepting the award *on behalf of* the whole class⟩

be·have \bi-'hāv\ *vb* **1** : to conduct oneself in a particular way ⟨*behaved* badly⟩ **2** : to conduct oneself in a proper manner ⟨please *behave*⟩ **3** : to act, function, or react in a particular way : exhibit reaction (as to an environment) [Middle English *be-* + *haven* "to have, hold"]

be·hav·ior \bi-'hā-vyər\ *n* : the way in which a person or thing behaves — **be·hav·ior·al** \-vyə-rəl\ *adj* — **be·hav·ior·al·ly** \-rə-lē\ *adv*

be·head \bi-'hed\ *vt* : to cut off the head of

be·he·moth \bi-'hē-məth, 'bē-ə-,mäth\ *n* **1** *often cap* : an animal described in the Bible that is probably the hippopotamus **2** : something of monstrous size or power [Hebrew *běhēmōth*]

be·hest \bi-'hest\ *n* : ORDER 5c, COMMAND [Old English *behǣs* "promise"]

¹be·hind \bi-'hīnd\ *adv* **1 a** : in a place, situation, or time that is being or has been departed from ⟨stay *behind*⟩ ⟨leaving years of poverty *behind*⟩ **b** : at, to, or toward the back ⟨look *behind*⟩ **2 a** : in a secondary or inferior position ⟨lag *behind* in competition⟩ **b** : in a state of failing to keep up to schedule ⟨*behind* in the car payments⟩

²behind *prep* **1 a** : at, to, or toward the back of ⟨look *behind* you⟩ ⟨a garden *behind* the house⟩ **b** : beyond in past time ⟨they put their worries *behind* them⟩ **2** : inferior to ⟨sales *behind* those of last year⟩ **3** : retarded in relation to ⟨*behind* the rest of the class⟩ **4 a** : in the background of ⟨the conditions *behind* the strike⟩ **b** : in support of ⟨solidly *behind* their candidate⟩

³behind *n* : BUTTOCKS

be·hind·hand \bi-'hīnd-,hand\ *adv or adj* : not keeping up : LATE ⟨*behindhand* with the rent⟩

be·hold \bi-'hōld\ *vb* **1** : SEE 1a **2** : to gaze upon : OBSERVE — **be·hold·er** *n*

be·hold·en \bi-'hōl-dən\ *adj* : being under obligation for a favor or gift : INDEBTED

be·hoof \bi-'hüf\ *n* : BENEFIT 1a [Old English *behōf*]

be·hoove \bi-'hüv\ *or* **be·hove** \-'hōv\ *vt* : to be necessary, fitting, or proper for ⟨it *behooves* a soldier to obey orders⟩ ⟨such behavior ill *behooves* you⟩

beige \'bāzh\ *n* : a light grayish yellowish brown [French] — **beige** *adj*

be·ing \'bē-ing\ *n* **1 a** : EXISTENCE 1 **b** : LIFE 1 **2** : the totality of existing things **3** : a living thing; *esp* : PERSON

bel \'bel\ *n* : ten decibels [Alexander Graham *Bell*]

be·la·bor \bi-'lā-bər\ *vt* **1** : to work on or at to absurd lengths ⟨*belabor* the obvious⟩ **2** : ASSAIL, ATTACK

be·lat·ed \bi-'lāt-əd\ *adj* : delayed beyond the usual time — **be·lat·ed·ly** *adv* — **be·lat·ed·ness** *n*

be·lay \bi-'lā\ *vb* **1** : to make fast (as a rope) by turns around a cleat or pin **2** : CEASE, STOP [Old English *belecgan* "to beset", from *be-* + *lecgan* "to lay"]

belch \'belch\ *vb* **1** : to expel gas suddenly from the stomach through the mouth **2** : to give off or issue forth violently ⟨smoke *belched* from the chimney⟩ [Old English *bealcian*] — **belch** *n*

bel·dam *or* **bel·dame** \'bel-dəm\ *n* : an old woman [Middle English *beldam* "grandmother", from Middle French *bel* "beautiful" + Middle English *dam* "lady"]

be·lea·guer \bi-'lē-gər\ *vt* **-guered; -guer·ing** \-gə-riŋ, -griŋ\ **1** : to surround with an army so as to prevent escape : BESIEGE **2** : to subject to troublesome forces : HARASS ⟨the pests that *beleaguer* farmers⟩ [Dutch *belegeren,* from *be-* "be-" + *leger* "camp"]

bel·em·nite \'bel-əm-ˌnīt\ *n* : a conical fossil shell of an extinct cephalopod [Greek *belemnon* "dart"] — **bel·em·noid** \'bel-əm-ˌnȯid\ *adj or n*

bel·fry \'bel-frē\ *n, pl* **belfries** : a tower or a room in a tower for a bell or set of bells [Middle French *berfrei*]

Bel·gae \'bel-ˌgī, -ˌjē\ *n pl* : a people occupying northern France and Belgium in Julius Caesar's time [Latin] — **Bel·gic** \-jik\ *adj*

Bel·gian hare \'bel-jən-\ *n* : any of a breed of slender dark red domestic rabbits

Belgian sheepdog *n* : any of a breed of hardy black or gray dogs developed in Belgium especially for herding sheep

be·lie \bi-'lī\ *vt* **-lied; -ly·ing** **1** : to give a false impression of ⟨a vigor that *belied* their years⟩ **2** : to show to be false ⟨your actions *belie* your promise⟩ — **be·li·er** *n*

be·lief \bə-'lēf\ *n* **1** : mental acceptance of something as real or true ⟨a *belief* in your own ability⟩ **2** : religious faith; *esp* : CREED 1 **3** : the thing that is believed : CONVICTION, OPINION ⟨political *beliefs*⟩ [Middle English *beleave*] □ SYN BELIEF, FAITH, CREDENCE mean the assent to the truth of something offered for acceptance. BELIEF may or may not imply certitude in the believer, whereas FAITH always does and implies trust and confidence even when there is no evidence or proof; CREDENCE implies intellectual acceptance but offers nothing about the soundness of the grounds for acceptance. SYN see in addition OPINION

be·lieve \bə-'lēv\ *vb* **1** : to have a firm religious faith **2** : to have a firm conviction as to the reality or goodness of something ⟨*believe* in fair play⟩ ⟨*believe* in magic⟩ **3** : to accept as true or honest ⟨*believe* the reports⟩ **4** : to hold as an opinion : THINK, SUPPOSE [Old English *belēfan,* from *be-* + *lēfan* "to allow, believe"] — **be·liev·a·ble** \-'lē-və-bəl\ *adj* — **be·liev·a·bly** \-və-blē\ *adv* — **be·liev·er** *n*

be·like \bi-'līk\ *adv, archaic* : most likely : PROBABLY

be·lit·tle \bi-'lit-l\ *vt* **-lit·tled; -lit·tling** \-'lit-liŋ, -'lit-l-iŋ\ : to speak of in a slighting way : DISPARAGE ⟨*belittle* the success of a rival⟩ — **be·lit·tle·ment** \-l-mənt\ *n* — **be·lit·tler** \-'lit-lər, -l-ər\ *n*

¹bell \'bel\ *n* **1** : a hollow usually cup-shaped metallic device that makes a ringing sound when struck **2** : the stroke or sound of a bell that tells the hour especially on shipboard **3 a** : the time indicated by the stroke of a bell **b** : a half hour period of a watch on shipboard **4** : something (as a flower) shaped like a bell **5** *pl* : BELL-BOTTOMS [Old English *belle*]

SHIP'S BELLS

NUMBER OF BELLS	HOUR (A.M. OR P.M.)		
1	12:30	4:30	8:30
2	1:00	5:00	9:00
3	1:30	5:30	9:30
4	2:00	6:00	10:00
5	2:30	6:30	10:30
6	3:00	7:00	11:00
7	3:30	7:30	11:30
8	4:00	8:00	12:00

²bell *vb* **1** : to provide with a bell ⟨*bell* a cat⟩ **2** : to take the form of a bell : FLARE

bel·la·don·na \ˌbel-ə-'dän-ə\ *n* **1** : a European poisonous herb of the potato family with reddish bell-shaped flowers, shining black berries, and root and leaves that yield atropine **2** : a drug or extract from the belladonna plant [Italian, literally, "beautiful lady"]

bell·bird \'bel-ˌbərd\ *n* : any of several birds whose notes are likened to the sound of a bell

bell–bot·toms \-'bät-əmz\ *n pl* : pants with legs that flare at the bottom — **bell–bottom** *or* bell–bot·tomed \-'bät-əmd\ *adj*

bell·boy \-ˌbȯi\ *n* : BELLHOP

belle \'bel\ *n* : a popular attractive girl or woman [French, from the feminine of *beau* "beautiful"]

belles let·tres \bel-'letr\ *n pl* : literature of primarily artistic interest and not simply practical or informative [French, literally, "fine letters"] — **bel·le·tris·tic** \ˌbel-ə-'tris-tik\ *adj*

bell·flow·er \'bel-ˌflaù-ər, -ˌflaùr\ *n* : CAMPANULA

bell·hop \'bel-ˌhäp\ *n* : a hotel or club employee who escorts guests to rooms, carries luggage, and runs errands [short for *bell-hopper*]

bel·li·cose \'bel-ə-ˌkōs\ *adj* : showing a readiness to quarrel or fight [Latin *bellicosus,* from *bellum* "war"] — **bel·li·cos·i·ty** \ˌbel-ə-'käs-ət-ē\ *n*

bel·lig·er·ence \bə-'lij-rəns, -ə-rəns\ *n* : a belligerent attitude or disposition

bel·lig·er·en·cy \-rən-sē\ *n* **1** : the status of a nation that is at war **2** : BELLIGERENCE

bel·lig·er·ent \bə-'lij-rənt, -ə-rənt\ *adj* **1** : waging war; *esp* : belonging to or recognized as a power at war and protected by and subject to the laws of war ⟨*belligerent* nations⟩ **2** : showing a readiness to fight [Latin *belligerare* "to wage war", from *bellum* "war" + *gerare* "to wage"] — **belligerent** *n* — **bel·lig·er·ent·ly** *adv*

bell jar *n* : a bell-shaped usually glass vessel designed to cover objects or to contain gases or a vacuum

bell·man \'bel-mən\ *n* **1** : one (as a town crier) who rings a bell **2** : BELLHOP

bel·low \'bel-ō\ *vb* **1** : to make the loud deep hollow sound characteristic of a bull **2** : to shout in a deep voice : BAWL [Old English *bylgian*] — **bellow** *n*

bel·lows \'bel-ōz, -əz\ *n sing or pl* **1** : a device (as for blowing fires or operating an organ) that by alternate expansion and contraction draws in air through a valve and expels it forcibly through a tube; *also* : any of various blowers or enclosures of variable volume **2** : the pleated expandable part of some cameras [Middle English *bely, below* "belly, bellows"]

bell pepper *n* : SWEET PEPPER

bell–pull \'bel-ˌpùl\ *n* : a cord or wire with a handle by which one rings a bell

bells and whistles *n pl* : items or features that are useful or decorative but not essential : FRILLS

bell·weth·er \'bel-'weth-ər\ *n* : one that takes the lead or initiative; *also* : an indicator of trends [Middle English, leading sheep of a flock, from *belle* "bell" + *wether*; from the practice of belling the leading sheep]

¹bel·ly \'bel-ē\ *n, pl* **bellies** **1 a** : ABDOMEN 1 **b** : the underside of an animal's body; *also* : hide from this part **c** : UTERUS **d** : STOMACH 1a **2** : an internal cavity : INTERIOR **3** : a surface or object curved or rounded like a human belly ⟨the *belly* of an airplane⟩ **4 a** : the part of a sail that swells out when filled with wind **b** : the enlarged fleshy body of a muscle [Middle English *bely* "bellows, belly", from Old English *belg* "bag"]

²belly *vb* **bel·lied; bel·ly·ing** : to swell or bulge out

¹bel·ly·ache \'bel-ē-ˌāk\ *n* : pain in the abdomen and especially in the bowels

²bellyache *vi* : to complain in a whining or peevish way

bel·ly·band \'bel-ē-ˌband\ *n* : a band around or across the belly: as **a** : GIRTH 1 **b** : BAND 4

belly button *n* : NAVEL 1

belly flop *n* : a dive in which the front of the body lands flat against a surface (as of water or the top of a coasting sled) — **belly flop** *vb*

bel·ly·ful \'bel-ē-ˌfùl\ *n* : an excessive amount

belly laugh *n* : a deep hearty laugh

be·long \bə-'lȯŋ\ *vi* **1** : to be suitable or appropriate : have a proper place ⟨this *belongs* on the table⟩ **2 a** : to

belfry

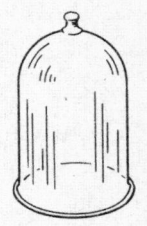

bell jar

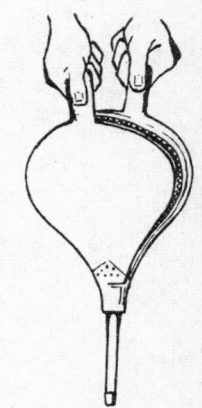

bellows 1

\ə\ abut	\ŋ\ sing
\ər\ further	\ō\ bone
\a\ mat	\ȯ\ saw
\ā\ take	\ȯi\ coin
\ä\ cot, cart	\th\ thin
\aù\ out	\th\ this
\ch\ chin	\ü\ food
\e\ pet	\ù\ foot
\ē\ easy	\y\ yet
\g\ go	\yü\ few
\i\ tip	\yù\ cure
\ī\ life	\zh\ vision
\j\ job	

be the property of a person or thing ⟨this book *belongs* to me⟩ **b** : to become attached or bound; *esp* : to be a member of an organization **3** : to be an attribute, part, adjunct, or function of a person or thing ⟨parts *belonging* to a watch⟩ **4** : to be properly classified ⟨whales *belong* among the mammals⟩ [Middle English *be-* + *longen* "to be suitable"]

be·long·ings \bə-'lȯng-ingz\ *n pl* : the things that belong to a person : POSSESSIONS

be·loved \bi-'ləvd, -'ləv-əd\ *adj* : dearly loved — **beloved** *n*

¹be·low \bə-'lō\ *adv* **1** : in or to a lower place **2 a** : on earth **b** : in or to Hades or hell **3** : on or to a lower floor or deck **4** : lower on the same page or on a following page

²below *prep* : lower than in place, rank, or value ⟨*below* sea level⟩ ⟨*below* average⟩ □ SYN UNDER, BENEATH: BELOW is opposed to *above* and implies only that one thing is on a lower level than another ⟨ten degrees *below* zero⟩ UNDER is opposed to *over* and implies a relation between two things such as contact, support, subjection, inferiority ⟨my legs doubled *under* me⟩ ⟨held the cup *under* the spout⟩ ⟨troops *under* their command⟩ BENEATH is chiefly poetical for UNDER or BELOW except when expressing moral or social inferiority ⟨actions *beneath* contempt⟩ ⟨thought manual labor was *beneath* them⟩

¹belt \'belt\ *n* **1** : a strip of flexible material (as leather or cloth) worn around a person's body for holding in or supporting clothing or weapons or for ornament **2** : something resembling a belt : BAND, CIRCLE ⟨a *belt* of trees⟩ **3 a** : a flexible endless band running around wheels or pulleys and used for moving or carrying something ⟨a fan *belt* on a car⟩ **b** : a band of strong reinforcing material laid beneath the tread of a tire **4** : a natural area marked by some distinctive feature, product, or activity ⟨the corn *belt*⟩ [Old English, from Latin *balteus*] — **belt·ed** \'bel-təd\ *adj* — **below the belt** : not fair : in an unfair manner — **under one's belt** : as part of one's experience ⟨100 hours of flying time *under my belt*⟩

²belt *vt* **1** : to put a belt on or around **2 a** : to beat with or as if with a belt **b** : to hit or strike powerfully ⟨*belted* a home run⟩ **3** : to mark with a band **4** : to sing in a forceful manner ⟨*belt* out a song⟩

³belt *n* **1** : a jarring blow **2** : DRINK 2 ⟨a *belt* of whiskey⟩

belt·ing \'bel-ting\ *n* : material for belts

belt·way \'belt-,wā\ *n* : a highway going around an urban area — called also *belt highway*

be·lu·ga \bə-'lü-gə\ *n* **1** : a sturgeon especially of the Black and Caspian seas **2** : a mammal of the dolphin family becoming about 3 meters long and white when adult [sense 1 from Russian *beluga*, from *belyĭ* "white"; sense 2 from Russian *belukha*, from *belyĭ*]

bel·ve·dere \'bel-və-,diər\ *n* : GAZEBO [Italian, literally, "beautiful view"]

be·mire \bi-'mīr\ *vt* **1** : to cover or soil with mire **2** : to sink in mire

be·moan \bi-'mōn\ *vt* **1** : to express grief over : LAMENT **2** : to look upon with regret or displeasure

be·muse \bi-'myüz\ *vt* : to make confused : BEWILDER

¹bench \'bench\ *n* **1** : a long seat for two or more persons **2** : a long table for holding work and tools ⟨a carpenter's *bench*⟩ **3 a** : the seat where a judge sits in a court of law **b** : the position or rank of a judge **c** : a person or persons sitting as judge **4** : a seat where the members of a team wait for an opportunity to play **5** : TERRACE 2, SHELF [Old English *benc*] — **bench·like** \-,līk\ *adj*

²bench *vt* **1** : to seat on a bench **2** : to remove from or keep out of a game

bench mark *n* **1** : a mark on a permanent object indicating elevation and serving as a reference in geological surveys **2** *usually* **benchmark** : something that serves as a standard by which others may be measured

bench·warm·er \'bench-,wȯr-mər\ *n* : a reserve player on an athletic team

¹bend \'bend\ *n* **1** : a diagonal band in heraldry **2** : a knot by which one rope is fastened to another or to some object [sense 1 from Middle French *bende, bande* "strip, band"; sense 2 from Old English *bend* "fetter"]

²bend *vb* bent \'bent\; **bend·ing** **1** : to pull taut or tense ⟨*bend* a bow⟩ **2** : to curve or cause a change of shape ⟨*bend* a wire into a circle⟩ **3** : to turn in a certain direction ⟨*bent* their steps toward town⟩ **4** : to force to yield ⟨*bent* the family to our will⟩ **5** : to apply or apply oneself closely ⟨*bend* your energy to the task⟩ **6** : to curve out of line ⟨the road *bends* to the left⟩ **7** : to curve downward : STOOP ⟨backs *bent* by age⟩ **8** : YIELD, SUBMIT [Old English *bendan*]

³bend *n* **1** : the act or process of bending : the state of being bent **2** : something that is bent; *esp* : a curved part of a stream **3** *pl* : CAISSON DISEASE

bend·er \'ben-dər\ *n* **1** : one that bends **2** : SPREE

¹be·neath \bi-'nēth\ *adv* **1** : in or to a lower position **2** : directly under [Old English *beneothan*, from *be-* + *neothan* "below"]

²beneath *prep* **1 a** : in or to a lower position than **b** : directly under ⟨the ground *beneath* one's feet⟩ **2** : unworthy of ⟨*beneath* our dignity⟩ SYN see BELOW

Ben·e·dic·tine \,ben-ə-'dik-tən, -,tēn\ *n* : a monk or a nun of a religious order following the rule of Saint Benedict and devoted especially to scholarship and liturgical worship — **Benedictine** *adj*

bene·dic·tion \,ben-ə-'dik-shən\ *n* : the invocation of a blessing; *esp* : a short blessing at the end of a religious service [Late Latin *benedicere* "to bless", from Latin, "to speak well of", from *bene* "well" + *dicere* "to say"] — **bene·dic·to·ry** \-'dik-tə-rē, -trē\ *adj*

Ben·e·dict's solution \'ben-ə-,diks-, -,dikts-\ *n* : a blue solution that yields a red, yellow, or orange precipitate upon warming with a sugar (as glucose or maltose) capable of reducing a mild oxidizing agent [Stanley R. *Benedict,* died 1936, American chemist]

Bene·dic·tus \,ben-ə-'dik-təs\ *n* **1** : a canticle from Matthew 21:9 beginning "Blessed is he that cometh in the name of the Lord" **2** : a canticle from Luke 1:68 beginning "Blessed be the Lord God of Israel" [Late Latin, "blessed"]

bene·fac·tion \'ben-ə-,fak-shən, ,ben-ə-'\ *n* **1** : the action of benefiting **2** : a benefit given; *esp* : a charitable donation [Late Latin *benefactio*, from Latin *bene facere* "to do good"]

bene·fac·tor \'ben-ə-,fak-tər\ *n* : one that gives help; *esp* : one that gives or bequeaths financial aid

bene·fac·tress \-,fak-trəs\ *n* : a woman who is a benefactor

ben·e·fice \'ben-ə-fəs\ *n* : a post held by a member of the clergy that gives the right to use certain property and to receive income from stated sources [Medieval Latin *beneficium*, from Latin, "benefit, favor, promotion"] — **benefice** *vt*

be·nef·i·cence \bə-'nef-ə-səns\ *n* **1** : the quality or state of being beneficent **2** : BENEFACTION

be·nef·i·cent \-sənt\ *adj* : doing or producing good; *esp* : performing acts of kindness and charity — **be·nef·i·cent·ly** *adv*

ben·e·fi·cial \,ben-ə-'fish-əl\ *adj* : producing good effects : HELPFUL, ADVANTAGEOUS [Latin *beneficium* "kindness, benefit", from *beneficus* "conferring benefits", from *bene* "well" + *facere* "to do"] — **ben·e·fi·cial·ly** \-'fish-ə-lē\ *adv* — **ben·e·fi·cial·ness** *n* □ SYN BENEFICIAL, ADVANTAGEOUS, PROFITABLE mean bringing good or gain. BENEFICIAL implies promoting health or well-being; ADVANTAGEOUS stresses a choice or preference that brings superiority or greater success in attaining an end; PROFITABLE implies the yielding of useful or lucrative returns.

ben·e·fi·ci·ary \-'fish-ē-,er-ē; -'fish-rē, -ə-rē\ *n, pl* **-ar·ies** : a person who benefits or is expected to benefit from something ⟨the *beneficiary* of a life insurance policy⟩

¹**ben·e·fit** \'ben-ə-,fit\ *n* **1 a** : something that promotes well-being : ADVANTAGE **b** : useful aid : HELP **2** : money paid (as by an insurance company or a public agency) at death or when one is sick, retired, or unemployed **3** : an entertainment or social event to raise funds for a person or cause [Anglo-French *benfet* "good deed", from Latin *bene factum,* literally, "thing well done"]

²**benefit** *vb* **-fit·ed** *or* **-fit·ted; -fit·ing** *or* **-fit·ting 1** : to be useful or profitable to **2** : to receive benefit

be·nev·o·lence \bə-'nev-ləns, -ə-ləns\ *n* **1** : disposition to do good **2 a** : an act of kindness **b** : a generous gift

be·nev·o·lent \-lənt\ *adj* **1** : having or showing goodwill : KINDLY **2** : freely or generously giving to charity **3** : existing or operated to help others and not for profit ⟨*benevolent* institutions⟩ [Latin *benevolens,* from *bene* "well" + *velle* "to wish"] — **be·nev·o·lent·ly** *adv* — **be·nev·o·lent·ness** *n*

Ben·gali \ben-'gȯ-lē, beng-\ *n* **1** : a native or inhabitant of Bengal **2** : the modern Indic language of Bengal — **Bengali** *adj*

ben·ga·line \'beng-gə-,lēn\ *n* : fabric with a crosswise rib [French, from *Bengal*]

be·night·ed \bi-'nīt-əd\ *adj* **1** : overtaken by night or darkness **2** : IGNORANT 1a, 2

be·nign \bi-'nīn\ *adj* **1** : of a gentle disposition : GRACIOUS **2 a** : showing kindness and gentleness ⟨a *benign* face⟩ **b** : FAVORABLE 2 ⟨a *benign* climate⟩ **3** : of a mild character; *esp* : not malignant ⟨a *benign* tumor⟩ [Latin *benignus* "good-natured", from *bene* "well" + *gigni* "to be born"] — **be·nig·ni·ty** \-'nig-nət-ē\ *n* — **be·nign·ly** \-'nīn-lē\ *adv* □ SYN BENIGN, BENIGNANT both mean kindly or favorable in appearance, but BENIGN suggests actual effect given by action or appearance ⟨the weather remained *benign*⟩ ⟨a frown on a usually *benign* face⟩ BENIGNANT tends to suggest conscious feeling or intention of kindliness ⟨giving out candy with a *benignant* smile for each child⟩

be·nig·nant \bi-'nig-nənt\ *adj* **1** : serenely mild and kind ⟨a *benignant* smile⟩ **2** : FAVORABLE 2, BENEFICIAL SYN see BENIGN — **be·nig·nan·cy** \-nən-sē\ *n* — **be·nig·nant·ly** *adv*

ben·i·son \'ben-ə-sən, -zən\ *n* : BLESSING 1, 2, 3; *also* : BENEDICTION [Old French *beneiçon,* from Late Latin *benedictio*]

ben·ny \'ben-ē\ *n, pl* **bennies** *slang* : a tablet of amphetamine [from *Benzadrine*]

¹**bent** \'bent\ *n* : any of a genus of mostly perennial pasture and lawn grasses with fine velvety or wiry herbage [Middle English]

²**bent** *adj* : strongly inclined : DETERMINED ⟨*bent* on winning⟩

³**bent** *n* **1 a** : strong inclination or interest **b** : a natural capacity : TALENT ⟨a *bent* for languages⟩ **2** : capacity for endurance [from ²*bend*]

ben·thic \'ben-thik, 'bent-\ *or* **ben·thon·ic** \ben-'thän-ik\ *adj* : of, relating to, or occurring in the depths of a body of water (as the ocean) or the bottom underlying these depths [Greek *benthos* "depths of the sea"]

ben·thos \'ben-,thäs\ *n* : organisms that live on or in the bottom of bodies of water

ben·ton·ite \'bent-n-,īt\ *n* : an absorptive and colloidal clay used especially as a filler (as in paper) [Fort *Benton,* Montana]

bent·wood \'bent-,wu̇d\ *adj* : made of wood that is bent rather than cut to shape ⟨*bentwood* furniture⟩

be·numb \bi-'nəm\ *vt* : to make numb especially by cold

Ben·ze·drine \'ben-zə-,drēn\ *trademark* — used for amphetamine

ben·zene \'ben-,zēn, ben-'\ *n* : a colorless volatile flammable toxic liquid hydrocarbon C_6H_6 used as a solvent and in making other chemicals (as dyes and drugs) — called also *benzol* [alteration of *benzine*]

benzene ring *n* : an arrangement of atoms held to exist in benzene and other aromatic compounds that is marked by six carbon atoms linked by alternate single and double bonds in a hexagon

ben·zine \'ben-,zēn, ben-'\ *n* **1** : BENZENE **2** : any of various volatile flammable petroleum distillates used especially as solvents for fatty substances or as motor fuels [from *benzoic acid*]

ben·zo·ic acid \ben-'zō-ik-\ *n* : a white crystalline acid $C_7H_6O_2$ found naturally (as in cranberries) or made synthetically and used especially as a preservative and as an antiseptic [from *benzoin*]

ben·zo·in \'ben-zə-wən, -,wēn; -,zȯin\ *n* : a hard fragrant yellowish resin from trees of southeastern Asia used especially in medicine, as a fixative in perfumes, and as incense [Middle French *benjoin,* from Catalan *benjui,* from Arabic *lubān jāwī,* literally, "frankincense of Java"]

ben·zol \'ben-,zȯl, -,zōl\ *n* : BENZENE; *also* : a mixture of benzene and other aromatic hydrocarbons

ben·zo·yl peroxide \'ben-zə-,wil-, -,zȯil-\ *n* : a white crystalline flammable compound $C_{14}H_{10}O_4$ used in bleaching and in medicine especially in the treatment of acne

be·queath \bi-'kwēth, -'kwēth\ *vt* **1** : to give or leave (personal property) by will **2** : to hand down ⟨ideas *bequeathed* by our ancestors⟩ [Old English *becwethan,* from *be-* + *cwethan* "to say"] — **be·queath·al** \-əl\ *n*

be·quest \bi-'kwest\ *n* **1** : the act of bequeathing **2** : something bequeathed : LEGACY

be·rate \bi-'rāt\ *vt* : to scold forcefully

Ber·ber \'bər-bər\ *n* **1** : a member of a people of northwestern Africa **2** : any of a group of languages spoken in northwestern Africa [Arabic *Barbar*] — **Berber** *adj*

be·reave \bi-'rēv\ *vt* **-reaved** \-'rēvd\ *or* **-reft** \-'reft\; **-reav·ing** *archaic* : to deprive of something [Old English *berēafian,* from *be-* + *rēafian* "to rob"]

¹**be·reaved** \bi-'rēvd\ *adj* : suffering the death of a loved one ⟨*bereaved* parents⟩

²**bereaved** *n, pl* **bereaved** : one who is bereaved

be·reave·ment \bi-'rēv-mənt\ *n* : the state or fact of being bereaved

be·reft \bi-'reft\ *adj* **1** : not having something needed, wanted, or expected **2** : BEREAVED

be·ret \bə-'rā\ *n* : a soft flat wool cap without a visor [French *béret,* from Provençal *berret*]

berg \'bərg\ *n* : ICEBERG

ber·ga·mot \'bər-gə-,mät\ *n* **1** : a pear-shaped orange whose rind yields an oil used in perfumery; *also* : the tree or oil **2** : any of several mints (as Oswego tea) [French *bergamote*]

beri·beri \,ber-ē-'ber-ē\ *n* : a deficiency disease marked by weakness, wasting, and damage to nerves and caused by a dietary lack of or inability to assimilate thiamine [Sinhalese *bæribæri*]

berke·li·um \'bər-klē-əm\ *n* : a radioactive chemical element produced by bombarding americium with helium ions — see ELEMENT table [New Latin, from *Berkeley,* California]

Berk·shire \'bərk-,shiər, -shər\ *n* : any of a breed of medium-sized swine that are black with white markings [*Berkshire,* England]

berm *or* **berme** \'bərm\ *n* : a narrow shelf, path, or ledge typically at the top or bottom of a slope [French *berme,* from Dutch *berm* "strip of ground along a dike"]

Ber·mu·da grass \bər-'myüd-ə-\ *n* : a trailing southern European grass widely grown in tropical and subtropical regions especially as a turf grass

Bermuda shorts *n pl* : knee-length walking shorts

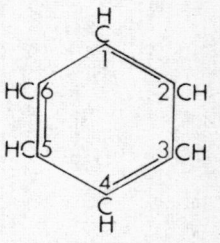

benzene ring

beret

\ə\ abut		\ng\ sing	
\ər\ further		\ō\ bone	
\a\ mat		\ȯ\ saw	
\ā\ take		\ȯi\ coin	
\ä\ cot, cart		\th\ thin	
\au̇\ out		\th\ this	
\ch\ chin		\ü\ food	
\e\ pet		\u̇\ foot	
\ē\ easy		\y\ yet	
\g\ go		\yü\ few	
\i\ tip		\yu̇\ cure	
\ī\ life		\zh\ vision	
\j\ job			

¹ber·ry \'ber-ē\ *n, pl* **berries** **1 a** : a small pulpy and usually edible fruit (as a strawberry or raspberry) **b** : a fruit (as a currant, grape, tomato, or banana) that develops from a single ovary and has the wall of the ripened ovary pulpy or fleshy **c** : the dry seed of some plants (as coffee) **2** : an egg of a fish or lobster [Old English *berie*] — **ber·ried** \'ber-ēd\ *adj*

²berry *vi* **ber·ried; ber·ry·ing** **1** : to bear or produce berries ⟨a *berrying* shrub⟩ **2** : to gather or seek berries

¹ber·serk \bər-'sərk, bə-, -'zərk, 'bər-, *or* **ber·serk·er** \-ər\ *n* : an ancient Scandinavian warrior frenzied in battle and held to be invulnerable [Old Norse *berserkr,* from *bjǫrn* "bear" + *serkr* "shirt"]

²berserk *adj* : FRENZIED, CRAZED — **berserk** *adv*

¹berth \'bərth\ *n* **1** : distance sufficient to maneuver a ship **2** : a place where a ship lies at anchor or at a wharf **3** : a place to sit or sleep on a ship or vehicle **4** : a job especially on a ship [probably from ²*bear* + *-th*]

²berth *vb* **1** : to bring or come into a berth **2** : to allot a berth to

ber·tha \'bər-thə\ *n* : a wide round collar covering the shoulders [French *berthe,* from *Berthe* (Bertha), died 783, queen of the Franks]

ber·yl \'ber-əl\ *n* : a mineral $Be_3Al_2Si_6O_{18}$ consisting of a silicate of beryllium and aluminum of great hardness and occurring in green, bluish green, yellow, pink, or white prisms [Greek *bēryllos,* of Indic origin]

be·ryl·li·um \bə-'ril-ē-əm\ *n* : a steel-gray light strong brittle metallic element — see ELEMENT table

be·seech \bi-'sēch\ *vb* **be·sought** \-'sȯt\ *or* **be·seeched; be·seech·ing** : to ask for earnestly : IMPLORE [Middle English *besechen,* from *be-* + *sechen* "to seek"] SYN see BEG

be·seem \bi-'sēm\ *vb, archaic* : to be fitting or becoming : BEFIT

be·set \bi-'set\ *vt* **-set; -set·ting** **1** : to place at intervals in or on : STUD ⟨a pin *beset* with gems⟩ **2** : to trouble with problems : HARASS **3 a** : to set upon : ASSAIL **b** : to hem in : SURROUND

be·set·ting *adj* : constantly present or attacking ⟨a *besetting* sin⟩

be·shrew \bi-'shrü\ *vt, archaic* : CURSE

¹be·side \bi-'sīd\ *adv, archaic* : BESIDES

²beside *prep* **1 a** : by the side of ⟨walk *beside* me⟩ **b** : in comparison with ⟨the kitten looks tiny *beside* the big dog⟩ **2** : BESIDES **3** : not relevant to ⟨*beside* the point⟩ — **beside oneself** : very upset

¹be·sides \bi-'sīdz\ *prep* **1** : other than **2** : in addition to

²besides *adv* : in addition : ALSO ⟨the play is excellent, and *besides* the tickets cost very little⟩

be·siege \bi-'sēj\ *vt* **1** : to surround with or as if with armed forces : lay siege to **2** : to press especially with questions or requests — **be·sieg·er** *n*

be·smear \bi-'smiər\ *vt* : SMEAR

be·smirch \bi-'smərch\ *vt* : to reduce the quality or purity of : SULLY

be·som \'bē-zəm\ *n* : a broom made of twigs [Old English *besma*]

be·sot \bi-'sät\ *vt* **be·sot·ted; be·sot·ting** : to make dull or stupid : STUPEFY; *esp* : to muddle with drink

be·spat·ter \bi-'spat-ər\ *vt* : SPATTER

be·speak \bi-'spēk\ *vt* **-spoke** \-'spōk\; **-spo·ken** \-'spō-kən\ **-speak·ing** **1 a** : to hire or arrange for beforehand **b** : REQUEST **2 a** : to give evidence of **b** : FORETELL

Bes·se·mer converter \'bes-ə-mər-\ *n* : the furnace used in the Bessemer process [Sir Henry *Bessemer*]

Bessemer process *n* : a process of making steel from pig iron by burning out impurities (as carbon) by means of a blast of air forced through the molten metal

¹best \'best\ *adj* **1** : good or useful in the highest degree : most excellent **2** : MOST, LARGEST ⟨the *best* part of a week⟩ [Old English *betst*]

²best *adv* **1** : in the best way **2** : to the highest degree : MOST ⟨*best* able to do the work⟩

³best *n* **1** : the best state or part **2** : one that is best ⟨trying to be the *best*⟩ **3** : one's maximum effort ⟨do your *best*⟩ **4** : best clothes ⟨wear your Sunday *best*⟩ — **at best 1** : under the most favorable conditions **2** : at most

⁴best *vt* : to get the better of : OUTDO

bes·tial \'bes-chəl, 'bēs-\ *adj* **1 a** : of or relating to beasts **b** : resembling a beast **2 a** : lacking intelligence or reason **b** : VICIOUS, BRUTAL [Latin *bestia* "beast"] — **bes·tial·ly** \-chə-lē\ *adv*

bes·ti·al·i·ty \,bes-chē-'al-ət-ē, ,bēs-\ *n* **1** : the condition or status of a lower animal **2** : display or indulgence of bestial traits or desires

bes·ti·ary \'bes-chē-,er-ē, 'bēs-\ *n, pl* **-ar·ies** : a medieval allegorical or moralizing work on the appearance and habits of animals

be·stir \bi-'stər\ *vt* : to stir up : rouse to action

best man *n* : a male friend who stands with the bridegroom at a wedding

be·stow \bi-'stō\ *vt* **1** : APPLY 1, USE **2** : QUARTER 2, LODGE **3** : to present as a gift : CONFER — **be·stow·al** \-'stō-əl\ *n*

be·stride \bi-'strīd\ *vt* **-strode** \-'strōd\; **-strid·den** \-'strid-n\; **-strid·ing** **1** : to ride, sit, or stand astride : STRADDLE **2** : to tower over : DOMINATE

best seller *n* : an article (as a book) whose sales are among the highest of its class

¹bet \'bet\ *n* **1 a** : an agreement based on the result of a contest or the outcome of an event requiring the person whose guess proves wrong to give something to a person whose guess proves right **b** : the making of such an agreement : WAGER **2** : the money or thing risked ⟨a *bet* of 10 cents⟩ [origin unknown]

²bet *vb* **bet** *or* **bet·ted; bet·ting** **1** : to risk in a bet **2** : to make a bet with **3** : to lay a bet

be·ta \'bāt-ə\ *n* **1** : the 2d letter of the Greek alphabet—B or β **2** : the second brightest star of a constellation

be·ta–car·o·tene \-'kar-ə-,tēn\ *n* : an isomer of carotene found in dark green and dark yellow vegetables and fruits

be·take \bi-'tāk\ *vt* **-took** \-'tůk\; **-tak·en** \-'tā-kən\; **-tak·ing** \-'tā-king\ : to cause (oneself) to go

beta particle *n* : an electron or positron ejected from the nucleus of an atom during radioactive decay; *also* : a high-speed electron or positron

beta ray *n* **1** : BETA PARTICLE **2** : a stream of beta particles

be·ta·tron \'bāt-ə-,trän\ *n* : a device that accelerates electrons by the inductive action of a rapidly varying magnetic field

be·tel \'bēt-l\ *n* : a climbing pepper whose dried leaves are chewed with betel nut and lime [Portuguese, from Tamil *verri-lai*]

Be·tel·geuse \'bet-l-,jüz, 'bēt-, -,jůz, -,jərz\ *n* : a variable red giant star near one shoulder of Orion [French *Bételgeuse,* from Arabic *bayt al-jawzā'* "Gemini", literally, "the house of the twins"]

betel nut *n* : the astringent seed of an Asian palm that is chewed with betel and lime as a stimulant especially by southeastern Asians

bête noire \,bet-'nwär, ,bāt-\ *n, pl* **bêtes noires** \,bet-'nwär, ,bāt-, -'nwärz\ : a person or thing strongly detested or avoided : BUGBEAR [French, literally, "black beast"]

beth·el \'beth-əl\ *n* : a place of worship especially for sailors [Hebrew *bēth'ēl* "house of God"]

be·think \bi-'thingk\ *vt* **-thought** \-'thȯt\; **-think·ing** **1 a** : REMEMBER, RECALL **b** : to cause (oneself) to be reminded **2** : to cause (oneself) to consider

be·tide \bi-'tīd\ *vb* : to happen or happen to : BEFALL

be·to·ken \bi-'tō-kən\ *vt* : to be a sign of : INDICATE

be·tray \bi-'trā\ *vt* **1** : to give over to an enemy by treachery or fraud **2** : to be unfaithful or treacherous to : FAIL ⟨*betray* a trust⟩ **3** : to reveal unintentionally

⟨*betray* one's ignorance⟩ **4 :** to tell in violation of a trust [Middle English *betrayen,* from *be-* + *trayen* "to betray", from Old French *traïr,* from Latin *tradere* "to hand over, betray"] — **be·tray·al** \-'trā-əl, -'trāl\ *n* — **be·tray·er** \-'trā-ər\ *n*

be·troth \bi-'träth, -'tróth, -'trōth, or with *th*\ *vt* **:** to promise to marry or give in marriage

be·troth·al \-'trōth-əl, -'tróth-, -'trōth-\ *n* **1 :** an engagement to be married **2 :** the act or ceremony of becoming engaged to be married

be·trothed *n* **:** the person to whom one is betrothed

bet·ta \'bet-ə\ *n* **:** any of a genus of small brilliantly colored long-finned freshwater fishes of southeastern Asia [New Latin]

¹**bet·ter** \'bet-ər\ *adj* **1 :** more than half ⟨the *better* part of a week⟩ **2 :** improved in health **3 :** of higher quality [Old English *betera*]

²**better** *adv* **1 :** in a more excellent manner **2 a :** to a higher or greater degree **b :** MORE ⟨*better* than an hour's drive⟩

³**better** *n* **1 a :** something better **b :** a superior especially in merit or rank **2 :** ADVANTAGE, VICTORY ⟨got the *better* of me⟩

⁴**better** *vt* **1 :** to make better **2 :** to surpass in excellence **:** EXCEL

bet·ter·ment \'bet-ər-mənt\ *n* **:** IMPROVEMENT

bet·tor *or* **bet·ter** \'bet-ər\ *n* **:** one that bets

¹**be·tween** \bi-'twēn\ *prep* **1 a :** by the common action of ⟨shared the work *between* the two of them⟩ **b :** with shares to each of **:** AMONG ⟨divided the fortune *between* the two heirs⟩ **2 :** in the time, space, or interval that separates ⟨*between* nine and ten o'clock⟩ ⟨*between* the desk and the wall⟩ **3 :** DISTINGUISHING ⟨the difference *between* soccer and football⟩ **4 :** by comparison of ⟨choose *between* the two coats⟩ **5 :** from one to the other or another of ⟨the bond *between* friends⟩ [Old English *betwēonum,* from *be-* + *-twēonum* "two"] □ SYN AMONG: BETWEEN indicates a relation of two objects in position, distribution, participation, or communication ⟨*between* two fires⟩ ⟨lost it *between* school and home⟩ but may be used of more than two if it brings them individually into the expressed relation ⟨the four children had only seven dollars *between* them⟩ ⟨a treaty *between* three countries⟩ AMONG always implies more than two objects which it brings less definitely or individually into the relationship ⟨scattered the corn *among* the chickens⟩ ⟨it was whispered *among* their friends that they were bankrupt⟩

²**between** *adv* **:** in an intermediate space or interval

be·tween·ness \-nəs\ *n* **:** the quality or state of an element that is between two others in an ordered set

be·twixt \bi-'twikst\ *adv or prep* **:** BETWEEN [Old English *be-twux*]

betwixt and between *adv or adj* **:** in an intermediate position or state

¹**bev·el** \'bev-əl\ *adj* **:** OBLIQUE 1, BEVELED [derived from Old French *baif* "with open mouth", from *baer* "to yawn"]

²**bevel** *n* **1 a :** the angle that one surface or line makes with another when they are not at right angles **b :** the slant or inclination of such a surface or line **2 :** an instrument consisting of two rules or arms jointed together and opening to any angle for drawing angles or adjusting surfaces to be given a bevel

³**bevel** *vb* **bev·eled** *or* **bev·elled; bev·el·ing** *or* **bev·el·ling** \'bev-ling, -ə-ling\ **1 :** to cut or shape (as an edge or surface) to a bevel **2 :** INCLINE 3, SLANT

bev·er·age \'bev-rij, -ə-rij\ *n* **:** a liquid for drinking; *esp* **:** one other than water [Middle French *bevrage,* from *beivre* "to drink", from Latin *bibere*]

bevy \'bev-ē\ *n, pl* **bev·ies :** CLUSTER 1, GROUP, COLLECTION ⟨a *bevy* of quail⟩ [Middle English *bevey*]

be·wail \bi-'wāl\ *vt* **1 :** to wail over **2 :** to express deep regret for

be·ware \bi-'waər, -'weər\ *vb* **:** to be wary or wary of [Middle English *been war,* from *been* "to be" + *war* "wary"]

be·wil·der \bi-'wil-dər\ *vt* **-dered; -der·ing** \-də-ring, -dring\ **1 :** to cause to lose one's bearings **2 :** to perplex or confuse especially by a complex variety or large number of objects or possibilities — **be·wil·der·ing·ly** \-də-ring-lē, -dring-lē\ *adv* — **be·wil·der·ment** \-dər-mənt\ *n*

be·witch \bi-'wich\ *vt* **1 :** to gain an influence over by means of magic or witchcraft **:** put under a spell **2 :** FASCINATE, CHARM — **be·witch·ery** \-ə-rē\ *n* — **be·witch·ment** \-mənt\ *n*

be·wray \bi-'rā\ *vt, archaic* **:** DIVULGE, BETRAY, REVEAL [Middle English *bewreyen,* from *be-* + *wreyen* "to accuse", from Old English *wrēgan*]

bey \'bā\ *n* **1 :** a provincial governor in the Ottoman Empire **2 :** the former native ruler of Tunis [Turkish, "gentleman, chief"]

¹**be·yond** \bē-'änd\ *adv* **:** on or to the farther side ⟨extending to the river and *beyond*⟩

²**beyond** *prep* **1 a :** on or to the farther side of ⟨*beyond* that tree⟩ **b :** later than ⟨*beyond* closing time⟩ **2 :** out of the reach or sphere of ⟨*beyond* help⟩ **3 :** out of the comprehension of ⟨these ideas are *beyond* me⟩

³**beyond** *n* **:** HEREAFTER

be·zel \'bē-zəl, 'bez-əl\ *n* **1 :** a sloping edge or face especially on a cutting tool **2 :** the top part of a ring setting that holds a stone or ornament; *also* **:** the top including the stone **3 :** the grooved rim that holds the crystal on a watch; *also* **:** a rim that holds a covering (as on a clock dial or headlight) [probably from French dialect]

be·zoar \'bē-,zōr, -,zór\ *n* **:** a hard mass of ingested material (as hair) that forms and lodges in the stomach or intestine of a ruminant (as a cow) and was formerly believed to possess magical properties [Spanish, from Arabic *bāzahr*]

bhang \'bang, 'bäng\ *n* **:** the leaves and flowering tips of hemp; *also* **:** a narcotic and intoxicant product from this — compare CANNABIS, HASHISH, MARIJUANA [Hindi *bhā̃g*]

B–horizon *n* **:** a soil layer immediately beneath the A-horizon from which it obtains material by leaching and from which it is usually distinguished by less weathering

bi- *prefix* **1 a :** two ⟨*bi*directional⟩ **b :** coming or occurring every two ⟨*bi*monthly⟩ ⟨*bi*weekly⟩ **c :** into two parts ⟨*bi*sect⟩ **2 a :** twice **:** doubly **:** on both sides ⟨*bi*convex⟩ **b :** coming or occurring two times ⟨*bi*monthly⟩ ⟨*bi*weekly⟩ — often disapproved in this sense because of the likelihood of confusion with sense 1b; compare SEMI- [Latin]

bi·an·nu·al \bī-'an-yə-wəl, 'bī-, -'an-yəl\ *adj* **:** occurring twice a year — compare BIENNIAL — **bi·an·nu·al·ly** \-ē\ *adv*

¹**bi·as** \'bī-əs\ *n* **1 :** a line diagonal to the grain of a fabric often utilized in the cutting of garments for smoother fit **2 :** an inclination of temperament or outlook; *esp* **:** such an inclination marked by strong prejudice **3 :** the tendency of a bowl in lawn bowling to swerve on the green; *also* **:** the uneven shape of the bowl causing this tendency **4 :** a voltage applied to a device (as the grid of an electron tube) to establish a reference level for operation [Middle French *biais*] SYN see PREJUDICE

²**bias** *adj* **:** DIAGONAL, SLANTING — used chiefly of fabrics and their cut

³**bias** *vt* **bi·ased** *or* **bi·assed; bi·as·ing** *or* **bi·as·sing :** to give a bias to **:** PREJUDICE

bi·ath·lon \bī-'ath-lən, -,län\ *n* **:** a contest consisting of cross-country skiing and rifle target shooting [*bi-* + Greek *athlon* "contest"]

bib \'bib\ *n* **1 :** a cloth, paper, or plastic shield tied under the chin (as of a child at mealtime) to protect

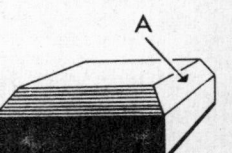

²bevel 1: A bevel

\ə\ abut	\ng\ sing
\ər\ **further**	\ō\ bone
\a\ mat	\ó\ saw
\ā\ take	\ói\ coin
\ä\ cot, cart	\th\ thin
\aú\ out	\th\ this
\ch\ chin	\ü\ food
\e\ pet	\ú\ foot
\ē\ easy	\y\ yet
\g\ go	\yü\ few
\i\ tip	\yú\ cure
\ī\ life	\zh\ vision
\j\ job	

BOOKS OF THE OLD TESTAMENT

ROMAN CATHOLIC CANON	PROTESTANT CANON	ROMAN CATHOLIC CANON	PROTESTANT CANON
Genesis	Genesis	Wisdom	
Exodus	Exodus	Sirach (Ecclesiasticus)	
Leviticus	Leviticus	Isaiah	Isaiah
Numbers	Numbers	Jeremiah	Jeremiah
Deuteronomy	Deuteronomy	Lamentations	Lamentations
Joshua	Joshua	Baruch	
Judges	Judges	Ezekiel	Ezekiel
Ruth	Ruth	Daniel	Daniel
1 & 2 Samuel (1 & 2 Kings)	1 & 2 Samuel	Hosea (Osee)	Hosea
1 & 2 Kings (3 & 4 Kings)	1 & 2 Kings	Joel	Joel
1 & 2 Chronicles (1 & 2 Paralipomenon)	1 & 2 Chronicles	Amos	Amos
Ezra (1 Esdras)	Ezra	Obadiah (Abdias)	Obadiah
Nehemiah (2 Esdras)	Nehemiah	Jonah	Jonah
Tobit		Micah	Micah
Judith		Nahum	Nahum
Esther	Esther	Habakkuk	Habakkuk
Job	Job	Zephaniah (Sophonias)	Zephaniah
Psalms	Psalms	Haggai (Aggeus)	Haggai
Proverbs	Proverbs	Zechariah	Zechariah
Ecclesiastes	Ecclesiastes	Malachi	Malachi
Song of Songs (Canticle of Canticles)	Song of Solomon	1 & 2 Maccabees	

JEWISH SCRIPTURE

Law	1 & 2 Kings	Nahum	Song of Songs
Genesis	Isaiah	Habakkuk	Ruth
Exodus	Jeremiah	Zephaniah	Lamentations
Leviticus	Ezekiel	Haggai	Ecclesiastes
Numbers	Hosea	Zechariah	Esther
Deuteronomy	Joel	Malachi	Daniel
Prophets	Amos	**Hagiographa**	Ezra
Joshua	Obadiah	Psalms	Nehemiah
Judges	Jonah	Proverbs	1 & 2 Chronicles
1 & 2 Samuel	Micah	Job	

PROTESTANT APOCRYPHA

1 & 2 Esdras	Additions of Esther	Baruch	Susanna
Tobit	Wisdom of Solomon	Prayer of Azariah and the	Bel and the Dragon
Judith	Ecclesiasticus or the Wisdom of Jesus Son of Sirach	Song of the Three Holy Children	The Prayer of Manasses 1 & 2 Maccabees

BOOKS OF THE NEW TESTAMENT

Matthew	1 & 2 Corinthians	1 & 2 Thessalonians	James
Mark	Galatians	1 & 2 Timothy	1 & 2 Peter
Luke	Ephesians	Titus	1, 2, 3 John
John	Philippians	Philemon	Jude
Acts of the Apostles	Colossians	Hebrews	Revelation *or* Apocalypse
Romans			

the clothes **2** : the part of an apron or of overalls extending above the waist in front [Middle English *bib-ben* "to drink"]

bib and tucker *n* : an outfit of clothing

bib·ber \'bib-ər\ *n* : TIPPLER — **bib·bery** \-ə-rē\ *n*

bi·be·lot \'bē-bə-ˌlō\ *n* : a small household ornament or decorative object [French]

Bi·ble \'bī-bəl\ *n* **1** : a book made up of the writings accepted by Christians as inspired by God and comprising the Old Testament and the New Testament **2** : a book containing the sacred writings of another religion (as Judaism) **3** *not cap* : a publication that is outstandingly authoritative [Medieval Latin *biblia,* from Greek, from *biblion* "book", from *byblos* "papyrus, book", from *Byblos,* ancient Phoenician city from which papyrus was exported)
SEE BIBLE TABLE ABOVE

bib·li·cal \'bib-li-kəl\ *adj* **1** : of, relating to, or in accord with the Bible **2** : suggestive of the Bible or Bible times — **bib·li·cal·ly** \-kə-lē, -klē\ *adv*

biblio- *combining form* : book [Greek *biblion*]

bib·li·og·ra·pher \ˌbib-lē-'äg-rə-fər\ *n* **1** : an expert in bibliography **2** : a compiler of bibliographies

bib·li·og·ra·phy \ˌbib-lē-'äg-rə-fē\ *n, pl* **-phies** **1** : the history, identification, or description of writings or publications **2** : a list often with descriptive or critical notes of writings relating to a particular subject, period, or author; *also* : a list of works written by an author or printed by a publishing house **3** : a list of the works referred to in a text or consulted by the author in its production — **bib·li·o·graph·ic** \ˌbib-lē-ə-'graf-ik\ *or* **bib·lio·graph·i·cal** \-'graf-i-kəl\ *adj* — **bib·li·o·graph·i·cal·ly** \-kə-lē, -klē\ *adv*

bib·lio·phile \'bib-lē-ə-ˌfīl\ *n* : a lover of books; *also* : a book collector

bib·u·lous \'bib-yə-ləs\ *adj* **1** : highly absorbent **2 a** : inclined to drink **b** : of or relating to drink or drinking [Latin *bibulus,* from *bibere* "to drink"] — **bib·u·lous·ly** *adv* — **bib·u·lous·ness** *n*

bi·cam·er·al \bī-'kam-rəl, 'bī-, -ə-rəl\ *adj* : having, consisting of, or based on two legislative chambers ⟨*bicameral* legislatures⟩ [Latin *camera* "room, chamber"] — **bi·cam·er·al·ism** \-rə-,liz-əm\ *n*

bi·car·bon·ate \bī-'kär-bə-,nāt, 'bī-, -nət\ *n* : an acid carbonate

bicarbonate of soda : SODIUM BICARBONATE

bi·cen·te·na·ry \,bī-sen-'ten-ə-rē, -'tē-nə-; bī-'sent-n-,er-ē\ *n* : BICENTENNIAL — **bicentenary** *adj*

bi·cen·ten·ni·al \,bī-sen-'ten-ē-əl\ *n* : a 200th anniversary or its celebration — **bicentennial** *adj*

bi·ceps \'bī-,seps\ *n* : a muscle having two heads; *esp* : a large flexor muscle of the front of the upper arm [Latin *biceps* "two-headed", from *bi-* + *caput* "head"]

bi·chlo·ride \bī-'klōr-,īd, 'bī-, -'klȯr-\ *n* : MERCURIC CHLORIDE — called also *bichloride of mercury*

bi·chro·mate \bī-'krō-,māt, 'bī-\ *n* : DICHROMATE

bick·er \'bik-ər\ *vi* **bick·ered; bick·er·ing** \'bik-ring, -ə-ring\ : to engage in an angry and often petty quarrel : WRANGLE [Middle English *bikeren*] — **bicker** *n*

bi·con·cave \bī-,kän-'kāv, bī-'kän-,, 'bī-\ *adj* : concave on both sides ⟨a *biconcave* lens⟩

bi·con·di·tion·al \,bī-kən-'dish-nəl, -ən-l\ *n* : a logical relationship between two propositions such that the truth of the first implies the second and the truth of the second implies the first; *also* : a statement of this kind ⟨the statement "*q* if and only if *p*" is a *biconditional*⟩

bi·con·vex \bī-,kän-'veks, bī-'kän-,, 'bī\ *adj* : convex on both sides ⟨a *biconvex* lens⟩

bi·cul·tur·al \bī-'kəl-chə-rəl\ *adj* : of, relating to, or including two distinct cultures ⟨*bicultural* education⟩ — **bi·cul·tur·al·ism** \-rə-,liz-əm\ *n*

¹bi·cus·pid \bī-'kəs-pəd, 'bī-\ *adj* : having or ending in two points [Latin *cuspis* "point, cusp"]

²bicuspid *n* : PREMOLAR

bicuspid valve *n* : a heart valve guarding the opening between the left auricle and ventricle and consisting of two triangular flaps — called also *mitral valve*

¹bi·cy·cle \'bī-,sik-əl\ *n* : a vehicle with two wheels one behind the other, a tubular metal frame, a steering handle, a saddle seat, and pedals by which it is propelled [Greek *kyklos* "wheel"] — **bi·cy·clist** \-,sik-ləst, -ə-ləst\ *n*

²bicycle *vi* **bi·cy·cled; bi·cy·cling** \-,sik-ling, -ə-ling\ : to ride a bicycle — **bi·cy·cler** \-,sik-lər, -ə-lər\ *n*

¹bid \'bid\ *vb* **bade** \'bad, 'bād\ *or* **bid; bid·den** \'bid-n\ *or* **bid** *also* **bade; bid·ding** **1 a** : to issue an order to : TELL ⟨did as I was *bidden*⟩ **b** : to request to come : INVITE **2** : to give expression to ⟨*bade* me farewell⟩ **3** *past* **bid a** : to offer (a price) for something (as at an auction) **b** : to make a bid of in a card game [partly from Old English *biddan* "to ask, pray"; partly from Old English *bēodan* "to offer, command"] — **bid·der** *n* — **bid fair** : to seem likely

²bid *n* **1** : an offer to pay a stated sum for something or to do something at a stated fee; *also* : the price or fee offered **2** : an opportunity or turn to bid **3** : INVITATION **4 a** : an announcement of what a card player will attempt to win **b** : the amount of such a bid **5** : an attempt or effort to win, achieve, or attract

bid·da·ble \'bid-ə-bəl\ *adj* **1** : OBEDIENT, DOCILE **2** : capable of being bid (as in a card game) — **bid·da·bly** \-blē\ *adv*

bide \'bīd\ *vb* **bode** \'bōd\ *or* **bid·ed; bid·ed; bid·ing** : to continue in a state or condition; *also* : WAIT ⟨*bide* a while⟩ [Old English *bīdan*] — **bid·er** *n* — **bide one's time** : to wait for an appropriate moment before acting

bi·di·rec·tion·al \,bī-də-'rek-shnel, 'bī-, -dī-, -shən-l\ *adj* : involving, moving, or taking place in two usually opposite directions ⟨*bidirectional* flow⟩

bi·en·ni·al \bī-'en-ē-əl, 'bī-\ *adj* **1** : occurring every two years — compare BIANNUAL **2 a** : continuing or lasting for two years **b** : growing vegetatively during the first year and fruiting and dying during the second — **biennial** *n* — **bi·en·ni·al·ly** \-ē-ə-lē\ *adv*

bi·en·ni·um \bī-'en-ē-əm\ *n, pl* **-ni·ums** *or* **-nia** \-ē-ə\ : a period of two years [Latin, from *bi-* + *annus* "year"]

bier \'biər\ *n* : a stand on which a corpse or coffin is placed; *also* : a coffin together with its stand [Old English *bǣr*]

bi·fid \'bī-,fid, -fəd\ *adj* : divided into two equal lobes or parts by a median cleft ⟨a *bifid* leaf⟩ [Latin *bifidus,* from *bi-* + *findere* "to split"]

¹bi·fo·cal \bī-'fō-kəl, 'bī-\ *adj* : having two focal lengths

²bifocal *n* **1** : a bifocal glass or lens **2** *pl* : eyeglasses with bifocal lenses

bi·fur·cate \'bī-fər-,kāt, bī-'fər-\ *vb* : to divide into two branches or parts [Latin *furca* "fork"] — **bi·fur·cate** \bī-'fər-kət, 'bī-, -,kāt; 'bī-fər-,kāt\ *adj* — **bi·fur·ca·tion** \,bī-fər-'kā-shən, -,fər-\ *n*

¹big \'big\ *adj* **big·ger; big·gest** **1** : of great force ⟨a *big* storm⟩ **2 a** : large in size, bulk, or extent ⟨a *big* house⟩ **b** : conducted on a large scale ⟨*big* government⟩ **c** : ¹CAPITAL 2 ⟨*big* letters⟩ **d** : being older ⟨my *big* sister⟩ **3 a** : PREGNANT ⟨*big* with child⟩ **b** : full to overflowing or bursting ⟨eyes *big* with tears⟩ **c** : being full and resonant ⟨a *big* voice⟩ **4 a** : of great importance or significance; *esp* : CHIEF, PREDOMINANT ⟨the *big* issue of the campaign⟩ **b** : IMPOSING, PRETENTIOUS; *also* : BOASTFUL ⟨*big* talk⟩ **c** : MAGNANIMOUS, GENEROUS ⟨a *big* heart⟩ [Middle English] SYN see LARGE — **big·ness** *n*

²big *adv* **1** : to a large amount or extent **2 a** : in an outstanding manner ⟨made it *big*⟩ **b** : POMPOUSLY, PRETENTIOUSLY

big·a·mist \'big-ə-məst\ *n* : a person who commits bigamy

big·a·my \'big-ə-mē\ *n* : the statutory offense of marrying one person while still legally married to another — **big·a·mous** \-məs\ *adj* — **big·a·mous·ly** *adv*

big bang theory *n* : a theory in astronomy : the universe originated billions of years ago from the explosion of a single mass of material so that the pieces are still flying apart — compare STEADY STATE THEORY

Big Dipper *n* : DIPPER 2a

big·eye \'big-,ī\ *n* : either of two small widely distributed marine reddish to silvery food fishes related to the perches

big·gish \'big-ish\ *adj* : somewhat big : comparatively big

big·horn \'big-,hȯrn\ *n, pl* **bighorn** *or* **bighorns** : a usually grayish brown wild sheep of mountainous western North America

bight \'bīt\ *n* **1 a** : the slack middle part of a rope when it is fastened at both ends **b** : a loop or double part of a bent rope **2** : a bend or curve especially in a river **3** : a bend in a coast or the bay it forms [Old English *byht* "bend"]

big·ot \'big-ət\ *n* : a person obstinately or intolerantly devoted to his or her own group, beliefs, or opinions [Middle French]

big·ot·ed \'big-ət-əd\ *adj* : obstinately attached to a belief or opinion and intolerant of the ideas and opinions of others

big·ot·ry \'big-ə-trē\ *n, pl* **-ries** : the state of mind of a bigot; *also* : behavior or beliefs arising from such a state of mind

big shot *n* : an important person

big stick *n* : coercive use or threat of military or political intervention [from Theodore Roosevelt's belief that "we must speak softly but carry a big stick"]

big time *n* : the top rank (as of a profession) where income and prestige are greatest

big toe *n* : the innermost and largest digit of the foot

big top *n* **1** : the main tent of a circus **2** : CIRCUS 2

bighorn

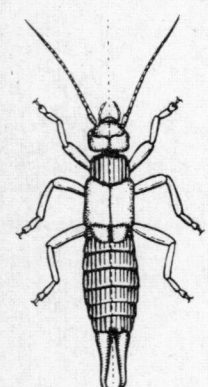

bilateral symmetry

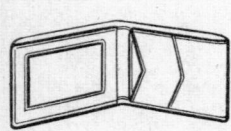

billfold

big tree *n* : a California evergreen of the pine family that often exceeds 90 meters in height — called also *giant sequoia, sequoia*; compare REDWOOD

big·wig \'big-,wig\ *n* : an important person

bike \'bīk\ *n or vi* : BICYCLE, MOTORCYCLE — **bik·er** *n*

bi·ki·ni \bə-'kē-nē\ *n* : a woman's scanty two-piece bathing suit [French, from *Bikini,* atoll of the Marshall islands]

bi·la·bi·al \bī-'lā-bē-əl, 'bī-\ *adj* : of, relating to, or produced with both lips ⟨a *bilabial* consonant⟩

bi·lat·er·al \bī-'lat-ə-rəl, 'bī-, -'la-trəl\ *adj* **I** : having or involving two sides; *esp* : affecting reciprocally two sides or parties ⟨a *bilateral* treaty⟩ **2** : characterized by bilateral symmetry — **bi·lat·er·al·ism** \-,iz-əm\ *n* — **bi·lat·er·al·ly** \-ē\ *adv*

bilateral symmetry *n* : a pattern of animal symmetry in which similar parts are arranged on opposite sides of a median axis so that one and only one plane can divide the individual into essentially identical halves — compare RADIAL SYMMETRY

bil·ber·ry \'bil-,ber-ē\ *n* : any of several blueberries with flowers and fruit borne in leaf axils; *also* : the sweet edible bluish fruit [probably of Scandinavian origin]

bile \'bīl\ *n* **I** : a thick bitter yellow or greenish fluid secreted by the liver and functioning in the duodenum in the digestion and absorption of fats **2** : tendency toward anger : ILL WILL [French, from Latin *bilis*]

bile duct *n* : a canal by which bile passes from the liver or gall bladder to the duodenum

bile salts *n pl* : a dry mixture of the principal salts of the gall of the ox used as a liver stimulant and as a laxative

bilge \'bilj\ *n* **I a** : the part of a ship's hull between the flat of the bottom and the vertical topsides **b** : the lowest point of a ship's inner hull **2** : stale or worthless remarks or ideas [probably from Middle French *boulge, bouge* "leather bag, curved part"]

bilge water *n* : water that collects in the bilge of a ship

bil·i·ary \'bil-ē-,er-ē\ *adj* : of, relating to, or conveying bile

bi·lin·gual \'bī-'ling-gwəl, 'bī-, -gyə-wəl\ *adj* : **I** : of, containing, expressed in, or involving the use of two languages ⟨a *bilingual* dictionary⟩ ⟨*bilingual* education⟩ **2** : able to use two languages especially with fluency [Latin *lingua* "tongue, language"] — **bilingual** *n* — **bi·lin·gual·ism** \-,iz-əm\ *n*

bil·ious \'bil-yəs\ *adj* **I a** : of or relating to bile **b** : marked by or suffering from disordered liver function **2** : of an irritable ill-natured disposition : PEEVISH — **bil·ious·ly** *adv* — **bil·iousness** *n*

bil·i·ru·bin \,bil-ə-'rü-bən, 'bil-ə-,\ *n* : a reddish yellow pigment occurring in bile, blood, urine, and gallstones [Latin *ruber* "red"]

bil·i·ver·din \-'vərd-n, -,vərd-\ *n* : a green pigment occurring in bile [obsolete French *verd* "green"]

bilk \'bilk\ *vt* : to cheat out of what is due : SWINDLE [perhaps alteration of ²*balk*]

¹**bill** \'bil\ *n* **I** : the jaws of a bird together with their horny covering **2** : a beak (as of a turtle) or a mouth structure resembling a bird's bill **3** : a projection of land like a beak **4** : the visor of a cap [Old English *bile*] — **billed** \'bild\ *adj* □ SYN BILL, BEAK mean the horny two-parted projection that serves a bird for jaws. In popular usage BEAK is applied especially to the strong triangular pointed or hooked shape associated with striking, tearing, or crushing ⟨an eagle's *beak*⟩ while BILL applies to the structure in any bird ⟨a duck's *bill*⟩

²**bill** *vi* **I** : to touch bill to bill **2** : to caress and kiss affectionately ⟨lovers *billing* and cooing⟩

³**bill** *n* : a weapon used up to the 18th century that consists of a long staff with a hook-shaped blade at one end [Old English]

⁴**bill** *n* **I** : a draft of a law presented to a legislature for enactment **2** : a written statement of a wrong one person has suffered from another or of a breach of law by some person ⟨a *bill* of complaint⟩ **3** : an itemized list : a detailed statement of items **4** : an itemized account of the cost of goods sold or work done : INVOICE **5 a** : an advertisement posted or distributed to announce an event (as a theatrical entertainment) **b** : an entertainment program or the entertainment presented on it **6** : NOTE 3a; *esp* : a piece of paper money [Medieval Latin *billa* "formal document", from *bulla* "seal, sealed document", from Latin, "bubble"]

⁵**bill** *vt* **I a** : to make a bill of ⟨*bill* the goods to my account⟩ **b** : to submit a bill of charges to ⟨*bill* a customer⟩ **2 a** : to advertise especially by posters or placards **b** : to arrange for the presentation of (as a play) — **bill·er** *n*

bill·board \'bil-,bōrd, -,bȯrd\ *n* : a flat surface on which bills are posted; *esp* : a large vertical panel designed to carry outdoor advertising

bill·bug \-,bəg\ *n* : a usually small dark weevil with larvae that eat the roots of grasses

¹**bil·let** \'bil-ət\ *n* **I** : an official order directing that a soldier be lodged (as in a private home) **2** : quarters assigned (as to a soldier) [Middle French *billette* "note, letter", derived from Medieval Latin *bulla* "document"]

²**billet** *vb* **I** : to assign lodging to by a billet : QUARTER **2** : to have quarters : LODGE

³**billet** *n* **I** : a short thick piece of wood (as for firewood) **2** : a bar of metal; *esp* : one of iron or steel [Middle French *billette,* from *bille* "log", of Celtic origin]

bil·let–doux \,bil-ā-'dü\ *n, pl* **bil·lets–doux** \-ā-'dü, -ā-'düz\ : a love letter [French *billet doux,* literally, "sweet note"]

bill·fold \'bil-,fōld\ *n* : a usually leather container for paper money and identification and credit cards that may have compartments for photographs and loose change and that can be folded and carried in a pocket or handbag

bill·head \-,hed\ *n* : a printed form usually headed with a business address and used for billing charges

bil·liard \'bil-yərd\ *n* : CAROM 1

bil·liards \-yərdz\ *n* : any of several games played on an oblong table by driving small balls against one another or into pockets with a cue; *esp* : a game in which one scores by causing a cue ball to hit in succession two object balls [Middle French *billard* "billiard cue, billiards", from *bille* "log"]

bil·lings·gate \'bil-ingz-,gāt\ *n* : coarsely abusive language [*Billingsgate,* a fish market in London, England]

bil·lion \'bil-yən\ *n* **I** — see NUMBER table **2** : a very large or indefinitely large number ⟨*billions* of dollars⟩ [French, from *bi-* "two" + *-llion* (as in *million*)] — **billion** *adj* — **-bil·lionth** \-yənth, -yəntth\ *adj or n*

bil·lion·aire \,bil-yə-'naər, -'neər, 'bil-yə-,\ *n* : one whose wealth is a billion or more

bill of exchange : a written order from one individual to another to pay a specified sum of money to a designated third : DRAFT 11a

bill of fare : MENU

bill of health : a certificate given to a ship's master on leaving port that indicates the state of health of the ship's company and of the port with regard to infectious diseases

bill of lad·ing \-'lād-ing\ : a receipt listing goods shipped that is signed by the agent of the owner of a ship or issued by a common carrier

bill of rights *often cap B&R* : a statement of fundamental rights and privileges guaranteed to a people against violation by the state; *esp* : the first 10 amendments to the United States Constitution

bill of sale : a formal document showing transfer of ownership of personal property

¹bil·low \'bil-ō\ *n* **1** : WAVE; *esp* : a great wave or surge of water **2** : a rolling mass (as of flame or smoke) like a high wave [probably from Old Norse *bylgja*] — **bil·lowy** \'bil-ə-wē\ *adj*

²billow *vb* **1** : to rise or roll in waves or surges ⟨the *billowing* ocean⟩ **2** : to bulge or swell out (as through action of the wind) ⟨sails *billowing* in the breeze⟩

bil·ly \'bil-ē\ *n, pl* **billies** : CLUB 1a; *esp* : a police officer's club — called also *billy club*

bil·ly goat \'bil-ē-\ *n* : a male goat

bi·lobed \'bī-'lōbd\ *adj* : divided into two lobes

bi·met·al \'bī-,met-l\ *adj* : BIMETALLIC

bi·me·tal·lic \,bī-mə-'tal-ik\ *adj* **1** : of or relating to bimetallism **2** : composed of two different metals — often used of devices having a part in which two metals that expand differently are bonded together — **bimetallic** *n*

bi·met·al·lism \bī-'met-l-,iz-əm, 'bī-\ *n* : the use of two metals (as gold and silver) jointly as a monetary standard — **bi·met·al·list** \-l-əst\ *n* — **bi·met·al·list·ic** \,bī-,met-l-'is-tik\ *adj*

¹bi·month·ly \bī-'mənth-lē, 'bī-, -'mənth-\ *adj* **1** : occurring every two months **2** : occurring twice a month : SEMIMONTHLY

²bimonthly *n* : a bimonthly publication

³bimonthly *adv* **1** : once every two months **2** : twice a month

bin \'bin\ *n* : an enclosed place (as a box or crib) used for storage [Old English *binn*]

¹bi·na·ry \'bī-nə-rē\ *adj* **1** : compounded or consisting of or characterized by two often similar things or parts **2** : relating to, being, or belonging to a system of numbers having two as its base **3** : relating two logical or mathematical elements (addition and multiplication are *binary* operations) [Latin *bini* "two each"]

²binary *n, pl* **-ries** : something constituted of two things or parts

binary fission *n* : reproduction of a cell by division into two approximately equal parts

binary notation *n* : expression of a number with a base of 2 using only the digits 0 and 1 with each digital place representing a power of 2 instead of a power of 10 as in decimal notation

binary star *n* : a system of two stars that revolve around each other under their mutual gravitation

bin·au·ral \bī-'nȯr-əl, 'bī-\ *adj* **1** : of, relating to, or used with two or both ears **2 a** : of, relating to, or constituting a three-dimensional effect of reproduced sound involving the use of two separate recording paths **b** : STEREOPHONIC [Latin *bini* "two each" + *auris* "ear"] — **bin·au·ral·ly** \-ə-lē\ *adv*

¹bind \'bīnd\ *vb* **bound** \'baund\; **bind·ing** **1 a** : to tie together or tie securely **b** : to confine, restrain, restrict, or attach by force, obligation, or strong feeling ⟨*bound* by friendship⟩ **c** : to hamper free movement of ⟨the tight jacket *bound* the hiker⟩ **2 a** : to wrap around with something so as to enclose, encircle, or cover ⟨a sash *bound* the child's waist⟩ **b** : BANDAGE ⟨*bound* up the wound⟩ **3 a** : to stick together **b** : to form a cohesive mass **c** : to take up and hold by chemical forces **4** : CONSTIPATE **5** : to make firm : ESTABLISH ⟨a deposit *binds* the sale⟩ **6 a** : to protect, strengthen, or decorate by a band or binding **b** : to apply the cover to (a book) **7** : INDENTURE, APPRENTICE [Old English *bindan*]

²bind *n* : something that binds — **in a bind** : in trouble

bind·er \'bīn-dər\ *n* **1** : one that binds something (as books) **2 a** : something used in binding **b** : a detachable cover or device for holding together sheets of paper or similar material **c** : a harvesting machine that cuts grain and ties it in bundles **3** : something (as tar or cement) that produces or promotes cohesion in loosely assembled substances

bind·ery \'bīn-də-rē, -drē\ *n, pl* **-er·ies** : a place where books are bound

bind·ing \'bīn-ding\ *n* **1** : the action of one that binds **2** : a material or device used to bind: as **a** : the cover and fastenings of a book **b** : a narrow fabric used to finish raw edges **c** : a device for securing a boot to a ski

binding energy *n* : the energy required to break up a molecule, atom, or atomic nucleus into its constituent particles

bind over *vt* : to put (a person) under a legal obligation to appear in court or to perform or refrain from some specific action

bind·weed \'bīnd-,wēd\ *n* : any of various twining plants especially of the morning-glory family that grow matted or interlaced with other plants

bine \'bīn\ *n* : a twining stem or flexible shoot (as of the hop) [alteration of ²*bind*]

binge \'binj\ *n* : a period of unrestrained indulgence ⟨a buying *binge*⟩ [English dialect *binge* "to drink heavily"]

bin·go \'bing-gō, -,gō\ *n* : a game of chance played with cards having numbered squares corresponding to numbered balls drawn at random and won by the player first covering five squares in a row [earlier *bingo*, interjection used to announce an unexpected event]

bin·na·cle \'bin-i-kəl\ *n* : a case, box, or stand containing a ship's compass and a lamp [Middle English *bitakille*, derived from Latin *habitaculum* "habitation"]

bin·oc·u·lar \bī-'näk-yə-lər, bə-\ *adj* : of, relating to, using, or adapted to the use of both eyes ⟨*binocular* vision⟩ [Latin *bini* "two each" + *oculus* "eye"] — **bin·oc·u·lar·ly** *adv*

bin·oc·u·lars \bə-'näk-yə-lərz, bī-\ *n pl* : a hand-held magnifying optical instrument similar to field glasses but having a set of prisms which increase the focal length and magnifying ability without increasing the size of the instrument — often used with *pair*; *also* : FIELD GLASSES

bi·no·mi·al \bī-'nō-mē-əl\ *n* **1** : a mathematical expression consisting of two terms connected by a plus sign or minus sign **2** : a biological species name consisting of two terms [Latin *bi-* + *nomen* "name, term"] — **binomial** *adj* — **bi·no·mi·al·ly** \-mē-ə-lē\ *adv*

binomial coefficient *n* : one of the coefficients obtained when the binomial $(x + y)^n$ is expanded according to the binomial theorem

binomial nomenclature *n* : a system of nomenclature in which each species of animal or plant receives a binomial name of which the first term identifies the genus to which it belongs and the second the species itself

binomial theorem *n* : a theorem that specifies the expansion of a binomial of the form $(x + y)^n$ in $n + 1$ terms of which the general term is of the form

$$\frac{n!}{k!(n-k)!} \, x^k \, y^{(n-k)}$$

bi·nu·cle·ate \bī-'nyü-klē-ət, 'bī-, -'nü-\ *adj* : having two nuclei

bio- *combining form* **1** : life ⟨*bio*sphere⟩ **2** : living organisms or tissue ⟨*bio*luminescence⟩ [Greek *bios* "life, mode of life"]

bio·as·say \,bī-ō-'as-,ā, -a'sā\ *n* : determination of relative strength (as of a drug) by comparison of effect on a test organism with that of a standard preparation — **bio·as·say** \-a-'sā, -'as-,ā\ *vt*

bio·avail·abil·i·ty \-ə-,vā-lə-'bil-ət-ē\ *n* : the degree and rate at which a substance (as a drug) is absorbed into a living system or is made available at the site of physiological activity — **bio·avail·able** \-'vā-lə-bəl\ *adj*

bio·chem·is·try \-'kem-ə-strē\ *n* : chemistry that deals with the chemical compounds and processes occurring in living things — **bio·chem·i·cal** \,bī-ō-'kem-i-kəl\ *adj* — **bio·chem·i·cal·ly** \-kə-lē, -klē\ *adv* — **bio·chem·ist** \-'kem-əst\ *n*

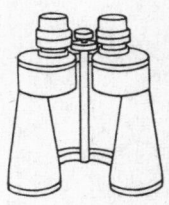

binoculars

\ə\ abut	\ng\ sing
\ər\ further	\ō\ bone
\a\ mat	\ȯ\ saw
\ā\ take	\ȯi\ coin
\ä\ cot, cart	\th\ thin
\aȯ\ out	\th\ this
\ch\ chin	\ü\ food
\e\ pet	\ u̇ \ foot
\ē\ easy	\y\ yet
\g\ go	\yü\ few
\i\ tip	\ yu̇ \ cure
\ī\ life	\zh\ vision
\j\ job	

bio·com·pat·i·bil·i·ty \-kəm-,pat-ə-'bil-ət-ē\ *n* : compatibility with living tissue or a living system by not being toxic or injurious and not causing immunological rejection — **bio·com·pat·i·ble** \-'pat-ə-bəl\ *adj*

bio·con·trol \,bī-ō-kən-'trōl\ *n* : BIOLOGICAL CONTROL

bio·de·grad·able \-di-'grād-ə-bəl\ *adj* : capable of being broken down especially into relatively harmless products by the action of living beings (as microorganisms) — **bio·de·grad·abil·i·ty** \-,grād-ə-'bil-ət-ē\ *n* — **bio·de·grade** \-di-'grād\ *vt*

bio·di·ver·si·ty \-də-'vər-sət-ē, -dī-\ *n* : biological diversity in an environment as indicated by numbers of different species of plants and animals

bio·en·er·get·ics \-,en-ər-'jet-iks\ *n* : the biology of energy transformations and energy exchanges (as in photosynthesis) within and between living things and their environments — **bio·en·er·get·ic** \-ik\ *adj*

bio·feed·back \-'fēd-,bak\ *n* : the technique of making unconscious or involuntary bodily processes (as heartbeat or brain waves) perceptible to the senses (as by the use of an oscilloscope) in order to manipulate them by conscious mental control

bio·gas \'bī-ō-,gas\ *n* : a mixture of methane and carbon dioxide produced by the bacterial decomposition of organic wastes and used as a fuel

bio·gen·e·sis \,bī-ō-'jen-ə-səs\ *n* : the development of life from preexisting life — **bio·gen·e·sist** \-ə-səst\ *n* — **bio·ge·net·ic** \-jə-'net-ik\ *adj*

biogenetic law *n* : a theory in biology : an organism passes through successive stages in development resembling the series of evolutionary ancestors from which it is descended

bio·ge·og·ra·phy \,bī-ō-jē-'äg-rə-fē\ *n* : a branch of biology that deals with the geographical distribution of animals and plants — **bio·ge·og·ra·pher** \-jē-'äg-rə-fər\ *n* — **bio·geo·graph·ic** \-,jē-ə-'graf-ik\ *or* **bio·geo·graph·i·cal** \-'graf-i-kəl\ *adj*

bi·og·ra·pher \bī-'äg-rə-fər, bē-\ *n* : a writer of a biography

bio·graph·i·cal \,bī-ə-'graf-i-kəl\ *or* **bio·graph·ic** \-'graf-ik\ *adj* **1** : of, relating to, or constituting biography ⟨a *biographical* sketch⟩ **2** : consisting of biographies ⟨a *biographical* dictionary⟩ — **bio·graph·i·cal·ly** \-'graf-i-kə-lē, -klē\ *adv*

bi·og·ra·phy \bī-'äg-rə-fē, bē-\ *n, pl* **-phies** **1** : a usually written history of a person's life **2** : biographical writings in general **3** : a life history ⟨the *biography* of a building⟩

bi·o·log·ic \,bī-ə-'läj-ik\ *or* **bi·o·log·i·cal** \-i-kəl\ *n* : a medicinal product of biological origin

bi·o·log·i·cal \,bī-ə-'läj-i-kəl\ *also* **bi·o·log·ic** \-'läj-ik\ *adj* : of or relating to biology or to life and living processes ⟨*biological* supplies⟩ — **bi·o·log·i·cal·ly** \-'läj-i-kə-lē, -klē\ *adv*

biological clock *n* : an inherent timing mechanism in a living being responsible for various cyclical physiological and behavioral responses

biological control *n* : elimination or reduction in numbers of pest organisms by interference with their ecological adjustment (as by the introduction of parasites or disease)

biological warfare *n* : warfare in which living organisms (as disease germs) are used to harm the enemy or his livestock and crops

bi·ol·o·gy \bī-'äl-ə-jē\ *n* **1** : a branch of knowledge that deals with living organisms and life processes **2** : the life processes of an organism or a group ⟨the *biology* of insects⟩ — **bi·ol·o·gist** \-jəst\ *n*

bio·lu·mi·nes·cence \,bī-ō-,lü-mə-'nes-nts\ *n* : the emission of light by living organisms — **bio·lu·mi·nes·cent** \-nt\ *adj*

bio·mass \'bī-ō-,mas\ *n* : the amount of living matter (as in a unit area of a natural habitat or in a unit volume of a liquid culture)

bi·ome \'bī-,ōm\ *n* : a major ecological community type ⟨the grassland *biome*⟩ [*bio-* + Latin *-oma* "group, mass"]

bio·med·i·cal \,bī-ō-'med-i-kəl\ *adj* : of, relating to, or involving biological, medical, and physical science (as in the development of artificial organs or the alteration of human genes)

bi·o·nom·ics \,bī-ə-'näm-iks\ *n sing or pl* : ECOLOGY [Greek *nomos* "law"] — **bi·o·nom·ic** \-ik\ *adj*

bio·phys·ics \,bī-ō-'fiz-iks\ *n* : a branch of knowledge concerned with the application of physical principles and methods to biological problems — **bio·phys·i·cal** \,bī-ō-'fiz-i-kəl\ *adj* — **bio·phys·i·cist** \-'fiz-ə-səst\ *n*

bi·op·sy \'bī-,äp-sē\ *n, pl* **-sies** : the removal and examination of tissue, cells, or fluids from the living body [*bio-* + Greek *opsis* "appearance"]

bio·re·ac·tor \,bī-ō-rē-'ak-tər\ *n* : a device or apparatus in which living organisms and especially bacteria synthesize useful substances or break down harmful ones

bio·sphere \'bī-ə-,sfiər\ *n* : the part of the world in which life can exist

bio·syn·the·sis \,bī-ō-'sin-thə-səs, -'sint-\ *n* : the production of a chemical compound by a living organism — **bio·syn·thet·ic** \-sin-'thet-ik\ *adj*

bi·o·ta \bī-'ōt-ə\ *n* : the flora and fauna of a region [New Latin, from Greek *biotē* "life"]

bio·tech·nol·o·gy \,bī-ō-tek-'näl-ə-jē\ *n* : applied biological science (as recombinant DNA technology) — **bio·tech·no·log·i·cal** \-,tek-nə-'läj-ə-kəl\ *adj* — **bio·tech·nol·o·gist** \-'näl-ə-jəst\ *n*

bi·ot·ic \bī-'ät-ik\ *adj* : of or relating to life; *esp* : composed of or caused by living things ⟨a *biotic* community⟩ [Greek *biōtikos,* from *bioun* "to live", from *bios* "life"]

biotic potential *n* : the inherent capacity of an organism or species to reproduce and survive

bi·o·tin \'bī-ə-tən\ *n* : a colorless crystalline growth vitamin of the vitamin B complex found especially in yeast, liver, and egg yolk [Greek *biotos* "life, sustenance"]

bi·o·tite \'bī-ə-,tīt\ *n* : a generally black or dark green mica containing iron, magnesium, potassium, and aluminum [Jean B. *Biot,* died 1862, French mathematician]

bi·par·ti·san \bī-'pärt-ə-zən, 'bī-\ *adj* : of, relating to, or involving members of two parties ⟨a *bipartisan* foreign policy⟩ — **bi·par·ti·san·ism** \-zə-,niz-əm\ *n* — **bi·par·ti·san·ship** \-zən-,ship\ *n*

bi·par·tite \bī-'pär-,tīt, 'bī-\ *adj* **1** : being in two parts **2** : shared by two ⟨a *bipartite* treaty⟩ — **bi·par·tite·ly** *adv* — **bi·par·ti·tion** \,bī-,pär-'tish-ən\ *n*

bi·ped \'bī-,ped\ *n* : a 2-footed animal [Latin *ped-, pes* "foot"] — **bi·ped·al** \bī-'ped-l, 'bī-\ *adj*

bi·pin·nate \bī-'pin-,āt, 'bī-\ *adj* : twice pinnate ⟨*bipinnate* leaves⟩ — **bi·pin·nate·ly** *adv*

bi·plane \'bī-,plān\ *n* : an airplane with two sets of wings usually placed one above the other

bi·po·lar \bī-'pō-lər, 'bī-\ *adj* **1** : having or involving two poles **2** : having or marked by two mutually repellent forces or wholly opposed natures or views — **bi·po·lar·i·ty** \,bī-pō-'lar-ət-ē\ *n*

bi·ra·mous \bī-'rā-məs, 'bī-\ *adj* : having two branches [*bi-* + *ramous* "having branches", from Latin *ramosus,* from *ramus* "branch"]

¹birch \'bərch\ *n* **1** : any of a genus of deciduous trees or shrubs having simple leaves with petioles and typically a membranous outer bark that occurs in layers and peels readily; *also* : its hard pale close-grained wood **2** : a birch rod or bundle of twigs for whipping [Old English *beorc*] — **birch** *adj*

²birch *vt* : to beat with or as if with a birch : WHIP

¹bird \'bərd\ *n* **1** : any of a class (Aves) of warm-blooded egg-laying vertebrate animals with the body covered with feathers and the forelimbs modified as wings **2** : FELLOW 4a; *esp* : a peculiar person **3** : SHUTTLECOCK

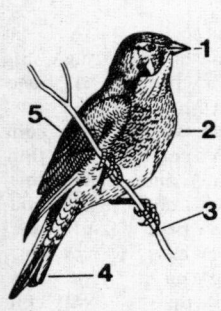
¹bird 1: *1* bill, 2 breast, 3 claw, 4 tail, 5 wing

[Old English *bridd*] — **bird·like** \-,līk\ *adj* — **for the birds** : being worthless or ridiculous

²**bird** *vi* : to observe or identify wild birds in their natural environment — **bird·er** *n*

bird-bath \'bərd-,bath, -,bȧth\ *n* : a basin set up for birds to bathe in

bird-brain \-,brān\ *n* : a flighty thoughtless person : SCATTERBRAIN

bird dog *n* : a dog trained to hunt or retrieve birds

bird-house \'bərd-,haús\ *n* : an artificial nesting place for birds; *also* : AVIARY

¹**bird·ie** \'bərd-ē\ *n* : a golf score of one stroke less than par on a hole

²**birdie** *vt* **bird·ied; bird·ie·ing** : to shoot (a hole in golf) in one stroke under par

bird·lime \'bərd-,līm\ *n* : a sticky substance smeared on twigs to catch and hold small birds

bird·man \'bərd-mən *also* -,man\ *n* **1** : one who deals with birds: as **a** : FOWLER **b** : ORNITHOLOGIST **2** : AVIATOR

bird of paradise : any of numerous brilliantly colored plumed birds related to the crows and found in the New Guinea area

bird of passage : a migratory bird

bird of prey : a carnivorous bird (as a hawk or owl) that feeds wholly or chiefly on meat taken by hunting

bird·seed \'bərd-,sēd\ *n* : a mixture of seeds (as of sunflowers or millet) used for feeding birds

bird's-eye \'bərd-,zī\ *adj* **1** : seen from above as if by a flying bird ⟨a *bird's-eye* view⟩ **2** : marked with spots resembling birds' eyes ⟨*bird's-eye* maple⟩; *also* : made of a bird's-eye wood

bird's-foot trefoil \'bərdz-,fút-\ *n* : a European legume with claw-shaped pods that is widely used as a forage and fodder plant

bi·reme \'bī-,rēm\ *n* : a galley with two banks of oars [Latin *remus* "oar"]

bi·ret·ta \bə-'ret-ə\ *n* : a square cap with three upright ridges on top worn especially by the Roman Catholic clergy [Italian *berretta*, from Provençal *berret* "cap"]

birth \'bərth\ *n* **1 a** : the emergence of a new individual from the body of its parent **b** : the act or process of bringing forth young from the womb **2** : a person's descent : LINEAGE ⟨one of noble *birth*⟩ **3** : a coming into existence : BEGINNING ⟨the *birth* of an idea⟩ [Old Norse *byrth*]

birth canal *n* : the channel formed by the cervix, vagina, and vulva through which the fetus passes during birth

birth control *n* : control of the number of children born especially by preventing or lessening the frequency of conception

birth·day \'bərth-,dā\ *n* **1** : the day of a person's birth **2** : a day of origin or beginning **3** : an anniversary of a birth ⟨our nation's 200th *birthday*⟩

birth·mark \-,märk\ *n* : an unusual mark or blemish on the skin at birth — **birthmark** *vt*

birth·place \-,plās\ *n* : the place where a person was born or something began

birth·rate \-,rāt\ *n* : the number of births for every hundred or every thousand persons in a given area or group during a given time

birth·right \-,rīt\ *n* : a right, privilege, or possession to which a person is entitled by birth

birth·stone \-,stōn\ *n* : a jewel associated symbolically with the month of one's birth

bis·cuit \'bis-kət\ *n, pl* **biscuits** *also* **biscuit 1** : a crisp flat cake; *esp, British* : CRACKER 2 **2** : earthenware or porcelain after the first firing and before glazing **3** : a small quick bread made from dough that has been rolled and cut or dropped from a spoon [Middle French *bescuit*, from *pain bescuit* "twice-cooked bread"] □ ORIGIN In earlier ages the preservation of food was often a great problem, especially on long journeys. One expedient was to preserve flat cakes of

bread by baking them a second time in order to dry them out. In Middle French, this bread was called *pain bescuit* "twice-cooked bread". The second element of the phrase was borrowed into English, and, the notion of cooking twice having been lost, *biscuit* came to be used for any of various hard or crisp, dry baked products, more often called crackers in the United States. A small quick bread of similar size and shape is also called *biscuit*.

bi·sect \'bī-,sekt, bī-'\ *vb* **1** : to divide into two usually equal parts ⟨the river *bisects* the town⟩ ⟨*bisect* an angle⟩ **2** : INTERSECT 2 [Latin *sect-*, *secare* "to cut"] — **bi·sec·tion** \'bī-,sek-shən, bī-'\ *n*

bi·sec·tor \'bī-,sek-tər, bī-'\ *n* : one that bisects; *esp* : a straight line that bisects an angle or a line segment

bi·sex·u·al \bī-'sek-shə-wəl, 'bī-, -shəl\ *adj* **1** : possessing characters of or sexually oriented toward both sexes **2** : of, relating to, or involving two sexes — **bisexual** *n* — **bi·sex·u·al·i·ty** \,bī-,sek-shə-'wal-ət-ē\ *n* — **bi·sex·u·al·ly** \-ē\ *adv*

bish·op \'bish-əp\ *n* **1 a** : a high-ranking member of the clergy typically governing a diocese **b** : a member of the clergy who oversees a church district **2** : a chess piece that can move diagonally across any number of unoccupied squares [Old English *bisceop*, from Late Latin *episcopus*, from Greek *episkopos*, literally, "overseer", from *epi-* "upon" + *skeptesthai* "to look at"]

bish·op·ric \'bish-ə-prik\ *n* **1** : DIOCESE **2** : the office of bishop [Old English *bisceop* + *rīce* "realm"]

bis·muth \'biz-məth\ *n* : a heavy brittle grayish white metallic element that is chemically like arsenic and antimony and is used in alloys and medicine — see ELEMENT table [German *wismut, bismut*]

bi·son \'bīs-n, 'bīz-\ *n, pl* **bison** : any of several large shaggy-maned usually gregarious recent or extinct mammals of the ox family with a large head, short horns, and heavy forequarters surmounted by a large fleshy hump: as **a** : WISENT **b** : BUFFALO 2a [Latin, of Germanic origin] — **bi·son·tine** \-n-,tīn\ *adj*

bisque \'bisk\ *n* **1** : a thick cream soup made of shellfish, meat, or vegetables **2** : ice cream containing powdered nuts or macaroons [French]

bis·ter *or* **bis·tre** \'bis-tər\ *n* : a grayish to yellowish brown [French *bistre*]

bis·tro \'bēs-,trō, 'bis-\ *n, pl* **bistros 1** : a small European wineshop or restaurant **2 a** : a small bar or tavern **b** : NIGHTCLUB [French]

bi·sul·fate \bī-'səl-,fāt, 'bī-\ *n* : an acid sulfate

bi·sul·fide \-,fīd\ *n* : DISULFIDE

bi·sul·fite \-,fīt\ *n* : an acid sulfite

¹**bit** \'bit\ *n* **1** : the part of a bridle inserted in the mouth of a horse **2** : the biting or cutting edge or part of a tool; *also* : a replaceable part of a compound tool that actually performs the function (as drilling or boring) for which the whole tool is designed **3** : something that curbs or restrains [Middle English *bitt*, from Old English *bite* "act of biting"]

²**bit** *vt* **bit·ted; bit·ting 1** : to put a bit in the mouth of (a horse) **2** : to control as if with a bit : CURB

³**bit** *n* **1** : a small piece or amount ⟨a *bit* of cheese⟩ ⟨a little *bit* of luck⟩ **2** : a short time : WHILE ⟨rest a *bit*⟩ **3** : one having a quality or nature to some extent ⟨a *bit* of a fool⟩ [Old English *bita* "piece bitten off"]

⁴**bit** *n* **1** : a unit of computer information equivalent to the result of a choice between two alternatives (as *yes* or *no, on* or *off*) **2** : the physical representation of a bit (as a hole on a card or a magnetized spot on a tape) whose presence or absence stands for data [*bi*nary digi*t*]

bitch \'bich\ *n* : a female dog [Old English *bicce*]

¹**bite** \'bīt\ *vb* **bit** \'bit\; **bit·ten** \'bit-n\; **bit·ing** \'bīt-ing\ **1** : to seize, grip, or cut into with or as if with teeth ⟨*bite* an apple⟩ ⟨a steam shovel *bites* into the earth⟩ **2** : to wound or pierce with or as if with fangs

biretta

\ə\ abut	\ng\ sing
\ər\ further	\ō\ bone
\a\ mat	\ȯ\ saw
\ā\ take	\ȯi\ coin
\ä\ cot, cart	\th\ thin
\aú\ out	\th\ this
\ch\ chin	\ü\ food
\e\ pet	\ú\ foot
\ē\ easy	\y\ yet
\g\ go	\yü\ few
\i\ tip	\yú\ cure
\ī\ life	\zh\ vision
\j\ job	

⟨*bitten* by a snake⟩ **3** : to make a gash or cut ⟨the sword *bit* into the soldier's arm⟩ **4** : to cause to smart : STING ⟨pepper *bites* the mouth⟩ **5** : to eat into : CORRODE **6** : to respond to a lure : take a bait ⟨the fish are really *biting*⟩ [Old English *bītan*] — **bit·er** *n* — **bite the dust** : to fall dead especially in battle

²bite *n* **1** : a seizing of something with the teeth or the mouth **2 a** : the amount of food taken at a bite **b** : a light informal meal : SNACK **3** : a wound made by biting **4** : a sharp penetrating quality or effect

bit·ing \'bīt-ing\ *adj* : causing bodily or mental distress : CUTTING ⟨*biting* remarks⟩ ⟨a *biting* wind⟩ SYN see INCISIVE — **bit·ing·ly** *adv*

bitt \'bit\ *n* : a post or pair of posts on the deck of a ship for securing mooring lines [perhaps from Old Norse *biti* "beam"]

¹bit·ter \'bit-ər\ *adj* **1** : being or inducing the one of the four basic taste sensations characterized by a disagreeable acrid taste ⟨*bitter* as quinine⟩ **2 a** : hard to bear : PAINFUL ⟨*bitter* disappointment⟩ **b** : being relentlessly determined : VEHEMENT ⟨*bitter* partisans⟩ **c** : sharp and resentful ⟨a *bitter* answer⟩ **d** : unpleasantly cold or raw ⟨a *bitter* wind⟩ **3** : expressing severe pain, grief, or regret ⟨*bitter* tears⟩ [Old English *biter*] — **bit·ter·ish** \'bit-ə-rish\ *adj* — **bit·ter·ly** \'bit-ər-lē\ *adv* — **bit·ter·ness** *n*

²bitter *adv* : BITTERLY ⟨it's *bitter* cold⟩

³bitter *n* **1** : bitter sensation or quality **2** *pl* : a usually alcoholic solution of bitter and often aromatic plant products used in mixing drinks and as a mild tonic

bit·tern \'bit-ərn\ *n* : any of various small or medium-sized nocturnal herons that have a characteristic booming cry [Middle French *butor*]

¹bit·ter·sweet \'bit-ər-‚swēt\ *n* **1** : something that is bittersweet **2 a** : a sprawling poisonous weedy nightshade with purple flowers and oval reddish orange berries **b** : a North American woody climbing plant with yellow capsules that open when ripe and disclose the scarlet seed covers

²bittersweet *adj* : being both bitter and sweet; *esp* : pleasant but marked by elements of suffering or regret ⟨*bittersweet* memories⟩ **2** : of or relating to a prepared chocolate containing little sugar

¹bit·ty \'bit-ē\ *adj* : containing or made up of bits

²bitty *adj* : very small ⟨a little *bitty* dog⟩

bi·tu·men \bə-'tyü-mən, bī-, -'tü-\ *n* : any of various dark or black mixtures of hydrocarbons (as asphalt, crude petroleum, or tar) [Latin, "asphalt"]

bi·tu·mi·nous \-mə-nəs\ *adj* : resembling, containing, or impregnated with bitumen

bituminous coal *n* : a coal that when heated yields considerable volatile bituminous matter — called also *soft coal*

bi·va·lent \bī-'vā-lənt, 'bī-\ *adj* : having a valence of two

¹bi·valve \'bī-‚valv\ *adj* : having a shell composed of two movable valves

²bivalve *n* : an animal (as a clam) with a bivalve shell

¹biv·ouac \'biv-‚wak, -ə-‚wak\ *n* **1** : a usually temporary encampment offering little or no shelter **2** : a camping out for a night [French, from Low German *biwake*, from *bi* "by, at" + *wake* "guard"]

²bivouac *vi* **biv·ouacked; biv·ouack·ing** : to encamp with little or no shelter

¹bi·week·ly \bī-'wē-klē, 'bī-\ *adj* **1** : occurring or produced every two weeks : FORTNIGHTLY **2** : occurring or produced twice a week — **biweekly** *adv*

²biweekly *n* : a biweekly publication

bi·year·ly \bī-'yiər-lē, 'bī-\ *adj* **1** : BIENNIAL 1 **2** : BIANNUAL

bi·zarre \bə-'zär\ *adj* : strikingly unusual or odd; *esp* : having sensational contrasts or incongruities ⟨*bizarre* costumes⟩ [French, from Italian *bizarro*] SYN see FANTASTIC — **bi·zarre·ly** *adv* — **bi·zarre·ness** *n*

¹blab \'blab\ *n* **1** : TATTLETALE **2** : idle or excessive talk : CHATTER [Middle English *blabbe*] — **blab·by** \'blab-ē\ *adj*

²blab *vb* **blabbed; blab·bing** **1** : to reveal (secrets) by careless talking : TATTLE **2** : BABBLE 1b

¹blab·ber \'blab-ər\ *vb* **blab·bered; blab·ber·ing** \'blab-ring, -ə-ring\ : BABBLE 1b [Middle English *blaberen*]

²blabber *n* : idle talk : BABBLE

³blabber *n* : BLABBERMOUTH

blab·ber·mouth \'blab-ər-‚mauth\ *n* : one that talks too much; *esp* : TATTLETALE

¹black \'blak\ *adj* **1 a** : of the color black **b** : very dark ⟨a face *black* with rage⟩ **2 a** : having dark skin, hair, and eyes : SWARTHY **b** *often cap* (1) : of or relating to the Negro race ⟨*black* Africans⟩ (2) : of or relating to black Afro-Americans or their culture ⟨*black* literature⟩ **3** : characterized by the absence of light ⟨a *black* night⟩ **4** : thoroughly sinister or evil : WICKED ⟨a *black* deed⟩ **5** : invoking evil supernatural powers ⟨a *black* curse⟩ **6 a** : very sad or gloomy ⟨*black* despair⟩ **b** : marked by disaster ⟨*black* Friday⟩ **7** : characterized by hostility or discontent : SULLEN ⟨*black* resentment⟩ [Old English *blæc*] — **black·ish** \-ish\ *adj* — **black·ly** *adv* — **black·ness** *n*

²black *n* **1** : a black pigment or dye; *esp* : one consisting largely of carbon **2** : the color of soot or coal **3** : something that is black; *esp* : black clothing **4** *often cap* : a person belonging to a dark-skinned race or one stemming in part from such a race; *esp* : NEGRO **5** : absence of light : DARKNESS ⟨the *black* of night⟩ **6** : the dark-colored pieces of a two-handed board game (as chess) **7** : the condition of making a profit ⟨operating in the *black*⟩

³black *vb* : BLACKEN

black–and–blue \‚blak-ən-'blü\ *adj* : darkly discolored (as from a bruise)

Black and Tan *n* : one recruited in England in 1920–21 into the Royal Irish Constabulary to suppress the Irish revolution [from the color of the uniform]

¹black·ball \'blak-‚bol\ *n* **1** : a small black ball used to cast a negative vote **2** : an adverse vote especially against admitting someone to membership in an organization

²blackball *vt* : to vote against; *esp* : to exclude from membership by casting a negative vote

black bass *n* : any of several freshwater sunfishes native to eastern and central North America

black bean *n* **1** : a black kidney bean commonly used in Latin American cuisine **2** : a black soybean commonly used in oriental cuisine

black bear *n* : the common usually largely black-furred bear of North America

black belt *n* **1** : an area characterized by rich black soil **2** *often cap both Bs* : an area inhabited by large numbers of blacks

black·ber·ry \'blak-‚ber-ē\ *n* **1** : the usually black or dark purple juicy but seedy edible fruit of various brambles **2** : a plant that bears blackberries

black·bird \'blak-‚bərd\ *n* : any of various birds of which the males are largely or entirely black: as **a** : a common and familiar British thrush **b** : any of several American birds (as the red-winged blackbird) related to the bobolink

black·board \'blak-‚bord, -‚bord\ *n* : CHALKBOARD

black·body \'blak-'bäd-ē\ *n* : a body or surface that completely absorbs all radiant energy falling upon it

black book *n* : a book containing a blacklist

black box *n* **1** : an electronic module (as for a spacecraft) **2** : a usually electronic device whose components are hidden from or mysterious to the user

black·cap \'blak-‚kap\ *n* **1** : any of several black-crowned birds (as the chickadee) **2** : BLACK RASPBERRY

black·cock \-‚käk\ *n* : BLACK GROUSE; *esp* : the male black grouse

black crappie *n* : a silvery black-mottled sunfish of the central and eastern United States

black death *n* **1** : PLAGUE 2b **2** : a severe epidemic of plague and especially bubonic plague that occurred in Asia and Europe in the 14th century [from the black patches on the skin of its victims]

black·en \'blak-ən\ *vb* **black·ened; black·en·ing** \'blak-ning, -ə-ning\ **1** : to make or become black **2** : to injure the reputation of — **black·en·er** \-nər, -ə-nər\ *n*

black eye *n* : a puffy darkening of the area about an eye caused by bruising (as from a blow)

black-eyed pea \'blak-ˌīd-\ *n* : COWPEA

black-eyed Su·san \-'süz-n\ *n* : an American daisy with deep yellow or orange petals and a dark center

black·face \'blak-ˌfās\ *n* : makeup for a performer playing a black person especially in a minstrel show

black·fish \-ˌfish\ **1** : any of numerous dark-colored fishes: as **a** : TAUTOG **b** : a small food fish of Alaska and Siberia that is especially resistant to cold **2** : any of several small toothed whales related to the dolphins

black flag *n* : JOLLY ROGER

black·fly \'blak-ˌflī\ *n* : any of several small dark-colored insects; *esp* : a two-winged biting fly whose larvae live in flowing streams

Black·foot \-ˌfút\ *n, pl* **Black·feet** \-ˌfēt\ *or* **Blackfoot** : a member of a people belonging to an Indian confederacy of Montana, Alberta, and Saskatchewan

black grouse *n* : a large grouse of Europe and western Asia of which the male is black with white wing patches and the female is barred and mottled

¹**black·guard** \'blag-ərd, -ˌärd; 'blak-ˌgärd\ *n* : a rude or unscrupulous person — **black·guard·ly** \-lē\ *adj or adv*

²**blackguard** *vt* : to abuse with bad language : REVILE

black gum *n* : an important timber tree of the southeastern United States with light and soft but tough wood

black hand *n, often cap B&H* : a lawless secret society engaged in crime [*Black Hand,* a Sicilian and Italian-American society of the late 19th and 20th centuries] — **black–hand·er** *n*

black·head \'blak-ˌhed\ *n* : a small oily plug blocking the duct of a sebaceous gland

black hole *n* : a hypothetical invisible region in space with a small diameter and intense gravitational field that is held to be caused by the collapse of a massive star

black·ing \'blak-ing\ *n* : a substance that makes things black; *esp* : a paste or liquid used in shining black shoes

black·jack \'blak-ˌjak\ *n* **1** : a small leather-covered club with a flexible handle **2** : a common often scrubby oak of the southern United States with black bark **3** : a card game the object of which is to be dealt cards having a higher count than those of the dealer up to but not exceeding 21 — called also *twenty-one*

black lead \-'led\ *n* : GRAPHITE

black·leg \'blak-ˌleg\ *n* : a usually fatal toxemia especially of young cattle

black light *n* : invisible ultraviolet or infrared light

black·list \-ˌlist\ *n* : a list of persons who are disapproved of and are to be punished or boycotted — **blacklist** *vt*

black lung *n* : a disease of the lungs caused by habitual inhalation of coal dust

black·mail \-ˌmāl\ *n* : the forcing of someone to pay money by threatening to reveal a secret that will bring trouble and disgrace; *also* : the money paid under threat of blackmail [Scots *mail* "payment", from Old English *māl* "agreement, pay", from Old Norse, "agreement"] — **blackmail** *vt* — **black·mail·er** *n*

Black Ma·ria \ˌblak-mə-'rī-ə\ *n* : PATROL WAGON

black market *n* : illicit trade in violation of official regulations; *also* : a place where such trade is carried on — **black–market** *vb* — **black mar·ke·teer** \-ˌmär-kə-'tiər\ *n*

black oak *n* : any of several American oaks having dark bark or foliage; *esp* : a large timber tree of the eastern and central United States having a yellow inner bark used for tanning

black·out \'blak-ˌaut\ *n* **1** : a period of darkness resulting from absence of artificial light; *esp* : one due to power failure **2** : a transient dulling or loss of vision or consciousness **3** : a blotting out by or as if by censorship ⟨a news *blackout*⟩

black out \blak-'aut, 'blak-\ *vb* **1** : to be affected by a blackout ⟨*black out* from exhaustion⟩ **2** : to cause a blackout of ⟨an ice storm *blacked* the city *out*⟩ ⟨*black out* the news⟩

black pepper *n* : a pungent seasoning that consists of the fruit of the East Indian pepper ground with the black husk still on

black power *n* : the political and economic power of black Americans especially when used to further racial equality

black racer *n* : an American blacksnake common in the eastern United States

black raspberry *n* : a raspberry with a purplish black fruit that is native to eastern North America

black sheep *n* : a disreputable member of an otherwise respectable group ⟨the *black sheep* of the family⟩

Black·shirt \'blak-ˌshərt\ *n* : a member of a fascist group having a black shirt as a distinctive part of its uniform; *esp* : a member of the Italian Fascist party

black·smith \'blak-ˌsmith\ *n* : a worker who shapes iron by heating and then hammering it [from the blacksmith's working with iron, which was known as "black metal" to distinguish it from tin, or "white metal"] — **black·smith·ing** *n*

black·snake \-ˌsnāk\ *n* **1** : any of several snakes largely black or dark in color; *esp* : a black racer or a related harmless snake **2** : a long tapering braided whip

black studies *n pl* : studies (as history and literature) relating to the culture of black Americans

black·thorn \'blak-ˌthórn\ *n* **1** : a European spiny plum with hard wood and small white flowers **2** : any of several American hawthorns

black tie *n* : semiformal evening dress for men — **black–tie** \ˌblak-'tī, 'blak-\ *adj*

black·top \'blak-ˌtäp\ *n* : a bituminous material used especially for surfacing roads; *also* : a surface paved with blacktop — **blacktop** *vt*

black walnut *n* : a walnut of eastern North America with hard strong heavy dark brown wood and oily edible nuts; *also* : its wood or nut

black widow *n* : a poisonous New World spider having the female black with an hourglass-shaped red mark on the underside of the abdomen

blad·der \'blad-ər\ *n* **1** : a membranous sac in an animal in which a liquid or gas is stored; *esp* : one in a vertebrate into which urine passes from the kidneys **2** : something resembling a bladder; *esp* : an inflatable bag or container [Old English *blǣdre*] — **blad·der·like** \-ˌlīk\ *adj*

bladder worm *n* : a bladderlike larval tapeworm

blad·der·wort \'blad-ər-ˌwərt, -ˌwórt\ *n* : any of several slender plants growing in water or on wet shores and having insect-catching bladders on the stem, scalelike leaves, and irregular yellow or purple flowers

blade \'blād\ *n* **1 a** : a leaf of a plant and especially of a grass **b** : the broad flat part of a leaf as distinguished from its stalk **2** : something resembling the blade of a leaf: as **a** : the broad flattened part of a paddle **b** : an arm of a propeller, electric fan, or steam turbine **c** : the upper flat part of the tongue immediately behind the tip **3 a** : the cutting part of an implement **b** (1) : SWORD 1 (2) : SWORDSMAN (3) : a dashing lively fellow **c** : the runner of an ice skate [Old English *blæd*] — **blad·ed** \'blād-əd\ *adj*

blah \'blä\ *adj* : lacking interest or excitement ⟨a *blah* winter day⟩ [imitative]

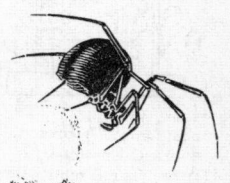

black widow

blahs \'blāz\ *n pl* : a feeling of boredom, discomfort, or general dissatisfaction ⟨the post-vacation *blahs*⟩

blain \'blān\ *n* : an inflammatory swelling or sore [Old English *blegen*]

¹blame \'blām\ *vt* **1** : to find fault with : CENSURE **2 a** : to hold responsible ⟨*blame* them for the failure⟩ **b** : to place responsibility for ⟨*blamed* the error on me⟩ [Old French *blamer*, from Late Latin *blasphemare* "to blaspheme"] — **blam·able** \'blā-mə-bəl\ *adj* — **blam·ably** \-ə-blē\ *adv* — **blam·er** *n* □ SYN BLAME, CENSURE, CONDEMN, CRITICIZE mean to find fault with openly. BLAME may imply simply the opposite of *praise* but often suggests an accusation or the placing of responsibility for something bad or unfortunate; CENSURE carries a stronger suggestion of authority and reprimanding than BLAME; CONDEMN usually suggests an unqualified and final unfavorable judgment; CRITICIZE implies finding fault especially with methods or policies or intentions.

²blame *n* **1** : expression of disapproval **2** : responsibility for something felt to deserve censure

blame·less \'blām-ləs\ *adj* : free from blame or fault — **blame·less·ly** *adv* — **blame·less·ness** *n*

blame·wor·thy \'blām-₁wər-t̶h̶ē\ *adj* : deserving blame — **blame·wor·thi·ness** *n*

blanch \'blanch\ *vb* **1** : to take the color out of : **a** : to bleach by excluding light ⟨*blanch* celery⟩ **b** : to scald in order to remove the skin from or whiten ⟨*blanch* almonds⟩ **2** : to become white or pale [Middle French *blanchir*, from *blanc* "white"] SYN see WHITEN — **blanch·er** *n*

blanc·mange \blə-'mänj, -'mäⁿzh\ *n* : a dessert made from gelatin or a starchy substance and milk usually sweetened and flavored [Middle French *blanc manger*, literally, "white food"]

bland \'bland\ *adj* **1** : smooth and soothing in manner : GENTLE ⟨a *bland* smile⟩ **2** : having soft and soothing qualities : not irritating ⟨a *bland* diet⟩ [Latin *blandus*] SYN see SUAVE — **bland·ly** *adv* — **bland·ness** \'bland-nəs, 'blan-\ *n*

blan·dish \'blan-dish\ *vt* : to coax with flattery : CAJOLE [Middle French *blandiss-*, stem of *blandir*, from Latin *blandiri*, from *blandus* "bland"] — **blan·dish·er** *n* — **blan·dish·ment** \-mənt\ *n*

¹blank \'blangk\ *adj* **1** : free from writing, printing, or marks ⟨*blank* sheets of paper⟩ **2** : having empty spaces to be filled in ⟨a *blank* form⟩ **3** : appearing dazed or confused : EXPRESSIONLESS ⟨a *blank* look⟩ **4** : lacking variety, change, or accomplishment : EMPTY ⟨a *blank* day⟩ **5** : ABSOLUTE 4, UNQUALIFIED ⟨a *blank* refusal⟩ **6** : not shaped into finished form ⟨a *blank* key⟩ [Middle French *blanc* "white", of Germanic origin] SYN see EMPTY — **blank·ly** *adv* — **blank·ness** *n*

²blank *n* **1 a** : an empty space (as on a paper) **b** : a paper with spaces for the entry of data **2** : an empty space or period ⟨my mind was a *blank* during the test⟩ **3** : the bull's-eye of a target **4 a** : a piece of material prepared to be made into something (as a key) by a further operation **b** : a cartridge loaded with powder but no bullet **5** : VOID 4

³blank *vt* **1 a** : to make obscure : OBLITERATE ⟨*blank* out a line⟩ **b** : to stop up : SEAL ⟨*blank* off a tunnel⟩ **2** : to keep from scoring ⟨*blanked* for eight innings⟩

blank check *n* **1** : a signed check with the amount unspecified **2** : complete freedom of action

¹blan·ket \'blang-kət\ *n* **1** : a usually heavy woven covering for a bed **2** : a covering layer ⟨a *blanket* of snow⟩ [Old French *blankete*, from *blanc* "white"]

²blanket *vt* : to cover with or as if with a blanket

³blanket *adj* : covering all members of a group ⟨*blanket* rules⟩

blank verse *n* : unrhymed verse; *esp* : unrhymed iambic pentameter verse

¹blare \'blaər, 'bleər\ *vb* **1** : to sound loud and harsh **2** : to utter in a harsh noisy way ⟨radios *blaring* advertisements⟩ [Middle English *bleren*]

²blare *n* : a harsh loud noise ⟨the *blare* of radios⟩

blar·ney \'blär-nē\ *n* : skillful flattery [*Blarney* stone, a stone in *Blarney* Castle near Cork, Ireland, held to make those who kiss it skilled in flattery] — **blarney** *vb*

bla·sé \blä-'zā\ *adj* : indifferent to pleasure or excitement as a result of excessive indulgence; *also* : SOPHISTICATED 2b [French]

blas·pheme \blas-'fēm, 'blas-₁\ *vb* **1 a** : to speak of or address with irreverence **b** : to utter blasphemy **2** : ABUSE 1, REVILE [Late Latin *blasphemare*, from Greek *blasphēmein*] — **blas·phem·er** *n*

blas·phe·my \'blas-fə-mē\ *n, pl* **-mies** : great disrespect shown to God or to sacred persons or things — **blas·phe·mous** \-məs\ *adj* — **blas·phe·mous·ly** *adv* — **blas·phe·mous·ness** *n* □ SYN PROFANITY: BLASPHEMY applies in strict use to an intentional utterance defying or offering indignity to God; PROFANITY includes all irreverent reference to holy persons or things; it is particularly applicable when the name of God is used lightly or irreverently

¹blast \'blast\ *n* **1** : a strong gust of wind **2** : a current of air or gas forced through an opening (as in an organ or furnace) **3** : the blowing that a charge of ore or metal receives in a blast furnace **4** : the sound made by a wind instrument (as a horn) or by a whistle **5 a** : EXPLOSION; *esp* : an explosion (as of dynamite) for shattering rock **b** : an explosive charge for this purpose **c** : the sudden air pressure produced in the vicinity of an explosion that has the effect of a violent wind **6** : a sudden harmful effect from or as if from a hot wind; *esp* : a withering blight of plants [Old English *blǣst*]

²blast *vb* **1** : BLARE ⟨music *blasting* from the radio⟩ **2 a** : to use an explosive **b** : SHOOT **3** : to injure or destroy ⟨seedlings *blasted* by the hot dry wind⟩ **4** : to shatter by or as if by an explosive **5** : to attack vigorously ⟨*blasted* by the local press⟩ **6** : to cause to blast off ⟨will *blast* themselves from the moon's surface⟩ — **blast·er** *n*

blast- *or* **blasto-** *combining form* : bud : germ : embryo in its early stages ⟨*blasto*coel⟩ [Greek *blastos* "bud, shoot, embryo"]

blast furnace *n* : a furnace in which combustion is forced by a current of air under pressure; *esp* : one for the reduction of iron ore

blas·to·coel *or* **blas·to·coele** \'blas-tə-₁sēl\ *n* : the cavity of a blastula — **blas·to·coe·lic** \₁blas-tə-'sē-lik\ *adj*

blas·to·cyst \'blas-tə-₁sist\ *n* : the modified blastula of a placental mammal

blas·to·derm \-tə-₁dərm\ *n* : a discoidal blastula formed especially in an egg with much yolk — **blas·to·der·mic** \-'dər-mik\ *adj*

blast off \blas-'tóf, 'blas-\ *vi* : to take off — used of rocket-propelled missiles and vehicles — **blast-off** \'blas-₁tóf\ *n*

blas·to·mere \'blas-tə-₁miər\ *n* : a cell produced during cleavage of an egg — **blas·to·mer·ic** \₁blas-tə-'miər-ik, -'mer-\ *adj*

blas·to·pore \'blas-tə-₁pōr, -₁pór\ *n* : the opening of the cavity of the gastrula

blas·tu·la \'blas-chə-lə\ *n, pl* **-las** *or* **-lae** \-₁lē, -₁lī\ : an early metazoan embryo typically having the form of a hollow fluid-filled rounded cavity bounded by a single layer of cells — compare GASTRULA, MORULA [New Latin, from Greek *blastos* "bud, embryo"] — **blas·tu·lar** \-lər\ *adj*

blat \'blat\ *vi* **blat·ted; blat·ting** : BLEAT 1 [imitative] — **blat** *n*

bla·tant \'blāt-nt\ *adj* **1** : noisy especially in a vulgar or offensive way : CLAMOROUS **2** : completely obvious or conspicuous especially in an offensive way [perhaps from Latin *blatire* "to chatter"] — **bla·tan·cy** \-n-sē\ *n* — **bla·tant·ly** *adv*

blast furnace: *A* coke,
B ore, *C* limestone,
D hot blast, *E* molten iron

blath·er \'bla<u>th</u>-ər\ *vi* **blath·ered; blath·er·ing** \-ring, -ə-ring\ : to talk foolishly [Old Norse *blathra*] — **blather** *n* — **blath·er·er** \-ər-ər\ *n*

blath·er·skite \'bla<u>th</u>-ər-ˌskīt\ *n* : a blustering talkative person [*blather* + Scots dialect *skate* "contemptible person"]

¹blaze \'blāz\ *n* **1 a** : an intensely burning fire **b** : intense direct light often accompanied by heat ⟨the *blaze* of the sun⟩ **c** : a sudden outburst of flame **2 a** : a dazzling display ⟨a *blaze* of color⟩ **b** : a sudden outburst (as of anger) [Old English *blǣse* "torch"]

²blaze *vi* **1 a** : to burn brightly **b** : to flare up : FLAME ⟨suddenly *blazed* with anger⟩ **2** : to be conspicuously brilliant ⟨fields *blazing* with flowers⟩ **3** : to shoot rapidly and repeatedly ⟨*blaze* away at a target⟩

³blaze *vt* : to make public : PROCLAIM ⟨*blaze* the news abroad⟩ [Middle Dutch *blāsen* "to blow"]

⁴blaze *n* **1** : a white mark usually running lengthwise on the face of an animal **2** : a mark made on a tree by chipping off a piece of the bark usually to leave a trail [German *blas*]

⁵blaze *vt* : to mark (as a trail) with blazes

blaz·er \'blā-zər\ *n* : a sports jacket often with notched collar and patch pockets [²*blaze*]

blazing star *n* : any of several plants having conspicuous flower clusters; *esp* : any of a genus of composite American herbs with slender grassy leaves and spikes of rose-purple or white flower heads

¹bla·zon \'blāz-n\ *n* **1 a** : COAT OF ARMS **b** : the proper description of a coat of arms **2** : ostentatious display : SHOW [Middle French *blason*]

²blazon *vt* **bla·zoned; bla·zon·ing** \'blāz-ning, -n-ing\ **1 a** : to describe (heraldic or armorial bearings) in technical terms **b** : to represent (armorial bearings) in a drawing or engraving **2** : to depict in colors **3** : to cover as if with blazons ⟨*blazoned* the building with posters⟩ — **bla·zon·er** \'blāz-nər, -n-ər\ *n*

bla·zon·ry \'blāz-n-rē\ *n, pl* **-ries 1 a** : BLAZON 1b **b** : COAT OF ARMS **2** : a dazzling display

¹bleach \'blēch\ *vb* **1** : to remove color or stains from **2** : to make or become whiter or lighter [Old English *blǣcean*] SYN see WHITEN

²bleach *n* **1** : the act or process of bleaching **2** : a preparation used in bleaching

bleach·er \'blē-chər\ *n* **1** : one that bleaches or is used in bleaching **2** : a usually uncovered stand of tiered planks providing seats for spectators — usually used in pl.

bleaching powder *n* : a mixture of calcium hydroxide, chloride, and hypochlorite used as a bleach, disinfectant, or deodorant

bleak \'blēk\ *adj* **1** : exposed to wind or weather ⟨a *bleak* coast⟩ **2** : lacking warmth or kindliness ⟨a *bleak* personality⟩ **3** : COLD 1, RAW ⟨a *bleak* day⟩ **4** : severely simple : AUSTERE [Middle English *bleke* "pale"] — **bleak·ly** *adv* — **bleak·ness** *n*

¹blear \'bliər\ *vt* **1** : to make (the eyes) sore or watery **2** : DIM 1, BLUR ⟨*bleared* sight⟩ [Middle English *bleren*]

²blear *adj* : dim with water or tears — used of the eyes — **blear–eyed** \-ˈīd\ *adj*

bleary \'bliər-ē\ *adj* **1** : dull or dimmed especially from fatigue or sleep ⟨*bleary* eyes⟩ **2** : poorly outlined or defined : DIM — **blear·i·ly** \'blir-ə-lē\ *adv* — **blear·i·ness** \'blir-ē-nəs\ *n*

¹bleat \'blēt\ *vb* **1** : to utter a bleat or similar sound **2** : to utter in a bleating manner [Old English *blǣtan*]

²bleat *n* : the characteristic cry of a sheep or goat

bleb \'bleb\ *n* : a small blister [perhaps alteration of *blob*] — **bleb·by** \-ē\ *adj*

bleed \'blēd\ *vb* **bled** \'bled\; **bleed·ing 1** : to lose blood ⟨a cut finger *bleeds*⟩ **2** : to be wounded ⟨fought and *bled* for their country⟩ **3** : to feel pain or deep sympathy ⟨my heart *bleeds* for them⟩ **4** : to flow from or as if from a wounded surface ⟨pitch *bleeding* from the broken bark⟩ **5** : to draw fluid (as blood or sap)

from ⟨*bleed* a patient⟩ ⟨*bleed* a tire⟩ **6** : to extort money from [Old English *blēdan*, from *blōd* "blood"]

bleed·er \'blēd-ər\ *n* : one that bleeds; *esp* : HEMOPHILIAC

bleeding heart *n* **1** : a garden plant of the poppy family with drooping spikes of deep pink heart-shaped flowers **2** : a person extravagantly sympathetic toward one felt to be abused

¹blem·ish \'blem-ish\ *vt* : to spoil by a flaw [Middle French *blesmiss-*, stem of *blesmir* "to make pale, wound", of Germanic origin]

²blemish *n* : something (as a mark) that impairs appearance or quality : FLAW □ SYN BLEMISH, DEFECT, FLAW mean an imperfection that mars or damages. BLEMISH suggests something, as a spot or stain, that mars the surface or appearance; DEFECT implies a lack, often hidden, of something essential to completeness ⟨a *defect* in the organs of vision⟩ FLAW suggests a defect in continuity or cohesion, as a crack, break, or fissure.

¹blench \'blench\ *vi* : to shrink back out of fear : FLINCH [Old English *blencan* "to deceive"]

²blench *vb* : to grow or make pale : BLANCH [alteration of *blanch*]

¹blend \'blend\ *vb* **1** : to mix so thoroughly that the separate things mixed cannot be distinguished **2** : to shade into each other : MERGE, HARMONIZE ⟨furniture that *blends* with the draperies⟩ [Old Norse *blanda*] SYN see MIX — **blend·er** *n*

²blend *n* **1** : a thorough mixture **2** : a product (as coffee) prepared by blending **3** : a word produced by combining parts of other words (as *motel* from *motor* and *hotel*)

blend·ing inheritance *n* : inheritance involving expression in the offspring of characters intermediate between those of the parents due especially to incomplete genetic dominance

blen·ny \'blen-ē\ *n, pl* **blennies** : any of numerous usually small and elongated and often scaleless fishes living about rocky seashores [Latin *blennius*, a sea fish, from Greek *blennos*]

bless \'bles\ *vt* **blessed** \'blest\ *also* **blest** \'blest\; **bless·ing 1** : to consecrate by religious rite or word ⟨*bless* an altar⟩ **2** : to make the sign of the cross upon or over **3** : to ask divine care or protection for **4** : PRAISE 2, GLORIFY **5** : ENDOW 2 ⟨*blessed* with good health⟩ [Old English *blētsian*, from *blōd* "blood"; from the use of blood in consecration]

bless·ed \'bles-əd, 'blest\ *also* **blest** \'blest\ *adj* **1** : honored in worship ⟨the *blessed* Trinity⟩ **2 a** : bringing or enjoying happiness ⟨a *blessed* relief from pain⟩ **b** : enjoying the bliss of heaven — used as a title for a beatified person — **bless·ed·ly** \'bles-əd-lē\ *adv* — **bless·ed·ness** \'bles-əd-nəs\ *n*

Bless·ed Sacrament \'bles-əd-\ *n* **1** : EUCHARIST **2** : the consecrated Host

bless·ing *n* **1 a** : the act of one that blesses **b** : APPROVAL ⟨give one's *blessing* to a plan⟩ **2** : something conducive to happiness or welfare **3** : grace said at a meal

blew *past of* BLOW

¹blight \'blīt\ *n* **1 a** : a disease or disorder of plants resulting in withering and death without rotting **b** : an organism that causes blight **2 a** : something that impairs or destroys ⟨the *blight* of totalitarianism⟩ **b** : an impaired or decayed condition ⟨urban *blight*⟩ [origin unknown]

²blight *vb* **1** : to affect with blight **2** : to cause to deteriorate **3** : to suffer from or become affected with blight

blimp \'blimp\ *n* : a nonrigid airship [imitative; from the sound made by striking the gas bag with the thumb]

¹blind \'blīnd\ *adj* **1 a** : SIGHTLESS **b** : having less than 1/10 normal vision in the best eye even with the aid of glasses **2** : lacking in judgment or understanding **3 a** : closed at one end ⟨a *blind* street⟩ **b** : having no opening ⟨a *blind* wall⟩ **4** : made or done without the aid of

blimp

sight; *esp* : performed solely by the aid of instruments within an airplane ⟨a *blind* landing⟩ [Old English] — **blind·ly** *adv* — **blind·ness** \'blīnd-nəs, 'blīn-\ *n*

²**blind** *vt* **1 a** : to make blind **b** : to make temporarily blind : DAZZLE ⟨*blinded* by oncoming headlights⟩ **2** : to deprive of judgment or understanding ⟨love may *blind* parents to a child's faults⟩ **3** : to make dim by comparison : OUTSHINE

³**blind** *n* **1** : a device to hinder sight or keep out light ⟨window *blinds*⟩ **2** : a place of concealment especially for hunters

⁴**blind** *adv* **1** : BLINDLY; *esp* : to the point of insensibility ⟨*blind* drunk⟩ **2** : without seeing outside of an airplane ⟨fly *blind* with the aid of instruments⟩

blind date *n* **1** : a date between two persons who have not previously met **2** : either participant in a blind date

blind·er \'blīn-dər\ *n* : either of two flaps on a horse's bridle to prevent sight of objects at its sides

¹**blind·fold** \'blīnd-,fōld, 'blīn-\ *vt* : to cover the eyes of with or as if with a piece of material [Middle English *blindfellen*, literally, "to strike blind", from *blind* + *fellen* "to fell"] — **blindfold** *adj*

²**blindfold** *n* : a covering for the eyes

blind·man's buff \'blīnd-,manz-'bəf, 'blīn-\ *also* **blindman's bluff** \-'bləf\ *n* : a group game in which a blindfolded player tries to catch and identify another player

blind spot *n* **1** : a point in the retina through which the optic nerve enters and which is insensitive to light **2** : an area of weakness (as in judgment) **3** : a locality in which radio reception is poor

blind·worm \'blīnd-,wərm\ *n* : a small burrowing limbless lizard with minute eyes

¹**blink** \'blingk\ *vb* **1 a** : to look with half-shut winking eyes **b** : to close and open the eyes involuntarily **2** : to wink repeatedly or rapidly ⟨*blink* back tears⟩ **3** : to shine dimly or intermittently **4 a** : to shut one's eyes to : IGNORE ⟨*blink* the facts⟩ **b** : to look with surprise or dismay [Middle English *blinken* "to open one's eyes"] SYN see WINK

²**blink** *n* **1** : GLIMMER, SPARKLE **2** : a usually involuntary shutting and opening of the eye — **on the blink** : not functioning properly : DISABLED

blink·er \'bling-kər\ *n* : one that blinks; *esp* : a light that flashes on and off (as for signaling)

blin·tze \'blin-sə, 'blint-\ *or* **blintz** \'blints\ *n* : a thin rolled pancake with a filling usually of cheese [Yiddish *blintse*]

blip \'blip\ *n* : an image on a radar screen [earlier *blip* "a short sound", of imitative origin]

bliss \'blis\ *n* : complete happiness and joy [Old English] — **bliss·ful** \-fəl\ *adj* — **bliss·ful·ly** \-fə-lē\ *adv* — **bliss·ful·ness** *n*

¹**blis·ter** \'blis-tər\ *n* **1** : a raised area of the outer skin containing watery liquid **2** : a raised spot (as in paint) resembling a blister **3** : any of various structures that bulge out (as a gunner's compartment on an airplane) [Dutch *bluyster*] — **blis·tery** \-tə-rē, -trē\ *adj*

²**blister** *vb* **blis·tered; blis·ter·ing** \-tə-ring, -tring\ **1** : to develop a blister : rise in blisters **2** : to raise a blister on

blister beetle *n* : any of a family of soft-bodied beetles including some whose dried bodies are used medicinally to blister the skin

blister copper *n* : metallic copper that has a black blistered surface, is the product of converting a crude smelted sulfur-containing ore, and is about 98.5 to 99.5 percent pure

blister rust *n* : any of several diseases of pines caused by rust fungi and marked by external blisters

blithe \'blīth, 'blīth\ *adj* **1** : of a happy lighthearted character or disposition **2** : HEEDLESS ⟨*blithe* unconcern⟩ [Old English *blīthe*] SYN see MERRY — **blithe·ly** *adv*

blithe·some \'blīth-səm, 'blīth-\ *adj* : GAY 1, MERRY — **blithe·some·ly** *adv*

blitz \'blits\ *n* **1** : an intensive series of air raids; *also* : AIR RAID **2 a** : a fast intensive campaign ⟨a publicity *blitz*⟩ **b** : a rush of the passer by the defensive linebackers in football [short for *blitzkrieg*] — **blitz** *vt*

blitz·krieg \'blits-,krēg\ *n* : a swift surprise offensive by coordinated air and ground forces [German, literally, "lightning war"] — **blitzkrieg** *vt*

bliz·zard \'bliz-ərd\ *n* **1** : a long severe snowstorm **2** : an intensely strong cold wind filled with fine snow **3** : an overwhelming rush or deluge ⟨a *blizzard* of fan mail⟩ [origin unknown]

¹**bloat** \'blōt\ *vb* : to swell by or as if by filling with water or air : puff up [Middle English *blout* "bloated"]

²**bloat** *n* : a disorder of cattle marked by abdominal bloating

bloat·er \'blōt-ər\ *n* : a large fat herring or mackerel lightly salted and briefly smoked [obsolete *bloat* "to cure"]

blob \'bläb\ *n* : a small lump or drop of something thick ⟨a *blob* of paste⟩ [Middle English]

bloc \'bläk\ *n* **1** : a group of legislators who act together on some issues regardless of party lines ⟨the farm *bloc* in Congress⟩ **2** : a combination of persons, groups, or nations united by treaty, agreement, or common interest ⟨the Soviet *bloc*⟩ [French, literally, "block"]

¹**block** \'bläk\ *n* **1 a** : a solid piece of material (as stone or wood) usually with one or more flat sides ⟨building *blocks*⟩; *also* : a hollow rectangular building unit **b** : a piece of wood on which condemned persons are beheaded **c** : a stand for something to be sold at auction **d** : a mold or form on which something is shaped ⟨a hat *block*⟩ **2 a** : OBSTACLE **b** : an obstruction of an opponent's play in sports **c** : interruption of normal function of body or mind ⟨heart *block*⟩ ⟨a mental *block*⟩ **3** : a wooden or metal case enclosing one or more pulleys **4** : a quantity, number, or section of things thought of as forming a group or unit ⟨a *block* of seats⟩ **5 a** : a large building divided into separate houses or shops : a number of houses or shops joined ⟨an apartment *block*⟩ **b** : a space enclosed by streets **c** : the length of one of the sides of such a block ⟨three *blocks* south⟩ **6** : a section of railroad track controlled by block signals **7** : a piece of material having a hand-cut design on its surface from which impressions are to be printed [Middle French *bloc*, from Dutch *blok*]

²**block** *vt* **1 a** : to stop up or close off : OBSTRUCT **b** : to hinder the progress or advance of; *esp* : to interfere with an opponent (as in football) **c** : to prevent normal functioning of ⟨*block* a nerve with an anesthetic⟩ **2** : to mark the chief lines of ⟨*block* out a sketch⟩ **3** : to shape on, with, or as if with a block **4** : to make (lines of writing or type) flush at the left or at both left and right **5** : to secure, support, or provide with a block — **block·er** *n*

block·ade \blä-'kād\ *n* : the isolation of an area by means of troops or warships to prevent passage of persons or supplies in or out — **blockade** *vt* — **block·ad·er** *n*

block·ade–run·ner \-,rən-ər\ *n* : a ship or person that attempts to sail through a blockade — **block·ade–run·ning** \-,rən-ing\ *n*

block·age \'bläk-ij\ *n* : an act or instance of obstructing : the state of being blocked ⟨*blockage* of blood flow in an artery⟩

block and tackle *n* : pulley blocks with associated rope or cable for hoisting or hauling

block·bust·er \'bläk-,bəs-tər\ *n* **1** : a very large high-explosive demolition bomb **2** : an enormously successful product or entertainment

block·head \'bläk-,hed\ *n* : a stupid person

block·house \-,haús\ *n* **1** : a building of heavy timbers or of concrete built with holes in its sides through

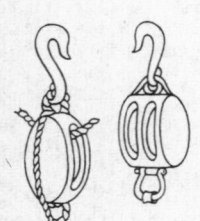

¹block 3

blockhouse 1

which persons inside may fire out at an enemy **2** : a building serving as an observation point for an operation likely to be accompanied by heat, blast, or radiation hazard

block·ish \\'bläk-ish\\ *adj* : lacking intelligence : STUPID — **block·ish·ly** *adv*

block letter *n* : a bold simple capital letter composed of strokes of uniform thickness

block printing *n* : printing from carved wooden or linoleum blocks

block signal *n* : a fixed signal at the entrance of a section of railroad track to govern trains entering and using it

blocky \\'bläk-ē\\ *adj* **block·i·er; -est** : resembling a block : solidly built ⟨a *blocky* physique⟩

bloke \\'blōk\\ *n, chiefly British* : MAN 1a [origin unknown]

¹blond *also* **blonde** \\'bländ\\ *adj* **1 a** : of a pale yellowish brown color ⟨*blond* hair⟩ **b** : of a pale white or rosy white color ⟨*blond* skin⟩ **c** : having blond hair ⟨a *blond* actor⟩ **2 a** : of a light color **b** : of the color blond [French] — **blond·ness** \\'bländ-nəs, 'blän-\\ *n*

²blond *or* **blonde** *n* **1** : a blond person **2** : a light yellowish brown to dark grayish yellow

¹blood \\'bləd\\ *n* **1** : the red fluid that circulates in the heart, arteries, capillaries, and veins of a vertebrate animal carrying nourishment and oxygen to and bringing away waste products from all parts of the body; *also* : a fluid resembling this **2 a** : LINEAGE 2, DESCENT; *esp* : royal lineage ⟨a prince or princess of the *blood*⟩ **b** : relationship by descent from a common ancestor : KINSHIP **c** : descent from parents of superior status or breeding **3** : ANGER [Old English *blōd*]

²blood *vt* : to give experience to ⟨troops *blooded* in battle⟩

blood bank *n* : a reserve supply of blood or plasma or the place where it is stored

blood·bath \\-,bath, -,báth\\ *n* : a great slaughter : MASSACRE

blood brother *n* **1** : a brother by birth **2** : one that is bound in ceremonial blood brotherhood

blood brotherhood *n* : a solemn friendship established between men by a ceremonial use of each other's blood

blood cell *n* : a cell normally present in blood

blood count *n* : the determination of the number of blood cells in a definite volume of blood; *also* : the number of cells so determined

blood·cur·dling \\'bləd-,kərd-liŋ\\ *adj* : arousing fear or horror : TERRIFYING, HORRIBLE ⟨*bloodcurdling* screams⟩

blood·ed \\'bləd-əd\\ *adj* : entirely or largely of pure blood or stock ⟨*blooded* horses⟩

blood feud *n* : a feud between different clans or families

blood fluke *n* : a flatworm (as a schistosome) parasitic in blood vessels

blood group *n* : one of the classes into which human beings can be separated on the basis of the presence or absence in their blood of specific antigens — called also *blood type* — **blood grouping** *n*

blood·guilt \\'bləd-,gilt\\ *n* : guilt resulting from bloodshed — **blood·guilt·i·ness** \\-,gil-tē-nəs\\ *n* — **blood·guilty** \\-tē\\ *adj*

blood·hound \\'bləd-,haùnd\\ *n* : a large powerful hound of a breed of European origin with a keen sense of smell

blood·less \\'bləd-ləs\\ *adj* **1** : deficient in blood **2** : not accompanied by loss of blood or by bloodshed ⟨a *bloodless* revolution⟩ **3** : lacking in spirit or feeling — **blood·less·ly** *adv* — **blood·less·ness** *n*

blood·let·ting \\-,let-iŋ\\ *n* **1** : the opening of a vein for removing or releasing blood **2** : BLOODSHED

blood·line \\-,līn\\ *n* : a sequence of direct ancestors especially in a pedigree; *also* : FAMILY

blood·mo·bile \\'bləd-mō-,bēl\\ *n* : a motor vehicle staffed and equipped for collecting blood from donors [*blood* + auto*mobile*]

blood money *n* **1** : money obtained at the cost of another's life **2** : money paid to the next of kin of a slain person by the slayer or his relatives

blood plasma *n* : the fluid part of whole blood — compare BLOOD SERUM

blood platelet *n* : one of the minute protoplasmic disks of vertebrate blood that assist in blood clotting

blood poisoning *n* : invasion of the bloodstream by virulent microorganisms from a local seat of infection accompanied especially by chills, fever, and prostration — called also *septicemia*; compare SEPSIS

blood pressure *n* : pressure of the blood on the walls of blood vessels and especially arteries that varies with physical condition and age

blood·red \\'bləd-'red\\ *adj* : having the color of blood

blood·root \\-,rüt, -,rút\\ *n* : a plant of the poppy family having a red root and sap and bearing a single lobed leaf and white flower in early spring

blood serum *n* : blood plasma from which the fibrin has been removed (as by clotting)

blood·shed \\'bləd-,shed\\ *n* **1** : the shedding of blood **2** : the taking of life : SLAUGHTER

blood·shot \\-,shät\\ *adj* : inflamed to redness ⟨*bloodshot* eyes⟩

blood·stain \\-,stān\\ *n* : a discoloration caused by blood — **blood·stained** \\-,stānd\\ *adj*

blood·stone \\-,stōn\\ *n* : a green quartz speckled with red jasper

blood·stream \\-,strēm\\ *n* : the flowing blood in a circulatory system

blood·suck·er \\-,sək-ər\\ *n* **1** : an animal that sucks blood; *esp* : LEECH **2** : a person who sponges or preys on another — **blood·suck·ing** \\-,sək-iŋ\\ *adj*

blood sugar *n* : the glucose in the blood; *also* : its concentration (as in milligrams per 100 milliliters)

blood test *n* : a test of the blood; *esp* : a serologic test for syphilis

blood·thirsty \\'bləd-,thər-stē\\ *adj* : eager for or marked by the shedding of blood — **blood·thirst·i·ly** \\-stə-lē\\ *adv* — **blood·thirst·i·ness** \\-stē-nəs\\ *n*

blood type *n* : BLOOD GROUP — **blood–type** *vt*

blood vessel *n* : a vessel (as an artery, vein, or capillary) in which blood circulates during life

blood·worm \\'bləd-,wərm\\ *n* : any of various reddish annelid worms often used as bait

bloody \\'bləd-ē\\ *adj* **blood·i·er; -est** **1** : smeared or stained with blood ⟨a *bloody* handkerchief⟩; *also* : BLEEDING ⟨a *bloody* nose⟩ **2** : causing or accompanied by bloodshed ⟨a *bloody* battle⟩ **3** : BLOODTHIRSTY, MURDEROUS ⟨a *bloody* band of pirates⟩ — **blood·i·ly** \\'bləd-l-ē\\ *adv* — **blood·i·ness** \\'bləd-ē-nəs\\ *n* — **bloody** *vt*

¹bloom \\'blüm\\ *n* **1** : a mass of wrought iron from a forge or puddling furnace **2** : a bar of iron or steel hammered or rolled from an ingot [Old English *blōma*]

²bloom *n* **1 a** : FLOWER ⟨a large yellow *bloom*⟩ **b** : flowers or amount of flowers ⟨the apple trees had a very light *bloom* this spring⟩ **c** : the flowering state ⟨the roses are in *bloom*⟩ **d** : a period of flowering ⟨the spring *bloom*⟩ **e** : an excessive growth of plankton **2** : a state or time of beauty, freshness, and vigor **3** : a surface coating or appearance: as **a** : a delicate powdery coating on some fruits and leaves **b** : a rosy appearance of the cheeks; *also* : an outward evidence of freshness or healthy vigor [Old Norse *blōm*] — **bloomy** \\'blü-mē\\ *adj*

³bloom *vi* **1** : to produce or yield flowers **2 a** : to be in a state of youthful beauty or freshness : FLOURISH **b** : SHINE, GLOW **3** : to appear unexpectedly in large quantities — **bloom·er** *n*

bloo·mers \\'blü-mərz\\ *n pl* : full loose trousers gathered at the knee formerly worn by women (as for athletics); *also* : underpants of similar design worn chiefly by girls [Amelia *Bloomer*, died 1894, American pioneer in feminism]

\\ə\\ abut	\\ŋ\\ sing	
\\ər\\ further	\\ō\\ bone	
\\a\\ mat	\\ó\\ saw	
\\ā\\ take	\\ói\\ coin	
\\ä\\ cot, cart	\\th\\ thin	
\\aù\\ out	\\th\\ this	
\\ch\\ chin	\\ü\\ food	
\\e\\ pet	\\ù\\ foot	
\\ē\\ easy	\\y\\ yet	
\\g\\ go	\\yü\\ few	
\\i\\ tip	\\yú\\ cure	
\\ī\\ life	\\zh\\ vision	
\\j\\ job		

bloop·er \'blü-pər\ *n* : an embarrassing blunder made in public [*bloop* "an unpleasing sound"]

¹blos·som \'bläs-əm\ *n* **I a** : the flower of a seed plant ⟨apple *blossoms*⟩ **b** : the state of flowering ⟨apple trees in *blossom*⟩ **2** : a peak period or stage of development [Old English *blōs-tm*]— **blos·somy** \-ə-mē\ *adj*

²blossom *vi* **I** : BLOOM 1 **2** : to unfold like a blossom: as **a** : to flourish and prosper markedly **b** : DEVELOP 5a, EXPAND **c** : to come into being

¹blot \'blät\ *n* **I** : SPOT, STAIN **2** : a flaw in morals or reputation [Middle English]

²blot *vb* **blot·ted; blot·ting I** : to spot, stain, or spatter with a discoloring substance **2** : to make obscure : DIM **3** : to bring shame to : DISGRACE **4** : to dry or remove with or as if with blotting paper **5** : to become marked with a blot

blotch \'bläch\ *n* **I** : FLAW, BLEMISH **2** : a spot or mark (as of color or ink) especially when large or irregular [probably alteration of *botch*] — **blotch** *vt* — **blotched** \'blächt\ *adj* — **blotchy** \'bläch-ē\ *adj*

blot out *vt* **I a** : to make unimportant or trivial **b** : to make obscure ⟨clouds *blotted out* the sun⟩ **2** : DESTROY 1, KILL

blot·ter \'blät-ər\ *n* **I** : a piece of blotting paper **2** : a book in which entries are made temporarily ⟨a police *blotter*⟩

blotting paper *n* : a soft spongy paper used to absorb wet ink

blouse \'blaùs *also* 'blaùz\ *n, pl* **blous·es** \'blaù-səz, -zəz\ **I** : a loose overgarment like a shirt or smock varying from hip-length to calf-length **2** : the jacket of a uniform **3** : a usually loose-fitting garment covering the body from the neck to the waist [French]

¹blow \'blō\ *vb* **blew** \'blü\; **blown** \'blōn\; **blow·ing I** : to move or become moved especially with speed or with power ⟨wind *blowing* from the north⟩ **2** : to send forth a strong current of air ⟨*blow* on one's hands⟩ **3** : to drive or become driven by a current of air ⟨a tree *blown* down in a storm⟩ **4** : to make a sound or cause to sound by blowing ⟨*blow* a horn⟩ ⟨*blew* a tune⟩ **5** : to breathe hard or rapidly : PANT **6 a** : to melt when overloaded ⟨the fuse *blew*⟩ **b** : to cause (a fuse) to blow **7 a** : to release suddenly the contained air through a rupture ⟨the tire *blew* out⟩ **b** : to rupture by too much pressure ⟨*blew* a gasket⟩ **8** : to clear of contents by forcing air through **9** : to produce or shape by the action of blown or injected air ⟨*blow* glass⟩ **10** : to shatter or destroy by explosion **II a** : to put out of breath with exertion **b** : to let (as a horse) pause to catch the breath **12** : to spend recklessly ⟨*blew* all my money⟩ [Old English *blāwan*]

²blow *n* **I** : a blowing of wind especially when violent : GALE **2** : a forcing of air from the mouth or nose or through some instrument

³blow *vi* **blew** \'blü\; **blown** \'blōn\; **blow·ing** : FLOWER 1, BLOOM [Old English *blōwan*]

⁴blow *n* **I** : a display of flowers **2** : ²BLOOM 1c ⟨lilacs in full *blow*⟩

⁵blow *n* **I** : a forcible stroke delivered with a part of the body or with an instrument **2** : a hostile act : COMBAT ⟨come to *blows*⟩ **3** : a forcible or sudden act or effort : ASSAULT **4** : a severe and sudden calamity ⟨a heavy *blow* to the nation⟩ [Middle English *blaw*] □ SYN STROKE: BLOW implies violence or force; STROKE suggests suddenness or definiteness or precision.

blow–by–blow \-bī-, -bə-\ *adj* : minutely detailed ⟨a *blow-by-blow* account⟩

blow·er \'blō-ər, 'blòr\ *n* **I** : one that blows **2** : a device for producing a current of air or gas

blow·fly \'blō-,flī\ *n* : any of various two-winged flies (as a bluebottle) that deposit their eggs or maggots on meat or in wounds

blow·gun \-,gən\ *n* : a tube from which an arrow or a dart may be shot by the force of the breath

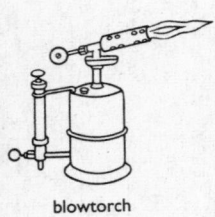

blowtorch

blow·hard \-,härd\ *n* : BRAGGART

blow·hole \-,hōl\ *n* **I** : a nostril in the top of the head of a whale or related animal **2** : a hole in the ice to which aquatic mammals (as seals) come to breathe

blown \'blōn\ *adj* **I** : SWOLLEN; *esp* : afflicted with bloat **2** : FLYBLOWN 1 **3** : being out of breath

blow·out \'blō-,aùt\ *n* **I** : a big social affair **2** : a bursting of a container (as a tire) by pressure of the contents on a weak spot **3** : an uncontrolled eruption of an oil or gas well

blow out \blō-'aùt, 'blō-\ *vb* **I** : to extinguish or become extinguished by a gust **2** : to dissipate (itself) by blowing — used of a storm

blow·pipe \'blō-,pīp\ *n* **I** : a small round tube for blowing a jet of gas (as air) into a flame so as to concentrate and increase the heat **2** : BLOWGUN

blow·sy *also* **blow·zy** \'blaù-zē\ *adj* : DISHEVELED, SLOVENLY; *also* : COARSE 3 [English dialect *blowse* "wench"]

blow·torch \'blō-,tòrch\ *n* : a small portable burner that intensifies combustion by means of a blast of air or oxygen and that usually includes a fuel tank pressurized by a hand pump

blow–up \'blō-,əp\ *n* **I** : EXPLOSION **2** : an outburst of temper **3** : a photographic enlargement

blow up *vb* **I a** : to destroy or become destroyed by explosion **b** : to become violently angry **2** : to build up, expand, or become expanded to unreasonable proportions **3** : to fill up with a gas ⟨*blow up* a balloon⟩ **4** : to make a photographic enlargement of

blowy \'blō-ē\ *adj* **blow·i·er; -est** : WINDY 1

¹blub·ber \'bləb-ər\ *n* **I a** : the fat of large sea mammals (as whales) **b** : excessive fat on the body **2** : the action of blubbering [Middle English *bluber* "bubble, foam"]

²blubber *vb* **blub·bered; blub·ber·ing** \'bləb-ring, -ə-ring\ **I** : to weep noisily **2** : to utter while weeping [Middle English *blubren* "to make a bubbling sound", from *bluber*]

³blub·ber \-ər\ *or* **blub·bery** \'bləb-rē, -ə-rē\ *adj* : puffed out : THICK ⟨*blubber* lips⟩

bludg·eon \'bləj-ən\ *n* : a short club with one end thicker and heavier than the other [origin unknown] — **bludgeon** *vt*

¹blue \'blü\ *adj* **I** : of the color blue **2 a** : BLUISH **b** : LIVID 1, 2 **c** : bluish gray **3 a** : low in spirits : MELANCHOLY **b** : tending to lower the spirits **4** : PURITANICAL [Old French *blou*, of Germanic origin] — **blue·ly** *adv* — **blue·ness** *n*

²blue *n* **I** : the color of the clear daytime sky : a color lying between green and violet in the spectrum **2** : blue clothing or cloth **3 a** : SKY 1 **b** : the far distance **c** : SEA 1a — **out of the blue** : UNEXPECTEDLY

³blue *vt* **blued; blue·ing** *or* **blu·ing I** : to make blue **2** : to add bluing to so as to make white ⟨*blue* the sheets⟩

blue baby *n* : an infant with a bluish tint because of insufficient oxygenation of the blood due to a congenital defect of the heart

blue·beard \'blü-,biərd\ *n* : a man who marries and kills one woman after another [Bluebeard, a fairy-tale character]

blue·bell \-,bel\ *n* : any of various plants (as a grape hyacinth) with blue bell-shaped flowers; *esp* : HAREBELL

blue·ber·ry \'blü-,ber-ē, -bə-rē, -brē\ *n* : the edible blue or blackish small-seeded berry of any of several plants of the heath family; *also* : a low or tall shrub producing these berries — compare HUCKLEBERRY

blue·bird \-,bərd\ *n* : any of several small North American songbirds related to the robin but with blue above especially in the male

blue blood *n* **I** \'blü-'bləd\ : aristocracy by birth **2** \-,bləd\ : a member of a noble or socially prominent family — **blue–blood·ed** \-'bləd-əd\ *adj*

blue·bon·net \'blü-ˌbän-ət\ *n* : a low-growing annual lupine of Texas with silky foliage and blue flowers

blue·bot·tle \-ˌbät-l\ *n* : any of several blowflies with the abdomen or the whole body iridescent blue in color

blue cheese *n* : cheese ripened by and marked with greenish blue mold

blue chip *n* : a stock issue that commands a high price because of public faith in its worth and stability [from the high value of blue chips in games of chance]

blue-col·lar \'blü-ˌkäl-ər\ *adj* : of, relating to, or constituting the wage-earning class

blue crab *n* : a largely blue edible crab of the Atlantic and Gulf coasts

blue·fin \'blü-ˌfin\ *n* : a very large tuna with short pectoral fins that is dark blue above and lighter colored below

blue·fish \-ˌfish\ *n* : an active saltwater food and sport fish that is related to the pompanos and is bluish above and silvery below; *also* : any of several bluish food fishes

blue flag *n* : a blue-flowered iris; *esp* : a common iris of the eastern United States with a root formerly used medicinally

blue·gill \'blü-ˌgil\ *n* : a common food and sport sunfish of the eastern and central United States

blue·grass \-ˌgras\ *n* 1 : a widely used pasture and lawn grass with bluish green stems 2 : country music played on unamplified stringed instruments (as banjos, fiddles, guitars, and mandolins) [sense 2 from the *Blue Grass Boys,* performing group, from the *Bluegrass* state, nickname of Kentucky]

blue-green alga \'blü-ˌgrēn-\ *n* : any of a major group (Cyanophyta) of algae having the chlorophyll masked by bluish green pigments

blue jay \-ˌjā\ *n* : any of several largely blue and usually crested American jays

blue jeans *n pl* : pants usually made of blue denim

blue law *n* 1 : one of many strict laws regulating morals and conduct in colonial New England 2 : a statute limiting work, commerce, and amusements on Sundays or holidays

blue line *n* : either of two wide blue lines that cross an ice hockey rink and divide it approximately into thirds

blue mold *n* : a fungus and especially a penicillium that produces blue or blue-green surface growths

blue moon *n* : a very long period of time ⟨once in a *blue moon*⟩

blue·nose \'blü-ˌnōz\ *n* : one who advocates a strict moral code

blue plate \-ˌplāt\ *n* : a main course (as of meat and vegetables) served as a single menu item

blue·point \-ˌpȯint\ *n* : a small oyster typically from the south shore of Long Island [*Blue Point,* Long Island]

¹blue·print \-ˌprint\ *n* 1 : a photographic print in white on a blue ground used especially for copying mechanical drawings and architects' plans 2 : a detailed plan or program of action

²blueprint *vt* : to make a blueprint of or for

blue racer *n* : a blacksnake of a bluish green subspecies occurring from Ohio to Texas

blue ribbon *n* 1 : a blue ribbon awarded the first-place winner in a competition 2 : an honor or award gained for outstanding performance

blues \'blüz\ *n pl* 1 : low spirits : MELANCHOLY 2 : a song expressing melancholy and composed in a style originating among the American Negroes 3 : a blue uniform

blue-sky law \'blü-ˈskī-\ *n* : a law providing for the regulation of the sale of securities [*blue-sky stock* "worthless stock"; from the emptiness of the sky]

blue spruce *n* : COLORADO BLUE SPRUCE

blue·stem \'blü-ˌstem\ *n* : either of two important hay and forage grasses of the western United States with smooth bluish leaf sheaths

blue·stock·ing \-ˌstäk-ing\ *n* : a woman having intellectual or literary interests [*Bluestocking* society, 18th century literary clubs]

blue streak *n* 1 : something that moves very fast 2 : a constant stream of words ⟨talked a *blue streak*⟩

blu·et \'blü-ət\ *n* : a small American herb with solitary bluish flowers and stems arranged in tufts

blue vitriol *n* : a hydrated copper sulfate $CuSO_4 \cdot 5H_2O$

blue whale *n* : a whale that may reach a weight of 90 metric tons and a length of 30 meters and is generally considered the largest living animal

¹bluff \'bləf\ *adj* 1 : rising steeply with a broad front (as from a plain or shore) ⟨a *bluff* coastline⟩ 2 : blunt and outspoken in a good-natured manner [Dutch *blaf* "flat"] — **bluff·ly** *adv* — **bluff·ness** *n*

²bluff *n* : a high steep bank : CLIFF

³bluff *vb* : to deceive or frighten by pretending to have strength or confidence that one does not really have [probably from Dutch *bluffen* "to boast"] — **bluff·er** *n*

⁴bluff *n* 1 **a** : an act or instance of bluffing **b** : the practice of bluffing 2 : one who bluffs

blu·ing *or* **blue·ing** \'blü-ing\ *n* : a preparation of blue or violet dyes used in washing clothes to prevent yellowing of white fabrics

blu·ish *or* **blue·ish** \'blü-ish\ *adj* : somewhat blue

¹blun·der \'blən-dər\ *vb* **blun·dered; blun·der·ing** \-də-ring, -dring\ 1 : to move unsteadily or blindly : STUMBLE 2 : to make a mistake (as through stupidity or carelessness) 3 : to say stupidly or thoughtlessly : BLURT [Middle English *blundren*] — **blun·der·er** \-dər-ər\ *n*

²blunder *n* : a mistake resulting especially from stupidity or carelessness SYN SEE ERROR

blun·der·buss \'blən-dər-ˌbəs\ *n* 1 : a short firearm usually with a flaring muzzle that was formerly used for firing at close range without taking precise aim 2 : a blundering person [obsolete Dutch *donderbus,* literally, "thunder gun"]

¹blunt \'blənt\ *adj* 1 **a** : lacking in feeling : INSENSITIVE **b** : slow in understanding or in making distinctions : DULL 2 : having an edge or point that is not sharp 3 : abrupt in speech or manner [Middle English] — **blunt·ly** *adv* — **blunt·ness** *n* □ SYN DULL, OBTUSE: BLUNT suggests an innate or inherent lack of sharpness or quickness of feeling or perception ⟨a *blunt* refusal⟩ DULL suggests lack or loss of keenness, zest, or pungency ⟨a *dull* report⟩ OBTUSE implies bluntness or insensitivity in perception or imagination ⟨an *obtuse* audience⟩

²blunt *vb* : to make or become blunt

¹blur \'blər\ *n* 1 : a smear or stain that dims but does not completely cover 2 : something vague or lacking definite outline ⟨saw only a *blur* of words through the tears⟩ [perhaps related to *blear*] — **blur·ry** \-ē\ *adj*

²blur *vb* **blurred; blur·ring** 1 : to make indistinct by or as if by smearing 2 : to make (as the senses) dim or confused 3 : to become vague, indistinct, or indefinite

blurb \'blərb\ *n* : a brief notice (as in advertising) praising a product extravagantly [coined by Gelett Burgess, died 1951, American humorist]

blurt \'blərt\ *vt* : to utter suddenly and thoughtlessly ⟨*blurt* out a secret⟩ [probably imitative]

¹blush \'bləsh\ *vi* 1 : to become red in the face especially from shame, modesty, or confusion 2 : to feel shame or embarrassment 3 : to have a rosy or fresh color : BLOOM [Old English *blyscan* "to redden", from *blysa* "flame"] — **blush·er** *n*

²blush *n* 1 : outward appearance : VIEW ⟨at first *blush*⟩ 2 : a reddening of the face especially from shame, modesty, or confusion 3 : a red or rosy tint — **blush·ful** \-fəl\ *adj*

¹blus·ter \'bləs-tər\ *vi* **blus·tered; blus·ter·ing** \-tə-ring, -tring\ 1 : to blow violently and noisily 2 : to talk or act in a noisy boastful way [Middle English *blustren*] — **blus·ter·er** \-tər-ər\ *n*

blue whale

blunderbuss 1

\ə\ abut	\ng\ sing
\ər\ further	\ō\ bone
\a\ mat	\ȯ\ saw
\ā\ take	\ȯi\ coin
\ä\ cot, cart	\th\ thin
\aů\ out	\th\ this
\ch\ chin	\ü\ food
\e\ pet	\ů\ foot
\ē\ easy	\y\ yet
\g\ go	\yü\ few
\i\ tip	\yů\ cure
\ī\ life	\zh\ vision
\j\ job	

²bluster *n* **1** : a violent noisy blowing **2** : noisy boisterous activity **3** : loudly boastful or threatening speech — **blus·tery** \-tə-rē, -trē\ *adj*

B lymphocyte *n* : B CELL

boa \'bō-ə\ *n* **1** : a large snake (as the boa constrictor or python) that crushes its prey **2** : a long fluffy scarf of fur, feathers, or delicate fabric [Latin, a kind of water snake]

boa con·stric·tor \-kən-'strik-tər\ *n* : a mottled brown tropical American boa

boar \'bōr, 'bȯr\ *n* **1** : a male swine; *also* : the male of any of several mammals **2** : WILD BOAR [Old English *bār*] — **boar·ish** \-ish\ *adj*

¹board \'bōrd, 'bȯrd\ *n* **1** : the side of a ship — often used in combination ⟨star*board*⟩ ⟨over*board*⟩ **2 a** : a thin flat relatively long piece of lumber **b** *pl* : STAGE 2a ⟨trod the *boards* for 40 years⟩ **3 a** : a dining table **b** : regular meals especially when furnished for pay ⟨room and *board*⟩ **c** : a group of persons who manage, direct, or investigate ⟨*board* of directors⟩ ⟨school *board*⟩ ⟨*board* of examiners⟩ **4 a** : a flat usually rectangular piece of material designed for a special purpose ⟨cutting *board*⟩: as (1) : a flat surface specially marked for the positioning and advancing of men or markers in certain games (2) : BACKBOARD (3) : SURFBOARD (4) : a sheet of insulating material carrying circuit elements and terminals that can be inserted in an electronic apparatus **b** : a surface, frame, or device for posting notices or listing market quotations **5 a** : a flat rectangular sheet formed of wood pulp or composition materials : PAPERBOARD **b** : a piece of stiff cardboard for the side of a book cover [Old English *bord*] — **by the board 1** : over the side of a ship **2** : into a state of discard, neglect, or ruin ⟨all our plans went *by the board*⟩ — **on board** : ABOARD

²board *vb* **1** : to go aboard : get on ⟨*boarded* the plane in New York⟩ **2** : to cover with boards ⟨*boarded* up a window⟩ **3** : to provide or be provided with regular meals and often lodging usually for pay

board·er \'bōrd-ər, 'bȯrd-\ *n* : one that boards; *esp* : one who boards at another's house for pay

board foot *n* : a unit of quantity for lumber equal to the volume of a board 12 × 12 × 1 inches (about 30.5 × 30.5 × 2.5 centimeters)

board game *n* : a game of strategy (as chess, checkers, or backgammon) played by moving pieces on a board

board·ing·house \'bōrd-ing-,haùs, 'bȯrd-\ *n* : a house at which persons are boarded

boarding school *n* : a school in which pupils are boarded and lodged as well as taught

board measure *n* : measurement in board feet

board of trade : an organization of business people to promote and protect business interests — compare CHAMBER OF COMMERCE

board·walk \'bōrd-,wȯk, 'bȯrd-\ *n* **1** : a walk constructed of planking **2** : a walk constructed along a beach

¹boast \'bōst\ *n* **1** : the act of boasting : BRAG **2** : a cause for pride [Middle English *boost*] — **boast·ful** \'bōst-fəl\ *adj* — **boast·ful·ly** \-fə-lē\ *adv* — **boast·ful·ness** *n*

²boast *vb* **1** : to praise oneself ⟨*boasting* of your ability⟩ **2** : to tell with extreme pride : BRAG ⟨*boasting* about their money⟩ **3** : to possess or display proudly ⟨our band *boasted* new uniforms⟩ — **boast·er** *n*

¹boat \'bōt\ *n* **1** : a small vessel propelled by oars or paddles or by sail or power **2** : SHIP **3** : a boat-shaped utensil or device ⟨gravy *boat*⟩ [Old English *bāt*] — **in the same boat** : in the same situation

²boat *vb* **1** : to place in or bring into a boat ⟨*boated* a large halibut⟩ **2** : to travel by boat — **boat·er** *n*

boat hook *n* : a hook with a point on the back fixed to a pole and used especially to pull or push a boat into place

boat·house \'bōt-,haùs\ *n* : a building to house and protect boats

bobwhite

boat·load \-,lōd\ *n* : a boat's full load or a quantity equal to such a load ⟨a *boatload* of passengers⟩

boat·man \'bōt-mən\ *n* : a person who manages, works on, or deals in boats — **boat·man·ship** \-,ship\ *n*

boat·swain *also* **bo·s'n** *or* **bo·sun** \'bōs-n\ *n* : a warrant officer on a warship or a petty officer on a merchant ship in charge of the hull and all related equipment [Middle English *boot* "boat" + *swein* "boy, servant"]

¹bob \'bäb\ *vb* **bobbed; bob·bing 1 a** : to move or cause to move up and down in a short quick movement ⟨a cork *bobbing* in the water⟩ **b** : to emerge or appear suddenly or unexpectedly ⟨this question *bobs* up often⟩ **2** : to grasp or make a grab with the teeth ⟨*bob* for apples⟩ [Middle English *boben*]

²bob *n* : a short jerky motion ⟨a *bob* of the head⟩

³bob *n* **1** : a woman's or child's short haircut **2** : a ball or weight hanging from a rod or line **3** : a device (as a cork) for buoying up the baited end of a fishing line [Middle English *bobbe* "bunch, cluster"]

⁴bob *vt* **bobbed; bob·bing 1** : to cut shorter : CROP **2** : to cut (hair) in the style of a bob

⁵bob *n, pl* **bob** *British* : SHILLING [perhaps from the name *Bob*]

⁶bob *n* : BOBSLED

bob·ber \'bäb-ər\ *n* : one that bobs

bob·bin \'bäb-ən\ *n* **1** : a cylinder or spindle on which yarn or thread is wound (as in a sewing machine) **2** : a coil of insulated wire or the reel it is wound on [origin unknown]

bob·ble \'bäb-əl\ *vb* **bob·bled; bob·bling** \'bäb-ling, -ə-ling\ **1** : ¹BOB 1a **2** : FUMBLE 2 [from ¹*bob*] — **bobble** *n*

bob·by \'bäb-ē\ *n, pl* **bobbies** *British* : POLICEMAN [*Bobby*, nickname for Robert, from Sir Robert Peel, died 1850, organizer of the London police force]

bob·by pin \'bäb-ē-\ *n* : a flat wire hairpin with prongs that press close together [perhaps from ³*bob*]

bobby socks *or* **bobby sox** *n pl* : girls' socks reaching above the ankle [perhaps from *bobby* pin]

bob·by–sox·er \'bäb-ē-,säk-sər\ *or* **bob·by–sock·er** \-,säk-ər\ *n* : an adolescent girl

bob·cat \'bäb-,kat\ *n* : a common usually rusty-colored North American lynx [³*bob*; from the stubby tail]

bob·o·link \'bäb-ə-,lingk\ *n* : an American migratory songbird related to the blackbirds [imitative]

bob·sled \'bäb-,sled\ *n* **1** : a short sled usually used as one of a joined pair **2** : a racing sled with two sets of runners in tandem, a seat for two or four riders, a steering device, and a brake — **bobsled** *vi* — **bob·sled·der** *n*

bob·stay \'bäb-,stā\ *n* : a stay used to hold a ship's bowsprit down

bob·tail \'bäb-,tāl\ *n* **1 a** : a bobbed tail **b** : a horse or dog with a bobbed tail **2** : something shortened or abbreviated — **bobtail** \-,tāl\ *or* **bob·tailed** \-,tāld\ *adj*

bob·white \bäb-'hwīt, 'bäb-, -'wīt\ *n* : any of several American quails; *esp* : a gray, white, and reddish game bird of the eastern and central United States — called *also partridge* [imitative]

boc·cie *or* **boc·ci** *or* **boc·ce** \'bäch-ē\ *n* : a game similar to lawn bowling played on a long narrow usually dirt court [Italian *bocce* "balls"]

bock \'bäk\ *n* : a heavy dark rich beer usually sold in the early spring [German]

¹bode \'bōd\ *vb* **1** : to indicate by signs **2** : to give promise of something : PRESAGE [Old English *bodian*] — **bode·ment** \-mənt\ *n*

²bode *past of* BIDE

bod·ice \'bäd-əs\ *n* : the part of a woman's dress that covers the body from neck to waist □ ORIGIN *Bodice* is derived from *body*. One sense of the word *body* is "the part of a garment covering the body or trunk". In the 17th and 18th centuries a woman's corset was often called a "pair of bodies". The plural *bodies*, or *bodice*, was eventually interpreted as a singular. *Bod-*

ice is now most often used to refer to the upper part of a woman's dress.

bod·ied \'bäd-ēd\ *adj* : having a body or such a body ⟨long-*bodied*⟩

bod·i·less \'bäd-i-ləs, 'bäd-l-əs\ *adj* : having no body or substance ⟨*bodiless* ghosts⟩ ⟨a *bodiless* rumor⟩

¹bod·i·ly \'bäd-l-ē\ *adj* **1** : having a body **2** : of or relating to the body ⟨*bodily* organs⟩ ⟨*bodily* comfort⟩

²bodily *adv* **1** : in the flesh **2** : as a whole : ALTOGETHER

bod·ing \'bōd-ing\ *n* : FOREBODING

bod·kin \'bäd-kən\ *n* **1 a** : DAGGER 1 **b** : a sharp slender instrument for making holes in cloth **2** : a blunt needle with a large eye for drawing tape or ribbon through a loop or hem [Middle English]

body \'bäd-ē\ *n, pl* **bod·ies** **1 a** : the physical whole of a living or dead organism **b** : the trunk or main part of a plant or animal body as distinguished from the head, appendages, or branches **c** : HUMAN BEING, PERSON **2** : the main or central part: as **a** : the box of a vehicle on or in which the load is placed **b** : the main part of a document **3** : the part of a garment covering the body or trunk **4** : a mass or portion of matter distinct from other masses ⟨a *body* of water⟩ ⟨a *body* of cold air⟩ **5 a** : a group of individuals united for some purpose ⟨a legislative *body*⟩ **b** : a unit formed of a number of persons or things : a collective whole ⟨a *body* of laws⟩ **6 a** : VISCOSITY ⟨paint with a good *body*⟩ **b** : richness of flavor (as of wine) [Old English *bodig*]

body cavity *n* : a cavity within an animal body; *esp* : COELOM

body English *n* : the instinctive attempt of a person to influence the movement of a propelled object (as a ball) by moving the body in the desired direction

body·guard \'bäd-ē-ˌgärd\ *n* : a person or group of persons whose duty it is to protect someone

body louse *n* : a sucking louse that lives in the clothing and feeds on the human body

body politic *n* : a group of persons politically organized under a single government

body snatcher *n* : one that steals corpses from graves usually for dissection

body·surf \'bäd-ē-ˌsərf\ *vi* : to ride a wave on the chest and stomach without a surfboard — **body·surf·er** *n*

Boer \'bōr, 'bor, 'bur\ *n* : a South African of Dutch or Huguenot descent [Dutch, literally, "farmer"]

¹bog \'bäg, 'bog\ *n* : wet spongy ground; *esp* : poorly drained acid soil that adjoins a body of water and is usually grown over by sedges, heaths, and sphagnum [of Celtic origin] — **bog·gy** \-ē\ *adj*

²bog *vb* **bogged**; **bog·ging** : to sink into or as if into a bog : MIRE — often used with *down*

¹bo·gey *or* **bo·gy** *or* **bo·gie** *n, pl* **bogeys** *or* **bogies** **1** \'bug-ē, 'bō-gē, 'bü-gē\ : GHOST 2, PHANTOM **2** \'bō-gē *also* 'bug-ē *or* 'bü-gē\ : a source of annoyance, perplexity, or harassment **3** \'bō-gē\ : one golf stroke over par on a hole [probably from English dialect *bogle* "terrifying apparition"]

²bo·gey \'bō-gē\ *vt* **bo·geyed**; **bo·gey·ing** : to shoot (a hole in golf) in one over par

bo·gey·man \'bug-ē-ˌman, 'bō-gē-, 'bü-gē-, 'bug-ər-\ *n* : a terrifying person or thing : MENACE; *esp* : a monstrous imaginary figure used especially in threatening children

bog·gle \'bäg-əl\ *vb* **bog·gled**; **bog·gling** \'bäg-ling, -ə-ling\ **1** : to start with fright or amazement **2** : to hesitate because of doubt, fear, or scruples **3** : to overwhelm with wonder or confusion [perhaps from English dialect *bogle* "terrifying apparition"] — **boggle** *n*

bo·gie *also* **bo·gey** *or* **bo·gy** \'bō-gē\ *n, pl* **bogies** *also* **bogeys** **1** : a low strong cart **2** : the driving-wheel assembly of a 6-wheel automotive truck consisting of the rear four wheels [origin unknown]

bo·gus \'bō-gəs\ *adj* : not genuine : SPURIOUS, SHAM [*bogus*, a machine for making counterfeit money]

bo·he·mia \bō-'hē-mē-ə\ *n, often cap* : a community of bohemians : the world of bohemians

Bo·he·mi·an \bō-'hē-mē-ən\ *n* **1 a** : a native or inhabitant of Bohemia **b** : the group of Czech dialects used in Bohemia **2** *often not cap* **a** : one who wanders from place to place; *esp* : GYPSY **b** : a writer or artist living an unconventional life — **bohemian** *adj, often cap* — **bo·he·mi·an·ism** \-mē-ə-ˌniz-əm\ *n, often cap*

¹boil \'boil\ *n* : a painful swollen inflamed area in the skin resulting from infection and usually ending with the discharge of pus and a hardened core — compare CARBUNCLE [Old English *bȳl*]

²boil *vb* **1 a** : to produce bubbles of vapor when heated ⟨the water is *boiling*⟩ **b** : to come or bring to the boiling point **2** : to become agitated like boiling water : SEETHE ⟨*boiling* flood waters⟩ **3** : to be excited or stirred up ⟨*boiling* with anger⟩ **4** : to subject to the action of a boiling liquid ⟨*boil* eggs⟩ [Old French *boillir*, derived from Latin *bulla* "bubble"]

³boil *n* : the act or state of boiling

boil·er \'boi-lər\ *n* **1** : a container in which something is boiled **2** : a tank holding hot water **3** : a strong metal container used in making steam for heating buildings or for driving engines

boil·er·mak·er \-ˌmā-kər\ *n* : a workman who makes, assembles, or repairs boilers

boiling point *n* : the temperature at which a liquid boils

bois·ter·ous \'boi-stə-rəs, -strəs\ *adj* **1 a** : noisily rough : ROWDY ⟨a *boisterous* crowd⟩ **b** : marked by exuberance and high spirits ⟨*boisterous* laughter⟩ **2** : vigorously active : VIOLENT ⟨*boisterous* winds⟩ [Middle English *boistous* "rough"] — **bois·ter·ous·ly** *adv* — **bois·ter·ous·ness** *n*

bo·la \'bō-lə\ *or* **bo·las** \-ləs\ *n, pl* **bo·las** \-ləz\ : a weapon consisting of two or more stone or iron balls attached to the ends of a cord for hurling at and entangling an animal [American Spanish *bolas*, from Spanish *bola* "ball"]

bold \'bōld\ *adj* **1 a** : fearless in meeting danger : INTREPID **b** : showing a courageous daring spirit ⟨a *bold* plan⟩ **2** : IMPUDENT, PRESUMPTUOUS **3** : very steep : SHEER ⟨*bold* cliffs⟩ **4** : standing out prominently : CONSPICUOUS ⟨*bold* colors⟩ [Old English *beald*] — **bold·ly** *adv* — **bold·ness** \'bōld-nəs, 'bōl-\ *n*

bold·face \'bōld-ˌfās, 'bōl-\ *n* : a typeface having thick dark lines

bold–faced \-'fāst\ *adj* **1** : bold in manner or conduct : FORWARD **2** : set in boldface

bole \'bōl\ *n* : the trunk of a tree [Old Norse *bolr*]

bo·le·ro \bə-'lear-ō\ *n, pl* **-ros** **1** : a Spanish dance in ¾ time; *also* : the music for it **2** : a loose waist-length jacket open at the front [Spanish]

bo·li·var \bə-'lē-ˌvär, 'bäl-ə-vər\ *n, pl* **bo·li·vars** *or* **bo·li·va·res** \ˌbäl-ə-'vär-ˌās, ˌbō-li-\ **1** : the basic monetary unit of Venezuela **2** : a coin representing one bolivar [Simón *Bolivar*]

bo·li·vi·a·no \bə-ˌliv-ē-'än-ō\ *n, pl* **-nos** **1** : a former monetary unit of Bolivia **2** : a coin or note representing one boliviano [Spanish]

boll \'bōl\ *n* : a seedpod or capsule of a plant (as cotton) [Middle English]

bol·lard \'bäl-ərd\ *n* **1** : a post on a wharf around which to fasten mooring lines **2** : BITT [perhaps from *bole*]

boll weevil *n* : a small grayish weevil whose larva lives in and feeds on the buds and bolls of the cotton plant

boll·worm \'bōl-ˌwərm\ *n* : CORN EARWORM; *also* : any of several other moths or the immature stages of moths that feed on cotton bolls as larvae

bo·lo \'bō-lō\ *n, pl* **bolos** : a long heavy single-edged knife used in the Philippines [Spanish]

bo·lo·gna \bə-'lō-nē *also* -nyə *or* -nə\ *n* : a large smoked sausage of beef, veal, and pork [*Bologna*, Italy]

bolero 2

\ə\ abut	\ng\ sing
\ər\ further	\ō\ bone
\a\ mat	\o\ saw
\ā\ take	\oi\ coin
\ä\ cot, cart	\th\ thin
\au\ out	\th\ this
\ch\ chin	\ü\ food
\e\ pet	\u\ foot
\ē\ easy	\y\ yet
\g\ go	\yü\ few
\i\ tip	\yu\ cure
\ī\ life	\zh\ vision
\j\ job	

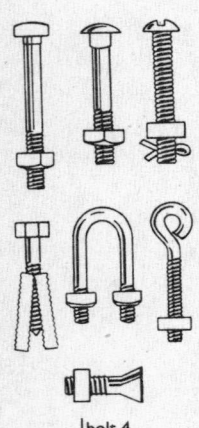

¹**bolt 4**

bo·lom·e·ter \bə-'läm-ət-ər\ *n* : a very sensitive thermometer based on varying electrical resistance and
used to measure feeble thermal radiation [Greek *bolē*
"stroke, beam of light"]

Bol·she·vik \'bōl-shə-ˌvik\ *n, pl* **Bolsheviks** *or* **Bol·she·vi·-
ki** \ˌbōl-shə-'vik-ē\ **1** : a member of the radical wing
of the Russian Social Democratic party that favored the
overthrow of capitalism by force and seized power in
Russia by the revolution of November 1917 **2** :
COMMUNIST [Russian *bol'shevik,* from *bol'she* "larger"]
— **Bolshevik** *adj*

Bol·she·vism \'bōl-shə-ˌviz-əm\ *n* : the doctrine or program of the Bolsheviks

Bol·she·vist \-vəst\ *n* : BOLSHEVIK — **Bolshevist** *adj*

¹**bol·ster** \'bōl-stər\ *n* **1** : a long pillow or cushion extending the full width of a bed **2** : a structural part
designed to eliminate friction or provide support [Old
English]

²**bolster** *vt* **bol·stered; bol·ster·ing** \-stə-riŋ, -striŋ\ :
to support with or as if with a bolster; *also* : REINFORCE
— **bol·ster·er** \-stər-ər\ *n*

¹**bolt** \'bōlt\ *n* **1 a** : a shaft or missile for a crossbow or
catapult **b** : a lightning stroke : THUNDERBOLT **2** : a sliding bar used to fasten a door **3** : the part of a lock
worked by a key **4** : a metal pin or rod usually with a
head at one end and a screw thread at the other that is
used to hold something in place **5** : a roll of cloth or
wallpaper of a specified length **6** : the breech closure
of a breech-loading firearm [Old English]

²**bolt** *vb* **1** : to move suddenly or nervously **2** : to move
rapidly : DASH ⟨reporters *bolted* for the door⟩ **3** : to run
away ⟨the horse shied and *bolted*⟩ **4** : to break away
from or oppose (as one's political party) **5** : to say
impulsively : BLURT **6** : to fasten with a bolt **7** : to
swallow hastily or without chewing ⟨*bolted* down our
dinner and rushed out⟩ — **bolt·er** *n*

³**bolt** *n* : an act of bolting

⁴**bolt** *vt* : to sift (as flour) usually through fine-meshed
cloth [Old French *buleter,* of Germanic origin] — **bolt·-
er** *n*

bo·lus \'bō-ləs\ *n* : a rounded mass: as **a** : a large pill
b : a soft mass of chewed food [Greek *bōlos* "lump"]

¹**bomb** \'bäm\ *n* **1** : an explosive device fused to detonate under planned conditions **2** : a container in
which a substance (as an insecticide) is stored under
pressure and from which it is released in the form of a
fine spray **3** : a rounded mass of lava exploded from a
volcano [French *bombe,* from Italian *bomba*]

²**bomb** *vb* : to attack with bombs

¹**bom·bard** \'bäm-ˌbärd\ *n* : a cannon used in late medieval times chiefly to hurl large stones [Middle French
bombarde]

²**bom·bard** \bäm-'bärd, bəm-\ *vt* **1** : to attack with artillery **2** : to attack vigorously or persistently (as with
questions) **3** : to subject to the impact of rapidly moving particles (as electrons or alpha rays) — **bom·bard·-
ment** \-mənt\ *n*

bom·bar·dier \ˌbäm-bə-'diər, -bər-\ *n* : a member of a
bomber crew whose duty is to release the bombs

bom·bast \'bäm-ˌbast\ *n* : pompous speech or writing
[obsolete *bombast* "padding", from Middle French
bombace "cotton", derived from Latin *bombyx* "silkworm, silk", from Greek] — **bom·bas·tic** \bäm-'bas-
tik\ *adj* — **bom·bas·ti·cal·ly** \-ti-kə-lē, -klē\ *adv*

bom·ba·zine \ˌbäm-bə-'zēn\ *n* : a twilled and usually
silk fabric used especially for mourning wear [Middle
French *bombasin,* derived from Latin *bombyx* "silk"]

bomb bay *n* : a bomb-carrying compartment in the underside of a combat airplane

bomb·er \'bäm-ər\ *n* : one that bombs; *esp* : an airplane designed for dropping bombs

bom·bi·nate \'bäm-bə-ˌnāt\ *vi* : DRONE, BUZZ [derived
from Latin *bombus* "deep hollow sound"] — **bom·bi·-
na·tion** \ˌbäm-bə-'nā-shən\ *n*

bomb·proof \'bäm-'prüf\ *adj* : safe against the explosive force of bombs

bomb·shell \'bäm-ˌshel\ *n* **1** : BOMB 1 **2** : a stunning or
upsetting surprise

bomb·sight \-ˌsīt\ *n* : a sighting device on an airplane
for aiming bombs

bo·na fide \'bō-nə-ˌfīd, 'bän-ə-; ˌbō-nə-'fīd-ē, -'fīd-ə\ **1
a** : made or carried out in good faith without fraud or
deceit ⟨a *bona fide* offer⟩ **b** : acting in good faith without fraud or deceit ⟨*bona fide* purchasers⟩ **2** : GENUINE
1 ⟨a *bona fide* cowboy⟩ [Latin, "in good faith"] SYN see
AUTHENTIC

bo·nan·za \bə-'nan-zə\ *n* **1** : a rich mass of ore in a
mine **2** : something that brings a rich return [Spanish,
literally, "fair weather", from Medieval Latin *bona-
cia,* alteration of Latin *malacia* "calm at sea", from
Greek *malakia,* literally, "softness", from *malakos*
"soft"]

Bo·na·part·ism \'bō-nə-ˌpärt-ˌiz-əm\ *n* : a political
movement associated chiefly with authoritarian rule
[Napoleon *Bonaparte*] — **Bo·na·part·ist** \-ˌpärt-əst\ *n*

bon·bon \'bän-ˌbän\ *n* : a candy with chocolate or fondant coating and a soft center with fruits and nuts
sometimes added [French, from *bon* "good"]

¹**bond** \'bänd\ *n* **1** : something that restrains : FETTER
2 : a binding agreement **3 a** : material or a device for
binding **b** : an attractive force that acts between atoms, ions, or groups of atoms and holds them together
in a molecule or crystal **c** : a cementing material that
combines, unites, or strengthens **4** : a tie of loyalty,
sentiment, or friendship **5 a** : a pledge to do an act or
pay a sum on or before a stated day or to forfeit a sum
if the pledge is not fulfilled **b** : one that gives bail or
acts as surety **c** : a certificate bearing interest and
promising payment of a certain sum on or before a
stated day and issued by a government or corporation
as an evidence of indebtedness **d** : insurance taken out
by a party (as a contractor) to insure another against
his failure to perform an obligation **6** : a binding or
connection made by overlapping parts of a structure
(as in laying brick) **7** : the state of goods manufactured, stored, or transported under the care of bonded
agencies until taxes on them are paid [Old Norse
band]

²**bond** *vb* **1** : to protect or secure by or operate under a
bond ⟨*bonded* locksmiths⟩; *esp* : to secure payment of
taxes on (goods) by giving a bond **2 a** : to cause to
adhere firmly **b** : to embed in a cementing material **c** :
to hold together or make solid by or as if by means of a
bond or binder — **bond·able** \'bän-də-bəl\ *adj* —
bond·er *n*

bond·age \'bän-dij\ *n* : involuntary personal servitude
(as serfdom or slavery) [Middle English *bonde* "peasant, serf", from Old English *bōnda* "householder",
from Old Norse *bōndi*]

bond·hold·er \'bänd-ˌhōl-dər\ *n* : the owner of a government or corporation bond

bond·man \'bänd-mən, 'bän-\ *n* : SERF, SLAVE

bond paper *n* : a strong durable paper used especially
for documents

bond servant *n* : a person bound to service without
wages; *also* : SLAVE

¹**bonds·man** \'bänz-mən\ *n* : BONDMAN

²**bondsman** *n* : SURETY 3

bond·wom·an \'bän-ˌdwum-ən\ *n* : a woman who is a
slave or serf

¹**bone** \'bōn\ *n* **1 a** : the hard largely calcareous connective tissue of which the skeleton of most vertebrate
animals is formed; *also* : one of the hard pieces in
which this tissue occurs ⟨break a *bone*⟩ **b** : a similar
hard animal substance (as whalebone or ivory) **2 a**
pl : something (as dice) usually or originally made
from bone **b** : STAY 1b **3** *pl* : an end man in a minstrel
show [Old English *bān*] — **bone·less** \-ləs\ *adj* —
bone to pick : a matter to argue or complain about

²bone *vb* **1** : to remove the bones from ⟨*bone* a fish⟩ **2** : to provide (a garment) with stays **3** : to study hard ⟨*bone* up on math⟩

bone black *n* : the black chiefly carbon residue of bones heated in a closed vessel that is used especially as a pigment or a decolorizing material — called also **bone char**

bone–dry \'bōn-'drī\ *adj* : very dry

bone·fish \'bōn-ˌfish\ *n* **1** : a slender silvery small=scaled fish that is a sport and food fish of warm seas **2** : LADYFISH

bone·head \-ˌhed\ *n* : a stupid person : NUMSKULL — **bone·head·ed** \-'hed-əd\ *adj*

bone meal *n* : fertilizer or feed made of crushed or ground bone

bon·er \'bō-nər\ *n* **1** : one that bones **2** : a stupid or ridiculous mistake

bon·fire \'bän-ˌfīr\ *n* : a large fire built in the open air [Middle English *bonefire* "fire of bones"]

bong \'bäng, 'bóng\ *n* : a deep resonant sound (as of a bell) [imitative] — **bong** *vb*

bon·go \'bäng-gō\ *n, pl* **bongos** *also* **bongoes** : one of a pair of small tuned drums played with the hands [American Spanish *bongó*]

bon·ho·mie *also* **bon·hom·mie** \ˌbän-ə-'mē, ˌbō-nə-\ *n* : good-natured easy friendliness : GENIALITY [French *bonhomie*, from *bonhomme* "good-natured man", from *bon* "good" + *homme* "man"]

bon·i·face \'bän-ə-fəs, -ˌfās\ *n* : the proprietor of a hotel, nightclub, or restaurant [*Boniface*, innkeeper in *The Beaux' Stratagem* (1707), play by George Farquhar]

bo·ni·to \bə-'nēt-ō, -'nēt-ə\ *n, pl* **bonitos** *or* **bonito** : any of various medium-sized tunas [Spanish, from *bonito* "pretty", from Latin *bonus* "good"]

bon mot \bōⁿ-'mō\ *n, pl* **bons mots** \bōⁿ-'mō, -'mōz\ *or* **bon mots** \-'mō, -'mōz\ : a clever remark : WITTICISM [French, literally, "good word"]

bon·net \'bän-ət\ *n* **1** : a head covering often tied under the chin by ribbons or strings and now worn mostly by small children **2** : a soft woolen cap worn by men in Scotland **3** : the headdress of an American Indian **4** *British* : an automobile hood [Middle French *bonet*]

bon·ny *also* **bon·nie** \'bän-ē\ *adj, chiefly British* : having a pleasing look or quality [Old French *bon* "good", from Latin *bonus*] — **bon·ni·ly** \'bän-l-ē\ *adv*

bon·sai \bōn-'sī, 'bōn-ˌ\ *n, pl* **bonsai** : a potted plant (as a tree) dwarfed by special methods of culture [Japanese]

bon·spiel \'bän-ˌspēl\ *n* : a match or tournament between curling clubs [perhaps from Dutch *bond* "league" + *spel* "game"]

bon ton \bän-'tän, 'bän-ˌ\ *n* **1** : fashionable manner or style **2** : the fashionable or proper thing [French, literally, "good tone"]

bo·nus \'bō-nəs\ *n* : something given in addition to what is usual or strictly due; *esp* : money given in addition to salary or wages [Latin, "good"]

bon vi·vant \ˌbän-vē-'vänt, ˌbōⁿ-vē-'väⁿ\ *n, pl* **bons vivants** \ˌbän-vē-'vänts; ˌbōⁿ-vē-'väⁿ, -'väⁿz\ *or* **bon vivants** *same*\ : a person having cultivated or refined tastes especially in food and drink [French, literally, "good liver"]

bon voy·age \ˌbōⁿv-ˌwī-'äzh, -ˌwä-'yäzh; ˌbōⁿ-ˌvói-'äzh, ˌbän-\ *n* : FAREWELL 1 — often used interjectionally [French, literally, "good trip"]

bony \'bō-nē\ *adj* **bon·i·er; -est** **1** : of or relating to bone ⟨the *bony* structure of the body⟩ **2** : full of bones **3** : resembling bone especially in hardness ⟨a *bony* substance⟩ **4** : having large or prominent bones ⟨a rugged *bony* face⟩ **5** : SCRAWNY, SKINNY ⟨*bony* underfed children⟩

bony fish *n* : any of a class (Teleostomi) comprising higher fishes with usually well-developed bony skeletons

¹boo \'bü\ *interj* — used to express contempt or disapproval or to startle or frighten [Middle English *bo*]

²boo *n* : a shout of disapproval or contempt — **boo** *vb*

boob \'büb\ *n* **1** : SIMPLETON **2** : BOOR 2b [short for *booby*]

boo-boo \'bü-ˌbü\ *n* **1** : a usually small bruise or scratch especially on a child **2** : a foolish mistake [probably alteration of *boohoo*, imitative of the sound of weeping]

boo·by \'bü-bē\ *n, pl* **boobies** **1** : a foolish person : DOPE **2** : any of several small tropical gannets [Spanish *bobo*, from Latin *balbus* "stammering"]

booby prize *n* : an award for the poorest performance in a game or competition

booby trap *n* : a trap for a careless or unwary person; *esp* : a concealed explosive device set to go off when some harmless-looking object is touched — **boo·by-trap** \'bü-bē-ˌtrap\ *vt*

boo·dle \'büd-l\ *n* **1** : a large group of people : CROWD **2** : bribe money [Dutch *boedel* "estate, lot"]

boo·gie-woo·gie \ˌbùg-ē-'wùg-ē, ˌbüg-ē-'wüg-ē\ *n* : a percussive style of playing blues on the piano characterized by a steady rhythmic bass and a simple often improvised melody — called also *boogie* [origin unknown]

¹book \'bùk\ *n* **1 a** : a set of written, printed, or blank sheets of paper bound together into a volume **b** : a long written or printed literary composition **c** : a major division of a literary work **d** : a volume of business records (as a ledger) **2** *cap* : BIBLE 1 **3** : something regarded as a source of enlightenment or instruction **4 a** : all the knowledge available about a task or problem ⟨tried every trick in the *book* to win⟩ **b** : the standards or authority relevant in a situation ⟨follow the *book* and you'll be all right⟩ **5** : all the charges that can be made against an accused person ⟨threw the *book* at them⟩ **6 a** : LIBRETTO **b** : the script of a play **7** : a packet of commodities bound together ⟨a *book* of matches⟩ **8** : the bets registered by a bookmaker **9** : the tricks a cardplayer must win before scoring [Old English *bōc*] — **in one's book** : in one's opinion — **in one's good books** : in favor with one — **one for the book** : an act or occurrence worth noting

²book *vb* **1 a** : to engage transportation or reserve lodgings **b** : to schedule engagements for ⟨*book* an entertainer⟩ **2** : to enter charges against in a police register — **book·er** *n*

³book *adj* **1** : derived from books ⟨*book* learning⟩ **2** : shown by books of account ⟨*book* value⟩

book·bind·ing \'bùk-ˌbīn-ding\ *n* **1** : the binding of a book **2** : the art or trade of binding books — **book·bind·er** *n* — **book·bind·ery** \-də-rē, -drē\ *n*

book·case \'bùk-ˌkās\ *n* : a piece of furniture consisting of shelves to hold books

book·end \'bùk-ˌend\ *n* : a support placed at the end of a row of books to hold them up

book·ie \'bùk-ē\ *n* : BOOKMAKER

book·ish \'bùk-ish\ *adj* **1** : fond of books and reading **2** : inclined to rely on knowledge from books rather than practical experience **3** : resembling or derived from the language of books : FORMAL ⟨many English words derived from Latin have a *bookish* tone⟩ — **book·ish·ly** *adv* — **book·ish·ness** *n*

book·keep·er \'bùk-ˌkē-pər\ *n* : a person who keeps accounts (as of a business) — **book·keep·ing** \-ping\ *n*

□ SYN ACCOUNTANT: a BOOKKEEPER keeps regular, concise, accurate records of business transactions by entering them in account books; an ACCOUNTANT is an expert bookkeeper who may be employed to organize or set up a system of records or to investigate or report upon the financial condition of an organization.

book·let \'bùk-lət\ *n* : a little book; *esp* : PAMPHLET

\ə\	abut	\ng\	sing
\ər\	further	\ō\	bone
\a\	mat	\ó\	saw
\ā\	take	\ói\	coin
\ä\	cot, cart	\th\	thin
\aù\	out	\th\	this
\ch\	chin	\ü\	food
\e\	pet	\ù\	foot
\ē\	easy	\y\	yet
\g\	go	\yü\	few
\i\	tip	\yù\	cure
\ī\	life	\zh\	vision
\j\	job		

book louse *n* : any of several tiny wingless insects (order Corrodentia) injurious especially to books

book lung *n* : a specialized breathing organ of spiders and related animals containing numerous thin folds of membrane arranged like the leaves of a book

book·mak·er \'bùk-,mā-kər\ *n* : one who determines odds and receives and pays off bets — **book·mak·ing** \-king\ *n*

book·mark \'bùk-,märk\ *or* **book·mark·er** \-,mär-kər\ *n* : a marker for keeping one's place in a book

book·mo·bile \'bùk-mō-,bēl\ *n* : a vehicle that serves as a traveling library [*book* + auto*mobile*]

Book of Common Prayer : the service book of the Anglican Communion

book·plate \'bùk-,plāt\ *n* : a label placed in a book showing who owns it

book review *n* : a critical estimate of a book

book·sell·er \'bùk-,sel-ər\ *n* : the proprietor of a bookstore

book·stall \-,stol\ *n* **1** : a stall where books are sold **2** *chiefly British* : NEWSSTAND

book·store \-,stōr, -,stòr\ *n* : a retail store where books are the main item for sale — called also *bookshop*

book·worm \-,wərm\ *n* **1** : any of various insect larvae that feed on the binding and paste of books **2** : a person unusually devoted to reading and study

Bool·ean algebra \'bü-lē-ən-\ *n* : a mathematical set together with two commutative operations (as the taking of unions and intersections of subsets) whose rules of combination can be described by any of various equivalent systems of postulates [George *Boole*, died 1864, English mathematician]

¹boom \'büm\ *n* **1** : a long pole; *esp* : one for stretching the bottom of a sail **2 a** : a long beam projecting from the mast of a derrick to support or guide the thing that is being lifted **b** : a long movable arm used to manipulate a microphone **3** : a line of connected floating timbers to hold logs together in a river [Dutch, "tree, beam, boom"]

²boom *vb* **1** : to make a deep hollow sound **2 a** : to increase in esteem or importance **b** : to experience a boom (as in growth) **3** : to cause to resound — often used with *out* 〈their voices *boomed* out the song〉 [imitative]

³boom *n* **1** : a booming sound or cry **2** : a rapid expansion or increase: as **a** : a general movement in support of a candidate for office **b** : rapid settlement and development of a town or district **c** : a rapid widespread expansion of business activity

boom box *n* : a large portable radio and often tape player with two attached speakers

boo·mer·ang \'bü-mə-,rang\ *n* **1** : a curved club or stick usually somewhat flat that can be thrown so as to return near the starting point **2** : an act or utterance that backfires on its originator [from an indigenous language of Australia] — **boomerang** *vi*

boom·town \'büm-,taun\ *n* : a town undergoing a sudden growth in business activity and population

¹boon \'bün\ *n* : FAVOR 2, KINDNESS: as **a** : one given in answer to a request **b** : a timely benefit : BLESSING [Old Norse *bōn* "petition"]

²boon *adj* : CONVIVIAL, MERRY 〈a *boon* companion〉 [Middle French *bon* "good", from Latin *bonus*]

boon·docks \'bün-,däks\ *n pl* **1** : rough country filled with dense brush **2** : a rural area : STICKS [Tagalog *bundok* "mountain"]

boon·dog·gle \'bün-,däg-əl, -,dòg-\ *n* : a trivial, useless, or wasteful activity [coined by Robert H. Link, died 1957, American scoutmaster] — **boondoggle** *vi* — **boon·dog·gler** \-,däg-lər, -ə-lər\ *n*

boor \'bùr\ *n* **1** : PEASANT 1 **2 a** : a rough clownish rustic : BUMPKIN **b** : a rude or insensitive person [Dutch *boer*]

boor·ish \'bùr-ish\ *adj* : resembling a boor : RUDE — **boor·ish·ly** *adv* — **boor·ish·ness** *n*

boomerang 1

bootjack

¹boost \'büst\ *vt* **1** : to push or shove up from below **2** : to make greater especially in amount 〈*boost* prices〉 〈*boost* morale〉 **3** : to promote enthusiastically the cause or interests of [origin unknown] SYN see LIFT

²boost *n* **1** : a push upward **2** : an increase in amount **3** : an act that brings help or encouragement

boost·er \'bü-stər\ *n* : one that boosts: as **a** : an enthusiastic supporter **b** : a device for strengthening radio or television signals **c** : a supplementary dose of an immunizing agent given to maintain or revive a previously established immunity **d** : the first stage of a multistage rocket providing thrust for the launching and the initial part of the flight

¹boot \'büt\ *n, chiefly dialect* : something to equalize a trade [Old English *bōt* "advantage, remedy"] — **to boot** : ²BESIDES

²boot *vb, archaic* : to be of use : HELP, PROFIT

³boot *n* **1** : a covering (as of leather or rubber) for the foot and leg **2** : a protective sheath or casing **3** : a navy or marine corps recruit undergoing basic training **4** *British* : an automobile trunk **5 a** : a kick with the foot **b** : an abrupt discharge or dismissal [Middle French *bote*]

⁴boot *vt* **1** : to put boots on **2 a** : KICK **b** : to eject or discharge abruptly — often used with *out* 〈was *booted* out of the office〉 **3 a** : to load (a program) into a computer from a disk **b** : to start or make ready for use especially by booting a program 〈*boot* a microcomputer〉

boot·black \'büt-,blak\ *n* : a person who shines boots and shoes

boot camp *n* : a camp for the basic training of navy or marine recruits

boot·ee *or* **boot·ie** \'büt-ē\ *n* : an infant's knitted or crocheted sock

Bo·ö·tes \bō-'ōt-ēz\ *n* : a northern constellation containing the bright star Arcturus [Greek *Boōtēs*, literally, "plowman", from *bous* "head of cattle"]

booth \'büth\ *n, pl* **booths** \'büthz, 'büths\ **1** : a temporary shelter **2 a** : a stall or stand (as at a fair) for the sale or exhibition of goods **b** (1) : a small enclosure affording privacy for one person at a time 〈voting *booth*〉 〈telephone *booth*〉 (2) : a small enclosure that separates its occupant from customers or patrons 〈a ticket *booth*〉 **c** : a restaurant accommodation consisting of a table between two backed benches [Middle English *bothe*, of Scandinavian origin]

boot·jack \'büt-,jak\ *n* : a V-shaped device used in pulling off boots

¹boot·leg \'büt-,leg\ *n* : something bootlegged; *esp* : MOONSHINE 3 — **bootleg** *adj*

²boot·leg *vb* **1** : to make or transport for sale alcoholic liquor contrary to law **2 a** : to produce or sell illicitly **b** : SMUGGLE 1 [from the carrying of illicit liquor concealed in the leg of a boot] — **boot·leg·ger** \-,leg-ər\ *n*

boot·less \'büt-ləs\ *adj* : FRUITLESS 2 — **boot·less·ly** *adv* — **boot·less·ness** *n*

boot·lick \-,lik\ *vb* : to fawn on : curry favor — **boot·lick·er** *n*

boo·ty \'büt-ē\ *n* **1** : SPOIL 1b; *esp* : goods seized from the enemy in war **2** : a rich gain or prize [Middle French *butin*]

¹booze \'büz\ *vi* : to drink intoxicating liquor to excess [Middle Dutch *būsen*] — **booz·er** \'bü-zər\ *n*

²booze *n* : intoxicating liquor — **booz·i·ly** \'bü-zə-lē\ *adv* — **boozy** \'bü-zē\ *adj*

bor·age \'bòr-ij, 'bär-\ *n* : a hairy blue-flowered European herb used medicinally and in salads [Middle French *bourage*]

bo·rate \'bōr-,āt, 'bòr-\ *n* : a salt or ester of a boric acid

bo·rax \'bōr-,aks, 'bòr-\ *n* : a crystalline slightly alkaline compound $Na_2B_4O_7 \cdot 10H_2O$ that is a borate of sodium, occurs as a mineral, and is used as a flux, cleansing agent, and antiseptic [Medieval Latin, from Arabic *būraq*, from Persian *būrah*]

Bo·ra·zon \'bȯr-ə-ˌzän, 'bȯr-\ *trademark* — used for a boron nitride abrasive

bor·deaux mixture \bȯr-'dō-\ *n, often cap B* : a fungicide made by reaction of copper sulfate, lime, and water

¹**bor·der** \'bȯrd-ər\ *n* **1** : an outer part or edge **2** : FRONTIER 1, BOUNDARY **3** : a narrow bed of plants along the edge of a garden or walk **4** : an ornamental design at the edge of a fabric or rug [Middle French *bordure*, from *border* "to border", from *bort* "border", of Germanic origin] — **bor·dered** \-ərd\ *adj* □ SYN BORDER, EDGE, MARGIN mean a line or narrow space marking the limit or outermost bound of something. A BORDER is that part of a surface lying along its boundary line; EDGE denotes specifically the terminating line made by two converging surfaces as of a blade or a box; MARGIN suggests a border of definite width or distinctive character ⟨the sandy *margin* of the sea⟩

²**border** *vb* **bor·dered; bor·der·ing** \'bȯrd-ring, -ə-ring\ **1** : to put a border on **2** : to touch at the edge or boundary : BOUND **3** : to lie on the border of something ⟨the town *borders* on the sea⟩ **4** : to approach the nature of a specified thing : VERGE ⟨*border* on the ridiculous⟩ — **bor·der·er** \-ər-ər\ *n*

bor·der·land \'bȯrd-ər-ˌland\ *n* **1** : territory at or near a border : FRONTIER **2** : a vague intermediate state or region ⟨the *borderland* between fantasy and reality⟩

bor·der·line \-ˌlīn\ *adj* **1** : situated at or near a border or boundary **2 a** : situated between two points or states : INTERMEDIATE **b** : not quite average, normal, or acceptable ⟨*borderline* intelligence⟩ ⟨a *borderline* joke⟩

¹**bore** \'bōr, 'bȯr\ *vb* **1** : to pierce with or as if with a rotary tool ⟨*bore* a piece of wood⟩ **2** : to make by piercing or drilling ⟨*bore* a well⟩ **3** : to make a hole by boring [Old English *borian*]

²**bore** *n* **1** : a hole made by or as if by boring **2** : an interior lengthwise cylindrical cavity; *esp* : the interior cavity of a gun **3 a** : the diameter of a hole or tube; *esp* : the interior diameter of a gun barrel **b** : the diameter of an engine cylinder

³**bore** *past of* BEAR

⁴**bore** *n* : a tidal flood with a high abrupt front [Old Norse *bāra* "wave"]

⁵**bore** *n* : one that causes boredom [origin unknown]

⁶**bore** *vt* : to weary by being dull or monotonous

bo·re·al \'bōr-ē-əl, 'bȯr-\ *adj* : of, relating to, or located or growing in northern or mountainous regions ⟨*boreal* coniferous forests⟩ [Greek *Boreas* "north wind, north"]

bore·dom \'bōrd-əm, 'bȯrd-\ *n* : the state of being bored

bor·er \'bōr-ər, 'bȯr-\ *n* : one that bores: as **a** : a tool used for boring **b** (1) : SHIPWORM (2) : an insect that as a larva or an adult bores in the woody parts of plants

bo·ric acid \'bōr-ik-, 'bȯr-\ *n* : a white crystalline weak acid H_3BO_3 easily obtained from its salts and used especially as a mild antiseptic

bor·ing \'bōr-ing, 'bȯr-\ *adj* : causing boredom : TIRESOME

born \'bȯrn\ *adj* **1 a** : brought into life by birth **b** : NATIVE 2 ⟨American-*born*⟩ **2** : having from birth special natural abilities or character ⟨a *born* leader⟩ **3** : destined from or as if from birth ⟨*born* to succeed⟩ [Old English *boren*, past participle of *beran* "to bear"]

borne *past participle of* BEAR

born·ite \'bȯr-ˌnīt\ *n* : a brittle metallic-looking mineral Cu_5FeS_4 consisting of a sulfide of copper and iron and constituting a valuable ore of copper [Ignaz von *Born*, died 1791, Austrian mineralogist]

bo·ron \'bōr-ˌän, 'bȯr-\ *n* : a metalloid element found in nature only in combination (as in borax) — see ELEMENT table [*borax* + *-on* (as in *carbon*)]

bor·ough \'bər-ō\ *n* **1 a** : a town or urban constituency in Great Britain that sends a member to Parliament **b** : a self-governing incorporated urban area in Great Britain **2 a** : a municipal corporation in some states corresponding to the incorporated town or village of the other states **b** : one of the five constituent political divisions of New York City **3** : a civil division of the state of Alaska corresponding to a county in most other states [Old English *burg* "fortified town"]

bor·row \'bär-ō\ *vb* **1** : to take or receive something with the promise or intention of returning it **2** : to take for one's own use ⟨*borrow* a phrase⟩ **3** : to take 1 from a digit of the minuend in subtraction and add it as 10 to the digit holding the next lower place [Old English *borgian*] — **bor·row·er** \'bär-ə-wər\ *n*

borscht \'bȯrsht, 'bȯrsh\ *also* **borsch** \'bȯrsh\ *n* : a soup made largely of beets and served hot or cold often with sour cream [Yiddish *borsht* or Russian *borshch*]

bor·zoi \'bȯr-ˌzȯi\ *n* : any of a breed of large long-haired dogs of the greyhound type developed in Russia especially for pursuing wolves [Russian *borzoĭ*, from *borzoĭ* "swift"]

bos·cage *also* **bos·kage** \'bäs-kij\ *n* : a growth of shrubs or trees : THICKET [Middle French *boscage*, from *bois, bosc* "forest"]

bosh \'bäsh\ *n* : foolish talk [Turkish *baş* "empty"]

bosky \'bäs-kē\ *adj* : covered with trees or shrubs [Middle English *bush, bosk* "bush"]

bo·s'n *or* **bo·sun** *variant of* BOATSWAIN

¹**bos·om** \'búz-əm\ *n* **1** : the front of the human chest; *esp* : the female breasts **2 a** : the center of secret thoughts and feelings **b** : intimate association ⟨something only whispered in the *bosom* of the family⟩ **3** : the part of a garment covering the breast [Old English *bōsm*] — **bos·omed** \-əmd\ *adj*

²**bosom** *adj* : CLOSE, INTIMATE ⟨*bosom* friends⟩

¹**boss** \'bäs, 'bȯs\ *n* : a projecting and typically rounded part; *also* : a raised or projecting ornament (as on a shield or a ceiling) [Old French *boce*]

²**boss** *vt* : to ornament with bosses : EMBOSS

³**boss** \'bȯs\ *n* **1** : one who has control or authority; *esp* : one who directs or supervises workers **2 a** : a politician who controls votes or dictates appointments or legislative measures **b** : an official having dictatorial authority over an organization [Dutch *baas* "master"] — **boss** *adj* — **boss·ism** \-ˌiz-əm\ *n*

⁴**boss** \'bȯs\ *vt* **1** : to exercise control of : DIRECT **2** : ORDER ⟨refused to be *bossed* around⟩

bos·sa no·va \ˌbäs-ə-'nō-və\ *n* **1** : a Brazilian dance characterized by the step pattern of the samba and a subtle bounce **2** : music influenced by jazz and rhythmically similar to the samba [Portuguese, literally, "new trend"]

¹**bossy** \'bȯ-sē\ *n, pl* **boss·ies** : COW 2 [English dialect *buss, boss* "young calf"]

²**bossy** *adj* **boss·i·er; -est** : inclined to act like a boss — **boss·i·ness** *n*

Bos·ton cream pie \'bȯ-stən-\ *n* : a rich cake that is usually split, filled with custard or cream, and often topped with icing [*Boston*, Massachusetts]

Boston fern *n* : a fern widely grown for its often drooping much-divided fronds

Boston ivy *n* : a woody Asian vine of the grape family with 3-lobed leaves that is often grown over walls

Boston terrier *n* : any of a breed of small smooth-coated brindle or black terriers with white markings — called also *Boston bull*

bot \'bät\ *n* : the larva of a botfly [perhaps from Scottish Gaelic *boiteag* "maggot"]

¹**bo·tan·i·cal** \bə-'tan-i-kəl\ *also* **bo·tan·ic** \-ik\ *adj* : of or relating to plants or botany — **bo·tan·i·cal·ly** \-i-kə-lē, -klē\ *adv*

²**botanical** *n* : a vegetable drug especially in the crude state

\ə\	abut	\ng\	sing
\ər\	further	\ō\	bone
\a\	mat	\ȯ\	saw
\ā\	take	\ȯi\	coin
\ä\	cot, cart	\th\	thin
\aú\	out	\th\	this
\ch\	chin	\ü\	food
\e\	pet	\ú\	foot
\ē\	easy	\y\	yet
\g\	go	\yü\	few
\i\	tip	\yú\	cure
\ī\	life	\zh\	vision
\j\	job		

bot·a·nize \'bät-n-ˌīz\ *vi* : to collect and study plants

bot·a·ny \'bät-n-ē, 'bät-nē\ *n* **1** : a branch of biology dealing with plant life **2 a** : plant life ⟨the *botany* of a region⟩ **b** : the biology of a plant or plant group [Greek *botanē* "pasture, herb", from *boskein* "to graze"] — **bot·a·nist** \'bät-n-əst, 'bät-nəst\ *n*

¹botch \'bäch\ *vt* **1** : to repair or patch poorly **2** : BUNGLE [Middle English *bocchen*]

²botch *n* : a botched job : BUNGLE, MESS — **botchy** \-ē\ *adj*

bot·fly \'bät-ˌflī\ *n* : any of various stout two-winged flies whose larvae are parasitic in cavities or tissues of various mammals

¹both \'bōth\ *adj* : being the two : involving the one and the other ⟨*both* feet⟩ [Old Norse *bāthir*]

²both *pron, pl in construction* : the one as well as the other ⟨*both* of us⟩ ⟨we are *both* well⟩

³both *conj* — used as a function word to indicate and stress the inclusion of each of two or more things specified by coordinated words, phrases, or clauses ⟨*both* New York and London⟩

¹both·er \'bäth-ər\ *vb* **both·ered; both·er·ing** \'bäth-ring, -ə-ring\ **1 a** : to upset with often minor annoyances : TRY **b** : to intrude upon : INTERRUPT **2 a** : to cause to be anxious or concerned : TROUBLE **b** : to feel concern or anxiety **3** : to take pains : make an effort ⟨don't *bother* to knock⟩ [perhaps from Irish Gaelic *bodhar* "bothered"]

²bother *n* **1 a** : a state of petty annoyance **b** : something that causes such a state **2** : FUSS 2, DISTURBANCE

both·er·some \'bäth-ər-səm\ *adj* : causing bother

¹bot·tle \'bät-l\ *n* **1 a** : a container typically of glass or plastic with a narrow neck and mouth and usually no handle **b** : a bag made of skin **c** : the quantity held by a bottle **2 a** : intoxicating drink ⟨hit the *bottle*⟩ **b** : bottled milk used in place of mother's milk [Middle French *bouteille*, derived from Late Latin *buttis* "cask"] — **bot·tle·ful** \-ˌfúl\ *n*

²bottle *vt* **bot·tled; bot·tling** \'bät-ling, -l-ing\ **1** : to put into a bottle **2** : to confine or hold back as if in a bottle — usually used with *up* — **bot·tler** \'bät-lər, -l-ər\ *n*

bottled gas *n* : gas under pressure in portable cylinders

bot·tle·neck \'bät-l-ˌnek\ *n* **1** : a narrow passageway **2** : a place, condition, or point where progress is held up ⟨a *bottleneck* for traffic⟩ **3** : a style of guitar playing using an object (as a metal bar) pressed against the strings

bot·tle–nosed dolphin \'bät-l-ˌnōz-\ *n* : any of various moderately large stout-bodied toothed whales with a prominent beak and sickle-shaped dorsal fin — called also **bottle-nosed porpoise**

¹bot·tom \'bät-əm\ *n* **1 a** : the under surface of something **b** : a supporting surface or part : BASE **c** : BUTTOCK 2 **2** : the bed of a body of water **3 a** : the part of a ship's hull lying below the water **b** : BOAT, SHIP **4** : the lowest part, place, or point ⟨the *bottom* of the page⟩ **5** : low land along a river ⟨the Mississippi river *bottoms*⟩ **6** *pl* : the trousers of pajamas **7** : the main plowing mechanism of a plow [Old English *botm*] — **bot·tomed** \-əmd\ *adj* — **at bottom** : BASICALLY, REALLY

²bottom *vb* : to rest on, bring to, or reach the bottom

bot·tom·land \'bät-əm-ˌland\ *n* : BOTTOM 5

bot·tom·less \-ləs\ *adj* **1** : having no bottom **2** : very deep — **bot·tom·less·ly** *adv* — **bot·tom·less·ness** *n*

bot·u·lism \'bäch-ə-ˌliz-əm\ *n* : an acute food poisoning caused by bacterial toxin formed by clostridia in food [from *Clostridium botulinum*, a species of bacterium]

bou·clé *or* **bou·cle** \bü-'klā\ *n* **1** : a yarn made of three plies one of which is looped at intervals **2** : a fabric made from bouclé yarn [French *bouclé* "curly"]

bou·doir \'büd-ˌwär, 'bùd-\ *n* : a dressing room, bedroom, or private sitting room [French, from *bouder* "to pout"]

bouf·fant \bü-'fänt, 'bü-ˌ\ *adj* : puffed out ⟨*bouffant* hairdos⟩ [French, from Middle French *bouffer* "to puff"]

bough \'baú\ *n* : a branch of a tree; *esp* : a main branch [Old English *bōg* "shoulder, bough"] — **boughed** \'baúd\ *adj*

bought *past of* BUY

bouil·la·baisse \ˌbü-yə-'bäs\ *n* : a highly seasoned fish stew made of at least two kinds of fish [French]

bouil·lon \'búl-ˌyän, -yən; 'bü-ˌyän, 'bù-\ *n* : a clear seasoned soup made usually from lean beef or chicken [French, from *bouillir* "to boil"]

boul·der *also* **bowl·der** \'bōl-dər\ *n* : a large detached and rounded or much-worn mass of rock [of Scandinavian origin] — **boul·dery** \-də-rē, -drē\ *adj*

bou·le·vard \'búl-ə-ˌvärd, 'bül-\ *n* : a broad often landscaped thoroughfare [French, from Dutch *bolwerc* "bulwark"]

¹bounce \'baúns\ *vb* **1** : to rebound or cause to rebound **2 a** : DISMISS 2, FIRE **b** : to throw out from a place by force **3** : to recover quickly from a blow or defeat — usually used with *back* **4** : to be returned by a bank as no good ⟨the check *bounced*⟩ **5** : to leap suddenly : BOUND [Middle English *bounsen*]

²bounce *n* **1 a** : a sudden leap or bound **b** : a bouncing back : REBOUND **2** : ENERGY 1, LIVELINESS

bounc·er \'baún-sər\ *n* : one that bounces; *esp* : a person employed in a public place to remove disorderly patrons

bounc·ing \-sing\ *adj* : enjoying good health : ROBUST ⟨a *bouncing* baby⟩ — **bounc·ing·ly** \-sing-lē\ *adv*

bouncing bet \ˌbaún-sing-'bet\ *n, often cap 2d B* : a European perennial herb of the pink family that is widely naturalized in the United States and has pink and white flowers and leaves which yield a detergent when bruised — called also *soapwort* [*Bet*, nickname for Elizabeth]

¹bound \'baúnd\ *adj* : going or intending to go ⟨*bound* for home⟩ [Middle English *boun*, from Old Norse *būinn* "ready", from *būa* "to dwell, prepare"]

²bound *n* **1** : a boundary line (as of a piece of property) **2** : a point or a line beyond which one cannot go : LIMIT ⟨out of *bounds*⟩ **3** : the land within specific bounds — usually used in pl. [Old French *bodne*, from Medieval Latin *bodina*]

³bound *vt* **1** : to set limits to : CONFINE **2** : to form a bound or boundary of : ENCLOSE; *also* : ADJOIN 2 **3** : to name the boundaries of ⟨*bound* the state of Ohio⟩

⁴bound *adj* **1 a** : fastened by or as if by a band : CONFINED ⟨desk-*bound*⟩ **b** : CERTAIN, SURE ⟨*bound* to rain soon⟩ **2 a** : OBLIGED ⟨duty-*bound*⟩ **b** : RESOLVED, DETERMINED ⟨*bound* to have your own way⟩ **3** : always occurring in combination with another linguistic form (as *un-* in *unknown*, *-er* in *speaker*) — compare FREE 14 [from past participle of *bind*]

⁵bound *n* **1** : LEAP 1a, JUMP **2** : BOUNCE 1b, REBOUND [Middle French *bond*, from *bondir* "to leap"]

⁶bound *vi* **1** : to move by leaping **2** : REBOUND 1, BOUNCE

bound·a·ry \'baún-də-rē, -drē\ *n, pl* **-ries** : a line or strip that marks or shows a limit or end (as of a region or a piece of land) : a line that bounds, divides, or separates

bound·en \'baún-dən\ *adj* : OBLIGATORY, BINDING ⟨our *bounden* duty⟩

bound·er \'baún-dər\ *n* **1** : one that bounds **2** *chiefly British* : a person of objectionable social behavior : CAD, BOOR

bound·less \'baúnd-ləs\ *adj* : having no boundaries or limits : VAST — **bound·less·ly** *adv* — **bound·less·ness** *n*

boun·te·ous \'baúnt-ē-əs\ *adj* **1** : BOUNTIFUL 1 **2** : liberally provided or bestowed : AMPLE — **boun·te·ous·ly** *adv* — **boun·te·ous·ness** *n*

boun·ti·ful \'baunt-i-fəl\ *adj* **1** : giving liberally : GEN-EROUS ⟨a *bountiful* contributor⟩ **2** : PLENTIFUL, ABUN-DANT ⟨a *bountiful* supply⟩ SYN see GENEROUS — **boun-ti·ful·ly** \-fə-lē, -flē\ *adv* — **boun·ti·ful·ness** \-fəl-nəs\ *n*

boun·ty \'baunt-ē\ *n, pl* **bounties** **1 a** : GENEROSITY 1a **b** : something given generously **2** : money given as a reward or inducement (as for the killing of vermin) [Old French *bonté* "goodness", from Latin *bonitas*, from *bonus* "good"]

bou·quet \bō-'kā, bü-\ *n* **1** : a bunch of flowers **2** : FRA-GRANCE ⟨the *bouquet* of good wine⟩ [French, from Mid-dle French, "thicket", derived from Old French *bosc* "forest"]

bour·bon \'bùr-bən, *usually* 'bər- *in sense 3* \ *n* **1** *cap* : a member of a French family to which belong many kings of France, Spain, Naples, and the kingdom of the Two Sicilies **2** *often cap* : a person who clings firmly to outmoded social and political ideas **3** : a whiskey distilled from corn mash; *esp* : one distilled from a mash of corn, malt, and rye [from *Bourbon*, seigniory in France; sense 3 from *Bourbon* county, Kentucky] — **bour·bon·ism** \-bə-,niz-əm\ *n, often cap*

¹bour·geois \'bùrzh-,wä, bùrzh-'\ *n, pl* **bour·geois** \-,wä, -,wäz, -'wä, -'wäz\ **1 a** : an inhabitant of a borough or a town **b** : a middle-class person **2** : a person whose so-cial behavior and political views are held to be influ-enced by interest in private property; *esp* : CAPITALIST **3** *pl* : BOURGEOISIE [Middle French, derived from Old French *borc* "town", from Late Latin *burgus* "forti-fied place", of Germanic origin]

²bourgeois *adj* **1** : of, relating to, or characteristic of town dwellers or of the middle class **2** : marked by a concern for material interests and respectability and a leaning toward mediocrity **3** : controlled by commer-cial and industrial interests : CAPITALISTIC

bour·geoi·sie \,bùrzh-,wä-'zē\ *n,* **1** : the middle class **2** : a social order controlled by bourgeois [French, from *bourgeois*]

¹bourn *or* **bourne** \'bōrn, 'bórn, 'bùrn\ *n* : STREAM 1, BROOK [Middle English *burn, bourne*]

²bourn *or* **bourne** *n* **1** *archaic* : BOUNDARY, LIMIT **2** *ar-chaic* : GOAL 2, DESTINATION [Middle French *bourne*, alteration of Old French *bodne*]

bour·rée \bù-'rā\ *n* : a lively 17th century French dance [French]

bourse \'bùrs\ *n* : EXCHANGE 5a; *esp* : a European stock exchange [French, literally, "purse", from Medieval Latin *bur·sa*]

bout \'baùt\ *n* : a spell of activity: as **a** : an athletic match (as of boxing) **b** : OUTBREAK, ATTACK ⟨a *bout* of measles⟩ **c** : SESSION 5 ⟨a drinking *bout*⟩ [English dia-lect, "a trip going and returning in plowing", from Middle English *bought* "bend"]

bou·tique \bü-'tēk\ *n* : a small fashionable specialty shop; *also* : a small shop within a large department store [French, "shop"]

bou·ton·niere \,büt-n-'iər, ,bü-tən-'yeər\ *n* : a flower or bouquet worn in a buttonhole [French *boutonnière* "buttonhole", from *bouton* "button"]

¹bo·vine \'bō-,vīn, -,vēn\ *adj* **1** : of, relating to, or re-sembling the ox or cow **2** : both sluggish and patient ⟨a *bovine* disposition⟩ [Latin *bov-, bos* "ox, cow"]

²bovine *n* : a bovine animal

¹bow \'baù\ *vb* **1** : to bend the head, body, or knee in greeting, reverence, respect, or submission **2** : SUBMIT, YIELD ⟨*bow* to authority⟩ **3** : BEND ⟨*bowed* with age⟩ **4** : to express by bowing ⟨*bow* one's thanks⟩ [Old English *būgan* "to bend, bow"]

²bow *n* : a bending of the head or body in respect, sub-mission, agreement, or greeting

³bow \'bō\ *n* **1** : RAINBOW 1 **2** : a weapon for shooting arrows that is made of a strip of elastic material (as wood) bent by a cord connecting the two ends **3** :

something shaped in a curve like a bow : BEND **4** : a wooden rod with horsehairs stretched from end to end used for playing a violin or similar instrument **5** : a knot formed by doubling a ribbon or string into loops [Old English *boga*]

⁴bow \'bō\ *vb* **1** : to bend into a curve **2** : to play a stringed instrument with a bow

⁵bow \'baù\ *n* : the forward part of a ship [probably from Danish *bov* "shoulder, bow"]

bowd·ler·ize \'bōd-lə-,rīz, 'baùd-\ *vt* : to clean up (as a book) by removing or altering parts considered objec-tionable [Thomas *Bowdler*, died 1825, English editor of Shakespeare] — **bowd·ler·i·za·tion** \,bōd-lə-rə-'zā-shən, ,baùd-\ *n*

bow·el \'baù-əl, 'baùl\ *n* **1 a** : INTESTINE, GUT — usually used in pl. **b** : a division of the intestine **2** *archaic* : the seat of pity or tenderness — usually used in pl. **3** *pl* : the interior parts ⟨the *bowels* of the earth⟩ [Old French *boel*, derived from Latin *botulus* "sausage"]

bow·er \'baù-ər, 'baùr\ *n* **1** : a place for rest : RETREAT **2** : a shelter (as in a garden) made with tree boughs or vines twined together : ARBOR [Old English *būr* "dwelling"] — **bow·ery** \-ē\ *adj*

bow·er·bird \-,bərd\ *n* : any of various birds especially of Australia and New Guinea that build chambers or passages arched over with twigs and grasses

bow·fin \'bō-,fin\ *n* : a predaceous dull green irides-cent American freshwater fish related to the sturgeons

bow·ie knife \'bü-ē-, 'bō-ē-\ *n* : a stout straight single-edged hunting knife [James *Bowie*, died 1836, Ameri-can soldier]

bow·knot \'bō-,nät, -'nät\ *n* : a knot with decorative loops

¹bowl \'bōl\ *n* **1** : a rounded hollow dish **2** : the con-tents of a bowl **3** : the bowl-shaped part of something (as a spoon or a tobacco pipe) **4** : a bowl-shaped am-phitheater; *esp* : STADIUM 2b [Old English *bolla*] — **bowled** \'bōld\ *adj*

²bowl *n* **1 a** : a ball shaped so as to curve to one side when rolled **b** *pl* : the game of lawn bowling **2** : a delivery of the ball in bowling or bowls [Middle French *boule* "ball", from Latin *bulla* "bubble"]

³bowl *vb* **1** : to roll a ball or participate in bowling or lawn bowling **2** : to travel smoothly and rapidly **3 a** : to strike with a swiftly moving object **b** : to stun with surprise ⟨the news *bowled* us over⟩

bowlder *variant of* BOULDER

bow·leg \'bō-,leg, -'leg\ *n* : a leg bowed outward at or below the knee — **bow·legged** \'bō-'leg-əd, -'legd\ *adj*

¹bowl·er \'bō-lər\ *n* : one that bowls

²bow·ler \'bō-lər\ *n* : DERBY 3 [*Bowler*, 19th century family of English hatters]

bowl game *n* : a football game played after the regular season between specially invited teams

bow·line \'bō-lən, -,līn\ *n* **1** : a rope used to keep the windward edge of a square sail pulled forward **2** : a knot used for making a loop that will not slip [Middle English *bouline*]

bowl·ing \'bō-ling\ *n* **1** : a game played by rolling balls so as to knock down wooden pins set up at the far end of an alley : ninepins or tenpins **2** : LAWN BOWLING

bow·man \'bō-mən\ *n* : ARCHER

Bow·man's capsule \'bō-mənz-\ *n* : a thin membranous double-walled structure enclosing each glomerulus of a vertebrate kidney [Sir William *Bowman*, died 1892, English surgeon]

bow·sprit \'baù-,sprit, 'bō-\ *n* : a large spar projecting forward from the bow of a ship [Middle English *bous-pret*]

bow·string \'bō-,string\ *n* : the cord connecting the two ends of a bow

bow tie \'bō-\ *n* : a short necktie tied in a bowknot

bow window \'bō-\ *n* : a curved bay window

bow·yer \'bō-yər\ *n* : one that makes shooting bows

\ə\ abut		\ng\ sing	
\ər\ further		\ō\ bone	
\a\ mat		\ó\ saw	
\ā\ take		\òi\ coin	
\ä\ cot, cart		\th\ thin	
\aù\ out		\th\ this	
\ch\ chin		\ü\ food	
\e\ pet		\ù\ foot	
\ē\ easy		\y\ yet	
\g\ go		\yü\ few	
\i\ tip		\yù\ cure	
\ī\ life		\zh\ vision	
\j\ job			

¹**box** \'bäks\ *n, pl* **box** *or* **box·es** : an evergreen shrub or small tree used especially for hedges [Old English, from Latin *buxus,* from Greek *pyxos*]

²**box** *n* **1 a** : a usually 4-sided receptacle with a bottom and often a cover **b** : the amount held by a box **2** : a small compartment for a group of spectators in a theater **3** : BOX STALL **4** : the driver's seat on a carriage **5** : a shed that protects ⟨sentry *box*⟩ **6** : a boxlike housing (as for a bearing) **7** : printed matter enclosed by rules or white space **8** : any of the spaces on a baseball diamond where a batter, coach, pitcher, or catcher stands [Old English, from Late Latin *buxis,* from Greek *pyxis,* from *pyxos* "box tree, boxwood"]

³**box** *vt* : to enclose in or as if in a box — **box the compass 1** : to name the 32 points of the compass in their order **2** : to make a complete reversal

⁴**box** *n* : a punch or slap especially on the ear [Middle English]

⁵**box** *vb* **1** : to strike with the hand **2** : to engage in boxing : fight with the fists

box camera *n* : a camera of simple box shape with a fixed focus and a single shutter speed

box·car \'bäk-ˌskär\ *n* : a railroad freight car with a roof and usually with sliding doors in the sides

box elder *n* : a North American maple with compound leaves

¹**box·er** \'bäk-sər\ *n* : one that engages in the sport of boxing

²**boxer** *n* : a compact medium-sized short-haired usually fawn or brindle dog of a breed originating in Germany

Box·er \'bäk-sər\ *n* : a member of a Chinese secret society that in 1900 attempted by violence to drive foreigners out of China and to force native converts to abandon Christianity [translation of Chinese (Beijing dialect) *yìhé juǎn,* literally, "righteous harmonious fist"] □ ORIGIN In the late 19th century, a group of Chinese who were opposed to the spread of Western customs in their country formed a secret society. Among the rituals they practiced were boxing and calisthenics, from which they believed they would gain supernatural strength. They named their policy *yìhé juǎn,* which means "righteous harmonious fist". English-speaking foreigners simplified the name in translating it and called the group *Boxers.* The rebellion which the Boxers led failed, and Western influence remained important in China.

box·ing *n* : the art of attack and defense with the fists practiced as a sport

Box·ing Day \'bäk-sing-\ *n* : the first weekday after Christmas observed as a legal holiday in parts of the British Commonwealth [from the giving of Christmas boxes on this day to service workers (as postmen)]

boxing glove *n* : one of a pair of padded leather mittens worn in boxing

box kite *n* : a tailless kite consisting of two or more open-ended connected boxes

box·like \'bäk-ˌslīk\ *adj* : resembling a box

box office *n* **1** : an office in a public place (as a theater) where tickets of admission are sold **2** : the financial results of an entertainment enterprise; *also* : something affecting these results

box pleat *n* : a pleat made by forming two folded edges one facing right and the other left

box score *n* : a printed summary of a game usually in the form of a table giving essential details of play

box seat *n* : an advantageous position for viewing something

box spring *n* : a bedspring that consists of spiral springs attached to a foundation and enclosed in a cloth-covered frame

box stall *n* : an individual enclosure for an animal

box turtle *n* : any of several North American land tortoises able to withdraw completely into the shell

box·wood \'bäk-ˌswůd\ *n* : the close-grained tough hard wood of the box; *also* : ¹BOX

box turtle

boy \'bȯi\ *n* **1** : a male child from birth to young manhood **2** : SON 1 **3** : a male servant [Middle English] — **boy·hood** \-ˌhůd\ *n* — **boy·ish** \-ish\ *adj* — **boy·ish·ly** *adv* — **boy·ish·ness** *n*

bo·yar \bō-'yär\ *n* : a member of a Russian aristocratic order next in rank below the ruling princes until its abolition by Peter the Great [Russian *boyarin*]

¹**boy·cott** \'bȯi-ˌkät\ *vt* : to jointly refuse to deal with (as a person or country) or use (as a product) usually to express disapproval or force concessions [Charles C. *Boycott,* died 1897, English land agent in Ireland who was ostracized for refusing to reduce rents]

²**boycott** *n* : the process or an instance of boycotting

boy·friend \'bȯi-ˌfrend\ *n* : a male friend or companion especially of a girl or woman

Boy Scout *n* : a member of any of various national scouting programs (as the Boy Scouts of America) for boys usually 11 to 17 years of age

boy·sen·ber·ry \'bȯiz-n-ˌber-ē, 'bȯis-\ *n* : the large edible fruit of a trailing hybrid bramble; *also* : this bramble [Rudolph *Boysen,* died 1950, American horticulturist]

bra \'brä\ *n* : BRASSIERE

¹**brace** \'brās\ *n, pl* **brac·es** *or* **brace 1** : two of a kind (several *brace* of quail) **2** : something (as a clasp) that connects or fastens **3** : a crank-shaped instrument for turning a wood-boring bit **4 a** : something that transmits, directs, resists, or supports weight or pressure; *esp* : an inclined timber used as a support **b** *pl* : SUSPENDERS **c** : a device for supporting a body part (as the shoulders) **d** *pl* : a dental appliance worn on the teeth to correct irregularities of growth and position **5 a** : a mark { or } used to connect words or items to be considered together **b** : this mark connecting two or more musical staffs the parts on which are to be performed simultaneously; *also* : the group of staffs so connected [Middle English, "pair, clasp", from Middle French, "two arms", from Latin *bracchia,* plural of *bracchium* "arm"]

²**brace** *vb* **1 a** : to make firm or taut ⟨*brace* a drum⟩ **b** : to get ready or set : STEEL ⟨*braced* themselves for the test⟩ **c** : INVIGORATE, FRESHEN **2 a** : to furnish or support with a brace **b** : to make stronger : REINFORCE **3** : to plant firmly ⟨*bracing* my feet⟩ **4** : to take heart ⟨*brace* up, all is not lost⟩

brace·let \'brā-slət\ *n* **1** : an ornamental band or chain worn around the wrist **2** : something (as handcuffs) resembling a bracelet [Middle French, from *bras* "arm", from Latin *bracchium*]

brac·er \'brā-sər\ *n* : an arm or wrist protector

brace root *n* : PROP ROOT

bra·chi·al \'brā-kē-əl\ *adj* : of or relating to the arm or a comparable structure [Latin *bracchium, brachium* "arm"]

brachial plexus *n* : a network of nerves lying mostly in the armpit and supplying nerves to the chest, shoulder, and arm

bra·chi·ate \'brā-kē-ˌāt\ *vi* : to progress by swinging from one hold to another by the arms ⟨a *brachiating* gibbon⟩ — **bra·chi·a·tion** \ˌbrā-kē-'ā-shən\ *n*

bra·chio·pod \'brā-kē-ə-ˌpäd\ *n* : any of a phylum (Brachiopoda) of marine invertebrate animals with bivalve shells and a pair of arms bearing tentacles — called also *lampshell* [Latin *bracchium* "arm" + Greek *pod-, pous* "foot"] — **brachiopod** *adj*

brachy- *combining form* : short ⟨*brachy*cephalic⟩ [Greek *brachys*]

brachy·ce·phal·ic \ˌbrak-i-sə-'fal-ik\ *adj* : having a head that is relatively short from front to back or relatively wide from side to side — **brachy·ceph·a·ly** \-i-'sef-ə-lē\ *n*

brac·ing \'brā-sing\ *adj* : giving strength or freshness ⟨a *bracing* wind⟩

brack·en \'brak-ən\ *n* : a large coarse branching fern; *also* : a growth of such ferns [Middle English *braken*]

¹brack·et \'brak-ət\ *n* **1** : an overhanging member or fixture that projects from a structure (as a wall) and is usually intended to support a vertical load or to strengthen an angle **2** : a short wall shelf **3 a** : one of a pair of marks [ ] used to enclose matter or in mathematics used as signs indicating that two or more terms are treated as one quantity — called also *square bracket* **b** : one of a pair of marks < > used to enclose matter — called also *angle bracket* **4** : a section of a continuously numbered or graded series; *esp* : one of a series of groups graded by income ⟨the $20,000 *bracket*⟩ [Middle French *braguette* "projecting part on breeches", from *brague* "breeches", derived from Latin *braca*, from Gaulish *brāca*]

²bracket *vt* **1** : to place within or as if within brackets **2** : to furnish with brackets **3** : to put into the same category : ASSOCIATE **4** : to get the range on (a target) by firing over and short

bracket fungus *n* : a basidiomycete that forms shelflike fruiting bodies

brack·ish \'brak-ish\ *adj* : somewhat salty ⟨*brackish* water⟩ [Dutch *brac* "salty"]

bract \'brakt\ *n* **1** : a leaf from the axil of which a flower or flower cluster arises **2** : a leaf that grows on a flower-bearing stem [Latin *bractea* "thin metal plate"] — **bract·ed** \'brak-təd\ *adj*

brad \'brad\ *n* : a slender nail with a small often indented head [Old Norse *broddr* "spike"]

brae \'brā\ *n, chiefly Scottish* : a hillside especially along a river [Old Norse *brā* "eyelash"]

¹brag \'brag\ *n* **1** : a pompous or boastful statement **2** : arrogant talk or manner : COCKINESS **3** : BRAGGART [Middle English]

²brag *vb* **bragged; brag·ging** : to talk or assert boastfully — **brag·ger** \'brag-ər\ *n*

brag·ga·do·cio \,brag-ə-'dō-shē-,ō, -shē-ō, -shō\ *n, pl* **-cios 1** : BRAGGART, BOASTER **2 a** : empty boasting **b** : COCKINESS [*Braggadochio*, personification of boasting in *Faerie Queene* by Edmund Spenser]

brag·gart \'brag-ərt\ *n* : a loud arrogant boaster — **braggart** *adj*

Brah·ma \'bräm-ə\ *n* : the ultimate ground of all being in Hinduism [Sanskrit *brahman*]

Brah·man *or* **Brah·min** \'bräm-ən; *2 is* 'bräm-, 'bräm-, 'bram-\ **1 a** : a Hindu of the highest and traditionally the priestly caste : BRAHMA **2** : ZEBU; *esp* : a large vigorous heat-resistant tick-resistant usually silvery gray animal developed in the southern United States by interbreeding Indian cattle [Sanskrit *brāhmaṇa*, from *brahman* "prayer, sacred lore"] — **Brahman** *or* **Brah·man·ic** \brä-'man-ik\ *adj*

Brah·man·ism \'bräm-ə-,niz-əm\ *n* : orthodox Hinduism that follows the Vedas in accepting the forces and laws of the universe as divine and in practicing ancient rites and ceremonies

Brah·min \'bräm-ən\ *n* : an aloof intellectually and socially cultivated person; *esp* : such a person from one of the older New England families — **Brah·min·i·cal** \brä-'min-i-kəl\ *adj* — **Brah·min·ism** \'bräm-ə-,niz-əm\ *n*

¹braid \'brād\ *vt* **1** : to form (three or more strands) into a braid **2** : to ornament especially with ribbon or braid [Old English *bregdan* "to move suddenly"] — **braid·er** *n*

²braid *n* **1** : a cord or ribbon with usually three or more strands forming a regular diagonal pattern down its length; *esp* : a narrow fabric of intertwined threads used especially for trimming **2** : a length of braided hair

braid·ing \'brād-ing\ *n* : something made of braided material

brail \'brāl\ *n* : a rope fastened to the leech of a sail for hauling the sail up or in [Old French *braiel* "strap"] — **brail** *vt*

braille \'brāl\ *n, often cap* : a system of writing for the blind that uses characters made up of raised dots [Louis *Braille*]

¹brain \'brān\ *n* **1 a** : the portion of the vertebrate central nervous system that is the organ of thought and nervous coordination, is made up of neurons and supporting and nutritive structures, is enclosed within the skull, and is continuous with the spinal cord **b** : a major nervous center in an invertebrate animal **2 a** (1) : INTELLECT ⟨has a clever *brain*⟩ (2) : INTELLIGENCE — often used in pl. **b** (1) : a very intelligent or intellectual person (2) : the chief planner of an enterprise — usually used in pl. [Old English *brægen*]

²brain *vt* **1** : to kill by smashing the skull **2** : to hit on the head

brain·case \-,kās\ *n* : the cranium enclosing the brain

brain·child \-,chīld\ *n* : a product of one's creative imagination

brain death *n* : final cessation of activity in the central nervous system especially as indicated by an electroencephalogram showing no brain waves for a predetermined length of time that is often used as a criterion for human death

brain·less \'brān-ləs\ *adj* : UNINTELLIGENT, SILLY — **brain·less·ly** *adv* — **brain·less·ness** *n*

brain stem *n* : the posterior and lower part of the brain including the midbrain, pons, and medulla oblongata

brain·storm \'brān-,störm\ *n* **1** : a temporary but violent mental upset or disturbance **2** : a sudden inspiration

brain trust *n* : a group of expert advisers dealing especially with planning and strategy and often lacking official status — **brain trust·er** \-,trəs-tər\ *n*

brain·wash·ing \'brān-,wȯsh-ing, -,wäsh-\ *n* : a forcible attempt by indoctrination to induce someone to give up basic political, social, or religious beliefs and attitudes and to accept contrasting regimented ideas — **brain·wash** *vb*

brain wave *n* : rhythmic fluctuations of voltage between parts of the brain resulting in the flow of an electric current

brainy \'brā-nē\ *adj* **brain·i·er; -est** : INTELLIGENT — **brain·i·ness** *n*

braise \'brāz\ *vt* : to cook slowly in fat and then in a little liquid in a closed pot [French *braiser*]

¹brake \'brāk\ *archaic past of* BREAK

²brake *n* : a coarse fern often growing up to a meter high : BRACKEN [Middle English]

³brake *n* **1** : a toothed instrument or machine for separating out the fiber of flax or hemp **2** : a machine for bending sheet metal [Low German]

⁴brake *n* : a device for slowing or stopping motion (as of a wheel, vehicle, or engine) especially by friction [Middle English]

⁵brake *vb* **1** : to slow or stop by or as if by a brake **2** : to operate a brake especially on a vehicle

⁶brake *n* : rough or marshy land overgrown usually with one kind of plant [Middle English *-brake*] — **braky** \'brā-kē\ *adj*

brake·man \'brāk-mən\ *n* : a freight or passenger train crew member who inspects the train and assists the conductor

bram·ble \'bram-bəl\ *n* : any of a large genus of usually prickly shrubs of the rose family including the raspberries and blackberries [Old English *brēmel*] — **bram·bly** \-bə-lē, -blē\ *adj*

bran \'bran\ *n* : the broken coat of the seed of cereal grain separated from the flour or meal by sifting or bolting [Old French]

¹branch \'branch\ *n* **1** : a natural subdivision (as a bough arising from a trunk or a twig from a bough) of a plant stem **2** : something (as a tributary of a river or a secondary road) forming a part of a larger whole in a manner suggesting the relation of a branch to a tree ⟨a *branch* of an antler⟩ ⟨the *branches* of an artery⟩: as **a** :

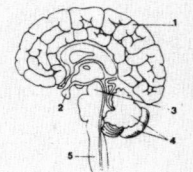

¹brain 1a: *1* cerebrum, 2 pituitary gland, 3 midbrain, 4 cerebellum, 5 spinal cord

\ə\ abut	\ng\ sing
\ər\ further	\ō\ bone
\a\ mat	\ȯ\ saw
\ā\ take	\ȯi\ coin
\ä\ cot, cart	\th\ thin
\au̇\ out	\th\ this
\ch\ chin	\ü\ food
\e\ pet	\u̇\ foot
\ē\ easy	\y\ yet
\g\ go	\yü\ few
\i\ tip	\yu̇\ cure
\ī\ life	\zh\ vision
\j\ job	

a division of a family descending from a particular ancestor **b** : a division of an organization ⟨executive *branch* of the government⟩ **c** : a subordinate office or part of a central system ⟨a *branch* of a bank⟩ **d** : a part of a mathematical curve separated from others [Old French *branche*, from Late Latin *branca* "paw"] — **branched** \'brancht\ *adj* — **branch·less** \'branch-ləs\ *adj* — **branchy** \'bran-chē\ *adj*

²branch *vi* **1** : to develop branches : spread or separate into branches ⟨an elm *branches* over the yard⟩ **2** : to spring out (as from a main stem) : DIVERGE ⟨streets *branching* off the highway⟩ **3** : to extend activities ⟨the business is *branching* out⟩

bran·chi·al \'brang-kē-əl\ *adj* : of, relating to, or situated near the gills [Latin *branchia* "gill", from Greek *branchion*]

¹brand \'brand\ *n* **1** : a charred or burning piece of wood **2** : SWORD **3 a** : a mark made by burning (as on cattle) to show ownership or origin **b** : a mark made (as on freight) with a stamp or stencil for similar purposes **c** : a mark put on criminals with a hot iron **d** : a mark of disgrace : STIGMA **4 a** : a class of goods identified by name as the product of a single firm or manufacturer **b** : a characteristic or distinctive kind : VARIETY [Old English, "torch, sword"]

²brand *vt* **1** : to mark with or as if with a brand **2** : to mark with disapproval : STIGMATIZE — **brand·er** *n*

bran·dish \'bran-dish\ *vt* **1** : to shake or wave (as a weapon) threateningly **2** : to display in a showy or aggressive manner [Middle French *brandiss-*, stem of *brandir*, from *brand* "sword", of Germanic origin] — **brandish** *n*

brand–new \'brand-'nü, -'nyü\ *adj* : conspicuously new and unused

¹bran·dy \'bran-dē\ *n, pl* **-dies** : an alcoholic liquor distilled from wine or fermented fruit juice (as of apples) [short for *brandywine*, from Dutch *brandewijn*, from *brant* "distilled" + *wijn* "wine"] □ ORIGIN An earlier English form of the word *brandy* is *brandywine*, which was borrowed from Dutch *brandewijn*. The second element of this compound is Dutch for "wine". The first means "burnt". The name "burnt wine" refers to wine that has been distilled over a fire.

²brandy *vt* **bran·died; bran·dy·ing** : to flavor, blend, or preserve with brandy ⟨*brandied* cherries⟩

brant \'brant\ *n, pl* **brant** or **brants** : a wild goose; *esp* : any of several small dark geese that breed in the Arctic [origin unknown]

brash \'brash\ *adj* **1** : IMPETUOUS, RASH ⟨a *brash* attack⟩ **2** : aggressively self-assertive : IMPUDENT ⟨a *brash* youth⟩ **3** : piercingly sharp : HARSH ⟨a *brash* squeal of brakes⟩ [origin unknown] — **brash·ly** *adv* — **brash·ness** *n*

brass \'bras\ *n* **1** : an alloy consisting essentially of copper and zinc; *also* : the reddish yellow color of this alloy **2 a** : brass musical instruments — often used in pl. **b** : a usually brass memorial tablet **c** : bright metal fittings or utensils **3** : brazen self-assurance : GALL **4** : BRASS HATS [Old English *bræs*] — **brass** *adj*

brass band *n* : a band consisting chiefly or solely of brass and percussion instruments

brass·bound \'bras-,baund, -'baund\ *adj* **1** : having trim made of brass ⟨a *brassbound* trunk⟩ **2** : strictly bound by tradition : INFLEXIBLE

brass hat *n* : a person (as a military officer) in a high-ranking position

bras·siere \brə-'ziər *also* ,bras-ē-'eər\ *n* : a woman's close-fitting undergarment with cups for bust support [obsolete French *brassière* "bodice", from Old French *braciere* "arm protector", from *bras* "arm"]

brass knuckles *n pl* : KNUCKLE 3

brass tacks *n pl* : details of immediate practical importance — usually used in the phrase *get down to brass tacks*

brassy \'bras-ē\ *adj* **brass·i·er; -est 1 a** : shamelessly bold **b** : UNRULY **2** : resembling brass especially in color **3** : resembling the sound of a brass instrument — **brass·i·ly** \'bras-ə-lē\ *adv* — **brass·i·ness** \'bras-ē-nəs\ *n*

brat \'brat\ *n* : CHILD; *esp* : an ill-mannered annoying child [perhaps from English dialect *brat* "ragamuffin"] — **brat·tish** \'brat-ish\ *adj* — **brat·ty** \'brat-ē\ *adj*

bra·va·do \brə-'väd-ō\ *n, pl* **-does** or **-dos 1** : blustering swaggering conduct **2** : a pretense of bravery [Middle French *bravade*, from Italian *bravata*, from *bravo* "courageous"]

¹brave \'brāv\ *adj* **1** : COURAGEOUS **2** : making a fine show : COLORFUL ⟨*brave* banners flying in the wind⟩ **3** : SPLENDID ⟨the business collapsed despite a *brave* start⟩ [Middle French, from Italian and Spanish *bravo* "wild, courageous", from Latin *barbarus* "barbarous"] — **brave·ly** *adv*

²brave *vt* : to face or endure with courage ⟨*braved* the taunts of the mob⟩

³brave *n* : one who is brave; *esp* : an American Indian warrior

brav·ery \'brāv-rē, -ə-rē\ *n, pl* **-er·ies 1 a** : fine clothes **b** : showy display **2** : the quality or state of being brave : FEARLESSNESS SYN see COURAGE

¹bra·vo \'bräv-ō\ *n, pl* **bravos** or **bravoes** : VILLAIN, DESPERADO; *esp* : a hired assassin [Italian, from *bravo* "wild, courageous"]

²bra·vo \'bräv-ō, brä-'vō\ *n, pl* **bravos** : a shout of approval — often used interjectionally in applauding a performance

³bra·vo \'bräv-ō, brä-'vō\ *vt* **bra·voed; bra·vo·ing** : to applaud by shouts of bravo

bra·vu·ra \brə-'vyur-ə, -'vur-\ *n* **1** : a florid brilliant musical style **2** : a musical passage requiring agility and skill to perform **3** : a show of daring or brilliance [Italian, literally, "bravery"]

braw \'brò\ *adj, chiefly Scottish* : GOOD, FINE; *also* : well dressed [Middle French *brave*]

¹brawl \'bròl\ *vi* **1** : to quarrel or fight noisily **2** : to make a loud confused noise ⟨the river *brawling* by⟩ [Middle English *brawlen*] — **brawl·er** *n*

²brawl *n* : a noisy quarrel or fight

brawn \'bròn\ *n* **1** : full strong muscles especially of the arm or leg **2** : muscular strength [Middle French *braon* "muscle", of Germanic origin]

brawny \'brò-nē\ *adj* **brawn·i·er; -est** : having large strong muscles — **brawn·i·ness** *n*

¹bray \'brā\ *vb* **1** : to utter a bray or similar sound **2** : to utter or play loudly, harshly, or discordantly [Old French *braire* "to cry"]

²bray *n* : the characteristic loud harsh cry of a donkey

bray·er \'brā-ər\ *n* : a hand roller for inking something (as a block) to be printed [Middle English *brayen* "to crush to powder", from Middle French *broiier*]

braze \'brāz\ *vb* : to solder with a nonferrous alloy having a relatively high melting point [French *braser*, from Old French *brese* "live coals"]

¹bra·zen \'brāz-n\ *adj* **1** : made of brass **2 a** : sounding harsh and loud like struck brass **b** : of the color of polished brass **3** : IMPUDENT, SHAMELESS ⟨a *brazen* violation of the rules⟩ [Old English *bræsen*, from *bræs* "brass"] — **bra·zen·ly** *adv* — **bra·zen·ness** \'brāz-nnəs, -əs\ *n*

²brazen *vt* **bra·zened; bra·zen·ing** \'brāz-ning, -n-ing\ : to face with defiance or impudence ⟨would the prisoner *brazen* it out or break down and confess⟩

bra·zen–faced \,brāz-n-'fāst\ *adj* : showing insolence and bold disrespect ⟨a *brazen-faced* liar⟩

¹bra·zier \'brā-zhər\ *n* : one that works in brass [Middle English *brasier*, from *bras* "brass"]

²brazier *n* **1** : a pan for holding burning coals **2** : a utensil on which food is exposed to heat (as from burning charcoal) through a grill [French *brasier,* derived from Old French *brese* "hot coals"]

Bra·zil nut \brə-'zil-\ *n* : one of the 3-sided oily edible nuts that occur packed inside the round fruit of a large Brazilian tree

¹**breach** \'brēch\ *n* **1** : violation of a law, duty, or tie ⟨a *breach* of trust⟩ **2 a** : a broken, ruptured, or torn condition or area **b** : a gap (as in a wall) made by battering **3 a** : a break in accustomed friendly relations **b** : a temporary gap in continuity : HIATUS [Old English *bryce*]

²**breach** *vb* **1** : to make a breach in ⟨*breach* the city walls⟩ **2** : BREAK, VIOLATE ⟨*breach* an agreement⟩ **3** : to leap out of water ⟨an otter *breaching*⟩

breach of promise : violation of a promise especially to marry

¹**bread** \'bred\ *n* **1** : a baked food made of a mixture whose basic constituent is flour or meal **2** : FOOD, SUSTENANCE ⟨our daily *bread*⟩ **3 a** : LIVELIHOOD ⟨earn one's *bread* as a laborer⟩ **b** *slang* : MONEY [Old English *brēad*]

²**bread** *vt* : to cover with bread crumbs ⟨*breaded* veal cutlet⟩

bread–and–but·ter \,bred-n-'bət-ər\ *adj* **1 a** : of, relating to, or affecting a means of livelihood ⟨unions concerned with *bread-and-butter* issues⟩ **b** : DEPENDABLE ⟨*bread-and-butter* products that always sell⟩; *also* : COMMONPLACE, EVERYDAY ⟨*bread-and-butter* language⟩ **2** : sent or given as thanks for hospitality ⟨a *bread-and-butter* letter⟩

bread and butter *n* : a means of livelihood

bread·bas·ket \'bred-,bas-kət\ *n* **1** *slang* : STOMACH **2** : a major cereal-producing region

bread·board \-,bōrd, -,bord\ *n* **1** : a board on which dough is kneaded or bread cut **2** : a board on which electric or electronic circuits may be laid out

bread·fruit \-,früt\ *n* : a round usually seedless fruit that resembles bread in color and texture when baked; *also* : a tall tropical tree of the mulberry family that bears this fruit

bread mold *n* : any of several molds (as a rhizopus) that are found especially on bread

bread·stuff \-,stəf\ *n* **1** : a cereal product (as grain or flour) **2** : BREAD

breadth \'bredth, 'breth, 'bretth\ *n* **1** : distance from side to side : WIDTH **2 a** : something of full width **b** : a wide expanse **3** : COMPREHENSIVENESS, SCOPE ⟨the remarkable *breadth* of a scholar's learning⟩ [Old English *brēdu,* from *brād* "broad"]

bread·win·ner \'bred-,win-ər\ *n* : a member of a family whose wages supply its livelihood

¹**break** \'brāk\ *vb* **broke** \'brōk\; **bro·ken** \'brō-kən\; **break·ing 1 a** : to separate suddenly or violently into parts : SHATTER ⟨*break* a dish⟩ **b** : FRACTURE **c** : MAIM **d** : RUPTURE **e** : to curl over and fall apart ⟨waves *breaking* against the shore⟩ **2** : VIOLATE, TRANSGRESS ⟨*broke* the law⟩ **3 a** : to force a way into, out of, or through ⟨burglars *broke* into the house⟩ **b** : to escape with sudden effort ⟨*broke* away from our captors⟩ **c** : to develop, appear, or burst forth with suddenness or force ⟨day *breaks* in the east⟩ ⟨*broke* into laughter⟩ **d** : to become fair ⟨waited for the weather to *break*⟩ **e** : to make a sudden dash ⟨*break* for cover⟩ **f** : to make or effect by cutting, forcing, or pressing ⟨*break* open a package⟩ **g** : PENETRATE, PIERCE **4** : LOOSEN, SUNDER ⟨*break* a hold⟩ **5** : to cut into and turn over the surface of : PLOW ⟨*break* ground for a new school⟩ **6 a** : to disrupt the order or uniformity of ⟨*break* ranks⟩ **b** : to end by or as if by dispersing ⟨police *broke* up the mob⟩ **c** : to give way in disorderly retreat ⟨the soldiers *broke* under fire⟩ **d** : to decline suddenly and sharply in price or value **e** : to end a relationship or accord — usually used with *with* **7 a** : to subdue completely : CRUSH ⟨*broke* the revolt⟩ **b** : to lose or cause to lose health, strength, or spirit ⟨*broke* under the strain⟩ **c** :

to become inoperative because of damage, wear, or strain ⟨the TV set is *broken*⟩ **d** : to ruin financially **e** : to reduce in rank **f** : to force (a strike) to end by measures outside bargaining practices **g** : to ruin the prospects of ⟨could make or *break* my career⟩ **8 a** : to bring to an end suddenly ⟨*break* a deadlock⟩ ⟨*broke* the silence⟩ **b** : INTERRUPT, SUSPEND ⟨*broke* in with a comment⟩ ⟨*broke* their tour for a rest⟩ **9 a** : to make (an animal) fit for use (as by training) **b** : to accustom to an activity or occurrence ⟨*break* in a new worker⟩ **10** : to make known ⟨*break* the news to them⟩ **11** : to check the force or intensity of ⟨the bushes *broke* my fall⟩ **12** : EXCEED, SURPASS ⟨*broke* all records⟩ **13** : OPEN ⟨*break* an electric circuit⟩ **14** : to split the surface of ⟨fish *breaking* water⟩ **15** : to cause to discontinue a habit ⟨*broke* the child of thumb-sucking⟩ **16** : SOLVE ⟨*broke* the enemy code⟩ **17 a** : to alter course sharply ⟨*broke* to the left⟩ **b** : to curve, drop, or rise sharply ⟨the pitch *broke* over the plate for a strike⟩ **c** : to alter sharply in tone, pitch, or intensity ⟨a voice *breaking* with emotion⟩ **d** : to shift abruptly from one register to another **18** : HAPPEN, DEVELOP ⟨everything *broke* right for us⟩ [Old English *brecan*] — **break·able** \'brā-kə-bəl\ *adj* — **break camp** : to pack up gear and leave a camp — **break cover** : to start from a covert or lair ⟨the hunted fox *broke cover*⟩ — **break one's heart** : to crush emotionally with sorrow — **break the back** : to subdue the main force ⟨*break the back* of inflation⟩ — **break the ice 1** : to make a beginning **2** : to get through the first difficulties in starting a conversation — **break wind** : to expel gas from the intestine

²**break** *n* **1 a** : an act or action of breaking **b** : the opening shot in a game of pool or billiards **2 a** : a condition produced by breaking ⟨a *break* in the clouds⟩ **b** : a gap in an electric circuit interrupting the flow of current **3** : an interruption in continuity: as **a** : a respite from work or duty **b** : a planned interruption in a radio or television program ⟨a commercial *break*⟩ **c** : a noticeable change (as in a surface, course, movement, or direction) **d** : a notable variation of pitch, intensity, or tone in the voice **e** : an abrupt run : DASH **f** : the act of separating after a boxing or wrestling clinch **4** : a rupture in previously friendly relations ⟨a *break* between the two countries⟩ **5** : a place or situation at which a break occurs: as **a** : the point where one musical register changes to another **b** : the place at which a word is divided **c** : CAESURA **6** : social blunder; *esp* : an indiscreet remark that causes embarrassment **7** : a stroke of luck ⟨a bad *break*⟩; *esp* : a stroke of good luck ⟨got all the *breaks*⟩

break·age \'brā-kij\ *n* **1 a** : the action of breaking **b** : a quantity broken ⟨a *breakage* of 10 percent⟩ **2** : loss due to or a charge for things broken

break·down \'brāk-,daún\ *n* **1 a** : a failure to function properly **b** : a physical, mental, or nervous collapse **2** : DECOMPOSITION **3** : division into categories : CLASSIFICATION

break down \brāk-'daún, 'brāk-\ *vb* **1 a** : to cause to fall or collapse by breaking or shattering **b** : to make ineffective **2 a** : to separate (as a protein) into simpler substances : DECOMPOSE **b** : to undergo decomposition **3** : to become subdivided or separated by analysis

break·er \'brā-kər\ *n* **1** : one that breaks **2** : a wave breaking into foam against the shore

break even *vi* : to end up with neither gain nor loss ⟨gamblers who barely *break even*⟩

break·fast \'brek-fəst\ *n* : the first meal of the day especially when taken in the morning — **breakfast** *vb*

break·neck \'brāk-,nek\ *adj* : very fast or dangerous ⟨*breakneck* speed⟩

break·out \'brāk-,aút\ *n* : a violent or forceful break from restraint

break out \brāk-'aút, 'brāk-\ *vb* : to be affected with a skin eruption

breadfruit

\ə\ abut		\ng\ sing	
\ər\ further		\ō\ bone	
\a\ mat		\o\ saw	
\ā\ take		\oi\ coin	
\ä\ cot, cart		\th\ thin	
\aú\ out		\th\ this	
\ch\ chin		\ü\ food	
\e\ pet		\ú\ foot	
\ē\ easy		\y\ yet	
\g\ go		\yü\ few	
\i\ tip		\yú\ cure	
\ī\ life		\zh\ vision	
\j\ job			

break·through \'brāk-,thrü\ *n* **1** : an act or point of breaking through an obstruction or defensive line **2** : an important advance in knowledge or technique

break·wa·ter \'brāk-,wȯt-ər, -,wät-\ *n* : an offshore structure (as a wall) to protect a harbor or beach from the force of waves

bream \'brim, 'brēm\ *n, pl* **bream** *or* **breams** : any of various mostly freshwater spiny-finned fishes; *esp* : any of several sunfishes [Middle French *breme*, of Germanic origin]

¹breast \'brest\ *n* **1** : either of two protuberant milk-producing glandular organs situated on the front of the chest in the human female and some other mammals; *also* : any mammary gland **2** : the front or ventral part of the body between the neck and the abdomen **3** : the center of emotion and thought : BOSOM **4** : something resembling a breast [Old English *brēost*] — **breast·ed** \'bres-təd\ *adj*

²breast *vt* : to face or oppose boldly : BRAVE

breast·bone \'brest-'bōn, 'bres-, -,bōn\ *n* : STERNUM

breast–feed \'brest-,fēd\ *vt* **-fed** \-,fed\; **-feed·ing** : to feed (a baby) from a mother's breast rather than from a bottle

breast·plate \'brest-,plāt, 'bres-\ *n* : a metal plate worn as defensive armor for the chest

breast·stroke \'brest-,strōk, 'bres-\ *n* : a swimming stroke performed by extending the arms in front of the head while drawing the knees forward and outward and then sweeping the arms back with palms out while kicking outward and backward

breast·work \'bres-,twərk\ *n* : an improvised or temporary fortification

breath \'breth\ *n* **1** : a slight indication : SUGGESTION **2 a** : the power of breathing **b** : an act of breathing **c** : RESPITE 2, BREATHER **3** : a slight breeze **4 a** : air inhaled and exhaled in breathing **b** : something (as moisture on a cold surface) produced by breathing **5** : a spoken sound : UTTERANCE **6** : expiration of air with the glottis wide open in the formation of speech sounds [Old English *brǣth*] — **out of breath** : breathing very rapidly (as from strenuous exercise)

breathe \'brēth\ *vb* **1** : to draw air into and expel it from the lungs : RESPIRE **2** : LIVE 1 **3** : to pause and rest before continuing **4 a** : to send out by exhaling **b** : to instill by or as if by breathing ⟨*breathe* new life into the movement⟩ **5** : to tell to someone ⟨don't *breathe* a word of it⟩ **6** : to allow to rest after exertion ⟨*breathe* a horse⟩ **7** : to take in in breathing — **breath·able** \'brē-thə-bəl\ *adj*

breathed \'bretht\ *adj* : VOICELESS 2

breath·er \'brē-thər\ *n* **1** : one that breathes **2** : a break in activity for rest

breath·ing \'brē-thing\ *n* : either of the marks ' and ' used in writing Greek to indicate an intial h-sound or its absence

breath·less \'breth-ləs\ *adj* **1 a** : not breathing **b** : DEAD **2** : gasping for breath : PANTING **b** : leaving one breathless — **breath·less·ly** *adv* — **breath·less·ness** *n*

breath·tak·ing \'breth-,tā-king\ *adj* **1** : making one out of breath ⟨a *breathtaking* climb⟩ **2** : of a kind to excite or thrill ⟨*breathtaking* beauty⟩ — **breath·tak·ing·ly** \-king-lē\ *adv*

brec·cia \'brech-ə, -ē-ə\ *n* : a rock consisting of sharp fragments embedded in a fine-grained material [Italian]

breech \'brēch; *"breeches" (garment) is usually* 'brich-əz\ *n* **1** *pl* **a** : short trousers fitting snugly at or just below the knee **b** : PANTS 1 **2** : BUTTOCK 2 **3** : the part of a firearm at the rear of the bore [Old English *brēc* "breeches", plural of *brōc* "leg covering"]

breech·es buoy \'brē-chəz- *also* 'brich-əz-\ *n* : a canvas sling in the form of a pair of short-legged breeches hung from a life buoy running along a rope that is used to take persons off a ship especially in rescue operations

breastplate

breech·load·er \'brēch-,lōd-ər\ *n* : a firearm that receives its ammunition at the breech

¹breed \'brēd\ *vb* **bred** \'bred\; **breed·ing 1 a** : BEGET 1 **b** : to be the source of ⟨wars *breed* depressions⟩ **2** : to propagate (plants or animals) sexually and usually under controlled conditions **3 a** : to bring up : NURTURE **b** : to instill by training **4** : to mate with **5** : to produce offspring sexually **6** : to produce (a fissionable element) by bombarding a nonfissionable element with neutrons from a radioactive element so that more fissionable material is produced than is used up [Old English *brēdan*] — **breed·er** *n*

²breed *n* **1** : a group of presumably related animals or plants visibly similar in most characters; *esp* : one differentiated from the wild type under the influence of humans **2** : CLASS 3a, KIND

breed·ing *n* **1** : ANCESTRY **2** : training or education especially in manners **3** : the sexual propagation of plants or animals

¹breeze \'brēz\ *n* **1 a** : a gentle wind **b** : a wind of from 1.6 to 13.8 meters per second **2** : something easily done : CINCH [Middle English *brise*]

²breeze *vi* : to proceed quickly and easily ⟨*breezed* through the report⟩

breeze·way \'brēz-,wā\ *n* : a roofed open passage connecting two buildings (as a house and garage) or parts of a building

breezy \'brē-zē\ *adj* **breez·i·er; -est 1** : swept by breezes **2** : both lively and informal ⟨a *breezy* manner⟩ — **breez·i·ly** \-zə-lē\ *adv* — **breez·i·ness** \-zē-nəs\ *n*

breth·ren \'breth-rən, -ərn, -ə-rən\ *pl of* BROTHER — used chiefly in formal or solemn address

Bret·on \'bret-n\ *n* **1** : a native or inhabitant of Brittany **2** : the Celtic language of the Bretons — **Breton** *adj*

breve \'brēv, 'brev\ *n* **1** : a mark ˘ placed over a vowel to show that the vowel is short **2** : a note equivalent to four half notes [Latin, neuter of *brevis* "brief"]

bre·via·ry \'brē-vyə-rē, -və-; -vē-,er-ē\ *n, pl* **-ries** : a book containing the prayers, hymns, and readings prescribed especially for priests for each day of the year [Latin *breviarium*, from *brevis* "brief"]

brev·i·ty \'brev-ət-ē\ *n* **1** : shortness of duration **2** : expression in few words : CONCISENESS

¹brew \'brü\ *vb* **1** : to prepare (as beer or ale) by steeping, boiling, and fermentation **2** : to form a plot or plan : CONTRIVE **3** : to prepare (as tea) by steeping in hot water **4** : to be forming ⟨a storm is *brewing*⟩ [Old English *brēowan*] — **brew·er** \'brü-ər, 'brù-ər, 'brùr\ *n*

²brew *n* **1** : a brewed beverage **2** : a product of brewing

brewer's yeast *n* : a yeast used or suitable for use in brewing; *also* : the dried pulverized cells of such a yeast used as a source of B-complex vitamins — compare BAKER'S YEAST

brew·ery \'brü-ə-rē, 'brù-ər-ē, 'brùr-ē\ *n, pl* **-er·ies** : a plant where malt liquors are manufactured

bri·ar *variant of* BRIER

¹bribe \'brīb\ *n* **1** : money or favor given or promised to influence improperly the judgment or conduct of a person in a position of trust **2** : something that serves to induce or influence [Middle English, "something stolen", from Middle French, "bread given to a beggar"]

²bribe *vb* : to influence by or as if by giving bribes — **brib·able** \'brī-bə-bəl\ *adj* — **brib·er** *n*

brib·ery \'brī-bə-rē, -brē\ *n, pl* **-er·ies** : the act or practice of giving bribes

bric-a-brac \'brik-ə-,brak\ *n* : small ornamental articles : KNICKKNACKS [French *bric-à-brac*]

¹brick \'brik\ *n* **1 a** : a building or paving material made from clay molded into blocks and hardened in the sun or baked **b** : a rectangular block made of brick **2** : a brick-shaped mass ⟨a *brick* of ice cream⟩ [Middle French *brique*, from Middle Dutch *bricke*]

²brick *vt* : to stop up, face, or pave with bricks

brick·bat \'brik-,bat\ *n* **1** : a piece of a broken brick; *esp* : one thrown as a missile **2** : an uncomplimentary remark

brick·lay·er \'brik-,lā-ər, -,le-ər, -,ler\ *n* : a person who builds or paves with bricks — **brick·lay·ing** \-,lā-ing\ *n*

brick·work \'brik-,wərk\ *n* : work of or with brick

brick·yard \-,yärd\ *n* : a place where bricks are made

¹brid·al \'brīd-l\ *n* : a marriage ceremony : WEDDING [Old English *brȳdealu*, from *brȳd* "bride" + *ealu* "ale, festival"]

²bridal *adj* : of or relating to a bride or a wedding : NUPTIAL

bridal wreath *n* : a spirea widely grown for its slender drooping branches and clusters of small white flowers borne in spring

bride \'brīd\ *n* : a woman newly married or about to be married [Old English *brȳd*]

bride·groom \-,grüm, -,grum\ *n* : a man newly married or about to be married [Old English *brȳdguma*, from *brȳd* "bride" + *guma* "man"]

brides·maid \'brīdz-,mād\ *n* : a woman who attends a bride at her wedding

¹bridge \'brij\ *n* **1** : a structure built over a depression or an obstacle (as a river or a railroad) to allow passage **2** : a platform above and across the deck of a ship for the captain or officer in charge **3** : something resembling a bridge in form or function: as **a** : the upper bony part of the nose **b** : an arch serving to raise the strings of a musical instrument **4** : something (as a partial denture anchored to adjacent teeth) that fills a gap [Old English *brycg*]

²bridge *vt* : to make a bridge over or across (*bridge* a gap) — **bridge·able** \-ə-bəl\ *adj*

³bridge *n* : any of various card games for four players developed from whist; *esp* : CONTRACT BRIDGE [earlier *biritch*, of unknown origin]

bridge·head \-,hed\ *n* **1** : a fortified position protecting a bridge **2** : a position seized in enemy territory as a foothold for further advance

bridge·work \-,wərk\ *n* : the dental bridges in a mouth

¹bri·dle \'brīd-l\ *n* **1** : the headgear with which a horse is controlled consisting of a headstall, a bit, and reins **2** : CURB 2, RESTRAINT [Old English *brīdel*]

²bridle *vb* **bri·dled; bri·dling** \'brīd-ling, -l-ing\ **1** : to put a bridle upon **2** : to restrain with or as if with a bridle **3** : to show hostility or resentment especially by drawing back the head and chin

bridle path *n* : a trail suitable for horseback riding

¹brief \'brēf\ *adj* **1** : short in duration or extent (a *brief* visit) **2 a** : expressed in few words : CONCISE **b** : CURT, ABRUPT [Middle French, from Latin *brevis*] — **brief·ly** *adv* — **brief·ness** *n*

²brief *n* **1 a** : a brief summary of an argument, set of facts, or document **b** : a concise statement of the case a lawyer will present in court **2** *pl* : short snug underpants

³brief *vt* **1** : to make a summary of **2 a** : to give final instructions to (*brief* a bombing crew) **b** : to give essential information to (*brief* reporters)

brief·case \-,kās\ *n* : an often flat flexible case (as of leather) for carrying papers

¹bri·er *or* **bri·ar** \'brī-ər, 'brīr\ *n* : a plant (as the blackberry or the wild rose) with a thorny or prickly woody stem [Old English *brēr*] — **bri·ery** \'brī-ər-ē, 'brīr-ē\ *adj*

²brier *or* **briar** *n* : a heath of southern Europe the root of which is used for making tobacco pipes [French *bruyère*]

¹brig \'brig\ *n* : a 2-masted square-rigged sailing vessel [short for *brigantine*]

²brig *n* : a place (as on a ship) for temporary confinement of offenders in the United States Navy

bri·gade \brig-'ād\ *n* **1** : a military unit composed of one or more units of infantry or armor with supporting units **2** : a group of people organized for special activity (fire *brigade*) [French, from Italian *brigata*, from *briga* "strife"]

brig·a·dier \,brig-ə-'diər\ *n* : BRIGADIER GENERAL

brigadier general *n* : an officer rank in the Army, Marine Corps, and Air Force above colonel and below major general

brig·and \'brig-ənd\ *n* : a person who lives by plunder usually as a member of a band : BANDIT [Middle French, from Italian *brigante*, from *briga* "strife", of Celtic origin] — **brig·and·age** \-ən-dij\ *n* — **brig·and·ism** \-,diz-əm\ *n*

brig·an·tine \'brig-ən-,tēn\ *n* : a 2-masted squarerigged sailing vessel differing from a brig in not carrying a square mainsail [Middle French *brigantin*, from Italian *brigantino*, from *brigante* "brigand"]

bright \'brīt\ *adj* **1** : shedding much light : SHINING, GLOWING (a *bright* fire) **2** : very clear or vivid in color (a *bright* red) **3** : quick in learning : INTELLIGENT **4** : full of life : CHEERFUL **5** : promising success (a *bright* future) [Old English *beorht*] — **bright** *adv* — **bright·ly** *adv* — **bright·ness** *n*

bright·en \'brīt-n\ *vb* **bright·ened; bright·en·ing** \'brītning, -n-ing\ : to make or become bright or brighter

Bright's disease \'brīts-\ *n* : kidney disease in which albumin appears in the urine [Richard *Bright*, died 1858, English physician]

brill \'bril\ *n, pl* **brill** : a European flatfish related to the turbot [perhaps from Cornish *brȳthel* "mackerel"]

¹bril·liant \'bril-yənt\ *adj* **1** : very bright : GLITTERING (*brilliant* jewels) **2 a** : outstandingly successful : DISTINGUISHED **b** : unusually keen or alert in mind [French *brillant*, from *briller* "to shine"] — **bril·liance** \-yəns\ *or* **bril·lian·cy** \-yən-sē\ *n* — **bril·liant·ly** *adv* — **bril·liant·ness** *n*

²brilliant *n* : a gem (as a diamond) cut with numerous facets so as to have particular brilliance

bril·lian·tine \'bril-yən-,tēn\ *n* **1** : a preparation for making hair glossy **2** : a light lustrous fabric similar to alpaca

¹brim \'brim\ *n* **1** : the rim especially of a cup, bowl, or depression (the *brim* of the crater) **2** : the projecting rim of a hat [Middle English *brimme*] SYN see RIM — **brim·ful** \-'fúl\ *adj* — **brim·less** \-ləs\ *adj*

²brim *vb* **brimmed; brim·ming** **1** : to fill or become filled to overflowing **2** : to reach or overflow a brim

brim·stone \'brim-,stōn\ *n* : SULFUR [Middle English *brinston*, probably from *brinnen* "to burn" + *ston* "stone"]

brin·dle \'brin-dl\ *n* : a brindled color or animal

brin·dled \-dld\ *or* **brin·dle** \-dl\ *adj* : having faint dark streaks or flecks on a gray or tawny ground [Middle English *brended*]

brine \'brīn\ *n* **1** : water containing a great deal of salt **2 a** : OCEAN **b** : the water of an ocean, sea, or salt lake [Old English *brȳne*]

brine shrimp *n* : any of a genus of crustaceans found in salt lakes and the brine of saltworks

bring \'bring\ *vt* **brought** \'brot\; **bring·ing** \'bringing\ **1** : to cause to come with one by carrying or leading (*bring* a lunch) (*bring* a friend) **2** : to cause to be, act, or move in a special way (their screams *brought* the neighbors) **3** : to cause to come into a particular state or condition (*bring* water to a boil) **4** : to cause to exist or occur (winter will *bring* snow) **5** : to sell for (apples will *bring* a good price) [Old English *bringan*] — **bring·er** \'bring-ər\ *n* □ SYN BRING, TAKE may denote identical action performed in opposite directions in relation to the speaker. BRING implies carrying, leading, transporting toward a point where the speaker is or will be; TAKE implies the same action away from the speaker (*take* this message to the superintendent and *bring* back an answer)

— **bring up the rear** : to come last or behind

bring about *vt* : to cause to take place : EFFECT

¹brig

\ə\ abut	\ng\ sing
\ər\ further	\ō\ bone
\a\ mat	\o\ saw
\ā\ take	\oi\ coin
\ä\ cot, cart	\th\ thin
\au\ out	\th\ this
\ch\ chin	\ü\ food
\e\ pet	\u\ foot
\ē\ easy	\y\ yet
\g\ go	\yü\ few
\i\ tip	\yu\ cure
\ī\ life	\zh\ vision
\j\ job	

Brittany spaniel

bring around *vt* **1** : to cause (someone) to adopt an opinion or a course of action : PERSUADE **2** : to restore to consciousness : REVIVE

bring forth *vt* : to bear or give birth to : PRODUCE

bring in *vt* **1** : to produce as profit or return **2** : INCLUDE 2, INTRODUCE ⟨*bring in* a new topic⟩ **3** : EARN 2 ⟨*brings in* a good salary⟩

bring off *vt* : to carry to a successful conclusion : ACHIEVE

bring out *vt* : to present to the public ⟨*bring out* a new book⟩

bring to *vt* : to restore to consciousness

bring up *vb* **1** : EDUCATE 2, REAR **2** : to stop suddenly **3** : to bring to attention : INTRODUCE

brink \'bringk\ *n* **1** : EDGE; *esp* : the edge at the top of a steep place **2** : the point of onset : VERGE ⟨at the *brink* of war⟩ [Middle English]

brink·man·ship \-mən-,ship\ *also* **brinksmanship** *n* : the practice of pushing a dangerous situation to the limit of safety before stopping

briny \'brī-nē\ *adj* **brin·i·er; -est** : of or resembling brine : SALTY — **brin·i·ness** *n*

brio \'brē-ō\ *n* : VIVACITY, SPIRIT [Italian]

bri·quette *or* **bri·quet** \brik-'et\ *n* : a compacted often brick-shaped mass of usually fine material ⟨charcoal *briquette*⟩ [French *briquette*, from *brique* "brick"]

¹brisk \'brisk\ *adj* **1** : very active or alert : LIVELY **2** : REFRESHING ⟨*brisk* autumn weather⟩ **3** : full of energy : QUICK ⟨a *brisk* pace⟩ [probably from Middle French *brusque*] — **brisk·ly** *adv* — **brisk·ness** *n*

²brisk *vb* : to make or become brisk

bris·ket \'bris-kət\ *n* : the breast or lower chest of a quadruped animal [Middle English *brusket*]

bris·ling *or* **bris·tling** \'briz-ling, 'bris-\ *n* : a small herring that resembles and is processed like a sardine [Norwegian *brisling*]

¹bris·tle \'bris-əl\ *n* : a short stiff coarse hair or filament [Old English *byrst*] — **bris·tled** \-əld\ *adj* — **bris·tly** \'bris-lē, -ə-lē\ *adj*

²bristle *vi* **bris·tled; bris·tling** \'bris-ling, -ə-ling\ **1** : to rise and stand stiffly erect ⟨quills *bristling* in all directions⟩ **2** : to show signs of anger or defiance ⟨people who *bristle* at criticism⟩ **3** : to appear as if covered with bristles ⟨a harbor *bristling* with the masts of ships⟩

bris·tle·cone pine \'bris-əl-,kōn-\ *n* : a pine of the western United States of which some specimens are held to be nearly 5000 years old

bris·tle·tail \'bris-əl-,tāl\ *n* : any of various wingless insects (orders Thysanura and Entotrophi) with two projecting tail bristles

bris·tol \'bris-tl\ *n* : cardboard with a smooth surface suitable for writing or printing — called also *bristol board* [*Bristol,* England]

brit *or* **britt** \'brit\ *n* : tiny sea animals important as fish food [Cornish *brȳthel* "mackerel"]

Bri·tan·nia metal \bri-'tan-yə-\ *n* : a silver-white alloy similar to pewter composed largely of tin, antimony, and copper [Latin *Britannia* "Great Britain"]

britch·es \'brich-əz\ *n pl* : BREECHES

Brit·i·cism \'brit-ə-,siz-əm\ *n* : a characteristic feature of British English [*Brit*ish + *-icism* (as in *gallicism*)]

¹Brit·ish \'brit-ish\ *n* **1** *pl in construction* : the people of Great Britain or their descendants **2** : British English

²British *adj* **1** : of, relating to, or characteristic of the original inhabitants of Britain **2 a** : of, relating to, or characteristic of Great Britain or the British **b** : ENGLISH

Brit·ish·er \'brit-i-shər\ *n* : BRITON 2

British thermal unit *n* : the quantity of heat required to raise the temperature of one pound of water one degree Fahrenheit at a specified temperature (as 39°F or 60°F) and equal to about 1055 joules — abbreviation *Btu*

Brit·on \'brit-n\ *n* **1** : a member of one of the peoples inhabiting Britain previous to the Anglo-Saxon invasions **2** : a native or subject of Great Britain

Brit·ta·ny spaniel \'brit-n-ē-\ *n* : a large active spaniel of a French breed developed by interbreeding pointers with spaniels of Brittany

brit·tle \'brit-l\ *adj* **1 a** : easily broken, cracked, or snapped ⟨*brittle* clay⟩ ⟨*brittle* glass⟩ **b** : not firm or substantial : FRAIL ⟨a *brittle* promise⟩ **2** : lacking warmth, depth, or generosity of spirit [Middle English *britil*] — **brit·tle·ness** *n* □ SYN BRITTLE, CRISP, FRIABLE, FRAGILE mean tending to break easily. BRITTLE implies hardness without toughness or elasticity and susceptibility to snapping or fracture; CRISP suggests the light firmness and brittleness desirable in some foods as opposed to limpness or sogginess ⟨*crisp* lettuce⟩ ⟨*crisp* crackers⟩ FRIABLE is applied to substances that are readily crumbled or pulverized ⟨*friable* soil⟩ FRAGILE is applicable to anything that must be handled with care and implies delicacy of material or structure.

brittle star *n* : any of a group (Ophiuroidea) of sea animals similar to the related starfishes but having slender flexible arms

¹broach \'brōch\ *n* **1** : any of various pointed or tapered tools, implements, or parts: as **a** : a spit for roasting meat **b** : a tool for tapping casks **c** : a cutting tool with a series of teeth in a straight line used especially for shaping a hole already bored **2** : BROOCH [Middle French *broche*, derived from Latin *broccus* "projecting"]

²broach *vb* **1** : to pierce (as a cask) in order to draw the contents : TAP **2** : to shape or enlarge (a hole) with a broach **3** : to introduce or make known for the first time ⟨*broach* a subject for discussion⟩ **4** : to break the surface from below ⟨saw a whale *broaching*⟩ — **broach·er** *n*

broad \'brȯd\ *adj* **1** : not narrow : WIDE ⟨a *broad* highway⟩ **2** : extending far and wide : SPACIOUS ⟨*broad* prairies⟩ **3** : being such to a full degree ⟨*broad* daylight⟩ **4** : UNMISTAKABLE ⟨a *broad* hint⟩ **5** : COARSE 3, INDELICATE **6** : liberal in thought ⟨*broad* religious views⟩ **7** : not limited : extended in range or amount ⟨a *broad* choice of topics⟩ ⟨education in its *broadest* sense⟩ **8** : being main and essential ⟨*broad* outlines of a problem⟩ **9** : ³LOW 12 — used specifically of *a* pronounced as in *father* [Old English *brād*] — **broad·ly** *adv* — **broad·ness** *n* □ SYN BROAD, WIDE mean having horizontal extent; they apply to a surface measured or viewed from side to side. BROAD is preferred when full horizontal extent is considered ⟨*broad* shoulders⟩ WIDE is commonly used with units of measure ⟨rugs eight feet *wide*⟩ or is applied when the distance between limits or the extent of an opening is in mind ⟨a *wide* view⟩ ⟨*wide* doorways⟩

broad-ax *or* **broad-axe** \'brȯ-,daks\ *n* : a broad-bladed ax

broad bean *n* : the large flat edible seed of an Old World upright vetch; *also* : this plant widely grown for its seeds and as fodder

¹broad·cast \'brȯd-,kast\ *adj* **1** : cast or scattered in all directions **2** : made public by means of radio or television — **broadcast** *adv*

²broadcast *n* **1** : the action of transmitting sound or images by radio or television **2** : a single radio or television program

³broadcast *vb* **-cast** *also* **-cast·ed; -cast·ing** **1** : to scatter or sow (as seed) broadcast **2** : to make widely known **3 a** : to send out a broadcast from a radio or television transmitting station **b** : to speak or perform on a broadcast program — **broad·cast·er** *n*

broad·cloth \'brȯd-,klȯth\ *n* **1** : a fine woolen cloth made compact and glossy in finishing **2** : a fine cloth (as of cotton or silk) with plain or ribbed weave

broad·en \'brȯd-n\ *vb* **broad·ened; broad·en·ing** \'brȯd-ning, -n-ing\ : to make or become broad or broader

broad jump *n* : LONG JUMP — **broad jumper** *n*

broad·leaf \'bròd-,lēf\ *adj* : BROAD-LEAVED

broad–leaved \-'lēvd\ *or* **broad·leaf** \-'lēf\ *also* **broad-leafed** \-'lēft\ *adj* **1** : having broad leaves; *esp* : having leaves that are not needles ⟨*broad-leaved* evergreens⟩ **2** : composed of broad-leaved plants ⟨*broad-leaved* forests⟩

broad·loom \-,lüm\ *adj* : woven on a wide loom ⟨*broadloom* carpets⟩ — **broadloom** *n*

broad–mind·ed \-'mīn-dəd\ *adj* **1** : tolerant of differing views **2** : inclined to tolerate minor departures from conventional behavior — **broad–mind·ed·ly** *adv* — **broad–mind·ed·ness** *n*

¹**broad·side** \'bròd-,sīd\ *n* **1** : the part of a ship's side above the waterline **2 a** : all the guns that can be fired from the same side of a ship **b** : a discharge of all these guns together **3** : a storm of abuse : a strongly worded attack **4** : a sheet of paper printed on one or both sides; *also* : something (as a ballad or an advertisement) printed on a broadside

²**broadside** *adv* **1 a** : with one side forward ⟨turn *broadside*⟩ **b** : from the side ⟨hit the car *broadside*⟩ **2** : in one volley — **broadside** *adj*

broad–spectrum *adj* : effective against various microorganisms ⟨*broad-spectrum* antibiotics⟩

broad·sword \'bròd-,sòrd, -,sòrd\ *n* : a broad-bladed sword for cutting rather than thrusting

broad·tail \-,tāl\ *n* : the fur or skin of a very young or premature karakul lamb characterized by a flat and wavy appearance resembling moiré silk — compare PERSIAN LAMB

Brob·ding·nag·ian \,bräb-ding-'nag-ē-ən, -dig-\ *adj* : very large : TREMENDOUS [*Brobdingnag,* country inhabited by giants in *Gulliver's Travels* by Jonathan Swift]

bro·cade \brō-'kād\ *n* : a heavy fabric (as of silk) with raised interwoven patterns [Spanish *brocado,* from Italian *broccato,* derived from *brocco* "small nail", from Latin *broccus* "projecting"] — **bro·cad·ed** \-'kād-əd\ *adj*

broc·co·li \'bräk-lē, -ə-lē\ *n* : an open branching form of cauliflower that bears young green flowering shoots used as a vegetable [Italian, from *brocco* "small nail, sprout"]

bro·chette \brō-'shet\ *n* : a small spit : SKEWER [French, derived from Old French *broche* "pointed tool"]

bro·chure \brō-'shùr\ *n* : PAMPHLET [French, from *brocher* "to sew", derived from Old French *broche* "pointed tool"]

brock \'bräk\ *n* : BADGER [Old English *broc,* of Celtic origin]

bro·gan \'brō-gən, brō-'gan\ *n* : a heavy shoe; *esp* : a work shoe reaching to the ankle [Irish Gaelic *brōgan*]

¹**brogue** \'brōg\ *n* **1** : a heavy shoe often with a hobnailed sole : BROGAN **2** : a sturdy oxford often with an ornamental toe cap [Irish and Scottish Gaelic *bróg*]

²**brogue** *n* : a marked dialect or regional pronunciation; *esp* : an Irish accent [Irish Gaelic *barróg* "accent, speech impediment", literally, "wrestling hold"]

broi·der \'bròid-ər\ *vt* : EMBROIDER — **broi·dery** \'bròid-rē, -ə-rē\ *n*

¹**broil** \'bròil\ *vb* : to cook or become cooked by direct exposure to radiant heat [Middle French *bruler* "to burn"]

²**broil** *vi* : BRAWL 1 [Middle French *brouiller* "to mix, confuse"]

³**broil** *n* : a confused or noisy disturbance; *esp* : a loud quarrel

broil·er \'bròi-lər\ *n* **1** : a rack and pan or an oven equipped with a rack and pan for broiling meats **2** : a young chicken suitable for broiling

¹**broke** *past of* BREAK

²**broke** \'brōk\ *adj* : having no money : PENNILESS [Middle English, from *broken*]

bro·ken \'brō-kən\ *adj* **1** : shattered into pieces ⟨*broken* glass⟩ **2 a** : RUGGED 1, ROUGH ⟨*broken* country⟩ **b** : having gaps or breaks ⟨a *broken* line⟩ **3** : not kept ⟨a *broken* promise⟩ **4** : SUBDUED, CRUSHED ⟨a *broken* spirit⟩ **5 a** : lacking continuity : FRAGMENTARY **b** : imperfectly spoken ⟨*broken* English⟩ **6** : FRACTURED ⟨a *broken* leg⟩ [Old English *brocen,* past participle of *brecan* "to break"] — **bro·ken·ly** *adv* — **bro·ken·ness** \-kən-nəs\ *n*

bro·ken·heart·ed \,brō-kən-'härt-əd\ *adj* : crushed by grief or despair

bro·ker \'brō-kər\ *n* : a person who acts as an agent in the purchase and sale of property [Middle English, "negotiator"]

bro·ker·age \'brō-kə-rij, -krij\ *n* **1** : the business of a broker **2** : the fee or commission charged by a broker

bro·me·li·ad \brō-'mē-lē-,ad\ *n* : any of a family of chiefly tropical American plants (as the pineapple and Spanish moss) that often grow on the surface of other plants [Olaf *Bromelius,* died 1705, Swedish botanist]

bro·mide \'brō-,mīd\ *n* **1** : any of various compounds of bromine with another element or a radical including some (as potassium bromide) used as sedatives **2** : a commonplace or trite expression or idea □ ORIGIN The word *bromide* is derived from *bromine.* Several compounds of bromine, especially potassium bromide, are used as sedatives. They can calm a nervous, restless person and help that person to get to sleep. *Bromide* has come to be used too for a boring or tiresome talker, who can often put listeners to sleep as effectively as any drug.

bro·mid·ic \brō-'mid-ik\ *adj* : DULL, TRITE ⟨*bromidic* remarks⟩

bro·mine \'brō-,mēn\ *n* : a chemical element that is a deep red corrosive toxic liquid giving off an irritating reddish brown vapor of disagreeable odor — see ELEMENT table [Greek *brōmos* "bad smell"]

brom·thy·mol blue \,brōm-'thī-,mòl-, -,mōl-\ *or* **bro·mo·thy·mol blue** \,brō-mō-'thī-,mòl-, -,mōl-\ *n* : a dye derived from thymol that is an acid-base indicator

bronc \'brängk\ *n* : BRONCO

bron·chi·al \'bräng-kē-əl\ *adj* : of, relating to, or involving the bronchi or their branches

bronchial tube *n* : a primary bronchus or any of its branches

bron·chi·ole \'bräng-kē-,ōl\ *n* : a tiny thin-walled branch of a bronchial tube

bron·chi·tis \brän-'kīt-əs, bräng-\ *n* : acute or chronic inflammation of the bronchial tubes or a disease marked by this — **bron·chit·ic** \-'kit-ik\ *adj*

bron·cho·pneu·mo·nia \,bräng-kō-nù-'mō-nyə, -nü-, ,brän-\ *n* : pneumonia involving many relatively small areas of lung tissue — called also *bronchial pneumonia*

bron·chus \'bräng-kəs\ *n, pl* **bron·chi** \'brän-,kī, 'bräng-, -,kē\ : either of the main divisions of the trachea each leading to a lung [Greek *bronchos* "windpipe"]

bron·co \'bräng-kō, 'brän-\ *n, pl* **broncos** : an unbroken or partly broken range horse of western North America; *also* : MUSTANG [Mexican Spanish, from Spanish, "rough, wild"]

bron·co·bust·er \-,bəs-tər\ *n* : a person who breaks wild horses to the saddle

bron·to·sau·rus \,bränt-ə-'sòr-əs\ *also* **bron·to·saur** \'bränt-ə-,sòr\ *n* : any of several very large four-footed and probably herbivorous dinosaurs — called also *thunder lizard* [Greek *brontē* "thunder" + *sauros* "lizard"]

Bronx cheer \'brängks-\ *n* : RASPBERRY 2

¹**bronze** \'bränz\ *vt* : to give the appearance of bronze to

²**bronze** *n* **1** : an alloy of copper and tin and sometimes other elements (as zinc) **2** : a work of art (as a statue, bust, or medallion) made of bronze **3** : a moderate yellowish brown [French, from Italian *bronzo*] — **bronzy** \'brän-zē\ *adj*

\ə\ abut		\ng\ sing	
\ər\ further		\ō\ bone	
\a\ mat		\ò\ saw	
\ā\ take		\òi\ coin	
\ä\ cot, cart		\th\ thin	
\aù\ out		\th\ this	
\ch\ chin		\ü\ food	
\e\ pet		\ù\ foot	
\ē\ easy		\y\ yet	
\g\ go		\yü\ few	
\i\ tip		\yù\ cure	
\ī\ life		\zh\ vision	
\j\ job			

Bronze Age *n* : a period of human culture characterized by the use of bronze tools and held to begin in Europe about 3500 B.C. and in western Asia and Egypt somewhat earlier

brooch \'brōch, 'brüch\ *n* : an ornamental clasp or pin ⟨wore a diamond *brooch* on the lapel⟩ [Middle English *broche* "pointed tool, brooch"]

¹**brood** \'brüd\ *n* **1** : a family of young animals or children; *esp* : the young (as of a bird) hatched or cared for at one time **2** : a group resembling (as in similarity of form or nature) a brood of young [Old English *brōd*]

²**brood** *vb* **1** : to sit on eggs in order to hatch them **2** : to cover young with the wings **3** : to think anxiously or moodily upon a subject : PONDER **4** : to hover over : LOOM ⟨*brooding* clouds⟩ — **brood·ing·ly** \-ing-lē\ *adv*

³**brood** *adj* : kept for breeding ⟨*brood* mare⟩ ⟨*brood* flock⟩

brood·er \'brüd-ər\ **1** : one that broods **2** : a heated structure used for raising young fowl

broody \'brüd-ē\ *adj* **1** : physiologically ready to brood **2** : inclined to brood : MOODY — **brood·i·ness** *n*

¹**brook** \'brùk\ *vt* : to put up with : BEAR, TOLERATE ⟨*brooks* no interference⟩ [Old English *brūcan* "to use, enjoy"]

²**brook** *n* : CREEK 2 [Old English *brōc*]

brook·let \'brùk-lət\ *n* : a small brook

brook trout *n* : a common speckled cold-water char of eastern North America

broom \'brüm, 'brùm\ *n* **1** : a plant of the pea family with long slender branches along which grow many drooping yellow flowers **2** : a usually long-handled brush used for sweeping and originally made from twigs of broom [Old English *brōm*]

broom·corn \-,kòrn\ *n* : a tall cultivated sorghum whose stiff branched flower cluster is used in brooms and brushes

broom·stick \-,stik\ *n* : the handle of a broom

broth \'bròth\ *n, pl* **broths** \'bròths, 'bròthz\ : liquid in which food has been cooked : STOCK [Old English]

broth·el \'bräth-əl, 'bròth-\ *n* : an establishment in which prostitutes are available [Middle English, "worthless fellow, prostitute", derived from Old English *brēothan* "to waste away"]

broth·er \'brəth-ər\ *n, pl* **brothers** *or* **breth·ren** \'breth-rən, -ərn, -ə-rən\ **1** : a male who has one or both parents in common with another **2** : KINSMAN **3** : a fellow member — used as a title for ministers in some evangelical denominations ⟨*Brother* Smith⟩ **4** : one related to another by common ties (as of race or interests) **5** *often cap* : a man who is a religious but not a priest ⟨a lay *brother*⟩ — often used as a title ⟨*Brother* John, S.J.⟩ [Old English *brōthor*]

broth·er·hood \'brəth-ər-,hùd\ *n* **1** : the state of being brothers or a brother **2** : an association (as a labor union) for a particular purpose **3** : the whole body of persons engaged in a business or profession : FRATERNITY

broth·er–in–law \'brəth-rən-,lò, -ə-rən-, 'brəth-ərn-,lò\ *n, pl* **broth·ers–in–law** \'brəth-ər-zən-\ **1** : the brother of one's spouse **2** : the husband of one's sister

broth·er·ly \'brəth-ər-lē\ *adj* **1** : of or relating to brothers **2** : natural or becoming to brothers ⟨*brotherly* love⟩ ⟨*brotherly* rivalry⟩ — **broth·er·li·ness** *n*

brougham \'brü-əm, 'brüm, 'brō-əm\ *n* **1** : a light closed horse-drawn carriage with seats inside for two or four **2** : a 2-door sedan or coupe [Henry Peter *Brougham*, Baron Brougham and Vaux, died 1868, Scottish jurist]

brought *past of* BRING

brou·ha·ha \'brü-,hä-,hä, ,brü-,hä-'hä; brü-'hä-,hä\ *n* : FUROR 2, HUBBUB [French]

brow \'braù\ *n* **1 a** : EYEBROW **b** : the ridge on which the eyebrow grows **c** : FOREHEAD 1 **2** : the edge or projecting upper part of a steep slope ⟨on the *brow* of a hill⟩ [Old English *brū*]

brow·beat \'braù-,bēt\ *vt* **-beat; -beat·en** \-,bēt-n\; **-beat·ing** : to frighten by a stern manner or threatening speech

¹**brown** \'braùn\ *adj* : of the color brown; *also* : of dark or tanned complexion [Old English *brūn*]

²**brown** *n* : any of a group of dull colors between red and yellow in hue — **brown·ish** \'braù-nish\ *adj*

³**brown** *vb* : to make or become brown

brown alga *n* : any of a division (Phaeophyta) of mostly marine algae with chlorophyll masked by brown pigment

brown coal *n* : LIGNITE

Brown·i·an movement \'braù-nē-ən-\ *n* : a random movement of microscopic particles suspended in liquids or gases that results from the impact of molecules of the fluid on the particles — called also *Brownian motion* [Robert *Brown,* died 1858, Scottish botanist]

brown·ie \'braù-nē\ *n* **1** : a good-natured sprite who performs helpful services at night **2** : a member of the Girl Scouts of the United States of America from six through eight years of age **3** : a small rectangle of rich chocolate cake containing nuts

brown·out \'braù-,naùt\ *n* : a reduction in the use or availability of electric power; *also* : a period of dimmed lighting resulting from such reduction

brown·stone \'braùn-,stōn\ *n* **1** : a reddish brown sandstone used for building **2** : a dwelling faced with brownstone

brown study *n* : a state of deep absorption in thought

brown sugar *n* : soft sugar whose crystals are covered by a film of refined dark syrup

brown–tail moth *n* : a tussock moth whose larva feeds on foliage and has hairs irritating to the skin

brown trout *n* : a speckled European trout widely introduced as a game fish

¹**browse** \'braùz\ *n* **1** : tender shoots, twigs, and leaves of trees and shrubs fit for food for cattle **2** : an act or instance of browsing [probably from Middle French *brouts* "sprouts"]

²**browse** *vb* **1** : to nibble or feed on leaves and shoots **2 a** : to skim a book reading random passages **b** : to look over a number of things casually in search of something of interest SYN see GRAZE — **brows·er** *n*

bru·cel·lo·sis \,brü-sə-'lō-səs\ *n, pl* **-lo·ses** \-,sēz\ : UNDULANT FEVER [*Brucella,* genus of bacteria]

bru·in \'brü-ən\ *n* : BEAR 1 [Dutch, name of the bear in the beast epic *Reynard the Fox*]

¹**bruise** \'brüz\ *vb* **1** : to inflict or cause a bruise on **2** : to break down (as leaves or berries) by rubbing or pounding : CRUSH **3** : to wound or hurt the feelings of **4** : to become bruised or show bruises [partly from Middle French *bruisier* "to break", of Celtic origin; partly from Old English *brȳsan* "to bruise"]

²**bruise** *n* : an injury (as from a blow) in which the skin is not broken but is discolored from the breaking of small underlying blood vessels : CONTUSION

bruis·er \'brü-zər\ *n* : a big husky person

¹**bruit** \'brüt\ *n, archaic* : REPORT, RUMOR [Old French, "noise"]

²**bruit** *vt* : to noise abroad : RUMOR

brum·ma·gem \'brəm-i-jəm\ *adj* : being showy and cheap [alteration of *Birmingham,* England, the source in the 17th century of counterfeit groats] — **brummagem** *n*

brunch \'brənch\ *n* : a late breakfast, an early lunch, or a combination of the two [*br*eakfast + l*unch*]

bru·net *or* **bru·nette** \brü-'net\ *adj* : of dark or relatively dark complexion; *esp* : having brown or black hair and eyes [French, from *brun* "brown", of Germanic origin]

brunt \'brənt\ *n* : the main force of a blow or an attack : the heaviest shock, stress, or strain ⟨coastal towns bore the *brunt* of the storm⟩ [Middle English]

brougham 1

¹brush \'brəsh\ *n* **1** : BRUSHWOOD **2** : scrubby vegetation; *also* : land covered with this [Middle French *broce* "brushwood"]

²brush *n* **1** : a device composed of bristles set into a handle and used especially for sweeping, scrubbing, or painting **2** : a bushy tail (as of a fox or squirrel) **3** : an electrical conductor that makes sliding contact between a moving and a nonmoving part of an electric motor or generator **4 a** : an act of brushing **b** : a quick light touch or momentary contact [Middle French *broisse,* from *broce* "brushwood"]

³brush *vb* **1 a** : to apply a brush to **b** : to apply with a brush **2 a** : to remove with or as if with a brush **b** : to dispose of in an offhand way ⟨*brushed* my protest aside⟩ **3** : to pass lightly across : touch gently in passing — **brush·er** *n*

⁴brush *n* : a brief encounter or skirmish [⁵*brush*]

⁵brush *vi* : to move quickly or without paying attention ⟨*brushed* past the receptionist⟩ [Middle French *brosser* "to dash through underbrush", from *broce* "brushwood"]

brush–off \'brəsh-,óf\ *n* : an abrupt or offhand dismissal

brush up *vb* : to refresh one's memory of : renew one's skill or knowledge

brush·wood \'brəsh-,wùd\ *n* **1** : small branches cut from trees or shrubs **2** : a thicket of shrubs and small trees

¹brushy \'brəsh-ē\ *adj* **brush·i·er**; **-est** : SHAGGY **1**, ROUGH

²brushy *adj* **brush·i·er**; **-est** : covered with or abounding in brush or brushwood

brusque \'brəsk\ *adj* : unpleasantly curt in manner or speech ⟨a *brusque* answer⟩ [French, from Italian *brusco,* from Medieval Latin *bruscus,* a kind of plant with stiff branches] — **brusque·ly** *adv* — **brusque·ness** *n*

brus·sels sprout \'brəs-əlz-\ *n, often cap B* : one of the edible small green heads borne on the stem of a plant related to the cabbage; *also* : this plant [*Brussels,* Belgium]

bru·tal \'brüt-l\ *adj* : befitting a brute: as **a** : lacking all mercy **b** : causing injury or misery **c** : HARSH 3, SEVERE — **bru·tal·ly** \-l-ē\ *adv* □ SYN BRUTE, BRUTISH: BRUTAL applies only to human behavior, stresses lack of humanity, and always implies moral condemnation; BRUTE stresses crude force or strength in contrast with skill or intelligence; BRUTISH stresses lack of refinement and sensitivity and often suggests stupidity rather than cruelty.

bru·tal·i·ty \brü-'tal-ət-ē\ *n, pl* **-ties** **1** : the quality or state of being brutal **2** : a brutal act or course of action

bru·tal·ize \'brüt-l-,īz\ *vt* **1** : to make brutal, unfeeling, or inhuman **2** : to treat brutally — **bru·tal·iza·tion** \,brüt-l-ə-'zā-shən\ *n*

¹brute \'brüt\ *adj* **1** : of, relating to, or typical of lower animals as distinguished from humans **2** : resembling an animal in quality, action, or instinct: as **a** : irrationally cruel : SAVAGE **b** : grossly sensual **c** : UNREASONING **d** : wholly physical ⟨moved the rock by *brute* strength⟩ [Middle French *brut,* from Latin *brutus* "stupid"] SYN see BRUTAL

²brute *n* **1** : BEAST 1 **2** : a brutal person

brut·ish \'brüt-ish\ *adj* **1** : of or resembling a beast **2 a** : grossly sensual : INSENSITIVE **b** : UNREASONING, IRRATIONAL SYN see BRUTAL — **brut·ish·ly** *adv* — **brut·ish·ness** *n*

bry·ol·o·gy \brī-'äl-ə-jē\ *n* : a branch of botany that deals with mosses and liverworts [Greek *bryon* "moss"]

bry·o·ny \'brī-ə-nē\ *n, pl* **-nies** : any of a genus of tendril-bearing vines of the gourd family with large leaves, red or black fruit, and a cathartic root [Greek *bryōnia*]

bry·o·phyl·lum \,brī-ə-'fil-əm\ *n* : a kalanchoe often grown as a foliage plant especially from leaf cuttings — called also *air plant, life plant*

bry·o·phyte \'brī-ə-,fīt\ *n* : any of a division (Bryophyta) of nonflowering green plants comprising the mosses and liverworts [Greek *bryon* "moss" + *phyton* "plant"] — **bry·o·phyt·ic** \,brī-ə-'fit-ik\ *adj*

bry·o·zo·an \,brī-ə-'zō-ən\ *n* : any of a phylum or class (Bryozoa) of aquatic invertebrate animals that usually form branching, flat, or mosslike colonies and reproduce by budding — **bryozoan** *adj* [Greek *bryon* "moss" + *zōion* "animal"]

¹bub·ble \'bəb-əl\ *vb* **bub·bled**; **bub·bling** \'bəb-ling, -ə-ling\ **1** : to form bubbles **2** : to flow out with a gurgling sound **3 a** : to utter as though giving off bubbles ⟨*bubbling* praise of the new teacher⟩ **b** : to be or become lively : EFFERVESCE ⟨*bubbling* with joy⟩ **4 a** : to cause to bubble **b** : BURP 2 [Middle English *bublen*]

²bubble *n* **1** : a small typically hollow and light globule: as **a** : a small body of gas within a liquid **b** : a thin film of liquid inflated with air or gas ⟨a soap *bubble*⟩ **c** : a globule in a transparent solid **2 a** : something that lacks firmness, solidity, or reality **b** : a delusive scheme **3** : a sound like that of bubbling **4** : MAGNETIC BUBBLE

bubble chamber *n* : a chamber of heated liquid in which the path of an ionizing particle is made visible by a string of vapor bubbles

bubble gum *n* : a chewing gum that can be blown into large bubbles

bubble memory *n* : a computer memory that uses magnetic bubbles to store information

bub·bler \'bəb-lər, -ə-lər\ *n* : a drinking fountain from which a stream of water bubbles upward

bub·bly \'bəb-lē, -ə-lē\ *adj* **bub·bli·er**; **-est** **1** : full of bubbles : EFFERVESCENT **2** : resembling a bubble

bu·bo \'bü-,bō, 'byü-\ *n, pl* **buboes** : an inflammatory swelling of a lymph node especially in the groin [Medieval Latin, from Greek *boubōn*] — **bu·bon·ic** \bü-'bän-ik, byü-\ *adj*

bubonic plague *n* : plague caused by a bacterium and characterized especially by the formation of buboes

buc·cal \'bək-əl\ *adj* : of, relating to, near, or being the surface of a tooth next to the cheek [Latin *bucca* "cheek"] — **buc·cal·ly** \-ē\ *adv*

buc·ca·neer \,bək-ə-'niər\ *n* : PIRATE [French *boucanier*] — **buccaneer** *vi*

¹buck \'bək\ *n, pl* **buck** or **bucks** **1** : a male animal; *esp* : a male deer or antelope **2 a** : a male human being : MAN **b** : DANDY **1** **3 a** : BUCKSKIN; *also* : an article made of buckskin **b** *slang* : DOLLAR 3b **4 a** : a supporting rack or frame **b** : a short thick leather-covered block for gymnastic vaulting [Old English *bucca* "stag, he-goat"]

²buck *vb* **1 a** : to spring with a quick plunging leap ⟨a *bucking* horse⟩ **b** : to throw (as a rider) by bucking **2 a** : to move or act forcefully in opposition to ⟨snowplows *bucking* the drifts⟩ **b** : to stand firm in opposition to : RESIST ⟨determined to *buck* city hall⟩ **3** : to start, move, or react jerkily **4** : to strive for advancement or promotion ⟨*bucking* for sergeant⟩ — **buck·er** *n*

³buck *adj* : of the lowest grade within a military category ⟨*buck* private⟩

buck·a·roo or **buck·er·oo** \,bək-ə-'rü\ *n, pl* **-aroos** or **-eroos** : COWBOY [Spanish *vaquero,* from *vaca* "cow", from Latin *vacca*]

buck·board \'bək-,bōrd, -,bórd\ *n* : a four-wheeled horse-drawn vehicle with a floor made of long springy boards [obsolete English *buck* "body of a wagon"]

¹buck·et \'bək-ət\ *n* **1** : a typically round vessel for catching, holding, or carrying liquids or solids **2** : an object resembling a bucket in collecting, scooping, or carrying something: as **a** : the scoop of an excavating machine **b** : one of the vanes of a turbine rotor **3 a** : BUCKETFUL **b** : a large quantity [Anglo-French *buket,* from Old English *būc* "pitcher"]

brussels sprout

\ə\ abut \ng\ sing
\ər\ **further** \ō\ bone
\a\ **mat** \ó\ saw
\ā\ **take** \ói\ **coin**
\ä\ **cot, cart** \th\ **thin**
\au̇\ **out** \t̲h̲\ **this**
\ch\ **chin** \ü\ **food**
\e\ **pet** \u̇\ **foot**
\ē\ **easy** \y\ **yet**
\g\ **go** \yü\ **few**
\i\ **tip** \yu̇\ **cure**
\ī\ **life** \zh\ **vision**
\j\ **job**

²**bucket** *vb* **1 :** to draw or lift in or as if in buckets **2 :** HUSTLE 2, HURRY **3 a :** to go about haphazardly or irresponsibly **b :** to move roughly or jerkily

bucket brigade *n* **:** a chain of persons acting to put out a fire by passing buckets of water from hand to hand

buck·et·ful \'bək-ət-ˌfül\ *n, pl* **buck·et·fuls** \-ət-ˌfülz\ *or* **buck·ets·ful** \-əts-ˌfül\ **:** the amount held by a bucket

bucket seat *n* **:** a low individual seat used chiefly in automobiles and airplanes

bucket shop *n* **:** a dishonest brokerage house [earlier, a saloon in which liquor was sold in buckets or pitchers]

buck·eye \'bək-ˌī\ *n* **:** a shrub or tree of the horse-chestnut family; *also* **:** its large nutlike seed

buck fever *n* **:** nervous excitement of an inexperienced hunter at the sight of game

¹**buck·le** \'bək-əl\ *n* **1 :** a fastening for two loose ends that is attached to one and holds the other by a catch **2 :** an ornamental device that suggests a buckle ⟨silver shoe *buckles*⟩ [Middle French *boucle* "boss of a shield, buckle", derived from Latin *bucca* "cheek"]
□ ORIGIN The literal meaning of Latin *buccula* was "little cheek", but *buccula* was also the name for the part of a helmet that protects the cheek. Its Middle French descendant, *boucle,* was the word for the boss of a shield, which looks a little like a small cheek on the face of the shield. The use of the word was later extended to belt fasteners. In this sense, the word was borrowed into English.

²**buckle** *vb* **buck·led; buck·ling** \'bək-ling, -ə-ling\ **1 :** to fasten with a buckle **2 :** to apply oneself with vigor ⟨*buckle* down to a job⟩ **3 :** to bend, warp, or kink usually under the influence of some external agency ⟨the pavement *buckled* in the heat⟩ ⟨knees *buckling* from fatigue⟩ **4 :** to give way : YIELD

³**buckle** *n* **:** a product of buckling : BEND

buck·ler \'bək-lər\ *n* **1 :** SHIELD 1; *esp* **:** a small round shield used to parry blows **2 :** one that shields and protects

buck passer *n* **:** a person who habitually evades responsibility — **buck–pass·ing** \'bək-ˌpas-ing\ *n*

buck·ram \'bək-rəm\ *n* **:** a stiff-finished heavily sized fabric of cotton or linen used in garments, millinery, and bookbindings [Old French *boquerant,* from Provençal *bocaran,* from *Bokhara,* city in central Asia] — **buckram** *adj*

buck·saw \'bək-ˌsȯ\ *n* **:** a saw set in a usually H-shaped frame and used for sawing wood on a sawhorse

buck·shot \-ˌshät\ *n* **:** a coarse lead shot used in shotgun shells

buck·skin \-ˌskin\ *n* **1 a :** the skin of a buck **b :** a soft pliable usually suede-finished leather **2** *pl* **:** buckskin breeches **3 :** a horse of a light yellowish dun color with black mane and tail

buck·thorn \-ˌthȯrn\ *n* **:** any of a genus of often thorny trees or shrubs some of which yield purgatives or pigments

buck·tooth \-ˈtüth\ *n* **:** a large projecting front tooth — **buck–toothed** \-ˈtütht\ *adj*

buck up *vb* **:** to become or cause to become encouraged : cheer up

buck·wheat \'bək-ˌhwēt\ *n* **:** any of several herbs with pinkish white flowers and triangular seeds; *also* **:** the seeds used as a cereal grain

¹**bu·col·ic** \byü-ˈkäl-ik\ *adj* **1 :** of or relating to shepherds or herdsmen : PASTORAL **2 :** RUSTIC 1 [Latin *bucolicus,* from Greek *boukolikos,* from *boukolos* "cowherd", from *bous* "cow" + *-kolos* "herd"] — **bu·col·i·cal·ly** \-i-kə-lē, -klē\ *adv*

²**bucolic** *n* **:** a pastoral poem : ECLOGUE

¹**bud** \'bəd\ *n* **1 :** a small growth at the tip or on the side of a plant stem that later develops into a flower, leaf, or new shoot **2 :** a flower that has not fully opened **3 :** a part that grows out from the body of an organism and develops into a new organism : GEMMA

¹buffalo 2a

4 : a stage of development in which something is not yet fully developed : an early stage or condition ⟨trees in *bud*⟩ ⟨a plan still in the *bud*⟩ [Middle English *budde*]

²**bud** *vb* **bud·ded; bud·ding** **1 a :** to set or put forth buds **b :** to reproduce asexually by forming and developing buds **2 :** to be or develop like a bud (as in freshness and promise of growth) ⟨a *budding* diplomat⟩ **3 :** to insert a bud from one plant into an opening cut in the bark of (another plant) in order to propagate a desired variety — **bud·der** *n*

Bud·dha \'büd-ə, 'bùd-\ *n* **1 :** a person who has attained the perfect spiritual fulfillment sought in Buddhism **2 :** a representation of Gautama Buddha [Sanskrit, "enlightened"]

Bud·dhism \'bü-ˌdiz-əm, 'bùd-ˌiz-\ *n* **:** a religion chiefly of eastern and central Asia growing out of the teaching of Gautama Buddha that suffering is inherent in life and that one can be liberated from it by mental and moral self-purification — **Bud·dhist** \'büd-əst, 'bùd-\ *n or adj* — **Bud·dhis·tic** \bü-ˈdis-tik, bù-\ *adj*

bud·dy \'bəd-ē\ *n, pl* **buddies :** COMPANION 1, PARTNER, PAL [probably baby talk for *brother*]

buddy system *n* **:** an arrangement in which two individuals are paired for safety (as in swimming)

budge \'bəj\ *vb* **:** to start to move; *esp* **:** to give or cause to give way [Middle French *bouger,* derived from Latin *bullire* "to boil"]

bud·ger·i·gar \'bəj-rē-ˌgär, -ə-rē-\ *n* **:** a small Australian parrot usually light green with black and yellow markings in the wild but bred under domestication in many colors [from an indigenous language of Australia]

¹**bud·get** \'bəj-ət\ *n* **1 :** a supply available or at hand **2 a :** a statement of estimated expenditures (as of a nation) during a period and of proposals to finance them **b :** a plan for using resources to finance expenditures **c :** the amount of money available for or assigned to some purpose ⟨a low-*budget* operation⟩ [Middle French *bougette,* from *bouge* "leather bag", from Latin *bulga,* of Gaulish origin]

²**budget** *vb* **1 :** to put in or on a budget ⟨*budget* money for food⟩ ⟨*budget* yourself carefully⟩ **2 :** to provide funds for in a budget ⟨*budget* a new car⟩ **3 :** to plan or provide for the use of ⟨*budget* your time wisely⟩

bud·get·ary \'bəj-ə-ˌter-ē\ *adj* **:** of or relating to a budget

bud·gie \'bəj-ē\ *n* **:** BUDGERIGAR

bud scale *n* **:** one of the leaves resembling scales that form the sheath of a plant bud

¹**buff** \'bəf\ *n* **1 :** a garment made of buff leather **2 :** the bare skin **3 a :** a light yellowish brown **b :** a light to moderate yellow **4 :** a device (as a stick or wheel) with a soft absorbent surface for applying polishing material **5 :** FAN, ENTHUSIAST [Middle French *buffle* "wild ox", from Italian *bufalo;* sense 5 from earlier *buff* "one enthusiastic about going to fires", from the buff overcoats worn by volunteer firemen in New York City about 1820]

²**buff** *adj* **:** of the color buff

³**buff** *vt* **:** to polish with or as if with a buff

¹**buf·fa·lo** \'bəf-ə-ˌlō\ *n, pl* **-lo** *or* **-loes** **1 :** WATER BUFFALO **2 a :** a large shaggy-maned North American wild ox with short horns and heavy forequarters bearing a large muscular hump — called also *American bison, American buffalo* **b :** any of a genus of wild oxen (as the wisent) of the northern hemisphere belonging to the same genus as the American buffalo [Italian *bufalo* and Spanish *búfalo,* derived from Greek *boubalos* "African gazelle"]

²**buffalo** *vt* **1 :** BAFFLE 1, BEWILDER **2 :** OVERAWE, INTIMIDATE

buffalo bug *n* **:** CARPET BEETLE

buffalo grass *n* **:** a low-growing native fodder grass of the American plains and prairies

¹**buff·er** \'bəf-ər\ *n* **:** one that buffs

²buffer *n* **1** : a device or material for reducing shock due to contact **2 a** : BUFFER STATE **b** : a person who shields another especially from annoying routine matters **3** : a substance capable in solution of neutralizing both acids and bases and thereby maintaining approximately the original pH of the solution **4** : a temporary storage unit (as for a computer) that can receive data at one rate and transmit it at a different rate [*buff* "to act like a soft body when struck"]

³buffer *vt* **1** : to lessen the shock of : CUSHION **2** : to treat (a solution) with a buffer; *also* : to prepare (aspirin) with an antacid **3** : to collect (as data) in a buffer

buffer state *n* : a small neutral state lying between two larger potentially rival powers

¹buf·fet \'bəf-ət\ *n* : a blow especially with the hand [Middle French]

²buffet *vb* **1** : STRIKE 2a: as **a** : CUFF, SLAP **b** : to pound repeatedly ⟨waves *buffeted* the cliff⟩ **2 a** : to contend against : STRUGGLE ⟨*buffeting* the wind⟩ **b** : to make one's way by fighting or struggling ⟨*buffeted* on through the storm⟩

³buf·fet \bə-'fā, bü-, 'bü-,\ *n* **1** : SIDEBOARD **2** : a cupboard or set of shelves for the display of tableware **3 a** : a counter for refreshments **b** *chiefly British* : a restaurant operated as a public convenience (as in a railway station) **c** : a meal set out on a buffet or table for guests to serve themselves [French]

buff leather *n* : a strong supple oil-tanned leather produced chiefly from cattle hides

buf·fle·head \'bəf-əl-,hed\ *n* : a small North American diving duck [archaic English *buffle* "buffalo"]

buf·foon \bə-'fün, ,bə-\ *n* **1** : a person who amuses others by tricks, jokes, and antics : CLOWN **2** : a coarse crude person [Middle French *bouffon,* from Italian *buffone,* derived from Latin *bufo* "toad"] — **buf·foon·ish** \-'fü-nish\ *adj*

buf·foon·ery \-'fün-rē, -ə-rē\ *n, pl* **-er·ies** : the art or the conduct of a buffoon; *esp* : coarse crude behavior

¹bug \'bəg\ *n* **1 a** : an insect or other creeping or crawling invertebrate; *esp* : an obnoxious insect (as a bedbug or head louse) **b** : any of an order (Hemiptera) of insects with sucking mouthparts and incomplete metamorphosis that includes many destructive plant pests — called also *true bug* **2** : an unexpected defect, fault, flaw, or imperfection **3** : a disease-producing germ or a disease caused by it **4 a** : FAD, ENTHUSIASM **b** : ENTHUSIAST **5** : a concealed listening device [origin unknown]

²bug *vt* **bugged; bug·ging 1** : ANNOY, BOTHER **2** : to plant a concealed microphone in

bug·a·boo \'bəg-ə-,bü\ *n, pl* **-boos** : BUGBEAR, BOGEY [origin unknown]

bug·bear \'bəg-,baər, -,beər\ *n* **1** : an imaginary goblin or specter used to cause fear **2** : an object or source of dread

¹bug·gy \'bəg-ē\ *adj* **bug·gi·er; -est 1** : infested with bugs **2** *slang* : CRAZY 2, SILLY

²buggy *n, pl* **buggies** : a light single-seated carriage usually drawn by one horse [origin unknown]

¹bug·house \'bəg-,haús\ *n, slang* : an insane asylum

²bughouse *adj, slang* : mentally deranged : CRAZY

¹bu·gle \'byü-gəl\ *n* : a European annual mint with spikes of blue flowers that is naturalized in the United States [Old French, from Late Latin *bugula*]

²bugle *n* : a brass musical instrument that resembles the trumpet but usually has no valves [Old French, "buffalo, instrument made from a buffalo horn, bugle", from Latin *buculus,* from *bos* "head of cattle"]

³bugle *vb* **bu·gled; bu·gling** \-gə-ling, -gling\ : to sound or summon by or as if by a bugle — **bu·gler** \-glər\ *n*

bu·gloss \'byü-,gläs, -,glós\ *n* : any of a genus of coarse hairy herbs of the borage family [Middle French *bu-glosse,* derived from Greek *bous* "head of cattle" + *glōssa* "tongue"]

buhr·stone \'bər-,stōn\ *n* : a siliceous rock used for millstones; *also* : a millstone of this rock [probably from *burr*]

¹build \'bild\ *vb* **built** \'bilt\; **build·ing 1** : to make by putting together parts or materials : CONSTRUCT ⟨*build* a bridge⟩ **2** : to produce or create gradually especially by effort ⟨*build* a winning team⟩ **3** : to cause to be constructed ⟨the city *built* a new station⟩ **4** : to engage in building **5** : to become greater ⟨costs are *building* rapidly⟩ **6** : to progress toward a peak ⟨tension *building* up⟩ [Old English *byldan*]

²build *n* : form or style of structure; *esp* : PHYSIQUE

build·ed \'bil-dəd\ *archaic past of* BUILD

build·er \'bil-dər\ *n* : one that builds; *esp* : a person whose business is the construction of buildings

build in *vt* : to construct as an integral part of something ⟨*build in* a bookcase⟩

build·ing \'bil-ding\ *n* **1** : a usually roofed and walled structure built for permanent use (as for a dwelling) **2** : the art, work, or business of assembling materials into a structure ⟨bridge *building*⟩

build·up \'bil-,dəp\ *n* **1** : an often gradual increase (as in amount or numbers) ⟨a *buildup* of resentment⟩ **2** : something (as publicity) intended to attract favorable attention (as to a politician)

built-in \'bil-'tin\ *adj* **1** : forming an integral part of a structure; *esp* : constructed as or in a recess in a wall ⟨*built-in* bookcases⟩ **2** : INHERENT

bulb \'bəlb\ *n* **1 a** : a plant underground resting stage consisting of a short stem base bearing one or more buds enclosed in thickened storage leaves — compare CORM, TUBER **b** : a fleshy structure (as a tuber or corm) resembling a bulb in appearance or function **c** : a plant having or developing from a bulb **2 a** : an incandescent electric lamp **b** : a rounded or swollen anatomical structure [Latin *bulbus,* from Greek *bolbos* "bulbous plant"] — **bulbed** \'bəlbd\ *adj*

bul·bar \'bəl-bər\ *adj* : of or relating to a bulb; *also* : involving the medulla oblongata

bul·bil \'bəl-bəl, -,bil\ *n* : a small or secondary plant bulb; *esp* : one produced in a leaf axil or replacing the flowers [French *bulbille,* from *bulbe* "bulb"]

bul·bous \'bəl-bəs\ *adj* **1** : having a bulb : growing from or bearing bulbs **2** : resembling a bulb : ROUNDED, SWOLLEN — **bul·bous·ly** *adv*

bul·bul \'búl-,búl\ *n* **1** : a Persian songbird that is probably a nightingale **2** : any of various social songbirds of Asia and Africa [Persian, from Arabic]

Bul·gar \'bəl-,gär, 'búl-\ *n* : BULGARIAN

Bul·gar·i·an \,bəl-'gar-ē-ən, ,búl-, -'ger-\ *n* **1** : a native or inhabitant of Bulgaria **2** : the Slavic language of the Bulgarians — **Bulgarian** *adj*

¹bulge \'bəlj\ *n* : a swelling or distended part; *also* : a part with an outward bend ⟨a *bulge* in a line⟩ [Middle French *boulge* "leather bag", from Latin *bulga*] — **bulgy** *adj*

²bulge *vb* : to become or cause to become bent or swollen outward

bu·lim·ia \bü-'lē-mē-ə, byü-, -'li-\ *n* : a serious eating disorder primarily of young women that is characterized by compulsive overeating usually followed by self-induced vomiting or laxative abuse and is often accompanied by depression [Greek *boulimia* "great hunger"] — **bu·lim·ic** \-'lē-mik, -'li-\ *adj*

¹bulk \'bəlk\ *n* **1** : greatness of size or extent : MAGNITUDE, VOLUME **2** : a large body or mass **3** : the main or greater part [Old Norse *bulki* "cargo"] □ SYN BULK, MASS, VOLUME mean the whole that makes up a body or unit with reference to its size or amount. BULK implies a whole that is large, heavy, or unwieldy; MASS suggests a whole made by piling things of the same kind; VOLUME applies to a whole without shape or outline and capable of flowing or fluctuating ⟨a large *volume* of water⟩ ⟨the *volume* of traffic⟩ — **in**

\ə\ abut	\ng\ sing
\ər\ **further**	\ō\ **bone**
\a\ **mat**	\ó\ **saw**
\ā\ **take**	\ói\ **coin**
\ä\ **cot, cart**	\th\ **thin**
\aú\ **out**	\th\ **this**
\ch\ **chin**	\ü\ **food**
\e\ **pet**	\ú\ **foot**
\ē\ **easy**	\y\ **yet**
\g\ **go**	\yü\ **few**
\i\ **tip**	\yú\ **cure**
\ī\ **life**	\zh\ **vision**
\j\ **job**	

bulk : in a mass : not divided into parts or packaged in separate units

²**bulk** vb **1** : to swell or bulge or cause to swell or bulge **2** : to appear as a consideration

bulk·head \'bəlk-,hed, 'bəl-,ked\ n **1** : an upright partition separating compartments on a ship **2** : a structure or partition to resist pressure or to shut off water, fire, or gas **3** : a framework projecting from the outside of a building that has a sloping door giving access to a cellar stairway

bulky \'bəl-kē\ adj **bulk·i·er; -est** : having bulk: as **a** : large of its kind; esp : both large and unwieldy **b** : having great volume in proportion to weight — **bulk·i·ly** \-kə-lē\ adv — **bulk·i·ness** \-kē-nəs\ n

¹**bull** \'bùl\ n **1 a** : an adult male bovine animal; also : a usually adult male of various large animals **b** : ELEPHANT **2** : one who buys commodities or securities in expectation of a price rise — compare BEAR **3** : one that resembles a bull **4** : BULLDOG **5** slang : POLICE OFFICER, DETECTIVE [Old English bula]

²**bull** adj **1 a** : MALE **b** : of, relating to, or resembling a bull **2** : large of its kind

³**bull** vb : to act or act on with the violence of a bull : FORCE ⟨bulling their way ahead⟩

⁴**bull** n : a papal pronouncement of the most formal and important kind [Medieval Latin bulla "papal seal, papal bull", from Latin, "bubble, amulet"]

⁵**bull** n **1** : a grotesque blunder in language **2** slang **a** : empty boastful talk **b** : NONSENSE

¹**bull·dog** \'bùl-,dòg\ n : a compact muscular short-haired dog of a breed developed in England to fight bulls and having forelegs set widely apart and an undershot lower jaw

²**bulldog** adj : suggestive of a bulldog ⟨bulldog courage⟩

³**bulldog** vt : to throw (a steer) by seizing the horns and twisting the neck

bull·doze \'bùl-,dōz\ vt **1** : BULLY, INTIMIDATE **2** : to move, clear, gouge out, or level off with a bulldozer **3** : to force as if by using a bulldozer ⟨bulldoze one's way through brush⟩ [perhaps from ¹bull + alteration of dose]

bull·doz·er \-,dō-zər\ n **1** : one that bulldozes **2** : a tractor-driven machine having a broad horizontal blade or ram for pushing (as in clearing land or road building)

bul·let \'bùl-ət\ n **1** : a shaped piece of metal made to be shot from a firearm **2** : something suggesting a bullet (as in form or vigor of action) [Middle French boulet, from boule "ball"]

bul·le·tin \'bùl-ət-n\ n **1** : a brief public notice usually from an authoritative source ⟨a weather bulletin⟩ **2** : a periodical publication; esp : one issued by an institution or association [French, from Italian bullettino, from bulla "papal bull"]

bulletin board n **1** : a board for posting notices **2** : a program on a computer system that allows users to read and write public notices and is accessed usually by modem

bul·let·proof \,bùl-ət-'prüf\ adj : so made as to prevent the passing through of bullets ⟨bulletproof glass⟩

bull fiddle n : DOUBLE BASS — **bull fiddler** n

bull·fight \'bùl-,fīt\ n : a spectacle in which persons ceremonially excite, fight with, and usually kill bulls in an arena for public entertainment — **bull·fight·er** n — **bull·fight·ing** \-iŋ\ n

bull·finch \-,finch\ n : a thick-billed red-breasted European songbird often kept as a cage bird

bull·frog \-,fròg, -,fräg\ n : FROG; esp : a large heavy frog that makes a booming or bellowing sound

bull·head \-,hed\ n : any of various large-headed fishes; esp : any of several common freshwater catfishes of the United States

bull·head·ed \'bùl-'hed-əd\ adj : stupidly stubborn : HEADSTRONG — **bull·head·ed·ly** adv — **bull·head·ed·ness** n

bul·lion \'bùl-yən\ n : gold or silver metal; esp : gold or silver in bars or ingots [Anglo-French, "mint"]

bull·ish \'bùl-ish\ adj **1** : suggestive of a bull **2 a** : marked by, tending to cause, or hopeful of rising prices (as in a stock market) **b** : OPTIMISTIC — **bull·ish·ly** adv — **bull·ish·ness** n

bull mastiff n : a large powerful dog of a breed developed by crossing bulldogs with mastiffs

Bull Moose \'bùl-'müs\ n : a follower of Theodore Roosevelt in the United States presidential campaign of 1912 [bull moose, emblem of the Progressive party of 1912]

bull neck n : a thick short powerful neck — **bull·necked** \'bùl-'nekt\ adj

bull·ock \'bùl-ək\ n **1** : a young bull **2** : a castrated bull : STEER — **bull·ocky** \-ə-kē\ adj

bull·pen \'bùl-,pen\ n **1** : a large cell where prisoners are held until brought into court **2 a** : a place on a baseball field where relief pitchers warm up **b** : the relief pitchers of a team

bull·ring \'bùl-,riŋ\ n : an arena for bullfights

bull session n : an informal rambling group discussion

bull's–eye \'bùl-,zī\ n **1** : a small thick disk of glass inserted (as in a deck) to let in light **2** : a very hard globular candy **3 a** : the center of a target; also : something central or critical **b** : a shot that hits a bull's-eye; also : a complete success **4** : a simple lens for concentrating rays of light

bull snake n : any of several large harmless North American snakes feeding chiefly on rodents

bull·ter·ri·er \'bùl-'ter-ē-ər\ n : a short-haired terrier of a breed originated in England by crossing the bulldog with terriers

bull·whip \'bùl-,hwip, -,wip\ n : a rawhide whip with a braided lash 4 to 7 meters long

¹**bul·ly** \'bùl-ē\ n, pl **bullies** : a rough browbeating person; esp : one habitually cruel to others who are weaker [probably from Dutch boel "lover"] □ ORIGIN The earliest meaning of English bully was "sweetheart". The word was probably borrowed from Dutch boel "lover". Later bully was used for anyone who seemed a good fellow, then for a blustering daredevil. Today, a bully is usually one whose claims to strength and courage are based on the intimidation of those who are weaker.

²**bully** adj : EXCELLENT, FIRST-RATE — often used interjectionally ⟨bully for you⟩

³**bully** vb **bul·lied; bul·ly·ing** : to play the bully toward : act like a bully

bul·ly·rag \'bùl-ē-,rag\ vt **1** : to make timid or fearful by bullying **2** : to annoy by teasing : BADGER [origin unknown]

bul·rush \'bùl-,rəsh\ n : any of several large sedges growing in wet land or water [Middle English bulrysche]

¹**bul·wark** \'bùl-wərk, -,wərk, -,wòrk; 'bəl-wərk, -,wərk\ n **1 a** : a solid wall built for defense **b** : BREAKWATER, SEAWALL **2** : a strong support or protection **3** : the side of a ship above the upper deck — usually used in pl. [Dutch bolwerc, from Middle High German, literally, "plank work"]

²**bulwark** vt : to strengthen or safeguard with a bulwark : PROTECT

¹**bum** \'bəm\ vb **bummed; bum·ming 1** : to go around in the manner of a bum : **a** : LOAF 1 **b** : to wander like a tramp **2** : to obtain by begging [probably derived from German bummler "loafer"]

²**bum** n **1** : a person who avoids work and tries to live off others **2** : TRAMP 1

³**bum** adj **1** : of poor quality : INFERIOR ⟨bum advice⟩ **2** : physically disabled ⟨a bum knee⟩

bum·ble·bee \'bəm-bəl-,bē\ n : any of numerous large robust hairy social bees [Middle English bomblen "to boom"]

bum·boat \'bəm-,bōt\ *n* : a boat that brings provisions and commodities for sale to ships in port or offshore [probably from Low German *bumboot,* from *bum* "tree" + *boot* "boat"]

bum·mer \'bəm-ər\ *n* **1** : an unpleasant experience (as a bad reaction to a hallucinogenic drug) **2** : FAILURE, FLOP

¹bump \'bəmp\ *vb* **1** : to strike or knock against something with force **2** : to collide with **3** : to proceed in a series of bumps : JOLT [imitative] — **bump into** : to meet especially by chance

²bump *n* **1** : a sudden forceful blow or jolt **2 a** : a rounded projection or bulge; *esp* : a swelling of tissue (as from a blow or sting) **b** : an irregularity in a road surface likely to cause a jolt

¹bump·er \'bəm-pər\ *n* : a cup or glass filled to the brim [probably from *bump* "to bulge"]

²bumper *adj* : unusually large or fine ⟨a *bumper* crop⟩

³bumper *n* : a device for absorbing shock or preventing damage (as in collision); *esp* : a metal bar at either end of a motor vehicle

bump·kin \'bəm-kən, 'bəmp-\ *n* : an awkward and crude rustic [perhaps from Flemish *bommekijn* "small cask"]

bump·tious \'bəm-shəs, 'bəmp-\ *adj* : stupidly and often noisily self-assertive : PRESUMPTUOUS [¹*bump* + *-tious* (as in *fractious*)] — **bump·tious·ly** *adv* — **bump·tious·ness** *n*

bumpy \'bəm-pē\ *adj* **bump·i·er; -est** : causing, having, or covered with bumps ⟨a *bumpy* ride⟩ ⟨a *bumpy* surface⟩ — **bump·i·ly** \-pə-lē\ *adv* — **bump·i·ness** \-pē-nəs\ *n*

bun \'bən\ *n* **1** : a sweet or plain small bread; *esp* : a round roll **2** : a knot of hair shaped like a bun [Middle English *bunne*]

¹bunch \'bənch\ *n* **1** : BULGE, SWELLING **2 a** : a number of things of the same kind : CLUSTER ⟨a *bunch* of grapes⟩ **b** : GROUP 2 ⟨a *bunch* of friends⟩ [Middle English *bunche*] — **bunch·i·ly** \'bən-chə-lē\ *adv* — **bunchy** \-chē\ *adj*

²bunch *vb* : to form in or gather into a group or cluster

bunch·ber·ry \'bənch-,ber-ē\ *n* : a creeping perennial herb related to the dogwood with whorled leaves and white floral bracts followed by clusters of red berries

bunch·grass \-,gras\ *n* : any of several grasses chiefly of the western United States that grow in tufts

bun·co *or* **bun·ko** \'bəng-kō\ *n, pl* **buncos** *or* **bunkos** : a swindling game or scheme [perhaps from Spanish *banca* "bench, bank"] — **bunco** *vt*

bund \'bund, 'bənd\ *n, often cap* : a political association; *esp* : a pro-Nazi German-American organization of the 1930s [German, "league"] — **bund·ist** \-əst\ *n, often cap*

¹bun·dle \'bən-dl\ *n* **1 a** : a group of things tied together **b** : PARCEL 4 **c** : a large sum of money **2 a** : a small band of mostly parallel fibers (as of nerve) **b** : VASCULAR BUNDLE [Dutch *bundel*]

²bundle *vb* **bun·dled; bun·dling** \'bən-dling, -dl-ing\ **1** : to make into a bundle : WRAP **2** : to hurry or send away unceremoniously ⟨*bundled* the children off to school⟩ **3** : to take part in bundling — **bun·dler** \-dlər, -dl-ər\ *n*

bundle up *vb* : to dress warmly

bun·dling \'bən-dling, -dl-ing\ *n* : a former custom in which a couple during courtship would occupy the same bed without undressing

¹bung \'bəng\ *n* **1** : the stopper in the bunghole of a cask; *also* : BUNGHOLE **2** : the cecum or anus especially of a slaughtered animal [Dutch *bonghe,* from Late Latin *puncta* "puncture", from Latin *pungere* "to prick"]

²bung *vt* : to plug with or as if with a bung

bun·ga·low \'bəng-gə-,lō\ *n* : a usually one-storied house with a low-pitched roof [Hindi *banglā,* literally, (house) "in the Bengal style"]

bun·gee cord \'bən-jē\ *n* : an elasticized cord used especially as a fastening device or to absorb shocks — called also **bungee** [origin unknown]

bung·hole \'bəng-,hōl\ *n* : a hole for emptying or filling a cask

bun·gle \'bəng-gəl\ *vb* **bun·gled; bun·gling** \-gə-ling, -gling\ : to act, make, or work in a clumsy manner [perhaps of Scandinavian origin] — **bungle** *n* — **bun·gler** \-gə-lər, -glər\ *n*

bung up *vt* : BATTER, BRUISE

bun·ion \'bən-yən\ *n* : an inflamed swelling on the first joint of the big toe [probably from *bunny* "swelling"]

¹bunk \'bəngk\ *n* **1** : a built-in bed (as on a ship) that is often one of a tier **2** : a sleeping place [probably short for *bunker*]

²bunk *vb* **1** : to occupy a bunk **2** : to provide with a bunk

³bunk *n* : NONSENSE 1 [short for *bunkum*]

bun·ker \'bəng-kər\ *n* **1** : a bin or compartment for storage (as for coal or oil on a ship) **2 a** : a protective dugout; *esp* : a fortified chamber mostly below ground **b** : a sand trap on a golf course [Scots *bonker* "chest, box"]

bunk·house \'bəngk-,haus\ *n* : a rough simple building providing sleeping quarters (as for construction workers)

bun·kum *or* **bun·combe** \'bəng-kəm\ *n* : NONSENSE 1 [*Buncombe* County, North Carolina; from the statement by its congressional representative in defending a seemingly irrelevant speech that he was speaking to Buncombe]

bun·ny \'bən-ē\ *n, pl* **bunnies** : RABBIT [English dialect *bun* "rabbit"]

Bun·sen burner \'bən-sən-\ *n* : a gas burner consisting typically of a tube with small holes at the bottom where air enters and mixes with the gas to produce a very hot blue flame [Robert W. *Bunsen,* died 1899, German chemist]

¹bunt \'bənt\ *n* : the middle part of a square sail [perhaps from Low German, "bundle"]

²bunt *n* : a destructive smut of wheat in which the grains are replaced by greasy masses of dark ill-smelling spores [origin unknown]

³bunt *vb* **1** : to strike or push with or as if with the head : BUTT **2** : to push or tap a baseball lightly without swinging the bat [alteration of ¹*butt*] — **bunt·er** *n*

⁴bunt *n* **1** : an act or instance of bunting **2** : a bunted ball

¹bun·ting \'bənt-ing\ *n* : any of various stout-billed finches of the size and habits of a sparrow [Middle English]

²bunting *n* **1** : a thin cloth used chiefly for making flags and decorations **2** : flags or decorations made of bunting [perhaps from English dialect *bunt* "to sift"]

bunt·line \'bənt-,līn, -lən\ *n* : one of the ropes attached to the foot of a square sail to haul the sail up to the yard for furling

¹buoy \'bü-ē, 'bȯi\ *n* **1** : a floating marker anchored in a body of water to point out a channel or warn of danger **2** : LIFE BUOY [Middle English *boye*]

²buoy *vt* **1** : to mark by or as if by a buoy **2 a** : to keep afloat **b** : to raise the spirits of : SUSTAIN ⟨*buoyed* up by the news⟩

buoy·an·cy \'bȯi-ən-sē, 'bü-yən-\ *n* **1 a** : the tendency of a body to float or to rise when submerged in a fluid ⟨the *buoyancy* of a cork in water⟩ **b** : the power of a fluid to exert an upward force on a body placed in it ⟨the *buoyancy* of seawater⟩ **2** : natural lightness of spirit : LIGHTHEARTEDNESS

buoy·ant \'bȯi-ənt, 'bü-yənt\ *adj* **1** : able to rise and float in the air or on the surface of a liquid **2** : able to keep a body afloat ⟨hawks gliding in *buoyant* currents of air⟩ **3** : LIGHTHEARTED SYN see ELASTIC — **buoy·ant·ly** *adv*

bur *variant of* BURR

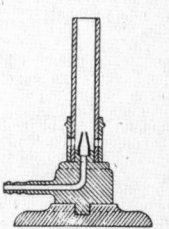

Bunsen burner

\ə\ abut	\ng\ sing
\ər\ further	\ō\ bone
\a\ mat	\ȯ\ saw
\ā\ take	\ȯi\ coin
\ä\ cot, cart	\th\ thin
\au̇\ out	\th\ this
\ch\ chin	\ü\ food
\e\ pet	\u̇\ foot
\ē\ easy	\y\ yet
\g\ go	\yü\ few
\i\ tip	\yu̇\ cure
\ī\ life	\zh\ vision
\j\ job	

bur·ble \'bər-bəl\ *vi* **bur·bled; bur·bling** \'bər-bə-ling, -bling\ **1** : to make a bubbling sound : GURGLE **2** : to talk constantly and enthusiastically : BABBLE [Middle English *burblen*] — **burble** *n* — **bur·bler** \-bə-lər, -blər\ *n* — **bur·bly** \-bə-lē, -blē\ *adj*

bur·bot \'bər-bət\ *n, pl* **burbot** *also* **burbots** : a northern freshwater fish related to the cod but somewhat resembling an eel [Middle French *bourbotte,* from *bourbe* "mud"]

¹**bur·den** \'bərd-n\ *n* **1 a** : something that is carried : LOAD **b** : something borne as a duty or responsibility often with labor or difficulty ⟨tax *burdens*⟩ **c** : the duty of doing or providing something ⟨*burden* of proof⟩ **2** : something hard to bear : ENCUMBRANCE **3 a** : the bearing of a load ⟨beasts of *burden*⟩ **b** : capacity for carrying cargo ⟨a ship of 100 tons *burden*⟩ [Old English *byrthen*]

²**burden** *vt* **bur·dened; bur·den·ing** \'bərd-ning, -n-ing\ : to put a burden on : LOAD, OPPRESS

³**burden** *n* **1** : the refrain or chorus of a song **2** : a main theme or central idea : GIST [Middle English *burdoun* "bass part", from Middle French *bourdon* "bass horn"]

bur·den·some \'bərd-n-səm\ *adj* : difficult to bear : OPPRESSIVE — **bur·den·some·ly** *adv* — **bur·den·some·ness** *n*

bur·dock \'bər-,däk\ *n* : any of a genus of coarse herbs related to the daisy that have globular flower heads with prickly bracts

bu·reau \'byür-ō\ *n, pl* **bu·reaus** *also* **bu·reaux** \-ōz\ **1 a** *British* : a writing desk; *esp* : one with drawers and a slant top **b** : a low chest of drawers with a mirror for use in a bedroom **2 a** : a subdivision of a governmental department performing a particular function ⟨Federal *Bureau* of Investigation⟩ **b** : a commercial agency providing services for the public or for other businesses ⟨a travel *bureau*⟩ [French, "desk, cloth covering for desks", derived from Late Latin *burra* "shaggy cloth"]

bu·reau·cra·cy \byü-'räk-rə-sē\ *n, pl* **-cies 1** : a body of appointed or hired government officials **2 a** : a system of administration characterized by specialization of functions, adherence to fixed rules, and a hierarchy of authority **b** : a system of administration marked by constant strivings for power and by ever increasing inefficiency and red tape

bu·reau·crat \'byür-ə-,krat\ *n* : a member of a bureaucracy; *esp* : one that carries out duties in a narrow routine way

bu·reau·crat·ic \,byür-ə-'krat-ik\ *adj* : of, relating to, or having the characteristics of a bureaucracy or a bureaucrat ⟨*bureaucratic* government⟩ — **bu·reau·crat·i·cal·ly** \-'krat-i-kə-lē, -klē\ *adv*

bu·rette *or* **bu·ret** \byü-'ret\ *n* : a graduated glass tube usually with a small opening at the bottom and a stopcock for delivering measured quantities of liquid or for measuring the liquid or gas received or discharged [French *burette,* from Middle French *buire* "pitcher", of Germanic origin]

burg \'bərg\ *n* **1** : a medieval fortress or walled town **2** : CITY, TOWN [Old English]

bur·gee \,bər-'jē\ *n* : a swallow-tailed flag used especially by ships for signals or identification [perhaps from French dialect *bourgeais* "shipowner"]

bur·geon \'bər-jən\ *vi* **1 a** : to put forth new growth (as buds) **b** : to burst into bloom : BLOSSOM **2** : to expand rapidly and widely [Middle English *burjon* "bud", from Old French, derived from Late Latin *burra* "shaggy cloth"]

bur·gess \'bər-jəs\ *n* **1** : a citizen of a British borough **2** : a representative in the lower house of the legislature of colonial Virginia [Middle English *burgeis* "burgher", from Old French *borjois*]

burgh \'bər-ō, 'bə-rō\ *n* : BOROUGH; *esp* : a Scottish town with certain local lawmaking rights [Old English *burg* "fortified town"]

bur·gher \'bər-gər\ *n* : an inhabitant of a borough or a town

bur·glar \'bər-glər\ *n* : a person who commits burglary : THIEF [Anglo-French *burgler,* from Medieval Latin *burglator*]

bur·glar·ize \'bər-glə-,rīz\ *vt* : to break into and steal from

bur·glary \'bər-glə-rē\ *n, pl* **-glar·ies** : the act of breaking into a building (as a house) especially at night and for the purpose of committing a crime (as stealing)

bur·go·mas·ter \'bər-gə-,mas-tər\ *n* : the chief magistrate of a town in some European countries [Dutch *burgemeester,* from *burg* "town" + *meester* "master"]

Bur·gun·dy \'bər-gən-dē\ *n* : a red or white table wine from parts of Burgundy; *also* : a similar wine made elsewhere

buri·al \'ber-ē-əl\ *n* : the act of burying

bu·rin \'byür-ən, 'bər-\ *n* **1** : a pointed steel cutting tool used by engravers **2** : a prehistoric flint tool with a point like that of a chisel [French]

¹**burl** \'bərl\ *n* **1** : a knot or lump in thread or cloth **2** : a gnarled woody outgrowth on a tree; *also* : veneer cut from this [Middle English *burle,* derived from Late Latin *burra* "shaggy cloth"]

²**burl** *vt* : to finish (cloth) especially by repairing burls — **burl·er** *n*

bur·lap \'bər-,lap\ *n* : a coarse fabric made usually from jute or hemp and used principally for bags and wrappings [earlier *borelapp*]

¹**bur·lesque** \bər-'lesk, ,bər-\ *n* **1 a** : a witty or derisive literary or dramatic imitation **b** : mockery usually by caricature **2** : theatrical entertainment consisting especially of low comedy skits and dance routines involving displays of partial nudity [French, "comical", from Italian *burlesco,* from *burla* "joke", from Spanish] SYN see CARICATURE — **burlesque** *adj*

²**burlesque** *vt* : to imitate in such a way as to make ridiculous — **bur·lesqu·er** *n*

bur·ly \'bər-lē\ *adj* **bur·li·er; -est** : strongly and heavily built : HUSKY [Middle English] — **bur·li·ness** *n*

bur marigold *n* : any of a genus of coarse herbs related to the daisies with burs that adhere to clothing

Bur·mese \,bər-'mēz, -'mēs\ *n, pl* **Burmese 1** : a native or inhabitant of Burma **2** : the language of the Burmese people — **Burmese** *adj*

¹**burn** \'bərn\ *n, British* : CREEK **2** [Old English]

²**burn** *vb* **burned** \'bərnd, 'bərnt\ *or* **burnt** \'bərnt\; **burn·ing 1 a** : BLAZE (the fire *burned* brightly) **b** : to undergo combustion; *also* : to undergo nuclear fission or fusion **2 a** : to feel hot (the *burning* sand) **b** : to become affected by or as if by the action of fire or heat; *esp* : SCORCH **c** : to give off light : GLOW (left the lights *burning*) **d** : to set on fire; *esp* : to destroy by fire (*burn* trash) **e** : to use as fuel (this furnace *burns* gas) **3** : to produce by the action of fire or heat (*burned* a hole in my shirt) **4** : to injure or alter by or as if by fire or heat (*burn* out a bearing) [Old English *byrnan* and *bærnan*] — **burn·able** \'bər-nə-bəl\ *adj* — **burn·ing·ly** \-ning-lē\ *adv* — **burn one's bridges** : to cut off all means of retreat — **burn the candle at both ends** : to be very wasteful of one's energy or resources

³**burn** *n* : injury, damage, or effect produced by or as if by burning

burn·er \'bər-nər\ *n* : one that burns; *esp* : the part of a fuel-burning device (as a stove or furnace) where the flame or heat is produced

burn–in \'bər-nin\ *n* : the continuous operation of a device (as a computer) as a test for defects or failure prior to putting it to use

¹**bur·nish** \'bər-nish\ *vt* : to make shiny or lustrous especially by rubbing : POLISH [Middle French *bruniss-,* stem of *brunir,* literally, "to make brown", from *brun* "brown"] — **bur·nish·er** *n* □ SYN BURNISH, POLISH

mean to smooth or brighten by rubbing. BURNISH applies chiefly to metals that are rubbed until they become lustrous; POLISH implies friction and usually the application of a substance (as wax) that gives a smooth and glossy surface.

²burnish *n* : LUSTER 1

bur·noose *or* **bur·nous** \bər-'nüs, ˌbər-\ *n* : a hooded cloak worn by Arabs and Berbers [French *burnous,* from Arabic *burnus*]

burn·out \'bər-ˌnaut\ *n* 1 : the stoppage of a jet or rocket engine; *also* : the point at which burnout occurs 2 : exhaustion of physical or emotional strength usually as a result of prolonged stress or frustation

burn out *vb* 1 : to drive out or destroy the property of by fire 2 : to cause to wear out or become exhausted especially from overwork or overuse

burn·sides \'bərn-ˌsīdz\ *n pl* : a beard consisting of side-whiskers and a mustache [Ambrose E. *Burnside*]

¹burp \'bərp\ *n* : the act or an instance of expelling stomach gas through the mouth : BELCH [imitative]

²burp *vb* 1 : BELCH 1 2 : to help (a baby) expel gas from the stomach especially by patting or rubbing the back

burp gun *n* : SUBMACHINE GUN

¹burr \'bər\ *n* 1 *usually* **bur a** : a rough or prickly envelope of a fruit **b** : a plant that bears burs 2 : BURL 2 3 : a roughness left by a tool in cutting or shaping metal 4 **a** : a trilled uvular \r\ as used by some speakers of English especially in northern England and in Scotland **b** : a tongue-point trill that is the usual Scottish \r\ 5 **a** : a small rotary cutting tool **b** *usually* **bur** : a bit used on a dental drill 6 : a rough humming sound : WHIR [Middle English *burre*] — **burred** \'bərd\ *adj*

²burr *vb* 1 : to speak or pronounce with a burr 2 : to make a whirring sound 3 **a** : to form into a rough edge **b** : to remove burrs from (as a sharp edge) — **burr·er** \'bər-ər\ *n*

bur reed *n* : any of a genus of plants with globe-shaped fruits resembling burs

bur·ri·to \bə-'rēt-ō\ *n, pl* **-tos** : a flour tortilla folded around a filling (as of meat or cheese) [American Spanish, from Spanish, "little donkey", diminutive of *burro*]

bur·ro \'bər-ō, 'bùr-; 'bə-rō\ *n, pl* **burros** : DONKEY; *esp* : a small one used as a pack animal [Spanish, from Late Latin *burricus* "small horse"]

¹bur·row \'bər-ō, 'bə-rō\ *n* : a hole in the ground made by an animal (as a rabbit) for shelter and habitation [Middle English *borow*]

²burrow *vb* 1 : to construct by tunneling 2 : to conceal oneself in or as if in a burrow 3 **a** : to make a burrow **b** : TUNNEL (they *burrowed* under the wall) 4 : to make a thorough search : DELVE (*burrowed* through the files) 5 : to make a motion suggestive of burrowing : NESTLE — **bur·row·er** *n*

bur·ry \'bər-ē\ *adj* : containing burs

bur·sa \'bər-sə\ *n, pl* **bur·sas** *or* **bur·sae** \-ˌsē, -ˌsī\ : a bodily pouch or sac; *esp* : a small serous sac between a tendon and a bone [Medieval Latin, "bag, purse", from Greek *byrsa* "animal skin"] — **bur·sal** \-səl\ *adj*

bur·sar \'bər-sər, -ˌsär\ *n* : a treasurer especially of a college or monastery [Medieval Latin *bursarius,* from *bursa* "bag, purse"]

bur·sa·ry \'bərs-rē, -ə-rē\ *n, pl* **-ries** : the treasury of a college or monastery

burse \'bərs\ *n* : a square cloth case for carrying the corporal in a Communion service [Medieval Latin *bursa* "bag, purse"]

bur·si·tis \ˌbər-'sīt-əs\ *n* : inflammation of a bursa especially of the shoulder or elbow

¹burst \'bərst\ *vb* **burst; burst·ing** 1 **a** : to break open, apart, or into pieces from or as if from impact or from or as if from pressure within (buds ready to *burst* open) **b** : to cause to burst (*burst* a balloon) 2 **a** : to give way from an excess of emotion (their hearts *burst* with grief) **b** : to give vent suddenly to an emotion (*burst* out laughing) 3 **a** : to emerge or spring suddenly (the sun *burst* through the clouds) **b** : LAUNCH, PLUNGE (*burst* into song) 4 : to be filled to the point of breaking or overflowing (*bursting* with pride) [Old English *berstan*]

²burst *n* 1 **a** : a sudden outbreak or outburst (a *burst* of laughter) **b** : a sudden intense effort or exertion (a *burst* of speed) **c** : a short quick volley of shots (fire a machine gun in *bursts*) 2 : an act of bursting 3 : a result of bursting; *esp* : a visible puff accompanying the explosion of a shell

bur·then \'bər-thən\ *archaic variant of* BURDEN

bur·weed \'bər-ˌwēd\ *n* : any of various plants with the fruit enclosed in a bur

bury \'ber-ē\ *vt* **bur·ied; bury·ing** 1 : to deposit (a dead body) in the earth, in a tomb, or in the sea especially with funeral ceremonies 2 : to place in the ground and cover over (*bury* treasure) 3 : CONCEAL, HIDE (*bury* one's face in one's hands) 4 : to remove from the world of action (*bury* oneself in a book) [Old English *byrgan*] — **bur·i·er** *n* — **bury the hatchet** : to settle a disagreement : become reconciled

¹bus \'bəs\ *n, pl* **bus·es** *or* **bus·ses** 1 **a** : a large motor vehicle for carrying passengers especially on an established route according to a schedule **b** *slang* : AUTOMOBILE 2 : a conductor for collecting electric currents and distributing them to outgoing feeders — called also *bus bar* [short for *omnibus*] □ ORIGIN Latin *omnibus,* the dative plural of *omnis* "all", means "for all". In English, *omnibus* has several meanings. An omnibus may be a public vehicle which carries all or a waiter's assistant who does all odd jobs. The shortening of *omnibus* has given us *bus,* the usual word for the vehicle.

²bus *vb* **bused** *or* **bussed; bus·ing** *or* **bus·sing** : to travel or transport by bus

bus·boy \'bəs-ˌbòi\ *n* : a person employed in a restaurant to remove dirty dishes and reset tables [*omnibus* "busboy"]

bus·by \'bəz-bē\ *n, pl* **busbies** 1 : a military full-dress fur hat with a bag hanging down on one side 2 : the bearskin worn by British guardsmen [probably from the name *Busby*]

bus girl *n* : a woman or girl employed as a busboy

bush \'bùsh\ *n* 1 : SHRUB; *esp* : a low densely branched shrub 2 : a large uncleared or sparsely settled area (as in Australia) 3 : a bushy tuft or mass; *esp* : BRUSH 2 [Middle English]

bush baby *n* : any of several small African lemurs

bushed \'bùsht\ *adj* : worn out with fatigue : EXHAUSTED

bush·el \'bùsh-əl\ *n* 1 : any of various units of dry capacity — see MEASURE table 2 : a container holding a bushel 3 : a large quantity : LOTS [Old French *boissel,* of Celtic origin]

Bu·shi·do \'bùsh-i-ˌdō, 'büsh-\ *n* : a Japanese code of feudal chivalry emphasizing loyalty and valuing honor above life [Japanese *bushidō*]

bush·ing \'bùsh-iŋ\ *n* 1 : a usually removable cylindrical lining in an opening of a mechanical part to limit the size of the opening, resist wear (as in a bearing for an axle), or serve as a guide 2 : an electrically insulating lining for a hole to protect a conductor [Dutch *bus* "bushing, box", from Late Latin *buxis* "box"]

Bush·man \'bùsh-mən\ *n* : a member of a nomadic hunting people of southern Africa

bush·mas·ter \-ˌmas-tər\ *n* : a tropical American pit viper that is the largest New World venomous snake

bush pilot *n* : a pilot who flies a small plane over uncleared or sparsely settled country especially away from regular commercial air routes

bush·whack \'bùsh-ˌhwak, -ˌwak\ *vb* 1 : to clear a path through woods by cutting bushes and low branches

busby 1

2 : to live or hide out in the woods **3** : to attack from a place of hiding : AMBUSH — **bush·whack·er** n — **bush·whack·ing** n

bushy \'bush-ē\ adj **bush·i·er; -est** **1** : full of or overgrown with bushes **2** : resembling a bush especially in thick spreading form or growth ⟨bushy eyebrows⟩ — **bush·i·ness** n

busi·ness \'biz-nəs, -nəz\ n **1 a** : an activity that takes a major part of the time, attention, or effort of a person or group **b** : a commercial or mercantile activity engaged in as a means of livelihood **2** : an immediate task or objective : MISSION ⟨get down to business⟩ **3 a** : a commercial or industrial enterprise **b** : the area of economic activity that usually includes trade, commerce, finance, and industry **c** : transactions of any sort; esp : PATRONAGE ⟨took their business elsewhere⟩ **4** : AFFAIR, MATTER ⟨a strange business⟩ **5** : personal concern ⟨none of your business⟩ [Middle English bisinesse, from bisy "busy"] □ SYN BUSINESS, COMMERCE, TRADE, INDUSTRY mean activity in supplying commodities. BUSINESS may be an inclusive term but specifically applies to the activities of all engaged in the sale and purchase of commodities or in related financial transactions; COMMERCE and TRADE apply to the exchange and transportation of commodities; INDUSTRY applies to the producing of commodities, especially by manufacturing or processing.

busi·ness·like \'biz-nəs-ˌlīk, -nəz-\ adj **1** : having or showing qualities desirable in business **2** : SERIOUS, PURPOSEFUL

busi·ness·man \'biz-nə-ˌsman\ n : a man engaged in a business enterprise especially on an executive level

busi·ness·wom·an \-ˌswúm-ən\ n : a woman engaged in a business enterprise especially on an executive level

bus·kin \'bəs-kən\ n **1** : a boot reaching halfway to the knee **2** : TRAGEDY 1; esp : tragedy resembling ancient Greek drama [perhaps from Spanish borcegui]

bus·man's holiday \'bəs-mənz-\ n : a holiday spent in doing something similar to one's usual occupation

buss \'bəs\ n : KISS 1 [probably imitative] — **buss** vt

¹bust \'bəst\ n **1** : a piece of sculpture representing the upper part of the human figure including the head and neck **2** : the upper portion of the human torso between neck and waist; esp : the breasts of a woman [French buste, from Italian busto, from Latin bustum "tomb"]

²bust vb **bust·ed** also **bust; bust·ing** **1** : HIT, PUNCH **2 a** : to break up or apart ⟨bust trusts⟩; also : FRACTURE **b** : to ruin financially **3** : to demote especially in military rank **4** : BURST ⟨laughing fit to bust⟩ **5** slang : ARREST 2 [alteration of burst] — **bust·er** n

³bust n **1** : ²PUNCH 2 **2** : a complete failure **3** : SPREE **4** slang : ARREST 2

bus·tard \'bəs-tərd\ n : any of various Old World and Australian game birds [Middle French bistarde, from Italian bistarda, from Latin aves tarda, literally, "slow bird"]

¹bus·tle \'bəs-əl\ vi **bus·tled; bus·tling** \'bəs-ling, -ə-ling\ **1** : to move about busily and noisily ⟨bustling about the house⟩ **2** : to be busily astir : SEETHE ⟨the wharf bustled with activity⟩ [probably from busk "to prepare"]

²bustle n : noisy or energetic activity

³bustle n : a pad or a light frame formerly worn by women just below the back waistline to give fullness to the skirt [origin unknown]

¹busy \'biz-ē\ adj **bus·i·er; -est** **1 a** : engaged in action : OCCUPIED ⟨too busy to eat⟩ **b** : being in use ⟨a busy telephone⟩ **2** : full of activity : BUSTLING ⟨a busy street⟩ **3** : OFFICIOUS, MEDDLING **4** : full of distracting detail ⟨a busy design⟩ [Old English bisig] — **bus·i·ly** \'biz-ə-lē\ adv

²busy vb **bus·ied; busy·ing** : to make or keep busy : OCCUPY

busy·body \'biz-ē-ˌbäd-ē\ n : a person who meddles in the affairs of others

busy·ness \'biz-ē-nəs\ n : the quality or state of being busy

¹but \bət, 'bət\ conj **1 a** : except that : UNLESS ⟨it never rains but it pours⟩ **b** : that . . . not ⟨not so stupid but you could learn⟩ **c** : THAT — used after a negative ⟨there is no doubt but we won⟩ **2 a** (1) : on the contrary ⟨not peace but a sword⟩ ⟨was called but did not answer⟩ (2) : despite that fact : YET ⟨was poor but honest⟩ ⟨we tried but we failed⟩ **b** : with this exception, namely ⟨no one but you may enter⟩ [Old English būtan "outside, except, except that"]

²but prep **1** : with the exception of ⟨no one came but us⟩ **2** : other than ⟨this letter is nothing but an insult⟩

³but adv **1** : no more than : ONLY ⟨we are but children⟩ **2** : otherwise than ⟨who knows but that we may succeed⟩

bu·ta·di·ene \ˌbyüt-ə-'dī-ˌēn, -ˌdī'-\ n : a flammable gaseous hydrocarbon C_4H_6 used in making synthetic rubbers [butane + di- + -ene]

bu·tane \'byü-ˌtān\ n : either of two flammable gaseous hydrocarbons C_4H_{10} obtained usually from petroleum or natural gas [butyric + -ane]

¹butch·er \'búch-ər\ n **1 a** : a person who slaughters animals or dresses their flesh **b** : a dealer in meat **2** : one that kills ruthlessly or brutally **3** : a vendor especially on a train or at a circus [Old French bouchier, from bouc "he-goat"]

²butcher vt **butch·ered; butch·er·ing** \'búch-ring, -ə-ring\ **1** : to slaughter and dress for meat ⟨butchered hogs last week⟩ **2** : to kill in a barbarous manner **3** : to make a mess of : BOTCH — **butch·er·er** \-ər-ər\ n

butch·er·bird \'búch-ər-ˌbərd\ n : any of various shrikes that impale their prey upon thorns

butch·ery \'búch-rē, -ə-rē\ n, pl **-er·ies** **1** chiefly British : SLAUGHTERHOUSE **2** : the business of a butcher **3** : brutal murder : great slaughter

bu·teo \'byüt-ē-ˌō\ n, pl **-te·os** : any of various hawks with broad rounded wings and soaring flight [Latin, a kind of hawk]

but·ler \'bət-lər\ n : the chief male servant of a household [Old French bouteillier "servant in charge of wine", from bouteille "bottle"]

butler's pantry n : a service room between kitchen and dining room

¹butt \'bət\ vb : to strike with the head or horns [Old French boter, of Germanic origin]

²butt n : a blow or thrust usually with the head or horns

³butt n **1 a** : a mound, bank, or structure for stopping missiles shot at a target **b** : TARGET 1a **c** pl : RANGE 5b **2** : a target of abuse or ridicule ⟨the butt of a joke⟩ [Middle French but "target", of Germanic origin]

⁴butt vb **1** : ABUT 1 **2** : to place end to end without overlapping

⁵butt n **1** : BUTTOCK 2 **2** : the large or thicker end of something; esp : the thicker or handle end of a tool or weapon **3** : an unused remainder ⟨a cigarette butt⟩ [Middle English]

⁶butt n **1** : a large cask especially for wine, beer, or water **2** : any of various units of liquid capacity; esp : a measure equal to 108 imperial gallons (about 491 liters) [Middle French botte, from Old Provençal bota, from Late Latin buttis]

butte \'byüt\ n : an isolated hill with steep sides usually having a smaller summit area than a mesa [French]

¹but·ter \'bət-ər\ n **1** : a solid yellow emulsion of fat, air, and water made by churning milk or cream and used as food **2** : a substance resembling butter in appearance, texture, or use ⟨apple butter⟩ [Old English butere, from Latin butyrum, from Greek boutyron, from bous "cow" + tyros "cheese"]

²butter vt : to spread with or as if with butter

but·ter–and–eggs \ˌbət-ə-rə-'negz, -'nāgz\ n sing or pl : a common European herb of the snapdragon fami-

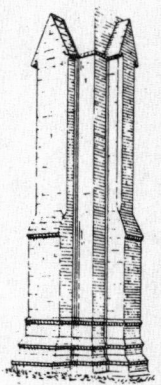

¹buttress 1

ly that has showy yellow and orange flowers and is a naturalized weed in much of North America — called also *toadflax*

but·ter bean *n* **1** : WAX BEAN **2** : LIMA BEAN **3** : a green shell bean especially as opposed to a snap bean

but·ter·cup \'bət-ər-ˌkəp\ *n* : any of a genus of yellow-flowered herbs with usually five petals and five sepals, usually lobed leaves, and fruits that are achenes

but·ter·fat \-ˌfat\ *n* : the natural fat of milk and chief constituent of butter

but·ter·fin·gered \'bət-ər-ˌfing-gərd\ *adj* : likely to let things fall or slip through the fingers

but·ter·fish \-ˌfish\ *n* : any of numerous fishes with a slippery coating of mucus

but·ter·fly \'bət-ər-ˌflī\ *n* **1** : any of numerous slender-bodied day-flying insects (order Lepidoptera) often with large broad usually brightly colored wings — compare MOTH **2** : a person who dresses gaudily or who is chiefly occupied in the pursuit of pleasure **3** : a swimming stroke performed by moving both arms together in a circular motion while kicking the legs up and down **4** *pl* : a queasy feeling caused by nervousness

butterfly fish *n* : any of various fishes having variegated colors, broad expanded fins, or both

butterfly weed *n* : a showy orange-flowered milkweed of eastern North America

but·ter·milk \'bət-ər-ˌmilk\ *n* **1** : the liquid left after the butterfat has been churned from milk or cream **2** : cultured milk made by the addition of certain organisms to sweet milk

but·ter·nut \-ˌnət\ *n* **1** : the edible oily nut of an American tree of the walnut family **2** : a butternut tree

butternut squash *n* : a smooth buff to yellow winter squash

but·ter·scotch \-ˌskäch\ *n* : a candy made from sugar, corn syrup, and water; *also* : the flavor of such candy — **butterscotch** *adj*

¹**but·tery** \'bət-ə-rē, 'bə-trē\ *n, pl* **-ter·ies** *chiefly dialect* : PANTRY [Middle French *boterie* "storeroom for liquors", from *botte* "cask, butt"]

²**but·tery** \'bət-ə-rē\ *adj* **1** : having the qualities of butter **2** : containing or spread with butter **3** : marked by flattery

butt hinge *n* : a hinge usually set flush into the edge of a door

butt in *vi* : to meddle in the affairs of others

butt joint *n* : a joint made by fastening the parts together end-to-end without overlap and often with reinforcement

but·tock \'bət-ək\ *n* **1** : the back of the hip which forms one of the fleshy parts on which a person sits **2** *pl* : the seat of the human body [Middle English *buttok*]

¹**but·ton** \'bət-n\ *n* **1** : a small knob or disk (as of shell, leather, or plastic) used for holding parts of a garment together or as an ornament **2** : something (as an immature mushroom) that resembles a button [Middle French *boton*, from *boter* "to thrust, butt"]

²**button** *vb* **but·toned; but·ton·ing** \'bət-ning, -n-ing\ : to close or fasten with buttons — **but·ton·er** \'bət-nər, -n-ər\ *n*

¹**but·ton·hole** \'bət-n-ˌhōl\ *n* : a slit or loop for fastening a button

²**buttonhole** *vt* **1** : to furnish with buttonholes **2** : to work with buttonhole stitch

³**buttonhole** *vt* : to hold in conversation by or as if by clutching the clothes — **but·ton·hol·er** *n*

buttonhole stitch *n* : a closely worked loop stitch used to make a firm edge (as on a buttonhole)

but·ton·hook \'bət-n-ˌhuk\ *n* : a hook for drawing small buttons through buttonholes

but·ton·wood \'bət-n-ˌwud\ *n* : PLANE TREE

¹**but·tress** \'bə-trəs\ *n* **1** : a projecting structure (as of masonry) that supports or stabilizes a wall or building

2 : something that supports, props, or strengthens [Middle French *bouterez* from *bouter* "to thrust"]

²**buttress** *vt* : to support with or as if with a buttress : PROP, STRENGTHEN (*buttress* an argument with facts)

bu·tyl alcohol \'byüt-l-\ *n* : any of four flammable alcohols C_4H_9OH derived from butanes and used in organic synthesis and as solvents [*but*yric + -*yl*]

bu·tyr·ic acid \byü-'tir-ik-\ *n* : an acid $C_4H_8O_2$ of unpleasant odor found in rancid butter and perspiration [Latin *butyrum* "butter"]

bux·om \'bək-səm\ *adj* : vigorously or healthily plump; *also* : having a large bosom [Middle English *buxsum* "obedient, tractable", from Old English *būgan* "to bend"] — **bux·om·ly** *adv* — **bux·om·ness** *n*

¹**buy** \'bī\ *vt* **bought** \'bot\; **buy·ing** **1** : to become owner of by giving money in exchange **2** : to obtain by sacrificing something (*buy* peace at the cost of freedom) **3** : to secure decisive control over by bribery (*buy* votes) **4** : to be sufficient to purchase ($5000 will *buy* this land) **5** : BELIEVE 3, ACCEPT [Old English *bycgan*]

²**buy** *n* **1** : an act of buying : PURCHASE **2** : something sold or for sale at a price favorable to a buyer : BARGAIN

buy·er \'bī-ər, 'bīr\ *n* : one that buys; *esp* : a person who purchases goods to be sold in a retail store

buyer's market *n* : a market with many goods at relatively low prices — compare SELLER'S MARKET

buy up *vt* : to buy all of the available supply of

¹**buzz** \'bəz\ *vb* **1** : to make a low continuous humming sound like that of a bee **2** : to be filled with a confused murmur (the room *buzzed* with excitement) **3** : to summon or signal with a buzzer **4** : to fly low and fast over (planes *buzzed* the crowd) [Middle English *bussen*]

²**buzz** *n* **1** : a persistent sound produced by or as if by rapid vibrations **2** : a confused murmur or flurry of activity **3 a** : a signal conveyed by buzzer **b** : a call on the telephone

buz·zard \'bəz-ərd\ *n* **1** *chiefly British* : BUTEO **2** : any of several vultures; *esp* : TURKEY BUZZARD [Old French *busard*, derived from Latin *buteo*, a kind of hawk]

buzz·er \'bəz-ər\ *n* : an electric signaling device that makes a buzzing sound

buzz saw *n* : CIRCULAR SAW

B vitamin *n* : any vitamin of the vitamin B complex

¹**by** \bī, 'bī, *especially before consonants* bə\ *prep* **1** : close to : NEAR (*by* the sea) **2 a** : ALONG, THROUGH (*by* a different route) (enter *by* the door) **b** : PAST (went right *by* us) **3 a** : during the course of (studied *by* night) **b** : not later than (be there *by* 2 p.m.) **4** : through the agency or instrumentality of (painted *by* a master) (a town taken *by* force) **5** : with the witness or sanction of (swear *by* all that is holy) **6 a** : in conformity with (*by* the rules) **b** : in terms of (sold *by* the pound) **7** : with respect to (a doctor *by* profession) **8** : in or to the amount or extent of (win *by* a nose) **9** — used as a function word to indicate a succession of units or groups (walk two *by* two) **10 a** — used as a function word in multiplication, in division, and in measurements (divide 12 *by* 4) (a room 4 meters *by* 6 meters) **b** : plus one point toward (north *by* northeast) [Old English *be, bī*] □ SYN BY, THROUGH, WITH are used in explaining or accounting for an action or effect. BY names the immediate agent or causative agency (a novel *by* Dickens) (destroyed *by* fire) THROUGH implies intermediateness and names a means or medium (express feelings *through* music) (money lost *through* carelessness) WITH names an instrument or instrumentality used in or accompanying an action (wrote *with* a pen) (amused them *with* a story)

²**by** \'bī\ *adv* **1 a** : close at hand : NEAR (standing *by*) **b** : at or to another's home (stop *by* for a chat) **2** : PAST

⟨saw them go *by*⟩ **3** : in reserve for future using ⟨putting some money *by*⟩

³by *or* **bye** \'bī\ *n, pl* **byes** \'bīz\ : something of secondary importance — **by the by** : by the way : INCIDENTALLY

by–and–by \,bī-ən-'bī\ *n* : a future time or occasion

by and by \,bī-ən-'bī\ *adv* : before long : SOON

by and large \,bī-ən-'lärj\ *adv* : on the whole : in general

bye–bye *or* **by–by** \'bī-,bī, bī-'bī\ *interj* — used to express farewell [from *goodbye*]

by–elec·tion \'bī-ə-,lek-shən\ *n* : a special election held between regular elections in order to fill a vacancy

by·gone \'bī-,gȯn *also* -,gän\ *adj* : gone by : PAST ⟨a *bygone* era⟩ — **bygone** *n*

by·law \'bī-,lȯ\ *n* : a rule adopted by an organization (as a club or municipality) for the regulation of its affairs [Middle English *bilawe*, probably from Old Norse *bȳr* "town" + *lǫg* "law"]

by·line \'bī-,līn\ *n* : a line at the head of a newspaper or magazine article giving the writer's name

¹by·pass \'bī-,pas\ *n* **1** : a passage to one side or around a congested area **2** : a channel through which a fluid passes around a particular part and back to the main stream

²bypass *vt* : to make a detour or circuit around ⟨*bypass* a city⟩

by·path \'bī-,path, -,pȧth\ *n* : BYWAY 1

by·play \-,plā\ *n* : action occurring on the side while the main action proceeds (as in a play)

by–prod·uct \'bī-,präd-əkt, -,əkt\ *n* **1** : something produced (as in manufacturing) in addition to the principal product **2** : a secondary and often unexpected or unintended result

byre \'bīr\ *n, chiefly British* : a cow barn [Old English *bȳre*]

by·road \'bī-,rōd\ *n* : BYWAY 1

By·ron·ic \bī-'rän-ik\ *adj* : of, relating to, or having the characteristics of the poet Byron or his writings — **By·ron·i·cal·ly** \-'rän-i-kə-lē, -klē\ *adv* — **By·ron·ism** \'bī-rə-,niz-əm\ *n*

bys·sus \'bis-əs\ *n* : a tuft of long tough filaments by which some mollusks (as mussels) attach themselves (as to rocks) [Greek *byssos* "flax", of Semitic origin]

by·stand·er \'bī-,stan-dər\ *n* : a person present or standing near but taking no part in something going on

by·street \'bī-,strēt\ *n* : a street off a main thoroughfare : a side street

byte \'bīt\ *n* : a group of adjacent binary digits often shorter than a word that a computer processes as a unit ⟨an 8-bit *byte*⟩ [perhaps alteration of ²*bite*]

by·way \'bī-,wā\ *n* **1** : a little-traveled side road **2** : a secondary or little known aspect or field

by·word \'bī-,wərd\ *n* **1** : a proverbial saying **2 a** : a person or thing typical especially of some bad class or quality **b** : an object of scorn or contempt

¹Byz·an·tine \'biz-n-,tēn *also* -,tīn\ *n* : a native or inhabitant of Byzantium or of the Byzantine Empire

²Byzantine *adj* **1** : of, relating to, or characteristic of the ancient city of Byzantium or the Eastern Roman Empire **2** : of or relating to a style of architecture developed in the Byzantine Empire especially in the 5th and 6th centuries characterized by a central dome over a square space and by much use of mosaics **3** : of or relating to the Eastern Orthodox Church **4** : intricately involved and often devious ⟨*Byzantine* political maneuvering⟩

Cc

c \'sē\ *n, pl* **c's** *or* **cs** \'sēz\ *often cap* **1** : the 3d letter of the English alphabet **2** : one hundred in Roman numerals **3** : the musical tone C **4** : a grade rating a student's work as fair or mediocre

cab \'kab\ *n* **1 a** : a light closed horse-drawn carriage (as a hansom) **b** : a carriage for hire **2** : TAXICAB **3 a** : the part of a locomotive that houses the engineer and operating controls **b** : a comparable shelter on a truck, tractor, or crane [short for *cabriolet*]

ca·bal \kə-'bal, -'bäl\ *n* : a small group of persons working together to promote their own plans or interests especially by intrigue [French *cabale*, from Medieval Latin *cabbala* "cabala", from Hebrew *qabbālāh*, literally, "received (lore)"]

ca·ba·la *or* **cab·ba·la** *or* **cab·ba·lah** *or* **kab·ba·la** *or* **kab·ba·lah** *or* **ka·ba·la** \'kab-ə-lə, kə-'bäl-ə\ *n, often cap* **1** : a system of Jewish mysticism and magic using a cipher method of interpreting Scripture **2** : a strange and abstruse doctrine or mysterious art [Medieval Latin *cabbala*] — **cab·a·lism** \'kab-ə-,liz-əm\ *n* — **ca·ba·list** \'kab-ə-ləst, kə-'bäl-əst\ *adj* — **cab·a·lis·tic** \,kab-ə-'lis-tik\ *adj*

ca·bal·le·ro \,kab-ə-'leər-ō, -əl-'yeər-, -ə-'yeər-\ *n, pl* **-ros** *chiefly Southwest* : HORSEMAN [Spanish, derived from Latin *caballus* "horse"]

ca·bana \kə-'ban-yə, -'ban-ə\ *n* : a shelter resembling a cabin usually with an open side facing a beach or swimming pool [Spanish *cabaña*, literally "hut", from Medieval Latin *capanna*]

cab·a·ret \,kab-ə-'rā\ *n* : a restaurant serving liquor and providing entertainment (as by singers or dancers) [French]

cab·bage \'kab-ij\ *n* : a garden plant related to the turnip but lacking a swollen root and producing a dense globular head of leaves used as a vegetable [Old North French *caboche* "head"]

cab·by *or* **cab·bie** \'kab-ē\ *n, pl* **cabbies** : a driver of a cab

cab·driv·er \'kab-,drī-vər\ *n* : a driver of a cab

cab·in \'kab-ən\ *n* **1 a** : a private room on a ship for one or a few persons **b** : a compartment below deck on a small boat for passengers or crew **c** : an airplane or airship compartment for cargo, crew, or passengers **2** : a small one-story dwelling usually of simple construction [Middle French *cabane*, from Provençal *cabana* "hut", from Medieval Latin *capanna*]

cabin boy *n* : a boy working as servant on a ship

cabin class *n* : a class of accommodations on a passenger ship superior to tourist class and inferior to first class

cabin cruiser *n* : CRUISER 3

cab·i·net \'kab-ə-nət, 'kab-nət\ *n* **1 a** : a case or cupboard usually having doors and shelves **b** : an upright case housing a radio, television, or phonograph : CONSOLE **2 a** : a group of ministers acting as advisers to a monarch or chief of state but constituting the real political executive in a cabinet government ⟨the British *cabinet*⟩ **b** : a body of advisers to the president of the United States consisting chiefly of the heads of the executive departments [Middle French, "small room", from Old North French *cabine* "gambling house"]

cabinet government *n* : a government in which the real executive and policy-making power is held by a cabinet of ministers who are responsible to the legislature

cab·i·net·mak·er \-,mā-kər\ *n* : a skilled woodworker who makes fine furniture — **cab·i·net·mak·ing** \-king\ *n*

cab·i·net·work \-,wərk\ *n* : the finished work of a cabinetmaker

¹ca·ble \'kā-bəl\ *n* **1 a** : a strong rope especially of 25 or more centimeters in circumference **b** : a wire rope or metal chain of great strength **c** : a wire or wire rope by which force is exerted to operate a mechanism **2** : CABLE LENGTH **3 a** : a bundle of electrical conductors insulated from each other but held together usually by being twisted around a central core **b** : CABLEGRAM [Old North French, from Medieval Latin *capulum* "lasso", from Latin *capere* "to take"]

²cable *vb* **ca·bled; ca·bling** \'kā-bling, -bə-ling\ **1** : to fasten or provide with a cable **2** : to telegraph by submarine cable

cable car *n* : a car moved on a railway by an endless cable or along an overhead cableway

ca·ble·gram \'kā-bəl-,gram\ *n* : a message sent by submarine cable

cable length *n* : a maritime unit of length variously reckoned as 100 fathoms, 120 fathoms, or 608 feet (about 183, 220, or 185 meters)

cable railway *n* : a railway on which the cars grip and are moved by an endless cable that is driven by a stationary engine

cable TV *n* : a system of television reception in which signals are picked up by a single antenna and sent by cable to the receivers of paying subscribers — called also *cable television*

ca·ble·way \'kā-bəl-,wā\ *n* : a suspended cable used as a track along which carriers can be pulled

cab·o·chon \'kab-ə-,shän\ *n* : a gem or bead cut in convex form and highly polished but not faceted [Middle French, from Old North French *caboche* "head"] — **cabochon** *adv*

ca·boose \kə-'büs\ *n* : a freight-train car attached usually to the rear mainly for the use of the train crew and railroad workers [probably from Dutch *kabuis* "ship's galley"]

cab·ri·o·let \,kab-rē-ə-'lā\ *n* **1** : a light 2-wheeled one-horse carriage with a folding leather top and upward-curving shafts **2** : a convertible coupe [French, from *cabriole* "caper", from Middle French *capriole*]

cab·stand \'kab-,stand\ *n* : a place for cabs to park while waiting for passengers

ca·cao \kə-'kaù, kə-'kā-ō\ *n, pl* **cacaos** **1** : a South American tree with small yellowish flowers followed by fleshy yellow pods with many seeds **2** : the dried partly fermented fatty seeds of the cacao from which cocoa and chocolate are made — called also *cacao bean, cocoa bean* [Spanish, from Nahuatl *cacahuatl* "cacao beans"]

¹cache \'kash\ *n* **1** : a place for hiding, storing, or safeguarding treasure or food and supplies **2** : the material hidden in a cache **3** : a computer memory

with very short access time used from storage of frequently used instructions or data [French, from *cacher* "to hide"]

²cache *vt* : to place, hide, or store in a cache

ca·chet \ka-'shā\ *n* **1** : a seal especially of official approval **2** : a characteristic feature or quality conferring prestige **3** : a design on an envelope commemorating an event important to stamp collectors ⟨a *cachet* on a first day cover⟩ [Middle French, from *cacher* "to press, hide"]

ca·chex·ia \kə-'kek-sē-ə, ka-\ *n* : general physical wasting and malnutrition usually associated with chronic disease [Late Latin, from Greek *kachexia* "bad condition", from *kakos* "bad" + *hexis* "condition"] — **ca·chec·tic** \-'kek-tik\ *adj*

ca·cique \kə-'sēk\ *n* : an Indian chief in Latin America [Spanish, of American Indian origin]

cack·le \'kak-əl\ *vi* **cack·led; cack·ling** \'kak-ling, -ə-ling\ **1** : to make the sharp broken noise or cry characteristic of a hen especially after laying **2** : to laugh or chatter noisily [Middle English *cakelen*, of imitative origin] — **cackle** *n* — **cack·ler** \'kak-lər, -ə-lər\ *n*

ca·coph·o·ny \kə-'käf-ə-nē, ka-\ *n, pl* **-nies** : harsh or discordant sound : DISSONANCE [Greek *kakophōnia*, from *kakos* "bad" + *phōnē* "sound"] — **ca·coph·o·nous** \-nəs\ *adj*

cac·tus \'kak-təs\ *n, pl* **cac·tus·es** *or* **cac·ti** \-,tī, -,tē, -tē\ : any of a large family of flowering plants able to live in dry regions and having fleshy stems and branches that bear scales or prickles instead of leaves [Latin, "cardoon", from Greek *kaktos*]

cad \'kad\ *n* : a person who behaves in a usually deliberately callous way [English dialect, "unskilled assistant", from Scottish *caddie*]

ca·dav·er \kə-'dav-ər\ *n* : a dead body especially of a human being : CORPSE [Latin, from *cadere* "to fall"] — **ca·dav·er·ic** \-'dav-rik, -ə-rik\ *adj*

ca·dav·er·ous \kə-'dav-rəs, -ə-rəs\ *adj* : of, relating to, or resembling a cadaver: as **a** : GHASTLY 2, PALE **b** : THIN 3, HAGGARD — **ca·dav·er·ous·ly** *adv*

¹cad·die *or* **cad·dy** \'kad-ē\ *n, pl* **caddies** : a person who carries a golfer's clubs [Scottish *caddie* "one who does odd jobs", from French *cadet* "military cadet"]

²caddie *or* **caddy** *vi* **-died; -dy·ing** : to work as a caddie

cad·dis fly \'kad-əs-\ *n* : any of an order (Trichoptera) of 4-winged insects with aquatic larvae — compare CADDISWORM

cad·dish \'kad-ish\ *adj* : resembling a cad or the behavior of a cad — **cad·dish·ly** *adv* — **cad·dish·ness** *n*

cad·dis·worm \'kad-əs-,wərm\ *n* : a caddis-fly larva that lives in and carries around a silken case covered with bits of debris [probably from obsolete *codworm*, from Middle English *cod* "bag"]

cad·dy \'kad-ē\ *n, pl* **caddies** : a small box, can, or chest; *esp* : one to keep tea in [Malay *kati*, a unit of weight]

ca·dence \'kād-ns\ *n* **1 a** : rhythmic flow of sounds in language **b** : the beat, time, or measure of rhythmical motion or activity **2** : the close of a musical strain; *esp* : a musical chord sequence moving to a harmonic close or point of rest [Italian *cadenza*, from *cadere* "to fall", from Latin] — **ca·denced** \-nst\ *adj*

ca·den·za \kə-'den-zə\ *n* **1** : an added flourish in a solo piece (as an aria) commonly just before the end **2** : a technically brilliant sometimes improvised solo passage toward the close of a movement of a concerto [Italian, "cadence, cadenza"]

ca·det \kə-'det\ *n* **1 a** : a younger brother or son **b** : a younger branch of a family or a member of it **2** : one in training for a military commission; *esp* : a student in a service academy **3** : a student at a military school **4** : a boy or girl in any of various organizations usually associated with an adult group organized on military lines [French, from French dialect *capdet* "chief",

\ə\ abut		\ng\ sing	
\ər\ **further**		\ō\ **bone**	
\a\ **mat**		\ò\ **saw**	
\ā\ **take**		\òi\ **coin**	
\ä\ **cot, cart**		\th\ **thin**	
\aù\ **out**		\t̶h̶\ **this**	
\ch\ **chin**		\ü\ **food**	
\e\ **pet**		\ù\ **foot**	
\ē\ **easy**		\y\ **yet**	
\g\ **go**		\yü\ **few**	
\i\ **tip**		\yù\ **cure**	
\ī\ **life**		\zh\ **vision**	
\j\ **job**			

from Late Latin *capitellum,* from *caput* "head"] — **ca·det·ship** \-,ship\ *n*

cadge \'kaj\ *vb* : BEG 1, SPONGE [back-formation from Scottish *cadger* "peddler", from Middle English *caggen* "to tie"] — **cadg·er** *n*

cad·mi·um \'kad-mē-əm\ *n* : a bluish white malleable ductile metallic element used especially in protective platings and in bearing metals — see ELEMENT table [Latin *cadmia* "calamine"; from the occurrence of its ores together with *calamine*]

cad·re \'kad-rē, 'käd-, -,rä\ *n* **1** : a nucleus of trained personnel capable of assuming leadership and control and of training others **2** : a member of a cadre [French, "frame, framework", from Italian *quadro,* from Latin *quadrum* "square"]

ca·du·ceus \kə-'dü-sē-əs, -'dyü-, -shəs\ *n, pl* **-cei** \-sē-,ī\ **1 a** : the symbolic staff of a herald **b** : a representation of a staff with two entwined snakes and two wings at the top **2** : an insignia bearing a caduceus and symbolizing a physician [Latin, from Greek *karykeion,* from *karyx, kēryx* "herald"] — **ca·du·cean** \-sē-ən, -shən\ *adj*

cae·cal, cae·cum *variant of* CECAL, CECUM

cae·ci·lian \si-'sil-yən, -'sēl-\ *n* : any of an order (Gymnophiona) of chiefly tropical burrowing amphibians resembling worms [Latin *caecilia,* a kind of lizard, from *caecus* "blind"] — **caecilian** *adj*

Cae·sar \'sē-zər\ *n* **1** : any of the Roman emperors succeeding Augustus Caesar — used as a title **2 a** *often not cap* : a powerful ruler : (1) : EMPEROR : DICTATOR 1b, AUTOCRAT **b** : the civil power : a temporal ruler [from Gaius Julius *Caesar;* sense 2b from the reference in Matthew 22: 21] — **Cae·sar·e·an** *or* **Cae·sar·i·an** \si-'zar-ē-ən, -'zer-\ *adj*

cae·sar·e·an *variant of* CESAREAN

cae·si·um *variant of* CESIUM

cae·su·ra *also* **ce·su·ra** \si-'zur-ə, -'zhur-\ *n, pl* **-su·ras** *or* **-su·rae** \-'zur-ē, -'zhur-\ : a break in the flow of sound usually in the middle of a line of verse [Latin, "act of cutting", from *caedere* "to cut"] — **cae·su·ral** \-'zur-əl, -'zhur-\ *adj*

ca·fé *also* **ca·fe** \ka-'fā, kə-\ *n* **1** : COFFEEHOUSE **2** : BARROOM, SALOON **3** : RESTAURANT; *also* : NIGHTCLUB [French *café* "coffee, café", from Turkish *kahve*]

ca·fé au lait \ka-,fā-ō-'lā\ *n* : coffee with usually hot milk in about equal parts [French, "coffee with milk"]

caf·e·te·ria \,kaf-ə-'tir-ē-ə\ *n* : a restaurant in which the customers serve themselves or are served at a counter but take the food to tables to eat [American Spanish *cafetería* "coffee store", from Spanish *café* "coffee", from French]

caf·feine \'ka-,fēn, ka-'fēn\ *n* : a bitter stimulating compound $C_8H_{10}N_4O_2$ found especially in coffee, tea, and kola nuts [German *kaffein,* from *kaffee* "coffee", from French *café*]

caf·tan *or* **kaf·tan** \kaf-'tan, 'kaf-,\ *n* : an ankle-length garment with long sleeves that is worn in the Levant; *also* : a comparable garment widely used as a housecoat [Russian *kaftan,* from Turkish, from Persian *qaftān*]

¹cage \'kāj\ *n* **1** : a largely openwork enclosure for confining or carrying an animal (as a bird) **2** : an enclosure like a cage in form or purpose **3** : a goal structure consisting of posts or a frame with a net attached (as in ice hockey) **4** : a large building with unobstructed interior for practicing outdoor sports [Old French, from Latin *cavea* "cavity, cage", from *cavus* "hollow" — see JAIL *origin*]

²cage *vt* : to confine or keep in or as if in a cage

cage·ling \'kāj-ling\ *n* : a caged bird

ca·gey *also* **ca·gy** \'kā-jē\ *adj* **ca·gi·er; -est** : wary of being trapped or deceived : SHREWD, CAUTIOUS [origin unknown] — **ca·gi·ly** \-jə-lē\ *adv* — **ca·gi·ness** \-jē-nəs\ *n*

ca·hoot \kə-'hüt\ *n* : PARTNERSHIP 1, LEAGUE — usually used in pl. ⟨in cahoots with the devil⟩ [perhaps from French *cahute* "cabin, hut"]

cai·man *or* **cay·man** \'kā-mən; kā-'man, kī-\ *n* : any of several Central and South American reptiles basically similar to alligators but often superficially resembling crocodiles [Spanish *caimán,* probably from Carib *cayman*]

ca·ï·que \kä-'ēk\ *n* **1** : a light skiff used on the Bosporus **2** : a Greek sailing vessel usually equipped with an auxiliary engine [Turkish *kayık*]

cairn \'kaərn, 'keərn\ *n* : a heap of stones piled up as a landmark or as a memorial [Scottish Gaelic *carn*]

cairn terrier *n* : a small compactly built terrier of Scottish origin with a weather resistant coat of harsh texture [from its use in hunting among cairns]

cais·son \'kā-,sän, 'käs-n\ *n* **1 a** : a chest for ammunition **b** : a 2-wheeled vehicle for artillery ammunition **2 a** : a watertight chamber used in construction work under water or as a foundation **b** : a float for raising a sunken vessel [French, from *caisse* "box", derived from Latin *capsa* "chest, case"]

caisson disease *n* : a severe disorder marked by pain (as in joints and limbs), distress in breathing, and often collapse and caused by release of gas bubbles in the tissues upon too rapid decrease in air pressure after a stay in a compressed atmosphere — called also *bends*

cai·tiff \'kāt-əf\ *adj* : being base, cowardly, or contemptible [Old North French *caitif* "captive, vile", from Latin *captivus* "captive"] — **caitiff** *n*

ca·jole \kə-'jōl\ *vt* : to coax or persuade especially by flattery or false promises : WHEEDLE [French *cajoler*] — **ca·jol·ery** \-'jōl-rē, -ə-rē\ *n*

¹Ca·jun \'kā-jən\ *n* : a Louisianian descended from French-speaking immigrants from Acadia [alteration of *Acadian*]

²Cajun *adj* **1** : of, relating to, or characteristic of the Cajuns **2** : of, relating to, or prepared in a style of cooking originating with the Cajuns and characterized by the use of hot seasonings (as cayenne pepper)

¹cake \'kāk\ *n* **1** : a small mass of food (as dough, meat, or fish) baked or fried **2** : a baked food made from a sweet batter or dough **3** : a substance hardened or molded into a solid mass ⟨a *cake* of soap⟩ [Old Norse *kaka*]

²cake *vb* **1** : ENCRUST **2** : to form or harden into a mass

cal·a·bash \'kal-ə-,bash\ *n* **1** : GOURD; *esp* : one whose hard shell is used for a utensil (as a bottle) **2** : a tropical American tree related to the trumpet creeper; *also* : its hard round fruit **3** : a utensil made from a calabash shell [Spanish *calabaza*]

cal·a·boose \'kal-ə-,büs\ *n, dialect* : JAIL [Spanish *calabozo* "dungeon"]

ca·la·di·um \kə-'lād-ē-əm\ *n* : any of a genus of tropical American herbs related to the arums and often grown for their brightly colored leaves [Malay *kĕladi,* a plant of the arum family]

cal·a·mine \'kal-ə-,mīn, -mən\ *n* : a mixture of zinc oxide and a small amount of ferric oxide used in lotions, liniments, and ointments in skin treatment [French, "zinc ore", from Medieval Latin *calamina,* from Latin *cadmia,* from Greek *kadmeia,* literally, "Theban (earth)", from *kadmeios* "Theban", from *Kadmos* "Cadmus", founder of Thebes]

cal·a·mite \'kal-ə-,mīt\ *n* : a Paleozoic fossil plant resembling a giant equisetum [Latin *calamus* "reed"]

ca·lam·i·ty \kə-'lam-ət-ē\ *n, pl* **-ties** **1** : a state of deep distress or misery caused by major misfortune or loss **2** : an extraordinarily grave event marked by great loss and lasting distress and affliction [Middle French *calamité,* from Latin *calamitas*] SYN see DISASTER — **ca·lam·i·tous** \-ət-əs\ *adj* — **ca·lam·i·tous·ly** *adv* — **ca·lam·i·tous·ness** *n*

cal·a·mus \'kal-ə-məs\ *n, pl* **-mi** \-,mī, -,mē\ **1** : the sweet flag or its aromatic root **2** : QUILL 2a [Latin, "reed, reed pen", from Greek *kalamos*]

ca·lash \kə-'lash\ *n* **1** : a light small-wheeled 4-passenger carriage with a folding top **2** : a large hood on a hoop frame worn by women in the 18th century [French *calèche*, from German *kalesche*, from Czech *kolesa* "wheels, carriage"]

calc- *or* **calci-** *or* **calco-** *combining form* : calcium : calcium salt ⟨*calci*fy⟩

cal·ca·ne·us \kal-'kā-nē-əs\ *n, pl* -**nei** \-nē-ˌī\ : a tarsal bone that in humans is the great bone of the heel [Late Latin, "heel", from Latin *calcaneum,* from *calx* "heel"]

cal·car·e·ous \kal-'kar-ē-əs, -'ker-\ *adj* **1** : resembling calcite or calcium carbonate especially in hardness **2** : consisting of or containing calcium carbonate; *also* : containing calcium — **cal·car·e·ous·ly** *adv* — **cal·car·e·ous·ness** *n*

cal·ce·o·lar·ia \ˌkal-sē-ə-'lar-ē-ə, -'ler-\ *n* : any of a genus of tropical American plants of the snapdragon family widely grown for their showy pouch-shaped flowers [Latin *calceolus* "small shoe", from *calceus* "shoe", from *calx* "heel"]

cal·ces *pl of* CALX

cal·cif·er·ol \kal-'sif-ə-ˌról, -ˌról\ *n* : a vitamin D prepared by irradiation of ergosterol

cal·cif·er·ous \kal-'sif-rəs, -ə-rəs\ *adj* : producing or containing calcium carbonate

cal·ci·fi·ca·tion \ˌkal-sə-fə-'kā-shən\ *n* **1** : the process of calcifying; *esp* : deposition of insoluble lime salts (as in tissue) ⟨bone formation by *calcification* of cartilage⟩ **2** : a calcified structure

cal·ci·fy \'kal-sə-ˌfī\ *vb* -**fied; -fy·ing** **1** : to make calcareous by deposit of calcium salts **2** : to become calcareous

cal·ci·mine *or* **kal·so·mine** \'kal-sə-ˌmīn\ *n* : a white or tinted wash of glue, whiting or zinc white, and water used especially on plastered surfaces [*calcimine* alteration of *kalsomine,* of unknown origin] — **calcimine** *vt*

cal·cine \kal-'sīn, 'kal-ˌ\ *vt* : to heat to a high temperature but without fusing in order to drive off volatile matter (as carbon dioxide from limestone) [Middle French *calciner,* from Latin *calx* "lime"] — **cal·ci·na·tion** \ˌkal-sə-'nā-shən\ *n*

cal·cite \'kal-ˌsīt\ *n* : a crystalline mineral $CaCO_3$ composed of calcium carbonate and found in numerous forms including limestone, chalk, and marble — **cal·cit·ic** \kal-'sit-ik\ *adj*

cal·ci·to·nin \ˌkal-sə-'tō-nən\ *n* : THYROCALCITONIN [*calc-* + ¹*ton*ic + *-in*]

cal·ci·um \'kal-sē-əm\ *n* : a silver-white bivalent soft metallic chemical element that is found only in combination with other chemical elements (as in limestone) and that is one of the essential parts of the bodies of most plants and animals — see ELEMENT table [New Latin, from Latin *calx* "lime"]

calcium carbide *n* : a usually dark gray crystalline compound CaC_2 used for the generation of acetylene

calcium carbonate *n* : a solid substance $CaCO_3$ found in nature as limestone and marble and in plant ashes, bones, and shells

calcium chloride *n* : a salt $CaCl_2$ that absorbs moisture from the air and that is used as a drying agent and in a hydrated state to control dust and melt ice on roads

calcium phosphate *n* : any of various phosphates of calcium: as **a** : the phosphate $Ca_3(PO_4)_2$ used as a fertilizer **b** : a naturally occurring phosphate containing other elements (as fluorine) and occurring as the chief constituent of phosphate rock, bones, and teeth

cal·cu·late \'kal-kyə-ˌlāt\ *vb* **1 a** : to determine by mathematical processes **b** : to reckon by an informed guess : ESTIMATE **2** : to make a calculation **3** : to plan by careful thought ⟨a program *calculated* to succeed⟩ **4** : RELY, DEPEND [Latin *calculare,* from *calculus* "pebble (used in reckoning)", from *calx* "stone used in

gaming, lime"] — **cal·cu·la·ble** \-kyə-lə-bəl\ *adj* — **cal·cu·la·bly** \-blē\ *adv*

cal·cu·lat·ed \-ˌlāt-əd\ *adj* : undertaken after estimating the probability of success or failure ⟨a *calculated* risk⟩ — **cal·cu·lat·ed·ly** *adv*

cal·cu·lat·ing \-ˌlāt-ing\ *adj* **1** : designed to make calculations ⟨*calculating* machine⟩ **2** : marked by shrewd analysis of one's own self-interest — **cal·cu·lat·ing·ly** \-ing-lē\ *adv*

cal·cu·la·tion \ˌkal-kyə-'lā-shən\ *n* **1 a** : the process or an act of calculating **b** : the result of an act of calculating **2** : studied care in analyzing or planning : CAUTION — **cal·cu·la·tive** \'kal-kyə-ˌlāt-iv\ *adj*

cal·cu·la·tor \'kal-kyə-ˌlāt-ər\ *n* : one that calculates; *esp* : a machine for performing mathematical operations mechanically or electronically

cal·cu·lus \'kal-kyə-ləs\ *n, pl* -**li** \-ˌlī, -ˌlē\ *also* -**lus·es** **1** : a mass usually of mineral salts deposited in or around organic material in a hollow organ or bodily duct **2 a** : a method of computation or calculation in a special symbolic notation **b** : the mathematical methods comprising differential and integral calculus [Latin, "pebble, stone"]

cal·de·ra \kal-'der-ə, kól-, -'dir-\ *n* : a large crater formed by the collapse or explosion of a volcanic cone [Spanish, literally, "caldron", from Late Latin *caldaria*]

cal·dron *also* **caul·dron** \'kól-drən\ *n* : a large kettle or boiler [Old North French *cauderon,* from Late Latin *caldaria,* from Latin, "warm bath", from *calidus* "warm"]

¹cal·en·dar \'kal-ən-dər\ *n* **1 a** : an arrangement of time into days, weeks, months, and years **b** : a record of such an arrangement for a certain period and usually for a year **2** : an orderly list: as **a** : a list of cases to be tried in court **b** : a list of bills to be considered by a legislative assembly **c** : a schedule of coming events [Medieval Latin *kalendarium,* from Latin *kalendae* "calends"]

²calendar *vt* -**dared; -dar·ing** \-də-ring, -dring\ : to enter in a calendar

¹cal·en·der \'kal-ən-dər\ *vt* -**dered; -der·ing** \-də-ring, -dring\ : to press (as cloth or paper) between rollers or plates in order to smooth and glaze or thin into sheets [Middle French *calendrer,* from *calandre* "calender", from Greek *kylindros* "cylinder"] — **cal·en·der·er** *n*

²calender *n* : a machine for calendering cloth or paper

cal·ends *or* **kal·ends** \'kal-ənz\ *n pl* : the first day of the ancient Roman month [Latin *kalendae*]

ca·len·du·la \kə-'len-jə-lə\ *n* : any of a small genus of yellow-rayed herbs related to the daisies — compare POT MARIGOLD [derived from Latin *kalendae* "calends"]

¹calf \'kaf, 'káf\ *n, pl* **calves** \'kavz, 'kávz\ **1 a** : the young of the domestic cow **b** : the young of various large animals (as the elephant or whale) **2** *pl* **calfs** : CALFSKIN **3** : a boy or youth held to be awkward or silly [Old English *cealf*]

²calf *n, pl* **calves** : the fleshy back part of the leg below the knee [Old Norse *kálfi*]

calf·skin \'kaf-ˌskin, 'káf-\ *n* : leather made of the skin of a calf

cal·i·ber *or* **cal·i·bre** \'kal-ə-bər\ *n* **1** : the diameter of a bullet or other projectile **2** : the diameter of the bore of a gun — usually expressed in hundredths or thousandths of an inch and as a decimal fraction ⟨.32 *caliber*⟩ **3 a** : mental ability or moral quality **b** : degree of excellence [Middle French *calibre,* from Italian *calibro,* from Arabic *qālib* "shoemaker's last"]

cal·i·brate \'kal-ə-ˌbrāt\ *vt* **1** : to measure the caliber of **2** : to determine, correct, or put the measuring marks on (as a thermometer tube) — **cal·i·bra·tion** \ˌkal-ə-'brā-shən\ *n* — **cal·i·bra·tor** \'kal-ə-ˌbrāt-ər\ *n*

California condor

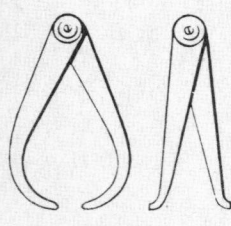

caliper

cal·i·co \'kal-i-ˌkō\ *n, pl* **-coes** *or* **-cos** **1** : cotton cloth; *esp* : cotton cloth with a colored pattern printed on one side **2** : a blotched or spotted animal (as a piebald horse) [*Calicut*, city in India] — **calico** *adj*

Cal·i·for·nia condor \ˌkal-ə-ˈfȯr-nyə-\ *n* : a large nearly extinct vulture of mountainous southern California that is related to the condor of South America — called also **condor**

California poppy *n* : any of a genus of herbs of the poppy family including one widely grown for its pale yellow to red flowers

cal·i·for·ni·um \ˌkal-ə-ˈfȯr-nē-əm\ *n* : an artificially prepared radioactive chemical element — see ELEMENT table [New Latin, from *California*, United States]

cal·i·per *or* **cal·li·per** \'kal-ə-pər\ *n* : a measuring instrument with two legs or jaws that can be adjusted to determine thickness, diameter, and distance between surfaces — usually used in pl. ⟨a pair of *calipers*⟩ [alteration of *caliber*]

ca·liph *or* **ca·lif** \'kā-ləf, 'kal-əf\ *n* : a successor of Muhammad as temporal and spiritual head of Islam — used as a title [Middle French *calife*, from Arabic *khalīfah* "successor"] — **ca·liph·ate** \-ˌāt\ *n*

cal·is·then·ics \ˌkal-əs-ˈthen-iks\ *n sing or pl* **1** : systematic rhythmic bodily exercises performed usually without apparatus **2** : the art or practice of calisthenics [Greek *kalos* "beautiful" + *sthenos* "strength"] — **cal·is·then·ic** \-ik\ *adj*

¹calk \'kȯk\ *variant of* CAULK

²calk *or* **caulk** *n* : a tapered piece projecting downward from a shoe (as of a horse) to prevent slipping [probably derived from Old North French *calcain* "heel", from Latin *calcaneum*, from *calx* "heel"]

³calk *or* **caulk** *vt* **1** : to furnish with calks **2** : to wound with a calk

¹call \'kȯl\ *vb* **1** : to speak in a loud distinct voice so as to be heard at a distance : SHOUT **2** : to utter in a loud clear voice ⟨*call* out a command⟩ **3** : to announce with authority : PROCLAIM **4 a** : to summon with or as if with a shout ⟨*call* the children to dinner⟩ **b** : to cause to come ⟨*call* to mind an old saying⟩ **5** : to bring into action or discussion ⟨*call* a case into court⟩ **6** : to make an appeal, request, or demand ⟨*call* on a person's sense of decency⟩ **7** : to get in touch with by telephone : make a telephone call **8** : SUMMON ⟨*call* a meeting⟩ **9** : to make a brief visit **10** : to give a name to : address by name **11** : to regard as being of a certain kind : CONSIDER **12** : to estimate as being ⟨*call* it an even dollar⟩ **13 a** : to utter a characteristic note or cry — used of an animal **b** : to attract (as game) by imitating the characteristic cry **14** : to make a demand in card games (as for a show of hands) **15** : to give temporary control of computer processing to a particular set of instructions [probably from Old Norse *kalla*] — **call·able** \'kȯ-lə-bəl\ *adj* — **call·er** *n* — **call in question** : to challenge the accuracy or truth of — **call it a day** : to stop at least for the present whatever one has been doing — **call the tune** : to be in charge or control — **call to account** : to hold responsible

²call *n* **1 a** : an act of calling with the voice; *also* : SHOUT **b** : a cry of an animal (as a bird); *also* : an imitation of this or a device used (as in calling game) to make such an imitation **2 a** : a request or command to assemble **b** : a signal on a drum or bugle **c** : an invitation to become the minister of a church or to accept a professional appointment **d** : a divine or inner prompting to a course of action : the attraction or appeal of a particular activity, condition, or place ⟨the *call* of the wild⟩ **3 a** : DEMAND, CLAIM **b** : NEED, JUSTIFICATION ⟨no *call* to apologize⟩ **c** : REQUEST ⟨many *calls* for the new toy⟩ **d** : a request that control of computer processing temporarily be given to a particular set of instructions **4** : a short visit **5** : a name or thing called ⟨the *call* was heads⟩ **6** : the act of calling in a card game **7** : the act of calling on the telephone **8** : a di-

rection or set of directions for a square dance rhythmically called to the dancers **9** : a decision or ruling made by an official of a sports contest

cal·la \'kal-ə\ *n* : a plant of the arum family often grown for its white showy spathe surrounding a fleshy spike of yellow florets — called also **calla lily** [Greek *kallaia* "rooster's wattles"]

call–board \'kȯl-ˌbȯrd, -ˌbȯrd\ *n* : BULLETIN BOARD 1

call–boy \'kȯl-ˌbȯi\ *n* : BELLHOP, PAGE

call down *vt* : REPRIMAND

cal·lig·ra·phy \kə-ˈlig-rə-fē\ *n* **1** : beautiful or elegant handwriting; *also* : the art of producing such writing **2** : PENMANSHIP 2 [Greek *kalligraphia*, from *kallos* "beauty" + *-graphia* "-graphy"] — **cal·lig·ra·pher** \-fər\ *n* — **cal·li·graph·ic** \ˌkal-ə-ˈgraf-ik\ *adj* — **cal·li·graph·i·cal·ly** \-ˈgraf-i-kə-lē, -klē\ *adv*

call·ing \'kȯ-ling\ *n* **1** : a strong inner impulse; *esp* : one toward the ministry or priesthood **2** : one's customary profession

cal·li·o·pe \kə-ˈlī-ə-ˌpē, 'kal-ē-ˌōp\ *n* : a keyboard musical instrument resembling an organ and consisting of a series of whistles sounded by steam or compressed air [*Calliope*, a Greek muse]

cal·li·op·sis \ˌkal-ē-ˈäp-səs\ *n* : COREOPSIS — used especially of annual forms [Greek *kallos* "beauty" + *opsis* "appearance"]

call letters *n pl* : CALL SIGN

call loan *n* : a loan payable on demand of either party

call number *n* : a combination of characters assigned to a library book to indicate its place on a shelf

call off *vt* **1** : to draw away : DIVERT ⟨*call off* your dog⟩ **2** : CANCEL ⟨*call off* a meeting⟩

cal·los·i·ty \ka-ˈläs-ət-ē, kə-\ *n, pl* **-ties** **1** : the quality or state of being callous **2** : CALLUS 1

¹cal·lous \'kal-əs\ *adj* **1** : so thickened and usually hardened as to form callus or a callus **2** : lacking in emotional response : UNFEELING ⟨a *callous* disregard for human rights⟩ [Middle French *calleux*, from Latin *callosus*, from *callus* "callous skin"] — **cal·lous·ly** *adv* — **cal·lous·ness** *n*

²callous *vt* : to make callous

cal·low \'kal-ō\ *adj* : lacking adult sophistication : IMMATURE [Old English *calu* "bald"] — **cal·low·ness** *n*

call sign *n* : the combination of identifying letters assigned to a radio or television station

call–up \'kȯl-ˌəp\ *n* : an order to report for military service

¹cal·lus \'kal-əs\ *n* **1** : a thickening of or a hard thickened area on skin or bark **2** : a mass of exudate and connective tissue that surrounds a break in a bone and is converted into bone in the healing of the break **3** : tissue that forms over an injured plant surface [Latin]

²callus *vi* : to form callus or a callus

¹calm \'käm, 'kälm\ *n* **1** : a period or condition of freedom from storm, wind, or rough activity of water **2** : a state of repose and freedom from turmoil or agitation : QUIET [Middle French *calme*, from Italian *calma*, derived from Greek *kauma* "heat"]

²calm *adj* **1** : marked by calm : STILL ⟨a *calm* sea⟩ **2** : free from agitation, excitement or disturbance ⟨a *calm* manner⟩ — **calm·ly** *adv* — **calm·ness** *n* □ SYN CALM, TRANQUIL, SERENE, PLACID mean quiet and free from whatever disturbs or hurts. CALM implies a contrast with a foregoing or nearby state of agitation or violence; TRANQUIL suggests a very deep quietude or composure; SERENE stresses an unclouded and lofty tranquillity; PLACID suggests an undisturbed appearance and often implies complacency.

³calm *vb* **1** : to become calm **2** : to make calm

ca·ló \kä-ˈlō\ *n* : any of several Spanish argots; *esp* : an argot used by Chicano youths in cities of the southwest United States [Spanish]

cal·o·mel \'kal-ə-məl, -ˌmel\ *n* : a white tasteless substance Hg_2Cl_2 that occurs as a mineral or is made chemically and that is used as a purgative, fungicide, and insecticide — called also *mercurous chloride* [Greek *kalos* "beautiful" + *melas* "black"]

¹**ca·lor·ic** \kə-'lȯr-ik, -'lōr, '-lär; 'kal-ə-rik\ *n* : a supposed form of matter formerly held responsible for the phenomena of heat and combustion

²**caloric** *adj* **1** : of or relating to heat **2** : of or relating to calories — **ca·lor·i·cal·ly** \-i-kə-lē, -i-klē\ *adv*

cal·o·rie *also* **cal·o·ry** \'kal-rē, -ə-rē\ *n, pl* **-ries** : a unit of heat: **a** : the heat energy required to raise the temperature of one gram of water one degree Celsius and equal to about 4.19 joules — called also *small calorie* **b** : the heat energy required to raise the temperature of one kilogram of water one degree Celsius and equal to 1000 small calories — used especially to indicate the value of foods in the production of heat and energy; called also *large calorie* [French *calorie,* from Latin *calor* "heat", from *calēre* "to be warm"]

cal·o·rif·ic \,kal-ə-'rif-ik\ *adj* : **CALORIC**

cal·o·rim·e·ter \,kal-ə-'rim-ət-ər\ *n* : an apparatus for measuring quantities of absorbed or evolved heat or for determining specific heats — **cal·o·ri·met·ric** \,kal-ə-rə-'me-trik\ *adj* — **cal·o·ri·met·ri·cal·ly** \-'me-tri-kə-lē, -klē\ *adv* — **cal·o·rim·e·try** \-'rim-ə-trē\ *n*

cal·u·met \'kal-yə-,met, -mət\ *n* : an ornamented shaft of reed or wood used as a peace pipe or ceremonial object by American Indians [American French, from French dialect, "straw", derived from Latin *calamus* "reed"]

ca·lum·ni·ate \kə-'ləm-nē-,āt\ *vt* : to speak falsely and maliciously about : **SLANDER** — **ca·lum·ni·a·tion** \-,ləm-nē-'ā-shən\ *n* — **ca·lum·ni·a·tor** \-'ləm-nē-,āt-er\ *n*

cal·um·ny \'kal-əm-nē\ *n, pl* **-nies** : a false charge made to injure another person's reputation; *also* : the uttering of such charges [Latin *calumnia,* from *calvi* "to deceive"] — **ca·lum·ni·ous** \kə-'ləm-nē-əs\ *adj* — **ca·lum·ni·ous·ly** *adv*

calve \'kav, 'kȧv\ *vb* **1** : to give birth to a calf; *also* : to produce offspring **2** *of an ice mass* : to let (as an iceberg) become detached

calves *pl of* **CALF**

Cal·vin·ism \'kal-və-,niz-əm\ *n* : the theological system of John Calvin and his followers emphasizing the absolute power of God and especially the doctrine of predestination to eternal life — **Cal·vin·ist** \-və-nəst\ *n or adj* — **Cal·vin·is·tic** \,kal-və-'nis-tik\ *adj*

calx \'kalks\ *n, pl* **calx·es** *or* **cal·ces** \'kal-,sēz\ : the crumbly residue left when a metal or mineral has been subjected to calcination or combustion [Latin, "lime"]

ca·lyp·so \kə-'lip-sō\ *n, pl* **-sos** : a ballad of West Indian origin having usually improvised lyrics set to an African rhythm [origin unknown] — **ca·lyp·so·ni·an** \kə-,lip-'sō-nē-ən, ,kal-ip-\ *adj or n*

ca·lyp·tra \kə-'lip-trə\ *n* : a covering of a plant reproductive structure suggestive of a cap or hood [Greek *kalyptra* "veil", from *kalyptein* "to cover"]

ca·lyx \'kā-liks *also* 'kal-iks\ *n, pl* **ca·lyx·es** *or* **ca·ly·ces** \'kā-lə-,sēz *also* 'kal-ə-\ **1** : the external usually green or leafy part of a flower consisting of sepals **2** : an animal structure shaped like a cup [Latin, from Greek *kalyx*]

cal·zo·ne \kal-'zōn, -'zō-nē, -zō-nā; käl-'zȯn-ā\ *n, pl* **calzone** *or* **calzones** : a baked or fried turnover of pizza dough with various fillings [Italian, from singular of *calzoni* "pants"]

cam \'kam\ *n* : a device that consists of a plate or cylinder on a revolving shaft and that transmits motion by means of its edge or a groove to another mechanical part (as a rod or lever) so that circular motion may be transformed into intermittent or back-and-forth motion [perhaps from French *came,* from German *kamm,* literally, "comb"]

ca·ma·ra·de·rie \,käm-'räd-ə-rē, -ə-'räd-, ,kam-, -'rad-\ *n* : good feeling existing between comrades [French, from *camarade* "comrade"]

cam·as *or* **cam·ass** \'kam-əs\ *n* : any of a genus of plants of the lily family of the western United States with edible bulbs — compare **DEATH CAMAS** [of American Indian origin]

¹**cam·ber** \'kam-bər\ *vb* **cam·bered; cam·ber·ing** \-bə-ring, -bring\ : to curve upward in the middle : arch slightly [French *cambrer,* derived from Latin *camur* "curved"]

²**camber** *n* **1** : a slight convexity, arching, or curvature (as of a beam, deck, or road) **2** : a setting of the wheels of an automotive vehicle closer together at the bottom than at the top

cam·bi·um \'kam-bē-əm\ *n, pl* **-bi·ums** *or* **-bia** \-bē-ə\ : a thin cell layer between the xylem and phloem of most vascular plants from which new cells (as of wood and bark) develop [Medieval Latin, "exchange", from Latin *cambiare* "to exchange"] — **cam·bi·al** \-bē-əl\ *adj*

Cam·bri·an \'kam-brē-ən\ *n* : the earliest period of the Paleozoic era marked by fossils of every great animal type except the vertebrate and by scarcely recognizable plant fossils; *also* : the corresponding system of rocks — see **GEOLOGIC TIME** table [Medieval Latin *Cambria* "Wales"] — **Cambrian** *adj*

cam·bric \'kām-brik\ *n* **1** : a fine thin white linen fabric **2** : a cotton fabric that resembles cambric [obsolete Flemish *Kameryk* "Cambrai", city in France]

came *past of* **COME**

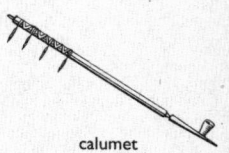
calumet

cam·el \'kam-əl\ *n* **1** : either of two large cud-chewing mammals used as draft and saddle animals in desert regions especially of Africa and Asia: **a** : **DROMEDARY** **2** **b** : a 2-humped camel of central Asian origin — called also *Bactrian camel* **2** : a light brown color [Latin *camelus,* from Greek *kamēlos,* of Semitic origin]

cam·el·back \-,bak\ *n* : the back of a camel

cam·el·eer \,kam-ə-'liər\ *n* : a camel driver

ca·mel·lia *also* **ca·me·lia** \kə-'mēl-yə\ *n* : any of several shrubs or trees of the tea family; *esp* : a greenhouse shrub with glossy evergreen leaves and showy roselike flowers [*Camellus* (Georg Josef Kamel), died 1706, Moravian Jesuit missionary]

camel 1b

Ca·mel·o·par·da·lis \kə-,mel-ə-'pärd-l-əs\ *n* : a northern constellation between Cassiopeia and Ursa Major [Latin, giraffe]

Cam·e·lot \'kam-ə-,lät\ *n* **1** : the site of King Arthur's palace in Arthurian legend **2** : a time or place of idyllic happiness

camel hair *n* : a fabric made of the hair of camels or of a mixture of this hair with wool

Cam·em·bert \'kam-əm-,beər\ *n* : a soft cheese with a thin grayish white rind and a yellow interior [*Camembert,* Normandy, France]

cam·eo \'kam-ē-,ō\ *n, pl* **-e·os** : a carved gem in which the design is higher than its background [Italian]

cam·era \'kam-rə, -ə-rə\ *n* **1** : a judge's private office ⟨hearings held in *camera*⟩ **2** : a lightproof box fitted with a lens through the opening of which the image of an object is recorded on a material that is sensitive to light **3** : the part of a television transmitting apparatus in which the image to be televised is formed for change into electrical impulses [Late Latin, "room, chamber"; sense 2 from New Latin *camera obscura,* literally, "dark chamber"]

cam·era·man \-,man, -mən\ *n* : the operator of a camera

cam·era·wom·an \-,wùm-ən\ *n* : a woman who operates a camera

cam·i·sole \'kam-ə-,sōl\ *n* : a short sleeveless undergarment for women [French]

cam·o·mile *variant of* **CHAMOMILE**

cam·ou·flage \'kam-ə-,fläzh, -,fläj\ *n* **1** : the disguising especially of military equipment or installations with paint, nets, or foliage; *also* : the disguise so applied **2** **a** : concealment by means of disguise **b** : behavior or a trick intended to deceive or hide [French, from *cam-*

\ə\ abut		\ng\ si**ng**	
\ər\ f**ur**ther		\ō\ b**o**ne	
\a\ m**a**t		\ȯ\ s**a**w	
\ā\ t**a**ke		\ȯi\ c**oi**n	
\ä\ c**o**t, c**a**rt		\th\ **th**in	
\aú\ **ou**t		\th\ **th**is	
\ch\ **ch**in		\ü\ f**oo**d	
\e\ p**e**t		\ù\ f**oo**t	
\ē\ **e**asy		\y\ **y**et	
\g\ **g**o		\yü\ f**ew**	
\i\ t**i**p		\yù\ c**ure**	
\ī\ l**i**fe		\zh\ vi**si**on	
\j\ **j**ob			

oufler "to disguise", from Italian *camuffare*] — **cam·ouflage** *vt*

¹camp \\'kamp\\ *n* **1 a** : ground on which tents or buildings for temporary residence are erected **b** : a group of buildings or tents erected on such ground **c** : a temporary shelter (as a cabin or tent) **d** : an open-air location where persons camp **e** : a new lumbering or mining town **2 a** : a body of persons encamped **b** (1) : a group of persons promoting a theory or doctrine ⟨liberal and conservative *camps*⟩ (2) : an ideological position **3** : military service or life [Middle French, derived from Latin *campus* "plain, field"]

²camp *vi* **1** : to make camp or occupy a camp **2** : to live temporarily in a camp or outdoors ⟨*camp* out overnight⟩

cam·paign \\kam-'pān\\ *n* **1** : a series of military operations forming a distinct phase of a war **2** : a series of operations designed to bring about a particular result ⟨an election *campaign*⟩ [French *campagne,* derived from Late Latin *campania* "level country"] — **campaign** *vi* — **cam·paign·er** *n*

cam·pa·nile \\,kam-pə-'nē-lē, *of United States structures also* -'nēl\\ *n, pl* **-niles** *or* **-ni·li** \\-'nē-lē\\ : a usually freestanding bell tower [Italian, from *campana* "bell", from Late Latin]

cam·pan·u·la \\kam-'pan-yə-lə\\ *n* : any of a large genus of herbs with regular bell-shaped flowers including several grown as ornamentals [Late Latin *campana* "bell"]

camp·er \\'kam-pər\\ *n* **1** : one that camps **2** : a portable dwelling (as a specially equipped automotive vehicle) for use during casual travel and camping

cam·pes·tral \\kam-'pes-trəl\\ *adj* : of or relating to fields or open country [Latin *campester,* from *campus* "field"]

camp·fire \\'kamp-,fīr\\ *n* : a fire built outdoors (as at a camp)

Camp Fire Girl *n* : a member of a national organization for girls from 7 to 18 [*Camp Fire Girls,* Incorporated]

cam·phor \\'kam-fər, 'kamp-\\ *n* : a tough gummy volatile fragrant crystalline compound $C_{10}H_{16}O$ obtained especially from the wood and bark of the camphor tree and used as a stimulant, as a plasticizer, and as an insect repellent [Medieval Latin *camphora,* from Arabic *kāfūr,* from Malay *kāpūr*]

cam·phor·ate \\-fə-,rāt\\ *vt* : to impregnate with camphor ⟨*camphorated* oil⟩

camphor tree *n* : a large evergreen tree of the laurel family

cam·pi·on \\'kam-pē-ən\\ *n* : any of various plants of the pink family [probably from obsolete *campion* "champion"]

camp meeting *n* : a series of evangelistic meetings usually held outdoors or in a tent

camp·o·ree \\,kam-pə-'rē\\ *n* : a gathering of Boy Scouts or Girl Scouts from a given area [*camp* + jamb*oree*]

camp·stool \\'kamp-,stül\\ *n* : a folding stool

cam·pus \\'kam-pəs\\ *n* : the grounds and buildings of a school (as a college) [Latin, "field, plain"]

cam·shaft \\'kam-,shaft\\ *n* : a shaft to which a cam is fastened

¹can \\kən, kan, 'kan\\ *auxiliary verb, past* **could** \\kəd, kud, 'kud\\; *present sing & pl* **can 1 a** : know how to ⟨you *can* read⟩ **b** : be physically or mentally able to ⟨I *can* swim⟩ **c** : be permitted by conscience or feeling ⟨you *can* hardly blame me⟩ **d** : be inherently able or designed to ⟨all that money *can* buy⟩ **e** : be enabled by law, agreement, or custom to **2** : have permission to — used interchangeably with *may* ⟨you *can* go now if you like⟩ [Old English, "know, knows, am able, is able"] □ **SYN** MAY: CAN primarily implies physical or mental ability ⟨I *can* run very fast⟩ or circumstantial possibility ⟨we *can* take an earlier train⟩ MAY expresses primarily permission or sanction, not capability ⟨you *may* leave when you wish⟩ but CAN is frequently used

in asking permission ⟨*can* I help you⟩ and normally used in denying it ⟨you *cannot* smoke here⟩

²can \\'kan\\ *n* **1** : a usually cylindrical container: **a** : a vessel for holding liquids; *esp* : a drinking vessel **b** : a container (as for milk, oil, or garbage) usually with an open top and often with a cover **c** : a container (as of tinplate) in which a perishable product (as food) is hermetically sealed **d** : a jar for packing or preserving fruit or vegetables **2** : the contents of a can [Old English *canne*]

³can \\'kan\\ *vt* **canned; can·ning 1** : to put in a can; *esp* : to preserve by sealing in an airtight can or jar **2** *slang* : to discharge from a job — **can·ner** *n*

Can·a·da balsam \\'kan-əd-ə-\\ *n* : a viscid yellowish resin exuded by the balsam fir that solidifies to a transparent mass and is used as a transparent cement especially in microscopy

Canada goose *n* : a common wild goose of North America that is mostly gray and brownish in color with black head and neck

Ca·na·di·an lynx \\kə-'nād-ē-ən-\\ *n* : LYNX C

ca·naille \\kə-'nī, -'nāl\\ *n* : RABBLE 2, RIFFRAFF [French, from Italian *canaglia,* from *cane* "dog", from Latin *canis*]

ca·nal \\kə-'nal\\ *n* **1** : a tubular anatomical passage or channel : DUCT **2** : an artificial waterway for navigation or for draining or irrigating land **3** *pl* : faint narrow markings on the planet Mars sometimes seen through telescopes [Latin *canalis* "pipe, channel", from *canna* "reed, cane"]

ca·nal·boat \\-,bōt\\ *n* : a boat for use on a canal

can·a·lic·u·lus \\,kan-l-'ik-yə-ləs\\ *n, pl* **-u·li** \\-yə-,lī, -,lē\\ : a minute bodily canal (as in bone) [Latin, from *canalis* "canal"]

can·a·li·za·tion \\,kan-l-ə-'zā-shən\\ *n* **1** : an act or instance of canalizing **2** : a system of channels

can·a·lize \\'kan-l-,īz\\ *vt* **1** : to provide with a canal **2** : to make into or like a canal

can·a·pé \\'kan-ə-pē, -,pā\\ *n* : an appetizer consisting of a piece of bread or toast or a cracker topped with a spread (as of fish or cheese) [French, literally, "sofa"]

ca·nard \\kə-'närd\\ *n* : a false or unfounded report or story; *esp* : one deliberately made up [French, literally, "duck", from Middle French *vendre des canards à moitié* "to cheat", literally, "to half-sell ducks"]

□ **ORIGIN** In 16th century France "vendre des canards à moitié" was a colorful way of saying "to cheat". The French phrase means, literally, "to half-sell ducks". Unfortunately, no one now knows just what was meant by "to half-sell"—vendre à moitié". The proverb was probably based on some story widely known at the time, but the details have not survived. At any rate, the proverbial duck, the *canard,* came to stand for any hoax, especially a made-up report. And French *canard,* in this sense, was borrowed into English.

ca·nary \\kə-'near-ē\\ *n, pl* **-nar·ies 1** : a sweet wine made in the Canary islands **2** : a small usually yellow or greenish finch native to the Canary islands that is kept as a cage bird □ **ORIGIN** The Canaries are a group of islands off the northwest coast of Africa. Early explorers from Africa reported that these islands were covered with dogs. Because of these reports the islands were given the Latin name *Canariae insulae,* "dog islands". In fact, the dogs that gave the islands their name had probably not always been there but had been brought by still earlier invaders from Africa. Native to the islands, however, were small greenish brown birds. Some of these were taken to Europe in the 16th century and were called *canary birds* in England. The yellow domestic canary is a descendant of the wild greenish birds of the dog islands.

canary yellow *n* : a light to a moderate yellow

can·can \\'kan-,kan\\ *n* : a woman's dance of French origin characterized by high kicking [French]

¹can·cel \'kan-səl\ *vb* **-celed** *or* **-celled; -cel·ing** *or* **-cel·ling** \-sə-ling, -sling\ *vb* **1 a :** to mark or strike out for deletion **b :** DELETE, OMIT **2 a :** to destroy the force, effectiveness, or validity of : ANNUL ⟨*cancel* a magazine subscription⟩ **b :** to match in force or effect : OFFSET — often used with *out* **c :** to call off usually without expecting to reschedule ⟨*cancel* a party because of bad weather⟩ **3 a :** to remove (a common divisor) from numerator and denominator **b :** to remove (equivalents) on opposite sides of an equation or account **4 :** to mark (a postage stamp or check) so as to prevent reuse [Middle French *canceller,* from Late Latin *cancellare,* from Latin, "to make like a lattice", from *cancelli* "latticework, grating"] SYN see ERASE — **can·cel·er** *or* **can·cel·ler** \-sə-lər, -slər\ *n* □ ORIGIN The original meaning of *cancel* is "to mark out or cross out". The cross-hatchings which sometimes cover a canceled document resemble a lattice. This resemblance was reflected in the formation of the Latin verb *cancellare* from the noun *cancelli* "lattice". *Cancelli* is a diminutive form of *cancer.* This *cancer* is not related to its homonym *cancer,* "crab, disease". Rather it is the word for the type of latticed barrier used to restrain a prisoner. It is an altered form of Latin *carcer,* "prison", the word which has also given us *incarcerate.*

²cancel *n* : CANCELLATION

can·cel·la·tion *also* **can·cel·ation** \,kan-sə-'lā-shən\ *n* **1 :** an act of canceling **2 :** a mark made to cancel something

can·cel·lous \'kan-sə-ləs\ *adj* : having a porous structure ⟨*cancellous* bone⟩ [Latin *cancelli* "lattice"]

can·cer \'kan-sər\ *n* **1 cap a :** a northern zodiacal constellation between Gemini and Leo **b :** the 4th sign of the zodiac; *also* : one born under this sign **2 :** a malignant tumor that tends to spread locally and to other parts of the body; *also* : an abnormal state marked by such tumors **3 :** a source of evil or anguish ⟨the *cancer* of hatred⟩ [Latin, "crab, Cancer, cancer"] — **can·cer·ous** \'kans-rəs, -ə-rəs\ *adj*

can·de·la \kan-'dē-lə, -'del-ə\ *n* : an international unit of luminous intensity in a given direction of a source that emits radiation only of 540×10^{12} hertz and has a radiant intensity in that direction of $1/683$ watt per unit of angular measurement in three-dimensional space [Latin, "candle"]

can·de·la·bra \,kan-də-'läb-rə *sometimes* -'lab-\ *n* : CANDELABRUM

can·de·la·brum \-rəm\ *n, pl* **-bra** \-rə\ *also* **-brums** : a candlestick or lamp with branches holding sockets for lights [Latin, from *candela* "candle"]

can·des·cent \kan-'des-nt\ *adj* : glowing or dazzling especially from great heat [Latin *candescere* "to grow light or bright", from *candēre* "to shine"] — **can·des·cence** \-ns\ *n*

can·did \'kan-dəd\ *adj* **1 :** free from prejudice : FAIR **2 a :** marked by honest sincere expression **b :** showing sincere honesty and absence of deception **3 :** relating to photography of subjects acting naturally or spontaneously without being posed ⟨a *candid* snapshot⟩ [French *candide,* from Latin *candidus* "shining, white", from *candēre* "to shine"] SYN see FRANK — **can·did·ly** *adv* — **can·did·ness** *n*

can·di·da·cy \'kan-dəd-ə-sē\ *n, pl* **-cies** : the state of being a candidate ⟨announce one's *candidacy* for office⟩

can·di·date \'kan-də-,dāt, -ə-, -dət\ *n* : one who offers oneself or is proposed by others for an office, membership, right, or honor ⟨the party's *candidate* for mayor⟩ [Latin *candidatus,* literally, "one clothed in white", from *candidus* "white"; from the white toga worn by candidates for office in ancient Rome]

can·died \'kan-dēd\ *adj* **1 :** encrusted or coated with sugar **2 :** baked with sugar or syrup until translucent

¹can·dle \'kan-dl\ *n* **1 :** a usually cylindrical mass of tallow or wax containing a loosely twisted linen or cotton wick that is burned to give light **2 :** CANDELA [Latin *candela,* from *candēre* "to shine"]

²candle *vt* **can·dled; can·dling** \'kan-dling, -dl-ing\ : to examine (an egg) by holding between the eye and a light — **can·dler** \-dlər, -dl-ər\ *n*

can·dle·light \'kan-dl-,līt, -,īt\ *n* **1 a :** the light of a candle **b :** a soft artificial light **2 :** the time when candles are lit : TWILIGHT

Can·dle·mas \'kan-dl-məs\ *n* : February 2 observed as a church festival in commemoration of the presentation of Christ in the temple and the purification of the Virgin Mary [Old English *candelmæsse,* from *candel* "candle" + *mæsse* "mass, feast"; from the candles blessed and carried in celebration of the feast]

can·dle·pin \'kan-dl-,pin\ *n* **1 :** a slender bowling pin tapering toward top and bottom **2** *pl* : a bowling game using candlepins and a smaller ball than that used in tenpins

can·dle·pow·er \-,pau̇-ər, -,pau̇r\ *n* : luminous intensity (as of a light bulb) expressed in candles or candelas

can·dle·stick \-,stik\ *n* : a holder with a socket for a candle

can·dor \'kan-dər\ *n* **1 :** freedom from prejudice **2 :** unreserved, honest, or sincere expression : FRANKNESS [Latin, literally, "whiteness", from *candēre* "to shine"]

¹can·dy \'kan-dē\ *n, pl* **-dies** **1 :** crystallized sugar formed by boiling down sugar syrup **2 a :** a rich food made largely of sugar often with flavoring and filling **b :** a piece of such food [Middle French *sucre candi,* from Italian *zucchero candi,* from *zucchero* "sugar" + Arabic *qandī* "candied", from *qand* "cane sugar"]

²candy *vb* **can·died; can·dy·ing** **1 :** to coat or become coated with sugar often by cooking **2 :** to make seem attractive : SWEETEN **3 :** to crystallize into sugar

can·dy·tuft \'kan-dē-,təft\ *n* : any of a genus of plants of the mustard family grown for their white, pink, or purple flowers [*Candy* (now *Candia*) "Crete", Greek island + English *tuft*]

¹cane \'kān\ *n* **1 a :** a hollow or pithy and usually slender, flexible, and jointed stem (as of a reed or bramble) **b :** any of various tall woody grasses or reeds; *esp* : SUGARCANE **2 a :** WALKING STICK 1; *esp* : a cane walking stick **b :** a rod for flogging **c :** RATTAN 1b; *esp* : split rattan for wickerwork or basketry [Middle French, derived from Latin *canna,* from Greek *kanna,* of Semitic origin]

²cane *vt* **1 :** to beat with a cane **2 :** to make or repair with cane ⟨*cane* the seat of a chair⟩

cane·brake \-,brāk\ *n* : a thicket of cane

cane sugar *n* : sugar from sugarcane commonly used at the dining table and in cooking : SUCROSE

¹ca·nine \'kā-,nīn\ *adj* **1 :** of or relating to dogs or to the family that includes the dogs, wolves, jackals, and foxes **2 :** resembling a dog [Latin *caninus,* from *canis* "dog"]

²canine *n* **1 :** a conical pointed tooth situated between the outer incisor and the first premolar — called also *cuspid*

Ca·nis Ma·jor \,kā-nəs-'mā-jər, ,kan-əs-\ *n* : a constellation to the southeast of Orion containing Sirius [Latin, literally, "greater dog"]

Canis Mi·nor \-'mī-nər\ *n* : a constellation to the east of Orion containing Procyon [Latin, literally, "lesser dog"]

can·is·ter \'kan-ə-stər\ *n* **1 :** a small box or can for holding a dry product (as tea) **2 :** a shell for close-range artillery fire consisting of a number of bullets enclosed in a lightweight case that is burst by the firing charge **3 :** a perforated box for gas masks that contains material to adsorb, filter, or make harmless a poisonous or irritating substance in the air [Latin *canistrum* "basket", from Greek *kanastron,* from *kanna* "reed"]

candelabrum

\ə\ abut   \ng\ sing
\ər\ further   \ō\ bone
\a\ mat   \ȯ\ saw
\ā\ take   \ȯi\ coin
\ä\ cot, cart   \th\ thin
\au̇\ out   \th\ this
\ch\ chin   \ü\ food
\e\ pet   \u̇\ foot
\ē\ easy   \y\ yet
\g\ go   \yü\ few
\i\ tip   \yu̇\ cure
\ī\ life   \zh\ vision
\j\ job

¹can·ker \'kang-kər\ *n* **1 a** : a spreading sore that eats into the tissue **b** : an area of necrosis in a plant **c** : any of various disorders of animals marked by chronic inflammatory changes **2** : a source of corruption or destruction [Old North French *cancre,* from Latin *cancer* "crab, cancer"] — **can·ker·ous** \'kang-kə-rəs, -krəs\ *adj*

²canker *vb* **can·kered; can·ker·ing** \'kang-kə-ring, -kring\ **1** : to become affected by canker **2** : to become or cause to become malignant ⟨a mind *cankered* by hate⟩

canker sore *n* : a small painful ulcer especially of the mouth

can·ker·worm \'kang-kər-,wərm\ *n* : a moth larva that injures plants especially by feeding on buds and foliage

can·na \'kan-ə\ *n* : a tall tropical herb with large leaves and an unbranched stem bearing bright-colored flowers at the end [Latin, "reed"]

can·na·bis \'kan-ə-bəs\ *n* : the dried flowering spikes of the pistillate plants of the hemp — compare BHANG, HASHISH, MARIJUANA [Latin, "hemp", from Greek *kannabis*]

canned \'kand\ *adj* **1** : preserved in a sealed can or jar **2** : recorded for radio or television use ⟨*canned* laughter⟩

can·nel coal \'kan-l-\ *n* : a bituminous coal containing much volatile matter that burns brightly [probably from English dialect *cannel* "candle"]

can·nery \'kan-rē, -ə-rē\ *n, pl* **-ner·ies** : a factory for the canning of food

can·ni·bal \'kan-ə-bəl\ *n* **1** : a human being who eats human flesh **2** : an animal that eats its own kind [Spanish *Caníbal* "Carib", of American Indian origin] — **cannibal** *adj* — **can·ni·bal·ism** \-bə-,liz-əm\ *n* — **can·ni·bal·is·tic** \,kan-ə-bə-'lis-tik\ *adj*

can·ni·bal·ize \'kan-ə-bə-,līz\ *vt* : to dismantle (a machine) for parts to be used as replacements in other machines

can·non \'kan-ən\ *n, pl* **cannons** or **cannon 1** : a heavy gun mounted on a carriage and fired from that position : a piece of artillery **2** : a heavy-caliber automatic gun on an airplane [Middle French *canon,* from Italian *cannone,* literally, "large tube", from *canna* "reed, tube", from Latin, "reed, cane"]

¹can·non·ade \,kan-ə-'nād\ *n* : a heavy firing of artillery

²cannonade *vb* : to attack with artillery

can·non·ball \'kan-ən-,bȯl\ *n* : a round solid missile made for firing from a cannon

cannon bone *n* : a bone in hoofed mammals that supports the leg from the hock joint to the fetlock

can·non·eer \,kan-ə-'niər\ *n* : an artillery gunner

can·not \'kan-ät, -ət; kə-'nät, ka-'\ : can not — **cannot but** : to be bound to : MUST

can·ny \'kan-ē\ *adj* **can·ni·er; -est** : being cautious and shrewd : watchful of one's own interests ⟨very *canny* with money⟩ [¹*can*] — **can·ni·ly** \'kan-l-ē\ *adv* — **can·ni·ness** \'kan-ē-nəs\ *n*

¹ca·noe \kə-'nü\ *n* : a long light narrow boat with sharp ends and curved sides that is usually paddled by hand [French, from Spanish *canoa,* of American Indian origin]

²canoe *vb* **ca·noed; ca·noe·ing** : to travel or transport in a canoe — **ca·noe·ist** *n*

ca·no·la \kə-'nō-lə\ *n* **1** : a rape plant of an improved variety having seeds that are the source of canola oil **2** : CANOLA OIL [*Can*ada *o*il—*l*ow *a*cid]

canola oil *n* : an edible vegetable oil obtained from the seeds of canola that is low in saturated and high in monounsaturated fatty acids

¹can·on \'kan-ən\ *n* **1** : a church law or decree **2** : the fundamental and unvarying part of the Mass including the consecration of the bread and wine **3** : an official or authoritative list (as of the saints or of the books of the Bible) **4** : an accepted principle or rule ⟨the *can-*

ons of good taste⟩ **5** : a musical composition in two or more voice parts in which the melody is imitated exactly and completely by the successive voices [Latin, "ruler, rule, model, standard", from Greek *kanōn*]

²canon *n* **1** : a member of the clergy who is on the staff of a cathedral **2** : CANON REGULAR

³ca·ñon \'kan-yən\ *variant of* CANYON

ca·non·i·cal \kə-'nän-i-kəl\ *adj* **1** : of, relating to, or complying with church law **2** : accepted as authoritative — **ca·non·i·cal·ly** \-kə-lē; -klē\ *adv*

canonical hour *n* **1** : a time of day canonically appointed for an office of devotion **2** : one of the daily offices in the breviary including matins with lauds, prime, terce, sext, none, vespers, and compline

ca·non·i·cals \kə-'nän-i-kəlz\ *n pl* : the vestments prescribed by church law for an officiating member of the clergy

can·on·ic·i·ty \,kan-ə-'nis-ət-ē\ *n* : the quality or state of being canonical

can·on·ize \'kan-ə-,nīz\ *vt* : to declare to be a saint and worthy of veneration [Late Latin *canon* "catalog of saints", from Latin, "standard"] — **can·on·i·za·tion** \,kan-ə-nə-'zā-shən\ *n*

canon law *n* : the body of laws governing a church

canon regular *n, pl* **canons regular** : a member of one of several Roman Catholic religious institutes of regular priests living in community

Ca·no·pus \kə-'nō-pəs\ *n* : a star of the first magnitude not visible north of 37° latitude [Latin, from Greek *Kanōpos*]

¹can·o·py \'kan-ə-pē\ *n, pl* **-pies 1 a** : a covering suspended over a bed, throne, or shrine or carried on poles over a person of high rank or over some sacred object **b** : an overhanging shade or shelter ⟨a *canopy* of chestnut trees⟩ **c** : the uppermost spreading branchy layer of a forest **2 a** : the transparent covering over an airplane cockpit **b** : the lifting or supporting surface of a parachute [Medieval Latin *canopeum* "mosquito net", from Latin *conopeum,* from Greek *kōnōpion,* from *kōnōps* "mosquito"] — **can·o·py·like** \-,līk\ *adj*

²canopy *vt* **-pied; -py·ing** : to cover with or as if with a canopy

canst \kənst, kanst, 'kanst\ *archaic present 2d sing of* CAN

¹cant \'kant\ *n* : a slanting surface or its slope [probably from Old North French, "edge, corner", from Latin *canthus, cantus* "iron tire"]

²cant *vt* : to give a slant to

³cant *vi* : to talk hypocritically [probably from Old North French *canter* "to tell", literally, "to sing", from Latin *cantare*]

⁴cant *n* **1 a** : ARGOT **b** : JARGON **2** : insincere speech; *esp* : insincerely pious words or statements

can't \'kant, 'kant, *especially South* 'känt\ : can not

can·ta·bi·le \kän-'täb-ə-,lā, kan-'tab-ə-lē\ *adv or adj* : in a singing smoothly flowing manner — used as a direction in music [Italian, from Latin *cantare* "to sing"]

Can·ta·bri·gian \,kant-ə-'brij-ən, -ē-ən\ *n* **1** : a student or graduate of Cambridge University **2** : a native or resident of Cambridge [Medieval Latin *Cantabrigia* "Cambridge"] — **Cantabrigian** *adj*

can·ta·loupe \'kant-l-,ōp\ *n* : MUSKMELON; *esp* : a muskmelon with a hard ridged or warty rind and reddish orange flesh [*Cantalupo,* former papal villa near Rome, Italy]

can·tan·ker·ous \kan-'tang-kə-rəs, kən-, -krəs\ *adj* : ILL-NATURED, QUARRELSOME [perhaps from obsolete *contack* "contention"] — **can·tan·ker·ous·ly** *adv* — **can·tan·ker·ous·ness** *n*

can·ta·ta \kən-'tät-ə\ *n* : a poem or narrative set to music to be sung by a chorus and soloists [Italian, from Latin, "sung mass", from *cantare* "to sing"]

can·teen \kan-'tēn\ *n* **1** : a store (as in a camp or a factory) in which food, drinks, and small supplies are sold **2** : a place of recreation and entertainment for military personnel **3** : a small container for carrying liquid (as drinking water) [French *cantine* "bottle case, sutler's shop", from Italian *cantina* "wine cellar", from *canto* "corner", from Latin *canthus* "iron tire"]

¹**can·ter** \'kant-ər\ *vb* : to move or cause to move at or as if at a canter [from *Canterbury,* England; from the supposed gait of pilgrims to Canterbury]

²**canter** *n* : a 3-beat gait (as of a horse) resembling but smoother and slower than the gallop

Can·ter·bury bell \'kant-ər-,ber-ē-, -ə-,ber-ē-\ *n* : a cultivated campanula

cant hook *n* : a stout wooden lever used especially in handling logs that has a blunt usually metal-clad end and a movable metal arm with a sharp spike [¹*cant*]

can·ti·cle \'kant-i-kəl\ *n* **1** : SONG **2** : any of several liturgical songs taken from the Bible [Latin *canticulum* "little song", from *canticum* "song", from *canere* "to sing"]

Canticle of Canticles — see BIBLE table

can·ti·le·ver \'kant-l-,ē-vər *also* -,ev-ər\ *n* **1** : a projecting beam or similar structure fastened (as by being built into a wall or pier) only at one end **2** : either of two beams or structures that project from piers toward each other and when joined form a span in a bridge [perhaps from ¹*cant* + *-i-* + *lever*]

can·tle \'kant-l\ *n* : the upwardly projecting rear part of a saddle [Old North French *cantel* "little corner, part cut off", from *cant* "edge, corner"]

can·to \'kan-,tō\ *n, pl* **cantos** : one of the major divisions of a long poem [Italian, from Latin *cantus* "song", from *canere* "to sing"]

¹**can·ton** \'kant-n, 'kan-,tän\ *n* **1** : a small division of a country; *esp* : one of the states of the Swiss confederation **2** : the top inner quarter of a flag [Middle French, from Italian *cantone,* from *canto* "corner", from Latin *canthur* "iron tire"] — **can·ton·al** \'kant-n-əl, kan-'tän-l\ *adj*

²**can·ton** \'kant-n, 'kan-,tän, *in sense 2 usually* kan-'tōn *or* -'tän\ *vt* **1** : to divide into parts; *esp* : to divide into cantons **2** : to allot quarters to (troops)

Can·ton·ese \,kant-n-'ēz, -'ēs\ *n, pl* **Cantonese** **1** : a native or inhabitant of Canton, China **2** : the dialect of Chinese spoken in and around Canton — **Cantonese** *adj*

can·ton flannel \'kan-,tän-\ *n, often cap C* : FLANNEL 1b [*Canton,* China]

can·ton·ment \kan-'tōn-mənt, -'tän-\ *n* : a group of temporary structures for housing troops

can·tor \'kant-ər\ *n* **1** : a choir leader **2** : a synagogue official who sings or chants the liturgy and leads the congregation in prayer [Latin, "singer", from *canere* "to sing"]

Ca·nuck \kə-'nək\ *n* **1** : CANADIAN **2** *chiefly Canadian* : FRENCH CANADIAN [origin unknown]

can·vas \'kan-vəs\ *n* **1** : a strong cloth of hemp, flax, or cotton that is used for making tents and sails and as a material on which oil paintings are made **2 a** : something made of canvas or on canvas **b** : OIL PAINTING **3** : the floor of a boxing ring [Old North French *canevas,* from Latin *cannabis* "hemp"]

can·vas·back \-,bak\ *n* : a North American wild duck with reddish head and grayish back

can·vass \'kan-vəs\ *vb* **1 a** : to examine in detail; *esp* : to investigate officially ⟨*canvass* election returns⟩ **b** : DISCUSS, DEBATE ⟨*canvass* a question⟩ **2 a** : to go through (an area) soliciting something (as information, contributions, or votes) **b** : to ask for information, money, or votes ⟨*canvass* faculty members for opinions⟩ [obsolete *canvass* "to toss in a canvas sheet, beat thoroughly"] — **canvass** *n* — **can·vass·er** *n*

can·yon *also* **ca·ñon** \'kan-yən\ *n* : a deep valley with high steep slopes and often with a stream flowing through it [American Spanish *cañón*]

caou·tchouc \'kaù-,chùk, -,chùk, -,chü\ *n* : RUBBER 2a [French, from obsolete Spanish *cauchuc*]

¹**cap** \'kap\ *n* **1** : a head covering; *esp* : one that has a visor and no brim **2** : something like a cap in appearance, position, or function ⟨a bottle *cap*⟩ ⟨the *cap* of a fountain pen⟩ **3** : a natural cover or top: as **a** : the umbrella-shaped part that bears the spores of a mushroom — called also *pileus* **b** : the top of a bird's head **4** : a paper or metal container holding an explosive charge (as for a toy pistol) **5** : the symbol ∩ indicating the intersection of two sets — compare CUP 6 [Late Latin *cappa* "head covering, cloak"]

²**cap** *vt* **capped; cap·ping** **1** : to provide with a cap **2** : to match with something better ⟨*cap* one story with another⟩

ca·pa·bil·i·ty \,kā-pə-'bil-ət-ē\ *n, pl* **-ties** **1** : the quality or state of being capable **2** : a feature or faculty that can be developed : POTENTIALITY

ca·pa·ble \'kā-pə-bəl\ *adj* **1** : having the ability, capacity, or power to do something ⟨a room *capable* of holding 50 people⟩ **2** : of such a nature as to permit : SUSCEPTIBLE ⟨a remark *capable* of being misunderstood⟩ **3** : having general ability [Late Latin *capabilis,* from Latin *capere* "to take"] SYN see ABLE — **ca·pa·bly** \-blē\ *adv*

ca·pa·cious \kə-'pā-shəs\ *adj* : able to contain a great deal : not narrow ⟨*capacious* pockets⟩ ⟨students with *capacious* minds⟩ [Latin *capax* "capacious, capable", from *capere* "to take"] — **ca·pa·cious·ly** *adv* — **ca·pa·cious·ness** *n*

ca·pac·i·tance \kə-'pas-ət-əns\ *n* : the property of a system of conductors and dielectrics that permits the storage of electrical energy; *also* : a measure of this property — **ca·pac·i·tive** \-ət-iv\ *adj*

ca·pac·i·tor \kə-'pas-ət-ər\ *n* : a device giving capacitance and usually consisting of conducting plates separated by layers of dielectric with the plates on opposite sides of the dielectric layers oppositely charged by a source of voltage — called also *condenser*

ca·pac·i·ty \kə-'pas-ət-ē, -'pas-tē\ *n, pl* **-ties** **1 a** : the ability to hold or accommodate ⟨the seating *capacity* of a room⟩ **b** : a measure of content : VOLUME ⟨a jug with a *capacity* of one gallon⟩ **c** : productive ability or potential ⟨a plant with a *capacity* of 50 metric tons a month⟩ **2** : ABILITY, CALIBER ⟨an individual of unknown *capacity*⟩ **3** : a position or character assigned or assumed ⟨in one's *capacity* as a judge⟩ [Middle French *capacité,* from Latin *capacitas,* from *capax* "capacious"]

ca·par·i·son \kə-'par-ə-sən\ *n* **1 a** : an ornamental covering for a horse **b** : decorative trappings and harness **2** : rich clothing : ADORNMENT [Middle French *caparaçon,* from Spanish *caparazón*] — **caparison** *vt*

¹**cape** \'kāp\ *n* : a point or extension of land jutting out into water either as a peninsula or as a projecting point [Middle French *cap,* from Provençal, from Latin *caput* "head"]

²**cape** *n* : a sleeveless outer garment or part of a garment that fits closely at the neck and hangs loosely from the shoulders [probably from Spanish *capa,* from Late Latin *cappa* "head covering, cloak"]

cap·e·lin \'kap-lən, -ə-lən\ *n* : a small northern sea fish related to the smelts and often used as cod bait [French *capelan* "codfish", derived from Medieval Latin *cappellanus* "chaplain"]

Ca·pel·la \kə-'pel-ə\ *n* : a bright star in Auriga [Latin, literally, "she-goat", from *caper* "he-goat"]

¹**ca·per** \'kā-pər\ *n* **1** : any of a genus of low prickly shrubs of the Mediterranean region; *esp* : one cultivated for its buds **2** : one of the flower buds or young berries of the caper pickled for use as a relish [Latin *capparis,* from Greek *kapparis*]

²**caper** *vi* **ca·pered; ca·per·ing** \-pə-riŋ, -priŋ\ : to leap about playfully or wildly [probably from *capriole*]

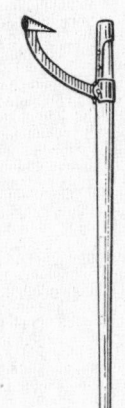

cant hook

³caper *n* **1** : an unrestrained bounding leap **2** : PRANK, ANTIC

cap·er·cail·lie \‚kap-ər-'kāl-yē, -ē\ *or* **cap·er·cail·zie** \-yē, -zē\ *n* : the largest Old World grouse [Scottish Gaelic *capalcoille,* literally, "horse of the woods"]

cape·skin \'kāp-‚skin\ *n* : a leather made from sheepskins with the natural grain retained [*Cape* of Good Hope]

Ca·pe·tian \kə-'pē-shən\ *adj* : of or relating to the French dynasty founded by Hugh Capet — **Capetian** *n*

cap·il·lar·i·ty \‚kap-ə-'lar-ət-ē\ *n* : the action by which the surface of a liquid where (as in a slender tube) it is in contact with a solid is raised or lowered depending upon the relative attraction of the molecules of the liquid for each other and for those of the solid

¹cap·il·lary \'kap-ə-‚ler-ē\ *adj* **1** : resembling a hair in having a slender elongated form; *esp* : having a very small bore ⟨a *capillary* tube⟩ **2** : involving, held by, or resulting from surface tension ⟨*capillary* water in the soil⟩ **3** : of or relating to capillaries or capillarity [Latin *capillaris,* from *capillus* "hair"]

²capillary *n, pl* **-lar·ies** : a capillary tube; *esp* : any of the tiny blood vessels connecting arterioles with venules and forming networks throughout the body

¹cap·i·tal \'kap-ət-l, 'kap-tl\ *adj* **1 a** : punishable by death ⟨a *capital* crime⟩ **b** : resulting in death ⟨*capital* punishment⟩ **2** : being a letter that belongs to or conforms to the series A, B, C, etc. rather than a, b, c, etc. **3** : being the seat of government ⟨the *capital* city⟩ **4** : of or relating to capital ⟨*capital* costs⟩ **5** : EXCELLENT ⟨a *capital* performance⟩ [Latin *capitalis,* from *caput* "head"]

²capital *n* **1 a** : accumulated goods on hand at a specified time in contrast to income received over a specified period; *also* : the value of such goods **b** : the excess of assets over liabilities **2 a** : capital goods and invested savings used in the process of production **b** : possessions (as money) used to bring in income **c** : persons owning or investing capital **d** : CAPITAL STOCK **3** : ADVANTAGE, GAIN ⟨make *capital* out of another's weakness⟩ **4** : a capital letter **5** : a capital city ⟨the *capital* of Vermont⟩ [Italian *capitale,* from *capitale,* adjective, "chief, principal", from Latin *capitalis* "capital"]

³capital *n* : the top part or piece of an architectural column [Old North French *capitel,* from Late Latin *capitellum* "small head, top of column", from Latin *caput* "head"]

³capital: *1* Doric, *2* Ionic, *3* Corinthian

capital goods *n pl* : machinery, tools, factories, and commodities used in the production of goods

cap·i·tal·ism \'kap-ət-l-‚iz-əm\ *n* : an economic system in which natural resources and means of production are privately owned, investments are determined by private decision rather than by state control, and prices, production, and the distribution of goods are determined mainly by competition in a free market — **cap·i·tal·ist** \-l-əst\ *or* **cap·i·tal·is·tic** \‚kap-ət-l-'is-tik\ *adj* — **cap·i·tal·is·ti·cal·ly** \-ti-kə-lē, -klē\ *adv*

cap·i·tal·ist \'kap-ət-l-əst, 'kap-tl-\ *n* **1** : a person who has capital; *esp* : one who has or controls a great amount of business capital **2** : a person who favors capitalism

cap·i·tal·i·za·tion \‚kap-ət-l-ə-'zā-shən, ‚kap-tl-\ *n* **1** : the act or process of capitalizing **2** : the amount of money used as capital in a business

cap·i·tal·ize \'kap-ət-l-‚īz, 'kap-tl-\ *vb* **1** : to write or print with an initial capital or in capitals **2 a** : to charge (an expenditure) to a capital account **b** (1) : to supply capital for ⟨*capitalize* an enterprise at $50,000⟩ (2) : to use as capital ⟨*capitalize* reserve funds⟩ **3** : to use to help oneself ⟨*capitalize* on an opponent's mistake⟩

cap·i·tal·ly \'kap-ət-l-ē, -tl-ē\ *adv* : in a capital manner : EXCELLENTLY ⟨got along *capitally* in school⟩

capstan

capital ship *n* : a warship (as a battleship or aircraft carrier) of the greatest size or offensive power

capital stock *n* : the amount invested by stockholders in a corporation as holders of its shares; *also* : the shares of stock held by these stockholders

cap·i·ta·tion \‚kap-ə-'tā-shən\ *n* : POLL TAX [Late Latin *capitatio,* from Latin *caput* "head"]

cap·i·tol \'kap-ət-l, 'kap-tl\ *n* **1** : a building in which a state legislative body meets **2** *cap* : the building in which the United States Congress meets in Washington [Latin *Capitolium,* a temple of Jupiter in Rome on the Capitoline hill]

Cap·i·to·line \'kap-ət-l-‚īn\ *adj* : of or relating to the smallest of the seven hills of ancient Rome, the temple on it, or the gods worshiped there [Latin *capitolinus,* from *Capitolium,* a temple of Jupiter]

ca·pit·u·late \kə-'pich-ə-‚lāt\ *vi* : to surrender usually on terms agreed upon in advance [Medieval Latin *capitulare* "to draw up under chapters, negotiate", from Late Latin *capitulum* "chapter", from Latin *caput* "head"]

ca·pit·u·la·tion \kə-‚pich-ə-'lā-shən\ *n* **1** : a set of terms or articles constituting an agreement between governments **2** : an act of capitulating : a surrender on agreed terms

ca·pit·u·lum \kə-'pich-ə-ləm\ *n, pl* **-la** \-lə\ **1** : a rounded knob (as on a bone) **2** : HEAD 7a [Latin, "small head", from *caput* "head"]

ca·pon \'kā-‚pän, -pən\ *n* : a castrated male chicken [Old English *capūn*]

ca·pric·cio \kə-'prē-chō, -chē-‚ō\ *n, pl* **-cios** : an instrumental piece in fanciful irregular form usually lively in tempo [Italian, "whim, capriccio"]

ca·price \kə-'prēs\ *n* **1** : a sudden unpredictable turn or change; *esp* : WHIM **2** : an inclination to change one's mind impulsively **3** : CAPRICCIO [French, from Italian *capriccio* "whim, shudder", literally, "head with hair standing on end", from *capo* "head" + *riccio* "hedgehog"] □ SYN CAPRICE, WHIM, VAGARY, CROTCHET mean an irrational or unpredictable idea or desire. CAPRICE stresses lack of apparent motivation and suggests a degree of willfulness; WHIM implies a fantastic, capricious turn or inclination; VAGARY stresses the erratic, irresponsible character of the notion or desire; CROTCHET implies an eccentric opinion or preference.

ca·pri·cious \kə-'prish-əs, -'prē-shəs\ *adj* : moved or controlled by caprice : apt to change suddenly : FICKLE, CHANGEABLE ⟨a *capricious* child⟩ ⟨*capricious* weather⟩ — **ca·pri·cious·ly** *adv* — **ca·pri·cious·ness** *n*

Cap·ri·corn \'kap-rə-‚kórn\ *also* **Cap·ri·cor·nus** \‚kap-rə-'kòr-nəs\ *n* **1** : a southern zodiacal constellation between Sagittarius and Aquarius **2** : the 10th sign of the zodiac; *also* : one born under this sign [Latin *Capricornus,* from *caper* "goat" + *cornu* "horn"]

cap·ri·ole \'kap-rē-‚ōl\ *n* : an upward leap of a horse with a backward kick of the hind legs at the height of the leap [Italian *capriola* "caper", from *capriolo* "roebuck", from Latin *capreolus* "goat, roebuck", from *caper* "he-goat"]

cap·si·cum \'kap-si-kəm\ *n* : any of a genus of tropical herbs and shrubs of the potato family widely cultivated for their many-seeded usually fleshy-walled fruits — called also *pepper* [New Latin, genus name]

cap·size \'kap-‚sīz, kap-'\ *vb* : to turn over : UPSET ⟨canoes *capsize* easily⟩ [origin unknown]

cap·stan \'kap-stən\ *n* : a mechanical device that consists of an upright drum to which a rope is fastened, is used on ships for moving or raising weights and for exerting pulling force, and is rotated manually or by steam or electric power [Middle English]

cap·su·lar \'kap-sə-lər\ *adj* : of, relating to, or resembling a capsule

cap·su·lat·ed \-‚lāt-əd\ *adj* : enclosed in a capsule

¹cap·sule \'kap-səl, -ˌsül\ *n* **1** : a membrane or sac enclosing a body part ⟨the *capsule* of a joint⟩ **2** : a closed receptacle containing spores or seeds: as **a** : a dry dehiscent usually many-seeded fruit composed of two or more carpels **b** : the spore sac of a moss **3** : an edible shell (as of gelatin) enclosing medicine **4** : an often polysaccharide envelope surrounding a microorganism (as some bacteria) **5** : an extremely brief condensation **6** : a small pressurized compartment for an aviator or astronaut for flight or emergency escape [French, from Latin *capsula* "small box", from *capsa* "box, case"]

²capsule *adj* **1** : extremely brief ⟨a *capsule* review of the news⟩ **2** : being small and very compact

¹cap·tain \'kap-tən\ *n* **1** : a leader of a group ⟨the *captain* of a team⟩ **2 a** : an officer rank in the Navy and Coast Guard above commander and below rear admiral **b** : an officer rank in the Army, Marine Corps, and Air Force above first lieutenant and below major **3** : the commanding officer of a ship **4** : a fire or police department officer usually ranking between a chief and a lieutenant [Middle French *capitain,* from Late Latin *capitaneus* "chief", from Latin *caput* "head"] — **cap·tain·ship** \-ˌship\ *n*

²captain *vt* : to be captain of : LEAD

cap·tain·cy \'kap-tən-sē\ *n, pl* **-cies** : a captain's rank or position

¹cap·tion \'kap-shən\ *n* **1** : the heading especially of an article or document **2** : the explanation accompanying a pictorial illustration **3** : a motion-picture subtitle [Latin *captio* "act of taking", from *capere* "to take"]

²caption *vt* : to furnish with a caption

cap·tious \'kap-shəs\ *adj* : quick to find fault especially over trifles [Latin *captiosus* "designed to entrap", from *captio* "act of taking, deception"] — **cap·tious·ly** *adv* — **cap·tious·ness** *n*

cap·ti·vate \'kap-tə-ˌvāt\ *vt* : to attract and win over : CHARM, FASCINATE ⟨music that *captivated* everybody who heard it⟩ — **cap·ti·va·tion** \ˌkap-tə-'vā-shən\ *n* — **cap·ti·va·tor** \'kap-tə-ˌvāt-ər\ *n*

cap·tive \'kap-tiv\ *adj* **1 a** : taken and held prisoner especially in war **b** : held or confined so as to prevent escape **c** : owned or controlled by a business to meet its own needs rather than to produce for the market ⟨a *captive* mine⟩ **2** : of or relating to captivity [Latin *captivus,* from *capere* "to take, capture"] — **captive** *n*

cap·tiv·i·ty \kap-'tiv-ət-ē\ *n, pl* **-ties** : the state of being captive

cap·tor \'kap-tər\ *n* : one that has captured a person or thing

¹cap·ture \'kap-chər\ *n* **1** : the act of catching or gaining control by force or trickery **2** : one that has been taken captive [Middle French, from Latin *captura,* from *capere* "to take"]

²capture *vt* **cap·tured; cap·tur·ing** \'kap-chə-ring, 'kap-shring\ **1 a** : to make captive : TAKE ⟨*capture* a city⟩ **b** : to preserve in a relatively permanent form ⟨*capture* a smile on film⟩ **c** : to captivate and hold the interest of ⟨*captured* their imagination⟩ **2** : to take according to rules of a game (as chess) SYN see CATCH

ca·pu·chin \'kap-yə-shən, -ə-, sense 2 also kə-'pü-shən, -'pyü-\ *n* **1** *cap* : a member of an austere branch of the first order of Saint Francis of Assisi engaged in missionary work and preaching **2** : a South American monkey with the forehead bare and fringed by dark hair [Middle French, from Italian *cappuccino,* from *cappuccio* "hood, cowl", from *cappa* "cloak", from Late Latin; from the cowl worn by members of this order]

cap·y·bara \ˌkap-i-'bar-ə, -'bär-\ *n* : a tailless largely aquatic South American rodent often exceeding a meter in length [Portuguese *capibara,* from Tupi]

car \'kär\ *n* **1** : a vehicle (as a railroad coach or an automobile) that moves on wheels **2** : the compartment of an elevator **3** : the part of a balloon or an airship in which passengers or equipment are carried [Anglo-French *carre,* from Latin *carrus,* of Celtic origin]

ca·ra·bao \ˌkar-ə-'baú, ˌkär-\ *n, pl* **-bao** or **-baos** : WATER BUFFALO [Philippine Spanish, from Eastern Bisayan (a language of the Visayan islands, Philippines) *karabáw*]

car·a·bi·neer or **car·a·bi·nier** \ˌkar-ə-bə-'niər\ *n* : a soldier armed with a carbine [French *carabinier,* from *carabine* "carbine"]

ca·ra·ca·ra \ˌkar-ə-'kär-ə, -ə-kə-'rä\ *n* : any of various large long-legged mostly South American hawks resembling vultures in habits [Spanish, from Tupi *caracará*]

car·a·cole \'kar-ə-ˌkōl\ *n* : a half turn to right or left performed by a mounted horse [French, from Spanish *caracol* "snail, spiral stair, caracole"] — **caracole** *vb*

car·a·cul \'kar-ə-kəl\ *n* : the pelt of a karakul lamb after the curl begins to loosen [alteration of *karakul*]

ca·rafe \kə-'raf, -'räf\ *n* : a bottle with a wide base and flaring lip used to hold water or beverages [French, from Italian *caraffa,* from Arabic *gharrāfah*]

car·a·mel \'kär-məl; 'kar-ə-mel, -ˌmel\ *n* **1** : a brittle brown and somewhat bitter substance obtained by heating sugar and used as a coloring and flavoring agent **2** : a firm chewy candy [French, from Spanish *caramelo,* from Portuguese, "icicle, caramel", from Late Latin *calamellus* "small reed", from *calamus* "reed"]

car·a·mel·ize \-mə-ˌlīz\ *vb* : to turn into caramel — **car·a·mel·i·za·tion** \ˌkär-mə-lə-'zā-shən, ˌkar-ə-mə-\ *n*

car·a·pace \'kar-ə-ˌpās\ *n* : a bony or chitinous case or shield covering all or part of the back of an animal (as a turtle or crayfish) [French, from Spanish *carapacho*]

¹carat *variant of* KARAT

²car·at \'kar-ət\ *n* : a unit of weight for precious stones (as diamonds) equal to 200 milligrams [probably from Medieval Latin *carratus,* from Arabic *qīrāt* "bean pod, a small weight", from Greek *keration,* from *keras* "horn"]

car·a·van \'kar-ə-ˌvan\ *n* **1 a** : a company of travelers on a journey through desert or hostile regions **b** : a train of pack animals or of vehicles traveling together **2** : a covered vehicle: as **a** : one equipped as traveling living quarters **b** *British* : TRAILER 2b [Italian *caravana,* from Persian *kārwān*]

car·a·van·sa·ry \ˌkar-ə-'van-sə-rē\ or **car·a·van·se·rai** \-sə-ˌrī\ *n, pl* **-ries** or **-rais** **1** : a lodging place in eastern countries for caravans **2** : HOTEL, INN [Persian *kārwānsarāī,* from *kārwān* "caravan" + *sarāī* "palace, inn"]

car·a·vel \'kar-ə-ˌvel, -vəl\ *n* : a small 15th and 16th century ship with broad bows, high narrow poop, and lateen sails [Middle French *caravelle,* from Portuguese *caravela*]

car·a·way \'kar-ə-ˌwā\ *n* **1** : a usually white-flowered aromatic herb of the carrot family **2** : the aromatic pungent fruit of the caraway used in seasoning and medicine — called also *caraway seed* [probably from Medieval Latin *carvi,* from Arabic *karawyā,* from Greek *karon*]

carb- or **carbo-** *combining form* : carbon : carbonic : carbonyl : carboxyl (*carb*ide) (*carbo*hydrate)

car·bide \'kär-ˌbīd\ *n* : a compound of carbon with another element; *esp* : CALCIUM CARBIDE

car·bine \'kär-ˌbēn, -ˌbīn\ *n* : a short light rifle [French *carabine*]

car·bo·hy·drase \ˌkär-bō-'hī-ˌdrās, -ˌdrāz\ *n* : an enzyme (as amylase) that promotes decomposition or synthesis of carbohydrate

car·bo·hy·drate \-ˌdrāt\ *n* : any of various neutral compounds of carbon, hydrogen, and oxygen (as sugars, starches, or celluloses) most of which are formed by green plants and which constitute a major class of animal foods

\ə\ abut	\ng\ sing
\ər\ further	\ō\ bone
\a\ mat	\ȯ\ saw
\ā\ take	\ȯi\ coin
\ä\ cot, cart	\th\ thin
\au̇\ out	\th\ this
\ch\ chin	\ü\ food
\e\ pet	\u̇\ foot
\ē\ easy	\y\ yet
\g\ go	\yü\ few
\i\ tip	\yu̇\ cure
\ī\ life	\zh\ vision
\j\ job	

car·bol·ic acid \,kär-'bäl-ik-\ *n* : PHENOL 1 [*carb-* + Latin *oleum* "oil"]

car·bon \'kär-bən\ *n* **1** : a nonmetallic chiefly tetravalent chemical element found native (as in the diamond and graphite) or as a constituent of coal, petroleum, and asphalt, of limestone and other carbonates, and of organic compounds or obtained artificially — see ELEMENT table **2 a** : a sheet of carbon paper **b** : CARBON COPY 1 **3** : a carbon rod used in an arc lamp [French *carbone,* from Latin *carbo* "ember, charcoal"]

car·bo·na·ceous \,kär-bə-'nā-shəs\ *adj* : relating to, containing, or composed of carbon

car·bo·na·do \,kär-bə-'nād-ō, -'näd-\ *n, pl* **-nados** : an impure opaque dark-colored fine-grained aggregate of diamond particles valuable for its superior toughness [Portuguese, literally, "carbonated"]

¹**car·bon·ate** \'kär-bə-,nāt, -nət\ *n* : a salt or ester of carbonic acid

²**car·bon·ate** \-,nāt\ *vt* **1** : to convert into a carbonate **2** : to impregnate with carbon dioxide ⟨a *carbonated* beverage⟩ — **car·bon·ation** \,kär-bə-'nā-shən\ *n*

carbon black *n* : any of various colloidal black substances consisting wholly or principally of carbon obtained as soot and used especially as pigments

carbon copy *n* **1** : a copy made by carbon paper **2** : DUPLICATE 1

carbon cycle *n* : the cycle of carbon in living beings in which carbon dioxide fixed by photosynthesis to form organic nutrients is ultimately restored to the inorganic state by respiration and decay

carbon dating *n* : the determination of age (as of an archaeological find) by means of the content of carbon 14

carbon dioxide *n* : a heavy colorless gas CO_2 that does not support combustion, dissolves in water to form carbonic acid, is formed especially by the combustion and decomposition of organic substances (as in animal respiration), is absorbed from the air by plants in photosynthesis, and is used in the carbonation of beverages

carbon disulfide *n* : a colorless flammable poisonous liquid CS_2 used as a solvent for rubber — called also *carbon bisulfide*

carbon 14 *n* : a heavy radioactive form of carbon that has mass number 14, is formed especially by the action of cosmic rays on nitrogen in the atmosphere, and is used as a tracer or for determining the age of very old specimens of formerly living materials (as bones or charcoal)

car·bon·ic \kär-'bän-ik\ *adj* : of, relating to, or derived from carbon, carbonic acid, or carbon dioxide

carbonic acid *n* : a weak acid H_2CO_3 that decomposes readily into water and carbon dioxide

carbonic an·hy·drase \-an-'hī-,drās, -,drāz\ *n* : a zinc-containing enzyme that occurs in living tissues (as red blood cells) and aids carbon-dioxide transport from the tissues and its release from the blood in the lungs by catalyzing the reversible hydration of carbon dioxide to carbonic acid

car·bon·if·er·ous \,kär-bə-'nif-rəs, -ə-rəs\ *adj* **1** : producing or containing carbon or coal **2** *cap* : of, relating to, or being the Carboniferous

Carboniferous *n* : the period of the Paleozoic era between the Devonian and the Permian during which reptiles first appeared in the fossil record and tremendous deposits of coal were formed; *also* : the corresponding system of rocks

car·bon·ize \'kär-bə-,nīz\ *vb* : to convert or become converted into carbon — **car·bon·i·za·tion** \,kär-bə-nə-'zā-shən\ *n*

carbon monoxide *n* : a colorless odorless very poisonous gas CO formed by the incomplete burning of carbon

carbon paper *n* : a thin paper faced with a transferable waxy pigmented coating so that when placed between two sheets of paper the pressure of writing or typing on the top sheet causes reproduction of the graphic material on the bottom sheet

carbon tetrachloride *n* : a colorless nonflammable poisonous liquid CCl_4 that has an odor resembling that of chloroform and is used as a solvent especially of grease and as a refrigerant

car·bon·yl \'kär-bə-,nil, -,nēl\ *n* : a bivalent radical CO occurring in aldehydes, ketones, esters, and amides

Car·bo·run·dum \,kär-bə-'rən-dəm\ *trademark* — used for various abrasives

car·box·yl \kär-'bäk-səl\ *n* : a univalent radical—COOH typical of organic acids — **car·box·yl·ic** \,kär-bäk-'sil-ik\ *adj*

car·box·yl·ase \kär-'bäk-sə-,lās, -,lāz\ *n* : an enzyme that catalyzes the addition or removal of carboxyl or carbon dioxide

car·boy \'kär-,bȯi\ *n* : a large bottle cushioned in a special container [Persian *qarāba,* from Arabic *qarrābah* "demijohn"]

car·bun·cle \'kär-,bəng-kəl\ *n* **1** : a cut cabochon garnet **2** : a painful inflammation of the skin and deeper tissues that discharges pus from several openings — compare BOIL [Middle French, from Latin *carbunculus* "small coal, carbuncle", from *carbo* "charcoal, ember"] — **car·bun·cled** \-kəld\ *adj* — **car·bun·cu·lar** \kär-'bəng-kyə-lər\ *adj*

car·bu·re·tor \'kär-bə-,rāt-ər, -byə-\ *n* : an apparatus for supplying an internal-combustion engine with vaporized fuel mixed with air in an explosive mixture [*carburet* "to combine with carbon", from obsolete *carburet* "carbide"]

car·case \'kär-kəs\ *British variant of* CARCASS

car·cass \'kär-kəs\ *n* **1** : a dead body; *esp* : the dressed body of a meat animal **2** : the living body **3** : the foundation structure of something (as a tire) [Middle French *carcasse*]

car·cin·o·gen \kär-'sin-ə-jən, 'kärs-n-ə-,jen\ *n* : a substance or agent producing or inciting cancer [Greek *karkinos* "crab, cancer"] — **car·ci·no·gen·ic** \,kärs-n-ō-'jen-ik\ *adj* — **car·ci·no·ge·nic·i·ty** \-jə-'nis-ət-ē\ *n*

car·ci·no·ma \,kärs-n-'ō-mə\ *n, pl* **-mas** *or* **-ma·ta** \-mət-ə\ : a malignant tumor originating in epithelium — **car·ci·no·ma·tous** \,kärs-n-'ō-mət-əs\ *adj*

¹**card** \'kärd\ *vt* : to clean and untangle (fibers) by combing with a card before spinning — **card·er** *n*

²**card** *n* : an instrument usually having bent wire teeth and used for combing fibers (as wool or cotton) [Middle French *carde,* from Latin *carduus* "thistle"]

³**card** *n* **1** : PLAYING CARD **2** *pl* **a** : a game played with cards **b** : card playing **3** : an amusing person : WAG **4 a** : a flat stiff usually small and rectangular piece of paper or thin paperboard (as a postcard) **b** : a sports program ⟨a racing *card*⟩ **c** (1) : a wine list (2) : MENU 1 **d** : a removable circuit board in a microcomputer) [Middle French *carte,* derived from Latin *charta* "leaf of papyrus", from Greek *chartēs* — see CARTEL origin]

⁴**card** *vt* **1** : to provide with a card **2** : to ask for identification (as in a bar)

car·da·mom \'kärd-ə-məm, -,mäm\ *n* : the aromatic capsular fruit of an East Indian herb of the ginger family with seeds used as a condiment and in medicine; *also* : this plant [Latin *cardamomum,* from Greek *kardamōmon*]

card·board \'kärd-,bȯrd, -,bȯrd\ *n* : a paperboard usually made from wood pulp

cardi- *or* **cardio-** *combining form* : heart ⟨*cardio*gram⟩ [Greek *kardia*]

¹**car·di·ac** \'kärd-ē-,ak\ *adj* **1** : of, relating to, situated near, or acting on the heart **2** : of, relating to, or being the part of the stomach into which the esophagus

opens [Latin *cardiacus,* from Greek *kardiakos,* from *kardia* "heart"]

²**cardiac** *n* : a person with heart disease

cardiac muscle *n* : striated muscle tissue that is found in the heart, is made up of contractile cells whose protoplasm is continuous from one cell to another, and is not under voluntary control — compare SMOOTH MUSCLE

car·di·gan \'kärd-i-gən\ *n* : a usually collarless sweater opening the full length of the front [James Thomas Brudenell, 7th earl of *Cardigan,* died 1868, English soldier]

Cardigan *n* : a Welsh corgi with rounded ears, slightly bowed forelegs, and long tail — called also *Cardigan Welsh Corgi* [*Cardigan* county, Wales]

¹**car·di·nal** \'kärd-nəl, -n-əl\ *adj* : of basic importance : MAIN, CHIEF, PRIMARY [Old French, from Late Latin *cardinalis,* from Latin *cardo* "hinge"] — **car·di·nal·ly** \-ē\ *adv*

²**cardinal** *n* **1** : one of the high officials of the Roman Catholic Church who rank next below the pope and who form his advisory and administrative council and elect his successor **2** : CARDINAL NUMBER — usually used in pl. **3** : any of several American finches of which the male is bright red with a black face and pointed crest [sense 3 from its color, resembling that of a cardinal's robes]

car·di·nal·ate \-ət, -ˌāt\ *n* : the office, rank, or dignity of a cardinal

cardinal flower *n* : the brilliant red flower of a North American lobelia; *also* : this plant

car·di·nal·i·ty \ˌkärd-n-'al-ət-ē\ *n, pl* **-ties** : the numbers of elements in a given mathematical set

cardinal number *n* : a number (as 1, 5, 15) that is used in simple counting and that indicates how many elements there are in a set but not the order in which they are arranged — compare ORDINAL NUMBER; see NUMBER table

cardinal point *n* : one of the four principal points of the compass: north, south, east, or west

car·dio·gram \'kärd-ē-ə-ˌgram\ *n* : the curve or tracing made by a cardiograph

car·dio·graph \-ˌgraf\ *n* : an instrument that records graphically the duration and character of the heart movements — **car·dio·graph·ic** \ˌkärd-ē-ə-'graf-ik\ *adj*

car·di·ol·o·gy \ˌkärd-ē-'äl-ə-jē\ *n* : the study of the heart and its action and diseases — **car·di·ol·o·gist** \-jəst\ *n*

car·dio·vas·cu·lar \-'vas-kyə-lər\ *adj* : of, relating to, or involving the heart and blood vessels

car·doon \kär-'dün\ *n* : a large perennial plant related to the artichoke and sometimes grown for its edible root and leafstalks [French *cardon,* from Late Latin *cardo* "thistle", from Latin *carduus*]

card·play·er \'kärd-ˌplā-ər\ *n* : one that plays cards

card·sharp \-ˌshärp\ *or* **card·sharp·er** \-ˌshär-pər\ *n* : a skilled cheater at cards

¹**care** \'keər, 'kaər\ *n* **1** : a heavy sense of responsibility : WORRY, ANXIETY, CONCERN **2** : painstaking or watchful attention : HEED ⟨take *care* in crossing streets⟩ **3** : SUPERVISION ⟨under a doctor's *care*⟩ **4** : an object of one's watchful attention ⟨the garden was his special *care*⟩ [Old English *caru*]

²**care** *vb* **1 a** : to feel trouble or anxiety **b** : to feel interest or concern ⟨*care* about freedom⟩ **2** : to give care ⟨*care* for the sick⟩ **3 a** : to have a liking, fondness, or taste ⟨don't *care* for sweets⟩ **b** : to have an inclination ⟨would you *care* for some pie⟩ — **car·er** *n*

ca·reen \kə-'rēn\ *vb* **1** : to cause a boat to lean or tilt over on one side for cleaning, caulking, or repairing **2** : to sway from side to side : LURCH [Middle French *carène* "keel", derived from Latin *carina* "keel", literally, "nutshell"]

¹**ca·reer** \kə-'riər\ *n* **1 a** : COURSE 1a **b** : speed in a course ⟨ran at full *career*⟩ **2** : a course of continued progress or activity **3** : a profession for which one trains and which is undertaken as a permanent calling [Middle French *carrière,* from Provençal *carriera* "street", from Medieval Latin *carraria* "road for vehicles", from Latin *carrus* "car"]

²**career** *vi* : to go at top speed especially in a headlong manner ⟨a car *careering* down the road⟩

care·free \'keər-ˌfrē, 'kaər-\ *adj* : free from care

care·ful \-fəl\ *adj* **1** : using or taking care ⟨a *careful* driver⟩ **2** : made, done, or said with care ⟨*careful* examination⟩ — **care·ful·ly** \-fə-lē, -flē\ *adv* — **care·ful·ness** \-fəl-nəs\ *n* □ SYN METICULOUS, SCRUPULOUS, PUNCTILIOUS: CAREFUL implies attentiveness and cautiousness in avoiding mistakes ⟨a *careful* worker⟩ ⟨*careful* nursing⟩ METICULOUS may imply either commendable extreme carefulness or a hampering finicky caution over small points; SCRUPULOUS applies to what is proper or fitting or ethical ⟨*scrupulous* honesty⟩ PUNCTILIOUS implies minute, even excessive attention to fine points.

care·less \'keər-ləs, 'kaər-\ *adj* **1** : CAREFREE **2** : not taking proper care : HEEDLESS ⟨*careless* of danger⟩ **3** : done, made, or said without due care ⟨a *careless* mistake⟩ — **care·less·ly** *adv* — **care·less·ness** *n*

¹**ca·ress** \kə-'res\ *n* : a tender or loving touch or embrace [French *caresse,* from Italian *carezza,* from *caro* "dear", from Latin *carus*] — **ca·res·sive** \-'res-iv\ *adj* — **ca·res·sive·ly** *adv*

²**caress** *vt* : to touch or stroke lightly in a loving manner — **ca·ress·er** *n*

car·et \'kar-ət\ *n* : a mark ∧ used to show where something is to be inserted in written or printed matter [Latin, "there is lacking", from *carēre* "to lack"]

care·tak·er \'keər-ˌtā-kər, 'kaər-\ *n* : one that takes care of buildings or land often for an absent owner

care·worn \-ˌwōrn, -ˌwȯrn\ *adj* : showing the effect of grief or anxiety

car·fare \'kär-ˌfaər, -ˌfeər\ *n* : the fare charged a passenger (as on a bus or streetcar)

car·go \'kär-ˌgō\ *n, pl* **cargoes** *or* **cargos** : the goods or merchandise carried in a ship, airplane, or vehicle : FREIGHT [Spanish, "load, charge", from *cargar* "to load, charge", from Late Latin *carricare*]

car·hop \'kär-ˌhäp\ *n* : one who serves customers at a drive-in restaurant [*car* + -*hop* (as in bellhop)]

Car·ib \'kar-əb\ *n* **1** : a member of an Indian people of northern South America and the Lesser Antilles **2** : the language of the Caribs [Spanish *Caribe,* of American Indian origin]

ca·ri·be \kə-'rē-bē\ *n* : PIRANHA [American Spanish, from Spanish, "Carib, cannibal"]

car·i·bou \'kar-ə-ˌbü\ *n, pl* **-bou** *or* **-bous** : any of several large deer of northern North America closely related to the reindeer [Canadian French, of American Indian origin]

car·i·ca·ture \'kar-i-kə-ˌchùr\ *n* **1** : exaggeration by means of comic distortion of parts or characteristics **2** : a representation especially in literature or art that has the qualities of caricature [Italian *caricatura,* literally, "act of loading", from *caricare* "to load", from Late Latin *carricare*] — **caricature** *vt* — **car·i·ca·tur·ist** \-əst\ *n* □ SYN CARICATURE, BURLESQUE, PARODY, TRAVESTY mean a comic or grotesque imitation. CARICATURE implies ludicrous exaggeration of the characteristic features of a subject; BURLESQUE implies the ridiculous effect resulting either from treating a trivial subject in a mock-heroic style or from giving a serious or lofty subject a frivolous treatment; PARODY applies to treatment of a trivial or ludicrous subject in the exactly imitated style of a particular author or work; TRAVESTY implies that the subject remains unaltered but that the style and effect is extravagant or absurd.

caribou

\ə\ abut	\ng\ sing
\ər\ further	\ō\ bone
\a\ mat	\ȯ\ saw
\ā\ take	\ȯi\ coin
\ä\ cot, cart	\th\ thin
\au̇\ out	\t̲h̲\ this
\ch\ chin	\ü\ food
\e\ pet	\u̇\ foot
\ē\ easy	\y\ yet
\g\ go	\yü\ few
\i\ tip	\yu̇\ cure
\ī\ life	\zh\ vision
\j\ job	

car·ies \'kaər-ēz, 'keər-\ *n, pl* **caries** : a progressive destruction of bone or tooth; *esp* : tooth decay [Latin, "decay"] — **car·i·ous** \'kar-ē-əs, 'ker-\ *adj*

car·il·lon \'kar-ə-,län, -lən\ *n* **1** : a set of bells sounded by hammers controlled by a keyboard **2** : a tune for the carillon [French, from Old French *quarregnon*, from Late Latin *quaternio* "set of four"]

car·il·lon·neur \,kar-ə-lə-'nər, ,kar-ē-ə-'nər\ *n* : a carillon player [French, from *carillon*]

ca·ri·na \kə-'rī-nə, -'rē-\ *n, pl* **-nas** *or* **-nae** \-'rī-,nē, -'rē-,nī\ : a keel-shaped anatomical part, ridge, or process [Latin, "keel"]

car·i·ole \'kar-ē-,ōl\ *n* : a dog-drawn toboggan [French *carriole* "light carriage", derived from Latin *carrus* "car"]

car·load \'kär-'lōd\ *n* : a load that fills a car

Car·mel·ite \'kär-mə-,līt\ *n* : a friar or nun of the Roman Catholic Order of Our Lady of Mount Carmel founded in the 12th century — **Carmelite** *adj*

car·mi·na·tive \kär-'min-ət-iv, 'kär-mə-,nāt-iv\ *adj* : helping to expel gas from the alimentary canal [French *carminatif*, from Latin *carminare* "to card, comb out knots in"] — **carminative** *n*

car·mine \'kär-mən, -,mīn\ *n* **1** : a rich crimson or scarlet coloring matter made from cochineal **2** : a vivid red [French *carmin*, from Medieval Latin *carminium*, from Arabic *qirmiz* "kermes" + Latin *minium* "red lead"]

car·nage \'kär-nij\ *n* : great and bloody slaughter (as in battle) [Middle French, from Medieval Latin *carnaticum* "tribute of animals or meat", from Latin *caro* "flesh"]

car·nal \'kärn-l\ *adj* **1** : of or relating to the body : CORPORAL **2** : marked by sexuality : SENSUAL **3** : characterized by physical rather than spiritual orientation [Late Latin *carnalis*, from Latin *carn-, caro* "flesh"] — **car·nal·i·ty** \kär-'nal-ət-ē\ *n* — **car·nal·ly** \'kärn-l-ē\ *adv*

car·nas·si·al \kär-'nas-ē-əl\ *adj* : of, relating to, or being teeth of a carnivore adapted for cutting rather than tearing [French *carnassier* "carnivorous", derived from Latin *caro* "flesh"] — **carnassial** *n*

car·na·tion \kär-'nā-shən\ *n* **1** : a moderate red **2** : any of the numerous cultivated usually double-flowered pinks derived from the common gillyflower [Middle French, "color of human flesh", derived from Latin *caro* "flesh"]

car·nau·ba \kär-'no-bə, -'naù; ,kär-nə-'ü-bə\ *n* **1** : a Brazilian palm that yields a brittle yellowish wax used especially in polishes — called also *carnauba palm* **2** : the wax produced by the carnauba — called also *carnauba wax* [Portuguese]

car·ne·lian \kär-'nēl-yən\ *n* : a hard tough reddish quartz used as a gem [Middle French *corneline*]

car·ni·val \'kär-nə-vəl\ *n* **1** : a season or festival of merrymaking before Lent **2** : a merrymaking, feasting, or masquerading **3 a** : a traveling enterprise offering amusements **b** : a program of entertainment ⟨a winter *carnival*⟩ [Italian *carnevale*, alteration of earlier *carnelevare*, literally, "removal of meat"]

car·niv·o·ra \kär-'niv-rə, -ə-rə\ *n pl* : carnivorous mammals [New Latin]

car·ni·vore \'kär-nə-,vōr, -,vor\ *n* : a flesh-eating animal; *esp* : any of an order (Carnivora) of flesh-eating mammals

car·niv·o·rous \kär-'niv-rəs, -ə-rəs\ *adj* **1** : subsisting or feeding on animal tissues **2** : of or relating to the carnivores [Latin *carnivorus*, from *carn-, caro* "flesh" + *vorare* "to devour"] — **car·niv·o·rous·ly** *adv* — **car·niv·o·rous·ness** *n*

car·no·tite \'kär-nə-,tīt\ *n* : a mineral consisting of a radioactive compound of potassium, uranium, vanadium, and oxygen [M. A. *Carnot*, died 1920, French inspector general of mines]

car·ob \'kar-əb\ *n* : one of the long pods of a Mediterranean tree of the pea family; *also* : its sweet pulp [Middle French *carobe*, from Medieval Latin *carrubium*, from Arabic *kharrūbah*]

¹car·ol \'kar-əl\ *n* **1** : an old round dance with singing **2** : a song of joy or mirth **3** : a popular song of religious joy ⟨Christmas *carol*⟩ [Old French *carole*, from Late Latin *choraula* "choral song", from Latin, "choral accompanist", from Greek *choraulēs*, from *choros* "chorus" + *aulein* "to play a reed instrument", from *aulos*, a kind of reed instrument]

²carol *vb* **-oled** *or* **-olled; -ol·ing** *or* **-ol·ling** **1** : to sing especially in a joyful way **2** : to sing carols — **car·ol·er** *or* **car·ol·ier** *n*

Car·o·line \'kar-ə-,līn, -lən\ *adj* : of or relating to Charles I or Charles II of England [Medieval Latin *Carolus* "Charles"]

Car·o·lin·gian \,kar-ə-'lin-jē-ən, -jən\ *adj* : of or relating to a Frankish dynasty dating from about A.D. 613 and ruling France from 751 to 987, Germany from 752 to 911, and Italy from 774 to 961 [French *carolingien*, from Medieval Latin *karolingi* "Carolingians", from *Karolus* "Charlemagne"] — **Carolingian** *n*

¹car·om \'kar-əm\ *n* **1** : a shot in billiards in which the cue ball strikes each of two object balls **2** : a rebounding especially at an angle [Spanish *carambola*]

²carom *vi* **1** : to make a carom **2** : to strike and rebound at an angle : GLANCE

car·o·tene \'kar-ə-,tēn\ *n* : any of several orange or red hydrocarbon pigments (as $C_{40}H_{56}$) that occur in plants and in the fatty tissues of plant-eating animals and are convertible to vitamin A [Late Latin *carota* "carrot"]

ca·rot·enoid \kə-'rät-n-,oid\ *n* : any of various usually yellow to red pigments (as carotenes) found widely in plants and animals and characterized chemically by a long chain of carbon atoms — **carotenoid** *adj*

ca·rot·id \kə-'rät-əd\ *n* : the chief artery or one of the pair of arteries that pass up each side of the neck and supply the head — called also *carotid artery* [Greek *karōtides* "carotid arteries"] — **carotid** *adj*

ca·rous·al \kə-'raù-zəl\ *n* : CAROUSE

¹ca·rouse \kə-'raùz\ *n* : a drunken revel [Middle French *carousse*, from *boire carous* "to empty the cup", from *boire* "to drink" + German *garaus* "all out"]

²carouse *vi* : to drink liquor freely — **ca·rous·er** *n*

car·ou·sel *or* **car·rou·sel** \,kar-ə-'sel *also* -'zel\ *n* : MERRY-GO-ROUND 1 [French *carrousel*, from Italian *carosello*]

¹carp \'kärp\ *vi* : to find fault : complain fretfully [of Scandinavian origin] — **carp·er** *n*

²carp *n, pl* **carp** *or* **carps** : a large variable Old World soft-finned freshwater fish noted for its longevity and often raised for food; *also* : any of various related or similar fishes [Middle French *carpe*, from Late Latin *carpa*]

-carp \,kärp\ *n combining form* **1** : part of a fruit ⟨meso*carp*⟩ **2** : fruit ⟨schizo*carp*⟩ [Greek *karpos* "fruit"]

¹car·pal \'kär-pəl\ *adj* : relating to the carpus

²carpal *n* : a carpal bone or cartilage

car·pel \'kär-pəl\ *n* : one of the structures of the innermost whorl of a flower that together form the ovary of a seed plant [New Latin *carpellum*, from Greek *karpos* "fruit"]

car·pen·ter \'kär-pən-tər, 'kärp-m-tər\ *n* : a worker who builds or repairs wooden structures [Old North French *carpentier*, from Latin *carpentarius* "carriage maker", from *carpentum* "carriage", of Celtic origin] — **carpenter** *vb* — **car·pen·try** \-trē\ *n*

car·pet \'kär-pət\ *n* **1 a** : a heavy often tufted fabric used as a floor covering **b** : a floor covering made of this fabric **2** : a surface resembling a carpet ⟨a *carpet* of leaves⟩ [Middle French *carpite*, from Italian *carpita*, from *carpire* "to pluck", from Latin *carpere*] — **carpet** *vt*

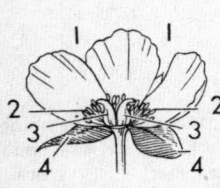

carpel: *1* petal, *2* stamen, *3* carpel, *4* sepal

¹car·pet·bag \-,bag\ *n* : a traveling bag made of carpeting common in the 19th century

²carpetbag *adj* : of, relating to, or characteristic of carpetbaggers

car·pet·bag·ger \-,bag-ər\ *n* : a Northerner in the South during the reconstruction period seeking private gain by taking advantage of unsettled conditions and political corruption [from their carrying their belongings in *carpetbags*] — **car·pet·bag·gery** \-,bag-rē, -ə-rē\ *n*

carpet beetle *n* : a small beetle whose larva damages woolen goods

car·pet·ing \'kär-pət-ing\ *n* : material for carpets; *also* : CARPET 1b

carp·ing *adj* : tending to carp — **carp·ing·ly** \'kär-ping-lē\ *adv*

car·po·go·ni·um \,kär-pə-'gō-nē-əm\ *n, pl* **-nia** \-nē-ə\ : the flask-shaped egg-bearing organ of some thallophytes [Greek *karpos* "fruit" + *gonos* "procreation, seed"] — **car·po·go·ni·al** \-nē-əl\ *adj*

car·port \'kär-,pōrt, -,pòrt\ *n* : an open-sided automobile shelter usually formed by extension of a roof from the side of a building

car·pus \'kär-pəs\ *n, pl* **car·pi** \-,pī, -,pē\ : the wrist or its bones [New Latin, from Greek *karpos* "wrist"]

car·rack \'kar-ək\ *n* : a large armed merchant ship chiefly of the 16th and 17th centuries [Middle French *caraque*, from Spanish *carraca*, from Arabic *qarāqīr*, plural of *qurqūr* "merchant ship"]

car·rel \'kar-əl\ *n* : a table that is often partitioned or enclosed for individual study in a library [Middle English *carole* "round dance, carol, ring", from Old French]

car·riage \'kar-ij\ *n* **1** : the act of carrying **2** : manner of bearing the body **3** : the cost of carrying **4 a** : a wheeled vehicle; *esp* : a horse-drawn vehicle for carrying persons **b** *British* : a railway passenger coach **5** : a wheeled support carrying a load ⟨a gun *carriage*⟩ **6** : a movable part of a machine for supporting or carrying some other movable object or part

carriage trade *n* : trade especially from well-to-do people

car·ri·er \'kar-ē-ər\ *n* **1** : one that carries **2 a** : a person or firm engaged in transporting passengers or goods **b** : a postal employee who delivers or collects mail **c** : one that delivers newspapers **3 a** : a bearer and transmitter of disease germs; *esp* : one that carries in his system germs of a disease (as typhoid fever) to which he is immune **b** : one having a specified gene and capable of transmitting it to his offspring but not exhibiting its typical expression **4** : a substance (as a catalyst) by means of which energy, a charged particle, or an ion is transferred from one source to another ⟨ATP is an energy *carrier*⟩ **5** : AIRCRAFT CARRIER **6** : an electric wave or alternating current whose modulations are used as signals in radio, telephonic, or telegraphic transmission

car·ri·on \'kar-ē-ən\ *n* : dead and decaying flesh [Anglo-French *caroine*, derived from Latin *caro* "flesh"]

car·rot \'kar-ət\ *n* : a biennial herb with a usually orange spindle-shaped edible root; *also* : its root [Middle French *carotte*, from Late Latin *carota*, from Greek *karōton*]

car·roty \-ət-ē\ *adj* : resembling carrots in color

¹car·ry \'kar-ē\ *vb* **car·ried; car·ry·ing 1 a** : to support and take from one place to another : TRANSPORT, CONVEY ⟨*carry* a package⟩ **b** : to act as a bearer — often used in the phrase *fetch and carry* **2** : to influence by mental or emotional appeal ⟨the speaker *carried* the audience⟩ **3** : to get possession or control of : CAPTURE ⟨*carry* off a prize⟩ **4** : to transfer from one place to another; *esp* : to transfer (a number) in adding columns of figures from the sum obtained in adding a single column to the next column on the left **5** : to contain and direct the course of : CONDUCT ⟨a pipe

carries water⟩ **6 a** : to wear or have on one's person ⟨*carries* a gun⟩ **b** : to bear upon or within one ⟨*carries* a scar⟩ ⟨*carry* an unborn child⟩ **c** : to include as a necessary or natural effect ⟨the crime *carries* a penalty⟩ **7** : to conduct oneself in a specified way **8** : to bear the weight of ⟨pillars *carry* an arch⟩ **9** : to sing in correct pitch ⟨*carry* a tune⟩ **10** : to keep in stock for sale ⟨*carries* three brands of tires⟩ **11** : to provide sustenance for ⟨land *carrying* 10 head of cattle⟩ **12** : to maintain on a list or record ⟨*carry* them on the payroll⟩ **13** : to prolong in space, time, or degree ⟨*carried* the argument too far⟩ **14 a** : to gain victory for; *esp* : to win adoption or the adoption of ⟨*carry* a bill⟩ **b** : to win a majority of votes in ⟨*carry* a state⟩ **15** : PUBLISH 2a ⟨the paper *carries* weather reports⟩ **16 a** : to bear the charges of holding (as merchandise) **b** : to keep on one's books as a debtor ⟨a merchant *carries* a customer⟩ **17** : to penetrate to a distance ⟨a voice that *carries* well⟩ [Old North French *carier* "to transport in a vehicle", from *car* "vehicle", from Latin *carrus*]

²carry *n, pl* **carries 1** : the range of a gun or projectile or of a struck or thrown ball **2 a** : the act or method of carrying ⟨one-hand *carry*⟩ **b** : PORTAGE 2

car·ry·all \'kar-ē-,ȯl\ *n* **1** : a light covered carriage for four or more persons **2** : a passenger automobile similar to a station wagon but with a higher body often on a truck chassis **3** : a capacious bag or case [by folk etymology from French *carriole*, derived from Latin *carrus* "car"]

carry away *vt* : to arouse to a high and often excessive degree of emotion or enthusiasm

carrying capacity *n* : the population (as of deer) that an area will support without undergoing ecological deterioration

carrying charge *n* : a charge added to the price of merchandise sold on the installment plan

carry on *vb* **1** : to oversee and make decisions about : CONDUCT ⟨*carries on* a dry cleaning business⟩ **2** : to behave in a foolish, excited, or improper manner ⟨embarrassed at the way they *carried on*⟩ **3** : to continue in spite of hindrance or discouragement

car·ry·out \'kar-ē-,aut\ *n* : a food product prepared to be eaten away from its place of sale

carry out *vt* **1** : to put into execution ⟨*carry out* a plan⟩ **2** : to bring to a successful conclusion

car·sick \'kär-,sik\ *adj* : affected with motion sickness especially in an automobile — **car sickness** *n*

¹cart \'kärt\ *n* **1** : a heavy usually horse-drawn 2-wheeled vehicle **2** : a light usually 2-wheeled vehicle drawn by a horse, pony, or dog **3** : a small wheeled vehicle ⟨a garden *cart*⟩ [Middle English]

²cart *vt* : to convey in or as if in a cart — **cart·er** *n*

cart·age \'kärt-ij\ *n* : the act of or rate charged for carting

carte blanche \'kärt-'bläⁿsh, -'blänch\ *n, pl* **cartes blanches** *same*\ : full discretionary power [French, literally, "blank document"]

car·tel \kär-'tel\ *n* : a combination of independent commercial enterprises designed to limit competition [Middle French, "letter of defiance", from Italian *cartello*, literally, "placard", from *carta* "leaf of paper"] SYN SEE MONOPOLY ☐ ORIGIN The literal meaning of Italian *cartello*, a derivative of *carta*, "leaf of paper", is "placard". The word is also used for a letter of defiance or a challenge. In this sense the Italian word was borrowed into Middle French as *cartel*, and the French word was borrowed into English. In English, a *cartel* was originally a letter of defiance. Later the word came to be used for a written agreement between warring nations to regulate such matters as the treatment and exchange of prisoners. Another type of agreement, a combination of commercial enterprises, is now called a *cartel*. *Cartel* is ultimately derived from Greek *chartēs* "leaf of papyrus" and is thus a relative of *card* and *chart*.

\ə\ abut	\ng\ sing
\ər\ further	\ō\ bone
\a\ mat	\ȯ\ saw
\ā\ take	\ȯi\ coin
\ä\ cot, cart	\th\ thin
\au̇\ out	\th\ this
\ch\ chin	\ü\ food
\e\ pet	\u̇\ foot
\ē\ easy	\y\ yet
\g\ go	\yü\ few
\i\ tip	\yu̇\ cure
\ī\ life	\zh\ vision
\j\ job	

Car·te·sian \kär-'tē-zhən\ *adj* : of or relating to René Descartes, his philosophy, or his mathematical methods [New Latin *Cartesius* "Descartes"]

Cartesian coordinate *n* : either of two coordinates that locate a point on a plane and measure its distance from one of two usually perpendicular axes along a line parallel to the other axis

Cartesian coordinate system *n* : a coordinate system based on Cartesian coordinates

Cartesian plane *n* : a plane whose points are labeled with Cartesian coordinates

Cartesian product *n* : a set that is constructed from two given sets and comprises all pairs of elements such that one element of the pair is from the first set and the other element is from the second set

Car·thu·sian \kär-'thü-zhən, -'thyü-\ *n* : a member of a religious order founded in 1084 and devoted to prayer and meditation [Medieval Latin *cartusiensis,* from Old French *Chartrouse,* motherhouse of the Carthusian order, near Grenoble, France]

car·ti·lage \'kärt-l-ij\ *n* **1** : a translucent elastic tissue that composes most of the skeleton of embryonic and very young vertebrates and becomes for the most part converted into bone in the higher vertebrates **2** : a part or structure composed of cartilage [Latin *cartilago*]

car·ti·lag·i·nous \,kärt-l-'aj-ə-nəs\ *adj* **1** : of, relating to, or resembling cartilage **2** : having a skeleton mostly of cartilage

car·tog·ra·phy \kär-'täg-rə-fē\ *n* : the making of maps [French *cartographie,* from *carte* "card, map"] — **car·tog·ra·pher** \-fər\ *n* — **car·to·graph·ic** \,kärt-ə-'graf-ik\ *adj*

car·ton \'kärt-n\ *n* : a paperboard box or container [French, from Italian *cartone* "pasteboard"]

car·toon \kär-'tün\ *n* **1** : a preparatory design, drawing, or painting **2 a** : a satirical drawing commenting on public and usually political matters **b** : COMIC STRIP **3** : ANIMATED CARTOON [Italian *cartone* "pasteboard, cartoon", from *carta* "leaf of paper", from Latin *charta* "piece of papyrus"] — **cartoon** *vb* — **car·toon·ist** \-'tü-nəst\ *n*

car·tridge \'kär-trij\ *n* : a case or container that holds a substance or device which is difficult, troublesome, or awkward to handle and that is easily interchangeable: as **a** : a tube containing a complete charge for a firearm **b** : a holder for photographic film **c** : a device on a phonograph that changes vibrations of the needle into electrical signals **d** : a case for holding a magnetic tape or disk **e** : a case for integrated circuitry containing a computer program ⟨a video-game *cartridge*⟩ [Middle French *cartouche* "scroll, cartridge", from Italian *cartoccio,* from *carta* "paper", from Latin *charta* "piece of papyrus"]

cart·wheel \'kärt-,hwēl, -,wēl\ *n* **1** : a large coin (as a silver dollar) **2** : a handspring performed to one side with arms and legs extended

car·un·cle \'kar-,əng-kəl, kə-'rəng-\ *n* : a fleshy outgrowth (as on a seed) [obsolete French *caruncule,* from Latin *caruncula* "little piece of flesh", from *caro* "flesh"]

carve \'kärv\ *vb* **1** : to cut with care or precision especially artistically ⟨*carve* a statue⟩ **2** : to make or get by cutting — often used with *out* **3** : to cut into pieces or slices **4** : to cut up and serve meat [Old English *ceorfan*] — **car·ver** *n*

carv·en \'kär-vən\ *adj* : made by carving

carv·ing \'kär-ving\ *n* **1** : the act or art of one who carves **2** : a carved object, design, or figure

cary·at·id \,kar-ē-'at-əd\ *n, pl* **-at·ids** *or* **-at·i·des** \-'at-ə-,dēz\ : a statue of a woman in flowing robes used as an architectural column [Latin *caryatides,* plural, from Greek *karyatides* "priestesses of Artemis at Caryae in Laconia, caryatids", from *Karyai* "Caryae"]

caryatid

cary·op·sis \,kar-ē-'äp-səs\ *n, pl* **-op·ses** \-'äp-,sēz\ *or* **-op·si·des** \-'äp-sə-,dēz\ : a small one-seeded dry indehiscent fruit in which the fruit and seed fuse in a single grain [Greek *karyon* "nut, kernel" + *opsis* "appearance"]

ca·sa·ba *or* **cas·sa·ba** \kə-'säb-ə\ *n* : any of several winter melons with yellow rind and sweet flesh — called also *casaba melon, cassaba melon* [*Kasaba* (now Turgutlu), Turkey]

¹cas·cade \kas-'kād\ *n* **1** : a steep usually small fall of water; *esp* : one of a series **2** : something arranged in a series or in a succession of stages so that each stage derives from or acts upon the product of the preceding ⟨a *cascade* amplifier⟩ **3** : something falling or rushing forth in quantity ⟨a *cascade* of sound⟩ [French, from Italian *cascata,* from *cascare* "to fall"]

²cascade *vi* : to fall in a cascade

cas·cara \kas-'kar-ə\ *n* : the dried laxative bark of a buckthorn tree that grows along the Pacific coast of the United States [Spanish *cáscara* "bark"]

¹case \'kās\ *n* **1** : a special set of circumstances or conditions **2 a** : a situation requiring investigation or action ⟨a *case* for the police⟩ **b** : an object of investigation or consideration **3 a** : a form of a noun, pronoun, or adjective indicating its grammatical relation to other words ⟨the word *child's* in "the child's shirt" is in the possessive *case*⟩ **b** : such a relation whether indicated by inflection or not ⟨the subject of a verb is in the nominative *case*⟩ **4** : what actually exists or happens : FACT ⟨if that's the *case*⟩ **5 a** : a legal suit or action **b** (1) : the evidence supporting a conclusion or judgment (2) : ARGUMENT; *esp* : a convincing argument **6 a** : an instance of disease or injury; *also* : PATIENT **b** : an instance that calls attention to or exemplifies a situation : EXAMPLE ⟨a clear *case* of negligence⟩ [Old French *cas,* from Latin *casus* "fall, chance", from *cadere* "to fall"] SYN see INSTANCE — **in any case** : without regard to or in spite of other considerations — **in case 1** : IF 1 **2** : as a precaution **3** : as a precaution against the event that

²case *n* **1 a** : a box or receptacle to contain something **b** : a box with its contents **c** : a set of like or related things; *esp* : PAIR ⟨a *case* of pistols⟩ **2** : an outer covering, sheath, or housing ⟨spore *cases*⟩ **3** : a shallow divided tray for printing type **4** : the frame of a door or window : CASING [Old North French *casse,* from Latin *capsa* "chest, case", from *capere* "to take"]

³case *vt* : to enclose in or cover with a case

case hard·en \'kās-,härd-n\ *vt* : to treat (an iron alloy) so that the outside is harder than the interior — **case·hard·ened** *adj*

case history *n* : a record of history, environment, and relevant details (as of individual behavior or condition) especially for use in analysis or illustration

ca·sein \'kā-,sēn, kā-'sēn\ *n* **1** : a phosphorus-containing protein that is precipitated from milk by heating with an acid or by lactic acid in souring and that is used in making paints and adhesives **2** : a phosphorus-containing protein that is produced when milk is curdled by rennet, that is one of the chief constituents of cheese, and that is used in making plastics [derived from Latin *caseus* "cheese"]

case knife *n* **1** : SHEATH KNIFE **2** : a table knife

case·mate \'kās-,māt\ *n* : a fortified position or enclosure from which guns are fired through openings [Middle French, from Italian *casamatta*]

case·ment \'kās-mənt\ *n* : a window sash opening on hinges like a door; *also* : a window with such a sash [Middle English, "hollow molding", probably from Old North French *encassement* "frame", from *en-* "in" + *casse* "case"]

case·work \'kās-,wərk\ *n* : social work involving direct consideration of the individual case including study of and treatment for its needs and problems — **case·work·er** *n*

¹cash \'kash\ *n* : ready money [Italian *cassa* "money box", from Latin *capsa* "case, chest"]

²cash *vt* : to pay or obtain cash for ⟨*cash* a check⟩

³cash *n, pl* **cash** : any of various coins of small value in China and India; *esp* : a Chinese coin with a square hole in the center [Portuguese *caixa*, from Tamil *kācu*, a small copper coin]

cash–and–carry \,kash-ən-'kar-ē\ *n* : the policy of selling for cash and without delivery service

cash·book \'kash-,buk\ *n* : a book in which records are kept of all cash received and paid out

cash·ew \'kash-ü, kə-'shü\ *n* : a tropical American tree of the sumac family grown for its edible kidney-shaped nut and receptacle and for the gum it yields; *also* : its nut [Portuguese *acajú, cajú*, of American Indian origin]

¹ca·shier \ka-'shiər, kə-\ *vt* : to discharge in disgrace from a position of responsibility or trust [Dutch *casseren*, from Middle French *casser* "to discharge, annul", from Latin *cassus* "void"]

²cash·ier \ka-'shiər\ *n* **1** : a high officer of a bank responsible for all money received and paid out **2** : one who receives and records payments ⟨a *cashier* in a supermarket⟩ [Middle French *cassier*, from *casse* "money box", from Italian *cassa*]

cashier's check *n* : a check drawn by a bank on its own funds and signed by its cashier

cash·mere \'kazh-,miər, 'kash-\ *n* **1** : fine wool from the undercoat of Kashmir goats; *also* : a yarn of this wool **2** : a soft twilled fabric made originally from cashmere wool [*Cashmere* "Kashmir"]

cash register *n* : a business machine that usually has a money drawer, records money received, and shows the amount of each sale

cas·ing \'kā-sing\ *n* : something that encases : material for encasing: as **a** : an enclosing frame especially around a door or window opening **b** : TIRE 2b **c** : a membranous case for processed meat (as bologna)

ca·si·no \kə-'sē-nō\ *n, pl* **-nos** **1** : a building or room used for social amusements; *esp* : one used for gambling **2** *or* **cas·si·no** : a card game in which players try to match cards in their hands with exposed cards on the table [Italian, from *casa* "house", from Latin, "cabin"]

cask \'kask\ *n* : a barrel-shaped container usually for liquids; *also* : the quantity contained in a cask [Middle French *casque* "helmet", from Spanish *casco* "potsherd, skull, helmet", from *cascar* "to break"]

cas·ket \'kas-kət\ *n* **1** : a small chest or box (as for jewels) **2** : a usually fancy coffin [Middle French *cassette*, from Old North French *casse* "case"]

casque \'kask\ *n* : a piece of armor for the head : HELMET [Middle French, from Spanish *casco*]

cas·sa·ba *variant of* CASABA

cas·sa·va \kə-'säv-ə\ *n* : any of several plants of the spurge family grown in the tropics for their fleshy rootstocks which yield a nutritious starch; *also* : the rhizome or its starch — compare TAPIOCA [Spanish *cazabe* "cassava bread", of American Indian origin]

cas·se·role \'kas-ə-,rōl\ *n* **1** : a dish in which food can be baked and served **2** : the food cooked and served in a casserole [French, "saucepan", from Middle French *casse* "ladle, dripping pan", derived from Greek *kyathos* "ladle"]

cas·sette \kə-'set\ *n* **1** : a lightproof container for holding film or plates for use in a camera **2** : a small plastic box containing two reels wound with magnetic tape in which the tape on one reel passes to the other during recording and playback [French, "casket"]

cas·sia \'kash-ə\ *n* **1** : a coarse cinnamon bark **2** : any of a genus of leguminous herbs, shrubs, and trees of warm regions some of which yield senna [Latin, from Greek *kassia*, of Semitic origin]

cas·si·mere \'kaz-ə-,miər, 'kas-\ *n* : a smooth twilled usually wool fabric [obsolete *Cassimere* "Kashmir"]

cas·si·no *variant of* CASINO

Cas·si·o·pe·ia \,kas-ē-ə-'pē-ə, -'pē-yə\ *n* : a northern constellation between Andromeda and Cepheus [*Cassiopeia*, mythical queen of Ethiopia and mother of Andromeda]

Cassiopeia's Chair *n* : a group of stars in the constellation Cassiopeia

cas·sit·er·ite \kə-'sit-ə-,rīt\ *n* : a brown or black mineral SnO₂ that consists of tin dioxide and is the chief source of tin [Greek *kassiteros* "tin"]

cas·sock \'kas-ək\ *n* : an ankle-length gown worn especially in Roman Catholic and Anglican churches by the clergy and by lay people assisting at services [Middle French *casaque*, from Persian *kazhāghand* "padded jacket", from *kazh* "raw silk" + *āghand* "stuffed"]

cas·so·wary \'kas-ə-,wer-ē\ *n, pl* **-war·ies** : any of several tall swift-running birds of New Guinea and Australia closely related to the emu [Malay *kĕsuari*]

¹cast \'kast\ *vb* **cast; cast·ing** **1 a** (1) : THROW 2 ⟨*cast* a stone⟩ (2) : to throw out a lure or line with a fishing rod **b** : to point or project in a specified direction : DIRECT ⟨*cast* a glance⟩ **c** : to place as if by throwing ⟨*cast* doubt on their integrity⟩ **d** : to deposit (a ballot) formally **e** : to throw off, out, or away ⟨the horse *cast* a shoe⟩: as (1) : to get rid of : DISCARD ⟨*cast* aside all restraint⟩ (2) : SHED, MOLT ⟨a snake *casts* its skin⟩ **2 a** : COMPUTE, FIGURE **b** : to calculate by astrology ⟨*cast* a horoscope⟩ **3 a** : to assign the parts of to actors ⟨*cast* a play⟩ **b** : to assign (an actor) to a part **4 a** : to give shape to (a substance) by pouring in liquid or plastic form into a mold or form and letting harden without pressure ⟨*cast* steel⟩ **b** : to form by this process ⟨*cast* machine parts⟩ [Old Norse *kasta*] — **cast lots** : to draw lots to determine a matter by chance

²cast *n* **1 a** : an act or instance of casting **b** : something that happens as a result of chance **2 a** : the form in which a thing is constructed **b** : the characters or the actors in a narrative or play **3** : the distance to which a thing can be thrown **4** : a turning of the eye in a particular direction; *also* : EXPRESSION **5** : something thrown or the quantity thrown **6 a** : something formed by casting in a mold or form : CASTING ⟨a bronze *cast* of a statue⟩ **b** : a rigid dressing of gauze impregnated with plaster of paris for immobilizing a diseased or broken part **7** : a forecast about future events or conditions ⟨to make a long *cast* ahead⟩ **8** : an overspread of a color : SHADE ⟨gray with a greenish *cast*⟩ **9** : physical form or character : APPEARANCE ⟨features of delicate *cast*⟩ **10** : something thrown out or off, shed, or ejected; *esp* : the excrement of an earthworm

cast about *vi* : to look around : SEEK ⟨*cast about* for a seat⟩

cas·ta·net \,kas-tə-'net\ *n* : a rhythm instrument that consists of two small ivory, wood, or plastic shells fastened to the thumb and clicked together by the fingers — usually used in pl. [Spanish *castañeta*, from *castaña* "chestnut", from Latin *castanea*]

cast·away \'kas-tə-,wā\ *adj* **1** : thrown away **2** : cast adrift or ashore as a survivor of a shipwreck — **castaway** *n*

caste \'kast\ *n* **1** : one of the hereditary classes formerly dividing Hindu society **2 a** : a division of society based on differences of wealth, inherited rank, or occupation **b** : the position conferred by caste standing : PRESTIGE **3** : a specialized form that carries out a particular function in the colony of a social insect (as the honeybee) [Portuguese *casta*, literally, "race, lineage", from *casto* "pure, chaste", from Latin *castus*]

cas·tel·lat·ed \'kas-tə-,lāt-əd\ *adj* : having battlements like a castle [Medieval Latin *castellare* "to fortify", from Latin *castellum* "castle, fortress"]

cast·er \'kas-tər\ *n* **1** : one that casts **2** : a small container with a perforated top for sprinkling food seasoning **3** : a small tray for condiment containers **4** *or* **cas-**

cashew

cassowary

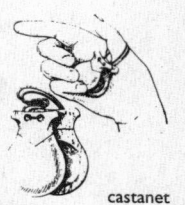

castanet

\ə\ abut		\ng\ sing
\ər\ further		\ō\ bone
\a\ mat		\o˙\ saw
\ā\ take		\o˙i\ coin
\ä\ cot, cart		\th\ thin
\au˙\ out		\th\ this
\ch\ chin		\ü\ food
\e\ pet		\u˙\ foot
\ē\ easy		\y\ yet
\g\ go		\yü\ few
\i\ tip		\yu˙\ cure
\ī\ life		\zh\ vision
\j\ job		

tor \'kas-tər\ : a wheel or set of wheels mounted in a swivel frame used for supporting furniture, trucks, and portable machines

cas·ti·gate \'kas-tə-ˌgāt\ vt : to punish, reprove, or criticize severely [Latin castigare "to correct, chasten, castigate", from castus "pure, chaste"] — **cas·ti·ga·tion** \ˌkas-tə-'gā-shən\ n — **cas·ti·ga·tor** \'kas-tə-ˌgāt-ər\ n

cas·tile soap \ˌkas-'tēl-\ n, often cap C : a hard bland soap made from olive oil and sodium hydroxide [Castile, region of Spain]

Cas·til·ian \ka-'stil-yən\ n **1 a** : a native or inhabitant of Castile **b** : SPANIARD **2** : the official and literary language of Spain based on the dialect of Castile — **Castilian** adj

cast·ing n **1** : the act of one that casts **2** : something cast in a mold ⟨a bronze casting⟩ **3** : something (as skin or excrement) that is cast out or off

casting vote n : a deciding vote cast by a presiding officer in case of a tied vote

cast iron n : a hard brittle alloy of iron, carbon, and silicon that is cast in a mold

1cas·tle \'kas-əl\ n **1 a** : a large fortified building or set of buildings **b** : a massive or imposing house **2** : 3ROOK [Old North French castel, from Latin castellum "fortress, castle", from castrum "fortified place"]

2castle vb **cas·tled; cas·tling** \'kas-ling, -ə-ling\ **1** : to establish in a castle **2** : to move a chess king two squares toward a rook and the rook to the square next past the king on a single move

castle in the air : an impracticable project : DAYDREAM — called also castle in Spain

cast–off \'kas-ˌtȯf\ adj : thrown away or aside — **castoff** n

cast off \'kas-'tȯf\ vi : to unfasten or untie a boat or a line securing a boat

cas·tor \'kas-tər\ n **1** : a bitter strong-smelling orange-brown substance obtained from the beaver and used by perfumers **2** : a beaver hat [Latin, "beaver", from Greek kastōr]

Cas·tor \'kas-tər\ n : the more northern of the two bright stars in Gemini

castor bean n : the very poisonous seed of the castor-oil plant; also : this plant

castor oil n : a thick yellowish oil extracted from castor beans and used as a lubricant, in soap, and as a cathartic [probably from its former use as a substitute for castor in medicine]

castor–oil plant n : a tropical Old World herb widely grown as an ornamental or for its oil-rich castor beans

1cas·trate \'kas-ˌtrāt\ vt : to deprive of the testes or ovaries [Latin castrare] — **cas·tra·tion** \ka-'strā-shən\ n

2castrate n : a castrated individual

ca·su·al \'kazh-wəl, -ə-wəl; 'kazh-əl\ adj **1** : subject to or occurring by chance **2** : occurring without regularity : OCCASIONAL **3 a** : feeling or showing little concern : NONCHALANT **b** : INFORMAL 1, 2 [Late Latin casualis, from Latin casus "fall, chance", from cadere "to fall"] SYN see ACCIDENTAL, RANDOM — **ca·su·al·ly** \-ē\ adv — **ca·su·al·ness** n

ca·su·al·ty \'kazh-əl-tē; 'kazh-wəl-, -ə-wəl-\ n, pl **-ties** **1** : serious or fatal accident : DISASTER **2 a** : a military person lost (as by death or capture) during warfare **b** : a person or thing injured, lost, or destroyed **3** : injury or death from accident

ca·su·ist·ry \'kazh-wə-strē, -ə-wə-\ n, pl **-ries** **1** : the study or resolution of questions of right and wrong in conduct **2** : false reasoning or application of principles especially with regard to morals or law [probably from Spanish casuista "casuist", from Latin casus "fall, chance", from cadere "to fall"] — **ca·su·ist** \'kazh-wəst, -ə-wəst\ n — **ca·su·is·tic** \ˌkazh-ə-'wis-tik\ adj

cat \'kat\ n **1 a** : a small flesh-eating mammal long domesticated and kept by humans as a pet or for catching

rats and mice **b** : an animal (as a lion, tiger, leopard, jaguar, cougar, wildcat, lynx, or cheetah) of the same family as the domestic cat **2** : CAT-O'-NINE-TAILS **3** : CATFISH [Old English catt]

ca·tab·o·lism \kə-'tab-ə-ˌliz-əm\ n : the part of metabolism concerned with the destruction of the substance of plants and animals involving the breakdown of complex materials and the release of energy — compare ANABOLISM [Greek katabolē "throwing down", from kataballein "to throw down", from kata "down" + ballein "to throw"] — **cat·a·bol·ic** \ˌkat-ə-'bäl-ik\ adj

cat·a·clysm \'kat-ə-ˌkliz-əm\ n **1** : a great flood : DELUGE **2** : a violent and destructive natural event (as an earthquake) **3** : a violent social or political upheaval [French cataclysme, from Latin cataclysmos, from Greek kataklysmos, from kataklyzein "to inundate", from kata "down" + klyzein "to wash"] SYN see DISASTER — **cat·a·clys·mal** \ˌkat-ə-'kliz-məl\ adj — **cat·a·clys·mic** \-'kliz-mik\ adj

cat·a·comb \'kat-ə-ˌkōm\ n : an underground burying place; esp : one that has passages with hollowed places in the sides for tombs — usually used in pl. [Middle French catacombe, derived from Late Latin catacumbae "catacombs"]

ca·tad·ro·mous \kə-'tad-rə-məs\ adj : living in fresh water and going to the sea to spawn ⟨catadromous eels⟩ — compare ANADROMOUS [Greek kata "down" + dramein "to run"]

cat·a·falque \'kat-ə-ˌfalk, -ˌfȯlk, -ˌfȯk\ n : a structure sometimes used in funerals to support the coffin [Italian catafalco]

Cat·a·lan \'kat-l-ən, -ˌan\ n **1** : a native or inhabitant of Catalonia **2** : the Romance language of Catalonia, Valencia, Andorra, and the Balearic islands — **Catalan** adj

cat·a·lase \'kat-l-ˌās, -ˌāz\ n : an enzyme that catalyzes the decomposition of hydrogen peroxide into water and oxygen and the oxidation by hydrogen peroxide of alcohols to aldehydes

cat·a·lep·sy \'kat-l-ˌep-sē\ n, pl **-sies** : a condition of suspended animation and loss of voluntary motion in which the limbs hold any position they are placed in [Medieval Latin catalepsia, from Greek katalēpsis, literally, "act of seizing", from katalambanein "to seize", from kata "down" + lambanein "to take"] — **cat·a·lep·tic** \ˌkat-l-'ep-tik\ adj or n

1cat·a·log or **cat·a·logue** \'kat-l-ˌȯg\ n **1** : a list of names, titles, or articles arranged according to a system **2 a** : a book or a file containing a catalog **b** : the items listed in such a book or file [Middle French catalogue, from Late Latin catalogus, from Greek katalogos, from katalegein "to list", from kata "down" + legein "to gather, speak"]

2catalog or **catalogue** vt **1** : to make a catalog of **2** : to enter in a catalog; esp : to classify (books or information) descriptively — **cat·a·log·er** or **cat·a·logu·er** n

ca·tal·pa \kə-'tal-pə, -'tȯl-\ n : a small tree of America and Asia with broad oval leaves, flowers brightly striped inside and spotted outside, and long narrow pods [Creek kutuhlpa, literally, "head with wings"]

ca·tal·y·sis \kə-'tal-ə-səs\ n : the change and especially increase in the rate of a chemical reaction brought about by a catalyst [Greek katalysis "dissolution", from katalyein "to dissolve", from kata "down" + lyein "to loosen, dissolve"] — **cat·a·lyt·ic** \ˌkat-l-'it-ik\ adj — **cat·a·lyt·i·cal·ly** \-'it-i-kə-lē, -klē\ adv

cat·a·lyst \'kat-l-əst\ n : a substance that changes the rate of a chemical reaction but is itself unchanged at the end of the process; esp : such a substance that speeds up a reaction or enables it to proceed under milder conditions than otherwise possible

catalytic converter n : a pollution-control device attached to the exhaust system of an automotive vehicle that contains a chemical catalyst which converts pollutants (as carbon monoxide and unburned hydrocarbons) to other products (as carbon dioxide and water)

cat·a·lyze \'kat-l-ˌīz\ *vt* : to bring about or produce by chemical catalysis — **cat·a·lyz·er** *n*

cat·a·ma·ran \ˌkat-ə-mə-'ran, 'kat-ə-mə-ˌran\ *n* **1** : a raft propelled by paddles or sails **2** : a boat with twin hulls side by side [Tamil *kaṭṭumaram*, from *kaṭṭu* "to tie" + *maram* "tree"]

cat·a·mount \'kat-ə-ˌmaùnt\ *n* : any of various wild cats: as **a** : COUGAR **b** : LYNX [Middle English *cat of the mountain*]

¹cat·a·pult \'kat-ə-ˌpəlt, -ˌpùlt\ *n* **1** : an ancient military device for hurling missiles **2** : a device for launching an airplane at flying speed (as from the deck of an aircraft carrier) [Latin *catapulta*, from Greek *katapaltēs*, from *kata* "down" + *pallein* "to hurl"]

²catapult *vb* **1** : to throw or launch by or as if by a catapult **2** : to become catapulted

cat·a·ract \'kat-ə-ˌrakt\ *n* **1** : a clouding of the lens of the eye or of its capsule obstructing the passage of light **2 a** : WATERFALL; *esp* : a large one over a precipice **b** : steep rapids in a river **c** : FLOOD 3 ⟨a *cataract* of words⟩ [Latin *cataracta* "waterfall, portcullis", from Greek *kataraktēs*, from *katarassein* "to dash down", from *kata* "down" + *arassein* "to strike, dash"]

ca·tarrh \kə-'tär\ *n* : inflammation of a mucous membrane; *esp* : one chronically affecting the human nose and air passages [Late Latin *catarrhus*, from Greek *katarrhous*, from *katarrhein* "to flow down", from *kata* "down" + *rhein* "to flow"] — **ca·tarrh·al** \-'tär-əl\ *adj*

ca·tas·tro·phe \kə-'tas-trə-fē\ *n* **1** : the final event of the dramatic action especially of a tragedy **2** : a momentous tragic event : DISASTER **3** : a violent and sudden change in a feature of the earth **4** : utter failure or ruin : FIASCO [Greek *katastrophē*, from *katastrephein* "to overturn", from *kata* "down" + *strephein* "to turn, twist"] SYN see DISASTER — **cat·a·stroph·ic** \ˌkat-ə-'sträf-ik\ *adj* — **cat·a·stroph·i·cal·ly** \-'sträf-i-kə-lē, -klē\ *adv*

catastrophe theory *n* : mathematical theory and conjecture that uses topology to explain events (as an earthquake or a stock market crash) characterized by major abrupt changes

ca·tas·tro·phism \kə-'tas-trə-ˌfiz-əm\ *n* : a geological doctrine that changes in the earth's crust have in the past been brought about suddenly by physical forces operating in ways that cannot be observed today — compare UNIFORMITARIANISM — **ca·tas·tro·phist** \-fəst\ *n*

cat·bird \'kat-ˌbərd\ *n* : a dark gray American songbird with black cap and reddish under tail coverts

cat·boat \-ˌbōt\ *n* : a sailboat with a single mast set far forward and a single large sail extended by a long boom

cat·call \-ˌkól\ *n* : a loud or raucous cry made to express disapproval (as at a sports event) — **catcall** *vb*

¹catch \'kach, 'kech\ *vb* **caught**; **catch·ing 1 a** : to capture or seize in flight or motion ⟨*catch* a thief⟩ ⟨*catch* a ball⟩ **b** : TRAP 1a ⟨*caught* in a lie⟩ **c** : DECEIVE 1, MISLEAD **2 a** : to discover unexpectedly ⟨was *caught* in the act⟩ **b** : to check suddenly ⟨*catch* oneself before giving away a secret⟩ **3 a** : to take in and retain ⟨a barrel to *catch* rainwater⟩ **b** : to take in with the mind or senses ⟨*catch* an explanation⟩ ⟨barely *caught* the whisper⟩ **4 a** : to get entangled ⟨*catch* a sleeve on a nail⟩ **b** : to engage firmly ⟨this lock will not *catch*⟩ **c** : to fasten in position **5** : to become affected by ⟨*catch* a cold⟩ **6** : to take or get momentarily or quickly ⟨*catch* a glimpse of a friend⟩ **7 a** : to come abreast of : OVERTAKE **b** : to get aboard in time ⟨*catch* a bus⟩ **8** : to play ball as a catcher [Old North French *cachier* "to hunt", from Latin *captare* "to chase", from *capere* "to take"] — **catch·able** \'kach-ə-bəl, 'kech-\ *adj* — **catch fire 1** :

to begin to burn **2** : to become excited or exciting — **catch it** : to incur blame, reprimand, or punishment — **catch one's breath** : to pause or rest briefly □ SYN CAPTURE, SNARE, TRAP: CATCH implies the seizing of something in motion or in flight or in hiding; CAPTURE adds an implication of overcoming resistance or difficulty; SNARE and TRAP imply using a device that catches by surprise and holds at the mercy of the captor.

²catch *n* **1** : something caught; *esp* : the total quantity (as of fish) caught at one time **2 a** : the act of catching **b** : a game in which a ball is thrown and caught **3** : something that checks or holds immovable ⟨a *catch* on a safety pin⟩ **4** : one worth catching or acquiring **5** : a round for three or more voices **6** : FRAGMENT 1 ⟨heard *catches* of a melody⟩ **7** : a concealed difficulty

catch·all \'kach-ˌól, 'kech-\ *n* : something to hold odds and ends

catch·er \'kach-ər, 'kech-\ *n* : one that catches; *esp* : a baseball player stationed behind home plate

catch·ing *adj* **1** : INFECTIOUS, CONTAGIOUS **2** : CATCHY 1

catch·ment \'kach-mənt, 'kech-\ *n* **1** : the action of catching water **2** : something that catches water

catch on *vi* **1** : to understand the nature of something ⟨*caught on* to the plot⟩ **2** : to become popular ⟨a tune that really *caught on*⟩

catch·pen·ny \'kach-ˌpen-ē, 'kech-\ *adj* : intended to appeal to the ignorant or unwary by cheap or sensational quality

catch·up \'kech-əp, 'kach-; 'kat-səp\ *variant of* CATSUP

catch·word \'kach-ˌwərd, 'kech-\ *n* **1** : GUIDE WORD **2** : a word or expression repeated until it becomes associated with a party, school, or viewpoint

catchy \'kach-ē, 'kech-ē\ *adj* **catch·i·er; -est 1** : likely to attract ⟨a *catchy* tune⟩ **2** : apt to entangle one : TRICKY ⟨a *catchy* question⟩

cat·e·chism \'kat-ə-ˌkiz-əm\ *n* **1** : a summary of religious doctrine often in the form of questions and answers **2** : a set of formal questions put as a test — **cat·e·chet·i·cal** \ˌkat-ə-'ket-i-kəl\ *adj* — **cat·e·chis·mal** \-'kiz-məl\ *adj* — **cat·e·chis·tic** \-'kis-tik\ *adj*

cat·e·chist \'kat-ə-ˌkist, -i-kəst\ *n* : one that catechizes

cat·e·chize \'kat-ə-ˌkīz\ *vt* **1** : to instruct systematically especially by questions, answers, and explanations and corrections; *esp* : to give religious instruction in this manner **2** : to question systematically or closely [Late Latin *catechizare*, from Greek *katēchein* "to teach", literally, "to din into", from *kata* "down" + *ēchein* "to resound", from *ēchē* "sound"]

cat·e·chu·men \ˌkat-ə-'kyü-mən\ *n* **1** : a convert to Christianity receiving training in doctrine and discipline before baptism **2** : one receiving instruction in the basic doctrines of Christianity before being admitted as a member of a church [Greek *katēchoumenos*, from *katēchein* "to teach, catechize"]

cat·e·gor·i·cal \ˌkat-ə-'gór-i-kəl, -'gär-\ *also* **cat·e·gor·ic** \-ik\ *adj* **1** : involving neither qualification nor reservation : ABSOLUTE ⟨a *categorical* denial⟩ **2** : of, relating to, or being a category [Late Latin *categoricus*, from Greek *katēgorikos*, from *katēgoria* "affirmation, category"] — **cat·e·gor·i·cal·ly** \-i-kə-lē, -klē\ *adv*

cat·e·go·rize \'kat-i-gə-ˌrīz\ *vt* : to put into a category : CLASSIFY — **cat·e·go·ri·za·tion** \ˌkat-i-gə-rə-'zā-shən\ *n*

cat·e·go·ry \'kat-ə-ˌgōr-ē, -ˌgór-\ *n, pl* **-ries 1** : a division in a system of classification ⟨courses in the liberal arts *category*⟩ **2** : a unit of a larger whole made up of members sharing one or more characteristics : CLASS ⟨a new *category* of computers⟩ [Late Latin *categoria*, from Greek *katēgoria* "predication, category", from *katēgorein* "to accuse, affirm, predicate", from *kata* "down" + *agora* "public assembly"]

cat·e·nate \'kat-ə-ˌnāt\ *vt* : to connect in a series : LINK [Latin *catenare*, from *catena* "chain"] — **cat·e·na·tion** \ˌkat-ə-'nā-shən\ *n*

catamaran 2

¹catapult 1

\ə\ abut	\ng\ sing
\ər\ further	\ō\ bone
\a\ mat	\ó\ saw
\ā\ take	\ói\ coin
\ä\ cot, cart	\th\ thin
\aú\ out	\th\ this
\ch\ chin	\ü\ food
\e\ pet	\ù\ foot
\ē\ easy	\y\ yet
\g\ go	\yü\ few
\i\ tip	\yù\ cure
\ī\ life	\zh\ vision
\j\ job	

caterpillar

ca·ter \'kāt-ər\ *vi* **1** : to provide a supply of food **2** : to supply what is required or desired ⟨*catered* to their whims⟩ [Anglo-French *acatour* "buyer of provisions", from Old North French *acater* "to buy"]

cat·er·cor·ner \,kat-ē-'kòr-nər, ,kat-ə-, ,kit-ē-\ *or* **cat·er–cor·nered** \-nərd\ *or* **cat·ty–cor·ner** *or* **kit·ty–cor·ner** \-nər\ *or* **cat·ty–cor·nered** *or* **kit·ty–cor·nered** \-nərd\ *adv or adj* : in a diagonal or oblique position : on a diagonal or oblique line [obsolete *cater* "four in cards or dice"]

ca·ter·er \'kāt-ər-ər\ *n* : one that caters; *esp* : one that provides food and service for a social affair

cat·er·pil·lar \'kat-ə-,pil-ər, 'kat-ər-,\ *n* : the wormlike larva of a butterfly or moth; *also* : any of various similar insect larvae (as of a sawfly) [Old North French *catepelose*, literally, "hairy cat"]

Caterpillar *trademark* — used for a tractor that travels on two endless belts for use on rough or soft ground

cat·er·waul \'kat-ər-,wòl\ *vi* : to utter the characteristic harsh cry of a rutting cat or a similar sound [Middle English *caterwawen*] — **caterwaul** *n*

cat·fish \'kat-,fish\ *n* : any of numerous usually stout-bodied large-headed fishes (order Ostariophysi) with long sensory barbels

cat·gut \-,gət\ *n* : a tough cord made usually from sheep intestines and used for strings of musical instruments and rackets and for sewing in surgery

ca·thar·sis \kə-'thär-səs\ *n, pl* **-thar·ses** \-'thär-,sēz\ **1** : a purification that brings about spiritual renewal or release from tension ⟨the *catharsis* of tears⟩ **2** : release from an emotional problem through expression of its unconscious basis [Greek *katharsis*, from *kathairein* "to purge", from *katharos* "pure"]

¹ca·thar·tic \-'thärt-ik\ *adj* : of or relating to catharsis or to a cathartic

²cathartic *n* : PURGATIVE, LAXATIVE

ca·the·dra \kə-'thē-drə\ *n* : a bishop's official throne [Latin, "chair", from Greek *kathedra*, from *kata* "down" + *hedra* "seat"]

¹ca·the·dral \kə-'thē-drəl\ *adj* **1** : of, relating to, or containing a bishop's throne **2** : of or relating to a cathedral

²cathedral *n* : a church that contains a bishop's throne and is the principal church of a diocese

ca·thep·sin \kə-'thep-sən\ *n* : a proteinase that functions inside the body cells [Greek *kathepsein* "to digest", from *kata* "down" + *hepsein* "to boil"]

cath·e·ter \'kath-ət-ər\ *n* : a slender tube for insertion (as for medication or removal of contents) into a bodily passage or cavity [Late Latin, from Greek *kathetēr*, from *kathienai* "to send down", from *kata* "down" + *hienai* "to send"]

cath·ode \'kath-,ōd\ *n* **1** : the negative electrode of an electrolytic cell to which the positive ions are attracted — compare ANODE **2** : the positive terminal of a primary cell or of a storage battery that is delivering current **3** : the electron-emitting electrode of an electron tube [Greek *kathodos* "way down", from *kata* "down" + *hodos* "way"] — **ca·thod·ic** \ka-'thäd-ik\ *adj*

cathode ray *n* **1** : one of the high-speed electrons projected in a stream from the heated cathode of a vacuum tube under the propulsion of a strong electric field **2** : a stream of cathode-ray electrons

cathode–ray tube *n* : a vacuum tube in which cathode rays usually in the form of a slender beam are projected upon a fluorescent screen and produce a luminous spot

cath·o·lic \'kath-lik, -ə-lik\ *adj* **1** : COMPREHENSIVE 1, UNIVERSAL; *esp* : broad in sympathies, tastes, or interests **2** *cap* **a** : of, relating to, or forming the church universal **b** : of or relating to the church of which the pope is head : Roman Catholic [Late Latin *catholicus*, from Greek *katholikos* "universal, general", from *katholou* "in general", from *kata* "by" + *holos*

"whole"] — **ca·thol·i·cal·ly** \kə-'thäl-i-kə-lē, -klē\ *adv* — **Ca·thol·i·cism** \kə-'thäl-ə-,siz-əm\ *n* — **ca·thol·i·cize** \kə-'thäl-ə-,sīz\ *vb*

Catholic *n* **1** : a person who belongs to the universal Christian church **2** : a member of a Catholic church; *esp* : ROMAN CATHOLIC

cath·o·lic·i·ty \,kath-ə-'lis-ət-ē\ *n* **1** *cap* : the character of being in conformity with a Catholic church **2 a** : liberality of sentiments or views **b** : comprehensive range

cat·ion \'kat-,ī-ən\ *n* : the ion in an electrolyzed solution that migrates to the cathode; *also* : a positively charged ion [Greek *kation*, from *katienai* "to go down", from *kata* "down" + *ienai* "to go"]

cat·kin \'kat-kən\ *n* : a flower cluster that is a usually long ament densely crowded with bracts [from its resemblance to a cat's tail]

cat·like \'kat-,līk\ *adj* : resembling a cat; *esp* : STEALTHY

cat·nap \-,nap\ *n* : a very short light nap — **catnap** *vi*

cat·nip \-,nip\ *n* : a common strong-scented mint of which cats are especially fond [*cat* + obsolete *nep* "catnip", from Old English *nepte*, from Latin *nepeta*]

cat·o'–nine–tails \,kat-ə-'nīn-,tālz\ *n, pl* **cat-o'–nine-tails** : a whip used in flogging and made of nine knotted cords fastened to a handle

cat's cradle *n* : a game in which a string looped on the fingers in such a way as to resemble a small cradle is transferred to the hands of another person

cat's–eye \'kats-,ī\ *n* **1** : any of various gems (as a chrysoberyl or a chalcedony) exhibiting opalescent reflections from within **2** : a glass playing marble with a colored area that resembles the eye of a cat

cat's–paw \'kats-,pò\ *n* **1** : a light breeze that ruffles the surface of the water in patches **2** : a person used by another person for his or her own ends

cat·sup *or* **ketch·up** *or* **catch·up** \'kech-əp, 'kach-; 'kat-səp\ *n* : a thick seasoned sauce usually with a tomato base [Malay *kĕchap* "spiced fish sauce"]

cat·tail \'kat-,tāl\ *n* : a tall reedy marsh plant with brown furry spikes of very tiny flowers

cat·tle \'kat-l\ *n, pl* **cattle** **1** : domesticated mammals held as property or raised for use; *esp* : bovine animals kept on a farm or ranch **2** : people held to be or treated as if of little importance or worth [Old North French *catel* "personal property", from Medieval Latin *capitale*, from Latin *capitalis* "of the head, capital"]

cattle egret *n* : a small white buff-backed egret that is native to the Old World but is now found in parts of the eastern United States

cattle guard *n* : a device that consists of a shallow ditch across which ties or rails are laid far enough apart to prevent livestock from crossing and that is often used instead of a gate at a fence opening

cat·tle·man \-mən, -,man\ *n* : a person who tends or raises cattle

cat·ty \'kat-ē\ *adj* **cat·ti·er; -est** : resembling or held to resemble a cat; *esp* : slyly spiteful — **cat·ti·ly** \'kat-l-ē\ *adv* — **cat·ti·ness** \'kat-ē-nəs\ *n*

cat·ty–cor·ner *or* **cat·ty–cor·nered** *variant of* CATER-CORNER

cat·walk \'kat-,wòk\ *n* : a narrow walk or way (as along a bridge or over some structure)

Cau·ca·sian \kò-'kā-zhən, -'kazh-ən\ *adj* **1** : of or relating to the Caucasus or its inhabitants **2 a** : of, relating to, or designating the white race of humankind as classified according to physical features **b** : of, relating to, or designating the white race as defined by law (as in South Africa) as composed of persons of European, North African, or southwest Asian ancestry — **Caucasian** *n* — **Cau·ca·soid** \'kò-kə-,sòid\ *adj or n*

cau·cus \'kò-kəs\ *n* : a closed meeting of members of the same political party or faction usually to select candidates or decide policy [origin unknown] — **caucus** *vi*

cau·dad \'ko·ˌdad\ *adv* : toward the tail or posterior end [Latin *cauda* "tail" + English *-ad*]

cau·dal \'kod·l\ *adj* **1** : of, relating to, or being a tail **2** : situated in or directed toward the hind part of the body [Latin *cauda* "tail"] — **cau·dal·ly** \-l-ē\ *adv*

caudal fin *n* : the unpaired fin at the posterior end of the body of a fish

cau·di·llo \kaú·'thē-yō, -'thēl-yō\ *n, pl* **-di·llos** : a Spanish or Latin-American military dictator [Spanish, from Late Latin *capitellum* "small head", from Latin *caput* "head"]

cau·dle \'kod·l\ *n* : a drink usually of warm ale or wine mixed with bread or gruel, eggs, sugar, and spices [Old North French *caudel*, from *caut* "warm", from Latin *calidus*]

caught *past of* CATCH

caul \'kol\ *n* **1** : the large fatty omentum covering the intestines **2** : the amnion especially when covering the head at birth [Middle French *cale*]

caul·dron *variant of* CALDRON

cau·li·flow·er \'ko·li·ˌflaú-ər, -ˌflaúr\ *n* : a garden plant closely related to the cabbage and grown for its compact edible head of usually white undeveloped flowers; *also* : the flower head used as a vegetable [Italian *cavolfiore*, from *cavolo* "cabbage" (from Latin *caulis* "stem, cabbage") + *fiore* "flower", from Latin *flor-, flos*]

cauliflower ear *n* : an ear deformed from injury and excessive growth of scar tissue

¹caulk *or* **calk** \'kók\ *vt* **1** : to waterproof the seams of by filling with a watertight substance **2** : to make tight against leakage [Old North French *cauquer* "to trample", from Latin *calcare*, from *calx* "heel"] — **caulk·er** *n*

²caulk *variant of* CALK

caus·al \'ko·zəl\ *adj* **1** : expressing or indicating cause **2** : of, relating to, or being a cause **3** : involving causation or a cause **4** : having a cause — **caus·al·ly** \-zə-lē\ *adv*

cau·sal·i·ty \ko·'zal·ət·ē\ *n, pl* **-ties** **1** : a causal quality or agency **2** : the relation between a cause and its effect or between regularly related events or facts

cau·sa·tion \ko·'zā-shən\ *n* **1 a** : the act or process of causing **b** : the act or agency by which an effect is produced **2** : CAUSALITY

caus·ative \'ko·zət-iv\ *adj* **1** : functioning as a cause or agent **2** : expressing causation — **caus·ative·ly** *adv*

¹cause \'koz\ *n* **1** : something or someone that brings about a result : one that is the source of an action or state **2** : a good reason ⟨a *cause* for anxiety⟩ **3 a** : a ground of legal action **b** : CASE 5a **c** : a matter or question to be decided (as by a court) **4** : a principle or movement strongly defended or supported [Old French, from Latin *causa*] — **cause·less** \-ləs\ *adj* ▫ SYN CAUSE, REASON, OCCASION mean something that produces an effect. CAUSE applies to any event, circumstance, or condition that brings about or helps bring about a result ⟨an icy road was the *cause* of the accident⟩ REASON applies to a traceable or explainable cause of a known effect or action ⟨the storm was the *reason* for the delay⟩ OCCASION applies to a particular time or situation at which underlying causes become effective ⟨the assassination was the *occasion* of the war⟩

²cause *vt* **1** : to serve as cause of ⟨fire *caused* the damage⟩ **2** : to bring about by command, authority, or force ⟨*caused* all offenders to appear⟩ — **caus·er** *n*

cause cé·lè·bre \ˌkoz-sā-'lebr, ˌkoz-\ *n, pl* **causes cé·lè·bres** *same*\ : something (as a scandalous affair or a controversial legal case) that attracts great interest [French, literally, "celebrated case"]

cau·se·rie \ˌkoz-'rē, -ə-rē\ *n* **1** : light informal talk **2** : a short informal composition [French, from *causer* "to chat", from Latin *causari* "to plead, discuss", from *causa* "cause"]

cause·way \'koz-ˌwā\ *n* : a raised way especially across wet ground or water [Middle English *cauciwey*, from *cauci* "causeway" (from Old North French *caucie*, from Medieval Latin *calciata* "paved highway", from *calciatus* "paved with limestone", from Latin *calx* "limestone") + *wey* "way"]

caus·tic \'ko·stik\ *adj* **1** : capable of eating away by chemical action : CORROSIVE **2** : CUTTING **3**, INCISIVE ⟨*caustic* wit⟩ [Latin *causticus*, from Greek *kaustikos*, from *kaiein* "to burn"] — **caustic** *n* — **caus·ti·cal·ly** \-sti-kə-lē, -klē\ *adv*

caustic potash *n* : POTASSIUM HYDROXIDE

caustic soda *n* : SODIUM HYDROXIDE

cau·ter·ize \'kót-ə-ˌrīz\ *vb* : to burn with a hot iron or a caustic substance usually to destroy infected tissue ⟨*cauterize* a wound⟩ [derived from Greek *kaiein* "to burn"] — **cau·ter·iza·tion** \ˌkot-ə-rə-'zā-shən\ *n*

¹cau·tion \'ko·shən\ *n* **1** : ADMONITION, WARNING **2** : careful avoidance of unnecessary risk [Latin *cautio* "precaution", from *cavēre* "to be on one's guard"]

²caution *vt* **cau·tioned; cau·tion·ing** \'ko·shə-ning, 'kosh-ning\ : to advise caution to SYN see WARN

cau·tion·ary \'ko·shə-ˌner-ē\ *adj* : serving as or offering a warning ⟨a *cautionary* tale⟩

cau·tious \'ko·shəs\ *adj* : marked by or given to caution ⟨a *cautious* reply⟩ ⟨a *cautious* driver⟩ — **cau·tious·ly** *adv* — **cau·tious·ness** *n*

cav·al·cade \ˌkav-əl-'kād, 'kav-əl-ˌ\ *n* **1 a** : a procession of riders or carriages **b** : a procession of vehicles or ships **2** : a sequence of dramatic scenes : PAGEANT ⟨a *cavalcade* of American history⟩ [Middle French, "horseback ride", from Italian *cavalcata*, from *cavalcare* "to go on horseback", from Latin *caballus* "horse"]

¹cav·a·lier \ˌkav-ə-'liər\ *n* **1** : a gentleman trained in arms and horsemanship **2** : a mounted soldier : KNIGHT **3** *cap* : an adherent of Charles I of England **4** : LADIES' MAN [Middle French, from Italian *cavaliere*, derived from Latin *caballus* "horse"]

²cavalier *adj* **1** : DEBONAIR **2** : treating important matters or the interests of other people with contemptuous disregard **3 a** *cap* : of or relating to the party of Charles I of England in his struggles with the Puritans and Parliament **b** : ARISTOCRATIC — **cav·a·lier·ly** *adv* — **cav·a·lier·ness** *n*

cav·al·ry \'kav-əl-rē\ *n, pl* **-ries** : a highly mobile army component mounted on horseback or moving in motor vehicles [Italian *cavalleria* "cavalry, chivalry", from *cavaliere* "cavalier"] — **cav·al·ry·man** \-rē-mən, -ˌman\ *n*

¹cave \'kāv\ *n* : a hollowed-out place in the earth and especially in the side of a hill or cliff; *esp* : a cavern that opens to the surface of the ground [Old French, from Latin *cava*, from *cavus* "hollow"]

²cave *vb* **1** : to fall or cause to fall in or down especially from being undermined : COLLAPSE ⟨the wall *caved* in⟩ **2** : to cease to resist : SUBMIT ⟨the defenders *caved* in and surrendered⟩

ca·ve·at \'kā-vē-ˌat, 'kav-ē-; 'käv-ē-ˌät\ *n* : WARNING **2** [Latin, "let him or her beware", from *cavēre* "to be on one's guard"]

caveat emp·tor \-'em-tər, -'emp-, -ˌtor\ *n* : a warning that without a warranty the buyer of goods takes the risk of their quality upon himself [New Latin, "let the buyer beware"]

cave dweller *n* : one (as a prehistoric human) that lives in a cave

cave-in \'kā-ˌvin\ *n* **1** : the action of caving in **2** : a place where earth has caved in

cave·man \'kāv-ˌman\ *n* **1** : a cave dweller especially of the Stone Age **2** : a man who acts with rough or violent directness especially toward women

cav·ern \'kav-ərn\ *n* : a usually natural underground chamber often of large or indefinite extent [Middle

\ə\ abut		\ng\ sing	
\ər\ further		\ō\ bone	
\a\ mat		\o\ saw	
\ā\ take		\oi\ coin	
\ä\ cot, cart		\th\ thin	
\aú\ out		\th\ this	
\ch\ chin		\ü\ food	
\e\ pet		\ú\ foot	
\ē\ easy		\y\ yet	
\g\ go		\yü\ few	
\i\ tip		\yú\ cure	
\ī\ life		\zh\ vision	
\j\ job			

French *caverne*, from Latin *caverna*, from *cavus* "hollow"]

cav·ern·ous \-ər-nəs\ *adj* **1** : having caverns or cavities **2** : constituting or suggesting a cavern **3** : composed largely of vascular spaces and capable of filling with blood to bring about the enlargement of a body part — **cav·ern·ous·ly** *adv*

cav·i·ar *or* **cav·i·are** \'kav-ē-,är *also* 'käv-\ *n* : processed salted roe of a large fish (as the sturgeon) prepared as an appetizer [obsolete Italian *caviaro*, from Turkish *havyar*]

cav·il \'kav-əl\ *vb* **cav·iled** *or* **cav·illed; cav·il·ing** *or* **cav·il·ling** \'kav-ling, -ə-ling\ : to raise trivial and frivolous objections : QUIBBLE [Latin *cavillari* "to jest, cavil", from *cavilla* "raillery"] — **cavil** *n* — **cav·il·er** *or* **cav·il·ler** \-lər, -ə-lər\ *n*

cav·ing \'kā-ving\ *n* : the sport of exploring caves : SPELUNKING

cav·i·ta·tion \,kav-ə-'tā-shən\ *n* : the formation of partial vacuums in a liquid by a swiftly moving body (as a propeller) or by high-frequency sound waves [*cavity* + *-ation*]

cav·i·ty \'kav-ət-ē\ *n, pl* **-ties** : an unfilled space within a mass : a hollow place : HOLE ⟨a *cavity* in a tooth⟩ [Middle French *cavité*, derived from Latin *cavus* "hollow"]

ca·vort \kə-'vort\ *vi* : to bound or frisk about : CAPER [perhaps alteration of *curvet*]

ca·vy \'kā-vē\ *n, pl* **cavies** : any of several short-tailed rough-haired South American rodents; *esp* : GUINEA PIG [obsolete Portuguese *çavia* (now *savia*), from Tupi *sawiya* "rat"]

caw \'ko\ *vi* : to utter the characteristic harsh raucous cry of a crow or a similar sound [imitative] — **caw** *n*

cay \'kē, 'kā\ *n* : a small low island or emergent reef of sand or coral : ISLET, KEY [Spanish *cayo*]

cay·enne pepper \'kī-,en-, 'kā-\ *n* : a pungent condiment consisting of the ground dried fruits or seeds of hot peppers; *also* : a plant bearing such fruits [Tupi *kyinha*]

cay·man *variant of* CAIMAN

Ca·yu·ga \kē-'ü-gə, kā-'yü-, kī-\ *n* : a member of an Iroquoian people of what is now western New York

cay·use \'kī-,üs, -,yüs; kī-'\ *n* **1** *cap* : a member of an Indian people of what is now northeastern Oregon **2** : a native range horse of the western United States

CCD \,sē-sē-'dē\ *n* : CHARGE-COUPLED DEVICE

C clef *n* : a movable clef indicating middle C by its placement on one of the lines of the staff

¹cease \'sēs\ *vb* : to come or bring to an end ⟨ordered the soldiers to *cease* firing⟩ [Old French *cesser*, from Latin *cessare* "to delay", from *cedere* "to withdraw, cede"] SYN see STOP

²cease *n* : CESSATION — usually used with *without*

cease-fire \'sēs-'fīr\ *n* **1** : a military order to cease firing **2** : a suspension of active hostilities

cease·less \'sē-sləs\ *adj* : continuing without end — **cease·less·ly** *adv* — **cease·less·ness** *n*

ce·cro·pia moth \si-'krō-pē-ə-\ *n* : a large silkworm moth that is the largest moth of the eastern United States [Latin *Cecropius* "Athenian", from Greek *Kekropios*, from *Kekrops* "Cecrops", legendary first king of Athens]

ce·cum *or* **cae·cum** \'sē-kəm\ *n, pl* **ce·ca** *or* **cae·ca** \-kə\ : a cavity open at one end; *esp* : the blind pouch in which the large intestine begins and into which the ileum opens from one side [Latin *intestinum caecum*, literally, "blind intestine"] — **ce·cal** \-kəl\ *adj*

ce·dar \'sēd-ər\ *n* **1 a** : any of a genus of usually tall trees of the pine family noted for their fragrant durable wood **b** : any of numerous coniferous trees (as some junipers or arborvitaes) resembling the true cedars especially in the fragrance and durability of their wood **2** : the wood of a cedar [Old French *cedre*, from Latin *cedrus*, from Greek *kedros*]

ce·dar·bird \'sēd-ər-,bərd\ *n* : CEDAR WAXWING

cedar waxwing *n* : a long-crested brown waxwing of temperate North America with a yellow band on the tip of the tail

cede \'sēd\ *vt* **1** : to give up or grant usually by treaty **2** : ASSIGN 1 ⟨*ceded* the farm to their children⟩ [Latin *cedere* "to go, withdraw, yield"] — **ced·er** *n*

ce·dil·la \si-'dil-ə\ *n* : a mark placed under the letter *c* (as ç) to show that the *c* is to be pronounced like *s* [Spanish, "the obsolete letter ç (actually a medieval form of the letter *z*), cedilla", from *ceda, zeda* "the letter *z*", from Late Latin *zeta* "zeta", from Greek *zēta*]

cei·ba \'sā-bə\ *n* : a massive tropical tree related to the silk-cotton tree that bears large pods containing a silky floss which yields the fiber kapok [Spanish]

ceil·ing \'sē-ling\ *n* **1** : the overhead inside surface of a room **2** : something that overhangs like a shelter **3 a** : the greatest height at which an airplane can maintain level flight or operate efficiently **b** : the height above the ground of the base of the lowest layer of clouds when over half of the sky is obscured **4** : an upper usually prescribed limit ⟨a price *ceiling*⟩ [Middle English *celen* "to furnish with a ceiling", probably from Latin *caelare* "to carve", from *caelum* "chisel", from *caedere* "to cut"]

cel *also* **cell** \'sel\ *n* : a transparent sheet of celluloid on which objects are drawn or painted in the making of animated cartoons [from *celluloid*]

cel·an·dine \'sel-ən-,dīn, -,dēn\ *n* **1** : a yellow-flowered biennial herb related to the poppy **2** : a perennial tuber-forming buttercup — called also *lesser celandine* [Middle French *celidoine*, from Latin *chelidonia*, derived from Greek *chelidōn* "swallow"]

cel·e·brant \'sel-ə-brənt\ *n* : one who celebrates; *esp* : the priest who is celebrating a mass

cel·e·brate \'sel-ə-,brāt\ *vb* **1** : to perform publicly and according to rule or form : officiate at ⟨*celebrate* a mass⟩ **2** : to honor or honor something (as a holiday or event) with special activities or festivities ⟨*celebrate* one's birthday with a party⟩ **3** : to praise or make known publicly [Latin *celebrare* "to frequent, celebrate", from *celeber* "much frequented, famous"] SYN see KEEP — **cel·e·bra·tion** \,sel-ə-'brā-shən\ *n* — **cel·e·bra·tor** \'sel-ə-,brāt-ər\ *n*

cel·e·brat·ed *adj* : widely known and often referred to : RENOWNED SYN see FAMOUS — **cel·e·brat·ed·ness** *n*

ce·leb·ri·ty \sə-'leb-rət-ē\ *n, pl* **-ties** **1** : the state of being celebrated **2** : a celebrated person ⟨television *celebrities*⟩

ce·le·ri·ac \sə-'ler-ē-,ak, -'lir-\ *n* : a celery grown for its thickened edible root [from *celery*]

ce·ler·i·ty \sə-'ler-ət-ē\ *n, pl* **-ties** : rapidity of motion or action [Middle French *célérité*, from Latin *celeritas*, from *celer* "swift"] □ SYN CELERITY, ALACRITY mean quickness of movement or action. CELERITY stresses speed in moving especially so as to accomplish work ⟨got ready with remarkable *celerity*⟩ ALACRITY stresses promptness in responding and often suggests readiness or eagerness ⟨they went with surprising *alacrity*⟩

cel·ery \'sel-rē, -ə-rē\ *n* : a European herb of the carrot family widely grown for its thick edible leafstalks; *also* : leafstalks of celery used for food [probably from Italian dialect *selero*, from Late Latin *selinon*, from Greek]

ce·les·ta \sə-'les-tə\ *n* : a keyboard instrument with hammers that strike steel plates producing a tone similar to that of a glockenspiel [French *célesta*, from *céleste*, literally, "heavenly", from Latin *caelestis*]

ce·les·tial \sə-'les-chəl\ *adj* **1** : of, relating to, or suggesting the spiritual heaven : HEAVENLY ⟨*celestial* beings⟩ **2** : of or relating to the sky or heavens ⟨a star is a *celestial* body⟩ [Middle French, from Latin *caelestis*, from *caelum* "sky, heaven"] — **ce·les·tial·ly** \-chə-lē\ *adv*

celestial equator *n* : the great circle on the celestial sphere midway between the celestial poles

celestial navigation *n* : navigation by observation of the positions of celestial bodies

celestial pole *n* : one of the two points on the celestial sphere around which the diurnal rotation of the stars appears to take place

celestial sphere *n* : an imaginary sphere of infinite radius against which the celestial bodies appear to be projected

ce·li·ac \'sē-lē-ak\ *adj* : of or relating to the abdominal cavity [Latin *coeliacus,* from Greek *koiliakos,* from *koilia* "cavity", from *koilos* "hollow"]

celiac disease *n* : a chronic nutritional disorder in young children in which fats are not digested and used in a normal way

cel·i·ba·cy \'sel-ə-bə-sē\ *n* : the state of not being married; *esp* : the state of one bound by vow not to marry

cel·i·bate \'sel-ə-bət\ *n* : one who lives in celibacy [Latin *caelibatus,* from *caelebs* "unmarried"] — **celibate** *adj*

cell \'sel\ *n* **1 a** : a one-room dwelling occupied by a solitary person (as a hermit) **b** : a single room (as in a convent or prison) usually for one person **2** : a small compartment (as in a honeycomb), receptacle (as for a polyp), cavity (as in a plant ovary), or bounded space (as in an insect wing) **3** : a tiny mass of protoplasm that includes a nucleus and is enclosed by a semipermeable membrane and that is the fundamental unit of living matter and the basic structural element of plants and animals **4 a** : a receptacle (as a jar) containing electrodes and an electrolyte either for generating electricity by chemical action or for use in electrolysis **b** : a single unit in a device for converting radiant energy into electrical energy or for varying the intensity of an electric current in accordance with radiation **5** : the basic and usually smallest unit of an organization or movement; *esp* : the primary unit of a Communist organization [derived from Latin *cella* "small room"] — **celled** \'seld\ *adj*

cel·lar \'sel-ər\ *n* **1** : BASEMENT 1 **2** : a stock of wines [Anglo-French *celer,* from Latin *cellarium* "storeroom", from *cella* "small room"]

cel·lar·age \'sel-ə-rij\ *n* **1** : a cellar especially for storage **2** : charge for storage in a cellar

cell body *n* : the nucleus-containing central part of a neuron exclusive of its axons and dendrites

cell division *n* : the process by which cells multiply involving both nuclear and cytoplasmic divisions — compare MEIOSIS, MITOSIS

cel·list \'chel-əst\ *n* : one that plays the cello

cell membrane *n* **1** : PLASMA MEMBRANE **2** : CELL WALL

cel·lo \'chel-ō\ *n, pl* **cellos** : the member of the violin family tuned an octave below the viola [short for *violoncello*]

cel·lo·phane \'sel-ə-ˌfān\ *n* : a thin transparent usually waterproof material made from cellulose and used especially as a wrapping [French, from *cellulose* + *-phane* (as in *diaphane* "diaphanous")]

cell plate *n* : the rudiment of a new cell wall that forms between dividing plant cells

cell sap *n* : the liquid consisting of a watery solution of nutrients and wastes that fills the vacuole of most plant cells

cell theory *n* : a generally accepted theory in biology that the cell is the fundamental structural and functional unit of living matter and that all cells come from preexisting cells

cel·lu·lar \'sel-yə-lər\ *adj* **1** : of, relating to, or consisting of cells **2** : containing cavities : having a porous texture **3** : of, relating to, or being a radiotelephone system in which a geographical area (as a city) is divided into small sections each served by a transmitter of limited range so that any available radio channels

can be used in different parts of the area simultaneously — **cel·lu·lar·i·ty** \ˌsel-yə-'lar-ət-ē\ *n*

cel·lu·lase \'sel-yə-ˌlās, -ˌlāz\ *n* : an enzyme that hydrolyzes cellulose

cel·lu·loid \'sel-yə-ˌlȯid, -ə-\ *n* **1** : a tough flammable thermoplastic composed essentially of cellulose nitrate and camphor **2** : a motion-picture film

cel·lu·lose \'sel-yə-ˌlōs\ *n* : a complex carbohydrate constituting the chief part of the cell walls of plants, yielding many fibrous products, and being commonly obtained from vegetable matter (as wood or cotton) as a white fibrous substance that is used in making various products (as rayon and cellophane) [French, from *cellule* "living cell", from New Latin *cellula,* from Latin *cella* "small room"]

cellulose acetate *n* : any of several compounds formed especially by the action of acetic acid, anhydride of acetic acid, and sulfuric acid on cellulose and used for making textile fibers, packaging sheets, photographic films, and varnishes

cellulose nitrate *n* : a compound formed by the action of nitric acid on cellulose in the presence of sulfuric acid and used for making explosives, plastics, rayon, and varnishes

cel·lu·los·ic \ˌsel-yə-'lō-sik, -zik\ *adj* : of, relating to, or made from cellulose ⟨*cellulosic* fibers⟩ — **cellulosic** *n*

cell wall *n* : the firm nonliving and usually chiefly cellulose wall that encloses and supports most plant cells

Cel·sius \'sel-sē-əs, 'sel-shəs\ *adj* : relating to, conforming to, or having the international thermometer scale on which the interval between the triple point and the boiling point of water is divided into 99.9 degrees with 0.01° representing the triple point and 100.00° the boiling point; *also* : CENTIGRADE ⟨10° *Celsius*⟩ — abbreviation C [Anders *Celsius,* died 1744, Swedish astronomer]

Celt \'kelt, 'selt\ *also* **Kelt** \'kelt\ *n* **1** : a member of a division of the early Indo-European peoples distributed from the British Isles and Spain to Asia Minor **2** : a modern Gael, Highland Scot, Irishman, Welshman, Cornishman, or Breton [French *Celte,* from Latin *Celtae* "Celts"]

¹Celt·ic \'kel-tik, 'sel-\ *or* **Kelt·ic** \'kel-\ *adj* : of, relating to, or characteristic of the Celts or their languages

²Celtic *or* **Keltic** *n* : a branch of the Indo-European language family containing Irish Gaelic, Scottish Gaelic, Manx, Welsh, Breton, and Cornish

Celt·i·cist \'kel-tə-səst, 'sel-\ *n* : a person who specializes in Celtic languages or culture

cem·ba·lo \'chem-bə-ˌlō\ *n, pl* **-los** *or* **-li** \-ˌlē\ : HARPSICHORD [Italian]

¹ce·ment \si-'ment\ *n* **1 a** : a powder of alumina, silica, lime, iron oxide, and magnesia burned together in a kiln and finely pulverized and used as an ingredient of mortar and concrete **b** (1) : CONCRETE (2) : MORTAR **2** : a binding element or agency: as **a** : a substance to make objects adhere to each other **b** : a notion or feeling serving to unite firmly **3** : CEMENTUM [Old French *ciment,* from Latin *caementum* "stone chips used in making mortar", from *caedere* "to cut"]

²cement *vb* **1** : to unite by or as if by cement **2** : to overlay with concrete — **ce·ment·er** *n*

ce·men·ta·tion \ˌsē-ˌmen-'tā-shən\ *n* : the act or process of cementing

ce·ment·ite \si-'ment-ˌīt\ *n* : a hard brittle carbide of iron Fe_3C in steel, cast iron, and iron-carbon alloys

ce·men·tum \si-'ment-əm\ *n* : a specialized external bony layer of the part of a tooth normally within the gum

cem·e·tery \'sem-ə-ˌter-ē\ *n, pl* **-ter·ies** : a burial ground [Middle French *cimitere,* from Late Latin *coemeterium,* from Greek *koimētērion* "sleeping chamber, burial place", from *koiman* "to put to sleep"]

cell 3: *1* nucleus, *2* nucleolus, *3* endoplasmic reticulum, *4* mitochondrion, *5* Golgi apparatus

\ə\ abut	\ng\ sing
\ər\ **further**	\ō\ bone
\a\ mat	\ȯ\ saw
\ā\ take	\ȯi\ coin
\ä\ cot, cart	\th\ thin
\au̇\ out	\th\ this
\ch\ chin	\ü\ food
\e\ pet	\u̇\ foot
\ē\ easy	\y\ yet
\g\ go	\yü\ few
\i\ tip	\yu̇\ cure
\ī\ life	\zh\ vision
\j\ job	

cen- *or* **ceno-** *combining form* : new : recent ⟨*Ceno*zoic⟩ [Greek *kainos*]

-cene \ˌsēn\ *adj combining form* : Cenozoic ⟨*Eo*cene⟩

cen·o·bite \'sen-ə-ˌbīt\ *or* **coe·no·bite** \'sē-nə-\ *n* : a member of a religious group living together [Late Latin *coenobita,* from *coenobium* "monastery", from Late Greek *koinobion,* from Greek *koinos* "common" + *bios* "life"] — **cen·o·bit·ic** \ˌsen-ə-'bit-ik\ *or* **cen·o·bit·i·cal** \-'bit-i-kəl\ *adj*

cen·o·taph \'sen-ə-ˌtaf\ *n* : a tomb or a monument erected in honor of a person whose body is elsewhere [French *cénotaphe,* from Latin *cenotaphium,* from Greek *kenotaphion,* from *kenos* "empty" + *taphos* "tomb"]

Ce·no·zo·ic \ˌsē-nə-'zō-ik, ˌsen-ə-\ *n* **1** : the most recent of the four eras of geological history that extends to the present time and is marked by a rapid evolution of mammals and birds and of grasses, shrubs, and various flowering plants — called also *Age of Mammals;* see GEOLOGIC TIME table **2** : the system of rocks corresponding to the Cenozoic — **Cenozoic** *adj*

cen·ser \'sen-sər\ *n* : a vessel for burning incense; *esp* : a covered incense burner swung on chains in a religious ritual [Middle English *censen* "to burn incense"]

censer

¹cen·sor \'sen-sər\ *n* **1** : one of two magistrates of ancient Rome acting as census takers, assessors, and inspectors of morals and conduct **2** : an official who examines publications or communications for objectionable matter [Latin, from *censēre* "to assess, tax"] — **cen·so·ri·al** \sen-'sōr-ē-əl, -'sȯr-\ *adj*

²censor *vt* **cen·sored; cen·sor·ing** \'sens-ring, -ə-ring\ : to examine in order to suppress or delete anything thought to be harmful or dangerous □ SYN CENSOR, CENSURE are not actually synonymous but are easily confused. CENSOR denotes examining officially in order to suppress or alter anything thought morally or politically objectionable; CENSURE denotes criticizing adversely and usually publicly or officially.

cen·so·ri·ous \sen-'sōr-ē-əs, -'sȯr-\ *adj* : marked by or given to censure : sternly critical — **cen·so·ri·ous·ly** *adv* — **cen·so·ri·ous·ness** *n*

cen·sor·ship \'sen-sər-ˌship\ *n* : the institution, system, or practice of censoring or of censors

¹cen·sure \'sen-chər\ *n* **1** : the act of blaming or condemning sternly **2** : an official reprimand [Latin *censura,* from *censēre* "to assess, tax"]

²censure *vt* **cen·sured; cen·sur·ing** \'sench-ring, -ə-ring\ : to find fault with : criticize as blameworthy SYN see BLAME, CENSOR — **cen·sur·able** \'sench-rə-bəl, -ə-rə-\ *adj* — **cen·sur·er** \'sen-chər-ər\ *n*

cen·sus \'sen-səs\ *n* **1** : a periodic governmental counting of population and usually gathering of related statistics **2** : COUNT 1, TALLY [Latin, from *censēre* "to assess, tax"]

cent \'sent\ *n* **1** : a unit of value equal to ¹/₁₀₀ part of a basic monetary unit (as of a dollar) **2** : a coin, token, or note representing one cent [Middle French, "hundred", from Latin *centum*]

cen·taur \'sen-ˌtȯr\ *n* : one of a race in Greek mythology who are half man and half horse [Latin *Centaurus,* from Greek *Kentauros*]

cen·ta·vo \sen-'täv-ō\ *n, pl* **-vos** **1** : a unit of value equal to ¹/₁₀₀ part of any of several basic monetary units (as the peso or cruzeiro) **2** : a coin representing one centavo [Spanish, literally, "hundredth", from Latin *centum* "hundred"]

cen·te·nar·i·an \ˌsent-n-'er-ē-ən\ *n* : a person who is 100 years old or older — **centenarian** *adj*

cen·ten·a·ry \sen-'ten-ə-rē, 'sent-n-ˌer-ē\ *n, pl* **-ries** : CENTENNIAL [Latin *centenarius* "of a hundred", from *centeni* "a hundred each", from *centum* "hundred"] — **centenary** *adj*

cen·ten·ni·al \sen-'ten-ē-əl\ *n* : a 100th anniversary or its celebration [Latin *centum* "hundred" + English

-ennial (as in *biennial*)] — **centennial** *adj* — **cen·ten·ni·al·ly** \-ē-ə-lē\ *adv*

¹cen·ter \'sent-ər\ *n* **1** : the point in the plane of a circle equidistant from all points on its circumference; *also* : the point within a sphere equidistant from all points on its surface **2 a** : a point, area, person, or thing that is most important in relation to an indicated activity, interest, or condition ⟨*center* of the controversy⟩ **b** : a group of nerve cells having a common function ⟨respiratory *center*⟩ **c** : a region of concentrated population **3 a** : a middle part (as of an army or stage) **b** *often cap* (1) : individuals holding moderate political views especially between those of conservatives and liberals (2) : the views of such individuals **4** : a player occupying a middle position on a team [Middle French *centre,* from Latin *centrum,* from Greek *kentron* "sharp point, center of a circle", from *kentein* "to prick"]

²center *vb* **cen·tered; cen·ter·ing** \'sent-ə-ring, 'sen-tring\ **1** : to place or fix at or around a center or central area or position **2** : to gather to a center : CONCENTRATE **3** : to adjust (as lenses) so that the axes coincide **4** : to have a center **5 a** : to pass (a ball or puck) from either side to or toward the middle of a playing area **b** : to snap (the ball) in football

cen·ter·board \'sent-ər-ˌbōrd, -ˌbȯrd\ *n* : a retractable keel used especially in sailboats

center field *n* **1** : the part of the baseball outfield between right and left field **2** : the position of the player defending center field — **center fielder** *n*

center of gravity 1 : CENTER OF MASS **2** : the point at which the entire weight of a body may be considered as concentrated so that if supported at this point the body would remain in equilibrium in any position

center of mass : the point in a body or system of bodies at which the whole mass may be considered as concentrated

cen·ter·piece \'sent-ər-ˌpēs\ *n* : an object occupying a central position; *esp* : an adornment in the center of a table

cen·tes·i·mal \sen-'tes-ə-məl\ *adj* : marked by or relating to division into hundredths [Latin *centesimus* "hundredth", from *centum* "hundred"]

¹cen·tes·i·mo \chen-'tez-ə-ˌmō\ *n, pl* **-mi** \-ˌmē\ **1** : a monetary unit equal to ¹/₁₀₀ lira **2** : a coin representing this unit [Italian]

²cen·tes·i·mo \sen-'tes-ə-ˌmō\ *n, pl* **-mos** **1** : a monetary unit equal to ¹/₁₀₀ part of any of several basic monetary units **2** : a coin representing this unit [Spanish *centésimo*]

centi- *combining form* : hundredth part ⟨*centi*meter⟩ [French, from Latin *centum* "hundred"]

cen·ti·grade \'sent-ə-ˌgrād, 'sänt-\ *adj* : relating to, conforming to, or having a thermometer scale on which the interval between the freezing point and the boiling point of water is divided into 100 degrees with 0° representing the freezing point and 100° the boiling point ⟨10° *centigrade*⟩ — abbreviation C; compare CELSIUS [French, from Latin *centum* "hundred" + *gradus* "step, degree"]

cen·ti·gram \-ˌgram\ *n* — see METRIC SYSTEM table

cen·ti·li·ter \-ˌlēt-ər\ *n* — see METRIC SYSTEM table

cen·time \'sän-ˌtēm, 'sen-\ *n* **1** : a unit of value equal to ¹/₁₀₀ franc **2** : a coin representing one centime [French, from *cent* "hundred", from Latin *centum*]

cen·ti·me·ter \'sent-ə-ˌmēt-ər, 'sänt-\ *n* — see METRIC SYSTEM table

centimeter–gram–second *adj* : of, relating to, or being a system of units based upon the centimeter as the unit of length, the gram as the unit of mass, and the second as the unit of time — abbreviation cgs

cen·ti·mo \'sent-ə-ˌmō\ *n, pl* **-mos** **1** : a unit of value equal to ¹/₁₀₀ part of any of several basic monetary units (as the peseta) **2** : a coin representing one centimo [Spanish *céntimo*]

cen·ti·pede \'sent-ə-ˌpēd\ *n* : any of a class (Chilopoda) of long flattened many-segmented arthropods with each segment bearing one pair of legs of which the foremost pair is modified into poison fangs — compare MILLIPEDE [Latin *centipeda,* from *centum* "hundred" + *ped-, pes* "foot"]

centr- *or* **centri-** *or* **centro-** *combining form* : center ⟨*centr*oid⟩ [Greek *kentron*]

¹**cen·tral** \'sen-trəl\ *adj* 1 : containing or constituting a center 2 : ESSENTIAL 3, PRINCIPAL 3 : situated at, in, or near the center 4 : controlling or directing local or branch activities 5 : holding to a middle between extremes : MODERATE 6 : of, relating to, or comprising the brain and spinal cord; *also* : originating within the central nervous system ⟨*central* deafness⟩ — **cen·tral·i·ty** \sen-'tral-ət-ē\ *n* — **cen·tral·ly** \'sen-trə-lē\ *adv*

²**central** *n* : a telephone exchange or operator

central angle *n* : an angle with its vertex at the center of a circle and with sides that are radii of the circle

central bank *n* : a national bank that operates to control money supply and interest rates

central committee *n* : a large central executive body of a Communist party that is elected to function between party congresses and that elects in turn from its own membership a powerful executive presidium

cen·tral·ism \'sen-trə-ˌliz-əm\ *n* : the concentration of power and control in the central authority especially of a nation — compare FEDERALISM — **cen·tral·ist** \-ləst\ *n or adj* — **cen·tral·is·tic** \ˌsen-trə-'lis-tik\ *adj*

cen·tral·ize \'sen-trə-ˌlīz\ *vt* : to concentrate (as authority) in a center or central organization — **cen·tral·i·za·tion** \ˌsen-trə-lə-'zā-shən\ *n* — **cen·tral·iz·er** \'sen-trə-ˌlī-zər\ *n*

central nervous system *n* : the part of the nervous system which in vertebrates consists of the brain and spinal cord, to which sensory impulses are transmitted and from which motor impulses pass out, and which supervises and coordinates the activity of the entire nervous system

central processing unit *n* : PROCESSOR 2

Central time *n* : the time of the 6th time zone west of Greenwich that includes the central United States

cen·tre \'sent-ər\ *chiefly British variant of* CENTER

cen·tric \'sen-trik\ *adj* : concentrated about or directed to a center — **cen·tri·cal·ly** \-tri-kə-lē, -klē\ *adv* — **cen·tric·i·ty** \sen-'tris-ət-ē\ *n*

-cen·tric \'sen-trik\ *adj combining form* : having (such) a center or (such or so many) centers : having (something specified) as its center ⟨helio*centric*⟩

cen·trif·u·gal \sen-'trif-yə-gəl, -'trif-i-gəl\ *adj* 1 : proceeding or acting in a direction away from a center or axis 2 : using or acting by centrifugal force ⟨a *centrifugal* pump⟩ [Latin *centrum* "center" + *fugere* "to flee"] — **cen·trif·u·gal·ly** \-gə-lē\ *adv*

centrifugal force *n* : the force that tends to impel a thing or parts of a thing outward from a center of rotation

¹**cen·tri·fuge** \'sen-trə-ˌfyüj, 'sän-\ *n* : a machine using centrifugal force for separating substances of different densities, for removing moisture, or for simulating gravitational effects — compare SEPARATOR

²**centrifuge** *vt* : to subject to centrifugal action especially in a centrifuge — **cen·trif·u·ga·tion** \ˌsen-ˌtrif-yə-'gā-shən, -ˌtrif-ə-, ˌsän-\ *n*

cen·tri·ole \'sen-trē-ˌōl\ *n* : one of a pair of cellular organelles that are adjacent to the nucleus, function in the formation of the mitotic apparatus, and consist of a cylinder with nine tiny tubules arranged peripherally in a circle [German *zentriol,* from *zentrum* "center"]

cen·trip·e·tal \sen-'trip-ət-l\ *adj* : proceeding or acting in a direction toward a center or axis [Latin *centrum* "center" + *petere* "to seek"] — **cen·trip·e·tal·ly** \-l-ē\ *adv*

centripetal force *n* : the force that tends to impel a thing or parts of a thing inward toward a center of rotation

cen·troid \'sen-ˌtroid\ *n* : the point of intersection of the medians of a triangle

cen·tro·mere \'sen-trə-ˌmiər\ *n* : the point on a chromosome by which it appears to attach to the spindle in mitosis — **cen·tro·mer·ic** \ˌsen-trə-'mer-ik, -'miər-\ *adj*

cen·tro·some \'sen-trə-ˌsōm\ *n* 1 : the centriole-containing region of clear cytoplasm adjacent to the cell nucleus 2 : CENTRIOLE

cen·trum \'sen-trəm\ *n, pl* **centrums** *or* **cen·tra** \-trə\ : the body of a vertebra [Latin, "center"]

cen·tu·ri·on \sen-'tùr-ē-ən, -'tyùr-\ *n* : an officer commanding a century in a Roman legion [Latin, from *centuria* "century"]

cen·tu·ry \'sench-rē, -ə-rē\ *n, pl* **-ries** 1 : a subdivision of the Roman legion 2 : a group, sequence, or series of 100 like things 3 : a Roman voting unit based on property qualifications 4 : a period of 100 years; *esp* : one of the 100-year divisions of the Christian era or of the preceding period [Latin *centuria,* from *centum* "hundred"]

century plant *n* : a commonly cultivated Mexican agave maturing and flowering only once in many years and then dying

cephal- *or* **cephalo-** *combining form* : head ⟨*cephalo*thorax⟩ [Greek *kephalē*]

ce·phal·ic \sə-'fal-ik\ *adj* 1 : of or relating to the head 2 : directed toward or situated on or in or near the head — **ce·phal·i·cal·ly** \-i-kə-lē, -klē\ *adv*

ceph·a·lo·pod \'sef-ə-lə-ˌpäd\ *n* : any of a class (Cephalopoda) of mollusks including the squids, cuttlefishes, and octopuses and having a tubular siphon under the head, a group of muscular sucker-bearing arms, highly developed eyes, and usually a bag of inky fluid which they can eject — **cephalopod** *adj* — **ceph·a·lop·o·dan** \ˌsef-ə-'läp-əd-ən\ *adj or n*

ceph·a·lo·tho·rax \ˌsef-ə-lō-'thōr-ˌaks, -'thȯr-\ *n* : a united head and thorax (as of a spider or crustacean) — **ceph·a·lo·tho·rac·ic** \-thə-'ras-ik\ *adj*

Ce·phe·id \'sē-fē-əd\ *n* : one of a class of pulsating stars whose light variations are very regular

Ce·pheus \'sē-ˌfyüs, -fē-əs\ *n* : a constellation between Cygnus and the north pole [Latin, from Greek *Kēpheus*]

ce·ra·mal \sə-'ram-əl, 'ser-ə-ˌmal\ *n* : CERMET [*ceram*ic *al*loy]

¹**ce·ram·ic** \sə-'ram-ik\ *adj* : of or relating to a product (as earthenware, porecelain, or brick) made essentially from a nonmetallic mineral by firing at high temperatures [Greek *keramikos,* from *keramos* "pottery"]

²**ceramic** *n* 1 *pl* : the art of making ceramic articles 2 : a product of ceramic manufacture

ce·ram·ist \sə-'ram-əst\ *or* **ce·ram·i·cist** \-'ram-ə-səst\ *n* : one that engages in ceramics

cer·car·ia \sər-'kar-ē-ə, -'ker-\ *n, pl* **-i·ae** \-ē-ˌē\ *also* **-i·as** : a usually tadpole-shaped larval trematode worm produced in a molluscan host by a redia [Greek *kerkos* "tail"] — **cer·car·i·al** \-ē-əl\ *adj*

cer·cus \'sər-kəs\ *n, pl* **cer·ci** \'sər-ˌsī\ : a many-jointed posterior appendage of an insect [Greek *kerkos* "tail"]

¹**ce·re·al** \'sir-ē-əl\ *adj* : relating to grain or to the plants that produce it; *also* : made of grain [Latin *cerealis,* literally, "of Ceres"]

²**cereal** *n* 1 : a plant (as a grass) yielding starchy grain suitable for food; *also* : its grain 2 : a prepared foodstuff of grain

cer·e·bel·lum \ˌser-ə-'bel-əm\ *n, pl* **-bel·lums** *or* **-bel·la** \-'bel-ə\ : a large part of the brain especially concerned with the coordination of muscles and the maintenance of bodily equilibrium and situated in front of and above the medulla which it partly overlaps [Medieval Latin, from Latin *cerebrum* "brain"] — **cer·e·bel·lar** \-'bel-ər\ *adj*

cerebr- *or* **cerebro-** *combining form* 1 : brain : cerebrum ⟨*cerebr*ation⟩ 2 : cerebral and ⟨*cerebro*spinal⟩ [Latin *cerebrum* "brain"]

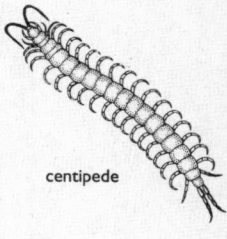

centipede

ce·re·bral \sə-'rē-brəl, 'ser-ə-\ *adj* **1 a** : of or relating to the brain or the intellect **b** : of, relating to, or being the cerebrum **2** : appealing to the intellect — **ce·re·bral·ly** \-brə-lē\ *adv*

cerebral cortex *n* : the surface layer of gray matter of each cerebral hemisphere that functions chiefly in the coordination of higher nervous activity

cerebral hemisphere *n* : either of the two hollow convoluted lateral halves of the cerebrum

cerebral palsy *n* : a disability resulting from damage to the brain usually before or during birth and outwardly manifested by muscular incoordination and speech disturbances

cer·e·brate \'ser-ə-,brāt\ *vi* : to use the mind : THINK — **cer·e·bra·tion** \,ser-ə-'brā-shən\ *n*

ce·re·bro·spi·nal \sə-,rē-brō-'spīn-l, ,ser-ə-brō-\ *adj* : of or relating to the brain and spinal cord or to these together with the cranial and spinal nerves that innervate voluntary muscles

cerebrospinal fluid *n* : a liquid comparable to serum that occupies the cavities of the brain and spinal cord and the space between these and the meninges

ce·re·brum \sə-'rē-brəm, 'ser-ə-brəm\ *n, pl* **-brums** *or* **-bra** \-brə\ **1** : BRAIN 1a **2** : an enlarged anterior or upper part of the brain; *esp* : the expanded anterior portion of the brain that consists of cerebral hemispheres and connecting structures and is held to be the seat of conscious mental processes [Latin]

cere·cloth \'siər-,klȯth\ *n* : cloth treated with melted wax or gummy matter and formerly used especially for wrapping a dead body [derived from Latin *cera* "wax"]

cer·e·ment \'ser-ə-mənt, 'siər-mənt\ *n* : a shroud for the dead; *esp* : CERECLOTH — usually used in pl.

¹cer·e·mo·ni·al \,ser-ə-'mō-nē-əl\ *adj* : of, relating to, or forming a ceremony — **cer·e·mo·ni·al·ism** \-nē-ə-,liz-əm\ *n* — **cer·e·mo·ni·al·ist** \-ləst\ *n* — **cer·e·mo·ni·al·ly** \-nē-ə-lē\ *adj* — **cer·e·mo·ni·al·ness** *n* □ SYN CEREMONIOUS: CEREMONIAL applies to things that are themselves ceremonies or an essential part of them ⟨*ceremonial* offerings⟩ ⟨a *ceremonial* gown⟩ CEREMONIOUS applies to a person overly careful to observe formalities or to acts performed elaborately or pompously ⟨the *ceremonious* courtier entered with a flourish⟩ ⟨took *ceremonious* leave⟩

²ceremonial *n* : a ceremonial act, action, or system

cer·e·mo·ni·ous \,ser-ə-'mō-nē-əs\ *adj* **1** : CEREMONIAL **2** : careful to observe forms and ceremony **3** : according to prescribed usage or procedures SYN see CEREMONIAL — **cer·e·mo·ni·ous·ly** *adv* — **cer·e·mo·ni·ous·ness** *n*

cer·e·mo·ny \'ser-ə-,mō-nē\ *n, pl* **-nies** **1** : a formal act or series of acts prescribed by ritual or custom ⟨graduation *ceremonies*⟩ **2** : a conventional act of politeness or etiquette ⟨went through the *ceremony* of introductions⟩ **3** : the social behavior required by strict etiquette : FORMALITY ⟨dined without *ceremony*⟩ [Middle French *cérémonie*, from Latin *caerimonia*]

Ce·res \'siər-,ēz\ *n* : the largest asteroid and the one first discovered

ce·re·us \'sir-ē-əs\ *n* : any of various cacti of the western United States and tropical America often with showy flowers [Latin, "wax candle", from *cera* "wax"]

ce·rise \sə-'rēs, -'rēz\ *n* : a moderate red [French, literally, "cherry"]

ce·ri·um \'sir-ē-əm\ *n* : a gray malleable ductile metallic element used especially in alloys — see ELEMENT table [*Ceres*, an asteroid]

cer·met \'sər-,met\ *n* : a strong alloy of a heat-resistant compound (as carbide of titanium) and a metal (as nickel) used especially for turbine blades — called also *ceramal* [ceramic *met*al]

cer·tain \'sərt-n\ *adj* **1 a** : FIXED 1c, SETTLED **b** : proved to be true **2** : implied as being specific but not named ⟨a *certain* town in Maine⟩ **3 a** : RELIABLE **b** : INDISPUTABLE **4 a** : INEVITABLE **b** : incapable of failing : DES-

TINED **5** : assured in mind or action [Old French, from Latin *certus,* from *cernere* "to sift, decide"] SYN see SURE — **cer·tain·ly** *adv*

cer·tain·ty \-tē\ *n, pl* **-ties** **1** : something that is certain **2** : the quality or state of being certain □ SYN CERTAINTY, CERTITUDE, CONVICTION mean a state of being free from doubt. CERTAINTY and CERTITUDE are frequently interchangeable but CERTAINTY may stress objective proof or evidence supporting a belief ⟨scientific *certainty*⟩ CERTITUDE stresses rather the strength of inner belief in something not needing or not capable of proof; CONVICTION applies especially to a strong individual belief concerned with moral or spiritual rather than merely factual matters.

¹cer·tif·i·cate \sər-'tif-i-kət\ *n* **1** : a document containing a certified statement especially as to the truth of something; *esp* : one certifying that a person has fulfilled the requirements of a school or profession ⟨a teaching *certificate*⟩ **2** : a document evidencing ownership or debt ⟨stock *certificates*⟩

²cer·tif·i·cate \-'tif-ə-,kāt\ *vt* : to testify to, furnish with, or authorize by a certificate — **cer·tif·i·ca·to·ry** \-'tif-i-kə-,tōr-ē, -,tȯr-\ *adj*

cer·ti·fi·ca·tion \,sərt-ə-fə-'kā-shən\ *n* **1** : the act of certifying : the state of being certified **2** : a certified statement

certified check *n* : a check drawn on a depositor's account for which the bank guarantees payment

certified mail *n* : uninsured first class mail for which the addressee signs a receipt as proof of delivery

certified milk *n* : milk of high quality produced under the rules and regulations of an authorized medical milk commission

certified public accountant *n* : an accountant who has met the requirements of state law and holds a state certificate

cer·ti·fy \'sərt-ə-,fī\ *vt* **-fied; -fy·ing** **1 a** : to attest formally or authoritatively **b** : to guarantee to be true or valid or as represented or meeting a standard **2** : GUARANTEE 1 **3** : to provide with a usually professional certificate or license ⟨*certify* a teacher⟩ [Middle French *certifier,* from Late Latin *certificare,* from Latin *certus* "certain"] — **cer·ti·fi·able** \-,fī-ə-bəl\ *adj* — **cer·ti·fi·er** \-,fī-ər, -,fīr\ *n*

cer·ti·tude \'sərt-ə-,tüd, -,tyüd\ *n* **1** : the state of being or feeling certain : CONFIDENCE **2** : an end, event, or concept that is certain and unfailing ⟨moral *certitudes*⟩ SYN see CERTAINTY — **cer·ti·tu·di·nous** \,sərt-ə-'tüd-n-əs, -'tyüd-\ *adj*

ce·ru·le·an \sə-'rü-lē-ən\ *adj* : resembling the blue of the sky : AZURE [Latin *caeruleus* "dark blue"]

ce·ru·men \sə-'rü-mən\ *n* : EARWAX [derived from Latin *cera* "wax"] — **ce·ru·mi·nous** \-mə-nəs\ *adj*

cer·vi·cal \'sər-vi-kəl\ *adj* : of or relating to a neck or cervix

cervical cap *n* : a contraceptive in the form of a thimble-shaped cap that fits over the uterine cervix to block sperm from entering the uterus

cer·vine \'sər-,vīn\ *adj* : of, relating to, or resembling deer [Latin *cervus* "stag, deer"]

cer·vix \'sər-viks\ *n, pl* **cer·vi·ces** \'sər-və-,sēz\ *or* **cer·vix·es** : a constricted portion of an organ or part; *esp* : the narrow outer end of the uterus [Latin, "neck"]

ce·sar·e·an *or* **ce·sar·i·an** *also* **cae·sar·e·an** \si-'zar-ē-ən, -'zer-\ *n* : surgical incision of the walls of the abdomen and uterus for delivery of offspring [from the belief that Julius Caesar was born this way] — **cesarean** *or* **cesarian** *also* **caesarean** *adj*

ce·si·um *also* **cae·si·um** \'sē-zē-əm\ *n* : a silver-white soft ductile element used as a getter in electron tubes and in photoelectric cells — see ELEMENT table [Latin *caesius* "bluish gray"]

ces·sa·tion \se-'sā-shən\ *n* : a temporary or final ceasing (as of action) : STOP [Middle French, from Latin

cessatio "delay, idleness", from *cessare* "to delay, be idle"]

ces·sion \'sesh-ən\ *n* : a giving up (as of territory or rights) to another [Middle French, from Latin *cessio,* from *cedere* "to withdraw, cede"]

cess·pool \'ses-ˌpül\ *n* : an underground pit or tank for liquid waste (as household sewage) [by folk etymology from Middle English *suspiral* "vent, cesspool", from Middle French *souspirail* "ventilator", from *soupirer* "to sigh, breathe", from Latin *suspirare*]

ces·ta \'ses-tə\ *n* : a narrow curved wicker basket used in jai alai [Spanish, literally, "basket", from Latin *cista* "box, basket"]

ces·tode \'ses-ˌtōd\ *n* : any of a group (Cestoda) of internally parasitic flatworms comprising the tapeworms [derived from Greek *kestos* "girdle"] — **cestode** *adj*

cesura *variant of* CAESURA

ce·ta·cean \si-'tā-shən\ *n* : any of an order (Cetacea) of aquatic mammals including the whales, dolphins, porpoises, and related forms [Latin *cetus* "whale", from Greek *kētos*] — **cetacean** *adj* — **ce·ta·ceous** \-shəs\ *adj*

Ce·tus \'sēt-əs\ *n* : an equatorial constellation south of Pisces and Aries [Latin, literally, "whale"]

cgs system \ˌsē-ˌjē-'es-\ *n* : a system of metric measure based on the centimeter, gram, and second as fundamental units

Chad \'chad\ *n* : a branch of the Afro-Asiatic language family comprising numerous languages of northern Nigeria and Cameroon

chae·tog·nath \'kēt-ˌäg-ˌnath, -əg-, -ə-\ *n* : any of a class (Chaetognatha) of small free-swimming marine worms with movable curved bristles on each side of the mouth [Greek *chaitē* "long hair" + *gnathos* "jaw"] — **chaetognath** *adj* — **chae·tog·na·than** \kē-'täg-nə-thən\ *adj or n*

¹chafe \'chāf\ *vb* **1 a** : IRRITATE 1, VEX **b** : to feel irritation or discontent : FRET **2** : to warm by rubbing **3 a** : to rub so as to wear away : ABRADE **b** : to make sore by or as if by rubbing ⟨a tight collar *chafed* the dog's neck⟩ [Middle French *chaufer* "to warm", from Latin *calefacere,* from *calēre* "to be warm" + *facere* "to make"]

²chafe *n* **1** : a state of vexation : RAGE **2** : injury or wear caused by friction; *also* : FRICTION

cha·fer \'chā-fər\ *n* : any of various large beetles [Old English *ceafor*]

¹chaff \'chaf\ *n* **1** : the debris (as seed coverings) separated from the seed in threshing grain **2** : something trivial or worthless [Old English *ceaf*] — **chaffy** \-ē\ *adj*

²chaff *n* : light jesting talk : BANTER

³chaff *vb* : to tease good-naturedly : BANTER

chaf·fer \'chaf-ər\ *vb* : HAGGLE 2, BARGAIN [Middle English *chaffare* "a dispute about price", from *chep* "trade" + *fare* "journey"] — **chaf·fer·er** *n*

chaf·finch \'chaf-ˌinch, -inch\ *n* : a European finch of which the male has reddish breast plumage and a cheerful song

chaf·ing dish \'chā-fing-\ *n* : a utensil for cooking or warming food at the table [Middle English *chafen* "to warm, chafe"]

¹cha·grin \shə-'grin\ *n* : a feeling of annoyance caused by failure or disappointment [French, from *chagrin* "sad"]

²chagrin *vt* **cha·grined** \-'grind\; **cha·grin·ing** \-'grin-\ : to cause to feel chagrin

¹chain \'chān\ *n* **1 a** : a series of connected usually metal links or rings **b** (1) : a measuring instrument of 100 links (about 20 meters) used in surveying (2) : a unit of length equal to 66 feet (about 20 meters) **2** : something that confines or restrains **3 a** : series of things linked, connected, or associated together **b** : a number of atoms or chemical groups united like links

in a chain ⟨a polypeptide *chain*⟩ [Old French *chaeine,* from Latin *catena*]

²chain *vt* : to fasten, bind, or connect with or as if with a chain

chain gang *n* : a group of convicts chained together

chain mail *n* : flexible armor of interlinked metal rings — called also *chain armor*

chain reaction *n* **1** : a series of events so related to each other that each one initiates the succeeding one **2** : a chemical or nuclear reaction yielding energy or products that cause further reactions of the same kind — **chain–re·act** \ˌchān-rē-'akt\ *vt*

chain saw *n* : a portable power saw that has teeth linked together to form an endless chain

chain–smoke \'chān-ˌsmōk\ *vb* : to smoke cigarettes one right after another — **chain–smok·er** *n*

chain stitch *n* : an ornamental stitch like the links of a chain

chain store *n* : one of numerous usually retail stores under the same ownership and general management and selling the same lines of goods

chair \'cheər, 'chaər\ *n* **1** : a seat with legs and a back for use by one person **2 a** : an official seat or a seat of authority or dignity **b** : an office or position of authority or dignity **c** : the presiding officer of a meeting or an organization or committee **3** : any of various supporting devices [Old French *chaiere,* from Latin *cathedra,* from Greek *kathedra,* from *kata* "down" + *hedra* "seat"]

chair lift *n* : a motor-driven conveyor for skiers consisting of a series of seats suspended from an overhead cable

chair·man \-mən\ *n* : CHAIR 2c — **chair·man·ship** \-ˌship\ *n*

chair·per·son \-ˌpərs-n\ *n* : CHAIR 2c

chair·wom·an \-ˌwu̇m-ən\ *n* : a woman who is the presiding officer of a meeting, organization, or committee

chaise \'shāz\ *n* **1** : a 2-wheeled carriage with a folding top **2** : a light carriage or pleasure cart [French, "chair, chaise", alteration of Old French *chaiere* "chair"]

chaise longue \'shāz-ˌlȯng\ *n, pl* **chaise longues** *also* **chaises longues** \'shāz-ˌlȯng, -ˌlȯngz\ : a long chair for reclining [French, literally, "long chair"]

chaise lounge \'shāz-ˌlau̇nj, 'chās-\ *n* : CHAISE LONGUE [by folk etymology from *chaise longue*]

chal·ce·do·ny \kal-'sed-n-ē, 'chal-sə-ˌdän-ē\ *n, pl* **-nies** : a translucent quartz commonly pale blue or gray with nearly waxy luster [Late Latin *chalcedonius,* a precious stone, from Greek *Chalkēdōn* "Chalcedon, former city in Turkey"]

chal·cid \'kal-səd\ *n* : any of a large group of mostly tiny insects related to the bees and ants and parasitic in the larval state on the larvae or pupae of other insects [derived from Greek *chalkos* "copper"] — **chalcid** *adj*

chal·co·cite \'kal-kə-ˌsīt\ *n* : a black or gray mineral Cu_2S of metallic luster that is an important ore of copper [derived from Greek *chalkos* "copper"]

chal·co·py·rite \ˌkal-kə-'pīr-ˌīt\ *n* : a yellow mineral $CuFeS_2$ consisting of copper-iron sulfide and constituting an important ore of copper

Chal·de·an \kal-'dē-ən\ *n* **1** : one of an ancient Semitic people founding the second Babylonian Empire in the 7th century B.C. **2** : the Semitic language of the Chaldeans [*Chaldea,* region of ancient Babylonia] — **Chal·da·ic** \kal-'dā-ik\ *adj or n* — **Chaldean** *adj*

Chal·dee \'kal-ˌdē\ *n* : CHALDEAN

cha·let \sha-'lā, 'shal-ˌā\ *n* **1** : a remote herdsman's hut in the Alps **2 a** : a Swiss dwelling with a wide roof overhang **b** : a cottage in chalet style [French]

chal·ice \'chal-əs\ *n* **1** : a drinking cup : GOBLET; *esp* : the liturgical vessel in which wine is consecrated **2** : a flower cup [Anglo-French, from Latin *calix*]

cesta

\ə\ abut   \ng\ sing
\ər\ further   \ō\ bone
\a\ mat   \ȯ\ saw
\ā\ take   \ȯi\ coin
\ä\ cot, cart   \th\ thin
\au̇\ out   \th\ this
\ch\ chin   \ü\ food
\e\ pet   \u̇\ foot
\ē\ easy   \y\ yet
\g\ go   \yü\ few
\i\ tip   \yu̇\ cure
\ī\ life   \zh\ vision
\j\ job

¹chalk \'chȯk\ *n* **1** : a soft white, gray, or buff lime-stone chiefly composed of the shells of foraminifers **2** : chalk or a chalky material especially when used in the form of a crayon [Old English *cealc*, from Latin *calx* "lime", from Greek *chalix* "pebble"] — **chalky** \'chȯ·ke\ *adj*

²chalk *vt* **1** : to rub, mark, write, or draw with chalk **2 a** : to make a rough sketch of **b** : to record with or as if with chalk

chalk·board \-,bōrd, -,bȯrd\ *n* : a dark smooth surface (as of slate) used for writing or drawing on with chalk

chalk up *vt* **1** : ASCRIBE, CREDIT ⟨*chalk* success *up* to hard work⟩ **2** : ATTAIN 1, ACHIEVE ⟨*chalk up* a victory⟩

¹chal·lenge \'chal-ənj\ *vb* **1** : to claim as due or deserved ⟨an act that *challenged* everyone's admiration⟩ **2** : to halt and demand the countersign from **3 a** : to take exception to : object to ⟨*challenge* a juror⟩ **b** : to question the legality or legal qualifications of ⟨*challenge* a vote⟩ **4 a** : to call out to duel or combat **b** : to invite into competition **5** : STIMULATE 1, EXCITE [Old French *chalengier* "to accuse", from Latin *calumniari* "to accuse falsely", from *calumnia* "calumny"] — **chal·leng·er** *n*

²challenge *n* **1** : an objection raised to something or someone **2** : a sentry's command to halt and prove identity **3** : an often threatening or provocative summons or invitation to compete; *esp* : a summons to a duel **4** : a test of immunity by exposure to virulent infective material after specific immunization

chal·lis \'shal-ē\ *n, pl* **chal·lises** \'shal-ēz\ : a light-weight soft clothing fabric especially of cotton or wool [probably from the name *Challis*]

¹cham·ber \'chām-bər\ *n* **1** : ROOM; *esp* : BEDROOM **2** : an enclosed space or compartment **3 a** : a meeting hall of a deliberative, legislative, or judicial body **b** : a room where a judge transacts business out of court **c** : the reception room of a person of rank or authority **4 a** : a legislative or judicial body; *esp* : either of the houses of a bicameral legislature **b** : a voluntary board or council (as of businessmen) **5 a** : the part of the bore of a gun that holds the cartridge **b** : a compartment in the cartridge cylinder of a revolver [Old French *chambre*, from Late Latin *camera*, from Latin, "vault", from Greek *kamara*] — **cham·bered** \-bərd\ *adj*

²chamber *vt* : to place or hold in or as if in a chamber

³chamber *adj* : intended for performance by a few musicians for a small audience ⟨*chamber* music⟩

chambered nautilus *n* : NAUTILUS 1

cham·ber·lain \'chām-bər-lən\ *n* **1** : a chief officer in the household of a sovereign or noble **2** : TREASURER [Old French *chamberlayn*, derived from Late Latin *camera* "chamber"]

cham·ber·maid \'chām-bər-,mād\ *n* : a maid who makes beds and does general cleaning of bedrooms (as in a hotel)

chamber of commerce : an association of business people to promote commercial and industrial interests

chamber pot *n* : a handled and often lidded bowl for urination and defecation

cham·bray \'sham-,brā, -,brē\ *n* : a lightweight clothing fabric with colored and white yarns [*Cambrai*, France]

cha·me·leon \kə-'mēl-yən\ *n* : a lizard that has the ability to vary the color of its skin [derived from Greek *chamaileōn*, from *chamai* "on the ground" + *leōn* "lion"]

¹cham·fer \'cham-fər, 'champ-\ *n* : a beveled edge [Middle French *chanfraindre* "to bevel", from *chant* "edge" (from Latin *canthus* "iron tire") + *fraindre* "to break", from Latin *frangere*]

²chamfer *vt* **1** : to cut a furrow in (as a column) : GROOVE **2** : to make a chamfer on : BEVEL

cham·ois \'sham-ē\ *n, pl* **cham·ois** *also* **cham·oix** \'sham-ēz\ **1** : a small goatlike mountain antelope of Europe and the Caucasus **2** *also* **cham·my** *or* **sham·my**

chamois 1

\'sham-ē\ : a soft pliant leather prepared from the skin of the chamois or from sheepskin [Middle French, from Late Latin *camox*]

cham·o·mile *or* **cam·o·mile** \'kam-ə-,mīl, -,mēl\ *n* : any of a genus of strong-scented herbs related to the daisies with flower heads that contain a bitter medicinal principle [Medieval Latin *camomilla*, derived from Greek *chamaimēlon*, from *chamai* "on the ground" + *mēlon* "apple"]

¹champ \'champ\ *vb* **1** : to bite and chew noisily ⟨a horse *champing* its bit⟩ **2** : to show impatience [perhaps imitative]

²champ *n* : CHAMPION 3

cham·pagne \sham-'pān\ *n* : a white sparkling wine made in Champagne, France; *also* : a similar wine made elsewhere

cham·paign \sham-'pān\ *n* : an expanse of level open country : PLAIN [Middle French *champagne*, from Late Latin *campania*, from Latin *campus* "field, plain"]

¹cham·pi·on \'cham-pē-ən\ *n* **1** : a militant advocate or defender **2** : one that fights for another's rights or honor **3 a** : a person formally acknowledged as better than all others in a sport or in a game of skill **b** : the winner of first place in a competition [Old French, "warrior", from Medieval Latin *campio*, of Germanic origin]

²champion *vt* : to protect or fight for as a champion

cham·pi·on·ship \-,ship\ *n* **1** : the act of defending as a champion ⟨her *championship* of civil rights⟩ **2 a** : the position or title of champion **b** : a contest held to determine a champion

¹chance \'chans\ *n* **1** : the way in which things happen without apparent cause or intent ⟨meet by *chance*⟩ ⟨the outcome depends on *chance*⟩ **2** : OPPORTUNITY ⟨had a *chance* to travel⟩ **3** : RISK, GAMBLE ⟨take *chances*⟩ **4 a** : the possibility of an indicated outcome in an uncertain situation ⟨a good *chance* of failure⟩ ⟨a 50–50 *chance*⟩ **b** : at least a slight possibility of a favorable outcome ⟨does stand a *chance* of winning⟩ **c** : the more likely of possible outcomes ⟨*chances* are they've already left⟩ **5** : a ticket in a raffle [Old French, derived from Latin *cadere* "to fall"] — **chance** *adj*

²chance *vb* **1 a** : to take place or come about by chance : HAPPEN **b** : to be found by chance **c** : to have good or bad luck ⟨*chanced* to miss the train⟩ **2** : to come casually and unexpectedly — used with *on* or *upon* **3** : to accept the hazard of : RISK SYN SEE HAPPEN

chan·cel \'chan-səl\ *n* : the part of a church containing the altar and seats for the clergy and choir [Middle French, from Latin *cancelli* "lattice"; from the lattice-work enclosing it]

chan·cel·lery *or* **chan·cel·lory** \'chan-sə-lə-rē, -slə-rē\ *n, pl* **-ler·ies** *or* **-lor·ies** **1 a** : the position or department of a chancellor **b** : the building or room where a chancellor's office is located **2** : the office or staff of an embassy or consulate

chan·cel·lor \'chan-sə-lər, -slər\ *n* **1** : the head of a university **2** : a judge in a court of chancery or equity **3** : the chief minister of state in some European countries [Old French *chancelier*, from Late Latin *cancellarius* "doorkeeper, secretary", from Latin *cancelli* "lattice"] — **chan·cel·lor·ship** \-,ship\ *n*

chancellor of the exchequer : a member of the British cabinet in charge of the public income and expenditure

chan·cery \'chans-rē, -ə-rē\ *n, pl* **-cer·ies** **1** : a court of equity **2** : a record office for public archives **3** : CHANCELLERY [Middle English *chancerie*, alteration of *chancellerie* "chancellery"]

chan·cre \'shang-kər\ *n* : a primary sore or ulcer at the site of entry of an infective agent (as of syphilis) [French, from Latin *cancer*] — **chan·crous** \-kə-rəs, -krəs\ *adj*

chancy \'chan-sē\ *adj* **chanc·i·er; -est** : uncertain in outcome or prospect : RISKY

chan·de·lier \,shan-də-'liər\ *n* : a branched often ornate lighting fixture usually suspended from a ceiling [French, from Latin *candelabrum* "candlestick"]

chan·dler \'chan-dlər\ *n* **1** : a maker or seller of candles **2** : a dealer in supplies or equipment especially for ships [Middle French *chandelier*, from Old French *chandelle* "candle", from Latin *candela*] — **chan·dlery** \-dlə-rē\ *n*

¹change \'chānj\ *vb* **1** : to make or become different : MODIFY **2 a** : to give a different position, course, or direction to **b** : REVERSE ⟨*change* one's vote⟩ **3** : to replace with another : SWITCH **4** : to put fresh clothes or covering on ⟨*change* a bed⟩ **5** : to shift one's means of transportation : TRANSFER **6** : to undergo transformation, transition, or substitution **7** : to give up one thing for something else in return : EXCHANGE ⟨*change* places⟩ [Old French *changier*, from Latin *cambiare* "to exchange", of Celtic origin] — **chang·er** *n* □ SYN ALTER, MODIFY, VARY: CHANGE implies making either an essential difference amounting to loss of original identity or a substitution of one thing for another; ALTER implies a difference in some respect without loss of identity; MODIFY suggests a difference that limits, restricts, or adapts to a new purpose; VARY stresses a breaking away from exact repetition. — **change hands** : to pass from the possession of one person to that of another

²change *n* **1** : the act, process, or result of changing: as **a** : ALTERATION ⟨a *change* in routine⟩ **b** : TRANSFORMATION ⟨a *change* of seasons⟩ **c** : SUBSTITUTION ⟨a *change* of jobs⟩ **2** : a fresh set of clothes **3 a** : money in small denominations received in exchange for an equivalent sum in larger denominations **b** : money returned when a payment exceeds the amount due **c** : COINS ⟨a pocketful of *change*⟩

change·able \'chān-jə-bəl\ *adj* **1** : capable of or given to change : VARIABLE ⟨*changeable* weather⟩ **2** : appearing different (as in color) from different points of view — **change·abil·i·ty** \,chān-jə-'bil-ət-ē\ *n* — **change·able·ness** *n* — **change·ably** \'chān-jə-blē\ *adv*

change·ful \'chānj-fəl\ *adj* : full of or given to change — **change·ful·ly** \-fə-lē\ *adv* — **change·ful·ness** *n*

change·less \'chānj-ləs\ *adj* : marked by the absence of change : CONSTANT — **change·less·ly** *adv* — **change·less·ness** *n*

change·ling \'chānj-ling\ *n* : a child secretly exchanged for another in infancy

change of life : MENOPAUSE; *also* : a corresponding period in the male

change ringing *n* : the art or practice of ringing a set of tuned bells in continually varying order

¹chan·nel \'chan-l\ *n* **1 a** : the bed of a stream **b** : the deeper part of a river, harbor, or strait **c** : a strait or narrow sea between two close landmasses ⟨the English *Channel*⟩ **2 a** : a means aiding communication or exchange ⟨trade *channels*⟩ **b** : a way or course of thought or action ⟨new *channels* of exploration⟩ **3** : a long gutter, groove, or furrow **4** : a range of frequencies of sufficient width for a single radio or television transmission [Old French *chanel*, from Latin *canalis* "pipe, channel, canal"]

²channel *vt* **-neled** *or* **-nelled**; **-nel·ing** *or* **-nel·ling** **1 a** : to form, cut, or wear a channel in **b** : GROOVE ⟨*channel* a chair leg⟩ **2** : to direct into or through a channel

chan·nel·ize \'chan-l-īz\ *vt* : CHANNEL — **chan·nel·iza·tion** \,chan-l-ə-'zā-shən\ *n*

chan·son \shän-'sōn\ *n, pl* **chan·sons** \-'sōn, -'sōnz\ : SONG; *esp* : a French song [French]

¹chant \'chant\ *vb* **1** : SING; *esp* : to sing a chant **2** : to recite in a monotonous repetitive tone [Middle French *chanter*, from Latin *cantare*, from *canere* "to sing"]

²chant *n* **1** : a melody in which several words or syllables are sung on one tone **2** : a rhythmic monotonous utterance

chan·te·relle \,shant-ə-'rel, ,shänt-\ *n* : an edible mushroom of rich yellow color and pleasant aroma [French]

chan·teuse \shän-'túz, -'tərz, shan-'tüz\ *n* : a woman concert or nightclub singer [French, from *chanter* "to sing"]

chan·tey *or* **chan·ty** \'shant-ē, 'chant-\ *n, pl* **chanteys** *or* **chanties** : a song sung by sailors in rhythm with their work [French *chanter* "to sing, chant"]

chan·ti·cleer \,chant-ə-'kliər, ,shant-\ *n* : ¹COCK 1 [Old French *Chantecler*, rooster in the beast epic *Reynard the Fox*]

cha·os \'kā-,äs\ *n* : a state of utter confusion ⟨the city-wide blackout caused *chaos*⟩ [Latin, from Greek] SYN see ANARCHY — **cha·ot·ic** \kā-'ät-ik\ *adj* — **cha·ot·i·cal·ly** \-i-kə-lē, -klē\ *adv*

¹chap \'chap\ *n* : FELLOW 4a [short for *chapman*]

²chap *vb* **chapped**; **chap·ping** : to open in slits : CRACK ⟨*chapped* lips⟩ [Middle English *chappen*]

³chap *n* : a crack in or a sore roughening of the skin from exposure

⁴chap \'chäp, 'chap\ *n* : JAW : the fleshy covering of a jaw; *also* : the forepart of the face — usually used in pl. [²*chap*]

chap·ar·ral \,shap-ə-'ral, -'rel\ *n* : a thicket of dwarf evergreen oaks; *also* : a dense impenetrable thicket [Spanish, from *chaparro* "dwarf evergreen oak", from Basque *txapar*]

chap·book \'chap-,búk\ *n* : a small book containing ballads, tales, or tracts [*chap*man + *book*]

cha·peau \sha-'pō\ *n, pl* **cha·peaus** \-'pōz\ *or* **cha·peaux** \-'pō, -'pōz\ : HAT [Middle French, derived from Medieval Latin *cappellus* "head covering", from Late Latin *cappa*]

chap·el \'chap-əl\ *n* **1** : a place of worship in a residence or institution **2** : a building or a room or recess for prayer or special religious services **3** : a service of worship in a school or college **4** : a place of worship used by British Nonconformists [Old French *chapele*, from Medieval Latin *cappella*, from Late Latin *cappa* "cloak"; from the preservation of the cloak of Saint Martin of Tours in a chapel built for that purpose]

¹chap·er·on *or* **chap·er·one** \'shap-ə-,rōn\ *n* : a person who accompanies and is responsible for (as at a dance) a young woman or a group of young people [French *chaperon*, literally, "hood", derived from Late Latin *cappa* "head covering, cloak"]

²chaperon *or* **chaperone** *vb* : to act as a chaperon : ESCORT — **chap·er·on·age** \-,rō-nij\ *n*

chap·fall·en \'chap-,fò-lən, 'chäp-\ *or* **chop·fall·en** \'chäp-\ *adj* : cast down in spirits : DEPRESSED

chap·lain \'chap-lən\ *n* **1** : a member of the clergy appointed to serve a dignitary, institution, or military force **2** : a person chosen to conduct religious exercises for an organization [Old French *chapelain* "clergyman in charge of a chapel", from Medieval Latin *cappellanus*, from *cappella* "chapel"] — **chap·lain·cy** \-sē\ *n* — **chap·lain·ship** \-,ship\ *n*

chap·let \'chap-lət\ *n* **1** : a wreath worn on the head **2 a** : a string of beads **b** : a part of a rosary comprising five decades [Middle French *chapelet*, derived from Late Latin *cappa* "head covering, cloak"]

chap·man \'chap-mən\ *n, British* : a traveling merchant [Old English *cēapman*, from *cēap* "trade" + *man*]

chaps \'shaps, 'chaps\ *n pl* : leather leggings resembling trousers without a seat that are worn especially by western ranch hands [Mexican Spanish *chaparreras*]

chap·ter \'chap-tər\ *n* **1** : a main division of a book or of a law code **2** : a local branch of a society or fraternity [Old French *chapitre*, from Late Latin *capitulum*, from Latin *caput* "head"]

¹char \'chär\ *n, pl* **char** *or* **chars** : any of a genus of small-scaled trouts including the common brook trout [origin unknown]

chaps

²**char** *vb* **charred; char·ring** I : to change to charcoal by burning 2 : to burn slightly : SCORCH 3 : to burn to a cinder [back-formation from *charcoal*]

³**char** *n* : a charred substance

⁴**char** *vi* **charred; char·ring** : to work as a charwoman

char·a·banc \'shar-ə-,bang\ *n, British* : a sight-seeing bus [French *char à bancs,* literally, "wagon with benches"]

char·a·cin \'kar-ə-sən\ *n* : any of a family of usually small brightly colored tropical fishes [derived from Greek *charax* "pointed stake, a kind of fish"] — **char·acin** *adj*

char·ac·ter \'kar-ik-tər\ *n* I **a** : a conventional marking indicating origin or ownership **b** : a mark or symbol (as a hieroglyph or a letter of an alphabet) used in writing or printing **c** : a symbol (as a letter or number) that represents information; *also* : something standing for such a character that may be accepted by a computer 2 **a** (1) : a distinguishing feature : CHARACTERISTIC (2) : the sum total of the distinguishing qualities of a person, group, or thing : NATURE **b** : the detectable result of the action of a gene or group of genes 3 : POSITION, STATUS (in their *character* of children) 4 : a person having notable traits or characteristics; *esp* : an odd or peculiar person 5 : a person in a story, novel, or play 6 : REPUTATION 1 7 : moral excellence and strength [Middle French *caractère,* from Latin *character* "mark, distinctive quality", from Greek *charaktēr,* from *charassein* "to scratch, engrave"] — **char·ac·ter·less** \-ləs\ *adj*

¹**char·ac·ter·is·tic** \,kar-ik-tə-'ris-tik\ *adj* : serving to mark the distinctive character of an individual, group, or class — **char·ac·ter·is·ti·cal·ly** \-ti-kə-lē, -klē\ *adv*

☐ SYN CHARACTERISTIC, INDIVIDUAL, DISTINCTIVE, PECULIAR mean indicating a special quality or identity. CHARACTERISTIC applies to something that marks a person or thing or class; INDIVIDUAL stresses qualities that distinguish one from all other members of the same kind or class; DISTINCTIVE indicates qualities that are distinguishing and uncommon and often superior or praiseworthy; PECULIAR applies to qualities possessed only by a particular individual or class.

²**characteristic** *n* I : a distinguishing trait, quality, or property 2 : the integral part of a common logarithm

char·ac·ter·iza·tion \,kar-ik-tə-rə-'zā-shən\ *n* I : the act of characterizing : description by a statement of characteristics 2 : the creation of characters in fiction or drama : the artistic representation of fictitious persons

char·ac·ter·ize \'kar-ik-tə-,rīz\ *vt* I : to indicate the character or characteristics of : DESCRIBE 2 : to be characteristic of

character sketch *n* : a usually short piece of writing dealing with a character of strongly marked individuality

char·ac·tery \'kar-ik-tə-rē, -trē\ *n* : characters or symbols used to express ideas

cha·rades \shə-'rādz\ *n pl* : a game in which each syllable of a word to be guessed is acted out by some of the persons playing the game while the others try to guess the word [French]

cha·ras \'chär-əs\ *n* : HASHISH [Hindi *caras*]

char·coal \'chär-,kōl\ *n* I : a dark or black porous carbon prepared from vegetable or animal substances (as from wood by charring in a kiln from which air is excluded) 2 **a** : a piece or pencil of fine charcoal used in drawing **b** : a charcoal drawing [Middle English *charcole*]

chard \'chärd\ *n* : a beet that lacks a swollen root and forms large leaves and succulent stalks often cooked as a vegetable — called also *Swiss chard* [French *carde,* from Provençal *cardo* "cardoon", from Latin *carduus* "thistle, artichoke"]

¹**charge** \'chärj\ *vb* I **a** : to place a charge (as of powder) in (*charge* the magazine with three rounds) **b** : to load or fill to capacity **c** (1) : to impart an electric charge to (2) : to restore the active materials in (a storage battery) by the passage of a direct current through in the opposite direction to that of discharge 2 **a** : to impose a task or responsibility on **b** : to command, instruct, or exhort with right or authority (*charge* a jury) 3 : ACCUSE, BLAME (*charged* them with murder) 4 : to rush against or bear down upon a place : ASSAULT, ATTACK 5 **a** : to impose a monetary charge upon a person (*charged* me $50) **b** : to fix or ask as fee or payment (*charge* $2.50 for a ticket) **c** : to ask or set a price (*charges* too much) [Old French *chargier* "to load", from Late Latin *carricare,* from Latin *carrus* "car, wheeled vehicle"] — **charge·able** \'chär-jə-bəl\ *adj* — **charge·able·ness** *n*

²**charge** *n* I : a figure borne on a heraldic field 2 **a** : the quantity of material that an apparatus (as a gun, furnace, or the cylinder of an internal-combustion engine) is intended to receive at one time **b** : a store or accumulation of force **c** : a definite quantity of electricity; *esp* : an excess or deficiency of electrons 3 **a** : OBLIGATION 2, REQUIREMENT **b** : MANAGEMENT 1, SUPERVISION **c** : a person or thing committed to the care of another 4 : INSTRUCTION, COMMAND (a *charge* to a jury) 5 **a** : EXPENSE 1, COST **b** : the price of something **c** : a debit to an account 6 **a** : an often formal accusation of a wrong or offense **b** : an expression of hostile criticism (made a *charge* of racism) 7 : a rush to attack an enemy : ASSAULT

charge account *n* : a customer's account with a creditor (as a merchant) to which the purchase of goods is charged

charge card *n* : CREDIT CARD

charge–coupled device *n* : a semiconductor device which senses light intensity and whose electrical output is used in conjunction with that of other such devices in the formation of images (as in a television camera) — called also *CCD*

char·gé d'af·faires \'shär-,zhäd-ə-'faər, -'feər\ *n, pl* **char·gés d'af·faires** \-,zhäd-ə-, -,zhäz-də-\ I : a diplomat who substitutes for an absent ambassador or minister 2 : a diplomat of inferior rank [French, literally, "one charged with affairs"]

¹**char·ger** \'chär-jər\ *n, archaic* : a large flat platter for carrying meat

²**charg·er** \'chär-jər\ *n* I : a cavalry horse 2 : a device for charging storage batteries

char·i·ot \'char-ē-ət\ *n* : a 2-wheeled horse-drawn battle car of ancient times used also in processions and races [Middle French, from *char* "car", from Latin *carrus*]

char·i·o·teer \,char-ē-ə-'tiər\ *n* I : a driver of a chariot 2 *cap* : the constellation Auriga

cha·ris·ma \kə-'riz-mə\ *n, pl* **-ma·ta** \-mət-ə\ I : an extraordinary power (as of healing) given a Christian by the Holy Spirit for the good of the church 2 **a** : a personal magic of leadership arousing popular loyalty or enthusiasm for a public figure **b** : a special magnetic charm or appeal [Greek, "favor, gift", from *charis* "grace"] — **char·is·mat·ic** \,kar-əz-'mat-ik\ *adj*

char·i·ta·ble \'char-ət-ə-bəl\ *adj* I : liberal with money or help for poor and needy persons : GENEROUS 2 : given for or serving the needy (*charitable* funds) 3 : generous and kindly in judging other people — **char·i·ta·bly** \-blē\ *adv*

char·i·ty \'char-ət-ē\ *n, pl* **-ties** I : love for one's fellow human beings 2 : kindliness in judging others 3 **a** : the giving of aid to the poor and suffering **b** : public aid for the poor **c** : an institution or fund for aiding the needy [Old French *charité,* from Latin *caritas* "dearness", from *carus* "dear"]

char·la·tan \'shär-lə-tən\ *n* : a person who pretends to have a particular knowledge or ability : QUACK [Italian *ciarlatano,* alteration of *cerretano,* literally, "inhabitant of Cerreto, village in Italy"] — **char·la·tan·ism**

chariot

\-tə-ˌniz-əm\ *n* — **char·la·tan·ry** \-tən-rē\ *n* □ ORI-GIN In the early 16th century quacks wandered through Italy, peddling medicines and treatments of doubtful value. Because the village of Cerreto seemed to produce so many of these unskilled practitioners of medicine, the name *Cerretano,* "inhabitant of Cerreto", came to mean "quack". Such quacks always have a ready line of glib talk to help them sell their wares. Thus, under the influence of *ciarlare,* "to chatter", *Cerretano* was altered to *ciarlatano,* from which we get our English *charlatan.*

Charles·ton \ˈchärl-stən\ *n* : a dance in which the knees are twisted in and out and the heels are swung sharply outward on each step [*Charleston,* South Carolina]

char·ley horse \ˈchär-lē-ˌhȯrs\ *n* : pain and stiffness from muscular strain especially in a leg [*Charley,* nickname for *Charles*]

char·lotte russe \ˌshär-lət-ˈrüs\ *n* : a dessert made with sponge cake or ladyfingers and a whipped-cream or custard-gelatin filling [French, from *charlotte,* "a kind of dessert" + *russe* "Russian"]

¹**charm** \ˈchärm\ *n* 1 : a word, action, or thing believed to have magic powers 2 : something worn or carried to keep away evil and bring good luck 3 : a small decorative object worn on a chain or bracelet 4 a : a quality that attracts and pleases b : physical grace or attractiveness [Old French *charme,* from Latin *carmen* "song, charm", from *canere* "to sing"]

²**charm** *vt* 1 : to affect or influence by or as if by magic : COMPEL 2 : to protect by or as if by a charm ⟨a *charmed* life⟩ 3 : to control (an animal) by charms (as the playing of music) ⟨*charm* a snake⟩ 4 : to attract by grace or beauty — **charm·er** *n*

charm·ing \ˈchär-miŋ\ *adj* : pleasant and attractive especially in manner ⟨a very *charming* person⟩

char·nel \ˈchärn-l\ *n* : a building or chamber in which dead bodies or bones are deposited [Middle French, from Medieval Latin *carnale,* from Late Latin *carnalis* "of the flesh", from Latin *caro* "flesh"] — **charnel** *adj*

charr *variant of* CHAR

¹**chart** \ˈchärt\ *n* 1 : MAP: as a : an outline map exhibiting something (as climatic or magnetic variations) in its geographical aspects b : a map with specific information for use by navigators 2 : a sheet giving information in the form of a table or of lists or by means of diagrams or graphs; *also* : GRAPH 3 : a sheet of paper ruled and graduated for use in a recording instrument [Middle French *charte,* from Latin *charta* "piece of papyrus, document", from Greek *chartēs* "piece of papyrus" — see CARTEL origin]

²**chart** *vt* 1 : to make a chart of ⟨set out to *chart* the coast⟩ 2 : to lay out a plan for ⟨*charting* campaign strategy⟩

¹**char·ter** \ˈchärt-ər\ *n* 1 a : an official document granting, guaranteeing, or defining the rights and duties of the body (as a municipality, corporation, or a local society) to which it is issued b : CONSTITUTION ⟨the United Nations *Charter*⟩ 2 : a special privilege or immunity 3 : a contract by which the owners of a ship lease it to others — called also *charter party* [Old French *chartre,* from Medieval Latin *chartula,* from Latin *charta* "document"]

²**charter** *vt* 1 : to grant a charter to 2 : to hire (as a ship or a bus) for one's own use — **char·ter·er** \ˈchärt-ər-ər\ *n*

Char·tism \ˈchärt-ˌiz-əm\ *n* : the principles and practices of a body of 19th century English political reformers advocating better social and industrial conditions for the working classes [Medieval Latin *charta* "charter", from Latin, "document"] — **Char·tist** \ˈchärt-əst\ *adj or n*

char·treuse \shär-ˈtrüz, -ˈtrüs\ *n* : a brilliant yellow green [*Chartreuse,* trademark used for a green or yellow liqueur]

char·wom·an \ˈchär-ˌwu̇m-ən\ *n* 1 *British* : a woman hired to do household work 2 : a cleaning woman usually in a large building [Middle English *char* "turn, piece of work", from Old English *cierr*]

chary \ˈchaər-ē, ˈcheər-\ *adj* **char·i·er; -est** 1 : cautiously sparing or frugal ⟨*chary* of giving praise⟩ 2 : cautiously watchful especially in preserving something ⟨*chary* of one's reputation⟩ [Old English *cearig* "sorrowful", from *caru* "sorrow, care"] — **char·i·ly** \ˈchar-ə-lē, ˈcher-\ *adv* — **char·i·ness** \ˈchar-ē-nəs, ˈcher-\ *n*

¹**chase** \ˈchās\ *vb* 1 : to follow rapidly : PURSUE 2 : to seek out 3 : to drive away or out ⟨*chase* a dog off the lawn⟩ [Middle French *chasser,* from Latin *captare,* from *capere* "to take"] □ SYN PURSUE, FOLLOW, TRAIL: CHASE implies going swiftly after and trying to overtake something running or fleeing usually in full view ⟨a dog *chasing* a cat⟩ PURSUE may add the suggestion of a continuing effort to overtake ⟨*pursue* a fox⟩ FOLLOW puts less emphasis upon speed and may not imply intent to overtake ⟨a stray dog *followed* me home⟩ TRAIL applies to a following of tracks or traces rather than a visible object ⟨*trail* a deer through the snow⟩

²**chase** *n* 1 a : the act of chasing : PURSUIT b : HUNTING — used with *the* 2 : something pursued 3 : a tract of unenclosed land used as a game preserve

³**chase** *vt* : to ornament (metal) by embossing or engraving ⟨*chased* bronze⟩ [Middle French *enchasser* "to set"]

⁴**chase** *n* : a channel (as in a wall) for something to lie in or pass through [French *chas* "eye of a needle", from Late Latin *capsus* "enclosed space", from Latin *capsa* "box"]

⁵**chase** *n* : a rectangular steel or iron frame into which letterpress matter is locked for printing or plating [probably from French *châsse* "frame", from Latin *capsa* "box"]

chas·er \ˈchā-sər\ *n* 1 : one that chases 2 : a mild drink (as water or beer) taken after hard liquor

Cha·sid or **Chas·sid** \ˈhas-əd, ˈkäs-\ *n, pl* **Cha·si·dim** or **Chas·si·dim** \ˈhas-əd-əm, kä-ˈsēd-\ *variant of* HASID

chasm \ˈkaz-əm\ *n* 1 : a deep cleft in the earth 2 : a marked division, separation, or difference [Latin *chasma,* from Greek]

chas·seur \sha-ˈsər\ *n* : one of a body of light cavalry or infantry trained for rapid maneuvering [French, from Middle French *chasser* "to chase"]

chas·sis \ˈshas-ē, ˈchas-ē\ *n, pl* **chas·sis** \-ēz\ : a supporting framework (as that bearing the body of an automobile or airplane or the parts of a radio or television receiving set) [French *châssis,* derived from Latin *capsa* "box"]

chaste \ˈchāst\ *adj* 1 a : innocent of unlawful sexual intercourse b : CELIBATE 2 : pure in thought and act : MODEST 3 : pure or severe in design and expression [Old French, from Latin *castus* "pure, chaste"] — **chaste·ly** *adv* — **chaste·ness** \ˈchās-nəs, ˈchāst-\ *n* □ SYN CHASTE, PURE, MODEST mean free from all taint of what is lewd or salacious. CHASTE implies a refraining from acts, thoughts, or desires that are not virginal or not sanctioned in marriage; it may suggest avoidance of anything that cheapens or debases; PURE implies innocence and absence of temptation; MODEST applies especially to behavior and dress as outward signs of chastity or purity.

chas·ten \ˈchās-n\ *vt* **chas·tened; chas·ten·ing** \ˈchās-niŋ, -n-iŋ\ 1 : to correct by punishment or suffering : DISCIPLINE 2 : to purify of excess, pretense, or falsity : REFINE [Old French *chastier,* from Latin *castigare,* from *castus* "pure, chaste"] — **chas·ten·er** \ˈchās-nər, -n-ər\ *n*

chas·tise \chas-ˈtīz\ *vt* 1 : to inflict punishment on (as by whipping) 2 : to censure severely : CASTIGATE [Middle English *chastisen,* alteration of *chasten*] SYN see

\ə\ abut   \ng\ sing
\ər\ further   \ō\ bone
\a\ mat   \ȯ\ saw
\ā\ take   \ȯi\ coin
\ä\ cot, cart   \th\ thin
\au̇\ out   \th\ this
\ch\ chin   \ü\ food
\e\ pet   \u̇\ foot
\ē\ easy   \y\ yet
\g\ go   \yü\ few
\i\ tip   \yu̇\ cure
\ī\ life   \zh\ vision
\j\ job

chasuble

PUNISH — **chas·tise·ment** \chas-'tīz-mənt, 'chas-təz-\ *n* — **chas·tis·er** \chas-'tī-zər\ *n*

chas·ti·ty \'chas-tət-ē\ *n* : the quality or state of being chaste; *esp* : personal purity and modesty

cha·su·ble \'chazh-ə-bəl, 'chaz-ə-, 'chas-ə-\ *n* : a sleeveless outer vestment worn by the officiating priest at mass [French, from Late Latin *casubla* "hooded garment"]

¹chat \'chat\ *vi* **chat·ted; chat·ting** 1 : CHATTER 2 2 : to talk in a light, informal, or familiar manner

²chat *n* 1 a : light familiar talk b : an informal conversation 2 : any of several songbirds with a chattering call

châ·teau \sha-'tō\ *n, pl* **châ·teaus** \-'tōz\ *or* **châ·teaux** \-'tō, -'tōz\ 1 : a feudal castle in France 2 : a large country house 3 : a French vineyard estate [French, from Latin *castellum* "castle"]

chat·e·laine \'shat-l-,ān\ *n* 1 : the mistress of a château or a household 2 : an ornamental clasp or hook for a watch, purse, or bunch of keys [French]

chat·tel \'chat-l\ *n* 1 : SLAVE 1, BONDMAN 2 : an item of property (as animals, furniture, money, or goods) other than real estate [Old French *chatel* "property", from Medieval Latin *capitale*, from Latin *capitalis* "of the head, capital"]

chat·ter \'chat-ər\ *vb* 1 : to utter rapidly succeeding sounds suggesting speech but lacking meaning ⟨squirrels *chattered* angrily⟩ 2 : to speak idly, continually, or rapidly : JABBER 3 a : to click repeatedly or uncontrollably ⟨*chattering* teeth⟩ b : to vibrate rapidly in cutting ⟨a *chattering* tool⟩ [Middle English *chatteren*] — **chatter** *n* — **chat·ter·er** \'chat-ər-ər\ *n*

chat·ter·box \'chat-ər-,bäks\ *n* : a person who talks continuously : a constant chatterer

chat·ty \'chat-ē\ *adj* **chat·ti·er; -est** 1 : fond of chatting : TALKATIVE 2 : having the style and manner of light informal conversation ⟨a *chatty* letter⟩ — **chat·ti·ly** \'chat-l-ē\ *adv* — **chat·ti·ness** \'chat-ē-nəs\ *n*

¹chauf·feur \'shō-fər, shō-'\ *n* : a person employed to drive an automobile for the transportation of persons or property [French, literally, "stoker", from *chauffer* "to heat", from Latin *calefacere*, from *calēre* "to be warm" + *facere* "to make"] □ ORIGIN The French verb *chauffer* means "to heat", so the literal meaning of the noun *chauffeur* is "heater, one that heats". *Chauffeur* is the French name for the stoker who heats a steam engine and keeps it going. In the early days of the automobile, the French gave the nickname *chauffeur* to motorists. As automobiles became more common, *chauffeur* came to be used especially for people hired to drive for others. This is the sense of English *chauffeur*, borrowed from the French.

²chauffeur *vb* 1 : to do the work of a chauffeur 2 : to transport as or as if a chauffeur ⟨*chauffeur* children to school⟩

chau·tau·qua \shə-'tȯ-kwə\ *n* : an institution of the late 19th and early 20th centuries offering educational entertainment (as lectures) in circuit performances often in a tent [*Chautauqua* lake, New York]

chau·vin·ism \'shō-və-,niz-əm\ *n* : excessive or blind patriotism or devotion to a group to which one belongs ⟨male *chauvinism*⟩ [French *chauvinisme*, from Nicolas *Chauvin*, 19th century French soldier excessively devoted to Napoleon and his regime] — **chau·vin·ist** \-və-nəst\ *n* — **chau·vin·is·tic** \,shō-və-'nis-tik\ *adj* — **chau·vin·is·ti·cal·ly** \-ti-kə-lē, -klē\ *adv*

cheap \'chēp\ *adj* 1 : of low cost or price ⟨a *cheap* watch⟩ 2 : worth little : of inferior quality ⟨*cheap* material wears out quickly⟩ 3 a : gained with little effort b : not worth gaining ⟨*cheap* applause⟩ 4 : lowered in one's own opinion : ABASHED ⟨feel *cheap*⟩ 5 a : charging low prices b : dealing in inferior goods 6 a : lowered in value or purchasing power (as by inflation) ⟨*cheap* dollars⟩ b : obtainable at a low rate of interest ⟨*cheap* money⟩ [obsolete *cheap* "bargain", from Old English *cēap* "trade", from Latin *caupo* "tradesman"] — **cheap** *adv* — **cheap·ly** *adv* — **cheap·ness** *n*

cheap·en \'chē-pən\ *vb* **cheap·ened; cheap·en·ing** \'chēp-ning, -ə-ning\ : to make or become cheap or cheaper

cheap·skate \-,skāt\ *n* : a mean or miserly person [*cheap* + *skate* "miserly person"]

¹cheat \'chēt\ *n* 1 : an act of cheating : DECEPTION, FRAUD 2 : one that cheats : DECEIVER [earlier *cheat* "forfeited property", from Middle English *eschete* "escheat"]

²cheat *vb* 1 : to rob by deceit or fraud ⟨*cheated* them out of a large sum⟩ 2 : to influence or lead astray by deceit, trick, or artifice 3 : to disappoint in a hope or purpose by deceit and trickery 4 a : to practice fraud or trickery b : to violate rules dishonestly (as at cards) □ SYN CHEAT, DEFRAUD, SWINDLE mean to get something from another by deception or dishonesty. CHEAT suggests using trickery that escapes observation; DEFRAUD stresses depriving one of legitimate rights and connotes deliberate lying or deception; SWINDLE implies cheating usually on a large scale by abuse of confidence.

¹check \'chek\ *n* 1 : exposure of a chess king to an attack 2 a : a stoppage of progress : ARREST, PAUSE b : the act of checking a hockey or lacrosse player 3 : something that arrests, limits, or restrains : RESTRAINT ⟨constitutional *checks* and balances⟩ 4 a : a standard for testing and evaluation : CRITERION b : EXAMINATION 1, INVESTIGATION, VERIFICATION; *also* : the sample used for testing 5 : an order directing a bank to pay out money in accordance with instructions written thereon 6 a : a ticket or token that shows that the bearer has a claim to property ⟨a baggage *check*⟩ or has made payment for a previous performance that did not take place ⟨a rain *check*⟩ b : a slip indicating the amount due : BILL 7 a : a pattern in squares that resembles a checkerboard b : a fabric with such a design 8 : a mark ✓ placed beside an item to show it has been noted 9 : CRACK, BREAK ⟨a *check* in wood or steel⟩ [Old French *eschec*, from Arabic *shāh*, from Persian, literally, "king"] — **in check** : under restraint or control

²check *vb* 1 : to put (a chess king) in check 2 a : to bring to a sudden pause : STOP b : to halt through caution, uncertainty, or fear : STOP 3 a : RESTRAIN 2, CURB b : to legally impede or interfere with a hockey or lacrosse player 4 a : to make sure of the correctness or satisfactoriness of b : to mark printing or writing with a check to show that something has been specially noted 5 : to mark with squares or checks ⟨a *checked* suit⟩ 6 : to leave or accept for safekeeping in a checkroom or for shipment as baggage 7 : to investigate conditions ⟨*check* up on things⟩ 8 : to correspond point for point : TALLY 9 : to develop small cracks

check·book \'chek-,bu̇k\ *n* : a book containing blank checks to be drawn on a bank

¹check·er \'chek-ər\ *n* 1 : a square or spot resembling the markings on a checkerboard 2 : a playing piece used in checkers [Middle English *cheker* "chessboard", from Old French *eschequier*, from *eschec* "check"]

²checker *vt* **check·ered; check·er·ing** \'chek-ring, -ə-ring\ 1 : to mark with colored squares ⟨a *checkered* tablecloth⟩ 2 : to subject to frequent changes (as of fortune) ⟨a *checkered* career⟩

³checker *n* : one that checks; *esp* : an employee who checks out purchases in a supermarket

check·er·ber·ry \'chek-ər-,ber-ē, 'chek-ə-,\ *n* : the spicy red fruit of an American wintergreen; *also* : this plant [*checker* "wild service tree" + *berry*]

check·er·board \-,bȯrd, -,bȯrd\ *n* : a board used in games (as checkers) and marked with 64 squares in 2 alternating colors

check·ers \'chek-ərz\ *n* : a game played on a checkerboard by two persons each having 12 playing pieces

check·ing account \'chek-ing-\ *n* : an account in a bank from which the depositor can draw money by writing checks — compare SAVINGS ACCOUNT

check·list \'chek-,list\ *n* : a list of items that may easily be referred to (as for verifying or comparing)

¹check·mate \'chek-,māt\ *vt* **1** : to arrest or frustrate completely **2** : to check (a chess opponent's king) so that escape is impossible [Middle English, interjection announcing checkmate, from Middle French *eschec mat,* from Arabic *shāh māt,* from Persian, literally, "the king is left unable to escape"]

²checkmate *n* **1 a** : the act of checkmating **b** : the situation of a checkmated king **2** : a thorough defeat

check·off \'chek-,òf\ *n* : an authorized practice of deducting union dues from a worker's paycheck by the employer

check out *vb* : to total or have totaled the cost of purchases in a self-service store (as a supermarket) and make or receive payment for them

check·point \'chek-,point\ *n* : a point at which traffic is halted for inspection or clearance

check·rein \-,rān\ *n* : a short rein fastened so that it prevents a horse from lowering its head

check·room \-,rüm, -,rùm\ *n* : a room at which baggage, parcels, or clothing is checked

check·up \'chek-,əp\ *n* : EXAMINATION; *esp* : a general physical examination

ched·dar \'ched-ər\ *n, often cap* : a hard pressed cheese of smooth texture [*Cheddar,* England]

cheek \'chēk\ *n* **1** : the fleshy side of the face below the eye and above and to the side of the mouth **2 a** : something suggesting the human cheek in position or form **b** : a lateral part or side (as of a structure or opening) **3** : saucy speech or behavior [Old English *cēace*] — **cheek by jowl** : in close proximity

cheek·bone \-'bōn, -,bōn\ *n* : the bone or the bony prominence below the eye

cheek pouch *n* : an enlargement of the cheeks in some monkeys and rodents that resembles a sac and is used for holding food

cheek tooth *n* : MOLAR

cheeky \'chē-kē\ *adj* **cheek·i·er; -est** : IMPUDENT, SAUCY — **cheek·i·ness** *n*

cheep \'chēp\ *vb* : ¹PEEP 1 [imitative] — **cheep** *n*

¹cheer \'chiər\ *n* **1** : state of mind or heart : SPIRIT ⟨be of good *cheer*⟩ **2** : GAIETY 2, ANIMATION **3** : food and drink for or fit for a feast **4** : something that gladdens **5** : a shout of applause or encouragement [Middle English *chere* "face, cheer," from Old French *chere* "face," from "face"]

²cheer *vb* **1** : to give hope to or make happier : COMFORT ⟨*cheer* a sick person⟩ **2** : to urge on especially with shouts or cheers ⟨*cheer* one's team to victory⟩ **3** : to shout with joy, approval, or enthusiasm ⟨the students *cheered* loudly⟩ **4** : to grow or be cheerful : REJOICE — usually used with *up*

cheer·ful \'chiər-fəl\ *adj* **1 a** : full of good spirits : HAPPY **b** : WILLING **3** ⟨*cheerful* obedience⟩ **2** : pleasantly bright : likely to dispel gloom or worry ⟨a sunny *cheerful* room⟩ — **cheer·ful·ly** \-fə-lē, -flē\ *adv* — **cheer·ful·ness** \-fəl-nəs\ *n* □ SYN CHEERY: CHEERFUL implies an inner contentment that may or may not be expressed outwardly ⟨*cheerful* cooperation⟩ CHEERY stresses the brightening or enlivening effect of behavior on others ⟨a *cheery* welcome⟩ ⟨*cheery* laughter⟩

cheer·lead·er \'chiər-,lēd-ər\ *n* : a person who directs organized cheering especially at a sports event

cheer·less \'chiər-ləs\ *adj* : lacking in warmth of kindliness : DEPRESSING, GLOOMY — **cheer·less·ly** *adv* — **cheer·less·ness** *n*

cheery \'chiər-ē\ *adj* **cheer·i·er; -est** : causing or suggesting cheerfulness : gay in manner or effect SYN see CHEERFUL — **cheer·i·ly** \'chir-ə-lē\ *adv* — **cheer·i·ness** \'chir-ē-nəs\ *n*

cheese \'chēz\ *n* : a food made from milk especially by separating out the curd and molding or pressing and usually ripening [Old English *cēse,* from Latin *caseus*]

cheese·bur·ger \-,bər-gər\ *n* : a hamburger with a slice of cheese

cheese·cake \-,kāk\ *n* **1** : a cake made by baking a mixture of cream cheese or cottage cheese, eggs, and sugar in a pastry shell or a mold **2** : photographs of attractive usually scantily clothed young women

cheese·cloth \-,klòth\ *n* : a thin loose-woven cotton cloth [from its use in making cheese]

cheesy \'chē-zē\ *adj* **1** : resembling or suggesting cheese (as in texture or odor) **2** *slang* : of poor quality

chee·tah \'chēt-ə\ *n* : a long-legged spotted swift-moving African and formerly Asian cat about the size of a small leopard that is often trained to run down game [Hindi *cītā,* from Sanskrit *citrakāya* "tiger", from *citra* "bright" + *kāya* "body"]

cheetah

chef \'shef\ *n* : COOK; *esp* : a head cook [French, short for *chef de cuisine* "head of the kitchen"]

chef d'oeu·vre \shā-'dœvr\ *n, pl* **chefs d'oeuvre** *same* \ : a masterpiece especially in art or literature [French *chef-d'oeuvre,* literally, "leading work"]

che·la \'kē-lə\ *n, pl* **che·lae** \-,lē\ : a pincerlike organ or claw on a limb of a crustacean or arachnid [Greek *chēlē* "claw"]

che·late \'kē-,lāt\ *adj* : resembling or having chelae

chela

che·lic·era \ki-'lis-ə-rə\ *n, pl* **-er·as** or **-er·ae** \-,rē\ : either of the front pair of appendages of an arachnid often specialized as fangs [French *chélicère,* from Greek *chēlē* "claw" + *keras* "horn"] — **che·lic·er·al** \-ə-rəl\ *adj*

che·li·ped \'kē-lə-,ped\ *n* : either of the pair of legs of a crustacean that bear chelae [Greek *chēlē* "claw" + Latin *ped-, pes* "foot"]

che·lo·ni·an \ki-'lō-nē-ən\ *adj* : of, relating to, or being a tortoise or turtle [Greek *chelōnē* "tortoise"] — **chelonian** *n*

chem- *or* **chemo-** *also* **chemi-** *combining form* : chemical : chemistry ⟨*chemo*reception⟩

¹chem·i·cal \'kem-i-kəl\ *adj* **1** : of, relating to, used in, or produced by chemistry **2** : acting or operated or produced by chemicals [New Latin *chimicus* "alchemist", from Medieval Latin *alchimicus,* from *alchymia* "alchemy"] — **chem·i·cal·ly** \-i-kə-lē, -klē\ *adv*

²chemical *n* : a substance (as an element or compound) obtained by a chemical process or used for producing a chemical effect

chemical engineering *n* : engineering dealing with the industrial application of chemistry

chemical warfare *n* : tactical warfare using smoke-producing substances or burning, poisonous, or smothering gases

che·mise \shə-'mēz, -'mēs\ *n* **1** : a woman's one-piece undergarment **2** : a loose straight-hanging dress [Old French, "shirt", from Late Latin *camisia*]

chem·ist \'kem-əst\ *n* **1** : one trained or working in chemistry **2** *British* : PHARMACIST [New Latin *chimista* "alchemist", from Medieval Latin *alchimista*]

chem·is·try \'kem-ə-strē\ *n* **1** : a science that deals with the composition, structure, and properties of substances and with the changes that they undergo **2** : chemical composition, properties, or processes ⟨the *chemistry* of iron⟩ ⟨the *chemistry* of blood⟩

che·mo·re·cep·tion \,kē-mō-ri-'sep-shən *also* ,kem-ō-\ *n* : the physiological reception of chemical stimuli — **che·mo·re·cep·tor** \-'sep-tər\ *n*

che·mo·syn·the·sis \-'sin-thə-səs, -'sint-\ *n* : formation of organic compounds (as in living cells) using energy derived from chemical reactions — **che·mo·syn·thet·ic** \-sin-'thet-ik\ *adj*

che·mo·tax·is \-'tak-səs\ *n* : orientation or movement of an organism in relation to chemical agents — **che·mo·tac·tic** \-'tak-tik\ *adj*

che·mo·ther·a·peu·tic \-,ther-ə-'pyüt-ik\ *adj* : of or relating to chemotherapy — **che·mo·ther·a·peu·ti·cal·ly** \-'pyüt-i-kə-lē, -klē\ *adv*

\ə\ abut	\ng\ sing
\ər\ further	\ō\ bone
\a\ mat	\ò\ saw
\ā\ take	\òi\ coin
\ä\ cot, cart	\th\ thin
\aù\ out	\th\ this
\ch\ chin	\ü\ food
\e\ pet	\ù\ foot
\ē\ easy	\y\ yet
\g\ go	\yü\ few
\i\ tip	\yù\ cure
\ī\ life	\zh\ vision
\j\ job	

che·mo·ther·a·py \-'ther-ə-pē\ *n* : the use of chemical agents in the treatment or control of disease

che·mot·ro·pism \ki-'mä-trə-ˌpiz-əm, ke-\ *n* : orientation of cells or organisms in relation to chemical stimuli

chem·ur·gy \'kem-ˌər-jē, -ər-; kə-'mər-\ *n* : chemistry that deals with industrial utilization of organic raw materials especially from farm products [*chem-* + Greek *ergon* "work"] — **chem·ur·gic** \kə-'mər-jik, ke-\ *adj* — **chem·ur·gi·cal·ly** \-ji-kə-lē, -klē\ *adv*

che·nille \shə-'nēl\ *n* : a fabric with a deep fuzzy pile often used for bedspreads and rugs [French, literally, "caterpillar", from Latin *canicula* "little dog", from *canis* "dog"]

cheque \'chek\ *chiefly British variant of* CHECK 5

cher·ish \'cher-ish\ *vt* **1 a** : to hold dear : feel or show affection for ⟨*cherished* their pet⟩ **b** : to keep with care and affection ⟨*cherish* your freedom⟩ **2** : to harbor in the mind ⟨*cherish* a hope⟩ [Middle French *cheriss-*, stem of *cherir* "to cherish", from *cher* "dear", from Latin *carus*]

cher·no·zem \ˌchər-nə-'zhȯm, -'zem\ *n* : a dark-colored zonal soil with a deep rich humus layer found in temperate to cool climates of rather low humidity [Russian, literally, "black earth"]

Cher·o·kee \'cher-ə-ˌkē\ *n* : a member of an Iroquoian people of the southern Appalachian mountains

Cherokee rose *n* : a climbing rose with fragrant usually white blossoms native to China and Japan but widely naturalized in the southern United States

cher·ry \'cher-ē\ *n, pl* **cherries** **1 a** : any of numerous trees and shrubs of the rose family that have rather small pale yellow to deep blackish red smooth-skinned fruits and include several grown for their edible fruits or showy flowers **b** : the fruit of a cherry **c** : the wood of a cherry **2** : a medium red color [Old North French *cherise* (understood as plural), from Late Latin *ceresia*, from Latin *cerasus* "cherry tree", from Greek *kerasos*] — **cherry** *adj*

chevron 2: *1* marine, *2* air force, *3* army

chert \'chərt, 'chat\ *n* : a rock resembling flint and consisting essentially of fibrous chalcedony and smaller amounts of very fine crystalline quartz and amorphous silica [origin unknown]

cherty \'chərt-ē, 'chat-\ *adj* **chert·i·er; chert·i·est** **1** : resembling flint **2** : full of flint ⟨a *cherty* soil⟩

cher·ub \'cher-əb\ *n* **1** *pl* **cher·u·bim** \'cher-yə-ˌbim, 'ker-, -ə-\ : an angel of high rank **2** *pl* **cherubs** **a** : a beautiful usually winged child in fine art **b** : a chubby rosy child [Latin, from Greek *cheroub*, from Hebrew *kĕrūbh*]

cher·vil \'chər-vəl\ *n* : an aromatic herb of the carrot family with finely divided leaves often used in soups and salads [Old English *cerfille*]

Ches·a·peake Bay retriever \'ches-ˌpēk-'bā-, -ə-ˌpēk-\ *n* : a large powerful sporting dog that was developed in Maryland and is distinguished by a short dense brown coat

Chesh·ire cat \'chesh-ər-\ *n* : a cat with a broad grin in Lewis Carroll's *Alice's Adventures in Wonderland* [*Cheshire*, England]

Cheshire cheese *n* : a cheese similar to cheddar made chiefly in Cheshire, England

chess \'ches\ *n* : a game of strategy for 2 players each of whom plays with 16 pieces on a checkerboard [Old French *esches*, plural of *eschec* "check"] — **chess·board** \-ˌbȯrd, -ˌbȯrd\ *n*

chess·man \-ˌman, -mən\ *n* : one of the 32 pieces used in chess

chest \'chest\ *n* **1** : a container for storage or shipping; *esp* : a box with a lid **2** : a public fund collected for some purpose **3** : the part of the body enclosed by the ribs and breastbone [Old English *cest*, from Latin *cista* "box, basket", from Greek *kistē* "basket, hamper"] — **chest·ed** \'ches-təd\ *adj*

ches·ter·field \'ches-tər-ˌfēld\ *n* : an overcoat with a velvet collar [from a 19th century Earl of *Chesterfield*]

Ches·ter White \'ches-tər-\ *n* : any of a breed of large white swine [*Chester* County, Pennsylvania]

¹chest·nut \'ches-ˌnət, -nət\ *n* **1** : an edible nut from several trees or shrubs of the beech family; *also* : a plant bearing chestnuts or its wood **2** : HORSE CHESTNUT **3** : a horse with the body colored pure or reddish brown and the mane, tail, and points of the same or a lighter shade — compare ²BAY 1, SORREL **4** : a callosity on the inner side of the leg of the horse **5** : an old joke or story [Middle French *chastaigne* "chestnut tree", from Latin *castanea*, from Greek *kastanea*]

²chestnut *adj* : of a grayish to reddish brown color

chestnut blight *n* : a destructive fungous disease of the American chestnut

chest of drawers : a piece of furniture containing a set of drawers (as for holding clothing)

che·val-de-frise \shə-ˌval-də-'frēz\ *n, pl* **che·vaux-de-frise** \shə-ˌvōd-ə-\ : a defense consisting of a timber or barrel covered with projecting spikes and often strung with barbed wire [French, literally, "horse from Friesland"]

che·val glass \shə-'val-\ *n* : a full-length mirror that may be tilted in a frame [French *cheval* "horse, support"]

chev·a·lier \ˌshev-ə-'liər, *especially for 2 also* shə-'val-ˌyā\ *n* **1** : CAVALIER 2 **2** : a member of any of various orders of knighthood or of merit (as the French Legion of Honor) [Middle French, from Late Latin *caballarius* "horseman"]

chev·i·ot \'shev-ē-ət, 'chev-\ *n* **1** : any of a breed of hardy hornless British sheep **2 a** : a heavy napped woolen or worsted fabric **b** : a sturdy cotton shirting [*Cheviot* hills, England and Scotland]

chev·ron \'shev-rən\ *n* **1** : a figure resembling an upside-down V **2** : a sleeve badge usually indicating rank or service (as in the armed forces) [Middle French, "rafter, chevron"]

¹chew \'chü\ *vb* : to crush or grind with the teeth [Old English *cēowan*] — **chew·able** \-ə-bəl\ *adj* — **chew·er** *n* — **chewy** \'chü-ē\ *adj*

²chew *n* **1** : the act of chewing **2** : something for chewing

chewing gum *n* : gum usually of sweetened and flavored chicle prepared for chewing

che·wink \chi-'wingk\ *n* : TOWHEE 1 [imitative]

Chey·enne \shī-'an, -'en\ *n* : a member of an Algonquian people of the western plains

chi \'kī\ *n* : the 22d letter of the Greek alphabet — X or χ

Chi·an·ti \kē-'änt-ē, -'ant-\ *n* : a dry usually red table wine [*Chianti* mountain area, Italy]

chiar·oscu·ro \kē-ˌär-ə-'skùr-ō, -'skyùr-\ *n* **1** : pictorial representation in terms of light and shade without regard to color **2** : the arrangement or treatment of light and dark parts in a pictorial work of art [Italian, from *chiaro* "clear, light" + *oscuro* "obscure, dark"] — **chiar·oscu·rist** \-'skùr-əst, -'skyùr-\ *n*

chi·as·mus \kī-'az-məs\ *n* : reversal in word order between the elements of parallel phrases (as in *we must not live to eat, but eat to live*) [Greek *chiasmos*, from *chiazein* "to mark with a chi"]

Chib·cha \'chib-ˌchä\ *n, pl* **Chibcha** *or* **Chibchas** : a member of an Indian people originally of central Colombia [Spanish, of American Indian origin]

¹chic \'shēk\ *n* : STYLE 5c [French]

²chic *adj* : cleverly stylish : SMART

chi·cane \shik-'ān, chik-\ *n* : CHICANERY [French]

chi·ca·nery \-'ān-rē, -ə-rē\ *n, pl* **-ner·ies** : artful trickery

Chi·ca·no \chi-'kän-ō, shi-, -'kán-\ *n, pl* **-nos** : an American of Mexican descent [Mexican Spanish, alteration of Spanish *mexicano* "Mexican"] — **Chicano** *adj*

chi·chi \'shē-ˌshē, 'chē-ˌchē\ *adj* **1** : elaborately ornamented **2** : ARTY ⟨a *chichi* film⟩ **3** : FASHIONABLE, CHIC ⟨*chichi* nightclubs⟩ [French] — **chichi** *n*

Chihuahua

chick \'chik\ *n* **l a** : CHICKEN; *esp* : one newly hatched **b** : the young of any bird **2** *slang* : a young woman

chick·a·dee \'chik-əd-ē\ *n* : any of several crestless American titmice usually with the crown of the head darker than the body [imitative]

chick·a·ree \'chik-ə-‚rē\ *n* : RED SQUIRREL [imitative]

Chick·a·saw \'chik-ə-‚sȯ\ *n* : a member of an Indian people of what is now northern Mississippi and Alabama and western Tennessee

chick·en \'chik-ən\ *n* **l** : the common domestic fowl especially when young; *also* : its flesh used as food **2** : any of various birds or their young **3** : COWARD [Old English *cicen* "young chicken"]

chicken hawk *n* : a hawk that preys or is said to prey on chickens

chick·en·heart·ed \‚chik-ən-'härt-əd\ *adj* : TIMID, COW-ARDLY

chicken pox *n* : a contagious virus disease especially of children marked by low fever and watery blisters on the skin

chicken snake *n* : any of several rat snakes

chick–pea \'chik-‚pē\ *n* : an Asiatic leguminous herb cultivated for its short pods with one or two edible seeds; *also* : its seed [by folk etymology from Middle English *chiche,* from Middle French, from Latin *cicer*]

chick·weed \'chik-‚wēd\ *n* : any of several low-growing small-leaved weedy plants of the pink family

chi·cle \'chik-əl, -lē\ *n* : a gum from the latex of the sapodilla used as the chief ingredient of chewing gum [Spanish, from Nahuatl *tzictli*]

chic·o·ry \'chik-rē, -ə-rē\ *n, pl* **-ries** : a thick-rooted usually blue-flowered European perennial herb related to the daisies and grown for its roots and as a salad plant; *also* : its dried ground roasted root used to flavor or adulterate coffee [Middle French *cichorée, chicorée,* from Latin *cichoreum,* from Greek *kichoreia*]

chide \'chīd\ *vb* **chid** \'chid\ *or* **chid·ed** \'chīd-əd\; **chid** *or* **chid·den** \'chid-n\ *or* **chided; chid·ing** \'chīd-ing\ : to speak disapprovingly to : SCOLD [Old English *cīdan* "to quarrel, chide", from *cīd* "strife"]

¹chief \'chēf\ *n* **l** : the upper part of a heraldic field **2** : the head of a group or organization : LEADER ⟨*chief* of police⟩ **3** : the principal part [Old French, "head, chief", from Latin *caput* "head"] — **in chief l** : held or holding rights or title directly from a paramount feudal lord ⟨tenure *in chief*⟩ **2** : in the chief position or place ⟨editor *in chief*⟩

²chief *adj* **l** : highest in rank, office, or authority **2** : of greatest importance, significance, or influence

chief executive *n* : a principal officer: as **a** : the president of a republic **b** : the governor of a state

chief justice *n* : the principal judge of a court of justice

¹chief·ly \'chē-flē\ *adv* **l** : most importantly : PRINCI-PALLY **2** : for the most part : MOSTLY

²chiefly *adj* : of or relating to a chief ⟨*chiefly* duties⟩

chief master sergeant *n* : an enlisted rank in the Air Force above senior master sergeant

chief of staff l : the ranking officer of a military staff and principal adviser to the commander **2** : the ranking office of the Army or Air Force

chief of state : the formal head of a national state as distinguished from the head of the government

chief petty officer *n* : an enlisted rank in the Navy and Coast Guard above petty officer first class and below senior chief petty officer

chief·tain \'chēf-tən\ *n* : a chief especially of a band, tribe, or clan [Middle French *chevetain,* from Late Latin *capitaneus* "chief"] — **chief·tain·cy** \-sē\ *n* — **chief·tain·ship** \-‚ship\ *n*

chief warrant officer *n* : any of the three warrant officer ranks in the Navy and Coast Guard and the three upper warrant officer ranks in the Army, Marine Corps, and Air Force

¹chif·fon \shif-'än, 'shif-‚\ *n* : a sheer usually silk fabric [French, literally, "rag", from Middle French *chipe* "old rag", from Middle English *chip* "chip"]

²chiffon *adj* : having a light soft texture ⟨a *chiffon* cake⟩

chif·fo·nier \‚shif-ə-'niər\ *n* : a high narrow chest of drawers often with a mirror [French *chiffonnier,* from *chiffon*]

chig·ger \'chig-ər, 'jig-\ *n* **l** : CHIGOE 1 **2** : a 6-legged larval mite that sucks the blood of vertebrates and causes intense irritation [of African origin]

chi·gnon \'shēn-‚yän\ *n* : a knot of hair worn at the back of the head [French]

Chi·hua·hua \chə-'wä-‚wä, shə-, -‚wə\ *n* : a very small round-headed large-eared dog held to antedate Aztec civilization [*Chihuahua,* Mexico]

chil·blain \'chil-‚blān\ *n* : an inflammatory swelling or sore caused by exposure (as of the feet or hands) to cold

child \'chīld\ *n, pl* **chil·dren** \'chil-drən, -dərn\ **l** : an unborn or recently born person **2 a** : a young person especially between infancy and youth **b** : a childlike or childish person **c** : a person not yet of legal age **3** *usually* **childe** \'chīld\ *archaic* : a youth of noble birth **4 a** : a son or daughter of human parents **b** : DE-SCENDANT 1 **5** : one strongly influenced by another or by a place or state of affairs ⟨a *child* of the times⟩ [Old English *cild*] — **child·less** \'chīl-ləs, -dləs\ *adj* — **with child** : PREGNANT

child·bear·ing \'chīl-‚bar-ing, 'chīld-, -‚ber-\ *adj* : of or relating to the process of conceiving, being pregnant with, and giving birth to children — **childbearing** *n*

child·bed fever \'chīl-‚bed-, 'chīld-\ *n* : PUERPERAL FEVER

child·birth \'chīl-‚bərth, 'chīld-\ *n* : the act or process of giving birth to offspring — called also *parturition*

child·hood \'chīld-‚hud\ *n* : the state or time of being a child

child·ish \'chīl-dish\ *adj* **l** : of, resembling, or suitable to a child ⟨*childish* games⟩ **2** : marked by the less pleasing qualities (as silliness) often felt to be characteristic of the young — **child·ish·ly** *adv* — **child·ish·ness** *n*

child·like \'chīl-‚līk, -‚dlīk\ *adj* **l** : of, relating to, or resembling a child or childhood **2** : marked by the more pleasing qualities (as simplicity, innocence, and trustfulness) often felt to be characteristic of the young — **child·like·ness** *n*

child's play *n* **l** : an extremely simple task **2** : something that is unimportant

child·proof \'chīld-‚prüf\ *adj* : made to prevent tampering by children ⟨a *childproof* bottle⟩

Chile saltpeter \'chil-ē-\ *n* : sodium nitrate especially occurring naturally [*Chile,* South America]

chili *or* **chile** *or* **chil·li** \'chil-ē\ *n, pl* **chil·ies** *or* **chil·es** *or* **chil·lies l** : HOT PEPPER 1 **2** : CHILI CON CARNE [Spanish *chile,* from Nahuatl *chilli*]

chili con car·ne \‚chil-ē-‚kän-'kär-nē, -ē-kən-\ *n* : a stew of ground beef, hot peppers or chili powder, and usually beans [Spanish *chile con carne* "chili with meat"]

chili dog *n* : a hot dog topped with chili

chili powder *n* : a seasoning made of ground hot peppers, oregano, garlic, cloves, and allspice

chili sauce *n* : a spiced tomato sauce usually made with red and green peppers

¹chill \'chil\ *vb* **l** : to make or become cold or chilly **2** : to harden the surface of (metal) by sudden cooling [Old English *cele* "cold, frost"] — **chill·er** *n* — **chill·ing·ly** \-ing-lē\ *adv*

²chill *adj* **l a** : fairly cold ⟨a *chill* night⟩ **b** : COLD 1, RAW ⟨a *chill* wind⟩ **2** : affected by cold **3** : cool in manner : DISTANT ⟨a *chill* greeting⟩ — **chill·ness** *n*

³chill *n* **l** : a sensation of cold accompanied by shivering **2** : a moderate but unpleasant degree of cold **3** : a depressing effect on the feelings

chill out *vi, slang* : to calm down : go easy — often used in the imperative

chilly \'chil-ē\ *adj* **chill·i·er; -est l** : noticeably cold **2** : unpleasantly affected by cold **3** : lacking warmth of

\ə\ abut		\ng\ sing	
\ər\ further		\ō\ bone	
\a\ mat		\ȯ\ saw	
\ā\ take		\ȯi\ coin	
\ä\ cot, cart		\th\ thin	
\aủ\ out		\th\ this	
\ch\ chin		\ü\ food	
\e\ pet		\u̇\ foot	
\ē\ easy		\y\ yet	
\g\ go		\yü\ few	
\i\ tip		\yu̇\ cure	
\ī\ life		\zh\ vision	
\j\ job			

feeling — **chill·i·ly** \'chil-ə-lē\ *adv* — **chill·i·ness** \'chil-ē-nəs\ *n*

¹**chime** \'chīm\ *n* **1** : a musically tuned set of bells **2 a** : the sound of a set of bells — usually used in pl. **b** : a musical sound suggesting that of bells [Middle English, "cymbal", from Old French *chimbe,* from Latin *cymbalum*]

²**chime** *vb* **1 a** : to make a musical and usually harmonious sound **b** : to make the sounds of a chime **c** : to cause to chime **2** : to be or act in accord **3** : to call or indicate by chiming ⟨a clock *chiming* midnight⟩ **4** : to utter repetitively — **chim·er** *n*

chime in *vb* : to break into or join in a conversation

chi·me·ra *or* **chi·mae·ra** \kī-'mir-ə, kə-\ *n* **1** *cap* : a fire-breathing she-monster in Greek mythology usually with a lion's head, a goat's body, and a serpent's tail **2** : an often grotesque creation of the imagination **3** : an individual, organ, or part with tissues of diverse genetic constitution [Latin *chimaera,* from Greek *chimaira* "she-goat, chimera"]

chi·mer·i·cal \kī-'mer-i-kəl, kə-, -'mir-\ *or* **chi·mer·ic** \-ik\ *adj* **1** : existing only in the imagination **2** : inclined to fantastic ideas or schemes — **chi·mer·i·cal·ly** \-i-kə-lē, -klē\ *adv*

chi·mi·chan·ga \,chim-ē-'chäng-gə\ *n* : a tortilla wrapped around a filling (as of meat) and fried in deep fat [Mexican Spanish, "trinket"]

chim·ney \'chim-nē\ *n, pl* **chimneys** **1** : a passage for smoke; *esp* : an upright structure (as of brick or stone) extending above the roof of a building **2** : a glass tube around a lamp flame [Middle French *cheminée,* from Late Latin *caminata,* from Latin *caminus* "furnace, fireplace", from Greek *kaminos*]

chim·ney·piece \'chim-nē-,pēs\ *n* : a decorative construction over and around a fireplace that includes the mantel

chimney pot *n* : a usually earthenware pipe at the top of a chimney to increase draft and carry off smoke

chimney sweep *n* : a person who cleans soot from chimneys

chimney swift *n* : a small sooty-gray bird with long narrow wings that often attaches its nest to the inside of an unused chimney

chimp \'chimp, 'shimp\ *n* : CHIMPANZEE

chim·pan·zee \,chim-,pan-'zē, ,shim-; chim-'pan-zē, shim-\ *n* : an African anthropoid ape that is smaller, weaker, and more arboreal than the gorilla [of African origin]

chimpanzee

¹**chin** \'chin\ *n* : the lower portion of the face lying below the lower lip and including the prominence of the lower jaw [Old English *cinn*]

²**chin** *vb* **chinned; chin·ning** **1** : to raise (oneself) while hanging by the hands until the chin is level with the support **2** *slang* : to talk idly : CHATTER

chi·na \'chī-nə\ *n* **1** : vitreous porcelain ware originally from the Orient; *also* : PORCELAIN **2** : articles (as dishes) of porcelain or earthenware for domestic use [Persian *chīnī* "Chinese porcelain"]

chi·na·ber·ry \'chī-nə-,ber-ē\ *n* **1** : a soapberry of the southern United States and Mexico **2** : a small Asiatic tree of the mahogany family naturalized in the southern United States where it is widely planted for shade or ornament

Chi·na·man \'chī-nə-mən\ *n* : CHINESE 1 — often taken to be offensive

Chi·na·town \-,taùn\ *n* : the Chinese quarter of a city

China tree *n* : CHINABERRY 2

chi·na·ware \'chī-nə-,waər, -,weər\ *n* : tableware made of china

chinch \'chinch\ *n* : BEDBUG [Spanish *chinche,* from Latin *cimex*]

chinch bug *n* : a small black-and-white bug very destructive to cereal grasses

chin·chil·la \chin-'chil-ə\ *n* **1** : a South American rodent the size of a large squirrel widely bred in captivi-

chipmunk

ty for its very soft fur of a pearly gray color; *also* : its fur **2** : a heavy twilled woolen coating [Spanish]

chine \'chīn\ *n* **1** : BACKBONE, SPINE; *also* : a cut of meat or fish including the backbone or part of it and the surrounding flesh **2** : CREST 2, RIDGE **3** : the intersection of the bottom and sides of a boat [Middle French *eschine,* of Germanic origin]

Chi·nese \chī-'nēz, -'nēs\ *n, pl* **Chinese** **1 a** : a native or inhabitant of China **b** : a person of Chinese descent **2 a** : a group of related languages used by the people of China that are often mutually unintelligible in their spoken form but share a single system of writing **b** : MANDARIN 2 — **Chinese** *adj*

Chinese cabbage *n* : either of two Asian plants related to the common cabbage and widely used as greens

Chinese checkers *n* : a game in which each player in turn transfers his or her pieces from a home point to the opposite point of a 6-pointed star by means of single moves and jumps

Chinese lantern *n* : a collapsible lantern of thin colored paper

Chinese liver fluke *n* : a common and destructive Asian liver fluke that invades the human liver

Chinese puzzle *n* **1** : an elaborate or clever puzzle **2** : something complex and hard to solve

Ching *or* **Ch'ing** \'ching\ *n* : a Manchu dynasty in China dated 1644–1912 and the last imperial dynasty

¹**chink** \'chingk\ *n* : a narrow slit or crack (as in a wall) [probably from Middle English *chin* "crack, fissure", from Old English *cine*]

²**chink** *vt* : to fill the chinks of (as by caulking)

³**chink** *n* : a short sharp sound [imitative]

⁴**chink** *vb* : to make or cause to make a short sharp sound

chi·no \'chē-nō, 'shē-\ *n, pl* **chinos** **1** : a usually khaki cotton twill fabric **2 a** : an article of clothing made of chino **b** *pl* : chino pants [origin unknown]

Chi·nook \shə-'nùk, chə-\ *n* **1** : a member of an Indian people of the shores of the Columbia river **2** *not cap* **a** : a warm moist southwest wind of the coast from Oregon northward **b** : a warm dry wind that descends the eastern slopes of the Rocky mountains

Chinook salmon *n* : a large commercially important salmon of the northern Pacific ocean usually with red flesh

chin·qua·pin \'ching-ki-,pin\ *n* : an American dwarf chestnut; *also* : its edible nut [of American Indian origin]

chintz \'chins\ *n* **1** : a printed calico from India **2** : a usually glazed printed cotton fabric [earlier *chints,* plural of *chint,* from Hindi *chīṭ*]

chintzy \'chin-sē\ *adj* **chintz·i·er; -est** **1** : decorated with or as if with chintz **2** : TAWDRY

chin–up \'chin-,əp\ *n* : the act or an instance of chinning oneself especially as a conditioning exercise

¹**chip** \'chip\ *n* **1 a** : a small piece (as of stone) broken off by a sharp blow : FLAKE **b** (1) : a thin crisp slice of potato (2) : FRENCH FRY **2 a** : a counter used in poker **b** *pl, slang* : MONEY 1, 2 **3** : a piece of dried dung ⟨cow *chip*⟩ **4** : a flaw left after a small piece has been broken off ⟨a cup with a *chip* in it⟩ **5** : INTEGRATED CIRCUIT [Middle English] — **chip off the old block** : a child that resembles his or her parent — **chip on one's shoulder** : a challenging or belligerent attitude

²**chip** *vb* **chipped; chip·ping** **1 a** : to cut with an edged tool ⟨*chip* ice from a sidewalk⟩ **b** (1) : to cut or break (a small piece) from something (2) : to cut or break a chip from ⟨*chip* a cup⟩ **2** : to break off in small pieces

chip in *vb* : CONTRIBUTE ⟨everyone *chipped in* to buy the gift⟩

chip·munk \'chip-,məngk\ *n* : any of numerous small striped largely terrestrial American squirrels [of American Indian origin]

chipped beef \'chipt-, 'chip-\ *n* : smoked dried beef sliced thin

Chip·pen·dale \\'chip-ən-ˌdāl\\ *adj* : of or relating to a late 18th century English furniture style characterized by graceful outline and often ornate ornamentation [Thomas *Chippendale,* died 1779, English cabinetmaker]

chip·per \\'chip-ər\\ *adj* : SPRIGHTLY, GAY (looks bright and *chipper* every morning) [perhaps from English dialect *kipper* "lively"]

Chip·pe·wa \\'chip-ə-ˌwȯ, -,-wä, -ˌwā\\ *n* : OJIBWA

chip·ping sparrow \\'chip-ing-\\ *n* : a small eastern North American sparrow whose song is a monotonous trill

chiro- *combining form* : hand (*chiro*practic) [Greek *cheir*]

chi·rog·ra·phy \\kī-'räg-rə-fē\\ *n* 1 : HANDWRITING 1, PENMANSHIP 2 : CALLIGRAPHY 1 — **chi·rog·ra·pher** \\-fər\\ *n* — **chi·ro·graph·ic** \\ˌkī-rə-'graf-ik\\ *adj*

chi·rop·o·dy \\kə-'räp-əd-ē\\ *n* : PODIATRY [*chir-* + *-pod,* from its original concern with both hands and feet] — **chi·rop·o·dist** \\-əd-əst\\ *n*

chi·ro·prac·tic \\'kī-rə-ˌprak-tik\\ *n* : a system of therapy based on manipulation and adjustment of body structures (as the spinal column) [*chir-* + Greek *praktikos* "practical, operative"] — **chi·ro·prac·tor** \\-tər\\ *n*

chi·rop·ter·an \\kī-'räp-tə-rən\\ *n* : ³BAT [Greek *cheir* "hand" + *pteron* "wing"]

chirp \\'chərp\\ *n* : the characteristic short sharp sound of a small bird or cricket [imitative] — **chirp** *vi*

chirr \\'chər\\ *n* : the characteristic vibrant or trilled sound of a cicada [imitative] — **chirr** *vi*

chir·rup \\'chər-əp, 'chir-\\ *n* : CHIRP [imitative] — **chirrup** *vb*

¹chis·el \\'chiz-əl\\ *n* : a metal tool with a cutting edge at the end of a blade used to shape or chip away stone, wood, or metal [Old North French, derived from Latin *caedere* "to cut"]

²chisel *vb* **-eled** *or* **-elled; -el·ing** *or* **-el·ling** \\'chiz-ling, -ə-ling\\ 1 : to cut or work with or as if with a chisel 2 a : to use shrewd sometimes unfair practices b : CHEAT — **chis·el·er** \\'chiz-lər, -ə-lər\\ *n*

chis·eled *or* **chis·elled** \\'chiz-əld\\ *adj* : appearing as if shaped with a chisel : finely cut (sharply *chiseled* features)

chi–square \\'kī-'skwaər, -'skweər\\ *n* : a statistic that is a sum of terms each of which is a quotient obtained by dividing the square of the difference between the observed and theoretical values of a quantity by the theoretical value

chit \\'chit\\ *n* 1 : CHILD 2a 2 : a pert young woman [Middle English *chitte* "kitten, cub"]

chit·chat \\'chit-ˌchat\\ *n* : SMALL TALK, GOSSIP [reduplication of *chat*]

chi·tin \\'kīt-n\\ *n* : a horny substance that forms part of the hard outer integument of some invertebrates (as insects and crustaceans) [French *chitine,* from Greek *chitōn* "chiton, tunic"] — **chi·tin·ous** \\-əs\\ *adj*

chi·ton \\'kīt-n, 'kī-ˌtän\\ *n* 1 : any of a class (Amphineura) of bilaterally symmetrical marine mollusks with a dorsal shell of calcareous plates 2 : a tunic worn in ancient Greece [Greek *chitōn* "tunic", of Semitic origin]

chit·ter \\'chit-ər\\ *vi* 1 : TWITTER 1, CHIRP 2 : CHATTER 1 [Middle English *chiteren*]

chit·ter·lings *or* **chit·lings** *or* **chit·lins** \\'chit-lənz\\ *n pl* : the intestines of hogs especially when prepared as food [Middle English *chiterling*]

chi·val·ric \\shə-'val-rik\\ *adj* : of or relating to chivalry : CHIVALROUS

chiv·al·rous \\'shiv-əl-rəs\\ *adj* 1 : VALIANT 2 : of or relating to chivalry 3 : having or displaying the qualities of an ideal knight of the age of chivalry: as a : marked by honor, generosity, and courtesy b : marked by especial courtesy and consideration to women — **chiv·al·rous·ly** *adv* — **chiv·al·rous·ness** *n*

chiv·al·ry \\-rē\\ *n, pl* **-ries** 1 : a body of knights (the *chivalry* of France) 2 : the system, spirit, ways, or customs of medieval knighthood 3 : the qualities (as bravery, honor, protection of the weak, and generous treatment of foes) held to characterize an ideal knight [Old French *chevalerie,* from *chevalier*]

chive \\'chīv\\ *n* : a perennial herb related to the onion and used for flavoring [Old North French, from Latin *cepa* "onion"]

chivy \\'chiv-ē\\ *vt* **chiv·ied; chivy·ing** : to annoy or bother repeatedly about little things [from *chivy* "hunt, chase"]

chla·my·do·spore \\klə-'mid-ə-ˌspōr, -ˌspȯr\\ *n* : a thick-walled usually resting spore [Greek *chlamyd-, chlamys* "mantle"]

chlor- *or* **chloro-** *combining form* 1 : green (*chlor*osis) 2 : chlorine (*chlor*tetracycline) [Greek *chlōros* "greenish yellow"]

chlo·ral hydrate \\'klōr-əl-, 'klȯr-\\ *n* : a bitter white crystalline drug $C_2H_3Cl_3O_2$ used to bring sleep — called also *chloral*

chlor·am·phen·i·col \\ˌklōr-am-'fen-i-ˌkōl, ˌklȯr-, -ˌkōl\\ *n* : a broad-spectrum antibiotic originally isolated from cultures of a soil microorganism or prepared synthetically

chlo·rate \\'klōr-ˌāt, 'klȯr-\\ *n* : a salt of chloric acid

chlor·dane \\'klȯr-ˌdān\\ *or* **chlor·dan** \\-ˌdan\\ *n* : a viscous volatile liquid insecticide $C_{10}H_6Cl_8$ [*chlor-* + *indane, indan* (C_9H_{10})]

chlor·di·az·epox·ide \\ˌklōr-dī-ˌaz-ə-'päk-ˌsīd, ˌklȯr-\\ *n* : a compound the hydrochloride of which is used as a tranquilizer — compare LIBRIUM

chlo·rel·la \\klə-'rel-ə\\ *n* : any of a genus of unicellular green algae potentially a cheap source of high-grade protein and B-complex vitamins [derived from Greek *chlōros* "greenish yellow"]

chlo·ren·chy·ma \\klōr-'eng-kə-mə, klȯr-\\ *n* : chlorophyll-containing tissue [*chlor-* + *-enchyma* (as in *parenchyma*)]

chlo·ric acid \\'klōr-ik-, 'klȯr-\\ *n* : a strong acid $HClO_3$ like nitric acid in oxidizing properties but far less stable

chlo·ride \\'klōr-ˌīd, 'klȯr-\\ *n* : a chemical compound of chlorine with another element or radical; *esp* : a salt or ester of hydrochloric acid

chloride of lime : BLEACHING POWDER

chlo·ri·nate \\'klōr-ə-ˌnāt, 'klȯr-\\ *vt* : to treat or cause to combine with chlorine especially for purifying — **chlo·ri·na·tion** \\ˌklōr-ə-'nā-shən, klȯr-\\ *n* — **chlo·ri·na·tor** \\'klōr-ə-ˌnāt-ər, 'klȯr-\\ *n*

chlorinated lime *n* : BLEACHING POWDER

chlo·rine \\'klōr-ˌēn, 'klȯr-, -ən\\ *n* : a chemical element that is a heavy greenish yellow irritating gas of pungent odor used especially as a bleach, oxidizing agent, and disinfectant in water purification — see ELEMENT table

chlo·rite \\'klōr-ˌīt, 'klȯr-\\ *n* : any of a group of usually green minerals associated with and resembling the micas

chlo·ro·flu·o·ro·car·bon \\ˌklōr-ō-ˌflùr-ō-'kär-bən, ˌklȯr-, -ˌflù-ər-\\ *n* : a compound containing carbon, chlorine, fluorine, and sometimes hydrogen that is used as a refrigerant, solvent, or aerosol propellant or in the manufacture of plastic foams

¹chlo·ro·form \\'klōr-ə-ˌfȯrm, 'klȯr-\\ *n* : a colorless volatile heavy poisonous liquid $CHCl_3$ with anesthetic properties that smells like ether and is used especially as a solvent [*chlor-* + *form*ic acid]

²chloroform *vt* : to treat with chloroform especially so as to produce anesthesia or death

chlo·ro·phyll \\'klōr-ə-ˌfil, 'klȯr-, -fəl\\ *n* : the green photosynthetic coloring matter of plants found in chloroplasts and made up chiefly of a bluish black ester $C_{55}H_{72}MgN_4O_5$ and a dark green ester $C_{55}H_{70}MgN_4O_6$ — called also respectively *chlorophyll a, chlorophyll*

\\ə\\ abut	\\ng\\ sing
\\ər\\ further	\\ō\\ bone
\\a\\ mat	\\ȯ\\ saw
\\ā\\ take	\\ȯi\\ coin
\\ä\\ cot, cart	\\th\\ thin
\\aù\\ out	\\th\\ this
\\ch\\ chin	\\ü\\ food
\\e\\ pet	\\ù\\ foot
\\ē\\ easy	\\y\\ yet
\\g\\ go	\\yü\\ few
\\i\\ tip	\\yù\\ cure
\\ī\\ life	\\zh\\ vision
\\j\\ job	

b [French *chlorophylle,* from *chlor-* "chlor-" + Greek *phyllon* "leaf"] — **chlo·ro·phyl·lose** \,klōr-ə-'fil-,ōs, ,klȯr-, -,fil-'\ *adj* — **chlo·ro·phyl·lous** \-'fil-əs\ *adj*

chlo·ro·plast \'klōr-ə-,plast, 'klȯr-\ *n* : a plastid that contains chlorophyll and is the seat of photosynthesis and starch formation in a plant cell

chlo·ro·quine \'klōr-ə-,kwēn, 'klȯr-\ *n* : a drug $C_{18}H_{26}ClN_3$ administered in the form of a phosphate for the treatment of malaria [*chlor-* + *quinine*]

chlo·ro·sis \klə-'rō-səs\ *n, pl* **-ro·ses** \-'rō-,sēz\ 1 : an anemia in which the skin is greenish 2 : a disorder of green plants marked by yellowing or blanching — **chlo·rot·ic** \-'rät-ik\ *adj*

chlor·prom·azine \klȯr-'präm-ə-,zēn, klȯr-, -zən\ *n* : a phenothiazine derivative $C_{17}H_{19}ClN_2S$ used as a tranquilizer in the form of its hydrochloride — compare THORAZINE

chlor·tet·ra·cy·cline \,klōr-,te-trə-'sī-,klēn, ,klȯr-\ *n* : a yellow crystalline antibiotic $C_{22}H_{23}ClN_2O_8$ produced by a soil actinomycete, used in the treatment of diseases, and added to animal feeds for stimulating growth

¹**chock** \'chäk\ *n* 1 : a wedge or block for steadying a body (as a cask) and holding it motionless, for filling in an unwanted space, or for blocking the movement of a wheel 2 : a metal fitting with two short arms curving inward between which ropes may pass for mooring or towing [origin unknown]

²**chock** *vt* : to stop or make fast with or as if with chocks

chock·a·block \'chäk-ə-,bläk\ *adj* : very full : CROWDED

chock–full \'chək-'ful, 'chäk-\ *or* **chuck–full** \'chək-\ *adj* : full to the limit [Middle English *chokkefull,* probably from *choken* "to choke" + *full*]

choc·o·late \'chäk-lət, 'chȯk-, -ə-lət\ *n* 1 : a food prepared from ground roasted cacao beans 2 : a beverage of chocolate in water or milk 3 : a candy with a chocolate coating 4 : a brownish gray color [Spanish, from Nahuatl *xocoatl*] — **chocolate** *adj*

Choc·taw \'chäk-,tȯ\ *n* 1 : a member of an Indian people of what is now Mississippi, Alabama, and Louisiana 2 : the language of the Choctaw and Chickasaw people [Choctaw *Chahta*]

¹**choice** \'chȯis\ *n* 1 : the act of choosing : SELECTION 2 : power of choosing : OPTION 3 a : a person or thing chosen b : the best part : CREAM 4 : a sufficient number and variety for wide or free selection [Old French *chois,* from *choisir* "to choose", of Germanic origin] □ SYN CHOICE, OPTION, ALTERNATIVE, PREFERENCE mean the act or opportunity of choosing or the thing chosen. CHOICE suggests the opportunity or privilege of choosing freely; OPTION implies a power to choose that is specifically granted or guaranteed; ALTERNATIVE implies a necessity to choose one and reject another possibility; PREFERENCE suggests the guidance of choice by one's judgment or inclinations.

²**choice** *adj* 1 : very fine : better than most ⟨*choice* fruits⟩ 2 : of a grade between prime and good ⟨*choice* meat⟩ — **choice·ly** *adv* — **choice·ness** *n*

choir \'kwīr\ *n* 1 : an organized group of singers especially in a church 2 : the part of a church assigned to the choir and usually located between the sanctuary and the nave 3 : any of the nine ranks of angels 4 : a group of instruments of the same class [Old French *cuer,* from Latin *chorus* "chorus"]

choir·boy \-,bȯi\ *n* : a boy member of a church choir

choir loft *n* : a gallery occupied by a church choir

choir·mas·ter \-,mas-tər\ *n* : the director of a choir (as in a church)

¹**choke** \'chōk\ *vb* 1 : to hinder normal breathing by cutting off the supply of air 2 : to have the windpipe stopped entirely or partly ⟨*choke* on a bone⟩ 3 : to check the growth or action of : SUPPRESS, SMOTHER ⟨*choke* a fire⟩ ⟨*choke* back tears⟩ 4 : to obstruct by clogging ⟨leaves *choked* the sewer⟩ 5 : to fill to the limit ⟨the store was *choked* with customers⟩ 6 : to de-

crease or shut off the air intake of the carburetor of a gasoline engine in order to make the fuel mixture richer [Old English *acēocian*]

²**choke** *n* : something that chokes: as **a** : a valve for choking a gasoline engine **b** : a narrowing toward the muzzle in the bore of a gun **c** : a coil of wire that provides inductance in an electric circuit and is used to impede the flow of current, to block surges of current, or to filter out unwanted frequencies — called also *choke coil*

choke·cher·ry \-,cher-ē, -'cher-\ *n* : any of several American wild cherries with bitter or astringent fruit; *also* : this fruit

choke up *vi* 1 : to become or feel choked (as from strong emotion) 2 : to become flustered and perform poorly

choky \'chō-kē\ *adj* : inclined to choke : having a tendency to choke ⟨grew *choky* with fear⟩

chol- *or* **chole-** *combining form* : bile : gall ⟨*chol*ine⟩ [Greek *cholē*]

cho·le·cys·ti·tis \,kō-lə-,sis-'tīt-əs\ *n* : inflammation of the gallbladder

cho·ler \'käl-ər, 'kō-lər\ *n* : a tendency toward sudden and often unreasonable irritability : IRASCIBILITY [Middle French *colere,* from Latin *cholera* "bilious disease", from Greek, from *cholē* "bile"]

chol·era \'käl-ə-rə\ *n* : any of several diseases usually marked by severe vomiting and dysentery; *esp* : ASIATIC CHOLERA [Latin, from Greek, from *cholē* "bile"] — **chol·e·ra·ic** \,käl-ə-'rā-ik\ *adj*

cho·ler·ic \'käl-ə-rik, kə-'ler-ik\ *adj* 1 : easily moved to anger : hot-tempered 2 : showing or expressing anger : IRATE SYN see IRASCIBLE

cho·les·ter·ol \kə-'les-tə-,rȯl, -,rōl\ *n* : a waxy substance $C_{27}H_{45}OH$ normally present in cells and tissues, important in many bodily processes, and possibly a contributing factor to arteriosclerosis when deposits in arteries are excessive [French *cholésterine,* from *chol-* "chol-" + Greek *stereos* "solid"]

cho·line \'kō-,lēn\ *n* : a basic substance $C_5H_{15}NO_2$ that is widely distributed in animal and plant products and is a vitamin of the vitamin B complex essential to liver function

cho·lin·er·gic \,kō-lə-'nər-jik\ *adj* : liberating or activated by acetylcholine ⟨a *cholinergic* nerve fiber⟩ [acetyl*choline* + Greek *ergon* "work"]

cho·lin·es·ter·ase \,kō-lə-'nes-tə-,rās, -,rāz\ *n* : ACETYLCHOLINESTERASE

chomp \'chämp, 'chȯmp\ *vb* : to chew or bite on noisily or vigorously [alteration of ¹*champ*]

choose \'chüz\ *vb* **chose** \'chōz\; **cho·sen** \'chōz-n\; **choos·ing** \'chü-zing\ 1 : to select according to preference especially after consideration ⟨*choose* a leader⟩ 2 **a** : DECIDE ⟨*chose* to go by train⟩ **b** : PREFER 3 : to see fit : INCLINE ⟨take them if you *choose*⟩ 4 : to make a choice [Old English *cēosan*] — **choos·er** *n*

choosy *or* **choos·ey** \'chü-zē\ *adj* **choos·i·er**; **-est** : inclined to be very selective : FASTIDIOUS, PARTICULAR

¹**chop** \'chäp\ *vt* **chopped**; **chop·ping** 1 : to cut by striking especially repeatedly with something sharp ⟨*chop* down a tree⟩ 2 : to cut into small pieces : MINCE ⟨*chopped* vegetables⟩ 3 : to strike (as a ball) with a short quick downward stroke [Middle English *chappen, choppen* "to chop, crack"] — **chop·per** *n*

²**chop** *n* 1 **a** : a forceful sudden stroke with a sharp instrument **b** : a sharp downward blow or stroke especially in sports 2 : a small cut of meat often including a part of a rib 3 : a short quick motion (as of a wave)

³**chop** *vi* **chopped**; **chop·ping** 1 : to change direction 2 : to veer with or as if with the wind [Old English *cēapian* "to barter"]

chop·fall·en *variant of* CHAPFALLEN

chop·house \'chäp-,haus\ *n* : RESTAURANT

chop·pi·ness \'chäp-ē-nəs\ *n* : the quality or state of being choppy

¹chop·py \'chäp-ē\ *adj* **chop·pi·er; -est** : subject to frequent changes : VARIABLE ⟨*choppy* winds⟩

²choppy *adj* **chop·pi·er; -est 1** : rough with small waves ⟨*choppy* seas⟩ **2** : JERKY, DISCONNECTED ⟨*choppy* sentences⟩

chops \'chäps\ *n pl* : the fleshy covering of the jaws ⟨the dog licked its *chops*⟩ [alteration of ⁴*chap*]

chop shop *n* : a place where stolen automobiles are stripped of salable parts

chop·stick \'chäp-ˌstik\ *n* : one of a pair of slender sticks used chiefly in oriental countries to lift food to the mouth [Pidgin English, from *chop* "fast", of Chinese origin]

chop su·ey \chäp-'sü-ē\ *n* : a dish prepared chiefly from bean sprouts, bamboo shoots, water chestnuts, onions, mushrooms, and meat or fish [Chinese (Cantonese) *shap sui* "odds and ends", from *shap* "miscellaneous" + *sui* "bits"]

cho·ral \'kōr-əl, 'kor-\ *adj* : of, relating to, or performed by a chorus or choir or in chorus — **cho·ral·ly** \-ə-lē\ *adv*

cho·rale \kə-'ral, -'räl\ *n* **1** : a hymn or psalm sung to a traditional or composed melody; *also* : a hymn tune or a harmonization of a traditional melody **2** : CHORUS 1c, CHOIR [German *choral*, short for *choralgesang* "choral song"]

¹chord \'kord\ *n* : a combination of tones that blend harmoniously when sounded together [Middle English *cord*, short for *accord*] — **chord·al** \-l\ *adj*

²chord *vi* : to play chords especially on a stringed instrument

³chord *n* **1** : CORD 3a **2** : a straight line joining two points on a curve **3** : an individual emotional response ⟨strike a familiar *chord*⟩ [alteration of ¹*cord*]

chor·date \'kor-ˌdāt, 'kord-ət\ *n* : any of a phylum or other major group (Chordata) of animals having at least at some stage of development a notochord, paired gill slits, and a dorsally situated central nervous system and including the vertebrates, amphioxi, and tunicates — compare HEMICHORDATE — **chordate** *adj*

chore \'chōr, 'chor\ *n* **1** *pl* : the routine duties of running a household or farm **2** : a difficult or disagreeable task ⟨reading should be fun, not a *chore*⟩ [Middle English *char* "turn, piece of work", from Old English *cierr*]

cho·rea \kə-'rē-ə\ *n* : a nervous disorder (as of humans or dogs) marked by spasmodic movements and lack of coordination [Latin, "dance", from Greek *choreia*, from *choros* "chorus"]

cho·re·og·ra·phy \ˌkōr-ē-'äg-rə-fē, ˌkor-\ *n, pl* **-phies** : the art of dancing or of composing or arranging dances and especially ballets [derived from Greek *choreia* "dance", from *choros* "chorus"] — **cho·reo·graph** \'kōr-ē-ə-ˌgraf, 'kor-\ *vt* — **cho·re·og·ra·pher** \ˌkōr-ē-'äg-rə-fər, ˌkor-\ *n* — **cho·reo·graphic** \-ē-ə-'graf-ik\ *adj* — **cho·reo·graph·i·cal·ly** \-'graf-i-kə-lē, -klē\ *adv*

cho·ric \'kōr-ik, 'kor-, 'kär-\ *adj* : of, relating to, or being in the style of a chorus and especially a Greek chorus

cho·rine \'kōr-ˌēn, 'kor-\ *n* : CHORUS GIRL

cho·rio·al·lan·to·is \ˌkōr-ē-ō-ə-'lant-ə-wəs, ˌkor-\ *n* : a vascular fetal membrane composed of the fused chorion and adjacent wall of the allantois — **cho·rio·al·lan·to·ic** \-ō-ˌal-ən-'tō-ik\ *adj*

cho·ri·on \'kōr-ē-ˌän, 'kor-\ *n* : the highly vascular outer embryonic membrane of higher vertebrates that in placental mammals joins the allantois in the formation of the placenta [Greek] — **cho·ri·on·ic** \ˌkōr-ē-'än-ik, ˌkor-\ *adj*

cho·ris·ter \'kōr-ə-stər, 'kor-, 'kär-\ *n* : a singer in a choir [Anglo-French *cueristre*, from Medieval Latin *chorista*, from Latin *chorus* "chorus"]

C-horizon *n* : the layer of a soil profile lying beneath the B–horizon and consisting essentially of more or less weathered parent rock

cho·roid \'kōr-ˌoid, 'kor-\ *also* **cho·ri·oid** \-ē-ˌoid\ *n* : a vascular pigmented membrane of the vertebrate eye lying between the sclera and the retina [Greek *chorioeidēs*, from *chorion* "chorion"] — **choroid** *adj*

choroid coat *n* : CHOROID

chor·tle \'chort-l\ *vi* **chor·tled; chor·tling** \'chort-ling, -l-ing\ : to express often smug satisfaction by or as if by a chuckling laugh [blend of *chuckle* and *snort*] — **chortle** *n* — **chor·tler** \'chort-lər, -l-ər\ *n*

¹cho·rus \'kōr-əs, 'kor-\ *n* **1 a** : a group of singers and dancers in Greek drama participating in or commenting on the action **b** : a character in Elizabethan drama who speaks the prologue and epilogue and comments on the action **c** : an organized group of singers : CHOIR; *esp* : a body of singers who sing the choral parts of a work (as in opera) **d** : a group of supporting dancers and singers in a musical comedy or revue **2 a** : a recurring part of a song or hymn **b** : the part of a drama sung or spoken by the chorus **c** : a composition to be sung by a chorus **3** : something uttered simultaneously by a number of persons ⟨a *chorus* of boos⟩ [Latin, from Greek *choros*] — **in chorus** : in unison

²chorus *vb* : to sing or utter in chorus

chorus girl *n* : a young woman who sings or dances in a chorus (as of a musical comedy) — called also *chorine*

chose *past of* CHOOSE

cho·sen \'chōz-n\ *adj* : selected or marked for favor or special privilege ⟨privileges granted to a *chosen* few⟩ [Middle English, from past participle of *choose* "to choose"]

Chou \'jō\ *n* : a Chinese dynasty traditionally dated 1122 to about 256 B.C. and marked by the development of the philosophical schools of Confucius and Lao-tzu

chough \'chəf\ *n* : an Old World black red-legged bird related to the crows [Middle English]

chow \'chaú\ *n, slang* : FOOD, VICTUALS [from *chow-chow*]

chow·chow \'chaù-ˌchaù\ *n* : a relish of chopped mixed pickles in mustard sauce [Chinese Pidgin English, "food"]

chow chow \'chaù-ˌchaù\ *n* : a thick-coated straight-legged muscular dog with a blue-black tongue and a short tail curled close to the back — called also *chow* [of Chinese origin]

chow·der \'chaúd-ər\ *n* : a soup or stew made of fish, clams, or a vegetable usually stewed in milk [French *chaudière* "kettle", from Late Latin *caldaria*, from Latin *calidus* "warm"]

chow mein \'chaù-'mān\ *n* : a thick stew of shredded or chopped meat, mushrooms, and vegetables usually served with fried noodles [Chinese (Pekingese) *ch'ao³ mien⁴*, from *ch'ao³* "to fry" + *mien⁴* "dough"]

chrism \'kriz-əm\ *n* : consecrated oil used especially in baptism, confirmation, and ordination [Late Latin *chrisma*, from Greek, "ointment", from *chriein* "to anoint"]

Christ \'krīst\ *n* **1** : MESSIAH 1 **2** : an ideal type of humanity [Latin *Christus*, from Greek *Christos*, literally, "anointed", from *chriein* "to anoint"]

chris·ten \'kris-n\ *vt* **chris·tened; chris·ten·ing** \'kris-ning, -n-ing\ **1 a** : BAPTIZE 1 **b** : to name at baptism **2** : to name or dedicate (as a ship) by a ceremony suggestive of baptism [Old English *cristnian*, from *cristen* "Christian", from Latin *christianus*]

Chris·ten·dom \'kris-n-dəm\ *n* **1** : the entire body of Christians **2** : all the countries or peoples that are predominantly Christian

chris·ten·ing *n* : the ceremony of baptizing and naming a child

¹Chris·tian \'kris-chən, 'krish-\ *n* **1** : a person who believes or professes belief in Jesus Christ and lives according to his teachings **2** : a member of a Christian church **3** : a member of a group (as the Disciples of

Christ or the Churches of Christ) seeking a return to New Testament Christianity

²Christian *adj* **I** : of or relating to Jesus Christ or the religion deriving from him **2** : of or relating to Christians ⟨a *Christian* nation⟩ **3 a** : befitting a Christian ⟨*Christian* charity⟩ **b** : KIND 1, MERCIFUL

Christian Brother *n* : a member of the Roman Catholic institute of Brothers of the Christian Schools founded in France in 1680 and devoted to primary and secondary education

Christian era *n* : the period dating from the birth of Christ

chris·ti·ania \,kris-chē-'an-ē-ə, ,krish-chē-, ,kris-tē-, -'än-\ *n* : CHRISTIE [*Christiania*, former name of Oslo, Norway]

Chris·ti·an·i·ty \,kris-chē-'an-ət-ē, ,krish-, -'chan-; ,kris-tē-'an-\ *n* **I** : the religion deriving from Jesus Christ **2** : Christian belief or practice

Chris·tian·ize \'kris-chə-,nīz, 'krish-\ *vt* : to make Christian — **Chris·tian·i·za·tion** \,kris-chə-nə-'zā-shən, ,krish-\ *n* — **Chris·tian·iz·er** *n*

christian name *n, often cap C* : the name given to a person at birth or christening as distinct from the family name

Christian Science *n* : a religion and system of healing founded by Mary Baker Eddy and taught by the Church of Christ, Scientist — **Christian Scientist** *n*

chris·tie *or* **chris·ty** \'kris-tē\ *n, pl* **christies** : a skiing turn made by shifting the body weight and skidding into a turn with the skis parallel — called also *christiania* [*Christiania*, former name of Oslo, Norway]

Christ·like \'krīst-,līk\ *adj* : resembling Christ in character or spirit

Christ·mas \'kris-məs\ *n* **I** : December 25 celebrated as a church festival in commemoration of the birth of Christ and observed as a legal holiday **2** : CHRISTMASTIDE [Old English *Cristes mæsse*, literally, "Christ's mass"]

Christmas club *n* : a savings account in which regular deposits are made throughout the year to provide money for Christmas shopping

Christmas fern *n* : a North American evergreen fern often used for winter decorations

Christ·mas·tide \'kris-mə-,stīd\ *n* : the festal season of Christmas

Christ·mas·time \-,stīm\ *n* : CHRISTMASTIDE

Christmas tree *n* : a usually evergreen tree decorated at Christmas

chrom- *or* **chromo-** *combining form* : color : colored ⟨*chromo*sphere⟩ [Greek *chrōma* "color"]

chro·ma \'krō-mə\ *n* : SATURATION 2

chromat- *or* **chromato-** *combining form* : color ⟨*chromat*in⟩ ⟨*chromato*graphy⟩ [Greek *chrōmat-, chrōma*]

chro·mate \'krō-,māt\ *n* : a salt or ester of chromic acid

¹chro·mat·ic \krō-'mat-ik\ *adj* **I** : of or relating to color or color phenomena; *esp* : being a shade other than black, gray, or white ⟨*chromatic* colors like green, red, blue⟩ **2** : of, relating to, or giving all the tones of the chromatic scale — **chro·mat·i·cal·ly** \-'mat-i-kə-lē, -klē\ *adv*

²chromatic *n* : ACCIDENTAL

chromatic aberration *n* : aberration caused by the differences in refraction of the colored rays of the spectrum

chromatic scale *n* : a musical scale that consists entirely of half steps

chro·ma·tid \'krō-mə-təd\ *n* : one of the paired longitudinal strands of a chromosome

chro·ma·tin \-tən\ *n* : a material present in chromosomes that contains the nuclear genes and stains deeply with basic dyes — **chro·ma·tin·ic** \,krō-mə-'tin-ik\ *adj*

chro·ma·to·gram \krō-'mat-ə-,gram, krə-\ *n* : the pattern formed on the adsorbent medium by the layers of components separated by chromatography

chro·ma·to·graph \krō-'mat-ə-,graf, krə-\ *n* : an instrument used in chromatography — **chromatograph** *vb*

chro·ma·tog·ra·phy \,krō-mə-'täg-rə-fē\ *n* : a separating especially of closely related compounds by allowing a solution or mixture of them to seep through an adsorbent (as clay or paper) so that each compound becomes adsorbed in a separate often colored layer — **chro·ma·to·graph·ic** \-,mat-ə-'graf-ik\ *adj* — **chro·ma·to·graph·i·cal·ly** \-i-kə-lē, -klē\ *adv*

chro·ma·to·phore \krō-'mat-ə-,fōr, -,fòr\ *n* : a pigment-bearing cell; *esp* : one capable of causing skin color changes in an animal by expanding or contracting

chrome \'krōm\ *n* **I a** : CHROMIUM **b** : a chromium pigment **2** : something plated with an alloy of chromium [French, from Greek *chrōma* "color"]

-chrome \,krōm\ *n or adj combining form* **I** : colored : colored thing : colored **2** : coloring matter

chrome green *n* : any of various brilliant green pigments containing or consisting of chromium compounds

chrome yellow *n* : any of various bright yellow pigments consisting essentially of a compound $PbCrO_4$ of lead, chromium, and oxygen

chro·mic \'krō-mik\ *adj* : of, relating to, or derived from chromium

chromic acid *n* : an acid H_2CrO_4 analogous to sulfuric acid but known only in solution

chro·mite \'krō-,mīt\ *n* : a mineral $FeCr_2O_4$ that consists of an oxide of iron and chromium and is an important ore of chromium

chro·mi·um \'krō-mē-əm\ *n* : a blue-white metallic element found naturally only in combination and used especially in alloys and in electroplating — see ELEMENT table [New Latin, from French *chrome*]

chro·mo·mere \'krō-mə-,miər\ *n* : one of the small bead-shaped and heavily staining concentrations of chromatin that are linearly arranged along the chromosome

chro·mo·ne·ma \,krō-mə-'nē-mə\ *n, pl* **-ne·ma·ta** \-'nē-mət-ə\ : the coiled filamentous core of a chromatid [*chrom-* + Greek *nēma* "thread"]

chro·mo·phore \'krō-mə-,fōr, -,fòr\ *n* : a group of atoms that gives rise to color in a molecule

chro·mo·plast \-,plast\ *n* : a colored plastid usually containing red or yellow pigment

chro·mo·some \'krō-mə-,sōm\ *n* : one of the usually elongated chromatin-containing bodies of a cell nucleus made up of chromatids, usually constant in number in any one kind of plant or animal, and seen especially during mitosis and meiosis — **chro·mo·som·al** \,krō-mə-'sō-məl\ *adj*

chromosome number *n* : the usually constant number of chromosomes characteristic of a particular kind of animal or plant

chro·mo·sphere \'krō-mə-,sfiər\ *n* : the inner part of the atmosphere of the sun composed chiefly of hydrogen

chron- *or* **chrono-** *combining form* : time ⟨*chrono*graph⟩ [Greek *chronos*]

chron·ic \'krän-ik\ *adj* **I a** : lasting a long time or recurring frequently ⟨*chronic* indigestion⟩ — compare ACUTE 5a **b** : suffering from a chronic disease **2 a** : constantly present or encountered ⟨*chronic* financial difficulties⟩ **b** : being such habitually ⟨a *chronic* complainer⟩ — **chron·i·cal·ly** \-i-kə-lē, -klē\ *adv* — **chron·ic·i·ty** \krä-'nis-ətē\ *n*

¹chron·i·cle \'krän-i-kəl\ *n* **I** : a historical account of events arranged in order of time without analysis or interpretation **2** : NARRATIVE 1 [Old French *chronique*, derived from Greek *chronos* "time"]

²chronicle *vt* **-cled**; **-cling** \-kəling, -kling\ : to record in or as if in a chronicle : tell the story of — **chron·i·cler** \-kə-lər, -klər\ *n*

Chron·i·cles \'krän-i-kəlz\ *n* — see BIBLE table

chro·no·graph \'krän-ə-ˌgraf, 'krō-nə-\ *n* : an instrument for measuring and recording time intervals with accuracy: as **a** : an instrument having a revolving drum on which a stylus makes marks **b** : a watch with a sweep-second hand — **chron·o·graph·ic** \ˌkrän-ə-'graf-ik, ˌkrō-nə-\ *adj* — **chro·nog·ra·phy** \krə-'näg-rə-fē\ *n*

chron·o·log·i·cal \ˌkrän-l-'äj-i-kəl, ˌkrōn-\ *adj* : arranged in or according to the order of time ⟨*chrono-logical* tables of American history⟩ — **chron·o·log·i·cal·ly** \-'äj-i-kə-lē, -klē\ *adv*

chro·nol·o·gy \krə-'näl-ə-jē\ *n, pl* **-gies 1** : the science that deals with measuring time by regular divisions and that assigns to events their proper dates **2** : a chronological table or list **3** : an arrangement (as of events) in order of occurrence — **chro·nol·o·gist** \-jəst\ *n*

chro·nom·e·ter \krə-'näm-ət-ər\ *n* : an instrument for measuring time; *esp* : one designed to keep time with great accuracy and used especially in navigation — **chron·o·met·ric** \ˌkrän-ə-'me-trik, ˌkrō-nə-\ *adj*

chro·no·scope \'krän-ə-ˌskōp, 'krō-nə-\ *n* : an instrument for precise measurement of small time intervals

chrys·a·lid \'kris-ə-ləd\ *n* : CHRYSALIS

chrys·a·lis \'kris-ə-ləs\ *n, pl* **chry·sal·i·des** \krə-'sal-ə-ˌdēz\ *or* **chrys·a·lis·es** \'kris-ə-lə-səz\ : the pupa of a butterfly [Latin *chrysallis* "gold-colored pupa of butterflies", from Greek, from *chrysos* "gold", of Semitic origin]

chry·san·the·mum \kris-'an-thə-məm, -ant-\ *n* **1** : any of a genus of plants related to the daisies that include weeds, ornamentals grown for their brightly colored often double flower heads, and important sources of medicinals and insecticides **2** : a flower head of an ornamental chrysanthemum [Latin, from Greek *chrysanthemon*, from *chrysos* "gold" + *anthemon* "flower"]

chrys·o·phyte \'kris-ə-ˌfīt\ *n* : GOLDEN-BROWN ALGA

chrys·o·prase \'kris-ə-ˌprāz\ *n* : a yellowish green chalcedony valued as a gem [derived from Greek *chrysoprasos*, from *chrysos* "gold" + *prason* "leek"]

chrys·o·tile \'kris-ə-ˌtīl\ *n* : a fibrous silky serpentine that is one kind of asbestos [derived from Greek *chrysos* "gold" + *tilos* "plucked hair", from *tillein* "to pluck"]

chub \'chəb\ *n, pl* **chub** *or* **chubs** : any of several small freshwater fishes related to the carp [Middle English *chubbe*]

chub·by \'chəb-ē\ *adj* **chub·bi·er; -est** : PLUMP ⟨*chubby* little children⟩ [*chub*] — **chub·bi·ness** *n*

¹chuck \'chək\ *vt* **1** : to give a pat or a tap to ⟨*chuck* a person under the chin⟩ **2** : THROW 2, TOSS ⟨*chuck* a ball back and forth⟩ **3** : DISCARD 2 [origin unknown]

²chuck *n* **1** : a pat or nudge under the chin **2** : THROW 1

³chuck *n* **1** : a portion of a side of dressed beef including most of the neck and the parts about the shoulder blade and the first three ribs **2** *chiefly West* : FOOD **3** : a device for holding work or a tool in a machine (as a drill press or lathe) [English dialect *chuck* "lump"]

chuck-full \'chək-ˈfùl\ *variant of* CHOCK-FULL

chuck·hole \'chək-ˌhōl, 'chəg-\ *n* : a hole or rut in a road [¹*chuck*]

chuck·le \'chək-əl\ *vi* **chuck·led; chuck·ling** \'chək-ling, -ə-ling\ : to laugh inwardly or quietly [probably from Middle English *chukken* "to cluck"] — **chuckle** *n*

chuck·le·head \'chək-əl-ˌhed\ *n* : BLOCKHEAD — **chuck·le·head·ed** \ˌchək-əl-'hed-əd\ *adj* [*chuckle* "lumpish", from English dialect *chuck* "lump"]

chuck wagon \'chək-\ *n* : a wagon carrying a stove and provisions for cooking (as on a ranch)

chuck·wal·la \'chək-ˌwäl-ə\ *n* : a large but harmless lizard of the desert regions of the southwestern United States [Mexican Spanish *chacahuala*, of American Indian origin]

chuck–will's–wid·ow \ˌchək-ˌwilz-'wid-ō\ *n* : a goatsucker of the southern United States [imitative]

¹chug \'chəg\ *n* : a dull explosive sound made by or as if by a laboring engine [imitative]

²chug *vi* **chugged; chug·ging** : to move or go with chugs ⟨a locomotive *chugging* along⟩

chuk·ka \'chək-ə\ *n* : a short usually ankle-length leather boot with two pairs of eyelets or a buckle and strap [alteration of *chukker*; from a similar polo player's boot]

chuk·ker *or* **chuk·kar** \'chək-ər\ *or* **chuk·ka** \'chək-ə\ *n* : a playing period of a polo game [Hindi *cakkar* "circular course", from Sanskrit *cakra* "wheel"]

¹chum \'chəm\ *n* : a close friend : PAL [perhaps by shortening and alteration from *chamber fellow* "roommate"]

²chum *vi* **chummed; chum·ming** : to be or become chums

chum·my \'chəm-ē\ *adj* **chum·mi·er; -est** : FAMILIAR 1, INTIMATE — **chum·mi·ly** \'chəm-ə-lē\ *adv* — **chum·mi·ness** \'chəm-ē-nəs\ *n*

chump \'chəmp\ *n* : DUPE [perhaps blend of *chunk* and *lump*]

chunk \'chəngk\ *n* **1** : a short thick piece : HUNK ⟨a *chunk* of meat⟩ **2** : a significant portion ⟨food takes a *chunk* out of the budget⟩ [perhaps alteration of English dialect *chuck* "lump"]

chunky \'chəng-kē\ *adj* **chunk·i·er; -est** : STOCKY — **chunk·i·ly** \-kə-lē\ *adv* — **chunk·i·ness** \-kē-nəs\ *n*

¹church \'chərch\ *n* **1** : a building for public and especially Christian worship **2 a** : a body or organization of religious believers **b** : the clergy of a religious body **3** : public worship especially in a church [Old English *cirice*, derived from Late Greek *kyriakon*, from Greek *kyriakos* "of the lord", from Greek *kyrios* "lord"] — **church·ly** \-lē\ *adj*

²church *vt* : to bring to church to receive one of its rites

church·go·er \-ˌgō-ər, -ˌgȯr\ *n* : one that goes to church especially regularly — **church·go·ing** \-ˌgō-ing\ *adj or n*

church·ing *n* : a ceremony in certain churches in which a woman is received in church with prayer and blessings after childbirth

church·man \-mən\ *n* **1** : CLERGYMAN **2** : a church member

Church of England : the established episcopal church of England

church·wom·an \-ˌwùm-ən\ *n* : a woman who is a church member

church·yard \'chərch-ˌyärd\ *n* : a yard that belongs to a church and is often used as a burial ground

churl \'chərl\ *n* **1** : a medieval peasant **2** : RUSTIC **3** : a rude or surly person [Old English *ceorl* "man, freeman of low rank"]

churl·ish \'chər-lish\ *adj* : offensive in action or manner : RUDE, SURLY — **churl·ish·ly** *adv* — **churl·ish·ness** *n*

¹churn \'chərn\ *n* : a vessel in which cream is agitated to separate the butterfat from the other parts [Old English *cyrin*]

²churn *vb* **1** : to agitate (milk or cream) in a churn in making butter : make (butter) by churning **2** : to work a churn in making butter **3** : to agitate or be agitated violently ⟨the wind *churned* up huge waves⟩

churr \'chər\ *vi* : to make a vibrant or whirring noise like that of a partridge [imitative] — **churr** *n*

chute \'shüt\ *n* **1** : a quick drop (as of a river) **2** : an inclined plane, trough, or passage down or through which things may pass ⟨a mail *chute*⟩ **3** : PARACHUTE 1 [French, "fall", from Old French, from *cheoir* "to fall", from Latin *cadere*]

chut·ney \'chət-nē\ *n, pl* **chutneys** : a relish of acid fruits, raisins, dates, and onions [Hindi *caṭnī*]

chyle \'kīl\ *n* : lymph milky from emulsified fats that is present especially in the lacteals during intestinal ab-

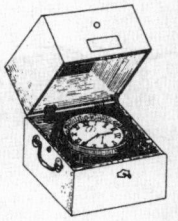

chronometer

sorption of fats [Late Latin *chylus,* from Greek *chylos* "juice, chyle", from *chein* "to pour"]

chyme \'kīm\ *n* : the semifluid mass of partly digested food that passes from the stomach into the duodenum [Late Latin *chymus* "chyle", from Greek *chymos* "juice", from *chein* "to pour"] — **chy·mous** \'kī-məs\ *adj*

chy·mo·tryp·sin \ˌkī-mō-'trip-sən\ *n* : a pancreatic enzyme that acts on proteins by breaking internal peptide bonds

ci·bo·ri·um \sə-'bōr-ē-əm, -'bòr-\ *n, pl* **-ria** \-ē-ə\ *or* **-riums 1** : a covered goblet-shaped vessel for holding eucharistic bread **2** : a vaulted canopy supported by four columns over a high altar [Latin, "cup", from Greek *kibōrion*]

ci·ca·da \sə-'kād-ə, -'käd-\ *n, pl* **-cadas** *also* **-ca·dae** \-'kād-ˌē, -ˌkäd-ˌē\ : any of a family of stout-bodied insects that are related to the bugs and have a wide blunt head and large transparent wings [Latin]

cicada

cic·a·trix \'sik-ə-ˌtriks, sə-'kā-triks\ *n, pl* **cic·a·tri·ces** \ˌsik-ə-'trī-ˌsēz, sə-'kā-trə-ˌsēz\ **1** : a scar resulting from formation and contraction of fibrous tissue in a flesh wound **2** : a scar marking the previous point of attachment of a part or organ (as a leaf or seed) [Latin] — **cic·a·tri·cial** \ˌsik-ə-'trish-əl\ *adj*

ci·ce·ro·ne \ˌsis-ə-'rō-nē, ˌchich-ə-\ *n, pl* **-ro·ni** \-ˌnē\ : GUIDE 1b [Italian, from *Cicerone* "Cicero"]

Cic·ero·nian \ˌsis-ə-'rō-nyən, -nē-ən\ *adj* : of, relating to, or characteristic of Cicero or his writings

cich·lid \'sik-ləd\ *n* : any of a family of mostly tropical spiny-finned freshwater fishes including several kept in tropical aquariums [derived from Greek *kichlē* "thrush, kind of fish"] — **cichlid** *adj*

-cide \ˌsīd\ *n combining form* **1** : killer ⟨insecti*cide*⟩ **2** : killing ⟨geno*cide*⟩ [Latin *-cida,* from *caedere* "to cut, kill"]

ci·der \'sīd-ər\ *n* : the fresh or fermented juice of fruit (as apples) used as a beverage or for making other products (as vinegar) [Old French *sidre,* from Late Latin *sicera* "strong drink", from Greek *sikera,* from Hebrew *shēkhār*]

ci·gar \sig-'är\ *n* : a roll of tobacco leaves for smoking [Spanish *cigarro*]

cig·a·rette *also* **cig·a·ret** \ˌsig-ə-'ret, 'sig-ə-ˌ\ *n* : a small roll of cut tobacco wrapped in paper for smoking

cil·i·ary \'sil-ē-ˌer-ē\ *adj* **1** : of or relating to cilia **2** : of, relating to, or being the muscular body supporting the lens of the eye

¹cil·i·ate \'sil-ē-ət, -ˌāt\ *or* **cil·i·at·ed** \-ˌāt-əd\ *adj* : provided with cilia

²ciliate *n* : any of a group (Ciliophora) of ciliate protozoans

cil·i·um \'sil-ē-əm\ *n, pl* **cil·ia** \-ē-ə\ **1** : EYELASH **2** : one of the tiny filaments of many cells that are capable of lashing movement [Latin, "eyelid"]

cim·me·ri·an \sə-'mir-ē-ən\ *adj, often cap* : very dark or gloomy [from *Cimmerians,* a mythical people in Homer dwelling in eternal gloom]

¹cinch \'sinch\ *n* **1** : a strong girth for a pack or saddle **2** : a tight grip **3 a** : a thing done or gained with ease **b** : a certainty to happen [Spanish *cincha,* from Latin *cingula* "girdle, girth", from *cingere* "to gird"]

²cinch *vt* **1** : to put a cinch on **2** : to make certain : ASSURE ⟨*cinched* the victory⟩

cin·cho·na \sing-'kō-nə, sin-'chō-\ *n* **1** : any of a genus of South American trees and shrubs **2** : the dried bark of a cinchona containing alkaloids (as quinine) and being used as a malaria remedy — called also *cinchona bark* [countess of *Chinchón,* died 1641, wife of the Peruvian viceroy] — **cin·chon·ic** \sing-'kän-ik, sin-'chän-\ *adj*

cinc·ture \'sing-chər, 'singk-\ *n* : BELT 1, GIRDLE [Latin *cinctura,* from *cingere* "to gird"]

cin·der \'sin-dər\ *n* **1** : waste matter from the smelting of metal ores : SLAG **2 a** : a piece of partly burned coal or wood in which fire is extinct **b** : a hot coal without flame **3** *pl* : ASH 2a **4** : a fragment of solidified lava from an erupting volcano [Old English *sinder*] — **cin·dery** \-də-rē, -drē\ *adj*

cinder block *n* : a building block made of concrete using coal cinders as aggregate

cine- *combining form* : motion picture [*cinema*]

cin·e·ma \'sin-ə-mə\ *n* **1** *chiefly British* : a motion-picture theater **2** : MOVIE [short for *cinematograph,* derived from Greek *kinēma* "motion", from *kinein* "to move"] — **cin·e·mat·ic** \ˌsin-ə-'mat-ik\ *adj* — **cin·e·mat·i·cal·ly** \-'mat-i-kə-lē, -klē\ *adv*

cin·e·mat·o·graph \ˌsin-ə-'mat-ə-ˌgraf\ *n, chiefly British* : a motion-picture camera, projector, theater, or show

cin·e·ma·tog·ra·phy \ˌsin-ə-mə-'täg-rə-fē\ *n* : the art or science of motion-picture photography — **cin·e·mat·o·graph·ic** \-ˌmat-ə-'graf-ik\ *adj*

cin·er·ar·ia \ˌsin-ə-'rer-ē-ə, -'rar-\ *n* : a pot plant related to the daisies that has heart-shaped leaves and clusters of bright flower heads [Latin *cinerarius* "of ashes", from *cinis* "ashes"]

cin·er·ar·i·um \-ē-əm\ *n, pl* **-ar·ia** \-ē-ə\ : a place to receive the ashes of the cremated dead [Latin, from *cinis* "ashes"] — **cin·er·ary** \'sin-ə-ˌrer-ē\ *adj*

cin·na·bar \'sin-ə-ˌbär\ *n* : a red mineral HgS that consists of a sulfide of mercury and is the only important ore of mercury [Latin *cinnabaris,* from Greek *kinnabari*]

cin·na·mon \'sin-ə-mən\ *n* **1 a** : the highly aromatic bark of any of several trees of the laurel family used as a spice **b** : a tree that yields cinnamon **2** : a light yellowish brown [Latin, from Greek *kinnamon*]

cinque·foil \'singk-ˌföil, 'sangk-\ *n* **1** : any of a genus of plants of the rose family with 5-lobed leaves **2** : a design consisting of five joined foils [Middle French *cincfoille,* from Latin *quinquefolium,* from *quinque* "five" + *folium* "leaf"]

ci·on *variant of* SCION

¹ci·pher \'sī-fər\ *n* **1 a** : ZERO 1 — see NUMBER table **b** : an insignificant individual : NONENTITY **2 a** : a method of transforming a text in order to conceal its meaning — compare CODE 4 **b** : a message in code **3** : ARABIC NUMERAL **4** : a combination of symbolic letters; *esp* : the interwoven initials of a name [Middle French *cifre,* from Medieval Latin *cifra,* from Arabic *ṣifr* "empty, cipher, zero"]

²cipher *vb* **ci·phered; ci·pher·ing** \-fə-ring, -fring\ **1** : to use figures in a mathematical process **2** : ENCIPHER **3** : to compute arithmetically ⟨a sum *ciphered* out⟩

cir·ca \'sər-kə, 'kiər-ˌkä\ *prep* : at, in, or of approximately — used with numerals and especially with dates ⟨born *circa* 1600⟩ [Latin, from *circum* "around"]

cir·ca·di·an \sər-'kād-ē-ən, -'kad-; ˌsər-kə-'dē-ən, -'dī-\ *adj* : being, having, or occurring in approximately 24-hour periods or cycles (as of biological activity or function) ⟨*circadian* rhythms in hatching⟩ [Latin *circa* "about" + *dies* "day" + English *-an*]

Cir·cas·sian walnut \sər-'kash-ən-\ *n* : the light brown irregularly black-veined wood of the English walnut much used for veneer and cabinetwork [*Circassia,* Russia]

cir·ci·nate \'sərs-n-ˌāt\ *adj* : COILED, ROUNDED; *esp* : rolled up on the axis with the apex as a center ⟨*circinate* fronds of ferns⟩ [Latin *circinare* "to round", from *circinus* "pair of compasses", from *circus* "circle, circus"] — **cir·ci·nate·ly** *adv*

¹cir·cle \'sər-kəl\ *n* **1 a** : HALO 1 **b** : a closed plane curve every point of which is equidistant from a fixed point within the curve **c** : the plane surface bounded by such a curve **2** : something in the form of a circle or section of a circle: as **a** : CIRCLET, DIADEM **b** : a balcony or tier of seats in a theater or opera house **c** : a circle on the surface of a sphere (as the earth) — compare GREAT CIRCLE, SMALL CIRCLE **d** : ROTARY 2 **3** :

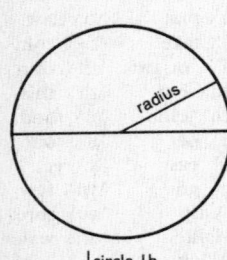
¹circle 1b

an area of action or influence : **REALM** **4 a** : **CYCLE** 2a, **ROUND** **b** : fallacious reasoning in which something apparently proved is really taken for granted **5** : a group bound by a common tie; *esp* : **COTERIE** [Old French *cercle,* from Latin *circulus,* from *circus* "circle, circus"]

²**circle** *vb* **cir·cled; cir·cling** \-kə-ling, -kling\ **I** : to enclose in or as if in a circle : **ENCIRCLE** **2** : to move or revolve around ⟨a spacecraft *circling* the earth⟩ **3** : to move in or as if in a circle — **cir·cler** \-kə-lər, -klər\ *n*

circle graph *n* : **PIE CHART**

cir·clet \'sər-klət\ *n* : a little circle; *esp* : a personal ornament (as a headband) in the form of a circle

cir·cuit \'sər-kət\ *n* **I** : a boundary line around an area; *also* : the space enclosed **2** : a moving or revolving around (as in a circle or orbit) : **CIRCLING** ⟨the *circuit* of the earth around the sun⟩ **3 a** : a regular tour (as by a judge or preacher) around an assigned territory **b** : the route traveled **4 a** : an association of similar groups : **LEAGUE** **b** : a group of establishments offering similar entertainment or presenting a series of contests; *esp* : a chain of theaters at which productions are successively presented **5 a** : the complete path of an electric current **b** : an assemblage of electronic elements : **HOOKUP** [Middle French *circuite,* from Latin *circuitus,* from *circuire* "to go around", from *circum* "around" + *ire* "to go"] — **circuit** *vb* — **cir·cuit·al** \-kət-l\ *adj*

circuit breaker *n* : a switch that automatically interrupts an electric circuit under an overload

circuit court *n* : a court that sits in two or more places in a judicial district

cir·cu·i·tous \sər-'kyü-ət-əs\ *adj* **I** : marked by a circular or winding course ⟨a *circuitous* route⟩ **2** : not being or going straight to the point : **INDIRECT** — **cir·cu·i·tous·ly** *adv* — **cir·cu·i·tous·ness** *n*

cir·cuit·ry \'sər-kə-trē\ *n, pl* **-ries** : the plan or the components of an electric circuit

cir·cu·i·ty \sər-'kyü-ət-ē\ *n* : **INDIRECTION** 1

¹**cir·cu·lar** \'sər-kyə-lər\ *adj* **I a** : having the form of a circle : **ROUND** ⟨a *circular* driveway⟩ **b** : having a circular base or bases ⟨a *circular* cone⟩ **2** : moving in or describing a circle or spiral **3** : relating to or forming part of a circle ⟨a *circular* arc⟩ **4** : **CIRCUITOUS, ROUNDABOUT** ⟨a *circular* explanation⟩ **5** : characterized by reasoning in a circle ⟨*circular* arguments⟩ **6** : sent around to a number of persons ⟨a *circular* letter⟩ — **cir·cu·lar·i·ty** \,sər-kyə-'lar-ət-ē\ *n* — **cir·cu·lar·ly** \'sər-kyə-lər-lē\ *adv* — **cir·cu·lar·ness** *n*

²**circular** *n* : a paper (as a leaflet containing an advertisement) intended for wide distribution

circular function *n* : **TRIGONOMETRIC FUNCTION**

cir·cu·lar·ize \'sər-kyə-lə-,rīz\ *vt* : to send circulars to — **cir·cu·lar·iza·tion** \,sər-kyə-lə-rə-'zā-shən\ *n*

circular saw *n* : a power saw having a revolving thin steel disk with teeth on its edge

cir·cu·late \'sər-kyə-,lāt\ *vb* **I** : to move or cause to move in a circle, circuit, or orbit; *esp* : to follow a course that returns to the starting point ⟨blood *circulates* through the body⟩ **2** : to pass from person to person or place to place: as **a** : to flow without obstruction ⟨air *circulating* through the house⟩ **b** : to become or cause to become well known or widespread ⟨*circulate* a rumor⟩ **c** : to come into the hands of readers ⟨a magazine that *circulated* widely⟩ — **cir·cu·la·tor** \-,lāt-ər\ *n*

cir·cu·la·tion \,sər-kyə-'lā-shən\ *n* **I** : orderly movement through a circuit; *esp* : the movement of blood through the vessels of the body caused by the pumping action of the heart **2 a** : passage or transmission from person to person or place to place; *esp* : the interchange of currency ⟨coins in *circulation*⟩ **b** : the extent of dissemination (as of copies of a publication sold over a given period) **3** : an active social life with different people ⟨back in *circulation* after the divorce⟩ — **cir·cu·la·tive** \'sər-kyə-,lāt-iv\ *adj*

cir·cu·la·to·ry \'sər-kyə-lə-,tōr-ē, -,tȯr-\ *adj* : of or relating to circulation (as of the blood) ⟨the *circulatory* system⟩

circum- *prefix* : around : about ⟨*circum*polar⟩ [Latin, from *circus* "circle"]

cir·cum·am·bi·ent \,sər-kəm-'am-bē-ənt\ *adj* : being on all sides : **ENCOMPASSING**

cir·cum·am·bu·late \-'am-byə-,lāt\ *vb* : to circle on foot especially as or as if part of a ritual

cir·cum·cen·ter \'sər-kəm-,sent-ər\ *n* : the point at which the perpendicular bisectors of the sides of a triangle intersect and which is equidistant from the three vertices

cir·cum·cise \'sər-kəm-,sīz\ *vt* : to cut off the foreskin of [Latin *circumcidere,* from *circum-* + *caedere* "to cut"]

cir·cum·ci·sion \,sər-kəm-'sizh-ən, 'sər-kəm-,\ *n* **I** : the act of circumcising or being circumcised; *esp* : a Jewish rite performed on male infants as a sign of inclusion in the covenant between God and Abraham **2** *cap* : January 1 observed as a church festival in commemoration of the circumcision of the infant Jesus

cir·cum·fer·ence \sər-'kəm-fərns, sə-, -'kəmp-, -fə-rəns, -frəns\ *n* **I** : the perimeter of a circle **2** : the external boundary or surface of a body : **PERIPHERY** [Middle French, from Latin *circumferentia,* from *circumferre* "to carry around", from *circum-* + *ferre* "to carry"] — **cir·cum·fer·en·tial** \-,kəm-fə-'ren-chəl, -,kəmp-\ *adj*

¹**cir·cum·flex** \'sər-kəm-,fleks\ *adj* **I a** : having the kind of sound indicated by a circumflex **b** : marked with a circumflex **2** : bending around ⟨a *circumflex* artery⟩ [Latin *circumflexus,* past participle of *circumflectere* "to bend around, mark with a circumflex", from *circum-* + *flectere* "to bend"]

²**circumflex** *n* : a mark ^, ˆ, or ˜ used chiefly to indicate length, contraction, or a specific vowel quality

cir·cum·lo·cu·tion \,sər-kəm-lō-'kyü-shən\ *n* : use of many words to express a relatively simple idea or to avoid stating one's position directly or clearly [Latin *circumlocutio,* from *circum-* + *locutio* "speech", from *loqui* "to speak"] — **cir·cum·loc·u·to·ry** \-'läk-yə-,tōr-ē, -,tȯr-\ *adj*

cir·cum·lu·nar \,sər-kəm-'lü-nər\ *adj* : revolving about or surrounding the moon

cir·cum·nav·i·gate \-'nav-ə-,gāt\ *vt* : to go completely around (as the earth) especially by water — **cir·cum·nav·i·ga·tion** \-,nav-ə-'gā-shən\ *n* — **cir·cum·nav·i·ga·tor** \-'nav-ə-,gāt-ər\ *n*

cir·cum·po·lar \,sər-kəm-'pō-lər\ *adj* **I** : continually visible above the horizon ⟨a *circumpolar* star⟩ **2** : surrounding or found in the vicinity of the north pole or south pole

cir·cum·scribe \'sər-kəm-,skrīb\ *vt* **I a** : to draw a line around **b** : to surround by a boundary **2 a** : to limit the range or activity of definitely and clearly **b** : to define or mark off carefully **3** : to construct or be constructed around ⟨a geometrical figure⟩ so as to touch at as many points as possible ⟨a triangle *circumscribed* about a circle⟩ [Latin *circumscribere,* from *circum-* + *scribere* "to write, draw"]

cir·cum·scrip·tion \,sər-kəm-'skrip-shən\ *n* **I** : something that circumscribes: as **a** : **BOUNDARY** **b** : **RESTRICTION** 1 **2** : the act of circumscribing : the state of being circumscribed **3** : a circumscribed area [Latin *circumscriptio,* from *circumscribere* "to circumscribe"]

cir·cum·spect \'sər-kəm-,spekt\ *adj* : careful to consider all circumstances and possible consequences [Latin *circumspectus,* from *circumspicere* "to look around, be cautious", from *circum-* + *specere* "to look"] — **cir·cum·spect·ly** *adv*

cir·cum·spec·tion \,sər-kəm-'spek-shən\ *n* : circumspect action or behavior

cir·cum·stance \'sər-kəm-,stans\ *n* **I** : a fact or event that must be considered along with another fact or

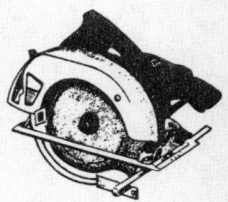

circular saw

\ə\ abut		\ng\ sing
\ər\ further		\ō\ bone
\a\ mat		\ȯ\ saw
\ā\ take		\ȯi\ coin
\ä\ cot, cart		\th\ thin
\au̇\ out		\th\ this
\ch\ chin		\ü\ food
\e\ pet		\u̇\ foot
\ē\ easy		\y\ yet
\g\ go		\yü\ few
\i\ tip		\yu̇\ cure
\ī\ life		\zh\ vision
\j\ job		

event **2** *pl* : surrounding conditions 〈under the *cir-cumstances*〉 **3** *pl* : condition or situation with respect to wealth 〈in easy *circumstances*〉 **4** : formal ceremony accompanying an event 〈pomp and *circumstance*〉 **5** : a happening or fact in a chain of events : DETAIL **6** : CHANCE 1, FATE 〈a victim of *circumstance*〉 [Middle French, from Latin *circumstantia*, from *circumstare* "to surround", from *circum-* + *stare* "to stand"]

cir·cum·stanced \-,stanst\ *adj* : placed in particular circumstances especially in regard to property or income

cir·cum·stan·tial \,sər-kəm-'stan-chəl\ *adj* **1** : consisting of or relating to circumstances : dependent on circumstances 〈*circumstantial* evidence〉 **2** : relating to a matter but not essential to it : INCIDENTAL **3** : containing full details 〈a *circumstantial* account of what happened〉 — **cir·cum·stan·tial·ly** \-'stanch-lē, -ə-lē\ *adv*
□ SYN PARTICULAR, MINUTE, DETAILED: CIRCUMSTANTIAL implies fullness of details that fixes something described in time and space 〈a *circumstantial* account of our visit〉 PARTICULAR implies a precise attention to every detail 〈a *particular* description of the scene of the crime〉 MINUTE implies close and searching attention to the smallest details 〈a *minute* examination of a fossil〉 DETAILED stresses abundance or completeness of detail 〈a *detailed* analysis of the event〉

cir·cum·vent \,sər-kəm-'vent\ *vt* **1** : to go around : BY-PASS 〈*circumvent* the town〉 **2** : to escape from or avoid especially by skill or trickery : get around 〈*circumvent* the law〉 〈*circumvent* difficulties〉 [Latin *circumvenire*, from *circum-* + *venire* "to come"] — **cir·cum·ven·tion** \-'ven-chən\ *n*

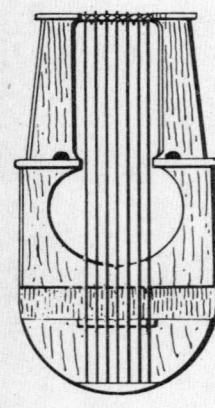

cithara

cir·cus \'sər-kəs\ *n* **1** : a large arena enclosed by tiers of seats and used for spectacles (as athletic contests or horse races) especially in ancient Rome **2 a** : a usually traveling public entertainment that features clowns, acrobats, and animal acts **b** : a performance of a circus **c** : the company of a circus including personnel and livestock **3** : an activity suggesting a circus especially in being a showy public display 〈turned the campaign into a political *circus*〉 **4** *British* : a usually circular area at the intersection of streets 〈Piccadilly *Circus*〉 [Latin, "circle, circus"]

cirque \'sərk\ *n* **1** : something round : CIRCLET, CIRCLE **2** : a deep steep-walled hollow on a mountain shaped like half a bowl [French, "circus, amphitheater", from Latin *circus*]

cir·rho·sis \sə-'rō-səs\ *n* : fibrosis and hardening especially of the liver [Greek *kirrhos* "orange-colored"] — **cir·rhot·ic** \-'rät-ik\ *adj or n*

cir·ri·ped \'sir-ə-,ped\ *or* **cir·ri·pede** \-,pēd\ *n* : any of a subclass (Cirripedia) of specialized marine crustaceans (as barnacles) that swim about as larvae but are permanently attached or parasitic as adults [Latin *cirrus* "curl" + *ped-, pes* "foot"] — **cirriped** *adj*

cir·ro·cu·mu·lus \,sir-ō-'kyü-myə-ləs\ *n* : a cloud form of small white rounded masses at a high altitude usually in regular groupings

cir·ro·stra·tus \-'strāt-əs, -'strat-\ *n* : a fairly uniform layer of high stratus darker than cirrus

cir·rus \'sir-əs\ *n, pl* **cir·ri** \'siər-,ī\ **1** : a plant tendril **2** : a slender usually flexible animal appendage **3** : a wispy white cloud usually of minute ice crystals formed at altitudes of 6 to 12 kilometers [Latin, "curl, ringlet, tuft, bird's crest, fringe"]

cis- *prefix* : on this side 〈*cis*lunar〉 [Latin]

cis·co \'sis-kō\ *n, pl* **ciscoes** : any of various whitefishes including important food fishes of the Great Lakes region [Canadian French *ciscoette*, of American Indian origin]

cis·lu·nar \'sis-'lü-nər\ *adj* : lying between the earth and the moon or the moon's orbit 〈*cislunar* space〉

Cis·ter·cian \sis-'tər-shən\ *n* : a member of a monastic order founded at Cîteaux, France in 1098 under an austere rule — **Cistercian** *adj* [Medieval Latin *Cistercium* "Cîteaux"]

cis·tern \'sis-tərn\ *n* **1** : an often underground artificial reservoir or tank for storing water and especially rainwater **2** : a fluid-containing sac or cavity in an organism [Old French *cisterne*, from Latin *cisterna*, from *cista* "box, chest"]

cit·a·del \'sit-əd-l, -ə-,del\ *n* **1** : a fortress that commands a city **2** : STRONGHOLD [Middle French *citadelle*, from Italian *cittadella*, from *cittade* "city", from Medieval Latin *civitas*]

ci·ta·tion \sī-'tā-shən\ *n* **1** : an official order to appear (as before a court) **2 a** : an act or instance of quoting **b** : a passage quoted : EXCERPT **3 a** : a formal statement of the achievements of a person (as one receiving an award) **b** : specific reference in a military dispatch to praiseworthy performance of duty

cite \'sīt\ *vt* **1** : to order to appear before a court **2** : to quote as an example, authority, or proof **3 a** : to refer to; *esp* : to mention formally in commendation or praise **b** : to name in a citation [Middle French *citer* "to cite, summon", from Latin *citare* "to rouse, summon", from *ciēre* "to stir, move"]

cith·a·ra \'sith-ə-rə, 'kith-\ *n* : an ancient Greek stringed instrument of the lyre class with a wooden sounding board [Latin, from Greek *kithara*]

cit·i·fy \'sit-i-,fī\ *vt* **-fied; -fy·ing** : to accustom to urban ways

cit·i·zen \'sit-ə-zən\ *n* **1** : an inhabitant of a city or town **2 a** : a member of a state **b** : a person who by birth or naturalization owes allegiance to a government and is entitled to protection from it **3** : CIVILIAN [Anglo-French *citezein*, alteration of Old French *citeien*, from *cité* "city"] — **cit·i·zen·ly** \-lē\ *adj* □ SYN CITIZEN, SUBJECT, NATIONAL mean a person owing allegiance to and entitled to the protection of a sovereign state. CITIZEN is preferred for one owing allegiance to a state in which sovereign power is retained by the people and sharing in the political rights of those people; SUBJECT implies allegiance to a personal sovereign such as a monarch; NATIONAL designates one who may claim the protection of a state whether or not he is an actual citizen or subject and applies especially to one living or traveling outside that state.

cit·i·zen·ess \-zə-nəs\ *n* : a woman who is a citizen

cit·i·zen·ry \-zən-rē\ *n, pl* **-ries** : the whole body of citizens

citizens band \-zənz-\ *n* : one of the frequency bands that in the United States is allocated officially for private radio communication

cit·i·zen·ship \-zən-,ship\ *n* **1** : possession of the rights and privileges of a citizen **2** : the quality of a person's response to membership in a community

cit·rate \'si-,trāt\ *n* : a salt or ester of citric acid

cit·ric acid \'si-trik-\ *n* : a pleasantly sour-tasting acid $C_6H_8O_7$ occurring in cellular metabolism and obtained especially from lemon and lime juices or by fermentation of sugars and used as a flavoring [derived from Latin *citrus* "citron tree"]

citric acid cycle *n* : KREBS CYCLE

cit·rine \'si-,trēn\ *adj* : resembling a citron or lemon especially in color [Middle French *citrin*, from Latin *citrus* "citron tree"]

cit·ron \'si-trən\ *n* **1 a** : a fruit like the lemon in appearance and structure but larger; *also* : the citrus tree producing this fruit **b** : the preserved rind of the citron used especially in fruitcake **2** : a small hard-fleshed watermelon used mostly in pickles and preserves [Middle French, from Provençal, from Latin *citrus* "citron tree"]

cit·ro·nel·la \,si-trə-'nel-ə\ *n* : a fragrant grass of southern Asia that yields an oil used in perfumery and as an insect repellent; *also* : its oil [French *citronelle* "lemon balm", from *citron* "citron"]

cit·rul·line \'si-trə-ˌlēn\ *n* : an amino acid $C_6H_{13}N_3O_3$ formed especially as an intermediate in the conversion of ornithine to arginine in the living system [New Latin *Citrullus*, genus name of the watermelon, derived from Latin *citrus* "citron tree"]

cit·rus \'si-trəs\ *n*, *pl* **citrus** *or* **cit·rus·es** : any of a genus of often thorny trees and shrubs of the rue family grown in warm regions for their fruits (as orange, grapefruit, or lemon) with firm usually thick rind and juicy pulp; *also* : the fruit of a citrus [Latin, "citron tree"] — **citrus** *adj*

city \'sit-ē\ *n*, *pl* **cit·ies** **1 a** : an inhabited place of greater size or importance than a town **b** : a usually large or important place in the United States governed under a charter granted by the state **2** : CITY-STATE **3** : the people of a city [Old French *cité* "capital city", from Medieval Latin *civitas*, from Latin, "citizenship, state, city of Rome", from *civis* "citizen"]

city hall *n* **1** : the chief administrative building of a city **2 a** : a municipal government **b** : city bureaucracy

city manager *n* : an official employed by an elected council to administer a city government

city–state \'sit-ē-ˈstāt, -ˌstāt\ *n* : a self-governing state (as of ancient Greece) consisting of a city and surrounding territory

civ·et \'siv-ət\ *n* : a thick yellowish musky-odored substance obtained from the civet cat and used in perfume [Middle French *civette*, from Italian *zibetto*, from Arabic *zabād* "civet perfume"]

civet cat *n* **1** : a long-bodied short-legged African mammal that produces most of the civet of commerce **2** : any of the small spotted skunks of western North America

civ·ic \'siv-ik\ *adj* : of or relating to a citizen, a city, or citizenship ⟨*civic* pride⟩ ⟨*civic* duty⟩ [Latin *civicus*, from *civis* "citizen"] — **civ·i·cal·ly** \'siv-i-kə-lē, -klē\ *adv*

civ·ics \'siv-iks\ *n* : the study of the rights and duties of citizens

civ·il \'siv-əl\ *adj* **1** : of or relating to citizens **2** : of or relating to the state as an organized political body ⟨*civil* institutions⟩ **3** : of or relating to the general population as distinguished from the military or the church **4** : marked by courtesy or politeness ⟨give a *civil* answer⟩ **5 a** : relating to legal proceedings in connection with private rights and obligations ⟨the *civil* code⟩ ⟨a *civil* suit⟩ **b** : of or relating to the civil law [Middle French, from Latin *civilis*, from *civis* "citizen"] □ SYN POLITE, COURTEOUS: CIVIL implies no more than barely meeting the requirements of good breeding and the avoidance of roughness or unpleasantness; POLITE implies showing good manners and thoughtfulness but may often suggest lack of warmth or cordiality; COURTEOUS implies more actively considerate or dignified politeness.

civil defense *n* : organized protective and emergency relief activities by civilians in case of attack or disaster

civil engineering *n* : engineering that deals with the designing and construction of public works (as roads or harbors) and of various private works — **civil engineer** *n*

ci·vil·ian \sə-ˈvil-yən\ *n* : one not on active duty in a military, police, or fire-fighting force — **civilian** *adj*

ci·vil·i·ty \sə-ˈvil-ət-ē\ *n*, *pl* **-ties** **1** : POLITENESS, COURTESY **2** : a polite act or expression

civ·i·li·za·tion \ˌsiv-ə-lə-ˈzā-shən\ *n* **1 a** : a relatively high level of cultural and technological development **b** : the special culture of a people or a period ⟨Greek *civilization*⟩ ⟨18th century *civilization*⟩ **2** : the process of becoming civilized **3 a** : refinement of thought, manners, or taste **b** : city life and comforts

civ·i·lize \'siv-ə-ˌlīz\ *vt* : to raise out of a savage state; *esp* : to bring to an advanced and ordered stage of cultural development — **civ·i·lized** *adj*

civil law *n*, *often cap C & L* **1** : a body of law developed from Roman law **2** : the law of civil or private rights

civil liberty *n* : freedom from governmental interference with rights (as of free speech) especially as guaranteed by a bill of rights

civ·il·ly \'siv-ə-lē, -əl-lē\ *adv* : in a civil manner : POLITELY

civil marriage *n* : a marriage performed by a magistrate

civil rights *n pl* : the rights of personal liberty guaranteed to United States citizens by the 13th and 14th amendments to the Constitution and by acts of Congress

civil servant *n* : a member of a civil service

civil service *n* : the administrative service of a government exclusive of the armed forces

civil war *n* : a war between opposing groups of citizens of the same country or nation

clab·ber \'klab-ər\ *n*, *chiefly dialect* : sour milk that has thickened or curdled [short for *bonnyclabber*, from Irish Gaelic *bainne clabair*, from *bainne* "milk" + *clabar* "sour thick milk"]

¹clack \'klak\ *vb* **1** : CHATTER 2, PRATTLE **2** : to make or cause to make a clatter [Middle English *clacken*] — **clack·er** *n*

²clack *n* **1** : CHATTER ⟨the *clack* of voices⟩ **2** : a sound of clacking ⟨the *clack* of a typewriter⟩

clad \'klad\ *adj* : CLOTHED, COVERED ⟨ivy-*clad* walls⟩ [past participle of *clothe*]

¹claim \'klām\ *vt* **1 a** : to ask for as one's right or property ⟨*claim* an inheritance⟩ ⟨*claim* one's bags⟩ **b** : to call for : REQUIRE ⟨this matter *claims* our attention⟩ **2 a** : to state as a fact : MAINTAIN ⟨*claimed* they'd been cheated⟩ **b** : PROFESS ⟨*claimed* to know nothing of the matter⟩ [Old French *clamer*, from Latin *clamare* "to cry out"] SYN see DEMAND — **claim·able** \'klā-mə-bəl\ *adj* — **claim·er** *n*

²claim *n* **1** : a demand for something due or believed to be due ⟨an insurance *claim*⟩ **2 a** : a right to something; *esp* : a title to something in the possession of another **b** : an assertion open to challenge ⟨a *claim* of authenticity⟩ **3** : something claimed; *esp* : a tract of land marked out by a settler or prospector

claim·ant \'klā-mənt\ *n* : a person who asserts a right to something ⟨a *claimant* to an estate⟩

clair·voy·ance \klaər-ˈvȯi-əns, kleər-\ *n* **1** : the professed power of seeing or knowing about things that are not present to the senses **2** : sharp insight : DISCERNMENT

¹clair·voy·ant \-ənt\ *adj* **1** : unusually perceptive : DISCERNING **2** : of or relating to clairvoyance [French, from *clair* "clear" + *voyant*, present participle of *voir* "to see"] — **clair·voy·ant·ly** *adv*

²clairvoyant *n* : a person held to have the power of clairvoyance

¹clam \'klam\ *n* **1** : any of numerous edible marine bivalve mollusks living in sand or mud **2** : a freshwater mussel **3** : the flesh of a clam used as food [earlier *clam* "clamp", from Old English *clamm* "bond, fetter"; from the clamping action of the shells]

²clam *vi* **clammed**; **clam·ming** : to gather clams especially by digging

clam·bake \'klam-ˌbāk\ *n* : a party or outing where food is cooked on heated rocks covered by seaweed; *also* : a usually loud and lively get-together

clam·ber \'klam-bər\ *vi* **clam·bered**; **clam·ber·ing** \'klam-bə-riŋ, -briŋ\ : to climb awkwardly (as by scrambling) ⟨*clamber* over steep rocks⟩ [Middle English *clambren*] — **clam·ber·er** \-bər-ər\ *n*

clam·my \'klam-ē\ *adj* **clam·mi·er**; **-est** : being damp, soft, sticky, and usually cool [Middle English, probably from *clammen* "to smear, stick", from Old English *clǣman*] — **clam·mi·ly** \'klam-ə-lē\ *adv* — **clam·mi·ness** \'klam-ē-nəs\ *n*

¹clam·or \'klam-ər\ *n* **1 a** : noisy shouting **b** : a loud continuous noise **2** : insistent protest or demand ⟨pub-

civet cat 1

¹clam 1

\ə\ abut	\ng\ sing
\ər\ further	\ō\ bone
\a\ mat	\ȯ\ saw
\ā\ take	\ȯi\ coin
\ä\ cot, cart	\th\ thin
\au̇\ out	\t͟h\ this
\ch\ chin	\ü\ food
\e\ pet	\u̇\ foot
\ē\ easy	\y\ yet
\g\ go	\yü\ few
\i\ tip	\yu̇\ cure
\ī\ life	\zh\ vision
\j\ job	

clarinet

lic *clamor* for a tax cut) [Middle French *clamour,* from Latin *clamor,* from *clamare* "to cry out"]

²clamor *vb* **clam·ored; clam·or·ing** \'klam-ring, -ə-ring\ **1** : to make a din (gulls *clamored* overhead) **2** : to express insistently and noisily (*clamoring* that they had been misunderstood)

clam·or·ous \'klam-rəs, -ə-rəs\ *adj* : full of clamor : NOISY — **clam·or·ous·ly** *adv* — **clam·or·ous·ness** *n*

¹clamp \'klamp\ *n* : a device that holds or presses two or more parts together firmly [probably from Dutch *klamp*]

²clamp *vt* **1 a** : to fasten with or as if with a clamp (*clamp* two boards together) **b** : to grip firmly (winter *clamped* the region) **2** : to place by decree : IMPOSE — often used with *on* (*clamped* on a curfew after the riots)

clamp down *vi* : to impose restrictions (*clamping down* on speeders)

clam·shell \'klam-,shel\ *n* **1** : the shell of a clam **2** : a bucket or grapple (as on a dredge) having two hinged jaws

clam up *vi* : to become silent; *esp* : to refuse to talk further (they *clammed up* when asked for details)

clam worm *n* : any of several large burrowing marine annelid worms often used as bait

clan \'klan\ *n* **1** : a group (as in the Scottish Highlands) made up of households whose heads claim descent from a common ancestor **2** : a group united by a common interest (the whole *clan* of actors) [Scottish Gaelic *clann* "offspring, clan", from Irish *cland* "plant, offspring", from Latin *planta* "plant"]

clan·des·tine \klan-'des-tən\ *adj* : held in or conducted with secrecy : FURTIVE (a *clandestine* meeting) [Latin *clandestinus,* derived from *clam* "secretly"] SYN see SECRET — **clan·des·tine·ly** *adv* — **clan·des·tine·ness** *n*

¹clang \'klang\ *vb* : to make or cause to make a clang [Latin *clangere*]

²clang *n* : a loud ringing metallic sound (the *clang* of a fire alarm)

clang·or \'klang-ər, -gər\ *n* : a resounding clang or series of clangs (the *clangor* of hammers) [Latin, from *clangere* "to clang"] — **clangor** *vi* — **clang·or·ous** \-ə-rəs, -gə-rəs\ *adj* — **clang·or·ous·ly** *adv*

¹clank \'klangk\ *vb* **1** : to make or cause to make a clank or series of clanks (the radiator hissed and *clanked*) **2** : to move with a clank (tanks *clanking* through the streets) [probably imitative] — **clank·ing·ly** \'klang-king-lē\ *adv*

²clank *n* : a sharp brief metallic ringing sound

clan·nish \'klan-ish\ *adj* **1** : of or relating to a clan **2** : tending to associate only with others of similar background or status (a *clannish* clique) — **clan·nish·ly** *adv* — **clan·nish·ness** *n*

clans·man \'klanz-mən\ *n* : a member of a clan

¹clap \'klap\ *vb* **clapped; clap·ping** **1** : to strike (as two flat hard surfaces) together to produce a sharp noise (the door *clapped* shut) **2** : to strike the hands together repeatedly in applause : APPLAUD **3** : to strike with the open hand (*clapped* a friend on the shoulder) **4** : to put usually hastily or energetically (*clap* on one's hat) [Old English *clæppan*]

²clap *n* **1** : a loud crash made by or as if by clapping (a *clap* of thunder) **2** : a firm slap (a *clap* on the shoulder) **3** : the sound of clapping hands; *esp* : APPLAUSE

³clap *n* : GONORRHEA [Middle French *clapoir* "bubo"]

clap·board \'klab-ərd; 'kla-,bōrd, 'klap-, -,bȯrd\ *n* : a narrow board thicker at one edge than at the other used as siding [Dutch *klaphout* "stave wood"] — **clapboard** *vt*

clap·per \'klap-ər\ *n* : one that makes a clapping sound: as **a** : the tongue of a bell **b** : a device that makes noise especially by the banging of one part against another **c** : a person who applauds

clap·trap \'klap-,trap\ *n* : pretentious nonsense [¹*clap;* from its being a trap for applause]

claque \'klak\ *n* **1** : a group hired to applaud at a performance **2** : a group of self-seeking flatterers [French, from *claquer* "to clap"]

clar·et \'klar-ət\ *n* **1** : a dry red table wine **2** : a dark purplish red [Middle French *vin claret* "clear wine"] — **claret** *adj*

clar·i·fy \'klar-ə-,fī\ *vb* **-fied; -fy·ing** **1** : to make or become pure or clear (*clarify* a liquid) **2** : to make or become more readily understandable (*clarify* an explanation) [Middle French *clarifier,* from Late Latin *clarificare,* from Latin *clarus* "clear"] — **clar·i·fi·ca·tion** \,klar-ə-fə-'kā-shən\ *n* — **clar·i·fi·er** \'klar-ə-,fī-ər,-,fīr\ *n*

clar·i·net \,klar-ə-'net, 'klar-ə-nət\ *n* : a single-reed woodwind instrument having a cylindrical tube with moderately flaring end [French *clarinette*] — **clar·i·net·ist** *or* **clar·i·net·tist** \,klar-ə-'net-əst\ *n*

¹clar·i·on \'klar-ē-ən\ *n* : a medieval trumpet with clear shrill tones [Medieval Latin *clario,* from Latin *clarus* "clear"]

²clarion *adj* : brilliantly clear (a *clarion* call to action)

clar·i·ty \'klar-ət-ē\ *n* : CLEARNESS (the *clarity* of the atmosphere) [Latin *claritas,* from *clarus* "clear"]

clary \'klaər-ē, 'kleər-\ *n, pl* **clar·ies** : an aromatic mint of southern Europe grown as a potherb and ornamental [Middle French *sclaree,* from Medieval Latin *sclareia*]

¹clash \'klash\ *vb* **1** : to make a clash (gears *clashed* as the truck moved on) **2** : to come into conflict (rebels *clashed* with the police) **3** : to cause to clash (*clashed* the cymbals together) [imitative] — **clash·er** *n*

²clash *n* **1** : a noisy usually metallic sound of collision (the *clash* of swords) **2 a** : a hostile encounter (a *clash* between two armies) **b** : a sharp conflict (a *clash* of opinion)

¹clasp \'klasp\ *n* **1** : a device (as a hook) for holding objects or parts together (the *clasp* of a necklace) **2** : a holding with or as if with the hands : EMBRACE, GRASP (the *clasp* of warm hands) [Middle English *claspe*]

²clasp *vt* **1** : to fasten with or as if with a clasp **2** : to enclose and hold with or as if with the arms; *esp* : EMBRACE **3** : to seize with or as if with the hand : GRASP — **clasp·er** *n*

¹class \'klas\ *n* **1 a** : a group sharing the same economic or social status (the working *class*) **b** *pl* : persons of high social or economic status (the *classes* as opposed to the masses) **c** : social rank or level (an awareness of *class*) **d** : high quality (the team was competent but lacked *class*) **2 a** : a course of instruction (a *class* in arithmetic) **b** : the group of pupils meeting regularly in a course (a big *class* this year) **c** : the period during which such a group meets **d** : a group of students or alumni whose year of graduation is the same (*class* of '81) **3 a** : a group or set alike in some way **b** : a major category in biological taxonomy ranking above the order and below the phylum or division **4** : a division or rating based on grade or quality (a *class* A movie) [French *classe,* from Latin *classis* "group called to arms, class of citizens"] — **class·less** \-ləs\ *adj*

²class *vt* : CLASSIFY

class–con·scious \'klas-,kän-chəs\ *adj* **1** : aware of one's common status with others in an economic or social class **2** : believing in and actively aware of class struggle — **class consciousness** *n*

¹clas·sic \'klas-ik\ *adj* **1 a** : serving as a standard of excellence **b** : belonging to the great accomplishments of humanity (*classic* products of the imagination) **c** : characterized by simple tailored lines in fashion year after year (*classic* apparel) **2** : of or relating to the ancient Greeks and Romans or their culture : CLASSICAL **3 a** : AUTHENTIC 1 (a *classic* folk dance) **b** : notable as the most typical instance (the *classic* study of American politics) [Latin *classicus* "of the highest class of Roman citizens, of the first rank", from *classis* "class"]

²classic *n* **1** : a literary work of ancient Greece or Rome **2** : a work of enduring excellence; *also* : its author **3** : something perfect of its kind : MODEL **4** : a traditional event ⟨a football *classic*⟩

clas·si·cal \'klas-i-kəl\ *adj* **1** : having recognized and permanent value : CLASSIC **2** : of or relating to the ancient Greek and Roman world and especially to its literature and art ⟨*classical* studies⟩ ⟨a *classical* scholar⟩ **3** : of, relating to, or being music in established European styles and forms (as the symphony and opera) **4 a** : regarded as of first historical significance : TRADITIONAL **b** : of or relating to the first developed form or system of a science, art, or discipline ⟨the *classical* economists⟩ **c** : conforming to a pattern of usage sanctioned by a body of literature rather than by everyday speech ⟨*classical* Latin⟩ **5** : concerned with a general study of the arts and sciences and not specializing in technical studies ⟨a *classical* high school⟩

clas·si·cal·ly \'klas-i-kə-lē, -klē\ *adv* : in a classic or classical manner

clas·si·cism \'klas-ə-,siz-əm\ *n* **1 a** : the principles or style embodied in the literature, art, or architecture of ancient Greece and Rome **b** : classical scholarship **c** : a classical idiom or expression **2** : adherence to traditional standards (as of simplicity, restraint, or proportion) that are universally and permanently valid

clas·si·cist \-səst\ *n* **1** : an advocate or follower of classicism **2** : a classical scholar — **clas·si·cis·tic** \,klas-ə-'sis-tik\ *adj*

clas·si·fi·ca·tion \,klas-ə-fə-'kā-shən, ,klas-fə-\ *n* **1** : the act or process of classifying **2 a** (1) : systematic arrangement in groups or categories according to established criteria (2) : TAXONOMY **2b b** : CLASS 3a, CATEGORY — **clas·si·fi·ca·to·ry** \'klas-ə-fə-kə-,tōr-ē, 'klas-fə-, -,tȯr-\ *adj*

clas·si·fied \'klas-ə-,fīd\ *adj* **1** : divided into classes or placed in a class ⟨*classified* ads⟩ **2** : withheld from general circulation for reasons of national security ⟨*classified* information⟩

clas·si·fy \'klas-ə-,fī\ *vt* **-fied; -fy·ing** : to arrange in or assign to a class or classes ⟨*classify* books according to subject matter⟩ — **clas·si·fi·able** \-,fī-ə-bəl\ *adj* — **clas·si·fi·er** \-,fī-ər, -,fīr\ *n*

class·mate \'klas-,māt\ *n* : a member of the same class in a school or college

class·room \-,rüm, -,rùm\ *n* : a room in a school or college in which classes meet

class struggle *n* : a basic conflict between social classes in Marxian theory — called also *class war*

¹clat·ter \'klat-ər\ *vb* **1** : to make or cause to make a rattling sound ⟨*clattering* the dishes⟩ **2** : to move or go with a clatter ⟨*clatter* down the stairs⟩ **3** : CHATTER 2 [Middle English *clatren*] — **clat·ter·er** \-ər-ər\ *n* — **clat·ter·ing·ly** \'klat-ə- riŋ-lē\ *adv*

²clatter *n* **1** : a rattling sound (as of hard bodies striking together) **2** : COMMOTION ⟨the midday *clatter* of the business district⟩ **3** : noisy chatter — **clat·tery** \'klat-ə-rē\ *adj*

clause \'klȯz\ *n* **1** : a separate section of an article or document ⟨a *clause* in a will⟩ **2** : a group of words having its own subject and predicate but forming only part of a compound or complex sentence (as "when it rained" or "they went inside" in the sentence "when it rained, they went inside") [Old French, from Medieval Latin *clausa* "close of a rhetorical period", from Latin *claudere* "to close"] — **claus·al** \'klȯ-zəl\ *adj*

claus·tro·pho·bia \,klȯ-strə-'fō-bē-ə\ *n* : abnormal fear of being in closed or narrow spaces [Latin *claustrum* "bar, bolt", from *claudere* "to close"] — **claus·tro·pho·bic** \-bik\ *adj*

clave *past of* CLEAVE

clav·i·chord \'klav-ə-,kȯrd\ *n* : an early keyboard instrument in use before the piano [Medieval Latin *clavi-*

chordium, from Latin *clavis* "key" + *chorda* "string"] — **clav·i·chord·ist** \-əst\ *n*

clav·i·cle \'klav-i-kəl\ *n* : a bone of the shoulder that joins the breastbone and the shoulder blade — called also *collarbone* [French *clavicule*, derived from Latin *clavis* "key"] — **cla·vic·u·lar** \kla-'vik-yə-lər\ *adj*

cla·vier \klə-'viər; 'klāv-ē-ər, 'klav-\ *n* **1** : the keyboard of a musical instrument **2** : an early keyboard instrument [French, from Old French, "key bearer", from Latin *clavis* "key"] — **cla·vier·ist** \-əst\ *n*

¹claw \'klȯ\ *n* **1 a** : a sharp usually slender and curved nail on the toe of an animal **b** : a sharp curved process especially if at the end of a limb (as of an insect); *also* : one of the pincerlike organs terminating some limbs of an arthropod (as a lobster or scorpion) **2** : something that resembles a claw; *esp* : the forked end of a tool (as a hammer) [Old English *clawu* "hoof, claw"] — **clawed** \'klȯd\ *adj*

²claw *vb* : to rake, seize, or dig with or as if with claws

clay \'klā\ *n* **1 a** : an earthy material that is plastic when moist but hard when fired, is composed chiefly of silicates of aluminum and water, and is used for brick, tile, and earthenware; *also* : soil composed chiefly of this material having particles less than a specified size **b** : earth especially when moist **2 a** : a plastic substance used for modeling **b** : the human body as distinguished from the spirit [Old English *clæg*] — **clay·ish** \'klā-ish\ *adj*

clay·ey \'klā-ē\ *adj* **clay·i·er; -est** : resembling clay or containing much clay ⟨a *clayey* soil⟩

clay loam *n* : a loam consisting of from 20 to 30 percent clay

clay·more \'klā-,mōr, -,mȯr\ *n* : a large 2-edged sword formerly used by Scottish Highlanders [Scottish Gaelic *claidheamh mōr*, literally, "great sword"]

clay pigeon *n* : a saucer-shaped target thrown from a trap in skeet and trapshooting

¹clean \'klēn\ *adj* **1 a** : free from dirt or pollution ⟨*clean* clothes⟩ ⟨*clean* air⟩ **b** : free from contamination or disease **2** : free from admixture : PURE **3 a** : characterized by moral integrity : HONORABLE ⟨a candidate with a *clean* record⟩ **b** : free from offensive treatment of sexual subjects and from the use of obscenity ⟨a *clean* joke⟩ **4** : ceremonially or spiritually pure **5 a** : so complete as to leave no remainder ⟨made a *clean* sweep⟩ **b** : well done : SKILLFUL ⟨a good *clean* job⟩ **6 a** : being trim and well-formed ⟨a ship with *clean* lines⟩ **b** : EVEN, SMOOTH ⟨a sharp knife makes a *clean* cut⟩ **7** : habitually neat [Old English *clǣne*] — **clean·ness** \'klēn-nəs\ *n*

²clean *adv* **1 a** : so as to clean ⟨a new broom sweeps *clean*⟩ **b** : in a clean manner ⟨fight *clean*⟩ **2** : all the way : COMPLETELY ⟨hit the ball *clean* out of the ball park⟩

³clean *vb* **1** : to make or become clean ⟨*clean* this room⟩ ⟨*cleaned* up for supper⟩ **2** : to remove or exhaust the contents or resources of ⟨*clean* a fish⟩ ⟨thieves *cleaned* out the safe⟩ — **clean·er** *n* □ SYN CLEAN, CLEANSE mean to remove dirt or impurities from. CLEAN applies to any removing of dirt, litter, dust; CLEANSE applies chiefly to washing with water or a solvent; it may also apply to figurative purification ⟨*cleansed* from sin⟩ —

clean house : to get rid of whatever is hampering, wrong, or degrading

clean–cut \'klēn-'kət\ *adj* **1** : CLEAR-CUT ⟨*clean-cut* features⟩ ⟨a *clean-cut* skyline⟩ **2** : of wholesome appearance

¹clean·ly \'klen-lē\ *adj* **clean·li·er; -est** **1** : careful to keep clean : FASTIDIOUS **2** : habitually kept clean ⟨*cleanly* surroundings⟩ — **clean·li·ness** \-nəs\ *n*

²clean·ly \'klēn-lē\ *adv* : in a clean manner

cleanse \'klenz\ *vt* : to make clean [Old English *clǣnsian* "to purify", from *clǣne* "clean"] SYN see CLEAN

clavichord

\ə\ abut		\ng\ sing	
\ər\ further		\ō\ bone	
\a\ mat		\ȯ\ saw	
\ā\ take		\ȯi\ coin	
\ä\ cot, cart		\th\ thin	
\aù\ out		\th\ this	
\ch\ chin		\ü\ food	
\e\ pet		\ù\ foot	
\ē\ easy		\y\ yet	
\g\ go		\yü\ few	
\i\ tip		\yù\ cure	
\ī\ life		\zh\ vision	
\j\ job			

cleans·er \'klen-zər\ *n* **1** : one that cleanses **2** : a preparation (as a scouring powder or a skin cream) used for cleaning

clean·up \'klē-,nəp\ *n* : an act or instance of cleaning

clean up \klē-'nəp\ *vi* : to make a lot of money ⟨*cleaned up* at the races⟩

¹clear \'kliər\ *adj* **1 a** : shining brightly : LUMINOUS ⟨*clear* sunlight⟩ **b** : free from clouds, haze, or mist ⟨a *clear* day⟩ **c** : SERENE 2 ⟨a *clear* gaze⟩ **2** : CLEAN, PURE: as **a** : free of blemishes ⟨a *clear* complexion⟩ **b** : easily seen through : TRANSPARENT ⟨*clear* glass⟩ **3 a** : easily heard ⟨the sound was quite *clear*⟩ **b** : easily visible : PLAIN **c** : easily understandable : UNMISTAKABLE ⟨the meaning was *clear*⟩ **4** : free from doubt : SURE ⟨a *clear* understanding of the issue⟩ **5** : free from guile or guilt : INNOCENT ⟨a *clear* conscience⟩ **6** : unhampered by restriction or limitation: as **a** : unencumbered by debts or charges **b** : NET ⟨a *clear* profit⟩ **c** : free from qualification : ABSOLUTE ⟨a *clear* case of treason⟩ **d** : free from obstruction or entanglement ⟨the coast is *clear*⟩ [Old French *cler,* from Latin *clarus* "clear, bright"] — **clear·ly** *adv* — **clear·ness** *n* □ SYN TRANSPARENT, TRANSLUCENT: CLEAR implies absence of cloudiness, haziness, or muddiness ⟨*clear* water⟩ TRANSPARENT implies being so clear that objects can be seen distinctly ⟨a *transparent* film of varnish⟩ TRANSLUCENT usually implies permitting the passage of light but not vision ⟨*translucent* frosted glass⟩ ⟨*translucent* shades for lamps⟩

²clear *adv* **1** : in a clear manner ⟨shout loud and *clear*⟩ **2** : all the way : COMPLETELY ⟨can see *clear* to the mountains on a day like this⟩

³clear *vb* **1 a** : to make or become clear or translucent ⟨*clear* the water by filtering⟩ ⟨the sky *cleared*⟩ **b** : to go away : DISPERSE ⟨clouds *cleared* away after the rain⟩ **2 a** : to free from accusation or blame ⟨*clear* one's name⟩ **b** : to certify as trustworthy ⟨*cleared* for top-secret work⟩ **3** : to make intelligible : EXPLAIN ⟨*cleared* the matter up for me⟩ **4** : to free from obstruction: as **a** : to submit for approval ⟨*clear* this with the boss⟩ **b** : to give approval to : AUTHORIZE **c** : to erase stored or displayed data from (as a computer or calculator) **5** : to make free especially from financial obligation : SETTLE ⟨*clear* an account⟩ **6** : to go through (customs) **7** : NET ⟨*cleared* a profit⟩ **8** : to get rid of : REMOVE ⟨*clear* away that trash⟩ **9 a** : to jump or go by without touching ⟨*cleared* the fence⟩ **b** : PASS 7a ⟨the bill *cleared* the legislature⟩ — **clear·able** \'klir-ə-bəl\ *adj* — **clear·er** *n* — **clear the air** : to remove tension or confusion ⟨*cleared the air* by discussing their differences⟩

⁴clear *n* : a clear space or part — **in the clear 1** : in inside measurement **2** : free of resistance or obstruction ⟨some nice blocking got the halfback *in the clear*⟩ **3** : free from suspicion **4** : not in code or cipher ⟨sent the message *in the clear*⟩

clear·ance \'klir-əns\ *n* **1** : an act or process of clearing: as **a** : the act of clearing a ship at the customhouse; *also* : the papers showing that a ship has cleared **b** : the passage of checks and claims among banks through a clearinghouse **c** : certification as clear of objection ⟨was given a security *clearance*⟩ **d** : a sale to clear out stock **2** : the distance by which one object clears another or the clear space between them

clear-cut \'kliər-'kət\ *adj* **1** : sharply outlined : DISTINCT ⟨a *clear-cut* pattern⟩ **2** : free from uncertainty : DEFINITE ⟨*clear-cut* victory⟩

clear·head·ed \-'hed-əd\ *adj* : having a clear understanding — **clear·head·ed·ly** *adv* — **clear·head·ed·ness** *n*

clear·ing \'kliər-ing\ *n* **1** : the act or process of making or becoming clear **2** : a tract of land cleared of wood and brush **3 a** : CLEARANCE 1b **b** *pl* : the gross amount of balances adjusted by clearance

clear·ing·house \-,haùs\ *n* **1** : an establishment maintained by banks for settling mutual claims and ac-

counts **2** : a central agency for collection, classification, and distribution especially of information

clear out *vi* : to go away : DEPART

clear–sight·ed \'kliər-'sīt-əd\ *adj* **1** : having clear vision **2** : DISCERNING — **clear–sight·ed·ly** *adv* — **clear–sight·ed·ness** *n*

¹cleat \'klēt\ *n* **1** : a wedge-shaped piece fastened to something and used as a support or check (as for a rope on the spar of a ship) **2** : a wooden or metal device usually with projecting arms at each end around which a rope may be made fast **3** : a strip or projecting piece fastened on or across something to give strength, to provide a grip, or to prevent slipping [Middle English *clete* "wedge"]

²cleat *vt* **1** : to fasten to or by a cleat **2** : to provide with a cleat

cleav·age \'klē-vij\ *n* **1** : the quality possessed by a crystallized substance or rock of splitting along definite planes **2** : the action of cleaving : the state of being cleft **3** : cell division; *esp* : the series of mitotic divisions of the egg that changes the single-celled zygote into a multicellular embryo

¹cleave \'klēv\ *vi* **cleaved** \'klēvd\ *or* **clove** \'klōv\ *also* **clave** \'klāv\; **cleav·ing** : CLING 1a, ADHERE [Middle English *clevien,* from Old English *clifian*]

²cleave *vb* **cleaved** \'klēvd\ *also* **cleft** \'kleft\ *or* **clove** \'klōv\; **cleaved** *also* **cleft** *or* **clo·ven** \'klō-vən\; **cleav·ing 1 a** : to split by or as if by a cutting blow ⟨some woods *cleave* along the grain easily⟩ **b** : to cause to separate ⟨the controversy *cleaved* the group into two camps⟩ **2** : to pass through : PENETRATE ⟨a ship's bow *cleaving* the waves⟩ [Middle English *cleven,* from Old English *clēofan*] — **cleav·able** \'klē-və-bəl\ *adj*

cleav·er \'klē-vər\ *n* : one that cleaves; *esp* : a heavy broad-bladed knife for chopping meat or cutting through bone

cleav·ers \'klē-vərz\ *n sing or pl* : any of several plants of the madder family with weak prickly stems [alteration of Old English *clife* "burdock, cleavers"]

clef \'klef\ *n* : a sign placed on the staff in music to show what pitch is represented by each line and space [French, literally, "key", from Latin *clavis*]

¹cleft \'kleft\ *n* **1** : a space or opening made by splitting : FISSURE **2** : a usually V-shaped indentation [Old English *geclyft*]

²cleft *adj* **1** : partially split or divided **2** : divided about halfway to the midrib ⟨a *cleft* leaf⟩

cleft graft *n* : a plant graft made by cutting the stock squarely across, splitting the cut end, and inserting one or two scions so that the cambiums of stock and scion are in contact

cleft palate *n* : congenital fissure of the roof of the mouth

clem·a·tis \'klem-ət-əs, kli-'mat-əs\ *n* : a vine or herb related to the buttercups that has leaves with three leaflets and is widely grown for its showy usually white or purple flowers [Latin, from Greek *klēmatis* "brushwood, clematis"]

clem·en·cy \'klem-ən-sē\ *n, pl* **-cies 1 a** : disposition to be merciful **b** : an act or instance of leniency **2** : mildness of weather SYN see MERCY

clem·ent \'klem-ənt\ *adj* **1** : inclined to be merciful : LENIENT ⟨a *clement* judge⟩ **2** : not harsh or severe ⟨*clement* weather⟩ [Latin *clemens*] — **clem·ent·ly** *adv*

¹clench \'klench\ *vb* **1** : CLINCH 1 **2** : to hold fast : CLUTCH **3** : to set or close tightly ⟨*clench* one's teeth⟩ ⟨hands *clenched* together⟩ [Old English *-clencan*]

²clench *n* **1** : the end of a nail that is turned back in clinching it **2** : an act or instance of clenching

clep·sy·dra \'klep-sə-drə\ *n, pl* **-dras** *or* **-drae** \-,drē, -,drī\ : WATER CLOCK [Latin, from Greek *klepsydra,* from *kleptein* "to steal" + *hydōr* "water"]

clere·sto·ry *or* **clear·sto·ry** \'kliər-,stōr-ē, -,stȯr-\ *n, pl* **-ries** : an outside wall of a room or building that rises

clef: left F clef, *right* C clef

above an adjoining roof and contains windows [Middle English, from *clere* "clear" + *story*]

cler·gy \'klər-jē\ *n, pl* **clergies** 1 : the body of religious officials (as priests, ministers, and rabbis) authorized to conduct services 2 : the official or priestly class of a religion [Old French *clergie* "knowledge, learning", from *clerc* "clergyman"]

cler·gy·man \-ji-mən\ *n* : a member of the clergy

cler·ic \'kler-ik\ *n* 1 : CLERGYMAN 2 : a member of a religious order lower than the priesthood [Late Latin *clericus*]

cler·i·cal \'kler-i-kəl\ *adj* 1 : of, relating to, or characteristic of the clergy, a clergyman, or a cleric 2 : of or relating to a clerk or office worker — **cler·i·cal·ly** \'kler-i-kə-lē, -klē\ *adv*

clerical collar *n* : a narrow stiffly upright white collar buttoned at the back of the neck and worn by clergymen

cler·i·cal·ism \'kler-i-kə-ˌliz-əm\ *n* : a policy of maintaining or increasing the worldly power of the church

¹clerk \'klərk\ *n* 1 : CLERIC 2 a : an official responsible for correspondence, records, and accounts ⟨town *clerk*⟩ b : one employed to keep records or accounts or to perform general office work c : SALESCLERK [Old English and Old French *clerc,* both from Late Latin *clericus,* from Late Greek *klērikos,* from Greek *klēros* "lot, inheritance"; from the statement in Deuteronomy 18:2 that the Lord is the inheritance of the Levite priests]

²clerk *vi* : to act or work as a clerk

clerk·ly \'klər-klē\ *adj* : of, relating to, or characteristic of a clerk

clerk·ship \'klərk-ˌship\ *n* : the position or business of a clerk

clev·er \'klev-ər\ *adj* 1 a : apt and skillful in using the hands or body b : quick in learning 2 : marked by wit or ingenuity [Middle English *cliver*] — **clev·er·ish** \'klev-rish, -ə-rish\ *adj* — **clev·er·ly** \-ər-lē\ *adv* — **clev·er·ness** \-ər-nəs\ *n* ☐ SYN CLEVER, INTELLIGENT, SMART, ALERT mean mentally quick or keen. CLEVER stresses quickness, deftness, or great aptitude; INTELLIGENT implies success in understanding and coping with the new situations and solving problems; SMART suggests alertness and quickness to learn, or it may imply pungency of wit tending often toward impudence; ALERT stresses quickness in perceiving and understanding.

clev·is \'klev-əs\ *n* : a usually U-shaped metal shackle with the ends drilled to receive a pin or bolt used for attaching or suspending parts [earlier *clevi,* probably of Scandinavian origin]

¹clew *or* **clue** \'klü\ *n* 1 : a ball of thread, yarn, or cord 2 *usually* **clue** : something that guides a person in solving a problem; *esp* : a piece of evidence in a crime 3 : a lower corner or the after corner of a sail [Old English *cliewen*]

²clew *or* **clue** *vt* **clewed** *or* **clued**; **clew·ing** *or* **clue·ing** *or* **clu·ing** 1 : to roll into a ball 2 *usually* **clue** : to provide with information or a clue ⟨*clue* me in on the situation⟩

cli·ché \kli-'shā\ *n* 1 : a trite phrase or expression; *also* : the idea expressed by it 2 : a hackneyed theme or situation [French, literally, "stereotype"] — **cliché** *adj*

¹click \'klik\ *n* : a slight sharp noise [probably imitative]

²click *vb* 1 a : to make or cause to make a click ⟨*click* one's tongue⟩ b : to move or strike with a click ⟨high heels *clicking* down the street⟩ ⟨*clicked* on the light⟩ 2 : to fit or work together smoothly 3 : SUCCEED 2 ⟨the idea *clicked*⟩

click beetle *n* : any of a family of elongated tapering beetles that are able when turned over to flip into the air by a sudden thoracic movement that produces a distinct click

cli·ent \'klī-ənt\ *n* 1 : a person under the protection of another : DEPENDENT 2 a : a person who engages the professional services of another b : CUSTOMER 1 [Latin *cliens*] — **cli·ent·age** \-ən-tij\ *n* — **cli·en·tal** \klī-'ent-l, 'klī-ənt-\ *adj*

cli·en·tele \ˌklī-ən-'tel\ *n* : a body of clients and especially of customers ⟨a store that caters to an exclusive *clientele*⟩ [French *clientèle,* from Latin *clientela,* from *cliens* "client"]

cliff \'klif\ *n* : a high steep face of rock [Old English *clif*]

cliff dweller *n, often cap C & D* : one of the people of the American Southwest who erected their dwellings on rock ledges or in the recesses of canyon walls and cliffs — **cliff dwelling** *n*

cliff–hang·er \'klif-ˌhang-ər\ *n* 1 : an adventure serial or melodrama; *esp* : one presented in installments each ending in suspense 2 : a contest whose outcome is in doubt up to the end

¹cli·mac·ter·ic \klī-'mak-tə-rik, ˌklī-ˌmak-'ter-ik\ *adj* 1 : being or relating to a critical period (as of life) 2 : CRUCIAL [Latin *climactericus,* from Greek *klimaktērikos,* from *klimaktēr* "critical point", literally, "rung of a ladder", from *klimax* "ladder"]

²climacteric *n* 1 : a major turning point or critical stage 2 : MENOPAUSE; *also* : a corresponding period in the male

cli·mac·tic \klī-'mak-tik\ *adj* : of, relating to, or being a climax — **cli·mac·ti·cal·ly** \-ti-kə-lē, -klē\ *adv*

cli·mate \'klī-mət\ *n* 1 a : a region with specified weather conditions b : the average weather conditions of a place or region over a long period 2 : the prevailing conditions or mood ⟨a favorable financial *climate*⟩ ⟨a *climate* of fear⟩ [Middle French *climat,* from Late Latin *clima,* from Greek *klima* "inclination, latitude, climate", from *klinein* "to lean"] — **cli·mat·ic** \klī-'mat-ik\ *adj* — **cli·mat·i·cal·ly** \-'mat-i-kə-lē, -klē\ *adv*

cli·ma·tol·o·gy \ˌklī-mə-'täl-ə-jē\ *n* : the science that deals with climates — **cli·ma·to·log·i·cal** \ˌklī-mət-l-'äj-i-kəl\ *adj* — **cli·ma·tol·o·gist** \ˌklī-mə-'täl-ə-jəst\ *n*

¹cli·max \'klī-ˌmaks\ *n* 1 a : a series of ideas or statements so arranged that they increase in force and power from the first to the last b : the highest or most forceful in a series c : the highest point : CULMINATION ⟨the storm had reached its *climax*⟩ 2 : ORGASM 3 : a relatively stable ecological stage or community; *esp* : the final stage of an ecological succession [Latin, from Greek *klimax* "ladder", from *klinein* "to lean"]

²climax *vb* : to come or bring to a climax

¹climb \'klīm\ *vb* 1 a : to go up or down by grasping or clinging with hands and feet ⟨*climb* down a ladder⟩ b : to ascend in growth (as by twining) ⟨a *climbing* vine⟩ 2 : to rise gradually to a higher point ⟨*climb* to power⟩ 3 : to slope upward ⟨the road *climbs* steeply⟩ [Old English *climban*] SYN see ASCEND — **climb·able** \'klī-mə-bəl\ *adj* — **climb·er** \'klī-mər\ *n*

²climb *n* 1 : a place where climbing is necessary 2 : the act of climbing

climbing iron *n* : a steel framework with spikes that may be attached to one's boots for climbing

clime \'klīm\ *n* : CLIMATE ⟨travel to warmer *climes*⟩ [Late Latin *clima*]

¹clinch \'klinch\ *vb* 1 a : to turn over or flatten the protruding end of (as a driven nail) b : to fasten by clinching 2 : CLENCH 2 3 : to make final or irrefutable ⟨*clinch* the deal⟩ 4 : to hold a boxing opponent [probably alteration of *¹clench*]

²clinch *n* 1 a : a fastening by means of a clinched nail, rivet, or bolt b : the clinched part of a nail, bolt, or rivet 2 : an act or instance of clinching in boxing

clinch·er \'klin-chər\ *n* : one that clinches; *esp* : a decisive fact, argument, act, or remark

\ə\ abut	\ng\ sing
\ər\ further	\ō\ bone
\a\ mat	\ȯ\ saw
\ā\ take	\ȯi\ coin
\ä\ cot, cart	\th\ thin
\au̇\ out	\th\ this
\ch\ chin	\ü\ food
\e\ pet	\u̇\ foot
\ē\ easy	\y\ yet
\g\ go	\yü\ few
\i\ tip	\yu̇\ cure
\ī\ life	\zh\ vision
\j\ job	

cline \'klīn\ *n* : a graded series of differences exhibited by a group of related organisms usually along a line of environmental or geographic change [Greek *klinein* "to lean"]

cling \'kling\ *vi* **clung** \'kləng\; **cling·ing** \'kling-ing\ **1 a** : to adhere firmly as if glued : STICK ⟨the burr *clung* to the dog's tail⟩ **b** : to hold or hold on tightly ⟨*clung* desperately to the ladder⟩ **2** : to have a strong emotional attachment or dependence ⟨*clings* to old friends⟩ [Old English *clingan*] SYN see STICK

cling·stone \'kling-ˌstōn\ *n* : a fruit (as a peach) whose flesh clings to the pit

clin·ic \'klin-ik\ *n* **1 a** : a class of medical instruction in which patients are examined and discussed **b** : a facility (as of a hospital) in which persons not bedridden are diagnosed or treated **2** : a class meeting devoted to the analysis and treatment of cases in some special field ⟨a writing *clinic* for poor students⟩ [French *clinique,* from Greek *klinikē* "medical practice at the sickbed", from *klinē* "bed", from *klinein* "to lean, recline"]

-clin·ic \'klin-ik\ *adj combining form* **1** : inclining : dipping **2** : having (so many) oblique intersections of the axes ⟨mono*clinic*⟩ ⟨tri*clinic*⟩ [Greek *klinein* "to lean"]

clin·i·cal \'klin-i-kəl\ *adj* **1 a** : of, relating to, or conducted in or as if in a clinic ⟨*clinical* examination⟩ **b** : involving or based on direct observation of the patient ⟨*clinical* studies⟩ **2** : coolly analytical and impersonal ⟨a *clinical* analysis of the program⟩ — **clin·i·cal·ly** \'klin-i-kə-lē, -klē\ *adv*

clinical thermometer *n* : a thermometer for measuring body temperature that continues to indicate the maximum temperature reached until the thermometer is reset

cli·ni·cian \klin-'ish-ən\ *n* : one qualified in clinical practice (as of medicine) as distinguished from a specialist in laboratory or research techniques

¹clink \'klingk\ *vb* : to make or cause to make a slight sharp short metallic sound [Middle English *clinken*]

²clink *n* : a clinking sound

clin·ker \'kling-kər\ *n* : stony matter fused by fire (as in a furnace from impurities in the coal) : SLAG [earlier *klincard,* a kind of brick, from obsolete Dutch *klinkaard,* from *klinken* "to clink"]

clin·ker–built \-ˌbilt\ *adj* : having the external planks or plates overlapping like clapboards on a house ⟨a *clinker-built* boat⟩ [*clinker* "clinch", from Middle English *clinken* "to clinch"]

cli·nom·e·ter \klī-'näm-ət-ər\ *n* : an instrument for measuring angles of elevation or inclination [Greek *klinein* "to lean"]

¹clip \'klip\ *vb* **clipped; clip·ping** : to clasp or fasten with a clip ⟨*clip* papers together⟩ [Old English *clyppan*]

²clip *n* **1** : a device that grips, clasps, or hooks **2** : a device to hold cartridges for charging the magazine of a rifle **3** : a piece of jewelry held in position by a spring clip

³clip *vb* **clipped; clip·ping** **1 a** : to cut or cut off or out with or as if with shears **b** : to cut off the tip or outer part of **2 a** : to make less ⟨*clip* one's influence⟩ **b** : to abbreviate in speech or writing **3** : PUNCH 2a ⟨*clip* one on the chin⟩ **4** : to block (an opposing player in football other than the ballcarrier) by hitting with the body from behind [Old Norse *klippa*]

⁴clip *n* **1** : a 2-bladed instrument for cutting especially the nails **2** : something that is clipped: as **a** : the sheared fleece of a sheep; *also* : a crop of wool **b** : a section of filmed material **3** : an act of clipping **4** : a sharp blow **5** : a rapid pace ⟨move along at a good *clip*⟩

clip·board \'klip-ˌbōrd, -ˌbord\ *n* : a small board with a clip at the top for holding papers

clip·per \'klip-ər\ *n* **1** : one that clips **2** *pl* : an implement for clipping especially hair, fingernails, or toe-nails **3** : a fast square-rigged ship with usually three masts, an overhanging bow, and a large sail area

clip·ping \'klip-ing\ *n* **1** : a cutting or shearing of something **2** : a piece clipped or cut out or off of something ⟨a newspaper *clipping*⟩ ⟨swept up the hair *clippings*⟩

clique \'klēk, 'klik\ *n* : a small exclusive group of people having a shared often selfish interest [French] — **cliqu·ey** \-ē\ *adj* — **cliqu·ish** \-ish\ *adj* — **cliqu·ish·ness** *n*

cli·tel·lum \klī-'tel-əm\ *n, pl* **-la** : a thickened glandular band about the body of an earthworm that secretes a sticky sac in which the eggs are deposited [Latin *clitellae* "packsaddle"]

cli·to·ris \'klit-ə-rəs, kli-'tór-əs\ *n, pl* **cli·to·ri·des** \kli-'tór-ə-ˌdēz\ *or* **cli·to·ris·es** : a small organ at the anterior or ventral part of the vulva homologous to the penis [Greek *kleitoris*] — **clit·o·ral** \'klit-ə-rəl\ *adj*

clo·a·ca \klō-'ā-kə\ *n, pl* **-cae** \-ˌkē, -ˌsē\ : a chamber into which the intestinal, urinary, and reproductive canals discharge in birds, reptiles, amphibians, and many fishes; *also* : a comparable chamber of an invertebrate [Latin, "sewer"] — **clo·a·cal** \-'ā-kəl\ *adj*

¹cloak \'klōk\ *n* **1** : a loose outer garment usually longer than a cape **2** : something that conceals or covers ⟨under the *cloak* of darkness⟩ [Old North French *cloque* "bell, cloak", from Medieval Latin *clocca* "bell"; from its shape] SYN see DISGUISE

²cloak *vt* : to cover or hide with a cloak

cloak–and–dag·ger \ˌklōk-ən-'dag-ər\ *adj* : of or relating to intrigue and spying

clob·ber \'kläb-ər\ *vt* **1** : to hit with great force : SMASH **2** : to defeat overwhelmingly [origin unknown]

cloche \'klōsh\ *n* : a woman's close-fitting hat usually having a deep rounded crown and narrow brim [French, literally, "bell", from Medieval Latin *clocca*]

¹clock \'kläk\ *n* **1** : a device for measuring or telling the time; *esp* : one not intended to be worn or carried about by a person **2** : a registering device (as a dial) attached to something (as a machine) to measure or record its performance **3** : TIME CLOCK **4** : BIOLOGICAL CLOCK **5** : a device (as in a computer) that sends out signals at regular intervals so that other events will happen in the right order [Dutch *clocke* "bell, clock", from Medieval Latin *clocca* "bell", of Celtic origin]

²clock *vt* **1** : to time with a stopwatch or by an electric device **2** : to register on a mechanical recording device

clock·wise \-ˌwīz\ *adv* : in the direction in which the hands of a clock rotate — **clockwise** *adj*

clock·work \-ˌwərk\ *n* : machinery (as in a mechanical toy) containing a train of small wheels

clod \'kläd\ *n* **1** : a lump or mass especially of earth or clay **2** : a dull or insensitive person : OAF [Middle English, alteration of *clot*] — **clod·dish** \-ish\ *adj* — **clod·dish·ness** *n* — **clod·dy** \'kläd-ē\ *adj*

clod·hop·per \'kläd-ˌhäp-ər\ *n* **1** : a clumsy and uncouth person **2** : a large heavy shoe

¹clog \'kläg\ *n* **1 a** : a weight attached especially to an animal to hinder motion or prevent escape **b** : something that hinders or restrains **2** : a shoe having a thick typically wooden sole [Middle English *clogge* "log"]

²clog *vb* **clogged; clog·ging** **1** : to impede with a clog : HINDER **2 a** : to obstruct passage through by filling beyond capacity ⟨heavy traffic *clogged* the roads⟩ **b** : to fill or become filled ⟨pipes *clogged* with grease⟩ **3** : to become filled with extraneous matter **4** : to dance a clog dance

clog dance *n* : a dance in which the performer wears clogs and beats out a clattering rhythm on the floor — **clog dancer** *n* — **clog dancing** *n*

cloi·son·né \ˌklóiz-n-'ā, klə-ˌwäz-\ *n* : a decoration made of colored enamels poured into divided areas in a design outlined with bent wire or metal strips [French, from *cloisonner* "to partition"]

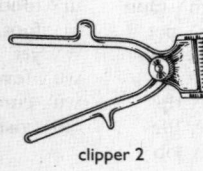

clipper 2

¹clois·ter \'klȯi-stər\ *n* **1 a** : a place (as a convent or a monastery) of religious seclusion **b** : life in religious seclusion **2** : a covered passage on the side of or around a court usually having one side walled and the other an open arcade or colonnade [Old French *cloistre*, from Medieval Latin *claustrum*, from Latin, "bar, bolt", from *claudere* "to close"] — **clois·tral** \-strəl\ *adj*

²cloister *vt* **1** : to shut away from the world in or as if in a cloister **2** : to surround with a cloister ⟨*cloistered* gardens⟩

¹clone \'klōn\ *n* : the whole asexual progeny of an individual (as a plant increased by grafting) [Greek *klōn* "twig, slip"] — **clon·al** \'klōn-l\ *adj* — **clon·al·ly** \-l-ē\ *adv*

²clone *vt* : to cause to grow as a clone

clop \'kläp\ *n* : a sound made by or as if by a hoof or wooden shoe against pavement [imitative] — **clop** *vi*

¹close \'klōz\ *vb* **1 a** : to move so as to bar passage through something ⟨*close* the gate⟩ **b** : to block against entry or passage ⟨*close* a street⟩ **2** : to suspend or stop the operations of ⟨*close* school⟩ **3** : to bring or come to an end : TERMINATE ⟨*close* a meeting⟩ **4 a** : to bring or bind together the parts or edges of ⟨a *closed* fist⟩ **b** : to fill or stop up ⟨*close* a crack with plaster⟩ **c** : to make complete by circling or enveloping or by making continuous ⟨*close* a circuit⟩ **5** : to fold, swing, or slide so as to leave no opening ⟨the door *closed*⟩ **6 a** : to draw near **b** : to engage in a struggle at close quarters : GRAPPLE ⟨*close* with the enemy⟩ **7** : to reach an agreement on ⟨*close* a deal⟩ [Old French *clos-*, stem of *clore*, frome Latin *claudere*] — **clos·able** \'klō-zə-bəl\ *adj* — **clos·er** *n* □ SYN CONCLUDE, TERMINATE, END: CLOSE implies shutting off from outside forces that could cause further development or change ⟨*close* an account⟩ CONCLUDE adds a suggestion of formality; TERMINATE implies setting a limit with or without completing; END stresses finality and usually implies an achievement of progress or concluding of a sequence ⟨an armistice *ended* hostilities⟩ ⟨the years *ending* the colonial period⟩

²close \'klōz\ *n* **1 a** : a coming or bringing to a conclusion **b** : CESSATION, END **2** : the last part (as of a speech or play)

³close \'klōs\ *n* : an enclosed area

⁴close \'klōs\ *adj* **1** : having no openings : CLOSED **2** : confined or confining strictly ⟨*close* arrest⟩ **3** : restricted (as in membership) to a privileged group **4 a** : OUT-OF-THE-WAY 1, SECLUDED **b** : SECRETIVE **5** : STRICT 2, RIGOROUS ⟨keep *close* watch⟩ **6** : hot and stuffy **7** : reluctant to give up money or possessions **8** : having little space between items or units ⟨flying in *close* formation⟩ **9 a** : fitting tightly or exactly ⟨a *close* gown⟩ **b** : very short or near to the surface ⟨a *close* haircut⟩ **c** : matching or blending without gap ⟨ideas in *close* harmony⟩ **10** : being near in time, space, effect, or degree : FAMILIAR ⟨*close* friends⟩ **12 a** : paying careful attention to details ⟨a *close* study⟩ **b** : marked by fidelity to an original **13** : having an even or nearly even score ⟨a *close* game⟩ SYN see NEAR, STINGY — **close·ly** *adv* — **close·ness** *n*

⁵close \'klōs\ *adv* : in a close position or manner : NEAR

close call \'klōs-\ *n* : a narrow escape

closed \'klōzd\ *adj* **1 a** : not open : ENCLOSED **b** : composed entirely of closed tubes or vessels ⟨a *closed* circulatory system⟩ **2 a** : forming a self-contained unit ⟨a *closed* association⟩ **b** : not subject to immigraton or emigration ⟨the *closed* ecosystem of a spacecraft⟩ **c** : traced by a moving point that returns to an arbitrary starting point ⟨a *closed* curve⟩; *also* : so formed that every plane section is a closed curve ⟨a *closed* solid⟩ **d** : having elements that when subjected to an operation produce only elements of the same set ⟨the whole numbers are *closed* under addition and multiplication⟩ **e** : containing its endpoints ⟨a *closed* interval⟩ **3** : con-

fined to a few ⟨a *closed* meeting⟩ **4** : ending in a consonant ⟨a *closed* syllable⟩

closed circuit *n* : a television installation in which the signal is transmitted by wire to a limited number of receivers

closed shop *n* : an establishment in which only union members in good standing are hired

close·fist·ed \'klōs-'fis-təd\ *adj* : STINGY 1, TIGHTFISTED

close–grained \-'grānd\ *adj* : having a firm smooth texture

close–hauled \-'hȯld\ *adj* : having the sails set for sailing as nearly against the wind as the vessel will go

close–mouthed \-'maú̇thd, -'maú̇tht\ *adj* : cautious in speaking or disclosing information

close·out \'klō-,zaú̇t\ *n* : a sale of leftover merchandise

close quarters \'klōs-\ *n pl* : direct contact or close range ⟨fought at *close quarters*⟩

close shave *n* : a narrow escape

¹clos·et \'kläz-ət\ *n* **1** : an apartment or small room for privacy **2** : a cabinet or recess for china, household utensils, or clothing **3** : WATER CLOSET [Middle French "small enclosure", from *clos* "enclosure", from *clore* "to close"]

²closet *vt* **1** : to shut up in or as if in a closet ⟨*closeted* myself in my study⟩ **2** : to take into a private room for an interview ⟨*closeted* for an hour with the governor⟩

closet drama *n* : drama suited primarily for reading

close–up \'klōs-,əp\ *n* **1** : a photograph or movie shot taken at close range **2** : an intimate view or examination

clos·ing \'klō-zing\ *n* **1** : a concluding part (as of a speech) **2** : a closable gap (as in a garment)

clos·trid·i·um \klä-'strid-ē-əm\ *n, pl* **-ia** \-ē-ə\ : any of various spore-forming mostly anaerobic soil or intestinal bacteria including some that produce deadly toxins — compare BOTULISM, TETANUS [derived from Greek *klōstēr* "spindle", from *klōthein* "to spin"]

clo·sure \'klō-zhər\ *n* **1** : an act of closing : the condition of being closed **2** : something that closes **3** : CLOTURE **4** : the property that a number system or a set has when it is mathematically closed under an operation

¹clot \'klät\ *n* : a mass or lump made by a portion of a liquid substance thickening and sticking together ⟨a *clot* of blood⟩ [Middle English, from Old English *clott*]

²clot *vb* **clot·ted; clot·ting** : to become or cause to become a clot : form clots

cloth \'klȯth\ *n, pl* **cloths** \'klȯthz, 'klȯths\ **1** : a pliable material made usually by weaving, felting, or knitting natural or synthetic fibers **2** : a piece of cloth used for a particular purpose; *esp* : TABLECLOTH **3** : distinctive dress of a profession or calling and especially of the clergy; *also* : CLERGY [Old English *clāth*]

clothe \'klōth\ *vt* **clothed** *or* **clad** \'klad\; **cloth·ing** **1 a** : to cover with or as if with cloth or clothing : DRESS **b** : to provide with clothes **2** : to express by suitable language : COUCH ⟨learn to *clothe* your thought effectively⟩ **3** : to endow especially with a quality ⟨*clothed* with dignity⟩ [Old English *clāthian*, from *clāth* "cloth, garment"]

clothes \'klōz, 'klōthz\ *n pl* **1** : CLOTHING **2** : BEDCLOTHES

clothes·horse \-,hȯrs\ *n* **1** : a frame on which to hang clothes **2** : one overly concerned with fashion

clothes moth *n* : any of several small dull-colored moths whose larvae eat wool, fur, or feathers

clothes·pin \-,pin\ *n* : a forked piece of wood or plastic or a clamp for holding clothes on a line

clothes·press \-,pres\ *n* : a receptacle for clothes

clothes tree *n* : an upright stand with hooks or pegs at the top on which to hang clothes

cloth·ier \'klōth-yər, 'klō-thē-ər\ *n* : one who makes or sells cloth or clothing

cloth·ing \'klō-thing\ *n* **1** : garments or an outfit of garments **2** : an outer or protective covering ⟨the trees' green *clothing*⟩

¹cloister 2

\ə\ abut		\ng\ sing	
\ər\ further		\ō\ bone	
\a\ mat		\ȯ\ saw	
\ā\ take		\ȯi\ coin	
\ä\ cot, cart		\th\ thin	
\aú̇\ out		\th\ this	
\ch\ chin		\ü\ food	
\e\ pet		\ú\ foot	
\ē\ easy		\y\ yet	
\g\ go		\yü\ few	
\i\ tip		\yú̇\ cure	
\ī\ life		\zh\ vision	
\j\ job			

¹cloud 1: *top* cumulus, *middle* nimbus, *bottom* stratus

clo·ture \'klō-chər\ *n* : the closing or limiting of debate in a legislative body especially by calling for a vote [French *clôture,* literally, "closure"] — **cloture** *vt*

¹**cloud** \'klaúd\ *n* **1** : a visible mass of particles of water or ice in the form of fog, mist, or haze suspended usually at a considerable height in the air **2 a** : a visible mass of minute particles in the air or a mass of obscuring matter in interstellar space **b** : an aggregate of charged particles (as electrons) **3** : a great crowd massed together : SWARM ⟨a *cloud* of mosquitoes⟩ **4** : something that appears dark or threatening ⟨war *clouds*⟩ **5** : something that obscures or blemishes ⟨worked under a *cloud* of secrecy⟩ **6** : a dark vein or spot (as in marble) [Old English *clūd* "rock, hill"] — **cloud·less** \-ləs\ *adj* — **cloud·less·ly** *adv* — **cloud·less·ness** *n*

²**cloud** *vb* **1** : to grow cloudy **2** : to make or become gloomy or ominous **3** : to envelop or hide with or as if with a cloud **4** : to make unclear : OBSCURE **5** : to make or become soiled or tainted

cloud·burst \-,bərst\ *n* : a sudden heavy rainfall

cloud chamber *n* : a vessel containing air saturated with water vapor whose sudden expansion reveals the passage of an ionizing particle (as an electron) by a trail of visible droplets

cloud forest *n* : a wet tropical mountain forest characterized by many plants that are epiphytes and by the presence of clouds even in the dry season

cloud·let \-lət\ *n* : a small cloud

cloudy \'klaúd-ē\ *adj* **cloud·i·er; -est 1** : of, relating to, or resembling cloud **2** : darkened by gloom or anxiety **3 a** : overcast with clouds; *esp* : six tenths to nine tenths covered with clouds **b** : having a cloudy sky **4** : obscure in meaning ⟨*cloudy* issues⟩ **5** : dimmed or dulled as if by clouds ⟨a *cloudy* mirror⟩ **6** : marked with veins or spots — **cloud·i·ly** \'klaúd-l-ē\ *adv* — **cloud·i·ness** \'klaúd-ē-nəs\ *n*

¹**clout** \'klaút\ *n* **1** : a blow especially with the hand; *also* : a hard hit **2** : a white cloth used as a target in long-distance archery **3** : PULL 2b ⟨political *clout*⟩ [Old English *clūt* "cloth, rag"]

²**clout** *vt* : to hit forcefully

¹**clove** \'klōv\ *n* : one of the small bulbs developed in the axils of the scales of a large bulb [Old English *clufu*]

²**clove** *past of* CLEAVE

³**clove** *n* : the dried flower bud of a tropical tree of the myrtle family that is a spice and the source of an oil used in perfumery and medicine; *also* : this tree [Old French *clou (de girofle),* literally, "nail (of clove)" from Latin *clavus* "nail"]

clo·ven \'klō-vən\ *past participle of* CLEAVE

cloven foot *n* **1** : a foot (as of a sheep) divided into two parts at its outer extremity **2** : the sign of devilish character [sense 2 from the traditional representation of Satan as cloven-footed] — **clo·ven-foot·ed** \,klō-vən-'fút-əd\ *adj*

cloven hoof *n* : CLOVEN FOOT — **cloven-hoofed** \,klō-vən-'húft, -'húvd, -'húft, -'húvd\ *adj*

clo·ver \'klō-vər\ *n* : any of a genus of leguminous herbs having leaves with three leaflets and flowers in dense heads and including many valuable forage and bee plants; *also* : any of various related plants [Old English *clāfre*] — **in clover** *or* **in the clover** : in prosperity or in pleasant circumstances

clo·ver·leaf \-,lēf\ *n* : a road plan that in shape resembles a four-leaf clover and that is used for passing one highway over another and routing traffic for turns by turnoffs that lead around to enter the other highway from the right

¹**clown** \'klaún\ *n* **1** : a rude ill-bred person : BOOR **2 a** : a fool, jester, or comedian in an entertainment; *esp* : a grotesquely dressed comedy performer in a circus **b** : one who habitually plays the buffoon : JOKER [earlier *clown* "countryman, farmer", perhaps from Middle French *coulon* "settler", from Latin *colonus* "colonist, farmer"]

²**clown** *vi* : to act like a clown

clown·ish \'klaú-nish\ *adj* : of or resembling a clown (as in foolishness or ignorance) — **clown·ish·ly** *adv* — **clown·ish·ness** *n*

cloy \'klói\ *vb* **1** : to weary or disgust with an excess usually of something once pleasing **2** : to cause weariness or disgust through being in excess [Middle English *acloien* "to lame", from Middle French *encloer* "to drive in a nail", from Medieval Latin *inclavare,* from Latin *in* "in" + *clavus* "nail"] — **cloy·ing·ly** \-ing-lē\ *adv*

¹**club** \'kləb\ *n* **1 a** : a heavy usually tapering staff especially of wood used as a weapon **b** : a stick or bat used for hitting a ball in a game **c** : a black figure resembling a clover leaf used to distinguish a suit of playing cards; *also* : a card of the suit bearing clubs **2 a** : an association of persons for some common object **b** : the meeting place of a club [Old Norse *klubba*]

²**club** *vb* **clubbed; club·bing 1** : to beat or strike with or as if with a club **2** : to unite or combine for a common cause — often used with *together*

club·foot \'kləb-,fút\ *n* : a misshapen foot twisted out of position from birth; *also* : this deformity — **club-foot·ed** \-əd\ *adj*

club fungus *n* : BASIDIOMYCETE

club·house \-,haús\ *n* **1** : a house occupied by a club or used for club activities **2** : locker rooms used by a ball team

club moss *n* : any of an order (Lycopodiales) of low often trailing evergreen vascular plants (as the ground pine) having branching stems covered with small mosslike leaves and reproducing by spores usually borne in club-shaped cones

club sandwich *n* : a sandwich of three slices of bread and two layers of meats and lettuce, tomato, and mayonnaise

club steak *n* : a small steak from just behind the ribs

¹**cluck** \'klək\ *vi* : to utter a cluck or a similar sound [imitative]

²**cluck** *n* **1** : the characteristic sound of a hen especially in calling her chicks **2** : a broody fowl

clue *variant of* CLEW

clum·ber spaniel \'kləm-bər-\ *n, often cap C & S* : a large massive heavyset spaniel with a dense silky largely white coat [*Clumber,* estate in Nottinghamshire, England]

¹**clump** \'kləmp\ *n* **1** : a group of things clustered together ⟨a *clump* of bushes⟩ **2** : a compact mass : LUMP **3** : a heavy tramping sound [probably from Low German *klump*] — **clumpy** \'kləm-pē\ *adj*

²**clump** *vb* **1** : to walk clumsily and noisily **2** : to form or cause to form clumps

clum·sy \'kləm-zē\ *adj* **clum·si·er; -est 1 a** : lacking dexterity, nimbleness, or grace ⟨*clumsy* fingers⟩ **b** : lacking tact or subtlety ⟨a *clumsy* joke⟩ **2** : awkwardly or poorly made : UNWIELDY [probably from obsolete English *clumse* "benumbed with cold"] SYN see AWKWARD — **clum·si·ly** \-zə-lē\ *adv* — **clum·si·ness** \-zē-nəs\ *n*

clung *past of* CLING

¹**clus·ter** \'kləs-tər\ *n* **1** : a number of similar things growing, collected, or grouped closely together : BUNCH **2** : two or more consecutive consonants or vowels in a segment of speech [Old English *clyster*]

²**cluster** *vb* **clus·tered; clus·ter·ing** \-tə-ring, -tring\ : to grow, collect, or assemble in a cluster

¹**clutch** \'kləch\ *vb* **1** : to grasp or hold with or as if with the hand or claws usually strongly, tightly, or suddenly **2** : to try to grasp and hold ⟨*clutch* at a railing⟩ [Old English *clyccan*]

²**clutch** *n* **1 a** : the claws or a hand in the act of grasping or seizing firmly **b** : an often cruel or unrelenting con-

trol **2** : a device for gripping an object **3 a** : a coupling used to connect and disconnect a driving and a driven part of a mechanism **b** : a lever operating a clutch **4** : a tight or critical situation : PINCH

³clutch *n* : a nest or batch of eggs or a brood of chicks [alteration of English dialect *cletch* "hatching, brood"]

¹clut·ter \'klət-ər\ *vt* : to fill or cover with a disorderly scattering of things ⟨*clutter* up a room⟩ [Middle English *clotteren* "to clot", from *clot*]

²clutter *n* : a crowded or disorderly collection ⟨a *clutter* of useless facts⟩

Clydes·dale \'klīdz-,dāl\ *n* : a heavy draft horse of a breed originally from Clydesdale, Scotland

clyp·e·us \'klip-ē-əs\ *n, pl* **-ei** \-ē-,ī, -ē-,ē\ : a plate on the front central part of an insect's head [Latin, "round shield"]

co- *prefix* **1** : with : together : joint : jointly ⟨*co*exist⟩ **2** : in or to the same degree ⟨*co*extensive⟩ **3** : fellow : partner ⟨*co*author⟩ [Latin, from *com-*]

See *co-* and 2d element

coact	cofounder	coprincipal
co-anchor	coheir	coprisoner
coauthor	coheiress	coproduce
cocaptain	coholder	coproducer
co–chairman	cohost	coproduction
co–chairperson	cohostess	copromote
cochampion	coinvent	copromoter
cocomposer	coinventor	coproprietor
coconspirator	coinvestigator	copublish
cocreator	coleader	copublisher
codefendant	comanagement	corecipient
codesign	comanager	coreligionist
codesigner	co–officiate	coresident
coedit	co–organizer	cosponsor
coeditor	co–own	cowinner
coexecutor	co–owner	co–worker
cofinance	copresident	cowrite
cofound		

co·ac·er·vate \kō-'as-ər-,vāt\ *n* : an aggregate of colloidal droplets held together by electrostatic forces [Latin *coacervatus,* past participle of *coacervare* "to heap up", from *co-* + *acervus* "heap"] — **co·ac·er·va·tion** \,kō-,as-ər-'vā-shən\ *n*

¹coach \'kōch\ *n* **1 a** : a large usually closed four‑wheeled carriage having doors in the sides and a raised seat in front for the driver **b** : a railroad passenger car intended primarily for day travel **c** : BUS 1a **d** : an automobile body especially of a closed model **e** : a class of passenger air transportation at a lower fare than first class **2 a** : a private tutor **b** : one who instructs or trains a performer or a team of performers; *esp* : one who instructs players in the fundamentals of a competitive sport and directs team strategy [Middle French *coche,* from German *kutsche;* sense 2 from the concept that the tutor conveys the student through his examinations]

²coach *vb* **1** : to go in a horse-drawn coach **2** : to instruct, direct, or prompt as a coach — **coach·er** *n*

coach dog *n* : DALMATIAN

coach·man \'kōch-mən\ *n* : a person whose business is driving a coach or carriage

co·ac·tion \kō-'ak-shən\ *n* : joint action

co·ad·ju·tor \,kō-ə-'jüt-ər, kō-'aj-ət-ər\ *n* **1** : one who works together with another : ASSISTANT **2** : a bishop assisting a diocesan bishop and often having the right of succession [Middle French *coadjuteur,* from Latin *coadjutor,* from *co-* + *adjutor* "helper", from *adjuvare* "to help"] — **coadjutor** *adj*

co·ag·u·la·ble \kō-'ag-yə-lə-bəl\ *adj* : capable of being coagulated — **co·ag·u·la·bil·i·ty** \-,ag-yə-lə-'bil-ət-ē\ *n*

co·ag·u·lant \-'ag-yə-lənt\ *n* : something that produces coagulation

co·ag·u·lase \-,lās, -,lāz\ *n* : an enzyme that promotes coagulation

co·ag·u·late \-,lāt\ *vb* : to become or cause to become viscous or thickened into a coherent mass : CLOT [Latin *coagulare* "to curdle", from *coagulum* "curdling agent", from *cogere* "to drive together", from *co-* + *agere* "to drive"] — **co·ag·u·la·tion** \,kō-,ag-yə-'lā-shən\ *n*

¹coal \'kōl\ *n* **1** : a piece of glowing or charred wood : EMBER **2** : a black or brownish black solid combustible mineral substance formed by the partial decay of vegetable matter under the influence of moisture and often increased pressure and temperature that is widely used as a natural fuel [Old English *col*]

²coal *vb* **1** : to supply with coal **2** : to take in coal

co·a·lesce \,kō-ə-'les\ *vi* : to unite by growth into one body [Latin *coalescere,* from *co-* + *alescere* "to grow"] SYN see MIX — **co·a·les·cence** \-'les-ns\ *n* — **co·a·les·cent** \-nt\ *adj*

coal·field \'kōl-,fēld\ *n* : a region where deposits of coal occur

coal gas *n* : gas from coal; *esp* : gas made by distilling bituminous coal and used for heating

co·a·li·tion \,kō-ə-'lish-ən\ *n* **1** : the union of separate items into a body or group; *also* : a body or group so formed : COMBINATION **2** : a temporary alliance of persons, parties, or countries for joint action [Middle French, from Latin *coalescere* "to coalesce"] — **co·a·li·tion·ist** \-'lish-nəst, -ə-nəst\ *n*

coal measures *n pl* : beds of coal with the associated rocks

coal oil *n* **1** : a refined oil prepared from petroleum : PETROLEUM **2** : KEROSENE

coal tar *n* : tar obtained by distilling bituminous coal and used in making drugs, dyes, and explosives

coam·ing \'kō-ming\ *n* : a raised frame around a hatchway to keep out water [probably derived from *comb*]

coarse \'kōrs, 'kȯrs\ *adj* **1** : of ordinary or inferior quality or appearance : COMMON **2 a** : made up of fairly large parts or particles ⟨*coarse* porous soil⟩ **b** : rough in texture ⟨*coarse* skin⟩ **c** : designed for heavy, fast, or less delicate work ⟨a *coarse* saw with large teeth⟩ **d** : not precise or detailed in adjustment or discrimination **3** : crude in taste, manner, or language ⟨*coarse* humor⟩ **4** : harsh or rough in tone ⟨a *coarse* voice⟩ [Middle English *cors,* from *course, cors* "course"] — **coarse·ly** *adv* — **coarse·ness** *n* □ SYN VULGAR, RIBALD, OBSCENE: COARSE implies roughness, rudeness, or crudeness of spirit, behavior, or language; VULGAR implies actual offensiveness to good taste or decency; RIBALD applies to what is amusingly or picturesquely vulgar or irreverent or mildly indecent; OBSCENE may apply to whatever strongly offends the sense of decency or propriety but especially implies flagrant violation of taboo in sexual matters.

coarse adjustment *n* : a knob on a microscope used for making relatively large changes in focus — compare FINE ADJUSTMENT

coarse–grained \-'grānd\ *adj* **1** : having a coarse grain or texture **2** : lacking in culture : CRUDE

coars·en \'kōrs-n, 'kȯrs-\ *vb* **coars·ened; coars·en·ing** \'kōrs-ning, 'kȯrs-, -n-ing\ : to make or become coarse ⟨hands *coarsened* by hard labor⟩

¹coast \'kōst\ *n* **1** : the land near a shore : SEASHORE **2** : a slope suited to sliding (as on a sled) downhill; *also* : a slide down such a slope [Middle French *coste,* from Latin *costa* "rib, side"]

²coast *vi* **1** : to sail along a coast **2 a** : to slide, run, or glide (as over snow on a sled) downhill by the force of gravity **b** : to move along (as on a bicycle when not pedaling) without applying power

coast·al \'kōst-l\ *adj* : of or relating to a coast : located on, near, or along a coast ⟨*coastal* waters⟩

coast·er \'kō-stər\ *n* **1** : one that coasts; *esp* : a ship engaged in coastal trade **2 a** : a tray often on wheels that is used for passing a decanter **b** : a shallow con-

\ə\ abut	\ng\ sing
\ər\ further	\ō\ bone
\a\ mat	\ȯ\ saw
\ā\ take	\ȯi\ coin
\ä\ cot, cart	\th\ thin
\au̇\ out	\t̶h̶\ this
\ch\ chin	\ü\ food
\e\ pet	\u̇\ foot
\ē\ easy	\y\ yet
\g\ go	\yü\ few
\i\ tip	\yu̇\ cure
\ī\ life	\zh\ vision
\j\ job	

tainer or a plate or mat to protect a surface ⟨tea *coasters*⟩ **c** : a small vehicle (as a sled) used in coasting

coaster brake *n* : a brake in the hub of the rear wheel of a bicycle operated by reverse pressure on the pedals

coast guard *n* : a military force concerned with enforcing marine laws and traffic regulations, maintaining aids to navigation, and performing rescue service — **coast·guards·man** \'kōst-ˌgärdz-mən, 'kōs-ˌ\ *or* **coast-guard·man** \-ˌgärd-mən\ *n*

coast·line \'kōst-ˌlīn\ *n* : the outline or shape of a coast

coast·ward \'kōs-twərd\ *or* **coast·wards** \-twərdz\ *adv* : toward the coast — **coastward** *adj*

¹coat \'kōt\ *n* **1** : an outer garment varying in length and style according to fashion and use **2** : the external growth (as of fur) on an animal **3** : a layer of one substance covering another ⟨a *coat* of paint⟩ [Old French *cote*, of Germanic origin] — **coat·ed** \-əd\ *adj*

²coat *vt* : to cover with a coat and especially with a finishing, protecting, or enclosing layer

co·a·ti \kə-'wät-ē, ˌkō-ə-'tē\ *n* : a tropical American mammal related to the raccoon but with a longer body and tail and a long flexible snout [Portuguese *coati*, from Tupi]

coati

coat·ing \'kōt-ing\ *n* **1** : a layer covering a surface : COAT ⟨a *coating* of ice on a pond⟩ **2** : cloth for coats

coat of arms : heraldic arms (as of a person or family) displayed on a shield or surface

coat of mail : a garment of metal scales or rings worn as armor

coax \'kōks\ *vb* **1** : to influence or influence a person by gentle urging, caressing, or flattering **2** : to gain by gentle persuasion or flattery ⟨*coax* a dollar from one's father⟩ [obsolete *cokes* "simpleton"] — **coax·er** *n*

co·ax·i·al \kō-'ak-sē-əl, 'kō-\ *adj* **1** : having coincident axes **2** : mounted on concentric shafts — **co·ax·i·al·ly** \-sē-ə-lē\ *adv*

coaxial cable *n* : a transmission line that consists of a central conductor surrounded by and insulated from a tube of conducting material

cob \'käb\ *n* **1** : a male swan **2** : CORNCOB 1 **3** : a short-legged stocky horse usually with a high stylish action [Middle English *cobbe* "leader"]

co·balt \'kō-ˌbȯlt\ *n* : a tough shiny silver-white magnetic metallic element found with iron and nickel — see ELEMENT table [German *kobalt*, from *kobold* "goblin"; from its occurrence in silver ore, once believed to be due to goblins] — **co·bal·tic** \kō-'bȯl-tik\ *adj* — **co·bal·tous** \-təs\ *adj*

cobalt chloride *n* : the dichloride of cobalt $CoCl_2$ that is blue when dehydrated but turns red in the presence of moisture

co·balt·ite \'kō-ˌbȯl-ˌtīt\ *or* **co·balt·ine** \-ˌtēn\ *n* : a grayish to silver-white mineral $CoAsS$ that consists of cobalt, arsenic, and sulfur and is an important ore of cobalt

cobalt 60 *n* : a heavy radioactive isotope of cobalt of the mass number 60 produced in nuclear reactors and used as a source of gamma rays

¹cob·ble \'käb-əl\ *vt* **cob·bled; cob·bling** \'käb-ling, -ə-ling\ : to make or put together roughly or hastily ⟨a shed *cobbled* up out of scraps⟩ [Middle English *coblen*]

²cobble *n* : a naturally rounded stone larger than a pebble and smaller than a boulder; *esp* : such a stone used in paving a street [back-formation from *cobblestone*]

³cobble *vt* : to pave with cobblestones

cob·bler \'käb-lər\ *n* **1** : one that mends or makes shoes **2** *archaic* : a clumsy worker **3** : a deep-dish fruit pie with a thick top crust [Middle English *cobelere*]

cob·ble·stone \'käb-əl-ˌstōn\ *n* : COBBLE [Middle English]

CO·BOL \'kō-ˌbȯl\ *n* : a language for programming a computer to work business problems [*co*mmon *bu*siness *o*riented *l*anguage]

co·bra \'kō-brə\ *n* : any of several venomous Asian and African snakes that when excited expand the skin of the neck into a hood; *also* : any of several related African snakes [Portuguese *cobra (de capello)*, literally, "serpent (with a hood)", from Latin *colubra* "snake"]

cob·web \'käb-ˌweb\ *n* **1** : the network spread by a spider; *also* : a single thread spun by a spider or insect larva **2** : something resembling a spiderweb ⟨*cobwebs* of intrigue⟩ [Middle English *coppeweb*, from *coppe* "spider" (from Old English *atorcoppe*) + *web*] — **cob·webbed** \-ˌwebd\ *adj* — **cob·web·by** \-ˌweb-ē\ *adj*

co·ca \'kō-kə\ *n* : a South American shrub with leaves that are chewed by the natives to impart endurance and are the source of cocaine; *also* : its dried leaves [Spanish, from Quechua *kúka*]

co·caine \kō-'kān\ *n* : a bitter drug obtained from coca leaves that is used as a local anesthetic and can result in psychological dependence

coc·cid \'käk-səd\ *n* : SCALE INSECT, MEALYBUG [derived from Greek *kokkos* "grain, kermes"]

coc·cus \'käk-əs\ *n, pl* **coc·ci** \'käk-ˌsī, -ˌī\ : a spherical bacterium [Greek *kokkos* "grain"] — **coc·cal** \'käk-əl\ *adj*

coc·cyx \'käk-siks\ *n, pl* **coc·cy·ges** \'käk-sə-ˌjēz\ *also* **coc·cyx·es** : the end of the vertebral column beyond the sacrum in humans and tailless apes that consists of four reduced fused vertebrae [Greek *kokkyx* "cuckoo, coccyx"; from its resemblance to a cuckoo's beak] — **coc·cyg·eal** \käk-'sij-ē-əl, -'sij-əl\ *adj*

coch·i·neal \ˌkäch-ə-ˌnēl, 'kō-chə-\ *n* : a red dyestuff consisting of the dried bodies of female cochineal insects used especially as a biological stain [Spanish *cochinilla* "wood louse, cochineal"]

cochineal insect *n* : a small bright red insect that is related to and resembles the mealybug, feeds on cactus, and yields cochineal

co·chlea \'kō-klē-ə, 'käk-lē-\ *n, pl* **co·chle·as** *or* **co·chle·ae** \'kō-klē-ē, 'käk-lē-, -ˌī\ : a part of the inner ear of higher vertebrates that is usually coiled like a snail shell and is the seat of the hearing organ [Latin, "snail, snail shell", from Greek *kochlias*, from *kochlos* "land snail"] — **co·chle·ar** \'kō-klē-ər, 'käk-lē-\ *adj*

¹cock \'käk\ *n* **1** : the adult male of a bird and especially the domestic fowl **2** : a device (as a faucet or valve) for regulating the flow of a liquid **3** : the cocked position of the hammer of a firearm [Old English *cocc*]

²cock *vt* **1 a** : to draw back the hammer of (a firearm) and set for firing **b** : to draw or bend back in preparation to throw or hit ⟨*cock* one's fist⟩ **c** : to set a mechanism (as a camera shutter) for tripping **2** : to turn, tip, or tilt usually to one side **3** : to turn up (as a hat brim)

³cock *n* : TILT 3a, SLANT ⟨a *cock* of the head⟩

⁴cock *n* : a small pile (as of hay) [Middle English *cok*, of Scandinavian origin]

⁵cock *vt* : to put (as hay) into cocks

cock·ade \kä-'kād\ *n* : an ornament (as a rosette) worn on the hat as a badge [French *cocarde*, from *cocard* "vain", from *coq* "cock"]

Cock·aigne \kä-'kān\ *n* : an imaginary land of great luxury and ease [Middle French *pais de cocaigne* "land of plenty"]

cock–and–bull story \ˌkäk-ən-'bül-\ *n* : an absurd, incredible, or highly improbable story told as true

cock·a·tiel \ˌkäk-ə-'tēl\ *n* : a small gray crested Australian parrot with a yellow head [Dutch *kaketielje*, from Malay *kakatua*]

cock·a·too \'käk-ə-ˌtü\ *n, pl* **-toos** : any of numerous large noisy usually showy and crested chiefly Australasian parrots [Malay *kakatua*]

cock·a·trice \'käk-ə-trəs, -ˌtrīs\ *n* : a legendary serpent with a deadly glance hatched by a reptile from a cock's egg [Middle French *cocatris* "ichneumon, cockatrice'', from Medieval Latin *cocatrix* "ichneumon"]

cock·crow \'käk-ˌkrō\ *n* : the time of day when roosters first crow : DAWN

cocked hat \'käkt-\ *n* : a hat with brim turned up to give a 3-cornered appearance

cock·er·el \'käk-rəl, -ə-rəl\ *n* : a young male domestic fowl [Old French dialect *kokerel* "small cock", from Old French *coc* "cock"]

cock·er spaniel \'käk-ər-\ *n* : a small spaniel with long ears, square muzzle, and silky coat [*cocking* "woodcock hunting"]

cock·eye \'käk-ˌī, -ˌī\ *n* : a squinting eye

cock·eyed \'käk-ˌīd\ *adj* 1 : having a cockeye 2 a : being out of line : ASKEW b : slightly foolish or absurd ⟨a *cockeyed* idea⟩ c : DRUNK 1, INTOXICATED

cock·fight \'käk-ˌfīt\ *n* : a combat of gamecocks usually fitted with metal spurs — **cock·fight·ing** \-ing\ *adj or n*

cock·horse \'käk-ˌhȯrs\ *n* : ROCKING HORSE [perhaps from *cock* "male" + *horse*]

¹cock·le \'käk-əl\ *n* : any of several grainfield weeds; *esp* : CORN COCKLE [Old English *coccel*]

²cockle *n* 1 : an edible mollusk with a heart-shaped 2-valved shell 2 : COCKLESHELL [Middle French *coquille* "shell", from Latin *conchylium*, from Greek *konchylion*, from *konchē* "conch"]

cock·le·bur \'käk-əl-ˌbər, 'kȯk-\ *n* : any of a genus of prickly-fruited plants related to the thistles; *also* : one of its fruits

cock·le·shell \'käk-əl-ˌshel\ *n* 1 a : a shell or shell valve of a cockle b : a shell (as a scallop) suggesting a cockleshell 2 : a light flimsy boat

cock·les of the heart \'käk-əlz-\ : the deepest part of one's being — usually used in the phrase *warm the cockles of the heart*

cock·ney \'käk-nē\ *n, pl* **cockneys** *often cap* 1 : a native of London and especially of the East End of London 2 : the dialect used by cockneys [Middle English *cokeney* "spoiled child", literally, "cocks' egg", from *cok* "cock" + *ey* "egg"] — **cockney** *adj*

cock·pit \'käk-ˌpit\ *n* 1 : a pit for cockfights 2 a : an open space aft of a decked area from which a boat or yacht is steered b : a space in the fuselage of an airplane for the pilot or the pilot and passengers or in large passenger planes the pilot and crew

cock·roach \'käk-ˌrōch\ *n* : any of an order (Blattaria) of mostly nocturnal insects which have flattened bodies and long antennae and some of which are domestic pests [by folk etymology from Spanish *cucaracha*, derived from *cuca* "caterpillar"]

cocks·comb \'käk-ˌskōm\ *n* 1 : COXCOMB 2 : a garden plant of the amaranth family grown for its showy flower clusters

cock·sure \'käk-'shu̇r\ *adj* 1 : perfectly sure : CERTAIN 2 : marked by overconfidence : COCKY — **cock·sure·ly** *adv* — **cock·sure·ness** *n*

cocktail *n* 1 : an iced drink of distilled liquor mixed with flavoring ingredients 2 : an appetizer (as tomato juice) served as a first course at a meal

cocky \'käk-ē\ *adj* **cock·i·er; -est** 1 : arrogantly self-confident 2 : jaunty in behavior or appearance — **cock·i·ly** \'käk-ə-lē\ *adv* — **cock·i·ness** \'käk-ē-nəs\ *n*

¹co·co \'kō-ˌkō\ *n, pl* **cocos** : the coconut palm or its fruit [Spanish, from Portuguese *côco*, literally, "bogeyman"]

²coco *adj* : made from the fibrous husk of the coconut

co·coa \'kō-ˌkō\ *n* 1 : a cacao tree 2 a : chocolate freed of some of its fat and ground b : a beverage made by heating cocoa powder with water or milk [Spanish *cacao*]

cocoa bean *n* : CACAO 2

cocoa butter *n* : a pale fat with a low melting point obtained from cacao beans and used in foods and cosmetics

co·co·nut *also* **co·coa·nut** \'kō-kə-ˌnət, -nət\ *n* : the fruit of the coconut palm with an outer fibrous husk yielding coir and a nut containing thick edible meat and coconut milk

coconut oil *n* : a nearly colorless oil or soft white fat extracted from coconuts or copra and used in soaps and foods

coconut palm *n* : a tall pinnate-leaved tropical palm probably of American origin

co·coon \kə-'kün\ *n* 1 a : a usually largely silken envelope which an insect larva (as a caterpillar) forms about itself and in which it passes the pupal stage b : any of various other protective coverings produced by animals 2 : a covering suggesting a cocoon [French *cocon*, from Provençal *coucoun*, from *coco* "shell", from Latin *coccum* "excrescence on a tree", from Greek *kokkos* "grain, seed, kermes berry"]

cod \'käd\ *n, pl* **cod** *also* **cods** : a soft-finned fish of the colder parts of the North Atlantic that is a major food fish; *also* : any of several related fishes [Middle English]

co·da \'kōd-ə\ *n* : a distinctive formal closing section in a musical composition [Italian, literally, "tail", from Latin *cauda*]

cod·dle \'käd-l\ *vt* **cod·dled; cod·dling** \'käd-ling, -l-ing\ 1 : to cook slowly in water just below the boiling point ⟨*coddle* eggs⟩ 2 : to treat with extreme care : PAMPER [perhaps from *caudle*] — **cod·dler** \'käd-lər, -l-ər\ *n*

¹code \'kōd\ *n* 1 : a systematic statement of a body of law; *esp* : one having the force of statute ⟨a criminal *code*⟩ 2 : a system of principles or rules ⟨moral *codes*⟩ 3 : a system of signals for communicating 4 : a system (as of letters or symbols) used to represent assigned and often secret meanings 5 : GENETIC CODE [Middle French, from Latin *codex* "tree trunk, wood writing tablet covered with wax, book"]

²code *vt* : to put into the form of a code — **cod·er** *n*

co·deine *or* **co·dein** \'kō-ˌdēn, 'kōd-ē-ən\ *n* : a drug that is obtained from opium, is weaker than morphine, and is used in cough remedies [French *codéine*, from Greek *kōdeia* "poppy capsule", from *kōos* "cavity"]

co·dex \'kō-ˌdeks\ *n, pl* **co·di·ces** \'kōd-ə-ˌsēz, 'käd-\ : a manuscript book (as of the Scriptures) [Latin]

cod·fish \'käd-ˌfish\ *n* : COD; *also* : its flesh used as food

cod·ger \'käj-ər\ *n* : an odd or cranky individual [probably alteration of *cadger*]

cod·i·cil \'käd-ə-səl, -ˌsil\ *n* : a supplementary document that modifies an earlier will [Middle French *codicille*, from Latin *codex* "book"]

cod·i·fy \'käd-ə-ˌfī, 'kōd-\ *vt* **-fied; -fy·ing** 1 : to reduce (as laws) to a code 2 : to arrange in a systematic and understandable order — **cod·i·fi·ca·tion** \ˌkäd-ə-fə-'kā-shən, ˌkōd-\ *n*

¹cod·ling \'käd-ling\ *n* 1 : a young cod 2 : HAKE

²cod·ling \'käd-ling\ *or* **cod·lin** \-lən\ *n* : a small immature apple; *also* : any of several elongated greenish English cooking apples [Middle English *querdlyng*]

codling moth *n* : a small moth whose larva lives in apples, pears, quinces, and English walnuts

cod–liver oil *n* : an oil obtained from the liver of the cod and related fishes and used as a source of vitamins A and D

co·don \'kō-ˌdän\ *n* : a triplet of nucleotides that is part of the genetic code and that specifies a particular amino acid in a protein or starts or stops protein synthesis

¹co·ed \'kō-ˌed\ *n* : a female student in a coeducational school

²coed *adj* 1 : COEDUCATIONAL ⟨a *coed* college⟩ 2 : of or relating to a coed

co·ed·u·ca·tion \ˌkō-ˌej-ə-'kā-shən\ *n* : the education of students of both sexes at the same school or college — **co·ed·u·ca·tion·al** \-'kā-shnəl, -shən-l\ *adj*

co·ef·fi·cient \ˌkō-ə-'fish-ənt\ *n* 1 : any of the factors of a product considered in relation to a specific factor;

cockroach

\ə\ abut	\ng\ sing
\ər\ further	\ō\ bone
\a\ mat	\ȯ\ saw
\ā\ take	\ȯi\ coin
\ä\ cot, cart	\th\ thin
\au̇\ out	\th\ this
\ch\ chin	\ü\ food
\e\ pet	\u̇\ foot
\ē\ easy	\y\ yet
\g\ go	\yü\ few
\i\ tip	\yu̇\ cure
\ī\ life	\zh\ vision
\j\ job	

esp : a constant factor of a term as distinguished from a variable ⟨in $5xy^2$, 5 is the *coefficient* of xy^2⟩ **2** : a number that serves as a measure of a property or characteristic (as of a substance or device)

coe·la·canth \'sē-lə-ˌkanth\ *n* : a fish or fossil of a family of mostly extinct fishes — compare LATIMERIA [Greek *koilos* "hollow" + *akantha* "thorn"] — **coelacanth** *adj*

-coele *or* **-coel** \ˌsēl\ *n combining form* : cavity : chamber ⟨blasto*coel*⟩ ⟨entero*coele*⟩ [Greek *koilos,* adjective, "hollow"]

coe·len·ter·ate \si-'lent-ə-ˌrāt, -rət\ *n* : any of a phylum (Coelenterata) of invertebrate animals that include the corals, sea anemones, jellyfishes, and hydroids and have radial body symmetry [Greek *koilos* "hollow" + *enteron* "intestine"] — **coelenterate** *adj*

coe·li·ac \'sē-lē-ˌak\ *adj* : of or relating to the abdominal cavity [Latin *coeliacus,* from Greek *koiliakos,* from *koilia* "cavity", from *koilos* "hollow"]

coe·lom \'sē-ləm\ *n, pl* **coe·loms** *or* **coe·lo·ma·ta** \si-'lō-mət-ə\ : the usually epithelium-lined body cavity of animals above the lower worms [German, from Greek *koilōma* "cavity", from *koilos* "hollow"] — **coe·lo·mate** \'sē-lə-ˌmāt\ *adj or n* — **coe·lo·mic** \si-'läm-ik, -'lō-mik\ *adj*

coen- *or* **coeno-** *combining form* : common : general ⟨*coeno*cytic⟩ [Greek *koinos*]

coe·no·bite \'sē-nə-ˌbīt\ *variant of* CENOBITE

coe·no·cyt·ic \ˌsē-nə-'sit-ik\ *adj* : containing several or many nuclei ⟨a *coenocytic* cell⟩

co·en·zyme \'kō-'en-ˌzīm\ *n* : a substance (as a vitamin) closely associated with an enzyme and essential for its normal function

coenzyme A *n* : a coenzyme $C_{21}H_{36}N_7O_{16}P_3S$ that occurs in all living cells and is essential to the metabolism of carbohydrates, fats, and some amino acids — compare ACETYL COENZYME A

co·equal \'kō-'ē-kwəl\ *adj* : equal with one another — **co·equal·i·ty** \ˌkō-ē-'kwäl-ət-ē\ *n* — **co·equal·ly** \'kō-'ē-kwə-lē\ *adv*

co·erce \kō-'ərs\ *vt* **1** : to restrain or dominate by negating individual will **2** : to compel to an act or a choice ⟨*coerced* them to cheat⟩ **3** : to enforce by force or threat ⟨*coerce* obedience to an order⟩ [Latin *coercēre,* from *co-* + *arcēre* "to shut up, enclose"] SYN see FORCE — **co·erc·ible** \-'ər-sə-bəl\ *adj*

co·er·cion \kō-'ər-zhən, -shən\ *n* : the act, process, or power of coercing

co·er·cive \-'ər-siv\ *adj* : serving or intended to coerce — **co·er·cive·ly** *adv* — **co·er·cive·ness** *n*

co·eval \kō-'ē-vəl\ *adj* : of the same or equal age or duration [Latin *coaevus,* from *co-* + *aevum* "age, lifetime"] — **coeval** *n*

co·ex·ist \ˌkō-ig-'zist\ *vi* **1** : to exist together or at the same time **2** : to live in peace with each other especially as a matter of policy — **co·ex·is·tence** \-'zis-təns\ *n* — **co·ex·is·tent** \-tənt\ *adj*

co·ex·ten·sive \ˌkō-ik-'sten-siv\ *adj* : having the same scope or extent in space or time — **co·ex·ten·sive·ly** *adv*

cof·fee \'kò-fē, 'käf-ē\ *n* **1** : a drink made from the roasted and ground or pounded seeds of a tropical tree or shrub of the madder family; *also* : these seeds or a plant producing them **2** : a cup of coffee ⟨two *coffees*⟩ [Italian *caffè,* from Turkish *kahve,* from Arabic *qahwah*]

cof·fee·house \-ˌhaùs\ *n* : a place where refreshments (as coffee) are sold

cof·fee·pot \-ˌpät\ *n* : a covered container for preparing or serving coffee

coffee shop *n* : a small restaurant

coffee table *n* : a low table usually placed in front of a sofa and used for serving refreshments

cof·fer \'kò-fər, 'käf-ər\ *n* **1** : a box or chest usually used for valuables; *esp* : STRONGBOX **2** : monetary funds : TREASURY — usually used in pl. **3** : COFFERDAM **4** : a recessed panel in a vault or ceiling [Old French *coffre,* from Latin *cophinus* "basket", from Greek *kophinos*]

cof·fer·dam \-ˌdam\ *n* : a watertight enclosure from which water is pumped to expose the bottom of a body of water and permit construction

cof·fin \'kò-fən\ *n* : a box into which a corpse is placed for burial [Middle English, "basket, receptacle", from Middle French *cofin,* from Latin *cophinus*]

coffin bone *n* : the bone enclosed within the hoof of the horse

co·func·tion \kō-'fəng-shən, -'fəngk-, 'kō-ˌ\ *n* : a trigonometric function whose value for the complement of an angle is equal to the value of a given trigonometric function for the angle itself ⟨the sine is the *cofunction* of the cosine⟩

cog \'käg\ *n* : a tooth on the rim of a wheel or gear [Middle English *cogge,* of Scandinavian origin]

co·gent \'kō-jənt\ *adj* **1** : having power to compel or constrain ⟨a *cogent* motive⟩ **2** : appealing forcibly to the mind or reason : CONVINCING ⟨*cogent* evidence⟩ [Latin *cogere* "to drive together, compel", from *co-* + *agere* "to drive"] SYN see VALID — **co·gen·cy** \-jən-sē\ *n* — **co·gent·ly** *adv*

cog·i·tate \'käj-ə-ˌtāt\ *vb* : to think over carefully or deeply : PONDER [Latin *cogitare* "to think, think about", from *co-* + *agitare* "to drive, agitate"] — **cog·i·ta·tion** \ˌkäj-ə-'tā-shən\ *n* — **cog·i·ta·tive** \'käj-ə-ˌtāt-iv\ *adj*

co·gnac \'kōn-ˌyak\ *n* : a French brandy [*Cognac,* district in France]

cog·nate \'käg-ˌnāt\ *adj* **1** : related by descent from the same ancestral language ⟨Spanish and French are *cognate* languages⟩ ⟨Spanish *madre* meaning "mother" and French *mère* meaning "mother" are *cognate* words⟩ **2 a** : related by processes of derivation within a single language ⟨English *boyish* and *boyhood* are *cognate* words⟩ **b** : related by adoption from one source language into two or more other languages ⟨English *tobacco* and French *tabac* are *cognate* words⟩ **3** : being a substantive that is related usually in derivation to the verb of which it is the object ⟨*song* in "sang the song" is a *cognate* object⟩ **4** : the same or similar nature ⟨illustrated books and *cognate* reference materials⟩ [Latin *cognatus* "related by birth", from *co-* + *gnatus, natus,* past participle of *nasci* "to be born"] — **cognate** *n* — **cog·nate·ly** *adv*

cog·ni·tion \käg-'nish-ən\ *n* **1** : the act or process of knowing including both awareness and judgment; *also* : something known by this process **2** : a cognitive activity [Latin *cognitio,* from *cognoscere* "to know, become acquainted with", from *co-* + *gnoscere* "to come to know"] — **cog·ni·tion·al** \-'nish-nəl, -'nish-ən-l\ *adj*

cog·ni·tive \'käg-nət-iv\ *adj* : of, relating to, or being conscious intellectual activities (as thinking, reasoning, imagining, learning words, or using language) — **cog·ni·tive·ly** *adv*

cog·ni·zance \'käg-nə-zəns\ *n* **1 a** : conscious recognition ⟨had no *cognizance* of the crime⟩ **b** : range of understanding or awareness ⟨an idea beyond a child's *cognizance*⟩ **c** : a noting of something : HEED ⟨take *cognizance* of what is happening⟩ **2 a** : the right and power to hear and decide controversies : JURISDICTION **b** : the judicial hearing of a matter [Old French *conoissance,* from *conoistre* "to know", from Latin *cognoscere*]

cog·ni·zant \-zənt\ *adj* : having cognizance

cog·no·men \käg-'nō-mən, 'käg-nə-\ *n, pl* **-nomens** *or* **-no·mi·na** \-'näm-ə-nə, -'nō-mə-\ **1** : SURNAME; *esp* : the third of the usual three names of an ancient Roman **2** : NAME 1; *esp* : NICKNAME [Latin, from *co-* + *nomen* "name"]

cog·no·scen·te \,kän-yə-'shent-ē, -ə-; ,käg-nə-\ *n, pl* **-scen·ti** \-'shent-ē\ : CONNOISSEUR [obsolete, Italian, from Latin *cognoscere* "to know"]

cog·wheel \'käg-,hwēl, -,wēl\ *n* : a wheel with cogs on the rim

co·hab·it \kō-'hab-ət\ *vi* : to live together as husband and wife [Late Latin *cohabitare,* from Latin *co-* + *habitare* "to inhabit"] — **co·hab·i·ta·tion** \,kō-,hab-ə-'tā-shən\ *n*

co·here \kō-'hiər\ *vi* **1** : to hold together firmly as parts of the same mass **2** : to consist of parts that cohere **3 a** : to become united in principles, relationships, or interests **b** : to be consistent [Latin *cohaerēre,* from *co-* + *haerēre* "to stick"] SYN see STICK — **co·her·ence** \-'hir-əns\ *or* **co·her·en·cy** \-ən-sē\ *n*

co·her·ent \kō-'hir-ənt, -'her-\ *adj* **1** : having the quality of cohering **2** : logically consistent — **co·her·ent·ly** *adv*

co·he·sion \kō-'hē-zhən\ *n* **1** : the action of sticking together tightly **2** : union between similar plant parts or organs **3** : molecular attraction by which the particles of a body are united throughout the mass [Latin *cohaerēre* "to cohere"]

co·he·sive \kō-'hē-siv, -ziv\ *adj* : exhibiting or producing cohesion — **co·he·sive·ly** *adv* — **co·he·sive·ness** *n*

co·ho \'kō-,hō\ *n, pl* **cohos** *or* **coho** : a small salmon with light-colored flesh [of American Indian origin]

co·hort \'kō-,hòrt\ *n* **1 a** : one of 10 divisions of an ancient Roman legion **b** : a group of warriors or followers **2** : ¹COMPANION 1 [Latin *cohors* "enclosure, throng, cohort"]

¹coif \'kòif, *in sense 2 usually* 'kwäf\ *n* **1** : a close-fitting cap **2** : COIFFURE [Middle French *coife,* from Latin *cofea*]

²coif \'kòif, 'kwäf\ *or* **coiffe** \'kwäf\ *vt* **coiffed** *or* **coifed; coiff·ing** *or* **coif·ing** : to provide with a coif

coif·fure \kwä-'fyùr\ *n* : a manner of arranging the hair [French, from *coiffer* "to cover with a coif, arrange (hair)", from *coife* "coif"]

coign of van·tage \,kòin-ə-'vant-ij\ : an advantageous position [Middle English *coyn, coigne* "projecting corner, coin"]

¹coil \'kòil\ *n* **1** : TUMULT 1 **2** : TROUBLE 1 [origin unknown]

²coil *vb* **1** : to wind into rings or spirals **2** : to move in a circular, spiral, or winding course **3** : to form or lie in a coil [Middle French *coillir* "to gather", from Latin *colligere* "to collect"]

³coil *n* **1 a** : a series of loops : SPIRAL **b** : a single loop of a coil **2** : a number of turns of wire especially in spiral form usually for electromagnetic effect or for providing electrical resistance **3** : a series of connected pipes in rows, layers, or windings

¹coin \'kòin\ *n* **1** : a piece of metal issued by governmental authority as money **2** : metal money [Middle English *coyn, coigne* "wedge, corner, coin", from Middle French *coing, coin* "wedge, corner", from Latin *cuneus* "wedge"]

²coin *vt* **1 a** : to make (a coin) especially by stamping : MINT **b** : to convert (metal) into coins **2** : INVENT ⟨*coin* a phrase⟩ — **coin·er** *n*

³coin *adj* **1** : of or relating to coins ⟨a *coin* show⟩ **2** : operated by coins ⟨a *coin* laundry⟩

coin·age \'kòi-nij\ *n* **1** : the act or process of coining **2 a** : COINS **b** : something (as a word) made up or invented

co·in·cide \,kō-ən-'sīd\ *vi* **1** : to occupy the same place in space or time **2** : to be the same shape and cover the same area **3** : to correspond or agree exactly ⟨an opinion that *coincides* with my own⟩ [Medieval Latin *coincidere,* from Latin *co-* + *incidere* "to fall on", from *in-* + *cadere* "to fall"]

co·in·ci·dence \kō-'in-səd-əns\ *n* **1** : the act or condition of coinciding **2** : two things that happen at the same time by accident but seem to have some connection; *also* : either one of these things

co·in·ci·dent \-səd-ənt\ *adj* **1** : occupying the same space or time ⟨*coincident* events⟩ **2** : of similar nature : HARMONIOUS SYN see CONTEMPORARY — **co·in·ci·dent·ly** *adv*

co·in·ci·den·tal \kō-,in-sə-'dent-l\ *adj* **1** : resulting from a coincidence **2** : occurring or existing at the same time — **co·in·ci·den·tal·ly** \-'dent-l-ē, -'dent-lē\ *adv*

coir \'kòir\ *n* : a stiff coarse fiber from the outer husk of the coconut [Tamil *kayal̮u* "rope"]

co·i·tus \'kō-ət-əs, kō-'ēt-\ *n* : sexual intercourse [Latin, from *coire* "to come together", from *co-* + *ire* "to go"]

¹coke \'kōk\ *n* : gray porous lumps of fuel made by heating soft coal in a closed chamber until some of its gases have passed off [Middle English]

²coke *vt* : to change into coke

³coke *n* : COCAINE

Coke *trademark* — used for a cola drink

coke·head \'kōk-,hed\ *n* : a compulsive user of cocaine

col- — see COM-

co·la \'kō-lə\ *n* : a carbonated soft drink containing sugar, caffeine, phosphoric acid or citric acid, caramel, and a characteristic flavoring [from *Coca-Cola,* a trademark]

col·an·der \'kəl-ən-dər, 'käl-\ *n* : a perforated utensil for draining food [Middle English *colyndore,* derived from Latin *colare* "to strain", from *colum* "sieve"]

col·chi·cine \'käl-chə-,sēn, 'käl-kə-\ *n* : a poisonous substance from the corms or seeds of the meadow saffron used to induce polyploidy in cells and to treat gout

col·chi·cum \'käl-chi-kəm, 'käl-ki-\ *n* : MEADOW SAFFRON; *also* : its dried corm or dried ripe seeds containing colchicine [Latin, a kind of plant with a poisonous root, from Greek *kolchikon,* literally, "product of Colchis"]

¹cold \'kōld\ *adj* **1** : having a low temperature or one decidedly below normal ⟨a *cold* day⟩ ⟨a *cold* drink⟩ **2** : lacking warmth of feeling : UNFRIENDLY ⟨a *cold* welcome⟩ **3** : suffering or uncomfortable from lack of warmth ⟨feel *cold*⟩ [Old English *ceald, cald*] — **cold·ly** *adv* — **cold·ness** \'kōld-nəs, 'kōl-\ *n* — **in cold blood** : with premeditation : DELIBERATELY

²cold *n* **1 a** : a condition of low temperature **b** : cold weather **2** : bodily sensation produced by loss or lack of heat : CHILL **3** : a bodily disorder popularly associated with chilling; *esp* : COMMON COLD

cold–blood·ed \'kōld-'bləd-əd, 'kōl-\ *adj* **1** : lacking or showing a lack of natural human feelings : not moved by sympathy ⟨a *cold-blooded* criminal⟩ **2** : having cold blood; *esp* : having a body temperature not internally regulated but approximating that of the environment **3** *or* **cold·blood** \-'bləd\ : of mixed or inferior breeding **4** : sensitive to cold — **cold–blood·ed·ly** *adv* — **cold–blood·ed·ness** *n*

cold chisel *n* : a strong steel chisel for chipping and cutting cold metal

cold cream *n* : a creamy preparation for cleansing, softening, and soothing the skin

cold cuts *n pl* : sliced assorted cold meats

cold frame *n* : a usually glass-covered frame without artificial heat used to protect plants and seedlings

cold front *n* : an advancing edge of a cold air mass

cold shoulder *n* : intentionally cold or unsympathetic treatment — **cold–shoulder** *vt*

cold sore *n* : a group of blisters about or within the mouth caused by a common virus

cold sweat *n* : concurrent perspiration and chill usually associated with fear, pain, or shock

cold war *n* : a conflict between nations carried on by methods (as propaganda or economic pressure) short

cogwheel

\ə\ abut		\ng\ sing
\ər\ further		\ō\ bone
\a\ mat		\ò\ saw
\ā\ take		\òi\ coin
\ä\ cot, cart		\th\ thin
\aù\ out		\th\ this
\ch\ chin		\ü\ food
\e\ pet		\ù\ foot
\ē\ easy		\y\ yet
\g\ go		\yü\ few
\i\ tip		\yù\ cure
\ī\ life		\zh\ vision
\j\ job		

of actual military action and usually without breaking off diplomatic relations

cold wave *n* : a period of unusually cold weather

cole \'kōl\ *n* : any of a genus of herbaceous plants that includes the cabbage and turnip [Old English *cāl*, from Latin *caulis* "stem, cabbage"]

cole·man·ite \'kōl-mə-,nīt\ *n* : a mineral $Ca_2B_6O_{11}\cdot 5H_2O$ consisting of a hydrous borate of calcium occurring in brilliant colorless or white massive crystals [William T. *Coleman*, died 1893, American mine owner]

co·le·op·tera \,kō-lē-'äp-tə-rə\ *n pl* : insects that are beetles [Greek *koleon* "sheath" + *pteron* "wing"] — **co·le·op·ter·ist** \-tə-rəst\ *n* — **co·le·op·ter·ous** \-tə-rəs\ *adj*

co·le·op·ter·an \-tə-rən\ *n* : ¹BEETLE 1 — **coleopteran** *adj*

co·le·op·tile \-'äp-tl\ *n* : the first leaf of a monocot seedling forming a protective sheath about the plumule [Greek *koleon* "sheath" + *ptilon* "down, feather"]

cole·slaw \'kōl-,slo\ *n* : a salad made of sliced or shredded raw cabbage [Dutch *koolsla*, from *kool* "cabbage" + *sla* "salad"]

co·le·us \'kō-lē-əs\ *n* : any of a large genus of herbs of the mint family often grown for their varicolored leaves [Greek *koleos, koleon* "sheath"]

col·ic \'käl-ik\ *n* : sharp sudden pain in the abdomen [Middle French *colique*, from Latin *colicus* "colicky", from Greek *kōlikos*, from *kolon* "colon"] — **col·icky** \'käl-i-kē\ *adj*

co·li·form \'kō-lə-,form\ *adj* : relating to, resembling, or being the colon bacillus [New Latin *Escherichia coli* "colon bacillus" + English *-form*] — **coliform** *n*

col·i·se·um \,käl-ə-'sē-əm\ *n* : a large building, amphitheater, or stadium for athletic contests or public entertainments [Medieval Latin *Colosseum, Coliseum* "the Colosseum"]

co·li·tis \kō-'līt-əs, kə-\ *n* : inflammation of the colon

col·lab·o·rate \kə-'lab-ə-,rāt\ *vi* **1** : to work jointly with others (as in writing a book) **2** : to cooperate with or assist an enemy force occupying one's country — **col·lab·o·ra·tion** \-,lab-ə-'rā-shən\ *n* — **col·lab·o·ra·tion·ist** \-shə-nəst, -shnəst\ *n* — **col·lab·o·ra·tor** \-'lab-ə-,rāt-ər\ *n*

col·lage \kə-'läzh, ko-, kō-\ *n* **1** : an artistic composition of fragments of materials (as printed matter) pasted on a surface **2** : the art of making collages [French, "gluing", from *coller* "to glue", from *colle* "glue", from Greek *kolla*]

col·la·gen \'käl-ə-jən\ *n* : an insoluble fibrous protein that is the chief constituent of connective tissue fibrils and yields gelatin and glue on prolonged heating with water [Greek *kolla* "glue"] — **col·lag·e·nous** \kə-'laj-ə-nəs\ *adj*

¹col·lapse \kə-'laps\ *vb* **1** : to break down completely : DISINTEGRATE **2** : to shrink together abruptly and completely (a *collapsed* balloon) **3** : to fall in : give way (the tunnel *collapsed*) **4** : to suddenly lose value or effectiveness (the country's currency *collapsed*) **5** : to break down physically or mentally through exhaustion or disease; *esp* : to fall helpless or unconscious **6** : to fold down into a more compact shape (*collapse* a card table) [Latin *collabi*, from *com-* + *labi* "to fall, slide"] — **col·laps·ible** \-'lap-sə-bəl\ *adj*

²collapse *n* : the act or an instance of collapsing : BREAKDOWN

¹col·lar \'käl-ər\ *n* **1 a** : a band, strip, or chain worn around the neck or the neckline of a garment **b** : a part of the harness of a draft animal fitted over the shoulders and taking strain when a load is drawn **2** : something resembling a collar (as a ring or round flange to restrain motion or hold something in place) [Old French *coler*, from Latin *collare*, from *collum* "neck"] — **col·lar·less** \-ər-ləs\ *adj*

²collar *vt* **1 a** : to seize by the collar **b** : to take prisoner : NAB **2** : to put a collar on

col·lar·bone \'käl-ər-,bōn, ,käl-ər-'\ *n* : CLAVICLE

collar cell *n* : a flagellated cell (as of a sponge) with a protoplasmic collar about the base of its flagellum

col·lard \'käl-ərd\ *n* : a stalked smooth-leaved kale — usually used in pl. [alteration of *colewort* "cole, kale"]

collared lizard *n* : a brightly colored iguana of the south-central United States and Mexico

col·late \kə-'lāt, kä-, kō-; 'käl-,āt, 'kōl-\ *vt* : to collect and compare carefully in order to verify and often to unify or arrange in order [back-formation from *collation*] — **col·la·tor** \-'lāt-ər, -,āt-\ *n*

¹col·lat·er·al \kə-'lat-ə-rəl, -'la-trəl\ *adj* **1** : associated but of secondary or supporting importance (a main question and *collateral* questions) **2** : descended from the same ancestors but not in the same line (cousins are *collateral* relatives) **3 a** : of, relating to, or being collateral used as security **b** : secured by collateral [Medieval Latin *collateralis*, from Latin *com-* + *lateralis* "lateral"] — **col·lat·er·al·ly** \-ē\ *adv*

²collateral *n* **1** : property (as stocks, bonds, or a mortgage) handed over or pledged as security for the repayment of a loan **2** : a branch of a bodily part (as a vein)

col·la·tion \kə-'lā-shən, kä-, kō-\ *n* **1** : a light meal **2** : the act, process, or result of collating [Medieval Latin *collatio*, from Latin, "bringing together, comparison", from *collatus*, past participle of *conferre* "to bring together", from *com-* + *ferre* "to carry"]

col·league \'käl-,ēg\ *n* : an associate in a profession or office; *also* : a fellow worker [Middle French *collegue*, from Latin *collega*, from *com-* + *legare* "to appoint, delegate"]

¹col·lect \'käl-ikt, -,ekt\ *n* : a short prayer consisting of an invocation, petition, and conclusion [Old French *collecte*, from Medieval Latin *collecta*, short for *oratio ad collectam* "prayer upon assembly"]

²col·lect \kə-'lekt\ *vb* **1 a** : to bring together into one body or place **b** : to gather from a number of sources (*collect* taxes) **2** : to gain or regain control of (*collect* one's thoughts) **3** : to claim as due and receive payment for **4 a** : ASSEMBLE (a crowd *collected* at the scene of the accident) **b** : ACCUMULATE (dust *collects* on the furniture) **5** : to simplify mathematically by carrying out addition and subtraction of (terms containing the same variables) (when terms are *collected* $8x - 3x + 5$ becomes $5x + 5$) [Latin *collectus*, past participle of *colligere* "to collect", from *com-* + *legere* "to gather"] SYN see GATHER — **col·lect·able** *or* **col·lect·ible** \-'lek-tə-bəl\ *adj*

³col·lect \kə-'lekt\ *adv or adj* : to be paid for by the receiver (we telephoned *collect*)

col·lect·ed \kə-'lek-təd\ *adj* : SELF-POSSESSED, CALM — **col·lect·ed·ly** *adv* — **col·lect·ed·ness** *n*

collecting tubule *n* : the part of a nephron by which urine is collected

col·lec·tion \kə-'lek-shən\ *n* **1** : the act or process of collecting **2** : something collected; *esp* : an accumulation of objects gathered for study, comparison, or exhibition **3** : a gathering of money (as for charitable purposes)

¹col·lec·tive \kə-'lek-tiv\ *adj* **1** : denoting a number of persons or things considered as one group (flock is a *collective* noun) **2** : formed by collecting : AGGREGATED **3** : of or relating to a group of individuals (*collective* needs) **4** : collectivized or characterized by collectivism **5** : shared or assumed by all members of the group (*collective* leadership) — **col·lec·tive·ly** *adv*

²collective *n* **1** : a collective body : GROUP **2** : a cooperative unit or organization; *esp* : COLLECTIVE FARM

collective bargaining *n* : negotiation between an employer and union representatives usually on wages, hours, and working conditions

collective farm *n* : a farm in a communist country formed from many small holdings collected into a single unit for joint operation under governmental supervision

collective fruit *n* : MULTIPLE FRUIT

collective mark *n* : a trademark or a service mark of a group (as a cooperative or other association)

col·lec·tiv·ism \kə-'lek-ti-ˌviz-əm\ *n* : a political or economic theory advocating collective control especially over production and distribution; *also* : a system marked by such control — **col·lec·tiv·ist** \-vəst\ *adj or n* — **col·lec·tiv·is·tic** \-ˌlek-ti-'vis-tik\ *adj*

col·lec·tiv·i·ty \kə-ˌlek-'tiv-ət-ē, ˌkäl-ek-\ *n, pl* **-ties** : a collective whole

col·lec·tiv·ize \kə-'lek-ti-ˌvīz\ *vt* : to organize under collective control — **col·lec·tiv·iza·tion** \-ˌlek-ti-və-'zā-shən\ *n*

col·lec·tor \kə-'lek-tər\ *n* : one that collects: as **a** : an official or agent who collects funds or money due **b** : one that makes a collection ⟨a stamp *collector*⟩ **c** : an object, device, or substance that collects — **col·lec·tor·ship** \-ˌship\ *n*

col·leen \kä-'lēn, 'käl-ˌēn\ *n* : an Irish girl [Irish Gaelic *cailín* "young girl"]

col·lege \'käl-ij\ *n* **1** : a building used for an educational or religious purpose **2 a** : a subordinate school in a university **b** : a school higher than a high school; *esp* : a 4-year school offering courses in the sciences and humanities leading to a bachelor's degree **c** : an institution offering instruction usually in a professional, vocational, or technical field ⟨business *college*⟩ ⟨barber *college*⟩ **3** : an organized body of persons having common interests or duties ⟨the *college* of cardinals⟩ [Middle French, "body of clergy", from Latin *collegium* "society", from *collega* "colleague"]

col·le·gian \kə-'lē-jən, -jē-ən\ *n* : a student or recent graduate of a college

col·le·giate \kə-'lē-jət, -jē-ət\ *adj* **1** : of or relating to a college **2** : of, relating to, or characteristic of college students ⟨*collegiate* clothes⟩

col·le·gi·um \kə-'leg-ē-əm, -'läg-\ *n, pl* **-gia** \-ē-ə\ *or* **-gi·ums** : a governing group in which each member has approximately equal power and authority [Russian *kollegya*, from Latin *collegium* "society"] — **col·le·gial** \-'lē-jē-əl, -jəl; -gē-əl\ *adj*

col·lem·bo·lan \kə-'lem-bə-lən\ *n* : SPRINGTAIL [Greek *kolla* "glue" + *embolos* "wedge, stopper"] — **collembolan** *adj*

col·len·chy·ma \kə-'leng-kə-mə\ *n* : a plant tissue of living usually elongated cells with thickened walls — compare SCLERENCHYMA [Greek *kolla* "glue" + *-enchyma* (as in par *enchyma*)] — **col·len·chy·ma·tous** \ˌkäl-ən-'kim-ət-əs, -'kī-mət-\ *adj*

col·lide \kə-'līd\ *vi* **1** : to come together with solid impact **2** : to come into conflict : CLASH [Latin *collidere*, from *com-* + *laedere* "to injure by striking"]

col·lie \'käl-ē\ *n* : a large dog of a breed developed in Scotland especially for herding sheep [probably from English dialect *colly* "black"]

col·lier \'käl-yər\ *n* **1** : a coal miner **2** : a ship for carrying coal [Middle English *colier*, from *col* "coal"]

col·liery \'käl-yə-rē\ *n, pl* **-lier·ies** : a coal mine and the buildings connected with it

col·li·mate \'käl-ə-ˌmāt\ *vt* : to make (as rays of light) parallel [Latin *collimare*, from *collineare* "to make straight", from *com-* + *linea* "line"] — **col·li·ma·tor** \-ˌmāt-ər\ *n*

col·lin·e·ar \kə-'lin-ē-ər, kä-\ *adj* : lying on the same straight line — **col·lin·ear·i·ty** \-ˌlin-ē-'ar-ət-ē\ *n*

col·li·sion \kə-'lizh-ən\ *n* : an act or instance of colliding : CRASH [Latin *collisio*, from *collidere* "to collide"]

col·lo·ca·tion \ˌkäl-ə-'kā-shən\ *n* : the act or result of placing together

col·lo·di·on \kə-'lōd-ē-ən\ *n* : a viscous solution of pyroxylin used especially as a coating for wounds and in cements [Greek *kollōdēs* "glutinous", from *kolla* "glue"]

col·loid \'käl-ˌóid\ *n* : a very finely divided substance that is scattered throughout another substance; *also* : a mixture (as smoke, gelatine, or marshmallow) consisting of such a substance together with the substance in which it is scattered [Greek *kolla* "glue"] — **col·loi·dal** \kə-'lóid-l, kä-\ *adj* — **col·loi·dal·ly** \-l-ē\ *adv*

col·lo·qui·al \kə-'lō-kwē-əl\ *adj* **1** : used in or characteristic of familiar and informal conversation **2** : using conversational style — **col·lo·qui·al·ly** \-kwē-ə-lē\ *adv*

col·lo·qui·al·ism \-kwē-ə-ˌliz-əm\ *n* **1** : a colloquial expression **2** : colloquial style

col·lo·qui·um \kə-'lō-kwē-əm\ *n, pl* **-qui·ums** *or* **-quia** \-kwē-ə\ : CONFERENCE; *esp* : a seminar that several lecturers take turns in leading [Latin, "colloquy"]

col·lo·quy \'käl-ə-kwē\ *n, pl* **-quies** : CONVERSATION; *esp* : a formal conversation or conference [Latin *colloquium*, from *colloqui* "to converse", from *com-* + *loqui* "to speak"]

col·lu·sion \kə-'lü-zhən\ *n* : secret agreement or cooperation for a deceitful purpose [Middle French, from Latin *collusio*, from *colludere* "to conspire", from *com-* + *ludere* "to play", from *ludus* "game"] — **col·lu·sive** \-'lü-siv, -ziv\ *adj* — **col·lu·sive·ly** *adv*

co·log·a·rithm \'kō-'lòg-ə-ˌrith-əm, -'läg-\ *n* : the logarithm of the reciprocal of a number

co·logne \kə-'lōn\ *n* : a perfumed toilet water composed of alcohol and aromatic oils [*Cologne*, Germany]

¹co·lon \'kō-lən\ *n* : the part of the large intestine that extends from the cecum to the rectum [Latin, from Greek *kolon*] — **co·lon·ic** \kō-'län-ik\ *adj*

²colon *n* : a punctuation mark : used chiefly to direct attention to what follows (as a list, explanation, or quotation) [Latin, "part of a poem", from Greek *kōlon* "limb, clause"]

³co·lon \kə-'lōn\ *n, pl* **co·lo·nes** \-'lō-ˌnās\ **1** : the basic monetary unit of Costa Rica and El Salvador **2** : a coin or note representing one colon [Spanish *colón*, from *Cristóbal Colón* "Christopher Columbus"]

colon bacillus *n* : a bacillus regularly present in the intestine and used as an index of fecal contamination (as of water)

col·o·nel \'kərn-l\ *n* : an officer rank in the Army, Marine Corps, and Air Force above lieutenant colonel and below brigadier general [from earlier *coronel*, from Middle French, from Italian *colonnello* "column of soldiers, colonel", from *colonna* "column", from Latin *columna*] — **col·o·nel·cy** \-l-sē\ *n* □ ORIGIN English *colonel* is pronounced the same as *kernel*. A review of the history of *colonel* shows how this difference between spelling and pronunciation came about. In many languages when a word contains two identical or similar sounds, one of these sounds will often change over a period of time. This kind of change is called *dissimilation*. When the Italian word *colonello* was taken into French, it became *coronel*; and the word was borrowed by the English from the French in this form. Later the spelling *colonel* came to be used in order to reflect the Italian origin of the word. But by then the pronunciation with *r* was well established.

¹co·lo·nial \kə-'lō-nē-əl, -nyəl\ *adj* **1** : of, relating to, or characteristic of a colony **2** *often cap* : of or relating to the original 13 colonies forming the United States **3** : possessing, forming, or composed of colonies ⟨a *colonial* nation and its *colonial* empire⟩ — **co·lo·nial·ize** \-ˌīz\ *vt* — **co·lo·nial·ly** \-ē\ *adv* — **co·lo·nial·ness** *n*

²colonial *n* : COLONIST 1

co·lo·nial·ism \-nē-ə-ˌliz-əm, -nyə-ˌliz-\ *n* : control by one power over a dependent area or people; *also* : a policy advocating or based on such control — **co·lo·nial·ist** \-ləst\ *n or adj*

collie

\ə\ abut		\ng\ sing
\ər\ further		\ō\ bone
\a\ mat		\ó\ saw
\ā\ take		\ói\ coin
\ä\ cot, cart		\th\ thin
\aú\ out		\th\ this
\ch\ chin		\ü\ food
\e\ pet		\ú\ foot
\ē\ easy		\y\ yet
\g\ go		\yü\ few
\i\ tip		\yú\ cure
\ī\ life		\zh\ vision
\j\ job		

colophon 2

columbine

col·o·nist \'käl-ə-nəst\ *n* **1** : an inhabitant or member of a colony **2** : a person who takes part in founding a colony

col·o·nize \'käl-ə-,nīz\ *vb* **1** : to establish a colony in or on ⟨England *colonized* Australia⟩ **2** : to establish in a colony **3** : to make or establish a colony : SETTLE — **col·o·ni·za·tion** \,käl-ə-nə-'zā-shən\ *n* — **col·o·niz·er** *n*

col·on·nade \,käl-ə-'nād\ *n* : a row of columns set at regular intervals and usually supporting the base of the roof structure [French, from Italian *colonnata,* from *colonna* "column", from Latin *columna*] — **col·on·nad·ed** \-'nād-əd\ *adj*

col·o·ny \'käl-ə-nē\ *n, pl* **-nies** **1 a** : a body of people sent out by a state to a new territory **b** : the territory inhabited by people sent to new territory **c** : a distant territory belonging to or under the control of a nation **2 a** : a distinguishable localized population within a species ⟨a *colony* of termites⟩ **b** : a circumscribed mass of microorganisms usually growing in or on a solid medium **c** : the aggregation of zooids of a compound animal **3** : a group of individuals with common characteristics or interests situated in close association; *also* : the section occupied by such a group ⟨an artist *colony*⟩ [Latin *colonia,* from *colonus* "farmer, colonist", from *colere* "to cultivate"]

col·o·phon \'käl-ə-fən, -,fän\ *n* **1** : an inscription placed at the end of a book with facts relative to its production **2** : an identifying device used by a printer or a publisher [Latin, from Greek *kolophōn* "summit, finishing touch"]

¹col·or \'kəl-ər\ *n* **1 a** : a phenomenon of light (as red, brown, pink, gray) or visual perception that enables one to differentiate otherwise identical objects **b** : the aspect of objects and light sources that may be described in terms of hue, lightness, and saturation for objects and hue, brightness, and saturation for light sources **c** : a hue as contrasted with black, white, or gray **2 a** : an outward often deceptive show : APPEARANCE ⟨the story has the *color* of truth⟩ **b** : an appearance of authenticity : PLAUSIBILITY **3 a** : COMPLEXION 2; *esp* : a healthy complexion **b** : BLUSH 2 **4** : vividness or variety of effects of language **5** : the use or combination of colors **6** *pl* **a** : an identifying flag, ensign, or pennant **b** : service in the armed forces ⟨a call to the *colors*⟩ **7** : VITALITY 2b, INTEREST **8** : something used to give color : PIGMENT **9** : skin pigmentation other than white characteristic of race ⟨overcome prejudice toward *color*⟩ [Old French *colour,* from Latin *color*]
□ SYN HUE, TINT, SHADE: COLOR is the general term for any distinguishable quality of light but specifically implies the property of things seen as red, yellow, blue, and so on as distinguished from white, black, or gray; HUE usually implies some modification of or a finer discrimination of a primary color ⟨a reddish orange *hue*⟩ TINT applies especially to a color modified toward white; SHADE to one modified toward black; but all four terms are frequently interchangeable.

²color *vb* **1 a** : to give color to ⟨the wind *colored* our cheeks⟩ **b** : to change the color of : PAINT **2** : MISREPRESENT, DISTORT ⟨a story *colored* by prejudice⟩ **3** : to take on or change color; *esp* : BLUSH — **col·or·er** \'kəl-ər-ər\ *n*

Col·o·ra·do blue spruce \,käl-ə-'rad-ō-, -'räd-\ *n* : a tall wide-spreading spruce usually with bluish green needles that is native to the Rocky Mountain region of the United States but is often planted elsewhere as an ornamental [*Colorado,* state of the United States]

Colorado potato beetle *n* : a black-and-yellow striped beetle that feeds on the leaves of the potato — called also *potato beetle, potato bug*

col·or·ation \,kəl-ə-'rā-shən\ *n* : use or arrangement of colors or shades : COLORING ⟨the *coloration* of a flower⟩

col·or·a·tu·ra \,kəl-ə-rə-'tùr-ə, -'tyùr-\ *n* **1** : showy style in singing (as in opera) **2** : a soprano specializing

in coloratura [obsolete Italian, literally, "coloring", from Latin *colorare* "to color", from *color* "color"]

col·or-blind \'kəl-ər-,blīnd\ *adj* : affected with partial or total inability to distinguish one or more chromatic colors — **color blindness** *n*

col·ored \'kəl-ərd\ *adj* **1** : having color ⟨*colored* pictures⟩ **2** : marked by exaggeration or bias : SLANTED **3 a** : of a race other than the white; *esp* : NEGRO **b** : of or relating to colored persons

col·or·fast \'kəl-ər-,fast\ *adj* : having color that does not fade or run — **col·or·fast·ness** \-,fas-nəs, -,fast-\ *n*

color filter *n* : FILTER 3b

col·or·ful \'kəl-ər-fəl\ *adj* **1** : having striking colors **2** : full of variety or interest — **col·or·ful·ly** \-fə-lē, -flē\ *adv* — **col·or·ful·ness** \-fəl-nəs\ *n*

color guard *n* : a guard of honor for the colors of an organization

col·or·im·e·ter \,kəl-ə-'rim-ət-ər\ *n* : a device for determining colors; *esp* : one used for chemical analysis by comparison of a liquid's color with standard colors — **col·or·i·met·ric** \,kəl-ə-rə-'me-trik\ *adj* — **col·or·i·met·ri·cal·ly** \-tri-kə-lē, -klē\ *adv* — **col·or·im·e·try** \,kəl-ə-'rim-ə-trē\ *n*

col·or·ing \'kəl-ə-ring\ *n* **1** : the act of applying colors **2** : something that produces color **3 a** : the effect produced by applying or combining colors **b** : natural color **c** : COMPLEXION 2, COLORATION **4** : a false appearance especially of something better ⟨an explanation that gave the lie a *coloring* of truth⟩

col·or·less \'kəl-ər-ləs\ *adj* **1** : lacking color **2** : DULL, UNINTERESTING ⟨a *colorless* story⟩ — **col·or·less·ly** *adv* — **col·or·less·ness** *n*

co·los·sal \kə-'läs-əl\ *adj* **1** : of, relating to, or resembling a colossus; *esp* : of very great size **2** : EXCEPTIONAL, ASTONISHING ⟨*colossal* growth⟩ — **co·los·sal·ly** \-ə-lē\ *adv*

col·os·se·um \,käl-ə-'sē-əm\ *n* **1** *cap* : an amphitheater built in Rome in the first century A.D. **2** : COLISEUM [Medieval Latin, from Latin *colosseus* "colossal", from *colossus* "colossus"]

Co·los·sians \kə-'läsh-ənz, -'läs-ē-ənz\ *n* — see BIBLE table

co·los·sus \kə-'läs-əs\ *n, pl* **-los·si** \-'läs-ī, -,ē\ **1** : a statue of gigantic size and proportions **2** : one that resembles a colossus in size or scope [Latin, from Greek *kolossos*]

co·los·trum \kə-'läs-trəm\ *n* : milk secreted for a few days after parturition and characterized by a high content of proteins and antibodies [Latin, "colostrum of a cow"]

col·our \'kəl-ər\ *chiefly British variant of* COLOR

colt \'kōlt\ *n* **1 a** : FOAL **b** : a young male horse **2** : a young untried person [Old English]

col·ter \'kōl-tər\ *n* : a cutter on a plow to cut the turf [Old English *culter* and Old French *coltre,* both from Latin *culter* "plowshare"]

colt·ish \'kōl-tish\ *adj* **1** : FRISKY, PLAYFUL **2** : of, relating to, or resembling a colt — **colt·ish·ly** *adv*

col·um·bine \'käl-əm-,bīn\ *n* : any of a genus of plants related to the buttercups that have showy flowers with usually five spurred petals [Medieval Latin *columbina,* from Latin *columba* "dove"]

co·lum·bi·um \kə-'ləm-bē-əm\ *n* : NIOBIUM [New Latin, from *Columbia* "United States", from *Christopher Columbus*]

Co·lum·bus Day \kə-'ləm-bəs-\ *n* : a day, formerly October 12 and now the second Monday in October, observed as a legal holiday in many states of the United States in commemoration of the landing of Columbus in the Bahamas in 1492

col·u·mel·la \,käl-yə-'mel-ə, ,käl-ə-\ *n, pl* **-mel·lae** \-'mel-ē, -,ī\ : any of various plant or animal parts resembling a column [Latin, "small column", from *columna* "column"]

col·umn \'käl-əm\ *n* **1 a** : a printed or written vertical arrangement of items ⟨a *column* of figures⟩ **b** : one of two or more vertical sections of a printed page **c** : a special department in a newspaper or periodical **2** : a supporting pillar; *esp* : one consisting of a usually round shaft, a capital, and a base **3** : something resembling a column in form, position, or function ⟨a *column* of water⟩ **4** : a long row (as of soldiers) **5** : one of the vertical lines of elements of a determinant or matrix [Middle French *colomne*, from Latin *columna*, from *columen* "top"] — **co·lum·nar** \kə-'ləm-nər\ *adj* — **col·umned** \'käl-əmd\ *adj*

col·um·nist \'käl-əm-nəst, -əm-əst\ *n* : a person who writes a newspaper or magazine column

col·za \'käl-zə, 'kōl-\ *n* : a cole (as rape) producing seed used as a source of oil [French, from Dutch *koolzaad*, literally, "cabbage seed"]

com- *or* **col-** *or* **con-** *prefix* : with : together : jointly — usually *com-* before *b*, *p*, or *m* ⟨*com*mingle⟩, *col-* before *l* ⟨*col*linear⟩, and *con-* before other sounds ⟨*con*centrate⟩ [Latin, "with, together, thoroughly"]

¹co·ma \'kō-mə\ *n* : a state of profound unconsciousness caused by disease, injury, or poison [Greek *kōma* "deep sleep"] — **co·ma·tose** \-,tōs\ *adj*

²coma *n, pl* **co·mae** \-,mē, -,mī\ : the head of a comet usually containing a nucleus [Latin, "hair", from Greek *komē*]

Co·man·che \kə-'man-chē\ *n* : a member of an Indian people of the southwestern plains having an Aztec-related language [Spanish, of American Indian origin]

Co·man·che·an \-chē-ən\ *n* : the period of the Mesozoic era between the Jurassic and the Upper Cretaceous; *also* : the corresponding system of rocks [*Comanche*, Texas] — **Comanchean** *adj*

¹comb \'kōm\ *n* **1 a** : a toothed implement to smooth and arrange the hair or worn in the hair to hold it in place **b** : a toothed instrument for separating fibers (as of wool or flax) **2** : a fleshy crest on the head of the domestic fowl and some related birds **3** : HONEYCOMB [Old English *camb*] — **combed** \'kōmd\ *adj*

²comb *vb* **1** : to smooth, arrange, or untangle with a comb ⟨*comb* one's hair⟩ ⟨*comb* wool⟩ **2** : to go over or through carefully in search of something : search thoroughly ⟨*combed* the woods for the lost child⟩

¹com·bat \kəm-'bat, 'käm-\ *vb* **-bat·ed** *or* **-bat·ted; bat·ing** *or* **-bat·ting** **1** : to fight with : BATTLE **2** : to struggle against; *esp* : to strive to reduce or eliminate ⟨*combat* disease⟩ [Middle French *combattre*, from Latin *com-* + *battuere* "to beat"]

²com·bat \'käm-,bat\ *n* **1** : a fight or contest between individuals or groups **2** : CONFLICT 2, CONTROVERSY **3** : active fighting in a war : ACTION

com·bat·ant \kəm-'bat-nt, 'käm-bət-ənt\ *adj* : engaging in or ready to engage in combat — **combatant** *n*

combat fatigue *n* : a neurotic or psychotic reaction to intense stress under combat conditions in wartime

com·bat·ive \kəm-'bat-iv\ *adj* : eager to fight : PUGNACIOUS — **com·bat·ive·ly** *adv* — **com·bat·ive·ness** *n*

comb·er \'kō-mər\ *n* **1** : one that combs fibers (as of wool or flax) **2** : a long curling wave rolling in from the ocean

com·bi·na·tion \,käm-bə-'nā-shən\ *n* **1** : a result or product of combining; *esp* : an alliance of persons or groups to achieve some end **2 a** : a sequence of letters or numbers chosen in setting a lock **b** : any of the different sets of individuals (as letters) that can be chosen from a population without regard to the order of the individuals within the set **3** : a one-piece undergarment for the upper and lower parts of the body **4 a** : the act or process of combining; *esp* : that of uniting to form a chemical compound **b** : the quality or state of being combined — **com·bi·na·tion·al** \-'nā-shnəl, -shən-l\ *adj*

com·bi·na·to·ri·al \,käm-bə-nə-'tōr-ē-əl, kəm-'bī-nə-, -'tōr-\ *adj* : of or relating to the arrangement, opera-

tion on, and selection of mathematical elements within finite sets and configurations ⟨*combinatorial* mathematics⟩

¹com·bine \kəm-'bīn\ *vb* **1 a** : to bring into close relationship : UNIFY **b** : to unite or cause to unite into a chemical compound **2** : to cause to mix together : BLEND **3** : to become one **4** : to act together [Middle French *combiner*, from Late Latin *combinare*, from Latin *com-* + *bini* "two by two"] SYN see JOIN — **com·bin·able** \-'bī-nə-bəl\ *adj* — **com·bin·er** *n*

²com·bine \'käm-,bīn\ *n* **1** : a combination to gain an often illicit end **2** : a harvesting machine that harvests, threshes, and cleans grain while moving over a field

³com·bine \'käm-,bīn\ *vt* : to harvest with a combine

comb·ings \'kō-mingz\ *n pl* : loose hairs or fibers removed by a comb

com·bin·ing form \kəm-'bī-ning-\ *n* : a linguistic form that occurs only in compounds or derivatives (as *electro-* in *electromagnetic* or *mal-* in *malodorous*)

comb jelly *n* : CTENOPHORE

com·bo \'käm-,bō\ *n, pl* **combos** **1** : COMBINATION **2** : a small jazz or dance band [alteration of *combination*]

com·bust \kəm-'bəst\ *vb* : BURN [Latin *combustus*, past participle of *comburere* "to burn up", from *com-* + *urere* "to burn"]

com·bus·ti·ble \kəm-'bəs-tə-bəl\ *adj* **1** : capable of being burned **2** : catching fire or burning easily — **com·bus·ti·bil·i·ty** \-,bəs-tə-'bil-ət-ē\ *n* — **combustible** *n* — **com·bus·ti·bly** \-'bəs-tə-blē\ *adv*

com·bus·tion \kəm-'bəs-chən\ *n* **1** : the process of burning **2 a** : a chemical process (as an oxidation) accompanied by the evolution of heat and light **b** : a slower oxidation — **com·bus·tive** \-'bəs-tiv\ *adj*

com·bus·tor \-'bəs-tər\ *n* : a chamber (as in a jet engine) in which combustion occurs

come \kəm, 'kəm\ *vi* **came** \'kām\; **come; com·ing** \'kəm-ing\ **1** : to move toward something : APPROACH ⟨*come* here⟩ **2** : to move toward or enter a scene of action or into a field of interest ⟨the police *came* to our rescue⟩ **3 a** : to reach the point of being or becoming ⟨the rope *came* untied⟩ **b** : AMOUNT ⟨the bill *came* to 10 dollars⟩ **4 a** : to take place ⟨the holiday *came* on Thursday⟩ **b** : to proceed as a consequence, effect, or conclusion ⟨our plans *came* to naught⟩ **5** : ORIGINATE, ARISE ⟨*comes* from sturdy stock⟩ **6** : to be obtainable ⟨an article that *comes* in three sizes⟩ **7** : to be attainable ⟨success *came* after hard work⟩ **8** : EXTEND, REACH ⟨a coat that *comes* to the knees⟩ **9 a** : to arrive at a particular place, end, result, or conclusion ⟨*came* home tired⟩ **b** : HAPPEN, OCCUR ⟨no harm will *come* to you⟩ **10** : to fall within a scope ⟨*comes* under the terms of the treaty⟩ **11** : BECOME ⟨things will *come* clear if we are patient⟩ [Old English *cuman*] — **come across** : to meet or find by chance — **come by** : ACQUIRE — **come into** : to acquire as an inheritance — **come into one's own** : to approach or reach one's appropriate level of importance, skill, or recognition — **come to be** : to arrive at or attain to being : BECOME — **come to pass** : HAPPEN — used with *it*

come about *vi* **1** : to come to pass : HAPPEN **2** : to change direction ⟨the wind has *come about* into the north⟩ **3** : to turn a boat onto a new tack

come around *vi* : to come round

come·back \'kəm-,bak\ *n* **1** : ²RETORT **2** : a return to a former position or condition (as of health or prosperity) : RECOVERY

co·me·di·an \kə-'mēd-ē-ən\ *n* **1** : an actor who plays in comedy **2** : a comical individual; *esp* : a professional entertainer who uses various physical or verbal means to be amusing

co·me·di·enne \kə-,mēd-ē-'en\ *n* : a woman who is a comedian [French *comédienne*, feminine of *comédien* "comedian", from *comédie* "comedy"]

com·e·do \'käm-ə-,dō\ *n, pl* **com·e·do·nes** \,käm-ə-'dō-,nēz\ : BLACKHEAD [Latin, "glutton", from *comedere* "to eat"]

¹comb 2

come·down \'kəm-,daun\ *n* : a descent in rank or dignity
come down \,kəm-'daun\ *vi* : to become sick ⟨*came
down* with the measles⟩
com·e·dy \'käm-əd-ē\ *n, pl* **-dies** **1 a** : a light amusing
play with a happy ending **b** : dramatic literature dealing with the comic or with the serious in a light or
satirical manner **2 a** : a medieval narrative that ends
happily ⟨Dante's Divine *Comedy*⟩ **b** : a literary work
written in a comic style or treating a comic theme **3** :
an amusing or ludicrous event [Middle French *come-
die*, from Latin *comoedia*, from Greek *kōmōidia*,
from *kōmos* "revel" + *aidein* "to sing"]
come in *vi* **1** : to be among the finishers (as of a race)
2 : to come into use or be useful **3** : to be the recipient
of — used with *for* **4** : to reach maturity, fruitfulness,
or production — **come in handy** : to be useful
come·ly \'kəm-lē\ *adj* **come·li·er; -est** : pleasing to look
at : good-looking ⟨*comely* people⟩ [Old English *cȳmlic*
"glorious", from *cȳme* "lively, fine"]
come-on \'kəm-,ón, -,än\ *n* : INDUCEMENT 2, LURE
come out *vi* **1** : to come into public view **2** : to declare
oneself ⟨*come out* for a candidate⟩ **3** : to turn out ⟨the
cake *came out* splendidly⟩ **4** : to make one's debut **5** :
SAY 1a — usually used with *with* ⟨*come out* with the
truth⟩
com·er \'kəm-ər\ *n* **1** : one that comes ⟨all *comers*⟩ **2** :
a promising newcomer
come round *vi* **1** : to return to a former condition; *esp* :
to regain consciousness **2** : to change direction or
opinion
¹co·mes·ti·ble \kə-'mes-tə-bəl\ *adj* : suitable for eating : EATABLE, EDIBLE [Middle French, derived from Latin *comedere* "to eat up", from *com-* + *edere* "to eat"]
²comestible *n* : FOOD 3 — usually used in pl.
com·et \'käm-ət\ *n* : a celestial body that orbits the
sun, that consists of a diffuse head usually surrounding
a bright nucleus, and that often when in the part of its
orbit near the sun develops a long tail which points
away from the sun [Latin *cometa*, from Greek
kométēs, literally, "long-haired", from *komē* "hair"]
come to *vi* : to recover consciousness
come-up·pance \kə-'məp-əns, ,kə-\ *n* : a deserved rebuke or penalty : DESERTS
com·fit \'kəm-fət, 'käm-, 'kəmp-, 'kämp-\ *n* : a confection consisting of a piece of fruit, a root, or a seed
coated and preserved with sugar [Middle French *con-
fit*, from *confire* "to prepare", from Latin *conficere*,
from *com-* + *facere* "to make"]
¹com·fort \'kəm-fərt, 'kəmp-\ *n* **1** : acts or words that
comfort **2** : the feeling of the one that is comforted
⟨find *comfort* in a parent's love⟩ **3** : something that
makes a person comfortable ⟨the *comforts* of home⟩
— **com·fort·less** \-ləs\ *adj*
²comfort *vt* **1** : to give strength and hope to : CHEER **2** :
to ease the grief or trouble of : CONSOLE [Old French
conforter, from Late Latin *confortare* "to strengthen
greatly", from Latin *com-* + *fortis* "strong"] □ SYN
CONSOLE, SOLACE: COMFORT implies giving cheer,
strength, or encouragement as well as lessening pain;
CONSOLE stresses the lessening of grief or sense of loss
rather than giving relief or pleasure; SOLACE may suggest relieving loneliness or despondency as well as
pain or grief.
com·fort·able \'kəm-fərt-ə-bəl, 'kəmp-; 'kəmf-tə-bəl,
'kəmp-, 'kəmpf-, 'kəm-, -tər-\ *adj* **1** : giving comfort;
esp : providing physical comfort **2** : more than adequate ⟨a *comfortable* income⟩ **3** : physically or mentally at ease — **com·fort·able·ness** *n* — **com·fort·ably**
\-blē\ *adv*
com·fort·er \'kəm-fərt-ər, 'kəmp-, -fət-\ *n* **1** : one that
gives comfort **2 a** : a long narrow neck scarf **b** : QUILT
1
com·fy \'kəm-fē, 'kəmp-\ : COMFORTABLE [alteration of
comfortable]

¹com·ic \'käm-ik\ *adj* **1 a** : of or relating to comedy **b** :
acting in comedies **2** : causing laughter or amusement : FUNNY **3** : of or relating to comic strips [Latin
comicus, from Greek *kōmikos*, from *kōmos* "revel"]
□ SYN COMIC, COMICAL mean causing laughter. COMIC
applies especially to what arouses thoughtful amusement and particularly applies to comedy as a literary
form ⟨a *comic* masterpiece of wit and satire⟩ COMICAL
suggests the provoking of unrestrained spontaneous
hilarity ⟨*comical* frustrations of a circus clown⟩
²comic *n* **1** : COMEDIAN 2 **2 a** : COMIC STRIP **b** *pl* : the
part of a newspaper devoted to comic strips
com·i·cal \'käm-i-kəl\ *adj* : provoking spontaneous
laughter or amusement : DROLL SYN see COMIC — **com·i-
cal·i·ty** \,käm-i-'kal-ət-ē\ *n* — **com·i·cal·ly** \'käm-i-kə-
lē, -klē\ *adv*
comic book *n* : a magazine made up of a series of comic
strips
comic opera *n* : a musical dramatic work with spoken
dialogue that is usually of light and amusing character
comic strip *n* : a sequence of cartoons that tell a story or
part of a story
com·ing \'kəm-ing\ *adj* **1** : APPROACHING, NEXT ⟨the
coming year⟩ **2** : gaining importance ⟨a *coming* young
star⟩
Com·in·tern \'käm-ən-,tərn\ *n* : the Communist International established in 1919 in an attempt to supersede the Second International of Socialist organizations [Russian *Komintern*, from *Kom*munisticheskiĭ
*Intern*atsional "Communist International"]
co·mi·ty \'käm-ət-ē, 'kō-mət-\ *n, pl* **-ties** : courteous behavior : CIVILITY [Latin *comitas*, from *comis* "courteous"]
comity of nations : the code of courtesy and friendship
by which nations get along together; *also* : the group
of nations observing such a code
com·ma \'käm-ə\ *n* : a punctuation mark , used chiefly
to show separation of words or word groups within a
sentence [Latin, "part of a sentence", from Greek
komma "segment, clause", from *koptein* "to cut"]
comma bacillus *n* : the bacterium that causes Asiatic
cholera
comma fault *n* : the careless or unjustified use of a
comma between coordinate main clauses not connected by a conjunction — called also *comma splice*
¹com·mand \kə-'mand\ *vb* **1 a** : to direct authoritatively : ORDER, GOVERN **b** : to have authority and control of
a military force or post : be commander of **2 a** : to
have at one's disposal **b** : to demand as one's due : EX-
ACT ⟨*commands* a high fee⟩ **c** : to overlook from a strategic position ⟨the hill *commands* the town⟩ [Old
French *comander*, from Latin *commendare* "to commit to one's charge, commend"]
²command *n* **1** : the act of commanding ⟨march on
command⟩ **2** : an order given **3 a** : the ability to control : MASTERY ⟨has *command* of the subject⟩ **b** : the
authority or right to command **c** : the power to dominate **d** : facility in using ⟨a good *command* of French⟩
4 : the personnel, area, or unit under a commander **5** :
a position from which military operations are directed
— called also *command post*
³command *adj* : done on command or request ⟨a *command* performance⟩
com·man·dant \'käm-ən-,dant, -,dänt\ *n* : COMMANDING
OFFICER
com·man·deer \,käm-ən-'diər\ *vt* : to take arbitrary or
forcible possession of especially for military purposes
[Afrikaans *kommandeer*, from French *commander*
"to command"]
com·mand·er \kə-'man-dər\ *n* **1** : one in official command; *esp* : COMMANDING OFFICER **2** : an officer rank in
the Navy and Coast Guard above lieutenant commander and below captain — **com·mand·er·ship** \-,ship\ *n*
commander in chief : one who holds the supreme command of an armed force

commanding officer *n* : a military or naval officer in command of a unit or post

com·mand·ment \kə-'man-mənt, -'mand-\ *n* : something commanded; *esp* : one of the biblical Ten Commandments

command module *n* : a space vehicle module designed to carry the crew, the chief communication equipment, and the equipment for reentry

com·man·do \kə-'man-dō\ *n, pl* **-dos** *or* **-does** **1** : a military unit trained and organized for surprise raids into enemy territory **2** : a member of a specialized raiding unit [Afrikaans *kommando*, from Dutch *commando* "command", from Spanish *comando*, from *comander* "to command", from French *commander*]

command sergeant major *n* : an enlisted rank in the Army above first sergeant

comme il faut \,kəm-ēl-'fō, -,ē-\ *adj* : conforming to accepted standards : PROPER [French, literally, "as it should be"]

com·mem·o·rate \kə-'mem-ə-,rāt\ *vt* **1** : to call to remembrance **2** : to mark by a ceremony : OBSERVE **3** : to be a memorial of [Latin *commemorare*, from *com-* + *memorare* "to remind of", from *memor* "mindful"] SYN see KEEP — **com·mem·o·ra·tor** \-,rāt-ər\ *n*

com·mem·o·ra·tion \kə-,mem-ə-'rā-shən\ *n* **1** : the act of commemorating **2** : something (as a ceremony) that commemorates

com·mem·o·ra·tive \kə-'mem-ə-,rāt-iv, -rət-\ *adj* : intended to commemorate ⟨a *commemorative* stamp⟩ — **commemorative** *n* — **com·mem·o·ra·tive·ly** *adv*

com·mence \kə-'mens\ *vb* : to bring or come into activity, being, or operation ⟨*commence* firing⟩ ⟨work will *commence* next week⟩ [Middle French *comencer*, from Latin *com-* + *initiare* "to initiate"] — **com·menc·er** *n*

com·mence·ment \-'mens-mənt\ *n* **1** : an act, instance, or time of commencing **2 a** : the ceremonies or the day for conferring degrees or diplomas on graduates of a school or college **b** : the period of activities at this time

com·mend \kə-'mend\ *vt* **1** : to give into another's care : ENTRUST **2** : to speak of with approval : PRAISE [Latin *commendare*, from *com-* + *mandare* "to entrust"] — **com·mend·able** \-'men-də-bəl\ *adj* — **com·mend·ably** \-də-blē\ *adv*

com·men·da·tion \,käm-ən-'dā-shən, -,en-\ *n* **1** : an act of commending **2** : something (as a formal citation) that commends — **com·men·da·to·ry** \kə-'men-də-,tōr-ē, -,tȯr-\ *adj*

com·men·sal \kə-'men-səl\ *adj* : relating to or living in a state of commensalism [Medieval Latin *commensalis* "of those who habitually eat together", from Latin *com-* + *mensa* "table"] — **commensal** *n* — **com·men·sal·ly** \-sə-lē\ *adv*

com·men·sal·ism \-sə-,liz-əm\ *n* : a relation between two kinds of organisms in which one obtains a benefit (as food) from the other without either damaging or benefiting it

com·men·su·ra·ble \kə-'mens-rə-bəl, -'mench-, -ə-rə-\ *adj* : having a common measure; *esp* : divisible by a common unit a whole number of times — **com·men·su·ra·bly** \-blē\ *adv*

com·men·su·rate \kə-'mens-rət, -'mench-, -ə-rət\ *adj* **1** : equal in measure or extent **2** : PROPORTIONATE ⟨a job *commensurate* with one's abilities⟩ [Late Latin *commensuratus*, from Latin *com-* + *mensura* "measure"] — **com·men·su·rate·ly** *adv* — **com·men·su·ra·tion** \-,men-sə-'rā-shən, -,mench-ə-'rā-\ *n*

¹com·ment \'käm-,ent\ *n* **1** : an expression of opinion either in speech or writing **2** : a usually critical or explanatory remark [Late Latin *commentum* "invention", from Latin *commentus*, past participle of *comminisci* "to invent"]

²comment *vi* : to make a comment : REMARK

com·men·tary \'käm-ən-,ter-ē\ *n, pl* **-tar·ies** : a series of comments or notes; *also* : a book composed of such material ⟨Caesar's *Commentaries*⟩

com·men·tate \'käm-ən-,tāt\ *vb* : to give a commentary on : act as a commentator

com·men·ta·tor \-,tāt-ər\ *n* : one that gives a commentary; *esp* : one who reports and discusses news on radio or television

com·merce \'käm-,ərs, -ərs\ *n* **1** : interchange of ideas, opinions, or sentiments **2** : the exchange or buying and selling of goods on a large scale involving transportation from place to place : TRADE [Middle French, from Latin *commercium*, from *com-* + *merx* "merchandise"] SYN see BUSINESS

¹com·mer·cial \kə-'mər-shəl\ *adj* **1 a** : of or relating to commerce **b** : engaged in commerce ⟨a *commercial* city⟩ **2 a** : viewed with regard to profit ⟨a *commercial* success⟩ **b** : designed for profit; *esp* : designed for mass appeal ⟨the *commercial* theater⟩ **3** : emphasizing skills and subjects useful in business ⟨*commercial* education⟩ **4** : paid for by advertisers ⟨*commercial* TV⟩ — **com·mer·cial·ly** \-'mərsh-lē, -ə-lē\ *adv*

²commercial *n* : an advertisement broadcast on radio or television

commercial bank *n* : a bank that accepts deposits withdrawable without notice and creates credit through short-term loans mainly to business

com·mer·cial·ism \kə-'mər-shə-,liz-əm\ *n* : a spirit, method, or practice characteristic of business — **com·mer·cial·is·tic** \-,mər-shə-'lis-tik\ *adj*

com·mer·cial·ize \kə-'mər-shə-,līz\ *vt* **1** : to manage on a business basis for profit **2** : to exploit for profit ⟨*commercialize* Christmas⟩ — **com·mer·cial·iza·tion** \-,mər-shə-lə-'zā-shən\ *n*

commercial paper *n* : short-term negotiable instruments arising out of commercial transactions

commercial traveler *n* : TRAVELING SALESMAN

com·mi·na·tion \,käm-ə-'nā-shən\ *n* : DENUNCIATION [Latin *comminatio*, from *comminari* "to threaten", from *com-* + *minari* "to threaten"] — **com·mi·na·to·ry** \'käm-ə-nə-,tōr-ē, -,tȯr-; kə-'min-ə-, -'mīn-\ *adj*

com·min·gle \kə-'ming-gəl\ *vb* : MINGLE 1, MIX ⟨*commingle* two liquids⟩

com·mi·nute \'käm-ə-,nüt, -nyüt\ *vt* : to reduce to minute particles : PULVERIZE [Latin *comminuere*, from *com-* + *minuere* "to lessen"] — **com·mi·nu·tion** \,käm-ə-'nü-shən, -'nyü-\ *n*

com·mis·er·ate \kə-'miz-ə-,rāt\ *vb* : to feel or express sorrow, compassion, or sympathy for : SYMPATHIZE [Latin *commiserari*, from *com-* + *miserari* "to pity", from *miser* "wretched"] — **com·mis·er·a·tion** \-,miz-ə-'rā-shən\ *n* — **com·mis·er·a·tive** \-'miz-ə-,rāt-iv\ *adj*

com·mis·sar \'käm-ə-,sär\ *n* **1** : a Communist party official assigned to a military unit to teach party principles and policies and to ensure party loyalty **2** : the head of a government department in the Soviet Union from 1917 to 1946 [Russian *komissar*, from German *kommissar* "commissary", from Medieval Latin *commissarius*]

com·mis·sar·i·at \,käm-ə-'ser-ē-ət, -'sar-, *especially for* 2 -'sär-\ *n* **1** : a system for supplying an army with food **2** : a government department in the Soviet Union from 1917 to 1946 [New Latin *commissariatus*, from Medieval Latin *commissarius* "commissary"; sense 2 from Russian *komissariat*, from German *kommissariat*, from New Latin *commissariatus*]

com·mis·sary \'käm-ə-,ser-ē\ *n, pl* **-sar·ies** **1** : a person to whom a duty or office is entrusted by a superior **2** : a store supplying provisions especially to military personnel and dependents **3** : a lunchroom in a motion picture studio [Medieval Latin *commissarius*, from Latin *commissus*, past participle of *committere* "to commit"]

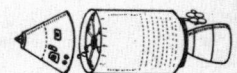

command module separating from service module

\ə\ **abut**		\ng\ **sing**	
\ər\ **further**		\ō\ **bone**	
\a\ **mat**		\ȯ\ **saw**	
\ā\ **take**		\ȯi\ **coin**	
\ä\ **cot, cart**		\th\ **thin**	
\au̇\ **out**		\th\ **this**	
\ch\ **chin**		\ü\ **food**	
\e\ **pet**		\u̇\ **foot**	
\ē\ **easy**		\y\ **yet**	
\g\ **go**		\yü\ **few**	
\i\ **tip**		\yu̇\ **cure**	
\ī\ **life**		\zh\ **vision**	
\j\ **job**			

¹com·mis·sion \kə-'mish-ən\ n **1 a** : a formal order granting the power to perform various acts or duties **b** : a certificate conferring military rank and authority; *also* : the rank and authority conferred **2** : an authorization or command to act in a prescribed manner or to perform prescribed acts **3 a** : authority to act as agent for another **b** : a task or matter entrusted to an agent **4 a** : a group of persons directed to perform a duty **b** : a government agency having administrative, legislative, or judicial powers **c** : a city council having legislative and executive functions **5** : an act of committing something (as a crime) **6** : a fee paid to an agent or employee for transacting a piece of business or performing a service ⟨a brokerage *commission*⟩ [Middle French, from Latin *commissio* "act of bringing together", from *committere* "to commit"] — **in commission 1** : ready for active service — used of a ship **2** : in use or ready for use — **out of commission 1** : out of service or use **2** : out of working order

²commission *vt* -**mis·sioned**; -**mis·sion·ing** \-'mish-ning, -ə-ning\ **1** : to confer a commission on **2** : to order to be made **3** : to put (a ship) in commission

com·mis·sion·aire \kə-,mish-ə-'naər, -'neər\ n, *chiefly British* : a uniformed attendant [French *commissionnaire*, from *commission* "commission"]

com·mis·sion·er \kə-'mish-nər, -ə-nər\ n **1** : a member of a commission **2** : an official in charge of a government department ⟨*Commissioner* of Public Safety⟩

commission merchant n : one who buys or sells another's goods for a commission

com·mis·sure \'käm-ə-,shùr\ n : a connecting band of nerve tissue in the brain or spinal cord [Latin *commissura* "a joining", from *committere* "to connect, commit"] — com·mis·sur·al \,käm-ə-'shùr-əl\ *adj*

com·mit \kə-'mit\ *vt* com·mit·ted; com·mit·ting **1 a** : to give in trust ⟨*commit* power to the legislature⟩ **b** : to place in a prison or mental institution **c** : to consign for preservation, disposal, or safekeeping ⟨*commit* it to memory⟩ **d** : to refer (as a legislative bill) to a committee for consideration and report **2** : to bring about : PERFORM ⟨*commit* a crime⟩ **3 a** : OBLIGATE, BIND ⟨was *committed* to defend them⟩ **b** : to pledge or assign to a particular course or use **c** : to express the opinion of ⟨refused to *commit* themselves on the issue⟩ [Latin *committere* "to connect, entrust", from *com-* + *mittere* "to send"] — com·mit·ta·ble \-'mit-ə-bəl\ *adj*

com·mit·ment \kə-'mit-mənt\ n **1** : an act of committing: as **a** : a consignment to a penal or mental institution **b** : an act of referring a matter to a legislative committee **2 a** : an agreement or pledge to do something in the future **b** : something pledged

com·mit·tal \kə-'mit-l\ n : COMMITMENT 1a

com·mit·tee \kə-'mit-ē\ n **1** : a body of persons delegated or elected to consider or take action on some matter **2** : a self-constituted organization for the promotion of a common goal

com·mit·tee·man \-mən, -,man\ n **1** : a member of a committee **2** : a party leader of a ward or precinct

committee of the whole : the whole membership of a legislative house sitting as a committee and operating under informal rules

com·mit·tee·wom·an \-,wùm-ən\ n **1** : a woman member of a committee **2** : a woman party leader of a ward or precinct

com·mix \kə-'miks, kä-\ *vb* : to mix or mingle together : BLEND

com·mix·ture \-chər\ n : MIXTURE 2a, COMPOUND

com·mode \kə-'mōd\ n **1 a** : a low chest of drawers **b** : a movable washstand with a cupboard underneath **2** : TOILET 2b [French *commode* "suitable, convenient", from Latin *commodus*, from *com-* + *modus* "measure"]

com·mo·di·ous \kə-'mōd-ē-əs\ *adj* **1** *archaic* : HANDY, SERVICEABLE **2** : comfortably or conveniently spacious : ROOMY [Middle French *commodieux*, from Me-

dieval Latin *commodiosus*, from Latin *commodum* "convenience", from *commodus* "convenient"] — com·mo·di·ous·ly *adv* — com·mo·di·ous·ness *n*

com·mod·i·ty \kə-'mäd-ət-ē\ n, *pl* -**ties** : an economic good: as **a** : a product of agriculture or mining **b** : an article exchanged in commerce [Middle French *commodité* "convenience, advantage", from Latin *commoditas*, from *commodus* "convenient"]

com·mo·dore \'käm-ə-,dōr, -,dòr\ n **1** : a commissioned officer in the Navy above captain and below rear admiral **2** : the senior captain of a line of merchant ships **3** : the chief officer of a yacht club [probably from Dutch *commandeur* "commander", from French]

¹com·mon \'käm-ən\ *adj* **1** : having to do with, belonging to, or used by everybody : PUBLIC ⟨work for the *common* good⟩ **2 a** : belonging to or shared by two or more individuals or by the members of a group ⟨a *common* ancestor⟩ **b** : belonging equally to two or more mathematical entities ⟨two angles with a *common* side⟩ **c** : formed of or dividing into two or more branches ⟨*common* carotid artery⟩ **3** : widely or generally known, met, or seen ⟨facts of *common* knowledge⟩ **4** : FREQUENT, FAMILIAR ⟨a *common* sight⟩ **5 a** : not above the average in rank, merit, or social position ⟨a *common* soldier⟩ ⟨the *common* people⟩ **b** : falling below ordinary standards : SECOND-RATE **c** : lacking refinement : VULGAR **6 a** : being either masculine or feminine ⟨*common* gender⟩ **b** : being a noun that designates any of a class of beings or things **c** : being a grammatical case used both for the subject and the object ⟨the word *man* in "the man is tall", "watch the man", and "with the man" is in the *common* case⟩ [Old French *commun*, from Latin *communis*] SYN see RECIPROCAL — com·mon·ly *adv* — com·mon·ness \-ən-nəs\ n

²common n **1** *pl* : the common people **2** *pl* : a dining hall **3** *pl, often cap* **a** : the political group or estate comprising the commoners **b** : the parliamentary representatives of the commoners **c** : HOUSE OF COMMONS **4** : a piece of land subject to common use especially for pasture — often used in pl. **5 a** : a religious service suitable for a festival **b** : the ordinary of the Mass — **in common** : shared together

com·mon·al·i·ty \,käm-ə-'nal-ət-ē\ *or* com·mon·al·ty \'käm-ə-nəl-tē\ n, *pl* -**ties** : the common people

common carrier n : an individual or corporation engaged in transporting persons, goods, or messages for money

common cold n : an acute virus disease of the upper respiratory tract marked by congestion and inflammation of mucous membranes and usually accompanied by excessive secretion of mucus and coughing and sneezing

common denominator n **1** : a common multiple of the denominators of a number of fractions **2** : a common trait or theme

common difference n : the difference between two consecutive terms of an arithmetic progression

common divisor n : a number or expression that divides two or more numbers or expressions without remainder — called also *common factor*

com·mon·er \'käm-ə-nər\ n : one of the common people : a person not of noble rank

common fraction n : a fraction in which both numerator and denominator are expressed as integers

common law n : the body of law developed in England primarily from judicial decisions based on custom and precedent, unwritten in statute or code, and forming the basis of the legal system in most jurisdictions of the United States and parts of the world under British control or influence

common–law marriage n : a marriage relationship created by agreement and usually cohabitation between a man and a woman without religious or civil ceremony

common logarithm *n* : a logarithm whose base is 10

common market *n* : an economic unit formed to remove trade barriers among member nations

common multiple *n* : a multiple of each of two or more numbers or expressions

common noun *n* : a noun (as *chair* or *fear*) that names a class of persons or things or any individual of a class

¹**com·mon·place** \'käm-ən-ˌplās\ *n* **1** : an obvious or trite remark **2** : a thing so commonly encountered as to be taken for granted

²**commonplace** *adj* : lacking originality, freshness, or interest

common ratio *n* : the ratio of each term of a geometric progression to the term preceding it

common room *n* **1** : a lounge available to all members of a residential community **2** : a room in a college for the use of the faculty

common salt *n* : SALT 1a

common school *n* : a free public school

common sense *n* : sound and prudent but often unsophisticated judgment

common stock *n* : capital stock other than preferred stock

common time *n* : four beats to a measure in music

common touch *n* : the gift of appealing to or arousing the sympathetic interest of people of all walks of life

com·mon·weal \'käm-ən-ˌwēl\ *n* **1** : the general welfare **2** *archaic* : COMMONWEALTH

com·mon·wealth \-ˌwelth\ *n* **1** : a political unit whose aim is the common good of all the people **2** *cap* : the English state from the death of Charles I in 1649 to the Restoration in 1660 **3** : a state of the United States — used officially of Kentucky, Massachusetts, Pennsylvania, and Virginia **4** *cap* : a federal union of states — used officially of Australia **5** *often cap* : an association of self-governing states having a common political and cultural background and united by a common allegiance (the British *Commonwealth*) **6** *often cap* : a political unit having local self-government but voluntarily united with the United States — used officially of Puerto Rico

com·mo·tion \kə-'mō-shən\ *n* **1** : disturbed or violent motion : AGITATION **2 a** : noisy excitement and confusion **b** : a confused noisy disturbance : TUMULT [Middle French, from Latin *commotio*, from *commovēre* "to agitate", from *com-* + *movēre* "to move"]

com·mu·nal \kə-'myün-l, 'käm-yən-l\ *adj* **1** : of or relating to a commune or community **2 a** : characterized by collective ownership and use of property **b** : shared, participated in, or used in common by members of a group or community

¹**com·mune** \kə-'myün\ *vi* **1** : to receive Communion **2** : to communicate intimately (went off into the woods to *commune* with nature) [Middle French *comunier* "to converse, administer or receive Communion", from Latin *communicare* "to impart, participate", from *communis* "common"]

²**com·mune** \'käm-ˌyün; kə-'myün, kä-\ *n* **1** : the smallest administrative district of many countries especially in Europe **2 a** : a medieval municipality **b** : a rural community (as the Russian mir) organized on a communal basis **3** *cap* **a** : the French government elected by representatives of the communes in 1792 **b** : a revolutionary government in Paris from March 18 to May 28, 1871 **4** : a large collectivized farm in the People's Republic of China [French, from Middle French *comugne*, from Medieval Latin *communia*, from Latin *communis* "common"]

com·mu·ni·ca·ble \kə-'myü-ni-kə-bəl\ *adj* : capable of being communicated : TRANSMITTABLE (*communicable* diseases) — **com·mu·ni·ca·bil·i·ty** \-ˌmyü-ni-kə-'bil-ət-ē\ *n* — **com·mu·ni·ca·ble·ness** \-'myü-ni-kə-bəl-nəs\ *n* — **com·mu·ni·ca·bly** \-blē\ *adv*

com·mu·ni·cant \kə-'myü-ni-kənt\ *n* **1 a** : a person who receives Communion **b** : a church member **2** : a person who communicates — **communicant** *adj*

com·mu·ni·cate \kə-'myü-nə-ˌkāt\ *vb* **1 a** : to make known (*communicate* the news) **b** : TRANSFER, TRANSMIT (*communicate* a disease) **2** : to receive Communion **3** : to be in communication **4** : JOIN, CONNECT (the rooms *communicate*) [Latin *communicare* "to impart, participate", from *communis* "common"] — **com·mu·ni·ca·tor** \-ˌkāt-ər\ *n*

com·mu·ni·ca·tion \kə-ˌmyü-nə-'kā-shən\ *n* **1** : an act or instance of transmitting **2 a** : information communicated **b** : MESSAGE 1 **3** : an exchange of information **4** *pl* **a** : a system (as of telephones) for communicating **b** : a system of routes for moving troops, supplies, and vehicles **5** *pl* : the business or technology of the transmission of information **6** : the interchange of ideas and opinions

com·mu·ni·ca·tive \kə-'myü-nə-ˌkāt-iv, -ni-kət-\ *adj* **1** : tending to communicate : TALKATIVE **2** : of or relating to communication — **com·mu·ni·ca·tive·ly** *adv* — **com·mu·ni·ca·tive·ness** *n*

com·mu·nion \kə-'myü-nyən\ *n* **1 a** *cap* : a Christian sacrament in which bread and wine are partaken of as a commemoration of the death of Christ **b** : the act of receiving the sacrament **c** *cap* : the part of a religious service in which the sacrament is received **2** : COMMUNICATION 1 **3** : a body of Christians having a common faith

com·mu·ni·qué \kə-'myü-nə-ˌkā, -ˌmyü-nə-'\ *n* : an official communication : BULLETIN [French, from *communiquer* "to communicate", from Latin *communicare*]

com·mu·nism \'käm-yə-ˌniz-əm\ *n* **1** : a social system in which property and goods are owned in common; *also* : a theory advocating such a system **2** *cap* **a** : a doctrine based upon revolutionary Marxian socialism and Marxism-Leninism that was the official ideology of the Union of Soviet Socialist Republics, the Chinese People's Republic, and several satellite nations **b** : a totalitarian system of government in which a single party controls state-owned means of production with the professed aim of establishing a stateless society

com·mu·nist \'käm-yə-nəst\ *n* **1** : an adherent or advocate of communism **2** *cap* : a member or adherent of a Communist party or movement — **communist** *adj, often cap* — **com·mu·nis·tic** \ˌkäm-yə-'nis-tik\ *adj, often cap* — **com·mu·nis·ti·cal·ly** \-ti-kə-lē, -klē\ *adv*

com·mu·ni·ty \kə-'myü-nət-ē\ *n, pl* **-ties** **1 a** : the people living in an area; *also* : the area itself **b** : an interacting population of various kinds of individuals (as species) in a common location **c** : a group of people with common interests living together within a larger society (the Christian *community*) **d** : a body of persons or nations having a history or social, economic, or political interests or policies in common (the European Coal and Steel *Community*) **2 a** : joint ownership or participation (*community* of goods) **b** : LIKENESS (their works showed a *community* of style) **c** : shared activity **d** : a social state or condition

community center *n* : a building or group of buildings for a community's educational and recreational activities

community chest *n* : a general fund made up of individual subscriptions in a community to provide public aid

community college *n* : a public junior college that designs its instruction to meet the needs of the community

com·mu·nize \'käm-yə-ˌnīz\ *vb* **1** : to place under common ownership **2** : to organize according to Communist principles — **com·mu·ni·za·tion** \ˌkäm-yə-nə-'zā-shən\ *n*

com·mu·ta·tion \ˌkäm-yə-'tā-shən\ *n* **1** : EXCHANGE 2; *esp* : a substitution of one form of payment for another **2** : a reduction of a legal penalty **3** : an act of commuting **4** : the process of reversing the direction of an electric circuit

commutation ticket *n* : a transportation ticket sold at a reduced rate for a fixed number of trips over the same route during a limited period

com·mu·ta·tive \kə-'myüt-ət-iv, 'käm-yə-ˌtāt-iv\ *adj* : combining elements or having elements that combine in such a manner that the result is independent of the order in which the elements are taken ⟨addition of the real numbers is *commutative* but subtraction is not⟩ — **com·mu·ta·tiv·i·ty** \kə-ˌmyüt-ə-'tiv-ət-ē\ *n*

com·mu·ta·tor \'käm-yə-ˌtāt-ər\ *n* : a device for reversing the direction of an electric current so that the alternating currents generated in the armature of a dynamo are converted to direct current

com·mute \kə-'myüt\ *vb* **I a** : INTERCHANGE, SUBSTITUTE **b** : CHANGE 1, ALTER **2** : to substitute one form of obligation for another **3** : to substitute a less severe penalty for a greater one ⟨*commute* a death sentence to life imprisonment⟩ **4 a** : to travel by use of a commutation ticket **b** : to travel back and forth regularly [Latin *commutare* "to change, exchange", from *com-* + *mutare* "to change"] — **com·mut·able** \-'myüt-ə-bəl\ *adj* — **com·mut·er** *n*

¹com·pact \kəm-'pakt, 'käm-,\ *adj* **I** : closely united, collected, or packed **2** : arranged or designed so as to save space ⟨a *compact* house⟩ **3** : not wordy : CONCISE **4** : not rangy or lanky in appearance ⟨a *compact* body⟩ [Latin *compactus* "firmly put together", from past participle of *compingere* "to put together", from *com-* + *pangere* "to fasten"] — **com·pact·ly** *adv* — **com·pact·ness** \-'pakt-nəs, -'pak-; -ˌpakt-, -ˌpak-\ *n*

²compact *vb* **I** : CONSOLIDATE 3 **2** : FORM 1, COMPOSE **3** : to make or become compact — **com·pac·tor** *or* **com·pact·er** *n*

³com·pact \'käm-ˌpakt\ *n* **I** : a small case for cosmetics **2** : a relatively small automobile

⁴com·pact \'käm-ˌpakt\ *n* : an agreement (as a treaty) between two or more parties [Latin *compactum*, from *compacisci* "to make an agreement", from *com-* + *pacisci* "to contract"]

com·pac·tion \kəm-'pak-shən\ *n* : the act or process of compacting : the state of being compacted

¹com·pan·ion \kəm-'pan-yən\ *n* **I** : one much in the company of another : COMRADE **2 a** : one of a pair of matching things **b** : one employed to live with and serve another [Old French *compagnon*, from Late Latin *companio*, from Latin *com-* + *panis* "bread, food"]

²companion *n* **I** : a covering at the top of a companionway **2** : COMPANIONWAY [by folk etymology from Dutch *kampanje* "poop deck"]

com·pan·ion·able \kəm-'pan-yə-nə-bəl\ *adj* : fitted to be a companion : SOCIABLE — **com·pan·ion·ably** \-blē\ *adv*

companion cell *n* : a living nucleated cell adjacent to a sieve tube of a vascular plant

com·pan·ion·ship \kəm-'pan-yən-ˌship\ *n* : FELLOWSHIP

com·pan·ion·way \-ˌwā\ *n* : a ship's stairway from one deck to another

com·pa·ny \'kəmp-nē, -ə-nē\ *n, pl* **-nies I a** : association with another : FELLOWSHIP **b** : persons with whom one regularly associates **c** : VISITORS **2 a** : a group of persons or things **b** : a body of soldiers; *esp* : a unit especially of infantry consisting usually of a headquarters and two or more platoons **c** : an organization of musical or dramatic performers ⟨an opera *company*⟩ **d** : the officers and men of a ship **e** : a firefighting unit **3 a** : an association of persons carrying on a commercial or industrial enterprise **b** : those members of a partnership whose names do not appear in the firm name ⟨Doe and *Company*⟩ [Old French *compagnie*, from *compain* "companion", from Late Latin *companio*]

company union *n* : an unaffiliated labor union of the employees of a single firm; *esp* : one dominated by the employer

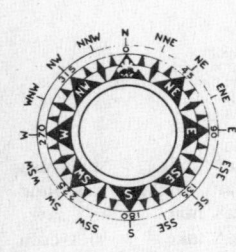

compass card

com·pa·ra·ble \'käm-pə-rə-bəl, -prə-\ *adj* **I** : capable of being compared **2** : EQUIVALENT, SIMILAR ⟨fabrics of *comparable* quality⟩ — **com·pa·ra·bly** \-blē\ *adv*

¹com·par·a·tive \kəm-'par-ət-iv\ *adj* **I** : of, relating to, or constituting the degree of grammatical comparison that denotes increase in the quality, quantity, or relation expressed by an adjective or adverb **2 a** : measured by comparison : RELATIVE ⟨a *comparative* stranger⟩ **b** : involving systematic study of comparable elements ⟨*comparative* anatomy⟩ — **com·par·a·tive·ly** *adv* — **com·par·a·tive·ness** *n*

²comparative *n* : the comparative degree or a comparative form in a language ⟨taller is the *comparative* of tall⟩

com·par·a·tor \kəm-'par-ət-ər, 'käm-pə-ˌrāt-\ *n* : an instrument for comparing something with a like thing or with a standard measure

¹com·pare \kəm-'paər, -'peər\ *vb* **I** : to represent as similar : LIKEN ⟨*compare* an anthill to a town⟩ **2** : to examine in order to discover likenesses or differences ⟨*compare* two bicycles⟩ **3** : to be worthy of comparison ⟨roller-skating does not *compare* with ice-skating⟩ **4** : to inflect or modify (an adjective or adverb) according to the degrees of comparison [Middle French *comparer*, from Latin *comparare* "to couple, compare", from *compar* "like", from *com-* + *par* "equal"] □ SYN COMPARE, CONTRAST mean to set side by side in order to show differences and likenesses. COMPARE implies an aim of showing relative values and stresses similarities; CONTRAST implies an emphasis on differences or especially opposite qualities.

²compare *n* : the possibility of comparing ⟨beauty beyond *compare*⟩

com·par·i·son \kəm-'par-ə-sən\ *n* **I** : the act of comparing : the state of being compared **2** : an examination of two or more objects to find the likenesses and differences between them **3** : change in the form of an adjective or an adverb (as by having *-er* or *-est* added or *more* or *most* prefixed) to show different levels of quality, quantity, or relation

com·part·ment \kəm-'pärt-mənt\ *n* **I** : one of the parts into which an enclosed space is divided **2** : a separate division or section — **com·part·ment·ed** \-ˌment-əd\ *adj*

com·part·men·tal·ize \kəm-ˌpärt-'ment-l-ˌīz\ *vt* : to separate into compartments — **com·part·men·tal·iza·tion** \-ˌment-l-ə-'zā-shən\ *n*

¹com·pass \'kəm-pəs, 'käm-\ *vt* **I** : to travel entirely around **2 a** : to bring about : ACHIEVE **b** : to get into one's power or possession : OBTAIN **3** : to understand fully : COMPREHEND [Old French *compasser* "to measure", from Latin *com-* + *passus* "pace"]

²compass *n* **I a** : an often rounded or curved boundary limit : CIRCUMFERENCE **b** : an enclosed space **c** : RANGE, SCOPE ⟨the *compass* of a voice⟩ **2 a** : a device for determining directions by means of a magnetic needle turning freely on a pivot and pointing to the magnetic north **b** : any of various nonmagnetic devices that indicate direction **c** : an instrument for making circles or transferring measurements that consists of two pointed branches joined at the top by a pivot — usually used in pl.; called also *pair of compasses*

compass card *n* : the circular card attached to the needles of a mariner's compass on which are marked 32 points of the compass and the 360° of the circle

com·pas·sion \kəm-'pash-ən\ *n* : sorrow or pity aroused by the suffering or misfortune of another : SYMPATHY, MERCY [Late Latin *compassio*, from *compati* "to sympathize", from Latin *com-* + *pati* "to suffer"]

com·pas·sion·ate \kəm-'pash-nət, -ə-nət\ *adj* : having or showing compassion : SYMPATHETIC — **com·pas·sion·ate·ly** *adv*

com·pat·i·ble \kəm-'pat-ə-bəl\ *adj* **I** : capable of existing together in harmony ⟨*compatible* colors⟩ **2** :

able to cross-fertilize freely ⟨*compatible* plants⟩ **3** : free from adverse or unwanted effects when present together ⟨*compatible* drugs⟩ [Middle French, from Medieval Latin *compatibilis* "sympathetic", from Latin *compati* "to sympathize"] — **com·pat·i·bil·i·ty** \-,pat-ə-'bil-ət-ē\ *n* — **com·pat·i·bly** \-'pat-ə-blē\ *adv*

com·pa·tri·ot \kəm-'pā-trē-ət, -,ät\ *n* **1** : a fellow countryman **2** : COLLEAGUE, COMPANION

com·pel \kəm-'pel\ *vt* **com·pelled; com·pel·ling 1** : to drive or urge forcefully or irresistibly : CONSTRAIN **2** : to cause to do or occur by overwhelming pressure ⟨*compel* obedience⟩ [Middle French *compellir*, from Latin *compellere*, from *com-* + *pellere* "to drive"] SYN see FORCE — **com·pel·ler** *n*

com·pend \'käm-,pend\ *n* : COMPENDIUM

com·pen·di·ous \kəm-'pen-dē-əs\ *adj* : marked by brief expression of a comprehensive matter : CONCISE — **com·pen·di·ous·ly** *adv* — **com·pen·di·ous·ness** *n*

com·pen·di·um \-dē-əm\ *n, pl* **-di·ums** *or* **-dia** \-dē-ə\ : a brief summary of a larger work or of a field of knowledge : ABSTRACT [Latin, "saving, shortcut", from *compendere* "to weigh together", from *com-* + *pendere* "to weigh"]

com·pen·sate \'käm-pən-,sāt\ *vb* **1** : to be equivalent to in value or effect : make up for : COUNTERBALANCE **2** : to make amends or amends to ⟨nothing can *compensate* for the loss of reputation⟩ **3** : to make equal return to : PAY ⟨*compensate* workers for their labor⟩ [Latin *compensare*, from *compensus*, past participle of *compendere* "to weigh together"] — **com·pen·sa·tor** \'käm-pən-,sāt-ər\ *n* — **com·pen·sa·to·ry** \kəm-'pen-sə-,tōr-ē, -,tȯr-\ *adj* □ SYN COMPENSATE, BALANCE, OFFSET mean to make up in one thing what is deficient or excessive in another. COMPENSATE implies making up a lack or making amends for loss or injury; BALANCE suggests the equalizing or adjusting of two things so that neither outweighs the other in effect; OFFSET implies neutralizing one thing's good or bad effect by something exerting an opposite effect. SYN see in addition PAY

com·pen·sa·tion \,käm-pən-'sā-shən\ *n* **1** : the act of compensating : the state of being compensated **2 a** : something that compensates; *esp* : payment to an unemployed or injured worker or his or her dependents **b** : SALARY, WAGES — **com·pen·sa·tion·al** \-shnəl, -shən-l\ *adj*

com·pete \kəm-'pēt\ *vi* : to vie with another for an objective (as position, profit, or a prize) [Late Latin *competere* "to seek together", from Latin *com-* + *petere* "to go to, seek"]

com·pe·tence \'käm-pət-əns\ *n* **1** : means sufficient for the necessities of life **2** : the quality or state of being competent

com·pe·ten·cy \-ən-sē\ *n* : COMPETENCE

com·pe·tent \'käm-pət-ənt\ *adj* **1** : having the necessary ability or qualities : FIT **2** : legally qualified [Latin *competens*, from *competere* "to come together, be suitable", from *com-* + *petere* "to go to, seek"] SYN see ABLE — **com·pe·tent·ly** *adv*

com·pe·ti·tion \,käm-pə-'tish-ən\ *n* **1** : the act or process of competing **2** : a contest between rivals; *also* : one's competitors **3** : the effort of two or more persons or firms acting independently to secure business by offering the most favorable terms **4** : active demand by two or more organisms or kinds of organisms for some environmental resource in short supply — **com·pet·i·to·ry** \kəm-'pet-ə-,tōr-ē, -,tȯr-\ *adj*

com·pet·i·tive \kəm-'pet-ət-iv\ *adj* : relating to, characterized by, or based on competition ⟨*competitive* sports⟩ — **com·pet·i·tive·ly** *adv* — **com·pet·i·tive·ness** *n*

com·pet·i·tor \kəm-'pet-ət-ər\ *n* : one that competes: as **a** : RIVAL 1a **b** : one selling or buying goods or services in the same market as another **c** : an organism that lives in competition with another

com·pi·la·tion \,käm-pə-'lā-shən\ *n* **1** : the act or process of compiling **2** : something compiled; *esp* : a book composed of materials gathered from other books or documents

com·pile \kəm-'pīl\ *vt* **1** : to collect into a volume **2** : to compose out of materials from other documents **3** : to translate (as a computer program) with a compiler [Middle French *compiler*, from Latin *compilare* "to plunder"]

com·pil·er \kəm-'pī-lər\ *n* **1** : one that compiles **2** : a computer program that automatically translates an entire set of instructions written in a computer language (as BASIC) into machine language

com·pla·cence \kəm-'plās-ns\ *n* : SELF-SATISFACTION

com·pla·cen·cy \-n-sē\ *n* : COMPLACENCE

com·pla·cent \kəm-'plās-nt\ *adj* **1** : SELF-SATISFIED ⟨a *complacent* smile⟩ **2** : feeling or showing complaisance [Latin *complacēre* "to please greatly", from *com-* + *placēre* "to please"] — **com·pla·cent·ly** *adv*

com·plain \kəm-'plān\ *vi* **1** : to express grief, pain, or discontent **2** : to make a formal accusation or charge [Middle French *complaindre*, from Latin *com-* + *plangere* "to lament"] — **com·plain·er** *n* — **com·plain·ing·ly** \-'plā-ning-lē\ *adv*

com·plain·ant \kəm-'plā-nənt\ *n* : one that makes a complaint in a legal action or proceeding

com·plaint \kəm-'plānt\ *n* **1** : expression of grief, pain, or resentment **2 a** : a cause or reason for complaining **b** : a bodily ailment or disease **3** : a formal charge against a person

com·plai·sance \kəm-'plās-ns, -'plāz-; ,käm-plā-'zans\ *n* : inclination to please or oblige

com·plai·sant \-nt; -'zant\ *adj* : marked by an inclination to please or oblige or consent to others' wishes [French, from Middle French *complaire* "to gratify, acquiesce", from Latin *complacēre* "to please greatly"] — **com·plai·sant·ly** *adv*

com·plect·ed \kəm-'plek-təd\ *adj* : COMPLEXIONED ⟨dark-*complected*⟩ [derived from *complexion*]

¹com·ple·ment \'käm-plə-mənt\ *n* **1** : something that fills up, completes, or makes perfect **2** : full quantity, number, or amount ⟨a ship's *complement* of officers and men⟩ **3 a** : an angle or arc that when added to a given angle or arc equals a right angle **b** : a subset that contains all the elements of a set that are not contained in a particular one of its subsets **4** : an added word or group of words by which the predicate of a sentence is made complete ⟨*president* in "they elected me president" and *good* in "that is good" are different kinds of *complements*⟩ **5** : a heat-sensitive substance in normal blood that in combination with antibodies destroys antigens [Latin *complementum*, from *complēre* "to complete"] □ SYN COMPLEMENT, COMPLIMENT are not synonyms but are easily confused. COMPLEMENT applies to a thing, quantity, or part required to make something complete or full; COMPLIMENT is an often formal expression of approval, praise, or greeting.

²com·ple·ment \-,ment\ *vt* : to be complementary to

com·ple·men·tal \,käm-plə-'ment-l\ *adj* : relating to or being a complement : COMPLEMENTARY

com·ple·men·ta·ry \,käm-plə-'ment-ə-rē, -'men-trē\ *adj* **1** : forming or serving as a complement **2** : of or relating to the precise pairing of purine to pyrimidine bases between strands of DNA and sometimes RNA through which the structure of one strand determines the other — **complementary** *n*

complementary angles *n pl* : two angles whose sum is 90 degrees

complementary colors *n pl* : a pair of colors that when mixed in proper proportions produce a neutral color

¹com·plete \kəm-'plēt\ *adj* **1 a** : possessing all necessary parts : ENTIRE **b** : having all four sets of floral organs **2** : brought to an end : CONCLUDED **3** : highly proficient ⟨a *complete* artist⟩ **4 a** : fully carried out : THOROUGH **b** : TOTAL, ABSOLUTE ⟨*complete* silence⟩ [Middle

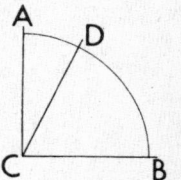

complementary angles
∠ ACD and ∠ DCB are
complementary

\ə\ abut	\ng\ sing
\ər\ further	\ō\ bone
\a\ mat	\ȯ\ saw
\ā\ take	\ȯi\ coin
\ä\ cot, cart	\th\ thin
\au̇\ out	\th\ this
\ch\ chin	\ü\ food
\e\ pet	\u̇\ foot
\ē\ easy	\y\ yet
\g\ go	\yü\ few
\i\ tip	\yu̇\ cure
\ī\ life	\zh\ vision
\j\ job	

French *complet*, from Latin *completus*, from *complēre* "to complete", from *com-* + *plēre* "to fill"] — **com·plete·ly** *adv* — **com·plete·ness** *n*

²**complete** *vt* **1** : to bring to an end : accomplish or achieve fully **2** : to make whole or perfect; *esp* : to provide with all lacking parts SYN see FINISH

com·ple·tion \kəm-'plē-shən\ *n* : the act or process of completing : the state of being complete ⟨a job near *completion*⟩

complete protein *n* : protein (as in meat, fish, milk, and eggs) supplying all the amino acids that are needed by the human body but cannot be made by it

¹**com·plex** \käm-'pleks, kəm-', 'käm-,\ *adj* **1** : composed of two or more parts ⟨a *complex* mixture⟩: as **a** : consisting of a main clause and one or more subordinate clauses ⟨*complex* sentence⟩ **b** : formed by union of simpler substances ⟨a *complex* protein⟩ **2** : having many interrelated parts, patterns, or elements that are hard to separate, analyze, or solve **3** : of or relating to complex numbers [Latin *complexus*, past participle of *complecti* "to embrace, comprise", from *com-* + *plectere* "to braid"] — **com·plex·ly** *adv* — **com·plex·ness** *n* □ SYN COMPLEX, COMPLICATED, INTRICATE, INVOLVED mean having confusingly interrelated parts. COMPLEX suggests an unavoidable and necessary lack of simplicity and does not imply a fault or failure in designing or arranging; COMPLICATED applies to what offers difficulty in understanding, explaining, or solving; INTRICATE implies an interlacing of parts that can scarcely be grasped or traced separately; INVOLVED implies extreme complication and often suggests disorder.

²**com·plex** \'käm-,pleks\ *n* **1** : a whole made up of complicated or interrelated parts ⟨the military-industrial *complex*⟩ **2 a** : a group of culture traits usually associated with a particular activity or process **b** : a system of repressed desires and memories that exerts a dominating influence upon the personality; *also* : an exaggerated reaction to a subject or situation **c** : a group of obviously related units of which the degree and nature of the relationship is imperfectly known

complex fraction *n* : a fraction with a fraction or mixed number in the numerator or denominator or both — compare SIMPLE FRACTION

com·plex·ion \kəm-'plek-shən\ *n* **1** : natural disposition : TEMPERAMENT **2** : the hue or appearance of the skin especially of the face **3** : general appearance or impression : CHARACTER [Middle French "combination of qualities that determines temperament", from Latin *complexio* "combination", from *complexus,* past participle of *complecti* "to comprise"] — **com·plex·ioned** \-shənd\ *adj*

com·plex·i·ty \kəm-'plek-sət-ē, käm-\ *n, pl* **-ties 1** : the quality or state of being complex **2** : something complex ⟨the *complexities* of the English language⟩

complex number *n* : a number (as $3 + 4\sqrt{-1}$) formed by adding a real number to the product of a real number and the square root of minus one

complex plane *n* : a plane whose points are identified by means of complex numbers

com·pli·ance \kəm-'plī-əns\ *n* **1** : the act or process of complying **2** : a readiness or disposition to yield to others — **in compliance with** : in accordance with : in obedience to

com·pli·an·cy \-ən-sē\ *n* : COMPLIANCE

com·pli·ant \-ənt\ *adj* : ready or disposed to comply : SUBMISSIVE — **com·pli·ant·ly** *adv*

com·pli·cate \'käm-plə-,kāt\ *vb* : to make or become complex, intricate, or difficult [Latin *complicare* "to fold together", from *com-* + *plicare* "to fold"]

com·pli·cat·ed *adj* **1** : consisting of parts intricately combined **2** : difficult to analyze, understand, or explain SYN see COMPLEX — **com·pli·cat·ed·ly** *adv* — **com·pli·cat·ed·ness** *n*

com·pli·ca·tion \,käm-plə-'kā-shən\ *n* **1 a** : a situation or a detail of character complicating the main thread

of a plot **b** : a making difficult, involved, or intricate **c** : a complex or intricate feature or element **d** : something that makes a situation more complicated or difficult **2** : a secondary disease or condition developing in the course of a primary disease

com·plic·i·ty \kəm-'plis-ət-ē\ *n, pl* **-ties** : association or participation in a wrongful act [French *complicité*, from *complice* "associate, accomplice", from Late Latin *complex* "partner", from *com-* + *plicare* "to fold"]

¹**com·pli·ment** \'käm-plə-mənt\ *n* **1** : an expression of esteem, respect, affection, or admiration; *esp* : a flattering remark **2** *pl* : best wishes : REGARDS [French, from Italian *complimento*, from Spanish *cumplimiento,* from *cumplir* "to comply, be courteous"] SYN see COMPLEMENT

²**com·pli·ment** \-,ment\ *vt* : to pay a compliment to

com·pli·men·ta·ry \,käm-plə-'ment-ə-rē, -'men-trē\ *adj* **1** : expressing or containing a compliment **2** : given free as a courtesy or favor ⟨a *complimentary* ticket⟩ — **com·pli·men·tar·i·ly** \-,men-'ter-ə-lē\ *adv*

com·pline \'käm-plən, -,plīn\ *n, often cap* : the last of the canonical hours [Old French *complie,* from Late Latin *completa,* from Latin *completus* "complete"]

com·ply \kəm-'plī\ *vi* **com·plied; com·ply·ing** : to conform or adapt one's actions to another's wishes, to a rule, or to necessity ⟨*comply* with a request⟩ [Italian *complire,* from Spanish *cumplir* "to perform what is due, comply, be courteous", from Latin *complēre* "to complete"] — **com·pli·er** \-'plī-ər,-'plīr\ *n*

¹**com·po·nent** \kəm-'pō-nənt, 'käm-,, käm-'\ *n* **1** : a constituent part : INGREDIENT ⟨the *components* of a solution⟩ **2 a** : any one of the vector terms added to form a vector sum or resultant **b** : a coordinate of a vector [Latin *componere* "to put together", from *com-* + *ponere* "to put"] SYN see ELEMENT — **com·po·nen·tial** \,käm-pə-'nen-chəl\ *adj*

²**component** *adj* : being or forming a part : CONSTITUENT ⟨the *component* parts of a machine⟩

com·port \kəm-'pōrt, -'pórt\ *vb* **1** : to be fitting : ACCORD ⟨acts that *comport* with ideals⟩ **2** : CONDUCT ⟨*comport* oneself with dignity⟩ [Middle French *comporter* "to bear, conduct", from Latin *comportare* "to bring together", from *com-* + *portare* "to carry"]

com·port·ment \kəm-'pōrt-mənt, -'pórt-\ *n* : BEHAVIOR, BEARING

com·pose \kəm-'pōz\ *vb* **1 a** : to form by putting together : FASHION **b** : to make up : CONSTITUTE ⟨a cake *composed* of many ingredients⟩ **c** : to assemble the characters of (text) in order for printing : SET **2** : to create by mental or artistic labor ⟨*compose* a song⟩ **3** : to reduce to a minimum ⟨*compose* their differences⟩ **4** : to arrange in proper form **5** : to free from agitation : CALM ⟨*composed* herself⟩ [Middle French *composer,* from Latin *componere,* from *com-* + *ponere* "to put"]

com·posed \-'pōzd\ *adj* : free from agitation : CALM; *esp* : SELF-POSSESSED — **com·pos·ed·ly** \-'pō-zəd-lē\ *adv* — **com·pos·ed·ness** \-'pō-zəd-nəs\ *n*

com·pos·er \kəm-'pō-zər\ *n* : one that composes; *esp* : a person who writes music

¹**com·pos·ite** \käm-'päz-ət, kəm-\ *adj* **1** : made up of various distinct parts or elements ⟨a *composite* photograph⟩ **2** : of or relating to a large family (Compositae) of dicotyledonous trees, shrubs, and herbs (as the dandelion, sunflower, and ragweed) often considered to be the most highly evolved plants and characterized by florets arranged in dense heads that resemble single flowers (the daisy and other *composite* plants) [Latin *compositus,* past participle of *componere* "to compose"] — **com·pos·ite·ly** *adv*

²**composite** *n* **1** : something that is made up of different parts : COMPOUND **2** : a composite plant

composite number *n* : an integer that can be factored into two or more whole numbers each greater than 1

com·po·si·tion \ˌkäm-pə-'zish-ən\ *n* **I** : a composing: as **a** : a putting words together to make sentences : the art or practice of writing **b** : the composing of matter to be printed **2** : the manner in which the parts of a thing are put together : MAKEUP ⟨the *composition* of a painting⟩ **3** : the makeup of a compound or mixture ⟨the *composition* of rubber⟩ **4** : a product of combining various ingredients : COMBINATION ⟨a *composition* made of several different metals⟩ **5** : a literary, musical, or artistic production; *esp* : a short piece of writing done as an educational exercise ⟨must write one *composition* each week⟩ — **com·po·si·tion·al** \-'zish-nəl, -ən-l\ *adj*

com·pos·i·tor \kəm-'päz-ət-ər\ *n* : one that composes matter to be printed

¹com·post \'käm-ˌpōst\ *n* : a mixture largely of decayed organic matter used for fertilizing and conditioning land [Middle French, from Medieval Latin *compostum,* from Latin *componere* "to put together"]

²compost *vt* : to convert (as plant debris) to compost

com·po·sure \kəm-'pō-zhər\ *n* : calmness or repose especially of mind, bearing, or appearance : SELF-POSSESSION

com·pote \'käm-ˌpōt\ *n* **I** : fruits cooked in syrup **2** : a bowl usually with a base and stem from which compotes, fruits, nuts, or sweets are served [French, from Old French *composte,* from Latin *componere* "to put together, compose"]

¹com·pound \käm-'paund, kəm-', 'käm-,\ *vb* **I** : to put together or be joined to form a whole : COMBINE **2** : to form by combining parts ⟨*compound* a medicine⟩ **3** : to settle peaceably : COMPROMISE **4 a** : to pay (interest) on both the accrued interest and the principal ⟨*compound* interest quarterly⟩ **b** : to add to **5** : to agree for a consideration not to prosecute (an offense) ⟨*compound* a felony⟩ [Middle French *compondre,* from Latin *componere* "to put together, compose"] — **compound·able** \-ə-bəl\ *adj* — **com·pound·er** *n*

²com·pound \'käm-,paund, käm-', kəm-'\ *adj* **I a** : made up of or by the union of separate elements or parts ⟨a *compound* substance⟩ **b** : composed of united similar elements especially of a kind usually independent ⟨a *compound* fruit⟩ **c** : having the blade divided to the midrib and forming two or more leaflets on a common axis ⟨a *compound* leaf⟩ **2** : involving or used in a combination : COMPOSITE **3 a** : being a word that is a compound ⟨the *compound* noun *steamboat*⟩ **b** : consisting of two or more main clauses ⟨a *compound* sentence⟩

³com·pound \'käm-,paund\ *n* **I a** : a word consisting of components that are words ⟨*rowboat, high school,* and *light-year* are *compounds*⟩ **b** : a word consisting of any of various combinations of words, word elements, or affixes ⟨*anthropology, kilocycle,* and *builder* are *compounds*⟩ **2** : something formed by a union of elements, ingredients, or parts; *esp* : a distinct substance formed by the union of two or more chemical elements in definite proportion by weight

⁴com·pound \'käm-,paund\ *n* **I** : an enclosure of European residences and commercial buildings especially in the Orient **2** : a large fenced or walled-in area [by folk etymology from Malay *kampong* "group of buildings, village"]

compound-complex *adj* : having two or more main clauses and one or more subordinate clauses ⟨*compound-complex* sentence⟩

compound eye *n* : an eye (as of an insect) made up of many separate visual units

compound fracture *n* : a breaking of a bone in such a way as to produce an open wound through which bone fragments stick out

compound interest *n* : interest paid or to be paid both on the principal and on accumulated interest

compound microscope *n* : a microscope consisting of an objective and an eyepiece mounted in a drawtube

com·pre·hend \ˌkäm-pri-'hend\ *vt* **I** : to grasp the meaning of : UNDERSTAND **2** : to take in : EMBRACE [Latin *comprehendere,* from *com-* + *prehendere* "to grasp"] SYN see COMPRISE, INCLUDE — **com·pre·hend·ible** \-'hen-də-bəl\ *adj*

com·pre·hen·si·ble \-'hen-sə-bəl\ *adj* : capable of being comprehended : INTELLIGIBLE — **com·pre·hen·si·bil·i·ty** \-ˌhen-sə-'bil-ət-ē\ *n* — **com·pre·hen·si·bly** \-'hen-sə-blē\ *adv*

com·pre·hen·sion \ˌkäm-pri-'hen-chən\ *n* **I a** : the act or process of including or comprising **b** : COMPREHENSIVENESS **2 a** : the act or action of grasping with the intellect **b** : knowledge gained by comprehending **c** : the capacity for understanding [Latin *comprehensio,* from *comprehendere* "to comprehend"]

com·pre·hen·sive \-'hen-siv\ *adj* **I** : covering broadly or completely : INCLUSIVE ⟨*comprehensive* insurance⟩ ⟨a *comprehensive* examination⟩ **2** : having wide mental comprehension — **com·pre·hen·sive·ly** *adv* — **com·pre·hen·sive·ness** *n*

¹com·press \kəm-'pres\ *vb* **I** : to press or become pressed together **2** : to reduce the volume of by pressure [Late Latin *compressare* "to press hard", from Latin *compressus,* past participle of *comprimere* "to compress", from *com-* + *premere* "to press"] SYN see CONDENSE

²com·press \'käm-,pres\ *n* **I** : a folded cloth or pad applied so as to press upon a body part ⟨a cold *compress*⟩ **2** : a machine for compressing cotton into bales

com·pressed \kəm-'prest, 'käm-,\ *adj* : flattened as though subjected to compression: **a** : flattened laterally ⟨petioles *compressed*⟩ **b** : narrow from side to side and deep in a dorsoventral direction

compressed air *n* : air under pressure greater than that of the atmosphere

com·press·ible \kəm-'pres-ə-bəl\ *adj* : capable of being compressed — **com·press·ibil·i·ty** \-ˌpres-ə-'bil-ət-ē\ *n*

com·pres·sion \kəm-'presh-ən\ *n* **I** : the act or process of compressing : the state of being compressed **2** : the process of compressing the fuel mixture in the cylinders of an internal-combustion engine (as of an automobile) — **com·pres·sion·al** \-'presh-nəl, -ən-l\ *adj* — **com·pres·sive** \-'pres-iv\ *adj*

com·pres·sor \-'pres-ər\ *n* **I** : one that compresses **2** : a machine that compresses gases and especially air

com·prise \kəm-'prīz\ *vt* **I** : to include especially within a particular scope : CONTAIN **2** : to be made up of **3** : to make up : CONSTITUTE [Middle French *compris,* past participle of *comprendre* "to include, comprehend", from Latin *comprehendere*] □ SYN COMPRISE, INCLUDE, COMPREHEND, EMBRACE mean to take in or contain within one unit or boundary. COMPRISE implies that the list of parts or members is complete ⟨New York City *comprises* the boroughs Manhattan, Brooklyn, Queens, Staten Island, and the Bronx⟩ INCLUDE does not imply that all constituent members are presently specified ⟨the United States now *includes* Alaska and Hawaii⟩ COMPREHEND implies that something falls within the scope of a whole ⟨true love *comprehends* loyalty and much more⟩ EMBRACE implies a gathering of several items into a whole ⟨their philosophy *embraced* several schools of thought⟩

¹com·pro·mise \'käm-prə-ˌmīz\ *n* **I** : a settlement of a dispute by mutual concessions **2** : a concession that is wrong or degrading ⟨a *compromise* of one's principles⟩ **3** : an agreement reached by mutual concessions ⟨the Missouri *Compromise*⟩ [Middle French *compromis,* from Latin *compromissum,* from *compromittere* "to promise mutually", from *com-* + *promittere* "to promise"]

²compromise *vb* **I** : to adjust or settle differences by mutual concessions **2** : to expose to discredit, suspicion, or danger **3** : to make unworthy concessions — **com·pro·mis·er** *n*

\ə\ abut	\ng\ sing
\ər\ further	\ō\ bone
\a\ mat	\ȯ\ saw
\ā\ take	\ȯi\ coin
\ä\ cot, cart	\th\ thin
\au̇\ out	\th\ this
\ch\ chin	\ü\ food
\e\ pet	\u̇\ foot
\ē\ easy	\y\ yet
\g\ go	\yü\ few
\i\ tip	\yu̇\ cure
\ī\ life	\zh\ vision
\j\ job	

comp·trol·ler \kən-'trō-lər, 'käm-ˌ, 'kämp-ˌ, käm-', kämp-'\ *n* **1** : a public official who audits government accounts and sometimes certifies expenditures **2** : CONTROLLER 1b [Middle English, alteration of *conter-roller* "controller"] — **comp·trol·ler·ship** \-ˌship\ *n*

com·pul·sion \kəm-'pəl-shən\ *n* **1 a** : an act of compelling : the sate of being compelled **b** : a force or agency that compels **2** : an irresistible impulse to do something [Late Latin *compulsio,* from Latin *compulsus,* past participle of *compellere* "to compel"]

com·pul·sive \-'pəl-siv\ *adj* **1** : having power to compel **2** : of, relating to, or caused by compulsion — **com·pul·sive·ly** *adv* — **com·pul·sive·ness** *n*

com·pul·so·ry \-'pəls-rē, -ə-rē\ *adj* **1** : required by authority **2** : having the power of compelling

com·punc·tion \kəm-'pəng-shən, -'pəngk-\ *n* **1** : sharp uneasiness caused by a sense of guilt : REMORSE **2** : a passing feeling of regret for some slight wrong [Middle French *componction,* from Late Latin *compunctio,* from Latin *compunctus,* past participle of *compungere* "to prick hard, sting", from *com-* + *pungere* "to prick"] SYN see QUALM — **com·punc·tious** \-shəs\ *adj*

com·pu·ta·tion \ˌkäm-pyu̇-'tā-shən\ *n* **1** : the act or action of computing : CALCULATION **2** : a system of reckoning **3** : an amount computed — **com·pu·ta·tion·al** \-shnəl, -shən-l\ *adj*

com·pute \kəm-'pyüt\ *vb* : to determine or calculate especially by mathematical means [Latin *computare,* from *com-* + *putare* "to consider"] — **com·put·able** \-'pyüt-ə-bəl\ *adj*

com·put·er \-'pyüt-ər\ *n* : one that computes; *esp* : an automatic electronic machine that can store, retrieve, and process data

com·put·er·ize \-ə-ˌrīz\ *vt* **1** : to carry out, control, or conduct by means of a computer **2** : to equip with computers **3 a** : to store in a computer **b** : to put into a form a computer can use — **com·put·er·iza·tion** \-ˌpyüt-ə-rə-'zā-shən\ *n*

com·rade \'käm-ˌrad, -rəd\ *n* **1 a** : an intimate friend or associate : COMPANION **b** : a fellow soldier : COMMUNIST [Middle French *camarade* "group of roommates, companion", from Spanish *camarada,* from *cámara* "room", from Late Latin *camera;* sense 2 from its use as a form of address by Communists]

com·rade·ship \-ˌship\ *n* : association as comrades : FELLOWSHIP, FRIENDSHIP

¹con \'kän\ *vt* **conned, con·ning 1** : to study carefully : PERUSE [Middle English *connen* "to know, study", alteration of *cunnen* "to know", infinitive of *can*]

²con *adv* : on the negative side : in opposition [short for *contra*]

³con *n* **1** : an opposing argument, person, or position **2** : the negative position or one holding it

⁴con *vt* **conned; con·ning 1** : SWINDLE **2** : COAX, CAJOLE [*confidence game*]

⁵con *n* : CONVICT [by shortening]

con- — see COM-

con amo·re \ˌkän-ə-'mōr-ē, ˌkō-nə-'mōr-ˌā, -'mȯr-\ *adv* **1** : with love, devotion, or zest **2** : TENDERLY — used as a direction in music [Italian, "with love"]

con·cat·e·nate \kän-'kat-ə-ˌnāt\ *vt* : to link together in a series or chain [Late Latin *concatenare,* from Latin *com-* + *catena* "chain"] — **con·cat·e·na·tion** \ˌkän-ˌkat-ə-'nā-shən\ *n*

con·cave \kän-'kāv, 'kän-ˌ\ *adj* : hollowed or rounded inward like the inside of a bowl [Middle French, from Latin *concavus,* from *com-* + *cavus* "hollow"] — **con·cave·ly** *adv* — **con·cave·ness** *n*

con·cav·i·ty \kän-'kav-ət-ē\ *n, pl* **-ties 1** : a concave surface or space : HOLLOW **2** : the quality or state of being concave

con·cavo–con·vex \kän-ˌkā-vō-kän-'veks, -kən-, -'kän-ˌveks\ *adj* : concave on one side and convex on the other **2** : having the concave side of greater curvature than the convex

con·ceal \kən-'sēl\ *vt* **1** : to hide from sight **2** : to keep secret [Middle French *conceler,* from Latin *concelare,* from *com-* + *celare* "to hide"] — **con·ceal·able** \-ə-bəl\ *adj*

con·ceal·ment \-mənt\ *n* **1** : the act of hiding : the state of being hidden **2** : a hiding place

con·cede \kən-'sēd\ *vb* **1** : to grant as a right or privilege **2** : to acknowledge or admit grudgingly : YIELD [Latin *concedere,* from *com-* + *cedere* "to yield, cede"] SYN see GRANT — **con·ced·ed·ly** \-'sēd-əd-lē\ *adv* — **con·ced·er** *n*

con·ceit \kən-'sēt\ *n* **1** : excessive pride in one's own worth or virtue **2 a** : a fanciful idea **b** : an elaborate metaphor [Middle English, "judgment", from *conceiven* "to conceive"]

con·ceit·ed \-'sēt-əd\ *adj* : having a very high opinion of oneself — **con·ceit·ed·ly** *adv* — **con·ceit·ed·ness** *n*

con·ceiv·able \kən-'sē-və-bəl\ *adj* : capable of being conceived : IMAGINABLE — **con·ceiv·ably** \-blē\ *adv*

con·ceive \kən-'sēv\ *vb* **1** : to become pregnant **2 a** : to take into the mind ⟨*conceived* a liking for the student⟩ **b** : to form an idea of : IMAGINE ⟨*conceive* a new system⟩ **3** : to have an opinion : THINK ⟨not likely to *conceive* of me as a genius⟩ [Middle English *conceiven,* from Old French *conceivre,* from Latin *concipere,* from *com-* + *capere* "to take"] — **con·ceiv·er** *n*

¹con·cen·trate \'kän-sən-ˌtrāt\ *vb* **1 a** : to bring, direct, or come toward a common center or objective **b** : to gather into one body, mass, or force **2** : to make stronger by removing something unwanted ⟨*concentrate* ore⟩ **3** : to fix one's powers, efforts, or attention on one thing ⟨*concentrate* on a problem⟩ [*com-* + Latin *centrum* "center"] — **con·cen·tra·tor** \-ˌtrāt-ər\ *n*

²concentrate *n* : something concentrated

con·cen·tra·tion \ˌkän-sən-'trā-shən\ *n* **1** : the act or process of concentrating : the state of being concentrated; *esp* : direction of attention on a single object **2** : a concentrated mass **3** : the relative amount of an ingredient : STRENGTH ⟨the *concentration* of salt in a solution⟩

concentration camp *n* : a camp where persons (as prisoners of war or political prisoners) are detained or confined

con·cen·tric \kən-'sen-trik, kän-\ *adj* : having a common center ⟨*concentric* circles⟩ [Medieval Latin *concentricus,* from Latin *com-* + *centrum* "center"] — **con·cen·tri·cal·ly** \-tri-kə-lē, -klē\ *adv* — **con·cen·tric·i·ty** \ˌkän-ˌsen-'tris-ət-ē\ *n*

con·cept \'kän-ˌsept\ *n* **1** : something conceived in the mind : THOUGHT, NOTION **2** : an abstract idea generalized from particular instances [Latin *conceptus,* past participle of *concipere* "to conceive"] SYN see IDEA

con·cep·ta·cle \kən-'sep-ti-kəl\ *n* : an external cavity containing reproductive cells in some algae [Latin *conceptaculum* "receptacle", from *concipere* "to take in, conceive"]

con·cep·tion \kən-'sep-shən\ *n* **1** : the beginning of pregnancy : the formation of a zygote **2 a** : the function or process of forming or understanding ideas or abstractions or their symbols **b** : a general idea : CONCEPT **3** : the originating of something (as a plan) in the mind SYN see IDEA — **con·cep·tion·al** \-shnəl, -shən-l\ *adj* — **con·cep·tive** \-'sep-tiv\ *adj*

con·cep·tu·al \kən-'sep-chə-wəl, -chəl\ *adj* : of, relating to, or consisting of concepts — **con·cep·tu·al·ly** \-ē\ *adv*

¹con·cern \kən-'sərn\ *vt* **1** : to relate to : be about ⟨the novel *concerns* three soldiers⟩ **2** : to be the business or affair of : AFFECT ⟨the problem *concerns* us all⟩ **3** : to make anxious or worried ⟨our mother's illness *concerns* us all⟩ **4** : to take up the interest or energies of : INVOLVE ⟨*concern* oneself with business⟩ [Medieval Latin *concernere,* from Late Latin, "to sift together, mingle", from Latin *com-* + *cernere* "to sift"]

²con·cern *n* **1** : something that relates to or involves one : AFFAIR ⟨the usual *concerns* of the day⟩ **2 a** : marked regard or care ⟨showed deep *concern* for their friend's welfare⟩ **b** : a state of uncertainty and apprehension ⟨public *concern* over the threat of war⟩ **3** : a business or manufacturing establishment

con·cerned \-'sərnd\ *adj* **1** : ANXIOUS 1 **2** : interestedly engaged

con·cern·ing \-'sər-ning\ *prep* : relating to ⟨news *concerning* friends⟩

con·cern·ment \-'sərn-mənt\ *n* **1** : something in which one is concerned **2** : IMPORTANCE 1

¹con·cert \kən-'sərt\ *vb* : to plan or arrange together : settle by agreement ⟨the allies *concerted* their tactics⟩ [Middle French *concerter,* from Italian *concertare,* from Late Latin, from Latin, "to contend", from *com-* + *certare* "to strive", from *certus* "determined, certain"]

²con·cert \'kän-,sərt, -sərt\ *n* **1** : agreement in design or plan ⟨work in *concert*⟩ **2** : musical harmony : CONCORD **3** : a musical performance of some length by several voices or instruments or both

con·cert·ed \kən-'sərt-əd\ *adj* **1 a** : mutually planned or agreed on ⟨*concerted* effort⟩ **b** : performed in unison ⟨*concerted* artillery fire⟩ **2** : arranged in parts for several voices ⟨*concerted* music⟩

con·cer·ti·na \,kän-sər-'tē-nə\ *n* : a musical instrument of the accordion family

con·cer·ti·no \,kän-chər-'tē-nō\ *n, pl* **-nos** : a short concerto

con·cert·mas·ter \'kän-sərt-,mas-tər\ *or* **con·cert·meis·ter** \-,mī-stər\ *n* : the leader of the first violins and assistant conductor

con·cer·to \kən-'chert-ō\ *n, pl* **-tos** *or* **-ti** \-ē\ : a piece for one or more soloists and orchestra usually in symphonic form with three contrasting movements [Italian, from *concerto* "concert"]

con·ces·sion \kən-'sesh-ən\ *n* **1** : the act or an instance of conceding **2** : something conceded: **a** : ACKNOWLEDGMENT, ADMISSION ⟨a *concession* of guilt⟩ **b** : a grant of property or of a right by a government ⟨a mining *concession*⟩ **c** : a lease of a part of premises for some purpose ⟨a soft-drink *concession*⟩; *also* : the part leased or the activities carried on [Latin *concessio,* from *concessus,* past participle of *concedere* "to concede"]

con·ces·sion·aire \kən-,sesh-ə-'naər, -'neər\ *n* : one that owns or operates a concession [French *concessionnaire,* from *concession* "concession"]

con·ces·sive \kən-'ses-iv\ *adj* : tending toward, expressing, or being a concession — **con·ces·sive·ly** *adv*

conch \'kängk, 'känch\ *n, pl* **conchs** \'kängks\ *or* **conch·es** \'kän-chəz\ **1** : a large spiral-shelled marine gastropod mollusk; *also* : its shell used especially for cameos **2** : CONCHA [Latin *concha* "mussel, mussel shell", from Greek *konchē*]

con·cha \'käng-kə\ *n, pl* **con·chae** \-,kē, -,kī\ : the largest and deepest concavity of the external ear [Latin, "shell"]

con·chol·o·gy \käng-'käl-ə-jē\ *n* : a branch of zoology that deals with shells

con·cierge \kōⁿ-'syerzh\ *n* : an attendant at the entrance of a building especially in France who oversees people coming or going, handles mail, and acts as a janitor or porter [French, from Latin *com-* + *serviens,* present participle of *servire* "to serve"]

con·cil·i·ate \kən-'sil-ē-,āt\ *vt* **1** : to bring into agreement or harmony : RECONCILE **2** : to gain the goodwill or favor of [Latin *conciliare* "to assemble, unite, win over", from *concilium* "assembly, council"] — **con·cil·i·a·tion** \-,sil-ē-'ā-shən\ *n* — **con·cil·i·a·tor** \-'sil-ē-,āt-ər\ *n* — **con·cil·ia·to·ry** \-'sil-yə-,tōr-ē, -'sil-ē-ə-, -,tȯr-\ *adj*

con·cise \kən-'sīs\ *adj* : marked by brevity of expression or statement ⟨a *concise* review of the year's work⟩ [Latin *concisus,* from *concidere* "to cut up", from *com-* + *caedere* "to cut"] — **con·cise·ly** *adv* — **con·cise·ness** *n*

con·clave \'kän-,klāv\ *n* **1** : a private meeting or secret assembly; *esp* : a meeting of Roman Catholic cardinals to choose a pope **2** : a gathering of a group : CONVENTION [Medieval Latin, from Latin, "room that can be locked up", from *com-* + *clavis* "key"] — **con·clav·ist** \-,klā-vəst\ *n*

con·clude \kən-'klüd\ *vb* **1** : to bring or come to an end : FINISH ⟨*conclude* a speech⟩ **2** : to form an opinion : decide by reasoning ⟨*conclude* that a statement is true⟩ **3** : to bring about as a result : ARRANGE ⟨*conclude* an agreement⟩ [Latin *concludere* "to shut up, end, infer", from *com-* + *claudere* "to shut"] SYN see CLOSE — **con·clud·er** *n*

con·clu·sion \kən-'klü-zhən\ *n* **1 a** : a reasoned judgment : INFERENCE **b** : the necessary consequence of two or more propositions taken as premises **2** : the last part of something: as **a** : a final result : OUTCOME **b** : a final summing up **3** : an act or instance of concluding [Middle French, from Latin *conclusio,* from *concludere* "to conclude"]

con·clu·sive \kən-'klü-siv, -ziv\ *adj* : involving a conclusion or decision : DECISIVE, FINAL ⟨*conclusive* proof⟩ — **con·clu·sive·ly** *adv* — **con·clu·sive·ness** *n*

con·coct \kən-'käkt, kän-\ *vt* **1** : to prepare by combining various ingredients ⟨*concoct* a stew⟩ **2** : to make up : INVENT ⟨*concoct* a likely story⟩ [Latin *concoquere* "to cook together", from *com-* + *coquere* "to cook"] — **con·coct·er** *n* — **con·coc·tion** \-'käk-shən\ *n* — **con·coc·tive** \-'käk-tiv\ *adj*

con·com·i·tant \kən-'käm-ət-ənt, kän-\ *adj* : accompanying especially in a subordinate or incidental way [Latin *concomitari* "to accompany", from *com-* + *comit-, comes* "companion"] — **concomitant** *n* — **con·com·i·tant·ly** *adv*

con·cord \'kän-,kȯrd, 'käng-\ *n* **1 a** : a state of agreement : HARMONY **b** : a harmonious combination of tones heard together **2** : agreement by covenant or treaty [Old French *concorde,* from Latin *concordia,* from *com-* + *cord-, cor* "heart"]

con·cor·dance \kən-'kȯrd-ns\ *n* **1** : an alphabetical index of the principal words in a book or in the works of an author with their contexts **2** : a state of concord

con·cor·dant \-nt\ *adj* : marked by harmony : CONSONANT — **con·cor·dant·ly** *adv*

con·cor·dat \kən-'kȯr-,dat\ *n* : a compact or covenant especially between a pope and a government about church affairs [French, derived from Latin *com-* + *cor* "heart"]

con·course \'kän-,kōrs, 'käng-, -,kȯrs\ *n* **1** : a gathering together ⟨a great *concourse* of people⟩ **2** : a place (as a boulevard, open area, or hall) where many people pass or congregate ⟨met in the *concourse* of the bus terminal⟩ [Latin *concursus,* from *concurrere* "to run together, concur"]

con·cres·cence \kən-'kres-ns, kän-\ *n* : a growing together : COALESCENCE [Latin *concrescentia,* from *concrescere* "to grow together"] — **con·cres·cent** \-nt\ *adj*

¹con·crete \kän-'krēt, 'kän,\ *adj* **1** : naming a real thing or class of things : not abstract ⟨a *concrete* noun⟩ **2 a** : belonging to or derived from actual experience ⟨*concrete* examples⟩ **b** : existing in fact : REAL ⟨*concrete* evidence⟩ **3** \'kän-,, 'kän-'\ : relating to or made of concrete ⟨a *concrete* mixer⟩ [Latin *concretus* "formed by coalition of particles, concrete", from *concrescere* "to grow together", from *com-* + *crescere* "to grow"] — **con·crete·ly** *adv* — **con·crete·ness** *n*

²con·crete \'kän-,krēt, kän-'\ *n* : a hard strong building material made by mixing cement, sand, and gravel

concertina

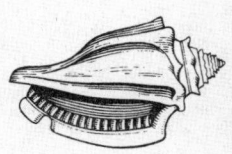

conch 1

\ə\ abut		\ng\ sing
\ər\ further		\ō\ bone
\a\ mat		\ȯ\ saw
\ā\ take		\ȯi\ coin
\ä\ cot, cart		\th\ thin
\aú\ out		\th\ this
\ch\ chin		\ü\ food
\e\ pet		\ú\ foot
\ē\ easy		\y\ yet
\g\ go		\yü\ few
\i\ tip		\yú\ cure
\ī\ life		\zh\ vision
\j\ job		

with sufficient water to cause the cement to set and bind the entire mass

³**con·crete** \'kän-ˌkrēt, kän-'\ *vb* 1 : to form into a solid mass : SOLIDIFY 2 : to cover with, form of, or set in concrete

con·cre·tion \kän-'krē-shən, kən-\ *n* 1 : the act or process of solidifying 2 : something solidified; *esp* : a hard usually inorganic mass formed in a living body — **con·cre·tion·ary** \-shə-ˌner-ē\ *adj*

con·cu·bine \'käng-kyə-ˌbīn, 'kän-\ *n* : a woman who lives with a man and among some peoples has a legally recognized position in his household less than that of a wife [Old French, from Latin *concubina*, from *com-* + *cubare* "to lie"] — **con·cu·bi·nage** \kän-'kyü-bə-nij, kən-\ *n*

con·cu·pis·cence \kän-'kyü-pə-səns, kən-\ *n* : ardent desire; *esp* : sexual desire [Middle French, derived from Latin *concupiscere* "to desire ardently", from *com-* + *cupere* "to desire"] — **con·cu·pis·cent** \-sənt\ *adj*

con·cur \kən-'kər, kän-\ *vi* **con·curred; con·cur·ring** 1 : to happen together : COINCIDE 2 : to act together to a common end or single effect 3 : to be in agreement : ACCORD ⟨four justices *concurred* in the decision⟩ [Latin *concurrere*, from *com-* + *currere* "to run"]

con·cur·rence \kən-'kər-əns, -'kə-rəns\ *n* 1 a : agreement in action, opinion, or intent : COOPERATION b : CONSENT 2 : a coming together : CONJUNCTION

con·cur·rent \-'kər-ənt, -'kə-rənt\ *adj* 1 a : coming together; *esp* : meeting in a point ⟨*concurrent* lines⟩ b : running parallel 2 : operating at the same time ⟨*concurrent* expeditions to the Antarctic⟩ 3 : acting in conjunction 4 : exercised over the same matter or area by two different authorities ⟨*concurrent* jurisdiction⟩ SYN see CONTEMPORARY — **concurrent** *n* — **con·cur·rent·ly** *adv*

concurrent resolution *n* : a resolution that is passed by both houses of a legislative body and lacks the force of law

con·cuss \kən-'kəs\ *vt* : to affect with concussion

con·cus·sion \kən-'kəsh-ən\ *n* 1 : a violent irregular motion 2 : a smart or hard blow or collision 3 : bodily injury especially of the brain resulting from a sudden sharp jar (as from a blow) [Latin *concussio*, from *concutere* "to shake violently", from *com-* + *quatere* "to shake"] — **con·cus·sive** \-'kəs-iv\ *adj*

con·demn \kən-'dem\ *vt* 1 : to declare to be wrong : CENSURE 2 a : to pronounce guilty : CONVICT b : SENTENCE 1a 3 : to declare officially to be unfit for use or consumption 4 : to take for public use under the right of eminent domain [Old French *condemner*, from Latin *condemnare*, from *com-* + *damnare* "to damn"] SYN see BLAME — **con·dem·nable** \-'dem-nə-bəl, -'dem-ə-bəl\ *adj* — **con·demn·er** *or* **con·dem·nor** \-'dem-ər\ *n*

con·dem·na·tion \ˌkän-ˌdem-'nā-shən, -dəm-\ *n* 1 : CENSURE 1 2 : the act of judicially condemning 3 : the state of being condemned — **con·dem·na·to·ry** \kən-'dem-nə-ˌtōr-ē, -ˌtor-\ *adj*

con·den·sa·tion \ˌkän-ˌden-'sā-shən, -dən-\ *n* 1 : the act or process of condensing 2 : a chemical reaction involving union between molecules often with elimination of a simple molecule (as water) to form a new and more complex compound 3 : the quality or state of being condensed 4 : a product of condensing; *esp* : an abridgment of a literary work — **con·den·sa·tion·al** \-shnəl, -shən-l\ *adj*

con·dense \kən-'dens\ *vb* 1 : to make or become more close, compact, concise, or dense : CONCENTRATE, COMPRESS ⟨*condense* a paragraph into a sentence⟩ 2 : to change from a less dense to a denser form ⟨steam *condenses* into water⟩ 3 : to subject to or undergo condensation ⟨a chemical that *condenses* to form a plastic⟩ [Middle French *condenser*, from Latin *condensare*, from *com-* + *densus* "dense"] — **con·dens·able**

\-'den-sə-bəl\ *adj* □ SYN CONDENSE, CONTRACT, CONSTRICT, COMPRESS mean to decrease in bulk or volume. CONDENSE implies reduction to greater compactness usually of material all of the same kind ⟨*condense* gas into liquid⟩ CONTRACT applies to the drawing together of surfaces or particles or a reduction of area or length ⟨molten iron *contracts* as it cools⟩ CONSTRICT implies a tightening that reduces diameter ⟨a *constricted* throat⟩ COMPRESS implies reduction by pressure from without ⟨*compress* a bale of cotton⟩

condensed milk *n* : evaporated milk with sugar added

con·dens·er \kən-'den-sər\ *n* 1 : one that condenses: as a : a lens or mirror used to concentrate light on an object b : an apparatus in which gas or vapor is condensed 2 : CAPACITOR

con·de·scend \ˌkän-di-'send\ *vi* 1 : to descend to a level considered less dignified or humbler than one's own 2 : to grant favors with a superior air [Middle French *condescendre*, from Late Latin *condescendere*, from Latin *com-* + *descendere* "to descend"] SYN see STOOP

con·de·scend·ing *adj* : showing or characterized by condescension : PATRONIZING — **con·de·scend·ing·ly** \-'sen-ding-lē\ *adv*

con·de·scen·sion \ˌkän-di-'sen-chən\ *n* : a patronizing attitude

con·dign \kən-'dīn, 'kän-\ *adj* : especially deserved or appropriate ⟨*condign* punishment⟩ [Middle French *condigne*, from Latin *condignus* "very worthy", from *com-* + *dignus* "worthy"] — **con·dign·ly** *adv*

con·di·ment \'kän-də-mənt\ *n* : something used to give an appetizing taste to food; *esp* : a pungent seasoning [Middle French, from Latin *condimentum*, from *condire* "to pickle", from *condere* "to build, store up"]

¹**con·di·tion** \kən-'dish-ən\ *n* 1 : a provision upon which the carrying out of an agreement depends : STIPULATION ⟨*conditions* of employment⟩ 2 : something essential to another : PREREQUISITE 3 : a restricting factor : LIMITATION 4 a : a state of being b : social status : RANK c *pl* : attendant circumstances 5 : state of health or fitness [Middle French *condicion*, from Latin *condicio* "items of agreement, condition", from *condicere* "to agree", from *com-* + *dicere* "to say"]

²**condition** *vt* **-di·tioned; -di·tion·ing** \-'dish-ning, -ə-ning\ 1 : to put into a proper or desired condition 2 a : to adapt, modify, or mold to respond in a particular way b : to modify the behavior of so that a response previously associated with one stimulus becomes associated with another — **con·di·tion·er** \-'dish-nər, -ə-nər\ *n*

¹**con·di·tion·al** \kən-'dish-nəl, -ən-l\ *adj* 1 : subject to, implying, or dependent upon a condition ⟨a *conditional* promise⟩ 2 : expressing, containing, or implying a supposition ⟨a *conditional* clause⟩ — **con·di·tion·al·ly** \-ē\ *adv*

²**conditional** *n* : IMPLICATION 3

con·di·tioned *adj* 1 : CONDITIONAL 1 2 : brought or put into a specified state 3 : determined or established by conditioning ⟨a *conditioned* response to a stimulus⟩

conditioned reflex *n* : a learned reflex reaction caused by repeated exposure to one stimulus in association with another for which the first comes to be a substitute ⟨a flow of saliva occurring in a dog when a bell is rung after the dog has learned to associate the sound with food is a classic *conditioned reflex*⟩

con·dole \kən-'dōl\ *vi* : to express sympathetic sorrow ⟨*condole* with a new-made orphan⟩ [Late Latin *condolēre* "to suffer with", from Latin *com-* + *dolēre* "to feel pain"]

con·do·lence \kən-'dō-ləns, 'kän-də-\ *n* : expression of sympathy with another in sorrow or grief ⟨sent our *condolences* to the family⟩

con·dom \'kän-dəm, 'kən-\ *n* : a flexible sheath worn over the penis during sexual intercourse to prevent pregnancy or venereal disease [origin unknown]

con·do·min·i·um \,kän-də-'min-ē-əm\ *n* **1** : joint sovereignty by two or more nations **2** : a politically dependent territory under condominium **3** : individual ownership of a unit in a multi-unit structure (as an apartment building); *also* : a unit so owned [Latin *com-* + *dominium* "domain"]

con·done \kən-'dōn\ *vt* : to pardon or overlook voluntarily ⟨*condone* a friend's faults⟩ [Latin *condonare* "to forgive", from *com-* + *donare* "to give"] SYN see EXCUSE — **con·do·na·tion** \,kän-dō-'nā-shən, -də-\ *n* — **con·don·er** \kən-'dō-nər\ *n*

con·dor \'kän-dər, -,dȯr\ *n* **1** : a very large South American vulture having the head and neck bare and the plumage dull black with a downy white neck ruff **2** : CALIFORNIA CONDOR [Spanish *cóndor,* from Quechua *kuntur*]

con·duce \kən-'düs, -'dyüs\ *vi* : to lead or tend to a usually desirable result [Latin *conducere* "to conduct, conduce", from *com-* + *ducere* "to lead"]

con·du·cive \kən-'dü-siv, -'dyü-\ *adj* : tending to promote or aid : CONTRIBUTING ⟨action *conducive* to success⟩ — **con·du·cive·ness** *n*

¹con·duct \'kän-dəkt, -dəkt\ *n* **1** : the act, manner, or process of carrying on : MANAGEMENT ⟨the *conduct* of foreign affairs⟩ **2** : personal behavior ⟨marked down for bad *conduct*⟩ [derived from Medieval Latin *conductus* "act of leading", from Latin *conducere* "to conduct, conduce"]

²con·duct \kən-'dəkt\ *vb* **1** : GUIDE 1, ESCORT **2** : to carry on or out usually from a position of command or control ⟨*conduct* a business⟩ **3 a** : to convey in a channel **b** : to act as a medium for conveying ⟨copper *conducts* electricity⟩ **4** : to cause (oneself) to act in an indicated manner ⟨*conducted* themselves badly⟩ **5** : to act as leader or director **6** : to have the quality of transmitting light, heat, sound, or electricity — **con·duct·i·bil·i·ty** \-,dək-tə-'bil-ət-ē\ *n* — **con·duct·ible** \-'dək-tə-bəl\ *adj* □ SYN MANAGE, CONTROL, DIRECT: CONDUCT implies guiding or leading in person ⟨*conduct* an orchestra⟩ ⟨selected to *conduct* negotiations⟩ MANAGE implies handling of details and maneuvering toward a desired result; CONTROL implies a regulating or restraining so as to keep on a desired course; DIRECT implies constant guidance and suggests the issuance of orders.

con·duc·tance \kən-'dək-təns\ *n* **1** : conducting power **2 a** : the readiness with which a conductor transmits an electric current **b** : the reciprocal of electrical resistance

con·duc·tion \kən-'dək-shən\ *n* **1** : the act of conducting or conveying **2** : transmission through a conductor; *also* : CONDUCTIVITY **3** : the transmission of excitation through living and especially nervous tissue

con·duc·tive \kən-'dək-tiv\ *adj* : having conductivity

con·duc·tiv·i·ty \,kän-,dək-'tiv-ət-ē\ *n, pl* **-ties** : the quality or power of conducting or transmitting

con·duc·tor \kən-'dək-tər\ *n* : one that conducts: as **a** : a person in charge of a public conveyance (as a bus or railroad train) **b** : the leader of a musical ensemble **c** : a substance or body capable of readily transmitting electricity, heat, or sound — **con·duc·to·ri·al** \,kän-,dək-'tōr-ē-əl, -'tȯr-\ *adj*

con·duc·tress \kən-'dək-trəs\ *n* : a woman who is a conductor

con·duit \'kän-,dü-ət, -,dyü-ət, -dət\ *n* **1** : a natural or artificial channel through which water or other fluid is conveyed **2** *archaic* : FOUNTAIN **3** : a pipe or tube for protecting electric wires or cables [Middle French, literally, "act of leading", from Medieval Latin *conductus*]

con·dy·larth \'kän-də-,lärth\ *n* : any of an order (Condylarthra) of primitive extinct ungulate mammals [Greek *kondylos* "knuckle, joint" + *arthron* "joint"]

con·dyle \'kän-,dīl, -dl\ *n* : a prominence at the end of a bone that forms part of a joint; *esp* : one of a pair like knuckles [Latin *condylus* "knuckle", from Greek *kondylos*]

cone \'kōn\ *n* **1** : a mass of overlapping woody scales that especially in trees of the pine family are arranged on an axis and bear seeds between them; *also* : any of several flower or fruit clusters resembling such cones **2** : a solid figure tapering evenly to a point from a closed curve (as a circle) in a plane; *esp* : a surface generated by a straight line through a fixed point as it moves along a closed curve (as a circle) in a plane — compare RIGHT CIRCULAR CONE **3** : something that resembles a cone in shape: as **a** : a sensory end organ of the retina that functions in color vision **b** : a crisp cone-shaped wafer for holding ice cream [Latin *conus,* from Greek *kōnos*]

cone·nose \'kōn-,nōz\ *n* : any of various large bloodsucking bugs

Con·es·to·ga \,kän-ə-'stō-gə\ *n* : a broad-wheeled covered wagon used by American pioneers especially for transporting freight across the prairies — called also *Conestoga wagon* [Conestoga, Pennsylvania]

co·ney *or* **co·ny** \'kō-nē\ *n, pl* **coneys** *or* **conies 1 a** (1) : RABBIT; *esp* : the common European rabbit (2) : PIKA **b** : HYRAX **c** : rabbit fur **2** : any of several fishes; *esp* : a dusky reddish-finned grouper of the tropical Atlantic [Old French *conil,* from Latin *cuniculus*]

con·fab \kən-'fab, 'kän-,\ *vi* **con·fabbed; con·fab·bing** : CONFABULATE — **con·fab** \'kän-,fab, kən-'\ *n*

con·fab·u·late \kən-'fab-yə-,lāt\ *vi* **con·fab·u·lat·ed 1** : CHAT 2 **2** : CONFER 2 [Latin *confabulari,* from *com-* + *fabulari* "to talk", from *fabula* "story"] — **con·fab·u·la·tion** \-,fab-yə-'lā-shən\ *n* — **con·fab·u·la·tor** \-'fab-yə-,lāt-ər\ *n*

con·fect \kən-'fekt\ *vt* : to put together from varied material [Latin *confectus,* past participle of *conficere* "to prepare", from *com-* + *facere* "to make"]

con·fec·tion \kən-'fek-shən\ *n* **1** : the act or process of confecting **2** : something confected: as **a** : a fancy dish or sweetmeat **b** : a piece of fine craftsmanship

con·fec·tion·er \-shə-nər, -shnər\ *n* : a manufacturer of or dealer in confections

con·fec·tion·ery \-shə-,ner-ē\ *n, pl* **-er·ies 1** : sweet edibles (as candy) **2** : the confectioner's art or business **3** : a confectioner's shop

con·fed·er·a·cy \kən-'fed-rə-sē, -ə-rə-\ *n, pl* **-cies 1** : a loose league of persons, parties, or states : ALLIANCE, CONFEDERATION **2** : a group united in a league; *esp, cap* : the Confederate States of America composed of the 11 southern states that seceded from the United States in 1860 and 1861 — **con·fed·er·al** \-'fed-rəl, -ə-rəl\ *adj*

¹con·fed·er·ate \kən-'fed-rət, -ə-rət\ *adj* **1** : united in a league : ALLIED **2** *cap* : of or relating to the Confederate States of America [Late Latin *confoederare* "to unite by a league", from Latin *com-* + *foedus* "compact"]

²confederate *n* **1** : ALLY 2a, ACCOMPLICE **2** *cap* : a soldier, citizen, or supporter of the Confederate States of America or their cause

³con·fed·er·ate \-'fed-ə-,rāt\ *vb* : to unite in a confederacy

Confederate Memorial Day *n* : any of several days appointed for the commemoration of servicemen of the Confederacy: **a** : April 26 in Alabama, Florida, Georgia, and Mississippi **b** : May 10 in North and South Carolina **c** : May 30 in Virginia **d** : June 3 in Kentucky, Louisiana, and Texas

con·fed·er·a·tion \kən-,fed-ə-'rā-shən\ *n* **1** : an act of confederating : a state of being confederated **2** : LEAGUE 1

con·fer \kən-'fər\ *vb* **con·ferred; con·fer·ring 1** : to grant from or as if from a position of superiority **2** : to compare views : CONSULT ⟨*confer* with the committee⟩ [Latin *conferre* "to bring together", from *com-* + *ferre* "to carry"] — **con·fer·al** \-'fər-əl\ *n* — **con·fer·rer** \-'fər-ər\ *n*

condor 1

Conestoga

\ə\ abut	\ng\ sing
\ər\ further	\ō\ bone
\a\ mat	\ȯ\ saw
\ā\ take	\ȯi\ coin
\ä\ cot, cart	\th\ thin
\au̇\ out	\th\ this
\ch\ chin	\ü\ food
\e\ pet	\u̇\ foot
\ē\ easy	\y\ yet
\g\ go	\yü\ few
\i\ tip	\yu̇\ cure
\ī\ life	\zh\ vision
\j\ job	

con·fer·ee \ˌkän-fə-'rē\ *n* **1** : one conferred with **2** : one on whom something (as a degree) is conferred

con·fer·ence \'kän-fə-rəns, -frəns, -fərns\ *n* **1** : a meeting for formal discussion or exchange of opinions; *also* : the discussion itself **2** : a meeting of members of the two branches of a legislature to adjust differences **3** : an association of athletic teams

con·fess \kən-'fes\ *vb* **1** : to tell of or make known (as something wrong) ⟨*confess* a crime⟩ **2 a** : to acknowledge one's sins to God or to a priest **b** : to receive the confession of ⟨the priest *confessed* the penitents⟩ **3** : to declare faith in : PROFESS [Middle French *confesser,* from Latin *confessus,* past participle of *confitēri* "to confess", from *com-* + *fatēri* "to confess"] SYN see ACKNOWLEDGE

con·fess·ed·ly \-'fes-əd-lē, -'fest-lē\ *adv* : by confession : ADMITTEDLY

con·fes·sion \kən-'fesh-ən\ *n* **1** : an act of confessing; *esp* : a disclosure of one's sins in the sacrament of penance **2** : a statement of something confessed: as **a** : a written acknowledgment of guilt by one accused of an offense **b** : a formal statement of religious beliefs : CREED **3** : an organized religious body having a common creed — **con·fes·sion·al** \-'fesh-nəl, -ən-l\ *adj*

con·fes·sion·al \-'fesh-nəl, -ən-l\ *n* **1** : a place where a priest hears confessions **2** : the practice of confessing to a priest

con·fes·sor \kən-'fes-ər\ *n* **1** : one that confesses **2** : a Christian who gives heroic evidence of faith but does not suffer martyrdom **3** : a priest who hears confessions

con·fet·ti \kən-'fet-ē\ *n* : small bits of brightly colored paper made for throwing (as at weddings) [Italian, plural of *confetto* "sweetmeat", from Medieval Latin *confectum,* from Latin *conficere* "to prepare"]

con·fi·dant \'kän-fə-ˌdant, -ˌdänt\ *n* : one to whom secrets are entrusted; *esp* : an intimate friend with whom one feels free to discuss private or secret matters [French *confident,* derived from Latin *confidere* "to confide"]

con·fi·dante \'kän-fə-ˌdant, -ˌdänt\ *n* : a female confidant [French *confidente,* feminine of *confident* "confidant"]

con·fide \kən-'fīd\ *vb* **1** : to have confidence : TRUST ⟨*confide* in a doctor's skill⟩ **2** : to show confidence by imparting secrets ⟨*confided* in one's mother⟩ **3** : to tell confidentially ⟨*confide* a secret to a friend⟩ **4** : ENTRUST 1 ⟨*confide* one's safety to the police⟩ [Latin *confidere,* from *com-* + *fidere* "to trust"] — **con·fid·er** *n*

con·fi·dence \'kän-fəd-əns, -fə-ˌdens\ *n* **1** : FAITH, TRUST ⟨had *confidence* in the leader⟩ **2** : consciousness of feeling sure : ASSURANCE ⟨spoke with great *confidence*⟩ **3 a** : reliance on another's discretion ⟨told a friend in *confidence*⟩ **b** : legislative support ⟨a vote of *confidence*⟩ **4** : a communication made in confidence : SECRET ⟨*confidences* between friends⟩

confidence game *n* : a swindle in which the swindler takes advantage of the trust he has persuaded the victim to place in him — called also *con game*

confidence man *n* : a swindler in a confidence game — called also *con man*

con·fi·dent \'kän-fəd-ənt, -fə-ˌdent\ *adj* : having or showing confidence; *esp* : SELF-ASSURED ⟨*confident* of their welcome⟩ — **con·fi·dent·ly** *adv*

con·fi·den·tial \ˌkän-fə-'den-chəl\ *adj* **1** : known only to a few people : PRIVATE ⟨*confidential* information⟩ **2** : marked by intimacy : FAMILIAR ⟨a *confidential* tone of voice⟩ **3** : trusted with secret matters ⟨a *confidential* secretary⟩ — **con·fi·den·tial·ly** \-'dench-lē, -ə-lē\ *adv* — **con·fi·den·tial·ness** \-'den-chəl-nəs\ *n*

con·fid·ing \kən-'fīd-iŋ\ *adj* : tending to confide : TRUSTFUL — **con·fid·ing·ly** \-iŋ-lē\ *adv*

con·fig·u·ra·ion \kən-ˌfig-yə-'rā-shən, -ˌfig-ə-\ *n* : relative arrangement of parts; *also* : something (as a figure, contour, or pattern) produced by such arrangement [Late Latin *configuratio* "similar formation", from Latin *configurare* "to form from or after", from *com-* + *figurare* "to form", from *figura* "figure"] — **con·fig·u·ra·tion·al** \-shnəl, -shən-l\ *adj* — **con·fig·u·ra·tion·al·ly** \-ē\ *adv* — **con·fig·u·ra·tive** \-'fig-yə-ˌrāt-iv, -'fig-ə-, -rət\ *adj*

con·fig·ure \kən-'fig-yər\ *vt* : to set up for operation especially in a particular way ⟨ships *configured* for spying⟩

con·fine \kən-'fīn\ *vt* **1** : to keep within limits : RESTRICT ⟨*confined* to quarters⟩ **2 a** : to shut up : IMPRISON ⟨*confined* for life⟩ **b** : to keep indoors ⟨*confined* with a cold⟩ — **con·fin·er** *n*

con·fine·ment \kən-'fīn-mənt\ *n* : an act of confining : the state of being confined; *esp* : LYING-IN

con·fines \'kän-ˌfīnz\ *n pl* **1** : BOUNDARY; *also* : outlying parts **2** : ²BOUND **3** [Latin *confine* "border", from *confinis* "adjacent", from *com-* + *finis* "end"]

con·firm \kən-'fərm\ *vt* **1** : to make firm or firmer (as in a habit, in faith, or in intention) **2** : to give approval to : RATIFY ⟨*confirm* a treaty⟩ **3** : to administer the rite of confirmation to **4** : to make sure of the truth of : VERIFY ⟨*confirm* a suspicion⟩ [Old French *confirmer,* from Latin *confirmare,* from *com-* + *firmus* "firm"] — **con·firm·able** \-'fər-mə-bəl\ *adj* □ SYN CONFIRM, CORROBORATE, AUTHENTICATE, VERIFY mean to support the truth or validity of something. CONFIRM implies removing doubts by an authoritative statement or an indisputable fact; CORROBORATE suggests the strengthening of what is already partly established; AUTHENTICATE implies establishing genuineness by showing legal or official documents or presenting expert opinion; VERIFY implies the authentication of something supposed or presumed with appropriate facts or events.

con·fir·ma·tion \ˌkän-fər-'mā-shən\ *n* **1** : an act or process of confirming: as **a** : a Christian rite or sacrament conferring the gifts of the Holy Spirit and also entitling the recipient to full church privileges **b** : a ceremony confirming Jewish youths in their ancestral faith **c** : the ratification of an executive act by a legislative body **2** : something that confirms : PROOF — **con·fir·ma·to·ry** \kən-'fər-mə-ˌtōr-ē, -ˌtor-\ *adj*

con·firmed \kən-'fərmd\ *adj* **1 a** : made firm : STRENGTHENED **b** : deeply ingrained ⟨*confirmed* distrust of change⟩ **c** : HABITUAL, CHRONIC ⟨a *confirmed* drunkard⟩ **2** : having received the rite of confirmation — **con·firm·ed·ly** \-'fər-məd-lē\ *adv*

con·fis·cate \'kän-fə-ˌskāt\ *vt* : to seize by or as if by authority ⟨smuggled goods may be *confiscated*⟩ [Latin *confiscare,* from *com-* + *fiscus* "treasury"] — **con·fis·ca·tion** \ˌkän-fə-'skā-shən\ *n* — **con·fis·ca·tor** \'kän-fə-ˌskāt-ər\ *n* — **con·fis·ca·to·ry** \kən-'fis-kə-ˌtōr-ē, -ˌtor-\ *adj*

con·fi·te·or \kən-'fēt-ē-ə-r\ *n* : a confession of fault or error; *esp* : a liturgical form in the Mass in which sinfulness is admitted [Latin, "I confess", from *confitēri* "to confess"]

con·fla·gra·tion \ˌkän-flə-'grā-shən\ *n* : FIRE; *esp* : a large disastrous fire [Latin *conflagratio,* from *conflagrare* "to burn up", from *com-* + *flagrare* "to burn"]

¹con·flict \'kän-ˌflikt\ *n* **1** : a hostile encounter : FIGHT, BATTLE **2** : a clashing or sharp disagreement (as between ideas, interests, or purposes) [Latin *conflictus* "act of striking together", from *confligere* "to strike together", from *com-* + *fligere* "to strike"]

²con·flict \kən-'flikt, 'kän-\ *vi* : to show antagonism : CLASH ⟨duty and desire often *conflict*⟩

con·flu·ence \'kän-ˌflü-əns\ *n* **1** : a coming or flowing together at one point ⟨the *confluence* of scholarship that produced the atomic bomb⟩ **2** : a flowing together or place of meeting especially of two or more streams

con·flu·ent \'kän-ˌflü-ənt, kən-'\ *adj* **1** : flowing or coming together ⟨*confluent* rivers⟩ **2** : run together ⟨a *confluent* rash⟩ [Latin *confluere* "to flow together", from *com-* + *fluere* "to flow"]

con·form \kən-'fȯrm\ *vb* **1** : to bring into harmony ⟨*conform* one's behavior to the circumstances⟩ **2** : to be similar or identical ⟨the data *conform* to the pattern⟩ **3** : to be obedient or compliant; *esp* : to adapt oneself to prevailing standards or customs ⟨found it easier to *conform* than rebel⟩ [Middle French *conformer*, from Latin *conformare*, from *com-* + *forma* "form"] **SYN** see **ADAPT** — **con·form·er** *n* — **con·form·ism** \-'fȯr-ˌmiz-əm\ *n* — **con·form·ist** \-məst\ *n*

con·form·able \kən-'fȯr-mə-bəl\ *adj* **1** : corresponding in form or character : **SIMILAR** — usually used with *to* **2** : giving compliance : **SUBMISSIVE** — **con·form·ably** \-blē\ *adv*

con·for·mal \kən-'fȯr-məl, kän-\ *adj* **1** : leaving the size of the angle between corresponding curves unchanged; *esp* : representing small areas in their true shape ⟨a *conformal* map⟩

con·form·ance \kən-'fȯr-məns\ *n* : **CONFORMITY** 2, 3

con·for·ma·tion \ˌkän-fȯr-'mā-shən, -fər-\ *n* **1** : the act of conforming or producing conformity : **ADAPTATION** **2** : formation of something by an assembling into a whole **3 a** : **STRUCTURE** ⟨*conformation* of the ocean bed⟩ **b** : the proportionate shape or contour especially of an animal

con·for·mi·ty \kən-'fȯr-mət-ē\ *n, pl* **-ties** **1** : correspondence in form, manner, or character : **AGREEMENT** ⟨behaved in *conformity* with his beliefs⟩ **2** : an act or instance of conforming **3** : action in accordance with some standard or authority : **OBEDIENCE** ⟨*conformity* to social custom⟩

con·found \kən-'faund, kän-\ *vt* **1** *archaic* : to bring to ruin : **DEFEAT** **2** : to put to shame : **DISCOMFIT** **3** : to swear at : **DAMN, CURSE** **4** : to throw into disorder : mix up : **CONFUSE** [Old French *confondre*, from Latin *confundere* "to pour together, confuse", from *com-* + *fundere* "to pour"]

con·found·ed \kən-'faun-dəd, 'kän-ˌfaun-\ *adj* **1** : filled with confusion : **PERPLEXED** **2** : **DAMNED** 1 — **con·found·ed·ly** *adv*

con·fra·ter·ni·ty \ˌkän-frə-'tər-nət-ē\ *n, pl* **-ties** : a society devoted to a religious or charitable cause

con·frere \'kȯⁿ-ˌfreər, 'kän-\ *n* : **COLLEAGUE, COMRADE** [Middle French, translation of Medieval Latin *confrater* "fellow, brother", from Latin *com-* + *frater* "brother"]

con·front \kən-'frənt\ *vt* **1** : to face especially in challenge : **OPPOSE** ⟨*confront* an enemy⟩ **2** : to bring face-to-face : cause to meet ⟨*confront* one with a problem⟩ [Middle French *confronter* "to border on, confront", derived from Latin *com-* + *frons* "forehead, front"] — **con·fron·ta·tion** \ˌkän-frən-'tā-shən, -ˌfrän-\ *n*

Con·fu·cian \kən-'fyü-shən\ *adj* : of or relating to the Chinese philosopher Confucius or his teachings or followers — **Confu·cian** *n* — **Con·fu·cian·ism** \-shə-ˌniz-əm\ *n* — **Con·fu·cian·ist** \-shə-nəst\ *n or adj*

con·fuse \kən-'fyüz\ *vt* **1 a** : to make embarrassed **b** : to disturb in mind or purpose : throw off ⟨this complicated problem *confused* me⟩ **2 a** : to make indistinct : **BLUR** ⟨stop *confusing* the issue⟩ **b** : to mix up : **JUMBLE** ⟨their motives were hopelessly *confused*⟩ **c** : to fail to distinguish between ⟨teachers always *confused* the twins⟩ [back-formation from Middle English *confused* "perplexed", from Middle French *confus*, from Latin *confusus*, past participle of *confundere* "to confuse, confound"] — **con·fused·ly** \-'fyüz-əd-lē\ *adv* — **con·fus·ing·ly** \-'fyü-zing-lē\ *adv*

con·fu·sion \kən-'fyü-zhən\ *n* **1** : an act or instance of confusing **2** : the quality or state of being confused — **con·fu·sion·al** \-'fyüzh-nəl, -'fyü-zhən-l\ *adj*

con·fute \kən-'fyüt\ *vt* : to overwhelm in argument : refute conclusively [Latin *confutare*] — **con·fu·ta·tion** \ˌkän-fyü-'tā-shən\ *n* — **con·fu·ta·tive** \kən-'fyüt-ət-iv\ *adj* — **con·fut·er** \kən-'fyüt-ər\ *n*

con·ga \'käng-gə\ *n* **1** : a Cuban dance of African origin performed by a group usually in single file **2** : a

tall narrow bass drum beaten with the hands [American Spanish, from *Congo*, region in Africa]

con game \'kän-\ *n* : **CONFIDENCE GAME**

con·gé \kōⁿ-'zhā, 'kän-ˌjā\ *n* **1** : **DISMISSAL** **2** : **FAREWELL** 2 [French]

con·geal \kən-'jēl\ *vb* **1** : to change from a fluid to a solid state by or as if by cold **2** : to make or become viscid or curdled : **COAGULATE** **3** : to make or become rigid or inflexible [Middle French *congeler*, from Latin *congelare*, from *com-* + *gelare* "to freeze"] — **con·geal·ment** \-mənt\ *n*

con·ge·ner \'kän-jə-nər, kən-'jē-\ *n* **1** : a member of the same taxonomic genus as another plant or animal **2** : a person or thing resembling another in nature or action [Latin, "of the same kind", from *com-* + *genus* "kind"] — **con·ge·ner·ic** \ˌkän-jə-'ner-ik\ *adj*

con·ge·nial \kən-'jē-nyəl\ *adj* **1** : having the same nature, disposition, or tastes **2 a** : existing together harmoniously **b** : **PLEASANT**; *esp* : agreeably suited to one's nature, tastes, or outlook **c** : characterized by friendly sociability : **GENIAL** ⟨the innkeeper was a most *congenial* host⟩ [*com-* + *genius*] — **con·ge·nial·i·ty** \-ˌjē-nē-'al-ət-ē, -ˌjēn-'yal-\ *n* — **con·ge·nial·ly** \-'jē-nyə-lē\ *adv*

con·gen·i·tal \kən-'jen-ə-tl\ *adj* **1** : existing at or dating from birth but usually not hereditary ⟨*congenital* disease⟩ **2** : being such by nature : **INHERENT** ⟨a *congenital* liar⟩ [Latin *congenitus*, from *com-* + *genitus*, past participle of *gignere* "to bring forth"] **SYN** see **INNATE** — **con·gen·i·tal·ly** \-tl-ē\ *adv*

con·ger eel \'käng-gər-\ *n* : a scaleless saltwater eel that sometimes grows to a length of eight feet and is an important food fish of Europe [Old French *congre*, from Latin *conger*, from Greek *gongros*]

con·ge·ries \'kän-jə-rēz, -ˌrēz\ *n, pl* **congeries** *same*\ : a collection of entities : **AGGREGATION** [Latin, from *congerere* "to bring together"]

con·gest \kən-'jest\ *vb* **1** : to cause an excessive fullness of the blood vessels of (as an organ) **2** : **CLOG** 2 ⟨traffic *congested* the streets⟩ **3** : to concentrate in a small or narrow space [Latin *congestus*, past participle of *congerere* "to bring together", from *com-* + *gerere* "to carry"] — **con·ges·tion** \-'jes-chən\ *n* — **con·ges·tive** \-'jes-tiv\ *adj*

¹con·glom·er·ate \kən-'gläm-rət, -ə-rət\ *adj* : made up of parts from various sources or of various kinds ⟨an ethnically *conglomerate* culture⟩ [Latin *conglomerare* "to roll together", from *com-* + *glomus* "ball"]

²con·glom·er·ate \-'gläm-ə-ˌrāt\ *vb* : to gather into a mass

³con·glom·er·ate \-'gläm-rət, -ə-rət\ *n* **1** : a composite mass or mixture; *esp* : rock composed of rounded fragments varying from small pebbles to large boulders in a cement (as of hardened clay) **2** : a widely diversified corporation

con·glom·er·a·tion \kən-ˌgläm-ə-'rā-shən, ˌkän-\ *n* **1** : the act of conglomerating : the state of being conglomerated **2** : something that is conglomerated

Con·go red \'käng-ˌgō-\ *n* : an azo dye red in alkaline and blue in acid solution [*Congo*, region in Africa]

con·go snake \'käng-ˌgō-\ *n* : a long bluish black amphibian of the southeastern United States that has two pairs of very short limbs — called also *congo eel*

con·grat·u·late \kən-'grach-ə-ˌlāt\ *vt* : to express pleasure to on account of success or good fortune ⟨*congratulated* the winner⟩ [Latin *congratulari* "to wish joy", from *com-* + *gratus* "pleasing"] — **con·grat·u·la·to·ry** \-'grach-lə-ˌtōr-ē, -ə-lə-, -ˌtȯr-\ *adj*

con·grat·u·la·tion \-ˌgrach-ə-'lā-shən\ *n* **1** : the act of congratulating **2** : an expression of pleasure at another's success, happiness, or good fortune — usually used in pl.

con·gre·gate \'käng-gri-ˌgāt\ *vb* : to collect into a group or crowd : **ASSEMBLE** [Latin *congregare*, from

\ə\ abut	\ng\ sing
\ər\ further	\ō\ bone
\a\ mat	\ȯ\ saw
\ā\ take	\ȯi\ coin
\ä\ cot, cart	\th\ thin
\au\ out	\th\ this
\ch\ chin	\ü\ food
\e\ pet	\u̇\ foot
\ē\ easy	\y\ yet
\g\ go	\yü\ few
\i\ tip	\yu̇\ cure
\ī\ life	\zh\ vision
\j\ job	

com- + greg-, grex "flock"] SYN see GATHER — **con·gre·ga·tor** \-ˌgāt-ər\ n

con·gre·ga·tion \ˌkäng-gri-'gā-shən\ n **1 a** : an assembly of persons; esp : one gathered for religious worship **b** : a religious community: as (1) : an organized body of believers in a particular locality (2) : a Roman Catholic religious society with only simple vows **2** : the action of congregation : the state of being congregated; also : a collection of separate things **3** : a body of cardinals and officials forming an administrative division of the papal curia

con·gre·ga·tion·al \-'gā-shnəl, -shən-l\ adj **1** : of or relating to a congregation **2** cap : of or relating to a body of Protestant churches affirming the essential importance and the autonomy of the local congregation **3** : of or relating to church government placing final authority in the assembly of the local congregation — **con·gre·ga·tion·al·ism** \-ˌiz-əm\ n, often cap — **con·gre·ga·tion·al·ist** \-əst\ n or adj, often cap

con·gress \'käng-grəs\ n **1 a** : the act or action of coming together and meeting **b** : COITUS **2** : a formal meeting of delegates for discussion and action **3** : the supreme legislative body of a nation and especially of a republic **4** : an association of constituent organizations **5** : a single meeting or session of a group [Latin congressus, from congredi "to come together", from com- + gradi "to step, go"] — **con·gres·sion·al** \kən-'gresh-nəl, -ən-l\ adj — **con·gres·sion·al·ly** \-ē\ adv

con·gress·man \'käng-grəs-mən\ n : a member of a congress; esp : a member of the United States House of Representatives

con·gress·wom·an \-ˌwum-ən\ n : a female member of a congress; esp : a female member of the United States House of Representatives

con·gru·ence \kən-'grü-əns, 'käng-grə-wəns\ n **1** : the quality or state of agreeing or coinciding **2** : a statement that two numbers are congruent with respect to a modulus

con·gru·en·cy \-ən-sē, -wən-sē\ n : CONGRUENCE 1

con·gru·ent \kən-'grü-ənt, 'käng-grə-wənt\ adj **1** : being in agreement ⟨the report proved to be congruent with the facts⟩ **2** : capable of being placed over one another so that all points of one correspond to all points of the other : having the same size and shape ⟨congruent triangles⟩ **3** : having the difference divisible by a given modulus ⟨12 is congruent to 2 with respect to a modulus of 5 since $12 - 2 = (2) \cdot (5)$⟩ [Latin congruere "to come together, agree"] — **con·gru·ent·ly** adv

con·gru·i·ty \kən-'grü-ət-ē, käng-\ n, pl **-i·ties 1** : the quality or state of being congruent or congruous : AGREEMENT **2** : a point of agreement

con·gru·ous \'käng-grə-wəs\ adj **1 a** : being in agreement, harmony, or correspondence **b** : conforming to the circumstances of a situation : APPROPRIATE **2** : marked by harmony among parts [Latin congruus, from congruere "to come together, agree"] — **con·gru·ous·ly** adv — **con·gru·ous·ness** n

¹con·ic \'kän-ik\ adj **1** : CONICAL **2** : of or relating to a cone

²conic n : CONIC SECTION

con·i·cal \'kän-i-kəl\ adj : resembling a cone especially in shape ⟨conical roots⟩ — **con·i·cal·ly** \-i-kə-lē, -klē\ adv

conic section n : a plane section of a cone : a curve (as an ellipse, parabola, hyperbola, or circle) generated by a point which always moves so that the ratio of its distance from a fixed point to its distance from a fixed line is constant

co·nid·io·phore \kə-'nid-ē-ə-ˌfōr, -ˌfor\ n : a plant structure (as a special hypha) that bears conidia

co·nid·i·um \kə-'nid-ē-əm\ n, pl **-ia** \-ē-ə\ : an asexual spore produced on a conidiophore [Greek konis "dust"] — **co·nid·i·al** \-ē-əl\ adj

co·ni·fer \'kän-ə-fər also 'kō-nə-\ n : any of an order (Coniferales) of mostly evergreen trees and shrubs that are gymnosperms and include forms (as pines) with true cones [Latin conifer "cone-bearing", from conus "cone"] — **co·nif·er·ous** \kō-'nif-rəs, kə-, -ə-rəs\ adj

con·jec·tur·al \kən-'jek-chə-rəl, -'jeksh-rəl\ adj **1** : of the nature of, involving, or based on conjecture **2** : given to conjectures — **con·jec·tur·al·ly** \-ē\ adv

¹con·jec·ture \kən-'jek-chər\ n **1** : inference from inadequate evidence **2** : a conclusion reached by surmise or guesswork ⟨a mistaken conjecture⟩ [Latin conjectura, from conjectus, past participle of conicere "to throw together, conjecture", from com- + jacere "to throw"]

²conjecture vb **-jec·tured; -jec·tur·ing** \-chə-ring, 'jek-shring\ **1** : to arrive at by conjecture **2** : to make conjectures as to : SURMISE — **con·jec·tur·er** \-'jek-chər-ər\ n ◻ SYN SURMISE, GUESS: CONJECTURE implies forming an opinion on what is recognized as insufficient evidence; SURMISE implies even slighter evidence and suggests the influence of suspicion or imagination; GUESS stresses hitting on a conclusion at random or from very uncertain evidence.

con·join \kən-'join, kän-\ vb : to join together for a common purpose

con·joint \-'joint\ adj **1** : being or coming together so as to unite **2** : related to, made up of, or carried on by two or more in combination : JOINT — **con·joint·ly** adv

con·ju·gal \'kän-ji-gəl, kən-'jü-\ adj : of or relating to the married state or matrimonial relations [Latin conjugalis, from conjux "spouse", from conjungere "to join, unite in marriage", from com- + jungere "to join"] SYN see MATRIMONIAL — **con·ju·gal·ly** adv

con·ju·gant \'kän-ji-gənt\ n : either of a pair of conjugating gametes or organisms

¹con·ju·gate \'kän-ji-gət, -jə-ˌgāt\ adj **1 a** : joined together especially in pairs **b** : acting or operating as if joined **2** : having features in common but opposite or inverse in some particular; esp : being complex numbers that are conjugates [Latin conjugare "to unite", from com- + jugum "yoke"] — **con·ju·gate·ly** adv — **con·ju·gate·ness** n

²con·ju·gate \'kän-jə-ˌgāt\ vb **1** : to give the various inflectional forms of (a verb) in a prescribed order **2** : to join together : COUPLE **3** : to pair and fuse in conjugation

³con·ju·gate \-gət, -ˌgāt\ n **1** : something conjugate : a product of conjugating **2** : one of two complex numbers (as $a + bi$ and $a - bi$) differing only in the sign of the imaginary part

conjugated protein n : a compound of a protein with a nonprotein

con·ju·ga·tion \ˌkän-jə-'gā-shən\ n **1** : the act of conjugating : the state of being conjugated **2 a** : an orderly arrangement of the inflectional forms of a verb **b** : verb inflection **c** : a class of verbs having the same type of inflectional forms ⟨the weak conjugation⟩ **3 a** : fusion of usually similar gametes that among lower thallophytes replaces the typical fertilization of higher forms **b** : temporary cytoplasmic union with exchange of nuclear material that is the usual sexual process in ciliated protozoans — **con·ju·ga·tion·al** \-shnəl, -shən-l\ adj — **con·ju·ga·tion·al·ly** \-ē\ adv — **con·ju·ga·tive** \'kän-jə-ˌgāt-iv\ adj

con·junct \kən-'jəngt, kän-, -'jəngkt\ adj : bound together : JOINED, UNITED [Latin conjunctus, past participle of conjungere "to join", from com- + jungere "to join"]

con·junc·tion \kən-'jəng-shən, -'jəngk-\ n **1** : the act or an instance of conjoining : the state of being conjoined **2** : occurrence together in time or space : CONCURRENCE **3** : the apparent meeting or passing of two or more celestial bodies in the same degree of the zodiac

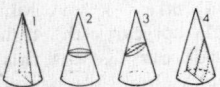

conic section: 1 straight lines, 2 circle, 3 ellipse, 4 parabola

4 : an uninflected word or expression that joins together sentences, clauses, phrases, or words **5** : a statement formed by joining two or more statements together with the word *and* that is true only if all its components are true — con·junc·tion·al \-'shnəl, -shən-l\ *adj* — con·junc·tion·al·ly \-ē-\ *adv*

con·junc·ti·va \,kän-,jəngk-'tī-və, -'tē-\ *n, pl* -tivas *or* -ti·vae \-'tī-,vē, -'tē-,vī\ : the mucous membrane that lines the inner surface of the eyelids and is continued over the front part of the eyeball [derived from Latin *conjungere* "to join"] — con·junc·ti·val \-vəl\ *adj*

con·junc·tive \kən-'jəng-tiv, -'jəngk-\ *adj* **1** : CONNECTIVE **2** : done or existing in conjunction : CONJUNCT **3** : being or functioning like a conjunction ⟨*conjunctive* adverbs such as *hence, however,* and *therefore*⟩ — conjunctive *n* — con·junc·tive·ly *adv*

con·junc·ti·vi·tis \kən-,jəng-ti-'vīt-əs, -,jəngk-\ *n* : inflammation of the conjunctiva

con·junc·ture \kən-'jəng-chər, -'jəngk-\ *n* **1** : CONJUNCTION 1, UNION **2** : a combination of circumstances usually producing a crisis : JUNCTURE

con·ju·ra·tion \,kän-jə-'rā-shən, ,kən-\ *n* **1** : the act of conjuring : INCANTATION **2** : an expression or trick used in conjuring

con·jure \'kän-jər, 'kən-; *in sense 1* kən-'jùr\ *vb* **1** : to entreat earnestly or solemnly : BESEECH **2 a** : to summon by invocation or incantation **b** : to create or bring about as if by magic ⟨*conjure* up a scheme⟩ **3 a** : to practice magical arts **b** : to use a conjuror's tricks [Old French *conjurer,* from Latin *conjurare* "to swear together", from *com-* + *jurare* "to swear"]

con·jur·er *or* con·ju·ror \'kän-jər-ər, 'kən-\ *n* **1** : one that practices magic arts : WIZARD **2** : one that performs tricks involving sleight of hand and illusion : MAGICIAN

conk *vi* : to break down; *esp* : STALL ⟨the motor *conked* out⟩ [probably imitative]

con man \'kän-\ *n* : CONFIDENCE MAN

con·nate \kä-'nāt, 'kän-,āt\ *adj* **1** : INNATE 1 **2** : agreeing in nature : CONGENIAL ⟨*connate* spirits⟩ **3** : born or originated together **4** : congenitally or firmly united ⟨*connate* leaves⟩ **5** : entrapped in sediments at the time of deposition ⟨*connate* water⟩ [Late Latin *connatus,* past participle of *connasci* "to be born together", from Latin *com-* + *nasci* "to be born"] — con·nate·ly *adv*

con·nect \kə-'nekt\ *vb* **1** : to join or link together directly or by something coming between ⟨*connect* two wires⟩ ⟨towns *connected* by a railroad⟩ **2** : to join by personal relationship or association ⟨*connected* by marriage⟩ **3** : to associate in the mind ⟨*connect* two ideas⟩ **4** : to be related (as by cause or logic) ⟨an event *connected* with the fire⟩ **5** : to meet at a time and place suitable for transferring passengers or freight ⟨*connecting* trains⟩ [Latin *connectere,* from *com-* + *nectere* "to bind"] SYN see JOIN — con·nec·tor \-'nek-tər\ *n*

connecting rod *n* : a rod that transmits power from one rotating part of a machine to another in reciprocating motion

con·nec·tion \kə-'nek-shən\ *n* **1** : the act of connecting **2** : the fact or condition of being connected : RELATIONSHIP ⟨the *connection* between two ideas⟩ **3 a** : a thing that connects : BOND, LINK ⟨a loose *connection* in a radio⟩ **b** : a means of communication **4 a** : a person connected with others especially by marriage or kinship ⟨an uncle and some family *connections*⟩ **b** : a social, professional, or commercial relationship ⟨business *connections* in the city⟩ **5** : a means of continuing a journey by transferring to another conveyance ⟨make a *connection* for New York at Chicago⟩ **6** : a set of persons associated together: as **a** : DENOMINATION 3 **b** : a large family : CLAN — con·nec·tion·al \-shnəl, -shən-l\ *adj*

¹con·nec·tive \kə-'nek-tiv\ *adj* : connecting or tending to connect — con·nec·tive·ly *adv* — con·nec·tiv·i·ty \,kä-,nek-'tiv-ət-ē\ *n*

²connective *n* : something that connects; *esp* : a word or expression (as a conjunction or a relative pronoun) that connects words or word groups

connective tissue *n* : a tissue of mesodermal origin with much intercellular substance or many interlacing processes that forms a supporting framework (as of bone, cartilage, and fibrous tissue) for the body and its parts

connector neuron *n* : an internuncial neuron

conn·ing tower \'kän-ing-\ *n* **1** : an armored pilothouse (as on a battleship) **2** : a raised structure on the deck of a submarine that contains observation and communications equipment for use when the submarine is on the surface [*conn* "to direct the steering of a ship", from Middle English *condien* "to conduct", from Middle French *conduire,* from Latin *conducere*]

con·nip·tion \kə-'nip-shən\ *n* : a fit of rage, hysteria, or alarm [origin unknown]

con·niv·ance \kə-'nī-vəns\ *n* : the act of conniving; *esp* : knowledge of and active or passive consent to wrongdoing

con·nive \kə-'nīv\ *vi* **1** : to pretend ignorance of something that one ought to oppose or stop **2** : to cooperate secretly or have a secret understanding **3** : PLOT 3, CONSPIRE [Latin *connivēre, connivēre* "to close the eyes, connive"] — con·niv·er *n*

con·nois·seur \,kän-ə-'sər *also* -'sùr\ *n* : a person qualified to act as a judge in matters involving taste and appreciation : EXPERT ⟨a *connoisseur* of French painting⟩ [obsolete French, from Old French *connoistre* "to know", from Latin *cognoscere,* from *com-* + *gnoscere, noscere* "to know"] — con·nois·seur·ship \-,ship\ *n*

con·no·ta·tion \,kän-ə-'tā-shən\ *n* **1** : a meaning or significance suggested by a word apart from and in addition to the thing it explicitly names or describes ⟨the word *home* with all its heart-warming *connotations*⟩ — compare DENOTATION 2 **2** : something implied : IMPLICATION ⟨a speech with political *connotations*⟩ — con·no·ta·tion·al \-shnəl, -shən-l\ *adj*

con·no·ta·tive \'kän-ə-,tāt-iv, kə-'nōt-ət-iv\ *adj* **1** : connoting or tending to connote **2** : relating to connotation — con·no·ta·tive·ly *adv*

con·note \kə-'nōt\ *vt* : to suggest or mean along with or in addition to the explicit meaning ⟨the word *home* usually *connotes* comfort and security⟩ [Medieval Latin *connotare,* from Latin *com-* + *notare* "to note"] SYN see DENOTE

con·nu·bi·al \kə-'nü-bē-əl, -'nyü-\ *adj* : of or relating to marriage : CONJUGAL [Latin *connubium* "marriage", from *com-* + *nubere* "to marry"] — con·nu·bi·al·ly \-bē-ə-lē\ *adv*

co·noid \'kō-,nòid\ *or* co·noi·dal \kō-'nòid-l\ *adj* : shaped like or nearly like a cone — conoid *n*

con·quer \'käng-kər\ *vb* con·quered; con·quer·ing \-kə-ring, -kring\ **1** : to gain or acquire by force of arms : SUBJUGATE ⟨*conquer* a country⟩ **2** : to overcome by force of arms : VANQUISH ⟨*conquered* all their enemies⟩ **3** : to master or win by overcoming obstacles or opposition ⟨*conquered* the mountain⟩ **4** : to overcome by mental or moral power ⟨*conquer* one's fear⟩ **5** : to be victorious [Old French *conquerre,* from Latin *conquirere* "to search for, collect", from *com-* + *quaerere* "to seek, ask"] — con·quer·or *n* □ SYN SUBDUE, SUBJUGATE, VANQUISH: CONQUER implies gaining mastery of after a prolonged effort and with more or less permanent result; SUBDUE implies overpowering and suppressing; SUBJUGATE stresses a bringing under oppressive or humiliating rule or control; VANQUISH implies a complete or final overpowering.

con·quest \'kän-,kwest, 'käng-\ *n* **1** : the act or process of conquering **2 a** : something conquered; *esp* : territory seized in war **b** : a person whose affections have

conning tower 2

\ə\ abut	\ng\ sing
\ər\ further	\ō\ bone
\a\ mat	\ò\ saw
\ā\ take	\òi\ coin
\ä\ cot, cart	\th\ thin
\aù\ out	\th\ this
\ch\ chin	\ü\ food
\e\ pet	\ù\ foot
\ē\ easy	\y\ yet
\g\ go	\yü\ few
\i\ tip	\yù\ cure
\ī\ life	\zh\ vision
\j\ job	

been won [Old French, from Latin *conquisitus,* past participle of *conquirere* "to search for, collect"] SYN see VICTORY

con·quis·ta·dor \kȯng-'kēs-tə-ˌdȯr; kän-'kis-, -'kwis-; kən-\ *n, pl* **con·quis·ta·do·res** \kȯng-ˌkēs-tə-'dȯr-ēz, -'dȯr-ˌās, -'dōr-; kän-ˌkis-, -ˌkwis-; kən-\ *or* **con·quis·ta·dors** : one that conquers; *esp* : a leader in the Spanish conquest of America and especially of Mexico and Peru in the 16th century [Spanish, from *conquista* "conquest"]

con·san·guin·e·ous \ˌkän-ˌsan-'gwin-ē-əs, -ˌsang-\ *adj* : of the same blood or origin; *esp* : descended from the same ancestor — **con·san·guin·e·ous·ly** *adv* — **con·san·guin·i·ty** \-'gwin-ət-ē\ *n*

con·science \'kän-chəns\ *n* : the sense or consciousness of the moral goodness or badness of one's own conduct, intentions, or character together with a feeling of obligation to do right or be good [Old French, from Latin *conscientia,* from *conscire* "to be conscious, be conscious of guilt", from *com-* + *scire* "to know"] — **in all conscience** *or* **in conscience** 1 : in all fairness 2 : beyond a doubt : to be sure

conscience money *n* : money paid to relieve the conscience by restoring what has been wrongfully acquired

con·sci·en·tious \ˌkän-chē-'en-chəs\ *adj* 1 : governed by or in accordance with one's conscience : SCRUPULOUS 2 : marked by or done with exactness and thought : CAREFUL ⟨*conscientious* workmanship⟩ — **con·sci·en·tious·ly** *adv* — **con·sci·en·tious·ness** *n*

conscientious objector *n* : a person who refuses to serve in the armed forces or bear arms on the grounds of moral or religious principles

con·scious \'kän-chəs\ *adj* 1 : perceiving or noticing facts or feelings 2 : personally felt ⟨*conscious* guilt⟩ 3 : capable of or marked by thought, will, design, or perception 4 : marked by self-consciousness 5 : mentally alert or active : AWAKE 6 : done or acting with critical awareness ⟨a *conscious* effort⟩ [Latin *conscius,* from *com-* + *scire* "to know"] — **con·scious·ly** *adv*

con·scious·ness \'kän-chəs-nəs\ *n* 1 : awareness of something ⟨*consciousness* of evil⟩ 2 : the condition of having ability to feel, think, and react : MIND 3 : the normal state of conscious life as distinguished from sleep or insensibility 4 : the part of mental life that is characterized by conscious thought and awareness

¹con·script \'kän-ˌskript\ *adj* 1 : enrolled into service by compulsion : DRAFTED 2 : made up of conscripted persons ⟨a *conscript* army⟩ [Middle French, from Latin *conscribere* "to enroll", from *com-* + *scribere* "to write"]

²conscript *n* : a person who has been conscripted

³con·script \kən-'skript\ *vt* : to enroll into service by compulsion : DRAFT

con·scrip·tion \kən-'skrip-shən\ *n* 1 : compulsory enrollment of persons especially for military service : DRAFT 2 : a forced contribution (as of money) imposed by a government in time of emergency (as war)

¹con·se·crate \'kän-sə-ˌkrāt\ *adj* : dedicated to a sacred purpose

²consecrate *vb* 1 : to induct into a permanent office with a religious rite; *esp* : to ordain to the office of bishop 2 : to make or declare sacred : set apart for the service of God 3 : to devote to a purpose with deep solemnity or dedication ⟨*consecrate* one's life to the dance⟩ 4 : to make inviolate or venerable ⟨rules *consecrated* by time⟩ [Latin *consecrare,* from *com-* + *sacrare* "to consecrate", from *sacer* "sacred"] — **con·se·cra·tor** \-ˌkrāt-ər\ *n*

con·se·cra·tion \ˌkän-sə-'krā-shən\ *n* 1 : the act or ceremony of consecrating 2 : the state of being consecrated 3 *often cap* : the part of a Communion rite in which the bread and wine are consecrated

con·sec·u·tive \kən-'sek-yət-iv, -ət-\ *adj* : following one after the other in order without gaps [Latin *conse-*

cutus, past participle of *consequi* "to follow along"] — **con·sec·u·tive·ly** *adv* — **con·sec·u·tive·ness** *n* □ SYN CONSECUTIVE, SUCCESSIVE mean following one after the other. CONSECUTIVE stresses immediacy in following and implies that no interruption or interval occurs in the series ⟨three *consecutive* terms in office⟩ SUCCESSIVE may apply to things of the same kind that follow each other regardless of length of interval between ⟨rain fell on three *successive* weekends⟩

con·sen·sus \kən-'sen-səs\ *n* 1 : general agreement (as in opinion or testimony) : ACCORD 2 : the trend of opinion [Latin, from *consentire* "to agree in feeling"]

¹con·sent \kən-'sent\ *vi* : to give assent or approval : AGREE [Latin *consentire* "to agree in feeling", from *com-* + *sentire* "to feel"]

²consent *n* : compliance in or approval of what is asked or proposed : ACQUIESCENCE

con·se·quence \'kän-sə-ˌkwens, -si-kwəns\ *n* 1 : something produced by a cause or necessarily following from a set of conditions 2 : a conclusion that results from reason or argument 3 **a** : importance with respect to power to produce an effect : MOMENT ⟨a mistake of no *consequence*⟩ **b** : social importance ⟨a person of *consequence*⟩ SYN see EFFECT

¹con·se·quent \-si-kwənt, -sə-ˌkwent\ *n* 1 : the conclusion of a conditional sentence 2 : the second term of a ratio

²consequent *adj* 1 : following as a result or effect 2 : observing logical sequence : RATIONAL [Middle French, from Latin *consequi* "to follow along", from *com-* + *sequi* "to follow"]

con·se·quen·tial \ˌkän-sə-'kwen-chəl\ *adj* 1 : of the nature of a consequence or result : following as a consequence 2 : having significant consequences 3 : having or displaying self-importance — **con·se·quen·tial·ly** \-'kwench-lē, -ə-lē\ *adv* — **con·se·quen·tial·ness** \-'kwen-chəl-nəs\ *n*

con·se·quent·ly \'kän-sə-ˌkwent-lē, -kwənt-\ *adv* : as a result : ACCORDINGLY

con·ser·van·cy \kən-'sər-vən-sē\ *n, pl* **-cies** : an organization or area designated to conserve and protect natural resources

con·ser·va·tion \ˌkän-sər-'vā-shən\ *n* : a careful preservation and protection of something; *esp* : planned management of a natural resource to prevent exploitation, destruction, or neglect — **con·ser·va·tion·al** \-shnəl, -shən-l\ *adj*

con·ser·va·tion·ist \-'vā-shə-nəst, -shnəst\ *n* : one who advocates conservation especially of natural resources

conservation of energy : a principle in physics: the total energy of an isolated system remains constant irrespective of whatever internal changes may take place

conservation of mass : a principle in classical physics: the total mass of any material system is neither increased nor diminished by reactions between the parts — called also *conservation of matter*

con·ser·va·tism \kən-'sər-və-ˌtiz-əm\ *n* 1 **a** : disposition in politics to preserve what is established **b** : a political philosophy supporting tradition, social stability, and established institutions and preferring gradual development to abrupt change 2 : the tendency to prefer an existing situation and to be suspicious of change

¹con·ser·va·tive \kən-'sər-vət-iv\ *adj* 1 : tending to conserve or preserve 2 **a** : of or relating to conservatism **b** *often cap* : of or constituting a political party professing conservatism 3 **a** : tending or disposed to maintain existing views, conditions, or institutions : TRADITIONAL **b** : MODERATE, CAUTIOUS ⟨a *conservative* investment⟩ **c** : marked by traditional standards of taste, elegance, or manners ⟨a *conservative* suit⟩ — **con·ser·va·tive·ly** *adv* — **con·ser·va·tive·ness** *n*

²conservative *n* 1 **a** : an adherent or advocate of conservatism **b** *often cap* : a member or supporter of a conservative political party **2** : a cautious or discreet person

Conservative Judaism *n* : a movement in Judaism that holds sacred the Torah and the religious traditions but accepts some liturgical and ritual change

con·ser·va·tor \kən-ˈsər-vət-ər, -və-ˌtȯr; ˈkän-sər-ˌvāt-ər\ *n* **1** : one that preserves or guards : PROTECTOR **2** : one designated to take over and protect the interests of an incompetent **3** : an official charged with the protection of something affecting public welfare and interests

con·ser·va·to·ry \kən-ˈsər-və-ˌtōr-ē, -ˌtȯr-\ *n, pl* **-ries** **1** : a greenhouse for growing or displaying plants **2** : a school specializing in one of the fine arts

¹con·serve \kən-ˈsərv\ *vt* **1** : to keep in a safe or sound state : PRESERVE ⟨*conserve* natural resources⟩ **2** : to preserve with sugar **3** : to maintain (a quantity) constant during a process of chemical, physical, or evolutionary change [Middle French *conserver*, from Latin *conservare*, from *com-* + *servare* "to keep, guard, observe"] — **con·serv·er** *n*

²con·serve \ˈkän-ˌsərv\ *n* **1** : CONFECTION; *esp* : a candied fruit **2** : PRESERVE; *esp* : one prepared from a mixture of fruits

con·sid·er \kən-ˈsid-ər\ *vb* **-sid·ered; -sid·er·ing** \-ˈsid-ring, -ə-ring\ **1** : to think over carefully : PONDER **2** : to regard highly : ESTEEM **3** : to think of in a certain way : regard as being [Middle French *considerer*, from Latin *considerare*, literally, "to observe the stars", from *com-* + *sider-, sidus* "star"]

con·sid·er·able \kən-ˈsid-ər-bəl, -ər-ə-bəl, -ˈsid-rə-bəl\ *adj* **1** : worth consideration : IMPORTANT **2** : large in extent or degree ⟨a *considerable* area⟩ ⟨a *considerable* number⟩ — **con·sid·er·ably** \-blē\ *adv*

con·sid·er·ate \kən-ˈsid-rət, -ə-rət\ *adj* **1** : marked by or given to careful consideration : CIRCUMSPECT **2** : thoughtful of the rights and feelings of others SYN see THOUGHTFUL — **con·sid·er·ate·ly** *adv* — **con·sid·er·ate·ness** *n*

con·sid·er·ation \kən-ˌsid-ə-ˈrā-shən\ *n* **1** : careful thought : DELIBERATION **2** : something considered as a ground : REASON **3** : thoughtfulness for other people **4** : RESPECT 3a, REGARD ⟨a person of *consideration* in that field⟩ **5** : a payment made in return for something : COMPENSATION

con·sid·er·ing \-ˈsid-ring, -ə-ring\ *prep* : in view of : taking into account

con·sign \kən-ˈsīn\ *vt* **1** : to give over to another's care : ENTRUST **2** : to give, transfer, or deliver formally ⟨*consign* a body to the grave⟩ **3** : to send or address to an agent to be cared for or sold [Middle French *consigner*, from Latin *consignare*, from *com-* + *signum* "sign, mark, seal"] — **con·sign·able** \-ˈsī-nə-bəl\ *adj* — **con·sign·ee** \kən-ˌsī-ˈnē, ˌkän-ˌsī-, ˌkän-sə-\ *n* — **con·sign·or** \kən-ˈsī-nər; ˌkən-ˌsī-ˈnȯr, ˌkän-ˌsī-, ˌkän-sə-\ *n*

con·sign·ment \kən-ˈsīn-mənt\ *n* **1** : the act or process of consigning **2** : something consigned especially in a single shipment

con·sist \kən-ˈsist\ *vi* **1** : to be contained : LIE — used with *in* ⟨honesty *consists* in telling the truth⟩ **2** : to be composed — used with *of* ⟨breakfast *consisted* of bacon and eggs⟩ [Latin *consistere*, literally, "to stand together", from *com-* + *sistere* "to take a stand"]

con·sis·tence \kən-ˈsis-təns\ *n* : CONSISTENCY

con·sis·ten·cy \kən-ˈsis-tən-sē\ *n, pl* **-cies** **1** : the degree of density, firmness, viscosity, or resistance to movement or separation of constituent particles ⟨mud with the *consistency* of glue⟩ **2 a** : agreement or harmony of parts or features to one another or a whole **b** : harmony of conduct or practice with past performance or stated aims

con·sis·tent \kən-ˈsis-tənt\ *adj* **1** : marked by harmony, regularity, or steady continuity ⟨*consistent* statements⟩ **2** : conforming steadily to one's own belief, profes-

sions, or character ⟨were *consistent* in their opposition⟩ **3** : having a common solution ⟨*consistent* linear equations⟩ — **con·sis·tent·ly** *adv*

con·sis·to·ry \kən-ˈsis-tə-rē, -trē\ *n, pl* **-ries** : a solemn meeting of Roman Catholic cardinals presided over by the pope [Medieval Latin *consistorium* "church tribunal", from Latin *consistere* "to stand together, consist"] — **con·sis·to·ri·al** \ˌkän-ˌsis-ˈtȯr-ē-əl, -ˈtȯr-, kən-\ *adj*

con·so·la·tion \ˌkän-sə-ˈlā-shən\ *n* **1** : the act or an instance of consoling : the state of being consoled : COMFORT **2** : a contest held for those who have lost early in a tournament — **con·sol·a·to·ry** \kən-ˈsō-lə-ˌtōr-ē, -ˈsäl-ə-, -ˌtȯr-\ *adj*

consolation prize *n* : a prize given to a runner-up or a loser in a contest

¹con·sole \kən-ˈsōl\ *vt* : to lessen the grief or sense of loss of [French *consoler*, from Latin *consolari*, from *com-* + *solari* "to console"] SYN see COMFORT — **con·sol·able** \-ˈsō-lə-bəl\ *adj*

²con·sole \ˈkän-ˌsōl\ *n* **1** : an architectural bracket used for ornament or support **2 a** : the desk from which an organ is played and which contains the keyboards, pedal board, and controls **b** : a panel or cabinet on which are mounted dials and switches used in controlling an electronic or mechanical device or system **3** : a cabinet (as for a radio or television set) designed to rest directly on the floor [French, from Middle French, short for *consolateur* "bracket in human shape", literally, "consoler", from Latin *consolator*, from *consolari* "to console"]

console table *n* **1** : a table fixed to a wall with its top supported by brackets or bracket-shaped legs **2** : a table designed to fit against a wall

con·sol·i·date \kən-ˈsäl-ə-ˌdāt\ *vb* **1** : MERGE 2 **2** : to make firm or secure : STRENGTHEN ⟨*consolidate* a beachhead⟩ **3** : to form into a compact mass [Latin *consolidare* "to make solid", from *com-* + *solidus* "solid"]

consolidated school *n* : a public school formed by merging other schools

con·sol·i·da·tion \kən-ˌsäl-ə-ˈdā-shən\ *n* **1** : the act or process of consolidating : the state of being consolidated **2** : the merger of two or more corporations into one

con·som·mé \ˌkän-sə-ˈmā\ *n* : a clear soup chiefly of meat stock [French, from *consommer* "to complete, boil down", from Latin *consummare* "to complete"]

con·so·nance \ˈkän-sə-nəns, -snəns\ *n* **1** : harmony or agreement of parts **2 a** : an agreeable combination or correspondence of musical tones or speech sounds **b** : a musical interval included in a major or minor triad and its inversions

¹con·so·nant \ˈkän-sə-nənt, -snənt\ *n* **1** : a speech sound (as \p\, \n\, or \s\) characterized by narrowing or stoppage at one or more points in the breath channel **2** : a letter representing a consonant; *esp* : any letter of the English alphabet except *a, e, i, o,* and *u* [Latin *consonans*, from *consonare* "to sound together, agree", from *com-* + *sonare* "to sound"]

²consonant *adj* **1** : being in agreement or harmony ⟨*consonant* with the truth⟩ **2** : marked by musical consonances **3** : having like sounds ⟨*consonant* words⟩ — **con·so·nant·ly** *adv*

con·so·nan·tal \ˌkän-sə-ˈnant-l\ *adj* : relating to, being, or marked by a consonant or group of consonants

¹con·sort \ˈkän-ˌsȯrt\ *n* **1** : a ship sailing in company with another ship **2** : a married person : SPOUSE [Middle French, "associate", from Latin *consors*, literally, "one who shares a common lot", from *com-* + *sors* "lot, share"]

²con·sort \kən-ˈsȯrt\ *vb* **1** : to keep company : ASSOCIATE ⟨*consorting* with criminals⟩ **2** : to be or come into accord : HARMONIZE

\ə\ abut		\ng\ sing	
\ər\ further		\ō\ bone	
\a\ mat		\ȯ\ saw	
\ā\ take		\ȯi\ coin	
\ä\ cot, cart		\th\ thin	
\au̇\ out		\th\ this	
\ch\ chin		\ü\ food	
\e\ pet		\u̇\ foot	
\ē\ easy		\y\ yet	
\g\ go		\yü\ few	
\i\ tip		\yu̇\ cure	
\ī\ life		\zh\ vision	
\j\ job			

con·sor·tium \kən-'sȯr-shē-əm, -shəm\ *n, pl* **-tia** \-shē-ə, -shə\ : an international business or banking agreement or combination [Latin, "fellowship", from *consors* "associate"]

con·spe·cif·ic \ˌkän-spi-'sif-ik\ *adj* : of the same species

con·spec·tus \kən-'spek-təs\ *n* **1** : a brief survey or summary **2** : a condensed version of a larger work : SYNOPSIS [Latin, "sight", from *conspicere* "to get sight of"]

con·spic·u·ous \kən-'spik-yə-wəs\ *adj* **1** : obvious to the eye or mind **2** : attracting attention : STRIKING **3** : noticeably violating good taste [Latin *conspicuus*, from *conspicere* "to get sight of", from *com-* + *specere* "to look"] — **con·spic·u·ous·ly** *adv* — **con·spic·u·ous·ness** *n*

con·spir·a·cy \kən-'spir-ə-sē\ *n, pl* **-cies** **1** : the act of conspiring together **2 a** : an agreement among conspirators **b** : a group of conspirators SYN see PLOT

con·spir·a·tor \kən-'spir-ət-ər\ *n* : one that conspires : PLOTTER

con·spir·a·to·ri·al \kən-ˌspir-ə-'tōr-ē-əl, -'tȯr-\ *adj* : of, relating to, or characteristic of a conspiracy — **con·spir·a·to·ri·al·ly** \-ē\ *adv*

con·spire \kən-'spīr\ *vi* **1** : to agree secretly to do an unlawful or wrongful act or to use such means to accomplish a lawful end ⟨*conspire* against the state⟩ **2** : to act in harmony ⟨events *conspired* to defeat their efforts⟩ [Middle French *conspirer*, from Latin *conspirare* "to breathe together, agree, conspire", from *com-* + *spirare* "to breathe"]

con·sta·ble \'kän-stə-bəl, 'kən-\ *n* **1** : a high officer of a medieval royal or noble household **2** : the warden of a royal castle or a fortified town **3 a** : a public officer responsible for keeping the peace **b** : a British policeman [Old French *conestable*, from Late Latin *comes stabuli*, literally, "officer of the stable"] □ ORIGIN When the word *constable* first came into English from French in the Middle Ages, a *conestable* was the chief officer of a king's household. His office was one of great power: he was commander of the army and supreme judge, subordinate only to the king himself. Latin *comes stabuli*, which is the ancestor of *constable*, means literally "officer of the stable". But the title was transferred from stable to court. The increase in prestige was not as great as it may seem. All the king's horses were scarcely less valuable to the king than all his men, and being in charge of them was a very important duty.

con·stab·u·lary \kən-'stab-yə-ˌler-ē\ *n, pl* **-lar·ies** **1** : an organized body of police **2** : an armed police force organized on military lines but distinct from the regular army

con·stan·cy \'kän-stən-sē\ *n* **1 a** : firmness in one's beliefs : STEADFASTNESS **b** : steadiness in attachments : LOYALTY **2** : freedom from change : STABILITY

¹con·stant \'kän-stənt\ *adj* **1** : marked by firm resolution or faithfulness : STEADFAST **2** : remaining unchanged : UNIFORM **3** : continually occurring or recurring : REGULAR [Middle French, from Latin *constans*, from *constare* "to stand firm", from *com-* + *stare* "to stand"] SYN see CONTINUAL, FAITHFUL — **con·stant·ly** *adv*

²constant *n* : something invariable or unchanging: as **a** : a number that has a fixed value (as the velocity of light) in a given situation or universally or that is a characteristic (as the refractive index of glass) of some substance or instrument **b** : a number whose value does not change in a given mathematical discussion

con·stan·tan \'kän-stən-ˌtan\ *n* : an alloy of copper and nickel used for electrical resistors and in thermocouples [from the fact that its resistance remains constant under change of temperature]

con·stel·la·tion \ˌkän-stə-'lā-shən\ *n* : any of 88 groups of stars forming patterns (as the Big Dipper) or an area of the heavens covering one of these groups [Middle French, from Late Latin *constellatio*, from Latin *com-* + *stella* "star"]

con·ster·nate \'kän-stər-ˌnāt\ *vt* : to fill with consternation

con·ster·na·tion \ˌkän-stər-'nā-shən\ *n* : amazement or dismay that hinders or throws into confusion [Latin *consternatio*, from *consternare* "to bewilder, alarm"]

con·sti·pate \'kän-stə-ˌpāt\ : to cause constipation in [Medieval Latin *constipare*, from Latin, "to crowd together", from *com-* + *stipare* "to press together"]

con·sti·pa·tion \ˌkän-stə-'pā-shən\ *n* : abnormally delayed or infrequent passage of dry hardened feces

con·stit·u·en·cy \kən-'stich-wən-sē, -ə-wən-\ *n, pl* **-cies** **1** : a body of citizens entitled to elect a representative to a legislative or other public body **2 a** : the residents in an electoral district **b** : an electoral district **3** : a group of supporters

¹con·stit·u·ent \kən-'stich-wənt, -ə-wənt\ *n* **1** : an essential part : COMPONENT, ELEMENT ⟨flour is the chief *constituent* of bread⟩ **2 a** : one of a group who elects another as a representative in public office **b** : a resident in a constituency [French *constituant*, from Middle French *constituer* "to constitute", from Latin *constituere*] SYN see ELEMENT

²constituent *adj* **1** : forming a part of a whole : COMPONENT **2** : having the power to create a government or to frame or amend a constitution ⟨a *constituent* assembly⟩ — **con·stit·u·ent·ly** *adv*

con·sti·tute \'kän-stə-ˌtüt, -ˌtyüt\ *vt* **1** : to appoint to an office or duty ⟨a duly *constituted* representative⟩ **2** : to set up : ESTABLISH ⟨a fund was *constituted* to help needy students⟩ **3** : to make up : FORM ⟨twelve months *constitute* a year⟩ [Latin *constituere* "to set up, constitute", from *com-* + *statuere* "to set, fix", from *status* "standing, status"]

con·sti·tu·tion \ˌkän-stə-'tü-shən, -'tyü-\ *n* **1** : the act of establishing, making, or setting up **2 a** : the physical makeup of an individual : PHYSIQUE **b** : the structure, composition, or nature of something **3 a** : the basic principles and laws of a nation, state, or social group that determine the powers and duties of the government and guarantee certain rights to the people in it **b** : a document containing a constitution

¹con·sti·tu·tion·al \-shnəl, -shən-l\ *adj* **1** : of, relating to, or affecting a person's physical or mental makeup **2** : of, relating to, or entering into the fundamental makeup of something : ESSENTIAL **3** : of, relating to, or in accordance with the constitution of a nation or state ⟨a *constitutional* amendment⟩ ⟨*constitutional* rights⟩ — **con·sti·tu·tion·al·ly** \-ē\ *adv*

²constitutional *n* : a walk taken for one's health

con·sti·tu·tion·al·ism \-ˌiz-əm\ *n* : adherence to or government according to constitutional principles — **con·sti·tu·tion·al·ist** \-əst\ *n*

con·sti·tu·tion·al·i·ty \ˌkän-stə-ˌtü-shə-'nal-ət-ē, -ˌtyü-\ *n* : the quality or state of being in accordance with the provisions of a constitution

con·sti·tu·tive \'kän-stə-ˌtüt-iv, -ˌtyüt-; kən-'stich-ət-iv\ *adj* : forming part of the structure of a thing : CONSTITUENT, ESSENTIAL — **con·sti·tu·tive·ly** *adv*

con·strain \kən-'strān\ *vt* **1** : to force by imposed restriction or limitation **2** : to force or produce in an unnatural or strained manner ⟨a *constrained* smile⟩ **3** : to secure by or as if by bond : CONFINE **4** : to hold back by force : RESTRAIN [Middle French *constraindre*, from Latin *constringere* "to constrict, constrain", from *com-* + *stringere* "to draw tight"] SYN see FORCE — **con·strained·ly** \-'strān-əd-lē, -'strān-dlē\ *adv*

con·straint \kən-'strānt\ *n* **1 a** : the act of constraining : the state of being constrained **b** : a constraining agency or force : CHECK ⟨legal *constraints*⟩ **2 a** : a holding back of one's feelings, behavior, or actions **b** : a sense of being constrained : EMBARRASSMENT

con·strict \kən-'strikt\ *vb* **1 a** : to make or become smaller in bulk or volume by means of compression;

also : SQUEEZE 1a, COMPRESS ⟨snakes that kill by *constricting* their prey⟩ **b** : to make or become narrow or narrower ⟨the pupil of the eye *constricts* in bright light⟩ **2** : to slow down, stop, or cause to falter : INHIBIT [Latin *constrictus,* past participle of *constringere* "to constrict, constrain"] — **con·stric·tive** \-'strik-tiv\ *adj*

con·stric·tion \kən-'strik-shən\ *n* **1** : an act of constricting : the state of being constricted **2** : something that constricts : a part that is constricted

con·stric·tor \kən-'strik-tər\ *n* **1** : one that constricts **2** : a snake that kills prey by compression in its coils

con·struct \kən-'strəkt\ *vt* **1** : to make or form by combining parts **2** : to draw (a geometrical figure) with suitable instruments and under specified conditions [Latin *constructus,* past participle of *construere* "to construct", from *com-* + *struere* "to build"] — **con·struct·ible** \-'strək-tə-bəl\ *adj* — **con·struc·tor** \-'strək-tər\ *n*

con·struc·tion \kən-'strək-shən\ *n* **1** : the arrangement and connection of words or groups of words in a sentence **2** : the process, art, or manner of constructing; *also* : a thing constructed : STRUCTURE **3** : an interpretation or explanation of a statement or a fact ⟨put the wrong *construction* on a remark⟩ — **con·struc·tion·al** \-shnəl, -shən-l\ *adj* — **con·struc·tion·al·ly** \-ē\ *adv*

con·struc·tion·ist \kən-'strək-shə-nəst, -shnəst\ *n* : one who construes a legal document (as the United States Constitution) in a specific way ⟨a strict *constructionist*⟩

construction paper *n* : a thick colored paper used especially for school art work

con·struc·tive \kən-'strək-tiv\ *adj* **1** : fitted for or given to constructing ⟨Edison was a *constructive* genius⟩ **2** : helping to develop or improve something ⟨*constructive* criticism⟩ — **con·struc·tive·ly** *adv* — **con·struc·tive·ness** *n*

con·strue \kən-'strü\ *vb* **1** : to explain the grammatical relationships of the words in a sentence, clause, or phrase **2** : to understand or explain the sense or intention of : INTERPRET [Late Latin *construere,* from Latin, "to construct"] — **con·stru·able** \-'strü-ə-bəl\ *adj*

con·sul \'kän-səl\ *n* **1** : either of two chief magistrates of the Roman republic **2** : an official appointed by a government to live in a foreign country to represent the commercial interests of citizens of the appointing country [Latin, from *consulere* "to consult"] — **con·sul·ar** \-sə-lər, -slər\ *adj* — **con·sul·ship** \-səl-,ship\ *n*

con·sul·ate \'kän-sə-lət, -slət\ *n* **1** : a government by consuls **2** : the office, term of office, or jurisdiction of a consul **3** : the residence or official premises of a consul

con·sult \kən-'səlt\ *vb* **1** : to ask the advice or opinion of ⟨*consult* a doctor⟩ **2** : to seek information from ⟨*consult* a dictionary⟩ **3** : to have regard to : CONSIDER ⟨*consult* one's best interests⟩ **4** : to deliberate together : CONFER [Latin *consultare,* from *consultus,* past participle of *consulere* "to deliberate, counsel, consult"] — **con·sult·er** *n*

con·sult·ant \kən-'səlt-nt\ *n* **1** : one who consults another **2** : one who gives professional advice or services

con·sul·ta·tion \,kän-səl-'tā-shən\ *n* **1** : CONFERENCE 1, COUNCIL; *esp* : a deliberation between physicians on a case or its treatment **2** : the act of consulting or conferring

con·sul·ta·tive \kən-'səl-tət-iv\ *adj* : of, relating to, or intended for consultation : ADVISORY

con·sul·tor \kən-'səl-tər\ *n* : one that consults or advises; *esp* : a member of a Roman Catholic diocesan advisory council

con·sume \kən-'süm\ *vb* **1** : to destroy or be destroyed by or as if by fire **2 a** : to spend wastefully : SQUANDER **b** : to use up : EXPEND ⟨hard work *consumed* our energy⟩ **3** : to eat or drink up **4** : to engage one's interest or

attention ⟨*consumed* with curiosity⟩ [Latin *consumere,* from *com-* + *sumere* "to take up, take", from *sub-* "up" + *emere* "to take"] — **con·sum·able** \-'sü-mə-bəl\ *adj*

con·sum·er \kən-'sü-mər\ *n* : one that consumes: as **a** : one that buys and uses economic goods **b** : an organism requiring complex organic compounds for food which it obtains by preying on other organisms or by eating particles of organic matter — compare PRODUCER 3

consumer credit *n* : credit granted to an individual especially to finance purchase of consumer goods or defray personal or family expenses

consumer goods *n pl* : goods that directly satisfy human wants

con·sum·er·ism \kən-'sü-mə-,riz-əm\ *n* : concern for or protection of the consumer's welfare — **con·sum·er·ist** \-rəst\ *n*

¹con·sum·mate \kən-'səm-ət, 'kän-sə-mət\ *adj* **1** : complete in every detail : PERFECT **2** : of the highest degree or quality ⟨*consummate* skill⟩ [Latin *consummare* "to sum up, finish", from *com-* + *summa* "sum"] — **con·sum·mate·ly** *adv*

²con·sum·mate \'kän-sə-,māt\ *vt* **1 a** : to bring to completion : FINISH ⟨*consummate* a deal⟩ **b** : to make perfect **2** : to make (marital union) complete by sexual intercourse — **con·sum·ma·tion** \,kän-sə-'mā-shən\ *n*

con·sump·tion \kən-'səm-shən, -'səmp-\ *n* **1 a** : the act or process of consuming **b** : the amount consumed ⟨yearly fuel *consumption*⟩ **2 a** : a progressive wasting away of the body especially from pulmonary tuberculosis **b** : TUBERCULOSIS [Latin *consumptio,* from *consumere* "to consume"]

¹con·sump·tive \kən-'səm-tiv, -'səmp-\ *adj* **1** : tending to consume **2** : of, relating to, or affected with consumption — **con·sump·tive·ly** *adv*

²consumptive *n* : a person affected with consumption

¹con·tact \'kän-,takt\ *n* **1 a** : union or junction of surfaces **b** (1) : the junction of two electrical conductors through which a current passes (2) : a special part made for such a junction or connection **2 a** : a social or business connection ⟨has *contacts* in the government⟩ **b** : a condition or instance of meeting, connecting, or communicating ⟨let's keep in *contact*⟩ **c** : direct visual observation of the earth's surface made from an airplane especially as an aid to navigation **d** : an establishing of communication with someone or an observing or receiving of a significant signal from a person or object [Latin *contactus,* from *contingere* "to have contact with", from *com-* + *tangere* "to touch"]

²con·tact \'kän-,takt, kən-'\ *vb* : to bring or come into contact

³con·tact \'kän-,takt\ *adj* : maintaining, involving, or caused by contact ⟨*contact* sports⟩

contact lens *n* : a thin lens designed to fit over the cornea

contact print *n* : a photographic print made with the negative in contact with the sensitized paper, plate, or film

con·ta·gion \kən-'tā-jən\ *n* **1** : the passing of a disease from one individual to another by direct or indirect contact **2** : a contagious disease or its causative agent **3 a** : rapid communication of an influence (as an idea or doctrine) **b** : an influence that spreads rapidly [Latin *contagio,* from *contingere* "to have contact with"]

con·ta·gious \kən-'tā-jəs\ *adj* **1** : communicable by contact : CATCHING **2** : bearing contagion ⟨a person who is *contagious*⟩ **3** : used for contagious diseases ⟨a *contagious* ward⟩ — **con·ta·gious·ly** *adv* — **con·ta·gious·ness** *n*

con·tain \kən-'tān\ *vt* **1** : to keep within limits : hold back : RESTRAIN ⟨*contain* one's anger⟩ **2 a** : to have within : HOLD **b** : COMPRISE, INCLUDE ⟨a gallon *contains* four quarts⟩ **3** : to be divisible by especially without a

contact lens

remainder ⟨12 *contains* 3⟩ [Old French *contenir,* from Latin *continēre* "to hold together, hold in, contain", from *com-* + *tenēre* "to hold"] — **con·tain·able** \-'tā-nə-bəl\ *adj* □ SYN HOLD, ACCOMMODATE: CONTAIN implies the actual presence of a specified substance or quantity within something; HOLD may imply only the capacity or usual function of containing or keeping; ACCOMMODATE stresses capacity to hold without crowding or inconvenience.

con·tain·er \kən-'tā-nər\ *n* : one that contains; *esp* : RECEPTACLE

con·tain·ment \kən-'tān-mənt\ *n* 1 : the act or process of containing 2 : the policy, process, or result of preventing the expansion of a hostile power or ideology

con·tam·i·nant \kən-'tam-ə-nənt\ *n* : something that contaminates

con·tam·i·nate \kən-'tam-ə-,nāt\ *vt* 1 : to soil, stain, or infect by contact or association 2 : to make unfit for use by introduction of unwholesome or undesirable elements [Latin *contaminare*] — **con·tam·i·na·tion** \-,tam-ə-'nā-shən\ *n* — **con·tam·i·na·tive** \-,nāt-iv\ *adj* — **con·tam·i·na·tor** \-'tam-ə-,nāt-ər\ *n*

con·temn \kən-'tem\ *vt* : to view or treat with contempt : SCORN [Middle French *contempner,* from Latin *contemnere,* from *com-* + *temnere* "to despise"] SYN see DESPISE — **con·tem·ner** \-'tem-ər, -'tem-nər\ *n*

con·tem·plate \'känt-əm-,plāt, 'kän-,tem-\ *vb* 1 : to consider long and carefully : MEDITATE 2 : to look forward to : have in mind : INTEND [Latin *contemplari,* from *com-* + *templum* "temple, space marked out for observation of auguries"] — **con·tem·pla·tor** \-,plāt-ər\ *n*

con·tem·pla·tion \,känt-əm-'plā-shən, ,kän-,tem-\ *n* 1 : concentration on spiritual things as a form of private devotion 2 : an act of considering with attention : STUDY 3 : the act of regarding steadily 4 : the act of considering a future event : EXPECTATION

con·tem·pla·tive \kən-'tem-plət-iv; 'känt-əm-,plāt-, 'kän-,tem-\ *adj* 1 : marked by or given to contemplation 2 : of or relating to a religious order devoted to prayer and penance — **con·tem·pla·tive·ly** *adv* — **con·tem·pla·tive·ness** *n*

con·tem·po·ra·ne·ous \kən-,tem-pə-'rā-nē-əs\ *adj* : existing, occurring, or originating during the same time [Latin *contemporaneus,* from *com-* + *tempor-, tempus* "time"] — **con·tem·po·ra·ne·ous·ly** *adv* — **con·tem·po·ra·ne·ous·ness** *n*

¹**con·tem·po·rary** \kən-'tem-pə-,rer-ē\ *adj* 1 : living or occurring during the same time : CONTEMPORANEOUS ⟨*contemporary* events in different countries⟩ 2 : of the same age 3 : existing in the present : CURRENT ⟨our *contemporary* writers⟩ [*com-* + Latin *tempor-, tempus* "time"] □ SYN CONTEMPORARY, SIMULTANEOUS, CONCURRENT, COINCIDENT mean existing or occurring at the same time. CONTEMPORARY applies chiefly to people and what relates to them and suggests indefinite lengths of time ⟨playwrights *contemporary* with Shakespeare⟩ SIMULTANEOUS implies correspondence in instant of time ⟨the two shots were almost *simultaneous*⟩ CONCURRENT implies beginning and ending together ⟨*concurrent* prison sentences⟩ COINCIDENT stresses simultaneousness of events and may emphasize lack of causal relation ⟨found that their birthdays were *coincident*⟩

²**contemporary** *n, pl* **-rar·ies** 1 : one that is contemporary with another 2 : one of about the same age as another

con·tempt \kən-'temt, -'tempt\ *n* 1 **a** : the act of despising **b** : the state of mind of one who despises : DISDAIN 2 : the state of being despised 3 : disobedience to or open disrespect for a court, judge, or legislative body [Latin *contemptus,* from *contemnere* "to contemn"]

con·tempt·ible \kən-'tem-tə-bəl, -'temp-\ *adj* : deserving contempt ⟨a *contemptible* lie⟩ — **con·tempt·**

ibly \-blē\ *adv* □ SYN DESPICABLE, SCURVY: CONTEMPTIBLE may apply to whatever is worthy of contempt; DESPICABLE implies arousing scornful often indignant moral disapproval; SCURVY implies extreme meanness and the arousing of disgust.

con·temp·tu·ous \kən-'tem-chə-wəs, -'temp-, -chəs; -'temsh-wəs, -'tempsh-\ *adj* : feeling or showing contempt ⟨a *contemptuous* sneer⟩ — **con·temp·tu·ous·ly** *adv* — **con·temp·tu·ous·ness** *n*

con·tend \kən-'tend\ *vb* 1 : to strive in opposition to someone or something ⟨*contending* against temptation⟩ 2 : MAINTAIN 2, ARGUE ⟨*contend* that their opinions are right⟩ 3 : RIVAL 2, COMPETE ⟨*contend* for a prize⟩ [Latin *contendere,* from *com-* + *tendere* "to stretch"] — **con·tend·er** *n*

¹**con·tent** \kən-'tent\ *adj* : being satisfied ⟨*content* to wait⟩ [Middle French, from Latin *contentus,* from *continēre* "to hold in, contain"]

²**content** *vt* : to appease the desires of : SATISFY

³**content** *n* : CONTENTMENT; *esp* : freedom from care of discomfort

⁴**con·tent** \'kän-,tent\ *n* 1 : something contained — usually used in pl. ⟨the *contents* of a jar⟩ 2 **a** : the topics or matter treated in a written work ⟨table of *contents*⟩ **b** : essential meaning or significance 3 : the amount of specified material contained : PROPORTION ⟨the sulfur *content* in a coal sample⟩ [Latin *contentus,* past participle of *continēre* "to contain"]

con·tent·ed \kən-'tent-əd\ *adj* : satisfied or showing satisfaction with one's possessions, status, or situation ⟨a *contented* smile⟩ — **con·tent·ed·ly** *adv* — **con·tent·ed·ness** *n*

con·ten·tion \kən-'ten-chən\ *n* 1 : an act or instance of contending : STRIFE, DISPUTE 2 : a point advanced or maintained in a debate or argument [Middle French *contencioun,* from Latin *contentio,* from *contendere* "to contend"]

con·ten·tious \kən-'ten-chəs\ *adj* : inclined to quarrels and disputes often over unimportant matters — **con·ten·tious·ly** *adv* — **con·ten·tious·ness** *n*

con·tent·ment \kən-'tent-mənt\ *n* : the state of being contented : peaceful satisfaction

con·ter·mi·nous \kən-'tər-mə-nəs, kän-\ *adj* 1 : having the same or a common boundary 2 : enclosed within one common boundary ⟨the 48 *conterminous* states of the United States⟩ [Latin *conterminus,* from *com-* + *terminus* "boundary"] — **con·ter·mi·nous·ly** *adv*

¹**con·test** \kən-'test, 'kän-,\ *vb* 1 : to make the subject of dispute or litigation; *esp* : CHALLENGE 3b ⟨*contest* a divorce⟩ 2 : to struggle over or for ⟨a *contested* territory⟩ 3 : RIVAL 2, VIE ⟨*contested* for the prize⟩ [Middle French *contester,* from Latin *contestari* "to call to witness, contest (a lawsuit)", from *com-* + *testis* "witness"] — **con·test·able** \-ə-bəl\ *adj* — **con·test·er** *n*

²**con·test** \'kän-,test\ *n* 1 : a struggle for victory or superiority ⟨a spelling *contest*⟩ 2 : COMPETITION, RIVALRY ⟨meet in friendly *contest*⟩

con·tes·tant \kən-'tes-tənt, 'kän-,tes-\ *n* : one that takes part in a contest

con·text \'kän-,tekst\ *n* 1 : the parts of a written or spoken passage that are near a certain word or group of words and that help to explain its meaning 2 : the circumstances surrounding an act or event [Latin *contextus* "connection of words, coherence", from *contexere* "to weave together", from *com-* + *texere* "to weave"] — **con·tex·tu·al** \kän-'teks-chə-wəl, -chəl\ *adj* — **con·tex·tu·al·ly** \-ē\ *adv*

con·ti·gu·i·ty \,känt-ə-'gyü-ət-ē\ *n, pl* **-ties** : the quality or state of being contiguous : PROXIMITY

con·tig·u·ous \kən-'tig-yə-wəs\ *adj* 1 : being in contact : TOUCHING 2 : very near though not in actual contact : NEIGHBORING 3 : CONTERMINOUS 2 [Latin *contiguus,* from *contingere* "to have contact with"] — **con·tig·u·ous·ly** *adv* — **con·tig·u·ous·ness** *n*

con·ti·nence \'känt-n-əns\ *n* : self-restraint especially in the face of bodily temptation

¹con·ti·nent \'känt-n-ənt\ *adj* : exercising continence [Middle French, from Latin *continens,* from *continēre* "to hold together, hold in, contain"] — **con·ti·nent·ly** *adv*

²con·ti·nent \'känt-n-ənt, 'känt-nənt\ *n* **1** : a continuous mass of land **2 a** : one of the great divisions of land (as North America, South America, Europe, Asia, Africa, Australia, or Antarctica) on the globe **b** *often cap* : the continent of Europe

¹con·ti·nen·tal \,känt-n-'ent-l\ *adj* **1** : of, relating to, or characteristic of a continent (*continental* waters); *esp* : of or relating to the continent of Europe **2** *often cap* : of or relating to the colonies later forming the United States (*Continental* Congress) — **con·ti·nen·tal·ly** \-l-ē\ *adv*

²continental *n* **1 a** *often cap* : an American soldier of the Revolution in the Continental army **b** : a piece of paper currency issued by the Continental Congress **c** : an inhabitant of a continent and especially the continent of Europe **2** : the least bit (not worth a *continental*) [sense 2 from the doubtful value of Continental currency]

continental drift *n* : a slow movement of the continents on a deep viscous zone within the earth : PLATE TECTONICS

continental shelf *n* : a shallow submarine plain of varying width forming a border to a continent and typically ending in a steep slope to the depths of the ocean

con·tin·gen·cy \kən-'tin-jən-sē\ *n, pl* **-cies 1** : the state of being contingent **2** : a chance happening or event **3** : a possible event or one foreseen as possible if another occurs

¹con·tin·gent \-jənt\ *adj* **1** : likely but not certain to happen : POSSIBLE **2 a** : happening by chance or unforeseen causes **b** : intended for use in circumstances not completely foreseen (*contingent* funds) **3** : dependent on or conditioned by something else (plans *contingent* on the weather) [Middle French, from Latin *contingere* "to have contact with, happen to"] — **con·tin·gent·ly** *adv*

²contingent *n* **1** : a chance occurrence : CONTINGENCY **2** : a number of persons representing or drawn from an area or group (a *contingent* of troops from each regiment)

con·tin·u·al \kən-'tin-yə-wəl, -'tin-yəl\ *adj* **1** : continuing indefinitely without interruption (*continual* fear) **2** : recurring in rapid succession (*continual* interruptions) **3** : forming a continuous series — **con·tin·u·al·ly** \-ē\ *adv* □ SYN CONTINUAL, CONTINUOUS, INCESSANT, CONSTANT mean marked by continued occurrence or recurrence. CONTINUAL implies prolonged succession or recurrence (*continual* showers) CONTINUOUS implies uninterrupted flow (*continuous* roar of the falls) INCESSANT implies ceaseless activity of varying intensity (*incessant* quarreling) CONSTANT implies uniform or persistent occurrence or recurrence (a *constant* supply of work)

con·tin·u·ance \kən-'tin-yə-wəns\ *n* **1** : the act of continuing in a state, condition, or course of action (during the *continuance* of the illness) **2** : unbroken succession : CONTINUATION **3** : postponement of court proceedings to a specified day

con·tin·u·a·tion \kən-,tin-yə-'wā-shən\ *n* **1** : continuance in or extension of a state or activity **2** : resumption after an interruption **3** : something that continues, increases, or adds (a *continuation* of last week's story)

con·tin·ue \kən-'tin-yü\ *vb* **1** : to remain in a place or a condition : STAY (*continue* in one's present job) **2** : ENDURE, LAST (rain *continued*) **3** : to go on or carry forward in a course (*continue* to study hard) **4** : to go on or carry on after an interruption : RESUME (play *continued* after a time-out) **5** : to postpone a legal pro-

ceeding to a later date **6** : to allow or cause to remain especially in a position (the town officials were *continued* in office) [Middle French *continuer,* from Latin *continuare,* from *continuus* "continuous"] — **con·tin·u·er** *n*

continued fraction *n* : an expression in the form of a fraction whose numerator is an integer and whose denominator is an integer plus a fraction whose numerator is an integer and whose denominator is an integer plus a fraction and so on

con·ti·nu·ity \,känt-n-'ü-ət-ē, -'yü-\ *n, pl* **-ties 1 a** : uninterrupted connection, succession, or union **b** : persistence without change **2 a** : a motion-picture, radio, or television script **b** : transitional spoken or musical matter for a radio or television program

con·tin·u·ous \kən-'tin-yə-wəs\ *adj* : being without break or interruption : UNBROKEN (a *continuous* line) [Latin *continuus,* from *continēre* "to hold together, contain"] SYN see CONTINUAL — **con·tin·u·ous·ly** *adv* — **con·tin·u·ous·ness** *n*

con·tin·u·um \-yə-wəm\ *n, pl* **-ua** \-wə\ *also* **-u·ums** : a coherent whole thought of as a collection, sequence, or progression of values or elements varying by minute degrees ("light" and "dark" stand at opposite ends of a *continuum*) [Latin, neuter of *continuus* "continuous"]

con·tort \kən-'tȯrt\ *vb* : to twist into an unusual appearance or unnatural shape : DEFORM, DISTORT [Latin *contortus,* past participle of *contorquēre* "to contort", from *com-* + *torquēre* "to twist"] — **con·tor·tion** \-'tȯr·shən\ *n*

con·tor·tion·ist \-shə·nəst, -shnəst\ *n* : one that contorts; *esp* : an acrobat who specializes in contortion of the body — **con·tor·tion·is·tic** \-,tȯr-shə-'nis-tik\ *adj*

¹con·tour \'kän-,tùr\ *n* **1** : the outline of a figure or body; *also* : a line or a drawing representing such an outline (sketch the *contour* of a coast) **2** : SHAPE, FORM (*contour* of the land) [French, from Italian *contorno,* from *contornare* "to round off, outline", from Latin *com-* + *tornare* "to turn in a lathe", from *tornus* "lathe"]

²contour *vt* **1** : to shape the contour of **2** : to shape to fit contours

³contour *adj* : following or fitted to the contour of something (*contour* farming)

contour feather *n* : one of the medium-sized feathers that form the general covering of a bird and determine the external contour

contour line *n* : a line (as on a map) connecting the points on a land surface that have the same elevation

contour map *n* : a map having contour lines

contra- *prefix* **1** : against : contrary : contrasting (*contra*distinction) **2** : pitched below normal bass [Latin, from *contra* "against, opposite"]

con·tra·band \'kän-trə-,band\ *n* **1** : goods or merchandise whose importation, exportation, or possession is forbidden **2** : smuggled goods [Italian *contrabbando,* from Medieval Latin *contrabannum,* from *contra-* + *bannum* "decree, ban"] — **contraband** *adj*

con·tra·bass \'kän-trə-,bās\ *n* : DOUBLE BASS

con·tra·bas·soon \,kän-trə-bə-'sün, -ba-\ *n* : the largest member of the oboe family an octave lower in pitch than the bassoon

con·tra·cep·tion \,kän-trə-'sep-shən\ *n* : voluntary prevention of conception [*contra-* + *conception*]

¹con·tra·cep·tive \-'sep-tiv\ *adj* : relating to or used for contraception

²contraceptive *n* : a contraceptive agent or device

¹con·tract \'kän-,trakt\ *n* **1 a** : a legally binding agreement between two or more persons or parties : COVENANT **b** : a document containing the terms and conditions of a contract **2** : an undertaking to win a specified number of tricks or points in bridge [Latin *contractus,* from *contrahere* "to draw together, make a

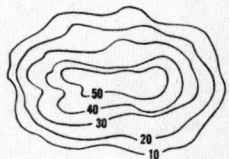

contour line

\ə\ abut	\ng\ sing
\ər\ further	\ō\ bone
\a\ mat	\ȯ\ saw
\ā\ take	\ȯi\ coin
\ä\ cot, cart	\th\ thin
\au̇\ out	\th\ this
\ch\ chin	\ü\ food
\e\ pet	\u̇\ foot
\ē\ easy	\y\ yet
\g\ go	\yü\ few
\i\ tip	\yu̇\ cure
\ī\ life	\zh\ vision
\j\ job	

contract, reduce in size'', from *com-* + *trahere* "to draw"]

²con·tract \kən-'trakt, *oftenest for 1* 'kän-,\ *vb* **1** : to enter into or undertake by contract ⟨*contract* to build a bridge⟩ **2** : to draw together or draw up so as to make or become shorter and broader ⟨*contract* a muscle⟩ **3 a** : to reduce to smaller size by or as if by squeezing or forcing together **b** : to make a contraction of (as a word) by omitting one or more sounds or letters **4 a** : GET, CATCH ⟨*contract* a cold⟩ **b** : FORM ⟨it is easier to *contract* a habit than to break one⟩ SYN *see* CONDENSE — **con·tract·ibil·i·ty** \kən-,trak-tə-'bil-ət-ē, ,kän-\ *n* — **con·tract·ible** \kən-'trak-tə-bəl, 'kän-,\ *adj*

contract bridge \'kän-,trakt-, -,trak-\ *n* : a card game for four players in two partnerships in which players bid for the right to name a trump suit and contract to win a specific number of tricks

con·trac·tile \kən-'trak-tl\ *adj* : having the power or property of contracting ⟨*contractile* fibers⟩ — **con·trac·til·i·ty** \,kän-,trak-'til-ət-ē\ *n*

contractile vacuole *n* : a vacuole in a unicellular organism that contracts regularly to discharge fluid from the body and that probably has an excretory or hydrostatic function

con·trac·tion \kən-'trak-shən\ *n* **1 a** : the act or process of contracting : the state of being contracted **b** : the shortening and thickening of a functioning muscle or muscle fiber **2** : a shortening of a word, syllable, or word group by omission of a sound or letter; *also* : a form produced by such shortening ⟨*aren't* is a contraction of *are not*⟩ — **con·trac·tion·al** \-'trak-shnəl, -shən-l\ *adj* — **con·trac·tive** \-'trak-tiv\ *adj*

con·trac·tor \'kän-,trak-tər, kən-'\ *n* : one that enters into a contract; *esp* : one that agrees to perform work or provide supplies at a given price or within a given time ⟨a building *contractor*⟩

con·trac·tu·al \kən-'trak-chə-wəl, kän-, -chəl\ *adj* : of, relating to, or constituting a contract ⟨*contractual* agreements⟩ — **con·trac·tu·al·ly** \-ē\ *adv*

con·tra·dict \,kän-trə-'dikt\ *vt* **1** : to deny the truth of ⟨*contradict* a story⟩ **2** : to state the opposite of what another has said **3** : to be contrary or opposed to ⟨your actions *contradict* your words⟩ [Latin *contradicere*, from *contra-* + *dicere* "to say"] — **con·tra·dict·able** \-'dik-tə-bəl\ *adj* — **con·tra·dic·tor** \-tər\ *n*

con·tra·dic·tion \-'dik-shən\ *n* **1 a** : a statement that contradicts another **b** : denial of the truth of something said **2** : opposition between things ⟨a *contradiction* between desire and reality⟩

con·tra·dic·to·ry \,kän-trə-'dik-tə-rē, -trē\ *adj* **1** : tending to contradict **2** : involving contradiction : OPPOSED ⟨*contradictory* statements⟩ SYN *see* CONTRARY — **con·tra·dic·to·ri·ly** \-tə-rə-lē, -trə-lē\ *adv* — **con·tra·dic·to·ri·ness** \-tə-rē-nəs, -trē-\ *n*

con·tra·dis·tinc·tion \,kän-trə-dis-'ting-shən, -'tingk-\ *n* : distinction by contrast ⟨painting in *contradistinction* to sculpture⟩ — **con·tra·dis·tinc·tive** \-'ting-tiv, -'tingk-\ *adj* — **con·tra·dis·tinc·tive·ly** *adv*

con·tra·dis·tin·guish \-'ting-gwish\ *vt* : to distinguish by contrast of qualities

con·trail \'kän-,trāl\ *n* : streaks of condensed water vapor created in the air by an airplane or rocket at high altitudes [*con*densation *trail*]

con·tral·to \kən-'tral-tō\ *n, pl* **-tos** **1 a** : the lowest female singing voice **b** : a singer having such a voice **2** : the part sung by a contralto [Italian, from *contra-* + *alto* "high"]

con·tra·pos·i·tive \,kän-trə-'päz-ət-iv, -'päz-tiv\ *n* : the statement obtained by interchanging the hypothesis and conclusion of a conditional statement and denying both clauses ⟨the *contrapositive* of "if A, then B" is "if not B, then not A"⟩

con·trap·tion \kən-'trap-shən\ *n* : CONTRIVANCE 2, GADGET [perhaps blend of *contrivance, trap,* and *invention*]

con·tra·pun·tal \,kän-trə-'pənt-l\ *adj* **1** : of or relating to counterpoint **2** : consisting of or relating to two or more melodies combined into a unified musical composition : POLYPHONIC [Italian *contrappunto* "counterpoint", from Medieval Latin *contrapunctus*] — **con·tra·pun·tal·ly** \-l-ē\ *adv*

con·tra·pun·tist \-'pənt-əst\ *n* : one who writes counterpoint

con·trari·wise \'kän-,trer-ē-,wīz, kən-'\ *adv* **1** : on the contrary **2** : vice versa : CONVERSELY **3** : in a contrary manner : PERVERSELY

¹con·trary \'kän-,trer-ē\ *n, pl* **-trar·ies** **1** : a fact or condition incompatible with another : OPPOSITE **2** : one of a pair of opposites **3** : a proposition in logic related to another in such a way that though both may be false they cannot both be true

²con·trary \'kän-,trer-ē, *4 is often* kən-'treər-ē\ *adj* **1** : exactly opposite : wholly different ⟨*contrary* opinions⟩ **2** : OPPOSED ⟨an act *contrary* to law⟩ **3** : UNFAVORABLE ⟨a *contrary* wind⟩ **4** : inclined to oppose or resist : WAYWARD ⟨a *contrary* child⟩ [Middle French *contraire*, from Latin *contrarius*, from *contra* "against, opposite"] — **con·trar·i·ly** \-,trer-ə-lē, -'trer-\ *adv* — **con·trar·i·ness** \-,trer-ē-nəs, -'trer-\ *n*

☐ SYN OPPOSITE, CONTRADICTORY: CONTRARY implies extreme divergence and often antagonism; OPPOSITE applies to things in sharp contrast or reversed positions; CONTRADICTORY implies the impossibility of two things being true or valid at the same time.

³con·trary *like* ²\ *adv* : in a contrary manner : CONTRARILY

¹con·trast \'kän-,trast\ *n* **1** : the act or process of contrasting : the state of being contrasted **2** : a person or thing that exhibits differences when contrasted **3** : difference especially when sharp or striking between associated things ⟨the *contrast* between light and dark⟩

²con·trast \kən-'trast, 'kän-,\ *vb* **1** : to show noticeable differences ⟨black and gold *contrast* sharply⟩ **2** : to compare especially so as to show differences ⟨*contrast* winter and summer⟩ [French *contraster*, derived from Latin *contra-* + *stare* "to stand"] SYN *see* COMPARE — **con·trast·able** \-ə-bəl\ *adj*

con·tra·vene \,kän-trə-'vēn\ *vt* **1** : to go or act contrary to ⟨*contravene* a law⟩ **2** : to oppose in argument : CONTRADICT ⟨*contravene* a proposition⟩ [Late Latin *contravenire*, from Latin *contra-* + *venire* "to come"] — **con·tra·ven·er** *n*

con·tra·ven·tion \,kän-trə-'ven-chən\ *n* : the act of contravening : VIOLATION [Middle French, from Late Latin *contravenire* "to contravene"]

con·tre·danse *or* **con·tra dance** \'kän-trə-,dans\ *n* **1** : a folk dance in which couples face each other in two lines or in a square **2** : a piece of music for a contredanse [French *contredanse*, by folk etymology (influenced by French *contre-* "counter-") from English *country-dance*]

con·tre·temps \'kän-trə-,tän\ *n, pl* **con·tre·temps** \-,tän, -,tänz\ : an untimely and embarrassing occurrence : MISHAP [French, from *contre-* "counter-" + *temps* "time"]

con·trib·ute \kən-'trib-yət\ *vb* **1** : to give along with others ⟨*contribute* to charities⟩ **2** : to have a share in something ⟨factors *contributing* to an accident⟩ **3** : to supply for publication ⟨*contributed* a poem to the school paper⟩ [Latin *contribuere*, from *com-* + *tribuere* "to grant"] — **con·trib·u·tive** \-yət-iv\ *adj* — **con·trib·u·tor** \-yət-ər\ *n*

con·tri·bu·tion \,kän-trə-'byü-shən\ *n* **1** : LEVY 1, TAX **2 a** : the act of contributing **b** : the sum or thing contributed **3** : a writing for publication especially in a periodical

con·trib·u·to·ry \kən-'trib-yə-,tōr-ē, -,tȯr-ē\ *adj* **1** : contributing or serving to contribute; *esp* : helping to accomplish a result ⟨carelessness *contributory* to an accident⟩ **2 a** : of, relating to, or forming a contribution **b** : supported by contributions ⟨a *contributory* pension plan⟩

con·trite \'kän-ˌtrīt, kən-'-\ *adj* **1** : sorrowful for a wrong that one has done : deeply repentant **2** : resulting from or expressing repentance ⟨*contrite* tears⟩ [Middle French *contrit*, from Medieval Latin *contritus*, from Latin *conterere* "to bruise", from *com-* + *terere* "to rub"] — **con·trite·ly** *adv* — **con·trite·ness** *n*

con·tri·tion \kən-'trish-ən\ *n* : the state of being contrite SYN see PENITENCE

con·triv·ance \kən-'trī-vəns\ *n* **1** : the act or faculty of contriving : the state of being contrived **2** : something contrived; *esp* : a mechanical device

con·trive \kən-'trīv\ *vb* **1** : PLAN, SCHEME ⟨*contrive* a means of escape⟩ **2** : to form or make in a skillful or ingenious way : INVENT **3** : to bring about : MANAGE ⟨*contriving* to make ends meet⟩ [Middle English *controven, contreven,* from Middle French *controver,* from Late Latin *contropare* "to compare"] — **con·triv·er** *n*

con·trived *adj* : ARTIFICIAL 3, UNNATURAL ⟨the *contrived* ending of a play⟩

¹con·trol \kən-'trōl\ *vt* **con·trolled; con·trol·ling 1** : to check, test, or verify by evidence or experiments **2 a** : to exercise restraining or directing influence over : REGULATE ⟨*control* one's temper⟩ **b** : to have power over : RULE ⟨*control* a territory⟩ [Middle French *contreroller,* from *contrerolle* "audit", from *contre-* "counter-" + *rolle* "roll, account"] SYN see CONDUCT — **con·trol·la·ble** \-'trō-lə-bəl\ *adj*

²control *n* **1** : the power or authority to control or command ⟨children under their parents' *control*⟩ **2** : ability to control ⟨lose *control* of a car⟩ **3** : a means or method of controlling : one that controls: as **a** (1) : CONTROL EXPERIMENT (2) : one (as an organism, culture, or group) that is part of a control **b** : a mechanism used to regulate or guide the operation of a machine, apparatus, or system ⟨the *controls* of an airplane⟩ ⟨price *controls*⟩ **c** : a personality or spirit believed to actuate the utterances or performances of a spiritualist medium

control experiment *n* : an experiment in which the subjects of experimentation are treated as in a parallel experiment except for omission of the procedure or agent under test and which is used as a standard of comparison in judging experimental effects

con·trol·ler \kən-'trō-lər, 'kän-,\ *n* **1 a** : COMPTROLLER 1 **b** : the chief accounting officer of a business or institution **2** : one that controls ⟨air traffic *controller*⟩ — **con·trol·ler·ship** \-,ship\ *n*

con·tro·ver·sial \,kän-trə-'vər-shəl, -'vər-sē-əl\ *adj* **1** : of, relating to, or arousing controversy ⟨a *controversial* public figure⟩ **2** : fond of controversy : ARGUMENTATIVE — **con·tro·ver·sial·ist** \-əst\ *n* — **con·tro·ver·sial·ly** \-ē\ *adv*

con·tro·ver·sy \'kän-trə-,vər-sē\ *n, pl* **-sies 1** : a discussion marked especially by expression of opposing views : DISPUTE **2** : QUARREL 2, STRIFE [Latin *controversia,* from *controversus* "disputable", literally, "turned opposite", from *contro-* "opposite" + *versus,* past participle of *vertere* "to turn"]

con·tro·vert \'kän-trə-,vərt, ,kän-trə-'-\ *vt* : to dispute or oppose by reasoning ⟨*controvert* a point in a discussion⟩ [derived from *controversy*] — **con·tro·vert·er** *n* — **con·tro·vert·ible** \-ə-bəl\ *adj*

con·tume·ly \'kän-tyü-mə-lē, -'tü-; 'kän-tyə-,mē-lē, -tə-; 'kän-tyüm-lē\ *n, pl* **-lies** : rude language or treatment arising from arrogance and contempt; *also* : an instance of such language or treatment [Middle French *contumelie,* from Latin *contumelia*]

con·tuse \kən-'tüz, -'tyüz\ *vt* : to injure (tissue) usually without breaking the skin : BRUISE [Middle French *contuser,* from Latin *contundere* "to crush, bruise", from

com- + *tundere* "to beat"] — **con·tu·sion** \-'tü-zhən, -'tyü-\ *n*

co·nun·drum \kə-'nən-drəm\ *n* **1** : a riddle whose answer is or involves a pun **2** : an intricate and difficult problem [origin unknown]

con·ur·ba·tion \,kän-ər-'bā-shən\ *n* : a continuous network of urban communities [*com-* + Latin *urbs* "city"]

co·nus ar·te·ri·o·sus \'kō-nəs-är-,tir-ē-'ō-səs\ *n* **1** : an extension of the ventricle of amphibians and some fishes that has a spiral valve separating venous blood going to the respiratory arteries from blood going to the aorta and systemic arteries **2** : a conical extension of the right ventricle in mammals from which the pulmonary arteries emerge — called also *conus* [New Latin, literally, "arterial cone"]

con·va·lesce \,kän-və-'les\ *vi* : to recover health and strength gradually after illness or weakness [Latin *convalescere,* from *com-* + *valescere* "to grow strong", from *valēre* "to be strong, be well"]

con·va·les·cence \,kän-və-'les-ns\ *n* : the process or period of convalescing — **con·va·les·cent** \-nt\ *adj or n*

con·vec·tion \kən-'vek-shən\ *n* : the circulatory motion that occurs in a gas or liquid at a nonuniform temperature owing to currents caused by differences in density with the warmer portions rising and the colder denser portions sinking; *also* : the transfer of heat by this automatic circulation of a fluid [Late Latin *convectio,* from Latin *convehere* "to bring together", from *com-* + *vehere* "to carry"] — **con·vec·tion·al** \-shnəl, -shən-l\ *adj* — **con·vec·tive** \-'vek-tiv\ *adj*

convection oven *n* : an oven with a fan that circulates hot air evenly and continuously around the food as it cooks

con·vec·tor \-'vek-tər\ *n* : a heating unit in which air heated by contact with a heating device in a casing circulates by convection

con·vene \kən-'vēn\ *vb* **1** : to come together in a body : MEET ⟨the legislature *convened* Tuesday⟩ **2** : to cause to assemble : call together ⟨the chairman *convened* the meeting⟩ [Middle French *convenir,* from Latin *convenire,* from *com-* + *venire* "to come"] — **con·ven·er** *n*

¹con·ve·nience \kən-'vē-nyəns\ *n* **1** : fitness or suitability for meeting a requirement **2** : personal comfort : EASE **3** : a suitable time : OPPORTUNITY ⟨come at your earliest *convenience*⟩ **4** : something (as a device or a service) that gives comfort or advantage ⟨a house with all modern *conveniences*⟩

²convenience *adj* : designed for quick easy preparation or use

convenience store *n* : a small market that is open long hours

con·ve·nient \kən-'vē-nyənt\ *adj* **1 a** : suited to personal comfort or to easy use ⟨a *convenient* location⟩ ⟨a *convenient* time⟩ **b** : suited to a particular situation ⟨found it *convenient* to ignore the remark⟩ **2** : near at hand : HANDY ⟨*convenient* parking⟩ [Latin *conveniens,* from *convenire* "to come together, agree, be suitable"] — **con·ve·nient·ly** *adv*

con·vent \'kän-vənt, -,vent\ *n* : a local community or house of a religious order or congregation; *esp* : an establishment of nuns [Old French *covent,* from Medieval Latin *conventus,* from Latin, "assembly", from *convenire* "to come together, agree, be suitable"] — **con·ven·tu·al** \kən-'vench-ə-wəl, kän-\ *adj*

con·ven·tion \kən-'ven-chən\ *n* **1** : AGREEMENT 2, COVENANT ⟨an international *convention* for treatment of prisoners of war⟩ **2** : generally accepted custom, practice, or belief; *also* : something accepted by convention as true, useful, or convenient ⟨the *convention* of driving on the right⟩ **3** : an assembly of persons met for a common purpose ⟨a constitutional *convention*⟩ **4** : a practice in bidding or playing that conveys information between partners in a card game (as bridge) [Latin *conventio,* from *convenire* "to convene, be suitable"]

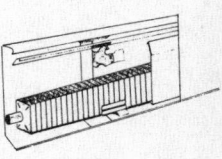

convector

\ə\ abut	\ng\ sing
\ər\ further	\ō\ bone
\a\ mat	\ȯ\ saw
\ā\ take	\ȯi\ coin
\ä\ cot, cart	\th\ thin
\au̇\ out	\t̲h̲\ this
\ch\ chin	\ü\ food
\e\ pet	\u̇\ foot
\ē\ easy	\y\ yet
\g\ go	\yü\ few
\i\ tip	\yu̇\ cure
\ī\ life	\zh\ vision
\j\ job	

con·ven·tion·al \kən-'vench-nəl, -'ven-chən-l\ *adj* **1** : behaving according to convention ⟨a very *conventional* person⟩ **2** : settled or prescribed by convention : CUSTOMARY ⟨*conventional* methods⟩ **3 a** : ORDINARY 1, COMMONPLACE ⟨*conventional* remarks⟩ **b** : conforming to established rules or traditions : not showing originality — **con·ven·tion·al·ly** \-ē\ *adv*

con·ven·tion·al·i·ty \kən-,ven-chə-'nal-ət-ē\ *n, pl* **-ties** **1** : the quality or state of being conventional especially in social behavior **2** : a conventional practice, custom, or rule

con·ven·tion·al·ize \kən-'vench-nə-,līz, -'ven-chən-l-,īz\ *vt* : to make conventional — **con·ven·tion·al·iza·tion** \-,vench-nə-lə-'zā-shən, -,ven-chən-l-ə-'zā-\ *n*

con·verge \kən-'vərj\ *vb* **1** : to tend or move toward one point or one another : MEET **2** : to come together and unite in a common interest or focus **3** : to cause to come together [Medieval Latin *convergere,* from Latin *com-* + *vergere* "to bend, incline"]

con·ver·gence \kən-'vər-jəns\ *n* **1** : the act or condition of converging especially toward union or uniformity **2** : independent development of similar characters (as of bodily structure or cultural traits) often associated with similarity of habits or environment — **con·ver·gent** \-jənt\ *adj*

convergent evolution *n* : convergence of two or more biological species — called also *parallel evolution*

con·ver·sant \kən-'vərs-nt\ *adj* : having knowledge or experience : FAMILIAR ⟨they were *conversant* with the facts⟩ — **con·ver·sant·ly** *adv*

con·ver·sa·tion \,kän-vər-'sā-shən\ *n* : oral exchange of sentiments, observations, opinions, or ideas; *also* : an instance of such exchange : TALK

con·ver·sa·tion·al \,kän-vər-'sā-shnəl, -shən-l\ *adj* **1** : of, relating to, or suitable for informal friendly talk ⟨written in *conversational* style⟩ **2** : fond of or given to conversation — **con·ver·sa·tion·al·ly** \-ē\ *adv*

con·ver·sa·tion·al·ist \-shnə-ləst, -shən-l-əst\ *n* : a person who is fond of or good at conversation

¹con·verse \kən-'vərs\ *vi* : to exchange thoughts and opinions in speech : TALK [Middle French *converser,* from Latin *conversari* "to live, keep company with", from *convertere* "to turn around, convert"] — **con·vers·er** *n*

²con·verse \'kän-,vərs\ *n* : CONVERSATION

³con·verse \kən-'vərs, 'kän-\ *adj* : reversed in order, relation, or action; *also* : being a converse ⟨a *converse* theorem in geometry⟩ [Latin *conversus,* past participle of *convertere* "to turn around"] — **con·verse·ly** *adv*

⁴con·verse \'kän-,vərs\ *n* : something that is the opposite of something else: as **a** : a theorem formed by the interchange of the hypothesis and the conclusion in a given theorem **b** : the statement obtained by interchanging the subject and predicate of a logical proposition

con·ver·sion \kən-'vər-zhən\ *n* **1** : the act of converting : the state of being converted **2** : a change in the nature or form of a thing ⟨the *conversion* of water into steam by boiling⟩ **3** : a spiritual change in a person associated with a change of religious belief or with the adoption of religion **4** : the taking and using of another's property without right as one's own **5** : the making of an extra point in football or a successful free throw in basketball — **con·ver·sion·al** \-'vərzh-nəl, -ən-l\ *adj*

¹con·vert \kən-'vərt\ *vb* **1** : to bring over from one belief, view, or party to another **2 a** : to change from one form or function to another : TRANSFORM ⟨*convert* starch into sugar⟩ **b** : to exchange for an equivalent ⟨*convert* diamonds into cash⟩ **3** : to take over without right **4** : to undergo conversion **5** : to make good on an extra point attempt, on a free throw, or on a penalty kick [Old French *convertir,* from Latin *convertere* "to turn around, convert", from *com-* + *vertere* "to turn"]

²con·vert \'kän-,vərt\ *n* : one that is converted

con·vert·er \kən-'vərt-ər\ *n* : one that converts: as **a** : the furnace used in the Bessemer process **b** *or* **con·ver·tor** \-'vərt-ər\ : a device employing mechanical rotation for changing alternating current to direct current **c** : CATALYTIC CONVERTER

¹con·vert·ible \kən-'vərt-ə-bəl\ *adj* **1** : capable of being converted **2** : having a top that may be lowered or removed ⟨a *convertible* coupe⟩ — **con·vert·ibil·i·ty** \-,vərt-ə-'bil-ət-ē\ *n* — **con·vert·ibly** \-'vərt-ə-blē\ *adv*

²convertible *n* : something convertible; *esp* : a convertible automobile

con·vex \kän-'veks, 'kän-, kən-'\ *adj* **1** : curved or rounded like the exterior of a sphere or circle **2** : being a set containing every straight line joining two points belonging to the set; *also* : having the property that the union of its perimeter and its interior comprises a convex set ⟨*convex* polygons⟩ [Latin *convexus*] — **con·vex·ly** *adv* — **con·vex·ness** *n*

con·vex·i·ty \kən-'vek-sət-ē, kän-\ *n, pl* **-ties** **1** : the quality or state of being convex **2** : a convex surface or part

con·vexo–con·cave \kən-,vek-sō-kän-'kāv, -'kän-,\ *adj* : having the convex side of greater curvature than the concave

con·vey \kən-'vā\ *vt* **con·veyed; con·vey·ing** **1** : to carry from one place to another : TRANSPORT ⟨*convey* passengers by bus⟩ **2** : to serve as a means of transferring ⟨an infection *conveyed* by insects⟩ **3** : to communicate or serve as a means of communicating ⟨a red light *conveys* a warning⟩ **4** : to transfer or deliver to another; *esp* : to transfer title to real estate by a legal document [Old French *conveier* "to accompany, escort", from Latin *com-* + *via* "way"]

con·vey·ance \kən-'vā-əns\ *n* **1** : the act of conveying **2** : a means or way of conveying: as **a** : a legal document by which title to property is conveyed **b** : a means of transport : VEHICLE

con·vey·er *or* **con·vey·or** \kən-'vā-ər\ *n* **1** : one that conveys **2** *usually* **conveyor** : a mechanical apparatus for carrying (as by an endless moving belt or a chain of receptacles) packages or bulk material from place to place

¹con·vict \kən-'vikt\ *vt* : to find or prove to be guilty [Latin *convictus,* past participle of *convincere* "to refute, convict", from *com-* + *vincere* "to conquer"]

²con·vict \'kän-,vikt\ *n* **1** : a person convicted of a crime **2** : a person serving a prison sentence usually for a long term

con·vic·tion \kən-'vik-shən\ *n* **1** : the act or process of convicting especially of a crime in a court of law : the state of being convicted **2** : the state of being convinced : CERTITUDE ⟨speaks with *conviction*⟩ **3** : a strong belief or opinion ⟨a person with firm *convictions*⟩ **SYN** see CERTAINTY, OPINION

con·vince \kən-'vins\ *vt* : to bring by argument or evidence to agreement or belief : overcome the disbelief or objections of ⟨*convinced* me that they were qualified⟩ [Latin *convincere* "to refute, convict, prove"] — **con·vinc·er** *n*

con·vinc·ing \-'vin-sing\ *adj* : having the power or the effect of overcoming objection or disbelief : strongly persuasive ⟨a *convincing* argument⟩ — **con·vinc·ing·ly** \-sing-lē\ *adv* — **con·vinc·ing·ness** *n*

con·viv·ial \kən-'viv-yəl, -'viv-ē-əl\ *adj* : relating to, occupied with, or fond of good company and festivity [Latin *convivium* "banquet", from *com-* + *vivere* "to live"] — **con·viv·i·al·i·ty** \-,viv-ē-'al-ət-ē\ *n* — **con·viv·ial·ly** \-ē\ *adv*

con·vo·ca·tion \,kän-və-'kā-shən\ *n* **1** : a summons to a meeting **2** : ASSEMBLY 1, MEETING — **con·vo·ca·tion·al** \-shnəl, -shən-l\ *adj*

con·voke \kən-'vōk\ *vt* : to call together to a meeting [Middle French *convoquer,* from Latin *convocare,* from *com-* + *vocare* "to call"]

con·vo·lute \'kän-və-ˌlüt\ *vb* : COIL 1, TWIST [Latin *convolutus,* past participle of *convolvere* "to roll up, enfold", from *com-* + *volvere* "to roll"]

con·vo·lut·ed *adj* 1 : having elaborately curved or twisted windings; *esp* : having convolutions 2 : elaborately organized : INTRICATE

con·vo·lu·tion \ˌkän-və-'lü-shən\ *n* 1 : one of the irregular ridges on the surface of the brain and especially of the cerebrum of higher mammals 2 : a convoluted form or structure — **con·vo·lu·tion·al** \-shnəl, -shən-l\ *adj*

con·vol·vu·lus \kən-'väl-vyə-ləs, -'vȯl-\ *n, pl* **-lus·es** or **-li** \-ˌlī, -ˌlē\ : any of a genus of erect, trailing, or twining herbs and shrubs of the morning-glory family [Latin *convolvere* "to roll up, enfold"]

¹con·voy \'kän-ˌvȯi, kän-'\ *vt* : to accompany for protection either by land or by sea : ESCORT ⟨a destroyer *convoying* merchant shipping⟩ [Middle French *conveier, convoier,* from Latin *com-* + *via* "way"]

²con·voy \'kän-ˌvȯi\ *n* 1 : a protective escort for ships, persons, or goods 2 : the act of convoying : the state of being convoyed ⟨ships traveling in *convoy*⟩ 3 : a group convoyed ⟨a *convoy* of freighters⟩

con·vulse \kən-'vəls\ *vt* : to shake or agitate violently; *esp* : to shake with or as if with irregular spasms ⟨*convulsed* with laughter⟩ ⟨land *convulsed* by an earthquake⟩ [Latin *convulsus,* past participle of *convellere* "to pluck up, convulse", from *com-* + *vellere* "to pluck"]

con·vul·sion \-'vəl-shən\ *n* 1 : an abnormal violent and involuntary contraction or series of contractions of the muscles 2 **a** : a violent disturbance **b** : an uncontrolled fit : PAROXYSM — **con·vul·sion·ary** \-shə-ˌner-ē\ *adj*

con·vul·sive \-'vəl-siv\ *adj* 1 : constituting or producing a convulsion 2 : accompanied by or affected with convulsions — **con·vul·sive·ly** *adv* — **con·vul·sive·ness** *n*

co·ny *variant of* CONEY

coo \'kü\ *vi* 1 : to utter the low soft cry characteristic of a dove or pigeon or a similar sound 2 : to talk fondly or amorously [imitative] — **coo** *n*

¹cook \'kuk\ *n* : one who prepares food for eating [Old English *cōc,* from Latin *coquus,* from *coquere* "to cook"]

²cook *vb* 1 : to prepare food for eating by a heating process 2 : to undergo cooking 3 **a** : to go on : HAPPEN ⟨what's *cooking*⟩ **b** : CONCOCT, DEVISE ⟨*cook* up a scheme⟩ 4 : to subject to the action of heat or fire — **cook·er** *n* — **cook one's goose** : to ruin (one) beyond recovery

cook·book \'kuk-ˌbuk\ *n* : a book of cooking directions and recipes

cook·ery \'kuk-rē, -ə-rē\ *n* : the art or practice of cooking

cook·ie *or* **cooky** \'kuk-ē\ *n, pl* **cook·ies** : any of various small sweet crisp or slightly raised cakes [Dutch *koekje* "small cake", from *koek* "cake"]

cook·out \'kuk-ˌaut\ *n* : an outdoor gathering at which a meal is cooked and served; *also* : such a meal

cook·stove \'kuk-ˌstōv\ *n* : a stove for cooking : RANGE

¹cool \'kül\ *adj* 1 : moderately cold : lacking in warmth 2 **a** : marked by steady calmness and self-control **b** : restrained in emotion 3 : WHOLE, FULL ⟨a *cool* million⟩ 4 : producing an impression of coolness ⟨blue is a *cool* color⟩ 5 *slang* : very good : EXCELLENT [Old English *cōl*] — **cool·ish** \'kü-lish\ *adj* — **cool·ly** \'kül-lē, -ē\ *adv* — **cool·ness** \'kül-nəs\ *n*

²cool *vb* 1 : to make or become cool 2 : to moderate or calm especially in emotional intensity ⟨allow tempers to *cool*⟩ — **cool it** : to calm down

³cool *n* : a cool time or place ⟨the *cool* of the night⟩

cool·ant \'kü-lənt\ *n* : a usually fluid cooling agent

cool·er \'kü-lər\ *n* : one that cools: as **a** : a container for cooling liquids **b** : REFRIGERATOR 2 : LOCKUP, JAIL

cool·head·ed \'kül-'hed-əd\ *adj* : not easily excited : CALM

coo·lie \'kü-lē\ *n* : an unskilled laborer or porter usually in or from the Far East [Hindi *kulī*]

coon \'kün\ *n* : RACCOON

coon·skin \-ˌskin\ *n* : the fur or pelt of the raccoon

¹coop \'küp, 'kup\ *n* 1 : a cage or small enclosure or building for housing poultry or small animals 2 : a confined place [Middle English *cupe*]

²coop *vt* : to place or keep in or as if in a coop : PEN

co–op \'kō-ˌäp, kō-'äp\ *n* : COOPERATIVE

¹coo·per \'kü-pər, 'kup-ər\ *n* : one that makes or repairs wooden casks or tubs [derived from Latin *cupa* "cask"]

²cooper *vb* : to work or work on as a cooper

coo·per·age \'kü-pə-rij, -prij; 'kup-rij, -ə-rij\ *n* 1 : a cooper's place of business 2 : a cooper's work or products

co·op·er·ate \kō-'äp-ˌrāt, -ə-ˌrāt\ *vi* : to act, work, or associate with others especially for mutual benefit [Late Latin *cooperari,* from Latin *co-* + *operari* "to work"]

co·op·er·a·tion \kō-ˌäp-ə-'rā-shən\ *n* 1 : the act or process of cooperating 2 : association of individuals or groups for mutual benefit

¹co·op·er·a·tive \kō-'äp-rət-iv, -ə-rət-, -ə-ˌrāt-\ *adj* 1 : marked by cooperation or a willingness to cooperate ⟨*cooperative* neighbors⟩ 2 : of, relating to, or organized as a cooperative ⟨a *cooperative* store⟩ — **co·op·er·a·tive·ly** *adv* — **co·op·er·a·tive·ness** *n*

²cooperative *n* : an association formed to enable its members to buy, sell, or perform other economic functions to better advantage

Coo·per's hawk \'kü-pərz-, 'kup-ərz-\ *n* : a common American hawk that has a rounded tail and is slightly smaller than a crow [William *Cooper,* died 1864, American naturalist]

co–opt \kō-'äpt\ *vt* 1 : to choose or elect as a fellow member or colleague 2 : ASSIMILATE 1a ⟨protesters were *co-opted* by the establishment⟩ [Latin *cooptare,* from *co-* + *optare* "to choose"] — **co–op·ta·tion** \ˌkō-ˌäp-'tā-shən\ *n* — **co–op·tion** \-'äp-shən\ *n*

¹co·or·di·nate \kō-'ȯrd-nət, -n-ət\ *adj* 1 : equal in rank or order ⟨*coordinate* branches of government⟩ 2 **a** : being of equal rank in a compound sentence ⟨*coordinate* clauses⟩ **b** : joining words or word groups of the same grammatical rank ⟨the word and is a *coordinate* conjunction⟩ [back-formation from *coordination*] — **co·or·di·nate·ly** *adv* — **co·or·di·nate·ness** *n*

²coordinate *n* 1 : one who has the same rank, authority, or importance as another 2 : any of a set of numbers used in specifying the location of a point on a line or surface or in space — compare ABSCISSA, ORDINATE

³co·or·di·nate \kō-'ȯrd-n-ˌāt\ *vb* 1 : to make or become coordinate 2 : to bring into a common action, movement, or condition ⟨*coordinated* the efforts of all three agencies⟩ — **co·or·di·na·tor** \-ˌāt-ər\ *n*

coordinate axis *n* : a line in a coordinate system along which coordinates are measured — compare X-AXIS, Y-AXIS

coordinate geometry *n* : ANALYTIC GEOMETRY

coordinate plane *n* 1 : a plane whose points are labeled by means of a coordinate system 2 : one of three mutually perpendicular planes in three-dimensional space with reference to which coordinates are measured

coordinate system *n* : any of various systems for locating points by means of lines; *esp* : CARTESIAN COORDINATE SYSTEM

co·or·di·nat·ing *adj* : COORDINATE 2b

co·or·di·na·tion \kō-ˌȯrd-n-'ā-shən\ *n* 1 : the act of coordinating 2 : the state of being coordinate : harmonious working together ⟨muscular *coordination*⟩ [Late Latin *coordinatio,* from Latin *co-* + *ordinatio* "arrangement", from *ordo* "order"]

coot \'küt\ *n* 1 : any of various sluggish slow-flying slaty-black birds of the rail family that somewhat re-

\ə\ abut	\ng\ sing
\ər\ further	\ō\ bone
\a\ mat	\ȯ\ saw
\ā\ take	\ȯi\ coin
\ä\ cot, cart	\th\ thin
\au\ out	\th\ this
\ch\ chin	\ü\ food
\e\ pet	\u̇\ foot
\ē\ easy	\y\ yet
\g\ go	\yü\ few
\i\ tip	\yu̇\ cure
\ī\ life	\zh\ vision
\j\ job	

semble ducks **2** : a North American scoter **3** : FELLOW 4a [Middle English *coote*]

coo·tie \'küt-ē\ *n* : BODY LOUSE [perhaps from Malay *kutu*]

¹cop \'käp\ *vt* **copped; cop·ping 1** *slang* : to get hold of : CATCH **2** *slang* : STEAL [perhaps from Dutch *kapen* "to steal"] — **cop a plea** : to plead guilty to a lesser charge in order to avoid standing trial for a more serious one

²cop *n* : POLICEMAN [short for ³*copper*]

co·pa·ce·tic *or* **co·pe·se·tic** \,kō-pə-'set-ik\ *adj* : very satisfactory [origin unknown]

co·pal \'kō-pəl, -,pal; kō-'pal\ *n* : a recent or fossil resin from various tropical trees used in making varnishes [Spanish, from Nahuatl *copalli* "resin"]

co·part·ner \'kō-'pärt-nər\ *n* : PARTNER — **co·part·ner·ship** \-,ship\ *n*

¹cope \'kōp\ *n* **1** : a long enveloping ecclesiastical vestment **2** : something (as the sky) resembling a cope (as in concealing or covering) [Old English -*cāp*, from Late Latin *cappa* "head covering, cloak"]

| ¹cope |

²cope *vt* : to cover or furnish with a cope or coping

³cope *vi* : to struggle or contend especially with some success ⟨a difficult situation to *cope* with⟩ [Middle English *copen* "to strike, fight with", from Middle French *couper* "to strike", from *coup* "blow, coup"]

co·pe·pod \'kō-pə-,päd\ *n* : any of a large group (Copepoda) of usually tiny freshwater and marine crustaceans [Greek *kōpē* "oar" + *pod-, pous* "foot"]

Co·per·ni·can \kō-'pər-ni-kən\ *adj* : of or relating to Copernicus or his theory that the earth rotates daily on its axis and the planets revolve in orbits round the sun

copi·er \'käp-ē-ər\ *n* : one that copies; *esp* : a machine for making copies of graphic matter

co·pi·lot \'kō-,pī-lət\ *n* : an assistant airplane pilot

cop·ing \'kō-ping\ *n* : the covering course of a wall usually with a sloping top [¹*cope*]

coping saw *n* : a handsaw with a very narrow blade held in a U-shaped frame for cutting curves in wood [from *cope* "to notch", probably from French *couper* "to cut"]

co·pi·ous \'kō-pē-əs\ *adj* **1 a** : full of thought, information, or matter **b** : profuse or exuberant in words, expression, or style **2** : very plentiful : ABUNDANT [Latin *copiosus*, from *copia* "abundance", from *co-* + *ops* "wealth"] SYN see PLENTIFUL — **co·pi·ous·ly** *adv* — **co·pi·ous·ness** *n*

co·pla·nar \'kō-'plā-nər\ *adj* : lying in the same plane ⟨*coplanar* lines⟩

co·pol·y·mer \'kō-'päl-ə-mər\ : a product of copolymerization

co·po·ly·mer·ize \,kō-pə-'lim-ə-,rīz, 'kō-'päl-ə-mə-\ *vb* : to polymerize (as two different monomers) together — **co·po·ly·mer·iza·tion** \,kō-pə-,lim-ə-rə-'zā-shən, ,kō-,päl-ə-mə-rə-\ *n*

cop-out \'käp-,aut\ *n* **1** : the act or an instance of copping out **2** : an excuse or means for copping out **3** : a person who cops out

cop out \käp-'aut, 'käp-\ *vi* : to withdraw from unwanted responsibility ⟨*cop out* on jury duty⟩

¹cop·per \'käp-ər\ *n* **1** : a reddish chiefly univalent and bivalent metallic element that is ductile and malleable and one of the best conductors of heat and electricity — see ELEMENT table **2** : a copper or bronze coin **3** : any of various small butterflies usually with copper-colored wings [Old English *coper*, from Late Latin *cuprum*, from Latin *aes Cyprium*, literally, "metal of Cyprus"] — **cop·pery** \'käp-rē, -ə-rē\ *adj*

²copper *vt* : to cover with copper

³copper *n* : POLICEMAN [¹*cop*]

cop·per·as \'käp-rəs, -ə-rəs\ *n* : a green sulfate of iron $FeSO_4 \cdot 7H_2O$ used in making inks and in dyeing [Middle French *coperose*, from Late Latin *cuprum* "copper" + Latin *rosa* "rose"]

cop·per·head \'käp-ər-,hed\ *n* **1** : a common largely coppery brown pit viper of the eastern United States **2** : a person in the northern states who sympathized with the South during the Civil War

cop·per·plate \,käp-ər-'plāt\ *n* : an engraved or etched copper printing plate; *also* : a print made from such a plate

cop·per·smith \'käp-ər-,smith\ *n* : a worker in copper

copper sulfate *n* : a crystalline compound $CuSO_4$ that is white when anhydrous but that is usually encountered in the blue hydrated form $CuSO_4 \cdot 5H_2O$ and that is used in solutions to destroy algae and fungi, in dyeing and printing, and in electric batteries

cop·pice \'käp-əs\ *n* **1** : a thicket, grove, or growth of small trees **2** : forest originating mainly from sprouts or root suckers [Middle French *copeiz*, from *couper* "to cut"]

co·pra \'kō-prə\ *n* : dried coconut meat yielding coconut oil [Portuguese, from Malayalam (a Dravidian language of India) *koppara*]

co·pro·ces·sor \,kō-'präs,es-ər, 'kō-, -'prōs-\ *n* : an extra processor in a computer that is designed to perform specialized tasks

cop·ro·lite \'käp-rə-,līt\ *n* : fossil excrement [derived from Greek *kopros* "dung"]

copse \'käps\ *n* : COPPICE 1 [by alteration]

Copt \'käpt\ *n* **1** : a member of a people descended from the ancient Egyptians **2** : a member of the ancient Christian church of Egypt [Arabic *qubṭ* "Copts", from Coptic *gyptios* "Egyptian", from Greek *aigyptios*] — **Coptic** \'käp-tik\ *adj*

cop·u·la \'käp-yə-lə\ *n* : a word or expression (as a form of the verb *to be*) that links a subject with its predicate [Latin, "bond"]

cop·u·late \'käp-yə-,lāt\ *vi* : to engage in sexual intercourse — **cop·u·la·tion** \,käp-yə-'lā-shən\ *n* — **cop·u·la·to·ry** \'käp-yə-lə-,tōr-ē, -,tòr-\ *adj*

¹cop·u·la·tive \'käp-yə-lət-iv, -,lāt-\ *adj* **1** : joining together coordinate words or word groups and indicating that their meanings are to be added ⟨*copulative* conjunctions⟩ **2** : being a copula ⟨a *copulative* verb⟩ — **cop·u·la·tive·ly** *adv*

²copulative *n* : a copulative word or expression

¹copy \'käp-ē\ *n, pl* **cop·ies 1** : an imitation, transcript, or reproduction of an original work **2** : one of the printed reproductions of an original text, engraving, or photograph **3** : text to be composed for printing [Middle French *copie*, from Medieval Latin *copia*, from Latin, "abundance"] SYN see DUPLICATE

²copy *vb* **cop·ied; copy·ing 1** : to make a copy : DUPLICATE **2** : to model oneself on : IMITATE

copy·book \-,buk\ *n* : a book containing copies especially of penmanship for learners to imitate

copy·boy \-,bòi\ *n* : one that carries copy and runs errands (as in a newspaper office)

copy·cat \-,kat\ *n* : a person who imitates the behavior or work of another

copy·desk \-,desk\ *n* : the desk at which newspaper copy is edited

copy·ist \'käp-ē-əst\ *n* **1** : a person who makes copies **2** : IMITATOR

copy·read·er \'käp-ē-,rēd-ər\ *n* **1** : one that edits and writes headlines for newspaper copy **2** : one that reads and corrects manuscript copy in a publishing house

¹copy·right \-,rīt\ *n* : the sole legal right to reproduce, publish, and sell the matter and form of a literary, musical, or artistic work — **copyright** *adj*

²copyright *vt* : to secure a copyright on

co·quet *or* **co·quette** \kō-'ket\ *vi* **co·quet·ted; co·quet·ting** : FLIRT 2a [French *coquet* "man who flirts", from *coq* "cock"]

co·que·try \'kō-kə-trē, kō-'ke-trē\ *n, pl* **-tries** : the conduct or art of a coquette : FLIRTATION

co·quette \kō-'ket\ *n* : FLIRT 2 — **co·quett·ish** \-'ket-ish\ *adj* — **co·quett·ish·ly** *adv* — **co·quett·ish·ness** *n*

co·qui·na \kō-ˈkē-nə\ *n* **1** : a small marine clam used for broth or chowder **2** : a soft whitish limestone formed of broken shells and corals used for building [Spanish]

cor·a·cle \ˈkȯr-ə-kəl, ˈkär-\ *n* : a boat made of horsehide or tarpaulin stretched over a wicker frame [Welsh *corwgl*]

cor·a·coid \ˈkȯr-ə-ˌkȯid, ˈkär-\ *adj* : of, relating to, or being a process or bone that in many vertebrates extends from the scapula to or toward the sternum [Greek *korax* "raven"] — **coracoid** *n*

cor·al \ˈkȯr-əl, ˈkär-\ *n* **1 a** : the stony or horny skeletal deposit produced by various polyps; *esp* : a richly red material used in jewelry **b** : a polyp or polyp colony together with its membranes and skeleton **2** : a deep pink [Middle French, from Latin *corallium,* from Greek *korallion*] — **coral** *adj*

¹cor·al·line \ˈkȯr-ə-ˌlīn, ˈkär-\ *adj* : of, relating to, or resembling coral or a coralline

²coralline *n* : any of various plants or animals (as some red algae and bryozoans) that resemble corals

coral reef *n* : a reef made up of corals, other organic deposits, and the solid limestone resulting from their fusion

coral snake *n* : any of several poisonous chiefly tropical New World snakes brilliantly banded in red, black, and yellow or white; *also* : any of several harmless snakes resembling the coral snakes

¹cor·bel \ˈkȯr-bəl\ *n* : a bracket-shaped architectural member that projects from a wall and supports a weight [Middle French, from *corp* "raven", from Latin *corvus*]

²corbel *vt* **-beled** *or* **-belled; -bel·ing** *or* **-bel·ling** : to furnish with or make into a corbel

¹cord \ˈkȯrd\ *n* **1** : a string or small rope consisting of several strands woven or twisted together **2** : a moral, spiritual, or emotional bond **3 a** : an anatomical structure (as a tendon or nerve) resembling a cord **b** : a small flexible insulated electrical cable with fittings for connecting an appliance (as a lamp) with a receptacle **4** : a unit of wood cut for fuel equal to a stack 4×4×8 feet or 128 cubic feet (about 3.6 cubic meters) **5 a** : a rib like a cord on a textile; *also* : a fabric with such ribs **b** *pl* : trousers made of this fabric [Old French *corde,* from Latin *chorda* "string", from Greek *chordē*]

²cord *vt* **1** : to furnish, bind, or connect with a cord **2** : to pile up (wood) in cords — **cord·er** *n*

cord·age \ˈkȯrd-ij\ *n* **1** : ropes or cords; *esp* : the ropes in the rigging of a ship **2** : the number of cords (as of wood) on a given area

cord·ed \ˈkȯrd-əd\ *adj* **1** : having or drawn into ridges or cords ⟨*corded* muscles⟩ **2** : bound or wound about with cords

¹cor·dial \ˈkȯr-jəl\ *adj* **1** : tending to revive, cheer, or invigorate **2** : HEARTFELT, HEARTY ⟨a *cordial* greeting⟩ [Medieval Latin *cordialis* "of the heart, hearty", from Latin *cord-, cor* "heart"] — **cor·di·al·i·ty** \ˌkȯr-jē-ˈal-ət-ē\ *n* — **cor·dial·ly** \ˈkȯrj-lē, -ə-lē\ *adv* — **cor·dial·ness** \ˈkȯr-jəl-nəs\ *n*

²cordial *n* **1** : a stimulating medicine or drink **2** : LIQUEUR

cor·dil·le·ra \ˌkȯrd-l-ˈyer-ə, -ˈer-; kȯr-ˈdil-ə-rə\ *n* : a system of mountain ranges often consisting of a number of more or less parallel chains [Spanish] — **cor·dil·le·ran** \-ˈyer-ən, -ˈer-ən; -ə-rən\ *adj*

cord·ite \ˈkȯr-ˌdīt\ *n* : a smokeless gunpowder composed of nitroglycerin, guncotton, and a stabilizing jelly

cor·do·ba \ˈkȯrd-ə-bə, -ə-və\ *n* **1** : the basic monetary unit of Nicaragua **2** : a note representing one cordoba [Spanish *córdoba,* from Francisco Fernández de *Córdoba,* died 1526, Spanish conquistador]

cor·don \ˈkȯrd-n, ˈkȯr-ˌdän\ *n* **1 a** : an ornamental cord used especially on costumes **b** : a cord or ribbon worn as a badge or decoration **2** : a line of persons or things around a person or place ⟨a *cordon* of police⟩ [French, from *corde* "cord"]

cor·do·van \ˈkȯrd-ə-vən\ *n* : a fine-grained colored leather [Spanish *Córdova* (now *Córdoba*), Spain] — **cordovan** *adj*

cor·du·roy \ˈkȯrd-ə-ˌrȯi\ *n, pl* **-roys 1 a** : a durable ribbed usually cotton fabric **b** *pl* : trousers of corduroy **2** : a road built of logs laid crosswise side by side [origin unknown] — **corduroy** *adj*

cord·wain·er \ˈkȯrd-ˌwā-nər\ *n* : SHOEMAKER [Middle English *cordwane* "cordovan leather"]

cord·wood \-ˌwu̇d\ *n* : wood cut for fuel and sold by the cord

¹core \ˈkōr, ˈkȯr\ *n* **1** : a central or most important part **2** : the usually inedible central part of some fruits (as a pineapple or apple) **3** : a part removed from the interior of a mass especially to find out the interior composition or a hidden condition ⟨took a *core* of rock⟩ **4 a** : a mass of iron used to concentrate and strengthen the magnetic field resulting from a current in a surrounding coil **b** : a tiny doughnut-shaped piece of magnetic material at one time commonly used in computer memories **c** : a computer memory made up of strings of cores **d** : the memory of a computer **5** : the central part of the earth having different properties from those of the surrounding parts; *also* : the central part of a heavenly body **6** : a system of studies that brings together material from subjects that are usually taught separately **7** : the place in a nuclear reactor where fission takes place [Middle English]

²core *vt* : to remove the core from — **cor·er** *n*

co·re·op·sis \ˌkōr-ē-ˈäsəs, ˌkȯr-\ *n* : any of a genus of herbs related to the daisies and widely grown for their showy flower heads [Greek *horis* "bedbug" + *opsis* "appearance"]

co·re·spon·dent \ˌkō-ri-ˈspän-dənt\ *n* : a person named as guilty of adultery with the defendant in a divorce suit

co·ri·an·der \ˈkōr-ē-ˌan-dər, ˈkȯr-\ *n* : an Old World herb of the carrot family with aromatic fruits; *also* : its dried ripened fruit used as a flavoring [Old French *coriandre,* from Latin *coriandrum,* from Greek *koriandron*]

Co·rin·thi·an \kə-ˈrin-thē-ən\ *adj* : of or relating to the lightest and most ornate of the three Greek types of architecture characterized especially by its bell‗shaped capital enveloped with acanthuses [*Corinth,* Greece]

Cor·in·thi·ans \-ənz\ *n* — see BIBLE table

Co·ri·o·lis force \ˌkōr-ē-ˌō-ləs-, ˌkȯr-\ *n* : an apparent force that as a result of the earth's rotation deflects moving objects (as projectiles) or air currents to the right in the northern hemisphere and to the left in the southern hemisphere [Gaspard G. *Coriolis,* died 1843, French civil engineer]

co·ri·um \ˈkōr-ē-əm, ˈkȯr-\ *n, pl* **-ria** \-ē-ə\ : DERMIS [Latin, "leather"]

¹cork \ˈkȯrk\ *n* **1 a** : the elastic tough outer tissue of a European oak used especially for stoppers and insulation **b** : the tissue of a woody plant making up most of the bark and arising from an inner cambium — called also *phellem* **2** : a usually cork stopper for a bottle or jug [Middle English, probably from Arabic *qurq,* from Latin *cortex* "bark, cork"]

²cork *vt* **1** : to furnish, fit, or seal with a cork **2** : to blacken with burnt cork

cork cambium *n* : PHELLOGEN

cork·er \ˈkȯr-kər\ *n* : an outstanding person or thing

cork·ing \ˈkȯr-king\ *adj* : extremely fine

cork oak *n* : an oak of southern Europe and northern Africa that is the source of the cork of commerce

¹cork·screw \ˈkȯrk-ˌskrü\ *n* : a pointed spiral piece of metal with a handle that is used to draw corks from bottles

\ə\	abut	\ng\	sing
\ər\	further	\ō\	bone
\a\	mat	\ȯ\	saw
\ā\	take	\ȯi\	coin
\ä\	cot, cart	\th\	thin
\au̇\	out	\t̲h̲\	this
\ch\	chin	\ü\	food
\e\	pet	\u̇\	foot
\ē\	easy	\y\	yet
\g\	go	\yü\	few
\i\	tip	\yu̇\	cure
\ī\	life	\zh\	vision
\j\	job		

cormorant 1

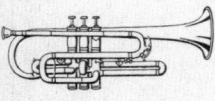

cornet 1

²**corkscrew** *adj* : resembling a corkscrew : SPIRAL

corky \'kȯr-kē\ *adj* **cork·i·er; -est** : resembling cork

corm \'kȯrm\ *n* : a thick fleshy underground stem (as of the crocus or gladiolus) that resembles a bulb and bears membranous or scaly leaves and buds — compare BULB, TUBER [Greek *kormos* "tree trunk"]

cor·mo·rant \'kȯrm-rənt, -ə-rənt\ *n* **1** : any of various dark-colored web-footed seabirds with a long neck, a wedge-shaped tail, a hooked bill, and a patch of bare often brightly colored skin under the mouth **2** : a greedy or gluttonous person [Middle French, from Old French *cormareng*, from *corp* "raven" + *marenc* "of the sea", from Latin *marinus*]

¹**corn** \'kȯrn\ *n* **1 a** : the seeds of a cereal grass and especially of the important cereal crop of a particular region (as in Britain wheat, in Scotland and Ireland oats, and in the New World and Australia Indian corn) **b** : sweet corn served as a vegetable while the kernels are still soft and milky **2** : a plant that produces corn **3** : corny actions or speech [Old English]

²**corn** *vb* : to preserve by packing with salt or by soaking in brine ⟨*corned* beef⟩

³**corn** *n* : a local hardening and thickening of skin (as on a toe) [Middle French *corne* "horn, corner", from Latin *cornu* "horn, point"]

corn borer *n* : any of several insects that bore in corn; *esp* : a moth whose larva is a major pest especially in the stems and crowns of Indian corn, dahlias, and potatoes

corn bread *n* : bread made with cornmeal

corn chip *n* : a piece of a dry crisp snack food prepared from a seasoned cornmeal batter

corn·cob \'kȯrn-ˌkäb\ *n* **1** : the woody axis on which the kernels of Indian corn are arranged **2** : a tobacco pipe with a bowl made from a hollowed out piece of corncob

corn cockle *n* : an annual hairy weed with purplish red flowers found in grainfields

corn·crib \'kȯrn-ˌkrib\ *n* : a crib for storing ears of Indian corn

corn dog *n* : a frankfurter dipped in cornmeal batter, fried, and served on a stick

cor·nea \'kȯr-nē-ə\ *n* : the transparent part of the coat of the eyeball that covers the iris and pupil and admits light to the interior [Medieval Latin, from Latin *corneus* "horny", from *cornu* "horn"] — **cor·ne·al** \-nē-əl\ *adj*

corn earworm *n* : a large striped yellow-headed moth larva especially destructive to the ear of Indian corn and to cotton bolls; *also* : any other stage of this insect

cor·nel \'kȯrn-l\ *n* : any of several shrubs or trees of the dogwood family; *esp* : DOGWOOD [derived from Latin *cornus*, a kind of dogwood]

¹**cor·ner** \'kȯr-nər, 'kȯ-nər\ *n* **1 a** : the point or place where converging lines, edges, or sides meet : ANGLE **b** : the place of intersection of two streets or roads **c** : a piece designed to form, mark, or protect a corner **2** : a usually remote area, region, or part **3** : a position from which escape or retreat is difficult or impossible **4** : control or ownership of enough of the available supply of something to control its price [Old French *cornere*, from *corne* "horn, corner", from Latin *cornu* "horn"] — **cor·nered** \-nərd\ *adj*

²**corner** *vb* **1** : to drive into a corner **2** : to get a corner on ⟨*corner* the wheat market⟩ **3** : to turn a corner ⟨a car that *corners* well⟩

³**corner** *adj* **1** : situated at a corner **2** : used or fitted for use in or on a corner

cor·ner·back \-ˌbak\ *n* : a defensive halfback in football who defends the flank

corner kick *n* : a free kick in soccer from the corner of the field awarded to the attacking team after the defending team drives the ball out of bounds over the goal line

cor·ner·stone \-ˌstōn\ *n* **1** : a stone forming part of a corner in a wall; *esp* : such a stone laid at the formal beginning of the erection of a building **2** : something of basic importance ⟨a *cornerstone* of foreign policy⟩

cor·net \kȯr-'net\ *n* **1** : a brass instrument resembling the trumpet but having a shorter tube and a more mellow tone **2** : something (as a piece of paper twisted for use as a container) shaped like a cone [Middle French, from *corn* "horn", from Latin *cornu*]

cor·net·ist *or* **cor·net·tist** \kȯr-'net-əst\ *n* : one that plays the cornet

corn-flow·er \'kȯrn-ˌflaù-ər, -ˌflaúr\ *n* **1** : CORN COCKLE **2** : BACHELOR'S BUTTON

cor·nice \'kȯr-nəs\ *n* **1** : the ornamental projecting piece that forms the top edge of the front of a building or of a pillar **2** : an ornamental molding placed where the walls meet the ceiling of a room **3** : a decorative band of metal or wood to conceal curtain fixtures [Middle French, from Italian]

¹**Cor·nish** \'kȯr-nish\ *adj* : of, relating to, or characteristic of Cornwall, Cornishmen, or Cornish

²**Cornish** *n* **1** : a Celtic language of Cornwall extinct since the late 18th century **2** : any of an English breed of domestic fowls much used in crossbreeding for meat production

Cor·nish·man \-mən\ *n* : a native or inhabitant of Cornwall, England

corn·meal \'kȯrn-ˌmēl, -ˌmēl\ *n* : meal ground from Indian corn

corn oil *n* : a yellow fatty oil obtained from the germ of Indian corn kernels and used chiefly in salad oil, in soft soap, and in margarine

corn pone *n, South & Midland* : CORN BREAD; *esp* : fried corn bread

corn smut *n* : a smut attacking Indian corn; *esp* : a common smut caused by a fungus and characterized by grayish white swellings that rupture to expose a black mass of spores

corn snow *n* : granular snow formed by alternate thawing and freezing

corn·stalk \'kȯrn-ˌstȯk\ *n* : a stalk of Indian corn

corn·starch \-ˌstärch\ *n* : a fine starch made from Indian corn and used in cooking as a thickening agent

corn sugar *n* : sugar made by hydrolysis of cornstarch

corn syrup *n* : a syrup made from cornstarch and used in baked goods and candy

cor·nu·co·pia \ˌkȯr-nyə-'kō-pē-ə, -nə-\ *n* **1** : a horn-shaped container overflowing with fruits and flowers used as a symbol of abundance **2** : a great abundance **3** : a container shaped like a horn or a cone [Late Latin, from Latin *cornu copiae* "horn of plenty"]

corn whiskey *n* : whiskey distilled from a mash made up of not less than 80 percent Indian corn

corny \'kȯr-nē\ *adj* **corn·i·er; -est** : tastelessly old-fashioned or countrified : tiresomely simple or sentimental ⟨a play full of *corny* jokes⟩

co·rol·la \kə-'räl-ə\ *n* : the inner floral envelope of a flower consisting of petals and enclosing the stamens and pistil [Latin, "small crown, garland", from *corona* "crown"] — **co·rol·late** \-'räl-ət\ *adj*

cor·ol·lary \'kȯr-ə-ˌler-ē, 'kär-\ *n, pl* **-lar·ies** **1** : something that follows directly from something that has been proved **2** : something that naturally follows : RESULT [Late Latin *corollarium*, from Latin, "money paid for a garland, gratuity", from *corolla* "crown, garland"] — **corollary** *adj*

co·ro·na \kə-'rō-nə\ *n* **1** : a usually colored circle often seen around and close to a luminous body (as the sun or moon) **2** : the outermost part of the atmosphere of the sun appearing as a gray halo around the moon's black disk during a total eclipse of the sun **3** : the upper portion of a body part (as a tooth or the skull) **4** : an appendage on the inner side of the corolla in some flowers (as the daffodil) **5** : a discharge of electricity seen as a faint glow adjacent to the surface of an electrical conductor at high voltage [Latin, "garland, crown"]

Co·ro·na Bo·re·al·is \-ˌbōr-ē-'al-əs, -ˌbȯr-\ *n* : a northern constellation between Hercules and Boötes [Latin, literally, "northern crown"]

cor·o·nach \'kȯr-ə-nək, 'kär-\ *n* : DIRGE [Scottish Gaelic *corranach* and Irish Gaelic *corānach*]

¹cor·o·nal \'kȯr-ən-l, 'kär-\ *n* : a circlet for the head

²cor·o·nal \'kȯr-ən-l, 'kär-; kə-'rōn-\ *adj* : of or relating to a corona or crown

¹cor·o·nary \'kȯr-ə-ˌner-ē, 'kär-\ *adj* : of, relating to, or being the arteries or veins that supply blood to the heart; *also* : of or relating to the heart

²coronary *n, pl* **-nar·ies** **1** : a coronary artery or vein **2** : CORONARY THROMBOSIS

coronary artery *n* : either of the two arteries, right and left, that arise from the aorta and supply the tissues of the heart

coronary occlusion *n* : the partial or complete blocking (as by a thrombus, by spasm, or by sclerosis) of a coronary artery

coronary sclerosis *n* : hardening of the coronary arteries of the heart

coronary thrombosis *n* : the blocking of an artery of the heart by a thrombus

coronary vein *n* : any of several veins that drain the tissues of the heart

cor·o·na·tion \ˌkȯr-ə-'nā-shən, ˌkär-\ *n* : the act or ceremony of crowning a sovereign or his consort

cor·o·ner \'kȯr-ə-nər, 'kär-\ *n* : a public officer whose chief duty is to discover the causes of any death possibly not due to natural causes [Middle English, "officer of the crown", from Old French *corone* "crown", from Latin *corona*]

cor·o·net \ˌkȯr-ə-'net, ˌkär-\ *n* **1** : a small crown worn by a person of noble but not of royal rank **2** : an ornamental wreath or band worn around the head

¹cor·po·ral \'kȯr-pə-rəl, -prəl\ *n* : a linen cloth on which the eucharistic elements are placed at mass [Middle French, derived from Latin *corporalis* "of the body"; from the doctrine that the bread of the Eucharist becomes or represents the body of Christ]

²corporal *adj* : of or relating to the body ⟨whipping and other *corporal* punishments⟩ [Middle French, from Latin *corporalis*, from *corpor-, corpus* "body"] — **cor·po·ral·ly** \-pə-rə-lē, -prə-lē\ *adv*

³corporal *n* : an enlisted rank in the Army above private first class and below sergeant and in the Marine Corps above lance corporal and below sergeant [Middle French, alteration of *caporal,* from Italian *caporale,* from *capo* "head", from Latin *caput*]

cor·po·rate \'kȯr-pə-rət, -prət\ *adj* **1 a** : INCORPORATED **b** : of or relating to a corporation **2** : of or relating to a whole composed of individuals : COLLECTIVE [Latin *corporare* "to form into a body", from *corpus* "body"] — **cor·po·rate·ly** *adv*

cor·po·ra·tion \ˌkȯr-pə-'rā-shən\ *n* **1** : the municipal authorities of a town or city **2** : a body authorized by law to carry on an activity (as a business enterprise) with the rights and duties of a single person although constituted by one or more persons and having an identity that survives its incorporators

cor·po·re·al \kȯr-'pōr-ē-əl, -'pȯr-\ *adj* : having, consisting of, or relating to a physical material body: as **a** : not spiritual **b** : not immaterial or intangible : SUBSTANTIAL **c** : of or relating to a human body : BODILY SYN see MATERIAL — **cor·po·re·al·i·ty** \-ˌpōr-ē-'al-ət-ē, -ˌpȯr-\ *n* — **cor·po·re·al·ly** \-'pōr-ē-ə-lē, -'pȯr-\ *adv* — **cor·po·re·al·ness** *n*

corps \'kōr, 'kȯr\ *n, pl* **corps** \'kōrz, 'kȯrz\ **1 a** : an organized branch of a military establishment ⟨Marine *Corps*⟩ **b** : a tactical unit consisting of two or more divisions and supporting forces **2** : a group of persons associated together or acting under common direction

⟨diplomatic *corps*⟩ [French, from Latin *corpus* "body"]

corps de bal·let \ˌkōrd-ə-ba-'lā, ˌkȯrd-\ *n, pl* **corps de ballet** *same*\ : the chorus of a ballet company [French]

corpse \'kȯrps\ *n* : a dead body [Middle French *corps* "body", from Latin *corpus*]

corps·man \'kōr-mən, 'kȯr-, 'kōrz-, 'kȯrz-\ *n* : an enlisted man in the Navy trained to give first aid

cor·pu·lent \'kȯr-pyə-lənt\ *adj* : having a large bulky body : OBESE [Latin *corpulentus,* from *corpus* "body"] — **cor·pu·lence** \-ləns\ *or* **cor·pu·lency** \-lən-sē\ *n* — **cor·pu·lent·ly** *adv*

cor·pus \'kȯr-pəs\ *n, pl* **cor·po·ra** \-pə-rə, -prə\ **1** : the main or central part of a bodily structure ⟨the *corpus* of the jaw⟩ **2** : the main body or principal substance (as of a field of study) [Latin, "body"]

Cor·pus Chris·ti \ˌkȯr-pəs-'kris-tē\ *n* : the Thursday after Trinity Sunday observed as a Roman Catholic festival in honor of the Eucharist [Medieval Latin, literally, "body of Christ"]

cor·pus·cle \'kȯr-ˌpəs-əl\ *n* **1** : a minute particle **2** : a living cell; *esp* : one (as a blood or cartilage cell) not aggregated into continuous tissues [Latin *corpusculum* "small body", from *corpus* "body"] — **cor·pus·cu·lar** \kȯr-'pəs-kyə-lər\ *adj*

cor·pus de·lic·ti \ˌkȯr-pəs-di-'lik-ˌtī, -ˌtē\ *n, pl* **cor·po·ra delicti** \ˌkȯr-pə-rə-, -prə-\ **1** : the substantial fact necessary to prove the commission of a crime **2** : the body of a murder victim [New Latin, literally, "body of the crime"]

cor·pus lu·te·um \ˌkȯr-pəs-'lüt-ē-əm\ *n, pl* **cor·po·ra lu·tea** \ˌkȯr-pə-rə-'lüt-ē-ə, -prə-\ : a yellowish mass of endocrine tissue formed in an ovarian follicle after the egg is shed [New Latin, literally, "yellowish body"]

¹cor·ral \kə-'ral\ *n* **1** : a pen or enclosure for confining or capturing livestock **2** : an enclosure made with wagons for defense of an encampment [Spanish, derived from Latin *currus* "cart", from *currere* "to run"]

²corral *vt* **cor·ralled; cor·ral·ling** **1** : to confine in or as if in a corral **2** : to arrange (as wagons) so as to form a corral **3** : to round up : GATHER

¹cor·rect \kə-'rekt\ *vt* **1 a** : to make or set right : AMEND **b** : COUNTERACT, NEUTRALIZE **c** : to alter or adjust so as to bring to some standard or required condition **2 a** : REBUKE, PUNISH **b** : to point out the errors or faults of ⟨*correct* a student's composition⟩ [Latin *correctus,* past participle of *corrigere* "to correct", from *com-* + *regere* "to lead straight"] — **cor·rect·able** \-'rek-tə-bəl\ *adj* — **cor·rec·tor** \-'rek-tər\ *n* □ SYN CORRECT, RECTIFY, AMEND, EMEND mean to make right what is wrong. CORRECT implies taking action to remove errors, faults, or deviations; RECTIFY suggests bringing into a straight line or one direction; AMEND implies improving or restoring by making slight changes; EMEND especially applies to the correction of a text.

²correct *adj* **1** : conforming to an approved or conventional standard **2** : agreeing with fact, logic, or known truth : ACCURATE — **cor·rect·ly** *adv* — **cor·rect·ness** \-'rek-nəs, -'rekt-\ *n* □ SYN CORRECT, ACCURATE, EXACT, PRECISE mean conforming to fact, truth, or standard. CORRECT implies little more than freedom from fault or error ⟨*correct* dress for the occasion⟩ ACCURATE implies greater fidelity to truth or fact attained by exercise of care ⟨*accurate* description of a situation⟩ EXACT stresses a very strict agreement with fact or truth ⟨a suit tailored to *exact* measurements⟩ PRECISE adds to EXACT an emphasis on sharpness of definition or delimitation ⟨*precise* terms of a contract⟩

cor·rec·tion \kə-'rek-shən\ *n* **1** : the action or an instance of correcting **2** : a change that corrects something **3** : punishment or discipline intended to correct faults of character or behavior **4** : the treatment of offenders through a program involving penal custody,

\ə\ abut		\ng\ sing	
\ər\ further		\ō\ bone	
\a\ mat		\ȯ\ saw	
\ā\ take		\ȯi\ coin	
\ä\ cot, cart		\th\ thin	
\au̇\ out		\th\ this	
\ch\ chin		\ü\ food	
\e\ pet		\u̇\ foot	
\ē\ easy		\y\ yet	
\g\ go		\yü\ few	
\i\ tip		\yu̇\ cure	
\ī\ life		\zh\ vision	
\j\ job			

parole, and probation — **cor·rec·tion·al** \-shnəl, -shən-l\ *adj*

cor·rec·tive \kə-'rek-tiv\ *adj* : serving to correct : having the power of making right, normal, or regular ⟨*corrective* exercises⟩ — **corrective** *n* — **cor·rec·tive·ly** *adv* — **cor·rec·tive·ness** *n*

cor·re·late \'kòr-ə-,lāt, 'kär-\ *vb* 1 : to have reciprocal or mutual relations 2 : to establish a mutual or reciprocal relation of 3 : to relate so that to each member of one set or series a corresponding member of another is assigned

cor·re·la·tion \,kòr-ə-'lā-shən, ,kär-\ *n* 1 : the act or process of correlating 2 : the state of being correlated; *esp* : a mutual relation existing between things ⟨the apparent *correlation* between the degree of poverty in a society and the crime rate⟩ [Medieval Latin *correlatio,* from Latin *com-* + *relatio* "relation"] — **cor·re·la·tion·al** \-shnəl, -shən-l\ *adj*

¹**cor·rel·a·tive** \kə-'rel-ət-iv\ *adj* 1 : mutually related 2 : having a mutual grammatical relation and regularly used together ⟨*either* and *or* are *correlative* conjunctions⟩ — **cor·rel·a·tive·ly** *adv*

²**correlative** *n* : either of two correlative things

cor·re·spond \,kòr-ə-'spänd, ,kär-\ *vi* 1 **a** : to be in conformity or agreement : **SUIT** **b** : to compare closely : **MATCH** **c** : to be equivalent or parallel **d** : to be in correspondence and especially in a one-to-one correspondence ⟨the real numbers *correspond* to points on the number line⟩ 2 : to communicate with a person by exchange of letters [Medieval Latin *correspondēre,* from Latin *com-* + *respondēre* "to respond"]

cor·re·spon·dence \-'spän-dəns\ *n* 1 **a** : the agreement of things with one another **b** : a particular similarity **c** : a relation between sets in which each member of one set is associated with one or more members of the other ⟨a one-to-one *correspondence*⟩ 2 : communication by letters; *also* : the letters exchanged

correspondence school *n* : a school that teaches nonresident students by mailing them lessons and exercises which upon completion are returned to the school for grading

¹**cor·re·spon·dent** \,kòr-ə-'spän-dənt, ,kär-\ *adj* 1 : **SIMILAR** 1 2 : being in agreement : **FITTING**

²**correspondent** *n* 1 : something that corresponds or conforms to something else 2 **a** : one who communicates with another by letter **b** : one who has regular commercial relations with another **c** : one who contributes news or comment to a newspaper often from a distant place

corresponding *adj* : having the same relationship (as kind, degree, position, or function) to the same or like wholes (as a geometric figure) ⟨*corresponding* parts of similar triangles⟩

cor·re·spond·ing·ly \-'spän-ding-lē\ *adv* : in a corresponding manner : in such a way as to correspond

cor·ri·da \kò-'rē-thə\ *n* : **BULLFIGHT** [Spanish, literally, "act of running"]

cor·ri·dor \'kòr-əd-ər, 'kär-, -ə-,dòr\ *n* 1 : a passageway into which compartments or rooms open (as in a hotel or school) 2 : a narrow strip of land especially through foreign-held territory 3 : an air route (as over a foreign country) to which aircraft are restricted [Middle French, from Italian *corridore,* from *correre* "to run", from Latin *currere*]

cor·ri·gen·dum \,kòr-ə-'jen-dəm, ,kär-\ *n, pl* **-da** \-də\ : an error in a printed work discovered after printing and shown with its correction on a separate sheet [Latin, "thing to be corrected", from *corrigere* "to correct"]

cor·ri·gi·ble \'kòr-ə-jə-bəl, 'kär-\ *adj* : capable of being set right [Middle French, derived from Latin *corrigere* "to correct"] — **cor·ri·gi·bil·i·ty** \,kòr-ə-jə-'bil-ət-ē, ,kär-\ *n* — **cor·ri·gi·bly** \'kòr-ə-jə-blē, 'kär-\ *adv*

cor·rob·o·rate \kə-'räb-ə-,rāt\ *vt* : to support with evidence or authority : make more certain [Latin *corroborare* "to strengthen", from *com-* + *robur* "strength"] **SYN** see **CONFIRM** — **cor·rob·o·ra·tor** \-,rāt-ər\ *n*

cor·rob·o·ra·tion \kə-,räb-ə-'rā-shən\ *n* 1 : the act of corroborating 2 : something that corroborates

cor·rob·o·ra·tive \kə-'räb-ə-,rāt-iv, -'räb-rət-, -ə-rət-\ *adj* : serving or tending to corroborate : **CONFIRMING** ⟨*corroborative* evidence⟩ — **cor·rob·o·ra·tive·ly** *adv*

cor·rob·o·ra·to·ry \kə-'räb-rə-,tōr-ē, -ə-rə-, -,tòr-\ *adj* : **CORROBORATIVE**

cor·rode \kə-'rōd\ *vb* : to destroy or be destroyed gradually as if by gnawing ⟨lungs *corroded* by disease⟩; *esp* : to wear away gradually usually by chemical action [Latin *corrodere* "to gnaw to pieces", from *com-* + *rodere* "to gnaw"] — **cor·rod·ible** \-'rōd-ə-bəl\ *adj*

cor·ro·sion \kə-'rō-zhən\ *n* : the action, process, or effect of corroding [Late Latin *corrosio* "act of gnawing", from Latin *corrodere* "to gnaw"]

¹**cor·ro·sive** \-'rō-siv, -ziv\ *adj* : tending or having the power to corrode ⟨*corrosive* acids⟩ — **cor·ro·sive·ly** *adv* — **cor·ro·sive·ness** *n*

²**corrosive** *n* : something corrosive

corrosive sublimate *n* : **MERCURIC CHLORIDE**

cor·ru·gate \'kòr-ə-,gāt, 'kär-\ *vb* : to form or shape into parallel wrinkles or folds or ridges and grooves ⟨*corrugated* paper⟩ [Latin *corrugare,* from *com-* + *ruga* "wrinkle"]

cor·ru·ga·tion \,kòr-ə-'gā-shən, ,kär-\ *n* 1 : the act of corrugating : the state of being corrugated 2 : a ridge or groove of a corrugated surface

¹**cor·rupt** \kə-'rəpt\ *vb* 1 **a** : to change from good to bad in morals, manners, or actions **b** : to influence a public official improperly : **BRIBE** 2 : **TAINT** 2, **ROT** 3 : to alter from an original or correct form or version ⟨*corrupt* a text⟩ 4 : to become debased [Latin *corruptus,* past participle of *corrumpere* "to corrupt", from *com-* + *rumpere* "to break"] **SYN** see **DEBASE** — **cor·rupt·er** *or* **cor·rup·tor** \-'rəp-tər\ *n*

²**corrupt** *adj* 1 : morally debased : **DEPRAVED** 2 : characterized by improper conduct (as the selling of political favors) ⟨a *corrupt* administration⟩ — **cor·rupt·ly** *adv* — **cor·rupt·ness** \-'rəpt-nəs, -'rəp-\ *n*

cor·rupt·ible \kə-'rəp-tə-bəl\ *adj* : capable of being corrupted — **cor·rupt·ibil·i·ty** \-,rəp-tə-'bil-ət-ē\ *n*

cor·rup·tion \kə-'rəp-shən\ *n* 1 **a** : physical decay or rotting **b** : moral debasement : **DEPRAVITY** **c** : inducement to do wrong by unlawful or improper means (as bribery) **d** : a departure from what is pure or correct 2 *archaic* : an agency or influence that corrupts

cor·rup·tive \kə-'rəp-tiv\ *adj* : producing corruption

cor·sage \kòr-'säzh, -'säj, 'kòr-,\ *n* 1 : the waist or bodice of a woman's dress 2 : an arrangement of flowers to be worn by a woman [French, "bust, bodice", from Old French, "bust", from *cors* "body", from Latin *corpus*]

cor·sair \'kòr-,saər, -,seər\ *n* : **PIRATE**; *esp* : a privateer of the Barbary coast [Middle French *corsaire,* derived from Medieval Latin *cursarius,* from Latin *cursus* "course"]

corse \'kòrs\ *n, archaic* : **CORPSE** [Old French *cors* "body"]

corse·let *n* 1 *or* **cors·let** \'kòr-slət\ : the body armor worn by a knight especially on the upper part of the body 2 \,kòr-sə-'let\ : a woman's undergarment somewhat like a corset [Middle French, from *cors* "body, bodice"]

¹**cor·set** \'kòr-sət\ *n* : a tight-fitting stiffened undergarment worn to support or give shape to waist and hips [Old French, a kind of jacket, from *cors* "body"]

²**corset** *vt* : to dress in or fit with a corset

cor·tege *also* **cor·tège** \kòr-'tezh, 'kòr-,\ *n* 1 : a train of attendants : **RETINUE** 2 : **PROCESSION**; *esp* : a funeral procession [French *cortège,* from Italian *corteggio,* from *corte* "court", from Latin *cohors* "throng"]

cor·tes \'kȯr-ˌtez, -ˌtes\ *n, pl* **cor·tes** \-ˌtez\ : a Spanish parliament [Spanish, plural of *corte* "court", from Latin *cohors* "throng"]

cor·tex \'kȯr-ˌteks\ *n, pl* **cor·ti·ces** \'kȯrt-ə-ˌsēz\ *or* **cor·tex·es** : an outer or surrounding layer of an organism or one of its parts ⟨the *cortex* of the kidney⟩: as **a** : the outer layer of gray matter of the brain **b** : the layer of tissue outside the vascular tissue and inside the corky or epidermal tissues of a vascular plant; *also* : all tissues external to the xylem [Latin *cortic-, cortex* "bark"] — **cor·ti·cal** \'kȯrt-i-kəl\ *adj* — **cor·ti·cal·ly** \-i-kə-lē, -klē\ *adv*

cor·ti·co·tro·pin \ˌkȯrt-i-kō-'trō-pən\ *n* : ACTH; *also* : a preparation of ACTH that is used especially in the treatment of rheumatoid arthritis and rheumatic fever

cor·tin \'kȯrt-n\ *n* : a hormone mixture from the adrenal cortex

cor·ti·sol \'kȯrt-ə-ˌsȯl, -ˌzȯl, -ˌsōl, -ˌzōl\ *n* : a hormone of the adrenal cortex that is derived from cortisone and has a similar use — called also *hydrocortisone*

cor·ti·sone \-ˌsōn, -ˌzōn\ *n* : a steroid hormone of the adrenal cortex used especially in the treatment of rheumatoid arthritis

co·run·dum \kə-'rən-dəm\ *n* : a very hard mineral Al_2O_3 that consists of aluminum oxide occurring in massive form and as variously colored crystals including the ruby and sapphire and that is used as an abrasive [Tamil *kuruntam*, from Sanskrit *kuruvinda* "ruby"]

cor·us·cate \'kȯr-ə-ˌskāt, 'kär-\ *vi* : to give off flashes of light : SPARKLE [Latin *coruscare*] — **cor·us·ca·tion** \ˌkȯr-ə-'skā-shən, ˌkär-\ *n*

cor·vée \'kȯr-ˌvā, kȯr-'\ *n* : unpaid labor on public works (as roads) required usually in place of taxes [Middle French *corvee*, from Medieval Latin *corrogata*, from Latin *corrogare* "to collect, requisition", from *com-* + *rogare* "to ask"]

cor·vette \kȯr-'vet\ *n* **1** : a warship of the old sailing navies smaller than a frigate **2** : a highly maneuverable armed escort ship smaller than a destroyer [French]

Cor·vus \'kȯr-vəs\ *n* : a small constellation adjoining Virgo on the south [Latin, literally, "raven"]

Cor·y·bant \'kȯr-ə-ˌbant, 'kär-\ *n, pl* **Cor·y·bants** *or* **Cor·y·ban·tes** \ˌkȯr-ə-'ban-ˌtēz, ˌkär-\ : one of the attendants or priests of the ancient goddess Cybele noted for their orgiastic rites [French *Corybante*, from Latin *Corybas*, from Greek *Korybas*] — **cor·y·ban·tic** \ˌkȯr-ə-'bant-ik, ˌkär-\ *adj*

cor·ymb \'kȯr-im, 'kär-\ *n* : a flat-topped indeterminate inflorescence in which the flower stalks arise at different levels on the main axis and reach about the same height [French *corymbe*, from Latin *corymbus* "cluster of fruit or flowers", from Greek *korymbos*]

co·se·cant \'kō-'sē-ˌkant, kō-, -kənt\ *n* : the trigonometric function that for an acute angle is the ratio between the hypotenuse of a right triangle of which the angle is considered part and the side opposite the angle — abbreviation *csc*

co·sig·na·to·ry \'kō-'sig-nə-ˌtōr-ē, -ˌtȯr-\ *n, pl* **-ries** : a joint signer

cosily, cosiness *variant of* COZILY, COZINESS

co·sine \'kō-ˌsīn\ *n* : the trigonometric function that for an acute angle is the ratio between the side adjacent to the angle when it is considered part of a right triangle and the hypotenuse — abbreviation *cos*

¹cos·met·ic \käz-'met-ik\ *n* : a cosmetic preparation for external use

²cosmetic *adj* **1** : intended to beautify the hair or complexion **2** : correcting defects especially of the face [Greek *kosmein* "to arrange, adorn", from *kosmos* "order"]

cos·me·tol·o·gist \ˌkäz-mə-'täl-ə-jəst\ *n* : a person who gives beauty treatments (as to skin and hair) — **cos·me·tol·o·gy** \-jē\ *n*

cos·mic \'käz-mik\ *adj* **1** : of or relating to the cosmos ⟨*cosmic* theories⟩ **2** : extremely vast : GRAND ⟨a topic of *cosmic* proportions⟩ — **cos·mi·cal·ly** \-mi-kə-lē, -klē\ *adv*

cosmic dust *n* : very fine particles of solid matter in any part of the universe and especially in interstellar space

cosmic ray *n* : a stream of atomic nuclei of extremely penetrating character that enter the earth's atmosphere from outer space at speeds approaching that of light

cosmic string *n* : any of a class of hypothetical astronomical objects of very high mass that are very thin but are millions of light years long

cos·mog·o·ny \käz-'mäg-ə-nē\ *n, pl* **-nies** **1** : the creation or origination of the world or universe **2** : a theory of the origin of the universe [Greek *kosmogonia*, from *kosmos* "order, universe" + *gonos* "offspring"] — **cos·mog·o·nist** \-nəst\ *n*

cos·mog·ra·phy \käz-'mäg-rə-fē\ *n, pl* **-phies** **1** : a general description of the world or of the universe **2** : the science that deals with the constitution of the whole order of nature — **cos·mog·ra·pher** \-fər\ *n* — **cos·mo·graph·ic** \ˌkäz-mə-'graf-ik\ *adj*

cos·mol·o·gy \käz-'mäl-ə-jē\ *n, pl* **-gies** : a study that deals with the origin, structure, and space-time relationships of the universe — **cos·mo·log·i·cal** \ˌkäz-mə-'läj-i-kəl\ *adj* — **cos·mol·o·gist** \käz-'mäl-ə-jəst\ *n*

cos·mo·naut \'käz-mə-ˌnȯt, -ˌnät\ *n* : a Soviet astronaut [Russian *kosmonavt*, from Greek *kosmos* "universe" + Russian *-navt* (as in *aeronavt* "aeronaut")]

cos·mo·pol·i·tan \ˌkäz-mə-'päl-ət-n\ *adj* **1** : having a worldwide scope or outlook : not limited or parochial ⟨*cosmopolitan* world travelers⟩ **2** : composed of persons or elements from many parts of the world ⟨a *cosmopolitan* city⟩ **3** : found in most parts of the world and under varied ecological conditions ⟨a *cosmopolitan* herb⟩ [derived from Greek *kosmos* "world, cosmos" + *politēs* "citizen", from *polis* "city, state"] — **cosmopolitan** *n* — **cos·mo·pol·i·tan·ism** \-n-ˌiz-əm\ *n*

cos·mop·o·lite \käz-'mäp-ə-ˌlīt\ *n* : a cosmopolitan person or organism

cos·mos \'käz-məs, *1 & 2 also* -ˌmōs, -ˌmäs\ *n* **1** : the orderly systematic universe **2** : a complex harmonious system **3** : a tall garden plant that is related to the daisies and has showy white, pink, or rose-colored flower heads with usually yellow centers [German *kosmos*, from Greek, "order, adornment, universe"]

cos·sack \'käs-ˌak, -ək\ *n* : a member of a group of frontiersmen of southern Russia organized as cavalry in the czarist army [Russian *kazak* and Ukrainian *kozak*, from Turkish *kazak* "free person"]

¹cos·set \'käs-ət\ *n* : a pet lamb; *also* : PET [origin unknown]

²cosset *vt* : to treat as a pet : PAMPER

¹cost \'kȯst\ *n* **1 a** : the amount paid or charged for something : PRICE **b** : the outlay made or loss suffered to achieve an object ⟨won the battle at the *cost* of many lives⟩ **2** *pl* : expenses charged to a party before a court of law ⟨fined $50 and *costs*⟩

²cost *vb* **cost; cost·ing** **1** : to have a price of : require payment ⟨each ticket *costs* one dollar⟩ **2** : to cause one to pay, spend, or lose ⟨selfishness *cost* them many friends⟩ [Middle French *coster*, from Latin *constare* "to stand firm, cost", from *com-* + *stare* "to stand"]

cos·ta \'käs-tə\ *n, pl* **cos·tae** \-ˌtē, -ˌtī\ : a rib or a body part (as the midrib of a leaf) resembling a rib [Latin, "rib, side"] — **cos·tal** \'käst-l\ *adj*

co-star \'kō-ˌstär\ *n* : a performer whose role (as in a play) is equal in importance to that of the star — **co-star** *vb*

cos·tard \'käs-tərd\ *n* **1** : any of several large English cooking apples **2** *archaic* : HEAD, NODDLE [Middle English]

cos·ter \'käs-tər\ *n, British* : COSTERMONGER

corymb

\ə\ abut	\ng\ sing
\ər\ further	\ō\ bone
\a\ mat	\ȯ\ saw
\ā\ take	\ȯi\ coin
\ä\ cot, cart	\th\ thin
\au̇\ out	\th\ this
\ch\ chin	\ü\ food
\e\ pet	\u̇\ foot
\ē\ easy	\y\ yet
\g\ go	\yü\ few
\i\ tip	\yu̇\ cure
\ī\ life	\zh\ vision
\j\ job	

cos·ter·mon·ger \\'käs-tər-ˌməŋg-gər, -ˌmäŋg-\ *n, British* : a person who sells fruit or vegetables in the street from a stand or cart [*costard*, a kind of apple + *monger*]

cos·tive \\'käs-tiv, 'kòs-\ *adj* **1** : CONSTIPATED **2** : causing constipation ⟨a *costive* diet⟩ [Middle French *costiver* "to constipate", from Latin *constipare*] — **cos·tive·ly** *adv* — **cos·tive·ness** *n*

cost·ly \\'kòst-lē\ *adj* **cost·li·er; -est 1** : very expensive or valuable ⟨*costly* furs⟩ **2** : gained at great cost or sacrifice ⟨a *costly* victory⟩ — **cost·li·ness** *n* □ SYN EXPENSIVE, VALUABLE, DEAR: COSTLY implies high price and may suggest luxury or rarity; EXPENSIVE may imply a price beyond the thing's value or the buyer's means; VALUABLE suggests worth measured in usefulness as well as price; DEAR implies a relatively high or excessive price often due to factors other than the thing's intrinsic value.

cost·mary \\'kòst-ˌmer-ē\ *n, pl* **-mar·ies** : an aromatic herb related to the daisies and used as a potherb and in flavoring [Middle English *coste* "costmary" + *Marie*, the Virgin Mary]

¹cos·tume \\'käs-ˌtüm, -ˌtyüm *also* -təm *or* -chəm\ *n* **1** : the prevailing fashion in hair style, jewelry, and apparel of a period, country, or class **2** : a suit or dress characteristic of a period, country, or class **3** : a person's ensemble of outer garments; *esp* : a woman's ensemble of dress with coat or jacket [French, from Italian, "custom, dress", from Latin *consuetudo* "custom"]

²cos·tume \käs-'tüm, -'tyüm *also* -'chüm; *or like* ¹\ *vt* **1** : to provide with a costume **2** : to design costumes for

³cos·tume *like* ¹\ *adj* **1** : characterized by use of costumes ⟨a *costume* ball⟩ **2** : suitable for or enhancing the effect of a particular costume ⟨a *costume* handbag⟩

cos·tum·er \\'käs-ˌtü-mər, -ˌtyü-\ *or* **cos·tu·mi·er** \käs-'tü-mē-ər, -'tyü-\ *n* **1** : one that makes, sells, or rents costumes **2** : CLOTHES TREE

co·sy \\'kō-zē\ *variant of* COZY

¹cot \\'kät\ *n* : a small house : COTTAGE [Old English]

²cot *n* : a small often collapsible bed usually of fabric stretched on a frame [Hindi *khāṭ* "bedstead"]

co·tan·gent \\'kō-'tan-jənt, kō-\ *n* : the trigonometric function that for an acute angle is the ratio between the side adjacent to the angle and the side opposite when the angle is considered part of a right triangle — abbreviation *cot*

cote \\'kōt, 'kät\ *n* : a shed or coop for small domestic animals (as sheep or pigeons) [Old English *cot, cote* "cottage"]

co·te·rie \\'kōt-ə-rē, ˌkōt-ə-'\ *n* : a small close group of persons with a shared interest or purpose [French, from Middle French, "tenants", from Medieval Latin *cotarius* "cotter"]

co·ter·mi·nal \\'kō-'tər-mən-l, kō-\ *adj* : having the same or coincident boundaries or sides ⟨*coterminal* angles⟩

co·ter·mi·nous \\'kō-'tər-mə-nəs, kō-\ *adj* **1** : having the same boundaries **2** : having the same scope or duration — **co·ter·mi·nous·ly** *adv*

co·til·lion *also* **co·til·lon** \kō-'til-yən, kə-\ *n* **1** : an elaborate dance with frequent changing of partners led by one couple at formal balls **2** : a formal ball [French *cotillon*, literally, "petticoat", from Old French, from *cote* "coat"]

co·to·neas·ter \kə-'tō-nē-ˌas-tər, 'kät-n-ˌēs-\ *n* : any of a genus of Old World flowering shrubs of the rose family often used in hedges [derived from Latin *cydonia, cotoneum* "quince"]

cot·ta \\'kät-ə\ *n* : a waist-length surplice [Medieval Latin, of Germanic origin]

cot·tage \\'kät-ij\ *n* **1** : a small usually frame one-family house **2** : a small house for vacation use [Middle English *cotage*, from *cot*]

cottage cheese *n* : a soft uncured cheese made from soured skim milk

cottage pudding *n* : plain cake covered with a hot sweet sauce

cot·tag·er \\'kät-ij-ər\ *n* : one who lives in a cottage; *esp* : one occupying a private house at a vacation resort

¹cot·ter *or* **cot·tar** \\'kät-ər\ *n* : a peasant or rural laborer occupying a small holding [Medieval Latin *cotarius*, from Middle English *cot* "cottage"]

²cot·ter \\'kät-ər\ *n* : a wedge-shaped or tapered piece used to fasten together parts of a structure [origin unknown]

cotter pin *n* : a half-round metal strip bent into a pin whose ends can be flared after insertion through a slot or hole

¹cot·ton \\'kät-n\ *n* **1 a** : a soft usually white fibrous substance composed of the hairs surrounding the seeds of various erect freely branching tropical plants of the mallow family **b** : a plant producing cotton **c** : a crop of cotton **2 a** : fabric made of cotton **b** : yarn spun from cotton [Middle French *coton*, from Arabic *quṭn*] — **cotton** *adj*

²cotton *vi* **cot·toned; cot·ton·ing** \\'kät-niŋ, -n-iŋ\ : to take a liking ⟨*cottoned* to them at first sight⟩

cotton candy *n* : a candy made of spun sugar

cotton gin *n* : a machine that separates the seeds, hulls, and foreign material from cotton

cot·ton·mouth \\'kät-n-ˌmau̇th\ *n* : WATER MOCCASIN — called also *cottonmouth moccasin*

cot·ton·seed \-ˌsēd\ *n* : the seed of the cotton plant which yields a protein-rich meal and a fixed oil used especially in cooking

cot·ton·tail \-ˌtāl\ *n* : any of several small brownish gray rabbits with white-tufted tail

cot·ton·wood \-ˌwu̇d\ *n* : a poplar that produces a tuft of cottony hairs on the seed; *esp* : one of the eastern and central United States noted for its rapid growth and luxuriant foliage

cotton wool *n* : raw cotton; *esp* : cotton batting

cot·tony \\'kät-nē, -n-ē\ *adj* : resembling cotton in appearance or character: as **a** : covered with soft hairs : DOWNY **b** : SOFT 1e

-cotyl \ˌkät-l\ *n combining form* : cotyledon ⟨epi*cotyl*⟩

cot·y·le·don \ˌkät-l-'ēd-n\ *n* **1** : a small lobe of a placenta **2** : the first leaf or one of the first pair or whorl of leaves developed by the embryo of a seed plant [Greek *kotylēdōn* "cup-shaped hollow", from *kotylē* "cup"] — **cot·y·le·don·ary** \-'ēd-n-ˌer-ē\ *adj*

cot·y·lo·saur \\'kät-l-ō-ˌsòr\ *n* : any of an order (Cotylosauria) of ancient extinct primitive reptiles that were probably the earliest truly terrestrial vertebrate animals [Greek *kotylē* "cup" + *sauros* "lizard"]

¹couch \\'kau̇ch\ *vb* **1** : to recline for rest or sleep **2** : to bring down : LOWER ⟨a knight charging with *couched* lance⟩ **3** : to phrase in a specified manner ⟨a letter *couched* in polite terms⟩ **4** : to lie in ambush [Middle French *coucher*, from Latin *collocare* "to set in place", from *com-* + *locus* "place"]

²couch *n* : a piece of furniture (as a sofa) for sitting or reclining

couch·ant \\'kau̇-chənt\ *adj* : lying down especially with the head up ⟨a heraldic lion *couchant*⟩

couch grass \\'kau̇ch-, 'ku̇ch-\ *n* : QUACK GRASS [*couch*, alteration of *quitch* "couch grass" from Old English *cwice*]

cou·gar \\'kü-gər, -ˌgär\ *n, pl* **cougars** *also* **cougar** : a large powerful tawny brown cat formerly widespread in the Americas but now extinct in many areas — called also *mountain lion, panther, puma* [French *couguar*, derived from Tupi *suasuarana*, literally, "false deer", from *suasú* "deer" + *rana* "false"]

¹cough \\'kòf\ *vb* **1** : to force air from the lungs with a sharp short noise or series of noises **2** : to get rid of by

cottontail

cougar

coughing ⟨*cough* up phlegm⟩ [Middle English *coughen*]

²**cough** *n* **1** : a condition marked by repeated or frequent coughing **2** : an act or sound of coughing

cough drop *n* : a medicated tablet or candy used to relieve coughing

cough up *vt* : DELIVER, PAY ⟨*cough up* the money⟩

could \kəd, 'kůd, 'kůd\ *past of* CAN — used as an auxiliary verb in the past ⟨we found we *could* go⟩ ⟨we said we would go if we *could*⟩ and as a polite or less forceful alternative to *can* ⟨*could* you do this for me⟩ [Old English *cūthe*]

could·est \'kůd-əst\ *archaic past 2d sing of* CAN

couldn't \'kůd-nt\ : could not

couldst \kədst, kůdst, 'kůdst\ *archaic past 2d sing of* CAN

cou·lee \'kü-lē\ *n* **1 a** : a dry creek bed **b** : a steep-walled valley **2** : a thick sheet or stream of lava [Canadian French *coulée*, from French, "flowing, flow of lava", from *couler* "to flow", from Latin *colare* "to strain", from *colum* "sieve"]

cou·lomb \'kü-,läm, -,lōm, kü-'\ *n* : the practical mks unit of electric charge equal to the quantity of electricity transferred by a current of one ampere in one second [Charles A. de *Coulomb*, died 1806, French physicist]

coun·cil \'kaůn-səl\ *n* **1** : a meeting for consultation, advice, or discussion **2** : an advisory or legislative body ⟨governor's *council*⟩ **3** : an administrative body (as of a town) **4** : deliberation in a council **5 a** : a federation of or a central body uniting a group of organizations or other bodies **b** : a local chapter of an organization **c** : CLUB 2a, SOCIETY [Old French *concile*, from Latin *concilium*, from *com-* + *calare* "to call"]

coun·cil·lor *or* **coun·cil·or** \'kaůn-sə-lər, -slər\ *n* : a member of a council — **coun·cil·lor·ship** \-,ship\ *n*

coun·cil·man \'kaůn-səl-mən\ *n* : a member of a council especially in a city government

¹**coun·sel** \'kaůn-səl\ *n* **1 a** : advice given especially as a result of consultation **b** : a policy or plan of action or behavior **2** : DELIBERATION, CONSULTATION ⟨take *counsel* together⟩ **3** *pl* **counsel** : a lawyer who gives advice in law or manages cases for clients in court [Old French *conseil*, from Latin *consilium*, from *consulere* "to consult"]

²**counsel** *vb* **-seled** *or* **-selled**; **-sel·ing** *or* **-sel·ling** \-sə-ling, -sling\ **1** : to give counsel : ADVISE ⟨*counsel* a student on a choice of studies⟩ **2** : to seek counsel : CONSULT ⟨*counsel* with friends⟩

coun·sel·or *or* **coun·sel·lor** \'kaůn-sə-lər, -slər\ *n* **1** : ADVISER **2** : LAWYER; *esp* : one that manages cases for clients in court **3** : a supervisor of campers or activities at a summer camp — **coun·sel·or·ship** \-,ship\ *n*

¹**count** \'kaůnt\ *vb* **1 a** : to find the total number of by naming units or groups ⟨*count* the apples in a box⟩ **b** : to name the consecutive numbers up to and including ⟨*count* ten⟩ **c** : to recite the numbers in order by units or groups ⟨*count* to one hundred by fives⟩ **d** : to include in a tally ⟨40 present, *counting* children⟩ **2 a** : CONSIDER ⟨*count* oneself lucky⟩ **b** : to include or exclude by or as if by counting ⟨*counted* themselves out⟩ **3 a** : RELY, DEPEND ⟨a person you can *count* on⟩ **b** : RECKON, PLAN ⟨*counted* on going⟩ **4** : to have value, significance, or importance ⟨every vote *counts*⟩ [Middle French *compter*, from Latin *computare*, from *com-* + *putare* "to consider"] — **count·able** \-ə-bəl\ *adj*

²**count** *n* **1** : the act or process of counting; *also* : a total obtained by counting : TALLY **2** : ALLEGATION, CHARGE; *esp* : one stating a separate cause of action in a legal declaration or indictment ⟨guilty on all *counts*⟩ **3 a** : the calling off of the seconds from one to ten when a boxer has been knocked down **b** : the number of balls and strikes called on a baseball batter

³**count** *n* : a European nobleman whose rank corresponds to that of a British earl [Middle French *comte*, from Late Latin *comes*, from Latin, "companion", from *com-* + *ire* "to go"]

count·down \'kaůnt-,daůn\ *n* : an audible backward counting off in fixed units (as seconds) from an arbitrary starting number to mark the time remaining before an event (as the launching of a rocket)

¹**coun·te·nance** \'kaůnt-n-əns, 'kaůnt-nəns\ *n* **1 a** : calm expression **b** : mental composure **c** : LOOK 2a, EXPRESSION **2** : FACE, VISAGE; *esp* : facial expression as an indication of mood, emotion, or character **3** : a show of approval ⟨gave no *countenance* to the plan⟩ [Middle French *contenance* "demeanor, bearing", from Latin *continentia* "restraint", from *continens* "continent"]

²**countenance** *vt* : TOLERATE 1, SANCTION ⟨refused to *countenance* such habitual lateness⟩

¹**count·er** \'kaůnt-ər\ *n* **1** : a piece (as of metal or plastic) used in counting or in games **2** : a level surface (as a table or board) over which transactions are conducted or food is served or on which goods are displayed

²**count·er** *n* : one that counts; *esp* : a device for indicating a number or amount

³**coun·ter** \'kaůnt-ər\ *vb* **coun·tered**; **coun·ter·ing** \'kaůnt-ə-ring, 'kaůn-tring\ **1** : to act in opposition to : OPPOSE ⟨*countering* the charges⟩ **2** : RETALIATE ⟨*countered* with a left hook⟩

⁴**coun·ter** *adv* : in a contrary manner or direction ⟨acted *counter* to our orders⟩ [Middle French *contre*, from Latin *contra* "against, opposite"]

⁵**coun·ter** *n* **1** : the after portion of a boat from the waterline to the extreme outward swell or overhang **2** : the act of giving a retaliatory blow; *also* : the blow given **3** : a stiffener giving shape to the upper of a shoe or boot around the heel

⁶**coun·ter** *adj* **1** : moving in an opposite direction ⟨ships slowed by *counter* tides⟩ **2** : designed to oppose

counter- *prefix* **1** : contrary : opposite ⟨*counter*clockwise⟩ **b** : opposing : retaliatory ⟨*counter*offensive⟩ **2** : complementary : corresponding ⟨*counter*weight⟩ **3** : duplicate : substitute ⟨*counter*foil⟩ [Middle French *contre*]

See *counter-* and 2d element

counteraccusation	counterevidence	counterraid
counteraggression	counterguerrilla	counterrally
counterargue	counterinflationary	counterresponse
counterassault	counterinfluence	counterretaliation
counterbid	countermeasure	counterstrategy
counterblockade	countermove	counterstyle
counterblow	countermovement	countersue
countercampaign	counteroffer	countersuggestion
countercharge	counterpetition	countersuit
countercomplaint	counterploy	countertendency
countercoup	counterpower	counterterror
countercriticism	counterpressure	counterterrorism
counter–demand	counterpropaganda	counterterrorist
counterdemonstration	counterproposal	counterthreat
counterdemonstrator	counterprotest	counterthrust
counter–effort	counterquestion	countertrend

coun·ter·act \,kaůnt-ər-'akt\ *vt* : to lessen the force of : OFFSET ⟨a drug that *counteracts* the effect of a poison⟩ ⟨*counteract* an evil influence⟩ — **coun·ter·ac·tion** \-'ak-shən\ *n* — **coun·ter·ac·tive** \-'rak-tiv\ *adj*

coun·ter·at·tack \'kaůnt-ər-ə-,tak\ *n* : an attack made against an enemy's attack — **counterattack** *vb*

¹**coun·ter·bal·ance** \'kaůnt-ər-,bal-əns, ,kaůnt-ər-'\ *n* **1** : a weight that balances another **2** : a force or influence that offsets or checks an opposing force

²**counterbalance** \,kaůnt-ər-', 'kaůnt-ər-,\ *vt* : to oppose with an equal weight or force

¹**coun·ter·check** \'kaůnt-ər-,chek\ *n* : a check or restraint often operating against something that is itself a check

²countercheck *vt* : to check a second time for verification

counter check *n* : a blank check obtainable at a bank; *esp* : one to be cashed at the bank by the drawer

coun·ter·claim \'kaùn-tər-ˌklām\ *n* : an opposing claim especially in law — **counterclaim** *vb*

coun·ter·clock·wise \ˌkaùnt-ər-'kläk-ˌwīz\ *adv* : in a direction opposite to that in which the hands of a clock rotate — **counterclockwise** *adj*

coun·ter·cur·rent \'kaùnt-ər-ˌkər-ənt, -ˌkə-rənt\ *n* : a current flowing in a direction opposite to that of another one

coun·ter·es·pi·o·nage \ˌkaùnt-ər-'es-pē-ə-ˌnäzh, -nij, -ˌnäj\ *n* : activities intended to discover and defeat enemy espionage

coun·ter·ex·am·ple \'kaùnt-ər-ig-ˌzam-pəl\ *n* : an example that disproves a theorem or proposition

¹coun·ter·feit \'kaùnt-ər-ˌfit\ *vb* **1** : to imitate or copy especially with intent to deceive ⟨*counterfeiting* money⟩ **2** : PRETEND 2 ⟨*counterfeit* an air of indifference⟩ — **coun·ter·feit·er** *n*

²counterfeit *adj* **1** : made in imitation of something else with intent to deceive ⟨*counterfeit* money⟩ **2** : not real : SHAM ⟨a *counterfeit* interest⟩ [Middle French *contrefait,* from *contrefaire* "to imitate", from *contre-* "counter-" + *faire* "to make", from Latin *facere*]

³counterfeit *n* **1** : something counterfeit : FORGERY **2** : something that is likely to be confused with the genuine thing

coun·ter·foil \'kaùnt-ər-ˌfoil\ *n* : a detachable stub usually serving as a record or receipt [*counter-* + *foil* "leaf"]

coun·ter·in·tel·li·gence \ˌkaùnt-ər-in-'tel-ə-jəns\ *n* : organized activities of an intelligence service intended to foil the activities of an enemy's intelligence service by blocking its sources of information and by deceiving the enemy through tricks and misinformation

coun·ter·ir·ri·tant \ˌkaùnt-ər-'ir-ə-tənt\ *n* : something (as a mustard plaster) used to produce surface inflammation in order to reduce inflammation in deeper nearby structures — **counterirritant** *adj*

count·er·man \'kaùnt-ər-ˌman, -mən\ *n* : one who tends a counter (as in a lunchroom)

coun·ter·mand \'kaùnt-ər-ˌmand, ˌkaùnt-ər-'\ *vt* **1** : to cancel (a command) by a contrary order **2** : to recall or order back by a superseding contrary order [Middle French *contremander,* from *contre-* "counter-" + *mander* "to command", from Latin *mandare*] — **countermand** *n*

coun·ter·march \'kaùnt-ər-ˌmärch\ *n* : a marching back; *esp* : a maneuver by which a unit of troops reverses direction but keeps the same order — **countermarch** *vi*

coun·ter·of·fen·sive \'kaùnt-ər-ə-ˌfen-siv\ *n* : a large-scale counterattack

coun·ter·pane \'kaùnt-ər-ˌpān\ *n* : BEDSPREAD [Middle English *countrepointe,* from Middle French *coute pointe,* literally, "embroidered quilt"]

coun·ter·part \'kaùnt-ər-ˌpärt\ *n* **1** : a part or thing corresponding to another ⟨the left arm is the *counterpart* of the right arm⟩ **2** : something that serves to complete something else : COMPLEMENT **3** : one closely resembling another ⟨the twins were *counterparts* of each other⟩

¹coun·ter·plot \-ˌplät\ *vb* : to plot against (a plot or plotter) : INTRIGUE

²counterplot *n* : a plot in opposition to another plot

coun·ter·point \'kaùnt-ər-ˌpoint\ *n* **1** : one or more melodies added above or below a given melody **2** : combination of two or more melodies into a single harmonic texture [Middle French *contrepoint,* from Medieval Latin *contrapunctus,* from Latin *contra-* "counter-" + Medieval Latin *punctus* "musical note, melody"]

¹coun·ter·poise \-ˌpoiz\ *vt* : COUNTERBALANCE

²counterpoise *n* **1** : COUNTERBALANCE **2** : a state of balance

Coun·ter-Ref·or·ma·tion \ˌkaùn-tər-ˌref-ər-'mā-shən\ *n* : the reform movement in the Roman Catholic Church following the Reformation

coun·ter·rev·o·lu·tion \-ˌrev-ə-'lü-shən\ *n* : a revolution intended to undo a current or earlier one — **coun·ter·rev·o·lu·tion·ary** \-shə-ˌner-ē\ *adj or n* — **coun·ter·rev·o·lu·tion·ist** \-shə-nəst, -shnəst\ *n*

coun·ter·shaft \'kaùnt-ər-ˌshaft\ *n* : a shaft that receives motion from a main shaft and transmits it to a working part

¹coun·ter·sign \-ˌsīn\ *n* **1** : a signature confirming the authenticity of a document already signed by another **2** : a sign used in reply to another; *esp* : a secret signal that must be given by one wishing to pass a guard

²countersign *vt* : to add one's signature to (a document) after another's to confirm authenticity — **coun·ter·sig·na·ture** \ˌkaùnt-ər-'sig-nə-ˌchùr, -chər\ *n*

¹coun·ter·sink \'kaùnt-ər-ˌsingk\ *vt* -**sunk** \-ˌsəngk\; -**sink·ing** **1** : to make a countersink on **2** : to set the head of (as a screw, bolt, or nail) at or below the surface

²countersink *n* **1** : a funnel-shaped enlargement at the outer end of a drilled hole **2** : a bit or drill for making a countersink

coun·ter·spy \-ˌspī\ *n* : a spy employed in counterintelligence

coun·ter·ten·or \-ˌten-ər\ *n* : a tenor with an unusually high range

coun·ter·weight \-ˌwāt\ *n* : COUNTERBALANCE 1 — **counterweight** *vt*

count·ess \'kaùnt-əs\ *n* **1** : the wife or widow of a count or an earl **2** : a woman who holds the rank of a count or an earl in her own right

count·ing·house \'kaùnt-ing-ˌhaùs\ *n* : a building, room, or office used for keeping books and transacting business

counting number *n* : NATURAL NUMBER

counting room *n* : COUNTINGHOUSE

count·less \'kaùnt-ləs\ *adj* : too numerous to be counted : INNUMERABLE SYN see MANY

coun·tri·fied *or* **coun·try·fied** \'kən-tri-ˌfīd\ *adj* : looking or acting as if from the country : RUSTIC

¹coun·try \'kən-trē\ *n, pl* **countries** **1** : an indefinite usually large or open stretch of land : REGION ⟨hill *country*⟩ **2 a** : the land of a person's birth, residence, or citizenship **b** : a political state or nation or its territory **3** : the people of a state or district : POPULACE **4** : rural as distinguished from urban areas ⟨lives out in the *country*⟩ [Old French *contrée,* from Medieval Latin *contrata,* from Latin *contra* "against, on the opposite side"] □ ORIGIN English *country* is derived from Latin *contra,* which means "against" or "on the opposite side". In Medieval Latin the noun *contrata* was formed from *contra. Contrata* was literally "that which is situated opposite the beholder". But that which is opposite the beholder is just what he or she sees. So *contrata* meant "landscape". It also came to mean "expanse of land, region". This was the original meaning of English *country,* which over the years has itself developed a number of new meanings.

²country *adj* : of, relating to, or characteristic of the country

country club *n* : a suburban club for social life and recreation

coun·try–dance \'kən-trē-ˌdans\ *n* : an English dance in which partners face each other especially in rows

coun·try·man \'kən-trē-mən, *3 is often* -ˌman\ *n* **1** : an inhabitant or native of a specified country ⟨a north *countryman*⟩ **2** : COMPATRIOT 1 **3** : one living in the country or marked by country ways : RUSTIC

country music *n* : music derived from or imitating the folk style of the southern United States or of the Western cowboy

coun·try·seat \ˌkən-trē-ˈsēt\ *n* : a mansion or estate in the country

coun·try·side \ˈkən-trē-ˌsīd\ *n* : a rural area or its people

coun·ty \ˈkaunt-ē\ *n, pl* **counties** **1** : the domain of a count **2 a** : one of the chief territorial divisions of Great Britain and Ireland for administrative, judicial, and political purposes **b** : the largest territorial division for local government within a state of the United States [Old French *conté*, from Medieval Latin *comitatus*, from Late Latin, "office of a count", from *comit-*, *comes* "count"]

county agent *n* : a government agent employed to provide information about agriculture and home economics in rural areas

county seat *n* : a town that is the seat of county administration

coup \ˈkü\ *n, pl* **coups** \ˈküz\ **1** : a brilliant, sudden, and usually highly successful act **2** : COUP D'ETAT [French, "blow, stroke", from Late Latin *colpus*, from Latin *colaphus*, from Greek *kolaphos* "slap"]

coup de grace \ˌküd-ə-ˈgräs\ *n, pl* **coups de grace** \ˈküd-ə-\ **1** : a death blow or shot administered to end the suffering of one mortally wounded **2** : a decisive finishing blow or event [French *coup de grâce*, literally, "stroke of mercy"]

coup d'e·tat \ˌküd-ə-ˈtä, ˌküd-ā-\ *n, pl* **coups d'e·tat** \-ˈtä, -ˈtäz\ : a sudden decisive political move; *esp* : the overthrow of an existing government by a small group [French *coup d'état*, literally, "stroke of state"]

cou·pé *or* **coupe** \kü-ˈpā, *2 is often* ˈküp\ *n* **1** : a four-wheeled closed horse-drawn carriage for two persons inside with an outside seat for the driver in front **2** *usually* **coupe a** : a closed 2-door automobile for usually two persons **b** : a usually closed 2-door automobile with a full-width rear seat [French *coupé*, from *couper* "to cut, strike", from *coup* "blow, coup"]

¹cou·ple \ˈkəp-əl\ *vb* **cou·pled; cou·pling** \ˈkəp-ling, -ə-ling\ **1** : to join together : CONNECT (freight cars *coupled* end to end) **2** : COPULATE **3** : to bring (two electric circuits) into such close proximity as to permit mutual influence

²couple *n* **1 a** : a man and woman married, engaged, or otherwise paired **b** : two persons paired together **2** : BRACE 1, PAIR **3** : two equal and opposite forces that act along parallel lines **4** : an indefinite small number ⟨a *couple* of days ago⟩ [Old French *cople* "pair, bond", from Latin *copula* "bond"]

³couple *adj* : TWO; *also* : SEVERAL 2 ⟨a *couple* days ago⟩

cou·pler \ˈkəp-lər, -ə-lər\ *n* **1** : one that couples **2** : a device on a keyboard instrument by which keyboards or keys are connected to play together

cou·plet \ˈkəp-lət\ *n* : two successive lines of verse forming a unit; *esp* : two rhyming lines of the same length — compare HEROIC COUPLET

cou·pling \ˈkəp-ling (usual for 2), -ə-ling\ *n* **1** : the act of bringing or coming together : PAIRING **2** : something that joins or connects two parts or things ⟨a car *coupling*⟩ ⟨a pipe *coupling*⟩ **3** : the joining of or the part of the body that joins the hindquarters to the forequarters of a quadruped

cou·pon \ˈkü-ˌpän, ˈkyü-\ *n* **1** : a statement of due interest to be cut from a bond and presented for payment on a stated date **2 a** : one of a series of attached tickets to be detached and presented as needed **b** : a ticket or form authorizing purchases of rationed commodities **c** : a certificate or similar evidence of a purchase redeemable in premiums **d** : a part of a printed advertisement to be cut off for use as an order blank or inquiry form [French, from *couper* "to cut"]

cour·age \ˈkər-ij, ˈkə-rij\ *n* : mental or moral strength to venture, persevere, and withstand danger, fear, or difficulty [Old French *corage*, from *cuer* "heart", from Latin *cor*] □ SYN COURAGE, BRAVERY, VALOR, HEROISM mean greatness of heart in facing danger or difficulty.

COURAGE implies strength in overcoming fear and in persisting against odds or difficulties; BRAVERY stresses bold and daring defiance of danger; VALOR applies especially to bravery in fighting a dangerous enemy; HEROISM suggests bravery and boldness in accepting risk or sacrifice for a noble or generous purpose.

cou·ra·geous \kə-ˈrā-jəs\ *adj* : having or characterized by courage : BRAVE — **cou·ra·geous·ly** *adv* — **cou·ra·geous·ness** *n*

cou·ri·er \ˈkur-ē-ər, ˈkər-ē-, ˈkə-rē-\ *n* : MESSENGER: as **a** : a member of a diplomatic service entrusted with bearing messages **b** : a member of the armed services who carries mail, information, or supplies [Middle French *courrier*, from Italian *corriere*, from *correre* "to run", from Latin *currere*]

¹course \ˈkōrs, ˈkors\ *n* **1 a** : the act or action of moving in a path from point to point **b** : LIFE HISTORY 2, CAREER **2** : the path over which something moves: as **a** : RACECOURSE **b** : the direction of flight of an airplane **c** : WATERCOURSE **d** : land laid out for golf **3 a** : accustomed procedure or action ⟨the law taking its *course*⟩ **b** : a manner of conducting oneself : BEHAVIOR ⟨the wisest *course* is to retreat⟩ **c** : progression through a series of acts or events or a development or period ⟨in the *course* of one's career⟩ **4 a** : an ordered process or succession **b** : a series of lectures or discussions dealing with a subject; *also* : a number of such courses constituting a curriculum **5 a** : a part of a meal served at one time **b** : ROW, LAYER; *esp* : a continuous level range of brick or masonry throughout a wall [Old French, from Latin *cursus*, from *currere* "to run"] — **of course** **1** : following the ordinary way or procedure ⟨did it as a matter *of course*⟩ **2** : as might be expected

²course *vb* **1 a** : to hunt or pursue (game) with hounds **b** : to cause (dogs) to run (as after game) **2** : to run through or over ⟨when buffalo *coursed* the plains⟩ **3** : to move rapidly : RACE ⟨blood *coursing* through the veins⟩

cours·er \ˈkōr-sər, ˈkor-\ *n* : a swift or spirited horse

¹court \ˈkōrt, ˈkort\ *n* **1 a** : the residence of a dignitary and especially a sovereign **b** : a sovereign's formal assembly of his or her councillors and officers **c** : the sovereign and his or her officials who constitute the governing power **d** : the family and retinue of a sovereign **e** : a reception held by a sovereign **2 a** : an open space wholly or partly surrounded by buildings **b** : a space arranged for playing any of various games with a ball ⟨a tennis *court*⟩ **c** : a short street or lane **3 a** : an assembly for the transaction of judicial business **b** : a session of a judicial assembly ⟨*court* is now adjourned⟩ **c** : a place (as a chamber) for the administration of justice **d** : a judge in session **e** : a faculty or agency of judgment or evaluation **4 a** : an assembly or board with legislative or administrative powers **b** : LEGISLATURE, PARLIAMENT **5** : attention designed to win favor or dispel hostility ⟨pay *court* to the king⟩ [Old French, from Latin *cohors* "enclosure, throng, cohort"]

²court *vb* **1 a** : to try to gain ⟨*courting* favor with the higher-ups⟩ **b** : to act so as to provoke ⟨was *courting* disaster⟩ **2** : to seek the affections of ⟨*courted* a college student⟩ **3** : to try to get the support of ⟨both candidates *courted* the independent voters⟩ **4 a** : to engage in social relationship and activities usually leading to marriage **b** : to engage in activity leading to mating ⟨a pair of robins *courting*⟩

cour·te·ous \ˈkərt-ē-əs\ *adj* **1** : marked by polished manners, gallantry, or ceremonial usage of a court **2** : marked by respect for and consideration of others SYN see CIVIL — **cour·te·ous·ly** *adv* — **cour·te·ous·ness** *n*

cour·te·san \ˈkōrt-ə-zən, ˈkort- *also* ˈkərt-\ *n* : a prostitute with an upper-class clientele [Middle French *courtisane*, from Italian *cortigiana* "female courtier", from *corte* "court", from Latin *cohors* "throng"]

cour·te·sy \ˈkərt-ə-sē\ *n, pl* **-sies** **1** : courtly politeness ⟨old-world *courtesy*⟩ **2** : a favor courteously per-

formed **3 :** consideration and generosity in providing
(flowers given through the *courtesy* of a florist)

courtesy title *n* **:** a title (as "Professor" for any teacher)
taken by the user and commonly accepted without
consideration of official right

court·house \'kōrt-,haůs, 'kórt-\ *n* **1 a :** a building in
which courts of law are held **b :** a building in which
county offices are housed **2 :** COUNTY SEAT

court·ier \'kōrt-ē-ər, 'kórt-\ *n* **1 :** a person in attendance at a royal court **2 :** a person who practices flattery

court·ly \'kōrt-lē, 'kórt-\ *adj* **court·li·er; -est 1 a :** of a
quality befitting a royal court **:** ELEGANT ⟨*courtly* man-
ners⟩ **b :** insincerely flattering **2 :** favoring the policy
or party of the court — **court·li·ness** *n*

¹**court–mar·tial** \'kōrt-,mär-shəl, 'kórt-\ *n, pl* **courts–
martial** *also* **court–martials 1 :** a military court for the
trial of members of the armed forces or others within
its jurisdiction **2 :** a trial by court-martial

²**court–martial** *vt* **-mar·tialed** *also* **-mar·tialled; -mar-
tial·ing** *also* **-mar·tial·ling** \-,märsh-ling, -ə-ling\ **:** to
subject to trial by court-martial

Court of St. James's \-sānt-'jāmz, -sənt-\ **:** the British
court [from *Saint James's Palace,* London, former seat
of the British court]

court plaster *n* **:** an adhesive plaster especially of silk
coated with isinglass and glycerin [from its use for
beauty spots by ladies at royal courts]

court·room \'kōrt-,rüm, 'kórt-, -,rům\ *n* **:** a room in
which a court of law is held

court·ship \-,ship\ *n* **:** the act, process, or period of
courting

court tennis *n* **:** a game similar to tennis played with a
ball and racket in an enclosed court

court·yard \'kōrt-,yärd, 'kórt-\ *n* **:** a court or enclosure
attached to a building

cous·in \'kəz-n\ *n* **1 a :** a child of one's uncle or aunt
b : a relative descended from a common ancestor in a
different line **2 :** a person belonging to an ethnically
or culturally related group ⟨our English *cousins*⟩ [Old
French *cosin,* from Latin *consobrinus,* from *com-* +
sobrinus "cousin on the mother's side", from *soror*
"sister"]

cous·in–ger·man \,kəz-n-'jər-mən\ *n, pl* **cousins–german** \,kəz-nz-\ **:** COUSIN 1a [Middle English *germain*
"closely related", derived from Latin *germanus* "having the same parents", from *germen* "bud, sprout,
germ"]

co·va·lence \'kō-'vā-ləns, kō-\ *or* **co·va·len·cy** \-lən-sē\
n **:** valence characterized by the sharing of electrons
in pairs by two atoms in a chemical compound; *also* **:**
the number of pairs of electrons an atom can share
with its neighbors — **co·va·lent** \-lənt\ *adj* — **co·va-
lent·ly** *adv*

cove \'kōv\ *n* **1 a :** an architectural member with a concave cross section **b :** a trough for concealed lighting
at the upper part of a wall **2 :** a small sheltered inlet or
bay **3 :** a level area sheltered by hills or mountains
[Old English *cofa* "den, cave"]

cov·en \'kəv-ən\ *n* **:** a meeting or band of witches [Mid-
dle French *covin* "band", derived from Latin *convenire* "to come together"]

¹**cov·e·nant** \'kəv-nənt, -ə-nənt\ *n* **1 :** a solemn and
binding agreement **:** COMPACT **2 a :** a written agreement or promise usually under seal between parties
b : a promise incidental to and contained in an agreement (as a deed) [Old French, from *covenir,* from Latin *convenire* "to come together, agree", from *com-* +
venire "to come"] — **cov·e·nan·tal** \,kəv-ə-'nant-l\
adj

²**cov·e·nant** \'kəv-nənt, -ə-nənt, -ə-nant\ *vb* **1 :** to
promise by a covenant **:** PLEDGE **2 :** to enter into a covenant **:** CONTRACT — **cov·e·nant·er** \-ə-,nant-ər\ *n*

Cov·en·try \'kəv-ən-trē, 'käv-\ *n* **:** a state of ostracism or
exclusion ⟨sent to *Coventry*⟩ [*Coventry,* England]

¹**cov·er** \'kəv-ər\ *vb* **cov·ered; cov·er·ing** \'kəv-ring, -ə-
ring\ **1 a :** to guard from attack **b :** to have within
gunshot range **c** (1) **:** to provide protection or security
to **:** INSURE ⟨this insurance *covers* the traveler in any
accident⟩ (2) **:** to provide protection against or compensation for ⟨the policy *covered* all water damage⟩
d : to maintain a check on especially by patrolling
⟨state police *covering* the highways⟩ **2 a :** to hide from
sight or knowledge ⟨*cover* up a scandal⟩ **b :** to conceal
something illicit, blameworthy, or embarrassing from
notice ⟨*cover* for a friend in an investigation⟩ **c :** to act
as a substitute or replacement during an absence ⟨*covered* for me during my vacation⟩ **3 :** to overlay so as to
protect or shelter ⟨*cover* the plants with mulch⟩ **4 a :**
to spread or lie over or on ⟨water *covered* the floor⟩
⟨snow *covering* the hills⟩ **b :** DOT 2 ⟨resort area *covered* with lakes⟩ **5 :** to put something protective or
concealing over ⟨*cover* your head⟩ **6 :** to sit on and
incubate (eggs) **7 :** to have sufficient scope to include
or take into account ⟨an exam *covering* a semester's
work⟩ **8 :** to have as one's territory or field of activity
⟨one salesperson *covers* the whole state⟩ **9 :** to pass
over or through ⟨*covering* 500 kilometers a day⟩ **10 :**
to accept an offered bet **11 :** to buy securities or commodities for delivery against (an earlier short sale)
[Old French *covrir,* from Latin *cooperire,* from *co-* +
operire "to close, cover"] — **cov·er·er** \-ər-ər\ *n*

²**cover** *n* **1 :** something that protects, shelters, or
guards: as **a :** natural shelter for an animal or the factors that provide such shelter **b :** a position or situation affording protection from enemy fire **2 :** something that is placed over or about another thing **: a :**
LID 1, TOP **b :** a binding or case for a book; *also* **:** the
front or back of such a binding **c :** an overlay or outer
layer especially for protection ⟨a mattress *cover*⟩ **d :**
tableware laid out for one person **e :** ROOF **f :** a cloth
(as a blanket or bedspread) used on a bed **g :** something (as vegetation or snow) that covers the ground
3 : something that conceals or obscures ⟨under *cover*
of darkness⟩ **4 :** an envelope or wrapper for mail

cov·er·age \'kəv-rij, -ə-rij\ *n* **1 :** the act or fact of covering or something that covers: as **a :** inclusion within
the scope of protection (as of an insurance policy) **b :**
inclusion within the scope of discussion or reporting
⟨*coverage* of a political convention⟩ **2 a :** the number
or amount covered **:** SCOPE **b :** all the risks covered by
the terms of an insurance contract ⟨a policy with an
extensive *coverage*⟩

cov·er·all \'kəv-ər-,ol\ *n* **:** a one-piece outer garment
worn to protect one's clothes — usually used in pl.

cover charge *n* **:** a charge made by a restaurant or nightclub in addition to the charge for food and drink

cover crop *n* **:** a crop planted to prevent soil erosion
and to provide humus

covered wagon *n* **:** a wagon with a canvas top supported
by bows

cover glass *n* **:** a piece of very thin transparent material
used to cover material mounted on a glass microscope
slide

cov·er·ing \'kəv-ring, -ə-ring\ *n* **:** something that covers
or conceals

cov·er·let \'kəv-ər-lət\ *n* **:** BEDSPREAD [Middle English,
alteration of *coverlite,* from Old French *covrir* "to
cover" + *lit* "bed"]

cov·er·slip \'kəv-ər-,slip\ *n* **:** COVER GLASS

¹**co·vert** \'kō-,vərt, -vərt, kō-'; 'kəv-ərt\ *adj* **1 :** not
openly shown, engaged in, or avowed ⟨a *covert* alli-
ance⟩ **2 :** covered over **:** SHELTERED ⟨a *covert* nook⟩
[Old French, past participle of *covrir* "to cover"] SYN
see SECRET — **cov·ert·ly** *adv* — **cov·ert·ness** *n*

²**co·vert** \'kəv-ər, -ərt; 'kō-vərt\ *n* **1 a :** hiding place **:**
SHELTER **b :** a thicket affording cover for game **2 :** a
feather covering the bases of the quills of the wings
and tail of a bird **3 :** a firm durable twilled sometimes
waterproofed cloth

cov·et \'kəv-ət\ *vb* : to wish enviously especially for what belongs to another [Old French *coveitier,* from *coveitié* "desire", from Latin *cupiditas* "desire, cupidity"] — **cov·et·able** \-ə-bəl\ *adj* — **cov·et·er** \-ər\ *n* — **cov·et·ing·ly** \-ing-lē\ *adv*

cov·et·ous \'kəv-ət-əs\ *adj* : marked by a too eager desire for wealth or possessions or for another's possessions — **cov·et·ous·ly** *adv* — **cov·et·ous·ness** *n* □ SYN AVARICIOUS, GREEDY, GRASPING: COVETOUS implies excessive desire especially for what belongs to another; AVARICIOUS implies a strong desire to gain and keep money; GREEDY stresses lack of restraint and often of discrimination in desire; GRASPING adds the implications of selfishness and ruthlessness.

cov·ey \'kəv-ē\ *n, pl* **coveys** 1 : a mature bird or pair of birds with a brood of young; *also* : a small flock 2 : COMPANY 2a, GROUP [Middle French *covee,* from *cover* "to sit on, brood over", from Latin *cubare* "to lie"]

¹cow \'kaů\ *n* 1 : the mature female of cattle or of any animal (as the moose) the male of which is called bull 2 : a domestic bovine animal regardless of sex or age [Old English *cū*] — **cowy** \-ē\ *adj*

²cow *vt* : to subdue the spirits or courage of : INTIMIDATE ⟨*cowed* by threats⟩ [probably of Scandinavian origin]

cow·ard \'kaů-ərd, 'kaůrd\ *n* : one who shows disgraceful fear or timidity [Old French *coart,* from *coe* "tail", from Latin *cauda*] — **coward** *adj* □ ORIGIN A frightened animal may draw its tail between its hind legs, or it may simply turn its tail and run. In such an animal as the hare, the white flash of the fleeing tail is especially remarkable. But even a tailless animal like a human being can turn tail and flee when afraid. And unless an army is in retreat, it is in the tail of the army that you can expect to find the cowards. Whether it is the idea of an animal's tail or an army's that is responsible, it is certain that the Old French *coart,* from which we get our *coward,* is a derivative of *coe,* "tail".

cow·ard·ice \-əs\ *n* : lack of courage or resolution

¹cow·ard·ly \-lē\ *adv* : in a cowardly manner

²cowardly *adj* 1 : disgracefully timid ⟨a *cowardly* rascal⟩ 2 : resembling or befitting a coward ⟨a *cowardly* retreat⟩ — **cow·ard·li·ness** *n*

cow·bane \'kaů-ˌbān\ *n* : any of several poisonous plants (as a water hemlock) of the carrot family

cow·bell \-ˌbel\ *n* : a bell hung about the neck of a cow to indicate its whereabouts

cow·bird \-ˌbərd\ *n* : a small North American blackbird that lays its eggs in the nests of other birds

cow·boy \-ˌbȯi\ *n* 1 : one who tends or drives cattle; *esp* : a usually mounted cattle ranch hand 2 : a participant in rodeos

cow·catch·er \-ˌkach-ər, -ˌkech-\ *n* : an inclined frame on the front of a railroad locomotive for throwing obstacles off the track

cow·er \'kaů-ər, 'kaůr\ *vi* : to shrink away or cringe (as from fear) ⟨*cowered* at the sight of a whip⟩ [Middle English *couren,* of Scandinavian origin]

cow·fish \'kaů-ˌfish\ *n* : any of various small brightly colored fishes with projections resembling horns over the eyes

cow·girl \-ˌgərl\ *n* : a girl or woman who works as a cowboy

cow·hand \-ˌhand\ *n* : COWBOY

cow·herd \-ˌhərd\ *n* : one who tends cows

¹cow·hide \-ˌhīd\ *n* 1 : the hide of a cow or leather made from it 2 : a coarse whip of rawhide or braided leather

²cowhide *vt* : to flog with a cowhide whip

cowl \'kaůl\ *n* 1 : a hood or long hooded cloak especially of a monk 2 a : a chimney covering for improving the draft b : the top portion of the front part of an automobile body forward of the two front doors to which are attached the windshield and instrument panel c : COWLING [Old English *cugele,* from Late Latin *cuculla* "monk's hood", from Latin *cucullus* "hood"] — **cowled** \'kaůld\ *adj*

cow·lick \'kaů-ˌlik\ *n* : a turned-up tuft of hair growing in a direction different from the rest of the hair [from its appearance of having been licked by a cow]

cowl·ing \'kaů-ling\ *n* : a removable metal covering for the engine and sometimes a portion of the fuselage or nacelle of an airplane; *also* : a metallic cover for any engine

cow·man \'kaů-mən, -ˌman\ *n* 1 : COWHERD, COWBOY 2 : a cattle owner or rancher

co–work·er \'kō-ˌwər-kər\ *n* : a fellow worker

cow·pea \'kaů-ˌpē\ *n* : a sprawling herb related to the bean and grown in the southern United States especially for forage and green manure; *also* : its edible seed

Cow·per's gland \'kaů-pərz-, 'kü-ˌpərz-, 'kůp-ərz-\ *n* : either of two small glands discharging into the male urethra [William *Cowper,* died 1709, English surgeon]

cow·poke \'kaů-ˌpōk\ *n* : COWBOY [*cow* + *poke* "to punch"]

cow pony *n* : a light saddle horse trained for herding cattle

cow·pox \'kaů-ˌpäks\ *n* : a mild rash-producing virus disease of the cow that when communicated to a human protects against smallpox

cow·punch·er \-ˌpən-chər\ *n* : COWBOY

cow·rie *or* **cow·ry** \'kaůr-ē\ *n, pl* **cowries** : any of numerous small snails of warm seas with glossy often brightly colored shells; *also* : the shell of a cowrie [Hindi *kaurī*]

cow·slip \'kaů-ˌslip\ *n* 1 : a common Old World primrose with fragrant yellow or purplish flowers 2 : MARSH MARIGOLD [Old English *cūslyppe,* literally, "cow dung"]

cox \'käks\ *n* : COXSWAIN 2 — **cox** *vb*

coxa \'käk-sə\ *n, pl* **cox·ae** \-ˌsē, -ˌsī\ : the segment of an arthropod limb nearest the body [Latin, "hip"] — **cox·al** \-səl\ *adj*

cox·comb \'käk-ˌskōm\ *n* : a conceited foppish person [Middle English *cokkes comb,* literally, "cock's comb"] — **cox·comb·ical** \käk-'skō-mi-kəl, -'käm-i-\ *adj*

cox·swain \'käk-sən, -ˌswän\ *n* 1 : a sailor who has charge of a ship's boat and its crew 2 : one who steers a racing shell [Middle English *cokswayne,* from *cok* "small boat" + *swain* "servant"]

coy \'kȯi\ *adj* 1 a : BASHFUL 1 b : pretending shy or demure reserve 2 : showing reluctance to make a definite commitment ⟨politicians *coy* about their plans⟩ [Middle French *coi* "quiet, calm", from Latin *quietus*] SYN see SHY — **coy·ly** *adv* — **coy·ness** *n*

coy·ote \'kī-ˌōt, kī-'ōt-ē\ *n, pl* **coyotes** *or* **coyote** : a small wolf native to western North America [Mexican Spanish, from Nahuatl *coyotl*]

coy·pu \'kȯi-ˌpü\ *n* 1 : a South American aquatic rodent with webbed feet, mammary glands on its back, and a fur of some commercial value 2 : NUTRIA 2 [American Spanish *coipú,* of American Indian origin]

coz·en \'kəz-n\ *vb* : to deceive by artful coaxing ⟨tried to *cozen* their opponent's supporters⟩ [obsolete Italian *cozzonare,* from Italian *cozzone* "horse trader", from Latin *cocio* "trader"] — **coz·en·age** \-n-ij\ *n* — **coz·en·er** *n*

¹co·zy \'kō-zē\ *adj* **co·zi·er; -est** 1 : enjoying or affording warmth and ease : SNUG 2 : marked by a cautious attitude ⟨a *cozy* waiting game⟩ [probably of Scandinavian origin] — **co·zi·ly** \-zə-lē\ *adv* — **co·zi·ness** \-zē-nəs\ *n*

²cozy *adv* : in a cautious manner ⟨play it *cozy*⟩

³cozy *n, pl* **coz·ies** : a padded covering for a vessel (as a teapot) to keep the contents hot

¹crab \'krab\ *n* 1 : a crustacean with a short broad usually flattened shell, a small abdomen curled forward beneath the body, and a front pair of limbs with strong pincers; *also* : any of various other crustaceans resem-

C cowl 1

coypu 1

¹crab 1

bling true crabs in having a small abdomen **2** : any of various machines for raising or hauling heavy weights [Middle English *crabbe*, from Old English *crabba*]

²crab *vi* **crabbed; crab·bing** : to fish for crabs — **crab·ber** *n*

³crab *vb* **crabbed; crab·bing** : to find fault : COMPLAIN

⁴crab *n* **1** : CRAB APPLE **2** : a disagreeable ill-tempered person [Middle English *crabbe*, perhaps from *crabbe* "¹crab"]

crab apple *n* **1** : a small wild sour apple **2** : a cultivated apple with small usually brightly colored acid fruit

crab·bed \'krab-əd\ *adj* **1** : CROSS 3 **2** : difficult to read or understand — **crab·bed·ly** *adv* — **crab·bed·ness** *n*

crab·by \'krab-ē\ *adj* **crab·bi·er; -est** : ILL-NATURED ⟨a *crabby* disposition⟩

crab·grass \'krab-ˌgras\ *n* : a weedy grass with creeping or sprawling stems that root freely at the nodes

crab louse *n* : a louse infesting the human pubic region

¹crack \'krak\ *vb* **1 a** : to break or cause to break with a sudden sharp sound : SNAP **b** : to make or cause to make such a sound ⟨*crack* a whip⟩ **2** : to break with or without total separation of parts ⟨the ice *cracked* in several places⟩ **3** : to tell especially in a clever or witty way ⟨*crack* jokes⟩ **4 a** : to lose control **b** : to fail in tone ⟨their voices *cracked*⟩ **c** : to give or receive a sharp blow ⟨*crack* one's head⟩ **5 a** : to puzzle out and solve or discover the secret of ⟨*crack* a code⟩ **b** : to break into ⟨*crack* a safe⟩ **c** : to break through (as a barrier) **6 a** : to subject (hydrocarbons) to cracking ⟨*crack* petroleum⟩ **b** : to produce by cracking ⟨*cracked* gasoline⟩ [Old English *cracian*]

²crack *n* **1** : a sudden sharp noise **2** : a sharp witty remark : QUIP **3 a** : a narrow break **b** : a narrow opening ⟨open the window a *crack*⟩ **4 a** : a weakness or flaw caused by decay, age, or shortcoming **b** : a broken tone of the voice **5** : MOMENT ⟨the *crack* of dawn⟩ **6** : a sharp resounding blow **7** : TRY ⟨take a *crack* at it⟩ **8** : highly purified cocaine in small chips used illicitly usually for smoking

³crack *adj* : of superior quality ⟨*crack* troops⟩

crack·brain \'krak-ˌbrān\ *n* : an erratic or unbalanced person — **crack·brained** \-ˌbrānd\ *adj*

crack·down \'krak-ˌdaùn\ *n* : an act or instance of cracking down ⟨a *crackdown* on gambling⟩

crack down \'krak-'daùn\ *vi* : to take positive disciplinary action

cracked \'krakt\ *adj* **1** : broken into coarse pieces ⟨*cracked* wheat⟩ **2** : mentally disturbed

crack·er \'krak-ər\ *n* **1** : something (as a firecracker) that makes a cracking noise **2** : a dry thin crisp bakery product made of flour and water **3** : the equipment in which cracking is carried out

crack·er·jack \'krak-ər-ˌjak\ *n* : something very excellent — **crackerjack** *adj*

Cracker Jack *trademark* — used for a candied popcorn confection

crack·ing *n* : a process in which relatively heavy hydrocarbons (as oils from petroleum) are broken up by heat into lighter products (as gasoline)

¹crack·le \'krak-əl\ *vi* **crack·led; crack·ling** \'krak-ling, -ə-ling\ **1 a** : to make small sharp sudden repeated noises **b** : to show spirit : SPARKLE **2** : to develop a surface network of fine cracks [derived from ¹*crack*]

²crackle *n* **1** : the noise of repeated small cracks **2** : a network of fine cracks on an otherwise smooth surface

crack·ling *n* **1** \'krak-ling, -ə-ling\ : a series of small sharp crackling sounds **2** \'krak-lən, -ling\ : the crisp remainder left after the fat has been separated from the fibrous tissue (as in frying the skin of pork) — usually used in pl.

crack·ly \'krak-lē, -ə-lē\ *adj* : inclined to crackle : CRISP

crack·nel \'krak-nl\ *n* **1** : a hard brittle biscuit **2** : CRACKLING 2 — usually used in pl. [Middle English *krakenelle*]

crack·pot \'krak-ˌpät\ *n* : a crazy or peculiar person — **crack·pot** *adj*

cracks·man \'krak-smən\ *n* : BURGLAR; *also* : SAFE-CRACKER

crack·up \'krak-ˌəp\ *n* : CRASH 2, WRECK

crack up *vb* **1** : to smash up a vehicle (as by losing control) ⟨*cracked up* on a curve⟩ **2** : to assert the excellence of : PRAISE ⟨it's not all it's *cracked up* to be⟩

-c·ra·cy \k-rə-sē\ *n combining form* **1** : form of government; *also* : state having such a government **2** : social or political class (as of powerful persons) [Middle French *-cratie*, from Greek *-kratia*, from *kratos* "strength, power"]

¹cra·dle \'krād-l\ *n* **1** : a bed for a baby usually on rockers **2** : place of origin **3** : something serving as a framework or support: as **a** : the support for a telephone receiver or handset **b** : an implement with rods like fingers attached to a scythe and used formerly for harvesting grain **c** : a low frame on casters on which mechanics lie while working under an automobile **4** : a rocking device used in panning for gold [Old English *cradol*]

²cradle *vt* **cra·dled; cra·dling** \'krād-ling, -l-ing\ **1 a** : to place or keep in or as if in a cradle **b** : to shelter in childhood : REAR **c** : to protect and cherish lovingly **2** : to cut (grain) with a cradle scythe **3** : to place, raise, support, or transport on a cradle **4** : to wash in a miner's cradle

cra·dle·land \'krād-l-ˌland, -ˌand\ *n* : region of origin : BIRTHPLACE

cra·dle·song \'krād-l-ˌsòng\ *n* : LULLABY

craft \'kraft\ *n* **1** : skill in planning, making, or executing **2** : an occupation or trade requiring artistic skill or ease in using the hands **3** : skill in deceiving to gain an end **4** : the members of a trade or trade association **5** *pl usually* **craft a** : a boat especially of small size **b** : AIRCRAFT [Old English *cræft* "strength, skill"] SYN see ART

crafts·man \'kraf-smən, 'kraft-\ *n* **1** : a worker who practices a trade or handicraft **2** : a highly skilled worker in any field — **crafts·man·ship** \-ˌship\ *n*

craft union *n* : a labor union with membership limited to workers of the same craft — compare INDUSTRIAL UNION

crafty \'kraf-tē\ *adj* **craft·i·er; -est** : skillful at deceiving others : CUNNING SYN see SLY — **craft·i·ly** \-tə-lē\ *adv* — **craft·i·ness** \-tē-nəs\ *n*

crag \'krag\ *n* : a steep rugged rock or cliff [Middle English, of Celtic origin] — **crag·gy** \-ē\ *adj*

crake \'krāk\ *n* : any of various rails; *esp* : one with a short bill [Middle English, probably from Old Norse *krāka* "crow" or *krākr* "raven"]

cram \'kram\ *vb* **crammed; cram·ming** **1** : to stuff or crowd in ⟨*cram* clothes into a bag⟩ **2** : to fill full ⟨barns *crammed* with hay⟩ **3** : to study hastily in preparation for an examination **4** : to eat greedily : STUFF [Old English *crammian*] — **cram·mer** *n*

¹cramp \'kramp\ *n* **1** : a sudden painful involuntary contraction of muscle **2** : a temporary paralysis of muscles from overuse — compare WRITER'S CRAMP **3** : sharp abdominal pain — usually used in pl. [Middle French *crampe*, of Germanic origin]

²cramp *n* **1** : a usually iron device bent at the ends and used to hold timbers or blocks of stone together **2** : ¹CLAMP [Low German or obsolete Dutch *krampe* "hook"] — **cramp** *adj*

³cramp *vt* **1** : to affect with or as if with cramp **2 a** : CONFINE ⟨felt *cramped* in the tiny room⟩ **b** : HAMPER — used in the phrase cramp one's style **3** : to turn (the front wheels of a vehicle) to right or left **4** : to fasten or hold with a cramp

cram·pon \'kram-ˌpän\ *n* **1** : a hooked clutch or dog for raising heavy objects — usually used in pl. **2** : a framework that fits the bottom of a climbing boot and has spikes which grip on slopes of hard ice or snow [Middle French *crampon*, of Germanic origin]

cran·ber·ry \'kran-‚ber-ē, -bə-rē, -brē\ *n* : the bright red sour berry of any of several trailing plants related to the blueberry; *also* : a plant producing these [Low German *kraanbere*, from *kraan* "crane" + *bere* "berry"]

cranberry bush *n* : a viburnum that has leaves with three lobes and bears red fruit

¹crane \'krān\ *n* 1 : any of a family of tall wading birds related to the rails 2 : any of several herons 3 a : a machine for raising, shifting, and lowering heavy weights by means of a projecting swinging arm or with the hoisting apparatus supported on an overhead track b : an iron arm in a fireplace for supporting kettles c : a long movable support for a motion-picture or television camera [Old English *cran*]

²crane *vb* 1 : to raise or lift by a crane 2 : to stretch one's neck forward to see better

crane fly *n* : any of numerous long-legged slender two=winged flies that resemble large mosquitoes but do not bite

cranes·bill \'krānz-‚bil\ *n* : GERANIUM 1

cra·ni·al \'krā-nē-əl\ *adj* 1 : of or relating to the cranium 2 : CEPHALIC — **cra·ni·al·ly** \-ə-lē\ *adv*

cranial nerve *n* : any of the paired nerves that arise from the lower surface of the brain and pass through openings in the skull

cra·ni·um \'krā-nē-əm\ *n, pl* **-ni·ums** *or* **-nia** \-nē-ə\ : SKULL; *esp* : the part that encloses the brain [Medieval Latin, from Greek *kranion*]

¹crank \'krangk\ *n* 1 : a bent part of an axle or shaft or an arm at right angles to the end of a shaft by which circular motion is imparted to or received from the axle or shaft 2 a : WHIM b : an eccentric person c : a bad-tempered person : GROUCH [Old English *cranc*- (as in *crancstæf*, a weaving instrument)]

²crank *vb* 1 : to move with a winding course : ZIGZAG 2 : to bend into the shape of a crank 3 : to start or operate by turning a crank

crank·case \'krangk-‚kās\ *n* : the housing of a crankshaft

crank·pin \-‚pin\ *n* : the cylindrical piece which forms the handle of a crank or to which the connecting rod is attached

crank·shaft \-‚shaft\ *n* : a shaft turning or driven by a crank

cranky \'krang-kē\ *adj* **crank·i·er; -est** 1 : not in good working order ⟨a *cranky* old tractor⟩ 2 : IRRITABLE — **crank·i·ness** *n*

cran·ny \'kran-ē\ *n, pl* **crannies** : a small break or slit [Middle French *cren, cran* "notch"]

crape \'krāp\ *n* 1 : CREPE 1 2 : a band of crepe worn on a hat or sleeve as a sign of mourning [alteration of French *crêpe*]

crape myrtle *n* : an East Indian shrub of the loosestrife family widely grown in warm regions for its showy flowers

crap·pie \'krap-ē\ *n* 1 : BLACK CRAPPIE 2 : WHITE CRAPPIE [Canadian French *crapet*]

craps \'kraps\ *n pl* : a gambling game played with two dice [French, from English *crabs* "lowest throw at hazard", from ¹*crab*]

crap·shoot·er \'krap-‚shüt-ər\ *n* : a person who plays craps — **crap·shoot·ing** \-‚shüt-ing\ *n*

¹crash \'krash\ *vb* 1 a : to break violently and noisily : SMASH b : to damage an airplane in landing 2 a : to make or cause to make a loud noise b : to force through with loud crashing noises 3 : to enter or attend without invitation or without paying ⟨*crash* a party⟩ 4 : to decline or fail suddenly [Middle English *crasschen*] — **crash·er** *n*

²crash *n* 1 : a loud sound (as of things smashing) 2 : a breaking to pieces by or as if by collision; *also* : an

instance of crashing 3 : a sudden decline or failure (as of a business or prices) ⟨stock-market *crash*⟩

³crash *adj* : effected hastily on an emergency basis with all available means ⟨a *crash* program⟩

⁴crash *n* : a coarse fabric used for draperies, toweling, and clothing [probably from Russian *krashenina* "colored linen"]

crash dive *n* : a dive made by a submarine in the least possible time — **crash–dive** \'krash-'dīv\ *vi*

crash helmet *n* : a padded helmet that is worn (as by motorcyclists) as protection against head injury

crash–land \'krash-'land\ *vb* : to land an aircraft under emergency conditions usually with damage to the craft — **crash landing** *n*

crass \'kras\ *adj* : GROSS, INSENSITIVE ⟨*crass* ignorance⟩ [Latin *crassus* "thick, gross"] — **crass·ly** *adv* — **crass·ness** *n*

-crat \‚krat\ *n combining form* 1 : advocate or partisan of a (specified) form of government 2 : member of a (specified) dominant class [French *-crate*, back-formation from *-cratie* "-cracy"]

¹crate \'krāt\ *n* 1 : a box usually ventilated and made of thin wooden slats for packing fruit or vegetables 2 : an enclosing framework for protecting something (as in shipment) [Latin *cratis* "wickerwork, hurdle"]

²crate *vt* : to pack in a crate

cra·ter \'krāt-ər\ *n* : a bowl-shaped depression: as a : one around the opening of a volcano b : one formed by the impact of a meteorite c : a hole in the ground made by the explosion of a bomb or shell [Latin, "mixing bowl, crater", from Greek *kratēr*, from *kerannynai* "to mix"]

cra·vat \krə-'vat\ *n* : NECKTIE [French *cravate*, from *Cravate* "Croatian"]

crave \'krāv\ *vb* 1 : to ask for earnestly : BEG 2 : to have a strong desire or need for [Old English *crafian*]

¹cra·ven \'krā-vən\ *adj* : COWARDLY [Middle English *cravant*] — **cra·ven·ly** *adv* — **cra·ven·ness** \-vən-nəs\ *n*

²craven *n* : COWARD

crav·ing \'krā-ving\ *n* : a great desire or longing; *esp* : an abnormal desire (as for a habit-forming drug)

craw \'krȯ\ *n* 1 : the crop of a bird or insect 2 : the stomach especially of a lower animal [Middle English *crawe*]

craw·fish \'krȯ-‚fish\ *n* 1 : CRAYFISH 1 2 : SPINY LOBSTER [by folk etymology from Middle English *crevis*]

¹crawl \'krȯl\ *vb* 1 : to move slowly with the body close to the ground : CREEP 2 : to drag along slowly or feebly 3 : to advance by cunning or servility 4 : to be swarming with or have the sensation of swarming with creeping things [Old Norse *krafla*] SYN see CREEP — **crawl·er** *n*

²crawl *n* 1 : the act or motion of crawling 2 : a racing stroke in which a swimmer lying flat in the water moves forward by overarm strokes and a flutter kick

³crawl *n* : an enclosure in shallow waters (as for confining lobsters) [Afrikaans *kraal* "pen"]

crawly \'krȯ-lē\ *adj* : having the sensation of being swarmed with crawling things

cray·fish \'krā-‚fish\ *n* 1 : any of numerous freshwater crustaceans resembling but usually much smaller than the lobster 2 : SPINY LOBSTER [by folk etymology from Middle English *crevis*, from Middle French *crevice*, of Germanic origin]

¹cray·on \'krā-‚än, -ən; 'kran\ *n* 1 : a stick of white or colored chalk or of colored wax used for writing or drawing 2 : a crayon drawing [French, "crayon, pencil", from *craie* "chalk", from Latin *creta*]

²crayon *vt* : to draw or color with a crayon — **cray·on·ist** \'krā-ə-nəst\ *n*

¹craze \'krāz\ *vb* 1 : to make or become insane 2 : to develop a network of fine cracks [Middle English *crasen* "to crush, craze", of Scandinavian origin]

¹crank 1

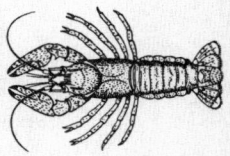

crayfish 1

\ə\	abut	\ng\	sing
\ər\	further	\ō\	bone
\a\	mat	\ȯ\	saw
\ā\	take	\ȯi\	coin
\ä\	cot, cart	\th\	thin
\au̇\	out	\th\	this
\ch\	chin	\ü\	food
\e\	pet	\u̇\	foot
\ē\	easy	\y\	yet
\g\	go	\yü\	few
\i\	tip	\yu̇\	cure
\ī\	life	\zh\	vision
\j\	job		

²craze \'krāz\ *n* **1** : a strong but temporary interest in something or the object of such an interest : FAD ⟨the latest *craze* among high school students⟩ **2** : a fine crack in glaze or enamel or on a painted surface

cra·zy \'krā-zē\ *adj* **cra·zi·er; -est 1 a** : full of cracks or flaws : UNSOUND **b** : CROOKED 1 **2 a** : mentally disordered : INSANE **b** (1) : wildly impractical (2) : ERRATIC **3** : distracted with desire or excitement SYN *see* INSANE — **cra·zi·ly** \-zə-lē\ *adv* — **cra·zi·ness** \-zē-nəs\ *n*

crazy bone *n* : FUNNY BONE 1

crazy quilt *n* : a patchwork quilt without a design

¹creak \'krēk\ *vi* : to make a prolonged grating or squeaking sound [Middle English *creken* "to croak"]

²creak *n* : a rasping or grating noise — **creak·i·ly** \'krē-kə-lē\ *adv* — **creaky** \'krē-kē\ *adj*

¹cream \'krēm\ *n* **1** : the yellowish part of milk containing butterfat **2 a** : a food prepared with cream **b** : something (as a food, or a medicinal or cosmetic preparation) having the consistency of cream **3** : the choicest part ⟨the *cream* of the crop⟩ **4** : a pale yellow [Middle French *craime,* from Late Latin *cramum,* of Celtic origin] — **creamy** \'krē-mē\ *adj*

²cream *vb* **1** : to form cream **2 a** : SKIM 1b **b** : to take the choicest part of something **3** : to furnish, prepare, or treat with cream **4 a** : to beat into a creamy froth **b** : to work or blend to the consistency of cream

cream cheese *n* : an unripened soft white cheese made from whole milk enriched with cream

cream·er \'krē-mər\ *n* **1** : a device for separating cream from milk **2** : a small pitcher or jug for serving cream

cream·ery \'krēm-rē, -ə-rē\ *n, pl* **-er·ies** : an establishment where butter and cheese are made or where milk and cream are sold or prepared

cream of tartar : a white crystalline salt $C_4H_5KO_6$ used especially in baking powder and in galvanic tinning of metals

cream puff *n* : a round shell of light pastry filled with whipped cream or a cream filling

cream sauce *n* : WHITE SAUCE

¹crease \'krēs\ *n* **1** : a line or mark made by or as if by folding **2** : a specially marked area around a goal (as in hockey) [probably from Middle English *creste* "crest"]

²crease *vb* **1** : to make a crease in or on **2** : to wound slightly especially by grazing **3** : to become creased — **creas·er** *n*

cre·ate \krē-'āt, 'krē-,\ *vt* **1** : to bring into existence **2** : to install in a new office or rank ⟨was *created* a lieutenant⟩ **3 a** : to bring about : CAUSE, MAKE, PRODUCE ⟨*create* a disturbance⟩ **b** : DESIGN ⟨*creates* evening dresses⟩ [Latin *creare*]

cre·atine \'krē-ə-ˌtēn, -ət-n\ *n* : a white crystalline nitrogenous substance $C_4H_9N_3O_2$ found especially in the muscles of vertebrates [Greek *kreat-, kreas* "flesh"]

cre·ation \krē-'ā-shən\ *n* **1** : the act of creating or fact of being created; *esp* : the bringing of the world into existence out of nothing **2** : something created **3** : all created things : WORLD

cre·ation·ism \-shə-ˌniz-əm\ *n* : a theory that matter, life, and the world were created by God from nothing as described in Genesis — **cre·ation·ist** \-shə-nəst, -shnəst\ *n or adj*

creation science *n* : CREATIONISM; *also* : scientific evidence or arguments put forth in support of creationism

cre·ative \krē-'āt-iv\ *adj* : able to create; *esp* : having or showing the power to produce original work (as in literature) — **cre·ative·ly** *adv* — **cre·ative·ness** *n*

cre·ativ·i·ty \ˌkrē-ā-'tiv-ət-ē, ˌkrē-ə-\ *n* : ability to create

cre·ator \krē-'āt-ər\ *n* **1** : one that creates or produces : MAKER **2** *cap* : GOD 1

crea·ture \'krē-chər\ *n* **1** : a created being **2 a** : a lower animal; *esp* : a farm animal **b** : a human being **c** : a being of abnormal or uncertain nature **3** : one who is

the obedient tool of another — **crea·tur·al** \'krēch-rəl, -ə-rəl\ *adj*

creature comfort *n* : something (as food or warmth) that gives bodily comfort

crèche \'kresh\ *n* **1** : a day nursery or foundling home **2** : a representation of the Nativity scene in the stable at Bethlehem [French, from Old French *creche* "manger, crib", of Germanic origin]

cre·dence \'krēd-ns\ *n* **1** : mental acceptance as true or real : BELIEF ⟨give *credence* to gossip⟩ **2** : a small table where the bread and wine rest before consecration [Medieval Latin *credentia,* from Latin *credere* "to believe, trust"]

cre·den·tial \kri-'den-chəl\ *n* **1** : something that gives a title to credit or confidence **2** *pl* : documents showing that a person is entitled to confidence or has a right to exercise official power

cre·den·za \kri-'den-zə\ *n* : a sideboard, buffet, or bookcase; *esp* : one without legs [Italian, literally, "belief, confidence", from Medieval Latin *credentia*]

cred·i·ble \'kred-ə-bəl\ *adj* : capable of being believed : deserving to be believed ⟨a *credible* story⟩ [Latin *credibilis,* from *credere* "to believe"] SYN *see* PLAUSIBLE — **cred·i·bil·i·ty** \ˌkred-ə-'bil-ət-ē\ *n* — **cred·i·bly** \'kred-ə-blē\ *adv*

¹cred·it \'kred-ət\ *n* **1 a** : a favorable balance in a bank account **b** : an entry in an account representing an addition of income or net worth ⟨debits and *credits*⟩ **c** : a sum of money placed at one's disposal by a bank **d** (1) : the right or privilege of taking present possession of money, goods, or services in exchange for a promise to pay for them at a future date ⟨long-term *credit*⟩ (2) : faith in the willingness of one to whom credit is extended to perform his or her promise ⟨buy on *credit*⟩ (3) : reputation for fulfilling financial obligations ⟨keep your *credit* good⟩ **2 a** : reliance on the truth or reality of something ⟨a story that deserves little *credit*⟩ **b** : reputation for honesty or integrity : good name **3** : something that adds to a person's reputation or honor ⟨give a person *credit* for a discovery⟩ **4** : a source of honor ⟨a *credit* to the school⟩ **5 a** : official certification of the completion of a course of study **b** : a unit of academic work for which such acknowledgment is made [Middle French, derived from Latin *creditum* "something entrusted to another, loan", from *credere* "to believe, trust"]

²credit *vt* **1** : to trust in the truth of : BELIEVE **2** : to enter upon the credit side of an account **3 a** : to give credit to **b** : to attribute to some person SYN *see* ASCRIBE

cred·it·able \'kred-ət-ə-bəl\ *adj* **1** : worthy of belief **2** : worthy of praise — **cred·it·abil·i·ty** \ˌkred-ət-ə-'bil-ət-ē\ *n* — **cred·it·ably** \'kred-ət-ə-blē\ *adv*

credit card *n* : a card authorizing purchases on credit

cred·i·tor \'kred-ət-ər\ *n* : a person to whom a debt is owed; *esp* : a person to whom money or goods are due

credit union *n* : a cooperative association that makes small loans to its members at low rates

cre·do \'krēd-ō, 'krād-\ *n, pl* **credos** : CREED [Latin, "I believe"]

cre·du·li·ty \kri-'dü-lət-ē, -'dyü-\ *n* : a willingness to believe especially on little or no evidence

cred·u·lous \'krej-ə-ləs\ *adj* : ready to believe especially on slight or uncertain evidence [Latin *credulus,* from *credere* "to believe"] — **cred·u·lous·ly** *adv* — **cred·u·lous·ness** *n*

Cree \'krē\ *n, pl* **Cree** *or* **Crees** : a member of an Algonquian people of what is now Manitoba and Saskatchewan [Canadian French *Cris* "Crees", short for *Cristinaux,* of American Indian origin]

creed \'krēd\ *n* **1** : a statement of the essential beliefs of a religious faith **2** : a set of guiding principles or beliefs [Old English *crēda,* from Latin *credo* "I believe" (first word of the Apostles' and Nicene creeds), from *credere* "to believe"] — **creed·al** *or* **cre·dal** \'krēd-l\ *adj*

creek \'krēk, 'krik\ *n* **1** *chiefly British* : a small narrow inlet extending farther inland than a cove **2** : a natural stream of water usually smaller than a river [Middle English *crike, creke*, from Old Norse *-kriki* "bend"]

Creek \'krēk\ *n* : a member of a confederacy of Indian peoples formerly occupying most of what is now Alabama and Georgia and parts of Florida

creel \'krēl\ *n* : a wicker basket (as for fish) [Middle English *creille, crele*]

¹creep \'krēp\ *vi* **crept** \'krept\; **creep·ing** **1** : to move along with the body prone and close to the ground; *also* : to move slowly on hands and knees **2** : to go slowly ⟨the hours *crept* by⟩ **3 a** : to move or stir slightly by swelling or shrinking ⟨the scream made my skin *creep*⟩ **b** : to spread or grow over a surface usually rooting at intervals ⟨*creeping* vines⟩ **4** : to slip or gradually shift position [Old English *crēopan*] □ SYN CREEP, CRAWL mean to move slowly in a prone or crouching posture. CREEP often suggests the furtive, noiseless movement of one capable of rapid movement ⟨the cat *crept* closer to the bird⟩ CRAWL suggests the laborious progress of legless insects or reptiles or of maimed animals. CREEP connotes stealth or insinuation ⟨*crept* into favor⟩ CRAWL often connotes abjectness or submission.

²creep *n* **1** : a creeping movement **2 a** : a distressing sensation like that of insects creeping over one's flesh **b** : a feeling of horror — usually used in pl. **3** : an enclosure that young animals (as calves) can enter while adults are excluded

creep·er \'krē-pər\ *n* **1** : one that creeps: as **a** : a creeping plant **b** : a bird that creeps about on trees or bushes searching for insects **2** : a device with iron points worn on a shoe to prevent slipping

creepy \'krē-pē\ *adj* **creep·i·er; -est** : feeling or producing nervous shivery apprehension ⟨a *creepy* horror story⟩ — **creep·i·ness** *n*

cre·mate \'krē-,māt, kri-'\ *vt* : to reduce (a corpse) to ashes by burning [Latin *cremare*] — **cre·ma·tion** \kri-'mā-shən\ *n*

cre·ma·to·ri·um \,krē-mə-'tōr-ē-əm, ,krem-ə-, -'tor-\ *n, pl* **-ri·ums** *or* **-ria** \-ē-ə\ : CREMATORY

cre·ma·to·ry \'krē-mə-,tōr-ē, 'krem-, -,tor-\ *n, pl* **-ries** : a furnace used for cremating; *also* : a structure containing such a furnace — **crematory** *adj*

crème de ca·cao \,krēm-də-'kō-kō, ,krem-də-kə-'kaù, -kə-'kā-ō\ *n* : a sweet liqueur flavored with cacao beans and vanilla [French, literally, "cream of cacao"]

crème de menthe \,krem-də-'menth, ,krēm-, -'mint\ *n* : a sweet mint-flavored liqueur [French, literally, "cream of mint"]

cre·nate \'krē-,nāt, 'kren-,āt\ *or* **cre·nat·ed** \-əd\ *adj* : having the margin (as of a leaf or a shrunken red blood cell) cut into rounded scallops [Medieval Latin *crena* "notch"] — **cre·na·tion** \kri-'nā-shən\ *n*

cren·el·ate *or* **cren·el·ate** \'kren-l-,āt\ *vt* : to furnish with battlements [Middle French *crenel* "embrasure in a battlement", from Old French *cren* "notch"] — **cren·el·la·tion** \,kren-l-'ā-shən\ *n*

cre·o·dont \'krē-ə-,dänt\ *n* : any of a group (Creodonta) of extinct primitive carnivorous mammals that form a link between modern carnivores and the ungulates [Greek *kreas* "flesh" + *odont-, odous* "tooth"] — **creodont** *adj*

Cre·ole \'krē-,ōl\ *n* **1** : a white person descended from early French or Spanish settlers in the United States Gulf states and preserving their speech and culture **2** : a person of mixed French or Spanish and Black descent speaking a dialect of French or Spanish **3 a** : a language evolved from a pidgin based on French that is spoken by blacks in southern Louisiana **b** *not cap* : a language that has evolved from a pidgin and serves as the native language of a speech community [French

créole, from Spanish *criollo*, from Portuguese *crioulo* "white person born in the colonies"] — **Creole** *adj*

¹cre·o·sote \'krē-ə-,sōt\ *n* **1** : a clear or yellowish oily liquid mixture of compounds obtained by the distillation of wood tar especially from beechwood **2** : a brownish oily liquid obtained by distillation of coal tar and used especially as a wood preservative [German *kreosot*, from Greek *kreas* "flesh" + *sōtēr* "preserver", from *sōzein* "to preserve", from *sōs* "safe"]

²creosote *vt* : to treat with creosote

creosote bush *n* : a desert shrub of the southwestern United States and adjacent Mexico with aromatic foliage and small bright yellow flowers

crepe *or* **crêpe** \'krāp\ *n* **1** : a thin crinkled fabric (as of silk, wool, or cotton) **2** : a small very thin pancake [French *crêpe*, from Middle French *crespe* "curly", from Latin *crispus*] — **crepe** *adj*

crepe de chine \,krāp-də-'shēn\ *n, often cap 2d C* : a soft fine clothing crepe [French *crêpe de Chine*, literally, "crepe of China"]

crepe paper *n* : paper with a crinkled or puckered texture

crepe rubber *n* : crude rubber in the form of nearly white to brown crinkled sheets used especially for shoe soles

crepe su·zette \,krāp-sù-'zet\ *n, pl* **crepes suzette** \,krāp-sù-, ,krāps-\ *or* **crepe suzettes** \,krāp-sù-'zets\ : a thin folded or rolled pancake in a hot orange-butter sauce that is sprinkled with a liqueur and set ablaze for serving [French *crêpe Suzette*, from *crêpe* "pancake" + *Suzette* "Susy"]

crept *past of* CREEP

cre·pus·cu·lar \kri-'pəs-kyə-lər\ *adj* **1** : of, relating to, or resembling twilight : DIM **2** : active in the twilight ⟨*crepuscular* insects⟩ [Latin *crepusculum* "twilight"]

cre·scen·do \kri-'shen-dō\ *n, pl* **-dos** *or* **-does** **1** : a gradual increase in volume of sound in music; *also* : a passage so performed **2** : a gradual increase (as in physical or emotional force); *also* : the peak of such an increase [Italian, from *crescendo* "increasing", from *crescere* "to increase", from Latin] — **crescendo** *adv or adj*

cres·cent \'kres-nt\ *n* **1 a** : the moon at any stage between new moon and first quarter and between last quarter and the succeeding new moon **b** : the figure of the moon defined by a convex and a concave edge **2** : an object shaped like a crescent [Middle French *creissant*, from *creistre* "to grow, increase", from Latin *crescere*] — **cres·cen·tic** \kre-'sent-ik\ *adj*

cre·sol \'krē-,sòl, -,sōl\ *n* : any of three isomeric poisonous colorless crystalline or liquid organic substances C_7H_8O obtained from coal tar and used as disinfectants or in making resins [derived from *creosote*]

cress \'kres\ *n* : any of numerous plants of the mustard family with leaves used in salads [Old English *cressa*]

¹crest \'krest\ *n* **1 a** : a showy tuft or process on the head of an animal (as a bird) **b** : a plume worn on a knight's helmet **c** : a heraldic design above the escutcheon in a coat of arms **2** : an upper part, edge, or limit ⟨the *crest* of a hill⟩ **3** : a high point of an action or process : CLIMAX, CULMINATION ⟨at the *crest* of their fame⟩ [Middle French *creste*, from Latin *crista*] — **crest·less** *adj*

²crest *vb* **1** : to furnish with a crest : CROWN **2** : to reach the crest of ⟨*crest* the hill⟩ **3** : to rise to a crest ⟨the river *crested* at eight feet⟩

crest·ed \'kres-təd\ *adj* : having a crest ⟨a *crested* bird⟩

crest·fall·en \'krest-,fò-lən, 'kres-\ *adj* : feeling shame or humiliation : DEJECTED — **crest·fall·en·ness** *n*

Cre·ta·ceous \kri-'tā-shəs\ *n* : the 3d and latest period of the Mesozoic era during which chalk and most of the coal of the United States west of the Great Plains were formed; *also* : the corresponding system of rocks — see GEOLOGIC TIME table [Latin *cretaceus* "chalky", from *creta* "chalk"] — **Cretaceous** *adj*

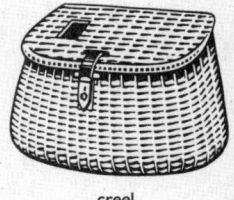

creel

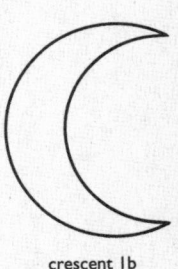

crescent 1b

\ə\ abut	\ng\ sing
\ər\ **further**	\ō\ **bone**
\a\ **mat**	\ò\ **saw**
\ā\ **take**	\òi\ **coin**
\ä\ **cot, cart**	\th\ **thin**
\aù\ **out**	\t̲h̲\ **this**
\ch\ **chin**	\ü\ **food**
\e\ **pet**	\ù\ **foot**
\ē\ **easy**	\y\ **yet**
\g\ **go**	\yü\ **few**
\i\ **tip**	\yù\ **cure**
\ī\ **life**	\zh\ **vision**
\j\ **job**	

cre·tin \'krēt-n\ *n* : one affected with cretinism; *also* : one having a marked mental deficiency [French *crétin*, from French dialect *cretin* "Christian, human being, kind of idiot found in the Alps", from Latin *christianus* "Christian"] — **cre·tin·ous** \-əs\ *adj* □ ORIGIN Most mountainous regions cannot provide an iodine‑rich diet. Iodine deficiency in a mother may result in the birth of mentally and physically retarded children, who become dwarfish idiots when fully grown. Such dwarfs were once common in certain Alpine valleys of French Switzerland. They were called *cretins* in the local dialect. A *cretin* was originally simply a "Christian". The term came to be used, as well, to differentiate human beings from other animals, since the possession of a Christian soul was considered to be what gave humans dominion over the rest of creation. The specific use of *cretin* for these unfortunate idiots emphasized their humanity.

cre·tin·ism \-,iz-əm\ *n* : a usually congenital abnormal condition marked by physical and mental stunting and caused by deficient functioning of the thyroid gland

cre·tonne \'krē-,tän, kri-'\ *n* : a strong unglazed cotton or linen cloth used especially for curtains and upholstery [French, from *Creton,* Normandy]

cre·vasse \kri-'vas\ *n* **1** : a deep crevice or fissure (as in a glacier) **2** : a breach in a levee [French, from Middle French *crevace*]

crev·ice \'krev-əs\ *n* : a narrow opening that results from a split or crack : FISSURE, CLEFT ⟨a *crevice* in a rock⟩ [Middle French *crevace,* from *crever* "to split", from Latin *crepare* "to crack"]

¹crew \'krü\ *chiefly British past of* CROW

²crew \'krü\ *n* **1** : a group of persons ⟨a happy *crew* on a picnic⟩ **2** : a group of people associated in joint work ⟨a train *crew*⟩ **3** : the group of persons who operate a ship **4 a** : the rowers and coxswain of a racing shell ⟨rowed on the college *crew*⟩ **b** : the sport of rowing **5** : the persons who operate an aircraft in flight [Middle English *crue,* literally, "reinforcement", from Middle French *creue* "increase", from *creistre* "to increase", from Latin *crescere*]

crew cut *n* : a very short haircut in which the hair resembles the bristles of a brush

crew·el \'krü-əl\ *n* : loosely twisted worsted yarn used for embroidery [Middle English *crule*]

¹crib \'krib\ *n* **1** : a manger for feeding animals **2** : a small child's bedstead with high enclosing usually slatted sides **3** : a building for storage **4** : the cards discarded in cribbage for the dealer to use in scoring **5 a** : a literal translation; *esp* : PONY 3 **b** : a device used for cheating in an examination **6** : ᴬˢˣcrècheᶠlᴬˢˣ 2 [Old English *cribb*]

²crib *vb* **cribbed; crib·bing 1** : to copy (as an idea or passage) and use as one's own : PLAGIARIZE **2** : to make use of a translation or notes dishonestly — **crib·ber** *n*

crib·bage \'krib-ij\ *n* : a card game for two players in which each player attempts to form various counting combinations of the cards [¹*crib*]

crick \'krik\ *n* : a painful spasm of muscles (as of the neck or back) [Middle English *cryk*] — **crick** *vt*

¹crick·et \'krik-ət\ *n* : any of a family of small leaping insects with leathery fore wings and thin hind wings that are related to the grasshoppers and are noted for the chirping notes of the males [Middle French *criquet*]

²cricket *n* **1** : a game played with a ball and bat by two sides of 11 players each on a large field centering upon 2 wickets **2** : fair and honorable behavior [Middle French *criquet* "goal stake in a bowling game"] — **crick·et·er** *n*

cri·er \'krī-ər, 'krīr\ *n* : one that cries; *esp* : one who proclaims orders or announcements

crime \'krīm\ *n* **1** : the doing of an act forbidden by law or the failure to do an act required by law **2** : a serious offense especially against morality **3** : criminal activity ⟨led a life of *crime*⟩ **4** : something shameful, foolish, or regrettable ⟨a *crime* to waste food⟩ [Middle French, from Latin *crimen* "accusation, fault, crime"]

¹crim·i·nal \'krim-ən-l\ *adj* **1** : involving or being a crime ⟨a *criminal* act⟩ **2** : relating to crime ⟨*criminal* courts⟩ **3** : guilty of crime [Late Latin *criminalis,* from Latin *crimen* "crime"] — **crim·i·nal·i·ty** \,krim-ə-'nal-ət-ē\ *n* — **crim·i·nal·ly** \'krim-ən-l-ē\ *adv*

²criminal *n* : one that has committed or has been convicted of a crime

crim·i·nol·o·gy \,krim-ə-'näl-ə-jē\ *n* : a scientific study of crime, criminals, and their punishment or correction — **crim·i·no·log·i·cal** \,krim-ən-l-'äj-i-kəl\ *adj* — **crim·i·nol·o·gist** \,krim-ə-'näl-ə-jəst\ *n*

¹crimp \'krimp\ *vt* **1** : to make wavy, bent, or warped **2** : to put a crimp in : INHIBIT [Dutch or Low German *krimpen* "to shrivel"] — **crimp·er** *n*

²crimp *n* **1** : something produced by or as if by crimping **2** : something that cramps or inhibits

¹crim·son \'krim-zən\ *n* : deep purplish red [Spanish *cremesin,* from Arabic *qirmizī,* from *qirmiz* "kermes"] — **crimson** *adj*

²crimson *vb* : to make or become crimson

¹cringe \'krinj\ *vi* **cringed; cring·ing 1** : to draw in or contract one's muscles involuntarily **2** : to shrink in fear : COWER **3** : to behave in a servile way [Middle English *crengen*] — **cring·er** *n*

²cringe *n* : an act of cringing

¹crin·kle \'kring-kəl\ *vb* **crin·kled; crin·kling** \-kə-ling, -kling\ **1** : to form many short bends or turns : RIPPLE **2** : to emit a thin crackling sound : RUSTLE ⟨*crinkling* silk⟩ [Middle English *crynkelen*]

²crinkle *n* : CREASE 1, WRINKLE ⟨*crinkles* around the eyes⟩ — **crin·kly** \-kə-lē, -klē\ *adj*

cri·noid \'krī-,noid\ *n* : any of a large class (Crinoidea) of echinoderms having usually a cup-shaped body with five or more feathery arms [Greek *krinon* "lily"] — **crinoid** *adj*

crin·o·line \'krin-l-ən\ *n* **1** : a cloth originally of horsehair and linen thread used for stiffening and lining **2 a** : HOOPSKIRT **b** : a full stiff skirt or underskirt [French, from Italian *crinolino,* from *crino* "horsehair" + *lino* "flax, linen"] — **crinoline** *adj*

¹crip·ple \'krip-əl\ *n* : a lame or partly disabled individual [Old English *crypel*]

²cripple *vt* **crip·pled; crip·pling** \'krip-ling, -ə-ling\ **1** : to deprive of the use of a limb and especially a leg **2** : to deprive of strength, efficiency, wholeness, or capability for service — **crip·pler** \-lər\ *n*

cri·sis \'krī-səs\ *n, pl* **cri·ses** \'krī-,sēz\ **1** : the turning point for better or worse in an acute disease or fever **2** : a decisive moment (as in the plot of a story) **3** : an unstable or crucial time or state of affairs ⟨a political *crisis*⟩ [Latin, from Greek *krisis,* literally, "decision", from *krinein* "to judge, decide"] SYN see JUNCTURE

¹crisp \'krisp\ *adj* **1** : CURLY 1, WAVY ⟨*crisp* hair⟩ **2** : easily crumbled : FLAKY ⟨*crisp* pastry⟩ **3** : being firm and fresh ⟨*crisp* lettuce⟩ **4 a** : being sharp, clean, and concise ⟨a *crisp* photo⟩ **b** : noticeably neat **c** : keenly alert and lively : INCISIVE ⟨a *crisp* retort⟩ **d** : SNAPPY 2b ⟨*crisp* weather⟩ [Old English, from Latin *crispus*] SYN see BRITTLE — **crisp·ly** *adv* — **crisp·ness** *n*

²crisp *vb* : to make or become crisp — **crisp·er** *n*

³crisp *n* : something crisp or brittle ⟨dinner burned to a *crisp*⟩

crispy \'kris-pē\ *adj* **crisp·i·er; -est** : CRISP 2 — **crisp·i·ness** *n*

¹criss·cross \'kris-,kròs\ *n* : a pattern formed by or as if by crossed lines [obsolete *christcross* "mark of a cross", from *Christ* + *cross*] — **crisscross** *adj or adv*

²crisscross *vb* **1** : to mark with intersecting lines **2** : to go or pass back and forth

cris·ta \'kris-tə\ *n, pl* **cris·tae** \-,tē, -,tī\ : any of the inwardly projecting ridges of the inner membrane of a mitochondrion [Latin, "crest"]

cri·te·ri·on \krī-'tir-ē-ən\ *n, pl* **-ria** \-ē-ə\ *also* **-ri·ons** : a standard on which a judgment or decision may be based [Greek *kritērion,* from *krinein* "to judge, decide"] **SYN** *see* **STANDARD**

crit·ic \'krit-ik\ *n* **1** : a person who judges the value, worth, beauty, or excellence of something; *esp* : one whose profession is to express trained judgment on work in art, music, drama, or literature **2** : one inclined to harsh or unfair criticism : **FAULTFINDER** [Latin *criticus,* from Greek *kritikos,* from *krinein* "to judge"]

crit·i·cal \'krit-i-kəl\ *adj* **1 a** : inclined to criticize harshly and unfavorably **b** : consisting of or involving criticism ⟨*critical* writings⟩ **c** : using or involving careful judgment **2 a** (1) : of, relating to, or being a turning point ⟨the *critical* phase of a fever⟩ (2) : critically ill **b** : relating to or being a state in which or a measurement or point at which a quality, property, or phenomenon suffers a definite change ⟨*critical* temperature⟩ **c** : **CRUCIAL** ⟨a *critical* test⟩ **3 a** : of sufficient size to sustain a chain reaction — used of a mass of fissionable material **b** : sustaining a chain reaction — used of a nuclear reactor — **crit·i·cal·ly** \-i-kə-lē, -klē\ *adv* — **crit·i·cal·ness** \-kəl-nəs\ *n*

critical angle *n* : the least angle of incidence at which total reflection takes place

crit·i·cism \'krit-ə-ˌsiz-əm\ *n* **1 a** : the act of criticizing; *esp* : **FAULTFINDING** **b** : a critical remark or observation **c** : **CRITIQUE** **2** : the art of judging expertly the merits and faults of works of art or literature

crit·i·cize \'krit-ə-ˌsīz\ *vb* **1** : to examine and judge as a critic : **EVALUATE** **2** : to express criticism especially of an unfavorable kind **3** : to find fault or find fault with ⟨some people are too quick to *criticize*⟩ — **crit·i·ciz·er** *n*

cri·tique \krə-'tēk\ *n* : an act or instance of criticizing; *esp* : a critical estimate or discussion

¹croak \'krōk\ *vb* **1 a** : to utter a croak or similar sound **b** : to speak in a hoarse throaty voice **2** : to grumble dourly : **COMPLAIN** **3** *slang* : **DIE** 1 [Middle English *croken*]

²croak *n* : the characteristic hoarse harsh cry of a frog

croak·er \'krō-kər\ *n* **1** : an animal that croaks **2** : any of various fishes that produce croaking or grunting noises **3** : one that habitually grumbles or predicts evil

Croat \'krōt, 'krō-ˌat\ *n* : **CROATIAN**

Cro·a·tian \krō-'ā-shən\ *n* **1** : a native or inhabitant of Croatia **2** : a south Slavic language spoken by the Croatian people and distinct from Serbian chiefly in its use of the Latin alphabet — **Croatian** *adj*

¹cro·chet \krō-'shā\ *n* : needlework consisting of interlocked looped stitches formed with a single thread and a hooked needle [French, from *croche* "hook", of Scandinavian origin]

²crochet *vb* : to make of or work with crochet — **cro·chet·er** \-'shā-ər\ *n*

¹crock \'kräk\ *n* : a thick earthenware pot or jar [Old English *crocc*]

²crock *n* : one that is broken down, disabled, or impaired [Middle English *crok,* probably of Scandinavian origin]

crock·ery \'kräk-rē, -ə-rē\ *n* : **EARTHENWARE**

croc·o·dile \'kräk-ə-ˌdīl\ *n* **1** : any of several large thick-skinned long-bodied aquatic reptiles of tropical and subtropical waters; *also* : **CROCODILIAN** — compare **ALLIGATOR** **2** : the skin or hide of a crocodile [Latin *crocodilus,* from Greek *krokodilos* "lizard, crocodile", from *krokē* "pebble" + *drilos* "worm"]

crocodile tears *n pl* : false or pretended tears : insincere sorrow [from the ancient belief that crocodiles weep in sympathy for their victims]

croc·o·dil·ian \ˌkräk-ə-'dil-ē-ən, -'dil-yən\ *n* : any of an order (Loricata) of reptiles including the crocodiles, alligators, and related extinct forms — **crocodilian** *adj*

cro·cus \'krō-kəs\ *n, pl* **cro·cus·es** **1** *pl also* **cro·ci** \-ˌkē, -ˌkī, -ˌsī\ : any of a large genus of small herbs of the iris family with showy solitary long-tubed flowers and slender linear leaves **2** : **SAFFRON** 1b [Latin, "saffron", from Greek *krokos,* of Semitic origin]

croft \'króft\ *n* **1** *chiefly British* : a small enclosed field **2** *chiefly British* : a small farm worked by a tenant [Old English] — **croft·er** *n, chiefly British*

crois·sant \krə-ˌwä-'sän, ˌkwä-\ *n, pl* **croissants** \-'sän, -'sänz\ : a rich crescent-shaped roll [French, literally, "crescent", from Middle French *creissant*]

Cro–Mag·non \krō-'mag-nən, -'man-yən\ *n* : any of a race of tall erect people known from skeletal remains chiefly from southern France and often placed in the same species as recent human beings [*Cro-Magnon,* a cave near Les Eyzies, France] — **Cro–Magnon** *adj*

crom·lech \'kräm-ˌlek\ *n* **1** : **DOLMEN** **2** : a circle of monoliths enclosing a dolmen [Welsh, literally, "bent stone"]

crone \'krōn\ *n* : **HAG** 2 [Old North French *carogne,* literally, "carrion"]

cro·ny \'krō-nē\ *n, pl* **cronies** : a close friend : **CHUM** [perhaps from Greek *chronios* "long-lasting", from *chronos* "time"]

¹crook \'krùk\ *n* **1** : an implement having a bent or hooked form: as **a** : a shepherd's staff **b** : **CROSIER** **2** : a dishonest person; *esp* : **CRIMINAL** **3** : **BEND** 2, **CURVE** **4** : a hook-shaped, curved, or bent part [Old Norse *krōkr* "hook"]

²crook *vb* : to turn from a straight line : **BEND, CURVE**

crook·ed \'krùk-əd\ *adj* **1** : having a crook or curve : **BENT** **2** : **DISHONEST** — **crook·ed·ly** *adv* — **crook·ed·ness** *n* ☐ **SYN** **CROOKED, AWRY, ASKEW** mean not straight. **CROOKED** applies to what is itself not straight but curving, bent, or twisted; **AWRY** applies to what is out of a straight line in relation to something else; **ASKEW** implies having a decided slant away from a straight course.

crook·neck \'krùk-ˌnek\ *n* : a squash with a long curved neck

croon \'krün\ *vb* : to hum or sing in a gentle murmuring way ⟨*croon* a lullaby⟩ [Dutch *cronen* "to bellow"] — **croon·er** *n*

¹crop \'kräp\ *n* **1** : the stock or handle of a whip; *also* : a riding whip with a short straight stock and a loop **2** : a pouched enlargement of the gullet of a bird or insect that receives food and prepares it for digestion **3 a** : an earmark on an animal; *esp* : one made by removing the upper part of the ear **b** : a close haircut **4 a** : a plant or animal or plant or animal product that can be grown and harvested **b** : the product or yield especially of a harvested crop **c** : **BATCH** 3, **LOT** ⟨a new *crop* of students⟩ [Old English *cropp* "craw, cluster, head of a plant"]

²crop *vb* **cropped; crop·ping** **1 a** : to remove the upper or outer parts of ⟨*crop* a hedge⟩ **b** : to cut off short : **CLIP** **2 a** : to cause (land) to bear produce; *also* : to grow as a crop **b** : **HARVEST** ⟨fishermen *cropped* a huge number of trout⟩ **3** : to feed by cropping something ⟨sheep *cropping* in the meadow⟩ **4** : to yield or make a crop ⟨the apple trees *cropped* well⟩ **5** : to appear unexpectedly or casually ⟨problems *crop* up daily⟩

crop·land \'kräp-ˌland\ *n* : land devoted to the production of plant crops

¹crop·per \'kräp-ər\ *n* : one that raises crops; *esp* : **SHARECROPPER**

²cropper *n* **1** : a severe fall **2** : a sudden or violent failure or collapse [probably from English dialect *crop* "neck", from ¹*crop*]

crop rotation *n* : the practice of growing different crops in succession on the same land chiefly to preserve the capacity of the soil to produce crops

cro·quet \krō-'kā\ *n* : a game in which the players use mallets to drive wooden balls through a series of

crocodile 1

\ə\ abut	\ng\ sing
\ər\ further	\ō\ bone
\a\ mat	\ò\ saw
\ā\ take	\oi\ coin
\ä\ cot, cart	\th\ thin
\aù\ out	\th\ this
\ch\ chin	\ü\ food
\e\ pet	\ù\ foot
\ē\ easy	\y\ yet
\g\ go	\yü\ few
\i\ tip	\yù\ cure
\ī\ life	\zh\ vision
\j\ job	

hoops set in the ground [French dialect, "hockey stick", from Old North French, "crook"]

cro·quette \krō-'ket\ *n* : a small roll or ball of minced meat, fish, or vegetables fried in deep fat [French, from *croquer* "to crunch"]

cro·sier *or* **cro·zier** \'krō-zhər\ *n* : a staff resembling a shepherd's crook carried by bishops and abbots as a symbol of office [Middle French *crossier* "crosier bearer", from *crosse* "crosier", of Germanic origin]

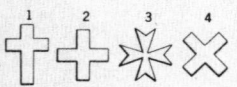

cross 4: *1* Latin, *2* Greek, *3* Maltese, *4* St Andrew's

¹cross \'krós\ *n* **1 a** : a structure consisting of an upright beam and a crossbar used especially by the ancient Romans for execution **b** *often cap* : the cross on which Jesus was crucified **2** : a trying affliction **3** : a cruciform sign made to invoke the blessing of Christ especially by touching the forehead, breast, and shoulders **4** : a cross-shaped mark or structure; *esp* : one used as a Christian emblem **5** : the intersection of two ways or lines : CROSSING **6 a** : an act of crossing unlike individuals **b** : a crossbred individual or kind **7** : a hook crossed over an opponent's lead in boxing [Old English, derived from Latin *crux*]

²cross *vb* **1 a** : to lie or be located across **b** : INTERSECT ⟨where two roads *cross*⟩ **2** : to make the sign of the cross on or over **3** : to cancel by marking a cross on or drawing a line through ⟨*cross* names off a list⟩ **4** : to place or fold crosswise one over the other ⟨*cross* the arms⟩ **5 a** : to run counter to : OPPOSE ⟨gets angry when *crossed*⟩ **b** : to turn against : BETRAY **6 a** : to extend across : TRAVERSE ⟨a highway *crossing* the state⟩ **b** : to go from one side to the other of ⟨*cross* a street⟩ **7** : to draw a line across ⟨*cross* a *t*⟩ **8** : INTERBREED, HYBRIDIZE **9** : to meet and pass on the way ⟨our letters *crossed* in the mail⟩

³cross *adj* **1** : lying or moving across ⟨*cross* traffic⟩ **2** : running counter : OPPOSITE ⟨*cross* winds⟩ **3** : marked by bad temper : GRUMPY — **cross·ly** *adv* — **cross·ness** *n*

cross·bar \'krós-ˌbär\ *n* : a transverse bar or stripe

cross·bill \-ˌbil\ *n* : any of a genus of finches with mandibles strongly curved and crossing each other

cross·bones \-ˌbōnz\ *n pl* : two leg or arm bones placed or depicted crosswise — compare SKULL AND CROSSBONES

cross·bow \-ˌbō\ *n* : a weapon that consists of a short bow mounted crosswise near the end of a wooden stock and that discharges stones or short arrows

cross·bow·man \-mən\ *n, pl* **-men** \-mən\ : a person who uses a crossbow

cross·bred \'krós-ˌbred\ *adj* : HYBRID; *esp* : produced by interbreeding two pure but different breeds, strains, or varieties — **cross·bred** \-ˌbred\ *n*

¹cross·breed \-ˌbrēd, -'brēd\ *vb* **1** : HYBRIDIZE; *esp* : to interbreed two varieties or breeds of the same species **2** : to engage in or undergo crossbreeding

²cross·breed \-ˌbrēd\ *n* : HYBRID 1

cross·coun·try \-'kən-trē\ *adj* **1** : extending across a country ⟨a *cross-country* tour⟩ **2** : proceeding over countryside and not by roads **3** : of or relating to racing over the countryside — **cross-country** *adv*

cross·cur·rent \-'kər-ənt, -'kə-rənt\ *n* **1** : a current running counter to another **2** : a conflicting tendency

¹cross·cut \-ˌkət, -'kət\ *vt* **-cut; -cut·ting** **1** : to cut with a crosscut saw **2** : to cut, go, or move across or through

²crosscut *adj* **1** : made or used for crosscutting ⟨a saw with *crosscut* teeth⟩ **2** : cut across or transversely ⟨a *crosscut* incision⟩

³cross·cut \-ˌkət\ *n* : something (as a walk) that cuts across or through ⟨took a *crosscut* through the park⟩

crosscut saw *n* : a saw designed chiefly to cut across the grain of wood

cross·dress·ing \'krós-ˌdres-ing\ *n* : the wearing of clothes designed for the opposite sex — **cross–dress·er** \-ˌdres-ər\ *n*

crosse \'krós\ *n* : the stick used in lacrosse [French, literally, "crosier"]

cross·ex·am·i·na·tion \ˌkrós-ig-ˌzam-ə-'nā-shən\ *n* : the questioning of a witness called by the opposing party to a legal action in order to check or discredit his or her testimony — **cross–ex·am·ine** \-'zam-ən\ *vt* — **cross–ex·am·in·er** *n*

cross–eye \'krós-ˌī\ *n* **1** : an abnormality in which the eye turns inward toward the nose **2** *pl* : eyes affected with cross-eye — **cross–eyed** \-'īd\ *adj*

cross–fer·til·i·za·tion \'krós-ˌfərt-l-ə-'zā-shən\ *n* **1** : fertilization between gametes produced by separate individuals or sometimes by individuals of different kinds **2** : CROSS-POLLINATION — **cross–fer·tile** \-'fərt-l\ *adj* — **cross–fer·til·ize** \-'fərt-l-ˌīz\ *vb*

cross fire *n* **1** : firing (as in combat) from two or more points so that the lines of fire cross; *also* : a situation in which forces of opposing factions meet or cross **2** : rapid or heated interchange (as of words)

cross–grained \'krós-'grānd\ *adj* **1** : having the grain or fibers running diagonally, transversely, or irregularly **2** : difficult to deal with : CONTRARY

cross hair *n* : one of the fine wires or threads in the focus of the eyepiece of an optical instrument used as a reference line

cross·hatch \'krós-ˌhach\ *vt* : to mark with a series of parallel lines that cross — **crosshatch** *n* — **crosshatch·ing** *n*

cross·ing \'kró-sing\ *n* **1 a** : the act or action of one that crosses **b** : a traversing or going across ⟨a channel *crossing*⟩ **c** : the act or process of interbreeding or hybridizing **2** : a place or structure (as on a street or over a river) where pedestrians or vehicles cross **3** : a point of intersection (as of streets)

cross·ing–over \ˌkró-sing-'ō-vər\ *n* : an exchange of genes or segments between associated parts of homologous chromosomes in synapsis during meiosis

cross–legged \'krós-'leg-əd, -'legd\ *adv or adj* **1** : with legs crossed and knees spread wide **2** : with one leg placed over and across the other

cross·over \'krós-ˌō-vər\ *n* **1** : CROSSING 2 **2** : an instance or product of genetic crossing-over

cross·piece \'krós-ˌpēs\ *n* : a horizontal member (as of a figure or a structure)

cross–pol·li·nate \-'päl-ə-ˌnāt\ *vt* : to subject to cross-pollination

cross–pol·li·na·tion \ˌkrós-ˌpäl-ə-'nā-shən\ *n* : the transfer of pollen from one flower to the stigma of another

cross product *n* : either of the two products obtained by multiplying together the two means or the two extremes of a proportion

cross–pur·pose \'krós-'pər-pəs\ *n* : an opposing or conflicting purpose ⟨working at *cross-purposes*⟩

cross–ques·tion \-'kwes-chən\ *vt* : to subject to close questioning; *esp* : CROSS-EXAMINE — **cross–question** *n*

cross–re·fer \ˌkrós-ri-'fər\ *vt* : to refer (a reader) by a notation or direction from one place to another (as in a book) — **cross–ref·er·ence** \'krós-'ref-ərns, -'ref-rəns, -ə-rəns\ *n*

cross·road \'krós-ˌrōd, -'rōd\ *n* **1** : a road that crosses a main road or runs cross-country between main roads **2** *usually pl* **a** : an intersection of two or more roads **b** : a small community located at a crossroads **3** : a crucial point where a decision must be made

cross·ruff \'krós-ˌrəf, -'rəf\ *n* : a series of plays in a card game (as bridge) in which partners alternately trump different suits — **crossruff** *vb*

cross section *n* **1 a** : a cutting made across something (as a log) **b** : a representation of a cutting made across something **c** : a section cut off at right angles to an axis by a plane ⟨a *cross section* of a right circular cone is a circle⟩ **2** : a number of persons or things selected to represent the general nature of a group ⟨a *cross sec-*

tion of society⟩ — **cross·sec·tion·al** \'krós-'sek-shnəl,
-shən-l\ *adj*

cross–stitch \'krós-,stich\ *n* 1 : a needlework stitch
that forms an X 2 : work done with cross-stitch —
cross–stitch *vb*

cross·town \'krós-,taùn, -'taùn\ *adj* 1 : situated at opposite points of a town 2 : extending or running
across a town ⟨a *crosstown* street⟩ — **crosstown** *adv*

cross·trees \'krós-,trēz\ *n pl* : two horizontal crosspieces near the top of a ship's mast to spread apart the
upper ropes that support the mast

cross·walk \'krós-,wòk\ *n* : a specially paved or marked
path for pedestrians crossing a street or road

cross·way \-,wā\ *n* : CROSSROAD 2a — often used in pl.

cross·ways \-,wāz\ *adv* : CROSSWISE 2, DIAGONALLY

¹**cross·wise** \-,wīz\ *adv* 1 *archaic* : in the form of a
cross 2 : so as to cross something : ACROSS

²**crosswise** *adj* : extended or lying across

cross·word puzzle \'krós-,wərd-\ *n* : a puzzle in which
words are filled into a pattern of numbered squares in
answer to similarly numbered clues and in such a way
that they read across and down

crotch \'kräch\ *n* 1 : an angle formed by the parting of
two branches or parts 2 : the region of the human
body between the legs where the legs join the trunk
[probably alteration of *crutch*]

crotch·et \'kräch-ət\ *n* : a peculiar opinion or habit
[Middle French *crochet* "small hook", from *croche*
"hook"] SYN see CAPRICE

crotch·ety \'kräch-ət-ē\ *adj* : marked by or given to
whims or ill temper — **crotch·et·i·ness** *n*

cro·ton \'krōt-n\ *n* : any of several herbs and shrubs of
the spurge family; *esp* : an East Indian plant yielding
an oil used as a strong purgative [Greek *krotōn* "castor-oil plant"]

Cro·ton bug \'krōt-n-\ *n* : a small active winged cockroach common where food and moisture are found
[*Croton* river, New York]

crouch \'kraùch\ *vb* 1 : to lower the body especially by
bending the legs 2 : to bend or bow servilely : CRINGE
[Middle English *crouchen*] — **crouch** *n*

¹**croup** \'krüp\ *n* : the rump of a four-footed animal
[Old French *croupe,* of Germanic origin]

²**croup** *n* : a laryngitis especially of infants marked by
episodes of difficult breathing and a hoarse metallic
cough [English dialect *croup* "to cry hoarsely,
cough"] — **croup·ous** \'krü-pəs\ *adj* — **croupy** \-pē\
adj

crou·pi·er \'krü-pē-ər, -pē-,ā\ *n* : an employee of a gambling casino who collects and pays bets at a gaming
table [French, literally, "rider on the croup of a
horse"]

crou·ton \'krü-,tän, krü-'\ *n* : a small crisp cube of
bread [French *croûton* "small crust", from *croûte*
"crust"]

¹**crow** \'krō\ *n* 1 : any of various large usually entirely
glossy black perching birds related to the jays 2 :
CROWBAR 3 : a member of a Siouan people of southeastern Montana [Old English *crāwe*] — **as the crow
flies** : in a straight line

²**crow** *vi* **crowed** \'krōd\ *also in sense 1 chiefly British*
crew \'krü\; **crow·ing** 1 : to utter the characteristic
loud shrill cry of a cock or a similar sound 2 : to utter
a sound expressive of pleasure 3 a : to exult gloatingly
especially over the distress of another b : to brag ex-
ultantly or blatantly [Old English *crāwan*]

³**crow** *n* 1 : the cry of a cock or a similar loud shrill
sound 2 : a triumphant cry

crow·bar \'krō-,bär\ *n* : a metal bar usually wedge=
shaped at the working end for use as a pry or lever

crow·ber·ry \'krō-,ber-ē\ *n* 1 : any of several low
shrubby evergreen plants; *esp* : a shrub of arctic and
alpine regions with an insipid black berry 2 : the fruit
of a crowberry

¹**crowd** \'kraùd\ *vb* 1 : to press onward : HURRY 2 : to
press close ⟨*crowd* around the speaker⟩ 3 : to collect
in numbers : THRONG 4 : to fill by pressing or thronging together : PACK ⟨*crowd* a room⟩ ⟨*crowd* children
into a bus⟩ [Old English *crūdan*]

²**crowd** *n* 1 : a large number of persons collected into a
body without order 2 : the great body of the people :
POPULACE ⟨books that appeal to the *crowd*⟩ 3 : a large
number of things close together 4 : a group of people
having a common interest SYN see MULTITUDE

crow·foot \'krō-,fùt\ *n, pl* **crow·feet** \-,fēt\ 1 *pl usually*
crowfoots : any of numerous plants having leaves with
cleft lobes; *esp* : BUTTERCUP 2 : CROW'S-FOOT 1 — usually used in pl.

¹**crown** \'kraùn\ *n* 1 : a wreath or band for the head;
esp : one worn as a mark of victory or honor 2 : a royal
headdress : DIADEM 3 : the highest part: as a : the topmost part of the skull or head b : the summit of a
mountain c : the head of foliage of a tree or shrub d :
the part of a hat covering the crown of the head e : the
part of a tooth external to the gum or an artificial substitute for this 4 : something (as the corona of a flower) resembling a crown 5 a (1) *often cap* : imperial
or regal power : SOVEREIGNTY (2) *often cap* : the government under a constitutional monarchy b : MON-
ARCH 1 6 : the highest point of development : CULMI-
NATION 7 a : a former British monetary unit equal to
five shillings b : any of several coins representing this
unit 8 a : the region of a seed plant in which stem and
root merge b : the thick arching end of the shank of an
anchor where the arms join it [Old French *corone,*
from Latin *corona* "wreath, crown", from Greek
korōnē "anything curved"] — **crown** *adj, often cap*
— **crowned** \'kraùnd\ *adj*

²**crown** *vt* 1 a : to place a crown on; *esp* : to invest with
regal dignity and power b : to recognize officially as
⟨was *crowned* champion⟩ 2 : IMBUE 2, ENDOW, ADORN
— usually used with *with* ⟨*crowned* with wisdom⟩ 3 :
SURMOUNT 1, TOP; *esp* : to top (a checker) with a
checker to make a king 4 : to bring to a successful
conclusion 5 : to put an artificial crown upon (a
tooth)

crown glass *n* : a very clear glass with a low index of
refraction that is used for optical instruments

crown prince *n* : the heir apparent to a crown or throne

crown princess *n* 1 : the wife of a crown prince 2 : a
woman who is an heir apparent to a crown or throne

crow's-foot \'krōz-,fùt\ *n, pl* **crow's-feet** \-,fēt\ 1 : any
of the wrinkles around the outer corners of the eyes
— usually used in pl. 2 : CROWFOOT 1

crow's nest *n* : a partly enclosed platform high on a
ship's mast for a lookout; *also* : any similar lookout

cro·zier *variant of* CROSIER

cruces *pl of* CRUX

cru·cial \'krü-shəl\ *adj* : of the utmost importance ⟨a
crucial moment in the game⟩; *esp* : DECISIVE 2 ⟨this
experiment would be *crucial*⟩ [French, literally, "cruciform", from Latin *cruc-, crux* "cross"] — **cru·cial·ly**
adv

cru·ci·ble \'krü-sə-bəl\ *n* 1 : a pot made of a heat-resistant material and used for holding a substance for
treatment in a process that requires high temperature
2 : a severe test [Medieval Latin *crucibulum,* from Old
French *croiseul*]

cru·ci·fer \'krü-sə-fər\ *n* 1 : one who carries a cross
especially at the head of a church procession 2 : any
of a family of plants (as the cabbage or mustard) that
produce flowers with four petals in the shape of a
cross and six stamens — **cru·cif·er·ous** \krü-'sif-rəs, -ə-
rəs\ *adj*

cru·ci·fix \'krü-sə-,fiks\ *n* : a representation of Christ on
the cross [Late Latin *crucifixus* "the crucified Christ",
from *crucifigere* "to crucify", from Latin *cruc-, crux*
"cross" + *figere* "to fasten, fix"]

¹crow 1

\ə\ abut	\ng\ sing
\ər\ further	\ō\ bone
\a\ mat	\ò\ saw
\ā\ take	\òi\ coin
\ä\ cot, cart	\th\ thin
\aù\ out	\th\ this
\ch\ chin	\ü\ food
\e\ pet	\ù\ foot
\ē\ easy	\y\ yet
\g\ go	\yü\ few
\i\ tip	\yù\ cure
\ī\ life	\zh\ vision
\j\ job	

cru·ci·fix·ion \,krü-sə-'fik-shən\ *n* : an act of crucifying; *esp, cap* : the crucifying of Christ

cru·ci·form \'krü-sə-,fórm\ *adj* : forming or arranged in a cross — **cru·ci·form·ly** *adv*

cru·ci·fy \'krü-sə-,fī\ *vt* **-fied; -fy·ing 1** : to put to death by nailing or binding the hands and feet to a cross **2** : to treat cruelly : TORTURE, PERSECUTE

crud \'krəd\ *n* **1** : a deposit of something filthy, greasy,or sticky ⟨machinery covered with *crud*⟩ **2** *slang* : something disagreeable or contemptible [Middle English *curd, crudd* "curd"]

¹**crude** \'krüd\ *adj* **1** : existing in a natural state and unaltered by processing : not refined ⟨*crude* oil⟩ **2** : lacking refinement, good manners, or tact; *esp* : marked by grossness or vulgarity **3** : rough in plan or execution : RUDE ⟨a *crude* shelter⟩ **4** : not concealed or glossed over : BARE ⟨the *crude* facts⟩ [Latin *crudus* "raw"] — **crude·ly** *adv* — **crude·ness** *n* — **cru·di·ty** \'krüd-ət-ē\ *n*

²**crude** *n* : a substance in its natural unprocessed state; *esp* : unrefined petroleum

cru·el \'krü-el\ *adj* **cru·el·er** *or* **cru·el·ler; cru·el·est** *or* **cru·el·lest 1** : disposed to inflict pain **2 a** : causing or helping to cause injury, grief, or pain **b** : devoid of leniency : MERCILESS [Old French, from Latin *crudelis,* from *crudus* "raw"] — **cru·el·ly** \'krü-ə-lē\ *adv* — **cru·el·ness** *n*

cru·el·ty \'krü-əl-tē\ *n, pl* **-ties 1** : the quality or state of being cruel **2 a** : a cruel action **b** : inhuman treatment

cru·et \'krü-ət\ *n* : a small glass bottle for holding vinegar, oil, or sauce [Anglo-French, from Old French *crue,* of Germanic origin]

¹**cruise** \'krüz\ *vb* **1** : to sail about touching at a series of ports **2** : to travel for the sake of traveling **3** : to go about the streets at random but on the lookout for possible developments **4** : to travel at an efficient operating speed ⟨the *cruising* speed of an airplane⟩ **5** : to travel over or about [Dutch *kruisen* "to make a cross, cruise", derived from Latin *crux* "cross"]

²**cruise** *n* : an act or an instance of cruising

cruis·er \'krü-zər\ *n* **1** : a boat or vehicle that cruises; *esp* : SQUAD CAR **2** : a warship intermediate in size between a battleship and a destroyer **3** : a motorboat with arrangements necessary for living aboard — called also *cabin cruiser*

crul·ler \'krəl-ər\ *n* **1** : a small sweet cake formed in a twisted strip and fried in deep fat **2** *North & Midland* : a doughnut made without yeast [Dutch *krulle,* a twisted cake, from *krul* "curly"]

¹**crumb** \'krəm\ *n* **1** : a small fragment especially of bread **2** : PARTICLE 2 ⟨not a *crumb* of comfort⟩ [Old English *cruma*]

²**crumb** *vt* **1** : to break into crumbs : CRUMBLE **2** : to cover or thicken with crumbs **3** : to remove crumbs from ⟨*crumb* a table⟩

crum·ble \'krəm-bəl\ *vb* **crum·bled; crum·bling** \-bə-ling, -bling\ : to break into small pieces : DISINTEGRATE ⟨*crumble* bread⟩ ⟨the wall *crumbled*⟩ [derived from Old English *cruma* "crumb"]

crum·bly \-bə-lē, -blē\ *adj* **crum·bli·er; -est** : easily crumbled — **crum·bli·ness** *n*

crum·my \'krəm-ē\ *adj* **crum·mi·er; -est 1** : MISERABLE 1a ⟨a *crummy* tenement⟩ **2** : CHEAP 2 ⟨a *crummy* piece of equipment⟩ [Middle English *crumme* "crumbly"]

crum·pet \'krəm-pət\ *n* : a small round cake made of unsweetened batter cooked on a griddle [perhaps from Middle English *crompid cake,* "wafer", literally, "curled-up cake"]

¹**crum·ple** \'krəm-pəl\ *vb* **crum·pled; crum·pling** \-pə-ling, -pling\ **1** : to press, bend, or crush out of shape **2** : to become crumpled **3** : to cause the collapse of or undergo collapse [Middle English *crumpen* "to curve, curl up", from *crump* "crooked", from Old English]

²**crumple** *n* : a wrinkle or crease made by crumpling

¹**crunch** \'krənch\ *vb* : to chew, grind, or press with a crushing or grinding noise [probably of imitative origin]

²**crunch** *n* : an act or sound of crunching — **crunchy** \'krən-chē\ *adj*

crup·per \'krəp-ər, 'krùp-\ *n* **1** : a leather loop passing under a horse's tail and buckled to the saddle of the harness **2** : the rump of a horse : CROUP [Old French *crupiere,* from *croupe* "croup"]

¹**cru·sade** \krü-'sād\ *n* **1** *cap* : any of the military expeditions undertaken by Christian powers in the 11th, 12th, and 13th centuries to win the Holy Land from the Muslims **2** : a campaign undertaken with zeal and enthusiasm ⟨a *crusade* against corruption⟩ [Middle French *croisade* and Spanish *cruzada,* both derived from Latin *crux* "cross"]

²**crusade** *vi* : to engage in a crusade — **cru·sad·er** *n*

cruse \'krüz, 'krüs\ *n* : a small vessel (as a jar or pot) for holding a liquid (as water or oil) [Middle English]

¹**crush** \'krəsh\ *vb* **1 a** : to squeeze or force by pressure so as to alter or destroy structure **b** : to squeeze together into a mass **2** : to embrace strongly : HUG **3** : to reduce to particles by pounding or grinding **4 a** : SUPPRESS 1 ⟨*crush* a rebellion⟩ **b** : to oppress or burden seriously ⟨a *crushing* burden of guilt⟩ **c** : to subdue completely : DEFEAT **5** : CROWD 4, PUSH ⟨people *crushed* into an elevator⟩ **6** : to become crushed [Middle French *cruisir,* of Germanic origin] — **crush·er** *n*

²**crush** *n* **1** : an act of crushing **2** : a tightly packed crowd **3** : an intense infatuation; *also* : the object of this

crust \'krəst\ *n* **1 a** : the hardened exterior surface of bread **b** : a piece of dry hard bread **2** : the pastry portion of a pie **3 a** : a hard external covering or surface layer ⟨*crust* of snow⟩ **b** : the outer part of the earth composed essentially of crystalline rocks **c** : SCAB 2 [Latin *crusta*] — **crust** *vb*

crus·ta·cea \,krəs-'tā-shē-ə, -shə\ *n pl* : CRUSTACEANS

crus·ta·cean \,krəs-'tā-shən\ *n* : any of a large class (Crustacea) of mostly aquatic arthropods (as lobsters, shrimps, crabs, wood lice, water fleas, and barnacles) that have an exoskeleton of chitin or of a compound of chitin and calcium [derived from Latin *crusta* "crust, shell"] — **crustacean** *adj*

crust·al \'krəst-l\ *adj* : relating to a crust and especially to that of the earth or the moon

crust·ose \'krəs-,tōs\ *adj* : forming a firm thin crust ⟨*crustose* lichens⟩ — compare FOLIOSE, FRUTICOSE

crusty \'krəs-tē\ *adj* **crust·i·er; -est 1** : having or being a crust **2** : giving an effect of bluff incivility — **crust·i·ly** \-tə-lē\ *adv* — **crust·i·ness** \-tē-nəs\ *n*

crutch \'krəch\ *n* **1** : a support typically fitting under the armpit for use by a disabled person in walking **2** : a usually forked support [Old English *crycc*]

crux \'krəks, 'krùks\ *n, pl* **crux·es** *also* **cru·ces** \'krü-,sēz\ **1 a** : a puzzling or difficult problem : an unsolved question **b** : a crucial or critical point ⟨the *crux* of the problem⟩ **2** : a main or central feature (as of an argument) [Latin, "cross, torture"]

cru·zei·ro \krü-'zeər-ō, -ü\ *n, pl* **-ros 1** : the basic monetary unit of Brazil **2** : a coin representing one cruzeiro [Portuguese]

¹**cry** \'krī\ *vb* **cried; cry·ing 1** : to call loudly : SHOUT **2** : WEEP 1, SOB **3** : to utter a characteristic sound or call **4** : BESEECH, BEG **5** : to proclaim publicly : call out [Old French *crier,* from Latin *quiritare* "to cry out to a citizen for help", from *Quirit-, Quiris* "Roman citizen"] — **cry havoc** : to sound an alarm — **cry wolf** : to give alarm without occasion

²**cry** *n, pl* **cries 1** : a loud call or shout (as of pain, fear, or joy) **2** : APPEAL ⟨the *cries* of the poor⟩ **3** : a fit of weeping **4** : the characteristic sound uttered by an animal (as a bird) **5** : SLOGAN, WATCHWORD — **a far cry** : a great distance : a great change — **in full cry** : in full pursuit

cry·ba·by \'krī-,bā-bē\ *n* : one who cries or complains easily or often

cry down *vt* : BELITTLE, DISPARAGE

cry·ing \'krī-ing\ *adj* **1** : calling for attention and correction ⟨a *crying* need⟩ **2** : NOTORIOUS ⟨a *crying* evil⟩

cryo·gen·ics \,krī-ə-'jen-iks\ *n* : a branch of physics that relates to the production and effects of very low temperatures [Greek *kryos* "cold, freezing"]

cryo·lite \'krī-ə-,līt\ *n* : a mineral Na_3AlF_6 consisting of sodium, aluminum, and fluorine found in Greenland and used in making aluminum

crypt \'kript\ *n* **1** : an underground vault or room; *esp* : one under the floor of a church used as a burial place **2** : a simple gland, glandular pit, or recess : FOLLICLE [Latin *crypta*, from Greek *kryptē*, from *kryptos* "hidden", from *kryptein* "to hide"]

cryp·tic \'krip-tik\ *adj* **1** : SECRET 1a, OCCULT **2** : having or seeming to have a hidden meaning ⟨a *cryptic* remark⟩ **3** : serving to conceal ⟨*cryptic* coloration in animals⟩ **4** : employing cipher or code SYN see OBSCURE — **cryp·ti·cal·ly** \-ti-kə-lē, -klē\ *adv*

cryp·to·gam \'krip-tə-,gam\ *n* : a plant (as a fern, moss, alga, or fungus) reproducing by spores and not producing flowers or seed [derived from Greek *kryptos* "hidden" + *-gamia* "-gamy"] — **cryp·to·gam·ic** \,krip-tə-'gam-ik\ *adj*

cryp·to·gram \'krip-tə-,gram\ *n* : a writing in cipher or code

cryp·to·graph \-,graf\ *n* : CRYPTOGRAM — **cryp·to·graph·ic** \,krip-tə-'graf-ik\ *adj* — **cryp·to·graph·i·cal·ly** \-'graf-i-kə-lē, -klē\ *adv*

cryp·tog·ra·phy \krip-'täg-rə-fē\ *n* : the enciphering and deciphering of messages in secret code — **cryp·tog·ra·pher** \-fər\ *n*

¹crys·tal \'kris-tl\ *n* **1** : quartz that is transparent or nearly so and that is either colorless or only slightly tinged **2** : something resembling crystal in transparency and colorlessness **3** : a body that is formed by the solidification of a substance or mixture and has a regularly repeating internal arrangement of its atoms and often external plane faces ⟨a *crystal* of quartz⟩ ⟨a snow *crystal*⟩ **4** : a clear colorless glass of superior quality **5** : the transparent cover over a watch or clock dial **6** : powdered methamphetamine [Old French *cristal*, from Latin *crystallum*, from Greek *krystallos* "ice, crystal"]

²crystal *adj* **1** : consisting of or resembling crystal : CLEAR **2** : relating to or using a crystal ⟨a *crystal* radio receiver⟩

crys·tal·line \'kris-tə-lən\ *adj* **1** : made of crystal or composed of crystals **2** : resembling crystal : TRANSPARENT **3** : of or relating to a crystal — **crys·tal·lin·i·ty** \,kris-tə-'lin-ət-ē\ *n*

crystalline lens *n* : the lens of the vertebrate eye

crys·tal·lize \'kris-tə-,līz\ *vb* **1** : to cause to form crystals or assume crystalline form **2** : to give a definite form to ⟨try to *crystallize* your thoughts⟩ **3** : to become crystallized — **crys·tal·liz·able** \-,lī-zə-bəl\ *adj* — **crys·tal·li·za·tion** \,kris-tə-lə-'zā-shən\ *n*

crys·tal·log·ra·phy \,kris-tə-'läg-rə-fē\ *n* : a science that deals with the form and structure of crystals — **crys·tal·log·ra·pher** \-fər\ *n* — **crys·tal·lo·graph·ic** \-tə-lō-'graf-ik\ *adj*

crys·tal·loid \'kris-tə-,lȯid\ *n* : a substance that forms a true solution and is capable of being crystallized

crystal set *n* : a radio receiver having a crystal for a detector and no vacuum tubes

cteno·phore \'ten-ə-,fōr, -,fȯr\ *n* : any of a phylum (Ctenophora) of nearly globe-shaped marine animals that superficially resemble jellyfishes but swim by means of eight bands of ciliated plates — called also *comb jelly* [derived from Greek *kten-, kteis* "comb" + *pherein* "to carry"] — **cte·noph·o·ran** \ti-'näf-ə-rən\ *adj or n*

cub \'kəb\ *n* **1 a** : a young flesh-eating mammal ⟨bear *cubs*⟩ ⟨lion *cubs*⟩ **b** : a young shark **2** : a young person **3** : APPRENTICE; *esp* : an inexperienced newspaper reporter [origin unknown]

cub·by·hole \'kəb-ē-,hōl\ *n* : a snug or confined place (as for hiding or storing things) [obsolete English *cub* "pen", from Dutch *kub* "thatched roof"]

¹cube \'kyüb\ *n* **1** : a regular solid that has six equal square sides **2** : the product obtained by taking a number three times as a factor ⟨the *cube* of 2 is 8⟩ [Latin *cubus*, from Greek *kybos*]

²cube *vt* **1** : to raise to the third power ⟨2 *cubed* is 8⟩ **2** : to form or cut into cubes

cu·beb \'kyü-,beb\ *n* : the dried unripe berry of a tropical shrub of the pepper family that was formerly used in medicine as a stimulant and diuretic [Middle French *cubebe*, from Medieval Latin *cubeba*, from Arabic *kubābah*]

cube root *n* : a number whose cube is a given number ⟨the *cube root* of 27 is 3⟩

cu·bic \'kyü-bik\ *also* **cu·bi·cal** \'kyü-bi-kəl\ *adj* **1** : having the shape of a cube **2** : having, being, or relating to volume; *esp* : being the volume of a cube whose edge is a specified unit ⟨a *cubic* inch⟩

cubic equation *n* : a polynomial equation in which the sum of the exponents of the variables in any term is no greater than three ⟨$x^3 + 2 x^2y + 5 xy^2 + 10 y^3 + 6 = 0$ is a *cubic equation*⟩ — called also *cubic*

cu·bi·cle \'kyü-bi-kəl\ *n* : a small partitioned compartment especially for sleeping [Latin *cubiculum*, from *cubare* "to lie, recline"]

cubic measure *n* : a unit (as a cubic inch or cubic centimeter) for measuring volume — see MEASURE table, METRIC SYSTEM table

cub·ism \'kyü-,biz-əm\ *n* : a 20th century art form characterized by the abstraction of natural forms into fragmented geometric shapes — **cub·ist** \-bəst\ *adj or n*

cu·bit \'kyü-bət\ *n* : a unit of length based on the length of the forearm from the elbow to the tip of the middle finger and usually equal to about 46 centimeters [Latin *cubitum* "elbow, cubit"]

cu·boi·dal \kyü-'bȯid-l\ *adj* : somewhat cubical : made up of nearly cubical elements ⟨*cuboidal* epithelium⟩

cub scout *n* : a member of the Boy Scouts of America program for boys of the age range 8-10

¹cuck·old \'kək-əld, -,ōld\ *n* : a man whose wife is unfaithful [Middle English *cokewold*] — **cuck·old·ry** \-əl-drē\ *n*

²cuckold *vt* : to make a cuckold of

¹cuck·oo \'kük-ü, 'kük-\ *n, pl* **cuckoos** **1** : a largely grayish brown European bird that lays its eggs in the nests of other birds for them to hatch; *also* : any of various related birds **2** : the call of a cuckoo [Middle English *cuccu*]

²cuckoo *adj* **1** : of or resembling the cuckoo **2** : SILLY 1, CRAZY

cuckoo spit *n* **1** : a frothy secretion exuded upon plants by the nymphs of spittlebugs **2** : SPITTLEBUG

cu·cum·ber \'kyü-,kəm-bər, -kəm-\ *n* : the long fleshy many-seeded fruit of a vine of the gourd family grown as a garden vegetable; *also* : this vine [Middle French *cocombre*, from Latin *cucumis*]

cu·cur·bit \kyü-'kər-bət\ *n* : a plant of the gourd family [Middle French *cucurbite*, from Latin *cucurbita* "gourd"]

cud \'kəd, 'kud\ *n* : food brought up into the mouth by a ruminating animal (as a cow) from its rumen to be chewed again [Old English *cwudu*]

cud·dle \'kəd-l\ *vb* **cud·dled; cud·dling** \'kəd-ling, -l-ing\ **1** : to hold close for warmth or comfort or in affection **2** : to lie close : SNUGGLE [origin unknown] — **cuddle** *n* — **cud·dly** \'kəd-lē, -l-ē\ *adj*

¹cud·gel \'kəj-əl\ *n* : a short heavy club [Old English *cycgel*]

¹crystal 3

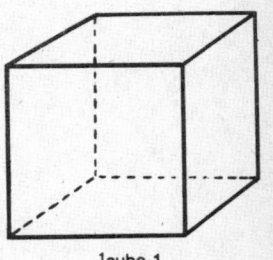
¹cube 1

\ə\ abut	\ng\ sing
\ər\ further	\ō\ bone
\a\ mat	\ȯ\ saw
\ā\ take	\ȯi\ coin
\ä\ cot, cart	\th\ thin
\aú\ out	\th\ this
\ch\ chin	\ü\ food
\e\ pet	\ú\ foot
\ē\ easy	\y\ yet
\g\ go	\yü\ few
\i\ tip	\yu̇\ cure
\ī\ life	\zh\ vision
\j\ job	

²cudgel *vt* **-geled** *or* **-gelled; -gel·ing** *or* **-gel·ling** : to beat with or as if with a cudgel

¹cue \'kyü\ *n* **1** : a word, phrase, or action in a play serving as a signal for the next actor to speak or act **2** : something serving as a signal or suggestion : HINT [probably from *qu,* abbreviation (used as a direction in actors' copies of plays) of Latin *quando* "when"]

²cue *n* **1** : QUEUE 2 **2 a** : a tapering rod for striking a ball in games (as billiards or pool) **b** : a long-handled stick with a concave head for shoving disks in shuffleboard [French *queue,* literally, "tail", from Latin *cauda*]

cue ball *n* : the ball struck with the cue and driven into the object ball in billiards and pool

¹cuff \'kəf\ *n* **1** : something (as a part of a sleeve) encircling the wrist **2** : the turned-back hem of a trouser leg [Middle English]

²cuff *vt* : to strike with or as if with the palm of the hand : SLAP

³cuff *n* : a blow with the hand especially when open : SLAP

cui·rass \kwi-'ras, kyü-\ *n* **1** : a piece of armor covering the body from neck to waist; *also* : the breastplate of such a piece **2** : something (as a plaster cast on the trunk and neck) resembling a cuirass [Middle French *curasse,* from Late Latin *coreaceus* "leathern", from Latin *corium* "skin, leather"]

cuir·as·sier \,kwir-ə-'siər, ,kyür-\ *n* : a mounted soldier wearing a cuirass

cui·sine \kwi-'zēn\ *n* : manner of preparing food; *also* : the food prepared [French, literally, "kitchen", from Late Latin *coquina,* from Latin *coquere* "to cook"]

cu·lex \'kyü-,leks\ *n* : any of a large cosmopolitan genus of mosquitoes that includes the mosquito commonly found in or about buildings in Europe and North America [Latin, "gnat"] — **cu·li·cine** \'kyü-lə-,sīn\ *adj or n*

cu·li·nary \'kəl-ə-,ner-ē, 'kyü-lə-\ *adj* : of or relating to the kitchen or cookery [Latin *culina* "kitchen", from *coquere* "to cook"]

¹cull \'kəl\ *vt* **1** : to select from a group : CHOOSE **2** : to identify and remove the culls from [Middle French *cuillir,* from Latin *colligere* "to bind together, collect"] — **cull·er** *n*

²cull *n* : something rejected as inferior or worthless

¹culm \'kəlm\ *n* : refuse coal screenings : SLACK [Middle English]

²culm *n* : the stem of a monocotyledonous plant [Latin *culmus* "stalk"]

cul·mi·nate \'kəl-mə-,nāt\ *vi* : to reach the highest or climactic point [Medieval Latin *culminare,* from Latin *culmen* "top, summit"]

cul·mi·na·tion \,kəl-mə-'nā-shən\ *n* **1** : the action of culminating **2** : the culminating position : CLIMAX

cu·lotte \'kü-,lät, 'kyü-; kü-', kyü-'\ *n* : a divided skirt or a garment with a divided skirt — often used in pl. [French, "breeches", from *cul* "backside"]

cul·pa·ble \'kəl-pə-bəl\ *adj* : deserving condemnation or blame ⟨*culpable* negligence⟩ [Middle French, from Latin *culpabilis,* from *culpare* "to blame", from *culpa* "fault, guilt"] — **cul·pa·bil·i·ty** \,kəl-pə-'bil-ət-ē\ *n* — **cul·pa·ble·ness** \'kəl-pə-bəl-nəs\ *n* — **cul·pa·bly** \-pə-blē\ *adv*

cul·prit \'kəl-prət, -,prit\ *n* **1** : one accused of or charged with a crime **2** : one guilty of a crime or fault [Anglo-French *cul.* (abbreviation of *culpable* "guilty") + *prest, prit* "ready" (that is, to prove it), from Latin *praestus*]

cult \'kəlt\ *n* **1** : formal religious veneration : WORSHIP **2** : a system of religious beliefs and ritual or those who practice it **3 a** : enthusiastic and usually temporary devotion to a person, idea, or thing **b** : a group of persons showing such devotion [Latin *cultus* "care, adoration", from *colere* "to cultivate, worship"] — **cult·ist** \'kəl-təst\ *n*

cul·ti·gen \'kəl-tə-jən\ *n* : a cultivated organism (as Indian corn) of a variety or species for which a wild ancestor is unknown

cul·ti·va·ble \'kəl-tə-və-bəl\ *adj* : capable of being cultivated

cul·ti·vate \'kəl-tə-,vāt\ *vt* **1 a** : to prepare or prepare and use for the raising of crops : TILL **b** : to loosen or break up the soil about (growing plants) **2 a** : to foster the growth of ⟨*cultivate* vegetables⟩ **b** : CULTURE 2 **c** : REFINE, IMPROVE ⟨*cultivate* the mind⟩ **3** : FURTHER, ENCOURAGE ⟨*cultivate* the arts⟩ **4** : to seek the society of [Medieval Latin *cultivare,* from *cultivus* "cultivated", from Latin *colere* "to cultivate"] — **cul·ti·vat·able** \-,vāt-ə-bəl\ *adj*

cul·ti·vat·ed *adj* **1** : subjected to or produced under cultivation ⟨*cultivated* farms⟩ ⟨*cultivated* fruits⟩ **2** : REFINED, EDUCATED ⟨*cultivated* speech⟩

cul·ti·va·tion \,kəl-tə-'vā-shən\ *n* **1** : the act or art of cultivating; *esp* : TILLAGE **2** : CULTURE 3, REFINEMENT

cul·ti·va·tor \'kəl-tə-,vāt-ər\ *n* : one that cultivates; *esp* : an implement to loosen the soil while crops are growing

cul·tur·al \'kəlch-rəl, -ə-rəl\ *adj* **1** : of or relating to culture **2** : produced by breeding ⟨a *cultural* variety⟩ — **cul·tur·al·ly** \-ē\ *adv*

cultural anthropology *n* : a division of anthropology that deals with human culture

¹cul·ture \'kəl-chər\ *n* **1** : CULTIVATION 1, TILLAGE **2 a** : the rearing or development of a particular product, stock, or crop ⟨bee *culture*⟩ ⟨the *culture* of grapes⟩ **b** : professional or expert care and training ⟨voice *culture*⟩ **3** : the state of being cultivated; *esp* : refinement in manners, taste, and thought **4** : the characteristic features of a civilization including its beliefs, its artistic and material products, and its social institutions ⟨ancient Greek *culture*⟩; *also* : a stage in the history of a civilization **5** : cultivation of living material in prepared nutrient media; *also* : a product of such cultivation [Middle French, from Latin *cultura,* from *colere* "to cultivate"]

²culture *vt* **cul·tured; cul·tur·ing** \'kəlch-ring, -ə-ring\ **1** : CULTIVATE 1 **2** : to grow in a prepared medium

cul·tured \'kəl-chərd\ *adj* **1** : CULTIVATED ⟨*cultured* fields⟩ ⟨*cultured* speech⟩ **2** : produced under artificial conditions ⟨*cultured* pearls⟩

cul·vert \'kəl-vərt\ *n* **1** : a drain crossing under a road or railroad **2** : a conduit for a culvert **3** : a bridge over a culvert [origin unknown]

cum·ber \'kəm-bər\ *vt* **cum·bered; cum·ber·ing** \-bə-ring, -bring\ **1** : to hinder by being in the way **2** : to clutter up ⟨rocks *cumbering* the yard⟩ [Middle English *cumbren*]

cum·ber·some \'kəm-bər-səm\ *adj* **1** : UNWIELDY, CLUMSY **2** : slow-moving : LUMBERING — **cum·ber·some·ly** *adv* — **cum·ber·some·ness** *n*

cum·brous \'kəm-brəs\ *adj* : CUMBERSOME — **cum·brous·ly** *adv* — **cum·brous·ness** *n*

cum·in \'kəm-ən\ *n* : a low plant of the carrot family grown for its aromatic seeds [Old English *cymen,* from Latin *cuminum,* from Greek *kyminon,* of Semitic origin]

cum lau·de \kum-'laud-ə, -ē; ,kəm-'lod-ē\ *adv or adj* : with academic distinction ⟨graduated *cum laude*⟩ [New Latin, "with praise"]

cum·mer·bund \'kəm-ər-,bənd\ *n* : a broad sash worn as a waistband [Hindi *kamarband,* from Persian, from *kamar* "waist" + *band* "band"]

cu·mu·late \'kyü-myə-,lāt\ *vb* : ACCUMULATE [Latin *cumulare,* from *cumulus* "mass, heap"] — **cu·mu·la·tion** \,kyü-myə-'lā-shən\ *n*

cu·mu·la·tive \'kyü-myə-lət-iv, -,lāt-\ *adj* **1 a** : increasing (as in force, strength, or amount) by successive additions **b** : composed of a series of increases ⟨*cumulative* evidence⟩ **2** : increasing in severity with repetition of the offense ⟨*cumulative* penalty⟩ **3** : bearing interest or dividends that must be added to a future payment if not paid when due ⟨*cumulative* stock⟩ **4** : formed by addition of new material of the same kind ⟨a *cumulative* book index⟩ — **cu·mu·la·tive·ly** *adv* — **cu·mu·la·tive·ness** *n*

cu·mu·lo·nim·bus \ˌkyü-myə-lō-'nim-bəs\ *n* : a cumulus often spread out in the shape of an anvil extending to great heights

cu·mu·lo·stra·tus \-'strāt-əs, -'strat-\ *n* : a cumulus whose base extends horizontally as a stratus cloud

cu·mu·lous \'kyü-myə-ləs\ *adj* : resembling a cumulus

cu·mu·lus \-ləs\ *n, pl* **cu·mu·li** \-ˌlī, -ˌlē\ **1** : HEAP 2, ACCUMULATION **2** : a massive cloud form having a flat base and rounded outlines often piled up like a mountain [Latin, "heap, mass"]

cu·ne·ate \'kyü-nē-ˌāt, -nē-ət\ *adj* : narrowly triangular with the acute angle toward the base ⟨a *cuneate* leaf⟩ [Latin *cuneatus,* from *cuneus* "wedge"]

¹cu·ne·i·form \kyù-'nē-ə-ˌform; 'kyü-nə-ˌform, -nē-ə-,\ *adj* **1** : having the shape of a wedge **2** : composed of or written in wedge-shaped characters ⟨*cuneiform* alphabet⟩ [derived from Latin *cuneus* "wedge"]

²cuneiform *n* : cuneiform writing (as of ancient Assyria and Babylonia)

cun·ner \'kən-ər\ *n* : a small American food fish that is abundant on the rocky shores of New England [origin unknown]

¹cun·ning \'kən-ing\ *adj* **1** : dexterous or crafty in the use of resources (as skill or knowledge) ⟨*cunning* schemers⟩ **2** : marked by wily artfulness ⟨a *cunning* plot⟩ **3** : prettily appealing : CUTE [Middle English, from *can* "know, can"] — **cun·ning·ly** \-ing-lē\ *adv*

²cunning *n* **1** : SKILL 1, DEXTERITY **2** : SLYNESS, CRAFTINESS

¹cup \'kəp\ *n* **1** : an open bowl-shaped drinking vessel usually with a handle **2 a** : the contents of a cup : CUPFUL **b** : the consecrated wine of the Communion **3** : a large ornamental cup offered as a prize **4 a** : something (as the corolla of a flower) resembling a cup **b** : a usually plastic-reinforced athletic supporter **c** : the metal case inside a hole in golf; *also* : the hole itself **5** : a food served in a cup-shaped vessel ⟨fruit *cup*⟩ **6** : the symbol ∪ indicating the union of two sets — compare CAP 5 [Old English *cuppe,* from Late Latin *cuppa,* from Latin *cupa* "tub"] — **cup·like** \'kəp-ˌlīk\ *adj* — **in one's cups** : DRUNK

²cup *vt* **cupped; cup·ping** **1** : to treat by cupping **2 a** : to curve into the shape of a cup ⟨*cupped* my hands⟩ **b** : to place in or as if in a cup — **cup·per** *n*

cup·bear·er \'kəp-ˌbar-ər, -ˌber-\ *n* : one who has the duty of filling and distributing cups of drink (as at a feast)

cup·board \'kəb-ərd\ *n* **1** : a closet with shelves for cups, dishes, or food **2** : a small closet

cup·cake \'kəp-ˌkāk\ *n* : a small cake baked in a cuplike mold

cu·pel \kyü-'pel, 'kyü-pəl\ *n* : a small shallow porous cup especially of bone ash used in assaying to separate precious metals from lead [French *coupelle* "small cup", from *coupe* "cup", from Late Latin *cuppa*]

cup·ful \'kəp-ˌfúl\ *n, pl* **cup·fuls** \-ˌfúlz\ *or* **cups·ful** \'kəps-ˌfúl\ **1** : the amount held by a cup **2** : a half pint : eight ounces (about 236 milliliters)

cup fungus *n* : any of an order of mostly saprophytic fungi bearing a cuplike fleshy or horny spore-bearing structure that is often colored

cu·pid \'kyü-pəd\ *n* : a winged naked figure of an infant often with a bow and arrow that represents the Roman god of love

cu·pid·i·ty \kyù-'pid-ət-ē\ *n* : excessive desire especially for wealth : GREED [Middle French *cupidité,* from Latin *cupiditas,* from *cupidus* "desirous", from *cupere* "to desire"]

cu·po·la \'kyü-pə-lə, -ˌlō\ *n* **1** : a rounded roof or ceiling **2** : a small structure built on top of a roof [Italian, from Latin *cupula* "small tub", from *cupa* "tub"]

cup·ping *n* : a technique formerly used for drawing blood to the surface of the body by application of a glass vessel from which air had been evacuated by heat forming a partial vacuum

cu·pric \'kü-prik, 'kyü-\ *adj* : of, relating to, or containing bivalent copper [Late Latin *cuprum* "copper"]

cu·prite \'kü-ˌprīt, 'kyü-\ *n* : a mineral Cu_2O that consists of oxide of copper and is an ore of copper

cu·prous \-prəs\ *adj* : of, relating to, or containing univalent copper

cur \'kər\ *n* **1** : a mongrel dog **2** : a low contemptible person [Middle English]

cur·able \'kyùr-ə-bəl\ *adj* : capable of being cured

cu·ra·cy \'kyùr-ə-sē\ *n, pl* **-cies** : the office or term of office of a curate

cu·ra·re \kyü-'rär-ē, kù-\ : a dried aqueous extract especially of a tropical American vine used in native arrow poisons and in medicine to produce muscular relaxation [Portuguese and Spanish, from Carib *kurari*]

cu·rate \'kyùr-ət\ *n* **1** : a clergyman in charge of a parish **2** : a clergyman serving as assistant (as to a rector) in a parish [Medieval Latin *curatus,* from *cura* "cure of souls", from Latin, "care"]

cu·ra·tive \'kyùr-ət-iv\ *adj* : relating to or used in the cure of diseases

cu·ra·tor \kyù-'rāt-ər, 'kyùr-ˌāt-\ *n* : one that has the care and supervision of something; *esp* : one in charge of a museum or zoo [Latin, from *curare* "to care", from *cura* "care"] — **cu·ra·to·ri·al** \ˌkyùr-ə-'tōr-ē-əl, -'tòr-\ *adj* — **cu·ra·tor·ship** \kyù-'rāt-ər-ˌship, 'kyùr-ət-\ *n*

¹curb \'kərb\ *n* **1** : a chain or strap on a bit used to restrain a horse **2** : RESTRAINT 2, CHECK ⟨price *curbs*⟩ **3** : a frame or a raised edge or margin to strengthen or confine ⟨the *curb* of a well⟩ **4** : an edging built along a street to form part of a gutter [Middle French *courbe* "curve, curved piece of wood or iron", from Latin *curvus* "curved"]

²curb *vt* **1** : to furnish with a curb **2** : to check or control with or as if with a curb ⟨*curb* your impulses⟩

curb·ing \'kər-bing\ *n* **1** : material for a curb **2** : CURB 3, 4

curb·stone \'kərb-ˌstōn\ *n* : a stone forming a curb

cur·cu·lio \kər-'kyü-lē-ˌō\ *n, pl* **-li·os** : any of various weevils; *esp* : one that injures fruit [Latin, "grain weevil"]

¹curd \'kərd\ *n* **1** : the thick casein-rich part of coagulated milk **2** : something resembling the curd of milk [Middle English] — **curdy** \-ē\ *adj*

²curd *vb* : COAGULATE, CURDLE

cur·dle \'kərd-l\ *vb* **cur·dled; cur·dling** \'kərd-ling, -l-ing\ **1** : to cause curds to form in **2** : to form curds : COAGULATE **3** : SOUR, SPOIL

¹cure \'kyùr\ *n* **1** : spiritual charge of a parish **2 a** : recovery or relief from a disease **b** : something (as a drug or treatment) that cures a disease **c** : a course, system, or period of treatment **3** : a process or method of curing ⟨a brine *cure* for meat⟩ [Old French, from Medieval Latin *cura* "cure of souls", from Latin, "care"] — **cure·less** \-ləs\ *adj*

²cure *vb* **1 a** : to restore to health, soundness, or normality **b** : to bring about recovery from **2** : to eliminate or free from something objectionable or harmful **3** : to prepare by or undergo chemical or physical processing for keeping or use ⟨*cure* bacon⟩ ⟨hay *curing* in the sun⟩ — **cur·er** \'kyùr-ər\ *n* □ SYN CURE, HEAL, REMEDY mean to rectify an unhealthy or undesirable condition. CURE applies to restoring to health after disease; HEAL may also apply to this but more commonly suggests restoring a wounded or sore part to soundness; REMEDY in extended use suggests correction or relief of a morbid or evil condition.

cu·ré \kyù-'rā, 'kyùr-ˌā\ *n* : a parish priest [Old French, from Medieval Latin *curatus*]

cure–all \'kyùr-ˌol\ *n* : a remedy for all ills : PANACEA

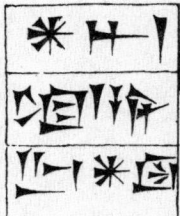

²cuneiform

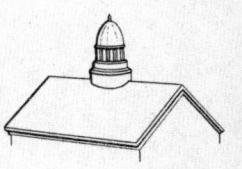

cupola 2

\ə\ abut		\ng\ sing	
\ər\ **further**		\ō\ bone	
\a\ mat		\o'\ saw	
\ā\ take		\oi\ coin	
\ä\ cot, cart		\th\ thin	
\aù\ out		\th\ this	
\ch\ chin		\ü\ food	
\e\ pet		\ù\ foot	
\ē\ easy		\y\ yet	
\g\ go		\yü\ few	
\i\ tip		\yù\ cure	
\ī\ life		\zh\ vision	
\j\ job			

cur·et·tage \ˌkyùr-ə-'täzh\ *n* : a surgical cleaning or scraping of a body part (as the uterus) [French, from *curette*, a surgical instrument]

cur·few \'kər-ˌfyü\ *n* **1** : a regulation requiring persons of a usually specified kind to be off the streets at a stated time **2** : a signal (as the ringing of a bell) to announce the beginning of a curfew **3 a** : the time when a curfew begins **b** : the period during which a curfew is in effect [Middle French *covrefeu* "signal given to bank the hearth fire, curfew", from *covrir* "to cover" + *feu* "fire"] □ ORIGIN In Europe in the Middle Ages people were required to put out or cover their hearth fires by a certain time in the evening. A hearth fire left unattended overnight might spread and destroy the house or even the town. A bell was rung to let people know they must cover their fires. In Middle French this signal was called *covrefeu*, a compound of *covrir*, "to cover", and *feu*, "fire". Even when hearth fires were no longer regulated, many towns had other rules that called for the ringing of an evening bell, and this signal was still called *covrefeu*. A common *covrefeu* regulation required that certain people be off the streets by a given time. The English borrowed *curfew* from the French *covrefeu*.

cu·ria \'kyùr-ē-ə, 'kùr-\ *n, pl* **cu·ri·ae** \'kyùr-ē-ˌē, 'kùr-ē-ˌī\ **1** : a division of an ancient Roman tribe **2** : a medieval royal court or court of justice **3** *often cap* : the group of administrative and judicial bodies through which the pope governs the Roman Catholic Church [Latin] — **cu·ri·al** \'kyùr-ē-əl\ *adj*

cu·rie \'kyùr-ˌē, kyù-'rē\ *n* **1** : a unit quantity of any radioactive element in which 37 billion disintegrations occur per second **2** : a unit of radioactivity equal to 37 billion disintegrations per second [Marie *Curie*]

cu·rio \'kyùr-ē-ˌō\ *n, pl* **-ri·os** : a rare or unusual article : CURIOSITY [short for *curiosity*]

cu·ri·os·i·ty \ˌkyùr-ē-'äs-ət-ē\ *n, pl* **-ties** **1** : an eager desire to learn and often to learn what does not concern one : INQUISITIVENESS **2** : something strange or unusual

cu·ri·ous \'kyùr-ē-əs\ *adj* **1** : eager to learn ⟨children are *curious* about everything⟩ **2** : overly eager to learn about others' concerns **3** : exciting attention as strange or novel ⟨a *curious* insect⟩ ⟨*curious* notions⟩ [Middle French *curios*, from Latin *curiosus* "careful, inquisitive", from *cura* "care"] — **cu·ri·ous·ly** *adv* — **cu·ri·ous·ness** *n* □ SYN INQUISITIVE, PRYING: CURIOUS implies an eager desire to learn or observe that may be either justifiable or objectionable; INQUISITIVE implies habitual curiosity especially about the personal affairs of others; PRYING implies officious, active inquisitiveness.

cu·ri·um \'kyùr-ē-əm\ *n* : a metallic radioactive element artificially produced — see ELEMENT table [New Latin, from Marie and Pierre *Curie*]

¹curl \'kərl\ *vb* **1** : to form into coils or ringlets **2** : to form into a curved shape : TWIST **3 a** : to grow in coils or spirals **b** : to move in curves or spirals **4** : to play the game of curling [Middle English *curlen*, from *crul* "curly"]

²curl *n* **1** : a lock of hair that coils : RINGLET **2** : something having a spiral or winding form : COIL **3** : the action of curling : the state of being curled **4** : an abnormal rolling or curling of leaves

curl·er \'kər-lər\ *n* **1** : one that curls; *esp* : a device for putting a curl into hair **2** : a player in the game of curling

cur·lew \'kər-ˌlü, 'kərl-ˌyü\ *n, pl* **curlews** *or* **curlew** : any of various largely brownish mostly migratory birds related to the woodcocks and distinguished by long legs and a long slender down-curved bill [Middle French *corlieu*]

curli·cue *also* **curly·cue** \'kər-li-ˌkyü\ *n* : a fancifully curved or spiral figure (as a flourish in handwriting) [*curly* + *cue* "braid of hair"]

curl·ing \'kər-ling\ *n* : a game in which two teams of four men each slide special stones over ice toward a target circle

curly \'kər-lē\ *adj* **curl·i·er; -est** **1** : tending to curl; *also* : having curls **2** : having the grain composed of wavy fibers that do not cross and that often form alternating light and dark lines ⟨*curly* maple⟩ — **curl·i·ness** *n*

cur·mud·geon \kər-'məj-ən\ *n* : a bad-tempered and often old man [origin unknown] — **cur·mud·geon·ly** *adj*

cur·rant \'kər-ənt, 'kə-rənt\ *n* **1** : a small seedless raisin grown chiefly in the Levant **2** : the acid edible fruit of any of several shrubs related to the gooseberries; *also* : a plant bearing currants [Middle English *raison of Coraunte*, literally, "raisin of Corinth"]

cur·ren·cy \'kər-ən-sē, 'kə-rən-\ *n, pl* **-cies** **1** : general use or acceptance ⟨a story that gained wide *currency*⟩ **2** : coins, government notes, and bank notes circulating as a medium of exchange : money in circulation

¹cur·rent \'kər-ənt, 'kə-rənt\ *adj* **1 a** : presently elapsing ⟨the *current* month⟩ **b** : occurring in or belonging to the present time ⟨the *current* crisis⟩ **2** : generally accepted, used, or practiced ⟨*current* theories of government⟩ [derived from Latin *currere* "to run"] SYN see PREVAILING — **cur·rent·ly** *adv* — **cur·rent·ness** *n*

²current *n* **1 a** : the part of a fluid body moving continuously in a certain direction **b** : the swiftest part of a stream **c** : a strong or forceful flow **2** : general course or movement : TREND ⟨changed the *current* of our lives⟩ **3** : a movement of electricity analogous to the flow of a stream of water; *also* : the rate of such movement

cur·ri·cle \'kər-i-kəl, 'kə-ri-\ *n* : a 2-wheeled chaise usually drawn by two horses [Latin *curriculum* "running, chariot"]

cur·ric·u·lum \kə-'rik-yə-ləm\ *n, pl* **-la** \-lə\ *or* **-lums** : a course of study; *esp* : the body of courses offered in a school or college or in one of its departments [Latin, "running, racecourse, chariot", from *currere* "to run"] — **cur·ric·u·lar** \-lər\ *adj*

¹cur·ry \'kər-ē, 'kə-rē\ *vt* **cur·ried; cur·ry·ing** **1** : to dress the coat of (as a horse) with a currycomb **2** : to treat (tanned leather) especially by incorporating oil or grease [Old French *correer* "to prepare, curry"] — **cur·ri·er** *n* — **curry fa·vor** \-'fā-vər\ : to seek to gain favor by flattery or attentions

²cur·ry *also* **cur·rie** \'kər-ē, 'kə-rē\ *n, pl* **curries** **1** : CURRY POWDER **2** : a food seasoned with curry powder ⟨shrimp *curry*⟩ [of Dravidian origin]

³curry *vt* **cur·ried; cur·ry·ing** : to flavor or cook with curry

cur·ry·comb \-ˌkōm\ *n* : a comb with rows of metallic teeth or ridges used especially to curry horses — **currycomb** *vt*

curry powder *n* : a sharp seasoning consisting of ground spices

¹curse \'kərs\ *n* **1** : a prayer that harm or injury may come upon someone or something **2** : a word or an expression used in cursing or swearing **3** : evil or misfortune that comes as if in answer to a curse : a cause of great harm or evil ⟨floods are the *curse* of this region⟩ [Old English *curs*]

²curse *vb* **1** : to call upon divine or supernatural power to send injury upon **2 a** : to use profanely insolent language against : BLASPHEME **b** : to utter profane or obscene words : SWEAR **3** : to bring great evil upon : AFFLICT

cursed \'kər-səd, 'kərst\ *also* **curst** \'kərst\ *adj* : being under or deserving a curse — **cursed·ly** *adv* — **cursed·ness** *n*

¹cur·sive \'kər-siv\ *adj* **1** : written or formed with the strokes of the letters joined together and most of the angles rounded ⟨*cursive* handwriting⟩ **2** : having a flowing easy character [Medieval Latin *cursivus*, literally, "running", from Latin *currere* "to run"] — **cur·sive·ly** *adv* — **cur·sive·ness** *n*

²**cursive** *n* : a style of printed letter imitating handwriting

cur·sor \'kər-sər\ *n* **1** : a part (as a transparent slide with a line) moved back and forth over a surface (as of a slide rule) to enable accurate readings to be made **2** : a mark (as a bright blinking spot) on a computer display screen that shows the place the user is working [Latin, "runner", from *currere* "to run"]

cur·so·ry \'kərs-rē, -ə-rē\ *adj* : rapidly and often superficially performed : HASTY ⟨a *cursory* reading of the book⟩ [Late Latin *cursorius* "of running", from Latin *currere* "to run"] SYN see SUPERFICIAL — **cur·so·ri·ly** \'kərs-rə-lē, -ə-rə-\ *adv* — **cur·so·ri·ness** \'kərs-rē-nəs, -ə-rē-\ *n*

curt \'kərt\ *adj* : rudely abrupt or brief ⟨a *curt* reply⟩ [Latin *curtus* "shortened"] — **curt·ly** *adv* — **curt·ness** *n*

cur·tail \kər-'tāl\ *vt* : to shorten or reduce by cutting away the end or another part of [derived from Latin *curtus* "shortened"] SYN see SHORTEN — **cur·tail·er** *n* — **cur·tail·ment** \-'tāl-mənt\ *n*

¹**cur·tain** \'kərt-n\ *n* **1 a** : a piece of material hung (as at a window) for decoration, privacy, or control of light and drafts **b** : the screen separating the stage from the auditorium of a theater **2 a** : the ascent or descent of a theater curtain **b** : the time at which a theatrical performance begins **3** : something that covers, conceals, or separates like a curtain **4** : CURTAIN WALL [Old French *curtine*, from Late Latin *cortina*, from Latin *cohors* "enclosure, court"] — **curtain** *vt*

curtain call *n* : an appearance by a performer usually at a final curtain (as of a play) in response to the applause of the audience

curtain raiser *n* **1** : a short play used to open a performance **2** : a usually short and unimportant preliminary to a main event

curtain wall *n* : an exterior enclosing wall (as of a skyscraper) that does not support any weight but its own

¹**curt·sy** *or* **curt·sey** \'kərt-sē\ *n, pl* **curtsies** *or* **curtseys** : a gesture of respect made chiefly by women that consists of a slight lowering of the body and bending of the knees [alteration of *courtesy*]

²**curtsy** *or* **curtsey** *vi* **curt·sied** *or* **curt·seyed; curt·sy·ing** *or* **curt·sey·ing** : to make a curtsy

cur·va·ceous \,kər-'vā-shəs\ *adj* : having a well-proportioned feminine figure marked by full curves

cur·va·ture \'kər-və-,chúr, -chər\ *n* **1** : the act of curving : the state of being curved **2** : a measure of the amount of curving of a curved line or surface **3 a** : an abnormal curving (as of a bodily structure) ⟨*curvature* of the spine⟩ **b** : a curved surface (as of an organ)

¹**curve** \'kərv\ *vb* **1** : to turn, change, or deviate gradually from a straight line **2** : to cause to curve : BEND [Latin *curvare*, from *curvus* "curved"]

²**curve** *n* **1** : a curving line or surface : BEND **2** : something curved ⟨a *curve* in the road⟩ **3** : a ball thrown so that it swerves from its normal course — called also *curve ball* **4** : a line connecting points on a graph or in a coordinate system that are determined by an equation or are plotted from data **5** : the path of a moving point — **curved** \'kərvd\ *adj*

¹**cur·vet** \,kər-'vet\ *n* : a prancing leap of a horse in which first the forelegs and then the hind are raised so that for an instant all the legs are in the air [Italian *corvetta*, from Middle French *courbette*, from *courber* "to curve", from Latin *curvare*]

²**curvet** *vi* **cur·vet·ted** *or* **cur·vet·ed; cur·vet·ting** *or* **cur·vet·ing** : to make a curvet; *also* : CAPER, PRANCE

cur·vi·lin·ear \,kər-və-'lin-ē-ər\ *adj* : consisting of, characterized by, or bounded by curved lines

¹**cush·ion** \'kúsh-ən\ *n* **1** : a soft pillow or pad to rest on or against **2** : something resembling a cushion in use, shape, or softness **3** : a pad of springy rubber along the inside of the rim of a billiard table **4** : something serving to lighten the effects of disturbances or disorders ⟨saved money as a *cushion* against hard times⟩ [Middle French *coissin*, derived from Latin *coxa* "hip"]

²**cushion** *vt* **cush·ioned; cush·ion·ing** \'kúsh-ning, -ə-ning\ **1** : to seat or place on a cushion **2** : to furnish with a cushion ⟨*cushion* the bench⟩ **3 a** : to lighten the effects of ⟨*cushion* the blow⟩ **b** : to shield from harm or injury : PROTECT ⟨*cushioned* the children from harsh realities⟩

Cush·it·ic \,kəsh-'it-ik, kúsh-\ *n* : a subfamily of the Afro-Asiatic language family comprising various languages spoken in East Africa and especially in Ethiopia and Somalia [*Cush* (Kush), ancient country in the Nile valley] — **Cushitic** *adj*

cushy \'kúsh-ē\ *adj* **cushi·er; cushi·est** : EASY ⟨a *cushy* job⟩ [Hindi *khush* "pleasant", from Persian *khūsh*] — **cushi·ly** \'kúsh-ə-lē\ *adv*

cusk \'kəsk\ *n, pl* **cusk** *or* **cusks** : a large edible marine fish related to the cod [probably alteration of *tusk*, a kind of codfish]

cusp \'kəsp\ *n* **1** : APEX 1, POINT: as **a** : either of the pointed ends of a crescent moon **b** : a pointed projection formed by or arising from the intersection of two arcs **c** : a point on the grinding surface of a tooth **d** : a fold or flap of a cardiac valve [Latin *cuspis* "point"]

cus·pid \'kəs-pəd\ *n* : CANINE 1 [back-formation from *bicuspid*]

cus·pi·dor \'kəs-pə-,dór\ *n* : SPITTOON [Portuguese *cuspidouro*, from *cuspir* "to spit", from Latin *conspuere*, from *com-* + *spuere* "to spit"]

¹**cuss** \'kəs\ *n* **1** : CURSE **2** : FELLOW ⟨an obstinate *cuss*⟩ [alteration of *curse*]

²**cuss** *vb* : CURSE 1, 2 — **cuss·er** *n*

cuss·ed \'kəs-əd\ *adj* **1** : CURSED **2** : PERVERSE 2, 3, OBSTINATE — **cuss·ed·ly** *adv*

cuss·ed·ness \-əd-nəs\ *n* : disposition to perversity : OBSTINACY

cus·tard \'kəs-tərd\ *n* : a usually sweetened mixture of milk and eggs baked, boiled, or frozen [Middle English, a kind of pie]

custard apple *n* **1** : any of several chiefly tropical American soft-fleshed edible fruits; *also* : a tree or shrub bearing such fruit **2** : PAPAW 2

cus·to·di·al \,kə-'stōd-ē-əl\ *adj* : of or relating to custody, custodians, or custodianship

cus·to·di·an \,kə-'stōd-ē-ən\ *n* : one that guards and protects or maintains: as **a** : one entrusted with guarding prisoners or inmates **b** : one entrusted with guarding and keeping property or records; *esp* : JANITOR — **cus·to·di·an·ship** \-,ship\ *n*

cus·to·dy \'kəs-təd-ē\ *n* : immediate charge and control (as of a ward or suspect) exercised by a person or an authority [Latin *custodia* "guarding", from *custos* "guardian"]

¹**cus·tom** \'kəs-təm\ *n* **1 a** : a usage or practice common to many or habitual with an individual **b** : long-established practice considered as unwritten law **2** *pl* : duties, tolls, or imposts imposed by the law of a country on imports or exports **3** : support given to a business by its customers : CUSTOMERS [Old French *costume, custume*, from Latin *consuetudo*, from *consuescere* "to accustom" from *com-* + *suescere* "to accustom"] SYN see HABIT

²**custom** *adj* **1** : made or performed according to personal order ⟨*custom* clothes⟩ **2** : specializing in custom work or operation

cus·tom·ary \'kəs-tə-,mer-ē\ *adj* **1** : based on or established by custom ⟨*customary* rent⟩ **2** : commonly practiced or observed : HABITUAL ⟨*customary* courtesy⟩ SYN see USUAL — **cus·tom·ar·i·ly** \,kəs-tə-'mer-ə-lē\ *adv* — **cus·tom·ar·i·ness** \'kəs-tə-,mer-ē-nəs\ *n*

cus·tom–built \,kəs-təm-'bilt\ *adj* : built to individual order

\ə\ abut	\ng\ sing
\ər\ further	\ō\ bone
\a\ mat	\ó\ saw
\ā\ take	\oi\ coin
\ä\ cot, cart	\th\ thin
\aú\ out	\th\ this
\ch\ chin	\ü\ food
\e\ pet	\ú\ foot
\ē\ easy	\y\ yet
\g\ go	\yü\ few
\i\ tip	\yú\ cure
\ī\ life	\zh\ vision
\j\ job	

cus·tom·er \'kəs-tə-mər\ *n* **1** : one that buys from or patronizes a business especially on a regular basis **2** : PERSON, FELLOW ⟨a queer *customer*⟩

cus·tom·house \'kəs-təm-ˌhaůs\ *also* **cus·toms·house** \-təmz-\ *n* : a building where customs are collected and where ships are entered and cleared at a port

cus·tom–made \ˌkəs-təm-'mād, -'ad\ *adj* : made to individual order

¹cut \'kət\ *vb* **cut; cut·ting** **1 a** : to penetrate with or as if with an edged instrument : GASH **b** : to function as or like an edged tool ⟨the knife *cuts* well⟩ **c** : to allow being shaped, penetrated, or divided with an edged tool ⟨cheese *cuts* easily⟩ **d** : to work with or as if with an edged tool ⟨a tailor busy *cutting*⟩ **e** : to experience the growth of (a tooth) through the gum **2 a** : to hurt emotionally **b** (1) : to strike sharply (2) : to strike or strike at (as a ball) with a glancing stroke **c** : to have validity or effect ⟨that argument *cuts* both ways⟩ **3 a** : to make less in amount ⟨cut costs⟩ **b** : to shorten by omissions ⟨cut a manuscript⟩ **c** : DILUTE ⟨cut whiskey with water⟩ **4 a** : TRIM 3a, PARE ⟨cut hair⟩ **b** : MOW, REAP ⟨cut hay⟩ **c** : to divide into parts with an edged tool ⟨cut the pie⟩ **d** : FELL, HEW ⟨cut timber⟩ **5** : to remove or separate from a group ⟨cut two players from the squad⟩ **6 a** : to turn sharply ⟨cut right to avoid a collision⟩ ⟨cut the wheels⟩ **b** : to move fast ⟨cut along the road⟩ **c** : to take a short or direct route ⟨cut across the campus⟩ **d** : INTERSECT, CROSS ⟨lines *cutting* other lines⟩ **e** : BREAK, INTERRUPT ⟨cut our supply line⟩ **f** : to divide a deck of cards or separate a group of cards from the deck **g** : to divide (as money) into shares : SPLIT **h** : to make a sudden transition from one sound or image to another (as in a film) **7 a** : CEASE, STOP ⟨cut the nonsense⟩ **b** : to refuse to recognize (an acquaintance) **c** : to fail to attend (as a meeting or class) **d** : to stop (a motor) by opening a switch **e** : to cease photographing a motion picture **8 a** : to make or give shape to with or as if with an edged tool ⟨cut a hole in the wall⟩ ⟨the floodwaters *cut* new channels⟩ ⟨cut a diamond⟩ **b** : to record sounds on (a phonograph record) **9 a** : to engage in : PERFORM ⟨cut a caper⟩ **b** : to give the appearance of ⟨cuts a fine figure⟩ [Middle English *cutten*] — **cut corners** : to reduce cost, time, or difficulty often at the expense of quality — **cut short** : to interrupt or end abruptly

²cut *n* **1** : something cut or cut off: as **a** : a yield of products cut especially during one harvest **b** : a part of a meat carcass ⟨a rib *cut*⟩ **c** : an allotted part : SHARE ⟨took our *cut* and left⟩ **2** : an effect produced by or as if by cutting: as **a** : a wound made by something sharp : GASH **b** : a surface or outline made by cutting ⟨a smooth *cut* in a board⟩ **c** : a passage made by cutting ⟨a railroad *cut*⟩ **d** : a grade or step especially in a social scale ⟨a *cut* above the neighbors⟩ **e** : a pictorial illustration **3** : the act or an instance of cutting: as **a** : a gesture or expression that wounds the feelings ⟨an unkind *cut*⟩ **b** : a straight path or course **c** : STROKE, BLOW ⟨took a *cut* at the ball⟩ **d** : the act of reducing or removing a part ⟨a *cut* in pay⟩ **e** : the act of or a turn at cutting cards ⟨it's your *cut*⟩ **4** : a voluntary absence from a class **5** : an abrupt transition from one sound or image to another in motion pictures, radio, or television **6** : the shape and style in which a thing is cut, formed, or made ⟨clothes of the latest *cut*⟩ **7** : BAND 5e

cut–and–dried \ˌkət-n-'drīd\ *also* **cut–and–dry** \-'drī\ *adj* : being or done according to a plan, set procedure, or formula : ROUTINE

cu·ta·ne·ous \kyů-'tā-nē-əs\ *adj* : of, relating to, or affecting the skin ⟨cutaneous infection⟩ [Latin *cutis* "skin"] — **cu·ta·ne·ous·ly** *adv*

¹cut·away \'kət-ə-ˌwā\ *adj* : having or showing parts removed ⟨a *cutaway* model of a beehive showing its inner structure⟩

²cutaway *n* **1** : a coat with skirts tapering from the front waistline to form tails at the back **2** : a cutaway picture or representation

cut·back \'kət-ˌbak\ *n* **1** : something cut back **2** : DECREASE ⟨a *cutback* in employment⟩

cut back \'kət-'bak, ˌkət-\ *vb* **1** : to shorten by cutting : PRUNE **2** : DECREASE, REDUCE ⟨cut back production⟩ **3** : to interrupt the sequence of a plot by introducing events prior to those last presented

cut down *vb* **1** : to remake in a smaller size ⟨cut down the coat⟩ **2** : to strike down by or as if by cutting **3 a** : REDUCE 1b ⟨cut down the accident rate⟩ **b** : to reduce or curtail volume or activity ⟨cut down on smoking⟩

cute \'kyüt\ *adj* **1** : SHREWD, WILY **2** : attractive or pretty especially in a dainty or delicate way **3** : obviously straining for effect [short for *acute*] — **cute·ly** *adv* — **cute·ness** *n*

cute·sy *also* **cute·sie** \'kyüt-sē\ *adj* **cute·si·er; -est** : self-consciously cute ⟨cutesy mannerisms⟩

cut glass *n* : glass ornamented with patterns cut into its surface and polished

cu·ti·cle \'kyüt-i-kəl\ *n* **1** : SKIN, PELLICLE: as **a** : an external sheathing layer secreted usually by epidermal cells **b** : the epidermis when it is the outermost layer **c** : a thin continuous fatty film on the external surface of many higher plants **2** : dead or horny epidermis [Latin *cuticula*, from *cutis* "skin"] — **cu·tic·u·lar** \kyů-'tik-yə-lər\ *adj*

cut·ie *or* **cut·ey** \'kyüt-ē\ *n, pl* **cuties** *or* **cuteys** : one that is cute; *esp* : a pretty girl

cu·tin \'kyüt-n\ *n* : an insoluble substance containing waxes, fatty acids, soaps, and resinous matter that forms a continuous layer on the outer epidermal wall of a plant [Latin *cutis* "skin"] — **cu·tin·ized** \-n-ˌīzd\ *adj*

cut in *vb* **1** : to thrust oneself into a position between others or belonging to another **2** : to join in something suddenly ⟨cut in on the conversation⟩ **3** : to interrupt a dancing couple and take one of them as a partner **4** : INCLUDE ⟨cut me *in* on the profits⟩

cut·lass \'kət-ləs\ *n* : a short curved sword formerly used by sailors on warships [Middle French *coutelas*, from *coutel* "knife", from Latin *culter* "knife, plowshare"]

cut·ler \'kət-lər\ *n* : one that makes, deals in, or repairs cutlery [Middle French *coutelier*, from Late Latin *cultellarius*, from Latin *cultellus* "knife"]

cut·lery \'kət-lə-rē\ *n* **1** : edged or cutting tools; *esp* : implements for cutting and eating food **2** : the business of a cutler

cut·let \'kət-lət\ *n* : a small slice of meat for broiling or frying [French *côtelette*, from Old French *costelette*, from *coste* "rib, side", from Latin *costa*]

cut·off \'kət-ˌof\ *n* **1** : the action of cutting off **2 a** : the channel formed when a stream cuts through the neck of an oxbow **b** : SHORTCUT 1 **3** : a device for cutting off — **cutoff** *adj*

cut off \ˌkət-'of, 'kət-\ *vt* **1** : to kill usually suddenly or prematurely **2** : to stop the passage of ⟨cut off our supplies⟩ **3** : SEPARATE, ISOLATE ⟨cut off by the sudden attack⟩ **4** : DISINHERIT **5 a** : to stop the operation of ⟨cut off a motor⟩ **b** : to stop or interrupt while in communication ⟨the operator *cut* me *off*⟩ **6** : INTERCEPT 2 ⟨an angle whose rays *cut off* an arc on a circle⟩

cut·out \'kət-ˌaůt\ *n* : something cut out or prepared for cutting out from something else ⟨a page of animal *cutouts*⟩ — **cutout** *adj*

¹cut out \ˌkət-'aůt, 'kət-\ *vb* **1** : to be all that one can handle ⟨they have their work *cut out* for them⟩ **2** : SUPPLANT 1 ⟨cut out a competitor⟩ **3** : to remove from a series or circuit : DISCONNECT **4** : to cease operating ⟨the engine *cut out*⟩ **5** : ELIMINATE ⟨cut out the waste⟩

²cut out *adj* : fitted by nature ⟨not *cut out* to be a lawyer⟩

cut·over \'kət-ˌō-vər\ *adj* : having most of its salable timber cut ⟨cutover land⟩

cut·purse \'kət-ˌpərs\ *n* : PICKPOCKET

cut–rate \'kət-'rāt\ *adj* **I** : selling or offered at a reduced rate or price ⟨a *cut-rate* store⟩ **2** : SECOND-RATE, CHEAP

cut·ter \'kət-ər\ *n* **I** : one that cuts ⟨a diamond *cutter*⟩ ⟨a cookie *cutter*⟩ **2 a** : a boat used by warships for carrying passengers and stores to and from the shore **b** : a small one-masted sailing boat that usually carries two headsails **c** : a small armed boat in the coast guard **3** : a small sleigh

¹**cut·throat** \'kət-ˌthrōt\ *n* : a murderous person : MURDERER

²**cutthroat** *adj* **I** : MURDEROUS, CRUEL ⟨a *cutthroat* rogue⟩ **2** : MERCILESS, RUTHLESS ⟨*cutthroat* competition⟩

cut time *n* : ALLA BREVE

¹**cut·ting** *n* **I** : something cut or cut off or out: as **a** : a section of a plant capable of developing into a new plant **b** : HARVEST 2 **2** : something made by cutting; *esp* : RECORD 4

²**cutting** *adj* **I** : designed for cutting : SHARP ⟨the *cutting* edge of a knife⟩ **2** : piercingly cold ⟨a *cutting* wind⟩ **3** : SARCASTIC SYN see INCISIVE — **cut·ting·ly** \-ing-lē\ *adv*

cut·tle·bone \'kət-l-ˌbōn\ *n* : the hard internal shell of cuttlefishes used for making polishing powder or for supplying birds housed in cages with lime and salts [Middle English *cotul* "cuttlefish"]

cut·tle·fish \-ˌfish\ *n* : a 10-armed marine mollusk differing from the related squid in having an internal shell composed of compounds of calcium [Middle English *cotul* "cuttlefish", from Old English *cudele*]

cut·up \'kət-ˌəp\ *n* : one who clowns or acts boisterously

cut up \ˌkət-'əp, 'kət-\ *vb* **I a** : to cut or be cut into parts or pieces **b** : to distress deeply ⟨*cut up* by the criticism⟩ **2** : to damage by or as if by cutting ⟨the truck *cut up* the lawn⟩ **3** : to clown or act boisterously

cut·wa·ter \'kət-ˌwȯt-ər, -ˌwät-\ *n* : the forepart of a ship's stem

cut·worm \-ˌwərm\ *n* : any of various smooth-bodied moth caterpillars that hide by day and feed especially on plant stems near ground level at night

-cy \sē\ *n suffix, pl* **-cies** : action : practice ⟨mendican*cy*⟩ : rank : office ⟨chaplain*cy*⟩ : body : class ⟨magistra*cy*⟩ : state : quality ⟨accura*cy*⟩ ⟨bankrupt*cy*⟩ — often replacing a final *-t* or *-te* of the base word [Old French *-cie,* from Latin *-tia*]

cyan- *or* **cyano-** *combining form* **I** : dark blue : blue ⟨*cyano*sis⟩ **2** : cyanogen ⟨*cyan*ide⟩ **3** : cyanide [Greek *kyanos* "dark blue enamel"]

cy·an·a·mide \sī-'an-ə-məd\ *n* **I** : a caustic acidic compound CH_2N_2 that consists of carbon, hydrogen, and nitrogen **2** : a grayish black lumpy or powdered substance $CaCN_2$ consisting of calcium, carbon, and nitrogen that is used as a fertilizer — called also *calcium cyanamide*

cy·a·nide \'sī-ə-ˌnīd, -nəd\ *n* : a compound of cyanogen with an element or another radical: as **a** : POTASSIUM CYANIDE **b** : SODIUM CYANIDE

cy·an·o·gen \sī-'an-ə-jən\ *n* **I** : a univalent radical –CN that consists of carbon and nitrogen and is present in simple and complex cyanides **2** : a colorless flammable poisonous gas $(CN)_2$

cy·a·no·sis \ˌsī-ə-'nō-səs\ *n* : a bluish or purplish discoloration (as of skin) due to lack of oxygen in the blood — **cy·a·not·ic** \ˌsī-ə-'nät-ik\ *adj*

cy·ber·net·ics \ˌsī-bər-'net-iks\ *n* : the science of communication and control theory that is concerned especially with the comparative study of automatic control systems (as the nervous system and brain and mechanical-electrical communication systems) [Greek *kybernētēs* "pilot, governor", from *kybernan* "to steer, govern"] — **cy·ber·net·ic** \-ik\ *adj*

cy·cad \'sī-kəd\ *n* : any of a family of tropical evergreen plants that resemble palms but are actually gymnosperms [New Latin *Cycad-, Cycas,* genus name]

cycl- *or* **cyclo-** *combining form* : circle ⟨*cyclo*meter⟩ [Greek *kyklos*]

cy·cla·men \'sī-klə-mən, 'sik-lə-\ *n* : any of a genus of plants of the primrose family grown as pot plants for their showy nodding flowers [Greek *kyklaminos*]

¹**cy·cle** \'sī-kəl, 6 *is also* 'sik-əl\ *n* **I** : a period of time taken up by a series of events or actions that repeat themselves regularly and in the same order ⟨the *cycle* of the seasons⟩ **2 a** : a course or series of events or activities that recur regularly and usually lead back to the starting point ⟨the *cycle* of the blood from the heart, through the blood vessels, and back again⟩ **b** : one complete performance of a series of recurring events: as (1) : one complete series of changes in voltage and current direction of an alternating electric current (2) : one complete set of consecutive changes in value of a sequence of numbers or digits which repeats itself **3** : a circular or spiral arrangement; *esp* : a whorl of floral leaves **4** : a long period of time : AGE **5 a** : a group of poems, plays, novels, or songs treating the same theme **b** : a series of narratives dealing typically with the exploits of a legendary hero **6 a** : BICYCLE **b** : TRICYCLE **c** : MOTORCYCLE [Late Latin *cyclus,* from Greek *kyklos* "circle, wheel, cycle"] — **cy·clic** \'sī-klik, 'sik-lik\ *or* **cy·cli·cal** \'sī-kli-kəl, 'sik-li-\ *adj* — **cy·cli·cal·ly** \-kə-lē, -klē\ *adv*

²**cy·cle** \'sī-kəl, 2 *is also* 'sik-əl\ *vb* **cy·cled; cy·cling** \'sī-kə-ling, -kling; 'sik-ling, -ə-ling\ **I a** : to pass or cause to go through a cycle **b** : to recur in cycles **2** : to ride a cycle — **cy·cler** \'sī-kə-lər, -klər; 'sik-lər, -ə-lər\ *n*

cyclic AMP *n* : a nucleotide formed from ATP that is believed to be an important message carrier to cells and a regulator of biological activities at the cellular level

cycling : the sport of bicycle riding and especially bicycle racing

cy·clist \'sī-kə-ləst, -kləst; 'sik-ləst, -ə-ləst\ *n* : one who rides a cycle and especially a bicycle

cy·cloid \'sī-ˌkloid\ *n* : a curve traced out by a point on the circumference of a circle that is rolling along a straight line — **cy·cloi·dal** \sī-'kloid-l\ *adj*

cy·clom·e·ter \sī-'kläm-ət-ər\ *n* : a device designed to record revolutions of a wheel and often used to register distance traversed by a wheeled vehicle

cy·clone \'sī-ˌklōn\ *n* **I** : a storm or system of winds that rotates about a center of low atmospheric pressure counterclockwise in the northern hemisphere, advances at a speed of 32 to 48 kilometers an hour, and often brings abundant rain **2** : TORNADO [Greek *kyklōma* "wheel, coil", from *kykloun* "to go around", from *kyklos* "circle"] — **cy·clon·ic** \sī-'klän-ik\ *adj* — **cy·clon·i·cal·ly** \-'klän-i-kə-lē, -klē\ *adv*

cy·clo·pe·an \ˌsī-klə-'pē-ən, sī-'klō-pē-\ *adj* **I** *often cap* : of, relating to, or characteristic of a Cyclops **2** : HUGE a, MASSIVE

cy·clo·pe·dia *or* **cy·clo·pae·dia** \ˌsī-klə-'pēd-ē-ə\ *n* : ENCYCLOPEDIA — **cy·clo·pe·dic** \-'pēd-ik\ *adj*

cy·clops \'sī-ˌkläps\ *n* **I** *pl* **cy·clo·pes** \sī-'klō-ˌpēz\ *cap* : one of a race of giants in Greek mythology with a single eye in the middle of the forehead **2** *pl* **cyclops** : any of a genus of small pear-shaped water fleas [Greek *Kyklōps,* from *kyklos* "circle" + *ōps* "eye"]

cy·clo·ra·ma \ˌsī-klə-'ram-ə, -'räm-\ *n* : a large pictorial representation encircling the spectator and often having real objects as a foreground [*cycl-* + *-orama* (as in *panorama*)] — **cy·clo·ram·ic** \-'ram-ik\ *adj*

cy·clo·sis \sī-'klō-səs\ *n* : the streaming of protoplasm within a cell

cy·clo·stome \'sī-klə-ˌstōm\ *n* : any of a class (Cyclostomi or Cyclostomata) of lower vertebrates with a large sucking mouth and no jaws [Greek *kyklos* "circle" + *stoma* "mouth"] — **cyclostome** *adj*

cy·clo·thy·mic \ˌsī-klə-'thī-mik\ *adj* : having a temperament marked by alternate lively and depressed moods [derived from Greek *kyklos* "circle" + *thymos* "mind"]

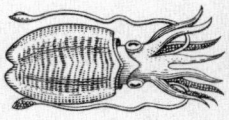

cuttlefish

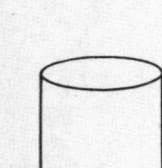

cylinder 1

cy·clo·tron \'sī-klə-ˌträn\ *n* : an accelerator in which charged particles (as protons or ions) are propelled by an alternating electric field in a constant magnetic field

cyg·net \'sig-nət\ *n* : a young swan [Middle French *cygne* "swan", from Latin *cygnus,* from Greek *kyknos*]

Cyg·nus \'sig-nəs\ *n* : a northern constellation between Lyra and Pegasus in the Milky Way [Latin, literally, "swan"]

cyl·in·der \'sil-ən-dər\ *n* **1** : the surface traced by a straight line moving parallel to a fixed straight line and intersecting a fixed curve; *also* : the space bounded by any such surface and two parallel planes cutting all the elements **2** : a long round solid or hollow body (as the piston chamber of an engine, the barrel of a pump, or the part of a revolver which turns and holds the cartridges) [Latin *cylindrus,* from Greek *kylindros,* from *kylindein* "to roll"] — **cyl·in·dered** \-dərd\ *adj*

cy·lin·dri·cal \sə-'lin-dri-kəl\ *or* **cy·lin·dric** \-drik\ *adj* : of, relating to, or having the form or properties of a cylinder — **cy·lin·dri·cal·ly** \-dri-kə-lē, -klē\ *adv*

cym·bal \'sim-bəl\ *n* : a brass plate that is struck with a drumstick or is used in pairs struck glancingly together to make a clashing sound [Old English, from Latin *cymbalum,* from Greek *kymbalon,* from *kymbē* "bowl"]

cym·bid·i·um \sim-'bid-ē-əm\ *n* : any of a genus of tropical Old World orchids with showy boat-shaped flowers [Latin *cymba* "boat", from Greek *kymbē* "bowl, boat"]

cyme \'sīm\ *n* : a broad branching often flat-topped cluster of flowers with a single flower at the end of each branch and with the individual flowers opening in sequence from the center toward the margin of the cluster [Latin *cyma* "cabbage sprout", from Greek *kyma* "swell, cabbage sprout", from *kyein* "to be pregnant"] — **cy·mose** \'sī-ˌmōs\ *adj*

¹Cym·ric \'kəm-rik, 'kim-\ *adj* **1** : of, relating to, or characteristic of the non-Gaelic Celtic people of Britain or their language **2** : WELSH [Welsh *Cymry* "Welshmen"]

²Cymric *n* **1** : the non-Gaelic Celtic languages **2** : WELSH 2

cyn·ic \'sin-ik\ *n* **1** *cap* : an adherent or advocate of the view held by some ancient Greek philosophers that virtue is the only good and that its essence lies in self-control and independence **2** : one who believes that human conduct is motivated wholly by self-interest [Latin *cynicus,* a member of a school of ancient Greek philosophers, from Greek *kynikos,* from *kynikos* "like a dog", from *kyōn* "dog"] — **cynic** *adj* □ ORIGIN The ancient Greek philosopher Antisthenes taught that virtue is the only goal worth striving for. He and his followers were devoted to an ascetic life and made great show of their contempt for wealth and pleasure. Such a philosopher was called *kynikos,* which means literally "doglike". It is likely that one reason for the name was that Antisthenes taught in a school outside Athens which was called *Kynosarges.* It is likely, however, that most Greeks who applied *kynikos* to these philosophers had been offended by their surly reproaches. *Cynic* has been used in English since the 16th century as a word for a philosopher of this school. The word had not been long in English before it was applied to any faultfinding critic, especially to one who doubts the sincerity of all human motives except self-interest.

cyn·i·cal \'sin-i-kəl\ *adj* : having the attitude or temper of a cynic; *esp* : contemptuously distrustful of human nature and motives ⟨*cynical* remarks about politicians⟩ — **cyn·i·cal·ly** \-kə-lē, -klē\ *adv*

cyn·i·cism \'sin-ə-ˌsiz-əm\ *n* **1** : cynical character or quality **2** : a cynical remark

cy·no·sure \'sī-nə-ˌshůr, 'sin-ə-\ *n* **1** *cap* : the northern constellation Ursa Minor; *also* : NORTH STAR **2** : a center of attraction or attention ⟨the *cynosure* of all eyes⟩ [Latin *cynosura,* from Greek *kynosoura,* from *kynos oura* "dog's tail"]

cy·pher *chiefly British variant of* CIPHER

cy·press \'sī-prəs\ *n* **1** : any of a genus of mostly evergreen trees of the pine family that have overlapping scalelike leaves **2** : either of two large swamp trees of the southern United States with hard red wood **3** : the wood of a cypress tree [Old French *ciprès,* from Latin *cyparissus,* from Greek *kyparissos*]

cyp·ri·pe·di·um \ˌsip-rə-'pēd-ē-əm\ *n* : any of a genus of leafy-stemmed terrestrial orchids that have large usually showy drooping flowers in the form of a pouch [Late Latin *Cypris,* a name for Venus + Greek *pedilon* "sandal"]

Cy·ril·lic \sə-'ril-ik\ *adj* : of, relating to, or constituting an alphabet used for Russian and various other Slavic languages [Saint *Cyril,* died 869, apostle of the Slavs, reputed inventor of the Cyrillic alphabet]

cyst \'sist\ *n* **1** : a closed sac developing abnormally in a cavity or structure of the body **2** : a covering (as of an internal parasite) resembling a cyst; *also* : a body (as a spore) with such a covering [Greek *kystis* "bladder, pouch"]

cyst- *or* **cysti-** *or* **cysto-** *combining form* : bladder ⟨*cyst*itis⟩ : sac [Greek *kystis*]

-cyst \ˌsist\ *n combining form* : bladder : sac ⟨blasto*cyst*⟩

cys·te·ine \'sis-tə-ˌēn\ *n* : a sulfur-containing amino acid $C_3H_7NO_2S$ that is readily oxidized to cystine [derived from *cystine*]

cys·tic \'sis-tik\ *adj* **1** : of, relating to, or containing cysts **2** : of or relating to the urinary bladder or the gallbladder

cys·ti·cer·cus \ˌsis-tə-'sər-kəs\ *n, pl* **-cer·ci** \-'sər-ˌsī\ : a tapeworm larva consisting of a head in a fluid-filled sac [*cyst*- + Greek *kerkos* "tail"]

cystic fibrosis *n* : a hereditary glandular disorder that appears usually in early childhood and is marked especially by defective functioning of the pancreas, respiratory disease, and excessive loss of salt in the sweat

cys·tine \'sis-ˌtēn\ *n* : an amino acid $C_6H_{12}N_2O_4S_2$ widespread in proteins (as keratins) [from its discovery in bladder stones]

cys·ti·tis \sis-'tīt-əs\ *n* : inflammation of the urinary bladder

cyt- *or* **cyto-** *combining form* : cell ⟨*cyto*logy⟩ [Greek *kytos* "hollow vessel"]

-cyte \ˌsīt\ *n combining form* : cell ⟨leuko*cyte*⟩

cy·to·chrome \'sīt-ə-ˌkrōm\ *n* : any of several iron-containing enzymes that function in the transport of electrons to molecular oxygen in the living cell by undergoing alternate oxidation and reduction

cy·to·ki·nin \ˌsīt-ə-'kī-nən\ *n* : any of various substances that promote growth in plants [*cyt*- + *kinin,* a plant growth factor, from Greek *kinein* "to move, stimulate"]

cy·tol·o·gy \sī-'täl-ə-jē\ *n* : a branch of biology dealing with cells — **cy·to·log·i·cal** \ˌsīt-l-'äj-i-kəl\ *or* **cy·to·log·ic** \-'äj-ik\ *adj* — **cy·to·log·i·cal·ly** \-'äj-i-kə-lē, -klē\ *adv* — **cy·tol·o·gist** \sī-'täl-ə-jəst\ *n*

cy·to·plasm \'sīt-ə-ˌplaz-əm\ *n* : the protoplasm of the living part of a cell outside the nucleus and its membrane — **cy·to·plas·mic** \ˌsīt-ə-'plaz-mik\ *adj* — **cy·to·plas·mi·cal·ly** \-mi-kə-lē, -klē\ *adv*

cy·to·plast \'sīt-ə-ˌplast\ *n* : the cytoplasmic part of a cell — compare PROTOPLAST

cy·to·sine \'sīt-ə-ˌsēn\ *n* : a pyrimidine base $C_4H_5N_3O$ that codes genetic information in the polynucleotide chain of DNA and RNA — compare ADENINE, GUANINE, THYMINE, URACIL

czar \'zär\ *n* **1** *or* **tsar** *also* **tzar** : the ruler of Russia until the 1917 revolution **2** *also* **tsar** : one having great power or authority ⟨baseball *czar*⟩ [Russian *tsar'*, from Gothic *kaisar* "emperor", from Latin *Caesar*] — **czar·dom** \'zärd-əm\ *n* — **czar·ism** \'zär-,iz-əm\ *n* — **czar·ist** \'zär-əst\ *adj or n*

czar·e·vitch \'zär-ə-,vich\ *n* : an heir of a Russian czar

cza·ri·na \zä-'rē-nə\ *n* **1** : the wife of a czar **2** : a woman who has the rank of czar in her own right

Czech \'chek\ *n* **1** : a native or inhabitant of Czechoslovakia; *esp* : a native or inhabitant of the provinces Bohemia, Moravia, or Silesia **2** : the Slavic language of the Czechs — **Czech** *adj* — **Czech·ish** \-ish\ *adj*

Dd

d \'dē\ *n, pl* **d's** *or* **ds** \'dēz\ *often cap* **1** : the 4th letter of the English alphabet **2** : five hundred in Roman numerals **3** : the musical tone D **4** : a grade rating a student's work as poor

'd \d, əd\ *vb* **1** : HAD ⟨they'*d* gone⟩ **2 a** : WOULD ⟨we'*d* go⟩ **b** : SHOULD ⟨I'*d* go⟩ **3** : DID ⟨where'*d* they go?⟩

-d *symbol* — used after the figure 2 or 3 to indicate the ordinal number second or third ⟨2*d*⟩ ⟨23*d*⟩

'dab \'dab\ *n* **1** : a sudden blow or thrust : POKE **2** : a gentle touch or stroke : PAT [Middle English *dabbe*]

'dab *vb* **dabbed; dab·bing 1** : to strike or touch lightly ⟨*dab* at one's eyes with a handkerchief⟩ **2** : to apply lightly or irregularly : DAUB — **dab·ber** *n*

'dab *n* : DAUB 1 **2** : a small amount

'dab *n* : FLATFISH; *esp* : any of several flounders [Anglo-French *dabbe*]

dab·ble \'dab-əl\ *vb* **dab·bled; dab·bling** \'dab-ling, -ə-ling\ **1** : to wet by splashing : SPATTER **2** : to paddle or play in or as if in water **3** : to work or concern oneself lightly or superficially [perhaps from *'dab*] — **dab·bler** \'dab-lər, -ə-lər\

da ca·po \dä-'käp-ō\ *adv or adj* : from the beginning — used as a direction in music to repeat [Italian]

dace \'dās\ *n, pl* **dace** : any of various small North American freshwater fishes related to the carp [Middle French *dars*, from Medieval Latin *darsus*]

da·cha \'däch-ə\ *n* : a Russian country house [Russian]

dachs·hund \'däks-,hunt, 'däk-sənt\ *n, pl* **dachs·hunds** *or* **dachs·hun·de** \-,hún-də\ : a small dog of a breed of German origin with a long body, short legs, and long drooping ears [German, from *dachs* "badger" + *hund* "dog"]

Da·cron \'dā-,krän, 'dak-,rän\ *trademark* — used for a synthetic polyester textile fiber

dac·tyl \'dak-tl\ *n* : a metrical foot consisting of one accented syllable followed by two unaccented syllables (as in *tenderly*) [Latin *dactylus* "foot of one long syllable followed by two short syllables", from Greek *daktylos*, literally, "finger"; from the fact that the three syllables have the first one longest like the joints of the finger] — **dac·tyl·ic** \dak-'til-ik\ *adj*

dad \'dad\ *n* : FATHER 1a [probably baby talk]

dad·dy \'dad-ē\ *n, pl* **daddies** : FATHER 1a

dad·dy long·legs \,dad-ē-'lóng-,legz\ *n* : any of various animals with long slender legs: as **a** : CRANE FLY **b** : an arachnid (order Phalangida) that resembles a true spider but has a small rounded body and long slender legs — called also *harvestman*

da·do \'dād-ō\ *n, pl* **dadoes 1** : the part of the pedestal of a column between the base and the top moldings **2** : the lower part of an interior wall when specially decorated or faced [Italian, "die, plinth"]

dae·mon *variant of* DEMON

daf·fo·dil \'daf-ə-,dil\ *n* : any of a genus of bulbous herbs with long slender leaves and yellow, white, or pinkish flowers borne in spring; *esp* : one with flowers whose inner parts are arranged to form a trumpet-shaped tube — compare JONQUIL [probably from Dutch *de affodil* "the asphodel"]

daf·fy \'daf-ē\ *adj* **daf·fi·er; -est 1** : CRAZY 2a, INSANE **2** : SILLY 1, 2, FOOLISH [obsolete English *daff* "fool"]

daft \'daft\ *adj* **1** : SILLY 1, 2, FOOLISH **2** : CRAZY 2a, INSANE [Middle English *dafte* "gentle, stupid"] — **daft·ly** *adv* — **daft·ness** \'daft-nəs, 'daf-\ *n*

dag·ger \'dag-ər\ *n* **1** : a short weapon for stabbing **2** : a character † used as a reference mark or to indicate a death date [Middle English]

da·guerre·o·type \də-'ger-ē-ə-,tīp, -'gər-ə-,\ *n* : an early photograph produced on a plate of silver or silver-covered copper; *also* : the process of producing such pictures [French *daguerréotype*, from L. J. M. *Daguerre*, died 1851, French painter]

dahl·ia \'dal-yə, 'däl-\ *n* : any of a genus of American tuberous-rooted herbs related to the daisies that have flower heads with brightly colored rays [Anders *Dahl*, died 1789, Swedish botanist]

'dai·ly \'dā-lē\ *adj* **1 a** : occurring, done, produced, or used every day or every weekday ⟨a *daily* newspaper⟩ **b** : of or relating to every day ⟨a *daily* visitor⟩ **2** : computed in terms of one day ⟨*daily* wages⟩ — **daily** *adv*

'daily *n, pl* **dailies** : a newspaper published every weekday

daily double *n* : a system of betting (as on horse races) in which the bettor must pick the winners of two stipulated races in order to win

dai·mon \'dī-,mōn\ *n, pl* **dai·mo·nes** \'dī-mə-,nēz\ *or* **daimons** : DEMON 1, 3 [Greek *daimōn*]

dai·myo *or* **dai·mio** \'dī-mē-ō, dī-'myō\ *n, pl* **daimyos** *or* **daimios** : a Japanese feudal baron [Japanese *daimyō*]

'dain·ty \'dānt-ē\ *n, pl* **dainties** : something that tastes delicious : DELICACY [Old French *deintié*, from Latin *dignitas* "dignity, worth"]

'dainty *adj* **dain·ti·er; -est 1** : TASTY 1, DELICIOUS **2** : delicately pretty ⟨a *dainty* flower⟩ **3** : having or showing delicate or discriminating taste : FASTIDIOUS ⟨a *dainty* eater⟩ — **dain·ti·ly** \'dānt-l-ē\ *adv* — **dain·ti·ness** \'dānt-ē-nəs\ *n*

dai·qui·ri \'dī-kə-rē, 'dak-ə-\ *n* : a cocktail made of rum, lime juice, and sugar [*Daiquirí*, Cuba]

dairy \'deər-ē, 'daər-\ *n, pl* **dair·ies 1** : a place where milk is kept and butter or cheese is made **2** : a farm devoted to the production of milk **3** : an establishment for the sale or distribution of milk and milk products [Middle English *deye* "dairymaid", from Old English *dǣge* "kneader of dough"] □ ORIGIN *Dairy* is related to *dough*. Old English *dǣge*, a relative of Old

dachshund

\ə\ abut	\ng\ sing
\ər\ further	\ō\ bone
\a\ mat	\ó\ saw
\ā\ take	\oi\ coin
\ä\ cot, cart	\th\ thin
\aú\ out	\th\ this
\ch\ chin	\ü\ food
\e\ pet	\ú\ foot
\ē\ easy	\y\ yet
\g\ go	\yü\ few
\i\ tip	\yú\ cure
\ī\ life	\zh\ vision
\j\ job	

English *dāg*, "dough", meant "a kneader of bread" or "a maid". The Middle English form *deye* meant "maid" or, more specifically, "dairymaid". A dairy, then, is the place where the (dairy)maid works.

dairy breed *n* : a cattle breed developed chiefly for milk production

dairy·ing \'der-ē-ing\ *n* : the business of operating a dairy

dairy·maid \-ē-,mād\ *n* : a woman employed in a dairy

dairy·man \-ē-mən, -,man\ *n* : one who operates a dairy farm or works in a dairy

da·is \'dā-əs, 'dī-\ *n* : a raised platform in a hall or large room [Old French *deis*, from Latin *discus* "dish, quoit"]

dai·sy \'dā-zē\ *n, pl* **daisies** 1 : any of numerous plants of the composite family having flower heads with well-developed ray flowers usually in one or a few whorls: as **a** : a low-growing European herb with white or pink ray flowers — called also *English daisy* **b** : a tall leafy-stemmed American wild flower with a yellow center and long white ray flowers — called also *oxeye daisy* 2 : the flower head of a daisy [Old English *dægesēage*, from *dæg* "day" + *ēage* "eye"]

daisy wheel *n* : a disk with spokes bearing type that serves as the printing element of an electric typewriter or printer; *also* : a printer that uses such a disk [from its resemblance to the flower]

Da·ko·ta \də-'kōt-ə\ *n, pl* **Dakotas** *also* **Dakota** : a member of a Siouan people of the northern Mississippi valley

Da·lai La·ma \,däl-,ī-'läm-ə\ *n* : the spiritual head of Lamaism [Mongolian *dalai* "ocean"]

dale \'dāl\ *n* : VALLEY 1 [Old English *dæl*]

dal·li·ance \'dal-ē-əns\ *n* : an act of dallying: as **a** : amorous play (as flirting or caressing) **b** : frivolous wasting of time : TRIFLING ⟨a short *dalliance* with radical ideas⟩

dal·ly \'dal-ē\ *vi* **dal·lied; dal·ly·ing** 1 **a** : to act playfully; *esp* : to play amorously **b** : to deal lightly : TOY ⟨*dally* with a problem⟩ 2 **a** : to waste time ⟨*dally* at one's work⟩ **b** : DAWDLE 2 ⟨*dally* on the way home⟩ [Anglo-French *dalier*] — **dal·li·er** *n*

dal·ma·tian \dal-'mā-shən\ *n, often cap* : a large dog of a breed characterized by a white short-haired coat with black or brown spots [from the supposed origin of the breed in Dalmatia]

dalmatian

dal·mat·ic \dal-'mat-ik\ *n* : a wide-sleeved vestment with slit sides worn by a deacon or prelate [Late Latin *dalmatica*, from Latin *dalmaticus* "of Dalmatia"]

dal se·gno \däl-'sān-yō\ *adv* : used as a direction in music to return to the sign that marks the beginning of a repeat [Italian, "from the sign"]

¹**dam** \'dam\ *n* : a female parent especially of a domestic animal [Middle English *dam, dame* "lady, dam"]

²**dam** *n* 1 : a barrier preventing the flow of water or of loose solid materials; *esp* : a barrier built across a watercourse 2 : a body of water confined by a dam [Middle English]

³**dam** *vt* **dammed; dam·ming** 1 : to provide or restrain with a dam ⟨*dam* a stream⟩ 2 : to stop up ⟨*dam* up an emotion⟩

¹**dam·age** \'dam-ij\ *n* 1 : a loss or harm resulting from injury to person, property, or reputation 2 *pl* : compensation in money imposed by law for loss or injury [Old French, from *dam* "damage", from Latin *damnum* "damage, penalty"] SYN see INJURY

²**damage** *vt* : to cause damage to

dam·a·scene \'dam-ə-,sēn\ *vt* : to ornament (as iron or steel) with wavy patterns or with inlaid work of precious metals [Middle French *damasquiner*, from *damasquin* "of Damascus"]

dam·ask \'dam-əsk\ *n* 1 : a firm lustrous reversible figured fabric used especially for household linen 2 : a tough steel having decorative wavy lines — called al-

so *damask steel* 3 : a grayish red [Medieval Latin *damascus*, from *Damascus*] — **damask** *adj*

damask rose *n* : a large hardy fragrant pink rose grown in Asia Minor as a source of attar of roses [obsolete *Damask* "of Damascus"]

dame \'dām\ *n* 1 : a woman of rank, station, or authority: as **a** *archaic* : the mistress of a household **b** : the wife or daughter of a lord **c** *often cap* : a woman who is a member of an order of knighthood — used as a title before a full name or a given name 2 **a** : an elderly woman **b** : WOMAN 1 [Middle English, from Old French, from Latin *domina*, feminine of *dominus* "master"]

dam·mar *or* **dam·ar** \'dam-ər\ *n* : a clear to yellow resin obtained from Malayan trees and used in varnishes and inks [Malay *damar*]

¹**damn** \'dam\ *vb* 1 : to condemn to a punishment or fate; *esp* : to condemn to hell 2 : to condemn as bad or as a failure 3 : to swear at : CURSE [Old French *dampner*, from Latin *damnare*, from *damnum* "damage, penalty"]

²**damn** *n* 1 : the utterance of the word *damn* as a curse 2 : the least bit ⟨not worth a *damn*⟩

³**damn** *adj or adv* : DAMNED

dam·na·ble \'dam-nə-bəl\ *adj* 1 : liable to or deserving condemnation ⟨*damnable* conduct⟩ 2 : very bad : DETESTABLE ⟨*damnable* weather⟩ — **dam·na·bly** \-blē\ *adv*

dam·na·tion \dam-'nā-shən\ *n* 1 : the act of damning 2 : the state of being damned

¹**damned** \'damd\ *adj* **damned·er** \'dam-dər\; **damned·est** *or* **damnd·est** \'dam-dəst\ 1 : DAMNABLE ⟨this *damned* smog⟩ 2 : COMPLETE, UTTER ⟨*damned* nonsense⟩ 3 : EXTRAORDINARY 1b — used in the superlative ⟨the *damnedest* thing I ever saw⟩

²**damned** \'damd, 'dam\ *adv* : VERY 1, EXTREMELY ⟨a *damned* good job⟩

¹**damp** \'damp\ *n* 1 : a harmful gas especially in a coal mine 2 : slight or moderate wetness 3 : DAMPER 2 [Dutch or Low German, "vapor"]

²**damp** *vb* 1 **a** : to lessen the activity or intensity of — often used with *down* ⟨failure *damped* their enthusiasm⟩ ⟨*damp* down a furnace⟩ **b** : to check the vibration or oscillation of 2 : DAMPEN 2

³**damp** *adj* 1 : lacking in vigor or spirit : DEPRESSED 2 : slightly or moderately wet : MOIST ⟨a *damp* cellar⟩ — **damp·ly** *adv* — **damp·ness** *n*

damp·en \'dam-pən\ *vb* **damp·ened; damp·en·ing** \'damp-ning, -ə-ning\ 1 : to check or diminish in activity or vigor : DEADEN 2 : to make or become damp — **damp·en·er** \'damp-nər, -ə-nər\ *n*

damp·er \'dam-pər\ *n* 1 : a device that damps: as **a** : a valve or plate (as in the flue of a furnace) for regulating the draft **b** : a small felted block to stop the vibration of a piano string **c** : a device for checking oscillation 2 : a dulling or deadening influence ⟨put a *damper* on the celebration⟩

dam·sel \'dam-zəl\ *n* : a young woman [Old French *dameisele*, derived from Latin *domina* "lady"]

dam·sel·fly \'dam-zəl-,flī\ *n* : any of numerous insects that are closely related to the dragonflies but have laterally projecting eyes and fold the wings over the body when at rest

dam·son \'dam-zən\ *n* : an Asian plum grown for its small acid purple fruit; *also* : this fruit [Latin *prunum damascenum*, literally, "plum of Damascus"]

¹**dance** \'dans\ *vb* 1 : to perform a rhythmic and patterned succession of bodily movements usually to music 2 : to move quickly up and down or about 3 : to perform or take part in as a dancer 4 : to cause to dance [Old French *dancier*] — **danc·er** *n*

²**dance** *n* 1 : an act or instance of dancing 2 : a social gathering for dancing 3 : a piece of music by which dancing may be guided 4 : the art of dancing

dan·de·li·on \'dan-dl-,ī-ən\ *n* : any of a genus of yellow-flowered herbs of the daisy family; *esp* : one with long deeply toothed stemless leaves sometimes grown as a potherb [Middle French *dent de lion,* literally, "lion's tooth"]

dan·der \'dan-dər\ *n* **1** : minute scales from hair, feathers, or skin that may cause allergy **2** : TEMPER 4d, ANGER (get one's *dander* up) [alteration of *dandruff*]

dan·di·fy \'dan-di-,fī\ *vt* **-fied; -fy·ing** : to cause to resemble a dandy — **dan·di·fi·ca·tion** \,dan-di-fə-'kā-shən\ *n*

dan·dle \'dan-dl\ *vt* **dan·dled; dan·dling** \-dling, -dl-ing\ : to move (as a baby) up and down in one's arms or on one's knee [origin unknown]

dan·druff \'dan-drəf\ *n* : a thin whitish flaky crust that forms especially on the scalp and is shed as scales [origin unknown]

¹dan·dy \'dan-dē\ *n, pl* **dandies 1** : a man who gives much attention to dress **2** : something excellent in its class [origin unknown] — **dan·dy·ish** \-dē-ish\ *adj* — **dan·dy·ish·ly** *adv*

²dandy *adj* **dan·di·er; -est** : very good : FIRST-RATE

Dane \'dān\ *n* **1** : a native or inhabitant of Denmark **2** : a person of Danish descent [Old Norse *Danr*]

dane·geld \'dān-,geld\ *n, often cap* : an annual tax once imposed in England supposedly to buy off Danish invaders or to maintain forces to oppose them [Middle English, from *Dan* "Dane" + *geld* "tribute, payment", from Old English *gield*]

Dane·law \'dān-,lȯ\ *n* **1** : the law in force in the part of England held by the Danes before the Norman Conquest **2** : the part of England under the Danelaw

dan·ger \'dān-jər\ *n* **1** : exposure or liability to injury, harm, or evil (their lives were in *danger*) **2** : a case or cause of danger (the *dangers* of mining) [Middle English *daungier* "jurisdiction, liability", from Old French *dongier, dangier* "jurisdiction", derived from Latin *dominium* "dominion, ownership"] □ SYN DANGER, PERIL, HAZARD, RISK mean a threat of loss, injury, or death. DANGER implies possible but not necessarily inescapable harm; PERIL suggests imminent danger and cause for fear; HAZARD implies danger from chance or something beyond one's control; RISK implies danger following on a chance voluntarily taken.

dan·ger·ous \'dānj-rəs, -ə-rəs\ *adj* **1** : exposing to or involving danger (a *dangerous* mission) **2** : able or likely to inflict injury (*dangerous* weapons) — **dan·ger·ous·ly** *adv* — **dan·ger·ous·ness** *n*

dan·gle \'dang-gəl\ *vb* **dan·gled; dan·gling** \-gə-ling, -gling\ **1** : to hang loosely especially with a swinging motion **2** : to be a hanger-on or dependent **3** : to be left without proper grammatical connection in a sentence (a *dangling* participle) **4** : to cause to dangle : SWING **5** : to keep hanging uncertainly : hold suspended [probably of Scandinavian origin] — **dan·gler** \-gə-lər, -glər\ *n* — **dan·gling·ly** \-gə-ling-lē, -gling-\ *adv*

Dan·iel \'dan-yəl\ *n* — see BIBLE table

¹Dan·ish \'dā-nish\ *adj* : of, relating to, or characteristic of Denmark, the Danes, or the Danish language

²Danish *n* : the Germanic language of the Danes

Danish pastry *n* : a pastry made of rich yeast-raised dough

dank \'dangk\ *adj* : unpleasantly moist or wet [Middle English *danke*] — **dank·ly** *adv* — **dank·ness** *n*

dan·seur \dän-'sər, dän-\ *n* : a male ballet dancer [French, from *danser* "to dance"]

dan·seuse \dän-'súz, -'sərz; dän-'süz\ *n* : a female ballet dancer [French, from *danser* "to dance"]

daph·nia \'daf-nē-ə\ *n* : any of a genus of tiny water fleas [New Latin, genus name]

dap·per \'dap-ər\ *adj* **1** : being neat and trim in dress or appearance : SPRUCE **2** : being alert and lively in movement and manners [Dutch, "quick, strong"] — **dap·per·ly** *adv* — **dap·per·ness** *n*

¹dap·ple \'dap-əl\ *n* **1** : a dappled state **2** : a dappled animal [Middle English *dappel-gray* "gray with spots of a different color"]

²dapple *vb* **dap·pled; dap·pling** \'dap-ling, -ə-ling\ : to mark or become marked with numerous usually cloudy and rounded spots of a color or shade different from their background (a *dappled* horse)

¹dare \'daər, 'deər\ *vb* **1 a** : to have sufficient courage : be bold enough to (try it if you *dare*) **b** — used as an auxiliary verb (no one *dared* say a word) **2** : to confront boldly (*dared* the dangerous crossing) **3** : to challenge to perform an action especially as proof of courage (I *dare* you) [Old English *dear* "I dare, he dares"]

²dare *n* : an act or instance of daring : CHALLENGE (dived from the bridge on a *dare*)

dare·dev·il \'daər-,dev-əl, 'deər-\ *n* : a recklessly bold person — **daredevil** *adj*

¹dar·ing *adj* : fearlessly ready to take risks — **dar·ing·ly** \-ing-lē\ *adv* — **dar·ing·ness** *n* □ SYN DARING, RASH, RECKLESS, FOOLHARDY mean exposing oneself to danger more than is sensible or courageous. DARING stresses fearlessness; RASH implies imprudent hastiness; RECKLESS implies complete heedlessness of consequences; FOOLHARDY suggests recklessness and foolish daring. SYN see in addition ADVENTUROUS

²daring *n* : venturesome boldness

¹dark \'därk\ *adj* **1 a** : being without light or without much light (in winter it gets *dark* early) **b** : not giving off light (the *dark* side of the moon) **2** : not light in color (a *dark* suit); *esp* : of low or very low lightness (*dark* blue) **3** : not bright and cheerful : GLOOMY (look on the *dark* side of things) **4** : lacking knowledge and culture **5** : not clear to the understanding (*dark* sayings) **6** : SWARTHY (their *dark* good looks) **7** : SECRET 1a (kept their plans *dark*) [Old English *deorc*] SYN see OBSCURE — **dark·ish** \'där-kish\ *adj* — **dark·ly** \-klē\ *adv* — **dark·ness** \'därk-nəs\ *n*

²dark *n* **1** : absence of light : DARKNESS **2 a** : a place or time of little or no light **b** : NIGHT, NIGHTFALL (get home before *dark*) **3** : a dark or deep color — **in the dark 1** : in secrecy **2** : in ignorance

dark adaptation *n* : the process by which the eye adapts to seeing in weak light — **dark–adapt·ed** \,därk-ə-'dap-təd\ *adj*

Dark Ages *n pl* : the period from about A.D. 476 to about 1000; *also* : MIDDLE AGES

dark·en \'där-kən\ *vb* **dark·ened; dark·en·ing** \'därk-ning, -ə-ning\ **1** : to make or grow dark or darker (*darken* a room) (the sky is *darkening*) **2** : to make less clear : OBSCURE (ignorance *darkens* the understanding) **3** : BESMIRCH, TARNISH (*darken* a reputation) **4** : to make or become gloomy or forbidding (*darkened* their hopes) (a face *darkened* in anger) — **dark·en·er** \'därk-ner, -ə-nər\ *n*

dark horse *n* : a contestant or a political figure whose abilities and chances as a contender are not known (the convention nominated a *dark horse*) □ ORIGIN Sometimes in a horse race a horse whose name and ability are not widely known puts on a surprisingly good show and defeats his more famous rivals. Such a horse is called *dark,* not because of his color (which might be anything), but because of his obscurity. The use of the term *dark horse* has been extended from racehorses to obscure competitors who do unexpectedly well in contests of other kinds. It is most often used to refer to a little known political candidate who will surprise people if he or she wins.

dark lantern *n* : a lantern that can be closed to conceal the light

darkling *adj* **1** : DARK 1a, 3 **2** : done or taking place in the dark

dark reaction *n* : the part of photosynthesis that does not require light and that uses carbon dioxide in the formation of carbohydrate

\ə\ abut		\ng\ si**ng**	
\ər\ f**ur**ther		\ō\ b**o**ne	
\a\ m**a**t		\ȯ\ s**a**w	
\ā\ t**a**ke		\ȯi\ c**oi**n	
\ä\ c**o**t, c**a**rt		\th\ **th**in	
\aú\ **ou**t		\t͟h\ **th**is	
\ch\ **ch**in		\ü\ f**oo**d	
\e\ p**e**t		\ú\ f**oo**t	
\ē\ **e**asy		\y\ **y**et	
\g\ **g**o		\yü\ f**ew**	
\i\ t**i**p		\yú\ c**ure**	
\ī\ l**i**fe		\zh\ vi**s**ion	
\j\ **j**ob			

dark·room \'därk-,rüm, -,rùm\ *n* : a usually small light-proof room used in developing sensitive photographic plates and film

dark·some \'därk-səm\ *adj* : gloomily somber : DARK

¹dar·ling \'där-ling\ *n* **1** : a dearly loved person **2** : FAVORITE [Old English *dēorling,* from *dēore* "dear"]

²darling *adj* **1** : dearly loved : FAVORITE **2** : very pleasing : CHARMING — **dar·ling·ly** \-ling-lē\ *adv*

¹darn \'därn\ *vb* : to mend with interlacing stitches ⟨*darn* socks⟩ [probably from French dialect *darner*]

²darn *n* : a place (as in a sock) that has been darned

³darn *vb* : DAMN 3 [euphemism] — **darn** \'därn\ *or* **darned** \'därnd, 'därn\ *adj or adv*

⁴darn *n* : ²DAMN 2 ⟨don't give a *darn*⟩

dar·nel \'därn-l\ *n* : any of several usually weedy grasses with bristly flower clusters [Middle English]

darning needle *n* **1** : a long needle with a large eye for use in darning **2** : DRAGONFLY, DAMSELFLY

¹dart \'därt\ *n* **1 a** : a small missile usually pointed at one end and feathered on the other **b** *pl* : a game in which darts are thrown at a target **2 a** : something projected with sudden speed; *esp* : a sharp glance **b** : something causing a sudden pain or distress ⟨*darts* of sarcasm⟩ **3** : a stitched tapering fold in a garment **4** : a quick movement ⟨made a *dart* for the door⟩ [Middle French, of Germanic origin]

¹dart 1a

²dart *vb* **1** : to throw with a sudden movement ⟨*dart* a javelin⟩ **2** : to thrust or move suddenly or rapidly

dart·er \'därt-ər\ *n* : any of numerous small American freshwater fishes closely related to the perches

Dar·win·ian \där-'win-ē-ən\ *adj* : of or relating to Charles Darwin, his theories, or his followers — **Darwinian** *n*

Dar·win·ism \'där-wə-,niz-əm\ *n* : a theory of evolution that explains how species of plants and animals arose and continue to arise by variation among offspring of a given plant or animal, by the survival of well-adapted variations in the process of natural selection, and by the gradual accumulation of differences over time — **Dar·win·ist** \-wə-nəst\ *n or adj*

¹dash \'dash\ *vb* **1** : to knock, hurl, or thrust violently ⟨the storm *dashed* the boat against a reef⟩ **2** : to break by striking or knocking ⟨the statue was *dashed* to pieces when it fell⟩ **3** : SPLASH 1b, SPATTER ⟨clothes *dashed* with mud⟩ **4 a** : FRUSTRATE 1 ⟨our hopes were *dashed* every time⟩ **b** : to lower in spirit or mood : DEPRESS **5** : to affect by mixing in something different ⟨oil *dashed* with vinegar⟩ **6** : to perform or finish hastily ⟨*dash* off a letter⟩ **7** : to move with sudden speed [Middle English *dasshen*] — **dash·er** *n*

²dash *n* **1** : a sudden burst or splash **2** : a punctuation mark — used chiefly to indicate a break in the thought or structure of a sentence **3** : a small usually distinctive addition **4** : a flashy display **5** : animation in style and action **6 a** : a sudden rush or attempt **b** : a short fast race **7** : a long click or buzz forming a letter or part of a letter (as in Morse code) **8** : DASHBOARD 2

dash·board \'dash-,bōrd, -,bòrd\ *n* **1** : a screen on the front of a vehicle (as a carriage) to keep out water, mud, or snow **2** : a panel extending across an automobile or aircraft below the windshield and usually containing dials and controls

da·shi·ki \də-'shē-kē\ *n* : a usually brightly colored loose-fitting pullover garment [Yoruba (a language of western Africa) *dànṣíkí*]

dash·ing *adj* **1** : marked by vigorous action ⟨a *dashing* attack⟩ **2** : marked by smartness especially in dress and manners ⟨made a *dashing* appearance⟩ — **dash·ing·ly** \-ing-lē\ *adv*

das·tard \'das-tərd\ *n* : COWARD; *esp* : one who commits dastardly acts [Middle English]

das·tard·ly \-lē\ *adj* : mean and treacherously cowardly — **das·tard·li·ness** *n*

da·ta \'dāt-ə, 'dat-, 'dät-\ *n sing or pl* **1** : factual information (as measurements or statistics) used as a basis for reasoning, discussion, or calculation **2** : DATUM [plural of *datum*]

data bank *n* : DATA BASE

data base *n* : a collection of data that is organized especially to be used by a computer

data processing *n* : the process of turning raw data into a form that a computer can use and then having the computer perform useful operations on the data

¹date \'dāt\ *n* : the oblong edible fruit of a tall Old World palm; *also* : this palm [Old French, derived from Latin *dactylus,* from Greek *daktylos,* literally, "finger"] □ ORIGIN The *date* that means "the fruit of the date palm" is not related to the *date* that means "a time". The earlier *date* is descended from Greek *dactylos*. The primary meaning of *daktylos* is "finger", but the word was also used for the fruit. The reason for this extension of meaning is debated. Some suggest that the pinnately divided leaves of the date palm look rather like fingers and that this fact gave the fruit its name. This account would be more convincing if the tree, rather than its fruit, had been named *daktylos*. It is more likely that the clustered dates themselves were felt to resemble fingers.

²date *n* **1 a** : the time at which an event occurs **b** : a statement giving the time of execution or making ⟨the *date* on the check⟩ **2** : DURATION 2 **3** : the period of time to which something belongs ⟨sculptures of an early *date*⟩ **4 a** : APPOINTMENT 3; *esp* : a social engagement between two persons **b** : a person with whom one has a social engagement [Middle French, from Late Latin *data,* from *data* "given" (as in *data Romae* "given at Rome"), from Latin *dare* "to give"] □ ORIGIN The English word *date* has nothing to do etymologically with *day* but is descended from Latin *dare,* "to give". In ancient Rome, the date of a letter was written in this manner: "Dabam Romae Kal. Aprilis." (I gave [this letter] at Rome April 1—the calends of April.) A later formula used *data Romae,* "given at Rome", instead of *dabam Romae,* "I gave at Rome". By the 6th century A.D., *data* had become a noun used for the date on a letter. In French its descendant *date* was used not only for the date on a letter, but also for the actual time that such a date indicated or indeed for any given point in time. — **to date** : up to the present moment

³date *vb* **1** : to determine the date of ⟨*date* an antique⟩ **2** : to record the date of or on ⟨*date* a letter⟩ **3** : to mark with characteristics typical of a particular period ⟨the architecture *dates* the house⟩ **4** : to make or have a date with **5** : ORIGINATE 2 ⟨that chair *dates* from the 16th century⟩ — **dat·able** *or* **date·able** \'dāt-ə-bəl\ *adj* — **dat·er** *n*

dat·ed *adj* **1** : having a date **2** : OLD-FASHIONED 1 ⟨*dated* formalities⟩ — **dat·ed·ly** *adv* — **dat·ed·ness** *n*

date·less \'dāt-ləs\ *adj* **1** : ENDLESS 1 **2** : having no date **3** : too ancient to be dated **4** : TIMELESS 1b, 2

date·line \'dāt-,līn\ *n* **1** : a line in a publication giving the date and place of composition or issue **2** *usually* **date line** : a hypothetical line approximately along the 180th meridian designated as the place where each calendar day begins — **dateline** *vt*

date rape *n* : rape committed by someone known to the victim

da·tive \'dāt-iv\ *adj* : of, relating to, or being the grammatical case that marks typically the indirect object of a verb or the object of some prepositions [Latin *dativus,* from *dare* "to give"] — **dative** *n*

da·tum \'dāt-əm, 'dat-, 'dät-\ *n, pl* **da·ta** \-ə\ *or* **datums** : a single piece of data : FACT [Latin, "something given", from *datus,* past participle of *dare* "to give"]

¹daub \'dòb, 'däb\ *vb* **1** : to cover with soft adhesive matter : PLASTER **2** : to coat with a dirty substance **3** : to apply (as paint) crudely [Old French *dauber*] — **daub·er** *n*

²daub n **1** : something daubed on **2** : a crudely painted picture

¹daugh·ter \'dȯt-ər\ n **1 a** : a female offspring especially of human beings **b** : woman or girl having a specified ancestor or belonging to a group of common ancestry **2** : something considered as a daughter **3** : an isotope that is the product of the radioactive decay of a given element [Old English *dohtor*] — **daugh·ter·ly** \-lē\ adj

²daughter adj **1** : having the characteristics or relationship of a daughter ⟨*daughter* cities⟩ **2** : belonging to the first generation of offspring, cells, parts of cells, or molecules produced by reproduction, division, or formation of replicas ⟨*daughter* cells⟩ ⟨*daughter* DNA molecules⟩

daugh·ter–in–law \'dȯt-ə-rən-ˌlȯ, -ərn-ˌlȯ\ n, pl **daughters–in–law** \-ər-zən-\ : the wife of one's son

daunt \'dȯnt, 'dänt\ vt : to lessen the courage of : make afraid [Old French *donter, danter,* from Latin *domitare* "to tame", from *domare* "to tame"]

daunt·less \-ləs\ adj : FEARLESS, UNDAUNTED ⟨a *dauntless* hero⟩ — **daunt·less·ly** adv — **daunt·less·ness** n

dau·phin \'dȯ-fən\ n, often cap : the eldest son of a king of France [Middle French *dalfin,* from Old French, title of lords of the Dauphiné, from *Dalfin,* a surname]

dav·en·port \'dav-ən-ˌpȯrt, 'dav-m-, -ˌpȯrt\ n : a large upholstered sofa [probably from the name *Davenport*]

da·vit \'dā-vət, 'dav-ət\ n : one of a pair of crane arms used for carrying small boats (as lifeboats or dinghies) aboard ships or yachts and for raising and lowering them to the water; *also* : a similar hoist (as over a hatchway) [probably from the name *David*]

Da·vy Jones's locker \'dā-vē-ˌjōnz, -ˌjōnz-əz-\ n : the bottom of the sea : a grave in the sea [*Davy Jones,* legendary spirit of the sea]

daw \'dȯ\ n : JACKDAW [Middle English *dawe*]

daw·dle \'dȯd-l\ vb **daw·dled; daw·dling** \-l-ing\ **1** : to spend time wastefully or idly : LINGER ⟨*dawdle* over homework⟩ **2** : to move lackadaisically : LOITER ⟨*dawdles* on the way back⟩ **3** : IDLE 3 ⟨*dawdle* the time away⟩ [origin unknown] — **daw·dler** \'dȯd-lər, -l-ər\ n

¹dawn \'dȯn, 'dän\ vi **1** : to become dawn : begin to grow light as the sun rises **2** : to begin to appear or develop ⟨the space age *dawned* with the first sputnik⟩ **3** : to begin to be perceived or understood ⟨the truth *dawned* on them⟩ [Middle English *dawnen*]

²dawn n **1** : the first appearance of light in the morning **2** : a first appearance : BEGINNING ⟨the *dawn* of a new era⟩

day \'dā\ n **1 a** : the time of light between one night and the next **b** : DAYLIGHT 1 **2** : the period of rotation of a planet (as earth) or a moon on its axis **3** : a period of 24 hours beginning at midnight **4** : a specified day or date ⟨the *day* of the picnic⟩ **5** : a specified time or period : AGE ⟨in our parents' *day*⟩ **6** : the conflict or contention of the day ⟨played hard and carried the *day*⟩ **7** : the time set apart by usage or law for work ⟨the 8-hour *day*⟩ [Old English *dæg*]

day·bed \'dā-ˌbed\ n : a couch with low head and foot pieces

day·book \-ˌbu̇k\ n : JOURNAL 1b, DIARY

day·break \-ˌbrāk\ n : DAWN 1

day–care \-ˌkeər, -ˌkaər\ adj : of, relating to, or providing care for preschool children during the day ⟨*day-care* centers⟩

¹day·dream \-ˌdrēm\ n : a dreamy sequence of usually happy or pleasant imaginings

²daydream vi : to have a daydream — **day·dream·er** n

day laborer n : one who works for daily wages especially as an unskilled laborer

day letter n : a telegram sent during the day that has a lower priority than a regular telegram — compare NIGHT LETTER

day·light \'dā-ˌlīt\ n **1** : the light of day **2** : DAYTIME **3** : DAWN 1 **4** : understanding of something that has been unclear ⟨began to see *daylight* on the problem⟩ **5** pl : mental soundness or stability : WITS ⟨scared the *daylights* out of them⟩

daylight saving time n : time usually one hour ahead of standard time — called also *daylight time*

day lily n : any of various plants of the lily family with short-lived flowers that are widespread in cultivation and naturalized in the wild

day–neutral adj : flowering or developing to maturity regardless of relative length of alternating light and dark periods — compare LONG-DAY, SHORT-DAY

day nursery n : a public center for the care and training of young children; *also* : NURSERY SCHOOL

Day of Atonement : YOM KIPPUR

days \'dāz\ adv : in the daytime repeatedly ⟨work *days*⟩

day school n : an elementary or secondary school held on weekdays; *esp* : a private school without boarding facilities

day·star \'dā-ˌstär\ n **1** : MORNING STAR **2** : SUN 1a

day·time \'dā-ˌtīm\ n : the time during which there is daylight

daze \'dāz\ vt **1** : to stupefy especially by a blow : STUN **2** : to dazzle with light [Old Norse *dasask* "to become exhausted"] — **daze** n

daz·zle \'daz-əl\ vt **daz·zled; daz·zling** \'daz-ling, -ə-ling\ **1** : to overpower with light ⟨the desert sunlight *dazzled* them⟩ **2** : to impress greatly or confound with brilliance ⟨*dazzled* the crowd with their performances⟩ [from *daze*] — **dazzle** n — **daz·zler** \'daz-lər, -ə-lər\ n — **daz·zling·ly** \'daz-ling-lē, -ə-ling-\ adv

D day n : a day set for launching an operation [*D,* abbreviation for *day*]

DDT \ˌdēd-ˌē-'tē\ n : a colorless odorless water‑insoluble compound formerly used widely as an insecticide that tends to accumulate in the environment and has toxic effects on many vertebrates [from the initial letters of its chemical components]

de- prefix **1 a** : do the opposite of ⟨*de*vitalize⟩ **b** : reverse of **2** : remove (a specified thing) from ⟨*de*louse⟩ : remove from (a specified thing) ⟨*de*throne⟩ **3** : reduce ⟨*de*value⟩ **4** : something derived from (a specified thing) : derived from something (of a specified nature) ⟨*de*nominative⟩ **5** : get off of (a specified thing) ⟨*de*plane⟩ [Latin *de-* "down, away, from"]

dea·con \'dē-kən\ n : a subordinate officer in a Christian church: as **a** : a clergyman next below a priest **b** : a clergyman or layman with particular duties in various Christian churches [Old English *dēacon,* from Late Latin *diaconus,* from Greek *diakonos,* literally, "servant"]

dea·con·ess \'dē-kə-nəs\ n : a woman chosen to assist in the church ministry; *esp* : one in a Protestant order

de·ac·ti·vate \dē-'ak-tə-ˌvāt\ vt : to make inactive or ineffective — **de·ac·ti·va·tion** \ˌdē-ˌak-tə-'vā-shən\ n

¹dead \'ded\ adj **1** : deprived of life : having died : LIFELESS **2 a** : having the appearance of death : DEATHLY ⟨in a *dead* faint⟩ **b** : lacking the power to move, feel, or respond : NUMB **c** : very tired **d** : UNRESPONSIVE ⟨*dead* to pity⟩ **e** : grown cold : burned out ⟨*dead* coals⟩ **3 a** : not naturally endowed with life : INANIMATE ⟨*dead* matter⟩ **b** : no longer producing or functioning ⟨a *dead* battery⟩ **4 a** : lacking power, significance, or effect ⟨a *dead* law⟩ **b** : no longer in use : OBSOLETE ⟨a *dead* language⟩ **c** : no longer active : EXTINCT ⟨a *dead* volcano⟩ **d** : lacking in gaiety or animation ⟨a *dead* party⟩ **e** (1) : lacking in commercial activity : QUIET (2) : commercially idle or unproductive ⟨*dead* capital⟩ **f** : lacking elasticity ⟨a *dead* tennis ball⟩ **g** : being out of action or out of use; *esp* : free from any connection to a source of voltage and free from electric charges ⟨a *dead* telephone line⟩ **h** : being out of play ⟨a *dead* ball⟩ ⟨*dead* cards⟩ **5 a** : not circulating :

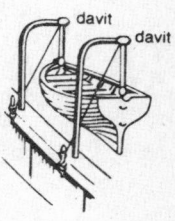

davit

davit

davit

\ə\ abut	\ng\ sing
\ər\ further	\ō\ bone
\a\ mat	\ȯ\ saw
\ā\ take	\ȯi\ coin
\ä\ cot, cart	\th\ thin
\au̇\ out	\th\ this
\ch\ chin	\ū\ food
\e\ pet	\u̇\ foot
\ē\ easy	\y\ yet
\g\ go	\yü\ few
\i\ tip	\yu̇\ cure
\ī\ life	\zh\ vision
\j\ job	

STAGNANT ⟨*dead* air⟩ **b** : lacking warmth, vigor, or taste ⟨a *dead* wine⟩ **6 a** : absolutely uniform ⟨the *dead* level of the prairie⟩ **b** : UNERRING, EXACT ⟨a *dead* shot⟩ ⟨*dead* center of the target⟩ **c** : SUDDEN 1a ⟨a *dead* stop⟩ **d** : ABSOLUTE 4, TOTAL ⟨a *dead* loss⟩ [Old English *dēad*]

²dead *n, pl* **dead** **I** : one that is dead — usually used collectively ⟨the living and the *dead*⟩ **2** : the time of greatest quiet ⟨the *dead* of night⟩

³dead *adv* **I** : WHOLLY 1 ⟨*dead* right⟩ **2** : suddenly and completely ⟨stopped *dead*⟩ **3** : DIRECTLY ⟨*dead* ahead⟩

dead·beat \'ded-ˌbēt\ *n* : one who persistently fails to pay debts

dead·en \'ded-n\ *vt* **dead·ened; dead·en·ing** \'ded-ning, -n-ing\ **I** : to impair in vigor or sensation : BLUNT ⟨*deaden* pain with drugs⟩ **2 a** : to deprive of brilliance or spirit **b** : to make (as a wall) soundproof

dead–end \'ded-'end\ *adj* : leading nowhere ⟨a *dead-end* job⟩ ⟨a *dead-end* street⟩

dead end *n* **I** : an end (as of a street) without an exit **2** : a position, situation, or course of action that leads to nothing further

dead·eye \'ded-ˌī\ *n* : an expert marksman

dead heat *n* : a contest in which two or more contestants tie (as by crossing the finish line simultaneously)

dead letter *n* **I** : something that has lost its force or authority without being formally abolished **2** : a letter that is undeliverable and unreturnable by the post office

dead·line \'ded-ˌlīn\ *n* : a date or time before which something must be done

dead·lock \'ded-ˌläk\ *n* : a stoppage of action because both sides in a struggle are equally powerful and neither will give in — **deadlock** *vt*

¹dead·ly \'ded-lē\ *adj* **dead·li·er; -est I** : likely to cause or capable of causing death ⟨a *deadly* disease⟩ **2 a** : aiming to kill or destroy : IMPLACABLE ⟨a *deadly* enemy⟩ **b** : very accurate : UNERRING ⟨a *deadly* marksman⟩ **3 a** : tending to deprive of force or vitality ⟨a *deadly* habit⟩ **b** : DEATHLY 2 ⟨a *deadly* chill⟩ **4** : very great : EXTREME ⟨a *deadly* bore⟩ — **dead·li·ness** *n* □ SYN DEADLY, MORTAL, FATAL, LETHAL mean causing or capable of causing death. DEADLY applies to an established or very likely cause of death ⟨a *deadly* disease⟩ MORTAL implies that death has occurred or is inevitable ⟨a *mortal* wound⟩ FATAL stresses the inevitability of what has in fact resulted in death or destruction ⟨*fatal* consequences⟩ LETHAL applies only to something that is bound to cause death or exists for the destruction of life ⟨*lethal* gas⟩

²deadly *adv* **I** : in a manner suggesting death ⟨*deadly* pale⟩ **2** : EXTREMELY, VERY ⟨*deadly* dull⟩

deadly nightshade *n* : the belladonna plant

deadly sin *n* : one of seven sins of pride, covetousness, lust, anger, gluttony, envy, and sloth believed to be fatal to spiritual progress

dead man's float *n* : a floating position in which a person lies face down in the water with the arms extended forward

dead march *n* : a solemn march for a funeral

dead·pan \'ded-ˌpan\ *adj* : marked by an impassive manner, style, or expression [English slang *pan* "face", from ¹*pan*] — **deadpan** *adv*

dead reckoning *n* : the determination without the aid of celestial observations of the position of a ship or aircraft from the record of the courses sailed or flown and the distance made from the last known position

dead·weight \'ded-'wāt\ *n* : the unrelieved weight of an inert mass

dead·wood \'ded-ˌwu̇d\ *n* **I** : wood dead on the tree : dead branches **2** : useless personnel or material

deaf \'def\ *adj* **I** : wholly or partly unable to hear **2** : unwilling to hear or listen ⟨*deaf* to all suggestions⟩ [Old English *dēaf*] — **deaf·ness** *n*

deaf·en \'def-ən\ *vb* **deaf·ened; deaf·en·ing** \'def-ning, -ə-ning\ **I** : to make deaf **2** : to cause deafness : stun one with noise — **deaf·en·ing·ly** \-lē\ *adv*

deaf–mute \'def-ˌmyüt\ *n* : a deaf person who cannot speak — **deaf–mute** *adj* — **deaf–mut·ism** \-ˌmyüt-ˌiz-əm\ *n*

¹deal \'dēl\ *n* **I** : a usually large or indefinite quantity or degree ⟨means a great *deal*⟩ ⟨a good *deal* faster⟩ **2 a** : the act or right of distributing cards to players in a card game **b** : HAND 11b [Old English *dǣl* "part, quantity"]

²deal *vb* **dealt** \'delt\; **deal·ing** \'dē-ling\ **I** : to give as one's portion : DISTRIBUTE ⟨*deal* out sandwiches⟩ ⟨*deal* the cards⟩ **2** : DELIVER 5, BESTOW ⟨*dealt* the dog a blow⟩ **3** : to have to do ⟨the book *deals* with art⟩ **4** : to take action ⟨*deal* with offenders⟩ **5 a** : to engage in bargaining : TRADE **b** : to sell or distribute something as a business ⟨*deals* in books⟩ — **deal·er** *n*

³deal *n* **I a** : an act of dealing : BARGAINING **b** : the result of bargaining : a mutual agreement ⟨make a *deal* for a used car⟩ **2** : treatment received ⟨a dirty *deal*⟩ **3** : a secret or underhand agreement **4** : a purchase at a fair or very low price : BARGAIN ⟨a good *deal* in a new car⟩

⁴deal *n* : wood or a board of fir or pine [Dutch or Low German *dele* "plank"] — **deal** *adj*

deal·ing *n* **I** *pl* : social or business interactions ⟨it's foolish to have *dealings* with such people⟩ **2** : a way of acting or of doing business ⟨believed in fair *dealing*⟩

de·am·i·nase \dē-'am-ə-ˌnās\ *n* : an enzyme that promotes removal of amino groups

de·am·i·nate \-ˌnāt\ *vt* : to remove the amino group from (a compound) — **de·am·i·na·tion** \ˌdē-ˌam-ə-'nā-shən\ *n*

dean \'dēn\ *n* **I a** : the head of the chapter of a collegiate or cathedral church **b** : a Roman Catholic priest who supervises one district of a diocese **2 a** : the head of a division, faculty, college, or school of a university **b** : a college or secondary school administrator in charge of counseling and disciplining students **3** : the senior member of a group ⟨the *dean* of the diplomatic corps⟩ [Middle French *deien*, from Late Latin *decanus*, literally, "chief of ten", from Latin *decem* "ten"] — **dean·ship** \-ˌship\ *n*

dean·ery \'dēn-rē, -ə-rē\ *n, pl* **-er·ies** : the office, jurisdiction, or official residence of a clerical dean

¹dear \'diər\ *adj* **I** : highly valued : PRECIOUS ⟨a *dear* memory⟩ **2** : feeling or expressing love : AFFECTIONATE **3** : EXPENSIVE **4** : HEARTFELT ⟨my *dearest* wish⟩ [Old English *dēore*] SYN see COSTLY — **dear** *adv* — **dear·ly** *adv* — **dear·ness** *n*

²dear *n* **I** : a loved one : DARLING **2** : a lovable person

dearth \'dərth\ *n* **I** : scarcity that makes dear; *esp* : FAMINE **2** : inadequate supply : LACK

death \'deth\ *n* **I** : a permanent cessation of all vital functions : the end of life **2** : the cause of loss of life **3** *often cap* : the destroyer of life represented usually as a skeleton with a scythe **4** : the state of being dead **5** : the passing or destruction of something inanimate or intangible ⟨the *death* of feudalism⟩ [Old English *dēath*] — **death·like** \-ˌlīk\ *adj*

death·bed \'deth-'bed\ *n* **I** : the bed in which a person dies **2** : the last hours of life — **on one's deathbed** : near death

death·blow \-'blō\ *n* : a destructive or killing stroke or event

death camas *n* : any of several plants of the lily family that cause poisoning of livestock in the western United States

death knell *n* : an action or event foretelling death or destruction

death·less \'deth-ləs\ *adj* : IMMORTAL 3 ⟨*deathless* fame⟩ — **death·less·ly** *adv* — **death·less·ness** *n*

death·ly \'deth-lē\ *adj* **I** : DEADLY 1, FATAL **2** : of, relating to, or suggestive of death ⟨a *deathly* pallor⟩ — **deathly** *adv*

death mask *n* : a cast taken from the face of a dead person

death ray *n* : a weapon that generates an intense beam of particles or radiation by which it destroys its target

death's–head \'deths-,hed\ *n* : a human skull symbolizing death

death trap *n* : a structure or situation that is potentially very dangerous to life

¹**death·watch** \'deth-,wäch\ *n* : any of several small insects that make a ticking sound [from the superstition that its ticking presages death]

²**deathwatch** *n* : a vigil kept with the dead or dying

deb \'deb\ *n* : DEBUTANTE

de·ba·cle \di-'bäk-əl, -'bak-\ *also* **dé·bâ·cle** *same, also* dä-'bäk-, -'bäk-lə\ *n* **1** : a tumultuous breaking up of ice in a river **2** : a violent disruption (as of an army) : ROUT **3 a** : a great disaster ⟨the stock market *debacle*⟩ **b** : a complete failure : FIASCO [French *débâcle*]

de·bar \di-'bär\ *vt* : to bar from having or doing something : PRECLUDE — **de·bar·ment** \-mənt\ *n*

de·bark \di-'bärk\ *vb* : DISEMBARK [Middle French *debarquer*, from *de-* "de-" + *barque* "bark"] — **de·bar·ka·tion** \,dē-,bär-'ka-shən\ *n*

de·base \di-'bās\ *vt* : to lower in status, dignity, value, quality, or character — **de·base·ment** \-mənt\ *n* — **de·bas·er** *n* □ SYN DEBASE, DEGRADE, CORRUPT, DEPRAVE mean to cause deterioration or lowering in quality or character. DEBASE implies loss of worth, value, or dignity; DEGRADE adds shamefulness or degeneracy to debasement; CORRUPT implies loss of soundness, purity, or integrity through forces that break down, pollute, or destroy; DEPRAVE implies moral deterioration or perversion.

de·bat·able \di-'bāt-ə-bəl\ *adj* **1** : open to debate : QUESTIONABLE ⟨a *debatable* conclusion⟩ **2** : capable of being debated

¹**de·bate** \di-'bāt\ *n* : a verbal argument: as **a** : the formal discussion of a motion before a deliberative body **b** : a regulated discussion of a proposition between two matched sides

²**debate** *vb* **1** : to discuss or examine a question by presenting and considering arguments on both sides **2** : to take part in a debate **3** : to present or consider the reasons for and against : CONSIDER [Middle French *debatre* "to fight, contend", from *de-* "de-" + *batre* "to beat", from Latin *battuere*] SYN see DISCUSS — **de·bat·er** *n*

¹**de·bauch** \di-'bóch, -'bäch\ *vt* : to lead away from virtue or morality : CORRUPT [Middle French *debaucher* "to make disloyal"] — **de·bauch·er** *n*

²**debauch** *n* **1** : an act or occasion of debauchery **2** : ORGY 2

de·bauch·ee \di-,bóch-'ē, -,bäch-\ *n* : one given to debauchery

de·bauch·ery \di-'bóch-rē, -'bäch-, -ə-rē\ *n, pl* **-er·ies** : extreme indulgence in sensual pleasure

de·ben·ture \di-'ben-chər\ *n* : a bond secured only by the general assets of the issuing government or corporation [Latin *debentur* "they are due", from *debēre* "to owe"]

de·bil·i·tate \di-'bil-ə-,tāt\ *vt* : to impair the strength of : WEAKEN — **de·bil·i·ta·tion** \di-,bil-ə-'tā-shən\ *n*

de·bil·i·ty \di-'bil-ət-ē\ *n, pl* **-ties** : an infirm or weakened state [Middle French *debilité*, from Latin *debilitas*, from *debilis* "weak"]

¹**deb·it** \'deb-ət\ *n* **1** : an entry in an account representing an amount paid out or owed **2** : something regarded as unfavorable : DRAWBACK [Latin *debitum* "debt"]

²**debit** *vt* : to enter as a debit : charge with or as a debt

debit card *n* : a card like a credit card but by which money is withdrawn from the holder's bank account immediately at the time of a transaction (as a purchase)

deb·o·nair \,deb-ə-'naər, -'neər\ *adj* : gaily and gracefully charming ⟨a *debonair* manner⟩ [Old French *debo-*

naire, from *de bon aire* "of good family or nature"] — **deb·o·nair·ly** *adv* — **deb·o·nair·ness** *n*

de·bouch \di-'büsh\ *vi* : to come out (as from a narrow passage) into an open area ⟨crowds *debouched* from side streets into the square⟩ [French *déboucher*, from *dé-* "de-" + *bouche* "mouth", from Latin *bucca* "cheek"] — **de·bouch·ment** \-mənt\ *n*

de·brief \di-'brēf, 'dē-\ *vt* : to interrogate (as an astronaut back from a mission) in order to obtain useful information

de·bris \də-'brē, 'dā-,brē\ *n, pl* **de·bris** \-'brēz, -,brēz\ **1** : the remains of something broken down or destroyed **2** : an accumulation of fragments of rock [French *débris*, from Old French *debrisier* "to break to pieces", from *de-* "de-" + *brisier* "to break"]

debt \'det\ *n* **1** : SIN 1, TRESPASS **2** : a state of owing ⟨hopelessly in *debt*⟩ **3** : something owed : OBLIGATION ⟨pay a *debt* of $10⟩ [Old French *dette* "something owed", from Latin *debitum*, from *debēre* "to owe", from *de-* + *habēre* "to have"]

debt·or \'det-ər\ *n* **1** : SINNER **2** : one that owes a debt

de·bug \'dē-'bəg, dē-\ *vt* : to eliminate errors or malfunctions in ⟨*debug* a computer program⟩

de·bunk \'dē-'bəngk, 'dē-\ *vt* : to expose the sham or falseness of ⟨*debunk* a hero legend⟩ — **de·bunk·er** *n*

de·but \'dā-,byü, dā-'\ *n* **1** : a first public appearance **2** : a formal entrance into society ⟨sixteen is the usual age for making one's *debut*⟩ [French *début*, from *débuter* "to begin"]

deb·u·tante \'deb-yü-,tänt\ *n* : a young woman making her formal entrance into society [French *débutante*, from *débuter* "to begin"]

deca- *or* **dec-** *or* **deka-** *or* **dek-** *combining form* : ten [Greek *deka*]

de·cade \'dek-,ād, -əd; de-'kād; *3 is usually* 'dek-əd\ *n* **1** : a group or set of 10 **2** : a period of 10 years **3** : a division of the rosary that is made up primarily of 10 Hail Marys

dec·a·dence \'dek-əd-əns, di-'kād-ns\ *n* **1** : the process of becoming decadent : the quality or state of being decadent **2** : a period of decline [Middle French, from Medieval Latin *decadentia*, from Late Latin *decadere* "to fall, sink", from Latin *de-* + *cadere* "to fall"]

dec·a·dent \'dek-əd-ənt, di-'kād-nt\ *adj* : marked by decay or decline — **decadent** *n* — **dec·a·dent·ly** *adv*

de·caf \'dē-,kaf\ *n* : decaffeinated coffee

de·caf·fein·at·ed \dē-'kaf-ə-,nāt-əd\ *adj* : having the caffeine removed ⟨*decaffeinated* coffee⟩

deca·gon \'dek-ə-,gän\ *n* : a polygon of 10 angles and 10 sides

deca·gram \'dek-ə-,gram\ *n* : DEKAGRAM

de·cal \'dē-,kal, di-'kal; *Canadian usually* 'dek-əl\ *n* : a picture or design made to be transferred (as to glass) from specially prepared paper [short for *decalcomania*]

de·cal·co·ma·nia \di-,kal-kə-'mā-nē-ə\ *n* **1** : the art or process of transferring or ornamenting with decals **2** : DECAL [French *décalcomanie*, from *décalquer* "to copy by tracing" + *manie* "mania"]

deca·li·ter \'dek-ə-,lēt-ər\ *n* : DEKALITER

deca·logue \'dek-ə-,lóg, -,läg\ *n* **1** *cap* : TEN COMMANDMENTS **2** : a basic set of rules carrying binding authority [Late Latin *decalogus*, from Greek *dekalogos*, from *deka* "ten" + *logos* "speech, word"]

deca·me·ter \'dek-ə-,mēt-ər\ *n* : DEKAMETER

de·camp \di-'kamp\ *vi* **1** : to break up a camp **2** : to depart suddenly : ABSCOND ⟨*decamped* with the funds⟩ — **de·camp·ment** \-mənt\ *n*

de·cant \di-'kant\ *vt* **1** : to pour from one vessel into another **2** : to draw off without disturbing any sediment ⟨*decant* wine⟩ [New Latin *decantare*, from Latin *de-* + Medieval Latin *cantus* "side", from Latin *canthus* "iron tire"] — **de·can·ta·tion** \,dē-,kan-'tā-shən\ *n*

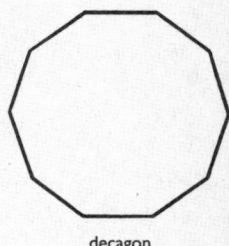

decagon

\ə\ abut	\ng\ sing
\ər\ further	\ō\ bone
\a\ mat	\ó\ saw
\ā\ take	\ói\ coin
\ä\ cot, cart	\th\ thin
\aú\ out	\th\ this
\ch\ chin	\ü\ food
\e\ pet	\ú\ foot
\ē\ easy	\y\ yet
\g\ go	\yü\ few
\i\ tip	\yú\ cure
\ī\ life	\zh\ vision
\j\ job	

de·cant·er \di-'kant-ər\ *n* : a vessel used to decant liquids or to receive decanted liquids; *esp* : an ornamental bottle used for serving wine

de·cap·i·tate \di-'kap-ə-,tāt\ *vt* : to cut off the head of : BEHEAD [Late Latin *decapitare*, from Latin *de-* + *caput* "head"] — **de·cap·i·ta·tion** \di-,kap-ə-'tā-shən\ *n*

deca·pod \'dek-ə-,päd\ *n* **1** : any of an order (Decapoda) of crustaceans (as shrimps, lobsters, crabs) with five pairs of appendages attached to the thorax one or more of which are modified into pincers **2** : any of an order (Decapoda) of cephalopod mollusks including forms (as the cuttlefishes and squids) with 10 arms — **decapod** *adj* — **de·cap·o·dan** \di-'kap-əd-ən\ *adj or n*

deca·syl·lab·ic \,dek-ə-sə-'lab-ik\ *adj* : having 10 syllables or composed of verses of 10 syllables — **decasyllabic** *n*

de·cath·lon \di-'kath-lən, -,län\ *n* : an athletic contest in which each competitor participates in each of a series of 10 track-and-field events [French *décathlon*, from *déca-* "deca-" + Greek *athlon* "contest"]

¹de·cay \di-'kā\ *vb* **1** : to decline from a sound or prosperous condition **2** : to decrease gradually in quantity, activity, or force **3** : to fall into ruin **4** : to decline in health, strength, or vigor **5** : to undergo or cause to undergo decomposition [Old North French *decaïr*, from Late Latin *decadere* "to fall, sink", from Latin *de-* + *cadere* "to fall"] □ SYN DECAY, DECOMPOSE, ROT, SPOIL mean to undergo disintegration or dissolution. DECAY implies a deterioration, often gradual, from soundness or perfection; DECOMPOSE stresses a breaking down into components or dissolution through corruption ⟨to *decompose* water into oxygen and hydrogen⟩ ⟨bacteria *decompose* organic products⟩ ROT implies decay with corruption and often suggests offensiveness; SPOIL applies chiefly to the decomposition of foods.

²decay *n* **1** : gradual decline in strength, soundness, prosperity, excellence, or value **2** : ROT; *esp* : decomposition of proteins in the presence of oxygen chiefly by bacteria **3** : a decline in health or vigor **4 a** : spontaneous decrease in the number of radioactive atoms in radioactive material **b** : spontaneous disintegration (as of an atom or a meson)

de·cease \di-'sēs\ *n* : DEATH 1 [Middle French *deces*, from Latin *decessus* "departure, death", from *decedere* "to depart, die", from *de-* + *cedere* "to go"] — **decease** *vi*

de·ceased \-'sēst\ *n, pl* **deceased** : a dead person

de·ce·dent \di-'sēd-nt\ *n* : a deceased person — used chiefly in law

de·ceit \di-'sēt\ *n* **1** : the act or practice of deceiving : DECEPTION **2** : a statement or act intended to deceive **3** : DECEITFULNESS [Old French *deceite*, derived from Latin *decipere* "to deceive"]

de·ceit·ful \-fəl\ *adj* **1** : using or tending to use deceit **2** : marked by deceit ⟨a *deceitful* answer⟩ — **de·ceit·ful·ly** \-fə-lē\ *adv* — **de·ceit·ful·ness** *n*

de·ceive \di-'sēv\ *vb* **1** : to cause to believe what is untrue : MISLEAD **2** : to use trickery [Old French *deceivre*, from Latin *decipere*, from *de-* + *capere* "to take"] — **de·ceiv·er** *n* — **de·ceiv·ing·ly** \-'sē-ving-lē\ *adv* □ SYN DECEIVE, MISLEAD, DELUDE, BEGUILE mean to lead astray or frustrate usually by underhandedness. DECEIVE implies imposing a false idea or belief that causes ignorance, bewilderment, or helplessness; MISLEAD implies a leading astray that may or may not be intentional; DELUDE implies deceiving so thoroughly that the truth is obscured; BEGUILE stresses the use of charm and persuasion in deceiving.

de·cel·er·ate \dē-'sel-ə-,rāt\ *vb* : to slow down or cause to slow down [*de-* + ac*celerate*] — **de·cel·er·a·tion** \,dē-,sel-ə-'rā-shən\ *n* — **de·cel·er·a·tor** \dē-'sel-ə-,rāt-ər\ *n*

De·cem·ber \di-'sem-bər\ *n* : the 12th month of the year [Old French *Decembre*, from Latin *December*, from *decem* "ten"; from its having been originally the tenth month of the Roman calendar]

de·cem·vir \di-'sem-vər\ *n* : one of a body of 10 magistrates in ancient Rome [Latin, from *decem* "ten" + *vir* "man"] — **de·cem·vi·rate** \-və-rət\ *n*

de·cen·cy \'dēs-n-sē\ *n, pl* **-cies** **1 a** : the quality or state of being decent **b** : conformity to standards of taste, propriety, or quality **2** : standard of propriety — usually used in pl.

de·cen·ni·al \di-'sen-ē-əl\ *adj* **1** : consisting of 10 years **2** : happening every 10 years ⟨*decennial* census⟩ [Latin *decennium* "period of 10 years", from *decem* "ten" + *annus* "year"] — **decennial** *n* — **de·cen·ni·al·ly** \-ē-ə-lē\ *adv*

de·cent \'dēs-nt\ *adj* **1 a** : conforming to standards of propriety, good taste, or morality **b** : modestly clothed **2** : free from immodesty or obscenity **3** : fairly good : ADEQUATE ⟨*decent* housing⟩ [Latin *decens*, present participle of *decēre* "to be fitting"] — **de·cent·ly** *adv*

de·cen·tral·ize \dē-'sen-trə-,līz\ *vt* **1** : to disperse or distribute among various regional or local authorities ⟨*decentralize* the administration of flood relief⟩ **2** : to cause to withdraw from urban centers to outlying areas ⟨*decentralize* industries⟩ — **de·cen·tral·i·za·tion** \,dē-,sen-trə-lə-'zā-shən\ *n*

de·cep·tion \di-'sep-shən\ *n* **1 a** : the act of deceiving **b** : the fact or condition of being deceived **2** : something that deceives : TRICK [Middle French, from Late Latin *deceptio*, from Latin *decipere* "to deceive"] □ SYN FRAUD, TRICKERY: DECEPTION may suggest deliberate cheating or merely legitimate tactical resource; FRAUD always implies guilt and often criminality; TRICKERY implies ingenious ways of fooling or cheating.

de·cep·tive \di-'sep-tiv\ *adj* : tending or having power to deceive — **de·cep·tive·ly** *adv* — **de·cep·tive·ness** *n*

deci- *combining form* : tenth part [Latin *decimus* "tenth", from *decem* "ten"]

deci·bel \'des-ə-,bel, -bəl\ *n* **1** : a unit for expressing the ratio of two amounts of electric or acoustic signal power equal to 10 times the common logarithm of this ratio **2** : a unit for measuring the relative intensity of sounds on a scale from zero for the average least perceptible sound to about 130 for the average pain level

de·cide \di-'sīd\ *vb* **1** : to arrive at a solution that ends uncertainty or dispute about ⟨*decided* the case in favor of the defendant⟩ **2** : to bring to a definitive end ⟨one blow *decided* the fight⟩ **3** : to induce to come to a choice ⟨what *decided* your mind⟩ **4** : to make a choice or judgment ⟨*decided* to go⟩ [Middle French *decider*, from Latin *decidere*, literally, "to cut off", from *de-* + *caedere* "to cut"] — **de·cid·able** \-'sīd-ə-bəl\ *adj* — **de·cid·er** *n*

de·cid·ed \-'sīd-əd\ *adj* **1** : free from ambiguity : CLEAR, UNMISTAKABLE ⟨a *decided* smell of gas⟩ **2** : free from doubt or wavering : DETERMINED ⟨a *decided* tone of voice⟩ — **de·cid·ed·ly** *adv* — **de·cid·ed·ness** *n*

de·cid·u·ous \di-'sij-ə-wəs\ *adj* **1** : falling off or shed (as at the end of a growing period or stage of development) ⟨antlers are *deciduous*⟩ ⟨the first or milk teeth are *deciduous*⟩ **2** : having deciduous parts or members with deciduous parts ⟨*deciduous* trees⟩ ⟨*deciduous* forests are typical of the temperate zones⟩ — compare EVERGREEN **3** : of only passing interest or importance [Latin *deciduus*, from *decidere* "to fall off", from *de-* + *cadere* "to fall"] — **de·cid·u·ous·ly** *adv* — **de·cid·u·ous·ness** *n*

deci·gram \'des-ə-,gram\ *n* — see METRIC SYSTEM table

deci·li·ter \'des-ə-,lēt-ər\ *n* — see METRIC SYSTEM table

de·cil·lion \di-'sil-yən\ *n* — see NUMBER table [Latin *decem* "ten" + English *-illion* (as in *million*)]

¹dec·i·mal \'des-məl, -ə-məl\ *adj* **1** : based on the number 10 ⟨a *decimal* system of writing numerals⟩ ⟨*decimal* coinage⟩ **2** : expressed as a decimal fraction ⟨¼ in *decimal* form is .25⟩ [derived from Latin *decimus* "tenth", from *decem* "ten"] — **dec·i·mal·ly** \-mə-lē\ *adv*

²decimal *n* **1** : a proper fraction in which the denominator is a power of 10 usually not expressed but signified by a point placed at the left of the numerator (as .2 = ²/₁₀, .25 = ²⁵/₁₀₀, .025 = ²⁵/₁₀₀₀) **2** : a mixed number (as 3.025) written as the combination of an integer and a decimal

decimal fraction *n* : DECIMAL

decimal notation *n* : expression of a number with a base of 10 using the first nine positive integers and 0 with each place representing a power of 10 — compare BINARY NOTATION

decimal place *n* : any of the places to the right of the decimal point in a number expressed in decimal notation

decimal point *n* : the dot at the left of a decimal fraction

dec·i·mate \'des-ə-ˌmāt\ *vt* **1** : to select by lot and kill every tenth man of **2** : to destroy a large part of ⟨disease *decimated* the population of the city⟩ [Latin *decimare*, from *decimus* "tenth"] — **dec·i·ma·tion** \ˌdes-ə-'mā-shən\ *n*

deci·me·ter \'des-ə-ˌmēt-ər\ *n* — see METRIC SYSTEM table

de·ci·pher \dē-'sī-fər\ *vt* **1 a** : to convert into intelligible form **b** : DECODE ⟨*decipher* a message⟩ **2** : to make out the meaning of despite indistinctness or obscurity ⟨*decipher* bad handwriting⟩ — **de·ci·pher·a·ble** \-fə-rə-bəl, -frə-\ *adj* — **de·ci·pher·ment** \-fər-mənt\ *n*

de·ci·sion \di-'sizh-ən\ *n* **1** : the act or result of deciding especially by giving judgment ⟨the *decision* of the court⟩ **2** : promptness and firmness in deciding : DETERMINATION ⟨people of courage and *decision*⟩ [Middle French, from Latin *decisio*, from *decidere* "to decide"]

de·ci·sive \di-'sī-siv\ *adj* **1** : having the power to decide ⟨the chairperson has the *decisive* vote⟩ **2** : of such nature as to settle a question or dispute ⟨a *decisive* victory⟩ **3** : marked by or showing decision ⟨a *decisive* manner⟩ — **de·ci·sive·ly** *adv* — **de·ci·sive·ness** *n*

¹deck \'dek\ *n* **1** : a platform within or over the hull of a boat or ship forming a structural element and serving as a floor or a covering (as for a cabin) **2** : something resembling the deck of a ship: as **a** : the roadway of a bridge **b** : a flat floored roofless area adjoining a house **3** : a pack of playing cards [probably derived from Low German *decken* "to cover"] — **on deck** : next in line

²deck *vt* **1 a** : to clothe elegantly : ARRAY ⟨*decked* out in a new suit⟩ **b** : DECORATE 1 **2** : to furnish with a deck **3** : to knock down forcibly [Dutch *dekken* "to cover"]

deck chair *n* : a folding chair often having an adjustable leg rest

deck·er \'dek-ər\ *n* : something having a deck or a specified number of levels, floors, or layers — often used in combination ⟨the buses are double-*deckers*⟩

deck·hand \'dek-ˌhand\ *n* : a sailor who performs manual duties

deck·le edge \'dek-əl-\ *n* : the rough untrimmed edge of paper [derived from German *decken* "to cover"] — **deck·le-edged** \-'ejd\ *adj*

de·claim \di-'klām\ *vb* : to speak or deliver in the manner of a formal oration [Latin *declamare*, from *de-* + *clamare* "to cry out"] — **de·claim·er** *n* — **dec·la·ma·tion** \ˌdek-lə-'mā-shən\ *n*

de·clam·a·to·ry \di-'klam-ə-ˌtōr-ē, -ˌtór-\ *adj* : of, relating to, or marked by declamation or rhetorical display

dec·la·ra·tion \ˌdek-lə-'rā-shən\ *n* **1** : the act of declaring : ANNOUNCEMENT **2 a** : something declared **b** : a document containing such a declaration ⟨the *Declaration* of Independence⟩

de·clar·a·tive \di-'klar-ət-iv\ *adj* : making a declaration or statement ⟨a *declarative* sentence⟩

de·clar·a·to·ry \di-'klar-ə-ˌtōr-ē, -ˌtór-\ *adj* : serving to declare or explain

de·clare \di-'klaər, -'kleər\ *vb* **1** : to make known formally or explicitly ⟨*declare* war⟩ **2** : to state emphatically : AFFIRM ⟨*declare* one's innocence⟩ **3** : to make a full statement of (taxable or dutiable property) [Middle French *declarer* "to make clear", from Latin *declarare*, from *de-* + *clarus* "clear"] □ SYN DECLARE, ANNOUNCE, PUBLISH, PROCLAIM mean to make known publicly or openly. DECLARE suggests a plainness and formality of statement ⟨the referee *declared* the contest a draw⟩ ANNOUNCE implies a declaration for the first time of something of interest or intended to satisfy curiosity ⟨*announce* an engagement⟩ ⟨*announce* the winner⟩ PUBLISH denotes a making public especially through print; PROCLAIM suggests a clear, forceful, and authoritative declaration ⟨the president *proclaimed* a national holiday⟩ SYN see in addition ASSERT

de·clar·er \-'klar-ər, -'kler-\ *n* **1** : one that declares **2** : the bridge player who plays both his or her own hand and that of the dummy

de·clas·si·fy \dē-'klas-ə-ˌfī, 'dē-\ *vt* : to remove or reduce the security classification of ⟨*declassify* a secret document⟩

de·clen·sion \di-'klen-chən\ *n* **1 a** : inflection of a noun, adjective, or pronoun especially in some prescribed order of the forms **b** : a class of nouns or adjectives having the same inflectional forms **2** : a falling off or away : DETERIORATION **3** : a downward slope [derived from Latin *declinare* "to inflect, turn aside"] — **de·clen·sion·al** \-'klench-nəl, -ən-l\ *adj*

dec·li·na·tion \ˌdek-lə-'nā-shən\ *n* **1** : angular distance north or south from the celestial equator measured along a great circle passing through the celestial poles ⟨the *declination* of a star⟩ **2** : DETERIORATION ⟨moral *declination*⟩ **3** : a bending downward : INCLINATION **4** : a formal refusal **5** : the angle that the magnetic needle makes with a true north and south line — **dec·li·na·tion·al** \-'nā-shnəl, -shən-l\ *adj*

¹de·cline \di-'klīn\ *vb* **1 a** : to slope downward : DESCEND **b** : to bend down : DROOP ⟨*decline* one's head⟩ **2** : to reach or pass toward a lower level : RECEDE **3** : to draw toward a close : WANE **4 a** : to withhold consent **b** : to refuse to undertake, engage in, or comply with **c** : to decide not to accept **5** : to give in a prescribed order the inflectional forms of a noun, pronoun, or adjective [derived from Latin *declinare* "to turn aside, inflect", from *de-* + *clinare* "to incline"] — **de·clin·able** \-'klī-nə-bəl\ *adj*

²decline *n* **1** : the process of declining: **a** : a gradual wasting away **b** : a change to a lower state or level ⟨business activity showed a sharp *decline* last month⟩ **2** : the time when something is approaching its end **3** : a downward slope : DECLIVITY **4** : a disease characterized by gradual loss of strength and health; *esp* : pulmonary tuberculosis

de·cliv·i·ty \di-'kliv-ət-ē\ *n, pl* **-ties** **1** : downward inclination **2** : a descending slope [Latin *declivitas*, from *declivis* "sloping down", from *de-* + *clivus* "slope"]

de·coc·tion \di-'käk-shən\ *n* : an extracting (as of a flavor or active principle) by boiling in water; *also* : a product of this process [Late Latin *decoctio*, from Latin *decoquere* "to cook down", from *de-* + *coquere* "to cook"]

de·code \dē-'kōd, 'dē-\ *vt* : to convert (a coded message) into ordinary language — **de·cod·er** *n*

dé·col·le·tage \ˌdā-ˌkäl-ə-'täzh, ˌdek-lə-\ *n* **1** : the low-cut neckline of a dress **2** : a décolleté dress [French]

dé·col·le·té \ˌdā-ˌkäl-ə-'tā, ˌdek-lə-\ *adj* **1** : wearing a strapless or low-necked dress **2** : having a low-cut neckline [French]

de·col·or·ize \dē-'kəl-ə-ˌrīz, 'dē-\ *vt* : to remove color from — **de·col·or·iza·tion** \ˌdē-ˌkəl-ə-rə-'zā-shən\ *n* — **de·col·or·iz·er** *n*

de·com·mis·sion \,dē-kə-'mish-ən\ *vt* : to take out of commission ⟨a *decommissioned* battleship⟩

de·com·pose \,dē-kəm-'pōz\ *vb* **1** : to separate into parts or elements or into simpler compounds **2** : to break down through chemical change : ROT SYN see DECAY — **de·com·pos·able** \-'pō-zə-bəl\ *adj* — **de·com·po·si·tion** \,dē-,käm-pə-'zish-ən\ *n*

de·com·pos·er \,dē-kəm-'pō-zər\ *n* : an organism (as a bacterium or a fungus) that breaks down dead protoplasm

de·com·press \,dē-kəm-'pres\ *vt* : to release (as a diver) from pressure or compression — **de·com·pres·sion** \-'presh-ən\ *n*

de·con·tam·i·nate \,dē-kən-'tam-ə-,nāt\ *vt* : to free from contamination — **de·con·tam·i·na·tion** \-,tam-ə-'nā-shən\ *n*

de·cor *or* **dé·cor** \dā-'kȯr, 'dā-,\ *n* : DECORATION; *esp* : the arrangement of accessories in interior decoration [French *décor*, from *décorer* "to decorate", from Latin *decorare*]

dec·o·rate \'dek-ə-,rāt\ *vt* **1** : to make more attractive by adding something beautiful or becoming ⟨*decorate* a room⟩ **2** : to award a decoration of honor to [Latin *decorare*, from *decor-, decus* "ornament"] SYN see ADORN

dec·o·ra·tion \,dek-ə-'rā-shən\ *n* **1** : the act or process of decorating **2** : something that adorns or beautifies **3** : a badge of honor (as a medal)

Decoration Day *n* : MEMORIAL DAY

dec·o·ra·tive \'dek-rət-iv, -ə-rət-; 'dek-ə-,rāt-\ *adj* : serving to decorate; *esp* : purely ornamental — **dec·o·ra·tive·ly** *adv* — **dec·o·ra·tive·ness** *n*

dec·o·ra·tor \'dek-ə-,rāt-ər\ *n* : one that decorates; *esp* : a person who designs or executes the interiors of buildings and their furnishings

dec·o·rous \'dek-ə-rəs; di-'kōr-əs, -'kȯr-\ *adj* : marked by propriety and good taste : CORRECT ⟨*decorous* conduct⟩ [Latin *decorus*, from *decor* "beauty, grace"] — **dec·o·rous·ly** *adv* — **dec·o·rous·ness** *n*

de·co·rum \di-'kōr-əm, -'kȯr-\ *n* **1** : conformity to accepted standards of conduct : proper behavior ⟨social *decorum*⟩ **2** : ORDERLINESS [Latin, from *decorus* "decorous"] □ SYN PROPRIETY, DIGNITY : DECORUM suggests conduct according with good taste often formally prescribed; PROPRIETY suggests an artificial standard of what is correct in conduct or speech; DIGNITY implies reserve or restraint in conduct prompted by a sense of personal integrity or social importance.

¹de·coy \'dē-,kȯi, di-'\ *n* **1** : something intended to lure into a trap; *esp* : an artificial bird used to attract live birds within shooting range **2** : a person used to lead another into a trap [probably from Dutch *de kooi*, literally, "the cage"]

²decoy *vt* : to lure by or as if by a decoy : ENTICE

¹de·crease \di-'krēs, 'dē-,\ *vb* : to become or cause to become less [Latin *decrescere*, from *de-* + *crescere* "to grow"] □ SYN DECREASE, LESSEN, DIMINISH, DWINDLE mean to grow or make less. DECREASE suggests progressive reduction in size, amount, or number; LESSEN suggests a decline in amount rather than in number; DIMINISH stresses loss, as in numbers or amount, and implies subtraction from the whole; DWINDLE implies progressive lessening, especially of things growing visibly smaller.

²de·crease \'dē-,krēs, di-'\ *n* **1** : a process of decreasing ⟨a *decrease* in automobile accidents⟩ **2** : the amount by which a thing decreases : REDUCTION ⟨a *decrease* of three dollars in wages⟩

¹de·cree \di-'krē\ *n* **1** : an order usually having the force of law : EDICT **2 a** : a religious ordinance enacted by a church assembly or head **b** : the will of the Deity **c** : something allotted by fate **3** : a judicial decision especially in an equity or probate court ⟨a divorce *decree*⟩ [Middle French *decré*, from Latin *decretum*, from *de-*

cernere "to decide", from *de-* + *cernere* "to sift, decide"]

²decree *vb* **de·creed; de·cree·ing** **1** : to order authoritatively ⟨*decree* an amnesty⟩ **2** : to determine or order judicially ⟨*decree* a punishment⟩ — **de·cre·er** \-'krē-ər\ *n*

dec·re·ment \'dek-rə-mənt\ *n* : DECREASE [Latin *decrementum*, from *decrescere* "to decrease"]

de·crep·it \di-'krep-ət\ *adj* : broken down or weakened by age [Middle French, from Latin *decrepitus*] — **de·crep·it·ly** *adv* — **de·crep·it·ness** *n*

de·crep·i·tude \di-'krep-ə-,tüd, -,tyüd\ *n* : the quality or state of being decrepit : infirmity especially from old age

¹de·cre·scen·do \,dā-krə-'shen-dō\ *adv or adj* : with diminishing volume — used as a direction in music [Italian, literally, "decreasing", from Latin *decrescere* "to decrease"]

²decrescendo *n, pl* **-dos** **1** : a lessening in volume of sound **2** : a decrescendo musical passage

de·cry \di-'krī\ *vt* **1** : to speak slightingly of : belittle publicly ⟨*decry* a hero's deeds⟩ **2** : to find fault with : express strong disapproval of ⟨*decried* the waste of natural resources⟩ [French *décrier*, from Old French *descrier*, from *des-* "de-" + *crier* "to cry"] — **de·cri·er** \-'krī-ər, -'krīr\ *n*

de·cum·bent \di-'kəm-bənt\ *adj* : lying down [Latin *decumbere* "to lie down", from *de-* + *-cumbere* "to lie down"] — **de·cum·ben·cy** \-bən-sē\ *n*

ded·i·cate \'ded-i-,kāt\ *vt* **1** : to set apart for some purpose and especially a sacred or serious purpose ⟨*dedicate* one's life to medicine⟩ **2** : to address or inscribe as a compliment ⟨*dedicate* a book to a friend⟩ [Latin *dedicare*, from *de-* + *dicare* "to proclaim, dedicate"] — **ded·i·ca·tor** \-,kāt-ər\ *n*

ded·i·ca·tion \,ded-i-'kā-shən\ *n* **1 a** : an act or rite of dedicating to a divine being or to a sacred use **b** : a setting aside for a particular purpose **2** : an inscription dedicating a literary work **3** : self-sacrificing devotion — **ded·i·ca·tive** \'ded-i-,kāt-iv\ *adj* — **ded·i·ca·to·ry** \'ded-i-kə-,tōr-ē, -,tȯr-\ *adj*

de·duce \di-'düs, -'dyüs\ *vt* **1** : to trace the course or derivation of **2** : to draw (an inevitable conclusion) from known facts [Latin *deducere*, literally, "to lead away", from *de-* + *ducere* "to lead"] — **de·duc·i·ble** \-'dü-sə-bəl, -'dyü-\ *adj*

de·duct \di-'dəkt\ *vt* : to take away (an amount) from a total : SUBTRACT [Latin *deductus*, past participle of *deducere* "to deduce, lead away"]

de·duct·ible \di-'dək-tə-bəl\ *adj* : capable of being deducted : allowable as a deduction — **de·duct·ibil·i·ty** \di-,dək-tə-'bil-ət-ē\ *n*

de·duc·tion \di-'dək-shən\ *n* **1** : an act of taking away **2 a** : the forming of a conclusion by reasoning; *esp* : inference in which the conclusion follows necessarily from the facts given **b** : a conclusion reached by mental deduction **3** : something that is or may be subtracted ⟨*deductions* from taxable income⟩ — **de·duc·tive** \-'dək-tiv\ *adj* — **de·duc·tive·ly** *adv*

¹deed \'dēd\ *n* **1** : something that is done : ACT; *esp* : a brave or noteworthy act ⟨judge them by their *deeds*⟩ **2** : a legal document by which one person transfers real property to another [Old English *dēd*] — **deed·less** \-ləs\ *adj*

²deed *vt* : to convey or transfer by legal deed

deem \'dēm\ *vb* : to come to think or judge : have an opinion : BELIEVE, SUPPOSE [Old English *dēman*]

¹deep \'dēp\ *adj* **1 a** : extending far downward ⟨a *deep* well⟩ : having a great distance between the top and bottom surfaces ⟨*deep* water⟩ : not shallow **b** : extending well inward from an outer surface ⟨a *deep* gash⟩ **c** : extending well back from a front surface ⟨a *deep* closet⟩ **d** : extending far outward from a center ⟨*deep* space⟩ **e** : occurring or located near the outer limits ⟨*deep* right field⟩ **2** : having a specified extension downward, inward, or backward ⟨a shelf 40 centimeters *deep*⟩ **3 a** : difficult to understand ⟨a *deep* book⟩ **b** : MYSTERIOUS, OBSCURE ⟨a *deep* dark secret⟩ **c** : WISE ⟨a *deep* thinker⟩ **d** : ABSORBED ⟨*deep* in thought⟩ **e** : of great intensity : PROFOUND ⟨*deep* sleep⟩ **4 a** : high in saturation and low in lightness ⟨a *deep* red⟩ **b** : having a low musical pitch or range ⟨a *deep* voice⟩ **5 a** : coming from or situated well within ⟨a *deep* sigh⟩ **b** : covered, enclosed, or filled often to a specified degree ⟨knee-*deep* in water⟩ [Old English *dēop*] — **deep·ly** *adv*

²**deep** *adv* **1** : to a great *depth* : DEEPLY **2** : far on : LATE ⟨*deep* in the night⟩

³**deep** *n* **1** : an extremely deep place or part; *esp* : OCEAN **2** : the middle or most intense part ⟨the *deep* of winter⟩

deep–dish pie *n* : a pie baked in a deep dish and having no bottom crust

deep·en \'dē-pən\ *vb* **deep·ened; deep·en·ing** \'dēp-ning, -ə-ning\ : to make or become deep or deeper

deep fat *n* : hot fat or oil deep enough in a cooking utensil to cover the food to be fried

deep–fry \'dēp-'frī\ *vt* : to cook in deep fat

deep–root·ed \'dēp-'rut-əd, -'rut-\ *adj* : deeply implanted or established ⟨a *deep-rooted* loyalty⟩

deep–sea \'dēp-'sē\ *adj* : of, relating to, or occurring in the deeper parts of the sea ⟨*deep-sea* fishing⟩

deep–seat·ed \'dēp-'sēt-əd\ *adj* **1** : situated far below the surface **2** : firmly established ⟨a *deep-seated* tradition⟩

deep–set \'dēp-'set\ *adj* : set far in ⟨*deep-set* eyes⟩

deep–sky \'dēp-'skī\ *adj* : relating to or existing in space outside the solar system ⟨*deep-sky* objects⟩

deep space *n* : space well outside the earth's atmosphere and especially that part lying beyond the earth-moon system

deer \'diər\ *n, pl* **deer** : any of a family of cloven-hoofed cud-chewing mammals with antlers borne by the males of nearly all and by the females of a few forms [Old English *dēor* "wild animal, beast"] □ ORIGIN The development of a word's meaning is often from the general to the specific. For instance, *deer* is used in modern English to denote numerous species, including white-tailed deer, reindeer, caribou, elk, and moose, all belonging to the same natural family. The Old English *dēor,* however, could refer to any beast or wild animal, or to wild animals in general. In time, *deer* came to be restricted to the animal that was the primary object of the hunt in England. From that usage the term has spread to other members of the same family and become somewhat more general again though not so general as once.

deer·hound \-,haund\ *n* : a large tall slender dog of a breed developed in Scotland and formerly used in hunting deer

deer mouse *n* : any of numerous North American mice occurring in fields and woods

deer·skin \'diər-,skin\ *n* : leather made from the skin of a deer; *also* : a garment of such leather

de·es·ca·late \dē-'es-kə-,lāt, 'dē-\ *vb* : to make less (as in extent or scope) — **de·es·ca·la·tion** \,dē-,es-kə-'lā-shən\ *n*

de·face \di-'fās\ *vt* : to destroy or mar the face or surface of [Middle French *desfacier,* from *des-* "de-" + *face* "face"] — **de·face·ment** \-'fās-mənt\ *n* — **de·fac·er** *n* □ SYN DEFACE, DISFIGURE mean to mar the appearance of. DEFACE suggests superficial injuries or the removal of some part or detail; DISFIGURE implies deeper or more permanent injury that impairs beauty or attractiveness.

de fac·to \di-'fak-,tō, dā-\ *adj or adv* **1** : ACTUAL 1a ⟨a *de facto* state of war⟩ **2** : actually exercising power ⟨a *de facto* government⟩ — compare DE JURE [New Latin, adverb, "in fact"]

de·fal·ca·tion \,dē-,fal-'kā-shən, -fol-; ,def-əl-\ *n* : a misuse or theft of money placed in one's keeping [Medieval Latin *defalcatio* "deduction", from *defalcare* "to deduct", from Latin *de-* + *falx* "sickle"] — **de·fal·cate** \di-'fal-,kāt, -'fol-, 'def-əl-\ *vi* — **de·fal·ca·tor** \-,kāt-ər\ *n*

def·a·ma·tion \,def-ə-'mā-shən\ *n* : the act of defaming : injury to the good name of another : SLANDER, LIBEL — **de·fam·a·to·ry** \di-'fam-ə-,tōr-ē, -,tòr-\ *adj*

de·fame \di-'fām\ *vt* : to injure or destroy the good name of : speak evil of SYN see SLANDER — **de·fam·er** *n*

¹**de·fault** \di-'folt\ *n* **1** : failure to do something required by law or duty **2** : a selection to be made automatically according to a computer program when the user does not specify a choice [Old French *defaute,* derived from Latin *de-* + *fallere* "to deceive"]

²**default** *vb* : to fail to carry out a contract, obligation, or duty; *also* : to forfeit something by such failure — **de·fault·er** *n*

¹**de·feat** \di-'fēt\ *vt* **1** : NULLIFY, FRUSTRATE ⟨*defeat* a hope⟩ **2** : to win victory over : BEAT [Middle French *deffait,* past participle of *deffaire* "to destroy", from Medieval Latin *disfacere,* from Latin *dis-* + *facere* "to do"]

²**defeat** *n* **1** : frustration by prevention of success ⟨the *defeat* of our plans⟩ **2 a** : an overthrow of an army in battle **b** : loss of a contest (as by a team)

de·feat·ism \-,iz-əm\ *n* : an attitude of expecting the defeat of one's own cause or of accepting such defeat on the ground that further effort would be useless or unwise — **de·feat·ist** \-əst\ *n or adj*

def·e·cate \'def-i-,kāt\ *vb* **1** : to free from impurity or corruption : REFINE **2** : to discharge feces from the bowels [Latin *defaecare,* from *de-* + *faex* "dregs, lees"] — **def·e·ca·tion** \,def-i-'kā-shən\ *n*

¹**de·fect** \'dē-,fekt, di-'\ *n* : a lack of something necessary for completeness or perfection [Middle French, from Latin *defectus* "lack", from *deficere* "to be wanting", from *de-* + *facere* "to do"] SYN see BLEMISH

²**de·fect** \di-'fekt\ *vi* : to desert a cause or party often in order to take up another — **de·fec·tion** \-'fek-shən\ *n* — **de·fec·tor** \-'fek-tər\ *n*

¹**de·fec·tive** \di-'fek-tiv\ *adj* **1** : lacking something essential : FAULTY **2** : lacking one or more of the usual forms of grammatical inflection ⟨*must* is a *defective* verb⟩ — **de·fec·tive·ly** *adv* — **de·fec·tive·ness** *n*

²**defective** *n* : a person who is subnormal physically or mentally

de·fend \di-'fend\ *vb* **1** : to repel danger or attack **2** : to act as attorney for **3** : to oppose the claim of another in a lawsuit : CONTEST **4** : to uphold against opposition ⟨*defend* an idea⟩ [Old French *defendre,* from Latin *defendere,* from *de-* + *-fendere* "to strike"] — **de·fend·er** *n* □ SYN DEFEND, PROTECT, SHIELD, GUARD mean to keep secure from danger or against attack. DEFEND denotes warding off actual or threatened attack; PROTECT implies something, as a covering, that serves as a bar to the admission or impact of that which may attack or injure ⟨*protect* one's eyes with dark glasses⟩ ⟨a bird sanctuary *protected* by state law⟩ SHIELD suggests protective intervention in imminent danger or actual attack; GUARD implies protecting with vigilance and force against expected danger.

de·fend·ant \di-'fen-dənt\ *n* : a person called on to answer an accusation in a legal action — compare PLAINTIFF

de·fense *or* **de·fence** \di-'fens\ *n* **1** : the act of defending : resistance against attack **2** : capability of resisting attack **3 a** : means or method of defending **b** : an argument in support or justification **4 a** : a defending party or group (as in a court of law) **b** : a defensive team **5** : the answer made by the defendant in a legal action [Old French, derived from Latin *defendere* "to defend"] — **de·fense·less** \-ləs\ *adj* — **de·fense·less·ly** *adv* — **de·fense·less·ness** *n*

deer mouse

\ə\ abut	\ng\ sing
\ər\ further	\ō\ bone
\a\ mat	\ȯ\ saw
\ā\ take	\ȯi\ coin
\ä\ cot, cart	\th\ thin
\au̇\ out	\t͟h\ this
\ch\ chin	\ü\ food
\e\ pet	\u̇\ foot
\ē\ easy	\y\ yet
\g\ go	\yü\ few
\i\ tip	\yu̇\ cure
\ī\ life	\zh\ vision
\j\ job	

defense mechanism *n* **I** : a defensive reaction by an organism **2** : a mental process (as rationalization or repression) by which one avoids becoming aware of unpleasant thoughts, feelings, or emotions

de·fen·si·ble \di-'fen-sə-bəl\ *adj* : capable of being defended — **de·fen·si·bil·i·ty** \-,fen-sə-'bil-ət-ē\ *n* — **de·fen·si·bly** \-'fen-sə-blē\ *adv*

¹de·fen·sive \di-'fen-siv\ *adj* : of or relating to defense: as **a** : serving or intended to defend or protect ⟨a *defensive* move⟩ **b** : of or relating to the attempt to keep an opponent from scoring in a game or contest — **de·fen·sive·ly** *adv* — **de·fen·sive·ness** *n*

²defensive *n* : a defensive position — **on the defensive** : in a state of readiness to oppose attack

¹de·fer \di-'fər\ *vt* **de·ferred; de·fer·ring** : to put off : DELAY ⟨*defer* payment for goods⟩ [Middle French *differer*, from Latin *differre* "to postpone, be different"] — **de·fer·ra·ble** \-'fər-ə-bəl\ *adj* — **de·fer·rer** *n* □ SYN DEFER, POSTPONE mean to delay an action or proceeding. DEFER may imply a deliberate putting off until a later usually indefinite time or may imply a delay in fulfillment ⟨*defer* college plans⟩ POSTPONE implies an intentional deferring usually to a definite time ⟨*postpone* the meeting until Monday⟩

²defer *vi* **de·ferred; de·fer·ring** : to yield to another's wish or opinion [Middle French *deferer*, from Latin *deferre* "to bring down", from *de-* + *ferre* "to carry"]

def·er·ence \'def-rəns, -ə-rəns\ *n* : courteous respectful regard for another or another's wishes □ SYN DEFERENCE, RESPECT, REVERENCE, HONOR mean esteem shown to another. DEFERENCE implies a courteous yielding of one's own opinion or preference to that of another; RESPECT implies regard for a person or quality or achievement as worthy of honor or confidence; REVERENCE implies profound respect mingled with awe or devotion; HONOR implies that the recognition shown is entirely due. — **in deference to** : in consideration of or out of respect for

def·er·en·tial \,def-ə-'ren-chəl\ *adj* : showing or expressing deference — **def·er·en·tial·ly** \-'rench-lē, -ə-lə\ *adv*

de·fer·ment \di-'fər-mənt\ *n* : the act of delaying; *esp* : official postponement of military service

de·fi·ance \di-'fī-əns\ *n* **I** : the act or an instance of defying **2** : disposition to resist : contempt of opposition — **in defiance of** : contrary to ⟨worked in *defiance* of doctor's orders⟩

de·fi·ant \-ənt\ *adj* : full of defiance — **de·fi·ant·ly** *adv*

de·fi·cien·cy \di-'fish-ən-sē\ *n, pl* **-cies I** : the quality or state of being deficient **2** : shortage of something needed; *esp* : a shortage of substances necessary to health

deficiency disease *n* : a disease (as scurvy) caused by a lack of essential dietary elements and especially a vitamin or mineral

¹de·fi·cient \di-'fish-ənt\ *adj* : lacking something necessary for completeness : DEFECTIVE ⟨a diet *deficient* in proteins⟩ [Latin *deficiens*, present participle of *deficere* "to be wanting, fail", from *de-* + *facere* "to do"] — **de·fi·cient·ly** *adv*

²deficient *n* : one that is deficient ⟨a mental *deficient*⟩

def·i·cit \'def-ə-sət\ *n* : a deficiency in amount; *esp* : an excess of expenses over income [French *déficit*, from Latin *deficit* "it is wanting", from *deficere* "to be wanting"]

¹de·file \di-'fīl\ *vt* **I** : to make filthy : DIRTY **2** : to corrupt the purity or perfection of: as **a** : RAPE **2**, VIOLATE **b** : DESECRATE ⟨invaders *defiled* the shrine⟩ **c** : TARNISH, ABASE ⟨*defile* a hero's record with lies⟩ [Old French *defouler* "to trample", from *de-* "de-" + *fouler* 'to trample'] — **de·file·ment** \-mənt\ *n* — **de·fil·er** *n*

²de·file \di-'fīl, 'dē-,\ *vi* : to march off in a single line [French *défiler*, from *dé-* "de-" + *filer* "to move in a column"]

³de·file \di-'fīl, 'dē-,\ *n* : a narrow passage or gorge

de·fine \di-'fīn\ *vt* **I a** : to fix or mark the limits of **b** : to make distinct in outline **2 a** : to determine the essential qualities of ⟨*define* the concept of loyalty⟩ **b** : to discover and set forth the meaning of ⟨*define* a word⟩ **c** : to assign a value or values to **d** : to specify (as a programming task) for a computer to use ⟨*define* a procedure⟩ [Latin *definire*, from *de-* + *finis* "boundary, end"] — **de·fin·able** \-'fī-nə-bəl\ *adj* — **de·fin·er** *n*

def·i·nite \'def-nət, -ə-nət\ *adj* **I** : having certain or distinct limits : FIXED ⟨a *definite* period of time⟩ **2** : clear in meaning : EXACT, EXPLICIT ⟨a *definite* answer⟩ **3** : typically designating an identified or immediately identifiable person or thing ⟨the *definite* article *the*⟩ [Latin *definitus,* past participle of *definire* "to define"] — **def·i·nite·ly** *adv* — **def·i·nite·ness** *n* □ SYN DEFINITE, DEFINITIVE are sometimes confused. DEFINITE denotes that which has limits so clearly fixed, defined, or stated there can be no doubt about the range or meaning ⟨a *definite* sum of money⟩ DEFINITIVE denotes supplying an answer as final and serving to end dispute and doubt ⟨a *definitive* statement of religious belief⟩ SYN see in addition EXPLICIT

def·i·ni·tion \,def-ə-'nish-ən\ *n* **I** : an act of determining or settling the limits **2 a** : a statement of the meaning of a word or word group or of a sign or symbol **b** : the action or process of defining **3 a** : the action or the power of making definite and clear **b** : the state of being clear ⟨the *definition* of the hills⟩ — **def·i·ni·tion·al** \-'nish-nəl, -'nish-ən-l\ *adj*

de·fin·i·tive \di-'fin-ət-iv\ *adj* **I** : providing a final solution : CONCLUSIVE ⟨a *definitive* victory⟩ **2** : authoritative and apparently completely informative ⟨the *definitive* book on the subject⟩ **3** : defining or limiting precisely SYN see DEFINITE — **de·fin·i·tive·ly** *adv* — **de·fin·i·tive·ness** *n*

de·flate \di-'flāt, 'dē-\ *vb* **I** : to release air or gas from **2** : to cause to contract from a high level : reduce from a state of inflation ⟨*deflate* the currency⟩ **3** : to become deflated : COLLAPSE [*de-* + *-flate* (as in *inflate*)] — **de·fla·tor** \-'flāt-ər\ *n*

de·fla·tion \di-'flā-shən, 'dē-\ *n* **I** : an act or instance of deflating : the state of being deflated **2** : a shrinking in the volume of available money or credit that results in a decline of the general price level — **de·fla·tion·ary** \-shə-,ner-ē\ *adj*

de·flect \di-'flekt\ *vb* : to take or cause to take a new course : turn aside ⟨*deflect* a stream from its bed⟩ ⟨do not let your mind *deflect* from reason⟩ [Latin *deflectere* "to bend down, turn aside", from *de-* + *flectere* "to bend"] — **de·flec·tion** \-'flek-shən\ *n*

de·fo·li·ant \'dē-'fō-lē-ənt\ *n* : a chemical applied to plants to cause the leaves to drop off prematurely

de·fo·li·ate \'dē-'fō-lē-,āt\ *vt* : to deprive of leaves especially prematurely [Latin *defoliare*, from *de-* + *folium* "leaf"] — **de·fo·li·a·tion** \,dē-,fō-lē-'ā-shən\ *n* — **de·fo·li·a·tor** \'dē-'fō-lē-,āt-ər\ *n*

de·for·est \'dē-'fȯr-əst, -'fär-\ *vt* : to clear of forests — **de·for·es·ta·tion** \,dē-,fȯr-ə-'stā-shən, -,fär-\ *n*

de·form \di-'fȯrm, 'dē-\ *vb* **I** : to spoil the form or natural appearance of : DISFIGURE ⟨a leg *deformed* by an injury⟩ ⟨a face *deformed* by grief⟩ **2** : to become misshapen or changed in shape — **de·for·ma·tion** \,dē-,fȯr-'mā-shən, ,def-ər-\ *n*

de·for·mi·ty \di-'fȯr-mət-ē\ *n, pl* **-ties I** : the state of being deformed **2** : a physical blemish or distortion **3** : a moral or aesthetic flaw

de·fraud \di-'frȯd\ *vt* : to deprive of something by trickery, deception, or fraud ⟨were *defrauded* of their money⟩ SYN see CHEAT — **de·fraud·er** \di-'frȯd-ər\ *n*

de·fray \di-'frā\ *vt* : to pay or provide for the payment of ⟨needs more money to *defray* expenses⟩ [Middle French *deffrayer*, from *des-* "de-" + *frayer* "to expend", derived from Latin *frangere* "to break"] — **de-**

fray·able \-'frā-ə-bəl\ *adj* — **de·fray·al** \-'frā-əl, -'frāl\ *n*

de·frost \di-'frȯst, 'dē-\ *vb* : to free from ice or a frozen state ⟨*defrost* meat⟩ ⟨*defrost* a refrigerator⟩ — **de·frost·er** *n*

deft \'deft\ *adj* : quick and neat in action : SKILLFUL ⟨dressing the wound with *deft* fingers⟩ [Middle English *defte*] SYN see DEXTEROUS — **deft·ly** *adv* — **deft·ness** *n*

de·funct \di-'fəŋt, -'fəŋkt\ *adj* : no longer living or existing ⟨a *defunct* factory⟩ [Latin *defunctus,* from *defungi* "to finish, die", from *de-* + *fungi* "to perform"]

de·fy \di-'fī\ *vt* **de·fied; de·fy·ing** **1** : to challenge to do something considered impossible ⟨the magician *defied* the audience to explain the trick⟩ **2** : to refuse boldly to yield or conform to ⟨*defy* public opinion⟩ ⟨*defy* the law⟩ **3** : to resist attempts at ⟨a scene that *defies* description⟩ [Old French *defier* "to renounce faith in, challenge", from *de-* "de-" + *fier* "to entrust", from Latin *fidere* "to trust"] — **de·fi·er** \-'fī-ər, -'fīr\ *n*

de·gas \'dē-'gas\ *vt* : to free from gas

de·gauss \'dē-'gȧus\ *vt* : DEMAGNETIZE

de·gen·er·a·cy \di-'jen-rə-sē, -ə-rə-\ *n, pl* **-cies** **1** : the state of being or process of becoming degenerate **2** : sexual perversion

¹de·gen·er·ate \di-'jen-rət, -ə-rət\ *adj* : having sunk to a lower state or level: as **a** : having declined (as in structure or function) from an ancestral or earlier state ⟨a *degenerate* eye⟩ **b** : fallen below what is normal or desirable; *esp* : fallen into a corrupt, evil, or vicious state [Latin *degeneratus,* past participle of *degenerare* "to deteriorate", from *de-* + *genus* "race, kind"]

²degenerate *n* : a degenerate person; *esp* : a sexual pervert

³de·gen·er·ate \di-'jen-ə-ˌrāt\ *vi* **1** : to pass from a higher to a lower type or condition ⟨the road *degenerated* into a rough track⟩ **2** : to undergo change toward an earlier or less highly organized biological type

de·gen·er·a·tion \di-ˌjen-ə-'rā-shən, ˌdē-\ *n* **1** : a lowering (as of power, vitality, or quality) to a feebler and poorer kind or state **2** : a change in a tissue or an organ resulting in lessened activity or usefulness ⟨fatty *degeneration* of the heart⟩; *also* : a condition marked by such changes and especially by loss of organs present in related forms ⟨tapeworms exhibit extreme *degeneration*⟩

de·gen·er·a·tive \di-'jen-ə-ˌrāt-iv\ *adj* : of, relating to, or tending to cause degeneration ⟨a *degenerative* disease⟩

deg·ra·da·tion \ˌdeg-rə-'dā-shən\ *n* **1** : a reduction in rank, dignity, or standing **b** : removal from office **2** : loss of honor or reputation : HUMILIATION **3** : moral or intellectual decay : DEGENERATION

de·grade \di-'grād\ *vb* **1** : DEMOTE; *also* : DEPOSE 1 **2** : to drag down in moral or intellectual character ⟨*degraded* by a life of crime⟩ **3** : to reduce the complexity of : DECOMPOSE SYN see DEBASE — **de·grad·er** *n*

de·gree \di-'grē\ *n* **1** : a step or stage in a process, course, or order of classification ⟨advance by *degrees*⟩ **2 a** : the extent, intensity, or scope of something especially as measured by a graded series ⟨murder in the first *degree*⟩ **b** : one of the forms or sets of forms used in the comparison of an adjective or adverb **3 a** : a rank or grade of official or social position **b** : the civil condition or status of a person **4 a** : a grade of membership attained in a ritualistic order or society **b** : the formal ceremonies observed in the awarding of a ritualistic distinction **c** : a title conferred upon students by a college, university, or professional school upon completion of a program of study **d** : an academic title conferred honorarily **5** : one of the divisions or intervals marked on a scale of a measuring instrument — symbol ° **6** : a 360th part of the circumference of a circle **7 a** : the sum of the exponents of the variable factors in a mathematical expression containing a sin-

gle term ⟨the *degree* of $3x^2y$ is 3⟩ **b** : the degree of the term of highest degree in a polynomial ⟨the *degree* of $3x^3 + 2x^2y + 5x$ is 3⟩ **8 a** : a line or space of the musical staff **b** : a step, note, or tone of a musical scale [Old French *degré* "step, stair", from Latin *de-* + *gradus* "step, grade"] — **to a degree** **1** : to a remarkable extent **2** : in a small way

degree–day *n* : a unit that represents one degree of departure from a given point (as 65°F or 18°C) in the mean daily outdoor temperature and is usually used to measure heat requirements

de·hisce \di-'his\ *vi* : to split open along a natural line especially with discharge of contents ⟨seedpods *dehiscing* at maturity⟩ [Latin *dehiscere* "to split open", from *de-* + *hiscere* "to gape"] — **de·his·cence** \-'his-ns\ *n* — **de·his·cent** \-nt\ *adj*

de·horn \dē-'hȯrn, 'dē-\ *vt* : to deprive of horns — **de·horn·er** *n*

de·hu·man·ize \dē-'hyü-mə-ˌnīz, dē-'yü-, 'dē-\ *vt* : to strip of human qualities or personality — **de·hu·man·iza·tion** \dē-ˌhyü-mə-nə-'zā-shən, dē-ˌyü-, 'dē-\ *n*

de·hu·mid·i·fy \ˌdē-hyü-'mid-ə-ˌfī, ˌdē-yü-\ *vt* : to remove moisture from (as the air) — **de·hu·mid·i·fi·ca·tion** \-ˌmid-ə-fə-'kā-shən\ *n* — **de·hu·mid·i·fi·er** \-'mid-ə-ˌfī-ər, -ˌfīr\ *n*

de·hy·drate \dē-'hī-ˌdrāt, 'dē-\ *vb* **1** : to remove water from (as foods) **2** : to lose water or body fluids — **de·hy·dra·tion** \ˌdē-ˌhī-'drā-shən\ *n*

de·hy·drog·e·nase \ˌdē-ˌhī-'dräj-ə-ˌnās, dē-'hī-drə-jə-\ *n* : an enzyme that accelerates the removal and transfer of hydrogen

de·hy·dro·ge·nate \ˌdē-ˌhī-'dräj-ə-ˌnāt, dē-'hī-drə-jə-\ *vt* : to remove hydrogen from — **de·hy·dro·ge·na·tion** \ˌdē-ˌhī-ˌdräj-ə-'nā-shən, dē-ˌhī-drə-jə-\ *n*

de·ice \dē-'īs, 'dē-\ *vt* : to keep free or rid of ice — **de·ic·er** *n*

de·i·fy \'dē-ə-ˌfī\ *vt* **-fied; -fy·ing** **1 a** : to make a god of **b** : to take as an object of worship **2** : to treat as an object of supreme regard ⟨*deify* money⟩ [Middle French *deifier,* from Late Latin *deificare,* from Latin *deus* "god"] — **de·i·fi·ca·tion** \ˌdē-ə-fə-'kā-shən\ *n*

deign \'dān\ *vi* : to condescend reluctantly ⟨barely *deigned* to acknowledge their greeting⟩ [Old French *deignier,* from Latin *dignare,* from *dignus* "worthy"] SYN see STOOP

de·ion·ize \dē-'ī-ə-ˌnīz, 'dē-\ *vt* : to remove ions from — **de·ion·iza·tion** \ˌdē-ˌī-ə-nə-'zā-shən\ *n*

de·ism \'dē-ˌiz-əm\ *n* : a movement or system of thought advocating natural religion based on human reason rather than revelation, emphasizing morality, and in the 18th century denying the interference of the Creator with the laws of the universe — **de·ist** \'dē-əst\ *n*

de·i·ty \'dē-ət-ē, 'dā-\ *n, pl* **-ties** **1 a** : DIVINITY 1 **b** *cap* : GOD 1 ⟨the *Deity*⟩ **2 a** : GOD 2 **b** : GODDESS 1 [Middle French *deité,* from Late Latin *deitas,* from Latin *deus* "god"]

de·ject·ed \di-'jek-təd\ *adj* : cast down in spirits : DEPRESSED ⟨*dejected* over a failure⟩ [Latin *dejectus,* past participle of *deicere* "to cast down", from *de-* + *jacere* "to throw"] — **de·ject·ed·ly** *adv* — **de·ject·ed·ness** *n*

de·jec·tion \di-'jek-shən\ *n* : lowness of spirits : SADNESS SYN see MELANCHOLY

de ju·re \dē-'jur-ē, dā-'yur-\ *adj or adv* : existing or exercising power by legal right ⟨*de jure* government⟩ — compare DE FACTO [New Latin, "by right"]

deka- *or* **dek-** — see DECA-

deka·gram \'dek-ə-ˌgram\ *n* — see METRIC SYSTEM table

deka·li·ter \-ˌlēt-ər\ *n* — see METRIC SYSTEM table

deka·me·ter \-ˌmēt-ər\ *n* — see METRIC SYSTEM table

de·lam·i·na·tion \dē-ˌlam-ə-'nā-shən\ *n* : separation or splitting into distinct layers — **de·lam·i·nate** \dē-'lam-ə-ˌnāt\ *vi*

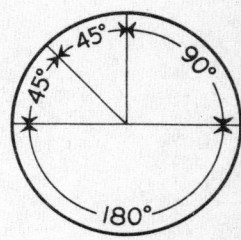

degree 5

\ə\	abut	\ŋ\	sing
\ər\	further	\ō\	bone
\a\	mat	\ȯ\	saw
\ā\	take	\ȯi\	coin
\ä\	cot, cart	\th\	thin
\aů\	out	\th\	this
\ch\	chin	\ü\	food
\e\	pet	\u̇\	foot
\ē\	easy	\y\	yet
\g\	go	\yü\	few
\i\	tip	\yu̇\	cure
\ī\	life	\zh\	vision
\j\	job		

Del·a·ware \'del-ə-ˌwaər, -ˌweər, -wər\ *n* : a member of an Algonquian people of the Delaware valley

¹de·lay \di-'lā\ *n* **1** : the act of delaying : the state of being delayed **2** : the time during which something is delayed

²delay *vb* **1** : to put off : POSTPONE **2** : to stop, detain, or hinder for a time ⟨*delayed* by a storm⟩ **3** : to move or act slowly [Old French *delaier,* from *de-* + *laier* "to leave", alteration of *laissier,* from Latin *laxare* "to slacken"] — **de·lay·er** *n*

de·lec·ta·ble \di-'lek-tə-bəl\ *adj* **1** : highly pleasing : DELIGHTFUL **2** : DELICIOUS ⟨a *delectable* meal⟩ [Middle French, from Latin *delectabilis,* from *delectare* "to delight"] — **de·lec·ta·bly** \-blē\ *adv*

de·lec·ta·tion \ˌdē-ˌlek-'tā-shən, di-; ˌdel-ək-\ *n* **1** : DELIGHT 1 **2** : something that gives pleasure

¹del·e·gate \'del-i-gət, -ˌgāt\ *n* : a person sent with power to act for another: as **a** : a representative to a convention, conference, or assembly **b** : a representative of a United States territory in the House of Representatives **c** : a member of the lower house of the legislature of Maryland, Virginia, or West Virginia [derived from Latin *delegare* "to delegate", from *de-* + *legare* "to send"]

²del·e·gate \-ˌgāt\ *vt* **1** : to entrust to another ⟨*delegate* responsibility⟩ **2** : to appoint as one's delegate

del·e·ga·tion \ˌdel-i-'gā-shən\ *n* **1** : the act of delegating (as power or authority) to another **2** : one or more persons chosen to represent others

de·lete \di-'lēt\ *vt* : to eliminate especially by blotting out, cutting out, or erasing [Latin *delēre* "to wipe out, destroy"]

del·e·te·ri·ous \ˌdel-ə-'tir-ē-əs\ *adj* : having a harmful effect [Greek *dēlētērios,* from *dēleisthai* "to hurt"] — **del·e·te·ri·ous·ly** *adv* — **del·e·te·ri·ous·ness** *n*

de·le·tion \di-'lē-shən\ *n* **1** : an act of deleting **2** : something deleted

delft \'delft\ *or* **delft·ware** \'delf-ˌtwaər, -ˌtweər\ *n* **1** : a Dutch pottery covered with an opaque white glaze upon which a predominantly blue decoration is painted **2** : glazed pottery especially when blue and white [*Delft,* Netherlands]

deli \'del-ē\ *n, pl* **del·is** : DELICATESSEN

¹de·lib·er·ate \di-'lib-rət, -ə-rət\ *adj* **1** : marked by or resulting from thorough and careful consideration ⟨a *deliberate* judgment⟩ **2** : showing awareness of the significance or nature of the thing done or said ⟨a *deliberate* lie⟩ **3** : weighing facts and arguments : careful and slow in deciding ⟨a *deliberate* person⟩ **4** : slow in action : not hurried ⟨*deliberate* movements⟩ [Latin *deliberatus,* past participle of *deliberare* "to weigh in mind", from *de-* + *libra* "scale, pound"] SYN see VOLUNTARY — **de·lib·er·ate·ly** *adv* — **de·lib·er·ate·ness** *n*

²de·lib·er·ate \di-'lib-ə-ˌrāt\ *vb* : to think about deliberately : CONSIDER ⟨*deliberate* before answering⟩

de·lib·er·a·tion \di-ˌlib-ə-'rā-shən\ *n* **1** : the act of deliberating **2** : a discussion and consideration of the reasons for and against a measure or question **3** : the quality of being deliberate : DELIBERATENESS

de·lib·er·a·tive \di-'lib-ə-ˌrāt-iv; -'lib-rət-, -ə-rət-\ *adj* : of or relating to deliberation : engaged in or devoted to deliberation ⟨a *deliberative* assembly⟩ — **de·lib·er·a·tive·ly** *adv* — **de·lib·er·a·tive·ness** *n*

del·i·ca·cy \'del-i-kə-sē\ *n, pl* **-cies** **1** : something pleasing to eat because it is rare or luxurious **2 a** : FINENESS, DAINTINESS ⟨lace of great *delicacy*⟩ **b** : FRAILTY 1 **3** : nicety or subtle expressiveness of touch (as in painting or music) **4 a** : precise and refined perception and discrimination **b** : extreme sensitivity : PRECISION **5** : SQUEAMISHNESS **6** : the quality or state of requiring delicate treatment ⟨the *delicacy* of a situation⟩

del·i·cate \'del-i-kət\ *adj* **1** : pleasing to the senses ⟨a *delicate* breeze⟩ ⟨a *delicate* aroma⟩ **2** : marked by keen sensitivity or fine discrimination **3** : exhibiting extreme sensitivity ⟨a *delicate* instrument⟩ **4** : calling for or involving extremely careful treatment ⟨a *delicate* balance of power⟩ **5** : marked by fineness of structure, workmanship, or texture ⟨*delicate* lace⟩ **6** : easily torn or hurt ⟨a *delicate* butterfly wing⟩; *also* : WEAK 1a, SICKLY **7** : marked by tact; *also* : requiring tact ⟨*delicate* negotiations⟩ [Latin *delicatus*] — **del·i·cate·ly** *adv* — **del·i·cate·ness** *n*

del·i·ca·tes·sen \ˌdel-i-kə-'tes-n\ *n pl* **1** : ready-to-eat food products (as cooked meats and prepared salads) **2** *sing, pl* **delicatessens** : a store where delicatessen are sold [obsolete German (now *delikatessen),* plural of *delicatesse* "delicacy", from French *délicatesse,* derived from Latin *delicatus* "delicate"] □ ORIGIN Near the end of the 19th century, the word *delicatessen* began to appear in English. Its earliest sense is "delicacies" or "ready-to-eat food products". In this sense *delicatessen* is a plural noun, reflecting its origin in a German word now spelled *Delikatessen,* the plural of *Delikatesse.* The German is a borrowing from French *délicatesse,* meaning "delicacy". In English a second sense of *delicatessen* developed when the word was understood as a singular noun used for a store where delicacies are sold. In spite of the widespread popular belief to the contrary, *delicatessen* has no etymological connection with the German verb *essen,* "to eat".

de·li·cious \di-'lish-əs\ *adj* : giving great pleasure : DELIGHTFUL; *esp* : very pleasing to the taste or smell [Old French, derived from Latin *delicere* "to allure"] — **de·li·cious·ly** *adv* — **de·li·cious·ness** *n*

¹de·light \di-'līt\ *n* **1** : extreme pleasure or satisfaction : JOY **2** : something that gives great pleasure

²delight *vb* **1** : to take great pleasure **2** : to give joy or satisfaction to : please greatly [Old French *delitier,* from Latin *delectare,* from *delicere* "to allure", from *de-* + *lacere* "to allure"]

de·light·ed *adj* : highly pleased : GRATIFIED — **de·light·ed·ly** *adv* — **de·light·ed·ness** *n*

de·light·ful \di-'līt-fəl\ *adj* : highly pleasing : giving delight ⟨a *delightful* vacation⟩ — **de·light·ful·ly** \-fə-lē\ *adv* — **de·light·ful·ness** *n*

de·lim·it \di-'lim-ət\ *vt* : to fix the limits of : BOUND — **de·lim·i·ta·tion** \-ˌlim-ə-'tā-shən\ *n* — **de·lim·i·ta·tive** \-'lim-ə-ˌtāt-iv\ *adj*

de·lin·eate \di-'lin-ē-ˌāt\ *vt* **1** : to indicate by lines drawn in the form or figure of : PORTRAY **2** : to describe in usually sharp or vivid detail ⟨*delineate* the characters in a story⟩ [Latin *delineare,* from *de-* + *linea* "line"] — **de·lin·ea·tion** \di-ˌlin-ē-'ā-shən\ *n* — **de·lin·ea·tor** \-ē-ˌāt-ər\ *n*

de·lin·quen·cy \di-'ling-kwən-sē\ *n, pl* **-cies** : the quality or state of being delinquent

¹de·lin·quent \-kwənt\ *n* : a delinquent person

²delinquent *adj* **1** : offending by neglect or violation of duty or of law **2** : overdue for payment ⟨a *delinquent* charge account⟩ [Latin *delinquere* "to fail, offend", from *de-* + *linquere* "to leave"] — **de·lin·quent·ly** *adv*

del·i·quesce \ˌdel-ə-'kwes\ *vi* : to melt away: **a** : to dissolve gradually by absorbing moisture from the air ⟨a *deliquescing* substance⟩ **b** : to become soft or liquid ⟨*deliquescing* mushrooms⟩ [Latin *deliquescere,* from *de-* + *liquēre* "to be fluid"] — **del·i·ques·cence** \-'kwes-ns\ *n*

del·i·ques·cent \-'kwes-nt\ *adj* **1** : marked by or undergoing deliquescence **2** : having repeated division into branches ⟨elms are *deliquescent* trees⟩ — compare EXCURRENT

de·lir·i·ous \di-'lir-ē-əs\ *adj* **1** : of or relating to delirium **2** : marked by delirium; *also* : wildly excited — **de·lir·i·ous·ly** *adv* — **de·lir·i·ous·ness** *n*

de·lir·i·um \-'lir-ē-əm\ *n* **1** : a mental disturbance characterized by confusion, disordered speech, and hallucinations **2** : frenzied excitement [Latin, from *delirare* "to deviate, be crazy", from *de-* + *lira* "furrow"]

delirium tre·mens \-'trē-mənz, -'trem-ənz\ *n* : a violent delirium with tremors that is induced by excessive and prolonged use of alcoholic liquors — called also *D.T.'s* [New Latin, literally, "trembling delirium"]

de·liv·er \di-'liv-ər\ *vb* **-liv·ered; -liv·er·ing** \-'liv-ring, -ə-ring\ **1** : to set free : SAVE **2** : to hand over : CONVEY, TRANSFER ⟨*deliver* a letter⟩ **3** : to assist in giving birth; *also* : to aid in the birth of **4** : UTTER, COMMUNICATE ⟨*deliver* a speech⟩ **5** : to send to an intended target or destination ⟨*deliver* a pitch⟩ **6** : to produce the promised, desired, or expected result ⟨*deliver* on a promise⟩ [Old French *delivrer*, from Late Latin *deliberare*, from Latin *de-* + *liberare* "to liberate"] SYN see RESCUE — **de·liv·er·able** \-'liv-rə-bəl, -ə-rə-\ *adj* — **de·liv·er·er** \-'liv-ər-ər\ *n*

de·liv·er·ance \di-'liv-rəns, -ə-rəns\ *n* **1** : a delivering or a being delivered : RESCUE **2** : something delivered or communicated; *esp* : a publicly expressed opinion

de·liv·ery \di-'liv-rē, -ə-rē\ *n, pl* **-er·ies** **1** : a delivering from restraint **2 a** : the act of handing over **b** : a legal conveyance of right or title **c** : something delivered at one time or in one unit **3** : the act of giving birth **4** : a delivering especially of a speech; *also* : manner or style of uttering in speech or song **5** : the act or manner of sending forth or throwing

dell \'del\ *n* : a secluded small valley usually covered with trees or turf [Middle English *delle*]

de·louse \dē-'laús, 'dē-, -'laúz\ *vt* : to remove lice from

Del·phi·an \'del-fē-ən\ *or* **Del·phic** \-fik\ *adj* **1** : of or relating to ancient Delphi or its oracle **2** : AMBIGUOUS, OBSCURE

del·phin·i·um \del-'fin-ē-əm\ *n* : any of a large genus of chiefly perennial erect branching herbs related to the buttercups and widely grown for their irregular flowers in showy spikes — compare LARKSPUR [Greek *delphinion* "larkspur", from *delphis* "dolphin"]

Del·phi·nus \del-'fī-nəs, -'fē-\ *n* : a northern constellation nearly west of Pegasus [Latin, literally, "dolphin"]

del·ta \'del-tə\ *n* **1** : the 4th letter of the Greek alphabet — Δ or δ **2** : something shaped like a capital Δ; *esp* : the triangular or fan-shaped piece of land made by deposits of mud and sand at the mouth of a river — **del·ta·ic** \del-'tā-ik\ *adj*

del·toid \'del-,tóid\ *n* : a large triangular muscle that covers the shoulder joint and serves to raise the arm laterally [Greek *deltoeidēs* "shaped like a delta"]

del·toi·de·us \del-'tóid-ē-əs\ *n, pl* **del·toi·dei** \-ē-,ī\ : DELTOID [New Latin, from Greek *deltoeidēs* "shaped like a delta"]

de·lude \di-'lüd\ *vt* : to mislead the mind or judgment of ⟨*deluded* by false promises⟩ [Latin *deludere*, from *de-* + *ludere* "to play"] SYN see DECEIVE — **de·lud·er** *n* — **de·lud·ing·ly** \-'lüd-ing-lē\ *adv*

¹del·uge \'del-,yüj\ *n* **1 a** : an overflowing of the land by water : FLOOD **b** : a drenching rain **2** : an overwhelming amount or number ⟨a *deluge* of Christmas mail⟩ [Middle French, from Latin *diluvium*, from *diluere* "to wash away", from *dis-* + *lavere* "to wash"]

²deluge *vt* **1** : to overflow with water : INUNDATE, FLOOD **2** : to overwhelm as if with a deluge ⟨was *deluged* with inquiries⟩

de·lu·sion \di-'lü-zhən\ *n* **1** : the act of deluding : the state of being deluded **2 a** : something that is falsely or delusively believed **b** : a false belief regarding the self or persons or objects outside the self that persists despite the facts and is common in some abnormal mental states [Latin *delusio*, from *deludere* "to delude"] — **de·lu·sion·al** \-'lüzh-nəl, -'lü-zhən-l\ *adj* □ SYN DELUSION, ILLUSION mean something accepted as true or real that is actually false or unreal. DELUSION implies persistent self-deception concerning facts or situations and usually suggests a disordered state of mind; ILLUSION implies an attributing of truth or reality to something that seems to normal perception to be true and real but in fact is not.

de·lu·sive \-'lü-siv, -'lü-ziv\ *adj* : deluding or apt to delude — **de·lu·sive·ly** *adv* — **de·lu·sive·ness** *n*

de·luxe \di-'lúks, -'ləks, -'lüks\ *adj* : notably luxurious or elegant ⟨a *deluxe* edition⟩ [French *de luxe*, literally, "of luxury"]

delve \'delv\ *vi* **1** : to dig or labor with a spade **2** : to make a careful or detailed search for information ⟨*delve* into the past⟩ [Old English *delfan*] — **delv·er** *n*

de·mag·ne·tize \dē-'mag-nə-,tīz\ *vt* : to deprive of magnetic properties — **de·mag·ne·ti·za·tion** \,dē-,mag-nət-ə-'zā-shən\ *n* — **de·mag·ne·tiz·er** \dē-'mag-nə-,tī-zər\ *n*

dem·a·gogue *or* **dem·a·gog** \'dem-ə-,gäg\ *n* : a person who appeals to the emotions and prejudices of people in order to arouse discontent and advance personal political ends [Greek *dēmagōgos*, from *dēmos* "people" + *agein* "to lead"] — **dem·a·gog·ic** \,dem-ə-'gäj-ik, -'gäg-\ *or* **dem·a·gog·i·cal** \-i-kəl\ *adj* — **dem·a·gogu·ery** \'dem-ə-,gäg-rē, -ə-rē\ *n* — **dem·a·gogy** \-,gäj-ē, -,gäg-ē\ *n*

¹de·mand \di-'mand\ *n* **1 a** : an act of demanding or asking especially with authority **b** : something claimed as due **2 a** : an expressed desire to own or use something ⟨the *demand* for new cars⟩ **b** : the ability and desire to purchase goods or services at a specified time and price **c** : the quantity of an article or service that is wanted at a stated price **3** : a seeking or state of being sought after ⟨tickets are in great *demand*⟩ **4** : a pressing need or requirement ⟨*demands* that tax one's energy⟩ — **on demand** : upon request for payment

²demand *vb* **1** : to ask or call for with authority : claim as one's right ⟨*demand* payment of a debt⟩ **2** : to ask earnestly or in the manner of a command ⟨the sentry *demanded* the password⟩ **3** : to call for : REQUIRE ⟨an illness that *demands* constant care⟩ [Middle French *demander*, from Medieval Latin *demandare*, from Latin *de-* + *mandare* "to enjoin"] — **de·mand·able** \-'man-də-bəl\ *adj* — **de·mand·er** *n* □ SYN DEMAND, CLAIM, REQUIRE, EXACT mean to ask or call for something as due or as necessary. DEMAND carries a suggestion of authoritativeness, insistence, and a right to make a request that is to be regarded as a command; CLAIM implies a demand for the concession of something due as one's own or one's right; REQUIRE strictly implies imperativeness arising from inner necessity or the compulsion of law or the urgency of the case; EXACT implies not only demanding but getting what one demands ⟨*exact* payment of an overdue debt⟩

de·mand·ing *adj* : EXACTING — **de·mand·ing·ly** \-'man-ding-lē\ *adv*

de·mar·cate \di-'mär-,kāt, 'dē-,mär-\ *vt* **1** : to mark the limits of **2** : to set apart : SEPARATE [back-formation from demarcation, derived from Spanish and Portuguese *demarcar* "to delimit", from *de-* "de-" + *marcar* "to mark"] — **de·mar·ca·tion** \,dē-,mär-'kā-shən\ *n*

deme \'dēm\ *n* : a unit of local government in ancient Attica [Greek *dēmos*, literally, "people"]

¹de·mean \di-'mēn\ *vt* **de·meaned; de·mean·ing** : to conduct or behave (oneself) usually in a proper manner [Old French *demener* "to conduct", from *de-* "de-" + *mener* "to drive", from Latin *minare*, from *minari* "to threaten"]

²demean *vt* **de·meaned; de·mean·ing** : DEGRADE, DEBASE ⟨refused to *demean* themselves by cheating⟩ [*de-* + *mean*]

de·mean·or \di-'mē-nər\ *n* : outward manner or behavior : CONDUCT, BEARING

de·ment·ed \di-'ment-əd\ *adj* : mentally disordered : INSANE — **de·ment·ed·ly** *adv* — **de·ment·ed·ness** *n*

de·men·tia \di-'men-chə\ *n* **1** : a condition of deteriorated mentality **2** : INSANITY 3a ⟨the *dementia* of racial hatred⟩ [Latin, from *demens* "mad", from *de-* + *mens* "mind"]

de·mer·it \di-'mer-ət\ *n* **1** : a quality that deserves blame : FAULT **2** : a mark placed against a person's record for some fault or offense

\ə\ abut		\ng\ sing	
\ər\ further		\ō\ bone	
\a\ mat		\ó\ saw	
\ā\ take		\ói\ coin	
\ä\ cot, cart		\th\ thin	
\aú\ out		\th\ this	
\ch\ chin		\ü\ food	
\e\ pet		\ú\ foot	
\ē\ easy		\y\ yet	
\g\ go		\yü\ few	
\i\ tip		\yú\ cure	
\ī\ life		\zh\ vision	
\j\ job			

demijohn

de·mesne \di-'mān, -'mēn\ *n* **1** : manorial land possessed by the lord and not held by free tenants **2 a** : the land attached to a mansion **b** : landed property : ESTATE **c** : a geographical area : REGION **3** : realm or range especially of interests or activity [Old French *demaine,* from Latin *dominium* "domain"]

demi- *prefix* **1** : half **2** : one that partly belongs to (a specified type or class) ⟨*demi*god⟩ [Middle French *demi,* from Latin *dimidius,* from *dis-* + *medius* "middle"]

demi·god \'dem-ē-,gäd\ *n* : a mythological being with more power than a mortal but less than a god

demi·john \-,jän\ *n* : a large bottle of glass or stoneware enclosed in wickerwork [by folk etymology from French *dame-jeanne,* literally, "Lady Jane"]

de·mil·i·ta·rize \dē-'mil-ə-tə-,rīz\ *vt* : to strip of military forces, weapons, or fortification ⟨a *demilitarized* zone⟩ — **de·mil·i·ta·ri·za·tion** \,dē-,mil-ə-tə-rə-'zā-shən\ *n*

demi·mon·daine \,dem-ē-,män-'dān\ *n* : a woman of the demimonde [French *demi-mondaine,* from *demimonde*]

demi·monde \'dem-ē-,mänd\ *n* **1** : a class of women on the fringes of respectable society supported by wealthy lovers **2** : a group engaged in activity of doubtful legality or propriety [French *demi-monde,* from *demi-* + *monde* "world", from Latin *mundus*]

de·mise \di-'mīz\ *n* **1** : a letting of property : LEASE **2** : transfer of sovereignty to a successor ⟨*demise* of the crown⟩ **3 a** : DEATH 1 **b** : an end of existence or activity [Middle French *demis,* past participle of *demettre* "to dismiss", from Latin *demittere* "to send down", from *de-* + *mittere* "to send"]

demi·tasse \'dem-ē-,tas, -,täs\ *n* : a small cup of black coffee; *also* : the cup used to serve it [French *demitasse,* from *demi-* + *tasse* "cup", from Arabic *ṭass,* from Persian *tast*]

de·mo·bi·lize \di-'mō-bə-,līz\ *vt* **1** : to discharge from military service ⟨*demobilize* an army⟩ **2** : to change from a state of war to a state of peace — **de·mo·bi·li·za·tion** \-,mō-bə-lə-'zā-shən\ *n*

de·moc·ra·cy \di-'mäk-rə-sē\ *n, pl* **-cies 1 a** : government by the people; *esp* : rule of the majority **b** : government in which the supreme power is vested in the people and exercised by them directly or indirectly through representation **2** : a political unit that has a democratic government **3 a** : the absence of hereditary or arbitrary class distinctions or privileges **b** : belief in or practice of social or economic equality for all people [Middle French *democratie,* derived from Greek *dēmokratia,* from *dēmos* "people" + *-kratia* "-cracy"]

dem·o·crat \'dem-ə-,krat\ *n* **1 a** : an adherent of democracy **b** : one who practices social equality **2** *cap* : a member of the Democratic party of the United States

dem·o·crat·ic \,dem-ə-'krat-ik\ *adj* **1** : of, relating to, or favoring political, social, or economic democracy **2** *often cap* : of or relating to a major United States political party evolving from the anti-federalists and the Democratic-Republican party and associated with policies of broad social reform and internationalism **3** : of, relating to, or appealing to the broad masses of the people ⟨*democratic* art⟩ **4** : favoring social equality : not snobbish — **dem·o·crat·i·cal·ly** \-i-kə-lē, -klē\ *adv*

Democratic–Republican *adj* : of or relating to an early 19th century American political party favoring strict interpretation of the constitution and emphasizing states' rights

de·moc·ra·tize \di-'mäk-rə-,tīz\ *vt* : to make democratic — **de·moc·ra·ti·za·tion** \-,mäk-rət-ə-'zā-shən\ *n*

de·mod·u·late \dē-'mäj-ə-,lāt\ *vt* : to extract from (a transmitted radio signal) the wave by which the sound or picture is reproduced — **de·mod·u·la·tion** \,dē-,mäj-ə-'lā-shən\ *n*

de·mog·ra·phy \di-'mäg-rə-fē\ *n* : the statistical study of human populations and especially their size and distribution and the number of births and deaths [French *démographie,* from Greek *dēmos* "people" + French *-graphie* "-graphy"] — **de·mog·ra·pher** \-fər\ *n* — **de·mo·graph·ic** \,dem-ə-'graf-ik, ,dē-mə-\ *adj* — **de·mo·graph·i·cal·ly** \-'graf-i-kə-lē, -klē\ *adv*

dem·oi·selle \,dem-wə-'zel, -ə-\ *n* : a young lady [French]

de·mol·ish \di-'mäl-ish\ *vt* **1 a** : to tear down : RAZE **b** : to break to pieces : SMASH **2** : to do away with : put an end to [Middle French *demoliss-,* stem of demolir, from Latin *demoliri,* from *de-* + *moliri* "to construct", from *moles* "mass"] SYN see DESTROY — **de·mol·ish·er** *n* — **de·mol·ish·ment** \-ish-mənt\ *n*

dem·o·li·tion \,dem-ə-'lish-ən, ,dē-mə-\ *n* : the act of demolishing; *esp* : destruction by means of explosives — **dem·o·li·tion·ist** \-'lish-nəst, -ə-nəst\ *n*

de·mon *or* **dae·mon** \'dē-mən\ *n* **1** *usually* daemon : an attendant power or spirit **2 a** : an evil spirit **b** : an evil or undesirable emotion, trait, or state **3** *usually* daemon : a demigod of Greek mythology [Latin *daemon* "divinity, spirit", from Greek *daimōn*]

de·mon·e·tize \dē-'män-ə-,tīz, -'mən-\ *vt* : to stop using as money or as a monetary standard ⟨*demonetize* silver⟩ [French *démonétiser,* from *dé-* "de-" + Latin *moneta* "coin"] — **de·mon·e·ti·za·tion** \dē-,män-ət-ə-'zā-shən, -,mən-\ *n*

¹de·mo·ni·ac \di-'mō-nē-,ak\ *also* **de·mo·ni·a·cal** \,dē-mə-'nī-ə-kəl\ *adj* **1** : possessed or influenced by a demon **2** : of, relating to, or suggestive of a demon : FIENDISH — **de·mo·ni·a·cal·ly** \,dē-mə-'nī-ə-kə-lē, -klē\ *adv*

²demoniac *n* : one held to be possessed by a demon

de·mon·ic \di-'män-ik\ *adj* : DEMONIAC 2

de·mon·ol·o·gy \,dē-mə-'näl-ə-jē\ *n* **1** : the study of demons **2** : belief in demons

de·mon·stra·ble \di-'män-strə-bəl, 'dem-ən-strə-\ *adj* **1** : capable of being demonstrated or proved **2** : APPARENT **2**, EVIDENT — **de·mon·stra·bil·i·ty** \di-,män-strə-'bil-ət-ē, ,dem-ən-strə-\ *n* — **de·mon·stra·ble·ness** \di-'män-strə-bəl-nəs, 'dem-ən-strə-\ *n* — **de·mon·stra·bly** \-blē\ *adv*

dem·on·strate \'dem-ən-,strāt\ *vb* **1** : to show clearly **2 a** : to prove or make clear by reasoning or evidence **b** : to illustrate and explain especially with many examples **3** : to show publicly the good qualities of a product ⟨*demonstrate* a new car⟩ **4** : to make a public display (as of feelings or military force) ⟨citizens *demonstrated* in protest⟩ [Latin *demonstrare,* from *de-* + *monstrare* "to show", from *monstrum* "portent, monster"]

dem·on·stra·tion \,dem-ən-'strā-shən\ *n* **1** : an outward expression or display ⟨a *demonstration* of joy⟩ **2** : an act, process, or means of demonstrating to the intelligence: **a** : convincing evidence : PROOF **b** : an explanation (as of a theory) by experiment **c** : a course of reasoning intended to prove that a conclusion must follow when certain conditions are accepted **d** : a showing to a prospective buyer of the merits of a product **3** : a show of armed force **4** : a public display of group feelings especially in support or protest — **dem·on·stra·tion·al** \-shnəl, -shən-l\ *adj*

¹de·mon·stra·tive \di-'män-strət-iv\ *adj* **1 a** : demonstrating as real or true **b** : characterized or established by demonstration ⟨*demonstrative* reasoning⟩ **2** : pointing out the one referred to and distinguishing it from others of the same class ⟨the *demonstrative* pronoun *this* in "this is my hat"⟩ ⟨the *demonstrative* adjective *that* in "that chair"⟩ **3** : marked by display of feeling ⟨a *demonstrative* greeting⟩ — **de·mon·stra·tive·ly** *adv* — **de·mon·stra·tive·ness** *n*

²demonstrative *n* : a demonstrative word; *esp* : a demonstrative pronoun

dem·on·stra·tor \'dem-ən-ˌstrāt-ər\ *n* **1** : a person who makes or takes part in a demonstration **2** : a product (as an automobile) used for purposes of demonstration

de·mor·al·ize \di-'mȯr-ə-ˌlīz, -'mär-\ *vb* **1** : to corrupt in morals : make bad **2** : to destroy the morale of : weaken in discipline or spirit ⟨fear *demoralized* the army⟩ — **de·mor·al·iza·tion** \di-ˌmȯr-ə-lə-'zā-shən, -ˌmär-\ *n* — **de·mor·al·iz·er** \-'mȯr-ə-ˌlī-zər, -'mär-\ *n*

de·mote \di-'mōt, 'dē-\ *vt* : to reduce to a lower grade or rank [*de-* + *-mote* (as in *promote*)] — **de·mo·tion** \-'mō-shən\ *n*

de·mot·ic \di-'mät-ik\ *adj* **1** : of or relating to the general public : POPULAR, COMMON **2** : of, relating to, or written in a simplified form of the ancient Egyptian writing **3** : of or relating to the form of Modern Greek that is based on conversational use [Greek *dēmotikos*, from *dēmos* "people"]

de·mount \dē-'maunt\ *vt* **1** : to remove from a mounted position **2** : DISASSEMBLE — **de·mount·able** \-ə-bəl\ *adj*

¹de·mul·cent \di-'məl-sənt\ *adj* : SOOTHING [Latin *demulcēre* "to soothe", from *de-* + *mulcēre* "to soothe"]

²demulcent *n* : a usually oily or somewhat thick and jellylike preparation used to soothe or protect an abraded mucous membrane

¹de·mur \di-'mər\ *vi* **de·murred; de·mur·ring** **1** : to enter a demurrer **2** : to take exception : OBJECT **3** *archaic* : DELAY **1**, HESITATE [Old French *demorer* "to linger", from Latin *demorari*, from *de-* + *morari* "to linger", from *mora* "delay"]

²demur *n* **1** : HESITATION **2** : the act of objecting : PROTEST ⟨accepted without *demur*⟩

de·mure \di-'myur\ *adj* **1** : marked by quiet modesty **2** : affectedly modest, reserved, or serious [Middle English] — **de·mure·ly** *adv* — **de·mure·ness** *n*

de·mur·rage \di-'mər-ij, -'mə-rij\ *n* **1** : the detention of a ship by the shipper or receiver beyond a time specified for loading, unloading, or sailing **2** : a charge for detaining a ship, freight car, or truck beyond a time specified for loading or unloading

¹de·mur·rer \di-'mər-ər, -'mə-rər\ *n* **1** : a claim by the defendant in a legal action that the pleadings of the plaintiff are insufficient or defective **2** : OBJECTION

²de·mur·rer \-'mər-ər\ *n* : one that demurs

¹den \'den\ *n* **1** : the shelter or resting place of a wild animal **2 a** : a hiding place (as for thieves) **b** : a center of secret activity ⟨a gambling *den*⟩ **3** : a small usually squalid dwelling ⟨*dens* of misery⟩ **4** : a quiet snug room; *esp* : one set apart for reading and relaxation **5** : a subdivision of a cub-scout pack [Old English *denn*]

²den *vb* **denned; den·ning** **1** : to live in or retire to a den **2** : to drive into a den

de·nar·i·us \di-'nar-ē-əs, -'ner-\ *n, pl* **de·nar·ii** \-ē-ˌī, -ē-ˌē\ : a small silver coin of ancient Rome; *also* : a gold coin equal to 25 silver denarii [Latin, a coin worth ten asses, from *deni* "ten each", from *decem* "ten"]

de·na·tion·al·ize \dē-'nash-nə-ˌlīz, -'nash-ən-l-ˌīz\ *vt* **1** : to strip of national character or rights **2** : to remove from ownership or control by the national government

de·nat·u·ral·ize \dē-'nach-rə-ˌlīz, -ə-rə-\ *vt* **1** : to make unnatural **2** : to deprive of the rights and duties of a citizen

de·na·tur·ant \dē-'nach-rənt, -ə-rənt\ *n* : a denaturing agent

de·na·ture \dē-'nā-chər\ *vt* **de·na·tured; de·na·tur·ing** \-'nāch-ring, -ə-ring\ : to deprive of natural qualities: as **a** : to make (alcohol) unfit for drinking without impairing usefulness for other purposes **b** : to modify (as a native protein) so as to diminish or destroy some of the original properties — **de·na·tur·ation** \ˌdē-ˌnā-chə-'rā-shən\ *n*

dendr- *or* **dendro-** *combining form* : tree ⟨*dendro*chronology⟩ : resembling a tree ⟨*dendr*ite⟩ [Greek *dendron* "tree"]

den·drite \'den-ˌdrīt\ *n* **1** : a branching figure (as in a mineral or stone) resembling a tree **2** : any of the usually branching processes of a nerve cell that conduct impulses toward its body — **den·drit·ic** \den-'drit-ik\ *adj*

den·dro·chro·nol·o·gy \ˌden-drō-krə-'näl-ə-jē\ *n* : the science of dating events by comparative study of growth rings in trees and aged wood — **den·dro·chron·o·log·i·cal** \-ˌkrän-l-'äj-i-kəl, -ˌkrōn-\ *adj* — **den·dro·chron·o·log·i·cal·ly** \-kə-lē, -klē\ *adv*

den·drol·o·gy \den-'dräl-ə-jē\ *n* : the study of trees

Den·eb \'den-ˌeb, -əb\ *n* : the brightest star in the constellation Cygnus [Arabic *dhanab al-dajāja*, literally, "tail of the hen"]

den·gue \'deng-gē, -ˌgā\ *n* : an acute virus disease characterized by headache, severe joint pain, and rash [Spanish]

de·ni·al \di-'nī-əl, -'nīl\ *n* **1** : a refusal to grant something asked for **2** : a refusal to admit the truth of a statement ⟨a flat *denial* of the charges⟩ **3** : a refusal to acknowledge something; *esp* : a statement of disbelief or rejection **4** : a cutting down or limiting : RESTRICTION ⟨*denial* of one's appetite⟩

¹de·ni·er \di-'nī-ər, -'nīr\ *n* : one that denies

²de·nier *n* **1** \də-'niər, dən-'yā\ : a small originally silver coin of France and western Europe from the 8th to the 19th century **2** \'den-yər\ : a unit of fineness for silk, rayon, or nylon yarn equal to the fineness of a yarn weighing one gram for each 9000 meters [Middle French, from Latin *denarius* "denarius"]

den·i·grate \'den-i-ˌgrāt\ *vt* : to cast aspersions on : DEFAME [Latin *denigrare*, from *de-* + *nigrare* "to blacken", from *niger* "black"] — **den·i·gra·tion** \ˌden-i-'grā-shən\ *n* — **den·i·gra·tor** \'den-i-ˌgrāt-ər\ *n* — **den·i·gra·to·ry** \-grə-ˌtōr-ē, -ˌtȯr-\ *adj*

den·im \'den-əm\ *n* **1** : a firm durable twilled usually cotton fabric **2** *pl* : overalls or trousers of usually blue denim [French *serge de Nîmes*, "serge of Nîmes, France"] □ ORIGIN Many fabrics have been named for the places where they originated or were manufactured. *Denim* comes from the French *de Nîmes*, meaning "of Nîmes". It was originally used in the phrase *serge de Nîmes*, which appeared in English in the 17th century as *serge denim*. *Serge*, from the Latin adjective *sericus*, "of silk", is a durable twilled fabric, and Nîmes is a city of southern France where textiles are still an important industry.

de·ni·tri·fy \dē-'nī-trə-ˌfī\ *vt* **1** : to remove nitrogen or its compound from **2** : to convert (a nitrate or a nitrite) into a compound of a lower state of oxidation especially as a step in the nitrogen cycle — **de·ni·tri·fi·ca·tion** \ˌdē-ˌnī-trə-fə-'kā-shən\ *n* — **de·ni·tri·fi·er** \ˌdē-'nī-trə-ˌfī-ər, -ˌfīr\ *n*

den·i·zen \'den-ə-zən\ *n* : INHABITANT; *esp* : a person, animal, or plant found or naturalized in a particular region or environment ⟨*denizens* of the forest⟩ [Middle French *denzein*, from Old French *denz* "within", from Late Latin *deintus*, from Latin *de-* + *intus* "within"]

de·nom·i·nate \di-'näm-ə-ˌnāt\ *vt* : to give a name to

de·nom·i·nate number \di-'näm-ə-nət-\ *n* : a number (as 7 in 7 *meters*) that specifies a quantity in terms of a unit of measurement

de·nom·i·na·tion \di-ˌnäm-ə-'nā-shən\ *n* **1** : an act of denominating **2** : NAME, DESIGNATION; *esp* : a general name for a class of things **3** : a religious body comprising a number of congregations with similar beliefs **4** : one of a series of related values each having a special name ⟨bills in $5 and $10 *denominations*⟩ — **de·nom·i·na·tion·al** \-shnəl, -shən-l\ *adj* — **de·nom·i·na·tion·al·ly** \-ē\ *adv*

de·nom·i·na·tion·al·ism \-shnəl-ˌiz-əm, -shən-l-ˌiz-\ *n* : devotion to the principles or interests of a denomination

\ə\ abut	\ng\ sing
\ər\ further	\ō\ bone
\a\ mat	\ȯ\ saw
\ā\ take	\ȯi\ coin
\ä\ cot, cart	\th\ thin
\au\ out	\th\ this
\ch\ chin	\ü\ food
\e\ pet	\u\ foot
\ē\ easy	\y\ yet
\g\ go	\yü\ few
\i\ tip	\yu\ cure
\ī\ life	\zh\ vision
\j\ job	

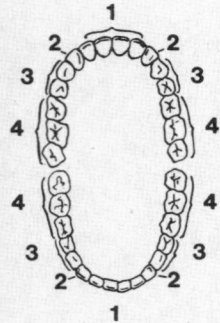

dentition 2: *top* upper jaw,
bottom lower jaw,
1 incisors, *2* canines,
3 premolars, *4* molars

de·nom·i·na·tive \di-'näm-nət-iv, -ə-nət-\ *adj* : derived from a noun or adjective 〈*denominative* verbs〉

de·nom·i·na·tor \di-'näm-ə-,nāt-ər\ *n* : the part of a fraction that is below the line signifying division and that in fractions with 1 as the numerator indicates into how many parts the unit is divided

de·no·ta·tion \,dē-nō-'tā-shən\ *n* **1** : an act or process of denoting **2** : MEANING; *esp* : a direct specific meaning as distinct from connotations **3** : a denoting term or label : NAME, SIGN

de·no·ta·tive \'dē-nō-,tāt-iv, di-'nōt-ət-iv\ *adj* **1** : denoting or tending to denote **2** : relating to denotation

de·note \di-'nōt\ *vt* **1** : to serve as an indication of 〈red flares *denoting* danger〉 **2** : to have the meaning of : MEAN, NAME 〈in the United States the word *corn denotes* Indian corn〉 □ SYN DENOTE and CONNOTE, when used of words, together equal *mean.* DENOTE implies all that strictly belongs to the definition of the word; CONNOTE implies all the ideas or emotions suggested by the word 〈home *denotes* the place where one lives, but it *connotes* the comforts, the privacy, and a whole range of experience one enjoys there〉

de·noue·ment \,dā-nü-'mäⁿ, -'nü-,\ *n* **1** : the final untangling of the conflicts or difficulties that make up the plot of a literary work **2** : a solution or working out especially of a complex or difficult situation [French *dénouement*, literally, "untying", derived from Old French *desnoer* "to untie", from *des-* "de-" + *noer* "to tie", from Latin *nodare*, from *nodus* "knot"]

de·nounce \di-'naúns\ *vt* **1** : to point out as deserving blame or punishment **2** : to inform against : ACCUSE **3** : to announce formally the ending of (as a treaty) [Old French *denoncier* "to proclaim", from Latin *denuntiare*, from *de-* + *nuntiare* "to report"] — **de·nounce·ment** \-mənt\ *n* — **de·nounc·er** *n*

de no·vo \di-'nō-vō, dā-\ *adv* : over again : ANEW [Latin]

dense \'dens\ *adj* **1** : marked by compactness or crowding together of parts 〈a *dense* forest〉 **2** : mentally dull **3** : having high opacity 〈*dense* fog〉 [Latin *densus*] SYN see STUPID — **dense·ly** *adv* — **dense·ness** *n*

den·si·ty \'den-sət-ē\ *n, pl* **-ties 1** : the quality or state of being dense **2** : the quantity of something per unit volume, unit area, or unit length: as **a** : the mass of a substance per unit volume 〈*density* expressed in grams per cubic centimeter〉 **b** : the average number of individuals or units in a unit of area or volume 〈population *density*〉 **3** : STUPIDITY 1 **4** : the degree of opacity of a translucent medium

¹dent \'dent\ *n* **1** : a hollow made by a blow or by pressure **2 a** : an impression or effect often having a weakening influence **b** : initial progress [Middle English, "blow", alteration of *dint*]

²dent *vb* **1** : to make a dent in or on **2** : to become marked by a dent

dent- *or* **denti-** *or* **dento-** *combining form* : tooth : teeth [Latin *dent-, dens* "tooth"]

¹den·tal \'dent-l\ *adj* **1** : of or relating to the teeth or to dentistry **2** : pronounced with the tip or blade of the tongue against or near the upper front teeth — **den·tal·ly** \-l-ē\ *adv*

²dental *n* : a dental consonant

dental floss *n* : a thread used to clean between the teeth

dental hygienist *n* : one who assists a dentist especially in cleaning teeth

den·tate \'den-,tāt\ *adj* : having pointed conical projections 〈a *dentate* margin of a leaf〉

den·til \'dent-l\ *n* : one of a series of small projecting rectangular blocks especially under a cornice [obsolete French *dentille*, from *dent* "tooth"]

dent corn *n* : an Indian corn having kernels that contain both hard and soft starch and that become indented at maturity

den·ti·cle \'dent-i-kəl\ *n* : a small conical pointed projection (as a tooth) [Latin *denticulus* "small tooth", from *dens* "tooth"]

den·ti·frice \'dent-ə-frəs\ *n* : a powder, paste, or liquid for cleaning the teeth [Latin *dentifricium*, from *dens* "tooth" + *fricare* "to rub"]

den·tine \'den-,tēn, den-'\ *also* **den·tin** \'dent-n\ *n* : a calcium-containing material like bone but harder and denser that composes the principal mass of a tooth — **den·tin·al** \den-'tēn-l, 'dent-n-əl\ *adj*

den·tist \'dent-əst\ *n* : one whose profession is the care and treatment of the teeth and gums and the fitting of false teeth

den·tist·ry \'dent-ə-strē\ *n* : the profession or practice of a dentist

den·ti·tion \den-'tish-ən\ *n* **1** : the development and cutting of teeth **2** : the number, kind, and arrangement of teeth (as of a person)

den·ture \'den-chər\ *n* **1** : a set of teeth **2** : an artificial replacement for one or more teeth; *esp* : a set of false teeth

de·nude \di-'nüd, -'nyüd\ *vt* : to strip of covering : lay bare 〈erosion that *denudes* the rocks of soil〉 — **de·nu·da·tion** \,dē-nü-'dā-shən, -nyü-; ,den-yü-'dā-\ *n* — **de·nu·da·tion·al** \-shnəl, -shən-l\ *adj* — **de·nud·er** \di-'nüd-ər, -'nyüd-\ *n*

de·nu·mer·a·ble \di-'nüm-rə-bəl, -'nyüm-, -ə-rə-\ *adj* : capable of being put into one-to-one correspondence with the positive integers — **de·nu·mer·a·bly** \-rə-blē\ *adv*

de·nun·ci·a·tion \di-,nən-sē-'ā-shən\ *n* : the act of denouncing; *esp* : a public accusation — **de·nun·ci·a·to·ry** \-'nən-sē-ə-,tōr-ē, -,tòr-\ *adj*

de·ny \di-'nī\ *vt* **de·nied; de·ny·ing 1** : to declare not to be true : CONTRADICT 〈*deny* a report〉 **2** : to refuse to acknowledge : DISOWN 〈*deny* one's faith〉 **3** : to refuse to grant 〈*deny* a request〉 **4** : to reject as false 〈*deny* a theory〉 [Old French *denier*, from Latin *denegare*, from *de-* + *negare* "to deny"] — **de·ny·ing·ly** \-'nī-ing-lē\ *adv*

de·o·dar \'dē-ə-,där\ *n* : an East Indian cedar valued as an ornamental and timber tree [Hindi *deodār*, from Sanskrit *devadāru*, literally, "timber of the gods"]

de·odor·ant \dē-'ōd-ə-rənt\ *n* : a preparation that eliminates or masks unpleasant odors — **deodorant** *adj*

de·odor·ize \dē-'ōd-ə-,rīz\ *vt* : to eliminate or prevent offensive odor of or in 〈*deodorize* a room〉 — **de·odor·iza·tion** \,dē-,ōd-ə-rə-'zā-shən\ *n* — **de·odor·iz·er** \dē-'ōd-ə-,rī-zər\ *n*

Deo vo·len·te \,dā-ō-və-'lent-ē, ,dē-\ : God being willing [Latin]

de·ox·i·dize \dē-'äk-sə-,dīz, 'dē-\ *vt* : to remove oxygen from — **de·ox·i·diz·er** *n*

de·oxy·gen·at·ed \-'äk-si-jə-,nāt-əd\ *adj* : having the hemoglobin in the reduced state

de·oxy·ri·bo·nu·cle·ic acid \,dē-,äk-sē-'rī-bō-nú-,klē-ik-, -nyú-, -,klā-\ *n* : DNA

de·oxy·ri·bose \dē-,äk-sē-'rī-,bōs\ *n* : a sugar that has five carbon atoms in the molecule and is a constituent of DNA

de·part \di-'pärt\ *vb* **1 a** : to go away or go away from : LEAVE **b** : DIE **2** : to turn aside : DEVIATE [Old French *departir* "to divide, go away", from *de-* "de-" + *partir* "to divide", from Latin *partire*, from *pars* "part"]

de·part·ed *adj* **1** : BYGONE **2** : no longer living

de·part·ment \di-'pärt-mənt\ *n* **1** : a distinct sphere : PROVINCE **2 a** : a major administrative division of a government or business **b** : a major territorial administrative division **c** : a division of a college or school giving instruction in a particular subject **d** : a section of a department store — **de·part·men·tal** \di-,pärt-'ment-l, ,dē-\ *adj* — **de·part·men·tal·ly** *adv*

de·part·men·tal·ize \di-,pärt-'ment-l-,īz, ,dē-\ *vt* : to divide into departments — **de·part·men·tal·iza·tion** \-,ment-l-ə-'zā-shən\ *n*

department store *n* : a store having separate departments for different kinds of goods

de·par·ture \di-'pär-chər\ *n* **1 a** : the act of going away **b** *archaic* : DEATH **2** : a setting out (as on a new course) **3** : DIVERGENCE 3

de·pend \di-'pend\ *vi* **1** : to be determined by or based on some action, condition, or variable ⟨success of the picnic will *depend* on the weather⟩ ⟨the value of the polynomial $x^2 + 2x + 2$ *depends* on the value of x⟩ **2** : to place reliance or trust ⟨you can *depend* on me⟩ **3** : to rely for support ⟨children *depend* on their parents⟩ **4** : to hang down ⟨a vine *depending* from a tree⟩ [Middle French *dependre*, from Latin *dependēre*, from *de-* + *pendēre* "to hang"]

de·pend·able \di-'pen-də-bəl\ *adj* : capable of being depended on : TRUSTWORTHY, RELIABLE — **de·pend·abil·i·ty** \-,pen-də-'bil-ət-ē\ *n* — **de·pend·ably** \-'pen-də-blē\ *adv*

de·pen·dence \di-'pen-dəns\ *n* **1** : the quality or state of being dependent; *esp* : the quality or state of being influenced by or subject to another **2** : RELIANCE, TRUST ⟨*dependence* on friends⟩ **3** : something on which one relies **4 a** : drug addiction **b** : HABITUATION 2

de·pen·den·cy \-dən-sē\ *n, pl* **-cies** **1** : DEPENDENCE 1, 4 **2** : something that is dependent on something else; *esp* : a territory under the jurisdiction of a nation but not formally annexed by it

¹de·pen·dent \di-'pen-dənt\ *adj* **1** : hanging down **2 a** : determined or conditioned by another **b** : relying on another for support ⟨*dependent* children⟩ **c** : subject to another's jurisdiction ⟨a *dependent* territory⟩ **3** : SUBORDINATE 3a — **de·pen·dent·ly** *adv*

²dependent *also* **de·pend·ant** *n* : one that is dependent; *esp* : a person who relies on another for support

de·pict \di-'pikt\ *vt* **1** : to represent by a picture **2** : to describe in words [Latin *depictus*, past participle of *depingere* "to depict", from *de-* + *pingere* "to paint"] — **de·pic·tion** \-'pik-shən\ *n*

dep·i·la·tion \,dep-ə-'lā-shən\ *n* : the removal of hair, wool, or bristles by chemical or mechanical methods [derived from Latin *depilare* "to remove hair from", from *de-* + *pilus* "hair"] — **dep·i·late** \'dep-ə-,lāt\ *vt*

de·pil·a·to·ry \di-'pil-ə-,tōr-ē, -,tȯr-\ *n, pl* **-ries** : a preparation for removing hair, wool, or bristles — **depilatory** *adj*

de·plane \'dē-'plān\ *vt* : to get off an airplane

de·plete \di-'plēt\ *vt* : to reduce in amount by using up : exhaust especially of strength or resources ⟨soil *depleted* of minerals⟩ ⟨a *depleted* treasury⟩ [Latin *deplēre*, from *de-* + *plēre* "to fill"] — **de·ple·tion** \-'plē-shən\ *n* — **de·ple·tive** \-'plēt-iv\ *adj*

de·plor·able \di-'plōr-ə-bəl, -'plȯr-\ *adj* **1** : deserving to be deplored : LAMENTABLE ⟨a *deplorable* accident⟩ **2** : very bad : WRETCHED ⟨*deplorable* conditions⟩ — **de·plor·able·ness** *n* — **de·plor·ably** \-blē\ *adv*

de·plore \di-'plōr, -'plȯr\ *vt* **1 a** : to feel or express grief for **b** : to regret strongly **2** : to consider unfortunate or deserving of disapproval [Latin *deplorare*, from *de-* + *plorare* "to wail"] — **de·plor·er** *n* — **de·plor·ing·ly** \-ing-lē\ *adv*

de·ploy \di-'plȯi\ *vb* : to spread out or place in position for some purpose ⟨troops *deployed* for battle⟩ [French *déployer*, from Latin *displicare* "to scatter", from *dis-* + *plicare* "to fold"] — **de·ploy·ment** \-mənt\ *n*

de·po·lar·ize \dē-'pō-lə-,rīz, 'dē-\ *vt* : to prevent, reduce, or remove polarization of (as a dry cell or the membrane of a nerve cell) — **de·po·lar·iza·tion** \,dē-,pō-lə-rə-'zā-shən\ *n* — **de·po·lar·iz·er** \dē-'pō-lə-,rī-zər, 'dē-\ *n*

¹de·po·nent \di-'pō-nənt\ *adj* : occurring with passive or middle voice forms but with active voice meaning ⟨*deponent* verbs in Latin and Greek⟩ [Late Latin *deponens*, from Latin *deponere* "to put down", from *de-* + *ponere* "to put"]

²deponent *n* **1** : a deponent verb **2** : one who gives evidence

de·pop·u·late \dē-'päp-yə-,lāt, 'dē-\ *vt* : to reduce greatly the population of (as a city or region) by destroying or driving away the inhabitants ⟨*depopulated* by a plague⟩ — **de·pop·u·la·tion** \,dē-,päp-yə-'lā-shən\ *n*

de·port \di-'pōrt, -'pȯrt\ *vt* **1** : CONDUCT, BEHAVE ⟨*deported* themselves with dignity⟩ **2** : to force (an alien whose presence is unlawful or harmful) to leave a country [Middle French *deporter*, from Latin *deportare* "to carry away", from *de-* + *portare* "to carry"] — **de·por·ta·tion** \,dē-,pōr-'tā-shən, -,pȯr-\ *n* — **de·por·tee** \,dē-,pōr-'tē, -,pȯr-\ *n*

de·port·ment \di-'pōrt-mənt, -'pȯrt-\ *n* : manner of conducting oneself : BEHAVIOR

de·pose \di-'pōz\ *vb* **1** : to remove from a throne or other high position **2** : to testify under oath or by affidavit [Old French *deposer*, derived from Latin *deponere* "to put down", from *de-* + *ponere* "to put"]

¹de·pos·it \di-'päz-ət\ *vb* **1** : to place for safekeeping; *esp* : to put money in a bank **2** : to give as a pledge that a purchase will be made or a service used ⟨*deposit* $10 on a new bicycle⟩ **3** : to lay down : PLACE, PUT ⟨*deposit* a parcel on a table⟩ **4** : to let fall or sink ⟨sand and silt *deposited* by a flood⟩ **5** : to become deposited : SETTLE [Latin *depositus*, past participle of *deponere* "to put down"] — **de·pos·i·tor** \-'päz-ət-ər, -'päz-tər\ *n*

²deposit *n* **1** : the state of being deposited ⟨money on *deposit*⟩ **2 a** : something placed for safekeeping; *esp* : money deposited in a bank **b** : money given as a pledge **3** : an act of depositing **4** : something laid or thrown down ⟨a *deposit* of silt left by the flood⟩ **5** : an accumulation of mineral matter (as iron ore, oil, or gas) in nature

de·pos·i·tary \di-'päz-ə-,ter-ē\ *n, pl* **-tar·ies** **1** : a person to whom something is entrusted **2** : DEPOSITORY 2

dep·o·si·tion \,dep-ə-'zish-ən, ,dē-pə-\ *n* **1** : the act of deposing a person from high office ⟨the *deposition* of the dictator⟩ **2** : a statement especially in writing made under oath **3** : the action or process of depositing ⟨the *deposition* of silt by a stream⟩ **4** : material deposited : SEDIMENT 2 — **dep·o·si·tion·al** \-'zish-nəl, -'zish-ən-l\ *adj*

de·pos·i·to·ry \di-'päz-ə-,tōr-ē, -,tȯr-\ *n, pl* **-ries** **1** : DEPOSITARY 1 **2** : a place where something is deposited especially for safekeeping

de·pot \ **1 & 2** are 'dep-,ō *also* 'dē-,pō, **3** is 'dē-,pō *sometimes* 'dep-,ō\ *n* **1** : a place where military supplies are kept or where troops are assembled and trained **2** : a place of deposit for goods : STOREHOUSE **3** : a building for railroad or bus passengers or freight : STATION [French *dépôt*, derived from Latin *deponere* "to put down"]

de·prave \di-'prāv\ *vt* : to make bad : corrupt the morals of : PERVERT [Middle French *depraver* "to speak ill of", from Latin *depravare* "to pervert", from *de-* + *pravus* "crooked, bad"] SYN see DEBASE

de·praved \-'prāvd\ *adj* : marked by corruption, unwholesomeness, or evil — **de·praved·ly** \-'prā-vəd-lē, -'prāv-dlē\ *adv* — **de·praved·ness** \-'prā-vəd-nəs, -'prāvd-nəs\ *n*

de·prav·i·ty \di-'prav-ət-ē\ *n, pl* **-ties** **1** : the quality or state of being depraved **2** : a depraved act or practice

dep·re·cate \'dep-ri-,kāt\ *vt* **1** : to express disapproval of **2** : DEPRECIATE 2 [Latin *deprecari* "to avert by prayer", from *de-* + *precari* "to pray"] — **dep·re·cat·ing·ly** \-,kāt-ing-lē\ *adv* — **dep·re·ca·tion** \,dep-ri-'kā-shən\ *n*

dep·re·ca·to·ry \'dep-ri-kə-,tōr-ē, -,tȯr-\ *adj* **1** : seeking to avert disapproval : APOLOGETIC **2** : serving to deprecate

de·pre·ci·ate \di-'prē-shē-,āt\ *vb* **1** : to lower the price or value of **2** : to represent as of little value : DISPARAGE **3** : to fall in value [Late Latin *depretiare*, from Latin *de-* + *pretium* "price"] — **de·pre·cia·tive** \-shē-

\ə\ abut		\ng\ sing	
\ər\ further		\ō\ bone	
\a\ mat		\ȯ\ saw	
\ā\ take		\ȯi\ coin	
\ä\ cot, cart		\th\ thin	
\au̇\ out		\th\ this	
\ch\ chin		\ü\ food	
\e\ pet		\u̇\ foot	
\ē\ easy		\y\ yet	
\g\ go		\yü\ few	
\i\ tip		\yu̇\ cure	
\ī\ life		\zh\ vision	
\j\ job			

derby 3

de·pre·ci·a·tion \di-ˌprē-shē-ˈā-shən\ n **1** : a decline in the purchasing power or exchange value of money **2** : the act of belittling : DISPARAGEMENT **3** : a decline (as from age or wear and tear) in the value of something

dep·re·da·tion \ˌdep-rə-ˈdā-shən\ n : the action or an act of plundering or laying waste : RAVAGING, PILLAGING [Late Latin *depraedatio*, from *depraedari* "to plunder", from Latin *de-* + *praedari* "to plunder"] — **dep·re·date** \ˈdep-rə-ˌdāt\ vb

de·press \di-ˈpres\ vt **1 a** : to press down **b** : to cause to sink to a lower position **2** : to lessen the activity or strength of **3** : to make sad or downcast : DISCOURAGE **4** : to lessen in price or value : DEPRECIATE [Middle French *depresser* "to repress", from Latin *depressus*, past participle of *deprimere* "to press down", from *de-* + *premere* "to press"] — **de·press·ible** \-ə-bəl\ adj — **de·press·ing·ly** \-ing-lē\ adv □ SYN DEPRESS, OPPRESS mean to press or weigh down heavily. DEPRESS stresses the resulting state of inactivity or dullness or dejection ⟨*depressed* by failure⟩ OPPRESS emphasizes the burden imposed that may or may not be successfully borne or withstood ⟨*oppressed* by the hot weather⟩

de·pres·sant \di-ˈpres-nt\ n : one that depresses; *esp* : an agent (as alcohol) that reduces activity of bodily functions — **depressant** adj

de·pressed adj **1 a** : low in spirits : SAD **b** : affected with psychological depression **2** : FLATTENED; *esp* : lying flat or prostrate ⟨a *depressed* shrub⟩ **3** : suffering from economic depression

de·pres·sion \di-ˈpresh-ən\ n **1** : an act of depressing : a state of being depressed: as **a** : a pressing down : LOWERING **b** : DEJECTION; *also* : a mental disorder marked by sadness, inactivity, difficulty in thinking and concentration, and feelings of dejection **c** (1) : a reduction in activity, amount, quality, or force (2) : a lowering of vitality or functional activity **2** : a depressed place or part : HOLLOW **3** : a region of low barometric pressure **4** : a period of low general economic activity with widespread unemployment SYN see MELANCHOLY

de·pres·sive \-ˈpres-iv\ adj : of or relating to psychological depression

de·pres·sor \-ˈpres-ər\ n : one that depresses: as **a** : a muscle that draws down a part — compare LEVATOR **b** : a device for pressing a part down or aside

de·pres·sur·ize \dē-ˈpresh-ə-ˌrīz, ˈdē-\ vt : to release (as a pressurized aircraft) from pressure

de·prive \di-ˈprīv\ vt **1** : to take something away from ⟨*deprive* a person of citizenship⟩ **2** : to stop from having something ⟨*deprived* of a college education by lack of funds⟩ [Medieval Latin *deprivare*, from Latin *de-* + *privare* "to deprive"] — **de·pri·va·tion** \ˌdep-rə-ˈvā-shən, dē-ˌprī-\ n

depth \ˈdepth\ n, pl **depths** \ˈdepts, ˈdeps, ˈdepths\ **1 a** (1) : something that is deep : a deep place or part (2) : ABYSS **b** : a part that is far from the outside or surface ⟨the *depths* of the woods⟩ **c** (1) : the middle of a time ⟨the *depth* of winter⟩ (2) : an extreme state (as of despair) (3) : the worst part **2** : the distance from top to bottom or from front to back **3** : the quality of being deep **4** : degree of intensity ⟨the *depth* of a color⟩ [Middle English, probably from *dep* "deep"] — **depth·less** \ˈdepth-ləs\ adj

depth charge n : an explosive device for underwater use especially against submarines that is designed to explode at a predetermined depth — called also **depth bomb**

dep·u·ta·tion \ˌdep-yə-ˈtā-shən\ n **1** : the act of appointing a deputy **2** : a group of people appointed to represent others

de·pute \di-ˈpyüt\ vt : DELEGATE [Middle French *deputer* "to appoint", from Late Latin *deputare* "to assign", from Latin *de-* + *putare* "to consider"]

dep·u·tize \ˈdep-yə-ˌtīz\ vb **1** : to appoint as deputy **2** : to act as deputy

dep·u·ty \ˈdep-yət-ē\ n, pl **-ties** **1** : a person appointed to act for or in place of another **2** : an assistant empowered to act as a substitute in the absence of his or her superior **3** : a member of a lower house of a legislative assembly — **deputy** adj

de·rail \di-ˈrāl\ vb : to leave or cause to leave the rails — **de·rail·ment** \-mənt\ n

de·rail·leur \di-ˈrā-lər\ n : a mechanism for shifting gears on a bicycle that operates by moving the chain from one set of exposed gears to another [French *dérailleur*, from *dérailler* "to throw off the track", from *dé-* "de-" + *rail* "rail", from English]

de·range \di-ˈrānj\ vt **1** : to put out of order : DISARRANGE, UPSET **2** : to disturb the operation or functions of **3** : to make insane [French *déranger*, from Old French *de-* "de-" + *reng* "place", of Germanic origin] — **de·range·ment** \-mənt\ n

der·by \ˈdər-bē, *especially British* ˈdär-\ n, pl **derbies** **1** : any of several horse races held annually and usually restricted to 3-year-olds **2** : a race or contest open to all comers **3** : a man's stiff felt hat with dome-shaped crown and narrow brim [Edward Stanley, died 1834, 12th earl of *Derby*]

¹der·e·lict \ˈder-ə-ˌlikt\ adj **1** : abandoned by the owner or occupant ⟨a *derelict* ship⟩ **2** : NEGLECTFUL, NEGLIGENT [Latin *derelictus*, past participle of *derelinquere* "to abandon", from *de-* + *relinquere* "to leave, relinquish"]

²derelict n **1** : something voluntarily abandoned; *esp* : a ship abandoned on the high seas **2** : a person without apparent means of support : VAGRANT

der·e·lic·tion \ˌder-ə-ˈlik-shən\ n **1** : the act of abandoning : the state of being abandoned ⟨the *dereliction* of a cause by its leaders⟩ **2** : neglect of one's duty : DELINQUENCY

de·ride \di-ˈrīd\ vt : to laugh at scornfully : make fun of [Latin *deridēre*, from *de-* + *ridēre* "to laugh"] SYN see RIDICULE — **de·rid·er** n — **de·rid·ing·ly** \-ˈrīd-ing-lē\ adv

de ri·gueur \də-ˌrē-ˈgər\ adj : prescribed or required by fashion, etiquette, or custom : PROPER [French]

de·ri·sion \di-ˈrizh-ən\ n **1** : scornful or contemptuous ridicule **2** : an object of ridicule [Middle French, from Late Latin *derisio*, from Latin *deridēre* "to deride"]

de·ri·sive \di-ˈrī-siv\ adj : expressing or characterized by derision ⟨*derisive* laughter⟩ — **de·ri·sive·ly** adv — **de·ri·sive·ness** n

de·ri·so·ry \di-ˈrī-sə-rē, -zə-\ adj : DERISIVE

der·i·va·tion \ˌder-ə-ˈvā-shən\ n **1 a** : the formation (as by the addition of an affix) of a word from an earlier word or root **b** : ETYMOLOGY 1 **2 a** : a point of origin : SOURCE **b** : development from a source : DESCENT **c** : an act or process of deriving — **der·i·va·tion·al** \-shnəl, -shən-l\ adj

¹de·riv·a·tive \di-ˈriv-ət-iv\ adj **1** : formed by derivation **2** : made up of or characterized by elements derived from something else ⟨*derivative* poetry⟩ — **de·riv·a·tive·ly** adv

²derivative n **1** : a word formed by derivation **2** : something derived **3** : a substance that can be made from another substance in one or more steps ⟨a *derivative* of coal tar⟩

de·rive \di-ˈrīv\ vb **de·rived**; **de·riv·ing** **1 a** : to receive or obtain from a source **b** : to obtain (as a chemical substance) from a parent substance **2** : to trace the origin, descent, or derivation of **3** : to come from a certain source **4** : INFER 1, DEDUCE [Middle French *deriver*, from Latin *derivare*, from *de-* + *rivus* "stream"] — **de·riv·able** \di-ˈrī-və-bəl\ adj

-derm \ˌdərm\ n *combining form* : skin : covering : layer ⟨ecto*derm*⟩ [Greek *derma* "skin", from *derein* "to skin"]

der·mal \'dər-məl\ *adj* : of or relating to the dermis or epidermis : CUTANEOUS

dermat- *or* **dermato-** *combining form* : skin ⟨*dermato*logy⟩ [Greek *dermat-, derma*]

der·ma·ti·tis \ˌdər-mə-'tīt-əs\ *n* : inflammation of the skin

der·ma·tol·o·gy \ˌdər-mə-'täl-ə-jē\ *n* : a branch of science dealing with the skin — **der·ma·to·log·ic** \-'mət-l-'äj-ik\ *or* **der·ma·to·log·i·cal** \-i-kəl\ *adj* — **der·ma·tol·o·gist** \ˌdər-mə-'täl-ə-jəst\ *n*

der·mes·tid \dər-'mes-təd\ *n* : any of a family of beetles that are very destructive to dried meat, fur, wool, and insect collections [derived from Greek *dermēstēs,* a leather-eating worm, literally, "skin-eater"] — **dermestid** *adj*

der·mis \'dər-məs\ *n* : the sensitive vascular inner layer of the skin — called also *corium* [New Latin, from Greek *derma* "skin"]

der·o·gate \'der-ə-ˌgāt\ *vb* **1** : to cause to seem inferior : BELITTLE **2** : to take away a part so as to impair : DETRACT [Latin *derogare* "to annul (a law), detract", from *de-* + *rogare* "to ask, propose (a law)"] — **der·o·ga·tion** \ˌder-ə-'gā-shən\ *n* — **de·rog·a·tive** \di-'räg-ət-iv, 'der-ə-ˌgāt-\ *adj*

de·rog·a·to·ry \di-'räg-ə-ˌtōr-ē, -ˌtȯr-\ *adj* : intended to lower the reputation of a person or thing : DISPARAGING — **de·rog·a·to·ri·ly** \-ˌräg-ə-'tōr-ə-lē, -'tȯr-\ *adv*

der·rick \'der-ik\ *n* **1** : any of various machines for moving or hoisting heavy weights by means of a long beam fitted with pulleys and ropes or cables **2** : a framework or tower built over a deep drill hole (as of an oil well) for supporting machinery [obsolete *derrick* "hangman, gallows", from *Derick,* name of a 17th century English hangman] □ ORIGIN In the reign of Queen Elizabeth I of England an executioner named *Derick* achieved some notoriety because of his position. The common people therefore named the gallows at London after Derick the hangman. This usage spread, and throughout the 17th century *derrick* was a term for both a hangman and a gallows. These senses eventually died out, but in the next century *derrick* began to be used for a hoisting apparatus resembling a gallows. Subsequently, *derrick* has become a term for a framework or tower over an oil well.

der·ri·ere *or* **der·ri·ère** \ˌder-ē-'eər\ *n* : BUTTOCK 2 [French *derrière,* derived from Latin *de retro* "behind"]

der·ring–do \ˌder-ing-'dü\ *n* : daring action : DARING [Middle English *dorring don* "daring to do"]

der·rin·ger \'der-ən-jər\ *n* : a short-barreled pocket pistol [Henry *Deringer,* 19th century American inventor]

der·ris \'der-əs\ *n* : any of a large genus of tropical Old World shrubs and woody vines of the pea family including commercial sources of rotenone; *also* : a derris insecticide [Greek, "skin"]

der·vish \'dər-vish\ *n* : a member of a Muslim religious order noted for devotional exercises (as bodily movements leading to a trance) [Turkish *derviş,* literally, "beggar", from Persian *darvēsh*]

de·sa·li·nate \dē-'sal-ə-ˌnāt\ *vt* : DESALT — **de·sa·li·na·tion** \ˌdē-ˌsal-ə-'nā-shən\ *n* — **de·sa·li·na·tor** \dē-'sal-ə-ˌnāt-ər\ *n*

de·salt \dē-'sȯlt, 'dē-\ *vt* : to remove salt from — **de·salt·er** *n*

¹des·cant \'des-ˌkant\ *n* **1** : a melody sung above a principal melody **2** : the art of composing or singing part music; *also* : a piece of music so composed **3** : a strain of melody : SONG **4** : a discourse or comment on a subject [Medieval Latin *discantus,* from Latin *dis-* + *cantus* "song"]

²des·cant \'des-ˌkant, des-'\ *vi* **1** : to sing or play a descant **2** : to talk or write at length

de·scend \di-'send\ *vb* **1 a** : to pass from a higher to a lower place or level **b** : to pass, move, or climb down or down along **2 a** : to come down from a stock or source : DERIVE **b** : to pass by inheritance **c** : to pass by transmission **3** : to incline, lead, or extend downward **4** : to swoop down in a sudden attack **5** : to sink in status or condition [Old French *descendre,* from Latin *descendere,* from *de-* + *scandere* "to climb"] — **de·scend·ible** \-'sen-də-bəl\ *adj*

¹de·scen·dant *or* **de·scen·dent** \di-'sen-dənt\ *adj* **1** : moving or directed downward **2** : proceeding from an ancestor or source

²descendant *or* **descendent** *n* **1** : one descended from another or from a common stock **2** : one deriving directly from a precursor or prototype

de·scent \di-'sent\ *n* **1** : the act or process of descending **2** : a downward step (as in status or value) : DECLINE **3** : derivation from an ancestor : BIRTH, LINEAGE **4 a** : an inclination downward : SLOPE **b** : a descending way (as a downgrade or stairway) **5** : a sudden hostile raid or assault

de·scribe \di-'skrīb\ *vt* **1** : to represent or give an account of in words **2** : to trace or traverse the outline of ⟨*describe* a circle⟩ [Latin *describere,* from *de-* + *scribere* "to write"] — **de·scrib·able** \-'skrī-bə-bəl\ *adj* — **de·scrib·er** *n*

de·scrip·tion \di-'skrip-shən\ *n* **1 a** : an act or instance of describing **b** : an account that presents a picture to a person who reads or hears it **2** : KIND, SORT ⟨people of every *description*⟩ [Latin *descriptio,* from *describere* "to describe"]

de·scrip·tive \-'skrip-tiv\ *adj* : serving to describe — **de·scrip·tive·ly** *adv* — **de·scrip·tive·ness** *n*

de·scry \di-'skrī\ *vt* **de·scried; de·scry·ing 1** : to catch sight of **2** : to discover or detect by observation or investigation [Old French *descrier* "to proclaim, decry"]

des·e·crate \'des-i-ˌkrāt\ *vt* : to violate the sanctity of : PROFANE — **des·e·crat·er** *or* **des·e·cra·tor** \-ˌkrāt-ər\ *n* — **des·e·cra·tion** \ˌdes-i-'krā-shən\ *n* [*de-* + -*secrate* (as in *consecrate*)]

de·seg·re·gate \dē-'seg-ri-ˌgāt, 'dē-\ *vb* : to eliminate segregation in or from — **de·seg·re·ga·tion** \dē-ˌseg-ri-'gā-shən\ *n*

de·sen·si·tize \dē-'sen-sə-ˌtīz, 'dē-\ *vt* : to make (an individual) insensitive or nonreactive to a sensitizing agent (as pollen) — **de·sen·si·ti·za·tion** \dē-ˌsen-sət-ə-'zā-shən\ *n* — **de·sen·si·tiz·er** *n*

¹des·ert \'dez-ərt\ *n* : an arid barren tract incapable of supporting a considerable population without an artificial water supply [Old French, from Late Latin *desertum,* from Latin *deserere* "to desert"]

²des·ert \'dez-ərt\ *adj* : of, relating to, or resembling a desert; *esp* : being barren and uninhabited ⟨a *desert* island⟩

³de·sert \di-'zərt\ *n* **1** : worthiness of reward or punishment ⟨rewarded according to their *deserts*⟩ **2** : a just reward or punishment [Old French *deserte,* from *deservir* "to deserve"]

⁴de·sert \di-'zərt\ *vb* **1** : to withdraw from : LEAVE **2** : to leave in the lurch : FORSAKE **3** : to fail one in time of need **4** : to quit one's post without permission especially with the intent to remain away permanently [French *déserter,* derived from Latin *deserere* "to desert", from *de-* + *serere* "to join together"] SYN see ABANDON — **de·sert·er** *n*

de·ser·tion \di-'zər-shən\ *n* **1** : an act of deserting; *esp* : the abandonment of a person (as a wife or child) to whom one has legal and moral duties and obligations **2** : a state of being deserted or forsaken : DESOLATION

de·serve \di-'zərv\ *vb* : to be worthy of ⟨*deserves* another chance⟩ [Old French *deservir,* from Latin *deservire* "to serve zealously", from *de-* + *servire* "to serve"] — **de·serv·er** *n*

de·serv·ed·ly \di-'zər-vəd-lē\ *adv* : according to merit

deserving *adj* : MERITORIOUS, WORTHY

des·ha·bille *variant of* DISHABILLE

des·ic·cant \'des-i-kənt\ *n* : a drying agent

derrick 2

\ə\ abut	\ng\ sing
\ər\ further	\ō\ bone
\a\ mat	\ȯ\ saw
\ā\ take	\ȯi\ coin
\ä\ cot, cart	\th\ thin
\au̇\ out	\th\ this
\ch\ chin	\ü\ food
\e\ pet	\u̇\ foot
\ē\ easy	\y\ yet
\g\ go	\yü\ few
\i\ tip	\yu̇\ cure
\ī\ life	\zh\ vision
\j\ job	

des·ic·cate \-,kāt\ *vb* **1** : to dry up or become dried up **2** : to preserve (a food) by drying : DEHYDRATE [Latin *desiccare,* from *de-* + *siccare* "to dry", from *siccus* "dry"] — **des·ic·ca·tion** \,des-i-'kā-shən\ *n* — **des·ic·ca·tor** \'des-i-,kāt-ər\ *n*

de·sid·er·a·tum \di-,sid-ə-'rät-əm, -,zid-, -'rāt-\ *n, pl* **-ta** \-ə\ : something sought for or aimed at [Latin]

¹de·sign \di-'zīn\ *vt* **1** : to conceive and plan out in the mind **2 a** : to have as a purpose or destiny : INTEND **b** : to devise for a specific function or end **3 a** : to make a pattern or sketch of **b** : to conceive and draw the plans for ⟨*design* an airplane⟩ [Middle French *designer,* from Latin *designare,* from *de-* + *signare* "to mark, mark out"] — **de·sign·er** *n*

²design *n* **1** : a project or scheme in which means to an end are laid down **2 a** : a planned purpose or intention ⟨my *design* is to write a trilogy⟩ **b** : goal-directed planning **3 a** : a secret project or scheme : PLOT **b** *pl* : aggressive or evil intent — used with *on* or *against* **4** : a sketch or plan showing the main features of something to be done **5** : the arrangement of elements that make up a structure or a work of art **6** : a decorative pattern SYN see INTENTION, PLAN

¹des·ig·nate \'dez-ig-,nāt, -nət\ *adj* : chosen for an office but not yet installed ⟨ambassador *designate*⟩

²des·ig·nate \-,nāt\ *vt* **1** : to mark or point out : INDICATE **2** : to appoint or choose by name for a special purpose ⟨*designate* someone as supervisor⟩ **3** : to call by a name or title [Latin *designare* "to design, designate"] — **des·ig·na·tive** \-,nāt-iv\ *adj* — **des·ig·na·tor** \-,nāt-ər\ *n* — **des·ig·na·to·ry** \-nə-,tōr-ē, -,tor-\ *adj*

designated hitter *n* : a baseball player designated at the start of a game to bat in place of the pitcher without causing the pitcher to be removed from the game

des·ig·na·tion \,dez-ig-'nā-shən\ *n* **1** : the act of designating or identifying **2** : a distinguishing name, sign, or title **3** : appointment to or selection for an office, post, or service

de·sign·ed·ly \di-'zī-nəd-lē\ *adv* : INTENTIONALLY, PURPOSELY ⟨came late *designedly*⟩

designer drug *n* : a synthetic version of a drug (as heroin) that is produced with a slightly altered molecular structure to avoid having it classified as an illicit drug

de·sign·ing *adj* : CRAFTY, SCHEMING

de·sir·able \di-'zī-rə-bəl\ *adj* **1** : having pleasing qualities or properties : ATTRACTIVE ⟨a *desirable* location⟩ **2** : worth seeking or doing as advantageous, beneficial, or wise ⟨*desirable* legislation⟩ — **de·sir·abil·i·ty** \-,zī-rə-'bil-ət-ē\ *n* — **de·sir·able·ness** \-'zī-rə-bəl-nəs\ *n* — **de·sir·ably** \-blē\ *adv*

¹de·sire \di-'zīr\ *vb* **1** : to long for : wish for earnestly ⟨*desire* peace⟩ **2** : to express a wish for : REQUEST ⟨the librarian *desires* us to return the books⟩ **3** : to have desire ⟨you can, if you *desire,* stay here⟩ [Old French *desirer,* from Latin *desiderare,* from *de-* + *sider-, sidus* "star"] □ SYN WISH, WANT: DESIRE usually emphasizes ardor and sometimes striving; WISH, less formal than DESIRE, often connotes longing for the unattainable; WANT may stress need or lack but is often used instead of WISH ⟨they *want* (or *wish*) to leave early⟩ ⟨do you *want* (or *wish*) tea or coffee?⟩

²desire *n* **1** : a strong wish : LONGING **2** : an expressed wish : REQUEST **3** : something desired

de·sir·ous \di-'zīr-əs\ *adj* : eagerly wishing : DESIRING ⟨*desirous* of an invitation⟩ — **de·sir·ous·ly** *adv*

de·sist \di-'zist, -'sist\ *vi* : to cease to proceed or act [Middle French *desister,* from Latin *desistere,* from *de-* + *sistere* "to stand, stop"] SYN see STOP

desk \'desk\ *n* **1 a** : a table, frame, or case with a flat or sloping surface especially for writing and reading **b** : a counter at which a person performs his or her duties **c** : a music stand **2** : a specialized division of an organization (as a newspaper) ⟨city *desk*⟩ [Medieval Latin *desca,* from Italian *desco* "table", from Latin *discus* "dish, disc"]

desk·top \'desk-,täp\ *adj* : of a size that can be conveniently used on a desk or table ⟨*desktop* computers⟩

des·mid \'dez-məd\ *n* : any of numerous one-celled or colonial green algae (order Zygnematales) [Greek *desmos* "bond, ligature"]

¹des·o·late \'des-ə-lət, 'dez-\ *adj* **1** : lacking inhabitants and visitors : DESERTED **2** : disconsolate from being left alone **3 a** : showing the effects of abandonment and neglect : DILAPIDATED **b** : lacking signs of life : BARREN ⟨a *desolate* landscape⟩ **c** : lacking warmth, comfort, or hope : GLOOMY [Latin *desolatus,* past participle of *desolare* "to abandon", from *de-* + *solus* "alone"] SYN see SOLITARY — **des·o·late·ly** *adv* — **des·o·late·ness** *n*

²des·o·late \-,lāt\ *vt* : to make desolate : **a** : to lay waste **b** : to make miserable

des·o·la·tion \,des-ə-'lā-shən, ,dez-\ *n* **1** : the action of desolating **2** : the condition of being desolated : DEVASTATION, RUIN **3** : a barren wasteland **4 a** : GRIEF 1, SADNESS **b** : LONELINESS

des·oxy·ri·bo·nu·cle·ic acid \de-,zäk-sē-'rī-bō-nu-,klē-ik-, -nyu-, -,klā-\ *n* : DNA

¹de·spair \di-'spaər, -'speər\ *vi* : to lose all hope or confidence [Middle French *desperer,* from Latin *desperare,* from *de-* + *sperare* "to hope"]

²despair *n* **1** : utter loss of hope **2** : a cause of hopelessness SYN see DESPONDENCY

de·spair·ing *adj* : given to, arising from, or marked by despair — **de·spair·ing·ly** \-ing-lē\ *adv*

des·patch \dis-'patch\ *variant of* DISPATCH

des·per·a·do \,des-pə-'räd-ō, -'rād-\ *n, pl* **-does** *or* **-dos** : a bold or reckless criminal [probably from *desperate*]

des·per·ate \'des-pə-rət, -prət\ *adj* **1** : being beyond or almost beyond hope ⟨a *desperate* illness⟩ **2** : reckless because of despair : RASH ⟨a *desperate* attempt⟩ **3** : extremely intense : OVERPOWERING ⟨*desperate* poverty⟩ [Latin *desperatus,* past participle of *desperare* "to despair"] — **des·per·ate·ly** *adv* — **des·per·ate·ness** *n*

des·per·a·tion \,des-pə-'rā-shən\ *n* **1** : a loss of hope and surrender to misery or dread **2** : a state of hopelessness leading to extreme recklessness SYN see DESPONDENCY

de·spi·ca·ble \di-'spik-ə-bəl, 'des-,pik-\ *adj* : deserving to be despised ⟨a *despicable* traitor⟩ [Late Latin *despicabilis,* from Latin *despicari* "to despise"] SYN see CONTEMPTIBLE — **de·spi·ca·ble·ness** *n* — **de·spi·ca·bly** \-blē\ *adv*

de·spise \di-'spīz\ *vt* **1** : to look down on with contempt or scorn ⟨*despised* liars⟩ **2** : to regard as negligible, worthless, or distasteful [Old French *despis-,* stem of *despire* "to despise", from Latin *despicere,* from *de-* + *specere* "to look"] — **de·spis·er** *n* □ SYN SCORN, DISDAIN, CONTEMN: DESPISE may cover a range of feeling from indifferent disdain to active loathing; SCORN suggests either a lively and indignant or a profound and passionate contempt; DISDAIN implies an arrogant or haughty aversion to what is regarded as unworthy; CONTEMN suggests vehement condemnation of a person or thing.

¹de·spite \di-'spīt\ *n* **1** : the feeling or attitude of despising : CONTEMPT **2** : MALICE, SPITE **3 a** : an act of contempt or defiance **b** : HARM 1, INJURY [Old French *despit,* from Latin *despectus,* from *despicere* "to despise"] — **in despite of** : in spite of

²despite *prep* : in spite of ⟨walked to town *despite* the rain⟩

de·spite·ful \di-'spīt-fəl\ *adj* : expressing malice or hate — **de·spite·ful·ly** \-fə-lē\ *adv* — **de·spite·ful·ness** *n*

de·spoil \di-'spoil\ *vt* : to strip of belongings, possessions, or value : PLUNDER, PILLAGE — **de·spoil·er** *n* — **de·spoil·ment** \-'spoil-mənt\ *n*

de·spo·li·a·tion \di-,spō-lē-'ā-shən\ *n* : the act of despoiling : the state of being despoiled

¹de·spond \di-'spänd\ *vi* : to become discouraged or disheartened [Latin *despondēre* "to give up, despond", from *de-* + *spondēre* "to promise solemnly"]

²despond *n* : DESPONDENCY

de·spon·den·cy \di-'spän-dən-sē\ *n* : the state of being despondent : DEJECTION, DISCOURAGEMENT □ SYN DESPAIR, DESPERATION: DESPONDENCY may imply a temporary mood of depression and apathy; DESPAIR implies utter loss of hope and suggests a final ceasing of effort or resistance; DESPERATION implies an urgency that drives one to any action offering immediate success regardless of consequences.

de·spon·dent \-dənt\ *adj* : feeling extreme discouragement, dejection, or depression — **de·spon·dent·ly** *adv*

des·pot \'des-pət, -,pät\ *n* 1 : a ruler with absolute power and authority 2 : a person exercising power abusively, oppressively, or tyrannously [Greek *despotēs* "master, lord"] — **des·pot·ic** \des-'pät-ik\ *adj* — **des·pot·i·cal·ly** \-i-kə-lē, -klē\ *adv*

des·po·tism \'des-pə-,tiz-əm\ *n* 1 **a** : rule by a despot : TYRANNY **b** : despotic exercise of power 2 : a state or a system of government in which the ruler has unlimited power

des·sert \di-'zərt\ *n* : a course of sweet food, fruit, or cheese served at the close of a meal [Middle French, from *desservir* "to clear the table", from *des-* "de-" + *servir* "to serve"]

des·ti·na·tion \,des-tə-'nā-shən\ *n* 1 : an act of appointing, setting aside for a purpose, or predetermining 2 : the purpose for which something is destined 3 : a place which is the goal of a journey or to which something is sent

des·tine \'des-tən\ *vt* 1 : to determine the fate of in advance ⟨a plan *destined* to fail⟩ 2 : to designate, assign, or dedicate in advance ⟨*destined* their children for college⟩ 3 : to be bound or directed ⟨a ship *destined* for New York⟩ [Old French *destiner,* from Latin *destinare*]

des·ti·ny \'des-tə-nē\ *n, pl* **-nies** 1 : something to which a person or thing is destined : FORTUNE 2 : a predetermined course of events often held to be an irresistible power or agency SYN see FATE

des·ti·tute \'des-tə-,tüt, -,tyüt\ *adj* 1 : lacking something needed or desirable ⟨*destitute* of common sense⟩ 2 : extremely poor : suffering great want ⟨a *destitute* family⟩ [Latin *destitutus,* past participle of *destituere* "to abandon, deprive", from *de-* + *statuere* "to set up"] — **des·ti·tute·ness** *n*

des·ti·tu·tion \,des-tə-'tü-shən, -'tyü-\ *n* : the state of being destitute; *esp* : extreme poverty

de·stroy \di-'stròi\ *vb* 1 : to ruin the structure, organic existence, or condition of ⟨a house *destroyed* by fire⟩ 2 : KILL ⟨have a sick animal *destroyed*⟩ [Old French *destruire,* from Latin *destruere,* from *de-* + *struere* "to build"] □ SYN DEMOLISH, ANNIHILATE: DESTROY implies any force that wrecks, kills, annihilates, or tears down or apart ⟨*destroy* a friendship by deceit⟩ DEMOLISH implies a pulling or smashing to pieces or a tearing down to the point of ruin ⟨*demolish* a building⟩ ANNIHILATE suggests destruction so complete as to make any restoration impossible ⟨*annihilate* a city by nuclear attack⟩

de·stroy·er \-'stròi-ər, -'stròir\ *n* 1 : a destroying agent or agency 2 : a small fast warship armed with guns, depth charges, torpedoes, and sometimes guided missiles

destroyer escort *n* : a warship similar to but smaller than a destroyer

de·struct \di-'strəkt\ *n* : the deliberate destruction of a rocket after launching

de·struc·ti·ble \di-'strək-tə-bəl\ *adj* : capable of being destroyed — **de·struc·ti·bil·i·ty** \-,strək-tə-'bil-ət-ē\ *n*

de·struc·tion \di-'strək-shən\ *n* 1 : the action or process of destroying something 2 : the state or fact of being destroyed : RUIN 3 : something that destroys [Middle French, from Latin *destructio,* from *destruere* "to destroy"]

de·struc·tive \di-'strək-tiv\ *adj* 1 : causing destruction : RUINOUS ⟨*destructive* storms⟩ 2 : designed or tending to destroy or discredit ⟨*destructive* criticism⟩ — **de·struc·tive·ly** *adv* — **de·struc·tive·ness** *n*

destructive distillation *n* : decomposition of a substance (as coal or oil) by heat in a closed container and collection of the volatile products produced

de·struc·tor \di-'strək-tər\ *n* 1 : a furnace for burning refuse : INCINERATOR 2 : a device for destroying a missile in flight

des·ue·tude \'des-wi-,tüd, -,tyüd, di-'sü-ə-,\ *n* : discontinuance from use or exercise : DISUSE [Latin *desuetudo,* from *desuescere* "to become unaccustomed", from *de-* + *suescere* "to become accustomed"]

des·ul·to·ry \'des-əl-,tōr-ē, -,tòr-\ *adj* : marked by lack of definite plan, regularity, or purpose : AIMLESS ⟨*desultory* reading⟩ [Latin *desultorius,* from *desilire* "to leap down", from *de-* + *salire* "to leap"] — **des·ul·to·ri·ly** \,des-əl-'tòr-ə-lē, -'tòr-\ *adv* — **des·ul·to·ri·ness** \'des-əl-,tòr-ē-nəs, -,tòr-\ *n*

de·tach \di-'tach\ *vt* 1 : to separate especially from a larger mass and usually without violence or damage 2 : DISENGAGE, WITHDRAW [French *détacher,* from Old French *destachier,* from *des-* "de-" + *-tachier* (as in *atachier* "to attach")] — **de·tach·able** \-ə-bəl\ *adj* — **de·tach·ably** \-blē\ *adv*

de·tached \-'tacht\ *adj* 1 : not joined or connected : SEPARATE ⟨a *detached* house⟩ 2 : UNBIASED, IMPARTIAL ⟨a *detached* appraisal⟩ 3 : ALOOF, UNCONCERNED — **de·tached·ly** \-'tach-əd-lē, -'tach-tlē\ *adv* — **de·tached·ness** \-'tach-əd-nəs; -'tacht-nəs, -'tach-\ *n*

de·tach·ment \di-'tach-mənt\ *n* 1 : the action or process of detaching : SEPARATION 2 **a** : the dispatching of a body of troops or part of a fleet from the main body for a special service **b** : the part so dispatched **c** : a small permanent military unit having a special task or function 3 **a** : indifference to worldly concerns : UNWORLDLINESS **b** : freedom from bias or prejudice

¹de·tail \di-'tāl, 'dē-,\ *n* 1 **a** : a dealing with something item by item ⟨go into *detail* about an adventure⟩ **b** : a small part : ITEM ⟨the *details* of a story⟩ 2 **a** : selection (as of a group of soldiers) for some special service **b** : a soldier or group of soldiers appointed for special duty [French *détail,* from Old French *detail* "slice, piece", from *detaillier* "to cut in pieces"]

²detail *vt* 1 : to report in detail 2 : ENUMERATE 2, SPECIFY 3 : to assign to a task — **de·tail·er** *n*

de·tailed \di-'tāld, 'dē-,\ *adj* 1 **a** : including many details **b** : marked by careful attention to details 2 : furnished with finely finished details ⟨beautifully *detailed* clothes⟩ SYN see CIRCUMSTANTIAL — **de·tailed·ly** \di-'tāl-əd-lē, -'tāld-lē, 'dē-,\ *adv* — **de·tailed·ness** \di-'tā-ləd-nəs, -'tāld-nəs, -'tāl-nəs-, 'dē-,\ *n*

de·tain \di-'tān\ *vt* 1 : to hold or keep in or as if in custody 2 : to keep back (as something due) : WITHHOLD 3 : to restrain especially from proceeding : STOP [Middle French *detenir,* from Latin *detinēre,* from *de-* + *tenēre* "to hold"] — **de·tain·ment** \-mənt\ *n*

de·tect \di-'tekt\ *vt* 1 : to discover the nature, existence, presence, or fact of ⟨*detect* smoke⟩ 2 : DEMODULATE [Latin *detectus,* past participle of *detegere* "to uncover"] — **de·tect·able** \-'tek-tə-bəl\ *adj*

de·tec·tion \di-'tek-shən\ *n* 1 : the act of detecting : the state or fact of being detected : DISCOVERY 2 : the extraction of information from a radio, laser, or computer signal

¹de·tec·tive \di-'tek-tiv\ *adj* 1 : fitted for or used in detecting something ⟨a *detective* device for coal gas⟩ 2 : of or relating to detectives or their work ⟨a *detective* story⟩

²detective *n* : an individual (as a policeman) whose business is solving crimes and catching criminals or gathering information that is not readily accessible

\ə\ abut		\ng\ sing	
\ər\ further		\ō\ bone	
\a\ mat		\ò\ saw	
\ā\ take		\òi\ coin	
\ä\ cot, cart		\th\ thin	
\aù\ out		\th\ this	
\ch\ chin		\ü\ food	
\e\ pet		\ù\ foot	
\ē\ easy		\y\ yet	
\g\ go		\yü\ few	
\i\ tip		\yù\ cure	
\ī\ life		\zh\ vision	
\j\ job			

de·tec·tor \di-'tek-tər\ *n* **1** : one that detects **2** : a device for demodulating a radio signal

de·tent \'dē-,tent, di-'\ *n* : a mechanism that locks or unlocks a movement : PAWL [French *détente,* from Old French *destendre* "to slacken", from *des-* "de-" + *tendre* "to stretch", from Latin *tendere*]

dé·tente \dā-'tänt, -'täⁿt\ *n* : a relaxation of strained relations or tensions (as between nations) [French]

de·ten·tion \di-'ten-chən\ *n* : the act of detaining : the state of being detained: as **a** : CONFINEMENT; *esp* : temporary custody preceding trial **b** : the punishment of being kept in after school [Late Latin *detentio,* from Latin *detinēre* "to detain"]

de·ter \di-'tər\ *vt* **de·terred; de·ter·ring** : to turn aside, discourage, or prevent from acting (as by fear) [Latin *deterrēre,* from *de-* + *terrēre* "to frighten"] — **de·ter·ment** \-'tər-mənt\ *n*

de·ter·gen·cy \di-'tər-jən-sē\ *n* : cleansing quality or power

¹de·ter·gent \-jənt\ *adj* : CLEANSING ⟨*detergent* oil for engines⟩ [Latin *detergēre* "to wash off", from *de-* + *tergēre* "to wipe"]

²detergent *n* : a cleansing agent; *esp* : any of numerous synthetic organic preparations that are chemically different from soaps but resemble them in the ability to emulsify oils and hold dirt in suspension

de·te·ri·o·rate \di-'tir-ē-ə-,rāt\ *vb* : to make or become worse or of less value : DEGENERATE [Late Latin *deteriorare,* from Latin *deterior* "worse"] — **de·te·ri·o·ra·tion** \-,tir-ē-ə-'rā-shən\ *n* — **de·te·ri·o·ra·tive** \-'tir-ē-ə-,rāt-iv\ *adj*

de·ter·min·able \di-'tərm-ə-nə-bəl, -'tərm-nə-\ *adj* : capable of being determined or ascertained — **de·ter·min·able·ness** *n* — **de·ter·min·ably** \-blē\ *adv*

de·ter·mi·nant \di-'tərm-ə-nənt, -'tərm-nənt\ *n* **1** : something that determines or conditions **2** : a square array of numbers bordered on either side by a straight line whose value is the algebraic sum of all the products that can be formed by taking as factors one element from each row and column such that no two elements in a given product are in the same row or column and giving the products a sign by rule **3** : GENE

de·ter·mi·nate \-mə-nət\ *adj* **1** : having fixed limits : DEFINITE **2** : definitely settled ⟨arranged in a *determinate* order⟩ **3** : having a single flower terminating the main or central stalk and opening before those below or around it : CYMOSE ⟨a *determinate* inflorescence⟩ — **de·ter·mi·nate·ly** *adv* — **de·ter·mi·nate·ness** *n*

de·ter·mi·na·tion \di-,tər-mə-'nā-shən\ *n* **1** : the act of coming to a decision; *also* : the decision or conclusion reached **2** : the act of fixing the extent, position, or character of something ⟨*determination* of the position of a ship⟩ **3** : accurate measurement (as of length or volume) **4** : firm or fixed purpose **5** : an identification of the taxonomic position of a plant or animal

¹de·ter·mi·na·tive \-'tər-mə-,nāt-iv\ *adj* : having power or tendency to determine — **de·ter·mi·na·tive·ly** *adv* — **de·ter·mi·na·tive·ness** *n*

²determinative *n* : one that serves to determine

de·ter·mine \di-'tər-mən\ *vb* **1 a** : to fix conclusively or authoritatively ⟨two points *determine* a straight line⟩ **b** : to bring about as a result ⟨demand *determines* the price⟩ **2** : to come to a decision : DECIDE ⟨*determine* whom to invite⟩ **3** : to find out the limits, nature, dimensions, or scope of : gain definite knowledge about ⟨*determine* the direction of the wind⟩ **4** : to be the cause of or reason for ⟨the quality of your work *determines* your mark⟩ **5** : to discover the taxonomic position or the generic and specific names of [Middle French *determiner,* from Latin *determinare,* from *de-* + *terminare* "to limit, terminate"]

de·ter·mined \-mənd\ *adj* **1** : marked by a decided purpose : RESOLVED ⟨*determined* to succeed⟩ **2** : marked by firmness or resoluteness ⟨a *determined* at-

tack⟩ — **de·ter·mined·ly** \-mən-dlē, -mə-nəd-lē\ *adv* — **de·ter·mined·ness** \-mənd-nəs, -mən-\ *n*

de·ter·min·er \-mə-nər\ *n* : one that determines: as **a** : GENE, DETERMINANT **b** : a word belonging to a group of noun modifiers characterized by occurrence before descriptive adjectives modifying the same noun ⟨*my* in "my new car" is a *determiner*⟩

de·ter·min·ism \-mə-,niz-əm\ *n* : a doctrine that acts of the will, natural events, or social changes are determined by preceding causes — **de·ter·min·ist** \-mə-nəst\ *n or adj* — **de·ter·min·is·tic** \-,tər-mə-'nis-tik\ *adj*

de·ter·rence \di-'tər-əns, -'ter-\ *n* : the act, process, or capacity of deterring

de·ter·rent \-ənt\ *adj* **1** : serving to deter **2** : relating to deterrence — **deterrent** *n* — **de·ter·rent·ly** *adv*

de·test \di-'test\ *vt* : to dislike intensely : LOATHE, ABHOR [Latin *detestari* "to curse while calling a deity to witness, detest", from *de-* + *testari* "to call to witness"] SYN see HATE — **de·test·er** *n*

de·test·able \di-'tes-tə-bəl\ *adj* : arousing or deserving intense dislike : ABOMINABLE — **de·test·able·ness** *n* — **de·test·ably** \-blē\ *adv*

de·tes·ta·tion \,dē-,tes-'tā-shən\ *n* **1** : intense hatred or dislike : LOATHING **2** : an object of hatred or contempt

de·throne \di-'thrōn\ *vt* : to remove from a throne : DEPOSE — **de·throne·ment** \-mənt\ *n* — **de·thron·er** *n*

det·o·nate \'det-n-,āt, 'det-ə-,nāt\ *vb* : to explode or cause to explode with sudden violence [Latin *detonare* "to thunder down", from *de-* + *tonare* "to thunder"] — **det·o·na·tion** \,det-n-'ā-shən, ,det-ə-'nā-shən\ *n*

det·o·na·tor \'det-n-,āt-ər, 'det-ə-,nāt-\ *n* : a device or small quantity of explosive used for detonating a high explosive

¹de·tour \'dē-,tùr, di-'\ *n* : a deviation from a direct course or the usual procedure; *esp* : a roundabout way temporarily replacing part of a regular route [French *détour,* from Old French *destorner* "to divert", from *des-* "de-" + *torner* "to turn"]

²detour *vb* **1** : to send or proceed by a detour ⟨*detour* around a pit⟩ **2** : to avoid by going around : BYPASS

de·tox \'dē-,täks, di-'täks\ *n* : detoxification from an intoxicating or an addictive substance — **detox** *vb*

de·tox·i·fy \dē-'täk-sə-,fī\ *vt* **-fied; -fy·ing** **1** : to remove a poison or toxin or the effect of such from **2** : to free (as a drug user or an alcoholic) from an intoxicating or an addictive substance in the body — **de·tox·i·fi·ca·tion** \,dē-,täk-sə-fə-'kā-shən\ *n*

de·tract \di-'trakt\ *vb* **1** : to lessen in importance, value, or praiseworthiness ⟨*detract* from a person's reputation⟩ **2** : DISTRACT 1 ⟨*detract* attention⟩ [Latin *detractus,* past participle of *detrahere* "to withdraw, disparage", from *de-* + *trahere* "to draw"] — **de·trac·tor** \-'trak-tər\ *n*

de·trac·tion \di-'trak-shən\ *n* : a lessening of reputation or esteem especially by malicious or petty criticism : BELITTLING — **de·trac·tive** \-'trak-tiv\ *adj* — **de·trac·tive·ly** *adv*

de·train \dē-'trān, 'dē-\ *vb* : to leave or cause to leave a railroad train — **de·train·ment** \-mənt\ *n*

det·ri·ment \'de-trə-mənt\ *n* : injury or damage or its cause : HURT [Latin *detrimentum,* from *deterere* "to wear away, impair", from *de-* + *terere* "to rub"]

det·ri·men·tal \,de-trə-'ment-l\ *adj* : causing detriment : DAMAGING — **det·ri·men·tal·ly** \-l-ē\ *adv*

de·tri·tus \di-'trīt-əs\ *n* **1** : loose material that results directly from rock disintegration or abrasion **2** : a product of disintegration or wearing away [French *détritus,* from Latin *detritus,* past participle of *deterere* "to wear away"] — **de·tri·tal** \-'trīt-l\ *adj*

¹deuce \'düs, 'dyüs\ *n* **1 a** (1) : the face of dice that bears two spots (2) : a playing card bearing the number two **b** : a cast of dice yielding a point of two **2** :

¹deuce 1a (2)

tie in tennis with each side having a score of 40 **3** : DEVIL 1, DICKENS — used chiefly as a mild oath [Middle French *deus* "two", derived from Latin *duo*; sense 3 from obsolete English *deuce* "bad luck"]

²deuce *vt* : to bring the score of (a tennis game or set) to deuce

deuc·ed \'dü-səd, 'dyü-\ *adj* : DAMNED, CONFOUNDED ⟨in a *deuced* fix⟩ — **deuced** *or* **deuc·ed·ly** *adv*

deu·te·ri·um \dü-'tir-ē-əm, dyü-\ *n* : the hydrogen isotope that is of approximately twice the mass of ordinary hydrogen and that occurs in water — called also *heavy hydrogen;* symbol *D* [New Latin, from Greek *deuteros* "second"]

deuterium oxide *n* : heavy water D_2O composed of deuterium and oxygen

deu·ter·on \'düt-ə-ˌrän, 'dyüt-\ *n* : the nucleus of the deuterium atom that consists of one proton and one neutron

Deu·ter·on·o·my \ˌdüt-ə-'rän-ə-mē, ˌdyüt-\ *n* — see BIBLE table [Greek *Deuteronomion*, from *deuteros* "second" + *nomos* "law"]

deut·sche mark \ˌdȯi-chə-'märk\ *n* **1** : the basic monetary unit of Germany **2** : a coin representing one deutsche mark [German]

de·val·ue \dē-'val-yü, 'dē-\ *vb* : to reduce the international exchange value of a currency — **de·val·u·a·tion** \ˌdē-ˌval-yə-'wā-shən\ *n*

dev·as·tate \'dev-ə-ˌstāt\ *vt* **1** : to reduce to ruin : lay waste **2** : OVERPOWER, OVERWHELM ⟨*devastated* by grief⟩ [Latin *devastare*, from *de-* + *vastare* "to lay waste"] SYN see RAVAGE — **dev·as·tat·ing·ly** \-ˌstāt-ing-lē\ *adv* — **dev·as·ta·tor** \-ˌstāt-ər\ *n*

dev·as·ta·tion \ˌdev-ə-'stā-shən\ *n* : the action of devastating : the state of being devastated : DESOLATION

de·vel·op \di-'vel-əp\ *vb* **1 a** : to unfold gradually or in detail **b** : to subject (exposed photographic material) especially to a chemical treatment to produce a visible image **c** : to elaborate (a musical theme) by working out rhythmic and harmonic changes **2** : to bring to a more advanced or more nearly perfect state ⟨study to *develop* the mind⟩ **3** : to make more available or usable ⟨*develop* resources⟩ **4** : to acquire gradually ⟨*develop* a taste for olives⟩ **5 a** : to go through a process of natural growth, differentiation, or evolution ⟨a blossom *develops* from a bud⟩ **b** : to acquire secondary sex characters **6** : to become apparent [French *développer*, from Old French *desvoloper*, from *des-* "de-" + *voloper* "to wrap"] — **de·vel·op·able** \-'vel-ə-pə-bəl\ *adj*

de·vel·oped \di-'vel-əpt\ *adj* : having a relatively high level of industrialization and standard of living ⟨a *developed* country⟩

de·vel·op·er \-'vel-ə-pər\ *n* : one that develops; as **a** : a chemical used to develop exposed photographic materials **b** : a person who develops real estate

de·vel·op·ment \di-'vel-əp-mənt\ *n* **1** : the act, process, or result of developing **2** : the state of being developed **3** : the elaboration of a musical theme, subject, or idea

de·vel·op·men·tal \-ˌvel-əp-'ment-l\ *adj* : of or relating to development ⟨*developmental* processes⟩ — **de·vel·op·men·tal·ly** \-l-ē\ *adv*

developmentally disabled *adj* : having a physical or mental handicap (as mental retardation) that hampers or prevents normal development

de·vi·ant \'dē-vē-ənt\ *adj* **1** : deviating especially from an accepted norm **2** : characterized by deviation — **de·vi·ance** \-əns\ *n* — **deviant** *n*

¹de·vi·ate \'dē-vē-ˌāt\ *vb* : to turn aside especially from an established way [Late Latin *deviare*, from Latin *de-* + *via* "way"]

²de·vi·ate \-vē-ət, -vē-ˌāt\ *adj* : DEVIANT — **deviate** *n*

de·vi·a·tion \ˌdē-vē-'ā-shən\ *n* : an act or instance of deviating: as **a** : the difference found by subtracting some fixed number (as the arithmetic mean of a series

of statistical data) from any item of the series **b** : departure from an established ideology or party line **c** : noticeable departure from accepted norms (as of behavior) — **de·vi·a·tion·ism** \-shə-ˌniz-əm\ *n* — **de·vi·a·tion·ist** \-shə-nəst, -shnəst\ *n*

de·vice \di-'vīs\ *n* **1 a** : a scheme to deceive : STRATAGEM **b** : a piece of equipment or a mechanism designed to serve a special purpose **2** *pl* : a way of doing or acting : unsupervised activities ⟨left to their own *devices*⟩ **3** : an emblematic design used especially as a heraldic bearing [Old French *devis* "division, intention", from *deviser* "to divide, regulate, tell"]

¹dev·il \'dev-əl\ *n* **1** *often cap* : the personified supreme spirit of evil often represented in Jewish and Christian belief as the ruler of hell — often used with *the* as a mild imprecation or expression of surprise, vexation, or emphasis **2** : DEMON 2a **3 a** : an extremely wicked person **b** : a reckless or dashing person **c** : a pitiable person — usually used in the phrase *poor devil* [Old English *dēofol*, from Late Latin *diabolus*, from Greek *diabolos*, literally, "slanderer", from *diaballein* "to throw across, slander", from *dia-* + *ballein* "to throw"]

²devil *vt* **dev·iled** *or* **dev·illed; dev·il·ing** *or* **dev·il·ling** \'dev-ling, -ə-ling\ **1** : ANNOY; *esp* : to press, beg, or urge persistently **2** : to season highly ⟨*deviled* eggs⟩

dev·il·fish \'dev-əl-ˌfish\ *n* **1** : any of several extremely large rays widely distributed in warm seas — called also *manta* **2** : OCTOPUS 1

devilfish 1

dev·il·ish \'dev-lish, -ə-lish\ *adj* **1** : characteristic of or resembling the devil ⟨*devilish* tricks⟩ **2** : EXTREME 1, EXCESSIVE ⟨in a *devilish* hurry⟩ — **devilish** *adv* — **dev·il·ish·ly** *adv* — **dev·il·ish·ness** *n*

dev·il–may–care \ˌdev-əl-mā-'keər, -'kaər\ *adj* : heedless of authority : RECKLESS

dev·il·ment \'dev-əl-mənt, -ˌment\ *n* : reckless mischief

dev·il·ry \'dev-əl-rē\ *or* **dev·il·try** \-əl-trē\ *n, pl* **-ries** *or* **-tries** **1** : action performed with the help of the devil : WITCHCRAFT **2** : reckless unrestrained conduct : MISCHIEF

devil's advocate *n* **1** : a Roman Catholic official whose duty is to examine critically the evidence on which a demand for beatification or canonization rests **2** : a person who supports a less accepted or approved cause for the sake of argument

devil's darning needle *n* **1** : DRAGONFLY **2** : DAMSELFLY

dev·il's food cake \'dev-əlz-ˌfüd-ˌkāk\ *n* : a rich chocolate cake

devil's paintbrush *n* : any of various hawkweeds found in the eastern United States

de·vi·ous \'dē-vē-əs\ *adj* **1** : deviating from a straight line : TWISTING **2 a** : ERRANT 2b **b** : UNDERHAND 1, SNEAKY [Latin *devius*, from *de-* + *via* "way"] — **de·vi·ous·ly** *adv* — **de·vi·ous·ness** *n*

de·vise \di-'vīz\ *vt* **1** : to form in the mind by new combinations or applications of ideas or principles : INVENT ⟨*devise* an engine⟩ **2** : to lay plans to obtain or bring about : PLOT ⟨*devise* the death of an enemy⟩ [Old French *deviser* "to divide, regulate, tell", derived from Latin *dividere* "to divide"] — **de·vis·er** *n*

de·vi·tal·ize \dē-'vīt-l-ˌīz, 'dē-\ *vt* : to deprive of life or vitality

de·void \di-'vȯid\ *adj* : wholly lacking : DESTITUTE ⟨a book *devoid* of interest⟩

de·voir \dəv-'wär, 'dev-\ *n* **1** : DUTY, RESPONSIBILITY **2** : RESPECT 3c — usually used in pl. [Old French *deveir*, from *devoir, deveir* "to owe, be obliged", from Latin *debēre*]

dev·o·lu·tion \ˌdev-ə-'lü-shən, ˌdē-və-\ *n* : transference (as of rights or powers) from one individual to another [Medieval Latin *devolutio*, from Latin *devolvere* "to roll down"] — **dev·o·lu·tion·ary** \-shə-ˌner-ē\ *adj* — **dev·o·lu·tion·ist** \-shə-nəst, -shnəst\ *n*

\ə\ abut   \ng\ sing
\ər\ further   \ō\ bone
\a\ mat   \ȯ\ saw
\ā\ take   \ȯi\ coin
\ä\ cot, cart   \th\ thin
\aú\ out   \th\ this
\ch\ chin   \ü\ food
\e\ pet   \ú\ foot
\ē\ easy   \y\ yet
\g\ go   \yü\ few
\i\ tip   \yú\ cure
\ī\ life   \zh\ vision
\j\ job

de·volve \di-'välv, -'vȯlv\ *vb* : to pass by transmission or succession from one person to another [Latin *devolvere* "to roll down", from *de-* + *volvere* "to roll"]

dev·on \'dev-ən\ *n, often cap* : any of a breed of vigorous red dual-purpose cattle of English origin [*Devon*, England]

De·vo·ni·an \di-'vō-nē-ən\ *n* 1 : the period of the Paleozoic era between the Silurian and Mississippian — called also *Age of Fishes*; see GEOLOGIC TIME table 2 : the system of rocks corresponding to the Devonian period [*Devon*, England] — **Devonian** *adj*

de·vote \di-'vōt\ *vt* 1 : to set apart for a special use ⟨*devote* land to farming⟩ 2 : to center the attention or activities of (oneself) ⟨*devoted* themselves to restoring the house⟩ [Latin *devotus*, past participle of *devovēre* "to dedicate, devote", from *de-* + *vovēre* "to vow"]

de·vot·ed *adj* 1 : dedicated to a purpose : DEVOUT, ZEALOUS ⟨*devoted* admirers⟩ 2 : LOVING ⟨*devoted* parents⟩ — **de·vot·ed·ly** *adv* — **de·vot·ed·ness** *n*

dev·o·tee \,dev-ə-'tē, -'tā\ *n* 1 : an ardent follower of a religion or deity 2 : a zealous follower, supporter, or enthusiast ⟨a *devotee* of sports⟩

de·vo·tion \di-'vō-shən\ *n* 1 **a** : religious fervor : PIETY **b** : an act of prayer — usually used in pl. **c** : a religious exercise or practice other than the regular worship of a church 2 **a** : the act of devoting or the quality of being devoted **b** : ardent love, affection, or dedication — **de·vo·tion·al** \-shnəl, -shən-l\ *adj* — **de·vo·tion·al·ly** \-ē\ *adv*

de·vo·tion·al \-shnəl, -shən-l\ *n* : a short worship service

de·vour \di-'vaùr\ *vt* 1 : to eat up greedily 2 : to seize upon and destroy : CONSUME ⟨fire *devoured* the building⟩ 3 : to enjoy avidly ⟨*devour* a book⟩ [Middle French *devourer*, from Latin *devorare*, from *de-* + *vorare* "to devour"]

de·vout \di-'vaùt\ *adj* 1 : devoted to religion or to religious duties or exercises 2 : expressing devotion or piety 3 : warmly devoted : SINCERE ⟨*devout* thanks⟩ [Old French *devot*, from Late Latin *devotus*, from Latin *devovēre* "to devote"] — **de·vout·ly** *adv* — **de·vout·ness** *n* □ SYN DEVOUT, PIOUS, RELIGIOUS mean showing fervor and reverence in religious practice. DEVOUT stresses an attitude that leads to frequent but not necessarily outward prayer and reverent worship; PIOUS emphasizes the faithful performance of one's religious duties; RELIGIOUS implies devoutness and piety but stresses faith in God or gods and adherence to a way of life conforming to that faith.

dew \'dü, 'dyü\ *n* 1 : moisture condensed upon cool surfaces at night 2 : something resembling dew in purity, freshness, or power to refresh 3 : moisture especially when appearing in minute droplets [Old English *dēaw*] — **dew** *vt*

dew·ber·ry \-,ber-ē\ *n* : any of several sweet edible berries related to and resembling blackberries; *also* : a trailing bramble that bears these

dew·claw \-,klȯ\ *n* : a vestigial digit on the foot of a mammal or a claw or hoof on such a digit — **dew·clawed** \-,klȯd\ *adj*

dew·drop \-,dräp\ *n* : a drop of dew

Dew·ey decimal classification \'dü-ē-, 'dyü-\ *n* : a system of classifying publications whereby main classes are designated by a 3-digit number and subdivisions are shown by numbers after a decimal point [Melvil *Dewey*, died 1931, American librarian]

dew·fall \'dü-,fȯl, 'dyü-\ *n* : formation of dew; *also* : the time when dew begins to form

dew·lap \-,lap\ *n* : a hanging fold of skin under the neck especially of a cud-chewing animal — **dew·lapped** \-,lapt\ *adj*

dew point *n* : the temperature at which the moisture in the air begins to condense

dewy \'dü-ē, 'dyü-\ *adj* **dew·i·er; -est** : moist with, affected by, or suggestive of dew ⟨eyes *dewy* with tears⟩

dhow

— **dew·i·ly** \'dü-ə-lē, 'dyü-\ *adv* — **dew·i·ness** \-ē-nəs\ *n*

Dex·e·drine \'dek-sə-,drēn, -drən\ *trademark* — used for dextroamphetamine

dex·ter \'dek-stər\ *adj* 1 : relating to or situated on the right 2 : being or related to the side of a heraldic shield at the right of the person bearing it [Latin, "dextral, skillful"] — **dexter** *adv*

dex·ter·i·ty \dek-'ster-ət-ē\ *n, pl* **-ties** 1 : readiness and grace in physical activity; *esp* : skill and ease in using the hands 2 : mental skill or quickness

dex·ter·ous *or* **dex·trous** \'dek-stə-rəs, -strəs\ *adj* 1 : skillful and competent with the hands 2 : mentally quick and skillful : EXPERT 3 : done with skillfulness — **dex·ter·ous·ly** *adv* — **dex·ter·ous·ness** *n* □ SYN DEXTEROUS, ADROIT, DEFT mean ready and skilled in physical or mental movement. DEXTEROUS implies expertness with facility and agility in manipulation or movement ⟨a *dexterous* pianist⟩ ⟨*dexterous* diplomacy⟩ ADROIT adds artfulness and resourcefulness to dexterity ⟨an *adroit* magician⟩ DEFT stresses lightness, neatness, and sureness of touch ⟨*deft* handling of suspense in a mystery novel⟩

dextr- *or* **dextro-** *combining form* 1 : right : on or toward the right 2 : turning the plane of polarization of light to the right ⟨*dextr*ose⟩ [Latin *dextr-*, *dexter*]

dex·tral \'dek-strəl\ *adj* : of, relating to, or inclined to the right; *esp* : RIGHT-HANDED — **dex·tral·i·ty** \dek-'stral-ət-ē\ *n* — **dex·tral·ly** \'dek-strə-lē\ *adv*

dex·trin \'dek-strən\ *also* **dex·trine** \-,strēn, -strən\ *n* : any of various soluble gummy substances obtained from starch by the action of heat, acids, or enzymes

dex·tro·am·phet·amine \'dek-,strō-am-'fet-ə-,mēn, -mən\ *n* : a stimulant of the central nervous system that is a derivative of amphetamine — compare DEXEDRINE

dex·trose \'dek-,strōs\ *n* : a sugar $C_6H_{12}O_6$ that is a kind of glucose, occurs in plants, fruits, and blood, is a source of energy for living things, may be obtained by hydrolysis of starch in acid solution, and is used in making candy [from the fact that it turns the plane of polarization of light to the right]

dey \'dā\ *n* : a ruling official of the Ottoman Empire in northern Africa [French, from Turkish *dayı*, literally, "maternal uncle"]

dhar·ma \'dər-mə\ *n* 1 : custom or law regarded as duty in Hinduism 2 **a** : the basic principles of cosmic or individual existence in Hinduism and Buddhism **b** : conformity to one's duty and nature in Hinduism and Buddhism [Sanskrit, from *dhārayati* "he holds"]

dhow \'daù\ *n* : any of a number of typically lateen-rigged Arab sailing vessels [Arabic *dāwa*]

di- *combining form* 1 : twice : twofold : double ⟨*di*chromatic⟩ 2 : containing two atoms, radicals, or groups ⟨*di*chromate⟩ [Greek]

dia- *also* **di-** *prefix* : through : across [Greek, "through, apart", from *dia*]

di·a·be·tes \,dī-ə-'bēt-ēz, -'bēt-əs\ *n* : any of various abnormal conditions characterized by the secretion and excretion of excessive amounts of urine; *esp* : DIABETES MELLITUS [Latin, from Greek *diabētēs*, from *diabainein* "to cross over", from *dia-* + *bainein* "to go"] — **di·a·bet·ic** \,dī-ə-'bet-ik\ *adj or n*

diabetes in·sip·i·dus \-in-'sip-əd-əs\ *n* : a disorder of the pituitary gland characterized by intense thirst and by the excretion of large amounts of urine [New Latin, literally, "insipid diabetes"]

diabetes mel·li·tus \-'mel-ət-əs\ *n* : an endocrine disorder characterized by inadequate secretion or utilization of insulin, by the discharge of abnormal amounts of urine, by large amounts of sugar in the blood and urine, and by thirst, hunger, and loss of weight [New Latin, literally, "honey-sweet diabetes"]

di·a·bol·ic \,dī-ə-'bäl-ik\ *adj* : of, relating to, or characteristic of the devil : FIENDISH [Middle French *diabo-*

lique, from Late Latin *diabolicus,* from *diabolus* "devil"] — **di·a·bol·i·cal** \-'bäl-i-kəl\ *adj* — **di·a·bol·i·cal·ly** \-i-kə-lē, -klē\ *adv* — **di·a·bol·i·cal·ness** \-i-kəl-nəs\ *n*

di·ac·o·nate \dī-'ak-ə-nət, dē-, -ˌnāt\ *n* **1** : the office or period of office of a deacon or deaconess **2** : an official body of deacons [Late Latin *diaconatus,* from *diaconus* "deacon"]

di·a·crit·ic \ˌdī-ə-'krit-ik\ *n* : a mark used with a letter or group of letters and indicating a sound value different from that given the unmarked or otherwise marked letter or combination of letters — called also *diacritical mark*

di·a·crit·i·cal \ˌdī-ə-'krit-i-kəl\ *also* **di·a·crit·ic** \-'krit-ik\ *adj* : serving as a diacritic [Greek *diakritikos* "separative", from *diakrinein* "to distinguish", from *dia-* + *krinein* "to separate"]

di·a·dem \'dī-ə-ˌdem, -əd-əm\ *n* **1** : CROWN; *esp* : an ornamental headband worn as a badge of royalty **2** : regal power or dignity [Old French *diademe,* derived from Greek *diadēma,* from *diadein* "to bind around", from *dia-* + *dein* "to bind"]

di·aer·e·sis \dī-'er-ə-səs\ *n, pl* **-e·ses** \-ˌsēz\ : a mark placed over a vowel to show that it is pronounced in a separate syllable (as in Brontë) [Late Latin, from Greek *diairesis,* from *diairein* "to divide", from *dia-* + *hairein* "to take"]

di·ag·nose \'dī-ig-ˌnōs, -ˌnōz, ˌdī-ig-'\ *vb* : to recognize (as a disease) by signs and symptoms : make a diagnosis ⟨*diagnose* a play in football⟩ [back-formation from *diagnosis*] — **di·ag·nos·able** \ˌdī-ig-'nō-sə-bəl, -zə-\ *adj*

di·ag·no·sis \ˌdī-ig-'nō-səs\ *n, pl* **-no·ses** \-'nō-ˌsēz\ **1 a** : the art or act of identifying a disease from its signs and symptoms **b** : the conclusion reached by diagnosis **2** : a concise technical description of a taxonomic group or entity **3 a** : a careful critical study of something especially to determine its nature or importance **b** : the conclusion reached after a critical study [Greek *diagnōsis,* from *diagignōskein* "to distinguish", from *dia-* + *gignōskein* "to know"] — **di·ag·nos·tic** \-'näs-tik\ *adj* — **di·ag·nos·ti·cal·ly** \-'näs-ti-kə-lē, -klē\ *adv* — **di·ag·nos·ti·cian** \-ˌnäs-'tish-ən\ *n*

¹di·ag·o·nal \dī-'ag-ən-l\ *adj* **1** : joining two nonadjacent corners of a plane figure composed of straight lines or of a solid bounded by plane faces in three dimensions **2 a** : running in a slanting direction **b** : having diagonal markings or parts ⟨a *diagonal* weave⟩ [Latin *diagonalis,* from Greek *diagōnios* "from angle to angle", from *dia-* + *gōnia* "angle"] — **di·ag·o·nal·ly** \-'ag-ən-l-ē, -'ag-nə-lē\ *adv*

²diagonal *n* **1** : a diagonal line or plane **2 a** : a diagonal direction **b** : a diagonal row, arrangement, or pattern **3** : a mark / used chiefly to denote "or" (as in *and/or*), "and or" (as in *straggler/deserter*), or "per" (as in *feet/second*) — called also *slant, slash, virgule*

¹di·a·gram \'dī-ə-ˌgram\ *n* : a drawing, sketch, plan, or chart that makes something clearer or easier to understand [Greek *diagramma,* from *diagraphein* "to mark out by lines", from *dia-* + *graphein* "to write"] — **di·a·gram·mat·ic** \ˌdī-ə-grə-'mat-ik\ *adj* — **di·a·gram·mat·i·cal·ly** \-'mat-i-kə-lē, -klē\ *adv*

²diagram *vt* **-gramed** *or* **-grammed** \-ˌgramd\; **-gram·ing** *or* **-gram·ming** \-ˌgram-ing\ : to represent by or put into the form of a diagram ⟨*diagram* a sentence⟩

¹di·al \'dī-əl, 'dīl\ *n* **1 a** : the face of a watch or clock **b** : SUNDIAL **2 a** : a face or scale upon which some measurement or other number is registered or indicated usually by means of numbers and a pointer ⟨the *dial* of a pressure gauge⟩ **b** : a disk usually with a knob or slots that may be turned to make electrical connections (as on a telephone) or to regulate the operation of a device (as a radio) and that usually has guiding marks around its border [Latin *dies* "day"]

²dial *vt* **di·aled** *or* **di·alled**; **di·al·ing** *or* **di·al·ling** **1** : to manipulate a dial so as to operate, regulate, or select **2** : to make a telephone call or connection

di·a·lect \'dī-ə-ˌlekt\ *n* **1** : a regional variety of a language usually transmitted orally and differing distinctively from the standard language ⟨the Lancashire *dialect* of English⟩ **2** : a special vocabulary or idiom used by the members of an occupational group **3** : a variety of language whose identity is fixed by a factor (as social class) other than geography [Middle French *dialecte,* from Latin *dialectus,* from Greek *dialektos* "conversation, dialect", from *dialegesthai* "to converse", from *dia-* + *legein* "to speak"] — **di·a·lec·tal** \ˌdī-ə-'lek-tl\ *adj* — **di·a·lec·tal·ly** \ˌdī-ə-'lek-tl-ē\ *adv* □ **SYN** DIALECT, LINGO, JARGON, SLANG mean language not recognized as standard. DIALECT applies to a form of language persisting regionally or among the uneducated; LINGO is mildly contemptuous for any language not readily understood; JARGON applies to a special or technical language used by a trade, profession, or cult, and may also be a stronger term than LINGO for language that sounds outlandish; SLANG designates a class of mostly recently coined and often short-lived terms or usages informally preferred to standard usage as being forceful, novel, or fashionable.

di·a·lec·tic \ˌdī-ə-'lek-tik\ *n* : a process of reasoning based on the clash of one idea with its opposite leading to a resolution of these ideas in the form of a truer or more comprehensive concept

di·a·lec·ti·cal \ˌdī-ə-'lek-ti-kəl\ *also* **di·a·lec·tic** \-tik\ *adj* **1** : of, relating to, or in accordance with dialectic **2** : of, relating to, or characteristic of a dialect — **di·a·lec·ti·cal·ly** \-ti-kə-lē, -klē\ *adv*

di·a·lec·tol·o·gy \ˌdī-ə-ˌlek-'täl-ə-jē\ *n* : the systematic study of dialect — **di·a·lec·tol·o·gist** \-jəst\ *n*

di·a·logue *or* **di·a·log** \'dī-ə-ˌlòg\ *n* **1 a** : a conversation between two or more persons **b** : an exchange of ideas and opinions **2** : the parts of a literary or dramatic composition that represent conversation [Middle French, from Latin *dialogus,* from Greek *dialogos,* from *dialegesthai* "to converse", from *dia-* + *legein* "to speak"]

di·al·y·sis \dī-'al-ə-səs\ *n, pl* **-y·ses** \-ə-ˌsēz\ : the separation of substances in solution by means of their unequal diffusion through semipermeable membranes; *esp* : such a separation of colloids from soluble substances [Greek, "separation", from *dialyein* "to dissolve", from *dia-* + *lyein* "to loosen"]

di·a·lyze \'dī-ə-ˌlīz\ *vt* : to subject to dialysis

dia·mag·net·ic \ˌdī-ə-ˌmag-'net-ik\ *adj* : slightly repelled by a magnet — **dia·mag·ne·tism** \-'mag-nə-ˌtiz-əm\ *n*

di·am·e·ter \dī-'am-ət-ər\ *n* **1** : a chord passing through the center of a figure or body **2** : the length of a straight line through the center of an object [Middle French *diametre,* from Latin *diametros,* from Greek, from *dia-* + *metron* "measure"] — **di·am·e·tral** \-'am-ə-trəl\ *adj*

di·a·met·ric \ˌdī-ə-'me-trik\ *or* **di·a·met·ri·cal** \-tri-kəl\ *adj* **1** : of, relating to, or being a diameter **2** : completely opposed or opposite ⟨a *diametric* contradiction⟩ — **di·a·met·ri·cal·ly** \-tri-kə-lē, -klē\ *adv*

di·a·mond \'dī-ə-mənd, 'dī-mənd\ *n* **1 a** : native crystalline carbon that is usually nearly colorless, that when transparent and free from flaws is highly valued as a precious stone, and that is used industrially as an abrasive powder and in rock drills; *also* : a piece of this substance especially when cut and polished **b** : crystallized carbon produced artificially **2** : a square or rhombus-shaped configuration usually upright or oriented on a diagonal axis **3** : a red diamond-shaped mark used to distinguish a suit of playing cards; *also* : a card of the suit so marked **4 a** : INFIELD 1 **b** : the entire playing field in baseball or softball [Middle

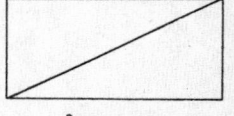

²diagonal 1

\ə\ abut	\ng\ sing
\ər\ further	\ō\ bone
\a\ mat	\ò\ saw
\ā\ take	\òi\ coin
\ä\ cot, cart	\th\ thin
\au̇\ out	\th\ this
\ch\ chin	\ü\ food
\e\ pet	\u̇\ foot
\ē\ easy	\y\ yet
\g\ go	\yü\ few
\i\ tip	\yu̇\ cure
\ī\ life	\zh\ vision
\j\ job	

diatom

French *diamant,* from Late Latin *diamas,* alteration of Latin *adamas* "hardest metal, diamond", from Greek]

¹**di·a·mond·back** \'dī-mənd-,bak, -ə-mənd-, -mən-\ *also* **di·a·mond–backed** \-'bakt\ *adj* : having marks like diamonds on the back

²**diamondback** *n* : a large and deadly rattlesnake of the southern United States

diamondback terrapin *n* : any of several edible terrapins of coastal salt marshes of the southeastern United States

di·a·pa·son \,dī-ə-'pāz-n, -'pās-\ *n* **1** : a full deep burst of harmonious sound **2** : one of two principal stops in an organ extending through the complete scale of the instrument **3** : the full range of musical tones [Latin, from Greek *(hē) dia pasōn (chordōn symphōnia)* "(the concord) through all (the notes)"]

dia·pause \'dī-ə-,pòz\ *n* : a period of dormancy (as in some insects) in which development slows down or in which activity decreases

¹**di·a·per** \'dī-pər, -ə-pər\ *n* **1** : a usually white linen or cotton fabric woven in a pattern formed by the repetition of a simple usually geometric design; *also* : the design on such cloth **2** : a basic garment for infants comprising a piece of absorbent material drawn up between the legs and fastened at the waist [Middle French *diapre,* from Medieval Latin *diasprum*]

²**diaper** *vt* **1** : to ornament with diaper designs **2** : to put a diaper on ⟨*diaper* a baby⟩

di·aph·a·nous \dī-'af-ə-nəs\ *adj* : having a very fine delicate texture : TRANSPARENT ⟨*diaphanous* chiffon⟩ [Medieval Latin *diaphanus,* from Greek *diaphanēs,* from *diaphainein* "to show through", from *dia-* + *phainein* "to show"] — **di·aph·a·nous·ly** *adv* — **di·aph·a·nous·ness** *n*

di·a·phragm \'dī-ə-,fram\ *n* **1** : a body partition of muscle and connective tissue; *esp* : the partition separating the chest and abdominal cavities in mammals **2** : a dividing membrane or thin partition (as in a tube) **3** : a device that limits (as in a camera) the aperture of a lens or optical system **4** : a thin flexible disk that vibrates (as in a microphone) **5** : a molded cap usually of thin rubber fitted over the cervix of the uterus to act as a contraceptive barrier [Late Latin *diaphragma,* from Greek, from *diaphrassein* "to barricade", from *dia-* + *phrassein* "to enclose"] — **di·a·phrag·mat·ic** \,dī-ə-,frag-'mat-ik\ *adj* — **di·a·phrag·mat·i·cal·ly** \-'mat-i-kə-lē, -klē\ *adv*

di·a·rist \'dī-ə-rəst\ *n* : one who keeps a diary

di·ar·rhea *or* **di·ar·rhoea** \,dī-ə-'rē-ə\ *n* : an abnormally frequent or abundant discharge of loose or fluid material from the bowels [Late Latin *diarrhoea,* from Greek *diarrhoia,* from *diarrhein* "to flow through", from *dia-* + *rhein* "to flow"] — **di·ar·rhe·al** \-'rē-əl\ *or* **di·ar·rhe·ic** \-'rē-ik\ *adj*

di·a·ry \'dī-ə-rē, 'dī-rē\ *n, pl* **-ries** : a daily record especially of personal experiences, observations, and thoughts; *also* : a book intended or used as a diary [Latin *diarium,* from *dies* "day"]

Di·as·po·ra \dī-'as-pə-rə, -prə\ *n* **1** : the settling of scattered colonies of Jews outside Palestine after the Babylonian exile **2** : the Jews living outside Palestine or modern Israel [Greek, "dispersion", from *diaspeirein* "to scatter", from *dia-* + *speirein* "to sow"]

di·a·stase \'dī-ə-,stās\ *n* : AMYLASE; *esp* : a mixture of amylases from malt [French, from Greek *diastasis* "separation", from *diistanai* "to separate", from *dia-* + *histanai* "to cause to stand"] — **di·a·stat·ic** \,dī-ə-'stat-ik\ *adj*

di·as·to·le \dī-'as-tə-,lē\ *n* : the relaxation of the heart during which its cavities fill with blood [Greek *diastolē* "stretching", from *diastellein* "to expand", from *dia-* + *stellein* "to send"] — **di·a·stol·ic** \,dī-ə-'stäl-ik\ *adj*

di·as·tro·phism \dī-'as-trə-,fiz-əm\ *n* : the process of deformation that produces in the earth's crust its continents and ocean basins, plateaus and mountains, folds of strata, and faults [Greek *diastrophē* "twisting", from *diastrephein* "to distort", from *dia-* + *strephein* "to twist"] — **di·a·stroph·ic** \,dī-ə-'sträf-ik\ *adj*

dia·ther·my \'dī-ə-,thər-mē\ *n* : the production of heat in tissue by electric currents for medical or surgical purposes — **dia·ther·mic** \,dī-ə-'thər-mik\ *adj*

di·ath·e·sis \dī-'ath-ə-səs\ *n, pl* **-e·ses** \-ə-,sēz\ : a constitutional predisposition toward an abnormality or disease [Greek, literally, "arrangement", from *diatithenai* "to arrange", from *dia-* + *tithenai* "to set"]

di·a·tom \'dī-ə-,täm\ *n* : any of a class (Bacillariophyceae) of minute floating single-celled or colonial algae that are abundant in fresh and salt water and in soil and have a cell wall of silica that persists as a skeleton after death [Greek *diatomos* "cut in half", from *diatemnein* "to cut through", from *dia-* + *temnein* "to cut"] — **di·a·to·ma·ceous** \,dī-ət-ə-'mā-shəs\ *adj*

diatomaceous earth *n* : DIATOMITE

di·atom·ic \,dī-ə-'täm-ik\ *adj* : having two atoms in the molecule

di·at·o·mite \dī-'at-ə-,mīt\ *n* : a light crumbly silica-containing material derived chiefly from diatom remains and used especially as a filter and as an adsorbent and for heat insulation

dia·ton·ic \,dī-ə-'tän-ik\ *adj* : relating to or being a standard major or minor scale of eight tones to the octave without chromatic deviation [Late Latin *diatonicus,* from Greek *diatonikos,* from *diatonos* "stretching", from *diateinein* "to stretch out", from *dia-* + *teinein* "to stretch"] — **dia·ton·i·cal·ly** \-'tän-i-kə-lē, -klē\ *adv*

di·a·tribe \'dī-ə-,trīb\ *n* : a bitter and abusive speech or writing [Latin *diatriba* "discourse", from Greek *diatribē* "pastime, discourse", from *diatribein* "to spend (time), wear away", from *dia-* + *tribein* "to rub"]

di·az·e·pam \dī-'az-ə-,pam\ *n* : a tranquilizer $C_{16}H_{13}ClN_2O$ used especially to relieve anxiety and tension and to relax muscles — compare VALIUM

di·ba·sic \dī-'bā-sik, 'dī-\ *adj* **1** : having two replaceable hydrogen atoms — used of acids **2** : having two hydroxyl groups — used of bases and basic salts

¹**dib·ble** \'dib-əl\ *n* : a small hand tool for making holes in the ground for plants, seeds, or bulbs [Middle English *debylle*]

²**dibble** *vt* **dib·bled; dib·bling** \'dib-ling, -ə-ling\ **1** : to plant with a dibble **2** : to make holes in (soil) with or as if with a dibble

¹**dice** \'dīs\ *n, pl* **dice** **1** : DIE 1 **2** : a gambling game played with dice [Middle English *dees, dyce,* pl. of *dee* "die"] — **no dice** : nothing doing : no use

²**dice** *vb* **1** : to cut into small cubes ⟨*dice* carrots⟩ **2** : to play games with dice — **dic·er** *n*

di·chlo·ride \dī-'klōr-,īd, -'klòr-\ *n* : a binary compound containing two atoms of chlorine combined with an element or radical — called also *bichloride*

di·chot·o·mous \dī-'kät-ə-məs\ *adj* **1** : dividing into two parts **2** : relating to, involving, or proceeding from dichotomy — **di·chot·o·mous·ly** *adv*

dichotomous key *n* : a key to biological classification based on successive choices between pairs of alternate characters

di·chot·o·my \dī-'kät-ə-mē\ *n, pl* **-mies** : a division or the process of dividing into two groups that are mutually exclusive or contradictory [Greek *dichotomia,* from *dicha* "in two" + *temnein* "to cut"]

di·chro·ic \dī-'krō-ik\ *adj* : having the property of dichroism [Greek *dichroos* "two-colored", from *di-* + *chrōs* "color"]

di·chro·ism \'dī-krə-,wiz-əm\ *n* **1** : the property according to which the colors are unlike when a crystal is viewed in the direction of two different axes **2** : the property of a surface of reflecting light of one color and transmitting light of other colors

di·chro·mate \dī-'krō-ˌmāt, 'dī-\ *n* : a usually orange to red chromium salt containing the radical Cr_2O_7 — called also *bichromate*

di·chro·mat·ic \ˌdī-krō-'mat-ik\ *adj* : having or exhibiting two colors

dick·cis·sel \dik-'sis-əl\ *n* : a common migratory black= throated finch of the central United States [imitative]

dick·ens \'dik-ənz\ *n* : DEVIL 1, DEUCE — used chiefly as a mild oath [euphemism]

Dick·en·si·an \dik-'en-zē-ən, -sē-\ *adj* : of, relating to, or characteristic of Charles Dickens or his writings

dick·er \'dik-ər\ *vi* **dick·ered; dick·er·ing** \'dik-ring, -ə-ring\ : HAGGLE 2, BARGAIN ⟨buyers *dickering* for lower prices⟩ [origin unknown] — **dicker** *n*

dick·ey *or* **dicky** \'dik-ē\ *n, pl* **dick·eys** *or* **dick·ies** 1 : any of various articles of clothing: as **a** : a separate or detachable shirtfront **b** : a small cloth insert worn to fill in a neckline 2 : a small bird [*Dicky*, nickname for *Richard*]

Dick test \'dik-\ *n* : a test to determine whether one can contract scarlet fever made by an injection of scar= let fever toxin [George F. *Dick*, died 1967, and Gladys H. *Dick*, died 1963, American physicians]

di·cli·nous \dī-'klī-nəs,'dī-\ *adj* : having the stamens and pistils in separate flowers — compare MONOCLI= NOUS [*di-* + Greek *klinē* "bed"]

di·cot \'dī-ˌkät\ *n* : DICOTYLEDON — **dicot** *adj*

di·cot·y·le·don \ˌdī-ˌkät-l-'ēd-n\ *n* : any of a group (Di= cotyledones) of flowering plants (as an aster, an oak, or a cabbage) having an embryo with two cotyledons and usually net-veined leaves and flower parts not in threes — **di·cot·y·le·don·ous** \-n-əs\ *adj*

Dic·ta·phone \'dik-tə-ˌfōn\ *trademark* — used for a dictating machine

¹dic·tate \'dik-ˌtāt\ *vb* 1 : to speak or read for a person to transcribe or for a machine to record ⟨*dictate* a let= ter⟩ 2 : to say or state with authority : give orders ⟨*dic= tate* terms of surrender⟩ [Latin *dictare*, from *dicere* "to say"]

²dictate *n* : an authoritative rule, prescription, or in= junction ⟨the *dictates* of conscience⟩ ⟨the *dictates* of good taste⟩

dictating machine *n* : a machine used especially for the recording of dictated matter

dic·ta·tion \dik-'tā-shən\ *n* 1 : the act or process of giving arbitrary commands 2 **a** : the dictating of words ⟨write from *dictation*⟩ **b** : something that is dictated or is taken down as dictated ⟨take *dictation*⟩

dic·ta·tor \'dik-ˌtāt-ər, dik-'\ *n* 1 **a** : a person given ab= solute emergency power by the ancient Roman senate **b** : one holding complete autocratic and often oppres= sive control 2 : one that dictates

dic·ta·to·ri·al \ˌdik-tə-'tōr-ē-əl, -'tȯr-\ *adj* 1 : of, relat= ing to, or characteristic of a dictator or a dictatorship ⟨a *dictatorial* manner⟩ ⟨a *dictatorial* regime⟩ 2 : op= pressive to or contemptuously overbearing toward others — **dic·ta·to·ri·al·ly** \-ē-ə-lē\ *adv* — **dic·ta·to= ri·al·ness** *n* ☐ SYN DICTATORIAL, DOGMATIC, DOCTRINAIRE mean imposing one's will or opinions on others. DICTATORIAL stresses autocratic, high-handed methods and a domineering manner; DOGMATIC im= plies being unduly and offensively positive in laying down principles and expressing opinions; DOCTRINAIRE implies a disposition to follow abstract theories in framing laws or policies affecting people.

dic·ta·tor·ship \dik-'tāt-ər-ˌship\ *n* 1 : the office or term of office of a dictator 2 : autocratic rule, control, or leadership 3 : a government, form of government, or country in which absolute power is held by a dicta= tor or a small clique

dictatorship of the proletariat : the assumption of po= litical power by the proletariat held in Marxism to be an essential part of the transition from capitalism to communism

dic·tion \'dik-shən\ *n* 1 : choice of words especially as to correctness, clearness, or effectiveness : WORDING ⟨careless *diction* in the essay⟩ 2 : quality of vocal ex= pression : ENUNCIATION ⟨a singer with excellent *dic= tion*⟩ [Latin *dictio* "speaking, style", from *dicere* "to say"] ☐ SYN STYLE: DICTION applies to choice of words in reference to their effectiveness in expressing ideas or emotions ⟨poetic *diction*⟩ STYLE refers to a manner of expression characteristic of its author and having artistic distinction ⟨Hemingway's terse *style*⟩

dic·tio·nary \'dik-shə-ˌner-ē\ *n, pl* **-nar·ies** 1 : a refer= ence book containing words usually alphabetically ar= ranged along with information about their forms, pro= nunciations, functions, etymologies, meanings, and syntactical and idiomatic uses 2 : a reference book listing alphabetically terms or names important to a particular subject or activity along with discussion of their meanings and applications ⟨a law *dictionary*⟩ 3 : a reference book giving for words of one language equivalents in another ⟨an English-French *dictionary*⟩ [Medieval Latin *dictionarium*, from Late Latin *dictio* "word", from Latin, "speaking"]

dic·tum \'dik-təm\ *n, pl* **dic·ta** \-tə\ *also* **dic·tums** : a formal authoritative statement : PRONOUNCEMENT [Lat= in, from *dictus*, past participle of *dicere* "to say"]

did *past of* DO

di·dac·tic \dī-'dak-tik\ *adj* 1 : intended primarily to in= struct rather than to entertain; *esp* : intended to teach a moral lesson ⟨*didactic* literature⟩ 2 : having or showing a tendency to instruct or lecture others ⟨a *di= dactic* manner⟩ [Greek *didaktikos*, from *didaskein* "to teach"] — **di·dac·ti·cal** \-ti-kəl\ *adj* — **di·dac·ti= cal·ly** \-ti-kə-lē, -klē\ *adv* — **di·dac·ti·cism** \-tə-ˌsiz= əm\ *n*

di·dac·tics \-tiks\ *n sing or pl* : systematic instruction : PEDAGOGY, TEACHINGS

didn't \'did-nt\ : did not

di·do \'dīd-ō\ *n, pl* **didoes** *or* **didos** 1 : a foolish or mis= chievous act ⟨cutting *didoes*⟩ 2 : something frivolous or showy [origin unknown]

didst \didst, 'didst\ *archaic past 2d sing of* DO

¹die \'dī\ *vi* **died; dy·ing** \'dī-ing\ 1 : to stop living : EXPIRE ⟨*died* of old age⟩ 2 **a** : to pass out of existence ⟨a *dying* race⟩ **b** : to disappear or subside gradually ⟨the wind *died* down⟩ 3 : to long keenly or desperately ⟨*dying* to go⟩ 4 : STOP ⟨the motor *died*⟩ [Middle English *dien*]

²die \'dī\ *n, pl* **dice** \'dīs\ *or* **dies** \'dīz\ 1 *pl* **dice** : a small cube marked on each face with from one to six spots and used usually in pairs in various games 2 *pl* **dies** : any of various tools or devices for imparting a desired shape, form, or finish to a material or for im= pressing an object or material: as **a** : the larger of a pair of cutting or shaping tools that when moved to= ward each other produce a certain desired form in or impress a desired device on an object **b** : a hollow screw-cutting tool for forming screw threads **c** : a per= forated block through which metal or plastic is drawn or extruded [Middle English *dee*, from Middle French *dé*]

die–hard \'dī-ˌhärd\ *n* : an irreconcilable opponent of change — **die–hard** *adj*

diel·drin \'dēl-drən\ *n* : a white crystalline chlorine= containing insecticide [*Diels-Alder* reaction, from Otto *Diels*, died 1954, and Kurt *Alder*, died 1958, German chemists]

di·elec·tric \ˌdī-ə-'lek-trik\ *n* : a nonconductor of direct electric current [*dia-* + *electric*] — **dielectric** *adj*

di·en·ceph·a·lon \ˌdī-ˌen-'sef-ə-ˌlän\ *n* : the posterior subdivision of the forebrain [*dia-* + *encephalon*] — **di= en·ce·phal·ic** \ˌdī-ˌen-sə-'fal-ik\ *adj*

die·sel \'dē-zəl, -səl\ *n* 1 : DIESEL ENGINE 2 : a vehicle driven by a diesel engine [Rudolf *Diesel*, died 1913, German engineer]

\ə\ abut	\ng\ sing
\ər\ further	\ō\ bone
\a\ mat	\ȯ\ saw
\ā\ take	\ȯi\ coin
\ä\ cot, cart	\th\ thin
\au̇\ out	\t̶h\ this
\ch\ chin	\ü\ foot
\e\ pet	\u̇\ foot
\ē\ easy	\y\ yet
\g\ go	\yü\ few
\i\ tip	\yu̇\ cure
\ī\ life	\zh\ vision
\j\ job	

diesel engine *n* : an internal-combustion engine in which air is compressed to a temperature sufficiently high to ignite fuel injected into the cylinder

Di·es Irae \,dē-,äs-'ē-,rā\ *n* : a medieval Latin hymn on the Day of Judgment sung in requiem masses [Medieval Latin, "day of wrath"; from the first words of the hymn]

¹**di·et** \'dī-ət\ *n* **1** : the food and drink that a person, animal, or group usually takes : customary nourishment **2** : the kind and amount of food selected for a person or animal for a special reason (as ill health or obesity) (a high-protein *diet*) **3** : something provided especially habitually (as for enjoyment) (a steady *diet* of television) [Old French *diete,* from Latin *diaeta* "prescribed diet", from Greek *diaita,* literally, "manner of living"]

²**diet** *vb* : to eat or cause to eat less or according to set rules — **di·et·er** *n*

³**diet** *n* : a formal deliberative assembly; *esp* : any of various national or provincial legislatures [Medieval Latin *dieta* "day's journey, assembly", from Latin *dies* "day"]

⁴**diet** *adj* : reduced in calories (a *diet* soft drink)

dietary *adj* : of or relating to a diet or to the rules of diet

di·e·tet·ic \,dī-ə-'tet-ik\ *adj* : of or relating to diet or dietetics — **di·e·tet·i·cal·ly** \-'tet-i-kə-lē, -klē\ *adv*

di·e·tet·ics \-'tet-iks\ *n* : the science or art of applying the principles of nutrition to feeding

di·e·ti·tian *or* **di·e·ti·cian** \,dī-ə-'tish-ən\ *n* : a person qualified in or practicing dietetics (a hospital *dietitian*)

dif·fer \'dif-ər\ *vi* **dif·fered; dif·fer·ing** \'dif-ring, -ə-ring\ **1** : to be not the same : be unlike (children who *differ* in looks) **2** : DISAGREE 1, 2 (they *differ* about what should be done) [Latin *differre* "to postpone, be different", from *dis-* + *ferre* "to carry"]

dif·fer·ence \'dif-ərns, 'dif-rəns, -ə-rəns\ *n* **1** : unlikeness between persons or things (the striking *difference* in the children's looks) **2** : the degree or amount by which things differ in quantity or measure; *esp* : the number or mathematical expression that is obtained by subtracting one number or expression from another (the *difference* between 4 and 6 is 2) **3** : a disagreement in opinion (we tried to settle our *differences*)

dif·fer·ent \'dif-ərnt, 'dif-rənt, -ə-rənt\ *adj* **1** : partly or totally unlike another in nature, form, or quality (this apple is *different* from the others) **2** : not the same: as **a** : DISTINCT (*different* age groups) **b** : VARIOUS (*different* members of the class) **c** : ANOTHER (switch to a *different* channel) □ SYN DIFFERENT, DIVERSE, DISPARATE, DIVERGENT mean unlike in kind or character. DIFFERENT often implies little more than separateness but may also suggest contrast or contrariness; DIVERSE implies both distinctness and marked contrast (a person of *diverse* interests) DISPARATE stresses incongruity or incompatibility; DIVERGENT implies movement apart or along different courses with little chance for an ultimate meeting.

dif·fer·en·tia \,dif-ə-'ren-chē-ə, -chə\ *n, pl* **-ti·ae** \-chē-,ē, -chē-,ī\ : the element, feature, or factor that distinguishes one thing, state, or class from another [Latin, "difference", from *differre* "to differ"]

¹**dif·fer·en·tial** \,dif-ə-'ren-chəl\ *adj* **1 a** : of, relating to, or constituting a distinction : DISTINGUISHING (the *differential* character of voice timbre) **b** : making a distinction between individuals or classes (*differential* legislation) **c** : based upon or resulting from a differential (*differential* freight charges) **d** : functioning or proceeding differently or at a different rate (*differential* melting in a glacier) **2** : relating to quantitative differences (*differential* readings on a scale) — **dif·fer·en·tial·ly** \-'rench-lē, -ə-lē\ *adv*

²**differential** *n* **1** : an amount or degree of difference between comparable individuals or classes **2** : DIFFERENTIAL GEAR

differential calculus *n* : a branch of mathematics dealing chiefly with the rate of change of functions with respect to their variables — compare INTEGRAL CALCULUS

differential gear *n* : an arrangement of gears in an automobile that allows one of the driving wheels to turn (as in going around a curve) faster than the other

dif·fer·en·ti·ate \,dif-ə-'ren-chē-,āt\ *vb* **1** : to make a person or a thing different in some way (the color of their eyes *differentiates* the twins) **2** : to undergo or cause differentiation in the course of development **3** : to recognize or state the difference or differences (*differentiate* between two plants)

dif·fer·en·ti·a·tion \-,ren-chē-'ā-shən\ *n* **1** : the act or process of differentiating **2** : development from the one to the many, the simple to the complex, or the homogeneous to the heterogeneous (the *differentiation* of Latin into the modern Romance languages) **3** : the developmental processes by which cells, tissues, and structures attain their specialized adult form and function; *also* : the result of these processes

dif·fer·ent·ly \'dif-ərnt-lē, 'dif-rənt-, -ə-rənt-\ *adv* **1** : in a different manner (they talk *differently* from us) **2** : to the contrary (thought they would win but learned *differently*)

dif·fi·cult \'dif-i-,kəlt, -kəlt\ *adj* **1** : hard to do, make, or carry out (a *difficult* climb) **2 a** : hard to deal with, manage, or overcome (a *difficult* child) **b** : hard to understand (*difficult* reading) [back-formation from *difficulty*] — **dif·fi·cult·ly** *adv*

dif·fi·cul·ty \-,kəl-tē, -kəl-\ *n, pl* **-ties** **1** : difficult nature (slowed up by the *difficulty* of a task) **2** : great effort (accomplish a task with *difficulty*) **3** : something that is hard to do or deal with (overcome *difficulties*) **4** : a difficult or distressing situation (in financial *difficulties*) **5** : a disagreement in opinion (finally cleared up their *difficulties*) [Latin *difficultas,* from *difficilis* "difficult", from *dis-* + *facilis* "easy"]

dif·fi·dent \-əd-ənt, -ə-,dent\ *adj* **1** : lacking confidence : TIMID **2** : RESERVED 1, UNASSERTIVE [Latin *diffidens,* present participle of *diffidere* "to distrust", from *dis-* + *fidere* "to trust"] — **dif·fi·dence** \-əd-əns, -ə-,dens\ *n* — **dif·fi·dent·ly** *adv*

dif·fract \dif-'rakt\ *vt* : to cause to undergo diffraction (*diffract* light) [back-formation from *diffraction*]

dif·frac·tion \dif-'rak-shən\ *n* : a modification which light undergoes in passing by the edges of opaque bodies or through narrow slits or in being reflected from ruled surfaces and in which the rays appear to be deflected and produce a series of parallel light and dark or colored bands; *also* : a similar modification of other waves [New Latin *diffractio,* from Latin *diffringere* "to break apart", from *dis-* + *frangere* "to break"]

diffraction grating *n* : GRATING 2

¹**dif·fuse** \dif-'yüs\ *adj* **1** : poured or spread out : SCATTERED **2** : marked by wordiness : VERBOSE (a *diffuse* writer) [Latin *diffusus,* past participle of *diffundere* "to spread out", from *dis-* + *fundere* "to pour"] — **dif·fuse·ly** *adv* — **dif·fuse·ness** *n*

²**dif·fuse** \dif-'yüz\ *vb* **1** : to pour out and spread freely **2** : to subject to or undergo diffusion (gases *diffuse* at different rates) — **dif·fus·er** *also* **dif·fu·sor** \-'yü-zər\ *n*

dif·fus·ible \dif-'yü-zə-bəl\ *adj* : capable of diffusing or of being diffused — **dif·fus·ibil·i·ty** \-,yü-zə-'bil-ət-ē\ *n*

dif·fu·sion \dif-'yü-zhən\ *n* **1** : a diffusing or a being diffused; *also* : the state of being diffused **2** : the intermingling of the particles of liquids, gases, or solids as a result of their spontaneous movement so that in dissolved substances they move from a region of higher to one of lower concentration **3** : the reflection of light from a rough surface or the transmission of light through a translucent material (as frosted glass) — **dif·fu·sion·al** \-'yüzh-nəl, -'yü-zhən-l\ *adj*

dif·fu·sive \dif-'yü-siv, -ziv\ *adj* : tending to diffuse : characterized by diffusion — **dif·fu·sive·ly** *adv* — **dif·fu·sive·ness** *n*

¹dig \'dig\ *vb* **dug** \'dəg\; **dig·ging** **1 a** : to turn up the soil (as with a spade) **b** : to hollow out or form by removing earth ⟨*dig* a hole⟩ ⟨*dig* a cellar⟩ **2** : to uncover or seek by turning up earth ⟨*dig* potatoes⟩ ⟨*dig* for gold⟩ **3** : to bring to light : DISCOVER ⟨*dig* up information⟩ **4** : JAB ⟨*dig* a person in the ribs⟩ **5** : to work hard **6** *slang* **a** : to pay attention to **b** : UNDERSTAND 1, GRASP [Middle English *diggen*] — **dig·ger** *n*

²dig *n* **1** : POKE 1, JAB **2** : a cutting remark : GIBE **3** : a place where an excavation is made for ancient relics; *also* : the excavation itself

¹di·gest \'dī-,jest\ *n* : a summary or condensation of a body of information or of a literary work ⟨a *digest* of the laws⟩ [Latin *digesta* "collection of writings arranged under headings", from *digerere* "to arrange, digest", from *dis-* + *gerere* "to carry"]

²di·gest \dī-'jest, də-\ *vb* **1** : to think over and arrange in the mind : take in mentally **2** : to convert food into simpler forms that can be taken in and used by the body **3** : to soften or decompose or to extract soluble ingredients from by heat and moisture **4** : to condense into a short summary **5** : to become digested — **di·gest·er** *n* — **di·gest·ible** \-'jes-tə-bəl\ *adj* — **di·gest·ibil·i·ty** \-,jes-tə-'bil-ət-ē\ *n*

di·ges·tion \dī-'jes-chən, də-, -'jesh-\ *n* : the process or power of digesting something and especially food

¹di·ges·tive \-'jes-tiv\ *n* : something that aids digestion

²digestive *adj* **1** : of or relating to digestion **2** : having the power to cause or promote digestion ⟨*digestive* enzymes⟩ — **di·ges·tive·ly** *adv*

digger wasp *n* : a burrowing wasp; *esp* : one that digs nest burrows in the soil and provisions them with insects or spiders paralyzed by stinging

dig·gings \'dig-ingz\ *n pl* **1** : a place where ore, metals, or precious stones are dug **2** *chiefly British* : LODGING 2

dight \'dīt\ *vt* **dight·ed** *or* **dight**; **dight·ing** *archaic* : DRESS, ADORN [Old English *dihtan* "to arrange, compose", from Latin *dictare* "to dictate, compose"]

dig in *vi* **1** : to dig and take position in defensive trenches **2** : to go to work **3** : to begin eating

dig·it \'dij-ət\ *n* **1 a** : any of the arabic numerals 1 to 9 and usually the symbol 0 **b** : one of the elements that combine to form numbers in a system other than the decimal system **2** : a finger or toe [Latin *digitus* "finger, toe"]

dig·i·tal \'dij-ət-l\ *adj* **1** : of or relating to the fingers or toes **2** : of, relating to, or using calculation directly with digits rather than through measurable physical quantities **3** : providing a readout in numerical digits ⟨a *digital* watch⟩ — **dig·i·tal·ly** \-l-ē\ *adv*

digital computer *n* : a computer that operates numbers in the form of digits — compare ANALOG COMPUTER

dig·i·tal·is \,dij-ə-'tal-əs\ *n* **1** : FOXGLOVE **2** : a powerful drug used as a heart stimulant and prepared from the dried leaves of the common foxglove [Latin, "of a finger", from *digitus* "finger, toe"; from its finger-shaped corolla]

dig·i·tate \'dij-ə-,tāt\ *adj* **1** : having digits **2** : having divisions arranged like fingers on a hand ⟨*digitate* leaves⟩

dig·i·ti·grade \'dij-ət-ə-,grād\ *adj* : walking on the toes with the back part of the foot raised [French, from Latin *digitus* "finger, toe" + *gradi* "to step, go"]

dig·i·tize \'dij-ə-,tīz\ *vt* : to convert (as data or an image) to digital form — **dig·i·tiz·er** *n*

dig·ni·fied \'dig-nə-,fīd\ *adj* : showing or expressing dignity

dig·ni·fy \-,fī\ *vt* **-fied**; **-fy·ing** : to give dignity or distinction to : HONOR [Middle French *dignifier*, from Late Latin *dignificare*, from Latin *dignus* "worthy"]

dig·ni·tary \'dig-nə-,ter-ē\ *n*, *pl* **-tar·ies** : a person of high position or honor ⟨*dignitaries* of the church⟩

dig·ni·ty \'dig-nət-ē\ *n*, *pl* **-ties** **1** : the quality or state of being worthy, honored, or esteemed **2** : high rank, office, or position **3** : formal reserve of manner or language [Old French *digneté*, from Latin *dignitas*, from *dignus* "worthy"] SYN see DECORUM

di·graph \'dī-,graf\ *n* : a group of two successive letters representing a single sound or a complex sound which is not a combination of the sounds ordinarily represented by each in other occurrences ⟨*ea* in *bread* and *ch* in *chin* are *digraphs*⟩ — **di·graph·ic** \dī-'graf-ik\ *adj*

di·gress \dī-'gres, də-\ *vi* : to turn aside especially from the main subject in writing or speaking [Latin *digressus*, past participle of *digredi* "to digress", from *dis-* + *gradi* "to step, go"] — **di·gres·sion** \-'gresh-ən\ *n*

di·gres·sive \-'gres-iv\ *adj* : characterized by digressions ⟨a *digressive* book⟩ — **di·gres·sive·ly** *adv* — **di·gres·sive·ness** *n*

di·he·dral angle \dī-'hē-drəl-\ *n* : the figure formed by two half planes meeting along a common line

di·hy·brid \dī-'hī-brəd, 'dī-\ *adj* : heterozygous with respect to two pairs of genes — **dihybrid** *n*

¹dike *or* **dyke** \'dīk\ *n* **1** : an artificial watercourse : DITCH **2** : a bank of earth constructed to control or confine water : LEVEE **3** : a long usually vertical body of igneous rock that has been forced while molten into a fissure [Old English *dīc* "ditch, dike"]

²dike *or* **dyke** *vt* : to surround or protect with a dike; *also* : to drain by a dike — **dik·er** *n*

di·lap·i·dat·ed \də-'lap-ə-,dāt-əd\ *adj* : partly ruined or decayed ⟨a *dilapidated* old house⟩ [Latin *dilapidare* "to destroy", from *dis-* + *lapidare* "to throw stones", from *lapis* "stone"]

di·lap·i·da·tion \də-,lap-ə-'dā-shən\ *n* : partial ruin (as from neglect)

di·la·ta·tion \,dil-ə-'tā-shən, ,dī-lə-\ *n* **1** : the condition of being stretched beyond normal dimensions especially as a result of overwork or disease ⟨*dilatation* of the heart⟩ **2** : the action of dilating an organ or part of the body **3** : a dilated part or formation — **di·la·ta·tion·al** \-shnəl, -shən-l\ *adj*

di·late \dī-'lāt, 'dī-,\ *vb* : to make or grow larger or wider ⟨eyes *dilated* with fear⟩ ⟨lungs *dilated* with air⟩ [Middle French *dilater*, from Latin *dilatare*, literally, "to spread wide", from *dis-* + *latus* "wide"] SYN see EXPAND — **di·lat·able** \dī-'lāt-ə-bəl\ *adj* — **di·la·tor** \dī-'lāt-ər, 'dī-,\ *n*

di·la·tion \dī-'lā-shən\ *n* : the act of dilating : the state of being dilated : EXPANSION ⟨*dilation* of the pupils of the eyes⟩

dil·a·to·ry \'dil-ə-,tōr-ē, -,tȯr-\ *adj* **1** : tending or intended to cause delay ⟨*dilatory* tactics⟩ **2** : characterized by dawdling or delay [Late Latin *dilatorius*, from Latin *dilatus*, past participle of *differre* "to postpone, differ", from *dis-* + *ferre* "to carry"] — **dil·a·to·ri·ly** \,dil-ə-'tōr-ə-lē, -'tȯr-\ *adv* — **dil·a·to·ri·ness** \'dil-ə-,tōr-ē-nəs, -,tȯr-\ *n*

di·lem·ma \də-'lem-ə *also* dī-\ *n* : a choice or a situation in which one has to choose between two or more things, ways, or plans that are equally unsatisfactory : a difficult choice [Late Latin, from Late Greek *dilēmma*, from Greek *di-* + *lēmma* "assumption"] SYN see PREDICAMENT

dil·et·tante \'dil-ə-,tänt, -,tant; ,dil-ə-'; -'tänt-ē, -'tant-ē\ *n*, *pl* **-tantes** *or* **-tan·ti** \-'tänt-ē, -'tant-ē\ **1** : an admirer or lover of the arts **2** : a person who engages usually superficially in an art or branch of knowledge as a pastime [Italian, from *dilettare* "to delight", from Latin *dilectare*] — **dilettante** *adj* — **dil·et·tan·tism** \-,tän-,tiz-əm, -,tan-, -'tän-, -'tan-\ *n*

¹dil·i·gence \'dil-ə-jəns\ *n* : careful and continued work : conscientious effort : INDUSTRY

²dil·i·gence \'dil-ə-,zhäⁿs, 'dil-ə-jəns\ *n* : STAGECOACH [French, "industry, haste, stagecoach"]

dil·i·gent \'dil-ə-jənt\ *adj* : characterized by steady, earnest, and energetic application and effort : PAINSTAKING [Middle French, from Latin *diligens*, from *dili-*

dihedral angle

gere "to esteem, love", from *di-* (from *dis-* "apart") + *legere* "to select"] — **dil·i·gent·ly** *adv*

dill \'dil\ *n* : any of several plants of the carrot family; *esp* : a European herb with aromatic foliage and seeds used especially in flavoring pickles [Old English *dile*]

dill pickle *n* : a pickle seasoned with dill or dill juice

dil·ly·dal·ly \'dil-ē-,dal-ē\ *vi* : to waste time by loitering or delay : DAWDLE ⟨*dillydallied* too long before making a decision⟩ [reduplication of *dally*]

dil·u·ent \'dil-yə-wənt\ *n* : a diluting agent

¹di·lute \dī-'lüt, də-\ *vt* **1** : to make more liquid by admixture (as with water) **2** : to lessen the strength, flavor, or quality of by admixture **3** : to make smaller or less ⟨*dilute* profits⟩ [Latin *diluere* "to wash away, dilute", from *dis-* + *lavere* "to wash"] — **di·lut·er** *or* **di·lu·tor** *n*

²dilute *adj* : that has been diluted ⟨a *dilute* acid⟩ — **di·lute·ness** *n*

di·lu·tion \dī-'lü-shən, də-\ *n* **1** : the action of diluting : the state of being diluted **2** : something (as a solution) that is diluted

di·lu·vi·al \də-'lü-vē-əl, dī-\ *or* **di·lu·vi·an** \-vē-ən\ *adj* : of, relating to, or brought about by a flood [Latin *diluvium* "deluge"]

¹dim \'dim\ *adj* **dim·mer; dim·mest** **1** : not bright or distinct : OBSCURE, FAINT ⟨a *dim* light⟩ **2** : being without luster : DULL **3 a** : not seen or understood clearly **b** : characterized by a skeptical or unfavorable attitude ⟨took a *dim* view of the proceedings⟩ **4** : not seeing or understanding clearly ⟨eyes grown *dim* with age⟩ [Old English] — **dim·ly** *adv* — **dim·ness** *n*

²dim *vb* **dimmed; dim·ming** **1** : to make or become dim **2** : to reduce the light from (headlights) by switching to the low beam

dime \'dīm\ *n* : a United States coin worth ¹/₁₀ dollar [Middle French, "tenth part", from Latin *decima,* from *decimus* "tenth", from *decem* "ten"]

¹di·men·sion \də-'men-chən *also* dī-\ *n* **1 a** : one of three or four coordinates determining a position in space or space and time **b** : magnitude of extension in one direction or in all directions ⟨find the *dimensions* of the rectangle⟩ **2** : the number of rows or columns in a matrix or determinant **3** : the range over which something extends : SCOPE [Middle French, from Latin *dimensio,* from *dimetiri* "to measure out", from *dis-* + *metiri* "to measure"] — **di·men·sion·al** \-'mench-nəl, -'men-chən-l\ *adj* — **di·men·sion·al·i·ty** \-,men-chə-'nal-ət-ē\ *n* — **di·men·sion·al·ly** \-'mench-nə-lē, -'men-chən-l-ē\ *adv* — **di·men·sion·less** \-'men-chən-ləs\ *adj*

²dimension *vt* **1** : to form to the required dimensions **2** : to indicate the dimensions on (a drawing)

dim·e·ter \'dim-ət-ər\ *n* : a line of verse consisting of two metrical feet [Late Latin, from Greek *dimetros* "being a dimeter", from *di-* + *metron* "measure"]

di·min·ish \də-'min-ish\ *vb* **1** : to make less or cause to appear less **2** : to lessen the authority, dignity, or reputation of : BELITTLE **3** : to become gradually less : DWINDLE ⟨interest in the project was *diminishing*⟩ [Middle English *deminishen,* alteration of *diminuen,* from Middle French *diminuer,* from Latin *deminuere,* from *de-* + *minuere* "to lessen"] SYN see DECREASE — **di·min·ish·able** \-ish-ə-bəl\ *adj* — **di·min·ish·ment** \-ish-mənt\ *n*

dingo

di·min·ished *adj* : made one half step less than perfect or minor ⟨the musical interval of a *diminished* fifth⟩

di·min·u·en·do \də-,min-yə-'wen-dō, -,min-ə-\ *adv or adj* : DECRESCENDO [Italian, literally, "diminishing", from Latin *deminuere* "to diminish"] — **diminuendo** *n*

dim·i·nu·tion \,dim-ə-'nü-shən, -'nyü-\ *n* : the act, process, or an instance of diminishing : DECREASE

¹di·min·u·tive \də-'min-yət-iv\ *n* **1** : a diminutive word or affix **2** : a diminutive individual

²diminutive *adj* **1** : indicating small size and sometimes the state or quality of being lovable, pitiable, or contemptible ⟨the *diminutive* suffixes *-ette* and *-ling*⟩ ⟨the *diminutive* nouns *kitchenette* and *duckling*⟩ **2** : extremely small : TINY — **di·min·u·tive·ly** *adv* — **di·min·u·tive·ness** *n*

dim·i·ty \'dim-ət-ē\ *n, pl* **-ties** : a sheer usually corded cotton fabric of plain weave in checks or stripes [Middle English *demyt*]

dim·mer \'dim-ər\ *n* **1** : a device for regulating the intensity of an electric lighting unit **2** : LOW BEAM

di·mor·phic \dī-'mòr-fik\ *adj* : DIMORPHOUS ⟨a *dimorphic* butterfly⟩

di·mor·phism \-,fiz-əm\ *n* : the condition or property of being dimorphous; *esp* : occurrence of individuals that might be expected to be similar or identical in two distinguishable forms ⟨sexual *dimorphism* in birds⟩

di·mor·phous \-fəs\ *adj* : occurring or crystallizing in two distinct forms

¹dim·ple \'dim-pəl\ *n* **1** : a slight natural indentation in the surface of some part of the human body **2** : a slight hollow [Middle English *dympull*]

²dimple *vb* **dim·pled; dim·pling** \-pə-ling, -pling\ : to mark with or form dimples ⟨you *dimple* when you smile⟩

¹din \'din\ *n* : a loud noise; *esp* : a jumble of confused or discordant sounds [Old English *dyne*]

²din *vb* **dinned; din·ning** **1 a** : to make a loud noise **b** : to deafen with loud noise **2** : to impress by insistent repetition ⟨*dinning* the lesson into their heads⟩

di·nar \di-'när, 'dē-\ *n* **1** : a gold coin formerly used in Muslim countries **2 a** : the basic monetary unit of Algeria, Bahrain, Iraq, Jordan, Kuwait, Libya, Tunisia, Southern Yemen, and Yugoslavia **b** : a coin or note representing one dinar **3** : an Irani monetary unit equal to ¹/₁₀₀ rial [Arabic *dīnār,* from Greek *dēnarion* "denarius", from Latin *denarius*]

dine \'dīn\ *vb* **1** : to eat dinner **2** : to give a dinner to : FEED ⟨wined and *dined* their friends⟩ [Old French *diner,* derived from Latin *dis-* + *jejunus* "fasting"]

din·er \'dī-nər\ *n* **1** : one that dines **2 a** : DINING CAR **b** : a restaurant usually in the shape of a railroad car

di·nette \dī-'net\ *n* : a small space usually off a kitchen used for dining

ding \'ding\ *vt* : to make a ringing sound [imitative]

¹ding·dong \'ding-,dòng, -,däng\ *n* : the sound of repeated strokes especially on a bell [imitative]

²dingdong *adj* **1** : of, relating to, or resembling the ringing sound made by a bell **2** : vigorously contested ⟨a *dingdong* battle⟩

din·ghy \'ding-ē, -gē, -kē\ *n, pl* **dinghies** **1** : an East Indian rowboat or sailboat **2** : a small sailboat **3** : a small boat used as a tender or lifeboat for a larger boat or yacht **4** : a rubber life raft [Bengali *diṅgi* and Hindi *ḍiṅgī*]

din·gle \'ding-gəl\ *n* : a small narrow wooded valley [Middle English, "abyss"]

din·go \'ding-,gō\ *n, pl* **dingoes** : a reddish brown bushy-tailed wild dog of Australia [from an indigenous language of Australia]

din·gus \'ding-gəs, -əs\ *n* : something whose common name is unknown or forgotten [Dutch *dinges*]

din·gy \'din-jē\ *adj* **din·gi·er; -est** **1** : not fresh or clean : GRIMY ⟨*dingy* wallpaper⟩ **2** : dull or drab in color ⟨a *dingy* room⟩ [origin unknown] — **din·gi·ly** \-jə-lē\ *adv* — **din·gi·ness** \-jē-nəs\ *n*

dining car *n* : a railroad car in which meals are served

din·key *or* **din·ky** \'ding-kē\ *n, pl* **dinkeys** *or* **dinkies** : a small locomotive used especially for hauling freight, logging, and shunting [probably from *dinky* "small"]

din·ky \'ding-kē\ *adj* **din·ki·er; -est** : SMALL, INSIGNIFICANT ⟨a *dinky* two-room apartment⟩ [Scottish *dink* "neat"]

din·ner \'din-ər\ *n* **1 a** : the main meal of the day **b** : the food provided for a dinner **2** : a formal banquet [Old French *diner*, from *diner* "to dine"]

dinner jacket *n* : a single-breasted or double-breasted usually black or blackish blue jacket

di·no·flag·el·late \,dī-nō-'flaj-ə-lət, -,lāt\ *n* : any of an order (Dinoflagellata) of chiefly marine floating organisms that resemble both algae and protozoa and are important in marine food chains [Greek *dinos* "rotation, eddy"]

di·no·saur \'dī-nə-,sȯr\ *n* : any of a group (Dinosauria) of extinct chiefly land-dwelling long-tailed reptiles with limbs adapted for walking [Greek *deinos* "terrible" + *sauros* "lizard"] — **di·no·sau·ri·an** \,dī-nə-'sȯr-ē-ən\ *adj or n*

1dint \'dint\ *n* **1** : FORCE, POWER — used chiefly in the phrase *by dint of* **2** : a mark left by a blow : DENT [Old English *dynt*]

2dint *vt* : DENT 1

di·oc·e·san \dī-'äs-ə-sən\ *n* : a bishop having jurisdiction over a diocese

di·o·cese \'dī-ə-səs, -,sēz, -,sēs\ *n, pl* **di·o·ces·es** \-sə-səz, -,sē-zəz, -,sē-səz; 'dī-ə-,sēz\ : the district over which a bishop has authority [Middle French *diocise*, derived from Greek *dioikēsis* "administration, administrative division", from *dia-* + *oikein* "to dwell, manage", from *oikos* "house"] — **di·oc·e·san** \dī-'äs-ə-sən\ *adj*

di·ode \'dī-,ōd\ *n* **1** : a 2-electrode electron tube having a cathode and an anode **2** : a rectifier consisting of a semiconducting crystal with two terminals

di·oe·cious \dī-'ē-shəs\ *adj* : having male and female flowers borne on different plants [Greek *di-* + *oikos* "house"] — **di·oe·cious·ly** *adv* — **di·oe·cism** \-'ē-,siz-əm\ *n*

Di·o·ny·sia \,dī-ə-'nizh-ē-ə, -'niz-, -'nish-, -'nis-\ *n pl* : any of the ancient Greek festivals held in honor of Dionysus; *esp* : an autumn festival from which the Greek drama is held to have developed

di·o·rama \,dī-ə-'ram-ə, -'räm-\ *n* : a scenic representation in which a partly transparent painting is seen from a distance through an opening or in which lifelike sculptured figures and surrounding details are realistically illuminated against a painted background [French, from *dia-* "dia-" + *-orama* (as in *panorama*, from English)]

di·o·rite \'dī-ə-,rīt\ *n* : a granular crystalline igneous rock [French, from Greek *diorizein* "to distinguish", from *dia-* + *horizein* "to define"]

di·ox·ide \dī-'äk-,sīd\ *n* : an oxide containing two atoms of oxygen in the molecule

1dip \'dip\ *vb* **dipped; dip·ping** **1 a** : to plunge momentarily or partially under the surface (as of a liquid) so as to moisten, cool, or coat **b** : to thrust in a way to suggest immersion **2** : to lift a portion of by reaching below the surface with something shaped to hold liquid : LADLE ⟨*dip* water from a pail⟩ **3** : to lower and then raise again ⟨*dip* a flag in salute⟩ **4 a** : to plunge into a liquid and quickly emerge ⟨oars *dipping* rhythmically⟩ **b** : to immerse something into a processing liquid or finishing material **5 a** : to suddenly drop down or out of sight ⟨the road *dipped* below the crest⟩ **b** : to decrease moderately and usually temporarily ⟨prices *dipped*⟩ **6** : to reach down inside or as if inside or below a surface especially to withdraw a part of the contents ⟨*dipped* into their savings⟩ **7** : to examine something casually or tentatively; *esp* : to read superficially ⟨*dip* into a book⟩ [Old English *dyppan*]

2dip *n* **1** : an act of dipping; *esp* : a brief plunge into the water for sport or exercise **2 a** : inclination downward **b** : a sharp or slight downward course : DROP **3** : something obtained by or used in dipping **4 a** : a sauce or soft mixture into which food may be dipped **b** : a liquid preparation into which an object may be dipped (as for coloring)

di·pep·tide \dī-'pep-,tīd\ *n* : a peptide composed of two molecules of amino acid

di·phos·pho·gly·cer·ic acid \dī-'fäs-fō-glis-,er-ik-\ *n* : a phosphate of glyceric acid that is important in photosynthesis and in glycolysis and fermentation

diph·the·ria \dif-'thir-ē-ə, dip-\ *n* : a contagious bacterial disease with fever in which the air passages become coated with a membranous layer that often obstructs breathing [French *diphthérie*, from Greek *diphthera* "leather"; from the toughness of the membranous layer] — **diph·the·rit·ic** \,dif-thə-'rit-ik, ,dip-\ *adj*

diph·thong \'dif-,thȯng, 'dip-\ *n* **1** : a 2-element speech sound that begins with the tongue position for one vowel and ends with the tongue position for another all within one syllable ⟨the sounds of *ou* in *out* and of *oy* in *boy* are *diphthongs*⟩ **2** : DIGRAPH [Middle French *diptongue*, from Late Latin *diphthongus*, from Greek *diphthongos*, from *di-* + *phthongos* "voice, sound"] — **diph·thon·gal** \dif-'thȯng-əl, dip-, -gəl\ *adj*

diph·thong·ize \-,thȯng-,īz\ *vb* : to change into or pronounce as a diphthong — **diph·thong·iza·tion** \,dif-,thȯng-ə-'zā-shən, dip-\ *n*

dipl- *or* **diplo-** *combining form* : double : twofold ⟨*dipl*oid⟩ [Greek *diploos*, from *di-* + *-ploos* "-fold"]

dip·lo·blas·tic \,dip-lō-'blas-tik\ *adj* : being an embryo or an invertebrate (as a hydra or a sponge) that has only two germ layers and lacks a true mesoderm

dip·lo·coc·cus \,dip-lō-'käk-əs\ *n, pl* **-coc·ci** \-'käk-,sī, -,ī, -,sē, -,ē\ : any of a genus of parasitic bacteria that occur usually in pairs in a capsule and include serious disease-causing agents — **dip·lo·coc·cal** \-'käk-əl\ *adj*

di·plod·o·cus \də-'pläd-ə-kəs, dī-\ *n* : any of a genus of very large plant-eating dinosaurs from what are now Colorado and Wyoming [*dipl-* + Greek *dokos* "beam"]

dip·loid \'dip-,lȯid\ *adj* : having or being the basic chromosome number doubled ⟨a *diploid* cell⟩ ⟨the *diploid* number of chromosomes⟩ — **diploid** *n* — **dip·loi·dy** \-,lȯid-ē\ *n*

di·plo·ma \də-'plō-mə\ *n* **1** : a document conferring a privilege or honor **2** : an official paper bearing record of graduation from or of a degree conferred by an educational institution [Latin, "passport, diploma", from Greek *diplōma* "folded paper, passport", from *diploun* "to double", from *diploos* "double"]

di·plo·ma·cy \də-'plō-mə-sē\ *n* **1** : the art and practice of conducting negotiations between nations **2** : skill in handling affairs without arousing hostility : TACT

dip·lo·mat \'dip-lə-,mat\ *n* : a person employed or skilled in diplomacy

dip·lo·mat·ic \,dip-lə-'mat-ik\ *adj* **1** : of, relating to, or concerned with diplomacy or diplomats ⟨*diplomatic* relations⟩ **2** : TACTFUL ⟨found a *diplomatic* way to say it⟩ [French *diplomatique*, from Latin *diploma* "document, diploma"] — **dip·lo·mat·i·cal·ly** \-'mat-i-kə-lē, -klē\ *adv*

dip·lo·ma·tist \də-'plō-mət-əst\ *n* : DIPLOMAT

di·pole \'dī-,pōl\ *n* **1 a** : a pair of equal and opposite electric charges or magnetic poles of opposite sign separated by a small distance **b** : a body (as a molecule) having such charges or poles **2** : a radio antenna consisting of two horizontal rods in line with each other with their ends slightly separated — **di·po·lar** \dī-'pō-lər, 'dī-\ *adj*

dip·per \'dip-ər\ *n* **1** : one that dips; *esp* : something (as a long-handled cup) used for dipping **2** *cap* **a** : the seven principal stars in the constellation of Ursa Major arranged in a form resembling a dipper **b** : the seven principal stars in Ursa Minor similarly arranged with the North Star forming the outer end of the handle **3** : any of several birds (as a bufflehead or water ouzel) skilled in diving

dip·so·ma·nia \,dip-sə-'mā-nē-ə, -nyə\ *n* : an uncontrollable craving for alcoholic liquors [Greek *dipsa*

dipper 1

\ə\ abut		\ng\ sing	
\ər\ further		\ō\ bone	
\a\ mat		\ȯ\ saw	
\ā\ take		\ȯi\ coin	
\ä\ cot, cart		\th\ thin	
\aů\ out		\th\ this	
\ch\ chin		\ü\ food	
\e\ pet		\u̇\ foot	
\ē\ easy		\y\ yet	
\g\ go		\yü\ few	
\i\ tip		\yu̇\ cure	
\ī\ life		\zh\ vision	
\j\ job			

"thirst"] — **dip·so·ma·ni·ac** \-nē-,ak\ *n* — **dip·so·ma·ni·a·cal** \,dip-sō-mə-'nī-ə-kəl\ *adj*

dip·stick \'dip-,stik\ *n* : a graduated rod for indicating depth (as of oil in a crankcase)

dip·tera \'dip-tə-rə\ *n pl* : insects that are two-winged flies

dip·ter·an \'dip-tə-rən\ *adj* : of, relating to, or being a two-winged fly — **dipteran** *n*

dip·ter·ous \-rəs\ *adj* : of or relating to the two-winged flies [Greek *dipteros* "two-winged", from *di-* + *pteron* "wing"]

dip·tych \'dip-tik\ *n* **1** : a picture or series of pictures (as an altarpiece) painted on two hinged tablets **2** : a work made up of two matching parts [derived from Greek *di-* + *ptychē* "fold"]

dire \'dīr\ *adj* **1** : exciting horror : DREADFUL ⟨*dire* suffering⟩ **2** : warning of disaster ⟨a *dire* forecast⟩ **3** : EXTREME ⟨*dire* poverty⟩ ⟨*dire* need⟩ [Latin *dirus*] — **dire·ly** *adv* — **dire·ness** *n*

¹di·rect \də-'rekt, dī-\ *vt* **1** : to mark with a name and address ⟨*direct* a letter⟩ **2** : to cause to turn, move, or point or to follow a straight course **3** : to point, extend, or project in a specified line, course, or direction **4** : to show or point out the way for **5 a** : to regulate the activities or course of ⟨*directed* the project⟩ **b** : to guide the organizing, supervising, or performance of ⟨*direct* a play⟩ ⟨*direct* an orchestra⟩ **6** : to request or instruct with authority ⟨use only as *directed*⟩ [Latin *directus,* past participle of *dirigere* "to set straight, direct", from *dis-* + *regere* "to lead straight"] SYN see CONDUCT

²direct *adj* **1** : proceeding from one point to another in time or space without deviation or interruption **2 a** : stemming immediately from a source ⟨a *direct* result⟩ **b** : being or passing in a straight line of descent from parent to offspring : LINEAL ⟨a *direct* ancestor⟩ **3** : NATURAL, STRAIGHTFORWARD ⟨a *direct* manner⟩ **4** : operating without an intervening agency or step ⟨*direct* action⟩ **5 a** : effected by the action of the people or the electorate and not by representatives **b** : consisting of or reproducing the exact words of a speaker ⟨a *direct* quotation⟩ — **direct** *adv* — **di·rect·ness** \-'rekt-nəs, -'rek-\ *n*

direct current *n* : an electric current flowing in one direction only — abbreviation *DC*

di·rect·ed *adj* : proceeding or measured in a direction designated as positive or negative ⟨a *directed* line segment⟩

di·rec·tion \də-'rek-shən, dī-\ *n* **1** : guidance or supervision of action or conduct **2** : the art and technique of directing an orchestra or a theatrical production **3** : an authoritative instruction, indication, or order **4** : the line or course along which something moves, lies, points, or is measured **5** : a course of progress or development : TREND

di·rec·tion·al \-shnəl, -shən-l\ *adj* **1** : relating to or indicating direction in space ⟨the *directional* signal lights on an automobile⟩ : **a** : suitable for sending out or receiving radio signals in one direction only ⟨a *directional* antenna⟩ **b** : operating in a particular direction ⟨a *directional* microphone⟩ **2** : relating to direction or guidance especially of thought or effort

¹di·rec·tive \də-'rek-tiv, dī-\ *adj* : serving to direct, guide, or influence ⟨the *directive* power of conscience⟩

²directive *n* : something that serves to direct, guide, and usually impel toward an action or goal; *esp* : an authoritative instruction issued by a high-level body or official

di·rec·tiv·i·ty \də-,rek-'tiv-ət-ē, ,dī-\ *n* : the property of being directional

di·rect·ly \də-'rek-tlē, dī-, -lē, *in sense 2 also* 'drek-lē\ *adv* **1** : in a direct manner ⟨spoke *directly*⟩ **2** : without delay : IMMEDIATELY ⟨go *directly* home⟩

direct object *n* : a grammatical object representing the primary goal or the result of the action of its verb ⟨*me* in "you hit me" and *house* in "we built a house" are *direct objects*⟩

di·rec·tor \də-'rek-tər, dī-\ *n* : one that directs: as **a** : the head of an organized group or administrative unit (as a school) **b** : one of a group of persons who direct the affairs of a corporation **c** : one that supervises the production of a show **d** : CONDUCTOR b — **di·rec·to·ri·al** \də-,rek-'tōr-ē-əl, ,dī-, -'tòr-\ *adj* — **di·rec·tor·ship** \də-'rek-tər-,ship, dī-\ *n*

di·rec·tor·ate \də-'rek-tə-rət, dī-, -trət\ *n* **1** : the office of director **2** : a board of directors (as of a corporation)

di·rec·to·ry \-tə-rē, -trē\ *n, pl* **-ries 1** : an alphabetical or classified list containing names and addresses **2** : a body of directors (as of a government)

direct primary *n* : a primary in which nominations of candidates for office are made by direct vote

di·rec·trix \də-'rek-triks, dī-\ *n* : a fixed curve with which a generatrix keeps a constant relationship as it traces out a geometric figure; *esp* : a straight line for which the distance from any point on a conic section is in fixed ratio to the distance from the same point to the focus

dire·ful \'dīr-fəl\ *adj* : producing dire effects — **dire·ful·ly** \-fə-lē\ *adv*

dire wolf *n* : a large extinct mammal related to the wolf whose remains are found in Pleistocene deposits of North America

dirge \'dərj\ *n* : a song or hymn of grief; *esp* : one intended for funeral or memorial rites [Latin *dirige* (the first word of a Late Latin antiphon), imperative of *dirigere* "to direct"] □ ORIGIN The meaning of English *dirge* is not directly related to the meaning of the Latin word it comes from. *Dirge* and its earlier form *dirige,* meaning "a song or hymn of lamentation", come from the first word of a Latin chant used in the church service for the dead: "Dirige, Domine deus meus, in conspectu tuo viam meam", (Direct, O Lord my God, my way in thy sight.) The first word of the Latin chant became the common English term for a funeral hymn and later for any slow, solemn, and mournful piece of music.

¹di·ri·gi·ble \'dir-ə-jə-bəl, də-'rij-ə-\ *adj* : capable of being steered [Latin *dirigere* "to direct"]

²dirigible *n* : AIRSHIP

dirk \'dərk\ *n* : a long straight-bladed dagger [Scottish *durk*] — **dirk** *vt*

dirndl \'dərn-dl\ *n* **1** : a dress with tight bodice and gathered skirt **2** : a full skirt with a tight waistband [short for German *dirndlkleid,* from German dialect *dirndl* "girl" + German *kleid* "dress"]

dirt \'dərt\ *n* **1 a** : a filthy or soiling substance (as mud, dust, or grime) **b** : a contemptible person **2** : loose or packed earth : SOIL **3 a** : CORRUPTION 1c **b** : obscene language or theme **4** : scandalous gossip [Old Norse *drit* "excrement"]

¹dirty \'dərt-ē\ *adj* **dirt·i·er; -est 1** : not clean : FILTHY, SOILED ⟨*dirty* clothes⟩ **2** : characterized by unfairness : LOW-DOWN ⟨a *dirty* trick⟩ **3** : OBSCENE 2, SMUTTY ⟨*dirty* talk⟩ **4** : STORMY 1 ⟨*dirty* weather⟩ **5** : not clear in color : DULL ⟨a *dirty* red⟩ **6** : conveying ill-natured resentment ⟨gave them a *dirty* look⟩ — **dirt·i·ly** \'dərt-l-ē\ *adv* — **dirt·i·ness** \'dərt-ē-nəs\ *n* □ SYN DIRTY, FILTHY, FOUL, NASTY mean conspicuously unclean or impure, literally or figuratively. DIRTY applies generally to whatever is soiled by dirt of any kind ⟨*dirty* hands⟩ or is capable of soiling ⟨*dirty* jokes⟩ FILTHY suggests offensiveness and a besmeared, cluttered state ⟨*filthy* rags⟩ FOUL adds to the offensiveness an implication of rottenness or loathsomeness ⟨*foul* sewers⟩ NASTY applies to something that is unpleasant or repugnant to one who is fastidious about cleanliness, sweetness, or freshness ⟨a *nasty* smell⟩ or it may imply mere disagreeableness ⟨received a *nasty* shock⟩

²dirty *vb* **dirt·ied; dirty·ing 1** : to make or become dirty **2** : to stain with dishonor : SULLY

dirty rice *n* : a Cajun dish of white rice cooked with chopped or ground giblets

dis- *prefix* **1 a** : do the opposite of ⟨*dis*establish⟩ **b** : deprive of (a specified quality, rank, or object) ⟨*dis*able⟩ ⟨*dis*mast⟩ **c** : exclude or expel from ⟨*dis*bar⟩ **2** : opposite or absence of ⟨*dis*union⟩ **3** : not ⟨*dis*agreeable⟩ **4** : DYS- [Latin, literally, "apart"; sense 4 by folk etymology from *dys-*]

dis·abil·i·ty \,dis-ə-'bil-ət-ē\ *n, pl* **-ties 1** : the condition of being disabled : lack of ability, power, or fitness to do something and especially to hold employment **2** : a source of disability (as a physical injury); *also* : a legal disqualification that prevents a person from doing something ⟨a law placing severe *disabilities* on immigrants⟩ SYN see INABILITY

dis·able \dis-'ā-bəl\ *vt* **dis·abled; dis·abling** \-bə-ling, -bling\ **1** : to disqualify legally **2** : to make unable or incapable; *esp* : to deprive of physical, moral, or intellectual strength : CRIPPLE — **dis·able·ment** \-bəl-mənt\ *n*

dis·abuse \,dis-ə-'byüz\ *vt* : to free from error (as in reasoning or judgment) : UNDECEIVE [French *désabuser*, from *dés-* "dis-" + *abuser* "to abuse"]

di·sac·cha·ride \dī-'sak-ə-,rīd\ *n* : any of a class of sugars (as sucrose) that yield on hydrolysis two monosaccharide molecules

dis·ac·cus·tom \,dis-ə-'kəs-təm\ *vt* : to make no longer accustomed

¹dis·ad·van·tage \,dis-əd-'vant-ij\ *n* **1** : loss or damage especially to reputation or finances ⟨the deal worked to our *disadvantage*⟩ **2 a** : an unfavorable or prejudicial condition ⟨was at a *disadvantage* in educated company⟩ **b** : HANDICAP ⟨the machine has two serious *disadvantages*⟩

²disadvantage *vt* : to place at a disadvantage : HARM

dis·ad·van·taged *adj* : lacking essentials (as standard housing or civil rights) held to be necessary for an equal position in society

dis·ad·van·ta·geous \,dis-,ad-,van-'tā-jəs, -vən-\ *adj* : constituting a disadvantage — **dis·ad·van·ta·geous·ly** *adv* — **dis·ad·van·ta·geous·ness** *n*

dis·af·fect \,dis-ə-'fekt\ *vt* : to alienate the affection or loyalty of : cause discontent in ⟨the troops were *disaffected*⟩ — **dis·af·fec·tion** \,dis-ə-'fek-shən\ *n*

dis·agree \,dis-ə-'grē\ *vi* **1** : to fail to agree ⟨the two accounts *disagree*⟩ **2** : to differ in opinion ⟨*disagree* over the price⟩ **3** : to be unsuitable ⟨fried foods *disagree* with me⟩

dis·agree·able \-'grē-ə-bəl\ *adj* **1** : causing discomfort : UNPLEASANT ⟨a *disagreeable* taste⟩ **2** : marked by ill temper — **dis·agree·able·ness** *n* — **dis·agree·ably** \-blē\ *adv*

dis·agree·ment \,dis-ə-'grē-mənt\ *n* **1** : the act of disagreeing **2 a** : the state of being different or at odds **b** : QUARREL 2

dis·al·low \,dis-ə-'laů\ *vt* : to refuse to admit or recognize : REJECT ⟨*disallow* a claim⟩ — **dis·al·low·ance** \-'laů-əns\ *n*

dis·ap·pear \,dis-ə-'piər\ *vi* **1** : to pass from view or thought **2** : to pass from existence ⟨dinosaurs *disappeared* ages ago⟩ — **dis·ap·pear·ance** \-'pir-əns\ *n*

dis·ap·point \,dis-ə-'pȯint\ *vt* : to fail to come up to the expectation or hope of [Middle French *desapointier*, from *des-* "dis-" + *apointier* "to arrange"]

dis·ap·point·ed *adj* : defeated in expectation or hope

dis·ap·point·ment \,dis-ə-'pȯint-mənt\ *n* **1** : the act or an instance of disappointing : the state of being disappointed **2** : one that disappoints ⟨the play was a *disappointment*⟩

dis·ap·pro·ba·tion \,dis-,ap-rə-'bā-shən\ *n* : DISAPPROVAL

dis·ap·prov·al \,dis-ə-'prü-vəl\ *n* **1** : the act of disapproving ⟨frowned in *disapproval*⟩ **2** : unfavorable opinion or judgment : CENSURE ⟨the plan met with *disapproval*⟩

dis·ap·prove \-'prüv\ *vb* **1** : to pass unfavorable judgment on : CONDEMN ⟨I *disapprove* your conduct⟩ **2** : to refuse approval to : REJECT ⟨*disapproved* the architect's plans⟩ **3** : to feel or express disapproval ⟨*disapproves* of smoking⟩ — **dis·ap·prov·ing·ly** \-'prü-ving-lē\ *adv*

dis·arm \dis-'ärm\ *vb* **1** : to deprive of arms : take arms or weapons from **2** : to disband or reduce the size and strength of the armed forces of a country **3** : to make harmless, peaceable, or friendly : remove dislike or suspicion ⟨a *disarming* smile⟩ — **dis·ar·ma·ment** \-'är-mə-mənt\ *n*

dis·ar·range \,dis-ə-'rānj\ *vt* : to disturb the arrangement or order of — **dis·ar·range·ment** \-mənt\ *n*

¹dis·ar·ray \,dis-ə-'rā\ *n* **1** : a lack of order or sequence : CONFUSION **2** : disorderly dress

²disarray *vt* : to throw into disorder

dis·as·sem·ble \,dis-ə-'sem-bəl\ *vt* : to take apart ⟨*disassemble* an engine⟩

dis·as·so·ci·ate \,dis-ə-'sō-shē-,āt, -sē-\ *vt* : to detach from association : DISSOCIATE — **dis·as·so·ci·a·tion** \-,sō-sē-'ā-shən, -,sō-shē-\ *n*

di·sas·ter \diz-'as-tər, dis-\ *n* : a sudden great misfortune; *esp* : one bringing with it destruction of life or property or causing complete ruin [Middle French *desastre* "unfavorable aspect of a star", from Italian *disastro*, from *dis-* "dis-" + *astro* "star", from Latin *astrum*] □ SYN DISASTER, CATASTROPHE, CALAMITY, CATACLYSM mean an event or situation that is a terrible misfortune. DISASTER is an unforeseen, ruinous, and often sudden misfortune that happens either through lack of foresight or through some hostile external agency; CATASTROPHE implies a disastrous conclusion, emphasizing finality; CALAMITY heightens the personal reaction to a great public loss; CATACLYSM, originally a deluge or geological convulsion, applies to an event or situation that produces an upheaval or complete reversal.

di·sas·trous \-'as-trəs\ *adj* : accompanied by or producing suffering or disaster : CALAMITOUS — **di·sas·trous·ly** *adv*

dis·avow \,dis-ə-'vaů\ *vt* : to refuse to acknowledge : deny responsibility for — **dis·avow·al** \-'vaů-əl, -'vaůl\ *n*

dis·band \dis-'band\ *vb* : to break up the organization of : DISPERSE ⟨*disband* an army⟩ — **dis·band·ment** \-'band-mənt, -'ban-\ *n*

dis·bar \dis-'bär\ *vt* **dis·barred; dis·bar·ring** : to deprive (a lawyer) of the rights and privileges of membership in the legal profession — **dis·bar·ment** \-'bär-mənt\ *n*

dis·be·lief \,dis-bə-'lēf\ *n* : the act of disbelieving : mental rejection of a statement as untrue SYN see UNBELIEF

dis·be·lieve \-'lēv\ *vb* **1** : to hold not to be true or real **2** : to withhold or reject belief — **dis·be·liev·er** *n*

dis·bud \dis-'bəd, 'dis-\ *vt* : to remove some flower buds from in order to improve the remaining flowers

dis·burse \dis-'bərs\ *vt* : to pay out : EXPEND [Middle French *desbourser*, from *des-* "dis-" + *bourse* "purse", from Medieval Latin *bursa*] — **dis·burs·er** *n*

dis·burse·ment \-'bər-smənt\ *n* : the act of disbursing; *also* : funds paid out

disc *variant of* DISK

¹dis·card \dis-'kärd, 'dis-\ *vb* **1 a** : to remove a playing card from one's hand **b** : to play (a card) from a suit other than trump but different from the one led **2** : to get rid of as useless or unwanted

²dis·card \'dis-,kärd\ *n* **1** : the act of discarding **2** : a person or thing cast off or rejected

disc brake *n* : a brake that operates by the friction of two plates pressing against the sides of a rotating disc

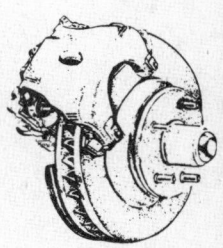

disc brake

\ə\	abut	\ng\	sing
\ər\	further	\ō\	bone
\a\	mat	\ȯ\	saw
\ā\	take	\ȯi\	coin
\ä\	cot, cart	\th\	thin
\aů\	out	\t̲h̲\	this
\ch\	chin	\ü\	food
\e\	pet	\ů\	foot
\ē\	easy	\y\	yet
\g\	go	\yü\	few
\i\	tip	\yů\	cure
\ī\	life	\zh\	vision
\j\	job		

dis·cern \dis-'ərn, diz-\ *vt* **1** : to detect with the eyes : DISTINGUISH ⟨*discern* an airplane in the clouds⟩ **2** : to come to know, recognize, or discriminate mentally ⟨*discern* the basic issue⟩ [Middle French *discerner*, from Latin *discernere* "to distinguish between", from *dis-* + *cernere* "to sift"] — **dis·cern·ible** \-'ər-nə-bəl\ *adj* — **dis·cern·ibly** \-blē\ *adv*

dis·cern·ing *adj* : revealing insight and understanding : PERCEPTIVE ⟨a *discerning* critic⟩ — **dis·cern·ing·ly** \-'ər-ning-lē\ *adv*

dis·cern·ment \dis-'ərn-mənt, diz-\ *n* : skill in discerning or discriminating : keenness of insight

¹dis·charge \dis-'chärj, 'dis-,\ *vb* **1** : to relieve of a charge, load, or burden : UNLOAD **2** : SHOOT ⟨*discharge* a gun⟩ **3** : to set free ⟨*discharge* a prisoner⟩ **4** : to dismiss from service or employment ⟨*discharge* a soldier⟩ **5** : to let go or let off ⟨*discharge* passengers⟩ **6** : to give forth fluid or other contents ⟨this river *discharges* into the ocean⟩ **7** : to get rid of by paying or doing ⟨*discharge* a debt⟩ SYN see FREE — **dis·charg·er** *n*

²dis·charge \'dis-,chärj, dis-'\ *n* **1 a** : the act of discharging, unloading, or releasing **b** : something that discharges; *esp* : a certification of release or payment **2** : a firing off of a weapon or missile **3 a** : a flowing or issuing out; *also* : a rate of flow **b** : something that is emitted **4 a** : release or dismissal especially from an office or employment **b** : complete separation from military service **5 a** : the equalization of electric potential between two points by a flow of electricity **b** : the conversion of the chemical energy of a battery into electrical energy

discharge tube *n* : an electron tube which contains gas or vapor at low pressure and through which electrical conduction takes place when a high voltage is applied

dis·ci·ple \dis-'ī-pəl\ *n* **1 a** : a pupil or follower who accepts and helps to spread the teachings of another **b** : a convinced adherent **2** *cap* : a member of the Disciples of Christ founded in the United States in 1809 [derived from Latin *discipulus* "pupil"] — **dis·ci·ple·ship** \-,ship\ *n*

dis·ci·pli·nar·i·an \,dis-ə-plə-'ner-ē-ən\ *n* : one that disciplines or enforces order — **disciplinarian** *adj*

dis·ci·plin·ary \'dis-ə-plə-,ner-ē\ *adj* : of or relating to discipline : CORRECTIVE ⟨take *disciplinary* action⟩

¹dis·ci·pline \'dis-ə-plən\ *n* **1** : a field of study : SUBJECT **2** : training that corrects, molds, or perfects **3** : PUNISHMENT 1 **4** : control gained by obedience or training : orderly conduct **5** : a system of rules governing conduct or practice [Latin *disciplina* "teaching, learning", from *discipulus* "pupil"]

²discipline *vt* **1** : to punish or penalize for the sake of discipline **2** : to train or develop by instruction and exercise especially in self-control **3** : to bring (a group) under control ⟨*discipline* troops⟩ SYN see PUNISH — **dis·ci·plin·er** *n*

disc jockey *n* : a person who conducts and announces a radio program of musical recordings often with interspersed comments not related to the music

dis·claim \dis-'klām\ *vt* : to deny having a connection with or responsibility for

dis·claim·er \-'klā-mər\ *n* : an act of disclaiming : a statement that disclaims : DENIAL

disc·like *variant of* DISKLIKE

dis·close \dis-'klōz\ *vt* : to expose to view : make known : REVEAL ⟨*disclose* secrets⟩ — **dis·clos·er** *n*

dis·clo·sure \-'klō-zhər\ *n* **1** : the act or an instance of disclosing : EXPOSURE **2** : something disclosed : REVELATION

dis·co \'dis-kō\ *n, pl* **discos** : DISCOTHEQUE

dis·cog·ra·phy \dis-'käg-rə-fē\ *n, pl* **-phies** : a descriptive list of phonograph recordings

dis·coid \'dis-,koid\ *adj* **1** : resembling a disk especially in being flat and circular **2** : relating to, forming, or being part of a disk or disk flower

dis·coi·dal \dis-'koid-l\ *adj* : of, resembling, or producing a disk ⟨a *discoidal* sponge⟩

dis·col·or \dis-'kəl-ər\ *vb* : to alter or change in hue or color — **dis·col·or·a·tion** \,dis-,kəl-ə-'rā-shən\ *n*

dis·com·bob·u·late \,dis-kəm-'bäb-yə-,lāt, -ə-\ *vt* : UPSET 4, CONFUSE [probably alteration of *discompose*]

dis·com·fit \dis-'kəm-fət, -'kəmp- *especially in the South* ,dis-kəm-'fit\ *vt* : to put into a state of perplexity and embarrassment ⟨hecklers *discomfited* the speaker⟩ [Old French *desconfit*, past participle of *desconfire* "to destroy, defeat", from *des-* "dis-" + *confire* "to prepare"] SYN see EMBARRASS — **dis·com·fi·ture** \dis-'kəm-fə-,chùr, -'kəmp-, -fə-chər\ *n*

¹dis·com·fort \dis-'kəm-fərt, -'kəmp-\ *vt* : to make uncomfortable or uneasy

²discomfort *n* : physical or mental uneasiness : DISTRESS

dis·com·mode \,dis-kə-'mōd\ *vt* : to cause inconvenience to [Middle French *discommoder*, from *dis-* "dis-" + *commode* "convenient"]

dis·com·pose \,dis-kəm-'pōz\ *vt* **1** : to disturb the calmness or peace of : AGITATE ⟨*discomposed* by the bad news⟩ **2** : DISARRANGE ⟨hair *discomposed* by the wind⟩ — **dis·com·po·sure** \-'pō-zhər\ *n*

dis·con·cert \,dis-kən-'sərt\ *vt* **1** : to throw into confusion ⟨the unexpected event *disconcerted* their plans⟩ **2** : to disturb the composure of ⟨the verdict *disconcerted* the defendant⟩ SYN see EMBARRASS — **dis·con·cert·ing·ly** *adv*

dis·con·nect \,dis-kə-'nekt\ *vt* : to undo or break the connection of ⟨*disconnect* two pipes⟩ ⟨*disconnect* a telephone⟩ — **dis·con·nec·tion** \-'nek-shən\ *n*

dis·con·nect·ed *adj* **1** : not connected : SEPARATE **2** : DISCURSIVE, INCOHERENT ⟨*disconnected* thoughts⟩ — **dis·con·nect·ed·ly** *adv* — **dis·con·nect·ed·ness** *n*

dis·con·so·late \dis-'kän-sə-lət\ *adj* **1 a** : DEJECTED, DOWNCAST ⟨the team was *disconsolate* after three straight losses⟩ **2** : causing or suggestive of dejection : CHEERLESS ⟨a *disconsolate* row of empty houses⟩ [Medieval Latin *disconsolatus*, from Latin *dis-* + *consolari* "to console"] — **dis·con·so·late·ly** *adv* — **dis·con·so·late·ness** *n*

¹dis·con·tent \,dis-kən-'tent\ *adj* : DISCONTENTED

²discontent *vt* : to make discontented — **dis·con·tent·ment** \-mənt\ *n*

³discontent *n* **1** : lack of contentment : UNEASINESS **2** : a yearning for improvement or perfection SYN see DISSATISFACTION

dis·con·tent·ed *adj* : not satisfied : MALCONTENT — **dis·con·tent·ed·ly** *adv* — **dis·con·tent·ed·ness** *n*

dis·con·tin·u·ance \,dis-kən-'tin-yə-wəns\ *n* : the act or an instance of discontinuing

dis·con·tin·ue \,dis-kən-'tin-yü\ *vb* **1** : to break the continuity of : cease to operate, use, or take **2** : END; *esp* : to cease publication

dis·con·tin·u·ous \,dis-kən-'tin-yə-wəs\ *adj* : not continuous : having interruptions or gaps : BROKEN ⟨*discontinuous* sleep⟩ — **dis·con·ti·nu·i·ty** \,dis-,känt-n-'ü-ət-ē, -'yü-\ *n* — **dis·con·tin·u·ous·ly** \,dis-kən-'tin-yə-wəs-lē\ *adv*

dis·cord \'dis-,kord\ *n* **1** : lack of agreement or accord : CONFLICT **2 a** : a harsh combination of musical sounds **b** : a harsh or unpleasant sound [derived from Latin *discordia*, from *discors* "discordant", from *dis-* + *cor* "heart"]

dis·cor·dance \dis-'kord-ns\ *n* **1** : the state or an instance of being discordant **2** : discordant sound or noises

dis·cor·dant \-nt\ *adj* **1 a** : being at variance : DISAGREEING **b** : QUARRELSOME **2** : relating to or producing a discord : JARRING SYN see DISSONANT — **dis·cor·dant·ly** *adv*

dis·co·theque \'dis-kə-,tek, ,dis-kə-'\ *n* : a nightclub for dancing to recorded music [French *discothèque*, from *disque* "disk, record" + *-othèque* (as in *bibliothèque* "library")]

¹dis·count \'dis-ˌkaȯnt\ *n* **1** : a reduction made from a regular or list price ⟨two percent *discount* for cash⟩ **2** : a deduction of interest in advance when lending money

²dis·count \'dis-ˌkaȯnt, dis-'\ *vt* **1 a** : to reduce or deduct from the amount of a bill, debt, or charge **b** : to sell or offer for sale at a discount **2** : to lend money on (a note) after deducting the discount **3 a** : MINIMIZE ⟨*discounted* the value of experience⟩ **b** : to make allowance for bias or exaggeration in ⟨*discount* a romantic tale⟩ **c** : to take into account (as a future event) in present calculations ⟨the stock market has already *discounted* the company's better prospects for next year⟩ — **dis·count·able** \-ə-bəl\ *adj*

dis·coun·te·nance \dis-'kaȯnt-n-əns, -'kaȯnt-nəns\ *vt* **1** : to put to shame : EMBARRASS **2** : to look with disfavor on

discount store *n* : a store where merchandise is sold at a discount from list price — called also *discount house*

dis·cour·age \dis-'kər-ij, -'kə-rij\ *vt* **1** : to lessen the courage or confidence of ⟨*discouraged* by a single failure⟩ **2 a** : to hinder by inspiring fear of consequences : DETER ⟨laws that *discourage* speeding⟩ **b** : to attempt to dissuade ⟨*discouraged* students from dropping out of school⟩ — **dis·cour·ag·ing·ly** \-'kər-i-jing-lē, -'kə-ri-\ *adv*

dis·cour·age·ment \-'kər-ij-mənt, -'kə-rij-\ *n* **1** : an act of discouraging : the state of being discouraged **2** : something that discourages

¹dis·course \'dis-ˌkōrs, -ˌkȯrs, dis-'\ *n* **1** : verbal interchange of ideas : CONVERSATION **2** : formal and orderly and usually extended expression of thought on a subject [Late Latin *discursus* "conversation", from Latin *discurrere* "to run about", from *dis-* + *currere* "to run"]

²dis·course \dis-'kōrs, -'kȯrs, 'dis-,\ *vi* **1** : to express oneself especially in oral discourse **2** : TALK 5, CONVERSE

dis·cour·te·ous \dis-'kərt-ē-əs\ *adj* : lacking courtesy : RUDE — **dis·cour·te·ous·ly** *adv* — **dis·cour·te·ous·ness** *n*

dis·cour·te·sy \-'kərt-ə-sē\ *n* **1** : rudeness of behavior or language **2** : a rude act

dis·cov·er \dis-'kəv-ər\ *vt* **dis·cov·ered; dis·cov·er·ing** \-'kəv-ring, -ə-ring\ **1** : to make known or visible **2 a** : to obtain sight or knowledge of for the first time **b** : to detect the presence of : FIND **c** : to find out — **dis·cov·er·able** \-'kəv-rə-bəl, -ə-rə-\ *adj* — **dis·cov·er·er** \-'kəv-ər-ər\ *n* □ SYN DISCOVER, INVENT mean to bring something new into being. DISCOVER implies the finding of something that preexisted but had been unknown ⟨Newton *discovered* the law of gravity⟩ INVENT suggests fabrication as a result of experiment, study, or ingenuity ⟨the cotton gin was *invented* by Eli Whitney⟩

dis·cov·ery \dis-'kəv-rē, -ə-rē\ *n, pl* **-er·ies 1** : the act or process of discovering **2** : something discovered

¹dis·cred·it \dis-'kred-ət\ *vt* **1** : to refuse to accept as true or accurate : DISBELIEVE ⟨*discredit* a rumor⟩ **2** : to cause disbelief in the accuracy or authority of ⟨*discredit* a witness⟩ **3** : to destroy the reputation of : DISGRACE ⟨involvement in graft *discredited* them⟩

²discredit *n* **1** : loss of credit or reputation ⟨knew something to their *discredit*⟩ **2** : lack or loss of belief or confidence : DOUBT ⟨bring a story into *discredit*⟩

dis·cred·it·able \-ə-bəl\ *adj* : injurious to reputation — **dis·cred·it·ably** \-blē\ *adv*

dis·creet \dis-'krēt\ *adj* : having or showing good judgment in conduct and especially in speech : PRUDENT; *esp* : capable of observing prudent silence [Middle French *discret*, from Latin *discretus*, past participle of *discernere* "to distinguish, discern"] — **dis·creet·ly** *adv* — **dis·creet·ness** *n*

dis·crep·an·cy \dis-'krep-ən-sē\ *n, pl* **-cies 1** : the quality or state of being discrepant : DIFFERENCE ⟨the extent of *discrepancy* between two reports⟩ **2** : an instance of being discrepant ⟨*discrepancies* in the firm's financial statements⟩

dis·crep·ant \-ənt\ *adj* : being at variance : DISAGREEING [Latin *discrepare* "to sound discordantly", from *dis-* + *crepare* "to rattle, creak"] — **dis·crep·ant·ly** *adv*

dis·crete \dis-'krēt, 'dis-,\ *adj* **1** : individually distinct : SEPARATE ⟨radiation composed of *discrete* particles⟩ **2** : consisting of unconnected elements : DISCONTINUOUS ⟨a *discrete* series⟩ [Latin *discretus*, past participle of *discernere* "to separate, distinguish, discern"] — **dis·crete·ly** *adv* — **dis·crete·ness** *n*

dis·cre·tion \dis-'kresh-ən\ *n* **1** : the quality of being discreet : PRUDENCE **2 a** : individual choice or judgment ⟨left the decision to your *discretion*⟩ **b** : power of free decision ⟨reached the age of *discretion*⟩ — **dis·cre·tion·ary** \-'kresh-ə-ner-ē\ *adj*

dis·crim·i·nant \dis-'krim-ə-nənt\ *n* : a mathematical expression from which it is possible to make statements about the value of another more complicated expression, relation, or set of relations

dis·crim·i·nate \dis-'krim-ə-ˌnāt\ *vb* **1 a** : to perceive the distinguishing features of ⟨*discriminate* the geological features of a terrain⟩ **b** : DIFFERENTIATE 3, DISTINGUISH ⟨*discriminate* hundreds of colors⟩ **2** : to see and note the differences ⟨*discriminate* among values⟩; *esp* : to distinguish one like object from another ⟨*discriminate* between a maple and an oak⟩ **3** : to make a distinction in favor of or against one person or thing as compared with others ⟨*discriminated* against because of race⟩ [Latin *discriminare*, from *discrimen* "distinction", from *discernere* "to distinguish, discern"] — **dis·crim·i·na·ble** \-'krim-nə-bəl, -ə-nə-\ *adj*

dis·crim·i·nat·ing *adj* : marked by discrimination; *esp* : DISCERNING, JUDICIOUS ⟨a *discriminating* taste⟩ — **dis·crim·i·nat·ing·ly** \-ˌnāt-ing-lē\ *adv*

dis·crim·i·na·tion \dis-ˌkrim-ə-'nā-shən\ *n* **1** : the act of perceiving distinctions **2** : the ability to make fine distinctions **3** : the act or practice of discriminating unfairly : prejudiced outlook or action ⟨racial *discrimination*⟩ — **dis·crim·i·na·tion·al** \-shnəl, -shən-l\ *adj*

dis·crim·i·na·tive \dis-'krim-ə-ˌnāt-iv\ *adj* **1** : making distinctions **2** : DISCRIMINATORY — **dis·crim·i·na·tive·ly** *adv*

dis·crim·i·na·to·ry \dis-'krim-nə-ˌtōr-ē, -ə-nə-, -ˌtȯr-\ *adj* : marked by unjust discrimination ⟨*discriminatory* treatment⟩

dis·cur·sive \dis-'kər-siv\ *adj* : passing from one topic to another : RAMBLING [Medieval Latin *discursivus*, from Latin *discurrere* "to run about", from *dis-* + *currere* "to run"] — **dis·cur·sive·ly** *adv* — **dis·cur·sive·ness** *n*

dis·cus \'dis-kəs\ *n, pl* **dis·cus·es** : a disk (as of wood or plastic) thicker in the center than at the edge that is hurled for distance in track-and-field competition [Latin, "disk, dish"]

dis·cuss \dis-'kəs\ *vt* **1** : to investigate or consider carefully by reasoning or argument ⟨*discuss* a proposal⟩ **2** : to talk about ⟨*discuss* the weather⟩ [Latin *discussus*, past participle of *discutere* "to shake apart, scatter", from *dis-* + *quatere* "to shake"] □ SYN DISCUSS, ARGUE, DEBATE, DISPUTE mean to talk about in order to reach conclusions or to convince others. DISCUSS implies a presentation of considerations pro and con and suggests an interchange of opinion for the sake of clarifying issues; ARGUE implies the marshaling of evidence and reasons to support a proposition or proposal; DEBATE stresses formal or public argument between opposing parties; DISPUTE implies quarrelsome or heated argument.

dis·cus·sion \dis-'kəsh-ən\ *n* **1** : consideration of a question in open usually informal debate **2** : a formal treatment of a topic

discus

\ə\ abut		\ng\ sing
\ər\ further		\ō\ bone
\a\ mat		\ȯ\ saw
\ā\ take		\ȯi\ coin
\ä\ cot, cart		\th\ thin
\aȯ\ out		\th\ this
\ch\ chin		\ü\ food
\e\ pet		\u̇\ foot
\ē\ easy		\y\ yet
\g\ go		\yü\ few
\i\ tip		\yu̇\ cure
\ī\ life		\zh\ vision
\j\ job		

¹dis·dain \dis-'dān\ *n* : a feeling of contempt for something regarded as beneath one : SCORN

²disdain *vt* **1** : to look with scorn on **2** : to reject or refrain from because of disdain [Middle French *desdeignier,* derived from Latin *dis-* + *dignare* "to deign"] SYN see DESPISE

dis·dain·ful \-fəl\ *adj* : full of or expressing disdain : SCORNFUL — **dis·dain·ful·ly** \-fə-lē\ *adv* — **dis·dain·ful·ness** *n*

dis·ease \diz-'ēz\ *n* **1** : a condition of the living animal or plant body in which the normal state is altered and the performance of the vital functions is impaired : ILLNESS **2** : a harmful development [Middle French *desaise* "trouble", from *des-* "dis-" + *aise* "ease"] — **diseased** \-'ēzd\ *adj*

dis·em·bark \‚dis-əm-'bärk\ *vb* **1** : to put ashore (as cargo) from a ship **2** : to leave a vehicle (as a ship or ·plane) — **dis·em·bar·ka·tion** \‚dis-‚em-‚bär-'kā-shən, -bər-\ *n*

dis·em·bar·rass \‚dis-əm-'bar-əs\ *vt* : to free from something troublesome or unnecessary

dis·em·body \‚dis-əm-'bäd-ē\ *vt* : to deprive of bodily existence

dis·em·bow·el \‚dis-əm-'baú-əl, -'baúl\ *vt* **-eled** *or* **-elled; -el·ing** *or* **-el·ling** : to take out the bowels of — **dis·em·bow·el·ment** \-mənt\ *n*

dis·en·chant \‚dis-n-'chant\ *vt* : to free from illusion — **dis·en·chant·ment** \-mənt\ *n*

dis·en·cum·ber \‚dis-n-'kəm-bər\ *vt* : to free from something that burdens or obstructs

dis·en·fran·chise \‚dis-n-'fran-‚chīz\ *vt* : to deprive of a franchise, a legal right, or a privilege or immunity; *esp* : to deprive of the right to vote — **dis·en·fran·chise·ment** \-‚chīz-mənt, -chəz-\ *n*

dis·en·gage \‚dis-n-'gāj\ *vb* : to free or release from an engagement, entanglement, or encumbrance ⟨*disengage* an automobile clutch⟩; *esp* : to remove oneself from military commitments, alliances, or positions — **dis·en·gage·ment** \-'gāj-mənt\ *n*

dis·en·tan·gle \‚dis-n-'tang-gəl\ *vb* : to free or become free from entanglement SYN see EXTRICATE — **dis·en·tan·gle·ment** \-mənt\ *n*

dis·equi·lib·ri·um \‚dis-‚ē-kwə-'lib-rē-əm, -‚ek-wə-\ *n* : loss or lack of equilibrium

dis·es·tab·lish \‚dis-ə-'stab-lish\ *vt* : to end the establishment of; *esp* : to deprive of the status and privileges of an established church — **dis·es·tab·lish·ment** \-mənt\ *n*

¹dis·es·teem \‚dis-ə-'stēm\ *vt* : to regard with disfavor

²disesteem *n* : lack of esteem : DISFAVOR, DISREPUTE

¹dis·fa·vor \dis-'fā-vər, 'dis-\ *n* **1** : DISAPPROVAL, DISLIKE ⟨practices looked on with *disfavor*⟩ **2** : the state or fact of being deprived of favor ⟨in *disfavor* at school⟩

²disfavor *vt* : to regard with disfavor

dis·fig·ure \dis-'fig-yər, *especially British* -'fig-ər\ *vt* : to spoil the appearance of ⟨*disfigured* by a scar⟩ SYN see DEFACE — **dis·fig·ure·ment** \-mənt\ *n*

dis·fran·chise \dis-'fran-‚chīz\ *vt* : DISENFRANCHISE — **dis·fran·chise·ment** \-‚chīz-mənt, -chəz-\ *n*

dis·gorge \dis-'górj, 'dis-\ *vb* **1** : VOMIT 1 **2** : to discharge violently, confusedly, or as a result of force **3** : to discharge contents

¹dis·grace \dis-'grās\ *vt* : to bring reproach or shame to — **dis·grac·er** *n*

²disgrace *n* **1** : the condition of being out of favor : loss of respect ⟨in *disgrace* with one's schoolmates⟩ **2** : SHAME, DISHONOR ⟨the *disgrace* of being a coward⟩ **3** : a cause of shame ⟨that child's manners are a *disgrace*⟩

dis·grace·ful \-fəl\ *adj* : bringing or involving disgrace — **dis·grace·ful·ly** \-fə-lē\ *adv* — **dis·grace·ful·ness** *n*

dis·grun·tle \dis-'grənt-l\ *vt* **dis·grun·tled; dis·grun·tling** \-'grənt-ling, -l-ing\ : to put in bad humor [*dis-* + Middle English *gruntlen* "to grumble", from *grunten* "to grunt"] — **dis·grun·tle·ment** \-l-mənt\ *n*

¹dis·guise \dis-'gīz\ *vt* **1** : to change the dress or looks of so as to conceal the identity or so as to resemble another ⟨*disguised* themselves with wigs⟩ **2 a** : HIDE, CONCEAL ⟨*disguised* their true feelings⟩ **b** : ALTER ⟨tried to *disguise* my voice⟩ — **dis·guis·ed·ly** \-'gīz-əd-lē, -'gīzd-lē\ *adv* — **dis·guis·er** \-'gī-zər\ *n*

²disguise *n* **1** : clothing put on to conceal one's identity or counterfeit another's **2 a** : an outward form hiding or misrepresenting the true nature or identity of a person or thing **b** : an artificial manner : PRETENSE **3** : the act of disguising □ SYN DISGUISE, CLOAK, MASK mean an appearance that hides one's true identity or nature. DISGUISE implies a change in appearance or behavior that misleads by presenting a different apparent identity; CLOAK suggests a means of hiding a movement or an intention completely; MASK suggests some usually obvious means of preventing recognition and does not always imply deception or pretense.

¹dis·gust \dis-'gəst\ *n* : marked aversion to something distasteful or loathsome : REPUGNANCE

²disgust *vt* : to provoke to loathing, repugnance, or aversion : be offensive to [Middle French *desgouster,* from *des-* "dis-" + *goust* "taste", from Latin *gustus*] — **dis·gust·ed** *adj* — **dis·gust·ed·ly** *adv* — **dis·gust·ing** \-'gəs-ting\ *adj* — **dis·gust·ing·ly** \-ting-lē\ *adv*

¹dish \'dish\ *n* **1 a** : a usually concave vessel from which food is served **b** : the contents of a dish ⟨ate a *dish* of strawberries⟩ **2** : food prepared in a particular way **3 a** : something resembling a dish especially in being shallow and concave **b** : a directional receiver having a concave usually parabolic reflector; *esp* : one used as a microwave antenna [Old English *disc* "plate", from Latin *discus* "quoit, disk, dish", from Greek *diskos,* from *dikein* "to throw"]

²dish *vt* **1** : to put into a dish or set of dishes **2** : to make concave like a dish ⟨a *dished* metal disk⟩

dis·ha·bille *or* **des·ha·bille** \‚dis-ə-'bēl\ *n* : the state of being dressed in a casual or careless style [French *déshabillé,* from *déshabiller* "to undress", from *dés-* "dis-" + *habiller* "to dress"]

dis·har·mo·ny \dis-'här-mə-nē\ *n* : lack of harmony : DISCORD

dish·cloth \'dish-‚klöth\ *n* : a cloth for washing dishes

dis·heart·en \dis-'härt-n\ *vt* : to deprive of courage and hope : DISCOURAGE — **dis·heart·en·ing** \-'härt-ning, -n-ing\ *adj* — **dis·heart·en·ing·ly** \-ning-lē, -n-ing-lē\ *adv* — **dis·heart·en·ment** \-'härt-n-mənt\ *n*

di·shev·el \dish-'ev-əl\ *vt* **di·shev·eled** *or* **di·shev·elled; di·shev·el·ing** *or* **di·shev·el·ling** \-'ev-ling, -ə-ling\ : to put into disorder or disarray [Middle French *descheveler* "to disarrange the hair", from *des-* "dis-" + *chevel* "hair", from Latin *capillus*] — **di·shev·el·ment** \-əl-mənt\ *n*

di·shev·eled *or* **di·shev·elled** *adj* : marked by disorder

dis·hon·est \dis-'än-əst, 'dis-\ *adj* **1** : not honest : UNTRUSTWORTHY **2** : marked by fraud : DECEITFUL, CORRUPT ⟨*dishonest* dealings⟩ — **dis·hon·est·ly** *adv*

dis·hon·es·ty \-ə-stē\ *n* : lack of honesty or integrity : disposition to defraud or deceive

¹dis·hon·or \dis-'än-ər, 'dis-\ *n* **1 a** : loss of honor or reputation **b** : the state of one who has lost honor or prestige **c** : a cause of disgrace **2** : the refusal to accept or pay (as a bill or check)

²dishonor *vt* **1** : to bring shame on : DISGRACE **2** : to refuse to accept or pay (as a bill or check) — **dis·hon·or·er** *n*

dis·hon·or·able \dis-'än-rə-bəl, -'än-ə-rə-bəl, -'än-ər-bəl\ *adj* : not honorable : SHAMEFUL — **dis·hon·or·ably** \-blē\ *adv*

dish·rag \'dish-‚rag\ *n* : DISHCLOTH

dish towel *n* : a cloth for drying dishes

dish·wash·er \'dish-‚wósh-ər, -‚wäsh-\ *n* : a person or a machine that washes dishes

dish·wa·ter \-‚wót-ər, -‚wät-\ *n* : water in which dishes have been or are to be washed

¹dis·il·lu·sion \\,dis-ə-'lü-zhən\\ *n* : the loss of illusions or hopes

²disillusion *vt* **-lu·sioned; -lu·sion·ing** \\-'lüzh-ning, -ə-ning\\ : to leave without illusion — **dis·il·lu·sion·ment** \\-'lü-zhən-mənt\\ *n*

dis·in·cline \\,dis-n-'klīn\\ *vb* : to make or be unwilling — **dis·in·cli·na·tion** \\,dis-,in-klə-'nā-shən, -,ing-\\ *n*

dis·in·fect \\,dis-n-'fekt\\ *vt* : to free from infection especially by destroying harmful germs; *also* : CLEANSE — **dis·in·fec·tion** \\-'fek-shən\\ *n*

dis·in·fec·tant \\-'fek-tənt\\ *n* : a substance that destroys harmful germs but not ordinarily spores of bacteria — **disinfectant** *adj*

dis·in·gen·u·ous \\,dis-n-'jen-yə-wəs\\ *adj* : lacking in candor : neither frank nor naive — **dis·in·gen·u·ous·ly** *adv* — **dis·in·gen·u·ous·ness** *n*

dis·in·her·it \\,dis-n-'her-ət\\ *vt* : to deprive of the right to inherit

dis·in·te·grate \\dis-'int-ə-,grāt\\ *vb* **1** : to break or decompose into constituent elements, parts, or particles **2 a** : to destroy the unity or integrity of **b** : to lose unity or integrity by or as if by breaking into parts **3** : to undergo a change in composition ⟨an atomic nucleus that *disintegrates* because of radioactivity⟩ — **dis·in·te·gra·tion** \\,dis-,int-ə-'grā-shən\\ *n* — **dis·in·te·gra·tor** \\dis-'int-ə-,grāt-ər\\ *n*

dis·in·ter \\,dis-n-'tər\\ *vt* **1** : to take out of the grave or tomb **2** : to bring to light : UNEARTH — **dis·in·ter·ment** \\-mənt\\ *n*

dis·in·ter·est·ed \\dis-'int-ə-,res-təd, 'dis-; -'in-trəs-, -,tres-; -'int-ərs-, -'int-ə-rəs-\\ *adj* **1** : not interested **2** : free from selfish motive or interest : UNBIASED ⟨a *disinterested* decision⟩ SYN see UNINTERESTED — **dis·in·ter·est·ed·ly** *adv* — **dis·in·ter·est·ed·ness** *n*

dis·join \\dis-'join, 'dis-\\ *vb* : to end the union of or become separated ⟨chromosome pairs *disjoin* in meiosis⟩

¹dis·joint \\dis-'join, 'dis-\\ *adj* : completely separate; *esp* : having no elements in common ⟨*disjoint* mathematical sets⟩

²disjoint *vb* **1** : to separate the parts of **2** : to take apart or become parted at the joints

dis·joint·ed *adj* **1** : separated at or as if at the joint **2** : lacking coherence or orderly sequence ⟨*disjointed* conversation⟩ — **dis·joint·ed·ly** *adv* — **dis·joint·ed·ness** *n*

dis·junc·tion \\dis-'jəng-shən, -'jəngk-\\ *n* **1** : DISUNION, SEPARATION **2** : a proposition composed of two or more statements joined by the connective *or* or its equivalent; *esp* : one in which one and only one of the statements is true at a time

¹dis·junc·tive \\-'jəng-tiv, -'jəngk-\\ *n* : a disjunctive conjunction

²disjunctive *adj* **1** : tending to disjoin **2** : expressing an alternative between the meanings of the words connected ⟨the *disjunctive* conjunction *or*⟩

¹disk *or* **disc** \\'disk\\ *n* **1** : the seemingly flat figure of a celestial body ⟨solar *disk*⟩ **2 a** : the central part of the flower head of a typical composite plant made up of closely packed tubular flowers **b** : any of various rounded and flattened animal anatomical structures **3 a** : a thin circular object : an object that appears to be thin and circular **b** *usually* **disc** : a phonograph record **c** : a round flat plate coated with a magnetic substance on which data for a computer may be stored **4** *usually* **disc** : a tilling implement (as a harrow or plow) with sharp-edged circular concave cutting blades; *also* : one of these blades [Latin *discus* "dish, disk"] — **disk·like** *or* **disc·like** \\-,līk\\ *adj*

²disk *or* **disc** *vt* : to cultivate (land) with a disc

disk·ette \\'dis-,ket, ,dis-'\\ *n* : : FLOPPY DISK

disk flower *n* : one of the tubular flowers in the disk of a composite plant — called also **disk floret**

¹dis·like \\dis-'līk, 'dis-\\ *vt* : to regard with dislike : DISAPPROVE

²dislike *n* : a feeling of aversion or disapproval

dis·lo·cate \\'dis-lō-,kāt, dis-'lō-\\ *vt* **1** : to put out of place; *esp* : to displace (a bone) from normal connections with another bone **2** : DISRUPT 2 — **dis·lo·ca·tion** \\,dis-,lō-'kā-shən\\ *n*

dis·lodge \\dis-'läj, 'dis-\\ *vt* **1** : to force out of a resting place **2** : to drive from a place of hiding or defense

dis·loy·al \\dis-'loi-əl, -'loil\\ *adj* : lacking in loyalty SYN see FAITHLESS — **dis·loy·al·ly** \\-'loi-ə-lē\\ *adv*

dis·loy·al·ty \\-'loi-əl-tē, -'loil-\\ *n* : lack of loyalty

dis·mal \\'diz-məl\\ *adj* : showing or causing gloom or depression ⟨a *dismal* voice⟩ ⟨*dismal* winter afternoons⟩ [derived from Medieval Latin *dies mali* "evil days"] — **dis·mal·ly** \\-mə-lē\\ *adv* ▢ ORIGIN Medieval calendars marked two days in every month as *dies mali*, "evil days". They were considered unlucky. English *dismal* was originally a noun meaning "the set of evil days". By the 15th century *dismal* was often being used before another noun. A "dismal day" was one of the 24 that belonged to the dismal. It was not long before the word was reinterpreted as an adjective, meaning at first "unlucky" but eventually "gloomy" or "depressing".

dis·man·tle \\dis-'mant-l\\ *vt* **dis·man·tled; dis·man·tling** \\-'mant-ling, -l-ing\\ **1** : to strip of furniture and equipment **2** : to take apart ⟨*dismantled* the engine to repair it⟩ [Middle French *desmanteler* "to strip of dress", from *des-* "dis-" + *mantel* "mantle"] — **dis·man·tle·ment** \\-'mant-l-mənt\\ *n*

dis·mast \\dis-'mast, 'dis-\\ *vt* : to remove or break off the mast of ⟨a ship *dismasted* in a storm⟩

¹dis·may \\dis-'mā, diz-\\ *vt* : to cause to lose courage or resolution through alarm or fear : DAUNT [Middle English *dismayen,* from Old French *des-* "dis-" + *-maii-er* (as in *esmaiier* "to dismay")] — **dis·may·ing·ly** \\-ing-lē\\ *adv*

²dismay *n* **1** : sudden loss of courage or resolution from alarm or fear **2** : a feeling of alarm or disappointment

dis·mem·ber \\dis-'mem-bər, 'dis-\\ *vt* **dis·mem·bered; dis·mem·ber·ing** \\-bə-ring, -bring\\ **1** : to cut off or separate the limbs, members, or parts of **2** : to break up or tear into pieces — **dis·mem·ber·ment** \\-bər-mənt\\ *n*

dis·miss \\dis-'mis\\ *vt* **1** : to permit or cause to leave ⟨*dismiss* the class⟩ **2** : to discharge from office, service, or employment **3** : to put aside or out of mind ⟨*dismiss* the thought⟩ **4** : to refuse further judicial consideration to ⟨the judge *dismissed* the charge⟩ [Latin *dimissus,* past participle of *dimittere* "to dismiss", from *dis-* "apart" + *mittere* "to send"]

dis·miss·al \\-'mis-əl\\ *n* : the act of dismissing : the fact or state of being dismissed

dis·mount \\dis-'maunt, 'dis-\\ *vb* **1** : to get down from something (as a horse or bicycle) **2** : to throw down from a horse : UNHORSE

dis·obe·di·ence \\,dis-ə-'bēd-ē-əns\\ *n* : neglect or refusal to obey — **dis·obe·di·ent** \\-ənt\\ *adj* — **dis·obe·di·ent·ly** *adv*

dis·obey \\,dis-ə-'bā\\ *vb* : to fail to obey : be disobedient

dis·oblige \\,dis-ə-'blīj\\ *vt* **1** : to go counter to the wishes of **2** : to cause inconvenience to

¹dis·or·der \\dis-'ord-ər, 'dis-\\ *vt* **1** : to disturb the order of **2** : to disturb the regular or normal functions of

²disorder *n* **1 a** : lack of order **b** : a disturbing, neglecting, or breaking away from a normal order **2** : an abnormal physical or mental condition : AILMENT — **dis·or·dered** \\-'ord-ərd\\ *adj*

dis·or·der·ly \\-ər-lē\\ *adj* **1 a** : UNRULY, TURBULENT **b** (1) : offensive to public order or decency ⟨*disorderly* behavior⟩ (2) : guilty of disorderly conduct ⟨*disorderly* persons⟩ **2** : not in an orderly condition : DISARRANGED ⟨a *disorderly* mass of papers⟩ — **dis·or·der·li·ness** *n*

dis·or·ga·nize \\'dis-'or-gə-,nīz\\ *vt* : to break up the regular arrangement or system of : throw into disorder :

1 **¹disk 2a**

\\ə\\ abut	\\ng\\ sing
\\ər\\ **further**	\\ō\\ bone
\\a\\ mat	\\ȯ\\ saw
\\ā\\ take	\\ȯi\\ coin
\\ä\\ cot, cart	\\th\\ thin
\\au̇\\ out	\\th\\ this
\\ch\\ chin	\\ü\\ food
\\e\\ pet	\\u̇\\ foot
\\ē\\ **easy**	\\y\\ yet
\\g\\ go	\\yü\\ few
\\i\\ tip	\\yu̇\\ cure
\\ī\\ life	\\zh\\ vision
\\j\\ job	

CONFUSE — **dis·or·ga·ni·za·tion** \,dis-,órg-ə-nə-'zā-shən, -,órg-nə-\ n

dis·ori·ent \dis-'ōr-ē-,ent, -'ór-\ vt : to cause to lose bearings : deprive of the normal sense of position or relationship — **dis·ori·en·ta·tion** \,dis-,ōr-ē-ən-'tā-shən, -,ór-\ n

dis·own \dis-'ōn, 'dis-\ vt : to refuse to acknowledge as one's own : REPUDIATE

dis·par·age \dis-'par-ij\ vt 1 : to lower in rank or reputation : DEGRADE 2 : to speak slightingly of : BELITTLE ⟨disparaged their achievements⟩ [Middle French desparagier "to marry below one's class", from des-"dis-" + parage "lineage", from per "peer"] — **dis·par·age·ment** \-mənt\ n — **dis·par·ag·ing·ly** \-ij-ing-lē\ adv

dis·par·ate \dis-'par-ət; 'dis-pə-rət, -prət\ adj : markedly distinct in quality or character [Latin disparatus, past participle of disparare "to separate", from dis- + parare "to prepare"] SYN see DIFFERENT — **dis·par·ate·ly** adv — **dis·par·ate·ness** n — **dis·par·i·ty** \dis-'par-ət-ē\ n

dis·pas·sion·ate \dis-'pash-nət, -ə-nət\ adj : not influenced by strong feeling : IMPARTIAL — **dis·pas·sion·ate·ly** adv

¹**dis·patch** or **des·patch** \dis-'pach\ vt 1 : to send away promptly or rapidly to a particular place or for a particular purpose ⟨dispatch a messenger⟩ ⟨dispatch a train⟩ 2 : KILL 1 3 : to attend to or dispose of speedily ⟨dispatch business⟩ [Spanish despachar or Italian dispacciare, from Provençal despacher "to get rid of", from Middle French despeechier "to set free"] — **dis·patch·er** n

²**dispatch** or **despatch** n 1 a : the sending of a message or messenger b : the shipment of goods 2 : MESSAGE; esp : an important official message 3 : the act of killing 4 : a news item sent in by a correspondent to a newpaper 5 : promptness and efficiency in performing a task

dis·pel \dis-'pel\ vt **dis·pelled; dis·pel·ling** : to drive away by or as if by scattering : DISSIPATE [Latin dispellere, from dis- + pellere "to drive, beat"] SYN see SCATTER

dis·pens·able \dis-'pen-sə-bəl\ adj : capable of being dispensed with : NONESSENTIAL — **dis·pens·abil·i·ty** \-,pen-sə-'bil-ət-ē\ n

dis·pen·sa·ry \dis-'pens-rē, -ə-rē\ n, pl **-ries** : a place where medical or dental aid is dispensed

dis·pen·sa·tion \,dis-pən-'sā-shən, -,pen-\ n 1 a : a system of rules for ordering affairs b : a particular arrangement or provision especially of nature 2 : an exemption from a rule or from a vow or oath 3 a : the act of dispensing b : something dispensed or distributed — **dis·pen·sa·tion·al** \-shnəl, -shən-l\ adj

dis·pen·sa·to·ry \dis-'pen-sə-,tōr-ē, -,tór-\ n, pl **-ries** : a book containing descriptions of medicines

dis·pense \dis-'pens\ vt 1 a : to deal out in portions b : ADMINISTER ⟨dispense justice⟩ 2 : to prepare and distribute (medication) [Latin dispensare "to distribute", from dispendere "to weigh out", from dis- + pendere "to weigh"] — **dispense with** 1 : to suspend the operation of 2 : to do or get along without

dis·pens·er \dis-'pen-sər\ n : one that dispenses; esp : a container that releases its contents in convenient amounts ⟨a soap dispenser⟩

dis·pers·al \dis-'pər-səl\ n : the act or result of dispersing

dis·perse \dis-'pərs\ vb 1 a : to cause to break up and go in different ways b : to cause to become spread widely c : to drive or clear away 2 a : to subject (as light) to dispersion b : to distribute more or less evenly throughout a medium ⟨disperse particles in water⟩ 3 : to move in different directions : SCATTER [Middle French disperser, from Latin dispergere "to scatter", from dis- + spargere "to scatter"] SYN see SCATTER — **dis·pers·ible** \-'pər-sə-bəl\ adj

dis·per·sion \dis-'pər-zhən\ n 1 : the act or process of dispersing : the state of being dispersed 2 : the separation of light into colors by refraction or diffraction with formation of a spectrum 3 a : a result or product of dispersing : something dispersed b : a system consisting of a dispersed substance and the medium in which it is dispersed ⟨a dispersion of fine particles in water⟩ — **dis·per·sive** \-'pər-siv, -ziv\ adj — **dis·per·sive·ly** adv — **dis·per·sive·ness** n

dis·pir·it \dis-'pir-ət, 'dis-\ vt : to deprive of morale or enthusiasm : DISHEARTEN [dis- + spirit] — **dis·pir·it·ed** adj — **dis·pir·it·ed·ly** adv — **dis·pir·it·ed·ness** n

dis·place \dis-'plās, 'dis-\ vt 1 : to remove from a usual or proper place; esp : to expel or force to flee from home or homeland ⟨displaced persons⟩ 2 a : to remove physically out of position ⟨water displaced by a floating object⟩ b : to take the place of : REPLACE — **dis·place·able** \-ə-bəl\ adj

dis·place·ment \-'plās-mənt\ n 1 : the act of displacing : the state of being displaced 2 a : the volume or weight of a fluid (as water) displaced by a floating body (as a ship) with the weight of the displaced fluid being equal to that of the displacing body ⟨a ship of 3000 tons displacement⟩ b : the difference between the initial position of an object and any later position c : the volume displaced by a piston (as in a pump or engine) in a single stroke; also : the total volume displaced in this way by all the pistons in an internal-combustion engine (as of an automobile)

¹**dis·play** \dis-'plā\ vb 1 a : to spread before the view ⟨display the flag⟩ b : to make evident : SHOW 2 : to make a display [Anglo-French despleier, from Latin displicare "to scatter", from dis- + plicare "to fold"] SYN see SHOW

²**display** n 1 a : a displaying of something ⟨a fireworks display⟩ b : unnecessary show especially for effect c : an eye-catching exhibition d : an electronic device (as a cathode-ray tube in a computer or radar receiver) that presents information in visual form; also : the information presented 2 : a pattern of behavior exhibited especially by male birds in the breeding season

dis·please \dis-'plēz, 'dis-\ vb 1 : to arouse the disapproval and dislike of 2 : to be offensive to 3 : to give displeasure

dis·plea·sure \dis-'plezh-ər, 'dis-, -'plāzh-\ n : the feeling of one who is displeased : DISSATISFACTION

dis·port \dis-'pōrt, -'pórt\ vb 1 a : DIVERT, AMUSE ⟨disporting themselves on the beach⟩ b : FROLIC 2 : DISPLAY 1b [Middle French desporter, from des- "dis-" + porter "to carry"]

dis·pos·al \dis-'pō-zəl\ n 1 : an orderly distribution : ARRANGEMENT 2 : MANAGEMENT 1, ADMINISTRATION 3 : a discarding or destroying especially in a systematic way 4 : the transfer of something into new hands 5 : the power to dispose of something : CONTROL, COMMAND 6 : a device used to reduce waste matter (as by grinding)

dis·pose \dis-'pōz\ vt 1 : to give a tendency to : INCLINE ⟨they were disposed to refuse⟩ 2 : to put in order : ARRANGE [Middle French disposer, from Latin disponere "to arrange", from dis- + ponere "to put"] — **dis·pos·able** \-'pō-zə-bəl\ adj — **dispose of** 1 : to settle or determine the fate, condition, or use of : deal with conclusively ⟨has the right to dispose of the personal property⟩ 2 a : to get rid of ⟨dispose of rubbish⟩ b : to treat or handle so as to finish with ⟨dispose of the morning's mail⟩ 3 : to transfer to the control of another ⟨we had to dispose of the house before we moved⟩

dis·po·si·tion \,dis-pə-'zish-ən\ n 1 a : the act or power of disposing : DISPOSAL b : a final settlement 2 : the giving up or transferring of something 3 : ARRANGEMENT 4 a : TENDENCY, INCLINATION b : natural attitude toward things

dis·pos·sess \,dis-pə-'zes\ vt : to deprive of possession or occupancy (as of land or houses) — **dis·pos·ses·sion** \-'zesh-ən\ n

dis·praise \dis-'prāz, 'dis-\ *vt* : to comment on with disapproval or censure — **dispraise** *n* — **dis·prais·er** *n* — **dis·prais·ing·ly** \-'prā-zing-lē\ *adv*

dis·proof \dis-'prüf, 'dis-\ *n* **1** : the action of disproving **2** : evidence that disproves

dis·pro·por·tion \,dis-prə-'pōr-shən, -'pȯr-\ *n* : lack of proportion, symmetry, or proper relation : DISPARITY; *also* : an instance of this — **disproportion** *vt* — **dis·pro·por·tion·al** \-shnəl, -shən-l\ *adj* — **dis·pro·por·tion·ate** \-shə-nət, -shnət\ *adj* — **dis·pro·por·tion·ate·ly** *adv*

dis·prove \dis-'prüv\ *vt* : to prove to be false : REFUTE — **dis·prov·able** \-'prü-və-bəl\ *adj*

dis·pu·ta·tion \,dis-pyù-'tā-shən\ *n* **1** : the act of disputing : DEBATE **2** : an oral defense of an academic thesis

dis·pu·ta·tious \,dis-pyù-'tā-shəs\ *adj* : inclined to dispute : ARGUMENTATIVE — **dis·pu·ta·tious·ly** *adv* — **dis·pu·ta·tious·ness** *n*

¹dis·pute \dis-'pyüt\ *vb* **1** : to engage in argument : DEBATE; *esp* : to argue irritably or with irritating persistence **2** : WRANGLE 1 **3 a** : to engage in controversy over : argue about **b** : to deny the truth or rightness of : QUESTION **4 a** : to struggle against : OPPOSE **b** : to struggle over : CONTEST [Old French *desputer,* from Latin *disputare* "to discuss", from *dis-* + *putare* "to think"] SYN see DISCUSS — **dis·put·able** \dis-'pyüt-ə-bəl, 'dis-pyət-\ *adj* — **dis·put·ably** \-blē\ *adv* — **dis·pu·tant** \dis-'pyüt-nt, 'dis-pyət-ənt\ *n* — **dis·put·er** *n*

²dispute *n* **1** : verbal controversy : DEBATE **2** : QUARREL 2

dis·qual·i·fy \dis-'kwäl-ə-,fī, 'dis-\ *vt* **1** : to deprive of necessary qualifications : make unfit (*disqualified* for military service by poor vision) **2** : to make or declare ineligible (*disqualify* voters who cannot read and write) — **dis·qual·i·fi·ca·tion** \,dis-,kwäl-ə-fə-'kā-shən\ *n*

¹dis·qui·et \dis-'kwī-ət\ *vt* : to make uneasy or restless : DISTURB — **dis·qui·et·ing** \-ing\ *adj* — **dis·qui·et·ing·ly** \-ing-lē\ *adv*

²disquiet *n* : DISQUIETUDE

dis·qui·etude \dis-'kwī-ə-,tüd, -,tyüd\ *n* : lack of peace and tranquillity : a state of unrest or anxiety

dis·qui·si·tion \,dis-kwə-'zish-ən\ *n* : a formal inquiry or discussion : DISCOURSE [Latin *disquisitio,* from *disquirere* "to inquire diligently", from *dis-* + *quaerere* "to seek"]

¹dis·re·gard \,dis-ri-'gärd\ *vt* : to pay no attention to : treat as unworthy of regard or notice

²disregard *n* : the act of disregarding : the state of being disregarded — **dis·re·gard·ful** \-fəl\ *adj*

¹dis·rel·ish \dis-'rel-ish\ *vt* : to find objectionable or distasteful

²disrelish *n* : lack of relish : DISTASTE, DISLIKE

dis·re·pair \,dis-ri-'paər, -'peər\ *n* : the state of being in need of repair

dis·rep·u·ta·ble \dis-'rep-yət-ə-bəl, 'dis-\ *adj* : not reputable; *esp* : having a bad reputation — **dis·rep·u·ta·ble·ness** *n* — **dis·rep·u·ta·bly** \-blē\ *adv*

dis·re·pute \,dis-ri-'pyüt\ *n* : loss or lack of esteem or reputation : DISCREDIT

dis·re·spect \,dis-ri-'spekt\ *n* : lack of respect : DISCOURTESY — **dis·re·spect·ful** \-fəl\ *adj* — **dis·re·spect·ful·ly** \-fə-lē\ *adv*

dis·robe \dis-'rōb, 'dis-\ *vb* : UNDRESS

dis·rupt \dis-'rəpt\ *vt* **1** : to break apart : RUPTURE **2** : to throw into disorder : break up **3** : to interrupt the unity or continuity of (the storm *disrupted* communications) [Latin *disruptus,* past participle of *disrumpere* "to break apart", from *dis-* + *rumpere* "to break"] — **dis·rupt·er** *n* — **dis·rup·tion** \-'rəp-shən\ *n* — **dis·rup·tive** \-'rəp-tiv\ *adj* — **dis·rup·tive·ly** *adv* — **dis·rup·tive·ness** *n*

dis·sat·is·fac·tion \,dis-,sat-əs-'fak-shən, ,dis-,at-\ *n* : the quality or state of being dissatisfied □ SYN DISCON-

TENT: DISSATISFACTION has usually a definite cause and is often temporary (*dissatisfaction* with the trend of business) DISCONTENT is more general, personal, and deep-rooted (the *discontent* of colonial peoples)

dis·sat·is·fac·to·ry \-'fak-tə-rē, -trē\ *adj* : causing dissatisfaction

dis·sat·is·fied \dis-'sat-əs-,fīd, 'dis-,-'at-\ *adj* : expressing or showing dissatisfaction (a *dissatisfied* look) (*dissatisfied* customers)

dis·sat·is·fy \dis-'sat-əs-,fī, 'dis-, -'at-\ *vt* : to fail to satisfy

dis·sect \dis-'ekt; dī-'sekt, 'dī-,\ *vt* **1** : to divide (as a plant or animal) into separate parts for examination and study **2** : to analyze thoroughly (*dissect* a proposed plan) [Latin *dissecare* "to cut apart", from *dis-* + *secare* "to cut"] — **dis·sec·tion** \dis-'ek-shən; dī-sek-, 'dī-,\ *n* — **dis·sec·tor** \-ər\ *n*

dis·sect·ed *adj* : cut deeply into fine lobes (a *dissected* leaf)

dis·sem·ble \dis-'em-bəl\ *vb* **-bled; -bling** \-bə-ling, -bling\ **1** : to hide under or put on a false appearance : conceal facts, intentions, or feelings under some pretense **2** : to put on the appearance of : SIMULATE [Middle French *dissimuler,* from Latin *dissimulare* "to dissimulate"] — **dis·sem·bler** \-bə-lər, -blər\ *n*

dis·sem·i·nate \dis-'em-ə-,nāt\ *vt* : to spread abroad as though sowing seed (*disseminate* ideas) [Latin *disseminare,* from *dis-* + *seminare* "to sow", from *semen* "seed"] — **dis·sem·i·na·tion** \-,em-ə-'nā-shən\ *n* — **dis·sem·i·na·tor** \-'em-ə-,nāt-ər\ *n*

dis·sen·sion \dis-'en-chən\ *n* : disagreement in opinion : DISCORD, QUARRELING [Middle French, from Latin *dissensio,* from *dissentire* "to dissent"]

¹dis·sent \dis-'ent\ *vi* **1** : to withhold assent **2** : to differ in opinion [Latin *dissentire,* from *dis-* + *sentire* "to feel"]

²dissent *n* **1** : difference of opinion; *esp* : religious nonconformity **2** : a written statement in which a justice disagrees with the opinion of the majority — called also *dissenting opinion*

dis·sent·er \dis-'ent-ər\ *n* **1** : one that dissents **2** *cap* : an English Nonconformist

dis·ser·ta·tion \,dis-ər-'tā-shən\ *n* : an extended usually written treatment of a subject; *esp* : one submitted for a doctorate [Latin *dissertatio* "discussion", derived from *disserere* "to discourse", from *dis-* + *serere* "to join, arrange"]

dis·ser·vice \dis-'sər-vəs, -'ər-\ *n* : an act that adversely affects someone or something : INJURY, HARM

dis·si·dence \'dis-əd-əns\ *n* : DISSENT 1, DISAGREEMENT

dis·si·dent \-ənt\ *adj* : openly differing with an opinion or a group : expressing dissent [Latin *dissidēre* "to sit apart, disagree", from *dis-* + *sedēre* "to sit"] — **dissident** *n*

dis·sim·i·lar \dis-'sim-ə-lər, -'im-\ *adj* : UNLIKE a — **dis·sim·i·lar·i·ty** \,dis-,sim-ə-'lar-ət-ē, -,im-\ *n* — **dis·sim·i·lar·ly** \dis-'sim-ə-lər-lē, -'im-\ *adv*

dis·sim·i·la·tion \,dis-,im-ə-'lā-shən\ *n* : the change or omission of one of two identical or closely related sounds in a word — **dis·sim·i·la·tive** \dis-'im-ə-,lāt-iv\ *adj*

dis·si·mil·i·tude \,dis-sə-'mil-ə-,tüd, ,dis-ə-, -,tyüd\ *n* : lack of resemblance

dis·sim·u·late \dis-'im-yə-,lāt\ *vb* : to hide under a false appearance : DISSEMBLE [Latin *dissimulare,* from *dis-* + *simulare* "to simulate"] — **dis·sim·u·la·tion** \,dis-,im-yə-'lā-shən\ *n* — **dis·sim·u·la·tor** \dis-'im-yə-,lāt-ər\ *n*

dis·si·pate \'dis-ə-,pāt\ *vb* **1 a** : to break up and drive off (as a crowd) **b** : to cause to spread out to the point of vanishing : DISSOLVE (the breeze *dissipated* the fog) **2 a** : to expend aimlessly or foolishly (*dissipate* our energies) **b** : SQUANDER (*dissipated* a fortune in gambling) **3** : to separate into parts and scatter or vanish **4** : to be extravagant or uncontrolled in the pursuit of

\ə\	abut	\ng\	sing
\ər\	further	\ō\	bone
\a\	mat	\ȯ\	saw
\ā\	take	\ȯi\	coin
\ä\	cot, cart	\th\	thin
\aù\	out	\th\	this
\ch\	chin	\ü\	food
\e\	pet	\ù\	foot
\ē\	easy	\y\	yet
\g\	go	\yü\	few
\i\	tip	\yù\	cure
\ī\	life	\zh\	vision
\j\	job		

pleasure; *esp* : to drink to excess [Latin *dissipare,* from *dis-* + *supare* "to throw"] SYN see SCATTER

dis·si·pat·ed *adj* : given to dissipation — **dis·si·pat·ed·ly** *adv* — **dis·si·pat·ed·ness** *n*

dis·si·pa·tion \,dis-ə-'pā-shən\ *n* : the act of dissipating : the state of being dissipated : **a** : DISPERSION 1 **b** : wasteful expenditure **c** : intemperate living; *esp* : excessive drinking

dis·so·ci·ate \dis-'ō-sē,āt, -shē-,āt\ *vb* **1** : to separate from association or union with another : DISCONNECT **2** : DISUNITE; *esp* : to subject to chemical dissociation **3** : to undergo dissociation (salts and acids *dissociate* in water) [Latin *dissociare,* from *dis-* + *sociare* "to join", from *socius* "companion"]

dis·so·ci·a·tion \,dis-,ō-sē-'ā-shən, -,ō-shē-\ *n* : the act or process of dissociating : the state of being dissociated; *esp* : the process by which a chemical combination breaks up into simpler constituents — **dis·so·cia·tive** \dis-'ō-sē-,āt-iv, -sē-,āt-, -shət-iv\ *adj*

dis·so·lute \'dis-ə-,lüt\ *adj* : lacking restraint; *esp* : loose in morals or conduct [Latin *dissolutus,* from *dissolvere* "to loosen, dissolve"] — **dis·so·lute·ly** *adv* — **dis·so·lute·ness** *n*

dis·so·lu·tion \,dis-ə-'lü-shən\ *n* **1** : the action or process of dissolving: as **a** : separation into component parts **b** : DECAY 1 **2** : the termination or breaking up of an assembly or a partnership or corporation

¹dis·solve \diz-'älv, -'olv\ *vb* **1** : to break up into component parts **2** : to pass or cause to pass into solution (sugar *dissolves* in water) **3** : to bring to an end : TERMINATE (*dissolve* parliament) **4** : to waste or fade away as if by breaking up or melting (their courage *dissolved* in the face of danger) **5** : to fade out (a motion-picture shot) in a dissolve **6** : to be overcome emotionally (*dissolved* into tears) [Latin *dissolvere,* from *dis-* + *solvere* "to loosen"] — **dis·solv·able** \-ə-bəl\ *adj* — **dis·solv·er** *n*

²dissolve *n* : a gradual superimposing of one motion-picture or television shot upon another on a screen

dis·so·nance \'dis-ə-nəns\ *n* **1** : a harsh or unpleasant sound or combination of sounds **2** : lack of agreement : DISCORD **3** : an unresolved musical note or chord

dis·so·nant \'dis-ə-nənt\ *adj* **1** : marked by dissonance in sound **2** : not being in harmony or agreement (*dissonant* viewpoints) [Latin *dissonare* "to be discordant", from *dis-* + *sonare* "to sound"] — **dis·so·nant·ly** *adv* □ SYN DISCORDANT: DISSONANT may apply to lack of harmony intended as a contrast to consonant sounds; DISCORDANT commonly suggests an unpleasant or disagreeable effect on the listener.

dis·suade \dis-'wād\ *vt* : to advise against a course of action : persuade or try to persuade not to do something [Latin *dissuadēre,* from *dis-* + *suadēre* "to urge"] — **dis·sua·sion** \-'wā-zhən\ *n* — **dis·sua·sive** \-'wā-siv, -ziv\ *adj* — **dis·sua·sive·ly** *adv* — **dis·sua·sive·ness** *n*

¹dis·taff \'dis-,taf\ *n, pl* **dis·taffs** \-,tafs, -,tavz\ **1** : a staff for holding the flax, tow, or wool in spinning **2** : the female branch or side of a family [Old English *distæf*] □ ORIGIN A *distaff* is a small staff used in spinning yarn or thread. Because spinning was in former times an important activity of most women, the *distaff* became a symbol for women's work. Activity that was felt to be proper to men rather than to women was symbolized by the spear, and the male side of a family was known as the "spear side". This term is now used very rarely, if at all, but the female side of a family is still commonly called the "distaff side" or simply the "distaff".

| ¹distaff |

²distaff *adj* : FEMALE

dis·tal \'dist-l\ *adj* **1** : far from the point of attachment or origin (as of a bone or limb) — compare PROXIMAL **2** : of, relating to, or being the surface of a tooth that is most distant from the middle of the front of the jaw and is usually next to the tooth behind it [*distant* + *-al*] — **dis·tal·ly** \-l-ē\ *adv*

¹dis·tance \'dis-təns\ *n* **1** : separation in time **2** : separation in space : the amount of space between two points, lines, surfaces, or objects (the *distance* from the earth to the moon) **3 a** : a measurable advance along a route or course (walked a *distance* of five kilometers) **b** : an amount or degree of progress (have come quite a *distance* toward achieving peace) **c** : a full course or extent (go the *distance*) **4** : the quality or state of being distant : **a** : remoteness in space (their parents sought to keep them at a *distance*) **b** : COLDNESS, RESERVE (they keep their *distance*) **5** : a distant point or region (saw a car off in the *distance*)

²distance *vt* : to leave far behind : OUTSTRIP

dis·tant \'dis-tənt\ *adj* **1 a** : separated in space : AWAY (a point 100 meters *distant*) **b** : situated at a great distance : FAR-OFF (travel to *distant* lands) **2** : not close in relationship (a *distant* cousin) **3** : reserved or aloof in personal relationship : COLD (they have recently been very *distant* toward me) **4** : coming from or going to a distance (*distant* voyages) [Middle French, from Latin *distare* "to stand apart, be distant", from *dis-* + *stare* "to stand"] — **dis·tant·ly** *adv* — **dis·tant·ness** *n* □ SYN DISTANT, FAR, REMOTE, REMOVED mean not close or near in space, time, or relationship. DISTANT is the opposite of *close* and implies separation in space or time; FAR is the opposite of *near* and implies a relatively long distance away; REMOTE applies to what is far removed especially from what is regarded as a center of interest (a *remote* corner of the world) REMOVED implies separateness and often a contrast in character or quality as well as time or space.

dis·taste \dis-'tāst, 'dis-\ *n* : DISLIKE (a *distaste* for work)

dis·taste·ful \-fəl\ *adj* : distinctly unpleasant : DISAGREEABLE — **dis·taste·ful·ly** \-fə-lē\ *adv* — **dis·taste·ful·ness** *n*

¹dis·tem·per \dis-'tem-pər\ **1** : a bad humor or temper **2** : a disordered or abnormal bodily state: as **a** : a highly contagious virus disease especially of dogs marked by fever and by respiratory and sometimes nervous symptoms **b** : PANLEUCOPENIA

²distemper *n* : a water-based paint in which the pigments are usually mixed with size or a casein binder and which is used for scene painting and mural decoration [Middle French *distemprer* "to dilute", from Latin *dis-* + *temperare* "to temper"]

dis·tend \dis-'tend\ *vb* : to stretch out or bulge out in all directions : SWELL [Latin *distendere,* from *dis-* + *tendere* "to stretch"] SYN see EXPAND

dis·ten·sion *or* **dis·ten·tion** \dis-'ten-chən\ *n* : the act of distending : the state of being distended especially unduly or abnormally

dis·till *also* **dis·til** \dis-'til\ *vb* **dis·tilled; dis·till·ing** **1** : to fall or let fall in drops **2 a** : to subject to or transform by distillation (*distill* water) **b** : to obtain by distillation (*distill* brandy from wine) **3** : to extract the essence of : CONCENTRATE (*distilled* the information in the report) **4** : to undergo distillation : condense from a still after distillation [Middle French *distiller,* from Latin *destillare,* from *de-* + *stilla* "drop"]

dis·til·late \'dis-tə-,lāt, dis-'til-ət\ *n* : a liquid product condensed from vapor during distillation

dis·til·la·tion \,dis-tə-'lā-shən\ *n* **1** : a process that consists of driving gas or vapor from liquids or solids by heating and condensing to liquid products and that is used especially for purification, separation, or the formation of new substances **2** : something obtained by or as if by a process of distilling : ESSENCE

dis·till·er \dis-'til-ər\ *n* : one that distills especially alcoholic liquors

dis·till·ery \dis-'til-rē, -ə-rē\ *n, pl* **-er·ies** : a place where distilling especially of alcoholic liquors is carried on

dis·tinct \dis-'tingt, -tingkt\ *adj* **1** : distinguished from others : SEPARATE ⟨guilty of three *distinct* crimes⟩ **2** : clearly seen, heard, or understood : UNMISTAKABLE ⟨*distinct* footprints⟩; *also* : NOTABLE ⟨a *distinct* improvement⟩ [Middle French, from Latin *distinctus*, from *distinguere* "to distinguish"] — **dis·tinct·ly** *adv* — **dis·tinct·ness** *n*

dis·tinc·tion \dis-'ting-shən, -'tingk-\ *n* **1** : the act of distinguishing a difference **2** : the quality or state of being different or distinct : DIFFERENCE ⟨the *distinction* between good and evil⟩ **3** : something that makes a difference : a distinguishing quality or mark ⟨the *distinction* of being the tallest building in town⟩ **4** : SIGNIFICANCE, EMINENCE ⟨a speaker of *distinction*⟩ **5** : special honor or recognition ⟨graduated with *distinction*⟩

dis·tinc·tive \dis-'ting-tiv, -'tingk-\ *adj* : clearly marking a person or a thing as different from others ⟨a *distinctive* way of speaking⟩ SYN see CHARACTERISTIC — **dis·tinc·tive·ly** *adv* — **dis·tinc·tive·ness** *n*

dis·tin·gué \,dēs-,tang-'gā\ *adj* : distinguished especially in manner or bearing [French, from *distinguer* "to distinguish"]

dis·tin·guish \dis-'ting-gwish, -wish\ *vb* **1** : to recognize as different by some mark or quality ⟨*distinguish* the sound of a piano in an orchestra⟩ **2** : to make distinctions ⟨*distinguish* between right and wrong⟩ **3** : to mark as different or distinct : set apart ⟨a church *distinguished* by the absence of a steeple⟩ **4** : to perceive clearly : make out ⟨*distinguish* a light in the distance⟩ **5** : to separate from others by a mark of honor : single out; *also* : to make (oneself) prominent ⟨*distinguished* themselves in Congress⟩ [Middle French *distinguer*, from Latin *distinguere*, literally, "to separate by pricking"] — **dis·tin·guish·able** \-ə-bəl\ *adj* — **dis·tin·guish·ably** \-ə-blē\ *adv*

dis·tin·guished *adj* **1** : marked by eminence, distinction, or excellence **2** : befitting an eminent person

dis·tort \dis-'tort\ *vt* **1** : to twist out of the true meaning : MISREPRESENT **2** : to twist out of a natural, normal, or original shape or condition [Latin *distortus*, past participle of *distorquēre* "to distort", from *dis-* + *torquēre* "to twist"] — **dis·tort·er** *n*

dis·tor·tion \dis-'tor-shən\ *n* **1** : the act of distorting **2** : the condition of being distorted or a product of distortion: as **a** : a misshapen condition of an image caused by defects in a lens **b** : inaccurate reproduction of a sound in radio or of an image in television — **dis·tor·tion·al** \-shnəl, -shən-l\ *adj*

dis·tract \dis-'trakt\ *vt* **1** : to turn aside : DIVERT; *esp* : to draw (the attention or mind) to a different object **2** : to stir up or confuse with conflicting emotions or motives : HARASS [Latin *distractus*, past participle of *distrahere* "to draw apart, distract", from *dis-* + *trahere* "to draw"]

dis·trac·tion \dis-'trak-shən\ *n* **1** : the act of distracting or the state of being distracted; *esp* : mental confusion **2** : something that distracts; *esp* : AMUSEMENT — **dis·trac·tive** \-'trak-tiv\ *adj*

dis·traught \dis-'trot\ *adj* **1** : troubled with doubt or mental conflict **2** : being or acting insane : CRAZED [Middle English, from Latin *distractus* "distracted"]

¹dis·tress \dis-'tres\ *n* **1** : great suffering of body or mind : PAIN, ANGUISH ⟨suffer *distress* from loss of a friend⟩ **2** : MISFORTUNE, TROUBLE ⟨unemployment and economic *distress*⟩ **3** : a condition of danger or desperate need ⟨a ship in *distress*⟩ [Old French *destresse*, derived from Latin *distringere* "to draw apart, detain"] □ SYN DISTRESS, SUFFERING, MISERY, AGONY mean the state of being in physical or mental anguish. DISTRESS implies conditions or circumstances that cause physical or mental stress or strain and suggests the need of assistance ⟨the *distress* of war orphans⟩ SUFFERING applies to human beings and connotes conscious awareness and endurance of pain; MISERY stresses the unhappy or wretched conditions attending distress or

suffering; AGONY suggests suffering too intense to be borne.

²distress *vt* **1** : to subject to great strain or difficulties **2** : to cause to worry or be troubled : UPSET — **dis·tress·ing·ly** \-ing-lē\ *adv*

dis·tress·ful \-fəl\ *adj* : causing distress : full of distress — **dis·tress·ful·ly** \-fə-lē\ *adv* — **dis·tress·ful·ness** *n*

dis·trib·u·tary \dis-'trib-yə-,ter-ē\ *n, pl* **-taries** : a river branch flowing away from the main stream

dis·trib·ute \dis-'trib-yət\ *vt* **1** : to divide among several or many : APPORTION ⟨*distribute* food packages to the needy⟩ **2 a** : to spread out so as to cover something : SCATTER ⟨*distribute* grass seed over a lawn⟩ **b** : to hand out : DELIVER ⟨*distributing* handbills to passersby⟩ **3** : to divide or separate especially into kinds **4** : to market (a line of goods) in a particular area usually as a wholesaler [Latin *distribuere*, from *dis-* + *tribuere* "to allot"] — **dis·trib·ut·able** \-yət-ə-bəl\ *adj*

dis·tri·bu·tion \,dis-trə-'byü-shən\ *n* **1** : the act or process of distributing **2 a** : the position, arrangement, or frequency of occurrence (as of the members of a group) over an area or throughout a space or unit of time ⟨the *distribution* of iron ore in the United States⟩ **b** : the natural geographic range of an organism **3 a** : something distributed **b** : FREQUENCY DISTRIBUTION **4** : the marketing or merchandising of commodities — **dis·tri·bu·tion·al** \-shnəl, -shən-l\ *adj*

dis·trib·u·tive \dis-'trib-yət-iv\ *adj* **1** : of or relating to distribution **2** : referring singly and without exception to the members of a group ⟨the *distributive* adjectives *each* and *every*⟩ **3 a** : being an operation (as multiplication in $a\,(b+c) = ab + ac$) that produces the same result when operating on the whole mathematical expression as when operating on each part and collecting the results **b** : being or relating to a rule or property concerning a distributive operation ⟨the *distributive* axiom for multiplication⟩ — **dis·trib·u·tive·ly** *adv* — **dis·trib·u·tive·ness** *n*

distributive education *n, often cap D & E* : a vocational program set up between schools and employers in which students receive both classroom instruction and on-the-job training

dis·trib·u·tor \dis-'trib-yət-ər\ *n* **1** : one that distributes **2** : an agent or agency for marketing goods **3** : a device for distributing electric current to the spark plugs of an engine

¹dis·trict \'dis-trikt\ *n* **1** : a territorial division marked off or defined (as for administrative or electoral purposes) ⟨school *districts*⟩ ⟨a judicial *district*⟩ **2** : a distinctive area or region ⟨residential *district*⟩ [French, from Medieval Latin *districtus* "jurisdiction, district", from Latin *distringere* "to draw apart, detain"]

²district *vt* : to divide or organize into districts

district attorney *n* : a public official who is the prosecuting officer for a judicial district

district court *n* : a trial court with jurisdiction over certain cases within a specified judicial district

¹dis·trust \dis-'trəst, 'dis-\ *vt* : to have no confidence in : SUSPECT

²distrust *n* : a lack of trust or confidence : SUSPICION, WARINESS SYN see DOUBT — **dis·trust·ful** \-fəl\ *adj* — **dis·trust·ful·ly** \-fə-lē\ *adv* — **dis·trust·ful·ness** *n*

dis·turb \dis-'tərb\ *vt* **1** : to interfere with : INTERRUPT **2 a** : to alter the position or arrangement of **2 a** : to destroy the tranquillity or composure of : make uneasy **b** : to throw into disorder **c** : to put to inconvenience [Latin *disturbare*, from *dis-* + *turbare* "to throw into disorder"] — **dis·turb·er** *n* □ SYN PERTURB: DISTURB implies the distracting or distorting effect of worry, conflict, or strain on mental processes; PERTURB applies to the deeper unsettling of the mind by uncertainty, disappointment, or danger.

dis·tur·bance \dis-'tər-bəns\ *n* **1** : the act of disturbing : the state of being disturbed **2** : mental confu-

\ə\ abut	\ng\ sing
\ər\ further	\ō\ bone
\a\ mat	\o\ saw
\ā\ take	\oi\ coin
\ä\ cot, cart	\th\ thin
\aù\ out	\th\ this
\ch\ chin	\ü\ food
\e\ pet	\ù\ foot
\ē\ easy	\y\ yet
\g\ go	\yü\ few
\i\ tip	\yù\ cure
\ī\ life	\zh\ vision
\j\ job	

sion : UPSET ⟨an emotional *disturbance*⟩ **3** : public disorder : COMMOTION

dis·turbed *adj* : showing symptoms of mental or emotional illness

di·sul·fide \dī-'səl-,fīd\ *n* : a compound containing two atoms of sulfur combined with an element or radical

dis·union \dish-'ü-nyən, dis-, -'yü-\ *n* : lack of union or agreement : SEPARATION

dis·unite \,dish-ü-'nīt, ,dis-, -yü-\ *vt* : DIVIDE 1, SEPARATE

dis·uni·ty \dish-'ü-nət-ē, dis-, -'yü-\ *n* : lack of unity; *esp* : DISSENSION

¹**dis·use** \dis-'yüz\ *vt* : to discontinue the use or practice of : ABANDON

²**dis·use** \dis-'yüs\ *n* : cessation of use or practice

di·syl·lab·ic \,dī-sə-'lab-ik\ *adj* : having two syllables — **di·syl·la·ble** \'dī-,sil-ə-bəl, dī-'\ *n*

¹**ditch** \'dich\ *n* : a long narrow excavation dug in the earth for defense, drainage, or irrigation [Old English *dīc* "dike, ditch"]

²**ditch** *vt* **1 a** : to enclose with a ditch **b** : to provide with ditches (as for drainage or irrigation) **2** : to drive (a car) into a ditch **3** : to get rid of : DISCARD **4** : to make a forced landing of (an airplane) on water

dith·er \'dith-ər\ *n* : a highly nervous, excited, or agitated state [Middle English *didderen*] — **dith·ery** \-ə-rē\ *adj*

dith·y·ramb \'dith-i-,ram\ *n* **1** : a short poem in a wild inspired strain **2** : an exalted or impassioned statement or writing [Greek *dithyrambos*] — **dith·y·ram·bic** \,dith-i-'ram-bik\ *adj*

dit·to \'dit-ō\ *n, pl* **dittos** **1** : SAME : more of the same : ANOTHER — used to avoid repeating a word ⟨lost: one shirt (white); *ditto* (blue)⟩ **2** : a mark composed of a pair of inverted commas or apostrophes used as a symbol for the word ditto [Italian dialect, past participle of Italian *dire* "to say", from Latin *dicere*]

dit·ty \'dit-ē\ *n, pl* **ditties** : SONG; *esp* : a short simple song [Old French *ditié* "poem", from *ditier* "to compose", from Latin *dictare* "to dictate, compose"]

dit·ty bag \'dit-ē-\ *n* : a small bag used especially by sailors to hold odds and ends of gear (as thread, needles, or tape) [origin unknown]

di·uret·ic \,dī-yù-'ret-ik\ *adj* : tending to increase the flow of urine [Late Latin *diureticus*, from Greek *diourētikos*, from *diourein* "to urinate", from *dia-* + *ourein* "to urinate"] — **diuretic** *n*

di·ur·nal \dī-'ərn-l\ *adj* **1 a** : recurring every day ⟨a *diurnal* task⟩ **b** : having a daily cycle ⟨*diurnal* rotation of the heavens⟩ **2 a** : of, relating to, occurring in, or active during the daytime ⟨a *diurnal* organism⟩ **b** : opening during the day and closing at night ⟨*diurnal* flowers⟩ [Latin *diurnalis*, from *diurnus* "of the day", from *dies* "day"] — **di·ur·nal·ly** \-l-ē\ *adv*

di·va \'dē-və\ *n, pl* **di·vas** *or* **di·ve** \-,vā\ : PRIMA DONNA 1 [Italian, literally, "goddess", from Latin, from *divus* "divine, god"]

di·va·gate \'dī-və-,gāt, 'div-ə-\ *vi* : to wander about : STRAY [Late Latin *divagari*, from Latin *dis-* + *vagari* "to wander"] — **di·va·ga·tion** \,dī-və-'gā-shən, ,div-ə-\ *n*

di·va·lent \dī-'vā-lənt, 'dī-\ *adj* : BIVALENT

di·van \di-'van, 'dī-,van\ *n* : a large couch or sofa usually without back or arms and often designed for use as a bed [Turkish, "council", from Persian *dīwān* "account book"]

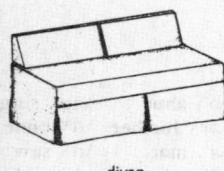
divan

¹**dive** \'dīv\ *vi* **dived** \'dīvd\ *or* **dove** \'dōv\; **div·ing** **1 a** : to plunge into water headfirst; *esp* : to execute a dive **b** : SUBMERGE **2 a** : PLUNGE 3b **b** : to descend in a dive **3** : to plunge into some matter or activity **4** : DART, LUNGE [Old English *dȳfan* "to dip" and *dūfan* "to dive"]

²**dive** *n* **1** : the act or an instance of diving: as **a** : a plunge into water executed in a prescribed manner **b** : a submerging of a submarine **c** : a steep descent of an airplane with or without power **2** : a sharp decline

dive–bomb \'dīv-,bäm\ *vt* : to bomb from an airplane by making a steep dive toward the target before releasing the bomb — **dive–bomb·er** *n*

div·er \'dī-vər\ *n* **1** : one that dives **2 a** : a person who stays under water for long periods by having air supplied from the surface or by carrying a supply of compressed air **b** : any of various diving birds; *esp* : LOON

di·verge \də-'vərj, dī-\ *vi* **1 a** : to move or extend in different directions from a common point : draw apart ⟨*diverging* rays of light⟩ **b** : to differ in character, form, or opinion **2** : to turn aside from a path or course : DEVIATE [Medieval Latin *divergere*, from Latin *dis-* + *vergere* "to incline"]

di·ver·gence \-'vər-jəns\ *n* **1** : a drawing apart (as of lines extending from a common center) **2** : DIFFERENCE 3, DISAGREEMENT **3** : a deviation from a course or standard

di·ver·gent \-jənt\ *adj* **1** : drawing apart from each other : SPREADING **2** : differing from each other or from a standard : DEVIANT SYN see DIFFERENT — **di·ver·gent·ly** *adv*

di·vers \'dī-vərz\ *adj* : VARIOUS 3 [Middle English *divers, diverse*]

di·verse \dī-'vərs, də-, 'dī-,\ *adj* **1** : differing from one another : UNLIKE **2** : having various forms or qualities ⟨a *diverse* personality⟩ [Middle English, from Latin *diversus*, from *divertere* "to divert"] SYN see DIFFERENT — **di·verse·ly** *adv* — **di·verse·ness** *n*

di·ver·si·fy \də-'vər-sə-,fī, dī-\ *vb* **-fied; -fy·ing** **1** : to make diverse : give variety to ⟨*diversify* an educational program by adding new subjects⟩ **2** : to produce variety; *esp* : to engage in a variety of operations ⟨manufacturers *diversifying* into new fields⟩ — **di·ver·si·fi·ca·tion** \də-,vər-sə-fə-'kā-shən, ,dī-\ *n*

di·ver·sion \də-'vər-zhən, dī-\ *n* **1** : the act or an instance of diverting from a course, activity, or use : DEVIATION **2** : something that diverts or amuses : PASTIME **3** : an attack made to draw the attention of an enemy from the point of a principal operation — **di·ver·sion·ary** \-zhə-,ner-ē\ *adj*

di·ver·si·ty \də-'vər-sət-ē, dī-\ *n, pl* **-ties** **1** : the condition of being different or having differences **2** : an instance or a point of difference **3** : VARIETY ⟨*diversity* of opinion⟩

di·vert \də-'vərt, dī-\ *vb* **1 a** : to turn from one course or use to another : DEFLECT **b** : DISTRACT **2** : to give pleasure to by causing the time to pass pleasantly [Latin *divertere* "to turn in opposite directions", from *dis-* + *vertere* "to turn"] SYN see AMUSE

di·ver·tic·u·lum \,dī-vər-'tik-yə-ləm\ *n, pl* **-la** \-lə\ : a pocket or closed branch opening off a main passage ⟨intestinal *diverticula*⟩ [Latin, "bypath", probably from *devertere* "to turn aside", from *de-* + *vertere* "to turn"]

di·ver·ti·men·to \di-,vərt-ə-'ment-ō, -,vert-\ *n, pl* **-men·ti** \-'ment-ē\ *or* **-men·tos** : a light instrumental musical work in several movements [Italian, literally, "diversion"]

di·vest \dī-'vest, də-\ *vt* **1** : to strip especially of clothing, ornament, or equipment **2** : to deprive especially of a right [Middle French *desvestir*, derived from Latin *dis-* + *vestire* "to clothe"]

¹**di·vide** \də-'vīd\ *vb* **1 a** : to separate into two or more parts, areas, or groups **b** : to separate into classes, categories, or divisions **2 a** : to give out in shares : DISTRIBUTE **b** : to possess or make use of in common : SHARE **3** : to cause to be separate, distinct, or apart from one another **4 a** : to subject (a number or quantity) to the operation of finding how many times it contains another number or quantity ⟨*divide* 42 by 14⟩ **b** : to use as a divisor ⟨*divide* 14 into 42⟩ **5 a** : to become separated into parts **b** : to branch out : DIVERGE [Latin *dividere*] SYN see SEPARATE

²**divide** *n* : a dividing ridge between drainage areas : WATERSHED

di·vid·ed *adj* **1 a :** separated into parts or pieces ⟨finely *divided* particles of iron⟩ **b :** cut into distinct parts by incisions extending to the base or to the midrib ⟨a *divided* leaf⟩ **c :** having a barrier (as a guardrail) to separate lanes of traffic going in opposite directions ⟨a 4=lane *divided* highway⟩ **2 a :** disagreeing with each other **: DISUNITED** ⟨sharply *divided* over the issue⟩ **b :** directed or moved toward conflicting goals ⟨*divided* loyalties⟩

div·i·dend \'div-ə-ˌdend, -əd-ənd\ *n* **1 :** a sum or amount to be distributed or an individual share of such a sum: **as a :** a share of profits distributed to stockholders or of surplus to an insurance policyholder **b :** interest paid on a bank account **2 : BONUS 3 :** a number to be divided by another

di·vid·er \də-'vīd-ər\ *n* **1 :** one that divides or separates ⟨a room *divider*⟩ **2** *pl* **:** an instrument that consists of two pointed branches joined at a pivot for measuring or marking (as in dividing lines and transferring dimensions)

div·i·na·tion \ˌdiv-ə-'nā-shən\ *n* **1 :** the art or practice that seeks to foresee or foretell future events or discover hidden knowledge usually by interpreting omens or by means of supernatural powers **2 :** unusual insight or intuitive perception

¹di·vine \də-'vīn\ *adj* **1 a :** of, relating to, or proceeding directly from deity ⟨*divine* law⟩ **b :** being deity ⟨the *divine* Savior⟩ **c :** directed to deity ⟨*divine* worship⟩ **2 a :** supremely good **: SUPERB** ⟨this pie is *divine*⟩ **b :** having a sublime quality ⟨*divine* beauty⟩ [Middle French *divin*, from Latin *divinus*, from *divus* "god"] **— di·vine·ly** *adv*

²divine *n* **1 : CLERGYMAN 2 : THEOLOGIAN**

³divine *vb* **1 :** to discover or perceive intuitively **: INFER 2 :** to practice divination [Latin *divinare*, from *divinus* "soothsayer", from *divinus*, adjective, "divine"] **— di·vin·er** *n*

Divine Liturgy *n* **:** the eucharistic rite of Eastern churches

Divine Office *n* **:** the daily devotional readings prescribed for priests

divine right *n* **:** a theory that a monarch receives his right to rule from God and not from the people

diving bell *n* **:** a diving apparatus consisting of a container open only at the bottom and supplied with compressed air by a hose

diving board *n* **:** a flexible board secured at one end and extending over water (as at a swimming pool or a lake) that is used to gain height in diving

diving duck *n* **:** any of various ducks that frequent deep waters and obtain their food by diving

diving suit *n* **:** a waterproof suit with a helmet that is worn for underwater work by a person who is supplied with air through a tube from the surface

divining rod *n* **:** a forked rod believed to indicate the presence of water or minerals by dipping downward when held over a vein

di·vin·i·ty \də-'vin-ət-ē\ *n, pl* **-ties 1 :** the quality or state of being divine **2 a** *often cap* **: GOD** 1 **b** (1) **: GOD** 2 (2) **: GODDESS** 1 **c : DEMIGOD**

di·vis·i·ble \də-'viz-ə-bəl\ *adj* **:** capable of being separated or divided **— di·vis·i·bil·i·ty** \-ˌviz-ə-'bil-ət-ē\ *n*

di·vi·sion \də-'vizh-ən\ *n* **1 a :** the act, process, or operation of dividing **:** the state of being divided **b : DISTRIBUTION** ⟨agreed on the *division* of profits⟩ **2 :** one of the parts, sections, or groupings into which a whole is divided: **as a :** a large self-contained military unit capable of independent action **b :** an administrative or operating unit of a governmental, business, or educational organization **3 :** a group of organisms forming part of a larger group; *esp* **:** a primary category of the plant kingdom **4 :** something that divides, separates, or marks off ⟨the *divisions* of the compass⟩ **5 :** difference in opinion or interest **: DISAGREEMENT** [Middle

French, from Latin *divisio*, from *dividere* "to divide"] **— di·vi·sion·al** \-'vizh-nəl, -ən-l\ *adj*

division of labor *n* **:** the distribution of tasks among members of a group or to different areas to increase efficiency

di·vi·sive \də-'vī-siv also -'viz-iv\ *adj* **:** creating disunity or dissension **— di·vi·sive·ly** *adv* **— di·vi·sive·ness** *n*

di·vi·sor \də-'vī-zər\ *n* **:** the number by which a dividend is divided

¹di·vorce \də-'vōrs, -'vȯrs\ *n* **1 :** a complete legal dissolution of a marriage **2 :** complete separation [Middle French *divorse*, from Latin *divortium*, from *divertere*, *divortere* "to divert, leave one's husband"]

²divorce *vt* **1 a :** to obtain a divorce from (one's spouse) **b :** to dissolve the marriage between (two spouses) **2 : SEPARATE, DISUNITE** ⟨*divorce* church from state⟩ **— di·vorce·ment** \-mənt\ *n*

di·vor·cée \də-ˌvōr-'sā, -ˌvȯr-, -'sē\ *n* **:** a divorced woman [French]

div·ot \'div-ət\ *n* **:** a piece of turf dug from a golf fairway in making a stroke [origin unknown]

di·vulge \də-'vəlj, dī-\ *vt* **:** to make known **: DISCLOSE, REVEAL** ⟨*divulge* a secret⟩ [Latin *divulgare*, from *dis-* + *vulgare* "to spread abroad", from *vulgus* "mob, common people"] **— di·vul·gence** \-'vəl-jəns\ *n*

Dix·ie \'dik-sē\ *n* **:** the southern states of the United States [name for the southern states in the song *Dixie* (1859) by Daniel D. Emmett]

Dix·ie·crat \-ˌkrat\ *n* **:** a dissident southern Democrat; *esp* **:** a supporter of a 1948 presidential ticket opposing the civil rights stand of the regular Democrats **— Dix·ie·crat·ic** \ˌdik-sē-'krat-ik\ *adj*

¹diz·zy \'diz-ē\ *adj* **diz·zi·er; -est 1 a :** having a whirling sensation in the head **: GIDDY b :** mentally confused **2 a :** causing or associated with a whirling sensation or a feeling of falling ⟨a *dizzy* height⟩ **b :** extremely rapid ⟨works at a *dizzy* pace⟩ [Old English *dysig* "stupid"] **— diz·zi·ly** \'diz-ə-lē\ *adv* **— diz·zi·ness** \'diz-ē-nəs\ *n*

²dizzy *vt* **diz·zied; diz·zy·ing :** to cause to feel dizzy

DNA \ˌdē-ˌen-'ā\ *n* **:** any of various nucleic acids that are found especially in cell nuclei, are the molecular basis of heredity in many organisms, and differ from RNA especially in containing a deoxyribose sugar and being constructed of a double helix composed of two nucleotide chains held together by hydrogen bonds in a pattern much like a flexible ladder twisted on its base — compare **RNA** [*d*eoxyribo*n*ucleic *a*cid]

DNA fingerprinting *n* **:** a method of identification (as for forensic purposes) by determining the unique pattern in an individual's DNA **— DNA fingerprint** *n*

¹do \dü, 'dü\ *vb* **did** \did, 'did, dəd\; **done** \'dən\; **do·ing** \'dü-ing\; **does** \dəz, 'dəz\ **1 a :** to carry out **: PERFORM** ⟨*do* some work⟩ ⟨*do* me a favor⟩ **b :** to work on ⟨*doing* a puzzle⟩ **2 : ACT, BEHAVE** ⟨*do* as I say, not as I *do*⟩ **3 a :** to affect in a usually specified way ⟨it might *do* you good⟩ **b :** to act so as to cause or create a feeling or sense of ⟨*do* honor to a soldier's memory⟩ **4 a :** to be successful **:** get along **: FLOURISH** ⟨not *doing* very well in school⟩ **b :** to be in regard to health **: FEEL** ⟨*doing* well after the operation⟩ **5 :** to carry on in one's affairs **: MANAGE** ⟨can *do* without your help⟩ **6 :** to take place **: HAPPEN** ⟨see what's *doing* tonight⟩ **7 :** to come or bring to an end **: FINISH** — used in the past participle ⟨the work is finally *done*⟩ **8 :** to put forth (as an effort) ⟨*do* your best to win⟩ **9 :** to be about one's work or duty ⟨up and *doing*⟩ **10 :** to produce by creative effort ⟨*do* a sketch⟩ **11 :** to deal with or treat in a sense of preparing, putting in order, or giving care and attention ⟨*did* the dishes⟩ ⟨must *do* my hair⟩ **12 : DECORATE, FURNISH** ⟨*did* the bedroom in blue⟩ **13 :** to work at as a vocation ⟨what *do* you *do* for a living⟩ **14 a :** to travel at a speed of ⟨I was only *doing* 55, officer⟩ **b :** to visit and explore as or as if sightseeing **:** enjoy the sights and attractions of ⟨*did* Europe last fall⟩ ⟨*doing*

\ə\ abut	\ng\ sing
\ər\ further	\ō\ bone
\a\ mat	\ȯ\ saw
\ā\ take	\ȯi\ coin
\ä\ cot, cart	\th\ thin
\au̇\ out	\th\ this
\ch\ chin	\ü\ food
\e\ pet	\u̇\ foot
\ē\ easy	\y\ yet
\g\ go	\yü\ few
\i\ tip	\yu̇\ cure
\ī\ life	\zh\ vision
\j\ job	

the town) **15** : to be suitable to the needs of : be adequate or fitting : SERVE ⟨worms will *do* us for bait⟩ **16** : to endure (as a term) in prison ⟨*doing* 20 years for armed robbery⟩ **17** : to be approved of especially by custom, propriety, or opinion : be fitting or appropriate — usually used in the negative ⟨it just won't *do* to be late⟩ **18** — used with so or a pronoun object as a substitute verb to avoid repetition ⟨if you must make a racket, *do* it somewhere else⟩ **19** — used as an auxiliary verb (1) before the subject of an interrogative sentence ⟨*do* you work?⟩ and after certain adverbs ⟨rarely *do* I go out⟩ ⟨they work and so *do* I⟩, (2) in a negative statement ⟨you *don't* look well⟩, (3) for emphasis ⟨*do* be careful⟩, and (4) as a substitute for a preceding verb or verb phrase ⟨this looks better than that *does*⟩ [Old English *dōn*] — **do away with 1** : to put an end to : ABOLISH **2** : to put to death : KILL — **do by** : to deal with : TREAT ⟨*did* well *by* us⟩ — **do for 1** : to bring about the death or ruin of **2** : to attend to the wants and needs of — **do one proud** : to give cause for pride or gratification — **do one's thing** : to engage in an activity or pursuit that is personally satisfying or rewarding

²do \'dō\ *n* : the 1st note of the diatonic scale [Italian]

do·able \'dü-ə-bəl\ *adj* : capable of being done

dob·bin \'däb-ən\ *n* **1** : a farm horse **2** : a quiet plodding horse [*Dobbin,* nickname for *Robert*]

Do·ber·man pin·scher \,dō-bər-mən-'pin-chər\ *n* : a short-haired medium-sized working dog of a breed of German origin [Ludwig *Dobermann,* 19th century German dog breeder]

dob·son \'däb-sən\ *n* : HELLGRAMMITE [probably from the name *Dobson*]

dob·son·fly \-,flī\ *n* : a large-eyed winged insect with a large carnivorous aquatic larva — compare HELLGRAMMITE

do·cent \'dōs-nt; dō-'sent, dōt-\ *n* : TEACHER, LECTURER [obsolete German, from Latin *docēre* "to teach"]

doc·ile \'däs-əl\ *adj* : easily taught, led, or managed : TRACTABLE ⟨a *docile* child⟩ [Latin *docilis,* from *docēre* "to teach"] — **doc·ile·ly** \'däs-əl-lē, -ə-lē\ *adv* — **do·cil·i·ty** \dä-'sil-ət-ē, dō-\ *n*

¹dock \'däk\ *n* : any of a genus of coarse weedy plants related to buckwheat that are used as potherbs and in folk medicine [Old English *docce*]

²dock *n* : the solid part of an animal's tail as distinguished from the hair [Old English *-docca* (as in *fingirdocca* "finger muscle")]

³dock *vt* **1** : to cut off the end of : cut short ⟨a *docked* tail⟩ **2** : to take away a part of : make a deduction from ⟨*dock* one's wages⟩

⁴dock *n* **1** : an artificial basin to receive ships that has gates to keep the water in or out **2** : a slip or waterway usually between two piers to receive ships **3** : a wharf or platform for the loading or unloading of materials ⟨a ship moored to the *dock*⟩ ⟨a loading *dock* for trucks⟩ **4** : a place or scaffolding for the inspection and repair of aircraft [probably from Dutch *docke* "dock, ditch", derived from Latin *ducere* "to lead"]

⁵dock *vb* **1** : to haul or guide into a dock **2** : to come or go into dock **3** : to join (as two spacecraft) mechanically while in space

⁶dock *n* : the place in a criminal court where a defendant stands or sits during trial [Flemish *docke* "cage"]

dock·age \'däk-ij\ *n* **1** : a charge for the use of a dock **2** : docking facilities **3** : the docking of ships

¹dock·et \'däk-ət\ *n* **1 a** : a formal abridged record of the proceedings in a legal action **b** : a register of such records **2** : a list of legal causes to be tried **3** : a calendar of matters to be acted on : AGENDA [Middle English *doggette* "brief summary, abstract"]

²docket *vt* **1** : to mark with an identifying statement : LABEL **2** : to make a brief abstract of (as a legal matter) and enter it in a list **3** : to place on the docket for legal action

dock·hand \'däk-,hand\ *n* : LONGSHOREMAN

dock·yard \'däk-,yärd\ *n* : SHIPYARD

¹doc·tor \'däk-tər\ *n* **1 a** : an eminent theologian declared a sound expounder of doctrine by the Roman Catholic Church — called also *doctor of the church* **b** : a learned or authoritative teacher **c** : a person holding one of the highest academic degrees (as a PhD) conferred by a university **2 a** : one skilled or specializing in healing; *esp* : a physician, surgeon, dentist, or veterinarian licensed to practice **b** : MEDICINE MAN [Medieval Latin, from Latin, "teacher", from *docēre* "to teach"] — **doc·tor·al** \-tə-rəl, -trəl\ *adj*

²doctor *vb* **doc·tored; doc·tor·ing** \-tə-ring, -tring\ **1 a** : to give medical treatment to **b** : to practice medicine **c** : to restore to good condition : REPAIR ⟨*doctor* an old clock⟩ **2 a** : to adapt or modify for a desired end ⟨*doctored* the play by abridging the last act⟩ **b** : to alter deceptively ⟨*doctored* the election returns⟩

doc·tor·ate \'däk-tə-rət, -trət\ *n* : the degree, title, or rank of a doctor

doc·tri·naire \,däk-trə-'naar, -'near\ *n* : one who attempts to put an abstract theory into effect without regard to practical difficulties [French, from *doctrine* "doctrine"] SYN see DICTATORIAL — **doctrinaire** *adj*

doc·trine \'däk-trən\ *n* **1** : something that is taught **2** : a principle or position or the body of principles in a branch of knowledge or system of belief **3** : a principle of law established through past decisions [Latin *doctrina* "teaching, instruction", from *doctor* "teacher"] — **doc·tri·nal** \-trən-l\ *adj* — **doc·tri·nal·ly** \-l-ē\ *adv* □ SYN DOCTRINE, DOGMA, TENET mean a principle accepted as authoritative. DOCTRINE strictly implies authoritative teaching accepted by a body of believers or adherents of a philosophy or school ⟨Christian *doctrine*⟩ ⟨a mathematical *doctrine*⟩ but also denotes a theory supported by evidence and proposed for acceptance ⟨the *doctrine* of evolution⟩ DOGMA implies a doctrine laid down as true and beyond dispute; TENET stresses acceptance and belief of a principle and implies a body of adherents ⟨the *tenets* of socialism are not identical with the *doctrines* of Marx⟩

docu·dra·ma \'däk-yə-,dräm-ə, -,dram-\ *n* : a drama for television, motion pictures, or theater dealing freely with historical events especially of a recent or controversial nature [*docu*mentary + *drama*]

¹doc·u·ment \'däk-yə-mənt\ *n* : a usually original or official paper furnishing information or used as proof of something [Middle French, from Latin *documentum* "lesson, proof", from *docēre* "to teach"] — **doc·u·men·tal** \,däk-yə-'ment-l\ *adj*

²doc·u·ment \'däk-yə-,ment\ *vt* : to furnish documentary evidence of ⟨*document* a case with an adversary's own statements⟩ — **doc·u·ment·able** \-ə-bəl, ,däk-yə-'ment-\ *adj*

¹doc·u·men·ta·ry \,däk-yə-'ment-ə-rē, -'men-trē\ *adj* **1** : consisting of or being documents; *also* : contained or certified in writing ⟨*documentary* proof⟩ **2** : giving factual material in artistic form ⟨a *documentary* film⟩ — **doc·u·men·tar·i·ly** \-mən-'ter-ə-lē, -,men-\ *adv*

²documentary *n, pl* **-ries** : a documentary presentation (as a film)

doc·u·men·ta·tion \,däk-yə-mən-'tā-shən, -,men-\ *n* **1** : the providing or the using of documents in proof of something **2** : evidence in the form of documents or references (as in footnotes) to documents **3** : written instructions for using a computer or computer program

¹dod·der \'däd-ər\ *n* : any of a genus of leafless herbs deficient in chlorophyll and parasitic on other plants [Middle English *doder*]

²dodder *vi* **dod·dered; dod·der·ing** \'däd-ring, -ə-ring\ **1** : to tremble from weakness or age **2** : to progress feebly [Middle English *dadiren*]

dod·der·ing *adj* : feeble and dull especially from age

do·deca·gon \dō-'dek-ə-,gän\ *n* : a polygon of 12 angles and 12 sides [Greek *dōdekagōnon*, from *dōdeka* "twelve" + *-gōnon* "-gon"]

do·deca·he·dron \,dō-,dek-ə-'hē-drən\ *n, pl* **-drons** or **-dra** \-drə\ : a solid having 12 plane faces

¹dodge \'däj\ *vb* **1 a** : to move suddenly aside **b** : to avoid by moving quickly aside ⟨*dodge* a batted ball⟩ **2** : to avoid by trickery or evasion ⟨*dodge* work⟩ [origin unknown]

²dodge *n* **1** : an act of evading by sudden bodily movement **2 a** : an artful device to evade, deceive, or trick ⟨crafty legal *dodges*⟩ **b** : EXPEDIENT 2

dodge ball *n* : a game in which players stand in a circle and attempt to hit a player within the circle with a large inflated ball

dodg·er \'däj-ər\ *n* **1** : one that dodges; *esp* : one that uses trickery **2** : a small handbill **3** : a cake made of cornmeal

do·do \'dōd-ō\ *n, pl* **dodoes** or **dodos** **1** : a large heavy flightless extinct bird related to the pigeons and formerly found on some of the islands of the Indian ocean **2 a** : a person hopelessly behind the times **b** : a stupid person [Portuguese *doudo*, from *doudo* "silly, stupid"]

doe \'dō\ *n, pl* **does** or **doe** : an adult female deer; *also* : the female especially when adult of any mammal (as an antelope or hare) of which the male is called buck [Old English *dā*]

do·er \'dü-ər\ *n* : one that does; *esp* : a person who gets things done

does *present 3d sing of* DO

doe·skin \'dō-,skin\ *n* **1** : the skin of does or leather made of it **2** : a soft firm cloth

doesn't \'dəz-nt\ : does not

do·est \'dü-əst\ *archaic present 2d sing of* DO

do·eth \'dü-əth\ *archaic present 3d sing of* DO

doff \'däf, 'dȯf\ *vt* **1** : to take off (one's clothes); *esp* : to take off or lift up (the hat) **2** : to rid oneself of : put aside [Middle English *doffen*, from *don* "to do" + *of* "off"]

¹dog \'dȯg\ *n* **1 a** : a variable flesh-eating domesticated mammal probably descended form the common wolf **b** : an animal of the family to which the domesticated dog belongs **c** : a male dog **2 a** : a worthless fellow **b** : FELLOW, CHAP ⟨a lazy *dog*⟩ **3** : any of various devices for holding, gripping, or fastening that consist of a spike, rod, or bar **4** : affected stylishness or dignity ⟨put on the *dog*⟩ **5** *pl, slang* : FEET **6** *pl* : RUIN ⟨go to the *dogs*⟩ [Old English *docga*] — **dog·like** \-,līk\ *adj*

²dog *vt* **dogged; dog·ging** **1** : to hunt or track like a hound **2** : HOUND ⟨*dogged* by bad luck⟩

dog·bane \'dȯg-,bān\ *n* : any of a genus of chiefly tropical and often poisonous plants with milky juice and small white or pink flowers

dog·cart \-,kärt\ *n* **1** : a cart drawn by a dog **2** : a light one-horse carriage with two seats back to back

dog·catch·er \-,kach-ər, -,kech-\ *n* : a community official assigned to catch and dispose of stray dogs

dog days *n pl* : the hot sultry period of summer between early July and early September [from their beginning at the date when the Dog Star (Sirius) rises just before the sun]

doge \'dōj\ *n* : the chief magistrate in the republics of Venice and Genoa [Italian dialect, from Latin *dux* "leader"]

dog-ear \'dȯg-,iər\ *n* : the turned-down corner of a page of a book — **dog-ear** *vt*

dog-eared \-,iərd\ *adj* **1** : having dog-ears ⟨a *dog-eared* book⟩ **2** : SHABBY 1, WORN, RUN-DOWN

dog-eat-dog \,dȯg-,ēt-'dȯg\ *adj* : marked by ruthless self-interest ⟨a *dog-eat-dog* business⟩

dog·face \'dȯg-,fās\ *n, slang* : SOLDIER; *esp* : INFANTRYMAN

dog·fight \-,fīt\ *n* : a fight between two or more fighter planes usually at close quarters

dog·fish \-,fish\ *n* : any of various small sharks that often appear in schools near shore

dog·ged \'dȯg-əd\ *adj* : stubbornly determined : TENACIOUS ⟨*dogged* persistence⟩ SYN see OBSTINATE — **dog·ged·ly** *adv* — **dog·ged·ness** *n*

¹dog·ger·el \'dȯg-rəl, 'däg-, -ə-rəl\ *adj* : loose in style and irregular in meter ⟨comic *doggerel* verse⟩ [Middle English *dogerel*]

²doggerel *n* : doggerel verse

¹dog·gone \'däg-'gän, 'dȯg-'gȯn\ *vb* : DAMN 3 [euphemism for *God damn*]

²doggone *n* : DAMN 2

dog·goned or **dog·gone** \'däg-'gän, -'gänd; 'dȯg-'gȯn, -'gȯnd\ *adj or adv* : DAMNED

¹dog·gy \'dȯg-ē\ *adj* **dog·gi·er; -est** **1** : of or resembling a dog **2** : STYLISH, SHOWY

²dog·gy or **dog·gie** \'dȯg-ē\ *n, pl* **doggies** : a small dog

dog·house \'dȯg-,haus\ *n* : a shelter for a dog — **in the doghouse** : in a state of disfavor

do·gie \'dō-gē\ *n, chiefly West* : a motherless calf in a range herd [origin unknown]

dog in the manger : a person who selfishly withholds from others something useless to himself or herself [from the fable of the dog who prevented an ox from eating hay which he did not want himself]

dog·ma \'dȯg-mə, 'däg-\ *n, pl* **dog·mas** also **dog·ma·ta** \-mət-ə\ **1 a** : something held as an established opinion; *esp* : a tenet set forth as authoritative **b** : a point of view or opinion set forth as authoritative without adequate grounds **2** : a doctrine or body of doctrines concerning faith or morals laid down by a church [Latin *dogmat-, dogma*, from Greek, from *dokein* "to seem, seem good"] SYN see DOCTRINE

dog·mat·ic \dȯg-'mat-ik, däg-\ *adj* **1** : characterized by or given to the use of dogmatism ⟨a *dogmatic* critic⟩ **2** : of or relating to dogma SYN see DICTATORIAL — **dog·mat·i·cal·ly** \-'mat-i-kə-lē, -klē\ *adv*

dog·ma·tism \'dȯg-mə-,tiz-əm, 'däg-\ *n* **1** : positiveness in assertion of opinion especially when unwarranted or arrogant **2** : a viewpoint or system of ideas based on inadequate study or knowledge

dog·ma·tist \-mət-əst\ *n* : one who dogmatizes

dog·ma·tize \-mə-,tīz\ *vb* : to speak or write dogmatically — **dog·ma·tiz·er** *n*

do-good·er \'dü-,gùd-ər\ *n* : an earnest usually impractical and often naive and ineffectual humanitarian or reformer

dog paddle *n* : an elementary form of swimming in which the head is kept out of the water and the arms paddle in the water while the legs maintain a kicking motion

Dog Star *n* **1** : SIRIUS **2** : PROCYON

dog tag *n* **1** : a tag worn on a dog's neck bearing a license registration number **2** : a military identification tag

dog·tooth violet \'dȯg-,tüth-\ *n* : any of a genus of small spring-flowering bulbous herbs of the lily family

¹dog·trot \'dȯg-,trät\ *n* : an easy gait suggesting that of a dog

²dogtrot *vi* : to move or progress at a dogtrot

dog watch *n* **1** : either of two shipboard watches from 4 to 6 and from 6 to 8 p.m. **2** : any of various night shifts; *esp* : the last shift

dog·wood \'dȯg-,wùd\ *n* : any of a genus of trees and shrubs with clusters of small flowers often surrounded by four broad leaves resembling petals

doi·ly \'dȯi-lē\ *n, pl* **doilies** **1** : a small napkin **2** : a small often decorative mat [*Doily* or *Doyley*, 18th century London draper]

do in *vt* **1** : to bring about the defeat or destruction of : RUIN ⟨*done in* by the stock-market crash⟩ **2** : KILL ⟨tried to *do* them *in* with a club⟩ **3** : to wear out : EXHAUST ⟨*done in* after work⟩

do·ing \'dü-ing\ *n* **1** : the act of performing or executing : ACTION ⟨it will take some *doing* to beat this re-

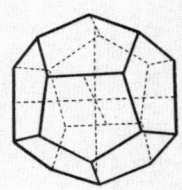
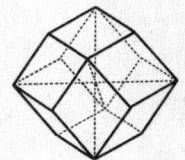

dodecahedron

\ə\ abut
\ər\ **further**
\a\ **mat**
\ā\ **take**
\ä\ **cot, cart**
\au\ **out**
\ch\ **chin**
\e\ **pet**
\ē\ **easy**
\g\ **go**
\i\ **tip**
\ī\ **life**
\j\ **job**

\ng\ sing
\ō\ **bone**
\ȯ\ **saw**
\ȯi\ **coin**
\th\ **thin**
\th\ **this**
\ü\ **food**
\ù\ **foot**
\y\ **yet**
\yü\ **few**
\yù\ **cure**
\zh\ **vision**

cord) **2** *pl* **a** : things that are done or that occur (everyday *doings*) **b** *dial* : social activities (big *doings* tonight)

doit \'dȯit\ *n* **1** : an old Dutch coin equal to about ¼ cent **2** : TRIFLE 1 [Dutch *duit*]

do-it-your·self \ˌdü-ə-chər-'self\ *adj* : of, relating to, or designed for use in construction, repair, or artistic work done by an amateur or hobbyist (*do-it-yourself* tools)

dol·ce \'dōl-chā\ *adv or adj* : SOFT 1b, SMOOTH — used as a direction in music [Italian, literally, "sweet", from Latin *dulcis*]

dol·ce far nien·te \ˌdōl-chē-ˌfär-nē-'ent-ē\ *n* : delightful relaxation in carefree idleness [Italian, literally, "a sweet doing nothing"]

dol·drums \'dōl-drəmz, 'däl-\ *n pl* **1** : a spell of listlessness or despondency **2** : a part of the ocean near the equator abounding in calms and light shifting winds **3** : a state of inactivity, stagnation, or slump [probably related to Old English *dol* "foolish"]

¹dole \'dōl\ *n* **1 a** (1) : a giving out of food, money, or clothing to the needy (2) : money, food, or clothing so given **b** : a grant of government funds to the unemployed **2** : something portioned out and distributed [Old English *dāl* "portion"]

²dole *vt* **1** : to distribute as charity (*doled* out blankets and clothing to the flood victims) **2** : to give out in small portions or gradually (*dole* out stories each evening)

³dole *n, archaic* : GRIEF 1, SORROW [Old French *dol,* from Latin *dolor*]

dole·ful \'dōl-fəl\ *adj* : full of grief : SAD — **dole·ful·ly** \-fə-lē\ *adv* — **dole·ful·ness** *n*

doll \'däl, 'dȯl\ *n* **1** : a small-scale figure of a human being used especially as a child's plaything **2 a** : a pretty but often scatterbrained young woman **b** *slang* : WOMAN 1 **c** *slang* : DARLING 1, SWEETHEART **d** : an attractive person [probably from *Doll,* nickname for *Dorothy*]

dol·lar \'däl-ər\ *n* **1** : TALER **2** : a coin (as a Spanish piece of eight) patterned after the taler **3 a** : a basic monetary unit (as of the United States and Canada) **b** : a coin, note, or token representing one dollar [Dutch or Low German *daler,* from German *taler*] □ ORIGIN In the mountains of northwestern Bohemia is the small town of Jáchymov. In the early 16th century the town was known by its German name, Sankt Joachimstal. At that time a silver mine was opened nearby, and coins were minted to which the name *joachimstaler* was applied. In German this was shortened to *taler.* Shortly afterward the Dutch or Low German form *daler* was borrowed into English to refer to the taler and other coins that were patterned after it. Our modern word *dollar* is a different spelling of this daler.

dollar diplomacy *n* : diplomacy held to be designed primarily to further private financial and commercial interests

dol·lop \'däl-əp\ *n* : LUMP 1, BLOB (a *dollop* of jelly) [origin unknown]

doll up *vb* : to dress or decorate formally or elegantly

¹dolly \'däl-ē, 'dȯ-lē\ *n, pl* **doll·ies** **1** : DOLL 1 **2** : a platform on a roller or on wheels for transporting heavy objects; *esp* : a wheeled platform for a television or motion-picture camera

²dolly *vi* **doll·ied; doll·y·ing** : to move a motion-picture or television dolly about while shooting a scene

dol·man \'dōl-mən, 'dȯl-, 'däl-\ *n* : a woman's coat made with dolman sleeves [French *doliman,* a kind of Turkish robe, from Turkish *dolama*]

dolman sleeve *n* : a sleeve that is very wide at the armhole and tight at the wrist

dol·men \'dōl-mən, 'dȯl-, 'däl-\ *n* : a prehistoric monument consisting of two or more upright stones supporting a horizontal stone slab [French, from Breton *tolmen,* from *tol* "table" + *men* "stone"]

do·lo·mite \'dō-lə-ˌmīt, 'däl-ə-\ *n* : a mineral $CaMg(CO_3)_2$ consisting of a calcium magnesium carbonate found in crystals and in extensive beds as a compact limestone [Déodat de *Dolomieu,* died 1801, French geologist] — **do·lo·mit·ic** \ˌdō-lə-'mit-ik, ˌdäl-ə-\ *adj*

do·lor \'dō-lər, 'däl-ər\ *n* : mental suffering or grief : SORROW [Middle French *dolour,* from Latin *dolor* "pain, grief", from *dolēre* "to feel pain, grieve"]

do·lor·ous \'dō-lə-rəs, 'däl-ə-\ *adj* : causing, marked by, or expressive of misery or grief — **do·lor·ous·ly** *adv* — **do·lor·ous·ness** *n*

dol·phin \'däl-fən, 'dȯl-\ *n* **1 a** : any of various small long-nosed toothed whales **b** : PORPOISE 1 **2** : either of two active spiny-finned marine food fishes noted for their brilliant colors when taken out of the water **3** *cap* : DELPHINUS [Middle French *dophin,* derived from Latin *delphinus,* from Greek *delphis*]

dolt \'dōlt\ *n* : a stupid person [probably related to Old English dol *"foolish"*] — **dolt·ish** \'dōl-tish\ *adj* — **dolt·ish·ly** *adv* — **dolt·ish·ness** *n*

Dom *n* **1** \ˌdäm\ — used as a title prefixed to the name of some monks and canons regular **2** \dōⁿ\ — used as a title prefixed to the Christian name of a Portuguese or Brazilian man of rank [Latin *dominus* "master"]

-dom \dəm\ *n suffix* **1 a** : dignity : office (duke*dom*) **b** : realm : jurisdiction (king*dom*) **2** : state or fact of being (free*dom*) **3** : those having a (specified) office, occupation, interest, or character (official*dom*) [Old English *-dōm*]

do·main \dō-'mān, də-\ *n* **1 a** : complete and absolute ownership of land — compare EMINENT DOMAIN **b** : land completely owned **2** : a territory over which dominion is exercised **3** : a sphere of influence or activity (the widening *domain* of science) **4** : the set of values to which a mathematical variable is limited; *esp* : the set on which a function is defined — compare RANGE 8 **5** : a small region of a magnetic substance that contains a group of atoms all aligned in the same direction so that each group has the effect of a tiny magnet pointing in one direction [Middle French *domaine,* from Latin *dominium,* from *dominus* "master"]

¹dome \'dōm\ *n* **1** *archaic* : a stately building : MANSION **2** : a large hemispherical roof or ceiling **3** : a natural formation that resembles the dome or cupola of a building (elevated rock *domes*) [Medieval Latin *domus* "church", from *Latin,* "house"]

²dome *vb* **1** : to cover with or as if with a dome **2** : to form into or swell upward or outward like a dome

¹do·mes·tic \də-'mes-tik\ *adj* **1** : of or relating to the household or the family (*domestic* life) **2** : of, relating to, produced, or carried on within one country (*domestic* trade) **3 a** : living near or about human habitations (*domestic* vermin) **b** : adapted to life with and to the advantage of humans : TAME **4** : devoted to home duties and pleasures [Middle French *domestique,* from Latin *domesticus,* from *domus* "house, home"] — **do·mes·ti·cal·ly** \-ti-kə-lē, -klē\ *adv*

²domestic *n* : a household servant

domestic animal *n* : any of various animals (as the horse or sheep) adapted by humans to live and breed in domestication

do·mes·ti·cate \də-'mes-ti-ˌkāt\ *vt* **1** : to bring into domestic use : ADOPT (European customs *domesticated* in America) **2** : to fit for domestic life **3** : to adapt to life in intimate association with and to the advantage of human beings (who *domesticated* the dog is unknown) — **do·mes·ti·ca·tion** \də-ˌmes-ti-'kā-shən\ *n*

do·mes·tic·i·ty \ˌdō-ˌmes-'tis-ət-ē, də-\ *n, pl* **-ties** **1** : the quality or state of being domestic or domesticated **2** : domestic activities or life **3** *pl* : domestic affairs

domestic prelate *n* : a priest having permanent honorary membership in the papal household

domestic science *n* : instruction in domestic management and the household arts (as cooking and sewing)

domestic system *n* : a system of manufacturing in the home with raw materials supplied by an employer

dom·i·cal \'dō-mi-kəl, 'däm-i-\ *adj* : relating to, shaped like, or having a dome

¹do·mi·cile \'däm-ə-ˌsīl, 'dō-mə-; 'däm-ə-səl\ *n* **1** : a dwelling place : place of residence : HOME **2** : a person's fixed, permanent, and principal home for legal purposes [Middle French, from Latin *domicilium*, from *domus* "house"] — **do·mi·cil·i·ary** \ˌdäm-ə-'sil-ē-ˌer-ē, ˌdō-mə-\ *adj*

²domicile *vt* : to establish in or provide with a domicile

do·mi·cil·i·ate \ˌdäm-ə-'sil-ē-ˌāt, ˌdō-mə-\ *vb* **1** : DOMICILE **2** : DOMESTICATE **3** : RESIDE

dom·i·nance \'däm-nəns, -ə-nəns\ *n* : the fact or state of being dominant: as **a** (1) : dominant position in an order of forcefulness (2) : the relative position of an individual in a social hierarchy (as a pecking order) **b** : the condition of being the one of a pair of contrasting genes or traits controlled by genes that is expressed in preference to the other when both are represented in the genetic material **c** : the influence or control exerted over an ecological community by a dominant organism

¹dom·i·nant \-nənt\ *adj* **1** : commanding, controlling, or prevailing over all others ⟨a *dominant* political figure⟩ **2** : overlooking from a higher elevation ⟨a *dominant* hill⟩ **3** : being the more effective or predominant in action of a pair of bodily structures ⟨*dominant* eye⟩ **4** : exhibiting genetic dominance — **dom·i·nant·ly** *adv*

²dominant *n* **1 a** : a dominant genetic gene or trait **b** : a kind of organism (as a species) that exerts a controlling influence on an ecological community **2** : the 5th note of the diatonic scale

dom·i·nate \'däm-ə-ˌnāt\ *vb* **1** : to exert dominance over : be dominant ⟨refuse to be *dominated* by friends⟩ **2** : to have a commanding position or controlling power over ⟨the rock of Gibraltar *dominates* the straits⟩ **3** : to rise high above ⟨the mountain range was *dominated* by a single snow-capped peak⟩ [Latin *dominari*, from *dominus* "master"] — **dom·i·na·tive** \-ˌnāt-iv\ *adj* — **dom·i·na·tor** \-ˌnāt-ər\ *n*

dom·i·na·tion \ˌdäm-ə-'nā-shən\ *n* **1** : supremacy over another **2** : exercise of authority or power

dom·i·neer \ˌdäm-ə-'niər\ *vb* **1** : to rule in a haughty manner **2** : to be overbearing

dom·i·neer·ing *adj* : inclined to domineer SYN see MASTERFUL — **dom·i·neer·ing·ly** \-ing-lē\ *adv* — **dom·i·neer·ing·ness** *n*

Do·min·i·can \də-'min-i-kən\ *n* : a member of a mendicant Order of Preachers founded in 1215 [Saint *Dominic*] — **Dominican** *adj*

do·mi·nie \ *1 oftenest* 'däm-ə-nē, *2 oftenest* 'dō-mə-\ *n* **1** *chiefly Scottish* : SCHOOLMASTER **2** : CLERGYMAN [derived from Latin *dominus* "master"]

do·min·ion \də-'min-yən\ *n* **1** : supreme authority **2** : DOMAIN 2 **3** *often cap* : a self-governing nation of the British Commonwealth other than the United Kingdom that acknowledges the British monarch as chief of state [Middle French, from Latin *dominium*, from *dominus* "master"]

Dominion Day *n* : July 1 observed in Canada as a legal holiday in commemoration of the proclamation of dominion status in 1867

dom·i·no \'däm-ə-ˌnō\ *n, pl* **-noes** *or* **-nos** **1** : a long loose hooded cloak usually worn with a half mask as a masquerade costume **2 a** : a small rectangular block (as of wood or plastic) whose face is divided into two equal parts that are blank or bear from one to usually six dots arranged as on dice faces **b** *pl* : any of several games played with a set of usually 28 dominoes [French, probably derived from Latin *dominus* "master"] □ ORIGIN English *domino* was borrowed from French but is ultimately derived from Latin *dominus*, which means "lord" or "master". The hooded cape worn in masquerades was given its French name of *domino* because it looks rather like the hooded capes worn by members of some religious orders. The name of the garment was probably derived from the Latin phrase "Benedicamus Domino" (Let us bless the Lord), used in prayers.   Another meaning of *domino* is "a rectangular block used in games". This *domino* came into our language from Italian, by way of French. Formerly, the winner of a game of dominoes would exclaim "Domino!" It is likely that this Italian exclamation originally meant "(I am) master!" Italian *domino*, meaning "master" or "lord", was derived from Latin dominus.

¹don \'dän\ *n* **1** : a Spanish nobleman or gentleman — used as a title prefixed to the Christian name **2** : a head, tutor, or fellow in a college of Oxford or Cambridge University [Spanish, from Latin *dominus* "master"]

²don *vt* **donned; don·ning** : to put on : dress oneself in ⟨*don* an apron for washing dishes⟩ [*do + on*]

do·ña \ˌdō-nyə\ *n* : a Spanish woman of rank — used as a title prefixed to the Christian name [Spanish, from Latin *domina* "lady", from *dominus* "master"]

do·nate \'dō-ˌnāt, dō-'\ *vb* : to make a gift of; *esp* : to contribute to a public or charitable cause ⟨*donate* a site for a park⟩ ⟨*donate* to the scholarship fund⟩ [backformation from *donation*] SYN see GIVE — **do·na·tor** \-ˌnāt-ər, -'nāt-\ *n*

do·na·tion \dō-'nā-shən\ *n* **1** : the action of donating something **2** : a free contribution : GIFT [Latin *donatio*, from *donare* "to present", from *donum* "gift"]

¹done \'dən\ *past participle of* DO

²done *adj* **1** : socially acceptable ⟨that's not the *done* thing⟩ **2** : physically exhausted : SPENT ⟨felt completely *done* at the end of the hike⟩ **3** : gone by : FINISHED **4** : doomed to failure, defeat, or death **5** : cooked sufficiently

do·nee \dō-'nē\ *n* : one that receives a gift [*don*or + *-ee*]

done for \'dən-ˌfȯr\ *adj* **1** : having no hope of surviving ⟨were *done for* when the boat sank⟩ **2** : WASHED-UP 1 ⟨that blunder means you are *done for* as a politician⟩

don·jon \'dän-jən, 'dən-\ *n* : a massive inner tower in a medieval castle [Middle French, derived from Latin *dominus* "lord"]

Don Juan \dän-'wän, -'hwän; dän-'jü-ən\ *n* : ⁵RAKE [*Don Juan*, unprincipled nobleman of Spanish legend]

don·key \'däng-kē, 'dəng-, 'dȯng-\ *n, pl* **donkeys** **1** : the domestic ass **2** : a stupid or stubborn person [perhaps from ¹*dun + -key* (as in *monkey*)]

donkey engine *n* **1** : a small usually portable auxiliary engine **2** : a small locomotive used in switching

don·na \ˌdän-ə\ *n, pl* **don·ne** \-ā\ : an Italian woman usually of rank — used as a title prefixed to the Christian name [Italian, from Latin *domina* "lady"]

don·nish \'dän-ish\ *adj* : suggestive of a university don ⟨a prim *donnish* greeting⟩ — **don·nish·ly** *adv* — **don·nish·ness** *n*

don·ny·brook \'dän-ē-ˌbrùk\ *n, often cap* : an uproarious brawl [*Donnybrook* Fair, annual Irish event known for its brawls]

do·nor \'dō-nər, -ˌnȯr\ *n* **1** : one that donates **2** : one used as a source of biological material ⟨a blood *donor*⟩ [Middle French *doneur*, from Latin *donator*, from *donare* "to present"] — **do·nor·ship** \-ˌship\ *n*

do–noth·ing \'dü-ˌnəth-ing\ *adj* : marked by inactivity; *esp* : marked by lack of ambition, unwillingness to disturb the existing state of affairs, or failure to make positive progress ⟨a *do-nothing* government⟩ — **do–nothing·ism** \-ing-ˌiz-əm\ *n*

don't \dōnt, 'dōnt\ : do not

do·nut *variant of* DOUGHNUT

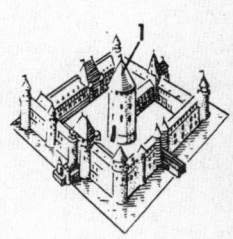

1 donjon

doo·dad \'dü-,dad\ *n* : a small article whose common name is unknown or forgotten [origin unknown]

¹doo·dle \'düd-l\ *vb* **doo·dled; doo·dling** \'düd-ling, -l̄ing\ : to draw or scribble aimlessly while occupied with something else [perhaps from earlier *doodle* "to ridicule", from *doodle* "fool"] — **doo·dler** \'düd-lər, -l-ər\ *n*

²doodle *n* : something produced by doodling

doo·dle·bug \'düd-l-,bəg\ *n* **1** : the larva of an ant lion **2** : a device (as a divining rod) used in attempting to locate underground gas, water, oil, or ores [probably from *doodle* "fool"]

doo·hick·ey \'dü-,hik-ē\ *n* : DOODAD [probably from *doo*dad + *hickey* "gadget", of unknown origin]

¹doom \'düm\ *n* **1 a** : a judicial decision; *esp* : a judicial sentence **b** (1) : a final determining of what is just (2) : JUDGMENT DAY **2 a** : an inevitable and usually calamitous state or end **b** : DEATH 2, RUIN [Old English *dōm* "law, judgment"] SYN see FATE

²doom *vt* **1** : to give judgment against : CONDEMN **2 a** : to fix the fate of : DESTINE **b** : to ensure the failure or destruction of

dooms·day \'dümz-,dā\ *n* : JUDGMENT DAY

door \'dōr, 'dȯr\ *n* **1 a** : a usually swinging or sliding barrier by which an entry (as in a building) is closed and opened **b** : a similar part of a piece of furniture **2** : DOORWAY **3** : a means of access (the *door* to success) [Old English *duru* "door" and *dor* "gate"]

door·bell \'dōr-,bel, 'dȯr-\ *n* : a bell, gong, or set of chimes to be rung usually by a push button at an outside door

door·jamb \-,jam\ *n* : an upright piece forming the side of a door opening

door·keep·er \-,kē-pər\ *n* : one that tends a door

door·knob \-,näb\ *n* : a knob that when turned releases a door latch

door·man \-,man, -mən\ *n* **1** : DOORKEEPER **2** : one who tends a door (as of a hotel) and assists people by calling taxis and helping them in and out of cars

door·mat \-,mat\ *n* : a mat placed before or inside a door for wiping dirt from the shoes

door·nail \-,nāl, -'nāl\ *n* : a large-headed nail — used chiefly in the phrase dead as a doornail

door·plate \-,plāt\ *n* : a nameplate on a door

door·post \-,pōst\ *n* : DOORJAMB

door·sill \-,sil\ *n* : SILL 1b

door·step \-,step\ *n* : a step or series of steps before an outer door

door·way \-,wā\ *n* **1** : the opening that a door closes **2** : a means of gaining access

door·yard \-,yärd\ *n* : a yard outside the door of a house

¹dope \'dōp\ *n* **1 a** : a thick liquid or pasty preparation **b** : a preparation for giving a desired quality to a substance or surface; *esp* : an antiknock added to gasoline **2 a** : a restricted or illicit drug (as heroin) **b** : a stupid person **3** : information especially from a reliable source [Dutch *doop* "sauce", from *dopen* "to dip"]

²dope *vt* **1** : to treat or affect with dope; *esp* : to give a narcotic to **2** *slang* : to guess the result of : predict (an outcome) especially by means of special information or skill (*dope* out which team will win) — **dop·er** *n*

dope·ster \'dōp-stər\ *n* : a forecaster of the outcome of future events (as sports contests or elections)

dop·ey \'dō-pē\ *adj* **dop·i·er; -est** **1** : dulled by or as if by alcohol or a narcotic **2** : DULL 1, 2, 3 — **dop·i·ness** *n*

Dopp·ler effect \'däp-lər-\ *n* : a change in the frequency with which waves (as of sound or light) from a given source reach an observer when the source and observer are moving rapidly toward or away from each other [Christian J. *Doppler*, died 1853, Austrian physicist and mathematician]

Do·ri·an \'dōr-ē-ən, 'dȯr-\ *n* : one of a Hellenic race that completed the overthrow of Mycenaean civiliza-

tion and settled especially in the Peloponnesus and Crete [*Doris*, region of ancient Greece] — **Dorian** *adj*

Dor·ic \'dȯr-ik, 'där-\ *adj* **1** : of, relating to, or characteristic of the Dorians **2** : belonging to the oldest and simplest Greek architectural order

dork \'dȯrk\ *n, slang* : JERK 3

dorky \'dȯr-kē\ *adj* **dork·i·er; -est** *slang* : foolishly stupid

dorm \'dȯrm\ *n* : DORMITORY 2

dor·mant \'dȯr-mənt\ *adj* **1** : not active but capable of resuming activity (a *dormant* volcano) **2 a** : sleeping or appearing to be asleep : SLUGGISH **b** : biologically inactive; *esp* : not actively growing (a *dormant* bud) **3** : of, relating to, or used during a period of inactivity or lack of growth (a *dormant* condition) (*dormant* sprays) [Middle French, "stationary", from *dormir* "to sleep", from Latin *dormire*] SYN see LATENT — **dor·man·cy** \-mən-sē\ *n*

dor·mer \'dȯr-mər\ *n* : a window placed upright in a sloping roof; *also* : a roofed structure containing such a window [Middle French *dormeor* "dormitory", from Latin *dormitorium*]

dor·mi·to·ry \'dȯr-mə-,tōr-ē, -,tȯr-\ *n, pl* **-ries** **1** : a room for sleeping; *esp* : a large room containing a number of beds **2** : a residence hall providing sleeping rooms [Latin *dormitorium*, from *dormire* "to sleep"]

dor·mouse \'dȯr-,maus\ *n, pl* **dor·mice** \-,mīs\ : any of numerous Old World rodents that resemble small squirrels [perhaps from Middle French *dormir* "to sleep"]

dors- *or* **dorsi-** *or* **dorso-** *combining form* : back : dorsal (*dors*ad) (*dorso*ventral) [Latin *dorsum*]

dor·sad \'dȯr-,sad\ *adv* : toward the back : DORSALLY

dor·sal \'dȯr-səl\ *adj* : relating to or situated near or on the back (as of an animal) — **dor·sal·ly** \-sə-lē\ *adv*

dorsal fin *n* : a fin on the ridge along the middle of the back of a fish

dorsal lip *n* : the dorsal margin of the blastopore of a gastrula

dor·so·ven·tral \,dȯr-sō-'ven-trəl\ *adj* : extending from the dorsal toward the ventral side — **dor·so·ven·tral·ly** \-trə-lē\ *adv*

dor·sum \'dȯr-səm\ *n, pl* **dor·sa** \-sə\ : the dorsal surface (as of an animal or one of its parts) [Latin, "back"]

do·ry \'dōr-ē, 'dȯr-\ *n, pl* **dories** : a flat-bottomed rowboat with a sharp bow and high sides that curve upward and outward [perhaps of American Indian origin]

dos·age \'dō-sij\ *n* **1 a** : the giving of medicine in doses **b** : the amount of a single dose **2 a** : the addition of a substance or the application of an agent in a measured dose **b** : the presence and relative representation or strength of a factor or agent

¹dose \'dōs\ *n* **1 a** : the measured amount of a medicine to be taken at one time **b** : the quantity of radiation administered or absorbed **2** : a portion of a substance added during a process **3** : an experience to which one is exposed (a *dose* of defeat) [French, from Late Latin *dosis*, from Greek, literally, "act of giving", from *didonai* "to give"]

²dose *vt* **1** : to give medicine to **2** : to divide (as a medicine) into doses **3** : to treat with an application or agent

do·sim·e·ter \dō-'sim-ət-ər\ *n* : an instrument for measuring doses of X rays or of radioactivity

dos·sier \'dȯs-,yā, 'dȯs-ē-,ā, 'däs-\ *n* : a file of papers containing a detailed report or detailed information [French, "bundle of documents labeled on the back, dossier", from *dos* "back", from Latin *dorsum*]

dost \dəst, 'dəst\ *archaic present 2d sing of* DO

¹dot \'dät\ *n* **1** : a small spot : SPECK **2 a** : a small point made with or as if with a pen **b** (1) : a point after a note or rest in music indicating increase of the time value by one half (2) : a point over or under a note indicating staccato **c** : DECIMAL POINT **d** : a centered point used as a sign of multiplication **3** : a precise point in time or space **4** : a short click or buzz forming a letter or part of a letter (as in the Morse code) [Old English *dott* "head of a boil"]

²dot *vt* **dot·ted; dot·ting 1** : to mark with a dot ⟨*dot* an i⟩ **2** : to cover with or as if with dots ⟨a lake *dotted* with boats⟩ — **dot·ter** *n*

dot·age \'dōt-ij\ *n* : SECOND CHILDHOOD, SENILITY

dot·ard \'dōt-ərd\ *n* : a person in his or her dotage

dote \'dōt\ *vi* **1** : to be feebleminded especially from old age **2** : to show excessive or foolish affection or fondness ⟨*doted* on their grandchildren⟩ [Middle English *doten*] — **dot·er** *n* — **dot·ing·ly** \-ing-lē\ *adv*

doth \dəth, 'dəth\ *archaic present 3d sing of* DO

dot matrix *n* : a rectangular arrangement of dots from which letters, numbers, and symbols can be formed (as by a computer printer or on a display screen)

dotted swiss *n* : a sheer light muslin ornamented with evenly spaced raised dots

dot·ter·el \'dät-ə-rəl, 'dä-trəl\ *n* : a Eurasian plover formerly common in England; *also* : any of several related birds [Middle English *dotrelle*, from *doten* "to dote"]

dot·tle \'dät-l\ *n* : unburned and partly burned tobacco caked in the bowl of a pipe [Middle English *dottel* "plug"]

dot·ty \'dät-ē\ *adj* **dot·ti·er; -est** : mentally unbalanced : CRAZY [Middle English *doten* "to dote"]

¹dou·ble \'dəb-əl\ *adj* **1** : TWOFOLD, DUAL ⟨serving a *double* function⟩ **2** : consisting of two members or parts **3** : being twice as great or as many **4** : DECEITFUL **1 5** : folded in two **6** : having more than the usual number of floral leaves ⟨*double* roses⟩ [Old French, from Latin *duplus*, from *duo* "two" + *-plus* "-fold"] — **dou·ble·ness** *n*

²double *n* **1 a** : something twice another ⟨12 is the *double* of 6⟩ **b** : a base hit in baseball that enables the batter to reach second base **2** : COUNTERPART; *esp* : a person who closely resembles another **3** : a sharp turn : REVERSAL **4** : something that is folded in two **5** *pl* : a game between two pairs of players **6** : an act of doubling in a card game

³double *adv* **1** : to twice the extent or amount : DOUBLY **2** : two together ⟨sleep *double*⟩

⁴double *vb* **dou·bled; dou·bling** \'dəb-ling, -ə-ling\ **1 a** : to make, be, or become twice as great or as many **b** : to make a call in bridge that increases the value of tricks over or less than (an opponent's bid) **2 a** : to make double by bending one part over another **b** : CLENCH **3** ⟨*double* one's fist⟩ **c** : to cause to stoop **d** : to become bent or folded usually in the middle **3** : to sail around (as a cape) by reversing direction **4** : to take the place of another **5** : to make a double in baseball **6** : to turn sharply and go back on one's course — **dou·bler** \'dəb-lər, -ə-lər\ *n*

double bar *n* : two vertical lines or a heavy single line separating principal sections of a musical composition

double bass *n* : the largest instrument of the viol family

double bassoon *n* : CONTRABASSOON

double bed *n* : a bed designed to sleep two persons

double boiler *n* : a cooking utensil consisting of two saucepans fitting into each other so that the contents of the upper can be cooked or heated by boiling water in the lower

double bond *n* : a chemical bond in which two pairs of electrons are shared by two atoms in a molecule — compare SINGLE BOND, TRIPLE BOND

dou·ble–breast·ed \,dəb-əl-'bres-təd\ *adj* : having one half of the front lapped over the other and usually two rows of buttons

dou·ble–check \,dəb-əl-'chek, 'dəb-əl-,\ *vb* : to make or subject to a double check

double check *n* : a careful checking to determine accuracy, condition, or progress especially of something already checked

double chin *n* : a fleshy or fatty fold under the chin — **dou·ble–chinned** \,dəb-əl-'chind\ *adj*

double cross *n* **1** : an act of betraying or cheating especially an associate **2** : a cross between first-generation hybrids of four separate inbred lines — **dou·ble–cross** \,dəb-əl-'kròs\ *vt* — **dou·ble–cross·er** *n*

double dagger *n* : a character ‡ used as a reference mark

dou·ble–deal·ing \,dəb-əl-'dē-ling\ *n* : DUPLICITY — **dou·ble–deal·er** *n* — **double–dealing** *adj*

dou·ble–deck·er \-'dek-ər\ *n* **1** : something (as a ship, bus, or bed) having two decks **2** : a 2-layered sandwich

double dribble *n* : an illegal action in basketball that occurs when a player resumes a dribble after stopping or dribbles the ball with both hands simultaneously

dou·ble entendre \,düb-,län-'tä[n]dr, ,dəb-, -ə-,län-\ *n, pl* **double entendres** \-'tä[n]dr, -'tä[n]d-rəz\ : a word or expression capable of two interpretations one of which is usually indelicate [obsolete French, literally, "double meaning"]

double entry *n* : a method of bookkeeping that debits the amount of a business transaction to one account and credits it to another so that the total debits equal the total credits

double fertilization *n* : fertilization characteristic of seed plants in which one of the two sperm nuclei fuses with the egg nucleus to form an embryo and the other fuses with the two separate or fused polar nuclei to form endosperm

dou·ble–head·er \,dəb-əl-'hed-ər\ *n* **1** : a train pulled by two locomotives **2** : two games, contests, or events held consecutively on the same program

double hyphen *n* : a punctuation mark ⸗ used in place of a hyphen at the end of a line to indicate that the word so divided is normally hyphenated

dou·ble–joint·ed \,dəb-əl-'jòint-əd\ *adj* : having a joint that permits an exceptional degree of freedom of motion of the parts joined

double knit *n* : a knitted fabric made with a double set of needles to produce a double thickness of fabric with each thickness joined by interlocking stitches

double negative *n* : a nonstandard syntactic construction that contains two negatives and is intended to have a negative meaning (as in "I didn't hear nothing" instead of "I didn't hear anything")

dou·ble–park \,dəb-əl-'pärk\ *vb* : to park beside a row of vehicles already parked parallel to the curb

double play *n* : a single play in baseball in which two players are put out

double pneumonia *n* : pneumonia involving both lungs

dou·ble–quick \'dəb-əl-,kwik\ *n* : DOUBLE TIME — **dou·ble–quick** *vi*

dou·ble–space \,dəb-əl-'spās\ *vb* **1** : to type (copy) leaving every other line blank **2** : to type on every second line

double star *n* **1** : BINARY STAR **2** : two stars that appear as one to the naked eye but can be seen as separate when viewed with a telescope

double sugar *n* : DISACCHARIDE

dou·blet \'dəb-lət\ *n* **1** : a close-fitting jacket worn by men of western Europe chiefly in the 16th century **2** : one of two similar or identical things **3** : one of two or more words in the same language derived by different routes from the same source ⟨dish and disk are *doublets*⟩ [Middle French, from *double* "double"]

dou·ble–talk \'dəb-əl-,tòk\ *n* **1** : language that appears to be meaningful but in fact is a mixture of sense and nonsense **2** : deliberately ambiguous language

dou·ble–time \'dəb-əl-,tīm\ *vt* : to move at double time

double time *n* **1** : a marching cadence of 180 36-inch steps per minute **2** : payment of a worker at twice the regular wage rate

double vision *n* : vision in which an object is seen as double due to unequal action of the eye muscles

dotterel

D doublet 1

\ə\ abut	\ng\ sing
\ər\ further	\ō\ bone
\a\ mat	\ò\ saw
\ā\ take	\òi\ coin
\ä\ cot, cart	\th\ thin
\aù\ out	\th\ this
\ch\ chin	\ü\ food
\e\ pet	\ù\ foot
\ē\ easy	\y\ yet
\g\ go	\yü\ few
\i\ tip	\yù\ cure
\ī\ life	\zh\ vision
\j\ job	

dou·bloon \ˌdə-ˈblün\ *n* : an old gold coin of Spain and Spanish America worth 16 pieces of eight [Spanish *doblón,* derived from Latin *duplus* "double"]

dou·bly \ˈdəb-lē\ *adv* **1** : to twice the degree **2** : in a twofold manner

¹doubt \ˈdau̇t\ *vb* **1** : to be uncertain about **2** : to lack confidence in : DISTRUST **3** : to consider unlikely [Old French *douter,* from Latin *dubitare*] — **doubt·able** \-ə-bəl\ *adj* — **doubt·er** *n* — **doubt·ing·ly** \-iŋ-lē\ *adv*

²doubt *n* **1** : uncertainty of belief or opinion **2** : a state of affairs that causes uncertainty or suspense ⟨the outcome is in *doubt*⟩ **3 a** : a lack of confidence : DISTRUST **b** : an inclination not to believe or accept □ SYN DOUBT, UNCERTAINTY, DISTRUST, SUSPICION mean lack of sureness about someone or something. DOUBT implies uncertainty about the truth or reality of something and an inability to make a decision; UNCERTAINTY may range from a falling short of certainty to an almost complete lack of knowledge about an outcome or result; DISTRUST implies lack of trust or confidence on vague or general grounds; SUSPICION stresses lack of faith in the truth or reality of someone or something and implies an often unfounded charge of wrongdoing.

doubt·ful \ˈdau̇t-fəl\ *adj* **1** : not clear or certain as to fact ⟨a *doubtful* claim⟩ **2** : questionable in character ⟨*doubtful* intentions⟩ **3** : not settled in opinion : UNDECIDED ⟨*doubtful* about what to do⟩ **4** : not certain in outcome ⟨a *doubtful* battle⟩ — **doubt·ful·ly** \-fə-lē\ *adv* — **doubt·ful·ness** *n*

doubting Thom·as \-ˈtäm-əs\ *n* : a habitually doubtful person [*Thomas,* apostle of Jesus who doubted Jesus' resurrection until he had proof of it (John 20:24–29)]

¹doubt·less \ˈdau̇t-ləs\ *adv* **1** : without doubt **2** : PROBABLY

²doubtless *adj* : free from doubt : CERTAIN

douche \ˈdüsh\ *n* **1 a** : a jet of fluid (as water) directed against a part or into a cavity of the body **b** : a cleansing with a douche **2** : a device for giving douches [French] — **douche** *vb*

dough \ˈdō\ *n* **1 a** : a soft mass of moistened flour or meal thick enough to knead or roll **b** : a comparably soft pasty mass **2** : MONEY 1, 2 [Old English *dāg*] — **doughy** \ˈdō-ē\ *adj*

dough·boy \ˈdō-ˌbȯi\ *n* : an American infantryman especially in World War I

dough·nut *or* **do·nut** \ˈdō-nət, -ˌnət\ *n* : a small usually ring-shaped cake fried in fat

dough·ty \ˈdau̇t-ē\ *adj* **dough·ti·er; -est** : being strong and valiant : BOLD [Old English *dohtig*] — **dough·ti·ly** \ˈdau̇t-l-ē\ *adv* — **dough·ti·ness** \ˈdau̇t-ē-nəs\ *n*

Doug·las fir \ˈdəg-ləs-\ *n* : a tall evergreen cone-bearing timber tree of the western United States; *also* : its wood [David *Douglas,* died 1834, Scottish botanist]

do up *vt* **1** : to put in order; *also* : REPAIR ⟨planned to *do up* the house⟩ **2** : WRAP 1b ⟨*do up* holiday packages⟩ **3** : ARRAY, CLOTHE ⟨all *done up* in a pirate costume⟩

dour \ˈdu̇r, ˈdau̇r\ *adj* **1** : STERN 3, HARSH **2** : MOROSE 1 [Latin *durus* "hard"] — **dour·ly** *adv* — **dour·ness** *n*

¹douse \ˈdau̇s\ *vt* : to take in ⟨*douse* a sail⟩ [earlier *douse* "blow, stroke"]

²douse \ˈdau̇s, ˈdau̇z\ *vt* **1 a** : to plunge into water **b** : to throw a liquid on : DRENCH **2** : to put out : EXTINGUISH

¹dove \ˈdəv\ *n* **1** : any of numerous pigeons; *esp* : a small wild pigeon **2** : a person who advocates negotiations and compromise in a dispute; *esp* : an opponent of war — compare HAWK [Middle English] — **dov·ish** \ˈdəv-ish\ *adj*

²dove \ˈdōv\ *past of* DIVE

dove·cote \ˈdəv-ˌkōt, -ˌkät\ *or* **dove·cot** \-ˌkät\ *n* : a small raised house or box with compartments for domestic pigeons

dove·kie \ˈdəv-kē\ *n* : a small short-billed auk breeding on arctic coasts and ranging south in winter [from *dove*]

¹dove·tail \ˈdəv-ˌtāl\ *n* : something resembling a dove's tail; *esp* : a flaring projection on a board and a slot into which it fits tightly making an interlocking joint between two pieces

²dovetail *vb* **1 a** : to join by means of dovetails **b** : to cut to a dovetail **2** : to fit skillfully together to form a whole

dow·a·ger \ˈdau̇-i-jər\ *n* **1** : a widow holding property or a title received from her deceased husband **2** : a dignified elderly woman [Middle French *douagiere,* from *douage* "dower", from *douer* "to endow", from Latin *dotare,* from *dot-, dos* "gift, dower"]

¹dowdy \ˈdau̇d-ē\ *n, pl* **dowd·ies** : a dowdy woman [Middle English *doude*]

²dowdy *adj* **dowd·i·er; -est** : not neatly or becomingly dressed or cared for : SHABBY; *also* : lacking in smartness or taste — **dowd·i·ly** \ˈdau̇d-l-ē\ *adv* — **dowd·i·ness** \ˈdau̇d-ē-nəs\ *n*

¹dow·el \ˈdau̇-əl, ˈdau̇l\ *n* : a pin or peg projecting from one of two parts or surfaces (as of wood) to be fastened together and fitting into a hole prepared in the other part; *also* : a rod for cutting into dowels [Middle English *dowle*]

²dowel *vt* **-eled** *or* **-elled; -el·ing** *or* **-el·ling** : to fasten by or furnish with dowels

¹dow·er \ˈdau̇-ər, ˈdau̇r\ *n* **1** : the part of or interest in the real estate of a deceased husband given by law to his widow during her life **2** : DOWRY

²dower *vt* : to supply with a dower or dowry : ENDOW

¹down \ˈdau̇n\ *n* : an undulating usually treeless upland with sparse soil — usually used in pl. [Old English *dūn* "hill"]

²down *adv* **1 a** (1) : toward or in a lower physical position (2) : to a lying or sitting position (3) : toward or to the ground, floor, or bottom **b** : in cash ⟨paid $10 *down*⟩ **2** : in a direction that is the opposite of up: as **a** : SOUTH **b** : away from a center (as of activity) ⟨went *down* to the country⟩ **3** : to or in a lower or worse condition, level, or status **4** : from a past time ⟨heirlooms handed *down*⟩ **5** : to or in a state of less activity ⟨excitement *died* down⟩ **6** : to a concentrated state ⟨boil *down* a report⟩ [Old English *dūne,* short for *adūne,* from *a-* "off, from" + *dūn* "hill"]

³down *adj* **1 a** : occupying a low position; *esp* : lying on the ground **b** : directed or going downward ⟨a *down* car⟩ **c** : being at a lower level ⟨sales were *down*⟩ **2 a** : being in a state of reduced or low activity **b** (1) : DEJECTED, DEPRESSED ⟨felt *down* after losing the game⟩ (2) : SICK ⟨*down* with flu⟩ (3) : having a low opinion or dislike ⟨was *down* on me for not helping⟩ **3** : DONE 3, FINISHED ⟨eight *down* and two to go⟩

⁴down *prep* : down along : down through : down toward : down in : down into : down on ⟨*down* the road⟩

⁵down *n* **1** : a low or falling period (as in activity, emotional life, or fortunes) ⟨have their ups and *downs*⟩ **2 a** : a complete play to advance the ball in football **b** : one of a series of four attempts to advance a football 10 yards

⁶down *vb* : to go or cause to go or come down

⁷down *n* **1** : a covering of soft fluffy feathers **2** : something soft and fluffy like down [Old Norse *dūnn*]

down·beat \ˈdau̇n-ˌbēt\ *n* : the downward stroke of a conductor indicating the principally accented note of a measure of music

down·cast \-ˌkast\ *adj* **1** : low in spirit : DISCOURAGED ⟨a *downcast* manner⟩ **2** : directed down ⟨*downcast* eyes⟩

down·draft \-ˌdraft\ *n* : a downward current of gas (as air in a chimney or during a thunderstorm)

down·er \ˈdau̇-nər\ *n* : a depressant drug; *esp* : BARBITURATE

down·fall \'daun-,fol\ *n* **1** : FALL 2c; *esp* : a sudden or heavy fall (as of rain) **2** : a sudden descent (as from a high position) : RUIN ⟨the *downfall* of the beaten champion⟩ **3** : the cause of a downfall ⟨*drink* was their downfall⟩ — **down·fall·en** \-,fo-lən\ *adj*

¹down·grade \-,grād\ *n* **1** : a downward grade or slope **2** : a decline toward a worse condition ⟨a neighborhood on the *downgrade*⟩ — **down·grade** \-'grād\ *adv*

²down·grade \-,grād\ *vt* : to lower in grade, rank, position, or status

down·heart·ed \'daun-'härt-əd\ *adj* : DEJECTED, DOWNCAST — **down·heart·ed·ly** *adv* — **down·heart·ed·ness** *n*

¹down·hill \'daun-'hil\ *adv* **1** : toward the bottom of a hill **2** : toward a lower state or level

²down·hill \-,hil\ *adj* : sloping downhill

³downhill *n* : a ski race in which individuals competing one at a time try to find the fastest most direct route down a long steep course

down·load \'daun-,lōd\ *vt* : to transfer (data) from a usually large computer to the memory of another device (as a smaller computer) — **down·load·able** \-,lōd-ə-bəl\ *adj*

down payment *n* : a part of the full price paid at the time of purchase with the balance to be paid later

down·pour \'daun-,pōr, -,pȯr\ *n* : a heavy rain

down·range \-'rānj\ *adv* : toward the target area of a firing range ⟨a missile landing 5000 kilometers *downrange*⟩ — **down·range** *adj*

¹down·right \-,rīt\ *adv* : OUTRIGHT 1 ⟨*downright* mean⟩

²downright *adj* **1** : ABSOLUTE 4, UTTER ⟨a *downright* lie⟩ **2** : PLAIN 4b, BLUNT ⟨a straightforward *downright* person⟩ — **down·right·ly** *adv* — **down·right·ness** *n*

Down's syndrome \'daunz-\ *n* : an inherited condition marked by moderate to severe mental deficiency, by distinctive physical characteristics (as slanting eyes and broad hands with short fingers), and by the presence of three chromosomes of the chromosome pair numbered 21 in human beings — called also *mongolism* [J.L.H. *Down,* died 1896, English physician]

down·stage \-'stāj\ *adv or adj* : toward or at the front of a theatrical stage

¹down·stairs \'daun-'staərz, -'steərz\ *adv* : down the stairs : on or to a lower floor

²down·stairs \-,staərz, -,steərz\ *adj* : located on the main, lower, or ground floor of a building

³down·stairs \'daun-', 'daun-,\ *n* : the lower floor of a building

down·stream \'daun-'strēm\ *adv or adj* : in the direction of flow of a stream

down·stroke \-,strōk\ *n* : a stroke made in a downward direction

down·swing \-,swing\ *n* **1** : a swing downward **2** : DOWNTURN 2

down–to–earth \,daun-tə-'ərth, -'wərth\ *adj* : free from frills or foibles : PRACTICAL

¹down·town \'daun-'taun\ *adv* : to, toward, or in the lower part or business center of a town or city — **downtown** *adj*

²down·town \-,taun\ *n* : an urban business center

down·trod·den \'daun-'träd-n\ *adj* : crushed by superior power : OPPRESSED

down·turn \-,tərn\ *n* **1** : a turning downward **2** : a decline especially in business activity

¹down·ward \'daun-wərd\ *also* **down·wards** \-wərdz\ *adv* **1** : from a higher to a lower place or condition **2 a** : from an earlier time **b** : from an ancestor or predecessor

²downward *adj* **1** : moving or extending downward **2** : descending from a head, origin, or source

down·wind \'daun-'wind\ *adv or adj* : in the direction that the wind is blowing

downy \'dau-nē\ *adj* **down·i·er; -est 1** : suggesting a bird's down (as in softness or lightness) **2** : covered with or made of down

downy mildew *n* : a parasitic mold that bears whitish masses of spore-producing bodies on the undersurface of the leaves of the host; *also* : a plant disease caused by a downy mildew

dow·ry \'daur-ē\ *n, pl* **dowries 1** : the property that a woman brings to her husband in marriage **2** : a gift of money or property by a man to or for his bride [Anglo-French *dowarie,* from Medieval Latin *dotarium,* from Latin *dot-, dos* "gift, dower"]

dowse \'dauz\ *vb* : to use a divining rod especially to find water [origin unknown] — **dows·er** *n*

dox·ol·o·gy \däk-'säl-ə-jē\ *n, pl* **-gies** : a usually liturgical expression of praise to God [Medieval Latin *doxologia,* from Late Greek, from Greek *doxa* "opinion, glory" + *-logia* "-logy"]

doze \'dōz\ *vi* : to sleep lightly [probably of Scandinavian origin] — **doze** *n* — **doz·er** *n*

doz·en \'dəz-n\ *n, pl* **dozens** *or* **dozen** : a group of twelve [Old French *dozaine,* from *doze* "twelve", from Latin *duodecim,* from *duo* "two" + *decem* "ten"] — **dozen** *adj* — **doz·enth** \-nth, -ntth\ *adj*

DP \'dē-'pē\ *n, pl* **DP's** *or* **DPs** : a displaced person

¹drab \'drab\ *n* : a light olive brown [Middle French *drap* "cloth", from Late Latin *drappus*]

²drab *adj* **drab·ber; drab·best 1** : of the color drab **2** : characterized by dullness and monotony : CHEERLESS ⟨they lead *drab* lives⟩ — **drab·ly** *adv* — **drab·ness** *n*

drachm \'dram\ *n* **1** : DRACHMA 2a **2** : DRAM 1, 2b

drach·ma \'drak-mə\ *n, pl* **drach·mas** *or* **drach·mae** \-,mē, -,mī\ *or* **drach·mai** \-,mī\ **1 a** : any of various ancient Greek units of weight **b** : any of various modern units of weight; *esp* : DRAM 1 **2 a** : an ancient Greek silver coin equivalent to 6 obols **b** : the basic monetary unit of modern Greece; *also* : a coin representing this unit [Latin, "drachma, dram", from Greek *drachmē*]

Dra·co \'drā-kō\ *n* : a northern circumpolar constellation between the Big Dipper and Little Dipper [Latin, literally, "dragon"]

¹draft \'draft, 'draft\ *n* **1** : the act of drawing a net; *also* : the quantity of fish taken at one drawing **2** : the act of moving loads by drawing or pulling **3 a** : the force required to pull an implement **b** : load-pulling capacity **4 a** : the act or an instance of drinking or inhaling; *also* : the portion drunk or inhaled **b** : a potion prepared for drinking : DOSE **5 a** : DELINEATION, REPRESENTATION; *esp* : a construction plan ⟨the *draft* of a future building⟩ **b** : a preliminary sketch, outline, or version ⟨a rough *draft* of a thesis⟩ **6** : the act or result of drawing out or stretching **7** : the act of drawing (as from a cask); *also* : a portion of liquid so drawn **8** : the depth of water a ship draws especially when loaded **9 a** : the selection of a person especially for compulsory military service **b** : a group of persons selected **10 a** : an order (as a check) issued by one party to another (as a bank) to pay money to a third party **b** : a heavy demand : STRAIN ⟨a *draft* on national resources⟩ **11 a** : a current of air in an enclosed space **b** : a device for regulating the flow of air (as in a fireplace) **12** : ANGLE, TAPER; *esp* : the taper given to a pattern or die so that the work can be easily withdrawn **13** : a narrow border along the edge of a stone or across its face serving as a stonecutter's guide **14** : a system whereby exclusive rights to selected new players are apportioned among professional teams [Middle English *draght*] — **on draft** : ready to be drawn from a receptacle ⟨beer *on draft*⟩

²draft *adj* **1** : used for drawing loads ⟨*draft* animals⟩ **2** : constituting a preliminary or tentative version, sketch, or outline ⟨a *draft* treaty⟩ **3** : being on draft ⟨*draft* beer⟩

³draft *vt* **1** : to select usually on a compulsory basis; *esp* : to conscript for military service **2 a** : to draw up a preliminary sketch, version, or plan of **b** : to draw

\ə\ abut		\ng\ sing	
\ər\ further		\ō\ bone	
\a\ mat		\ȯ\ saw	
\ā\ take		\oi\ coin	
\ä\ cot, cart		\th\ thin	
\au\ out		\th\ this	
\ch\ chin		\ü\ food	
\e\ pet		\u̇\ foot	
\ē\ easy		\y\ yet	
\g\ go		\yü\ few	
\i\ tip		\yu̇\ cure	
\ī\ life		\zh\ vision	
\j\ job			

up : COMPOSE ⟨*draft* a constitution⟩ **3** : to draw off or away ⟨water *drafted* by pumps⟩ — **draft·er** *n*

draft·ee \draf-'tē, draf-\ *n* : a person who is drafted especially into the armed forces

drafts·man \'draf-smən, 'draf-, 'draft-, 'draft-\ *n* : one who draws plans and sketches (as for machinery) — **drafts·man·ship** \-,ship\ *n*

drafty \'draf-tē, 'draf-\ *adj* **draf·ti·er; -est** : having or exposed to a draft ⟨a *drafty* hall⟩ — **draft·i·ly** \-tə-lē\ *adv* — **draft·i·ness** \-tē-nəs\ *n*

¹drag \'drag\ *n* **1** : something that is dragged, pulled, or drawn along or over a surface: as **a** : HARROW **b** : a sledge for carrying heavy loads **2** : something used to drag with; *esp* : a device for dragging under water to detect or obtain objects **3 a** : something that retards motion **b** : the retarding force acting on a body (as an airplane) moving through a fluid (as air) **c** : friction between engine parts **d** : something that hinders or obstructs progress **4 a** : the act or an instance of dragging or drawing **b** : a drawing along or over a surface with effort or pressure **c** : motion achieved with slowness or difficulty; *also* : the condition of having or seeming to have such motion **d** : a draw on a pipe, cigarette, or cigar : PUFF; *also* : a draft of liquid **5** : a movement, inclination, or retardation caused by or as if by dragging **6** *slang* : influence securing special favor **7** *slang* : STREET **1**, ROAD ⟨the main *drag*⟩ **8** : one that is boring ⟨the movie was a *drag*⟩

²drag *vb* **dragged; drag·ging** **1 a** : to draw slowly or heavily : HAUL **b** : to move or cause to move with painful slowness or difficulty ⟨*drags* one leg⟩ ⟨the story *drags*⟩ **c** : to bring by force or compulsion ⟨*dragged* them to the theater⟩ **d** : to pass (time) in lingering pain, tedium, or unhappiness **e** : PROTRACT ⟨*drag* a story out⟩ **2** : to hang or lag behind **3** : to trail along a surface **4** : to explore, search, or fish with a drag **5** : to inhale deeply ⟨*drag* on a cigarette⟩ [Old Norse *draga* or Old English *dragan*]

drag·ger \'drag-ər\ *n* : one that drags; *esp* : a fishing boat operating a trawl or dragnet

drag·gle \'drag-əl\ *vb* **drag·gled; drag·gling** \'drag-ling, -ə-ling\ **1** : to make or become wet and dirty by dragging **2 a** : to follow slowly : STRAGGLE **b** : to move along slowly [derived from *drag*]

drag·gy \'drag-ē\ *adj* **drag·gi·er; -est 1** : DULL 3 **2** : TEDIOUS

drag·net \'drag-,net\ *n* **1 a** : a net drawn along the bottom of a body of water : TRAWL **b** : a net used (as to capture small game) on the ground **2** : a network of planned actions for pursuing and catching a criminal

drag·o·man \'drag-ə-mən\ *n, pl* **-mans** *or* **-men** \-mən\ : an interpreter chiefly of Arabic, Turkish, or Persian employed especially in the Near East [Middle French *drogman*, from Italian *dragomanno*, from Middle Greek *dragomanos*, from Arabic *tarjumān*, from Aramaic *tūrgĕmānā*]

drag·on \'drag-ən\ *n* **1** : an imaginary animal usually represented as a huge winged and scaly serpent or lizard with a crested head and enormous claws **2** *cap* : DRACO **3** : a fierce or very strict person [Old French, from Latin *draco* "serpent, dragon", from Greek *drakōn* "serpent"]

drag·on·fly \-,flī\ *n* : any of an order (Odonata) of large harmless insects that have four long wings and feed especially on flies, gnats, and mosquitoes — compare DAMSELFLY

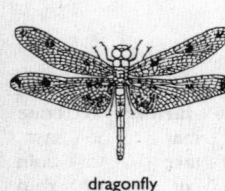

dragonfly

¹dra·goon \drə-'gün, dra-\ *n* : a cavalry soldier [French *dragon* "dragon, dragoon"]

²dragoon *vt* : to force or attempt to force into submission by violent measures

drag race *n* : an acceleration contest between motor vehicles

¹drain \'drān\ *vb* **1 a** : to draw off or flow off gradually or completely ⟨*drain* water from a tank⟩ **b** : to cause the gradual disappearance of **c** : to exhaust physically

or emotionally **2 a** : to make or become gradually dry or empty ⟨let the dishes *drain*⟩ **b** : to carry away the surface water of : discharge surface or surplus water [Old English *drēahnian*] — **drain·er** *n*

²drain *n* **1** : a means by which usually liquid matter is drained **2 a** : the act of draining **b** : a gradual outflow or withdrawal : DEPLETION **3** : something that causes depletion : BURDEN ⟨a *drain* on one's resources⟩ — **down the drain** : used wastefully or brought to nothing

drain·age \'drā-nij\ *n* **1** : the act, process, or mode of draining; *also* : something drained off **2** : a means for draining; *also* : a system of drains **3** : an area drained

drain·pipe \'drān-,pīp\ *n* : a pipe for drainage

drake *n* : a male duck [Middle English]

dram \'dram\ *n* **1 a** — see MEASURE table **b** : FLUID DRAM **2 a** : a small portion of something to drink **b** : a small amount [Late Latin *dragma* "dram, drachma", from Latin *drachma*, from Greek *drachmē*, literally, "handful", from *drassesthai* "to grasp"]

DRAM \'dram *also* 'dē-,ram\ *n* : a computer memory chip that must be continuously supplied with power in order to retain data [*d*ynamic + *RAM* (*r*andom-*a*ccess *m*emory)]

dra·ma \'dräm-ə, 'dram-\ *n* **1** : a composition telling a story through action and dialogue and designed for theatrical performance : PLAY **2** : dramatic art, literature, or affairs **3 a** : a series of events involving interesting or intense conflict of forces ⟨the *drama* of a hockey game⟩ **b** : dramatic effect or quality [Late Latin *dramat-, drama*, from Greek, "deed, drama", from *dran* "to do"]

Dram·a·mine \'dram-ə-,mēn\ *trademark* — used for a crystalline compound used in the prevention or treatment of motion sickness

dra·mat·ic \drə-'mat-ik\ *adj* **1** : of or relating to the drama **2 a** : suitable to or characteristic of the drama **b** : striking in appearance or effect — **dra·mat·i·cal·ly** \-'mat-i-kə-lē, -klē\ *adv* □ SYN DRAMATIC, THEATRICAL, HISTRIONIC, MELODRAMATIC mean having a character or an effect like that of acted plays. DRAMATIC applies to situations in life and literature when they give evidence of power to stir the imagination and emotions deeply ⟨a *dramatic* meeting of leaders⟩ THEATRICAL implies a crude appeal through artificiality or exaggeration in gesture or vocal expression ⟨a *theatrical* oration⟩ HISTRIONIC applies to tones, gestures, and motions and suggests a deliberate affectation or staginess ⟨a *histrionic* show of grief⟩ MELODRAMATIC suggests an exaggerated emotionalism or an inappropriate theatricalism ⟨making a *melodramatic* scene in public⟩

dra·mat·ics \-iks\ *n sing or pl* **1 a** : performance of plays especially as an extracurricular activity in school or college **b** : theatrical technique ⟨studying *dramatics*⟩ **2** : dramatic behavior or expression

dra·ma·tis per·so·nae \,dram-ət-əs-pər-'sō-,nē, ,dräm-, -,nī\ *n pl* : the characters or actors in a drama [New Latin]

dra·ma·tist \'dram-ət-əst, 'dräm-\ *n* : PLAYWRIGHT

dra·ma·tize \'dram-ə-,tīz, 'dräm-\ *vt* **1** : to adapt for theatrical presentation **2** : to present or represent in a dramatic manner — **dra·ma·ti·za·tion** \,dram-ət-ə-'zā-shən, ,dräm-\ *n*

dra·ma·tur·gy \'dram-ə-,tər-jē, 'dräm-\ *n* : the art or technique of dramatic composition and theatrical representation [German *dramaturgie*, from Greek *dramatourgia* "dramatic composition", derived from *drama* "drama" + *ergon* "work"] — **dra·ma·tur·gic** \,dram-ə-'tər-jik, ,dräm-\ *adj*

drank *past of* DRINK

¹drape \'drāp\ *vb* **1** : to cover or adorn with or as if with folds of cloth **2** : to cause to hang or stretch out loosely or carelessly ⟨*drape* oneself over a chair⟩ **3** : to arrange or become arranged in flowing lines or folds ⟨a cleverly *draped* suit) [Middle French *draper* "to weave", from *drap* "cloth", from Late Latin *drappus*]

²drape *n* **1** : a drapery especially for a window : CURTAIN **2** : arrangement in or of folds **3** : the cut or hang of clothing ⟨the *drape* of a jacket⟩

drap·er \'drā-pər\ *n, chiefly British* : a dealer in cloth and sometimes also in clothing and dry goods

drap·ery \'drā-pə-rē, -prē\ *n, pl* **-er·ies 1** *British* : DRY GOODS **2 a** : a decorative fabric usually hung in loose folds and arranged in a graceful design **b** : a hanging of heavy fabric used as a curtain **3** : the draping or arranging of materials

dras·tic \'dras-tik\ *adj* **1** : acting rapidly or violently ⟨a *drastic* purgative⟩ **2** : extreme in effect : SEVERE ⟨*drastic* changes in the law⟩ [Greek *drastikos*, from *dran* "to do"] — **dras·ti·cal·ly** \-ti-kə-lē, -klē\ *adv*

draught \'draft, 'dráft\ *chiefly British variant of* DRAFT

draughts \'drafs, 'dráfs, 'drafts, 'dráfts\ *n, British* : CHECKERS [Middle English *draghtes*, from *draght* "draft, move in chess"]

Dra·vid·i·an \drə-'vid-ē-ən\ *n* **1** : a member of an ancient people of southern India **2** : any of several languages of India, Sri Lanka, and Pakistan constituting a language family [Sanskrit *Draviḍa*] — **Dravidian** *adj*

¹draw \'dró\ *vb* **drew** \'drü\; **drawn** \'drón\; **draw·ing 1** : to cause to move continuously toward or after a force applied in advance : HAUL, DRAG **2 a** : to cause to go in a certain direction (as by leading) ⟨*drew* us aside⟩ **b** : to move or go steadily or gradually ⟨night *draws* near⟩ **3 a** : ATTRACT, ENTICE ⟨honey *draws* flies⟩ **b** : to bring on oneself : PROVOKE ⟨*drew* enemy fire⟩ **4** : INHALE ⟨*drew* a deep breath⟩ **5 a** : to bring or pull out by effort ⟨*draw* a sword⟩ **b** : to extract the essence from ⟨*draw* tea⟩ **c** : EVISCERATE ⟨a *drawn* and plucked hen⟩ **6** : to require (a specified depth) to float in ⟨a ship that *draws* four meters of water⟩ **7 a** : ACCUMULATE, GAIN ⟨*draw* interest⟩ **b** : to take (money) from a place of deposit : WITHDRAW **c** : to receive regularly from a source ⟨*draw* a salary⟩ **8 a** : to take (cards) from a stack or the dealer **b** : to receive or take at random ⟨*drew* a winning number⟩ **9** : to bend (a bow) by pulling back the string **10 a** : to cause to shrink or tighten **b** : to change shape by or as if by pulling or stretching ⟨a face *drawn* with fatigue⟩ **11** : to strike (a ball) so as to impart a backward spin **12** : to leave (a contest) undecided : TIE **13 a** : to produce a likeness of by or as if by making lines on a surface : DELINEATE **b** : to write out in due form : DRAFT ⟨*draw* up a will⟩ **c** : express in detail : FORMULATE ⟨*draw* comparisons⟩ **14** : to infer from evidence or premises ⟨*draw* a conclusion⟩ **15** : to spread or elongate (metal) by hammering or by pulling through dies **16 a** : to produce or allow a draft or current of air ⟨the furnace *draws* well⟩ **b** : to swell out in a wind ⟨all sails *drawing*⟩ [Old English *dragan*] — **draw a bead on** : to take aim at

²draw *n* **1** : the act, process, or result of drawing **2** : a lot or chance drawn at random ⟨a win at the first *draw*⟩ **3** : the movable part of a drawbridge **4** : a contest left undecided or deadlocked : TIE **5** : something that draws attention or patronage **6** : a gully shallower than a ravine

draw away *vi* : to move ahead (as of an opponent in a race) ⟨the brown horse soon *drew away* from the others⟩

draw·back \'dró-,bak\ *n* : an objectionable feature

draw·bar \-,bär\ *n* : a beam across the rear of a tractor to which implements are hitched

draw·bridge \-,brij\ *n* : a bridge made to be raised up, let down, or drawn aside so as to permit or hinder passage

draw·ee \dró-'ē\ *n* : the party (as a bank) ordered to pay a draft

draw·er \'dró-ər, 'drór\ *n* **1** : one that draws: as **a** : a person who draws liquor **b** : DRAFTSMAN **c** : one who executes a draft or makes a promissory note **2** : a sliding box or receptacle (as in a table or desk) opened by pulling out and closed by pushing in **3** *pl* : an undergarment for the lower part of the body

draw·ing \'dró-ing\ *n* **1 a** : an act or instance of drawing **b** : the deciding of something by drawing lots **2** : the act, art, or technique of representing an object by means of lines **3** : something drawn or capable of being drawn; *esp* : a representation formed by drawing

drawing board *n* : a board on which paper to be drawn on is fastened

drawing card *n* : something or someone that attracts attention or patronage

drawing room *n* **1 a** : a formal reception room **b** : a private room on a railroad passenger car with three berths and an enclosed toilet **2** : a formal reception ⟨at the queen's *drawing room*⟩ [short for *withdrawing room*]

draw·knife \'dró-,nīf\ *n* : a woodworker's tool having a blade with a handle at each end used to shave off surfaces

¹drawl \'dról\ *vb* : to speak slowly with vowels greatly prolonged : utter in a slow lengthened tone [probably from *draw*] — **drawl·er** *n* — **drawl·ing·ly** \'dró-ling-lē\ *adv*

²drawl *n* : a drawling manner of speaking

drawn butter *n* : melted and often seasoned butter

drawn·work \'drón-,wərk\ *n* : decoration on cloth made by drawing out threads according to a pattern

draw on *vb* **1 a** : APPROACH 1a ⟨night *draws on*⟩ **b** : to bring on : CAUSE **2** : to take funds from ⟨*draw on* a bank account⟩

draw out *vt* **1** : EXTRACT 1 ⟨*draw out* a confession⟩ **2** : to cause to speak freely ⟨tried to *draw* them *out* on the subject⟩ **3** : PROLONG 1 ⟨refused to *draw out* the interview⟩

draw·shave \'dró-,shāv\ *n* : DRAWKNIFE

draw·string \-,string\ *n* : a string, cord, or tape run through a hem, a casing, or eyelets and used to close a bag or to control fullness in garments and curtains

draw·tube \-,tüb, -,tyüb\ *n* : a telescoping tube (as for the eyepiece of a microscope)

draw up *vb* **1** : to arrange (as troops) in order **2** : to straighten (oneself) to an erect posture **3** : to bring or come to a halt

¹dray \'drā\ *n* : a vehicle used to haul goods; *esp* : a strong low cart or wagon without sides [Middle English *draye*, a wheelless vehicle, from Old English *dræge* "dragnet"]

²dray *vt* : to carry or transport on a dray

dray·age \'drā-ij\ *n* : the work or cost of draying

dray·man \'drā-mən\ *n* : one whose work is draying

¹dread \'dred\ *vb* **1 a** : to fear greatly : be apprehensive or fearful **b** *archaic* : to regard with awe **2** : to feel extreme reluctance to meet or face [Old English *drædan*]

²dread *n* **1 a** : great fear especially in the face of impending evil or harm **b** *archaic* : AWE 1 **2** : one causing fear syn see FEAR

³dread *adj* : causing dread : DREADFUL

dread·ful \'dred-fəl\ *adj* **1** : inspiring dread or awe : FRIGHTENING **2** : extremely distasteful, unpleasant, or shocking — **dread·ful·ly** \-fə-lē, -flē\ *adv* — **dread·ful·ness** \-fəl-nəs\ *n*

dread·nought \'dred-,nót, -,nät\ *n* : a battleship whose main armament consists entirely of big guns all of the same caliber [*Dreadnought*, a British battleship]

¹dream \'drēm\ *n* **1** : a series of thoughts, images, or emotions occurring during sleep **2 a** : a visionary creation of the imagination : DAYDREAM **b** : a state of mind in which a person is lost in fancies or reveries **c** : an object seen in a dreamlike state : VISION **3** : something notable for its beauty, excellence, or enjoyable quality **4** : a goal or purpose strongly desired [Old English *drēam* "noise, joy"] — **dream·like** \-,līk\ *adj* □ ORIGIN Not until the 13th century was our word *dream*

drawbridge

\ə\ abut	\ng\ sing
\ər\ further	\ō\ bone
\a\ mat	\ó\ saw
\ā\ take	\ói\ coin
\ä\ cot, cart	\th\ thin
\aú\ out	\th\ this
\ch\ chin	\ü\ food
\e\ pet	\ú\ foot
\ē\ easy	\y\ yet
\g\ go	\yü\ few
\i\ tip	\yú\ cure
\ī\ life	\zh\ vision
\j\ job	

used in the sense of "a series of thoughts, images, or emotions occurring during sleep". But the word itself is considerably older. In Old English *dream* means "joy", "noise", or "music". Yet the shift in sense did not come simply from the development of a more specialized sense. Rather it appears that after many Scandinavian conflicts, conquests, and settlements in Britain the Old Norse *draumr,* meaning "a dream during sleep", influenced the meaning of the similar and probably related English word. By the end of the 14th century the earlier meanings had been entirely replaced.

²dream \'drēm\ *vb* **dreamed** \'dremt, 'drēmd\ *or* **dreamt** \'dremt\; **dream·ing** \'drē-ming\ **1** : to have a dream **2** : to indulge in daydreams : pass (time) in reverie **3** : to conceive as possible, fitting, or proper : IMAGINE ⟨*dreamed* of success⟩

dream·er \'drē-mər\ *n* **1** : one that dreams **2 a** : one that lives in a world of fancy and imagination **b** : one that constantly conceives of impractical projects

dream·land \'drēm-,land\ *n* : an unreal delightful country existing only in imagination or in dreams

dream·world \-,wərld\ *n* : DREAMLAND; *also* : a world of illusion or fantasy

dreamy \'drē-mē\ *adj* **dream·i·er; -est** **1** : full of dreams ⟨*dreamy* sleep⟩ **2** : given to or marked by dreaming or fantasy **3 a** : having the quality or characteristics of a dream **b** : quiet and soothing ⟨*dreamy* music⟩ **c** : DELIGHTFUL ⟨a *dreamy* car⟩ — **dream·i·ly** \-mə-lē\ *adv* — **dream·i·ness** \-mē-nəs\ *n*

drea·ry \'driər-ē\ *adj* **drea·ri·er** \'drir-ē-ər\; **-est** : causing feelings of cheerlessness : GLOOMY ⟨a *dreary* landscape⟩ [Old English *drēorig* "sad, bloody", from *drēor* "gore"] — **drea·ri·ly** \'drir-ə-lē\ *adv* — **drea·ri·ness** \'drir-ē-nəs\ *n*

¹dredge \'drej\ *n* **1** : an oblong iron frame with an attached bag net used especially for gathering fish and shellfish **2** : a machine for removing earth usually by buckets on an endless chain or by a suction tube **3** : a barge used in dredging [probably from Scottish *dreg-* (in *dregbot* "dredge boat")]

²dredge *vb* **1** : to dig, gather, or pull out with or as if with a dredge ⟨*dredge* a channel⟩ ⟨*dredge* up something from one's memory⟩ **2** : to search with or as if with a dredge ⟨*dredging* for oysters⟩ — **dredg·er** *n*

³dredge *vt* : to coat (food) by sprinkling (as with flour) [Middle English *drage, drege* "sweetmeat", from Middle French *dragie,* from Latin *tragemata* "sweetmeats", from Greek *tragēmata,* pl. of *tragēma* "sweetmeat", from *trōgein* "to gnaw"] — **dredg·er** *n*

dreg \'dreg\ *n* **1** : sediment contained in a liquid or precipitated from it : LEES — usually used in pl. **2** : the most undesirable part — usually used in pl. ⟨the *dregs* of society⟩ **3** : the last remaining part : VESTIGE [Old Norse *dregg*]

¹drench \'drench\ *n* **1** : a medicinal potion for a domestic animal **2 a** : something that drenches **b** : a quantity sufficient to drench or saturate

²drench *vt* **1 a** *archaic* : to force to drink **b** : to administer a drench to (an animal) **2** : to wet thoroughly : SATURATE [Old English *drencan*]

¹dress \'dres\ *vb* **1** : to make or set straight (as troops in formation) : ALIGN **2 a** : to put clothes on **b** : to provide with clothing **c** : to put on or wear formal or fancy clothes **3** : to add decorative details to : EMBELLISH ⟨*dress* a store window⟩ **4** : to prepare for use or service **5 a** : to apply dressings or medication to **b** : to arrange (the hair) by combing, brushing, or curling **c** : to prepare (an animal) by grooming and currying **d** : to kill and prepare for market ⟨*dress* a chicken⟩ **e** : CULTIVATE, TEND; *esp* : to apply manure or fertilizer to **6** : SMOOTH, FINISH ⟨*dress* timber⟩ [Middle French *dresser,* derived from Latin *directus* "straight, direct"]

²dress *n* **1** : APPAREL, CLOTHING **2** : an outer garment with a skirt used by women or girls **3** : covering, adornment, or appearance appropriate or peculiar to a particular time **4** : the particular style in which something is presented : GUISE

³dress *adj* **1** : relating to or used for a dress ⟨*dress* goods⟩ **2** : suitable for a formal occasion ⟨*dress* clothes⟩ **3** : requiring or permitting formal dress ⟨a *dress* affair⟩

dres·sage \drə-'säzh, dre-\ *n* : the execution by a horse of complex maneuvers in response to barely perceptible movements of a rider's hands, legs, and weight

dress circle *n* : the first or lowest curved tier of seats in a theater

dress down *vt* : to reprove severely

¹dress·er \'dres-ər\ *n* **1** *obsolete* : a table or sideboard for preparing and serving food **2** : a cupboard to hold dishes and cooking utensils **3** : a chest of drawers or bureau with a mirror

²dresser *n* : one that dresses ⟨a window *dresser*⟩

dress·ing *n* **1 a** : the act or process of one that dresses **b** : an instance of dressing **2 a** : a sauce for adding to a dish **b** : a seasoned mixture usually used as a stuffing (as for poultry) **3 a** : material used to cover an injury **b** : fertilizing material

dressing gown *n* : a loose robe worn especially while dressing or resting

dressing room *n* : a room used chiefly for dressing; *esp* : a room in a theater for changing costumes and makeup

dressing station *n* : a station for giving first aid to the wounded

dressing table *n* : a low table with a mirror at which one sits while dressing

dress·mak·er \'dres-,mā-kər\ *n* : one that does dressmaking

dress·mak·ing \-king\ *n* : the process or occupation of making dresses

dress rehearsal *n* : a full rehearsal of a play in costume and with stage properties shortly before the first performance

dress shirt *n* : a man's shirt especially for wear with evening dress

dress suit *n* : a suit worn for full dress

dress uniform *n* : a uniform for formal wear

dressy \'dres-ē\ *adj* **dress·i·er; -est** **1** : showy in dress **2** : SMART 6a, STYLISH

drew *past of* DRAW

¹drib·ble \'drib-əl\ *vb* **drib·bled; drib·bling** \'drib-ling, -ə-ling\ **1** : to fall or flow or let fall in drops : TRICKLE **2** : DROOL 1, SLOBBER **3** : to come or issue little by little ⟨replies *dribbled* in⟩ **4** : to propel by tapping, bouncing, or kicking ⟨*dribble* a basketball⟩ [from *drib* "to dribble", probably alteration of *drip*] — **drib·bler** \'drib-lər, -ə-lər\ *n*

²dribble *n* **1 a** : a small trickling stream or flow **b** : a drizzling shower **2** : a tiny or insignificant quantity **3** : an act or instance of dribbling a ball or puck

drib·let \'drib-lət\ *n* **1** : a small amount **2** : a drop of liquid

dri·er *also* **dry·er** \'drī-ər, 'drīr\ *n* **1** : something that extracts or absorbs moisture **2** : a substance that accelerates drying (as of oils, paints, and printing inks) **3** *usually dryer* : a device for drying (as clothes) by heat or air

¹drift \'drift\ *n* **1 a** : the act of driving something along **b** : the flow of a river or ocean stream **2 a** : wind-driven snow, rain, or smoke usually near the ground surface **b** : a mass of matter (as sand) deposited together by or as if by wind or water **c** : a deposit of clay, sand, gravel, and boulders transported by a glacier or by running water from a glacier **3 a** : a general underlying design or tendency **b** : the meaning, import, or purport of what is spoken or written **4 a** : a ship's deviation from its course caused by currents **b** : the lateral motion of an airplane due to air currents **5**

a : a gradual shift in attitude, opinion, or position **b** : an aimless course [Middle English] **SYN** see TENDENCY

²drift *vb* **1 a** : to be or cause to be driven or carried along by a current (as of water or air) **b** : to move or float smoothly and effortlessly **2 a** : to move along a line of least resistance **b** : to travel about in a random way especially in search of work **c** : to become carried along subject to no guidance or control (the conversation *drifted* from one topic to another) **3 a** : to accumulate or cause to accumulate in a mass (*drifting* snow blocked the road) **b** : to cover or become covered with a drift (the road was *drifted* shut) **4 a** : to vary or deviate from a set adjustment **b** : to vary sluggishly — **drift·er** *n* — **drift·ing·ly** \'drif-ting-lē\ *adv*

drift·age \'drif-tij\ *n* **1** : a drifting of some object especially through action of wind or water **2** : deviation from a set course due to drifting **3** : something that drifts

drift·wood \'drift-,wùd\ *n* **1** : wood drifted or floated by water **2** : someone or something that drifts aimlessly

¹drill \'dril\ *vb* **1** : to pierce or bore with or as if with a drill (*drill* a tooth) (*drill* a hole) **2 a** : to instruct thoroughly (*drill* a class) **b** : to impart or communicate by repetition (*drill* some sense into their heads) **c** : to train or exercise in military skill and discipline (*drill* soldiers) [Dutch *drillen*] — **drill·er** *n*

²drill *n* **1** : a tool for making holes in hard substances by revolving or by a succession of blows **2** : the training of soldiers in military skill and discipline **3** : a physical or mental exercise regularly and repeatedly practiced **4** : a marine snail that destroys oysters by boring through their shells and feeding on the soft parts

³drill *n* : a west African baboon closely related to the typical mandrills [origin unknown]

⁴drill *n* **1** : a shallow furrow or trench into which seed is sown **2** : a planting implement that opens a drill, drops in seed, and covers it with earth [perhaps from earlier *drill* "small brook"]

⁵drill *vt* : to sow with or as if with a drill

⁶drill *n* : a durable cotton fabric in twill weave [derived from German *drillich*, from Middle High German *drilich* "fabric woven with a threefold thread", from Latin *trilix* "made up of three threads", from *tri-* + *licium* "thread"]

drill·mas·ter \'dril-,mas-tər\ *n* : one who drills; *esp* : an instructor in military drill

drill press *n* : an upright drilling machine in which the drill is pressed to the work by a hand lever or by power

drily *variant of* DRYLY

¹drink \'dringk\ *vb* **drank** \'drangk\; **drunk** \'drəngk\ *or* **drank; drink·ing** **1 a** : to swallow liquid : IMBIBE **b** : to take in or suck up **c** : to take in or receive avidly (*drink* in the scenery) **2** : to give or join in a toast (*drink* to success) **3 a** : to drink alcoholic beverages **b** : to spend in or waste on consumption of alcoholic beverages (*drank* the day away) **c** : to bring to a specified state by taking drink [Old English *drincan*]

²drink *n* **1 a** : liquid suitable for swallowing : BEVERAGE **b** : alcoholic liquor **2** : a draft or portion of liquid **3** : excessive consumption of alcoholic beverages

¹drink·able \'dring-kə-bəl\ *adj* : suitable or safe for drinking

²drinkable *n* : a liquid suitable for drinking : BEVERAGE

drink·er \'dring-kər\ *n* **1** : one that drinks **2** : one that drinks alcoholic beverages especially to excess

¹drip \'drip\ *vb* **dripped; drip·ping** **1** : to fall or let fall in drops **2 a** : to let fall drops of moisture or liquid (a *dripping* faucet) **b** : to overflow with or as if with moisture [Old English *dryppan*] — **drip·per** *n*

²drip *n* **1 a** : a falling in drops **b** : liquid that falls, overflows, or is extruded in drops **2** : the sound made by or as if by falling drops **3** : a part of a cornice or other member that projects to throw off rainwater; *also* : an

overlapping metal strip serving the same purpose **4** *slang* : a dull or unattractive person

drip–dry \'drip-'drī\ *vi* : to dry with few or no wrinkles when hung dripping wet — **drip–dry** \-,drī\ *adj*

drip·ping \'drip-ing\ *n* : fat and juices that drip from meat during cooking — often used in pl.

¹drive \'drīv\ *vb* **drove** \'drōv\; **driv·en** \'driv-ən\; **driv·ing** \'drī-ving\ **1 a** : to urge, push, or force onward **b** : to cause to penetrate with force (*drive* a nail) (1) : to direct the movement or course of (*drive* a car) (2) : to operate a vehicle (learn how to *drive*) **b** : to convey or transport in a vehicle (*drove* us to the airport) **c** : to ride in a vehicle (we *drove* into town) **3** : to set or keep in motion (*drive* machinery by electricity) **4** : to carry through strongly (*drive* a hard bargain) **5 a** : to force to act (*driven* by hunger to steal) **b** : to project, inject, or impress forcefully (*drove* the lesson home) **6** : to bring into a specified condition (the noise is *driving* me crazy) **7** : to produce by opening a way (as by drilling) (*drive* a well) **8** : to rush and press with violence **9** : to hit a golf ball from the tee [Old English *drīfan*] **SYN** see MOVE, RIDE

²drive *n* **1** : an act of driving or being driven: as **a** : a trip in a vehicle (as an automobile) **b** : a driving together of animals **c** : the guiding of logs downstream to a mill **d** : the act of driving a ball **e** : the flight of a ball **2 a** : DRIVEWAY 2 **b** : a public road for driving **3 a** : an offensive or aggressive move; *esp* : a strong sustained military attack **b** : an intensive group effort (a membership *drive*) **4** : the state of being hurried and under pressure **5 a** : an urgent, basic, or instinctual need or longing (the sex *drive*) **b** : dynamic quality (full of *drive*) **6 a** : the means for giving motion to a machine or machine part (a chain *drive*) **b** : the means by which the motive power of an automotive vehicle is applied to the road (front wheel *drive*) **7** : a device for reading and writing on a magnetic medium (as magnetic tape or disks)

drive–in \'drīv-,in\ *adj* : arranged and equipped to accommodate patrons while they remain in their vehicles (a *drive-in* theater) (*drive-in* banks) — **drive–in** *n*

¹driv·el \'driv-əl\ *vb* **driv·eled** *or* **driv·elled; driv·el·ing** *or* **driv·el·ling** \'driv-ling, -ə-ling\ **1** : to let saliva dribble from the mouth : SLAVER **2** : to talk or utter stupidly, carelessly, or in an infantile way [Old English *dreflian*] — **driv·el·er** *or* **driv·el·ler** \'driv-lər, -ə-lər\ *n*

²drivel *n* : NONSENSE 1

driv·er \'drī-vər\ *n* : one that drives: as **a** : the operator of a motor vehicle **b** : a golf club having a usually wooden head with a nearly straight face used in driving

driver ant *n* : ARMY ANT

driver's seat *n* : the position of top authority or dominance

drive shaft *n* : a shaft that transmits mechanical power

drive·way \'drīv-,wā\ *n* **1** : a road or way along which animals are driven **2** : a short private road leading from a public street to a house, barn, garage, or parking lot

driving iron *n* : a golf iron with a nearly vertical head for distance and little loft

¹driz·zle \'driz-əl\ *vb* **driz·zled; driz·zling** \'driz-ling, -ə-ling\ **1** : to rain in very small drops : SPRINKLE **2** : to shed in minute drops or particles [perhaps from Middle English *drysnen* "to fall"]

²drizzle *n* : a fine misty rain — **driz·zly** \'driz-lē, -ə-lē\ *adj*

drogue \'drōg\ *n* : a small attached parachute for slowing down or stabilizing something (as an astronaut's capsule) [probably alteration of ¹*drag*]

droll \'drōl\ *adj* : having a humorous, whimsical, or odd quality (a *droll* expression) [French *drôle*] — **droll·ness** \'drōl-nəs\ *n* — **drol·ly** \'drōl-lē\ *adv*

droll·ery \'drōl-rē, -ə-rē\ *n, pl* **-er·ies** **1** : something droll; *esp* : an amusing story or gesture **2** : droll behavior **3** : whimsical humor

²drill 1

dromedary 2

-drome \ˌdrōm\ *n combining form* **1** : racecourse **2** : large specially prepared place ⟨aero*drome*⟩ [*hippo-drome*]

drom·e·dary \'dräm-ə-ˌder-ē *also* 'drəm-\ *n, pl* **-dar·ies** **1** : a camel of unusual speed bred and trained especially for riding **2** : the one-humped camel of western Asia and northern Africa [Middle French *dromedaire*, from Late Latin *dromedarius*, from Latin *dromas*, from Greek, "running"]

¹drone \'drōn\ *n* **1** : the stingless male bee (as of the honeybee) that gathers no honey **2** : one that lives on the labors of others : PARASITE **3** : a pilotless airplane or ship controlled by radio signals [Old English *drān*]

²drone *vb* : to make or speak with a low dull monotonous humming sound

³drone *n* **1** : one of the pipes on a bagpipe that sound fixed continuous tones **2** : a deep monotonous sound : HUM

drone fly *n* : a large two-winged fly resembling a honeybee

drool \'drül\ *vb* **1 a** : to water at the mouth **b** : to let saliva or some other substance flow from the mouth : SLAVER **2 a** : to talk foolishly **b** : to express in a sentimental or effusive way [perhaps alteration of *drivel*]

¹droop \'drüp\ *vb* **1** : to hang or incline downward **2** : to sink gradually **3** : to become depressed or weakened **4** : to let droop [Old Norse *drūpa*] — **droop·ing·ly** \'drü-ping-lē\ *adv*

²droop *n* : the condition or appearance of drooping

droopy \'drü-pē\ *adj* **droop·i·er; -est** **1** : drooping or tending to droop **2** : GLOOMY 2, DOWNCAST

¹drop \'dräp\ *n* **1 a** (1) : the quantity of fluid that falls in one spherical mass (2) *pl* : a dose of medicine measured by drops **b** : a small quantity of drink **c** : the smallest practical unit of liquid measure **2** : something (as a hanging ornament on jewelry) shaped like a drop **3 a** : the act or an instance of dropping : FALL **b** : a decline in quantity or quality ⟨a *drop* in water pressure⟩ **c** : a descent by parachute; *also* : the persons or equipment dropped by parachute **4** : the distance through which something drops **5** : a slot into which something is to be dropped **6** : an unframed piece of cloth scenery in a theater [Old English *dropa*]

²drop *vb* **dropped; drop·ping** **1** : to fall or let fall in drops **2 a** : to let fall ⟨*drop* a book⟩ **b** : to let fall gradually : LOWER ⟨*drop* one's voice⟩ **3** : SEND ⟨*drop* me a letter⟩ **4** : to let go : DISMISS ⟨*drop* the subject⟩ ⟨*drop* several workers⟩ **5** : to knock down : cause to fall ⟨*drop* an opponent in a fight⟩ **6** : to go lower ⟨prices *dropped*⟩ **7** : to come or go unexpectedly or informally ⟨*drop* in for a chat⟩ **8** : to pass into a less active state ⟨*drop* off to sleep⟩ **9** : to move downward or with a current **10** : to withdraw from participation or membership : QUIT — usually used with *out* ⟨*drop* out of school⟩ **11** : to leave (a letter representing a speech sound) unsounded ⟨*drop* the first *r* in *surprise*⟩ **12** : to give birth to ⟨the cow *dropped* a fine calf⟩ **13** : to draw from an external point (as from a point to a line or plane) ⟨*drop* a perpendicular to a plane⟩

drop-forge \'dräp-ˈfōrj, -ˈfȯrj\ *vt* : to forge between dies by a drop hammer or punch press — **drop forger** *n*

drop hammer *n* : a power hammer raised and then released to drop (as on metal resting on an anvil or die)

drop-kick \'dräp-ˈkik\ *n* : a kick made by dropping a football to the ground and kicking it at the moment it starts to rebound — **drop-kick** *vb* — **drop-kick·er** *n*

drop leaf *n* : a hinged leaf on a table that can be folded down

drop·let \'dräp-lət\ *n* : a very small drop

droplet infection *n* : infection transmitted by airborne droplets of sputum containing infectious organisms

drop·out \'dräp-ˌaút\ *n* : one who drops out (as from school)

dropped egg *n* : a poached egg

drop·per \'dräp-ər\ *n* **1** : one that drops **2** : a short glass or plastic tube with a rubber bulb used to measure out liquids by drops

drop·pings \'dräp-ingz\ *n pl* : animal dung

drop·sy \'dräp-sē\ *n* : EDEMA [Old French *ydropesie*, from Latin *hydropisis*, from Greek *hydrōps*, from *hydōr* "water"] — **drop·si·cal** \-si-kəl\ *adj*

dro·soph·i·la \drō-ˈsäf-ə-lə\ *n* : any of a genus of small two-winged flies used especially in the study of inheritance [Greek *drosos* "dew" + *-philos* "-phil"]

dross \'dräs, 'drȯs\ *n* **1** : the scum that forms on the surface of molten metal **2** : waste or foreign matter : IMPURITY [Old English *drōs* "dregs"]

drought *or* **drouth** \'draúth, 'draút\ *n* : a long period of dry weather [Old English *drūgath*, from *drūgian* "to dry up"] — **droughty** \-ē\ *adj*

drove \'drōv\ *n* **1** : a group of animals driven or moving in a body **2** : a crowd of people moving or acting together [Old English *drāf*, from *drīfan* "to drive"]

drov·er \'drō-vər\ *n* : one that drives cattle or sheep

drown \'draún\ *vb* **1 a** : to suffocate by submersion especially in water **b** : to become drowned **2** : to cover with water : INUNDATE **3** : OVERWHELM 1, OVERPOWER [Middle English *drounen*]

drowse \'draúz\ *vi* : to sleep lightly : DOZE [probably related to Old English *drūsian* "to droop, become sluggish"] — **drowse** *n*

drowsy \'draú-zē\ *adj* **drows·i·er; -est** **1** : ready to fall asleep **2** : making one sleepy — **drows·i·ly** \-zə-lē\ *adv* — **drows·i·ness** \-zē-nəs\ *n*

drub \'drəb\ *vt* **drubbed; drub·bing** **1** : to beat severely with or as if with a stick **2** : to defeat decisively [perhaps from Arabic *daraba*]

¹drudge \'drəj\ *vi* : to do hard, menial, or monotonous work [Middle English *druggen*] — **drudg·er** *n*

²drudge *n* : one engaged in drudgery

drudg·ery \'drəj-rē, -ə-rē\ *n, pl* **-er·ies** : tiresome or menial work

¹drug \'drəg\ *n* **1** : a substance used as a medicine or in making medicines **2** : something for which there is little demand ⟨a *drug* on the market⟩ **3** : a narcotic substance or preparation [ME *drogge*]

²drug *vb* **drugged; drug·ging** **1** : to affect or treat with a drug; *esp* : to stupefy by a narcotic drug **2** : to lull or stupefy as if with a drug

drug·gist \'drəg-əst\ *n* : one who sells or dispenses drugs and medicines: as **a** : PHARMACIST **b** : an owner or manager of a drugstore

drug·store \'drəg-ˌstōr, -ˌstȯr\ *n* : a retail shop where medicines and miscellaneous articles are sold : PHARMACY

dru·id \'drü-əd\ *n, often cap* : one of an ancient Celtic priesthood of Gaul, Britain, and Ireland appearing in legends as magicians and wizards [Latin *druides* "druids", from Gaulish] — **dru·id·ic** \drü-ˈid-ik\ *adj, often cap* — **dru·id·ism** \'drü-ə-ˌdiz-əm\ *n, often cap*

¹drum \'drəm\ *n* **1** : a musical percussion instrument usually consisting of a hollow cylinder with a skin head stretched over each end that is beaten with a stick or pair of sticks in playing **2** : EARDRUM **3** : the sound of a drum; *also* : a similar sound **4** : a drum-shaped object: as **a** : a cylindrical machine or mechanical device or part **b** : a cylindrical container; *esp* : a metal barrel with a capacity of 45 to 416 liters **c** : a disk-shaped magazine for an automatic weapon **5** : any of various spiny-finned fishes that make a drumming noise [probably from Dutch *trom*]

²drum *vb* **drummed; drum·ming** **1** : to beat a drum **2** : to sound rhythmically **3** : to stir up interest : SOLICIT — usually used with *up* ⟨*drum up* customers⟩ **4** : to dismiss dishonorably : EXPEL — usually used with *out* **5** : to drive or force by steady effort or reiteration ⟨*drum* a lesson into one's head⟩ **6** : to strike or tap repeatedly so as to produce rhythmic sounds

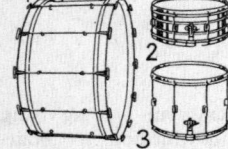

¹drum 1: *1* bass drum, *2,3* snare drums

drum·beat \'drəm-,bēt\ *n* : a stroke on a drum or its sound

drum·lin \'drəm-lən\ *n* : a long or oval hill of glacial drift [Irish Gaelic *druim* "back, ridge"]

drum major *n* : the marching leader of a band or drum corps

drum ma·jor·ette \'drəm-,mā-jə-'ret\ *n* : a girl who is a drum major

drum·mer \'drəm-ər\ *n* **1** : one that plays a drum **2** : TRAVELING SALESMAN

drum·stick \'drəm-,stik\ *n* **1** : a stick for beating a drum **2** : the lower segment of a fowl's leg

¹drunk \'drəngk\ *adj* **1** : having the faculties impaired by alcohol **2** : controlled by an intense feeling ⟨*drunk* with power⟩ **3** : DRUNKEN 2 [Middle English *drunke,* alteration of *drunken*]

²drunk *n* **1 a** : a person who is drunk **b** : DRUNKARD **2** : a period of excessive drinking : SPREE

drunk·ard \'drəng-kərd\ *n* : one who is habitually drunk

drunk·en \'drəng-kən\ *adj* **1 a** : DRUNK 1 **b** : given to habitual excessive use of alcohol **2** : of, relating to, or resulting from intoxication ⟨a *drunken* brawl⟩ **3** : unsteady or lurching as if from intoxication [Old English *druncen,* from past participle of *drincan* "to drink"] — **drunk·en·ly** *adv* — **drunk·en·ness** \-kən-nəs\ *n*

drupe \'drüp\ *n* : a fruit (as the plum, cherry, or peach) having one seed in a hard bony stone that is usually covered by pulpy flesh with a firm skin [Latin *drupa* "overripe olive," from Greek *dryppa* "olive"] — **dru·pa·ceous** \drü-'pā-shəs\ *adj*

drupe·let \'drüp-lət\ *n* : a small drupe; *esp* : one of the individual parts of an aggregate fruit (as the raspberry)

¹dry \'drī\ *adj* **dri·er** \'drī-ər, 'drīr\; **dri·est** \'drī-əst\ **1** : free or freed from water or liquid **2** : characterized by loss or lack of water: as **a** : lacking precipitation and humidity ⟨a *dry* climate⟩ **b** : lacking freshness : STALE **c** : low in or deprived of tissue moisture ⟨*dry* hay⟩ ⟨achenes and other *dry* fruits⟩ **3** : not being in or under water ⟨*dry* land⟩ **4 a** : THIRSTY 1 **b** : marked by the absence of alcoholic beverages **c** : no longer liquid or sticky ⟨the ink is *dry*⟩ **5** : containing or employing no liquid (as water) ⟨a *dry* creek⟩ ⟨*dry* heat⟩ **6** : not giving milk ⟨a *dry* cow⟩ **7** : lacking natural lubrication ⟨a *dry* cough⟩ **8** : solid as opposed to liquid ⟨*dry* groceries⟩ **9** : not productive **10** : marked by a matter-of-fact, ironic, or terse manner of expression ⟨*dry* humor⟩ **11** : UNINTERESTING, WEARISOME ⟨*dry* reading⟩ **12** : not sweet ⟨*dry* wines⟩ **13** : relating to, favoring, or practicing prohibition of alcoholic beverages ⟨a *dry* state⟩ [Old English *drȳge*] — **dry·ly** *adv* — **dry·ness** *n*

²dry *vb* **dried; dry·ing** : to make or become dry

³dry *n, pl* **drys** : PROHIBITIONIST

dry·ad \'drī-əd, -,ad\ *n* : WOOD NYMPH [Latin *dryas,* from Greek, from *drys* "tree"]

dry cell *n* : a small battery whose contents are not spillable

dry–clean \'drī-,klēn\ *vt* : to subject to dry cleaning — **dry–clean·able** \-,klē-nə-bəl\ *adj* — **dry clean·er** \-,klē-nər\ *n*

dry clean·ing \-,klē-ning\ *n* : the cleansing of fabrics with organic solvents (as naphtha)

dry dock \'drī-,däk\ *n* : a dock that can be kept dry for use during the construction or repairing of ships

dry·er *variant of* DRIER

dry farm \'drī-'färm\ *n* : a farm on dry land operated without irrigation on the basis of moisture-conserving tillage and drought-resistant crops — **dry–farm** *vt* — **dry farmer** *n* — **dry farming** *n*

dry fly *n* : an artificial angling fly designed to float upon the surface of the water

dry goods \'drī-,gudz\ *n pl* : textiles, ready-to-wear clothing, and notions as distinguished from other goods

dry ice *n* : solidified carbon dioxide usually in the form of blocks that at −78.5° C changes directly to a gas and that is used chiefly as a refrigerant

drying oil *n* : an oil (as linseed oil) that changes readily to a hard tough elastic substance when exposed in a thin film to air

dry measure *n* : a series of units of capacity for dry commodities — see MEASURE table, METRIC SYSTEM table

dry·point \'drī-,point\ *n* : an engraving made with a pointed instrument on the metal plate without the use of acid

dry rot *n* : a fungous decay of seasoned timber in which the cellulose of wood is consumed leaving a soft skeleton readily reduced to powder — **dry–rot** *vb*

dry run *n* **1** : a practice firing without ammunition **2** : a practice exercise : REHEARSAL

dry·wall \'drī-,wol\ *n* : PLASTERBOARD

dry wash *n, West* : WASH 3d

d.t.'s \dē-'tēz\ *n pl, often cap D&T* : DELIRIUM TREMENS

du·al \'dü-əl, 'dyü-\ *adj* **1** : consisting of two parts or elements : having two like parts **2** : having a double character or nature [Latin *dualis,* from *duo* "two"] — **du·al·i·ty** \dü-'al-ət-ē, dyü-\ *n* — **du·al·ly** \'dü-ə-lē, 'dyü-\ *adv*

du·al·ism \'dü-ə-,liz-əm, 'dyü-\ *n* : a doctrine that the universe is made up of or governed by two opposing principles (as good and evil) — **du·al·ist** \-ləst\ *n*

du·al–pur·pose \,dü-əl-'pər-pəs, ,dyü-\ *adj* : intended for or serving two purposes ⟨*dual-purpose* cattle⟩

¹dub \'dəb\ *vt* **dubbed; dub·bing 1** : to confer knighthood upon **2** : to call by a descriptive name [Old English *dubbian*]

²dub *vt* **dubbed; dub·bing 1** : to provide (a motion-picture film) with a new sound track **2** : to add (sound effects) to a film or broadcast [from *double*]

du·bi·ous \'dü-bē-əs, 'dyü-\ *adj* **1** : causing doubt : UNCERTAIN **2** : feeling doubt : UNDECIDED **3** : of doubtful promise or uncertain outcome ⟨a *dubious* battle⟩ **4** : of questionable value, quality, or propriety ⟨a *dubious* bargain⟩ ⟨won by *dubious* means⟩ [Latin *dubius,* from *dubare* "to vacillate"] — **du·bi·ous·ly** *adv* — **du·bi·ous·ness** *n*

du·bi·ta·ble \'dü-bət-ə-bəl, 'dyü-\ *adj* : open to doubt or question

du·cal \'dü-kəl, 'dyü-\ *adj* : of or relating to a duke or duchy

duc·at \'dək-ət\ *n* : a gold coin formerly used in Austria, Czechoslovakia, and the Netherlands [Middle French, from Italian *ducato* "coin with the doge's portrait on it", from *duca* "doge", from Late Greek *doux* "leader", from Latin *dux*]

duch·ess \'dəch-əs\ *n* **1** : the wife or widow of a duke **2** : a woman who is sovereign ruler of a duchy [Middle French *duchesse,* from *duc* "duke"]

duchy \'dəch-ē\ *n, pl* **duch·ies** : the territory of a duke or duchess : DUKEDOM [Middle French *duché,* from *duc* "duke"]

¹duck \'dək\ *n, pl* **duck** *or* **ducks** : any of various swimming birds with the neck and legs short, the body heavy, the bill often broad and flat, and the sexes almost always different from each other in plumage; *also* : a female duck — compare DRAKE [Old English *dūce*]

²duck *vb* **1** : to thrust or plunge under water **2** : to lower the head or body suddenly **3 a** : to move quickly : DODGE **b** : to evade a duty, question, or responsibility ⟨*duck* the issue⟩ [Middle English *douken*] — **duck·er** *n*

³duck *n* **1** : a durable closely woven usually cotton fabric **2** *pl* : clothes made of duck [Dutch *doek* "cloth"]

⁴duck *n* : an amphibious truck [*DUKW,* its code designation]

duck·bill \'dək-,bil\ *n* : PLATYPUS

¹duck: *1* drake feathers, *2* primaries, *3* secondaries, *4* bill, *5* coverts

\ə\ abut	\ng\ sing	
\ər\ further	\ō\ bone	
\a\ mat	\o\ saw	
\ā\ take	\oi\ coin	
\ä\ cot, cart	\th\ thin	
\au\ out	\th\ this	
\ch\ chin	\ü\ food	
\e\ pet	\u\ foot	
\ē\ easy	\y\ yet	
\g\ go	\yü\ few	
\i\ tip	\yu\ cure	
\ī\ life	\zh\ vision	
\j\ job		

duck·billed dinosaur \'dək-'bild-\ *n* : any of numerous plant-eating dinosaurs with the front part of the jaws covered by a horny bill resembling that of a bird

duckbilled platypus *n* : PLATYPUS

duck·board \'dək-,bōrd, -,bȯrd\ *n* : a boardwalk or slatted flooring laid on a wet, muddy, or cold surface — usually used in pl.

duck·ling \'dək-liŋ\ *n* : a young duck

duck·pin \'dək-,pin\ *n* **1** : a small bowling pin shorter and wider in the middle than a tenpin **2** *pl* : a bowling game using duckpins

ducks and drakes *n* : the pastime of skimming flat stones or shells along the surface of calm water

duck·weed \-,wēd\ *n* : a tiny free-floating stemless plant that grows on the surface of bodies of still water (as a pond)

duct \'dəkt\ *n* **1** : a tube or vessel carrying a bodily fluid (as the secretion of a gland) **2 a** : a pipe, tube, or channel that conveys a fluid (as air or water) **b** : a pipe or tubular passage for conductors (as an electric power line or telephone cables) [Latin *ductus* "act of leading", from *ducere* "to lead"] — **duct·less** \'dək-tləs\ *adj*

duc·tile \'dək-tl, -,tīl\ *adj* **1** : capable of being drawn out (as into a wire) or hammered thin ⟨*ductile* metal⟩ **2** : easily led or influenced — **duc·til·i·ty** \,dək-'til-ət-ē\ *n*

ductless gland *n* : ENDOCRINE GLAND

duc·tus ar·te·ri·o·sus \'dək-təs-är-,tir-ē-'ō-səs\ *n* : a short broad vessel in the fetus that conducts most of the blood directly from the right ventricle to the aorta bypassing the lungs [New Latin, literally, "arterial duct"]

dud \'dəd\ *n* **1** *pl* **a** : CLOTHES 1 **b** : personal belongings **2** : one that fails completely **3** : a missile (as a bomb or shell) that fails to explode [Middle English *dudde*]

dude \'düd, 'dyüd\ *n* **1** : an extremely fastidious man : DANDY **2** : a city man; *esp* : an Easterner in the West **3** : FELLOW 4a, MAN [origin unknown] — **dud·ish** \'düd-ish, 'dyüd-\ *adj* — **dud·ish·ly** *adv*

dude ranch *n* : a vacation resort offering horseback riding and other activities typical of western ranches

¹due \'dü, 'dyü\ *adj* **1** : owed or owing as a debt or right **2** : according to accepted notions or procedures : APPROPRIATE **3 a** : SUFFICIENT, ADEQUATE ⟨arrived in *due* time⟩ **b** : REGULAR, LAWFUL ⟨*due* process of law⟩ **4** : ATTRIBUTABLE, ASCRIBABLE — used with *to* ⟨an accident *due* to negligence⟩ **5** : having reached the date at which payment is required : PAYABLE **6** : required or expected to happen : SCHEDULED ⟨*due* to arrive any time⟩ [Middle French *deu*, past participle of *devoir* "to owe", from Latin *debēre*]

²due *n* **1** : something owed : DEBT ⟨pay them their *due*⟩ **2** *pl* : a regular or legal charge or fee ⟨membership *dues*⟩

³due *adv* : DIRECTLY, EXACTLY ⟨*due* north⟩

¹du·el \'dü-əl, 'dyü-\ *n* **1** : a combat between two persons; *esp* : one fought with weapons in the presence of witnesses **2** : a conflict between antagonistic persons, ideas, or forces [Medieval Latin *duellum*, from Latin *duellum, bellum* "war"]

²duel *vb* **du·eled** *or* **du·elled; du·el·ing** *or* **du·el·ling** : to fight in a duel — **du·el·er** *n* — **du·el·ist** \'dü-ə-ləst, 'dyü-\ *n*

du·en·na \dü-'en-ə, dyü-\ *n* **1** : an elderly woman in charge of the younger ladies in a Spanish or Portuguese family **2** : GOVERNESS, CHAPERON [Spanish *dueña*, from Latin *domina* "mistress, lady"]

du·et \dü-'et, dyü-\ *n* : a composition for or performance by two performers [Italian *duetto*, from *duo*, from Latin, "two"]

due to *prep* : because of

duff \'dəf\ *n* **1** : a steamed pudding usually containing raisins and currants **2** : partly decayed organic matter

on the forest floor [English dialect, alteration of *dough*]

duf·fel \'dəf-əl\ *n* : an outfit of supplies (as for camping) : KIT [Dutch *duffel*, a kind of cloth, from *Duffel*, Belgium]

duffel bag *n* : a large cylindrical fabric bag for personal belongings

duf·fer \'dəf-ər\ *n* : an incompetent or clumsy person [origin unknown]

¹dug *past of* DIG

²dug \'dəg\ *n* : UDDER 1, BREAST; *also* : TEAT 1, NIPPLE [perhaps of Scandinavian origin]

du·gong \'dü-,gäŋ, -,gȯŋ\ *n* : an aquatic plant-eating mammal related to the manatees but having a 2-lobed tail and tusks in the male — called also *sea cow* [Malay and Tagalog *duyong*]

dug·out \'dəg-,aút\ *n* **1** : a boat made by hollowing out a large log **2** : a shelter dug in a hillside or in the ground or in the side of a trench **3** : a low shelter facing a baseball diamond and containing the players' bench

dui·ker \'dī-kər\ *n* : any of several small African antelopes [Afrikaans, literally, "diver"]

duke \'dük, 'dyük\ **1** : a sovereign ruler of a duchy **2** : a noble of the highest rank; *esp* : a member of the highest grade of the British peerage **3** *slang* : FIST 1, HAND — usually used in pl. [Old French *duc*, from Latin *duc-, dux* "leader", from *ducere* "to lead"] — **duke·dom** \-dəm\ *n*

dul·cet \'dəl-sət\ *adj* : sweet to the ear : MELODIOUS [Middle French *doucet* "sweet to the taste", from *douz* "sweet", from Latin *dulcis*]

dul·ci·mer \'dəl-sə-mər\ *n* **1** : a wire-stringed instrument played with light hammers held in the hands **2** *or* **dul·ci·more** \-,mōr, -,mȯr\ : an American folk instrument with three or four strings stretched over an elongate fretted sound box held on the lap and played by strumming or plucking [Middle French *doulcemer*, from Italian *dolcimelo*]

dulcimer 1

¹dull \'dəl\ *adj* **1** : mentally slow : STUPID **2 a** : slow in perception or sensibility ⟨were *dull* to what went on around them⟩ **b** : lacking zest or vivacity : LISTLESS **3** : slow in action : SLUGGISH ⟨a *dull* market⟩ **4** : lacking sharpness of edge or point **5** : lacking brilliance or luster **6** : not resonant or ringing **7** : CLOUDY 3a, OVERCAST **8** : TEDIOUS, UNINTERESTING ⟨*dull* sermons⟩ **9** : low in saturation and lightness ⟨a *dull* shade of blue⟩ [Middle English *dul*] SYN see BLUNT, STUPID — **dull·ness** *or* **dul·ness** \'dəl-nəs\ *n* — **dul·ly** \'dəl-lē, -ē\ *adv*

²dull *vb* : to make or become dull

dull·ard \'dəl-ərd\ *n* : a stupid person

dulse \'dəls\ *n* : any of several coarse red seaweeds especially of northern seas that are used as food [Scottish Gaelic and Irish Gaelic *duilseag*]

du·ly \'dü-lē, 'dyü-\ *adv* : in a due manner, time, or degree ⟨*duly* authorized⟩ ⟨will be *duly* considered⟩

du·ma \'dü-mə\ *n* : a representative council in Russia; *esp* : the principal legislative assembly in czarist Russia [Russian]

dumb \'dəm\ *adj* **1 a** : lacking the normal power of speech ⟨deaf and *dumb* from birth⟩ **b** : naturally incapable of speech **2** : not willing to speak **3** : STUPID 1, FOOLISH [Old English] — **dumb·ly** \'dəm-lē\ *adv* — **dumb·ness** *n* □ SYN MUTE, SPEECHLESS: DUMB stresses lack of power to speak that may be natural and permanent ⟨*dumb* animals⟩ or temporary ⟨struck *dumb* with wonder⟩ MUTE stresses the fact of not speaking from whatever cause ⟨stood *mute* and ashamed before the accusers⟩ SPEECHLESS implies especially inability to find words because of shock or confusion of mind.

dumb·bell \'dəm-,bel\ *n* **1** : a weight consisting of a short bar with a sphere or weighted disk at each end and used usually in pairs for calisthenic exercise **2** : a dull or stupid person

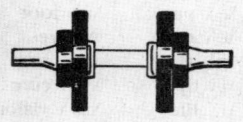

dumbbell 1

dumb down *vt* : to lower the level of difficulty and the intellectual content of (as a textbook)

dumb·found *or* **dum·found** \ˌdəm-ˈfau̇nd\ *vt* : to astonish greatly [*dumb* + *-found* (as in confound)]

dumb show *n* : signs and gestures without words

dumb·wait·er \ˈdəm-ˈwāt-ər\ *n* **1** : a portable serving table **2** : a small elevator for conveying food and dishes or small goods from one story of a building to another

dum·dum \ˈdəm-ˌdəm\ *n* : a soft-nosed bullet that expands when it hits [*Dum-Dum,* arsenal near Calcutta, India]

¹dum·my \ˈdəm-ē\ *n, pl* **dum·mies 1** : a person who lacks or seems to lack the power of speech **2** : one (as a person or group) that though seeming to act independently is actually a front for another **3** : a stupid person **4** : an imitation of something to be used as a substitute or model ⟨the *dummies* in a store window⟩ **5 a** : an exposed hand in bridge played by one of the players in addition to his own hand **b** : a bridge player whose hand is a dummy **6** : a set of pages (as for a magazine) with the position of text and artwork indicated for the printer

²dummy *adj* : resembling a dummy; *esp* : having the appearance of being real but lacking ability to function ⟨*dummy* wooden guns⟩

¹dump \ˈdəmp\ *vb* **1 a** : to let fall in a heap or mass : UNLOAD **b** : to get rid of quickly or unceremoniously **c** : to dump refuse **2** : to sell in quantity at a very low price **3** : to copy (data in a computer's internal storage) into external storage; *also* : to print out (data) from a computer's internal storage [perhaps from Dutch *dompen* "to immerse, topple"] — **dump·er** *n*

²dump *n* **1** : a place where discarded materials are dumped **2** : a place where reserve military supplies are stored **3** : a disorderly, slovenly, or dilapidated place **4** : an instance of dumping data stored in a computer

dump·ling \ˈdəm-pliŋ\ *n* **1** : a small mass of dough cooked by boiling or steaming **2** : a dessert of fruit baked in biscuit dough [perhaps alteration of *lump*]

dumps \ˈdəmps\ *n pl* : a dull gloomy state of mind : low spirits ⟨in the *dumps*⟩ [probably from Dutch *domp* "haze"]

dump truck *n* : a truck for transporting and dumping loose materials

dumpy \ˈdəm-pē\ *adj* **dump·i·er; -est** : short and thick in build : SQUAT [English dialect *dump* "lump"] — **dump·i·ness** *n*

¹dun \ˈdən\ *adj* **1** : having a dun color **2** : marked by dullness and drabness [Old English *dunn*] — **dun·ness** \ˈdən-nəs\ *n*

²dun *n* **1** : a pale horse usually with a dark mane and tail and a dorsal stripe **2** : a nearly neutral slightly brownish dark gray **3** : an immature winged mayfly

³dun *vt* **dunned; dun·ning 1** : to make persistent demands upon for payment **2** : to plague or pester constantly ⟨*dunned* by financial problems⟩ [origin unknown]

⁴dun *n* **1** : a person who duns another **2** : an urgent request; *esp* : a demand for payment

dunce \ˈdəns\ *n* : a dull-witted and stupid person [John *Duns* Scotus, died about 1308, Scottish scholastic theologian, whose once accepted writings were ridiculed in the 16th century]

dun·der·head \ˈdən-dər-ˌhed\ *n* : DUNCE, BLOCKHEAD [perhaps from Dutch *donder* "thunder" — **dun·der·head·ed** \ˌdən-dər-ˈhed-əd\ *adj*

dune \ˈdün, ˈdyün\ *n* : a hill or ridge of sand piled up by the wind [French, from Old French, from Middle Dutch]

¹dung \ˈdəŋ\ *n* : the excrement of an animal : MANURE [Old English] — **dungy** \ˈdəŋ-ē\ *adj*

²dung *vt* : to fertilize or dress with manure

dun·ga·ree \ˌdəŋ-gə-ˈrē\ *n* **1** : blue denim **2** *pl* : clothing made of blue denim [Hindi *d̆ugrī*]

dung beetle *n* : a beetle (as a tumblebug) that rolls balls of dung in which it lays eggs and on which the larvae feed

dun·geon \ˈdən-jən\ *n* **1** : DONJON **2** : a close dark usually underground prison [Middle French *donjon,* derived from Latin *dominus* "lord, master"]

dung·hill \ˈdəŋ-ˌhil\ *n* : a manure pile

dunk \ˈdəŋk\ *vb* **1** : to dip (as bread or cake) into liquid while eating **2** : to dip or submerge temporarily in liquid **3** : to submerge oneself in water [Pennsylvania German *dunke,* from Old High German *dunkōn*]

dunk shot *n* : a shot in basketball made by leaping high into the air and throwing the ball down through the basket

dun·lin \ˈdən-lən\ *n, pl* **dunlins** *or* **dunlin** : a widely distributed small sandpiper largely brown above and white below with a black patch on the belly [¹*dun* + *-lin* (alteration of *-ling*)]

dun·nage \ˈdən-ij\ *n* **1** : loose materials used around a cargo to prevent damage; *also* : padding in a shipping container **2** : baggage or personal effects especially of a sailor [origin unknown]

duo \ˈdü-ō, ˈdyü-\ *n, pl* **du·os 1** : DUET; *esp* : a composition for two performers at two pianos **2** : PAIR **3** [Italian, from Latin, "two"]

duo·dec·i·mal \ˌdü-ə-ˈdes-ə-məl, ˌdyü-\ *adj* **1** : of, relating to, or proceeding by 12 **2** : relating to, expressed in, or being a system of numeration with a base of 12 [Latin *duodecim* "twelve"] — **duo·decimal** *n*

du·o·de·num \ˌdü-ə-ˈdē-nəm, ˌdyü-; du̇-ˈäd-n-əm, dyu̇-\ *n, pl* **-de·na** \-ˈdē-nə, -n-ə\ *or* **-denums** : the first part of the small intestine extending from the pylorus to the jejunum [Medieval Latin, from Latin *duodeni* "twelve each", from *duodecim* "twelve"; from its length, about 12 fingers' breadth] — **du·o·de·nal** \-ˈdēn-l, -n-əl\ *adj*

duo·logue \ˈdü-ə-ˌlȯg, ˈdyü-\ *n* : a dialogue between two persons

¹dupe \ˈdüp, ˈdyüp\ *n* : one who is easily deceived or cheated [French]

²dupe *vt* : to make a dupe of : DECEIVE — **dup·er** *n*

du·ple \ˈdü-pəl, ˈdyü-\ *adj* **1** : taken by twos : TWOFOLD **2** : having two beats or a multiple of two beats per measure of music ⟨*duple* time⟩ [Latin *duplus* "double"]

¹du·plex \ˈdü-ˌpleks, ˈdyü-\ *adj* **1** : DOUBLE 2, TWOFOLD; *esp* : having two parts that act at the same time or in the same way **2** : allowing telecommunication in opposite directions at the same time [Latin, from *duo* "two" + *-plex* "-fold"]

²duplex *n* : something duplex; *esp* : a 2-family house

duplex apartment *n* : an apartment having rooms on two floors

¹du·pli·cate \ˈdü-pli-kət, ˈdyü-\ *adj* **1** : having or being two corresponding or identical parts or examples **2** : being the same as another **3** : of or relating to a card game in which players play identical hands in order to compare scores ⟨*duplicate* bridge⟩ [Latin *duplicare* "to double", from *duplex* "double"]

²duplicate *n* **1** : a thing that exactly resembles another in appearance, pattern, or content : COPY **2** : two copies both alike ⟨typed in *duplicate*⟩ □ SYN DUPLICATE, COPY, FACSIMILE, REPRODUCTION mean a thing made to resemble another or an original closely. DUPLICATE suggests exact sameness of pattern and usually of material; COPY applies to anything reproduced mechanically or without intentional changes; FACSIMILE implies exact and detailed reproduction of pattern that may differ in scale or material; REPRODUCTION implies an exact or very close imitation of an original in all respects.

³**du·pli·cate** \'dü-pli-ˌkāt, 'dyü-\ *vt* **1** : to make double **2** : to make a duplicate of — **du·pli·ca·tive** \-ˌkāt-iv\ *adj*

du·pli·ca·tion \ˌdü-pli-'kā-shən, ˌdyü-\ *n* **1 a** : an act or process of duplicating **b** : the quality or state of being duplicated **2** : DUPLICATE, COUNTERPART

duplication of the cube : the mathematical problem of constructing the edge of a cube having twice the volume of a cube whose edge is given

du·pli·ca·tor \'dü-pli-ˌkāt-ər, 'dyü-\ *n* : one that duplicates; *esp* : a machine for making copies of graphic matter

du·plic·i·ty \dù-'plis-ət-ē, dyù-\ *n, pl* **-ties** : deception by pretending to feel and act one way while acting another

du·ra·ble \'dùr-ə-bəl\ *adj* : able to last a long time ⟨*durable* clothing⟩ [Middle French, from Latin *durare* "to last"] SYN see LASTING — **du·ra·bil·i·ty** \ˌdùr-ə-'bil-ət-ē, ˌdyùr-\ *n* — **du·ra·ble·ness** *n* — **du·ra·bly** \'dùr-ə-blē, 'dyùr-\ *adv*

du·ral·u·min \dù-'ral-yə-mən, dyù-; ˌdùr-ə-'lü-mən, ˌdyùr-\ *n* : a strong light alloy of aluminum, copper, manganese, and magnesium [German, from *Dür*en, Germany + *alumin*ium "aluminum"]

du·ra ma·ter \'dùr-ə-ˌmāt-ər, 'dyùr-, -ˌmät-\ *n* : the outermost and tough fibrous membrane that envelops the brain and spinal cord [Medieval Latin, literally, "hard mother"]

du·rance \'dùr-əns, 'dyùr-\ *n* : IMPRISONMENT [Middle French, "endurance", from *durer* "to endure"]

du·ra·tion \dù-'rā-shən, dyù-\ *n* **1** : continuance in time ⟨a storm of short *duration*⟩ **2** : the time during which something lasts ⟨the *duration* of the war⟩ [Medieval Latin *duratio*, from Latin *durare* "to last"]

du·ress \dù-'res, dyù-\ *n* **1** : forcible restraint **2** : compulsion by threat ⟨a confession obtained under *duress*⟩ [Middle French *duresce* "hardness, severity", from Latin *duritia*, from *durus* "hard"]

Dur·ham \'dər-əm, 'də-rəm, 'dùr-əm\ *n* : SHORTHORN [County *Durham,* England]

du·ri·an \'dùr-ē-ən, 'dyùr-\ *n* : a large oval tasty but foul-smelling fruit with a prickly rind and soft pulp; *also* : the East Indian tree that bears it [Malay]

dur·ing \'dùr-ing, 'dyùr-\ *prep* **1** : throughout the duration of ⟨*during* their whole lifetimes⟩ **2** : at some time or times in the course of ⟨occasional showers *during* the day⟩ [Middle English, from *duren* "to last", from Old French *durer,* from Latin *durare,* from *durus* "hard"]

dur·ra \'dùr-ə\ *n* : any of several grain sorghums grown in warm dry regions [Arabic *dhurah*]

du·rum wheat \'dùr-əm-, 'dyùr-\ *n* : a wheat that yields a flour that is rich in gluten and is used especially in macaroni and spaghetti — called also *durum* [Latin *durum,* neuter of *durus* "hard"]

¹**dusk** \'dəsk\ *vb* : to make or become dark or gloomy [Middle English *dosk* "dusky", alteration of Old English *dox*]

²**dusk** *n* **1** : the darker part of twilight especially at night **2** : GLOOM

dusky \'dəs-kē\ *adj* **dusk·i·er; -est** **1** : somewhat dark in color; *esp* : having dark skin **2** : marked by slight or deficient light — **dusk·i·ly** \-kə-lē\ *adv* — **dusk·i·ness** \-kē-nəs\ *n*

¹**dust** \'dəst\ *n* **1** : fine particles (as of earth or in space); *also* : a fine powder **2** : the earthy remains of bodies once alive; *esp* : the human corpse **3 a** : a place (as in the earth) of burial **b** : the surface of the ground **4 a** : something worthless **b** : a low or miserable condition : state of humiliation [Old English *dūst*] — **dust·less** \'dəst-ləs\ *adj*

²**dust** *vb* **1 a** : to free from dust **b** : to brush or wipe away dust **2** : to sprinkle with fine particles or in the form of dust ⟨*dust* a pan with flour⟩ ⟨*dust* an insecticide on plants⟩

Dutchman's-breeches

dust·bin \'dəst-ˌbin, 'dəs-\ *n, British* : a trash or garbage can

dust bowl *n* : a region that suffers from prolonged droughts and dust storms

dust devil *n* : a small whirlwind containing sand or dust

dust·er \'dəs-tər\ *n* **1** : one that removes dust **2 a** : a light outer garment to protect clothing from dust **b** : a dress-length housecoat **3** : a device for applying insecticidal or fungicidal dusts to crops

dust jacket *n* : a removable usually decorative paper cover for a book

dust·man \'dəst-mən, 'dəs-\ *n, British* : a trash or garbage collector

dust·pan \-ˌpan\ *n* : a shovel-shaped pan for sweepings

dust storm *n* : strong turbulent winds bearing clouds of dust across a dry region

dusty \'dəs-tē\ *adj* **dust·i·er; -est** **1** : filled or covered with dust **2** : consisting of or resembling dust : POWDERY — **dust·i·ly** \-tə-lē\ *adv* — **dust·i·ness** \-tē-nəs\ *n*

dutch \'dəch\ *adv, often cap* : with each person paying his or her own way

¹**Dutch** \'dəch\ *adj* **1** *slang* : GERMAN **2** : of or relating to the Netherlands, its inhabitants, or their language

²**Dutch** *n* **1** : the Germanic language of the Netherlands **2** *pl in construction* : the people of the Netherlands **3** : DISFAVOR, TROUBLE ⟨was in *Dutch* with the teacher⟩ [Middle English *Duche,* from Dutch *duutsch*]

Dutch clover *n* : WHITE CLOVER

Dutch door *n* : a door divided horizontally so that the lower part can be shut while the upper part remains open

Dutch elm disease *n* : a fungous disease of elms characterized by yellowing of the foliage, loss of leaves, and death

Dutch·man \'dəch-mən\ *n* **1 a** : a native or inhabitant of the Netherlands **b** : a person of Dutch descent **2** *slang* : GERMAN

Dutch·man's–breech·es \'dəch-mənz-'brich-əz\ *n pl* : a delicate spring-flowering herb of the eastern United States resembling the related bleeding heart but having white double-spurred flowers

Dutch oven *n* **1** : a metal shield for roasting before an open fire **2** : a brick oven in which cooking is done by the preheated walls **3 a** : a cast-iron kettle with a tight cover used for baking in an open fire **b** : a heavy pot with a tight-fitting domed cover

Dutch treat *n* : something (as a meal) for which each participant pays his or her own way

Dutch uncle *n* : one who admonishes sternly and bluntly

du·te·ous \'düt-ē-əs, 'dyüt-\ *adj* : DUTIFUL, OBEDIENT — **du·te·ous·ly** *adv* — **du·te·ous·ness** *n*

du·ti·able \'düt-ē-ə-bəl, 'dyüt-\ *adj* : subject to a duty ⟨*dutiable* imports⟩

du·ti·ful \'düt-i-fəl, 'dyüt-\ *adj* **1** : motivated by a sense of duty **2** : coming from or showing a sense of duty ⟨*dutiful* affection⟩ — **du·ti·ful·ly** \-fə-lē\ *adv* — **du·ti·ful·ness** *n*

du·ty \'düt-ē, 'dyüt-\ *n, pl* **duties** **1** : conduct due to parents and superiors : RESPECT **2 a** : the action required by one's position or occupation **b** : assigned service or business; *esp* : active military service **3 a** : a moral or legal obligation **b** : the force of moral obligation ⟨obey the call of *duty*⟩ **4** : TAX; *esp* : a tax on imports **5** : USE ⟨a drill designed to withstand heavy *duty*⟩ [Anglo-French *dueté,* from Old French *deu* "due"] SYN see TASK

du·um·vir \dù-'əm-vər, dyü-\ *n* : either of two Roman officers or magistrates jointly constituting a board or court [Latin, from *duum* (genitive of *duo* "two") + *vir* "man"]

du·um·vi·rate \-və-rət\ *n* **1** : two people associated in high office **2** : government or control by two people

¹**dwarf** \'dwórf\ *n, pl* **dwarfs** \'dwórfs\ *also* **dwarves** \'dwórvz\ **1** : a person, lower animal, or plant much

below normal size **2** : a small legendary humanlike being usually misshapen and ugly and skilled at metalwork **3** : a star (as the sun) that gives off a relatively ordinary or small amount of energy and has relatively small mass and size [Old English *dweorg, dweorh*] — **dwarf** *adj* — **dwarf·ish** \'dwȯr-fish\ *adj* — **dwarf·ness** *n*

²dwarf *vb* **1** : to restrict the growth or development of : STUNT ⟨*dwarf* a tree⟩ **2** : to cause to appear smaller

dwarf·ism \'dwȯr-ˌfiz-əm\ *n* : a condition of stunted growth

dwell \'dwel\ *vi* **dwelt** \'dwelt\ *or* **dwelled** \'dweld, 'dwelt\; **dwell·ing** **1** : to remain for a time **2** : to live as a resident : RESIDE **3 a** : to linger over something (as with the eyes or mind) : keep the attention directed ⟨*dwelt* on the scene before them⟩ **b** : to write or speak at length or insistently [Old English *dwellan* "to go astray, hinder"] — **dwell·er** *n*

dwell·ing \'dwel-ing\ *n* : a building or other shelter in which people live : HOUSE

dwin·dle \'dwin-dl\ *vb* **dwin·dled; dwin·dling** \'dwin-dling, -dl-ing\ : to make or become gradually less ⟨a *dwindling* supply of coal⟩ [probably from *dwine* "to waste away"] SYN see DECREASE

dyb·buk \'dib-ək\ *n* : a wandering soul believed in Jewish folklore to enter and control a person [Hebrew *dibbūq*]

¹dye \'dī\ *n* **1** : color from dyeing **2** : a material used for dyeing or staining [Old English *dēah, dēag*]

²dye *vb* **dyed; dye·ing** **1** : to stain or color usually permanently **2** : to impart (a color) by dyeing **3** : to take up or impart color in dyeing — **dy·er** \'dī-ər, 'dīr\ *n*

dyed–in–the–wool \ˌdīd-n-thə-ˈwu̇l\ *adj* : THOROUGHGOING, UNCOMPROMISING ⟨a *dyed-in-the-wool* conservative⟩

dye·stuff \'dī-ˌstəf\ *n* : DYE 2

dy·ing \'dī-ing\ *adj* **1** : being about to die : being in the act of dying or dying out ⟨a *dying* fire⟩ **2** : of or relating to dying or death ⟨a *dying* wish⟩ [from present participle of *die*]

dyke *variant of* DIKE

dy·nam·ic \dī-ˈnam-ik\ *adj* **1 a** : of or relating to physical force or energy **b** : of or relating to dynamics : ACTIVE **2 a** : marked by continuous activity or change **b** : marked by energy : FORCEFUL ⟨a *dynamic* personality⟩ [French *dynamique*, from Greek *dynamis* "power", from *dynasthai* "to be able"] — **dy·nam·i·cal** \-ˈnam-i-kəl\ *adj* — **dy·nam·i·cal·ly** \-i-kə-lē, -klē\ *adv*

dy·nam·ics \dī-ˈnam-iks\ *n sing or pl* **1** : a branch of mechanics that deals with the motion of bodies and the action of forces in producing or changing their motion **2** : physical, moral, or intellectual forces or the laws relating to them **3** : the pattern of change or growth typical of something **4** : variation and contrast in force or intensity (as in music)

dy·na·mism \'dī-nə-ˌmiz-əm\ *n* **1 a** : a theory that explains the universe in terms of forces and their interplay **b** : DYNAMICS 3 **2** : a dynamic quality

¹dy·na·mite \'dī-nə-ˌmīt\ *n* : a blasting explosive that is made chiefly of nitroglycerin absorbed in a porous material; *also* : any of various blasting explosives that contain no nitroglycerin

²dynamite *vt* : to blow up with dynamite — **dy·na·mit·er** *n*

dy·na·mo \'dī-nə-ˌmō\ *n, pl* **-mos** **1** : GENERATOR 3 **2** : a forceful energetic person [short for *dynamoelectric machine*]

dy·na·mom·e·ter \ˌdī-nə-ˈmäm-ət-ər\ *n* : an apparatus for measuring mechanical power (as of an engine) — **dy·na·mo·met·ric** \ˌdī-nə-mō-ˈme-trik\ *adj* — **dy·na·mom·e·try** \ˌdī-nə-ˈmäm-ə-trē\ *n*

dy·na·mo·tor \'dī-nə-ˌmōt-ər\ *n* : a motor generator combining the electric motor and generator

dy·nas·ty \'dī-nə-stē, -ˌnas-tē\ *n, pl* **-ties** **1** : a succession of rulers of the same line of descent **2** : a powerful group or family that maintains its position for a considerable time [Greek *dynasteia* "power, lordship," from *dynastēs* "ruler", from *dynasthai* "to be able"] — **dy·nas·tic** \dī-ˈnas-tik\ *adj* — **dy·nas·ti·cal·ly** \-ti-kə-lē, -klē\ *adv*

dyne \'dīn\ *n* : the unit of force in the cgs system equal to the force that would give a free mass of one gram an acceleration of one centimeter per second per second that is equivalent to 10^{-5} newton [French, from Greek *dynamis* "power"]

dys- *combining form* **1** : abnormal **2** : difficult ⟨*dys*menorrhea⟩ — compare EU- **3** : impaired ⟨*dys*function⟩ [Greek, "bad, difficult"]

dys·en·tery \'dis-n-ˌter-ē\ *n* **1** : a disease characterized by severe diarrhea with passage of mucus and blood and usually caused by infection **2** : DIARRHEA [Latin *dysenteria*, from Greek, from *dys-* + *enteron* "intestine"] — **dys·en·ter·ic** \ˌdis-n-ˈter-ik\ *adj*

dys·func·tion \dis-ˈfəng-shən, -ˈfəngk-\ *n* : impaired or abnormal functioning — **dys·func·tion·al** \-shnəl, -shən-l\ *adj*

dys·lex·ia \dis-ˈlek-sē-ə\ *n* : a disturbance of the ability to read [*dys-* + Greek *lexis* "word, speech"] — **dys·lex·ic** \-sik\ *adj*

dys·men·or·rhea \ˌdis-ˌmen-ə-ˈrē-ə\ *n* : painful menstruation [*dys-* + *meno-* "menstruation" + *-rrhea*] — **dys·men·or·rhe·ic** \-ˈrē-ik\ *adj*

dys·pep·sia \dis-ˈpep-shə, -sē-ə\ *n* : INDIGESTION [Latin, from Greek, from *dys-* + *pepsis* "digestion", from *peptein, pessein* "to cook, digest"]

dys·pep·tic \-ˈpep-tik\ *adj* **1** : relating to or having dyspepsia **2** : GLOOMY 2, CROSS — **dys·pep·ti·cal·ly** \-ti-kə-lē, -klē\ *adv*

dys·pro·si·um \dis-ˈprō-zē-əm\ *n* : a chemical element that forms highly magnetic compounds — see ELEMENT table [New Latin, from Greek *dysprositos* "hard to get at", from *dys-* + *prositos* "approachable"]

dys·tro·phy \'dis-trə-fē\ *n, pl* **-phies** : imperfect nutrition; *esp* : any of several disorders involving nerves and muscles — compare MUSCULAR DYSTROPHY — **dys·tro·phic** \dis-ˈtrō-fik\ *adj*

\ə\ abut	\ng\ sing
\ər\ **further**	\ō\ bone
\a\ mat	\ȯ\ saw
\ā\ take	\ȯi\ coin
\ä\ cot, cart	\th\ thin
\au̇\ out	\th\ this
\ch\ chin	\ü\ food
\e\ pet	\u̇\ foot
\ē\ easy	\y\ yet
\g\ go	\yü\ few
\i\ tip	\yu̇\ cure
\ī\ life	\zh\ vision
\j\ job	

Ee

e \'ē\ *n, pl* **e's** *or* **es** \'ēz\ *often cap* **1** : the 5th letter of the English alphabet **2** : the musical tone E **3** : the base of the system of natural logarithms having the approximate numerical value 2.71828 **4** : a grade rating a student's work as poor and usually constituting a conditional pass

e- \'ē, 'ē, i\ *prefix* **1** : not **2** : out, forth, away [Latin, "out, forth, away", from *ex-*]

¹each \'ēch\ *adj* : being one of two or more distinct individuals [Old English *ǣlc*]

²each *pron* : each one ⟨*each* of us had a twin⟩

³each *adv* : to or for each : APIECE

each other *pron* : each of two or more in reciprocal action or relation ⟨looked at *each other*⟩

ea·ger \'ē-gər\ *adj* : marked by enthusiastic or sharply expectant desire or interest [Old French *aigre* "keen, sharp", from Latin *acer*] — **ea·ger·ly** *adv* — **ea·ger·ness** *n* □ SYN ANXIOUS: EAGER implies ardor and enthusiasm and suggests impatience at delay or restraint; ANXIOUS stresses fear of frustration or failure or disappointment.

eager beaver *n* : one who is unduly zealous in performing his assigned duties and in volunteering for more

ea·gle \'ē-gəl\ *n* **1** : any of various large day-flying sharp-eyed predatory birds that have a powerful flight and are related to the hawks **2** : a seal or standard or an insignia shaped like or bearing an eagle **3** : a 10-dollar gold coin of the United States bearing an eagle on the reverse **4** : a golf score of two strokes less than par on a hole [Old French *aigle,* from Latin *aquila*]

eagle 1

ea·glet \'ē-glət\ *n* : a young eagle

-ean — see -AN

¹ear \'iər\ *n* **1 a** : the vertebrate organ of hearing and balance consisting in the typical mammal of a sound-collecting outer ear separated by a membranous drum from a sound-transmitting middle ear that in turn is separated from a sensory inner ear **b** : the outer ear **c** : any of various organs capable of detecting vibrations **2 a** : the sense or act of hearing **b** : sensitivity to musical tone and pitch **3** : ATTENTION; *esp* : sympathetic attention **4** : something resembling an ear in shape or position [Old English *ēare*] — **eared** \'iərd\ *adj* — **ear·less** \'iər-ləs\ *adj*

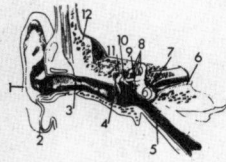

¹ear 1a: *1* pinna, *2* lobe, *3* auditory canal, *4* eardrum, *5* eustachian tube, *6* auditory nerve, *7* colchea, *8* semicircular canals, *9* stapes, *10* incus, *11* malleus, *12* bones of skull

²ear *n* : the fruiting spike of a cereal (as Indian corn) including both the seeds and protective structures [Old English *ēar*] — **ear** *vi*

ear·ache \'iər-,āk\ *n* : an ache or pain in the ear

ear·drum \-,drəm\ *n* : the thin membrane that separates the outer and middle ear and transmits sound waves as vibrations to the chain of tiny bones in the middle ear

eared seal *n* : any of a family of seals including the sea lions and fur seals and having small well-developed external ears

ear·ful \-,fúl\ *n* **1** : an outpouring of news or gossip **2** : a sharp reprimand

earl \'ərl\ *n* : a member of the British peerage ranking below a marquess and above a viscount [Old English *eorl* "warrior, nobleman"] — **earl·dom** \-dəm\ *n*

earless seal *n* : any of a family of seals with hairy coats and no external ears

ear·lobe \'iər-,lōb\ *n* : the pendent part of the ear of human beings or some fowls

¹ear·ly \'ər-lē\ *adv* **ear·li·er; -est 1** : near the beginning of a period of time or of a process or series **2** : before the usual or expected time [Old English *ǣrlīce,* from *ǣr* "early, soon"]

²early *adj* **ear·li·er; -est 1 a** : of, relating to, or occurring near the beginning of a period of time, a development, or a series **b** : PRIMITIVE ⟨*early* art forms⟩ **2 a** : occurring before the usual or expected time ⟨spring was *early* this year⟩ **b** : occurring in the near future **c** : maturing or producing sooner than related forms ⟨an *early* peach⟩ — **ear·li·ness** *n*

early on *adv* : at or during an early point on stage ⟨had decided *early on* not to accept⟩

¹ear·mark \'iər-,märk\ *n* **1** : a mark of identification on the ear of an animal **2** : a distinguishing characteristic ⟨all the *earmarks* of poverty⟩

²earmark *vt* **1** : to mark with or as if with an earmark **2** : to set aside (as funds) for a specific use

ear·muff \'iər-,məf\ *n* : one of a pair of ear coverings connected by a flexible band and worn as protection against cold or noises

earn \'ərn\ *vt* **1 a** : to get for services given ⟨*earn* a good salary⟩ **b** : RETURN 6, YIELD ⟨investments *earning* 8%⟩ **2** : to deserve as a result of labor or service ⟨you *earned* every cent you were paid⟩ [Old English *earnian*] — **earn·er** *n*

¹ear·nest \'ər-nəst\ *n* : a serious and intent state of mind ⟨in *earnest*⟩ [Old English *eornost*]

²earnest *adj* **1** : characterized by or proceeding from a serious state of mind **2** : not trivial : IMPORTANT SYN see SERIOUS — **ear·nest·ly** *adv* — **ear·nest·ness** \-nəst-nəs, -nəs-nəs\ *n*

³earnest *n* **1** : something of value given by a buyer to a seller to bind a bargain **2** : a token of what is to come : PLEDGE [Old French *erres,* pl. of *erre* "earnest," from Latin *arra,* short for *arrabo,* from Greek *arrhabōn,* from Hebrew *ʿērābhōn*]

earn·ings \'ər-ningz\ *n pl* : something earned: as **a** : WAGE **b** : revenue after deduction of expenses

ear·phone \'iər-,fōn\ *n* : a device that converts electrical energy into sound waves and is worn over or inserted into the ear

ear·piece \-,pēs\ *n* : a part of an instrument (as a telephone or hearing aid) that is applied to the ear; *esp* : EARPHONE

ear·ring \'iər-,ring\ *n* : an ornament for the earlobe

ear·shot \'iər-,shät\ *n* : the range within which the unaided voice may be heard

ear·split·ting \-,split-ing\ *adj* : intolerably loud or shrill

¹earth \'ərth\ *n* **1** : the soft or granular material composing part of the surface of the globe; *esp* : cultivable soil **2** : the sphere of mortal life as distinguished from heaven and hell **3** : areas of land as distinguished from sea and air : GROUND **4** *often cap* : the planet on which we live and which is 3d in order of distance from the sun — see PLANET table **5** : the lair of a burrowing animal **6** : any of several metallic oxides (as alumina) [Old English *eorthe*] — **earth·like** \-,līk\ *adj* □ SYN EARTH, WORLD, UNIVERSE mean the entire area in which humanity thinks of itself as living. EARTH denotes the material global body, the planet of the sun, but often means the immediate sphere of human action in contrast to the religious concepts of heaven and hell; WORLD often equals EARTH but may apply to space, earth, and all visible celestial bodies within our present range of knowledge; UNIVERSE denotes the entire system of created things and physical phenomena regarded as a unit in its arrangement and operation.

²**earth** *vt* : to draw soil about (plants)

earth·en \'ər-thən, -thən\ *adj* : made of earth or of baked clay ⟨an *earthen* floor⟩ ⟨*earthen* dishes⟩

earth·en·ware \-,waər, -,weər\ *n* : articles (as utensils or ornaments) made of baked clay

earth·ling \'ərth-ling\ *n* : an inhabitant of the earth

earth·ly \'ərth-lē\ *adj* **1 a** : of, relating to, or characteristic of the earth **b** : relating to human life on the earth ⟨*earthly* joys⟩ **2** : POSSIBLE, IMAGINABLE ⟨that tool is of no *earthly* use⟩ — **earth·li·ness** *n* □ SYN WORLDLY, MUNDANE: EARTHLY often implies contrast with heavenly or spiritual ⟨*earthly* love⟩ WORLDLY and MUNDANE both imply a relation to the immediate concerns and activities of human beings, WORLDLY suggesting tangible personal gain or gratification ⟨*worldly* goods⟩ and MUNDANE suggesting reference to the immediate and practical ⟨a *mundane* discussion of finances⟩

earth·quake \'ərth-,kwāk\ *n* : a shaking or trembling of a portion of the earth caused by movement of rock masses or by volcanic shocks

earth science *n* : any of the sciences (as geology or geography) that deal with the earth or one of its parts

earth·shine \-,shīn\ *n* : sunlight reflected by the earth that illuminates the dark part of the moon — called also *earthlight*

earth·work \-,wərk\ *n* : an embankment or other construction of earth; *esp* : one made as a fortification

earth·worm \-,wərm\ *n* : a long slender worm with segmented body that lives in damp earth and moves with the aid of setae

earthy \'ər-thē, -thē\ *adj* **earth·i·er; -est** **1** : consisting of or resembling earth ⟨an *earthy* flavor⟩ **2 a** : DOWN-TO-EARTH, PRACTICAL **b** : CRUDE ⟨*earthy* humor⟩ — **earth·i·ness** *n*

ear·wax \'iər-,waks\ *n* : a brownish yellow or orange waxlike substance produced by the glands of the external ear — called also *cerumen, wax*

ear·wig \-,wig\ *n* : any of numerous insects (order Dermaptera) with slender many-jointed antennae and a pair of large terminal appendages arranged like forceps [Old English *ēarwicga*, from *ēare* "ear" + *wicga* "insect"]

¹**ease** \'ēz\ *n* **1** : the state of being comfortable: as **a** : freedom from pain or discomfort **b** : freedom from care **c** : freedom from a sense of difficulty or embarrassment : NATURALNESS ⟨speak with *ease*⟩ **2** : EFFORTLESSNESS ⟨rides a horse with *ease*⟩ [Old French *aise* "convenience, comfort", from Latin *adjacens* "neighborhood", from *adjacēre* "to lie near", from *ad-* + *jacēre* "to lie"] — **ease·ful** \-fəl\ *adj*

²**ease** *vb* **1** : to free from something that disquiets or burdens ⟨*ease* you of your troubles⟩ **2** : to make less painful : ALLEVIATE ⟨*ease* your suffering⟩ **3** : to make less tight or difficult : LOOSEN, SLACKEN ⟨*ease* credit⟩ ⟨*ease* up on a rope⟩

ea·sel \'ē-zəl\ *n* : a frame for supporting something (as an artist's canvas) [Dutch *ezel* "ass", from Latin *asinus*] □ ORIGIN An *easel* is a frame for supporting something, such as an artist's painting or a blackboard. The word was borrowed into English from the Dutch *ezel*, which was used for the same piece of equipment.

This sense of *ezel* was a metaphorical extension of the literal meaning "ass, donkey", probably because an *easel*, like a beast of burden, is used to hold things.

eas·i·ly \'ēz-lē, -ə-lē\ *adv* **1** : in an easy manner ⟨won the game *easily*⟩ **2** : by far ⟨*easily* the best candidate⟩

¹**east** \'ēst\ *adv* : to, toward, or in the east [Old English *ēast*]

²**east** *adj* **1** : situated toward or at the east **2** : coming from the east

³**east** *n* **1 a** : the general direction of sunrise **b** : the compass point directly opposite to west **2** *cap* : regions or countries east of a specified or implied point **3** : the altar end of a church

east·bound \'ēst-,baund, 'ēs-\ *adj* : headed east

Eas·ter \'ē-stər\ *n* : a feast that commemorates Christ's resurrection and is observed on the first Sunday after the full moon on or next after March 21 or one week later if the full moon falls on Sunday [Old English *ēastre*]

Easter lily *n* : any of several white cultivated lilies that bloom in early spring

east·er·ly \'ē-stər-lē\ *adv or adj* **1** : from the east **2** : toward the east

east·ern \'ē-stərn\ *adj* **1** *often cap* : of, relating to, or characteristic of a region conventionally designated East **2** *cap* **a** : of, relating to, or being the Christian churches originating in the church of the Eastern Roman Empire **b** : Eastern Orthodox **3** : lying toward or coming from the east [Old English *ēasterne*] — **east·ern·most** \-,mōst\ *adj*

East·ern·er \'ē-stər-nər, -stə-nər\ *n* : a native or inhabitant of the East (as of the United States)

eastern hemisphere *n* : the half of the earth to the east of the Atlantic ocean including Europe, Asia, and Africa

Eastern Orthodox *adj* : of or consisting of the Eastern churches that form a loose federation according primacy of honor to the patriarch of Constantinople and adhering to the decisions of the first seven ecumenical councils and to one rite

Eastern time *n* : the time of the 5th time zone west of Greenwich that includes the eastern United States

East Goth *n* : OSTROGOTH

east·ing \'ē-sting\ *n* **1** : difference in longitude to the east from the last preceding point of reckoning **2** : easterly progress

east–northeast *n* : two points north of east : N67°30′E

east–southeast *n* : two points south of east : S67°30′E

¹**east·ward** \'ēs-twərd\ *adv or adj* : toward the east — **east·wards** \-twərdz\ *adv*

²**eastward** *n* : eastward direction or part

easy \'ē-zē\ *adj* **eas·i·er; -est** **1** : not hard to do ⟨an *easy* lesson⟩ **2 a** : not severe : LENIENT ⟨an *easy* teacher⟩ **b** : not steep or abrupt ⟨*easy* slopes⟩ **3 a** : marked by peace and comfort **b** : not hurried ⟨an *easy* pace⟩ **4 a** : free from pain, trouble or worry **b** : showing ease : NATURAL ⟨an *easy* manner⟩ **5 a** : giving comfort or relaxation ⟨an *easy* chair⟩ **b** : not imposing hardship ⟨buying on *easy* terms⟩ SYN see SIMPLE — **eas·i·ness** *n*

easy·go·ing \,ē-zē-'gō-ing\ *adj* : taking life easily : CAREFREE — **easy·go·ing·ness** *n*

easy street *n* : a situation with no financial worries

eat \'ēt\ *vb* **ate** \'āt\; **eat·en** \'ēt-n\; **eat·ing** **1** : to take into the mouth as food : chew and swallow in turn **2** : to take a meal **3** : to destroy, use up, or waste by or as if by eating ⟨locusts *ate* the country bare⟩ **4 a** : to affect something by gradual destruction or consumption — used with *into* ⟨acid *ate* into the metal⟩ **b** : BOTHER ⟨what's *eating* you⟩ [Old English *etan*] — **eat·er** *n* — **eat crow** : to accept what one has fought against — **eat one's heart out** : to suffer deep distress (as from grief or envy) — **eat one's words** : to take back what one has said

¹**eat·able** \'ēt-ə-bəl\ *adj* : fit to be eaten

²**eatable** *n* **1** : something to eat **2** *pl* : FOOD 2

\ə\	abut	\ng\	sing
\ər\	further	\ō\	bone
\a\	mat	\ȯ\	saw
\ā\	take	\ȯi\	coin
\ä\	cot, cart	\th\	thin
\aủ\	out	\th\	this
\ch\	chin	\ü\	food
\e\	pet	\ủ\	foot
\ē\	easy	\y\	yet
\g\	go	\yü\	few
\i\	tip	\yủ\	cure
\ī\	life	\zh\	vision
\j\	job		

eaves

echidna

eau de cologne \ˌōd-ə-kə-'lōn\ *n, pl* **eaux de cologne** \ˌōd-ə-, ˌōzd-ə-\ : COLOGNE [French, literally, "water from Cologne"]

eau–de–vie \ˌōd-ə-'vē\ *n, pl* **eaux–de–vie** \ˌōd-ə-, ˌōzd-ə-\ : BRANDY [French, literally, "water of life"]

eaves \'ēvz\ *n sing or pl* : the overhanging lower edge of a roof projecting beyond the wall of a building [Old English *efes,* singular]

eaves·drop \'ēvz-ˌdräp\ *vi* : to listen secretly to what is said in private [probably back-formation from *eavesdropper,* literally, "one standing under the drip from the eaves"] — **eaves·drop·per** *n* □ ORIGIN The verb *eavesdrop* is probably a back-formation from the noun *eavesdropper.* In Middle English the water that falls from the eaves of a house was called *evesdrop,* spelled *eavesdrop* in modern English (the noun is now very rare). *Eavesdropper* was originally used for a person who stood close to a house, in the area where water, or eavesdrop, falls from the eaves, in order to overhear what was going on inside.

eaves trough *n* : GUTTER 1a

¹ebb \'eb\ *n* **1** : the recession of the tide toward the sea **2 a** : a passing from a high to a low point **b** : a period or state of decline ⟨relations were at a low *ebb*⟩ [Old English *ebba*]

²ebb *vi* **1** : to recede from the flood **2** : to decline from a higher level or a better state

ebb tide *n* **1** : the tide while ebbing **2** : EBB 2b

EBCDIC \'eps-ə-ˌdik, 'ebs-\ *n* : a computer code for representing letters, numerals, and symbols [*e*xtended *b*inary *c*oded *d*ecimal *i*nterchange *c*ode]

eb·o·nite \'eb-ə-ˌnīt\ *n* : hard rubber especially when black

¹eb·o·ny \'eb-ə-nē\ *n, pl* **-nies** : a hard heavy wood yielded by various Old World tropical trees related to the persimmon; *also* : a tree yielding ebony [derived from Greek *ebenos,* from Egyptian *hbnj*]

²ebony *adj* **1** : made of or resembling ebony **2** : BLACK 1, DARK

ebul·lient \i-'bùl-yənt\ *adj* **1** : intensely agitated **2** : characterized by enthusiastic expression of thoughts or feelings [Latin *ebullire* "to bubble out", from *e-* + *bullire* "to bubble, boil"] — **ebul·lience** \-yəns\ *n* — **ebul·lient·ly** *adv*

eb·ul·li·tion \ˌeb-ə-'lish-ən\ *n* : the process or state of boiling or bubbling up

¹ec·cen·tric \ik-'sen-trik, ek-\ *adj* **1** : not having the same center ⟨*eccentric* spheres⟩ **2** : deviating from some established pattern or from accepted usage or conduct **3 a** : deviating from a circular path ⟨an *eccentric* orbit⟩ **b** : located elsewhere than at the geometrical center [Medieval Latin *eccentricus,* from Greek *ekkentros,* from *ex* "out of" + *kentron* "center"] — **ec·cen·tri·cal·ly** \-tri-kə-lē, -klē\ *adv*

²eccentric *n* **1** : a disklike device that turns around a shaft not at its center and is used in machinery for changing circular motion into back-and-forth motion **2** : an eccentric person

ec·cen·tric·i·ty \ˌek-ˌsen-'tris-ət-ē\ *n, pl* **-ties** **1 a** : the quality or state of being eccentric **b** : deviation from an established pattern, rule, or norm; *esp* : odd or whimsical behavior **2** : the degree of deviation from a circular path □ SYN ECCENTRICITY, IDIOSYNCRASY mean a peculiar trait, trick, or habit. ECCENTRICITY stresses divergence from the usual or customary and suggests whimsicality or mild mental aberration; IDIOSYNCRASY stresses the following of one's particular bent or temperament and connotes strong individuality and independence of action.

Ec·cle·si·as·tes \ik-ˌlē-zē-'as-ˌtēz\ *n* — see BIBLE table [Greek *Ekklēsiastēs,* literally, "preacher"]

ec·cle·si·as·tic \-'as-tik\ *n* : a member of the clergy

ec·cle·si·as·ti·cal \-ti-kəl\ *or* **ec·cle·si·as·tic** \-tik\ *adj* : of or relating to a church especially as an established institution ⟨*ecclesiastical* law⟩ [Late Latin *ecclesiasti-*

cus, derived from Greek *ekklēsia* "assembly of citizens, church", from *ekkalein* "to summon", from *ex* "out of" + *kalein* "to call"] — **ec·cle·si·as·ti·cal·ly** \-ti-kə-lē, -klē\ *adv*

Ec·cle·si·as·ti·cus \-ti-kəs\ *n* — see BIBLE table

ec·dy·sis \'ek-də-səs\ *n, pl* **-dy·ses** \-də-ˌsēz\ : the act of molting or of shedding (as by insects and crustaceans) an outer layer of cuticle [Greek *ekdysis* "act of getting out"]

ech·e·lon \'esh-ə-ˌlän\ *n* **1 a** : a formation of units (as troops or airplanes) resembling a series of steps **b** : any of several military units in echelon formation **2 a** : one of a series of levels or grades especially of authority **b** : the individuals at such a level [French *échelon,* literally, "rung of a ladder"]

echid·na \i-'kid-nə\ *n* : a spiny-coated toothless burrowing egg-laying mammal of Australia with a tapering snout and long tongue for eating ants [Latin, "viper", from Greek]

echi·no·derm \i-'kī-nə-ˌdərm\ *n* : any of a phylum (Echinodermata) of marine animals (as the starfishes and sea urchins) that have true coeloms and have similar parts arranged symmetrically around a central axis [*echin-* "prickle" (from Greek *echinos* "sea urchin") + Greek *derma* "skin"] — **echi·no·der·ma·tous** \i-ˌkī-nə-'dər-mət-əs\ *adj*

echi·noid \i-'kī-ˌnòid, 'ek-ə-ˌnòid\ *n* : SEA URCHIN

echi·nus \i-'kī-nəs\ *n, pl* **-ni** \-ˌnī\ : SEA URCHIN [Latin, from Greek *echinos* "hedgehog, sea urchin"]

¹echo \'ek-ō\ *n, pl* **ech·oes** **1** : the repetition of a sound caused by reflection of sound waves **2 a** : a repetition or imitation of another **b** : REPERCUSSION, RESULT ⟨the economic collapse had political *echoes*⟩ **3** : one who closely imitates or repeats another **4 a** : the repetition of a received radio signal due especially to reflection **b** (1) : the reflection of transmitted radar signals by an object (2) : the visual indication of this reflection on a radarscope [Latin, from Greek *ēchō*] — **echo·ic** \i-'kō-ik, e-\ *adj*

²echo *vb* **1** : to resound with echoes **2** : to produce an echo : send back or repeat a sound **3** : REPEAT, IMITATE ⟨*echoing* the words of the teacher⟩

echo·lo·ca·tion \ˌek-ō-lō-'kā-shən\ *n* : a process for locating distant or invisible objects by means of sound waves reflected back to the sender by the objects

echo sounder *n* : an instrument for determining the depth of a body of water or of an object below the surface by means of sound waves

éclair \ā-'klaər, -'kleər, 'ā-ˌ\ *n* : an oblong cream puff with whipped cream or custard filling [French, literally "lightning"]

eclamp·sia \e-'klam-sē-ə, -'klamp-\ *n* : a convulsive state; *esp* : an attack of convulsions during pregnancy or during the process of giving birth [Greek *eklampsis* "sudden flashing", from *eklampein* "to shine forth", from *ex* "out" + *lampein* "to shine"]

éclat \ā-'klä\ *n* **1** : brilliance especially in performance or achievement **2** : demonstration of approval : ACCLAIM [French, "splinter, burst, éclat"]

eclec·tic \e-'klek-tik, i-\ *adj* **1** : selecting what appears to be best from various doctrines, methods, or styles **2** : composed of elements drawn from various sources [Greek *eklektikos,* from *eklegein* "to select", from *ex* "out" + *legein* "to gather"] — **eclectic** *n* — **eclec·ti·cal·ly** \-ti-kə-lē, -klē\ *adv* — **eclec·ti·cism** \-tə-ˌsiz-əm\ *n*

¹eclipse \i-'klips\ *n* **1** : a complete or partial hiding or darkening of one celestial body by another **2** : a falling into obscurity or decline [Old French, from Latin *eclipsis,* from Greek *ekleipsis,* from *ekleipein* "to omit, suffer eclipse", from *ex-* "out" + *leipein* "to leave"]

²eclipse *vt* **1** : to cause an eclipse of **2** : to reduce in fame **3** : to surpass greatly : OUTSHINE

¹eclip·tic \i-'klip-tik\ *n* : the great circle of the celestial sphere that is the apparent path of the sun among the

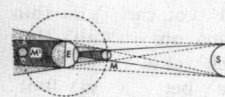

¹eclipse 1: S sun, E earth, M moon in solar eclipse, M¹ moon in lunar eclipse

stars [Late Latin *ecliptica linea,* literally, "line of eclipses"]

²eclip·tic *adj* : of or relating to the ecliptic or an eclipse

ec·logue \'ek-,lóg\ *n* : a poem in which shepherds converse [Latin *Eclogae,* title of Vergil's pastorals, literally, "selections"]

eco- *combining form* **1** : habitat or environment ⟨*eco*system⟩ **2** : ecology [Greek *oikos* "house"]

eco·log·i·cal \,ē-kə-'läj-i-kəl, ,ek-ə-\ *also* **eco·log·ic** \-ik\ *adj* : of, relating to, concerned with, or affecting ecology or the ecology of a particular group of organisms or an environment — **eco·log·i·cal·ly** \-i-kə-lē,-klē\ *adv*

ecol·o·gy \i-'käl-ə-jē, e-\ *n* **1** : a branch of science concerned with the interrelationship of organisms and their environments **2** : the pattern of relations between one or more organisms and the environment [German *ökologie,* from *öko-* "eco-" + *-logie* "-logy"] — **ecol·o·gist** \i-'käl-ə-jəst, e-\ *n*

ec·o·nom·ic \,ek-ə-'näm-ik, ,ē-kə-\ *adj* **1 a** : of or relating to economics **b** : of, relating to, or based on the production, distribution, and consumption of goods and services **c** : of or relating to an economy **2** : having practical or industrial significance or uses : affecting material resources ⟨*economic* pests⟩

ec·o·nom·i·cal \-'näm-i-kəl\ *adj* **1** : given to thrift : FRUGAL **2** : operating with little waste or at a saving ⟨an *economical* car⟩ — **ec·o·nom·i·cal·ly** \-'näm-i-kə-lē, -klē\ *adv*

ec·o·nom·ics \,ek-ə-'näm-iks, ,ē-kə-\ *n sing or pl* **1** : a social science concerned chiefly with description and analysis of the production, distribution, and consumption of goods and services **2** : economic aspect or significance ⟨the *economics* of buying a small car⟩ — **econ·o·mist** \i-'kän-ə-məst\ *n*

econ·o·mize \i-'kän-ə-,mīz\ *vb* **1** : to practice economy : be frugal ⟨*economize* on fuel⟩ **2** : to use more economically : SAVE — **econ·o·miz·er** *n*

econ·o·my \i-'kän-ə-mē\ *n, pl* **-mies 1 a** : thrifty use of material resources : frugality in expenditures; *also* : an act of economizing **b** : efficient and sparing use of nonmaterial resources (as effort or language) **2** : systematic arrangement of something : ORGANIZATION **3** : the structure of economic life in a country, area, or period; *esp* : an economic system [Middle French *yconomie,* from Medieval Latin *oeconomia,* from Greek *oikonomia,* derived from *oikos* "house" + *nemein* "to manage"]

eco·sys·tem \'ē-kō-,sis-təm, 'ek-ō-\ *n* : a complex system composed of an ecological community of organisms interacting with their environment

ec·ru \'ek-rü, 'ā-krü\ *adj* : BEIGE [French *écru* "unbleached"]

ec·sta·sy \'ek-stə-sē\ *n, pl* **-sies 1** : a state of being beyond reason and self-control **2** : a state of overwhelming emotion; *esp* : rapturous delight [Middle French *ecstasie,* derived from Greek *ekstasis,* from *existanai* "to derange", from *ex* "out" + *histanai* "to cause to stand"]

ec·stat·ic \ek-'stat-ik\ *adj* : of, relating to, or marked by ecstasy — **ec·stat·i·cal·ly** \-i-kə-lē, -klē\ *adv*

ect- *or* **ecto-** *combining form* : outside : external ⟨*ecto*derm⟩ — compare END-, EXO- [Greek *ektos,* from *ex* "out, out of"]

ec·to·derm \'ek-tə-,dərm\ *n* **1** : the outer cellular layer of a 2-layered animal (as a jellyfish) **2** : the outermost of the three primary germ layers of an embryo; *also* : a tissue (as skin or nerve) derived from this — **ec·to·der·mal** \,ek-tə-'dər-məl\ *adj*

ec·to·mor·phic \,ek-tə-'mór-fik\ *adj* : having a light and slender body build — **ec·to·morph** \'ek-tə-,mórf\ *n* — **ec·to·mor·phy** \'ek-tə-,mór-fē\ *n*

-ec·to·my \'ek-tə-mē\ *n combining form, pl* **-mies** : surgical removal ⟨tonsil*ectomy*⟩ [Greek *ektemnein* "to cut out", from *ex-* "out" + *temnein* "to cut"]

ec·to·plasm \'ek-tə-,plaz-əm\ *n* **1** : the outer relatively rigid layer of the cytoplasm usually held to be reversibly convertible from a gel to a sol — compare ENDOPLASM **2** : a substance held to be the material form of a ghost — **ec·to·plas·mic** \,ek-tə-'plaz-mik\ *adj*

ec·u·men·i·cal \,ek-yə-'men-i-kəl\ *adj* **1** : worldwide or general in extent, influence, or application **2** : of, relating to, or representing the whole of a body of churches **3** : promoting Christian unity or cooperation [Late Latin *oecumenicus,* derived from Greek *oikoumenē* "the inhabited world", from *oikein* "to inhabit", from *oikos* "house"] — **ec·u·men·i·cal·ly** \-i-kə-lē, -klē\ *adv* — **ec·u·me·nic·i·ty** \-mə-'nis-ət-ē\ *n*

ec·ze·ma \ig-'zē-mə, 'ek-sə-mə, 'eg-zə-\ *n* : a skin inflammation marked by redness, itching, and scaly or crusted lesions [Greek *ekzema,* from *ekzein* "to erupt", from *ex* "out" + *zein* "to boil"] — **ec·zem·a·tous** \ig-'zem-ət-əs\ *adj*

¹-ed \d *after a vowel or* b, g, j, l, m, n, ng, r, *th,* v, z, zh; əd, id *after* d, t; t *after other sounds; exceptions are pronounced at their subentries or entries* \ *vb suffix or adj suffix* **1** — used to form the past participle of regular weak verbs ⟨end*ed*⟩ ⟨fad*ed*⟩ ⟨tri*ed*⟩ ⟨patt*ed*⟩ **2** — used to form adjectives of identical meaning from Latin-derived adjectives ending in *-ate* ⟨umbilicat*ed*⟩ **3 a** : having : characterized by ⟨cultur*ed*⟩ ⟨two-fac*ed*⟩ **b** : having the characteristics of ⟨bigot*ed*⟩ [Old English *-ed, -od, -ad*]

²-ed *vb suffix* — used to form the past tense of regular weak verbs ⟨judg*ed*⟩ ⟨deni*ed*⟩ ⟨dropp*ed*⟩ [Old English *-de, -ede, -ode, -ade*]

Edam \'ēd-əm, 'ē-,dam\ *n* : a Dutch pressed cheese of yellow color and mild flavor [*Edam,* Netherlands]

edaph·ic \i-'daf-ik\ *adj* : of, relating to, or resulting from the soil [Greek *edaphos* "bottom, ground"] — **edaph·i·cal·ly** \-'daf-i-kə-lē, -klē\ *adv*

Ed·dic \'ed-ik\ *adj* : of, relating to, or resembling the Old Norse Edda which is a 13th century collection of chiefly mythological poems in alliterative verse

¹ed·dy \'ed-ē\ *n, pl* **eddies 1** : a current of air or water running contrary to the main current; *esp* : a current moving in a circle like a whirlpool **2** : a substance moving like an eddy ⟨*eddies* of dust⟩ [Middle English (Scottish dialect) *ydy*]

²eddy *vb* **ed·died; ed·dy·ing** : to move in an eddy or so as to form an eddy ⟨the stream *eddied* about a large rock⟩

eddy current *n* : an electric current induced by an alternating magnetic field

edel·weiss \'ād-l-,wīs\ *n* : a small perennial woolly herb that is related to the thistles and grows high in the Alps [German, from *edel* "noble" + *weiss* "white"]

ede·ma \i-'dē-mə\ *n* : abnormal accumulation of watery fluid in a bodily tissue or cavity [Greek *oidēma* "swelling", from *oidein* "to swell"] — **edem·a·tous** \i-'dem-ət-əs\ *adj*

Eden \'ēd-n\ *n* : PARADISE 3 [from *Eden,* the garden where Adam and Eve are held to have lived first, from Late Latin, from Hebrew *'Edhen*] — **Eden·ic** \i-'den-ik\ *adj*

eden·tate \ē-'den-,tāt\ *n* : any of an order (Edentata) of mammals having few or no teeth and including the sloths, armadillos, and New World anteaters — **edentate** *adj*

¹edge \'ej\ *n* **1 a** : the cutting side of a blade **b** : the sharpness of a blade **c** : penetrating power : KEENNESS ⟨a voice with a sarcastic *edge*⟩ **2 a** : the line where an object or surface begins or ends; *also* : the narrow adjacent part **b** : the intersection of two plane faces of a solid or of two planes **3** : a favorable margin : ADVANTAGE [Old English *ecg*] SYN see BORDER — **edged** \'ejd\ *adj* — **on edge** : ANXIOUS 1, NERVOUS

²edge *vb* **1** : to give an edge to ⟨*edge* an axe⟩ ⟨a voice *edged* with anger⟩ **2** : to move or advance slowly or by short moves ⟨the crowd *edged* along⟩ **3** : to incline (a ski) sideways

edelweiss

edge tool *n* : a tool (as a chisel, knife, plane, or gouge) with a sharp cutting edge

edge·ways \'ej-ˌwāz\ *adv* : with the edge foremost : SIDEWAYS

edge·wise \-ˌwīz\ *adv* : EDGEWAYS

edg·ing \'ej-ing\ *n* : something that forms an edge or border ⟨a lace *edging*⟩

edgy \'ej-ē\ *adj* **edg·i·er; -est** **1** : having an edge : SHARP ⟨an *edgy* tone⟩ **2** : being on edge : TENSE — **edg·i·ly** \'ej-ə-lē\ *adv* — **edg·i·ness** \'ej-ē-nəs\ *n*

ed·i·ble \'ed-ə-bəl\ *adj* : fit or safe to be eaten [Late Latin *edibilis,* from Latin *edere* "to eat"] — **ed·i·bil·i·ty** \ˌed-ə-'bil-ət-ē\ *n* — **edible** *n* — **ed·i·ble·ness** *n*

edict \'ē-ˌdikt\ *n* : a decree or order proclaimed by an authority (as a sovereign) that has the force of law [Latin *edictum,* from *edicere* "to decree", from *e-* + *dicere* "to say"] — **edic·tal** \i-'dik-tl\ *adj*

ed·i·fice \'ed-ə-fəs\ *n* : BUILDING; *esp* : a large or impressive building (as a church) [Middle French, from Latin *aedificium,* from *aedificare* "to erect a house"]

ed·i·fy \'ed-ə-ˌfī\ *vt* **-fied; -fy·ing** : to instruct and improve especially by good example : benefit morally or spiritually ⟨plays that *edify* the audience⟩ [Middle French *edifier,* from Late Latin *aedificare,* from Latin, "to erect a house", from *aedes* "temple, house"] — **ed·i·fi·ca·tion** \ˌed-ə-fə-'kā-shən\ *n*

ed·it \'ed-ət\ *vt* **1 a** : to correct, revise, and prepare especially for publication ⟨*edit* Poe's works⟩ **b** : to assemble (as a motion-picture film or tape recording) for use or publication by cutting and rearranging **2** : to supervise the publication of [back-formation from *editor*]

edi·tion \i-'dish-ən\ *n* **1** : the form in which a text (as a printed book) is published **2** : the whole number of copies printed or published at one time ⟨a third *edition*⟩ **3** : one of the several issues of a newspaper for a single day [Middle French, from Latin *editio* "publication, edition", from *edere* "to bring forth, publish"]

ed·i·tor \'ed-ət-ər\ *n* **1** : a person who edits **2** : a person who writes editorials **3** : a computer program that permits the user to create or change a program in a computer system [Late Latin, "publisher", from Latin *edere* "to bring forth, publish"] — **ed·i·tor·ship** \-ˌship\ *n*

¹ed·i·to·ri·al \ˌed-ə-'tōr-ē-əl, -'tȯr-\ *adj* **1** : of or relating to an editor ⟨an *editorial* staff⟩ **2** : being or resembling an editorial ⟨an *editorial* statement⟩ — **ed·i·to·ri·al·ly** \-ē-ə-lē\ *adv*

²editorial *n* : a newspaper or magazine article that gives the opinions of its editors or publishers

ed·i·to·ri·al·ist \-ē-ə-ləst\ *n* : a writer of editorials

ed·i·to·ri·al·ize \ˌed-ə-'tōr-ē-ə-ˌlīz, -'tȯr-\ *vi* **1** : to express an opinion in the form of an editorial **2** : to introduce opinion into the reporting of facts — **ed·i·to·ri·al·iza·tion** \-ˌtōr-ē-ə-lə-'zā-shən, -ˌtȯr-\ *n* — **ed·i·to·ri·al·iz·er** \-'tōr-ē-ə-ˌlī-zər, -'tȯr-\ *n*

ed·u·ca·ble \'ej-ə-kə-bəl\ *also* **ed·u·cat·able** \-ˌkāt-ə-bəl\ *adj* : capable of being educated

ed·u·cate \'ej-ə-ˌkāt\ *vt* **1** : to provide schooling for **2 a** : to develop mentally and morally especially by formal instruction **b** : TRAIN [Latin *educare* "to rear, educate"] SYN see TEACH — **ed·u·ca·tor** \-ˌkāt-ər\ *n*

ed·u·cat·ed *adj* **1** : having an education; *esp* : having an education beyond the average **2** : giving evidence of education ⟨*educated* speech⟩ **3** : based on some knowledge of fact ⟨an *educated* guess⟩

ed·u·ca·tion \ˌej-ə-'kā-shən\ *n* **1 a** : the action or process of educating or of being educated **b** : the knowledge and development resulting from an educational process ⟨a person of little *education*⟩ **2** : the field of study that deals mainly with methods and problems of teaching — **ed·u·ca·tion·al** \-shnəl, -shən-l\ *adj* — **ed·u·ca·tion·al·ly** \-ē\ *adv* □ SYN TRAINING: EDUCATION is the general term for institutional learning and implies the guidance and training intended to develop

a person's full capacities and intelligence; TRAINING suggests exercise or practice to gain skill, endurance, or facility in a specific field.

ed·u·ca·tive \'ej-ə-ˌkāt-iv\ *adj* **1** : tending to educate : INSTRUCTIVE **2** : of or relating to education ⟨improvements in *educative* procedures⟩

educe \i-'düs, -'dyüs\ *vt* **1** : to bring out : draw forth : ELICIT **2** : to arrive at (as a solution or conclusion) [Latin *educere* "to draw out", from *e-* + *ducere* "to lead"] — **educ·ible** \-'dü-sə-bəl, -'dyü-\ *adj* — **educ·tion** \-'dək-shən\ *n* — **educ·tor** \-'dək-tər\ *n*

Ed·war·di·an \ed-'wärd-ē-ən\ *adj* : of, relating to, or characteristic of Edward VII of England or his age — **Edwardian** *n*

¹-ee \'ē, ˌē, ē\ *n suffix* **1** : recipient or beneficiary of (a specified action or thing) ⟨appoint*ee*⟩ ⟨grant*ee*⟩ ⟨patent*ee*⟩ **2** : one who performs (a specified action) ⟨escap*ee*⟩ [Middle French *-é,* from *-é,* past participle ending, from Latin *-atus*]

²-ee *n suffix* **1** : a particular especially small kind of ⟨boot*ee*⟩ **2** : one resembling or suggestive of ⟨goat*ee*⟩ [probably alteration of *-y*]

eel \'ēl\ *n, pl* **eels** *or* **eel** **1** : any of numerous long snakelike fishes with smooth slimy skin and no pelvic fins **2** : EELWORM [Old English *ǣl*] — **eel·like** \'ēl-ˌlīk\ *adj* — **eely** \'ē-lē\ *adj*

eel·grass \'ēl-ˌgras\ *n* : a plant that grows underwater and has long narrow leaves

eel·pout \-ˌpau̇t\ *n* **1** : any of various marine fishes resembling blennies **2** : BURBOT

eel·worm \-ˌwərm\ *n* : a nematode worm; *esp* : one living in soil or parasitic on plants

e'en \ēn, 'ēn\ *adv* : EVEN

-eer \'iər\ *n suffix* : one that is concerned with professionally, conducts, or produces ⟨auction*eer*⟩ ⟨pamphlet*eer*⟩ — often in words with derogatory meaning ⟨profit*eer*⟩ [Middle French *-ier,* from Latin *-arius*]

e'er \eər, 'eər, aər, 'aər\ *adv* : EVER

ee·rie *also* **ee·ry** \'iər-ē\ *adj* **ee·ri·er; -est** **1** : frightening because of strangeness or gloominess **2** : STRANGE, MYSTERIOUS ⟨*eerie* lights shone from the swamp⟩ [Old English *earg* "cowardly, wretched"] SYN see WEIRD — **ee·ri·ly** \'ir-ə-lē\ *adv* — **ee·ri·ness** \'ir-ē-nəs\ *n*

ef·face \i-'fās, e-\ *vt* **1** : to wipe out : OBLITERATE **2** : to make indistinct by or as if by rubbing out : ERASE ⟨*efface* an inscription⟩ **3** : to make (oneself) inconspicuous or modestly unnoticeable [Middle French *effacer,* from *ex-* "ex-" + *face* "face"] — **ef·face·able** \-'fā-sə-bəl\ *adj* — **ef·face·ment** \-'fās-mənt\ *n* — **ef·fac·er** *n*

¹ef·fect \i-'fekt\ *n* **1** : an event, condition, or state of affairs that is produced by a cause **2** : EXECUTION, OPERATION ⟨the law went into *effect* today⟩ **3** : REALITY, FACT ⟨an excuse that was in *effect* a plain refusal⟩ **4** : the act of making a particular impression ⟨talked merely for *effect*⟩ **5** : INFLUENCE ⟨the *effect* of climate on growth⟩ **6** *pl* : GOODS, POSSESSIONS ⟨household *effects*⟩ [Latin *effectus,* from *efficere* "to bring about", from *ex-* + *facere* "to make, do"] □ SYN EFFECT, CONSEQUENCE, RESULT mean a condition or occurrence traceable to a cause. EFFECT designates something that necessarily and directly follows or occurs by reason of a cause ⟨the *effect* of the medicine was drowsiness⟩ CONSEQUENCE implies a looser or remoter connection with a cause that may no longer be operating ⟨the loss of prestige was a *consequence* of this ill-advised action⟩ RESULT often applies to the last in a series of effects.

²effect *vt* : to bring about : ACCOMPLISH SYN see AFFECT — **ef·fect·er** *n*

¹ef·fec·tive \i-'fek-tiv\ *adj* **1 a** : producing a decided, decisive, or desired effect **b** : IMPRESSIVE, STRIKING ⟨an *effective* window display⟩ **2** : ready for service or action **3** : being in effect : OPERATIVE — **ef·fec·tive·ly** *adv* — **ef·fec·tive·ness** *n* □ SYN EFFECTUAL, EFFICIENT, EFFICACIOUS: EFFECTIVE stresses the actual production of an effect when in use or force ⟨the law becomes *effective* immediately) EFFECTUAL suggests the decisive accomplishment of a result or fulfillment of an intention ⟨*effectual* methods of pest control⟩ EFFICIENT suggests having given proof of power to produce maximum results with minimum effort ⟨an *efficient* worker⟩ ⟨an *efficient* machine⟩ EFFICACIOUS implies possession of special qualities giving effective power ⟨this fluid is *efficacious* in removing ink spots⟩

²**effective** *n* : one that is effective; *esp* : a soldier equipped for duty

ef·fec·tor \i-'fek-tər\ *n* : a bodily organ (as a gland or muscle) that becomes active in response to stimulation

ef·fec·tu·al \i-'fek-chə-wəl, -'fek-chəl, -'feksh-wəl\ *adj* : producing or capable of producing a desired effect : ⟨an *effectual* remedy⟩ SYN see EFFECTIVE — **ef·fec·tu·al·ly** \-ē\ *adv* — **ef·fec·tu·al·ness** *n*

ef·fec·tu·ate \i-'fek-chə-ˌwāt\ *vt* : to bring about : EFFECT

ef·fem·i·nate \ə-'fem-ə-nət\ *adj* **1** : having feminine qualities not typical of a man : UNMANLY **2** : marked by weakness and love of ease ⟨an *effeminate* civilization⟩ [Latin *effeminatus,* from *effeminare* "to make effeminate", from *ex-* + *femina* "woman"] — **ef·fem·i·na·cy** \-nə-sē\ *n* — **ef·fem·i·nate·ly** *adv* — **ef·fem·i·nate·ness** *n*

ef·fen·di \e-'fen-dē, ə-\ *n* : a man of property, authority, or education in an eastern Mediterranean country [Turkish *efendi* "master", derived from Greek *authentēs*]

ef·fer·ent \'ef-ə-rənt; 'ef-ˌer-ənt, 'ē-fer-\ *adj* : conducting outward from a part or organ; *esp* : conveying nervous impulses to an effector — compare AFFERENT [French *efférent,* from Latin *efferre* "to carry outward", from *ex-* + *ferre* "to carry"] — **efferent** *n*

ef·fer·vesce \ˌef-ər-'ves\ *vi* **1** : to bubble, hiss, and foam as gas escapes ⟨ginger ale *effervesces*⟩ **2** : to show liveliness or exhilaration ⟨*effervesced* with excitement⟩ [Latin *effervescere,* from *ex-* + *fervescere* "to begin to boil", from *fervēre* "to boil"] — **ef·fer·ves·cence** \-'ves-nts\ *n* — **ef·fer·ves·cent** \-nt\ *adj* — **ef·fer·ves·cent·ly** *adv*

ef·fete \e-'fēt, i-\ *adj* **1** : no longer productive **2** : worn out : EXHAUSTED; *also* : marked by weakness or decadence ⟨an *effete* civilization⟩ [Latin *effetus,* from *ex-* + *fetus* "fruitful"] — **ef·fete·ly** *adv* — **ef·fete·ness** *n*

ef·fi·ca·cious \ˌef-ə-'kā-shəs\ *adj* : having the power to produce a desired effect ⟨an *efficacious* remedy⟩ [Latin *efficax,* from *efficere* "to bring about"] SYN see EFFECTIVE — **ef·fi·ca·cious·ly** *adv* — **ef·fi·ca·cious·ness** *n*

ef·fi·ca·cy \'ef-i-kə-sē\ *n, pl* **-cies** : power to produce effects : EFFECTIVENESS ⟨a medicine of tested *efficacy*⟩

ef·fi·cien·cy \i-'fish-ən-sē\ *n, pl* **-cies 1** : the quality or degree of being efficient **2 a** : efficient operation **b** : effective operation as measured by a comparison of production with cost (as in energy, time, and money) **3** : the ratio of the useful energy delivered by a dynamic system (as a machine) to the energy supplied to it

efficiency engineer *n* : one who analyzes methods, procedures, and jobs in order to secure maximum efficiency

ef·fi·cient \i-'fish-ənt\ *adj* : capable of producing desired effects ⟨an *efficient* worker⟩; *esp* : productive without waste ⟨*efficient* machinery⟩ [Latin *efficiens,* from *efficere* "to bring about"] SYN see EFFECTIVE — **ef·fi·cient·ly** *adv*

ef·fi·gy \'ef-ə-jē\ *n, pl* **-gies** : an image or likeness especially of a person: as **a** : a sculptured image on a tomb **b** : a crude figure representing a hated person [Latin *effigies,* from *effingere* "to form", from *ex-* + *fingere* "to shape"]

ef·flo·resce \ˌef-lə-'res\ *vi* **1** : to burst forth or appear as if by flowering **2 a** : to change to a powder from loss of water of crystallization ⟨a salt that *effloresces*⟩ **b** : to form or become covered with a powdery crust ⟨a brick that *effloresces*⟩ [Latin *efflorescere,* from *ex-* + *florescere* "to begin to blossom"]

ef·flo·res·cence \-'res-ns\ *n* **1** : the act, process, period, or result of developing or unfolding **2** : fullness of manifestation : CULMINATION **3** : the process or product of efflorescing chemically **4** : a redness of the skin : ERUPTION — **ef·flo·res·cent** \-nt\ *adj*

ef·flu·ence \'ef-ˌlü-əns; e-'flü-, ə-'\ *n* **1** : something that flows out **2** : an action or process of flowing out [Latin *effluere* "to flow out", from *ex-* + *fluere* "to flow"] — **ef·flu·ent** \-ənt\ *adj or n*

ef·flu·vi·um \e-'flü-vē-əm\ *n, pl* **-via** \-vē-ə\ *or* **-vi·ums** : an invisible emanation; *esp* : an offensive exhalation or smell [Latin, "act of flowing out", from *effluere* "to flow out"]

ef·fort \'ef-ərt, -ˌȯrt\ *n* **1** : conscious exertion of power **2** : a serious attempt : TRY **3** : something produced especially by creative or artistic exertion **4** : effective force as distinguished from the possible resistance called into action by such force [Middle French, from Old French *esfort,* from *esforcier* "to force", from *ex-* "ex-" + *forcier* "to force"] □ SYN EFFORT, EXERTION, PAINS, TROUBLE mean the active use of energy in producing a result. EFFORT stresses the calling up or directing of energy by the conscious will and suggests a single action or attempt; EXERTION suggests sustained, laborious, or exhausting effort; PAINS implies toilsome or solicitous effort; TROUBLE suggests that the effort inconveniences one.

ef·fort·less \'ef-ərt-ləs\ *adj* : showing or requiring little or no effort : EASY — **ef·fort·less·ly** *adv* — **ef·fort·less·ness** *n*

ef·fron·tery \i-'frənt-ə-rē, e-\ *n, pl* **-ter·ies** : shameless boldness : INSOLENCE ⟨had the *effrontery* to deny all guilt⟩ [French *effronterie,* derived from Late Latin *effrons* "shameless", from Latin *ex-* + *frons* "forehead"]

ef·ful·gence \i-'fu̇l-jəns, e-, -'fəl-\ *n* : radiant splendor : BRILLIANCE [Late Latin *effulgentia,* from Latin *effulgēre* "to shine forth", from *ex-* + *fulgēre* "to shine"] — **ef·ful·gent** \-jənt\ *adj*

¹**ef·fuse** \i-'fyüz, e-\ *vb* **1** : to pour out (a liquid) **2** : to give off : RADIATE **3** : to flow out : EMANATE [Latin *effusus,* past participle of *effundere* "to pour out", from *ex-* + *fundere* "to pour"]

²**ef·fuse** \-'fyüs\ *adj* : poured out freely : OVERFLOWING

ef·fu·sion \i-'fyü-zhən, e-\ *n* **1** : an act of effusing **2** : unrestrained expression of words or feelings **3 a** : escape of a fluid from containing vessels (as a blood vessel) **b** : the fluid that escapes

ef·fu·sive \i-'fyü-siv, e-, -ziv\ *adj* **1** : excessively demonstrative or emotional ⟨*effusive* thanks⟩ **2** : characterized or formed by a nonexplosive outpouring of lava — **ef·fu·sive·ly** *adv* — **ef·fu·sive·ness** *n*

eft \'eft\ *n* : NEWT [Old English *efete*]

egad \i-'gad\ *interj* — used as a mild oath [probably euphemism for *oh God*]

egal·i·tar·i·an \i-ˌgal-ə-'ter-ē-ən\ *adj* : asserting, promoting, or marked by egalitarianism [French *égalitaire,* from *égalité* "equality", from Latin *aequalitas,* from *aequalis* "equal"] — **egalitarian** *n*

egal·i·tar·i·an·ism \-ē-ə-ˌniz-əm\ *n* **1** : a belief in human equality especially in social, political, and economic affairs **2** : a social philosophy advocating the removal of social, political and economic inequalities

egest \i-'jest\ *vt* : to rid the body of (waste); *esp* : DEFECATE [Latin *egestus,* past participle of *egerere* "to carry outside, discharge", from *e-* + *gerere* "to carry"] — **eges·tion** \-'jes-chən\ *n* — **eges·tive** \-'jes-tiv\ *adj*

¹**egg** \'eg\ *vt* : to incite to action : URGE — usually used with *on* ⟨bystanders *egged* them on to fight⟩ [Old Norse *eggja*]

²**egg** *n* **1 a** : the hard-shelled reproductive body produced by a bird and especially by domestic poultry **b** : an animal reproductive body consisting of an ovum

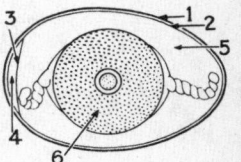

²egg 1a: *1* shell, *2* outer shell membrane, *3* inner shell membrane, *4* air space, *5* albumen or white, *6* yoke

\ə\ **abut**	\ng\ **sing**
\ər\ **further**	\ō\ **bone**
\a\ **mat**	\ȯ\ **saw**
\ā\ **take**	\ȯi\ **coin**
\ä\ **cot, cart**	\th\ **thin**
\au̇\ **out**	\t̲h̲\ **this**
\ch\ **chin**	\ü\ **food**
\e\ **pet**	\u̇\ **foot**
\ē\ **easy**	\y\ **yet**
\g\ **go**	\yü\ **few**
\i\ **tip**	\yu̇\ **cure**
\ī\ **life**	\zh\ **vision**
\j\ **job**	

with its nutritive and protective envelopes and being capable of development into a new individual **c** : OVUM **2** : something resembling an egg **3** : PERSON, INDIVIDUAL ⟨a good *egg*⟩ [Old Norse]

egg·beat·er \'eg-,bēt-ər\ *n* : a rotary beater operated by hand for beating eggs or liquids (as cream)

egg cell *n* : OVUM

egg·head \'eg-,hed\ *n* : INTELLECTUAL, HIGHBROW

egg·nog \-,näg\ *n* : a drink consisting of eggs beaten up with sugar, milk or cream, and often alcoholic liquor

egg·plant \-,plant\ *n* : a widely cultivated perennial herb that is related to the potato and yields edible fruit; *also* : its usually smooth and purple ovoid fruit

¹**egg·shell** \-,shel\ *n* : the hard exterior covering of an egg

²**eggshell** *adj* **1** : being thin and fragile ⟨*eggshell* china⟩ **2** : slightly glossy

egg tooth *n* : a hard sharp prominence on the beak of an unhatched bird or the nose of an unhatched reptile that is used to break through the eggshell

eg·lan·tine \'eg-lən-,tīn, -,tēn\ *n* : SWEETBRIER [Middle French *aiglent*]

ego \'ē-gō\ *n, pl* **egos 1** : the self especially as contrasted with another self or the world **2 a** : EGOTISM 2 **b** : SELF-ESTEEM 1 **3** : the one of the three divisions of the personality in psychoanalytic theory that acts as a go-between between demands of the outside world and basic inner drives — compare ID, SUPEREGO [Latin, "I"]

ego·cen·tric \,ē-gō-'sen-trik\ *adj* : overly concerned with the self; *esp* : SELF-CENTERED, SELFISH — **egocentric** *n*

ego·ism \'ē-gə-,wiz-əm\ *n* **1** : excessive interest in oneself : a self-centered attitude **2** : EGOTISM

ego·ist \'ē-gə-wəst\ *n* : a self-centered person — **ego·is·tic** \,ē-gə-'wis-tik\ *adj* — **ego·is·ti·cal·ly** \-'wis-ti-kə-lē, -klē\ *adv* □ SYN EGOTIST: EGOIST implies a person whose self-centered concentration on his own desires and aspirations excludes interest in others; EGOTIST may indicate a tendency to attract attention and center interest on oneself and one's achievements.

ego·ism \'ē-gə-,tiz-əm\ *n* **1** : too frequent reference (as by use of the word *I*) to oneself **2** : an exaggerated sense of self-importance : CONCEIT [Latin *ego* "I" + English -*tiṣm* (as in *idiotism* "idiocy", from *idiot* + -*ism*)]

ego·tist \'ē-gə-təst\ *n* : a conceited person SYN see EGO-IST — **ego·tis·tic** \,ē-gə-'tis-tik\ *or* **ego·tis·ti·cal** \-'tis-ti-kəl\ *adj* — **ego·tis·ti·cal·ly** \-'tis-ti-kə-lē, -klē\ *adv*

ego trip *n* : an act that satisfies one's ego

egre·gious \i-'grē-jəs\ *adj* : conspicuously bad : FLAGRANT ⟨*egregious* errors⟩ [Latin *egregius* "distinguished", from *e-* + *greg-, grex* "herd"] — **egre·gious·ly** *adv* — **egre·gious·ness** *n* □ ORIGIN English *egregious* comes from Latin *egregius,* which means "distinguished" or "eminent". The Latin word was derived from *e-,* "out of", and *grex* "herd, flock". An egregious person, then, has some quality that sets him or her apart from others. Originally this was a remarkably good quality that placed one above others. In 16th century English, however, *egregious* began to be used for one that was conspicuously bad. This shift to a pejorative sense may have resulted from the ironic use of the original sense. In any case, the pejorative meaning is the one that persists in common use today.

egress \'ē-,gres\ *n* **1** : the act or right of going or coming out **2** : a place or means of going out : EXIT [Latin *egressus,* from *egredi* "to go out", from *e-* + *gradi* "to go"]

egret \'ē-grət, i-'gret, 'ē-,gret, 'eg-rət\ *n* : any of various herons that bear long plumes during the breeding season [Middle French *aigrette*]

Egyp·tian \i-'jip-shən\ *n* **1** : a native or inhabitant of Egypt **2** : the language spoken by the ancient Egyptians from earliest times to about the 3d century A. D. — **Egyptian** *adj*

egret

Egyptian cotton *n* : a fine often somewhat brownish cotton with relatively long fibers that is grown chiefly in Egypt

Egyp·tol·o·gy \,ē-jip-'täl-ə-jē\ *n* : the study of Egyptian antiquities — **Egyp·tol·o·gist** \-jəst\ *n*

eh \'ā, 'e, 'a, 'ai, *also with* h *preceding and/or with nasalization* \ *interj* — used to ask for confirmation or to express inquiry [Middle English *ey*]

ei·der \'īd-ər\ *n* **1** : any of several large northern sea ducks having fine soft down that is used by the female for lining the nest — called also *eider duck* **2** : EIDER-DOWN 1 [derived from Old Norse *æthr*]

ei·der·down \-,daùn\ *n* **1** : the down of the eider **2** : a comforter filled with eiderdown

ei·det·ic \ī-'det-ik\ *adj* : marked by or involving peculiarly vivid recall especially of visual images ⟨an *eidetic* memory⟩ [Greek *eidētikos* "of a form", from *eidos* "form"]

eight \'āt\ *n* **1** : one more than seven; *also* : a symbol representing this — see NUMBER table **2** : the eighth in a set or series **3** : something having eight units or members: as **a** : an 8-oared racing boat or crew **b** : an 8-cylinder engine or automobile [Old English *eahta*] — **eight** *adj or pron*

eight ball *n* **1** : a black pool ball numbered 8 **2** : a pool game in which the eight ball is to be pocketed last — **behind the eight ball** : in a highly disadvantageous position or baffling situation

eigh·teen \ā-'tēn, āt-, 'ā-, 'āt-\ *n* : one more than 17; *also* : a symbol representing this — see NUMBER table [Old English *eahtatīene*] — **eighteen** *adj or pron* — **eigh·teenth** \-'tēnth, -'tēntth\ *adj or n*

eighth \'ātth\ *n, pl* **eighths** \'āts, 'ātths\ : number eight in a countable series — see NUMBER table — **eighth** *adj or adv*

eighth note *n* : a musical note with the time value of one eighth of a whole note

eighty \'āt-ē\ *n, pl* **eight·ies** : ten more than 70; *also* : a symbol representing this — see NUMBER table [Old English *eahtatig*] — **eighty** *adj or pron* — **eight·i·eth** \'āt-ē-əth\ *adj or n*

ein·stei·ni·um \īn-'stī-nē-əm\ *n* : a radioactive element produced artificially — see ELEMENT table [New Latin, from Albert *Einstein*]

¹**ei·ther** \'ē-thər *also* 'ī-\ *adj* **1** : the one and the other of two : EACH ⟨flowers blooming on *either* side of the walk⟩ **2** : the one or the other of two ⟨take *either* road⟩ [Old English *ǣghwæther* "both, each"]

²**either** *pron* : the one or the other

³**either** *conj* — used before the first of two or more words or word groups of which the last is preceded by or to indicate that they represent alternatives ⟨a statement is *either* true or false⟩

⁴**either** *adv* **1** : LIKEWISE 2, MOREOVER — used for emphasis after a negative ⟨not wise or handsome *either*⟩ **2** : as far as that is concerned — used for emphasis after an alternative following a question or conditional clause especially where negation is implied ⟨if their father had come or their mother *either* all would have gone well⟩

ejac·u·late \i-'jak-yə-,lāt\ *vb* **1** : to utter or eject suddenly and vigorously **2** : to eject a fluid and especially semen [Latin *ejaculari* "to throw out", from *e-* + *jaculari* "to throw", from *jaculum* "dart", from *jacere* "to throw"] — **ejac·u·la·to·ry** \-yə-lə-,tōr-ē, -,tȯr-\ *adj*

ejac·u·la·tion \i-,jak-yə-'lā-shən\ *n* **1** : an act or process of ejaculating; *esp* : a sudden discharging of a fluid from a duct **2** : something ejaculated; *esp* : a short sudden emotional utterance (as an exclamation)

eject \i-'jekt\ *vt* **1 a** : to drive out especially by physical force **b** : to evict from property **2** : to throw out or off from within [Latin *ejectus,* past participle of *eicere* "to eject", from *e-* + *jacere* "to throw"] — **ejec·tion** \-'jek-shən\ *n* — **ejec·tor** \-'jek-tər\ *n* □ SYN EJECT, EXPEL, EVICT, OUST mean to drive or force out. EJECT carries a strong implication of throwing or thrusting out from within as a physical action ⟨hot lava *ejected* from a volcano⟩ **EXPEL** stresses a thrusting out or driving away especially permanently ⟨*expelled* from school⟩ **EVICT** chiefly applies to turning out of house and home; **OUST** implies removal or dispossession by power of the law or by compulsion of necessity.

ejection seat *n* : an emergency escape seat for propelling an occupant out and away from an airplane by means of an explosive charge

eke out \ˌē-ˈkaut\ *vt* **1 a** : **SUPPLEMENT** ⟨*eked out* a small income by doing odd jobs⟩ **b** : to make (a supply) last by economy **2** : to make (a living) by difficult or uncertain means [Old English *īecan, ēcan* "to increase, lengthen"]

el \ˈel\ *n* : **ELEVATED RAILROAD**

¹elab·o·rate \i-ˈlab-rət, -ə-rət\ *adj* **1** : planned or carried out with great care ⟨*elaborate* preparations⟩ **2** : marked by complexity, fullness of detail, or ornateness ⟨an *elaborate* design⟩ [Latin *elaboratus,* from *elaborare* "to work out", from *e-* + *laborare* "to work"] — **elab·o·rate·ly** *adv* — **elab·o·rate·ness** *n*

²elab·o·rate \i-ˈlab-ə-ˌrāt\ *vb* **1** : to build up (complex organic compounds) from simple ingredients ⟨a substance *elaborated* by a gland⟩ **2** : to work out in detail : **DEVELOP** ⟨*elaborate* an idea⟩ **3** : to give especially additional details ⟨*elaborate* on a story⟩ — **elab·o·ra·tion** \-ˌlab-ə-ˈrā-shən\ *n* — **elab·o·ra·tive** \-ˈlab-ə-ˌrāt-iv\ *adj*

élan \ā-ˈlän\ *n* : vigorous spirit or enthusiasm [French]

eland \ˈē-lənd\ *n* : either of two large African antelopes resembling oxen and having short spirally twisted horns in both sexes [Afrikaans, "elk", from Dutch]

elapse \i-ˈlaps\ *vi* : to slip or glide away : **PASS** ⟨years *elapsed*⟩ [Latin *elapsus,* past participle of *elabi* "to elapse", from *e-* + *labi* "to slip"]

elas·mo·branch \i-ˈlaz-mə-ˌbrangk\ *n, pl* **-branchs** : any of a class (Chondrichthyes) of fishes (as a shark or ray) with skeletons of cartilage and with platelike gills [Greek *elasmos* "metal plate" + Latin *branchia* "gill"] — **elasmobranch** *adj*

¹elas·tic \i-ˈlas-tik\ *adj* **1 a** : capable of recovering shape or size after being stretched, pressed, or squeezed together : **SPRINGY** ⟨sponges are *elastic*⟩ **b** : capable of indefinite expansion — used of a gas **2** : able to recover quickly especially from depression or fatigue ⟨a youthful, *elastic* spirit⟩ **3** : **FLEXIBLE, ADAPTABLE** ⟨a plan *elastic* enough to be changed at any time⟩ [Late Greek *elastos* "ductile, beaten", from Greek *elaunein* "to beat out"] — **elas·ti·cal·ly** \-ti-kə-lē, -klē\ *adv* □ **SYN ELASTIC, RESILIENT, BUOYANT** mean quick to recover from depression or a setback. **ELASTIC** may indicate an ability to recover quickly from discouragement or dejection ⟨an *elastic* power of throwing off painful memories⟩ **RESILIENT** may stress speed of return to usual good or high spirits after strain, depression, or setback ⟨the *resilient* energy of the storm-wracked villagers⟩ **BUOYANT** may stress a lightness of spirit incapable of lasting dejection.

²elastic *n* **a** : an elastic fabric usually made of yarns containing rubber **b** : something made from elastic fabric **2** : easily stretched rubber; *esp* : a rubber band

elas·tic·i·ty \i-ˌlas-ˈtis-ət-ē, ˌē-ˈlas-\ *n, pl* **-ties** : the quality or state of being elastic : **RESILIENCE, ADAPTABILITY**

elas·ti·cized \i-ˈlas-tə-ˌsīzd\ *adj* : made with elastic thread or inserts

elas·to·mer \i-ˈlas-tə-mər\ *n* : any of various elastic substances resembling rubber [*elastic* + *-o-* + Greek *meros* "part"] — **elas·to·mer·ic** \i-ˌlas-tə-ˈmer-ik\ *adj*

elate \i-ˈlāt\ *vt* : to fill with joy or pride [Latin *elatus,* past participle of *efferre* "to carry out, elevate", from *e-* + *ferre* "to carry"]

elat·ed \i-ˈlāt-əd\ *adj* : marked by high spirits : **EXULTANT** ⟨*elated* over the victory⟩ — **elat·ed·ly** *adv* — **elat·ed·ness** *n*

el·a·ter \ˈel-ət-ər\ *n* : **CLICK BEETLE** [Greek *elatēr* "driver", from *elaunein* "to beat out, drive"]

ela·tion \i-ˈlā-shən\ *n* : the quality or state of being elated ⟨alternating moods of *elation* and despair⟩

E layer *n* : a layer of the ionosphere that occurs at about 100 kilometers above the earth's surface and is capable of reflecting radio waves

¹el·bow \ˈel-ˌbō\ *n* **1 a** : the joint of the arm; *also* : the outer curve of a bent arm **b** : a corresponding joint in the front limb of an animal **2** : something resembling an elbow; *esp* : an angular pipe fitting [Old English *elboga*]

²elbow *vb* **1** : to push or shove aside with the elbow : **JOSTLE** **2** : to force or advance by or as if by pushing with the elbow ⟨*elbowed* their way through the crowd⟩

elbow grease *n* : energy vigorously exerted especially in physical labor

el·bow·room \-ˌrüm, -ˌrùm\ *n* **1** : room for moving the elbows freely **2** : enough space for work or operation

¹el·der \ˈel-dər\ *n* : any of a genus of shrubs or trees of the honeysuckle family with flat clusters of small white or pink flowers and black or red drupes resembling berries [Old English *ellærn*]

²elder *adj* : of earlier birth or greater age : **OLDER** [Old English *ieldra,* comparative of *eald* "old"]

³elder *n* **1** : one who is older : **SENIOR** **2** : a person having authority by virtue of age and experience ⟨the village *elders*⟩ **3** : any of various church officers — **el·der·ship** \-ˌship\ *n*

el·der·ber·ry \ˈel-dər-ˌber-ē, -də-\ *n* **1** : the edible fruit of an elder **2** : **¹ELDER**

el·der·ly \ˈel-dər-lē\ *adj* **1** : rather old; *esp* : past middle age **2** : of, relating to, or characteristic of later life ⟨*elderly* pursuits⟩ — **el·der·li·ness** *n*

elder statesman *n* : an eminent senior member of a group or organization; *esp* : a retired statesman who unofficially advises current leaders

el·dest \ˈel-dəst\ *adj* : **OLDEST**

El Dorado \ˌel-də-ˈräd-ō, -ˈrad-\ *n* **1** : a city or country of fabulous riches held by 16th century explorers to exist in South America **2** : a place of great wealth, abundance, or opportunity [Spanish, literally, "the gilded one"]

ele·cam·pane \ˌel-i-ˌkam-ˈpān\ *n* : a coarse yellow-flowered European herb related to the daisies and naturalized in the United States [Medieval Latin *enula campana,* literally, "field elecampane", from *enula* "elecampane" + *campana* "of the field"]

¹elect \i-ˈlekt\ *adj* **1** : carefully selected : **CHOSEN** **2** : chosen for salvation through divine mercy **3** : chosen for office or position but not yet installed ⟨president-*elect*⟩ [Latin *electus* "choice", from *eligere* "to select", from *e-* + *legere* "to choose"]

²elect *n pl* : a carefully chosen group — usually used with *the*

³elect *vb* **1** : to select usually by vote for an office, position, or membership **2** : to choose especially by preference

elec·tion \i-ˈlek-shən\ *n* **1 a** : an act or process of electing; *esp* : the process of voting to choose a person for office **b** : the fact of being elected **2** : predestination to salvation **3** : the power or privilege of making a choice

elec·tion·eer \i-ˌlek-shə-ˈniər\ *vi* : to work for the election of a candidate or party

¹elec·tive \i-ˈlek-tiv\ *adj* **1** : chosen by election ⟨an *elective* official⟩ **2** : filled by a person who is elected ⟨the presidency is an *elective* office⟩ **3** : of, relating to, or based on elections ⟨an *elective* government⟩ **4** : followed or taken by choice : not required ⟨an *elective* course in school⟩ — **elec·tive·ly** *adv* — **elec·tive·ness** *n*

²elective *n* : an elective course or subject in school

eland

¹elbow 2

\ə\ abut	\ng\ sing
\ər\ further	\ō\ bone
\a\ mat	\ò\ saw
\ā\ take	\òi\ coin
\ä\ cot, cart	\th\ thin
\au\ out	\th\ this
\ch\ chin	\ü\ food
\e\ pet	\u\ foot
\ē\ easy	\y\ yet
\g\ go	\yü\ few
\i\ tip	\yu\ cure
\ī\ life	\zh\ vision
\j\ job	

elec·tor \i-'lek-tər, -,tȯr\ *n* **1** : one qualified to vote in an election **2 a** : one of the German princes entitled to take part in choosing the Holy Roman emperor **b** : a member of the electoral college in the United States

elec·tor·al \i-'lek-tə-rəl, -trəl\ *adj* : of or relating to an election or electors

electoral college *n* : a body of electors; *esp* : one that elects the president and vice-president of the United States

elec·tor·ate \i-'lek-tə-rət, -trət\ *n* **1** : the territory or jurisdiction of a German elector **2** : a body of people entitled to vote

electr- *or* **electro-** *combining form* **1 a** : electricity ⟨*electro*meter⟩ **b** : electric ⟨*electro*de⟩ **c** : electric and ⟨*electro*chemical⟩ **2** : electron ⟨*electro*valence⟩

¹elec·tric \i-'lek-trik\ *adj or* **elec·tri·cal** \-tri-kəl\ **1** : of, relating to, operated by, or produced by electricity **2** : EXCITING, THRILLING ⟨an *electric* performance⟩ [New Latin *electricus* "produced from amber by friction, electric", from Latin *electrum* "amber", from Greek *ēlektron*] — **elec·tri·cal·ly** \-tri-kə-lē, -klē\ *adv*
□ ORIGIN Only in modern times has practical use been made of electricity, but some electrical phenomena have been known since ancient times. Certain philosophers of ancient Greece found that, by rubbing amber with a piece of cloth, they could enable the amber to pick up light objects, such as feathers. In the 17th century, students of natural science began to discover that other natural phenomena were related to the effect of friction on amber. The word *electric,* used to refer to such phenomena, is derived from the Greek word for amber, *ēlektron.*

²electric *n* : something operated by electricity; *esp* : an electric automobile

electrical engineering *n* : engineering that deals with the practical applications of electricity — **electrical engineer** *n*

electrical storm *n* : THUNDERSTORM — called also *electric storm*

electrical transcription *n* **1** : a phonograph record or tape recording especially designed for use in radiobroadcasting **2** : a radio program broadcast from an electrical transcription

electric chair *n* **1** : a chair used in legal electrocution **2** : the penalty of death by electrocution

electric eel *n* : a large South American eel-shaped fish able to give a severe electric shock

electric eye *n* : PHOTOELECTRIC CELL

elec·tri·cian \i-,lek-'trish-ən\ *n* : one who installs, operates, or repairs electrical equipment

elec·tric·i·ty \i-,lek-'tris-ət-ē, -'tris-tē\ *n* **1 a** : a fundamental phenomenon of nature consisting of negative and positive kinds composed respectively of electrons and protons, observable in the attractions and repulsions of bodies electrified by friction and in natural phenomena (as lightning), and usually utilized as a source of energy in the form of electric currents **b** : electric current **2** : a science that deals with the phenomena and laws of electricity **3** : keen contagious excitement

electric ray *n* : any of various round-bodied short-tailed rays of warm seas able to give a severe electric shock

elec·tri·fy \i-'lek-trə-,fī\ *vt* **-fied; -fy·ing 1 a** : to charge with electricity **b** (1) : to equip for use of electric power (2) : to supply with electric power **2** : to excite intensely or suddenly : THRILL ⟨the acrobat *electrified* the audience⟩ — **elec·tri·fi·ca·tion** \i-,lek-trə-fə-'kā-shən\ *n*

elec·tro·car·dio·gram \i-,lek-trō-'kärd-ē-ə-,gram\ *n* : the tracing made by an electrocardiograph

elec·tro·car·dio·graph \-,graf\ *n* : an instrument for recording the changes of electrical potential occurring during the heartbeat — **elec·tro·car·dio·graph·ic** \-,kärd-ē-ə-'graf-ik\ *adj* — **elec·tro·car·dio·graph·i·cal·**

ly \-'graf-i-kə-lē, -klē\ *adv* — **elec·tro·car·di·og·ra·phy** \-ē-'äg-rə-fē\ *n*

elec·tro·chem·is·try \i-,lek-trō-'kem-ə-strē\ *n* : a science that deals with the relation of electricity to chemical changes and with the mutual conversion of chemical and electrical energy — **elec·tro·chem·i·cal** \-'kem-i-kəl\ *adj* — **elec·tro·chem·i·cal·ly** \-i-kə-lē, -klē\ *adv*

elec·tro·con·vul·sive therapy \i-,lek-trō-kən-'vəl-siv-\ *n* : ELECTROSHOCK THERAPY

elec·tro·cute \i-'lek-trə-,kyüt\ *vt* : to kill by electric shock; *esp* : to execute (a criminal) in this way [*electr-* + *-cute* (as in *execute*)] — **elec·tro·cu·tion** \i-,lek-trə-'kyü-shən\ *n*

elec·trode \i-'lek-,trōd\ *n* : a conductor (as a metal or carbon) used to establish electrical contact with a nonmetallic part of a circuit (as in a storage battery, electron tube, or arc lamp)

elec·tro·de·pos·it \i-,lek-trō-di-'päz-ət\ *vt* : to deposit (as metal or rubber) by electrolysis — **elec·tro·dep·o·si·tion** \-,dep-ə-'zish-ən, -,dē-pə-\ *n*

elec·tro·dy·nam·ics \-dī-'nam-iks\ *n* : physics that deals with the effects arising from the interactions of electric currents with magnets, with other currents, or with themselves — **elec·tro·dy·nam·ic** \-ik\ *adj*

elec·tro·en·ceph·a·lo·gram \-en-'sef-ə-lō-,gram\ *n* : the tracing of brain waves that is made by an electroencephalograph

elec·tro·en·ceph·a·lo·graph \-,graf\ *n* : an apparatus for detecting and recording brain waves — **elec·tro·en·ceph·a·lo·graph·ic** \-en-,sef-ə-lō-'graf-ik\ *adj* — **elec·tro·en·ceph·a·log·ra·phy** \-,sef-ə-'läg-rə-fē\ *n*

elec·trol·y·sis \i-,lek-'träl-ə-səs\ *n* **1 a** : the producing of chemical changes by passage of an electric current through an electrolyte with the ions carrying the current by migrating to the electrodes where they may form new substances that are given off as gases or deposited as solids **b** : subjection to this action **2** : the destruction of hair roots with an electric current

elec·tro·lyte \i-'lek-trə-,līt\ *n* **1** : a nonmetallic electric conductor in which current is carried by the movement of ions **2** : a substance that when dissolved in a suitable solvent or when fused becomes an ionic conductor

elec·tro·lyt·ic \i-,lek-trə-'lit-ik\ *adj* : of or relating to electrolysis or an electrolyte — **elec·tro·lyt·i·cal·ly** \-i-kə-lē, -klē\ *adv*

elec·tro·lyze \i-'lek-trə-,līz\ *vt* : to subject to chemical electrolysis

elec·tro·mag·net \i-,lek-trō-'mag-nət\ *n* : a core of magnetic material (as soft iron) surrounded by a coil of wire through which an electric current is passed to magnetize the core

electromagnetic radiation *n* : a series of electromagnetic waves

electromagnetic spectrum *n* : the entire range of wavelengths or frequencies of electromagnetic waves extending from gamma rays to the longest radio waves and including visible light

electromagnetic wave *n* : a wave (as a radio wave, infrared wave, wave of visible light, or X ray) that travels at the speed of light and that consists of an associated magnetic and electric effect

elec·tro·mag·ne·tism \i-,lek-trō-'mag-nə-,tiz-əm\ *n* **1** : magnetism developed by a current of electricity **2** : physical science that deals with the physical relations between electricity and magnetism — **elec·tro·mag·net·ic** \-mag-'net-ik\ *adj* — **elec·tro·mag·net·i·cal·ly** \-'net-i-kə-lē, -klē\ *adv*

elec·tro·me·chan·i·cal \i-,lek-trō-mə-'kan-i-kəl\ *adj* : of, relating to, or being a mechanical process or device put into motion or controlled electrically

elec·trom·e·ter \i-,lek-'träm-ət-ər\ *n* : an instrument for detecting or measuring electric-potential differ-

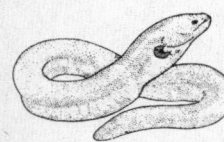

electric eel

ences or ionizing radiations — **elec·tro·met·ric** \i-ˌlek-trə-ˈme-trik\ *adj*

elec·tro·mo·tive force \i-ˌlek-trə-ˈmōt-iv-\ *n* : the work per unit charge required to carry a positive charge around a closed path (as a complete circuit) in an electric field — abbreviation *emf*

elec·tron \i-ˈlek-ˌträn\ *n* : a negatively charged elementary particle that revolves around the nucleus of an atom and that is of the kind of particles whose flow along a conductor is an electric current

elec·tro·neg·a·tive \i-ˌlek-trō-ˈneg-ət-iv\ *adj* **1** : charged with negative electricity **2** : capable of acting as the negative electrode of a voltaic cell **3** : having a tendency to attract electrons — **elec·tro·neg·a·tiv·i·ty** \-ˌneg-ə-ˈtiv-ət-ē\ *n*

electron gun *n* : the part of a cathode-ray tube that produces, accelerates, and focuses a stream of electrons

¹**elec·tron·ic** \i-ˌlek-ˈträn-ik\ *adj* **1** : of or relating to electrons **2** : of, relating to, or utilizing devices constructed or working by principles of electronics — **elec·tron·i·cal·ly** \-ˈträn-i-kə-lē, -klē\ *adv*

²**electronic** *n* : an electronic device or circuit

electronic mail *n* : messages sent and received electronically (as between computer terminals linked by telephone lines)

elec·tron·ics \-ˈträn-iks\ *n* : a branch of physics that deals with the emission, behavior, and effects of electrons (as in electron tubes and transistors) and with electronic devices

electron micrograph *n* : a micrograph made with an electron microscope

electron microscope *n* : an instrument in which a beam of electrons is used to produce an enlarged image of a minute object in a way similar to that in which light is used to form the image in an ordinary microscope

electron tube *n* : a device in which a controlled electron current flows through a vacuum or a gas within a sealed glass or metal container and which has various common uses (as in radio and television)

electron volt *n* : a unit of energy equal to the energy gained by an electron in passing from a point of low potential to a point one volt higher in potential that is equivalent to 1.60 x 10⁻¹⁹ joule

elec·tro·pho·re·sis \i-ˌlek-trə-fə-ˈrē-səs\ *n* : the movement of suspended particles through a fluid under the action of an electromotive force applied to electrodes in contact with the suspension [Greek *phorein* "to carry"] — **elec·tro·pho·ret·ic** \-ˈret-ik\ *adj*

elec·tro·plate \i-ˈlek-trə-ˌplāt\ *vt* : to cover with a coating (as of metal or rubber) by means of electrolysis

elec·tro·pos·i·tive \i-ˌlek-trō-ˈpäz-ət-iv, -ˈpäz-tiv\ *adj* **1 a** : charged with positive electricity **b** : capable of acting as the positive electrode of a voltaic cell **2** : having a tendency to release electrons (an *electropositive* atom)

elec·tro·scope \i-ˈlek-trə-ˌskōp\ *n* : any of various instruments for detecting the presence of an electric charge on a body, for determining whether the charge is positive or negative, or for indicating and measuring intensity of radiation

elec·tro·shock therapy \-ˌshäk-\ *n* : the treatment of mental disorder by the induction of coma with an electric current — called also *electroconvulsive therapy, electroshock*

elec·tro·stat·ic \i-ˌlek-trə-ˈstat-ik\ *adj* : of or relating to static electricity or electrostatics — **elec·tro·stat·i·cal·ly** \-ˈstat-i-kə-lē, -klē\ *adv*

electrostatic generator *n* : an apparatus for the production of electrical discharges at high voltage commonly consisting of an insulated hollow conducting sphere on which is accumulated large quantities of electric charge

electrostatic precipitator *n* : an electrostatic device in a chimney flue that removes particles from escaping gases

elec·tro·stat·ics \i-ˌlek-trə-ˈstat-iks\ *n* : physics that deals with phenomena due to attractions or repulsions of electric charges but not dependent upon their motion

elec·tro·ther·mal \-ˈthər-məl\ *or* **elec·tro·ther·mic** \-mik\ *adj* : relating to the generation of heat by electricity

elec·tro·type \i-ˈlek-trə-ˌtīp\ *n* : a plate for use in printing made by electroplating — **elec·tro·typ·er** \-ˌtī-pər\ *n*

elec·tro·va·lence \i-ˌlek-trō-ˈvā-ləns\ *or* **elec·tro·va·len·cy** \-lən-sē\ *n* : valence characterized by the transfer of electrons from one atom to another with the formation of ions; *also* : the number of charges acquired by an atom by the loss or gain of electrons — **elec·tro·va·lent** \-lənt\ *adj*

elec·trum \i-ˈlek-trəm\ *n* : a naturally occurring pale yellow alloy of gold and silver [Latin, "amber, electrum", from Greek *ēlektron*]

elec·tu·ary \i-ˈlek-chə-ˌwer-ē\ *n, pl* **-ar·ies** : a medicinal preparation made with honey or syrup [Latin *electuarium*]

el·ee·mos·y·nary \ˌel-i-ˈmäs-n-ˌer-ē, -ˈmäz-\ *adj* : of, relating to, or supported by charity [Medieval Latin *eleemosynarius,* from Late Latin *eleemosyna* "alms", from Greek *eleēmosynē* "mercy, alms", from *eleein* "to have mercy"]

el·e·gance \ˈel-i-gəns\ *n* **1** : refined gracefulness **2** : tasteful richness of design or decoration

el·e·gan·cy \-gən-sē\ *n, pl* **-cies** : ELEGANCE

el·e·gant \ˈel-i-gənt\ *adj* **1** : marked by elegance **2** : EXCELLENT, FIRST-RATE [Latin *elegans*] — **el·e·gant·ly** *adv*

el·e·gy \ˈel-ə-jē\ *n, pl* **-gies** **1** : a poem expressing sorrow for one who is dead **2** : a poem that is sad or mournful [Latin *elegia,* from Greek *elegeia,* from *elegos* "song of mourning"] — **el·e·gi·ac** \ˌel-ə-ˈjī-ək, i-ˈlē-jē-ˌak\ *adj* — **el·e·gize** \ˈel-ə-ˌjīz\ *vb*

el·e·ment \ˈel-ə-mənt\ *n* **1 a** : one of the four substances air, water, fire, or earth formerly believed to compose the physical universe **b** *pl* : forces of nature; *esp* : stormy or cold weather **c** : the state or sphere natural or suited to a person or thing **2** : a constituent part: as **a** *pl* : the simplest principles of a subject of study : RUDIMENTS **b** (1) : a generator of a geometric figure (as a cone) (2) : a member of a mathematical set (3) : one of the numbers that make up a matrix or determinant **c** : any of more than 100 fundamental substances that consist of atoms of only one kind (gold and carbon are *elements*) **d** : a distinct part of a composite device **e** : a subdivision of a military unit **3** *pl* : the bread and wine used in the sacrament of Communion [Latin *elementum*] □ SYN COMPONENT, CONSTITUENT, INGREDIENT: ELEMENT applies to anything that is a part of a compound or complex whole and often connotes irreducible simplicity; COMPONENT and CONSTITUENT are often interchangeable in designating any of the substances or qualities that enter into a compound or complex product; COMPONENT applies to one of the parts that make up a compounded or complex thing (the *components* of a carburetor) CONSTITUENT implies the essential or formative character of the parts (atoms are the *constituents* of molecules) INGREDIENT is applicable to any substance that combines with others to form something else and may also apply to intangible matters (*ingredients* of a chocolate cake) (*ingredients* of successful comedy)

\ə\	abut	\ng\	sing
\ər\	further	\ō\	bone
\a\	mat	\o͝\	saw
\ā\	take	\oi\	coin
\ä\	cot, cart	\th\	thin
\au̇\	out	\th\	this
\ch\	chin	\ü\	food
\e\	pet	\u̇\	foot
\ē\	easy	\y\	yet
\g\	go	\yü\	few
\i\	tip	\yu̇\	cure
\ī\	life	\zh\	vision
\j\	job		

CHEMICAL ELEMENTS

Those weights shown in parentheses are for the most stable or best known isotopes

ELEMENT & SYMBOL	ATOMIC NUMBER	ATOMIC WEIGHT (C = 12)
actinium (Ac)	89	227.0278
aluminum (Al)	13	26.89154
americium (Am)	95	(243)
antimony (Sb)	51	121.75
argon (Ar)	18	39.948
arsenic (As)	33	74.9216
astatine (At)	85	(210)
barium (Ba)	56	137.33
berkelium (Bk)	97	(247)
beryllium (Be)	4	9.01218
bismuth (Bi)	83	208.9804
boron (B)	5	10.81
bromine (Br)	35	79.904
cadmium (Cd)	48	112.41
calcium (Ca)	20	40.08
californium (Cf)	98	(251)
carbon (C)	6	12.011
cerium (Ce)	58	140.12
cesium (Cs)	55	132.9054
chlorine (Cl)	17	35.453
chromium (Cr)	24	51.996
cobalt (Co)	27	58.9332
columbium (Cb)	(see niobium)	
copper (Cu)	29	63.546
curium (Cm)	96	(247)
dysprosium (Dy)	66	162.50
einsteinium (Es)	99	(254)
erbium (Er)	68	167.26
europium (Eu)	63	151.96
fermium (Fm)	100	(257)
fluorine (F)	9	18.998403
francium (Fr)	87	(223)
gadolinium (Gd)	64	157.25
gallium (Ga)	31	69.72
germanium (Ge)	32	72.59
gold (Au)	79	196.9665
hafnium (Hf)	72	178.49
helium (He)	2	4.00260
holmium (Ho)	67	164.9304
hydrogen (H)	1	1.0079
indium (In)	49	114.82
iodine (I)	53	126.9045
iridium (Ir)	77	192.22
iron (Fe)	26	55.847
krypton (Kr)	36	83.80
lanthanum (La)	57	138.9055
lawrencium (Lr)	103	(260)
lead (Pb)	82	207.2
lithium (Li)	3	6.941
lutetium (Lu)	71	174.967
magnesium (Mg)	12	24.305
manganese (Mn)	25	54.9380
mendelevium (Md)	101	(258)
mercury (Hg)	80	200.59
molybdenum (Mo)	42	95.94
neodymium (Nd)	60	144.24
neon (Ne)	10	20.179
neptunium (Np)	93	237.0482
nickel (Ni)	28	58.69
niobium (Nb)	41	92.9064
nitrogen (N)	7	14.0067
nobelium (No)	102	(259)
osmium (Os)	76	190.2
oxygen (O)	8	15.9994
palladium (Pd)	46	106.42

ELEMENT & SYMBOL	ATOMIC NUMBER	ATOMIC WEIGHT (C = 12)
phosphorus (P)	15	30.97376
platinum (Pt)	78	195.08
plutonium (Pu)	94	(244)
polonium (Po)	84	(210)
potassium (K)	19	39.0983
praseodymium (Pr)	59	140.9077
promethium (Pm)	61	(145)
protactinium (Pa)	91	231.0359
radium (Ra)	88	226.0254
radon (Rn)	86	(222)
rhenium (Re)	75	186.207
rhodium (Rh)	45	102.9055
rubidium (Rb)	37	85.4678
ruthenium (Ru)	44	101.07
samarium (Sm)	62	150.36
scandium (Sc)	21	44.9559
selenium (Se)	34	78.96
silicon (Si)	14	28.0855
silver (Ag)	47	107.868
sodium (Na)	11	22.98977
strontium (Sr)	38	87.62
sulfur (S)	16	32.06
tantalum (Ta)	73	180.9479
technetium (Tc)	43	(99)
tellurium (Te)	52	127.60
terbium (Tb)	65	158.9254
thallium (Tl)	81	204.383
thorium (Th)	90	232.0381
thulium (Tm)	69	168.9342
tin (Sn)	50	118.69
titanium (Ti)	22	47.88
tungsten (W)	74	183.85
unnilhexium (Unh)	106	
unnilpentium (Unp)	105	
unnilquadium (Unq)	104	
uranium (U)	92	238.0289
vanadium (V)	23	50.9415
wolfram (W)	(see tungsten)	
xenon (Xe)	54	131.29
ytterbium (Yb)	70	173.04
yttrium (Y)	39	88.9059
zinc (Zn)	30	65.38
zirconium (Zr)	40	91.225

el·e·men·tal \ˌel-ə-'ment-l\ *adj* **1 a** : of, relating to, or being an element; *esp* : existing as an uncombined chemical element **b** : of, relating to, or being an ultimate constituent : FUNDAMENTAL **c** : ELEMENTARY 1a **d** : forming an integral part : INHERENT **2** : of, relating to, or resembling a great force of nature — **el·e·men·tal·ly** \-l-ē\ *adv*

el·e·men·ta·ry \ˌel-ə-'ment-ə-rē, -'men-trē\ *adj* **1 a** : of or relating to the simplest principles of something (as a subject) **b** : of or relating to an elementary school 〈an *elementary* curriculum〉 **2** : ELEMENTAL 1a

elementary particle *n* : any of the ultimate constituents (as the electron, proton, or neutron) of matter

elementary school *n* : a school usually including the first six or sometimes the first four or eight grades

el·e·phant \'el-ə-fənt\ *n* : any of several huge thickset nearly hairless mammals having the snout prolonged as a trunk and two upper incisors developed into long outward-curving pointed tusks which furnish ivory : **a** : one with large ears that occurs in tropical Africa **b** : one with relatively small ears that occurs in southeastern Asia [Latin *elephantus,* from Greek *elephas*]

elephant bird *n* : a gigantic extinct flightless bird of Madagascar

el·e·phan·ti·a·sis \ˌel-ə-fən-'tī-ə-səs, -ˌfan-\ *n, pl* **-a·ses** \-ə-ˌsēz\ : enlargement and thickening of tissues

elephant a, b: *1* Asian, 2 African

caused by obstruction (as by filarial worms) of vessels that carry lymph [Latin, a kind of leprosy, from Greek, from *elephas* "elephant"]

el·e·phan·tine \,el-ə-'fan-,tēn, -,tīn, 'el-ə-fən-\ *adj* **1** : of or relating to an elephant **2 a** : **IMMENSE** 1, **HUGE** **b** : lacking grace or ease : **PONDEROUS**

el·e·vate \'el-ə-,vāt\ *vt* **1** : to lift up : **RAISE** **2** : to raise in rank or status : **EXALT** **3** : to improve morally, intellectually, or culturally **4** : to raise the spirits of : **ELATE** [Latin *elevare,* from *e-* + *levare* "to raise"]

el·e·vat·ed \-,vāt-əd\ *adj* **1** : raised especially above the ground ⟨an *elevated* freeway⟩ **2 a** : being on a high plane morally or intellectually ⟨an *elevated* mind⟩ **b** : **FORMAL, DIGNIFIED** ⟨*elevated* diction⟩

elevated railroad *n* : a railroad supported by a structure of trestles and girders high enough to permit movement of traffic underneath — called also *elevated railway*

el·e·va·tion \,el-ə-'vā-shən\ *n* **1** : the height to which something is elevated: as **a** : the angular distance of a celestial object above the horizon **b** : the degree to which a gun is aimed above the horizon **c** : the height above sea level : **ALTITUDE** **2** : an act or instance of elevating **3 a** : something that is elevated **b** : an elevated place or station **4** : the quality or state of being elevated **5** : a scale drawing showing a vertical section (as of a building) **SYN** see **HEIGHT**

el·e·va·tor \'el-ə-,vāt-ər\ *n* **1 a** : an endless belt or chain conveyor with cleats, scoops, or buckets for raising material **b** : a cage or platform and its hoisting machinery for conveying something to different levels **c** : a building for elevating, storing, discharging, and sometimes processing grain **2** : a movable airfoil usually attached to the tail plane of an airplane for producing motion up or down

elev·en \i-'lev-ən\ *n* **1** : one more than 10; *also* : a symbol representing this — see **NUMBER** table **2** : the 11th in a set or series **3** : something having 11 units or members [Old English *endleofan*] — **eleven** *adj or pron* — **elev·enth** \-ənth, -əntth\ *n* — **eleventh** *adj or adv*

eleventh hour *n* : the latest possible time ⟨was saved at the *eleventh hour*⟩

el·e·von \'el-ə-,vän\ *n* : an airplane control surface that combines the functions of elevator and aileron [*elev*ator + ail*eron*]

elf \'elf\ *n, pl* **elves** \'elvz\ : a small legendary humanlike being [Old English *ælf*] — **elf·ish** *adj* — **elf·ish·ly** \'el-fish-lē\ *adv*

elf·in \'el-fən\ *adj* **1** : of or relating to an elf or elves **2** : resembling an elf; *esp* : having a strange beauty or charm

elic·it \i-'lis-ət\ *vt* : to draw forth or bring out often by skillful questioning or discussion ⟨*elicit* the truth from an unwilling witness⟩ [Latin *elicitus,* past participle of *elicere* "to elicit", from *e-* + *lacere* "to allure"] — **elic·i·ta·tion** \i-,lis-ə-'tā-shən\ *n* — **elic·i·tor** \i-'lis-ət-ər\ *n*

elide \i-'līd\ *vt* **1** : to suppress or alter (as a vowel) by elision **2** : to leave out of consideration : **IGNORE** [Latin *elidere* "to strike out", from *e-* + *laedere* "to injure by striking"]

el·i·gi·ble \'el-ə-jə-bəl\ *adj* **1** : qualified to be chosen or to serve ⟨*eligible* candidates for office⟩ **2** : having a right to something : **ENTITLED** ⟨*eligible* for benefits⟩ [Late Latin *eligibilis,* from Latin *eligere* "to choose"] — **el·i·gi·bil·i·ty** \,el-i-jə-'bil-ət-ē\ *n* — **eligible** *n* — **el·i·gi·bly** \'el-i-jə-blē\ *adv*

elim·i·nate \i-'lim-ə-,nāt\ *vt* **1 a** : to cast out or get rid of : **REMOVE** **b** : to set aside as unimportant : **IGNORE** **2** : to expel (as waste) from the living body **3** : to cause (a variable) to disappear by combining two or more equations [Latin *eliminare,* from *e-* + *limen* "threshold"] — **elim·i·na·tion** \i-,lim-ə-'nā-shən\ *n* — **elim·i·**

na·tive \i-'lim-ə-,nāt-iv\ *adj* — **elim·i·na·tor** \-,nāt-ər\ *n*

eli·sion \i-'lizh-ən\ *n* **1 a** : the omission of a final or initial sound of a word ⟨*is* has become *'s* in *there's* by *elision*⟩ **b** : the omission of an unstressed vowel or syllable in a verse to achieve a uniform rhythm **2** : the act or an instance of dropping out or omitting something [Late Latin *elisio,* from Latin *elidere* "to strike out"]

elite \ā-'lēt, i-\ *n* **1 a** : the choice part; *esp* : a socially superior group **b** : a powerful minority group ⟨a power *elite* inside the government⟩ **2** : a typewriter type providing 12 characters to the inch [French *élite,* from Old French *eslite,* from *eslire* "to choose", from Latin *eligere*] — **elite** *adj*

elix·ir \i-'lik-sər\ *n* **1 a** : a substance held to be capable of changing metals into gold **b** : a substance held to be capable of prolonging life indefinitely **c** : **CURE-ALL** **2** : a sweetened usually alcoholic liquid used as a vehicle for medicinal agents [Medieval Latin, from Arabic *al-iksīr* "the elixir"]

Eliz·a·be·than \i-,liz-ə-'bē-thən\ *adj* : of, relating to, or characteristic of Elizabeth I of England or her age — **Elizabethan** *n*

elk \'elk\ *n, pl* **elk** *or* **elks** **1 a** : the largest existing deer of Europe and Asia resembling but not so large as the moose of North America **b** : a large North American deer with curved antlers having many branches — called also *wapiti* **c** : any of various large Asian deer **2** *cap* : a member of a major benevolent and fraternal order [Middle English]

elk 1b

¹ell \'el\ *n* : a former English unit of length for cloth equal to 45 inches (about 1.14 meters) [Old English *eln*]

²ell *n* : an extension at right angles to a building [from the resulting shape like the letter *L*]

el·lipse \i-'lips, e-\ *n* **1** : an elongated circle : **OVAL** **2** : a closed plane curve generated by a point moving in such a way that the sums of its distances from two fixed points is a constant : a conic section that is a closed curve but not a circle [Greek *elleipsis*]

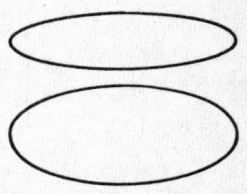

ellipse 1

el·lip·sis \i-'lip-səs, e-\ *n, pl* **-lip·ses** \-'lip-,sēz\ **1** : the omission of one or more words from a phrase when such omission does not affect its meaning ("fire when ready" for "fire when you are ready" is an example of *ellipsis*) **2** : marks or a mark (as . . . or *** or —) used to show the omission especially of letters or words [Latin, from Greek *elleipsis* "ellipsis, ellipse", from *elleipein* "to leave out, fall short", from *en-* "in-" + *leipein* "to leave"]

el·lip·soid \i-'lip-,sȯid, e-\ *n* : a surface all plane sections of which are ellipses or circles; *esp* : **SPHEROID** — **ellipsoid** *or* **el·lip·soi·dal** \i-,lip-'sȯid-l\ *adj*

el·lip·tic \i-'lip-tik, e-\ *or* **el·lip·ti·cal** \-ti-kəl\ *adj* **1** : of, relating to, or shaped like an ellipse **2** : of, relating to, or marked by ellipsis — **el·lip·ti·cal·ly** \-ti-kə-lē, -klē\ *adv*

elm \'elm\ *n* **1** : any of a genus of large trees that have alternate toothed leaves, small flowers without petals, and nearly circular one-seeded winged fruits and are often grown as shade trees **2** : the wood of an elm [Old English]

El Ni·ño \el-'nē-nyō\ *n, pl* **El Niños** : an irregularly occurring flow of unusually warm surface water along the western coast of South America that is accompanied by abnormally high rainfall in usually dry areas and a decline in the regional fish population [Spanish literally, "the child" (i.e., the Christ child); from the appearance of the flow at the Christmas season]

el·o·cu·tion \,el-ə-'kyü-shən\ *n* **1** : the art of effective public speaking **2** : a style of speaking especially in public [Latin *elocutio,* from *eloqui* "to speak out"] — **el·o·cu·tion·ary** \-shə-,ner-ē\ *adj* — **el·o·cu·tion·ist** \-shə-nəst, -shnəst\ *n*

\ə\ abut		\ng\ sing	
\ər\ further		\ō\ bone	
\a\ mat		\ȯ\ saw	
\ā\ take		\ȯi\ coin	
\ä\ cot, cart		\th\ thin	
\au̇\ out		\th\ this	
\ch\ chin		\ü\ food	
\e\ pet		\u̇\ foot	
\ē\ easy		\y\ yet	
\g\ go		\yü\ few	
\i\ tip		\yu̇\ cure	
\ī\ life		\zh\ vision	
\j\ job			

elo·dea \i-'lōd-ē-ə\ *n* : any of a small genus of American aquatic herbs [Greek *helōdēs* "marshy", from *helos* "marsh"]

¹elon·gate \i-'lóng-,gāt\ *vb* 1 : to extend the length of 2 : to grow in length — **elon·ga·tion** \,ē-,lóng-'gā-shən\ *n*

²elongate *adj* 1 : stretched out : LENGTHENED 2 : long in proportion to width

elon·gat·ed *adj* : ELONGATE

elope \i-'lōp\ *vi* 1 : to run away secretly with the intention of getting married usually without parental consent 2 : to slip away : ESCAPE [Anglo-French *aloper*] — **elope·ment** \-mənt\ *n* — **elop·er** *n*

el·o·quence \'el-ə-kwəns\ *n* : discourse marked by force and persuasiveness; *also* : the art or power of using such discourse

el·o·quent \-kwənt\ *adj* 1 : marked by forceful and fluent expression 2 : vividly or movingly expressive or revealing [Middle French, from Latin *eloquens*, from *eloqui* "to speak out", from *e-* + *loqui* "to speak"] — **el·o·quent·ly** *adv*

¹else \'els\ *adv* 1 **a** : in a different manner or place or at a different time ⟨how *else* can we act⟩ ⟨when *else* can they come⟩ **b** : in an additional place or manner or at an additional time 2 : if not : OTHERWISE [Old English *elles*]

²else *adj* : OTHER : **a** : being different in identity ⟨somebody *else*⟩ **b** : being in addition ⟨what *else*⟩

else·where \-,hweər, -,hwaər, -,weər, -,waər\ *adv* : in or to another place

elu·ci·date \i-'lü-sə-,dāt\ *vt* : to make clear or plain : EXPLAIN [Late Latin *elucidare*, from Latin *e-* + *lucidus* "lucid"] — **elu·ci·da·tion** \i-,lü-sə-'dā-shən\ *n* — **elu·ci·da·tive** \i-'lü-sə-,dāt-iv\ *adj* — **elu·ci·da·tor** \-,dāt-ər\ *n*

elude \ē-'lüd\ *vt* : to avoid or escape adroitly; *esp* : to evade by baffling ⟨the identity of the disease *eluded* researchers⟩ [Latin *eludere*, from *e-* + *ludere* "to play"] SYN see EVADE

elu·sion \ē-'lü-zhən\ *n* : an act of eluding : ESCAPE, EVASION [Medieval Latin *elusio*, derived from Latin *eludere* "to elude"]

elu·sive \ē-'lü-siv, -ziv\ *adj* 1 : tending to elude : EVASIVE 2 : hard to comprehend or define ⟨an *elusive* idea⟩ — **elu·sive·ly** *adv* — **elu·sive·ness** *n*

elute \ē-'lüt\ *vt* : to extract especially by means of a solvent [Latin *eluere* "to wash out", from *e-* + *lavere* "to wash"]

elu·vi·al \ē-'lü-vē-əl\ *adj* : of or relating to eluvium

elu·vi·um \-vē-əm\ *n* 1 : fine material produced where found by weathering of rock 2 : fine soil material deposited by wind [New Latin, from Latin *eluere* "to wash out"]

el·ver \'el-vər\ *n* : a young eel [alteration of *eelfare* "migration of eels"]

elves *pl of* ELF

elv·ish \'el-vish\ *adj* : MISCHIEVOUS 2, 3

Ely·si·um \i-'lizh-ē-əm, -'liz-\ *n* 1 : the abode of the good after death in classical mythology 2 : PARADISE 3 [Latin, from Greek *Elysion*] — **Ely·sian** \i-'lizh-ən\ *adj*

el·y·tron \'el-ə-,trän\ *also* **el·y·trum** \-trəm\ *n, pl* **-tra** \-trə\ : one of the thick modified front wings in beetles and some other insects that protect the pair of functional hind wings [Greek *elytron* "sheath, wing cover", from *eilyein* "to roll, wrap"]

em \'em\ *n* 1 : the width of a piece of type about as wide as it is tall used as a unit of measure of printed matter 2 : PICA 2 [from the size of the quad used for the letter *m*]

em- — see EN-

ema·ci·ate \i-'mā-shē-,āt\ *vt* 1 : to cause to lose flesh so as to become very thin 2 : to make feeble [Latin *emaciare*, from *e-* + *macies* "leanness", from *macer* "lean"] — **ema·ci·a·tion** \i-,mā-shē-'ā-shən, -sē-'ā-\ *n*

E-mail \'ē-,māl\ *n* : ELECTRONIC MAIL

em·a·nate \'em-ə-,nāt\ *vb* 1 : to come out from a source 2 : to give out : EMIT [Latin *emanare*, from *e-* + *manare* "to flow"]

em·a·na·tion \,em-ə-'nā-shən\ *n* 1 : the action of emanating 2 : something that emanates or is produced by emanation — **em·a·na·tion·al** \-shnəl, -shən-l\ *adj* — **em·a·na·tive** \'em-ə-,nāt-iv\ *adj*

eman·ci·pate \i-'man-sə-,pāt\ *vt* : to free from restraint, control, or the power of another; *esp* : to free from slavery [Latin *emancipare*, from *e-* + *mancipare* "to transfer ownership of", from *manceps* "purchaser", from *manus* "hand" + *capere* "to take"] — **eman·ci·pa·tion** \i-,man-sə-'pā-shən\ *n* — **eman·ci·pa·tor** \i-'man-sə-,pāt-ər\ *n*

emas·cu·late \i-'mas-kyə-,lāt\ *vt* 1 : CASTRATE 2 : to deprive of vigor or spirit : WEAKEN [Latin *emasculare*, from *e-* + *masculus* "male"] — **emas·cu·la·tion** \i-,mas-kyə-'lā-shən\ *n* — **emas·cu·la·tor** \i-'mas-kyə-,lāt-ər\ *n*

em·balm \im-'bäm, -'bälm\ *vb* 1 : to treat a corpse with special preparations to preserve it from decay 2 : to preserve as if by embalming [Middle French *embaumer*, from Old French *embasmer*, from *en-* + *basme* "balm"] — **em·balm·er** *n* — **em·balm·ment** \-'bäm-mənt, -'bälm-\ *n*

em·bank \im-'bangk\ *vt* : to enclose or confine by an embankment

em·bank·ment \-mənt\ *n* 1 : the action of embanking 2 : a raised bank or wall to carry a roadway or to hold back water

em·bar·go \im-'bär-gō\ *n, pl* **-goes** 1 : an order of a government prohibiting the departure of commercial ships from its ports 2 : legal prohibition or restriction of commerce 3 : IMPEDIMENT 1, STOPPAGE; *esp* : PROHIBITION 2 [Spanish, from *embargar* "to bar"] — **embargo** *vt*

em·bark \im-'bärk\ *vb* 1 : to go or put on board a ship or airplane 2 : to enter into an enterprise or undertaking ⟨*embark* on a career⟩ [Middle French *embarquer*, from Provençal *embarcar*, from *em-* "en-" + *barca* "bark"] — **em·bar·ka·tion** \,em-,bär-'kā-shən\ *n* — **em·bark·ment** \im-'bärk-mənt\ *n*

em·bar·rass \im-'bar-əs\ *vt* 1 : to hinder the freedom of movement of : IMPEDE ⟨soldiers *embarrassed* by heavy packs⟩ 2 **a** : to involve in financial difficulties **b** : to make confused or upset in mind : cause a feeling of uneasiness in : DISCONCERT ⟨unexpected laughter *embarrassed* the speaker⟩ [French *embarrasser*, from Spanish *embarazar*, from Portuguese *embaraçar*] — **em·bar·rass·ing·ly** \-ə-sing-lē\ *adv* □ SYN ABASH, DISCONCERT, DISCOMFIT: EMBARRASS implies an influence or circumstance that checks or constrains one's freedom of action, speech, or choice and causes uneasiness or confusion of mind; ABASH suggests producing feelings of shame, shyness, or unworthiness by suddenly destroying self-confidence; DISCONCERT implies producing uncertainty, hesitancy, or confusion especially through an unexpected discovery or turn of events; DISCOMFIT implies a hampering or frustrating accompanied by confusion.

em·bar·rass·ment \im-'bar-ə-smənt\ *n* 1 : the state of being embarrassed: as **a** : confusion or discomposure of mind **b** : difficulty arising from a lack of money to pay debts 2 **a** : something that embarrasses : IMPEDIMENT **b** : an excessive quantity from which to select — used especially in the phrase *embarrassment of riches*

em·bas·sy \'em-bə-sē\ *n, pl* **-sies** 1 : the function or position of an ambassador 2 : a mission abroad undertaken by an ambassador 3 : a body of diplomatic representatives 4 : the official residence or office of an ambassador [Middle French *ambassee*, of Germanic origin]

em·bat·tle \im-'bat-l\ *vt* **1** : to arrange in battle order : prepare for battle **2** : FORTIFY a

em·bed *or* **im·bed** \im-'bed\ *vb* **1** : to enclose closely in or as if in a surrounding mass : set solidly in or as if in a bed ⟨*embed* a post in concrete⟩ **2** : to become embedded

em·bel·lish \im-'bel-ish\ *vt* **1** : to make beautiful with ornamentation : DECORATE **2** : to heighten the attractiveness of by adding ornamental details [Middle French *embeliss-,* stem of *embelir* "to embellish", from *en-* + *bel* "beautiful"] SYN see ADORN — **em·bel·lish·ment** \-mənt\ *n*

em·ber \'em-bər\ *n* **1** : a glowing piece of coal or wood from a fire; *esp* : such a piece smoldering in ashes **2** *pl* : smoldering remains (as of a fire or a romance) [Old Norse *eimyrja*]

em·ber day \'em-bər-\ *n* : a Wednesday, Friday, or Saturday following the first Sunday in Lent, Whitsunday, September 14, or December 13 and set apart for fasting and prayer [Old English *ymbrendæg,* from *ymbrene* "anniversary" + *dæg* "day"]

em·bez·zle \im-'bez-əl\ *vt* **em·bez·zled; em·bez·zling** \-'bez-ling, -ə-ling\ : to take (property entrusted to one's care) dishonestly for one's own use [Anglo-French *embeseiller,* from Middle French *en-* + *besillier* "to destroy"] — **em·bez·zle·ment** \-'bez-əl-mənt\ *n* — **em·bez·zler** \-'bez-lər, -ə-lər\ *n*

em·bit·ter \im-'bit-ər\ *vt* : to make bitter or more bitter; *esp* : to arouse bitter feeling in — **em·bit·ter·ment** \-mənt\ *n*

em·bla·zon \im-'blāz-n\ *vt* **1** : to inscribe or ornament with markings or emblems in heraldry **2 a** : to deck in bright colors **b** : CELEBRATE 3, EXTOL

em·blem \'em-bləm\ *n* **1** : an object or a likeness used to suggest a thing that cannot be pictured : SYMBOL ⟨the flag is the *emblem* of one's country⟩ **2** : a device, symbol, design, or figure used as an identifying mark [Latin *emblema* "inlaid work", from Greek *emblēma,* from *emballein* "to insert", from *en-* + *ballein* "to throw"]

em·blem·at·ic \,em-blə-'mat-ik\ *also* **em·blem·at·i·cal** \-'mat-i-kəl\ *adj* : of, relating to, or constituting an emblem : SYMBOLIC

em·bod·i·ment \im-'bäd-i-mənt\ *n* **1** : the act of embodying : the state of being embodied **2** : one that embodies something

em·body \im-'bäd-ē\ *vt* **-bod·ied; -body·ing** **1** : to make a part of a body or system : INCORPORATE ⟨*embodied* a tax provision in the new law⟩ **2** : to express in a concrete or definite form ⟨*embody* one's ideas in words⟩ **3** : to represent in visible form ⟨a person who *embodies* courage⟩ — **em·bod·i·er** *n*

em·bold·en \im-'bōl-dən\ *vt* : to make bold

em·bo·lism \'em-bə-,liz-əm\ *n* **1** : the sudden obstruction of a blood vessel by an embolus **2** : EMBOLUS — **em·bol·ic** \em-'bäl-ik\ *adj*

em·bo·lus \'em-bə-ləs\ *n, pl* **-li** \-,lī, -,lē\ : an abnormal particle (as an air bubble) circulating in the blood — compare THROMBUS [Greek *embolos* "wedge-shaped object, stopper", from *emballein* "to insert, intercalate"]

em·bos·om \im-'bùz-əm\ *vt* : to shelter closely : ENCLOSE

em·boss \im-'bäs, -'bȯs\ *vt* : to ornament with a raised pattern or design [Middle French *embocer,* from *en-* + *boce* "boss"] — **em·boss·er** *n* — **em·boss·ment** \-mənt\ *n*

em·bou·chure \,äm-bù-'shùr\ *n* **1** : the position and use of the lips in producing a musical tone on a wind instrument **2** : the mouthpiece of a musical instrument [French, from *(s')emboucher* "to flow into", from *en-* + *bouche* "mouth"]

em·bow·er \im-'baù-ər, -'baùr\ *vt* : to shelter or enclose in or as if in a bower

¹em·brace \im-'brās\ *vb* **1** : to clasp in the arms : HUG **2** : ENCIRCLE 1, ENCLOSE **3 a** : to take up readily or gladly ⟨*embrace* a cause⟩ **b** : to avail oneself of : WELCOME ⟨*embrace* an opportunity⟩ **4** : to take in : INCLUDE [Middle French *embracer,* from Old French *embracier,* from *en-* + *brace* "two arms", from Latin *bracchia,* plural of *bracchium* "arm"] SYN see COMPRISE — **em·brace·able** \-'brā-sə-bəl\ *adj* — **em·brace·ment** \-'brās-mənt\ *n* — **em·brac·er** *n*

²embrace *n* : a gathering into one's arms and holding close

em·bra·sure \im-'brā-zhər\ *n* **1** : a recess of a door or window **2** : an opening with sides flaring outward in a wall or parapet usually for allowing the firing of cannon [French]

em·bro·ca·tion \,em-brə-'kā-shən\ *n* : LINIMENT [Latin *embrocare* "to rub with a lotion", from Greek *embrochē* "lotion"]

em·broi·der \im-'brȯid-ər\ *vb* **em·broi·dered; em·broi·der·ing** \-'brȯid-ring, -ə-ring\ **1** : to make or fill in a design with needlework **2** : to ornament with needlework **3** : to elaborate with often fictitious details : EXAGGERATE [Middle French *embroder*] — **em·broi·der·er** \-'brȯid-ər-ər\ *n*

em·broi·dery \im-'brȯid-rē, -ə-rē\ *n, pl* **-der·ies** **1 a** : the process or art of embroidering **b** : decorative needlework **2** : elaboration in details

em·broil \im-'brȯil\ *vt* **1** : to throw into disorder or confusion **2** : to involve in conflict or difficulties [French *embrouiller,* from *en-* + *brouiller* "to broil"] — **em·broil·ment** \-mənt\ *n*

em·bryo \'em-brē-,ō\ *n, pl* **em·bry·os** **1** : an animal in the early stages of development that are characterized by cleavage, the laying down of fundamental tissues, and the formation of primitive organs and organ systems — compare FETUS **2** : a rudimentary plant within a seed **3** : a beginning or undeveloped stage — used especially in the phrase *in embryo* [Medieval Latin, from Greek *embryon,* from *en-* + *bryein* "to swell"]

em·bry·ol·o·gy \,em-brē-'äl-ə-jē\ *n* **1** : a branch of biology dealing with embryos and their development **2** : the events and processes involved in the formation and development of an embryo — **em·bry·o·log·ic** \,em-brē-ə-'läj-ik\ *or* **em·bry·o·log·i·cal** \-'läj-i-kəl\ *adj* — **em·bry·o·log·i·cal·ly** \-i-kə-lē, -klē\ *adv* — **em·bry·ol·o·gist** \,em-brē-'äl-ə-jəst\ *n*

em·bry·on·ic \,em-brē-'än-ik\ *adj* **1** : of or relating to an embryo **2** : being in an early or undeveloped stage : being in embryo ⟨an *embryonic* idea⟩ — **em·bry·on·i·cal·ly** \-i-kə-lē, -klē\ *adv*

embryo sac *n* : the individual that produces female germ cells in the sexually reproducing generation of a seed plant and that consists of a thin-walled sac containing the egg nucleus and other nuclei which form nutritive tissue upon fertilization

¹em·cee \'em-'sē\ *n* : MASTER OF CEREMONIES [*M.C.*]

²emcee *vb* **em·ceed; em·cee·ing** : to act as master of ceremonies : HOST

emend \ē-'mend\ *vt* : to correct usually by textual changes [Latin *emendare* "to emend, amend"] SYN see CORRECT — **emend·able** \-'men-də-bəl\ *adj*

emen·da·tion \,ē-,men-'dā-shən, ,em-ən-\ *n* **1** : the act of emending **2** : a change designed to correct or improve

¹em·er·ald \'em-rəld, -ə-rəld\ *n* **1** : a rich green beryl prized as a gemstone **2** : a green gemstone (as synthetic corundum) [Middle French *esmeralde,* from Latin *smaragdus,* from Greek *smaragdos*]

²emerald *adj* : brightly or richly green

emerald green *n* **1** : a clear bright green resembling that of the emerald **2** : a strong green

emerge \i-'mərj\ *vt* **1** : to rise from or as if from an enveloping fluid : come out into view **2** : to become known or apparent **3** : to rise from an obscure or infe-

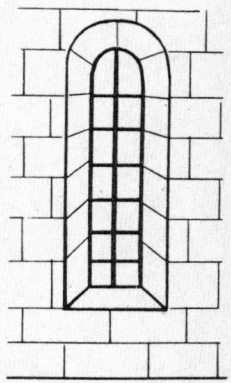

embrasure 1

rior condition [Latin *emergere*, from *e-* + *mergere* "to plunge"]

emer·gence \i-'mər-jəns\ *n* : the act or an instance of emerging

emer·gen·cy \i-'mər-jən-sē\ *n, pl* **-cies** **1** : an unforeseen combination of circumstances or the resulting state that calls for immediate action **2** : a pressing need SYN SEE JUNCTURE

¹emer·gent \i-'mər-jənt\ *adj* : rising out of or as if out of a fluid ⟨cattails are *emergent* plants⟩

²emergent *n* : a plant rooted in shallow water and having most of its growth above water

emer·i·tus \i-'mer-ət-əs\ *adj* **1** : holding after retirement an honorary title corresponding to that held last during active service ⟨professor *emeritus*⟩ **2** : retired from an office or position [Latin, past participle of *emereri* "to serve out one's term", from *e-* + *mereri, merēre* "to earn, serve"] — **emeritus** *n*

emer·sion \ē-'mər-zhən\ *n* : an act of emerging : EMERGENCE [Latin *emersus*, past participle of *emergere* "to emerge"]

em·ery \'em-rē, -ə-rē\ *n, pl* **em·er·ies** : a dark corundum used especially in the form of powder or grains for grinding and polishing [Middle French *emeri*, from Italian *smiriglio*, from Medieval Latin *smiriglum*, from Greek *smyris* "powdered emery"]

emet·ic \i-'met-ik\ *n* : an agent that induces vomiting [Latin *emetica*, from Greek *emetikē*, from *emein* "to vomit"] — **emetic** *adj* — **emet·i·cal·ly** \-'met-i-kə-lē, -klē\ *adv*

-emia *or* **-ae·mia** \'ē-mē-ə\ *n combining form* **1** : condition of having (such) blood ⟨septic*emia*⟩ **2** : condition of having (a specified thing) in the blood ⟨ur*emia*⟩ [Greek *haima* "blood"]

em·i·grant \'em-i-grənt\ *n* **1** : one that emigrates **2** : a migrant plant or animal — **emigrant** *adj* □ SYN EMIGRANT, IMMIGRANT mean one who leaves his or her country to settle in another. EMIGRANT applies to the person leaving a country; IMMIGRANT applies to the same person entering and settling in another country.

em·i·grate \'em-ə-grāt\ *vi* : to leave one's residence or country to live or reside elsewhere [Latin *emigrare*, from *e* + *migrare* "to migrate"] — **em·i·gra·tion** \,em-ə-'grā-shən\ *n*

émi·gré *or* **em·i·gré** \'em-i-grā, ,em-i-'\ *n* : EMIGRANT; *esp* : a person forced to emigrate for political reasons [French *émigré*, from *émigrer* "to emigrate", from Latin *emigrare*]

em·i·nence \'em-ə-nəns\ *n* **1** : a condition or station of prominence or superiority **2** *often cap* — used as a title for a Roman Catholic cardinal **3 a** : a person of high rank or achievement **b** : a natural elevation : HEIGHT

em·i·nent \-nənt\ *adj* : standing above all others especially in rank, merit, or virtue : NOTABLE ⟨an *eminent* physician⟩ [Latin *eminens*, from *eminēre* "to stand out"] — **em·i·nent·ly** *adv*

eminent domain *n* : a right of a government to buy private property for public use even if the owner is unwilling to sell

emir \i-'mir, ā-\ *n* : a ruler, chief, or commander in Islamic countries [Arabic *amīr* "commander" — see ADMIRAL *origin*]

emir·ate \'e-mar-at, -,āt\ *n* : the state or jurisdiction of an emir

em·is·sary \'em-ə-,ser-ē\ *n, pl* **-sar·ies** **1** : one sent on a mission as the agent of another **2** : a secret agent [Latin *emissarius*, from *emittere* "to send out"]

emis·sion \ē-'mish-ən\ *n* **1** : an act or instance of emitting **2** : DISCHARGE 6 — **emis·sive** \ē-'mis-iv\ *adj*

emit \ē-'mit\ *vt* **emit·ted; emit·ting** **1 a** : to throw or give off or out (as light) **b** : to send out : EJECT **2** : to issue (as a decree) with authority **3** : to give voice to : EXPRESS ⟨*emitted* a groan⟩ [Latin *emittere* "to send out", from *e* + *mittere* "to send"] — **emit·ter** *n*

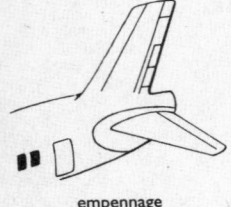

empennage

em·mer \'em-ər\ *n* : a hard red wheat having spikelets with two kernels [German]

Em·my \'em-ē\ *n, pl* **Emmys** : a statuette awarded annually for notable achievement in television [from *Immy*, nickname for *image orthicon*, a camera tube used in television]

¹emol·lient \i-'mäl-yənt\ *adj* : making soft or supple; *also* : soothing especially to the skin or mucous membrane [Latin *emollire* "to soften", from *e-* + *mollis* "soft"]

²emollient *n* : something that softens or soothes

emol·u·ment \i-'mäl-yə-mənt\ *n* : profit from one's employment or from an office held : SALARY, WAGES [Latin *emolumentum*, literally, "miller's fee", from *emolere* "to grind up", from *e-* + *molere* "to grind"]

emote \i-'mōt\ *vi* : to express emotion in or as if in a play [back-formation from *emotion*]

emo·tion \i-'mō-shən\ *n* **1** : strong feeling : EXCITEMENT ⟨spoke with *emotion*⟩ **2** : a mental and bodily reaction (as anger or fear) marked by strong feeling and physiological responses that prepare the body for action [Middle French, from *emouvoir* "to stir up", from Latin *exmovēre* "to move away, disturb", from *ex-* + *movēre* "to move"] SYN SEE FEELING

emo·tion·al \i-'mō-shnəl, -shən-l\ *adj* **1** : of or relating to the emotions ⟨an *emotional* upset⟩ **2** : inclined to show or express emotion : easily moved ⟨an *emotional* person⟩ **3** : appealing to or arousing emotion — **emo·tion·al·ly** \-ē\ *adv*

emo·tive \i-'mōt-iv\ *adj* **1** : EMOTIONAL 1 **2** : EMOTIONAL 3 — **emo·tive·ly** *adv*

em·pa·thy \'em-pə-thē\ *n* : the capacity for experiencing as one's own the feelings of another — **em·path·ic** \em-'path-ik\ *adj* — **em·pa·thize** \'em-pə-,thīz\ *vi*

em·pen·nage \,äm-pə-'näzh, ,em-\ *n* : the tail assembly of an airplane [French, "feathers of an arrow, empennage"]

em·per·or \'em-pər-ər, -prər\ *n* : the sovereign ruler of an empire — compare MONARCH [Old French *empereor*, from Latin *imperator*, literally, "commander", from *imperare* "to command", from *in-* + *parare* "to prepare, arrange"]

em·pery \'em-pə-rē, -prē\ *n* : wide dominion : EMPIRE

em·pha·sis \'em-fə-səs, 'emp-\ *n, pl* **-pha·ses** \-fə-,sēz\ **1 a** : forcefulness of expression ⟨spoke with *emphasis*⟩ **b** : prominence given to a word or syllable in reading or speaking **2** : special stress or insistence on something ⟨put great *emphasis* on cleanliness⟩ [Latin, from Greek, "exposition, emphasis", from *emphainein* "to indicate", from *en-* + *phainein* "to show"]

em·pha·size \'em-fə-,sīz, 'emp-\ *vt* : to place emphasis on : STRESS

em·phat·ic \im-'fat-ik, em-\ *adj* **1** : uttered with or marked by emphasis **2** : tending to express oneself in forceful speech or action **3** : attracting special attention ⟨an *emphatic* contrast⟩ **4** : constituting or belonging to a set of verb forms in English that have the auxiliary *do* and are used rarely for emphasis and regularly to take the place of a simple verb form in questions or negative statements ⟨the *emphatic* form "do know" or "do. . .know" in "but I tell you I do know him", "do you know him?", and "I do not know him"⟩ [Greek *emphatikos*, from *emphainein* "to indicate"] — **em·phat·i·cal·ly** \-'fat-i-kə-lē, -klē\ *adv*

em·phy·se·ma \,em-fə-'sē-mə, ,emp-, -'zē-\ *n* : a disorder marked by air-filled expansions of tissues especially of the lung [Greek *emphysēma* "bodily inflation"] — **em·phy·se·ma·tous** \-mət-əs\ *adj*

em·pire \'em-,pīr\ *n* **1 a** (1) : a major political unit with a great extent of territory or a number of territories or peoples under one sovereign authority; *esp* : one having an emperor as chief of state (2) : the territory of such a unit **b** : something held to resemble a political empire; *esp* : an extensive territory or enterprise under one control **2** : imperial sovereignty, rule, or dominion [Old French, from Latin *imperium,* from *imperare* "to command"]

Em·pire \ˈäm-ˌpiər, ˈem-ˌpīr\ *adj* : of or relating to an early 19th century French style (as of clothing or furniture) characterized by elaborateness and formality [French, from *le premier Empire* "the first Empire (of France)"]

em·pir·ic \im-ˈpir-ik, em-\ *n* : one who relies on practical experience [Latin *empiricus* "doctor relying on experience alone", from Greek *empeirikos,* from *empeiria* "experience", from *en-* + *peiran* "to attempt"]

em·pir·i·cal \-ˈpir-i-kəl\ *or* **em·pir·ic** \-ˈpir-ik\ *adj* **1** : relying on experience or observation usually without due regard for system and theory ⟨*empirical* medicine⟩ **2** : originating in or based on observation or experience **3** : capable of being verified or disproved by observation or experiment ⟨*empirical* laws⟩ — **em·pir·i·cal·ly** \-ˈpir-i-kə-lē, -klē\ *adv*

empirical formula *n* : a chemical formula showing the simplest ratio of elements in a compound

em·pir·i·cism \im-ˈpir-ə-ˌsiz-əm, em-\ *n* **1** : reliance on observation and experiment especially in the natural sciences **2** : a theory that knowledge originates in experience — **em·pir·i·cist** \-səst\ *adj or n*

em·place \im-ˈplās\ *vt* : to put into place

em·place·ment \im-ˈplā-smənt\ *n* **1** : a prepared position for weapons or military equipment **2** : a putting into position : PLACEMENT

¹em·ploy \im-ˈplȯi\ *vt* **1 a** : to make use of **b** : to occupy (as time) advantageously **2 a** : to use or engage the services of **b** : to provide with a job that pays wages or a salary **3** : to devote (as time or energy) to or direct toward a particular activity or person [Middle French *emploier,* from Latin *implicare* "to enfold, involve, implicate"] SYN see HIRE, USE — **em·ploy·able** \-ə-bəl\ *adj*

²employ *n* : the state of being employed especially for wages or a salary ⟨generous to workers in their *employ*⟩

em·ploy·ee *or* **em·ploye** \im-ˌplȯi-ˈē, -ˌem-; im-ˈplȯi-ˌē\ *n* : one employed by another usually for wages or a salary

em·ploy·er \im-ˈplȯi-ər, -ˈplȯir\ *n* : one that employs others

em·ploy·ment \im-ˈplȯi-mənt\ *n* **1** : USE 1a, PURPOSE; *also* : the action of using **2 a** : the act of engaging a person for work : HIRING **b** : the work at which one is employed : OCCUPATION **c** : the state of being employed ⟨*employment* in the machine trade⟩ **d** : the extent or degree to which a labor force is employed ⟨*employment* is high⟩

em·po·ri·um \im-ˈpȯr-ē-əm, em-, -ˈpȯr-\ *n, pl* **-ri·ums** *or* **-ria** \-ē-ə\ **1** : a place of trade : MARKETPLACE; *esp* : a commercial center **2** : a store carrying a wide variety of merchandise [Latin, from Greek *emporion,* from *emporos* "traveler, trader", from *en* "in" + *poros* "passage"]

em·pow·er \im-ˈpaù-ər, -ˈpaùr\ *vt* : to give official authority or legal power to SYN see ENABLE

em·press \ˈem-prəs\ *n* **1** : the wife or widow of an emperor **2** : a woman who holds an imperial title in her own right

em·prise \em-ˈprīz\ *n* : UNDERTAKING 1, ENTERPRISE; *esp* : a chivalric enterprise [Middle French, from Old French, from *emprendre* "to undertake"]

¹emp·ty \ˈem-tē, ˈemp-\ *adj* **emp·ti·er; -est** **1** : containing nothing ⟨an *empty* box⟩ **2** : UNOCCUPIED, VACANT ⟨an *empty* house⟩ **3** : being without reality or substance ⟨*empty* dreams⟩ **4** : lacking in value, sense, effect, or sincerity ⟨*empty* pleasures⟩ **5** : HUNGRY ⟨feel *empty* before dinner⟩ **6** : NULL 4 [Old English *ǣmettig* "unoccupied", from *ǣmetta* "leisure"] — **emp·ti·ly** \-tə-lē\ *adv* — **emp·ti·ness** \-tē-nəs\ *n* □ SYN VACANT, VOID, BLANK: EMPTY implies a complete lack or absence of usual content or significance ⟨*empty* jars⟩

⟨an *empty* promise⟩ VACANT implies lack of what is considered as or intended to be the usual occupant, tenant, or attribute ⟨a *vacant* store⟩ ⟨a *vacant* look⟩ VOID intensifies emptiness ⟨*void* of compassion⟩ BLANK stresses what is free from writing or marking and implies lack of signs of expression, comprehension, or meaning ⟨a *blank* page⟩ ⟨*blank* surprise⟩

²empty *vb* **emp·tied; emp·ty·ing** **1** : to make or become empty by removal of contents ⟨*empty* a barrel⟩ ⟨the theater *emptied* quickly⟩ **2** : to transfer by emptying ⟨*empty* the trash⟩ **3** : to discharge its contents ⟨the river *empties* into the ocean⟩

³empty *n, pl* **empties** : an empty container

emp·ty-hand·ed \ˌem-tē-ˈhan-dəd, ˌemp-\ *adj* **1** : having nothing in the hands **2** : having acquired or gained nothing

em·pur·ple \im-ˈpər-pəl\ *vb* **em·pur·pled; em·pur·pling** \-ˈpər-pə-ling, -pling\ : to tinge or color purple

em·py·re·an \ˌem-ˌpī-ˈrē-ən, -pə-; em-ˈpir-ē-ən, -ˈpī-rē-\ *n* **1** : the highest heaven or heavenly sphere **2** : FIRMAMENT, HEAVENS [Late Latin *empyreus* "celestial", from Late Greek *empyrios,* from Greek *en* "in" + *pyr* "fire"] — **em·py·re·al** \-əl\ *adj* — **empyrean** *adj*

emu \ˈē-ˌmyü\ *n* : a swift-running Australian bird with undeveloped wings that is related to but smaller than the ostrich [Portuguese *ema* "rhea"]

emu

em·u·late \ˈem-yə-ˌlāt\ *vt* **1** : to strive to equal or excel **2** : to equal or approach equality with : RIVAL [Latin *aemulari,* from *aemulus* "rivaling"] — **em·u·la·tor** \-ˌlāt-ər\ *n*

em·u·la·tion \ˌem-yə-ˈlā-shən\ *n* : effort or desire to equal or excel — **em·u·la·tive** \ˈem-yə-ˌlāt-iv\ *adj*

em·u·lous \ˈem-yə-ləs\ *adj* : eager or ambitious to equal or excel another — **em·u·lous·ly** *adv* — **em·u·lous·ness** *n*

emul·si·fi·er \i-ˈməl-sə-ˌfī-ər, -ˌfīr\ *n* : an agent (as a soap) promoting the formation and stabilization of an emulsion

emul·si·fy \-ˌfī\ *vt* **-fied; -fy·ing** : to convert (as an oil) into an emulsion — **emul·si·fi·able** \-ˌfī-ə-bəl\ *adj* — **emul·si·fi·ca·tion** \i-ˌməl-sə-fə-ˈkā-shən\ *n*

emul·sion \i-ˈməl-shən\ *n* **1** : a material consisting of a mixture of liquids that do not dissolve in each other and having droplets of one liquid dispersed throughout the other ⟨an *emulsion* of oil in water⟩ **2** : a light-sensitive coating on photographic plates, film, or paper consisting of particles of a silver salt suspended in a thick substance (as a gelatin solution) [Latin *emulsus,* past participle of *emulgēre* "to milk out", from *e-* + *mulgēre* "to milk"] — **emul·sive** \-siv\ *adj*

emul·soid \-ˌsȯid\ *n* : a colloid consisting of one liquid dispersed in another

en \ˈen\ *n* : one half of an em [from the size of the quad used for the letter *n*]

¹en- *also* **em-** \e *also occurs in these prefixes although only* i *may be shown as in* "engage"\ *prefix* **1** : put into or onto ⟨*en*throne⟩ : go into or onto ⟨*en*train⟩ — in verbs formed from nouns **2** : cause to be ⟨*en*able⟩ ⟨*en*slave⟩ — in verbs formed from adjectives or nouns **3** : provide with ⟨*em*power⟩ — in verbs formed from nouns **4** : so as to cover ⟨*en*wrap⟩ : thoroughly ⟨*en*tangle⟩ — in verbs formed from verbs; in all senses usually *em-* before *b, m,* or *p* [Old French, from Latin *in-*]

²en- *also* **em-** *prefix* : in : within ⟨*em*pathy⟩ — usually *em-* before *b, m,* or *p* [Greek, from *en* "in"]

¹-en \ən, ᵊn\ *also* **-n** \n\ *adj suffix* : made of : consisting of ⟨earth*en*⟩ ⟨silver*n*⟩ ⟨wool*en*⟩ [Old English]

²-en *vb suffix* **1** : become or cause to be ⟨sharp*en*⟩ **2** : cause or come to have ⟨strength*en*⟩ [Old English *-nian*]

en·able \in-ˈā-bəl\ *vt* **en·abled; en·abling** \-bə-ling, -bling\ **1 a** : to make able ⟨glasses *enable* me to read⟩ **b** : to make possible, practical, or easy **2** : to give a legal power or right to □ SYN ENABLE, EMPOWER mean to make one able to do something. ENABLE implies pro-

\ə\ abut	\ng\ sing
\ər\ further	\ō\ bone
\a\ mat	\ȯ\ saw
\ā\ take	\ȯi\ coin
\ä\ cot, cart	\th\ thin
\aù\ out	\th\ this
\ch\ chin	\ü\ food
\e\ pet	\ù\ foot
\ē\ easy	\y\ yet
\g\ go	\yü\ few
\i\ tip	\yù\ cure
\ī\ life	\zh\ vision
\j\ job	

vision of the means or opportunity for doing; EMPOWER implies the granting of power or delegation of authority to do.

en·act \in-'akt\ *vt* **1** : to make (as a bill) into law **2** : to act out : REPRESENT — **en·ac·tor** \-'ak-tər\ *n*

en·act·ment \-'akt-mənt, -'ak-\ *n* **1** : the act of enacting : the state of being enacted **2** : something (as a law) that has been enacted

¹**enam·el** \in-'am-əl\ *vt* **enam·eled** *or* **enam·elled; enam·el·ing** *or* **enam·el·ling** \-'am-ling, -ə-ling\ **1** : to cover or inlay with enamel **2** : to form a glossy surface on [Middle French *enamailler,* from *en-* + *esmail* "enamel", of Germanic origin]

²**enamel** *n* **1** : a usually opaque glassy composition applied by fusion to the surface of metal, glass, or pottery **2** : a surface that resembles enamel **3** : a usually glossy paint that flows out to a smooth hard coat when applied **4** : a very hard outer layer covering the crown of a tooth

enam·el·ware \-,waər, -,weər\ *n* : metal utensils (as pots and pans) coated with enamel

en·am·or \in-'am-ər\ *vt* : to fill with love or delight ⟨*enamored* with the charm of the scene⟩ [Old French *enamourer,* from *en-* + *amour* "love"]

en bloc \äⁿ-'bläk\ *adv or adj* : as a whole : in a mass [French]

en·camp \in-'kamp\ *vb* **1** : to set up and occupy a camp : CAMP **2** : to place or establish in a camp ⟨*encamp* troops⟩

en·camp·ment \-mənt\ *n* **1** : the act of encamping : the state of being encamped **2** : CAMP 1a, b, d, 2a

en·cap·su·late \in-'kap-sə-,lāt\ *vb* **1** : to encase in a capsule **2** : to become encapsulated ⟨parasites that *encapsulate* in muscle⟩ — **en·cap·su·la·tion** \-,kap-sə-'lā-shən\ *n*

en·case *also* **in·case** \in-'kās\ *vt* : to enclose in or as if in a case — **en·case·ment** \-'kā-smənt\ *n*

en·caus·tic \in-'kò-stik\ *n* : a paint mixed with melted beeswax and after application fixed by heat [derived from Greek *enkaustos* "painted in encaustic", from *enkaiein* "to burn in, paint in encaustic", from *en-* + *kaiein* "to burn"]

-ence \əns, ³ns\ *n suffix* **1** : action or process : instance of an action or process ⟨emerg*ence*⟩ ⟨refer*ence*⟩ **2** : quality or state ⟨coexist*ence*⟩ [Old French, from Latin *-entia,* from *-ent-, -ens,* resent participle ending + *-ia* "-y"]

encephal- *or* **encephalo-** *combining form* : brain ⟨*encephal*itis⟩ [Greek *enkephalos,* from *en* "in" + *kephalē* "head"]

en·ceph·a·li·tis \,en-,sef-ə-'līt-əs\ *n* : inflammation of the brain — **en·ceph·a·lit·ic** \-'lit-ik\ *adj*

en·ceph·a·lo·my·e·li·tis \en-,sef-ə-lō-,mī-ə-'līt-əs\ *n* : concurrent inflammation of the brain and spinal cord

en·ceph·a·lon \en-'sef-ə-,län, -lən\ *n, pl* **-la** \-lə\ : the vertebrate brain — **en·ce·phal·ic** \,en-sə-'fal-ik\ *adj*

en·chain \in-'chān\ *vt* : to bind or hold with or as if with chains — **en·chain·ment** \-mənt\ *n*

en·chant \in-'chant\ *vt* **1** : to influence by charms and incantation : BEWITCH **2** : THRILL 1 [Middle French *enchanter,* from Latin *incantare,* from *in-* + *cantare* "to sing"]

en·chant·er \-ər\ *n* : one that enchants; *esp* : SORCERER

en·chant·ing *adj* : ATTRACTIVE, CHARMING — **en·chant·ing·ly** \-ing-lē\ *adv*

en·chant·ment \in-'chant-mənt\ *n* **1** : the act or art of enchanting : the state of being enchanted **2** : something that enchants : SPELL, CHARM

en·chant·ress \in-'chan-trəs\ *n* **1** : a woman who practices magic : SORCERESS **2** : a fascinating woman

enchase \in-'chās\ *vt* **1** : SET ⟨*enchase* a gem⟩ **2** : ORNAMENT: as **a** : to cut or carve in relief **b** : INLAY [Middle French *enchasser* "to enshrine, set", from *en* + *chasse* "reliquary", from Latin *capsa* "case"]

en·chi·la·da \,en-chə-'läd-ə\ *n* : a tortilla rolled with meat or cheese filling and served with tomato sauce seasoned with chili [American Spanish]

en·ci·pher \in-'sī-fər, en-\ *vt* : to convert (a message) into cipher

en·cir·cle \in-'sər-kəl\ *vt* **1** : to form a circle around : SURROUND **2** : to pass completely around — **en·cir·cle·ment** \-kəl-mənt\ *n*

en·clave \'en-,klāv, 'än-, 'äng-\ *n* : a territorial or culturally distinct unit enclosed within foreign territory [French, from Middle French *enclaver* "to enclose", from Latin *in-* + *clavis* "key"]

en·clit·ic \en-'klit-ik\ *adj* : being without independent accent and treated in pronunciation as forming a part of the preceding word ⟨*thee* in *prithee* and *not* in *cannot* are *enclitic*⟩ [Latin *encliticus,* from Greek *enklitikos,* from *enklinesthai* "to lean on", from *en-* + *klinein* "to lean"] — **enclitic** *n*

en·close *or* **in·close** \in-'klōz\ *vt* **1 a** : to close in : SURROUND; *esp* : to mark off (land) by or as if by a fence **b** : to hold in : CONFINE **2** : to place in a parcel or envelope

en·clo·sure *or* **in·clo·sure** \in-'klō-zhər\ *n* **1** : the act of enclosing : the state of being enclosed **2** : an enclosed space **3** : something (as a fence) that encloses **4** : something enclosed ⟨a letter with two *enclosures*⟩

en·code \in-'kōd\ *vt* : to transfer from one system of communication into another; *esp* : to put (a message) in the form of a code

en·co·mi·ast \en-'kō-mē-,ast, -mē-əst\ *n* : one that praises — **en·co·mi·as·tic** \-,kō-mē-'as-tik\ *adj*

en·co·mi·um \en-'kō-mē-əm\ *n, pl* **-mi·ums** *or* **-mia** \-mē-ə\ : warm or high praise especially when formally expressed [Latin, from Greek *enkōmion,* from *en* "in" + *kōmos* "celebration"]

en·com·pass \in-'kəm-pəs, -'käm-\ *vt* **1** : to form a circle about : ENCLOSE **2 a** : ENVELOP **b** : INCLUDE ⟨a plan that *encompasses* a number of aims⟩ — **en·com·pass·ment** \-mənt\ *n*

¹**en·core** \'än-,kōr, -,kòr\ *n* : a demand for repetition or reappearance made by an audience; *also* : a further performance in response to such a demand [French, "again"]

²**encore** *vt* : to call for a further performance or appearance of or by

¹**en·coun·ter** \in-'kaunt-ər\ *vt* **en·coun·tered; en·coun·ter·ing** \-'kaunt-ə-ring, -'kaun-tring\ **1** : to meet as an enemy : engage in conflict with **2** : to come upon face to face **3** : to come upon unexpectedly ⟨*encounter* difficulties⟩ [Old French *encontrer,* derived from Latin *in-* + *contra* "against"]

²**encounter** *n* **1 a** : a meeting between unfriendly factions or persons **b** : a sudden often violent clash : COMBAT **2 a** : a chance meeting **b** : a meeting face to face

en·cour·age \in-'kər-ij, -'kə-rij\ *vt* **1** : to inspire with courage, spirit, or hope : HEARTEN **2** : to spur on **3** : to give help to : FOSTER — **en·cour·ag·ing·ly** \-ing-lē\ *adv*

en·cour·age·ment \-mənt\ *n* **1** : the act of encouraging : the state of being encouraged **2** : something that encourages

en·croach \in-'krōch\ *vi* **1** : to enter or force oneself gradually upon another's property or rights : TRESPASS **2** : to advance beyond the usual or proper limits ⟨the gradually *encroaching* sea⟩ [Middle French *encrochier* "to get, seize", from *en-* + *croche* "hook"] — **en·croach·ment** \-mənt\ *n*

en·crust *also* **in·crust** \in-'krəst\ *vb* **1** : to cover with a crust **2** : to form a crust

en·crus·ta·tion \in-,krəs-'tā-shən, ,en-\ *variant of* INCRUSTATION

en·cum·ber *also* **in·cum·ber** \in-'kəm-bər\ *vt* **en·cum·bered; en·cum·ber·ing** \-bə-ring, -bring\ **1** : to weigh down : BURDEN **2** : to hamper the function or activity of : HINDER **3** : to burden with a legal claim (as a mortgage) ⟨*encumber* an estate⟩ [Middle French *encombrer*]

en·cum·brance \in-'kəm-brəns\ *n* **1** : something that encumbers : LOAD, BURDEN **2** *or* **in·cum·brance** : a legal claim (as a mortgage) against property

-en·cy \ən-sē, ᵊn-sē\ *n suffix* : quality or state ⟨despond*ency*⟩ [Latin *-entia* "-ency, -ence"]

¹en·cyc·li·cal \in-'sik-li-kəl, en-\ *adj* : addressed to all the individuals of a group : GENERAL [Late Latin *encyclicus*, from Greek *enkyklios* "circular, general", from *en* "in" + *kyklos* "circle"]

²encyclical *n* : an encyclical letter; *esp* : a papal letter to the bishops of the church as a whole or to those in one country

en·cy·clo·pe·dia *also* **en·cy·clo·pae·dia** \in-ˌsī-klə-'pēd-ē-ə\ *n* : a work that contains information on all branches of knowledge or treats comprehensively a particular branch of knowledge usually in articles arranged alphabetically by subject [Medieval Latin *encyclopaedia* "course of general education", from Greek *enkyklios paideia* "general education"]

en·cy·clo·pe·dic *also* **en·cy·clo·pae·dic** \-'pēd-ik\ *adj* **1** : of or relating to an encyclopedia **2** : covering a wide range of subjects ⟨*encyclopedic* knowledge⟩ — **en·cy·clo·pe·di·cal·ly** \-'pēd-i-kə-lē, -klē\ *adv*

en·cyst \in-'sist, en-\ *vi* : to form or become enclosed in a cyst — **en·cyst·ment** \-'sist-mənt, -'sis-\ *n*

¹end \'end\ *n* **1 a** : the part of an area that lies at the boundary **b** : a point that marks the extent or limit of something **c** : the point where something ceases to exist ⟨world without *end*⟩ **d** : the extreme or last part lengthwise : TIP **e** : a football lineman whose position is at the extremity of the line **2 a** : cessation of a course of action or activity **b** : DEATH, DESTRUCTION ⟨meet one's *end* bravely⟩ **c** (1) : the final state (2) : RESULT, ISSUE **d** : the complex of events, parts, or sections that forms a finish **3** : something left over **4** : the goal toward which an agent acts or should act **5** : a particular phase of an undertaking [Old English *ende*] — **end·ed** \'en-dəd\ *adj* □ SYN END, TERMINATION, ENDING mean the point or line beyond which a thing does not or cannot go. END implies the final limit in time, space, extent, influence, or range of possibility; TERMINATION applies to the end of something complete or finished or having a set limit ⟨the *termination* of the treaty⟩ ENDING also includes the portion leading to the actual final point ⟨the *ending* of a play⟩ ⟨a long *ending* to a symphony⟩

²end *vb* **1 a** : to bring or come to an end : STOP **b** : DESTROY **1 2** : to make up the end of SYN see CLOSE

end- *or* **endo-** *combining form* **1** : within : inside ⟨*endo*-skeleton⟩ — compare ECT-, EXO- **2** : taking in ⟨*endo*thermal⟩ [Greek *endon* "within"]

en·dan·ger \in-'dān-jər\ *vt* **en·dan·gered; en·dan·ger·ing** \-'dānj-ring, -ə-ring\ : to bring into danger or peril

en·dan·gered *adj* : threatened with extinction ⟨an *endangered* species of bird⟩

end brush *n* : END PLATE

en·dear \in-'diər\ *vt* : to cause to become dear or beloved

en·dear·ment \-mənt\ *n* : a word or an act (as a caress) showing love or affection

¹en·deav·or \in-'dev-ər\ *vb* **en·deav·ored; en·deav·or·ing** \-'dev-riŋ, -ə-riŋ\ : to make an effort : work for a particular end : TRY ⟨*endeavor* to do better⟩ [Middle English *en-* + *dever* "duty", from Old French *devoir* "to owe", from Latin *debēre*]

²endeavor *n* : a serious determined effort

¹en·dem·ic \en-'dem-ik\ *adj* : restricted or peculiar to a locality or region ⟨*endemic* diseases⟩ ⟨an *endemic* plant⟩ [French *endémique*, derived from Greek *endēmos*, from *en* "in" + *dēmos* "people, populace"] SYN see NATIVE — **en·dem·i·cal·ly** \-'dem-i-kə-lē, -klē\ *adv* — **en·de·mic·i·ty** \ˌen-ˌdem-'is-ət-ē, -də-'mis-\ *n*

²endemic *n* : NATIVE 2b

end·er·gon·ic \ˌen-dər-'gän-ik\ *adj* : requiring outlay of energy ⟨an *endergonic* biochemical reaction⟩ [*end-* + Greek *ergon* "work"]

end·ing \'en-diŋ\ *n* **1** : CONCLUSION, END ⟨a novel with a happy *ending*⟩ **2** : one or more sounds or letters added at the end of a word especially in inflection SYN see END

en·dive \'en-ˌdīv\ *n* **1** : an annual or biennial herb closely related to chicory and widely grown as a salad plant — called also *escarole* **2** : the developing crown of chicory when blanched for use as salad [Middle French, from Late Latin *endivia*, from Late Greek *entubion*, from Latin *intubus*]

endive 1

end·less \'en-dləs, -ləs\ *adj* **1** : being or seeming to be without end **2** : joined at the ends : CONTINUOUS ⟨an *endless* belt⟩ SYN see ETERNAL — **end·less·ly** *adv* — **end·less·ness** *n*

end line *n* : a line at each end of a playing area (as a court or field) perpendicular to the sidelines marking a boundary

end man *n* : a comedian at either end of the line of performers in a minstrel show

end·most \'end-ˌmōst, 'en-\ *adj* : situated at the very end : FARTHEST

en·do·car·di·tis \ˌen-dō-kär-'dīt-əs\ *n* : inflammation of the lining of the heart and its valves

en·do·car·di·um \ˌen-dō-'kärd-ē-əm\ *n* : a thin membrane lining the cavities of the heart [New Latin, from *end-* + Greek *kardia* "heart"]

en·do·carp \'en-də-ˌkärp\ *n* : the inner layer of the pericarp of a fruit (as the stony wall enclosing the seed of a peach) — compare EPICARP, MESOCARP

¹en·do·crine \'en-də-krən, -ˌkrīn, -ˌkren\ *adj* **1** : of, relating to, being, or resembling that of an endocrine gland **2** : HORMONAL [*end-* + Greek *krinein* "to separate"]

²endocrine *n* **1** : HORMONE **2** : ENDOCRINE GLAND

endocrine gland *n* : any of various glands (as the thyroid) that have no duct and pour their secretions directly into the blood or lymph

en·do·cri·nol·o·gy \ˌen-də-kri-'näl-ə-jē, -krī-\ *n* : a science dealing with the endocrine glands — **en·do·cri·no·log·i·cal** \-krin-l-'äj-i-kəl, -ˌkrīn-\ *adj* — **en·do·cri·nol·o·gist** \-kri-'näl-ə-jəst, -krī-\ *n*

en·do·derm \'en-də-ˌdərm\ *n* : the innermost of the three primary germ layers of an embryo giving rise to the epithelium of the digestive tract and its derivatives; *also* : a tissue derived from this layer

en·do·der·mal \ˌen-də-'dər-məl\ *adj* : of or derived from endoderm or from endodermis

en·do·der·mis \ˌen-də-'dər-məs\ *n* : the innermost tissue of the cortex in many roots and stems

en·dog·a·my \en-'däg-ə-mē\ *n* : mating between members of a social group or population usually consisting of genetically related individuals — **en·dog·a·mous** \-məs\ *adj*

en·dog·e·nous \en-'däj-ə-nəs\ *adj* : developing or originating within the cell or body — **en·dog·e·nous·ly** *adv*

en·do·lymph \'en-də-ˌlimf, -ˌlimpf\ *n* : the watery fluid in the inner ear

en·do·me·tri·um \ˌen-dō-'mē-trē-əm\ *n, pl* **-tria** \-trē-ə\ : the mucous membrane lining the uterus [New Latin, from *end-* + Greek *mētra* uterus]

en·do·mor·phic \ˌen-də-'mór-fik\ *adj* : broad and heavy in build [*endo*derm + *-morphic* from the predominance in such people of structures developed from the endoderm] — **en·do·morph** \'en-də-ˌmórf\ *n* — **en·do·mor·phy** \-ˌmór-fē\ *n*

en·do·plasm \'en-də-ˌplaz-əm\ *n* : the inner relatively fluid part of the cytoplasm — compare ECTOPLASM — **en·do·plas·mic** \ˌen-də-'plaz-mik\ *adj*

endoplasmic reticulum *n* : a system of cavities and minute connecting canals that occupy much of the cyto-

\ə\ abut		\ng\ sing	
\ər\ further		\ō\ bone	
\a\ mat		\ò\ saw	
\ā\ take		\ói\ coin	
\ä\ cot, cart		\th\ thin	
\aú\ out		\th\ this	
\ch\ chin		\ü\ food	
\e\ pet		\ú\ foot	
\ē\ easy		\y\ yet	
\g\ go		\yü\ few	
\i\ tip		\yù\ cure	
\ī\ life		\zh\ vision	
\j\ job			

plasm of the cell and are studded with ribosomes in some places

end organ *n* : a structure forming the end of a path of nerve conduction and consisting of an effector or a receptor with its associated nerve terminations

en·dorse *or* **in·dorse** \in-'dȯrs\ *vt* **1** : to sign the back of (a commercial document) for some special purpose ⟨*endorse* a check⟩ **2** : to express approval of publicly ⟨*endorse* a candidate⟩ [Middle French *endosser* from Old French, "to put on the back", from *en-* + *dos* "back", from Latin *dorsum*] SYN SEE APPROVE — **en·dors·ee** \in-,dȯr-'sē, ,en-\ *n* — **en·dors·er** \in-'dȯr-sər\ *n*

en·dorse·ment *or* **in·dorse·ment** \in-'dȯr-smənt\ *n* **1** : the act or process of endorsing **2** : something written in the process of endorsing **3** : APPROVAL ⟨*endorsement* of a plan⟩

en·do·skel·e·ton \,en-dō-'skel-ət-n\ *n* : an internal skeleton or supporting framework in an animal — compare EXOSKELETON — **en·do·skel·e·tal** \-ət-l\ *adj*

en·do·sperm \'en-də-,spərm\ *n* : a nutritive tissue in seed plants formed within the embryo sac

en·do·spore \'en-də-,spōr, -,spȯr\ *n* : an asexual spore developed within the cell especially in bacteria

en·do·the·li·um \,en-də-'thē-lē-əm\ *n, pl* **-lia** \-lē-ə\ : an inner layer (as of epithelium or of a seed coat) [*end-* + epi*thelium*] — **en·do·the·li·al** \-lē-əl\ *adj*

en·do·ther·mic \,en-də-'thər-mik\ *or* **en·do·ther·mal** \-məl\ *adj* : characterized by or formed with absorption of heat ⟨*endothermic* chemical reactions⟩

en·do·tox·in \,en-dō-'täk-sən\ *n* : a poisonous substance of a bacterium (as one causing typhoid fever) separable from the cell only on its disintegration

en·dow \in-'dau̇\ *vt* **1** : to furnish with money for support or maintenance ⟨*endow* a hospital⟩ **2** : to furnish with something freely or naturally ⟨human beings are *endowed* with reason⟩ [Anglo-French *endouer* from Middle French *en-* + *douer* "to endow", from Latin *dotare* from *dot-, dos* "gift"]

en·dow·ment \-mənt\ *n* **1** : the providing of a permanent fund for support or the fund provided ⟨a college with a large *endowment*⟩ **2** : natural ability or talent

end·pa·per \'end-,pā-pər, 'en-\ *n* : a sheet of paper folded once with one half pasted flat against the inside of the front or back cover of a book and the other pasted to the base of the front or last page

end plate *n* : a treelike ending of a motor nerve fiber

end·point \'end-,pȯint, 'en-\ *n* **1** : a point marking the end of a process or a stage in a process **2** : either of two points that mark the ends of a line segment or a point that marks the end of a ray

end product *n* : the final product of a series of processes or activities

end run *n* : a football play in which the ballcarrier attempts to run wide around the end

end table *n* : a small table used beside a larger piece of furniture

en·due *also* **in·due** \in-'dü, -'dyü\ *vt* : to provide with a quality or power ⟨*endued* with grace⟩ [Middle French *enduire* "to bring in, introduce", from Latin *inducere* from *in-* + *ducere* "to lead"]

en·dur·ance \in-'dur-əns, -'dyur-\ *n* **1** : PERMANENCE, DURATION **2** : the ability to withstand hardship, misfortune, or stress **3** : TRIAL 3, SUFFERING

en·dure \in-'dur, -'dyur\ *vb* **1** : to continue in the same state : LAST **2 a** : to remain firm under suffering or misfortune without yielding **b** : to bear patiently : SUFFER **3** : to put up with : PERMIT [Middle French *endurer* from Latin *indurare* "to harden", from *in-* + *durare* "to harden, endure"] — **en·dur·able** \-ə-bəl\ *adj* — **en·dur·ably** \-ə-blē\ *adv*

en·dur·ing *adj* : LASTING, DURABLE — **en·dur·ing·ly** \-ing-lē\ *adv* — **en·dur·ing·ness** *n*

end user *n* : the ultimate consumer of a finished product

end·ways \'en-,dwāz\ *adv or adj* **1** : with the end forward **2** : in or toward the direction of the ends : LENGTHWISE **3** : on end : UPRIGHT

end·wise \-,dwīz\ *adv or adj* : ENDWAYS

end zone *n* : the area at each end of a football field bounded by the end line, the goal line, and the sidelines

-ene \,ēn\ *n suffix* : unsaturated carbon compound ⟨benz*ene*⟩; *esp* : carbon compound with one double bond ⟨ethyl*ene*⟩ [Greek *-ēnē* feminine of *-ēnos* adj. suffix]

en·e·ma \'en-ə-mə\ *n* : the injection of liquid into the intestine by way of the anus; *also* : the material injected [Late Latin, from Greek, from *enienai* "to inject", from *en-* + *hienai* "to send"]

en·e·my \'en-ə-mē\ *n, pl* **-mies** **1** : one that hates another : one that attacks or tries to harm another **2** : something that harms **3 a** : a nation with which a country is at war **b** : a hostile unit or force [Old French *enemi*, from Latin *inimicus*, from *in-* "¹in-" + *amicus* "friend"] □ SYN ENEMY, FOE mean one who shows hostility or ill will. ENEMY stresses antagonism showing itself in hatred or destructive attitude or action; FOE stresses active fighting or struggle and is used poetically for an enemy in war

en·er·get·ic \,en-ər-'jet-ik\ *adj* : having or showing energy : ACTIVE, FORCEFUL ⟨an *energetic* salesman⟩ [Greek *energētikos* from *energein* "to be active", from *energos* "active"] SYN SEE VIGOROUS — **en·er·get·i·cal·ly** \-'jet-i-kə-lē, -klē\ *adv*

en·er·gize \'en-ər-,jīz\ *vb* **1** : to put forth energy : ACT **2 a** : to impart energy to **b** : to make energetic or vigorous **3** : to apply voltage to — **en·er·giz·er** *n*

en·er·gy \'en-ər-jē\ *n, pl* **-gies** **1** : power or capacity to be active : strength of body or mind to do things or to work ⟨a person of great intellectual *energy*⟩ **2** : natural power vigorously exerted : vigorous action ⟨work with *energy*⟩ **3** : the capacity for performing work : usable power; *also* : the resources for producing such power — compare KINETIC ENERGY, POTENTIAL ENERGY [Late Latin *energia*, from Greek *energeia* "activity", from *energos* "active", from *en* "in" + *ergon* "work"] SYN SEE POWER

energy level *n* : one of the stable states of constant energy that may be assumed by a physical system — used especially of electrons in atoms

en·er·vate \'en-ər-,vāt\ *vt* : to cause to lose strength or vigor : WEAKEN [Latin *enervare*, from *e-* + *nervus* "sinew"] — **en·er·va·tion** \,en-ər-'vā-shən\ *n*

en·fant ter·ri·ble \äⁿ-,fäⁿ-te-'rēbl\ *n* : a person whose remarks or actions cause embarrassment [French, literally, "terrifying child"]

en·fee·ble \in-'fē-bəl\ *vt* **en·fee·bled; en·fee·bling** \-bə-ling, -bling\ : to make feeble — **en·fee·ble·ment** \-bəl-mənt\ *n*

¹en·fi·lade \'en-fə-,lād, -,läd\ *n* : gunfire directed along the length of an enemy battle line [French, from *enfiler* "to thread, enfilade", from *en-* + *fil* "thread"]

²enfilade *vt* : to rake or be in a position to rake with gunfire in a lengthwise direction

en·fold \in-'fōld\ *vt* **1 a** : to cover with folds **b** : to surround with a covering : CONTAIN **2** : to clasp within the arms

en·force \in-'fōrs,-'fȯrs\ *vt* **1** : FORCE, COMPEL ⟨*enforce* obedience⟩ **2** : to carry out effectively ⟨*enforce* the law⟩ — **en·force·able** \-ə-bəl\ *adj* — **en·force·ment** \-mənt\ *n* — **en·forc·er** *n*

en·fran·chise \in-'fran-,chīz\ *vt* **1** : to set free (as from slavery) **2** : to grant the privileges of a citizen to; *esp* : to grant the right of suffrage to [Middle French *enfranchiss-,* stem of *enfranchir* "to enfranchise", from *en-* + *franc* "free"] — **en·fran·chise·ment** \-,chīz-mənt, -chəz-\ *n*

en·gage \in-'gāj\ *vb* **1** : to interlock with : MESH; *also* : to cause to mesh **2** : to bind oneself to do some-

thing; *esp* : to bind by a pledge to marry **3 a** : to arrange to obtain the use or services of : HIRE **b** :
ENGROSS, OCCUPY (the task *engaged* my attention) **4** : to
enter into contest with (*engage* the enemy) **5 a** : to
begin and carry on an enterprise (*engaged* in sales) **b** :
PARTICIPATE [Middle French *engagier,* from *en-* + *gage*
"*gage*"]

en·gaged \in-'gājd\ *adj* **1** : OCCUPIED, EMPLOYED, BUSY
(*engaged* in conversation) **2** : pledged to be married

en·gage·ment \in-'gāj-mənt\ *n* **1 a** : the act of engaging : the state of being engaged **b** : an agreement to
marry **2** : PLEDGE, OBLIGATION (financial *engagements*
to fulfill) **3 a** : a promise to be present at a specified
time and place **b** : employment especially for a stated
time **4** : the state of being in gear **5** : a hostile encounter between military forces

en·gag·ing \in-'gā-jing\ *adj* : ATTRACTIVE, PLEASING —
en·gag·ing·ly \-jing-lē\ *adv*

en·gen·der \in-'jen-dər\ *vt* **en·gen·dered; en·gen·der-
ing** \-də-ring, -dring\ **1** : BEGET **2** : to cause to exist :
PRODUCE (angry words *engender* strife) [Middle French
engendrer, from Latin *ingenerare,* from *in-* + *generare* "to generate"]

en·gine \'en-jən\ *n* **1 a** : a mechanical tool (as an instrument of war or torture) **b** : a mechanical appliance
— compare FIRE ENGINE **2** : a machine for converting
energy into mechanical force and motion **3** : a railroad
locomotive [Old French *engin* "ingenuity", from Latin
ingenium "natural disposition, talent", from *in-* +
gignere "to beget"]

¹en·gi·neer \,en-jə-'niər\ *n* **1** : a member of a military
group devoted to engineering work **2 a** : a designer or
builder of engines **b** : a person who is trained in or
follows as a profession a branch of engineering **c** : a
person who skillfully carries out an enterprise **3** : a
person who runs or supervises an engine or an apparatus

²engineer *vt* **1** : to plan, build, or manage as an engineer **2** : to guide the course of (*engineer* a fund-raising campaign)

en·gi·neer·ing *n* **1** : the art of managing engines **2** : the
application of science and mathematics by which the
properties of matter and the sources of energy in nature are made useful to human beings

¹En·glish \'ing-glish also 'ing-lish\ *adj* : of, relating to,
or characteristic of England, the English people, or the
English language [Old English *englisc,* from *Engle*
"Angles"] — **En·glish·man** \-mən\ *n* — **En·glish·wom-
an** \-,wum-ən\ *n*

²English *n* **1 a** : the language of the people of England,
the United States, and many areas now or formerly under British control **b** : English language, literature, or
composition as a subject of study **2** *pl in construction* : the people of England **3** : a sideways spin given
to a ball

³English *vt* : to translate into English

English daisy *n* : DAISY 1a

English horn *n* : a double-reed woodwind instrument
similar to the oboe but a fifth lower in pitch

English ivy *n* : IVY 1

English setter *n* : any of a breed of bird dogs with a flat
silky coat of white or white with color

English shepherd *n* : any of a breed of medium-sized
dogs with a long and glossy black coat and usually tan
to brown markings

English sonnet *n* : a sonnet consisting of three quatrains
and a couplet with a rhyme scheme of *abab cdcd efef
gg*

English sparrow *n* : an Old World sparrow widely naturalized in the New World — called also *house sparrow*

English walnut *n* : an Old World walnut valued for its
large edible nut and its hard richly figured wood;
also : its nut

en·gorge \in-'gorj\ *vb* **1** : GORGE, GLUT **2** : to fill with
blood : CONGEST — **en·gorge·ment** \-mənt\ *n*

en·grave \in-'grāv\ *vt* **1 a** : to form (as letters or devices) by cutting into a surface **b** : to impress deeply
(the incident was *engraved* in my memory) **2 a** : to cut
figures, letters, or devices upon especially for printing; *also* : to print from an engraved plate **b** : PHOTO-
ENGRAVE — **en·grav·er** *n*

en·grav·ing \in-'grā-ving\ *n* **1** : the art of cutting figures, letters, or devices in wood, stone, or metal **2** :
something engraved: as **a** : an engraved printing
surface **b** : engraved work **3** : a print made from an
engraved surface

en·gross \in-'grōs\ *vt* **1 a** : to copy or write in a large
hand **b** : to prepare the usually final handwritten or
printed text of (an official document) **2** : to take up
the whole interest of : occupy fully : ABSORB [sense 1
from Anglo-French *engrosser,* probably from Medieval
Latin *ingrossare,* from Latin *in* "in" + Medieval Latin
grossa "large handwriting", from Latin *grossus*
"thick"; sense 2 from Middle French *en gros* "in large
quantities", from *gros* "thick", from Latin *grossus*] —
en·gross·er *n* — **en·gross·ment** \-'grō-smənt\ *n*

en·gulf \in-'gəlf\ *vt* : to flow over and enclose; *also* : to
take in (food) by such means — **en·gulf·ment** \-mənt\
n

en·hance \in-'hans\ *vt* : to make greater (as in value,
desirability, or attractiveness) : HEIGHTEN [Anglo-
French *enhauncer,* from Old French *enhaucier,* derived from Latin *in* "in" + *altus* "high"] SYN see IN-
TENSIFY — **en·hance·ment** \-mənt\ *n*

enig·ma \i-'nig-mə\ *n* : something hard to understand
or explain : PUZZLE [Latin *aenigma,* from Greek *ainig-
mat-, ainigma,* from *inissesthai* "to speak in riddles", *ainos* "fable, riddle"] SYN see MYSTERY — **enig-
mat·ic** \,en-ig-'mat-ik *also* ,ē-nig-\ *or* **enig·mat·i·cal**
\-'mat-i-kəl\ *adj* — **enig·mat·i·cal·ly** \-i-kə-lē, -klē\
adv

en·isle \in-'īl\ *vt* **1** : ISOLATE 1 **2** : to make an island of

en·jamb·ment *or* **en·jambe·ment** \in-'jam-mənt\ *n* : the
running over of a sentence from one verse or couplet
into another so that closely related words fall in different lines [French *enjambement,* from *enjamber* "to
straddle", from *en-* + *jambe* "leg"]

en·join \in-'join\ *vt* **1** : to direct or impose by authoritative order **2** : FORBID 1, PROHIBIT

en·joy \in-'joi\ *vt* **1** : to take pleasure or satisfaction in
2 : to have for one's use, benefit, or lot — **en·joy·able**
\-ə-bəl\ *adj* — **en·joy·able·ness** *n* — **en·joy·ably** \-ə-
blē\ *adv*

en·joy·ment \in-'joi-mənt\ *n* **1** : the condition of enjoying something : possession and use of something
with satisfaction (the *enjoyment* of good health) **2** :
PLEASURE, SATISFACTION (find *enjoyment* in skating) **3** :
something that gives pleasure

en·kin·dle \in-'kin-dl\ *vb* : KINDLE 1, 2

en·lace \in-'lās\ *vt* **1** : ENCIRCLE, ENFOLD **2** : ENTWINE,
INTERLACE

en·large \in-'lärj\ *vb* **1** : to make or grow larger **2** :
ELABORATE (*enlarge* on a story) — **en·larg·er** *n*

en·large·ment \in-'lärj-mənt\ *n* **1** : an act or instance
of enlarging : the state of being enlarged **2** : a photographic print that is larger than the negative and is
made by projecting an image of the negative upon a
photographic printing surface

en·light·en \in-'līt-n\ *vt* **en·light·ened; en·light·en·ing**
\-'līt-ning, -n-ing\ **1** : to furnish knowledge to : IN-
STRUCT **2** : to give spiritual insight to — **en·light·en·
ment** \-'līt-n-mənt\ *n*

en·list \in-'list\ *vb* **1** : to enroll for military or naval
service; *esp* : to join one of the armed services voluntarily **2** : to obtain the help or support of (*enlisted*
friends in the campaign); *also* : to participate heartily
(as in a cause) — **en·list·ment** \-'list-mənt, -'lis-\ *n*

English horn

en·list·ed *adj* : of, relating to, or constituting the part of a military or naval force below commissioned or warrant officers

en·liv·en \in-'lī-vən\ *vt* : to give life, action, or spirit to : ANIMATE

en masse \än-'mas, än-\ *adv* : in a body : as a whole [French]

en·mesh \in-'mesh\ *vt* : to entangle in or as if in meshes ⟨was *enmeshed* in disputes with his neighbors⟩

en·mi·ty \'en-mət-ē\ *n, pl* **-ties** : positive, active, and typically mutual hatred or ill will [Middle French *enemité*, from *enemi* "enemy"] □ SYN HOSTILITY, ANIMOSITY, ANTAGONISM: ENMITY suggests positive hatred which may be open or concealed; HOSTILITY suggests enmity showing itself in attacks or aggression; ANIMOSITY implies intense ill will and vindictiveness that threaten to kindle hostility; ANTAGONISM suggests a clash of temperaments leading readily to hostility.

en·no·ble \in-'ō-bəl\ *vt* **-bled; -bling** \-bə-ling, -bling\ **1** : to make noble : ELEVATE **2** : to raise to the rank of nobility — **en·no·ble·ment** \-bəl-mənt\ *n*

en·nui \'än-'wē\ *n* : a feeling of weariness and dissatisfaction : BOREDOM [French, from Old French *enui* "annoyance", from *enuier* "to annoy"]

enor·mi·ty \i-'nor-mət-ē\ *n, pl* **-ties 1** : great wickedness : OUTRAGEOUSNESS ⟨the *enormity* of the offense⟩ **2** : an outrageous act or offense **3** : very large size; *also* : something very large

enor·mous \i-'nor-məs\ *adj* **1** *archaic* **a** : ABNORMAL, INORDINATE **b** : exceedingly wicked : OUTRAGEOUS **2** : very great in size, number, or degree [Latin *enormis*, from *e, ex* "out of" + *norma* "norm"] — **enor·mous·ly** *adv* — **enor·mous·ness** *n* □ SYN IMMENSE, HUGE, VAST: ENORMOUS implies exceeding ordinary bounds in size, amount, or degree ⟨the *enormous* expenditures for war⟩ IMMENSE suggests size far in excess of ordinary measurements or concepts ⟨an *immense* waste of natural resources⟩ HUGE suggests immensity of bulk, size, or capacity ⟨*huge* wine vats⟩ VAST usually suggests immensity of extent ⟨*vast* stretches of desert⟩

¹enough \i-'nəf; *after* t, d, s, z *often* n-'əf\ *adj* : occurring in such quantity, quality, or scope as to fully satisfy demands or needs [Middle English *ynough*, from Old English *genōg*] SYN SEE SUFFICIENT

²enough *adv* **1** : in sufficient amount or degree : SUFFICIENTLY ⟨ran fast *enough*⟩ **2** : FULLY, QUITE ⟨ready *enough* to admit it⟩ **3** : PASSABLY, TOLERABLY ⟨sang well *enough*⟩

³enough *n* : a sufficient quantity ⟨we have *enough* to eat⟩

enow \i-'naù\ *adv or adj, archaic* : ENOUGH [Middle English *inow*, from Old English *genōg*]

en·plane \in-'plān\ *vi* : to board an airplane

en·quire \in-'kwīr\, **en·qui·ry** \'in-,kwīr-ē, in-'; 'in-kwə-rē, 'ing-\ *variant of* INQUIRE, INQUIRY

en·rage \in-'rāj\ *vt* : to fill with rage : MADDEN

en·rapt \in-'rapt\ *adj* : RAPT 1, ENRAPTURED

en·rap·ture \in-'rap-chər\ *vt* **-rap·tured; -rap·tur·ing** \-'rap-chə-ring, -'rap-shring\ : to fill with delight

en·rich \in-'rich\ *vt* **1** : to make rich or richer ⟨*enrich* the mind⟩ **2** : ADORN, ORNAMENT **3 a** : to make (soil) more fertile **b** : to improve (a food) in nutritive value by adding vitamins and minerals in processing **4** : to expand (a course of study) by increasing the variety of subjects and depth of treatment — **en·rich·ment** \-mənt\ *n*

en·robe \in-'rōb\ *vt* : to invest or adorn with a robe

en·roll *or* **en·rol** \in-'rōl\ *vb* **en·rolled; en·roll·ing 1** : to enter in a list, catalog, or roll **2** : ENTER, JOIN ⟨*enroll* in school⟩ — **en·roll·ment** \-'rōl-mənt\ *n*

en route \än-'rüt, en-, in-\ *adv* : on or along the way [French]

en·sconce \in-'skäns\ *vt* **1** : to place or hide securely : CONCEAL **2** : to establish comfortably : settle snugly

en·sem·ble \än-'säm-bəl, än-\ *n* : a group constituting a whole or producing a single effect: as **a** : SET 3 **b** : concerted music of two or more parts or the musicians that perform it **c** : a complete costume of harmonizing clothes **d** : a group of supporting performers [French, from *ensemble* "together", from Latin *insimul* "at the same time", from *in-* + *simul* "at the same time"]

en·sheathe \in-'shēth\ *vt* : to cover with or as if with a sheath

en·shrine \in-'shrīn\ *vt* **1** : to enclose in or as if in a shrine **2** : to preserve or cherish as sacred

en·shroud \in-'shraùd\ *vt* : SHROUD

en·sign \'en-sən, *in senses 1 & 2 also* 'en-,sīn\ *n* **1** : a flag flown as the symbol of nationality **2** : a badge of office, rank, or power **3** : an officer rank in the Navy and Coast Guard below lieutenant junior grade [Middle French *enseigne*, from Latin *insignia* "insignia, flags"]

en·si·lage \'en-sə-lij\ *n* : SILAGE

en·sile \en-'sīl, in-\ *vt* : to prepare and store (fodder) for silage [French *ensiler*, from *en-* + *silo* "silo", from Spanish]

en·slave \in-'slāv\ *vt* : to reduce to slavery : SUBJUGATE — **en·slave·ment** \-mənt\ *n* — **en·slav·er** *n*

en·snare \in-'snaər, -'sneər\ *vt* : SNARE 1, ENTRAP

en·sue \in-'sü\ *vi* : to come after in time or as a result ⟨*ensuing* effects⟩ [Middle French *ensuivre*, from *en-* + *suivre* "to follow"] SYN SEE FOLLOW

en·sure \in-'shùr\ *vt* : to make sure, certain, or safe : GUARANTEE [Anglo-French *enseurer*]

en·tab·la·ture \in-'tab-lə-,chùr, -chər\ *n* : the upper section of a wall or story usually supported on columns or pilasters and in classical orders consisting of architrave, frieze, and cornice [obsolete French, derived from Latin *in-* + *tabula* "board, table"]

¹en·tail \in-'tāl\ *vt* **1** : to limit the inheritance of (property) to the owner's direct descendants or to a class of these **2** : to impose, involve, or imply as a necessary accompaniment or result [derived from Middle French *taille* "limitation", from Old French *taillier* "to cut, limit"] — **en·tail·ment** \-mənt\ *n*

²en·tail \'en-,tāl, in-'tāl\ *n* **1 a** : an entailing especially of lands **b** : an entailed estate **2** : the rule by which the descent of property is fixed

en·tan·gle \in-'tang-gəl\ *vt* **1** : to make tangled, complicated, or confused **2** : to involve in or as if in a tangle — **en·tan·gle·ment** \-gəl-mənt\ *n*

en·tente \än-'tänt\ *n* **1** : an international understanding providing for a common course of action **2** : a coalition of parties to an entente [French, from Old French, "intent, understanding"]

en·ter \'ent-ər\ *vb* **en·tered; en·ter·ing** \'ent-ə-ring, 'en-tring\ **1** : to go or come into : go or come in ⟨*enter* a room⟩ ⟨*enter* and leave by the same door⟩ **2** : to pass into or through usually by overcoming resistance : PIERCE **3** : to cause to be admitted to ⟨*enter* a child in kindergarten⟩ **4** : to become a member of : JOIN ⟨*enter* the hikers' club⟩ **5** : to make a beginning ⟨*enter* into business⟩ **6** : to take part or play a part ⟨*enter* into a discussion⟩ **7** : to take possession ⟨*entered* upon their inheritance⟩ **8** : to put in : INSERT ⟨*enter* the new data into the computer⟩ **9** : to make a report to customs officials of (a ship or its cargo) upon arrival in port **10** : to put formally on record ⟨*enter* a complaint⟩ [Old French *entrer*, from Latin *intrare*, from *intra* "within"] — **en·ter·able** \'ent-ə-rə-bəl\ *adj* □ SYN ENTER, PENETRATE, PIERCE mean to make way into something. ENTER is the general term and may imply going in or forcing a way in; PENETRATE carries a strong implication of an impelling force or compelling power that achieves entrance; PIERCE adds an implication of running through with a sharp-pointed instrument.

enter- *or* **entero-** *combining form* : intestine ⟨*enter*itis⟩ [Greek *enteron*]

en·ter·ic \en-'ter-ik\ *adj* : of or relating to the alimentary canal : INTESTINAL

en·ter·i·tis \ˌent-ə-'rīt-əs\ *n* : inflammation of the intestine or a disease marked by this

en·tero·coc·cus \ˌent-ə-rō-'käk-əs\ *n* : STREPTOCOCCUS; *esp* : one normally present in the intestine — **en·tero·coc·cal** \-'käk-əl\ *adj*

en·tero·coele *or* **en·tero·coel** \'ent-ə-rō-ˌsēl\ *n* : a coelom originating by outgrowth from the cavity of the gastrula — **en·tero·coe·lic** \ˌent-ə-rō-'sē-lik\ *adj* — **en·tero·coe·lous** \-ləs\ *adj*

en·tero·ki·nase \ˌent-ə-rō-'kīn-ˌās, -ˌnāz\ *n* : an intestinal enzyme that converts trypsinogen to trypsin [*enter-* + *kin*etic + *-ase*]

en·ter·on \'ent-ə-ˌrän, -rən\ *n* : an embryonic alimentary canal

en·ter·prise \'ent-ər-ˌprīz, 'ent-ə-ˌ\ *n* **1** : a difficult, complicated, or risky project or undertaking **2** : a business organization **3** : readiness to engage in daring or difficult action : INITIATIVE [Middle French *entreprise*, from *entreprendre* "to undertake", from *entre-* "inter-" + *prendre* "to take", from Latin *prehendere* "to seize"] — **en·ter·pris·er** \-ˌprī-zər\ *n*

en·ter·pris·ing \-ˌprī-zing\ *adj* : marked by an independent energetic spirit and by readiness to undertake or experiment

en·ter·tain \ˌent-ər-'tān\ *vb* **1** : to receive and provide for as host : have as a guest ⟨*entertain* friends over the weekend⟩ **2** : to provide entertainment especially for guests **3** : to have in mind : CONSIDER ⟨*entertained* thoughts of quitting the job⟩ **4** : to provide entertainment for ⟨*entertain* the class with a play⟩ [Middle French *entretenir*, from *entre-* "inter-" + *tenir* "to hold", from Latin *tenēre*] SYN see AMUSE

en·ter·tain·er \-'tā-nər\ *n* : one that entertains; *esp* : one that gives or takes part in public entertainments

en·ter·tain·ment \-'tān-mənt\ *n* **1** : provision for guests especially in public places (as hotels and inns) **2** : AMUSEMENT 3, RECREATION **3** : a means of amusement or recreation; *esp* : a public performance

en·thrall *or* **en·thral** \in-'thról\ *vt* **en·thralled; en·thrall·ing 1** : ENSLAVE **2** : to hold spellbound : CHARM — **en·thrall·ment** \-'thról-mənt\ *n*

en·throne \in-'thrōn\ *vt* **1** : to seat ceremonially on a throne **2** : to regard as of supreme virtue or value : EXALT — **en·throne·ment** \-mənt\ *n*

en·thuse \in-'thüz, -'thyüz\ *vb* **1** : to make or grow enthusiastic **2** : to show enthusiasm [back-formation from *enthusiasm*]

en·thu·si·asm \in-'thü-zē-ˌaz-əm, -'thyü-\ *n* **1** : strong excitement of feeling : FERVOR **2** : something inspiring zeal or fervor [Greek *enthousiasmos*, from *enthousiazein* "to be inspired", from *entheos* "inspired", from *en-* + *theos* "god"] SYN see ZEAL

en·thu·si·ast \-zē-ˌast, -əst\ *n* : a person filled with enthusiasm

en·thu·si·as·tic \in-ˌthü-zē-'as-tik, -ˌthyü-\ *adj* : filled with or marked by enthusiasm ⟨an *enthusiastic* welcome⟩ — **en·thu·si·as·ti·cal·ly** \-ti-kə-lē, -klē\ *adv*

en·tice \in-'tīs\ *vt* : to attract by arousing hope or desire : TEMPT [Old French *enticier*] — **en·tice·ment** \-mənt\ *n*

en·tire \in-'tīr, 'en-ˌ\ *adj* **1** : having no element or part left out **2** : COMPLETE, TOTAL ⟨an *entire* regiment was lost⟩ **3** : consisting of one piece **4** : having the margin continuous and free from indentations ⟨an *entire* leaf⟩ [Middle French *entir*, from Latin *integer*, literally, "untouched", from *in-* + *tangere* "to touch"] SYN see WHOLE — **entire** *adv* — **en·tire·ly** *adv* — **en·tire·ness** *n*

en·tire·ty \in-'tī-rət-ē, -'tīrt-ē\ *n* **1** : the state of being entire or complete **2** : sum total : WHOLE

en·ti·tle \in-'tīt-l\ *vt* **en·ti·tled; en·ti·tling** \-'tīt-ling, -l-ing\ **1** : to give a title to : DESIGNATE **2 a** : to give a legal right to **b** : to qualify for something — **en·ti·tle·ment** \-'tīt-l-mənt\ *n*

en·ti·ty \'ent-ət-ē\ *n, pl* **-ties** : something existing or thought of as existing : BEING [Medieval Latin *entitas*, from Latin *ent-, ens* "existing thing", from coined present participle of *esse* "to be"]

en·tomb \in-'tüm\ *vt* : to place in a tomb : BURY — **en·tomb·ment** \-'tüm-mənt\ *n*

en·to·mol·o·gy \ˌent-ə-'mäl-ə-jē\ *n* : a branch of zoology that deals with insects [French *entomologie*, from Greek *entomon* "insect", from *entomos* "cut up", from *en-* + *temnein* "to cut"] — see INSECT origin — **en·to·mo·log·i·cal** \ˌent-ə-mə-'läj-i-kəl\ *adj* — **en·to·mo·log·i·cal·ly** \-i-kə-lē, -klē\ *adv* — **en·to·mol·o·gist** \ˌent-ə-'mäl-ə-jəst\ *n*

en·tou·rage \ˌän-tu̇-'räzh\ *n* : one's attendants or associates : RETINUE [French]

en·tr'acte \'än-ˌtrakt, 'änᵊ-; än-ˌ; änᵊ-'\ *n* **1** : the interval between two acts of a play **2** : a dance, piece of music, or interlude performed between two acts of a play [French, from *entre-* "inter-" + *acte* "act"]

en·trails \'en-trəlz, -ˌtrālz\ *n pl* : internal parts : VISCERA; *esp* : INTESTINES [Middle French *entrailles*, from Medieval Latin *intralia*, alteration of Latin *interanea* from *interaneus* "interior"]

en·train \in-'trān\ *vb* : to put or go aboard a railroad train

¹en·trance \'en-trəns\ *n* **1** : the act of entering **2** : the means or place of entry **3** : power or permission to enter : ADMISSION

²en·trance \in-'trans\ *vt* **1** : to put into a trance **2** : to fill with delight, wonder, or rapture — **en·trance·ment** \-mənt\ *n*

en·trant \'en-trənt\ *n* : one that enters; *esp* : one that enters a contest

en·trap \in-'trap\ *vt* **1** : to catch in or as if in a trap **2** : to lure into a compromising statement or act — **en·trap·ment** \-mənt\ *n*

en·treat \in-'trēt\ *vb* : to ask earnestly or urgently : PLEAD [Middle French *entraitier* "to treat", from *en-* + *traitier* "to treat"] SYN see BEG — **en·treat·ing·ly** \-ing-lē\ *adv*

en·treaty \in-'trēt-ē\ *n, pl* **-treat·ies** : an earnest request : PLEA

en·trée *or* **en·tree** \'än-ˌtrā\ *n* **1 a** : the act or manner of entering : ENTRANCE **b** : freedom of entry or access **2** : the principal dish of a meal in the United States [French *entrée*]

en·trench *or* **in·trench** \in-'trench\ *vb* **1 a** : to dig, place within, surround with, or occupy a trench especially for defense **b** : to establish solidly **2** : to cut into : FURROW; *esp* : to erode downward so as to form a trench **3** : ENCROACH 1 — used with *on* or *upon*

en·trench·ment \in-'trench-mənt\ *n* **1** : the act of entrenching : the state of being entrenched **2** : DEFENSE; *esp* : a defensive work consisting of a trench and a wall of earth

en·tre·pre·neur \ˌän-trə-prə-'nər, -pə-, -'nu̇r, -'nyu̇r\ *n* : one who organizes, manages, and assumes the risks of a business or enterprise [French]

en·tro·py \'en-trə-pē\ *n* **1** : a measure of the unavailable energy in a closed thermodynamic system **2** : the degradation of the matter and energy in the universe to an ultimate state of inert uniformity [German *entropie*, from Greek *en-* + *trepein* "to turn, change"]

en·trust *or* **in·trust** \in-'trəst\ *vt* **1** : to give into the care of another (as for safekeeping) **2** : to give custody, care, or charge of something to as a trust ⟨*entrusted* a bank with their savings⟩ — **en·trust·ment** \-'trəst-mənt, -'trəs-\ *n*

en·try \'en-trē\ *n, pl* **entries 1** : the act of entering : ENTRANCE **2** : a place through which entrance is made : HALL 3a, VESTIBULE **3 a** : the act of making (as in a book or list) a written record of something **b** : the thing thus recorded: as (1) : HEADWORD (2) : a head-

\ə\ abut   \ng\ sing
\ər\ further   \ō\ bone
\a\ mat   \ȯ\ saw
\ā\ take   \ȯi\ coin
\ä\ cot, cart   \th\ thin
\au̇\ out   \th\ this
\ch\ chin   \ü\ food
\e\ pet   \u̇\ foot
\ē\ easy   \y\ yet
\g\ go   \yü\ few
\i\ tip   \yu̇\ cure
\ī\ life   \zh\ vision
\j\ job

word with its definition or identification (3) : VOCABU-LARY ENTRY **4** : a person, thing, or group entered in a contest or race

en·twine \in-'twīn\ *vb* : to twine together or around

enu·mer·ate \i-'nü-mə-ˌrāt, -'nyü-\ *vt* **1** : to ascertain the number of : COUNT **2** : to specify one after anoth-er : LIST [Latin *enumerare,* from *e-* + *numerare* "to count", from *numerus* "number"] — **enu·mer·a·ble** \-'nüm-rə-bəl, 'nyüm-, -ə-rə-\ *adj* — **enu·mer·a·tion** \-ˌnü-mə-'rā-shən, -ˌnyü-\ *n* — **enu·mer·a·tor** \-'nü-mə-ˌrāt-ər, -'nyü-\ *n*

enun·ci·ate \ē-'nən-sē-ˌāt\ *vt* **1** : to make known pub-licly : PROCLAIM ⟨*enunciate* the aims of a program⟩ **2** : to utter distinctly : PRONOUNCE ⟨*enunciate* your words clearly⟩ [Latin *enuntiare* "to report, declare", from *e-* + *nuntiare* "to report", from *nuntius* "messenger"] — **enun·ci·a·tion** \-ˌnən-sē-'ā-shən\ *n*

en·ure·sis \ˌen-yů-'rē-səs\ *n* : involuntary discharge of urine : bed wetting [New Latin, from Greek *enourein* "to urinate in, wet the bed", from *en-* + *ourein* "to urinate"] — **en·uret·ic** \-'ret-ik\ *adj or n*

en·vel·op \in-'vel-əp\ *vt* : to enclose or enfold com-pletely with or as if with a covering [Middle French *enveloper,* from Old French *envoloper,* from *en-* + *vo-loper* "to wrap"] — **en·vel·op·ment** \-mənt\ *n*

en·ve·lope \'en-və-ˌlōp, 'än-\ *n* **1** : something that en-velops **2** : a flat usually paper container (as for a let-ter) **3** : the bag containing the gas in a balloon or air-ship **4** : a natural enclosing covering (as a membrane)

en·ven·om \in-'ven-əm\ *vt* **1** : to taint or fill with poi-son **2** : EMBITTER

en·vi·a·ble \'en-vē-ə-bəl\ *adj* : highly desirable — **en·vi·a·ble·ness** *n* — **en·vi·a·bly** \-blē\ *adv*

en·vi·ous \'en-vē-əs\ *adj* : feeling or showing envy ⟨*en-vious* of a friend's wealth⟩ — **en·vi·ous·ly** *adv* — **en·vi·ous·ness** *n* □ SYN JEALOUS: ENVIOUS suggests a spiteful or malicious grudging of another's possessions and ac-complishments; JEALOUS implies a grudging of some-thing regarded as properly belonging to oneself; it may also indicate a vigilant guarding ⟨*jealous* of one's good name and honor⟩

en·vi·ron·ment \in-'vī-rən-mənt, -'vī-ərn-, -'vīrn-\ *n* **1** : the circumstances, objects, or conditions by which one is surrounded **2** : surrounding conditions or forces that influence or change: as **a** : the whole com-plex of factors (as soil, climate, and living things) that determine the form and survival of an organism or eco-logical community **b** : the social and cultural condi-tions that influence the life of a person or human com-munity [*environ* "to surround", from Middle French *environner,* from *environ* "around", from *en* "in" + *viron* "circle"] — **en·vi·ron·men·tal** \in-ˌvī-rən-'ment-l, -ˌvī-ərn-, -ˌvīrn-\ *adj* — **en·vi·ron·men·tal·ly** \-l-ē\ *adv*

en·vi·ron·men·tal·ist \-ˌvī-rən-'ment-l-əst, -ˌvī-ərn-, -ˌvīrn-\ *n* : one concerned about the quality of the hu-man environment

en·vi·rons \in-'vī-rənz, -'vī-ərnz, -'vīrnz\ *n pl* **1** : the districts around a city **2** : ENVIRONMENT 1

en·vis·age \in-'viz-ij\ *vt* : to have a mental picture of especially in advance of realization : VISUALIZE

en·vi·sion \in-'vizh-ən\ *vt* : to picture to oneself

en·voy \'en-ˌvȯi, 'än-\ *n* **1 a** : a diplomatic representa-tive who ranks between an ambassador and a minister **b** : a representative sent by one government to another **2** : REPRESENTATIVE 2a, MESSENGER [French *envoyé,* from *envoyer* "to send", from Latin *in-* + *via* "way"]

¹en·vy \'en-vē\ *n, pl* **envies** **1** : painful or resentful awareness of an advantage enjoyed by another joined with a desire to possess the same advantage **2** : an ob-ject of envy ⟨their new car was the *envy* of the neigh-borhood⟩ [Old French *envie,* from Latin *invidia,* from *invidus* "envious", from *invidēre* "to look askance at, envy", from *in-* + *vidēre* "to see"]

²envy *vt* **en·vied; en·vy·ing** : to feel envy toward or on account of — **en·vi·er** *n* — **en·vy·ing·ly** \-ing-lē\ *adv*

en·wrap \in-'rap\ *vt* **1** : to wrap in a covering : ENFOLD **2** : to hold one's interest : ENGROSS

en·zy·mat·ic \ˌen-zə-'mat-ik\ *adj* : of, relating to, or produced by an enzyme — **en·zy·mat·i·cal·ly** \-i-kə-lē, -klē\ *adv*

en·zyme \'en-ˌzīm\ *n* : any of various complex proteins produced by living cells that bring about or accelerate reactions (as in the digestion of food at body tempera-tures) without being permanently altered [German *en-zym,* derived from Greek *en-* + *zymē* "leaven"]

en·zy·mic \en-'zī-mik\ *adj* : ENZYMATIC — **en·zy·mi·cal-ly** \-mi-kə-lē, -klē\ *adv*

eo- *combining form* : earliest : oldest ⟨*Eo*cene⟩ [Greek *ēōs* "dawn"]

Eo·cene \'ē-ə-ˌsēn\ *n* : the epoch of the Tertiary be-tween the Paleocene and the Oligocene; *also* : the corresponding system of rocks — **Eocene** *adj*

eo·hip·pus \ˌē-ō-'hip-əs\ *n* : any of a genus of small primitive horses from the Lower Eocene of the west-ern United States with four toes on each forelimb [Greek *hippos* "horse"]

eo·lian *also* **ae·o·lian** \ē-'ō-lē-ən, -'ōl-yən\ *adj* : borne, deposited, produced, or eroded by the wind ⟨*eolian* sand⟩ [Latin *Aeolus,* god of the winds]

eo·lith \'ē-ə-ˌlith\ *n* : a very crudely chipped flint from the earliest phase of human culture

Eo·lith·ic \ˌē-ə-'lith-ik\ *adj* : of or relating to the early period of the Stone Age marked by the use of eoliths — compare NEOLITHIC, PALEOLITHIC

eon *variant of* AEON

eo·sin \'ē-ə-sən\ *or* **eo·sine** \-sən, -ˌsēn\ *n* : a red syn-thetic fluorescent dye used especially in cosmetics and as a toner; *also* : a salt of this dye used chiefly in red pigments and as a stain for biological tissue [Greek *ēōs* "dawn"]

-eous *adj suffix* : like : resembling [Latin *-eus*]

ep·au·let *also* **ep·au·lette** \ˌep-ə-'let\ *n* : a shoulder or-nament on a uniform especially of a military or naval officer [French *épaulette,* from *épaule* "shoulder", from Late Latin *spatula* "shoulder blade, spoon", from Latin *spatha* "spoon, sword"]

épée \'ep-ˌā, ā-'pā\ *n* : a fencing or dueling sword hav-ing a bowl-shaped guard and a tapering rigid blade with no cutting edge [French, from Latin *spatha* "spoon, sword"]

ephah \'ē-fə, 'ef-ə\ *n* : an ancient Hebrew unit of dry measure equal to a little more than a bushel (about 35 liters) [Hebrew *ēphāh,* from Egyptian *'pt*]

ephed·rine \i-'fed-rən\ *n* : a crystalline basic substance extracted from Chinese woody plants or synthesized and used as a salt in relieving hay fever, asthma, and nasal congestion [New Latin *Ephedra,* genus of shrubs]

ephem·era \i-'fem-rə, -ə-rə\ *n pl* : ephemeral things

ephem·er·al \i-'fem-rəl, -ə-rəl\ *adj* **1** : lasting one day only **2** : lasting a very short time [Greek *ephēmeros* "lasting a day, daily", from *epi-* + *hēmera* "day"] — **ephem·er·al·ly** \-rə-lē\ *adv*

ephem·er·is \-rəs\ *n, pl* **eph·e·mer·i·des** \ˌef-ə-'mer-ə-ˌdēz\ : a tabular statement of the assigned places of a celestial body for regular intervals [Latin, "diary, ephemeris", from Greek *ephēmeris,* from *ephēmeros* "daily"]

Ephe·sians \i-'fē-zhənz\ *n* — see BIBLE table

eph·or \'ef-ər, -ˌȯr\ *n* : one of five ancient Spartan mag-istrates having power over the king [Latin *ephorus,* from Greek *ephoros,* from *ephoran* "to oversee", from *epi-* + *horan* "to see"]

epi- *or* **ep-** *prefix* : upon ⟨*epi*phyte⟩ : near to : over ⟨*epi*center⟩ : outer ⟨*epi*carp⟩ : after ⟨*epi*genesis⟩ [Greek, from *epi* "on"]

¹ep·ic \'ep-ik\ *adj* **1** : of, relating to, or having the char-acteristics of an epic **2** : unusually long especially in size or scope [Latin *epicus*, from Greek *epikos*, from *epos* "word, speech, poem"]

²epic *n* **1** : a long serious narrative poem in a dignified style relating the deeds of a legendary or historical hero **2** : a work of art that resembles or suggests an epic **3** : a series of events or body of tradition held to form the proper subject of an epic ⟨the winning of the West was a great American *epic*⟩

epi·carp \'ep-ə-,kärp\ *n* : the usually thin membranous outermost layer of the pericarp of a fruit (as the skin of a peach) — compare ENDOCARP, MESOCARP

epi·cen·ter \'ep-ə-,sent-ər\ *n* **1** : the part of the earth's surface directly above the focus of an earthquake **2** : CENTER 2a ⟨the *epicenter* of cultural activity⟩

ep·i·cot·yl \'ep-ə-,kät-l\ *n* : the part of a plant embryo or seedling above the cotyledons

ep·i·cure \'ep-i-,kyür\ *n* : a person with sensitive and discriminating tastes in food or wine [*Epicurus*, died 270 B.C., Greek philosopher]

¹ep·i·cu·re·an \,ep-i-kyü-'rē-ən, -'kyür-ē-\ *adj* **1** *cap* : of or relating to Epicurus or Epicureanism **2** : of, relating to, or suited to an epicure

²epicurean *n* **1** *cap* : a follower of Epicurus **2** : EPICURE

Ep·i·cu·re·an·ism \-ə-,niz-əm\ *n* : the philosophy of Epicurus that pleasure is the only good and the pleasures of wise, just, and moderate living are the best

¹ep·i·dem·ic \,ep-ə-'dem-ik\ *adj* **1** : affecting many individuals at one time ⟨an *epidemic* disease⟩ **2** : widespread especially to an excessive degree ⟨crime was *epidemic*⟩ [French *épidémique*, erived from Greek *epidēmia* "visit, epidemic", from *epi-* + *dēmos* "people"] — **ep·i·dem·i·cal·ly** \-'dem-i-kə-lē, -klē\ *adv* — **ep·i·de·mic·i·ty** \-,dem-'is-ət-ē\ *n*

²epidemic *n* **1** : an outbreak of epidemic disease **2** : a sudden rapidly spreading outbreak

ep·i·de·mi·ol·o·gy \,ep-ə-,dē-mē-'äl-ə-jē\ *n* **1** : a branch of medical science that deals with the rate of occurrence, distribution, and control of disease in a population **2** : the sum of the factors controlling the presence or absence of a particular disease — **ep·i·de·mi·o·log·ic** \-mē-ə-'läj-ik\ *or* **ep·i·de·mi·o·log·i·cal** \-'läj-i-kəl\ *adj* — **ep·i·de·mi·o·log·i·cal·ly** \-i-kə-lē, -klē\ *adv* — **ep·i·de·mi·ol·o·gist** \-mē-'äl-ə-jəst\ *n*

epi·der·mis \,ep-ə-'dər-məs\ *n* **1** : the thin outer layer of the animal body that in vertebrates forms an insensitive covering over the dermis **2** : a thin surface layer of protecting cells in seed plants and ferns **3** : any of various covering layers resembling the epidermis of the skin [Late Latin, from Greek, from *epi-* + *derma* "skin"] — **epi·der·mal** \-məl\ *adj*

ep·i·did·y·mis \,ep-ə-'did-ə-məs\ *n, pl* **-mi·des** \-mə-,dēz\ : a mass at the back of the testis composed of coiled tubes in which sperms are stored [Greek, from *epi-* + *didymos* "testicle", from *dyo* "two"] — **epi·did·y·mal** \-'did-ə-məl\ *adj*

epi·gen·e·sis \,ep-ə-'jen-ə-səs\ *n, pl* **-e·ses** \-,sēz\ : development in which an initially unspecialized entity (as a spore) gradually develops specialized characters (as of a whole plant) — **ep·i·ge·net·ic** \-jə-'net-ik\ *adj*

epi·glot·tis \,ep-ə-'glät-əs\ *n* : a thin plate of flexible cartilage in front of the glottis that folds back over and protects the glottis during swallowing — **epi·glot·tal** \-'glät-l\ *adj*

ep·i·gram \'ep-ə-,gram\ *n* **1** : a short often satirical poem ending with a clever turn of thought **2** : a brief witty saying [Latin *epigramma*, from Greek, from *epigraphein* "to write on, inscribe", from *epi-* + *graphein* " to write"] — **ep·i·gram·ma·tist** \,ep-ə-'gram-ət-əst\ *n*

ep·i·gram·mat·ic \,ep-i-grə-'mat-ik\ *adj* **1** : of, relating to, or resembling an epigram **2** : marked by or given to the use of epigrams — **ep·i·gram·mat·i·cal** \-'mat-i-kəl\ *adj* — **ep·i·gram·mat·i·cal·ly** \-i-kə-lē, -klē\ *adv*

epig·ra·phy \i-'pig-rə-fē, e-\ *n* : the study of inscriptions and especially of ancient inscriptions [Greek *epigraphein* "to inscribe", from *epi-* + *graphein* "to write"]

epig·y·nous \i-'pij-ə-nəs, e-\ *adj* **1** : grown to and appearing to arise from the top of a plant ovary ⟨*epigynous* stamens⟩ **2** : having epigynous floral organs

ep·i·lep·sy \'ep-ə-,lep-sē\ *n* : a disorder marked by disturbed electrical rhythms of the central nervous system and characterized by convulsive fits and loss of consciousness [Middle French *epilepsie*, from Late Latin *epilepsia*, from Greek *epilēpsia*, from *epilambanein* "to seize", from *epi-* + *lambanein* "to take, seize"] — **ep·i·lep·tic** \,ep-ə-'lep-tik\ *adj or n*

ep·i·logue \'ep-ə-,lóg, -,läg\ *n* **1** : a concluding section that rounds out the design of a literary work **2** : a speech often in verse addressed to the audience by an actor at the end of a play **3** : a concluding event or development [Middle French, from Latin *epilogus*, from Greek *epilogos*, from *epilegein* "to say in addition", from *epi-* + *legein* "to say"]

epi·neph·rine *also* **epi·neph·rin** \,ep-ə-'nef-rən\ *n* : a hormone of the adrenal gland acting especially on smooth muscle, causing narrowing of blood vessels, and raising blood pressure — called also *adrenaline* [derived from Greek *epi-* + *nephros* "kidney"]

epiph·a·ny \i-'pif-ə-nē\ *n, pl* **-nies 1** *cap* : January 6 observed as a church festival in commemoration of the coming of the three wise men to Jesus at Bethlehem **2** : an appearance or manifestation especially of a divine being [Middle French *epiphanie*, from Late Latin *epiphania*, from Late Greek, plural, probably from Greek *epiphaneia* "appearance, manifestation", from *epi-* + *phainein* "to show"]

epiph·y·sis \i-'pif-ə-səs\ *n, pl* **-y·ses** \-ə-,sēz\ : the end of a long bone [Greek, "growth", from *epi-* + *physesthai* "to grow"] — **epiph·y·se·al** \i-,pif-ə-'sē-əl\ *adj*

ep·i·phyte \'ep-ə-,fīt\ *n* : a plant that derives its moisture and nutrients from the air and rain and grows usually on another plant

ep·i·phyt·ic \,ep-ə-'fit-ik\ *adj* **1** : of, relating to, or being an epiphyte **2** : living on the surface of plants ⟨*epiphytic* algae on kelps⟩ — **ep·i·phyt·i·cal·ly** \-'fit-i-kə-lē, -klē\ *adv*

epi·scia \i-'pish-ē-ə, -'pish-ə\ *n* : any of a genus of tropical American herbs often grown for their showy hairy foliage and reddish flowers [Greek *episkios* "shaded", from *epi-* + *skia* "shadow"]

epis·co·pa·cy \i-'pis-kə-pə-sē\ *n, pl* **-cies 1** : government of the church by bishops **2** : EPISCOPATE 2

epis·co·pal \i-'pis-kə-pəl\ *adj* **1** : of or relating to a bishop or episcopacy **2** *cap* : of or relating to the Protestant Episcopal Church [Late Latin *episcopalis*, from *episcopus* "bishop", from Greek *episkopos*, literally, "overseer", from *epi-* + *skeptesthai* "to look at"] — **epis·co·pal·ly** \-pə-lē, -plē\ *adv*

Epis·co·pa·lian \i-,pis-kə-'pāl-yən\ *n* **1** : an adherent of episcopacy **2** : a member of the Protestant Episcopal Church — **Episcopalian** *adj* — **Epis·co·pa·lian·ism** \-yə-,niz-əm\ *n*

epis·co·pate \i-'pis-kə-pət\ *n* **1** : the rank, office, or term of office of a bishop **2** : the whole body of bishops

ep·i·sode \'ep-ə-,sōd\ *n* **1 a** : a developed situation integral to but separable from a continuous narrative : INCIDENT **b** : one of a series of loosely connected stories or scenes **2** : an event that is distinctive and separate especially in history or in a life ⟨an *episode* of the war⟩ ⟨an *episode* of coughing⟩ **3** : a digressive subdivision in a musical composition [Greek *epeisodion*, from *epeisodios* "coming in besides", from *epi-* + *eisodios* "coming in", from *eis* "into" + *hodos* "road"] SYN see OCCURRENCE — **ep·i·sod·ic** \,ep-ə-'säd-ik\ *also* **ep·i·sod·i·cal** \-'säd-i-kəl\ *adj* — **ep·i·sod·i·cal·ly** \-i-kə-lē, -klē\ *adv*

epis·tle \i-'pis-əl\ *n* **1** *cap* **a** : any of the letters of the New Testament **b** : a liturgical reading usually from one of the New Testament Epistles **2 :** LETTER 2; *esp* **:** a formal or elegant letter [Old French, literally, "letter", from Latin *epistula, epistola,* from Greek *epistolē,* from *epi-* + *stellein* "to send"]

epis·to·lary \i-'pis-tə-ˌler-ē\ *adj* **1 :** of, relating to, or suitable to a letter **2 :** contained in or carried on by letters **3 :** written in the form of a series of letters ⟨an *epistolary* novel⟩

ep·i·taph \'ep-ə-ˌtaf\ *n* **:** an inscription (as on a tombstone) in memory of a dead person [Middle French *epitaphe,* from Latin *epitaphium* "funeral oration", from Greek *epitaphion,* from *epi-* + *taphos* "tomb, funeral"]

ep·i·the·li·um \ˌep-ə-'thē-lē-əm\ *n, pl* **-lia** \-lē-ə\ **1 :** a membranous cellular tissue that covers a free surface or lines a tube or cavity of an animal body and usually encloses parts of the body, produces secretions and excretions, or functions in assimilation **2 :** a usually thin layer of parenchyma that lines a cavity or tube of a plant [*epi-* + Greek *thēlē* "nipple"] — **ep·i·the·li·al** \-lē-əl\ *adj* — **ep·i·the·li·oid** \-lē-ˌoid\ *adj*

ep·i·thet \'ep-ə-ˌthet\ *n* **1 :** a word or phrase (as *Lion-Hearted* in "Richard the Lion-Hearted") that expresses a quality held to be characteristic of a person or thing **2 :** a disparaging or abusive word or phrase **3 :** the part of a taxonomic name identifying a subunit (as a species or variety) within a genus [Latin *epitheton,* from Greek, from *epitithenai* "to put on, add", from *epi-* + *tithenai* "to put"] — **ep·i·thet·ic** \ˌep-ə-'thet-ik\ *adj*

epit·o·me \i-'pit-ə-mē\ *n* **1 :** a summary of a written work **2 :** a typical or ideal example : EMBODIMENT ⟨the *epitome* of good taste⟩ [Latin, from Greek *epitomē,* from *epitemnein* "to cut short", from *epi-* + *temnein* "to cut"]

epit·o·mize \i-'pit-ə-ˌmīz\ *vt* **1 :** to form or give an epitome of : SUMMARIZE **2 :** TYPIFY 2, EXEMPLIFY

¹epi·zo·ot·ic \ˌep-ə-zə-'wät-ik\ *adj* **:** of, relating to, or being a disease that affects many animals of one kind at the same time

²epizootic *n* **:** an epizootic disease

e plu·ri·bus unum \ˌē-ˌplu̇r-ə-bəs-'yü-nəm; ˌā-ˌplu̇r-, -bə-'sü-\ **:** one composed of many — used on the seal of the United States and on several United States coins [Latin, "one out of many"]

ep·och \'ep-ək, -ˌäk\ *n* **1 :** an instant of time selected as a point of reference in astronomy **2 a :** an event or a time that begins a new period or development **b :** a memorable event or date **3 a :** an extended period of time characterized by a distinctive development or by a memorable series of events **b :** a division of geologic time less than a period and greater than an age [Medieval Latin *epocha,* from Greek *epochē* "cessation, fixed point", from *epechein* "to pause, hold back", from *epi-* + *echein* "to hold"] SYN see PERIOD — **ep·och·al** \-əl\ *adj* — **ep·och·al·ly** \-ə-lē\ *adv*

epon·y·mous \i-'pän-ə-məs, e-\ *adj* **:** of, relating to, or being the person for whom something is named or is believed to be named [Greek *epōnymos,* from *epi-* + *onyma* "name"]

ep·oxy resin \ˌep-'äk-sē-\ *n* **:** a flexible usually thermosetting resin made by polymerization of an oxygen-containing compound and used chiefly in coatings and adhesives — called also *epoxy* [*epi-* + *oxy*gen]

ep·si·lon \'ep-sə-ˌlän, -lən\ *n* **:** the 5th letter of the Greek alphabet — E or ε

Ep·som salt \'ep-səm-\ *n* **:** a bitter colorless or white crystalline salt $MgSO_4 \cdot 7H_2O$ that is a hydrated sulfate of magnesium and is used especially as a cathartic — usually used in pl. [*Epsom,* England]

eq·ua·ble \'ek-wə-bəl, 'ē-kwə-\ *adj* **:** EVEN 2, UNIFORM; *esp* **:** free from extremes or sudden or harsh changes ⟨an *equable* temper⟩ ⟨an *equable* climate⟩ [Latin *aequabilis,* from *aequare* "to make level or equal", from *aequus* "level, equal"] — **eq·ua·bly** \-blē\ *adv*

¹equal \'ē-kwəl\ *adj* **1 a** (1) **:** of the same measure, quantity, amount, or number as another : LIKE (2) **:** identical in value : EQUIVALENT **b :** like in quality, nature, or status **c :** like for all; *esp* **:** not restricted to a particular ethnic, social, or sexual group ⟨*equal* job opportunities⟩ **d :** not varying : UNIFORM **2 :** FAIR 5a, IMPARTIAL **3 a :** free from extremes **b :** tranquil of mind or mood **4 :** capable of meeting requirements ⟨was *equal* to the task⟩ [Latin *aequalis,* from *aequus* "level, equal"]

²equal *n* **1 :** one that is equal ⟨has no *equal* at chess⟩ **2 :** an equal quantity

³equal *vt* **equaled** *or* **equalled; equal·ing** *or* **equal·ling** **1 :** to be equal to; *esp* **:** to be identical in value to **2 :** to produce something equal to : MATCH

equal–area *adj* **:** preserving the true extent of area of the forms represented although with distortion of shape ⟨*equal-area* maps⟩

equal·i·ty \i-'kwäl-ət-ē\ *n, pl* **-ties 1 :** the quality or state of being equal **2 :** EQUATION 2a

equal·ize \'ē-kwə-ˌlīz\ *vt* **1 :** to make equal **2 :** to make uniform; *esp* **:** to distribute evenly or uniformly : BALANCE — **equal·iza·tion** \ˌē-kwə-lə-'zā-shən\ *n* — **equal·iz·er** \'ē-kwə-ˌlī-zər\ *n*

equal·ly \'ē-kwə-lē\ *adv* **1 :** in an equal manner : EVENLY **2 :** to an equal degree : ALIKE

equa·nim·i·ty \ˌē-kwə-'nim-ət-ē, ˌek-wə-\ *n* **:** evenness of emotion or temper ⟨accept misfortunes with *equanimity*⟩ [Latin *aequanimitas,* from *aequo animo* "with even mind"]

equate \i-'kwāt\ *vt* **:** to make or treat as equal : represent or express as equal or equivalent

equa·tion \i-'kwā-zhən, -shən\ *n* **1 a :** the act or process of equating **b :** a state of being equated; *esp* **:** the regarding of two or more things as identical or similar **2 a :** a statement of the equality of two mathematical expressions ⟨solve the *equation* $x^2 - 6x + 9 = 0$ for x⟩ **b :** an expression representing a chemical reaction by means of chemical symbols

equa·tion·al \i-'kwāzh-nəl, -'kwāsh-, -ən-l\ *adj* **:** of, using, or involving equations or the equating of elements

equa·tor \i-'kwāt-ər, 'ē-ˌkwāt-\ *n* **1 :** the great circle of the celestial sphere whose plane is perpendicular to the axis of the earth **2 :** a great circle of the earth that is everywhere equally distant from the two poles and divides the earth's surface into the northern and southern hemispheres **3 :** a circle or roughly circular cross section dividing a body into two usually equal and symmetrical parts ⟨chromosomes move to the *equator* of a dividing cell⟩ [Medieval Latin *aequator,* literally, "equalizer", from Latin *aequare* "to make equal"; from its containing the equinoxes]

equa·to·ri·al \ˌē-kwə-'tōr-ē-əl, ˌek-wə-, -'tȯr-\ *adj* **1 :** of, relating to, or located at the equator or an equator **2 :** of, originating in, or suggesting the region around the geographic equator ⟨*equatorial* heat⟩

equatorial plate *n* **:** METAPHASE PLATE

eq·uer·ry \'ek-wə-rē, i-'kwer-ē\ *n, pl* **-ries 1 :** an officer in charge of the horses of a prince or noble **2 :** a personal attendant of a member of the British royal family [Middle French *escuirie* "office of a squire, stable", from *escuier* "squire"]

¹eques·tri·an \i-'kwes-trē-ən\ *adj* **1 :** of, relating to, or featuring horseback riding **2 :** representing a person on horseback ⟨an *equestrian* statue⟩ [Latin *equester* "of a horseman", from *eques* "horseman", from *equus* "horse"]

²equestrian *n* **:** one who rides on horseback

equi- *combining form* **:** equal : equally ⟨*equi*poise⟩ ⟨*equi*potential⟩ [Latin *aequus* "equal"]

equi·an·gu·lar \ˌē-kwi-'ang-gyə-lər, ˌek-wi-\ *adj* **:** having all or corresponding angles equal ⟨an *equiangular* triangle⟩

equi·ca·lor·ic \,ē-kwa-ka-'lȯr-ik, ,ek-wa-, -'lär-\ *adj* : capable of yielding equal amounts of energy in the body ⟨*equicaloric* diets⟩

equi·dis·tant \,ē-kwə-'dis-tənt, ,ek-wə-\ *adj* : equally distant ⟨two points *equidistant* from a line⟩

equi·lat·er·al \,ē-kwə-'lat-ə-rəl, ,ek-wə-, -'la-trəl\ *adj* : having all sides or all faces equal ⟨*equilateral* triangle⟩

equil·i·brate \i-'kwil-ə-,brāt\ *vb* 1 : to bring into or keep in equilibrium 2 : to bring about, come to, or be in equilibrium — **equil·i·bra·tion** \i-,kwil-ə-'brā-shən\ *n*

equi·lib·ri·um \,ē-kwə-'lib-rē-əm, ,ek-wə-\ *n, pl* **-ri·ums** *or* **-ria** \-rē-ə\ 1 : a static or dynamic state of balance between opposing forces or actions 2 : a state of intellectual or emotional balance : POISE 3 : the normal oriented state of the animal body in respect to the ground beneath it [Latin *aequilibrium,* from *aequi-* "equi-" + *libra* "weight, balance"]

equine \'ē-,kwīn, 'ek-,wīn\ *adj* : of, relating to, or resembling a horse or the horse family [Latin *equinus,* from *equus* "horse"] — **equine** *n*

¹**equi·noc·tial** \,ē-kwə-'näk-shəl, ,ek-wə-\ *adj* 1 : of, relating to, or occurring at or near an equinox ⟨*equinoctial* storms⟩ 2 : of or relating to the regions or climate of the equator ⟨*equinoctial* lands⟩ ⟨*equinoctial* heat⟩

²**equinoctial** *n* 1 : EQUATOR 1 2 : an equinoctial storm

equinoctial circle *n* : EQUATOR 1 — called also *equinoctial line*

equi·nox \'ē-kwə-,näks, 'ek-wə-\ *n* 1 : either of the two times each year when the sun crosses the equator and day and night are everywhere of equal length that occur about March 21 and September 23 2 : either of the two points on the celestial sphere where the celestial equator intersects the ecliptic [Medieval Latin *equinoxium,* from Latin *aequinoctium,* from *aequi-* "equi-" + *noct-, nox* "night"]

equip \i-'kwip\ *vt* **equipped; equip·ping** : to provide with what is necessary for service or action [Middle French *equiper,* from Old French *eschiper* "to equip a ship", of Germanic origin]

eq·ui·page \'ek-wə-pij\ *n* 1 : material or articles used in equipment : OUTFIT 2 : a horse-drawn carriage with its attendants or the carriage alone

equip·ment \i-'kwip-mənt\ *n* 1 a : the equipping of a person or thing b : the state of being equipped 2 a : the articles or resources serving to equip a person or thing: as (1) : the implements used in an operation or activity : APPARATUS (2) : the rolling stock of a railway b : a piece of such equipment

eq·ui·poise \'ek-wə-,pȯiz, 'ē-kwə-\ *n* 1 : a state of balance : EQUILIBRIUM 2 : a weight used to balance another weight

equi·pon·der·ate \,ē-kwə-'pän-də-,rāt\ *vb* : to be or make equal in weight or force

equi·po·ten·tial \-pə-'ten-chəl\ *adj* : having the same electrical potential ⟨*equipotential* points⟩ : of uniform potential throughout

equi·prob·a·ble \'präb-ə-bəl, 'präb-bəl\ *adj* : having the same degree of logical or mathematical probability ⟨*equiprobable* alternatives⟩

eq·ui·se·tum \,ek-wə-'sēt-əm\ *n* : any of a genus of primitive perennial vascular plants with leaves reduced to sheaths at the nodes on the hollow jointed grooved shoots — called also *horsetail, scouring rush* [Latin *equisaetum,* from *equus* "horse" + *saeta* "bristle"]

eq·ui·ta·ble \'ek-wət-ə-bəl\ *adj* : having or exhibiting equity : JUST SYN see FAIR — **eq·ui·ta·ble·ness** *n* — **eq·ui·ta·bly** \-blē\ *adv*

eq·ui·ta·tion \,ek-wə-'tā-shən\ *n* : the act or art of riding on horseback [Latin *equitare* "to ride on horseback", from *eques* "horseman", from *equus* "horse"]

eq·ui·ty \'ek-wət-ē\ *n, pl* **-ties** 1 : fairness or justice in dealings between persons 2 : a system of law that is a more flexible supplement to common and statute law and is intended to protect legal rights and enforce legal duties 3 : the value of an owner's interest in a property in excess of claims against it

equivalence relation *n* : a relation (as equality) that for a given set of elements (as the real numbers) is symmetric, reflexive, and transitive and for any two elements may or may not hold

equiv·a·lent \i-'kwiv-lənt, -ə-lənt\ *adj* 1 a : alike or equal in number, numerical value, or meaning ⟨*equivalent* fractions⟩ b : having the same solution set ⟨*equivalent* equations⟩ c : equal in area or volume but not capable of superposition ⟨a square *equivalent* to a triangle⟩ 2 : corresponding or virtually identical in effect or function 3 : having the same chemical combining capacity [Late Latin *aequivalēre* "to have equal power", from Latin *aequi-* "equi-" + *valēre* "to be strong"] — **equiv·a·lence** \-ləns\ *n* — **equivalent** *n* — **equiv·a·lent·ly** *adv*

equiv·o·cal \i-'kwiv-ə-kəl\ *adj* 1 : having two or more possible meanings : AMBIGUOUS ⟨an *equivocal* answer⟩ 2 : DOUBTFUL 1, 4, UNCERTAIN ⟨an *equivocal* result⟩ 3 : QUESTIONABLE 2, SUSPICIOUS ⟨*equivocal* behavior⟩ [Late Latin *aequivocus,* from Latin *aequi-* "equi-" + *voc-, vox* "voice"] — **equiv·o·cal·ly** \-kə-lē, -klē\ *adv* — **equiv·o·cal·ness** \-kəl-nəs\ *n*

equiv·o·cate \i-'kwiv-ə-,kāt\ *vi* 1 : to use equivocal language especially with intent to deceive : QUIBBLE 2 : to avoid committing oneself in what one says — **equiv·o·ca·tion** \i-,kwiv-ə-'kā-shən\ *n* — **equiv·o·ca·tor** \i-'kwiv-ə-,kāt-ər\ *n*

¹**-er** \ər; *after some vowels, often* r; *after ng, usually* gər\ *adj suffix or adv suffix* — used to form the comparative degree of adjectives and adverbs of one syllable ⟨hott*er*⟩ ⟨dri*er*⟩ and of some adjectives and adverbs of two syllables ⟨kindli*er*⟩ and sometimes of longer ones [Old English *-ra* (in adjectives), *-or* (in adverbs)]

²**-er** \ər; *after some vowels, often* r *also* **-ier** \ē-ər, yər\ *or* **-yer** \yər\ *n suffix* 1 a : a person occupationally connected with ⟨furri*er*⟩ ⟨hatt*er*⟩ ⟨lawy*er*⟩ b : person or thing belonging to or associated with ⟨oldtim*er*⟩ c : native of : resident of ⟨cottag*er*⟩ ⟨New York*er*⟩ d : one that has ⟨three-deck*er*⟩ e : one that produces or yields ⟨pork*er*⟩ 2 a : one that does or performs ⟨a specified action⟩ ⟨report*er*⟩ — sometimes added to both elements of a compound ⟨build*er*-upp*er*⟩ b : one that is a suitable object of ⟨a specified action⟩ ⟨fry*er*⟩ 3 : one that is ⟨foreign*er*⟩ [Middle English, partly from Old English *-ere,* partly from Old French *-ier,* both from Latin *-arius* "-ary"]

era \'ir-ə, 'er-ə, 'ē-rə\ *n* 1 : a period of time reckoned from a special date or event ⟨the Christian *era* is computed from the birth of Christ⟩ 2 : an important or distinctive period of history ⟨the Revolutionary *era*⟩ 3 : one of the five major divisions of geologic time [Late Latin *aera,* from Latin, "counters", plural of *aer-, aes* "copper, money"] SYN see PERIOD

erad·i·cate \i-'rad-ə-,kāt\ *vt* : to remove by or as if by uprooting ⟨*eradicate* weeds⟩ [Latin *eradicare,* from *e-* + *radix* "root"] — **erad·i·ca·ble** \-'rad-i-kə-bəl\ *adj* — **erad·i·ca·tion** \-,rad-ə-'kā-shən\ *n* — **erad·i·ca·tor** \-'rad-ə-,kāt-ər\ *n*

erase \i-'rās\ *vb* 1 a : to rub or scrape out (as something written) b : to remove (recorded matter) from a magnetic tape 2 : to remove as if by erasing ⟨*erased* the event from their memories⟩ 3 : to yield to being erased [Latin *erasus,* past participle of *eradere* "to erase", from *e-* + *radere* "to scratch, scrape"] — **eras·abil·i·ty** \-,rā-sə-'bil-ət-ē\ *n* — **eras·able** \-'rā-sə-bəl\ *adj* □ SYN CANCEL, OBLITERATE, EXPUNGE: ERASE implies rubbing or wiping out symbols or impressions often for correction or insertion of new matter; CANCEL implies an action (as marking, revoking, or neutralizing) that makes a thing no longer effective or usable; OBLITERATE implies a covering up or defacing that re-

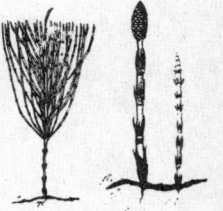

equisetum

\ə\ abut	\ng\ sing
\ər\ **further**	\ō\ **bone**
\a\ mat	\ȯ\ **saw**
\ā\ take	\ȯi\ **coin**
\ä\ cot, cart	\th\ **thin**
\au̇\ **out**	\t͟h\ **this**
\ch\ **chin**	\ü\ **food**
\e\ **pet**	\ẏ\ **foot**
\ē\ **easy**	\y\ **yet**
\g\ **go**	\yü\ **few**
\i\ **tip**	\yu̇\ **cure**
\ī\ **life**	\zh\ **vision**
\j\ **job**	

moves all distinct traces of a thing's existence; **EX-PUNGE** stresses a removal or destruction that leaves no trace.

eras·er \i-'rā-sər\ *n* : one that erases; *esp* : a device used to erase marks (as of chalk or ink)

era·sure \i-'rā-shər, -zhər\ *n* : an act or instance of erasing

er·bi·um \'ər-bē-əm\ *n* : a soft rare earth element that occurs with yttrium — see ELEMENT table [New Latin, from *Ytterby*, Sweden]

¹ere \,eər, ,aər\ *prep* : ²BEFORE 2 [Old English *ǣr* "early, soon"]

²ere *conj* : ³BEFORE 2

¹erect \i-'rekt\ *adj* **1 a** : vertical in position : UPRIGHT ⟨an *erect* pole⟩ **b** : straight in posture ⟨*erect* bearing⟩ **c** : standing up or out from the body ⟨a porcupine with quills *erect*⟩ **2** : directed upward ⟨a tree with *erect* branches⟩ **3** : being in a state of physiological erection [Latin *erectus*, past participle of *erigere* "to erect", from *e-* + *regere* "to lead straight"] — **erect·ly** *adv* — **erect·ness** \-'rekt-nəs, -'rek-\ *n*

²erect *vt* **1 a** : to put up by the fitting together of materials : BUILD ⟨*erect* a building⟩ **b** : to fix in an upright position ⟨*erect* a flagpole⟩ **c** : to cause to stand up or out **2** : to elevate in status **3** : to set up : ESTABLISH ⟨*erect* social barriers⟩ **4** : to construct (as a perpendicular) upon a given base — **erec·tor** \-'rek-tər\ *n*

erec·tile \i-'rek-tl, -,tīl\ *adj* : capable of becoming erect ⟨*erectile* tissue⟩ ⟨*erectile* feathers of a bird⟩

erec·tion \i-'rek-shən\ *n* **1** : the process of erecting : the state of being erected **2 a** : a state marked by firm turgid form and erect position of a previously limp and flabby bodily part whose tissue becomes dilated with blood **b** : an occurrence of such a state **3** : something erected

ere·long \eər-'lȯŋ, aər-\ *adv* : before long : SOON

er·e·mite \'er-ə-,mīt\ *n* : HERMIT 1 [Middle English]

erep·sin \i-'rep-sən\ *n* : a mixture of peptide-digesting enzymes from the intestinal juice [*er-* (probably from Latin *eripere* "to sweep away") + *pepsin*]

erg \'ərg\ *n* : a cgs unit of work equal to the work done by a force of one dyne acting through a distance of one centimeter and equivalent to 10^{-7} joule [Greek *ergon* "work"]

er·go \'eər-,gō, 'ər-\ *adv* : THEREFORE, HENCE [Latin]

er·gos·ter·ol \,ər-'gäs-tə-,rȯl, -,rōl\ *n* : a steroid alcohol that occurs especially in yeast, molds, and ergot and is converted by ultraviolet irradiation into vitamin D [*ergot* + *sterol*]

er·got \'ər-gət, -,gät\ *n* **1 a** : the dark club-shaped fruiting body of several fungi that replaces the seed of a grass (as rye) **b** : a disease of cereals (as rye) caused by ergot-producing fungi **2** : dried ergots that are used medicinally for their contractile effect on smooth muscle [French, literally, "cock's spur"]

er·got·ism \'ər-gət-,iz-əm\ *n* : a toxic condition caused by consumption of ergot (as in grain or bread)

Erie \'iər-ē\ *n* : a member of an Iroquoian people of the Lake Erie region

Er·len·mey·er flask \'ər-lən-,mī-ər-, 'er-lən-, -,mīr-\ *n* : a flat-bottomed conical laboratory flask [Emil *Erlenmeyer*, died 1909, German chemist]

er·mine \'ər-mən\ *n, pl* **ermine** *or* **ermines** **1 a** : any of several weasels that assume a white winter coat usually with more or less black on the tail **b** : the white fur of an ermine **2** : a rank or office whose robe is ornamented with ermine [Old French, of Germanic origin] — **er·mined** \-mənd\ *adj*

erne *or* **ern** \'ərn, 'eərn\ *n* : EAGLE; *esp* : a white-tailed sea eagle [Old English *earn*]

erode \i-'rōd\ *vb* **1** : to diminish or destroy by degrees : **a** : to eat into or away by slow destruction of substance : CORRODE **b** : to wear away by or as if by the action of water, wind, or glacial ice ⟨corruption that *eroded* confidence in government⟩ **2** : to undergo ero-

ermine 1a

sion [Latin *erodere* "to eat away", from *e-* + *rodere* "to gnaw"] — **erod·ible** \-'rōd-ə-bəl\ *adj*

ero·sion \i-'rō-zhən\ *n* : the process of eroding : the state of being eroded [Middle French, from Latin *erosio*, from *erodere* "to erode"] — **ero·sion·al** \-'rōzh-nəl, -'rō-zhən-l\ *adj*

ero·sive \i-'rō-siv, -ziv\ *adj* : eating or wearing away ⟨the *erosive* effect of water⟩ ⟨an *erosive* ulcer⟩ — **ero·sive·ness** *n* — **ero·siv·i·ty** \i-,rō-'siv-ət-ē\ *n*

erot·ic \i-'rät-ik\ *adj* : of, relating to, or marked by sexual love or desire [Greek *erōtikos*, from *erōt-*, *erōs* "love"] — **erot·i·cal·ly** \-i-kə-lē, -klē\ *adv* — **erot·i·cism** \-'rät-ə-,siz-əm\ *n*

err \'eər, 'ər\ *vi* **1** : to make a mistake ⟨*err* in one's calculations⟩ **2** : to violate an accepted standard of conduct [Old French *errer* "to stray", from Latin *errare*]

er·ran·cy \'er-ən-sē\ *n, pl* **-cies** : the state or an instance of erring

er·rand \'er-ənd\ *n* : a short trip taken to do something often for another; *also* : the object or purpose of such a trip [Old English *ǣrend* "message, business"]

er·rant \'er-ənt\ *adj* **1** : wandering especially in search of adventure ⟨an *errant* knight⟩ **2 a** : straying outside the proper bounds ⟨an *errant* calf⟩ **b** : deviating from an accepted pattern or standard ⟨an *errant* child⟩ — **er·rant·ry** \-ən-trē\ *n*

er·ra·ta \e-'rät-ə, -'rāt-, -'rat-\ *n* : a list of corrigenda [from plural of *erratum*]

er·rat·ic \ir-'at-ik\ *adj* **1** : having no fixed course : WANDERING ⟨an *erratic* comet⟩ **2** : marked by lack of consistency or regularity : ECCENTRIC ⟨*erratic* behavior⟩ [Latin *erraticus*, from *errare* "to stray"] — **er·rat·i·cal·ly** \-i-kə-lē, -klē\ *adv*

er·ra·tum \e-'rät-əm, -'rāt-, -'rat-\ *n, pl* **-ta** \-ə\ : CORRIGENDUM [Latin, from *errare* "to stray"]

er·ro·ne·ous \ir-'ō-nē-əs, e-'rō-\ *adj* : containing or characterized by error [Latin *erroneus* "wandering", from *erro* "wanderer", from *errare* "to stray"] — **er·ro·ne·ous·ly** *adv* — **er·ro·ne·ous·ness** *n*

er·ror \'er-ər\ *n* **1 a** : deviation from a code of behavior ⟨saw the *error* of their ways⟩ **b** : an act involving an unintentional deviation from truth or accuracy ⟨an arithmetic *error*⟩ **c** : an act that through ignorance, deficiency, or accident fails to achieve what should be done ⟨an *error* in judgment⟩ **d** : a defensive misplay made by a baseball player **2** : the quality or state of erring **3** : a false belief or a set of false beliefs **4** : something produced by mistake **5** : the difference between an observed or calculated value and the true value; *esp* : variation in measurements, calculations, or observations of a quantity due to mistakes or to uncontrollable factors [Old French *errour*, from Latin *error*, from *errare* "to stray"] — **er·ror·less** \-ləs\ *adj*

☐ SYN **ERROR, MISTAKE, BLUNDER, SLIP** mean a departure from what is true, right, or proper. **ERROR** is a deviation from what is right, correct, or sanctioned ⟨an *error* in reasoning⟩ ⟨an *error* in addition⟩ **MISTAKE** implies misunderstanding or an oversight or unintentional wrongdoing and connotes less severe judgment than **ERROR**; **BLUNDER** suggests ignorance, stupidity, carelessness, or lack of foresight and sometimes implies blame; **SLIP** carries a strong implication of inadvertence or accident producing trivial mistakes.

er·satz \'er-,zäts, er-'\ *adj* : being a usually artificial and inferior substitute ⟨*ersatz* cream⟩ [German, noun, "substitute"] SYN see ARTIFICIAL

Erse \'ərs\ *n* **1** : SCOTTISH GAELIC **2** : IRISH GAELIC [Middle English *Erisch* "Irish", alteration of *Irish*] — **Erse** *adj*

erst·while \'ərst-,hwīl, -,wīl\ *adv* : in the past : FORMERLY [Old English *ǣrest*, superlative of *ǣr* "early"] — **erstwhile** *adj*

eruct \i-'rəkt\ *vb* : BELCH [Latin *eructare*, from *e-* + *ructare* "to belch"] — **eruc·ta·tion** \i-,rək-'tā-shən, ,ē-,rək-\ *n*

er·u·dite \'er-yə-ˌdīt, -ə-\ *adj* : characterized by erudition [Latin *eruditus*, from *erudire* "to instruct", from *e-* + *rudis* "rude, ignorant"] — **er·u·dite·ly** *adv*

er·u·di·tion \ˌer-yə-'dish-ən, -ə-\ *n* : extensive knowledge gained chiefly from books : LEARNING

erupt \i-'rəpt\ *vi* **1 a** : to force out or release suddenly and often violently something pent up ⟨the volcano *erupted*⟩ **b** (1) : to burst from limits or restraint (2) : to break through a surface ⟨teeth *erupting* from the gum⟩ **c** : to become active or violent : EXPLODE ⟨riots *erupted*⟩ **2** : to break out [Latin *eruptus*, past participle of *erumpere* "to burst forth", from *e-* + *rumpere* "to break"]

erup·tion \i-'rəp-shən\ *n* **1 a** : an act, process, or instance of erupting **b** : the breaking out of a rash on the skin **2** : a product (as a skin rash) of erupting — **erup·tive** \-'rəp-tiv\ *adj*

-ery \ə-rē, -rē\ *n suffix, pl* **-eries 1** : qualities collectively : character : -HOOD 1 ⟨snobb*ery*⟩ **2** : art : practice ⟨cook*ery*⟩ **3** : place of doing, keeping, producing, or selling (a specified thing) ⟨bak*ery*⟩ ⟨fish*ery*⟩ **4** : collection : aggregate ⟨fin*ery*⟩ **5** : state or condition ⟨slav*ery*⟩ [Old French *-erie*, from *-ier* "-er" + *-ie* "-y"]

er·y·sip·e·las \ˌer-ə-'sip-ləs, ˌir-, -ə-ləs\ *n* : an acute disease marked by fever and intense local inflammation of the skin and underlying tissues and caused by a streptococcus [Latin, from Greek]

eryth·ro·cyte \i-'rith-rə-ˌsīt\ *n* : RED BLOOD CELL [Greek *erythros* "red"] — **eryth·ro·cyt·ic** \-ˌrith-rə-'sit-ik\ *adj*

eryth·ro·my·cin \i-ˌrith-rə-'mīs-n\ *n* : an antibiotic produced by an actinomycete and active against some bacteria

¹-es \əz, iz *after* s, z, sh, ch; z *after* v *or a vowel*\ *n pl suffix* **1** — used to form the plural of most nouns that end in s ⟨glass*es*⟩, z ⟨fuzz*es*⟩, sh ⟨bush*es*⟩, ch ⟨peach*es*⟩, or a final *y* that changes to *i* ⟨ladi*es*⟩ and of some nouns ending in *f* that changes to *v* ⟨loav*es*⟩ — compare ¹-s 1 **2** : ¹-s 2 [Old English *-as*, nominative and accusative plural ending of some masculine nouns]

²-es *vb suffix* — used to form the third person singular present of most verbs that end in s ⟨bless*es*⟩, z ⟨fizz*es*⟩, sh ⟨hush*es*⟩, ch ⟨catch*es*⟩, or a final *y* that changes to *i* ⟨defi*es*⟩ — compare ²-s [Old English *-es*, *-as*]

es·ca·drille \'es-kə-ˌdril, -ˌdrē\ *n* : a unit of a European air command containing usually six airplanes [French, "flotilla, escadrille", from Spanish *escuadrilla*, from *escuadra* "squadron, squad"]

es·ca·late \'es-kə-ˌlāt\ *vb* : to increase or be increased in extent, number, intensity, or scope [back-formation from *escalator*] — **es·ca·la·tion** \ˌes-kə-'lā-shən\ *n*

¹es·ca·la·tor \'es-kə-ˌlāt-ər\ *n* : a power-driven set of stairs arranged like an endless belt that ascend or descend continuously [from *Escalator*, a former trademark]

²escalator *adj* : providing for a periodic proportional upward or downward adjustment (as of prices or wages)

es·cal·lop \is-'käl-əp, -'kal-\ *variant of* SCALLOP

es·cap·able \is-'kā-pə-bəl\ *adj* : capable of being escaped : AVOIDABLE

es·ca·pade \'es-kə-ˌpād\ *n* : an unconventional adventure or experience : PRANK

¹es·cape \is-'kāp\ *vb* **1 a** : to get away (as by flight) ⟨*escape* from prison⟩ **b** : to leak out from confinement ⟨gas is *escaping*⟩ **c** : to run wild from cultivation **2** : to get out of the way of : AVOID ⟨*escaped* the plague by moving to the country⟩ **3** : to fail to be noticed or recallable by ⟨the name *escapes* me⟩ **4** : to issue from or be uttered involuntarily by ⟨a sigh *escaped* me⟩ [Old North French *escaper*, derived from Latin *ex-* + Late Latin *cappa* "head covering, cloak"] — **es·cap·er** *n*

□ **ORIGIN** A fugitive may sometimes get away from pursuers, even if they are close enough to clutch the fugitive, by slipping out of a coat or cloak and leaving the would-be captors holding an empty garment. This is the idea behind the word *escape*. *Escape* is derived from Latin *ex*, which means "out of", and Late Latin *cappa*, which means "head covering" or "cloak". This *cappa* is also the ancestor of English *cap* and *cape*.

²escape *n* **1** : an act or instance of escaping **2** : a means of escaping **3** : a cultivated plant run wild

³escape *adj* : providing a means of escape ⟨an *escape* hatch⟩ ⟨an *escape* clause⟩

es·cap·ee \ˌes-ˌkā-'pē, is-ˌkā-, ˌes-kə-\ *n* : one that has escaped; *esp* : an escaped prisoner

escape mechanism *n* : a mode of behavior or thinking adopted to evade unpleasant facts or responsibilities

es·cape·ment \is-'kāp-mənt\ *n* **1** : a device in a timepiece through which the energy of the weight or spring is transmitted to the pendulum or balance by means of impulses that permit one tooth on a wheel to escape from a projecting part at regular intervals **2** : a device (as the spacing mechanism of a typewriter) that permits motion in one direction only and in equal steps

escapement 1

escape velocity *n* : the minimum velocity that a moving body (as a rocket) must have to escape from the gravitational field of the earth or of a celestial body and move outward into space

es·cap·ism \is-'kā-ˌpiz-əm\ *n* : habitual thinking about imaginary or entertaining things in order to escape from reality or routine — **es·cap·ist** \-pəst\ *adj or n*

es·ca·role \'es-kə-ˌrōl\ *n* : ENDIVE 1 [French, from Late Latin *escariola*, from Latin *esca* "food", from *edere* "to eat"]

es·carp·ment \is-'kärp-mənt\ *n* **1** : a steep slope in front of a fortification **2** : a long cliff [French *escarpement*, from *escarper* "to cut so as to form a scarp"]

-escent \'es-nt\ *adj suffix* **1** : beginning : beginning to be : slightly ⟨irid*escent*⟩ **2** : reflecting or emitting light (in a specified way) ⟨opal*escent*⟩ ⟨phosphor*escent*⟩ [Latin *-escent-*, *-escens*, present participle ending of verbs in *-escere*]

¹es·cheat \is-'chēt\ *n* : the reversion of property to the state when there are no persons (as heirs) legally entitled to hold it; *also* : the property that reverts [Middle English *eschete*, from Old French, from *escheoir* "to fall, devolve", derived from Latin *ex-* + *cadere* "to fall"]

²escheat *vb* : to revert or cause to revert by escheat — **es·cheat·able** \-ə-bəl\ *adj*

es·chew \is-'chü, ish-\ *vt* : to abstain or refrain from : SHUN [Middle French *eschiuver*, of Germanic origin]

¹es·cort \'es-ˌkȯrt\ *n* **1 a** : a person or group of persons accompanying another to give protection or show courtesy **b** : the man who goes on a date with a woman **c** : a protective screen of vehicles, warships, or airplanes **2** : accompaniment by a person or an armed protector [French *escorte*, from Italian *scorta*, from *scorgere* "to guide", from Latin *ex-* + *corrigere* "to make straight, correct"]

²es·cort \is-'kȯrt, es-', 'es-,\ *vt* : to accompany as an escort

es·crow \'es-ˌkrō, es-'\ *n* : something (as a deed or a sum of money) delivered by one person to another to be delivered by the second to a third party only upon the fulfillment of a condition [Middle French *escroue* "scroll"] — **in escrow** : in trust as an escrow

es·cu·do \is-'küd-ō\ *n, pl* **-dos 1** : any of various former gold or silver coins of Hispanic countries **2 a** : the basic monetary unit of Portugal **b** : a coin representing this unit [Spanish and Portuguese, literally, "shield"]

es·cu·lent \'es-kyə-lənt\ *adj* : fit to be eaten : EDIBLE [Latin *esculentus*, from *esca* "food", from *edere* "to eat"] — **esculent** *n*

escutcheon

es·cutch·eon \is-'kəch-ən\ *n* : the usually shield=shaped surface on which a coat of arms is shown [Middle French *escuchon,* from Latin *scutum* "shield"]

Es·dras \'ez-drəs\ *n* — see BIBLE table

¹**-ese** \'ēz, 'ēs\ *adj suffix* : of, relating to, or originating in (a specified place or country) ⟨Japan*ese*⟩ [Portuguese *-ês* and Italian *-ese,* from Latin *-ensis*]

²**-ese** *n suffix, pl* **-ese** **1** : native or resident of (a specified place or country) ⟨Chin*ese*⟩ **2 a** : language of (a specified place, country, or nationality) ⟨Japan*ese*⟩ **b** : speech, literary style, or diction peculiar to (a specified place, person, or group) — usually in words applied in depreciation ⟨journal*ese*⟩

es·ker \'es-kər\ *n* : a long narrow mound of material deposited by a stream flowing on, within, or beneath a stagnant glacier [Irish Gaelic *eiscir* "ridge"]

Es·ki·mo \'es-kə-,mō\ *n* **1** : a member of a group of peoples of what is now northern Canada, Greenland, Alaska, and eastern Siberia **2** : the language of the Eskimo people [of American Indian origin]

Eskimo dog *n* **1** : a broad-chested powerful dog native to Greenland and Labrador that has a heavy double coat **2** : a sled dog of American origin

esoph·a·gus *also* **oesoph·a·gus** \i-'säf-ə-gəs\ *n, pl* **-gi** \-,gī, -,jī, -,gē\ : a muscular tube that leads from the pharynx to the stomach in vertebrates; *also* : a part of the muscular tube between the mouth and the stomach in some invertebrates [Greek *oisophagos,* from *oisein* "to be going to carry" + *phagein* "to eat"] — **esoph·a·ge·al** \i-,säf-ə-'jē-əl\ *adj*

es·o·ter·ic \,es-ə-'ter-ik\ *adj* **1** : designed for or understood by the specially initiated alone ⟨an *esoteric* ritual⟩ **2** : of or relating to knowledge that is restricted to a small group : RECONDITE ⟨*esoteric* writings⟩ **3** : PRIVATE 2b, CONFIDENTIAL ⟨an *esoteric* purpose⟩ [Late Latin *esotericus,* from Greek *esōterikos,* from *esōterō,* comparative of *eisō, esō* "within"] — **es·o·ter·i·cal·ly** \-'ter-i-kə-lē, -klē\ *adv*

ESP \,ē-,es-'pē\ *n* : EXTRASENSORY PERCEPTION

es·pa·drille \'es-pə-,dril\ *n* : a flat sandal usually having a fabric upper and a flexible sole [French]

es·pal·ier \is-'pal-yər, -,yā\ *n* : a plant (as a fruit tree) trained to grow flat against a support (as a wall or trellis) [French] — **espalier** *vt*

es·par·to \is-'pärt-ō\ *n, pl* **-tos** : either of two Spanish and Algerian grasses from which cordage, shoes, baskets, and paper are made — called also *esparto grass* [Spanish]

es·pe·cial \is-'pesh-əl\ *adj* : SPECIAL 1, 2 — **es·pe·cial·ly** \-'pesh-lē, -ə-lē\ *adv*

Es·pe·ran·to \,es-pə-'rant-ō, -'ränt-\ *n* : an artificial international language based as far as possible on words common to the chief European languages [Dr. *Esperanto,* pseudonym of L. L. Zamenhof, died 1917, Polish oculist, its inventor]

es·pi·al \is-'pī-əl, -'pīl\ *n* **1** : an act of spying or watching **2** : an act of noticing

es·pi·o·nage \'es-pē-ə-,näzh, -nij, -,näj\ *n* : the practice of spying or the use of spies to obtain information about the plans and activities (as of a foreign government or a business competitor) [French *espionnage,* from Middle French *espionner* "to spy", from *espion* "spy", from Italian *spione,* from *spia* "spy", of Germanic origin]

es·pla·nade \'es-plə-,näd, -,nād\ *n* : a level open stretch or area; *esp* : one designed for walking or driving along a shore [French]

es·pous·al \is-'paù-zəl *also* -səl\ *n* **1 a** : BETROTHAL **b** : WEDDING 1 **c** : MARRIAGE 2a; *also* : a union resembling marriage **2** : a taking up of a cause or belief

es·pouse \is-'paùz *also* -'paùs\ *vt* **1** : MARRY 1b, c **2** : to take up the cause of : SUPPORT — **es·pous·er** *n*

espres·so \e-'spres-ō\ *n* : coffee brewed by forcing steam through finely ground darkly roasted coffee beans [Italian *caffè espresso,* literally, "pressed out coffee"]

es·prit \is-'prē\ *n* : vivacious cleverness or wit [French, from Latin *spiritus* "spirit"]

es·prit de corps \is-,prēd-ə-'kōr, -'kòr\ *n* : the common spirit existing in the members of a group and inspiring enthusiasm, devotion, and strong regard for the honor of the group [French]

es·py \is-'pī\ *vt* **es·pied** \-'pīd\; **es·py·ing** : to catch sight of [Old French *espier* "to spy", of Germanic origin]

-esque \'esk\ *adj suffix* : in the manner or style of : like ⟨Roman*esque*⟩ ⟨statu*esque*⟩ [French, from Italian *-esco,* of Germanic origin]

es·quire \'es-,kwīr, is-'\ *n* **1** : a member of the English gentry ranking immediately below a knight **2** : a candidate for knighthood serving as attendant to a knight **3** *often cap* — used as a courtesy title usually placed in its abbreviated form after a surname (as of an attorney) ⟨John M. Doe, *Esq.*⟩ [Middle French *esquier* "squire"]

-ess \əs, is *also* ,es\ *n suffix* : female ⟨poet*ess*⟩ [Old French *-esse,* from Late Latin *-issa,* from Greek]

¹**es·say** \e-'sā, 'es-,ā\ *vt* : to make an often tentative effort to perform ⟨*essayed* the role of mediator⟩

²**es·say** \'es-,ā, *in sense 1 also* e-'sā\ *n* **1** : ATTEMPT; *esp* : an initial tentative effort **2** : a nonfictional usually short literary composition dealing with its subject from a limited or personal point of view [Middle French *essai,* from Late Latin *exagium* "act of weighing", from Latin *ex-* + *agere* "to drive"]

es·say·ist \'es-,ā-əst\ *n* : a writer of essays

es·sence \'es-ns\ *n* **1** : the basic nature of a thing : the quality or qualities that make a thing what it is ⟨the *essence* of honesty is truthfulness⟩ **2** : a substance extracted (as from a plant or drug) that retains the special qualities of its source ⟨*essence* of peppermint⟩ **3** : PERFUME 1, SCENT [Latin *essentia,* from *esse* "to be"]

Es·sene \is-'ēn, 'es-,\ *n* : a member of a monastic brotherhood of Jews in Palestine from the 2d century B. C. to the 2d century A. D. [Greek *Essēnos*]

¹**es·sen·tial** \i-'sen-chəl\ *adj* **1** : forming or belonging to the fundamental nature of a thing ⟨free speech is an *essential* right of citizenship⟩ **2** : containing or having the character of a volatile essence ⟨*essential* oils⟩ **3** : important in the highest degree : NECESSARY ⟨food is *essential* to life⟩ — **es·sen·ti·al·i·ty** \-,sen-chē-'al-ət-ē\ *n* — **es·sen·tial·ly** \-'sench-lē, -ə-lē\ *adv* — **es·sen·tial·ness** \-əl-nəs\ *n* □ SYN ESSENTIAL, FUNDAMENTAL, VITAL mean so important as to be indispensable. ESSENTIAL implies belonging to the very nature of a thing and therefore being incapable of removal without destroying the thing itself or its character; FUNDAMENTAL suggests something that is of the nature of a foundation without which an entire system or complex whole would collapse ⟨the *fundamental* principles of a democracy⟩ VITAL suggests that which is as necessary to continuance as air, food, and water are to living things ⟨resources *vital* to security⟩ SYN see in addition NECESSARY

²**essential** *n* : something basic, necessary, or indispensable ⟨the *essentials* for success⟩

essential amino acid *n* : an amino acid that is necessary for proper growth of the animal body and that cannot be manufactured by the body unassisted but must be obtained from protein food

¹**-est** \əst, ist\ *adj suffix or adv suffix* — used to form the superlative degree of adjectives and adverbs of one syllable ⟨fatt*est*⟩ ⟨lat*est*⟩, of some adjectives and adverbs of two syllables ⟨lucki*est*⟩, and less often of longer ones [Old English]

²**-est** \əst, ist\ *or* **-st** \st\ *vb suffix* — used to form the archaic second person singular of verbs (with *thou*) ⟨gett*est*⟩ ⟨did*st*⟩ [Old English]

es·tab·lish \is-'tab-lish\ *vb* **1** : to make firm or stable ⟨*establish* a gun on its base⟩ **2** : to enact permanently ⟨*establish* a constitution⟩ **3 a** : to bring into existence : FOUND ⟨*establish* a republic⟩ **b** : to bring about : EFFECT ⟨*establish* a good relationship⟩ **4 a** : to set on a firm basis ⟨*establish* one's children in business⟩ **b** : to put into a favorable position ⟨the *established* order⟩ **c** : to gain full recognition or acceptance of ⟨*establish* a claim⟩ **5** : to put beyond doubt : PROVE ⟨*establish* one's innocence⟩ **6** : to become naturalized ⟨a grass that *establishes* on poor soil⟩ [Middle French *establiss-*, stem of *establir* "to establish", from Latin *stabilire*, from *stabilis* "stable"] — **es·tab·lish·er** *n*

established church *n* : a church recognized by law as the official church of a nation

es·tab·lish·ment \is-'tab-lish-mənt\ *n* **1 a** : the act of establishing : the state or fact of being established **b** : the granting of a privileged position ⟨*establishment* of a church⟩ **2** : a permanent civil or military organization **3** : a place of business or residence with its furnishings and staff ⟨a dry-cleaning *establishment*⟩ **4** : an established order of society; *also, often cap* : the social, economic, and political leaders of such an order

es·tate \is-'tāt\ *n* **1** : STATE 1a, CONDITION **2** : social standing or rank especially of a high order **3** : a social or political class; *esp* : one of the great classes (as the nobility, clergy, and commons) formerly having distinct political powers **4 a** : the nature and extent of one's interest in property **b** : POSSESSIONS, PROPERTY; *esp* : a person's property in land and tenements **c** : the assets and liabilities left by a person at death **5** : a usually extensive landed property often with a large house [Middle French *estat*, from Latin *status* "state"]

¹es·teem \is-'tēm\ *n* : high regard

²esteem *vt* **1 a** : to view as : CONSIDER ⟨*esteem* it a privilege⟩ **b** : THINK 3a, BELIEVE **2** : to set a high value on : PRIZE [Middle French *estimer* "to estimate", from Latin *aestimare*] SYN see REGARD

es·ter \'es-tər\ *n* : an organic compound formed by the reaction between an acid and an alcohol [German, from *essigäther* "ethyl acetate", from *essig* "vinegar" + *äther* "ether"]

es·ter·ase \'es-tə-,rās\ *n* : an enzyme that accelerates the breakdown or synthesis of esters

es·ter·i·fy \e-'ster-ə-,fī\ *vt* **-fied; -fy·ing** : to convert into an ester — **es·ter·i·fi·ca·tion** \-,ster-ə-fə-'kā-shən\ *n*

Es·ther \'es-tər\ *n* — see BIBLE table

esthete, esthetic, esthetics *variant of* AESTHETE, AESTHETIC, AESTHETICS

es·ti·ma·ble \'es-tə-mə-bəl\ *adj* : worthy of esteem — **es·ti·ma·ble·ness** *n*

¹es·ti·mate \'es-tə-,māt\ *vt* **1** : to judge or determine tentatively or approximately the value, size, or cost of ⟨*estimate* a painting job⟩ **2** : to form an opinion of : JUDGE, CONCLUDE [Latin *aestimare* "to value, estimate"] — **es·ti·ma·tor** \-,māt-ər\ *n* □ SYN ESTIMATE, APPRAISE, EVALUATE, ASSESS mean to judge a thing with respect to its worth. ESTIMATE implies a judgment, considered or casual, that precedes or takes the place of actual measuring, counting, or testing; APPRAISE implies the fixing of the monetary worth of a thing by an expert; EVALUATE suggests an attempt to determine the relative or intrinsic worth of something in terms other than of money ⟨*evaluate* a new novel⟩ ASSESS implies a critical appraisal for the purpose of understanding or interpreting or as a guide in taking action ⟨*assess* the deterrent effect of punishment⟩ ⟨*assess* taxable real estate⟩

²es·ti·mate \'es-tə-mət\ *n* **1** : the act of appraising or valuing **2** : an opinion or judgment of the nature, character, or quality of a thing **3** : a rough or approximate calculation **4** : a statement of the cost of a job

es·ti·ma·tion \,es-tə-'mā-shən\ *n* **1** : an opinion formed or expressed **2 a** : the act of estimating **b** : ESTIMATE **3** : ESTEEM, HONOR

estivate, estivation *variant of* AESTIVATE, AESTIVATION

Es·to·nian \e-'stō-nē-ən, -nyən\ *n* **1** : a member of a Finno-Ugric-speaking people chiefly of Estonia **2** : the Finno-Ugric language of the Estonians — **Estonian** *adj*

estr- *or* **estro-** *or* **oestr-** *or* **oestro-** *combining form* : estrus ⟨*estro*gen⟩

es·tra·di·ol \,es-trə-'dī-,ȯl, -,ōl\ *n* : a powerful estrogenic hormone usually made synthetically for medicinal use

es·trange \is-'trānj\ *vt* **1** : to remove from customary environment or associations **2** : to destroy the affection of : ALIENATE ⟨friends *estranged* by gossip⟩ [Middle French *estranger*, from Medieval Latin *extraneare*, from Latin *extraneus* "strange"] — **es·trange·ment** \-mənt\ *n*

es·trin \'es-trən\ *n* : an estrogenic hormone

es·tri·ol \'es-,trī-,ȯl, e-'strī-, -,ōl\ *n* : an estrogenic hormone usually obtained from the urine of pregnant women

es·tro·gen \'es-trə-jən\ *n* : a substance (as a sex hormone) tending to promote estrus and stimulate the development of secondary sex characteristics in the female — **es·tro·gen·ic** \,es-trə-'jen-ik\ *adj*

es·trone \'es-,trōn\ *n* : an estrogenic hormone from the urine of pregnant females

estrous cycle *n* : the series of physiological changes of the endocrine and reproductive systems of a female mammal from the beginning of one period of estrus to the beginning of the next

es·trus \'es-trəs\ *or* **es·trum** \-trəm\ *n* **1** : a regularly recurrent state of sexual excitability during which the female of most mammals will accept the male and is capable of conceiving : HEAT **2** : ESTROUS CYCLE [Latin *oestrus* "gadfly, frenzy", from Greek *oistros*] — **es·trous** \-trəs\ *adj*

es·tu·a·rine \'es-chə-wə-,rīn\ *adj* : of, relating to, or formed in an estuary

es·tu·ary \'es-chə-,wer-ē\ *n, pl* **-ar·ies** : a water passage where the tide meets a river current; *esp* : an arm of the sea at the lower end of a river [Latin *aestuarium*, from *aestus* "boiling, time"]

-et \'et, ,et, ət, it\ *n suffix* **1** : small one : lesser one ⟨baron*et*⟩ ⟨isl*et*⟩ **2** : group ⟨oct*et*⟩ [Old French, from Latin *-itus*]

eta \'āt-ə\ *n* : the 7th letter of the Greek alphabet — H or η

et cetera \et-'set-ə-rə, -'se-trə\ : and others especially of the same kind : and so forth [Latin]

etch \'ech\ *vt* **1** : to produce (as a design) especially on metal or glass by the corrosive action of an acid; *also* : to subject to such etching **2** : to impress (as on the mind) sharply or clearly [Dutch *etsen*, from German *ätzen*, literally, "to feed"] — **etch·er** *n*

etch·ing *n* **1** : the art of producing pictures or designs by printing from an etched metal plate **2** : an impression from an etched plate

eter·nal \i-'tərn-l\ *adj* **1** : having no beginning and no end : lasting forever **2** : continuing without interruption : UNCEASING ⟨that dog's *eternal* barking⟩ [Middle French, from Late Latin *aeternalis*, from Latin *aeternus* "eternal"] — **eter·nal·ly** \-l-ē\ *adv* — **eter·nal·ness** *n* □ SYN ETERNAL, EVERLASTING, ENDLESS mean continuing on and on without end. ETERNAL implies being without either beginning or end and so unaffected by time or change ⟨*eternal* truths⟩ EVERLASTING and ENDLESS apply to what exists and endures in time without end or limit, EVERLASTING stressing the quality of permanence or the fact of duration and ENDLESS frequently suggesting a wearisome stretching out without conclusion or final rest ⟨*endless* arguments about money⟩ ⟨*endless* punishment⟩

Eternal *n* : GOD 1 — used with *the*

eter·ni·ty \i-'tər-nət-ē\ *n, pl* **-ties** **1** : the quality or state of being eternal **2** : infinite time **3** : the state after death : IMMORTALITY **4** : a seemingly endless time :

\ə\ abut		\ng\ sing	
\ər\ further		\ō\ bone	
\a\ mat		\ȯ\ saw	
\ā\ take		\ȯi\ coin	
\ä\ cot, cart		\th\ thin	
\au̇\ out		\th\ this	
\ch\ chin		\ü\ food	
\e\ pet		\u̇\ foot	
\ē\ easy		\y\ yet	
\g\ go		\yü\ few	
\i\ tip		\yu̇\ cure	
\ī\ life		\zh\ vision	
\j\ job			

AGE [Middle French *eternité,* from Latin *aeternitas,* from *aeternus* "eternal"]

¹-eth \əth, ith\ *or* **-th** \th\ *vb suffix* — used to form the archaic 3d person sing. present of verbs ⟨go*eth*⟩ ⟨do*th*⟩ [Old English]

²-eth — see **-TH**

eth·ane \'eth-ān\ *n* : a colorless odorless gas C_2H_6 that consists of carbon and hydrogen, is found in natural gas, and is used especially as a fuel [*eth*yl + *-ane*]

eth·a·nol \'eth-ə-nȯl, -nōl\ *n* : ALCOHOL 1a

eth·ene \'eth-ēn\ *n* : ETHYLENE

ether \'ē-thər\ *n* **1** : the upper regions of space : HEAVENS **2 a** : a medium formerly held to permeate all space and transmit transverse waves (as light) **b** : the medium that transmits radio waves **3 a** : a light volatile flammable liquid $C_4H_{10}O$ obtained by the distillation of alcohol with sulfuric acid and used chiefly as a solvent especially of fats and as an anesthetic **b** : any of various organic compounds characterized by an oxygen atom attached to two carbon atoms [Latin *aether,* from Greek *aithēr,* from *aithein* "to ignite"]

ethe·re·al \i-'thir-ē-əl\ *adj* **1** : HEAVENLY 1 ⟨*ethereal* spirits⟩ **2** : being light and airy : DELICATE ⟨*ethereal* music⟩ — **ethe·re·al·i·ty** \i-ˌthir-ē-'al-ət-ē\ *n* — **ethe·re·al·ly** \-'thir-ē-ə-lē\ *adv* — **ethe·re·al·ness** *n*

ether·ize \'ē-thə-ˌrīz\ *vt* : to treat or anesthetize with ether — **ether·iza·tion** \ˌē-thə-rə-'zā-shən\ *n* — **ether·iz·er** *n*

eth·i·cal \'eth-i-kəl\ *or* **eth·ic** \-ik\ *adj* **1** : of or relating to ethics **2** : conforming to accepted and especially professional standards of conduct ⟨*ethical* practices⟩ **3** : sold only on a doctor's prescription ⟨*ethical* drugs⟩ [Latin *ethicus,* from Greek *ēthikos,* from *ēthos* "character"] SYN see MORAL — **eth·i·cal·ly** \'eth-i-kə-lē, -klē\ *adv*

eth·ics \'eth-iks\ *n sing or pl* **1** : a branch of philosophy dealing with what is good and bad and with moral duty and obligation **2** : the principles of moral conduct governing an individual or a group

Ethi·o·pi·an \ˌē-thē-'ō-pē-ən\ *n* **1** : a member of any of the mythical or actual peoples usually described by the ancient Greeks as dark-skinned and living far to the south **2** : a native or inhabitant of Ethiopia — **Ethiopian** *adj*

Ethi·op·ic \-'äp-ik, -'ō-pik\ *n* : a Semitic language formerly spoken in Ethiopia and still used in church services there

eth·moid \'eth-ˌmȯid\ *or* **eth·moi·dal** \eth-'mȯid-l\ *adj* : of, relating to, adjoining, or being one or more bones of the walls of the nasal cavity [French *ethmoïde,* from Greek *ēthmoeidēs,* literally, "like a strainer", from *ēthmos* "strainer"] — **ethmoid** *n*

¹eth·nic \'eth-nik\ *adj* : of or relating to races or large groups of people classed according to common traits and customs ⟨*ethnic* minorities⟩ [Late Latin *ethnicus* "heathen", from Greek *ethnikos* "national", from *ethnos* "nation"] — **eth·ni·cal·ly** \-ni-kə-lē, -klē\ *adv*

²ethnic *n* : a member of an ethnic group; *esp* : one retaining traditional customs, outlook, and language

ethno- *combining form* : race : people : cultural group ⟨*ethno*centric⟩ [Greek *ethnos* "nation"]

eth·no·cen·tric \ˌeth-nō-'sen-trik\ *adj* : favoring especially one's own ethnic group ⟨*ethnocentric* views⟩

eth·nol·o·gy \eth-'näl-ə-jē\ *n* **1** : a science that deals with the origin, distribution, relations, and characteristics of human races **2** : the comparative study of cultures — **eth·no·log·ic** \ˌeth-nə-'läj-ik\ *or* **eth·no·log·i·cal** \-i-kəl\ *adj* — **eth·no·log·i·cal·ly** \-i-kə-lē, -klē\ *adv* — **eth·nol·o·gist** \eth-'näl-ə-jəst\ *n*

ethol·o·gy \ē-'thäl-ə-jē\ *n* : the scientific study of animal behavior [Latin *ethologia* "art of depicting character", from Greek *ēthologia,* from *ēthos* "character" + *-logia* "-logy"] — **etho·log·i·cal** \ˌē-thə-'läj-i-kəl, ˌeth-ə-\ *adj* — **ethol·o·gist** \ē-'thäl-ə-jəst\ *n*

Eton jacket

eth·yl \'eth-əl\ *n* : a chemical radical C_2H_5 consisting of carbon and hydrogen [*eth*er + *-yl*]

ethyl alcohol *n* : ALCOHOL 1a

ethyl cellulose *n* : any of various thermoplastic substances used especially in plastics and lacquers

eth·yl·ene \'eth-ə-ˌlēn\ *n* **1** : a colorless flammable gas C_2H_4 found in coal gas or obtained from petroleum hydrocarbons and used to ripen fruits or as an anesthetic **2** : a bivalent hydrocarbon radical C_2H_4 derived from ethane — **eth·yl·en·ic** \ˌeth-ə-'lē-nik\ *adj*

ethylene gly·col \-'glī-ˌkȯl, -ˌkōl\ *n* : a thick liquid alcohol $C_2H_6O_2$ used especially as an antifreeze

eth·yne \'eth-ˌīn, eth-'\ *n* : ACETYLENE

-et·ic \'et-ik\ *adj suffix* : -IC ⟨limn*etic*⟩ — often in adjectives corresponding to nouns ending in *-esis* ⟨gen*etic*⟩ [Greek *-etikos, -ētikos,* from *-etos, -ētos,* ending of certain verbals]

eti·o·late \'ēt-ē-ə-ˌlāt\ *vt* **1** : to make (a green plant) pale and spindling by lack of light **2** : to make pale and sickly [French *étioler*] — **eti·o·la·tion** \ˌēt-ē-ə-'lā-shən\ *n*

eti·ol·o·gy \ˌēt-ē-'äl-ə-jē\ *n* : the cause or origin especially of a disease [Medieval Latin *aetiologia* "statement of causes", from Greek *aitiologia,* from *aitia* "cause"] — **eti·o·log·ic** \ˌēt-ē-ə-'läj-ik\ *or* **eti·o·log·i·cal** \-i-kəl\ *adj* — **eti·o·log·i·cal·ly** \-i-kə-lē, -i-klē\ *adv*

et·i·quette \'et-i-kət, -ˌket\ *n* : the body of rules governing the way in which people behave socially, ceremonially, or in public life [French *étiquette,* literally, "ticket"] □ ORIGIN The primary meaning of French *étiquette* is "ticket, label attached to something for description or identification". It was once the practice in royal palaces of France to post notices that set down the proper forms to be observed at court. Such notices were called *étiquettes*. The word came to be used for the court ceremonial itself as well as the document that described it. It was this sense of French *étiquette* that English borrowed.

Eton collar \'ēt-n-\ *n* : a large stiff turnover collar [*Eton* College, English public school]

Eton jacket *n* : a short black jacket with long sleeves, wide lapels, and an open front

Etrus·can \i-'trəs-kən\ *n* **1** : a native or inhabitant of ancient Etruria **2** : the language of the Etruscans — **Etruscan** *adj*

-ette \'et, ˌet, ət, it\ *n suffix* **1** : little one ⟨kitchen*ette*⟩ **2** : female ⟨drum major*ette*⟩ [Middle French, feminine of *-et*]

étude \'ā-ˌtüd, -ˌtyüd\ *n* **1** : a piece of music for practice to develop technical skill **2** : a composition built on a technical motif but played for its artistic value [French, literally, "study", from Middle French *estude, estudie*]

et·y·mol·o·gy \ˌet-ə-'mäl-ə-jē\ *n, pl* **-gies** **1** : the history of a word as shown by identifying its related forms in other languages and tracing these to their origin in a common form in an earlier parent language or by tracing the transmission of a word from one language to another **2** : a branch of language study concerned with etymologies [Latin *etymologia,* from Greek, from *etymon* "the literal meaning of a word according to its origin", from *etymos* "true"] — **et·y·mo·log·i·cal** \-mə-'läj-i-kəl\ *adj* — **et·y·mo·log·i·cal·ly** \-'läj-i-kə-lē, -klē\ *adv* — **et·y·mol·o·gist** \ˌet-ə-'mäl-ə-jəst\ *n*

eu- *combining form* **1** : well : easily : good — compare DYS- **2** : true, truly ⟨*eu*caryote⟩ [Greek, "well, good"]

eu·ca·lypt \'yü-kə-ˌlipt\ *n* : EUCALYPTUS

eu·ca·lyp·tus \ˌyü-kə-'lip-təs\ *n, pl* **-ti** \-ˌtī, -ˌtē\ *or* **-tus·es** : any of a genus of mostly Australian evergreen trees of the myrtle family including many that are widely cultivated for their gums, resins, oils, and useful woods [*eu-* + Greek *kalyptos* "covered", from *kalyp-*

tein "to conceal"; from the conical covering of the buds]

Eu·cha·rist \'yü-kə-rəst, -ˌkrəst\ *n* : COMMUNION 1a; *esp* : a Roman Catholic sacrament renewing Christ's sacrifice of his body and blood [Middle French *eucharistie,* from Late Latin *eucharistia;* from Greek, "gratitude, Eucharist", from *eu-* + *charis* "favor, grace, gratitude"] — **eu·cha·ris·tic** \ˌyü-kə-'ris-tik\ *adj, often cap*

eu·chre \'yü-kər\ *n* : a card game in which each player is dealt five cards and the player making trump must take three tricks to win a hand [origin unknown]

eu·clid·e·an \yü-'klid-ē-ən\ *adj, often cap* : of or relating to the geometry of Euclid

eu·gen·ic \yü-'jen-ik\ *adj* 1 : relating to or fitted for the production of good offspring 2 : of or relating to eugenics — **eu·gen·i·cal·ly** \-'jen-i-kə-lē, -klē\ *adv*

eu·gen·ics \yü-'jen-iks\ *n* : a science that deals with the improvement of hereditary qualities of a race or breed and especially of human beings — **eu·gen·ist** \yü-'jen-əst, 'yü-jə-nəst\ *also* **eu·gen·i·cist** \yü-'jen-ə-səst\ *n*

eu·gle·na \yü-'glē-nə\ *n* : any of a large genus of green freshwater flagellates often classed as algae [*eu-* + Greek *glēnē* "eyeball"] — **eu·gle·noid** \-ˌnȯid\ *adj or n*

euglenoid movement *n* : writhing protoplasmic movement typical of some euglenoid flagellates

eu·kary·ote *also* **eu·cary·ote** \yü-'kar-ē-ˌōt, -ē-ət\ *n* : an organism composed of one or more cells with visibly evident nuclei — compare PROKARYOTE [*eu-* + *kary-* + *-ote* (as in *zygote*)] — **eu·kary·ot·ic** \ˌyü-ˌkar-ē-'ät-ik\ *adj*

eu·lo·gize \'yü-lə-ˌjīz\ *vt* : to speak or write in high praise of : EXTOL — **eu·lo·gist** \-jəst\ *n* — **eu·lo·gis·tic** \ˌyü-lə-'jis-tik\ *adj* — **eu·lo·gis·ti·cal·ly** \-ti-kə-lē, -klē\ *adv*

eu·lo·gy \'yü-lə-jē\ *n, pl* **-gies** 1 : a speech or a writing in praise of a person or thing; *esp* : a formal speech in praise of a dead person 2 : high praise

eu·nuch \'yü-nək\ *n* : a castrated man; *esp* : one placed in charge of a harem or employed as a court official [Latin *eunuchus,* from Greek *eunouchos,* from *eunē* "bed" + *echein* "to have, have charge of"]

eu·on·y·mus \yü-'än-ə-məs\ *n* : any of a genus of shrubs and small trees often grown as ornamentals [Latin *euonymos,* from Greek *euōnymos,* literally, "having an auspicious name", from *eu-* + *onyma* "name"]

eu·phe·mism \'yü-fə-ˌmiz-əm\ *n* : the substitution of an agreeable or inoffensive expression for one that may offend or suggest something unpleasant; *also* : an expression so substituted (pass away is a widely used *euphemism* for die) [Greek *euphēmismos,* from *eu-* + *phēmē* "speech", from *phanai* "to speak"] — **eu·phe·mis·tic** \ˌyü-fə-'mis-tik\ *adj* — **eu·phe·mis·ti·cal·ly** \-ti-kə-lē, -klē\ *adv*

eu·pho·ni·ous \yü-'fō-nē-əs\ *adj* : pleasing to the ear — **eu·pho·ni·ous·ly** *adv* — **eu·pho·ni·ous·ness** *n*

eu·pho·ni·um \-nē-əm\ *n* : a tenor tuba like a baritone but mellower in tone

eu·pho·ny \'yü-fə-nē\ *n, pl* **-nies** : pleasing or sweet sound; *esp* : the effect of words so combined as to please the ear [French *euphonie,* from Late Latin *euphonia,* from Greek *euphōnia,* from *eu-* + *phōnē* "voice"] — **eu·phon·ic** \yü-'fän-ik\ *adj* — **eu·phon·i·cal·ly** \-'fän-i-kə-lē, -klē\ *adv*

eu·phor·bia \yü-'fȯr-bē-ə\ *n* : any of a genus of spurges that have milky juice and flowers without a calyx [Latin *euphorbea,* from *Euphorbus,* 1st century A.D. physician]

eu·pho·ria \yü-'fōr-ē-ə, -'fȯr-\ *n* : a strong feeling of well-being or elation [Greek, from *euphoros* "healthy", from *eu-* + *pherein* "to bear"] — **eu·phor·ic** \-'fȯr-ik, -'fär-\ *adj*

Eur·asian \yü-'rā-zhən, -shən\ *adj* 1 : of or relating to Eurasia 2 : of mixed European and Asian origin — **Eurasian** *n*

eu·re·ka \yü-'rē-kə\ *interj* — used to express triumph on a discovery [Greek *heurēka* "I have found", from *heuriskein* "to find"; from the exclamation attributed to Archimedes on his discovering a method for determining the purity of gold]

Eu·ro·cur·ren·cy \ˌyu̇r-ō-'kar-an-sē, -'kə-rən-\ *n* : moneys (as of the United States and Japan) held outside their countries of origin and used in the money markets of Europe

Eu·ro·dol·lar \'yu̇r-ō-ˌdäl-ər\ *n* : a United States dollar held as Eurocurrency

Eu·ro·pe·an \ˌyu̇r-ə-'pē-ən\ *n* 1 : a native or inhabitant of Europe 2 : a person of European descent — **European** *adj*

European corn borer *n* : an Old World moth whose larva is a major pest in eastern North America especially in the stems and crowns of Indian corn, dahlias, and potatoes

European plan *n* : a hotel plan whereby the daily rate covers only the cost of the room — compare AMERICAN PLAN

eu·ro·pi·um \yü-'rō-pē-əm\ *n* : a gray soft rare earth element — see ELEMENT table [New Latin, from *Europa* "Europe"]

eury- *combining form* : broad : wide ⟨*eury*haline⟩ [Greek *eurys*]

eu·ry·ha·line \ˌyu̇r-i-'hā-ˌlīn, -'hal-ˌīn\ *adj* : able to live in waters of a wide range of salinity

eu·ryp·ter·id \yü-'rip-tə-rəd\ *n* : any of an order (Eurypterida) of usually large aquatic Paleozoic arthropods related to the horseshoe crabs [derived from Greek *eurys* "broad" + *pteron* "wing"] — **eurypterid** *adj*

eu·sta·chian tube \yü-'stā-shən- *also* -'stā-kē-ən-\ *n, often cap E* : a tube connecting the middle ear with the throat and equalizing air pressure on both sides of the eardrum [Bartolommeo *Eustachio,* died 1574, Italian anatomist]

eu·stat·ic \yü-'stat-ik\ *adj* : relating to or characterized by worldwide change of sea level

eu·tha·na·sia \ˌyü-thə-'nā-zhə, -zhē-ə\ *n* : MERCY KILLING [Greek, "easy death", from *eu-* + *thanatos* "death"]

eu·tro·phic \yü-'trō-fik\ *adj* : being a body of water rich in dissolved nutrients (as phosphates) but often shallow and seasonally deficient in oxygen [derived from Greek *eutrophos* "well nourished, nourishing", from *eu-* + *trephein* "to nourish"] — **eu·tro·phi·ca·tion** \-ˌtrō-fə-'kā-shən\ *n*

evac·u·ate \i-'vak-yə-ˌwāt\ *vb* 1 : to make empty 2 : to discharge waste matter from the body : VOID 3 : to remove something from especially by pumping 4 a : to remove or withdraw from a military or occupation zone or from a dangerous area b : VACATE 2 [Latin *evacuare,* from *e-* + *vacuus* "empty"] — **evac·u·a·tion** \i-ˌvak-yə-'wā-shən\ *n* — **evac·u·a·tive** \i-'vak-yə-ˌwāt-iv\ *adj*

evac·u·ee \i-ˌvak-yə-'wē\ *n* : an evacuated person

evade \i-'vād\ *vb* 1 : to get away or avoid by skill or trickery ⟨*evade* a question⟩ 2 : to avoid facing up to ⟨*evade* responsibility⟩ 3 : BAFFLE, FOIL ⟨the problem *evades* all efforts at solution⟩ [Latin *evadere,* from *e-* + *vadere* "to go, walk"] — **evad·able** \i-'vād-ə-bəl\ *adj* — **evad·er** *n* □ SYN ELUDE: EVADE implies adroitness, ingenuity, or lack of scruple in escaping or avoiding a pursuer or attacker; ELUDE implies a slippery or elusive quality that baffles attempts to seize or keep or identify the person or thing that escapes.

evag·i·nate \i-'vaj-ə-ˌnāt\ *vt* : to turn inside out [Latin *evaginare* "to unsheathe", from *e-* + *vagina* "sheath"] — **evag·i·na·tion** \i-ˌvaj-ə-'nā-shən\ *n*

eval·u·ate \i-'val-yə-ˌwāt\ *vt* 1 : to determine or fix the value of 2 : to examine and judge the quality or degree of SYN see ESTIMATE — **eval·u·a·tion** \-ˌval-yə-'wā-shən\ *n* — **eval·u·a·tive** \-'val-yə-ˌwāt-iv\ *adj*

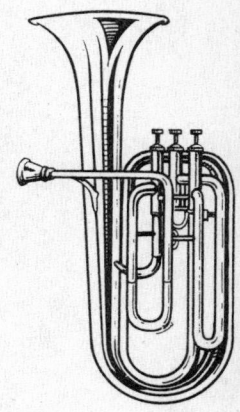

euphonium

\ə\ abut	\ng\ sing
\ər\ further	\ō\ bone
\a\ mat	\ȯ\ saw
\ā\ take	\ȯi\ coin
\ä\ cot, cart	\th\ thin
\au̇\ out	\th\ this
\ch\ chin	\ü\ food
\e\ pet	\u̇\ foot
\ē\ easy	\y\ yet
\g\ go	\yü\ few
\i\ tip	\yu̇\ cure
\ī\ life	\zh\ vision
\j\ job	

ev·a·nesce \,ev-ə-'nes\ *vi* : to dissipate like vapor [Latin *evanescere,* from *e-* + *vanus* "empty"]

ev·a·nes·cence \,ev-ə-'nes-ns\ *n* **1** : the process or fact of evanescing **2** : evanescent quality

ev·a·nes·cent \-nt\ *adj* : tending to vanish like vapor : not lasting : quickly passing ⟨*evanescent* pleasures⟩

evan·gel \i-'van-jəl\ *n* : GOSPEL [Middle French *evangile,* from Late Latin *evangelium,* from Greek *euangelion* "good news, gospel", from *eu-* + *angelos* "messenger"]

evan·gel·i·cal \,ē-,van-'jel-i-kəl, ,ev-ən-\ *also* **evan·gel·ic** \-'jel-ik\ *adj* **1** : of, relating to, or in agreement with the Christian gospel especially as it is presented in the four Gospels **2** : PROTESTANT 1b **3** : emphasizing salvation by faith in the atoning death of Jesus Christ through personal conversion, the authority of Scripture, and the importance of preaching as contrasted with ritual **4** *often cap* **a** : FUNDAMENTALIST **b** : Low Church **5** : ZEALOUS — **Evan·gel·i·cal·ism** \-i-kə-,liz-əm\ *n* — **evan·gel·i·cal·ly** \-i-kə-lē, -klē\ *adv*

Evangelical *n* : one holding evangelical principles or belonging to an evangelical party or church

evan·ge·lism \i-'van-jə-,liz-əm\ *n* **1** : the winning or revival of personal commitments to Christ **2** : militant or crusading zeal — **evan·ge·lis·tic** \i-,van-jə-'lis-tik\ *adj* — **evan·ge·lis·ti·cal·ly** \-ti-kə-lē\ *adv*

evan·ge·list \i-'van-jə-ləst\ *n* **1** *often cap* : a writer of any of the four Gospels **2** : one who evangelizes; *esp* : a preacher who goes about from place to place trying to awake religious enthusiasm

evan·ge·lize \i-'van-jə-,līz\ *vb* **1** : to preach the gospel **2** : to convert to Christianity — **evan·ge·li·za·tion** \-,van-jə-lə-'zā-shən\ *n* — **evan·ge·liz·er** \-'van-jə-,līzər\ *n*

evap·o·rate \i-'vap-ə-,rāt\ *vb* **1** : to change into vapor ⟨ether *evaporates* rapidly in air⟩; *also* : to pass off or cause to pass off in usually invisible minute particles **2 a** : to pass off or away : DISAPPEAR **b** : to diminish quickly **3** : to expel moisture from (as by heat) ⟨*evaporate* apples⟩ — **evap·o·ra·tion** \-,vap-ə-'rā-shən\ *n* — **evap·o·ra·tive** \-'vap-ə-,rāt-iv\ *adj* — **evap·o·ra·tor** \-,rāt-ər\ *n*

evaporated milk *n* : milk concentrated by evaporation without the addition of sugar to one half or less of its bulk

evap·o·rite \i-'vap-ə-,rīt\ *n* : a sedimentary rock (as gypsum) that originates by evaporation of seawater in an enclosed basin

eva·sion \i-'vā-zhən\ *n* **1** : the act or an instance of evading : ESCAPE ⟨tax *evasion*⟩ **2** : a means of evading [Late Latin *evasio,* from Latin *evadere* "to evade"]

eva·sive \i-'vā-siv, -ziv\ *adj* : tending or intended to evade : EQUIVOCAL — **eva·sive·ly** *adv* — **eva·sive·ness** *n*

eve \'ēv\ *n* **1** : EVENING **2** : the evening or the day before a special day ⟨Christmas *Eve*⟩ **3** : the period immediately preceding an event [Middle English *even, eve*]

¹even \'ē-vən\ *n, archaic* : EVENING [Middle English, from Old English *ǣfen*]

²even *adj* **1 a** : having a horizontal surface : FLAT ⟨*even* ground⟩ **b** : being without break or irregularity : SMOOTH **c** : being in the same plane or line ⟨houses *even* with each other⟩ **2** : being without variation : UNIFORM **3 a** : EQUAL, FAIR ⟨an *even* exchange⟩ **b** : leaving nothing due on either side : SQUARE **c** : BALANCED; *esp* : showing neither profit nor loss **4** : being exactly divisible by 2 ⟨*even* numbers⟩ **5** : EXACT, PRECISE ⟨an *even* dozen⟩ **6** : FIFTY-FIFTY 2 ⟨stands an *even* chance of winning⟩ [Old English *efen*] SYN see STEADY — **even·ly** *adv* — **even·ness** \-vən-nəs\ *n*

³even *adv* **1 a** : PRECISELY, EXACTLY ⟨*even* as you and I⟩ **b** : at the very time ⟨*even* as the clock struck⟩ **2 a** — used as an intensive to indicate something unexpected ⟨respected *even* by their enemies⟩ **b** — used as an intensive to stress the comparative degree ⟨did *even* better⟩

⁴even *vb* **evened; even·ing** \'ēv-ning, -ə-ning\ : to make or become even — **even·er** \'ēv-nər, -ə-nər\ *n*

even·hand·ed \,ē-vən-'han-dəd\ *adj* : FAIR 5a, IMPARTIAL

eve·ning \'ēv-ning\ *n* **1** : the latter part and close of the day and early part of the night **2** : the latter part ⟨the *evening* of life⟩ [derived from Old English *ǣfen* "evening"]

evening dress *n* : conventional dress for formal or semiformal evening social occasions

evening prayer *n, often cap E&P* : an evening service of the Anglican liturgy

evening primrose *n* : a coarse biennial herb with yellow flowers that open in the evening; *also* : any of several related plants

eve·nings \'ēv-ningz\ *adv* : in the evening repeatedly ⟨goes bowling *evenings*⟩

evening star *n* : a bright planet (as Venus) seen in the western sky at or after sunset

even·song \'ē-vən-,song\ *n, often cap* **1** : VESPERS 1 **2** : EVENING PRAYER

event \i-'vent\ *n* **1 a** : something that happens : OCCURRENCE **b** : a noteworthy happening **c** : a social occasion or activity **2** : CASE 4, EVENTUALITY ⟨in the *event* of rain the picnic will be postponed⟩ **3** : any of the contests in a program of sports **4** : a subset of the possible outcomes of a statistical experiment ⟨7 is an *event* in the throwing of two dice⟩ [Latin *eventus,* from *evenire* "to happen", from *e-* + *venire* "to come"] SYN see OCCURRENCE — **at all events** : in any case — **in any event** : in any case

event·ful \-fəl\ *adj* **1** : full of or rich in events ⟨an *eventful* day⟩ **2** : MOMENTOUS — **event·ful·ly** \-fə-lē\ *adv* — **event·ful·ness** *n*

even·tide \'ē-vən-,tīd\ *n* : EVENING

even·tu·al \i-'vench-wəl, -ə-wəl; -'ven-chəl\ *adj* : taking place at an unspecified later time : ULTIMATE ⟨*eventual* success⟩ — **even·tu·al·ly** \-ē\ *adv*

even·tu·al·i·ty \i-,ven-chə-'wal-ət-ē\ *n, pl* **-ties** : something that may happen : POSSIBILITY

even·tu·ate \i-'ven-chə-,wāt\ *vt* : to come out finally

ev·er \'ev-ər\ *adv* **1** : ALWAYS ⟨*ever* faithful⟩ **2 a** : at any time ⟨seldom if *ever* home⟩ **b** : in any way ⟨how can I *ever* repay you⟩ **3** — used as an intensive especially with *so* ⟨*ever* so angry⟩ [Old English *ǣfre*]

ev·er·bloom·ing \,ev-ər-'blü-ming\ *adj* : blooming more or less continuously throughout the growing season

ev·er·glade \'ev-ər-,glād\ *n* : a low-lying tract of swampy or marshy land [the *Everglades,* Florida]

¹ev·er·green \'ev-ər-,grēn\ *adj* : having foliage that remains green and functional through more than one growing season ⟨most conifers are *evergreen* trees⟩ — compare DECIDUOUS

²evergreen *n* **1** : an evergreen plant; *also* : CONIFER **2** *pl* : twigs and branches of evergreen plants used for decoration

¹ev·er·last·ing \,ev-ər-'las-ting\ *adj* **1** : lasting or enduring through all time : ETERNAL **2 a** (1) : continuing long or indefinitely : PERPETUAL (2) : retaining form or color when dried ⟨*everlasting* flowers⟩ **b** : tediously persistent **3** : wearing indefinitely : DURABLE SYN see ETERNAL — **ev·er·last·ing·ly** \-ting-lē\ *adv* — **ev·er·last·ing·ness** *n*

²everlasting *n* **1** *cap* : GOD 1 — used with *the* **2** : ETERNITY ⟨from *everlasting*⟩ **3 a** : a plant especially of the daisy family with everlasting flowers **b** : an everlasting flower

ev·er·more \,ev-ər-'mōr, -'mȯr\ *adv* : at all times : FOREVER

evert \i-'vərt\ *vt* : to turn outward or inside out [Latin *evertere* "to overturn" (past participle *eversus*), from *e-* + *vertere* "to turn"] — **ever·si·ble** \-'vər-sə-bəl\ *adj* — **ever·sion** \-'vər-zhən\ *n*

ev·ery \'ev-rē\ *adj* **1** : being each individual or part of a group without exception **2** : COMPLETE, ENTIRE ⟨I have *every* confidence in you⟩ [Middle English *everich, every,* from Old English *ǣfre ǣlc,* from *ǣfre* "ever" + *ǣlc* "each"]

ev·ery·body \'ev-ri-,bäd-ē, -bəd-\ *pron* : every person

ev·ery·day \'ev-rē-'dā\ *adj* : encountered or used routinely or typically : ORDINARY ⟨*everyday* clothes⟩

ev·ery·one \'ev-rē-wən, -,wən\ *pron* : EVERYBODY

ev·ery·thing \'ev-rē-,thing\ *pron* **1 a** : all that exists **b** : all that relates to the subject ⟨tell *everything*⟩ **2** : something that is most important or excellent : all that counts ⟨money isn't *everything*⟩

ev·ery·where \-,hwear, -,hwaar\ *adv* : in every place or part

evict \i-'vikt\ *vt* : to put (an occupant) out from property by legal process [Late Latin *evictus,* past participle of *evincere* "to evict", from Latin, "to vanquish", from *e-* + *vincere* "to conquer"] SYN see EJECT — **evic·tion** \-'vik-shən\ *n* — **evic·tor** \-'vik-tər\ *n*

¹ev·i·dence \'ev-əd-əns, -ə-,dens\ *n* **1 a** : an outward sign : INDICATION **b** : something that furnishes proof : TESTIMONY; *esp* : material legally submitted to a tribunal to determine the truth of a matter **2** : one who bears witness; *esp* : one who voluntarily confesses a crime and testifies for the prosecution against his accomplices — **ev·i·den·tial** \,ev-ə-'den-chəl\ *adj* — **in evidence** : to be seen : CONSPICUOUS

²evidence *vt* : to offer evidence of : PROVE

ev·i·dent \'ev-əd-ənt, -ə-,dent\ *adj* : clear to the sight or understanding : PLAIN ⟨was *evident* that the children were twins⟩ [Middle French, from Latin *evidens,* from *e-* + *videns,* present participle of *vidēre* "to see"] SYN see APPARENT — **ev·i·dent·ly** *adv*

¹evil \'ē-vəl\ *adj* **evil·er** *or* **evil·ler; evil·est** *or* **evil·lest 1 a** : not good morally : WICKED **b** : arising from bad character or conduct ⟨a person of *evil* reputation⟩ **2 a** : causing discomfort or repulsion : OFFENSIVE **b** : DISAGREEABLE ⟨in an *evil* temper⟩ **3 a** : causing harm : PERNICIOUS **b** : marked by misfortune : UNLUCKY ⟨an *evil* day⟩ [Old English *yfel*] — **evil·ly** \-vəl-lē, -və-\ *adv*

²evil *n* **1** : something that brings sorrow, distress, or calamity **2** : the fact of suffering, misfortune, and wrongdoing — **evil·do·er** \,ē-vəl-'dü-ər\ *n* — **evil·do·ing** \-'dü-ing\ *n*

evil eye *n* : an eye or glance held to be capable of inflicting harm

evil–mind·ed \,ē-vəl-'mīn-dəd\ *adj* : having an evil disposition or evil thoughts

evince \i-'vins\ *vt* **1** : to be evidence of : SHOW **2** : to display clearly : REVEAL [Latin *evincere* "to vanquish, win a point", from *e-* + *vincere* "to conquer"] — **ev·inc·i·ble** \i-'vin-sə-bəl\ *adj*

evis·cer·ate \i-'vis-ə-,rāt\ *vt* **1** : to take out the entrails of **2** : to deprive of vital content or force — **evis·cer·a·tion** \i-,vis-ə-'rā-shən\ *n*

evo·ca·tion \,ē-vō-'kā-shən, ,ev-ə-\ *n* : the act or fact of evoking

evoke \i-'vōk\ *vt* **1** : to call forth or up: as **a** : CONJURE 2a ⟨*evoke* evil spirits⟩ **b** : to cite especially with approval : INVOKE **c** : to bring to mind ⟨this place *evokes* happy memories⟩ **2** : to recreate imaginatively [French *évoquer,* from Latin *evocare,* from *e-* + *vocare* "to call"] — **evo·ca·ble** \'ev-ə-kə-bəl, i-'vō-kə-\ *adj* — **evoc·a·tive** \i-'väk-ət-iv\ *adj* — **evoc·a·tive·ly** *adv* — **evoc·a·tor** \'ē-vō-,kāt-ər, 'ev-ə-\ *n*

ev·o·lu·tion \,ev-ə-'lü-shən, ,ē-və-\ *n* **1 a** : a process of evolving or emitting ⟨*evolution* of a gas⟩ **b** : a process of change especially from a lower to a higher state : GROWTH **c** : something evolved **2** : one of a set of prescribed movements (as of a dancer) **3** : the process of working out or developing something (as an idea) **4** : the extraction of a mathematical root **5 a** : PHYLOGENY **b** : a theory that the various types of animals and plants have their origin in other preexisting types and that

the distinguishable differences are due to changes in successive generations **6** : a process in which the whole universe is a progression of interrelated phenomena [Latin *evolutio* "unrolling", from *evolvere* "to unroll"] — **ev·o·lu·tion·ary** \-shə-,ner-ē\ *adj* — **ev·o·lu·tion·ism** \-shə-,niz-əm\ *n* — **ev·o·lu·tion·ist** \-shə-nəst, -shnəst\ *n or adj*

evolve \i-'välv, -'vȯlv\ *vb* **1** : to give off : EMIT **2 a** : to arrive at through thought or study : work out ⟨*evolve* a plan⟩ **b** : to produce by natural evolutionary processes ⟨insects *evolved* wings⟩ **3** : to undergo evolutionary change ⟨species *evolve* continuously⟩ [Latin *evolvere* "to unroll", from *e-* + *volvere* "to roll"] — **evolve·ment** \-mənt\ *n*

ewe \'yü, 'yō\ *n* : the female of the sheep or a related animal especially when mature [Old English *ēowu*]

ew·er \'yü-ər, 'yü-ər, 'yùr\ *n* : a vase-shaped pitcher or jug [Anglo-French, from Old French *evier,* from Latin *aquarius* "of water", from *aqua* "water"]

ewer

ex \eks, ,eks\ *prep* **1 a** : out of : FROM ⟨goods supplied *ex* stock⟩ **b** : from a specified dam ⟨a promising colt by Ranger *ex* Margot⟩ **2** : without an indicated value or right — used especially of securities ⟨*ex* dividend⟩ [Latin]

¹ex- *prefix* **1** \e *also occurs in this prefix where only* i *is shown in entries below and* ks *sometimes occurs where only* gz *is shown* \ : out of : outside ⟨*ex*urb⟩ **2** \eks, ,eks, 'eks\ : former ⟨*ex*-president⟩ [Latin, "out, out of, thoroughly", from *ex* "out of, from"]

²ex- — see EXO-

ex·ac·er·bate \ig-'zas-ər-,bāt, ek-'sas-\ *vt* : to make more violent, bitter, or severe [Latin *exacerbare,* from *ex-* + *acerbus* "harsh, bitter", from *acer* "sharp"] — **ex·ac·er·ba·tion** \ig-,zas-ər-'bā-shən, ek-,sas-\ *n*

¹ex·act \ig-'zakt\ *vt* **1** : to call for forcibly or urgently and obtain ⟨*exact* the full penalty of the law⟩ **2** : to call for as necessary, appropriate, or desirable [Latin *exactus,* past participle of *exigere* "to drive out, demand", from *ex-* + *agere* "to drive"] SYN see DEMAND — **ex·act·able** \-'zak-tə-bəl\ *adj*

²exact *adj* **1** : showing strict, particular, and complete accordance with fact ⟨*exact* knowledge⟩ **2 a** : marked by thorough consideration or minute measurement of small factual details ⟨build an *exact* replica⟩ **b** : not incomplete or approximate ⟨*exact* measurements⟩ SYN see CORRECT — **exact·ness** \-'zakt-nəs -'zak-\ *n*

ex·act·ing \ig-'zak-ting\ *adj* **1** : making severe demands upon a person : TRYING ⟨an *exacting* teacher⟩ **2** : requiring precise accuracy ⟨*exacting* work⟩ — **ex·act·ing·ly** \-ting-lē\ *adv* — **ex·act·ing·ness** *n*

ex·ac·tion \ig-'zak-shən\ *n* **1** : the act or process of exacting especially by way of extortion **2** : something exacted; *esp* : something demanded with compelling force

ex·ac·ti·tude \ig-'zak-tə-,tüd, -,tyüd\ *n* : the quality or an instance of being exact

ex·act·ly \ig-'zak-tlē, -lē\ *adv* **1 a** : in an exact manner : PRECISELY ⟨copy *exactly*⟩ **b** : ALTOGETHER ⟨not *exactly* what I had in mind⟩ **2** : quite so — used to express agreement

exact science *n* : a science (as physics, chemistry, or astronomy) whose laws are capable of expression in accurately measured quantities

ex·ag·ger·ate \ig-'zaj-ə-,rāt\ *vb* **1** : to enlarge a fact beyond what is actual or true : OVERSTATE **2** : to enlarge or increase especially beyond the normal [Latin *exaggerare,* literally, "to heap up", from *ex-* + *agger* "heap"] — **ex·ag·ger·at·ed·ly** \-,rāt-əd-lē\ *adv* — **ex·ag·ger·a·tion** \-,zaj-ə-'rā-shən\ *n* — **ex·ag·ger·a·tor** \-'zaj-ə-,rāt-ər\ *n*

ex·alt \ig-'zȯlt\ *vt* **1** : to raise high : ELEVATE **2** : to raise in rank, power, or character **3** : to elevate by praise or in estimation : GLORIFY [Latin *exaltare,* from *ex-* + *altus* "high"] — **ex·alt·er** *n*

\ə\	abut	\ng\	sing
\ər\	further	\ō\	bone
\a\	mat	\ȯ\	saw
\ā\	take	\ȯi\	coin
\ä\	cot, cart	\th\	thin
\aú\	out	\th\	this
\ch\	chin	\ü\	food
\e\	pet	\ú\	foot
\ē\	easy	\y\	yet
\g\	go	\yü\	few
\i\	tip	\yú\	cure
\ī\	life	\zh\	vision
\j\	job		

ex·al·ta·tion \,eg-,zȯl-'tā-shən\ *n* **I** : the act of exalting : the state of being exalted **2** : a greatly heightened sense of well-being, power, or importance

ex·am \ig-'zam\ *n* : EXAMINATION

ex·am·i·na·tion \ig-,zam-ə-'nā-shən\ *n* **I** : the act or process of examining : the state of being examined **2** : an exercise designed to examine progress or test qualification or knowledge **3** : a formal interrogation — **ex·am·i·na·tion·al** \-shnəl, -shən-l\ *adj*

ex·am·ine \ig-'zam-ən\ *vb* **I a** : to inspect closely ⟨*examine* rock specimens⟩ **b** : to test the condition of ⟨have your eyes *examined*⟩ **c** : to inquire into carefully : INVESTIGATE **2** : to question closely in order to determine progress, fitness, or knowledge ⟨*examine* a class in arithmetic⟩ [Middle French *examiner,* from Latin *examinare,* from *examen* "tongue of a balance, examination", from *exigere* "to drive out, weigh"] SYN see SCRUTINIZE — **ex·am·in·er** *n*

ex·am·ple \ig-'zam-pəl\ *n* **I** : a sample of something taken to show what the whole is like ⟨a striking *example* of scientific method⟩ **2** : something to be imitated : MODEL ⟨a good *example*⟩ ⟨avoid bad *examples*⟩ **3** : punishment inflicted on someone as a warning to others **4** : a problem to be solved in order to show how a rule works ⟨an *example* in arithmetic⟩ [Middle French, from Latin *exemplum,* from *eximere* "to take out", from *ex-* + *emere* "to take"] SYN see INSTANCE

ex·arch \'ek-,särk\ *n* : an Eastern bishop ranking below a patriarch and above a metropolitan; *esp* : the head of an independent church [Late Latin *exarchus,* from Greek *exarchos* "leader", from *ex-* "ex-" + *archein* "to begin, rule"] — **ex·ar·chal** \ek-'sär-kəl\ *adj* — **ex·arch·ate** \'ek-,sär-kət\ *n* — **ex·ar·chy** \'ek-,sär-kē\ *n*

ex·as·per·ate \ig-'zas-pə-,rāt\ *vt* **I** : to make angry : ENRAGE **2** : to cause irritation or annoyance to [Latin *exasperare,* from *ex-* + *asper* "rough"] SYN see IRRITATE

ex·as·per·a·tion \ig-,zas-pə-'rā-shən\ *n* **I** : the state of being exasperated **2** : the action or an instance of exasperating

Ex·cal·i·bur \ek-'skal-ə-bər\ *n* : the legendary sword of King Arthur [Old French *Escalibor,* from Medieval Latin *Caliburnus*]

ex ca·the·dra \,eks-kə-'thē-drə\ *adv or adj* : officially and with authority ⟨*ex cathedra* pronouncements⟩ [New Latin, literally, "from the chair"]

ex·ca·vate \'ek-skə-,vāt\ *vt* **I** : to hollow out : form a hole in ⟨*excavate* a hillside⟩ **2** : to make by hollowing out ⟨*excavate* a tunnel⟩ **3** : to dig out and remove ⟨*excavate* sand⟩ **4** : to uncover by digging away covering earth [Latin *excavare,* from *ex-* + *cavare* "to make hollow", from *cavus* "hollow"] — **ex·ca·va·tor** \-,vātər\ *n*

ex·ca·va·tion \,ek-skə-'vā-shən\ *n* **I** : the act or process of excavating **2** : a hollowed-out place formed by excavating

ex·ceed \ik-'sēd\ *vt* **I** : to extend outside of ⟨the river will *exceed* its banks⟩ **2** : to be greater than or superior to : SURPASS ⟨the cost *exceeded* our funds⟩ **3** : to go beyond a limit set by ⟨*exceed* one's authority⟩ [Middle French *exceder,* from Latin *excedere,* from *ex-* + *cedere* "to go"] □ SYN EXCEL, SURPASS, TRANSCEND: EXCEED implies going beyond a limit or standard set by authority, custom, or previous achievement ⟨*exceed* last year's production⟩ EXCEL implies preeminence in achievement or quality ⟨*excelling* in athletics⟩ ⟨*excels* in writing dialogue⟩ SURPASS suggests superiority in quality, merit, or skill; TRANSCEND implies a rising or extending notably above or beyond ordinary limits ⟨writing that *transcends* prosaic statement⟩

ex·ceed·ing *adj* : exceptional in amount, quality, or degree

ex·ceed·ing·ly \ik-'sēd-ing-lē\ *or* **ex·ceed·ing** *adv* : to an extreme degree : EXTREMELY

ex·cel \ik-'sel\ *vb* **ex·celled; ex·cel·ling** : to outdo others (as in good qualities or ability) : SURPASS ⟨*excel* in

math⟩ ⟨a jump *excelling* the previous record⟩ [Latin *excellere,* from *ex-* + *-cellere* "to rise, project"] SYN see EXCEED

ex·cel·lence \'ek-sə-ləns, -sləns\ *n* **I** : the quality of being excellent **2** : an excellent or valuable quality : VIRTUE **3** *cap* : EXCELLENCY 2

ex·cel·len·cy \-sə-lən-sē, -slən-\ *n, pl* **-cies** **I** : outstanding or valuable quality — usually used in pl. **2** *cap* — used as a form of address for a high dignitary of state (as a foreign ambassador) or church (as a Roman Catholic bishop) ⟨Your *Excellency*⟩ ⟨His *Excellency*⟩ ⟨Her *Excellency*⟩

ex·cel·lent \'ek-sə-lənt, -slənt\ *adj* : very good of its kind : FIRST-CLASS — **ex·cel·lent·ly** *adv*

ex·cel·si·or \ik-'sel-sē-ər\ *n* : fine curled wood shavings used especially for packing fragile items [trade name, from Latin, "higher", from *excelsus* "high", from *excellere* "to excel"]

¹ex·cept \ik-'sept\ *vt* : to take or leave out from a number or a whole : EXCLUDE [Middle French *excepter,* from Latin *exceptare,* from *excipere* "to take out, except", from *ex-* + *capere* "to take"]

²except *also* **ex·cept·ing** *prep* : with the exclusion or exception of ⟨everybody *except* you⟩

³except *also* **excepting** *conj* **I** : UNLESS ⟨*except* you repent⟩ **2** : ³ONLY 2 ⟨I would go *except* it's too far⟩

ex·cep·tion \ik-'sep-shən\ *n* **I** : the act of excepting : EXCLUSION **2** : one that is excepted **3** : something offered as objection or taken as objectionable

ex·cep·tion·able \ik-'sep-shə-nə-bəl, -shnə-\ *adj* : likely to cause objection : OBJECTIONABLE — **ex·cep·tion·ably** \-blē\ *adv*

ex·cep·tion·al \ik-'sep-shnəl, -shən-l\ *adj* **I** : forming an exception : RARE **2** : better than average : SUPERIOR **3** : deviating from the norm; *esp* : below average ⟨schools for *exceptional* children⟩ — **ex·cep·tion·al·ly** \-ē\ *adv* — **ex·cep·tion·al·ness** *n*

¹ex·cerpt \ek-'sərpt, eg-'zərpt, 'ek-,, 'eg-,\ *vt* : to select (a passage) for quoting : EXTRACT [Latin *excerpere,* from *ex-* + *carpere* "to gather, pluck"]

²ex·cerpt \'ek-,sərpt, 'eg-,zərpt\ *n* : a passage selected or copied : EXTRACT

¹ex·cess \ik-'ses, 'ek-,\ *n* **I a** : the state or an instance of surpassing usual limits : SUPERFLUITY **b** : the amount or degree by which one thing or quantity exceeds another **2** : INTEMPERANCE [Late Latin *excessus,* from Latin *excedere* "to exceed"]

²excess *adj* : being more than the usual, proper, or specified amount ⟨charges for *excess* baggage⟩

ex·ces·sive \ik-'ses-iv\ *adj* : exceeding the usual, proper, or normal — **ex·ces·sive·ly** *adv* — **ex·ces·sive·ness** *n* □ SYN EXCESSIVE, EXORBITANT, INORDINATE, EXTRAVAGANT mean going beyond a normal limit. EXCESSIVE implies an amount or degree too great to be reasonable or acceptable ⟨*excessive* bail was required⟩ EXORBITANT applies to what is grossly excessive ⟨*exorbitant* demands⟩ INORDINATE implies an exceeding of the limits dictated by reason or good judgment ⟨an *inordinate* appetite⟩ ⟨*inordinate* desire for power⟩ EXTRAVAGANT implies an indifference to restraints imposed by truth, prudence, or good taste ⟨*extravagant* purchases⟩

¹ex·change \iks-'chānj, 'eks-,\ *n* **I** : a giving or taking one thing in return for another : TRADE **2** : the act of substituting one thing for another **3** : something offered, given, or received in an exchange **4 a** : funds payable currently at a distant point in foreign or domestic currency **b** (1) : interchange of two kinds of money (as money of two different countries) with allowance for difference in value (2) : the amount of one currency that will buy a given amount of another **5** : a place where things or services are exchanged: as **a** : an organized market or center for trading in securities or commodities **b** : a central office in which telephone lines are connected to permit communication

²exchange *vt* **1 a** : to give in exchange : TRADE ⟨*exchange* a knife for a book⟩ **b** : to replace by other merchandise ⟨*exchange* this shirt for one in a larger size⟩ **2** : to part with for a substitute ⟨*exchange* future security for immediate pleasure⟩ — **ex·change·able** \-ə-bəl\ *adj* — **ex·chang·er** *n*

exchange student *n* : a student from a usually foreign country received into an educational institution in exchange for a student sent to that foreign country

ex·che·quer \'eks-,chek-ər, iks-'\ *n* **1** : the department of the British government concerned with the receipt and care of the national revenue **2** : TREASURY; *esp* : a national or royal treasury **3** : money available : FUNDS [Anglo-French *escheker,* from Old French *eschequier* "chessboard, counting table", from *eschec* "check"]

¹ex·cise \'ek-,sīz, -,sīs\ *n* : an internal tax levied on the manufacture, sale, or consumption of a commodity within a country [obsolete Dutch *excijs*]

²ex·cise \ek-'sīz\ *vt* : to remove by cutting out ⟨*excise* a tumor⟩ [Latin *excisus,* past participle of *excidere* "to excise", from *ex-* + *caedere* "to cut"] — **ex·ci·sion** \-'sizh-ən\ *n*

ex·cit·able \ik-'sīt-ə-bəl\ *adj* : readily roused into action or an active state; *esp* : capable of activation by and reaction to stimuli — **ex·cit·abil·i·ty** \-,sīt-ə-'bil-ət-ē\ *n*

ex·ci·ta·tion \,ek-,sī-'tā-shən, ,ek-sə-\ *n* : EXCITEMENT; *esp* : the irritability induced in protoplasm by a stimulus

ex·cit·ato·ry \ik-'sīt-ə-,tōr-ē, -,tȯr-\ *adj* : tending to produce or marked by usually physiological excitation

ex·cite \ik-'sīt\ *vt* **1 a** : to call to activity **b** : to rouse to feeling **2 a** : ENERGIZE **b** : to produce a magnetic field in **3 a** : to increase the activity of (as nervous tissue) **b** : to arouse (as an emotional response) by appropriate stimuli **4** : to raise (as an atom) to a higher energy level [Middle French *exciter,* from Latin *excitare,* from *ex-* + *citare* "to rouse"] SYN see PROVOKE — **ex·cit·er** \-'sīt-ər\ *n*

ex·cit·ed \-'sīt-əd\ *adj* : having or showing strong feeling : worked up — **ex·cit·ed·ly** *adv*

ex·cite·ment \ik-'sīt-mənt\ *n* **1** : the act of exciting : the state of being excited **2** : something that excites

ex·cit·ing \-'sīt-ing\ *adj* : causing excitement : STIRRING — **ex·cit·ing·ly** \-ing-lē\ *adv*

ex·claim \iks-'klām\ *vb* **1** : to speak or cry out in strong or sudden emotion **2** : to speak loudly or forcefully [Middle French *exclamer,* from Latin *exclamare,* from *ex-* + *clamare* "to cry out"]

ex·cla·ma·tion \,eks-klə-'mā-shən\ *n* **1** : a sharp or sudden utterance : OUTCRY **2** : forceful expression of protest or complaint

exclamation point *n* : a punctuation mark ! used chiefly after an exclamation to show forceful utterance or strong feeling

ex·clam·a·to·ry \iks-'klam-ə-,tōr-ē, -,tȯr-\ *adj* : containing, expressing, using, or relating to exclamation

ex·clude \iks-'klüd\ *vt* **1 a** : to shut out **b** : to bar from participation, consideration, or inclusion **2** : to put out : EXPEL [Latin *excludere* (past participle *exclusus*), from *ex-* + *claudere* "to close"] — **ex·clud·able** \-'klüd-ə-bəl\ *adj* — **ex·clud·er** *n* — **ex·clu·sion** \-'klü-zhən\ *n*

ex·clu·sive \iks-'klü-siv, -ziv\ *adj* **1** : excluding or inclined to exclude certain persons or classes (as from ownership, membership, or privileges) : catering to a distinct and especially a fashionable class ⟨an *exclusive* neighborhood⟩ **2** : SOLE, SINGLE ⟨*exclusive* use of a beach⟩ **3** : COMPLETE, UNDIVIDED ⟨give me your *exclusive* attention⟩ **4** : not taking account : not inclusive ⟨for five days *exclusive* of today⟩ — **ex·clu·sive·ly** *adv* — **ex·clu·sive·ness** *n*

ex·cog·i·tate \eks-'käj-ə-,tāt\ *vt* : to think out : DEVISE — **ex·cog·i·ta·tion** \,eks-,käj-ə-'tā-shən\ *n* — **ex·cog·i·ta·tive** \eks-'käj-ə-,tāt-iv\ *adj*

ex·com·mu·ni·cate \,eks-kə-'myü-nə-,kāt\ *vt* : to deprive officially of the rights of church membership — **ex·com·mu·ni·ca·tion** \-,myü-nə-'kā-shən\ *n* — **ex·com·mu·ni·ca·tor** \-'myü-nə-,kāt-ər\ *n*

ex·co·ri·ate \ek-'skōr-ē-,āt, -'skȯr-\ *vt* **1** : to wear off the skin of : ABRADE **2** : to censure scathingly [Late Latin *excoriare,* from Latin *ex-* + *corium* "skin, hide"] — **ex·co·ri·a·tion** \ek-,skōr-ē-'ā-shən, -,skȯr-\ *n*

ex·cre·ment \'ek-skrə-mənt\ *n* : waste matter discharged from the body and especially from the alimentary canal [Latin *excrementum,* from *excernere* "to discharge"] — **ex·cre·men·tal** \,ek-skrə-'ment-l\ *adj*

ex·cres·cence \ek-'skres-ns\ *n* : OUTGROWTH; *esp* : an abnormal outgrowth (as a wart) on the body

ex·cres·cent \-nt\ *adj* : being or forming an excrescence [Latin *excrescere* "to grow out", from *ex-* + *crescere* "to grow"] — **ex·cres·cent·ly** *adv*

ex·cre·ta \ek-'skrēt-ə\ *n pl* : waste matter eliminated or separated from an organism

ex·crete \ek-'skrēt\ *vt* : to separate and eliminate (waste) from the blood or tissues or from the active protoplasm usually in the form of sweat or urine [Latin *excretus,* past participle of *excernere* "to sift out, discharge", from *ex-* + *cernere* "to sift"] — **ex·cret·er** *n*

ex·cre·tion \ek-'skrē-shən\ *n* **1** : the act or process of excreting **2** : excreted matter

ex·cre·to·ry \'ek-skrə-,tōr-ē, -,tȯr-\ *adj* : of, relating to, or functioning in excretion

ex·cru·ci·ate \ik-'skrü-shē-,āt\ *vt* : to subject to intense pain or mental distress [Latin *excruciare,* from *ex-* + *cruciare* "to crucify", from *cruc-, crux* "cross"] — **ex·cru·ci·a·tion** \-,skrü-shē-'ā-shən, -sē-'ā-\ *n*

ex·cru·ci·at·ing \-'skrü-shē-,āt-ing\ *adj* **1** : causing great pain or mental distress : AGONIZING **2** : very intense : EXTREME — **ex·cru·ci·at·ing·ly** \-ing-lē\ *adv*

ex·cul·pate \'ek-skəl-,pāt, -,skəl-, ek-'\ *vt* : to clear from alleged fault or guilt [derived from Latin *ex-* + *culpa* "blame"] — **ex·cul·pa·tion** \,ek-skəl-'pā-shən, -,skəl-\ *n* — **ex·cul·pa·to·ry** \ek-'skəl-pə-,tōr-ē, -,tȯr-\ *adj*

ex·cur·rent \ek-'skər-ənt, -'skə-rənt\ *adj* **1** : having a straight main stem that extends without forking to the top ⟨the spruce is an *excurrent* tree⟩ — compare DELIQUESCENT **2** : characterized by a current that flows outward ⟨*excurrent* canals of a sponge⟩

ex·cur·sion \ik-'skər-zhən\ *n* **1 a** : a going out or forth : EXPEDITION **b** : a usually brief pleasure trip; *esp* : such a trip at special reduced rates **2** : departure from a direct or proper course; *esp* : DIGRESSION [Latin *excursio,* from *excurrere* "to run out", from *ex-* + *currere* "to run"]

ex·cur·sion·ist \ik-'skərzh-nəst, -ə-nəst\ *n* : a person who goes on an excursion

ex·cur·sive \ik-'skər-siv\ *adj* : constituting a digression : characterized by digression — **ex·cur·sive·ly** *adv* — **ex·cur·sive·ness** *n*

ex·cur·sus \ik-'skər-səs\ *n, pl* **ex·cur·sus·es** *also* **ex·cur·sus** \-səs, -,süs\ : an appendix or a digression containing further exposition of some point or topic [Latin, "digression", from *excurrere* "to run out"]

¹ex·cuse \ik-'skyüz\ *vt* **1** : to make apology for : try to remove blame from ⟨*excuse* oneself for being late⟩ **2** : to accept an excuse for : PARDON **3** : to free or let off from doing something ⟨*excuse* a person from a debt⟩ **4** : to serve as an acceptable reason or explanation for (something said or done) : JUSTIFY ⟨nothing can *excuse* dishonesty⟩ [Old French *excuser,* from Latin *excusare,* from *ex-* + *causa* "cause, explanation"] — **ex·cus·able** \-'skyü-zə-bəl\ *adj* — **ex·cus·ably** \-blē\ *adv* — **ex·cus·er** *n* □ SYN CONDONE, PARDON, FORGIVE: EXCUSE implies an overlooking of a fault, omission, or failure without censure or due punishment; CONDONE suggests accepting without protest or censure a reprehensible act or condition ⟨*condone* the use of drugs⟩ PARDON implies freeing from penalty due for admitted or proved offense; FORGIVE implies a sincere change of

\ə\ abut	\ng\ si**ng**
\ər\ fur**ther**	\ō\ b**o**ne
\a\ m**a**t	\ȯ\ s**aw**
\ā\ t**a**ke	\ȯi\ c**oi**n
\ä\ c**o**t, c**a**rt	\th\ **th**in
\aú\ **ou**t	\t̷h\ **th**is
\ch\ **ch**in	\ü\ f**oo**d
\e\ p**e**t	\ú\ f**oo**t
\ē\ **ea**sy	\y\ **y**et
\g\ **g**o	\yü\ f**ew**
\i\ t**i**p	\yú\ c**u**re
\ī\ l**i**fe	\zh\ vi**s**ion
\j\ **j**ob	

feeling that makes no claim to retaliation and gives up resentment or desire for revenge.

²**ex·cuse** \ik-'skyüs\ *n* **1** : the act of excusing **2 a** : something offered as justification or as grounds for being excused **b** : a note of explanation of an absence **3** : JUSTIFICATION 2b, REASON SYN see APOLOGY

ex·ec \ig-'zek\ *n* : EXECUTIVE OFFICER

ex·e·cra·ble \'ek-si-krə-bəl\ *adj* : DETESTABLE — **ex·e·cra·ble·ness** *n* — **ex·e·cra·bly** \-blē\ *adv*

ex·e·crate \'ek-sə-,krāt\ *vt* **1** : to declare to be evil or detestable **2** : to detest utterly [Latin *exsecrari* "to put under a curse", from *ex-* + *sacer* "sacred"] — **ex·e·cra·tion** \,ek-sə-'krā-shən\ *n* — **ex·e·cra·tor** \'ek-sə-,krāt-ər\ *n*

ex·e·cute \'ek-sə-,kyüt\ *vt* **1** : to put into effect : carry out : PERFORM **2** : to do what is provided or required by ⟨*execute* a decree⟩ **3** : to put to death according to legal orders **4** : to make or produce especially by carrying out a design **5** : to perform what is required to give legal force to ⟨*execute* a deed⟩ [Middle French *executer,* derived from Latin *exsequi,* from *ex-* + *sequi* "to follow"]

ex·e·cu·tion \,ek-sə-'kyü-shən\ *n* **1** : the act or process of executing : PERFORMANCE ⟨put a plan into *execution*⟩ **2** : a putting to death as a legal penalty **3** : a judicial writ empowering an officer to carry out a judgment **4** : the act or mode or result of performance in something requiring special skill **5** : effective or destructive action

ex·e·cu·tion·er \-'kyü-shə-nər, -shnər\ *n* : one that executes; *esp* : one who puts into effect a sentence of death

¹**ex·ec·u·tive** \ig-'zek-yət-iv, -'zek-ət-\ *adj* **1** : designed for or relating to the execution of affairs ⟨*executive* ability⟩ **2** : of or relating to the execution of the laws and the conduct of public affairs **3** : of or relating to an executive

²**executive** *n* **1** : the executive branch of a government **2** : an individual or group that directs an organization **3** : one who holds a position of administrative or managerial responsibility

executive officer *n* : the officer second in command of a military or naval unit

executive session *n* : a usually closed session (as of a legislative body)

ex·ec·u·tor \ig-'zek-yət-ər, -'zek-ət-, *in sense 1 also* 'ek-sə-,kyüt-\ *n* **1** : one that executes something **2** : the person named in a will to carry out its provisions

ex·ec·u·trix \ig-'zek-yə-,triks, -'zek-ə-\ *n, pl* **ex·ec·u·trix·es** *or* **ex·ec·u·tri·ces** \-,zek-yə-'trī-,sēz, -,zek-ə-\ : a woman who is an executor

ex·e·ge·sis \,ek-sə-'jē-səs\ *n, pl* **-ge·ses** \-'jē-,sēz\ : explanation or critical interpretation of a text [Greek *exēgēsis,* from *exēgeisthai* "to explain, interpret", from *ex-* "ex-" + *hēgeisthai* "to lead"] — **ex·e·get·ic** \-'jet-ik\ *or* **ex·e·get·i·cal** \-'jet-i-kəl\ *adj* — **ex·e·get·i·cal·ly** \-i-kə-lē, -klē\ *adv*

ex·e·gete \'ek-sə-,jēt\ *n* : one who practices exegesis

ex·em·plar \ig-'zem-,plär, -plər\ *n* **1 a** : one that serves as a model or pattern; *esp* : an ideal model **b** : ARCHETYPE **2** : a typical instance : EXAMPLE; *esp* : a typical or standard specimen [Latin, from *exemplum* "example"]

ex·em·pla·ry \ig-'zem-plə-rē\ *adj* **1 a** : serving as a pattern **b** : deserving imitation **2** : serving as a warning **3** : serving as an example, instance, or illustration — **ex·em·plar·i·ly** \,eg-zəm-'pler-ə-lē\ *adv* — **ex·em·pla·ri·ness** \ig-'zem-plə-rē-nəs\ *n*

ex·em·pli·fy \ig-'zem-plə-,fī\ *vt* **-fied; -fy·ing 1** : to show or illustrate by example **2** : to serve as an example of — **ex·em·pli·fi·ca·tion** \-,zem-plə-fə-'kā-shən\ *n*

ex·em·pli gra·tia \ig-,zem-plē-'grät-ē-,ä\ *adv* : for example [Latin]

¹**ex·empt** \ig-'zempt\ *adj* : free or released from an obligation or requirement to which others are subject [Latin *exemptus,* past participle of *eximere* "to take out", from *ex-* + *emere* "to take"]

²**exempt** *vt* : to make exempt

ex·emp·tion \ig-'zem-shən, -'zemp-\ *n* **1** : the act of exempting : the state of being exempt **2** : something exempted; *esp* : a source or an amount of income exempted from taxation

ex·e·quy \'ek-sə-kwē\ *n, pl* **-quies** : a funeral rite — usually used in pl. [Latin *exsequiae,* plural, from *exsequi* "to follow out"]

¹**ex·er·cise** \'ek-sər-,sīz\ *n* **1** : the act of bringing into play or realizing in action : USE **2 a** : regular or repeated use of a mental faculty or bodily organ **b** : bodily exertion for the sake of physical fitness **3** : something performed or practiced in order to develop, improve, or display a specific power or skill : EXAMPLE ⟨10 *exercises* for math homework⟩ **4 a** : a drill carried out for training and discipline **b** *pl* : a program including speeches, announcements of awards and honors, and various traditional practices [Middle French *exercice,* from Latin *exercitium,* from *exercēre* "to drive on, keep busy", from *ex-* + *arcēre* "to hold off"]

²**exercise** *vb* **1** : to bring to bear : EXERT ⟨*exercise* patience⟩ **2 a** : to use repeatedly in order to strengthen or develop ⟨*exercise* one's wits⟩ **b** : to train (as troops) by drills **c** : to go or put through exercises : give or take exercise ⟨*exercise* a dog⟩ **3** : to engage the attention of; *esp* : to cause anxiety, alarm, or indignation in ⟨citizens *exercised* about pollution⟩ — **ex·er·cis·able** \-'sī-zə-bəl\ *adj* — **ex·er·cis·er** *n*

ex·ert \ig-'zərt\ *vt* **1** : to put forth (as strength, force, power, or influence) : bring into play **2** : to put (oneself) into action or to tiring effort [Latin *exsertus,* past participle of *exserere* "to thrust out", from *ex-* + *serere* "to join"]

ex·er·tion \ig-'zər-shən\ *n* : the act or an instance of exerting; *esp* : laborious or perceptible effort SYN see EFFORT

ex·e·unt \'ek-sē-ənt, -sē-,ənt\ — used as a stage direction to specify that all or certain named characters leave the stage [Latin, "they go out", from *exire* "to go out", from *ex-* + *ire* "to go"]

ex·fo·li·ate \eks-'fō-lē-,āt, 'eks-\ *vb* : to shed or remove in thin layers or scales — **ex·fo·li·a·tion** \,eks-,fō-lē-'ā-shən\ *n* — **ex·fo·li·a·tive** \eks-'fō-lē-,āt-iv\ *adj*

ex·hal·ant \eks-'hā-lənt\ *adj* : bearing out or outward ⟨an *exhalant* siphon of a clam⟩

ex·ha·la·tion \,eks-ə-'lā-shən, -hə-'lā-\ *n* : an act or product of exhaling

ex·hale \eks-'hāl\ *vb* **1** : to breathe out **2** : to send forth (as gas or odor) : EMIT ⟨the fragrance that flowers *exhale*⟩ **3** : to rise or be given off as vapor [Latin *exhalare,* from *ex-* + *halare* "to breathe"]

¹**ex·haust** \ig-'zost\ *vb* **1 a** : to draw off or let out completely ⟨*exhaust* the air from the jar⟩ **b** : to empty by drawing something from; *esp* : to create a vacuum in **2 a** : to use up the whole supply of **b** : to deprive wholly of (as strength, patience, or resources) **3 a** : to develop (a subject) completely **b** : to try out the whole number of ⟨had *exhausted* all possibilities⟩ **4** : to destroy the fertility of (soil) **5** : to pass or flow out : EMPTY [Latin *exhaustus,* past participle of *exhaurire* "to exhaust", from *ex-* + *haurire* "to draw"] — **ex·haust·er** *n* — **ex·haust·ibil·i·ty** \-,zo-stə-'bil-ət-ē\ *n* — **ex·haust·ible** \-'zo-stə-bəl\ *adj*

²**exhaust** *n* **1 a** : the escape of used steam or gas from an engine **b** : the gas thus escaping **2 a** : a conduit through which used gases escape **b** : an arrangement for withdrawing fumes, dusts, or odors from an enclosure

ex·haus·tion \ig-'zos-chən\ *n* **1** : the act or process of exhausting **2** : the state of being exhausted; *esp* : extreme weariness or fatigue

ex·haus·tive \ig-'zȯ-stiv\ *adj* **1** : serving or tending to exhaust **2** : THOROUGH 1, COMPLETE ⟨an *exhaustive* discussion⟩ — **ex·haus·tive·ly** *adv* — **ex·haus·tive·ness** *n*

ex·haust·less \ig-'zȯst-ləs\ *adj* : INEXHAUSTIBLE

¹**ex·hib·it** \ig-'zib-ət\ *vt* **1** : to show outwardly ⟨*exhibit* an interest in music⟩ **2** : to put on display ⟨*exhibit* a collection of paintings⟩ **3** : to present in legal form (as to a court) [Latin *exhibitus,* past participle of *exhibēre* "to exhibit", from *ex-* + *habēre* "to have, hold"] SYN see SHOW — **ex·hib·i·tor** \-ət-ər\ *n*

²**exhibit** *n* **1** : an act or instance of exhibiting **2** : something exhibited; *esp* : a document or material object produced and identified (as in a court) for use as evidence

ex·hi·bi·tion \,ek-sə-'bish-ən\ *n* **1** : an act or instance of exhibiting **2** *British* : a grant drawn from the funds of a school or university to help maintain a student **3** : a public showing (as of works of art, objects of manufacture, or athletic skill)

ex·hi·bi·tion·er \-'bish-nər, -ə-nər\ *n, British* : one who holds an exhibition (sense 2)

ex·hi·bi·tion·ism \-'bish-ə-,niz-əm\ *n* **1 a** : a compulsive tendency to expose one's body and especially the sex organs in a public place where such exposure is regarded as indecent **b** : an act of such exposure **2** : the act or practice of behaving so as to attract attention to oneself — **ex·hi·bi·tion·ist** \-'bish-nəst, -ə-nəst\ *n or adj* — **ex·hi·bi·tion·is·tic** \-,bish-ə-'nis-tik\ *adj*

ex·hil·a·rate \ig-'zil-ə-,rāt\ *vt* **1** : to make cheerful **2** : to fill with a lively sense of well-being ⟨an *exhilarating* autumn day⟩ [Latin *exhilarare,* from *ex-* + *hilarare* "to gladden", from *ex-* + *hilarus* "cheerful"] — **ex·hil·a·ra·tive** \-,rāt-iv\ *adj*

ex·hil·a·ra·tion \ig-,zil-ə-'rā-shən\ *n* **1** : the action of exhilarating **2** : the state or the feeling of being exhilarated : high spirits : LIVELINESS

ex·hort \ig-'zȯrt\ *vb* : to arouse by words (as of advice, encouragement, or warning) : urge or appeal strongly [Middle French *exhorter,* from Latin *exhortari,* from *ex-* + *hortari* "to incite"] — **ex·hort·er** *n*

ex·hor·ta·tion \,eks-,ȯr-'tā-shən, ,egz-\ *n* **1** : an act or instance of exhorting **2** : a speech intended to exhort : earnestly spoken words of urgent advice or warning

ex·hor·ta·tive \ig-'zȯrt-ət-iv\ *adj* : serving to exhort

ex·hor·ta·to·ry \-ə-,tōr-ē, -,tȯr-\ *adj* : giving exhortation

ex·hume \igz-'üm, -'yüm; iks-'yüm, -'hyüm\ *vt* **1** : to dig out of the ground; *esp* : to uncover and take out of a place of burial **2** : to bring back from neglect or obscurity [Medieval Latin *exhumare,* from Latin *ex* "out of" + *humus* "earth"] — **ex·hu·ma·tion** \,eks-yü-'mā-shən, -hyü-; ,egz-ü-, -yü-\ *n* — **ex·hum·er** *n*

ex·i·gence \'ek-sə-jəns\ *n* : EXIGENCY

ex·i·gen·cy \'ek-sə-jən-sē, ig-'zij-ən-\ *n, pl* **-cies** **1** : a case or a state of affairs demanding immediate action or remedy **2** : an urgent need SYN see NEED

ex·i·gent \'ek-sə-jənt\ *adj* **1** : requiring immediate aid or action : URGENT **2** : requiring or calling for much : DEMANDING, EXACTING [Latin *exigere* "to demand", from *ex-* + *agere* "to drive"] — **ex·i·gent·ly** *adv*

ex·ig·u·ous \eg-'zig-yə-wəs\ *adj* : scanty in amount [Latin *exiguus,* from *exigere* "to demand"] — **ex·i·gu·ity** \,ek-sə-'gyü-ət-ē\ *n* — **ex·ig·u·ous·ly** \eg-'zig-yə-wəs-lē\ *adv* — **ex·ig·u·ous·ness** *n*

¹**ex·ile** \'eg-,zīl, 'ek-,sīl\ *n* **1** : forced removal or voluntary absence from one's native country; *also* : the state of one so absent **2** : a person expelled from his or her country by authority [Middle French *exil,* from Latin *exilium*]

²**exile** *vt* : to expel from one's own country or home

ex·ist \ig-'zist\ *vi* **1** : to have actuality or reality : be real : BE ⟨do unicorns *exist*⟩ **2** : to continue to be : LIVE ⟨earn hardly enough to *exist* on⟩ **3** : to be found : OCCUR ⟨a disease that no longer *exists*⟩ [Latin *exsistere*

"to come into being, exist", from *ex-* + *sistere* "to stand"]

ex·is·tence \ig-'zis-təns\ *n* **1 a** : the fact or the state of being real and not imaginary ⟨believed in the *existence* of dragons⟩ **b** : objective reality : BEING ⟨the largest animal in *existence*⟩ **2** : continuance in living or way of living : LIFE ⟨a happy *existence*⟩ **3** : actual occurrence ⟨recognized the *existence* of a state of war⟩ **4 a** : the sum total of existing things **b** : a particular being

ex·is·tent \-tənt\ *adj* **1** : having being : EXISTING **2** : existing now : PRESENT

ex·is·ten·tial \,eg-zis-'ten-chəl, ,ek-sis-\ *adj* **1** : of, relating to, or dealing with existence **2 a** : grounded in existence or the experience of existence **b** : having being in time and space **3** : concerned with or involving human existence or its nature

¹**ex·it** \'eg-zət, 'ek-sət\ — used as a stage direction to specify who goes off stage [Latin, "he, she, or it goes out", from *exire* "to go out", from *ex-* + *ire* "to go"]

²**exit** *n* **1** : a departure from a stage **2** : the act of going out or going away **3** : a way out of an enclosed place or space

³**exit** *vi* : to go out : LEAVE

ex li·bris \eks-'lē-brəs\ *n, pl* **ex libris** : BOOKPLATE [New Latin, "from the books"; used before the owner's name on bookplates]

exo- *or* **ex-** *combining form* : outside ⟨*exo*gamy⟩ : outer ⟨*exo*skeleton⟩ — compare ECT-, END- [Greek *exō* "out, outside", from *ex* "out of"]

exo·bi·ol·o·gy \,ek-sō-bī-'äl-ə-jē\ *n* : a branch of biology concerned with the search for life outside the earth and with effects of extraterrestrial environments on living organisms — **exo·bi·o·log·i·cal** \-,bī-ə-'läj-i-kəl\ *adj* — **exo·bi·ol·o·gist** \-bī-'äl-ə-jəst\ *n*

exo·crine \'ek-sə-krən, -,krīn, -,krēn\ *adj* : secreting or secreted externally [*exo-* + Greek *krinein* "to separate"]

exocrine gland *n* : a gland (as a salivary gland or a sweat gland) that produces an exocrine secretion

exo·dus \'ek-səd-əs\ *n* **1** *cap* — see BIBLE table **2** : a mass departure [Latin, from Greek *Exodos,* literally, "road out", from *ex-* + *hodos* "road"]

ex of·fi·cio \,eks-ə-'fish-ē-,ō\ *adv or adj* : because of an office ⟨*ex officio* chairman⟩ [Late Latin]

ex·og·a·my \ek-'säg-ə-mē\ *n* : marriage outside a specific group especially as required by custom or law — **ex·og·a·mous** \-məs\ *adj*

ex·og·e·nous \ek-'säj-ə-nəs\ *adj* : developing or originating outside the cell or body — **ex·og·e·nous·ly** *adv*

ex·on·er·ate \ig-'zän-ə-,rāt\ *vt* : to clear from a charge of wrongdoing or from blame : declare innocent [Latin *exonerare* "to unburden", from *ex-* + *oner-, onus* "load"] — **ex·on·er·a·tion** \ig-,zän-ə-'rā-shən\ *n* — **ex·on·er·a·tive** \ig-'zän-ə-,rāt-iv\ *adj*

ex·or·bi·tant \ig-'zȯr-bət-ənt\ *adj* : going beyond the limits of what is fair, reasonable, or expected ⟨*exorbitant* prices⟩ [Middle French, from Late Latin *exorbitare* "to deviate", from Latin *ex-* + *orbita* "track, rut"] SYN see EXCESSIVE — **ex·or·bi·tance** \-bət-əns\ *n* — **ex·or·bi·tant·ly** *adv*

ex·or·cise \'ek-,sȯr-,sīz, -sər-\ *vt* **1 a** : to drive (an evil spirit) off or out by religious exercises or spells **b** : to get rid of (something that troubles or menaces) **2** : to free (a person or place) from an evil spirit [Middle French *exorciser,* from Late Latin *exorcizare,* from Greek *exorkizein,* from *ex-* + *horkizein* "to bind by oath", from *horkos* "oath"] — **ex·or·cis·er** *n*

ex·or·cism \-,siz-əm\ *n* **1** : the act or practice of exorcising **2** : a spell or formula used in exorcising — **ex·or·cist** \-,sist, -səst\ *n*

exo·skel·e·ton \,ek-sō-'skel-ət-n\ *n* : a hard supporting or protective structure (as of a crustacean) developed on the outside of the body — compare ENDOSKELETON — **exo·skel·e·tal** \-ət-l\ *adj*

\ə\ abut	\ng\ sing
\ər\ further	\ō\ bone
\a\ mat	\ȯ\ saw
\ā\ take	\ȯi\ coin
\ä\ cot, cart	\th\ thin
\au̇\ out	\th\ this
\ch\ chin	\ü\ food
\e\ pet	\u̇\ foot
\ē\ easy	\y\ yet
\g\ go	\yü\ few
\i\ tip	\yu̇\ cure
\ī\ life	\zh\ vision
\j\ job	

exo·sphere \'ek-sō-,sfiər\ *n* : the outermost region of the atmosphere of the earth or a planet

exo·ther·mic \,ek-sō-'thər-mik\ *or* **exo·ther·mal** \-məl\ *adj* : characterized by or formed by the giving off of heat ⟨an *exothermic* chemical reaction⟩

¹ex·ot·ic \ig-'zät-ik\ *adj* **1** : introduced from another country ⟨*exotic* plants⟩ **2** : strikingly or excitingly different or unusual (as in color or design) [Latin *exoticus,* from Greek *exōtikos,* from *exō* "outside", from *ex* "out of"] — **ex·ot·i·cal·ly** \-'zät-i-kə-lē, -klē\ *adv* — **ex·ot·ic·ness** \-ik-nəs\ *n*

²exotic *n* : something (as a plant) that is exotic

exo·tox·in \,ek-sō-'täk-sən\ *n* : a soluble poisonous substance given off by a microorganism

ex·pand \ik-'spand\ *vb* **1** : to open wide : UNFOLD ⟨a bird with wings *expanded*⟩ **2** : to take up or cause to take up more space ⟨metals *expand* under heat⟩ **3** : to develop more fully : work out in greater detail ⟨*expand* an argument⟩ **4** : to state in enlarged form or in the form of a series : write out in full ⟨*expand* an equation⟩ **5** : to increase in quantity or scope ⟨*expand* a business⟩ [Latin *expandere,* from *ex-* + *pandere* "to spread"] — **ex·pand·able** \-'span-də-bəl\ *adj* — **ex·pand·er** *n* □ SYN EXPAND, DILATE, DISTEND, INFLATE mean to increase in size or volume. EXPAND applies to any enlarging that comes from within or outside or in any way, as in growth, unfolding, or addition of parts; DILATE suggests expansion of diameter or circumference ⟨the pupil of the eye *dilates* in dim light⟩ DISTEND implies swelling or stretching caused by pressure from within forcing extension outward ⟨*distended* nostrils⟩ INFLATE implies distension by the introduction of air or something insubstantial and suggests a liability to sudden collapse ⟨an *inflated* balloon⟩ ⟨*inflated* currency⟩

ex·panse \ik-'spans\ *n* : a wide space, area, or stretch ⟨the vast *expanse* of the ocean⟩ [Latin *expansus,* past participle of *expandere* "to expand"]

ex·pan·si·ble \ik-'span-sə-bəl\ *adj* : capable of being expanded

ex·pan·sion \ik-'span-chən\ *n* **1** : the act or process of expanding **2** : the quality or state of being expanded **3 a** : an expanded part **b** : something that results from an act of expanding **4** : the result of an indicated operation : the result of expanding a mathematical expression or function (as into a sequence of terms)

ex·pan·sive \ik-'span-siv\ *adj* **1** : having a capacity or a tendency to expand ⟨gases are *expansive*⟩ **2** : causing or tending to cause expansion ⟨an *expansive* force⟩ **3** : characterized by high spirits or benevolent inclinations ⟨in an *expansive* mood⟩ **4** : having considerable extent : BROAD ⟨too *expansive* a subject for brief treatment⟩ — **ex·pan·sive·ly** *adv* — **ex·pan·sive·ness** *n*

ex par·te \ek-'spärt-ē, 'ek-\ *adj or adv* : from a one-sided or partisan point of view [Medieval Latin, "on behalf"]

ex·pa·ti·ate \ek-'spā-shē-,āt\ *vi* : to speak or write at length or in detail [Latin *exspatiari* "to wander, digress", from *ex-* + *spatium* "space, course"] — **ex·pa·ti·a·tion** \ek-,spā-shē-'ā-shən\ *n*

¹ex·pa·tri·ate \ek-'spā-trē-,āt\ *vb* **1** : to drive into exile : BANISH **2** : to leave one's native country; *esp* : to renounce allegiance to one's native country [Medieval Latin *expatriare* "to leave one's country", from Latin *ex-* + *patria* "native country", derived from *pater* "father"] — **ex·pa·tri·a·tion** \ek-,spā-trē-'ā-shən\ *n*

²ex·pa·tri·ate \ek-'spā-trē-,āt, -trē-ət\ *adj* : living in a foreign country : EXPATRIATED — **expatriate** *n*

ex·pect \ik-'spekt\ *vb* **1** : to anticipate or look forward to the coming or occurrence of ⟨*expect* rain⟩ ⟨*expect* a phone call⟩ **2** : to be pregnant **3** : SUPPOSE 2, THINK **4 a** : to consider probable or certain ⟨*expect* to be forgiven⟩ **b** : to consider reasonable, due, or necessary ⟨*expect* an honest day's work⟩ **c** : to consider obligated or in duty bound ⟨*expect* you to pay your dues⟩ [Latin *ex-*

spectare "to look forward to", from *ex-* + *spectare* "to look at", from *specere* "to look"] — **ex·pect·able** \-'spek-tə-bəl\ *adj* — **ex·pect·ably** \-blē\ *adv*

ex·pect·ance \ik-'spek-təns\ *n* : EXPECTATION

ex·pect·an·cy \ik-'spek-tən-sē\ *n, pl* **-cies** **1** : EXPECTATION 1 **2 a** : EXPECTATION 3 **b** : the expected amount (as of years of life) based on statistical probability

ex·pect·ant \-tənt\ *adj* **1** : characterized by or being in a state of expectation **2** : expecting the birth of a child ⟨*expectant* parents⟩; *esp* : PREGNANT — **expectant** *n* — **ex·pect·ant·ly** *adv*

ex·pec·ta·tion \,ek-,spek-'tā-shən, ik-\ *n* **1** : the act or state of expecting : a looking forward to or waiting for something **2** : prospect of good or bad fortune; *esp* : prospects of inheriting — usually used in pl. **3** : something expected

ex·pec·to·rant \ik-'spek-tə-rənt\ *adj* : tending to promote discharge of mucus from the respiratory tract — **expectorant** *n*

ex·pec·to·rate \ik-'spek-tə-,rāt\ *vb* **1** : to discharge (as phlegm) from the throat or lungs by coughing and spitting **2** : SPIT 1a [Latin *expectorare* "to cast out of the mind", from *ex-* + *pector, pectus* "breast, soul"] — **ex·pec·to·ra·tion** \-,spek-tə-'rā-shən\ *n*

ex·pe·di·ence \ik-'spēd-ē-əns\ *n* : EXPEDIENCY

ex·pe·di·en·cy \ik-'spēd-ē-ən-sē\ *n, pl* **-cies** **1** : the quality or state of being suited to the end in view : SUITABILITY **2** : the use of means and methods advantageous to oneself without regard to principles of fairness and rightness

¹ex·pe·di·ent \ik-'spēd-ē-ənt\ *adj* **1** : appropriate to and efficient in attaining an end **2** : seeking or concerned with immediate advantage rather than with what is just or right [Latin *expediens,* present participle of *expedire* "to extricate, be advantageous", from *ex-* + *ped-, pes* "foot"] — **ex·pe·di·ent·ly** *adv* □ SYN POLITIC, ADVISABLE: EXPEDIENT usually applies to what is immediately advantageous often without regard for ethics; POLITIC may apply to what is judicious and of tactical value and sometimes suggests an artful ulterior motive ⟨thought it *politic* to keep out of that argument⟩ ADVISABLE applies to what is practical, prudent, or advantageous without derogatory implication ⟨*advisable* to drive carefully⟩

²expedient *n* **1** : something expedient **2** : a means to accomplish an end; *esp* : one used in place of a better means that is not available

ex·pe·dite \'ek-spə-,dīt\ *vt* **1** : to carry out rapidly : execute promptly **2** : to accelerate the process or progress of **3** : to send out : DISPATCH [Latin *expedire* "to extricate, arrange, be advantageous"]

ex·pe·dit·er *also* **ex·pe·di·tor** \-,dīt-ər\ *n* : one that expedites; *esp* : one employed to ensure adequate supplies of raw materials and equipment or to coordinate the flow of materials, tools, parts, and processed goods within a plant

ex·pe·di·tion \,ek-spə-'dish-ən\ *n* **1 a** : a journey or trip undertaken for a specific purpose (as war or exploring) **b** : a group making such a journey **2** : efficient promptness : SPEED

ex·pe·di·tion·ary \-'dish-ə-,ner-ē\ *adj* : of, relating to, or constituting an expedition; *esp* : sent on military service abroad ⟨an *expeditionary* force⟩

ex·pe·di·tious \,ek-spə-'dish-əs\ *adj* : characterized by or acting with promptness and efficiency : SPEEDY — **ex·pe·di·tious·ly** *adv* — **ex·pe·di·tious·ness** *n*

ex·pel \ik-'spel\ *vt* **ex·pelled; ex·pel·ling** **1** : to drive or force out ⟨*expel* air from the lungs⟩ **2** : to drive away; *esp* : DEPORT **3** : to cut off from membership ⟨*expelled* from college⟩ [Latin *expellere,* from *ex-* + *pellere* "to drive"] SYN see EJECT — **ex·pel·la·ble** \-'spel-ə-bəl\ *adj*

ex·pend \ik-'spend\ *vt* **1** : to pay out : SPEND **2** : to consume by use : use up ⟨*expend* hours on the study⟩ [Latin *expendere* "to weigh out, expend", from *ex-* + *pendere* "to weigh, pay"]

ex·pend·able \ik-'spen-də-bəl\ *adj* : that may be used up in an ordinary way or sacrificed to accomplish a mission ⟨*expendable* ammunition⟩ — **ex·pend·abil·i·ty** \-,pen-də-'bil-ət-ē\ *n* — **expendable** *n* — **ex·pend·ably** \-'pen-də-blē\ *adv*

ex·pen·di·ture \ik-'spen-di-chər, -də-,chùr\ *n* : the act or process of expending 2 : an amount (as of money or time) expended

ex·pense \ik-'spens\ *n* 1 a : something expended to secure a benefit or bring about a result b : financial burden or outlay : COST 2 : a cause of expenditure ⟨a car is a great *expense*⟩ 3 : SACRIFICE 3 — usually used in the phrase *at the expense of* [Late Latin *expensa*, from Latin *expendere* "to expend"]

expense account *n* : an account of expenses reimbursable to an employee

ex·pen·sive \ik-'spen-siv\ *adj* 1 : involving expense ⟨an *expensive* journey⟩ 2 : high-priced : DEAR SYN see COSTLY — **ex·pen·sive·ly** *adv* — **ex·pen·sive·ness** *n*

¹**ex·pe·ri·ence** \ik-'spir-ē-əns\ *n* 1 a : the usually conscious perception or understanding of reality or of an event b : the sum total of the conscious events that make up an individual life or the past of a community, nation, or humankind generally 2 a : the actual living through an event or series of events ⟨learn by *experience*⟩ b : something that one has actually done or lived through ⟨a soldier's *experiences* in war⟩ 3 a : the skill or knowledge gained by actually doing or feeling a thing ⟨a job that requires *experience*⟩ b : the amount or kind of work one has done or the time during which work has been done ⟨a person with five years' *experience*⟩ [Middle French, from Latin *experientia* "act of trying", from *experiri* "to try"] — **ex·pe·ri·en·tial** \-,spir-ē-'en-chəl\ *adj*

²**experience** *vt* 1 : to have experience of : UNDERGO 2 : to learn by experience

ex·pe·ri·enced \ik-'spir-ē-ənst\ *adj* : having experience : made skillful or wise through experience ⟨an *experienced* pilot⟩

¹**ex·per·i·ment** \ik-'sper-ə-mənt\ *n* 1 a : TEST 1a, TRIAL b : a tentative procedure or policy c : an operation carried out under controlled conditions in order to discover an unknown effect or law, to test or establish a hypothesis, or to illustrate a known law 2 : the process of testing : EXPERIMENTATION [Middle French, from Latin *experimentum*, from *experiri* "to try"]

²**ex·per·i·ment** \-,ment\ *vi* : to make experiments — **ex·per·i·men·ta·tion** \ik-,sper-ə-mən-'tā-shən, -,men-\ *n* — **ex·per·i·ment·er** \-'sper-ə-,ment-ər\ *n*

¹**ex·per·i·men·tal** \ik-,sper-ə-'ment-l\ *adj* 1 : of, relating to, or based on experience 2 : founded on or derived from experiment ⟨an *experimental* finding⟩ 3 : serving the ends of or used for experimentation ⟨*experimental* apparatus⟩ 4 : relating to or having the characteristics of experiment : TENTATIVE ⟨*experimental* flights⟩ — **ex·per·i·men·tal·ly** \-l-ē\ *adv*

²**experimental** *n* : a plant or animal actually subjected to an experimental condition as contrasted to one kept for a control

experiment station *n* : an establishment for scientific research (as in agriculture) especially of practical application and for the spread of information

¹**ex·pert** \'ek-,spərt, ik-'\ *adj* : having, involving, or displaying special skill or knowledge derived from training or experience [Latin *expertus*, from *experiri* "to try"] SYN see PROFICIENT — **ex·pert·ly** *adv* — **ex·pert·ness** *n*

²**ex·pert** \'ek-,spərt\ *n* : one who has acquired special skill in or knowledge of a subject

ex·per·tise \,ek-spər-'tēz, -,spər-, *also* -'tēs\ *n* 1 : expert opinion or commentary 2 : skill in a particular field : KNOW-HOW [French, from *expert* "expert"]

expert system *n* : computer software that attempts to mimic the reasoning of a human specialist

ex·pi·ate \'ek-spē-,āt\ *vt* 1 : to atone for : pay the penalty for 2 : to make amends for [Latin *expiare* "to atone for", from *ex-* + *piare* "to appease"] — **ex·pi·a·ble** \-spē-ə-bəl\ *adj* — **ex·pi·a·tor** \-,āt-ər\ *n*

ex·pi·a·tion \,ek-spē-'ā-shən\ *n* 1 : the act of making atonement 2 : the means by which atonement is made

ex·pi·a·to·ry \'ek-spē-ə-,tōr-ē, -,tòr-\ *adj* : serving to expiate

ex·pi·ra·tion \,ek-spə-'rā-shən\ *n* 1 a : the expelling of air from the lungs in breathing b : air or vapor expelled from the lungs 2 : the fact of coming to an end : TERMINATION

ex·pi·ra·to·ry \ek-'spī-rə-,tōr-ē, -,tòr-\ *adj* : of, relating to, or used in respiratory expiration

ex·pire \ik-'spīr, *oftenest for 3* ek-\ *vb* 1 : DIE 1 2 : to come to an end : STOP 3 a : to emit the breath b : to breathe out from or as if from the lungs [Latin *exspirare*, from *ex-* + *spirare* "to breathe"]

ex·pi·ry \ik-'spīr-ē, 'ek-spə-rē\ *n, pl* **-ries** 1 : DEATH 1 2 : TERMINATION; *esp* : the termination of a time or period fixed by law, contract, or agreement

ex·plain \ik-'splān\ *vb* 1 : to make plain or understandable 2 : to give the reason for or cause of 3 : to show the logical development or relationships of [Latin *explanare*, literally, "to make level", from *ex-* + *planus* "level"] — **ex·plain·able** \-'splā-nə-bəl\ *adj* — **ex·plain·er** *n* □ SYN EXPOUND, EXPLICATE, INTERPRET: EXPLAIN implies making plain or intelligible; EXPOUND implies a careful, often elaborate explanation ⟨*expounding* one's philosophy of life⟩ EXPLICATE adds the idea of a developed or detailed analysis ⟨*explicate* the plot of a novel⟩ INTERPRET adds the use of the imagination, sympathy, or special knowledge to clarify something of more than obvious difficulty ⟨*interpret* a poem⟩ ⟨*interpret* the law⟩

ex·pla·na·tion \,ek-splə-'nā-shən\ *n* 1 : the act or process of explaining 2 : something that explains; *esp* : a statement that makes something clear

ex·plan·a·to·ry \ik-'splan-ə-,tōr-ē, -,tòr-\ *adj* : serving to explain ⟨*explanatory* notes⟩ — **ex·plan·a·to·ri·ly** \-,splan-ə-'tōr-ə-lē, -'tòr-\ *adv*

ex·plant \ek-'splant, 'ek-\ *vt* : to remove (living tissue) especially to a tissue culture medium

ex·ple·tive \'ek-splət-iv\ *n* 1 : a syllable, word, or phrase inserted to fill a vacancy (as in a sentence or a line of verse) without adding to the sense; *esp* : a word that occupies the position of the subject or object of a verb in normal English word order and anticipates a subsequent word or phrase that supplies the needed meaningful content ⟨*it* in "it is easy to say so" and in "make it clear which you prefer" is an *expletive*⟩ 2 : an exclamatory word or phrase; *esp* : one that is obscene or profane [Late Latin *expletivus* "serving to fill up", from Latin *explēre* "to fill out", from *ex-* + *plēre* "to fill"] — **expletive** *adj*

ex·pli·cate \'ek-splə-,kāt\ *vt* : to give a detailed explanation of [Latin *explicare*, literally, "to unfold", from *ex-* + *plicare* "to fold"] SYN see EXPLAIN — **ex·pli·ca·ble** \ek-'splik-ə-bəl, 'ek-splik-\ *adj* — **ex·pli·ca·tion** \,ek-splə-'kā-shən\ *n* — **ex·pli·ca·tive** \ek-'splik-ət-iv, 'ek-splə-,kāt-\ *adj* — **ex·pli·ca·tor** \'ek-splə-,kāt-ər\ *n* — **ex·pli·ca·to·ry** \ek-'splik-ə-,tōr-ē, 'ek-splik-, -,tòr-\ *adj*

ex·plic·it \ik-'splis-ət\ *adj* : so clear in statement that there is no doubt about the meaning : fully stated ⟨*explicit* instructions⟩ — compare IMPLICIT [Medieval Latin *explicitus*, from *explicare* "to explicate"] — **ex·plic·it·ly** *adv* — **ex·plic·it·ness** *n* □ SYN EXPLICIT, DEFINITE, EXPRESS, SPECIFIC mean perfectly clear in meaning. EXPLICIT implies such verbal plainness and distinctness that there is no room for doubt or difficulty in understanding; DEFINITE stresses precise, clear statement or arrangement that leaves no doubt or inde-

\ə\ abut   \ng\ sing
\ər\ further   \ō\ bone
\a\ mat   \ò\ saw
\ā\ take   \òi\ coin
\ä\ cot, cart   \th\ thin
\aú\ out   \th\ this
\ch\ chin   \ü\ food
\e\ pet   \ù\ foot
\ē\ easy   \y\ yet
\g\ go   \yü\ few
\i\ tip   \yù\ cure
\ī\ life   \zh\ vision
\j\ job

cision; EXPRESS implies explicitness and utterance with directness and positiveness ⟨*express* denial of the charges⟩ SPECIFIC applies to what is precisely and fully treated in detail or particular.

ex·plode \ik-'splōd\ *vb* **1** : to cause to be given up or rejected : DISCREDIT ⟨science has *exploded* many old ideas⟩ **2 a** : to burst or cause to burst violently and noisily **b** : to burn suddenly so that there is a violent expansion of hot gases with great disruptive force and a loud noise; *also* : to undergo an atomic nuclear reaction with similar but more violent effects **3** : to burst forth (as with anger or laughter) [Latin *explodere* "to drive off the stage by clapping", from *ex-* + *plaudere* "to clap"] □ ORIGIN A modern audience often expresses its disapproval of a performance by hissing, but in ancient Rome audiences showed their low opinion of an actor, and might even drive him from the stage, by loud clapping. Latin *explodere,* a compound of *ex,* "out of, from", and *plaudere,* "to clap", means "to drive off by clapping". The Latin verb was borrowed into English with the meaning "to drive from the stage by noisy disapproval". From this sense developed the now current senses "to reject or discredit" and "to burst noisily". *Explode* is no longer used in its original sense.

ex·plod·ed *adj* : showing the parts separated but in correct relationship to each other ⟨an *exploded* view of a carburetor⟩

¹ex·ploit \'ek-₁splȯit, ik-'\ *n* : a deed notable especially for heroism [Old French, "outcome, success", derived from Latin *explicare* "to explicate, unfold"] SYN see FEAT

²ex·ploit \ik-'splȯit, 'ek-₁\ *vt* **1** : to extract value or use from : UTILIZE ⟨*exploit* a mine⟩ **2** : to make use of unfairly for one's own advantage — **ex·ploit·able** \-ə-bəl\ *adj* — **ex·ploi·ta·tion** \₁ek-₁splȯi-'tā-shən\ *n* — **ex·ploit·er** \ik-'splȯit-ər, 'ek-₁\ *n*

ex·plo·ra·tion \₁ek-splə-'rā-shən\ *n* : the act or an instance of exploring — **ex·plor·a·tive** \ik-'splōr-ət-iv, -'splȯr-\ *adj* — **ex·plor·a·to·ry** \-ə-₁tōr-ē, -₁tȯr-\ *adj*

ex·plore \ik-'splōr, -'splȯr\ *vb* **1 a** : to search through or into **b** : to examine carefully and in detail especially for diagnostic purposes ⟨*explore* a wound⟩ **c** : to penetrate into or range over for purposes of discovery ⟨*explore* an uncharted sea⟩ **2** : to make or conduct a systematic search ⟨*explore* for oil⟩ [Latin *explorare* "to seek for", from *ex-* + *plorare* "to cry out"; probably from the outcry of hunters on sighting game]

ex·plor·er \ik-'splōr-ər, -'splȯr-\ *n* **1** : one that explores; *esp* : a person who travels in search of geographical or scientific information **2** *cap* : a member of the scouting program of the Boy Scouts of America for young people 14 to 20 years of age

ex·plo·sion \ik-'splō-zhən\ *n* **1** : the act or an instance of exploding **2** : a large-scale, rapid, and spectacular expansion, outbreak, or upheaval **3** : a violent outburst of feeling [Latin *explosio* "act of driving off by clapping", from *explodere* "to drive off by clapping"]

¹ex·plo·sive \ik-'splō-siv, -ziv\ *adj* **1** : relating to, characterized by, or operated by explosion **2** : likely to explode — **ex·plo·sive·ly** *adv* — **ex·plo·sive·ness** *n*

²explosive *n* : an explosive substance

ex·po·nent \ik-'spō-nənt, 'ek-₁\ *n* **1** : a symbol written above and to the right of a mathematical expression to indicate the operation of raising to a power (in the expression a^3, the *exponent* 3 indicates that *a* is to be taken as a factor three times) **2 a** : one that expounds or interprets **b** : one that champions or advocates [Latin *exponere* "to set forth, explain", from *ex-* + *ponere* "to put"]

ex·po·nen·tial \₁ek-spə-'nen-chəl\ *adj* **1 a** : of or relating to an exponent **b** : expressed in a form using exponents **2** : involving a variable exponent ⟨a function of the form $y=10^x$ is an *exponential* function⟩ — **ex·po·nen·tial·ly** \-'nench-lē, -ə-lē\ *adv*

¹ex·port \ek-'spōrt, -'spȯrt, 'ek-₁\ *vt* : to carry or send (as a commodity) to another country or place especially for sale [Latin *exportare,* from *ex-* + *portare* "to carry"] — **ex·port·able** \-ə-bəl\ *adj* — **ex·por·ta·tion** \₁ek-₁spȯr-'tā-shən, -₁spȯr-, -spər-\ *n* — **ex·port·er** \ek-'spȯrt-ər, -'spȯrt-, 'ek-₁\ *n*

²ex·port \'ek-₁spȯrt, -₁spȯrt\ *n* **1** : something exported; *esp* : a commodity conveyed from one country or region to another for purposes of trade **2** : an act of exporting : EXPORTATION

³export \'ek-₁\ *adj* **1** : of or relating to exportation or exports ⟨*export* duties⟩ **2** : intended for export ⟨*export* goods⟩

ex·pose \ik-'spōz\ *vt* **1 a** : to deprive of shelter, protection, or care ⟨*expose* troops needlessly⟩ **b** : to submit or subject to an action or influence; *esp* : to subject (a sensitive photographic film, plate, or paper) to the action of radiant energy (as light) **c** : to abandon (an infant) especially in the open **2** : to lay open to view : DISPLAY **3** : to bring to light : UNMASK ⟨*expose* a murderer⟩ [Middle French *exposer,* from Latin *exponere* "to set forth, explain", from *ex-* + *ponere* "to put, place"] — **ex·pos·er** *n*

ex·po·sé \₁ek-spō-'zā\ *n* : an exposure of something discreditable ⟨a newspaper *exposé* of illegal gambling⟩ [French, from *exposer* "to expose"]

ex·po·si·tion \₁ek-spə-'zish-ən\ *n* **1** : an explaining of the meaning or purpose of something (as a piece of writing) **2** : a composition that explains something **3** : a public exhibition or show **4** : the first part of a musical composition in sonata form in which the thematic material of the movement is presented — **ex·pos·i·to·ry** \ik-'späz-ə-₁tōr-ē, -₁tȯr-\ *adj*

ex·pos·i·tor \ik-'späz-ət-ər\ *n* : one that expounds or explains [Middle French *expositeur,* from Late Latin *expositor,* from Latin *exponere* "to set forth, explain"]

ex post fac·to \₁eks-₁pōst-'fak-tō\ *adj* : affecting something (as status or an action) having prior existence [Late Latin, "from a thing done afterward"]

ex·pos·tu·late \ik-'späs-chə-₁lāt\ *vi* : to reason earnestly with a person for purposes of dissuasion or protest [Latin *expostulare* "to demand, dispute", from *ex-* + *postulare* "to ask for"] — **ex·pos·tu·la·tion** \-₁späs-chə-'lā-shən\ *n* — **ex·pos·tu·la·to·ry** \-'späs-chə-lə-₁tōr-ē, -₁tȯr-\ *adj*

ex·po·sure \ik-'spō-zhər\ *n* **1** : the act or an instance of exposing: as **a** : disclosure to view **b** : disclosure of something usually shameful or criminal **c** : an act of abandoning especially in the open **d** (1) : a section of a film for a single picture (2) : the time during which a sensitive photographic film is exposed **2 a** : a condition or an instance of being exposed; *esp* : the condition of being exposed to the elements **b** : a position with respect to direction or to weather conditions ⟨a southern *exposure*⟩

ex·pound \ik-'spau̇nd\ *vt* **1 a** : to set forth : STATE **b** : to defend (as a theory) with argument **2** : to make clear the meaning of : INTERPRET [Middle French *expondre,* from Latin *exponere* "to explain"] SYN see EXPLAIN — **ex·pound·er** *n*

¹ex·press \ik-'spres\ *adj* **1 a** : directly and distinctly stated : EXPLICIT **b** : exactly represented : PRECISE **2** : of a particular sort : SPECIAL **3 a** : traveling at high speed; *esp* : traveling with few or no stops ⟨an *express* train⟩ **b** : adapted or suitable for travel at high speed ⟨an *express* route⟩ [Middle French *expres,* from Latin *expressus,* past participle of *exprimere* "to press out", from *ex-* + *premere* "to press"] SYN see EXPLICIT

²express *adv* : by express ⟨send a package *express*⟩

³express *n* **1 a** : a system for the prompt transportation of goods at an extra charge **b** : a company operating such a service **c** : the goods or shipments so transported **2** : an express vehicle

⁴express *vt* **1 a :** to represent especially in words or symbols **b :** to give expression to the opinions, feelings, or abilities of (oneself) **c : SYMBOLIZE** ⟨the sign = *expresses* equality⟩ **2 :** to press or squeeze out ⟨*express* juice from a lemon⟩ **3 :** to send by express — **ex·press·er** *n* — **ex·press·ible** \-ə-bəl\ *adj*

ex·pres·sion \ik-'spresh-ən\ *n* **1 :** the act or process of expressing especially in words or symbols **2 a :** a word, phrase, or sign that expresses a thought, feeling, or quality; *esp :* a significant word or phrase **b :** a mathematical symbol or a combination of symbols and signs representing a quantity or operation **3 :** a way of speaking or of singing or playing an instrument so as to show mood or feeling **4 : LOOK 2a, APPEARANCE** ⟨a pleased *expression*⟩ **5 :** the detectable effect of a gene **6 :** an act or product of pressing out — **ex·pres·sion·less** \-ləs\ *adj*

ex·pres·sion·ism \ik-'spresh-ə-ˌniz-əm\ *n* **:** a theory or practice in art of trying to depict the artist's personal responses to objects and events — **ex·pres·sion·ist** \-'spresh-nəst, -ə-nəst\ *n or adj* — **ex·pres·sion·is·tic** \-ˌspresh-ə-'nis-tik\ *adj*

ex·pres·sive \ik-'spres-iv\ *adj* **1 :** of or relating to expression **2 :** serving to express **3 :** full of expression : **SIGNIFICANT** — **ex·pres·sive·ly** *adv* — **ex·pres·sive·ness** *n*

ex·press·ly \ik-'spres-lē\ *adv* **1 :** in an express manner : **EXPLICITLY 2 :** for the express purpose : **PARTICULARLY**

ex·press·way \ik-'spres-ˌwā\ *n* **:** a high-speed divided highway with controlled access

ex·pro·pri·ate \ek-'sprō-prē-ˌāt\ *vt* **:** to take away from a person the possession of or right to (property) [Medieval Latin *expropriare,* from Latin *ex-* + *proprius* "own"] — **ex·pro·pri·a·tion** \-ˌek-ˌsprō-prē-'ā-shən\ *n* — **ex·pro·pri·a·tor** \ek-'sprō-prē-ˌāt-ər\ *n*

ex·pul·sion \ik-'spəl-shən\ *n* **:** the act of expelling : the state of being expelled [Latin *expulsio,* from *expellere* "to expel"] — **ex·pul·sive** \-'spəl-siv\ *adj*

ex·punge \ik-'spənj\ *vt* **1 :** to strike out, obliterate, or mark for deletion **2 :** to efface completely [Latin *expungere* "to mark for deletion by dots", from *ex-* + *pungere* "to prick"] **SYN see ERASE** — **ex·pung·er** *n*

ex·pur·gate \'ek-spər-ˌgāt\ *vt* **:** to clear of something wrong or objectionable; *esp :* to clear (as a book) of objectionable words or passages [Latin *expurgare,* from *ex-* + *purgare* "to purge"] — **ex·pur·ga·tion** \ˌek-spər-'gā-shən\ *n* — **ex·pur·ga·tor** \'ek-spər-ˌgāt-ər\ *n*

ex·quis·ite \ek-'skwiz-ət; 'ek-skwiz-, -ˌskwiz-\ *adj* **1 :** marked by flawless craftsmanship or delicate execution **2 :** keenly appreciative : **DISCRIMINATING 3 :** pleasing through beauty or excellence **4 : ACUTE 3, INTENSE** [Latin *exquisitus,* from *exquirere* "to search out", from *ex-* + *quaerere* "to seek"] — **ex·quis·ite·ly** *adv* — **ex·quis·ite·ness** *n*

ex·tant \'ek-stənt, ek-'stant\ *adj* **:** currently existing : not destroyed or lost [Latin *exstare* "to stand out, be in existence", from *ex-* + *stare* "to stand"]

ex·tem·po·ra·ne·ous \ek-ˌstem-pə-'rā-nē-əs\ *adj* **1 :** composed, performed, or uttered on the spur of the moment : **IMPROMPTU 2 :** carefully prepared but delivered without notes or text **3 :** provided, made, or put to use as an expedient : **MAKESHIFT** [Late Latin *extemporaneus,* from Latin *ex tempore* "on the spur of the moment"] — **ex·tem·po·ra·ne·ous·ly** *adv* — **ex·tem·po·ra·ne·ous·ness** *n*

ex·tem·po·rary \ik-'stem-pə-ˌrer-ē\ *adj* **: EXTEMPORANEOUS** — **ex·tem·po·rar·i·ly** \-ˌstem-pə-'rer-ə-lē\ *adv*

ex·tem·po·re \ik-'stem-pə-rē\ *adv* **: EXTEMPORANEOUSLY**

ex·tem·po·rize \ik-'stem-pə-ˌrīz\ *vb* **:** to do, make, or utter extemporaneously : **IMPROVISE** — **ex·tem·po·ri·za·tion** \ik-ˌstem-pə-rə-'zā-shən\ *n* — **ex·tem·po·riz·er** \-'stem-pə-ˌrī-zər\ *n*

ex·tend \ik-'stend\ *vb* **1 :** to spread out or stretch forth ⟨*extend* one's arm⟩ **2 :** to exert (oneself) to full capacity ⟨*extended* themselves to meet the deadline⟩ **3 :** to increase the bulk of (a product) by the addition of a cheaper substance **4 a :** to make the offer of : **PROFFER b :** to make available **5 :** to cause to be longer; *esp :* to prolong in time **6 a :** to cause to be of greater area or volume : **ENLARGE b :** to increase the scope, meaning, or application of : **BROADEN 7 :** to stretch out in distance, space, or time : **REACH** ⟨the bridge *extends* across the river⟩ **8 :** to span an interval of distance, space, or time [Latin *extendere,* from *ex-* + *tendere* "to stretch"] — **ex·ten·si·ble** \-'sten-sə-bəl\ *or* **ex·tend·ible** \-'sten-də-bəl\ *adj* □ **SYN EXTEND, LENGTHEN, PROLONG, PROTRACT** mean to draw out or add to so as to increase in length. **EXTEND** and **LENGTHEN** imply a drawing out in space or time; **EXTEND** may also imply increase in width, scope, area, or range ⟨*extend* a vacation⟩ ⟨*extend* welfare services⟩ ⟨*lengthen* a skirt⟩ ⟨*lengthen* the workweek⟩ **PROLONG** suggests chiefly increase in duration especially beyond usual limits ⟨*prolonged* illness⟩ **PROTRACT** adds to **PROLONG** implications of needlessness, vexation, or indefiniteness ⟨*protracted* litigation⟩

ex·tend·er \ik-'sten-dər\ *n* **:** something added to another thing usually to dilute or modify

ex·ten·sion \ik-'sten-chən\ *n* **1 a :** the act of extending : the state of being extended **b :** something extended **2 :** the total range over which something extends : **COMPASS 3 :** the property of occupying space **4 :** an increase in time; *esp :* a granting of extra time to fulfill an obligation **5 :** an educational program with special arrangements for persons unable to attend a school **6 a :** a part constituting an addition **b :** a section forming an additional length **c :** an extra telephone connected to the principal line [Late Latin *extensio,* from Latin *extendere* "to extend"]

extension cord *n* **:** an electric cord fitted with a plug at one end and a receptacle at the other

ex·ten·sive \ik-'sten-siv\ *adj* **:** having wide or considerable extent — **ex·ten·sive·ly** *adv* — **ex·ten·sive·ness** *n*

ex·ten·sor \ik-'sten-sər\ *n* **:** a muscle serving to extend a bodily part (as a limb) — compare **FLEXOR**

ex·tent \ik-'stent\ *n* **1 a :** the range, distance, or space over which something extends : **SCOPE b :** the point, degree, or limit to which something extends ⟨using talents to the greatest *extent*⟩ **2 :** an extended tract or region [Middle French *extente* "area", from *extendre* "to extend", from Latin *extendere*]

ex·ten·u·ate \ik-'sten-yə-ˌwāt\ *vt* **:** to lessen or try to lessen the seriousness or extent of by making partial excuses ⟨pleading the youth of the offender to *extenuate* the offense⟩ [Latin *extenuare,* from *ex-* + *tenuis* "thin"] — **ex·ten·u·a·tion** \-ˌsten-yə-'wā-shən\ *n* — **ex·ten·u·a·tor** \-'sten-yə-ˌwāt-ər\ *n* — **ex·ten·u·a·to·ry** \-wə-ˌtōr-ē, -ˌtȯr-\ *adj*

¹ex·te·ri·or \ek-'stir-ē-ər\ *adj* **1 : EXTERNAL 2, OUTER 2 a :** happening or coming from outside **b :** suitable for use on outside surfaces ⟨*exterior* paint⟩ [Latin, comparative of *exter, exterus* "being on the outside", from *ex* "out of"] — **ex·te·ri·or·ly** *adv*

²exterior *n* **1 a :** an exterior part or surface : **OUTSIDE b :** outward manner or appearance **2 :** a representation of an outdoor scene

exterior angle *n* **1 :** the angle between a side of a polygon and an extended adjacent side **2 :** an angle formed by a transversal cutting two lines and lying outside them

ex·ter·mi·nate \ik-'stər-mə-ˌnāt\ *vt* **:** to destroy utterly : **ANNIHILATE** [Latin *exterminare,* from *ex-* + *terminus* "boundary"] — **ex·ter·mi·na·tion** \-ˌstər-mə-'nā-shən\ *n* — **ex·ter·mi·na·tor** \-'stər-mə-ˌnāt-ər\ *n*

¹ex·ter·nal \ek-'stərn-l\ *adj* **1 a :** outwardly visible ⟨*external* signs⟩ **b :** having only the outward appearance

\ə\ abut		\ng\ sing	
\ər\ further		\ō\ bone	
\a\ mat		\ȯ\ saw	
\ā\ take		\ȯi\ coin	
\ä\ cot, cart		\th\ thin	
\au̇\ out		\th\ this	
\ch\ chin		\ü\ food	
\e\ pet		\u̇\ foot	
\ē\ easy		\y\ yet	
\g\ go		\yü\ few	
\i\ tip		\yu̇\ cure	
\ī\ life		\zh\ vision	
\j\ job			

/ extrados

of : SUPERFICIAL **2 a** : of, relating to, or connected with the outside or an outer part **b** : applied or applicable to the outside **3 a** (1) : situated outside, apart, or beyond (2) : arising or acting from outside ⟨*external* force⟩ **b** : of or relating to relationships with foreign countries [Latin *externus,* from *exter* "being on the outside"] — **ex·ter·nal·ly** \-l-ē\ *adv*

²**external** *n* : an external feature or aspect — usually used in pl.

external-combustion engine *n* : a heat engine (as a steam engine) that derives its heat from fuel consumed outside the engine cylinder

external ear *n* : the outer part of the ear consisting of the sound-collecting pinna and the canal leading from this to the eardrum

external respiration *n* : exchange of gases between the external environment and a distributing system of the animal body (as gills or lungs) or between the alveoli of the lungs and the blood — compare INTERNAL RESPIRATION

ex·tinct \ik-'stingt, 'ek-„ -'stingkt\ *adj* **1** : no longer burning : EXTINGUISHED **2** : no longer active ⟨an *extinct* volcano⟩ **3** : no longer existing ⟨an *extinct* animal⟩ [Latin *extinctus,* past participle of *extinguere* "to extinguish"] — **ex·tinc·tion** \ik-'sting-shən, -'stingk-\ *n*

ex·tin·guish \ik-'sting-gwish\ *vt* **1 a** : to put out (as a fire or a light) **b** : EXTERMINATE, ANNIHILATE **c** : to dim the brightness of : ECLIPSE **2** : to cause to be void : NULLIFY ⟨*extinguish* a claim⟩ [Latin *extinguere* (from *ex-* + *stinguere* "to extinguish") + English *-ish* (as in *abolish*)] — **ex·tin·guish·able** \-ə-bəl\ *adj* — **ex·tin·guish·er** \-ər\ *n* — **ex·tin·guish·ment** \-mənt\ *n*

ex·tir·pate \'ek-stər-„pāt, ek-'\ *vt* **1** : to pull up by the roots **2 a** : to eradicate (as by surgery) **b** : to destroy wholly [Latin *exstirpare,* from *ex-* + *stirps* "trunk, root"]

ex·tol *also* **ex·toll** \ik-'stōl\ *vt* **ex·tolled; ex·tol·ling** : to praise highly : GLORIFY [Latin *extollere,* from *ex-* + *tollere* "to lift up"] — **ex·tol·ler** *n* — **ex·tol·ment** \-'stōl-mənt\ *n*

ex·tort \ik-'stórt\ *vt* : to obtain (as money or a confession) from a person by force or threats [Latin *extortus,* past participle of *extorquēre* "to wrench out, extort", from *ex-* + *torquēre* "to twist"] — **ex·tort·er** *n* — **ex·tor·tive** \-'stórt-iv\ *adj*

ex·tor·tion \ik-'stór-shən\ *n* **1** : the act or practice of extorting; *esp* : the offense committed by an official engaging in this practice **2** : something extorted; *esp* : a gross overcharge — **ex·tor·tion·er** \-'stór-shə-nər, -shnər\ *n* — **ex·tor·tion·ist** \-shə-nəst, -shnəst\ *n*

ex·tor·tion·ate \ik-'stór-shə-nət, -shnət\ *adj* **1** : characterized by extortion **2** : grossly excessive : EXORBITANT ⟨*extortionate* prices⟩ — **ex·tor·tion·ate·ly** *adv*

¹**ex·tra** \'ek-strə\ *adj* **1 a** : more than is due, usual, or necessary : ADDITIONAL ⟨*extra* work⟩ **b** : subject to an additional charge **2** : SUPERIOR ⟨*extra* quality⟩ [probably short for *extraordinary*]

²**extra** *n* : something extra or additional: as **a** : an added charge **b** : a special edition of a newspaper **c** : an additional worker; *esp* : one hired to act in a group scene in a motion picture or stage production

³**extra** *adv* : beyond the usual size, extent, or degree ⟨*extra* long⟩

extra- *prefix* : outside : beyond ⟨*extra*curricular⟩ [Latin, from *extra* "outside, except, beyond"]

extra-base hit *n* : a base hit in baseball that enables the batter to take more than one base

ex·tra·cel·lu·lar \„ek-strə-'sel-yə-lər\ *adj* : situated, acting, or occurring outside a cell or the cells of the body ⟨*extracellular* digestion⟩ — **ex·tra·cel·lu·lar·ly** *adv*

¹**ex·tract** \ik-'strakt, *oftenest in sense 5* 'ek-,\ *vt* **1 a** : to draw forth ⟨the magician *extracted* a rabbit from the hat⟩ **b** : to pull out forcibly ⟨*extract* a tooth⟩ **c** : to obtain by effort from or as if from someone unwilling ⟨*extract* a confession⟩ ⟨*extract* information from a

book⟩ **2** : to separate or otherwise obtain (as a juice or a constituent element) by physical or chemical process **3** : to separate (a metal) from an ore **4** : to determine (a mathematical root) by calculation **5** : to select (excerpts) and copy out or cite [Latin *extractus,* past participle of *extrahere* "to extract", from *ex-* + *trahere* "to draw"] — **ex·tract·able** \-ə-bəl\ *adj* — **ex·trac·tor** \-ər\ *n*

²**ex·tract** \'ek-,strakt\ *n* **1** : a selection from a writing or discourse : EXCERPT **2** : a product (as an essence or concentrate) prepared by extracting; *esp* : a solution of essential constituents of a complex material (as meat or an aromatic plant)

ex·trac·tion \ik-'strak-shən\ *n* **1** : the act or process of extracting ⟨a tooth *extraction*⟩ **2** : ANCESTRY 1, LINEAGE **3** : something extracted

¹**ex·trac·tive** \ik-'strak-tiv\ *adj* **1 a** : of, relating to, or involving extraction ⟨*extractive* processes⟩ **b** : capable of being extracted ⟨*extractive* by-products of coal tar⟩ **2** : drawing on natural and especially irreplaceable resources ⟨*extractive* industries such as mining and lumbering⟩

²**extractive** *n* : an extractive substance

ex·tra·cur·ric·u·lar \„ek-strə-kə-'rik-yə-lər\ *adj* **1** : not falling within a regular curriculum; *esp* : of, relating to, or being those activities (as athletics) connected with school but usually not carrying academic credit **2** : being outside one's regular duties or routine

ex·tra·dite \'ek-strə-„dīt\ *vt* **1** : to deliver up to extradition **2** : to obtain the extradition of [back-formation from *extradition*] — **ex·tra·dit·able** \-„dīt-ə-bəl\ *adj*

ex·tra·di·tion \„ek-strə-'dish-ən\ *n* : the surrender of an alleged criminal by one authority (as a state) to another for trial [French, from *ex-* "ex-" + Latin *traditio* "act of handing over"]

ex·tra·dos \'ek-strə-„däs, -„dō; ek-'strā-„däs\ *n, pl* **extrados** \-„dōz, -„däs\ *or* **ex·tra·dos·es** \-„däs-əz\ : the exterior curve of an arch [French, from Latin *extra* "outside" + French *dos* "back"]

ex·tra·em·bry·on·ic \„ek-strə-„em-brē-'än-ik\ *adj* : situated outside the embryo proper; *esp* : developed from the fertilized egg but not part of the embryo itself ⟨*extraembryonic* membranes⟩

ex·tra·le·gal \„ek-strə-'lē-gəl\ *adj* : not regulated or sanctioned by law — **ex·tra·le·gal·ly** *adv*

ex·tra·mar·i·tal \„ek-strə-'mar-ət-l\ *adj* : of or relating to sexual intercourse by a married person with someone other than his or her spouse

ex·tra·ne·ous \ek-'strā-nē-əs\ *adj* **1** : existing or coming from the outside **2 a** : not forming an essential or vital part **b** : having no relevance [Latin *extraneus* "external, strange", from *extra* "outside"] — **ex·tra·ne·ous·ly** *adv* — **ex·tra·ne·ous·ness** *n*

ex·traor·di·nary \ik-'strórd-n-,er-ē, „ek-strə-'órd-\ *adj* **1 a** : going beyond what is usual, regular, or customary ⟨*extraordinary* powers⟩ **b** : very exceptional : REMARKABLE ⟨*extraordinary* beauty⟩ **2** : employed for or sent on a special function or service ⟨an ambassador *extraordinary*⟩ — **ex·traor·di·nar·i·ly** \ik-,strórd-n-'er-ə-lē, „ek-strə-'órd-\ *adv* — **ex·traor·di·nar·i·ness** \ik-'strórd-n-,er-ē-nəs, „ek-strə-'órd-\ *n*

extra point *n* **1** : a point scored in football after a touchdown by drop-kicking or placekicking **2** *pl* : a score of two points scored after a touchdown by advancing the ball across the goal line in one play

ex·trap·o·late \ik-'strap-ə-,lāt\ *vb* : to infer or infer facts and data from known facts and data [Latin *extra* "outside" + English *-polate* (as in *interpolate*)] — **ex·trap·o·la·tion** \-„strap-ə-'lā-shən\ *n*

ex·tra·sen·so·ry perception \„ek-strə-'sens-rē-, -ə-rē-\ *n* : an awareness of events or facts held to involve communication outside all the known senses

ex·tra·ter·res·tri·al \„ek-strə-tə-'res-trē-əl, -'resh-chəl\ *adj* : originating, existing, or taking place outside the earth or its atmosphere ⟨*extraterrestrial* life⟩ — **extraterrestrial** *n*

ex·tra·ter·ri·to·ri·al \-ˌter-ə-ˈtōr-ē-əl, -ˈtȯr-\ *adj* : located outside the territorial limits of a jurisdiction — **ex·tra·ter·ri·to·ri·al·ly** \-ē-ə-lē\ *adv*

ex·tra·ter·ri·to·ri·al·i·ty \-ˌtōr-ē-ˈal-ət-ē, -ˌtȯr-\ *n* : exemption from the application or jurisdiction of local law or tribunals ⟨diplomats enjoy *extraterritoriality*⟩

ex·trav·a·gance \ik-ˈstrav-i-gəns\ *n* **1 a** : an extravagant act; *esp* : excessive spending of money **b** : something extravagant **2** : the quality or fact of being extravagant

ex·trav·a·gant \-gənt\ *adj* **1** : going beyond what is reasonable or suitable ⟨*extravagant* praise⟩ **2** : wasteful especially of money **3** : too high in price [Middle French, from Medieval Latin *extravagans*, from Latin *extra-* + *vagari* "to wander about"] SYN see EXCESSIVE — **ex·trav·a·gant·ly** *adv* □ ORIGIN *Extravagant* is derived from Medieval Latin *extravagans*, formed from the prefix *extra-*, meaning "outside" or "beyond", and the verb *vagari*, "to wander about". Something that is *extravagant*, then, wanders beyond the borders of its usual home. Developing from its literal sense, "wandering", *extravagant* came to mean "exceeding the limits of reason or necessity" and "lacking in moderation, balance, and restraint". From these is derived the related wasteful sense of *extravagant*, that is, "spending much more than necessary".

ex·trav·a·gan·za \ik-ˌstrav-ə-ˈgan-zə\ *n* **1** : a literary or musical work marked by extreme freedom of style and structure **2** : a spectacular show [Italian *estravaganza*, literally, "extravagance"]

ex·tra·ve·hic·u·lar \ˌek-strə-vē-ˈhik-yə-lər\ *adj* : taking place outside a vehicle (as a spacecraft)

¹ex·treme \ik-ˈstrēm\ *adj* **1 a** : existing in a very high degree ⟨*extreme* poverty⟩ **b** : going to great or exaggerated lengths **c** : exceeding the ordinary, usual, or expected ⟨*extreme* measures⟩ **2** : most distant from a center ⟨an *extreme* outpost⟩ **3** : farthest advanced : UTMOST ⟨the *extreme* edge of the cliff⟩ [Middle French, from Latin *extremus*, superlative of *exter, exterus* "being on the outside"] — **ex·treme·ly** *adv* — **ex·treme·ness** *n*

²extreme *n* **1** : an extreme state, condition, or degree **2 a** : something situated at or marking one end or the other of a range ⟨*extremes* of heat and cold⟩ **b** : the first term or the last term of a mathematical proportion **3** : highest degree : MAXIMUM **4** : an extreme measure or expedient ⟨go to *extremes*⟩

extremely high frequency *n* : a ratio frequency in the range between 30,000 and 300,000 megahertz — abbreviation *EHF*

extreme unction *n* : ANOINTING OF THE SICK

ex·trem·ism \ik-ˈstrē-ˌmiz-əm\ *n* : advocacy or practice of extreme measures especially in politics; *esp* : RADICALISM — **ex·trem·ist** \-məst\ *n or adj*

ex·trem·i·ty \ik-ˈstrem-ət-ē\ *n, pl* **-ties 1 a** : the farthest or most remote part, section, or point **b** : a limb of the body; *esp* : a human hand or foot **2 a** : extreme danger or critical need **b** : a moment of such danger or need **3** : the utmost degree (as of emotion or pain) **4** : a drastic or desperate act or measure

ex·tri·cate \ˈek-strə-ˌkāt\ *vt* : to free or remove from an entanglement or difficulty [Latin *extricare*, from *ex-* + *tricae* "trifles, perplexities"] — **ex·tri·ca·ble** \ek-ˈstrik-ə-bəl, ˈek-strik-\ *adj* — **ex·tri·ca·tion** \ˌek-strə-ˈkā-shən\ *n* □ SYN EXTRICATE, DISENTANGLE, UNTANGLE mean to free from what binds or holds back. EXTRICATE implies the use of care or ingenuity in freeing from a difficult position or situation; DISENTANGLE implies a painstaking separating of two or more things that are confused together or closely interrelated; UNTANGLE suggests straightening out something whose parts are confusingly tangled or disordered.

ex·trin·sic \ek-ˈstrin-zik, -ˈstrin-sik\ *adj* **1 a** : not forming part of or belonging to a thing : EXTRANEOUS **b** : originating from or on the outside **2** : EXTERNAL 2a [Latin *extrinsecus* "from without"] — **ex·trin·si·cal·ly** \-zi-kə-lē, -si, -klē\ *adv*

ex·tro·vert *or* **ex·tra·vert** \ˈek-strə-ˌvərt\ *n* : a person whose attention and interests are directed wholly or predominantly toward what is outside the self — **ex·tro·ver·sion** \ˌek-strə-ˈvər-zhən, -shən\ *n* — **extrovert** *adj* — **ex·tro·vert·ed** \ˈek-strə-ˌvərt-əd\ *adj*

ex·trude \ik-ˈstrüd\ *vb* **1** : to force, press, or push out ⟨volcanoes *extrude* lava⟩ **2** : to shape (as metal) by forcing through a die **3** : to become extruded [Latin *extrudere*, from *ex-* + *trudere* "to thrust"] — **ex·trud·er** *n*

ex·tru·sion \ik-ˈstrü-zhən\ *n* : the act or process of extruding; *also* : a form produced by this process [Medieval Latin *extrusio*, from Latin *extrudere* "to extrude"]

ex·tru·sive \-ˈstrü-siv, -ziv\ *adj* : formed by crystallization of lava poured out on the earth's surface ⟨*extrusive* rock⟩

ex·u·ber·ant \ig-ˈzü-bə-rənt, -brənt\ *adj* **1** : joyously unrestrained and enthusiastic **2** : extreme or excessive in degree, size, or extent **3** : produced in great abundance [Middle French, from Latin *exuberare* "to be abundant", from *ex-* + *uber* "fruitful", from *uber* "udder"] — **ex·u·ber·ance** \-bə-rəns, -brənts\ *n* — **ex·u·ber·ant·ly** *adv*

ex·u·date \ˈeks-ə-ˌdāt, ˈegz-\ *n* : exuded matter

ex·ude \ig-ˈzüd\ *vb* **1** : to discharge slowly through pores or cuts : OOZE ⟨*exude* sweat⟩ ⟨sap *exuding* from a cut stem⟩ **2** : to give off or out conspicuously or abundantly ⟨*exuded* charm⟩ [Latin *exsudare*, from *ex-* + *sudare* "to sweat"] — **ex·u·da·tion** \ˌek-sù-ˈdā-shən, -syù-, -shù-\ *n* — **ex·u·da·tive** \ig-ˈzüd-ət-iv\ *adj*

ex·ult \ig-ˈzəlt\ *vi* : to be extremely and often triumphantly joyful [Middle French *exulter*, from Latin *exsultare*, literally, "to leap up", from *ex-* + *saltare* "to leap"] — **ex·ult·ing·ly** \-ˈzəl-ting-lē\ *adv*

ex·ult·ant \ig-ˈzəlt-nt\ *adj* : filled with or expressing great joy : JUBILANT — **ex·ult·ant·ly** *adv*

ex·ul·ta·tion \ˌeks-əl-ˈtā-shən, ˌegz-, -ˌəl-\ *n* : the act of exulting : the state of being exultant

ex·urb \ˈek-ˌsərb, ˈeg-ˌzərb\ *n* : a region or district outside a city and usually beyond its suburbs inhabited chiefly by well-to-do families [*ex-* + *-urb* (as in suburb)] — **ex·ur·bia** \ek-ˈsər-bē-ə, eg-ˈzər-\ *n*

ex·ur·ban·ite \ek-ˈsər-bə-ˌnīt, eg-ˈzər-\ *n* : one who lives in an exurb

-ey — see -Y

¹eye \ˈī\ *n* **1 a** : an organ of sight; *esp* : a rounded hollow organ lined with a sensitive retina and lodged in a bony orbit in the vertebrate skull **b** : the ability to see with the eyes **c** : the ability to perceive or appreciate ⟨an *eye* for beauty⟩ **d** : LOOK, GLANCE ⟨gave them the *eye*⟩ **e** : very close watching or observation ⟨kept an *eye* on them⟩ **f** : POINT OF VIEW, JUDGMENT — often used in pl. ⟨guilty in the *eyes* of the law⟩ **2** : something suggestive of an eye: as **a** : the hole through the head of a needle **b** : a loop to receive a hook **c** : an undeveloped bud (as on a potato) **3** : something central : CENTER ⟨the *eye* of a hurricane⟩ [Old English *ēage*] — **eyed** \ˈīd\ *adj* — **eye·less** \ˈī-ləs\ *adj* — **eye·like** \ˈī-ˌlīk\ *adj*

²eye *vt* **eyed; eye·ing** *or* **ey·ing** : to watch closely

eye·ball \ˈī-ˌbȯl\ *n* : the vertebrate eye

eye·brow \ˈī-ˌbraù\ *n* : the ridge over the eye or hair growing on it

eye–catch·er \ˈī-ˌkach-ər, -ˌkech-\ *n* : something that strongly attracts the eye — **eye–catch·ing** \-ing\ *adj*

eye·cup \ˈī-ˌkəp\ *n* : a small oval cup with a rim curved to fit the orbit of the eye used for applying liquid remedies to the eyes

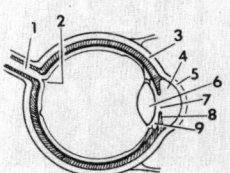

¹eye 1a: *1* optic nerve, *2* blind spot, *3* sclera, *4* anterior chamber, *5* cornea, *6* lens, *7* pupil, *8* iris, *9* posterior chamber

\ə\ abut	\ng\ sing
\ər\ **further**	\ō\ bone
\a\ mat	\ȯ\ saw
\ā\ take	\ȯi\ coin
\ä\ cot, cart	\th\ thin
\aù\ out	\th\ this
\ch\ chin	\ü\ food
\e\ pet	\ù\ foot
\ē\ easy	\y\ yet
\g\ go	\yü\ few
\i\ tip	\yù\ cure
\ī\ life	\zh\ vision
\j\ job	

eye doctor *n* : a specialist (as an optometrist or oph-thalmologist) in the examination, treatment, or care of the eyes

eye·drop·per \'ī-ˌdräp-ər\ *n* : DROPPER 2

eye·ful \'ī-ˌfül\ *n* 1 : a satisfying view 2 : one that is visually attractive

eye·glass \'ī-ˌglas\ *n* 1 a : a glass lens used to improve faulty eyesight b *pl* : GLASS 2c 2 : EYEPIECE

eye·lash \'ī-ˌlash\ *n* 1 *pl* : the fringe of hair edging the eyelid 2 : a single hair of the eyelashes

eye lens *n* : the lens nearest the eye in an eyepiece

eye·let \'ī-lət\ *n* 1 : a small hole designed to receive a cord or used for decoration (as in embroidery) 2 : GROMMET 2

eye·lid \'ī-ˌlid\ *n* : one of the movable lids of skin and muscle that can be closed over the eyeball

eye·lin·er \'ī-ˌlī-nər\ *n* : makeup used to emphasize the contour of the eyes

eye–open·er \'ī-ˌōp-nər, -ə-nər\ *n* : something startling or surprising — **eye–open·ing** \-ning\ *adj*

eye·piece \'ī-ˌpēs\ *n* : the lens or combination of lenses at the eye end of an optical instrument

eye shadow *n* : tinted makeup applied to the eyelids to accent the eyes

eye·sight \'ī-ˌsīt\ *n* : SIGHT, VISION ⟨keen *eyesight*⟩

eye socket *n* : ORBIT 1

eye·sore \'ī-ˌsōr, -ˌsȯr\ *n* : something displeasing to the sight

eye·spot \'ī-ˌspät\ *n* : a simple or primitive visual organ

eye·stalk \'ī-ˌstȯk\ *n* : a movable stalk bearing an eye at the tip in a crustacean

eye·strain \'ī-ˌstrān\ *n* : weariness or a strained state of the eye

eye·tooth \'ī-ˌtüth\ *n* : a canine tooth of the upper jaw

eye·wash \'ī-ˌwȯsh, -ˌwäsh\ *n* 1 : an eye lotion 2 : misleading or deceptive statements, actions, or proce-dures

eye·wit·ness \'ī-ˈwit-nəs\ *n* : a person who sees an oc-currence and is able to give a firsthand account of it ⟨an *eyewitness* to an accident⟩

ey·rie \'ī ər-ē, *or like* AERIE\ *variant of* AERIE

Eze·kiel \i-ˈzē-kyəl, -kē-əl\ *n* — see BIBLE table

Ez·ra \'ez-rə\ *n* — see BIBLE table

Ff

f \'ef\ *n*, *pl* **f's** *or* **fs** \'efs\ *often cap* 1 : the 6th letter of the English alphabet 2 : the musical tone F 3 : a grade rating a student's work as failing

fa \'fä\ *n* : the 4th note of the diatonic scale [Medieval Latin]

Fa·bi·an \'fā-bē-ən\ *adj* : of, relating to, or being a soci-ety of socialists organized in England in 1884 to spread socialist principles gradually [the *Fabian* Soci-ety, from Quintus *Fabius* Maximus, died 203 B.C., Ro-man general] — **Fabian** *n* — **Fa·bi·an·ism** \-ə-ˌniz-əm\ *n*

¹**fa·ble** \'fā-bəl\ *n* : a fictitious narrative or statement: as **a** : a legendary story of supernatural happenings **b** : a story meant to teach a lesson; *esp* : one in which ani-mals speak and act like human beings **c** : FALSEHOOD 1, LIE [Middle French, from Latin *fabula* "conversation, story", from *fari* "to speak"] SYN see MYTH

²**fable** *vt* **fa·bled; fa·bling** \-bə-ling, -bling\ : to talk or write about as if true — **fa·bler** \-bə-lər, -blər\ *n*

fa·bled \'fā-bəld\ *adj* 1 : FICTITIOUS 2 : told or men-tioned in fable : LEGENDARY

fab·ric \'fab-rik\ *n* 1 : underlying structure : FRAME-WORK ⟨the *fabric* of society⟩ 2 a : CLOTH 1 b : a materi-al that resembles cloth [Middle French *fabrique,* from Latin *fabrica* "workshop, structure", from *faber* "arti-san, smith"]

fab·ri·cate \'fab-ri-ˌkāt\ *vt* 1 : to construct especially from standardized parts 2 : to make up in order to de-ceive SYN see FICTION — **fab·ri·ca·tion** \ˌfab-ri-ˈkā-shən\ *n* — **fab·ri·ca·tor** \'fab-ri-ˌkāt-ər\ *n*

fab·u·list \'fab-yə-ləst\ *n* : a creator or teller of fables

fab·u·lous \'fab-yə-ləs\ *adj* 1 : told about in fable ⟨*fab-ulous* animals⟩ 2 : resembling a fable especially in in-credible, marvelous, or exaggerated quality ⟨the *fabu-lous* adventures of an explorer⟩ 3 : especially pleasing or satisfactory ⟨had a *fabulous* meal⟩ — **fab·u·lous·ly** *adv* — **fab·u·lous·ness** *n* □ SYN FABULOUS,

LEGENDARY, MYTHICAL mean having the character of what is invented or imagined. FABULOUS stresses mar-velousness or incredibility often without implying ac-tual nonexistence or impossibility ⟨the company made *fabulous* profits⟩ LEGENDARY suggests having a fabu-lous character created by the distortions or exaggera-tions of historical fact by popular tradition ⟨*legendary* deeds of Robin Hood⟩ MYTHICAL applies to what is or has been popularly believed but does not in fact exist ⟨*mythical* wood nymphs⟩

fa·cade *also* **fa·çade** \fə-ˈsäd\ *n* 1 : the front of a build-ing especially when given special architectural treat-ment 2 : a false, superficial, or artificial appearance ⟨a *facade* of wealth⟩ [French *façade*]

¹**face** \'fās\ *n* 1 : the front part of the head including the chin, mouth, nose, cheeks, eyes, and usually the forehead 2 : PRESENCE ⟨brave in the *face* of danger⟩ 3 **a** : LOOK 2a, EXPRESSION ⟨put a sad *face* on⟩ **b** : GRIMACE 4 **a** : outward appearance ⟨suspicious on the *face* of it⟩ **b** : ASSURANCE 2, CONFIDENCE **c** : DIGNITY, PRESTIGE ⟨afraid to lose *face*⟩ 5 : SURFACE: **a** : a front, upper, or outer surface; *esp* : an exposed surface of rock **b** : any of the plane surfaces that bound a geometric solid or a dihedral angle **c** : a surface or side that is marked or specially prepared ⟨the *face* of a clock⟩ 6 : an end or wall (as of a mine tunnel) at which work is progress-ing [Old French, derived from Latin *facies* "make, form, face", from *facere* "to make"]

²**face** *vb* 1 : to confront brazenly ⟨*face* out a compromis-ing situation⟩ 2 **a** : to line near the edge especially with a different material **b** : to cover the front or surface of ⟨*faced* the building with marble⟩ 3 : to bring face to face ⟨*face* one with the evidence⟩ 4 **a** : to stand or sit with the face toward ⟨*face* the class⟩ **b** : to front on ⟨a house *facing* the park⟩ 5 **a** : to oppose firm-ly ⟨*faces* danger bravely⟩ **b** : to master by confronting with determination ⟨*faced* down the critics of their

facade 1

policy) **6** : to turn or cause to turn the face or body in a specified direction

face card *n* : a playing card that is a king, queen, or jack

-faced \\fāst\ *adj combining form* : having (such) a face or (so many) faces

face·down \\'fās-ˌdȧun\ *adv* : with the face downward

face–lift·ing \\'fās-ˌlif-ting\ *n* **1** : plastic surgery for removal of facial defects (as wrinkles or sagging) **2** : an alteration intended to modernize

face–off \\'fā-ˌsȯf\ *n* : a method of putting the puck in play in ice hockey by dropping it between two opposing players

face·plate \\'fā-ˌsplāt\ *n* : a disk fixed with its face at right angles to the live spindle of a lathe for the attachment of the work

fac·et \\'fas-ət\ *n* **1** : a small plane surface (as on a cut gem) **2** : ASPECT 2, PHASE **3** : the external surface of a unit of a compound eye (as of an insect) [French *facette,* from *face* "face"] — **fac·et·ed** \\'fas-ət-əd\ *adj*

fa·ce·tious \\fə-'sē-shəs\ *adj* **1** : joking or jesting often inappropriately ⟨just being *facetious*⟩ **2** : meant to be humorous or funny : not serious ⟨a *facetious* remark⟩ [Middle French *facetieux,* from *facetie* "jest", from Latin *facetia*] — **fa·ce·tious·ly** *adv* — **fa·ce·tious·ness** *n*

face–to–face *adj* : being within each other's sight or presence ⟨a *face–to–face* interview⟩

face value *n* **1** : the value indicated on the face (as of a bill or a stock certificate) **2** : the apparent worth ⟨can't take a braggart's statements at *face value*⟩

¹fa·cial \\'fā-shəl\ *adj* : of or relating to the face — **fa·cial·ly** \\-shə-lē\ *adv*

²facial *n* : a facial treatment or massage

facial nerve *n* : either of the 7th pair of cranial nerves that control facial and ear movements and transmit sensations of taste

fa·cies \\'fā-shēz, -shē-ˌēz\ *n, pl* **facies** : a particular form or appearance; *esp* : a rock or group of rocks that can be distinguished (as by composition) in a single rock mass [Latin, "face"]

fac·ile \\'fas-əl\ *adj* **1 a** : easily accomplished or attained ⟨a *facile* success⟩ **b** : SPECIOUS, SUPERFICIAL ⟨too *facile* a solution to a complex problem⟩ **c** : easily produced and often insincere ⟨*facile* tears⟩ **2** : mild or yielding in disposition : PLIANT **3** : READY, FLUENT ⟨a *facile* writer⟩ [Middle French, from Latin *facilis,* from *facere* "to do, make"] — **fac·ile·ly** \\-əl-lē, -ə-lē\ *adv* — **fac·ile·ness** \\-əl-nəs\ *n*

fa·cil·i·tate \\fə-'sil-ə-ˌtāt\ *vt* : to make easier — **fa·cil·i·ta·tion** \\-ˌsil-ə-'tā-shən\ *n*

fa·cil·i·ty \\fə-'sil-ət-ē\ *n, pl* **-ties** **1** : the quality of being easily performed **2** : ease in performance : APTITUDE **3** : readiness to be influenced : PLIANCY **4 a** : something that makes an action, operation, or course of conduct easier — usually used in pl. ⟨*facilities* for graduate study⟩ **b** : something built, installed, or established to serve a particular purpose ⟨a hospital *facility*⟩

fac·ing \\'fā-sing\ *n* **1 a** : a lining along an edge (as of a garment) **b** *pl* : the collar, cuffs, and trimmings of a uniform coat **2** : an ornamental or protective layer ⟨a frame house with brick *facing*⟩ **3** : material for facing

fac·sim·i·le \\fak-'sim-ə-lē\ *n* **1** : an exact copy **2** : the transmission of graphic matter by wire or radio and its reproduction [Latin *fac simile* "make similar"] SYN see DUPLICATE

fact \\'fakt\ *n* **1 a** : a thing done : DEED **b** : CRIME 1 **2** : something that exists, happens, or has objective reality ⟨spaceflight is now a *fact*⟩ **3** : information or an item of information that is accurate and true ⟨they do not know *fact* from fancy⟩ [Latin *factum,* from *facere* "to make, do"] — **in fact** : in truth : ACTUALLY

fac·tion \\'fak-shən\ *n* **1** : a group or combination acting together within and usually against a larger body (as in a state, political party, or church) : CLIQUE **2** :

dissension within a group [Latin *factio* "act of making, faction", from *facere* "to make, do"] — **fac·tion·al** \\-shnəl, -shən-l\ *adj* — **fac·tion·al·ism** \\-ˌiz-əm\ *n* — **fac·tion·al·ist** \\-shnəl-əst, -shən-l-\ *n*

fac·tious \\'fak-shəs\ *adj* **1** : of, relating to, or caused by faction ⟨*factious* disputes⟩ **2** : inclined to faction or the formation of factions ⟨*factious* politicians⟩ — **fac·tious·ly** *adv* — **fac·tious·ness** *n*

fac·ti·tious \\fak-'tish-əs\ *adj* : not natural or genuine : ARTIFICIAL ⟨a *factitious* display of grief⟩ [Latin *facticius,* from *facere* "to make, do"] SYN see FICTITIOUS — **fac·ti·tious·ly** *adv* — **fac·ti·tious·ness** *n*

fac·toid \\'fak-ˌtȯid\ *n* **1** : an invented fact thought to be true due to its appearance in print **2** : a brief often trivial news item

¹fac·tor \\'fak-tər\ *n* **1 a** : one that buys or sells property for another **b** : an agent in charge of a trading post **2** : something that actively contributes to the production of a result ⟨hard work was a *factor* in their success⟩ **3** : GENE **4** : any of two or more numbers or mathematical expressions that when multiplied together form a product [Middle French *facteur,* from Latin *factor* "doer", from *facere* "to do, make"] — **fac·tor·ship** \\-ˌship\ *n*

²factor *vb* **fac·tored; fac·tor·ing** \\-tə-ring, -tring\ **1** : to resolve into factors **2** : to work as a factor — **fac·tor·able** \\-tə-rə-bəl, -trə-\ *adj*

¹fac·to·ri·al \\fak-'tōr-ē-əl, -'tȯr-\ *n* **1** : the product of all the positive integers from 1 to a given number **2** : the quantity that is obtained by substituting 0 in the notation for a factorial and that is arbitrarily defined as equal to 1

²factorial *adj* : of or relating to factors, factoring, or factorials

fac·tor·iza·tion \\ˌfak-tə-rə-'zā-shən\ *n* : the process or result of taking factors

fac·to·ry \\'fak-tə-rē, -trē\ *n, pl* **-ries** **1** : a trading station where resident factors trade **2** : a building or set of buildings used or suitable for manufacturing

factory system *n* : a system of manufacturing based on concentration of industry into large establishments that began with the Industrial Revolution

fac·to·tum \\fak-'tōt-əm\ *n* : an employee with numerous varied duties [Latin *fac* "do" + *totum* "everything"]

fac·tu·al \\'fak-chə-wəl, -chəl\ *adj* **1** : of or relating to fact or facts ⟨*factual* evidence⟩ **2** : restricted to or based on fact ⟨little *factual* knowledge of ancient civilizations⟩ — **fac·tu·al·i·ty** \\ˌfak-chə-'wal-ət-ē\ *n* — **fac·tu·al·ly** \\'fak-chə-wə-lē, -chə-lē\ *adv* — **fac·tu·al·ness** *n*

fac·u·la \\'fak-yə-lə\ *n, pl* **-lae** \\-ˌlē, -ˌlī\ : any of the brighter regions of the sun's photosphere [New Latin, from Latin *fac-, fax* "torch"]

fac·ul·ta·tive \\'fak-əl-ˌtāt-iv\ *adj* **1** : taking place under some conditions but not under others ⟨*facultative* diapause⟩ **2** : showing the typical mode of life under some environmental conditions but not under others ⟨*facultative* anaerobes⟩ — **fac·ul·ta·tive·ly** *adv*

fac·ul·ty \\'fak-əl-tē\ *n, pl* **-ties** **1** : ability to do something : TALENT ⟨a *faculty* for making friends⟩ **2** : one of the powers of the mind or body ⟨the *faculty* of hearing⟩ **3** : the teachers in a school or college or in one of its departments **4** : the members of a profession [Middle French *faculté,* from Latin *facultas,* from *facilis* "facile"]

fad \\'fad\ *n* : a practice or interest followed for a time with great zeal : CRAZE [origin unknown] — **fad·dist** \\'fad-əst\ *n*

¹fade \\'fād\ *vb* **1** : to lose freshness or vitality : WITHER **2** : to lose or cause to lose freshness or brilliance of color **3** : to grow dim or disappear gradually ⟨their hopes *faded*⟩ **4** : to change gradually in loudness or visibility — used of a motion-picture image or of an electronics signal and usually with *in* or *out* [Middle

\ə\ abut		\ng\ sing	
\ər\ further		\ō\ bone	
\a\ mat		\ȯ\ saw	
\ā\ take		\ȯi\ coin	
\ä\ cot, cart		\th\ thin	
\au̇\ out		\th\ this	
\ch\ chin		\ü\ food	
\e\ pet		\u̇\ foot	
\ē\ easy		\y\ yet	
\g\ go		\yü\ few	
\i\ tip		\yu̇\ cure	
\ī\ life		\zh\ vision	
\j\ job			

French *fader,* from *fade* "feeble, insipid", derived from Latin *fatuus* "fatuous, insipid"]

²**fade** *n* : a gradual changing of one picture to another in a motion-picture or television sequence

fade·less \'fād-ləs\ *adj* : not susceptible to fading

fae·cal, fae·ces *variant of* FECAL, FECES

fa·er·ie *also* **fa·ery** \'fā-rē, 'fā-ə-rē, 'faər-ē, 'feər-ē\ *n, pl* **fa·er·ies** 1 : FAIRYLAND 2 : FAIRY [Middle French *faerie*] — **faery** *adj*

¹**fag** \'fag\ *vb* **fagged; fag·ging** 1 : DRUDGE 2 : to act as a fag 3 : to tire by strenuous activity : EXHAUST [obsolete *fag* "to droop"]

²**fag** *n* 1 : an English public-school boy who acts as servant to another 2 : MENIAL, DRUDGE

³**fag** *n* : CIGARETTE [*fag end*]

fag end *n* 1 **a** : the last part or coarser end of a web of cloth **b** : the untwisted end of a rope 2 **a** : a poor or worn-out end **b** : the extreme end [Middle English *fagge* "flap"]

fag·ot *or* **fag·got** \'fag-ət\ *n* : a bundle of sticks or twigs used especially for fuel [Middle French *fagot*]

fag·ot·ing *or* **fag·got·ing** \'fag-ət-ing\ *n* : an embroidery produced by tying threads in hourglass-shaped clusters

Fahr·en·heit \'far-ən-,hīt\ *adj* : relating or conforming to a temperature scale on which under standard atmospheric pressure the boiling point of water is at 212 degrees above the zero of the scale and the freezing point is at 32 degrees above zero — abbreviation F [Gabriel D. *Fahrenheit*]

fa·ience *or* **fa·ïence** \fā-'äns\ *n* : earthenware decorated with opaque colored glazes [French, from *Faenza,* Italy]

¹**fail** \'fāl\ *vb* 1 **a** : to lose strength : WEAKEN (as one's eyesight *fails*) **b** : to stop functioning (the engine *failed*) 2 **a** : to fall short (*failed* in their duty) **b** : to prove inadequate : give way or break down (the water supply *failed*) **c** (1) : to be unsuccessful in passing (*failed* the exam) (2) : to grade as not passing (*fail* a student) **d** : to become insolvent (the bank *failed*) 3 : DISAPPOINT, DESERT (*fail* a friend) 4 **a** : to be such as not (the play *failed* to excite me) **b** : to act, behave, or exist so as not (the valve *failed* to function) (*failed* to see the red light) [Old French *faillir,* from Latin *fallere* "to deceive, disappoint"]

²**fail** *n* : FAILURE — usually used in the phrase *without fail*

¹**fail·ing** \'fā-ling\ *n* : a slight defect in character or conduct SYN *see* FAULT

²**failing** *prep* : in the absence or lack of (*failing* specific instructions, use your own judgment)

faille \'fīl\ *n* : a somewhat shiny closely woven ribbed fabric [French]

fail–safe \'fāl-,sāf\ *adj* : incorporating some feature for automatically counteracting the effect of an anticipated possible failure

fail·ure \'fāl-yər\ *n* 1 **a** : a failing to do or perform (their *failure* to appear) **b** : a state of inability to perform a normal function adequately (heart *failure*) 2 **a** : lack of satisfactory performance or effect (our *failure* in the campaign) **b** : a lack of commercial or financial success (a business *failure*) 3 **a** : a falling short : DEFICIENCY (crop *failure*) **b** : DETERIORATION, BREAKDOWN (a *failure* of memory) 4 : one that has failed

¹**fain** \'fān\ *adj* 1 *archaic* : GLAD 2 *archaic* : INCLINED 1 3 *archaic* : OBLIGED [Old English *fægen*]

²**fain** *adv* 1 *archaic* : WILLINGLY 2 *archaic* : RATHER 1

¹**faint** \'fānt\ *adj* 1 : lacking courage and spirit : COWARDLY (*faint* heart) 2 : being weak, dizzy, and likely to faint (feel *faint* at the sight of blood) 3 : lacking strength : FEEBLE (a *faint* attempt) 4 : lacking distinctness : barely perceptible (a *faint* sound) [Old French *feint, faint,* from *feindre, faindre* "to feign, shirk"] — **faint·ly** *adv* — **faint·ness** *n*

²**faint** *vi* 1 *archaic* : to lose courage or spirit 2 : to lose consciousness because of a temporary decrease in the blood supply to the brain

³**faint** *n* : an act or condition of fainting

faint·heart·ed \'fānt-'härt-əd\ *adj* : lacking courage or resolution : TIMID — **faint·heart·ed·ly** *adv* — **faint·heart·ed·ness** *n*

¹**fair** \'faər, 'feər\ *adj* 1 : attractive in appearance : BEAUTIFUL (our *fair* city) 2 : deceptively agreeable : SPECIOUS (*fair* promises) 3 **a** : CLEAN, PURE (sully a *fair* name) **b** : CLEAR, LEGIBLE (a *fair* copy) 4 : not stormy or cloudy (*fair* weather) 5 **a** : marked by impartiality and honesty : JUST **b** : conforming with the rules : ALLOWED (*fair* play) **c** : open to legitimate pursuit or attack (*fair* game) 6 **a** : PROMISING, LIKELY (a *fair* chance of winning) **b** : favorable to a ship's course (a *fair* wind) 7 : not dark (a *fair* complexion) 8 : moderately good (made a *fair* grade) [Old English *fæger*] — **fair·ness** *n*

☐ SYN FAIR, EQUITABLE, IMPARTIAL, UNBIASED mean free from favor toward either or any side. FAIR implies eliminating one's own feelings, prejudices, or desires so as to achieve a proper balance of conflicting interests (a *fair* settlement of property claims) EQUITABLE stresses equal treatment of all concerned (*equitable* sharing in the profits of a venture) IMPARTIAL implies absence or suppression of favor or prejudice in making a judgment (an *impartial* referee) UNBIASED stresses more definitely complete absence of prejudice or predisposition (*unbiased* history) SYN *see in addition* BEAUTIFUL

²**fair** *adv* 1 : in a fair way 2 : so as to be a fair ball

³**fair** *n* 1 : a gathering of buyers and sellers at a particular place and time for trade 2 : a competitive exhibition (as of farm products) usually with accompanying entertainment and amusements 3 : a sale of a collection of articles usually for a charitable purpose [Old French *feire,* from Medieval Latin *feria,* from Latin *feriae* (plural) "holidays"]

fair ball *n* : a batted baseball that settles within the foul lines in the infield, that first touches the ground within the foul lines in the outfield, or that is within the foul lines when bounding to the outfield past first or third base or when going beyond the outfield for a home run

fair catch *n* : a catch of a kicked football by a player who having given a prescribed signal gives up his right to advance the ball and may not be tackled

fair·ground \'faər-,graund, 'feər-\ *n* : an area set aside for the holding of fairs

¹**fair·ing** \'faər-ing, 'feər-\ *n, British* : GIFT; *esp* : a present bought or given at a fair

²**fairing** *n* : a structure (as on an aircraft or missile) whose function is to produce a smooth outline and reduce resistance to motion through the air

fair·ish \'faər-ish, 'feər-\ *adj* : fairly good or large

fair·lead \'faər-,lēd, 'feər-\ *n* : a block or ring that serves as a guide for a line on board a boat or ship and prevents it from chafing

fair·ly \'faər-lē, 'feər-\ *adv* 1 : HANDSOMELY, FAVORABLY (*fairly* situated) 2 : QUITE, COMPLETELY (*fairly* bursting with pride) 3 : in a fair manner : JUSTLY (treat each person *fairly*) 4 : MODERATELY (a *fairly* easy job)

fair–spo·ken \'faər-,spō-kən, 'feər-\ *adj* : pleasant and courteous in speech

fair–trade \-'trād\ *adj* : of, relating to, or being an agreement between a producer and a seller of an item that it will not be sold below a certain price — **fair–trade** *vt*

fair·way \-,wā\ *n* 1 : a navigable part of a river, bay, or harbor 2 : a path or line of travel 3 : the mowed part of a golf course between a tee and a green

fair–weather *adj* : loyal only when things are going well (a *fair-weather* friend)

fairy \'faər-ē, 'feər-\ *n, pl* **fairies** : a usually small humanlike being of folklore and romance endowed with magical powers [Old French *faerie* "fairyland, fairy people", from *feie, fee* "fairy", from Latin *Fata,* goddess of fate, from *fatum* "fate"] — **fairy·like** \-,līk\ *adj*

fairy·land \-,land\ *n* **1** : a land of fairies **2** : a place of delicate beauty or magical charm

fairy ring *n* : a ring of mushrooms in a lawn or meadow growing outward from a central point

fairy shrimp *n* : any of several delicate transparent freshwater crustaceans (order Anostraca)

fairy tale *n* **1** : a simple children's story about supernatural beings — called also *fairy story* **2** : a made-up story usually meant to mislead

fait ac·com·pli \'fāt-,ak-,ōⁿ-'plē, fe-,tak-, -,ōⁿm-\ *n, pl* **faits accomplis** *same, or* -'plēz\ : a thing accomplished and presumably irreversible [French, "accomplished fact"]

faith \'fāth\ *n* **1 a** : allegiance to duty or a person : LOYALTY **b** : fidelity to one's promises **2 a** (1) : belief and trust in and loyalty to God (2) : belief in the traditional doctrines of a religion **b** (1) : firm belief in something for which there is no proof (2) : complete confidence **3** : something that is believed especially with strong conviction; *also* : a system of religious beliefs [Old French *feid, foi,* from Latin *fides*] SYN see BELIEF — **in faith** : by my faith : TRULY

¹faith·ful \'fāth-fəl\ *adj* **1** : full of faith especially in God **2** : steadfast in keeping promises or in fulfilling duties ⟨a *faithful* worker⟩ **3** : steady, firm, and dependable in allegiance or devotion : LOYAL ⟨a *faithful* friend⟩ **4** : true to the facts : ACCURATE ⟨a *faithful* copy⟩ — **faith·ful·ly** \-fə-lē\ *adv* — **faith·ful·ness** *n* □ SYN LOYAL, CONSTANT, STEADFAST: FAITHFUL implies unswerving adherence to a person or to an oath or promise; LOYAL implies a firm resistance to any temptation to desert or betray; CONSTANT implies continuing firmness of emotional attachment; STEADFAST stresses a steady and unwavering adherence.

²faithful *n, pl* **faith·ful** *or* **faith·fuls** : one that is faithful: as **a** : a member of a religious body ⟨the *faithful* observe the holy days⟩ **b** : a loyal follower or member ⟨party *faithfuls* gather on election night⟩

faith·less \'fāth-ləs\ *adj* **1** : not having faith **2** : not worthy of trust or reliance : DISLOYAL — **faith·less·ly** *adv* — **faith·less·ness** *n* □ SYN FALSE, DISLOYAL, PERFIDIOUS: FAITHLESS may apply to any failure to keep a promise or pledge or to any breach of allegiance or loyalty; FALSE often implies a degree of premeditation and deception in betrayal or treachery ⟨*false* friends⟩ DISLOYAL implies a lack of complete faithfulness to a friend, cause, leader, or country ⟨*disloyal* officers⟩ PERFIDIOUS implies an inability to be faithful or reliable.

¹fake \'fāk\ *vt* **1** : to treat so as to falsify : DOCTOR ⟨*faked* the statistics to prove a point⟩ **2** : COUNTERFEIT ⟨*fake* a rare edition⟩ **3** : PRETEND, SIMULATE ⟨*fake* surprise⟩ [origin unknown] — **fak·er** \'fā-kər\ *n* — **fak·ery** \-kə-rē, -krē\ *n*

²fake *n* **1** : an imitation that is passed off as genuine : FRAUD, COUNTERFEIT ⟨the supposed antique was a *fake*⟩ **2** : IMPOSTOR, CHARLATAN

³fake *adj* : COUNTERFEIT, PHONY

fa·kir \fə-'kiər, fā-, fa-, 'fā-kər\ *n* **1** : a Muslim beggar : DERVISH **2** : a wandering Hindu ascetic or wonder₌worker [Arabic *faqīr,* literally, "poor man"]

fal·chion \'fȯl-chən\ *n* : a broad-bladed slightly curved medieval sword [Old French *fauchon,* from *fauchier* "to mow", from Latin *falc-, falx* "sickle, scythe"]

fal·con \'fal-kən *also* 'fȯl- *sometimes* 'fȯ-kən\ *n* **1** : a hawk trained for use in falconry; *esp* : a female peregrine falcon — compare TIERCEL **2** : any of various hawks with long wings and a notch and tooth on the upper half of the bill [Old French, from Late Latin *falco*]

fal·con·er \-kə-nər\ *n* : one that hunts with hawks or breeds or trains hawks for hunting

fal·con·ry \'fal-kən-rē *also* 'fȯl- *sometimes* 'fȯ-kən-\ *n* **1** : the art of training falcons to pursue game **2** : the sport of hunting with falcons

fal·de·ral \'fäl-də-,räl\ *variant of* FOLDEROL

¹fall \'fȯl\ *vi* **fell** \'fel\; **fall·en** \'fȯ-lən\; **fall·ing 1 a** : to descend freely by the force of gravity **b** : to hang freely ⟨the drapes *fall* quite gracefully⟩ **c** : to drop oneself to a lower position ⟨*fall* to one's knees⟩ **d** : to come as if by descending ⟨darkness *falls* early in winter⟩ **2 a** : to go down ⟨the temperature *fell* 10 degrees⟩ **b** : to drop in pitch or volume **c** : to become uttered ⟨as the words *fell* from my lips⟩ **d** : to become lowered ⟨her eyes *fell*⟩ **3 a** : to tip over from an erect position ⟨the lamp *fell* on its side⟩ **b** : to enter as if unaware : STUMBLE ⟨*fell* into error⟩ **c** : to drop down wounded or dead; *esp* : to die in battle **d** : to become captured or defeated ⟨the fortress *fell*⟩ **e** : to suffer ruin or failure **4** : to commit a wrong or immoral act **5 a** : to move or extend in a downward direction ⟨the ground *falls* away to the east⟩ **b** : SUBSIDE 4, ABATE **c** : to decline in quality, activity, quantity, or value **d** : to lose weight — used with *off* or *away* **e** : to assume a look of shame or dejection ⟨my face *fell* when I lost⟩ **6 a** : to occur at a certain time **b** : to come by chance ⟨*fell* in with a bad crowd⟩ **c** : DEVOLVE ⟨it *fell* to us to break the news⟩ **d** : to have the proper place or station ⟨the accent *falls* on the second syllable⟩ **7** : to come within the scope of something **8** : to pass from one condition of body or mind to another ⟨*fall* ill⟩ ⟨*fall* asleep⟩ **9** : to set about heartily or actively ⟨*fell* to work⟩ [Old English *feallan*] — **fall flat** : to produce no response or result : FAIL — **fall for 1** : to fall in love with **2** : to become a victim of — **fall foul 1** : to have a collision — used chiefly of ships **2** : to have a quarrel : CLASH — often used with *of* — **fall from grace 1** : to lapse morally : SIN **2** : BACKSLIDE — **fall into line** : to comply with a certain course of action — **fall over oneself** : to display excessive eagerness — **fall short 1** : to be deficient **2** : to fail to attain

²fall *n* **1** : the act of falling by the force of gravity ⟨a *fall* from a horse⟩ **2 a** : a falling out, off, or away : DROPPING ⟨the *fall* of the leaves⟩ **b** : AUTUMN **c** : a thing or quantity that falls ⟨a heavy *fall* of snow⟩ **3 a** : loss of greatness : COLLAPSE **b** : the surrender or capture of a besieged place **c** : lapse or departure from innocence or goodness; *esp, often cap* : the act of Adam and Eve in eating the forbidden fruit **d** : loss of chastity **4 a** : the downward slope of a hill **b** : WATERFALL — usually used in pl. **5** : a decrease in size, quantity, degree, activity, or value **6** : the distance which something falls **7 a** : an act of forcing a wrestler's shoulders to the mat **b** : a bout of wrestling

fal·la·cious \fə-'lā-shəs\ *adj* **1** : embodying a fallacy ⟨a *fallacious* argument⟩ **2** : DELUSIVE, MISLEADING ⟨cherish a *fallacious* hope⟩ — **fal·la·cious·ly** *adv* — **fal·la·cious·ness** *n*

fal·la·cy \'fal-ə-sē\ *n, pl* **-cies 1** : a false or mistaken idea ⟨the popular *fallacy* that poets are impractical⟩ **2** : false or illogical reasoning or an instance of this [Latin *fallacia,* from *fallac-, fallax* "deceptive", from *fallere* "to deceive"]

fall back *vi* : RETREAT 1, RECEDE

fall·er \'fȯ-lər\ *n* : a logger who fells trees

fall guy *n* **1** : one that is easily duped **2** : SCAPEGOAT 2

fal·li·ble \'fal-ə-bəl\ *adj* : liable to err or be erroneous ⟨even experts are *fallible*⟩ ⟨a *fallible* generalization⟩ [Medieval Latin *fallibilis,* from Latin *fallere* "to deceive"] — **fal·li·bil·i·ty** \,fal-ə-'bil-ət-ē\ *n* — **fal·li·bly** \'fal-ə-blē\ *adv*

fall in *vi* : to take one's proper place in a military formation

fall·ing–out \,fȯ-ling-'aut\ *n, pl* **fallings–out** *or* **falling–outs** : QUARREL 2

\ə\ abut		\ng\ sing	
\ər\ further		\ō\ bone	
\a\ mat		\ȯ\ saw	
\ā\ take		\ȯi\ coin	
\ä\ cot, cart		\th\ thin	
\aú\ out		\th\ this	
\ch\ chin		\ü\ food	
\e\ pet		\ú\ foot	
\ē\ easy		\y\ yet	
\g\ go		\yü\ few	
\i\ tip		\yú\ cure	
\ī\ life		\zh\ vision	
\j\ job			

falling star *n* : METEOR

fal·lo·pi·an tube \fə-'lō-pē-ən-\ *n, often cap F* : either of the pair of tubes that conduct the egg from the ovary to the uterus [Gabriel *Follopius*, died 1562, Italian anatomist]

fall·out \'fò-,laút\ *n* : the often radioactive particles resulting from a nuclear explosion and descending through the atmosphere

fall out \,fò-'laút, fò-\ *vi* **1** : CHANCE 1, HAPPEN **2** : to have a quarrel **3 a** : to leave one's place in the ranks **b** : to leave a building to take one's place in a military formation

¹fal·low \'fal-ō\ *adj* : of a light yellowish brown [Old English *fealu*]

²fallow *n* **1** : land for crops allowed to lie idle during the growing season **2** : the state or period of being fallow ⟨fields in summer *fallow*⟩ [Old English *fealg* "plowed land"]

³fallow *vt* : to till (land) without seeding

⁴fallow *adj* **1** : left untilled or if tilled left unsown **2** : DORMANT 1, INACTIVE — **fal·low·ness** *n*

fallow deer *n* : a small European deer with broad antlers and a pale yellow coat spotted white in the summer

fallow dear

¹false \'fòls\ *adj* **1** : ARTIFICIAL 1 ⟨*false* teeth⟩ **2 a** : intentionally untrue ⟨*false* testimony⟩ **b** : adjusted or made so as to deceive ⟨*false* scales⟩ **c** : tending to mislead ⟨a *false* promise⟩ **3** : not genuine or sincere ⟨*false* modesty⟩ ⟨a *false* prophet⟩ **4** : not faithful or loyal : TREACHEROUS **5** : not essential to structure ⟨a *false* ceiling⟩ **6** : inaccurate in pitch ⟨a *false* note⟩ **7 a** : based on mistaken ideas ⟨*false* pride⟩ **b** : inconsistent with the true facts ⟨a *false* sense of security⟩ [Latin *falsus*, from *fallere* "to deceive"] SYN see FAITHLESS — **false·ly** *adv* — **false·ness** *n*

²false *adv* : in a false or faithless manner : TREACHEROUSLY ⟨they played us *false*⟩

false·hood \'fòls-,húd\ *n* **1** : an untrue statement : LIE **2** : absence of truth or accuracy **3** : the practice of lying

false rib *n* : a rib whose cartilages unite indirectly or not at all with the sternum — compare FLOATING RIB

¹fal·set·to \fòl-'set-ō\ *n, pl* **-tos** **1** : an artifically high voice; *esp* : an artificial singing voice that extends above the range of the full voice especially of a tenor **2** : a singer who uses falsetto [Italian, from *falso* "false", from Latin *falsus*]

²falsetto *adv* : in falsetto

fal·si·fy \'fòl-sə-,fī\ *vb* **-fied; -fy·ing** **1** : to make false : change so as to deceive ⟨*falsify* financial accounts⟩ **2 a** : to tell lies : LIE **b** : MISREPRESENT **3** : to prove to be false ⟨promises *falsified* by events⟩ — **fal·si·fi·ca·tion** \,fòl-sə-fə-'kā-shən\ *n* — **fal·si·fi·er** \'fòl-sə-,fī-ər, -,fīr\ *n*

fal·si·ty \'fòl-sət-ē, -stē\ *n, pl* **-ties** **1** : something false : LIE **2** : the quality or state of being false

falt·boat \'fält-,bōt\ *n* : FOLDBOAT [German *faltboot*, from *falten* "to fold" + *boot* "boat"]

¹fal·ter \'fòl-tər\ *vb* **fal·tered; fal·ter·ing** \'fòl-tə-ring, -tring\ **1** : to move unsteadily : WAVER **2** : to stumble or hesitate in speech : STAMMER **3** : to hesitate in purpose or action ⟨courage that never *falters*⟩ [Middle English *falteren*] SYN see HESITATE — **fal·ter·er** \-tər-ər\ *n* — **fal·ter·ing·ly** \-tə-ring-lē, -tring-\ *adv*

¹fan 2a

²falter *n* : an act or instance of faltering

fame \'fām\ *n* : the fact or condition of being known to the public : RENOWN [Old French, from Latin *fama* "report, fame"]

famed \'fāmd\ *adj* : FAMOUS 1, WELL-KNOWN, RENOWNED

fa·mil·ial \fə-'mil-yəl\ *adj* : of, relating to, or characteristic of a family

¹fa·mil·iar \fə-'mil-yər\ *n* **1** : an intimate associate : COMPANION **2** : a spirit held to attend and serve or guard a person — called also *familiar spirit* **3** : one that frequents a place

²familiar *adj* **1** : closely acquainted : INTIMATE ⟨*familiar* friends⟩ **2** : INFORMAL 1, CASUAL ⟨spoke in a *familiar* manner⟩ **3** : overly intimate : FORWARD **4 a** : frequently seen or experienced **b** : of everyday occurrence **5** : having a good knowledge ⟨*familiar* with the rules of soccer⟩ [Old French *familier*, from Latin *familiaris*, from *familia* "family"] — **fa·mil·iar·ly** *adv*

fa·mil·iar·i·ty \fə-,mil-'yar-ət-ē, -,mil-ē-'ar-\ *n, pl* **-ties** **1** : close friendship : INTIMACY **2** : close acquaintance with or knowledge of something ⟨acquire a *familiarity* with French⟩ **3** : lack of formality : freedom and ease in personal relations **4** : an unduly bold or forward act or expression

fa·mil·iar·ize \fə-'mil-yə-,rīz\ *vt* **1** : to make thoroughly acquainted : ACCUSTOM ⟨*familiarize* oneself with a new job⟩ **2** : to make well known ⟨advertising *familiarizes* the name of a product⟩ — **fa·mil·iar·iza·tion** \-,mil-yə-rə-'zā-shən\ *n*

fam·i·ly \'fam-lē, -ə-lē\ *n, pl* **-lies** **1** : a group of persons of common ancestry : CLAN **2** : a group of individuals living under one roof and under one head : HOUSEHOLD **3** : a group of things having common characteristics or properties; *esp* : a closely related series of chemical elements or componds **4** : a social group composed of parents and their children **5** : a group of related plants or animals ranking in biological classification above a genus and below an order [Latin *familia* "household (including servants as well as kin of the householder)", from *famulus* "servant"]

family name *n* : SURNAME

family planning *n* : planning intended to determine the number and spacing of one's children through birth control

family tree *n* **1** : GENEALOGY 1 **2** : a diagram showing family relationships

fam·ine \'fam-ən\ *n* **1** : an extreme general scarcity of food **2** : a great shortage [Middle French, from Latin *fames* "hunger"]

fam·ish \'fam-ish\ *vb* **1** : to suffer or cause to suffer from extreme hunger **2** : to suffer for lack of something ⟨*famished* for news from home⟩ — **fam·ish·ment** \-mənt\ *n*

fa·mous \'fā-məs\ *adj* **1** : widely and favorably known ⟨a *famous* explorer⟩ **2** : deserving to be remembered : EXCELLENT □ SYN RENOWNED, CELEBRATED: FAMOUS may imply no more than being widely and favorably known for any reason and any length of time; RENOWNED implies glory and acclamation ⟨heroes *renowned* in song and story⟩ CELEBRATED stresses frequent public notice and mention especially in print ⟨a *celebrated* murder trial⟩

fa·mous·ly \'fā-məs-lē\ *adv* : very well ⟨got along *famously* together⟩

¹fan \'fan\ *n* **1** : any of various devices for winnowing grain **2** : a device for producing a current of air: as **a** : a device that consists of material (as paper or silk) often in the shape of a segment of a circle and is waved to and fro by hand **b** : a device that consists of a series of vanes radiating from a hub rotated on its axle by a motor **3** : something shaped like or suggesting a hand fan [Old English *fann*, from Latin *vannus*]

²fan *vb* **fanned; fan·ning** **1** : to drive away the chaff from grain by winnowing **2** : to move or impel air with a fan **3 a** : to direct a current of air upon with a fan **b** : to stir up to activity as if by fanning : STIMULATE **4** : to spread out or move like a fan **5** : to strike out in baseball **6** : to fire a gun by squeezing the trigger and striking the hammer to the rear with the free hand — **fan·ner** *n*

³fan *n* **1** : an enthusiastic follower of a sport or entertainment **2** : an enthusiastic admirer (as of an athlete or movie star) [probably short for *fanatic*]

fa·nat·ic \fə-'nat-ik\ *adj* : marked or moved by excessive enthusiasm and intense uncritical devotion [Latin *fanaticus* "inspired by a deity, frenzied", from *fanum* "temple"] — **fanatic** n — **fa·nat·i·cal** \-i-kəl\ adj — **fa·nat·i·cal·ly** \-i-kə-lē, -klē\ adv — **fa·nat·i·cism** \-'nat-ə-ˌsiz-əm\ n □ ORIGIN The Latin adjective *fanaticus,* a derivative of the noun *fanum,* "temple", originally meant "of or relating to a temple". It was later used to refer to those pious individuals who were thought to have been inspired by a god or goddess. In time the sense "frantic, frenzied, mad" arose because it was thought that persons behaving in such a manner were possessed by a deity. This was the first meaning of the English word *fanatic.* This sense is now obsolete, but it led to the development of the sense "excessively enthusiastic, especially about religious matters". The word later became less specific, meaning simply "excessively enthusiastic or unreasonable". The noun *fan,* meaning "enthusiast", is probably a shortening of *fanatic.*

fan·ci·er \'fan-sē-ər\ n : one with a special liking or interest; *esp* : a person who breeds or grows a particular animal or plant for points of excellence

fan·ci·ful \'fan-si-fəl\ adj 1 a : full of fancy ⟨a *fanciful* tale of an imaginary kingdom⟩ b : guided by fancy ⟨a *fanciful* impractical person⟩ 2 : coming from the fancy rather than from the reason ⟨a *fanciful* scheme for getting rich⟩ 3 : curiously made or shaped ⟨*fanciful* forms of ice on a windowpane⟩ — **fan·ci·ful·ly** \-fə-lē, -flē\ adv — **fan·ci·ful·ness** \-fəl-nəs\ n

¹**fan·cy** \'fan-sē\ n, pl **fancies** 1 : the power of the mind to think of things not present : IMAGINATION 2 : LIKING ⟨take a *fancy* to a person⟩ 3 : WHIM, NOTION ⟨changed plans at the slightest *fancy*⟩ 4 : taste or judgment especially in art, literature, or decoration 5 : enthusiasts over something (as an art or pursuit) : FANCIERS [Middle English *fantasie, fantsy* "fantasy, fancy", from Middle French *fantasie*]

²**fancy** vt **fan·cied; fan·cy·ing** 1 : to have a fancy for : LIKE 2 : to form a conception of : IMAGINE 3 : to believe without evidence

³**fancy** adj **fan·ci·er; -est** 1 : based on fancy : WHIMSICAL 2 a : not plain : SHOWY b : of particular excellence c : bred primarily for showiness 3 : executed with technical skill and superior grace ⟨*fancy* diving⟩ — **fan·ci·ly** \'fan-sə-lē\ adv — **fan·ci·ness** \-sē-nəs\ n

fancy dress n : a costume (as for a masquerade) chosen to suit the wearer's fancy — **fancy–dress** adj

fan·cy–free \'fan-sē-'frē\ adj : not centering the attention on any one person or thing; *esp* : not in love

fan·cy·work \-ˌwərk\ n : ornamental needlework (as embroidery)

fan·dan·go \fan-'dang-gō\ n, pl **-gos** : a lively Spanish or Spanish-American dance [Spanish]

fane \'fān\ n : a place of worship [Latin *fanum*]

fan·fare \'fan-ˌfaər, -ˌfeər\ n 1 : a flourish of trumpets 2 : a showy outward display [French]

fang \'fang\ n : a long sharp tooth: as a : one by which an animal's prey is seized and held or torn b : one of the long hollow or grooved poison-injecting teeth of a venomous snake [Old English] — **fanged** \'fangd\ adj

fan–jet \'fan-ˌjet\ n 1 : a jet engine having a fan that operates in a duct and draws in extra air whose compression and expulsion provide extra thrust 2 : an airplane powered by a fan-jet engine

fan·light \'fan-ˌlīt\ n : a semicircular window with radiating sash bars like the ribs of a fan placed over a door or window

fan mail n : letters sent to a public figure by admirers

fan·ny pack \'fan-ē-ˌpak\ n : a pack for carrying personal articles that straps to the waist

fan·tail \'fan-ˌtāl\ n 1 : a fan-shaped tail or end 2 a : a domestic pigeon having a broad rounded tail b : a fancy goldfish with the tail fins double 3 : an architectural part resembling a fan 4 : the part of the stern of a ship that overhangs the water

fan–tan \'fan-ˌtan\ n 1 : a Chinese gambling game 2 : a card game in which players play in sequence upon sevens [Chinese (Pekingese dialect) *fan¹-t'an¹*]

fan·ta·sia \fan-'tā-zhə, ˌfant-ə-'zē-ə\ n : an instrumental composition in a form determined by the composer's fancy [Italian *fantasia,* literally, "fancy"]

fan·ta·size \'fant-ə-ˌsīz\ vb : to create mental images by daydreaming

fan·tas·tic \fan-'tas-tik, fən-\ also **fan·tas·ti·cal** \-ti-kəl\ adj 1 : produced or seemingly produced by unrestrained fancy ⟨*fantastic* dreams⟩ ⟨a *fantastic* scheme⟩ 2 : going beyond belief : incredible or hardly credible ⟨airplanes now travel at *fantastic* speeds⟩ 3 : extremely individual or eccentric ⟨*fantastic* behavior⟩ [Late Latin *phantasticus,* from Greek *phantastikos* "producing mental images", from *phantazein* "to present to the mind"] — **fan·tas·ti·cal·ly** \-ti-kə-lē, -klē\ adv □ SYN FANTASTIC, BIZARRE, GROTESQUE mean conceived or produced without reference to reality, truth, or common sense. FANTASTIC may connote unrestrained extravagance in conception ⟨a *fantastic* theory⟩ ⟨*fantastic* prices⟩ or merely elaborateness of decorative invention; BIZARRE implies strangeness produced by violence of contrast or incongruity of combination ⟨*bizarre* architecture of an amusement park⟩ GROTESQUE implies violent distortion of the natural with a comic, startling, or pathetic result ⟨*grotesque* masks⟩ ⟨made *grotesque* attempts at operatic roles⟩

fan·ta·sy or **phan·ta·sy** \'fant-ə-sē, -ə-zē\ n, pl **-sies** 1 : IMAGINATION 1, FANCY 2 : something produced by a person's imagination: as a : a mental image produced to fill a psychological need : DAYDREAM b : FANTASIA [Middle French *fantasie* "fancy", from Latin *phantasia,* from Greek, "imagination", from *phantazein* "to present to the mind", from *phainein* "to show"]

¹**far** \'fär\ adv **far·ther** \-thər\ or **fur·ther** \'fər-\; **far·thest** or **fur·thest** \-thəst\ 1 : at or to a considerable distance in space or time ⟨*far* from home⟩ ⟨*far* in the future⟩ 2 : by a broad interval : WIDELY ⟨this is *far* better⟩ 3 : to or at a definite distance, point, or degree ⟨as *far* as I know⟩ 4 : to an advanced point or extent : a long way ⟨a field in which one can go *far*⟩ [Middle English *fer,* from Old English *feorr*] — **by far** : GREATLY — **far and away** : DECIDEDLY

²**far** adj **farther** or **further; farthest** or **furthest** 1 : remote in space or time 2 : LONG 1 ⟨a *far* journey⟩ 3 : the more distant of two ⟨on the *far* side of the lake⟩ SYN see DISTANT

far·ad \'far-ˌad, -əd\ n : the unit of capacitance equal to the capacitance of a capacitor between whose plates there appears a potential of one volt when it is charged by one coulomb of electricity [Michael *Faraday*]

far·away \'fär-ə-ˌwā\ adj 1 : DISTANT 1 ⟨*faraway* lands⟩ 2 : PENSIVE 1, DREAMY ⟨a *faraway* look⟩

farce \'färs\ n 1 : a play about ridiculous and absurd situations intended to make people laugh 2 : humor characteristic of a farce 3 : a ridiculous action, display, or pretense [Middle French, "stuffing, farce", from Latin *farcire* "to stuff"] — **far·ci·cal** \'fär-si-kəl\ adj

far·ceur \fär-'sər\ n : a writer or actor of farce [French]

¹**fare** \'faər, 'feər\ vi 1 : GO, TRAVEL ⟨*fare* forth on a journey⟩ 2 : to get along : SUCCEED ⟨how did you *fare*⟩ 3 : EAT 2, DINE [Old English *faran*]

²**fare** n 1 : the money a person pays to travel on a public conveyance 2 : a person paying a fare 3 : FOOD 3

¹**fare·well** \faər-'wel, feər-\ imperative verb : get along well — used interjectionally to or by one departing

²**farewell** n 1 : a wish of welfare at parting : GOOD-BYE 2 : an act of departure : LEAVE-TAKING

³**fare·well** \'faər-ˌwel, 'feər-\ adj : FINAL

far–fetched \'fär-'fecht\ adj : not natural or plausible : IMPROBABLE

far–flung \'fär-'fləng\ adj : covering a great area ⟨a *far-flung* empire⟩

fa·ri·na \fə-'rē-nə\ n : a fine meal (as of nuts or a cereal grain) used especially as a breakfast cereal [Latin, "meal, flour", from *far* "spelt"]

\ə\ abut   \ng\ sing
\ər\ further   \ō\ bone
\a\ mat   \ȯ\ saw
\ā\ take   \ȯi\ coin
\ä\ cot, cart   \th\ thin
\au̇\ out   \th\ this
\ch\ chin   \ü\ food
\e\ pet   \u̇\ foot
\ē\ easy   \y\ yet
\g\ go   \yü\ few
\i\ tip   \yu̇\ cure
\ī\ life   \zh\ vision
\j\ job

far·i·na·ceous \ˌfar-ə-'nā-shəs\ *adj* **1** : containing or rich in starch **2** : having a mealy texture or surface

¹farm \'färm\ *n* **1 a** : a tract of land devoted to raising crops or livestock **b** : a tract of water used for the cultivation of aquatic animals ⟨oyster *farms*⟩ **2** : a minor-league subsidiary of a major-league baseball club to which recruits are assigned for training [Middle English *ferme* "rent, lease", from Old French, "lease", from *fermer* "to make a contract", from Latin *firmare* "to make firm", from *firmus* "firm"]

²farm *vb* **1** : to turn over for performance or use usually on contract or for an agreed payment — usually used with *out* **2 a** : to devote to agriculture ⟨*farm* 60 hectares⟩ **b** : to engage in raising crops or livestock — **farm·er** *n*

farm·hand \'färm-ˌhand\ *n* : a farm laborer

farm·house \-ˌhaus\ *n* : a dwelling on a farm

farm·ing \'fär-ming\ *n* : the occupation or business of a person who farms : AGRICULTURE

farm·land \'färm-ˌland\ *n* : land used or suitable for farming

farm·stead \-ˌsted\ *n* : the building and adjacent service areas of a farm

farm·yard \-ˌyärd\ *n* : space around or enclosed by farm buildings

faro \'faər-ō, 'feər-\ *n, pl* **far·os** : a gambling game in which players bet on cards drawn from a dealing box [probably alteration of earlier *pharaoh*]

far–off \'fär-'óf\ *adj* : remote in time or space

fa·rouche \fə-'rüsh\ *adj* : marked by shyness and lack of polish; *also* : UNRESTRAINED 1, WILD [French, "wild, shy", from Late Latin *forasticus* "belonging outside", from Latin *foras* "outdoors"]

far–out \'fär-'aut\ *adj* : departing considerably from the conventional or traditional : EXTREME

far·ra·go \fə-'räg-ō, -'rā-gō\ *n, pl* **-goes** : a confused collection : MIXTURE [Latin, "mixed fodder, mixture", from *far* "spelt"]

far–reach·ing \'fär-'rē-ching\ *adj* : having a wide range, influence, or effect ⟨a *far-reaching* decision⟩

far·ri·er \'far-ē-ər\ *n* : a blacksmith who shoes horses [Middle French *ferrour*, derived from Latin *ferrum* iron]

¹far·row \'far-ō\ *vb* : to give birth to pigs [Middle English *farwen*, derived from Old English *fearh* "young pig"]

²farrow *n* : a litter of pigs

far·see·ing \'fär-'sē-ing\ *adj* : FARSIGHTED

Far·si \'fär-sē\ *n* : PERSIAN 2b

far·sight·ed \-'sīt-əd\ *adj* **1** : able to see distant things more clearly than near ones **2** : able to judge how something will work out in the future — **far·sight·ed·ly** *adv* — **far·sight·ed·ness** *n*

¹far·ther \'fär-thər\ *adv* **1** : at or to a greater distance or more advanced point **2** : more completely [Middle English *ferther*, alteration of *further*]

²farther *adj* **1** : more distant : REMOTER **2** : ²FURTHER 2

far·ther·most \-ˌmōst\ *adj* : most distant : FARTHEST

¹far·thest \'fär-thəst\ *adj* : most distant in space or time

²farthest *adv* **1** : to or at the greatest distance in space or time : REMOTEST **2** : to the most advanced point **3** : by the greatest degree or extent : MOST

far·thing \'fär-thing\ *n* : a former British monetary unit equal to ¼ of a penny; *also* : a coin representing this unit [Old English *feorthung*]

far·thin·gale \'fär-thən-ˌgāl, -thing-\ *n* : a support (as of hoops) worn especially in the 16th century to swell out a skirt [Middle French *verdugale*, from Spanish *verdugado*, from *verdugo* "young shoot of a tree", from *verde* "green", from Latin *viridis*]

fas·ces \'fas-ˌēz\ *n sing or pl* : a bundle of rods surrounding an ax with projecting blade borne before ancient Roman magistrates as a badge of authority [Latin, from plural of *fascis* "bundle"]

fas·cia \'fash-ə, 'fash-ē-ə, 'fāsh-\ *n, pl* **fas·ci·ae** \-ē-ˌē\ *or* **fas·cias** : a sheet of connective tissue covering or binding together body structures [Latin, "band, bandage"]

fas·ci·cle \'fas-i-kəl\ *n* **1** : a small bundle or cluster (as of flowers or roots) **2** : one of the divisions of a book published in parts [Latin *fasciculus*, from *fascis* "bundle"] — **fas·ci·cled** \-kəld\ *adj* — **fas·cic·u·lar** \fə-'sik-yə-lər, fa-\ *adj* — **fas·cic·u·late** \-lət\ *adj*

fas·ci·nate \'fas-n-ˌāt\ *vb* **1** : to grip the attention of especially so as to take away the power to move, act, or think for oneself **2** : to allure and hold by charming qualities : CAPTIVATE [Latin *fascinare*, from *fascinum* "witchcraft"] — **fas·ci·na·tion** \ˌfas-n-'ā-shən\ *n*

fas·ci·na·tor \'fas-n-ˌāt-ər\ *n* **1** : one that fascinates **2** : a crocheted head covering for women

fas·cine \fa-'sēn, fə-\ *n* : a long bundle of sticks of wood bound together and used for such purposes as filling ditches and making parapets [French, from Latin *fascina*, from *fascis* "bundle"]

fas·cism \'fash-ˌiz-əm\ *n, often cap* **1** : the principles of an Italian political organization headed by Mussolini that governed Italy 1922–1943 and that advocated nationalism, a centralized dictatorial regime, severe economic and social regimentation, and forcible suppression of opposition; *also* : the movement advocating or the regime following these principles **2** : a political philosophy, movement, or regime (as Nazism) similar to Fascism [Italian *fascismo*, from *fascio* "bundle, fasces, group", from Latin *fascis* "bundle" and *fasces* "fasces"] — **fas·cist** \'fash-əst\ *n or adj, often cap* — **fas·cis·tic** \fa-'shis-tik\ *adj, often cap* □ ORIGIN The English words *fascism* and *fascist* are borrowings from Italian *fascismo* and *fascista,* derivatives of *fascio,* "bundle, fasces, group". *Fascista* was first used in 1919, when Benito Mussolini organized a political group, the *Partito Nazionale Fascista* ("National Fascist Party"), to oppose communism. The fasces, a bundle of rods with an ax among them, was taken to symbolize the power of many people united and obedient to the single authority of the state. The English word *fascist* was first used for members of the Italian Fascisti, but it has since been generalized to those of similar beliefs.

Fa·sci·sta \fä-'shē-stä\ *n, pl* **-sti** \-stē\ : a member of the Italian Fascist movement [Italian]

¹fash·ion \'fash-ən\ *n* **1** : the make or form of something **2** : MANNER, WAY ⟨behaving in a strange *fashion*⟩ **3 a** : a prevailing custom, usage, or style **b** : the prevailing style (as in dress) during a particular time or among an especially innovative group ⟨*fashions* in women's hats⟩ [Old French *façon* "shape, manner", from Latin *factio* "act of making, faction"] □ SYN STYLE, MODE, VOGUE: FASHION may apply to any way of dressing, behaving, writing, or performing that is favored at any one time or place; STYLE often implies the fashion approved by the wealthy or socially prominent; MODE suggests the fashion among those anxious to appear elegant and sophisticated; VOGUE applies to a temporary widespread style. — **after a fashion** : in a rough or approximate way ⟨did the job after a *fashion*⟩

²fashion *vt* **fash·ioned; fash·ion·ing** \'fash-ning, -ə-ning\ : to give shape or form to : MOLD, CONSTRUCT — **fash·ion·er** \'fash-nər, -ə-nər\ *n*

fash·ion·able \'fash-nə-bəl, -ə-nə-\ *adj* **1 a** : following the fashion or established style : STYLISH ⟨*fashionable* clothes⟩ **b** : dressing or behaving according to fashion ⟨*fashionable* people⟩ **2** : of or relating to the world of fashion : popular among those who conform to fashion ⟨*fashionable* stores⟩ — **fash·ion·able·ness** *n* — **fash·ion·ably** \-blē\ *adj*

¹fast \'fast\ *adj* **1 a** : firmly fixed or bound **b** : tightly shut **c** : adhering firmly **d** : UNCHANGEABLE ⟨hard and *fast* rules⟩ **2** : firmly loyal ⟨became *fast* friends⟩ **3 a** : characterized by quick motion, operation, or effect :

fasces

(1) : moving or able to move rapidly : SWIFT (2) : taking a comparatively short time ⟨a *fast* trip⟩ (3) : imparting quickness of motion ⟨a *fast* bowler⟩ **b** : conducive to rapidity of play or action ⟨a *fast* track⟩ **c** (1) : indicating ahead of the correct time (2) : according to daylight saving time **d** : contributing to a shortening of photographic exposure time ⟨a *fast* lens⟩ **4** : not easily loosened or disturbed **5 a** : permanently dyed **b** : proof against fading by a particular agency **6 a** : DISSIPATED, WILD **b** : daringly unconventional especially in sexual matters [Old English *fæst*] □ SYN RAPID, SWIFT, FLEET: FAST and RAPID are very close in meaning but FAST applies especially to the thing that moves ⟨a *fast* horse⟩ and RAPID to the movement ⟨a series of *rapid* blows⟩ SWIFT suggests great rapidity together with ease of movement ⟨*swift* play of the imagination⟩ FLEET adds an implication of lightness and nimbleness ⟨*fleet* little ponies⟩

²fast *adv* **1** : in a fast or fixed manner ⟨stuck *fast* in the mud⟩ **2** : SOUNDLY, DEEPLY ⟨*fast* asleep⟩ **3 a** : in a rapid manner **b** : in quick succession **4** : in a dissipated manner : RECKLESSLY

³fast *vi* **1** : to eat no food **2** : to eat sparingly or avoid some foods [Old English *fæstan*]

⁴fast *n* **1** : the act or practice of fasting **2** : a time of fasting

fast·back \'fast-,bak, 'fas-\ *n* : an automobile roof with a long curving downward slope to the rear; *also* : an automobile with such a roof

fast·ball *n* : a baseball pitch thrown at full speed

fast break *n* : a quick offensive drive toward a goal (as in basketball) in an attempt to score before the defense can get into position

fas·ten \'fas-n\ *vb* **fas·tened**; **fas·ten·ing** \'fas-ning, -n-ing\ **1** : to attach or join by or as if by pinning, tying, or nailing ⟨*fastened* clothes on a line⟩ ⟨*fastened* the blame on the runaway⟩ **2** : to make fast : fix securely ⟨*fasten* a door⟩ **3** : to fix or set steadily ⟨*fasten* one's eyes on the view⟩ **4** : to become fixed or joined ⟨a shoe that *fastens* with a buckle⟩ — **fas·ten·er** \'fas-nər, -n-ər\ *n*

fas·ten·ing \'fas-ning, -n-ing\ *n* : something that fastens : FASTENER

¹fast–forward \,fast-'fȯr-wərd\ *n* **1** : a function of a tape recorder that advances a tape at a speed that is higher than normal **2** : a state of rapid advancement

²fast–forward *vb* **1** : to advance (a tape) at a speed that is higher than normal **2** : to proceed rapidly especially in time

fas·tid·i·ous \fa-'stid-ē-əs\ *adj* : very difficult to please especially in matters of taste or cleanliness [Latin *fastidiosus* "disgusted, fastidious", from *fastidium* "disgust"] — **fas·tid·i·ous·ly** *adv* — **fas·tid·i·ous·ness** *n*

fast lane *n* **1** : a traffic lane used by vehicles moving at higher speeds **2** : a way of life marked by a fast pace and the pursuit of immediate gratification **3** : FAST TRACK — **fast–lane** *adj*

fast·ness \'fast-nəs, 'fas-\ *n* **1** : the quality or state of being fast **2** : a fortified or secure place : STRONGHOLD

¹fast–track \'fast-,trak, 'fas-\ *adj* : of, relating to, or moving along a fast track

²fast–track *vb* : to speed up the processing or production of in order to meet a goal — **fast–track·er** \-,trak-ər\ *n*

fast track *n* : a course leading to rapid advancement or success

¹fat \'fat\ *adj* **fat·ter**; **fat·test** **1 a** : PLUMP, FLESHY **b** : OILY 2, GREASY **2** : well stocked : ABUNDANT ⟨a *fat* purse⟩ **3** : richly rewarding : PROFITABLE [Old English *fætt*, from *fætan* "to cram"] — **fat·ness** *n*

²fat *n* **1** : animal tissue consisting chiefly of cells containing much greasy or oily matter **2 a** : any of numerous compounds of carbon, hydrogen, and oxygen that are esters of glycerol and fatty acids, the chief constituents of plant and animal fat, and a major class of ener-

gy-rich food, and that are soluble in organic solvents but not in water **b** : a solid or semisolid fat (as lard) as distinguished from an oil **3** : the best or richest part ⟨lived on the *fat* of the land⟩ **4** : excess matter

³fat *vt* **fat·ted**; **fat·ting** : to make fat : FATTEN

fa·tal \'fāt-l\ *adj* **1** : causing death or ruin ⟨a *fatal* accident⟩ **2** : determining one's fate ⟨a *fatal* day in our lives⟩ [Latin *fatalis*, from *fatum* "fate"] SYN see DEADLY — **fa·tal·ly** \-l-ē\ *adv*

fa·tal·ism \'fāt-l-,iz-əm\ *n* : the belief that events are determined in advance by powers beyond human control; *also* : the attitude of mind of a person holding this belief — **fa·tal·ist** \-l-əst\ *n* — **fa·tal·is·tic** \,fāt-l-'is-tik\ *adj* — **fa·tal·is·ti·cal·ly** \-'is-ti-kə-lē, -klē\ *adv*

fa·tal·i·ty \fā-'tal-ət-ē, fə-\ *n, pl* **-ties** **1 a** : the quality or state of causing death : DEADLINESS **b** : the quality or condition of being destined for disaster **2** : FATE 1a **3** : a death resulting from a disaster or accident

fat·back \'fat-,bak\ *n* : a fatty strip from the back of the hog usually cured by salting and drying

fat body *n* : a mass of fatty tissue attached to each germ-cell producing gland in amphibians

¹fate \'fāt\ *n* **1 a** : a power beyond human control that is held to determine what happens : DESTINY ⟨blamed the failure on *fate*⟩ **b** *cap* : any of three goddesses of classical mythology who determine the course of human life **2** : something that happens as though determined by fate : FORTUNE ⟨it was their *fate* to outlive their children⟩ **3** : an unavoidable and often unpleasant outcome, condition, or end ⟨awaited news of the *fate* of the polar expedition⟩ **4** : DISASTER; *esp* : DEATH [Latin *fatum*, literally, "what has been spoken", from *fari* "to speak"] □ SYN FATE, DESTINY, LOT, DOOM mean a predetermined state or end. FATE implies an inevitable and usually adverse outcome or end; DESTINY implies something foreordained and usually suggests a great or notable course or end; LOT implies a distribution of success or happiness by fate or destiny according to blind chance; DOOM implies a grim or calamitous fate.

²fate *vt* : DESTINE 1; *also* : DOOM

fate·ful \'fāt-fəl\ *adj* **1** : having or marked by serious consequences : IMPORTANT ⟨a *fateful* decision⟩ ⟨that *fateful* day⟩ **2** : OMINOUS, PROPHETIC ⟨the *fateful* circling of the vultures overhead⟩ — **fate·ful·ly** \-fə-lē\ *adv* — **fate·ful·ness** *n*

¹fa·ther \'fäth-ər, 'fȧth-\ *n* **1 a** : a male parent **b** *cap* (1) : GOD 1 (2) : the first person of the Trinity **2** : FOREFATHER **3 a** : one who cares for another as a father might **b** : one deserving the respect and love given to a father **4** *often cap* : a pre-Scholastic Christian writer accepted by the church as an authoritative witness to its teaching and practice **5** : AUTHOR 2, ORIGINATOR **6** *often cap* : PRIEST — used especially as a title ⟨*Father* Smith⟩ **7** : one of the leading men (as of a city) — usually used in pl. [Old English *fæder*]

²father *vt* **fa·thered**; **fa·ther·ing** \'fäth-ring, 'fȧth-, -ə-ring\ **1 a** : BEGET **b** : to be the founder, producer, or author of **2** : to treat or care for as a father

fa·ther·hood \'fäth-ər-,hu̇d, 'fȧth-\ *n* : the condition of being a father

fa·ther–in–law \'fäth-rən-,lȯ, 'fȧth-, -ə-rən-,lȯ, -ərn-,lȯ\ *n, pl* **fathers–in–law** \'fäth-ər-zən-\ : the father of one's spouse

fa·ther·land \'fäth-ər-,land, 'fȧth-\ *n* **1** : one's native land **2** : the native land of one's ancestors

fa·ther·less \-ləs\ *adj* : having no father : ORPHAN

fa·ther·ly \-lē\ *adj* **1** : of or resembling a father ⟨a *fatherly* old man⟩ **2** : showing the affection or concern of a father ⟨*fatherly* advice⟩ — **fa·ther·li·ness** *n*

Father's Day *n* : the 3d Sunday in June appointed for the honoring of fathers

¹fath·om \'fath-əm\ *n* : a unit of length equal to 6 feet (about 1.83 meters) that is used especially for measur-

\ə\ abut		\ng\ sing
\ər\ further		\ō\ bone
\a\ mat		\ȯ\ saw
\ā\ take		\ȯi\ coin
\ä\ cot, cart		\th\ thin
\au̇\ out		\th\ this
\ch\ chin		\ü\ food
\e\ pet		\u̇\ foot
\ē\ easy		\y\ yet
\g\ go		\yü\ few
\i\ tip		\yu̇\ cure
\ī\ life		\zh\ vision
\j\ job		

ing the depth of water [Old English *fæthm* "outstretched arms, length of the outstretched arms"]

²**fathom** *vb* **1** : to measure by a sounding line : take
soundings; *also* : PROBE **2** : to penetrate and come to
understand (failed to *fathom* the problem) — **fath·om·
able** \'fath-ə-mə-bəl\ *adj*

Fa·thom·e·ter \fa-'thäm-ət-ər; 'fath-əm-ˌmēt-, 'fath-ə-ˌ\
trademark — used for a sonic depth finder

fath·om·less \'fath-əm-ləs\ *adj* : incapable of being fa-
thomed

¹**fa·tigue** \fə-'tēg\ *n* **1 a** : weariness from labor or exertion **b** : temporary loss of power to respond (as of a
sense organ) after prolonged stimulation **2 a** : manual
or menial work performed by military personnel **b** *pl* :
the uniform or work clothing worn on fatigue and in
the field **3** : the tendency of a material (as metal) to
break under repeated stress (as bending) [French,
from *fatiguer* "to fatigue", from Latin *fatigare*]

²**fatigue** *vb* **1** : to weary or become weary with labor or
exertion **2** : to induce a condition of fatigue in

fat·ling \'fat-ling\ *n* : a young animal fattened for
slaughter

fats·hed·era \fats-'hed-ə-rə, -'ed-\ *n* : a hybrid plant
grown as a houseplant for its glossy deeply lobed
leaves [New Latin *Fatsia,* genus of shrubs + *Hedera,*
genus of vines, from Latin, "ivy"]

fat–soluble *adj* : soluble in fats or fat solvents

fat·ten \'fat-n\ *vb* **fat·tened; fat·ten·ing** \'fat-ning, -n-
ing\ **1 a** : to make or become fat or fatter (cattle *fattening* on the range) **b** : to make larger (*fatten* profits)
2 : to make (as land) fertile : ENRICH — **fat·ten·er** \'fat-
nər, -n-ər\ *n*

fat·ty \'fat-ē\ *adj* **fat·ti·er; -est 1** : containing fat especially in unusual amounts; *also* : unduly stout **2** :
GREASY — **fat·ti·ly** \'fat-l-ē\ *adv* — **fat·ti·ness** \'fat-ē-
nəs\ *n*

fatty acid *n* : any of numerous saturated or unsaturated
acids that contain only carbon, hydrogen, and oxygen
and that occur naturally in the form of glycerides in
fats and various oils

fa·tu·ity \fə-'tü-ət-ē, fa-, -'tyü-\ *n, pl* **-ities** : FOOLISHNESS,
STUPIDITY (the *fatuity* of such a remark)

fat·u·ous \'fach-wəs, -ə-wəs\ *adj* : complacently or
inanely foolish : SILLY [Latin *fatuus*] — **fat·u·ous·ly**
adv — **fat·u·ous·ness** *n*

fau·bourg \fō-'bur\ *n* **1** : SUBURB 1; *esp* : a suburb of a
French city **2** : a city quarter [Middle French *faux-
bourg,* from Old French *forsborc,* from *fors* "outside" + *borc* "town"]

fau·ces \'fo-ˌsēz\ *n pl* : the narrow passage between the
soft palate and the base of the tongue that joins the
mouth to the pharynx [Latin, "throat, fauces"] — **fau-
cial** \'fo-shəl\ *adj*

fau·cet \'fo-sət, 'fäs-ət\ *n* : a fixture for drawing a liquid
(as from a pipe or cask) [Middle French *fausset*
"bung", from *fausser* "to damage", from Late Latin
falsare "to falsify", from *falsus* "false"] □ ORIGIN English *faucet* is descended from Latin *falsus,* "false". In
Late Latin a verb was formed from this adjective, *falsare,* "to falsify". In course of time it became French
fausser. In medieval French the verb developed new
meanings. As well as "to falsify", *fausser* could mean
"to be false to" or even "to damage or break". A cask
which is made to hold liquids usually has a hole
through which it may be emptied. Although this bunghole is present by intention, the stopper that plugs it
may be looked on a bit fancifully as piercing or breaking into the cask. So such a stopper was called a *fausset.* The English borrowing, *faucet,* was used not only
for the stopper in a cask but also for a fixture used to
draw liquid from a cask, pipe, or other container.

¹**fault** \'folt\ *n* **1 a** : a weakness in character : FAILING;
esp : a moral weakness less serious than a vice **b** : a
physical or intellectual imperfection or impairment
c : an error in a service in tennis **2 a** : a trivial misdeed

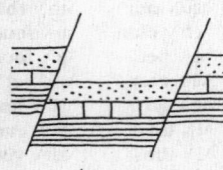

¹**fault 4**

b : MISTAKE 2 **3** : responsibility for wrongdoing or failure **4** : a fracture in the earth's crust accompanied by a
displacement of rock masses in a direction parallel to
the fracture [Old French *faute,* derived from Latin *fallere* "to deceive, disappoint"] □ SYN FAULT, FAILING,
FOIBLE, FRAILTY mean a weakness or imperfection of
character. FAULT applies to any failure, serious or trivial, to attain a standard of perfection in action, disposition, or habit; FAILING suggests a minor shortcoming in
character; FOIBLE implies a harmless or even endearing
weakness; FRAILTY implies weakness in the face of
temptation. — **at fault** : open to blame : RESPONSIBLE
— **to a fault** : EXCESSIVELY (generous *to a fault*)

²**fault** *vb* **1** : to commit a fault : ERR **2** : to fracture so as
to produce a geologic fault **3** : to find a fault in (could
not *fault* that argument)

fault·find·er \'folt-ˌfīn-dər\ *n* : a person who is inclined
to complain or criticize — **fault·find·ing** \-ding\ *n or
adj*

fault·less \'folt-ləs\ *adj* : free from fault : including no
error or imperfection : PERFECT — **fault·less·ly** *adv* —
fault·less·ness *n*

faulty \'fol-tē\ *adj* **fault·i·er; -est** : marked by fault,
blemish, or defect : IMPERFECT — **fault·i·ly** \-tə-lē\ *adj*
— **fault·i·ness** \-tē-nəs\ *n*

faun \'fon, 'fän\ *n* : an ancient Italian deity of fields and
herds represented as part goat and part man [Latin *faunus,* from *Faunus,* god of animals]

fau·na \'fon-ə, 'fän-\ *n, pl* **faunas** *also* **fau·nae** \-ˌē, -ˌī\ :
animals or animal life especially of a region, period, or
environment — compare FLORA [Late Latin *Fauna,* sister of Faunus, god of animals] — **fau·nal** \'fon-l, 'fän-\
adj — **fau·nal·ly** \-l-ē\ *adv*

fau·vism \'fō-ˌviz-əm\ *n, often cap* : a movement in
painting typified by the work of Matisse and characterized by vivid colors, free treatment of form, and a resulting vibrant and decorative effect [French *fau-
visme,* from *fauve* "wild animal"] — **fau·vist** \-vəst\
n, often cap

faux pas \fō-'pä\ *n, pl* **faux pas** \-'pä, -'päz\ : BLUNDER;
esp : a social blunder [French, literally, "false step"]

fa·va bean \'fäv-ə-\ *n* : BROAD BEAN [Italian *fava,* from
Latin *faba* "bean"]

fav·ism \'fäv-ˌiz-əm\ *n* : a hereditary condition especially of males of Mediterranean descent that involves
a severe allergic reaction to the broad bean or its pollen

¹**fa·vor** \'fā-vər\ *n* **1 a** : friendly regard shown toward
another especially by a superior (enjoyed the *favor* of
the king) **b** : APPROVAL, APPROBATION (look with *favor*
on a project) **c** : PARTIALITY (the judge showed *favor* to
the defendant) **d** : POPULARITY (a fad loses *favor* quickly) **2** : gracious kindness (treated the child with
favor); *also* : an act of such kindness **3 a** : a token of
love (as a ribbon) usually worn conspicuously **b** : a
small gift or decorative item given out at a party **4** : a
special privilege or right granted or conceded **5** *archaic* : LETTER **6** : BEHALF, INTEREST [Old French,
"friendly regard", from Latin, from *favēre* "to be favorable"] — **in favor of 1** : in accord or sympathy with
2 : in support of — **out of favor** : not now popular
(study seems *out of favor* today)

²**favor** *vt* **fa·vored; fa·vor·ing** \'fāv-ring, -ə-ring\ **1 a** : to
regard or treat with favor **b** (1) : to do a kindness for :
OBLIGE (2) : ENDOW (*favored* by nature) **c** : to treat
gently or carefully : SPARE (*favor* a lame leg) **2** : PREFER
1 **3 a** : to give support to : SUSTAIN **b** : to offer chances
for success to : FACILITATE (darkness *favors* attack) **4** :
to bear a resemblance to (children who *favor* their
parents) — **fa·vor·er** \'fā-vər-ər\ *n*

fa·vor·able \'fāv-rə-bəl, -ə-rə-, 'fā-vər-bəl\ *adj* **1** :
showing favor : APPROVING (a *favorable* opinion) **2** :
tending to promote or advance something (*favorable*
weather for the fair) — **fa·vor·able·ness** *n* — **fa·vor-
ably** \-blē\ *adv*

¹fa·vor·ite \'fāv-rət, -ə-rət\ *n* **1** : a person or a thing that is favored above others **2** : the contestant regarded as having the best chance to win [Italian *favorito*, past participle of *favorire* "to favor", from *favore* "favor", from Latin *favor*]

²favorite *adj* : being a favorite; *esp* : best-liked ⟨our *favorite* show⟩

favorite son *n* : a candidate supported by the delegates of his state at a presidential nominating convention

fa·vor·it·ism \'fāv-rət‚iz-əm, -ə-rət-\ *n* : unfairly favorable treatment of one or some to the neglect of others : PARTIALITY

¹fawn \'fȯn, 'fän\ *vt* **1** : to show affection — used especially of a dog **2** : to try to win favor by behavior that shows lack of self-respect [Old English *fagnian* "to rejoice", from *fægen* "glad, fain"] — **fawn·er** *n* — **fawn·ing·ly** \-ing-lē\ *adv*

²fawn *n* **1** : a young deer; *esp* : one in its first year **2** : a light grayish brown [Middle French *feon, faon* "young of an animal", derived from Latin *fetus* "offspring"]

fax \'faks\ *n* **1** : FACSIMILE **2** : a machine used to send or receive facsimile communications **3** : a facsimile communication — **fax** *vb*

¹fay \'fā\ *n* **1** : FAIRY **2** : ELF [Middle French *feie, fee*]

²fay *adj* : ELFIN 2

faze \'fāz\ *also* **feaze** \'fēz, 'fāz\ *vt* : to disturb the composure or courage of : DAUNT [Old English *fēsian* "to drive away"]

F clef *n* : BASS CLEF

fe·al·ty \'fē-əl-tē, 'fēl-\ *n* **1** : the loyalty of a feudal vassal to his lord **2** : ALLEGIANCE 2 [Old French *feelté, fealté*, from Latin *fidelitas* "fidelity"] SYN see FIDELITY

¹fear \'fiər\ *n* **1 a** : an unpleasant often strong emotion caused by expectation or awareness of danger **b** : an instance of fear or a state marked by fear **2** : anxious concern : WORRY **3** : reverential awe especially toward God [Old English *fǣr* "sudden danger"] □ SYN FEAR, DREAD, FRIGHT, PANIC mean a painful emotion in the presence or expectation of danger. FEAR is the general term and implies great anxiety and usually loss of courage; DREAD adds the idea of intense aversion and reluctance to face something; FRIGHT suggests the shock of sudden, startling appearance of danger or threat; PANIC implies completely dominating fear that causes hysterical activity.

²fear *vb* **1** : to have a reverential awe of ⟨*fear* God⟩ **2** : to be afraid of : have fear **3** : to be apprehensive ⟨*feared* they would miss the train⟩ — **fear·er** *n*

fear·ful \'fiər-fəl\ *adj* **1** : causing fear ⟨the *fearful* roar of a lion⟩ **2** : filled with fear ⟨*fearful* of danger⟩ **3** : showing or caused by fear ⟨a *fearful* glance⟩ **4** : extremely bad, large, or intense ⟨*fearful* cold⟩ — **fear·ful·ly** \-fə-lē\ *adv* — **fear·ful·ness** *n*

fear·less \'fiər-ləs\ *adj* : free from fear : BRAVE — **fear·less·ly** *adv* — **fear·less·ness** *n*

fear·some \'fiər-səm\ *adj* **1** : causing fear **2** : TIMID — **fear·some·ly** *adv* — **fear·some·ness** *n*

fea·si·ble \'fē-zə-bəl\ *adj* **1** : capable of being done or carried out ⟨a *feasible* plan⟩ **2** : capable of being used or dealt with successfully : SUITABLE ⟨a *feasible* new energy source⟩ **3** : PLAUSIBLE 1, LIKELY ⟨a *feasible* story⟩ [Middle French *faisible*, from *fais-*, stem of *faire* "to make, do", from Latin *facere*] SYN see POSSIBLE — **fea·si·bil·i·ty** \‚fē-zə-'bil-ət-ē\ *n* — **fea·si·ble·ness** \'fē-zə-bəl-nəs\ *n* — **fea·si·bly** \-blē\ *adv*

¹feast \'fēst\ *n* **1 a** : an elaborate meal : BANQUET **b** : something that gives great pleasure ⟨a *feast* of wit⟩ **2** : a religious festival : HOLY DAY [Old French *feste* "festival", from Latin *festum*, from *festus* "solemn, festal"]

²feast *vb* **1** : to eat plentifully : participate in a feast **2** : to entertain with rich and plentiful food — **feast·er** *n* — **feast one's eyes on** : to take pleasure in (something seen) ⟨*feast one's eyes on* autumn colors⟩

¹feat \'fēt\ *adj* **1** *archaic* : BECOMING, NEAT **2** *archaic* : SKILLFUL, DEXTEROUS [Middle French *fait*, past participle of *faire* "to make, do"]

²feat *n* **1** : ACT 1, DEED **2 a** : a deed notable especially for courage **b** : an act or product of skill, endurance, or ingenuity [Middle French *fait*, from Latin *factum*, from *facere* "to make, do"] □ SYN FEAT, EXPLOIT, ACHIEVEMENT mean a remarkable deed. FEAT implies strength or dexterity or daring in achieving; EXPLOIT applies to an adventurous or heroic act that brings fame; ACHIEVEMENT implies hard-won success in the face of difficulty or opposition.

¹feath·er \'feth-ər\ *n* **1 a** : one of the light horny outgrowths that form the external covering of the body of a bird **b** : the vane of an arrow **2 a** : KIND 1b, SORT **b** : CLOTHING, DRESS **c** (1) : CONDITION 5 (2) : MOOD **3** : a feathery tuft or fringe of hair **4** : a projecting strip, rib, fin, or flange **5** : the act of feathering an oar [Old English *fether*] — **feath·ered** \-ərd\ *adj* — **feath·er·less** \'feth-ər-ləs\ *adj* — **a feather in one's cap** : a mark of distinction : HONOR

²feather *vb* **feath·ered; feath·er·ing** \'feth-ring, -ə-ring\ **1 a** : to furnish (as an arrow) with feathers **b** : to cover, clothe, or adorn with feathers **2 a** : to turn (an oar blade) almost horizontal when lifting from the water at the end of a stroke in order to reduce air resistance while moving it forward for the next stroke **b** : to rotate (the blades of an aircraft propeller) about their base-to-tip axis in order to decrease wind resistance **3** : to grow or form feathers **4** : to move, spread, or grow like feathers — **feather one's nest** : to provide for oneself especially by taking advantage of a position of trust

feath·er bed \'feth-ər-‚bed\ *n* : a mattress filled with feathers; *also* : a bed with such a mattress

feath·er·bed·ding \-‚bed-ing\ *n* : the requiring of an employer usually under a union rule or safety statute to employ more workers than are needed or to limit production

feath·er·brain \'feth-ər-‚brān\ *n* : a foolish scatterbrained person — **feath·er·brained** \‚feth-ər-'brānd\ *adj*

feath·er·edge \'feth-ə-‚rej, ‚feth-ə-'\ *n* : a very thin sharp edge; *esp* : one that is easily broken or bent — **featheredge** *vt*

feath·er·weight \-ər-‚wāt\ *n* **1** : one that is very light in weight; *esp* : a boxer in a weight division having the approximate range of 54 to 57 kilograms **2** : a person of limited intelligence or effectiveness

feath·ery \'feth-re, -ə-rē\ *adj* : resembling, suggesting, or covered with feathers

¹fea·ture \'fē-chər\ *n* **1 a** : the shape or appearance of the face ⟨stern of *feature*⟩ **b** : a single part of the face (as the nose or the mouth) **2** : something especially noticeable : a prominent part or detail : CHARACTERISTIC ⟨such earth *features* as mountains⟩ **3** : a main or outstanding attraction: as **a** : the principal motion picture on a program **b** : a special column or section in a newspaper or magazine [Middle French *feture*, from Latin *factura* "act of making", from *facere* "to make, do"]

²feature *vb* **fea·tured; fea·tur·ing** \'fēch-ring, -ə-ring\ **1** : to picture in the mind : IMAGINE ⟨*feature* wearing such a hat⟩ **2** : to give special prominence to ⟨*feature* a story in a newspaper⟩ **3** : to play an important part

fea·ture·less \'fē-chər-ləs\ *adj* : having no distinctive features

feaze \'fēz, 'fāz\ *variant of* FAZE

feb·ri·fuge \'feb-rə-‚fyüj\ *n* : a medicine for relieving fever [French *fébrifuge*, derived from Latin *febris* "fever" + *fugare* "to put to flight"] — **febrifuge** *adj*

fe·brile \'feb-‚rīl *also* 'fēb-\ *adj* : affected with or as if with fever : FEVERISH [Medieval Latin *febrilis*, from Latin *febris* "fever"]

Feb·ru·ary \'feb-yə-‚wer-ē, 'feb-ə-, 'feb-rə-\ *n* : the 2d month of the year [Latin *Februarius*, from *Februa*, a festival held during the month]

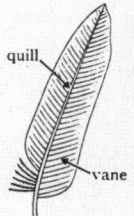

¹feather 1a

quill

vane

\ə\ abut	\ng\ sing
\ər\ further	\ō\ bone
\a\ mat	\ȯ\ saw
\ā\ take	\ȯi\ coin
\ä\ cot, cart	\th\ thin
\au̇\ out	\th\ this
\ch\ chin	\ü\ food
\e\ pet	\u̇\ foot
\ē\ easy	\y\ yet
\g\ go	\yü\ few
\i\ tip	\yu̇\ cure
\ī\ life	\zh\ vision
\j\ job	

fe·ces *also* **fae·ces** \'fē-ˌsēz\ *n pl* : bodily waste discharged through the anus : EXCREMENT [Middle English, "sediment, dregs", from Latin *faeces,* pl. of *faex*] — **fe·cal** \'fē-kəl\ *adj*

feck·less \'fek-ləs\ *adj* **1** : INEFFECTUAL, WEAK **2** : lacking qualities needed for efficiency or success [Scottish *feck* "effect", from Middle English *fek,* alteration of *effect*] — **feck·less·ly** *adv* — **feck·less·ness** *n*

fe·cund \'fek-ənd, 'fēk-\ *adj* **1** : fruitful in offspring or vegetation : PROLIFIC **2** : intellectually creative to a marked degree [Middle French *fecond,* from Latin *fecundus*] SYN see FERTILE — **fe·cun·di·ty** \fi-'kən-dət-ē\ *n*

fe·cun·date \'fek-ən-ˌdāt, 'fē-kən-\ *vt* : FERTILIZE — **fe·cun·da·tion** \ˌfek-ən-'dā-shən, ˌfē-kən-\ *n*

fed·er·al \'fed-rəl, -ə-rəl\ *adj* **1 a** : formed by a compact between political units that give up individual sovereignty to a central authority but retain certain limited powers **b** : of or being a form of government in which power is distributed between a central authority and constituent territorial units **c** : of or relating to the central government of a federation **2** *often cap* : FEDERALIST **3** *often cap* : of, relating to, or loyal to the federal government or the Union armies of the United States in the American Civil War [Latin *foeder-, foedus* "compact, league"] — **fed·er·al·ly** \-ē\ *adv*

Federal *n* **1** : a supporter of the government of the United States in the Civil War; *esp* : a soldier in the federal armies **2** : a federal agent or officer

federal district *n* : a district (as the District of Columbia) set apart as the seat of the central government of a federation

fed·er·al·ism \'fed-rə-ˌliz-əm, -ə-rə-\ *n* **1 a** *often cap* : the federal principle of organization **b** : support or advocacy of this principle **2** *cap* : the principles of the Federalists

fed·er·al·ist \-ləst\ *n* **1** : an advocate of federalism; *esp, often cap* : an advocate of a federal union between the American colonies after the Revolution and of the adoption of the United States Constitution **2** *cap* : a member of a major political party in the early years of the United States favoring a strong centralized national government — **federalist** *adj, often cap*

fed·er·al·ize \'fed-rə-ˌliz, -ə-rə-\ *vt* **1** : to unite in or under a federal system **2** : to bring under the jurisdiction of a federal government — **fed·er·al·i·za·tion** \ˌfed-rə-lə-'zā-shən, -ə-rə-\ *n*

Federal Reserve Bank *n* : a bank of the Federal Reserve system

Federal Reserve system *n* : a system of 12 central banks in the United States that serve as a depository for reserves of affiliated banks, engage in rediscounting, and serve as a clearinghouse for checks

fed·er·ate \'fed-ə-ˌrāt\ *vb* : to join in a federation

fed·er·a·tion \ˌfed-ə-'rā-shən\ *n* **1** : the act of federating; *esp* : the formation of a federal union **2** : something formed by federation: as **a** : a federal government **b** : a union of organizations

fed·er·a·tive \'fed-ə-ˌrāt-iv, 'fed-rət-, -ə-rət-\ *adj* : involving or arising from federation

fe·do·ra \fi-'dōr-ə, -'dȯr-\ *n* : a low soft felt hat with the crown creased lengthwise [*Fédora* (1882), drama by V. Sardou in which a type of fedora was introduced]

fed up *adj* : utterly worn out and disgusted ⟨*fed up* with their mistakes⟩

fedora

fee \'fē\ *n* **1 a** : an estate in land held from a feudal lord in return for homage and service paid him **b** : an inherited or heritable estate in land **2 a** : a fixed charge ⟨an admission *fee*⟩ ⟨license *fees*⟩ **b** : a charge for a professional service ⟨a doctor's *fees*⟩ **c** : GRATUITY, TIP [Old French *fé, fief,* of Germanic origin] SYN see WAGE

fee·ble \'fē-bəl\ *adj* **fee·bler** \-bə-lər, -blər\; **-blest** \-bə-ləst, -bləst\ **1 a** : greatly deficient in physical strength ⟨a *feeble* invalid⟩ **b** : showing weakness ⟨*feeble* steps⟩ **2** : not strong or effective (as in quality,

character, or mind) : INADEQUATE ⟨*feeble* imagery⟩ ⟨a *feeble* attempt⟩ [Old French *feble,* from Latin *flebilis* "lamentable, wretched", from *flere* "to weep"] — **fee·ble·ness** \-bəl-nəs\ *n* — **fee·bly** \-blē\ *adv*

fee·ble-mind·ed \ˌfē-bəl-'mīn-dəd\ *adj* : lacking normal intelligence : mentally deficient — **fee·ble-mind·ed·ness** *n*

¹feed \'fēd\ *vb* **fed** \'fed\; **feed·ing** **1 a** : to give food to **b** : to give as food **c** : to consume food : EAT **d** : PREY — used with *on, upon,* or *off* **2 a** : to furnish with something essential to growth, sustenance, or operation **b** : to become nourished or satisfied as if by food **3** : to give satisfaction to : GRATIFY ⟨praise only *fed* their vanity⟩ **4 a** : to supply (as material) for use or consumption **b** : to supply (a signal) to an electronic circuit **5** : to supply (a performer) with cues and situations that make a role more effective [Old English *fēdan*]

²feed *n* **1 a** : an act of eating **b** : MEAL; *esp* : a large meal **2 a** : food for livestock **b** : the amount given at one feeding **3 a** : material supplied (as to a furnace) **b** : a mechanism by which the action of feeding is effected

feed·back \'fēd-ˌbak\ *n* **1** : the return to the input of a part of the output of a machine, system, or process **2** : transmission to the original or controlling source of information about an action or process ⟨asked for student *feedback* about course content⟩; *also* : the information so transmitted

feed·er \'fēd-ər\ *n* : one that feeds: as **a** : a device or apparatus for supplying food **b** : TRIBUTARY **c** : a source of supply **d** : an animal being fattened or suitable for fattening **e** : an actor or role that serves as a foil for another — **feeder** *adj*

feed·lot \'fēd-ˌlät\ *n* : a plot of land on which cattle are fattened for market

feed·stuff \-ˌstəf\ *n* : FEED 2a; *also* : any of the nutrients in an animal ration

¹feel \'fēl\ *vb* **felt** \'felt\; **feel·ing** **1 a** : to perceive as a result of physical contact ⟨*feel* a blow⟩ **b** : to examine or test by touching : HANDLE ⟨*feel* a fabric with one's fingers⟩ **2 a** : EXPERIENCE ⟨*felt* their scorn⟩ **b** : to suffer from ⟨*feel* the heat⟩ **3** : to ascertain by cautious trial — often used with *out* **4 a** : to be aware or aware of ⟨*feel* the joy of victory⟩ **b** : BELIEVE 4, THINK **5** : to search for something with the fingers **6** : to seem especially to the sense of touch ⟨*feels* like wool⟩ **7** : to have sympathy or pity ⟨I *feel* for you⟩ [Old English *fēlan*] — **feel in one's bones** : to be sure for no evident reason

²feel *n* **1** : the sense of touch **2** : SENSATION, FEELING ⟨success brought them a *feel* of power⟩ **3** : the quality of a thing as imparted through touch

feel·er \'fē-lər\ *n* **1** : one that feels; *esp* : a movable organ (as an antenna) of an animal that usually functions for touch **2** : a proposal or remark made to find out the views of other people

feel-good \'fēl-ˌgůd\ *adj* : relating to or promoting an often false sense of satisfaction or well-being

¹feel·ing \'fē-ling\ *n* **1 a** : a sense whose receptors are chiefly in the skin and by which the hardness or softness, hotness or coldness, or heaviness or lightness of things is determined; *esp* : TOUCH 3 **b** : a sensation experienced through this sense **2 a** : an often indefinite state of mind ⟨a *feeling* of loneliness⟩; *also* : such a state with regard to someone or something ⟨a *feeling* of dislike⟩ **b** *pl* : general emotional condition : SENSIBILITIES ⟨hurt one's *feelings*⟩ **3 a** : the overall quality of one's awareness : conscious recognition : SENSE **4 a** : OPINION, BELIEF ⟨it's my *feeling* we will win⟩ **b** : unreasoned attitude : SENTIMENT ⟨public *feeling* was aroused by the crime⟩ **5** : capacity to respond emotionally especially with the higher emotions : SYMPATHY **6** : the quality of a work of art that conveys the emotion of the artist □ SYN EMOTION, SENTIMENT, PASSION: FEELING applies to any response or awareness marked by pleasure, pain, attraction, or repulsion; it may suggest the existence of a response without implying anything definite about its nature or intensity; EMOTION implies a clearly defined feeling and usually greater excitement or agitation; SENTIMENT may imply emotion inspired by an idea or belief ⟨argued more from grounds of moral *sentiment* than cold logic⟩ PASSION suggests a very powerful or controlling emotion.

²**feeling** *adj* : SENSITIVE 1; *esp* : easily moved emotionally — **feel·ing·ly** \'fē-ling-lē\ *adv* — **feel·ing·ness** *n*

feet *pl of* FOOT

feet·first \'fēt-'fərst\ *adv* : with the feet foremost ⟨jumped into the water *feetfirst*⟩

feign \'fān\ *vb* 1 : to give a false appearance of : SHAM ⟨*feign* illness⟩ 2 : to assert as if true : PRETEND ⟨*feign* an excuse⟩ [Old French *feindre*, from Latin *fingere* "to shape, feign"] — **feign·er** *n*

feint \'fānt\ *n* : something feigned; *esp* : a mock blow or attack at one point in order to distract attention from the point one really intends to attack [French *feinte*, from *feindre* "to feign"] — **feint** *vi*

feist \'fīst\ *n, chiefly dialect* : a small dog [obsolete *fisting hound*, from obsolete *fist* "to break wind"]

feisty \'fī-stē\ *adj* **feist·i·er; -est** : SCRAPPY

feld·spar \'feld-,spär, 'fel-\ *n* : any of a group of crystalline minerals that consist of silicates of aluminum with either potassium, sodium, calcium, or barium and that are an essential constituent of nearly all crystalline rocks [German *feldspat*, from *feld* "field" + *spat* "spar"]

fe·lic·i·tate \fi-'lis-ə-,tāt\ *vt* : to offer congratulations to — **fe·lic·i·ta·tion** \-,lis-ə-'tā-shən\ *n* — **fe·lic·i·ta·tor** \-'lis-ə-,tāt-ər\ *n*

fe·lic·i·tous \fi-'lis-ət-əs\ *adj* 1 : suitably expressed : APT ⟨*felicitous* wording⟩ 2 : having a talent for apt expression ⟨a *felicitous* speaker⟩ — **fe·lic·i·tous·ly** *adv* — **fe·lic·i·tous·ness** *n*

fe·lic·i·ty \fi-'lis-ət-ē\ *n, pl* **-ties** 1 : the quality or state of being happy; *esp* : great happiness 2 : something that causes happiness 3 **a** : a talent for apt expression **b** : an apt expression [Middle French *félicité*, from Latin *felicitas*, from *felix* "fruitful, happy"]

fe·line \'fē-,līn\ *adj* 1 **a** : belonging to the family of soft-furred flesh-eating mammals that includes the cats, lions, tigers, leopards, pumas, and lynxes **b** : of or resembling a cat : characteristic of cats 2 **a** : SLY 1, TREACHEROUS **b** : STEALTHY 1 [Latin *felinus*, from *felis* "cat"] — **feline** *n*

¹**fell** \'fel\ *n* : ²HIDE, PELT [Old English]

²**fell** *vt* 1 **a** : to cut, beat, or knock down ⟨*fell* trees for lumber⟩ **b** : KILL 1 2 : to sew (a seam) by folding one edge under the other [Old English *fellan*] — **fell·able** \-ə-bəl\ *adj*

³**fell** *past of* FALL

⁴**fell** *adj* : FIERCE 1, CRUEL; *also* : GRAVE 1b [Old French *fel*, from Medieval Latin *fello* "villain, felon"]

fel·lah \'fel-ə, fə-'lä\ *n, pl* **fel·la·hin** \,fel-ə-'hēn, fə-,lä-'hēn\ : a peasant or agricultural laborer in Arab countries (as Egypt or Syria) [Arabic *fallāḥ*]

fel·low \'fel-ō\ *n* 1 : COMRADE 1a, ASSOCIATE 2 **a** : an equal in rank, power, or character : PEER **b** : one of a pair : MATE 3 : a member of an incorporated literary or scientific society 4 **a** : a male human being ⟨played cards with the *fellows*⟩ **b** : INDIVIDUAL 2, PERSON ⟨won't give a *fellow* a chance⟩ **c** : BOYFRIEND ⟨on a date with her *fellow*⟩ 5 : a person granted funds for advanced study [Old English *fēolaga*, from Old Norse *fēlagi*, from *fēlag* "partnership", from *fē* "cattle, money" + *lag* "act of laying"] — **fellow** *adj* □ ORIGIN The Old Norse word for a partner, *fēlagi*, means literally "fee-layer". Such people were those who laid together their property (fee) for some common purpose. Old English borrowed *fēlagi* from Old Norse and called a partner a *fēolaga*. This word has come down to us, through several centuries and the development of a number of senses, as modern English *fellow*. Perhaps

its most common use today is its very general one, in which it is applied to any boy or man.

fel·low·man \,fel-ō-'man\ *n* : a kindred human being

fel·low·ship \'fel-ō-,ship\ *n* 1 : the condition of friendly relationship existing among persons 2 : a community of interest, activity, or feeling 3 : a group with similar interests 4 **a** : the position of a fellow (as of a university) **b** : the funds granted a fellow

fellow traveler *n* : a person who sympathizes with and often furthers the ideals and program of an organized group (as the Communist party) without joining it or regularly participating in its activities [translation of Russian *poputchik*]

fel·ly \'fel-ē\ *or* **fel·loe** \-ō\ *n, pl* **fellies** *or* **felloes** : the outside rim or a part of the rim of a wheel supported by the spokes [Old English *felg*]

fel·on \'fel-ən\ *n* 1 : one who has committed a felony 2 : a deep inflammation of the finger or toe especially near the end or around the nail and usually with pus [Old French *felon, fel* "villain, inflammation", from Medieval Latin *fello* "evildoer, villain"]

fel·o·ny \'fel-ə-nē\ *n, pl* **-nies** : a serious crime usually punishable by a sentence heavier than that for a misdemeanor — **fe·lo·ni·ous** \fə-'lō-nē-əs\ *adj* — **fe·lo·ni·ous·ly** *adv* — **fe·lo·ni·ous·ness** *n*

¹**felt** \'felt\ *n* 1 : an unwoven cloth (as of wool and fur) made by matting the fibers with heat, moisture, and pressure 2 : an article made of felt 3 : a material resembling felt [Old English]

²**felt** *vt* 1 : to make into felt 2 : to cause to adhere and mat together 3 : to cover with felt

³**felt** *past of* FEEL

felt·ing \'fel-ting\ *n* 1 : the process by which felt is made 2 : FELT 1

fe·luc·ca \fə-'lü-kə, -'lək-ə\ *n* : a narrow fast lateen=rigged sailing vessel of the Mediterranean [Italian *feluca*]

¹**fe·male** \'fē-,māl\ *n* : a female plant or animal [Middle English *femelle*, from Medieval Latin *femella*, from Latin, "girl", from *femina* "woman"] □ ORIGIN In the 14th century *female* appeared in English with spellings such as *femel, femelle,* and *female*. It is derived from the Latin *femella*, "young woman, girl", which is a diminutive of *femina*, "woman". In English the similarity in form and pronunciation between the words *female* and *male* led to the retention only of the spelling *female*. It also gave rise to the popular belief that *female* is derived from or somehow related to male. Apart from the influence on the spelling, however, there is no etymological connection between them.

²**female** *adj* 1 **a** : of, relating to, or being the sex that bears young or produces eggs **b** : having only seed=producing flowers : PISTILLATE ⟨a *female* holly⟩ 2 **a** : of, relating to, or characteristic of the female sex **b** : made up of females ⟨the *female* population⟩ 3 : designed with a hollow into which a corresponding male part fits ⟨a *female* hose coupling⟩ — **fe·male·ness** *n*

¹**fem·i·nine** \'fem-ə-nən\ *adj* 1 : of the female sex 2 : characteristic of or belonging to women : WOMANLY 3 : of, relating to, or constituting the class of words that ordinarily includes most of those referring to females ⟨a *feminine* noun⟩ ⟨the *feminine* gender⟩ 4 : having or occurring in an unstressed extra final syllable ⟨*feminine* rhyme⟩ [Middle French *feminin*, from Latin *femininus*, from *femina* "woman"]

²**feminine** *n* 1 : a word or form of the feminine gender 2 : the feminine gender

fem·i·nin·i·ty \,fem-ə-'nin-ət-ē\ *n* 1 : the quality or nature of the female sex 2 : EFFEMINACY 3 : female human beings : WOMANKIND

fem·i·nism \'fem-ə-,niz-əm\ *n* 1 : a doctrine advocating political, economic, and social equality of the sexes 2 : organized activity on behalf of women's rights and interests — **fem·i·nist** \-nəst\ *n or adj* — **fem·i·nis·tic** \,fem-ə-'nis-tik\ *adj*

\ə\	abut	\ng\	sing
\ər\	further	\ō\	bone
\a\	mat	\ȯ\	saw
\ā\	take	\ȯi\	coin
\ä\	cot, cart	\th\	thin
\au̇\	out	\t͟h\	this
\ch\	chin	\ü\	food
\e\	pet	\u̇\	foot
\ē\	easy	\y\	yet
\g\	go	\yü\	few
\i\	tip	\yu̇\	cure
\ī\	life	\zh\	vision
\j\	job		

fem·o·ral \'fem-rəl, -ə-rəl\ *adj* : of, relating to, or situated in or near the femur or thigh ⟨*femoral* artery⟩

femto- \,fem-tō\ *combining form* : one quadrillionth (10⁻¹⁵) part of [Danish or Norwegian *femten* "fifteen"]

fe·mur \'fē-mər\ *n, pl* **fe·murs** *or* **fem·o·ra** \'fem-rə, -ə-rə\ **1** : the long bone of the hind or lower limb extending from the hip to the knee and supporting the thigh — called also *thighbone* **2** : the segment of an insect's leg that is third from the body [Latin *femor-, femur* "thigh"]

fen \'fen\ *n* : low land covered naturally in whole or in part with water [Old English *fenn*]

¹fence \'fens\ *n* **1** : a barrier intended to prevent escape or intrusion or to mark a boundary **2** : a person who receives stolen goods or a shop where stolen goods are disposed of [Middle English *fens* "defense", short for *defens*] — **fence·less** \-ləs\ *adj* — **on the fence** : being neutral or undecided

²fence *vb* **1 a** : to enclose with a fence **b** : to keep in or out with a fence **2** : to engage in fencing — **fenc·er** *n*

fence·row \'fens-,rō\ *n* : the land occupied by a fence including the uncultivated land on each side

fenc·ing *n* **1** : the art or sport of attack and defense with a foil, épée, or saber **2 a** : the fences of a property or region **b** : material used for building fences

fend \'fend\ *vb* **1** : to keep or ward off : REPEL **2** : to try to get along without help : SHIFT ⟨*fend* for yourself⟩ [Middle English *fenden*, short for *defenden*]

fend·er \'fen-dər\ *n* : a device that protects: as **a** : a cushion hung over the side of a boat to protect it when two boats are together or when alongside a dock **b** : RAILING **c** : a device in front of a locomotive or streetcar to lessen injury to animals or pedestrians in case of collision **d** : a guard over the wheel of a motor vehicle **e** : a screen or a low metal frame before an open fireplace

fe·nes·tra \fi-'nes-trə\ *n, pl* **-trae** \-,trē, -,trī\ : a small opening; *esp* : either of two membrane-covered apertures in the bone between the middle and inner ear [Latin, "window"] — **fe·nes·tral** \-trəl\ *adj*

fen·es·tra·tion \,fen-əs-'trā-shən\ *n* : the arrangement, proportioning, and design of windows and doors in a building

Fe·ni·an \'fē-nē-ən\ *n* **1** : one of a legendary band of Irish warriors of the 2d and 3d centuries A.D. **2** : a member of a secret 19th century Irish and Irish-American organization dedicated to the overthrow of British rule in Ireland [Irish Gaelic *Fiann*, legendary band of warriors] — **Fenian** *adj*

fen·nec \'fen-ik\ *n* : a small large-eared African fox [Arabic *fanak*]

fennec

fen·nel \'fen-l\ *n* : a perennial European herb of the carrot family grown for its aromatic seeds and foliage; *also* : its seed [Old English *finugl*, from Latin *feniculum*, from *fenum* "hay"]

¹ferret

fen·ny \'fen-ē\ *adj* **1** : characteristic of a fen : BOGGY **2** : peculiar to or found in a fen

fen·u·greek \'fen-yə-,grēk\ *n* : a white-flowered Old World legume with aromatic seeds once used in medicine [Middle French *fenugrec*, from Latin *fenum Graecum*, literally, "Greek hay"]

-fer \fər\ *n combining form* : one that bears ⟨aqui*fer*⟩ [Latin, from *ferre* "to carry, bear"]

fe·ral \'fir-əl, 'fer-\ *adj* **1** : of, relating to, or suggestive of a wild beast : SAVAGE **2** : having escaped from domestication and become wild [Medieval Latin *feralis*, from Latin *fera* "wild animal", from *ferus* "wild"]

fer-de-lance \,ferd-l-'ans, -'äns\ *n, pl* **fer-de-lance** : a large extremely poisonous pit viper of Central and South America [French, literally, "lance iron"]

fe·ria \'fir-ē-ə, 'fer-\ *n* : a weekday of a church calendar on which no feast is celebrated [Medieval Latin, "weekday, fair"] — **fe·ri·al** \-ē-əl\ *adj*

¹fer·ment \fər-'ment\ *vb* : to undergo or cause to undergo fermentation — **fer·ment·able** \-ə-bəl\ *adj* — **fer·ment·er** *n*

²fer·ment \'fər-,ment\ *n* **1** : an agent (as an enzyme or a yeast) capable of bringing about fermentation **2 a** : FERMENTATION 1 **b** : a state of intense activity or unrest : AGITATION [Latin *fermentum* "yeast"]

fer·men·ta·tion \,fər-mən-'tā-shən, -,men-\ *n* **1** : chemical breaking down of an organic substance (as in the souring of milk or the formation of alcohol from sugar) produced by an enzyme and often accompanied by the evolution of a gas; *esp* : such an energy-yielding reaction proceeding without the aid of free oxygen **2** : FERMENT 2b — **fer·men·ta·tive** \fər-'ment-ət-iv\ *adj*

fer·mi·um \'fer-mē-əm, 'fər-\ *n* : a radioactive metallic element artificially produced (as by bombardment of plutonium with neutrons) — see ELEMENT table [Enrico *Fermi*, died 1954, Italian physicist]

fern \'fərn\ *n* : any of a class (Filicineae) of flowerless seedless vascular plants; *esp* : any of an order (Filicales) resembling seed plants in having root, stem, and leaflike fronds but reproducing by spores [Old English *fearn*] — **fern·like** \-,līk\ *adj* — **ferny** \'fər-nē\ *adj*

fern·ery \'fərn-rē, -ə-rē\ *n, pl* **-er·ies** **1** : a place for growing ferns **2** : a collection of growing ferns

fe·ro·cious \fə-'rō-shəs\ *adj* **1** : showing or given to extreme fierceness, violence, and brutality **2** : unbearably intense ⟨*ferocious* heat⟩ [Latin *feroc-, ferox*] SYN see FIERCE — **fe·ro·cious·ly** *adv* — **fe·ro·cious·ness** *n*

fe·roc·i·ty \fə-'räs-ət-ē\ *n, pl* **-ties** : the quality or state of being ferocious

-f·er·ous \f-rəs, f-ə-rəs\ *adj combining form* : bearing : producing ⟨carboni*ferous*⟩

fer·re·dox·in \,fer-ə-'däk-sən\ *n* : an iron-containing plant protein that functions as an electron carrier especially in photosynthesis [Latin *ferrum* "iron" + English *redox* + *-in*]

¹fer·ret \'fer-ət\ *n* : a partially domesticated usually albino European polecat used especially for hunting rodents [Middle French *furet*, from Latin *fur* "thief"]

²ferret *vb* **1** : to hunt game with ferrets **2 a** : to drive out of a hiding place **b** : to find and bring to light by searching — usually used with *out* — **fer·ret·er** *n*

fer·ric \'fer-ik\ *adj* **1** : of, relating to, or containing iron **2** : being or containing iron usually with a valence of three [Latin *ferrum* "iron"]

ferric oxide *n* : the red or black oxide of iron Fe₂O₃ that is found in nature as hematite and as rust, is obtained synthetically, and is used as a pigment and for polishing

Fer·ris wheel \'fer-əs-\ *n* : an amusement device consisting of a large upright power-driven wheel carrying seats around its rim [G. W. G. *Ferris*, died 1896, American engineer]

ferro- *combining form* : iron : iron and ⟨*ferro*magnetic⟩ [Latin *ferrum*]

fer·ro·mag·net·ic \,fer-ō-mag-'net-ik\ *adj* : of or relating to substances (as iron and nickel) that are easily magnetized

fer·ro·type \'fer-ə-,tīp\ *vt* : to give a gloss to (a photographic print) by pressing with the face down while wet on a metal plate and allowing to dry

fer·rous \'fer-əs\ *adj* **1** : of, relating to, or containing iron **2** : being or containing bivalent iron

ferrous oxide *n* : the monoxide of iron FeO

ferrous sulfate *n* : a salt FeSO₄ that consists of iron, sulfur, and oxygen and is used in making pigments and ink, in treating industrial wastes, and in medicine

fer·ru·gi·nous \fə-'rü-jə-nəs, fe-\ *adj* **1** : of, relating to, or containing iron **2** : resembling iron rust in color [Latin *ferruginus*, from *ferrugo* "iron rust", from *ferrum* "iron"]

fer·rule \'fer-əl\ *n* : a metal ring or cap placed around the end of a slender shaft of wood (as a cane) or around a tool handle to prevent splitting or to provide a strong well-fitting joint [Middle English *virole,* from Middle French, from Latin *viriola* "little bracelet", from *viria* "bracelet", of Celtic origin]

¹fer·ry \'fer-ē\ *vb* **fer·ried; fer·ry·ing 1 a** : to carry by boat over a body of water (as a river) **b** : to cross by a ferry **2 a** : to fly (an airplane) from the shipping point to a delivery point **b** : to transport in an airplane [Old English *ferian* "to carry, convey"]

²ferry *n, pl* **ferries 1** : a place where persons or things are carried across a body of water in a boat **2** : FERRY-BOAT **3** : an organized service and route for flying airplanes — **fer·ry·man** \-mən\ *n*

fer·ry·boat \-,bōt\ *n* : a boat used to ferry passengers, vehicles, or goods

fer·tile \'fərt-l\ *adj* **1** : producing or bearing fruit in great quantities : PRODUCTIVE **2 a** (1) : favorable to plant growth (2) : affording abundant possibilities for development ⟨a *fertile* area for research⟩ **b** : capable of growing or developing ⟨a *fertile* egg⟩ **c** : capable of reproducing or of producing reproductive cells ⟨a *fertile* bull⟩ ⟨*fertile* fungous hyphae⟩ [Latin *fertilis,* from *ferre* "to bear"] — **fer·tile·ly** \-l-lē, -l-ē\ *adv* — **fer·tile·ness** \-l-nəs\ *n* — **fer·til·i·ty** \fər-'til-ət-ē\ *n* ☐
SYN FRUITFUL, PROLIFIC, FECUND: FERTILE implies having the inherent power to reproduce in kind or to assist in reproduction and growth ⟨*fertile* soil⟩ FRUITFUL adds the implication of actually producing desirable and useful results ⟨*fruitful* methods⟩ PROLIFIC stresses the power of multiplying and spreading rapidly ⟨*prolific* rabbits⟩ or of creating freely ⟨a *prolific* writer⟩ FECUND emphasizes abundance or rapidity in bearing fruit or offspring.

fer·til·iza·tion \,fərt-l-ə-'zā-shən\ *n* : an act or process of making fertile: as **a** : the application of fertilizer **b** : union of male and female germ cells to form a zygote

fer·til·ize \'fərt-l-,īz\ *vt* : to make fertile: as **a** : to cause the fertilization of **b** : to apply a fertilizer to ⟨*fertilize* land⟩ — **fer·til·iz·able** \-,ī-zə-bəl\ *adj*

fer·til·iz·er \-,ī-zər\ *n* : one that fertilizes; *esp* : a substance (as manure or a chemical mixture) used to make soil more fertile

fer·ule \'fer-əl\ *n* : a rod or ruler used in punishing children [Latin *ferula*]

fer·ven·cy \'fər-vən-sē\ *n* : FERVOR 2

fer·vent \'fər-vənt\ *adj* **1** : very hot : GLOWING **2** : marked by great warmth of feeling : ARDENT [Latin *fervens,* present participle of *fervēre* "to boil, glow"] — **fer·vent·ly** *adv*

fer·vid \'fər-vəd\ *adj* : FERVENT [Latin *fervidus,* from *fervēre* "to boil, glow"] — **fer·vid·ly** *adv* — **fer·vid·ness** *n*

fer·vor \'fər-vər\ *n* **1** : intense heat **2** : warm steady intensity of feeling or expression [Latin, from *fervēre* "to boil, glow"] SYN see PASSION

fes·cue \'fes-kyü\ *n* : any of numerous tufted perennial grasses [Middle French *festu* "stalk, straw", derived from Latin *festuca*]

-fest \,fest\ *n combining form* : meeting or occasion marked by (such) activity ⟨gab*fest*⟩ [German *fest* "celebration", from Latin *festum*]

fes·tal \'fest-l\ *adj* : of or relating to a feast or festival : FESTIVE [Latin *festum* "feast, festival"] — **fes·tal·ly** \-l-ē\ *adv*

¹fes·ter \'fes-tər\ *n* : a pus-filled sore : PUSTULE [Middle French *festre,* from Latin *fistula* "pipe, fistula"]

²fester *vb* **fes·tered; fes·ter·ing** \-tə-ring, -tring\ **1** : to form pus **2** : PUTREFY, ROT **3** : to grow or cause to grow increasingly more irritating : RANKLE ⟨let resentment *fester* in one's mind⟩

fes·ti·val \'fes-tə-vəl\ *n* **1** : a time of celebration marked by special observances **2** : a periodic season or program of cultural events or entertainment ⟨a music *festival*⟩ — **festival** *adj*

fes·tive \'fes-tiv\ *adj* **1** : of, relating to, or suitable for a feast or festival **2** : GAY 1, MERRY — **fes·tive·ly** *adv* — **fes·tive·ness** *n*

fes·tiv·i·ty \fe-'stiv-ət-ē\ *n, pl* **-ties 1** : FESTIVAL 1 **2** : the quality or state of being festive : GAIETY **3** : festive activity

¹fes·toon \fe-'stün\ *n* **1** : a decorative chain or strip hanging between two points **2** : a carved, molded, or painted ornament representing a decorative chain [French *feston,* from Italian *festone,* from *festa* "festival", from Latin *festum*]

²festoon *vt* **1** : to hang or form festoons on **2** : to shape into festoons

fe·tal \'fēt-l\ *adj* : of, relating to, or being a fetus

fetal alcohol syndrome *n* : a variable group of birth defects including mental retardation and deficient growth that tend to occur in the infants of women who drink large amounts of alcohol during pregnancy

¹fetch \'fech\ *vb* **1** : to go after and bring back ⟨*fetch* a glass of water⟩ **2** : to cause to come ⟨*fetch* tears to one's eyes⟩ **3** : to bring as a price : sell for **4** : to arrive at [Old English *feccan*] — **fetch·er** *n*

²fetch *n* : an act or instance of fetching

fetch·ing *adj* : ATTRACTIVE, PLEASING ⟨a *fetching* smile⟩ — **fetch·ing·ly** \-ing-lē\ *adv*

¹fete *or* **fête** \'fāt, 'fet\ *n* **1** : FESTIVAL 1 **2** : a lavish entertainment or party [French *fête,* from Old French *feste*]

²fete *or* **fête** *vt* **1** : to honor or commemorate with a fete **2** : to pay high honor to

fet·id \'fet-əd\ *adj* : having an offensive smell [Latin *foetidus,* from *foetēre* "stink"] — **fet·id·ly** *adv* — **fet·id·ness** *n*

fet·ish *also* **fet·ich** \'fet-ish, 'fēt-\ *n* **1** : an object (as an idol or image) believed to have supernatural or magical powers **2** : an object of unreasoning devotion or concern ⟨make a *fetish* of secrecy⟩ [French *fétiche,* from Portuguese *feitiço,* from *feitiço* "artificial", from Latin *facticius* "factitious"] — **fet·ish·ism** \-,iz-əm\ *n*

fet·lock \'fet-,läk\ *n* **1** : a projection with a tuft of hair on the back of a horse's leg above the hoof **2** : the tuft of hair growing out of the fetlock [Middle English *fitlok*]

¹fet·ter \'fet-ər\ *n* **1** : a chain or shackle for the feet **2** : something that confines : RESTRAINT [Old English *feter*]

²fetter *vt* **1** : to put fetters on : SHACKLE **2** : to restrain from motion or action : CONFINE SYN see HAMPER

fet·tle \'fet-l\ *n* : a state of fitness or order : CONDITION ⟨in fine *fettle*⟩ [Middle English *fetlen*]

fe·tus *also* **foe·tus** \'fēt-əs\ *n* : a young animal while in the body of its mother or in the egg especially in the later stages of development — compare EMBRYO [Latin, "act of bearing young, offspring"]

¹feud \'fyüd\ *n* : a prolonged quarrel; *esp* : a lasting conflict between families or clans marked by violent attacks undertaken for revenge [Middle French *feide,* of Germanic origin] — **feud** *vi*

²feud *n* : FEE 1a [Medieval Latin *feodum, feudum,* of Germanic origin]

feu·dal \'fyüd-l\ *adj* **1** : of, relating to, or having the characteristics of a medieval fee **2** : of, relating to, or characteristic of feudalism — **feu·dal·ly** \-l-ē\ *adv*

feu·dal·ism \-,iz-əm\ *n* : a system of political organization in medieval Europe in which a vassal gave service to a lord and received protection and land in return; *also* : any of various similar political or social systems — **feu·dal·is·tic** \,fyüd-l-'is-tik\ *adj*

¹feu·da·to·ry \'fyüd-ə-,tōr-ē, -,tor-\ *adj* : owing feudal allegiance

²feudatory *n, pl* **-ries 1** : one who holds lands by feudal law or usage **2** : FIEF

fe·ver \'fē-vər\ *n* **1 a** : a rise of body temperature above the normal **b** : a disease of which fever is a prominent symptom **2 a** : a state of heightened or intense emotion or activity **b** : CRAZE 1 [Old English *fēfer,* from Latin *febris*] — **fe·vered** \-vərd\ *adj*

fever blister *n* : COLD SORE

fe·ver·few \'fē-vər-ˌfyü\ *n* : a perennial European herb related to the daisies [Late Latin *febrifugia,* a plant related to the gentians]

fe·ver·ish \'fēv-rish, -ə-rish\ *adj* **1 a** : having a fever **b** : relating to or indicative of fever **c** : tending to cause fever **2** : marked by intense emotion, activity, or instability — **fe·ver·ish·ly** *adv* — **fe·ver·ish·ness** *n*

¹few \'fyü\ *pron, pl in construction* : not many persons or things ⟨*few* were present⟩ ⟨*few* cars on the road⟩ [Old English *fēawa*]

²few *adj* **1** : consisting of or amounting to a small number ⟨one of our *few* pleasures⟩ **2** : not many but some ⟨caught a *few* fish⟩ — **few·ness** *n*

³few *n pl* **1** : a small number of units or individuals ⟨a *few* of them⟩ **2** : a special limited number ⟨the discriminating *few*⟩

¹few·er \'fyü-ər\ *pron, pl in construction* : a smaller number of persons or things ⟨*fewer* came than were expected⟩

²few·er *adj, comparative of* FEW ☐ SYN LESS: FEWER is applied to countable things ⟨*fewer* dollars⟩ ⟨*fewer* hours⟩ LESS may refer to amount, degree, or value ⟨*less* pay⟩ ⟨*less* heat⟩ ⟨*less* beauty⟩

fey \'fā\ *adj* **1** *chiefly Scottish* : fated to die; *also* : marked by a foreboding of death or calamity **2** : CRAZY 2, TOUCHED **3** : having an unworldly air : ELFIN [Old English *fǣge*]

fez \'fez\ *n, pl* **fez·zes** : a brimless flat-crowned hat that usually has a tassel, is made of red felt, and is worn especially by men in eastern Mediterranean countries [French, from *Fez,* Morocco]

fez

fi·an·cé \ˌfē-ˌän-'sā, fē-'än-ˌsā\ *n* : a man engaged to be married [French, from *fiancer* "to betroth"]

fi·an·cée \ˌfē-ˌän-'sā, fē-'än-ˌsā\ *n* : a woman engaged to be married [French, feminine of *fiancé*]

fi·as·co \fē-'as-kō\ *n, pl* **-coes** : a complete and often ridiculous failure [French, from Italian, literally, "bottle"]

fi·at \'fē-ət, -ˌat, -ˌät; 'fī-ət, -ˌat\ *n* : an authoritative often arbitrary order or decree [Latin, "let it be done", from *fieri* "to be done, become"]

¹fib \'fib\ *n* : a trivial or harmless lie [perhaps from *fable*]

²fib *vi* **fibbed; fib·bing** : to tell a fib — **fib·ber** *n*

fi·ber *or* **fi·bre** \'fī-bər\ *n* **1** : a thread or a structure or object resembling a thread: as **a** : a slender root (as of a grass) **b** : a long tapering thick-walled plant cell especially of vascular tissue **c** (1) : a strand of nerve tissue : AXON, DENDRITE (2) : a muscle cell **d** : a slender and greatly elongated natural or synthetic unit of material (as wool, cotton, glass, or rayon) typically capable of being spun into yarn **2** : material made of fibers **3 a** : an element that gives texture or substance **b** : basic toughness : STRENGTH [French *fibre,* from Latin *fibra*]

fi·ber·board \'fī-bər-ˌbōrd, -ˌbord\ *n* : a material made by compressing fibers (as of wood) into stiff sheets

fi·ber·glass \'fī-bər-ˌglas\ *n* : glass in fibrous form used in making various products (as yarn and insulation)

fiber optics *n* **1** *pl* : thin transparent enclosed fibers of glass or plastic that carry light by internal reflections; *also* : a bundle of such fibers used in an instrument **2** : the technique of the use of fiber optics

fibr- *or* **fibro-** *combining form* : fiber : fibrous tissue : fibrous and ⟨*fibr*oid⟩ [Latin *fibra*]

fi·bril \'fīb-rəl, 'fib-\ *n* : a small filament or fiber (as a root hair) — **fi·bril·lar** \-rə-lər\ *adj* — **fi·bril·lose** \-rə-ˌlōs\ *adj*

fi·bril·la·tion \ˌfib-rə-'lā-shən, ˌfīb-\ *n* : rapid irregular contractions of muscle fibers of the heart

fi·brin \'fī-brən\ *n* : a white insoluble fibrous protein formed in the clotting of blood — **fi·brin·ous** \'fib-rə-nəs, 'fīb-\ *adj*

fi·brin·o·gen \fī-'brin-ə-jən\ *n* : a soluble protein produced in the liver, present especially in blood plasma, and converted into fibrin during clotting of blood

fi·bro·blast \'fī-brə-ˌblast\ *n* : a cell giving rise to connective tissue [Greek *blastos* "bud, shoot"] — **fi·bro·blas·tic** \ˌfī-brə-'blas-tik\ *adj*

fi·broid \'fī-ˌbroid\ *adj* : resembling, forming, or consisting of fibrous tissue ⟨*fibroid* tumors⟩

fi·bro·sis \fī-'brō-səs\ *n* : an abnormal condition in which increased amounts of fibrous tissue form in other tissues — **fi·brot·ic** \-'brät-ik\ *adj*

fi·brous \'fī-brəs\ *adj* **1** : containing, consisting of, or resembling fibers **2** : TOUGH 1, STRINGY

fibrous root *n* : one of many slender roots branching directly from the base of the stem of a plant — compare TAPROOT

fibrous tissue *n* : a connective tissue rich in fibers that forms in and supports body structures and is prominent in healing wounds

fi·bro·vas·cu·lar bundle \ˌfī-brō-'vas-kyə-lər-\ *n* : VASCULAR BUNDLE

fib·u·la \'fib-yə-lə\ *n, pl* **-lae** \-ˌlē, -ˌlī\ *or* **-las** : the outer and usually the smaller of the two bones of the hind limb below the knee [Latin, "clasp, brace"] — **fib·u·lar** \-lər\ *adj*

-fic \fik\ *adj suffix* : making : causing ⟨sudori*fic*⟩ [Latin *-ficus,* from *facere* "to make, do"]

-fi·ca·tion \fə-'kā-shən\ *n suffix* : making : production ⟨syllabi*fication*⟩ [Latin *-fication-, -ficatio,* from *-ficare* "-fy"]

fichu \'fish-ü\ *n* : a woman's light triangular scarf draped over the shoulders and fastened in front [French]

fick·le \'fik-əl\ *adj* : not firm or steadfast in attitude or character : INCONSTANT ⟨*fickle* friends⟩ [Old English *ficol* "deceitful"] — **fick·le·ness** *n*

fic·tion \'fik-shən\ *n* **1** : something told or written that is not fact : something made up **2** : a made-up story about real or imaginary persons or events; *also* : such stories as a class [Middle French, from Latin *fictio* "act of fashioning, fiction", from *fingere* "to shape, fashion, feign"] — **fic·tion·al** \'fik-shnəl, -shən-l\ *adj* — **fic·tion·al·ly** \-ē\ *adv* ☐ SYN FICTION, FIGMENT, FABRICATION mean something that is an invention of the human mind. FICTION implies imaginative creation of events, characters, or circumstances with or more often without intent to deceive ⟨King Arthur belongs to *fiction* rather than to history⟩ FIGMENT suggests a creation of the imagination that deceives its own creator ⟨this *figment* of a fevered brain⟩ FABRICATION implies something deliberately made up to deceive or mislead ⟨their story of being robbed was pure *fabrication*⟩

fic·tion·al·ize \'fik-shnəl-ˌīz, -shən-l-\ *vb* : to make into fiction ⟨*fictionalize* a war diary⟩ — **fic·tion·al·iza·tion** \ˌfik-shnəl-ə-'zā-shən, -shən-l-\ *n*

fic·tion·ize \'fik-shə-ˌnīz\ *vt* : FICTIONALIZE — **fic·tion·iza·tion** \ˌfik-shə-nə-'zā-shən\ *n*

fic·ti·tious \fik-'tish-əs\ *adj* **1** : of, relating to, or suggestive of fiction : IMAGINARY ⟨*fictitious* values⟩ **2** : not genuinely felt or expressed : SIMULATED [Latin *ficticius* "artificial, feigned", from *fingere* "to feign"] ☐ SYN FICTITIOUS, FACTITIOUS are easily confused. FICTITIOUS applies to what is invented by the imagination ⟨a child's *fictitious* playmate⟩ ⟨*fictitious* characters in a novel⟩ FACTITIOUS applies to what has actual existence but an artificial rather than natural origin or cause ⟨a *factitious* show of enthusiasm⟩ ⟨a *factitious* scarcity of goods created by unfounded rumors⟩

fid \'fid\ *n* : a pin usually of hard wood that tapers to a point and is used in opening the strands of rope [origin unknown]

¹fid·dle \'fid-l\ *n* : VIOLIN [Old English *fithele*]

²fiddle *vb* **fid·dled; fid·dling** \'fid-ling, -l-ing\ **1** : to play on a fiddle **2 a** : to move the hands or fingers restlessly **b** : to spend time in aimless activity : PUTTER **c** : TAMP-

ER 2, MEDDLE — usually used with *with* — **fid·dler**
\'fid-lər, -l-ər\ *n*

fid·dle·head \'fid-l-,hed\ *n* : one of the young unfurling
fronds of some ferns that are often eaten as greens

fiddler crab *n* : any of numerous burrowing crabs with
one claw much larger than the other in the male

fid·dle·sticks \'fid-l-,stiks\ *n pl* : NONSENSE — used as
an interjection

fi·del·i·ty \fə-'del-ət-ē, fī-\ *n, pl* **-ties** **1 a** : the quality
or state of being faithful **b** : accuracy in details :
EXACTNESS **2** : the degree to which an electronic device (as a radio or phonograph) accurately reproduces
its effect (as sound) [Middle French *fidelité*, from Latin *fidelitas*, from *fidelis* "faithful", from *fides* "faith"]
□ SYN ALLEGIANCE, FEALTY, LOYALTY: FIDELITY implies
strict and continuous faithfulness to an obligation,
trust, or duty; ALLEGIANCE implies the formal obedient
adherence of a subject to a sovereign or a citizen to a
state; FEALTY implies an individual compelling fidelity; LOYALTY implies personal steadfast adherence in
the face of any temptation to desert or betray.

¹fidg·et \'fij-ət\ *n* **1** *pl* : uneasiness or restlessness as
shown by nervous movements **2** : one that fidgets
[Scottish *fidge* "to fidget"] — **fidg·ety** \-ət-ē\ *adj*

²fidget *vb* : to move or cause to move or act nervously
or restlessly

¹fi·du·cia·ry \fə-'dü-shē-,er-ē, fī-, -'dyü-, -shə-rē\ *n, pl*
-ries **1** : one that acts as a trustee for another **2** : one
that acts in a confidential capacity

²fiduciary *adj* **1** : involving a confidence or trust ⟨em-
ployed in a *fiduciary* capacity⟩ **2** : held or holding in
trust for another ⟨*fiduciary* accounts⟩ [Latin *fiduciar-
ius*, from *fiducia* "confidence, trust", from *fidere* "to
trust"]

fie \'fī\ *interj* — used to express mild disapproval or
feigned shock [Old French *fi*]

fief \'fēf\ *n* : a feudal estate : FEE [French, from Old
French *fief, fé*, of Germanic origin]

¹field \'fēld\ *n* **1 a** : open country — usually used in
pl. **b** : a piece of open land **c** : a piece of land put to a
special use or yielding a special product ⟨an athletic
field⟩ ⟨a gas *field*⟩ **d** : a place where a battle is fought :
the region in which military operations are carried on
e : an open space or expanse ⟨a *field* of ice⟩ **2** : a
sphere or range of activity or influence ⟨the *field* of
science⟩ **3** : a background on which something is
drawn, painted, or mounted ⟨the American flag has
white stars on a blue *field*⟩ **4** : the individuals that
make up all or part of a sports activity: as **a** : all the
participants in a contest or sporting event (as a golf
tournament) **b** : the baseball team not at bat **5** : a region or space in which a given effect (as gravity, electricity, or magnetism) exists **6** : the area visible
through the lens of an optical instrument [Old English
feld]

²field *vb* **1** : to catch, stop, or throw a ball as a fielder
⟨*field* a ground ball⟩ **2** : to put into the field ⟨*field* an
army⟩

³field *adj* : of or relating to a field: as **a** : growing or
living in open country ⟨*field* flowers⟩ **b** : made, conducted, used, or operating in the field

field artillery *n* : artillery other than antiaircraft artillery
used with armies in the field

field corn *n* : an Indian corn with starchy kernels grown
for feeding livestock or for market grain

field day *n* **1** : a day devoted to outdoor sports and athletic competition **2** : a time of unusual pleasure or unexpected success

field·er \'fēl-dər\ *n* : one that fields; *esp* : a baseball
player stationed in the outfield

field event *n* : an event in a track meet other than a race

field glasses *n pl* : a hand-held magnifying optical instrument consisting of two simple telescopes mounted
side-by-side in a frame which permits simultaneous focusing; *also* : BINOCULARS

field goal *n* **1** : a score of three points in football made
by drop-kicking or place-kicking the ball over the
crossbar from ordinary play **2** : a score of two points
in basketball on a goal made while the ball is in play

field hockey *n* : a game played on a field between two
teams of 11 players whose object is to knock a ball
into the opponent's goal with a curved stick

field magnet *n* : a magnet for producing and maintaining a magnetic field especially in a generator or electric motor

field marshal *n* : an officer (as in the British army) of
the highest rank

field mouse *n* : any of various mice that inhabit open
fields

field pea *n* : a small-seeded pea widely grown chiefly
for forage

field piece \'fēld-,pēs\ *n* : a gun or howitzer for use in
the field

field·stone \'fēld-,stōn\ *n* : stone used in building in
usually unchanged form as taken from the field

field trial *n* : a trial of sporting dogs in actual performance

field trip *n* : a visit (as to a factory, farm, or museum)
made by students and usually a teacher for purposes of
firsthand observation

fiend \'fēnd\ *n* **1 a** : DEVIL 1 **b** : DEMON 2a **2** : an extremely wicked or cruel person **3 a** : a person excessively devoted to a pursuit : FANATIC ⟨a golf *fiend*⟩ **b** : a
person who uses immoderate quantities of something :
ADDICT ⟨a dope *fiend*⟩ [Old English *fiend*, literally,
"enemy"]

fiend·ish \'fēn-dish\ *adj* : extremely cruel or wicked :
DIABOLICAL — **fiend·ish·ly** *adv* — **fiend·ish·ness** *n*

fierce \'fiərs\ *adj* **1 a** : violently hostile or aggressive in
temperament **b** : given to fighting or killing : PUGNA-
CIOUS **2** : marked by unrestrained zeal or vehemence :
INTENSE **3** : furiously active or determined **4** : wild or
menacing in aspect [Old French *fiers*, from Latin *ferus*
"wild, savage"] — **fierce·ly** *adv* — **fierce·ness** *n* □
SYN FEROCIOUS: FIERCE implies inspiring fear because of
a wild and menacing aspect or display of fury in attack
⟨*fierce* mountain tribes⟩ FEROCIOUS implies extreme
fierceness and unrestrained violence and brutality.

fi·ery \'fī-rē, -ə-rē\ *adj* **fi·eri·er; -est** **1 a** : consisting of
fire **b** : BURNING, BLAZING ⟨a *fiery* furnace⟩ **c** : FLAMMA-
BLE ⟨a *fiery* vapor⟩ **2 a** : hot like fire **b** (1) : INFLAMED
⟨a *fiery* boil⟩ (2) : feverish and flushed **3 a** : of the
color of fire : RED **b** : intensely or unnaturally red **4 a** :
full of emotion or spirit **b** : easily provoked : IRRITABLE
— **fi·eri·ness** *n*

fi·es·ta \fē-'es-tə\ *n* : FESTIVAL; *esp* : a saint's day celebrated in Spain and Latin America with processions
and dances [Spanish, from Latin *festa*, pl. of *festum*]

fife \'fīf\ *n* : a small shrill musical instrument resembling a flute [German *pfeife* "pipe, fife"]

fif·teen \fif-'tēn, 'fif-\ *n* **1** : one more than 14; *also* : a
symbol representing this — see NUMBER table **2** : the
1st point scored by a side in a game of tennis — called
also *five* [Old English *fīftēne*] — **fifteen** *adj or pron*
— **fif·teenth** \-'tēnth, -'tēntth\ *adj or n*

fifth \'fifth, 'fiftth\ *n, pl* **fifths** \'fifths, 'fiftths, 'fifts, 'fifs\
1 : number five in a countable series — see NUMBER
table **2 a** : the musical interval embracing five diatonic degrees **b** : the harmonic combination of two tones
at this interval **3** : a unit of measure for liquor equal to
one fifth of a United States gallon (about .75 liter) —
fifth *adj or adv* — **fifth·ly** *adv*

fifth column *n* : a group of secret sympathizers or supporters of a nation's enemy that engage in espionage
or sabotage within the country [name applied to rebel
sympathizers in Madrid in 1936 when four rebel columns were advancing on the city] — **fifth columnist** *n*

fifth wheel *n* : one that is unnecessary or superfluous

fif·ty \'fif-tē\ *n, pl* **fifties** : ten more than 40; *also* : a
symbol representing this — see NUMBER table [Old En-

fiddler crab

\ə\ abut	\ng\ sing
\ər\ further	\ō\ bone
\a\ mat	\o\ saw
\ā\ take	\oi\ coin
\ä\ cot, cart	\th\ thin
\au\ out	\th\ this
\ch\ chin	\ü\ food
\e\ pet	\u\ foot
\ē\ easy	\y\ yet
\g\ go	\yü\ few
\i\ tip	\yu\ cure
\ī\ life	\zh\ vision
\j\ job	

glish *fiftig*] — **fifty** *adj or pron* — **fif·ti·eth** \-tē-əth\ *adj or n*

fif·ty–fif·ty \ˌfif-tē-ˈfif-tē\ *adj* **1** : shared equally ⟨a *fifty-fifty* proposition⟩ **2** : half favorable and half unfavorable ⟨a *fifty-fifty* chance to live⟩ — **fifty–fifty** *adv*

fig \ˈfig\ *n* **1** : the usually edible oblong or pear-shaped fruit of a tree of the mulberry family; *also* : a tree bearing figs **2** : TRIFLE 1 [Old French *fige, figue,* derived from Latin *ficus* "fig tree, fig"]

¹fight \ˈfīt\ *vb* **fought** \ˈfȯt\; **fight·ing** **1 a** : to contend against another in battle or physical combat **b** : to engage in boxing : BOX **2** : to try hard **3 a** : to act in opposition : STRUGGLE ⟨*fight* for the right⟩ **b** : to attempt to prevent the success or effectiveness of **4** : to carry on : WAGE ⟨*fight* a war⟩ **5** : to gain by struggle ⟨*fought* our way through⟩ [Old English *feohtan*]

²fight *n* **1 a** : a hostile encounter : BATTLE **b** : a boxing match **c** : a verbal disagreement **2** : a struggle for a goal or an objective **3** : strength or disposition for fighting ⟨full of *fight*⟩

fight·er \ˈfīt-ər\ *n* : one that fights : **a** : SOLDIER 1, WARRIOR **b** : ¹BOXER **c** : an airplane of high speed and maneuverability with armament for destroying enemy aircraft

fig·ment \ˈfig-mənt\ *n* : something imagined or made up ⟨a *figment* of a fevered imagination⟩ [Latin *figmentum,* from *fingere* "to shape, feign"] SYN SEE FICTION

fig·u·ra·tion \ˌfig-yə-ˈrā-shən, ˌfig-ə-ˈ\ *n* **1** : OUTLINE 1, FORM **2** : an act or instance of representation in figures and shapes

fig·u·ra·tive \ˈfig-yə-rət-iv, ˈfig-ə-; ˈfig-yərt-iv, -ərt-\ *adj* **1** : representing by a figure : EMBLEMATIC **2 a** : expressing one thing in terms normally denoting another : METAPHORICAL **b** : characterized by figures of speech — **fig·u·ra·tive·ly** *adv* — **fig·u·ra·tive·ness** *n*

¹fig·ure \ˈfig-yər, *especially British* ˈfig-ər\ *n* **1 a** : a number symbol : NUMERAL **b** *pl* : arithmetical calculations **c** : a written or printed character **d** : value especially as expressed in numbers : PRICE **2 a** : the shape or outline of something **b** : bodily shape especially of a person **c** : an object noticeable only as a shape ⟨*figures* moving in the dusk⟩ **3 a** : the graphic representation of a form especially of a person **b** : a diagram or pictorial illustration of a text **c** : a combination of points, lines, or surfaces in geometry ⟨a circle is a closed plane *figure*⟩ **4** : FIGURE OF SPEECH **5** : PATTERN 5a, 6, DESIGN **6** : impression produced ⟨the couple cut quite a *figure*⟩ **7 a** : a series of movements in a dance **b** : an outline representation of a form traced by a series of evolutions (as with skates on ice) **8** : a prominent personality : PERSONAGE [Old French, from Latin *figura,* from *fingere* "to shape, feign"] SYN SEE FORM

²figure *vb* **1** : to represent by or as if by a figure or outline : PORTRAY **2** : to decorate with a pattern **3 a** : to indicate or represent by numerals **b** : CONCLUDE, DECIDE ⟨*figured* there was no use⟩ **c** : REGARD, CONSIDER ⟨*figure* oneself a good candidate⟩ **4** : to be or appear important or conspicuous ⟨*figure* in the news⟩ **5** : COMPUTE, CALCULATE — **fig·ur·er** \-yər-ər, -ər-ər\ *n* — **figure on** **1** : to take into consideration **2** : to rely on **3** : PLAN 2

fig·ured *adj* **1** : being represented : PORTRAYED **2** : adorned with, formed into, or marked with a figure **3** : indicated by figures

figure eight *n* : something (as a skating figure) resembling the Arabic numeral 8 in shape

fig·ure·head \ˈfig-yər-ˌhed, -ər-\ *n* **1** : a figure, statue, or bust on the bow of a ship **2** : a head or chief in name only

figure of speech : a form of expression (as a simile or metaphor) in which words are intentionally used in other than a plain or literal way so as to produce fresh, vivid, or poetic effects

figure out *vt* : SOLVE

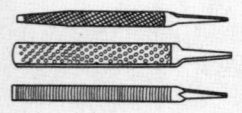

¹file

figure skating *n* : skating in which the skater performs figures and special jumps and turns

fig·u·rine \ˌfig-yə-ˈrēn, ˌfig-ə-\ *n* : a small carved or molded figure

fig·wort \ˈfig-ˌwərt, -ˌwȯrt\ *n* : any of a genus of chiefly erect herbs with toothed leaves and clustered flowers

fil·a·ment \ˈfil-ə-mənt\ *n* : a single thread or a thin flexible threadlike object, process, or appendage: as **a** : a wire (as in an electric lamp) made incandescent by the passage of an electric current; *esp* : a cathode in the form of a metal wire in an electron tube **b** : the anther-bearing stalk of a stamen [Middle French, from Medieval Latin *filamentum,* from Late Latin *filare* "to spin", from Latin *filum* "thread"] — **fil·a·men·tous** \ˌfil-ə-ˈment-əs\ *adj*

fi·lar·ia \fə-ˈlar-ē-ə, -ˈler-\ *n, pl* **-i·ae** \-ē-ˌē, -ē-ˌī\ : any of numerous slender threadlike nematodes that as adults are parasites in the blood or tissues of mammals and as larvae usually develop in biting insects [derived from Latin *filum* "thread"] — **fi·lar·i·al** \-ē-əl\ *adj*

fil·a·ri·a·sis \ˌfil-ə-ˈrī-ə-səs\ *n, pl* **-a·ses** \-ˌsēz\ : infestation with or disease caused by filariae

fil·bert \ˈfil-bərt\ *n* **1** : either of two European hazels; *also* : the sweet thick-shelled nut of a filbert **2** : HAZELNUT [Anglo-French *philber,* from Saint *Philibert,* died 684, Frankish abbot whose feast day falls in the nutting season]

filch \ˈfilch\ *vt* : to steal furtively : PILFER [Middle English *filchen*]

¹file \ˈfīl\ *n* : a usually steel tool with sharp ridges or teeth on its surface for smoothing or rubbing down a hard substance (as metal) [Old English *fēol*]

²file *vt* : to rub, smooth, or cut away with a file

³file *vb* **1** : to arrange in order for preservation or reference **2 a** : to enter or record as prescribed by law ⟨*file* a mortgage⟩ **b** : to send (copy) to a newspaper ⟨*file* a story⟩ **3** : to register as a candidate especially in a primary election [Middle French *filer* "to string documents on a string or wire", from *fil* "thread", from Latin *filum*]

⁴file *n* **1** : a device (as a folder, case, or cabinet) in which records are kept in order **2 a** : a collection of material kept in a file **b** : a collection of related data records (as for a computer)

⁵file *n* : a row of persons, animals, or things arranged one behind the other [Middle French, derived from Latin *filum* "thread"]

⁶file *vi* : to march or proceed in file

file·fish \ˈfīl-ˌfish\ *n* : any of various fishes with rough granular leathery skins

fi·let \fi-ˈlā\ *n* : a lace with a square mesh and geometric designs [French, literally, "net"]

fi·let mi·gnon \ˌfil-ˌā-mēn-ˈyōⁿ, fi-ˌlā-\ *n, pl* **filets mignons** *same or* -ˈyōⁿz\ : a fillet of beef cut from the thick end of a beef tenderloin [French, literally, "dainty fillet"]

fil·ial \ˈfil-ē-əl, ˈfil-yəl\ *adj* **1** : of, relating to, or befitting a son or daughter **2** : having or assuming the relation of a child or offspring [Late Latin *filialis,* from Latin *filius* "son"] — **fil·ial·ly** \-ē\ *adv*

filial generation *n* : a generation of offspring in a breeding experiment that is produced by the parents in the original cross by their offspring

¹fil·i·bus·ter \ˈfil-ə-ˌbəs-tər\ *n* **1** : an irregular mercenary; *esp* : an American engaged in stirring up rebellions in Latin America in the mid-19th century **2 a** : the use of delaying tactics (as extremely long speeches) in an attempt to delay or prevent action in a legislative assembly **b** : an instance of this practice [Spanish *filibustero,* derived from English *freebooter*]
□ ORIGIN The Dutch word *vrijbuiter,* "plunderer", has left its mark on the English vocabulary not once but twice. It first appeared in the 16th century as *freebooter.* Though the spelling had changed, the meaning remained the same. From English it passed into

Spanish and became *filibustero.* In the middle of the 19th century bands of adventurers organized in the United States were active in Central America and the West Indies stirring up revolutions. Such an adventurer came to be called in English a *filibuster,* from the Spanish *filibustero,* and so *vrijbuiter* made its second appearance in a very different guise. Later in the 19th century, the use of delaying tactics became very common in the United States Senate. Senators who practiced such tactics were compared with the troublesome *filibusters* and were said to be *filibustering.*

²**filibuster** *vb* **fil·i·bus·tered; fil·i·bus·ter·ing** \-tə-ring, -tring\ **1** : to carry out revolutionary activities in a foreign country **2** : to engage in a legislative filibuster — **fil·i·bus·ter·er** \-tər-ər\ *n*

fil·i·form \'fil-ə-ˌfórm, 'fī-lə-\ *adj* : shaped like a thread

fil·i·gree \'fil-ə-ˌgrē\ **1** : ornamental work especially of fine wire applied chiefly to gold and silver surfaces **2 a** : ornamental openwork of delicate or intricate design **b** : a pattern or design resembling this openwork [French *filigrane,* from Italian *filigrana,* from Latin *filum* "thread" + *granum* "grain"]

fil·ing \'fī-ling\ *n* **1** : the act of one who files **2** : a small piece scraped off by a file ⟨iron *filings*⟩

Fil·i·pi·no \ˌfil-ə-'pē-nō\ *n, pl* **-nos 1** : a native or inhabitant of the Philippines **2** : a person of Filipino descent [Spanish] — **Filipino** *adj*

¹**fill** \'fil\ *vb* **1** : to put into as much as can be held or conveniently contained **2** : to become full **3** : FULFILL 2 ⟨*fill* all requirements⟩ **4** : to take up whatever space there is **5** : to spread through ⟨laughter *filled* the room⟩ **6** : to stop up (as crevices or holes) : PLUG ⟨*fill* a crack with putty⟩ ⟨*fill* a tooth⟩ **7 a** : to have and perform the duties of : OCCUPY ⟨*fill* the office of president⟩ **b** : to put a person in ⟨*filled* several vacancies⟩ **8** : to supply according to directions ⟨*fill* a prescription⟩ [Old English *fyllan*] — **fill one's shoes** : to take one's place or position — **fill the bill** : to serve the purpose satisfactorily

²**fill** *n* **1** : a full supply; *esp* : a quantity that satisfies or satiates **2** : material used especially for filling a ditch or hollow in the ground

fill·er \'fil-ər\ *n* : one that fills: as **a** : a substance added to a product (as to increase bulk, weight, opacity, or strength) **b** : a material used for filling cracks and pores in wood before painting **c** : a pack of paper for insertion in a binder

¹**fil·let** \'fil-ət *also* fi-let \fi-'lā, 'fil-ā\ *n* **1** : a narrow strip of material (as a ribbon) used as a headband **2 a** : a thin narrow strip of material **b** : a piece or slice of boneless meat or fish **3 a** : a flat molding separating other moldings **b** : the space between two flutings in a shaft [Middle French *filet,* from *fil* "thread", from Latin *filum*]

²**fillet** *vt* **1** : to bind or adorn with or as if with a fillet **2** : to cut into fillets

fill in *vb* **1** : to furnish with specified information ⟨*fill in* an application⟩ **2** : to fill a vacancy usually temporarily : SUBSTITUTE ⟨*filled in* during the emergency⟩

fill·ing \'fil-ing\ *n* **1** : material that is used to fill something ⟨a *filling* for a tooth⟩ **2** : something that completes: as **a** : the yarn interlacing the warp in a fabric **b** : a food mixture used to fill pastry or sandwiches

filling station *n* : SERVICE STATION

¹**fil·lip** \'fil-əp\ *n* **1** : a blow or gesture made by the sudden forcible straightening of a finger curled up against the thumb **2** : something tending to arouse or excite [probably imitative]

²**fillip** *vt* **1** : to tap with the finger by flicking the fingernail outward across the end of the thumb **2** : to urge on : STIMULATE

fill out *vi* : to put on flesh

fil·ly \'fil-ē\ *n, pl* **fillies** : a young female horse usually less than four years old [Old Norse *fylja*]

¹**film** \'film\ *n* **1** : a thin skin or membrane **2** : a thin coating or layer **3** : a roll or strip of thin flexible transparent material coated with a chemical substance sensitive to light and used in taking pictures **4** : MOVIE [Old English *filmen*]

²**film** *vb* **1** : to cover or become covered with film ⟨eyes *filmed* with tears⟩ **2** : to photograph on film; *esp* : to make a motion picture of ⟨*film* a battle scene⟩

film·ic \'fil-mik\ *adj* : of, relating to, or resembling motion pictures

film·strip \'film-ˌstrip\ *n* : a strip of usually 35 millimeter film bearing photographs, diagrams, or graphic matter for still projection upon a screen

filmy \'fil-mē\ *adj* **film·i·er; -est 1** : of, resembling, or composed of film **2** : covered with a haze or film — **film·i·ness** *n*

fi·lo·plume \'fil-ə-ˌplüm, 'fī-lə-\ *n* : a slender threadlike feather with a tuft at the end [Latin *filum* "thread" + English *-o-* + *plume*]

¹**fil·ter** \'fil-tər\ *n* **1** : a porous article or mass through which a gas or liquid is passed to separate out matter in suspension **2** : an apparatus containing a filter medium **3 a** : a device or material for suppressing or minimizing waves or oscillations of certain frequencies (as of electricity, light, or sound) **b** : a transparent material (as colored glass) that absorbs light of certain colors and is used for modifying the light which reaches a sensitized photographic material [Medieval Latin *filtrum* "piece of felt used as a filter", of Germanic origin]

²**filter** *vb* **fil·tered; fil·ter·ing** \-tə-ring, -tring\ **1** : to subject to the action of a filter **2** : to remove by means of a filter **3** : to pass through or as if through a filter

fil·ter·able *also* **fil·tra·ble** \'fil-tə-rə-bəl, -trə-bəl\ *adj* : capable of being separated by or of passing through a filter ⟨*filterable* microorganisms⟩ ⟨a *filterable* liquid⟩ — **fil·ter·abil·i·ty** \ˌfil-tə-rə-'bil-ət-ē, -trə-\ *n*

filterable virus *n* : VIRUS 1a

filter bed *n* : a bed of sand or gravel for filtering water or sewage

filter paper *n* : porous paper used for filtering

filter tip *n* : a cigar or cigarette with a tip designed to filter the smoke

filth \'filth\ *n* **1** : foul or putrid matter; *esp* : disgusting dirt or refuse **2 a** : moral corruption **b** : something that tends to corrupt or disgust [Old English *fylth,* from *ful* "foul"]

filthy \'fil-thē\ *adj* **filth·i·er; -est 1** : covered with or containing filth : disgustingly dirty **2 a** : morally polluted : EVIL ⟨*filthy* politics⟩ **b** : OBSCENE SYN see DIRTY — **filth·i·ly** \-thə-lē\ *adv* — **filth·i·ness** \-thē-nəs\ *n*

fil·trate \'fil-ˌtrāt\ *n* : fluid that has passed through a filter

fil·tra·tion \fil-'trā-shən\ *n* : the act or process of filtering

fin \'fin\ *n* **1** : a thin external process of an aquatic animal (as a fish or whale) used in propelling or guiding the body **2 a** : a fin-shaped part (as on an airplane, boat, or automobile) **b** : FLIPPER 2 **c** : a projecting rib on a radiator or an engine cylinder [Old English *finn*] — **fin·like** \-ˌlīk\ *adj* — **finned** \'find\ *adj*

fi·na·gle \fə-'nā-gəl\ *vb* **fi·na·gled; fi·na·gling** \-'nā-gə-ling, -gling\ : WANGLE 1a [perhaps from *fainaigue* "to renege"] — **fi·na·gler** \-gə-lər, -glər\ *n*

¹**fi·nal** \'fīn-l\ *adj* **1 a** : bringing something (as conflict or uncertainty) to an end ⟨the *final* war that destroyed life⟩ **b** : not to be altered or undone ⟨reached a *final* decision⟩ ⟨all sales are *final*⟩ **2** : being the last stage of a series or process ⟨paid their *final* debt to nature⟩ **3** : being or relating to an end or purpose ⟨*final* causes⟩ **4** : coming after all others ⟨the *final* chapter of a book⟩ [Middle French, from Latin *finalis,* from *finis* "end, boundary"] SYN see LAST — **fi·nal·ly** \'fīn-l-ē, 'fīn-lē\ *adv*

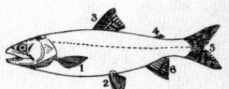

fin 1: *1* pectoral, 2 pelvic, 3,4 dorsal, 5 caudal, 6 anal

\ə\ abut		\ng\ sing	
\ər\ **further**		\ō\ bone	
\a\ mat		\ó\ saw	
\ā\ take		\ói\ coin	
\ä\ cot, cart		\th\ thin	
\au̇\ out		\t͟h\ this	
\ch\ chin		\ü\ food	
\e\ pet		\u̇\ foot	
\ē\ easy		\y\ yet	
\g\ go		\yü\ few	
\i\ tip		\yu̇\ cure	
\ī\ life		\zh\ vision	
\j\ job			

²**final** *n* : something final: as **a** : a deciding match, game, or trial **b** : the last examination in a course — usually used in pl.

fi·na·le \fə-'nal-ē, fi-'näl-\ *n* : the close or termination of something; *esp* : the last section of an instrumental musical composition [Italian, from Latin *finalis* "final"]

fi·nal·ist \'fīn-l-əst\ *n* : a contestant in the finals of a competition

fi·nal·i·ty \fī-'nal-ət-ē, fə-\ *n, pl* **-ties** **1** : the character or condition of being final, settled, or complete **2** : something final

fi·nal·ize \'fīn-l-ˌīz\ *vt* : to put in final or finished form

¹**fi·nance** \fə-'nans, 'fī-ˌ, fī-'\ *n* **1** *pl* : liquid resources (as money) of a government, business, group, or individual **2** : the system that includes the circulation of money, the granting of credit, the making of investments, and the provision of banking facilities **3** : the obtaining of funds or capital : FINANCING [Middle English, "payment, ransom", from Middle French, from *finer* "to end, pay", from *fin* "end", from Latin *finis*]

²**finance** *vt* **1** : to raise or provide funds or capital for ⟨*finance* a new car⟩ **2** : to sell to or supply on credit ⟨*finance* farmers until harvest⟩

finance company *n* : a company that specializes in making small loans usually to individuals

fi·nan·cial \fə-'nan-chəl, fī-\ *adj* : having to do with finance or with finances — **fi·nan·cial·ly** \-'nanch-lē, -ə-lē\ *adv* □ SYN MONETARY, PECUNIARY, FISCAL: FINANCIAL implies money matters involving a large scale or some degree of complexity ⟨*financial* aspects of a business⟩ MONETARY refers to money as coined, distributed, or circulating ⟨*monetary* reform⟩ PECUNIARY implies reference to money matters affecting the individual ⟨*pecuniary* rewards of an office⟩ FISCAL applies to the financial affairs of a corporation, institution, or state.

fin·an·cier \ˌfin-ən-'siər, fə-ˌnan-, ˌfī-ˌnan-\ *n* : a person who deals with finance and investment on a large scale

fin·back \'fin-ˌbak\ *n* : RORQUAL; *esp* : a large whale of the Atlantic

finch \'finch\ *n* : any of numerous songbirds (as sparrows, grosbeaks, crossbills, goldfinches, and buntings) having a short stout conical bill adapted for crushing seeds [Old English *finc*]

¹**find** \'fīnd\ *vb* **found** \'faùnd\; **find·ing** **1** : to encounter someone or something by chance ⟨*find* a kitten on the porch⟩ **2** : to come upon by searching or study : DISCOVER **3** : to obtain by effort or management ⟨*find* time to do it⟩ **4** : to arrive at : REACH ⟨*find* one's place in the world⟩ **5** : to make a decision and declare it ⟨*find* a verdict⟩ **6** : to know by experience ⟨people *found* them honest⟩ **7** : to gain or regain the use of ⟨*find* one's feet after an illness⟩ **8** : PROVIDE, SUPPLY ⟨*find* room for a guest⟩ [Old English *findan*] — **find fault** : to criticize unfavorably

²**find** *n* **1** : an act or instance of finding **2** : something found; *esp* : a valuable item of discovery

find·er \'fīn-dər\ *n* : one that finds: as **a** : a small telescope attached to a larger one for finding an object **b** : a lens on a camera that shows the view being photographed by the camera

fin de siè·cle \ˌfaⁿ-də-sē-'ekl\ *adj* : of, relating to, or characteristic of the close of the 19th century [French, "end of the century"]

find·ing *n* **1 a** : the act of one that finds **b** : FIND 2 **2** : the result of a judicial proceeding or investigation

find out *vt* **1** : to learn by study or observation **2** : DETECT 1, DISCOVER

¹**fine** \'fīn\ *n* : a sum of money imposed as punishment for an offense [Old French *fin* "end, fine", from Latin *finis* "end, limit, boundary"]

²**fine** *vt* : to impose a fine on : punish by a fine

³**fine** *adj* **1 a** : free from impurity **b** : having a stated proportion of pure metal in the composition ⟨silver 800/1000 *fine*⟩ **2 a** : very thin in gauge or texture ⟨*fine* thread⟩ **b** : not coarse ⟨*fine* sand⟩ **c** : very small ⟨*fine* print⟩ **3** : subtle or sensitive in perception or discrimination ⟨a *fine* distinction⟩ **4** : superior in quality, conception, or appearance : EXCELLENT ⟨a *fine* musician⟩ **5** : marked by or affecting elegance or refinement ⟨*fine* manners⟩ **6** : to one's liking : AGREEABLE ⟨that's *fine* with me⟩ [Old French *fin*, from Latin *finis* "end, limit"] — **fine·ly** *adv* — **fine·ness** \'fīn-nəs\ *n*

⁴**fine** *adv* : FINELY

⁵**fi·ne** \'fē-ˌnā\ *n* : END — used as a direction in music to mark the closing point after a repeat [Italian, from Latin *finis* "end"]

fine adjustment *n* : a knob on a microscope used for making small changes in focus — compare COARSE ADJUSTMENT

fine art *n* : art (as sculpture or music) concerned primarily with the creation of beautiful objects — usually used in pl.

fin·ery \'fīn-rē, -ə-rē\ *n, pl* **-er·ies** : ORNAMENT 1, DECORATION; *esp* : showy clothing and jewels

fines \'fīnz\ *n pl* : finely crushed or powdered material (as ore or coal)

¹**fi·nesse** \fə-'nes\ *n* **1** : refinement or delicacy of workmanship or composition ⟨a painting done with *finesse*⟩ **2** : skillful handling of a situation : CUNNING, SUBTLETY **3** : the withholding of one's highest card or trump in the hope that a lower card will take the trick because the only opposing higher card is in the hand of an opponent who has already played [Middle French, from *fin* "fine"]

²**finesse** *vb* **1 a** : to make a finesse in playing cards **b** : to play (a card) as a finesse **2 a** : to bring about by shrewd maneuvering **b** : to get the better of : TRICK

¹**fin·ger** \'fiÌ„ng-gər\ *n* **1** : one of the five divisions of the end of the hand; *esp* : one other than the thumb **2 a** : something that resembles or does the work of a finger **b** : a part of a glove into which a finger is inserted **3** : the breadth of a finger [Old English] — **fin·ger·like** \-ˌlīk\ *adj*

²**finger** *vb* **fin·gered; fin·ger·ing** \'fing-gə-ring, -gring\ **1** : to touch with the fingers : HANDLE **2** : to perform with the fingers or with a certain fingering **3** : to mark the notes of a piece of music to show what fingers are to be used **4** : to point out : IDENTIFY

fin·ger·board \'fing-gər-ˌbōrd, -ˌbord\ *n* : the part of a stringed instrument against which the fingers press the strings to vary the pitch

finger bowl *n* : a small bowl to hold water for rinsing the fingers at the table

finger hole *n* : a hole in a wind instrument by means of which the pitch of the tone is changed when it is left open or closed by the finger

fin·ger·ing *n* **1** : the act or process of handling or touching with the fingers **2 a** : the act or method of using the fingers in playing an instrument **b** : the marking of the method of fingering

fin·ger·ling \'fing-gər-ling\ *n* : a young fish especially up to one year of age

fin·ger·nail \'fing-gər-ˌnāl, ˌfing-gər-'\ *n* : the nail of a finger

finger painting *n* **1** : a technique of spreading pigment on paper with the fingertips **2** : a picture produced by finger painting

fin·ger·post \'fing-gər-ˌpōst\ *n* : a post bearing one or more signs often terminating in a pointing finger

fin·ger·print \'fing-gər-ˌprint\ *n* : the pattern of marks made by pressing the tip of a finger or thumb on a surface; *esp* : an ink impression of the lines on the tip of a finger or thumb taken for the purpose of identification — **fingerprint** *vt*

fin·ger·tip \-ˌtip\ *n* : the tip of a finger

fin·i·al \'fin-ē-əl\ *n* : an ornamental projection or end (as on a spire or topping a lamp shade) [Middle English, from *final, finial* "final"]

finial

fin·icky \'fin-i-kē\ *adj* : very particular or exacting in taste or standards : FUSSY [probably derived from ³*fine*] — **fin·ick·i·ness** *n*

fi·nis \'fin-əs, 'fī-nəs\ *n* : END 1b, CONCLUSION [Latin]

¹**fin·ish** \'fin-ish\ *vb* **1 a** : to bring or come to an end : TERMINATE **b** : to use or dispose of entirely **2 a** : to bring to completion : PERFECT **b** : to put a final coat or surface on **3** : to bring about the death of **4** : to come to the end of a course, task, or undertaking [Middle French *finiss-*, stem of *finir* "to finish", from Latin *finire*, from *finis* "end"] — **fin·ish·er** *n* □ SYN COMPLETE: FINISH implies accomplishing the final act or stage in producing, performing, or perfecting something (needed more paint to *finish* the job) COMPLETE stresses a bringing of something to a state of wholeness, fullness, or soundness (one more link was needed to *complete* the circle)

²**finish** *n* **1** : END 1b, CONCLUSION (a close *finish* in a race) **2** : the final treatment or coating of a surface **3** : cultivation in manners and speech : social polish

finishing school *n* : a private school for girls that emphasizes cultural studies and prepares students especially for social activities

finish line *n* : a line marking the end of a racecourse

fi·nite \'fī-nīt\ *adj* **1** : having definite or definable limits : limited in scope or nature **2** : not infinite but limited in number or extent; *esp* : having the number of elements or terms equal to zero or some positive integer (a *finite* set) **3** : showing distinction of grammatical person and number (a *finite* verb) [Latin *finitus*, past participle of *finire* "to limit, finish"] — **fi·nite·ly** *adv* — **fi·nite·ness** *n*

Finn \'fin\ *n* **1** : a member of a people speaking Finnish or a related language **2 a** : a native or inhabitant of Finland **b** : a person of Finnish descent [Swedish *Finne*]

¹**Finn·ish** \'fin-ish\ *adj* : of, relating to, or characteristic of Finland, the Finns, or Finnish

²**Finnish** *n* : a Finno-Ugric language spoken in Finland, Karelia, and small areas of Sweden and Norway

Fin·no–Ugric \,fin-ō-'yü-grik, -'ü-\ *adj* **1** : of or relating to any of various peoples including the Finnish and Hungarian peoples and the Lapps and Estonians **2** : of, relating to, or constituting a subfamily of the Uralic family of languages comprising various languages spoken in Hungary, Finland, Estonia, and northwestern Russia [derived from *Finn* + Old Russian *Ugre* "Hungarians"] — **Finno–Ugric** *n*

fin·ny \'fin-ē\ *adj* **1** : resembling or having fins **2** : of, relating to, or full of fish

fiord *variant of* FJORD

fip·ple flute \'fip-əl-\ *n* : a wind instrument (as the recorder) in which air is blown through a flue in the mouthpiece [origin unknown]

fir \'fər\ *n* **1** : any of various usually large symmetrical evergreen trees of the pine family which have cones growing upward on the branches and some of which yield useful lumber or resins **2** : the wood of a fir [Old English *fyrh*]

¹**fire** \'fīr\ *n* **1** : the light and heat and especially the flame produced by burning **2** : fuel that is burning (as in a fireplace or stove) **3** : the destructive burning of something (as a building or a forest) **4** : ardent liveliness : ENTHUSIASM **5** : the discharge of firearms [Old English *fyr*] — **on fire 1 a** : in a state of combustion **b** : very hot **2** : EAGER — **under fire 1** : exposed to the firing of an enemy's guns **2** : under attack

²**fire** *vb* **1 a** : to set on fire : KINDLE, IGNITE **b** : STIR, ENLIVEN (*fire* the imagination) **2** : to dismiss from employment **3** : to cause to explode (*fire* dynamite) **4** : to propel from or as if from a gun (*fire* an arrow): **a** : DISCHARGE (*fire* a gun) **b** : LAUNCH (*fire* a rocket) **c** : to throw with speed : HURL (*fired* the ball to first base) **5 a** : to subject to intense heat (*fire* pottery) **b** : to feed or serve the fire of (*fire* a furnace) **6 a** : to take fire :

KINDLE **b** : to have the explosive charge ignite at the proper time (a cylinder that does not *fire* right) **7 a** : to discharge a firearm **b** : to emit or let fly an object — **fir·er** *n*

fire·arm \'fīr-,ärm\ *n* : a weapon from which a shot is discharged by gunpowder — usually used only of a small arm (as a rifle or pistol)

fire·ball \-,bȯl\ *n* **1** : a ball of fire **2** : a brilliant meteor **3** : the highly luminous cloud of vapor and dust created by a nuclear explosion (as of an atom bomb)

fire blight *n* : a destructive highly infectious disease especially of apples and pears that is caused by a bacterium

fire·boat \'fīr-,bōt\ *n* : a boat or ship equipped with apparatus (as pumps) for fighting fire

fire·bomb \-,bäm\ *n* : an incendiary bomb — **firebomb** *vt*

fire·box \-,bäks\ *n* **1** : a chamber (as of a furnace or steam boiler) that contains a fire **2** : a box containing an apparatus for transmitting an alarm to a fire station

fire·brand \-,brand\ *n* **1** : a piece of burning wood **2** : a person who creates unrest or strife : AGITATOR

fire·break \-,brāk\ *n* : a barrier of cleared or plowed land intended to check a forest or grass fire

fire·brick \-,brik\ *n* : a brick capable of withstanding great heat and used for lining furnaces or fireplaces

fire·bug \-,bəg\ *n* : a person who deliberately sets destructive fires : ARSONIST

fire·clay \-,klā\ *n* : clay capable of withstanding high temperatures and used especially for firebrick and crucibles

fire·crack·er \-,krak-ər\ *n* : a paper cylinder containing an explosive and a fuse that is usually set off for amusement to make a noise

fire·damp \-,damp\ *n* : a combustible mine gas that consists chiefly of methane; *also* : the explosive mixture of this gas with air

fire·dog \-,dȯg\ *n, chiefly Southern & Midland* : ANDIRON

fire drill *n* : a practice drill in extinguishing fires or in the conduct and manner of exit in case of fire

fire engine *n* : an apparatus for directing water or an extinguishing chemical on fires; *esp* : a motortruck equipped with such an apparatus

fire escape *n* : a stairway or ladder for escape from a burning building

fire extinguisher *n* : something used to put out a fire; *esp* : a portable apparatus for ejecting fire-extinguishing chemicals

fire fighter *n* : one that fights fires : FIREMAN — **fire fighting** *n*

fire·fly \'fīr-,flī\ *n* : a winged nocturnal insect producing a bright soft flashing light; *esp* : the male of various long flat beetles — called also *lightning bug*

fire·house \-,haüs\ *n* : FIRE STATION

fire irons *n pl* : implements for tending a fire especially in a fireplace

fire·light \'fīr-,līt\ *n* : the light of a fire (as in a fireplace)

fire·man \-mən\ *n* **1** : a member of a company organized to fight fires **2** : one who tends or feeds fires : STOKER

fire·place \-,plās\ *n* : a structure (as a recess opening into a chimney) with a hearth on which an open fire can be built for heat or especially outdoors for cooking

fire·plug \-,pləg\ *n* : HYDRANT

fire·pow·er \-,paü-ər, -,paur\ *n* : the ability (as of a military unit) to deliver gunfire or missiles on a target

¹**fire·proof** \-'prüf\ *adj* : proof against or resistant to fire

²**fireproof** *vt* : to make fireproof

fire sale *n* : a sale of merchandise damaged by fire

fire screen *n* : a protecting screen before a fireplace

fire·side \'fīr-,sīd\ *n* **1** : a place near the fire or hearth **2** : HOME 1a

\ə\ abut	\ng\ sing
\ər\ further	\ō\ bone
\a\ mat	\ȯ\ saw
\ā\ take	\ȯi\ coin
\ä\ cot, cart	\th\ thin
\aü\ out	\th\ this
\ch\ chin	\ü\ food
\e\ pet	\u̇\ foot
\ē\ easy	\y\ yet
\g\ go	\yü\ few
\i\ tip	\yu̇\ cure
\ī\ life	\zh\ vision
\j\ job	

firkin 1

fire station *n* : a building housing fire apparatus and usually fire fighters

fire tower *n* : a tower (as in a forest) from which a watch for fires is kept

fire·trap \'fīr-ˌtrap\ *n* : a place (as a building) apt to catch on fire or difficult to escape from in case of fire

fire wall *n* : a wall for preventing the spread of fire

fire·wa·ter \-ˌwȯt-ər, -ˌwät\ *n* : intoxicating liquor

fire·weed \-ˌwēd\ *n* **1** : a tall perennial with long spikes of pinkish purple flowers that is related to the evening primrose and tends to spring up in clearings or burned areas **2** : any of several plants similar or related to the fireweed

fire·wood \-ˌwu̇d\ *n* : wood cut for fuel

fire·work \-ˌwərk\ *n* **1** : a device for producing a striking display (as of light, noise, or smoke) by the combustion of explosive or flammable compositions **2** *pl* : a display of fireworks **3** *pl* : a display of temper or hostility

firing line *n* **1** : a line from which gunfire is directed at a target **2** : the forefront of an activity

firing pin *n* : a pin that strikes the cartridge primer in the breech mechanism of a firearm

firing squad *n* **1** : a detachment detailed to fire volleys over the grave of one buried with military honors **2** : a detachment detailed to carry out a death sentence by shooting

fir·kin \'fər-kən\ *n* **1** : a small wooden vessel or cask **2** : any of various British units of capacity usually equal to ¼ barrel [derived from Dutch *veerdel* "fourth"]

¹firm \'fərm\ *adj* **1 a** : securely or solidly fixed in place **b** : not weak or uncertain : VIGOROUS **c** : having a solid or compact texture **2 a** : not subject to change or fluctuation (a *firm* price) **b** : not easily moved or disturbed : STEADFAST **c** : WELL-FOUNDED **3** : indicating firmness or resolution (a *firm* mouth) [Middle French *ferm*, from Latin *firmus*] — **firm·ly** *adv* — **firm·ness** *n*

²firm *vb* **1 a** : to make secure (*firm* one's grip on a racket) **b** : to make solid or compact (*firm* the soil) **2** : to become firm

³firm *n* **1** : the name under which a company does business **2** : a business partnership of two or more persons **3** : a business enterprise [German *firma*, from Italian, "signature", derived from Latin *firmare* "to make firm, confirm", from *firmus* "firm"]

fir·ma·ment \'fər-mə-mənt\ *n* : the arch of the sky : HEAVENS [Latin *firmamentum* "support", from *firmare* "to make firm"]

firm·ware \'fərm-ˌwaər, -ˌweər\ *n* : computer programs contained permanently in a hardware device

firn \'firn\ *n* : NÉVÉ [German]

¹first \'fərst\ *adj* **1** : being number one in a countable series (the *first* day of spring) **2** : preceding all others (as in time, order, or importance) **3** : being the lowest forward gear or speed of a motor vehicle **4** : highest or most prominent in carrying the melody (*first* violin) [Old English *fyrst*]

²first *adv* **1 a** : before any other (we got there *first*) **b** : for the first time **2** : in preference to something else : SOONER

³first *n* **1** : number one in a countable series (the *first* of the month) — see NUMBER table **2** : something that is first: as **a** : the lowest gear or speed of a motor vehicle **b** : the winning place in a competition or contest

first aid *n* : emergency care or treatment given to an ill or injured person — **first–aid·er** \'fərst-'ād-ər\ *n*

first base *n* **1** : the base that must be touched first by a base runner in baseball **2** : the position of the player defending the area around first base **3** : the first step or stage in a course of action (the plan never got to *first base*)

first base·man \'bā-smən\ *n* : the player defending the area around first base

first·born \'fərst-'bȯrn, 'fərs-\ *adj* : born first : ELDEST — **firstborn** *n*

first class *n* : the best or highest group in a classification: as **a** : the highest class of travel accommodations **b** : a class of mail that comprises letters, postcards, or matter sealed against inspection — **first–class** *adj or adv*

first day cover *n* : a stamp collector's cover bearing a newly issued postage stamp that is postmarked on the first day of issue at a city officially chosen for the first day of sale

first down *n* **1** : the first of a series of four downs in football in which a team must make a net gain of 10 yards (about 9.1 meters) **2** : a gain of 10 or more yards within four downs that permits a team to start a new series of four downs

first·hand \'fərst-'hand\ *adj* : coming directly from the original source — **firsthand** *adv*

first lady *n, often cap F&L* **1** : the wife or hostess of a male chief executive of a country or jurisdiction **2** : the leading woman of an art or profession

first lieutenant *n* : an officer rank in the Army, Marine Corps, and Air Force above second lieutenant and below captain

first·ling \'fərst-liŋ\ *n* : one that comes or is produced first

first·ly \-lē\ *adv* : in the first place

first person *n* **1** : a set of words or forms (as pronouns or verb forms) referring to the speaker or writer of the utterance in which they occur; *also* : a word or form belonging to such a set **2** : a writing style marked by general use of the first person

first–rate \'fərst-'rāt\ *adj* : of the first order of size, importance, or quality — **first–rate** *adv* — **first–rat·er** \-'rāt-ər\ *n*

First Reader *n* : a Christian Scientist chosen to conduct meetings for a specified time and specifically to read aloud from the writings of Mary Baker Eddy

first sergeant *n* **1** : a noncommissioned officer serving as chief enlisted assistant to the commander (as of a company) **2** : an enlisted rank in the Army above a platoon sergeant and below command sergeant major and in the Marine Corps above gunnery sergeant and below sergeant major

first–string \'fərst-'striŋ, 'fərs-\ *adj* : being a regular as distinguished from a substitute (as on a football team)

first water *n* **1** : the purest luster — used of gems **2** : the highest grade, degree, or quality (a novel of the *first water*)

firth \'fərth\ *n* : a narrow arm of the sea; *also* : ESTUARY [Old Norse *fjörthr*]

fis·cal \'fis-kəl\ *adj* **1** : of or relating to taxation, public revenues, or public debt **2** : of or relating to financial matters [Latin *fiscalis*, from *fiscus* "basket, treasury"] SYN see FINANCIAL — **fis·cal·ly** \-kə-lē\ *adv*

¹fish \'fish\ *n, pl* **fish** *or* **fish·es** **1 a** : an aquatic animal — usually used in combination (star*fish*) (cuttle*fish*) **b** : any of numerous cold-blooded aquatic water-breathing vertebrates with a usually long scaly body, limbs developed as fins, and a vertical tail fin **2** : the flesh of fish used as food **3** : INDIVIDUAL 2 (an odd *fish*) **4** : a piece of wood or iron fastened alongside another member to strengthen it [Old English *fisc*] — **fish·like** \'fish-ˌlīk\ *adj*

²fish *vb* **1** : to catch fish **2** : to catch or try to catch fish in (*fish* the stream) **3** : to search (as with a hook) for something underwater **4** : to seek something by or as if by groping or feeling

fish–and–chips \ˌfish-ən-'chips\ *n pl* : fried fish and french fried potatoes

fish cake *n* : a round fried cake made of shredded fish and mashed potato — called also *fish ball*

fish·er \'fish-ər\ *n* **1** : one that fishes **2** : a large dark brown North American flesh-eating mammal related to the weasels; *also* : its valuable fur or pelt

¹fish 1b: *1* operculum, *2* scales, *3* lateral line

fish·er·man \-mən\ *n* **1** : one who engages in fishing as an occupation or for pleasure **2** : a ship used in commercial fishing

fish·ery \'fish-rē, -ə-rē\ *n, pl* **-er·ies** **1** : the activity or business of taking fish or other aquatic animals **2** : a place or establishment for catching fish or other aquatic animals

fish hawk *n* : OSPREY

fish·hook \'fish-ˌhu̇k\ *n* : a usually barbed hook for catching fish

fish·ing *n* : the sport or business of catching fish

fish ladder *n* : a series of pools arranged like steps by which fishes can pass over or around a dam in going upstream

fish meal *n* : ground dried fish and fish waste used as fertilizer and animal food

fish·mon·ger \'fish-ˌməng-gər, -ˌmäng-\ *n, chiefly British* : a fish dealer

fish·net \-ˌnet\ *n* : netting fitted with floats and weights or a supporting frame for catching fish

fish·plate \-ˌplāt\ *n* : a steel plate used to lap a butt joint

fish·pond \-ˌpänd\ *n* : a pond stocked with edible fish

fish stick *n* : a small elongated breaded fillet of fish

fish story *n* : an extravagant or incredible story

fish·wife \'fish-ˌwīf\ *n* **1** : a woman who sells fish **2** : a coarsely abusive woman

fishy \'fish-ē\ *adj* **fish·i·er; -est** **1** : of, relating to, or resembling fish ⟨a *fishy* odor⟩ **2** : creating doubt or suspicion : QUESTIONABLE ⟨that story sounds *fishy* to me⟩

fis·sile \'fis-əl, -ˌīl\ *adj* **1** : capable of being split or divided along the grain or along planes ⟨a *fissile* crystal⟩ **2** : FISSIONABLE

¹fis·sion \'fish-ən *also* 'fizh-\ *n* **1** : a splitting or breaking up into parts **2** : reproduction by spontaneous division of a body or a cell into two or more parts each of which grows into a complete individual **3** : the splitting of an atomic nucleus resulting in the release of large amounts of energy [Latin *fissio,* from *findere* "to split"]

²fission *vb* : to undergo or cause to undergo fission

fis·sion·able \'fish-nə-bəl, 'fizh, -ə-nə-\ *adj* : capable of undergoing fission ⟨*fissionable* material⟩

fis·sip·a·rous \fis-'ip-ə-rəs\ *adj* : tending to break something up into parts : DIVISIVE [Latin *fissus,* past participle of *findere* "to split" + *parere* "to give birth to, produce"]

¹fis·sure \'fish-ər\ *n* : a narrow opening or crack of some length and depth ⟨a *fissure* in rock⟩

²fissure *vb* **1** : to break into fissures : CLEAVE **2** : CRACK 2, DIVIDE

fist \'fist\ *n* **1** : the hand clenched with fingers doubled into the palm **2** : CLUTCH 1a, GRASP **3** : INDEX 5 [Old English *fȳst*]

fist·ic \'fis-tik\ *adj* : of or relating to boxing or to fist fighting

fist·i·cuffs \'fis-ti-ˌkəfs\ *n pl* : a fight with the fists [alteration of *fisty cuff,* from *fisty* "fistic" + *cuff*]

fis·tu·la \'fis-chə-lə\ *n, pl* **-las** *or* **-lae** \-ˌlē, -ˌlī\ : an abnormal passage leading from an abscess or hollow organ to the body surface or from one hollow organ to another [Latin, "reed, pipe, fistula"] — **fis·tu·lous** \-ləs\ *adj*

¹fit \'fit\ *n* **1** : a sudden violent attack of a disorder (as epilepsy) especially when marked by convulsions or loss of consciousness **2** : a sudden flurry (as of activity) ⟨completed the assignment in a *fit* of efficiency⟩ **3** : an emotional outburst ⟨a *fit* of anger⟩ [Old English *fitt* "strife"] — **by fits** *or* **by fits and starts** : in an impulsive and irregular manner

²fit *adj* **fit·ter; fit·test** **1 a** : adapted to an end or design : APPROPRIATE ⟨water *fit* for drinking⟩ **b** : adapted to the environment so as to be capable of surviving **2** : SEEMLY 3, PROPER **3** : put into a suitable state ⟨a house *fit* to

live in⟩ **4** : QUALIFIED 1, COMPETENT **5** : sound physically and mentally : HEALTHY [Middle English] — **fit·ly** *adv* — **fit·ness** *n* □ SYN FIT, SUITABLE, PROPER, APPROPRIATE mean right with respect to the nature, condition, or use of the thing qualified. FIT stresses adaptability to the end in view or special readiness for a particular activity ⟨*fit* to teach young children⟩ SUITABLE implies answering the demands or requirements of an occasion ⟨*suitable* clothes for the reception⟩ PROPER suggests a suitability through essential nature ⟨a *proper* diet⟩ or in accordance with custom ⟨a request made in *proper* form⟩ APPROPRIATE implies a marked or distinctive fitness or suitability ⟨*appropriate* words of congratulation⟩

³fit *vb* **fit·ted; fit·ting** **1** : to be suitable for or to : BEFIT **2 a** : to be correctly adjusted to or shaped for **b** : to insert or adjust until correctly in place **c** : to make a place or room for **3** : to be in agreement or accord with ⟨the theory *fits* the facts⟩ **4 a** : to make ready : PREPARE **b** : to bring to a required form and size : ADJUST **c** : to cause to conform to or suit something else **5** : SUPPLY, EQUIP ⟨*fit* her with new shoes⟩ **6** : to be in harmony or accord : BELONG [Middle English *fitten*] — **fit·ter** \'fit-ər\ *n*

⁴fit *n* **1** : the quality, state, or manner of being fitted **2** : the manner in which clothing fits the wearer **3** : the degree of closeness with which surfaces are brought together in an assembly of parts

fitch \'fich\ *or* **fitch·ew** \'fich-ü\ *n* : POLECAT 1; *also* : its fur or pelt [Middle French *fichau,* from Dutch *vitsau*]

fit·ful \'fit-fəl\ *adj* : not regular : INTERMITTENT ⟨a *fitful* breeze⟩ — **fit·ful·ly** \-fə-lē\ *adv* — **fit·ful·ness** *n*

¹fit·ting *adj* : of a kind appropriate to the situation : SUITABLE — **fit·ting·ly** \-ing-lē\ *adv* — **fit·ting·ness** *n*

²fitting *n* **1 a** : the action or act of one that fits **b** : a trying on of clothes being made or altered **2** : a small often standardized accessory ⟨an electrical *fitting*⟩

five \'fīv\ *n* **1** : one more than four; *also* : a symbol representing this — see NUMBER table **2** : the fifth in a set or series **3** : something having five units or members; *esp* : a basketball team **4** : a 5-dollar bill **5** : FIFTEEN 2 [Old English *fīf*] — **five** *adj or pron*

five–and–ten \ˌfī-vən-'ten\ *also* **five–and–dime** \-'dīm\ *n* : a variety store that carries chiefly inexpensive items

five–year plan *n* : one of a series of detailed plans for development (as economic) each of which covers a 5-year period

¹fix \'fiks\ *vb* **1 a** : to make firm, stable, or fast **b** : to give a permanent or final form to: as (1) : to change into a stable or available form ⟨bacteria that *fix* nitrogen⟩ (2) : to kill, harden, and preserve for microscopic study (3) : to make the image of (a photographic film or print) permanent by chemical treatment **c** : AFFIX 1, ATTACH **2** : to hold or direct steadily ⟨*fixed* their eyes on the horizon⟩ **3 a** : to set or place definitely : ESTABLISH ⟨*fix* the date of a meeting⟩ **b** : ASSIGN ⟨*fix* blame⟩ **4** : to set in order : ADJUST **5** : to get ready : PREPARE ⟨*fix* lunch⟩ **6 a** : to make sound or whole again: (1) : REPAIR, MEND ⟨*fix* the clock⟩ (2) : RESTORE, CURE ⟨the doctor *fixed* me up⟩ **b** : SPAY, CASTRATE **7** : to influence the actions, outcome, or effect of by improper or illegal methods ⟨*fix* a horse race⟩ [Latin *fixus,* past participle of *figere* "to fasten"] — **fix·able** \'fik-sə-bəl\ *adj* □ SYN FIX, REPAIR mean to restore to sound condition or working order. FIX tends to stress the arranging, straightening out, or adjusting of parts ⟨*fix* a clock⟩ ⟨get one's teeth *fixed*⟩ REPAIR usually stresses the replacing or remaking of damaged or lost parts ⟨*repair* a damaged automobile⟩

²fix *n* **1** : a position of difficulty or embarrassment : PREDICAMENT **2** : the position (as of a ship) determined by bearings, observations, or radio; *also* : a precise determination of one's position **3** : a shot of a narcotic

\ə\ abut		\ng\ sing
\ər\ further		\ō\ bone
\a\ mat		\o̅\ saw
\ā\ take		\oi\ coin
\ä\ cot, cart		\th\ thin
\au̇\ out		\th\ this
\ch\ chin		\ü\ food
\e\ pet		\u̇\ foot
\ē\ easy		\y\ yet
\g\ go		\yü\ few
\i\ tip		\yu̇\ cure
\ī\ life		\zh\ vision
\j\ job		

fix·ate \'fik-ˌsāt\ *vb* **1** : to make unchanging : FIX **2 a** : to focus one's eyes upon **b** : to concentrate one's attention

fix·a·tion \fik-'sā-shən\ *n* **1** : the act, process, or result of fixing or fixating ⟨*fixation* of nitrogen⟩ **2** : an unhealthy or abnormally persistent state of concern or attachment

fix·a·tive \'fik-sət-iv\ *n* : something that stabilizes or sets: as **a** : a substance added to a perfume especially to prevent too rapid evaporation **b** : a varnish used especially for the protection of pencil or charcoal drawings — **fixative** *adj*

fixed \'fikst\ *adj* **1 a** : securely placed or fastened : STATIONARY **b** (1) : NONVOLATILE ⟨*fixed* oil⟩ (2) : COMBINED ⟨*fixed* nitrogen⟩ **c** : not subject to change or fluctuation : SETTLED ⟨a *fixed* income⟩ **d** : recurring on the same date from year to year ⟨*fixed* holidays⟩ **e** : INTENT ⟨a *fixed* stare⟩ **2** : supplied with something (as money) needed or desirable — **fix·ed·ly** \'fix-səd-lē\ *adv* — **fix·ed·ness** \'fik-səd-nəs\ *n*

fixed–point *adj* : involving or being a mathematical notation (as in a decimal system) in which the point separating integers and fractions is fixed — compare FLOATING-POINT

fix·er \'fik-sər\ *n* **1** : one that fixes **2** : ¹HYPO

fixed star *n* : a star so distant that its motion can be measured only by very precise long-term observations

fix·ing \'fik-siŋ, *2 is often* -sənz\ *n* **1** : a putting in permanent form **2** *pl* : TRIMMINGS ⟨a turkey dinner with all the *fixings*⟩

fix·i·ty \'fik-sət-ē\ *n* : the quality or state of being fixed or stable

fix·ture \'fiks-chər\ *n* **1** : the act of fixing : the state of being fixed **2** : something attached to another thing as a permanent part ⟨bathroom *fixtures*⟩ **3** : one firmly established in a place

¹fizz \'fiz\ *vi* : to make a hissing or sputtering sound [probably imitative]

²fizz *n* **1** : a hissing sound **2** : an effervescent beverage — **fizzy** \'fiz-ē\ *adj*

¹fiz·zle \'fiz-əl\ *vi* **fiz·zled; fiz·zling** \'fiz-liŋ, -ə-liŋ\ **1** : FIZZ **2** : to fail or end feebly especially after a promising start [probably alteration of *fist* "to break wind"]

²fizzle *n* : an abortive effort : FAILURE

fjord *or* **fiord** \fē-'ord\ *n* : a narrow inlet of the sea between cliffs or steep slopes [Norwegian, from Old Norse *fjörthr*]

flab·ber·gast \'flab-ər-ˌgast\ *vt* : to overwhelm with shock, surprise, or wonder : ASTOUND [origin unknown]

flab·by \'flab-ē\ *adj* **flab·bi·er; -est 1** : lacking resilience or firmness **2** : being weak and ineffective : FEEBLE [alteration of *flappy* "tending to flap"] SYN see LIMP — **flab·bi·ly** \'flab-ə-lē\ *adv* — **flab·bi·ness** \'flab-ē-nəs\ *n*

flac·cid \'flak-səd, 'flas-əd\ *adj* : FLABBY ⟨a *flaccid* muscle⟩; *also* : deficient in turgor ⟨*flaccid* stems⟩ [Latin *flaccidus*] SYN see LIMP — **flac·cid·i·ty** \flak-'sid-ət-ē, fla-\ *n* — **flac·cid·ly** \'flak-səd-lē, 'flas-əd-\ *adv*

flac·on \'flak-ən, -ˌän; fla-'kōⁿ\ *n* : a small usually ornamental bottle with a tight cap [French]

¹flag \'flag\ *n* : any of various plants with long narrow leaves: as **a** : IRIS; *esp* : a wild iris **b** : SWEET FLAG [Middle English *flagge* "reed, rush"]

²flag *n* **1** : a hard stone that is composed of even layers and splits into flat pieces suitable for paving **2** : a thin piece of flag used for paving [Old Norse *flaga* "slab"]

³flag *vt* **flagged; flag·ging** : to pave (as a walk) with flags

⁴flag *n* **1** : a usually rectangular piece of fabric of distinctive design that is used as a symbol (as of a nation) or as a signaling device **2 a** : something used like a flag to attract attention **b** : one of the cross strokes of a musical note less than a quarter note in value [perhaps from ¹*flag*]

⁵flag *vt* **flagged; flag·ging 1** : to put a flag on ⟨*flagged* the important pages with red tabs⟩ **2** : to signal with or as if with a flag; *esp* : to signal to stop ⟨*flag* a taxi⟩

⁶flag *vi* **flagged; flag·ging 1** : to hang loose without stiffness; *also* : to droop especially from lack of water ⟨plants *flagging* under the summer sun⟩ **2 a** : to become weak ⟨our interest *flagged*⟩ **b** : to decline in interest or attraction ⟨the topic *flagged*⟩ [origin unknown]

Flag Day *n* : June 14 observed in various states in commemoration of the adoption in 1777 of the official United States flag

fla·gel·lant \'flaj-ə-lənt, flə-'jel-ənt\ *n* : one that whips; *esp* : a person who scourges himself as a public penance

¹fla·gel·late \'flaj-ə-ˌlāt\ *vt* : to punish by whipping : WHIP [Latin *flagellare*, from *flagellum* "small whip", from *flagrum* "whip"] — **fla·gel·la·tion** \ˌflaj-ə-'lā-shən\ *n*

²fla·gel·late \'flaj-ə-lət, -ˌlāt; flə-'jel-ət\ *adj* **1 a** *or* **flag·el·lat·ed** \'flaj-ə-ˌlāt-əd\ : having flagella **b** : resembling a flagellum **2** : of, relating to, or caused by flagellates

³flagellate *like* ²\ *n* : a protozoan or alga having flagella

fla·gel·lum \flə-'jel-əm\ *n, pl* **-gel·la** \-'jel-ə\ *also* **-gel·lums** : a tapering process that projects singly or in groups from a cell and is the primary organ of motion of many microorganisms [Latin, "whip, shoot of a plant"] — **fla·gel·lar** \-'jel-ər\ *adj*

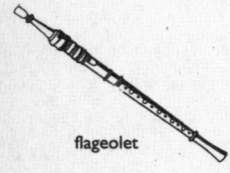

flageolet

fla·geo·let \ˌflaj-ə-'let\ *n* : a small woodwind instrument belonging to the flute class [French]

flag football *n* : a variation of football in which a player pulls a flag or handkerchief from the ballcarrier's clothing to stop play instead of tackling

flag·ging \'flag-iŋ\ *n* : a pavement of flagstones

fla·gi·tious \flə-'jish-əs\ *adj* : marked by outrageous or scandalous crime or vice : VILLAINOUS [Latin *flagitiosus*, from *flagitium* "shameful thing"] — **fla·gi·tious·ly** *adv* — **fla·gi·tious·ness** *n*

flag·man \'flag-mən\ *n* : one who signals with or as if with a flag

flag of truce : a white flag carried or displayed to an enemy to signal a desire to negotiate or surrender

flag·on \'flag-ən\ *n* : a container for liquids that has a handle, spout, and often a lid [Middle French *flascon*, *flacon* "bottle", from Late Latin *flasco*]

flag·pole \'flag-ˌpōl\ *n* : a pole on which to display a flag

flag rank *n* : any of the ranks in the Navy or Coast Guard above captain

fla·grant \'flā-grənt\ *adj* : conspicuously bad or objectionable : OUTRAGEOUS, NOTORIOUS ⟨*flagrant* abuse of power⟩ [Latin *flagrare* "to blaze, burn"] — **fla·gran·cy** \-grən-sē\ *n* — **fla·grant·ly** *adv* □ SYN FLAGRANT, GLARING, GROSS, RANK mean conspicuously bad or objectionable. FLAGRANT applies to behavior, errors, or offenses so bad that they cannot escape notice or be excused ⟨*flagrant* disobedience⟩ GLARING suggests painful or damaging obtrusiveness ⟨*glaring* imperfection⟩ GROSS applies to utterly inexcusable faults or offenses ⟨*gross* dishonesty⟩ ⟨*gross* carelessness⟩ RANK applies to what is openly and extremely objectionable and utterly condemned ⟨*rank* corruption in politics⟩

fla·gran·te de·lic·to \flə-ˌgrant-ē-di-'lik-ˌtō\ *adv* : in the very act of committing a misdeed [Medieval Latin, literally, "while the crime is blazing"]

flag·ship \'flag-ˌship\ *n* **1** : the ship that carries the commander of a fleet or subdivision thereof and flies his flag **2** : the finest, largest, or most important of a series or group

flag·staff \-ˌstaf\ *n* : FLAGPOLE

flag·stone \-ˌstōn\ *n* : ²FLAG 2

flag–wav·ing \'flag-ˌwā-viŋ\ *n* : passionate appeal to patriotic or partisan sentiment : political chauvinism

¹flail \'flāl\ *n* : a hand threshing tool consisting of a wooden handle with a free-swinging stout short stick at the end [Middle French *flaiel,* from Latin *flagellum* "whip"]

²flail *vb* : to strike with or as if with a flail

flair \'flaər, 'fleər\ *n* **1** : instinctive discernment ⟨relying on *flair* more than careful study⟩ **2** : natural aptitude : BENT **3** : a uniquely attractive quality ⟨a car with real *flair*⟩ [French, literally, "sense of smell", from Old French, "odor", from *flairier* "to give off an odor", from Late Latin *flagrare,* alteration of Latin *fragrare*] SYN SEE PENCHANT

flak \'flak\ *n* **1** : antiaircraft guns or the bursting shells fired from them **2** : severe criticism [German, from *flieger*abwehr*kanonen,* from *flieger* "flyer" + *abwehr* "defense" + *kanonen* "cannons"]

¹flake \'flāk\ *n* : a thin flattened usually loose piece ⟨a *flake* of snow⟩ ⟨soap *flakes*⟩ [Middle English, of Scandinavian origin]

²flake *vb* : to form or separate into flakes : make or become flaky ⟨this paint *flakes* badly⟩

flaky \'flā-kē\ *adj* **flak·i·er; -est 1** : consisting of flakes **2** : tending to flake ⟨pie with a crisp *flaky* crust⟩ — **flak·i·ness** *n*

flam·beau \'flam-,bō\ *n, pl* **flam·beaux** \-,bōz\ *or* **flambeaus** : a flaming torch [French]

flam·boy·ant \flam-'bȯi-ənt\ *adj* **1** *often cap* : characterized by waving curves suggesting flames ⟨*flamboyant* window tracery⟩ **2** : FLORID 1, ORNATE; *also* : brightly colored **3** : given to dashing display : SHOWY [French, from *flamboyer* "to flame", from Old French, from *flambe* "flame"] — **flam·boy·ance** \-əns\ *also* **flam·boy·an·cy** \-ən-sē\ *n* — **flam·boy·ant·ly** *adv*

¹flame \'flām\ *n* **1** : the glowing gaseous part of a fire **2 a** : a state of blazing combustion **b** : a condition or appearance suggesting a flame **3** : burning zeal or passion **4** : SWEETHEART [Middle French *flamme, flambe,* derived from Latin *flamma*]

²flame *vb* **1** : to burn with a flame : BLAZE **2** : to burst or break out violently or passionately ⟨*flaming* with anger⟩ **3** : to shine brightly : GLOW **4** : to treat or affect with flame — **flam·er** *n*

flame cell *n* : a hollow excretory cell of various lower invertebrates that has a tuft of cilia

fla·men·co \flə-'meng-kō\ *n, pl* **-cos** : a vigorous rhythmic dance style of the Andalusian Gypsies [Spanish, "Flemish, like a Gypsy", from Dutch *Vlaminc* "Fleming"] □ ORIGIN The Spanish homonyms *Flamenco,* "Fleming", and *flamenco,* "flamingo", are not related. From the first of these we get our English word *flamenco,* "a vigorous dance style of Gypsy origin". In the early 16th century the Holy Roman Emperor Charles V, who was also King Charles I of Spain, had several Flemish ministers unpopular with the king's Spanish subjects. It was probably because these particular Flemings were so detestable that *Flamenco,* the Spanish word for *Fleming,* became a disparaging term for any foreigner. Inhabitants of southern Spain used the term derisively for the Gypsies who came into that region in the 16th century. *Flamenco* was also applied to the dance style typical of these Gypsies.

flame·out \'flā-,maut\ *n* : the unintentional cessation of operation of a jet airplane engine

flame·proof \'flām-'prüf\ *adj* **1** : resistant to the action of flame **2** : not burning on contact with flame

flame·throw·er \-,thrō-ər, -,thrȯr\ *n* : a device that expels from a nozzle a burning stream of liquid or semiliquid fuel under pressure

flam·ing \'flā-ming\ *adj* **1** : producing flames **2** : suggesting a flame in brilliance or wavy outline **3** : ARDENT 1, PASSIONATE — **flam·ing·ly** \-ming-lē\ *adv*

fla·min·go \flə-'ming-gō\ *n, pl* **-gos** *also* **-goes** : any of several aquatic long-legged and long-necked birds with a broad bill bent downward at the end and usually rosy-white plumage with scarlet on the wings [Portuguese, from Spanish *flamenco,* derived from Latin *flamma* "flame"] □ ORIGIN English *flamingo* is a derivative, by way of Portuguese, of Spanish *flamenco,* "flamingo". This *flamenco* comes from Latin *flamma* "flame". Most flamingos are pale pink or rosy white. When standing at rest or wading about in search of food, they do not seem to justify their vivid name. But when they take flight, the sudden flash of their scarlet wing coverts against the coal black of their quill feathers is like a burst of flame.

flam·ma·ble \'flam-ə-bəl\ *adj* : capable of being easily ignited and of burning with extreme rapidity — **flam·ma·bil·i·ty** \,flam-ə-'bil-ət-ē\ *n* — **flam·mable** *n*

fla·neur \flä-'nər\ *n* : an aimless person: as **a** : MAN-ABOUT-TOWN **b** : an intellectual trifler [French *flâneur* "idler"]

¹flange \'flanj\ *n* : a rib or rim used for strength, for guiding, or for attachment to another object ⟨a *flange* on a pipe⟩ [perhaps derived from Middle French *flanche* "flank", from *flanc*]

²flange *vt* : to furnish with a flange

¹flank \'flangk\ *n* **1 a** : the fleshy part of the side between the ribs and the hip; *also* : the side of a four-footed animal **b** : a cut of meat from this part of an animal **2 a** : SIDE **b** : the right or left of a formation [Old French *flanc,* of Germanic origin]

²flank *vt* **1 a** : to attack or threaten the flank of **b** : to turn the flank of **2** : to be situated at the side of : BORDER

flank·er \'flang-kər\ *n* **1** : one that flanks **2** : a football player stationed wide of the formation; *esp* : an offensive halfback who lines up on the flank and serves chiefly as a pass receiver — called also *flanker back*

flan·nel \'flan-l\ *n* **1 a** : a soft twilled wool or worsted fabric with a napped surface **b** : a stout cotton fabric napped on one side **2** *pl* : flannel underwear or trousers [Middle English *flaunneol* "woolen cloth or garment"]

flan·nel·ette \,flan-l-'et\ *n* : a cotton flannel napped on one or both sides

¹flap \'flap\ *n* **1** : a stroke with something broad : SLAP **2** : something broad, limber, or flat and usually thin that hangs loose: as **a** : a piece on a garment that hangs free **b** : an extended part forming the closure (as of an envelope) **3** : the motion of something broad and limber **4** : a movable auxiliary airfoil attached to the trailing edge of an airplane wing permitting a steeper gliding angle in landing **5** : a state of excitement or agitation : UPROAR ⟨created a *flap* by denying the workers their raises⟩ [Middle English *flappe*]

²flap *vb* **flapped; flap·ping 1** : to beat with something broad and flat **2** : to move or cause to move with a beating motion ⟨birds *flapping* their wings⟩ **3** : to sway loosely usually with a noise of striking ⟨the flag *flapped* in the wind⟩ **4** : to talk foolishly and persistently

flap·jack \'flap-,jak\ *n* : PANCAKE

flap·per \'flap-ər\ *n* **1** : one that flaps **2** : a young woman especially of the 1920s who shows bold freedom from conventions in conduct and dress

¹flare \'flaər, 'fleər\ *vb* **1** : to burn with an unsteady flame **2 a** : to shine with a sudden light **b** : to become suddenly excited or angry ⟨*flare* up⟩ **3** : to open or spread outward [origin unknown]

²flare *n* **1** : an unsteady glaring light **2 a** : a fire or blaze of light used to signal, illuminate, or attract attention; *also* : a device or composition used to produce such a flare **b** : a temporary outburst of energy from a small area of the sun's surface **3** : a sudden outburst (as of sound, excitement, or anger) **4** : a spreading outward; *also* : a place or part that spreads ⟨the *flare* of a skirt⟩ ⟨the *flare* of a trumpet⟩

flare–up \-,əp\ *n* : a sudden burst (as of flame or anger)

flamingo

\ə\ abut		\ng\ sing	
\ər\ further		\ō\ bone	
\a\ mat		\ȯ\ saw	
\ā\ take		\ȯi\ coin	
\ä\ cot, cart		\th\ thin	
\au\ out		\th\ this	
\ch\ chin		\ü\ food	
\e\ pet		\u̇\ foot	
\ē\ easy		\y\ yet	
\g\ go		\yü\ few	
\i\ tip		\yu̇\ cure	
\ī\ life		\zh\ vision	
\j\ job			

¹flash \'flash\ *vb* **1** : to shine in or like a sudden flame ⟨lightning *flashed*⟩ **2** : to send out in or as if in flashes ⟨*flash* a message⟩ **3** : to appear or pass very suddenly ⟨a car *flashed* by⟩ **4** : to make a sudden display (as of brilliance or feeling) ⟨their eyes *flashed* with excitement⟩ **5** : to give off light suddenly or in brief bursts **6** : to expose briefly to view ⟨*flash* a badge⟩ [Middle English *flaschen*] □ SYN FLASH, GLANCE, GLINT, SPARKLE mean to send forth light. FLASH implies a sudden brief outburst of bright light; GLANCE suggests a darting light reflected from a quickly moving surface ⟨sunlight *glancing* from the ripples⟩ GLINT suggests a cold glancing light; SPARKLE implies innumerable moving points of bright light

²flash *n* **1 a** : a sudden burst of light **b** : a movement of a flag in signaling **2** : a sudden and brilliant burst (as of wit) **3** : a brief time **4 a** : SHOW 2, DISPLAY **b** : one that attracts notice; *esp* : an outstanding athlete **5** : something flashed: as **a** : GLIMPSE 1, LOOK **b** : a first brief news report **c** : a device for producing a brief and very bright flash of light for taking photographs **d** : a quick-spreading flame or momentary intense outburst of radiant heat

³flash *adj* **1** : FLASHY, SPORTY **2** : of sudden origin and short duration ⟨a *flash* fire⟩

flash·back \'flash-,bak\ *n* : introduction into the chronological sequence of events in a literary or theatrical work of an event of earlier occurrence; *also* : an event so introduced

flash·bulb \-,bəlb\ *n* : an electric bulb in which metal foil or wire is burned to produce a brief and very bright flash of light for taking photographs

flash card *n* : a card bearing words, numbers, or pictures briefly displayed by a teacher to a class during drills (as in reading, spelling, or arithmetic)

flash·cube \'flash-,kyüb\ *n* : a cubical device incorporating four flashbulbs for taking four pictures in succession

flash·er \'flash-ər\ *n* : one that flashes; *esp* : BLINKER

flash flood *n* : a local flood of great volume and short duration generally resulting from nearby heavy rainfall

flash·gun \'flash-,gən\ *n* : a device for holding and operating a flashbulb

flash·ing \'flash-ing\ *n* : sheet metal used in waterproofing roof valleys or the angle between a chimney or wall and a roof

flash lamp *n* : a usually electric lamp for producing a brief but intense flash of light for taking photographs

flash·light \'flash-,līt\ *n* **1** : a flash of light or a light that flashes **2** : a small battery-operated portable electric light

flash·over \-,ō-vər\ *n* : an abnormal electrical discharge (as through the air to the ground) from a high potential source

flash point *n* : the lowest temperature at which vapors above a volatile combustible substance ignite in air when exposed to flame

flash·tube \'flash-,tüb, -,tyüb\ *n* : a gas discharge tube that produces very brief intense flashes of light and is used especially in photography

flashy \'flash-ē\ *adj* **flash·i·er; -est 1** : momentarily dazzling **2 a** : superficially attractive : BRIGHT **b** : tastelessly showy SYN see GAUDY — **flash·i·ly** \'flash-ə-lē\ *adv* — **flash·i·ness** \'flash-ē-nəs\ *n*

flask \'flask\ *n* : a bottle-shaped container often somewhat narrowed toward the outlet and often fitted with a closure: **a** : a broad flat container (as for liquor) sometimes curved to fit a hip pocket **b** : a round or conical glass container with a narrow opening used in a laboratory [Middle French *flasque* "powder flask", derived from Late Latin *flasco* "bottle", of Germanic origin]

¹flat \'flat\ *adj* **flat·ter; flat·test 1** : having a smooth level horizontal surface ⟨*flat* ground⟩ **2** : being smooth and even or having a smooth even surface ⟨a *flat* rock⟩

3 : spread out on or along a surface ⟨was *flat* on the ground⟩ **4** : having opposite major surfaces essentially parallel ⟨a *flat* board⟩ **5** : DOWNRIGHT, POSITIVE ⟨a *flat* refusal⟩ **6** : FIXED, UNCHANGING ⟨charge a *flat* rate⟩ **7** : EXACT ⟨a *flat* four minutes⟩ **8** : DULL, UNINTERESTING, INSIPID ⟨a *flat* story⟩ ⟨water that tastes *flat*⟩ **9** : DEFLATED — used of tires **10 a** : lower than the true pitch **b** : lower by a half step ⟨tone of A *flat*⟩ **c** : having a flat in the signature ⟨key of B *flat*⟩ **11** : pronounced like the vowel of *hat* ⟨a *flat* a⟩ **12** : being an adverb with no distinctive ending **13 a** : having little or no illusion of depth ⟨a *flat* painting⟩ **b** : lacking contrast ⟨a *flat* photographic negative⟩ **c** : free from gloss ⟨*flat* paint⟩ [Old Norse *flatr*] — **flat·ly** *adv* — **flat·ness** *n*

²flat *n* **1** : a level surface of land with little or no relief : PLAIN **2** : a flat part or surface **3 a** : a musical note or tone one half step lower than a specified note or tone **b** : a character *b* on a line or space of the staff indicating such a note or tone **4** : something flat: as **a** : a flat piece of theatrical scenery **b** : a shoe or slipper having a flat heel or no heel **5** : a deflated tire

³flat *adv* : in a flat manner: as **a** : on or against a flat surface ⟨lie *flat*⟩ **b** : EXACTLY ⟨four minutes *flat*⟩ **c** : below the true musical pitch ⟨sing *flat*⟩

⁴flat *vb* **flat·ted; flat·ting 1** : FLATTEN **2 a** : to lower in pitch especially by a half step **b** : to sing or play below the true pitch

⁵flat *n* **1** : a floor or story in a building **2** : an apartment on one floor

flat·bed \'flat-,bed\ *n* : a motortruck or trailer with a body in the form of a platform or shallow box

flat·boat \-,bōt\ *n* : a large flat-bottomed boat with square ends used for transporting heavy freight on rivers

flat·car \-,kär\ *n* : a railroad freight car without permanent sides, ends, or covering

flat·fish \-,fish\ *n* : any of an order (Heterosomata) of marine fishes (as halibuts, flounders, or soles) that as adults swim on one side of the laterally compressed body and have both eyes on the upper side

flat·foot \-,fut, 1,2 also -'fut\ *n, pl* **flat·feet 1** : a condition in which the main arch of the foot is so flattened that the entire sole rests upon the ground **2** : a foot affected with flatfoot **3** *or pl* **flatfoots** *slang* : POLICE OFFICER; *esp* : PATROLMAN — **flat·foot·ed** \-'fut-əd\ *adj*

flat·iron \'flat-,ī-ərn, -,īrn\ *n* : an iron for pressing clothes

flat·ten \'flat-n\ *vb* **flat·tened; flat·ten·ing** \'flat-ning, -n-ing\ : to make or become flat

flat·ter \'flat-ər\ *vt* **1** : to praise too much or without sincerity especially out of self-interest **2** : to represent too favorably ⟨the picture *flatters* us⟩ **3** : to judge (oneself) favorably or too favorably especially in respect to an accomplishment or ability ⟨I *flatter* myself on my skill as a swimmer⟩ [Middle English *flateren*, from Old French *flater* "to lick, flatter", of Germanic origin] — **flat·ter·er** \'flat-ər-ər\ *n* — **flat·ter·ing·ly** \'flat-ə-ring-lē\ *adv*

flat·tery \'flat-ə-rē\ *n, pl* **-ter·ies 1** : the act of flattering **2** : flattering speech or attentions : insincere or excessive praise

flat·top \'flat-,täp\ *n* : AIRCRAFT CARRIER

flat·u·lent \'flach-ə-lənt\ *adj* **1 a** : marked by or affected with gases formed in the intestine or stomach **b** : likely to cause such gases to form **2** : pretentious without real worth or substance : POMPOUS [Middle French, from Latin *flatus* "act of blowing, wind", from *flare* "to blow"] — **flat·u·lence** \-ləns\ *n* — **flat·u·lent·ly** *adv*

fla·tus \'flāt-əs\ *n* : gas formed in the intestine or stomach

flat·ware \'flat-,waər, -,weər\ *n* **1** : ceramic objects (as plates or saucers) that have little depth and are usually formed or cast in a single piece **2** : eating and serving utensils (as forks, spoons, and knives)

flask b

flat·ways \-ˌwāz\ *adv* : FLATWISE

flat·wise \-ˌwīz\ *adv* : with the flat side downward or next to another object

flat·worm \-ˌwərm\ *n* : any of a phylum (Platyhelminthes) of flat bilaterally symmetrical unsegmented worms (as a planaria, a liver fluke, or a tapeworm) that lack a body cavity

flaunt \ˈflȯnt, ˈflänt\ *vb* **1** : to wave or flutter showily **2** : to call public attention to onself **3** : to display ostentatiously or boldly : PARADE ⟨he *flaunted* his victory⟩ [probably of Scandinavian origin] — **flaunt** *n* — **flaunt·ing·ly** \-ing-lē\ *adv* □ SYN FLAUNT, FLOUT are often confused. FLAUNT implies displaying something shamelessly, boastfully, or offensively ⟨*flaunts* her exploits to friends⟩ FLOUT implies scoffing or jeering at in contempt or defiance ⟨openly *flouting* the law⟩

flau·tist \ˈflȯt-əst, ˈflaut-\ *n* : FLUTIST [Italian *flautista*, from *flauto* "flute"]

fla·vo·pro·tein \ˌflā-vō-ˈprō-ˌtēn, -ˈprōt-ē-ən\ *n* : an enzyme that serves in the removal and transport of hydrogen and plays a major role in biological oxidations [derived from Latin *flavus* "yellow"]

¹fla·vor \ˈflā-vər\ *n* **1 a** : the quality of something that affects the sense of taste : SAVOR **b** : the blend of taste and smell sensations evoked by a substance in the mouth **2** : a substance that flavors **3** : characteristic or predominant quality [Middle French *flaor, flavor*, from Latin *flare* "to blow"] — **fla·vored** \-vərd\ *adj* — **fla·vor·ful** \-vər-fəl\ *adj* — **fla·vor·less** \-ləs\ *adj*

²flavor *vt* **fla·vored; fla·vor·ing** \ˈflāv-ring, -ə-ring\ : to give or add flavor to

fla·vor·ing *n* : FLAVOR 2

fla·vour \ˈflā-vər\ *chiefly British variant of* FLAVOR

¹flaw \ˈflȯ\ *n* **1** : an often hidden defect that may cause failure ⟨a *flaw* in a plan⟩ **2** : a marred or imperfect part ⟨a diamond with a *flaw*⟩ [Middle English] SYN see BLEMISH — **flaw·less** \-ləs\ *adj* — **flaw·less·ly** *adv* — **flaw·less·ness** *n*

²flaw *vb* : to make or become defective

flax \ˈflaks\ *n* : a slender erect blue-flowered plant grown for its fiber and seeds; *also* : its fiber especially prepared for spinning — compare LINEN [Old English *fleax*]

flax·en \ˈflak-sən\ *adj* **1** : made of flax **2** : resembling flax especially in pale soft straw color

flax·seed \ˈflak-ˌsēd\ *n* : the seed of flax used as a source of linseed oil and medicinally

flay \ˈflā\ *vt* **1** : to strip off the skin or surface of : SKIN **2** : to criticize harshly : SCOLD [Old English *flēan*]

F layer *n* : the highest and most densely ionized regular layer of the ionosphere

flea \ˈflē\ *n* : any of an order (Siphonaptera) of wingless blood-sucking insects with a hard laterally compressed body and legs adapted to leaping [Old English *flēa*]

flea·bane \-ˌbān\ *n* : any of various plants related to the daisies

flea beetle *n* : any of various small beetles that leap like fleas, feed on foliage, and sometimes transmit virus diseases of plants

flea–bit·ten \ˈflē-ˌbit-n\ *adj* : bitten by or infested with fleas

flea collar *n* : a collar for an animal (as a dog or a cat) that contains insecticide for killing fleas

flea market *n* : a usually open-air market for second-hand articles and antiques [translation of French *Marché aux Puces*, a market in Paris]

¹fleck \ˈflek\ *vt* : STREAK, SPOT ⟨hair *flecked* with gray⟩ [back-formation from *flecked* "spotted", from Middle English]

²fleck *n* **1** : SPOT 2a, MARK **2** : FLAKE, PARTICLE

flec·tion \ˈflek-shən\ *n* : FLEXION — **flec·tion·al** \-shnəl, -shən-l\ *adj*

fledge \ˈflej\ *vb* **1** : to develop the feathers necessary for flying **2** : to furnish with feathers ⟨*fledge* an arrow⟩ [Old English *-flycge* "capable of flying"]

fledg·ling \ˈflej-ling\ *n* **1** : a young bird just fledged **2** : an immature or inexperienced person

flee \ˈflē\ *vb* **fled** \ˈfled\; **flee·ing 1 a** : to run away from danger or evil : FLY **b** : to run away from : SHUN **2** : to pass away swiftly : VANISH [Old English *flēon*]

¹fleece \ˈflēs\ *n* **1** : the coat of wool covering an animal (as a sheep) **2** : a soft or woolly covering [Old English *flēos*]

²fleece *vt* **1** : to remove the fleece from : SHEAR **2** : to rob by fraud or extortion

fleecy \ˈflē-sē\ *adj* **fleec·i·er; -est** : covered with, made of, or resembling fleece — **fleec·i·ness** *n*

¹fleet \ˈflēt\ *vi* : to fly swiftly : pass rapidly ⟨time is *fleeting*⟩ [Old English *flēotan* "to float, flow"]

²fleet *n* **1** : a group of warships under one command **2** : a group of ships or vehicles that move together or are operated under one management ⟨a *fleet* of trucks⟩ ⟨a *fleet* of airplanes⟩ [Old English *flēot* "ship", from *flēotan* "to float"]

³fleet *adj* **1** : swift in motion : NIMBLE **2** : not enduring : MOMENTARY [probably from ¹*fleet*] SYN see FAST — **fleet·ly** *adv* — **fleet·ness** *n*

Fleet Admiral *n* : a commissioned officer of highest rank in the Navy whose insignia is five stars

fleet–foot·ed \ˈflēt-ˌfut-əd\ *adj* : swift of foot — **fleet–foot·ed·ness** *n*

Flem·ing \ˈflem-ing\ *n* : a member of the Germanic people inhabiting northern Belgium and a small section of northern France bordering on Belgium [Dutch *Vlaminc*]

Flem·ish \ˈflem-ish\ *n* **1** : the Germanic language of the Flemings that is made up of dialects of Dutch **2** *pl in construction* : FLEMINGS — **Flemish** *adj*

¹flesh \ˈflesh\ *n* **1 a** : the soft parts of the body of an animal; *esp* : skeletal muscle of a vertebrate **b** : sleek well-fatted condition of body **2** : parts of an animal used as food **3** : the physical being of a person as distinguished from the soul **4 a** : HUMAN BEINGS **b** : living beings **c** : STOCK 5b, KINDRED **5** : a fleshy plant part used as food; *esp* : the fleshy part of a fruit [Old English *flǣsc*] — **fleshed** \ˈflesht\ *adj*

²flesh *vb* **1** : to give substance to ⟨*flesh* out a story with details⟩ **2** : to remove flesh from **3** : to become fleshy — often used with *up* or *out*

flesh fly *n* : a two-winged fly whose maggots feed on flesh

flesh·ing \ˈflesh-ing\ *n* : the distribution of the lean and fat on an animal

flesh·ly \ˈflesh-lē\ *adj* **1** : CORPOREAL c, BODILY **2 a** : CARNAL, SENSUAL ⟨*fleshly* desires⟩ **b** : not spiritual : WORLDLY

flesh wound *n* : an injury involving penetration of body muscles without damage to other soft parts or to bones

fleshy \ˈflesh-ē\ *adj* **flesh·i·er; -est 1 a** : resembling or consisting of flesh **b** : having abundant flesh; *esp* : FAT **2** : SUCCULENT 1 ⟨*fleshy* fruits⟩ — **flesh·i·ness** *n*

fleur-de-lis *or* **fleur-de-lys** \ˌflərd-l-ˈē, ˌflurd-\ *n, pl* **fleurs-de-lis** *or* **fleur-de-lis** *or* **fleurs-de-lys** *or* **fleur-de-lys** \same *or* -ˈēz\ **1** : IRIS 3 **2** : a conventionalized iris in art and heraldry [Middle French *flor de lis*, literally, "lily flower"]

flew *past of* FLY

flews \ˈflüz\ *n pl* : the drooping lateral parts of a dog's upper lip [origin unknown]

flex \ˈfleks\ *vb* : to bend especially repeatedly : cause flexion of [Latin *flexus*, past participle of *flectere* "to bend, flex"]

flex·a·gon \ˈflek-sə-ˌgän\ *n* : a folded paper figure that can be flexed along its folds to expose various arrangements of its faces

flex·i·ble \ˈflek-sə-bəl\ *adj* **1** : capable of being flexed : PLIANT **2** : readily changed or changing : ADAPTABLE — **flex·i·bil·i·ty** \ˌflek-sə-ˈbil-ət-ē\ *n* — **flex·i·bly** \ˈflek-sə-blē\ *adv*

fleur-de-lis 2

\ə\ abut		\ng\ sing	
\ər\ further		\ō\ bone	
\a\ mat		\ȯ\ saw	
\ā\ take		\ȯi\ coin	
\ä\ cot, cart		\th\ thin	
\au̇\ out		\th\ this	
\ch\ chin		\ü\ food	
\e\ pet		\u̇\ foot	
\ē\ easy		\y\ yet	
\g\ go		\yü\ few	
\i\ tip		\yu̇\ cure	
\ī\ life		\zh\ vision	
\j\ job			

³flicker

flex·ion \'flek-shən\ *n* : muscular movement that lessens the angle between bones or parts; *also* : the resulting state or relation of parts

flex·or \'flek-sər\ *n* : a muscle that produces flexion — compare EXTENSOR — **flexor** *adj*

flex·ure \'flek-shər\ *n* **1** : the quality or state of being flexed **2** : TURN, FOLD — **flex·ur·al** \-shə-rəl, -shrəl\ *adj*

¹flick \'flik\ *n* **1** : a light sharp jerky stroke or movement **2** : a sound produced by a flick **3** : DAUB 1, SPLOTCH [imitative]

²flick *vb* **1** : to strike lightly with a quick sharp motion ⟨*flicked* a speck off the table⟩ **2** : FLICKER 1

³flick *n, slang* : MOVIE [short for ²*flicker*]

¹flick·er \'flik-ər\ *vb* **flick·ered; flick·er·ing** \'flik-ring, -ə-ring\ **1** : to move irregularly or unsteadily : FLUTTER **2** : to burn fitfully or with a fluctuating light ⟨a *flickering* candle⟩ [Old English *flicorian*]

²flicker *n* **1** : a brief interval of brightness **2** : a flickering light **3** : a brief stirring ⟨a *flicker* of interest⟩ — **flick·ery** \'flik-rē, -ə-rē\ *adj*

³flicker *n* : a common large brightly marked woodpecker of eastern North America; *also* : a related bird of the southern and western United States [imitative]

flied *past of* ³FLY

fli·er *or* **fly·er** \'flī-ər, 'flīr\ *n* **1** : one that flies; *esp* : AVIATOR **2** : a speculative undertaking; *esp* : an attempt to gain large profits in a business venture by one who is inexperienced or uninformed **3** : a printed notice or message (as an advertising leaflet) distributed in large numbers

¹flight \'flīt\ *n* **1** : an act or instance of passing through the air by the use of wings ⟨a *flight* in a plane⟩ ⟨the *flight* of birds⟩ **2 a** : a passing through the air or through space outside the earth's atmosphere ⟨the *flight* of a bullet⟩ ⟨a moon *flight*⟩ **b** : the distance covered in a flight **c** : swift movement **3** : an airplane making a scheduled flight **4** : a group of similar things flying through the air together ⟨a *flight* of ducks⟩ ⟨a *flight* of bombers⟩ **5** : a brilliant, imaginative, or unrestrained exercise or display ⟨a *flight* of fancy⟩ **6** : a continuous series of stairs from one landing or floor to another [Old English *flyht*]

²flight *n* : an act or instance of running away [Middle English *fliht*]

flight control *n* : the control from a ground station of an airplane or spacecraft especially by radio

flight engineer *n* : a member of a flight crew responsible for mechanical operation

flight feather *n* : one of the quills of a bird's wing or tail that support it in flight

flight·less \'flīt-ləs\ *adj* : unable to fly ⟨*flightless* birds⟩

flight line *n* : a parking and servicing area for airplanes

flight path *n* : the path made or followed by something (as a spacecraft, airplane, or particle) in flight

flighty \'flīt-ē\ *adj* **flight·i·er; -est** **1** : easily upset : VOLATILE **2** : easily excited : SKITTISH **3** : SCATTERBRAINED, SILLY — **flight·i·ly** \'flīt-l-ē\ *adv* — **flight·i·ness** \'flīt-ē-nəs\ *n*

flim·flam \'flim-,flam\ *n* **1** : DECEPTION 1, FRAUD **2** : HANKY-PANKY [probably of Scandinavian origin] — **flimflam** *vb*

flim·sy \'flim-zē\ *adj* **flim·si·er; -est** **1 a** : lacking strength or substance **b** : of inferior materials and workmanship **2** : having little worth or plausibility ⟨a *flimsy* excuse⟩ [perhaps derived from ¹*film*] — **flim·si·ly** \-zə-lē\ *adv* — **flim·si·ness** \-zē-nəs\ *n*

flinch \'flinch\ *vi* : to shrink from or as if from physical pain : WINCE [Middle French *flenchir* "to bend"] — **flinch** *n* — **flinch·er** *n*

¹fling \'fling\ *vb* **flung** \'fləng\; **fling·ing** \'fling-ing\ **1** : to move in a brusque or headlong manner ⟨*flung* out of the room⟩ **2** : to kick or plunge vigorously **3 a** : to throw or swing with force or recklessness **b** : to cast aside : DISCARD **4** : to place or put suddenly and unexpectedly into a state or condition ⟨*flung* the troops into confusion⟩ [Middle English *flingen*, of Scandinavian origin] SYN see THROW — **fling·er** \'fling-ər\ *n*

²fling *n* **1** : an act or instance of flinging **2** : a casual try : ATTEMPT **3** : a period of self-indulgence

flint \'flint\ *n* **1** : a grayish or dark hard quartz that produces a spark when struck by steel **2** : an alloy (as of iron and cerium) used for producing a spark in cigarette lighters [Old English]

flint glass *n* : heavy glass that contains an oxide of lead and is used for optical structures (as lenses)

flint·lock \'flint-,läk\ *n* **1** : a lock for a 17th and 18th century firearm using a flint to ignite the charge **2** : a firearm fitted with a flintlock

flinty \'flint-ē\ *adj* **flint·i·er; -est** **1** : composed of or covered with flint **2 a** : notably hard ⟨*flinty* seeds⟩ **b** : UNYIELDING, STERN ⟨a strong *flinty* character⟩ — **flint·i·ly** \'flint-l-ē\ *adv* — **flint·i·ness** \'flint-ē-nəs\ *n*

¹flip \'flip\ *vb* **flipped; flip·ping** **1** : to turn by tossing ⟨*flip* a coin⟩ **2** : to turn quickly ⟨*flip* the dial⟩ **3** : FLICK ⟨*flip* a light switch⟩ **4** : to lose self-control [probably imitative]

²flip *n* **1** : an act or instance of flipping : TOSS, FLICK **2** : a somersault performed in the air

³flip *adj* : FLIPPANT

flip·pant \'flip-ənt\ *adj* : treating lightly something serious or worthy of respect : lacking earnestness [probably from ¹*flip*] — **flip·pan·cy** \-ən-sē\ *n* — **flip·pant·ly** *adv*

flip·per \'flip-ər\ *n* **1** : a broad flat limb (as of a seal) adapted for swimming **2** : a flat rubber shoe with the front expanded into a paddle used in skin diving

¹flirt \'flərt\ *vi* **1** : to move erratically : FLIT **2 a** : to behave amorously without serious intent **b** : TOY ⟨*flirted* with the idea of getting a job⟩ [origin unknown] — **flir·ta·tion** \,flər-'tā-shən\ *n* — **flir·ta·tious** \-shəs\ *adj* — **flir·ta·tious·ness** *n* — **flirt·er** \'flərt-ər\ *n*

²flirt *n* **1** : an act or instance of flirting **2** : a person who flirts

flit \'flit\ *vi* **flit·ted; flit·ting** : to move in quick erratic darts [Middle English *flitten*, of Scandinavian origin] — **flit** *n*

flit·ter \'flit-ər\ *vi* : FLUTTER 1, FLICKER [derived from *flit*]

fliv·ver \'fliv-ər\ *n* : a small cheap usually old automobile [origin unknown]

¹float \'flōt\ *n* **1** : an act or instance of floating **2** : something that floats in or on the surface of a fluid: as **a** : a cork or bob buoying up the baited end of a fishing line **b** : a floating platform anchored near a shoreline for use by swimmers or boats **c** : a hollow ball that controls the flow or level of the liquid it floats on (as in a tank or cistern) **d** : a watertight structure giving an airplane buoyancy on water **3** : a vehicle carrying an exhibit in a parade **4** : a drink consisting of ice cream floating in a beverage [Middle English *flote* "boat, float", from Old English *flota* "ship"]

²float *vb* **1** : to rest or cause to rest in or on the surface of a fluid **2 a** : to drift or cause to drift on or through or as if on or through a fluid ⟨dust *floating* through the air⟩ ⟨*float* logs down a river⟩ **b** : WANDER ⟨*floating* from town to town⟩ **3 a** : to offer (an issue of stocks or bonds) in order to finance an enterprise **b** : to finance (an enterprise) by floating an issue of stocks or bonds **c** : to arrange for ⟨*float* a loan⟩

float·er \'flōt-ər\ *n* **1 a** : one that floats **b** : a person who floats something **2** : a person without a permanent home or job : VAGRANT

float·ing *adj* **1** : buoyed on or in a fluid **2 a** : not settled or committed : not established ⟨*floating* capital⟩ ⟨a *floating* population⟩ **b** : short-term and usually not funded ⟨a *floating* debt⟩ **3** : connected or constructed so as to operate and adjust smoothly ⟨a *floating* axle⟩

floating–point *adj* : involving or being a mathematical notation in which a quantity is denoted by one number multiplied by a power of the number base ⟨the fixed-point value 99.9 could be expressed in a *floating-point* system as .999 × 10²⟩ — compare FIXED=POINT

floating rib *n* : a rib (as one of the last two pairs in human beings) that has no attachment to the sternum — compare FALSE RIB

floc·cu·late \'fläk-yə-ˌlāt\ *vb* : to collect or cause to collect into a flocculent mass — **floc·cu·la·tion** \ˌfläk-yə-'lā-shən\ *n*

floc·cu·lent \'fläk-yə-lənt\ *adj* : resembling wool especially in loose fluffy texture [Latin *floccus* "flock of wool"]

¹**flock** \'fläk\ *n* **1** : a group of birds or mammals assembled or herded together **2** : a group under the guidance of a leader **3** : a large number [Old English *flocc* "crowd, band"]

²**flock** *vi* : to gather or move in a crowd ⟨they *flocked* to the beach⟩

³**flock** *n* **1** : a tuft of wool or cotton fiber **2** : woolen or cotton refuse used for stuffing furniture and mattresses **3** : very short or pulverized fiber used to form a pattern on cloth or paper or a protective covering on metal [Middle English]

⁴**flock** *vt* **1** : to fill with flock **2** : to decorate with flock

flock·ing \'fläk-ing\ *n* : a design in flock

floe \'flō\ *n* : a sheet or mass of floating ice [probably from Norwegian *flo* "flat layer"]

flog \'fläg\ *vt* **flogged; flog·ging** : to beat severely with a rod or whip [perhaps from Latin *flagellare* "to whip"] — **flog·ger** *n*

¹**flood** \'fləd\ *n* **1 a** : a great flow of water that rises and spreads over the land **b** *cap* : a flood described in the Bible as covering the earth in the time of Noah **2** : the flowing in of the tide **3** : an overwhelming quantity or volume ⟨a *flood* of mail⟩ [Old English *flōd*]

²**flood** *vb* **1** : to cover or become filled with a flood ⟨the river *flooded* the lowlands⟩ ⟨the cellar *floods* after a rain⟩ **2** : to fill abundantly or excessively ⟨a room *flooded* with light⟩ ⟨*flood* a carburetor⟩ **3** : to pour forth in a flood

flood·gate \'fləd-ˌgāt\ *n* **1** : a gate (as in a canal) for shutting out, admitting, or releasing a body of water : SLUICE **2** : something serving to restrain an outburst

flood·light \-ˌlīt\ *n* **1** : artificial illumination in a broad beam **2** : a lighting unit for projecting a beam of light — **floodlight** *vt*

flood·plain \-ˌplān\ *n* **1** : low flat land along a stream that may flood **2** : a plain built up by deposits of earth from floodwaters

flood tide *n* **1** : the tide while rising or at its greatest height **2 a** : an overwhelming quantity **b** : a high point : PEAK ⟨our success was at *flood tide*⟩

flood·wa·ter \'fləd-ˌwot-ər, -ˌwät-\ *n* : the water of a flood

flood·way \-ˌwā\ *n* : a channel for diverting floodwaters

¹**floor** \'flōr, 'flor\ *n* **1** : the part of a room on which one stands **2 a** : the lower inside surface of a hollow structure **b** : a ground surface ⟨the ocean *floor*⟩ ⟨the *floor* of a forest⟩ **3 a** : a structure dividing a building into stories **b** : STORY ⟨they live on the first *floor*⟩ **c** : the occupants of a story **4** : the surface of a structure on which one travels ⟨the *floor* of a bridge⟩ **5 a** : a main level space (as in a legislative chamber) distinguished from a platform or gallery **b** : the right to speak from one's place in an assembly ⟨the senator has the *floor*⟩ **6** : a lower limit (as of prices) [Old English *flōr*]

²**floor** *vt* **1** : to cover with a floor or flooring **2 a** : to knock to the floor **b** : SHOCK, OVERWHELM ⟨the news *floored* us⟩

floor·board \'flōr-ˌbōrd, 'flor-ˌbord\ *n* **1** : a board in a floor **2** : the floor of an automobile

floor exercise *n* : a gymnastic event in which participants perform various ballet and tumbling feats on a floor mat

floor·ing \'flōr-ing, 'flor-\ *n* **1** : FLOOR 1 **2** : material for floors

floor lamp *n* : a tall lamp that stands on the floor

floor leader *n* : a member of a legislative body chosen by a party to have charge of its organization and strategy on the floor

floor show *n* : a series of acts presented in a nightclub

floor·walk·er \'flōr-ˌwo-kər, 'flor-\ *n* : a person employed in a retail store to oversee the sales force and aid customers

floo·zy \'flü-zē\ *n, pl* **floozies** : a tawdry or immoral woman [origin unknown]

¹**flop** \'fläp\ *vb* **flopped; flop·ping** **1** : to swing or bounce loosely : flap about ⟨a hat brim *flopping* in the wind⟩ **2 a** : to throw oneself down heavily, clumsily, or in a completely relaxed manner ⟨*flop* into the chair⟩ **b** : to throw or drop suddenly and usually heavily or noisily ⟨*flopped* the bundles onto the table⟩ **3** : to fail completely ⟨the play *flopped*⟩ [alteration of ²*flap*]

²**flop** *n* **1** : an act or sound of flopping **2** : a complete failure : DUD ⟨the play was a *flop*⟩

³**flop** *adv* : RIGHT, SQUARELY ⟨fall *flop* on one's face⟩

flop·house \-ˌhaus\ *n* : a cheap rooming house or hotel

flop·py \'fläp-ē\ *adj* **flop·pi·er; -est** : tending to flop; *esp* : being soft and flexible ⟨a hat with a *floppy* brim⟩

floppy disk *n* : a small flexible disk with a magnetic coating on which data for a computer can be stored

flo·ra \'flōr-ə, 'flor-\ *n, pl* **floras** *also* **flo·rae** \-ˌē, -ˌī\ : plants or plant life especially of a region, period, or environment — compare FAUNA [Latin *Flora*, Roman goddess of flowers]

flo·ral \'flōr-əl, 'flor-\ *adj* : of or relating to flowers or a flora [Latin *flor-, flos* "flower"] — **flo·ral·ly** \-ə-lē\ *adv*

Flor·ence flask \'flor-əns-, 'flär-\ *n* : a round usually flat-bottomed glass laboratory vessel with a long neck [*Florence*, Italy; from the use of flasks of this shape for Italian wines]

flo·res·cence \flo-'res-ns, flə-\ *n* : a state or period of being in bloom or flourishing ⟨the highest *florescence* of a civilization⟩ [Latin *florescere* "to begin to bloom", from *florēre* "to blossom, flourish"] — **flo·res·cent** \-nt\ *adj*

flo·ret \'flōr-ət, 'flor-\ *n* : a small flower; *esp* : one of the small flowers forming the head of a plant of the daisy family

flori- *combining form* : flower or flowers ⟨*flori*gen⟩ [Latin *flor-, flos* "flower"]

flor·id \'flor-əd, 'flär-\ *adj* **1** : excessively flowery in style : ORNATE ⟨*florid* writing⟩ **2** : tinged with red : RUDDY ⟨a *florid* complexion⟩ [Latin *floridus* "blooming, flowery", from *florēre* "to blossom, flourish"] — **flo·rid·i·ty** \flə-'rid-ət-ē, flo-\ *n* — **flor·id·ly** \'flor-əd-lē, 'flär-\ *adv* — **flor·id·ness** *n*

flo·rif·er·ous \flo-'rif-rəs, -ə-rəs\ *adj* : bearing flowers; *esp* : blooming freely — **flo·rif·er·ous·ness** *n*

flo·ri·gen \'flor-ə-jən, 'flor-, 'flär-\ *n* : a plant hormone that promotes flowering

flor·in \'flor-ən, 'flär-, 'flor-\ *n* **1 a** : an old gold coin first struck at Florence in 1252 **b** : any of various former gold coins of European countries patterned after the Florentine florin **2 a** : a former British silver coin worth two shillings **b** : any of several similar coins issued in British Commonwealth countries **3** : GULDEN [Middle French, from Italian *fiorino*, from *fiore* "flower", from Latin *flor-, flos;* from the lily on the first *florins*]

flo·rist \'flōr-əst, 'flor-, 'flär-\ *n* : a seller of flowers and ornamental plants

flo·ris·tic \flo-'ris-tik\ *adj* : of or relating to flowers or a flora — **flo·ris·ti·cal·ly** \-ti-kə-lē, -klē\ *adv*

¹**floss** \'fläs, 'flos\ *n* **1** : waste or short silk fibers that cannot be reeled **2 a** : soft thread of silk or mercerized cotton used for embroidery **b** : DENTAL FLOSS **c** : a

\ə\ abut		\ng\ sing	
\ər\ further		\ō\ bone	
\a\ mat		\o\ saw	
\ā\ take		\oi\ coin	
\ä\ cot, cart		\th\ thin	
\au\ out		\th\ this	
\ch\ chin		\ü\ food	
\e\ pet		\u\ foot	
\ē\ easy		\y\ yet	
\g\ go		\yü\ few	
\i\ tip		\yu\ cure	
\ī\ life		\zh\ vision	
\j\ job			

lightweight knitting yarn **3** : fluffy fibrous material; *esp* : SILK COTTON [Dutch *vlos*]

²floss *vb* : to use or clean with dental floss ⟨*floss* daily⟩

flossy \'fläs-ē, 'flȯs-\ *adj* **floss·i·er; -est 1 a** : of, relating to, or having the characteristics of floss **b** : DOWNY 2 **2** : stylish or glamorous especially at first impression ⟨slick *flossy* writing⟩

flo·ta·tion \flō-'tā-shən\ *n* **1** : the act, process, or state of floating **2** : the separation of the particles of a mass of pulverized ore according to their relative capacity for floating on a given liquid

flo·til·la \flō-'til-ə\ *n* : a fleet of ships; *esp* : a fleet of small ships [Spanish, from *flota* "fleet", from Old French *flote,* from Old Norse *floti*]

flot·sam \'flät-səm\ *n* : floating wreckage of a ship or its cargo [Anglo-French *floteson,* from Old French *floter* "to float", of Germanic origin]

¹flounce \'flaúns\ *vi* **1** : to move with exaggerated jerky motions **2** : to go with sudden determination ⟨*flounced* out of the room in anger⟩ [perhaps of Scandinavian origin]

²flounce *n* : an act or instance of flouncing

³flounce *n* : a strip of fabric attached by the upper edge ⟨a wide *flounce* at the bottom of the skirt⟩ [alteration of Middle English *frouncen* "to curl"]

⁴flounce *vt* : to trim or finish with a flounce

¹floun·der \'flaún-dər\ *n, pl* **flounder** or **flounders** : FLATFISH; *esp* : any of various important marine food fishes [Middle English, of Scandinavian origin]

²flounder *vi* **floun·dered; floun·der·ing** \-də-riŋ, -driŋ\ : to struggle or proceed clumsily ⟨*flounder* in the deep mud⟩ [probably alteration of *founder*]

¹flour \'flaúr\ *n* **1 a** : finely ground powdery meal of wheat usually largely freed from bran **b** : a similar meal of any cereal grain or edible seed **2** : a fine soft powder [Middle English, "flower, best of anything, flour"] □ SYN FLOUR, MEAL mean the product of grinding cereal grain or other seeds. FLOUR used alone denotes wheat kernels finely ground and sifted to remove the bran; MEAL applies to any grain or seed coarsely ground and unsifted.

²flour *vt* : to coat with flour

flour beetle *n* : any of several usually elongated flattened brown beetles that are economic pests especially in flour or meal

¹flour·ish \'flər-ish, 'flə-rish\ *vb* **1** : to grow luxuriantly : THRIVE **2 a** : to achieve success : PROSPER **b** : to be active or prominent ⟨*flourished* around 1850⟩ **3** : to make bold and sweeping gestures **4** : to wield with dramatic gestures : BRANDISH ⟨*flourish* a sword⟩ [Middle French *floriss-,* stem of *florir* "to flourish", from Latin *florēre,* from *flor-, flos* "flower"]

²flourish *n* **1** : a period of thriving **2 a** : a flowery embellishment or passage ⟨handwriting with *flourishes*⟩ **b** : an act or instance of brandishing : WAVE ⟨gave a *flourish* of the cane⟩ **c** : a dramatic action ⟨introduced them with a *flourish*⟩

floury \'flaúr-ē\ *adj* **1** : of, relating to, or resembling flour **2** : covered with flour

flout \'flaút\ *vb* **1** : to treat with contemptuous disregard : SCORN ⟨*flouting* their parents' advice⟩ **2** : to indulge in scornful behavior [probably from Middle English *flouten* "to play the flute", from *floute* "flute"] SYN see FLAUNT — **flout·er** *n*

¹flow \'flō\ *vi* **1 a** : to issue or move in a stream **b** : to move with a continual shifting of the constituent particles ⟨the molasses *flowed* slowly⟩ **2** : RISE ⟨the tide ebbs and *flows*⟩ **3** : ABOUND ⟨a land that *flows* with milk and honey⟩ **4 a** : to proceed smoothly and readily ⟨the words *flowed* from my mouth⟩ **b** : to have a smooth uninterrupted continuity **5** : to hang loose and billowing ⟨a flag *flowing* in the breeze⟩ **6** : to come from as a source **7** : MENSTRUATE [Old English *flōwan*] — **flow·ing·ly** \-iŋ-lē\ *adv*

²flow *n* **1** : an act of flowing **2** : FLOOD 1a, 2 **3 a** : a smooth uninterrupted movement **b** : a stream of fluid; *also* : a mass of matter that has flowed ⟨a lava *flow*⟩ **4** : the quantity that flows in a certain time ⟨the *flow* of water over a dam⟩ **5 a** : MENSTRUATION **b** : OUTPUT 1, YIELD **6** : a continuous transfer of energy ⟨a *flow* of electricity⟩

flow chart *n* : a diagram showing step-by-step progression through a procedure or system

¹flow·er \'flaú-ər, 'flaúr\ *n* **1 a** : BLOSSOM, INFLORESCENCE **b** : a shoot of the spore-producing generation of a higher plant that is specialized for reproduction and consists of a shortened axis bearing modified leaves (as petals and sporophylls) **c** : a plant cultivated or valued for its blossoms **2 a** : the best part or example ⟨the *flower* of the family⟩ **b** : the finest most vigorous period **c** : a state of blooming or flourishing ⟨when knighthood was in *flower*⟩ **3** *pl* : a finely divided powder produced especially by condensation or sublimation ⟨*flowers* of sulfur⟩ [Middle English *flour,* from Old French, from Latin *flor-, flos*] — **flow·er·less** \-ləs\ *adj* — **flow·er·like** \-,līk\ *adj*

²flower *vb* **1** : to produce flowers : BLOOM **2 a** : DEVELOP ⟨*flowered* into a real scholar⟩ **b** : FLOURISH 2 **3** : to decorate with floral designs

flow·ered \'flaú-ərd, 'flaúrd\ *adj* **1** : having or bearing flowers **2** : decorated with flowers or flowerlike figures ⟨*flowered* silk⟩

flow·er·et \'flaú-ə-rət, 'flaúr-ət\ *n* : FLORET

flower girl *n* : a little girl who carries flowers at a wedding

flower head *n* : a tight cluster of small stemless flowers that looks like a single flower

flowering plant *n* : any of a major group (Angiospermae) of higher plants that comprises those which produce flowers, fruits, and seeds with the seeds in a closed ovary — called also *angiosperm;* compare SEED PLANT

flow·er·pot \'flaú-ər-,pät, 'flaúr-\ *n* : a pot in which to grow plants

flow·ery \'flaú-ər-ē, flaúr-\ *adj* **flow·er·i·er; -est 1** : full of or covered with flowers **2** : full of fine words or phrases : FLORID ⟨*flowery* language⟩ — **flow·er·i·ness** *n*

flown *past participle of* FLY

flu \'flü\ *n* **1** : INFLUENZA 1 **2** : any of several virus diseases marked especially by respiratory symptoms

flub \'fləb\ *vb* **flubbed; flub·bing 1** : to make a mess of : BOTCH ⟨the actor *flubbed* the line⟩ **2** : BLUNDER 2 [origin unknown] — **flub** *n*

fluc·tu·ate \'flək-chə-,wāt\ *vi* **1** : to move up and down or back and forth like a wave **2** : to be changing constantly and irregularly (as between points, levels, or conditions) ⟨the market *fluctuated* wildly⟩ ⟨one's health may *fluctuate* with the weather⟩ [Latin *fluctuare,* from *fluctus* "flow, wave", from *fluere* "to flow"] — **fluc·tu·a·tion** \,flək-chə-'wā-shən\ *n*

flue \'flü\ *n* : an enclosed passageway for directing a current: as **a** : a channel in a chimney for conveying flame and smoke to the outer air **b** : a pipe for conveying flame and hot gases around or through water in a steam boiler **c** : FLUE PIPE [origin unknown]

flu·en·cy \'flü-ən-sē\ *n* : the quality or state of being fluent especially in speech

flu·ent \'flü-ənt\ *adj* **1** : capable of flowing : FLUID **2 a** : ready or easy in speech ⟨*fluent* in Spanish⟩ **b** : effortlessly smooth and rapid : POLISHED ⟨*fluent* speech⟩ [Latin *fluere* "to flow"] — **flu·ent·ly** *adv*

flue pipe *n* : an organ pipe whose tone is produced by an air current striking the lip and causing the air within to vibrate

flue stop *n* : an organ stop made up of flue pipes

¹fluff \'fləf\ *n* **1** : ³NAP, DOWN ⟨soft *fluff* from a pillow⟩ **2** : something fluffy **3** : something unimportant **4** : BLUNDER; *esp* : an actor's lapse of memory [probably

¹flower 1a: *1* filament, *2* anther, *3* stigma, *4* style, *5* petal, *6* ovary, *7* sepal, *8* pedicel, *9* stamen, *10* pistil, *11* perianth

alteration of *flue* "fluff", from Flemish *vluwe*, from French *velu* "shaggy"]

²**fluff** *vb* **I** : to make or become fluffy ⟨*fluff* up a pillow⟩ **2** : to spoil by or make a mistake : BOTCH **3** : to deliver badly or fail to remember ⟨one's lines in a play⟩

fluffy \'fləf-ē\ *adj* **fluff·i·er; -est I a** : having, covered with, or resembling fluff or down ⟨*fluffy* fur⟩ **b** : being light and soft or airy ⟨a *fluffy* omelet⟩ **2** : SILLY **3** — **fluff·i·ness** *n*

¹**flu·id** \'flü-əd\ *adj* **I a** : capable of flowing like a liquid or gas **b** : likely or tending to change or move **2** : characterized by or employing a smooth easy style **3 a** : available for various uses **b** : easily converted into cash ⟨*fluid* assets⟩ [Latin *fluidus*, from *fluere* "to flow"] — **flu·id·i·ty** \flü-'id-ət-ē\ *n* — **flu·id·ly** \'flü-əd-lē\ *adv* — **flu·id·ness** *n*

²**fluid** *n* : a substance tending to flow or conform to the outline of its container ⟨liquids and gases are *fluids*⟩

fluid dram *n* : a unit of liquid capacity equal to 1/8 fluid ounce (about 3.7 milliliters) — see MEASURE table

fluid mechanics *n sing or pl* : a branch of mechanics that deals with the properties of liquids and gases

fluid ounce *n* : a unit of liquid capacity equal to 1/16 pint (about 29.6 milliliters) — see MEASURE table

¹**fluke** \'flük\ *n* **I** : FLATFISH **2** : any of a group of trematodes; *also* : TREMATODE [Old English *flōc*]

²**fluke** *n* **I** : the part of an anchor that digs into the ground **2** : a barbed head (as of a harpoon) **3** : one of the lobes of a whale's tail

³**fluke** *n* **I** : an accidentally successful stroke at billiards or pool **2** : a stroke of luck ⟨won by a *fluke*⟩ [origin unknown]

fluky \'flü-kē\ *adj* **fluk·i·er; -est I** : happening by or depending on chance **2** : being unsteady or uncertain : CHANGEABLE ⟨a *fluky* wind⟩

flume \'flüm\ *n* **I** : a ravine or gorge with a stream running through it **2** : an inclined channel for conveying water (as for power) [probably from Middle English *flum* "river", from Old French, from Latin *flumen*, from *fluere* "to flow"]

flum·mery \'fləm-rē, -ə-rē\ *n, pl* **-mer·ies I a** : a soft jelly or porridge made with flour or meal **b** : any of several sweet desserts **2 a** : something trashy **b** : empty compliment : HUMBUG [Welsh *llymru*]

flum·mox \'fləm-əks, -iks\ *vt* : CONFUSE 1 [origin unknown]

flung *past of* FLING

flunk \'fləngk\ *vb* **I** : to fail an examination or course **2** : to give a failing grade to [perhaps blend of *flinch* and *funk*] — **flunk** *n*

flunk out *vb* : to dismiss or be dismissed from a school or college for failure

flun·ky *or* **flun·key** \'fləng-kē\ *n, pl* **flunkies** *or* **flunkeys I a** : a servant in livery **b** : one doing menial duties **2** : TOADY, YES-MAN [Scottish]

fluor- *or* **fluoro-** *combining form* **I** : fluorine ⟨*fluor*ide⟩ **2** *also* **fluori-** : fluorescence ⟨*fluoro*scope⟩

flu·o·resce \flù-'es, ,flü-ər-\ *vi* : to produce, undergo, or exhibit fluorescence [back-formation from *fluorescence*]

flu·o·res·ce·in \-'es-ē-ən\ *n* : a yellow or red crystalline dye with a bright yellow-green fluorescence in alkaline solution

flu·o·res·cence \-'es-ns\ *n* : the property of a substance of emitting radiation usually as visible light when exposed to radiation from another source; *also* : the radiation emitted — **flu·o·res·cent** \-nt\ *adj*

fluorescent lamp *n* : an electric lamp in which light is produced on the inside fluorescent coating of a glass tube by the action of ultraviolet light

flu·o·ri·date \'flùr-ə-,dāt\ *vt* : to add a fluoride to ⟨*fluori*date drinking water⟩ — **flu·o·ri·da·tion** \,flùr-ə-'dā-shən\ *n*

flu·o·ride \'flù-ər-,īd, 'flùr-,\ *n* : a compound of fluorine with another chemical element or a radical

flu·o·ri·nate \'flùr-ə-,nāt\ *vt* : to treat or cause to combine with fluorine or a compound of fluorine — **flu·o·ri·na·tion** \,flùr-ə-'nā-shən\ *n*

flu·o·rine \'flùr-,ēn, 'flù-ər-\ *n* : a nonmetallic univalent chemical element that is normally a pale yellowish flammable irritating toxic gas — see ELEMENT table [French, from New Latin *fluor* "mineral belonging to a group including fluorite and used as fluxes", from Latin, "flow", from *fluere* "to flow"]

flu·o·rite \'flùr-,īt, 'flù-ər-\ *n* : a transparent or translucent mineral CaF₂ of different colors that consists of a fluoride of calcium and is used as a flux and in making glass

flu·o·ro·car·bon \'flùr-ō-,kär-bən, 'flù-ər-\ *n* : any of various inert compounds of carbon and fluorine used chiefly as lubricants and refrigerants

¹**flu·o·ro·scope** \'flùr-ə-,skōp\ *n* : an instrument that is used especially in examining inner parts of the body (as the lungs) by observing light and dark shadows produced on a screen by the action of X rays — **flu·o·ro·scop·ic** \,flùr-ə-'skäp-ik\ *adj* — **flu·o·ros·co·py** \,flùr-'äs-kə-pē, ,flù-ər-'\ *n*

²**fluoroscope** *vt* : to examine by a fluoroscope

flu·or·spar \'flùr-,spär, 'flù-ər-\ *n* : FLUORITE

¹**flur·ry** \'flər-ē, 'flə-rē\ *n, pl* **flurries I a** : a gust of wind **b** : a brief light snowfall **2** : nervous commotion **3** : a brief outburst of activity ⟨a *flurry* of trading in the stock exchange⟩ [probably from *flurr* "to strew"]

²**flurry** *vb* **flur·ried; flur·ry·ing** : to become or cause to become agitated and confused

¹**flush** \'fləsh\ *vb* : to take flight or cause to take flight suddenly ⟨*flushed* a covey of quail⟩ [Middle English *flusshen*]

²**flush** *n* **I** : a sudden flow (as of water) **2 a** : a sudden increase (as of growth) ⟨a spring *flush* of grass⟩ **b** : a surge of emotion ⟨a *flush* of anger⟩ **3 a** : a tinge of red : BLUSH **b** : a fresh and vigorous state ⟨in the *flush* of youth⟩ **4** : a brief sensation of extreme heat [perhaps from Latin *fluxus* "flow"]

³**flush** *vb* **I** : to flow and spread suddenly and freely **2 a** : to glow brightly **b** : BLUSH 1, 3 **3** : to pour liquid over or through; *esp* : to wash out with a rush of liquid **4** : INFLAME, EXCITE ⟨troops *flushed* with victory⟩ **5** : to make red or hot ⟨a face *flushed* with fever⟩

⁴**flush** *adj* **I a** : filled to overflowing **b** : fully supplied especially with money **2 a** : full of life and vigor : LUSTY **b** : of a ruddy healthy color **3** : readily available : ABUNDANT **4 a** : having an unbroken continuous surface ⟨*flush* paneling⟩ **b** : directly abutting or immediately adjacent **c** : set even with an edge of a type page or column — **flush·ness** *n*

⁵**flush** *adv* **I** : in a flush manner **2** : SQUARELY ⟨was hit *flush* on the chin⟩

⁶**flush** *vt* : to make flush ⟨*flush* the headings on a page⟩

⁷**flush** *n* : a hand of playing cards all of the same suit [Middle French *flus*, from Latin *fluxus* "flow"]

¹**flus·ter** \'fləs-tər\ *vt* **flus·tered; flus·ter·ing** \-tə-riŋ, -triŋ\ **I** : BEFUDDLE 1 **2** : to make nervous and unsure : UPSET ⟨*flustered* by their rudeness⟩ [probably of Scandinavian origin]

²**fluster** *n* : a state of agitated confusion

¹**flute** \'flüt\ *n* **I a** : RECORDER 3 **b** : a woodwind instrument consisting of a tube with keys that is played by blowing across a hole near the closed end **2 a** : a grooved pleat **b** : a rounded groove; *esp* : one of the vertical parallel grooves on a classical architectural column [Middle English *floute*, from Middle French *flahute*, from Provençal *flaut*] — **flute·like** \-,līk\ *adj*

²**flute** *vb* **I** : to play a flute **2** : to make a sound like that of a flute **3** : to form flutes in ⟨*fluted* columns⟩

flut·ing \'flüt-iŋ\ *n* : fluted decoration

flut·ist \'flüt-əst\ *n* : a flute player

¹flute 1b

\ə\ abut	\ng\ sing
\ər\ further	\ō\ bone
\a\ mat	\ò\ saw
\ā\ take	\òi\ coin
\ä\ cot, cart	\th\ thin
\aù\ out	\t̵h\ this
\ch\ chin	\ü\ food
\e\ pet	\ù\ foot
\ē\ easy	\y\ yet
\g\ go	\yü\ few
\i\ tip	\yù\ cure
\ī\ life	\zh\ vision
\j\ job	

l flying buttress

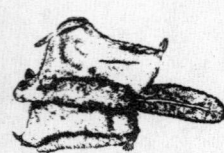

flying squirrel

¹flut·ter \'flət-ər\ *vb* **1** : to move or cause the wings to move rapidly without flying or in short flights ⟨butterflies *flutter*⟩ **2 a** : to move with quick wavering or flapping motions ⟨flags *fluttered* in the breeze⟩ **b** : to vibrate in irregular spasms ⟨a *fluttering* pulse⟩ **3** : to move about or behave in an agitated aimless way [Old English *floterian,* from *flotian* "to float"] — **flut·tery** \'flət-ə-rē\ *adj*

²flutter *n* **1** : an act of fluttering **2 a** : a state of nervous confusion or excitement **b** : FLURRY **3 3** : a distortion in reproduced sound similar to but of a higher pitch than wow

flutter kick *n* : an alternating whipping motion of the legs used in various swimming strokes (as the crawl)

flu·vi·al \'flü-vē-əl\ *adj* : produced by stream action ⟨a *fluvial* plain⟩ [Latin *fluvialis,* from *fluvius* "river", from *fluere* "to flow"]

¹flux \'fləks\ *n* **1** : an excessive fluid discharge from the body and especially the bowels **2 a** : a flowing in ⟨*flux* of the tide⟩ **b** : a series of changes : a state of continuous change **3** : a substance used to promote fusion especially of metals or minerals **4** : the rate of flow of fluid, particles, or energy across a given surface [Latin *fluxus* "flow", from *fluere* "to flow"]

²flux *vb* **1** : to become or cause to become fluid : FUSE **2** : to treat with a flux

¹fly \'flī\ *vb* **flew** \'flü\; **flown** \'flōn\; **fly·ing 1 a** : to move in or pass through the air with wings **b** : to move through the air or before the wind **c** : to float or cause to float, wave, or soar in the air ⟨flags *flying*⟩ **2 a** : to take flight : FLEE **b** : to fade and disappear : VANISH **3** : to move or pass swiftly ⟨time *flies*⟩ **4** : to become spent or wasted rapidly ⟨our money just *flew*⟩ **5 a** : to operate or travel in an aircraft **b** : to journey over by flying ⟨to *fly* the Atlantic⟩ **c** : to transport by aircraft ⟨to *fly* passengers⟩ [Old English *flēogan*] — **fly at** : to assail suddenly and violently — **fly blind** : to fly an airplane solely by instruments — **fly contact** : to fly an airplane with the aid of visible landmarks or reference points — **fly high** : to be elated — **fly in the face of** *or* **fly in the teeth of** : to act forthrightly or brazenly in defiance or disobedience of

²fly *n, pl* **flies 1** : the action or process of flying : FLIGHT **2** : a horse-drawn public coach or delivery wagon **3** *pl* : the space over a theater stage **4** : something attached by one edge: as **a** : a garment closing concealed by a fold of cloth extending over the fastener **b** : the outer fabric of a tent with a double top **c** : the length of an extended flag from its staff or support; *also* : the outer or loose end of a flag **5** : a baseball hit high into the air — **on the fly 1** : continuously active : very busy **2** : while still in the air

³fly *vi* **flied; flying** : to hit a fly in baseball

⁴fly *n, pl* **flies 1** : a winged insect **2** : a winged or rarely wingless insect (order Diptera) : TWO-WINGED FLY; *esp* : one (as a housefly or horsefly) that is relatively large and stout-bodied — compare GNAT **3** : a fishhook dressed to suggest an insect [Old English *flēoge*] — **fly in the ointment** : a detracting factor or element

fly·able \'flī-ə-bəl\ *adj* : suitable for flying or being flown

fly agaric *n* : a poisonous mushroom with a usually bright red cap

fly ash *n* : fine solid particles of noncombustible ash carried out of a bed of burning solid fuel by the draft

fly ball *n* : ²FLY 5

fly·blown \'flī-,blōn\ *adj* **1** : infested with the eggs or young larvae of a flesh fly or blowfly **2** : not pure : TAINTED, CORRUPT

fly·by \-,bī\ *n, pl* **flybys 1** : a usually low-altitude flight past a chosen place by one or more aircraft **2 a** : a flight of a spacecraft past a heavenly body (as Mars) close enough to obtain scientific data **b** : a spacecraft that makes a flyby

fly-by-night \'flī-bə-,nīt\ *adj* **1** : given to making quick profits by shady or irresponsible acts **2** : SHORT-LIVED, TRANSITORY

fly casting *n* : the casting of artificial flies (as in fly-fishing)

fly·catch·er \'flī-,kach-ər, -,kech-\ *n* : a small bird that feeds on insects that it captures in the air

fly·er *variant of* FLIER

fly-fishing \'flī-,fish-ing\ *n* : fishing with artificial flies cast by means of a large flexible pole and a relatively heavy line

¹fly·ing \'flī-ing\ *adj* **1 a** : rapidly moving **b** : HASTY 1a ⟨a *flying* visit⟩ **2** : ready to move or act quickly : MOBILE

²flying *n* **1** : travel by air **2** : the operation of an aircraft or spacecraft

flying boat *n* : a seaplane with a hull adapted for floating

flying buttress *n* : a projecting arched structure to support a wall or building

flying colors *n pl* : complete success ⟨passed the exam with *flying colors*⟩

flying fish *n* : any of numerous sea fishes that have long fins suggesting wings and are able to glide for a distance through the air

flying fox *n* : FRUIT BAT

flying jib *n* : a sail forward of the jib set on an extension of the jibboom

flying machine *n* : AIRCRAFT

flying saucer *n* : any of various unidentified moving objects repeatedly reported as seen in the air and usually represented as being saucer-shaped or disk-shaped

flying squirrel *n* : a squirrel with folds of skin connecting the forelegs and hind legs and enabling it to make long gliding leaps

flying start *n* : a start in racing in which the participants are moving when they receive the starting signal

fly·leaf \'flī-,lēf\ *n* : the half of the endpaper of a book that is not pasted down to the cover

fly·pa·per \-,pā-pər\ *n* : paper poisoned or coated with a sticky substance for killing or catching flies

fly·speck \-,spek\ *n* **1** : a speck of fly dung **2** : something small and insignificant — **flyspeck** *vt*

fly·swat·ter \-,swät-ər\ *n* : a device for killing insects that consists of a flat piece of perforated rubber or plastic or fine-mesh wire netting attached to a handle

fly·way \-,wā\ *n* : an established air route of migratory birds

fly·weight \-,wāt\ *n* : a boxer in a weight division having the approximate range of 48 to 51 kilograms

fly·wheel \-,hwēl, -,wēl\ *n* : a heavy wheel attached to the shaft of a revolving machine that reduces fluctuation in shaft speed through its inertia

FM \'ef-,em\ *n* : a system of broadcasting using frequency modulation; *also* : a receiver of radio waves broadcast by such a system [frequency modulation] — **FM** *adj*

f-number \'ef-,nəm-bər\ *n* : a number following the symbol f/ that expresses the ratio of the focal length of a camera or telescope lens to the aperture and that determines the range of sharpness and the brightness of the image so that the smaller the number the brighter the image but the larger the number the greater the range of sharpness [focal length]

¹foal \'fōl\ *n* : a young animal of the horse family; *esp* : one under one year [Old English *fola*]

²foal *vb* : to give birth to a foal

¹foam \'fōm\ *n* **1** : a light frothy mass of fine bubbles formed in or on a liquid **2** : a froth formed (as by a horse) in salivating or sweating **3** : a stabilized froth produced chemically and used especially in fighting oil fires **4** : a material (as rubber) in a lightweight cellular form resulting from introduction of gas bubbles during manufacture [Old English *fām*]

²foam *vb* **1 a** : to produce or form foam **b** : to froth at the mouth especially in anger; *also* : to be angry **2** : to gush out in foam **3** : to cause to form foam; *esp* : to cause air bubbles to form in **4** : to convert (as a plastic) into a foam

foam rubber *n* : spongy rubber of fine texture made from latex by foaming before vulcanization

foamy \'fō-mē\ *adj* **foam·i·er; -est 1** : covered with foam : FROTHY **2** : full of, consisting of, or resembling foam — **foam·i·ly** \-mə-lē\ *adv* — **foam·i·ness** \-mē-nəs\ *n*

fob \'fäb\ *n* **1** : a short strap, chain, or ribbon attached especially to a pocket watch **2** : a small ornament worn on a watch chain

fob off *vt* **1** : to put off with a trick or excuse **2** : to offer as genuine **3** : to put aside [Middle English *fobben* "to cheat"]

fo·cal \'fō-kəl\ *adj* : of, relating to, or having a focus — **fo·cal·ly** \-kə-lē\ *adv*

focal infection *n* : a persistent localized infection especially when causing symptoms elsewhere in the body

focal length *n* : the distance of the focus from the surface of a lens or concave mirror

focal point *n* : ¹FOCUS 1, 4

fo'·c'sle *variant of* FORECASTLE

¹fo·cus \'fō-kəs\ *n, pl* **fo·cus·es** *or* **fo·ci** \-ˌsī\ **1** : a point at which rays (as of light, heat, or sound) converge or from which they diverge or appear to diverge; *esp* : the point at which an image is formed by a mirror, lens, or optical system **2 a** : FOCAL LENGTH **b** : adjustment (as of the eye or field glasses) for distinct vision; *also* : the area that may be seen distinctly or resolved into a clear image **3** : a fixed point or one of the fixed points used in defining a circle, ellipse, parabola, or hyperbola **4** : a center of activity, attraction, or attention **5** : the place of origin of an earthquake [Latin, "hearth"]

²focus *vb* **fo·cused** *also* **fo·cussed; fo·cus·ing** *also* **fo·cus·sing 1** : to bring to a focus ⟨*focus* rays of light⟩ **2** : to cause to be concentrated ⟨*focus* public attention on a problem⟩ **3** : to adjust the focus of ⟨*focus* the eyes⟩ ⟨*focus* a telescope⟩ **4** : to come to a focus **5** : to adjust one's eye or a camera to a particular range ⟨*focus* at 3 meters⟩

fod·der \'fäd-ər\ *n* : coarse dry food (as cornstalks) for livestock [Old English *fōdor*] — **fodder** *vt*

foe \'fō\ *n* **1** : one who hates another : ENEMY **2** : an enemy in war : ADVERSARY **3** : one who opposes on principle ⟨a *foe* to waste⟩ **4** : something injurious ⟨a *foe* to health⟩ [Old English *fāh*] SYN see ENEMY

foehn *or* **föhn** \'fœn, 'fərn, 'fän\ *n* : a warm dry wind blowing down the side of a mountain [German *föhn*]

foe·tal, foe·tus *variant of* FETAL, FETUS

¹fog \'fòg, 'fäg\ *n* **1 a** : fine particles of water suspended in the lower atmosphere that differ from cloud only in being near the ground **b** : a fine spray or a foam for fire fighting **2** : a murky condition of the atmosphere or a substance causing it **3** : a state of mental confusion **4** : cloudiness in a developed photographic image [probably of Scandinavian origin]

²fog *vb* **fogged; fog·ging 1** : to cover or become covered with or as if with fog **2** : to make obscure or confusing **3** : to make confused

fog·bound \'fòg-ˌbaund, 'fäg-\ *adj* **1** : covered with or surrounded by fog ⟨a *fogbound* coast⟩ **2** : unable to move because of fog ⟨*fogbound* ships⟩

fog·gy \'fòg-ē, 'fäg-\ *adj* **fog·gi·er; -est 1 a** : filled or abounding with fog **b** : covered or made opaque by moisture or grime **2** : VAGUE 2 — **fog·gi·ly** \-ə-lē\ *adv* — **fog·gi·ness** \-ē-nəs\ *n*

fog·horn \'fòg-ˌhòrn, 'fäg-\ *n* : a horn (as on a ship) sounded in foggy weather to give warning

fo·gy *also* **fo·gey** \'fō-gē\ *n, pl* **fogies** *also* **fogeys** : a person with old-fashioned ideas — usually used with *old*

[origin unknown] — **fo·gy·ish** \-gē-ish\ *adj* — **fo·gy·ism** \-gē-ˌiz-əm\ *n*

foi·ble \'fòi-bəl\ *n* : a minor flaw or shortcoming in personal character or behavior : WEAKNESS [obsolete French, from Old French *feble* "feeble"] SYN see FAULT

¹foil \'fòil\ *vt* : to prevent from attaining an end : DEFEAT ⟨*foil* a plot⟩ [Middle English *foilen* "to trample, full cloth", from Middle French *fouler*] SYN see FRUSTRATE

²foil *n* **1** : a fencing weapon with a flat guard and a light flexible blade tapering to a blunt point **2** : the art or practice of fencing with foils — often used in pl.

³foil *n* **1** : a leaf-shaped architectural ornamentation or one of the arcs or rounded spaces between its projections **2** : a very thin sheet of metal ⟨tin or aluminum *foil*⟩ **3** : a thin leaf of polished and colored metal placed under an inferior or paste gem to add color and brilliance **4** : one that serves as a contrast to another ⟨acted as a *foil* for a comedian⟩ [Middle French, from Latin *folium* "leaf"]

foils·man \'fòilz-mən\ *n* : one that fences with a foil

foist \'fòist\ *vt* : to pass off as genuine or worthy [probably from Dutch *vuisten* "to take into one's hand", from *vuist* "fist"]

¹fold \'fōld\ *n* **1** : an enclosure for sheep **2 a** : a flock of sheep **b** : a group of people with a common faith, belief, or interest [Old English *falod, fald*]

²fold *vt* : to pen up or confine (as sheep) in a fold

³fold *vb* **1** : to lay one part over or against another part ⟨*fold* a blanket⟩ **2** : to clasp together ⟨*fold* one's hands⟩ **3** : EMBRACE 1 **4** : to incorporate (a food ingredient) into a mixture by overturning repeatedly without stirring or beating **5** : to become doubled or pleated ⟨the map *folds* into its case⟩ **6** : to fail completely ⟨the business *folded*⟩ [Old English *fealdan*]

⁴fold *n* **1** : a doubling or folding over **2** : a part doubled or laid over another part

-fold \ˌfōld, 'fōld\ *adj suffix or adv suffix* **1** : multiplied by (a specified number) : times ⟨a twelve*fold* increase⟩ ⟨repay you ten*fold*⟩ **2** : having (so many) parts ⟨three*fold* solution to the problem⟩ [Old English *-feald*]

fold·boat \'fōld-ˌbōt, 'fōl-\ *n* : a collapsible kayak made of rubberized fabric stretched over a framework

fold·er \'fōl-dər\ *n* **1** : one that folds **2** : a printed circular of folded sheets **3** : a folded cover or large envelope for holding loose papers

fol·de·rol *also* **fal·de·ral** \'fäl-də-ˌräl\ *n* **1** : a useless trifle **2** : NONSENSE 1 [*fol-de-rol*, a refrain in some old songs]

fo·li·a·ceous \ˌfō-lē-'ā-shəs\ *adj* : of, relating to, or resembling a plant leaf

fo·li·age \'fō-lē-ij, -lyij, -lij\ *n* : the mass of leaves of a plant : LEAFAGE [Middle French *fuellage*, from *foille* "leaf", from Latin *folium*] — **fo·li·aged** \-lē-ijd, -lyjd, -lijd\ *adj*

foliage plant *n* : a plant grown for its decorative foliage

fo·li·ar \'fō-lē-ər\ *adj* : consisting of or relating to leaves

¹fo·li·ate \'fō-lē-ət\ *adj* : having or made up of leaves ⟨3-*foliate*⟩

²fo·li·ate \-lē-ˌāt\ *vb* **1** : to number the leaves of (as a manuscript) **2** : to ornament with foils **3** : to divide into layers or leaves — **fo·li·at·ed** \-ˌāt-əd\ *adj*

fo·li·a·tion \ˌfō-lē-'ā-shən\ *n* **1** : the leafing out of a plant : the state of being in leaf **2** : the act of numbering the leaves of a book; *also* : the total count of leaves numbered **3** : a decoration resembling a leaf **4** : foliated texture

fo·lic acid \'fō-lik-\ *n* : a vitamin of the B complex used especially in the treatment of nutritional anemias [Latin *folium* "leaf"]

fo·lio \'fō-lē-ˌō\ *n, pl* **fo·li·os 1** : a leaf of a manuscript or book **2 a** : a book made of sheets of paper each

\ə\ abut		\ng\ sing	
\ər\ further		\ō\ bone	
\a\ mat		\ò\ saw	
\ā\ take		\òi\ coin	
\ä\ cot, cart		\th\ thin	
\au̇\ out		\th\ this	
\ch\ chin		\ü\ food	
\e\ pet		\u̇\ foot	
\ē\ easy		\y\ yet	
\g\ go		\yü\ few	
\i\ tip		\yu̇\ cure	
\ī\ life		\zh\ vision	
\j\ job			

folded once to make two leaves or four pages **b** : a very large book [Latin, ablative of *folium* "leaf"]

fo·li·o·late \'fō-lē-ə-ˌlāt\ *adj* : having or made up of leaflets — usually used in combination [Late Latin *foliolum* "leaflet", from Latin *folium* "leaf"]

fo·li·ose \'fō-lē-ˌōs\ *adj* : suggesting a leaf or an arrangement of leaves ⟨*foliose* lichens⟩ — compare CRUSTOSE, FRUTICOSE

¹folk \'fōk\ *n, pl* **folk** *or* **folks** **1** : a group of people forming a tribe or nation; *also* : the largest number or most characteristic part of such a group **2** *pl* : people of a specified kind or class ⟨country *folk*⟩ ⟨old *folks*⟩ **3** *folks pl* : people generally **4** *folks pl* : the persons of one's own family ⟨visit your *folks*⟩ [Old English *folc*]

²folk *adj* : of, relating to, or originating among the common people ⟨*folk* dances⟩

folk etymology *n* : the transformation of words so as to give them an apparent relationship to other better-known or better-understood words (as the change of *chaise longue* to *chaise lounge*)

folk·lore \'fōk-ˌlōr, -ˌlȯr\ *n* : customs, beliefs, stories, and sayings of a people handed down from generation to generation — **folk·lor·ist** \-ˌlōr-əst, -ˌlȯr-\ *n*

folk medicine *n* : traditional medicine involving especially the empirical and nonprofessional use of vegetable remedies

folk song *n* : a song originated or traditional among the common people of a country or region — **folk·sing·er** \'fōk-ˌsing-ər\ *n*

folksy \'fōk-sē\ *adj* **folks·i·er; -est** **1** : SOCIABLE 1, FRIENDLY **2** : informal, casual, or familiar in manner or style — **folks·i·ly** \-sə-lē\ *adv* — **folks·i·ness** \-sē-nəs\ *n*

folk·tale \'fōk-ˌtāl\ *n* : an anonymous tale circulated orally among a people

folk·way \'fōk-ˌwā\ *n* : a way of thinking, feeling, or acting common to a people or to a social group

fol·li·cle \'fäl-i-kəl\ *n* **1 a** : a small anatomical cavity or deep narrow-mouthed depression (as from which a hair grows) **b** : GRAAFIAN FOLLICLE **2** : a dry one-celled fruit (as in the peony, larkspur, or milkweed) that splits open by only one seam [Latin *folliculus* "small bag", from *follis* "bellows, bag"] — **fol·lic·u·lar** \'fə-'lik-yə-lər, fä-\ *adj*

follicle–stimulating hormone *n* : a hormone from the pituitary gland that stimulates the growth of ovarian follicles

¹fol·low \'fäl-ō\ *vb* **1** : to go or come after or behind **2** : to accept as authority : OBEY ⟨*follow* your conscience⟩ ⟨*follow* instructions⟩ **3** : to go after or on the track of ⟨*follow* that car⟩ **4** : to proceed along ⟨*follow* a path⟩ **5** : to engage in as a calling or a way of life ⟨*follow* the sea⟩ **6** : to come after in order of rank or natural sequence ⟨two *follows* one⟩ **7** : to result from something ⟨disaster *followed* the blunder⟩ **8** : to keep one's eyes or attention fixed on ⟨*follow* a lesson⟩ [Old English *folgian*] □ SYN FOLLOW, SUCCEED, ENSUE mean to come after or later than something or someone. FOLLOW may apply to a coming after in time, position, or logical sequence ⟨continue the sentence on the *following* page⟩ ⟨the punishment that *follows* crime⟩ SUCCEED may add a stronger implication of displacing or replacing ⟨hoped to *succeed* the president in office⟩ ENSUE commonly suggests a logical consequence or naturally expected development ⟨after the talk a lively debate *ensued*⟩ SYN see in addition CHASE — **follow suit 1** : to play a card of the same suit as the card led **2** : to follow an example set

²follow *n* : the act or process of following

fol·low·er \'fäl-ə-wər\ *n* **1** : one in the service of another : RETAINER **2** : one that follows the opinions or teachings of another **3** : one that imitates another

¹fol·low·ing \'fäl-ə-wing\ *adj* **1** : next after : SUCCEEDING ⟨the *following* day⟩ **2** : that immediately follows ⟨trains will leave at the *following* times⟩

²following *n* : a group of followers, adherents, or partisans

³following *prep* : subsequent to ⟨*following* dinner was dessert⟩

follow out *vt* **1** : to follow to the end or to a conclusion **2** : to carry out : EXECUTE

fol·low–through \'fäl-ō-ˌthrü, ˌfäl-ō-', -ə-\ *n* **1** : the act or an instance of following through **2** : the part of a stroke or swing following the striking of an object

follow through *vi* **1** : to continue a stroke or swing to the end of its arc **2** : to press on in an activity to a conclusion ⟨*follow through* with a study⟩

fol·low–up \'fäl-ə-ˌwəp\ *n* **1** : the act or an instance of following up **2** : something that follows up — **follow–up** *adj*

follow up \ˌfäl-ə-'wəp\ *vt* : to follow with something similar, related, or additional ⟨*follow up* an idea with action⟩

fol·ly \'fäl-ē\ *n, pl* **follies** **1** : lack of good sense or normal prudence and foresight **2 a** : a foolish act or idea **b** : foolish actions or conduct **3** : an excessively costly or unprofitable undertaking [Old French *folie*, from *fol* "fool"]

Fol·som \'fōl-səm\ *adj* : of or relating to a prehistoric culture of North America on the east side of the Rocky mountains characterized especially by a leaf-shaped flint projectile point [*Folsom*, New Mexico]

fo·ment \fō-'ment\ *vt* : to stir up : ROUSE, INSTIGATE ⟨*foment* rebellion⟩ [Late Latin *fomentare*, from Latin *fomentum* "fomentation", from *fovēre* "to warm, fondle, foment"] SYN see INCITE — **fo·ment·er** \fō-'ment-ər\ *n*

fo·men·ta·tion \ˌfō-mən-'tā-shən, -ˌmen-\ *n* **1** : a warm or hot moist material (as a hot damp cloth) applied to the body to ease pain **2** : the act of fomenting : INSTIGATION

fond \'fänd\ *adj* **1** : FOOLISH, SILLY ⟨*fond* pride⟩ **2 a** : prizing highly : DESIROUS ⟨*fond* of praise⟩ **b** : having an affection or liking ⟨*fond* of music⟩ **3** : LOVING, AFFECTIONATE ⟨a *fond* family⟩ **4** : doted on : DEAR ⟨their *fondest* hopes⟩ [Middle English, from *fonne* "fool"] — **fond·ly** *adv* — **fond·ness** \'fänd-nəs, 'fän-\ *n*

fon·dant \'fän-dənt\ *n* **1** : a creamy preparation of sugar used as a basis for candies or icings **2** : a candy consisting chiefly of fondant [French, from *fondre* "to melt"]

fon·dle \'fän-dl\ *vt* **fon·dled; fon·dling** \-dling, -dl-ing\ : to touch or handle in a tender or loving manner : CARESS [derived from *fond*] — **fon·dler** \-dlər, -dl-ər\ *n*

fon·due \fän-'dü, -'dyü\ *n* **1** : a preparation of melted cheese flavored with wine or brandy **2** : a dish consisting of small pieces of food (as meat) cooked in or dipped into a hot liquid [French, from *fondre* "to melt"]

¹font \'fänt\ *n* **1** : a basin for baptismal or holy water **2** : a point from which something originates : SOURCE ⟨a *font* of wisdom⟩ [Old English, from Latin *font-, fons* "fountain"]

²font *n* : an assortment of type all of one size and style [Middle French *fonte* "act of founding", derived from Latin *fundere* "to found, pour"]

fon·ta·nel *also* **fon·ta·nelle** \ˌfänt-n-'el\ *n* : a membrane-covered opening in bone or between bones; *esp* : one between the bones of a fetal or young skull [Middle English *fontinelle* "bodily hollow or pit", from Middle French *fontenele* "little spring", from *fontaine* "spring, fountain"]

food \'füd\ *n* **1 a** : material containing or consisting of carbohydrates, fats, proteins, and supplementary substances (as minerals) used in the body of an animal to sustain growth, repair, and vital processes and to furnish energy **b** (1) : inorganic substances absorbed by plants in gaseous form or in water solution (2) : organic material produced by green plants and used by them as building material and as a source of energy **2** : nourishment in solid form **3** : something that nourishes, sustains, or supplies [Old English *fōda*] — **food·less** \-ləs\ *adj* — **food·less·ness** *n*

food chain *n* : a sequence of the organisms of an ecological community in which each uses the next usually lower member of the sequence for food

food·ie \ˈfüd-ē\ *n* : a person having an avid interest in the latest food fads

food poisoning *n* : an acute digestive disorder caused by bacteria or their toxic products or by chemicals in food

food pyramid *n* : a system of ecological food relationships arranged by levels in which a chief predator is at the top, each level preys on the next lower level, and usually green plants are at the bottom

food stamp *n* : a government-issued coupon that can be used as currency to buy food

food·stuff \ˈfüd-ˌstəf\ *n* : a substance with food value; *esp* : a specific nutrient (as protein or fat)

food vacuole *n* : a vacuole (as in an amoeba) in which ingested food is digested

food web *n* : the totality of interacting food chains in an ecological community

¹**fool** \ˈfül\ *n* **1** : a person who lacks sense or judgment **2 a** : a person formerly kept in a noble or royal household for casual entertainment — called also *jester* **b** : DUPE **3** : a person lacking in common powers of understanding [Old French *fol*, derived from Latin *follis* "bellows, bag"]

²**fool** *vb* **1 a** : to spend time idly or aimlessly **b** : to meddle or tamper thoughtlessly or ignorantly ⟨don't *fool* with that gun⟩ **2** : to speak or act in jest : JOKE ⟨I was only *fooling*⟩ **3** : to make a fool of : DECEIVE **4** : to spend on trifles or without advantage : FRITTER — used with *away*

fool·ery \ˈfül-rē, -ə-rē\ *n, pl* **-er·ies 1** : foolish behavior **2** : a foolish act, utterance, or belief

fool·har·dy \ˈfül-ˌhärd-ē\ *adj* : foolishly adventurous and bold : RASH SYN see DARING — **fool·har·di·ly** \-ˌhärd-l-ē\ *adv* — **fool·har·di·ness** \-ˌhärd-ē-nəs\ *n*

fool·ish \ˈfü-lish\ *adj* **1** : lacking in sense, judgment, or discretion **2** : amusingly absurd ⟨a *foolish* little hat⟩ — **fool·ish·ly** *adv* — **fool·ish·ness** *n*

fool·proof \ˈfül-ˈprüf\ *adj* : so simple, plain, or reliable as to leave no opportunity for error, misuse, or failure

fool's gold *n* **1** : PYRITE **2** : CHALCOPYRITE

fool's paradise *n* : a state of delusory happiness

¹**foot** \ˈfut\ *n, pl* **feet** \ˈfēt\ *also* **foot 1 a** : the terminal part of the vertebrate leg upon which an individual stands **b** : an invertebrate organ of locomotion or attachment; *esp* : a ventral muscular part of a mollusk **2** : any of various units of length based on the length of the human foot; *esp* : a unit equal to ⅓ yard and comprising 12 inches (.3048 meter) ⟨a 10-*foot* pole⟩ ⟨6 *feet* tall⟩ — see MEASURE table **3** : the basic unit of verse meter consisting of a group of accented and unaccented syllables **4** : something resembling an animal's foot in position or use or in being opposite to the head ⟨the *foot* of a mountain⟩ ⟨the *foot* of a bed⟩ **5** : the lower edge (as of a sail) **6 foots** *pl* : material deposited especially on aging or refining : DREGS [Old English *fōt*] — **footlike** \ˈfut-ˌlīk\ *adj* — **on foot 1** : by walking **2** : under way : in progress

²**foot** *vb* **1** : DANCE 1 — often used with *it* **2** : to go on foot **3 a** : to add up **b** : to pay or provide for paying ⟨*foot* the bill⟩

foot·age \ˈfut-ij\ *n* : length expressed in feet

foot–and–mouth disease *n* : an acute virus disease especially of cattle marked by fever and by ulcers in the mouth, about the hooves, and on the udder

foot·ball \ˈfut-ˌbol\ *n* **1** : any of several games that are played with an inflated ball on a rectangular field having two goalposts at each end by two teams whose object is to get the ball over a goal line or between goal posts by running, passing, or kicking: as **a** *British* : SOCCER **b** *British* : RUGBY **c** : an American game played between two teams of 11 players each in which the ball is advanced by running or passing **2** : the ball used in football **3** : something shifted rapidly from one party to another with no one wanting responsibility for it ⟨a political *football*⟩

foot·board \ˈfut-ˌbōrd, -ˌbord\ *n* **1** : a narrow platform on which to stand or brace the feet **2** : a board at the foot of a bed

foot·bridge \-ˌbrij\ *n* : a bridge for pedestrians

foot·can·dle \ˈfut-ˈkan-dl\ *n* : a unit for measuring illumination that equals the illumination on a surface all parts of which are one foot from a light having an intensity of one candle and that amounts to about 10.76 lux

foot·ed \ˈfut-əd\ *adj* : having a foot or feet especially of a specified kind or number ⟨a *footed* stand⟩ ⟨a four-*footed* animal⟩

foot·fall \ˈfut-ˌfol\ *n* : FOOTSTEP 1a; *also* : the sound of a footstep

foot·gear \-ˌgiər\ *n* : FOOTWEAR

foot·hill \-ˌhil\ *n* : a hill at the foot of higher hills or mountains

foot·hold \-ˌhōld\ *n* **1** : a hold for the feet : FOOTING **2** : a position usable as a base for further advance

foot·ing \ˈfut-ing\ *n* **1** : the placing of one's feet in a stable position **2** : the act of moving on foot **3 a** : a place for standing : FOOTHOLD **b** : position with respect to one another : STATUS ⟨nations on a friendly *footing*⟩ **c** : BASIS ⟨put the enterprise on a firm *footing*⟩ **4** : the sum of a column of figures

foot·lights \ˈfut-ˌlīts\ *n pl* **1** : a row of lights set across the front of a stage floor **2** : the stage as a profession

foot·ling \-ling\ *adj* **1** : INEPT ⟨*footling* amateurs⟩ **2** : TRIVIAL **2** [*footle* "to trifle"]

foot·lock·er \-ˌläk-ər\ *n* : a small trunk designed to be placed at the foot of a bed (as in barracks)

foot·loose \-ˌlüs\ *adj* : having no ties : free to roam

foot·man \ˈfut-mən\ *n* : a male servant who attends a carriage, waits on table, admits visitors, and runs errands

foot·mark \-ˌmärk\ *n* : FOOTPRINT

foot·note \-ˌnōt\ *n* **1** : a note of reference, explanation, or comment often placed below the text on a printed page **2** : something that is subordinately related to a larger event or work — **footnote** *vt*

foot·pad \-ˌpad\ *n* : a flattish foot on the leg of a spacecraft to minimize sinking into a surface

foot·path \-ˌpath, -ˌpath\ *n* : a narrow path for pedestrians

foot–pound \-ˈpaund\ *n, pl* **foot–pounds** : a unit of work that equals the work done by a force of one pound acting through a distance of one foot and that amounts to about 1.36 joule

foot–pound–second *adj* : being or relating to a system of units based upon the foot as the unit of length, the pound as the unit of weight, and the second as the unit of time — abbreviation *fps*

foot·print \ˈfut-ˌprint\ *n* : an impression left by a foot

foot·race \-ˌrās\ *n* : a race run by humans on foot

foot·rest \-ˌrest\ *n* : a support for the feet

foot soldier *n* : INFANTRYMAN

foot·sore \ˈfut-ˌsōr, -ˌsor\ *adj* : having sore or tender feet (as from much walking)

foot·step \-ˌstep\ *n* **1 a** : a step of the foot **b** : distance covered by a step : PACE **2** : the mark of the foot : TRACK **3** : a step on which to ascend or descend **4** : a way of life, conduct, or action

foot·stone \-ˌstōn\ *n* : a stone placed at the foot of a grave

foot·stool \-ˌstül\ *n* : a low stool to support the feet

foot·way \-ˌwā\ *n* : a narrow way or path for pedestrians

\ə\ abut	\ng\ sing
\ər\ further	\ō\ bone
\a\ mat	\o͝\ saw
\ā\ take	\oi\ coin
\ä\ cot, cart	\th\ thin
\au̇\ out	\th\ this
\ch\ chin	\ü\ food
\e\ pet	\u̇\ foot
\ē\ easy	\y\ yet
\g\ go	\yü\ few
\i\ tip	\yu̇\ cure
\ī\ life	\zh\ vision
\j\ job	

foot·wear \-,waər, -,weər\ *n* : covering (as shoes) for the feet

foot·work \-,wərk\ *n* : the movement of the feet (as in boxing)

foo·zle \'fü-zəl\ *vt* **foo·zled; foo·zling** \'füz-ling, -ə-ling\ : to manage or play awkwardly : BUNGLE [perhaps from German dialect *fuseln* "to work carelessly"] — **foozle** *n*

fop \'fäp\ *n* : a man who is vain about his dress or appearance : DANDY [Middle English] — **fop·pish** \'fäp-ish\ *adj* — **fop·pish·ly** *adv* — **fop·pish·ness** *n*

fop·pery \'fäp-rē, -ə-re\ *n, pl* **-per·ies** **1** : foolish character or action : FOLLY **2** : the behavior or dress of a fop

¹for \fər, fŏr, 'fŏr\ *prep* **1** — used as a function word to indicate purpose ⟨money *for* studying⟩, intended destination ⟨left *for* home⟩, or an object of one's desire ⟨now *for* a good rest⟩ **2** : as being ⟨do you take me *for* a fool⟩ **3** : because of ⟨cried *for* joy⟩ **4 a** : in support of ⟨fighting *for* their country⟩ **b** — used as a function word to indicate appropriateness or belonging ⟨medicine *for* a cold⟩ **c** : so as to bring about a certain state ⟨shouted the news *for* all to hear⟩ **5 a** : in place of ⟨Doe batting *for* Roe⟩ **b** : as the equal or equivalent of ⟨paid $10 *for* a hat⟩ **6** : in spite of ⟨unconvinced *for* all the clever arguments⟩ **7** : CONCERNING ⟨a stickler *for* detail⟩ **8** — used as a function word to indicate equality or proportion ⟨point *for* point⟩ ⟨tall *for* their age⟩ **9** — used as a function word to indicate duration of time or extent of space ⟨waited *for* several hours⟩ **10** : ²AFTER 3b ⟨named *for* my grandfather⟩ [Old English]

²for *conj* : for this reason : on this ground

for- *prefix* **1** : so as to involve prohibition, exclusion, omission, failure, neglect, or refusal ⟨*for*bid⟩ **2** : destructively or detrimentally ⟨*for*do⟩ **3** : completely : excessively : to exhaustion : to pieces ⟨*for*lorn⟩ [Old English]

fora *pl of* FORUM

¹for·age \'fŏr-ij, 'fär-\ *n* **1** : food for animals especially when taken by browsing or grazing **2** : the act of foraging : search for provisions [Middle French, from *forre* "fodder", of Germanic origin]

²forage *vb* **1** : to collect forage from **2** : to seek forage or provisions ⟨*forage* through the refrigerator⟩ **3** : to get by foraging ⟨*forage* a chicken⟩ — **for·ag·er** *n*

fo·ram \'fōr-əm, 'fŏr-\ *n* : FORAMINIFER

fo·ra·men \fə-'rā-mən\ *n, pl* **-ram·i·na** \-'ram-ə-nə\ *or* **-ra·mens** \-'rā-mənz\ : a small opening, perforation, or orifice [Latin *foramin-, foramen,* from *forare* "to bore"]

fo·ra·men mag·num \fə-,rā-mən-'mag-nəm\ *n* : the opening in the skull through which the spinal cord joins the brain [New Latin, literally, "great opening"]

foramen ova·le \-ō-'val-ē, -'väl-, -'vāl-\ *n* : a small opening between the two atria of the heart that is normally present only in the fetus [New Latin, literally, "oval opening"]

for·a·min·i·fer \,fŏr-ə-'min-ə-fər, ,fär-\ *n* : any of an order (Foraminifera) of large chiefly marine amoeboid protozoans usually having perforated shells containing calcium that are important sources of chalk and limestone — **fo·ra·mi·nif·er·al** \fə-,ram-ə-'nif-rəl, -ə-rəl; ,fŏr-ə-mə-'nif-, ,fär-\ *adj* — **fo·ra·mi·nif·er·an** \-rən\ *adj or n*

for·as·much as \'fŏr-əz-,məch-əz\ *conj* : in view of the fact that : SINCE

for·ay \'fŏr-,ā\ *vb* : to raid often in search of plunder : PILLAGE [Middle French *forrer,* from *forre* "fodder"] — **foray** *n*

forb \'fŏrb\ *n* : an herb other than a grass [Greek *phorbe* "fodder, food", from *pherbein* "to graze"]

¹for·bear \fŏr-baər, fər-, -'beər\ *vb* **-bore** \-'bōr, -'bŏr\; **-borne** \-'bōrn, -'bŏrn\; **-bear·ing** **1** : to refrain or desist from : ABSTAIN **2** : to control oneself when provoked : be patient [Old English *forberan* "to endure, do without", from *for-* + *beran* "to bear"] SYN see REFRAIN — **for·bear·er** *n*

²forbear *variant of* FOREBEAR

for·bear·ance \fŏr-'bar-əns, fər-, -'ber-\ *n* **1** : the act of forbearing **2** : the quality of being forbearing : PATIENCE

for·bid \fər-'bid, fŏr-\ *vt* **-bade** \-'bad, -'bād\ *or* **-bad** \-'bad\; **-bid·den** \-'bid-n\; **-bid·ding** **1** : to order not to do something or not to be done or used : PROHIBIT ⟨they *forbade* us to leave⟩ ⟨loitering is *forbidden*⟩ **2** : to hinder or prevent as if by command ⟨space *forbids* quoting in full⟩ [Old English *forbēodan,* from *for-* + *bēodan* "to bid"] — **for·bid·der** *n* □ SYN PROHIBIT, INHIBIT, BAN: FORBID implies absolute proscription with expectation of obedience; PROHIBIT implies more generality and suggests the effect of statutes or ordinances; INHIBIT implies hampering or restricting by authority or more often by circumstances or involuntary self-restraint; BAN adds the implication of condemnation or disapproval along with prohibition.

for·bid·ding *adj* : frightening away : REPELLENT, UNPLEASANT ⟨a stern *forbidding* manner⟩ ⟨a *forbidding* task⟩ — **for·bid·ding·ly** \-ing-lē\ *adv*

forbode *variant of* FOREBODE

¹force \'fōrs, 'fŏrs\ *n* **1 a** : strength or energy exerted : active power ⟨*forces* of nature⟩ **b** : moral or mental strength **c (1)** : capacity to persuade or convince ⟨the *force* of this argument⟩ **(2)** : legal effectiveness ⟨that law is still in *force*⟩ **2 a** : military strength **b (1)** : a body (as of troops or ships) assigned to a military purpose **(2)** *pl* : ARMED FORCES **c** : a body of persons available for a particular end ⟨the labor *force*⟩ **3** : violence, compulsion, or constraint exerted on or against a person or thing **4** : an influence (as a push or pull) that if applied to a material free body results chiefly in an acceleration of the body and sometimes in other effects (as deformation) [Middle French, derived from Latin *fortis* "strong"] SYN see POWER — **force·less** \-ləs\ *adj*

²force *vt* **1** : to compel by force : COERCE ⟨*forced* them to quit⟩ **2** : to make or cause through natural or logical necessity ⟨*forced* to admit I am wrong⟩ **3** : to attain to or effect against resistance ⟨*force* a bill through the legislature⟩ **4 a** : to gain by struggle or violence ⟨*force* one's way in⟩ **b** : to break open or through ⟨*force* a lock⟩ **5 a** : to raise or accelerate to the utmost ⟨*forcing* the pace⟩ **b** : to produce with unnatural effort ⟨*forced* a laugh⟩ **6 a** : to hasten the rate of progress or growth of **b** : to bring (as plants) to maturity out of the normal season ⟨*forcing* lilies for the Easter trade⟩ — **forc·er** *n* □ SYN COMPEL, COERCE, CONSTRAIN: FORCE implies the use of physical power to overcome resistance of persons or things ⟨*forced* them to submit⟩ ⟨*forced* the door with a crowbar⟩ COMPEL and COERCE take only personal objects, COMPEL implying the working of an irresistible force ⟨hunger *compelled* them to surrender⟩ and COERCE suggesting the use of threatened violence or other injury; CONSTRAIN suggests the effect of a force or circumstance that limits action or choice ⟨*constrained* by hunger to yield⟩

forced \'fōrst, 'fŏrst\ *adj* **1** : compelled by force : INVOLUNTARY ⟨a *forced* landing⟩ **2** : done or produced with effort, exertion, or pressure ⟨*forced* laughter⟩ — **forc·ed·ly** \'fōr-səd-lē, 'fŏr-\ *adv*

force·ful \'fōrs-fəl, 'fŏrs-\ *adj* : possessing much force : VIGOROUS — **force·ful·ly** \-fə-lē\ *adv* — **force·ful·ness** *n*

force·meat \'fōrs-,mēt, 'fŏrs-\ *n* : chopped and seasoned meat or fish served alone or used as a stuffing [*force* (alteration of *farce* "stuffing") + *meat*]

for·ceps \'fŏr-səps, -,seps\ *n, pl* **forceps** : an instrument for grasping, holding, or moving objects especially for delicate operations (as by jewelers or surgeons) [Latin, from *formus* "warm" + *capere* "to take"] — **for·ceps·like** \-,līk\ *adj*

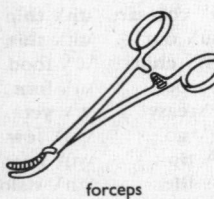
forceps

forc·ible \'fȯr-sə-bəl, 'fȯr-\ *adj* **1** : got, made, or done by force or violence ⟨a *forcible* entrance⟩ **2** : showing force or energy — **forc·ibly** \-blē\ *adv*

¹ford \'fōrd, 'fȯrd\ *n* : a shallow part of a body of water that may be crossed by wading [Old English]

²ford *vt* : to cross (a body of water) by wading — **ford·able** \-ə-bəl\ *adj*

for·do *or* **fore·do** \fȯr-'dü, fōr-\ *vt* **-did** \-'did\; **-done** \-'dən\; **-do·ing** : to overcome with fatigue : EXHAUST [Old English *fordōn* "to destroy", from *for-* + *dōn* "to do"]

¹fore \'fōr, 'fȯr\ *adv* : in, toward, or adjacent to the front : FORWARD ⟨the shell hit *fore* of the mast⟩ [Old English]

²fore *adj* : being or coming before in time, order, or space

³fore *n* : something that occupies a front position — **to the fore** : in or into a prominent position

⁴fore *interj* — used by a golfer to warn anyone within range of the probable line of flight of the ball [probably short for *before*]

fore- *combining form* **1** : earlier : beforehand ⟨*fore*named⟩ ⟨*fore*see⟩ **2 a** : situated at the front : in front ⟨*fore*leg⟩ **b** : front part of (something specified) ⟨*fore*brain⟩ [Old English, from *fore,* adv.]

fore–and–aft \ˌfōr-ə-'naft, ˌfȯr-\ *adj* **1** : lying, running, or acting in the general line of the length of a construction (as a ship) ⟨*fore-and-aft* sails⟩ **2** : having no square sails

fore and aft *adv* : lengthwise of a ship : from stem to stern

fore–and–aft·er \-'naf-tər\ *n* : a ship with a fore-and-aft rig; *esp* : SCHOONER

fore–and–aft rig *n* : a sailing-ship rig in which most or all of the sails are not attached to yards but are bent to gaffs or set on the masts or on stays in a fore-and-aft line — **fore–and–aft rigged** *adj*

¹fore·arm \fōr-'ärm, 'fōr-, 'fȯr-\ *vt* : to arm in advance : PREPARE

²fore·arm \'fōr-ˌärm, 'fȯr-\ *n* : the part of the arm between the elbow and the wrist

fore·bear *or* **for·bear** \'fōr-ˌbaer, 'fȯr-, -ˌbeər\ *n* : ANCESTOR 1, FOREFATHER [Middle English *forebear,* from *fore-* + *-bear* "one that is", from *been* "to be"]

fore·bode *also* **for·bode** \fōr-'bōd, fȯr-\ *vb* **1** : FORETELL, PORTEND ⟨such heavy air *forebodes* a storm⟩ **2** : to have a premonition of (as misfortune) — **fore·bod·er** *n*

¹fore·bod·ing *n* : an omen, prediction, or presentiment especially of coming evil : PORTENT

²foreboding *adj* : indicative of or marked by foreboding — **fore·bod·ing·ly** \-ing-lē\ *adv* — **fore·bod·ing·ness** *n*

fore·brain \'fōr-ˌbrān, 'fȯr-\ *n* : the front division of the embryonic vertebrate brain or the parts (as the cerebrum and olfactory lobes) developed from it

¹fore·cast \'fōr-ˌkast, 'fȯr-\ *vb* **forecast** *or* **fore·cast·ed; fore·cast·ing** **1** : to calculate or predict (a future event or condition) usually as a result of study and analysis of data; *esp* : to predict (weather conditions) on the basis of meteorological observations **2** : to indicate as likely to occur ⟨*forecast* an easy victory at the polls⟩ SYN see FORETELL — **fore·cast·er** *n*

²forecast *n* : a prophecy, estimate, or prediction of a future happening or condition ⟨weather *forecasts*⟩

fore·cas·tle \'fōk-səl; 'fōr-ˌkas-əl, 'fȯr-\ *or* **fo'·c's'le** \'fōk-səl\ *n* **1** : the forward part of the upper deck of a ship **2** : the part of a ship where the crew is housed

fore·close \fōr-'klōz, fȯr-\ *vb* **1** : to rule out ⟨didn't *foreclose* the possibility of a second term⟩ **2** : to take legal measures to end a mortgage and take possession of the mortgaged property because the conditions of the mortgage have not been met by the mortgagor [Old French *forclore,* from *fors* "outside" + *clore* "to close"]

fore·clo·sure \-'klō-zhər\ *n* : the act of foreclosing; *esp* : the legal procedure of foreclosing a mortgage

fore·deck \'fōr-ˌdek, 'fȯr-\ *n* : the forepart of a ship's main deck

foredo *variant of* FORDO

fore·doom \fōr-'düm, fȯr-\ *vt* : to doom beforehand ⟨efforts *foredoomed* to failure⟩

fore·fa·ther \'fōr-ˌfäth-ər, 'fȯr-, -ˌfȧth-\ *n* **1** : ANCESTOR 1 **2** : a person of an earlier period and common heritage

fore·fin·ger \'fōr-ˌfing-gər, 'fȯr-\ *n* : the finger next to the thumb

fore·foot \-ˌfu̇t\ *n* **1** : one of the front feet of a four-footed animal **2** : the forward part of a ship where the stem and keel meet

fore·front \-ˌfrənt\ *n* : the foremost part or place : the place of greatest activity or interest ⟨an event in the *forefront* of the news⟩

foregather *variant of* FORGATHER

¹fore·go \fōr-'gō, fȯr-\ *vb* **-went** \-'went\; **-gone** \-'gȯn, -'gän\; **-go·ing** \-'gō-ing\ : to go before : PRECEDE — **fore·go·er** \-'gō-ər, -'gōr\ *n*

²forego *variant of* FORGO

fore·go·ing \fōr-'gō-ing, fȯr-\ *adj* : going before; *esp* : said, written, or listed before or above SYN see PRECEDING

fore·gone \'fōr-ˌgȯn, 'fȯr-, -ˌgän\ *adj* : determined or settled in advance ⟨success was a *foregone* conclusion⟩

fore·ground \'fōr-ˌgrau̇nd, 'fȯr-\ *n* **1** : the part of a scene or representation that is nearest to and in front of the spectator **2** : a position of prominence : FOREFRONT

fore·gut \-ˌgət\ *n* : the part of the alimentary canal of a vertebrate embryo that develops into the pharynx, esophagus, stomach, and first part of the intestine

¹fore·hand \'fōr-ˌhand, 'fȯr-\ *n* : a stroke made with the palm of the hand turned in the direction of movement

²forehand *adv* : with a forehand

³forehand *adj* : using or made with a forehand

fore·hand·ed \'fōr-'han-dəd, 'fȯr-\ *adj* **1** : mindful of the future : THRIFTY, PRUDENT **2** : FOREHAND — **fore·hand·ed·ly** *adv* — **fore·hand·ed·ness** *n*

fore·head \'fȯr-əd, 'fär-; 'fōr-ˌhed, 'fȯr-\ *n* **1** : the part of the face above the eyes **2** : the front or forepart of something

for·eign \'fȯr-ən, 'fär-\ *adj* **1** : situated outside a place or country; *esp* : situated outside one's own country ⟨*foreign* nations⟩ **2** : born in, belonging to, or characteristic of some place or country other than the one under consideration ⟨a *foreign* language⟩ **3** : alien in character : not connected or pertinent ⟨material *foreign* to the topic under discussion⟩ **4** : related to or dealing with other nations ⟨*foreign* affairs⟩ **5** : occurring in an abnormal situation in the living body and commonly introduced from outside ⟨a *foreign* body in the eye⟩ [Old French *forein,* from Late Latin *foranus* "being outside", from Latin *foris* "outside"] — **for·eign·ness** \-ən-nəs\ *n*

for·eign·er \'fȯr-ə-nər, 'fär-\ *n* : a person belonging to or owing allegiance to a foreign country : ALIEN

foreign exchange *n* **1** : a process of settling accounts or debts between persons living in different countries **2** : foreign currency or current short-term credit instruments payable in such currency

for·eign·ism \'fȯr-ə-ˌniz-əm, 'fär-\ *n* : something peculiar to a foreign language or people; *esp* : a foreign idiom or custom

foreign minister *n* : a governmental minister for foreign affairs

fore·know \fōr-'nō, fȯr-, 'fōr-, 'fȯr-\ *vt* **-knew** \-'nu, -'nyu\; **-known** \-'nōn\; **-know·ing** : to have previous knowledge of : know beforehand SYN see FORESEE — **fore·knowl·edge** \-'näl-ij\ *n*

fore·la·dy \'fōr-ˌlād-ē, 'fȯr-\ *n* : a woman in charge of a group of workers

fore·land \-lənd\ *n* : PROMONTORY, HEADLAND

\ə\ abut		\ng\ sing	
\ər\ further		\ō\ bone	
\a\ mat		\ȯ\ saw	
\ā\ take		\ȯi\ coin	
\ä\ cot, cart		\th\ thin	
\au̇\ out		\th\ this	
\ch\ chin		\ü\ food	
\e\ pet		\u̇\ foot	
\ē\ easy		\y\ yet	
\g\ go		\yü\ few	
\i\ tip		\yu̇\ cure	
\ī\ life		\zh\ vision	
\j\ job			

fore·leg \-ˌleg\ *n* : a front leg

fore·limb \-ˌlim\ *n* : an arm, fin, wing, or leg that is one of a front pair of limbs

fore·lock \-ˌläk\ *n* : a lock of hair growing from the front of the head

fore·man \'fōr-mən, 'fȯr-\ *n* 1 : a member of a jury who acts as chairperson and spokesperson 2 : a person in charge of a group of workers

fore·mast \-ˌmast, -məst\ *n* : the mast nearest the bow of a ship

¹**fore·most** \'fōr-ˌmōst, 'fȯr-\ *adj* : first in time, place, or order; *also* : most important [Old English *formest*, superlative of *forma* "first"]

²**foremost** *adv* : in the first place

fore·name \-ˌnām\ *n* : a first name

fore·named \-ˌnāmd\ *adj* : previously named : AFORE-SAID

fore·noon \'fōr-ˌnün, 'fȯr-\ *n* : the early part of the day ending with noon : MORNING

¹**fo·ren·sic** \fə-'ren-sik, -'ren-zik\ *adj* : belonging to, used in, or suitable to courts of law or to public discussion and debate [Latin *forensis*, from *forum* "forum"] — **fo·ren·si·cal·ly** \-si-kə-lē, -zi-, -klē\ *adv*

²**forensic** *n* 1 : an argumentative exercise 2 *pl* : the art or study of argumentative discourse

fore·or·dain \ˌfōr-ȯr-'dān, ˌfȯr-\ *vt* : to ordain or decree in advance : PREDESTINE ⟨a *foreordained* course of events⟩ — **fore·or·di·na·tion** \-ˌȯrd-n-'ā-shən\ *n*

fore·part \'fōr-ˌpärt, 'fȯr-\ *n* : the part most advanced or first in place or in time ⟨the *forepart* of the day⟩

fore·paw \-ˌpȯ\ *n* : the paw of a foreleg

fore·quar·ter \-ˌkwȯrt-ər, -ˌkwȯt-\ *n* : the left or right half of the front half of the body or carcass of a four-footed animal ⟨a *forequarter* of beef⟩

fore·reach \fōr-'rēch, fȯr-\ *vb* 1 : to gain ground in tacking 2 : to gain on or overhaul and go ahead of (a ship) when close-hauled

fore·run·ner \'fōr-ˌrən-ər, 'fȯr-\ *n* 1 : one that precedes and indicates the approach of another ⟨the dark clouds were *forerunners* of a storm⟩ 2 : one that precedes another (as in office or an activity) ⟨*forerunners* of the modern cartoon⟩

fore·sail \'fōr-ˌsāl, 'fȯr-, -səl\ *n* 1 : the lowest sail on the foremast of a square-rigged ship 2 : the lower sail set on the foremast of a schooner

fore·see \fōr-'sē, fȯr-\ *vt* **-saw** \-'sȯ\; **-seen** \-'sēn\; **-seeing** : to see or realize (as a development) beforehand : EXPECT — **fore·see·able** \-ə-bəl\ *adj* — **fore·se·er** \-'sē-ər\ *n* □ SYN FORESEE, FOREKNOW, ANTICIPATE mean to know beforehand. FORESEE may apply to ordinary reasoning and of itself implies nothing concerning either action or feeling; FOREKNOW usually implies the involvement of supernatural forces; ANTICIPATE implies responding emotionally to or taking action about something before it happens.

fore·shad·ow \-'shad-ō\ *vt* : to give a hint of beforehand ⟨clouds *foreshadowed* snow⟩ — **fore·shad·ow·er** *n*

fore·sheet \-ˌshēt\ *n* 1 : one of the sheets of a foresail 2 *pl* : the forward part of an open boat

fore·shore \-ˌshōr, -ˌshȯr\ *n* : the part of a seashore between high-water and low-water marks

fore·short·en \fōr-'shȯrt-n, fȯr-\ *vt* : to shorten (a detail) in a drawing or painting so that the composition appears to have depth

fore·show \-'shō\ *vt* : FORETELL, FORESHADOW

fore·side \'fōr-ˌsīd, 'fȯr-\ *n* : the front side or part : FRONT

fore·sight \'fōr-ˌsīt, 'fȯr-\ *n* 1 : the act or power of foreseeing : knowledge of something before it happens 2 : the act of looking forward; *also* : a view forward 3 : care or provision for the future : PRUDENCE — **fore·sight·ed** \-ˌsīt-əd\ *adj* — **fore·sight·ed·ly** *adv* — **fore·sight·ed·ness** *n*

¹ foresail ¹

fore·skin \-ˌskin\ *n* : a fold of skin that covers the end of the penis — called also *prepuce*

for·est \'fȯr-əst, 'fär-\ *n* 1 : a dense growth of trees and underbrush covering a large tract; *also* : an area covered by forest 2 : something resembling a forest especially in profusion ⟨a *forest* of masts⟩ [Old French "forest, hunting preserve", from Medieval Latin *forestis*, from Latin *foris* "outside"] — **for·est·ed** \'fȯr-ə-stəd, 'fär-\ *adj*

fore·stage \'fōr-ˌstāj, 'fȯr-\ *n* : APRON 2

fore·stall \fōr-'stȯl, fȯr-\ *vt* : to keep out, hinder, or prevent by measures taken in advance ⟨*forestall* unnecessary questions by giving careful directions⟩ SYN see PREVENT — **fore·stall·er** *n* — **fore·stall·ment** \-'stȯl-mənt\ *n*

for·es·ta·tion \ˌfȯr-ə-'stā-shən, ˌfär-\ *n* : the planting and care of a forest

fore·stay \'fōr-ˌstā, 'fȯr-\ *n* : a stay from the top of a ship's foremast to the deck

for·est·er \'fȯr-ə-stər, 'fär-\ *n* : a person who practices or is trained in forestry

forest floor *n* : the upper layer of mixed soil and organic debris typical of forested land

forest green *n* : a dark yellowish or moderate olive green

forest ranger *n* : an officer in charge of forest protection (as by preventing, detecting, and fighting fires) and management (as supervision of lumbering and recreation)

for·est·ry \'fȯr-ə-strē, 'fär-\ *n* : scientific management of forests including development, care, and often economic harvesting

foreswear *variant of* FORSWEAR

¹**fore·taste** \'fōr-ˌtāst, 'fȯr-\ *n* : a preliminary or partial experience of something that will not be fully experienced until later ⟨through maneuvers a soldier gets a *foretaste* of war⟩

²**fore·taste** \fōr-'tāst, fȯr-', 'fōr-ˌ, 'fȯr-\ *vt* : to have a foretaste of

fore·tell \fōr-'tel, fȯr-\ *vt* **-told** \-'tōld\; **-tell·ing** : to tell of or describe beforehand — **fore·tell·er** *n* □ SYN FORETELL, PREDICT, FORECAST, PROPHESY mean to tell beforehand. FORETELL often implies seeing the future through occult or unexplained powers ⟨a sorcerer *foretold* their evil end⟩ PREDICT implies often exact foretelling through scientific methods ⟨*predict* an eclipse⟩ FORECAST commonly deals in probabilities and eventualities rather than certainties ⟨*forecasting* the week's weather⟩ PROPHESY suggests the presence of inspired or mystic knowledge in predicting ⟨*prophesying* the end of the world⟩

fore·thought \'fōr-ˌthȯt, 'fȯr-\ *n* 1 : a thinking or planning out in advance : PREMEDITATION 2 : thoughtful care for the future — **fore·thought·ful** \-fəl\ *adj*

¹**fore·to·ken** \'fōr-ˌtō-kən, 'fȯr-\ *n* : a premonitory sign

²**fore·to·ken** \fōr-'tō-kən, fȯr-\ *vt* **-to·kened; -to·ken·ing** \-'tōk-ning, -ə-ning\ : to indicate in advance ⟨the bright sunset *foretokened* good weather⟩

fore·top \'fōr-ˌtäp, 'fȯr-; -'təp\ *n* : the platform at the head of the ship's foremast

for·ev·er \fə-'rev-ər, fȯ-\ *adv* 1 : for a limitless time : EVERLASTINGLY 2 : at all times : CONSTANTLY ⟨a dog that was *forever* chasing cars⟩

for·ev·er·more \-ˌrev-ər-'mōr, -ˌrev-ə-', -'mȯr\ *adv* : FOREVER 1

fore·warn \fōr-'wȯrn, fȯr-\ *vt* : to warn in advance ⟨*forewarned* of danger⟩

fore wing *n* : either of the front wings of a 4-winged insect

fore·wom·an \'fōr-ˌwu̇m-ən, 'fȯr-\ *n* 1 : FORELADY 2 : a woman member of a jury who acts as foreman

fore·word \'fōr-wərd, 'fȯr-, -ˌwərd\ *n* : PREFACE 2

¹**for·feit** \'fȯr-fət\ *n* 1 : something lost by or taken away from a person because of an offense or error committed : PENALTY, FINE 2 *pl* : a game in which the players

redeem personal articles by paying amusing or embar- rassing penalties [Middle French *forfait,* from *forfaire* "to commit a crime, forfeit"]

²for·feit *vt* : to lose or lose the right to by some error, offense, or crime — **for·feit·er** *n*

³for·feit *adj* : forfeited or subject to forfeiture ⟨the spy's life was *forfeit*⟩

for·fei·ture \'fȯr-fə-ˌchu̇r, -chər\ *n* **1** : the act of forfeit- ing **2** : something forfeited : PENALTY

for·fend \fȯr-'fend\ *vt* **1 a** *archaic* : FORBID 1 **b** : to ward off **2** : PRESERVE 1, PROTECT

for·gath·er *or* **fore·gath·er** \fȯr-'gath-ər, fōr-\ *vi* **1** : to come together : ASSEMBLE **2** : to meet someone usually by chance

¹forge \'fōrj, 'fȯrj\ *n* **1** : a furnace or a shop with its furnace where metal is heated and worked **2** : a work- shop where wrought iron is produced or where iron is made malleable [Old French, from Latin *fabrica* "workshop", from *faber* "artisan, smith"]

²forge *vt* **1 a** : to form (as metal) by heating and ham- mering **b** : to form (metal) by a mechanical or hydrau- lic press **2** : to form or shape in any way : FASHION ⟨*forge* ties of friendship⟩ **3** : to make or imitate falsely especially with intent to defraud : COUNTERFEIT ⟨*forge* a check⟩

³forge *vi* : to move forward steadily but gradually ⟨*forge* ahead in the election⟩

forg·er \'fōr-jər, 'fȯr-\ *n* : one that forges; *esp* : a person guilty of forgery

forg·ery \'fōrj-rē, 'fȯrj-, -ə-rē\ *n, pl* **-er·ies 1** : the crime of falsely making or changing a written paper or sign- ing someone else's name **2** : something (as a signa- ture) that has been forged

for·get \fər-'get, fȯr-\ *vb* **-got** \-'gät\; **-got·ten** \-'gät-n\ *or* **-got**; **-get·ting 1** : to be unable to think of or recall ⟨*forgot* the address⟩ **2 a** : to fail to recall at the proper time ⟨*forgot* about paying the bill⟩ **b** : NEGLECT ⟨*forget* old friends⟩ [Old English *forgietan*] — **for·get·ter** *n* — **forget oneself** : to lose one's dignity, temper, or self-control

for·get·ful \-'get-fəl\ *adj* **1** : having a poor memory **2** : CARELESS, NEGLECTFUL ⟨*forgetful* of responsibilities⟩ — **for·get·ful·ly** \-'get-fə-lē\ *adv* — **for·get·ful·ness** *n*

for·get-me-not \fər-'get-mē-ˌnät, fȯr-\ *n* : any of a ge- nus of small herbs with bright blue, pink, or white flowers usually in a curved spike

for·get·ta·ble \-'get-ə-bəl\ *adj* : likely to be forgotten

forg·ing \'fōr-jing, 'fȯr-\ *n* : a piece of forged work ⟨alu- minum *forgings*⟩

for·give \fər-'giv, fȯr-\ *vb* **-gave** \-'gāv\; **-giv·en** \-'giv- ən\; **-giv·ing 1** : to cease to feel resentment against (an offender) : PARDON ⟨*forgive* your enemies⟩ **2 a** : to give up resentment of or claim to requital for ⟨*forgive* an insult⟩ **b** : to grant relief from payment of ⟨*forgive* a debt⟩ [Old English *forgifan,* from *for-* + *gifan* "to give"] SYN see EXCUSE — **for·giv·able** \-'giv-ə-bəl\ *adj* — **for·giv·er** *n*

for·give·ness \-'giv-nəs\ *n* : the act of forgiving : PAR- DON

for·giv·ing \-'giv-ing\ *adj* : showing forgiveness : in- clined or ready to forgive ⟨a person with a *forgiving* nature⟩ — **for·giv·ing·ly** \-ing-lē\ *adv* — **for·giv·ing- ness** *n*

for·go *or* **fore·go** \fȯr-'gō, fōr-\ *vt* **-went** \-'went\; **-gone** \-'gȯn, -'gän\; **-go·ing** \-'gō-ing\ : to give up : let pass : go without ⟨*forgo* lunch⟩ ⟨*forgo* an opportunity⟩ [Old English *forgān* "to pass by, forgo", from *for-* + *gān* "to go"]

¹fork \'fȯrk\ *n* **1** : an implement with two or more prongs used especially for taking up (as in eating), pitching, or digging **2** : a forked part, tool, or piece of equipment **3 a** : a dividing into branches or the place where something divides into branches ⟨a *fork* in the road⟩ **b** : a branch of a fork ⟨take the left *fork* at the

crossroads⟩ [Old English *forca* and Old North French *forque,* both from Latin *furca*]

²fork *vb* **1** : to divide into two or more branches ⟨the road *forks*⟩ **2** : to give the form of a fork to ⟨*fork* one's fingers⟩ **3** : to raise or pitch with a fork ⟨*fork* hay⟩ — **fork·er** *n*

forked \'fȯrkt, 'fȯr-kəd\ *adj* : having a fork : shaped like a fork ⟨*forked* lightning⟩

fork·ful \'fȯrk-ˌfu̇l\ *n, pl* **forkfuls** \'fȯrk-ˌfu̇lz\ *or* **forks- ful** \'fȯrks-ˌfu̇l\ : as much as a fork will hold

fork·lift \'fȯrk-ˌlift\ *n* : a machine for hoisting and trans- porting heavy objects by means of steel fingers insert- ed under the load

for·lorn \fər-'lȯrn\ *adj* **1** : seeming sad and lonely es- pecially because empty or abandoned **2** : being or feeling deserted or neglected : WRETCHED **3** : nearly hopeless ⟨a *forlorn* cause⟩ [Old English *forloren,* past participle of *forlēosan* "to lose, abandon", from *for-* + *lēosan* "to lose"] SYN see SOLITARY — **for·lorn·ly** *adv* — **for·lorn·ness** \-'lȯrn-nəs\ *n*

forlorn hope *n* **1** : a body of men selected to perform a perilous service **2** : a desperate or extremely difficult enterprise [by folk etymology from Dutch *verloren hoop,* literally, "lost band"]

¹form \'fȯrm\ *n* **1 a** : the shape and structure of some- thing as distinguished from its material **b** : a body (as of a person) especially in its external appearance or as distinguished from the face **2** : the essential nature of a thing as distinguished from its matter **3** : an estab- lished manner of doing or saying something ⟨the *forms* of worship⟩ **4** : a printed or typed document with blank spaces for insertion of required information ⟨a tax *form*⟩ **5 a** : conduct regulated by custom or eti- quette : CEREMONY, CONVENTION; *also* : show without substance ⟨outward *forms* of mourning⟩ **b** : manner of performing according to recognized standards ⟨such behavior is bad *form*⟩ **6** : a long seat : BENCH **7 a** : a supporting frame model of the human figure used for displaying clothes **b** : a mold in which concrete is placed to set **8** : printing type or matter arranged and secured ready for printing **9** : one of the different manifestations of a particular thing or substance ⟨coal is a *form* of carbon⟩ **10 a** : orderly method of arrange- ment (as in the presentation of ideas or artistic ele- ments); *also* : a particular kind or instance of such ar- rangement ⟨the sonnet is a poetical *form*⟩ **b** : the structural element, plan, or design of a work of art **c** : a visible and measurable unit defined by a contour : a bounded surface or volume **11** : a grade in a British secondary school or in some American private schools **12 a** : known ability to perform **b** : condition suitable for performing (as in athletic competition) **13 a** : a meaningful unit of speech (as a morpheme, word, or sentence) **b** : any of the different pronunciations or spellings a word may take in inflection or compound- ing **14** : a particular kind of mathematical expression ⟨the number 2.5 can be written in fractional *form* as ⁵⁄₂⟩ [Old French *forme,* from Latin *forma*] □ SYN FIG- URE, SHAPE: FORM may refer both to internal structure and external outline and often suggests the principle giving unity to the whole ⟨early *forms* of animal life⟩ FIGURE applies chiefly to the bounding or enclosing lines of a form ⟨cutting doll *figures* out of paper⟩ SHAPE may also suggest an outline, but carries a strong- er implication of a three-dimensional body ⟨the *shape* of the monument was pyramidal⟩

²form *vb* **1** : to give form or shape to : FASHION, MAKE ⟨*form* a letter of the alphabet⟩ **2** : TRAIN, INSTRUCT ⟨ed- ucation *forms* the mind⟩ **3** : DEVELOP, ACQUIRE ⟨*form* a habit⟩ **4** : to make up : CONSTITUTE ⟨bonds *formed* the bulk of the estate⟩ **5** : to arrange in order ⟨*form* a bat- tle line⟩ **6** : to take form : ARISE ⟨fog *forms* in the val- leys⟩ **7** : to take a definite form, shape, or arrangement ⟨each column of soldiers marched away as soon as it *formed*⟩ — **form·er** *n*

\ə\ abut	\ng\ sing	
\ər\ further	\ō\ bone	
\a\ mat	\ȯ\ saw	
\ā\ take	\ȯi\ coin	
\ä\ cot, cart	\th\ thin	
\au̇\ out	\th\ this	
\ch\ chin	\ü\ food	
\e\ pet	\u̇\ foot	
\ē\ easy	\y\ yet	
\g\ go	\yü\ few	
\i\ tip	\yu̇\ cure	
\ī\ life	\zh\ vision	
\j\ job		

-form \,form\ *adj combining form* : in the form or shape of : resembling ⟨reni*form*⟩ [Latin *-formis,* from *forma* "form"]

¹**for·mal** \'for-məl\ *adj* **1** : relating to, concerned with, or constituting the outward form of something as distinguished from its content ⟨the *formal* features of a thing can be misleading⟩ **2 a** : CONVENTIONAL 2 ⟨paying *formal* attention to his hostess⟩ ⟨a *formal* dinner⟩ **b** : done in due or lawful form ⟨a *formal* contract⟩ **3** : characterized by punctilious respect for form ⟨very *formal* in all their dealings⟩ **4** : NOMINAL 3a ⟨a purely *formal* requirement⟩ — **for·mal·ly** \-mə-lē\ *adv*

²**formal** *n* : something (as a social event) formal in character

form·al·de·hyde \for-'mal-də-,hīd, fər-\ *n* : a colorless gas CH₂O that consists of carbon, hydrogen, and oxygen, has a sharp irritating odor, and is used as a disinfectant and preservative [*form*ic acid + *aldehyde*]

for·ma·lin \'for-mə-lən, -,lēn\ *n* : a clear water solution of formaldehyde containing a small amount of methanol

for·mal·ism \'for-mə-,liz-əm\ *n* : the strict observance of forms or conventions (as in religion or art) — **for·mal·ist** \-ləst\ *n* — **for·mal·is·tic** \,for-mə-'lis-tik\ *adj* — **for·mal·is·ti·cal·ly** \-ti-kə-lē, -klē\ *adv*

for·mal·i·ty \for-'mal-ət-ē\ *n, pl* **-ties 1** : the quality or state of being formal **2** : compliance with formal or conventional rules : CEREMONY **3** : an established form that is required or conventional

for·mal·ize \'for-mə-,līz\ *vt* **1** : to make formal **2** : to give formal status or approval to — **for·mal·iz·er** *n*

for·mat \'for-,mat\ *n* **1** : the shape, size, and general makeup of a publication **2** : the general plan of organization or arrangement of something [German, from Latin *formare* "to form", from *forma* "form"]

for·ma·tion \for-'mā-shən\ *n* **1** : a forming of something ⟨the *formation* of good habits during childhood⟩ **2** : something that is formed ⟨new word *formations*⟩ **3** : the manner in which a thing is formed : STRUCTURE, SHAPE ⟨an abnormal *formation* of the jaw⟩ **4** : an arrangement or grouping of persons, ships, or airplanes ⟨battle *formation*⟩ ⟨planes flying in *formation*⟩ **5** : a bed of rocks or series of beds recognizable as a unit — **for·ma·tion·al** \-shnəl, -shən-l\ *adj*

for·ma·tive \'for-mət-iv\ *adj* **1** : giving or capable of giving form : CONSTRUCTIVE ⟨a *formative* influence⟩ **2** : of, relating to, or characterized by important growth or formation ⟨*formative* years⟩ — **for·ma·tive·ly** *adv* — **for·ma·tive·ness** *n*

form class *n* : a class of linguistic forms that can be used in the same position in a construction and that have one or more morphological or syntactical features in common

for·mer \'for-mər\ *adj* **1** : coming before in time; *esp* : of, relating to, or occurring in the past ⟨our *former* correspondence⟩ **2** : preceding in place or arrangement : FOREGOING ⟨the *former* part of the chapter⟩ **3** : first mentioned or in order of two things mentioned or understood ⟨of these two evils the *former* is the lesser⟩ [Middle English, from *forme* "first", from Old English *forma*]

for·mer·ly \-mər-lē, -mə-lē\ *adv* : at an earlier time : PREVIOUSLY

form·fit·ting \'form-,fit-ing\ *adj* : conforming to the outline of the body ⟨a *formfitting* sweater⟩

For·mi·ca \for-'mī-kə, fər-\ *trademark* — used for any of various laminated plastic products used especially for surface finish

for·mic acid \'for-mik-\ *n* : a colorless strong-smelling liquid acid CH₂O₂ that irritates the skin, is found in insects (as ants) and in many plants, and is used chiefly in dyeing and finishing textiles [Latin *formica* "ant"]

for·mi·cary \'for-mə-,ker-ē\ *n, pl* **-car·ies** : an ant nest

for·mi·da·ble \'for-məd-ə-bəl, for-'mid-\ *adj* **1** : arousing fear ⟨a *formidable* foe⟩ **2** : imposing serious difficulties or hardships ⟨the mountains were a *formidable* barrier⟩ **3** : tending to inspire awe or wonder ⟨the *formidable* accomplishments of science⟩ [Latin *formidabilis,* from *formidare* "to fear", from *formido* "fear"] — **for·mi·da·bil·i·ty** \,for-məd-ə-'bil-ət-ē, for-,mid-\ *n* — **for·mi·da·ble·ness** *n* — **for·mi·da·bly** \-blē\ *adv*

form·less \'form-ləs\ *adj* : having no regular form or shape — **form·less·ly** *adv* — **form·less·ness** *n*

for·mu·la \'for-myə-lə\ *n, pl* **-las** *also* **-lae** \-,lē, -,lī\ **1** : a set form of words for use in a ceremony or ritual **2 a** : RECIPE, PRESCRIPTION ⟨our *formula* for happiness⟩ **b** : a milk mixture or substitute for a baby **3 a** : a symbolic expression of the composition or constitution of a substance ⟨the *formula* for water is H₂O⟩ **b** : a group of mathematical symbols used to express briefly a single concept **4** : a prescribed or set form or method [Latin, "small form", from *forma* "form"] — **for·mu·la·ic** \,for-myə-'lā-ik\ *adj* — **for·mu·la·ical·ly** \-'lā-ə-kə-lē, -klē\ *adv*

for·mu·la·rize \'for-myə-lə-,rīz\ *vt* : to state in or reduce to a formula : FORMULATE — **for·mu·la·riz·er** *n*

for·mu·lary \'for-myə-,ler-ē\ *n, pl* **-lar·ies 1** : a book or collection of stated and prescribed forms **2** : a prescribed form or model : FORMULA **3** : a book containing a list of medicinal substances and formulas — **formulary** *adj*

for·mu·late \'for-myə-,lāt\ *vt* **1** : to express in a formula **2** : to put in systematic form : state definitely and clearly ⟨*formulate* a plan⟩ — **for·mu·la·tion** \,for-myə-'lā-shən\ *n* — **for·mu·la·tor** \'for-myə-,lāt-ər\ *n*

for·ni·cate \'for-nə-,kāt\ *vi* : to commit fornication [Late Latin *fornicare,* from Latin *fornix* "arch, vaulted basement, brothel"] — **for·ni·ca·tor** \-,kāt-ər\ *n*

for·ni·ca·tion \,for-nə-'kā-shən\ *n* : human sexual intercourse other than between a husband and wife and especially between unmarried persons — used in some translations (as AV, DV) of the Bible (as in Matthew 5:32) for *unchastity* (as in RSV) or *immorality* (as in NCE) to cover all sexual intercourse except between husband and wife or concubine; compare ADULTERY

for·nix \'for-niks\ *n, pl* **for·ni·ces** \-nə-,sēz\ : an anatomical arch or fold [Latin, "arch"]

for·sake \fər-'sāk, for-\ *vt* **for·sook** \-'suk\; **for·sak·en** \-'sā-kən\; **for·sak·ing 1** : to give up : RENOUNCE **2** : to quit or leave entirely : withdraw from ⟨*forsook* the theater for other work⟩ ⟨*forsaken* by false friends⟩ [Old English *forsacan,* from *for-* + *sacan* "to dispute"] SYN see ABANDON

for·sooth \fər-'süth\ *adv* : in truth : INDEED

for·swear *or* **fore·swear** \for-'swaər, fōr-, -'sweər\ *vb* **-swore** \-'swōr, -'swor\; **-sworn** \-'swōrn, -'sworn\; **-swear·ing 1** : to swear falsely : commit perjury **2** : to pledge oneself to give up ⟨*forswear* gambling⟩

for·syth·ia \fər-'sith-ē-ə\ *n* : any of a genus of shrubs of the olive family widely grown for their yellow bell-shaped flowers appearing before the leaves in early spring [William *Forsyth,* died 1804, British botanist]

fort \'fōrt, 'fort\ *n* **1** : a strong or fortified place; *esp* : a place surrounded with defenses and occupied by soldiers **2** : a permanent army post [Middle French, from *fort* "strong", from Latin *fortis*]

¹**forte** \'fōrt, 'fort, 'for-,tā\ *n* : something in which a person shows special ability : a strong point ⟨music was always your *forte*⟩ [Middle French *fort,* from *fort* "strong"]

²**for·te** \'for-,tā, 'fort-ē\ *adv or adj* : LOUDLY, POWERFULLY — used as a direction in music [Italian, from *forte* "strong", from Latin *fortis*]

forth \'fōrth, 'forth\ *adv* **1** : FORWARD, ONWARD ⟨from that time forth⟩ ⟨and so *forth*⟩ ⟨back and *forth*⟩ **2** : out into view : OUT ⟨plants putting *forth* leaves⟩ [Old English]

¹forth·com·ing \fōrth-'kəm-ing, fórth-\ *adj* **1** : being about to appear : APPROACHING ⟨the *forthcoming* holidays⟩ **2 a** : readily available ⟨the needed supplies were *forthcoming*⟩ **b** : RESPONSIVE 2

²forthcoming *n* : a coming forth : APPROACH

forth·right \'fōrth-,rīt, 'fórth-\ *adj* : STRAIGHTFORWARD, DIRECT ⟨a *forthright* answer⟩ — **forth·right·ly** *adv* — **forth·right·ness** *n*

forth·with \fōrth-'with, fórth-, -'with\ *adv* : IMMEDIATE-LY ⟨expect an answer *forthwith*⟩

for·ti·fi·ca·tion \,fórt-ə-fə-'kā-shən\ *n* **1** : the act of fortifying **2 a** : a construction built for the defense of a place : FORT **b** *pl* : defensive works

for·ti·fy \'fórt-ə-,fī\ *vt* **-fied; -fy·ing** : to make strong: as **a** : to strengthen and secure by military defenses ⟨*fortify* a town⟩ **b** : to give physical strength, courage, or endurance to ⟨*fortify* the body against illness⟩ **c** : to add mental or moral strength to : ENCOURAGE **d** : to add material to for strengthening or improving : ENRICH ⟨*fortify* a soil with fertilizer⟩ [Middle French *fortifier,* from Late Latin *fortificare,* from Latin *fortis* "strong"] — **for·ti·fi·er** \-,fī-ər, -,fīr\ *n*

for·tis·si·mo \fór-'tis-ə-,mō\ *adv or adj* : very loudly — used as a direction in music [Italian, superlative of *forte* "strong"]

for·ti·tude \'fórt-ə-,tüd, -,tyüd\ *n* : strength of mind that enables a person to meet danger or bear pain or adversity with courage [Latin *fortitudo* "strength", from *fortis* "strong"]

fort·night \'fórt-,nīt, 'fórt-\ *n* : the space of 14 days : two weeks [Middle English *fourtenight,* alteration of *fourtene night* "fourteen nights"]

¹fort·night·ly \-lē\ *adj* : occurring or appearing once in a fortnight

²fortnightly *adv* : once in a fortnight

³fortnightly *n, pl* **-lies** : a publication issued fortnightly

FOR·TRAN \'fór-,tran\ *n* : an algebraic and logical language for programming a computer [*for*mula *tran*slation]

for·tress \'fór-trəs\ *n* : a fortified place; *esp* : a large and permanent fortification sometimes including a town [Middle French *forteresce,* derived from Latin *fortis* "strong"]

for·tu·i·tous \fór-'tü-ət-əs, fər-, -'tyü-\ *adj* : occurring by chance [Latin *fortuitus*] SYN see ACCIDENTAL — **for·tu·i·tous·ly** *adv* — **for·tu·i·tous·ness** *n*

for·tu·i·ty \-ət-ē\ *n, pl* **-ties** **1** : the quality or state of being fortuitous **2** : a chance event or occurrence

for·tu·nate \'fórch-nət, -ə-nət\ *adj* **1** : coming or happening by good luck : bringing a benefit or good that was not expected or was not forseen as certain **2** : receiving some unexpected good : LUCKY SYN see LUCKY — **for·tu·nate·ly** *adv* — **for·tu·nate·ness** *n*

for·tune \'fór-chən\ *n* **1** : an apparent cause of something that happens to one suddenly and unexpectedly : CHANCE, LUCK **2** : what happens to a person : good or bad luck ⟨the *fortunes* of war⟩ ⟨have the good *fortune* to be elected class president⟩ **3** : a person's destiny or fate ⟨tell one's *fortune*⟩ **4 a** : possession of material goods : WEALTH ⟨people of *fortune*⟩ **b** : a store of material possessions : RICHES ⟨the family *fortune*⟩ [Middle French, from Latin *fortuna*]

fortune cookie *n* : a thin folded cookie containing a slip of paper on which is printed a fortune, proverb, or humorous statement

fortune hunter *n* : a person who seeks wealth especially by marriage

for·tune–tell·er \-,tel-ər\ *n* : a person who professes to foretell future events — **for·tune–tell·ing** \-,tel-ing\ *n or adj*

for·ty \'fórt-ē\ *n, pl* **forties** **1** : ten more than 30; *also* : a symbol representing this — see NUMBER table **2** : the 3d point scored by a side in a game of tennis [Old English *fēowertig*] — **for·ti·eth** \-ē-əth\ *adj or n* — **forty** *adj or pron*

for·ty–five \,fórt-ē-'fīv\ *n* **1** : a .45 caliber pistol — usually written .45 **2** : a phonograph record for play at 45 revolutions per minute

Forty Hours *n sing or pl* : a Roman Catholic devotion in which the churches of a diocese in two-day turns maintain continuous daytime prayer before the exposed Blessed Sacrament

for·ty–nin·er \,fórt-ē-'nī-nər\ *n* : a person in California in the gold rush of 1849

forty winks *n sing or pl* : a short sleep : NAP

fo·rum \'fōr-əm, 'fór-\ *n, pl* **forums** *also* **fo·ra** \-ə\ **1 a** : the marketplace or public place of an ancient Roman city serving as the center of judicial and public business **b** : a medium of open discussion **2** : a judicial body or assembly : COURT **3 a** : a public meeting or lecture involving audience discussion **b** : a program (as on radio or television) involving discussion of a problem usually by several authorities [Latin]

¹for·ward \'fór-wərd\ *adj* **1** : near, being at, or belonging to the front **2 a** : strongly inclined : READY **b** : tending to push oneself : BRASH **3** : notably advanced or developed **4** : moving, tending, or leading toward a position in front ⟨*forward* movement⟩ **5** : of, relating to, or getting ready for the future ⟨*forward* buying of produce⟩ [Old English *foreweard,* from *fore-* + *-weard* "-ward"] — **for·ward·ly** *adv* — **for·ward·ness** *n*

²forward *adv* : to or toward what is before or in front

³forward *n* : a mainly offensive player in a game (as basketball or soccer) who plays at the front of the team's formation

⁴forward *vt* **1** : to help onward : ADVANCE ⟨*forward* a friend's career⟩ **2 a** : to send forward **b** : to send or ship onward from an intermediate post or station in transit

for·ward·er \'fór-wərd-ər\ *n* : one that forwards; *esp* : an agent who forwards goods ⟨a freight *forwarder*⟩

for·ward·ing \-wərd-ing\ *n* : the act of one that forwards; *esp* : the business of a forwarder of goods

forward pass *n* : a pass in football thrown in the direction of the opponents' goal

for·wards \'fór-wərdz\ *adv* : FORWARD

fos·sa \'fäs-ə\ *n, pl* **fos·sae** \'fäs-,ē, -,ī\ : an anatomical pit or depression [Latin, "ditch"]

fosse *or* **foss** \'fäs\ *n* : DITCH, MOAT [Old French *fosse,* from Latin *fossa,* from *fodere* "to dig"]

¹fos·sil \'fäs-əl\ *n* **1** : a trace or impression or the remains of a plant or animal of a past age preserved in the earth's crust **2 a** : a person whose ideas are out-of-date **b** : something that has become rigidly fixed [Latin *fossilis* "dug up", from *fodere* "to dig"]

²fossil *adj* : being or resembling a fossil ⟨*fossil* plants⟩

fossil fuel *n* : a fuel (as coal, oil, or natural gas) that is formed in the earth from plant or animal remains

fos·sil·if·er·ous \,fäs-ə-'lif-rəs, -ə-rəs\ *adj* : containing fossils

fos·sil·ize \'fäs-ə-,līz\ *vb* **1** : to convert or become converted into a fossil **2** : to make outmoded, rigid, or fixed — **fos·sil·iza·tion** \,fäs-ə-lə-'zā-shən\ *n*

fos·so·ri·al \fä-'sōr-ē-əl, -'sór-\ *adj* : adapted to or occupied in digging ⟨a *fossorial* foot⟩ ⟨*fossorial* animals⟩

¹fos·ter \'fós-tər, 'fäs-\ *adj* : affording, receiving, or sharing nurture or parental care though not related by blood or legal ties ⟨*foster* parent⟩ ⟨*foster* child⟩ [Old English *fōstor-,* from *fōstor* "food, feeding"]

²foster *vt* **fos·tered; fos·ter·ing** \-tə-ring, -tring\ **1** : to give parental care to : NURTURE **2** : to promote the growth or development of : ENCOURAGE — **fos·ter·er** \-tər-ər\ *n*

fos·ter·age \'fós-tə-rij, 'fäs-\ *n* : the act of fostering

foster home *n* : a household in which an orphaned, neglected, or delinquent child or a mentally ill person is placed for care

fos·ter·ling \-tər-ling\ *n* : a foster child

Fou·cault pendulum \,fü-'kō-\ *n* : a pendulum that consists of a heavy weight hung by a long wire and that

\ə\ abut		\ng\ sing	
\ər\ further		\ō\ bone	
\a\ mat		\ó\ saw	
\ā\ take		\ói\ coin	
\ä\ cot, cart		\th\ thin	
\aú\ out		\th\ this	
\ch\ chin		\ü\ food	
\e\ pet		\ú\ foot	
\ē\ easy		\y\ yet	
\g\ go		\yü\ few	
\i\ tip		\yú\ cure	
\ī\ life		\zh\ vision	
\j\ job			

swings in a constant direction which appears to change showing that the earth rotates [J. B. L. *Foucault*, died 1868, French physicist]

fought *past of* FIGHT

¹foul \'faùl\ *adj* **1 a** : offensive to the senses ⟨a *foul* sewer⟩ **b** : clogged or covered with dirt **2** : morally or spiritually odious : DETESTABLE ⟨*foul* crimes⟩ **3** : OBSCENE, ABUSIVE ⟨*foul* language⟩ **4** : being wet and stormy ⟨*foul* weather⟩ **5 a** : grossly unfair : DISHONORABLE **b** : violating a rule in a game or sport ⟨a *foul* blow in boxing⟩ **6** : being outside the foul lines in baseball ⟨a *foul* grounder⟩ [Old English *fūl*] SYN see DIRTY — **foul·ly** \'faùl-lē, faù-\ *adv*

²foul *n* **1** : an entanglement or collision especially in angling or sailing **2** : an infringement of the rules in a game or sport **3** : FOUL BALL

³foul *adv* : FOULLY

⁴foul *vb* **1** : to make or become foul or filthy ⟨*foul* the air⟩ ⟨*foul* a stream⟩ **2** : DISGRACE ⟨*foul* one's good name⟩ **3 a** : to commit a violation of the rules in a sport or game **b** : to hit a foul ball **4** : to entangle or become entangled ⟨*foul* a rope⟩ **5** : to collide with ⟨*foul* a launch in moving away from the dock⟩

fou·lard \fù-'lärd\ *n* **1** : a lightweight plain-woven or twilled silk usually decorated with a printed pattern **2** : an article of clothing (as a scarf) made of foulard [French]

foul ball *n* : a baseball hit into foul territory

foul line *n* **1** : either of two straight lines extending from the rear corner of home plate through the outer corners of first and third bases and continued to the boundary of a baseball field **2** : a line across a bowling alley that a player must not step over when delivering the ball **3** : either of 2 lines on a basketball court behind which a player stands to shoot a free throw

foul·mouthed \'faùl-'maùthd, -'maùtht\ *adj* : inclined to use dirty, profane, or abusive language

foul·ness \'faùl-nəs\ *n* **1** : the quality or state of being foul **2** : something that is foul

foul play *n* : unfair play or dealing : dishonest conduct; *esp* : VIOLENCE ⟨a victim of *foul play*⟩

foul shot *n* : a free throw in basketball

foul tip *n* : a pitched baseball that is slightly deflected by the bat

foul-up \'faùl-,ləp\ *n* **1** : a state of confusion caused by bungling, carelessness, or mismanagement **2** : a mechanical difficulty

foul up \faùl-'ləp, 'faùl-\ *vb* **1** : to make dirty **2** : to spoil by making mistakes or using poor judgment : CONFUSE **3** : to become confused : get into difficulty : BUNGLE

¹found \'faùnd\ *past of* FIND

²found *vt* **1** : to take the first steps in building ⟨*found* a colony⟩ **2** : to set or ground on something solid : BASE ⟨a house *founded* on rock⟩ **3** : to establish and often to provide for the future maintenance of ⟨*found* a college⟩ [Old French *fonder*, from Latin *fundare*, from *fundus* "bottom"]

³found *vt* : to melt (metal) and pour into a mold [Middle French *fondre* "to pour, melt", from Latin *fundere*]

foun·da·tion \faùn-'dā-shən\ *n* **1** : the act of founding **2** : the base or basis upon which something stands or is supported ⟨a house with a cinder-block *foundation*⟩ ⟨suspicions with no *foundation* in fact⟩ **3** : funds given for the permanent support of an institution : ENDOWMENT; *also* : an organization or institution so endowed — **foun·da·tion·al** \-shnəl, -shən-l\ *adj*

¹found·er \'faùn-dər\ *n* : one that founds or establishes something ⟨the *founders* of the town⟩

²foun·der \'faùn-dər\ *vb* **foun·dered; foun·der·ing** \-dəring, -dring\ **1** : to go or cause to go lame ⟨the horse *foundered*⟩ **2** : to give way ⟨the building *foundered* in the fire⟩ **3** : to sink or cause to sink below the surface of the water ⟨a *foundering* ship⟩ **4** : to come or cause to come to grief : FAIL ⟨their efforts all *foundered*⟩

[Middle French *fondrer* "to send to the bottom, collapse", derived from Latin *fundus* "bottom"]

³found·er *n* : one that founds metal

found·ling \'faùn-dling\ *n* : an infant found after its unknown parents have abandoned it

foundry \'faùn-drē\ *n, pl* **foundries** **1** : the act, process, or art of casting metals; *also* : CASTINGS **2** : an establishment where founding is carried on

fount \'faùnt\ *n* : SOURCE 1b ⟨a *fount* of information⟩

foun·tain \'faùnt-n\ *n* **1** : a spring of water issuing from the earth **2** : SOURCE 1b **3** : an artificially produced jet of water; *also* : the structure from which it rises **4** : a reservoir containing a liquid that can be drawn off as needed [Middle French *fontaine*, from Late Latin *fontana*, derived from Latin *font-, fons*]

foun·tain·head \-,hed\ *n* **1** : a fountain or spring that is the source of a stream **2** : a primary source : ORIGIN

fountain pen *n* : a pen with a reservoir that automatically feeds the writing point with ink

four \'fōr, 'fòr\ *n* **1** : one more than three; *also* : a symbol representing this — see NUMBER table **2** : the 4th in a set or series **3** : something having four units or members [Old English *fēower*] — **four** *adj or pron*

four–dimensional *adj* : relating to or having four dimensions; *esp* : consisting of or relating to mathematical elements requiring four coordinates to determine them

four–flush \'fōr-,fləsh, 'fòr-\ *vi* : to make a false claim : BLUFF [earlier *four-flush* "to bluff in poker holding four cards of the same suit in a five-card hand"] — **four–flush·er** *n*

four–fold \-,fōld, -'fōld\ *adj* **1** : having four units or members **2** : being four times as great or as many — **fourfold** *adv*

four–foot·ed \-'fùt-əd\ *adj* : having four feet : QUADRUPED

4–H \-'āch\ *adj* : of or relating to a program set up by the United States Department of Agriculture to help young people become productive citizens by instructing them in useful skills, community service, and personal development ⟨*4-H* club⟩ [from the fourfold aim of improving the head, heart, hands, and health] — **4–H'er** \-'ā-chər\ *n*

four–hand \'fōr-,hand, 'fòr-\ *adj* : FOUR-HANDED

four–hand·ed \-'han-dəd\ *adj* **1** : designed for four hands **2** : engaged in by four persons ⟨a *four-handed* card game⟩

Four Horsemen *n pl* : war, famine, pestilence, and death personified as the four major plagues of mankind [from the apocalyptic vision in Revelation 6:2–8]

Four Hundred *or* **400** *n* : the exclusive social set of a community — used with *the* [from the idea that a social elite must necessarily be small in number]

four–in–hand \'fōr-ən-,hand, 'fòr-\ *n* **1 a** : a team of four horses driven by one person **b** : a vehicle drawn by such a team **2** : a necktie tied in a slipknot with long ends overlapping vertically in front

four–letter word *n* : any of a group of dirty or abusive words typically made up of four letters

four–o'clock \-ə-,kläk\ *n* : an American garden plant with fragrant yellow, red, or white flowers opening late in the afternoon

four–post·er \-'pō-stər\ *n* : a bed with tall corner posts originally designed to support curtains or a canopy

four·ra·gère \,fùr-ə-'zheər\ *n* : a braided cord worn (as by a soldier in uniform) usually around the left shoulder [French]

four·score \'fōr-,skōr, 'fòr-,skòr\ *adj* : being four times twenty : EIGHTY

four·some \'fōr-səm, 'fòr-\ *n* **1** : a group of four members **2** : a group of four golfers playing together

four·square \-'skwaər, -'skwər\ *adj* **1** : SQUARE 1a **2** : marked by boldness and conviction : FORTHRIGHT — **foursquare** *adv*

four·teen \fōr-ˈtēn, fȯr-, fōrt-, fȯrt-, ˈfōr-, ˈfȯr-, ˈfōrt-, ˈfȯrt-\ *n* : one more than 13; *also* : a symbol representing this — see NUMBER table [Old English *fēowertīene*] — **fourteen** *adj or pron* — **fourteenth** \-ˈtēnth, -ˈtēntth\ *adj or n*

four·teen·er \-ˈtē-nər\ *n* : a verse consisting of 14 syllables or especially of 7 iambic feet

fourth \ˈfōrth, ˈfȯrth\ *n* **1** : number four in a countable series — see NUMBER table **2 a** : the musical interval embracing four diatonic degrees **b** : the harmonic combination of two tones a fourth apart **3** : the 4th forward gear or speed of a motor vehicle — **fourth** *adj or adv* — **fourth·ly** *adv*

fourth class *n* **1** : a class or group ranking fourth in a series **2** : a class of mail in the United States that comprises merchandise and non-second-class printed matter and is not sealed against inspection

fourth dimension *n* **1** : a dimension in addition to length, width, and depth; *esp* : a coordinate in addition to three rectangular coordinates **2** : something outside the range of ordinary experience

fourth estate *n, often cap F&E* : the public press
☐ ORIGIN In Europe, in earlier days, the people who participated in the government of a country were generally divided into three classes or estates. In England the three traditional estates were the nobility, the clergy, and the commons. Occasionally the term *fourth estate* was used for some other group, like the mob or the public press, that had unofficial but often great influence on government. In time *fourth estate* came to refer exclusively to the press.

Fourth of July : INDEPENDENCE DAY

four–wheel \ˈfōr-ˌhwēl, ˈfȯr-, -ˌwēl\ *or* **four–wheeled** \-ˈhwēld, -ˈwēld\ *adj* **1** : having four wheels **2** : acting on or by means of four wheels of an automotive vehicle ⟨*four-wheel* drive⟩

fo·vea \ˈfō-vē-ə\ *n, pl* **-ve·ae** \-vē-ˌē, -vē-ˌī\ : an area of the retina containing only cones and affording acute vision [Latin, "pit"] — **fo·ve·al** \-vē-əl\ *adj* — **fo·ve·ate** \-vē-ˌāt\ *adj*

¹fowl \ˈfaùl\ *n, pl* **fowl** *or* **fowls 1** : BIRD 1: as **a** : a domestic cock or hen; *esp* : an adult hen **b** : any of several domesticated or wild birds related to the common domestic cock and hen **2** : the flesh of fowls used as food [Middle English *foul*, from Old English *fugel*]

²fowl *vi* : to seek, catch, or kill wildfowl — **fowl·er** *n*

fowling piece *n* : a light gun for shooting birds or small mammals

¹fox \ˈfäks\ *n, pl* **fox·es** *or* **fox 1 a** : any of various flesh-eating mammals related to the wolves but smaller and with shorter legs and more pointed muzzle **b** : the fur of a fox **2** : a clever crafty person [Old English]

²fox *vt* : to trick by cleverness or cunning : OUTWIT

foxed \ˈfäkst\ *adj* : discolored with yellowish brown stains ⟨the *foxed* pages of an old book⟩

fox fire *n* : an eerie phosphorescent light (as of decaying wood); *also* : a luminous fungus that causes decaying wood to glow

fox·glove \ˈfäks-ˌgləv\ *n* : any of a genus of erect herbs of the snapdragon family; *esp* : a common biennial or perennial plant that bears showy spikes of dotted white or purple tubular flowers and is a source of digitalis

fox grape *n* : any of several native grapes of eastern North America with sour or musky fruit

fox·hole \ˈfäks-ˌhōl\ *n* : a pit dug hastily during combat for individual cover against enemy fire

fox·hound \-ˌhaùnd\ *n* : any of various large swift powerful hounds used in hunting foxes

fox·tail \ˈfäk-ˌstāl\ *n* : any of several grasses with spikes resembling brushes

foxtail millet *n* : a coarse drought-resistant but frost-sensitive annual grass grown for grain, hay, and forage

fox terrier *n* : a small lively terrier formerly used to dig out foxes and known in smooth-haired and wirehaired varieties

fox–trot \ˈfäks-ˌträt\ *n* **1** : a short broken slow trotting gait of the horse **2** : a ballroom dance in duple time that includes slow walking steps and quick running steps — **fox–trot** *vi*

foxy \ˈfäk-sē\ *adj* **fox·i·er; -est 1 a** : resembling a fox in appearance or disposition : WILY **b** : being alert and knowing : CLEVER **2** : having the color of a fox **3** : FOXED **4** : being good-looking : ATTRACTIVE — **fox·i·ly** \-sə-lē\ *adv* — **fox·i·ness** \-sē-nəs\ *n*

foy·er \ˈfȯi-ər, ˈfȯi-ˌā; ˈfȯi-ˌā, -ˌyā\ *n* : an anteroom òr lobby especially of a theater; *also* : an entrance hallway [French, literally, "fireplace", from Medieval Latin *focarius*, from Latin *focus* "hearth"]

fra·cas \ˈfrā-kəs, ˈfrak-əs\ *n* : a noisy quarrel : BRAWL [French]

frac·tion \ˈfrak-shən\ *n* **1** : a mathematical expression (as 1/2 or 3/4) that represents one or more equal parts or the division of one number by another; *also* : a number (as 3.323) consisting of a decimal or a whole number and a decimal **2 a** : a piece broken off : FRAGMENT **b** : PORTION, SECTION ⟨a small *fraction* of the voters⟩ [Late Latin *fractio* "act of breaking", from Latin *frangere* "to break"]

frac·tion·al \-shnəl, -shən-l\ *adj* **1** : of, relating to, or being a fraction **2** : relatively small : INCONSIDERABLE **3** : of, relating to, or involving a separating of components from a mixture through differences in physical or chemical properties ⟨*fractional* distillation⟩ — **frac·tion·al·ly** \-ē\ *adv*

fractional equation *n* : an equation containing the unknown in the denominator of one or more terms ⟨$a/x + b/x + 1 = c$ is a *fractional equation*⟩

frac·tion·ate \ˈfrak-shə-ˌnāt\ *vt* : to separate into different portions; *esp* : to subject to fractional distillation — **frac·tion·ation** \ˌfrak-shə-ˈnā-shən\ *n*

frac·tious \ˈfrak-shəs\ *adj* **1** : hard to handle or control ⟨a *fractious* horse⟩ **2** : QUARRELSOME [*fraction* ("discord") + -*ous*] — **frac·tious·ly** *adv* — **frac·tious·ness** *n*

¹frac·ture \ˈfrak-chər\ *n* **1** : the act or process of breaking or the state of being broken; *esp* : the breaking of a bone — compare SIMPLE FRACTURE, COMPOUND FRACTURE **2** : the result of fracturing; *esp* : an injury resulting from the fracture of a bone [Latin *fractura*, from *frangere* "to break"] ☐ SYN FRACTURE, RUPTURE mean a break in tissue. FRACTURE applies to the cracking of hard substance ⟨*fractured* bones⟩ RUPTURE applies to the tearing or bursting of soft tissues ⟨a *ruptured* blood vessel⟩

²fracture *vb* **frac·tured; frac·tur·ing** \-chə-ring, -shring\ **1** : to cause a fracture in : BREAK **2** : to damage or destroy as if by breaking ⟨*fractured* families⟩ **3** : to undergo fracture

frae \frā, ˈfrā\ *prep, Scottish* : FROM [Old Norse *frā*]

frag·ile \ˈfraj-əl, -ˌīl\ *adj* **1** : easily broken or destroyed : DELICATE **2** : TENUOUS, SLIGHT ⟨*fragile* evidence⟩ [Middle French, from Latin *fragilis*, from *frangere* "to break"] SYN see BRITTLE — **fra·gil·i·ty** \frə-ˈjil-ət-ē\ *n*

frag·ment \ˈfrag-mənt\ *n* **1** : a part broken off, detached, or incomplete **2** : SENTENCE FRAGMENT [Latin *fragmentum*, from *frangere* "to break"] — **frag·ment** \-ˌment\ *vb*

frag·men·tal \frag-ˈment-l\ *adj* : FRAGMENTARY — **frag·men·tal·ly** \-l-ē\ *adv*

frag·men·tary \ˈfrag-mən-ˌter-ē\ *adj* : consisting of fragments : INCOMPLETE ⟨*fragmentary* evidence⟩ ⟨a *fragmentary* report⟩ — **frag·men·tar·i·ness** *n*

frag·men·tate \ˈfrag-mən-ˌtāt\ *vb* : to break or fall into pieces [back-formation from *fragmentation*] — **frag·men·ta·tion** \ˌfrag-mən-ˈtā-shən, -ˌmen-\ *n*

frag·men·tize \ˈfrag-mən-ˌtīz\ *vb* : FRAGMENTATE

fra·grance \ˈfrā-grəns\ *n* **1** : a sweet, pleasing and often flowery or fruity odor — compare AROMA **2** : a particular odor (as of a perfume or toilet water)

foxhound

\ə\ abut		\ng\ **sing**	
\ər\ **further**		\ō\ **bone**	
\a\ **mat**		\ȯ\ **saw**	
\ā\ **take**		\ȯi\ **coin**	
\ä\ **cot, cart**		\th\ **thin**	
\aù\ **out**		\th\ **this**	
\ch\ **chin**		\ü\ **food**	
\e\ **pet**		\ù\ **foot**	
\ē\ **easy**		\y\ **yet**	
\g\ **go**		\yü\ **few**	
\i\ **tip**		\yù\ **cure**	
\ī\ **life**		\zh\ **vision**	
\j\ **job**			

fra·grant \-grənt\ *adj* : having fragrance [Latin *fragrans,* from *fragrare* "to be fragrant"] — **fra·grant·ly** *adv*

frail \'frāl\ *adj* **1** : morally weak ⟨*frail* humanity⟩ **2** : FRAGILE 1 **3 a** : physically weak **b** : UNSUBSTANTIAL [Middle French *fraile,* from Latin *fragilis* "fragile"] — **frail·ly** \'frāl-lē\ *adv* — **frail·ness** *n*

frail·ty \'frā-əl-tē, 'frāl-\ *n, pl* **frailties 1** : the quality or state of being frail **2** : a fault due to weakness especially of moral character SYN see FAULT

¹frame \'frām\ *vt* **1 a** : PLAN 1, CONTRIVE **b** : to give expression to : FORMULATE **c** : SHAPE 1, CONSTRUCT **d** : to draw up ⟨*frame* a constitution⟩ **2** : to fit or adjust for a purpose **3** : to construct by fitting and uniting the parts of the skeleton of (a structure) **4** : to enclose in a frame ⟨*frame* a picture⟩ **5** : to make (an innocent person) appear guilty [Old English *framian* "to benefit, make progress"] — **fram·er** *n*

²frame *n* **1 a** : something composed of parts fitted together and united **b** : the physical makeup of an animal and especially a human body : PHYSIQUE **2 a** : an arrangement of structural parts that gives form or support to something ⟨the *frame* of a cart⟩ ⟨the bony *frame* of the body⟩; *esp* : one (as of girders, beams, and joists) that forms the main support of a structure (as a building) **b** : a structural unit on or in which something rests ⟨the *frame* of a bucksaw⟩; *also* : a machine built on or in a frame **c** : a supporting or enclosing border or open case (as for a window or a picture) **d** : matter or an area enclosed by a border: as (1) : one of the squares in which scores for each round are recorded (as in bowling); *also* : a turn in bowling (2) : one picture of the series on a length of film (3) : a complete image being transmitted by television **3** : a particular state of mind

³frame *adj* : having a wood frame ⟨*frame* houses⟩

frame of reference : a set or system (as of facts or ideas) serving to orient or give particular meaning

frame–up \'frā-,məp\ *n* : a scheme to cause an innocent person to be accused of a crime; *also* : the result of such a scheme

frame·work \'frām-,wərk\ *n* **1** : a structural or skeletal frame **2** : a basic structure (as of ideas)

fram·ing \'frā-ming\ *n* : FRAME 2, FRAMEWORK

franc \'frangk\ *n* **1** : the basic monetary unit of any of several countries (as France, Belgium, or Switzerland) **2** : a coin representing one franc [French, from Medieval Latin *Francorum Rex* "king of the French", words on 14th century francs]

fran·chise \'fran-,chīz\ *n* **1 a** : a special privilege or exemption granted (as by a government); *esp* : the right to exist and function as a corporation **b** : a right or license to market a company's goods or services in a particular territory; *also* : the territory covered by such a right or license **2** : a legal right or privilege; *esp* : the right to vote [Old French, "freedom from a restriction", from *franchir* "to free", from *franc* "free, frank"]

¹Fran·cis·can \fran-'sis-kən\ *adj* : of or relating to Saint Francis of Assisi or one of the orders under his monastic rule [Medieval Latin *Franciscus* "Francis"]

²Franciscan *n* : a member of a religious order established by Saint Francis of Assisi and engaging chiefly in preaching and in missionary and charitable work

fran·ci·um \'fran-sē-əm\ *n* : a radioactive chemical element obtained artificially by the bombardment of thorium with protons — see ELEMENT table [New Latin, from *France*]

Franco- *combining form* **1** : French and ⟨*Franco*-American⟩ **2** : French ⟨*Franco*phile⟩ [Medieval Latin *Francus* "Frenchman", from Late Latin, "Frank"]

fran·co·lin \'frang-kə-lən\ *n* : any of various African or Asian partridges [French, from Italian *francolino*]

Fran·co·phile \'frang-kə-,fīl\ *adj* : admiring or favoring France or French culture — **Francophile** *n*

fran·gi·ble \'fran-jə-bəl\ *adj* : easily broken : FRAGILE [Medieval Latin *frangibilis,* from Latin *frangere* "to break"] — **fran·gi·bil·i·ty** \,fran-jə-'bil-ət-ē\ *n*

fran·gi·pani *also* **fran·gi·pan·ni** \,fran-jə-'pan-ē\ *n, pl* **-pani** *or* **-pan·is** *also* **-pan·ni** *or* **-pan·nis** : a perfume derived from or imitating the odor of the flower of the red jasmine; *also* : red jasmine or a related tropical American shrub or small tree [Italian *frangipane,* from Marquis Muzio *Frangipane,* 16th century Italian nobleman]

¹frank \'frangk\ *adj* **1** : free and forthright in expressing one's feelings and opinions : OUTSPOKEN **2** : unmistakably evident : DOWNRIGHT ⟨*frank* treason⟩ [Old French *franc* "free, frank", from Medieval Latin *francus* "Frank"] — **frank·ly** *adv* — **frank·ness** *n* □ ORIGIN The word *frank* comes from the name of the Franks, a West Germanic people who lived long ago. In the early Middle Ages the Franks were in power in France. (It was from them that the country got its name.) At that time the Franks were the only people in the country who enjoyed complete freedom. So their name (*Francus* in Latin) came to mean "free". From the English adjective *frank,* which means "free" or "forthright", we get the verb *frank,* which means "to mark mail with an official sign so that it may be mailed free". □ SYN FRANK, CANDID, OPEN, PLAIN mean showing willingness to tell one's thoughts or feelings. FRANK implies absence of the evasiveness that springs from considerations of tact or of expedience ⟨*frank* declaration of selfish motives⟩ CANDID stresses sincerity and honesty of expression especially in offering unwelcome criticism or opinion ⟨gave a *candid* appraisal of my faults⟩ OPEN implies frankness but suggests more indiscretion than frank and less earnestness than CANDID ⟨*open* betrayal of a friend⟩ PLAIN suggests outspokenness and freedom from affectation or subtlety in expression ⟨*plain* talk⟩

²frank *vt* : to mark (a piece of mail) with an official signature or sign indicating the right of the sender to free mailing; *also* : to mail in this manner

³frank *n* **1** : a signature, mark, or stamp on a piece of mail indicating that it can be mailed free **2** : the privilege of sending mail free of charge

Frank \'frangk\ *n* : a member of a West Germanic people entering the Roman provinces in A.D. 253 and establishing themselves in the Netherlands, in Gaul, and along the Rhine [Old French *Franc,* from Late Latin *Francus,* of Germanic origin] — **Frank·ish** \'frang-kish\ *adj*

Fran·ken·stein \'frang-kən-,stīn, -,stēn\ *n* **1** : a work or agency that ruins its originator **2** : a monster in the shape of a man [from *Frankenstein,* a student of physiology in Mary W. Shelley's novel *Frankenstein* whose life is ruined by a monster he creates]

frank·furt·er *or* **frank·fort·er** \'frangk-fərt-ər, -fət-ər\ **frank·furt** *or* **frank·fort** \-fərt\ *n* : a seasoned beef or beef and pork sausage [German *frankfurter* "of Frankfurt", from *Frankfurt am Main,* Germany]

frank·in·cense \'frang-kən-,sens\ *n* : a fragrant gum resin from African or Arabian trees that is burned as incense [Middle English *frank* "frank, free, pure" + *incense*]

frank·lin \'frang-klən\ *n* : a free medieval English landowner not of noble birth [Anglo-French *fraunclein,* from Old French *franc* "free"]

Frank·lin stove \'frangklən-\ *n* : a metal heating stove resembling an open fireplace but designed to conserve and radiate heat [Benjamin *Franklin,* its inventor]

fran·tic \'frant-ik\ *adj* : wildly or uncontrollably excited ⟨*frantic* with pain⟩ ⟨*frantic* cries for help⟩ [Middle English *frenetik, frantik* "insane", from Middle French *frenetique,* from Latin *phreneticus,* from Greek *phrenitikos,* from *phrenitis* "inflammation of

Franklin stove

the brain", from *phrēn* "mind"] — **fran·ti·cal·ly** \-i-kə-lē, -klē\ *adv* — **fran·tic·ly** \-i-klē\ *adv* — **fran·tic·ness** *n*

frap·pé \fra-'pā\ *or* **frappe** \'frap, fra-'pā\ *n* **1** : an iced or frozen mixture or drink **2** : a thick milk shake [French *frappé* "iced, chilled", from *frapper* "to strike, chill"] — **frappé** *adj*

fra·ter·nal \frə-'tərn-l\ *adj* **1 a** : of, relating to, or involving brothers **b** : of, relating to, or being a fraternity or society **2** : BROTHERLY 2, FRIENDLY [Medieval Latin *fraternalis,* from Latin *fraternus,* from *frater* "brother"] — **fra·ter·nal·ism** \-l-,iz-əm\ *n* — **fra·ter·nal·ly** \-l-ē\ *adv*

fraternal twin *n* : either member of a pair of twins that are produced from different fertilized egg cells, usually differ in some or many genes, and are often not physically similar

fra·ter·ni·ty \frə-'tər-nət-ē\ *n, pl* **-ties 1** : a social, honorary, or professional organization; *esp* : a social club of male college students **2** : BROTHERHOOD 1, BROTHERLINESS **3** : persons of the same class, profession, character, or tastes ⟨the legal *fraternity*⟩

frat·er·nize \'frat-ər-,nīz\ *vi* **1** : to associate or mingle as brothers or friends **2** : to associate on friendly terms with citizens or troops of a hostile nation — **frat·er·ni·za·tion** \,frat-ər-nə-'zā-shən\ *n* — **frat·er·niz·er** \'frat-ər-,nī-zər\ *n*

frat·ri·cide \'fra-trə-,sīd\ *n* **1** : one who murders his or her own brother or sister **2** : the act of a fratricide [derived from Latin *fratr-, frater* "brother"] — **frat·ri·cid·al** \,fra-trə-'sīd-l\ *adj*

Frau \'frau̇\ *n, pl* **Frau·en** \'frau̇-ən\ — used by German-speaking people as a courtesy title equivalent to *Mrs.* [German]

fraud \'frȯd\ *n* **1 a** : DECEIT; *esp* : misrepresentation intended to induce another to part with something of value or to surrender a legal right **b** : an act of deceiving or misrepresenting : TRICK **2 a** : one who is not what he pretends to be : IMPOSTOR **b** : one who defrauds : CHEAT [Middle French *fraude,* from Latin *fraus*] SYN see DECEPTION

fraud·u·lent \'frȯ-jə-lənt\ *adj* : characterized by, based on, or done by fraud : DECEITFUL ⟨*fraudulent* claims of injury⟩ — **fraud·u·lence** \-ləns\ *n* — **fraud·u·lent·ly** *adv* — **fraud·u·lent·ness** *n*

fraught \'frȯt\ *adj* : full of or accompanied by something specified ⟨a situation *fraught* with danger⟩ [Middle English, "laden", from *fraughten* "to load", from *fraught* "freight, load", from Dutch or Low German *vracht, vrecht*]

Fräu·lein \'frȯi-,līn\ *n* — used by German-speaking people as a courtesy title equivalent to *Miss* [German]

¹fray \'frā\ *n* **1** : a noisy quarrel or fight : BRAWL **2** : a heated dispute [Middle English, short for *affray*]

²fray *vb* **1 a** : to wear (as an edge of cloth) by rubbing **b** : to separate the threads at the edge of **c** : to wear out or into shreds **2** : STRAIN, IRRITATE ⟨tempers were *frayed*⟩ [Middle French *frayer* "to rub", from Latin *fricare*]

fraz·zle \'fraz-əl\ *vb* **fraz·zled; fraz·zling** \'fraz-ling, -ə-ling\ **1** : FRAY 1 **2** : to exhaust physically or emotionally ⟨*frazzled* by hard work⟩ [alteration of English dialect *fazle* "to tangle, fray"] — **frazzle** *n*

¹freak \'frēk\ *n* **1 a** : WHIM **b** : a seemingly capricious action or event **2** : one that is very unusual or abnormal; *esp* : a person with a physical oddity who appears in a circus sideshow **3** *slang* : a person who uses an illicit drug **4** *slang* : an ardent enthusiast [origin unknown] — **freak·ish** \'frē-kish\ *adj* — **freak·ish·ly** *adv* — **freak·ish·ness** *n*

²freak *adj* : having the character of a freak; *esp* : very unusual ⟨a *freak* accident⟩

freak–out \'frē-,kau̇t\ *n* : a drug-induced state of mind characterized by nightmarish hallucinations; *also* : a person in such a state

freak out \frē-'kau̇t\ *vb* **1** : to experience a freak-out **2** : to behave irrationally under or as if under the influence of drugs **3** : to put into a state of intense excitement

¹freck·le \'frek-əl\ *n* : a small brownish spot in the skin usually due to precipitation of pigment on exposure to sunlight [Middle English *freken, frekel,* of Scandinavian origin] — **freck·ly** \'frek-lē, -ə-lē\ *adv*

²freckle *vb* **freck·led; freck·ling** \'frek-ling, -ə-ling\ : to mark or become marked with freckles or small spots

¹free \'frē\ *adj* **fre·er** \'frē-ər\; **fre·est** \'frē-əst\ **1 a** : having liberty : not being a slave or prisoner **b** : not controlled by others : INDEPENDENT ⟨a *free* state⟩ **2** : not subject to a duty, tax, or other charge **3** : released or not suffering from something unpleasant or painful ⟨*free* from worry⟩ **4** : given without charge ⟨*free* tickets⟩ **5** : made or done voluntarily ⟨a *free* choice⟩ **6** : LAVISH ⟨a *free* spender⟩ **7** : PLENTIFUL, COPIOUS ⟨a *free* flow of goods⟩ **8** : not held back by fear or distrust : OPEN, FRANK ⟨*free* expression of opinion⟩ **9** : not restricted by conventional forms ⟨*free* verse⟩ **10** : not literal or exact ⟨a *free* translation⟩ **11 a** : not obstructed : CLEAR ⟨a road *free* of ice⟩ **b** : not being used or occupied ⟨*free* time⟩ **c** : not fastened or bound : able to act, move, or turn ⟨*free* electrons⟩ **12** : not restricted or interfered with by an opponent ⟨a *free* kick⟩ ⟨let a player get *free*⟩ **13** : chemically uncombined ⟨*free* oxygen⟩ **14** : capable of being used meaningfully apart from another linguistic form ⟨the word *hats* is a *free* form⟩ — compare BOUND [Old English *frēo*] — **free·ly** *adv* □ SYN FREE, INDEPENDENT, SOVEREIGN mean not subject to the rule or control of another. FREE stresses the complete absence of external rule and the full right to make decisions ⟨a *free* society of equals⟩ INDEPENDENT implies standing alone; applied to a state it implies that no other state has power to interfere with its citizens, laws, or policies; SOVEREIGN stresses supremacy within one's own domain or sphere and implies the absence of any superior power.

²free *adv* **1** : in a free manner **2** : without charge ⟨was admitted *free*⟩

³free *vt* **freed; free·ing 1** : to cause to be free : set free ⟨*free* a prisoner⟩ **2** : RELIEVE, RID ⟨was *freed* from pain⟩ **3** : to clear of obstacles ⟨*free* a road of debris⟩ □ SYN FREE, RELEASE, LIBERATE, DISCHARGE mean to set loose from restraint or constraint. FREE implies usually permanent removal from whatever binds, entangles, or oppresses; RELEASE suggests a setting loose from confinement or from a state of pressure or tension; LIBERATE stresses the state resulting from freeing or releasing; DISCHARGE may imply removing from a lighter degree of restraint or constraint.

free association *n* **1** : expression of thoughts as they come to mind without control or censorship **2** : the reporting of the first thought that comes to mind in response to a given stimulus and especially a word

¹free·base \'frē-,bās\ *vb* : to prepare or use cocaine as freebase

²freebase *n* : cocaine freed from impurities and heated to produce vapors for inhalation or smoked as crack

free·board \'frē-,bōrd, -,bȯrd\ *n* : the vertical distance between the waterline and the deck of a ship or the upper edge of the side of a boat

free·boo·ter \'frē-,büt-ər\ *n* : PIRATE, PLUNDERER [Dutch *vrijbuiter,* from *vrijbuit* "plunder", from *vrij* "free" + *buit* "booty" — see FILIBUSTER origin]

free·born \'frē-'bȯrn\ *adj* **1** : not born in vassalage or slavery **2** : relating to or befitting one that is freeborn

freed·man \'frēd-mən\ *n* : a person freed from slavery

free·dom \'frēd-əm\ *n* **1** : the quality or state of being free: as **a** : the absence of necessity, coercion, or constraint in choice or action **b** : liberation from slavery or restraint or from the power of another : INDEPENDENCE **c** : EXEMPTION, RELEASE ⟨*freedom* from care⟩ **d** : EASE, FACILITY ⟨*freedom* of movement⟩ **e** : the quality

\ə\ abut		\ng\ sing	
\ər\ further		\ō\ bone	
\a\ mat		\ȯ\ saw	
\ā\ take		\ȯi\ coin	
\ä\ cot, cart		\th\ thin	
\au̇\ out		\th\ this	
\ch\ chin		\ü\ food	
\e\ pet		\u̇\ foot	
\ē\ easy		\y\ yet	
\g\ go		\yü\ few	
\i\ tip		\yu̇\ cure	
\ī\ life		\zh\ vision	
\j\ job			

of being outspoken **f** : unrestricted use ⟨the dog had the *freedom* of the yard⟩ **2** : PRIVILEGE, RIGHT; *esp* : one guaranteed by fundamental law □ SYN FREEDOM, LIBERTY, LICENSE mean the power or condition of acting without compulsion. FREEDOM has a broad range of application from total absence of restraint to merely a sense of not being unduly hampered or frustrated; LIBERTY suggests release from former restraint or compulsion; LICENSE implies freedom specially granted or conceded and may connote an abuse of freedom.

freed·wom·an \'frēd-ˌwüm-ən\ *n* : a woman freed from slavery

free enterprise *n* : freedom of private business to organize and operate for profit in competition with other businesses with a minimum of interference by the government; *also* : an economic system providing this freedom

free–fire zone \'frē-ˌfīr-\ *n* : a combat area in which any moving thing is a legitimate target

free–for–all \'frē-fə-ˌról\ *n* : a competition, dispute, or fight open to all comers and usually with no rules

free·hand \'frē-ˌhand\ *adj* : done without mechanical aids or devices ⟨*freehand* drawing⟩ — **freehand** *adv*

free hand \-'hand\ *n* : freedom of action or decision ⟨given a *free hand* to get the job done⟩

free–hand·ed \-'han-dəd\ *adj* : OPENHANDED, GENEROUS

free·hold \'frē-ˌhōld\ *n* : ownership of real estate for life usually with the right of leaving it to one's heirs; *also* : an estate so owned — **free·hold·er** \-ˌhōl-dər\ *n*

free lance *n* **1** : a knight whose services could be bought by any ruler or state **2** : one who pursues a profession (as writing, art, or acting) without being committed to work for one employer for a long period — **free–lance** *adj* — **free–lance** *vb* — **free–lanc·er** *n*

free–liv·ing \'frē-'liv-ing\ *adj* : being neither parasitic nor symbiotic

free·load \-'lōd\ *vi* : SPONGE 3 — **free·load·er** *n*

free·man \'frē-mən\ *n* **1** : a person enjoying civil or political liberty **2** : one having the full rights of a citizen

free market *n* : an economic market operating by free competition

free·mar·tin \-ˌmärt-n\ *n* : a sexually imperfect usually sterile female calf born in the same birth with a male [origin unknown]

Free·ma·son \-'mās-n\ *n* : a member of a secret fraternal society called Free and Accepted Masons

free·ma·son·ry \-rē\ *n* **1** *cap* : the principles, institutions, or practices of Freemasons — called also *Masonry* **2** : natural or instinctive fellowship or sympathy

free on board *adv or adj* : delivered without charge onto a means of transportation

free port *n* **1** : a port or section of a port where goods are received and shipped free of customs duty **2** : a port open to all vessels on equal terms

free·sia \'frē-zhə, -zhē-ə\ *n* : any of a genus of sweet-scented African herbs with showy red, white, or yellow flowers [F.H.T. *Freese,* died 1876, German physician]

free silver *n* : the free coinage of silver often at a fixed ratio with gold

free–soil *adj* **1** : characterized by free soil **2** *cap F&S* : of, relating to, or constituting a minor United States political party prior to the Civil War opposing the extension of slavery into United States territories and the admission of slave states into the Union — **Free–Soil·er** \-ˌsói-lər\ *n*

free soil *n* : United States territory where slavery was prohibited before the Civil War

free–spo·ken \'frē-'spō-kən\ *adj* : OUTSPOKEN

free·stand·ing \-'stan-ding\ *adj* : standing alone or on its own foundation free of attachment or support

free·stone \'frē-ˌstōn\ *n* **1** : a stone that may be cut without splitting **2 a** : a fruit stone to which the flesh does not cling **b** : a fruit (as a peach or cherry) having a freestone

free·style \-ˌstīl\ *n* : competition in which each competitor is free to use a style, method, or performance of his or her choice

free·think·er \-'thing-kər\ *n* : one who forms opinions independently and on the basis of reason; *esp* : one who doubts or denies religious dogma SYN see ATHEIST — **free·think·ing** \-king\ *n or adj*

free throw *n* : an unhindered shot in basketball made from behind a fixed line and awarded because of a foul by an opponent

free trade *n* : trade based on the unrestricted international exchange of goods without high tariffs

free·way \'frē-ˌwā\ *n* **1** : an expressway with fully controlled access **2** : a toll-free highway

free·wheel \'frē-'hwēl, -'wēl\ *vi* : to move or live freely or irresponsibly

free·will \ˌfrē-wil\ *adj* : VOLUNTARY ⟨a *freewill* offering⟩

free will *n* : the power of directing one's own actions without restraint by necessity or fate

free world *n* : the part of the world where political democracy and capitalism or moderate socialism rather than totalitarian or Communist political and economic systems prevail

¹freeze \'frēz\ *vb* **froze** \'frōz\; **fro·zen** \'frōz-n\; **freez·ing** **1** : to harden into or be hardened into ice or a like solid by loss of heat ⟨the river *froze* over⟩ ⟨*freeze* cream⟩ **2 a** : to chill or become chilled with cold ⟨almost *froze* to death⟩ **b** : to become coldly formal in manner **c** : to act toward in a stiff and formal way **3 a** : to act on usually destructively by frost ⟨*froze* the tomato plants⟩ **b** : to anesthetize by cold **4 a** : to adhere solidly by freezing **b** : to cause to grip tightly or remain in immovable contact ⟨fear *froze* the driver to the wheel⟩ **5** : to clog or become clogged with ice ⟨the water pipes *froze*⟩ **6** : to become fixed or motionless; *esp* : to make or become incapable of acting or speaking ⟨fear *froze* them in their tracks⟩ **7** : to fix at a certain stage or level ⟨*freeze* rents⟩ [Old English *frēosan*]

²freeze *n* **1** : a state of weather marked by low temperature **2 a** : an act or instance of freezing **b** : the state of being frozen

freeze–dry \'frēz-ˌdrī\ *vt* : to dry in a frozen state under high vacuum especially for preservation

freez·er \'frē-zər\ *n* : one that freezes or keeps cool; *esp* : an insulated compartment or room for keeping food at a temperature below freezing or for freezing perishable food rapidly

freezing point *n* : the temperature at which a liquid solidifies ⟨the *freezing* point of water is 0°C or 32°F⟩

F region *n* : the highest region of the atmosphere occurring from 140 to more than 400 kilometers above the earth

¹freight \'frāt\ *n* **1** : the amount paid to a common carrier for carrying goods **2** : goods or cargo carried by a common carrier; *also* : the ordinary carrying of goods from one place to another by a common carrier especially as distinguished from express **3** : a train that carries freight [Dutch or Low German *vracht, vrecht*]

²freight *vt* **1 a** : to load with goods for transportation **b** : to weigh down : BURDEN ⟨*freighted* with fear⟩ **2** : to transport or ship by freight

freight·er \'frāt-ər\ *n* **1** : one that loads or charters and loads a ship **2** : SHIPPER **3** : a ship or airplane used chiefly to carry freight

¹French \'french\ *adj* : of, relating to, or characteristic of France, its people, or their language [Old English *frencisc,* from *Franca* "Frank"] — **French·man** \-mən\ *n* — **French·wom·an** \-ˌwùm-ən\ *n*

²French *n* **1** : a Romance language developing out of the Vulgar Latin of Transalpine Gaul and becoming the literary and official language of France **2** *pl in construction* : the French people

French Canadian *n* : one of the descendants of French settlers in Lower Canada — **French–Canadian** *adj*

French cuff *n* : a shirt cuff that is made by turning back part of a wide cuff and is fastened with a cuff link

French door *n* : a door with glazed rectangular panels extending the full length; *also* : one of a pair of such doors in a single frame

¹french fry *vt, often cap 1st F* : to fry (as strips of potato) in deep fat until brown

²french fry *n, often cap 1st F* : a strip of potato fried in deep fat — usually used in pl.

French horn *n* : a brass wind instrument consisting of a long curved conical tube with a narrow funnel-shaped mouthpiece at one end and a flaring bell at the other

French leave *n* : an informal, hasty, or secret departure [from an 18th century French custom of leaving a reception without taking leave of the host or hostess]

French toast *n* : bread dipped in a mixture of egg and milk and then fried

French window *n* **1** : a French door placed in an outside wall **2** : a casement window

fre·net·ic \fri-'net-ik\ *adj* : HECTIC 4, FRANTIC [Middle French *frenetique* "insane", from Latin *phreneticus* "insane, frantic"] — **fre·net·i·cal·ly** \-'net-i-kə-lē, -klē\ *adv*

fre·num \'frē-nəm\ *n, pl* **frenums** *or* **fre·na** \-nə\ : a fold of membrane (as beneath the tongue) that supports or restrains [Latin, literally, "bridle"]

fren·zied \'fren-zēd\ *adj* : marked by frenzy : wildly excited — **fren·zied·ly** *adv*

fren·zy \'fren-zē\ *n, pl* **frenzies** **1** : a temporary madness or violent agitation **2** : intense and usually wild activity [Middle French *frenesie*, derived from Latin *phrenesis*, from *phreneticus* "insane, frantic"] — **frenzy** *vt*

Fre·on \'frē-,än\ *trademark* — used for any of various nonflammable gaseous and liquid fluorocarbons used as refrigerants

fre·quen·cy \'frē-kwən-sē\ *n, pl* **-cies** **1** : the fact or condition of occurring frequently **2 a** : rate or proportion of occurrence ⟨*frequency* of a gene in a population⟩ **b** : the number of individuals or objects in a particular class when classified according to variation in one or more qualities **3** : the number of repetitions of a periodic process in a unit of time: as **a** : the number of times per second that an electric current flowing in one direction changes direction then changes back ⟨a current having a *frequency* of 60 hertz⟩ **b** : the number of waves (as of sound or electromagnetic energy) that pass a fixed point each second ⟨a sound having a *frequency* of 1500 hertz⟩ ⟨the *frequency* of a radio wave⟩ ⟨the *frequency* of yellow light⟩

frequency distribution *n* : an arrangement of statistical data that exhibits the frequency of the occurrence of the values of a variable

frequency modulation *n* : modulation of the frequency of a carrier wave in accordance with speech or a signal; *esp* : a system of broadcasting using this method of modulation

¹fre·quent \'frē-kwənt\ *adj* **1** : happening often or at short intervals ⟨made *frequent* trips to town⟩ **2** : HABITUAL, CONSTANT ⟨a *frequent* visitor⟩ [Latin *frequens* "crowded, frequent"] — **fre·quent·ly** *adv* — **fre·quent·ness** *n*

²fre·quent \frē-'kwent, 'frē-kwənt\ *vt* : to visit often : associate with, be in, or resort to habitually ⟨*frequented* the library⟩ — **fre·quent·er** *n*

fres·co \'fres-,kō\ *n, pl* **frescoes** *or* **frescos** **1** : the art of painting on freshly spread moist lime plaster with pigments suspended in water **2** : a painting executed in fresco [Italian, from *fresco* "fresh", of Germanic origin] — **fresco** *vt*

¹fresh \'fresh\ *adj* **1 a** : not salt ⟨*fresh* water⟩ **b** : PURE, INVIGORATING ⟨*fresh* air⟩ **c** : fairly strong : BRISK ⟨a *fresh* breeze⟩ **2 a** : not stored, cured, or preserved ⟨*fresh*

vegetables⟩ **b** : having its original qualities unimpaired: as (1) : full of or renewed in vigor : REFRESHED (2) : not stale, sour, or decayed ⟨*fresh* bread⟩ (3) : not faded (4) : not worn or rumpled **3 a** (1) : experienced, made, or received newly or anew (2) : ADDITIONAL, ANOTHER ⟨make a *fresh* start⟩ **b** : not trite or hackneyed **c** : INEXPERIENCED, RAW **d** : newly arrived ⟨*fresh* out of college⟩ **4** : showing disrespect : IMPUDENT [Old French *freis*, of Germanic origin] SYN see NEW — **fresh·ly** *adv* — **fresh·ness** *n*

²fresh *adv* : just recently : FRESHLY ⟨a *fresh* laid egg⟩

fresh·en \'fresh-ən\ *vb* **fresh·ened**; **fresh·en·ing** \'fresh-ning, -ə-ning\ **1** : to make or become fresh: as **a** : to become brisk or strong ⟨the wind *freshened*⟩ **b** : to make or become fresh in appearance or vitality ⟨*freshen* up with a shower⟩ **2** : to begin giving milk ⟨when the cow *freshens*⟩ — **fresh·en·er** \'fresh-nər, -ə-nər\ *n*

fresh·et \'fresh-ət\ *n* : a great rise or overflowing of a stream caused by heavy rains or melted snow [from *fresh* "increased flow, freshet, stream of fresh water", from ¹*fresh*]

fresh·man \'fresh-mən\ *n* **1** : a newcomer to an occupation or activity : NOVICE **2** : a student in the first year (as of high school or college)

fresh·wa·ter \'fresh-'wȯt-ər, -'wät-\ *adj* **1** : of, relating to, or living in fresh water **2** : accustomed to navigating only in fresh waters ⟨a *freshwater* sailor⟩

¹fret \'fret\ *vb* **fret·ted**; **fret·ting** **1** : to suffer or cause to suffer emotional strain : WORRY, VEX ⟨*fretted* over petty problems⟩ **2 a** : to eat into or wear away ⟨rock *fretted* by rainwater⟩ **b** : FRAY 1a **c** : to cause by wearing away ⟨the stream *fretted* a channel⟩ **3** : to affect something as if by gnawing or biting : GRATE ⟨the siren *fretted* at their nerves⟩ **4** : to cause (water) to ripple [Old English *fretan* "to devour"]

²fret *n* : an irritated or worried state ⟨be in a *fret*⟩

³fret *vt* **fret·ted**; **fret·ting** : to decorate with interlaced designs [Middle French *freter* "to bind with a ferrule, fret", from *frete* "ferrule"]

⁴fret *n* : ornamental work consisting of small straight intersecting bars

⁵fret *n* : one of a series of ridges fixed across the fingerboard of a stringed musical instrument [probably from Middle French *frete* "ferrule"] — **fret·ted** \'fret-əd\ *adj*

⁶fret *vt* **fret·ted**; **fret·ting** : to press (the strings of a stringed instrument) against the frets

fret·ful \'fret-fəl\ *adj* **1** : inclined to fret : IRRITABLE **2 a** : marked by turbulence : TROUBLED ⟨*fretful* waters⟩ **b** : GUSTY ⟨a *fretful* wind⟩ — **fret·ful·ly** \-fə-lē\ *adv* — **fret·ful·ness** *n*

fret·saw \'fret-,sȯ\ *n* : a narrow-bladed fine-toothed saw for cutting curved outlines

fret·work \-,wərk\ *n* **1** : decoration consisting of work adorned with frets **2** : ornamental openwork or work in relief

Freud·ian \'frȯid-ē-ən\ *adj* : of, relating to, or according with the theories of psychology or practices of psychotherapy of Sigmund Freud — **Freudian** *n* — **Freud·ian·ism** \-ē-ə-,niz-əm\ *n*

fri·a·ble \'frī-ə-bəl\ *adj* : easily crumbled or pulverized [Latin *friabilis*, from *friare* "to crumble"] SYN see BRITTLE — **fri·a·bil·i·ty** \,frī-ə-'bil-ət-ē\ *n* — **fri·a·ble·ness** \'frī-ə-bəl-nəs\ *n*

fri·ar \'frī-ər, 'frīr\ *n* : a member of one of several Roman Catholic religious orders for men in which monastic life is combined with preaching and other priestly duties — compare MONK [Old French *frere*, literally, "brother", from Latin *frater*]

fri·ary \'frī-ə-rē, 'frīr-ē\ *n, pl* **-ar·ies** : a monastery of friars

¹fric·as·see \'frik-ə-,sē, ,frik-ə-'\ *n* : a dish of meat (as chicken or veal) cut into pieces and stewed in a gravy [Middle French]

²fricassee *vt* **-seed**; **-see·ing** : to cook as a fricassee

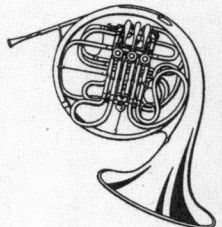

French horn

\ə\ abut		\ng\ sing	
\ər\ further		\ō\ bone	
\a\ mat		\ȯ\ saw	
\ā\ take		\ȯi\ coin	
\ä\ cot, cart		\th\ thin	
\au̇\ out		\th\ this	
\ch\ chin		\ü\ food	
\e\ pet		\u̇\ foot	
\ē\ easy		\y\ yet	
\g\ go		\yü\ few	
\i\ tip		\yu̇\ cure	
\ī\ life		\zh\ vision	
\j\ job			

fric·a·tive \\'frik-ət-iv\\ *n* : a consonant characterized by frictional passage of the expired breath through a narrowing at some point in the mouth or throat (\\f v th th s z sh zh h\\ are *fricatives*) [Latin *fricare* "to rub"] — **fricative** *adj*

fric·tion \\'frik-shən\\ *n* **1 a** : the rubbing of one body against another **b** : the force that resists motion between two bodies in contact (the *friction* of a box sliding along the floor) **2** : discord between two persons or parties [Latin *frictio*, from *fricare* "to rub"] — **fric·tion·less** \\-ləs\\ *adj*

fric·tion·al \\'frik-shnəl, -shən-l\\ *adj* **1** : of or relating to friction **2** : moved or produced by friction — **fric·tion·al·ly** \\-ē\\ *adv*

friction tape *n* : a usually cloth tape impregnated with insulating material and an adhesive and used especially to protect and insulate electrical conductors

Fri·day \\'frīd-ē\\ *n* : the 6th day of the week [Old English *frigedæg*, derived from a translation of Latin *Veneris dies* "day of Venus"; from the fact that Frig, or Fria, was the Germanic goddess of love]

fried cake \\'frīd-,kāk\\ *n* : DOUGHNUT, CRULLER

friend \\'frend\\ *n* **1 a** : one attached to another by affection or esteem **b** : ACQUAINTANCE 2 **2** : one who is not hostile (are you *friend* or foe) **3** : one who supports or favors something (a *friend* of liberal education) **4** *cap* : a member of a Christian group that stresses Inner Light, rejects ostentation, outward rites, and an ordained ministry, and opposes war — called also *Quaker* [Old English *frēond*] — **friend·less** \\'fren-dləs\\ *adj* — **friend·less·ness** *n*

friend·ly \\'fren-dlē, -lē\\ *adj* **friend·li·er; -est** : of, relating to, or befitting a friend: as **a** : showing kindly interest and goodwill (a *friendly* gesture) **b** : not hostile (*friendly* natives) **c** : serving a beneficial or helpful purpose : FAVORABLE (a *friendly* breeze) **d** : COMFORTING, CHEERFUL (the *friendly* glow of the fire) — **friend·li·ness** *n*

friend·ship \\'frend-,ship, 'fren-\\ *n* **1** : the state of being friends **2** : a friendly feeling : FRIENDLINESS

fri·er *variant of* FRYER

¹frieze \\'frēz, frē-'zā\\ *n* : a woolen cloth with a shaggy surface [Middle French *frise*, from Dutch *vriese*]

²frieze \\'frēz\\ *n* **1** : the part of an entablature between the architrave and the cornice **2** : a sculptured or richly ornamented band (as around a building) [Middle French *frise*, perhaps derived from Latin *Phrygius* "Phrygian"]

frig·ate \\'frig-ət\\ *n* **1** : a square-rigged warship intermediate between a corvette and a ship of the line **2** : a warship that is smaller than a destroyer and that is used for escort, antisubmarine, and patrol duties [Middle French, from Italian *fregata*]

frigate bird *n* : any of several chiefly tropical seabirds noted for their power of flight and the habit of robbing other birds of fish — called also *man-o'-war bird*

¹fright \\'frīt\\ *n* **1** : fear or alarm caused by sudden danger (cry out in *fright*) **2** : something that frightens **3** : something that is grotesque or shocking (you look a *fright*) [Old English *fyrhto, fryhto*] SYN see FEAR

²fright *vt* : to alarm suddenly : FRIGHTEN

fright·en \\'frīt-n\\ *vb* **fright·ened; fright·en·ing** \\'frīt-ning, -n-ing\\ **1** : to make afraid : TERRIFY **2** : to drive away or out by frightening **3** : to become frightened — **fright·en·ing·ly** \\-ning-lē, -n-ing-\\ *adv*

fright·ful \\'frīt-fəl\\ *adj* **1** : causing fear or alarm : TERRIFYING **2** : causing shock or horror : STARTLING (the cost in lives was *frightful*) **3** : EXTREME (a *frightful* thirst) — **fright·ful·ly** \\-fə-lē\\ *adv* — **fright·ful·ness** *n*

frig·id \\'frij-əd\\ *adj* **1** : intensely cold : lacking warmth or ardor : INDIFFERENT [Latin *frigidus*, from *frigēre* "to be cold"] — **fri·gid·i·ty** \\frij-'id-ət-ē\\ *n* — **frig·id·ly** \\'frij-əd-lē\\ *adv* — **frig·id·ness** *n*

frigid zone *n* : the area or region between the arctic circle and the north pole or between the antarctic circle and the south pole

fri·jol \\frē-'hōl\\ *also* **fri·jo·le** \\-'hō-lē\\ *n, pl* **fri·jo·les** \\-'hō-lēz\\ *chiefly Southwest* : BEAN 1b [American Spanish *frijol*]

¹frill \\'fril\\ *vt* : to provide or decorate with a frill

²frill *n* **1** : a gathered, pleated, or ruffled edging (as of lace) **2** : a ruff of hair or feathers about the neck of an animal **3** : something decorative but not essential [perhaps from Flemish *frul*] — **frilly** \\'fril-ē\\ *adj*

¹fringe \\'frinj\\ *n* **1** : an ornamental border consisting of short straight or twisted threads or strips hanging from cut or raveled edges or from a separate band **2** : something resembling a fringe : BORDER **3 a** : something that is secondary or supplementary to what is basic **b** : a group with marginal or extremist views [Middle French *frenge*, from Latin *fimbriae* (pl.) "fibers, fringe"]

²fringe *vt* **1** : to furnish or adorn with a fringe **2** : to serve as a fringe for : BORDER

fringe area *n* : a region in which reception from a broadcasting station is weak or subject to serious distortion

fringe benefit *n* : an employment benefit paid for by an employer without affecting basic wage rates

frip·pery \\'frip-rē, -ə-rē\\ *n, pl* **-per·ies** **1** : cheap showy finery **2** : affected elegance : pretentious display [Middle French *friperie* "cast-off clothes", derived from Medieval Latin *faluppa* "piece of straw"] — **frippery** *adj*

Fris·bee \\'friz-bē\\ *trademark* — used for a plastic disk sailed between players in games of catch

Fri·sian \\'frizh-ən, 'frē-zhən\\ *n* **1** : a member of a people that inhabit principally the Netherlands province of Friesland and the Frisian islands in the North sea **2** : the Germanic language of the Frisian people [Latin *Frisii* "Frisians"] — **Frisian** *adj*

frisk \\'frisk\\ *vb* **1** : to leap, skip, or dance in a lively or playful way : GAMBOL **2** : to search (a person) rapidly especially for concealed weapons by running the hand over the clothing [obsolete *frisk* "lively", from Middle French *frisque*, of Germanic origin] — **frisk·er** *n*

frisky \\'fris-kē\\ *adj* **frisk·i·er; -est** : inclined to frisk : FROLICSOME — **frisk·i·ly** \\-kə-lē\\ *adv* — **frisk·i·ness** \\-kē-nəs\\ *n*

frit·il·lar·ia \\,frit-l-'er-ē-ə, -'ar-\\ *n* : any of a genus of bulbous herbs of the lily family with mottled or checkered flowers [Latin *fritillus* "dice cup"; from its spotted markings]

frit·il·lary \\'frit-l-,er-ē\\ *n, pl* **-laries** **1** : FRITILLARIA **2** : any of numerous butterflies that are usually orange spotted with black

¹frit·ter \\'frit-ər\\ *n* : a small quantity of fried or sautéed batter often containing fruit, vegetables, or meat [Middle French *friture*, derived from Latin *frigere* "to fry"]

²fritter *vb* **1** : to reduce or waste little by little (*frittering* away their time) **2** : to break into small fragments **3** : to dwindle away [*fritter*, n., "fragment"] — **frit·ter·er** \\-ər-ər\\ *n*

fri·vol·i·ty \\friv-'äl-ət-ē\\ *n, pl* **-ties** **1** : the quality or state of being frivolous **2** : a frivolous act or thing

friv·o·lous \\'friv-ləs, -ə-ləs\\ *adj* **1** : of little importance : TRIVIAL **2** : not serious or practical (a *frivolous* attitude) [Latin *frivolus*] — **friv·o·lous·ly** *adv* — **friv·o·lous·ness** *n*

¹frizz \\'friz\\ *vb* : to curl in small tight curls [French *friser*]

²frizz *n* : a small tight curl or hair that is tightly curled — **frizzy** \\'friz-ē\\ *adj*

¹friz·zle \\'friz-əl\\ *vb* **friz·zled; friz·zling** \\'friz-ling, -ə-ling\\ : FRIZZ, CURL [probably related to Old English *fris* "curly"] — **frizzle** *n* — **friz·zly** \\'friz-lē, -ə-lē\\ *adj*

²frizzle *vb* **1** : to fry until crisp and curled **2** : to cook with a sizzling noise [*fry* + *sizzle*]

fro \'frō\ *adv* : BACK 2a, AWAY — used in the phrase *to and fro* [Middle English *fra, fro* "from", from Old Norse *frā*]

frock \'fräk\ *n* **1** : a friar's habit **2** : an outer garment worn by men **3** : a woman's or child's dress [Middle French *froc,* of Germanic origin]

frock coat *n* : a man's usually double-breasted knee=length coat

frog \'frȯg, 'fräg\ *n* **1 a** : any of various smooth-skinned web-footed largely aquatic tailless leaping amphibians — compare TOAD **b** : a condition in the throat that produces hoarseness ⟨a *frog* in one's throat⟩ **2** : the triangular elastic horny pad on the sole of the hoof of a horse **3** : an ornamental braiding for fastening the front of a garment by a loop through which a button passes **4** : a device permitting the wheels on one rail of a track to cross an intersecting rail **5** : a small holder with perforations or spikes for holding flowers in place in a bowl or vase [Old English *frogga*]

frog kick *n* : a kick used in swimming in which the legs are moved up, out, and back in the manner of a frog

frog·man \-ˌman, -mən\ *n* : a swimmer having equipment (as face mask, flippers, and air supply) that permits an extended stay under water usually for observation or demolition; *esp* : a member of a military unit so equipped

frog spit *n* : CUCKOO SPIT 1 — called also *frog spittle*

¹frol·ic \'fräl-ik\ *vi* **frol·icked; frol·ick·ing 1** : to make merry **2** : to play about boisterously : ROMP ⟨children *frolicking* on the beach⟩ [Dutch *vroolijk,* from earlier Dutch *vro* "happy"]

²frolic *n* **1** : a playful mischievous action **2** : GAIETY 2, MERRIMENT

frol·ic·some \'fräl-ik-səm\ *adj* : full of gaiety : PLAYFUL

from \frəm, 'frəm, 'främ\ *prep* **1** — used as a function word to indicate a starting point ⟨came here *from* the city⟩ ⟨cost *from* $5 to $10⟩ ⟨an avid reader *from* childhood⟩ **2** — used as a function word to indicate separation: as (1) physical separation ⟨a child taken *from* its mother⟩ (2) an act or condition of removal, abstention, exclusion, release, or differentiation ⟨refrain *from* interrupting⟩ ⟨far *from* safe⟩ **3** — used as a function word to indicate the source, cause, agent, or basis ⟨reading aloud *from* a book⟩ ⟨suffering *from* a cold⟩ [Old English]

frond \'fränd\ *n* : a leaf or leaflike part: as **a** : a palm leaf **b** : a fern leaf **c** : a leaflike thallus or shoot (as of a lichen or seaweed) [Latin *frond-, frons* "foliage"] — **frond·ed** \'frän-dəd\ *adj*

¹front \'frənt\ *n* **1 a** : FOREHEAD; *also* : the whole face **b** : DEMEANOR, BEARING **c** : external often feigned appearance ⟨put up a good *front*⟩ **2 a** : a region in which active warfare is taking place **b** : a sphere of activity **c** : the lateral space occupied by a military unit ⟨advanced on a 4-kilometer *front*⟩ **3** : the side of a building containing the principal entrance **4 a** : the forward part or surface ⟨the *front* of a shirt⟩ **b** : FRONTAGE 1 **c** : the boundary between two dissimilar air masses **5 a** : a position directly before or ahead of something else **b** : a position of leadership or superiority ⟨at the *front* of the profession⟩ **6** : a person, group, or thing used to mask the identity or true character or activity of the actual controlling agent ⟨the candy store was a *front* for a bookie joint⟩ **7** : a political coalition [Old French, from Latin *front-, frons*]

²front *vb* **1** : FACE ⟨the cottage *fronts* on the lake⟩ ⟨the house *fronts* the street⟩ **2** : to serve as a front **3** : CONFRONT

³front *adj* **1** : of, relating to, or situated at the front **2** : pronounced with closure or narrowing at or toward the front of the oral passage ⟨the *front* vowels \i\ and \e\⟩ — **front** *adv*

front·age \'frənt-ij\ *n* **1 a** : a piece of land that fronts something (as on a river or road) **b** : the front side of a building **2** : the extent or measure of a frontage ⟨the

United States has an Atlantic *frontage* of over 3000 kilometers⟩

front·al \'frənt-l\ *adj* **1** : of, relating to, or adjacent to the forehead or the frontal bone **2 a** : of, relating to, or situated at the front **b** : directed against the front or at the main point or issue ⟨a *frontal* assault⟩ — **fron·tal·ly** \-l-ē\ *adv*

frontal bone *n* : either of a pair of bones that unite to form the human forehead and the upper part of the cavities of the eye and nose

frontal lobe *n* : the front part of each cerebral hemisphere

fron·tier \ˌfrən-'tiər, frän-\ *n* **1** : a border between two countries **2 a** : a region that forms the margin of settled territory in a country being populated **b** : the outer limits of knowledge or achievement ⟨the *frontiers* of science⟩ [Middle French *frontiere,* from *front* "front"] — **frontier** *adj*

fron·tiers·man \-'tiərz-mən\ *n* : a person living on a frontier

fron·tiers·wom·an \-ˌwu̇m-ən\ *n* : a woman living on a frontier

fron·tis·piece \'frənt-ə-ˌspēs\ *n* : an illustration preceding and usually facing the title page of a book [Middle French *frontispice* "front of a building", from Late Latin *frontispicium,* from Latin *front-, frons* "front" + *specere* "to look at"] □ ORIGIN The process of folk etymology changes unfamiliar words to give them an apparent relationship to more familiar ones. This obscured the true origin of *frontispiece,* which has nothing to do with the word *piece* at all. The earliest known form of the word in English is *frontispice.* Latin *frons, frontis* originally meant "forehead" or "brow" and then came to mean "front" in general. This word combined with *specere,* "to look at", is the source of *frontispiece.* The earliest sense of *frontispice* was architectural: "the part of a building most easily seen, front". The word came to be used as well for the title page of a book, probably because of the once common practice of decorating title pages with columns and other architectural details. From this sense developed its current meaning.

front·let \'frənt-lət\ *n* **1** : a band worn on the forehead **2** : the forehead especially of a bird when distinctively marked

front man *n* : a person serving as a front or figurehead

front–run·ner \-'rən-ər\ *n* **1** : a competitor who is most effective when running in the lead **2** : the leader in a contest

¹frost \'frȯst\ *n* **1 a** : the process of freezing **b** : the temperature that causes freezing **c** : a covering of minute ice crystals on a cold surface **2** : coldness of manner or feeling : INDIFFERENCE [Old English]

²frost *vb* **1 a** : to cover with or as if with frost; *esp* : to put icing on (as cake) **b** : to produce a fine-grained slightly roughened surface on (as glass) **2** : to injure or kill by frost : FREEZE

¹frost·bite \'frȯst-ˌbīt, 'frȯs-\ *vt* : to blight or nip with frost

²frostbite *n* : the freezing or the local effect of a partial freezing of some part of the body

frost·ed \'frȯ-stəd\ *adj* **1** : covered with frost or with something resembling frost ⟨*frosted* glass⟩ **2** : decorated with frosting ⟨a *frosted* cake⟩ **3** : QUICK-FROZEN ⟨*frosted* foods⟩

frost heave *n* : an upthrust of ground or pavement caused by freezing of moist soil — called also *frost heaving*

frost·ing \'frȯ-stiŋ\ *n* **1** : ¹ICING 2 **2** : dull finish on metal or glass

frosty \'frȯ-stē\ *adj* **frost·i·er; -est 1** : attended with or producing frost : FREEZING ⟨a *frosty* night⟩ **2** : covered or appearing as if covered with frost **3** : marked by coolness or extreme reserve in manner ⟨a *frosty* recep-

frog 3

\ə\ abut	\ng\ sing
\ər\ further	\ō\ bone
\a\ mat	\ȯ\ saw
\ā\ take	\ȯi\ coin
\ä\ cot, cart	\th\ thin
\au̇\ out	\th\ this
\ch\ chin	\ü\ food
\e\ pet	\u̇\ foot
\ē\ easy	\y\ yet
\g\ go	\yü\ few
\i\ tip	\yu̇\ cure
\ī\ life	\zh\ vision
\j\ job	

tion) — **frost·i·ly** \-stə-lē\ *adv* — **frost·i·ness** \-stē-nəs\ *n*

¹froth \'frȯth\ *n, pl* **froths** \'frȯths, 'frȯthz\ **1 a** : bubbles formed in or on a liquid by fermentation or agitation **b** : the foam produced by saliva that sometimes accompanies disease or exhaustion **2** : something light or frivolous and of little value [Old Norse *frotha*]

²froth \'frȯth, 'frȯth\ *vb* **1** : to cause to foam **2** : to cover with froth **3** : to produce or throw up froth

frothy \'frȯ-thē, -thē\ *adj* **froth·i·er; -est 1** : full of or consisting of froth **2** : gaily frivolous or light in content or treatment — **froth·i·ly** \-thə-lē, -thə-\ *adv* — **froth·i·ness** \-thē-nəs, -thē-\ *n*

frou-frou \'frü-ˌfrü\ *n* **1** : a rustling especially of a woman's skirts **2** : frilly ornamentation especially in clothing [French]

fro·ward \'frō-wərd, -ərd\ *adj* : inclined to disobey and oppose : CONTRARY [Middle English, "turned away, froward", from *fro* + *-ward*] — **fro·ward·ly** *adv* — **fro·ward·ness** *n*

frown \'fraŭn\ *vb* **1** : to wrinkle the forehead (as in anger, displeasure, or concentration) **2** : to look with disapproval ⟨parents *frown* on rudeness⟩ **3** : to express with a frown ⟨*frown* one's disapproval⟩ [Middle French *froigner* "to snort, frown"] — **frown** *n* — **frown·er** *n* — **frown·ing·ly** \'fraŭ-ning-lē\ *adv*

frow·sy *also* **frow·zy** \'fraŭ-zē\ *adj* **frow·si·er** *also* **frow·zi·er; -est** : having a slovenly or uncared-for appearance [origin unknown]

froze *past of* FREEZE

fro·zen \'frōz-n\ *adj* **1 a** : affected or crusted over by freezing **b** : subject to long and severe cold ⟨the *frozen* north⟩ **2 a** : expressing or characterized by cold unfriendliness ⟨a *frozen* stare⟩ **b** : incapable of being changed, moved, or undone ⟨wages were *frozen*⟩ **c** : not available for present use ⟨*frozen* capital⟩ — **fro·zen·ly** *adv* — **fro·zen·ness** \-n-nəs, -əs\ *n*

frozen food *n* : food that has been subjected to rapid freezing and is kept frozen until used

fruc·ti·fy \'frək-tə-ˌfī, 'frük-\ *vb* **-fied; -fy·ing 1** : to bear fruit **2** : to make fruitful or productive [Middle French *fructifier*, derived from Latin *fructus* "fruit"] — **fruc·ti·fi·ca·tion** \ˌfrək-tə-fə-'kā-shən, ˌfrük-\ *n*

fruc·tose \'frək-ˌtōs, 'frük-\ *n* : a very sweet soluble sugar $C_6H_{12}O_6$ that occurs especially in fruit juices and honey [Latin *fructus* "fruit"]

fru·gal \'frü-gəl\ *adj* : characterized by or reflecting economy in the use of resources : THRIFTY [Latin *frugalis* "virtuous, frugal", derived from *frux* "fruit, value"] — **fru·gal·i·ty** \frü-'gal-ət-ē\ *n* — **fru·gal·ly** \'frü-gə-lē\ *adv*

¹fruit \'früt\ *n* **1 a** : a usually useful product of plant growth (as grain, vegetables, or cotton) ⟨*fruits* of the earth⟩ **b** : the usually edible reproductive body of a seed plant; *esp* : one (as a strawberry) having a sweet pulp **c** : a product of fertilization in a plant with its envelopes or appendages; *esp* : the ripened ovary of a seed plant, its contents, and inseparably associated parts (as the pod of a pea) **2** : CONSEQUENCE, RESULT ⟨the *fruits* of their labors⟩ [Old French, from Latin *fructus* "fruit, use", from *frui* "to enjoy, have the use of"] — **fruit·ed** \-əd\ *adj*

²fruit *vb* : to bear or cause to bear fruit

fruit·age \'früt-ij\ *n* **1** : the condition or process of bearing fruit **2** : yield or amount of fruit

fruit bat *n* : any of numerous large Old World fruit-eating bats of warm regions — called also *flying fox*

fruit·cake \'früt-ˌkāk\ *n* : a rich cake containing nuts, dried or candied fruits, and spices

fruit·er·er \'früt-ər-ər\ *n* : one that deals in fruit

fruit fly *n* : any of various small two-winged flies (as a drosophila) whose larvae feed on fruit or decaying vegetable matter

fruit·ful \'früt-fəl\ *adj* **1** : yielding or producing fruit **2** : abundantly productive : bringing results SYN see FERTILE — **fruit·ful·ly** \-fə-lē\ *adv* — **fruit·ful·ness** *n*

fruiting body *n* : a plant organ specialized for producing spores

fru·i·tion \frü-'ish-ən\ *n* **1** : the state of bearing fruit **2** : REALIZATION, ACCOMPLISHMENT ⟨brought the project to *fruition*⟩ [Late Latin *fruitio* "enjoyment", derived from Latin *frui* "to enjoy"]

fruit·less \'früt-ləs\ *adj* **1** : lacking or not bearing fruit **2** : producing no good effect : UNSUCCESSFUL ⟨a *fruitless* attempt⟩ — **fruit·less·ly** *adv* — **fruit·less·ness** *n*

fruit sugar *n* : FRUCTOSE

fruity \'früt-ē\ *adj* **fruit·i·er; -est** : relating to or suggesting fruit

frus·trate \'frəs-ˌtrāt\ *vt* **1** : to prevent from carrying out a purpose ⟨*frustrate* a person⟩ **2** : to make ineffective ⟨*frustrate* a plan⟩ [Latin *frustrare*, from *frustra* "in vain"] — **frus·tra·tion** \ˌfrəs-'trā-shən, frəs-\ *n* □ SYN THWART, BAFFLE, FOIL: FRUSTRATE implies making even the best or most persistent efforts vain and ineffectual; THWART implies frustrating or checking especially by deliberately crossing or opposing; BAFFLE implies frustrating by confusing or puzzling; FOIL implies checking or defeating so as to discourage further effort.

frus·tum \'frəs-təm\ *n, pl* **frustums** *or* **frus·ta** \-tə\ : the part of a cone or pyramid formed by cutting off the top by a plane parallel to the base [Latin, "piece, bit"]

fru·ti·cose \'früt-i-ˌkōs\ *adj* : having a shrubby bushy thallus with flattened or cylindrical branches ⟨*fruticose* lichens⟩ — compare CRUSTOSE, FOLIOSE [Latin *fruticosus*, from *frutex* "shrub"]

¹fry \'frī\ *vb* **fried; fry·ing** : to cook in a pan or on a griddle over a fire especially in fat [Old French *frire*, from Latin *frigere*]

²fry *n, pl* **fries 1** : a dish of something fried **2** : a social gathering where fried food is eaten

³fry *n, pl* **fry 1 a** : recently hatched fishes **b** : the young of animals other than fish **2** : very small adult fishes **3** : members of a group or class : PERSONS ⟨small *fry*⟩ [Middle English, probably from Old North French *fri*, from Old French *frier* "to rub, spawn"]

fry bread *n* : quick bread cooked in deep fat

fry·er *also* **fri·er** \'frī-ər, 'frīr\ *n* : something intended for or used in frying: as **a** : a young chicken **b** : a deep utensil for frying foods

f-stop \'ef-ˌstäp\ *n* : a camera lens aperture setting indicated by an f-number

fuch·sia \'fyü-shə\ *n* **1** : any of a genus of shrubs of the evening-primrose family that have showy nodding flowers usually in deep pinks, reds, and purples **2** : a vivid reddish purple [Leonhard *Fuchs*, died 1566, German botanist]

fuch·sin *or* **fuch·sine** \'fyük-sən, -ˌsēn\ *n* : a synthetic dye that yields a brilliant bluish red [French *fuchsine*, probably from *fuchsia* "fuchsia"]

fu·co·xan·thin \ˌfyü-kō-'zan-thən\ *n* : a brown pigment occurring especially in the ova of brown algae [derived from Greek *phykos* "seaweed" + *xanthos* "yellow"]

fu·cus \'fyü-kəs\ *n* : ROCKWEED [Latin, a kind of lichen, from Greek *phykos* "seaweed"]

fud·dle \'fəd-l\ *vt* **fud·dled; fud·dling** \'fəd-ling, -l-ing\ : to make confused : MUDDLE [origin unknown]

fud·dy–dud·dy \'fəd-ē-ˌdəd-ē\ *n, pl* **-dies** : one that is old-fashioned, pompous, unimaginative, or concerned about trifles [perhaps reduplication of Scottish *fuddy* "short-tailed animal, tail", from *fud* "tail"]

¹fudge \'fəj\ *vb* **1** : to act dishonestly **2** : to avoid commitment : HEDGE **3 a** : to devise as a substitute : FAKE **b** : FALSIFY ⟨*fudged* the figures⟩ [origin unknown]

²fudge *n* **1** : foolish nonsense **2** : a soft creamy candy of sugar, milk, butter, and flavoring

¹fu·el \'fyü-əl\ *n* **1 a** : a material used to produce heat or power by burning **b** : a material from which atomic energy can be produced especially in a reactor **2** : a source of support : REINFORCEMENT [Old French *fou-*

aille, from feu "fire", derived from Latin focus
"hearth"]

²**fuel** vb **-eled** or **-elled; -el·ing** or **-el·ling** 1 : to provide
with or take in fuel 2 : SUPPORT, STIMULATE ⟨fuel
research with federal grants⟩

fuel cell n : a cell that continuously changes the chemical energy of a fuel and oxidant to electrical energy

fuel oil n : an oil that is used for fuel and that usually
ignites at a higher temperature than kerosene

¹**fu·gi·tive** \'fyü-jət-iv\ adj 1 : running away or trying to
escape ⟨a fugitive slave⟩ 2 : likely to vanish suddenly :
not fixed or lasting ⟨fugitive thoughts⟩ [Latin fugitivus,
from fugere "to flee"] — **fu·gi·tive·ly** adv — **fu·gi-
tive·ness** n

²**fugitive** n 1 : one that flees or tries to escape 2 : something elusive or hard to find

fugue \'fyüg\ n : a musical composition in which one
or two themes are repeated or imitated by successively
entering voices and developed in a continuous interweaving of the voice parts [probably from Italian fuga
"flight, fugue", from Latin, "flight", from fugere "to
flee"] — **fu·gal** \'fyü-gəl\ adj

füh·rer or **fueh·rer** \'fyur-ər, 'fir-\ n : LEADER 2c — used
chiefly of the leader of the German Nazis [German]

¹**-ful** \fəl\ adj suffix, sometimes **-ful·ler;** sometimes **-ful-
lest** 1 : full of ⟨eventful⟩ 2 : characterized by
⟨peaceful⟩ 3 : having the qualities of ⟨masterful⟩ 4 :
tending, given, or liable to ⟨mournful⟩

²**-ful** \ˌful\ n suffix : number or quantity that fills or
would fill ⟨roomful⟩

ful·crum \'ful-krəm, 'fəl-\ n, pl **fulcrums** or **ful·cra**
\-krə\ : the support about which a lever turns [Latin,
"bedpost", from fulcire "to prop"]

ful·fill or **ful·fil** \ful-'fil\ vt **ful·filled; ful·fill·ing** 1 : to put
into effect ⟨fulfill a promise⟩ 2 : to measure up to :
SATISFY ⟨fulfill a need⟩ [Old English fullfyllan, from
full + fyllan "to fill"] — **ful·fill·er** n — **ful·fill·ment**
\-mənt\ n

¹**full** \'ful\ adj 1 : containing as much or as many as is
possible or normal ⟨a bin full of corn⟩ 2 a : complete
as to number, amount, or duration ⟨a full share⟩ b :
having all the distinguishing characteristics ⟨a full
member⟩ c : being at the highest degree : MAXIMUM
⟨full strength⟩ 3 a : plump and rounded in outline ⟨a
full figure⟩ b : having an abundance of material ⟨a full
skirt⟩ 4 a : possessing or containing an abundance ⟨a
full life⟩ b : rich in detail ⟨a full report⟩ 5 : satisfied
especially with food or drink 6 : having both parents
in common ⟨full sisters⟩ 7 : having volume or depth of
sound ⟨full tones⟩ 8 : completely occupied especially
with a thought or plan ⟨full of one's own concerns⟩
[Old English] — **full·ness** also **ful·ness** n

²**full** adv 1 a : VERY, EXTREMELY ⟨knew full well they
were lying⟩ b : ENTIRELY ⟨fill a glass full⟩ 2 : EXACTLY,
SQUARELY ⟨was hit full in the face⟩

³**full** n 1 a : the utmost extent ⟨enjoy life to the full⟩ b :
the highest or fullest state or degree ⟨the full of the
moon⟩ 2 : the requisite or complete amount ⟨paid in
full⟩

⁴**full** vt : to shrink and thicken (woolen cloth) by moistening, heating, and pressing [Middle French fouler,
from Latin fullo "fuller"]

full·back \'ful-ˌbak\ n 1 : an offensive football back
who usually lines up between the halfbacks 2 : a primarily defensive player (as in soccer or field hockey)
who usually plays near the goal to be defended

full–blood·ed \'ful-'bləd-əd\ adj : of unmixed ancestry : PUREBRED — **full–blood·ed·ness** n

full–blown \-'blōn\ adj 1 : being at the height of bloom
⟨a full-blown rose⟩ 2 : fully mature or developed

full–bod·ied \-'bäd-ēd\ adj : marked by richness and
fullness

full–dress \-'dres\ adj 1 : complete to the last detail ⟨a
full-dress rehearsal⟩ 2 : carried out by all possible
means

full dress n : formal or ceremonial dress

full·er \'ful-ər\ n : one that fulls cloth

fuller's earth n : a clayish earthy substance used for filtering and as an absorbent

fuller's teasel n : TEASEL 1a

full–fledged \'ful-'flejd\ adj 1 : fully developed : MA-
TURE 2 : having full plumage

full–grown \-'grōn\ adj : having reached full growth or
development : MATURE

full house n : a poker hand containing three cards of
one rank plus a pair of cards of another rank

full moon n : the moon with its whole apparent disk
illuminated

full–scale \'ful-'skāl\ adj 1 : identical to an original in
proportion and size ⟨full-scale drawing⟩ 2 : involving
full use of available resources ⟨a full-scale biography⟩

full tilt adv : at high speed

full time n : the standard working time for a given job or
period — **full–time** adj

ful·ly \'ful-lē, -ē\ adv 1 : in a full manner or degree :
COMPLETELY 2 : at least ⟨fully nine tenths of us⟩

ful·mar \'ful-mər, -ˌmär\ n : an Arctic seabird closely
related to the petrels [of Scandinavian origin]

ful·mi·nate \'ful-mə-ˌnāt, 'fəl-\ vb 1 : to utter or send
out censure or condemnation 2 : to make a sudden
loud noise : EXPLODE [Medieval Latin fulminare, from
Latin, "to flash with lightning, strike with lightning",
from fulmen "lightning"] — **ful·mi·na·tion** \ˌful-mə-
'nā-shən, ˌfəl-\ n — **ful·mi·na·tor** \-ˌnāt-ər\ n

ful·some \'ful-səm\ adj 1 : marked by abundance : CO-
PIOUS ⟨described in fulsome detail⟩ 2 : offensive especially from insincerity or baseness of motive ⟨a fulsome politeness⟩ ⟨fulsome praise⟩ [Middle English fulsome "copious, cloying", from ful "full" + -som
"-some"] — **ful·some·ly** adv — **ful·some·ness** n

fu·ma·role \'fyü-mə-ˌrōl\ n : a hole in a volcanic region
from which hot gases and vapors issue [Italian fuma-
rola, derived from Latin fumus "fume"]

¹**fum·ble** \'fəm-bəl\ vb **fum·bled; fum·bling** \-bə-ling,
-bling\ 1 : to feel or grope about clumsily ⟨fumbled
for the key⟩ 2 : to handle or manage something clumsily : fail to grasp firmly; esp : to fail to hold, catch, or
handle the ball properly in a game (as baseball or football) [probably of Scandinavian origin] — **fum·bler**
\-bə-lər, -blər\ n

²**fumble** n 1 : an act or instance of fumbling 2 : a fum-
bled ball

¹**fume** \'fyüm\ n 1 : a usually irritating or offensive
smoke, vapor, or gas — usually used in pl. ⟨exhaust
fumes⟩ ⟨acid fumes⟩ 2 : a state of excited irritation or
anger [Middle French fum, from Latin fumus "smoke,
fume"] — **fumy** \'fyü-mē\ adj

²**fume** vb 1 : to expose to or treat with fumes 2 : to give
off fumes 3 a : to be in a fume b : to express irritable
annoyance ⟨fume at a delay⟩

fu·mi·gant \'fyü-mi-gənt\ n : a substance used for fumigating

fu·mi·gate \'fyü-mə-ˌgāt\ vt : to apply smoke, vapor, or
gas to especially for the purpose of disinfecting or of
destroying pests [Latin fumigare, from fumus "fume"]
— **fu·mi·ga·tion** \ˌfyü-mə-'gā-shən\ n — **fu·mi·ga·tor**
\'fyü-mə-ˌgāt-ər\ n

fu·mi·to·ry \'fyü-mə-ˌtōr-ē, -ˌtòr-\ n, pl **-ries** : any of a
genus of erect or climbing herbs with showy irregular
flowers [Middle French fumeterre, from Medieval Latin fumus terrae, literally, "smoke of the earth"]

¹**fun** \'fən\ n 1 : something that provides amusement or
enjoyment; esp : playful boisterous action or speech
2 : AMUSEMENT, ENJOYMENT ⟨sickness takes the fun out
of life⟩ [English dialect fun "to hoax"]

²**fun** vi **funned; fun·ning** : to indulge in banter or play :
JOKE

¹**func·tion** \'fəng-shən, 'fəngk-\ n 1 : professional position or duties : OCCUPATION 2 : the action for which a
person or thing is specially fitted or used or for which

F fulcrum

\ə\ abut		\ng\ sing	
\ər\ further		\ō\ bone	
\a\ mat		\ò\ saw	
\ā\ take		\òi\ coin	
\ä\ cot, cart		\th\ thin	
\au̇\ out		\th\ this	
\ch\ chin		\ü\ food	
\e\ pet		\u̇\ foot	
\ē\ easy		\y\ yet	
\g\ go		\yü\ few	
\i\ tip		\yu̇\ cure	
\ī\ life		\zh\ vision	
\j\ job			

a thing exists **3** : an impressive, elaborate, or formal ceremony or social gathering **4** : one of a group of related actions contributing to a larger action; *esp* : the normal and specific contribution of a bodily part to the economy of a living organism **5 a** : a mathematical relationship that assigns to each element of one set one and usually only one element of the same or another set **b** : quality, trait, or fact dependent on and varying with another [Latin *functio* "performance", from *fungi* "to perform"] — **func·tion·less** \-ləs\ *adj*

²function *vi* **func·tioned; func·tion·ing** \-shə-ning, -shning\ **1** : to have a function : SERVE **2** : to be in action : OPERATE

func·tion·al \'fəng-shnəl, 'fəngk-, -shən-l\ *adj* **1 a** : of, connected with, or being a function **b** : affecting functions but not structure ⟨*functional* heart disease⟩ — compare ORGANIC 1b **2** : serving in a larger whole; *also* : designed or developed chiefly from the point of view of use ⟨*functional* architecture⟩ **3** : performing or able to perform a regular function **4** : organized by functions — **func·tion·al·ly** \-ē\ *adv*

functional illiterate *n* : a person having had some schooling but not meeting a minimum standard of literacy — **functionally illiterate** *adj*

func·tion·ary \'fəng-shə-,ner-ē, 'fəngk-\ *n, pl* **-ar·ies** : a person charged with the performance of a certain function; *esp* : OFFICIAL

function word *n* : a word expressing primarily grammatical relationship

¹fund \'fənd\ *n* **1** : an available quantity of material or intangible resources : SUPPLY **2 a** : a sum of money or other resources the principal or interest of which is set apart for a specific objective **b** *pl* : available money **3** : an organization administering a special fund [Latin *fundus* "bottom, piece of landed property"]

²fund *vt* **1** : to provide funds for ⟨the government *funded* the project⟩ **2** : to convert (a short-term obligation) into a debt payable at a distant date or at no definite date and bearing a fixed interest ⟨*fund* a debt⟩

fun·da·ment \'fən-də-mənt\ *n* **1** : FOUNDATION 2, BASE **2** : BUTTOCK 2 [Old French *fondement*, from Latin *fundamentum*, from *fundare* "to found", from *fundus* "bottom"]

¹fun·da·men·tal \,fən-də-'ment-l\ *adj* **1 a** : serving as an origin or source : PRIMARY **b** : serving as a basic support or essential structure or function : BASIC **2** : of or relating to essential structure or function : RADICAL ⟨a *fundamental* change⟩ **3** : of, relating to, or produced by the lowest part of a complex vibration **4** : of central importance : PRINCIPAL ⟨the *fundamental* aim of our trip⟩ SYN see ESSENTIAL — **fun·da·men·tal·ly** \-l-ē\ *adv*

²fundamental *n* **1** : something fundamental; *esp* : one of the basic constituents essential to a thing or system **2** : the part of a complex wave that has the lowest frequency and usually the greatest amplitude

fun·da·men·tal·ism \-l-,iz-əm\ *n* **1** *often cap* : a movement in 20th century Protestantism emphasizing the literally interpreted Bible as fundamental to Christian life and teaching **2 a** : the beliefs associated with fundamentalism **b** : adherence to such beliefs — **fun·da·men·tal·ist** \-l-əst\ *adj or n*

fundamental particle *n* : ELEMENTARY PARTICLE

¹fu·ner·al \'fyün-rəl, -ə-rəl\ *adj* **1** : of, relating to, or constituting a funeral **2** : FUNEREAL 2 [Late Latin *funeralis*, from Latin *funer-, funus*, n., "funeral"]

²funeral *n* **1** : a ceremony held for a dead person usually before burial or cremation **2** : a funeral party in transit

funeral director *n* : a person who manages funerals and is usually an embalmer

funeral home *n* : a set of rooms with facilities for the preparation of the dead for burial or cremation, for the viewing of the body, and for funerals — called also *funeral parlor*

¹funnel 1

fu·ne·re·al \fyù-'nir-ē-əl\ *adj* **1** : of or relating to a funeral **2** : suggesting a funeral ⟨*funereal* gloom⟩ [Latin *funereus*, from *funer-, funus* "funeral"] — **fu·ne·re·al·ly** \-ē-ə-lē\ *adv*

fun·gal \'fəng-gəl\ *adj* : FUNGOUS

fungi- *combining form* : fungus ⟨*fungi*cide⟩

fun·gi·cide \'fən-jə-,sīd, 'fəng-gə-\ *n* : a substance that destroys fungi or inhibits their growth — **fun·gi·cid·al** \,fən-jə-'sīd-l, fəng-gə-\ *adj* — **fun·gi·cid·al·ly** \-l-ē\ *adv*

fun·go \'fəng-gō\ *n, pl* **fungoes** : a fly ball hit by a player who tosses a ball in the air and hits it as it comes down [origin unknown]

fun·goid \'fəng-,goid\ *adj* : resembling, characteristic of, or being a fungus — **fungoid** *n*

fun·gous \'fəng-gəs\ *adj* **1** : of, relating to, or resembling fungi **2** : caused by a fungus

fun·gus \'fəng-gəs\ *n, pl* **fun·gi** \'fən-,jī, 'fəng-,gī\ *also* **fun·gus·es** **1** : any of a major group (Fungi) of lower plants (as molds, rusts, mildews, smuts, mushrooms, and yeasts) that lack chlorophyll and are saprophytic or parasitic **2** : infection with a fungus [Latin] — **fungus** *adj*

fu·nic·u·lar \fyù-'nik-yə-lər, fə-\ *n* : a cable railway ascending a mountain; *esp* : one in which an ascending car counterbalances a descending car [derived from Latin *funiculus* "small rope"]

¹funk \'fəngk\ *n* **1** : a state of paralyzing fear **2** : a depressed state of mind [probably from obsolete Flemish *fonck*]

²funk *vb* **1** : to become frightened and shrink back **2** : to be afraid of : DREAD

¹fun·nel \'fən-l\ *n* **1** : a utensil usually shaped like a hollow cone with a tube extending from the point to catch and direct a downward flow (as of liquid) **2** : a stack or flue (as of a ship) for the escape of smoke or for ventilation [Provençal *fonilh*, from Medieval Latin *fundibulum*, from Latin *infundibulum*, from *infundere* "to pour in", from *in-* + *fundere* "to pour"]

²funnel *vb* **-neled** *also* **-nelled; -nel·ing** *also* **-nel·ling** **1** : to form, take, or give the shape of a funnel ⟨*funneling* clouds⟩ **2** : to pass through or as if through a funnel ⟨funds were *funneled* into the project⟩

fun·ny \'fən-ē\ *adj* **fun·ni·er; -est** **1 a** : affording light mirth and laughter : AMUSING **b** : seeking or intended to amuse **2** : differing from the ordinary in a suspicious way : QUEER **3** : involving trickery or deception — **fun·ni·ly** \'fən-l-ē\ *adv* — **fun·ni·ness** \'fən-ē-nəs\ *n*

funny bone *n* **1** : a place at the back of the elbow where a blow may compress a nerve and cause a painful tingling sensation **2** : a sense of humor ⟨a joke that tickles my *funny bone*⟩

¹fur \'fər\ *vt* **furred; fur·ring** : to cover, line, trim, or clothe with fur [Middle French *fourrer*, from Old French *fuerre* "sheath", of Germanic origin] □ ORIGIN The hairy coat of a mammal is called *fur*. But originally this coat could not be called *fur* until it had been removed from the animal and used to adorn a human being. The well-to-do of the late Middle Ages wore robes *furred* (lined and trimmed) with the pelts of animals. These trimmings and linings were called *furs*. The word was soon used for the soft hair of animals, even of living animals. But when robes were first *furred*, it was the act of lining rather than the material used that the verb *fur* suggested. Middle French *fourrer*, "to line a garment", which is the source of English *fur*, originally meant "to encase". *Fourrer* was derived from the noun *fuerre*, a Germanic loanword in Old French which meant "sheath".

²fur *n* **1** : a piece of the dressed pelt of an animal used to make, trim, or line wearing apparel **2** : an article of clothing made of or with fur **3** : the hairy coat of a mammal especially when fine, soft, and thick **4** : a coating (as on the tongue) resembling fur — **fur·less** \'fər-ləs\ *adj* — **furred** \'fərd\ *adj*

fur·bear·er \'fər-ˌbar-ər, -ˌber-\ *n* : an animal that bears fur especially of a commerically desired quality

fur·be·low \'fər-bə-ˌlō\ *n* **1** : a pleated or gathered piece of material (as a ruffle or flounce) **2** : showy trimming [by folk etymology from French dialect *farbella*]

fur·bish \'fər-bish\ *vt* **1** : to make lustrous : POLISH **2** : to give a new look to : RENOVATE [Middle French *fourbiss-*, stem of *fourbir* "to furbish", of Germanic origin]

fu·ri·ous \'fyùr-ē-əs\ *adj* **1** : being in a fury : FIERCE, ANGRY **2** : VIOLENT ⟨a *furious* wind⟩ — **fu·ri·ous·ly** *adv*

¹furl \'fərl\ *vt* : to wrap or roll (as a sail or a flap) close to or around something [Middle French *ferler*, from Old North French *ferlier* "to tie tightly", from Old French *ferm, fer* "tight" (from Latin *firmus* "firm") + *lier* "to tie", from Latin *ligare*]

²furl *n* **1** : the act of furling **2** : something that is furled

fur·long \'fər-ˌlòng\ *n* : a unit of distance equal to 220 yards (about 201.2 meters) [Old English *furlang*, from *furh* "furrow" + *lang* "long"]

¹fur·lough \'fər-lō\ *n* : a leave of absence from duty; *esp* : one granted to a soldier [Dutch *verlof*, literally, "permission"]

²furlough *vt* **1** : to grant a furlough to **2** : to lay off from work

fur·nace \'fər-nəs\ *n* : an enclosed structure in which heat is produced (as for heating a house or melting metals) [Old French *fornaise*, from Latin *fornax*]

fur·nish \'fər-nish\ *vt* **1** : to provide with what is needed; *esp* : to equip with furniture **2** : SUPPLY, GIVE ⟨*furnished* them with food⟩ [Middle French *fourniss-*, stem of *fournir* "to complete, equip", of Germanic origin] — **fur·nish·er** *n*

fur·nish·ings \-nish-ingz\ *n pl* **1** : articles or accessories of dress **2** : objects that tend to increase comfort or utility; *esp* : articles of furniture for a room

fur·ni·ture \'fər-ni-chər\ *n* : equipment that is necessary, useful, or desirable; *esp* : movable articles (as chairs, tables, or beds) needed to fit a room for use [Middle French *fourniture*, from *fournir* "to equip"]

fu·ror \'fyùr-ˌór, -ˌōr\ *n* **1** : a fit of anger : RAGE **2** : a fashionable craze : VOGUE **3** : an outburst of public excitement or indignation : UPROAR [Latin, from *furere* "to rage"]

fu·rore \-ˌōr, -ˌòr\ *n* : FUROR 2, 3

fur·ri·er \'fər-ē-ər\ *n* : a person who prepares or deals in furs — **fur·ri·ery** \-ē-ə-rē\ *n*

fur·ring \'fər-ing\ *n* **1** : a fur trimming or lining **2** : the application of thin wood, brick, or metal to joists, studs, or walls to form a level surface or an air space; *also* : the material used in this process

¹fur·row \'fər-ō, 'fə-rō\ *n* **1** : a trench in the earth made by or as if by a plow **2** : something (as a groove or wrinkle) that resembles the track of a plow [Old English *furh*]

²furrow *vb* **1** : to make furrows in **2** : to form furrows

fur·ry \'fər-ē\ *adj* **fur·ri·er; -est 1** : consisting of or resembling fur **2** : covered with fur

fur seal *n* : any of various seals with a dense soft undercoat used as a fur — compare HAIR SEAL

¹fur·ther \'fər-thər\ *adv* **1** : ¹FARTHER 1 **2** : in addition : MOREOVER **3** : to a greater degree or extent [Old English *furthor*, comparative of *forth*]

²further *adj* **1** : ²FARTHER 1 **2** : going or extending beyond : ADDITIONAL ⟨*further* education⟩

³further *vt* **fur·thered; fur·ther·ing** \'fərth-ring, -ə-ring\ : to help forward : PROMOTE ⟨*furthered* medical research⟩ — **fur·ther·er** \'fər-thər-ər\ *n*

fur·ther·ance \'fərth-rəns, -ə-rəns\ *n* : the act of furthering : ADVANCEMENT

fur·ther·more \'fər-thər-ˌmōr, -thə-, -ˌmór\ *adv* : in addition to what precedes : BESIDES

fur·ther·most \-ˌmōst\ *adj* : most distant : FARTHEST

fur·thest \'fər-thəst\ *adv or adj* : FARTHEST

fur·tive \'fərt-iv\ *adj* : done by stealth : SLY, SECRET ⟨a *furtive* look⟩ [Latin *furtivus*, from *furtum* "theft", from *fur* "thief"] — **fur·tive·ly** *adv* — **fur·tive·ness** *n*

fu·run·cle \'fyùr-ˌəng-kəl\ *n* : BOIL [Latin *furunculus* "petty thief, sucker, furuncle", derived from *fur* "thief"]

fu·ry \'fyùr-ē\ *n, pl* **furies 1** : an intense and often destructive rage **2 a** *cap* : one of the avenging spirits in classical mythology **b** : a violent, angry, or spiteful person **3** : extreme fierceness or violence ⟨the *fury* of the storm⟩ [Latin *furia*, from *furere* "to rage"] SYN see ANGER

furze \'fərz\ *n* : a prickly evergreen shrub of the pea family with yellow flowers [Old English *fyrs*]

¹fuse \'fyüz\ *n* **1** : a continuous train (as of gunpowder) enclosed in a cord or cable for setting off an explosive charge by transmitting fire to it **2** *usually* **fuze** : a mechanical or electrical detonating device for setting off the bursting charge of a projectile, bomb, or torpedo [Italian *fuso* "spindle", from Latin *fusus*]

²fuse *or* **fuze** *vt* : to equip with a fuse

³fuse *vb* **1** : to reduce to a liquid or plastic state by heat **2** : to become fluid with heat **3** : to unite by or as if by melting together : BLEND, INTEGRATE [Latin *fusus*, past participle of *fundere* "to pour, melt"]

⁴fuse *n* : an electrical safety device consisting of or including a wire or strip of fusible metal that melts and interrupts the circuit when the current becomes too strong

fu·see *or* **fu·zee** \fyù-'zē\ *n* **1** : a friction match with a bulbous head not easily blown out **2** : a red signal flare used especially for protecting stalled trains and trucks

fu·se·lage \'fyü-sə-ˌläzh, 'fyü-zə-\ *n* : the central body portion of an airplane which holds the crew, passengers, and cargo [French, from *fuselé* "spindle-shaped", derived from Latin *fusus* "spindle"]

fu·sel oil \'fyü-zəl-\ *n* : an acrid oily liquid occurring in insufficiently distilled alcoholic liquors and consisting chiefly of amyl alcohol [German *fusel* "bad liquor"]

fus·ible \'fyü-zə-bəl\ *adj* : capable of being fused and especially liquefied by heat — **fus·ibil·i·ty** \ˌfyü-zə-'bil-ət-ē\ *n*

fu·si·form \'fyü-zə-ˌfórm\ *adj* : tapering toward each end ⟨*fusiform* swelling of the fingers⟩ [Latin *fusus* "spindle"]

fu·sil \'fyü-zəl\ *n* : a light flintlock musket [French, "steel for striking fire, fusil", derived from Late Latin *focus* "fire", from Latin, "hearth"]

fu·sil·ier *or* **fu·sil·eer** \ˌfyü-zə-'liər\ *n* **1** : a soldier armed with a fusil **2** : a member of a British regiment formerly armed with fusils

fu·sil·lade \'fyü-sə-ˌlād, -zə-, -ˌläd\ *n* **1** : a number of shots fired simultaneously or in rapid succession **2** : a spirited outburst especially of criticism

fu·sion \'fyü-zhən\ *n* **1** : the act or process of making fluid by heat **2** : union by or as if by melting; *esp* : a merging of diverse elements into a unified whole **3** : the union of atomic nuclei to form heavier nuclei resulting in the release of enormous quantities of energy when certain light elements unite

¹fuss \'fəs\ *n* **1 a** : needless bustle or excitement : COMMOTION **b** : a show of flattering attention ⟨made a big *fuss* over their grandchildren⟩ **2** : a state of agitation especially over a trivial matter [perhaps of imitative origin]

²fuss *vi* **1 a** : to create or be in a state of restless activity; *esp* : to shower flattering attentions **b** : to pay undue attention to small details **2** : to become upset : WORRY — **fuss·er** *n*

fuss·budg·et \'fəs-ˌbəj-ət\ *n* : one who fusses about trifles

\ə\ abut	\ng\ sing
\ər\ further	\ō\ bone
\a\ mat	\ó\ saw
\ā\ take	\òi\ coin
\ä\ cot, cart	\th\ thin
\aù\ out	\th\ this
\ch\ chin	\ü\ food
\e\ pet	\ù\ foot
\ē\ easy	\y\ yet
\g\ go	\yü\ few
\i\ tip	\yù\ cure
\ī\ life	\zh\ vision
\j\ job	

fussy \'fəs-ē\ *adj* **fuss·i·er; -est 1** : easily upset : IRRITA-BLE **2 a** : requiring or giving close attention to details **b** : too particular : FINICKY ⟨*fussy* about food⟩ — **fuss·i·ly** \'fəs-ə-lē\ *adv* — **fuss·i·ness** \'fəs-ē-nəs\ *n*

fus·tian \'fəs-chən\ *n* **1** : a strong cotton and linen fabric **2** : pretentious writing or speech [Old French *fustaine,* from Medieval Latin *fustaneum*] — **fustian** *adj*

fus·tic \'fəs-tik\ *n* : the wood of a tropical American tree of the mulberry family that yields a yellow dye; *also* : a tree yielding fustic [Middle French *fustoc,* from Arabic *fustuq,* from Greek *pistakē* "pistachio tree"]

fus·ty \'fəs-tē\ *adj* **fus·ti·er; -est 1** : saturated with dust and stale odors **2** : rigidly conservative : OLD-FASH-IONED [Middle English, from *fust* "wine cask", from Middle French, "club, cask", from Latin *fustis* "club, staff"] — **fus·ti·ly** \-tə-lē\ *adv* — **fus·ti·ness** \-tē-nəs\ *n*

fu·tile \'fyüt-l, 'fyü-,tīl\ *adj* : having no result or effect : useless ⟨a *futile* struggle⟩ **2** : UNIMPORTANT, TRIVIAL ⟨*futile* pleasures⟩ [Latin *futilis,* literally, "that pours out easily"] SYN see VAIN — **fu·tile·ly** \-l-lē, -,tīl-lē\ *adv* — **fu·til·i·ty** \fyü-'til-ət-ē\ *n*

¹fu·ture \'fyü-chər\ *adj* **1 a** : that is to be **b** : existing after death **2** : of, relating to, or constituting a verb tense formed in English with *will* and *shall* and expressive of time yet to come [Latin *futurus* "about to be"]

²future *n* **1 a** : time that is to come **b** : what is going to happen **2** : expectation of advancement or development ⟨a promising *future*⟩ **3** : something (as a com-modity) bought or sold for delivery at a future time — usually used in pl. **4 a** : the future tense **b** : a verb form in the future tense

fu·ture·less \-ləs\ *adj* : having no prospect of future success or accomplishment ⟨a *futureless* job⟩

future perfect *adj* : of, relating to, or constituting a verb tense formed in English with *will have* and *shall have* and expressing completion of an action by a specified time that is yet to come — **future perfect** *n*

fu·tur·ism \'fyü-chə-,riz-əm\ *n* : a movement in art, music, and literature begun in Italy about 1910 and marked especially by an effort to give formal expres-sion to the dynamic energy and movement of mechani-cal processes — **fu·tur·ist** \'fyüch-rəst, -ə-rəst\ *n*

fu·tur·is·tic \,fyü-chə-'ris-tik\ *adj* : of or relating to the future or to futurism — **fu·tur·is·ti·cal·ly** \-ti-kə-lē, -klē\ *adv*

fu·tu·ri·ty \fyü-'tur-ət-ē, -'tyur-, -'chur-\ *n, pl* **-ties 1** : FUTURE 1 **2** : the quality or state of being future **3** *pl* : future events or prospects

fuze, fuzee *variant of* FUSE, FUSEE

fuzz \'fəz\ *n* : fine light particles or fibers (as of down or fluff) [probably back-formation from *fuzzy*]

fuzzy \'fəz-ē\ *adj* **fuzz·i·er; -est 1** : covered with or re-sembling fuzz **2** : not clear : INDISTINCT [perhaps from Low German *fussig* "loose, spongy"] — **fuzz·i·ly** \'fəz-ə-lē\ *adv* — **fuzz·i·ness** \'fəz-ē-nəs\ *n*

-fy \,fī\ *vb suffix* **-fied; -fying 1** : make : form into ⟨dandi*fy*⟩ **2** : invest with the attributes of : make simi-lar to ⟨citi*fy*⟩ [Old French *-fier,* from Latin *-ficare,* from *-ficus* "-fic"]

Gg

g \'jē\ *n, pl* **g's** *or* **gs** \'jēz\ *often cap* **1** : the 7th letter of the English alphabet **2** : the musical tone G **3** : the acceleration that a body experiences at the earth's surface due to gravitational attraction; *also* : a unit of force equal to the force exerted by gravity on a body at rest and used to express the force to which a body is subjected when accelerated ⟨a force of three *G's*⟩ [sense 3 from *g*ravity]

G *trademark* — used to certify that a motion picture is of such a nature that persons of all ages may be al-lowed admission; compare NC-17, PG, PG-13, R

gab \'gab\ *vi* **gabbed; gab·bing** : to talk idly : CHATTER [probably short for *gabble*] — **gab** *n*

gab·ar·dine \'gab-ər-,dēn\ *n* **1** : GABERDINE 1 **2 a** : a firm durable twilled fabric having diagonal ribs **b** : a garment of gabardine [Middle French *gaverdine*]

gab·ble \'gab-əl\ *vb* **gab·bled; gab·bling** \'gab-ling, -ə-ling\ : to talk fast or foolishly : JABBER, BABBLE [proba-bly imitative] — **gabble** *n* — **gab·bler** \'gab-lər, -ə-lər\ *n*

gab·bro \'gab-rō\ *n, pl* **gabbros** : a granular igneous rock containing much magnesium and little quartz [Italian] — **gab·bro·ic** \ga-'brō-ik\ *adj*

gab·by \'gab-ē\ *adj* **gab·bi·er; -est** : TALKATIVE, GARRU-LOUS

gab·er·dine \'gab-ər-,dēn\ *n* **1 a** : a long smock worn chiefly by Jews in medieval times **b** : an English labor-er's smock **2** : GABARDINE 2 [Middle French *gaverdine*]

gab·fest \'gab-,fest\ *n* **1** : an informal gathering for general talk **2** : a long conversation

ga·ble \'gā-bəl\ *n* : the triangular part of an outside wall of a building formed by the sides of the roof slop-ing down from the ridgepole to the eaves; *also* : a sim-ilar triangular structure [Middle French, of Germanic origin] — **ga·bled** \-bəld\ *adj*

gable roof *n* : a roof having two sides sloping from a ridge and forming a gable at each end

¹gad \'gad\ *vi* **gad·ded; gad·ding** : to be on the go with little purpose — usually used with *about* [Middle En-glish *gadden*]

²gad *interj* — used as a mild oath [euphemism for *God*]

gad·about \'gad-ə-,baut\ *n* : a person who flits about in social activity — **gadabout** *adj*

gad·fly \'gad-,flī\ *n* **1** : any of various flies (as a horse-fly or botfly) that bite or harass livestock **2** : a person who annoys or criticizes others in an attempt to pro-voke or stimulate them [Middle English *gad* "spike", from Old Norse *gaddr*]

gad·get \'gaj-ət\ *n* : DEVICE 1b, CONTRIVANCE ⟨a *gadget* for peeling potatoes⟩ [origin unknown] — **gad·ge·teer** \,gaj-ə-'tiər\ *n* — **gad·get·ry** \'gaj-ə-trē\ *n*

gad·o·lin·i·um \,gad-l-'in-ē-əm\ *n* : a magnetic metallic chemical element occurring in several minerals — see ELEMENT table [Johann *Gadolin,* died 1852, Finnish chemist]

gad·wall \'gad-ˌwȯl\ *n, pl* **gadwalls** *or* **gadwall** : a grayish brown duck about the size of the mallard [origin unknown]

Gael \'gāl\ *n* **1** : a Scottish Highlander **2** : a Celtic especially Gaelic-speaking inhabitant of Ireland, Scotland, or the Isle of Man [Scottish Gaelic *Gàidheal* and Irish Gaelic *Gaedheal*]

Gael·ic \'gā-lik\ *adj* **1** : of or relating to the Gaels and especially the Celtic Highlanders of Scotland **2** : of, relating to, or constituting the Goidelic speech of the Celts in Ireland, the Isle of Man, and the Scottish Highlands — **Gaelic** *n*

¹gaff \'gaf\ *n* **1 a** : a spear or spearhead for taking fish or turtles **b** : a handled hook for holding or lifting heavy fish **c** : a metal spur for a gamecock **2** : the spar upon which the head of a fore-and-aft sail is extended **3** : rough treatment : ABUSE [French *gaffe*]

²gaff *vt* : to strike, take, or handle with a gaff

gaffe \'gaf\ *n* : a social blunder [French, "gaff, gaffe"]

gaf·fer \'gaf-ər\ *n* : an old man [probably alteration of *godfather*]

¹gag \'gag\ *vb* **gagged; gag·ging 1 a** : to prevent from speaking or crying out by stopping up the mouth **b** : to prevent from speaking freely **2** : to retch or cause to retch **3** : to make quips [Middle English *gaggen* "to strangle"]

²gag *n* **1 a** : something thrust into the mouth especially to prevent speech or outcry **b** : CLOTURE **c** : a check to free speech **2** : a laugh-provoking remark or act **3** : something (as a story or an action) intended to deceive : HOAX

ga·ga \'gä-ˌgä\ *adj* **1** : CRAZY **2**, FOOLISH **2** : INFATUATED [French, from *gaga* "fool"]

¹gage \'gāj\ *n* **1** : a token of defiance; *esp* : a glove or cap cast on the ground as a pledge of combat **2** : PLEDGE 2a [Middle French, of Germanic origin]

²gage *variant of* GAUGE

gag·man \'gag-ˌman\ *n* **1** : a writer of gags **2** : a comedian who uses gags

gag rule *n* : a rule restricting freedom of debate or expression especially in a legislative body

gag·ster \'gag-stər\ *n* : GAGMAN

gai·ety *or* **gay·ety** \'gā-ət-ē\ *n, pl* **-ties 1** : MERRYMAKING **1 2** : gay spirits or manner **3** : bright showy appearance

gail·lar·dia \gə-'lärd-ē-ə, -'lärd-ə\ *n* : any of a genus of chiefly western American herbs of the sunflower family with showy flower heads [*Gaillard* de Marentonneau, 18th century French botanist]

gai·ly *or* **gay·ly** \'gā-lē\ *adv* : in a gay manner

¹gain \'gān\ *n* **1** : resources or advantage acquired or increased : PROFIT **2** : the obtaining of profit or possessions **3** : an increase in amount, magnitude, or degree [Middle French *gaigne*, from Old French *gaaignier* "to till, earn, gain", of Germanic origin]

²gain *vb* **1 a** : to get possession of : PROCURE **b** : to win in competition or conflict ⟨*gain* a victory⟩ **c** : to get by a natural development or process : ACHIEVE ⟨*gain* strength⟩ **d** : to arrive at ⟨*gained* the river that night⟩ **2** : to win to one's side : PERSUADE **3** : to increase in ⟨*gain* momentum⟩ **4** : to run fast ⟨my watch *gains* a minute a day⟩ **5** : to get advantage : PROFIT ⟨hoped to *gain* from their crime⟩ **6 a** : INCREASE 1 **b** : to improve in health — **gain ground** : to make progress

gain·er \'gā-nər\ *n* **1** : one that gains **2** : a fancy dive in which the diver from a forward position rotates backward and enters the water feetfirst and facing away from the board

gain·ful \'gān-fəl\ *adj* : producing gain : PROFITABLE ⟨*gainful* employment⟩ — **gain·ful·ly** \-fə-lē\ *adv* — **gain·ful·ness** *n*

gain·say \gān-'sā\ *vt* **gain·said** \-'sād, -'sed\; **gain·saying** \-'sā-ing\ **1** : DENY 4, DISPUTE **2** : to speak against : CONTRADICT [Middle English *gainsayen*, from *gain-* "against" + *sayen* "to say"] — **gain·say·er** *n*

gait \'gāt\ *n* : manner of moving on foot ⟨a slow unsteady *gait*⟩; *also* : a particular pattern or style of such movement ⟨the walk, trot, and canter are *gaits* of the horse⟩ [Middle English *gate* "way, path", from Old Norse *gata*] — **gait·ed** \-əd\ *adj*

gai·ter \'gāt-ər\ *n* **1** : a cloth or leather leg covering reaching from the instep to ankle, mid calf, or knee **2 a** : an ankle-high shoe with elastic gores in the sides **b** : an overshoe with fabric upper [French *guêtre*]

ga·la \'gā-lə, 'gal-ə\ *n* : a gay celebration : FESTIVITY [Italian, from Middle French *gale* "festivity, pleasure"] — **gala** *adj*

ga·lac·tic \gə-'lak-tik\ *adj* : of or relating to a galaxy

ga·lac·tose \gə-'lak-ˌtōs\ *n* : a sugar $C_6H_{12}O_6$ less soluble and less sweet than glucose [French, from Greek *galakt-, gala* "milk"]

ga·la·go \gə-'lä-gō, -'läg-ō\ *n, pl* **-gos** : any of several small active leaping African primates with long ears, a long tail, and long hind limbs [perhaps from Wolof (a language of western Africa) *golokh* "monkey"]

galago

Ga·la·tians \gə-'lā-shənz\ *n* — see BIBLE table

ga·lax \'gā-ˌlaks\ *n* : an evergreen herb related to the heaths that has shiny leaves used in decorations [probably from Greek *galaxias* "Milky Way, galaxy"]

gal·axy \'gal-ək-sē\ *n, pl* **-ax·ies 1** *often cap* : MILKY WAY GALAXY **b** : one of billions of systems each including stars, nebulae, clusters of stars, gas, and dust that make up the universe **2** : an assemblage of brilliant or notable persons or things [Late Latin *galaxias*, from Greek, from *galakt-, gala* "milk"] □ ORIGIN The system of stars that includes our sun looks, in the night sky, like a broad band of light. We call this band the *Milky Way*. The idea of the whiteness of the Milky Way being similar to that of milk is much older than the English language, however. *Galaxias,* the Greek word for the Milky Way, was derived from the Greek *gala,* "milk". English *galaxy,* derived from Greek *galaxias,* was not used until the 19th century as a generic term for other star systems as well as the one in which we live.

gale \'gāl\ *n* **1** : a strong current of air; *esp* : a wind of from 13.9 to 24.4 meters per second **2** : an emotional outburst ⟨*gales* of laughter⟩ [origin unknown]

ga·le·na \gə-'lē-nə\ *n* : a bluish gray mineral PbS with metallic luster consisting of sulfide of lead and constituting the principal ore of lead [Latin, "lead ore"]

¹gall \'gȯl\ *n* **1** : BILE 1 **2** : something hard to bear **3** : EFFRONTERY, IMPUDENCE [Old English *gealla*]

²gall *n* **1** : a skin sore (as on a horse's back) caused by chronic irritation **2** : a cause or state of exasperation [Old English *gealla*, from Latin *galla* "gall on a plant"]

³gall *vb* **1 a** : to fray and wear away by friction : CHAFE **b** : to become sore or worn by rubbing **2** : IRRITATE 1, VEX **3** : HARASS ⟨*galled* by enemy fire⟩

⁴gall *n* : a swelling or growth of plant tissue usually caused by fungi or insect parasites [Middle French *galle,* from Latin *galla*]

¹gal·lant \gə-'lant, gə-'länt, 'gal-ənt\ *n* **1** : a fashionable young man **2 a** : LADIES' MAN **b** : SUITOR **3**

²gal·lant \'gal-ənt (*usual in sense 2b*); gə-'lant, gə-'länt (*usual in sense 3*)\ *adj* **1** : showy in dress or bearing : SMART **2** : SPLENDID, STATELY ⟨a *gallant* ship⟩ **b** : SPIRITED, BRAVE **c** : CHIVALROUS 3a, NOBLE **3** : polite and attentive to women [Middle French *galant,* from *galer* "to have a good time", from *gale* "pleasure", of Germanic origin] — **gal·lant·ly** *adv*

gal·lant·ry \'gal-ən-trē\ *n, pl* **-ries 1** *archaic* : gallant appearance **2 a** : an act of marked courtesy **b** : courteous attention to a woman **3** : conspicuous bravery

gall·blad·der \'gȯl-ˌblad-ər\ *n* : a membranous muscular sac in which bile from the liver is stored

gal·le·on \'gal-ē-ən\ *n* : a heavy square-rigged sailing ship of the 15th to early 18th centuries used for war or commerce especially by the Spanish [Spanish *ga-*

galleon

\ə\ abut	\ng\ sing
\ər\ further	\ō\ bone
\a\ mat	\ȯ\ saw
\ā\ take	\ȯi\ coin
\ä\ cot, cart	\th\ thin
\au̇\ out	\th\ this
\ch\ chin	\ü\ food
\e\ pet	\u̇\ foot
\ē\ easy	\y\ yet
\g\ go	\yü\ few
\i\ tip	\yu̇\ cure
\ī\ life	\zh\ vision
\j\ job	

león, from Middle French *galion,* from Old French *galie* "galley"]

gal·lery \'gal-rē, -ə-rē\ *n, pl* **gal·ler·ies** **1 a** : a roofed promenade : COLONNADE **b** : an outdoor balcony **c** *South & Midland* : PORCH, VERANDA **d** : a structure projecting from one or more interior walls of an auditorium to seat additional people; *esp* : the highest such structure in a theater or the people who sit there **e** : a body of spectators at a tennis or golf match **2 a** : a long narrow room, hall, or passage; *esp* : one having windows along one side **b** : a subterranean passageway (as in a mine) **c** : a passage (as in earth or wood) made by an animal and especially an insect **3 a** : a room or building devoted to the exhibition of works of art **b** : an institution or business exhibiting or dealing in works of art **4** : a photographer's studio [Medieval Latin *galeria*] — **gal·ler·ied** \-rēd\ *adj*

gal·ley \'gal-ē\ *n, pl* **galleys** **1** : a large low ship propelled by oars and sails and used in ancient times and in the Middle Ages chiefly in the Mediterranean sea **2** : the kitchen of a ship or airplane **3 a** : an oblong tray with upright sides to hold printer's type that has been set **b** : a proof from type in a galley [Old French *galie,* derived from Middle Greek *galea*]

galley slave *n* **1** : a slave or criminal acting as a rower on a galley **2** : DRUDGE

gall·fly \'gȯl-ˌflī\ *n* : an insect (as a gall wasp) that deposits its eggs in plants and causes galls in which the larvae feed

Gal·lic \'gal-ik\ *adj* : of or relating to Gaul or France [Latin *Gallicus,* from *Gallia* "Gaul"]

gal·li·cism \'gal-ə-ˌsiz-əm\ *n, often cap* : a characteristic French idiom, expression, or trait

gal·li·gas·kins \ˌgal-i-'gas-kənz\ *n pl* **1** : loose wide breeches worn in the 16th and 17th centuries **2** : chiefly dialect : LEGGINGS [probably from Middle French *garguesques,* from Spanish *gregüescos,* from *griego* "Greek"]

gal·li·na·ceous \ˌgal-ə-'nā-shəs\ *adj* : of or relating to an order (Galliformes) of heavy-bodied largely land-dwelling birds including the pheasants, turkeys, grouse, and the common domestic fowl [Latin *gallinaceus* "of domestic fowl", from *gallina* "hen", from *gallus* "cock"]

gall·ing \'gȯ-ling\ *adj* : very irritating : VEXING

gal·li·nip·per \'gal-ə-ˌnip-ər\ *n* : a large American mosquito [origin unknown]

gal·li·nule \'gal-ə-ˌnül, -ˌnyül\ *n* : any of several aquatic birds related to the rails but having unlobed feet and a shield on the front of the head [Latin *gallinula* "pullet", from *gallina* "hen"]

gallinule

gal·li·um \'gal-ē-əm\ *n* : a rare bluish white metallic chemical element that is hard and brittle at low temperatures but melts just above room temperature — see ELEMENT table [Latin *gallus* "cock" (intended as translation of Paul *Lecoq* de Boisbaudran, died 1912, French chemist)]

gal·li·vant \'gal-ə-ˌvant\ *vi* : to travel or roam about for pleasure [perhaps derived from *gallant*]

gal·lon \'gal-ən\ *n* — see MEASURE table [Middle English *galon,* a liquid measure, from Old North French, from Medieval Latin, literally, "pail"]

gal·lon·age \'gal-ə-nij\ *n* : amount in gallons

¹gal·lop \'gal-əp\ *n* **1** : a springing gait of a four-footed animal in which all four feet are off the ground at one time once in each stride; *esp* : a fast natural 3-beat gait of the horse — compare CANTER **2** : a ride or run at a gallop [Middle French *galop*]

²gallop *vb* **1** : to move or ride at a gallop **2** : to run fast **3** : to cause to gallop — **gal·lop·er** *n*

gal·lows \'gal-ōz\ *n, pl* **gallows** *or* **gal·lows·es** : a frame usually of two upright posts and a crosspiece from which criminals are hanged — called also *gallows tree* [Middle English *galwes,* pl. of *galwe,* from Old English *gealga*]

gall·stone \'gȯl-ˌstōn\ *n* : a hard mass formed in the gallbladder or bile passages

gall wasp *n* : a wasp that is a gallfly

ga·loot \gə-'lüt\ *n, slang* : a person who is odd or foolish [origin unknown]

ga·lore \gə-'lōr, -'lȯr\ *adj* : ABUNDANT, PLENTIFUL — used after the word it modifies ⟨bargains *galore*⟩ [Irish Gaelic *go leor* "enough"]

ga·losh \gə-'läsh\ *n* : a high overshoe worn especially in snow and slush [Middle French *galoche,* a kind of heavy-soled shoe]

gal·van·ic \gal-'van-ik\ *adj* **1** : of, relating to, or producing a direct current of electricity ⟨a *galvanic* cell⟩ **2** : having an electric effect : STIMULATING ⟨a *galvanic* personality⟩ [Luigi *Galvani,* died 1798, Italian physician and physicist] — **gal·van·i·cal·ly** \-i-kə-lē, -klē\ *adv*

gal·va·nize \'gal-və-ˌnīz\ *vt* **1 a** : to subject to the action of an electric current **b** : to stimulate or excite by or as if by an electric shock **2** : to coat (as iron) with zinc for protection — **gal·va·ni·za·tion** \ˌgal-və-nə-'zā-shən\ *n*

gal·va·nom·e·ter \ˌgal-və-'näm-ət-ər\ *n* : an instrument for detecting or measuring a small electric current by movements of a magnetic needle or of a coil in a magnetic field — **gal·va·no·met·ric** \ˌgal-və-nō-'me-trik\ *adj*

gal·vano·scope \gal-'van-ə-ˌskōp\ *n* : an instrument for detecting the presence and direction of an electric current by the deflection of a magnetic needle

gam·bit \'gam-bət\ *n* **1** : a chess opening in which a player risks one or more minor pieces to gain an advantage in position **2** : a carefully thought-out move : STRATAGEM [Italian *gambetto,* literally, "act of tripping someone", from *gamba* "leg", from Late Latin *gamba, camba,* from Greek *kampē* "bend"]

¹gam·ble \'gam-bəl\ *vb* **gam·bled; gam·bling** \-bə-ling, -bling\ **1 a** : to play a game for money or other stakes **b** : to bet on an uncertain outcome **2** : to stake something on a doubtful event : BET, WAGER **3** : RISK 1, HAZARD [probably derived from obsolete English *gamen* "to play", from *game*] — **gam·bler** \-blər\ *n*

²gamble *n* : a risky undertaking

gam·boge \gam-'bōj, -'büzh\ *n* : an orange to brown gum resin from southeast Asian trees that is used as a yellow pigment and purgative [derived from *Cambodia*]

gam·bol \'gam-bəl\ *vi* **-boled** *or* **-bolled; -bol·ing** *or* **-bol·ling** \-bə-ling, -bling\ : to skip about in play : FRISK [Middle French *gambade* "spring of a horse, gambol"] — **gambol** *n*

gam·brel roof \'gam-brəl-\ *n* : a roof having a double slope on each side with a lower steeper slope and an upper flatter one [Old North French *gamberel* "stick for suspending slaughtered animals", from *gambe* "leg", from Late Latin *gamba*]

gam·bu·sia \gam-'byü-zhē-ə, -zhə\ *n* : any of several topminnows used to exterminate mosquito larvae in warm fresh waters [American Spanish *gambusino*]

¹game \'gām\ *n* **1 a** : activity engaged in for amusement **b** : FUN 1, SPORT **c** : the equipment for a game **2 a** : a procedure for gaining an end **b** : a line of work ⟨the newspaper *game*⟩ **3 a** (1) : a physical or mental contest (2) : a division of a larger contest (3) : the number of points necessary to win (4) : the manner of playing in a contest **b** : a situation that involves contest, rivalry, or struggle **4 a** (1) : animals pursued or taken in hunting especially for sport or food (2) : the flesh of game animals **b** : an object of ridicule or attack — often used in the phrase *fair game* [Old English *gamen*]

²game *vb* : to play for a stake : GAMBLE

³game *adj* **1** : having a resolute unyielding spirit ⟨*game* to the end⟩ **2** : of, relating to, or being game ⟨*game* laws⟩ ⟨a *game* bird⟩ — **game·ly** *adv* — **game·ness** *n*

⁴game *adj* : LAME ⟨a *game* leg⟩

game·cock \'gām-ˌkäk\ *n* : a male game fowl

game fish *n* : a fish of the trout family; *also* : a fish regularly sought by anglers for sport

game fowl *n* : a domestic fowl of a strain developed for the production of fighting cocks

game·keep·er \'gām-ˌkē-pər\ *n* : a person who has charge of the breeding and protection of game animals or birds on a private preserve

game of chance : a game (as a dice game) in which chance rather than skill determines the outcome

game show *n* : a television program on which contestants compete for prizes in a game (as a quiz)

game·ster \'gām-stər\ *n* : a person who plays games; *esp* : GAMBLER

gam·etan·gi·um \ˌgam-ə-'tan-jē-əm\ *n, pl* **-gia** \-jē-ə\ : a cell or organ in which gametes are developed [*gamete* + Greek *angeion* "vessel"]

ga·mete \gə-'mēt, 'gam-ˌēt\ *n* : a mature germ cell capable of developing into a new individual upon uniting with another such cell [Greek *gametēs* "husband," from *gamein* "to marry," from *gamos* "marriage"] — **ga·met·ic** \gə-'met-ik\ *adj* — **ga·met·i·cal·ly** \-'met-i-kə-lē, -klē\ *adv*

ga·me·to·cyte \gə-'mēt-ə-ˌsīt\ *n* : a cell that divides to produce gametes

ga·me·to·gen·e·sis \gə-ˌmēt-ə-'jen-ə-səs\ *n* : the production of gametes

ga·me·to·phyte \gə-'mēt-ə-ˌfīt\ *n* : the individual or generation of a plant with alternating sexual and asexual generations that produces the gametes from which the asexual sporophyte develops — **ga·me·to·phyt·ic** \-ˌmēt-ə-'fit-ik\ *adj*

gam·in \'gam-ən\ *n* **1** : a boy who hangs out on the streets **2** : URCHIN 2 **3** : GAMINE 2 [French]

ga·mine \ga-'mēn\ *n* **1** : a girl who hangs out on the streets **2** : a girl of typically slight build and elfish charm [French, feminine of *gamin*]

gam·ing \'gā-ming\ *n* : the practice of gambling

gam·ma \'gam-ə\ *n* : the 3d letter of the Greek alphabet — Γ or γ

gamma globulin *n* : any of several proteins of blood plasma that include most antibodies

gamma radiation *n* : a continuous stream of gamma rays

gamma ray *n* : a very penetrating radiation of the same nature as X rays but of shorter wavelength emitted by various radioactive atomic nuclei

gam·mer \'gam-ər\ *n* : an old woman [probably alteration of *godmother*]

gam·ut \'gam-ət\ *n* **1** : the whole series of recognized musical notes **2** : an entire range or series [Medieval Latin *gamma,* lowest note of a medieval musical scale (from Late Latin, 3d letter of the Greek alphabet) + *ut,* lowest note of each group of six notes in the scale]
□ **ORIGIN** In the 11th century, Guido d'Arezzo, a musician and former Benedictine monk, devised a system of musical notation that was later adopted throughout Europe. Guido's system consisted of groups of six notes, which he named *ut, re, mi, fa, sol,* and *la.* Guido called the first line of the bass staff *gamma,* and we can assume that *gamma ut* was the term his followers used for the note falling on this line, that is, the first note of the lowest group of six. This was later contracted to *gamut* and used for the whole scale as well as the lowest note. The term was further generalized to mean the whole range of a voice or instrument. Eventually *gamut* came to be used for an entire range of any sort.

gamy \'gā-mē\ *adj* **gam·i·er; -est 1** : ³GAME, PLUCKY **2** : having the flavor of game especially when slightly tainted ⟨*gamy* meat⟩ — **gam·i·ly** \'gā-mə-lē\ *adv* — **gam·i·ness** \'gā-mē-nəs\ *n*

-g·a·my \g-ə-mē\ *n combining form, pl* **-gamies 1** : marriage ⟨exo*gamy*⟩ **2** : union for propagation or re-production ⟨syn*gamy*⟩ [Greek *-gamia,* from *gamos* "marriage"]

Gan·da \'gän-də\ *n, pl* **Ganda** or **Gandas 1** : a member of a Bantu-speaking people of Uganda **2** : the Bantu language of the Ganda people

¹gan·der \'gan-dər\ *n* : a male goose [Old English *gandra*]

²gander *n, slang* : a usually appraising look [probably from ¹*gander*; from the outstretched neck of a person craning to look at something]

gan·dy dancer \'gan-dē-\ *n* : a laborer in a railroad section gang [perhaps from the *Gandy* Manufacturing Company, Chicago, Illinois, toolmakers]

¹gang \'gang\ *n* **1** : a group of persons working or going about together ⟨a *gang* of laborers⟩ ⟨a *gang* of children playing⟩ **2** : a group of persons associated together for unlawful or antisocial purposes ⟨a *gang* of thieves⟩ **3** : two or more similar implements or devices arranged to work together ⟨a *gang* of saws⟩ [Middle English, "journey, set of things or persons", from Old English, "act of going, journey"]

²gang *vi* : to form into or move or act as a gang

³gang *vi, Scottish* : GO, WALK [Old English *gangan*]

gang·land \'gang-ˌland\ *n* : the world of organized crime

gan·gling \'gang-gling, -glən\ *adj* : LANKY, SPINDLY [perhaps from Scottish *gangrel* "vagrant, lanky person"]

gan·gli·on \'gang-glē-ən\ *n, pl* **-glia** \-glē-ə\ *also* **-glions** : a mass of neural tissue lying outside the brain or spinal cord and containing nerve cells; *also* : NUCLEUS c [Greek] — **gan·gli·on·at·ed** \'gang-glē-ə-ˌnāt-əd\ *adj* — **gan·gli·on·ic** \ˌgang-glē-'än-ik\ *adj*

gan·gly \'gang-glē\ *adj* **gan·gli·er; -est** : LANKY, GANGLING

gang·plank \'gang-ˌplangk\ *n* : a movable bridge used in boarding or leaving a ship at a pier [English dialect *gang* "passage, journey"]

gang·plow \-ˌplau̇\ *n* : a plow designed to turn two or more furrows at one time

¹gan·grene \'gang-ˌgrēn, gang-', 'gan-ˌ, gan-'\ *n* : local death of soft tissues due to loss of blood supply [Latin *gangraena,* from Greek *gangraina*] — **gan·gre·nous** \'gang-grə-nəs\ *adj*

²gangrene *vb* : to make or become gangrenous

gang·ster \'gang-stər\ *n* : a member of a gang of criminals — **gang·ster·ism** \-stə-ˌriz-əm\ *n*

gangue \'gang\ *n* : the rock or earth in which valuable metals or minerals occur [French, from German *gang* "vein of metal"]

gang up *vi* : to combine for a specific and often hostile purpose — often used with *on*

gang·way \'gang-ˌwā\ *n* **1** : a passage into, through, or out of an enclosed place **2** : GANGPLANK **3** : a clear passage through a crowd — often used as an interjection

gan·net \'gan-ət\ *n, pl* **gannets** *also* **gannet** : any of several large fish-eating seabirds that remain at sea for long periods and breed chiefly on offshore islands [Old English *ganot*]

gan·oid \'gan-ˌȯid\ *adj* : of or relating to a group (Ganoidei) of teleost fishes with usually hard enameled scales [derived from Greek *ganos* "brightness"] — **ganoid** *n*

gant·let \'gȯnt-lət, 'gänt-\ *variant of* GAUNTLET

gan·try \'gan-trē\ *n, pl* **gantries 1** : a platform made to carry a traveling crane and supported by towers or side frames running on parallel tracks; *also* : a movable structure with platforms at different levels used for erecting and servicing rockets before launching **2** : a structure spanning several railroad tracks and displaying signals for each [perhaps from Old North French *gantier* "frame for supporting barrels", from Latin *cantherius* "trellis"]

gaol \'jāl\, **gaol·er** *chiefly British variant of* JAIL, JAILER

gamecock

gantry 2

\ə\ abut		\ng\ sing	
\ər\ further		\ō\ bone	
\a\ mat		\ȯ\ saw	
\ā\ take		\ȯi\ coin	
\ä\ cot, cart		\th\ thin	
\au̇\ out		\th\ this	
\ch\ chin		\ü\ food	
\e\ pet		\u̇\ foot	
\ē\ easy		\y\ yet	
\g\ go		\yü\ few	
\i\ tip		\yu̇\ cure	
\ī\ life		\zh\ vision	
\j\ job			

gap \'gap\ *n* **1** : an opening made by a break or a parting : BREACH, CLEFT **2** : a mountain pass **3** : a break in continuity : a blank space ⟨a *gap* where the tooth had been⟩ **4** : a wide difference (as in amount, character, or attitude) [Old Norse, "chasm, hole"] — **gap** *vb*

¹gape \'gāp\ *vi* **1 a** : to open the mouth wide **b** : to open or part widely **2** : to stare openmouthed **3** : YAWN 2 [Old Norse *gapa*] — **gap·er** *n* — **gap·ing·ly** *adv*

²gape *n* **1** : an act of gaping **2** : the line along which the mandibles of a bird close **3** *pl* : a disease of young birds in which gapeworms invade and irritate the trachea

gape·worm \'gāp-,wərm\ *n* : a nematode worm that causes gapes in birds

gar \'gär\ *n* : any of various fishes with a long body like that of a pike and long narrow jaws; *esp* : any of several predatory North American freshwater ganoid fishes with edible but tough flesh [short for *garfish*]

¹ga·rage \gə-'räzh, -'räj\ *n* : a building where automobiles are housed or repaired [French] — **ga·rage·man** \-,man\ *n*

²garage *vt* : to keep or put in a garage

garage sale *n* : a sale of used household or personal articles held in the seller's own yard

¹garb \'gärb\ *n* **1** : a style of clothing **2** : APPAREL, CLOTHING [Middle French *garbe* "grace", from Italian *garbo*]

²garb *vt* : CLOTHE 1a, ARRAY

gar·bage \'gär-bij\ *n* : unwanted or useless material; *esp* : food waste [Middle English, "animal entrails"]

gar·ble \'gär-bəl\ *vt* **gar·bled; gar·bling** \-bə-ling, -bling\ : to distort the meaning or sound of ⟨*garble* a story⟩ ⟨*garble* words⟩ [Middle English *garbelen* "to cull", from Italian *garbellare* "to sift", from Arabic *ghirbāl* "sieve", from Late Latin *cribellum*] — **gar·bler** \-bə-lər, -blər\ *n*

gar·çon \gär-'sōⁿ\ *n, pl* **garçons** \-'sōⁿ, -'sōⁿz\ : WAITER 1 [French, "boy, servant"]

¹gar·den \'gärd-n\ *n* **1** : a plot of ground where herbs, fruits, flowers, or vegetables are grown **2** : a public recreation area or park; *esp* : one for the exhibition of plants or animals ⟨a botanical *garden*⟩ [Old North French *gardin*, of Germanic origin]

²garden *vb* **gar·dened; gar·den·ing** \'gärd-ning, -n-ing\ **1** : to lay out or work in a garden **2** : to make into a garden — **gar·den·er** \'gärd-nər, -n-ər\ *n*

³garden *adj* **1** : of, relating to, or frequenting gardens **2** : of a kind grown under cultivation especially in the open **3** : ORDINARY, COMMONPLACE

garden heliotrope *n* : a tall Old World valerian widely grown for its fragrant tiny flowers and for its roots which yield the drug valerian

gar·de·nia \gär-'dē-nyə\ *n* : any of various Old World tropical trees and shrubs of the madder family with leathery leaves and fragrant white or yellow flowers; *also* : one of the flowers [Alexander *Garden*, died 1791, Scottish naturalist]

gar·fish \'gär-,fish\ *n* : GAR [Middle English *garfysshe*]

gar·gan·tu·an \gär-'ganch-wən, -ə-wən\ *adj, often cap* : of tremendous size or volume : GIGANTIC [*Gargantua*, gigantic king in the novel *Gargantua* by Rabelais]

¹gar·gle \'gär-gəl\ *vb* **gar·gled; gar·gling** \-gə-ling, -gling\ : to rinse the throat with a liquid kept in motion by air forced through it from the lungs [Middle French *gargouiller*]

²gargle *n* **1** : a liquid used in gargling **2** : a gargling sound

gar·goyle \'gär-,gȯil\ *n* : a spout in the form of a grotesque human or animal figure projecting from a roof gutter to throw rainwater away from a building [Middle French *gargouille*] — **gar·goyled** \-,gȯild\ *adj*

gar·ish \'gaər-ish, 'geər-\ *adj* **1 a** : excessively vivid : FLASHY ⟨*garish* colors⟩ **b** : offensively bright : GLARING

gargoyle

⟨*garish* lighting⟩ **2** : tastelessly showy ⟨a *garish* display of wealth⟩ [origin unknown] SYN see GAUDY — **gar·ish·ly** *adv* — **gar·ish·ness** *n*

¹gar·land \'gär-lənd\ *n* : a wreath or rope of leaves or flowers [Middle French *garlande*]

²garland *vt* : to form into or deck with a garland

gar·lic \'gär-lik\ *n* : a European bulbous herb of the lily family widely grown for its pungent compound bulbs used in cooking; *also* : one of the bulbs [Old English *gārlēac*, from *gār* "spear" + *lēac* "leek"] — **gar·licky** \-li-kē\ *adj*

¹gar·ment \'gär-mənt\ *n* : an article of clothing [Middle French *garnement*, from Old French *garnir* "to equip"]

²garment *vt* : to clothe with or as if with a garment

¹gar·ner \'gär-nər\ *n* : a bin or building for storing grain [Old French *grenier*, from Latin *granarium*, from *granum* "grain"]

²garner *vt* **1** : to gather into or as if into a granary **2 a** : to acquire by effort : EARN ⟨*garnered* notoriety with displays of temper⟩ **b** : ACCUMULATE, COLLECT ⟨*garnered* many souvenirs on their travels⟩

gar·net \'gär-nət\ *n* **1** : a brittle and more or less transparent usually red silicate mineral that occurs mainly in crystals and is used as a semiprecious stone and as an abrasive **2** : a deep red color [Middle French *grenat*, from *grenat*, adj., "red like a pomegranate", from *pomme grenate* "pomegranate"]

garnet paper *n* : a paper that has crushed garnet glued on one side and is used for smoothing and polishing

¹gar·nish \'gär-nish\ *vt* **1** : DECORATE 1, EMBELLISH **2** : to add decorative or savory touches to (food) **3** : GARNISHEE [Middle French *garniss-*, stem of *garnir* "to warn, equip, garnish", of Germanic origin]

²garnish *n* **1** : ORNAMENT 1, EMBELLISHMENT **2** : a savory and usually decorative accompaniment to food

gar·nish·ee \,gär-nə-'shē\ *vt* **-eed; -ee·ing** : to take (as a debtor's wages) by legal authority

gar·nish·ment \'gär-nish-mənt\ *n* **1** : GARNISH 2 : a legal warning to a party holding property of a debtor to give it to a creditor; *also* : the attachment of such property (as a bank account or pending wages) to satisfy a creditor

gar·ni·ture \'gär-ni-chər, -nə-,chür\ *n* : a decorative accessory : EMBELLISHMENT [Middle French, "equipment", from Old French *garnesture*, from *garnir* "to equip, garnish"]

gar·ret \'gar-ət\ *n* : a room or unfinished part of a house just under the roof [Middle French *garite* "watchtower"]

¹gar·ri·son \'gar-ə-sən\ *n* **1** : a military post; *esp* : a permanent military installation **2** : the troops stationed at a garrison [Old French *garison* "protection", from *garir* "to protect", of Germanic origin]

²garrison *vt* **1** : to furnish (as a fort, town, or region) with troops or military installations for defense **2** : to assign as a garrison

garrison house *n* **1** : a house fortified against Indian attack **2** : a house having the second story overhanging the first in the front

¹gar·rote *or* **ga·rotte** \gə-'rät, -'rōt; 'gar-ət\ *n* **1 a** : a method of execution by strangling **b** : the apparatus used **2** : an implement (as a wire with a handle at each end) for strangling [Spanish *garrote*]

²garrote *or* **garotte** *vt* : to strangle with or as if with a garrote — **gar·rot·er** *n*

gar·ru·lous \'gar-ə-ləs\ *adj* : very talkative especially about trifles : WORDY [Latin *garrulus*, from *garrire* "to chatter"] SYN see TALKATIVE — **gar·ru·li·ty** \gə-'rü-lət-ē\ *n* — **gar·ru·lous·ly** \'gar-ə-ləs-lē\ *adv* — **gar·ru·lous·ness** *n*

¹gar·ter \'gärt-ər\ *n* : a band or strap worn to hold up a stocking or sock [Old North French *gartier*, from *garet* "bend of the knee", of Celtic origin]

²garter *vt* : to support with or as if with a garter

garter snake

garter snake *n* : any of numerous harmless viviparous American snakes with stripes along the back

¹gas \'gas\ *n, pl* **gas·es** *also* **gas·ses** **1** : a fluid (as hydrogen or air) that has neither independent shape nor volume but tends to expand indefinitely **2 a** : a gas or gaseous mixture used as a fuel or as an anesthetic **b** : a gaseous, liquid, or solid substance (as tear gas or mustard gas) that can be used to produce a poisonous, asphyxiating, or irritant atmosphere **3** *slang* : empty talk **4** : GASOLINE [New Latin, alteration of Latin *chaos* "space, chaos"]

²gas *vb* **gassed; gas·sing** **1 a** : to treat chemically with gas **b** : to poison with gas **2** : to supply with gas or especially gasoline (*gas* up the automobile) **3** *slang* : to talk idly

gas chamber *n* : a room in which people are executed by poison gas

gas·con \'gas-kən\ *n* **1** *cap* : a native of Gascony **2** : a boastful swaggering person — **Gascon** *adj*

gas·con·ade \,gas-kə-'nād\ *n* : arrogant boastful talk [French *gasconnade*, from *gasconner* "to boast", from *gascon* "gascon, boaster"] — **gasconade** *vi*

gas·eous \'gas-ē-əs, 'gash-əs\ *adj* **1** : having the form of or being gas; *also* : of or relating to gas **2** : lacking substance or solidity

gas fitter *n* : a worker who installs or repairs gas pipes and appliances

gas gangrene *n* : progressive gangrene marked by gas in the dead and dying tissue and caused by toxin-producing bacteria

gas–guz·zler \'gas-'gəz-lər, -'gəz-ə-\ *n* : a usually large automobile that gets relatively poor mileage — **gas–guz·zling** \-ling\ *adj*

gash \'gash\ *vb* : to make a long deep cut in : CUT [Old North French *garser,* derived from Greek *charassein* "to scratch, engrave"] — **gash** *n*

gas·hold·er \'gas-,hōl-dər\ *n* : a large cylindrical tank for storing fuel gas under pressure

gas·ify \'gas-ə-,fī\ *vb* **-fied; -fy·ing** **1** : to convert into gas **2** : to become gaseous — **gas·ifi·ca·tion** \,gas-ə-fə-'kā-shən\ *n*

gas·ket \'gas-kət\ *n* **1** : a line or band used to lash a furled sail **2** : material (as asbestos, rubber, or metal) used to make a joint leakproof [probably from French *garcette*]

gas·light \'gas-,līt\ *n* **1** : light made by burning illuminating gas **2 a** : a gas flame **b** : a gas lighting fixture — **gas·light·ing** \-ing\ *n* — **gas·lit** \-,lit\ *adj*

gas mask *n* : a mask connected to a chemical air filter and used to protect the face and lungs against harmful gases

gas·o·gene \'gas-ə-,jēn\ *n* **1** : an apparatus carried by a vehicle to produce gas for fuel by partial burning of charcoal or wood **2** : a portable apparatus for carbonating liquids [French *gazogène,* from *gaz* "gas" + *-o-* + *-gène* "-gen"]

gas·o·hol \'gas-ə-,hȯl\ *n* : a fuel consisting of 10 percent ethyl alcohol and 90 percent gasoline [blend of *gasoline* and *alcohol*]

gas·o·line \'gas-ə-,lēn, ,gas-ə-'\ *n* : a flammable liquid that evaporates easily, consists of a mixture of hydrocarbons produced by blending products from natural gas and petroleum, and is used especially as a motor fuel [*gas* + *-ol* + *-ine*]

gasp \'gasp\ *vb* **1** : to draw in a breath sharply with shock or other emotion **2** : to breathe laboriously : PANT **3** : to utter in a gasping manner [Middle English *gaspen*] — **gasp** *n*

gas station *n* : SERVICE STATION

gas·sy \'gas-ē\ *adj* **gas·si·er; -est** **1** : full of or containing gas **2** : having the characteristics of gas **3** : FLATULENT 1a — **gas·si·ness** *n*

gastr- *or* **gastro-** *also* **gastri-** **1** : belly : stomach (*gastr*itis) **2** : gastric and (*gastro*intestinal) [Greek *gastr-, gastēr*]

gas·tral \'gas-trəl\ *adj* : of, relating to, or serving as a stomach or digestive tract (the *gastral* cavity of a sponge)

gas·tric \'gas-trik\ *adj* : of, relating to, or located near the stomach

gastric gland *n* : a gland secreting gastric juice

gastric juice *n* : a watery acid digestive fluid secreted by glands in the walls of the stomach

gas·trin \'gas-trən\ *n* : a hormone that induces secretion of gastric juice

gas·tri·tis \ga-'strīt-əs\ *n* : inflammation of the stomach and especially of its mucous membrane

gas·troc·ne·mi·us \,gas-träk-'nē-mē-əs, -trək-\ *n* : the largest muscle of the calf of the leg [Greek *gastroknēmē* "calf of the leg", from *gastēr* "belly" + *knēmē* "shank"]

gas·tro·in·tes·ti·nal \,gas-trō-in-'tes-tən-l, -'tes-nəl\ *adj* : of, relating to, or including both stomach and intestine

gas·tron·o·my \ga-'strän-ə-mē\ *n* : the art of appreciating fine food [French *gastronomie,* from Greek *gastronomia,* from *gastēr* "belly" + *nomos* "law"] — **gas·tro·nom·ic** \,gas-trə-'näm-ik\ *adj* — **gas·tro·nom·i·cal** \-'näm-i-kəl\ *adj*

gas·tro·pod \'gas-trə-,päd\ *n* : any of a large class (Gastropoda) of mollusks (as snails) having a muscular ventral foot and usually a distinct head bearing sensory organs — **gastropod** *adj*

gas·tro·trich \'gas-trə-,trik\ *n* : any of a small group (Gastrotricha) of minute freshwater many-celled animals that resemble infusorians [derived from Greek *gastēr* "belly" + *trich-, thrix* "hair"]

gas·tro·vas·cu·lar \,gas-trō-'vas-kyə-lər\ *adj* : functioning in both digestion and circulation (the *gastrovascular* cavity of a starfish)

gas·tru·la \'gas-trə-lə\ *n, pl* **-las** *or* **-lae** \-,lē, -,lī\ : an early embryo typically consisting of a double cup-shaped layer of cells produced by a folding in of the wall of the blastula [New Latin, from *gastr-*] — **gas·tru·lar** \-lər\ *adj*

gas·tru·late \-,lāt\ *vi* : to become or form a gastrula — **gas·tru·la·tion** \,gas-trə-'lā-shən\ *n*

gas turbine *n* : an internal-combustion engine in which expanding gases from the combustion chamber drive the blades of a turbine

gas·works \'gas-,wərks\ *n pl* : a plant for manufacturing gas

¹gat \gat, 'gat\ *archaic past of* GET

²gat \'gat\ *n, slang* : PISTOL [short for *Gatling gun*]

gate \'gāt\ *n* **1** : an opening in a wall or fence **2** : a city or castle entrance often with towers or other defensive structures **3** : the frame or door that closes a gate **4** : a means of entrance or exit **5** : a door, valve, or other device for controlling the passage especially of fluid **6** : the total admission receipts or the number of spectators at a sports event **7** *slang* : DISMISSAL (got the *gate* for loafing) [Old English *geat*]

gate–crash·er \'gāt-,krash-ər\ *n* : one who enters without paying admission or attends without invitation — **gate–crash·ing** \-ing\ *n*

gate–leg table \'gāt-'leg-\ *n* : a table with drop leaves supported by movable paired legs

gate–post \'gāt-,pōst\ *n* : the post to which a gate is hung or the one against which it closes

gate·way \-,wā\ *n* **1** : an opening for a gate in a wall or fence **2** : a passage into or out of a place or state (Gibraltar is the *gateway* to the Mediterranean) (knowledge is the *gateway* to wisdom)

¹gath·er \'gath-ər, 'geth-\ *vb* **gath·ered; gath·er·ing** \'gath-ring, 'geth-, -ə-ring\ **1** : to come together in a body **2** : to bring together : COLLECT (*gather* a crowd) **3 a** : PICK 2b, HARVEST (*gather* flowers) **b** : to pick up little by little (*gather* souvenirs) **c** : to accumulate and place in order or readiness (*gathered* up their tools) **4 a** : GROW, INCREASE (the storm *gathered* in intensity as it advanced) **b** : to swell and fill with pus **5 a** : to summon up ⟨*gather* courage to dive⟩ **b** : to prepare (as oneself) by mustering strength **c** : to gain by gradual increase ⟨*gather* speed⟩ **6** : GUESS 1, INFER **7 a** : to draw about or close to something ⟨*gather* a cloak about oneself⟩ **b** : to pull (fabric) along a line of stitching into puckers [Old English *gaderian*] □ SYN COLLECT, ASSEMBLE, CONGREGATE: GATHER is the general term for bringing or coming together from a spread-out or scattered state ⟨a crowd *gathered* at the scene of the accident⟩ ⟨*gather* all the leaves into one pile⟩ COLLECT often implies careful selection or orderly arrangement ⟨*collect* rare coins⟩ ASSEMBLE implies an ordered gathering for a definite purpose often into a unified whole ⟨*assembled* a team of experts for an antarctic expedition⟩ CONGREGATE implies a spontaneous flocking together into a crowd or huddle ⟨people *congregating* on street corners⟩

²**gather** *n* : a drawing together; *esp* : a puckering in cloth made by gathering

gath·er·ing *n* **1 a** : the action or an instance of gathering **b** : ASSEMBLY 1, MEETING **c** : a pus-filled swelling (as an abscess) **2** : the collecting of food and raw materials from the wild **3** : something that is gathered: as **a** : COLLECTION 3 **b** : COMPILATION 2 **c** : a gather in cloth

Gat·ling gun \'gat-liŋ-\ *n* : an early machine gun with a revolving cluster of barrels fired once each per revolution [Richard J. *Gatling,* died 1903, American inventor]

gauche \'gōsh\ *adj* : lacking social experience or grace : CRUDE [French, literally, "left"] SYN see AWKWARD — **gauche·ness** *n*

gau·che·rie \ˌgōsh-'rē, -ə-'rē\ *n* : a tactless or awkward action

gau·cho \'gaù-chō\ *n, pl* **gauchos** : a cowboy of the South American pampas [American Spanish]

gaud \'gȯd, 'gäd\ *n* : a showy ornament or trinket [Middle English *gaude*]

gaudy \-ē\ *adj* **gaud·i·er; -est** : showily or tastelessly ornamented — **gaud·i·ly** \-l-ē\ *adv* — **gaud·i·ness** \-ē-nəs\ *n* □ SYN GARISH, FLASHY, TAWDRY: GAUDY implies a tasteless use of overly bright colors or lavish ornamentation; GARISH stresses an unpleasant brightness; FLASHY applies to what is momentarily dazzling but soon revealed to be shallow and vulgar; TAWDRY implies both gaudiness and cheapness of quality.

¹**gauge** *or* **gage** \'gāj\ *n* **1 a** : measurement according to some standard or system **b** : SIZE 1, DIMENSIONS **2** : an instrument for measuring, testing, or registering ⟨a steam *gauge*⟩ **3** : the distance between the rails of a railroad **4** : the size of a shotgun expressed as the number of lead balls of the same size as the interior diameter of the barrel required to make a pound ⟨a 12-*gauge* shotgun⟩ **5** : the thickness of sheet metal or the diameter of wire or a screw **6** : the fineness of a knitted fabric in loops per 1½ inch (3.81 centimeters) [Old North French] SYN see STANDARD

²**gauge** *or* **gage** *vt* **1 a** : to measure exactly the size, dimensions, or other measurable quantity of **b** : to determine the capacity or contents of **2** : JUDGE 5, ESTIMATE ⟨*gauge* the response of the audience⟩ — **gauge·able** \'gā-jə-bəl\ *adj* — **gaug·er** *n*

Gaul \'gȯl\ *n* **1** : a Celt of ancient Gaul **2** : FRENCHMAN

¹**Gaul·ish** \'gȯ-lish\ *adj* : of or relating to the ancient Gauls or their language or land

²**Gaulish** *n* : the Celtic language of the ancient Gauls

gaunt \'gȯnt, 'gänt\ *adj* **1** : excessively thin and angular often as a result of suffering or weariness **2** : grim and forbidding : DESOLATE [Middle English] SYN see LANK — **gaunt·ly** *adv* — **gaunt·ness** *n*

¹**gaunt·let** \'gȯnt-lət, 'gänt-\ *n* **1** : a protective glove worn with medieval armor **2** : a protective glove used in industry **3** : a dress glove extending above the wrist

[Middle French *gantelet,* from *gant* "glove", of Germanic origin — **gaunt·let·ed** \-lət-əd\ *adj*

²**gaunt·let** *or* **gant·let** \'gȯnt-lət, 'gänt-\ *n* **1** : a double row of people armed with clubs who strike at a person forced to run between them **2** : CROSS FIRE 1; *also* : ORDEAL 2 [by folk etymology from earlier *gantelope,* from Swedish *gatlopp*]

gaur \'gaùr\ *n* : an East Indian wild ox [Hindi, from Sanskrit *gaura*]

gauss \'gaùs\ *n, pl* **gauss** *also* **gauss·es** : a cgs unit of magnetic induction that is equal to 1×10^{-4} tesla [Karl F. *Gauss*]

gauze \'gȯz\ *n* **1** : a thin often transparent fabric **2** : a loosely woven cotton surgical dressing **3** : a woven fabric of metal or plastic filaments [Middle French *gaze*] — **gauz·i·ness** \'gȯ-zē-nəs\ *n* — **gauzy** \'gȯ-zē\ *adj*

gave *past of* GIVE

gav·el \'gav-əl\ *n* : the mallet of a presiding officer or auctioneer [origin unknown]

ga·votte \gə-'vät\ *n* : a lively dance in $\frac{4}{4}$ time of French peasant origin [French] — **gavotte** *vi*

¹**gawk** \'gȯk\ *n* : a clumsy stupid person : LOUT [probably from English dialect *gawk* "left-handed"]

²**gawk** *vi* : to gape or stare stupidly [perhaps from obsolete *gaw* "to stare"]

gawky \'gȯ-kē\ *adj* **gawk·i·er; -est** : CLUMSY 1a, AWKWARD ⟨a tall *gawky* youth⟩ — **gawk·i·ly** \-kə-lē\ *adv* — **gawk·i·ness** \-kē-nəs\ *n*

gay \'gā\ *adj* **1** : happily excited : MERRY **2 a** : BRIGHT ⟨a *gay* sunny meadow⟩ **b** : brilliant in color **3** : given to social pleasures; *also* : LICENTIOUS **4** : HOMOSEXUAL [Middle French *gai*] — **gay·ness** *n*

gay·e·ty *variant of* GAIETY

gay·ly *variant of* GAILY

gaze \'gāz\ *vi* : to fix the eyes in a steady intent look [Middle English *gazen*] — **gaze** *n* — **gaz·er** *n*

ga·ze·bo \gə-'zā-bō, -'zē-\ *n, pl* **-bos** : a freestanding roofed structure usually open on the sides [perhaps from *gaze* + Latin *-ebo* (as in *videbo* "I shall see")]

gaze·hound \'gāz-ˌhaùnd\ *n* : a dog that hunts chiefly by sight; *esp* : GREYHOUND

ga·zelle \gə-'zel\ *n, pl* **gazelles** *also* **gazelle** : any of numerous small graceful swift antelopes [French, from Arabic *ghazāl*]

¹**ga·zette** \gə-'zet\ *n* **1** : NEWSPAPER **2** : an official journal [French, from Italian *gazetta*]

²**gazette** *vt, chiefly British* : to announce or publish in a gazette

gaz·et·teer \ˌgaz-ə-'tiər\ *n* : a geographical dictionary [from *The Gazetteer's: or, Newsman's Interpreter* (1693), a geographical index, from earlier *gazetteer* "journalist"]

G clef *n* : TREBLE CLEF

ge- *or* **geo-** *combining form* **1** : earth : ground : soil ⟨*geo*centric⟩ **2** : geographical : geography and ⟨*geo*politics⟩ [Greek *gē-, geo-,* from *gē* "earth"]

¹**gear** \'giər\ *n* **1** : CLOTHING, GARMENTS **2** : EQUIPMENT, PARAPHERNALIA ⟨camping *gear*⟩ ⟨electronic *gear*⟩ **3** : the rigging of a ship or boat **4 a** (1) : a mechanism that performs a specific function in a complete machine ⟨steering *gear*⟩ (2) : a toothed wheel : COGWHEEL (3) : working relation or adjustment ⟨in *gear*⟩ **b** : one of two or more adjustments of a motor-vehicle transmission that determine the direction of travel and the relative speed between the engine and the motion of the vehicle [probably from Old Norse *gervi*] — **gearless** \-ləs\ *adj*

²**gear** *vb* **1 a** : to provide with gearing **b** : to connect by gearing **c** : to put into gear **2 a** : to make ready for effective operation ⟨*gear* up for a new season⟩ **b** : to adjust or become adjusted so as to match or satisfy something ⟨*geared* to the needs of the blind⟩ **3** : to be in or come into gear

gear·box \'giər-ˌbäks\ *n* : TRANSMISSION

gear·ing *n* **1** : the act or process of providing or fitting with gears **2** : the parts by which motion is transmitted from one portion of machinery to another; *esp* : a train of gear wheels

gear·shift \\'giər-,shift\\ *n* : a mechanism by which the transmission gears in a power-transmission system are engaged and disengaged

gear wheel *n* : a toothed wheel that gears with another piece of a mechanism; *esp* : COGWHEEL

Geat \\'gēt, 'yaət\\ *n* : a member of a Scandinavian people of southern Sweden subjugated by the Swedes in the 6th century [Old English *Gēat*] — **Geat·ish** \\-ish\\ *adj*

gecko \\'gek-ō\\ *n, pl* **geck·os** *or* **geck·oes** : any of numerous small harmless chiefly tropical and nocturnal insect-eating lizards [Malay *ge'kok*]

¹gee \\'jē\\ *imperative verb* — used as a direction to turn to the right or move ahead; compare ⁴HAW [origin unknown]

²gee *interj* — used to express surprise or enthusiasm [euphemism for *Jesus*]

geese *pl of* GOOSE

gee whiz \\jē-'hwiz, 'jē-, -'wiz\\ *interj* : ²GEE

gee·zer \\'gē-zər\\ *n* : FELLOW 4a, GUY [probably from Scottish *guiser* "one in disguise"]

Ge·hen·na \\gi-'hen-ə\\ *n* **1** : HELL 2 **2** : a place or state of misery [Late Latin, from Greek *Geenna*, from Hebrew *Gê' Hinnōm*, literally, "valley of Hinnom"]

Gei·ger counter \\'gī-gər-\\ *or* **Geiger–Mül·ler counter** \\-'myül-ər-, -'mil-, -'məl-\\ *n* : an electronic instrument for detecting the presence of cosmic rays or radioactive substances [Hans *Geiger,* died 1945, German physicist, and W. Müller, 20th century German physicist]

gei·sha \\'gā-shə, 'gē-\\ *n, pl* **geisha** *or* **geishas** : a Japanese girl who is trained to entertain men usually with music, dancing, or conversation [Japanese, from *gei* "art" + *-sha* "person"]

¹gel \\'jel\\ *n* : a solid jellylike colloid (as gelatin dessert) [*gelatin*]

²gel *vi* **gelled; gel·ling** : to change into or take on the form of a gel — **gel·able** \\'jel-ə-bəl\\ *adj*

gel·ate \\'jel-,āt\\ *vi* : GEL — **ge·la·tion** \\ji-'lā-shən\\ *n*

gel·a·tin *also* **gel·a·tine** \\'jel-ət-n\\ *n* **1** : gummy or sticky material obtained from animal tissues by boiling; *esp* : a colloidal protein used as a food, in photography, and in medicine **2 a** : any of various substances resembling gelatin **b** : an edible jelly formed with gelatin **c** : a thin colored transparent sheet used to color a stage light [French *gélatine*, from Italian *gelatina*, from *gelare* "to freeze", from Latin]

ge·lat·i·nous \\jə-'lat-nəs, -n-əs\\ *adj* **1** : resembling gelatin or jelly ⟨a *gelatinous* precipitate⟩ **2** : of, relating to, or containing gelatin — **ge·lat·i·nous·ly** *adv* — **ge·lat·i·nous·ness** *n*

geld \\'geld\\ *vt* : CASTRATE; *also* : SPAY [Old Norse *gelda*]

geld·ing \\'gel-ding\\ *n* : a castrated animal; *esp* : a castrated male horse

¹gem \\'jem\\ *n* **1 a** : JEWEL 3 **b** : a precious or sometimes semiprecious stone cut and polished for ornament **2** : something usually small or brief that is prized for great beauty or perfection [Middle French *gemme*, from Latin *gemma* "bud, gem"]

²gem *vt* **gemmed; gem·ming** : to adorn with or as if with gems

Ge·ma·ra \\gə-'mär-ə, -'mor-\\ *n* : a commentary on the Mishnah forming the second part of the Talmud [Aramaic *gĕmārā* "completion"]

gem·i·nate \\'jem-ə-,nāt\\ *vb* : DOUBLE 1a [Latin *geminare*, from *geminus* "twin"] — **gem·i·na·tion** \\,jem-ə-'nā-shən\\ *n*

Gem·i·ni \\'jem-ə-nē, -,nī\\ *n* **1** : the 3d zodiacal constellation pictorially represented as the twins Castor and Pollux sitting together and located on the opposite side of the Milky Way from Taurus and Orion **2** : the 3d sign of the zodiac; *also* : one born under this sign [Latin, literally, "the twins" (Castor and Pollux)]

gem·ma \\'jem-ə\\ *n, pl* **gem·mae** \\'jem-,ē\\ : BUD; *also* : a many-celled asexual reproductive body that becomes detached from a parent plant [Latin] — **gem·ma·tion** \\je-'mā-shən\\ *n*

gem·ol·o·gy *or* **gem·mol·o·gy** \\je-'mäl-ə-jē\\ *n* : the science of gems — **gem·olog·i·cal** *or* **gem·mo·log·i·cal** \\,jem-ə-'läj-i-kəl\\ *adj*

gem·mule \\'jem-yül\\ *n* : a small bud; *esp* : an internal reproductive bud (as of a sponge) [French, from Latin *gemmula*, from *gemma* "bud"]

gems·bok \\'gemz-,bäk\\ *n, pl* **gemsbok** *also* **gemsboks** : a large oryx formerly abundant in southern Africa [Afrikaans, literally, "male chamois", from German *gemsbock*, from *gems* "chamois" + *bock* "male goat"]

gem·stone \\'jem-,stōn\\ *n* : a mineral or petrified material that when cut and polished can be used in jewelry

¹gen- *or* **geno-** *combining form* **1** : race ⟨*geno*cide⟩ **2** : genus : kind [Greek *genos* "birth, race, kind"]

²gen- *or* **geno-** *combining form* : gene ⟨*geno*type⟩

-gen \\jən, ,jen\\ *also* **-gene** \\,jēn\\ *n combining form* **1** : producer ⟨andro*gen*⟩ **2** : one that is (so) produced ⟨culti*gen*⟩ ⟨phos*gene*⟩ [Greek *-genēs* "born"]

gen·darme \\'zhän-,därm *also* 'jän-\\ *n* : a police officer especially in France [French, derived from Middle French *gent d'armes*, literally, "armed people"]

gen·dar·mer·ie *or* **gen·dar·mery** \\jän-'därm-ə-rē, zhän-, -'däm-\\ *n, pl* **-mer·ies** : a body of gendarmes [French *gendarmerie*, from *gendarme*]

gen·der \\'jen-dər\\ *n* **1** : SEX 1 **2** : any of two or more classes of words (as nouns or pronouns) or of forms of words (as adjectives) that are usually partly based on sex and that determine agreement with other words or grammatical forms [Middle French *genre, gendre,* from Latin *gener-, genus* "birth, race, kind, gender"]

gene \\'jēn\\ *n* : a specific sequence of nucleotides in DNA or sometimes RNA that transmits a hereditary character and is usually located in a chromosome in the cell nucleus [German *gen,* short for *pangen,* from *pan-* + *-gen*]

ge·ne·al·o·gy \\,jē-nē-'äl-ə-jē, ,jen-ē-, -'al-\\ *n, pl* **-gies** **1** : a history of the descent of a person or family from an ancestor **2** : the descent of a person or family from an ancestor : PEDIGREE, LINEAGE **3** : the study of family pedigrees [Middle French *genealogie,* from Late Latin *genealogia,* from Greek, from *genea* "race, family" + *-logia* "-logy"] — **ge·ne·a·log·i·cal** \\,jē-nē-ə-'läj-i-kəl, ,jen-ē-\\ *adj* — **ge·ne·a·log·i·cal·ly** \\-'läj-i-kə-lē, -klē\\ *adv* — **ge·ne·al·o·gist** \\-'äl-ə-jəst, -'al-\\ *n*

gene pool *n* : the whole body of genes in an interbreeding population

genera *pl of* GENUS

¹gen·er·al \\'jen-rəl, -ə-rəl\\ *adj* **1** : of or relating to the whole : not local ⟨a *general* election⟩ **2** : taken as a whole ⟨the *general* body of citizens⟩ **3** : relating to or covering all instances or individuals of a class or group ⟨a *general* conclusion⟩ **4** : not limited in meaning : not specific or in detail ⟨a *general* outline⟩ **5** : common to many ⟨a *general* custom⟩ **6** : not special or specialized ⟨a *general* surgeon⟩ **7** : not precise or definite ⟨*general* comments⟩ **8** : superior in rank ⟨*general* manager⟩ ⟨inspector *general*⟩ [Middle French, from Latin *generalis,* from *gener-, genus* "kind, class"] SYN *see* UNIVERSAL

²general *n* **1** : something that involves or is applicable to the whole **2 a** : GENERAL OFFICER **b** : an officer rank in the Army, Marine Corps, and Air Force above lieutenant general — **in general** : for the most part : GENERALLY

general assembly *n* **1** : a legislative assembly; *esp* : a United States state legislature **2** *cap G&A* : the supreme deliberative body of the United Nations

gecko

gemsbok

General Court *n* : the state legislature in Massachusetts and New Hampshire

general delivery *n* : a department of a post office that can be used by individuals as a mailing address

gen·er·a·lis·si·mo \,jen-rə-'lis-ə-,mō, -ə-rə-\ *n, pl* **-mos** : the chief commander of an army : COMMANDER IN CHIEF [Italian, from *generale* "general"]

gen·er·al·i·ty \,jen-ə-'ral-ət-ē\ *n, pl* **-ties** 1 : the quality or state of being general 2 **a** : GENERALIZATION 2 **b** : a vague or inadequate statement 3 : the greatest part : BULK

gen·er·al·i·za·tion \,jen-rə-lə-'zā-shən, -ə-rə-\ *n* 1 : the act or process of generalizing 2 : a general statement, law, principle, or proposition

gen·er·al·ize \'jen-rə-,līz, -ə-rə-\ *vb* 1 : to make general : give a general form to 2 : to draw general conclusions from ⟨*generalized* their experiences⟩ 3 : to reach a general conclusion especially from particular instances — **gen·er·al·iz·er** *n*

gen·er·al·ized *adj* : made general; *esp* : not highly specialized biologically nor strictly adapted (as to an environment)

gen·er·al·ly \'jen-rə-lē, -ə-rə-, 'jen-ər-lē\ *adv* : in a general manner: as **a** : in disregard of specific instances and with regard to an overall picture ⟨*generally* speaking⟩ **b** : as a rule : USUALLY

general officer *n* : an officer ranking above a colonel in the Army, Marine Corps, or Air Force

General of the Air Force : a commissioned officer of highest rank in the Air Force whose insignia is five stars

General of the Army : a commissioned officer of highest rank in the Army whose insignia is five stars

general paresis *n* : insanity caused by syphilis of the brain that leads to dementia and paralysis

general practitioner *n* : a physician or veterinarian who does not limit his or her practice to a specialty

gen·er·al·ship \'jen-rəl-,ship, -ə-rəl-\ *n* 1 : office or tenure of office of a general 2 : military skill as a high commander 3 : LEADERSHIP

general staff *n* : a group of officers who assist a high-level commander in planning, coordinating, and supervising military operations

general store *n* : a retail store that carries a wide variety of goods but is not divided into departments

general strike *n* : a strike by workers in all industries and enterprises of an area

gen·er·ate \'jen-ə-,rāt\ *vt* : to bring into existence: as **a** : to originate especially by a vital or chemical process : PRODUCE ⟨*generate* an electric current⟩ ⟨heat *generated* by friction⟩ **b** : to trace out mathematically (a line, surface, or solid) by a moving point, line, or surface [Latin *generare*, from *gener-*, *genus* "birth, kind"] — **gen·er·a·tive** \-ə-,rāt-iv, -rət-\ *adj*

gen·er·a·tion \,jen-ə-'rā-shən\ *n* 1 **a** : a group of living beings constituting a single step in the line of descent from an ancestor **b** : a group of individuals born and living at the same time **c** : a type or class of objects developed from an earlier type 2 : the average span of time between the birth of parents and that of their offspring 3 : the action or process of generating ⟨*generation* of an electric current⟩ — **gen·er·a·tion·al** \-shnəl, -shən-l\ *adj*

generative nucleus *n* : the nucleus of a developing pollen grain that produces sperm nuclei — compare TUBE NUCLEUS

gen·er·a·tor \'jen-ə-,rāt-ər\ *n* 1 : one that generates 2 : an apparatus in which vapor or gas is formed 3 : a machine by which mechanical energy is changed into electrical energy

gen·er·a·trix \,jen-ə-'rā-triks\ *n, pl* **-tri·ces** \-trə-,sēz\ : a point, line, or surface whose motion generates a line, surface, or solid

ge·ner·ic \jə-'ner-ik\ *adj* 1 **a** : of, relating to, or characteristic of a whole group or class : not specific : GENERAL **b** : not protected by a trademark registration ⟨*ge-*

neric drugs⟩ 2 : of, relating to, or ranking as a biological genus — **ge·ner·i·cal·ly** \-'ner-i-kə-lē, -klē\ *adv*

gen·er·os·i·ty \,jen-ə-'räs-ət-ē\ *n, pl* **-ties** 1 **a** : liberality in spirit or act; *esp* : liberality in giving **b** : a generous act 2 **a** : ABUNDANCE 1 **b** : LARGENESS

gen·er·ous \'jen-rəs, -ə-rəs\ *adj* 1 : free in giving or sharing : not mean or stingy ⟨a *generous* giver⟩ 2 : HIGH-MINDED, NOBLE ⟨*generous* in dealing with a defeated enemy⟩ 3 : ABUNDANT, PLENTIFUL, AMPLE ⟨a *generous* supply⟩ [Latin *generosus* "highborn, magnanimous", from *gener-*, *genus* "birth, family, kind"] — **gen·er·ous·ly** *adv* — **gen·er·ous·ness** *n* □ SYN GENEROUS, BOUNTIFUL, MUNIFICENT mean giving freely and unstintingly. GENEROUS stresses unselfish warmheartedness in giving rather than the size or importance of the gift; BOUNTIFUL implies giving lavishly from ample means or an inexhaustible source of supply; MUNIFICENT suggests a scale of giving appropriate to lords and princes.

gen·e·sis \'jen-ə-səs\ *n, pl* **-e·ses** \-ə-,sēz\ : the origin or coming into being of something [Latin, from Greek, from *gignesthai* "to be born"]

Genesis — see BIBLE table

gene–splic·ing \'jēn-,splī-sing\ *n* : any of various techniques by which recombinant DNA is produced and made to function in an organism

gen·et \'jen-ət\ *n* : an Old World flesh-eating mammal related to the civets [Middle French *genete*, from Arabic *jarnayṭ*]

gene therapy *n* : the insertion of normal or genetically altered genes into cells usually to replace defective genes especially in the treatment of genetic disorders

ge·net·ic \jə-'net-ik\ *adj* 1 : of or relating to the origin, development, or causes of something 2 **a** : of, relating to, or involving genetics **b** : GENIC — **ge·net·i·cal** \-i-kəl\ *adj* — **ge·net·i·cal·ly** \-i-kə-lē, -klē\ *adv*

genetic code *n* 1 : the chemical basis of heredity consisting of specific chemical groupings which make up DNA and RNA and each kind of which determines a particular amino acid in proteins or controls a genetic process (as starting or stopping protein synthesis) 2 : the specific arrangement of the chemical groupings of the genetic code in the hereditary material of an organism

genetic engineering *n* : the alteration of genetic material by intervention in genetic processes; *esp* : GENE-SPLICING — **genetically engineered** *adj* — **genetic engineer** *n*

ge·net·ics \jə-'net-iks\ *n* 1 : a branch of biology that deals with heredity and variation of organisms 2 : the heredity and genetic processes of an organism, a group of organisms, or a condition (as a disease) — **ge·net·i·cist** \-'net-ə-səst\ *n*

ge·nial \'jē-nyəl\ *adj* 1 : favorable to growth or comfort ⟨a *genial* climate⟩ 2 : being cheerful and cheering : FRIENDLY [Latin *genialis*, from *genius*] — **ge·nial·i·ty** \,jē-nē-'al-ət-ē, jēn-'yal-\ *n* — **ge·nial·ly** \'jē-nyə-lē\ *adv* — **ge·nial·ness** *n*

gen·ic \'jēn-ik, 'jen-\ *adj* : of, relating to, produced by, or being a gene — **gen·i·cal·ly** \-i-kə-lē, -klē\ *adv*

-gen·ic \'jen-ik *sometimes* 'jē-nik\ *adj combining form* 1 : producing : forming ⟨carcino*genic*⟩ 2 : produced by : formed from ⟨nephro*genic*⟩ 3 : suitable for production or reproduction by (such) a medium ⟨tele*genic*⟩ [*-gen* and *-geny* + *-ic*; sense 3 from *photogenic*]

ge·nie \'jē-nē *also* 'jen-ē\ *n, pl* **genies** : JINN [French *génie*, from Arabic *jinnīy*]

¹**gen·i·tal** \'jen-ə-tl\ *adj* : of or relating to reproduction or the sexual organs [Latin *genitalis*, from *genitus*, past participle of *gignere* "to beget"]

²**genital** *n* : one of the genitalia

genital herpes *n* : herpes simplex of the type typically affecting the genitalia

gen·i·ta·lia \‚jen-ə-'tāl-yə\ *n pl* : reproductive organs; *esp* : the external genital organs [Latin, from *genitalis* "genital"] — **gen·i·tal·ic** \-'tal-ik, -'tāl-\ *adj*

gen·i·tive \'jen-ət-iv\ *adj* : of, relating to, or being a grammatical case marking typically a relationship especially of possessor or source — compare POSSESSIVE [Latin *genitivus*, literally "of generation", from *genitus*, past participle of *gignere* "to beget"] — **gen·i·ti·val** \‚jen-ə-'tī-vəl\ *adj* — **genitive** *n*

gen·i·to·uri·nary \‚jen-ə-tō-'yùr-ə-‚ner-ē\ *adj* : of or relating to the genital and urinary organs or functions

ge·nius \'jē-nyəs, -nē-əs\ *n, pl* **ge·nius·es** *or* **ge·nii** \-nē-‚ī\ **1** *pl* **genii** : an attendant spirit of a person or place **2** : a strong leaning or inclination : PENCHANT **3 a** : a peculiar, distinctive, or identifying character or spirit **b** : the associations and traditions of a place **4** *pl* **genii a** : JINN **b** : a person who influences another for good or bad ⟨my cousin was my evil *genius*⟩ **5** *pl* **geniuses a** : a single strongly marked capacity or aptitude **b** : extraordinary intellectual power especially as manifested in creative activity **c** : a person endowed with such power; *esp* : one with a very high intelligence quotient [Latin, "tutelary spirit, fondness for social enjoyment", from *gignere* "to beget"] SYN see TALENT □ ORIGIN According to ancient mythology, there are supernatural beings whose nature is intermediate between that of a god and that of humans. It was believed that at birth each person is assigned one of these spirits to act as a guardian throughout life. The Latin name for such a spirit was *genius*, from *gignere* "to beget". *Genius,* in the sense of "attendant spirit", was borrowed from Latin into English in the early 15th century. Part of the role of such a *genius* was to guard a person's character, and in the 16th century *genius* came to be used for a person's inclination or character. Later this led to the sense of "a strongly marked aptitude", and eventually *genius* came to mean "an extraordinary native intellectual power".

geno- — see GEN-

geno·cide \'jen-ə-‚sīd\ *n* : the deliberate and systematic destruction of a racial, political, or cultural group — **geno·cid·al** \‚jen-ə-'sīd-l\ *adj*

ge·nome \'jē-‚nōm\ *or* **ge·nom** \-‚näm\ *n* : one haploid set of chromosomes with the genes they contain [German *genom*, from *gen* "gene" + chromos*om* "chromosome"] — **ge·no·mic** \ji-'nō-mik, -'näm-ik\ *adj*

ge·no·type \'jē-nə-‚tīp, 'jen-ə-\ *n* : the genetic constitution of an individual or group — **ge·no·typ·ic** \‚jē-nə-'tip-ik, ‚jen-ə-\ *adj* — **ge·no·typ·i·cal·ly** \-i-kə-lē, -klē\ *adv*

-ge·nous \j-ə-nəs\ *adj combining form* **1** : producing : yielding **2** : having (such) an origin ⟨endo*genous*⟩ [-*gen* + -*ous*]

genre \'zhän-rə, 'zhä^n-, 'zhäng-; 'zhä^nr, 'zhän-ər\ *n* **1** : KIND 1b, SORT **2** : paintings that depict scenes or events from everyday life usually realistically; *also* : the style of painting featuring such subject matter **3** : a distinctive type or category of literary or musical composition [French, from Middle French, "kind, gender"]

gens \'jenz, 'gens\ *n, pl* **gen·tes** \'jen-‚tēz, 'gen-‚tās\ : a Roman clan embracing the families of the same stock in the male line [Latin]

gent \'jent\ *n* : FELLOW 4a [short for *gentleman*]

gen·teel \jen-'tēl\ *adj* **1** : of or relating or appropriate to an upper class (as in elegance, refinement, or style) **2 a** : maintaining the appearance of superior or middle-class social status or respectability **b** : marked by false delicacy, prudery, or affectation [Middle French *gentil* "gentle"] — **gen·teel·ly** \-'tēl-lē\ *adv* — **gen·teel·ness** *n*

gen·tian \'jen-chən\ *n* : any of various herbs with opposite smooth leaves and showy usually blue flowers [Middle French *gentiane*, from Latin *gentiana*]

gentian violet *n, often cap G&V* : a violet dye in the form of a green powder produced chemically and used as a biological stain and as an antiseptic in bacterial and fungus infections

gen·tile \'jen-‚tīl\ *n* **1** *often cap* : a person who is not Jewish **2** : HEATHEN 1, PAGAN **3** *often cap* : a person who is not a Mormon [Late Latin *gentilis* "heathen", from Latin *gent-, gens* "clan, nation"] — **gentile** *adj, often cap*

gen·til·i·ty \jen-'til-ət-ē\ *n, pl* **-ties** **1** : good birth and family **2 a** : the qualities and manners characteristic of a well-bred person **b** : affectedly delicate or prudish attitude or behavior **3** : maintenance of the appearance of superior or middle-class social status

¹gen·tle \'jent-l\ *adj* **gen·tler** \'jent-lər, -l-ər\; **gen·tlest** \'jent-ləst, -l-əst\ **1 a** : belonging or suitable to a family of high social station **b** : NOBLE, DISTINGUISHED ⟨of *gentle* blood⟩ **c** : AMIABLE, KIND ⟨*gentle* reader⟩ **2 a** : TRACTABLE 1, DOCILE ⟨a *gentle* horse⟩ **b** : not harsh or stern ⟨*gentle* words⟩ **3** : SOFT, DELICATE ⟨a *gentle* touch⟩ **4** : MODERATE ⟨a *gentle* slope⟩ [Old French *gentil*, from Latin *gentilis* "of a clan, of the same clan", from *gent-, gens* "clan, nation"] — **gen·tle·ness** \'jent-l-nəs\ *n* — **gent·ly** \'jent-lē\ *adv*

²gentle *vt* **gen·tled; gen·tling** \'jent-ling, -l-ing\ **1** : to make mild, docile, soft, or moderate **2** : PLACATE, MOLLIFY

gen·tle·folk \'jent-l-‚fōk\ *also* **gen·tle·folks** \-‚fōks\ *n pl* : persons of good family and breeding

gen·tle·man \'jent-l-mən\ *n* **1** : a man of good family **2 a** : a well-bred man of good education and social position **b** : a thoughtful, polite, well-mannered male **3** : MAN — used in the pl. as a form of address in speaking to a group of men

gen·tle·man·ly \-lē\ *adj* : characteristic of or having the character of a gentleman — **gen·tle·man·li·ness** *n*

gentleman's agreement *n* : an unwritten agreement secured only by the honor of the participants — called also *gentlemen's agreement*

gen·tle·wom·an \'jent-l-‚wùm-ən\ *n* **1** : a woman of good family or breeding **2** : a woman attending a lady of rank

gen·try \'jen-trē\ *n* **1** : people of good birth, breeding, and education : ARISTOCRACY **2** : the class of British people between the nobility and the yeomanry **3** : PEOPLE; *esp* : persons of a designated class ⟨the academic *gentry*⟩ [Old French *genterise*, alteration of *gentelise*, from *gentil* "gentle"]

gen·u·flect \'jen-yə-‚flekt\ *vi* : to kneel on one knee and then rise again especially as an act of reverence [Late Latin *genuflectere*, from Latin *genu* "knee" + *flectere* "to bend"] — **gen·u·flec·tion** \‚jen-yə-'flek-shən\ *n*

gen·u·ine \'jen-yə-wən\ *adj* **1** : being actually what it seems to be : REAL ⟨*genuine* gold⟩ **2** : SINCERE, HONEST ⟨a *genuine* interest⟩ [Latin *genuinus* "native, genuine"] SYN see AUTHENTIC — **gen·u·ine·ly** *adv* — **gen·u·ine·ness** *n*

ge·nus \'jē-nəs\ *n, pl* **gen·era** \'jen-ə-rə\ **1** : a category of biological classification ranking between the family and the species, comprising structurally or genetically related species and being designated by a capitalized singular noun formed in Latin **2** : a class of objects divided into several subordinate groups [Latin *gener-, genus* "birth, race, kind"]

-ge·ny \j-ə-nē\ *n combining form, pl* **-genies** : generation : production ⟨phylo*geny*⟩ [Greek -*geneia* "act of being born", from -*genēs* "born"]

geo — see GE-

geo·cen·tric \‚jē-ō-'sen-trik\ *adj* **1** : relating to or measured from the earth's center **2** : having or relating to the earth as a center — compare HELIOCENTRIC

geo·chem·is·try \-'kem-ə-strē\ *n* : a science that deals with the chemical composition of and chemical changes in the crust of the earth — **geo·chem·i·cal** \-'kem-i-kəl\ *adj*

geo·chro·nol·o·gy \‚jē-ō-krə-'näl-ə-jē\ *n* : the chronology of the past as indicated by geologic data — **geo·chro·no·log·i·cal** \-‚krän-l-'äj-i-kəl, -‚krōn-\ *adj*

\ə\ abut		\ng\ sing	
\ər\ further		\ō\ bone	
\a\ mat		\ò\ saw	
\ā\ take		\òi\ coin	
\ä\ cot, cart		\th\ thin	
\aù\ out		\t͟h\ this	
\ch\ chin		\ü\ food	
\e\ pet		\ù\ foot	
\ē\ easy		\y\ yet	
\g\ go		\yü\ few	
\i\ tip		\yù\ cure	
\ī\ life		\zh\ vision	
\j\ job			

GEOLOGIC TIME

EON	ERA	PERIOD AND SYSTEMS	EPOCHS AND SERIES	BEGINNING OF INTERVAL*	BIOLOGICAL FORMS
Phanerozoic	Cenozoic	Quaternary	Holocene	0.01	
			Pleistocene	1.6	Earliest humans
		Tertiary	Pliocene	5	
			Miocene	24	Earliest hominids
			Oligocene	37	
			Eocene	58	Earliest grasses
			Paleocene	65	Earliest large mammals
		Cretaceous-Tertiary boundary (65 million years ago): extinction of dinosaurs			
	Mesozoic	Cretaceous	Upper	98	
			Lower	144	Earliest flowering plants; dinosaurs in ascendancy
		Jurassic		208	Earliest birds & mammals
		Triassic		245	Age of Dinosaurs begins
	Paleozoic	Permian		286	
		Carboniferous			
		Pennsylvanian		320	Earliest reptiles
		Mississippian		360	Earliest winged insects
		Devonian		408	Earliest vascular plants (as ferns & mosses) & amphibians
		Silurian		438	Earliest land plants & insects
		Ordovician		505	Earliest corals
		Cambrian		570	Earliest fish
Proterozoic	Precambrian			2500	Earliest colonial algae & soft-bodied invertebrates
Archean				4000	Life appears: earliest algae & primitive bacteria

*In millions of years before the present

ge·ode \'jē-ˌōd\ *n* : a nodule of stone having a cavity lined with crystals or mineral matter; *also* : the cavity in a geode [Latin *geodes,* a kind of gem, from Greek *geōdēs* "earthlike", from *gē* "earth"]

¹ge·o·de·sic \ˌjē-ə-'des-ik, -'dēs-, -'dez-, -'dēz-\ *adj* : made of a framework of light straight-sided polygons in tension ⟨a *geodesic* dome⟩ [derived from Greek *geōdaisia* "measuring or surveying of land", from *geō-* "ge-" + *daiesthai* "to divide"]

²geodesic *n* : the shortest line between two points on a surface

geo·det·ic survey \ˌjē-ə-'det-ik-\ *n* : a survey of a large land area in which corrections are made for the curvature of the earth's surface [*geodetic* derived from Greek *geōdaisia* "land measuring"] — **geodetic surveying** *n*

ge·og·ra·pher \jē-'äg-rə-fər\ *n* : a specialist in geography

ge·o·graph·ic \ˌjē-ə-'graf-ik\ *or* **geo·graph·i·cal** \-i-kəl\ *adj* **1** : of or relating to geography **2** : belonging to or characteristic of a particular region ⟨*geographic* features of the plains⟩ — **ge·o·graph·i·cal·ly** \-i-kə-lē, -klē\ *adv*

geographical mile *n* : NAUTICAL MILE

ge·og·ra·phy \jē-'äg-rə-fē\ *n, pl* **-phies 1** : a science that deals with the distribution and interaction of the diverse physical and cultural features of the earth's surface **2** : the natural features of an area

geologic time *n* : the long period of time marked by the sequence of events in the earth's geological history SEE GEOLOGIC TIME CHART ABOVE

ge·ol·o·gy \jē-'äl-ə-jē\ *n, pl* **-gies 1 a** : a science that deals with the history of the earth and its life especially as recorded in rocks **b** : a study of the features of a celestial body (as the moon) **2** : the geologic features of an area — **geo·log·ic** \ˌjē-ə-'läj-ik\ *or* **geo·log·i·cal** \-i-kəl\ *adj* — **geo·log·i·cal·ly** \-i-kə-lē, -klē\ *adv* — **ge·ol·o·gist** \jē-'äl-ə-jəst\ *n*

geo·mag·net·ic \ˌjē-ō-mag-'net-ik\ *adj* : of or relating to the magnetism of the earth — **geo·mag·ne·tism** \-'mag-nə-ˌtiz-əm\ *n*

geom·e·ter \jē-'äm-ət-ər\ *n* : a specialist in geometry

geo·met·ric \ˌjē-ə-'me-trik\ *also* **geo·met·ri·cal** \-'me-tri-kəl\ *adj* **1** : of, relating to, or based on the methods or principles of geometry **2** : utilizing rectilinear or simple curvilinear motifs or outlines in design — **geo·met·ri·cal·ly** \-tri-kə-lē, -klē\ *adv*

geo·me·tri·cian \jē-ˌäm-ə-'trish-ən, ˌjē-ə-mə-\ *n* : GEOMETER

geometric mean *n* **1** : the square root of the product of two terms; *also* : the *n*th root of the product of *n* numbers **2** : a term between any two terms of a geometric progression

geometric progression *n* : a progression (as 1, ½, ¼) in which the ratio of a term to the preceding one is always the same

geo·met·rid \jē-'äm-ə-trəd, ˌjē-ə-'me-trəd\ *n* : any of a family of medium-sized moths with large wings and larvae that are loopers — **geometrid** *adj*

ge·om·e·try \jē-'äm-ə-trē\ *n* **1 a** : a branch of mathematics that deals with the measurement, properties, and relationships of points, lines, angles, surfaces, and solids **b** : a particular type or system of geometry **2 a** : the arrangement of the parts of a device ⟨the *geometry* of an electron tube⟩ **b** : SHAPE ⟨the *geometry* of a crystal⟩ [Middle French *geometrie,* from Latin *geometria,* from Greek *geōmetria,* from *geōmetrein* "to measure the earth", from *geō-* "ge-" + *metron* "measure"]

geo·mor·phol·o·gy \ˌjē-ə-mȯr-'fäl-ə-jē\ *n* : a science that deals with the land and submarine relief features of the earth's surface — **geo·mor·pho·log·i·cal** \-ˌmȯr-fə-'läj-i-kəl\ *adj*

geo·phys·ics \ˌjē-ə-'fiz-iks\ *n* : the physics of the earth including the fields of meteorology, hydrology, oceanography, seismology, volcanology, magnetism, and geodesy — **geo·phys·i·cal** \-'fiz-i-kəl\ *adj* — **geo·phys·i·cist** \-'fiz-ə-səst\ *n*

geo·pol·i·tics \,jē-ō-'päl-ə-,tiks\ *n* : study of the influence of such factors as geography, economics, and population on the politics and especially the foreign policy of a state — **geo·po·lit·i·cal** \-pə-'lit-i-kəl\ *adj*

geor·gette \jòr-'jet\ *n* : a thin strong clothing crepe having a dull pebbly surface [from *Georgette*, a former trademark]

¹**Geor·gian** \'jòr-jən\ *adj* **1** : of, relating to, or characteristic of the reigns of the first four Georges of Great Britain ⟨*Georgian* architecture⟩ **2** : of, relating to, or characteristic of the reign of George V of Great Britain

²**Georgian** *n* : one belonging to either of the Georgian periods

geo·syn·cline \-'sin-,klīn\ *n* : a great elongate subsidence of the earth's crust

geo·tax·is \-'tak-səs\ *n* : a taxis in which the force of gravity is the controlling stimulus — **geo·tac·tic** \-'tak-tik\ *adj* — **geo·tac·ti·cal·ly** \-ti-kə-lē, -klē\ *adv*

geo·ther·mal \-'thər-məl\ *or* **geo·ther·mic** \-mik\ *adj* : of or relating to the heat of the earth's interior; *also* : produced by such heat ⟨*geothermal* steam⟩

ge·ot·ro·pism \jē-'ä-trə-,piz-əm\ *n* : a tropism involving turning or movement toward the earth — **geo·tro·pic** \,jē-ə-'trō-pik, -'träp-ik\ *adj* — **geo·tro·pi·cal·ly** \-'trō-pi-kə-lē, -'träp-i-, -klē\ *adv*

ge·ra·ni·um \jə-'rā-nē-əm\ *n* **1** : any of a widely distributed genus of herbs with usually deeply cut leaves, regular flowers in which glands alternate with the petals, and long slender dry fruits **2** : any of a genus of herbs that are distinguished by clusters of scarlet, pink, or white flowers with the sepals joined at the base into a hollow spur and that are popular as window plants — called also *pelargonium* [Latin, from Greek *geranion*, from *geranos* "crane"]

ger·bil *also* **ger·bille** \'jər-bəl\ *n* : any of numerous Old World burrowing desert rodents with long hind legs adapted for leaping [French *gerbille*]

ger·i·at·ric \,jer-ē-'a-trik\ *adj* : of or relating to geriatrics, the old, or the process of aging [Greek *gēras* "old age" + *iatros* "physician"]

ger·i·at·rics \,jer-ē-'a-triks\ *n* : a branch of medicine that deals with the problems and diseases of old age and aging people — compare GERONTOLOGY — **ger·i·a·tri·cian** \,jer-ē-ə-'trish-ən\ *n*

germ \'jərm\ *n* **1** : a small mass of living substance capable of developing into an organism or one of its parts **2** : something that serves or may serve as an origin : RUDIMENT ⟨the *germ* of an idea⟩ **3** : MICROBE; *esp* : one causing disease [French *germe*, from Latin *germen*, from *gignere* "to beget"]

Ger·man \'jər-mən\ *n* **1 a** : a native or inhabitant of Germany **b** : a person of German descent **2** : the Germanic language of Germany, Austria, and parts of Switzerland **3** *often not cap* **a** : a dance consisting of capriciously involved figures intermingled with waltzes **b** *chiefly Midland* : a dancing party; *esp* : one at which the german is danced [Latin *Germanus*, any member of the Germanic peoples] — **German** *adj*

ger·man·der \jər-'man-dər, -jər-\ *n* : a plant of the mint family with dense spikes of purple flowers [derived from Greek *chamaidrys*, from *chamai* "on the ground" + *drys* "tree"]

ger·mane \jər-'mān, -jər-\ *adj* : having a significant connection : PERTINENT [Middle English *germain* "closely related", derived from Latin *germanus* "having the same parents", from *germen* "bud, sprout, germ"] — **ger·mane·ly** *adv*

¹**Ger·man·ic** \jər-'man-ik, -jər-\ *adj* **1** : GERMAN **2** : of, relating to, or characteristic of the Germanic-speaking peoples **3** : of, relating to, or constituting Germanic

²**Germanic** *n* : a branch of the Indo-European language family containing English, German, Dutch, Afrikaans, Flemish, Frisian, the Scandinavian languages, and Gothic

ger·ma·ni·um \jər-'mā-nē-əm, -jər-\ *n* : a grayish white hard brittle chemical element that resembles silicon and is used as a semiconductor — see ELEMENT table [New Latin, from Medieval Latin *Germania* "Germany"]

ger·man·ize \'jər-mə-,nīz\ *vt, often cap* : to cause to acquire German characteristics — **ger·man·iza·tion** \,jər-mə-nə-'zā-shən\ *n, often cap*

German measles *n sing or pl* : an acute contagious virus disease that is usually milder than typical measles but is likely to cause damage to the fetus when occurring early in pregnancy

Ger·mano- \jər-'man-ō, -jər-\ *combining form* **1** : German **2** : German and

German shepherd *n* : a large erect-eared dog of a breed originating in northern Europe that is often used in police work and as a guide dog for the blind

German silver *n* : NICKEL SILVER

germ cell *n* : an egg or sperm or one of the cells from which they arise

ger·mi·cid·al \,jər-mə-'sīd-l\ *adj* : of or relating to a germicide; *also* : destroying germs

ger·mi·cide \'jər-mə-,sīd\ *n* : an agent that destroys germs

ger·mi·nal \'jər-mən-l\ *adj* **1** : of or relating to a germ or germ cell; *also* : EMBRYONIC **2** : CREATIVE ⟨*germinal* ideas⟩ — **ger·mi·nal·ly** \-l-ē\ *adv*

ger·mi·nate \'jər-mə-,nāt\ *vb* **1** : to cause to sprout or develop **2** : to begin to grow : SPROUT **3** : to come into being : EVOLVE ⟨an idea that *germinated* slowly⟩ [Latin *germinare* "to sprout", from *germin-, germen* "bud, sprout, germ"] — **ger·mi·na·tion** \,jər-mə-'nā-shən\ *n*

ger·mi·na·tive \'jər-mə-,nāt-iv\ *adj* : having the power to germinate or to develop

germ layer *n* : any of the three primary layers of cells formed in most embryos during and immediately following gastrulation — called also *primary germ layer*; compare ECTODERM, ENDODERM, MESODERM

germ plasm *n* **1** : germ cells viewed as the bearers of hereditary material **2** : GENES

germ theory *n* : a theory that infectious and contagious disorders result from the action of living organisms

germ warfare *n* : the use of harmful microorganisms (as bacteria) as weapons in war

ger·on·tol·o·gy \,jer-ən-'täl-ə-jē\ *n* : a branch of knowledge dealing with aging and the problems of the old — compare GERIATRICS [Greek *geront-, gerōn* "old man"] — **ger·on·to·log·i·cal** \,jer-,änt-l-'äj-i-kəl\ *adj* — **ger·on·tol·o·gist** \,jer-ən-'täl-ə-jəst\ *n*

¹**ger·ry·man·der** \,jer-ē-'man-dər, 'jer-ē-, *also* ,ger-, 'ger-\ *n* **1** : the act or method of gerrymandering **2** : a district or pattern of districts varying greatly in size or population as a result of gerrymandering [Elbridge *Gerry*, died 1814, American statesman + -*mander* (as in *salamander*); from the shape of an election district formed during Gerry's governorship of Massachusetts]

²**gerrymander** *vt* -**dered**; -**der·ing** \-də-ring, -dring\ : to divide (as a state or county) into election districts so as to give one political party an advantage over its opponents

ger·und \'jer-ənd\ *n* **1** : a verbal noun in Latin that expresses generalized or uncompleted action **2** : an English verbal noun in -*ing* used as a substantive and at the same time capable of taking adverbial modifiers and having an object [Late Latin *gerundium*, from Latin *gerere* "to carry, carry on"]

ge·run·dive \jə-'rən-div\ *n* : a Latin verbal adjective that expresses necessity or fitness and has the same suffix as the gerund

ges·so \'jes-ō\ *n* : plaster of paris or gypsum mixed with a binder for use as a surface for painting or in making bas-reliefs [Italian, literally, "gypsum", from Latin *gypsum*]

gest *or* **geste** \'jest\ *n* **1** : a remarkable deed : EXPLOIT **2** : a tale of adventures; *esp* : a medieval tale in verse

¹gerrymander 2

\ə\ abut   \ng\ sing
\ər\ further   \ō\ bone
\a\ mat   \ó\ saw
\ā\ take   \ói\ coin
\ä\ cot, cart   \th\ thin
\aù\ out   \th̷\ this
\ch\ chin   \ü\ food
\e\ pet   \ú\ foot
\ē\ easy   \y\ yet
\g\ go   \yü\ few
\i\ tip   \yù\ cure
\ī\ life   \zh\ vision
\j\ job

[Old French *geste,* from Latin *gesta* "exploits", from *gerere* "to carry, carry on, perform"]

Ge·sta·po \gə-'stäp-ō\ *n* **1** : the state secret police of Nazi Germany **2** : a group whose tactics resemble those of the Gestapo [German, from *Ge*heime *Sta*atspo lizei, literally, "secret state police"]

ges·tate \'jes-,tāt\ *vt* **1** : to carry in the uterus during pregnancy **2** : to conceive and gradually develop in the mind [back-formation from *gestation*]

ges·ta·tion \je-'stā-shən\ *n* **1** : the carrying of young in the uterus : PREGNANCY **2** : conception and development especially in the mind [Latin *gestatio,* from *gestare* "to bear", from *gestus,* past participle of *gerere* "to bear, carry"] — **ges·ta·tion·al** \-shnəl, -shən-l\ *adj*

ges·tic·u·late \je-'stik-yə-,lāt\ *vi* : to make gestures especially when speaking [Latin *gesticulari,* from *gestus,* past participle of *gerere* "to carry"] — **ges·tic·u·la·tor** \-,lāt-ər\ *n*

ges·tic·u·la·tion \je-,stik-yə-'lā-shən\ *n* **1** : the action of making gestures **2** : GESTURE; *esp* : an expressive gesture made in showing strong feeling or in enforcing an argument

ges·tic·u·la·tive \je-'stik-yə-,lāt-iv\ *adj* : inclined to or marked by gesticulation

¹ges·ture \'jes-chər, 'jesh-\ *n* **1** : the use of motions of the limbs or body as a means of communication; *also* : an instance of such communication **2** : something said or done by way of formality or courtesy, as a symbol or token, or for its effect on the attitudes of others (a political *gesture*) [Medieval Latin *gestura* "mode of action", from Latin *gestus,* past participle of *gerere* "to carry, carry on"]

²gesture *vb* **1** : to make a gesture **2** : to express or direct by a gesture

ge·sund·heit \gə-'zùnt-,hīt\ *interj* — used to wish good health especially to one who has just sneezed [German, literally, "health"]

¹get \'get, 'get; often git, *without stress, when a heavily stressed syllable follows, as in* "get up"\ *vb* got \'gät, 'gät\; got *or* got·ten \'gät-n\; get·ting **1 a** : to gain possession of (as by receiving, acquiring, earning, buying, or winning) (*get* a present) (*got* first prize) (*get* a dog) **b** : to seek out and obtain (planned to *get* dinner at the inn) **c** : FETCH (*get* your father his slippers) **d** : to acquire wealth (those that have, *get*) **2 a** : to succeed in coming or going (*got* to the city on time) (*got* home early) **b** : to cause to come or go (*got* the dog out in a hurry) **3** : BEGET 1 **4 a** : to cause to be in a certain condition (*got* his hair cut) (*got* his feet wet) **b** : BECOME (*get* sick) (*get* better) **c** : PREPARE (started *getting* dinner) **5 a** : SEIZE (*got* the thief by the leg) **b** : to move emotionally (a song that always *got* them) **c** : BAFFLE, PUZZLE (the third question *got* everybody) **d** : IRRITATE (don't let it *get* you) **e** : HIT (*got* the dog in the leg) **f** : KILL (swore to *get* a deer) **6 a** : to be subjected to (*got* a broken nose) **b** : to receive as punishment (*got* six months for larceny) **7 a** : to find out by calculation (*got* the right answer) **b** : to hear correctly (I didn't *get* your name) **c** : UNDERSTAND 1 **8** : PERSUADE, INDUCE (couldn't *get* them to agree) **9 a** : HAVE — used in the present perfect form with present meaning (I've *got* no money) **b** : to be obliged — used in the present perfect form with present meaning (we have *got* to leave) **10** : to establish communication with (*got* me on the telephone) **11** : to be able : CONTRIVE, MANAGE (never *got* to go to college) **12** : to leave at once : clear out (told them to *get*) [Old Norse *geta* "to get, beget"] — **get ahead** : to achieve success — **get around 1** : to get the better of **2** : EVADE — **get at 1** : to reach effectively **2** : to influence corruptly **3** : to turn one's attention to **4** : to try to prove or make clear (what are you *getting* at) — **get away with** : to perform without suffering unpleasant consequences — **get back at** : to get even with — **get even** : to get

revenge — **get even with** : to repay in kind — **get into** : to become strongly involved with or deeply interested in — **get it** : to receive a scolding or punishment — **get one's goat** : to make one angry or annoyed — **get over 1** : OVERCOME (*get over* difficulties) **2** : to recover from — **get through 1** : to reach the end of : COMPLETE **2** : to while away — **get to 1** : BEGIN **2** : to have an effect on : INFLUENCE — **get together 1** : to bring together : ACCUMULATE **2** : to come together : ASSEMBLE **3** : to reach agreement — **get wind of** : to become aware of

²get \'get\ *n* **1** : something begotten : OFFSPRING, PROGENY **2** : a difficult return of a shot in tennis

get along *vi* **1 a** : PROGRESS **b** : to approach old age **2** : to meet one's needs : MANAGE **3** : to be or remain on congenial terms

get·at·able \get-'at-ə-bəl\ *adj* : ACCESSIBLE

get·away \'get-ə-,wā\ *n* **1** : the action or fact of getting away : ESCAPE **2** : the action of starting or getting under way (as in a race)

get by *vi* **1** : to avoid failure or catastrophe : barely succeed **2** : to proceed without being discovered, criticized, or punished

Geth·sem·a·ne \geth-'sem-ə-nē\ *n* : a place or occasion of great suffering especially in mind or spirit [from *Gethsemane,* the garden outside Jerusalem mentioned in the New Testament as the scene of the agony and arrest of Jesus, from Greek *Gethsēmanē*]

get off *vb* **1** : UTTER (*get off* a joke) **2** : START 5a, LEAVE **3** : to escape or help to escape **4** : to leave work with permission

get on *vi* **1** : to get along (they *get on* well) **2** : to gain knowledge or understanding (*got on* to the racket)

get out *vb* **1** : to escape or cause to escape (hoping to *get out* alive) (*get* oneself *out* of trouble) **2** : to become or cause to become known or public (let a secret *get out*); *esp* : PUBLISH

get·ter \'get-ər\ *n* **1** : one that gets **2** : a substance introduced into a vacuum tube or incandescent electric lamp to remove traces of gas

get-to·geth·er \'get-tə-,geth-ər\ *n* : MEETING; *esp* : an informal social gathering

get·up \'get-,əp\ *n* : COSTUME 3, OUTFIT

get up \get-'əp, git-\ *vb* **1 a** : to arise from bed **b** : to rise to one's feet **2** : to go ahead or faster — used as a command to a horse **3** : to make preparations for : ORGANIZE **4** : to arrange as to external appearance : DRESS (was *got up* as a pirate)

gew·gaw \'gü-,gó, 'gyü-\ *n* : a showy trifle : BAUBLE, TRINKET [origin unknown]

gey·ser \'gī-zər\ *n* : a spring that throws forth intermittent jets of heated water and steam [Icelandic *geysir* "gusher"]

gey·ser·ite \'gī-zə-,rīt\ *n* : a variety of opal that is deposited around some hot springs and geysers

¹ghast·ly \'gast-lē\ *adj* **ghast·li·er; -est 1** : terrifyingly horrible to the mind or senses (a *ghastly* crime) **2** : resembling a ghost : DEATHLIKE, PALE (a *ghastly* face) [Middle English *gastly,* from *gasten* "to terrify"] — **ghast·li·ness** *n* □ SYN GHASTLY, GRUESOME, GRIM, LURID mean horrifying and repellent in appearance or aspect. GHASTLY suggests the horrifying aspects of corpses or skeletons; GRUESOME suggests additionally the effects of cruelty or extreme violence; GRIM implies a fierce and forbidding aspect; LURID adds to GRUESOME the suggestion of shuddering fascination with violent death and especially with murder.

²ghastly *adv* : in a ghastly manner (turned *ghastly* pale)

ghat \'gót, 'gät\ *n* : a landing place with stairs descending to a river in India [Hindi *ghāt*]

gher·kin \'gər-kən\ *n* **1** : a small prickly cucumber used for pickling; *also* : the vine that bears it **2** : the immature fruit of the common cucumber [Dutch *gurken,* pl. of *gurk* "cucumber"]

ghet·to \'get-ō\ *n, pl* **ghettos** *or* **ghettoes** **I** : a quarter of a city in which Jews were formerly required to live **2** : a quarter of a city in which members of a minority group live because of social, legal, or economic pressure [Italian]

ghillie *variant of* GILLIE

¹ghost \'gōst\ *n* **I** : the seat of life : SOUL ⟨give up the *ghost*⟩ **2** : a disembodied soul; *esp* : the soul of a dead person believed to be an inhabitant of the unseen world or to appear to the living in bodily likeness **3** : SPIRIT 2b, DEMON **4** : a faint shadowy trace or suggestion ⟨a *ghost* of a smile⟩ **5** : a false image in a photographic negative or on a television screen caused especially by reflection **6** : one who ghostwrites [Old English *gāst*] — **ghost·like** \-,līk\ *adj* — **ghosty** \'gōstē\ *adj*

²ghost *vb* **I** : to haunt like a ghost **2** : to move silently like a ghost **3** : GHOSTWRITE

ghost·ly \'gōst-lē\ *adj* **ghost·li·er; -est** **I** : of or relating to the soul : SPIRITUAL **2** : of, relating to, or having the characteristics of a ghost : SPECTRAL — **ghost·li·ness** *n*

ghost town *n* : a once flourishing town deserted or nearly so usually after exhaustion of some natural resource

ghost·write \'gōst-,rīt\ *vb* : to write for and in the name of another [back-formation from *ghost-writer*] — **ghost·writ·er** *n*

ghoul \'gül\ *n* **I** : a legendary evil being that robs graves and feeds on corpses **2** : a person (as a grave robber) whose activities suggest those of a ghoul [Arabic *ghūl*] — **ghoul·ish** \'gü-lish\ *adj* — **ghoul·ish·ly** *adv* — **ghoul·ish·ness** *n*

¹GI \jē-'ī, 'jē-\ *adj* **I** : provided by an official United States military supply department ⟨*GI* shoes⟩ **2** : of, relating to, or characteristic of United States military personnel **3** : conforming to military regulations or customs ⟨a *GI* haircut⟩ [galvanized *iron*; from abbreviation used in listing such articles as garbage cans, but taken as abbreviation for *government issue*]

²GI *n* : a member or former member of the United States forces; *esp* : an enlisted person

³GI *vt* **GI'd; GI'ing** : to prepare for military inspection by cleaning

¹gi·ant \'jī-ənt\ *n* **I** : a legendary being of great stature and strength and of more than mortal but less than godlike power **2 a** : a living being of great size **b** : a person of extraordinary powers ⟨a literary *giant*⟩ **3** : something unusually large or powerful [Middle French *geant*, from Latin *gigant-, gigas,* from Greek]

²giant *adj* : characterized by extremely large size, proportion, or power

giant cactus *n* : SAGUARO

gi·ant·ess \'jī-ənt-əs\ *n* : a female giant; *esp* : an unusually large woman

gi·ant·ism \'jī-ənt-,iz-əm\ *n* **I** : the quality or state of being a giant **2** : GIGANTISM 2

giant panda *n* : PANDA 2

giant sequoia *n* : BIG TREE

giant squid *n* : any of a group of very large squids that include the largest mollusks known with some being 12 meters long including the arms

giant star *n* : a star of great luminosity and of large mass

giaour \'jaur\ *n* : one outside the Muslim faith : INFIDEL [Turkish *gâvur*]

gib \'gib\ *n* : a plate (as of metal) machined to hold other parts in place, to afford a bearing surface, or to take up wear [origin unknown]

gib·ber \'jib-ər\ *vi* **gib·bered; gib·ber·ing** \'jib-ring, -ə-ring\ : to speak gibberish : CHATTER [imitative] — **gib·ber** *n*

gib·ber·el·lic acid \,jib-ə-'rel-ik-\ *n* : a crystalline organic acid associated with and similar in effect to the gibberellins

gib·ber·el·lin \-'rel-ən\ *n* : any of several plant-growth regulators that in low concentrations promote shoot growth [New Latin *Gibberella,* genus of fungi]

gib·ber·ish \'jib-rish, 'gib-, -ə-rish\ *n* : obscure, confused, or meaningless speech or language [probably from *gibber*]

¹gib·bet \'jib-ət\ *n* **I** : GALLOWS **2** : an upright post with a projecting arm for hanging the bodies of executed criminals as a warning [Old French *gibet*]

²gibbet *vt* **I a** : to hang on a gibbet **b** : to expose to public scorn **2** : to execute by hanging

gib·bon \'gib-ən\ *n* : any of several tailless apes of southeastern Asia and the East Indies that are the smallest and most arboreal anthropoid apes [French]

gib·bos·i·ty \jib-'äs-ət-ē, gib-\ *n, pl* **-ties** : PROTUBERANCE, SWELLING

gib·bous \'jib-əs, 'gib-\ *adj* **I** : convexly rounded **2** : seen with more than half but not all of the apparent disk illuminated ⟨*gibbous* moon⟩ [Middle French *gibbeux* "protuberant, gibbous", from Late Latin *gibbosus* "humpbacked", from Latin *gibbus* "hump"]

¹gibe *or* **jibe** \'jīb\ *vb* : to utter or reproach with taunting or sarcastic words [perhaps from Middle French *giber* "to shake, handle roughly"] — **gib·er** *n*

²gibe *or* **jibe** *n* : JEER, TAUNT

gib·lets \'jib-ləts\ *n pl* : the edible viscera of a bird [Middle English *gibelet* "entrails, garbage", from Middle French, "stew of wildfowl"] — **gib·let** \-lət\ *adj*

gid \'gid\ *n* : a disease usually of sheep caused by a tapeworm larva in the brain [back-formation from *giddy*]

gid·dap \gid-'ap\ *imperative vb* : a command to a horse to go ahead or go faster [alteration of *get up*]

gid·dy \'gid-ē\ *adj* **gid·di·er; -est** **I** : having a feeling of whirling or reeling about : DIZZY **2** : causing dizziness ⟨a *giddy* height⟩ **3** : lightheartedly silly : FRIVOLOUS [Old English *gydig* "possessed, mad"] — **gid·di·ly** \'gid-l-ē\ *adv* — **gid·di·ness** \'gid-ē-nəs\ *n*

gie \'gē\ *chiefly Scottish variant of* GIVE

gift \'gift\ *n* **I** : the act or power of giving ⟨the appointment was not in my *gift*⟩ **2** : something given : PRESENT **3** : a special ability : TALENT ⟨a *gift* for music⟩ [Old Norse, "something given, talent"]

gift·ed \'gif-təd\ *adj* : having great natural ability ⟨a class for *gifted* children⟩

gift wrap *vt* : to wrap (merchandise intended as a gift) in specially attractive or fancy wrappings

¹gig \'gig\ *n* **I a** : a long light ship's boat propelled by oars, sail, or motor and usually reserved for use by the captain **b** : a rowboat designed for speed rather than for work **2** : a light 2-wheeled one-horse carriage [earlier *gig* "something that whirls, top", from Middle English *gigg* "top"]

²gig *n* : a pronged spear for catching fish [short for earlier *fizgig, fishgig,* of unknown origin]

³gig *vb* **gigged; gig·ging** : to spear or fish with a gig

⁴gig *n* : a military demerit [origin unknown]

⁵gig *vt* **gigged; gig·ging** : to give a military gig to ⟨*gigged* for dirty shoes⟩

giga- \'jig-ə, 'gig-ə\ *combining form* : billion [Greek *gigas* "giant"]

giga·byte \-,bīt\ *n* : 1,073,741,824 bytes

gi·gan·tesque \,jī-,gan-'tesk, -gən-\ *adj* : of huge proportions

gi·gan·tic \jī-'gant-ik\ *adj* : extremely large or great : HUGE ⟨*gigantic* industry⟩ [Greek *gigantikos,* from *gigant-, gigas* "giant"] — **gi·gan·ti·cal·ly** \-'gant-i-kə-lē, -klē\ *adv*

gi·gan·tism \jī-'gan-,tiz-əm, jə-; 'jī-gən-\ *n* **I** : GIANTISM 1 **2** : development to abnormally large size; *esp* : excessive bodily growth with delayed or inhibited reproduction

¹gig·gle \'gig-əl\ *vi* **gig·gled; gig·gling** \'gig-ling, -ə-ling\ : to laugh in a silly way [imitative] — **gig·gler** \'gig-lər, -ə-lar\ *n*

gibbon

\ə\ abut	\ng\ sing
\ər\ further	\ō\ bone
\a\ mat	\ȯ\ saw
\ā\ take	\oi\ coin
\ä\ cot, cart	\th\ thin
\au̇\ out	\th\ this
\ch\ chin	\ü\ food
\e\ pet	\u̇\ foot
\ē\ easy	\y\ yet
\g\ go	\yü\ few
\i\ tip	\yu̇\ cure
\ī\ life	\zh\ vision
\j\ job	

Gila monster

²gig·gle *n* : the act of giggling : a light silly laugh

gig·gly \'gig-lē, -ə-lē\ *adj* : given to giggling

gig·o·lo \'jig-ə-,lō\ *n, pl* **-los** **1** : a man supported by a woman in return for sexual favors **2** : a professional dancing partner or male escort [French]

gi·got \'jig-ət, zhē-'gō\ *n, pl* **gigots** \-əts, -'gō, -'gōz\ **1** : a leg (as of lamb) especially when cooked **2** : a leg-of-mutton sleeve [Middle French, from *gigue* "fiddle"; from its shape]

Gi·la monster \'hē-lə-\ *n* : a large orange and black venomous lizard of the southwestern United States; *also* : a related Mexican lizard [*Gila* river, Arizona]

¹gild \'gild\ *vt* **gild·ed** *or* **gilt** \'gilt\; **gild·ing** **1** : to cover with or as if with a thin coating of gold **2** : to give a falsely attractive appearance to [Old English *gyldan*] — **gild·er** *n* — **gild the lily** : to add unnecessary ornamentation to something beautiful in its own right

²gild *variant of* GUILD

¹gill \'jil\ *n* — see MEASURE table [Middle English *gille*]

²gill \'gil\ *n* **1** : an organ (as of a fish) for obtaining oxygen from water **2** *pl* : the flesh under or about the chin or jaws **3** : one of the radiating plates forming the undersurface of the cap of a mushroom [Middle English *gile, gille*] — **gilled** \'gild\ *adj*

gill arch *n* : one of the several bars of bone or cartilage that are paired on either side of the throat and support the gills of water-breathing vertebrates

gill filament *n* : one of the threadlike processes making up a gill

gil·lie *or* **gil·ly** *or* **ghil·lie** \'gil-ē\ *n, pl* **gillies** *or* **ghillies** **1** : a male attendant on a Scottish Highland chief **2** *Scottish & Irish* : a fishing and hunting guide **3** *usually* **ghillie** : a low-cut shoe with decorative lacing [Scottish Gaelic *gille* "boy"]

gill net *n* : a net that allows the head of a fish to pass but entangles it as it seeks to withdraw — **gill·net** \'gil-,net\ *vt*

gill raker *n* : one of the bony processes on each gill arch that divert debris

gill slit *n* **1** : any of the openings in vertebrates with gills through which water taken in at the mouth moves to the outside bathing the gills **2** : a rudiment of a gill slit that occurs at some stage of development in all vertebrate embryos

gil·ly·flow·er \'jil-ē-,flaú-ər, -,flaúr\ *n* : an Old World pink that is grown for its clove-scented flowers and is the source of garden carnations [by folk etymology from Middle English *gilofre* "clove", from Middle French *girofle, gilofre*, from Latin *caryophyllum*, from Greek *karyophyllon*, from *karyon* "nut" + *phyllon* "leaf"]

¹gilt \'gilt\ *adj* : of the color of gold [from past participle of **¹gild**]

²gilt *n* **1** : gold or something that resembles gold laid on a surface **2** : superficial brilliance

³gilt *n* : a young female swine [Old Norse *gyltr*]

gilt-edged \'gilt-'ejd\ *or* **gilt-edge** \-'ej\ *adj* **1** : having a gilt edge **2** : of the best quality (*gilt-edged* securities)

gim·bal \'gim-bəl, 'jim-\ *n* : a device that permits a body to incline freely in any direction or suspends something (as a ship's compass) so that it will remain level when its support is tipped — usually used in pl.; called also *gimbal ring* [from obsolete *gemel* "double hinge", derived from Latin *geminus* "twin"]

gim·crack \'jim-,krak\ *n* : a showy object of little use or value : GEWGAW [origin unknown] — **gimcrack** *adj* — **gim·crack·ery** \-,krak-rē, -ə-rē\ *n*

gim·let \'gim-lət\ *n* : a small tool with a screw point, grooved shank, and cross handle for boring holes [Middle French *guimbelet*]

gim·mick \'gim-ik\ *n* **1** : an ingenious or novel mechanical device : GADGET **2 a** : an important feature that is not immediately apparent : CATCH **b** : a new and ingenious scheme [origin unknown]

giraffe

¹gimp \'gimp\ *n* : an ornamental flat braid or round cord used as a trimming [perhaps from Dutch]

²gimp *n* : CRIPPLE; *also* : LIMP — **gimpy** \'gim-pē\ *adj*

¹gin \'jin\ *n* : a mechanical tool or device: as **a** : a snare or trap for game **b** : COTTON GIN [Old French *engin* "engine"]

²gin *vt* **ginned; gin·ning** **1** : SNARE 1 **2** : to separate (cotton fiber) from seeds and waste material — **gin·ner** *n*

³gin *n* **1** : a usually colorless alcoholic liquor flavored with juniper berries **2 a** : GIN RUMMY **b** : the act of laying down a full hand of matched cards in gin rummy [from earlier *geneva*, from obsolete Dutch *genever*, literally, "juniper", derived from Latin *juniperus*]

gin·ger \'jin-jər\ *n* **1** : any of a genus of tropical Old World herbs with pungent aromatic underground stems used for flavoring and in medicine; *also* : the underground stem **2** : high spirit : PEP [Old English *gingifer*, from Medieval Latin *gingiber*, from Latin *zingiber*, from Greek *zingiberi*] — **gin·gery** \'jinj-rē, -ə-rē\ *adj*

ginger ale *n* : a carbonated nonalcoholic drink flavored with ginger extract

ginger beer *n* : a carbonated nonalcoholic drink heavily flavored with ginger or capsicum or both

gin·ger·bread \'jin-jər-,bred\ *n* **1** : a cake made with molasses and flavored with ginger **2** : lavish or superfluous ornament — **gin·ger·bready** \-ē\ *adj*

gin·ger·ly \'jin-jər-lē\ *adj* : very cautious or careful [perhaps from *ginger*] — **gin·ger·li·ness** *n* — **gingerly** *adv*

gin·ger·snap \-,snap\ *n* : a thin brittle cookie flavored with ginger

ging·ham \'ging-əm\ *n* : a fabric usually of yarn-dyed cotton in plain weave [Malay *genggang* "checkered cloth"]

gin·gi·vi·tis \,jin-jə-'vīt-əs\ *n* : inflammation of the gums [Latin *gingiva* "gum"]

gink·go \'ging-kō\ *n, pl* **ginkgoes** *or* **ginkgos** : a large Chinese tree with fan-shaped leaves and foul-smelling fruit that is often grown as a shade tree — called also *maidenhair tree* [Japanese *ginkyo*]

gin rummy *n* : a rummy game for two players in which each player is dealt 10 cards and a player may win by matching all cards in the hand in sets or may end play when unmatched cards count up to less than 10 [**³gin**]

gin·seng \'jin-,sang, -,seng\ *n* **1** : a perennial Chinese herb with small greenish flowers in a rounded cluster and scarlet berries; *also* : a closely related North American herb **2** : the forked aromatic root of the ginseng used as a medicine in China [Chinese (Pekingese dialect) *jen²-shen¹*]

Gipsy *variant of* GYPSY

gi·raffe \jə-'raf\ *n, pl* **giraffe** *or* **giraffes** : a large fleet African ruminant mammal that is the tallest living four-footed animal and that has a very long neck and a short coat with dark blotches separated by pale lines [Italian *giraffa*, from Arabic *zirāfah*] — **gi·raff·ish** \-'raf-ish\ *adj*

gird \'gərd\ *vb* **gird·ed** *or* **girt** \'gərt\; **gird·ing** **1** : to encircle or fasten with or as if with a belt (*gird* on a sword) **2** : to invest especially with power or authority **3** : to get ready (*girded* themselves for a fight) [Old English *gyrdan*]

gird·er \'gərd-ər\ *n* : a horizontal main supporting beam

¹gir·dle \'gərd-l\ *n* : something that encircles or confines: as **a** : a belt or sash encircling the waist **b** : a woman's supporting undergarment that extends from the waist to below the hips **c** : a bony arch for the support of a limb : (1) : PECTORAL GIRDLE (2) : PELVIC GIRDLE [Old English *gyrdel*]

²girdle *vt* **gir·dled; gir·dling** \'gərd-ling, -l-ing\ **1** : to encircle with a girdle **2** : to move around : CIRCLE **3** :

to cut away the bark and cambium in a ring around (a plant)

girl \\'gərl\\ *n* **1 a** : a female child **b** : a typically young woman **2** : a female servant or employee **3** : GIRLFRIEND 2 [Middle English *girle* "young person of either sex"] — **girl·hood** \\-ˌhůd\\ *n*

girl·friend \\'gərl-ˌfrend\\ *n* **1** : a female friend **2** : a frequent or regular female companion of a boy or man

Girl Guide *n* : a member of a worldwide scouting movement for girls 7 to 18 years of age

girl·ish \\'gər-lish\\ *adj* : of, relating to, or having the characteristics of a female child — **girl·ish·ly** *adv* — **girl·ish·ness** *n*

Girl Scout *n* : a member of any of the scouting programs of the Girl Scouts of the United States of America for girls 6 through 17 years of age

Gi·rond·ist \\jə-'rän-dəst\\ *n* : a member of the moderate republican party in the French legislative assembly in 1791 [French *girondiste*, from *Gironde*, a political party, from *Gironde*, department of France]

girt \\'gərt\\ *vt* **1** : GIRD 1, 2 **2** : to fasten by means of a girth [Middle English *girten*, alteration of *girden*]

¹girth \\'gərth\\ *n* **1** : a band or strap that encircles the body of an animal to fasten something (as a saddle) upon its back **2** : a measure around a body [Old Norse *gjörth*]

²girth *vt* **1** : ENCIRCLE 2 **2** : to bind or fasten with a girth

gist \\'jist\\ *n* : the main point of a matter : ESSENCE [Anglo-French, "it lies" (in *cest action gist* "this action lies", statement laying the foundation of a legal action)]

¹give \\'giv\\ *vb* **gave** \\'gāv\\; **giv·en** \\'giv-ən\\; **giv·ing** **1** : to make a present of **2 a** : GRANT, ACCORD (*give* citizens the right to vote) **b** : to offer or yield to another (*gave* them my confidence) **3 a** : to put into the possession or keeping of another **b** : to offer to another : PROFFER (*give* one's hand to a visitor) **4 a** : to present in public performance (*give* a concert) **b** : to present to view (*gave* the signal) **5** : to provide by way of entertainment (*give* a party) **6** : to designate as a share or portion : ALLOT **7** : ATTRIBUTE, ASCRIBE (*gave* all the glory to God) **8** : to grant as true : ASSUME **9** : to yield as a product or result (cows *give* milk) **10** : PAY (*give* a fair price) **11 a** : to deliver by bodily action (*gave* it a push) **b** : to carry out (a movement) : EXECUTE (*gave* a sudden leap) **c** : to award by formal verdict (*give* judgment) **12** : to offer for consideration or acceptance (*give* a reason) **13** : to apply fully : DEVOTE (*give* oneself to a cause) **14** : to cause one to have or receive (*gave* pleasure to the reader) **15** : to make gifts or presents **16 a** : to yield to physical force or strain **b** : to collapse from the application of force or pressure [Middle English *given*, of Scandinavian origin] — **giv·er** \\'giv-ər\\ *n* □ SYN PRESENT, DONATE: GIVE is the general term applying to delivering, passing over, or transmitting in any manner; PRESENT implies more ceremony or formality and suggests a degree of complexity or value in what is given; DONATE implies a free but usually publicized giving, as to charity. — **give ground** : to withdraw before superior force : RETREAT — **give it to** : to attack vigorously — **give the lie to** : to show to be false — **give way 1 a** : RETREAT **b** : to yield the right of way **2** : to yield oneself without restraint or control **3 a** : COLLAPSE 3, FAIL **b** : CONCEDE 2

²give *n* **1** : capacity or tendency to yield to force or strain **2** : the quality or state of being springy

give-and-take \\ˌgiv-ən-'tāk\\ *n* **1** : the practice of making mutual concessions **2** : good-natured exchange of ideas

give·away \\'giv-ə-ˌwā\\ *n* **1** : an unintentional revelation or betrayal **2** : something given away free; *esp* : PREMIUM

give away \\ˌgiv-ə-'wā\\ *vt* **1** : to deliver (a bride) to the bridegroom at a wedding **2 a** : to expose to detection or ridicule : BETRAY **b** : REVEAL 1, DISCLOSE

give back *vb* **1** : RETREAT 1 **2** : RETURN 5, RESTORE

give in *vi* : YIELD 5, SURRENDER

giv·en \\'giv-ən\\ *adj* **1** : DISPOSED, INCLINED (*given* to gossiping) **2** : FIXED 1c, SPECIFIED (at a *given* time) **3** : granted as true : ASSUMED

given name *n* : CHRISTIAN NAME

give off *vt* : EMIT 1a

give out *vb* **1** : EMIT 1a **2** : ISSUE 2b **3** : to become exhausted : COLLAPSE **4** : to break down

give up *vb* **1** : to hand over to another : SURRENDER **2** : to abandon (oneself) to a feeling, influence, or activity **3** : to withdraw from an activity or course of action

giz·mo *or* **gis·mo** \\'giz-mō\\ *n, pl* **gizmos** *or* **gismos** : CONTRIVANCE 2, GADGET [origin unknown]

giz·zard \\'giz-ərd\\ *n* : a muscular enlargement of the digestive canal (as of a bird) that usually follows the crop and has a horny lining for grinding the food [Middle English *giser*, from Old North French *guisier*, from Latin *gigeria* "giblets"]

gla·brous \\'glā-brəs\\ *adj* : having a surface without hairs or projections : SMOOTH [Latin *glaber* "smooth, bald"] — **gla·brous·ness** *n*

gla·cé \\gla-'sā\\ *adj* **1** : made or finished so as to have a smooth glossy surface **2** : coated with a glaze : CANDIED [French, from *glacer* "to freeze, ice, glaze", derived from Latin *glacies* "ice"]

gla·cial \\'glā-shəl\\ *adj* **1 a** : extremely cold : FRIGID **b** : lacking warmth and cordiality **2 a** : of, relating to, or produced by glaciers **b** (1) : of, relating to, or being any of those parts of geologic time when a large portion of the earth was covered by glaciers (2) *cap* : PLEISTOCENE — **gla·cial·ly** \\-shə-lē\\ *adv*

gla·ci·ate \\'glā-shē-ˌāt\\ *vt* **1** : to cover with a glacier **2** : to subject to glacial action; *also* : to produce glacial effects in or on — **gla·ci·a·tion** \\ˌglā-shē-'ā-shən, -sē-\\ *n*

gla·cier \\'glā-shər\\ *n* : a large body of ice moving slowly down a slope or valley or spreading outward on a land surface [French dialect, from Middle French *glace* "ice", from Latin *glacies*]

gla·ci·ol·o·gy \\ˌglā-shē-'äl-ə-jē, -sē-\\ *n* : a branch of geology dealing with snow or ice accumulation, glaciation, and glacial epochs — **gla·ci·ol·o·gist** \\-jəst\\ *n*

¹glad \\'glad\\ *adj* **glad·der; glad·dest** **1 a** : experiencing pleasure, joy, or delight : made happy **b** : very willing (*glad* to do it) **2** : causing happiness and joy : PLEASANT (*glad* tidings) **3** : full of brightness and cheerfulness [Old English *glæd* "shining, glad"] — **glad·ly** *adv* — **glad·ness** *n*

²glad *n* : GLADIOLUS

glad·den \\'glad-n\\ *vt* **glad·dened; glad·den·ing** \\'glad-ning, -n-ing\\ : to make glad

glade \\'glād\\ *n* : a grassy open space in a forest [perhaps from ¹*glad*]

glad·i·a·tor \\'glad-ē-ˌāt-ər\\ *n* **1** : a person engaged in a fight to the death for public entertainment in ancient Rome **2** : a person engaging in a fierce fight or controversy [Latin, from *gladius* "sword", of Celtic origin] — **glad·i·a·to·ri·al** \\ˌglad-ē-ə-'tōr-ē-əl, -'tȯr-\\ *adj*

glad·i·o·lus \\ˌglad-ē-'ō-ləs\\ *n, pl* **-o·li** \\-lē, -ˌlē, -ˌlī\\ *or* **-o·lus** *or* **-o·lus·es** : any of a genus of chiefly African plants of the iris family with erect sword-shaped leaves and spikes of brilliantly colored irregular flowers [Latin, from *gladius* "sword"]

glad·some \\'glad-səm\\ *adj* : giving or showing joy : CHEERFUL — **glad·some·ly** *adv* — **glad·some·ness** *n*

glad·stone \\'glad-ˌstōn\\ *n, often cap* : a traveling bag with flexible sides on a rigid frame that opens flat into two compartments [W. E. *Gladstone*, died 1898, British statesman]

glam·or·ize \\'glam-ə-ˌrīz\\ *vt* **1** : to make glamorous **2** : to look upon as glamorous — **glam·or·iza·tion** \\ˌglam-ə-rə-'zā-shən\\ *n* — **glam·or·iz·er** *n*

glam·or·ous \\'glam-rəs, -ə-rəs\\ *adj* : full of glamour — **glam·or·ous·ly** *adv* — **glam·or·ous·ness** *n*

gladiolus

glam·our *or* **glam·or** \'glam-ər\ *n* : a romantic, exciting, and often illusory attractiveness; *esp* : alluring or fascinating personal attraction [Scottish *glamour* "magic spell", alteration of English *grammar*] □ ORIGIN In the Middle Ages the meaning of *grammar* was not restricted to the study of language but included learning in general. Since almost all learning was couched in language not spoken or understood by the unschooled populace, it was commonly believed that such subjects as magic and astrology were included in this broad sense of *grammar*. Scholars were often viewed with awe and more than a little suspicion by ordinary people. This connection between *grammar* and magic was evident in a number of languages, and in Scotland by the 18th century a form of *grammar*, altered to *glamer* or *glamour,* meant "a magic spell or enchantment". As *glamour* passed into more extended English usage, it came to mean "an elusive, mysteriously exciting attractiveness".

¹**glance** \'glans\ *vi* **1** : to strike something and fly off at an angle ⟨the bullet *glanced* off the wall⟩ **2** : to flash or gleam with quick intermittent rays of light ⟨the pond *glanced* in the sunlight⟩ **3 a** : to take a quick or hasty look ⟨*glanced* up from the book⟩ **b** : to refer briefly to a subject [Middle English *glencen, glenchen*] SYN see FLASH — **glanc·ing·ly** \-ing-lē\ *adv*

²**glance** *n* **1** : a quick intermittent flash or gleam **2** : a deflected impact or blow **3 a** : a swift movement of the eyes **b** : a quick or cursory look — **at first glance** : on first consideration □ SYN GLANCE, GLIMPSE are not synonymous even though both mean a brief view or viewing. GLANCE implies that one looks at something only briefly when he or she could have looked longer ⟨gave the paper hardly a *glance*⟩ GLIMPSE implies that only a brief look is possible ⟨got a *glimpse* of the deer before it vanished into the woods⟩

gland \'gland\ *n* **1** : a cell or group of cells that prepares and secretes a product for further use in or for elimination from the plant or animal body **2** : LYMPH GLAND [French *glande,* derived from Latin *gland-, glans* "acorn"] — **gland** *adj*

glan·ders \'glan-dərz\ *n sing or pl* : a destructive bacterial disease especially of horses characterized by nodules that tend to ulcerate [Middle French *glandre* "glandular swelling on the neck", derived from Latin *glans* "acorn"] — **glan·dered** \-dərd\ *adj*

glan·du·lar \'glan-jə-lər\ *adj* **1** : of, relating to, or involving glands, gland cells, or their products **2** : having the characteristics or function of a gland — **glan·du·lar·ly** *adv*

glans \'glanz\ *n, pl* **glan·des** \'glan-,dēz\ : the conical vascular extremity of the penis or clitoris [Latin, literally, "acorn"]

glans cli·to·ri·dis \-klə-'tór-əd-əs\ *n* : the glans of the clitoris

glans penis *n* : the glans of the penis

¹**glare** \'glaər, 'gleər\ *vb* **1** : to shine with a harsh uncomfortably brilliant light **2 a** : to stare angrily or fiercely **b** : to express (as hostility) by staring angrily [Middle English *glaren*]

²**glare** *n* **1** : a harsh uncomfortably bright light; *esp* : painfully bright sunlight **2** : an angry or fierce stare

³**glare** *n* : a smooth slippery surface or sheet of ice

glar·ing *adj* **1** : having a fixed look of hostility, fierceness, or anger **2 a** : shining with or reflecting an uncomfortably bright light **b** (1) : GARISH 1b (2) : vulgarly ostentatious **3** : painfully obvious ⟨a *glaring* error⟩ SYN see FLAGRANT — **glar·ing·ly** \-ing-lē\ *adv* — **glar·ing·ness** *n*

glary \'glaər-ē, 'gleər-\ *adj* **glar·i·er; -est** : having a dazzling brightness : GLARING

¹**glass** \'glas\ *n* **1 a** : a hard brittle usually transparent or translucent noncrystalline inorganic substance formed by melting a mixture (as of silica sand and metallic oxides) and cooling to a rigid condition **b** : a substance (as a rock formed by the rapid cooling of molten minerals) resembling glass **2 a** : something (as a water tumbler, lens, mirror, barometer, or telescope) that is made of glass or has a glass lens **b** *pl* : BINOCULARS **c** *pl* : a pair of glass lenses used to correct defects of vision — called also *eyeglasses, spectacles* **3** : the quantity held by a glass container [Old English *glæs*]

²**glass** *vt* : to fit or protect with glass

glass·blow·ing \-,blō-ing\ *n* : the art of shaping a mass of glass that has been softened by heat by blowing air into it through a tube — **glass·blow·er** \-,blō-ər, -,blor\ *n*

glass ceiling *n* : an intangible barrier within the hierarchy of a company that prevents women or minorities from obtaining upper-level positions

glass·ful \'glas-,fúl\ *n* : the quantity held by a glass

glass·mak·ing \-,mā-king\ *n* : the art or process of manufacturing glass

glass snake *n* : a limbless lizard of the southern United States resembling a snake and having a fragile tail that readily breaks into pieces

glass sponge *n* : a sponge with a glassy skeleton of silica

glass·ware \'glas-,waər, -,weər\ *n* : articles made of glass

glass wool *n* : glass fibers in a mass resembling wool used especially for thermal insulation and air filters

glassy \'glas-ē\ *adj* **glass·i·er; -est** **1** : resembling glass **2** : DULL, LIFELESS ⟨*glassy* eyes⟩ — **glass·i·ly** \'glas-ə-lē\ *adv* — **glass·i·ness** \'glas-ē-nəs\ *n*

Glau·ber's salt \'glaú-bərz-\ *also* **Glau·ber salt** \'glaú-bər-\ *n* : a colorless crystalline sulfate of sodium $Na_2SO_4 \cdot 10H_2O$ used especially as a cathartic [Johann R. *Glauber,* died 1668, German chemist]

glau·co·ma \glaú-'kō-mə, gló-\ *n* : an abnormal condition of the eye marked by increased pressure within the eye that causes damage to the retina and gradual loss of vision [Latin, "cataract", from Greek *glaukōma,* from *glaukos* "gray"]

glau·cous \'gló-kəs\ *adj* **1 a** : of a pale yellow green color **b** : of a light bluish gray or bluish white color **2** : having a powdery or waxy coating ⟨*glaucous* fruits like plums or grapes⟩ [Latin *glaucus* "gleaming, gray", from Greek *glaukos*] — **glau·cous·ness** *n*

¹**glaze** \'glāz\ *vb* **1** : to furnish or fit with glass **2 a** : to coat with or as if with glass **b** : to apply a glaze to **3** : to give a smooth glossy surface to **4** : to become glazed [Middle English *glasen,* from *glas* "glass"] — **glaz·er** *n*

²**glaze** *n* **1** : a smooth slippery coating of thin ice **2 a** : a transparent or translucent substance used as a coating (as on food or pottery) to produce a gloss **b** : a smooth glossy or lustrous surface or finish

gla·zier \'glā-zhər, -zē-ər\ *n* : a person who sets glass in window frames

glaz·ing \'glā-zing\ *n* : GLAZE

¹**gleam** \'glēm\ *n* **1 a** : a transient subdued or partly obscured light **b** : a small bright light : GLINT **2** : a brief or faint appearance : TRACE ⟨a *gleam* of hope⟩ [Old English *glæm*]

²**gleam** *vi* **1** : to shine with subdued light or moderate brightness **2** : to appear briefly or faintly

glean \'glēn\ *vb* **1** : to gather from a field or vineyard what has been left by harvesters **2** : to gather little by little ⟨*glean* knowledge from books⟩ [Middle French *glener,* from Late Latin *glennare*] — **glean·er** *n*

glean·ings \'glē-ningz\ *n pl* : things gotten by gleaning

glee \'glē\ *n* **1** : exultant high-spirited joy : HILARITY **2** : an unaccompanied song for three or more voices [Old English *gléo* "entertainment, music"] SYN see MIRTH

glee club *n* : a chorus organized for singing usually short choral pieces

glee·ful \'glē-fəl\ *adj* : full of glee : MERRY — **glee·ful·ly** \-fə-lē\ *adv* — **glee·ful·ness** *n*

gleet \'glēt\ *n* : chronic inflammation about a bodily opening accompanied by an abnormal discharge; *also* : this discharge [Middle French *glete* "mucous matter", from Latin *glittus* "viscous"]

glen \'glen\ *n* : a small secluded narrow valley [Middle English (Scottish dialect), "valley", of Scottish Gaelic origin]

glen·gar·ry \glen-'gar-ē\ *n, often cap* : a woolen cap of Scottish origin [*Glengarry,* valley in Scotland]

glib \'glib\ *adj* **glib·ber; glib·best** : marked by careless ease and fluency and often trickiness in speaking or writing ⟨a *glib* talker⟩ ⟨a *glib* excuse⟩ [probably from Low German *glibberig* "slippery"] — **glib·ly** *adv* — **glib·ness** *n*

¹glide \'glīd\ *vi* **1** : to move smoothly, continuously, and effortlessly **2** : to pass gradually and imperceptibly ⟨hours *gliding* by⟩ **3** : to descend gradually without engine power sufficient for level flight ⟨*glide* in an airplane⟩ [Old English *glīdan*]

²glide *n* **1** : the act or action of gliding **2 a** : PORTAMENTO **b** : a transitional sound produced by the passing of the vocal organs to or from the position for the articulation of a speech sound

glid·er \'glīd-ər\ *n* : one that glides: as **a** : an aircraft without an engine that glides on air currents **b** : a porch seat suspended from a frame by short chains or straps

¹glim·mer \'glim-ər\ *vi* **glim·mered; glim·mer·ing** \'glim-ring, -ə-ring\ : to shine faintly or unsteadily [Middle English *glimeren*]

²glimmer *n* **1 a** : a feeble or intermittent light **b** : a soft shimmer **2 a** : a faint idea : INKLING **b** : a small amount : BIT

¹glimpse \'glimps\ *vb* : to take a brief look : see momentarily or incompletely [Middle English *glimsen*] — **glimps·er** *n*

²glimpse *n* **1** : a short hurried view ⟨catch a *glimpse* of someone rushing by⟩ **2** : GLIMMER 2a SYN see GLANCE

¹glint \'glint\ *vi* **1** *archaic* : GLANCE 1 **2** : to shine by reflection : **a** : to shine with small bright flashes : SPARKLE **b** : GLITTER 1a **c** : GLEAM 1 **3** : to appear briefly or faintly ⟨fear *glinted* in their eyes⟩ [Middle English *glinten* "to dart obliquely, glint", of Scandinavian origin] SYN see FLASH

²glint *n* **1** : a small bright flash of light : SPARKLE **2** : a brief or faint manifestation ⟨a *glint* of interest⟩

glis·san·do \gli-'sän-dō\ *n, pl* **-di** \-,dē\ *or* **-dos** : a rapid sliding up or down the musical scale [probably from French *glissade* "slide", from *glisser* "to slide"]

glis·ten \'glis-n\ *vi* **glis·tened; glis·ten·ing** \'glis-ning, -n-ing\ : to shine by reflection with a soft luster or sparkle [Old English *glisnian*] — **glisten** *n* □ SYN GLISTEN, GLITTER, SCINTILLATE mean to give out bright flashes of light. GLISTEN implies a subdued shining as from a wet or oily surface; GLITTER implies a dancing brightness often with a suggestion of coldness or evil ⟨eyes *glittering* with greed⟩; SCINTILLATE suggests a series of quick flashes caused by or as if by the emission of sparks ⟨clear sky with *scintillating* stars⟩ ⟨*scintillating* conversation⟩

glis·ter \'glis-tər\ *vi* **glis·tered; glis·ter·ing** \-tə-ring, -tring\ : GLISTEN [Middle English *glistren*] — **glister** *n*

glitch \'glich\ *n* **1 a** : a usually minor malfunction; *also* : BUG 2 **b** : a minor problem that causes a temporary setback : SNAG **2** : a false electronic signal [perhaps from Yiddish *glitsh* "slippery place"]

¹glit·ter \'glit-ər\ *vi* **1 a** : to shine with brilliant or metallic luster ⟨*glittering* sequins⟩ **b** : to shine with a cold glassy brilliance ⟨eyes *glittered* cruelly⟩ **2** : to be brilliantly attractive especially in a superficial way [Old Norse *glitra*] SYN see GLISTEN

²glitter *n* **1** : sparkling brilliancy, showiness, or attractiveness **2** : small glittering objects used for decoration — **glit·tery** \'glit-ə-rē\ *adj*

glitz \'glits\ *n* : extravagant showiness : GLITTER — **glitzy** \'glit-sē\ *adj* [perhaps from German *glitzern* to glitter]

gloam·ing \'glō-ming\ *n* : DUSK 1, TWILIGHT [Old English *glōming,* from *glōm* "twilight"]

gloat \'glōt\ *vi* : to think about something with great and often malicious delight [probably of Scandinavian origin] — **gloat·er** *n* — **gloat·ing·ly** \-ing-lē\ *adv*

glob \'gläb\ *n* : a small drop : BLOB [perhaps blend of *globe* and *blob*]

glob·al \'glō-bəl\ *adj* **1** : GLOBULAR **2** : WORLDWIDE ⟨a *global* communications system⟩ **3** : of, relating to, or applying to the whole of something ⟨as a computer program⟩ ⟨a *global* search through the data⟩ — **glob·al·ly** \-bə-lē\ *adv*

globe \'glōb\ *n* : something spherical or rounded: as **a** : a spherical representation of the earth or heavens **b** : EARTH 4 [Middle French, from Latin *globus*]

globe·fish \-,fish\ *n* : PUFFER 2

globe–trot·ter \-,trät-ər\ *n* : one that travels widely — **globe–trot·ting** \-,trät-ing\ *n or adj*

glob·u·lar \'gläb-yə-lər\ *adj* : having the shape of a globe

glob·ule \'gläb-yül\ *n* : a tiny globe or ball ⟨*globules* of fat⟩

glob·u·lin \'gläb-yə-lən\ *n* : any of a class of simple proteins insoluble in pure water but soluble in dilute salt solutions that occur widely in plant and animal tissues

glock·en·spiel \'gläk-ən-,shpēl, -,spēl\ *n* : a percussion instrument consisting of a series of graduated metal bars tuned to the chromatic scale and played with two hammers [German, from *glocke* "bell" + *spiel* "play"]

glo·mer·u·lus \glä-'mer-ə-ləs, -yə-ləs\ *n, pl* **-li** \-,lī, -,lē\ : a clump of capillaries surrounded by the expanded sac-shaped end of each functional tubule of the vertebrate kidney [New Latin, from Latin *glomus* "ball"] — **glo·mer·u·lar** \-lər\ *adj*

¹gloom \'glüm\ *vi* **1** : to look sullen or despondent **2** : to be or become overcast [Middle English *gloumen*]

²gloom *n* **1** : partial or total darkness **2 a** : lowness of spirits : DEJECTION **b** : an atmosphere of despondency

gloomy \'glü-mē\ *adj* **gloom·i·er; -est** **1** : dismally dark ⟨a *gloomy* cave⟩ **2** : low in spirits **3 a** : causing gloom ⟨*gloomy* weather⟩ ⟨*gloomy* news⟩ **b** : PESSIMISTIC 1 — **gloom·i·ly** \-mə-lē\ *adv* — **gloom·i·ness** \-mē-nəs\ *n*

Glo·ria \'glōr-ē-ə, 'glȯr-\ *n* : either of two Christian doxologies: **a** *or* **Gloria in Ex·cel·sis** \-,in-eks-'chel-səs, -ek-'shel-\ : one beginning "Glory be to God on high" **b** *or* **Gloria Pa·tri** \-'pä-trē\ : one beginning "Glory be to the Father" [Latin *gloria* "glory"]

glo·ri·fy \'glōr-ə-,fī, 'glȯr-\ *vt* **-fied; -fy·ing** **1** : to make glorious by bestowing honor, praise, or admiration **2** : to present in a highly often overly favorable light ⟨*glorify* war⟩ **3** : to give glory to ⟨as in worship⟩ — **glo·ri·fi·ca·tion** \,glōr-ə-fə-'kā-shən, ,glȯr-\ *n* — **glo·ri·fi·er** \'glōr-ə-,fī-ər, 'glȯr-, -,fīr\ *n*

glo·ri·ous \'glōr-ē-əs, 'glȯr-\ *adj* **1 a** : having or deserving glory **b** : conferring glory ⟨a *glorious* victory⟩ **2** : marked by great beauty, excellence, or splendor ⟨*glorious* weather⟩ **3** : extremely pleasant ⟨had a *glorious* time⟩ SYN see SPLENDID — **glo·ri·ous·ly** *adv* — **glo·ri·ous·ness** *n*

¹glo·ry \'glōr-ē, 'glȯr-\ *n, pl* **glories** **1 a** : praise, honor, or distinction extended by common consent : RENOWN **b** : worshipful praise, honor, and thanksgiving ⟨giving *glory* to God⟩ **2 a** : something that brings praise or renown **b** : a brilliant asset ⟨was a *glory* to the profession⟩ **3 a** : RESPLENDENCE, MAGNIFICENCE ⟨the *glory* of ancient Greece⟩ **b** : the splendor and bliss of heaven **4** : a height of prosperity, achievement, or gratification ⟨in your *glory* when you're acting⟩ [Latin *gloria*]

²glory *vi* : to rejoice proudly or intensely : EXULT

gloss \'gläs, 'glȯs\ *n* **1** : brightness from a smooth surface : LUSTER, SHEEN **2** : a deceptively attractive ap-

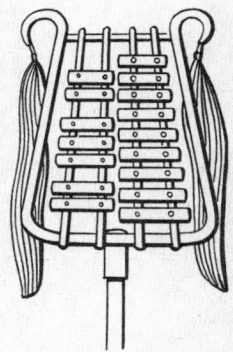

glockenspiel

pearance ⟨a *gloss* of good manners⟩ [probably of Scandinavian origin]

²gloss *vt* **1** : to give a false appearance of acceptableness or adequacy to ⟨*gloss* over faults⟩ **2** : to make glossy

³gloss *n* **1** : a brief explanation (as in the margin of a text) of a hard or unusual word or expression **2 a** : GLOSSARY **b** : an interlinear translation **c** : a continuous commentary accompanying a text [Old French *glose*, from Latin *glossa* "unusual word requiring explanation", from Greek *glōssa*, *glōtta*, literally, "tongue, language"]

⁴gloss *vt* : to furnish glosses for

glos·sa·ry \'gläs-rē, 'glȯs-, -ə-rē\ *n*, *pl* **-ries 1** : a list in the back of a book of the hard or unusual words found in the text **2** : a dictionary of the special terms found in a particular field of study — **glos·sar·i·al** \gläs-'sar-ē-əl, -'ser-\ *adj*

glos·so·pha·ryn·geal nerve \ˌgläs-ō-ˌfar-ən-'jē-əl-, ˌglȯs-; -fə-'rin-jē-əl-, -jəl-\ *n* : either of a pair of cranial nerves that supply chiefly the pharynx, posterior tongue, and parotid gland — called also *glossopharyngeal* [Greek *glōssa* "tongue"]

glossy \'gläs-ē, 'glȯs-\ *adj* **gloss·i·er; -est 1** : having surface luster ⟨*glossy* leather⟩ **2** : superficially sophisticated and attractive ⟨*glossy* advertisements⟩ — **gloss·i·ness** *n*

glot·tis \'glät-əs\ *n*, *pl* **glot·tis·es** *or* **glot·ti·des** \'glät-ə-ˌdēz\ : the elongated space in the larynx between the vocal cords; *also* : the structures that surround this space — compare EPIGLOTTIS [Greek *glōttis*, from *glōtta* "tongue"] — **glot·tal** \'glät-l\ *adj*

glove \'gləv\ *n* **1 a** : a covering for the hand having separate sections for each finger **b** : GAUNTLET 1 **2 a** : a padded leather covering for the hand used in baseball **b** : BOXING GLOVE [Old English *glōf*] — **gloved** \'gləvd\ *adj*

¹glow \'glō\ *vi* **1 a** : to shine with or as if with an intense heat **b** (1) : to have a rich warm usually ruddy color (2) : FLUSH, BLUSH **2 a** : to experience a sensation of heat **b** : to show exuberance or elation ⟨*glow* with pride⟩ [Old English *glōwan*]

²glow *n* **1** : brightness or warmth of color; *esp* : REDNESS **2 a** : warmth of feeling or emotion **b** : a sensation of warmth **3** : light that is emitted by something intensely hot but not flaming ⟨the *glow* of embers⟩

glow·er \'glau̇-ər, 'glau̇r\ *vi* : to stare angrily [Middle English *glowren*] — **glower** *n*

glow·worm \'glō-ˌwərm\ *n* : an insect or insect larva that gives off light

glox·in·ia \gläk-'sin-ē-ə\ *n* : any of a genus of Brazilian tuberous herbs related to the African violets; *esp* : one often grown for its showy bell-shaped or slipper-shaped flowers [B. P. *Gloxin*, 18th century German botanist]

gloze \'glōz\ *vt* : ²GLOSS 1 [Middle English *glosen* "to gloss, flatter", from *glose* "gloss"]

glu·ca·gon \'glü-kə-ˌgän\ *n* : a protein hormone secreted by the pancreas that increases the content of sugar in the blood [derived from *glucose*]

glu·cose \'glü-ˌkōs\ *n* **1** : a sugar $C_6H_{12}O_6$ known in three different forms; *esp* : DEXTROSE **2** : CORN SYRUP [French, from Greek *gleukos* "must, sweet wine"]

glu·co·side \'glü-kə-ˌsīd\ *n* : GLYCOSIDE

¹glue \'glü\ *n* **1** : any of various strong adhesive substances; *esp* : a hard protein substance that absorbs water to form a viscous solution with strong adhesive properties **2** : a solution of glue used to stick things together [Middle French *glu*, from Late Latin *glus*] — **glu·ey** \'glü-ē\ *adj* — **glu·i·ly** \'glü-ə-lē\ *adv*

²glue *vt* **glued; glu·ing** *also* **glue·ing** : to make fast with or as if with glue

glum \'gləm\ *adj* **glum·mer; glum·mest 1** : SULLEN 1 **2** : DREARY, GLOOMY [probably related to Middle English *gloumen* "to gloom"] — **glum·ly** *adv* — **glum·ness** *n*

glume \'glüm\ *n* : either of two empty bracts at the base of the spikelet in a grass [Latin *gluma* "hull, husk"]

¹glut \'glət\ *vt* **glut·ted; glut·ting 1** : to fill especially with food to excess : STUFF **2** : to flood with goods so that supply exceeds demand ⟨the market was *glutted* with fruit⟩ [Middle English *glouten*]

²glut *n* : an excessive quantity : OVERSUPPLY

glu·ta·mate \'glüt-ə-ˌmāt\ *n* : a salt or ester of glutamic acid

glu·tam·ic acid \glü-'tam-ik-\ *n* : an amino acid $C_5H_9NO_4$ widely distributed in plant and animal proteins and used in the form of a sodium salt as a seasoning [*glut*en + *am*ino + -*ic*]

glu·ta·mine \'glüt-ə-ˌmēn\ *n* : an amino acid that is found in plant and animal proteins and that yields glutamic acid and ammonia on hydrolysis

glu·ten \'glüt-n\ *n* : a tough elastic protein substance in flour especially from wheat that holds dough together and makes it sticky [Latin, "glue"] — **glu·ten·ous** \'glüt-nəs, -n-əs\ *adj*

glu·te·us \'glüt-ē-əs\ *n*, *pl* **-tei** \-ē-ˌī\ : any of the large muscles of the buttocks [New Latin, from Greek *gloutos* "buttock"] — **glu·te·al** \-ē-əl\ *adj*

glu·ti·nous \'glüt-nəs, -n-əs\ *adj* : resembling glue : STICKY [Latin *glutinosus*, from *gluten* "glue"] — **glu·ti·nous·ly** *adv*

glut·ton \'glət-n\ *n* **1** : one that eats too much **2** : WOLVERINE [Old French *gloton*, from Latin *glutto*] — **glut·ton·ous** \'glət-nəs, -n-əs\ *adj* — **glut·ton·ous·ly** *adv*

glut·tony \'glət-nē; -n-ē\ *n*, *pl* **-ton·ies** : excess in eating or drinking

glyc·er·al·de·hyde \ˌglis-ə-'ral-də-ˌhīd\ *n* : a sweet crystalline compound $C_3H_6O_3$ that is formed as an intermediate in carbohydrate metabolism by the breakdown of sugars

gly·cer·ic acid \glis-'er-ik-\ *n* : a syrupy acid $C_3H_6O_4$ obtainable by oxidation of glycerol

glyc·er·ide \'glis-ə-ˌrīd\ *n* : an ester of glycerol especially with fatty acids — **glyc·er·id·ic** \ˌglis-ə-'rid-ik\ *adj*

glyc·er·in *or* **glyc·er·ine** \'glis-rən, -ə-rən\ *n* : GLYCEROL [French *glycérine*, from Greek *glykeros* "sweet"]

glyc·er·ol \'glis-ə-ˌrȯl, -ˌrōl\ *n* : a sweet colorless syrupy alcohol $C_3H_8O_3$ usually obtained by the hydrolysis of fats and oils and used especially as a solvent and plasticizer

gly·cine \'glī-ˌsēn, 'glīs-n\ *n* : a sweet amino acid $C_2H_5NO_2$ formed especially by hydrolysis of proteins [Greek *glykys* "sweet"]

gly·co·gen \'glī-kə-jən\ *n* : a white tasteless substance that is the chief storage carbohydrate of animals — called also *animal starch* [Greek *glykys* "sweet"]

gly·col·y·sis \glī-'käl-ə-səs\ *n* : energy-producing breakdown of carbohydrate (as glucose) by enzymes by way of phosphate derivatives — **gly·co·lyt·ic** \ˌglī-kə-'lit-ik\ *adj*

gly·co·side \'glī-kə-ˌsīd\ *n* : any of numerous derivatives of sugars that on hydrolysis yield a sugar (as glucose) — **gly·co·sid·ic** \ˌglī-kə-'sid-ik\ *adj*

gly·cos·uria \ˌglī-kō-'shu̇r-ē-ə, -kəs-'yu̇r-\ *n* : the presence of abnormal amounts of sugar in the urine [derived from Greek *glykys* "sweet" + *ouron* "urine"]

G-man \'jē-ˌman\ *n* : a special agent of the Federal Bureau of Investigation [probably from *g*overnment *man*]

gnarl \'närl\ *n* : a hard knob with twisted grain on a tree [probably from *knurl*] — **gnarled** \'närld\ *adj* — **gnarly** \'när-lē\ *adj*

gnash \'nash\ *vt* : to strike or grind (the teeth) together [Middle English *gnasten*]

gnat \'nat\ *n* : any of various small usually biting two-winged flies — compare ³FLY 2 [Old English *gnætt*]

gnaw \'nȯ\ *vb* **1 a** : to bite or chew with the teeth; *esp* : to wear away by persistent biting or nibbling ⟨a dog *gnawing* a bone⟩ **b** : to make by gnawing ⟨rats *gnawed* a hole⟩ **2 a** : to be a source of vexation to : PLAGUE **b** : to affect like gnawing ⟨*gnawing* hunger⟩ **3** : ERODE 1a, CORRODE [Old English *gnagan*]— **gnaw·er** \'nȯ-ər, 'nȯr\ *n*

gneiss \'nīs\ *n* : a metamorphic rock occurring in layers that is similar in composition to granite or feldspar [German *gneis*]

gnome \'nōm\ *n* : a legendary dwarf living inside the earth and guarding precious ore or treasure [French] — **gnom·ish** \'nō-mish\ *adj*

gno·mon \'nō-ˌmän, -mən\ *n* : an object that by the position or length of its shadow serves as an indicator of the hour of the day : *esp* : the style of an ordinary sundial [Latin, from Greek *gnōmōn* "interpreter, pointer on a sundial", from *gignōskein* "to know"]

gnu \'nü, 'nyü\ *n, pl* **gnu** *or* **gnus** : any of several large African antelopes with a head like that of an ox, short mane, long tail, and horns in both sexes that curve downward and outward [Bushman *nqu*]

¹go \'gō\ *vb* **went** \'went\; **gone** \'gȯn, 'gän\; **go·ing** \'gō-ing\; **goes** \'gōz\ **1** : to move on a course : PROCEED ⟨*go* slow⟩ **2** : to move away from one point to or toward another : LEAVE, DEPART **3 a** : to take a certain course or follow a certain procedure ⟨reports *go* through channels⟩ **b** : to pass by a process like journeying ⟨the message *went* by wire⟩ **c** (1) : EXTEND, RUN ⟨our land *goes* to the river⟩ (2) : to give access : LEAD ⟨that door *goes* to the cellar⟩ **4** : to be habitually in a certain state ⟨*goes* bareheaded⟩ **5 a** : to become lost, consumed, or spent **b** : ELAPSE, PASS ⟨the evening *went* well⟩ **c** : to pass by sale ⟨*went* for a good price⟩ **d** : to become impaired or weakened ⟨my hearing started to *go*⟩ **e** : to give way under force or pressure : BREAK **6 a** : to be in general or on an average ⟨cheap, as yachts *go*⟩ **b** : to become especially as the result of a contest ⟨the decision *went* against them⟩ **7 a** : to apply oneself ⟨*went* to fighting among themselves⟩ **b** : to put or subject oneself ⟨*went* to great expense⟩ **8** : to have recourse : RESORT ⟨*go* to court to recover damages⟩ **9 a** : to begin or maintain an action or motion ⟨drums *going* strong⟩ **b** : to function properly ⟨get the motor to *go*⟩ **10** : to have currency : CIRCULATE ⟨the report *goes*⟩ **11 a** : to act in accordance ⟨a good rule to *go* by⟩ **b** : to come to be applied ⟨part of the budget *goes* for schools⟩ **c** : to pass by award, assignment, or lot ⟨the prize *went* to a sophomore⟩ **d** : to contribute to a result ⟨qualities that *go* to make a hero⟩ **12 a** : to be about, intending, or expecting something ⟨is *going* to leave town⟩ **b** : to come or arrive at a certain state or condition ⟨*go* to sleep⟩ **c** : to come to be ⟨the tire *went* flat⟩ **13 a** : FIT 2a ⟨these clothes will *go* in your suitcase⟩ **b** : to have a usual or proper place or position : BELONG ⟨these books *go* on the top shelf⟩ **c** : to be contained in another quantity when used as a divisor ⟨5 *goes* into 60 12 times⟩ **14** : TEND, CONDUCE ⟨*goes* to show they can be trusted⟩ **15** : to be acceptable : DO ⟨any kind of dress *goes*⟩ **16 a** : to proceed along or according to : FOLLOW ⟨if I was *going* your way⟩ **b** : TRAVERSE 2 **17** : to make a wager or offer of ⟨willing to *go* $50⟩ **18 a** : to assume the function or obligation of ⟨*go* bail for a friend⟩ **b** : to participate to the extent of ⟨*go* halves⟩ **19** : WEIGH 1b [Old English *gan*]— **go at 1** : to make an attack on **2** : UNDERTAKE 1 — **go back on 1** : ABANDON 2, 3 **2** : BETRAY 2 **3** : FAIL 2a — **go by the board** : to be discarded — **go down the line** : to give wholehearted support — **go for 1** : to pass for or serve as **2** : to be attracted to : LIKE **3** : ATTACK 1 — **go one better** : SURPASS 1, OUTDO — **go over 1 a** : CONSIDER 1 **b** : EXAMINE 1 **2 a** : REPEAT 1a **b** : REVIEW 1 — **go places** : to be on the way to success — **go steady** : to date one person exclusively — **go through 1** : to subject to thorough examination, consideration, or study **2** : EXPERIENCE 1, UNDERGO **3** : to carry out : PERFORM ⟨*went through* the act perfectly⟩ — **go to bat for** : to

give active support or help to — **go to one's head** : to cause one to become conceited or overconfident — **go to pieces** : to become shattered (as in nerves or health) — **go to town 1** : to act rapidly or efficiently **2** : to be very successful — **go with** : DATE 4 — **go without saying** : to be self-evident

²go *n, pl* **goes 1** : the act or manner of going **2** : the height of fashion **3** : an often unexpected turn of affairs **4** : ENERGY 1 **5** : TRY ⟨give it a *go*⟩ **6** : a spell of activity — **no go** : to no avail : USELESS — **on the go** : constantly or restlessly active

³go *adj* : ready to go ⟨declared all systems *go*⟩

⁴go *n* : an Oriental board game played between two players who alternately place black and white stones on a board checkered by 19 vertical and 19 horizontal lines in an attempt to enclose the opponent's stones [Japanese]

goad \'gōd\ *n* **1** : a pointed rod used to urge an animal on **2** : something that urges : SPUR [Old English *gād* "spear, goad"]— **goad** *vt*

go–ahead \'gō-ə-ˌhed\ *n* : GREEN LIGHT

goal \'gōl, *in children's games sometimes* 'gül\ *n* **1** : the terminal point of a race **2** : the end toward which effort is directed : AIM **3 a** : an area or object toward which players in various games attempt to advance a ball or puck to score points **b** : the score resulting from such an act [Middle English *gol* "boundary, limit"]

goal·ie \'gō-lē\ *n* : GOALKEEPER

goal·keep·er \'gōl-ˌkē-pər\ *n* : a player who defends the goal in various games

goal line *n* : a line at or near one end of the playing area which marks the goal or on which the goal sits

goal·post \'gōl-ˌpōst\ *n* : one of two vertical posts that with a crossbar constitute the goal in various games

goal·ten·der \'gōl-ˌten-dər\ *n* : GOALKEEPER

goat \'gōt\ *n, pl* **goat** *or* **goats 1** : any of various hollow-horned ruminant mammals related to the sheep but of lighter build and with backwardly arching horns, a short tail, and usually straight hair **2** : SCAPEGOAT 2 [Old English *gāt*]— **goat·like** \-ˌlīk\ *adj*

goa·tee \gō-'tē\ *n* : a small pointed or tufted beard on a man's chin [from its resemblance to the beard of a he-goat]

goat·fish \'gōt-ˌfish\ *n* : MULLET 2

goat·skin \-ˌskin\ *n* **1** : the skin of a goat **2** : leather made from goatskin

goat·suck·er \-ˌsək-ər\ *n* : any of various medium-sized long-winged nocturnal birds (as the whippoorwills and nighthawks) having a short wide bill, short legs, and soft mottled plumage and feeding on insects which they catch on the wing [from the belief that it sucks milk from goats]

¹gob \'gäb\ *n* **1** : LUMP 1, MASS **2** : a large amount — usually used in pl. ⟨*gobs* of money⟩ [Middle French *gobe* "large piece of food", from *gobet*]

²gob *n* : SAILOR 1a [origin unknown]

gob·bet \'gäb-ət\ *n* : LUMP 1, MASS [Middle French *gobet* "mouthful, piece"]

¹gob·ble \'gäb-əl\ *vt* **gob·bled; gob·bling** \'gäb-ling, -ə-ling\ **1** : to swallow or eat greedily **2** : to take eagerly : GRAB — usually used with up [probably from ¹*gob*]

²gobble *vi* : to utter the characteristic guttural cry of a male turkey [imitative]— **gobble** *n*

gob·ble·dy·gook *or* **gob·ble·de·gook** \'gäb-əl-dē-ˌgùk\ *n* : wordy and generally unintelligible jargon [from *gobble, n.*]

gob·bler \'gäb-lər\ *n* : a male turkey

go–be·tween \'gō-bə-ˌtwēn\ *n* : a person who acts as a messenger or an intermediary between two parties

gob·let \'gäb-lət\ *n* : a drinking glass with a foot and stem — compare TUMBLER [Middle French *gobelet*]

goblet cell *n* : a mucus-secreting cell swollen at the free end by secretion [from its shape]

gnu

gob·lin \'gäb-lən\ *n* : an ugly grotesque sprite with evil or mischievous ways [Middle French *gobelin,* from Medieval Latin *gobelinus,* derived from Greek *kobalos* "rogue"]

go·by \'gō-bē\ *n, pl* **gobies** *also* **goby** : any of numerous spiny-finned fishes with the pelvic fins often united to form a sucking disk [Latin *gobius,* a kind of fish, from Greek *kōbios*]

go-cart \'gō-,kärt\ *n* **1** : STROLLER 2 **2** : a light open carriage

god \'gäd *also* 'gȯd\ *n* **1** *cap* : the supreme or ultimate reality; *esp* : the Being perfect in power, wisdom, and goodness whom humans worship as creator and ruler of the universe **2** : a being held to possess more than human powers 〈ancient peoples worshipped many *gods*〉 **3** : a natural or man-made physical object (as an image or idol) worshipped as divine **4** : something held to be the most important thing in existence 〈make a *god* of money〉 [Old English]

god·child \-,chīld\ *n* : a person for whom another person stands as sponsor at baptism

god·daugh·ter \-,dȯt-ər\ *n* : a female godchild

god·dess \'gäd-əs\ *n* **1** : a female god **2** : a woman whose great charm or beauty arouses adoration

god·fa·ther \'gäd-,fäth-ər *also* 'gȯd-\ *n* : a man who stands as sponsor for a child at its baptism

god·head \-,hed\ *n* **1** : divine nature or essence : DIVINITY **2** *cap* **a** : GOD 1 **b** : the nature of God especially as existing in three persons — used with *the* [Middle English *godhed,* from *god* + *-bed* "-hood"]

god·hood \-,hu̇d\ *n* : DIVINITY 1

god·less \'gäd-ləs *also* 'gȯd-\ *adj* : not acknowledging a deity or divine law — **god·less·ness** *n*

god·like \-,līk\ *adj* : resembling or having the qualities of God or a god : DIVINE — **god·like·ness** *n*

god·ling \-ling\ *n* : an inferior or local god

god·ly \-lē\ *adj* **god·li·er; -est** : PIOUS, DEVOUT 〈*godly* people〉 — **god·li·ness** *n*

god·moth·er \-,məth-ər\ *n* : a woman who stands as sponsor for a child at its baptism

god·par·ent \-,par-ənt, -,per-\ *n* : a sponsor at baptism

God's acre *n* : CHURCHYARD; *esp* : a churchyard burial ground

god·send \'gäd-,send *also* 'gȯd-\ *n* : a desirable or needed thing or event that comes unexpectedly [back-formation from *god-sent*]

god·son \-,sən\ *n* : a male godchild

God·speed \-'spēd\ *n* : a prosperous journey : SUCCESS 〈wished them *Godspeed*〉 [Middle English *god speid,* from the phrase *God spede you* "God prosper you"]

god·wit \'gäd-,wit\ *n* : any of a genus of long-billed wading birds related to the snipes but similar to curlews [origin unknown]

go·er \'gō-ər, 'gȯr\ *n* : one that goes

go-get·ter \'gō-,get-ər\ *n* : an aggressively enterprising person : HUSTLER — **go-get·ting** \-,get-ing\ *adj or n*

¹gog·gle \'gäg-əl\ *vi* **gog·gled; gog·gling** \'gäg-ling, -ə-ling\ : to stare with wide or protuberant eyes [Middle English *gogelen* "to squint"] — **gog·gler** \'gäg-lər, -ə-lər\ *n*

²goggle *adj* : PROTUBERANT, STARING 〈*goggle* eyes〉 — **gog·gly** \'gäg-lē, -ə-lē\ *adj*

gog·gle-eyed \,gäg-əl-'īd\ *adj* : having bulging or rolling eyes

gog·gles \'gäg-əlz\ *n pl* : protective eyeglasses typically with shields at the side

Goi·del·ic \gȯi-'del-ik\ *n* : a branch of the Celtic languages that includes Irish Gaelic, Scottish Gaelic, and Manx [Irish *Gōidel* "Gael"] — **Goidelic** *adj*

go in *vi* : to enter some place — **go in for** **1** : to make one's particular interest or specialty **2** : to take part in out of interest or liking 〈*go in* for track〉

¹go·ing \'gō-ing\ *n* **1** : the condition of the ground especially for walking or driving **2** : advance toward an objective : PROGRESS

²going *adj* **1** : EXISTING, LIVING 〈the best novelist *going*〉 **2** : CURRENT, PREVAILING 〈*going* prices〉 **3** : being successful and likely to remain so 〈a *going* concern〉

go·ing-over \,gō-ing-'ō-vər\ *n* **1** : a thorough examination or investigation **2** : a severe scolding or beating : DRUBBING

go·ings-on \,gō-ingz-'ȯn, -'än\ *n pl* : usually undesirable actions or events

goi·ter *also* **goi·tre** \'gȯit-ər\ *n* : an enlargement of the thyroid gland visible as a swelling of the front of the neck — compare HYPERTHYROIDISM, HYPOTHYROIDISM [French *goitre,* from Middle French *goitron* "throat", from Latin *guttur*] — **goi·trous** \'gȯi-trəs, 'gȯit-ə-rəs\ *adj*

gold \'gōld\ *n* **1** : a malleable ductile yellow metallic element that occurs chiefly free but also in a few minerals and is used especially in coins and jewelry — see ELEMENT table **2 a** : gold coins **b** : RICHES, MONEY **3** : a deep yellow [Old English] — **gold** *adj*

¹gold-brick \'gōld-,brik, 'gōl-\ *n* : a person who habitually shirks assigned work [earlier *goldbrick* "worthless brick that appears to be of gold"]

²goldbrick *vi* : to shirk duty or responsibility

gold digger *n* : a woman who uses her charm to get money or gifts from men

gold·en \'gōl-dən\ *adj* **1** : consisting of, relating to, or containing gold **2** : having the color of gold 〈*golden* hair〉 **3** : FLOURISHING, PROSPEROUS 〈a *golden* age〉 **4** : radiantly youthful and vigorous **5** : of precious rarity 〈a *golden* opportunity〉 **6** : MELLOW, RESONANT 〈a smooth *golden* tenor〉 — **gold·en·ly** *adv* — **gold·en·ness** \-dən-nəs\ *n*

golden-brown alga *n* : any of a major group (Chrysophyta) of algae with golden brown pigments usually hiding the chlorophyll — called also *golden alga*

gold·en·eye \'gōl-də-,nī\ *n* **1** : a northern diving duck having the male strikingly marked in black and white **2** : LACEWING

golden glow *n* : a tall branching herb related to the daisies that has showy yellow very double flower heads

golden mean *n* : the medium between extremes : MODERATION

gold·en·rod \'gōl-dən-,räd\ *n* : any of numerous chiefly North American biennial or perennial plants that are related to the daisies and that have stems resembling wands and heads of small yellow or sometimes white flowers usually in loosely branched clusters

golden rule *n* : a rule that one should do to others as one would do to oneself

gol·den·seal \'gōl-dən-,sēl\ *n* : a perennial American herb of the buttercup family with a thick knotted yellow rhizome and large rounded leaves

golden section *n* : division of a line segment such that the ratio of the smaller part to the larger is equal to the ratio of the larger to the whole segment

gold·field \'gōld-,fēld, 'gōl-\ *n* : a gold-mining district

gold-filled \-'fild\ *adj* : covered with a layer of gold

gold·finch \-,finch\ *n* **1** : a small largely red, black, and yellow European finch often kept as a cage bird **2** : any of several small American finches usually having the male in summer plumage yellow with black wings, tail, and crown

gold·fish \-,fish\ *n* : a small usually golden yellow or orange carp much used as an aquarium and pond fish

gold leaf *n* : a thin sheet of gold used especially for gilding

gold·smith \'gōld-,smith, 'gōl-\ *n* : a maker of or dealer in articles of gold

gold standard *n* : a monetary standard under which the basic unit of currency is defined by a stated quantity of gold

golf \'gälf, 'gȯlf, 'gäf, 'gȯf\ *n* : a game in which a player using special clubs tries to sink a ball into each of 9 or 18 holes around a course using as few strokes as possible [Middle English (Scottish dialect)] — **golf** *vi* — **golf·er** *n*

Gol·gi apparatus \\'gȯl-jē-\\ *n* : a cytoplasmic component that probably plays a part in the formation and secretion of cell products — called also *Golgi complex* [Camillo *Golgi,* died 1926, Italian physician]

Golgi body *n* : a single particle of the Golgi apparatus

golly \\'gäl-ē\\ *interj* — used as a mild oath or to express surprise [euphemism for *God*]

gon- *or* **gono-** *combining form* : sexual : generative : semen : seed ⟨*gono*coccus⟩ [Greek *gonos* "procreation, seed", from *gignesthai* "to be born"]

-gon \\ˌgän *also* gən\\ *n combining form* : figure having (so many) angles ⟨nona*gon*⟩ [Greek *-gōnon,* from *gōnia* "angle"]

go·nad \\'gō-ˌnad\\ *n* : a sperm- or egg-producing gland ⟨testes and ovaries are *gonads*⟩ [New Latin *gonad-, gonas,* from Greek *gonos*] — **go·nad·al** \\gō-'nad-l\\ *adj*

go·nad·o·tro·phic \\gō-ˌnad-ə-'trō-fik\\ *or* **go·nad·o·trop·ic** \\-'träp-ik\\ *adj* : acting on or stimulating the gonads ⟨a *gonadotropic* hormone⟩

go·nad·o·tro·phin \\-'trō-fən\\ *or* **go·nad·o·tro·pin** \\-pən\\ *n* : a gonadotrophic hormone

gon·do·la \\'gän-də-lə (*usual for sense 1*), gän-'dō-\\ *n* **1** : a long narrow flat-bottomed boat with a high bow and stern used on the canals of Venice **2** : a railroad car with flat bottom, fixed sides, and no top used chiefly for hauling heavy bulk commodities **3 a** : an elongated car attached to the underside of an airship **b** : an enclosure or metal-frame basket suspended from a balloon for carrying passengers or instruments **c** : an enclosed car suspended from a cable used especially as a ski lift [Italian]

gon·do·lier \\ˌgän-də-'liər\\ *n* : one who propels a gondola.

gone \\'gȯn, 'gän\\ *adj* **1** : PAST 2 **2 a** : ADVANCED, ABSORBED ⟨far *gone* in hysteria⟩ **b** : INFATUATED ⟨they're *gone* on each other⟩ **c** : PREGNANT 1a **3 a** : DEAD 1 **b** : WEAK 1a ⟨a *gone* feeling from hunger⟩ [from past participle of *go*]

gon·er \\'gȯn-ər, 'gän-\\ *n* : one whose case is hopeless

gon·fa·lon \\'gän-fə-ˌlän\\ *n* **1** : the ensign of certain princes or states (as the medieval republics of Italy) **2** : a flag that hangs from a crosspiece or frame [Italian *gonfalone*]

gong \\'gäng, 'gȯng\\ *n* **1** : a metallic disk that produces a resounding tone when struck **2** : a flat saucer-shaped bell [Malay]

go·nid·i·um \\gō-'nid-ē-əm\\ *n, pl* **-ia** \\-ē-ə\\ : an asexual reproductive cell or group of cells of a gametophyte — **go·nid·i·al** \\-ē-əl\\ *adj*

gono·coc·cus \\ˌgän-ə-'käk-əs\\ *n, pl* **-coc·ci** \\-'käk-ˌsī, -ˌī, -sē, -ē\\ : the bacterium that causes gonorrhea [gon- + Greek *kokkos* "grain, seed, berry"] — **gono·coc·cal** \\-'käk-əl\\ *or* **gono·coc·cic** \\-'käk-sik, -ik\\

gon·or·rhea \\ˌgän-ə-'rē-ə\\ *n* : a contagious inflammatory disease of the genitourinary tract caused by the gonococcus — called also *clap* — **gon·or·rhe·al** \\-'rē-əl\\ *adj*

-g·o·ny \\g-ə-nē\\ *n combining form, pl* **-gonies** : reproduction [Greek *-gonia,* from *gonos* "procreation, seed"]

goo \\'gü\\ *n* : a viscid or sticky substance [perhaps alteration of *glue*] — **goo·ey** \\'gü-ē\\ *adj*

goo·ber \\'gü-bər, 'güb-ər\\ *n, South & Midland* : PEANUT 1 [of African origin]

¹good \\'gůd\\ *adj* **bet·ter** \\'bet-ər\\; **best** \\'best\\ **1 a** (1) : of a favorable character or tendency ⟨*good* news⟩ (2) : BOUNTIFUL, FERTILE ⟨*good* land⟩ (3) : COMELY, ATTRACTIVE ⟨*good* looks⟩ **b** (1) : SUITABLE, FIT ⟨*good* to eat⟩ (2) : SOUND, WHOLE ⟨one *good* arm⟩ (3) : not depreciated ⟨bad money drives out *good*⟩ (4) : commercially reliable ⟨a *good* risk⟩ (5) : certain to last or live ⟨*good* for another year⟩ (6) : certain to pay or contribute

ute ⟨*good* for a hundred dollars⟩ (7) : certain to elicit a specified result ⟨always *good* for a laugh⟩ **c** (1) : AGREEABLE, PLEASANT ⟨a *good* time⟩ (2) : SALUTARY, WHOLESOME ⟨*good* for a cold⟩ **d** (1) : CONSIDERABLE, AMPLE ⟨a *good* margin⟩ (2) : FULL ⟨a *good* four hours⟩ **e** (1) : WELL-FOUNDED, COGENT ⟨*good* reasons⟩ (2) : TRUE ⟨holds *good* for society at large⟩ (3) : recognized or valid especially in law ⟨members in *good* standing⟩ ⟨a *good* title⟩ **f** (1) : ADEQUATE, SATISFACTORY ⟨*good* care⟩ (2) : conforming to a standard ⟨*good* English⟩ (3) : DISCRIMINATING, CHOICE ⟨*good* taste⟩ **2 a** (1) : COMMENDABLE, VIRTUOUS, JUST ⟨a *good* man⟩ (2) : RIGHT ⟨*good* conduct⟩ (3) : KIND, BENEVOLENT ⟨*good* intentions⟩ **b** : UPPER-CLASS ⟨a *good* family⟩ **c** : COMPETENT, SKILLFUL ⟨a *good* doctor⟩ **d** : LOYAL, FAITHFUL ⟨a *good* member of the party⟩ ⟨a *good* Catholic⟩ **3** : containing less fat and being less tender than higher grades — used of meat and especially beef [Old English *gōd*] — **as good as** : in effect : VIRTUALLY ⟨*as good as* dead⟩ — **good and** : VERY, ENTIRELY ⟨was *good and* mad⟩

²good *n* **1 a** : what is good or moral ⟨know *good* from evil⟩ **b** : praiseworthy character : GOODNESS **2** : PROSPERITY, BENEFIT, WELFARE ⟨for the *good* of the community⟩ **3 a** : something that has economic utility or satisfies an economic need or desire **b** *pl* : PERSONAL PROPERTY **c** *pl* : CLOTH 1 **d** *pl* : WARES, COMMODITIES ⟨canned *goods*⟩ **4** : good persons — used with *the* ⟨the *good* die young⟩ **5** *pl* : proof of wrongdoing ⟨got the *goods* on them⟩

³good *adv* : WELL

good book *n, often cap G&B* : BIBLE 1

good-bye *or* **good-by** \\gůd-'bī, gəd-, gə-\\ *n* : a concluding remark at parting ⟨said their *good-byes* and left⟩ — often used interjectionally as a farewell [alteration of *God be with you*]

good day *interj* — used as a greeting or farewell in the daytime

good evening *interj* — used as a greeting or farewell in the evening

good fellow *n* : an affable companionable person — **good-fel·low·ship** *n*

¹good-for-nothing \\'gůd-fər-ˌnəth-ing\\ *adj* : of no use or value

²good-for-nothing *n* : a good-for-nothing person

Good Friday *n* : the Friday before Easter observed as the anniversary of the crucifixion of Christ [from its special sanctity]

good-heart·ed \\'gůd-'härt-əd\\ *adj* : having a kindly generous disposition — **good-heart·ed·ly** *adv* — **good-heart·ed·ness** *n*

good-hu·mored \\-'hyü-mərd, -'yü-\\ *adj* : AMIABLE, CHEERFUL — **good-hu·mored·ly** *adv* — **good-hu·mored·ness** *n*

good·ish \\'gůd-ish\\ *adj* **1** : fairly good **2** : fairly large or long

good-looking \\'gůd-lůk-ing\\ *adj* : having an attractive appearance — **good-looker** *n*

good·ly \\'gůd-lē\\ *adj* **good·li·er; -est 1** : of pleasing appearance **2** : LARGE, CONSIDERABLE ⟨a *goodly* number⟩

good·man \\'gůd-mən\\ *n* **1** *archaic* : the head of a household : HUSBAND **2** *archaic* : MISTER 1

good morning *interj* — used as a greeting or farewell in the morning

good-na·tured \\'gůd-'nā-chərd\\ *adj* : of a pleasant cheerful disposition — **good-na·tured·ly** *adv* — **good-na·tured·ness** *n*

good-neighbor policy *n* : a policy of friendship, cooperation, and noninterference in the affairs of another country

good·ness \\'gůd-nəs\\ *n* **1** : the quality or state of being good; *esp* : excellence of character **2** : the nutritious, flavorful, or beneficial portion or element

good-sized \\'gůd-'sīzd\\ *adj* : fairly large

good-tem·pered \\-'tem-pərd\\ *adj* : having an even temper — **good-tem·pered·ly** *adv* — **good-tem·pered·ness** *n*

gondola 1

\ə\ abut	\ng\ sing	
\ər\ further	\ō\ bone	
\ā\ take	\ȯ\ saw	
\ä\ cot, cart	\òi\ coin	
\aů\ out	\th\ thin	
\ch\ chin	\th\ this	
\e\ pet	\ü\ food	
\ē\ easy	\ů\ foot	
\g\ go	\y\ yet	
\i\ tip	\yü\ few	
\ī\ life	\yů\ cure	
\j\ job	\zh\ vision	

good·wife \'gud-,wīf\ n I archaic : the mistress of a household 2 archaic : MRS. 1

good·will \'gud-'wil\ n I : kindly feeling : BENEVOLENCE 2 : the value of the custom a business has built up over a period of time 3 a : cheerful consent b : willing effort

¹**goody** \'gud-ē\ n, pl good·ies : something that is particularly good to eat or otherwise attractive

²**goody** interj — used as an expression of delight especially by children

goody-goody \,gud-ē-'gud-ē\ adj : affectedly or self=righteously good — **goody-goody** n

goo·ey \'gü-ē\ adj goo·i·er; -est I : STICKY 1 2 : very emotional or sentimental

goof \'güf\ vb : BUNGLE [earlier goof "ridiculous or stupid person", probably from English dialect goff "simpleton"] — **goof** n

goof·ball \'güf-,bol\ n I slang : a barbiturate sleeping pill 2 slang : a goofy person

go off vi I : EXPLODE 2 2 : to undergo decline or deterioration 3 : to follow the expected or desired course

goofy \'gü-fē\ adj goof·i·er; -est : CRAZY 2b, SILLY — **goof·i·ly** \-fə-lē\ adv — **goof·i·ness** n

goon \'gün\ n I : a stupid person 2 : a man hired to terrorize or eliminate opponents [probably from English dialect gooney "simpleton"]

goo·ney \'gü-nē\ n, pl gooneys : an albatross of the Pacific that is chiefly blackish with a dusky bill and black feet and legs — called also gooney bird [probably from English dialect gooney "simpleton"]

goose \'güs\ n, pl geese \'gēs\ I a : any of numerous long-necked birds intermediate in size between the related swans and ducks b : a female goose as distinguished from a gander 2 : SIMPLETON, DOLT 3 pl goos·es : a tailor's smoothing iron with a gooseneck handle [Old English gōs]

goose Ia

goose·ber·ry \'güs-,ber-ē, 'güz-\ n : the acid usually prickly fruit of any of several shrubs related to the currant

goose bumps n pl : GOOSEFLESH

goose·flesh \'güs-,flesh\ n : a roughening of the skin caused usually by cold or fear

goose·foot \-,fut\ n, pl goosefoots : any of numerous mostly weedy smooth herbs with branched clusters of small petalless greenish or whitish flowers — compare BEET, SPINACH

goose·neck \-,nek\ n : something (as a flexible or jointed metal tube) curved like the neck of a goose or U=shaped — **goose·necked** \-,nekt\ adj

goose pimples n pl : GOOSEFLESH

gorilla I

goose step n : a straight-legged stiff-kneed step used by troops of some armies when passing in review — **goose-step** \'güs-,step\ vi

go out vi I : to go forth; esp : to leave one's house 2 : to become extinguished ⟨the hall light went out⟩ 3 : to go on strike 4 : to become a candidate ⟨went out for the football team⟩

go·pher \'gō-fər\ n I : a burrowing American land tortoise — called also gopher tortoise 2 a : any of several burrowing American rodents with large cheek pouches — called also pocket gopher b : a small striped ground squirrel of the prairie region of the United States [origin unknown]

Gor·di·an knot \'gord-ē-ən-\ n : a very intricate and difficult problem or task [Gordius, king of Phrygia, who tied a knot held to be capable of being untied only by the future ruler of Asia, and cut by Alexander the Great with his sword]

¹**gore** \'gōr, 'gor\ n : BLOOD; esp : clotted blood [Old English gor "filth"]

²**gore** n : a tapering or triangular piece (as of cloth in a skirt) [Old English gāra "triangular piece of land"]

³**gore** vt I : to cut into a tapering triangular form 2 : to provide with a gore

⁴**gore** vt : to pierce or wound with a horn or tusk [Middle English goren]

¹**gorge** \'gorj\ n I : THROAT 1 2 : a narrow passage (as between two mountains) [Middle French, from Late Latin gurges, from Latin, "whirlpool"] ☐ ORIGIN Gurges, the Latin word for "whirlpool", came in Late Latin to mean "throat" as well. The notions of downward passage and of voraciousness must have suggested to speakers of Late Latin that a word meaning "whirlpool" was an apt term for the throat. Gurges eventually became Middle French gorge, which was borrowed into English in the late 14th century, later developing such familiar meanings as "a ravine with steep, rocky walls", by metaphorical extension from the original "throat".

²**gorge** vb : to eat greedily : stuff to capacity : — **gorg·er** n

gor·geous \'gor-jəs\ adj : resplendently beautiful ⟨a gorgeous sunset⟩ [Middle French gorgias "elegant", from gorgias "wimple", from gorge "throat"] SYN see SPLENDID — **gor·geous·ly** adv — **gor·geous·ness** n ☐ ORIGIN In the late Middle Ages, a standard article of feminine dress was the wimple, a cloth headdress that surrounded the neck and head, leaving only the face uncovered. Middle French gorgias, derived from gorge, "throat", was, strictly speaking, the name for the part of this garment that covered the throat and shoulders. But the word was also applied to the whole wimple. An elegant and elaborate wimple, or gorgias, was so much the mark of a well-to-do and fashionable lady that gorgias became an adjective meaning "elegant" or "fond of dress". In English it gradually came to emphasize "beauty" more than "elegance".

gor·get \'gor-jət\ n : a piece of armor protecting the throat and shoulders [Middle French, from gorge "throat"]

gor·gon \'gor-gən\ n I cap : any of three snaky-haired sisters in Greek mythology capable of turning to stone any who behold them 2 : an ugly or repulsive woman [Greek Gorgōn]

Gor·gon·zo·la \,gor-gən-'zō-lə\ n : a blue cheese of Italian origin usually made of cow's milk [Gorgonzola, Italy]

go·ril·la \gə-'ril-ə\ n I : an anthropoid ape of west equatorial Africa related to but much larger than the chimpanzee 2 : THUG, GOON [Greek Gorillai, African creatures believed to be hairy women]

gor·man·dize \'gor-mən-,dīz\ vb : to eat greedily or ravenously [gormand, alteration of gourmand] — **gor·man·diz·er** n

gorse \'gors\ n : FURZE [Old English gorst] — **gorsy** \'gor-sē\ adj

gory \'gōr-ē, 'gor-\ adj gor·i·er; -est I : covered with blood : BLOODSTAINED 2 : involving much bloodshed ⟨a gory fight⟩ 3 : BLOODCURDLING

gosh \'gäsh also 'gosh\ interj — used as a mild oath or to express surprise [euphemism for God]

gos·hawk \'gäs-,hok\ n : any of several long-tailed short-winged hawks noted for their powerful flight, activity, and vigor [Old English gōshafoc, from gōs "goose" + hafoc "hawk"]

gos·ling \'gäz-ling, 'goz-, -lən\ n : a young goose [Middle English, from gos "goose"]

¹**gos·pel** \'gäs-pəl\ n I a often cap : the Christian message concerning Christ, the kingdom of God, and salvation b cap : any of the first four New Testament books that tell of the life, death, and resurrection of Jesus Christ; also : a similar apocryphal book 2 cap : a liturgical reading from one of the New Testament Gospels 3 : the message or teachings of a religious teacher 4 : something accepted as infallible truth or as a guiding principle [Old English gōdspel, from gōd "good" + spell "tale, news"]

²**gospel** adj I : relating to or in accordance with the gospel : EVANGELICAL 2 : EVANGELISTIC ⟨a gospel team⟩

3 : of or relating to religious songs associated with evangelism and popular devotion ⟨a *gospel* singer⟩

gospel truth *n* : something absolutely and completely true

Gos·plan \'gäs-ˌplan, 'gȯs-ˌplän\ *n* : a Soviet governmental agency that made long-term economic and social plans [Russian *Gos*udarstvennaya *Plan*ovaya Komissiya "State Planning Commission"]

gos·sa·mer \'gäs-ə-mər, 'gäz-\ *n* **1** : a film of cobwebs floating in air **2** : something light, delicate, or tenuous [Middle English *gossomer,* from *gos* "goose" + *somer* "summer"] — **gossamer** *adj* — **gos·sa·mery** \-mə-rē\ *adj*

¹gos·sip \'gäs-əp\ *n* **1** : a person who habitually reveals personal or sensational facts **2 a** : rumor or report of an intimate nature **b** : chatty talk **c** : the subject matter of gossip [Middle English *gossib* "crony, godparent", from Old English *godsibb* "godparent", from *god* + *sibb* "kinsman"] — **gos·sipy** \-ə-pē\ *adj* □ ORIGIN Old English *sibb,* meaning "relative" or "kinsman", came from the adjective *sibb,* "related by blood" (the ancestor of modern English *sibling*). Old English *godsibb* was a person spiritually related to another, specifically by being a sponsor at baptism. Today we call such a person a *godparent.* Over the centuries *godsibb* changed both in form and in meaning. Middle English *gossib* came to be used for a close friend or crony as well as for a godparent. From there it was only a short step to the *gossip* of today, a person no longer necessarily friend, relative, or sponsor, but someone filled with irresistible tidbits of rumor.

²gossip *vi* : to relate gossip — **gos·sip·er** *n*

got *past of* GET

Goth \'gäth\ *n* : a member of a Germanic people that in the early centuries of the Christian era overran the Roman Empire [Late Latin *Gothi* "Goths"]

¹Goth·ic \'gäth-ik\ *adj* **1** : of, relating to, or resembling the Goths, their civilization, or their language **2** : of or relating to a style of architecture prevalent in western Europe from the middle 12th to the early 16th century and characterized by weights and stresses converging at isolated points on slender vertical piers and counterbalancing buttresses and by pointed arches and vaulting **3** *often not cap* : of or relating to a literary style characterized by the use of desolate or remote settings and macabre, mysterious, or violent incidents — **goth·i·cal·ly** \-i-kə-lē, -klē\ *adv* — **Goth·ic·ness** *n*

²Gothic *n* **1** : the Germanic language of the Goths **2** : the Gothic architectural style or decoration

gotten *past participle of* GET

gouache \'gwäsh\ *n* **1** : painting with watercolors that have been mixed with white pigment to produce an opaque effect **2** : a picture painted by gouache [French]

Gou·da \'gaud-ə, 'güd-\ *n* : a mild cheese of Dutch origin resembling Edam but containing more fat [*Gouda,* Netherlands]

¹gouge \'gauj\ *n* **1** : a chisel with a curved blade for scooping or cutting holes **2** : a hole or groove made with or as if with a gouge [Middle French, from Late Latin *gulbia,* of Celtic origin]

²gouge *vt* **1** : to cut holes or grooves in with or as if with a gouge **2** : to force out (an eye) with the thumb **3** : to charge excessively : DEFRAUD, CHEAT — **goug·er** *n*

gou·lash \'gü-ˌläsh, -ˌlash\ *n* : a beef stew usually with onion, paprika, and caraway [Hungarian *gulyás* "herdsman, herdsman's stew"]

gourd \'gōrd, 'gȯrd, 'gurd\ *n* **1** : any of a family of chiefly herbaceous tendril-bearing vines including the cucumber, melon, squash, and pumpkin **2** : the fruit of a gourd; *esp* : any of various hard-shelled inedible fruits often used for ornament or for vessels and utensils [Middle French *gourde,* from Latin *cucurbita*]

gourde \'gurd\ *n* **1** : the basic monetary unit of Haiti **2** : a coin representing one gourde [American French]

gour·mand \'gur-ˌmänd\ *n* **1** : one who is excessively fond of eating and drinking **2** : a person heartily interested in good food and drink [Middle French *gourmant*] — **gour·mand·ism** \'gur-ˌmän-ˌdiz-əm, -mən-\ *n*

gour·met \-ˌmā\ *n* : a connoisseur of food and drink [French, from Middle French *gromet* "groom, wine merchant's assistant", from Middle English *grom* "groom"]

gout \'gaut\ *n* **1** : a metabolic disease marked by a painful inflammation and swelling of the joints with deposits of salts of uric acid in and around the joints **2** : a drop or clot (as of blood) [Old French *goute* "drop, gout", from Latin *gutta* "drop"] — **gouty** \-ē\ *adj*

gov·ern \'gəv-ərn\ *vb* **1** : to exercise authority or authority over : RULE; *esp* : to control and direct the making and administration of policy in **2** : to control the speed of by automatic means **3 a** : to control, direct, or strongly influence the actions and conduct of **b** : to hold in check : RESTRAIN **4** : to require a word to be in a certain case or mood ⟨in English a transitive verb *governs* a pronoun in the objective case⟩ **5** : to constitute a rule or law for [Old French *governer,* from Latin *gubernare* "to steer, govern", from Greek *kybernan*] — **gov·ern·able** \-ər-nə-bəl\ *adj* □ SYN GOVERN, RULE mean to exercise power or authority over others. GOVERN implies the aim of keeping in a straight course or smooth operation for the common good; RULE more often suggests the exercise of arbitrary or despotic power.

gov·ern·ance \'gəv-ər-nəns\ *n* : the exercise of control

gov·ern·ess \'gəv-ər-nəs\ *n* : a woman who teaches and trains a child especially in a private home

gov·ern·ment \'gəv-ər-mənt; 'gəb-m-ənt, 'gəv-; 'gəvərn-mənt\ *n* **1** : the act or process of governing; *esp* : authoritative direction or control **2 a** : the exercise of authority over a political unit : RULE **b** : the making of policy as distinguished from the administration of policy decisions **3 a** : the organization, machinery, or agency through which a political unit exercises authority and performs functions **b** : manner of governing : the institutions, laws, and customs through which a political unit is governed ⟨republican *government*⟩ **4** : the body of persons that constitutes the governing authority of a political unit: as **a** : the officials comprising the governing body of a political unit **b** *cap* : the executive branch of the United States federal government **5** : POLITICAL SCIENCE — **government** *adj* — **gov·ern·men·tal** \ˌgəv-ərn-'ment-l, -ər-\ *adj* — **gov·ern·men·tal·ly** \-l-ē\ *adv*

gov·er·nor \'gəv-ə-nər, -ər-\ *n* **1** : one that governs: as **a** : one that exercises authority especially over an area or group **b** : an official elected or appointed to act as ruler, chief executive, or nominal head of a political unit (as a colony, state, or province) **c** : COMMANDANT ⟨*governor* of a fortress⟩ **d** : the managing director and usually the principal officer of an institution or organization ⟨the *governor* of a bank⟩ **e** : a member of a group that directs or controls an institution or society **2** : TUTOR **3** : an attachment to a machine for automatic control of speed

gov·er·nor-gen·er·al \ˌgəv-ə-nər-'jen-rəl, -ər-nər, -ə-rəl\ *n, pl* **governors-general** *or* **governor-generals** : a governor of high rank; *esp* : one who governs a large territory or has deputy governors under him

governor's council *n* : an executive or legislative council chosen to advise or assist a governor

gov·er·nor·ship \'gəv-ə-nər-ˌship, -ər-nər-\ *n* **1** : the office or position of governor **2** : the term of office of a governor

gown \'gaun\ *n* **1 a** : a loose flowing outer garment formerly worn by men **b** : an official robe worn espe-

\ə\ abut	\ng\ sing
\ər\ further	\ō\ bone
\a\ mat	\o\ saw
\ā\ take	\oi\ coin
\ä\ cot, cart	\th\ thin
\au\ out	\th\ this
\ch\ chin	\ü\ food
\e\ pet	\u\ foot
\ē\ easy	\y\ yet
\g\ go	\yü\ few
\i\ tip	\yu\ cure
\ī\ life	\zh\ vision
\j\ job	

cially by a judge, clergyman, or teacher **c** : a woman's dress; *esp* : one suitable for afternoon or evening wear **d** : a loose robe (as a nightgown) **e** : a coverall worn in an operating room **2 a** : an office or profession symbolized by a distinctive robe **b** : a body of college students and faculty [Middle French *goune,* from Late Latin *gunna,* a kind of fur garment] — **gown** *vt*

Graaf·ian follicle \\'gräf-ē-ən-, 'graf-\\ *n* : a fluid-filled sac in a mammal ovary enclosing a developing egg — called also *follicle*

¹grab \\'grab\\ *vb* **grabbed; grab·bing** : to take hastily : SNATCH [obsolete Dutch or Low German *grabben*] — **grab·ber** *n*

²grab *n* **l a** : a sudden snatch **b** : an unlawful seizure (a land *grab*) **c** : something grabbed **2 a** : a device for clutching an object **b** : CLAMSHELL 2

¹grace \\'grās\\ *n* **l a** : help held to be given man by God especially in overcoming temptation or in leading a good life **b** : a state of freedom from sin and of love for God held to be enjoyed through divine grace **2** : a short prayer at a meal asking a blessing or giving thanks **3 a** : a disposition to kindness or mercy **b** : a temporary delay granted from the performance of an obligation (as the payment of a debt) **c** : APPROVAL, ACCEPTANCE (stay in one's *good* graces) **4 a** : a charming trait or accomplishment **b** (1) : BEAUTY, ATTRACTIVENESS (2) : fitness or proportion of line or expression (3) : ease of movement : charm of bearing **5** : a musical trill, turn, or appoggiatura **6** *cap* — used as a form of address for a duke, a duchess, or an archbishop **7** *cap* : any of three sister goddesses who personify charm and beauty in Greek mythology [Old French, from Latin *gratia* "favor, thanks", from *gratus* "pleasing, grateful"] — **grace·ful** \\-fəl\\ *adj* — **grace·ful·ly** \\-fə-lē\\ *adv* — **grace·ful·ness** *n*

²grace *vt* **l** : HONOR 1b **2** : ADORN, EMBELLISH

grace·less \\'grās-ləs\\ *adj* : lacking grace, charm, or elegance; *esp* : showing lack of feeling for what is fitting (*graceless* behavior) — **grace·less·ly** *adv* — **grace·less·ness** *n*

grace note *n* : a musical note added as an ornament; *esp* : APPOGGIATURA

gra·cious \\'grā-shəs\\ *adj* **l a** : marked by kindness and courtesy **b** : GRACEFUL **c** : characterized by charm, good taste, and urbanity (*gracious* living) **2** : MERCIFUL, COMPASSIONATE — used conventionally of royalty and high nobility — **gra·cious·ly** *adv* — **gracious·ness** *n*

grack·le \\'grak-əl\\ *n* **l** : any of various Old World starlings **2** : any of several rather large American blackbirds with glossy iridescent black plumage [derived from Latin *graculus* "jackdaw"]

grackle 2

gra·da·tion \\grā-'dā-shən, grə-\\ *n* **l a** : a series forming successive stages **b** : a step, degree, or stage in a series **2** : an advance by regular degrees **3** : the act or process of arranging in grades — **gra·da·tion·al** \\-shnəl, -shən-l\\ *adj* — **gra·da·tion·al·ly** \\-ē\\ *adv*

¹grade \\'grād\\ *n* **l** : a stage, step, or degree in a series, order, or ranking **2** : position in a scale of rank, quality, or order (the *grade* of sergeant) (leather of the highest *grade*) **3** : a class of things that are of the same rank, quality, or order **4 a** : a division of the school course representing a year's work (finish the fourth *grade*) **b** : the pupils in a school division **c** *pl* : the elementary school system (teach in the *grades*) **5** : a mark or rating especially of accomplishment in school (a *grade* of 90 in a test) **6** : a standard of quality (government *grades* for meat) **7 a** : the degree of slope (as of a road, railroad track, or embankment); *also* : a sloping road **b** : ground level **8** : a domestic animal with only one parent purebred [French, from Latin *gradus* "step, degree"]

²grade *vb* **l** : to arrange in grades : SORT (*grade* apples) **2** : to make level or evenly sloping (*grade* a highway) **3** : to give a grade to (*grade* a pupil in arithmetic) **4** :

to assign to a grade or assign a grade to (*grade* lumber) **5** : to form a series having only slight differences (colors that *grade* into one another)

grade crossing *n* : a crossing (as of highways, railroad tracks, or pedestrian walks) on the same level

grad·er \\'grād-ər\\ *n* **l** : one that grades **2** : a machine for leveling earth **3** : a pupil in a school grade (a 5th *grader*)

grade school *n* : a public school including usually the first six or the first eight grades

gra·di·ent \\'grād-ē-ənt\\ *n* **l a** : the rate of ascent or descent : INCLINATION (the *gradient* of a rock layer) **b** : a part (as of a road) sloping upward or downward : GRADE 2 : change in the value of a quantity per unit distance in a specified direction (vertical temperature *gradient*) [Latin *gradiens,* present participle of *gradi* "to step, go"]

¹grad·u·al \\'graj-ə-wəl, 'graj-əl\\ *n, often cap* **l** : a response following the Epistle in the Mass **2** *or* **gra·du·a·le** \\,gräd-ə-'wäl-,ā\\ : a book containing the choral parts of the Mass [Medieval Latin *graduale,* from Latin *gradus* "step"; from its being sung on the steps of the altar]

²gradual *adj* **l** : proceeding by steps or degrees **2** : moving or changing by slight degrees [Medieval Latin *gradualis,* from Latin *gradus* "degree, step"] — **grad·u·al·ly** \\'graj-ə-lē, -ə-wə-lē\\ *adv* — **grad·u·al·ness** \\'graj-ə-wəl-nəs, 'graj-əl-\\ *n*

grad·u·al·ism \\'graj-ə-wə-,liz-əm, -ə-,liz-\\ *n* : the policy of approaching a desired end by gradual stages — **grad·u·al·ist** \\-ləst\\ *n or adj*

¹grad·u·ate \\'graj-ə-wət, -,wāt\\ *n* **l** : a holder of an academic degree or diploma **2** : a graduated cup, cylinder, or flask for measuring contents

²graduate *adj* **l** : holding an academic degree or diploma **2** : of, relating to, or engaged in studies beyond the bachelor's degree

³grad·u·ate \\'graj-ə-,wāt\\ *vb* **l** : to grant or receive an academic degree or diploma **2** : to admit to a particular standing or grade **3 a** : to mark with degrees of measurement (*graduate* a thermometer) **b** : to divide into grades, classes, or intervals (a *graduated* income tax) **4** : to change gradually [Medieval Latin *graduare,* from Latin *gradus* "step, degree"] — **grad·u·a·tor** \\-,wāt-ər\\ *n*

grad·u·at·ed cylinder *n* : a tall narrow container with a volume scale used especially for measuring liquids

graduate school *n* : a division of a university or college devoted entirely to studies beyond the bachelor's degree and having authority to grant advanced degrees

grad·u·a·tion \\,graj-ə-'wā-shən\\ *n* **l** : a mark or the marks on an instrument or vessel indicating degrees or quantity **2 a** : an act or process of graduating **b** : the ceremony or exercises marking the completion by a student of a course of study at a school or college : COMMENCEMENT **3** : arrangement in degrees or ranks

Graeco- — see GRECO-

graf·fi·to \\grə-'fēt-ō\\ *n, pl* **-ti** \\-ē\\ : an inscription or drawing made on a rock or wall [Italian]

¹graft \\'graft\\ *vb* **l a** : to unite (plants or scion and stock) to form a graft; *also* : to insert a shoot from a plant into (a different plant) to grow **b** : to join as if by grafting **2** : to implant (living tissue) surgically (*graft* skin over a scar) **3** : to gain money or advantage by dishonest means [Middle English *graffen, graften,* from *graffe* "grafted plant", from Middle French *grafe,* from Latin *graphium* "stylus", from Greek *grapheion,* from *graphein* "to write"] — **graft·er** *n*

²graft *n* **l a** : a grafted plant **b** : the point of insertion of a scion upon a stock **2 a** : the act of grafting **b** : something used in grafting: as (1) : SCION 1 (2) : living tissue used in surgical grafting **3** : the getting of money or advantage through misuse of an official position; *also* : the money or advantage gained

gra·ham cracker \'grā-əm-, 'gram-\ *n* : a slightly sweet cracker made chiefly of whole wheat flour

graham flour *n* : whole wheat flour [Sylvester *Graham*, died 1851, American dietary reformer]

Grail \'grāl\ *n* : the cup or platter used according to medieval legend by Christ at the Last Supper and thereafter the object of knightly quests — called also *Holy Grail* [Middle French *graal* "bowl, grail", from Medieval Latin *gradalis*]

¹**grain** \'grān\ *n* **1 a** : a seed or fruit of a cereal grass **b** : the seeds or fruits of various food plants and especially the cereal grasses **c** : plants producing grain **2** : a small hard particle or crystal (as of sand) **3 a** : a granulated surface or appearance **b** : the outer or hair side of a skin or hide **4** : a unit of weight based on the weight of a grain of wheat — see MEASURE table **5 a** : the arrangement of fibers in wood **b** : appearance or texture due to constituent particles or fibers **c** : the direction of threads in cloth **6** : natural disposition : TEMPER [Middle French, from Latin *granum*] — **grained** \'grānd\ *adj*

²**grain** *vt* **1** : to form into grains : GRANULATE **2** : to paint in imitation of the grain of wood or stone — **grain·er** *n*

grain alcohol *n* : ALCOHOL 1a

grain elevator *n* : ELEVATOR 1c

grain·field \'grān-ˌfēld\ *n* : a field where grain is grown

grain sorghum *n* : any of several sorghums cultivated primarily for grain — compare SORGO

grainy \'grā-nē\ *adj* **grain·i·er; -est** **1** : consisting of or resembling grains : GRANULAR **2** : resembling the grain of wood — **grain·i·ness** *n*

gram *or* **gramme** \'gram\ *n* : a metric unit of mass equal to ¹⁄₁₀₀₀ kilogram and nearly equal to one cubic centimeter of water at its maximum density — see METRIC SYSTEM table [French *gramme*, from Late Latin *gramma*, a small weight, from Greek *gramma* "letter, writing, a small weight"]

-gram \ˌgram\ *n combining form* : drawing : writing : record ⟨spectro*gram*⟩ ⟨tele*gram*⟩ [Greek *gramma* "letter, writing", from *graphein* "to write"]

grama \'gram-ə\ *n* : a pasture grass of the western United States — called also *grama grass* [Spanish]

gram atom *n* : the quantity of an element that has a weight in grams numerically equal to the atomic weight — called also *gram-atomic weight*

gra·mer·cy \grə-'mər-sē\ *interj, archaic* — used to express gratitude or astonishment [Middle French *grand merci* "great thanks"]

gram·i·ci·din \ˌgram-ə-'sīd-ən\ *n* : a toxic crystalline antibiotic produced by a soil bacterium and used against bacteria in local infections [*gram*-positive + -*i*- + -*cide* + -*in*]

gram·mar \'gram-ər\ *n* **1** : the study of the structure of a language **2** : the facts of language with which grammar deals **3 a** : a grammar textbook **b** : speech or writing evaluated according to its conformity to grammatical rules ⟨bad *grammar*⟩ [Middle French *gramaire*, from Latin *grammatica*, from Greek *grammatikē*, from *gramma* "letter, writing", from *graphein* "to write"] — **gram·mar·i·an** \grə-'mer-ē-ən, -'mar-\ *n*

grammar school *n* **1 a** : a secondary school emphasizing Latin and Greek in preparation for college **b** : a British college preparatory school **2** : an elementary school

gram·mat·i·cal \grə-'mat-i-kəl\ *adj* **1** : of or relating to grammar **2** : conforming to the rules of grammar — **gram·mat·i·cal·ly** \-kə-lē, -klē\ *adv*

gram molecule *n* : the quantity of a chemical compound or element that has a weight in grams numerically equal to the molecular weight — called also *gram-molecular weight*

gram–neg·a·tive \'gram-'neg-ət-iv\ *adj* : not holding the purple dye when stained by the Gram stain

gram·o·phone \'gram-ə-ˌfōn\ *n* : PHONOGRAPH [from *Gramophone*, a former trademark]

gram–pos·i·tive \'gram-'päz-ət-iv, -'päz-tiv\ *adj* : holding the purple dye when stained by the Gram stain

gram·pus \'gram-pəs\ *n* **1** : a sea mammal that is a dolphin with teeth in the lower jaw only **2** : KILLER WHALE [Middle French *graspeis*, from *gras* "fat" + *peis* "fish"]

Gram stain \'gram-\ *also* **Gram's stain** *n* : a technique of staining bacteria with gentian violet such that some bacteria retain the stain and others do not — compare GRAM-NEGATIVE, GRAM-POSITIVE [Hans C. J. *Gram*, died 1938, Danish physician]

grana *pl of* GRANUM

gran·a·dil·la \ˌgran-ə-'dil-ə\ *n* : the edible fruit of a tropical American passionflower [Spanish]

gra·na·ry \'grān-rē, 'gran-, -ə-rē\ *n, pl* **-ries** **1** : a storehouse for threshed grain **2** : a region producing grain in abundance [Latin *granarium*, from *granum* "grain"]

¹**grand** \'grand\ *adj* **1** : higher in rank than others of the same class : FOREMOST, PRINCIPAL ⟨the *grand* prize⟩ **2** : INCLUSIVE, COMPLETE ⟨a *grand* total⟩ **3** : of great size, scope, or extent ⟨*grand* ideas⟩ **4 a** : marked by magnificence or splendor **b** : tending to impress (as by wealth, dignity, or rank) ⟨a *grand* lady⟩ **5** : making a fine show : STATELY ⟨a *grand* palace⟩ **6** : very good : FINE ⟨have a *grand* old time⟩ [Middle French, "large, great, grand", from Latin *grandis*] — **grand·ly** \'grandlē, -lē\ *adv* — **grand·ness** \'grand-nəs, 'gran-\ *n* ☐ SYN MAGNIFICENT, MAJESTIC, GRANDIOSE: GRAND often adds to greatness of size implications of handsomeness and dignity; MAGNIFICENT implies an impressive largeness achieved without sacrifice of dignity or taste ⟨*magnificent* paintings⟩ MAJESTIC adds to MAGNIFICENT connotations of awe-inspiring grandeur or loftiness ⟨a *majestic* waterfall⟩ GRANDIOSE commonly implies inflated pretension or pomposity ⟨*grandiose* schemes of world conquest⟩

²**grand** *n* **1** : GRAND PIANO **2** *pl* **grand**, *slang* : a thousand dollars

gran·dam \'gran-ˌdam, -dəm\ *or* **gran·dame** \-ˌdām, -dəm\ *n* **1** : GRANDMOTHER **2** : an old woman [Anglo-French *graund dame*, literally, "great lady"]

grand·aunt \'gran-'dant, -'dänt\ *n* : an aunt of one's father or mother

grand·child \'grand-ˌchīld, 'gran-\ *n* : a child of one's son or daughter

grand·daugh·ter \'gran-ˌdȯt-ər\ *n* : a daughter of one's son or daughter

grand duchess *n* **1** : the wife or widow of a grand duke **2** : a woman who rules a grand duchy in her own right

grand duchy *n* : the territory or dominion of a grand duke or grand duchess

grand duke *n* **1** : the sovereign duke of any of various European states **2** : a son or male descendant of a Russian czar

grande dame \gräⁿd-'dam, grän-\ *n, pl* **grandes dames** *or* **grande dames** *same or* -'damz\ : a usually elderly woman of great prestige [French, literally, "great lady"]

gran·dee \gran-'dē\ *n* : a man of high rank or station; *esp* : a high-ranking Spanish or Portuguese nobleman [Spanish *grande*, from *grande* "large, great", from Latin *grandis*]

gran·deur \'gran-jər\ *n* : the quality or state of being grand : awe-inspiring magnificence [Middle French, from *grand*]

grand·fa·ther \'grand-ˌfäth-ər, 'gran-\ *n* : the father of one's father or mother; *also* : ANCESTOR 1

grandfather clock *n* : a tall pendulum clock standing on the floor — called also *grandfather's clock*

gran·dil·o·quence \gran-'dil-ə-kwəns\ *n* : lofty or pompous eloquence : BOMBAST [derived from Latin *grandiloquus* "using lofty language", from *grandis*

grandfather clock

\ə\ abut		\ng\ sing	
\ər\ further		\ō\ bone	
\a\ mat		\ȯ\ saw	
\ā\ take		\ȯi\ coin	
\ä\ cot, cart		\th\ thin	
\au̇\ out		\th\ this	
\ch\ chin		\ü\ food	
\e\ pet		\u̇\ foot	
\ē\ easy		\y\ yet	
\g\ go		\yü\ few	
\i\ tip		\yu̇\ cure	
\ī\ life		\zh\ vision	
\j\ job			

"grand" + *loqui* "to speak"] — **gran·dil·o·quent** \-kwənt\ *adj* — **gran·dil·o·quent·ly** *adv*

gran·di·ose \'gran-dē-ˌōs\ *adj* **1** : impressive because of uncommon largeness, scope, effect, or grandeur **2** : characterized by affectation of grandeur or splendor or by absurd exaggeration [French, from Italian *grandioso,* from *grande* "great", from Latin *grandis*] SYN see GRAND — **gran·di·ose·ly** *adv* — **gran·di·os·i·ty** \ˌgran-dē-'äs-ət-ē\ *n*

grand jury *n* : a jury that chiefly examines accusations made against persons and if the evidence warrants makes formal charges on which the accused persons are tried

grand·ma \'grand-ˌmä, 'gran-, -ˌmȯ; 'gram-ˌä, -ˌȯ\ *n* : GRANDMOTHER

grand mal \'grand-ˌmäl, 'gran-\ *n* : severe epilepsy [French, literally, "great illness"]

grand march *n* : a march at the opening of a ball in which all the guests participate

grand·moth·er \'grand-ˌməth-ər, 'gran-\ *n* : the mother of one's father or mother; *also* : a female ancestor

grand·neph·ew \-'nef-yü\ *n* : a grandson of one's brother or sister

grand·niece \-'nēs\ *n* : a granddaughter of one's brother or sister

grand opera *n* : opera in which the plot is elaborated as in serious drama and the entire text set to music

grand·pa \'grand-ˌpä, 'gran-, -ˌpȯ; 'gram-ˌpä, -ˌpȯ\ *n* : GRANDFATHER

grand·par·ent \'grand-ˌpar-ənt, 'gran-, -ˌper-\ *n* : a parent of one's father or mother

grand piano *n* : a piano with horizontal frame and strings

grand·sire \'grand-ˌsīr, 'gran-\ *or* **grand·sir** \'gran-sər\ *n* **1** *dialect* : GRANDFATHER **2** *archaic* : an aged man

grand slam *n* **1** : the winning of all the tricks of one hand in a card game (as bridge) **2** : a clean sweep or total success (as in winning all of a number of specified contests) **3** : a home run made with the bases loaded

grand·son \'grand-ˌsən, 'gran-\ *n* : a son of one's son or daughter

grand·stand \-ˌstand\ *n* : a usually roofed stand for spectators at a racecourse or stadium

grand tour *n* : an extended European tour once a part of the education of aristocratic British youth

grand·un·cle \'gran-ˌdəng-kəl\ *n* : an uncle of one's father or mother

grange \'grānj\ *n* **1** : FARM; *esp* : a farmhouse with out-buildings **2** *cap* : one of the lodges of a national fraternal association of farmers; *also* : the association itself [Middle French, "granary", from Medieval Latin *granica,* from Latin *granum* "grain"]

grang·er \'grān-jər\ *n* : a member of a Grange

gran·ite \'gran-ət\ *n* : a very hard igneous rock formed essentially of quartz and orthoclase or microcline and used for building and for monuments [Italian *granito,* from *granire* "to granulate", from *grano* "grain", from Latin *granum*] — **gra·nit·ic** \gra-'nit-ik\ *adj*

gran·ite·ware \'gran-ət-ˌwaər, -ˌweər\ *n* : enameled ironware

gran·ny *or* **gran·nie** \'gran-ē\ *n, pl* **grannies** : GRANDMOTHER [by shortening and alteration]

granny knot *n* : an insecure knot often made instead of a square knot

¹grant \'grant\ *vt* **1 a** : to consent to : ALLOW **b** : to permit as a right, privilege, or favor **2** : to give the possession or benefit of formally or legally ⟨*grant* a pardon⟩ **3** : to concede (something not yet proved) to be true [Old French *creanter, graanter,* derived from Latin *credere* "to believe, trust"] — **grant·er** \-ər\ *n* — **grant·or** \'grant-ər, grant-'ȯr\ *n* □ SYN GRANT, CONCEDE mean to give as a favor or a right. GRANT implies giving voluntarily something that could be as well withheld or denied ⟨*grant* one's assistant a week's leave⟩ CONCEDE implies yielding with reluctance to a rightful or compelling claim ⟨forced to *concede* that they were right⟩

²grant *n* **1** : the act of granting ⟨land ceded by *grant*⟩ **2** : something granted; *esp* : a gift (as of money) for a particular purpose ⟨a research *grant*⟩ **3 a** : a transfer of property by deed or writing **b** : the instrument by which such a transfer is made; *also* : the property so transferred

grant·ee \grant-'ē\ *n* : one to whom a grant is made

gran·tia \'grant-ē-ə\ *n* : a small cylindrical sponge with a skeleton containing calcium [Robert E. *Grant,* died 1874, Scottish anatomist]

grant–in–aid \ˌgrant-n-'ād\ *n, pl* **grants–in–aid** \ˌgrant-sə-'nād\ **1** : a grant from public funds paid to a local government in aid of a public undertaking **2** : a grant to a school or individual for an educational or artistic project

gran·u·lar \'gran-yə-lər\ *adj* : consisting of or appearing to consist of granules : having a grainy texture — **gran·u·lar·i·ty** \ˌgran-yə-'lar-ət-ē\ *n*

gran·u·late \'gran-yə-ˌlāt\ *vb* **1** : to form or crystallize into grains or granules **2** : to collect into grains or granules

gran·u·la·tion \ˌgran-yə-'lā-shən\ *n* **1** : the act or process of granulating or the condition of being granulated **2** : a product of granulating (as a tiny knot of vascular tissue in a healing wound)

granulation tissue *n* : tissue made up of granulations that temporarily replaces lost tissue in a wound

gran·ule \'gran-yül\ *n* : a small grain or particle ⟨*granules* of sugar⟩ [Late Latin *granulum,* from Latin *granum* "grain"]

gra·num \'grā-nəm\ *n, pl* **gra·na** \-nə\ : one of the laminated stacks of chlorophyll-containing material in plant chloroplasts [Latin, "grain, seed"]

grape \'grāp\ *n* **1** : a smooth-skinned juicy greenish white to deep red or purple berry eaten dried or fresh as a fruit or used to make wine **2** : a climbing woody vine whose clustered fruits are grapes **3** : GRAPESHOT [Old French] — **grapy** \'grā-pē\ *adj*

grape·fruit \'grāp-ˌfrüt\ *n* : a large citrus fruit with a bitter yellow rind and a highly flavored somewhat acid juicy pulp; *also* : a tree that bears grapefruit [from its growing in clusters like grapes]

grape hyacinth *n* : any of several small bulbous spring-flowering herbs of the lily family bearing spikes of clustered usually blue flowers

grape·shot \'grāp-ˌshät\ *n* : a cluster of small iron balls used as shot for a cannon

grape sugar *n* : DEXTROSE

grape·vine \'grāp-ˌvīn\ *n* **1** : GRAPE 2 **2 a** : an informal means of circulating information, rumor, or gossip **b** : a secret source of information

¹graph \'graf\ *n* **1** : a diagram that represents change in one variable factor in comparison with that of one or more other factors **2** : a pictorial representation of a set of points (as a line or curve) that satisfy a mathematical equation or belong to a given set [short for *graphic* formula]

²graph *vt* **1** : to represent by a graph **2** : to plot on a graph

-graph \ˌgraf\ *n combining form* **1** : something written ⟨mono*graph*⟩ **2** : instrument for making or transmitting records ⟨chrono*graph*⟩ [Greek *graphein* "to write"]

-g·ra·pher \g-rə-fər\ *n combining form* : one that writes about (specified) material or in a (specified) way ⟨biogra*pher*⟩

¹graph·ic \'graf-ik\ *or* **graph·i·cal** \-i-kəl\ *adj* **1** : being written, drawn, or engraved **2 a** : described or related with vivid clarity or striking imaginative power **b** : sharply outlined or detailed **3** : of or relating to the graphic arts **4** : of, relating to, or represented by a graph **5** : of or relating to writing [Latin *graphicus,*

¹graph ¹

from Greek *graphikos,* from *graphein* "to write"] —
graph·i·cal·ly \-i-kə-lē, -klē\ *adv* — **graph·ic·ness** *n*

☐ SYN GRAPHIC, VIVID, PICTURESQUE mean giving a clear visual impression through words. GRAPHIC stresses the evoking of a lifelike picture especially of an action; VIVID suggests conveying a strong or lasting impression of reality; PICTURESQUE implies the presenting of a striking or effective picture often without regard to reality ⟨a *picturesque* account of their adventures⟩

²graphic *n* **I a** : a product of graphic art **b** *pl* : the graphic media **2** : a picture, map, or graph used for illustration or demonstration **3** *pl* : a display (as of pictures or graphs) generated by a computer on a screen, printer, or plotter

graphic arts *n pl* : the fine and applied arts of representation, decoration, and writing or printing on flat surfaces together with the techniques and crafts associated with each

graphic equalizer *n* : an electronic device for adjusting the frequency response of an audio system by means of a number of slides that each control the response for a band centered on a particular frequency

graphics tablet *n* : a device by which pictures, graphs, or maps are put into a computer in a manner similar to drawing

graph·ite \'graf-ˌīt\ *n* : a soft black carbon with a metallic luster that conducts electricity and is used in making lead pencils, as a dry lubricant, and for electrodes [German *graphit,* from Greek *graphein* "to write"] — **gra·phit·ic** \gra-'fit-ik\ *adj*

graph·i·tize \'graf-ə-ˌtīz\ *vt* **I** : to convert into graphite **2** : to impregnate or coat with graphite — **graph·it·iza·tion** \ˌgraf-ˌīt-ə-'zā-shən\ *n*

gra·phol·o·gy \gra-'fäl-ə-jē\ *n* : the study of handwriting especially to analyze character — **gra·phol·o·gist** \-jəst\ *n*

graph paper *n* : paper ruled (as into small squares) for drawing graphs or making diagrams

-g·ra·phy \g-rə-fē\ *n combining form, pl* **-graphies I** : writing or representation in a (specified) manner or by a (specified) means or of a (specified) object ⟨phonog*raphy*⟩ ⟨photog*raphy*⟩ ⟨stenog*raphy*⟩ **2** : writing on a (specified) subject or in a (specified) field ⟨lexicog*raphy*⟩

grap·nel \'grap-nᵊl\ *n* : a small anchor with four or five claws or curved flukes used in dragging or grappling operations and for anchoring a small boat [Middle English *grapenel,* derived from Middle French *grape* "hook"]

¹grap·ple \'grap-əl\ *n* **I** : an implement used or designed for grappling; *esp* : GRAPNEL **2** : the act of grappling or seizing [Middle French *grappelle* "small hook", from *grape* "hook"]

²grapple *vb* **grap·pled; grap·pling** \'grap-ling, -ə-ling\ **I** : to seize or hold with or as if with a hooked implement **2** : to struggle in or as if in a close fight **3** : to attempt to deal : COPE ⟨*grapple* with a problem⟩ — **grap·pler** \'grap-lər, -ə-lər\

grappling iron *n* : a hooked iron for anchoring a boat, grappling ships to each other, or recovering sunken objects

grap·to·lite \'grap-tə-ˌlīt\ *n* : any of numerous Paleozoic fossil colonial animals having individual animals in cups arranged along a support of chitin [Greek *graptos* "painted", from *graphein* "to write, paint"]

¹grasp \'grasp\ *vb* **I** : to make the effort of seizing with or as if with the hand : CLUTCH ⟨*grasping* at straws⟩ **2** : to clasp or embrace with or as if with the fingers or arms ⟨*grasp* a bat⟩ **3** : UNDERSTAND 1, COMPREHEND ⟨*grasp* a new idea⟩ [Middle English *graspen*] SYN see TAKE — **grasp·able** \'gras-pə-bəl\ *adj* — **grasp·er** *n*

²grasp *n* **I a** : HANDLE 1 **b** : EMBRACE 2 : HOLD, CONTROL ⟨in the tyrant's *grasp*⟩ **3** : the power of seizing and holding ⟨success within our *grasp*⟩ **4** : UNDERSTANDING 2, COMPREHENSION

grasp·ing *adj* : ruthlessly avaricious SYN see COVETOUS — **grasp·ing·ly** \'gras-ping-lē\ *adv* — **grasp·ing·ness** *n*

¹grass \'gras\ *n* **I** : herbage suitable or used for grazing animals **2** : any of a large family of mostly herbaceous plants with jointed stems, slender sheathing leaves, and fruits consisting of seedlike grains **3** : grass-covered land **4** : MARIJUANA [Old English *græs*] — **grass·like** \-ˌlīk\ *adj*

²grass *vt* : to seed with grass

grass·hop·per \'gras-ˌhäp-ər\ *n* : any of numerous plant-eating insects (order Orthoptera) having the hind legs adapted for leaping

grass·land \-ˌland\ *n* : land covered naturally or under cultivation with grasses and other low-growing herbs

grass roots *n pl* : society at the local and popular level especially in rural areas as distinguished from the centers of political leadership ⟨*grass roots* support⟩

grass widow *n* **I** : a woman divorced or separated from her husband **2** : a woman whose husband is temporarily away

grass widower *n* **I** : a man divorced or separated from his wife **2** : a man whose wife is temporarily away

grassy \'gras-ē\ *adj* **grass·i·er; -est I** : covered or abounding with grass **2** : resembling grass ⟨a *grassy* odor⟩

¹grate \'grāt\ *n* **I** : a frame containing parallel or crossed bars (as in a prison window) **2** : a frame or basket of iron bars for holding burning fuel (as in a furnace or a fireplace) [Medieval Latin *crata, grata* "hurdle", from Latin *cratis*]

²grate *vt* : to furnish with a grate

³grate *vb* **I** : to make into small particles by rubbing against something rough ⟨*grate* cheese⟩ **2** : to grind or rub against something with a rasping noise ⟨a door that *grates* on its hinges⟩ **3** : to have a harsh or rasping effect ⟨a noise that *grates* on one's nerves⟩ [Middle French *grater* "to scratch", of Germanic origin] — **grat·er** *n*

grate·ful \'grāt-fəl\ *adj* **I a** : appreciative of benefits received **b** : expressing gratitude **2** : affording pleasure or contentment; *esp* : pleasing by reason of comfort supplied or discomfort alleviated ⟨*grateful* warmth of a fire on a frosty day⟩ [obsolete *grate* "pleasing, thankful", from Latin *gratus*] — **grate·ful·ly** \-fə-lē\ *adv* — **grate·ful·ness** *n* ☐ SYN GRATEFUL, THANKFUL mean feeling or expressing gratitude. GRATEFUL applies to an appropriate sense of having received favors from other persons ⟨I was very *grateful* for your help⟩ THANKFUL suggests a more generalized acknowledgement of what is vaguely felt to be providential ⟨*thankful* for a good harvest⟩

grat·i·fi·ca·tion \ˌgrat-ə-fə-'kā-shən\ *n* **I** : the act of gratifying : the state of being gratified **2** : a source of satisfaction or pleasure

grat·i·fy \'grat-ə-ˌfī\ *vt* **-fied; -fy·ing I** : to give or be a source of pleasure or satisfaction to **2** : to give in to : INDULGE ⟨*gratify* a whim⟩ [Middle French *gratifier,* from Latin *gratificari,* literally, "to make oneself pleasing", from *gratus* "pleasing" + *-ificari,* passive of *-ificare* "-ify"]

grat·ing \'grāt-ing\ *n* **I** : a partition, covering, or frame of parallel bars or crossbars : GRATE **2** : a system of close parallel lines on a polished surface used to produce spectra by diffraction

gra·tis \'grat-əs, 'grāt-\ *adv or adj* : without charge or recompense : FREE [Latin *gratiis, gratis,* from *gratia* "favor"]

grat·i·tude \'grat-ə-ˌtüd, -ˌtyüd\ *n* : the state of being grateful : THANKFULNESS [Medieval Latin *gratitudo,* from Latin *gratus* "grateful"]

gra·tu·i·tous \grə-'tü-ət-əs, -'tyü-\ *adj* **I** : done or provided without return or expectation of return or payment; *also* : acting without compensation **2** : not called for by the circumstances : UNWARRANTED ⟨a *gra-*

grapnel

\ə\ abut   \ng\ sing
\ər\ further   \ō\ bone
\a\ mat   \ȯ\ saw
\ā\ take   \ȯi\ coin
\ä\ cot, cart   \th\ thin
\au̇\ out   \th\ this
\ch\ chin   \ü\ food
\e\ pet   \u̇\ foot
\ē\ easy   \y\ yet
\g\ go   \yü\ few
\i\ tip   \yu̇\ cure
\ī\ life   \zh\ vision
\j\ job

tuitous insult) [Latin *gratuitus*, from *gratus* "pleasing, grateful"] — **gra·tu·i·tous·ly** *adv* — **gra·tu·i·tous·ness** *n*

gra·tu·i·ty \grə-'tü-ət-ē, -'tyü-\ *n, pl* **-ties** : something given freely; *also* : something given in return for a favor or service : TIP

gra·va·men \grə-'vām-ən\ *n, pl* **-vamens** *or* **-va·mi·na** \-'vam-ə-nə\ : the significant part (as of a grievance or complaint) : BASIS [Late Latin, "burden", from Latin *gravare* "to burden", from *gravis* "heavy"]

¹grave \'grāv\ *vt* **graved; grav·en** \'grā-vən\ *or* **graved; grav·ing** **1 a** : to carve or shape with a chisel : SCULPTURE **b** : to carve or cut (as letters or figures) into a hard surface : ENGRAVE **2** : to impress or fix (as a thought) deeply [Old English *grafan* "to dig, engrave"]

²grave *n* **1 a** : an excavation for burial of a body **b** : TOMB **2 1** : DEATH 1 — used with *the* [Old English *græf*]

³grave \'grāv, *in sense 4 also* 'gräv\ *adj* **1 a** : meriting serious consideration : IMPORTANT ⟨a *grave* issue⟩ **b** : threatening great harm or danger : MORTAL ⟨*grave* risks⟩ **2** : dignified in appearance or demeanor : SERIOUS **3** : drab in color : SOMBER **4** : of, marked by, or being an accent mark having the form ` [Middle French, from Latin *gravis* "heavy, grave"] SYN *see* SERIOUS — **grave·ly** *adv* — **grave·ness** *n*

⁴gra·ve \'gräv-ā\ *adv or adj* : in a slow and solemn manner — used as a direction in music [Italian, from Latin *gravis* "grave"]

grave·clothes \'grāv-ˌklōz, -ˌklō*thz*\ *n pl* : the clothes in which a dead person is buried

¹grav·el \'grav-əl\ *n* **1** : loose rounded fragments of rock coarser than sand **2** : a deposit of small hard masses in the kidneys and urinary bladder [Middle French *gravele*, from *grave, greve* "pebbly ground"]

²gravel *adj* : GRAVELLY 2

³gravel *vt* **grav·eled** *or* **grav·elled; grav·el·ing** *or* **grav·el·ling** \'grav-ling, -ə-ling\ : to cover or spread with gravel

grave·less \'grāv-ləs\ *adj* **1** : not buried ⟨*graveless* bones⟩ **2** : not requiring graves : DEATHLESS ⟨the *graveless* home of the blessed⟩

grav·el·ly \'grav-lē, -ə-lē\ *adj* **1** : of, containing, or covered with gravel **2** : having a harsh grating sound ⟨a *gravelly* voice⟩

grav·er \'grā-vər\ *n* **1** : SCULPTOR, ENGRAVER **2** : any of various cutting or shaving tools

grave·stone \'grāv-ˌstōn\ *n* : a stone marking a grave

grave·yard \-ˌyärd\ *n* : CEMETERY

grav·id \'grav-əd\ *adj* : PREGNANT 1a [Latin *gravidus*, from *gravis* "heavy"]

grav·i·tate \'grav-ə-ˌtāt\ *vi* **1** : to move or tend to move under the influence of gravitation **2** : to be attracted to or toward something

grav·i·ta·tion \ˌgrav-ə-'tā-shən\ *n* **1** : a force of attraction between two material particles or bodies that is proportional to the product of their masses and inversely proportional to the square of the distance between them **2** : the action or process of gravitating — **grav·i·ta·tion·al** \-shnəl, -shən-l\ *adj* — **grav·i·ta·tion·al·ly** \-ē\ *adv* — **grav·i·ta·tive** \'grav-ə-ˌtāt-iv\ *adj*

gravitational lens *n* : a massive celestial object (as a galaxy) that bends and focuses the light of another more distant object (as a quasar) by gravity

grav·i·ty \'grav-ət-ē\ *n, pl* **-ties** **1 a** : dignity or sobriety of bearing **b** : IMPORTANCE 1; *esp* : SERIOUSNESS ⟨the *gravity* of the crime⟩ **2** : WEIGHT — used chiefly in the phrase *center of gravity* **3 a** : the gravitational attraction of the earth's mass for bodies at or near its surface **b** : GRAVITATION 1 **c** : ACCELERATION OF GRAVITY [Latin *gravitas*, from *gravis* "heavy, grave"] — **gravity** *adj*

gra·vure \grə-'vyùr, grā-\ *n* : PHOTOGRAVURE [French, from *graver* "to grave", of Germanic origin]

gra·vy \'grā-vē\ *n, pl* **gravies** **1** : a sauce made from the thickened and seasoned juices of cooked meat **2** : something over and above what is ordinarily earned or expected [Middle French *gravé*]

¹gray *or* **grey** \'grā\ *adj* **1** : of the color gray; *also* : dull in color **2** : having gray hair **3** : dull or cheerless in mood or outlook : DISMAL ⟨a *gray* day⟩ [Old English *grǣg*] — **gray·ish** \'grā-ish\ *adj* — **gray·ness** *n*

²gray *n* **1** : something of a gray color **2** : one of the series of shades formed by a blending of black and white

³gray *vb* : to make or become gray

gray·beard \'grā-ˌbiərd\ *n* : an old man

gray·ling \'grā-ling\ *n, pl* **grayling** *also* **graylings** : any of several freshwater fishes related to the trouts and valued for food and sport

gray matter *n* **1** : neural tissue especially of the brain and spinal cord that contains nerve-cell bodies as well as nerve fibers and has a brownish gray color **2** : BRAINS, INTELLECT ⟨use one's *gray matter*⟩

gray squirrel *n* : a common light gray to black squirrel native to eastern North America and introduced into England

gray trout *n* : a common weakfish of the Atlantic coast of the United States

¹graze \'grāz\ *vb* **1** : to feed on growing herbage or the herbage of **2** : to put cattle to feed on the herbage of **3** : to put to graze [Old English *grasian*, from *græs* "grass"] □ SYN GRAZE, BROWSE mean to feed on growing vegetation. GRAZE applies especially to animals wandering freely on open grassland; BROWSE implies specifically feeding on leaves and shoots of trees or shrubs.

²graze *n* **1** : an act of grazing **2** : herbage for grazing

³graze *vt* **1** : to rub or touch lightly in passing : touch against and glance off **2** : to scratch or scrape by rubbing against something [perhaps from ¹*graze*]

⁴graze *n* : a scraping along a surface or an abrasion made by it; *esp* : a superficial skin injury

¹grease \'grēs\ *n* **1** : rendered animal fat **2** : oily matter **3** : a thick lubricant [Old French *craisse, graisse*, from Latin *crassus*, adj., "fat"]

²grease \'grēs, 'grēz\ *vt* **1** : to smear or daub with grease **2** : to lubricate with grease — **greas·er** *n*

grease·paint \'grēs-ˌpānt\ *n* : theater makeup

grease pencil *n* : a pencil with a lead like crayon for marking on hard surfaces (as glass)

grease·wood \-ˌwùd\ *n* : a low stiff shrub of the goosefoot family common in alkaline soils in the western United States

greasy \'grē-sē, -zē\ *adj* **greas·i·er; -est** **1** : smeared with grease **2** : containing grease ⟨*greasy* food⟩ **3** : resembling grease or oil : SMOOTH, SLIPPERY — **greas·i·ly** \-sə-lē, -zə-\ *adv* — **greas·i·ness** \-sē-nəs, -zē-\ *n*

great \'grāt, *in South also* 'grēət, 'grēt\ *adj* **1** : very large in size or extent ⟨a *great* expanse of land⟩ **2** : large in number ⟨4 is *greater* than 2⟩ **3** : being much beyond the average or ordinary ⟨in *great* pain⟩ ⟨once in a *great* while⟩ **4** : EMINENT, DISTINGUISHED ⟨a *great* artist⟩ **5** : remarkable for knowledge of or skill in something ⟨*great* at arithmetic⟩ **6** : much favored or much used ⟨a *great* joke of my friend's⟩ **7** : EXCELLENT, FINE ⟨a *great* time at the beach⟩ **8** : more distant in relationship by one generation ⟨*great*-grandchildren⟩ [Old English *grēat*] SYN *see* LARGE — **great·ly** *adv* — **great·ness** *n*

great ape *n* : any of the recent anthropoid apes

great auk *n* : an extinct large flightless auk formerly abundant along North Atlantic coasts

great–aunt *n* : GRANDAUNT

Great Bear *n* : URSA MAJOR

great blue heron *n* : a large grayish blue American heron with a crested head

great circle *n* : a circle formed on the surface of a sphere by the intersection of a plane that passes through the center of the sphere; *esp* : such a circle on the surface of the earth an arc of which constitutes the shortest distance between any two points on the earth's surface — compare SMALL CIRCLE

great·coat \'grāt-ˌkōt\ *n* : a heavy overcoat

Great Dane *n* : any of a breed of tall massive powerful smooth-coated dogs

great divide *n* **1** : a watershed between major drainage systems **2** : a significant point of division; *esp* : DEATH

greatest common divisor *n* : the largest integer that is an exact divisor of each of two or more integers — called also *greatest common factor*

great·heart·ed \'grāt-'härt-əd\ *adj* **1** : COURAGEOUS **2** : MAGNANIMOUS **2** — **great·heart·ed·ly** *adv* — **great·heart·ed·ness** *n*

great–nephew *n* : GRANDNEPHEW

great–niece *n* : GRANDNIECE

great power *n* : one of the nations that figure most decisively in international affairs

Great Russian *n* : a member of the Russian-speaking people of central and northeastern Russia

great–uncle *n* : GRANDUNCLE

great white shark *n* : a large man-eating shark that is bluish gray when young but becomes whitish when older and is widespread in warm and tropical seas

greave \'grēv\ *n* : armor for the leg below the knee [Middle French *greve*]

grebe \'grēb\ *n* : any of a family of swimming and diving birds closely related to the loons [French *grèbe*]

Gre·cian \'grē-shən\ *adj* : GREEK 1 [Latin *Graecia* "Greece"] — **Grecian** *n*

Greco- *or* **Graeco-** \'grek-ō, 'grē-kō\ *combining form* **1** : Greece : Greeks **2** : Greek and [Latin *Graecus*]

greed \'grēd\ *n* : excessive or blameworthy acquisitiveness : AVARICE [back-formation from *greedy*]

greedy \'grēd-ē\ *adj* **greed·i·er; -est** **1** : having a driving appetite for food or drink : very hungry **2** : having an eager and often selfish desire or longing ⟨*greedy* for praise⟩ **3** : wanting more than one needs or more than one's fair share (as of food or wealth) [Old English *grǣdig*] SYN see COVETOUS — **greed·i·ly** \'grēd-l-ē\ *adv* — **greed·i·ness** \'grēd-ē-nəs\ *n*

¹Greek \'grēk\ *n* **1 a** : a native or inhabitant of ancient or modern Greece **b** : a person of Greek descent **2 a** : the Indo-European language used by the Greeks from prehistoric times to the present **b** : ancient Greek as used from the time of the earliest records to the end of the 2d century A.D. [Old English *Grēca,* from Latin *Graecus,* from Greek *Graikos*]

²Greek *adj* **1** : of, relating to, or characteristic of Greece, the Greeks, or Greek ⟨*Greek* architecture⟩ **2 a** : Eastern Orthodox **b** : of or relating to the Orthodox church of Greece **3** : of or relating to the Eastern rite of the Roman Catholic Church

Greek cross *n* : an upright cross with all arms of equal length

Greek fire *n* : a composition of uncertain ingredients that burns even in water [from the Byzantine Greeks who used it in warfare]

Greek Orthodox *adj* : Eastern Orthodox; *esp* : GREEK 2b

¹green \'grēn\ *adj* **1** : of the color green **2 a** : covered by green foliage or herbage ⟨*green* hills⟩ **b** : consisting of green plants or of the leafy part of a plant ⟨a *green* salad⟩ **3** : YOUTHFUL, VIGOROUS **4** : not fully grown or ripe **5** : appearing sickly or pale ⟨scared *green*⟩ **6** : not fully processed, treated, or seasoned ⟨*green* lumber⟩ **7 a** : lacking training, knowledge, or experience ⟨*green* troops⟩ **b** : GULLIBLE, NAIVE ⟨too *green* to suspect a trick⟩ [Old English *grēne*] — **green·ish** \'grē-nish\ *adj* — **green·ly** *adv* — **green·ness** \'grēn-nəs\ *n*

²green *vb* : to make or become green

³green *n* **1** : a color whose hue is somewhat less yellow than that of growing fresh grass or of the emerald or is that of the part of the spectrum lying between blue and yellow **2** : something of a green color **3 a** : green

vegetation **b** *pl* : leafy parts of plants used for some purpose (as ornament or food) **4** : a grassy plain or plot; *esp* : PUTTING GREEN — **greeny** \'grē-nē\ *adj*

green alga *n* : an alga (especially group Chlorophyta) in which the chlorophyll is not masked by other pigments

green·back \'grēn-ˌbak\ *n* : a piece of paper currency issued by the United States government; *esp* : one without gold or silver backing issued during the Civil War

Green·back·er \-ər\ *n* : a member of a post-Civil War American political party opposing reduction in the amount of greenbacks in circulation

green bean *n* : a kidney bean that is used as a snap bean while the pods are green

green·belt \'grēn-ˌbelt\ *n* : a belt of parkways, parks, or farmlands that encircles a community

green·bri·er \'grēn-ˌbrī-ər, -ˌbrīr\ *n* : a prickly vine of the lily family of the eastern United States with thick leaves and clusters of small greenish flowers

green·ery \'grēn-rē, -ə-rē\ *n, pl* **-er·ies** : green foliage or plants : VERDURE

green gland *n* : a greenish excretory organ in the head of some crustaceans (as a lobster)

green·gro·cer \'grēn-ˌgrō-sər\ *n, chiefly British* : a retailer of fresh vegetables and fruit — **green·gro·cery** \-ˌgrōs-rē, -ə-rē\ *n*

green·horn \'grēn-ˌhórn\ *n* : an inexperienced person; *esp* : one easily tricked or cheated [obsolete *greenhorn* "animal with young horns"]

¹green·house \-ˌhaús\ *n* : a glassed enclosure used for the cultivation or protection of plants

²greenhouse *adj* : of, relating to, or caused by the greenhouse effect ⟨*greenhouse* warming⟩

greenhouse effect *n* : warming of the lower atmosphere as a result of absorption by carbon dioxide and water vapor of radiation received from the sun and reemitted by the earth

green light *n* : authority or permission to undertake a project [from the green traffic light which signals permission to proceed]

green·ling \'grēn-ling\ *n* : any of several spiny-finned food fishes of the rocky coasts of the northern Pacific

green manure *n* : an herbaceous crop (as clover) plowed under while green to enrich the soil

green mold *n* : a green or green-spored mold (as a penicillium)

green onion *n* : a young onion pulled before the bulb has enlarged especially for use in salad

green pepper *n* : a sweet pepper before it turns red at maturity

green revolution *n* : the great increase in the production of food grains resulting from improved plant varieties and farming methods

green·room \'grēn-ˌrüm, -ˌrùm\ *n* : a room in a theater or concert hall where actors or musicians relax before, between, or after appearances

green snake *n* : either of two bright green harmless largely insect-eating North American snakes

green soap *n* : a soft soap made from vegetable oils and used especially to treat skin diseases

green·stick fracture \'grēn-'stik-\ *n* : a bone fracture in the young in which the bone is partly broken and partly bent

green·sward \'grēn-ˌswórd\ *n* : turf green with growing grass

green thumb *n* : an unusual ability to make plants grow — **green–thumbed** \'grēn-'thəmd\ *adj*

green turtle *n* : a large edible sea turtle with a smooth greenish shell

Green·wich time \'grin-ij-, 'gren-, -ich-\ *n* : the time of the meridian of Greenwich used as the basis of standard time throughout the world [*Greenwich,* England]

green·wood \'grēn-ˌwùd\ *n* : a forest green with foliage

Great Dane

greet \\'grēt\ *vt* **1** : to address with expressions of kind wishes : HAIL **2** : to meet or react to in a specified manner 〈*greeted* the team with cheers〉 **3** : to be perceived by 〈offensive odors *greeted* the nose〉 [Old English *grētan*] — **greet·er** *n*

greet·ing *n* **1** : a salutation at meeting **2** : an expression of good wishes : REGARDS — usually used in pl.

gre·gar·i·ous \gri-'gar-ē-əs, -'ger-\ *adj* **1** : tending to associate with others of one's kind : SOCIAL **2** : habitually living or moving with others of one's own kind : tending to flock together 〈*gregarious* insects〉 [Latin *gregarius* "of a flock or herd", from *greg-, grex* "flock, herd"] — **gre·gar·i·ous·ly** *adv* — **gre·gar·i·ous·ness** *n*

Gre·go·ri·an calendar \gri-'gōr-ē-ən-, -'gȯr-\ *n* : a calendar in general use introduced in 1582 by Pope Gregory XIII as a revision of the Julian calendar that was marked by the initial dropping of 10 days as well as the 366th day in any century year not divisible by 400 (as 1700, 1800, and 1900) and that was adopted by Great Britain and the American colonies in 1752

Gregorian chant *n* : a rhythmically free unaccompanied melody sung in unison in services of the Roman Catholic Church

grem·lin \\'grem-lən\ *n* : a small sprite held to be responsible for malfunction of equipment especially in an airplane [probably from *grem-* (of unknown origin) + *-lin* (as in *goblin*)]

gre·nade \grə-'nād\ *n* **1** : a small bomb filled with a destructive agent (as gas, high explosive, or incendiary chemicals) and made to be hurled **2** : a device containing a gaseous or volatile substance (as tear gas) that when hurled releases its contents on impact [Middle French, "pomegranate", from Late Latin *granata*, from Latin *granum* "grain"]

gren·a·dier \,gren-ə-'diər\ *n* : a member of a European regiment formerly armed with grenades

gren·a·dine \,gren-ə-'dēn, 'gren-ə-,\ *n* : a syrup flavored with pomegranates and used in mixed drinks [French, from *grenade* "pomegranate"]

Gret·na Green \,gret-nə-'grēn\ *n* : a place where many eloping couples are married [*Gretna* Green, village in Scotland near the English border]

grew *past of* GROW

grey *variant of* GRAY

grey friar *n, often cap G & F* : a Franciscan friar

grey·hound \\'grā-,haund\ *n* : a tall slender graceful smooth-coated dog noted for swiftness and keen sight and used for pursuing game and for racing [Old English *grīghund*]

greyhound

grey·lag \-,lag\ *n* : the common gray wild goose of Europe [probably from *gray* + *lag* "last", from *lag* "to fall behind"]

grid \\'grid\ *n* **1** : GRATING 1 **2** : a perforated or ridged metal plate used as a conductor in a storage battery **3** : an electrode consisting of a mesh or a spiral of fine wire placed between two other elements of an electron tube so as to control the amount of current that flows between them **4 a** : a network of horizontal and perpendicular lines for locating points by means of coordinates 〈a *grid* of longitude and latitude lines on a map〉 **b** : GRIDIRON 2 [back-formation from *gridiron*]

grid·dle \\'grid-l\ *n* : a flat surface or pan on which food is cooked by dry heat [Old North French *gredil* "gridiron", from Latin *craticulum*, from *cratis* "wickerwork, hurdle"]

griddle cake *n* : PANCAKE

grid·iron \\'grid-,ī-ərn, -,īrn\ *n* **1** : a grate for broiling food **2** : something consisting of or covered with a network; *esp* : a football field [Middle English *gredire*]

grief \\'grēf\ *n* **1** : deep sorrow : SADNESS, DISTRESS **2** : a cause of sorrow **3** : MISHAP, DISASTER 〈the boat came to *grief* on the rocks〉 [Old French, "heavy, grave", from Latin *gravis* SYN see SORROW

griffin

griev·ance \\'grē-vəns\ *n* **1** : a cause of distress (as an unsatisfactory working condition) affording reason for complaint or resistance **2** : the formal expression of a grievance : COMPLAINT

grieve \\'grēv\ *vb* **1** : to cause grief or sorrow to : cause to suffer : DISTRESS **2** : to feel grief : SORROW [Old French *grever*, from Latin *gravare* "to burden", from *gravis* "heavy, grave"] — **griev·er** *n*

griev·ous \\'grē-vəs\ *adj* **1** : causing suffering or sorrow : DISTRESSING 〈*grievous* poverty〉 **2** : SERIOUS, GRAVE 〈a *grievous* fault〉 — **griev·ous·ly** *adv* — **griev·ous·ness** *n*

grif·fin *or* **grif·fon** *also* **gryph·on** \\'grif-ən\ *n* : a fabulous animal typically half eagle and half lion [Middle French *grifon*, from Latin *gryphus*, from Greek *gryps*, from *grypos* "curved"]

¹grill \\'gril\ *vt* **1** : to broil on a grill **2** : to question intensely 〈police *grilled* the suspect〉

²grill *n* **1** : a cooking utensil of parallel bars on which food is exposed to radiant heat (as from charcoal) **2** : food that is broiled usually on a grill **3** : a usually informal restaurant [French *gril*, from Latin *craticulum*, from *cratis* "wickerwork, hurdle"]

grille *or* **grill** \\'gril\ *n* **1** : a grating forming a barrier or screen **2** : an opening covered with a grille [French *grille*, from Latin *craticula* "fine wickerwork, gridiron", from *cratis* "wickerwork, hurdle"]

grill·work \\'gril-,wərk\ *n* : work constituting or resembling a grille

grilse \\'grils\ *n, pl* **grilse** : a young mature Atlantic salmon returning from the sea to spawn for the first time [Middle English *grills*]

grim \\'grim\ *adj* **grim·mer; grim·mest** **1** : SAVAGE, FIERCE 〈a *grim* battle〉 **2 a** : harsh and forbidding in appearance **b** : ghastly, repellent, or sinister in character **3** : UNFLINCHING, UNYIELDING 〈*grim* determination〉 [Old English *grimm*] SYN see GHASTLY — **grim·ly** *adv* — **grim·ness** *n*

grim·ace \\'grim-əs, grim-'ās\ *n* : a twisting or distortion of the face or features expressive usually of disgust or disapproval [French] — **grimace** *vi*

gri·mal·kin \grim-'ȯl-kən, -'ō-kən, -'al-kən\ *n* : CAT 1a; *esp* : an old female cat [*gray* + English dialect *malkin* "cat"]

grime \\'grīm\ *n* : soot, smut, or dirt adhering to or embedded in a surface; *also* : accumulated dirtiness and disorder [Flemish *grijm*] — **grime** *vt*

grimy \\'grī-mē\ *adj* **grim·i·er; -est** : full of or covered with grime : DIRTY — **grim·i·ness** *n*

grin \\'grin\ *vi* **grinned; grin·ning** : to draw back the lips so as to show the teeth especially in amusement or laughter [Old English *grennian*] — **grin** *n*

¹grind \\'grīnd\ *vb* **ground** \\'graund\; **grind·ing** **1** : to reduce to powder or small fragments by crushing (as in a mill or with the teeth) **2** : to wear down, polish, or sharpen by friction **3** : to press with a grating noise : GRIT 〈*grind* the teeth〉 **4** : OPPRESS, HARASS 〈*grinding* down the peasantry〉 **5** : to operate or produce by or as if by turning a crank **6** : to move with difficulty or friction especially so as to make a grating noise 〈gears *grinding* in an automobile〉 [Old English *grindan*]

²grind *n* **1** : an act of grinding **2 a** : monotonous labor or routine; *esp* : intensive study **b** : one who works or studies excessively **3** : the result of grinding; *esp* : the size of particle obtained by grinding

grind·er \\'grīn-dər\ *n* **1 a** : MOLAR **b** *pl* : TEETH **2** : one that grinds **3** : ²SUBMARINE 2

grind out *vt* : to produce steadily but mechanically as if by turning a crank 〈*ground out* three novels a year for 20 years〉

grind·stone \\'grīn-,stōn\ *n* : a flat circular stone of natural sandstone that revolves on an axle and is used for grinding, shaping, or smoothing

griot \'grē-ˌō\ *n* : any of a class of musician-entertainers of western Africa whose performances include tribal histories and genealogies [French]

¹**grip** \'grip\ *vt* **gripped; grip·ping 1** : to seize firmly **2** : to hold strongly the interest of ⟨the story *grips* the reader⟩ [Old English *grippan*]

²**grip** *n* **1 a** : a strong or tight grasp **b** : strength in gripping **c** : manner or style of gripping; *esp* : a way of clasping the hand by which members of a secret order recognize or greet one another **2 a** : CONTROL 1, 2, MASTERY **b** : mental grasp : UNDERSTANDING **3** : a part or device for gripping **4** : a part by which something is grasped; *esp* : HANDLE **5** : SUITCASE

¹**gripe** \'grīp\ *vb* **1** : CLUTCH 1, 2 : IRRITATE, VEX ⟨these rules *gripe* me⟩ **3** : to cause or experience spasms of pain in the bowels **4** : COMPLAIN 1 [Old English *grīpan*] — **grip·er** *n*

²**gripe** *n* **1 a** : GRIP 1a **b** : CONTROL 1, MASTERY **2 a** : painful distress **b** : COMPLAINT 1 **3** : a spasm of intestinal pain **4** : HANDLE 1, GRIP

grippe \'grip\ *n* : an acute virus disease identical with or resembling influenza [French, literally, "seizure"] — **grippy** \'grip-ē\ *adj*

grip·sack \'grip-ˌsak\ *n* : TRAVELING BAG

gris–gris \'grē-ˌgrē\ *n, pl* **gris–gris** \-ˌgrēz\ : an amulet or incantation used chiefly by people of African ancestry [French, of African origin]

gris·ly \'griz-lē\ *adj* **gris·li·er; -est** : GHASTLY 1, GRUESOME [Old English *grislic*] — **gris·li·ness** *n*

grist \'grist\ *n* : grain to be ground or already ground [Old English *grist*]

gris·tle \'gris-əl\ *n* : tough tissue of fiber or cartilage especially in table meats [Old English] — **gris·tli·ness** \'gris-lē-nəs, -ə-lē-\ *n* — **gris·tly** \'gris-lē, -ə-lē\ *adj*

grist·mill \'grist-ˌmil\ *n* : a mill for grinding grain

¹**grit** \'grit\ *n* **1** : a hard sharp granule (as of sand); *also* : material (as an abrasive) composed of such granules **2** : firmness of mind or spirit [Old English *grēot*]

²**grit** *vb* **grit·ted; grit·ting** : to grind or cause to grind : GRATE

grits \'grits\ *n pl* : coarsely ground hulled grain [Old English *grytt*]

grit·ty \'grit-ē\ *adj* **grit·ti·er; -est 1** : containing or resembling grit **2** : courageously persistent : PLUCKY — **grit·ti·ness** *n*

griz·zled \'griz-əld\ *adj* : sprinkled, streaked, or mixed with gray [Middle French *grisel* "gray", from *gris,* of Germanic origin]

¹**griz·zly** \'griz-lē\ *adj* **griz·zli·er; -est** : GRIZZLED

²**grizzly** *n, pl* **grizzlies** : GRIZZLY BEAR

grizzly bear *n* : a large powerful usually brownish yellow bear of the uplands of western North America

groan \'grōn\ *vi* **1** : to utter a deep moan of pain, grief, or annoyance **2** : to make a harsh sound under sudden or prolonged strain ⟨the floor *groaned* under the weight⟩ [Old English *grānian*] — **groan** *n* — **groan·er** *n*

¹**groat** \'grōt\ *n* **1** : hulled grain broken into fragments larger than grits **2** : a grain (as of oats) exclusive of the hull [Old English *grot*]

²**groat** *n* : a former British coin worth four pennies [Middle English *groot*]

gro·cer \'grō-sər\ *n* : a dealer in staple foodstuffs and household supplies [Middle French *grossier* "wholesaler", from *gros,* adj., "gross, wholesale"]

gro·cery \'grōs-rē, -ə-rē\ *n, pl* **-cer·ies 1** *pl* : commodities sold by a grocer **2** : a grocer's store

grog \'gräg\ *n* : alcoholic liquor; *esp* : liquor (as rum) cut with water [Old *Grog,* nickname of Edward Vernon, died 1757, English admiral who ordered the sailors' rum to be diluted] — **grog·shop** \-ˌshäp\ *n* □ ORIGIN The 18th century English admiral Edward Vernon is said to have been in the habit of wearing a cloak made of a kind of coarsely woven fabric called *gro-*

gram. For this reason, the sailors under his command gave him the nickname "Old Grog". The Royal Navy in the West Indies had been given by custom a daily ration of rum, but in 1740 Vernon, alarmed at the damage to the physical and moral health of his men, ordered that the rum should be diluted with water. This mixture was christened *grog,* after its godfather. *Grog* is now sometimes used as a general term for any liquor, even undiluted.

grog·gy \'gräg-ē\ *adj* **grog·gi·er; -est** : weak and unsteady on the feet or in action [*grog*] — **grog·gi·ly** \'gräg-ə-lē\ *adv* — **grog·gi·ness** \'gräg-ē-nəs\ *n*

¹**groin** \'grȯin\ *n* **1** : the fold or depression marking the junction of the lower abdomen and the thigh; *also* : the region of this junction **2** : the projecting curved line along which two intersecting structural vaults meet [Middle English *grynde,* from Old English, "abyss"]

²**groin** *vt* : to build or equip with groins

grom·met \'gräm-ət, 'grəm-\ *n* **1** : a ring of rope **2** : a small usually metal ring used to reinforce an eyelet or to protect something passed through it [perhaps from obsolete French *gormette* "curb of a bridle"]

¹**groom** \'grüm, 'grüm\ *n* **1 a** : *archaic* : a male servant **b** : a person in charge of horses **2** : BRIDEGROOM [Middle English *grom* "man, servant"; sense 2 short for *bridegroom*]

²**groom** *vt* **1** : to clean and care for (an animal) **2** : to make neat, attractive, or acceptable

grooms·man \'grümz-mən, 'grümz-\ *n* : a male attendant of a bridegroom at his wedding

groove \'grüv\ *n* **1** : a long narrow channel or depression **2** : a fixed routine : RUT [Middle English *groof*] — **groove** *vt* — **in the groove** : in top form

groovy \'grü-vē\ *adj* **groov·i·er; -est** : MARVELOUS 3, WONDERFUL ⟨had a *groovy* time at the beach⟩

grope \'grōp\ *vi* **1** : to feel about or cast about blindly or uncertainly in search ⟨*grope* for the right word⟩ **2** : to feel one's way by groping ⟨*grope* along a wall⟩ [Old English *grāpian*]

gros·beak \'grōs-ˌbēk\ *n* : any of several finches of Europe or America having large stout conical bills [French *grosbec,* from *gros* "gross, thick" + *bec* "beak"]

gro·schen \'grō-shən, 'grȯ-\ *n, pl* **groschen 1** : a unit of value equal to ¹/₁₀₀ schilling **2** : an Austrian coin representing one groschen [German]

gros·grain \'grō-ˌgrān\ *n* : a silk or rayon fabric with crosswise cotton ribs [French *gros grain* "coarse texture"]

¹**gross** \'grōs\ *adj* **1 a** : glaringly noticeable usually because of inexcusable badness ⟨a *gross* error⟩ **b** : OUT-AND-OUT, UTTER ⟨a *gross* fool⟩ **2 a** : BIG, BULKY; *esp* : excessively fat **b** : excessively luxuriant **3 a** : GENERAL 4, BROAD **b** : consisting of an overall total before any deductions ⟨*gross* earnings⟩ — compare NET **4** : EARTHY, CARNAL ⟨*gross* pleasures⟩ **5** : lacking knowledge or culture **6** : crudely vulgar ⟨*gross* epithets⟩ [Middle French *gros* "thick, coarse", from Latin *grossus*] SYN see FLAGRANT — **gross·ly** *adv* — **gross·ness** *n*

²**gross** *n* : a whole amount before any deductions

³**gross** *vt* : to earn before deductions

⁴**gross** *n, pl* **gross** : a total of 12 dozen things ⟨a *gross* of pencils⟩ [Middle French *grosse,* from *gros* "thick, coarse"]

gross national product *n* : the total value of the goods and services produced in a nation during a year

¹**gro·tesque** \grō-'tesk\ *n* **1** : decorative art featuring fanciful human and animal forms often interwoven with foliage **2** : one that is grotesque [Italian *pittura grottesca,* literally, "cave painting", from *grotta* "cave"] □ ORIGIN During the Italian Renaissance the remaining buildings of the ancient city of Rome were heavily excavated, exposing chambers that became

grizzly bear

\ə\ abut	\ng\ sing
\ər\ further	\ō\ bone
\a\ mat	\ȯ\ saw
\ā\ take	\ȯi\ coin
\ä\ cot, cart	\th\ thin
\au̇\ out	\th\ this
\ch\ chin	\ü\ food
\e\ pet	\u̇\ foot
\ē\ easy	\y\ yet
\g\ go	\yü\ few
\i\ tip	\yu̇\ cure
\ī\ life	\zh\ vision
\j\ job	

known, familiarly, as *grotte,* "caves" (the plural of *grotta*). The walls of many *grotte* were covered with exotic paintings. *Pittura grottesca,* or simply *grottesca,* the term for such a painting, became the name for a later but similar type of painting representing fantastic combinations of human and animal forms interwoven with strange fruits and flowers. The word was soon borrowed into English. The adjective *grotesque,* first applied only to decorative art of this kind, is now used to describe anything fanciful or bizarre.

²**grotesque** *adj* : of, relating to, or characteristic of the grotesque: as **a** : FANCIFUL 3, BIZARRE **b** : absurdly awkward or incongruous SYN see FANTASTIC — **gro·tesque·ly** *adv* — **gro·tesque·ness** *n*

grot·to \'grät-ō\ *n, pl* **grottoes** *also* **grottos** 1 : CAVE 2 : an artificial recess or structure made to resemble a natural cave [Italian *grotta, grotto,* from Latin *crypta* "cavern, crypt"]

grouch \'graûch\ *n* 1 : a fit of bad temper 2 : an habitually irritable or complaining person [probably from English dialect *grutch* "grudge", from Middle English *grucchen* "to grumble"] — **grouch** *vi* — **grouch·i·ly** \'graû-chə-lē\ *adv* — **grouch·i·ness** \-chē-nəs\ *n* — **grouchy** \-chē\ *adj*

¹**ground** \'graûnd\ *n* **1 a** : the bottom of a body of water ⟨the boat struck *ground*⟩ **b** *pl* : sediment at the bottom of a liquid : LEES 2 : a basis for belief, action, or argument ⟨*grounds* for divorce⟩ **3 a** : a surrounding area : BACKGROUND ⟨a picture on a gray *ground*⟩ **b** : material that serves as a base : FOUNDATION **4 a** : the surface of the earth **b** : an area used for a particular purpose ⟨parade *ground*⟩ **c** *pl* : the area around and belonging to a building ⟨the capitol *grounds*⟩ 5 : SOIL 2, EARTH **6 a** : an object that makes an electrical connection with the earth **b** : a large conducting body (as the earth) used as a common return for an electric circuit [Old English *grund*]

²**ground** *vb* 1 : to bring to or place on the ground ⟨*ground* a rifle⟩ **2 a** : to provide a reason or justification for **b** : to instruct in fundamentals ⟨well *grounded* in math⟩ 3 : to connect electrically with a ground 4 : to restrict to the ground ⟨*ground* a pilot⟩ 5 : to run aground ⟨the ship *grounded* on a reef⟩ 6 : to hit a ground ball

³**ground** *past of* GRIND

ground ball *n* : a baseball hit along the ground

ground–cher·ry \'graûnd-'cher-ē, 'graûn-\ *n* : a plant related to the nightshades that is sometimes grown for its edible yellow fruits enclosed in papery husks; *also* : its fruit

ground cover *n* : low-growing plants that cover the ground (as in a forest or in place of turf); *also* : a plant used as ground cover

ground crew *n* : the mechanics and technicians who maintain and service an airplane

ground·er \'graûn-dər\ *n* : GROUND BALL

ground finch *n* : any of several dull-colored large-billed finches of the Galapagos islands

ground floor *n* : the floor of a building most nearly on a level with the ground

ground glass *n* : glass with a roughened light-diffusing nontransparent surface

ground·hog \'graûnd-,hòg, -,häg\ *n* : WOODCHUCK

Groundhog Day *n* : February 2 that traditionally indicates six more weeks of winter if sunny or an early spring if cloudy [from the legend that the groundhog comes out and is frightened back into hibernation if he sees his shadow]

ground·less \'graûn-dləs\ *adj* : being without basis or reason ⟨*groundless* fears⟩ — **ground·less·ly** *adv* — **ground·less·ness** *n*

ground·ling \'graûn-dling\ *n* 1 : a member of the masses : PLEBEIAN 2 : one that lives or works on or near the ground

¹grouse

ground loop *n* : a sharp uncontrollable turn made by an airplane in landing, taking off, or taxiing

ground·mass \'graûnd-,mas, 'graûn-\ *n* : the fine-grained base of a rock in which larger crystals are embedded

ground·nut \-,nət\ *n* : a North American vine of the pea family with brownish purple fragrant flowers and an edible tuberous root; *also* : its root

ground pine *n* : any of several club mosses with long creeping stems and erect branches

ground plan *n* 1 : a plan of a floor of a building 2 : a basic plan

ground rule *n* 1 : a sports rule adopted to modify play on a particular field, court, or course 2 : a basic rule of procedure

ground·sel \'graûnd-səl, 'graûn-\ *n* : any of a large genus of plants of the daisy family which have mostly yellow flower heads and some of which are poisonous [Old English *grundeswelge,* from *grund* "ground" + *swelgan* "to swallow"]

ground·sheet \-,shēt\ *n* : a waterproof sheet placed on the ground for protection from moisture

ground squirrel *n* : any of numerous burrowing rodents (as the gophers and chipmunks) differing from true squirrels in having cheek pouches and shorter fur

ground state *n* : the energy level of a system (as of elementary particles) having the least energy of all its possible states

ground swell *n* 1 : a broad deep ocean swell caused by a distant storm or earthquake 2 : a rapid spontaneous growth (as of political opinion)

ground·wa·ter \'graûn-,dwòt-ər, -,dwät-\ *n* : water within the earth that supplies wells and springs

ground wave *n* : a radio wave that is propagated along the surface of the earth

ground·work \'graûn-,dwərk\ *n* : FOUNDATION 2, BASIS

¹**group** \'grüp\ *n* 1 : two or more figures forming a complete unit (as in a painting) **2 a** : a number of individuals assembled together or having common interests **b** : a number of objects regarded as a unit **3 a** : an assemblage of related organisms **b** : an assemblage of atoms forming part of a molecule ⟨a methyl *group* (CH_3)⟩ [French *groupe,* from Italian *gruppo,* of Germanic origin]

²**group** *vb* 1 : to combine in a group 2 : to assign to a group : CLASSIFY 3 : to form a group

grou·per \'grü-pər\ *n, pl* **groupers** *also* **grouper** 1 : any of numerous mostly large solitary bottom fishes of warm seas related to the sea basses 2 : any of several rockfishes [Portuguese *garoupa*]

group·ie \'grü-pē\ *n* : a female fan of a rock group who usually follows it on tour

¹**grouse** \'graûs\ *n, pl* **grouse** : any of numerous lump-bodied game birds usually protectively colored and less brilliant in plumage than the related pheasants [origin unknown]

²**grouse** *vi* : COMPLAIN 1, GRUMBLE [origin unknown] — **grous·er** *n*

grout \'graût\ *n* 1 : thin mortar 2 : PLASTER 2 [Old English *grūt* "coarse meal"] — **grout** *vt*

grove \'grōv\ *n* : a small wood; *esp* : a group of trees without underbrush [Old English *grāf*]

grov·el \'gräv-əl, 'grəv-\ *vi* **grov·eled** *or* **grov·elled; grov·el·ing** *or* **grov·el·ling** \'gräv-ling, 'grəv-, -ə-ling\ 1 : to lie or creep with the body prostrate especially as a sign of humbleness or abasement 2 : to abase oneself : CRINGE [back-formation from *groveling* "prone", from Middle English *gruf* "on the face" + ²*-ling*] — **grov·el·er** *or* **grov·el·ler** \-lər, -ə-lər\ *n*

grow \'grō\ *vb* **grew** \'grü\; **grown** \'grōn\; **grow·ing** 1 **a** : to spring up and develop to maturity **b** : to be able to grow in some place or situation ⟨rice *grows* in water⟩ **c** : to assume some relation through or as if through a process of natural growth ⟨a tree with limbs *grown* together⟩ **2 a** : to become larger and often more complex by addition of material either by assimilation into the living organism or by accretion in a natural inorganic process (as crystallization) **b** : INCREASE, EXPAND ⟨the city is *growing* rapidly⟩ ⟨*grow* in wisdom⟩ **3** : ORIGINATE ⟨the project *grew* out of a mere suggestion⟩ **4 a** : to pass into a condition : BECOME ⟨*grew* pale⟩ **b** : to obtain influence ⟨habit *grows* on a person⟩ **5** : to cause to grow : CULTIVATE, RAISE ⟨*grow* wheat⟩ [Old English *grōwan*] — **grow·er** \'grō-ər, 'grōr\ *n*

growing pains *n pl* **1** : pains in the legs of growing children having no demonstrable relation to growth **2** : the stresses and strains attending a new project or development

growing point *n* : the tip of a plant shoot from which additional shoot tissues differentiate

growl \'graúl\ *vb* **1 a** : RUMBLE 1 **b** : to utter a deep guttural threatening sound ⟨a *growling* dog⟩ **2** : to complain angrily [probably imitative] — **growl** *n* — **growl·er** *n*

grown \'grōn\ *adj* : ADULT 1, MATURE

grown–up \'grō-,nəp\ *adj* : ADULT ⟨*grown-up* behavior⟩ — **grown–up** *n*

growth \'grōth\ *n* **1 a** : stage or condition attained in growing : SIZE ⟨reach one's full *growth*⟩ **b** : a process of growing: as (1) : an increase in the size or amount of something (as an organism, a crystal, or wealth) (2) : progressive development ⟨the *growth* of civilization⟩ **2** : a result or product of growing: as **a** : vegetation or a cover of vegetation ⟨a *growth* of new rye⟩ **b** : an abnormal mass of tissue (as a tumor) **3** : a producing especially by growing ⟨fruits of one's own *growth*⟩

growth factor *n* : a substance (as a vitamin) that promotes the growth of an organism

growth hormone *n* **1** : a hormone that is secreted by the pituitary gland and regulates growth — called also *somatotrophic hormone* **2** : any of various plant substances (as gibberellin) that regulate growth

growth ring *n* : a layer of wood (as an annual ring) produced during a single period of growth

¹**grub** \'grəb\ *vb* **grubbed; grub·bing** **1** : to clear or root out by digging ⟨*grub* land for planting⟩ **2** : to work hard : DRUDGE **3 a** : to dig in the ground usually for a hidden object ⟨*grub* for potatoes⟩ **b** : to search about : RUMMAGE ⟨*grubbing* through the drawer⟩ [Middle English *grubben*] — **grub·ber** *n*

²**grub** *n* **1** : a soft thick wormlike larva of an insect **2** : a dull plodding person **3** : FOOD 2 [Middle English *grubbe*, from *grubben* "to grub"]

grub·by \'grəb-ē\ *adj* **grub·bi·er; -est** **1** : DIRTY 1, GRIMY **2** : IGNOBLE 2 — **grub·bi·ly** \'grəb-ə-lē\ *adv* — **grub·bi·ness** \'grəb-ē-nəs\ *n*

grub·stake \'grəb-,stāk\ *n* **1** : supplies or funds furnished a mining prospector on promise of a share in his finds **2** : material assistance advanced for a project — **grubstake** *vt* — **grub·stak·er** *n*

¹**grudge** \'grəj\ *vt* : BEGRUDGE 1 [Middle English *grucchen, grudgen* "to grumble, complain", from Old French *groucier*, of Germanic origin] — **grudg·er** *n* — **grudg·ing·ly** \'grəj-ing-lē\ *adv*

²**grudge** *n* : a feeling of deep-seated resentment or ill will

gru·el \'grü-əl\ *n* : a thin porridge [Middle French, of Germanic origin]

gru·el·ing *or* **gru·el·ling** \'grü-ə-ling\ *adj* : taxing to the point of exhaustion : making severe demands : PUNISHING ⟨a *grueling* race⟩ [from obsolete *gruel* "to exhaust"]

grue·some \'grü-səm\ *adj* : inspiring horror or repulsion : GRISLY [Middle English *gruen* "to shiver"] SYN see GHASTLY — **grue·some·ly** *adv* — **grue·some·ness** *n*

gruff \'grəf\ *adj* **1** : rough or stern in manner, speech, or look ⟨a *gruff* reply⟩ **2** : being deep and harsh : HOARSE ⟨a *gruff* voice⟩ [Dutch *grof*] — **gruff·ly** *adv* — **gruff·ness** *n*

grum·ble \'grəm-bəl\ *vb* **grum·bled; grum·bling** \-bə-ling, -bling\ **1** : to mutter in discontent **2 a** : to make low indistinct noises **b** : RUMBLE 1 [probably from Middle French *grommeler*] — **grumble** *n* — **grum·bler** \-bə-lər, -blər\ *n*

grump \'grəmp\ *n* **1** *pl* : a fit of bad humor **2** : a person given to complaining [obsolete *grumps* "snubs, slights"] — **grump** *vi* — **grump·i·ly** \'grəm-pə-lē\ *adv* — **grump·i·ness** \-pē-nəs\ *n* — **grumpy** \-pē\ *adj*

grun·ion \'grən-yən\ *n* : a small fish of the California coast that regularly comes inshore to spawn at nearly full moon [probably from Spanish *gruñón* "grunter"]

¹**grunt** \'grənt\ *vb* **1** : to utter a grunt **2** : to utter with a grunt [Old English *grunnettan*] — **grunt·er** *n*

²**grunt** *n* **1** : the characteristic deep short sound of a hog or a similar sound **2** : any of numerous marine fishes related to the snappers

gryph·on *variant of* GRIFFIN

G suit *n* : an aviator's or astronaut's suit designed to counteract the physiological effects of acceleration [*g*ravity *suit*]

gua·na·co \gwə-'näk-ō\ *n, pl* **-cos** *also* **-co** : a South American mammal that has a soft thick fawn-colored coat and is related to the camel [Spanish, from Quechua *huanacu*]

gua·nine \'gwän-,ēn\ *n* : a purine base $C_5H_5N_5O$ that codes genetic information in the polynucleotide chain of DNA and RNA — compare ADENINE, CYTOSINE, THYMINE, URACIL [*guano* + *-ine*; from its being found in guano]

gua·no \'gwän-ō\ *n, pl* **guanos** : a substance composed chiefly of the excrement of seabirds and used as a fertilizer [Spanish, from Quechua *huanu* "dung"]

gua·ra·ni \,gwär-ə-'nē\ *n, pl* **-nis** *or* **-nies** : the basic monetary unit of Paraguay; *also* : a note representing this unit [Spanish]

¹**guar·an·tee** \,gar-ən-'tē, ,gär-\ *n* **1** : GUARANTOR **2** : an agreement by which a person or firm guarantees something or someone **3** : something given as security : PLEDGE

²**guarantee** *vt* **-teed; -tee·ing** **1** : to undertake to answer to (a party) for the debt, failure to perform, or faulty performance of another **2** : to undertake an obligation to establish, perform, or continue ⟨*guaranteed* annual wage⟩ **3** : SECURE 1c

guar·an·tor \,gar-ən-'tor, 'gar-ən-tər, ,gär-, 'gär-\ *n* : one that gives a guarantee

¹**guar·an·ty** \'gar-ən-tē, 'gär-\ *n, pl* **-ties** : GUARANTEE [Middle French *garantie*, from *garantir* "to guarantee", from *garant* "warrant", of Germanic origin]

²**guaranty** *vt* **-tied; -ty·ing** : GUARANTEE

¹**guard** \'gärd\ *n* **1** : a defensive position (as in boxing) **2 a** : the act or duty of defending **b** : PROTECTION 1 **3 a** : a person or a body of persons on sentinel duty **b** *pl* : troops attached to the person of a sovereign **4 a** : either of two football players who line up inside the tackles and next to the center **b** : either of two players stationed usually away from the basket in basketball **5** : a protective or safety device (as on a machine) [Middle French *garde*, from *garder* "to guard", of Germanic origin]

²**guard** *vb* **1** : to protect from danger : DEFEND **2 a** : to watch over so as to prevent escape, disclosure, or indiscretion ⟨*guard* a prisoner⟩ ⟨*guard* a secret⟩ **b** : to attempt to prevent (an opponent) from playing effectively or scoring **3** : to be on guard : take precautions ⟨*guard* against infection⟩ SYN see DEFEND

guard cell *n* : one of the two crescent-shaped epidermal cells that border and open and close a plant stoma

guard·ed \'gärd-əd\ *adj* : CAUTIOUS, CIRCUMSPECT ⟨a *guarded* answer⟩ — **guard·ed·ly** *adv*

guard hair *n* : one of the long coarse hairs forming a protective coating over the underfur of a mammal

guanaco

\ə\ abut	\ng\ sing
\ər\ further	\ō\ bone
\a\ mat	\ȯ\ saw
\ā\ take	\ȯi\ coin
\ä\ cot, cart	\th\ thin
\aú\ out	\th\ this
\ch\ chin	\ü\ food
\e\ pet	\ú\ foot
\ē\ easy	\y\ yet
\g\ go	\yü\ few
\i\ tip	\yú\ cure
\ī\ life	\zh\ vision
\j\ job	

guard·house \'gärd-ˌhaus\ n 1 : a building occupied by a guard or used as a headquarters by soldiers on guard duty 2 : a military jail

guard·i·an \'gärd-ē-ən\ n 1 : one that guards : CUSTODIAN 2 : one having the care of the person or property of another — **guard·i·an·ship** \-ˌship\ n

guard of honor : a guard assigned to greet or accompany a distinguished person or to accompany a casket at a military funeral — called also *honor guard*

guard·rail \'gär-ˌdrāl\ n : a railing for guarding against danger or trespass; *esp* : a barrier placed at dangerous points along a highway

guard·room \'gär-ˌdrüm, -ˌdrum\ n 1 : a room used by a military guard while on duty 2 : a room where military prisoners are confined

guards·man \'gärdz-mən\ n : a member of a military body organized as guards

gua·va \'gwäv-ə\ n 1 : any of several tropical American shrubs or small trees of the myrtle family; *esp* : one widely grown for its sweet-to-acid yellow fruit 2 : the fruit of a guava [Spanish *guayaba*, of American Indian origin]

gua·yu·le \gwī-'ü-lē, wī-\ n : a low shrubby plant of the daisy family that is found in Mexico and the southwestern United States and has been grown as a source of rubber [American Spanish, from Nahuatl *cuauhuli*]

gu·ber·na·to·ri·al \ˌgü-bər-nə-'tōr-ē-əl, ˌgyü-, -bə-, -'tor-\ *adj* : of or relating to a governor [Latin *gubernator* "governor", from *gubernare* "to govern"]

guern·sey \'gərn-zē\ n, *pl* **guernseys** *often cap* : any of a breed of fawn and white dairy cattle that are larger than jerseys and produce rich yellowish milk [*Guernsey*, Channel Islands]

guer·ril·la *or* **gue·ril·la** \gə-'ril-ə\ n : one who engages in irregular warfare especially as a member of an independent unit carrying out harassment and sabotage [Spanish *guerrilla*, from *guerra* "war", of Germanic origin]

guess \'ges\ *vb* 1 : to form an opinion from little or no evidence 2 : to arrive at a correct conclusion about by conjecture ⟨*guessed* the answer⟩ 3 : BELIEVE, SUPPOSE ⟨I *guess* you're right⟩ [Middle English *gessen*] SYN see CONJECTURE — **guess** n — **guess·er** n — **guess·work** \'ges-ˌwərk\ n

guest \'gest\ n 1 a : a person entertained in one's house b : a person to whom hospitality is extended c : a patron of a commercial establishment (as a hotel or restaurant) 2 : an organism that lives in close association with another kind of organism [Old Norse *gestr*]

guf·faw \gə-'fȯ, ˌgə-\ n : a loud boisterous burst of laughter [imitative] — **guf·faw** *vi*

guid·ance \'gīd-ns\ n 1 : the act or process of guiding 2 : advice on vocational or educational problems given to students

¹**guide** \'gīd\ n 1 a : one who leads or directs another on a course b : one who exhibits and explains points of interest c : something that provides guiding information ⟨a city *guide*⟩ d : one (as a teacher) that directs a person in the conduct or course of life 2 a : a device for steadying or directing the motion of something b : a sheet or a card with a projecting tab for labeling that is inserted in a card index to facilitate reference [Middle French, from Provençal *guida*, of Germanic origin]

²**guide** *vt* 1 : to act as a guide for : CONDUCT 2 a : MANAGE, DIRECT ⟨*guide* a car through traffic⟩ b : to superintend the training of — **guid·able** \'gīd-ə-bəl\ *adj*

guide·book \'gīd-ˌbuk\ n : a book of information for travelers

guided missile n : a missile whose course toward a target may be changed (as by radio signals or a built-in target-seeking device) during flight

guide word n : either of the terms at the head of a page of an alphabetical reference work (as a dictionary) indicating the alphabetically first and last words on the page

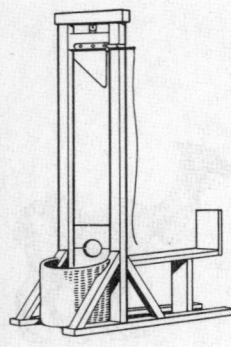

guillotine

guitar

gui·don \'gīd-ˌän, -n\ n 1 : a small flag; *esp* : one carried by a military unit as a unit marker 2 : one who carries a guidon [Middle French]

guild *also* **gild** \'gild\ n : an association of people with similar interests or pursuits; *esp* : a medieval association of merchants or craftsmen [Old Norse *gildi* "payment, guild"] — **guild·ship** \-ˌship\ n

guil·der \'gil-dər\ n : GULDEN [Dutch *gulden*]

guild·hall \'gild-ˌhȯl\ n : a hall where a guild or corporation usually assembles

guile \'gīl\ n : deceitful cunning : DUPLICITY [Old French] — **guile·ful** \-fəl\ *adj* — **guile·ful·ly** \-fə-lē\ *adv* — **guile·ful·ness** n

guile·less \'gīl-ləs\ *adj* : free from deceit or cunning : NAIVE — **guile·less·ly** *adv* — **guile·less·ness** n

guil·le·mot \'gil-ə-ˌmät\ n : any of several narrow-billed auks of northern seas [French, from *Guillaume* "William"]

guil·lo·tine \'gil-ə-ˌtēn; ˌgē-ə-', 'gē-ə-ˌ, -yə-\ n : a device for beheading by means of a heavy blade that slides down between vertical guides [French, from Joseph *Guillotin*, died 1814, French physician] — **guillotine** *vt*

guilt \'gilt\ n 1 : the fact of having committed an offense and especially one that is punishable by law 2 : the state of deserving blame 3 : a feeling of responsibility for offenses [Old English *gylt* "delinquency"] — **guilt·less** \-ləs\ *adj*

guilty \'gil-tē\ *adj* **guilt·i·er; -est** 1 : having committed a breach of conduct 2 a : suggesting or involving guilt ⟨a *guilty* look⟩ b : aware of or suffering from guilt — **guilt·i·ly** \-tə-lē\ *adv* — **guilt·i·ness** \-tē-nəs\ n

guin·ea \'gin-ē\ n 1 : a former monetary unit equal to 21 shillings 2 : a British gold coin representing this unit [*Guinea*, West Africa, supposed source of the gold from which it was made]

guinea fowl n : an African bird related to the pheasants, widely raised for food, and marked by a bare neck and head and white-speckled usually gray plumage

guinea hen n : a female guinea fowl; *also* : GUINEA FOWL

guinea pig n 1 : a small stout-bodied short-eared nearly tailless rodent often kept as a pet and widely used in biological research — called also *cavy* 2 : one that is the subject of a scientific experiment

guinea worm n : a slender nematode worm attaining a length of several feet and occurring as an adult under the skin of various mammals including humans

guise \'gīz\ n 1 : a form or style of dress : COSTUME ⟨appeared in the *guise* of a shepherd⟩ 2 : external appearance : SEMBLANCE ⟨swindled them under the *guise* of friendship⟩ [Old French, of Germanic origin]

gui·tar \gə-'tär, gi-\ n : a flat-bodied stringed instrument with a long fretted neck and usually six strings plucked with a pick or with the fingers [French *guitare*, from Spanish *guitarra*, from Arabic *gītār*, from Greek *kithara* "cithara"]

gu·lar \'gü-lər, 'gyü-\ *adj* : of, relating to, or situated on the throat [Latin *gula* "throat"]

gulch \'gəlch\ n : RAVINE, COULEE [perhaps from English dialect *gulch* "to gulp"]

gul·den \'gül-dən, 'gul-\ n, *pl* **guldens** *or* **gulden** 1 : the basic monetary unit of the Netherlands 2 : a coin or note representing one gulden [Dutch *gulden florijn* "golden florin"]

gulf \'gəlf\ n 1 : a part of an ocean or sea extending into the land 2 : a deep hollow in the earth : CHASM, ABYSS 3 : WHIRLPOOL 4 : an unbridgeable gap [Middle French *golfe*, from Italian *golfo*, from Late Latin *colpus*, from Greek *kolpos* "bosom, gulf"] □ SYN BAY: GULF implies a body of water of considerable size and importance and usually suggests deep penetration of the land and a relatively narrow entrance; BAY commonly implies a shallow penetration and wide entrance but may apply to a body of water of almost any size or shape that is connected with or is part of a larger one.

gulf·weed \\'gəlf-ˌwēd\ *n* : any of several marine brown algae; *esp* : a branching olive-brown seaweed of tropical American seas with numerous air-filled sacs suggesting berries

¹gull \\'gəl\ *n* : any of numerous mostly white or gray long-winged web-footed aquatic birds [Middle English, of Celtic origin]

²gull *vt* : take advantage of : DUPE [obsolete *gull* "gullet"]

³gull *n* : a person easily deceived or cheated : DUPE

gul·let \\'gəl-ət\ *n* **1 a** : a tube that leads from the back of the mouth to the stomach : ESOPHAGUS **b** : THROAT 1 **2** : a tubular infolding of the protoplasm in various protozoans (as a paramecium) that sometimes functions in the intake of food **3** : the space between adjacent saw teeth [Middle French *goulet* "narrow passage", from *goule* "throat", from Latin *gula*]

gull·ible \\'gəl-ə-bəl\ *adj* : easily cheated or duped — **gull·ibil·i·ty** \ˌgəl-ə-'bil-ət-ē\ *n* — **gull·ibly** \\'gəl-ə-blē\ *adv*

gul·ly \\'gəl-ē\ *n, pl* **gullies** : a trench worn in the earth by rainwater [obsolete *gully* "gullet"] — **gully** *vb*

gully erosion *n* : soil erosion produced by running water

gulp \\'gəlp\ *vb* **1** : to swallow hurriedly or greedily or in one swallow **2** : to keep back as if by swallowing ⟨*gulp* down a sob⟩ **3** : to catch the breath as if in taking a long drink [Middle English *gulpen*] — **gulp** *n* — **gulp·er** *n*

¹gum \\'gəm\ *n* : the tissue along the jaws of animals that surrounds the necks of the teeth [Old English *gōma* "palate"]

²gum *vt* **gummed; gum·ming** **1** : to enlarge gullets of (a saw) **2** : to chew with the gums

³gum *n* **1** : any of numerous complex colloidal substances (as gum arabic) that are exuded by plants or are extracted from them by solvents, that are thick or sticky when moist but harden on drying and are either soluble in water or swell up in contact with water, and that are used in pharmacy (as for emulsifiers), for adhesives, as food thickeners, and in inks; *also* : any of various gummy plant exudates including natural resins, oleoresins, rubber, and rubberlike substances **2** : a substance or deposit resembling a plant gum (as in sticky quality) **3 a** (1) : BLACK GUM (2) : SWEET GUM **b** *Australian* : EUCALYPTUS **4** : the wood of a gum **5** : CHEWING GUM [Old French *gomme*, from Latin *cummi, gummi*, from Greek *kommi*, from Egyptian *gmy·t*]

⁴gum *vt* **gummed; gum·ming** : to smear, seal, or clog with or as if with gum ⟨*gum* up the works⟩

gum arabic *n* : a water-soluble gum obtained from several acacias and used especially in adhesives, in confectionery, and in pharmacy

gum·bo \\'gəm-ˌbō\ *n, pl* **gumbos** **1** : OKRA **2** : a soup thickened with okra pods **3** : any of various silty soils that when wet become very sticky [American French *gombo*, of Bantu origin]

gum·drop \-ˌdräp\ *n* : a sugar-coated candy made usually from corn syrup with gelatin or gum arabic

gum·ma \\'gəm-ə\ *n, pl* **gummas** *also* **gum·ma·ta** \\'gəm-ət-ə\ : a gummy or rubbery tumor associated especially with late stages of syphilis [Late Latin *gummat-, gumma* "gum", from Latin *gummi*] — **gum·ma·tous** \-ət-əs\ *adj*

gum·my \\'gəm-ē\ *adj* **gum·mi·er; -est** **1** : consisting of, containing, or covered with gum **2** : VISCOUS 1, STICKY — **gum·mi·ness** *n*

gump·tion \\'gəm-shən, 'gəmp-\ *n* **1** : shrewd common sense **2** : ENTERPRISE 3, INITIATIVE [origin unknown]

gum resin *n* : a plant product consisting essentially of a mixture of gum and resin

gum·shoe \\'gəm-ˌshü\ *n* : DETECTIVE — **gumshoe** *vi*

gum tragacanth *n* : TRAGACANTH

gum turpentine *n* : TURPENTINE 2a

gum·wood \\'gəm-ˌwùd\ *n* : ³GUM 4

¹gun \\'gən\ *n* **1 a** : a piece of artillery usually with high muzzle velocity and comparatively flat trajectory : CANNON **b** : a portable firearm (as a rifle or pistol) **c** : a device that throws a projectile **2 a** : a discharge of a gun **b** : a signal marking a beginning or ending ⟨the opening *gun* of a campaign⟩ **3** : one who is skilled with a gun ⟨a hired *gun*⟩ **4** : something suggesting a gun in shape or function ⟨a grease *gun*⟩ **5** : THROTTLE 2 [Middle English *gunne*] — **gunned** \\'gənd\ *adj*

²gun *vb* **gunned; gun·ning** **1** : to hunt or shoot with a gun **2** : to open up the throttle of quickly so as to increase speed ⟨*gun* the engine⟩

gun·boat \\'gən-ˌbōt\ *n* : a small armed ship for patrolling coastal waters

gun·cot·ton \-ˌkät-n\ *n* : an explosive that consists of cellulose nitrate with a high nitrogen content and is used chiefly in smokeless powder

gun·fight \-ˌfīt\ *n* : a duel with guns — **gun·fight·er** *n*

gun·fire \-ˌfīr\ *n* : the firing of guns

gung ho \\'gəng-'hō\ *adj* : very enthusiastic [*Gung ho!*, motto (supposed to mean "work together") of a United States Marine battalion in World War II, from Chinese (Pekingese dialect) *kung¹-ho²*, short for *chung¹-kuo² kung¹-yeh⁴ ho²-tso⁴ she⁴* "Chinese Industrial Cooperatives Society"] □ ORIGIN The Chinese Industrial Cooperatives Society, whose Chinese name was chung¹-kuo² kung¹-yeh⁴ ho²-tso⁴ she⁴, was founded in 1938. Its long name was soon abbreviated to *kung¹-ho²*. In 1942 Lt. Col. Evans Fordyce Carlson of the United States Marine Corps was in China organizing the Second Raider Battalion. Trying to instill a sense of unity and purpose in his men, Carlson told them that *Gung ho* was the motto of the Chinese cooperatives, whose ardent spirit he admired, and that it meant "work together". In fact, although *kung¹* may be translated "work" and *ho²* "together", the two do not form a Chinese phrase meaning "work together", but are only a shortened form of an unwieldy name. But the misinterpreted motto caught on and members of the battalion were soon proudly calling themselves and their spirit *gung ho*.

gun·lock \\'gən-ˌläk\ *n* : a device on a firearm by which the charge is ignited

gun·man \-mən\ *n* : a man armed with a gun; *esp* : a professional killer

gun·ner \\'gən-ər\ *n* **1** : a person (as a soldier) who operates a gun **2** : one that hunts with a gun

gun·nery \\'gən-rē, -ə-rē\ *n* : the use of guns; *esp* : the science of the flight of projectiles and of the effective use of guns

gunnery sergeant *n* : an enlisted rank in the Marine Corps above staff sergeant and below master sergeant

gun·ny \\'gən-ē\ *n, pl* **gunnies** **1** : coarse jute sacking **2** : BURLAP [Hindi *ganī*]

gun·ny·sack \-ˌsak\ *n* : a sack made of gunny

gun·point \\'gən-ˌpòint\ *n* : the point of a gun — **at gunpoint** : under a threat of death by being shot

gun·pow·der \-ˌpaùd-ər\ *n* : an explosive mixture of potassium nitrate, charcoal, and sulfur used in gunnery and blasting; *also* : any of various explosive powders used in guns

gun·shot \-ˌshät\ *n* **1** : shot or a projectile fired from a gun **2** : the range of a gun ⟨within *gunshot*⟩ **3** : the firing of a gun

gun·shy \-ˌshī\ *adj* **1** : afraid of loud noise (as that of a gun) **2** : markedly distrustful

gun·smith \-ˌsmith\ *n* : one whose business is to design, make, or repair small firearms

gun·wale *or* **gun·nel** \\'gən-l\ *n* : the upper edge of a ship's side [from its former use as a support for guns]

gup·py \\'gəp-ē\ *n, pl* **guppies** : a small tropical topminnow frequently kept as an aquarium fish [R. J. L. *Guppy*, died 1916, Trinidadian naturalist]

\ə\ abut	\ng\ sing
\ər\ **further**	\ō\ **bone**
\a\ **mat**	\ȯ\ **saw**
\ā\ **take**	\ȯi\ **coin**
\ä\ **cot, cart**	\th\ **thin**
\aú\ **out**	\th\ **this**
\ch\ **chin**	\ü\ **food**
\e\ **pet**	\ù\ **foot**
\ē\ **easy**	\y\ **yet**
\g\ **go**	\yü\ **few**
\i\ **tip**	\yù\ **cure**
\ī\ **life**	\zh\ **vision**
\j\ **job**	

gur·gle \\'gər-gəl\\ *vi* **gur·gled; gur·gling** \\'gər-gə-ling, -gling\\ **1** : to flow in a broken irregular current **2** : to make a sound like that of a gurgling liquid [probably imitative] — **gurgle** *n*

gur·nard \\'gər-nərd\\ *n, pl* **gurnard** *or* **gurnards** : any of various marine spiny-finned fishes with a spiny armored head and modified fins used especially in crawling [Middle French *gornart*]

gu·ru \\gə-'rü, 'gür-ü\\ *n* **1** : a personal religious teacher and spiritual guide in Hinduism **2** : an acknowledged leader or teacher [Hindi *gurū*, from Sanskrit *guru*, from *guru* "heavy, venerable"]

gush \\'gəsh\\ *vb* **1** : to issue or pour forth copiously or violently : SPOUT ⟨oil *gushed* from the well⟩ **2** : to make an exaggerated display of affection or enthusiasm ⟨*gushed* over the movie star⟩ [Middle English *guschen*] — **gush** *n*

gush·er \\'gəsh-ər\\ *n* : one that gushes; *esp* : an oil well with a large natural flow

gushy \\'gəsh-ē\\ *adj* **gush·i·er; -est** : marked by exaggerated sentimentality — **gush·i·ly** \\'gəsh-ə-lē\\ *adv* — **gush·i·ness** \\'gəsh-ē-nəs\\ *n*

gus·set \\'gəs-ət\\ *n* : a usually triangular or diamond-shaped insert (as in a glove) to give width or strength [Middle English, "piece of armor covering the joints in a suit of armor", from Middle French *gousset*]

gust \\'gəst\\ *n* **1** : a sudden brief rush of wind **2** : a sudden outburst : SURGE ⟨a *gust* of rage⟩ [probably from Old Norse *gustr*] — **gust·i·ly** \\'gəs-tə-lē\\ *adv* — **gust·i·ness** \\-tē-nəs\\ *n* — **gusty** \\-tē\\ *adj*

gus·ta·tion \\,gəs-'tā-shən\\ *n* : the act or sensation of tasting [Latin *gustatio*, from *gustare* "to taste"]

gus·ta·to·ry \\'gəs-tə-,tōr-ē, -,tȯr-\\ *adj* : relating to, associated with, or being the sense or sensation of taste

gus·to \\'gəs-,tō\\ *n* **1** : enthusiastic vigorous enjoyment or appreciation ⟨eat with *gusto*⟩ **2** : very great vitality [Spanish, from Latin *gustus* "taste"] SYN SEE TASTE

¹gut \\'gət\\ *n* **1 a** : VISCERA, ENTRAILS — usually used in pl. **b** : the alimentary canal or part of it **c** : ABDOMEN 1, BELLY **2** *pl* : the inner essential parts ⟨the *guts* of a car⟩ **3** *pl* : COURAGE [Old English *guttas*, pl.]

²gut *vt* **gut·ted; gut·ting** **1** : EVISCERATE 1 **2** : to destroy the inside of ⟨fire *gutted* the building⟩

gutsy \\'gət-sē\\ *adj* **guts·i·er; -est** : COURAGEOUS ⟨a *gutsy* fighter⟩

gut·ta–per·cha \\,gət-ə-'pər-chə\\ *n* : a tough plastic substance from the latex of several Malaysian trees that resembles but contains more resin than rubber and that is used especially as insulation and in dentistry [Malay *gětah-pěrcha*]

gut·ta·tion \\,gə-'tā-shən\\ *n* : physiological oozing of drops of water from a plant [Latin *gutta* "drop"]

¹gut·ter \\'gət-ər\\ *n* **1 a** : a trough along the eaves to catch and carry off water from a roof **b** : a low area (as at a roadside) to carry off surface water **2** : a narrow channel or groove [Old French *goutiere*, from *goute* "drop", from Latin *gutta*]

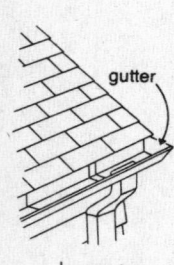

gutter

¹gutter 1a

²gutter *vb* **1** : to form gutters in **2 a** : to flow in small streams **b** : to melt away rapidly by becoming channeled down the sides ⟨a *guttering* candle⟩ **3** : to flicker in a draft ⟨a flame *guttering* in the breeze⟩

gut·ter·snipe \\-,snīp\\ *n* : a person of the lowest moral or economic station; *esp* : a street urchin

gut·tur·al \\'gət-ə-rəl\\ *adj* **1** : of or relating to the throat **2 a** : formed or pronounced in the throat ⟨*guttural* sounds⟩ **b** : VELAR 2 **c** : being or marked by an utterance that is strange or disagreeable [Middle French, derived from Latin *guttur* "throat"] — **guttural** *n* — **gut·tur·al·ly** \\-rə-lē\\ *adv* — **gut·tur·al·ness** *n*

gut·ty \\'gət-ē\\ *adj* **gut·ti·er; -est** **1** : COURAGEOUS ⟨a *gutty* fighter⟩ **2** : having a vigorous challenging quality ⟨*gutty* realism⟩

¹guy \\'gī\\ *n* : a rope, chain, or wire attached to something as a brace or guide [probably from Dutch *gei* "brail"]

²guy *vt* **guyed; guy·ing** : to steady or reinforce with a guy

³guy *n* : FELLOW 4a [*guy* "grotesque effigy of Guy Fawkes paraded and burned in England on November 5", from *Guy* Fawkes, died 1606, English conspirator who plotted to blow up the Houses of Parliament]

☐ **ORIGIN** On 4 November 1605 in London, Guy Fawkes was arrested for having planted gunpowder in the cellars of the Houses of Parliament as his part in a conspiracy to blow up the Parliament buildings on the following day. He was later executed. The failure of the conspiracy is still celebrated in England on November 5, Guy Fawkes Day. On this day fireworks are displayed and effigies of Guy Fawkes are burned on bonfires. These effigies came to be called *guys*. The use of the word was extended to other similar effigies and then to people of grotesque appearance. In the United States the word was generalized to mean simply "man" or "fellow".

⁴guy *vt* : to make fun of : RIDICULE

guy·ot \\'gē-ō\\ *n* : a flat-topped seamount [Arnold H. *Guyot*, died 1884, American geographer and geologist]

guz·zle \\'gəz-əl\\ *vb* **guz·zled; guz·zling** \\'gəz-ling, -ə-ling\\ : to drink greedily [origin unknown] — **guz·zler** \\-lər, -ə-lər\\ *n*

gybe \\'jīb\\ *variant of* JIBE

gym \\'jim\\ *n* : GYMNASIUM 1

gym·kha·na \\jim-'kän-ə, -'kan-\\ *n* : a meet featuring sports contests (as horseback-riding events) [probably from Hindi *gendkhāna*, court for a game similar to tennis]

gymn- *or* **gymno-** *combining form* : naked : bare ⟨*gymn*osperm⟩ [Greek *gymnos*]

gym·na·si·um *in sense 1* jim-'nā-zē-əm, *in sense 2* gim-'nä-zē-əm\\ *n, pl* **-si·ums** *or* **-sia** \\-zē-ə\\ **1** : a room or building for indoor sports activities **2** : a German secondary school preparing students for the university [Latin, "exercise ground, school", from Greek *gymnasion*, from *gymnazein* "to exercise naked", from *gymnos* "naked"]

gym·nast \\'jim-,nast, -nəst\\ *n* : one trained in gymnastics

gym·nas·tics \\jim-'nas-tiks\\ *n sing or pl* : physical exercises developing or exhibiting skill, strength, and control in the use of the body; *also* : a sport in which such exercises are performed — **gym·nas·tic** \\-tik\\ *adj* — **gym·nas·ti·cal·ly** \\-ti-kə-lē, -klē\\ *adv*

gym·no·din·i·um \\,jim-nō-'din-ē-əm\\ *n* : any of a genus of marine dinoflagellates some of which cause red tides [*gymn-* + Greek *dinein* "to whirl"]

gym·no·sperm \\'jim-nə-,spərm\\ *n* : any of a group (Gymnospermae) of woody vascular seed plants that produce naked seeds not enclosed in a true fruit [*gymn-* + Greek *sperma* "seed"] — **gym·no·sper·mous** \\,jim-nə-'spər-məs\\ *adj*

gyn·an·dro·morph \\gīn-'an-drə-,mȯrf, jin-\\ *n* : an abnormal individual exhibiting characters of both sexes in various parts of the body [Greek *gynē* "woman" + *andr-*, *anēr* "man" + *morphē* "form"] — **gyn·an·dro·mor·phic** \\-,an-drə-'mȯr-fik\\ *adj* — **gyn·an·dro·mor·phism** \\-,fiz-əm\\ *n* — **gyn·an·dro·mor·phy** \\-'an-drə-,mȯr-fē\\ *n*

gy·ne·col·o·gy \\,gīn-i-'käl-ə-jē, ,jin-\\ *n* : a branch of medicine that deals with women, their diseases, and their hygiene [Greek *gynaik-*, *gynē* "woman"] — **gy·ne·co·log·ic** \\-kə-'läj-ik\\ *or* **gy·ne·co·log·i·cal** \\-'läj-i-kəl\\ *adj* — **gy·ne·col·o·gist** \\-'käl-ə-jəst\\ *n*

gy·noe·ci·um \\jin-'ē-sē-əm, gīn-, -shē-\\ *n, pl* **-cia** \\-sēə, -shē-ə\\ : the carpels in a flower [Latin *gynaeceum* "women's apartments", from Greek *gynaikeion*, from *gynaik-*, *gynē* "woman"]

-g·y·nous \\j-ə-nəs\\ *adj combining form* **1** : of, relating to, or having (such or so many) females ⟨poly*gynous*⟩ **2** : situated (in a specified place) in relation to

gyp-
habit

447

a female organ of a plant ⟨hypo*gynous*⟩ [Greek *gynē* "woman"]

¹gyp \'jip\ *n* **1 :** CHEAT 2, SWINDLER **2 :** FRAUD 1b, SWIN-DLE [probably short for *Gypsy*]

²gyp *vb* **gypped; gyp·ping : CHEAT 1, 4, SWINDLE**

gyp·soph·i·la \jip-'säf-ə-lə\ *n* **:** any of a large genus of Old World herbs of the pink family having loosely branched clusters of tiny flowers [Latin *gypsum* + *-phila* "-phil"]

gyp·sum \'jip-səm\ *n* **:** a colorless mineral $CaSO_4.2H_2O$ that consists of hydrous sulfate of calcium occurring in crystals or masses and that is used especially as a soil improver and in making plaster of paris [Latin, from Greek *gypsos*, of Semitic origin]

Gyp·sy *or* **Gip·sy** \'jip-sē\ *n, pl* **Gypsies** *or* **Gipsies 1 :** one of a dark Caucasoid people coming originally from India to Europe in the 14th or 15th century and living and maintaining a migratory way of life chiefly in Europe and the United States **2 :** ROMANY 2 **3** *not cap* **:** one that resembles a Gypsy **:** WANDERER [alteration of *Egyptian*] ☐ ORIGIN In the early years of the 16th century there began to appear in Britain some members of a wandering race of people who were ultimately of Hindu origin and who called themselves and their language *Romany*. In Britain, however, it was popularly believed that they came from Egypt, so they were called *Egipcyans* or *Egyptians*. This was soon shortened to *Gipcyan*, and by 1600 the further altered form *Gipsy, Gypsey* began to appear in print.

gypsy moth *n* **:** an Old World tussock moth introduced about 1869 into the United States that has a hairy caterpillar which is a destructive defoliator of many trees

gyr- *or* **gyro-** *combining form* **1 :** ring **:** circle **:** spiral **2 :** gyroscope ⟨*gyro* compass⟩ [Greek *gyros*]

gy·rate \'jī-,rāt\ *vi* **1 :** to revolve around a point or axis **2 :** to oscillate with or as if with a circular or spiral motion — **gy·ra·tion** \jī-'rā-shən\ *n* — **gy·ra·tion·al** \-shnəl, -shən-l\ *adj*

gyr·fal·con \'jər-,fal-kən *also* -,fol- *sometimes* -,fo-kən\ *n* **:** an arctic falcon that occurs in several forms, is the largest of all falcons, and is more powerful though less active than the peregrine falcon [Middle French *gir-faucon*]

gy·ro \'jī-rō\ *n, pl* **gyros 1 :** GYROSCOPE **2 :** GYROCOM-PASS

gy·ro·com·pass \'jī-rō-,kəm-pəs, -,käm-\ *n* **:** a compass in which the horizontal axis of a constantly spinning gyroscope points to the north and which is often used instead of a magnetic compass where metal in the vicinity (as on a ship) would interfere with the working of a magnetic compass

gy·ro·scope \'jī-rə-,skōp\ *n* **:** a wheel or disk mounted to spin rapidly about an axis that is free to turn in various directions [from its original use to illustrate the rotation of the earth] — **gy·ro·scop·ic** \,jī-rə-,skäp-ik\ *adj*

gy·rus \'jī-rəs\ *n, pl* **gy·ri** \-,rī\ **:** a convoluted ridge between anatomical grooves [Latin, "circle", from Greek *gyros*]

gyve \'jīv\ *n* **:** FETTER 1 [Middle English] — **gyve** *vt*

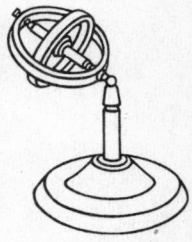

gyroscope

Hh

h \'āch\ *n, pl* **h's** *or* **hs** \'ā-chəz\ *often cap* **:** the 8th letter of the English alphabet

ha *or* **hah** \'hä\ *interj* — used especially to express surprise or joy [Middle English *ha*]

Hab·ak·kuk \'hab-ə-,kək, hə-'bak-ək\ *n* — see BIBLE table

ha·ba·ne·ra \,häb-ə-'ner-ə, ,äb-\ *n* **1 :** a Cuban dance in slow duple time **2 :** the music for the habanera [Spanish *danza habanera,* literally, "dance of Havana"]

hab·da·lah \,häv-də-'lä, häv-'dò-lə\ *n, often cap* **:** a Jewish ceremony that marks the close of a Sabbath or holy day [Hebrew *habbdālāh* "separation"]

ha·be·as cor·pus \,hä-bē-əs-'kòr-pəs\ *n* **1 :** any of several writs issued to bring a person before a court; *esp* **:** one ordering an inquiry to determine whether or not a person has been lawfully imprisoned **2 :** the right of a citizen to obtain a writ of habeas corpus as a protection against illegal imprisonment [Medieval Latin, literally, "you should have the body" (the opening words of the writ)]

hab·er·dash·er \'hab-ər-,dash-ər, 'hab-ə-,\ *n* **:** a dealer in menswear [Anglo-French *hapertas* "petty merchandise"]

hab·er·dash·ery \-,dash-rē, -ə-rē\ *n, pl* **-er·ies 1 :** goods sold by a haberdasher **2 :** a haberdasher's shop

ha·bil·i·ment \hə-'bil-ə-mənt\ *n* **1 :** the dress characteristic of an occupation or occasion — usually used in pl. ⟨the *habiliments* of a priest⟩ **2 :** CLOTHING — usually used in pl. [Middle French *habillement,* from *habiller* "to dress a log, dress", from *bille* "log"]

¹hab·it \'hab-ət\ *n* **1 :** a costume characteristic of a calling, rank, or function ⟨riding *habit*⟩ **2 :** bodily appearance or physical makeup **:** PHYSIQUE **3 :** the prevailing disposition or character of a person's thoughts and feelings **:** mental makeup **4 :** a usual manner of behavior **:** CUSTOM **5 a :** a behavior pattern acquired and fixed by frequent repetition — compare REFLEX **b :** an acquired mode of behavior that has become nearly or completely involuntary **c :** ADDICTION **6 :** characteristic mode of growth or occurrence ⟨elms have a spreading *habit*⟩ [Old French, from Latin *habitus* "condition, custom, dress", from *habēre* "to have, hold"] ☐ SYN HABIT, PRACTICE, USAGE, CUSTOM mean a way of acting that has become fixed through repetition. HABIT implies doing something unconsciously, often involuntarily or without forethought, and as a result of much repetition ⟨*habits* of speech⟩ ⟨pocketed the car keys by force of *habit*⟩ PRACTICE suggests an act performed with regularity and usually by choice; USAGE suggests a customary action or practice followed so generally that it has become a social norm; CUSTOM applies to practice or usage so long and continuously associated with an individual or group as to have the force of unwritten law ⟨by *custom* Saturday was bath night⟩

²habit *vt* **:** CLOTHE 1, DRESS

\ə\ abut		\ng\ si**ng**	
\ər\ fur**ther**		\ō\ b**o**ne	
\a\ m**a**t		\ò\ s**aw**	
\ā\ t**a**ke		\òi\ c**oi**n	
\ä\ c**o**t, c**a**rt		\th\ **th**in	
\aú\ **ou**t		\th\ **th**is	
\ch\ **ch**in		\ü\ f**oo**d	
\e\ p**e**t		\ú\ f**oo**t	
\ē\ **ea**sy		\y\ **y**et	
\g\ **g**o		\yü\ f**ew**	
\i\ t**i**p		\yú\ c**u**re	
\ī\ l**i**fe		\zh\ vi**si**on	
\j\ **j**ob			

hab·it·able \'hab-ət-ə-bəl\ *adj* : suitable or fit to live in ⟨the *habitable* parts of the earth⟩ — **hab·it·abil·i·ty** \,hab-ət-ə-'bil-ət-ē\ *n* — **hab·it·able·ness** \'hab-ət-ə-bəl-nəs\ *n* — **hab·it·ably** \-blē\ *adv*

ha·bi·tant *n* **1** \'hab-ət-ənt\ : INHABITANT, RESIDENT **2** \,hab-i-'tän, ,ab-\ : a French settler or a farmer of French origin in Canada

hab·i·tat \'hab-ə-,tat\ *n* **1** : the place or type of site where a plant or animal naturally or normally lives or grows **2** : the place where something is commonly found [Latin, "it inhabits", from *habitare* "to inhabit"]

hab·i·ta·tion \,hab-ə-'tā-shən\ *n* **1** : the act of inhabiting : OCCUPANCY **2** : a dwelling place : RESIDENCE

hab·it–form·ing *adj* : causing addiction

ha·bit·u·al \hə-'bich-ə-wəl, -'bich-wəl\ *adj* **1** : having the nature of a habit ⟨*habitual* tardiness⟩ **2** : doing or acting by force of habit ⟨*habitual* smokers⟩ **3** : done, followed, or used often or regularly ⟨took our *habitual* path⟩ SYN see USUAL — **ha·bit·u·al·ly** \-ē\ *adv* — **ha·bit·u·al·ness** *n*

ha·bit·u·ate \hə-'bich-ə-,wāt, ha-\ *vt* : to make used to : ACCUSTOM

ha·bit·u·a·tion \-,bich-ə-'wā-shən\ *n* **1** : the act or process of habituating **2** : psychological dependence on a drug after a period of use — compare ADDICTION

hab·i·tude \'hab-ə-,tüd, -,tyüd\ *n* **1** : habitual disposition or mode of behavior or procedure **2** : CUSTOM 1b

ha·bi·tué \hə-'bich-ə-,wā, ha-\ *n* : one who frequents a place or type of place [French, from *habituer* "to frequent", derived from Latin *habitus* "habit"]

hab·i·tus \'hab-ət-əs\ *n, pl* **habitus** \-ət-əs, -ə-,tüs\ : bodily habit; *also* : HABIT 6 [Latin]

Habs·burg \'haps-,bərg 'häps-, -,bùrg\ *variant of* HAPSBURG

ha·chure \ha-'shùr\ *n* : a short line used for shading and in representing surfaces in relief (as in map drawing) [French]

ha·ci·en·da \,häs-ē-'en-də, ,äs-\ *n* **1** : a large estate especially in a Spanish-speaking country : PLANTATION **2** : the main building of a farm or ranch [Spanish]

¹hack \'hak\ *vb* **1 a** : to cut with repeated irregular or unskillful blows **b** : to sever with repeated blows : CHOP **2** : to cough in a short dry manner **3** : to manage successfully ⟨tried sales work but couldn't *hack* it⟩ [Old English *-haccian*]

²hack *n* **1** : an implement for hacking **2** : NICK 1, NOTCH **3** : a short dry cough **4** : a hacking blow

³hack *n* **1 a** (1) : a horse let out for common hire (2) : a horse used in all kinds of work **b** : a horse worn out in service **c** : a light easy saddle horse; *esp* : a saddle horse trained to walk, trot, and canter **2 a** : HACKNEY 2 **b** (1) : TAXICAB (2) : CABDRIVER **3** : one who gives up individual freedom of action or professional integrity in exchange for money or other reward; *esp* : a writer who works mainly for hire [short for *hackney*]

⁴hack *adj* **1** : working for hire **2** : done by or characteristic of a hack ⟨*hack* writing⟩ **3** : HACKNEYED, TRITE

⁵hack *vi* **1** : to ride or drive at an ordinary pace or over the roads especially as distinguished from racing or hunting **2** : to operate a taxicab

hack·a·more \'hak-ə-,mōr, -,mòr\ *n* : a bridle (as of rope) that controls by a slip noose about the nose or a loop about the lower jaw (as of a horse) [by folk etymology from Spanish *jaquima*]

hack·ber·ry \'hak-,ber-ē\ *n* : any of a genus of trees and shrubs of the elm family with small often edible berries; *also* : its wood [alteration of *hagberry*, a kind of cherry]

hack·er \'hak-ər\ *n* **1** : one that hacks **2** : a person who is unskilled at a particular activity **3** : an expert at programming and solving problems with a computer **4** : a person who illegally gains access to information in a computer system

hack·ie \'hak-ē\ *n* : CABDRIVER

¹hack·le \'hak-əl\ *n* **1** : a comb for dressing fibers (as flax or hemp) **2** : one of the long narrow feathers on the neck or lower back of a bird **3** *pl* **a** : hairs that can be raised to an erect position along the neck and back especially of a dog **b** : TEMPER 4d, DANDER [Middle English *hakell*]

²hackle *vt* **hack·led; hack·ling** \'hak-ling, -ə-ling\ : to chop up or chop off roughly : HACK [derived from *¹hack*]

hack·man \'hak-mən\ *n* : CABDRIVER

hack·ma·tack \'hak-mə-,tak\ **1** : TAMARACK **2** : BALSAM POPLAR [of American Indian origin]

¹hack·ney \'hak-nē\ *n, pl* **hack·neys** **1 a** : a horse suitable for ordinary riding or driving **b** : any of a breed of rather compact English horses with a flashy high-stepping action while trotting **2** : a carriage or automobile kept for hire [Middle English *hackeney*]

²hackney *adj* **1** : kept for public hire **2** : HACKNEYED

³hackney *vt* **1** : to make common or frequent use of **2** : to make trite, vulgar, or commonplace

hack·neyed \'hak-nēd\ *adj* : lacking in freshness or originality ⟨a *hackneyed* expression⟩ SYN see TRITE

hack·saw \'hak-,sò\ *n* : a fine-tooth saw with blade under tension in a bow-shaped frame for cutting hard materials (as metal)

hack·work \-,wərk\ *n* : literary, artistic, or professional work done on order usually according to formula and in conformity with commercial standards

had *past of* HAVE

had·dock \'had-ək\ *n, pl* **haddock** *also* **haddocks** : an important Atlantic food fish usually smaller than the related common cod [Middle English *haddok*]

ha·des \'hād-ēz\ *n, often cap* : HELL 1 [Greek *Haidēs*, god of the underworld, abode of the dead in Greek mythology]

hadn't \'had-nt\ : had not

hadst \hadst, 'hadst, hədst, ədst\ *archaic past 2d sing of* HAVE

hae \hā, 'hā\ *chiefly Scottish variant of* HAVE

haem- *or* **haemo-** — see HEM-

haemat- *or* **haemato-** — see HEMAT-

haf·ni·um \'haf-nē-əm\ *n* : a metallic chemical element that resembles zirconium chemically and is useful because of its ready emission of electrons — see ELEMENT table [New Latin, from *Hafnia* (Copenhagen), Denmark]

¹haft \'haft\ *n* : the handle of a weapon or tool (as a sword or file) [Old English *hæft*]

²haft *vt* : to set in or furnish with a haft

haf·ta·rah *or* **haf·to·rah** \,häf-tə-'rä, häf-'tò-rə\ *n* : one of the biblical selections from the Books of the Prophets read at the conclusion of the Jewish synagogue service [Hebrew *haphṭārāh* "conclusion"]

hag \'hag\ *n* **1** : WITCH 1 **2** : an ugly, slatternly, or evil-looking old woman [Middle English *hagge*]

hag·fish \'hag-,fish\ *n* : an eellike fish related to the lampreys

Hag·ga·dah \hə-'gäd-ə, -'gòd-\ *n, pl* **Hag·ga·doth** \-'gäd-,ōt, -'gòd-, -,ōth\ **1** : ancient Jewish lore forming especially the nonlegal part of the Talmud **2** : the Jewish ritual for the seder [Hebrew *haggadhah*] — **hag·gad·ic** \-'gad-ik, -'gäd-, -'gòd-\ *adj, often cap*

Hag·gai \'hag-ē-,ī, 'hag-,ī\ *n* — see BIBLE table

hag·gard \'hag-ərd\ *adj* **1** : wild in appearance **2** : having a worn or emaciated look : GAUNT [Middle French *hagard*]

hag·gis \'hag-əs\ *n* : a pudding popular especially in Scotland made of the heart, liver, and lungs of a sheep or a calf minced with suet, onions, oatmeal, and seasonings and boiled in the stomach of the animal [Middle English *hagese*]

¹hag·gle \'hag-əl\ *vb* **hag·gled; hag·gling** \'hag-ling, -ə-ling\ **1** : to cut roughly or clumsily : HACK **2** : to argue especially over a price [derived from Middle English *haggen* "to hew"] — **hag·gler** \-lər, -ə-lər\ *n*

²haggle *n* : an act or instance of haggling

Hag·i·og·ra·pha \,hag-ē-'äg-rə-fə, ,hä-jē-\ *n sing or pl* : the third part of the Jewish scriptures — compare LAW 3b, PROPHETS [Late Latin, from Late Greek, literally, "holy writings"]

hag·i·og·ra·phy \-fē\ *n* **1** : biography of saints or venerated persons **2** : idealizing or idolizing biography [Greek *hagios* "saint", from *hagios* "holy"] — **hag·i·og·ra·pher** \-fər\ *n*

hah *variant of* HA

ha-ha \hä-'hä, 'hä-\ *interj* — used to express amusement or derision [Old English *ha ha*]

¹hail \'hāl\ *n* : precipitation in the form of small balls or lumps usually consisting of concentric layers of clear ice and compact snow **2** : something that gives the effect of falling hail ⟨a *hail* of bullets⟩ [Old English *hægl*]

²hail *vb* **1** : to precipitate hail **2** : to pour down like hail **3** : to hurl forcibly ⟨*hailed* curses on them⟩

³hail *interj* **1** — used to express acclamation **2** *archaic* — used as a greeting [Old Norse *heill*, from *heill* "healthy, hale"]

⁴hail *vb* **1 a** : SALUTE 1, GREET **b** : to greet with enthusiastic approval : ACCLAIM ⟨*hailed* the book as a masterpiece⟩ **2** : to greet or summon by calling ⟨*hail* a taxi⟩ **3** : to call out; *esp* : to call a greeting to a passing ship — **hail from** : to come from ⟨they *hail from* New York⟩

⁵hail *n* **1** : an exclamation of greeting or acclamation **2** : a calling to attract attention **3** : hearing distance ⟨stayed within *hail*⟩

hail-fel·low \'hāl-,fel-ō\ *or* **hail-fellow-well-met** \-,wel-'met\ *adj* : heartily informal [from the archaic salutation "Hail, fellow! Well met!"]

Hail Mary *n* : a Roman Catholic prayer to the Virgin Mary [translation of Medieval Latin *Ave, Maria*]

hail·stone \'hāl-,stōn\ *n* : a pellet of hail

hail·storm \-,storm\ *n* : a storm accompanied by hail

hair \'haər, 'heər\ *n* **1 a** : a slender threadlike outgrowth of the epidermis of an animal; *esp* : one of the usually pigmented filaments that form the characteristic coat of a mammal **b** : the hairy covering of an animal or a body part **2** : HAIRCLOTH **3 a** : a minute distance or amount ⟨won by a *hair*⟩ **b** : a precise degree : NICETY ⟨aligned to a *hair*⟩ **4** : a threadlike structure that resembles hair ⟨leaf *hairs*⟩ [Old English *hær*] — **haired** \'haərd, 'heərd\ *adj* — **hair·less** \'haər-ləs, 'heər-\ *adj* — **hair·like** \-,līk\ *adj*

¹hair·breadth \'haər-,bredth, 'heər-\ *or* **hairs·breadth** \'haərz-, 'heərz-\ *n* : a very small distance or margin

²hairbreadth *adj* : very narrow : CLOSE ⟨a *hairbreadth* escape⟩

hair·brush \'haər-,brəsh, 'heər-\ *n* : a brush for the hair

hair cell *n* : a sensory cell (as of the organ of hearing) bearing hairlike processes

hair·cloth \-,kloth\ *n* : any of various stiff wiry fabrics especially of horsehair or camel's hair used for upholstery or stiffening in garments

hair·cut \-,kət\ *n* : the act, process, or result of cutting and shaping the hair — **hair·cut·ter** \-,kət-ər\ *n* — **hair·cut·ting** \-,kət-ing\ *n*

hair·do \-,dü\ *n, pl* **hairdos** : a way of dressing a person's hair : COIFFURE

hair·dress·er \-,dres-ər\ *n* : one that dresses or cuts hair — **hair·dress·ing** \-,dres-ing\ *n*

hair follicle *n* : the tubular sheath surrounding the lower part of a hair shaft

hair·line \-,līn\ *n* **1 a** : a very slender line **b** : a very thin crack on a surface ⟨a *hairline* bone fracture⟩ **2** : the line at which the hair meets the scalp ⟨a receding *hairline*⟩ — **hairline** *adj*

hair·pin \-,pin\ *n* **1** : a 2-pronged U-shaped pin to hold the hair in place **2** : something shaped like a hairpin; *esp* : a sharp turn in a road — **hairpin** *adj*

hair·rais·er \'haər-,rā-zər, 'heər-\ *n* : THRILLER

hair-rais·ing \-,rā-zing\ *adj* : causing terror, excitement, or astonishment ⟨a *hair-raising* adventure⟩ — **hair-rais·ing·ly** \-zing-lē\ *adv*

hair seal *n* : any of a family of seals with coarse hairy coats and no external ears — compare FUR SEAL

hair shirt *n* : a shirt made of rough animal hair worn next to the skin as a penance

hair·split·ter \'haər-,split-ər, 'heər-\ *n* : one that makes excessively fine distinctions in reasoning — **hair·split·ting** \-,split-ing\ *adj or n*

hair·spring \-,spring\ *n* : a slender spiraled spring that regulates the motion of the balance wheel of a timepiece

hair·streak \-,strēk\ *n* : any of various small usually dark butterflies with filaments projecting from the hind wings

hair-trig·ger \-'trig-ər\ *adj* **1** : immediately responsive to the slightest stimulus ⟨a *hair-trigger* temper⟩ **2** : delicately adjusted or easily disrupted

hair·worm \'haər-,wərm, 'heər-\ *n* : any of various very slender worms (as a horsehair worm)

hairy \'haər-ē, 'heər-\ *adj* **hair·i·er; -est** **1** : bearing or covered with or as if with hair **2** : made of or resembling hair **3** : tending to cause nervous tension (as from danger, difficulty, or fear) ⟨a *hairy* experience⟩ — **hair·i·ness** *n*

hake \'hāk\ *n* : any of several marine food fishes related to the cod [Middle English]

hal- *or* **halo-** *combining form* **1** : salt ⟨*halo*phyte⟩ **2** : halogen ⟨*hal*ide⟩ [Greek *hals* "salt, sea"]

ha·la·kah \hä-'läk-ə, ,hä-lə-'kä\ *n, often cap* : the body of Jewish law supplementing the scriptural law and forming especially the legal part of the Talmud [Hebrew *hălākhāh*, literally, "way"] — **ha·lak·ic** \hə-'lak-ik, -'läk-\ *adj, often cap*

ha·la·tion \hā-'lā-shən\ *n* : the spreading (as in a developed photographic image) of light beyond its proper boundaries [*halo* + *-ation*]

hal·berd \'hal-bərd, 'hol-\ *or* **hal·bert** \-bərt\ *n* : a long-handled weapon used both as a spear and as a battle-ax especially in the 15th and 16th centuries [Middle French *hallebarde*] — **hal·berd·ier** \,hal-bər-'diər, ,hol-\ *n*

¹hal·cy·on \'hal-sē-ən\ *n* **1** : a bird identified with the kingfisher and held in ancient legend to nest at sea about the time of the winter solstice and to calm the waves during incubation **2** : KINGFISHER [Latin, from Greek *halkyōn*]

²halcyon *adj* **1** : of or relating to the halcyon or its nesting period **2 a** : CALM 2, PEACEFUL **b** : HAPPY, GOLDEN ⟨the *halcyon* days of youth⟩

¹hale \'hāl\ *adj* : free from defect, disease, or infirmity : SOUND, HEALTHY ⟨still *hale* at the age of 80⟩ [partly from Old English *hāl* "whole"; partly from Old Norse *heill*]

²hale *vt* **1** : HAUL 1a, PULL **2** : to compel to go ⟨*haled* them into court⟩ [Middle French *haler*]

¹half \'haf, 'hàf\ *n, pl* **halves** \'havz, 'hàvz\ **1 a** (1) : one of two equal parts into which a thing is divisible; *also* : a part of a thing approximately equal to the remainder (2) : a number which when multiplied by 2 is equal to a given number **b** : half an hour **2** : one of a pair: as **a** : PARTNER **b** : SEMESTER, TERM **c** : one of the two equal periods that together make up the playing time of various games [Old English *healf*] — **by half** : by a great deal — **by halves** : in part : HALFHEARTEDLY — **in half** : into two equal or nearly equal parts

²half *adj* **1 a** : being one of two equal parts **b** (1) : amounting to nearly half (2) : PARTIAL ⟨a *half* smile⟩ **2** : of half the usual size or extent — **half·ness** *n*

³half *adv* **1 a** : to the extent of half ⟨*half* full⟩ **b** : PARTIALLY ⟨*half* persuaded⟩ **2** : at all : by any means — used with preceding negative ⟨the song wasn't *half* bad⟩

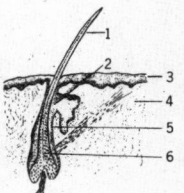

hair 1a: *1* shaft, *2* sebaceous gland, *3* epidermis, *4* dermis, *5* follicle, *6* root

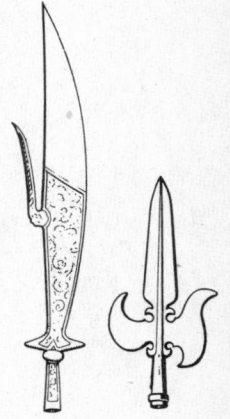

halberd

\ə\ abut	\ng\ sing
\ər\ further	\ō\ bone
\a\ mat	\o'\ saw
\ā\ take	\oi\ coin
\ä\ cot, cart	\th\ thin
\aů\ out	\th\ this
\ch\ chin	\ü\ food
\e\ pet	\ů\ foot
\ē\ easy	\y\ yet
\g\ go	\yü\ few
\i\ tip	\yů\ cure
\ī\ life	\zh\ vision
\j\ job	

half-and-half \,haf-ən-'haf, ,håf-ən-'håf\ *n* : something that is half one thing and half another: as **a** : a mixture of two malt beverages **b** : a mixture of cream and whole milk — **half-and-half** *adj or adv*

half-back \'haf-,bak, 'håf-\ *n* **1** : a football back who lines up on or near either flank **2** : a player stationed behind the forward line in field games (as soccer or field hockey)

half-baked \-'bākt\ *adj* **1** : imperfectly baked : UNDER-DONE **2 a** : not well planned ⟨a *half-baked* scheme⟩ **b** : lacking judgment, intelligence, or common sense

half blood *n* : the relation of individuals with but one parent or parent strain in common; *also* : one related in the half blood — **half-blood-ed** \-'bləd-əd\ *adj*

half boot *n* : a boot with a top reaching above the ankle

half-breed \'haf-,brēd, 'håf-\ *n* : the offspring of parents of different races; *esp* : the offspring of an American Indian and a white person — **half-breed** *adj*

half brother *n* : a brother related through one parent only

half-caste \'haf-,kast, 'håf-\ *n* : a person of mixed racial descent : HALF-BREED — **half-caste** *adj*

half cock *n* **1** : the position of the hammer of a firearm when it is partly drawn back and locked in position so that it cannot be operated by a pull on the trigger **2** : a state of inadequate preparation or mental confusion — **half-cocked** \'haf-'käkt, 'håf-\ *adj*

half crown *n* : a former British coin worth two shillings and sixpence

half-dol-lar \'haf-'däl-ər, 'håf-\ *n* **1** : a coin representing one half of a dollar **2** : the sum of fifty cents

half eagle *n* : a 5-dollar gold piece issued by the United States 1795–1916 and in 1929

half gainer *n* : a gainer in which the diver executes a half-backward somersault and enters the water headfirst and facing the board

half-heart-ed \'haf-'härt-əd, 'håf-\ *adj* : lacking spirit or interest — **half-heart-ed-ly** *adv* — **half-heart-ed-ness** *n*

half hitch *n* : a simple knot so made as to be easily unfastened

half hour *n* **1** : thirty minutes **2** : the middle point of an hour — **half-hour-ly** \'haf-'aur-lē, 'håf-\ *adv or adj*

half-knot \'haf-,nät, 'håf-\ *n* : a knot joining the ends of two cords and used in tying other knots

half-life \-,līf\ *n* : the time required for half of the atoms of a radioactive substance to disintegrate

half line *n* : a straight line extending from a point in one direction only

half-mast \'haf-'mast, 'håf-\ *n* : a point some distance but not necessarily halfway down below the top of a mast or staff or the peak of a gaff ⟨flags flying at *half-mast*⟩

half-moon \-,mün\ *n* **1** : the moon when half its disk appears illuminated **2** : something shaped like a crescent **3** : the lunule of a fingernail

half note *n* : a musical note equal in value to one half of a whole note

half-pen-ny \'hāp-nē, -ə-nē, United States also 'haf-,pen-ē, 'håf-\ *n, pl* **half-pence** \'hā-pəns, United States also 'haf-,pens, 'håf-\ *or* **halfpennies** **1** : a former British coin worth one half of a penny **2** : the sum of half a penny **3** : a small amount — **halfpenny** *adj*

half plane *n* : a part of a plane on one side of an indefinitely extended straight line drawn in the plane

half sister *n* : a sister related through one parent only

half-slip \'haf-,slip, 'håf-\ *n* : an underskirt with an elasticized waistband

half sole *n* : a shoe sole extending from the shank forward — **half-sole** \'haf-'sōl, 'håf-\ *vt*

half sovereign *n* : a former British gold coin worth 10 shillings

half-staff \'haf-'staf, 'håf-\ *n* : HALF-MAST

half step *n* : the pitch interval between any two adjacent tones on a keyboard instrument — called also *semitone*

half-tim-ber \'haf-'tim-bər, 'håf-\ *or* **half-tim-bered** \-bərd\ *adj* : constructed of wood framing with spaces filled with masonry ⟨a *half-timbered* house⟩

half-time \-,tīm\ *n* : an intermission marking the completion of half of a game

half-tone \-,tōn\ *n* **1** : HALF STEP **2 a** : any of the shades of gray between the darkest and the lightest parts of a photographic image **b** : a photoengraving made from an image photographed through a screen so that the details of the image are reproduced in dots

half-track \-,trak\ *n* **1** : one of the endless-chain tracks used in place of rear wheels on a heavy-duty vehicle **2** : a motor vehicle propelled by half-tracks; *esp* : such a vehicle lightly armored for military use — **half-track** *or* **half-tracked** \-,trakt\ *adj*

half-truth \-,trüth\ *n* : a statement that is only partially true; *esp* : one that mingles truth and falsehood with deliberate intent to deceive

half-way \-'wā\ *adj* **1** : midway between two points ⟨stop at the *halfway* mark⟩ **2** : PARTIAL **3** ⟨*halfway* measures⟩ — **halfway** *adv*

half-wit \-,wit\ *n* : a foolish or imbecilic person — **half-wit-ted** \-'wit-əd\ *adj*

hal-i-but \'hal-ə-bət, 'hàl-\ *n, pl* **halibut** *also* **halibuts** : a marine food fish that is the largest flatfish of both the Atlantic and Pacific oceans [Middle English *halybutte*, from *haly* "holy" + *butte* "flatfish"; from its being eaten on holy days]

ha-lide \'hal-,īd, 'hā-,līd\ *n* : a compound of a halogen with another element or a radical

hal-i-dom \'hal-əd-əm\ *or* **hal-i-dome** \-ə-,dōm\ *n, archaic* : a holy place or relic [Old English *hāligdōm*, from *hālig* "holy"]

ha-lite \'hal-,īt, 'hā-,līt\ *n* : native salt : ROCK SALT

hal-i-to-sis \,hal-ə-'tō-səs\ *n* : a condition of having breath with an offensive odor [Latin *halitus* "breath", from *halare* "to breathe"]

hall \hȯl\ *n* **1 a** : a large or imposing residence; *esp* : MANOR HOUSE **b** : a large building used for public purposes ⟨city *hall*⟩ **c** : one of the buildings of a college or university set apart for a special purpose ⟨Science *Hall*⟩ ⟨residence *halls*⟩ **d** : a college or a division of a college at some universities **e** : the common dining room of an English college **2** : the chief living room in a medieval castle **3 a** : the entrance room of a building : LOBBY **b** : a corridor or passage in a building **4** : a large room for assembly : AUDITORIUM **5** : a place used for public entertainment [Old English *heall*]

Hal-lel \hä-'lāl\ *n* : a selection comprising Psalms 113–118 chanted during a Jewish feast (as the Passover) [Hebrew *hallēl* "praise"]

¹hal-le-lu-jah \,hal-ə-'lü-yə\ *interj* — used to express praise, joy, or thanks [Hebrew *hallĕlūyāh* "praise ye the Lord"]

²hallelujah *n* : a shout or song of praise or thanksgiving

halliard *variant of* HALYARD

¹hall-mark \'hȯl-,märk\ *n* **1 a** : an official mark stamped on gold and silver articles in England to attest their purity **b** : a mark placed on an article to indicate origin, purity, or genuineness **2** : a distinguishing characteristic or feature [Goldsmiths' *Hall*, London, England, where gold and silver articles were assayed and stamped]

²hallmark *vt* : to stamp with a hallmark

hal-lo \hə-'lō, ha-\ *or* **hal-loo** \-'lü\ *variant of* HOLLO

Hall of Fame 1 : a structure housing memorials to famous individuals **2** : a group of individuals selected as particularly distinguished in a field or category (as a sport) — **Hall of Fam-er**

hal-low \'hal-ō\ *vt* **1** : to make holy or set apart for holy use **2** : to respect greatly [Old English *hālgian*, from *hālig* "holy"]

hal-lowed \'hal-ōd, -əd, in the Lord's Prayer also 'hal-ə-wəd\ *adj* : SACRED ⟨*hallowed* traditions⟩

Hal·low·een \,hal-ə-'wēn, ,häl-\ *n* : October 31 observed especially by children wearing costumes and getting treats and by the displaying of jack-o'-lanterns [short for *All Hallow even,* the eve of All Saints' Day]

Hal·low·mas \'hal-ō-,mas, -məs\ *n* : ALL SAINTS' DAY

hal·lu·ci·na·tion \hə-,lüs-n-'ā-shən\ *n* : the perceiving of objects or the experiencing of feelings that have no cause outside one's mind especially as the result of a mental disorder or as the effect of a drug; *also* : something so perceived or experienced [Latin *hallucinatio,* from *hallucinari* "to wander in mind"] — **hal·lu·ci·nate** \-'lüs-n-,āt\ *vb* — **hal·lu·ci·na·to·ry** \-'lüs-n-ə-,tōr-ē, -,tȯr-\ *adj*

hal·lu·ci·no·gen \hə-'lüs-n-ə-jən\ *n* : a substance (as LSD) that induces hallucinations — **hal·lu·ci·no·gen·ic** \-,lüs-n-ə-'jen-ik\ *adj*

hal·lux \'hal-əks\ *n, pl* **hal·lu·ces** \'hal-ə-,sēz, -yə-\ : BIG TOE [Latin]

hall·way \'hȯl-,wā\ *n* 1 : an entrance hall 2 : CORRIDOR 1

¹**ha·lo** \'hā-lō\ *n, pl* **halos** *or* **haloes** 1 : a circle of light around the sun or moon caused by the presence of tiny ice crystals in the air 2 : something resembling a halo: as **a** : NIMBUS 1, 2 **b** : a differentiated zone surrounding a central object 3 : the glory surrounding an idealized person or thing [Latin *halos,* from Greek *halōs* "threshing floor, disk, halo"]

²**halo** *vt* : to form into or surround with a halo

halo- — see HAL-

hal·o·gen \'hal-ə-jən\ *n* : any of the five elements fluorine, chlorine, bromine, iodine, and astatine existing in the free state normally as diatomic molecules

hal·o·ge·ton \,hal-ə-'jē-,tän\ *n* : a coarse annual herb related to the goosefoots that is a noxious weed in western North America [*hal-* + Greek *geitōn* "neighbor"]

hal·o·phyte \'hal-ə-,fīt\ *n* : a plant that thrives in salty soil — **hal·o·phyt·ic** \,hal-ə-'fit-ik\ *adj*

¹**halt** \'hȯlt\ *adj* : LAME [Old English *healt*]

²**halt** *vi* 1 : to walk or proceed lamely : LIMP 2 : to stand in perplexity or doubt between alternate courses 3 : to display weakness or fault

³**halt** *n* : STOP ⟨call a *halt*⟩ [German, derived from Old High German *haltan* "to hold"]

⁴**halt** *vb* 1 : to cease marching or journeying 2 : to bring or come to a stop : END

¹**hal·ter** \'hȯl-tər\ *n* 1 **a** : a rope or strap for leading or tying an animal **b** : a headstall to which a lead may be attached 2 : a rope for hanging criminals : NOOSE 3 : a woman's blouse that is typically held in place by straps around the neck and across the back and leaves the back, arms, and midriff bare [Old English *hælftre*]

²**halter** *vt* **hal·tered; hal·ter·ing** \-tə-ring, -tring\ 1 : to catch with or as if with a halter; *also* : to put a halter on 2 : RESTRAIN 1, HAMPER

hal·tere \'hȯl-,tiər, 'hal-\ *also* **hal·ter** \-tər\ *n, pl* **hal·teres** \-,tiərz; hȯl-'tir-ēz, hal-\ : one of a pair of club-shaped organs that are the modified second pair of wings of a two-winged fly and serve to maintain balance in flight [Latin *halter* "jumping weight", from Greek *haltēr,* from *hallesthai* "to jump"]

halt·ing \'hȯl-ting\ *adj* 1 : marked by a limp 2 : UNCERTAIN, FALTERING ⟨the witness spoke in a *halting* manner⟩ — **halt·ing·ly** \-ting-lē\ *adv*

hal·vah *or* **hal·va** \häl-'vä, 'häl-,vä, -və\ *n* : a flaky candy made of crushed sesame seeds in a base of syrup (as of honey) [Yiddish *halva,* derived from Arabic *ḥalwā* "sweetmeat"]

halve \'hav, 'hav\ *vt* 1 **a** : to divide into two equal parts **b** : to reduce to one half ⟨*halving* the cost⟩ **c** : to share equally 2 : to play (a hole) in the same number of strokes as one's opponent at golf

halv·ers \'hav-ərz, 'hav-\ *n pl* : half shares : HALVES

halves *pl of* HALF

hal·yard *or* **hal·liard** \'hal-yərd\ *n* : a rope or tackle for hoisting and lowering [Middle English *halier,* from *halen* "to pull, haul"]

¹**ham** \'ham\ *n* 1 : a buttock with its associated thigh — usually used in pl. 2 : a cut of meat consisting of a thigh; *esp* : one from a hog 3 **a** : an unskillful but showy performer **b** : an operator of an amateur radio station [Old English *hamm* "hollow of the knee"; sense 3 short for *hamfatter,* from "The Ham-Fat Man," minstrel song] — **ham** *adj*

²**ham** *vb* **hammed; ham·ming** : to execute with exaggerated speech or gestures : OVERACT

hama·dry·ad \,ham-ə-'drī-əd, -,ad\ *n* : WOOD NYMPH [Latin *hamadryas,* from Greek, from *hama* "together with" + *dryas* "dryad"]

ham·burg·er \'ham-,bər-gər\ *or* **ham·burg** \-,bərg\ *n* 1 **a** : ground beef **b** : a cooked patty of ground beef 2 : a sandwich consisting of a patty of hamburger in a split round bun [German *Hamburger* "of Hamburg"]

hame \'hām\ *n* : one of two curved supports which are attached to the collar of a draft horse and to which the traces are fastened [Middle English]

Ham·ite \'ham-,īt\ *n* : a member of a mainly Caucasoid group of chiefly northern African peoples [*Ham,* son of Noah, their supposed ancestor]

Ham·it·ic \ha-'mit-ik, hə-\ *adj* : of, relating to, or characteristic of the Hamites or one of the Hamitic languages

Hamitic languages *n pl* : the Berber, Cushitic, and sometimes Egyptian branches of the Afro-Asiatic languages

ham·let \'ham-lət\ *n* : a small group of houses in a rural area [Middle French *hamelet,* from *ham* "village", of Germanic origin]

¹**ham·mer** \'ham-ər\ *n* 1 **a** : a hand tool that consists of a solid head set crosswise on a handle and is used for pounding (as in driving nails) **b** : a power tool that substitutes a metal block or a drill for the head for pounding (as in driving posts or breaking rock) 2 : something that resembles a hammer in shape or action: as **a** : an implement consisting of a handle or lever and a striking head used to sound a musical instrument (as a bell, the strings of a piano, or a xylophone) **b** : the part of a gun whose striking action causes explosion of the charge 3 : MALLEUS 4 : a metal sphere weighing about 7.26 kilograms that is attached to a wire handle and is hurled in an athletic event [Old English *hamor*]

²**hammer** *vb* **ham·mered; ham·mer·ing** \'ham-ring, -ə-ring\ 1 : to strike blows especially repeatedly with or as if with a hammer : POUND 2 **a** : to make repeated efforts **b** : to emphasize (as an opinion) by repetition 3 **a** : to beat, drive, or shape with repeated blows of a hammer **b** : to fasten or build with a hammer 4 : to produce or bring about as if by repeated blows ⟨*hammer* out a policy⟩

hammer and sickle *n* : an emblem consisting of a crossed hammer and sickle used chiefly as a symbol of Soviet Communism

hammer and tongs *adv* : with great force and violence

ham·mered *adj* : having surface indentations produced or appearing to have been produced by hammering

ham·mer·head \'ham-ər-,hed\ *n* 1 : the striking part of a hammer 2 : BLOCKHEAD 3 : any of several sharks with the eyes on lateral extensions of the flat head

ham·mer·lock \-,läk\ *n* : a wrestling hold in which an opponent's arm is held bent behind the back

ham·mer·toe \-,tō\ *n* : a toe and especially the second deformed by having the end part permanently bent

¹**ham·mock** \'ham-ək\ *n* : a swinging couch or bed usually made of netting or canvas and slung by cords from supports at each end [Spanish *hamaca,* of American Indian origin]

²**hammock** *n* : HUMMOCK 1 [origin unknown]

hammerhead 3

\ə\ abut	\ng\ sing
\ər\ further	\ō\ bone
\a\ mat	\ȯ\ saw
\ā\ take	\ȯi\ coin
\ä\ cot, cart	\th\ thin
\aü\ out	\th\ this
\ch\ chin	\ü\ food
\e\ pet	\ů\ foot
\ē\ easy	\y\ yet
\g\ go	\yü\ few
\i\ tip	\yů\ cure
\ī\ life	\zh\ vision
\j\ job	

ham·my \'ham-ē\ *adj* **ham·mi·er; -est** : characteristic of a ham actor

¹ham·per \'ham-pər\ *vt* **ham·pered; ham·per·ing** \-pə-ring, -pring\ **1** : to restrict or interfere with the movement or operation of ⟨fog *hampered* the traffic⟩ **2** : to interfere with : ENCUMBER [Middle English *hamperen*] □ SYN FETTER, SHACKLE, MANACLE: HAMPER may imply the effect of any hindering or restraining influence; FETTER suggests a restraining so severe that freedom to move or progress is almost lost; SHACKLE and MANACLE are still stronger and suggest total loss of freedom to act or to move from one position.

²hamper *n* : a large basket usually with a cover ⟨a clothes *hamper*⟩ [Middle French *hanapier* "case to hold goblets", from *hanap* "goblet", of Germanic origin]

ham·ster \'ham-stər, 'hamp-\ *n* : any of various stocky short-tailed Old World rodents with large cheek pouches [German, of Slavic origin]

¹ham·string \'ham-,string\ *n* **1 a** : either of two groups of tendons at the back of the human knee **b** : HAMSTRING MUSCLE **2** : a large tendon above and behind the hock of a four-footed animal

²hamstring *vt* **-strung** \-,strəng\; **-string·ing** \-,string-ing\ **1** : to cripple by cutting the leg tendons **2** : to make ineffective or powerless : CRIPPLE

hamstring muscle *n* : any of three muscles at the back of the thigh that function to extend the thigh when the leg is flexed

Han \'hän\ *n* : a Chinese dynasty dated 207 B.C.–A.D. 220 and marked by centralized bureaucratic control, a revival of learning, and the penetration of Buddhism

¹hand \'hand\ *n* **1 a** : the free end part of the forelimb when modified (as in man) for handling, grasping, and holding **b** : any of various anatomical parts (as the hind foot of an ape or the chela of a crab) that are like the hand in origin or function **2** : something resembling a hand: as **a** : an indicator or pointer on a dial ⟨the *hands* of a clock⟩ **b** : a figure of a hand with forefinger extended to point a direction or call attention to something **c** : a cluster of bananas developed from a single flower group **3** : personal possession : CONTROL ⟨in the *hands* of the enemy⟩ **4 a** : SIDE, DIRECTION ⟨fighting on either *hand*⟩ **b** : a side or aspect of an issue or argument ⟨on the one *hand* . . . on the other *hand*⟩ **5** : a pledge especially of marriage **6 a** : style of penmanship : HANDWRITING **b** : SIGNATURE ⟨some legal orders require a judge's *hand*⟩ **7 a** : SKILL, ABILITY ⟨try one's *hand* at chess⟩ **b** : a part or share in doing something ⟨take a *hand* in the work⟩ **c** : ASSISTANCE, AID ⟨lend a *hand*⟩ **8** : SOURCE ⟨learn at first *hand*⟩ **9** : a unit of measure equal to 10.16 centimeters used especially for the height of horses **10** : a round of applause **11 a** (1) : a player in a card game or board game (2) : the cards or pieces held by a player **b** : a single round in a game **12 a** : one who performs or executes a particular work ⟨two portraits by the same *hand*⟩ **b** : a hired worker : LABORER **c** : a member of a ship's crew ⟨all *hands* on deck⟩ **d** : one skilled in a particular activity or field **13 a** : HANDIWORK 1 **b** : style of execution : WORKMANSHIP ⟨the *hand* of a master⟩ **c** : the touch or feel of something [Old English] — **at hand** : near in time or place — **by hand** : with the hands — **in hand** **1** : in one's possession or control **2** : in preparation — **off one's hands** : out of one's care or charge — **on all hands** *or* **on every hand** — EVERYWHERE — **on hand** **1** : in present possession ⟨goods *on hand*⟩ **2** : about to appear **3** : in attendance : PRESENT — **out of hand** **1** : without delay : FORTHWITH **2** : done with **3** : out of control — **to hand** **1** : into possession **2** : within reach **3** : into control or subjection

²hand *vt* **1** : to lead, guide, or assist with the hand : CONDUCT **2 a** : to give or pass with the hand ⟨*hand* a person a letter⟩ **b** : PRESENT, PROVIDE ⟨*handed* them a surprise⟩

hand and foot *adv* : TOTALLY 1, COMPLETELY ⟨waited on them *hand and foot*⟩

hand ax *n* : a prehistoric stone tool having one end pointed for cutting and the other end rounded for holding in the hand

hand·bag \'hand-,bag, 'han-\ *n* **1** : TRAVELING BAG **2** : a bag for carrying small personal articles and money

hand·ball \-,bȯl\ *n* : a game played in a walled court or against a single wall or board by two or four players who use their hands to strike a small rubber ball; *also* : the ball used in this game

hand·bar·row \-,bar-ō\ *n* : a flat rectangular frame with handles at both ends that is carried by two persons

hand·bill \-,bil\ *n* : a small printed sheet to be distributed by hand

hand·book \-,bůk\ *n* : a small book of facts or useful information usually about a particular subject : MANUAL

hand·breadth \-,bredth\ *or* **hands·breadth** \'hanz-\ *n* : any of various units of length based on the breadth of a hand varying from about 6 to 10 centimeters

hand·car \'hand-,kär, 'han-\ *n* : a small four-wheeled railroad car propelled by a hand-operated mechanism or a small motor

hand·cart \-,kärt\ *n* : a cart drawn or pushed by hand

hand·clasp \-,klasp\ *n* : HANDSHAKE

¹hand·craft \-,kraft\ *n* : HANDICRAFT

²handcraft *vt* : to fashion by handicraft

¹hand·cuff \-,kəf\ *vt* : to apply handcuffs to : MANACLE

²handcuff *n* : a metal fastening that can be locked around a wrist and that is usually connected by a chain or bar with another handcuff

hand down *vt* **1** : to transmit in succession ⟨*handed down* from generation to generation⟩ **2** : to make official formulation of and express ⟨the opinion of a court⟩

hand·ed \'han-dəd\ *adj* : having or using such or so many hands ⟨a right-*handed* person⟩ — **hand·ed·ness** *n*

hand·ful \'hand-,fůl, 'han-\ *n, pl* **handfuls** \-,fůlz\ *or* **handsful** \'hanz-,fůl\ **1** : as much as or as many as the hand will grasp **2** : a small quantity or number **3** : as much as one can control or manage

hand·glass *n* : a small mirror with a handle

hand·grip \'hand-,grip, 'han-\ *n* **1** : a grasping with the hand **2** : HANDLE 1

hand·gun \'hand-,gən, 'han-\ *n* : a firearm held and fired with one hand

hand·hold \'hand-,hōld\ *n* **1** : GRIP 1a **2** : HOLD 5

¹hand·i·cap \'han-di-,kap\ *n* **1 a** : a race or contest in which an artificial advantage is given to or disadvantage imposed on a contestant to equalize chances of winning **b** : the advantage given or disadvantage imposed **2** : a disadvantage that makes progress or success more difficult [obsolete *handicap*, a game in which forfeits were held in a cap, from hand in cap] □ ORIGIN *Handicap*, from *hand in cap*, was an old form of barter. Two people who wished to make an exchange asked a third to act as umpire. All three put forfeit money in a cap, into which each of the two barterers put a hand. The umpire described the goods to be traded and set the additional amount the owner of the inferior article should pay the other in order that the exchange might be fair. The barterers withdrew their hands from the cap empty to signify refusal of the umpire's decision, or full to indicate acceptance. If both hands were full, the exchange was made and the umpire pocketed the forfeit money. If both were empty, the umpire took the money but there was no exchange. Otherwise, each barterer kept his own property, and the one who had accepted the umpire's decision took the forfeit money as well. Later, horse races arranged in accordance with the rules of *handicap* were called *handicap races*. The umpire decided how much extra weight the better horse should carry.

The term was eventually extended to other contests, and the advantage or disadvantage imposed was called *handicap.*

²hand·i·cap *vt* **-capped; -cap·ping 1 a :** to give a handicap to **b :** to assign handicaps to **2 :** to put at a disadvantage

hand·i·craft \\'han-di-ˌkraft\\ *n* **1 :** an occupation (as weaving or pottery making) requiring skill with the hands **2 :** articles fashioned by those engaged in handicraft [alteration of *handcraft*] — **hand·i·craft·er** \\-ˌkraf-tər\\ *n* — **hand·i·crafts·man** \\-ˌkrafs-mən\\ *n*

hand·i·ly \\'han-də-lē\\ *adv :* in a handy manner **: EASILY, CONVENIENTLY**

hand·i·ness \\-dē-nəs\\ *n :* the quality or state of being handy

hand in glove *or* **hand and glove** *adv :* in extremely close relationship or agreement

hand in hand *adv* **1 :** with one's hand clasping another's hand **2 :** in close association

hand·i·work \\'han-di-ˌwərk\\ *n :* work done by the hands or personally ⟨showed the *handiwork* of a master criminal⟩ [Old English *handgeweorc*, from *hand* + *geweorc* "work", from *ge-*, collective prefix + *weorc* "work"]

hand·ker·chief \\'hang-kər-chəf, -ˌchif, -ˌchēf\\ *n, pl* **-chiefs** *also* **-chieves** \\-chəfs, -ˌchifs, -ˌchēvz *(used by many who have sing* -chəf *or* -ˌchif), -ˌchēfs, -ˌchəvz, -ˌchivz\\ **1 :** a small piece of cloth used especially for wiping the face, nose, or eyes **2 : KERCHIEF 1**

hand language *n :* communication by means of a manual alphabet

¹han·dle \\'han-dl\\ *n* **1 :** a part that is designed especially to be grasped by the hand **2 :** something that resembles a handle **3** *slang :* **NAME** [Old English] — **han·dled** \\-dld\\ *adj* — **off the handle :** into a state of sudden and violent anger

²handle *vb* **han·dled; han·dling** \\-dling, -dl-ing\\ **1 a :** to affect with the hand (as by touching or feeling) **b :** to manage with the hands ⟨*handle* a horse⟩ **2 a :** to deal with in writing or speaking or in the plastic arts **b : CONTROL, DIRECT** ⟨a lawyer *handles* my affairs⟩ **c :** to train and act as second for (a prizefighter) **3 :** to deal with or act on ⟨*handle* a problem⟩ **4 :** to deal or trade in ⟨a store that *handles* rugs⟩ **5 :** to act, behave, or feel in a certain way when managed or directed ⟨a car that *handles* well⟩ [Old English *handlian*]

han·dle·able \\'han-dl-ə-bəl\\ *adj :* capable of being handled

handlebar mustache *n :* a heavy mustache with long sections that curve upward at each end

han·dle·bars \\'han-dl-ˌbärz\\ *n pl :* a straight or bent bar with a handle (as for steering a bicycle) at each end

hand lens *n :* a magnifying glass to be held in the hands

han·dler \\'han-dlər, -dl-ər\\ *n* **1 :** one that handles **2 :** one that helps to train a prizefighter or acts as his second during a match

hand·made \\'hand-'mād, 'han-\\ *adj :* made by hand and not by machine

hand·maid \\-ˌmād\\ *or* **hand·maid·en** \\-ˌmād-n\\ *n :* a female servant or attendant

hand–me–down \\'hand-mē-ˌdaün, 'han-\\ *adj :* worn or put in use by one person or group after being discarded by another — **hand–me–down** *n*

hand–off \\'han-ˌdof\\ *n :* a football play in which the ball is handed by one player to another nearby

hand on *vt :* to pass along in succession : hand down

hand organ *n :* a barrel organ operated by a hand crank

hand·out \\'han-ˌdaüt\\ *n* **1 :** a portion of food, clothing, or money given to or as if to a beggar **2 :** an information sheet for free distribution **3 :** a prepared statement released to the press

hand over *vt :* to give up possession or control of

hand·pick \\'hand-'pik, 'han-\\ *vt :* to select personally

hand·rail \\'han-ˌdrāl\\ *n :* a narrow rail for grasping with the hand as a support (as on a staircase)

hand·saw \\'hand-ˌso, 'han-\\ *n :* a saw used with one hand; *esp :* a woodworker's ripsaw or crosscut saw

hands·breadth \\'handz-ˌbredth\\ *variant of* **HANDBREADTH**

hands down *adv :* without question **: EASILY**

hand·sel \\'han-səl\\ *n* **1 :** a gift made as a token of good wishes or luck especially at the beginning of a new year **2 : ³EARNEST, FORETASTE** [Middle English *hansell*]

hand·set \\'hand-ˌset, han-\\ *n :* a combined telephone transmitter and receiver mounted on a handle

hand·shake \\-ˌshāk\\ *n :* a clasping (as in greeting or farewell) of right hands by two people

hands–off \\'han-'zof\\ *adj :* marked by noninterference

hand·some \\'han-səm\\ *adj* **1 :** fairly large **: SIZABLE** ⟨a *handsome* fortune⟩ **2 :** marked by graciousness or generosity ⟨a *handsome* tribute⟩ **3 :** having a pleasing and often impressive or dignified appearance ⟨a *handsome* young lad⟩ ⟨a *handsome* building⟩ [Middle English *handsom* "easy to manipulate"] — **hand·some·ly** *adv* — **hand·some·ness** *n*

hand·spike \\'han-ˌspīk\\ *n :* a bar used as a lever (as in working a windlass on a boat) [by folk etymology from Dutch *handspaak*, from *hand* "hand" + *spaak* "pole"]

hand·spring \\-ˌspring\\ *n :* a tumbling feat in which the body turns forward or backward in a full circle from a standing position and lands first on the hands and then on the feet

hand·stand \\-ˌstand\\ *n :* an act of balancing the body on the hands with the trunk and legs in the air

hand–to–hand \\'han-tə-ˌhand, -də-\\ *adj :* involving physical contact — **hand to hand** \\-'hand\\ *adv*

hand–to–mouth \\-tə-'maüth\\ *adj :* having or providing nothing to spare ⟨a *hand-to-mouth* existence⟩

hand·wheel \\'hand-ˌhwēl, 'han-, -ˌwēl\\ *n :* a wheel worked by hand

hand·work \\'han-ˌdwərk\\ *n :* work done with the hands and not by machine

hand·wo·ven \\'han-ˌdwō-vən\\ *adj :* produced on a hand-operated loom

hand·writ·ing \\'han-ˌdrīt-ing\\ *n* **1 :** writing done by hand; *esp :* the cast or form of writing peculiar to a particular person **2 :** something written by hand **: MANUSCRIPT** — **hand·writ·ten** \\-ˌdrit-n\\ *adj*

handy \\'han-dē\\ *adj* **hand·i·er; -est 1 a :** conveniently near **b :** convenient for use ⟨a *handy* reference book⟩ **c :** easily handled ⟨a *handy* sloop⟩ **2 :** clever in using the hands **: DEXTEROUS** ⟨*handy* with a needle⟩

handy·man \\-dē-ˌman\\ *n :* a person who does odd jobs

¹hang \\'hang\\ *vb* **hung** \\'həng\\ *also* **hanged** \\'hangd\\; **hang·ing** \\'hang-ing\\ **1 a :** to fasten or be fastened to some elevated point without support from below **b :** to put to death or be put to death by hanging from a rope tied round the neck ⟨sentenced to be *hanged*⟩ **c :** to fasten so as to allow free motion upon a point of suspension ⟨*hang* a door⟩ **d :** to adjust the hem of (a skirt) so as to hang evenly and at a proper height when worn **2 :** to cover, decorate, or furnish by hanging pictures, trophies, or drapery **3 :** to hold or bear in a suspended or inclined manner **: DROOP** ⟨*hang* your head in shame⟩ **4 :** to fasten to a wall ⟨*hang* wallpaper⟩ **5 :** to display (pictures) in a gallery **6 :** to remain poised or stationary in the air ⟨clouds *hanging* low overhead⟩ **7 :** to stay with persistence **8 :** to hover threateningly ⟨evils *hang* over the nation⟩ **9 : DEPEND** ⟨election *hangs* on one vote⟩ **10 a :** to take hold for support **: CLING** ⟨*hang* on my arm⟩ **b :** to be burdensome or oppressive ⟨time *hung* on our hands⟩ **11 :** to be in suspense : suffer delay ⟨the decision is still *hanging*⟩ **12 :** to lean, incline, or jut over or downward **13 :** to be in a state of close attention ⟨*hung* on their every word⟩ **14 :** to fit or fall from the figure in easy lines ⟨the coat *hangs* loosely⟩ [Old English *hōn* (v.t.) and *hanglan* (v.i. and v.t.)] — **hang·able** \\'hang-ə-bəl\\ *adj* — **hang**

\\ə\\ abut	\\ng\\ sing
\\ər\\ further	\\ō\\ bone
\\a\\ mat	\\o\\ saw
\\ā\\ take	\\oi\\ coin
\\ä\\ cot, cart	\\th\\ thin
\\aü\\ out	\\th\\ this
\\ch\\ chin	\\ü\\ food
\\e\\ pet	\\u\\ foot
\\ē\\ easy	\\y\\ yet
\\g\\ go	\\yü\\ few
\\i\\ tip	\\yu\\ cure
\\ī\\ life	\\zh\\ vision
\\j\\ job	

together 1 : to remain united : stand by one another **2 :** to form a consistent or coherent whole

²hang *n* **1 :** the manner in which a thing hangs ⟨the *hang* of a skirt⟩ **2 a :** peculiar and significant meaning ⟨the *hang* of an argument⟩ **b :** the special method of doing, using, or dealing with something : KNACK ⟨get the *hang* of driving a car⟩

¹hang·ar \'hang-ər, 'hang-gər\ *n* : SHELTER, SHED; *esp* : a covered and usually enclosed area for housing and repairing aircraft [French]

²hangar *vt* : to place in a hangar

hang around *vb* **1 :** to pass time or stay aimlessly : loiter idly ⟨*hang around* the park⟩ **2 :** to spend one's time in company

hang back *vi* **1 :** to lag behind others **2 :** to be reluctant : HESITATE

hang·dog \'hang-,dȯg\ *adj* **1 :** ASHAMED 1, GUILTY ⟨a *hangdog* look⟩ **2 :** ABJECT 3, COWED

hang·er \'hang-ər\ *n* **1 :** one that hangs or causes to be hung or hanged **2 :** a device by which or to which something is hung or hangs; *esp* : a device for hanging a garment from a hook or rod

hang·er–on \'hang-ər-,ȯn, -,än\ *n, pl* **hangers–on :** one that hangs around a person, place, or institution in hope of personal gain

hang glider *n* : a small glider made usually in the form of a kite from which a person hangs in soaring — **hang gliding** *n*

¹hang·ing \'hang-ing\ *n* **1 :** an execution by strangling or breaking the neck by a suspended noose **2 :** something hung (as a curtain or tapestry) — usually used in pl. **3 :** a downward slope

²hanging *adj* **1 :** situated or lying on steeply sloping ground ⟨*hanging* gardens⟩ **2 a :** jutting out or over **b :** supported only by the wall on one side ⟨a *hanging* staircase⟩ **3 :** adapted for sustaining a hanging object **4 :** punishable by death by hanging ⟨a *hanging* offense⟩

hang·man \'hang-mən\ *n* : a person who hangs condemned criminals

hang·nail \-,nāl\ *n* : a bit of skin hanging loose at the side or base of a fingernail [by folk etymology from earlier *agnail,* from Old English *angnægl* "corn on the foot or toe"] □ ORIGIN Old English *angnægl* meant "a corn on the foot". The second element of the word, *-nægl,* meant "nail", but it referred to an iron nail rather than to a toenail or fingernail. A hard corn was likened to the head of a nail. The first element, *ang-,* is related to Old English *ange,* "painful". Over the centuries *angnægl* became *agnail* and was used for a variety of ailments of the fingers or toes. This usage led to the belief that the *-nail* of *agnail* meant "toenail" or "fingernail". By then the adjective *ange* was obsolete, and the first element of *agnail* was not easy to interpret. So the compound was transformed to make sense to ordinary speakers of the language. The new form, *hangnail,* was used specifically for a bit of loose skin at the base of a fingernail.

hang on *vi* **1 :** to keep hold : hold onto something **2 :** to persist stubbornly ⟨a cold that *hung on* all spring⟩ — **hang on to :** to hold, grip, or keep persistently ⟨*hang on to* your money⟩

hang·out \'hang-,aut\ *n* : a favorite or usual meeting place

hang out \'hang-'aut, hang-\ *vi* : to habitually spend one's time idly ⟨*hangs out* in poolrooms⟩

hang·over \'hang-,ō-vər\ *n* **1 :** something (as a surviving custom) that remains from what is past **2 :** disagreeable aftereffects following great excitement or excess (as in consumption of alcohol)

hang–up \'hang-,əp\ *n* : a source of mental or emotional difficulty

hang up \'hang-'əp, hang-\ *vb* **1 a :** to place on a hook or hanger ⟨*hang up* your coat⟩ **b :** to replace (a telephone receiver) on the cradle so that the connection is broken; *also* : to terminate a telephone conversation

2 : to snag or cause to snag so as to be immovable ⟨the ship *hung up* on a sandbar⟩

hank \'hangk\ *n* : SKEIN [Middle English, of Scandinavian origin]

han·ker \'hang-kər\ *vi* **han·kered; han·ker·ing** \-kə-ring, -kring\ : to have an eager or persistent desire ⟨*hanker* after fame and fortune⟩ [probably from Flemish *hankeren,* from *hangen* "to hang"] SYN see LONG — **han·ker·er** \-kər-ər\ *n*

han·ky–pan·ky \,hang-kē-'pang-kē\ *n* : questionable or underhand activity [alteration of *hocus-pocus*]

Han·o·ve·ri·an \,han-ə-'vir-ē-ən, -'ver-\ *adj* : of, relating to, or supporting the German ducal house of Hanover or the descendant British royal house furnishing sovereigns from 1714 to 1901 [*Hanover,* Germany] — **Hanoverian** *n*

Han·sen's disease \'han-sənz-\ *n* : LEPROSY [Armauer *Hansen,* died 1912, Norwegian physician]

han·som \'han-səm\ *n* : a light 2-wheeled covered carriage with the driver's seat elevated behind [Joseph A. *Hansom,* died 1882, English architect]

Ha·nuk·kah \'k̲än-ə-kə, 'hän-\ *n* : an 8-day Jewish festival of lights celebrated in November or December in commemoration of the rededication of the Temple of Jerusalem after its defilement by Antiochus of Syria [Hebrew *hănukkāh* "dedication"]

hao·le \'hau̇-lā\ *n* : one who is not a member of the native race of Hawaii; *esp* : WHITE [Hawaiian]

¹hap \'hap\ *n* **1 :** HAPPENING **2 :** CHANCE 1, FORTUNE [Old Norse *happ* "good luck"]

²hap *vb* **happed; hap·ping :** HAPPEN 3, 4a

hap·haz·ard \hap-'haz-ərd, 'hap-\ *adj* : marked by lack of plan, order, or direction : AIMLESS SYN see RANDOM — **haphazard** *adv* — **hap·haz·ard·ly** *adv* — **hap·haz·ard·ness** *n*

hap·less \'hap-ləs\ *adj* : having no luck : UNFORTUNATE ⟨a *hapless* child⟩ — **hap·less·ly** *adv* — **hap·less·ness** *n*

hap·loid \'hap-,loid\ *adj* : having the number of chromosomes characteristic of germ cells or half the number characteristic of body cells [Greek *haploeidēs* "single", from *haploos* "single"] — **haploid** *n* — **hap·loi·dy** \-,loid-ē\ *n*

hap·pen \'hap-ən, 'hap-m\ *vi* **hap·pened; hap·pen·ing** \'hap-ning, -ə-ning\ **1 :** to occur by chance **2 :** to take place **3 :** to have occasion or opportunity without intention : CHANCE ⟨*happened* to overhear⟩ **4 a :** to find something by chance ⟨*happened* on the right answer⟩ **b :** to appear casually or by chance **5 :** to come especially by way of injury or harm ⟨I promise nothing will *happen* to you⟩ [Middle English *happenen,* from *hap*] □ SYN HAPPEN, CHANCE, OCCUR, TRANSPIRE mean to come about. HAPPEN applies to whatever comes about without cause or intention; CHANCE stresses lack of plan or apparent cause; OCCUR, often interchangeable with HAPPEN, stresses a being brought to sight or to mind or attention ⟨theoretically possible, but not *occurring* in reality⟩ ⟨it never *occurred* to them that we would object⟩ TRANSPIRE can imply a coming out or becoming known ⟨what happened that day only *transpired* much later⟩ but is often equal to OCCUR.

hap·pen·ing *n* **1 :** something that happens : OCCURRENCE **2 a :** an event or series of events designed to evoke a spontaneous reaction to sensory, emotional, or spiritual stimuli **b :** something (as an event) of special interest or importance

hap·pi·ly \'hap-ə-lē\ *adv* **1 :** FORTUNATELY, LUCKILY ⟨*happily,* no one was injured⟩ **2 :** in a happy manner or state ⟨lived *happily* ever after⟩ **3 :** APTLY, SUCCESSFULLY ⟨the remarks were *happily* worded⟩

hap·pi·ness \'hap-i-nəs\ *n* **1 a :** a state of well-being and contentment : JOY **b :** a pleasurable satisfaction **2 :** FELICITY 1, APTNESS

hap·py \'hap-ē\ *adj* **hap·pi·er; -est** **1 :** favored by fortune : FORTUNATE **2 :** notably well adapted or fitting ⟨a *happy* choice for governor⟩ **3 a :** enjoying well-being

hang glider

and contentment ⟨*happy* in their work⟩ **b** : expressing or suggestive of happiness : PLEASANT ⟨*happy* laughter⟩ **c** : feeling satisfaction ⟨*happy* to escape⟩ [Middle English, from *hap*]

hap·py–go–lucky \ˌhap-ē-gō-ˈlək-ē\ *adj* : blithely unconcerned : CAREFREE

Haps·burg *also* **Habs·burg** \ˈhaps-ˌbərg, ˈhäps-ˌbürg\ *adj* : of or relating to a princely German family furnishing the rulers of Austria from 1278 to 1918 and of Spain from 1516 to 1700 and many of the Holy Roman emperors [*Habsburg,* Aargau, Switzerland] — **Hapsburg** *n*

hap·ten \ˈhap-ˌten\ *n* : a substance that does not cause formation of antibodies by itself but reacts with specific chemical groups on antibodies and may stimulate antibody formation when joined with a protein [German, from Greek *haptesthai* "to touch"]

hara–kiri \ˌhar-i-ˈkir-ē, -ˈkar-ē\ *n* : suicide by disembowelment formerly practiced by the Japanese samurai [Japanese *harakiri*]

ha·rangue \hə-ˈrang\ *n* **1** : a speech addressed to a public assembly **2** : a ranting speech or writing [Middle French, from Italian *aringa*] — **harangue** *vb* — **ha·rangu·er** \-ˈrang-ər\ *n*

ha·rass \hə-ˈras, ˈhar-əs\ *vt* **1** : to tire out by persistent efforts : worry or annoy with repeated attacks **2** : to lay waste : HARRY [French *harasser,* from Middle French *harer* "to set a dog on", from Old French *hare,* interj. used to incite dogs, of Germanic origin] SYN see ANNOY — **ha·rass·ment** \-mənt\ *n*

¹har·bin·ger \ˈhär-bən-jər\ *n* : one that announces or shows what is coming : FORERUNNER ⟨robins are *harbingers* of spring⟩ [Middle English *herbergere* "host, one sent ahead to provide lodgings", from Old French, "host", from *herberge* "inn", of Germanic origin]

□ ORIGIN The modern *harbinger* is simply a forerunner. But in late medieval and early modern times a *harbinger,* or *herbergere,* was the person sent before an army, a royal progress, or the like, to find lodgings for the whole company. Still earlier English *herbergeres* were hosts, the actual providers of lodgings. The Old French word from which the English was borrowed was itself derived from an early Germanic loanword. Old French *herberge* took from its Germanic ancestor both the literal meaning, "army encampment", and the figurative extension, "hostelry, inn". Modern English *harbor* is another descendant of the same old Germanic word.

²harbinger *vt* : to be a harbinger of : PRESAGE

¹har·bor \ˈhär-bər\ *n* **1** : a place of security : REFUGE **2** : a protected part of a body of water deep enough to furnish anchorage; *esp* : one with port facilities [Middle English *herberge*] — see HARBINGER origin — **har·bor·less** \-ləs\ *adj*

²harbor *vb* **har·bored; har·bor·ing** \-bə-ring, -bring\ **1** **a** : to give shelter or refuge to **b** : to be the home or habitat of : CONTAIN **2** : to hold a thought or feeling of **3** : to take shelter in or as if in a harbor — **har·bor·er** *n*

har·bor·age \ˈhär-bə-rij\ *n* : SHELTER 1, HARBOR

har·bour \ˈhär-bər\ *chiefly British variant of* HARBOR

¹hard \ˈhärd\ *adj* **1** : not easily penetrated, cut, or divided into parts : not soft **2 a** : strong in alcoholic content ⟨*hard* liquor⟩ **b** : characterized by the presence of salts that prevent lathering with soap ⟨*hard* water⟩ **3 a** : having high penetrating power ⟨*hard* X rays⟩ **b** : having or producing relatively great photographic contrast ⟨a *hard* negative⟩ **4 a** : metallic as distinct from paper ⟨*hard* money⟩ **b** : convertible into gold : stable in value ⟨*hard* currency⟩ **5 a** : physically fit ⟨in good *hard* condition⟩ **b** : free of weakness or flaw **6 a** (1) : FIRM, DEFINITE ⟨a *hard* agreement⟩ (2) : FACTUAL, ACTUAL ⟨*hard* evidence⟩ **b** : CLOSE, SEARCHING ⟨a *hard* look⟩ **c** : free from sentimentality or illusion : REALISTIC ⟨good *hard* sense⟩ **d** : lacking sympathy or senti-

ment ⟨a *hard* heart⟩ **7 a** : difficult to bear or endure : HARSH, SEVERE ⟨*hard* times⟩ **b** : RESENTFUL ⟨*hard* feelings⟩ **c** : making no concessions ⟨drive a *hard* bargain⟩ **d** : INCLEMENT ⟨a *hard* winter⟩ **e** : intense in force, manner, or degree ⟨a *hard* blow⟩ **f** : physically or mentally difficult ⟨*hard* work⟩ ⟨a *hard* question⟩ **8** : DILIGENT, ENERGETIC ⟨a *hard* worker⟩ **9 a** : sharply or harshly defined : STARK ⟨*hard* shadows⟩ **b** : sounding as in *cow* and *gun* respectively — used of *c* and *g* **10 a** : difficult to accomplish or resolve : TROUBLESOME ⟨a *hard* problem⟩ **b** : difficult to comprehend or explain ⟨*hard* words⟩ **11** : being both addictive and harmful to health ⟨*hard* drugs⟩ **12** : persisting in the environment for a long time without breaking down ⟨*hard* insecticides⟩ [Old English *heard*] — **hard up 1** : short of money : POOR ⟨family was *hard up* for years⟩ **2** : poorly provided ⟨*hard up* for friends⟩

²hard *adv* **1 a** : with great effort or energy : STRENUOUSLY ⟨try *hard*⟩ **b** : VIOLENTLY, FIERCELY ⟨the wind is blowing *hard*⟩ **c** : to the full extent — used in nautical directions **d** : in a searching, close, or concentrated manner ⟨stared *hard* at the sign⟩ **2 a** : HARSHLY, SEVERELY ⟨the recession hit them *hard*⟩ **b** : with rancor, bitterness, or grief ⟨took the defeat *hard*⟩ **3** : TIGHTLY, FIRMLY ⟨hold *hard* to something⟩ **4** : to the point of hardness **5** : close in time or space ⟨the school stood *hard* by a church⟩

hard–and–fast \ˌhärd-n-ˈfast\ *adj* : rigidly binding : STRICT ⟨a *hard-and-fast* rule⟩

hard·back \ˈhärd-ˌbak\ *n* : a book bound in hard covers

hard·ball \-ˌból\ *n* : BASEBALL

hard–bit·ten \-ˈbit-n\ *adj* : seasoned or strengthened by difficult experience : TOUGH ⟨*hard-bitten* campaigners⟩

hard·board \-ˌbōrd, -ˌbord\ *n* : a very dense fiberboard usually smooth on one side

hard–boiled \-ˈbóild\ *adj* **1** : boiled until both white and yolk become solid ⟨*hard-boiled* eggs⟩ **2 a** : lacking sentiment ⟨a *hard-boiled* drill sergeant⟩ **b** : HARDHEADED 2

hard candy *n* : a candy made of sugar and corn syrup boiled without crystallizing and often fruit-flavored

hard coal *n* : ANTHRACITE

hard copy *n* : a copy of information (as words, numbers, or pictures) in normal size on paper (as from computer storage)

hard–core \ˈhärd-ˌkōr, -ˌkor\ *adj* **1** : fanatically loyal, devoted, or committed ⟨*hard-core* supporters⟩ **2** : barely capable of being or willing to be reformed ⟨a *hard-core* criminal⟩ **3** : continuing for a long time ⟨*hard-core* unemployment⟩ — **hard core** *n*

hard·en \ˈhärd-n\ *vb* **hard·ened; hard·en·ing** \ˈhärd-ning, -n-ing\ **1** : to make or become hard or harder **2** : to make or become hardy or strong ⟨muscles *hardened* by exercise⟩ **3 a** : to make or become stubborn, unfeeling, or unsympathetic ⟨*harden* one's heart⟩ **b** : to become confirmed or strengthened **c** : to protect from blast, heat, or radiation ⟨*harden* a missile site⟩ — **hard·en·er** \ˈhärd-nər, -n-ər\ *n*

hard·hack \ˈhärd-ˌhak\ *n* : a shrubby American spirea with rusty hairy leaves and dense terminal clusters of pink or occasionally white flowers

hard·head·ed \-ˈhed-əd\ *adj* **1** : STUBBORN 1 **2** : marked by sound judgment : REALISTIC ⟨a *hardheaded* reappraisal⟩ — **hard·head·ed·ly** *adv* — **hard·head·ed·ness** *n*

hard·heart·ed \-ˈhärt-əd\ *adj* : lacking in sympathetic understanding — **hard·heart·ed·ly** *adv* — **hard·heart·ed·ness** *n*

hard labor *n* : compulsory labor of imprisoned criminals that is a part of the prison discipline

hard·ly \ˈhärd-lē\ *adv* **1** : in a severe manner : HARSHLY **2** : with difficulty : PAINFULLY **3** : almost not : BARELY ⟨it *hardly* ever rains⟩ **4** : certainly not ⟨that news is *hardly* surprising⟩

\ə\ abut		\ng\ sing	
\ər\ further		\ō\ bone	
\a\ mat		\ó\ saw	
\ā\ take		\ói\ coin	
\ä\ cot, cart		\th\ thin	
\aú\ out		\th\ this	
\ch\ chin		\ū\ food	
\e\ pet		\ú\ foot	
\ē\ easy		\y\ yet	
\g\ go		\yū\ few	
\i\ tip		\yú\ cure	
\ī\ life		\zh\ vision	
\j\ job			

hard·ness *n* **1** : the quality or state of being hard **2** : the cohesion of the particles on the surface of a mineral as determined by its capacity to scratch another or be itself scratched

hard-of-hearing \,härd-əv-'hiər-ing, -ə-'\ *adj* : of or relating to a defective but functional sense of hearing

hard palate *n* : the bony front part of the palate

hard·pan \'härd-,pan\ *n* **1** : a cemented or compacted and often clayey layer in soil that roots cannot readily penetrate **2** : a fundamental part : BASIS

hard put *adj* : barely able ⟨*hard put* to find an explanation⟩

hard rubber *n* : a firm rubber or rubber product that is relatively incapable of being stretched

hard sell *n* : aggressive high-pressure salesmanship

hard·ship \'härd-,ship\ *n* **1** : PRIVATION 2, DISTRESS **2** : something that causes or involves distress or privation

hard·stand \-,stand\ *n* : a hard-surfaced area for parking an airplane

hard–sur·face \-'sər-fəs\ *vt* : to provide (as a road) with a paved surface

hard·tack \'härd-,tak\ *n* : a hard biscuit or bread made of flour and water without salt

hard·top \-,täp\ *n* : an automobile styled to resemble a convertible but having a rigid top of metal or plastic

hard·ware \'här-,dwaər, -,dweər\ *n* **1** : articles (as fittings, cutlery, tools, utensils, or parts of machines) made of metal **2** : major items of equipment used for a particular purpose; *esp* : sophisticated electronic or military equipment

hardware cloth *n* : galvanized screening of steel wire woven with a close mesh commonly ⅛ to ¾ inch (3 to 19 millimeters)

hard wheat *n* : a wheat with hard flinty kernels high in gluten that yield a flour especially suitable for bread and macaroni

hard·wired \'härd-,wīrd\ *adj* : implemented in the form of permanent electronic circuits; *also* : having permanent electrical connections ⟨a *hardwired* ⟩

¹hard·wood \'här-,dwud\ *n* **1** : the wood of a deciduous broad-leaved tree **2** : a tree that yields hardwood

²hardwood *adj* **1** : having or made of hardwood ⟨*hardwood* floors⟩ **2** : consisting of mature woody tissue ⟨a *hardwood* cutting⟩

hard–wood·ed \'här-'dwud-əd\ *adj* **1** : having wood that is hard ⟨a *hard-wooded* pine⟩ **2** : HARDWOOD 1

hard·work·ing \'här-'dwər-king\ *adj* : INDUSTRIOUS

har·dy \'härd-ē\ *adj* **har·di·er; -est 1** : BOLD 1, BRAVE **2** : full of confidence or brashness : BRAZEN **3 a** : used to fatigue or hardships : ROBUST **b** : able to withstand adverse conditions (as of weather) ⟨a *hardy* rose⟩ [Old French *hardi,* of Germanic origin] — **har·di·ly** \'härd-l-ē\ *adv* — **har·di·ness** \'härd-ē-nəs\ *n*

Har·dy–Wein·berg law \,härd-ē-'wīn-,bərg-\ *n* : a fundamental principle of population genetics: population gene frequencies remain constant from generation to generation if mating is random and if mutation, selection, immigration, and emigration do not occur — called also *Hardy-Weinberg principle* [G. H. *Hardy,* died 1947, English mathematician and W. *Weinberg,* 20th century German scientist]

hare \'haər, 'heər\ *n, pl* **hare** *or* **hares** : any of various swift timid long-eared mammals (order Lagomorpha) with a divided upper lip, long hind legs, a short cocked tail, and the young open-eyed and furred at birth — compare RABBIT [Old English *hara*]

hare and hounds *n* : a game in which some of the players scatter bits of paper for a trail and others try to find and catch them

hare·bell \'haər-,bel, 'heər-\ *n* : a slender herb with bright blue bell-shaped flowers

hare·brained \-'brānd\ *adj* : FLIGHTY, FOOLISH

hare·lip \-'lip\ *n* : a deformity in which the upper lip is divided like that of a hare — **hare·lipped** \-'lipt\ *adj*

hare

harmonica

har·em \'har-əm, 'her-\ *n* **1 a** : the rooms assigned to the women in a Muslim household **b** : the women of a Muslim household **2** : a group of female animals (as fur seals) associated with one male [Arabic *ḥarīm*]

hark \'härk\ *vi* : to pay close attention [Middle English *herken*]

hark back *vi* : to turn back to an earlier topic or circumstance

har·le·quin \'här-li-kən, -kwən\ *n* **1** : BUFFOON 1, CLOWN **2** : a variegated pattern (as of a textile) [Italian *arlecchino,* a character in comedy and pantomime with a shaved head, masked face, variegated tights, and wooden sword, from Middle French *Helquin,* a demon]

har·lot \'här-lət\ *n* : PROSTITUTE [Old French *herlot* "rogue"]

har·lot·ry \-lə-trē\ *n, pl* **-ries** : PROSTITUTION

¹harm \'härm\ *n* **1** : physical or mental damage : INJURY **2** : MISCHIEF 2, HURT [Old English *hearm*] SYN see INJURY

²harm *vt* : to cause harm to

harm·ful \'härm-fəl\ *adj* : INJURIOUS, DAMAGING — **harm·ful·ly** \-fə-lē\ *adv* — **harm·ful·ness** *n*

harm·less \'härm-ləs\ *adj* **1** : free from harm, liability, or loss **2** : lacking capacity or intent to injure ⟨a *harmless* joke⟩ — **harm·less·ly** *adv* — **harm·less·ness** *n*

¹har·mon·ic \här-'män-ik\ *adj* **1** : of or relating to musical harmony as opposed to melody or rhythm **2** : HARMONIOUS 2 — **har·mon·i·cal·ly** \-'män-i-kə-lē, -klē\ *adv*

²harmonic *n* **1 a** : OVERTONE 1; *esp* : one whose frequency is a multiple of the fundamental **b** : a flutelike tone produced (as on a violin) by lightly touching a vibrating string with a finger **2** : a component frequency of a harmonic motion (as of an electromagnetic wave) that is an integral multiple of the fundamental frequency

har·mon·i·ca \här-'män-i-kə\ *n* : a small rectangular wind instrument with free metallic reeds sounded by exhaling and inhaling — called also *mouth organ*

harmonic motion *n* : a periodic motion that has a single frequency or amplitude (as of a sounding violin string or swinging pendulum) or a vibratory motion that is composed of two or more such simple periodic motions

har·mon·ics \här-'män-iks\ *n* : the study of the physical characteristics of musical sounds

har·mo·ni·ous \här-'mō-nē-əs\ *adj* **1** : musically concordant ⟨a *harmonious* song⟩ **2** : having the parts agreeably related : CONGRUOUS ⟨*harmonious* colors⟩ **3** : marked by accord in sentiment or action ⟨a *harmonious* family⟩ — **har·mo·ni·ous·ly** *adv* — **har·mo·ni·ous·ness** *n*

har·mo·ni·um \-nē-əm\ *n* : REED ORGAN

har·mo·nize \'här-mə-,nīz\ *vb* **1** : to play or sing in harmony **2** : to be in harmony **3** : to bring into harmony or agreement **4** : to provide or accompany with harmony ⟨*harmonize* a melody⟩ — **har·mo·ni·za·tion** \,här-mə-nə-'zā-shən\ *n* — **har·mo·niz·er** \'här-mə-,nī-zər\ *n*

har·mo·ny \'här-mə-nē\ *n, pl* **-nies 1** *archaic* : tuneful sound **2 a** : the combination of simultaneous musical notes in a chord **b** : the structure of music with respect to the composition and progression of chords **c** : the science of the structure, relation, and progression of chords **3 a** : pleasing or congruent arrangement of parts ⟨a picture showing *harmony* of color and design⟩ **b** : ACCORD, AGREEMENT ⟨live in *harmony* with one's neighbors⟩ **c** : internal calm : TRANQUILLITY [Middle French *armonie,* from Latin *harmonia,* from Greek, "fastening, harmony", from *harmos* "joint, fastening"]

¹har·ness \'här-nəs\ *n* **1 a** : the gear of a draft animal other than a yoke **b** : TACKLE 1, EQUIPMENT; *esp* : military equipment for man or horse **c** : something felt to resemble an animal's harness (shoulder *harness* for a motorist) **2 a** : occupational surroundings or routine (back in *harness* after a vacation) **b** : close association 〈doesn't work well in *harness*〉 [Old French *herneis* "baggage, gear"]

²**harness** *vt* **I a** : to put a harness on **b** : to attach by means of a harness **2** : to join together : YOKE **3** : to put to work : UTILIZE 〈*harness* a waterfall〉

harness horse *n* : a horse for racing or working in harness

harness racing *n* : the sport of racing standardbred horses harnessed to 2-wheeled sulkies

¹**harp** \'härp\ *n* : an instrument having strings of graded length stretched across an open triangular frame with a curving top and played by plucking with the fingers [Old English *hearpe*] — **harp·ist** \'här-pəst\ *n*

²**harp** *vi* **I** : to play on a harp **2** : to dwell on or come back to a subject tiresomely or monotonously 〈always *harping* on my shortcomings〉 — **harp·er** \'här-pər\ *n*

har·poon \här-'pün\ *n* : a barbed spear used especially in hunting large fish or whales [probably from Dutch *harpoen*, from Middle French *harpon* "clamp"] — **harpoon** *vt* — **har·poon·er** *n*

harp·si·chord \'härp-si-ˌkȯrd\ *n* : a keyboard instrument resembling the grand piano and producing tones by the plucking of wire strings with quills or leather points [Italian *arpicordo*, from *arpa* "harp" + *corda* "string"]

har·py \'här-pē\ *n, pl* **harpies** **I** *cap* : a foul malign creature in Greek mythology that is part woman and part bird **2 a** : a greedy or grasping person : LEECH **b** : a shrewish woman [Latin *Harpyia*, from Greek]

har·que·bus \'här-kwi-bəs, -ˌbəs\ *or* **ar·que·bus** \'är-\ *n* : a portable firearm of the 15th and 16th centuries later replaced by the musket [Middle French *harquebuse*, *arquebuse*]

har·ri·dan \'har-əd-n\ *n* : a scolding old woman [perhaps from French *haridelle* "old horse, gaunt woman"]

¹**har·ri·er** \'har-ē-ər\ *n* **I** : a hunting dog that resembles a small foxhound and is used especially for hunting rabbits **2** : a runner on a cross-country team [derived from *hare*]

²**harrier** *n* **I** : one that harries **2** : any of various slender long-legged hawks

¹**har·row** \'har-ō\ *n* : a cultivating implement set with spikes, spring teeth, or disks and used primarily for pulverizing and smoothing the soil [Middle English *harwe*]

²**harrow** *vt* **I** : to cultivate with a harrow **2** : TORMENT, VEX 〈*harrowed* by grief〉 — **har·row·er** \'har-ə-wər\ *n*

har·ry \'har-ē\ *vt* **har·ried; har·ry·ing** **I** : to make a raid on : PILLAGE **2** : to torment by or as if by constant attack 〈*harried* by cares〉 [Old English *hergian*]

harsh \'härsh\ *adj* **I** : having a coarse uneven surface unpleasant to the touch **2** : disagreeable to one of the senses 〈a *harsh* light〉; *also* : physically discomforting : PAINFUL 〈a *harsh* wind〉 **3** : unduly exacting : SEVERE 〈*harsh* discipline〉 **4** : lacking in aesthetic appeal or refinement : CRUDE 〈*harsh* colors〉 [Middle English *harsk*, of Scandinavian origin] SYN SEE ROUGH — **harsh·en** \'här-shən\ *vb* — **harsh·ly** *adv* — **harsh·ness** *n*

hart \'härt\ *n, chiefly British* : a male red deer especially over five years old : STAG — compare HIND [Old English *heort*]

harte·beest \'härt-ˌbēst, -ə-ˌbēst\ *n* : a large nearly extinct African antelope with ringed horns [obsolete Afrikaans, from Dutch, from *hart* "deer" + *beest* "beast"]

har·um–scar·um \ˌhar-əm-'skar-əm, ˌher-əm-'sker-\ *adj* : casually or heedlessly careless [perhaps alteration of *helter-skelter*] — **harum–scarum** *n* — **harum–scarum** *adv*

ha·rus·pex \hə-'rəs-ˌpeks, 'har-əs-\ *n, pl* **ha·rus·pi·ces** \hə-'rəs-pə-ˌsēz\ : a diviner in ancient Rome basing

predictions on inspection of the entrails of animals [Latin]

¹**har·vest** \'här-vəst\ *n* **I** : the season when grains and fruits are gathered **2** : the gathering of a crop **3** : a ripe crop; *also* : the quantity of a crop gathered in a single season **4** : the product or reward of effort [Old English *hærfest*]

²**harvest** *vb* **I a** : to gather in a crop : REAP **b** : to gather as if by harvesting **2** : to win by achievement — **har·vest·able** \-və-stə-bəl\ *adj* — **har·vest·er** *n*

har·vest·man \'här-vəst-mən, -vəs-\ *n* : DADDY LONGLEGS

harvest moon *n* : the full moon nearest the time of the September equinox

has *present 3d sing of* HAVE

has–been \'haz-ˌbin\ *n* : one that has passed the peak of ability, power, effectiveness, or popularity

ha·sen·pfef·fer \'häz-n-ˌpfef-ər, -ˌfef-\ *n* : a stew made of marinated rabbit meat [German, from *hase* "hare" + *pfeffer* "pepper"]

¹**hash** \'hash\ *vt* **I a** : to chop into small pieces **b** : CONFUSE 1, MUDDLE **2** : to talk about : REVIEW 〈*hash* over the evidence〉 [French *hacher*, from *hache* "ax", of Germanic origin]

²**hash** *n* **I** : chopped food; *esp* : chopped meat mixed with potatoes and browned **2** : a restatement of something that is already known **3** : JUMBLE, HODGEPODGE

³**hash** *n* : HASHISH

Hash·em·ite *or* **Hash·im·ite** \'hash-ə-ˌmīt\ *n* : a member of an Arab family having common ancestry with Muhammad and founding dynasties in countries of the eastern Mediterranean [*Hashim*, great-grandfather of Muhammad]

hash·ish \'hash-ˌēsh, ha-'shēsh\ *n* : the resin from the flowering tops of the female hemp plant that is smoked, chewed, or drunk for its intoxicating effect — called also *charas*; compare BHANG, CANNABIS, MARIJUANA [Arabic *hashīsh*]

Ha·sid *or* **Cha·sid** *or* **Has·sid** *or* **Chas·sid** \'has-əd, 'käs-\ *n, pl* **Ha·si·dim** *or* **Has·si·dim** \'has-əd-əm, kə-'sēd-\ : a member of a Jewish mystical sect founded in Poland about 1750 in opposition to rationalism and ritual laxity [Hebrew *hāsīdh* "pious"] — **Ha·sid·ic** \hə-'sid-ik, ha-\ *adj* — **Has·i·dism** \'has-ə-ˌdiz-əm\ *n*

Has·mo·nae·an *or* **Has·mo·ne·an** \ˌhaz-mə-'nē-ən\ *n* : a member of the Maccabees [*Hasmon*, ancestor of the Maccabees] — **Hasmonaean** *or* **Hasmonean** *adj*

hasn't \'haz-nt\ : has not

hasp \'hasp\ *n* : any of several devices for fastening; *esp* : a fastener (as for a door or lid) consisting of a hinged metal strap that fits over a staple and is secured by a pin or padlock [Old English *hæsp*]

has·sle \'has-əl\ *n* **I** : a heated argument : WRANGLE **2** : a violent skirmish : FIGHT [perhaps blend of *haggle* and *tussle*] — **hassle** *vi*

has·sock \'has-ək\ *n* **I** : a tuft of bog grass or sedge **2 a** : a cushion to kneel on in prayer **b** : a cushion that serves as a seat or as a leg rest [Old English *hassuc* "coarse grass"]

hast \'hast, 'hast, əst, həst\ *archaic present 2d sing of* HAVE

has·tate \'has-ˌtāt\ *adj* : shaped like an arrow with flaring barbs 〈a *hastate* leaf〉 [Latin *hasta* "spear"]

¹**haste** \'hāst\ *n* **I** : rapidity of motion or action : SWIFTNESS **2** : rash or headlong action **3** : undue eagerness to act : URGENCY [Old French, of Germanic origin] □ SYN HASTE, HURRY, SPEED mean quickness in movement or action. HASTE implies quickness impelled by urgency, eagerness, or rashness; HURRY suggests agitation, bustle, or confusion; SPEED stresses swiftness without confusion and often with success (increase the *speed* of social progress)

²**haste** *vb* : to move or act swiftly : HASTEN, HURRY

has·ten \'hās-n\ *vb* **has·tened; has·ten·ing** \'hās-ning, -n-ing\ **I** : to urge on **2** : to speed up : ACCELERATE

¹harp

\ə\ abut	\ng\ sing
\ər\ further	\ō\ bone
\a\ mat	\ȯ\ saw
\ā\ take	\ȯi\ coin
\ä\ cot, cart	\th\ thin
\au̇\ out	\th\ this
\ch\ chin	\ü\ food
\e\ pet	\u̇\ foot
\ē\ easy	\y\ yet
\g\ go	\yü\ few
\i\ tip	\yu̇\ cure
\ī\ life	\zh\ vision
\j\ job	

hasty \'hā-stē\ *adj* **hast·i·er; -est** **1 a** : done or made in a hurry ⟨made a *hasty* sketch of the scene⟩ **b** : fast and often superficial ⟨a *hasty* survey of the plan⟩ **2** : acting or done without forethought : RASH **3** : quick to anger : IRRITABLE ⟨a *hasty* temper⟩ — **hast·i·ly** \-stə-lē\ *adv* — **hast·i·ness** \-stē-nəs\ *n*

hasty pudding *n* **1** *British* : a porridge of oatmeal or flour boiled in water **2** *New England* : cornmeal mush

hat \'hat\ *n* : a covering for the head usually having a shaped crown and brim [Old English *hæt*] — **hat in the ring** : an announcement of entry especially into a political contest

hat·box \'hat-ˌbäks\ *n* : a round piece of luggage especially for carrying hats

¹hatch \'hach\ *n* **1** : an opening in the deck of a ship or in the floor or roof of a building; *also* : a small door or opening (as in an airplane) ⟨an escape *hatch*⟩ ⟨a cargo *hatch*⟩ **2** : the covering for a hatch [Old English *hæc* "lower part of a divided door"]

²hatch *vb* **1 a** : to produce (young) from the egg by applying heat ⟨the hen *hatched* chicks⟩ **b** : INCUBATE 1 ⟨the hen *hatched* the eggs⟩ **2 a** : to emerge from an egg, pupa, or chrysalis ⟨the chicks *hatched* today⟩ **b** : to give forth young ⟨the eggs *hatched* today⟩ **3** : to bring into being : ORIGINATE; *esp* : to concoct in secret ⟨*hatch* a plot⟩ [Middle English *hacchen*] — **hatch·abil·i·ty** \ˌhach-ə-'bil-ət-ē\ *n* — **hatch·able** \'hach-ə-bəl\ *adj*

³hatch *n* : a brood of hatched young

⁴hatch *vt* **1** : to inlay in fine lines **2** : to mark (as the shading in a picture) with fine closely spaced lines [Middle French *hacher* "to chop up, hatch", from *hache* "ax"]

⁵hatch *n* : a line used to give the effect of shading

hatch·ery \'hach-rē, -ə-rē\ *n, pl* **-er·ies** : a place for hatching eggs

hatch·et \'hach-ət\ *n* **1** : a short-handled ax for use with one hand **2** : TOMAHAWK [Middle French *hachette*, from *hache* "ax"]

hachet face *n* : a thin sharp face — **hatch·et-faced** \ˌhach-ət-'fāst\ *adj*

hatchet man *n* : one hired for murder, coercion, or attack

hatch·ment \'hach-mənt\ *n* : a panel on which a coat of arms of a deceased person is temporarily displayed [perhaps alteration of *achievement*]

hatch·way \'hach-ˌwā\ *n* : a passage giving access to an enclosed space (as a cellar) and usually having a ladder or stairs

¹hate \'hāt\ *n* **1 a** : intense hostility and aversion **b** : distaste coupled with sustained ill will **c** : a very strong dislike : ANTIPATHY **2** : an object of hatred [Old English *hete*]

²hate *vt* **1** : to feel extreme enmity toward ⟨*hate* one's enemies⟩ **2 a** : to have a strong aversion to : DETEST ⟨*hate* hypocrisy⟩ **b** : to find distasteful : DISLIKE ⟨*hates* cold weather⟩ — **hat·er** *n* □ **SYN** DETEST, ABHOR, LOATHE: HATE implies strong dislike coupled with enmity or malice; DETEST suggests violent or intense dislike but may lack the hostility implied in HATE; ABHOR suggests a deep often shuddering repugnance; LOATHE implies utter disgust and intolerance.

hate·ful \'hāt-fəl\ *adj* **1** : full of hate : MALICIOUS ⟨*hateful* enemies⟩ **2** : exciting or deserving hate ⟨a *hateful* crime⟩ — **hate·ful·ly** \-fə-lē\ *adv* — **hate·ful·ness** *n*

hath \hath, 'hath, əth, həth\ *archaic present 3d sing of* HATE

ha·tred \'hā-trəd\ *n* **1** : HATE 1 **2** : prejudiced hostility or animosity [Middle English, from *hate* + Old English *rǣden* "condition"]

hat·ter \'hat-ər\ *n* : one that makes, sells, or cleans and repairs hats

hat trick *n* : the scoring of three goals in one game by one player (as in hockey or soccer)

hau·berk \'hȯ-bərk\ *n* : a tunic of chain mail worn as armor from the 12th to the 14th century [Old French *hauberc,* of Germanic origin]

haugh·ty \'hȯt-ē, 'hät-\ *adj* **haugh·ti·er; -est** : disdainfully proud [Middle French *haut,* literally, "high", from Latin *altus*] — **haugh·ti·ly** \-l-ē\ *adv* — **haugh·ti·ness** \-ē-nəs\ *n*

¹haul \'hȯl\ *vb* **1 a** : to exert traction : DRAW, PULL ⟨the horse *hauled* a cart⟩ **b** : to obtain or move by or as if by hauling **c** : to transport in a vehicle **2** : SHIFT ⟨the wind *hauled* around to the south⟩ [Old French *haler* "to pull, draw", of Germanic origin] — **haul·er** *n*

²haul *n* **1 a** : the act or process of hauling **b** : a device for hauling **2 a** : an amount collected : TAKE ⟨a burglar's *haul*⟩ **b** : the fish taken in a single draft of a net **3 a** : transportation by hauling **b** : the distance or route over which a load is transported ⟨a long *haul*⟩ **c** : a quantity transported : LOAD

haul·age \'hȯ-lij\ *n* **1** : the act or process of hauling **2** : a charge made for hauling

haulm \'hȯm\ *n* : the stems or tops of a plant (as peas or potatoes) especially after the crop is gathered; *also* : a plant stem [Old English *healm*]

haunch \'hȯnch, 'hänch\ *n* **1 a** : HIP 1 **b** : HINDQUARTER 2 — usually used in pl. **2** : HINDQUARTER 1 [Old French *hanche,* of Germanic origin]

¹haunt \'hȯnt, 'hänt\ *vb* **1 a** : to visit often : FREQUENT **b** : to continually seek the company of **c** : to stay around or persist : LINGER **2 a** : to recur constantly and spontaneously to ⟨the tune *haunted* me all day⟩ **b** : to reappear continually in **3** : to visit or inhabit as a ghost [Old French *hanter*]

²haunt \'hȯnt, 'hänt, 2 is usually 'hant\ *n* **1** : a place habitually frequented or repeatedly visited ⟨a favorite *haunt* of birds⟩ **2** *chiefly dialect* : GHOST 2

haunt·ing \-ing\ *adj* : not easily forgotten ⟨a *haunting* melody⟩ — **haunt·ing·ly** \-ing-lē\ *adv*

haus·to·ri·um \hȯ-'stȯr-ē-əm, -'stȯr-\ *n, pl* **-ria** \-ē-ə\ : a food-absorbing outgrowth of a plant organ [New Latin, from Latin *haustus,* past participle of *haurire* "to drink, drain"] — **haus·to·ri·al** \-ē-əl\ *adj*

haut·bois *or* **haut·boy** \'ō-ˌbȯi, 'hō-\ *n, pl* **hautbois** \-ˌbȯiz\ *or* **hautboys** : OBOE [Middle French *hautbois,* from *haut* "high" + *bois* "wood"]

haute cou·ture \ˌōt-kü-'tür\ *n* : the establishments or designers that create high fashions for women; *also* : the fashions created [French, literally, "high sewing"]

hau·teur \hȯ-'tər\ *n* : ARROGANCE, HAUGHTINESS [French, from *haut* "high", from Latin *altus*]

¹have \hav, 'hav, həv, əv, v; *before "to" usually* 'haf\ *vb, past & past participle* **had** \had, 'had, həd, əd, d\; *present participle* **hav·ing** \'hav-ing\; *present 3d sing* **has** \haz, 'haz, həz, əz, z, s; *before "to" usually* 'has\ **1 a** : POSSESS, OWN ⟨*have* a car⟩ **b** : to hold in one's use, service, or affection or at one's disposal ⟨can't *have* your cake and eat it too⟩ **c** : to consist of : CONTAIN ⟨April *has* 30 days⟩ **2** : to feel obligation or necessity in regard to ⟨*have* to go⟩ **3** : to stand in relationship to ⟨*have* enemies⟩ **4 a** : to get possession of : OBTAIN ⟨best to be *had*⟩ **b** : RECEIVE ⟨*had* bad news⟩ **c** : ACCEPT; *esp* : to accept in marriage **5 a** : to be marked or characterized by ⟨*have* red hair⟩ **b** : SHOW ⟨*had* the gall to refuse⟩ **c** : USE, EXERCISE ⟨*have* mercy on us⟩ **6 a** : to experience especially by submitting to, undergoing, or suffering ⟨*have* a cold⟩ **b** : to carry on : PERFORM, TAKE ⟨*have* a look at this⟩ ⟨*have* a fight⟩ **c** : to entertain in the mind ⟨*have* an opinion⟩ **7 a** : to cause to by persuasive or forceful means ⟨please *have* them stay⟩ **b** : to cause to be ⟨*have* the house painted⟩ **8** : ALLOW ⟨we'll *have* no more of that⟩ **9** : to be competent in ⟨I *have* no French⟩ **10 a** : to hold an advantage over ⟨we *have* them now⟩ **b** : TRICK, FOOL ⟨was *had* by a partner⟩ **11** : to be able to exercise ⟨I *have* my rights⟩ **12** : BEGET 1,

BEAR ⟨*have* a baby⟩ **13** : to partake of ⟨*have* dinner⟩
14 : BRIBE ⟨can be *had* for a price⟩ **15** — used as an
auxiliary verb with the past participle to form the
present perfect, past perfect, or future perfect ⟨*has*
gone home⟩ ⟨*had* already eaten⟩ ⟨will *have* finished⟩
[Old English *habban*] — **have at** : to go at or deal
with : ATTACK — **have done** : FINISH 1a, STOP — **have it
in for** : to intend to do harm to — **have it out** : to settle
a matter of contention by discussion or fighting —
have to do with 1 : to deal with ⟨the program *has* to *do
with* rare animals⟩ **2** : to have a specified relationship
with or effect on ⟨size *has* nothing *to do with* intelli-
gence⟩
²have \ˈhav\ *n* : one that has material wealth — compare HAVE-NOT
ha·ven \ˈhā-vən\ *n* **1** : HARBOR 2, PORT **2 a** : place of
safety : ASYLUM [Old English *hæfen*]
have-not \ˈhav-ˌnät, -ˈnät\ *n* : one that is poor in material wealth — compare HAVE
haven't \ˈhav-ənt\ : have not
hav·er·sack \ˈhav-ər-ˌsak\ *n* : a bag similar to a knapsack but worn over one shoulder [French *havresac*,
from German *habersack* "bag for oats", from *haber*
"oats" + *sack* "bag"]
Ha·ver·sian canal \hə-ˈvər-zhən-\ *n* : any of the small
canals by which blood vessels traverse bone [Clopton
Havers, died 1702, English physician]
hav·oc \ˈhav-ək\ *n* **1** : wide and general destruction :
DEVASTATION **2** : great confusion and disorder [Anglo-
French *havok*, from Old French *havot* "plunder"]
¹haw \ˈhȯ\ *n* **1** : a hawthorn berry **2** : HAWTHORN [Old
English *haga*]
²haw *vi* : to utter the sound represented by *haw*
⟨hemmed and *hawed* before answering⟩ [imitative]
³haw *n* : a vocalized pause in speaking or an instance of
uttering this sound [imitative]
⁴haw *imperative verb* — used as a direction to turn to
the left; compare GEE [origin unknown]
Ha·waii–Aleu·tian time \hə-ˈwä-ē-ə-ˈlü-shən-, -ˈwī-,
-ˈwȯ-, -yē\ *n* : the time of the 10th time zone west of
Greenwich that includes the Hawaiian islands and the
Aleutians west of the Fox group
Ha·wai·ian \hə-ˈwä-yən; -ˈwī-yən, -ən-; -ˈwȯ-yən\ *n* **1** :
a native or resident of Hawaii; *esp* : one of Polynesian
ancestry **2** : the Polynesian language of the Hawaiians
— **Hawaiian** *adj*
Hawaiian guitar *n* : a usually electric stringed instrument consisting of a long soundboard and six to eight
steel strings that are plucked while being pressed with
a movable steel bar
¹hawk \ˈhȯk\ *n* **1** : any of numerous birds of prey including all the smaller members of this group active
mostly by day — compare OWL **2** : a person who advocates immediate vigorous action in a dispute; *esp* : a
supporter of a war or warlike policy — compare DOVE
[Old English *hafoc*] — **hawk·ish** \ˈhȯ-kish\ *adj*
²hawk *vb* **1** : to hunt birds by means of a trained hawk
2 : to hunt on the wing like a hawk
³hawk *vt* : to offer for sale by calling out in the street
⟨*hawk* vegetables⟩ [back-formation from ²*hawker*]
⁴hawk *vb* **1** : to utter a harsh guttural sound in or as if in
clearing the throat **2** : to raise by hawking ⟨*hawk* up
phlegm⟩ [imitative]
¹hawk·er \ˈhȯ-kər\ *n* : FALCONER
²hawker *n* : one that hawks wares [Low German *höker*,
from *höken* "to peddle"]
hawk·moth \ˈhȯk-ˌmȯth\ *n* : any of numerous stout-
bodied swift-flying moths with long strong narrow
pointed fore wings and small hind wings
hawks·bill \ˈhȯks-ˌbil\ *n* : a flesh-eating sea turtle
whose shell yields the best tortoiseshell of commerce
hawk·weed \ˈhȯ-ˌkwēd\ *n* : any of several plants of the
daisy family that usually have flower heads with red or
orange rays

hawse \ˈhȯz\ *n* **1 a** : HAWSEHOLE **b** : the part of a ship's
bow that contains the hawseholes **2** : the distance between a ship's bow and her anchor [Old Norse *hals*
"neck, hawse"]
hawse·hole \-ˌhōl\ *n* : a hole in the bow of a ship
through which a cable passes
haw·ser \ˈhȯ-zər\ *n* : a large rope for towing, mooring,
or securing a ship [Anglo-French *hauceour*, from Middle French *haucier* "to hoist", derived from Latin
altus "high"]
haw·thorn \ˈhȯ-ˌthȯrn\ *n* : any of a genus of spring-
flowering spiny shrubs or small trees of the rose family
with glossy and often lobed leaves, white or pink fragrant flowers, and small red fruits
¹hay \ˈhā\ *n* : herbage (as grass) mowed and cured for
fodder [Old English *hīeg*]
²hay *vb* **1** : to cut, cure, and store herbage for hay **2** : to
feed with hay — **hay·er** *n*
hay·cock \ˈhā-ˌkäk\ *n* : a conical pile of hay
hay fever *n* : an acute allergic reaction of the mucous
membranes of the eyes, nose, and throat characterized
especially by secretion of tears, itching, inflammation
of the mucous membranes, and sneezing
hay·fork \ˈhā-ˌfȯrk\ *n* : a fork operated mechanically or
by hand to load or unload hay
hay·loft \-ˌlȯft\ *n* : the upper part of a barn where hay
is stored
hay·mak·er \-ˌmā-kər\ *n* **1** : one that cures or cuts and
cures hay **2** : a powerful blow (as in boxing)
hay·mow \-ˌmau̇\ *n* : HAYLOFT
hay·rack \-ˌrak\ *n* **1 a** : a frame mounted on the running gear of a wagon and used especially in hauling
hay or straw **b** : a wagon mounted with a hayrack **2** : a
feeding rack that holds hay for livestock
hay·rick \-ˌrik\ *n* : a large sometimes thatched outdoor
stack of hay
hay·seed \-ˌsēd\ *n* **1 a** : seed shattered from hay **b** :
clinging bits of straw or chaff from hay **2** : BUMPKIN,
YOKEL
hay·stack \-ˌstak\ *n* : a stack of hay : HAYRICK
hay·wire \-ˌwīr\ *adj* **1** : hastily or shoddily made **2** :
being out of order ⟨the radio is *haywire*⟩ **3** : emotionally or mentally upset : CRAZY ⟨went *haywire* after the
accident⟩ [from the use of baling wire for makeshift
repairs]
ha·zan \ḵə-ˈzän, ˈḵäz-n\ *n, pl* **ha·za·nim** \ḵə-ˈzän-əm\ :
CANTOR 2 [Hebrew *ḥazzān*]
¹haz·ard \ˈhaz-ərd\ *n* **1** : a game of chance played with
two dice **2** : a source of danger **3 a** : ACCIDENT 1b,
CHANCE **b** : chance that is likely to result unfavorably
4 : a golf-course obstacle [Middle French *hasard*, from
Arabic *az-zahr* "the die"] SYN see DANGER □ ORIGIN
Hazard was originally a game played with dice. The
English word comes from Middle French *hasard*,
which was most likely borrowed from Arabic *az-zahr*,
"the die" ("one of the dice"). *Hazard* was borrowed
from the French by the medieval English, and within a
few centuries what had been a venture on the outcome of a throw of the dice could be any venture or
risk. Now "chance" or "venture" and "risk" or "peril" are the primary meanings of *hazard*. The game of
hazard is only infrequently played, and the modern
player probably assumes that the game is so called because of the chances taken in play.
²hazard *vt* : VENTURE, RISK ⟨*hazard* a guess⟩
haz·ard·ous \ˈhaz-ərd-əs\ *adj* : DANGEROUS, RISKY —
haz·ard·ous·ly *adv* — **haz·ard·ous·ness** *n*
¹haze \ˈhāz\ *n* **1** : fine dust, smoke, or light vapor causing lack of transparency in the air **2** : a vague uncertain state of mind or mental perception
²haze *vb* : to make or become hazy or cloudy [probably
back-formation from *hazy*]
³haze *vt* **1** : to harass needlessly (as by exacting hard or
disagreeable work or by mockery) **2** : to play abusive

hawksbill

\ə\ **abut**		\ng\ **sing**	
\ər\ **further**		\ō\ **bone**	
\a\ **mat**		\ȯ\ **saw**	
\ā\ **take**		\ȯi\ **coin**	
\ä\ **cot, cart**		\th\ **thin**	
\au̇\ **out**		\th\ **this**	
\ch\ **chin**		\ü\ **food**	
\e\ **pet**		\u̇\ **foot**	
\ē\ **easy**		\y\ **yet**	
\g\ **go**		\yü\ **few**	
\i\ **tip**		\yu̇\ **cure**	
\ī\ **life**		\zh\ **vision**	
\j\ **job**			

and humiliating tricks on by way of initiation [origin unknown] — **haz·er** *n*

ha·zel \'hā-zəl\ *n* **1** : any of a genus of shrubs or small trees of the birch family bearing edible nuts enclosed in a leafy case **2** : a light brown to a strong yellowish brown [Old English *hæsel*] — **hazel** *adj*

ha·zel·nut \'hā-zəl-,nət\ *n* : the nut of a hazel

hazy \'hā-zē\ *adj* **haz·i·er; -est 1** : obscured or darkened by or as if by haze ⟨a *hazy* view⟩ **2** : VAGUE ⟨a *hazy* idea⟩ [origin unknown] — **haz·i·ly** \-zə-lē\ *adv* — **haz·i·ness** \-zē-nəs\ *n*

H–bomb \'āch-,bäm\ *n* : HYDROGEN BOMB

¹he \hē, 'hē, ē\ *pron* **1** : that male one who is neither speaker nor hearer ⟨*he* is my father⟩ — compare HIM, HIS, IT, SHE, THEY **2** — used in generic sense or when the sex of the person is not specified ⟨*he* who hesitates is lost⟩ ⟨one should do the best *he* can⟩ [Old English *hē*]

²he \'hē\ *n* : a male person or animal

¹head \'hed\ *n* **1** : the upper or front division of the body (as of a man or an insect) that contains the brain, the chief sense organs, and the mouth **2 a** : MIND, UNDERSTANDING ⟨a good *head* for figures⟩ **b** : mental or emotional control : POISE ⟨a level *head*⟩ **3** : the obverse of a coin **4 a** : PERSON, INDIVIDUAL ⟨count *heads*⟩ **b** *pl* **head** : a unit of number (as of livestock) **5 a** : the end that is upper or higher or opposite the foot ⟨the *head* of the bed⟩ **b** : the source of a stream **c** : either end of something (as a drum) whose two ends need not be distinguished **d** : a horizontal passage in a coal mine **6 a** : HEADMASTER **b** : a person responsible for directing the actions and duties of others : CHIEF, LEADER ⟨the *head* of a company⟩ **7 a** : an inflorescence (as of a dandelion or daisy) in the form of a rounded or flattened cluster of stemless flowers — called also *capitulum* **b** : a compact mass of plant parts (as leaves or flowers) ⟨a *head* of cabbage⟩ **8 a** : the leading element of a military column or a procession **b** : HEADWAY 1a **9 a** : the uppermost extremity or projecting part of an object : TOP **b** : the striking part of a weapon or tool **10** : a body of water kept in reserve at a height **11 a** : the difference in elevation between two points in a body of fluid **b** : the resulting pressure of the fluid at the lower point expressible as this height; *also* : pressure of a fluid ⟨a *head* of steam⟩ **12 a** : the bow and adjacent parts of a ship **b** : a ship's toilet **13** : the place of leadership or command ⟨the one at the *head* of the group⟩ **14 a** (1) : a word often in larger letters placed above a passage in order to introduce or categorize (2) : a separate part or topic **b** : a portion of a page or sheet that is above the first line of printing **15** : the foam that rises on an effervescing liquid **16 a** : the part of a boil, pimple, or abscess at which it is likely to break **b** : CRISIS ⟨events came to a *head*⟩ **17** : a part of a machine or machine tool containing a device (as a cutter, drill) ⟨a machine with a grinding *head*⟩; *also* : the part of an apparatus that performs the chief function or a particular function ⟨a shower *head*⟩ [Old English *hēafod*] — **off one's head** : CRAZY, DISTRACTED — **out of one's head** : DELIRIOUS — **over one's head 1** : beyond one's comprehension **2** : so as to pass over one's superior standing or authority

²head *adj* **1** : of, relating to, or used for the head **2** : PRINCIPAL, CHIEF ⟨*head* cook⟩ **3** : situated at the head **4** : coming from in front ⟨*head* sea⟩

³head *vb* **1** : to cut back or off the upper or terminal growth of (a plant or plant part) **2 a** : to provide with or form a head ⟨*head* an arrow⟩ ⟨this cabbage *heads* early⟩ **b** : to form the head or top of ⟨a tower *headed* by a spire⟩ **3** : to put oneself at the head of : act as leader to ⟨*head* a revolt⟩ **4 a** : to get in front of so as to hinder, stop, or turn back ⟨*head* them off at the pass⟩ **b** : to take a lead over (as in a race) **c** : to pass (a stream) by going round above the source **5 a** : to put something at the head of (as a list) **b** : to stand as the

first or leading member of ⟨*heads* the list⟩ **6** : to take or cause to take a specified course ⟨*head* for home⟩

head·ache \'hed-,āk\ *n* **1** : pain in the head **2** : an annoying or baffling situation or problem — **head·achy** \-,ā-kē\ *adj*

head·band \-,band\ *n* : a band worn on or around the head

head·board \-,bōrd, -,bȯrd\ *n* : a board forming the head (as of a bed)

head·cheese \-,chēz\ *n* : a jellied loaf or sausage made from the edible parts of the head, feet, and sometimes the tongue and heart especially of a pig

head cold *n* : a common cold centered in the nasal passages and adjacent mucous tissues

head·dress \'hed-,dres, 'he-\ *n* : a covering or ornament for the head

head·ed \'hed-əd\ *adj* **1** : having a head or a heading ⟨a *headed* bolt⟩ **2** : having such a head or so many heads ⟨curly-*headed*⟩ ⟨three-*headed* monster⟩

head·er \'hed-ər\ *n* **1** : one that removes heads; *esp* : a grain-harvesting machine that cuts off the grain heads and lifts them into a wagon **2 a** : a brick or stone laid in a wall with its end toward the face of the wall **b** : a beam fitted between trimmers and across the ends of tailpieces in a building frame **3** : a fall or dive head foremost **4** : a shot or pass made in soccer by hitting the ball with the head

head·first \'hed-'fərst\ *also* **head·fore·most** \-'fōr-,mōst, -fȯr-\ *adv* : with the head foremost : HEADLONG — **headfirst** *adj*

head gate *n* : a gate for controlling the water flowing into a channel (as an irrigation ditch)

head·gear \'hed-,giər\ *n* **1** : a covering or protective device for the head **2** : harness for a horse's head

head·hunt·ing \-,hənt-ing\ *n* : the practice of cutting off and preserving the heads of enemies as trophies — **head·hunt·er** *n*

head·ing \'hed-ing\ *n* **1** : the compass direction in which the longitudinal axis of a ship or aircraft points **2** : something that forms or serves as a head; *esp* : an inscription, headline, or title standing at the top or beginning (as of a letter or chapter)

head·land \'hed-lənd, -,land\ *n* : a point of usually high land jutting out into the sea : PROMONTORY

head·less \-ləs\ *adj* **1** : having no head **2** : having no leader **3** : lacking good sense or prudence : FOOLISH — **head·less·ness** *n*

head·light \-,līt\ *n* : a light on the front of a vehicle

¹head·line \-,līn\ *n* **1** : the title over an item or article in a newspaper **2** : a line at the top of a page (as in a book) giving a title or heading

²headline *vt* **1** : to provide with a headline **2** : to publicize highly **3** : to be a leading performer or attraction in

head·lin·er \-,lī-nər\ *n* : a performer whose name is given prominent billing : STAR

head·lock \'hed-,läk\ *n* : a wrestling hold in which one encircles the opponent's head with one arm

¹head·long \-'lȯng\ *adv* **1** : HEADFIRST **2** : without deliberation : RECKLESSLY ⟨dash *headlong* into traffic⟩ **3** : without pause or delay [Middle English *hedlong*, alteration of *hedling*, from *hed* "head" + *-ling*]

²head·long \-,lȯng\ *adj* **1** : PRECIPITATE, RASH ⟨*headlong* flight⟩ **2** : plunging headfirst ⟨a *headlong* dive into the pool⟩

head louse *n* : a louse that lives on the human scalp

head·man \'hed-'man, -,man\ *n* : one who is a leader (as of a tribe, clan, or village) : CHIEF

head·mas·ter \'hed-,mas-tər\ *n* : a man heading the staff of a private school

head·mis·tress \-,mis-trəs\ *n* : a woman heading the staff of a private school

head·most \-,mōst\ *adj* : most advanced : LEADING

head–on \'hed-'ȯn, -'än\ *adj* **1** : having the front facing in the direction of initial contact or line of sight **2** : FRONTAL 2b — **head–on** *adv*

head over heels *adv* **1** : in or as if in a somersault ⟨fell *head over heels* down the hill⟩ **2** : very much ⟨*head over heels* in love⟩

head·phone \'hed-ˌfōn\ *n* : an earphone held over the ear by a band worn on the head

head·piece \-ˌpēs\ *n* **1** : a protective or defensive covering for the head **2** : INTELLIGENCE 1a, BRAINS

head·pin \-ˌpin\ *n* : a pin that stands at the apex in a triangular arrangement of bowling pins

head·quarter \'hed-ˌkwȯrt-ər, -ˌkwȯt-, hed-'\ *vb* **1** : to make one's headquarters **2** : to place in headquarters

head·quar·ters \-ərz\ *n sing or pl* **1** : a place from which a commander exercises command **2** : the administrative center of an enterprise

head·rest \'hed-ˌrest\ *n* : a support for the head

head·sail \-ˌsāl, -səl\ *n* : a sail set forward of the mast

head·set \-ˌset\ *n* : a pair of headphones

head·ship \-ˌship\ *n* : the position, office, or dignity of a head

heads·man \'hedz-mən\ *n* : one that beheads : EXECUTIONER

head·stall \'hed-ˌstȯl\ *n* : a part of a bridle or halter that encircles the head

head·stand \-ˌstand\ *n* : the gymnastic feat of standing on one's head usually with support from the hands

head start *n* **1** : an advantage allowed at the start of a race **2** : a favorable or promising beginning

head·stock \'hed-ˌstäk\ *n* : a part of a lathe that holds the revolving spindle and its attachments

head·stone \-ˌstōn\ *n* : a memorial stone placed at the head of a grave

head·strong \-ˌstrȯng\ *adj* **1** : not easily restrained : WILLFUL ⟨a *headstrong* child⟩ **2** : directed by ungovernable will ⟨violent *headstrong* actions⟩

head·wait·er \'hed-ˌwāt-ər\ *n* : the head of the dining-room staff of a restaurant or hotel

head·wa·ters \-ˌwȯt-ərz, -ˌwät-\ *n pl* : the source and upper part of a stream

head·way \-ˌwā\ *n* **1 a** : motion or rate of motion (as of a ship) in a forward direction **b** : ADVANCE, PROGRESS ⟨made *headway* in scientific research⟩ **2** : clear space (as under an arch) **3** : the time interval between two vehicles traveling in the same direction on the same route

head wind *n* : a wind blowing in a direction opposite to a course especially of a ship or aircraft

head·word \'hed-ˌwərd\ *n* : a word or term placed at the beginning (as of a chapter or entry)

head·work \-ˌwərk\ *n* : mental work : THINKING

heady \'hed-ē\ *adj* **head·i·er; -est 1** : WILLFUL, RASH ⟨*heady* opinions⟩ **2** : tending to make giddy ⟨*heady* wine⟩ — **head·i·ly** \'hed-l-ē\ *adv* — **head·i·ness** \'hed-ē-nəs\ *n*

heal \'hēl\ *vb* **1** : to make healthy or whole **2** : to return to a sound or healthy condition ⟨the arm *healed*⟩ ⟨the wound *healed*⟩ [Old English *hǣlan*] SYN see CURE

heal·er \'hē-lər\ *n* : one that heals

health \'helth\ *n* **1 a** : the condition of being sound in body, mind, or spirit; *esp* : freedom from physical disease or pain **b** : general condition of an individual ⟨in poor *health*⟩ **2** : flourishing condition ⟨the economic *health* of a country⟩ **3** : a toast to someone's health or prosperity [Old English *hǣlth*, from *hāl* "whole, hale"]

health·ful \-fəl\ *adj* **1** : beneficial to health of body or mind ⟨*healthful* exercise⟩ **2** : HEALTHY 1 — **health·ful·ly** \-fə-lē\ *adv* — **health·ful·ness** *n* □ SYN HEALTHFUL, WHOLESOME, SALUBRIOUS, SALUTARY mean favorable to the health of mind or body. HEALTHFUL implies a positive contribution to a healthy condition ⟨a *healthful* diet⟩ WHOLESOME applies to what benefits, builds up, or sustains physically, mentally, or spiritually ⟨*wholesome* meals⟩ ⟨*wholesome* literature⟩ SALUBRIOUS applies chiefly to the helpful effects of climate or air; SALUTARY describes something corrective or benefi-

cially effective, even though it may in itself be unpleasant ⟨the *salutary* influence of constructive criticism⟩

healthy \'hel-thē\ *adj* **health·i·er; -est 1** : enjoying or typical of good health : WELL **2** : conducive to health **3 a** : PROSPEROUS, FLOURISHING ⟨a *healthy* economy⟩ **b** : not small or feeble : CONSIDERABLE ⟨a *healthy* serving⟩ — **health·i·ly** \-thə-lē\ *adv* — **health·i·ness** \-thē-nəs\ *n* □ SYN WELL, SOUND: HEALTHY implies full strength and vigor as well as freedom from disease; WELL implies merely freedom from disease or illness; SOUND stresses perfect health, absence of all defects, disease, or morbidity ⟨a *sound* mind in a *sound* body⟩

¹heap \'hēp\ *n* **1** : a collection of things thrown one on another : PILE ⟨a rubbish *heap*⟩ **2** : a great number or large quantity : LOT ⟨*heaps* of people⟩ ⟨a *heap* of fun⟩ [Old English *hēap*]

²heap *vt* **1** : to throw or lay in a heap : PILE ⟨*heap* up leaves⟩ **2** : to cast or bestow in large quantities ⟨*heaped* scorn on them⟩ **3** : to fill (a measure or container) more than even full

hear \'hiər\ *vb* **heard** \'hərd\; **hear·ing** \'hiər-ing\ **1** : to perceive or grasp by the ear ⟨*hear* music⟩; *also* : to have the power of perceiving sound ⟨doesn't *hear* well⟩ **2** : to gain knowledge of by hearing : LEARN ⟨*heard* you're leaving⟩ **3** : to listen to : HEED ⟨*hear* me out⟩ **4 a** : to give a legal hearing to ⟨*hear* a case⟩ **b** : to take testimony from ⟨*hear* witnesses⟩ **5 a** : to get news ⟨*heard* from them yesterday⟩ **b** : to have knowledge ⟨had *heard* of them⟩ **6** : to entertain the idea ⟨wouldn't *hear* of it⟩ [Old English *hīeran*] — **hear·er** \'hir-ər\ *n* □ SYN LISTEN: HEAR implies the actual sensation and response of the auditory nerves to a stimulus; LISTEN implies the conscious or voluntary effort to hear.

hear·ing *n* **1 a** : the process, function, or power of perceiving sound; *esp* : the special sense by which noises and tones are received as stimuli **b** : EARSHOT ⟨stay within *hearing*⟩ **2 a** : a chance to present one's case **b** : a listening to arguments or testimony **c** : a session in which testimony is heard ⟨a public *hearing* on the bill⟩

hearing aid *n* : an electronic device for amplifying sound usually worn by a person to assist poor hearing

hear·ken \'här-kən\ *vi* **hear·kened; hear·ken·ing** \'härk-ning, -ə-ning\ **1** : LISTEN 1 **2** : to give respectful attention [Old English *heorcnian*]

hear·say \'hiər-ˌsā\ *n* : something heard from another : RUMOR

hearsay evidence *n* : evidence based not on a witness's personal knowledge but on information given the witness by another

hearse \'hərs\ *n* : a vehicle for conveying the dead to the grave [Middle French *herce* "harrow, frame for holding candles", from Latin *hirpex* "harrow"] □ ORIGIN In Middle French the word *herce*, meaning "harrow", was applied to a triangular frame that was used for holding candles and was similar to the ancient form of a harrow. Both the literal and extended senses were used in English when the word was borrowed. It was a widespread practice to erect an elaborate framework over the coffin or tomb of a distinguished person. Because such frameworks were often decorated with lighted candles, the term *hearse* was applied to them. A series of extensions led to the use of *hearse* for a bier and then for a vehicle to carry the dead to the grave.

heart \'härt\ *n* **1 a** : a hollow muscular organ of vertebrate animals that by its rhythmic contraction acts as a force pump maintaining the circulation of the blood **b** : a structure in an invertebrate animal similar in function to the vertebrate heart **2** : something resembling a heart in shape **3 a** : a red stylized heart used to distinguish a suit of playing cards; *also* : a card of the suit bearing hearts **b** *pl* : a card game in which the object is to avoid taking tricks containing hearts or win

headset

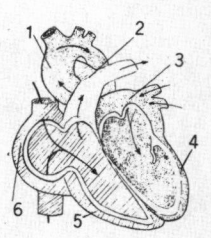

heart 1a: *1* aorta,
2 pulmonary artery, *3* left
auricle, *4* left ventricle,
5 right ventricle, *6* right
auricle

\ə\ abut	\ng\ sing
\ər\ further	\ō\ bone
\a\ mat	\ȯ\ saw
\ā\ take	\ȯi\ coin
\ä\ cot, cart	\th\ thin
\aú\ out	\t͟h\ this
\ch\ chin	\ü\ food
\e\ pet	\ú\ foot
\ē\ easy	\y\ yet
\g\ go	\yü\ few
\i\ tip	\yú\ cure
\ī\ life	\zh\ vision
\j\ job	

all of the hearts **4 a** : the whole personality including intellectual and emotional functions or traits **b** : generous disposition : KINDNESS ⟨a person without a *heart*⟩ **c** : COURAGE, SPIRIT ⟨take *heart*⟩ **5 a** : the central part ⟨the *heart* of the forest⟩ **b** : the most important part ⟨the *heart* of the issue⟩ [Old English *heorte*] — **by heart** : by rote — **to heart** : with deep concern

heart·ache \'härt-ˌāk\ *n* : mental anguish : SORROW

heart attack *n* : an acute episode of heart disease especially when caused by a coronary thrombosis or occlusion

heart·beat \'härt-ˌbēt\ *n* : one complete pulsation of the heart

heart block *n* : lack of coordination of the heartbeat so that the atria and ventricles beat independently

heart·break \'härt-ˌbrāk\ *n* : crushing grief

heart·break·ing \-ˌbrā-kiŋ\ *adj* : causing crushing grief — **heart·break·ing·ly** \-kiŋ-lē\ *adv*

heart·bro·ken \-ˌbrō-kən\ *adj* : overcome by grief

heart·burn \-ˌbərn\ *n* : a burning discomfort that seems to be localized about the heart and is usually related to spasm of the lower esophagus or the upper stomach

heart·burn·ing \-ˌbər-niŋ\ *n* : intense or rancorous jealousy or resentment

heart disease *n* : an abnormal condition of the heart or of the heart and circulation

heart·ed \'härt-əd\ *adj* : having a heart especially of a specified kind ⟨stout*hearted*⟩

heart·en \'härt-n\ *vt* **heart·ened; heart·en·ing** \'härt-niŋ, -n-iŋ\ : to cheer up : ENCOURAGE

heart·felt \'härt-ˌfelt\ *adj* : deeply felt : EARNEST

hearth \'härth\ *n* **1 a** : a brick, stone, or cement area in front of a fireplace **b** : the floor of a fireplace **c** (1) : the lowest section of a blast furnace (2) : the floor of a metal-processing furnace **2** : HOME 1a, FIRESIDE [Old English *heorth*]

hearth·stone \-ˌstōn\ *n* : stone forming a hearth

heart·i·ly \'härt-l-ē\ *adv* **1** : with sincerity, goodwill, or enthusiasm ⟨set to work *heartily*⟩ ⟨eat *heartily*⟩ **2** : CORDIALLY ⟨made them *heartily* welcome⟩ **3** : COMPLETELY, THOROUGHLY

heart·land \'härt-ˌland\ *n* : a central land area; *esp* : one thought of as economically and militarily self-sufficient

heart·less \-ləs\ *adj* : lacking feeling or compassion : PITILESS — **heart·less·ly** *adv* — **heart·less·ness** *n*

heart·rend·ing \-ˌren-diŋ\ *adj* : causing heartbreak

hearts·ease \'härt-ˌsēz\ *n* **1** : peace of mind : TRANQUILLITY **2** : any of various violas; *esp* : WILD PANSY

heart·sick \'härt-ˌsik\ *adj* : very despondent : DEPRESSED — **heart·sick·ness** *n*

heart·sore \-ˌsōr, -ˌsȯr\ *adj* : HEARTSICK

heart·string \-ˌstriŋ\ *n* : the deepest emotions or affections

heart·throb \-ˌthräb\ *n* **1** : the throb of a heart **2 a** : sentimental emotion : PASSION **b** : SWEETHEART 2

heart-to-heart \'härt-tə-'härt\ *adj* : SINCERE, FRANK ⟨a *heart-to-heart* talk⟩

heart·wood \'härt-ˌwu̇d\ *n* : the older harder usually darker wood in the central portion of a woody stem — compare SAPWOOD

¹hearty \'härt-ē\ *adj* **heart·i·er; -est 1 a** : giving unqualified support : THOROUGHGOING ⟨*hearty* agreement⟩ **b** : enthusiastically cordial ⟨a *hearty* welcome⟩ **c** : UNRESTRAINED ⟨*hearty* laughter⟩ **2 a** : exhibiting vigorous good health **b** : abundant and satisfying ⟨a *hearty* meal⟩ **c** : NOURISHING ⟨a *hearty* beef stew⟩ **3** : ENERGETIC, STRONG ⟨gave a *hearty* pull⟩ — **heart·i·ness** *n*

²hearty *n, pl* **heart·ies** : a bold brave fellow

¹heat \'hēt\ *vb* **1** : to make or become warm or hot **2** : to make or become excited or angry [Old English *hǣtan*]

²heat *n* **1 a** : a condition of being hot : WARMTH **b** : a high degree of hotness **c** : a hot place or period **d** : a

form of energy that causes substances to rise in temperature, fuse, evaporate, expand, or undergo any of various other changes and that flows to a body by contact with or radiation from bodies at higher temperatures **2 a** : intensity of feeling; *esp* : ANGER ⟨answered with some *heat*⟩ **b** : the height of an action or condition ⟨the *heat* of battle⟩ **c** : sexual excitement especially in a female mammal; *esp* : ESTRUS **3** : pungency of flavor **4** : a single continuous effort: as **a** : a single course in a race **b** : one of several preliminary races held to eliminate less competent contenders **5 a** *slang* : POLICE FORCE — usually used with *the* **b** : PRESSURE, COERCION ⟨the *heat* was on to get the job done⟩ — **heat·less** \'hēt-ləs\ *adj*

heat·ed \'hēt-əd\ *adj* : marked by anger ⟨*heated* words⟩ — **heat·ed·ly** *adv*

heat engine *n* : a mechanism for converting heat energy into mechanical energy

heat·er \'hēt-ər\ *n* : a device that imparts heat or holds something to be heated

heat exchanger *n* : a device (as an automobile radiator) for transferring heat from one fluid to another without allowing them to mix

heat exhaustion *n* : a condition marked by weakness, nausea, dizziness, and profuse sweating that results from physical exertion in a hot environment — called also *heat prostration*; compare HEATSTROKE

heath \'hēth\ *n* **1** : any of a family of shrubby often evergreen plants that thrive on open barren usually acid and poorly drained soil; *esp* : a low evergreen shrub with whorls of needlelike leaves and clusters of small flowers **2** : a tract of usually level and poorly drained wasteland commonly overgrown with low shrubs [Old English *hǣth*] — **heath·like** \-ˌlīk\ *adj* — **heathy** \'hē-thē\ *adj*

¹hea·then \'hē-thən\ *adj* : of or relating to heathens [Old English *hǣthen*]

²heathen *n, pl* **heathens** *or* **heathen 1** : an unconverted member of a people or nation that does not acknowledge the God of the Bible **2** : an uncivilized or irreligious person — **hea·then·dom** \-dəm\ *n* — **hea·then·ism** \-ˌthə-ˌniz-əm\ *n*

hea·then·ish \'hē-thə-nish\ *adj* : resembling or characteristic of heathens : BARBAROUS — **hea·then·ish·ly** *adv*

¹heath·er \'heth-ər\ *n* : HEATH 1; *esp* : a common evergreen heath of northern and alpine regions with small crowded stemless leaves and tiny usually purplish pink flowers in one-sided spikes [Middle English *hather*] — **heath·ery** \'heth-rē, -ə-rē\ *adj*

²heather *adj* **1** : of, relating to, or resembling heather **2** : having flecks of various colors ⟨a soft *heather* tweed⟩

heath hen *n* : an extinct grouse of the northeastern United States related to the prairie chicken

heat island *n* : an urban area in which significantly more heat is absorbed and retained (as by buildings and streets) than in surrounding areas

heat lightning *n* : flashes of light without thunder caused by distant lightning reflected by high clouds

heat pump *n* : a device for heating or cooling a building by transferring heat contained in a fluid to or from the building

heat rash *n* : PRICKLY HEAT

heat shield *n* : a barrier of insulation to protect a space capsule from heat on its return to earth

heat·stroke \'hēt-ˌstrōk\ *n* : a condition marked especially by cessation of sweating, high fever, and collapse that results from prolonged exposure to high temperature — compare HEAT EXHAUSTION

heat wave *n* : a period of unusually hot weather

¹heave \'hēv\ *vb* **heaved** *or* **hove** \'hōv\; **heav·ing 1** : to raise with an effort : LIFT ⟨*heave* a trunk onto a truck⟩ **2** : THROW, HURL ⟨*heave* a rock⟩ **3** : to utter with effort ⟨*heave* a sigh⟩ **4** : to rise and fall repeatedly ⟨the runner's chest was *heaving*⟩ **5** : to be thrown up or raised ⟨the ground *heaved* during the earthquake⟩ **6** : RETCH [Old English *hebban*] — **heav·er** *n* — **heave to** : to bring a ship to a stop

²heave *n* **1 a** : an effort to heave or raise **b** : a forceful throw : CAST **2** : an upward motion; *esp* : a rhythmical rising (as of the chest in breathing)

heav·en \'hev-ən\ *n* **1** : SKY 1 — usually used in pl. **2 a** *often cap* : the dwelling place of God **b** : a spiritual state of everlasting communion with God **3** *cap* : GOD 1 **4** : a place or condition of utmost happiness [Old English *heofon*]

heav·en·ly \'hev-ən-lē\ *adj* **1** : of or relating to heaven or the heavens **2** : DIVINE, SACRED ⟨*heavenly* grace⟩ **3** : supremely delightful ⟨a *heavenly* day⟩ — **heav·en·li·ness** *n*

heav·en·ward \'hev-ən-wərd\ *adv or adj* : toward heaven

heav·en·wards \-wərdz\ *adv* : HEAVENWARD

heav·i·ly \'hev-ə-lē\ *adv* **1** : in a heavy manner **2** : in a slow and laborious manner ⟨breathe *heavily*⟩ **3** : to a great degree : SEVERELY ⟨*heavily* punished⟩

¹heavy \'hev-ē\ *adj* **heav·i·er; -est 1 a** : having great weight **b** : weighty in proportion to bulk : having a high specific gravity ⟨gold is a *heavy* metal⟩ **2** : hard to bear; *esp* : GRIEVOUS ⟨a *heavy* sorrow⟩ **3** : of great import : SERIOUS ⟨words *heavy* with meaning⟩ **4 a** : borne down by something oppressive : BURDENED **b** : PREGNANT 1a; *esp* : approaching the time for giving birth **5 a** : slow or dull from loss of vitality or resiliency : SLUGGISH **b** : lacking sparkle or vivacity ⟨a *heavy* writing style⟩ **c** : lacking mirth or gaiety : DOLEFUL **6** : dulled with weariness : DROWSY **7** : greater in volume or force than the average ⟨*heavy* traffic⟩ ⟨*heavy* seas⟩ **8 a** : OVERCAST ⟨*heavy* skies⟩ **b** : full of clay and inclined to hold water ⟨*heavy* soils⟩ **c** : coming as if from a depth : LOUD **d** : THICK ⟨a *heavy* growth of timber⟩ **e** : OPPRESSIVE ⟨a *heavy* odor⟩ **f** : STEEP, ACUTE ⟨a *heavy* grade⟩ **g** : LABORIOUS, DIFFICULT ⟨a *heavy* task⟩ **h** : using or consuming much : IMMODERATE ⟨a *heavy* smoker⟩ **9** : very rich and hard to digest ⟨a *heavy* dessert⟩ **10** : producing goods (as coal or steel) used in the production of other goods ⟨*heavy* industry⟩ **11** : heavily armed or armored ⟨*heavy* tank⟩ **12** : having stress [Old English *hefig*] — **heav·i·ness** *n*

²heavy *adv* : in a heavy manner : HEAVILY

³heavy *n, pl* **heav·ies 1** : HEAVYWEIGHT 2 **2 a** : a theatrical role or an actor representing a dignified or imposing person **b** : VILLAIN 4

heavy–du·ty \,hev-ē-'düt-ē, -'dyüt-\ *adj* : able or designed to withstand unusual strain

heavy–foot·ed \-'fut-əd\ *adj* : heavy and slow in movement

heavy–hand·ed \-'han-dəd\ *adj* **1** : CLUMSY 1 **2** : OPPRESSIVE 1,2 — **heavy–hand·ed·ly** *adv* — **heavy–hand·ed·ness** *n*

heavy–heart·ed \-'härt-əd\ *adj* : SAD 1, MELANCHOLY — **heavy–heart·ed·ly** *adv* — **heavy–heart·ed·ness** *n*

heavy hydrogen *n* : DEUTERIUM

heavy·set \,hev-ē-'set\ *adj* : being stocky and compact and sometimes tending to stoutness in build

heavy water *n* : water containing more than the usual proportion of heavy isotopes; *esp* : water enriched with deuterium

heavy·weight \'hev-ē-,wāt\ *n* **1** : one above average in weight **2** : one in the heaviest class of contestants; *esp* : a boxer weighing over 81 kilograms

He·bra·ic \hi-'brā-ik\ *adj* : of, relating to, or characteristic of the Hebrews or their language or culture

He·bra·ism \'hē-brā-,iz-əm\ *n* **1** : a characteristic feature of Hebrew occurring in another language **2** : the thought, spirit, or practice characteristic of the Hebrews

He·bra·ist \-,brā-əst\ *n* : a specialist in Hebrew and Hebraic studies

He·brew \'hē-,brü\ *n* **1** : a member of or descendant from one of a group of northern Semitic peoples including the Israelites; *esp* : ISRAELITE **2 a** : the Semitic language of the ancient Hebrews **b** : any of various later forms of this language [derived from Greek *Hebraios*, from Aramaic *'Ebrai*] — **Hebrew** *adj*

He·brews \'hē-,brüz\ *n* — see BIBLE table

hec·a·tomb \'hek-ə-,tōm\ *n* **1** : an ancient Greek and Roman sacrifice of 100 oxen or cattle **2** : a great slaughter [Latin *hecatombe,* from Greek *hekatombē,* from *hekaton* "hundred" + *bous* "cow"]

heck·le \'hek-əl\ *vt* **heck·led; heck·ling** \'hek-ling, -ə-ling\ : to interrupt with questions or comments usually in order to annoy or hinder : BADGER [Middle English *hekelen,* from *heckele* "hackle"] — **heck·ler** \-lər, -ə-lər\ *n*

hect- *or* **hecto-** *combining form* : hundred [French, derived from Greek *hekaton*]

hect·are \'hek-,taər, -,teər, -,tär\ *n* — see METRIC SYSTEM table

hec·tic \'hek-tik\ *adj* **1** : of, relating to, or being a fluctuating but persistent fever (as in tuberculosis) **2** : having a hectic fever **3** : RED, FLUSHED **4** : filled with excitement or confusion [derived from Late Latin *hecticus,* from Greek *hektikos* "habitual, consumptive", from *echein* "to have, hold"] — **hec·ti·cal·ly** \-ti-kə-lē, -klē\ *adv*

hec·to·gram \'hek-tə-,gram\ *n* — see METRIC SYSTEM table

hec·to·graph \-,graf\ *n* : a machine for making copies of a writing or drawing — **hectograph** *vt* — **hec·to·graph·ic** \,hek-tə-'graf-ik\ *adj*

hec·to·li·ter \'hek-tə-,lēt-ər\ *n* — see METRIC SYSTEM table

hec·to·me·ter \'hek-tə-,mēt-ər\ *n* — see METRIC SYSTEM table

hec·tor \'hek-tər\ *vb* **hec·tored; hec·tor·ing** \-tə-ring, -tring\ **1** : to act like a bully : SWAGGER **2** : to intimidate by bluster or personal pressure [*Hector,* Trojan champion]

he'd \hēd, ,hēd, ēd\ : he had : he would

hed·dle \'hed-l\ *n* : one of the sets of parallel cords or wires that with their mounting compose the harness used to guide warp threads in a loom [probably derived from Old English *hefeld*]

¹hedge \'hej\ *n* **1 a** : a fence or boundary formed by a dense row of shrubs or low trees **b** : a fence or wall marking a boundary or forming a barrier **2** : a protection against financial loss **3** : a statement that intentionally avoids a direct answer or a promise [Old English *hecg*]

²hedge *vb* **1** : to enclose or protect with or as if with a hedge **2** : to obstruct with or as if with a barrier : HINDER ⟨*hedged* in by restrictions⟩ **3** : to protect oneself from losing by making a second balancing transaction ⟨*hedge* on a bet⟩ **4** : to avoid giving a direct or definite answer or promise ⟨*hedged* when asked their opinion⟩ — **hedg·er** *n*

³hedge *adj* : of, relating to, or designed for a hedge

hedge·hog \'hej-,hog, -,häg\ *n* **1** : an Old World insect-eating mammal having sharp spines mixed with the hair on its back and able to roll itself up into a spiny ball **2** : PORCUPINE

hedge·hop \-,häp\ *vi* : to fly an airplane so low that it is sometimes necessary to climb to avoid obstacles (as trees) [back-formation from *hedgehopper*] — **hedge·hop·per** *n*

hedge·row \-,rō\ *n* : HEDGE 1a; *esp* : one bounding or separating fields

he·do·nism \'hēd-n-,iz-əm\ *n* **1** : a doctrine that pleasure or happiness is the sole or chief good in life **2** : a way of life based on hedonism [Greek *hēdonē* "pleasure"] — **he·do·nist** \-n-əst\ *n* — **he·do·nis·tic** \,hēd-n-'is-tik\ *adj*

hedgehog 1

\ə\ abut		\ng\ sing	
\ər\ further		\ō\ bone	
\a\ mat		\ȯ\ saw	
\ā\ take		\ȯi\ coin	
\ä\ cot, cart		\th\ thin	
\au̇\ out		\th\ this	
\ch\ chin		\ü\ food	
\e\ pet		\u̇\ foot	
\ē\ easy		\y\ yet	
\g\ go		\yü\ few	
\i\ tip		\yu̇\ cure	
\ī\ life		\zh\ vision	
\j\ job			

-he·dral \'hē-drəl\ *adj combining form* : having (such) a surface or (such or so many) surfaces ⟨di*hedral*⟩ [Greek *hedra* "seat"]

-he·dron \'hē-drən\ *n combining form, pl* **-hedrons** or **-he·dra** \-drə\ : crystal or geometric figure having a (specified) form or number of surfaces ⟨rhombo*hedron*⟩ [Greek *hedra* "seat"]

hee·bie-jee·bies \ˌhē-bē-'jē-bēz\ *n pl* : JITTERS, WILLIES [coined by Billy DeBeck, died 1942, American cartoonist]

¹heed \'hēd\ *vb* **1** : to pay attention **2** : to concern oneself with : MIND [Old English *hēdan*]

²heed *n* : ATTENTION 1, NOTICE ⟨give *heed* to my words⟩

heed·ful \'hēd-fəl\ *adj* : taking heed ⟨*heedful* of the rights of others⟩ — **heed·ful·ly** \-fə-lē\ *adv* — **heed·ful·ness** *n*

heed·less \-ləs\ *adj* : not taking heed : INATTENTIVE ⟨*heedless* of danger⟩ — **heed·less·ly** *adv* — **heed·less·ness** *n*

hee-haw \'hē-ˌhȯ\ *n* **1** : the bray of a donkey **2** : a loud rude laugh : GUFFAW [imitative] — **hee-haw** *vi*

¹heel \'hēl\ *n* **1 a** : the back part of the human foot behind the arch and below the ankle; *also* : the corresponding part of a lower vertebrate **b** : the part of the palm of the hand nearest the wrist **2 a** : a part (as of a shoe) that covers the human heel **b** : a solid attachment of a shoe or boot forming the back of the sole under the heel of the foot **3** : something resembling a heel in form, function, or position: as **a** (1) : one of the crusty ends of a loaf of bread (2) : one of the rind ends of a cheese **b** (1) : the after end of a ship's keel (2) : the lower end of a mast **c** : the base of a tuber or cutting of a plant used for propagation **d** : the base of a ladder **4** : a contemptible person [Old English *hēla*] — **heeled** \'hēld\ *adj* — **heel·less** \'hēl-ləs\ *adj* — **on the heels of** : immediately following — **to heel** **1** : close behind **2** : into agreement or into line

²heel *vt* **1** : to furnish with a heel **2** : to supply especially with money ⟨a well-*heeled* customer⟩ **3** : to follow closely ⟨a dog *heeling* his master⟩ — **heel·er** *n*

³heel *vb* : to tilt or cause to tilt to one side : TIP ⟨a boat *heeling* badly⟩ [Old English *hieldan*]

⁴heel *n* : a tilt to one side

heel-and-toe \ˌhē-lən-'tō\ *adj* : marked by a stride in which the heel of one foot touches the ground before the toe of the other foot leaves it ⟨a *heel-and-toe* walking race⟩

heel·tap \'hēl-ˌtap\ *n* **1** : a lift for the heel of a shoe **2** : a small quantity of liquor remaining (as in a glass after drinking)

¹heft \'heft\ *n* : physical or figurative weight [derived from *heave*]

²heft *vt* **1** : to heave up : HOIST **2** : to test the weight of by lifting

hefty \'hef-tē\ *adj* **heft·i·er; -est** **1** : quite heavy **2 a** : marked by bigness, bulk, and usually strength **b** : POWERFUL, MIGHTY **c** : impressively large : SUBSTANTIAL — **heft·i·ly** \-tə-lē\ *adv* — **heft·i·ness** \-tē-nəs\ *n*

he·gem·o·ny \hi-'jem-ə-nē, 'hej-ə-ˌmō-nē\ *n* : dominant influence or authority especially of one nation over others [Greek *hēgemonia*, from *hēgemōn* "leader", from *hēgeisthai* "to lead"]

he·gi·ra *or* **he·ji·ra** \hi-'jī-rə, 'hej-ə-rə\ *n* : a journey especially when undertaken to seek refuge away from a dangerous or undesirable environment [the *Hegira*, flight of Muhammad from Mecca in A.D. 622, from Medieval Latin, from Arabic *hijrah*, literally, "flight"]

heif·er \'hef-ər\ *n* : a young cow; *esp* : one that has not had a calf [Old English *hēahfore*]

heigh-ho \'hī-'hō,'hā-\ *interj* — used typically to express boredom, weariness, or sadness or sometimes as a cry of encouragement

height \'hīt, 'hītth\ *n* **1 a** : the highest part : SUMMIT **b** : the highest or most advanced point or level ⟨the *height* of stupidity⟩ **2 a** : the distance from the bottom to the top of something standing upright **b** : the extent of elevation above a level : ALTITUDE **3** : the condition of being tall or high **4 a** : an extent of land rising to a considerable degree above the surrounding country **b** : a high point or position [Old English *hiehthu*] □ SYN ELEVATION, ALTITUDE: HEIGHT refers to something measured vertically whether high or low ⟨a wall 2 meters in *height*⟩ ⟨lettering not more than one centimeter in *height*⟩ ELEVATION and ALTITUDE suggest reckoning of height by angular measurement or atmospheric pressure; ALTITUDE is preferable when referring to vertical distance above the surface of the earth or above sea level and ELEVATION is used especially in reference to vertical height on land ⟨fly at an *altitude* of 10,000 meters⟩ ⟨Mexico City has a high *elevation*⟩

height·en \'hīt-n\ *vb* **height·ened; height·en·ing** \'hīt-ning, -n-ing\ **1 a** : to increase the amount or degree of : AUGMENT ⟨*heightened* the citizens' awareness⟩ **b** : to make or become brighter or more intense : DEEPEN ⟨excitement *heightened* the pinkness of their cheeks⟩ **c** : to bring out more strongly : point up ⟨*heighten* a contrast⟩ **2 a** : to raise high or higher : ELEVATE **b** : to raise above the ordinary or trite SYN see INTENSIFY

hei·nous \'hā-nəs\ *adj* : hatefully or shockingly evil : ABOMINABLE [Middle French *haineus*, from *haine* "hate", from *hair* "to hate", of Germanic origin] SYN see OUTRAGEOUS — **hei·nous·ly** *adv* — **hei·nous·ness** *n*

heir \'aər, 'eər\ *n* **1** : a person who inherits or is entitled to inherit property **2** : a person who has legal claim to a title or a throne when the person holding it dies [Old French, from Latin *heres*] — **heir·ship** \-ˌship\ *n*

heir apparent *n, pl* **heirs apparent** : an heir who cannot legally be deprived of the right to succeed (as to a throne or a title)

heir·ess \'ar-əs, 'er-\ *n* : a woman who is an heir; *also* : one who is wealthy through inheritance

heir·loom \'aər-ˌlüm, 'eər-\ *n* : a piece of personal property handed down by inheritance for several generations [Middle English *heirlome*, from *heir* + *lome* "implement"]

heir presumptive *n, pl* **heirs presumptive** : an heir whose present right to inherit could be lost through the birth of a nearer relative

¹heist \'hīst\ *vt* **1** *chiefly dialect* : HOIST **2** *slang* **a** : to commit armed robbery on **b** : STEAL 2a [alteration of *hoist*]

²heist *n, slang* : armed robbery : HOLDUP; *also* : THEFT

held *past of* HOLD

heli- *or* **helio-** *combining form* : sun ⟨*helio*centric⟩ [Greek *hēlios*]

helic- *or* **helico-** *combining form* : helix : spiral ⟨*helic*al⟩ [Greek *helik-*, *helix* "spiral"]

hel·i·cal \'hel-i-kəl, 'hē-li-\ *adj* : of, relating to, or having the form of a helix; *also* : SPIRAL 1 — **hel·i·cal·ly** \-kə-lē, -klē\ *adv*

hel·i·con \'hel-ə-ˌkän, -i-kən\ *n* : a large circular bass tuba used in military bands [probably derived from Greek *helix* "spiral"]

¹he·li·cop·ter \'hel-ə-ˌkäp-tər, 'hē-lə-\ *n* : an aircraft that is supported in the air by propellers revolving on a vertical axis [French *hélicoptère*, from Greek *helix* "helix" + *pteron* "wing"]

²helicopter *vb* : to travel or transport by helicopter

he·lio·cen·tric \ˌhē-lē-ō-'sen-trik\ *adj* **1** : referred to or measured from the sun's center or appearing as if seen from it ⟨a *heliocentric* position⟩ **2** : having or relating to the sun as a center ⟨a *heliocentric* theory of the solar system⟩ — compare GEOCENTRIC

he·lio·graph \'hē-lē-ə-ˌgraf\ *n* : an apparatus for signaling by means of the sun's rays reflected from a mirror — **heliograph** *vb*

he·lio·trope \'hēl-yə-ˌtrōp\ *n* **1** : any of a genus of herbs or shrubs related to the forget-me-not — compare GARDEN HELIOTROPE **2** : BLOODSTONE **3 a** : a mod-

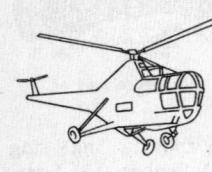

¹helicopter

erate purple **b** : a moderate reddish purple [Latin *he-liotropium*, from Greek *hēliotropion*, from *hēlios* "sun" + *tropos* "turn"; from its flowers turning toward the sun]

he·li·ot·ro·pism \,hē-lē-'ä-trə-,piz-əm\ *n* : phototropism in which sunlight is the orienting stimulus — **he·lio·tro·pic** \,hē-lē-ə-'trōp-ik, -'träp-\ *adj*

he·li·port \'hel-ə-,pōrt, 'hē-lə-, -,pȯrt\ *n* : a landing and takeoff place for a helicopter

he·li·um \'hē-lē-əm\ *n* : a light colorless nonflammable gaseous chemical element found in various natural gases — see ELEMENT table [New Latin, from Greek *hēlios* "sun"; from its first being observed in the sun's atmosphere]

he·lix \'hē-liks\ *n, pl* **he·li·ces** \'hel-ə-,sēz, 'hē-lə-\ *also* **he·lix·es** \'hē-lik-səz\ **1** : something (as a wire coiled around a cylinder, a cone-shaped wire spring, or a corkscrew) spiral in form **2** : the incurved rim of the external ear **3** : a curve traced on a cylinder by a point moving at a constant angle to the straight lines parallel to the axis and lying in the surface; *also* : SPIRAL 1b [Latin, from Greek]

hell \'hel\ *n* **1** : a nether world in which the dead are held to continue to exist : HADES **2** : a place or state of punishment for the wicked after death : the home of evil spirits **3** : a place or condition of misery or wickedness **4** : something that causes torment; *esp* : a severe scolding [Old English]

he'll \hēl, ,hēl, hil, ēl, il\ : he shall : he will

hell·ben·der \'hel-,ben-dər\ *n* : a large aquatic salamander of the Ohio valley

hell–bent \-,bent\ *adj* **1** : stubbornly and often recklessly determined **2** : moving at full speed

hell·cat \-,kat\ *n* : a violently temperamental person; *esp* : SHREW 2

hel·le·bore \'hel-ə-,bōr, -,bȯr\ *n* **1 a** : any of a genus of herbs of the buttercup family **b** : the dried root of a hellebore formerly used in medicine **2** : a poisonous herb of the lily family; *also* : its dried root or a product of this containing alkaloids used in medicine and insecticides [Latin *helleborus*, from Greek *helleboros*]

Hel·lene \'hel-,ēn\ *n* : GREEK 1 [Greek *Hellēn*] — **Hel·len·ic** \he-'len-ik, hə-\ *adj*

Hel·le·nism \'hel-ə-,niz-əm\ *n* **1** : devotion to or imitation of especially ancient Greek thought, customs, or styles **2** : Greek civilization **3** : a body of humanistic and classical ideals associated with ancient Greece

Hel·le·nist \-nəst\ *n* **1** : a person living in Hellenistic times Greek in language, outlook, and way of life but not in ancestry; *esp* : a hellenized Jew **2** : a specialist in the language or culture of ancient Greece

Hel·le·nis·tic \,hel-ə-'nis-tik\ *adj* **1** : of or relating to the cosmopolitan culture with blended Greek and eastern elements that followed the conquests of Alexander the Great **2** : of or relating to the Hellenists — **Hel·le·nis·ti·cal·ly** \-ti-kə-lē, -klē\ *adv*

hel·le·nize \'hel-ə-,nīz\ *vb, often cap* : to make or become Greek or Hellenistic in form or culture — **hel·le·ni·za·tion** \,hel-ə-nə-'zā-shən\ *n, often cap*

hell·er \'hel-ər\ *n, chiefly dialect* : HELLION

hell·eri \'hel-ə-,rī, -rē\ *n* : a brightly colored hybrid tropical fish [C. *Heller*, 20th century tropical fish collector]

hell·gram·mite \'hel-grə-,mīt\ *n* : the aquatic larva of a dobsonfly much used as fish bait [origin unknown]

hel·lion \'hel-yən\ *n* : a troublesome or mischievous person [probably from earlier *hallion* "scamp"]

hell·ish \'hel-ish\ *adj* : of, resembling, or befitting hell : DEVILISH — **hell·ish·ly** *adv* — **hell·ish·ness** *n*

hel·lo \hə-'lō, he-\ *n, pl* **hellos** : an expression or gesture of greeting — used interjectionally in greeting, in answering the telephone, or to express surprise [alteration of *hollo*]

¹helm \'helm\ *n* : HELMET 1 [Old English]

²helm *vt* : to cover or furnish with a helmet

³helm *n* **1** : a lever or wheel controlling the rudder of a ship for steering; *also* : the entire apparatus for steering a ship **2** : a position of control ⟨at the *helm* of the business⟩ [Old English *helma*]

hel·met \'hel-mət\ *n* **1** : a covering or enclosing headpiece of ancient or medieval armor **2** : any of various protective head coverings usually made of a hard material to resist impact **3** : something resembling a helmet [Middle French, from *helme* "helmet", of Germanic origin] — **hel·met·like** \-,līk\ *adj*

hel·minth \'hel-,minth, -,mintth\ *n* : a parasitic worm; *esp* : an intestinal worm (as a tapeworm) [Greek *helminth-, helmis*] — **hel·min·thic** \hel-'min-thik, -'mint-\ *adj*

hel·min·thi·a·sis \,hel-,min-'thī-ə-səs\ *n* : infestation with or disease caused by parasitic worms

hel·min·thol·o·gy \-'thäl-ə-jē\ *n* : a branch of zoology concerned with the study of parasitic worms

helms·man \'helmz-mən\ *n* : the person at the helm : STEERSMAN

hel·ot \'hel-ət\ *n* **1** *cap* : a member of a class of serfs of ancient Sparta **2** : SLAVE 1 [Latin *Helotes*, pl., from Greek *Heilōtes*] — **hel·ot·ism** \'hel-ət-,iz-əm\ *n* — **hel·ot·ry** \-ə-trē\ *n*

¹help \'help, *South also* 'hep\ *vb* **1** : to give aid or assistance ⟨*help* a child with a lesson⟩ **2 a** : REMEDY, RELIEVE ⟨rest *helps* a cold⟩ **b** : to get (oneself) out of a difficulty ⟨you must learn to *help* yourself⟩ **3** : to further the advancement of : PROMOTE ⟨*helping* industrial development with loans⟩ **4 a** : to change for the better ⟨learn to live with what you can't *help*⟩ **b** : to refrain from ⟨couldn't *help* laughing⟩ **c** : to keep from occurring : PREVENT ⟨they couldn't *help* the accident⟩ **5** : to serve with food or drink especially at a meal — often used with *to* **6** : to appropriate for the use of (oneself) [Old English *helpan*] — **cannot help but** : cannot but — **so help me** : on my word : believe it or not

²help *n* **1** : an act or instance of helping : AID, ASSISTANCE ⟨give *help*⟩ **2** : the state of being helped : RELIEF ⟨a situation beyond *help*⟩ **3** : a person or a thing that helps ⟨a *help* in time of trouble⟩ **4** : a hired helper or a body of hired helpers ⟨hire additional *help* in a business⟩

help·er \'hel-pər\ *n* : one that helps; *esp* : a relatively unskilled worker who assists a skilled worker usually by manual labor

helper T cell *n* : a T cell that participates in an immune response by recognizing a foreign antigen and secreting substances promoting lymphocyte proliferation, that carries molecular markers on its surface to which HIV attaches, and that is reduced to 20 percent or less of normal numbers in AIDS — called also *helper cell*

help·ful \'help-fəl\ *adj* : furnishing help ⟨a *helpful* friend⟩ ⟨a *helpful* book⟩ — **help·ful·ly** \-fə-lē\ *adv* — **help·ful·ness** *n*

help·ing \'hel-ping\ *n* : a portion of food : SERVING

helping verb *n* : an auxiliary verb

help·less \'hel-pləs\ *adj* **1** : lacking protection or support : DEFENSELESS **2** : lacking strength or effectiveness : POWERLESS ⟨was *helpless* to prevent them from going⟩ — **help·less·ly** *adv* — **help·less·ness** *n*

help·mate \'help-,māt\ *n* : one that is a companion and helper [by folk etymology from *helpmeet*]

help·meet \-,mēt\ *n* : HELPMATE [²*help* + *meet*, adj.]

¹hel·ter–skel·ter \,hel-tər-'skel-tər\ *adv* **1** : in headlong disorder : PELL-MELL **2** : in random order : HAPHAZARDLY [perhaps from Middle English *skelten* "to come, go"]

²helter–skelter *n* : a disorderly confusion : TURMOIL

³helter–skelter *adj* **1** : confusedly hurried : PRECIPITATE ⟨*helter-skelter* rush-hour traffic⟩ **2** : HIT-OR-MISS, HAPHAZARD ⟨does things in a *helter-skelter* manner⟩

helve \'helv\ *n* : a handle of a tool or weapon : HAFT [Old English *hielfe*]

hellbender

helmet 2

\ə\ abut	\ng\ sing
\ər\ further	\ō\ bone
\a\ mat	\ȯ\ saw
\ā\ take	\ȯi\ coin
\ä\ cot, cart	\th\ thin
\au̇\ out	\th\ this
\ch\ chin	\ü\ food
\e\ pet	\u̇\ foot
\ē\ easy	\y\ yet
\g\ go	\yü\ few
\i\ tip	\yu̇\ cure
\ī\ life	\zh\ vision
\j\ job	

Hel·ve·tian \hel-'vē-shən\ *adj* : of or relating to the Helvetii or Helvetia : SWISS — **Helvetian** *n*

Hel·ve·tii \-shē-,ī\ *n pl* : an early Celtic people of western Switzerland in the time of Julius Caesar [Latin]

¹**hem** \'hem\ *n* : a border of a garment or cloth; *esp* : one made by folding back an edge and sewing it down [Old English]

²**hem** *vb* **hemmed; hem·ming 1** : to finish with or make a hem in sewing **2** : to surround in a restrictive manner : CONFINE ⟨*hemmed* in by the enemy⟩ — **hem·mer** *n*

³**hem** *vi* **hemmed; hem·ming 1** : to utter the sound represented by *hem* **2** : EQUIVOCATE ⟨*hemmed* and hawed and refused to act⟩

⁴**hem** *usually read as* 'hem\ *interj* — often used to indicate a vocalized pause in speaking [imitative]

hem- *or* **hemo-** *or* **haem-** *or* **haemo-** *combining form* : blood ⟨*hemo*cyanin⟩ [Greek *haima*]

he–man \'hē-'man\ *n* : a strong virile man

hemat- *or* **hemato-** *or* **haemat-** *or* **haemato-** *combining form* : blood ⟨*hemato*logy⟩ [Greek *haimat-*, *haima*]

he·ma·tite \'hē-mə-,tīt\ *n* : a mineral Fe$_2$O$_3$ consisting of ferric oxide, constituting an important iron ore, and occurring in crystals or in a red earthy form

he·ma·tol·o·gy \,hē-mə-'täl-ə-jē\ *n* : a branch of biology that deals with the blood and blood-forming organs — **he·ma·to·log·ic** \'hē-mət-l-'äj-ik\ *adj* — **he·ma·tol·o·gist** \,hē-mə-'täl-ə-jəst\ *n*

he·ma·to·ma \,hē-mə-'tō-mə\ *n, pl* **-mas** *or* **-ma·ta** : a blood-containing tumor or swelling

he·ma·tox·y·lin \,hē-mə-'täk-sə-lən\ *n* : a crystalline compound found in logwood and used chiefly as a biological stain [New Latin *Haematoxylon*, genus of plants that includes the logwood]

heme \'hēm\ *n* : a deep red iron-containing pigment obtained from hemoglobin [derived from Greek *haima* "blood"]

hem·ero·cal·lis \,hem-ə-rō-'kal-əs\ *n* : DAY LILY [Greek *hēmerokalles*, from *hēmera* "day" + *kallos* "beauty"]

hemi- *prefix* : half — compare SEMI [Greek *hēmi-*]

hemi·chor·date \,hem-i-'kórd-ət, -'kór-,dāt\ *n* : any of a small group (Hemichordata) of lowly marine animals (as an acorn worm) resembling worms but having a proboscis that contains a structure held to be a degenerate notochord — compare CHORDATE

he·mip·ter·an \hi-'mip-tə-rən\ *n* : any of a large order (Hemiptera) of insects including the true bugs (as the bedbug and chinch bug) and sometimes related forms (as the plant lice) and having flattened bodies, two pairs of wings, and heads with piercing and sucking organs [Greek *pteron* "wing"] — **he·mip·ter·ous** \-tə-rəs\ *adj*

hemi·sphere \'hem-ə-,sfier\ *n* **1** : the northern or southern half of the earth divided by the equator or the eastern or western half divided by a meridian **2** : one of two half spheres formed by a plane through the sphere's center **3** : CEREBRAL HEMISPHERE — **hemi·spher·ic** \,hem-ə-'sfiər-ik, -'sfer-\ *or* **hemi·spher·i·cal** \-'sfir-i-kəl, -'sfer-\ *adj*

hemi·stich \'hem-i-,stik\ *n* : half a poetic line usually divided by a caesura [Latin *hemistichium*, from Greek *hēmistichion*, from *hēmi-* + *stichos* "line, verse"]

hem·line \'hem-,līn\ *n* : the line formed by the lower edge of a dress, skirt, or coat

hem·lock \'hem-,läk\ *n* **1** : any of several poisonous herbs of the carrot family having finely cut leaves and small white flowers **2** : any of a genus of evergreen trees of the pine family; *also* : the soft light splintery wood of a hemlock [Old English *hemlic*]

hemo- — see HEM-

he·mo·cy·a·nin \,hē-mō-'sī-ə-nən\ *n* : a copper-containing respiratory pigment in the blood of some mollusks and arthropods

he·mo·glo·bin \'hē-mə-,glō-bən\ *n* : an iron-containing protein that is the chief means of oxygen transport in the vertebrate body where it occurs in the red blood cells and is able to combine loosely with oxygen in regions (as the lungs) of high concentration and release it in regions (as the visceral tissues) of low concentration; *also* : any of various similar iron-containing compounds [derived from Greek *haima* "blood" + Latin *globus* "globe"]

hemoglobin S *n* : a hemoglobin that occurs in the red blood cells in sickle-cell anemia and sickle-cell trait

he·mo·phil·ia \,hē-mə-'fil-ē-ə\ *n* : a usually hereditary tendency to uncontrollable bleeding — **he·mo·phil·i·ac** \-ē-,ak\ *adj or n*

hem·or·rhage \'hem-rij, -ə-rij\ *n* : a copious discharge of blood from the blood vessels [Latin *haemorrhagia*, from Greek *haimorrhagia*, from *haima* "blood" + *rhēgnyai* "to break"] — **hemorrhage** *vi* — **hem·or·rhag·ic** \,hem-ə-'raj-ik\ *adj*

hem·or·rhoid \'hem-,róid, -ə-,róid\ *n* : a swollen mass of dilated veins situated at or just within the anus — usually used in pl.; called also *piles* [derived from Greek *haimorrhoides* "hemorrhoids", from *haima* "blood" + *rhein* "to flow"] — **hem·or·rhoid·al** \,hem-ə-'roid-l\ *adj*

hemp \'hemp\ *n* : a tall Asiatic herb of the mulberry family widely grown for its tough bast fiber that is used especially in cordage or for its flowers and leaves that yield hashish and marijuana [Old English *hænep*] — **hemp·en** \'hem-pən\ *adj*

¹**hem·stitch** \'hem-,stich\ *vt* : to embroider (fabric) by drawing out parallel threads and stitching the exposed threads in groups to form various designs — **hem·stitch·er** *n*

²**hemstitch** *n* **1** : decorative needlework **2** : a stitch used in hemstitching

hen \'hen\ *n* **1** : a female domestic fowl especially over a year old; *also* : a female bird **2** : the female of various mostly aquatic animals (as lobsters or fish) [Old English *henn*]

hen·bane \'hen-,bān\ *n* : a poisonous sticky-leaved Old World herb related to the nightshades

hence \'hens\ *adv* **1** : from this place : AWAY **2** : from this time ⟨a week *hence*⟩ **3** : CONSEQUENTLY, THEREFORE ⟨was a newcomer and *hence* had no close friends in the city⟩ [Middle English *hennes, henne*, from Old English *heonan*]

hence·forth \-,fōrth, -,fórth\ *adv* : from this point on

hence·for·ward \hens-'fór-wərd\ *adv* : HENCEFORTH

hench·man \'hench-mən\ *n* : a trusted follower or supporter ⟨a gangster's *henchman*⟩ [Middle English *hengestman* "groom", from *hengest* "stallion" + *man*]

hen·e·quen \'hen-i-kən, ,hen-i-'kən\ *n* : a strong hard cordage fiber from the leaves of a tropical American agave; *also* : this plant [Spanish *henequén*]

¹**hen·na** \'hen-ə\ *n* **1** : an Old World tropical shrub with clusters of fragrant white flowers **2** : a reddish brown dye obtained from leaves of the henna and used especially on hair [Arabic *ḥinnā'*]

²**henna** *vb* **hen·naed** \'hen-əd\; **hen·na·ing** : to treat or dye with henna

hen·nery \'hen-ə-rē\ *n, pl* **-ner·ies** : a poultry farm; *also* : a poultry enclosure or house

hen party *n* : a party for women only

hen·peck \'hen-,pek\ *vt* : to subject (one's husband) to persistent nagging and domination

hen·ry \'hen-rē\ *n, pl* **henries** *also* **henrys** : the mks unit of inductance equal to the self-inductance of a circuit or the mutual inductance of two circuits in which the variation of one ampere per second results in an induced electromotive force of one volt [Joseph *Henry*, died 1878, American physicist]

hep \'hep\ *variant of* HIP

hep·a·rin \'hep-ə-rən\ *n* : a compound found especially in liver that slows the clotting of blood and is used medically [Greek *hēpar* "liver"]

he·pat·ic \hi-'pat-ik\ *adj* : of, relating to, affecting, or conveying to or away from the liver ⟨*hepatic* veins⟩

⟨*hepatic* arteries⟩ [Latin *hepaticus,* from Greek *hēpatikos,* from *hēpar* "liver"]

he·pat·i·ca \hi-ˌpat-i-kə\ *n* : any of a genus of herbs of the buttercup family with lobed leaves and delicate white, pink, or bluish flowers; *also* : one of these flowers [Medieval Latin, from Latin *hepaticus* "hepatic"]

hep·a·ti·tis \ˌhep-ə-ˈtīt-əs\ *n, pl* **-tit·i·des** \-ˈtit-ə-ˌdēz\ : inflammation of the liver; *also* : an acute virus disease marked by hepatitis, jaundice, fever, and gastrointestinal symptoms

hepped up \ˈhep-ˈtəp\ *adj* : ENTHUSIASTIC ⟨all *hepped up* about the new job⟩

Hep·ple·white \ˈhep-əl-ˌhwīt, -ˌwīt\ *adj* : of or relating to a style of furniture originating in late 18th century England [George *Hepplewhite,* died 1786, English cabinetmaker]

hepta- *or* **hept-** *combining form* : seven ⟨*hepta*meter⟩ [Greek *hepta*]

hep·ta·gon \ˈhep-tə-ˌgän\ *n* : a polygon of seven angles and seven sides — **hep·tag·o·nal** \hep-ˈtag-ən-l\ *adj*

hep·tam·e·ter \hep-ˈtam-ət-ər\ *n* : a line of verse consisting of seven metrical feet

¹her \hər, ər, ˌhər\ *adj* : of or relating to her or herself especially as possessor, agent, or object of an action ⟨*her* house⟩ ⟨*her* research⟩ ⟨*her* rescue⟩ — compare ¹SHE 1 [Old English *hiere,* genitive of *hēo* "she"]

²her \ər, hər, ˈhər\ *pron, objective case of* SHE

¹her·ald \ˈher-əld\ *n* **1 a** : an official at a medieval tournament **b** : an officer acting as messenger between leaders of warring parties **c** : an officer responsible for granting and registering coats of arms **2** : an official crier or messenger **3** : one that precedes or foreshadows : HARBINGER [Middle French *hiraut,* of Germanic origin]

²herald *vt* **1** : to give notice of : ANNOUNCE **2** : to greet especially with enthusiasm : HAIL

he·ral·dic \he-ˈral-dik\ *adj* : of or relating to heralds or heraldry — **he·ral·di·cal·ly** \-di-kə-lē, -klē\ *adv*

her·ald·ry \ˈher-əl-drē\ *n, pl* **-ries** **1** : the art or science of tracing a person's family history and determining its coat of arms **2** : PAGEANTRY 2

herb \ˈərb, ˈhərb\ *n* **1** : an annual, biennial, or perennial seed plant that does not develop persistent woody tissue but dies down at the end of a growing season — compare SHRUB **2** : a plant or plant part used in medicine or for seasoning [Old French *herbe,* from Latin *herba* "grass, herb"] — **her·ba·ceous** \ˌər-ˈbā-shəs, ˌhər-\ *adj* — **herb·like** \ˈərb-ˌlīk, ˈhərb-\ *adj* — **herby** \ˈər-bē, ˈhər-\ *adj*

herb·age \ˈər-bij, ˈhər-\ *n* **1** : herbaceous vegetation (as grass) especially when used for grazing **2** : the juicy parts of herbaceous plants

¹herb·al \ˈər-bəl, ˈhər-\ *n* : a book about plants and especially their medical properties

²herbal *adj* : of, relating to, or made of herbs

herb·al·ist \ˈər-bə-ləst, ˈhər-\ *n* : one that collects, grows, or deals in herbs

her·bar·i·um \ˌər-ˈbar-ē-əm, ˌhər-, -ˈber-\ *n, pl* **-ia** \-ē-ə\ **1** : a collection of dried plant specimens **2** : a place that houses an herbarium

her·bi·cide \ˈər-bə-ˌsīd, ˈhər-\ *n* : an agent used to destroy or inhibit plant growth — **her·bi·cid·al** \ˌər-bə-ˈsīd-l, ˌhər-\ *adj*

her·biv·o·ra \ˌər-ˈbiv-ə-rə, ˌhər-\ *n pl* : animals that are herbivores

her·bi·vore \ˈər-bə-ˌvōr, ˈhər-, -ˌvȯr\ *n* : a plant-eating animal; *esp* : UNGULATE [derived from Latin *herba* "grass" + *vorare* "to devour"] — **her·biv·o·rous** \ˌər-ˈbiv-ə-rəs, ˌhər-\ *adj*

her·cu·le·an \ˌhər-kyə-ˈlē-ən, ˌhər-ˈkyü-lē-\ *adj, often cap* : of extraordinary power, size, or difficulty ⟨a *herculean* task⟩ [*Hercules,* mythical hero]

Her·cu·les \ˈhər-kyə-ˌlēz\ *n* : a northern constellation between Corona Borealis and Lyra

Her·cu·les'–club \ˌhər-kyə-ˌlēz-ˈkləb\ *n* : a small prickly tree of the eastern United States that is related to the ginseng

¹herd \ˈhərd\ *n* **1** : a number of animals of one kind kept or living together **2** : CROWD 2 [Old English *heord*]

²herd *vb* : to keep, assemble, or move in or as if in a herd — **herd·er** *n*

herds·man \ˈhərdz-mən\ *n* : a manager, breeder, or tender of livestock

¹here \ˈhiər\ *adv* **1 a** : in or at this place ⟨turn *here*⟩ **b** : NOW ⟨*here* it's morning already⟩ **2** : at or in this point or particular ⟨*here* we agree⟩ **3** : in the present life or state **4** : to this place ⟨come *here*⟩ **5** — used interjectionally in rebuke or encouragement ⟨*here,* that's enough⟩ [Old English *hēr*]

²here *n* : this place ⟨get away from *here*⟩

here·abouts \ˈhir-ə-ˌbaùts\ *or* **here·about** \-ˌbaùt\ *adv* : in this vicinity

¹here·af·ter \hir-ˈaf-tər\ *adv* **1** : after this **2** : in some future time or state

²hereafter *n, often cap* **1** : FUTURE 1a **2** : an existence beyond earthly life ⟨belief in the *hereafter*⟩

here and there *adv* : in one place and another

here·by \hir-ˈbī\ *adv* : by this means

her·e·dit·a·ment \ˌher-ə-ˈdit-ə-mənt\ *n* : heritable property [Medieval Latin *hereditamentum,* from Late Latin *hereditare* "to inherit", from Latin *heres* "heir"]

he·red·i·tary \hə-ˈred-ə-ˌter-ē\ *adj* **1** : genetically transmitted from parent to offspring ⟨*hereditary* traits⟩ **2 a** : received or passing by inheritance ⟨*hereditary* rank⟩ **b** : having title or possession through inheritance ⟨*hereditary* rulers⟩ **3** : of a kind established by tradition **4** : of or relating to inheritance or heredity

he·red·i·ty \hə-ˈred-ət-ē\ *n, pl* **-ties** **1** : the genetic traits including both genes and their expressed characters derived from one's ancestors **2** : the transmission of qualities from ancestor to descendant through genes [Middle French *heredité* "inheritance", from Latin *hereditas,* from *hered-, heres* "heir"]

Her·e·ford \ˈhər-fərd sometimes ˈher-ə-\ *n* : any of an English breed of hardy red white-faced beef cattle widely raised in the western United States [*Hereford* county, England]

here·in \hir-ˈin\ *adv* : in this

here·of \hir-ˈəv, -ˈäv\ *adv* : of this

here·on \-ˈȯn, -ˈän\ *adv* : on this

her·e·sy \ˈher-ə-sē\ *n, pl* **-sies** **1** : religious opinion contrary to the doctrines of a church **2** : opinion or doctrine contrary to a dominant or generally accepted belief [Old French *heresie,* from Late Latin *haeresis,* from Greek *hairesis* "action of taking, choice, sect", from *hairein* "to take"]

her·e·tic \ˈher-ə-ˌtik\ *n* : a person who believes or teaches heretical doctrines

he·ret·i·cal \hə-ˈret-i-kəl\ *also* **her·e·tic** \ˈher-ə-ˌtik, hə-ˈret-ik\ *adj* : of, relating to, or characterized by heresy : UNORTHODOX SYN see HETERODOX — **he·ret·i·cal·ly** \hə-ˈret-i-kə-lē, -klē\ *adv* — **he·ret·i·cal·ness** \-kəl-nəs\ *n*

here·to \hir-ˈtü\ *adv* : to this document

here·to·fore \ˈhirt-ə-ˌfōr, -ˌfȯr\ *adv* : up to this time : HITHERTO

here·un·der \hir-ˈən-dər\ *adv* : under or in accordance with this document or agreement

here·un·to \hir-ˈən-tü\ *adv* : to this

here·up·on \ˈhir-ə-ˌpȯn, -ˌpän\ *adv* : on this : immediately after this

here·with \hir-ˈwith, -ˈwith\ *adv* : with this : enclosed in this

her·i·ot \ˈher-ē-ət\ *n* : a feudal duty or tribute due under English law to a lord on the death of a tenant [Old English *heregeatwe* "military equipment", from *here* "army" + *geatwe* "equipment"]

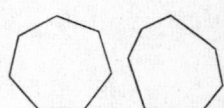

heptagon

her·i·ta·ble \'her-ət-ə-bəl\ *adj* : HEREDITARY 1, 2 — **her·i·ta·bil·i·ty** \,her-ət-ə-'bil-ət-ē\ *n*

her·i·tage \'her-ət-ij\ *n* **1** : property that descends to an heir **2** : something transmitted by or acquired from a predecessor : LEGACY **3** : TRADITION (America's Puritan *heritage*) [Middle French, from *heriter* "to inherit", from Late Latin *hereditare*, from Latin *heres* "heir"] □ SYN INHERITANCE: HERITAGE may imply anything passed on to heirs or succeeding generations, but applies usually to something other than actual property or material things (our *heritage* of freedom) INHERITANCE applies to anything acquired by an heir (received a large *inheritance* from an aunt) (this optimistic nature was considered a maternal *inheritance*)

her·maph·ro·dite \hər-'maf-rə-,dīt\ *n* : one that has both male and female reproductive organs [Latin *hermaphroditus*, from Greek *hermaphroditos*, from *Hermaphroditos* "Hermaphroditus"] — **her·maph·ro·dit·ic** \hər-,maf-rə-'dit-ik\ *adj*

her·met·ic \hər-'met-ik\ *adj* **1** : AIRTIGHT 1 **2** : completely resistant to outside influence [New Latin *hermeticus*, from *Hermes Trismegistus*, legendary inventor of a magic seal to keep vessels airtight] — **her·met·i·cal** \-'met-i-kəl\ *adj* — **her·met·i·cal·ly** \-i-kə-lē, -klē\ *adv*

her·mit \'hər-mət\ *n* **1** : one that lives in solitude especially for religious reasons **2** : a spiced molasses cookie [Old French *eremite*, from Late Latin *eremita*, from Late Greek *erēmitēs*, from Greek *erēmia* "solitude, desert", from *erēmos* "lonely"]

her·mit·age \'hər-mət-ij\ *n* **1** : the habitation of a hermit **2** : a secluded residence : RETREAT

hermit crab *n* : any of various marine crustaceans having soft asymmetrical abdomens and occupying empty mollusk shells

hermit crab

her·nia \'hər-nē-ə\ *n, pl* **her·ni·as** *or* **her·ni·ae** \-nē-,ē, -nē-,ī\ : a protrusion of an organ or part through connective tissue or through a wall of the cavity in which it is normally enclosed — called also *rupture* [Latin] — **her·ni·al** \-nē-əl\ *adj* — **her·ni·ate** \-nē-,āt\ *vi*

he·ro \'hē-rō, 'hiər-ō\ *n, pl* **heroes** **1 a** : a mythological or legendary figure often of divine descent endowed with great strength or ability **b** : an illustrious warrior **c** : a person admired for achievements and qualities **d** : one that shows great courage (the *hero* of a rescue) **2 a** : the chief male figure in a literary work or in an event or period [Latin *heros*, from Greek *hērōs*]

he·ro·ic \hi-'rō-ik\ *adj* **1** : of, relating to, or resembling heroes especially of antiquity (the *heroic* age) (*heroic* legends) **2** : exhibiting or marked by courage, daring, or desperate enterprise (a *heroic* rescue) **3** : large or impressive in size or range — **he·ro·i·cal** \-'rō-i-kəl\ *adj* — **he·ro·i·cal·ly** \-i-kə-lē, -klē\ *adv*

heroic couplet *n* : a rhyming couplet in iambic pentameter

he·ro·ics \hi-'rō-iks\ *n pl* **1** : heroic behavior **2** : showy behavior

heroic verse *n* : the iambic pentameter used in English poetry (as epic) during the 17th and 18th centuries

her·o·in \'her-ə-wən\ *n* : a strongly addictive narcotic derived from the opium poppy and more potent than morphine [from *Heroin*, a former trademark] — **her·o·in·ism** \-wə-,niz-əm\ *n*

her·o·ine \'her-ə-wən\ *n* **1** : a woman of courage and daring **2** : a woman admired for her achievements and qualities **3** : the chief female figure in a literary work or in an event or period [Latin *heroina*, from Greek *hērōinē*, feminine of *hērōs* "hero"]

her·o·ism \'her-ə-,wiz-əm\ *n* **1** : heroic conduct or qualities **2** : great self-sacrificing courage SYN see COURAGE

her·on \'her-ən\ *n, pl* **herons** *also* **heron** : any of various long-necked wading birds with a long tapering bill, large wings, and soft plumage [Middle French *hairon*, of Germanic origin]

hero worship *n* **1** : veneration of a hero **2** : foolish or excessive praise for an individual

her·pes \'hər-pēz\ *n* : any of several virus diseases marked by the formation of blisters on the skin or mucous membranes [Latin, from Greek *herpēs*, from *herpein* "to creep"] — **her·pet·ic** \hər-'pet-ik\ *adj*

herpes sim·plex \-'sim-,pleks\ *n* : a virus disease marked by groups of watery blisters on the skin or mucous membranes (as of the lips or genitals) [New Latin, literally, "simple herpes"]

her·pe·tol·o·gy \,hər-pə-'täl-ə-jē\ *n* : a branch of zoology dealing with reptiles and amphibians [Greek *herpeton* "reptile", from *herpein* "to creep"] — **her·pe·tol·o·gist** \,hər-pə-'täl-ə-jəst\ *n*

Herr \heər, 'heər\ *n, pl* **Her·ren** \,her-ən, heərn, ,heərn\ — used by or to German-speaking people as a courtesy title equivalent to *Mr.* [German]

her·ring \'her-ing\ *n, pl* **herring** *or* **herrings** : a valuable soft-rayed food fish abundant in the temperate and colder parts of the north Atlantic; *also* : any of various similar and related fishes [Old English *hǣring*]

her·ring·bone \'her-ing-,bōn\ *n* **1** : a pattern made up of rows of parallel lines with neighboring rows slanting in opposite directions **2** : a twilled fabric with a herringbone pattern

herring gull *n* : a common large gull of the northern hemisphere that as an adult is largely white and gray with dark wing tips

hers \'hərz\ *pron, sing or pl in construction* : that which belongs to her : those which belong to her — used without a following noun as an equivalent in meaning to the adjective *her*

her·self \hər-'self, ər-\ *pron* **1** : that identical female one — used reflexively or for emphasis (she considers *herself* lucky) (she *herself* did it); compare SHE 1 **2** : her normal, healthy, or sane condition or self (was *herself* again after a good night's sleep)

hertz \'hərts, 'heərts\ *n* : a unit of frequency equal to one cycle per second — abbreviation *Hz* [Heinrich R. *Hertz*, died 1894, German physicist]

he's \hēz, ,hēz, ēz\ : he is : he has

hes·i·tance \'hez-ə-təns\ *n* : HESITANCY

hes·i·tan·cy \-tən-sē\ *n, pl* **-cies** **1** : the quality or state of being hesitant **2** : an act or instance of hesitating

hes·i·tant \'hez-ə-tənt\ *adj* : tending to hesitate — **hes·i·tant·ly** *adv*

hes·i·tate \'hez-ə-,tāt\ *vi* **1** : to stop or pause because of forgetfulness, uncertainty, or indecision (*hesitate* before answering) **2** : to be reluctant (never *hesitated* to ask a favor) **3** : to falter in speaking : STAMMER [Latin *haesitare* "to stick fast, hesitate", from *haesus*, past participle of *haerēre* "to stick"] — **hes·i·tat·er** *n* — **hes·i·tat·ing·ly** \-,tat-ing-lē\ *adv* — **hes·i·ta·tion** \,hez-ə-'tā-shən\ *n* □ SYN HESITATE, WAVER, VACILLATE, FALTER mean to show irresolution or uncertainty. HESITATE implies a pause before deciding, acting, or choosing; WAVER implies hesitation after a decision and connotes weakness or a retreat; VACILLATE implies prolonged hesitation from inability to reach a decision; FALTER suggests a wavering or stumbling due to emotional stress, lack of courage, or fear.

Hes·per·us \'hes-pə-rəs, -prəs\ *n* : Venus when appearing as an evening star [Latin, from Greek *Hesperos*]

Hes·sian \'hesh-ən\ *n* **1** : a native or inhabitant of Hesse **2** : a German mercenary serving in the British forces during the American Revolution

Hessian fly *n* : a small two-winged fly destructive in America especially to wheat

heter- *or* **hetero-** *combining form* : other than usual : other : different (*hetero*gamete) [Greek *heteros* "other"]

het·ero·cyst \'het-ə-rō-,sist\ *n* : a large transparent thick-walled cell that resembles a spore and occurs at intervals along the filament of some blue-green algae

het·er·o·dox \'het-ə-rə-ˌdäks\ *adj* **1** : differing from or contrary to prevailing opinions, beliefs, or standards; *esp* : not orthodox in religion **2** : holding or expressing unorthodox beliefs or opinions [Late Latin *heterodoxus,* from Greek *heterodoxos,* from *heteros* "other" + *doxa* "opinion"] □ SYN HERETICAL: HETERODOX implies only not being in conformity with orthodox teachings; HERETICAL implies that such divergence is regarded as destructive of truth.

het·er·o·doxy \-ˌdäk-sē\ *n, pl* **-dox·ies 1** : the quality or state of being heterodox **2** : a heterodox opinion or doctrine

het·er·o·dyne \'het-ə-rə-ˌdīn\ *vt* : to combine (a radio frequency) with a different frequency so that a beat is produced — **heterodyne** *adj*

het·ero·ga·mete \ˌhet-ə-rō-gə-'mēt, -'gam-ˌēt\ *n* : either of a pair of gametes (as egg and sperm) that differ in form, size, or behavior — **het·ero·ga·met·ic** \-gə-'met-ik\ *adj*

het·er·o·ge·ne·ity \ˌhet-ə-rō-jə-'nē-ət-ē\ *n* : the quality or state of being heterogeneous

het·er·o·ge·neous \ˌhet-ə-rə-'jē-nē-əs, -nyəs\ *adj* : differing in kind : consisting of dissimilar ingredients or constituents : MIXED (a *heterogeneous* population) [Medieval Latin *heterogeneus,* from Greek *heterogenēs,* from *heteros* "other" + *genos* "kind"] — **het·er·o·ge·neous·ly** *adv* — **het·er·o·ge·neous·ness** *n*

het·er·ol·o·gous \ˌhet-ə-'räl-ə-gəs\ *adj* : derived from a different species (a *heterologous* organ transplant) [*heter-* + Greek *logos* "proportion, word"]

het·er·op·ter·ous \ˌhet-ə-'räp-tə-rəs\ *adj* : of or relating to a group (Heteroptera) of insects comprising the true bugs [*heter-* + Greek *pteron* "wing"] — **het·er·op·ter·an** \-tə-rən\ *adj or n*

het·ero·sex·u·al \ˌhet-ə-rō-'sek-shə-wəl, -shəl\ *adj* : of, relating to, or marked by sexual orientation toward members of the opposite sex — **heterosexual** *n* — **het·ero·sex·u·al·i·ty** \-ˌsek-shə-'wal-ət-ē\ *n*

het·er·o·sis \ˌhet-ə-'rō-səs\ *n* : the exceptional vigor or capacity for growth often exhibited by hybrid animals or plants — called also *hybrid vigor* — **het·er·ot·ic** \-'rät-ik\ *adj*

het·ero·troph \'het-ə-rə-ˌtrōf, -ˌträf\ *n* : an organism that is unable to live and grow without complex compounds of nitrogen and carbon — **het·ero·tro·phic** \ˌhet-ə-rə-'trō-fik\ *adj* — **het·ero·tro·phi·cal·ly** \-fi-kə-lē, -klē\ *adv*

het·ero·zy·gote \-'zī-ˌgōt\ *n* : a plant or animal with at least one gene pair containing different genes — **het·ero·zy·gos·i·ty** \-ˌzī-'gäs-ət-ē\ *n* — **het·ero·zy·gous** \ˌhet-ə-rō-'zī-gəs\ *adj*

hew \'hyü\ *vb* **hewed; hewed** *or* **hewn** \'hyün\; **hew·ing 1** : to chop down : CHOP (*hew* logs) (*hew* trees) **2** : to make or shape by or as if by cutting with an ax (a cabin built of rough-*hewn* logs) **3** : to conform strictly : ADHERE (*hew* to the line) [Old English *hēawan*] — **hew·er** *n*

¹hex \'heks\ *vt* **1** : to put a hex on **2** : to affect as if by an evil spell : JINX [German *hexen,* from *hexe* "witch"] — **hex·er** *n*

²hex *n* **1** : ¹SPELL 1, JINX **2** : a person who practices witchcraft

³hex *adj* : HEXAGONAL (a bolt with a *hex* head)

⁴hex *n* : a hexadecimal number system

hexa- *or* **hex-** *combining form* : six (*hex*ose) [Greek *hex*]

hexa·dec·i·mal \ˌhek-sə-'des-ə-məl, -'des-məl\ *adj* : of, relating to, or being a number system with a base of 16

hex·a·gon \'hek-sə-ˌgän\ *n* : a polygon of six angles and six sides

hex·ag·o·nal \hek-'sag-ən-l\ *adj* **1** : having six angles and six sides **2** : relating to or being a crystal system characterized by three equal lateral axes intersecting at angles of 60 degrees and a vertical axis of variable length at right angles (quartz occurs in *hexagonal* crystals) — **hex·ag·o·nal·ly** \-l-ē\ *adv*

hex·a·gram \'hek-sə-ˌgram\ *n* : a figure consisting of two equilateral triangles forming a 6-pointed star

hex·a·he·dron \ˌhek-sə-'hē-drən\ *n, pl* **-drons** *also* **-dra** \-drə\ : a polyhedron of six faces

hex·am·e·ter \hek-'sam-ət-ər\ *n* : a line consisting of six metrical feet

hex·ane \'hek-ˌsān\ *n* : any of five isomeric volatile liquid hydrocarbons C_6H_{14} found in petroleum

¹hex·a·pod \'hek-sə-ˌpäd\ *n* : INSECT 2

²hexapod *adj* **1** : having six feet **2** : of or relating to insects

hex·ose \'hek-ˌsōs\ *n* : a saccharide $C_6H_{12}O_6$ containing six carbon atoms in the molecule

hey \'hā\ *interj* — used especially to call attention or to express doubt, surprise, or joy [Middle English]

hey·day \'hā-ˌdā\ *n* : the time of greatest strength or vigor

hi \'hī, 'hī-ē\ *interj* — used especially as a greeting [Middle English *hy*]

hi·a·tus \hī-'āt-əs\ *n* **1** : a gap in space or in time; *esp* : a break where a part is missing (a *hiatus* in an old manuscript) **2** : the occurrence of two vowel sounds without pause or intervening consonantal sound [Latin, from *hiare* "to gape, yawn"]

hi·ba·chi \hi-'bäch-ē\ *n* : a charcoal brazier [Japanese]

hi·ber·nate \'hī-bər-ˌnāt\ *vi* : to pass the winter in a torpid or resting state [Latin *hibernare* "to pass the winter", from *hibernus* "of winter"] — **hi·ber·na·tion** \ˌhī-bər-'nā-shən\ *n* — **hi·ber·na·tor** \'hī-bər-ˌnāt-ər\ *n*

hi·bis·cus \hī-'bis-kəs, hə-\ *n* : any of a large genus of herbs, shrubs, or small trees of the mallow family with toothed leaves and large showy flowers [Latin, "marshmallow plant"]

¹hic·cup *also* **hic·cough** \'hik-ˌəp, -əp\ *n* : a spasmodic drawing in of breath that is stopped by sudden closure of the glottis and is accompanied by a peculiar sound [imitative]

²hiccup *also* **hiccough** *vi* **hic·cuped** *also* **hic·cupped; hic·cup·ing** *also* **hic·cup·ping** : to make a hiccup or be affected with hiccups

hick \'hik\ *n* : an awkward unsophisticated person : BUMPKIN [*Hick,* nickname for Richard]

hick·o·ry \'hik-rē, -ə-rē\ *n, pl* **-ries 1** : any of a genus of North American hardwood trees of the walnut family that often produce hard-shelled sweet edible nuts **2** : the usually tough pale wood of a hickory [of American Indian origin]

hi·dal·go \hid-'al-gō, ē-'thäl-\ *n, pl* **-gos** : a member of the lower nobility of Spain [Spanish]

¹hide \'hīd\ *vb* **hid** \'hid\; **hid·den** \'hid-n\ *or* **hid; hid·ing** \'hīd-ing\ **1** : to put or get out of sight (*hide* a treasure) (*hid* in a closet) **2** : to keep secret (*hide* their grief) **3** : to screen from view (a house *hidden* by trees) **4** : to seek protection or evade responsibility (*hides* behind dark glasses) [Old English *hȳdan*] — **hid·er** \'hīd-ər\ *n*

²hide *n* : the skin of an animal whether raw or dressed [Old English *hȳd*]

³hide *vt* **hid·ed; hid·ing** : to give a beating to : FLOG

hide–and–go–seek \ˌhīd-n-gō-'sēk\ *n* : HIDE-AND-SEEK

hide–and–seek \-n-'sēk\ *n* : a children's game in which one player gives the others time to hide and then tries to find them before they can return safely to the goal

hide·away \'hīd-ə-ˌwā\ *n* : RETREAT 2, HIDEOUT

hide·bound \'hīd-ˌbaúnd\ *adj* **1** : having a dry skin lacking in pliancy and adhering closely to the underlying flesh (a *hidebound* horse) **2** : stubbornly conservative

hid·eous \'hid-ē-əs\ *adj* : horribly ugly or disgusting : FRIGHTFUL [Old French *hidous,* from *hisde, hide* "terror"] — **hid·eous·ly** *adv* — **hid·eous·ness** *n*

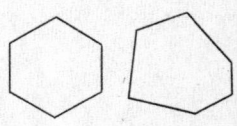

hexagon

hide·out \'hīd-ˌau̇t\ *n* : a place of refuge or concealment

¹hid·ing \'hīd-iŋ\ *n* : a state or place of concealment ⟨go into *hiding*⟩

²hiding *n* : WHIPPING, FLOGGING ⟨got a severe *hiding*⟩

hie \'hī\ *vb* **hied; hy·ing** *or* **hie·ing** : HURRY 1, HASTEN [Old English *hīgian*]

hi·er·arch \'hī-ˌrärk, -ə-ˌrärk\ *n* **1** : a religious leader in a position of authority **2** : a person high in a hierarchy [Medieval Latin *hierarcha,* from Greek *hierarchēs,* from *hieros* "holy" + *archos* "ruler, leader"] — **hi·erar·chal** \ˌhī-'rär-kəl, -ə-'rär-\ *adj*

hi·er·ar·chy \'hī-ˌrär-kē, -ə-ˌrär-\ *n, pl* **-chies 1** : a ruling body especially of clergy organized into ranks each subordinate to the one above it **2 a** : arrangement into a graded series **b** : persons or things arranged in ranks or classes — **hi·er·ar·chi·cal** \ˌhī-'rär-ki-kəl, -ə-'rär-\ *or* **hi·er·ar·chic** \-'rär-kik\ *adj* — **hi·er·ar·chi·cal·ly** \-'rär-ki-kə-lē, -klē\ *adv* □ ORIGIN The earliest examples of the use of *hierarchy* in English are found in works of the late 14th century and refer to the ranks or orders of angels. The first element of the word is from Greek *hieros,* "holy, sacred". The second element comes from Greek *archos,* "leader, ruler". A second sense of the word, appearing only slightly later than the first, is "a form of government administered by a priesthood". Later the term was extended from government to the classification of groups of people and then to the arrangement of objects, elements, or values in graduated series.

hi·er·o·glyph \'hī-rə-ˌglif, -ə-rə-\ *n* : a character used in a system of hieroglyphic writing [French *hiéroglyphe,* from Middle French *hieroglyphique,* adj., "hieroglyphic", from Late Latin *hieroglyphicus,* from Greek *hieroglyphikos,* from *hieros* "holy" + *glyphein* "to carve"]

hi·ero·glyph·ic \ˌhī-rə-'glif-ik, -ə-rə-\ *n* **1** : HIEROGLYPH **2** : a system of hieroglyphic writing; *esp* : the picture script of the ancient Egyptian priesthood **3** : characters that resemble a hieroglyphic especially in being hard to decipher — **hieroglyphic** *adj*

hieroglyphic 2

hi–fi \'hī-'fī\ *n* **1** : HIGH FIDELITY **2** : equipment for reproduction of sound with high fidelity

hig·gle·dy–pig·gle·dy \ˌhig-əl-dē-'pig-əl-dē\ *adv* : in confusion : TOPSY–TURVY [origin unknown] — **higgledy–piggledy** *adj*

¹high \'hī\ *adj* **1 a** : extending or raised up ⟨a *high* building⟩ **b** : having a specified elevation ⟨six meters *high*⟩ **2** : advanced toward fullness or culmination ⟨*high* summer⟩ **3** : elevated in pitch ⟨a *high* note⟩ **4** : relatively far from the equator ⟨*high* latitudes⟩ **5** : exalted in character : NOBLE ⟨a person of *high* purpose⟩ **6** : of greater degree, size, amount, or content than average or ordinary ⟨*high* pressure⟩ ⟨*high* prices⟩ **7** : of relatively great importance: as **a** : foremost in rank, dignity, or standing ⟨*high* society⟩ **b** : SERIOUS, GRAVE ⟨*high* crimes⟩ **8** : FORCIBLE, STRONG ⟨*high* winds⟩ **9 a** : showing elation or excitement ⟨*high* spirits⟩ **b** : INTOXICATED 1b **10** : advanced in complexity or development ⟨*higher* mathematics⟩ ⟨*higher* algae⟩ **11** : pronounced with some part of the tongue close to the palate ⟨\ē\ is a *high* vowel⟩ [Old English *hēah*]

²high *adv* **1** : at or to a high place, altitude, or degree ⟨hit the ball *high* into the bleachers⟩ **2** : RICHLY, LUXURIOUSLY ⟨lived *high* after winning the lottery⟩

³high *n* **1** : an elevated place or region: as **a** : HILL 1, KNOLL **b** : SKY 1, HEAVEN ⟨birds wheeling on *high*⟩ **2** : a region of high barometric pressure **3 a** : a high point or level ⟨prices reached a new *high*⟩ **b** : the transmission gear of an automotive vehicle giving the highest ratio of propeller-shaft to engine-shaft speed and consequently the highest speed of travel **4** : an excited or stupefied state produced by or as if by a drug

high·ball \'hī-ˌbȯl\ *n* : a drink of alcoholic liquor (as whiskey) with water or a carbonated beverage [earlier

highball "fast train, signal for a train to proceed at full speed"]

high beam *n* : the point of aim of a vehicle headlight for long distances

high·bind·er \-ˌbīn-dər\ *n* **1** : a professional killer operating in the Chinese quarter of an American city **2** : a corrupt or scheming politician [the *Highbinders,* gang of vagabonds in New York City about 1806]

high blood pressure *n* : blood pressure that is abnormally high especially in the arteries; *also* : the bodily condition accompanying high blood pressure

high·born \'hī-'bȯrn\ *adj* : of noble birth

high·boy \'hī-ˌbȯi\ *n* : a tall chest of drawers mounted on a base with long legs

high·bred \-'bred\ *adj* : coming from superior stock

high·brow \-ˌbrau̇\ *n* : a person of superior learning or culture : INTELLECTUAL — **highbrow** *adj*

high chair *n* : a child's chair with long legs, a feeding tray, and a footrest

High Church *adj* : tending to stress the ceremonial, traditional, and Catholic elements especially in Anglican worship — compare LOW CHURCH

high command *n* **1** : the supreme headquarters of a military force **2** : the highest leaders in an organization

high commissioner *n* : a principal or high-ranking commissioner; *esp* : an ambassadorial representative of the government of one country stationed in another

higher education *n* : education provided by a college or university

high·er–up \ˌhī-ər-'əp\ *n* : a superior officer or official

high explosive *n* : an explosive (as TNT) that generates gas with extreme rapidity and has a shattering effect

high·fa·lu·tin \ˌhī-fə-'lüt-n\ *adj* **1** : PRETENTIOUS 1 **2** : POMPOUS **3**, BOMBASTIC ⟨*highfalutin* talk⟩ [perhaps from *high* + *fluting,* present participle of flute]

high fidelity *n* : the reproduction of sound with a high degree of faithfulness to the original

high five *n* : a slapping of upraised right hands by two people (as in celebration) — **high–five** \'hī-'fīv\ *vb*

high–flown \'hī-'flōn\ *adj* : FLOWERY 2, EXTRAVAGANT ⟨*high-flown* language⟩

high–fly·ing \-'flī-iŋ\ *adj* **1** : rising to considerable height **2** : marked by extravagance, pretension, or excessive ambition

high frequency *n* : a radio frequency in the range between 3 and 30 megahertz — abbreviation HF

High German *n* : German as natively used in southern and central Germany

high–grade \'hī-'grād\ *adj* : of superior grade or quality

high–hand·ed \-'han-dəd\ *adj* : DOMINEERING, OVERBEARING ⟨*high-handed* actions⟩ — **high–hand·ed·ly** *adv* — **high–hand·ed·ness** *n*

high–hat \'hī-'hat\ *adj* : snobbish and supercilious in attitude — **high–hat** *vt*

High Holiday *n* : either of two important Jewish holidays: **a** : ROSH HASHANAH **b** : YOM KIPPUR

high horse *n* : an arrogant mood or attitude ⟨get off your *high horse* and start treating your classmates as equals⟩

high jump *n* : a jump for height in a track-and-field contest — **high jumper** *n*

¹high·land \'hī-lənd\ *n* : elevated or mountainous land

²highland *adj* **1** : of or relating to a highland **2** *cap* : of or relating to the Highlands of Scotland

high·land·er \-lən-dər\ *n* **1** : an inhabitant of a highland **2** *cap* : an inhabitant of the Highlands of Scotland

Highland fling *n* : a lively Scottish folk dance

¹high·light \'hī-ˌlīt\ *n* **1 a** : one of the points or areas on an object that reflect the most light **b** : the brightest spot (as in a painting or drawing) **2** : an event or scene of major interest ⟨the *highlights* of a trip⟩

²highlight *vt* **1** : to throw a strong light on **2 a** : to center attention on : EMPHASIZE **b** : to be a highlight of ⟨a bullfight *highlighted* their trip to Mexico⟩

high·ly \'hī-lē\ *adv* **1** : to a high degree : EXTREMELY ⟨*highly* pleased⟩ **2** : with much approval ⟨speak *highly* of a person⟩

high mass *n, often cap H & M* : a mass that is sung in full ceremonial form — compare LOW MASS

high–mind·ed \'hī-'mīn-dəd\ *adj* : having or marked by elevated principles and feelings — **high–mind·ed·ly** *adv* — **high–mind·ed·ness** *n*

high–muck–a–muck \,hī-,mək-i-'mək\ *or* **high–muck·e·ty–muck** \,hī-mək-ət-ē-'mək\ *n* : an important and often arrogant person [by folk etymology from Chinook Jargon (a pidgin language used in northwestern America) *hiu muckamuck* "plenty to eat"]

high·ness \'hī-nəs\ *n* **1** : the quality or state of being high **2** *often cap* — used as a form of address for persons (as a prince, a princess, a duke, or a duchess) of exalted rank and usually of royal blood ⟨Her *Highness* Princess Anne⟩ ⟨His *Highness* the Duke of Edinburgh⟩ ⟨Your *Highness*⟩ ⟨Their *Highnesses*⟩

high–octane *adj* : having a high octane number and hence good antiknock properties ⟨*high-octane* gasoline⟩

¹high–pressure *adj* **1 a** : having or involving a high or comparatively high pressure especially greatly exceeding that of the atmosphere **b** : having a high atmospheric pressure **2 a** : using or involving aggressive and insistent sales techniques **b** : imposing or involving severe strain or tension ⟨a *high-pressure* job⟩

²high–pressure *vt* : to sell or influence by high-pressure tactics

high relief *n* : sculptural relief in which at least half the thickness of the represented form is raised from the background — compare BAS-RELIEF

high–rise \'hī-'rīz\ *adj* : having many stories and being equipped with elevators ⟨*high-rise* apartment buildings⟩

high·road \'hī-,rōd\ *n* **1** : HIGHWAY **2** : the easiest course

high school *n* : a school usually including grades 9–12 or 10–12

high seas *n pl* : the open part of a sea or ocean especially outside territorial waters

high–sound·ing \'hī-'saùn-ding\ *adj* : PRETENTIOUS 1, IMPOSING

high–spir·it·ed \'hī-'spir-ət-əd\ *adj* : characterized by a bold or energetic spirit — **high–spir·it·ed·ly** *adv* — **high–spir·it·ed·ness** *n*

high–strung \-'strəng\ *adj* : having an extremely nervous or sensitive temperament

high·tail \'hī-,tāl\ *vi* : to retreat at full speed ⟨*hightailed* it for home⟩

high–tension *adj* : having a high voltage; *also* : relating to apparatus to be used at high voltage

high–test *adj* : meeting a high standard; *esp* : HIGH-OCTANE ⟨*high-test* gasoline⟩

high tide *n* **1** : the tide when the water is at its greatest height **2** : the culminating point : CLIMAX

high–toned \'hī-'tōnd\ *adj* **1** : high in social, moral, or intellectual quality **2** : pretentiously fashionable

high–top \'hī-,täp\ *adj* : extending up over the ankle ⟨*high-top* sneakers⟩ — **high–tops** \-,täps\ *n pl*

high treason *n* : TREASON 2

high·way \'hī-,wā\ *n* : a public way; *esp* : a main direct road

high·way·man \-mən\ *n* : a person who robs travelers on a road

hi·jack *or* **high–jack** \'hī-,jak\ *vt* **1** : to steal by stopping a vehicle on the highway ⟨*hijack* a load of furs⟩; *also* : to stop and steal from (a vehicle in transit) **2** : to commandeer a flying airplane (as by coercing the pilot at gunpoint) [origin unknown] — **hi·jack·er** *n*

¹hike \'hīk\ *vb* **1 a** : to move or raise up often with a sudden motion **b** : to increase (as prices) usually sharply or suddenly **2** : to go on a hike [perhaps related to ¹*hitch*] — **hik·er** *n*

²hike *n* **1** : a long walk especially for pleasure or exercise **2** : an upward movement : RISE ⟨a price *hike*⟩

hi·lar·i·ous \hil-'ar-ē-əs, -'er-; hī-'lar-, -'ler-\ *adj* : marked by or causing hilarity [Latin *hilarus, hilarus* "cheerful", from Greek *hilaros*] — **hi·lar·i·ous·ly** *adv* — **hi·lar·i·ous·ness** *n*

hi·lar·i·ty \-ət-ē\ *n* : high spirits usually marked by boisterous conviviality or merriment SYN see MIRTH

¹hill \'hil\ *n* **1** : a usually rounded natural elevation of land lower than a mountain **2** : an artificial heap or mound (as of earth) **3** : several seeds or plants planted in a group rather than a row ⟨a *hill* of beans⟩ [Old English *hyll*]

²hill *vt* **1** : to form into a heap **2** : to draw earth around the roots or base of — **hill·er** *n*

hill·bil·ly \'hil-,bil-ē\ *n, pl* **-lies** : a person from a backwoods area [¹*hill* + *Billy*, nickname for *William*]

hillbilly music *n* : COUNTRY MUSIC

hill·ock \'hil-ək\ *n* : a small hill — **hill·ocky** \-ə-kē\ *adj*

hill·side \'hil-,sīd\ *n* : the side of a hill

hill·top \'hil-,täp\ *n* : the highest part of a hill

hilly \'hil-ē\ *adj* **hill·i·er; -est** **1** : having many hills ⟨a *hilly* city⟩ **2** : STEEP ⟨a *hilly* climb⟩

hilt \'hilt\ *n* : a handle especially of a sword or dagger [Old English] — **to the hilt** : to the very limit : COMPLETELY

hi·lum \'hī-ləm\ *n, pl* **hi·la** \-lə\ **1** : a scar on a seed (as a bean) at the point of attachment of the ovule **2** : a notch in or opening from a bodily part suggesting the hilum of a bean [Latin, "trifle"] — **hi·lar** \-lər\ *adj*

him \im, him, 'him\ *pron, objective case of* HE

Hi·ma·la·yan \,him-ə-'lā-ən; him-'äl-yən, -ə-yən\ *n* : any of a breed of small white domesticated rabbits with black nose, feet, tail, and ear tips — called also *Himalayan rabbit* [*Himalaya* mountains]

him·self \im-'self, him-\ *pron* **1 a** : that identical male one — used reflexively or for emphasis ⟨he considers *himself* lucky⟩ ⟨he *himself* did it⟩; compare ¹HE **b** — used reflexively when the sex of the antecedent is unspecified ⟨everyone must look out for *himself*⟩ **2** : his normal, healthy, or sane condition or self ⟨he's *himself* again⟩

¹hind \'hīnd\ *n, pl* **hinds** *also* **hind** **1** : a female red deer — compare HART **2** : any of various usually spotted groupers [Old English]

²hind *adj* : located behind : REAR ⟨*hind* legs⟩ [Middle English]

hind·brain \'hīnd-,brān, 'hīn-\ *n* : the posterior division of the embryonic vertebrate brain or the parts developed from it

hin·der \'hin-dər\ *vb* **hin·dered; hin·der·ing** \-də-ring, -dring\ **1** : to make slow or difficult : HAMPER ⟨bad weather *hindered* the progress of the climbers⟩ **2** : to hold back : CHECK [Old English *hindrian*]

hind·gut \'hīnd-,gət, 'hīn-\ *n* : the posterior part of the alimentary canal

Hin·di \'hin-dē\ *n* **1** : a literary and official language of northern India **2** : a complex of Indic dialects of northern India for which Hindi is the usual literary language [Hindi *hindi*, from *Hind* "India", from Persian] — **Hindi** *adj*

hind·most \'hīnd-,mōst, 'hīn-\ *adj* : farthest to the rear

hind·quar·ter \-,kwórt-ər, -,kwót-\ *n* **1** : the back half of a lateral half of the body or carcass of a four-footed animal ⟨a *hindquarter* of beef⟩ **2** *pl* : the part of a four-footed animal lying behind the attachment of the hind legs to the trunk

hin·drance \'hin-drəns\ *n* **1** : the state of being hindered **2** : the action of hindering **3** : something that hinders : IMPEDIMENT

hind·sight \'hīnd-,sīt, 'hīn-\ *n* : the understanding of the importance of an event only after it has happened ⟨*hindsight* is easier than foresight⟩

\ə\ abut	\ng\ sing
\ər\ further	\ō\ bone
\a\ mat	\ó\ saw
\ā\ take	\ói\ coin
\ä\ cot, cart	\th\ thin
\aù\ out	\th\ this
\ch\ chin	\ü\ food
\e\ pet	\ú\ foot
\ē\ easy	\y\ yet
\g\ go	\yü\ few
\i\ tip	\yú\ cure
\ī\ life	\zh\ vision
\j\ job	

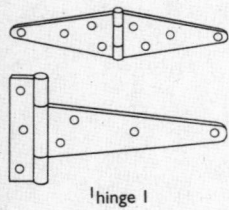

¹hinge I

hippopotamus

¹Hin·du also **Hin·doo** \'hin-,dü\ *n* **I** : an adherent of Hinduism **2** : a native or inhabitant of India [Persian *Hindū* "inhabitant of India", from *Hind* "India"]

²Hindu also **Hindoo** *adj* : of, relating to, or characteristic of the Hindus or Hinduism

Hin·du·ism \-,iz-əm\ *n* : a body of social, cultural, and religious beliefs and practices native to the Indian subcontinent

Hin·du·stani also **Hin·do·stani** \,hin-du̇-'stan-ē, -'stän-ē\ *n* : a group of Indic dialects of northern India of which literary Hindi and Urdu are considered diverse written forms [Hindi *Hindūstānī*, from Persian *Hindūstān* "India"] — **Hindustani** *adj*

¹hinge \'hinj\ *n* **I** : a jointed piece on which one surface (as a door, gate, or lid) turns or swings on another **2** : the joint between valves of a bivalve's shell — compare HINGE JOINT [Middle English *heng*]

²hinge *vb* **I** : to attach by or furnish with hinges **2** : to hang or turn as if on a hinge ⟨success *hinges* on the decision⟩

hinge joint *n* : a joint between bones (as at the elbow) that permits motion in but one plane

hin·ny \'hin-ē\ *n, pl* **hinnies** : a hybrid between a stallion and a female donkey — compare MULE [Latin *hinnus*]

¹hint \'hint\ *n* **I a** : a suggestion for action given briefly or in an indirect manner ⟨*hints* on lawn care⟩ **b** : a statement that communicates delicately and indirectly rather than directly **2 a** : a slight indication of the existence or nature of something **b** : SMIDGEN, BIT [probably from *hent* "to seize", from Old English *hentan*]

²hint *vb* : to convey by or make a hint SYN see SUGGEST — **hint·er** *n*

hin·ter·land \'hint-ər-,land\ *n* **I** : a region lying inland from a coast **2** : a region remote from urban areas or cultural centers [German, from *hinter* "hind" + *land* "land"]

¹hip \'hip\ *n* : the fruit of a rose [Old English *hēope*]

²hip *n* **I** : the part of the body that curves outward below the waist on either side and is formed by the side part of the pelvis and the upper part of the thigh **2** : HIP JOINT [Old English *hype*]

³hip also **hep** \'hep\ *adj* **hip·per; hip·pest** : characterized by a keen informed awareness of or interest in the newest developments [origin unknown]

hip·bone \'hip-'bōn, -,bōn\ *n* : either of two large flaring compound bones that make lateral halves of the pelvis in mammals, provide points of attachment for the skeleton of the leg, and fuse together in front and with the backbone in the rear to form a closed bony ring which supports the lower part of the trunk and the abdominal organs

hip girdle *n* : PELVIC GIRDLE

hip–hop \'hip-,häp\ *n* : a subculture especially of inner-city youths whose amusements include rap music and characteristic dance steps [perhaps from ³*hip* + ¹*hop*]

hip joint *n* : the articulation between the femur and the hipbone

hip·par·i·on \hip-'ar-ē-,än, -'er-\ *n* : any of a genus of extinct Miocene and Pliocene 3-toed horses [Greek, "pony", from *hippos* "horse"]

¹hipped \'hipt\ *adj* : having hips or such hips ⟨a *hipped* roof⟩ ⟨broad-*hipped*⟩

²hipped *adj* : DEPRESSED 1a [derived from *hypochondria*]

³hipped *adj* : extremely absorbed or interested ⟨*hipped* on astrology⟩ [*hip* "to make aware", from ³*hip*]

hip·pie *or* **hip·py** \'hip-ē\ *n, pl* **hippies** : a usually young person who rejects the values and practices of established society (as by dressing unconventionally or favoring communal living); *also* : a long-haired unconventionally dressed young person [³*hip* + *-ie*]

hip·po \'hip-ō\ *n, pl* **hippos** : HIPPOPOTAMUS

Hip·po·crat·ic oath \,hip-ə-'krat-ik-\ *n* : an oath embodying a code of medical ethics usually taken by those about to begin medical practice [*Hippocrates,* died about 377 B.C., Greek physician believed to have formulated it]

hip·po·drome \'hip-ə-,drōm\ *n* **I** : an oval stadium for horse and chariot races in ancient Greece **2** : an arena for spectacles (as horse shows or circuses) [Middle French, from Latin *hippodromos,* from Greek, from *hippos* "horse" + *dromos* "racecourse"]

hip·po·pot·a·mus \,hip-ə-'pät-ə-məs\ *n, pl* **-mus·es** *or* **-mi** \-,mī, -mē\ : any of several large plant-eating 4-toed chiefly aquatic African mammals related to the swine and characterized by an extremely large head and mouth, very thick hairless skin, and short legs [Latin, from Greek *hippopotamos,* from *hippos* "horse" + *potamos* "river"] □ ORIGIN *Hippopotamos* was the name invented by the Greeks to describe the bulky, barrel-shaped animal that spends most of the day bathing in the rivers of Africa. The two elements of the word are *hippos,* "horse", and *potamos,* "river". In fact, however, the hippopotamus is more closely related to the hog than to the horse.

hip roof *n* : a roof having sloping ends and sloping sides

hip·ster \'hip-stər\ *n* **I** : a person who is hip **2** : HIPPIE

¹hire \'hīr\ *n* **I a** : payment for temporary use **b** : payment for services : WAGES **2 a** : the act of hiring **b** : the state of being hired : EMPLOYMENT [Old English *hȳr*] — **for hire** : available for use or service at a price

²hire *vb* **I a** : to engage the personal services of for a set sum ⟨*hire* a new crew⟩ **b** : to engage the temporary use of for a fixed sum ⟨*hire* a hall⟩ **2** : to grant the personal services of for a fixed sum ⟨*hire* themselves out⟩ **3** : to take employment ⟨*hire* out as a cook⟩ — **hir·er** *n* □ SYN HIRE, LET, LEASE, RENT mean to engage or grant for use at a price. HIRE and LET, strictly speaking, are complementary terms. HIRE implying the act of engaging or taking for use and LET the granting of use ⟨we *hired* a car for the summer⟩ ⟨decided to *let* the cottage to a young couple⟩ LEASE strictly implies a letting under the terms of a contract but is often applied to hiring on a lease ⟨the diplomat *leased* an apartment for a year⟩ ⟨the landlord refused to *lease* to tenants with pets⟩ RENT stresses the payment of money for the full use of property and may imply either hiring or letting. □ SYN HIRE, EMPLOY mean to engage for work. HIRE stresses the act of engaging a person's services for pay; EMPLOY stresses the continued or regular use of a person's services.

hire·ling \'hīr-ling\ *n* : a person who serves for pay and usually for no other reason

hiring hall *n* : a union-operated placement office where registered applicants are referred in rotation to jobs

hir·sute \'hər-,süt, 'hiər-\ *adj* : HAIRY; *esp* : having coarse stiff hairs [Latin *hirsutus*] — **hir·sute·ness** *n*

¹his \iz, hiz, ,hiz\ *adj* : of or relating to him or himself especially as possessor, agent, or object of an action ⟨*his* house⟩ ⟨*his* writings⟩ ⟨*his* confirmation⟩ — compare ¹HE [Old English, genitive of *hē* "he"]

²his \'hiz\ *pron, sing or pl in construction* : that which belongs to him : those which belong to him — used without a following noun as an equivalent in meaning to the adjective *his*

¹His·pan·ic \his-'pan-ik\ *adj* : of, relating to, or derived from the people, speech, or culture of Spain or Latin America [Latin *Hispania* "Iberian peninsula, Spain"]

²Hispanic *n* : a Hispanic person

his·pid \'his-pəd\ *adj* : rough or covered with bristles, stiff hairs, or minute spines ⟨*hispid* leaf⟩ [Latin *hispidus*] — **his·pid·i·ty** \his-'pid-ət-ē\ *n*

hiss \'his\ *vb* **I** : to utter the characteristic prolonged sibilant sound of an alarmed animal (as a snake or cat) or a similar sound **2** : to express disapproval by hissing [Middle English *hissen*] — **hiss** *n* — **hiss·er** *n*

hist \s *often prolonged and usually with* p *preceding and* t *following*; *often read as* 'hist\ *interj* — used to attract attention [origin unknown]

hist- *or* **histo-** *combining form* : tissue ⟨*hist*amine⟩ [Greek *histos* "mast, loom, beam, web", from *histanai* "to cause to stand"]

his·tam·i·nase \his-'tam-ə-ˌnās, 'his-tə-mə-\ *n* : an enzyme that breaks down histamine

his·ta·mine \'his-tə-ˌmēn, -mən\ *n* : a compound occurring in many animal tissues that is believed to play an important part in allergic reactions (as hives, asthma, and hay fever) and in some respiratory diseases

his·ti·dine \'his-tə-ˌdēn\ *n* : a crystalline basic amino acid $C_6H_9N_3O_2$ formed in the splitting of most proteins

his·to·gram \'his-tə-ˌgram\ *n* : a representation of a frequency distribution by means of rectangles whose widths represent the different values included in the class and whose heights represent the number of items found within the class [Greek *histos* "mast, pole, web"]

his·tol·o·gy \his-'täl-ə-jē\ *n, pl* **-gies** **1** : a branch of anatomy that deals with the structure of animal and plant tissues as revealed by the microscope **2** : tissue structure or organization — **his·to·log·i·cal** \ˌhis-tə-'läj-i-kəl\ *adj* — **his·tol·o·gist** \his-'täl-ə-jəst\ *n*

his·to·plas·mo·sis \ˌhis-tə-plaz-'mō-səs\ *n* : a disease that is caused by a fungus infection of the lungs and is endemic in the Mississippi and Ohio River valleys of the United States

his·to·ri·an \his-'tōr-ē-ən, -'tȯr-\ *n* **1** : a student or writer of history; *esp* : one that produces a scholarly historical study **2** : a writer of chronicles : CHRONICLER

his·tor·ic \his-'tȯr-ik, -'tär-\ *adj* : HISTORICAL; *esp* : famous in history ⟨*historic* events⟩

his·tor·i·cal \-i-kəl\ *adj* **1 a** : of, relating to, or having the character of history ⟨*historical* fact⟩ **b** : based on history ⟨*historical* novels⟩ **2** : famous in history ⟨*historical* personages⟩ — **his·tor·i·cal·ly** \-i-kə-lē, -klē\ *adv* — **his·tor·i·cal·ness** \-kəl-nəs\ *n*

historical present *n* : the present tense used to relate past events

his·to·ric·i·ty \ˌhis-tə-'ris-ət-ē\ *n* : historical actuality : FACT

his·to·ri·og·ra·pher \his-ˌtōr-ē-'äg-rə-fər, -ˌtȯr-\ *n* : a usually official writer of history : HISTORIAN — **his·to·rio·graph·ic** \-ē-ə-'graf-ik\ *or* **his·to·rio·graph·i·cal** \-'graf-i-kəl\ *adj* — **his·to·rio·graph·i·cal·ly** \-i-kə-lē, -klē\ *adv* — **his·to·ri·og·ra·phy** \-ē-'äg-rə-fē\ *n*

his·to·ry \'his-tə-rē, -trē\ *n, pl* **-ries** **1** : STORY 1a, TALE **2 a** : a chronological record of significant events usually with an explanation of their causes **b** : an account of a sick person's medical background **3** : a branch of knowledge that records and explains past events **4 a** : events that form the subject matter of a history **b** : past events [Latin *historia* from Greek, "inquiry, history", from *istōr, histōr* "knowing, learned"]

his·tri·on·ic \ˌhis-trē-'än-ik\ *adj* **1** : of or relating to actors, acting, or the theater **2** : deliberately affected : THEATRICAL [Late Latin *histrionicus,* from Latin *histrio* "actor"] SYN see DRAMATIC — **his·tri·on·i·cal·ly** \-'än-i-kə-lē, -klē\ *adv*

his·tri·on·ics \-'än-iks\ *n sing or pl* **1** : theatrical performances **2** : deliberate display of emotion for effect

¹hit \'hit\ *vb* **hit**; **hit·ting** **1 a** : to strike usually with force ⟨*hit* a ball⟩ ⟨the ball *hit* against the house⟩ **b** : to make usually forceful contact with something ⟨fell and *hit* the ground⟩ **2 a** : ATTACK ⟨tried to guess when and where the enemy would *hit*⟩ **b** : to affect unfavorably ⟨the loss of the contract *hit* the company hard⟩ **3** : OCCUR, HAPPEN ⟨when the storm *hit*⟩ **4 a** : COME, STUMBLE ⟨*hit* upon the solution⟩ **b** : to experience or find especially by chance ⟨*hit* a run of bad luck⟩ **c** : to get to : REACH ⟨*hit* town that night⟩ ⟨prices *hit* a new high⟩ **d** : to accord with accurately ⟨styles that *hit* modern taste⟩

5 : to fire the charge in the cylinders ⟨an automobile engine not *hitting*⟩ [Old Norse *hitta* "to meet with, hit"] — **hit·ter** *n*

²hit *n* **1 a** : a blow striking an object aimed at **b** : COLLISION **2 a** : a stroke of luck **b** : something that is conspicuously successful ⟨the show was a *hit*⟩ **3** : a telling remark **4** : BASE HIT

hit–and–miss \ˌhit-n-'mis\ *adj* : sometimes successful and sometimes not : HAPHAZARD

hit–and–run \-'rən\ *adj* **1** : being or relating to a baseball play in which a base runner starts for the next base as the pitcher starts to pitch and the batter attempts to hit the ball **2** : being or involving a motor-vehicle driver who does not stop after being involved in an accident

¹hitch \'hich\ *vb* **1** : to move by jerks ⟨*hitch* a chair toward the table⟩ **2 a** : to catch or fasten by or as if by a hook or knot ⟨*hitch* a horse to a rail⟩ **b** : to connect to or with a hitch **3** : HITCHHIKE [Middle English *hytchen*] — **hitch·er** *n*

²hitch *n* **1** : a jerky movement or pull **2** : a sudden stop : an unforeseen obstacle : HALT ⟨the plan went off without a *hitch*⟩ **3** : the connection between something towed (as a plow or trailer) and its mover (as a tractor, automobile, or animal) **4** : a knot used for a temporary fastening ⟨barrel *hitch*⟩ **5** : a period of time in a specified state or activity ⟨a *hitch* in the infantry⟩

hitch·hike \'hich-ˌhīk\ *vb* : to travel by or secure free rides — **hitch·hik·er** *n*

hitch up *vi* : to harness and hitch a draft animal or team

¹hith·er \'hith-ər\ *adv* : to this place ⟨come *hither*⟩ [Old English *hider*]

²hither *adj* : being on the near or adjacent side ⟨the *hither* side of the hill⟩

hith·er·most \-ˌmōst\ *adj* : nearest on this side

hith·er·to \-ˌtü\ *adv* : up to this time

hith·er·ward \'hith-ər-wərd, -ə-\ *adv* : HITHER

hit off *vb* **1** : to characterize precisely and usually satirically **2** : HARMONIZE, AGREE

hit–or–miss \ˌhit-ər-'mis\ *adj* : marked by a lack of care, forethought, system, or plan

hit or miss *adv* : in a hit-or-miss manner : HAPHAZARDLY

Hit·tite \'hi-ˌtīt\ *n* **1** : a member of a conquering people in Asia Minor and Syria ruling an empire in the 2d millennium B.C. **2** : an Indo-European language of the Hittite people known from cuneiform texts [Hebrew *Ḥittī,* from Hittite *ḫatti*] — **Hittite** *adj*

HIV \ˌāch-ˌī-'vē\ *n* : any of a group of retroviruses that infect and destroy helper T cells of the immune system causing the marked reduction in their numbers that is diagnostic of AIDS — called also *AIDS virus, human immunodeficiency virus*

¹hive \'hīv\ *n* **1 a** : a container for housing honeybees **b** : a colony of bees **2** : a place swarming with busy occupants [Old English *hȳf*] — **hive·less** \-ləs\ *adj*

²hive *vb* **1 a** : to collect (as bees) into a hive **b** : to enter and take over a hive **2** : to store up in or as if in a hive ⟨*hive* honey⟩ **3** : to live in close association

hives *n sing or pl* : an allergic disorder in which the skin or mucous membrane is affected by itching swellings [origin unknown]

ho \'hō\ *interj* — used especially to attract attention [Middle English]

hoar \'hōr, 'hȯr\ *adj, archaic* : HOARY [Old English *hār*]

hoard \'hōrd, 'hȯrd\ *n* : a supply or fund stored up usually in secret [Old English *hord*] — **hoard** *vt* — **hoard·er** *n*

hoar·frost \'hōr-ˌfrȯst, 'hȯr-\ *n* : FROST 1c

hoarse \'hōrs, 'hȯrs\ *adj* **1** : harsh in sound ⟨a crow's *hoarse* caw⟩ **2** : having a rough grating voice ⟨*hoarse* from a cold⟩ [Middle English *hos, hors,* from Old English *hās*] — **hoarse·ly** *adv* — **hoarse·ness** *n*

hoary \'hōr-ē, 'hȯr-\ *adj* **hoar·i·er; -est** **1** : grayish or whitish especially from age ⟨an old dog's *hoary* muz-

histogram

zle) **2** : very old : ANCIENT ⟨*hoary* legends⟩ — **hoar·i·ness** *n*

¹**hoax** \'hōks\ *vt* : to trick into believing or accepting as genuine something false and often preposterous [probably from *hocus*] — **hoax·er** *n*

²**hoax** *n* **1** : an act intended to trick or fool **2** : something false passed off or accepted as genuine

¹**hob** \'häb\ **1** *English dialect* : HOBGOBLIN 1, ELF **2** : MISCHIEF, TROUBLE ⟨raise *hob*⟩ [Middle English *hobbe*, from *Hobbe*, nickname for *Robert*]

²**hob** *n* **1** : a projection at the back or side of a fireplace on which something may be kept warm **2** : a cutting tool used for cutting the teeth of worm wheels or gear wheels [origin unknown]

³**hob** *vt* **hobbed; hob·bing 1** : to furnish with hobnails **2** : to cut with a hob

¹**hob·ble** \'häb-əl\ *vb* **hob·bled; hob·bling** \'häb-ling, -ə-ling\ **1 a** : to move along unsteadily or with difficulty; *esp* : to limp along ⟨*hobble* on crutches⟩ **b** : to cause to limp : make lame : CRIPPLE ⟨*hobbled* by an ankle injury⟩ **2 a** : to keep (as a horse) from straying by joining two legs with a short length (as of rope) **b** : to place under handicap : HAMPER, IMPEDE [Middle English *hoblen*] — **hob·bler** \'häb-lər, -ə-lər\ *n*

²**hobble** *n* **1** : a hobbling movement **2** : something used to hobble an animal

hob·ble·de·hoy \'häb-əl-di-,hȯi\ *n* : an awkward gawky youth [origin unknown]

hobble skirt *n* : a skirt very narrow at the ankles

hob·by \'häb-ē\ *n, pl* **hobbies** : an interest or activity which is outside a person's regular occupation and is pursued for pleasure [short for *hobbyhorse*] — **hob·by·ist** \-ē-əst\ *n*

hob·by·horse \'häb-ē-,hȯrs\ *n* **1** : a stick with an imitation horse's head at one end which children pretend to ride **2 a** : a toy horse **b** : ROCKING HORSE **3** : a topic to which one constantly returns [Middle English *hoby* "small light horse"]

hob·gob·lin \'häb-,gäb-lən\ *n* **1** : a mischievous elf or goblin **2** : BOGEY 2, BUGABOO

hob·nail \'häb-,nāl\ *n* : a short large-headed nail used to stud the soles of heavy shoes as a protection against wear [²*hob*] — **hob·nailed** \-,nāld\ *adj*

hob·nob \-,näb\ *vi* **hob·nobbed; hob·nob·bing** : to associate familiarly ⟨*hobnobbing* with royalty⟩ [from the obsolete phrase drink *hobnob* "to drink alternately to one another"] — **hob·nob·ber** *n*

ho·bo \'hō-bō\ *n, pl* **hoboes** *also* **hobos 1** : a migratory worker **2** : TRAMP 1 [perhaps from *ho, boy*] — **hobo** *vi*

Hob·son's choice \'häb-sənz-\ *n* : apparently free choice with no real alternative [Thomas *Hobson*, died 1631, English liveryman, who required every customer to take the horse nearest the door]

¹**hock** \'häk\ *n* : the tarsal joint or region in the hind limb of a four-footed animal (as the horse) corresponding to the human ankle [Old English *hōh* "heel"]

²**hock** *n, often cap, chiefly British* : RHINE WINE [German *hochheimer*, from *Hochheim*, Germany]

³**hock** *n* : ¹PAWN 2 ⟨got the watch out of *hock*⟩ [Dutch *hok* "pen, prison"]

⁴**hock** *vt* : PAWN ⟨*hocked* the silverware⟩

hock·ey \'häk-ē\ *n* **1** : FIELD HOCKEY **2** : ICE HOCKEY [perhaps from Middle French *hoquet* "shepherd's crook", from *hoc* "hook", of Germanic origin]

ho·cus \'hō-kəs\ *vt* **ho·cused** *or* **ho·cussed; ho·cus·ing** *or* **ho·cus·sing 1** : to play a trick on : DECEIVE **2** : DRUG 1, DOPE [from *hocus-pocus*]

ho·cus-po·cus \,hō-kə-'spō-kəs\ *n* **1** : a set form of words used by those skilled in tricks of illusion **2** : nonsense that serves as a means of deception [probably from *hocus pocus*, imitation Latin phrase used by jugglers]

hod \'häd\ *n* **1** : a long-handled wooden tray or trough used for carrying mortar or bricks on the shoulder **2** :

hogan

a bucket for holding or carrying coal [probably from Dutch *hodde*]

hod carrier *n* : a laborer who carries supplies to bricklayers, stonemasons, cement finishers, or plasterers on the job

hodge·podge \'häj-,päj\ *n* : MISHMASH, JUMBLE [alteration of *hotchpotch*] □ ORIGIN An earlier form of *hodgepodge*, and still a form used commonly in Britain, is *hotchpotch*. This in turn is a rhyming alteration of Middle English *hochepot*. The Old French *hochepot*, from which the English is derived, is formed from *hochier*, "to shake", and *pot*, which has the same meaning as English *pot*. *Hochepot*, then, was a stew with many different ingredients all shaken (and presumably cooked) together in the same pot. This mixture of many ingredients in one pot prompted the extension of meaning to any heterogeneous mixture.

Hodg·kin's disease \'häj-kənz-\ *n* : a disease characterized by progressive enlargement of the lymph glands, spleen, and liver and by progressive anemia [Thomas *Hodgkin*, died 1866, English physician]

hoe \'hō\ *n* : a farm or garden tool with a thin flat blade at nearly a right angle to a long handle that is used for weeding, loosening the earth about plants, and hilling [Middle French *houe*, of Germanic origin] — **hoe** *vb* — **ho·er** \'hō-ər, 'hȯr\ *n*

hoe·cake \'hō-,kāk\ *n* : a small cornmeal cake [from its formerly being baked on the blade of a *hoe*]

hoe·down \-,daȯn\ *n* **1** : SQUARE DANCE **2** : a gathering featuring hoedowns

¹**hog** \'hȯg, 'häg\ *n, pl* **hogs** *also* **hog 1** : a domestic swine especially when weighing more than 120 pounds; *also* : any of various animals related to the domestic swine **2** : a selfish, gluttonous, or filthy person [Old English *hogg*]

²**hog** *vt* **hogged; hog·ging** : to take more than one's share of

ho·gan \'hō-,gän\ *n* : an earth-covered dwelling of the Navajo Indians [Navajo]

hog·back \'hȯg-,bak, 'häg-\ *n* **1** : a ridge of land formed by the outcropping edges of tilted strata **2** : a ridge with a sharp summit and steeply sloping sides

hog cholera *n* : a highly infectious often fatal virus disease of swine

hog·gish \'hȯg-ish, 'häg-\ *adj* : very selfish, gluttonous, or filthy — **hog·gish·ly** *adv* — **hog·gish·ness** *n*

hog·nose snake \'hȯg-,nōz-, 'häg-\ *or* **hog–nosed snake** \-,nōz-, -,nōzd-\ *n* : any of several rather small harmless stout-bodied North American snakes that protect themselves when disturbed first by a threat display and then by playing dead — called also *puff adder*

hogs·head \'hȯgz-,hed, 'hägz-\ *n* **1** : a large cask or barrel; *esp* : one containing from 63 to 140 gallons (about 238 to 530 liters) **2** : a United States measure for liquids equal to 63 gallons (about 238 liters)

hog–tie \'hȯg-,tī, 'häg-\ *vt* **1** : to tie together the feet of ⟨*hog-tie* a calf⟩ **2** : to make helpless ⟨*hog-tied* by red tape⟩

hog·wash \-,wȯsh, -,wäsh\ *n* **1** : SWILL 1, SLOP 4a **2** : worthless or nonsensical language

Ho·hen·stau·fen \'hō-ən-,shtaȯ-fən, -,staȯ-\ *adj* : of or relating to the German royal family furnishing monarchs of the Holy Roman Empire from 1138 to 1254 and of Sicily from 1194 to 1266 — **Hohenstaufen** *n*

Ho·hen·zol·lern \'hō-ən-,zäl-ərn\ *adj* : of or relating to the German royal family furnishing kings of Prussia from 1701 to 1918 and German emperors from 1871 to 1918 — **Hohenzollern** *n*

hoi polloi \,hȯi-pə-'lȯi\ *n pl* : the common people : MASSES [Greek, "the many"]

hoise \'hȯiz\ *vt* **hoised** \'hȯizd\ *or* **hoist** \'hȯist\; **hoising** \'hȯi-zing\ : HOIST [origin unknown] — **hoist with one's own petard** : affected or hurt by one's own scheme

¹hoist \ˈhȯist\ *vb* : to raise or become raised into position by or as if by means of tackle [alteration of *hoise*] SYN see LIFT — **hoist·er** *n*

²hoist *n* **1** : an act of hoisting : LIFT **2** : an apparatus for hoisting heavy loads

hoi·ty-toi·ty \ˌhȯit-ē-ˈtȯit-ē, ˌhīt-ē-ˈtīt-ē\ *adj* **1** : GIDDY 3, FLIGHTY **2** : HAUGHTY, PATRONIZING [derived from English dialect *hoit* "to play the fool"]

ho·key-po·key \ˌhō-kē-ˈpō-kē\ *n* : HOCUS-POCUS 2

ho·kum \ˈhō-kəm\ *n* **1** : a stock technique for evoking a desired response (as laughter or sentiment) from an audience **2** : pretentious nonsense : BUNKUM [probably from *ho*cus-pocus + bun*kum*]

hol- *or* **holo-** *combining form* : complete : total : completely : totally ⟨*Holo*cene⟩ [Greek *holos* "whole"]

¹hold \ˈhōld\ *vb* **held** \ˈheld\; **hold·ing 1 a** : to maintain possession of : HAVE ⟨*hold* title to property⟩ **b** : to retain by force ⟨the soldiers *held* the bridge⟩ **2 a** : to impose restraint upon especially by keeping back ⟨*hold* your temper⟩ **b** : DELAY ⟨*held* the plane⟩ **c** : to keep from advancing or succeeding in attack **d** : to bind legally or morally : CONSTRAIN ⟨I'll *hold* you to your word⟩ **3 a** : to have or keep in the grasp **b** : to cause to be or remain in a particular situation, position, or relation ⟨*hold* a ladder steady⟩ **c** : SUPPORT, SUSTAIN ⟨the floor will *hold* 10 metric tons⟩ **d** : to keep in custody **e** : to have in one's keeping : RESERVE ⟨*hold* a room⟩ **4** : BEAR, CARRY, COMPORT ⟨*hold* oneself proudly⟩ **5 a** : to keep up without interruption or flagging ⟨*hold* silence⟩ **b** : to keep the uninterrupted interest, attention, or devotion of **6 a** : to receive and retain : CONTAIN, ACCOMMODATE ⟨the can *holds* 20 liters⟩ **b** : to have in store ⟨what the future *holds*⟩ **7 a** : HARBOR, ENTERTAIN ⟨*hold* a theory⟩ **b** : CONSIDER, REGARD, JUDGE ⟨truths *held* to be self-evident⟩ **8** : to schedule and carry out (as a social event or a conference) **9 a** : to have (as an office) by election or appointment ⟨*holds* a captaincy in the navy⟩ **b** : to have earned or been awarded ⟨*holds* a Ph.D.⟩ **10** : to handle (as reins or a gun) so as to guide or manage **11 a** : to maintain position : not retreat **b** (1) : to continue in the same way or state : LAST ⟨hope the weather *holds*⟩ (2) : to endure a test or trial ⟨their courage *held* against all odds⟩ **c** : to remain steadfast or faithful ⟨*held* to their beliefs⟩ **12** : to maintain a grasp on something : remain fastened to something ⟨the anchor *held* in the rough sea⟩ **13** : to bear or carry oneself ⟨asked them to *hold* still⟩ **14** : to be or remain valid : APPLY ⟨the rule *holds* in most cases⟩ **15** : to forbear an intended or threatened action : HALT, PAUSE [Old English *healdan*] SYN see CONTAIN — **hold forth** : to talk or preach at length — **hold one's own** : to prove at least equal to opposition — **hold the bag 1** : to be left empty-handed **2** : to bear alone a responsibility that should have been shared by others — **hold water** : to stand up under criticism or analysis — **hold with** : to agree with or approve of

²hold *n* **1** : STRONGHOLD 1 **2** : the act or manner of holding : SEIZURE, GRASP ⟨took a firm *hold* on the rope⟩ **3** : a manner of grasping the opponent in wrestling **4** : the authority to take or keep : POWER ⟨had a strong *hold* over their children⟩ **5** : something that may be grasped or held **6** : a prolonged note or rest in music; *also* : a sign ⌢ or ⌣ denoting a hold **7** : an order or indication that something is to be reserved or delayed

³hold *n* **1** : the interior of a ship below decks; *esp* : the cargo deck of a ship **2** : the cargo compartment of an airplane [alteration of *hole*]

hold·all \ˈhōl-ˌdȯl\ *n, chiefly British* : an often cloth traveling case or bag

hold·er \ˈhōl-dər\ *n* **1** : a person that holds: **a** (1) : OWNER — often used in combination ⟨job*holder*⟩ (2) : TENANT 1 **b** : a person in possession of and legally entitled to receive payment of a bill, note, or check **2** : a device that holds

hold·fast \ˈhōld-ˌfast, ˈhōl-\ *n* : a part by which a plant or animal clings (as to a flat surface or the body of a host)

hold·ing \ˈhōl-ding\ *n* **1 a** : land held (as for farming or residence) **b** : property (as bonds or stocks) owned — usually used in pl. **2** : a ruling of a court especially on an issue of law raised in a case

holding company *n* : a company that owns part or all of other companies for purposes of control

holding pattern *n* : the course flown (as over an airport) by an aircraft awaiting permission to land

hold out \hōl-ˈdaŭt, ˈhōl-\ *vb* **1** : PROFFER ⟨*held out* little chance of success⟩ **2** : REPRESENT 4 ⟨*hold* oneself *out* to be a scholar⟩ **3** : to remain unsubdued or operative : continue to cope **4** : to refuse to come to an agreement — **hold·out** \ˈhōl-ˌdaŭt\ *n*

hold over \hōl-ˈdō-vər, ˈhōl-\ *vb* **1** : to continue (as in office) beyond the normal term **2** : to prolong the engagement or tenure of — **hold·over** \ˈhōl-ˌdō-vər\ *n*

hold up \hōl-ˈdəp, ˈhōl-\ *vt* **1** : DELAY, IMPEDE ⟨only *holding* things *up*⟩ **2** : to rob at gunpoint — **hold·up** \ˈhōl-ˌdəp\ *n*

hole \ˈhōl\ *n* **1** : an opening into or through a thing ⟨a *hole* in a wall⟩ **2 a** : a hollow place (as a pit or cave) **b** : a deep place in a body of water ⟨trout *holes*⟩ **3** : an underground habitation : BURROW ⟨a fox in its *hole*⟩ **4** : FLAW, FAULT ⟨a big *hole* in your argument⟩ **5 a** : a cavity in the putting green of a golf course into which the ball is played **b** : the play or the part of the course from the tee to the hole **6** : a mean or dingy place ⟨lives in a real *hole*⟩ **7** : an awkward position : FIX [Old English *hol* and *holh*] — **hole** *vb* — **hol·ey** \ˈhō-lē\ *adj* — **in the hole 1** : in debt **2** : having a score below zero

hol·i·day \ˈhäl-ə-ˌdā\ *n* **1** : HOLY DAY **2** : a day of freedom from work; *esp* : a day of celebration or commemoration fixed by law **3** : a period of relaxation : VACATION [Old English *hāligdæg*, from *hālig* "holy" + *dæg* "day"] — **holiday** *vi* — **hol·i·day·er** *n*

ho·li·ness \ˈhō-lē-nəs\ *n* **1** : the quality or state of being holy **2** *cap* — used as a form of address for various high religious dignitaries ⟨His *Holiness* Pope John Paul II⟩ ⟨Your *Holiness*⟩

hol·land \ˈhäl-ənd\ *n* : a cotton or linen fabric in plain weave usually heavily sized or glazed and used especially for window shades [Middle English *Holand*, county in the Netherlands, from Dutch *Holland*]

hol·lan·daise sauce \ˌhäl-ən-ˈdāz-\ *n* : a sauce made of butter, yolks of eggs, and lemon juice or vinegar [French sauce *hollandaise*, literally, "Dutch sauce"]

¹hol·ler \ˈhäl-ər\ *vb* **hol·lered; hol·ler·ing** \ˈhäl-ring, -ə-ring\ **1** : to cry or call out : SHOUT **2** : COMPLAIN 1 [alteration of *hollo*, of unknown origin]

²holler *n* **1** : SHOUT, CRY **2** : COMPLAINT 1

hol·lo \hä-ˈlō, hə-; ˈhäl-ō\ *or* **hal·lo** \hə-ˈlō, ha-\ *or* **hal·loo** \-ˈlü\ *interj* **1** — used to attract attention **2** — used as a call of encouragement or jubilation

¹hol·low \ˈhäl-ō\ *adj* **1** : curved inward : SUNKEN ⟨*hollow* cheeks⟩ **2** : having a hole inside : not solid throughout ⟨a *hollow* tree⟩ **3 a** : FALSE, DECEITFUL ⟨*hollow* promises⟩ **b** : apparently but not really valuable or significant ⟨a *hollow* victory⟩ **4** : echoing like a sound made in a large empty enclosure or by beating on a hollow object [Middle English *holh, holw,* from *holh* "hole, den", from Old English, "hole, hollow"] — **hol·low·ly** *adv* — **hol·low·ness** *n*

²hollow *vb* : to make or become hollow

³hollow *n* **1** : a low spot in a surface; *esp* : VALLEY **2** : an empty space within something : HOLE ⟨the *hollow* of a tree⟩

hol·low·ware *or* **hol·lo·ware** \ˈhäl-ə-ˌwaər, -ˌweər\ *n* **1** : vessels (as cups or vases) usually of pottery or glass that have significant depth **2** : domestic metalware and especially tableware other than flatware

\ə\	abut	\ng\	sing
\ər\	further	\ō\	bone
\a\	mat	\ȯ\	saw
\ā\	take	\ȯi\	coin
\ä\	cot, cart	\th\	thin
\aŭ\	out	\th\	this
\ch\	chin	\ü\	food
\e\	pet	\ u̇ \	foot
\ē\	easy	\y\	yet
\g\	go	\yü\	few
\i\	tip	\yu̇\	cure
\ī\	life	\zh\	vision
\j\	job		

holly

hol·ly \'häl-ē\ *n, pl* **hollies** : any of a genus of trees and shrubs with thick glossy spiny-margined leaves and usually bright red berries; *also* : the foliage or branches of a holly [Old English *holegn*]

hol·ly·hock \'häl-ē-,häk, -,hȯk\ *n* : a tall widely grown perennial Chinese herb of the mallow family with large coarse rounded leaves and tall spikes of showy flowers [Middle English *holihoc*, from *holi* "holy" + *hoc* "mallow", from Old English]

Hol·ly·wood bed \'häl-ē-,wu̇d-\ *n* : a mattress on a box spring supported by low legs sometimes with an upholstered headboard [*Hollywood,* district of Los Angeles, California]

hol·mi·um \'hōl-mē-əm, 'hō-\ *n* : a metallic element that occurs with yttrium and forms highly magnetic compounds — see ELEMENT table [New Latin, from *Holmia* (Stockholm), Sweden]

holo- — see HOL-

ho·lo·caust \'häl-ə-,kȯst, 'hō-lə- also 'hȯ-lə-\ *n* **1** : a sacrifice consumed by fire **2** : a thorough destruction especially by fire [Old French *holocauste,* from Late Latin *holocaustum,* from Greek *holokauston,* from *holokaustos* "burnt whole", from *holos* "whole" + *kaustos* "burnt", from *kaiein* "to burn"]

Ho·lo·cene \'hō-lə-,sēn, 'häl-ə-\ *adj* : of, relating to, or being the present epoch of the Quaternary which is dated from the close of the Pleistocene — **Holocene** *n*

ho·lo·gram \'hō-lə-,gram, 'häl-ə-\ *n* : a three-dimensional image reproduced from a pattern of interference produced by a laser; *also* : the pattern of interference itself

ho·lo·graph \'hō-lə-,graf, 'häl-ə-\ *n* : a document wholly in the handwriting of its author — **holograph** *adj* — **ho·lo·graph·ic** \,hō-lə-'graf-ik, ,häl-ə-\ *adj*

ho·log·ra·phy \hō-'läg-rə-fē\ *n* : the process of making or using a hologram — **ho·lo·graph** \'hō-lə-,graf, 'häl-ə-\ *vt* — **ho·lo·graph·ic** \,hō-lə-'graf-ik, ,häl-ə-\ *adj* — **ho·lo·graph·i·cal·ly** \-i-kə-lē, -klē\ *adv*

ho·lo·thu·ri·an \,hō-lə-'thu̇r-ē-ən, ,häl-ə-, -'thyu̇r-\ *n* : SEA CUCUMBER [derived from Greek *holothourion,* a water polyp] — **holothurian** *adj*

hol·stein \'hōl-,stēn, -,stīn\ *n* : any of a breed of large black-and-white dairy cattle that produce large quantities of comparatively low-fat milk [short for *holstein-friesian*]

hol·stein–frie·sian \-'frē-zhən\ *n* : HOLSTEIN [*Holstein,* Germany + *Friesian,* variant of Frisian]

hol·ster \'hōl-stər, 'hōlt-\ *n* : a usually leather case for carrying a pistol [Dutch]

ho·ly \'hō-lē\ *adj* **ho·li·er; -est** **1** : set apart to the service of God or a god : SACRED **2 a** : commanding absolute adoration and reverence **b** : spiritually pure : SAINTLY **3 a** : evoking or meriting veneration or awe **b** : being awesome, frightening, or beyond belief ⟨a *holy* terror⟩ [Old English *hālig*]

Holy Communion *n* : COMMUNION 1a

holy day *n* : a day observed as a religious feast or fast

holy day of obligation : a feast on which Roman Catholics are obliged to hear mass

Holy Father *n* : POPE

Holy Ghost *n* : HOLY SPIRIT

Holy Grail *n* : GRAIL

holy order *n, often cap H&O* **1 a** : MAJOR ORDER — usually used in pl. **b** : one of the orders of the ministry in the Anglican or Episcopal church **2** : the rite or sacrament of ordination — usually used in pl.

Holy Roman Empire *n* : a loose confederation of German and Italian territories under an emperor that existed from the 9th or 10th century to 1806

Holy Saturday *n* : the Saturday before Easter

Holy See *n* : the see of the pope

Holy Spirit *n* : the active presence of God in human life constituting the third person of the Trinity

ho·ly·stone \'hō-lē-,stōn\ *n* : a soft sandstone used to scrub a ship's decks — **holystone** *vb*

Holy Thursday *n* : MAUNDY THURSDAY

holy water *n* : water blessed by a priest and used as a purifying sacramental

Holy Week *n* : the week before Easter

Holy Writ *n* : BIBLE 1, 2

hom- *or* **homo-** *combining form* : one and the same : similar : alike ⟨*homo*graph⟩ [Greek *homos* "same"]

hom·age \'äm-ij, 'häm-\ *n* **1** : a ceremony in which a person pledged allegiance to a lord and became his vassal **2** : something done or given as an acknowledgment of a vassal's duty to his lord **3 a** : respectful admiration : HONOR **b** : flattering attention : TRIBUTE [Old French *hommage,* from *homme* "man, vassal", from Latin *homo* "man"]

hom·bre \'äm-brē, -,brä\ *n* : FELLOW 4a [Spanish, "man", from Latin *homo*]

hom·burg \'häm-,bərg\ *n* : a man's felt hat with a stiff curled brim and a high crown creased lengthwise [*Homburg,* Germany]

¹home \'hōm\ *n* **1 a** : the house in which one lives or in which one's family lives **b** : a dwelling house ⟨new *homes* for sale⟩ **2** : the social unit formed by a family living together in one dwelling ⟨a city of 20,000 *homes*⟩ **3** : the country or place where one lives or where one's ancestors lived **4** : the place where something is usually or naturally found : HABITAT ⟨the *home* of the elephant⟩ **5** : a place for the care of persons unable to care for themselves ⟨a *home* for old people⟩ **6** : the goal or point to be reached in some games [Old English *hām* "village, home"]

²home *adv* **1** : to or at home ⟨go *home*⟩ ⟨stay *home*⟩ **2** : to a final, closed, or standard position ⟨drive a nail *home*⟩ **3** : to a vital core ⟨the truth struck *home*⟩

³home *vb* **1 a** : to go or return home **b** : to return home accurately from a distance ⟨a pigeon *homes* to its loft⟩ **c** : to proceed to or toward a source of radiated energy used as a guide ⟨missiles *home* in on radar⟩ **2** : to have a home **3** : to send to or provide with a home

home- *or* **homeo-** *also* **homoi-** *or* **homoio-** *combining form* : like : similar ⟨*homeo*stasis⟩ ⟨*homoio*thermic⟩ [Greek *homoios,* from *homos* "same"]

home·body \'hōm-,bäd-ē\ *n* : one whose life centers around the home

home·boy \'hōm-,bȯi\ *n* **1** : a boy or man from one's neighborhood, home town, or region **2** : a fellow member of a youth gang

home·bred \-'bred\ *adj* : produced at home : INDIGENOUS

home brew *n* : an alcoholic beverage made at home

home·com·ing \'hōm-,kəm-ing\ *n* **1** : a return home **2 a** : the return of a group of people especially on a special occasion to a place formerly frequented **b** : an annual celebration for alumni at a college or university

home computer *n* : a small inexpensive microcomputer

home economics *n* : the study of the various arts and skills involved in running a household — **home economist** *n*

home front *n* : the sphere of civilian activity in war

home·grown \'hōm-'grōn\ *adj* **1** : grown or produced at home or nearby **2** : INDIGENOUS ⟨*homegrown* politicians⟩

home·land \'hōm-,land\ *n* : native land : FATHERLAND

home·less \'hōm-ləs\ *adj* : having no home or permanent place of residence

home·like \-,līk\ *adj* : having qualities suggestive of a home or family living

home·ly \'hōm-lē\ *adj* **home·li·er; -est** **1** : characteristic of home life : PLAIN, SIMPLE ⟨*homely* meals⟩ **2** : lacking polish or refinement ⟨*homely* manners⟩ **3** : not handsome ⟨a *homely* person⟩ — **home·li·ness** *n*

home·made \'hōm-'mād, 'hō-\ *adj* : made in the home, on the premises, or by one's own efforts ⟨*homemade* bread⟩

home·mak·er \'hōm-,mā-kər\ *n* : a person who manages a household especially as a wife and mother — **home·mak·ing** \-king\ *n or adj*

ho·me·op·a·thy \,hō-mē-'äp-ə-thē\ *n* : a system of medical practice that treats disease especially with minute doses of material that would in healthy persons produce symptoms of the disease treated — **ho·meo·path** \'hō-mē-ə-,path\ *n* — **ho·meo·path·ic** \,hō-mē-ə-'path-ik\ *adj*

ho·meo·sta·sis \,hō-mē-ō-'stā-səs\ *n* : a tendency toward keeping a relatively stable internal environment in the bodies of higher animals by means of complex physiological interactions — **ho·meo·stat·ic** \-mē-ō-'stat-ik\ *adj*

home plate *n* : the rubber slab at the apex of a baseball diamond that the batter stands beside and must return to in order to score

hom·er \'hō-mər\ *n* **1** : HOMING PIGEON **2** : HOME RUN

home range *n* : the area to which an animal confines its activities — compare TERRITORY

Ho·mer·ic \hō-'mer-ik\ *adj* : of, relating to, or characteristic of the Greek poet Homer, his age, or his writings — **Ho·mer·i·cal·ly** \-i-kə-lē, -klē\ *adv*

home·room \'hōm-,rüm, -,rüm\ *n* : a schoolroom where pupils of the same class report at the opening of school

home rule *n* : self-government in internal affairs by the people of a dependent political unit

home run *n* : a hit in baseball that enables the batter to round all the bases and score a run — called also *homer*

home·sick \'hōm-,sik\ *adj* : longing for home and family while absent from them — **home·sick·ness** *n*

¹home·spun \-,spən\ *adj* **1 a** : spun or made at home **b** : made of homespun **2** : SIMPLE 3a(1), HOMELY ⟨*homespun* humor⟩

²homespun *n* : a loosely woven usually woolen or linen fabric originally made from homespun yarn

¹home·stead \'hōm-,sted\ *n* **1 a** : the home and adjoining land occupied by a family **b** : an ancestral home **2** : a tract of land acquired from United States public lands by filing a record and living on and cultivating it

²homestead *vb* : to acquire or settle on land for use as a homestead ⟨*homesteaded* in Alaska⟩

home·stead·er \-,sted-ər\ *n* : one that holds a homestead; *esp* : a person with a homestead acquired under laws authorizing the sale of public lands in parcels of about 64.75 hectares to settlers

home·stretch \'hōm-'strech\ *n* **1** : the part of a racecourse between the last curve and the winning post **2** : a final stage (as of a project)

home·ward \'hōm-wərd\ *or* **home·wards** \-wərdz\ *adv* : toward or in the direction of home — **homeward** *adj*

home·work \-,wərk\ *n* : work and especially school lessons to be done at home

hom·ey \'hō-mē\ *adj* **hom·i·er; -est** : HOMELIKE, INTIMATE — **hom·ey·ness** *or* **hom·i·ness** *n*

ho·mi·cid·al \,häm-ə-'sīd-l, ,hō-mə-\ *adj* : having or showing tendencies toward homicide : MURDEROUS — **ho·mi·cid·al·ly** \-l-ē\ *adv*

ho·mi·cide \'häm-ə-,sīd, 'hō-mə-\ *n* **1** : a person who kills another **2** : a killing of one human being by another [Middle French, from Latin *homicida*, from *homo* "man" + *-cida* "-cide"]

hom·i·let·ic \,häm-ə-'let-ik\ *adj* **1** : of the nature of a homily **2** : of or relating to homiletics — **hom·i·let·i·cal** \-i-kəl\ *adj* — **hom·i·let·i·cal·ly** \-i-kə-lē, -klē\ *adv*

hom·i·let·ics \-'let-iks\ *n* : the art of preaching

hom·i·ly \'häm-ə-lē\ *n, pl* **-lies** **1** : SERMON; *esp* : an informal explanation of Scripture **2** : a moral lecture [Middle French *omelie,* from Late Latin *homilia,* from Greek, "conversation, discourse", from *homilein* "to consort with, address", from *homilos* "crowd, assembly"]

homing pigeon *n* : a racing pigeon trained to return home

hom·i·nid \'häm-ə-nəd\ *n* : any of a family (Hominidae) of 2-footed primate mammals comprising recent human beings, their immediate ancestors, and related extinct forms [derived from Latin *homin-, homo* "man"] — **hominid** *adj*

hom·i·noid \'häm-ə-,nòid\ *adj* : resembling or related to the biological family to which human beings belong — **hominoid** *n*

hom·i·ny \'häm-ə-nē\ *n* : hulled corn with the germ removed [of American Indian origin]

ho·mo \'hō-mō\ *n* : any of a genus (Homo) of primate mammals that includes modern humans (*H. sapiens*) and several extinct related species [Latin, "man"]

homo- — see HOM-

ho·mog·e·nate \hō-'mäj-ə-,nāt\ *n* : a product of homogenizing

ho·mo·ge·ne·i·ty \,hō-mə-jə-'nē-ət-ē, -'nā-ət-\ *n* : the quality or state of being homogeneous

ho·mo·ge·neous \-'jē-nē-əs, -nyəs\ *adj* **1** : of the same or a similar kind or nature **2** : of uniform structure or composition throughout [Medieval Latin *homogeneus,* from Greek *homogenēs,* from *homos* "same" + *genos* "kind"] — **ho·mo·ge·neous·ly** *adv* — **ho·mo·ge·neous·ness** *n*

ho·mog·e·nize \hə-'mäj-ə-,nīz, hō-\ *vt* **1** : to make homogeneous **2 a** : to reduce to small particles of uniform size and distribute evenly ⟨*homogenize* paint⟩ **b** : to break up the fat globules of (milk) into very fine particles especially by forcing through minute openings — **ho·mog·e·ni·za·tion** \-,mäj-ə-nə-'zā-shən\ *n* — **ho·mog·e·niz·er** \-'mäj-ə-,nī-zər\ *n*

ho·mog·e·nous \-'mäj-ə-nəs\ *adj* : HOMOGENEOUS

ho·mo·graph \'häm-ə-,graf, 'hō-mə-\ *n* : one of two or more words alike in spelling but different in origin or meaning or pronunciation ⟨the noun conduct and the verb conduct are *homographs*⟩ — **ho·mo·graph·ic** \,häm-ə-'graf-ik, ,hō-mə-\ *adj*

homoi- *or* **homoio-** — see HOME-

ho·moio·ther·mic \hō-,mòi-ə-'thər-mik\ *or* **ho·moio·ther·mal** \-məl\ *adj* : WARM-BLOODED — **ho·moio·therm** \-'mòi-ə-,thərm\ *n*

ho·mol·o·gous \hō-'mäl-ə-gəs, hə-\ *adj* **1 a** : having the same relative position, value, or structure **b** (1) : corresponding in structure because of derivation from the same or a similar part of a remote ancestor ⟨arms and wings are *homologous* structures⟩ (2) : having the same or allelic genes with corresponding genes arranged in the same order ⟨*homologous* chromosomes⟩ **2** : derived from or developed in response to organisms of the same species ⟨*homologous* tissue graft⟩ [Greek *homologos* "agreeing", from *homos* "same" + *legein* "to say"]

ho·mo·logue *or* **ho·mo·log** \'hō-mə-,lóg, 'häm-ə-, -,läg\ *n* : something that is homologous

ho·mol·o·gy \hō-'mäl-ə-jē, hə-\ *n, pl* **-gies** **1** : a similarity often attributable to common origin **2 a** : structural likeness between corresponding parts of different organisms due to evolution from a remote common ancestor — compare ANALOGY **b** : structural likeness between different parts of the same individual

hom·onym \'häm-ə-,nim, 'hō-mə-\ *n* **1 a** : HOMOPHONE **b** : HOMOGRAPH **2** : one of two or more words spelled and pronounced alike but different in meaning ⟨*pool* of water and *pool* (the game) are *homonyms*⟩ [Latin *homonymum,* from Greek *homōnymon,* from *homōnymos* "having the same name", from *homos* "same" + *onyma, onoma* "name"] — **hom·onym·ic** \,häm-ə-'nim-ik, ,hō-mə-\ *adj*

ho·mo·phone \'häm-ə-,fōn, 'hō-mə-\ *n* : one of two or more words pronounced alike but different in meaning or derivation or spelling ⟨*to, too,* and *two* are *homophones*⟩ — **ho·moph·o·nous** \hō-'mäf-ə-nəs\ *adj*

ho·mo·phon·ic \,häm-ə-'fän-ik, ,hō-mə-\ *adj* : of, relating to, or being music consisting of a single accompanied melodic line — **ho·moph·o·ny** \hō-'mäf-ə-nē\ *n*

\ə\ abut		\ng\ sing	
\ər\ further		\ō\ bone	
\a\ mat		\ó\ saw	
\ā\ take		\òi\ coin	
\ä\ cot, cart		\th\ thin	
\aů\ out		\th\ this	
\ch\ chin		\ü\ food	
\e\ pet		\ů\ foot	
\ē\ easy		\y\ yet	
\g\ go		\yü\ few	
\i\ tip		\yů\ cure	
\ī\ life		\zh\ vision	
\j\ job			

ho·mop·ter·ous \hō-'mäp-tə-rəs\ *adj* : of or relating to a group (Homoptera) of insects (as cicadas, aphids, or scale insects) having sucking mouthparts [derived from Greek *homos* "same" + *pteron* "wing"] — **ho·mop·ter·an** \-rən\ *adj or n*

Ho·mo sa·pi·ens \‚hō-mō-'sap-ē-ənz, -'sā-pē-, -‚enz\ *n* : HUMANITY 4 [New Latin, species name, from Latin *homo* "man" + *sapiens* "wise, intelligent"]

ho·mo·sex·u·al \‚hō-mə-'sek-shə-wəl, -shəl\ *adj* : of, relating to, or exhibiting sexual desire toward a member of one's own sex — **homosexual** *n* — **ho·mo·sex·u·al·i·ty** \-‚sek-shə-'wal-ət-ē\ *n*

ho·mo·zy·gote \-'zī-‚gōt\ *n* : a plant or animal with at least one gene pair containing identical genes — **ho·mo·zy·gos·i·ty** \-‚zī-'gäs-ət-ē\ *n* — **ho·mo·zy·gous** \-'zī-gəs\ *adj*

hone \'hōn\ *vt* : to sharpen or smooth with or as if with a fine abrasive stone — **hon·er** *n*

hon·est \'än-əst\ *adj* **1 a** : free from fraud or deception : TRUTHFUL ⟨an *honest* plea⟩ **b** : GENUINE, REAL ⟨made an *honest* mistake⟩ **c** : free from ornament or pretense : PLAIN **2** : virtuous in the eyes of society : RESPECTABLE **3** : of a creditable nature : PRAISEWORTHY ⟨do an *honest* job⟩ **4 a** : marked by integrity : UPRIGHT **b** : marked by frankness or sincerity : STRAIGHTFORWARD **c** : INNOCENT 4, SIMPLE [Old French *honeste*, from Latin *honestus* "honorable", from *honos, honor* "honor"] — **hon·est·ly** *adv*

hon·es·ty \'än-ə-stē\ *n* **1** : fairness and straightforwardness of conduct : INTEGRITY **2** : TRUTHFULNESS, SINCERITY ⟨*honesty* is the best policy⟩

¹hon·ey \'hən-ē\ *n, pl* **honeys** **1** : a thick sugary material prepared by bees from floral nectar and stored by them in a honeycomb for food **2 a** : SWEETHEART, DEAR — often used as a term of endearment **b** : something superlative ⟨a *honey* of a play⟩ **3** : the quality or state of being sweet : SWEETNESS [Old English *hunig*] — **honey** *adj*

²honey *vb* **hon·eyed** *also* **hon·ied**; **hon·ey·ing** **1** : to sweeten with or as if with honey **2** : to speak ingratiatingly : FLATTER

hon·ey·bee \'hən-ē-‚bē\ *n* : a social honey-producing bee; *esp* : a European bee widely kept for its honey and wax

¹hon·ey·comb \-‚kōm\ *n* **1** : a mass of 6-sided wax cells built by honeybees in their nest for rearing larvae and storing honey **2** : something that resembles a honeycomb in structure or appearance

²honeycomb *vb* : to make or become full of holes like a honeycomb

hon·ey·dew \'hən-ē-‚dü, -‚dyü\ *n* : a sugary deposit secreted on the leaves of plants by aphids, scale insects, or fungus

honeydew melon *n* : a pale smooth-skinned muskmelon with sweet greenish flesh

honey locust *n* : a tall usually spiny North American tree of the pea family with hard durable wood and long flat twisted pods

hon·ey·moon \'hən-ē-‚mün\ *n* **1** : the time immediately after marriage **2** : the holiday spent by a newly-married couple [from the idea that the first month of marriage is the sweetest] — **honeymoon** *vi* — **hon·ey·moon·er** *n*

hon·ey·suck·le \-‚sək-əl\ *n* : any of a genus of shrubs with opposite leaves and often showy flowers rich in nectar; *also* : any of various plants (as a columbine or azalea) with tubular flowers rich in nectar [Old English *hunisūce*, from *hunig* "honey" + *sūcan* "to suck"]

honk \'hängk, 'hȯngk\ *vb* : to utter the characteristic cry of a goose or a similar sound [imitative] — **honk** *n*

hon·ky–tonk \'häng-kē-‚tängk, 'hȯng-kē-‚tȯngk\ *n* : a cheap nightclub or dance hall [origin unknown]

¹hon·or \'än-ər\ *n* **1 a** : good name : public esteem : REPUTATION **b** : a showing of usually merited respect ⟨a

honeybee: *left* worker, *middle* queen, *right* drone

leader worthy of all possible *honor*⟩ **2** : PRIVILEGE ⟨whom have I the *honor* of addressing⟩ **3** *cap* — used especially as a title for a holder of high usually judicial office ⟨if Your *Honor* please⟩ **4** : one whose worth brings respect or fame : CREDIT ⟨an *honor* to your profession⟩ **5** : an evidence or symbol of distinction: as **a** : an exalted title or rank **b** : BADGE 3, DECORATION **c** : a ceremonial rite or observance ⟨buried with full military *honors*⟩ **d** *pl* : an academic distinction conferred on a superior student **e** : an award in a contest or field of competition **6** : CHASTITY, PURITY **7 a** : a keen sense of ethical conduct : INTEGRITY ⟨a person of *honor*⟩ **b** : one's word given as a guarantee of performance **8** *pl* : social courtesies or civilities extended by a host ⟨did the *honors* at the table⟩ [Old French, from Latin *honos, honor*] SYN see DEFERENCE

²honor *vt* **hon·ored; hon·or·ing** \'än-ring, -ə-ring\ **1 a** : to regard or treat with honor : RESPECT ⟨*honor* your parents⟩ **b** : to confer honor on **2** : to live up to or fulfill the terms of; *esp* : to accept and pay when due ⟨*honor* a check⟩ **3** : to salute with a bow in square dancing

hon·or·able \'än-rə-bəl, -ə-rə-; 'än-ər-bəl\ *adj* **1** : deserving of honor and respect **2** : performed or accompanied with marks of honor or respect ⟨an *honorable* burial⟩ **3 a** : of great renown : ILLUSTRIOUS **b** *cap* — used as a title usually preceded by the and placed before the names of various high-ranking persons ⟨the *Honorable* John M. Doe⟩ ⟨the *Honorable* Jane M. Doe⟩ ⟨met the *Honorable* Mr. Doe⟩ ⟨met the *Honorable* Ms. Doe⟩ **4 a** : doing credit to the possessor **b** : consistent with an untarnished reputation **5** : characterized by integrity : ETHICAL — **hon·or·ably** \-blē\ *adv*

hon·o·rar·i·um \‚än-ə-'rer-ē-əm\ *n, pl* **-ia** \-ē-ə\ *also* **-iums** : a reward usually for professional services on which custom forbids a price to be set [Latin, from *honorarius* "honorary"]

hon·or·ary \'än-ə-‚rer-ē\ *adj* **1 a** : having or conferring distinction **b** : COMMEMORATIVE ⟨an *honorary* plaque⟩ **2** : conferred in recognition of achievement or service without the usual requirements or obligations ⟨an *honorary* degree⟩ **3** : UNPAID, VOLUNTARY ⟨*honorary* chairman⟩ [Latin *honorarius*, from *honor* "honor"] — **hon·or·ar·i·ly** \‚än-ə-'rer-ə-lē\ *adv*

honor guard *n* : GUARD OF HONOR

¹hon·or·if·ic \‚än-ə-'rif-ik\ *adj* **1** : conferring or conveying honor **2** : belonging to or constituting a class of grammatical forms used in speaking to or about a social superior

²honorific *n* : an honorific word, phrase, or form

hon·our \'än-ər\ *chiefly British variant of* HONOR

¹hood \'hud\ *n* **1 a** : a flexible covering for the head and neck often attached to a coat or cape **b** : a protective covering for the head and face **2 a** (1) : an ornamental scarf worn over an academic gown (2) : an ornamental fold at the back of an ecclesiastical vestment **b** : a color marking, crest, or expandable fold on the head of an animal **3 a** : a covering that resembles a hood **b** : a cover for parts of mechanisms; *esp* : the movable metal covering over the engine of an automobile **c** : an enclosure provided with a draft for carrying off disagreeable or harmful fumes, sprays, or dust [Old English *hōd*] — **hood** *vt* — **hood·like** \-‚līk\ *adj*

²hood \'hud, 'hud\ *n* : HOODLUM

-hood \‚hud\ *n suffix* **1** : state : condition : quality : character ⟨child*hood*⟩ ⟨hardi*hood*⟩ **2** : instance of a (specified) state or quality ⟨false*hood*⟩ **3** : individuals sharing a (specified) state or character ⟨brother*hood*⟩ [Old English *-hād*]

hood·ed \'hud-əd\ *adj* : having or shaped like a hood — **hood·ed·ness** *n*

hood·lum \'hud-ləm\ *n* **1** : THUG, MOBSTER **2** : a young ruffian [origin unknown]

hoo·doo \'hud-ü\ *n, pl* **hoodoos** **1** : VOODOO 1 **2** : something that brings bad luck [of African origin] — **hoodoo** *vt* — **hoo·doo·ism** \-‚iz-əm\ *n*

hood·wink \'hùd-,wingk\ *vt* **1** *archaic* : BLINDFOLD **2** : DECEIVE, CHEAT [¹*hood* + *wink*]

hoo·ey \'hü-ē\ *n* : NONSENSE **1** [origin unknown]

¹**hoof** \'hùf, 'hüf\ *n, pl* **hooves** \'hùvz, 'hüvz\ *or* **hoofs** **1** : a curved covering of horn that protects the front of or encloses the ends of the toes of some mammals and that corresponds to a nail or claw **2** : a hoofed foot especially of a horse [Old English *hōf*] — **hoofed** \'hùft, 'hüft, 'hùvd, 'hüvd\ *adj* — **on the hoof** : LIVING ⟨meat animals bought *on the hoof*⟩

²**hoof** *vb* **1** : to move or traverse on foot : WALK **2** : DANCE **1, 3**

hoof–and–mouth disease *n* : FOOT-AND-MOUTH DISEASE

hoof·beat \'hùf-,bēt, 'hüf-\ *n* : the sound of a hoof striking a hard surface (as the ground)

¹**hook** \'hùk\ *n* **1** : a curved or bent implement for catching, holding, or pulling **2** : something curved or bent like a hook **3** : a path of a ball that deviates from a straight course in a direction opposite to the dominant hand of the player propelling it **4** : a short blow delivered with a circular motion by a boxer while the elbow remains bent and rigid [Old English *hōc*] — **by hook or by crook** : by any means — **off the hook** : out of trouble — **on one's own hook** : by oneself : INDEPENDENTLY

²**hook** *vb* **1** : to form into a hook : CROOK, CURVE **2 a** : to seize, make fast, or connect by or as if by a hook **b** : to become secured or connected by or as if by a hook **3** : to strike or pierce as if with a hook **4** : to make (as a rug) by drawing loops of thread, yarn, or cloth through a coarse fabric with a hook **5** : to propel (a ball) so that a hook results

hoo·kah \'hùk-ə, 'hü-kə\ *n* : a tobacco pipe with a water vessel and a long flexible tube so that the smoke is drawn through the water and cooled [Arabic *ḥuqqah* "bottle of a hookah"]

hook and eye *n* : a 2-part fastening device (as on a garment or a door) consisting of a wire hook that catches over a bar or into a loop of wire

hooked \'hùkt\ *adj* **1** : shaped like or furnished with a hook **2** : made by hooking ⟨a *hooked* rug⟩ **3 a** : addicted to narcotics **b** : fascinated by or devoted to something ⟨*hooked* on skiing⟩

¹**hook·er** \'hùk-ər\ *n* : one that hooks

²**hooker** *n* **1** : a one-masted fishing boat **2** : an outmoded or clumsy boat [Dutch *hoeker*, derived from *hoec* "fishhook"]

hook·up \'hùk-,əp\ *n* **1** : an assemblage (as of circuits) used for a specific purpose (as in radio); *also* : the plan of such an assemblage **2** : an arrangement of mechanical parts

hook·worm \'hùk-,wərm\ *n* **1** : any of several parasitic nematode worms which have strong hooks or plates about the mouth and some of which are serious blood-sucking pests **2** : a disordered state marked by blood loss, paleness, and weakness due to hookworms in the intestine — called also *hookworm disease*

hooky *or* **hook·ey** \'hùk-ē\ *n, pl* **hook·ies** *or* **hookeys** : TRUANT — used chiefly in the phrase *play hooky* [probably from slang *hook, hook it* "to make off"]

hoo·li·gan \'hü-li-gən\ *n* : RUFFIAN, HOODLUM [perhaps from Patrick *Hooligan*, 19th century Irish hoodlum in London] — **hoo·li·gan·ism** \-gə-,niz-əm\ *n*

¹**hoop** \'hùp, 'hüp\ *n* **1** : a circular strip used especially for holding together the staves of containers **2** : a circular figure or object : RING **3** : a circle or series of circles of flexible material used to expand a woman's skirt [Old English *hōp*]

²**hoop** *vt* : to bind or fasten with or as if with a hoop — **hoop·er** *n*

hoop·la \'hü-,plä\ *n* : great commotion and excitement : FUSS, BALLYHOO ⟨*hoopla* and fanfare of the bicentennial⟩ [French *houp-là*, *interj.*]

hoop·skirt \'hùp-,skərt, 'hüp-\ *n* : a skirt stiffened with or as if with hoops

hoo·ray \hù-'rā\ *variant of* HURRAH

hoose·gow \'hüs-,gaù\ *n, slang* : JAIL [Spanish *juzgado* "panel of judges, courtroom", from *juzgar* "to judge", from Latin *judicare*]

¹**hoot** \'hüt\ *vb* **1** : to utter a loud shout usually in contempt **2** : to make the characteristic cry of an owl or a similar cry **3** : to assail or drive out by hooting ⟨*hooted* the speaker off the stage⟩ **4** : to express in or by hoots ⟨*hooted* disapproval⟩ [Middle English *houten*] — **hoot·er** *n*

²**hoot** *n* **1** : the cry of an owl or a similar sound **2** : the least bit ⟨don't care a *hoot* about the book⟩

hoo·te·nan·ny \'hüt-n-,an-ē\ *n, pl* **-nies** : a gathering at which folksingers entertain often with the audience joining in [origin unknown]

¹**hop** \'häp\ *vb* **hopped; hop·ping** **1** : to move by a quick springy leap or in a series of leaps; *esp* : to jump on one foot **2** : to jump over ⟨*hop* a puddle⟩ **3** : to get aboard by or as if by hopping ⟨*hop* a train⟩ **4** : to make a quick trip especially by air [Old English *hoppian*]

²**hop** *n* **1 a** : a short brisk leap especially on one leg **b** : BOUNCE, REBOUND ⟨fielded the ball on the first *hop*⟩ **2** : DANCE, BALL ⟨the junior *hop*⟩ **3 a** : a flight in an airplane **b** : a short trip

³**hop** *n* **1** : a twining vine of the mulberry family with lobed leaves and female flowers in cone-shaped catkins **2** *pl* : the ripe dried catkins of a hop used especially to impart a bitter flavor to malt liquors [Dutch *hoppe*]

⁴**hop** *vt* **hopped; hop·ping** **1** : to flavor with hops **2** : to increase the power of beyond an original rating — used with up ⟨*hop* up an engine⟩

¹**hope** \'hōp\ *vb* **1** : to cherish a desire with expectation of fulfillment ⟨*hope* to succeed⟩ ⟨*hope* for peace⟩ **2** : to long for with expectation of obtainment **3** : to expect with desire : TRUST ⟨*hope* you'll accept the invitation⟩ [Old English *hopian*]

²**hope** *n* **1** : TRUST, RELIANCE ⟨our *hope* is in the Lord⟩ **2 a** : desire accompanied by expectation of or belief in fulfillment ⟨in *hope* of an early recovery⟩ **b** : someone or something on which hopes are centered ⟨a fast halfback was the team's only *hope* for victory⟩ **c** : something hoped for

hope chest *n* : a young woman's accumulation of clothes and domestic furnishings (as silver or linen) kept in or as if in a chest in anticipation of her marriage; *also* : a chest for such an accumulation

¹**hope·ful** \'hōp-fəl\ *adj* **1** : full of or inclined to hope **2** : having qualities which inspire hope ⟨a *hopeful* sign⟩ — **hope·ful·ly** \-fə-lē\ *adv* — **hope·ful·ness** *n*

²**hopeful** *n* : a person who has hopes or is considered promising especially as a political candidate

hope·less \'hō-pləs\ *adj* **1 a** : having no expectation of good or success **b** : not susceptible of remedy or cure : INCURABLE **2 a** : giving no ground for hope : DESPERATE ⟨a *hopeless* situation⟩ **b** : incapable of solution, management, or accomplishment : IMPOSSIBLE ⟨a *hopeless* task⟩ — **hope·less·ly** *adv* — **hope·less·ness** *n*

Ho·pi \'hō-pē\ *n, pl* **Hopi** *also* **Hopis** **1** : a member of an Indian people of what is now northeastern Arizona **2** : the Aztec-related language of the Hopi people [Hopi *Hópi*, literally, "good, peaceful"]

hop·lite \'häp-,līt\ *n* : a heavily armed infantry soldier of ancient Greece [Greek *hoplitēs*, from *hoplon* "tool, weapon"]

hop·per \'häp-ər\ *n* **1** : one that hops or leaps; *esp* : an immature hopping form of an insect (as a grasshopper) **2 a** : a usually funnel-shaped receptacle for delivering material (as grain or coal) **b** : a tank holding liquid and having a device for releasing its contents through a pipe **3** : a box in which a bill to be considered by a legislative body is dropped [sense 2 from the shaking motion of hoppers used to feed grain into a mill]

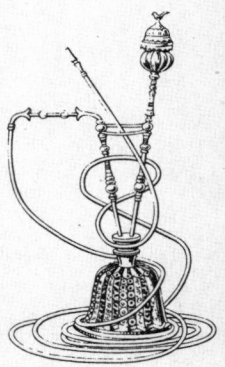

hookah

hop·scotch \'häp-,skäch\ *n* : a child's game in which a player tosses an object (as a stone) into areas of a figure outlined on the ground and hops through the figure and back to regain the object

ho·ra *also* **ho·rah** \'hōr-ə, 'hȯr-ə\ *n* : a circle dance of Rumania and Israel [Modern Hebrew *hōrāh,* from Rumanian *horă*]

horde \'hȯrd, 'hȯrd\ *n* **1 a** : a tribal group of Mongolian nomads **b** : a nomadic people or tribe **2** : a great multitude : THRONG, SWARM ⟨*hordes* of tourists⟩ [Polish *horda,* of Mongolic origin]

hore·hound \'hōr-,haund, 'hȯr-\ *n* : an aromatic bitter mint with hoary downy leaves; *also* : an extract or confection made from this plant [Old English *bārhūne,* from *bār* "hoary" + *hūne* "horehound"]

ho·ri·zon \hə-'rīz-n\ *n* **1** : the apparent junction of earth and sky **2** : the limit or range of a person's outlook or experience ⟨reading broadens our *horizons*⟩ **3 a** : the geological deposit of a particular time **b** : a distinct layer of soil or its underlying material in a vertical section of land [Late Latin *horizont-, horizon,* from Greek *horizont-, horizōn,* from *horizein* "to bound", from *horos* "boundary"] — **ho·ri·zon·al** \-'rīz-nəl, -n-əl\ *adj*

¹hor·i·zon·tal \,hȯr-ə-'zänt-l, ,här-\ *adj* **1 a** : of, relating to, or situated near the horizon **b** : parallel to, in the plane of, or operating in a plane parallel to the horizon or to a base line : LEVEL ⟨*horizontal* distance⟩ ⟨*horizontal* engine⟩ **2** : relating to or consisting of individuals or groups of similar level in a hierarchy ⟨*horizontal* labor unions⟩ — **hor·i·zon·tal·ly** \-l-ē\ *adv*

²horizontal *n* : something (as a line or plane) that is horizontal

horizontal bar *n* : a steel bar supported horizontally above the ground and used for swinging feats in gymnastics

hor·mone \'hȯr-,mōn\ *n* : a product of living cells that circulates in body fluids or sap and produces a specific and usually stimulatory effect on cells at a distance from the point of origin [Greek *hormōn,* present participle of *horman* "to stir up, set in motion"] — **hor·mon·al** \hȯr-'mōn-l\ *adj* — **hor·mon·al·ly** \-l-ē\ *adv*

horn \'hȯrn\ *n* **1 a** : one of the hard growths of bone or keratin on the head of many hoofed animals: as (1) : one of the permanent paired hollow sheaths of keratin usually present in both sexes of cattle and their relatives that function chiefly for defense and arise from a bony core anchored to the skull (2) : ANTLER **b** : a tough fibrous material that consists chiefly of keratin and forms the sheath of a true horn and horny parts (as hooves or nails) **2** : a hollow animal's horn used to hold something (as gunpowder) **3** : something resembling or suggestive of a horn: as **a** : one of the curved ends of a crescent **b** : the knob on the pommel of a western-style saddle **4** : a manufactured product (as a plastic) resembling horn **5 a** : an animal's horn used as a musical instrument **b** : a brass wind instrument; *esp* : FRENCH HORN **c** : a usually electrical device that makes a noise like that of a horn ⟨an automobile *horn*⟩ [Old English] — **horned** \'hȯrnd\ *adj* — **horn·less** \'hȯrn-ləs\ *adj* — **horn·less·ness** *n* — **horn·like** \-,līk\ *adj*

horn·beam \'hȯrn-,bēm\ *n* : any of a genus of trees of the birch family having smooth gray bark and hard white wood

horn·bill \-,bil\ *n* : any of a family of large Old World birds with enormous bills

horn·blende \-,blend\ *n* : a black, dark green, or brown mineral that occurs as distinct crystals and in columnar, fibrous, and granular form [German]

horn·book \-,buk\ *n* **1** : an early primer for children consisting of a sheet of parchment or paper containing the alphabet, numbers, and often religious verses or prayers protected by a transparent sheet of horn **2** : a treatise of basic principles or skills

hornbill

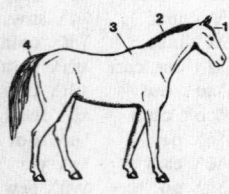

¹horse 1a (1): *1* forelock, *2* mane, *3* withers, *4* tail

horned owl *n* : any of several owls with conspicuous tufts of feathers on the head

horned pout *n* : a common bullhead of the eastern United States

horned toad *n* : any of several small harmless insect-eating lizards of the western United States and Mexico having hornlike spines

hor·net \'hȯr-nət\ *n* : any of the larger social wasps — compare YELLOW JACKET [Old English *byrnet*]

horn·fels \'hȯrn-,felz\ *n* : a fine-grained rock produced by the action of heat especially on slate [German, from *horn* "horn" + *fels* "cliff, rock"]

horn in *vi* : to participate without invitation or consent : INTRUDE ⟨*horn in* on a conversation⟩

horn of plenty : CORNUCOPIA 1

horn·pipe \'hȯrn-,pīp\ *n* **1** : a single-reed wind instrument consisting of a wooden or bone pipe with holes at intervals and a bell and mouthpiece usually of horn **2** : a lively folk dance of the British Isles originally accompanied by hornpipe playing

horn·tail \-,tāl\ *n* : any of a family of insects closely related to the sawflies

horn·worm \-,wərm\ *n* : a hawkmoth caterpillar having a hornlike tail process

horn·wort \-,wȯrt, -,wȯrt\ *n* : any of an order (Anthocerotales) of mostly aquatic plants related to the liverworts

horny \'hȯr-nē\ *adj* **horn·i·er; -est 1** : made of horn or of something resembling horn **2** : HARD, CALLOUS ⟨*horny* hands⟩

hor·o·scope \'hȯr-ə-,skōp, 'här-\ *n* **1** : a diagram of the relative positions of planets and signs of the zodiac at a specific time (as that of a person's birth) used by astrologers to infer character traits and foretell events **2** : an astrological forecast [Middle French, from Latin *horoscopus,* from Greek *horoskopos,* from *hora* "time, hour" + *skopein* "to look at"]

hor·ren·dous \hȯ-'ren-dəs, hä-\ *adj* : DREADFUL, HORRIBLE [Latin *horrendus,* from *horrēre* "to shudder"] — **hor·ren·dous·ly** *adv*

hor·ri·ble \'hȯr-ə-bəl, 'här-\ *adj* **1** : marked by or conducive to horror ⟨*horrible* scenes of death and destruction⟩ **2** : extremely unpleasant or disagreeable ⟨*had* horrible weather in July⟩ — **hor·ri·bly** \-blē\ *adv*

hor·rid \'hȯr-əd, 'här-\ *adj* **1** : HIDEOUS, SHOCKING ⟨the *horrid* rite of human sacrifice⟩ **2** : REPULSIVE 2, OFFENSIVE ⟨a *horrid* example⟩ [Latin *horridus,* from *horrēre* "to shudder"] — **hor·rid·ly** *adv* — **hor·rid·ness** *n*

hor·rif·ic \hȯ-'rif-ik, hä-\ *adj* : causing horror

hor·ri·fy \'hȯr-ə-,fī, 'här-\ *vt* **-fied; -fy·ing 1** : to cause to feel horror **2** : to fill with distaste : SHOCK

hor·ror \'hȯr-ər, 'här-\ *n* **1 a** : painful and intense fear, dread, or dismay **b** : intense aversion or repugnance **2 a** : the quality of inspiring horror **b** : something that inspires horror ⟨the war was a *horror*⟩ **3** *pl* : a state of extreme depression or apprehension [Middle French, from Latin, "action of trembling", from *horrēre* "to tremble, shudder"]

hors de combat \,ȯrd-ə-kōⁿ-'bä\ *adv or adj* : out of combat : disabled especially from fighting [French]

hors d'oeuvre \ȯr-'dərv\ *n, pl* **hors d'oeuvres** *also* **hors d'oeuvre** \-'dərvz, -'dərv\ : any of various savory foods usually served as appetizers at the beginning of a meal [French *hors-d'œuvre,* literally, "outside of work"]

¹horse \'hȯrs\ *n, pl* **hors·es** *also* **horse 1 a** (1) : a large solid-hoofed plant-eating mammal domesticated by man since a prehistoric period and used as a beast of burden, a draft animal, or for riding — compare PONY (2) : RACEHORSE ⟨play the *horses*⟩ **b** : a male horse : STALLION **2 a** : a frame that supports something (as wood while being cut or clothes while being dried) **b** : a piece of gymnasium equipment used for balancing and swinging movements or for vaulting exercises **3** *slang* : HEROIN [Old English *hors*] — **from the horse's mouth** : from the original source

²**horse** *vt* **1** : to provide with a horse **2** : to lift, pull, or push by brute force

³**horse** *adj* **1 a** : of or relating to the horse **b** : hauled or powered by a horse ⟨a *horse* barge⟩ **2** : large or coarse of its kind ⟨*horse* corn⟩ **3** : mounted on horses ⟨*horse* guards⟩

horse around *vi* : to engage in horseplay

¹**horse·back** \'hórs-‚bak\ *n* : the back of a horse

²**horseback** *adv* : on horseback

horse·car \'hór-‚skär\ *n* **1** : a streetcar drawn by horses **2** : a car for transporting horses

horse chestnut *n* : a large Asian tree that has palmate leaves and erect clusters of showy flowers and is widely grown as an ornamental and shade tree; *also* : its large glossy brown seed

horse·flesh \'hórs-‚flesh\ *n* : horses for riding, driving, or racing

horse·fly \-‚flī\ *n* : any of a family of swift usually large two-winged flies with bloodsucking females

horse·hair \-‚haər, -‚heər\ *n* **1** : the hair of a horse especially from the mane or tail **2** : cloth made from horsehair

horsehair worm *n* : any of various long slender worms whose adults live in water and whose larvae are parasites of insects — called also *horsehair snake*

horse·hide \'hórs-‚hīd\ *n* : a horse's hide or leather made from it

horse latitudes *n pl* : either of two belts or regions in the neighborhood of 30° north and 30° south latitude characterized by high pressure, calms, and light changeable winds

horse·laugh \'hór-‚slaf, -‚slaf\ *n* : a loud boisterous laugh

horse·less carriage \'hór-sləs-\ *n* : AUTOMOBILE

horse mackerel *n* : any of several large fishes (as a bluefin tuna)

horse·man \'hór-smən\ *n* **1 a** : a rider on horseback **b** : one skilled in managing horses **2** : a breeder or raiser of horses — **horse·man·ship** \-‚ship\ *n*

horse·mint \'hór-‚smint\ *n* : any of various coarse mints

horse nettle *n* : a coarse prickly weed with bright yellow fruit that is related to the nightshades

horse opera *n* : WESTERN 2

horse·play \'hór-‚splā\ *n* : rough or boisterous play

horse·pow·er \'hór-‚spaů-ər, -‚spaur\ *n* : a unit of power equal in the United States to 746 watts

horse·rad·ish \'hórs-‚rad-ish\ *n* : a tall coarse white-flowered herb of the mustard family; *also* : its pungent root used as a seasoning

horse sense *n* : COMMON SENSE

horse·shoe \'hórs-‚shü, 'hórsh-\ *n* **1** : a shoe for horses usually consisting of a narrow plate of iron shaped to fit the rim of a horse's hoof **2** : something (as a valley) shaped like a horseshoe **3** *pl* : a game in which horseshoes or horseshoe-shaped pieces of metal are tossed at a stake in the ground in an attempt to encircle the stake or come closer than one's opponent — **horseshoe** *vt* — **horse·sho·er** \-‚shü-ər\ *n*

horseshoe crab *n* : any of several closely related marine arthropods with a broad crescent-shaped cephalothorax — called also *king crab, limulus*

horse·tail \'hór-‚stāl\ *n* : EQUISETUM

horse trade *n* : negotiation accompanied by shrewd bargaining and concessions on both sides — **horse-trade** *vi* — **horse trader** *n*

horse·whip \'hór-‚swip, 'hórs-‚hwip\ *vt* : to flog with or as if with a whip made to be used on a horse

horse·wom·an \'hór-‚swům-ən\ *n* **1** : a woman horseback rider **2** : a woman skilled in riding horseback or in caring for or managing horses

hors·ey *or* **horsy** \'hór-sē\ *adj* **hors·i·er; -est 1** : of, relating to, or suggesting a horse **2 a** : having to do with horses or horse racing ⟨the *horsey* set⟩ **b** : characteristic of horsemen and horsewomen — **hors·i·ness** *n*

hor·ta·to·ry \'hórt-ə-‚tōr-ē, -‚tór-\ *adj* : given to or characterized by strong urging or encouragement [Late Latin *hortatorius*, from Latin *hortari* "to urge, exhort"]

hor·ti·cul·ture \'hórt-ə-‚kəl-chər\ *n* : the science and art of growing fruits, vegetables, flowers, or ornamental plants [Latin *hortus* "garden"] — **hor·ti·cul·tur·al** \‚hórt-ə-'kəlch-rəl, -ə-rəl\ *adj* — **hor·ti·cul·tur·al·ly** \-rə-lē\ *adv* — **hor·ti·cul·tur·ist** \-'kəlch-rəst, -ə-rəst\ *n*

ho·san·na \hō-'zan-ə\ *interj* — used as a cry of acclamation and adoration [Late Latin *osanna*, from Greek *hōsanna*, from Hebrew *hōshī ‘āh-nnā* "pray, save (us)!"]

¹**hose** \'hōz\ *n, pl* **hose** *or* **hos·es 1** *pl* **hose a** (1) : a cloth leg covering that sometimes covers the foot (2) : STOCKING 1, SOCK **b** (1) : a close-fitting garment covering the legs and waist that is usually attached to a doublet by points (2) : short breeches reaching to the knee **2** : a flexible tube for conveying a fluid (as from a faucet) [Old English *hosa* "stocking, husk"]

²**hose** *vt* : to spray, water, or wash with a hose

Ho·sea \hō-'zē-ə, -'zā-\ *n* — see BIBLE table

ho·siery \'hōzh-rē, 'hōz-, -ə-rē\ *n* : HOSE 1a

hos·pice \'häs-pəs\ *n* **1** : an inn for travelers; *esp* : one kept by a religious order **2** : a place or program for caring for dying persons [French, from Latin *hospitium* "lodging", from *hospit-, hospes* "host"]

hos·pi·ta·ble \hä-'spit-ə-bəl, 'häs-pit-\ *adj* **1 a** : showing hospitality : generous and cordial in receiving guests **b** : promising or suggesting generous and cordial welcome **c** : offering a pleasant or sustaining environment **2** : readily receptive : OPEN ⟨*hospitable* to new ideas⟩ — **hos·pi·ta·bly** \-blē\ *adv*

hos·pi·tal \'häs-‚pit-l\ *n* **1** : an institution where the sick or injured are given medical or surgical care **2** : a repair shop for specified small objects ⟨doll *hospital*⟩ [Old French, derived from Late Latin *hospitale* "hospice", from Latin, "guest room", from *hospit-, hospes* "host, guest"]

Hos·pi·tal·er *or* **Hos·pi·tal·ler** \-l-ər\ *n* : a member of a religious military order established in Jerusalem in the 12th century

hos·pi·tal·i·ty \‚häs-pə-'tal-ət-ē\ *n, pl* **-ties 1** : cordial reception and entertainment (as of guests) **2** : an instance of hospitality

hos·pi·tal·ize \'häs-‚pit-l-‚īz\ *vt* : to place in a hospital for care and treatment — **hos·pi·tal·iza·tion** \‚häs-‚pit-l-ə-'zā-shən\ *n*

¹**host** \'hōst\ *n* **1** : ARMY 1a **2** : a great number : MULTITUDE [Old French, from Late Latin *hostis*, from Latin, "stranger, enemy"]

²**host** *n* **1** : one who receives or entertains guests socially or as a business **2** : a living animal or plant that provides food and living space to a parasite [Old French *hoste* "host, guest", from Latin *hospit-, hospes*, from *hostis* "stranger"] — **host** *vt* — **host·al** \'hōst-l\ *adj*

³**host** *n, often cap* : the bread or wafer consecrated in the Mass [Middle French *hoiste*, from Latin *hostia* "sacrifice"]

hos·tage \'häs-tij\ *n* : a person held by one party in a conflict as a pledge that promises will be kept or terms met by the other party [Old French, from *hoste* "host, guest"]

hos·tel \'häst-l\ *n* **1** : INN 1 **2** : a supervised lodging for usually young travelers — called also *youth hostel* [Old French, from Late Latin *hospitale* "hospice"]

hos·tel·er \'häs-tə-lər\ *n* **1** : one that lodges guests or strangers **2** : a young traveler who stops at hostels

hos·tel·ry \'häst-l-rē\ *n, pl* **-ries** : INN 1, HOTEL

host·ess \'hō-stəs\ *n* : a woman who acts as host; *esp* : one who greets and provides service for patrons

hos·tile \'häst-l, 'häs-‚tīl\ *adj* **1** : of or relating to an enemy ⟨*hostile* troops⟩ **2** : marked by open antagonism : UNFRIENDLY **3** : not hospitable ⟨a *hostile* envi-

\ə\ abut	\ng\ sing
\ər\ further	\ō\ bone
\a\ mat	\ó\ saw
\ā\ take	\ói\ coin
\ä\ cot, cart	\th\ thin
\aů\ out	\t͟h\ this
\ch\ chin	\ü\ food
\e\ pet	\ů\ foot
\ē\ easy	\y\ yet
\g\ go	\yü\ few
\i\ tip	\yů\ cure
\ī\ life	\zh\ vision
\j\ job	

ronment) [Latin *hostilis,* from *hostis* "enemy"] — **hos-tile-ly** \-l-lē, -,tīl-lē\ *adv*

hos-til-i-ty \hä-'stil-ət-ē\ *n, pl* -ties **1 a** : a hostile state **b** (1) : hostile action (2) *pl* : overt acts of warfare **2** : antagonism, opposition, or resistance in thought or principle SYN see ENMITY

hos-tler \'äs-lər, 'häs-\ *also* **ost-ler** \'äs-\ *n* **1** : one who takes care of horses or mules **2** : one who services a vehicle (as a locomotive or truck) or machine (as a crane) [Middle English, "innkeeper, hostler", from *hostel*]

1hot \'hät\ *adj* **hot-ter; hot-test** **1 a** : having a relatively high temperature **b** : capable of burning, scalding, or searing **2** : having or showing intense feeling: as **a** : FIERY, VEHEMENT ⟨a *hot* temper⟩ **b** : VIOLENT 1 ⟨a *hot* battle⟩ **c** : LUSTFUL **d** : ZEALOUS ⟨*hot* for reform⟩ **3** : feeling or causing an uncomfortable degree of body heat **4 a** : NEW, FRESH ⟨*hot* off the press⟩ **b** : close to an objective ⟨guess again, you're getting *hotter*⟩ **c** : in close pursuit ⟨police were *hot* on their heels⟩ **5** : PUNGENT, SPICY ⟨*hot* sauces⟩ **6 a** : causing a sensation ⟨a *hot* scandal⟩ **b** : currently popular ⟨cotton is the *hot* item for spring clothes⟩ **c** : temporarily capable of unusual performances ⟨felt *hot* with the dice⟩ **d** — used as a generalized term of approval ⟨a *hot* new lawyer⟩ **7 a** : electrically charged especially with high voltage **b** : RADIOACTIVE **8** : recently stolen ⟨the jewels are *hot*⟩ **9** : dangerously unsafe ⟨police made the town too *hot* for them⟩ [Old English *hāt*] — **hot-ly** *adv* — **hot-ness** *n*

2hot *adv* : HOTLY

hot air *n* : empty talk

hot-bed \'hät-,bed\ *n* **1** : a bed of soil enclosed in glass, heated usually by fermenting manure, and used for forcing or for raising seedlings **2** : an environment that favors rapid growth or development ⟨a *hotbed* of dissent⟩

hot-blood-ed \-'bləd-əd\ *adj* : easily roused or excited : PASSIONATE — **hot-blood-ed-ness** *n*

hot-box \'hät-,bäks\ *n* : a bearing (as of a railroad car) overheated by friction

hot-cake \-,kāk\ *n* : PANCAKE

hotch-potch \'häch-,päch\ *n* : HODGEPODGE [Middle French *hochepot* "stew", from *hochier* "to shake" + *pot* "pot"]

hot cross bun *n* : a sweet bun that is marked with a cross on the top and often contains fruit (as raisins)

hot dog \'hät-,dȯg\ *n* : FRANKFURTER; *esp* : a cooked frankfurter usually served in a long split roll

ho-tel \hō-'tel\ *n* : an establishment that provides lodging and usually meals, entertainment, and various personal services for the public [French *hôtel,* from Old French *hostel*]

1hot-foot \'hät-,fu̇t\ *adv* : in haste

2hotfoot *vi* : to go quickly : HURRY ⟨*hotfooted* it home⟩

3hotfoot *n, pl* **hotfoots** : a practical joke in which a match is secretly inserted into the side of a victim's shoe and lighted

hot-head \'hät-,hed\ *n* : a hotheaded person

hot-head-ed \-'hed-əd\ *adj* : RASH 2, HEADSTRONG — **hot-head-ed-ly** *adv* — **hot-head-ed-ness** *n*

hot-house \'hät-,hau̇s\ *n* : a heated greenhouse — **hothouse** *adj*

hot line *n* : a communications line for direct emergency use (as between heads of governments or to a counseling service)

hot pepper *n* **1** : a pungent often thin-walled and small capsicum fruit **2** : a pepper plant bearing hot peppers

hot plate *n* : a small portable appliance for heating or for cooking

hot rod *n* : an automobile rebuilt or modified for high speed and fast acceleration — **hot-rod-der** \'hät-'räd-ər\ *n*

hot-shot \'hät-,shät\ *n* : a spectacularly skillful or successful person

hourglass

hot spring *n* : THERMAL SPRING; *esp* : a spring with water above 36.7°C

Hot-ten-tot \'hät-n-,tät\ *n* : a member of a people of southern Africa apparently akin to both the Bushmen and the Bantus [Afrikaans]

hot water *n* : a distressing predicament : TROUBLE ⟨got in *hot water* at school⟩

hot-wire \'hät-,wīr\ *vt* : to start (as an automobile) by short-circuiting the ignition system

1hound \'hau̇nd\ *n* **1 a** : DOG 1a **b** : a dog of any of various hunting breeds typically having large drooping ears and a deep voice and following its prey by scent **2** : ENTHUSIAST, FAN ⟨autograph *hounds*⟩ [Old English *hund*]

2hound *vt* **1** : to pursue with or as if with hounds **2** : HARASS 1

hour \'au̇r\ *n* **1** : a time or office for daily devotion; *esp* : CANONICAL HOUR **2** : one of the 24 divisions of a day : 60 minutes **3 a** : the time of day reckoned in two 12-hour periods ⟨the *hour* is now 10:00 a.m.⟩ **b** *pl* : the time reckoned in one 24-hour period ⟨in the military 4:00 p.m. is called 1600 *hours*⟩ **4 a** : a customary time ⟨the lunch *hour*⟩ **b** : a particular time ⟨in your *hour* of need⟩ **5** : the work done or distance traveled at normal rate in an hour ⟨two *hours* away by car⟩ **6** : the time (as 50 minutes) taken up by a class ⟨I have math this *hour*⟩ [Old French *heure,* from Latin *hora* "hour of the day", from Greek *hōra*]

hour-glass \-,glas\ *n* : an instrument for measuring time in which sand, water, or mercury runs from the upper to the lower part of a glass container in an hour — **hourglass** *adj*

hou-ri \'hu̇r-ē, 'hu̇-rē\ *n* : one of the beautiful maidens that in Muslim belief live with the blessed in paradise [French, from Persian *hūri,* from Arabic *ḥūrīyah*]

hour-ly \'au̇r-lē\ *adj* **1** : occurring hour by hour **2** : computed in terms of one hour ⟨*hourly* wages⟩ — **hourly** *adv*

1house \'hau̇s\ *n, pl* **hous-es** \'hau̇-zəz\ **1** : a building that serves as living quarters for one or more families **2 a** : an animal's shelter or habitation **b** : a building in which something is housed ⟨carriage *house*⟩ **3 a** : one of the 12 equal sectors in which the celestial sphere is divided in astrology **b** : a zodiacal sign that is the seat of a planet's greatest influence **4 a** : HOUSEHOLD **b** : FAMILY 1; *esp* : a royal or noble family ⟨the *house* of Windsor⟩ **5 a** : a residence for a religious community or for students **b** : the community or students in residence **6 a** : a legislative, deliberative, or consultative assembly; *esp* : one constituting a division of a bicameral body **b** : the place where an assembly meets **7 a** : a place of business or entertainment ⟨the *house* was full for the opening⟩ **b** (1) : a business organization ⟨a publishing *house*⟩ (2) : the operator of a gambling establishment ⟨a percentage of the bets always goes to the *house*⟩ **c** : the audience in a theater or concert hall ⟨played to small *houses*⟩ [Old English *hūs*] — **house-ful** \'hau̇s-,fu̇l\ *n* — **on the house** : at the expense of the management

2house \'hau̇z\ *vb* **1 a** : to provide with living quarters or shelter **b** : to store in a house **2** : to encase, enclose, or shelter as if by putting in a house **3** : to take shelter : LODGE

house-boat \'hau̇s-,bōt\ *n* : a usually flat-bottomed shallow-draft vessel with a structure resembling a house built on deck for use as a dwelling on the water

house-boy \-,bȯi\ *n* : a boy or man hired to act as a general household servant

house-break \-,brāk\ *vt* : to make housebroken

house-break-ing \-,brā-king\ *n* : the act of breaking into and entering a person's dwelling house with the intent of committing a felony — **house-break-er** \-kər\ *n*

house-bro-ken \-,brō-kən\ *adj* : trained to excretory habits acceptable in indoor living

house·clean \\'haù-ˌsklēn\\ *vb* **1** : to clean a house and its furniture **2** : to clean the surfaces and furnishings of (as a room) **3** : to get rid of unwanted or undesirable items or people — **house·clean·ing** *n*

house·coat \\'haù-ˌskōt\\ *n* : a woman's one-piece and often long garment for wear around the house

house·fly \\'haùs-ˌflī\\ *n* : a two-winged fly that is common about human habitations and can act as a carrier of disease-producing organisms

¹house·hold \\'haùs-ˌhōld, 'haù-ˌsōld\\ *n* : those who dwell under the same roof and compose a family; *also* : a social unit made up of those living together in the same dwelling

²household *adj* **1** : of or relating to a household : DOMESTIC **2** : FAMILIAR, COMMON ⟨a *household* name⟩

house·hold·er \\'haùs-ˌhōl-dər, 'haù-ˌsōl-\\ *n* : one who occupies a dwelling alone or as the head of a household

house·keep \\'haù-ˌskēp\\ *vi* **-kept** \\-ˌskept\\; **-keep·ing** : to care for and run a home [back-formation from *housekeeper*]

house·keep·er \\-ˌskē-pər\\ *n* : a person employed to housekeep

house·keep·ing \\-ˌping\\ *n* : the care and management of a house and home affairs

house·lights \\'haù-ˌslīts\\ *n pl* : the lights that illuminate the parts of a theater occupied by the audience

house·maid \\-ˌsmād\\ *n* : a woman or girl employed to do housework

housemaid's knee *n* : a swelling over the knee due to an enlargement of the bursa in the front of the kneecap

house·man \\'haù-smən, -ˌsman\\ *n* : a man who performs general work about a house : HOUSEBOY

house·moth·er \\'haù-ˌsməth-ər\\ *n* : a woman acting as hostess, chaperon, and often supervisor in a residence for young people

House of Burgesses : the representative assembly of colonial Virginia

House of Commons : the lower house of the British and Canadian parliaments

house of correction : an institution where persons are confined who have committed a minor offense and are considered capable of being reformed

House of Lords : the upper house of the British Parliament composed of the peers temporal and spiritual

house of representatives : the lower house of a legislative body (as the United States Congress)

house organ *n* : a periodical distributed by a business concern among its employees, sales personnel, and customers

house party *n* : a party lasting over one or more nights at a residence (as a home or fraternity house)

house·plant \\'haù-ˌsplant\\ *n* : a plant grown or kept indoors

house–rais·ing \\'haùs-ˌrā-zing\\ *n* : the putting up of a house or its framework by a gathering of neighbors

house sparrow *n* : ENGLISH SPARROW

house·top \\'haù-ˌstäp\\ *n* : ROOF 1

house·warm·ing \\-ˌswor-ming\\ *n* : a party to celebrate moving into a house or premises

house·wife \\'haù-ˌswīf, *2 is often* 'həz-əf, 'həs-əf\\ *n* **1** : a usually married woman in charge of a household **2** : a small container for small articles (as thread) — **house·wife·li·ness** \\'haù-ˌswī-flē-nəs\\ *n* — **house·wife·ly** \\-flē\\ *adj* — **house·wif·ery** \\-ˌswī-fə-rē, -frē\\ *n*

house·work \\'haù-ˌswərk\\ *n* : the work of housekeeping

¹hous·ing \\'haù-zing\\ *n* **1 a** : SHELTER 1, LODGING **b** : dwellings provided for people ⟨*housing* for the elderly⟩ **2 a** : something that covers or protects **b** : a support (as a frame) for mechanical parts

²housing *n* : a usually ornamental covering for the back and sides of a horse : CAPARISON [Middle French *housse,* of Germanic origin]

hove *past of* HEAVE

hov·el \\'həv-əl, 'häv-\\ *n* **1** : an open shed or shelter **2** : a small mean house : HUT [Middle English]

hov·er \\'həv-ər, 'häv-\\ *vb* **hov·ered; hov·er·ing** \\'həv-ring, 'häv-, -ə-ring\\ **1** : to hang fluttering in the air or on the wing ⟨hawks *hovering* over their prey⟩ **2 a** : to move to and fro near a place ⟨waiters *hovered* about⟩ **b** : to be in a state of uncertainty, irresolution, or suspense ⟨*hovering* between life and death⟩ **3** : to brood over ⟨a hen *hovers* her chicks⟩ [Middle English *hoveren*] — **hover** *n* — **hov·er·er** \\-ər-ər\\ *n*

¹how \\'haù, 'haù\\ *adv* **1 a** : in what manner or way ⟨learn *how* to study⟩ **b** : with what meaning : to what effect ⟨*how* do you mean that⟩ **c** : by what name or title **d** : for what reason : WHY ⟨*how* can you do that⟩ **2** : to what degree or extent ⟨*how* do you like that⟩ **3** : in what state or condition ⟨*how* are you⟩ **4** : at what price ⟨*how* do you sell your eggs⟩ [Old English *hū*] — **how about** : what do you say to or think of ⟨*how about* another game⟩ — **how come** : why is it that ⟨*how come* you're so early⟩ — **how do you do** — used to express a polite greeting

²how *conj* **1** : in what manner or condition ⟨remember *how* they fought⟩ ⟨asked *how* they were⟩ **2** : in whatever way or manner ⟨do it *how* you think⟩

³how \\'haù\\ *n* : MANNER, METHOD ⟨the *hows* and whys⟩

¹how·be·it \\haù-'bē-ət\\ *adv* : NEVERTHELESS

²howbeit *conj* : ALTHOUGH

how·dah \\'haùd-ə\\ *n* : a seat or covered pavilion on the back of an elephant or camel [Hindi *hauda*]

how·dy \\'haù-dē\\ *interj* — used to express a greeting [from *how do you do*]

¹how·ev·er \\haù-'ev-ər\\ *conj* : in whatever way or manner ⟨go *however* you like⟩

²however *adv* **1 a** : to whatever degree or extent **b** : in whatever manner or way **2** : in spite of that : on the other hand : BUT ⟨still seems possible, *however,* that conditions will improve⟩ **3** : how in the world ⟨*however* did you do it⟩

how·it·zer \\'haù-ət-sər\\ *n* : a short cannon used to fire projectiles in a high trajectory [Dutch *houwitser,* from German *haubitze,* from Czech *houfnice,* a machine for hurling missiles]

howl \\'haùl\\ *vb* **1** : to make a loud sustained doleful sound ⟨the wind *howled* all night⟩ **2** : to cry out or exclaim without restraint under strong impulse (as pain, grief, or rage) **3** : to utter with unrestrained outcry **4** : to affect, effect, or drive by adverse outcry ⟨*howl* down all opposition⟩ [Middle English *houlen*] — **howl** *n*

howl·er \\'haù-lər\\ *n* **1 a** : one that howls **b** : HOWLER MONKEY **2** : a stupid and ridiculous blunder

howler monkey *n* : any of a genus of South and Central American monkeys that have a long grasping tail and are able to make loud howling noises

how·so·ev·er \\ˌhaù-sə-'wev-ər\\ *adv* **1** : in whatever manner **2** : to whatever degree or extent

hoy·den \\'hoid-n\\ *n* : a girl or woman of saucy, boisterous, or carefree behavior [perhaps from obsolete Dutch *heiden* "country lout", from Dutch, "heathen"] — **hoy·den·ish** \\-ish\\ *adj*

hua·ra·che \\wə-'räch-ē, hə-\\ *n* : a low-heeled sandal having an upper made of interwoven leather thongs [Mexican Spanish]

hub \\'həb\\ *n* **1** : the central part of a wheel, propeller, or fan **2** : a center of activity ⟨the *hub* of the universe⟩ [probably alteration of ²*hob*]

hub·bub \\'həb-ˌəb\\ *n* **1** : a noisy confusion of sound : UPROAR **2** : TURMOIL [probably of Celtic origin]

hu·bris \\'hyü-brəs\\ *n* : bold or unreasonable pride or self-confidence : ARROGANCE [Greek *hybris*]

huck·le·ber·ry \\'hək-əl-ˌber-ē\\ *n* **1** : an American shrub related to the blueberry; *also* : its edible dark blue to black usually acid berry **2** : BLUEBERRY [perhaps alteration of *hurtleberry* "whortleberry, huckleberry"]

howdah

\ə\ abut		\ng\ sing
\ər\ further		\ō\ bone
\a\ mat		\ó\ saw
\ā\ take		\oi\ coin
\ä\ cot, cart		\th\ thin
\aù\ out		\th\ this
\ch\ chin		\ü\ food
\e\ pet		\u̇\ foot
\ē\ easy		\y\ yet
\g\ go		\yü\ few
\i\ tip		\yu̇\ cure
\ī\ life		\zh\ vision
\j\ job		

huck·ster \'hək-stər\ *n* **1** : ²HAWKER, PEDDLER **2** : a writer of advertising especially for radio or television [Dutch *hoekester,* from *hoeken* "to peddle"]

¹hud·dle \'həd-l\ *vb* **hud·dled; hud·dling** \'həd-ling, -l-ing\ **1** *British* : to throw together, arrange, or complete carelessly or hurriedly **2** : to crowd, push, or pile together ⟨*huddled* in a doorway⟩ **3** : to gather in a group for conference : CONFER; *esp* : to gather in a huddle during a football game **4** : to curl up : CROUCH ⟨a child *huddled* in its crib⟩ [probably from Middle English *hoderen*] — **hud·dler** \'həd-lər, -l-ər\ *n*

²huddle *n* **1** : a close-packed group : BUNCH **2 a** : CONFERENCE 1 **b** : a brief gathering of football players behind the line of scrimmage before each play to receive instructions

Hud·son seal \'həd-sən-\ *n* : the fur of the muskrat dressed to resemble seal [*Hudson* bay, sea in Canada]

hue \'hyü\ *n* **1** : outward appearance : ASPECT **2 a** : gradation of color **b** : the attribute of colors that permits them to be classed as red, yellow, green, blue, or an intermediate between any neighboring pair of these colors [Old English *hīw*] SYN see COLOR — **hued** \'hyüd\ *adj*

hue and cry *n* **1** : a loud outcry formerly used in the pursuit of felons **2** : a clamor of protest [earlier *hue* "outcry", from Old French *hue,* from *huer* "to shout, hoot"]

¹huff \'həf\ *vi* **1** : PUFF 1a, b ⟨tourists *huffing* up the steps behind their guide⟩ **2 a** : BLUSTER 2, RANT **b** : to react indignantly ⟨*huffed* off in a fit of anger⟩

²huff *n* : a fit of anger or pique

huffy \'həf-ē\ *adj* **huff·i·er; -est** **1** : HAUGHTY **2 a** : aroused to indignation : OFFENDED **b** : easily offended : TOUCHY — **huff·i·ly** \'həf-ə-lē\ *adv* — **huff·i·ness** *n*

hug \'həg\ *vb* **hugged; hug·ging** **1** : to press tightly especially in the arms : EMBRACE **2** : to hold fast : CHERISH ⟨*hugged* their fancied grievances⟩ **3** : to stay close to ⟨drives along *hugging* the curb⟩ [perhaps of Scandinavian origin] — **hug** *n*

huge \'hyüj, 'yüj\ *adj* : very large or extensive: as **a** : of great size or area **b** : of sizable scale or degree ⟨a *huge* success⟩ **c** : of limitless scope or character ⟨*huge* talent⟩ [Old French *ahuge*] SYN see ENORMOUS — **huge·ly** *adv* — **huge·ness** *n*

hug·ger–mug·ger \'həg-ər-,məg-ər\ *n* **1** : SECRECY 2 **2** : a disorderly jumble [origin unknown] — **hugger–mugger** *adj*

Hu·gue·not \'hyü-gə-,nät\ *n* : a French Protestant of the 16th and 17th centuries [Middle French, from Middle French dialect, "adherent of a Swiss political movement", from Besançon *Hugues,* died 1532, Swiss political leader + *eidgnot* "confederate", from German dialect *eidgnoss*]

huh \a snort or a strong h-*sound followed with varying intonation by an* m-*sound or by* ə\; *often read as* 'hə \ *interj* — used to express surprise, disbelief, disgust, or interrogation [probably imitative]

hu·la \'hü-lə\ *or* **hu·la–hu·la** \,hü-lə-'hü-lə\ *n* : a Polynesian dance usually accompanied by chants and rhythmic drumming [Hawaiian]

¹hulk \'həlk\ *n* **1** : a heavy clumsy ship **2** : the body of an old ship unfit for service or of an abandoned wreck **3** : a bulky, unwieldy, or clumsy person or thing [Old English *hulc,* from Medieval Latin *holcas,* from Greek *holkas,* from *helkein* "to pull, drag"]

²hulk *vi* : to appear impressively large : BULK

hulk·ing \'həl-king\ *adj* : MASSIVE 2a, PONDEROUS

¹hull \'həl\ *n* **1 a** : the outer covering of a fruit or seed **b** : the persistent calyx or involucre that clings to the base of some fruits **2** : the frame or body of a ship, flying boat, or airship **3** : COVERING, CASING [Old English *hulu*]

²hull *vt* : to remove the hulls of — **hull·er** *n*

hul·la·ba·loo \'həl-ə-bə-,lü\ *n, pl* **-loos** : a confused noise : UPROAR [perhaps from *hallo,* interj. used to at-

tract attention + Scottish *balloo,* interj. used to hush children]

hum \'həm\ *vb* **hummed; hum·ming** **1 a** : to utter a sound like that of the speech sound \m\ prolonged **b** : to make the characteristic buzzing sound of an insect in motion or a similar sound **c** : to give forth a low continuous blend of sound **2** : to sing with the lips closed and without articulation **3** : to be busily active [Middle English *hummen*] — **hum** *n* — **hum·mer** *n*

hu·man \'hyü-mən, 'yü-\ *adj* **1** : of, relating to, or characteristic of human beings ⟨the *human* body⟩ ⟨*human* history⟩ ⟨to err is *human*⟩ **2** : consisting of human beings ⟨the *human* race⟩ **3** : having human form or attributes ⟨the dog's expression was almost *human*⟩ [Middle French *humain,* from Latin *humanus*] — **human** *n* — **hu·man·ness** \-mən-nəs\ *n* □ SYN HUMANE: HUMAN applies to any feeling or quality shared by humanity in general ⟨*human* love⟩ ⟨*human* achievements⟩ HUMANE suggests the gentler side of human nature and implies compassion for people or animals in difficulty or need ⟨the growth of the *humane* treatment of prisoners in recent history⟩

human being *n* : an individual of the species of primate mammal that walks on two feet, is related to the great apes, and is distinguished by a greatly developed brain with capacity for speech and abstract reasoning

hu·mane \hyü-'mān, yü-\ *adj* **1** : marked by compassion, sympathy, or consideration for others **2** : characterized by broad humanistic culture ⟨*humane* studies⟩ [Middle French *humain* "human, humane"] SYN see HUMAN — **hu·mane·ly** *adv* — **hu·mane·ness** \-'mān-nəs\ *n*

human immunodeficiency virus *n* : HIV

hu·man·ism \'hyü-mə-,niz-əm, 'yü-\ *n* **1** : a revival of classical letters, an individualistic and inquiring spirit, and an emphasis on secular concerns characteristic of the Renaissance **2** : a doctrine or way of life centered on human interests or values; *esp* : a philosophy that asserts the dignity and worth of human beings and their capacity for self-realization through reason and that often rejects supernaturalism — **hu·man·ist** \-nəst\ *n or adj* — **hu·man·is·tic** \,hyü-mə-'nis-tik, ,yü-\ *adj*

hu·man·i·tar·i·an \,hyü-,man-ə-'ter-ē-ən, ,yü-\ *n* : a person promoting human welfare and social reform : PHILANTHROPIST — **humanitarian** *adj* — **hu·man·i·tar·i·an·ism** \-ē-ə-,niz-əm\ *n*

hu·man·i·ty \hyü-'man-ət-ē, yü-\ *n, pl* **-ties** **1** : the quality or state of being humane : COMPASSION **2** : the quality or state of being human ⟨the common *humanity* of all peoples⟩ **3** *pl* : the branches of learning having primarily a cultural character **4** : the totality of human beings both past and present : MANKIND 1

hu·man·ize \'hyü-mə-,nīz, 'yü-\ *vb* **1** : to represent as human or with human attributes **2** : to make or become humane or more humane ⟨*humanize* industry⟩ — **hu·man·iza·tion** \,hyü-mə-nə-'zā-shən, ,yü-\ *n*

hu·man·kind \'hyü-mən-,kīnd, 'yü-\ *n* : HUMANITY 4

hu·man·like \-,līk\ *adj* : resembling a human being

hu·man·ly \'hyü-mən-lē, 'yü-\ *adv* **1 a** : from the viewpoint of human beings **b** : within the range of human capacity ⟨a task not *humanly* possible⟩ **2** : in a human manner

hu·man·oid \-mə-,nȯid\ *adj* : HUMANLIKE — **humanoid** *n*

¹hum·ble \'həm-bəl, 'əm-\ *adj* **hum·bler** \-bə-lər, -blər\; **hum·blest** \-bə-ləst, -bləst\ **1** : modest or meek in spirit or manner : not proud or assertive **2** : expressing a spirit of deference or submission ⟨a *humble* apology⟩ **3** : low in rank or status : UNPRETENTIOUS ⟨*humble* birth⟩ ⟨a *humble* position⟩ [Old French, from Latin *humilis* "low, humble", from *humus* "earth"] — **hum·bly** \-blē\ *adv*

²humble *vt* **hum·bled; hum·bling** \-bə-ling, -bling\ **1** : to make humble in spirit or manner **2** : to destroy the power or prestige of ⟨*humbled* their opponents with a crushing attack⟩ — **hum·bler** \-bə-lər, -blər\ *n*

hum·ble-bee \'həm-bəl-ˌbē\ *n* : BUMBLEBEE [Middle English *humbylbee*]

hum·bug \'həm-ˌbəg\ *n* **1 a** : something designed to deceive and mislead : FRAUD ⟨took their fervent denials as *humbug*⟩ **b** : CHARLATAN **2** : DRIVEL, NONSENSE ⟨the speech was full of *humbug*⟩ [origin unknown] — **humbug** *vb* — **hum·bug·gery** \-ˌbəg-rē, -ə-rē\ *n*

hum·ding·er \'həm-'diŋ-ər\ *n* : a striking or extraordinary one of its kind [probably alteration of *hummer*]

hum·drum \'həm-ˌdrəm\ *adj* : BANAL, ORDINARY [reduplication of *hum*]

hu·mec·tant \hyü-'mek-tənt\ *n* : a substance that promotes retention of moisture [Latin *humectare* "to moisten", from *humectus* "moist", from *humēre* "to be moist"]

hu·mer·al \'hyüm-rəl, -ə-rəl\ *adj* : of, relating to, or used or located in the region of the humerus or shoulder or an analogous region — **humeral** *n*

humeral veil *n* : an oblong vestment worn around the shoulders and over the hands by a priest or subdeacon holding a sacred vessel

hu·mer·us \'hyüm-rəs, -ə-rəs\ *n, pl* **hu·meri** \'hyü-mə-ˌrī, -ˌrē\ : the long bone of the upper arm or forelimb extending from the shoulder to the elbow [Latin, "upper arm, shoulder"]

hu·mic \'hyü-mik, 'yü-\ *adj* : of, relating to, or derived from humus ⟨a *humic* acid⟩

hu·mid \'hyü-məd, 'yü-\ *adj* : containing or characterized by perceptible moisture ⟨a *humid* day⟩ ⟨a *humid* climate⟩ [Latin *humidus*, from *humēre* "to be moist"] — **hu·mid·ly** *adv*

hu·mid·i·fy \hyü-'mid-ə-ˌfī, yü-\ *vt* **-fied; -fy·ing** : to make (as the air of a room) humid — **hu·mid·i·fi·ca·tion** \-ˌmid-ə-fə-'kā-shən\ *n* — **hu·mid·i·fi·er** \-'mid-ə-ˌfī-ər, -ˌfīr\ *n*

hu·mid·i·ty \-'mid-ət-ē\ *n, pl* **-ties** : DAMPNESS, MOISTURE; *esp* : the amount of moisture in the air — compare RELATIVE HUMIDITY

hu·mi·dor \'hyü-mə-ˌdor, 'yü-\ *n* : a case usually for storing cigars in which the air is kept properly humidified [*humid* + -*or* (as in cuspidor)]

hu·mil·i·ate \hyü-'mil-ē-ˌāt, yü-\ *vt* : to reduce to a lower position in one's own eyes or others' eyes : MORTIFY ⟨the public reprimand *humiliated* the general⟩ [Late Latin *humiliare*, from Latin *humilis* "low, humble"] — **hu·mil·i·a·tion** \-ˌmil-ē-'ā-shən\ *n*

hu·mil·i·ty \hyü-'mil-ət-ē, yü-\ *n* : the quality or state of being humble

hum·ming·bird \'həm-iŋ-ˌbərd\ *n* : any of numerous tiny brightly colored American birds related to the swifts and having narrow swiftly beating wings, a slender bill, and a long tongue for sipping nectar

hum·mock \'həm-ək\ *n* **1** : a rounded mound of earth : KNOLL **2** : a ridge or pile of ice [alteration of *²hammock*] — **hum·mocky** \-ə-kē\ *adj*

¹hu·mor \'hyü-mər, 'yü-\ *n* **1** : a normal functioning bodily semifluid or fluid (as the blood or lymph) — compare AQUEOUS HUMOR, VITREOUS HUMOR **2** : an often temporary state of mind induced especially by circumstances **3** : WHIM 1, FANCY **4** : the amusing quality of things ⟨the *humor* of a situation⟩ **5** : the power to see or tell about the amusing side of things : a keen perception of the comic or the ridiculous **6** : something comical or amusing [Middle French *humeur*, from Latin *humor* "moisture"] SYN see MOOD, WIT — **hu·mor·less** \-ləs\ *adj* — **hu·mor·less·ness** *n* □ ORIGIN In the Middle Ages it was believed that everything on Earth was made of different combinations of four elements: earth, air, fire, and water. These elements in turn were thought to be composed of combinations of what were known as the Four Contraries: hot, cold, moist, and dry. In people these same four contraries were thought to combine into the four humors: cho-

ler, blood, melancholy, and phlegm. The balance or imbalance of these humors determined a person's temperament. Coming from a Latin word meaning "moisture", *humor* originally reflected the combinations of heat and moisture that accounted for a person's disposition. *Humor* became a general term for "disposition" and soon came to mean "a mood or state of mind". From this developed the sense of "whim or fancy", from which are derived the senses of *humor* which refer to the comical or amusing.

²humor *vt* **hu·mored; hu·mor·ing** \'hyüm-riŋ, 'yüm-, -ə-riŋ\ : to comply with the wishes or mood of

hu·mor·al \'hyüm-rəl, 'yüm-, -ə-rəl\ *adj* : of, relating to, proceeding from, or involving a bodily humor and especially a hormone

hu·mor·esque \ˌhyü-mə-'resk, ˌyü-\ *n* : a typically whimsical or fanciful musical composition [German *humoreske*, from *humor* "humor", from English]

hu·mor·ist \'hyüm-rəst, 'yüm-, -ə-rəst\ *n* : a person specializing in or noted for humor

hu·mor·ous \'hyüm-rəs, 'yüm-, -ə-rəs\ *adj* : full of, characterized by, or expressive of humor : DROLL ⟨a *humorous* story⟩ — **hu·mor·ous·ly** *adv* — **hu·mor·ous·ness** *n*

hu·mour *chiefly British variant of* HUMOR

¹hump \'həmp\ *n* **1** : a rounded bulge or lump (as on the back of a camel) **2** : KNOLL, HUMMOCK **3** : a difficult phase [related to Low German *hump* "bump"] — **humped** \'həmpt\ *adj* — **humpy** \'həm-pē\ *adj*

²hump *vb* **1** : to exert oneself vigorously : HUSTLE **2** : to make hump-shaped : HUNCH

hump·back \'həmp-ˌbak\ *n* **1** : a humped or crooked back **2** : HUNCHBACK 2 **3** : a large whalebone whale with very long flippers

hump·backed \-'bakt\ *or* **hump·back** \-ˌbak\ *adj* : having a humped back

hu·mus \'hyü-məs, 'yü-\ *n* : the brown or black organic portion of soil formed by partial decomposition of plant or animal matter [Latin, "earth"]

Hun \'hən\ *n* **1** : a member of a nomadic Mongolian people gaining control of a large part of central and eastern Europe under Attila about A.D. 450 **2** *often not cap* : a person who is wantonly destructive [Late Latin *Hunni* "Huns"]

¹hunch \'hənch\ *vb* **1** : to thrust oneself forward ⟨*hunch* nearer the fire⟩ **2** : to assume a bent or crooked posture ⟨sat *hunched* over the table⟩ **3** : to thrust into a hump ⟨*hunch* one's shoulders⟩ [origin unknown]

²hunch *n* **1** : HUMP 1 **2** : a strong intuitive feeling

hunch·back \'hənch-ˌbak\ *n* **1** : HUMPBACK 1 **2** : a person with a humpback — **hunch·backed** \-ˌbakt\ *adj*

hun·dred \'hən-drəd, -dərd\ *n, pl* **hundreds** *or* **hundred** **1** : ten more than 90; *also* : a symbol representing this — see NUMBER table **2** : a great number ⟨*hundreds* of times⟩ [Old English] — **hundred** *adj*

hundreds digit *n* : the numeral (as 4 in 456) occupying the hundreds place in a number expressed in the Arabic system of writing numbers

hundreds place *n* : the place three to the left of the decimal point in a number expressed in the Arabic system of writing numbers

hun·dredth \'hən-drədth, -drəth\ *n* **1** : one of 100 equal parts of something **2** : one numbered 100 in a countable series — see NUMBER table — **hundredth** *adj*

hun·dred·weight \'hən-drə-ˌdwāt, -dər-ˌdwāt\ *n, pl* **-weight** *or* **-weights** **1** : a unit of weight equal to 100 pounds (about 45.6 kilograms) — called also *short hundredweight*; see MEASURE table **2** *British* : a unit of weight equal to 112 pounds (about 50.8 kilograms) — called also *long hundredweight*

hung *past of* HANG

Hun·gar·i·an \ˌhəŋ-'ger-ē-ən, -'gar-\ *n* **1 a** : a native or inhabitant of Hungary : MAGYAR **b** : a person of Hungarian descent **2** : MAGYAR 2 — **Hungarian** *adj*

hummingbird

\ə\ abut	\ng\ sing
\ər\ further	\ō\ bone
\a\ mat	\o\ saw
\ā\ take	\oi\ coin
\ä\ cot, cart	\th\ thin
\au\ out	\th\ this
\ch\ chin	\ü\ food
\e\ pet	\u\ foot
\ē\ easy	\y\ yet
\g\ go	\yü\ few
\i\ tip	\yu\ cure
\ī\ life	\zh\ vision
\j\ job	

¹hun·ger \'həŋ-gər\ *n* **1** : a desire or a need for food; *also* : an uneasy feeling or weakened condition resulting from lack of food **2** : a strong desire : CRAVING ⟨a *hunger* for praise⟩ [Old English *hungor*] — **hunger** *adj*

²hunger *vi* **hun·gered; hun·ger·ing** \-gə-riŋ, -griŋ\ **1** : to feel or suffer hunger **2** : to have an eager desire

hunger strike *n* : refusal (as by a prisoner) to eat enough to sustain life

hung jury *n* : a jury that fails to reach a verdict

hun·gry \'həŋ-grē\ *adj* **hun·gri·er; -est** **1** : feeling or showing hunger **2** : EAGER, AVID **3** : not rich or fertile : BARREN — **hun·gri·ly** \-grə-lē\ *adv* — **hun·gri·ness** \-grē-nəs\ *n*

hunk \'həŋk\ *n* **1** : a large lump or piece **2** : a male who is physically very attractive [Flemish *hunke*]

hun·ker \'həŋ-kər\ *vi* : CROUCH 1, SQUAT [perhaps of Scandinavian origin]

hun·kers \-kərz\ *n pl* : HINDQUARTER 2

hun·ky–do·ry \,həŋ-kē-'dōr-ē, -'dȯr-\ *adj* : quite satisfactory : FINE [obsolete English dialect *hunk* "home base" + *-dory*, of unknown origin]

¹hunt \'hənt\ *vb* **1 a** : to seek out and pursue (game) for food or sport ⟨*hunt* deer⟩ **b** : to use in hunting game ⟨*hunts* a pack of dogs⟩ **2** : to pursue with intent to capture **3 a** : to attempt to find something **b** : to search out : SEEK **4** : to drive or chase especially by harrying ⟨*hunt* a criminal out of town⟩ **5** : to search through in quest of prey ⟨*hunts* the woods⟩ **6** : to take part in a hunt [Old English *huntian*]

²hunt *n* **1** : the act, the practice, or an instance of hunting **2** : a group of hunters; *esp* : persons with horses and dogs engaged in hunting (as foxes)

hunt·er \'hənt-ər\ *n* **1 a** : a person who hunts game **b** : a dog or horse used or trained for hunting **2** : a person who searches for something

hunt·er–gath·er·er \'hənt-ər-'gath-ər-ər, -'geth-\ *n* : a member of a culture in which food is obtained by hunting, fishing, and gathering (as fruits) rather than by agriculture

hunt·ing *n* : the act of one that hunts; *esp* : the pursuit of game

hunt·ress \'hən-trəs\ *n* : a woman who is a hunter

hunts·man \'həns-mən\ *n* **1** : HUNTER 1a **2** : a person who manages the hounds in a hunt

¹hur·dle \'hərd-l\ *n* **1** : a movable panel used for enclosing land or livestock **2** : a barrier to be jumped in a race **3** : OBSTACLE [Old English *hyrdel*]

²hurdle *vt* **hur·dled; hur·dling** \'hərd-liŋ, -l-iŋ\ **1** : to leap over while running **2** : OVERCOME 1, SURMOUNT — **hur·dler** \'hərd-lər, -l-ər\ *n*

¹hurdle 2

·hur·dy–gur·dy \,hərd-ē-'gərd-ē\ *n, pl* **-dies** : a musical instrument in which the sound is produced by turning a crank; *esp* : BARREL ORGAN [probably imitative]

hurl \'hərl\ *vb* **1** : to throw violently or powerfully ⟨*hurl* a spear⟩ **2** : PITCH 2 [Middle English *hurlen*] SYN see THROW — **hurl·er** *n*

hur·ly–bur·ly \,hər-lē-'bər-lē\ *n, pl* **-lies** : UPROAR, TUMULT [probably derived from *hurl*]

Hu·ron \'hyùr-ən, 'hyùr-,än\ *n* : a member of an Iroquoian people originally of the St. Lawrence valley and what is now Ontario [French, literally, "boor"]

¹hur·rah \hù-'rȯ, -'rä\ *or* **hoo·ray** \-'rā\ *also* **hur·ray** \-'rā\ *interj* — used to express joy, approval, or encouragement [perhaps from German *hurra*]

²hur·rah \hù-'rȯ, -'rä, 'hü-\ *also* **hoo·ray** \-'rā\ *n* **1** : FANFARE 2, EXCITEMENT **2** : FUSS 2, CONTROVERSY

hur·ri·cane \'hər-ə-,kān, -i-kən, 'hə-rə-, 'hə-ri-\ *n* : a tropical cyclone with winds of 33.1 meters per second or greater but rarely exceeding 65 meters per second usually accompanied by rain, thunder, and lightning [Spanish *huracán*, of American Indian origin]

hurricane deck *n* : PROMENADE DECK

hurricane lamp *n* : a candlestick or an electric lamp with a glass chimney

hur·ried \'hər-ēd, 'hə-rēd\ *adj* **1** : going or working at speed ⟨the *hurried* life of the city⟩ **2** : done in a hurry : HASTY ⟨a *hurried* meal⟩ — **hur·ried·ly** *adv*

¹hur·ry \'hər-ē, 'hə-rē\ *vb* **hur·ried; hur·ry·ing** **1 a** : to carry or cause to go with haste ⟨*hurry* them to the airport⟩ **b** : to move or act with haste ⟨had to *hurry* to arrive in time⟩ **2 a** : to impel to greater speed : PROD **b** : EXPEDITE ⟨*hurry* a repair job⟩ **c** : to perform with undue haste [perhaps from Middle English *horyen*] — **hur·ri·er** *n*

²hurry *n, pl* **hurries** **1** : DISTURBANCE 3, COMMOTION **2** : a recurrent agitation of sound ⟨a *hurry* of voices⟩ **3 a** : agitated and often bustling or disorderly haste **b** : a state of eagerness or urgency : RUSH ⟨in a *hurry* to get there⟩ SYN see HASTE

¹hurt \'hərt\ *vb* **hurt; hurt·ing** **1 a** : to afflict with physical pain **b** : to do physical harm to : DAMAGE ⟨the storm didn't *hurt* the house⟩ **2 a** : to cause anguish to : OFFEND **b** : HAMPER ⟨the scandal *hurt* their election chances⟩ **3** : to feel or be a source of pain ⟨I *hurt* all over⟩ ⟨my tooth *hurts*⟩ [Middle English *hurten*] — **hurt·er** *n*

²hurt *n* **1 a** : a bodily injury or wound **b** : mental distress : SUFFERING **2** : WRONG 1a, HARM

hurt·ful \'hərt-fəl\ *adj* : causing injury or suffering : DAMAGING — **hurt·ful·ly** \-fə-lē\ *adv* — **hurt·ful·ness** *n*

hur·tle \'hərt-l\ *vb* **hur·tled; hur·tling** \'hərt-liŋ, -l-iŋ\ **1** : to move with or as if with a rushing sound ⟨boulders *hurtled* down the hill⟩ **2** : HURL, FLING ⟨*hurtled* the stone through the air⟩ [Middle English *hurtlen* "to collide", from *hurten* "to cause to strike, hurt"]

¹hus·band \'həz-bənd\ *n* : a married man [Old English *hūsbonda* "master of a house", from Old Norse *hūsbōndi*, from *hūs* "house" + *bōndi* "householder"]

²husband *vt* **1** : to manage prudently and economically : use carefully : CONSERVE ⟨*husbanded* their resources⟩ **2** *archaic* : to be a husband to : MARRY — **hus·band·er** *n*

hus·band·man \'həz-bənd-mən, -bən-\ *n* : FARMER; *also* : a specialist in farm husbandry

hus·band·ry \-bən-drē\ *n* **1** : the management or careful use of resources **2** : ECONOMY 2 : FARMING, AGRICULTURE; *esp* : the technical and scientific aspects of farming and especially of the care and production of domestic animals — compare ANIMAL HUSBANDRY

¹hush \'həsh\ *vb* **1** : to make quiet, calm, or still : SOOTHE ⟨*hush* a baby⟩ **2** : to become quiet **3** : to keep from public knowledge : SUPPRESS ⟨*hush* up a scandal⟩ [Middle English *huissht*, interj. used to enjoin silence]

²hush *n* : a silence or calm especially following noise : QUIET

hush–hush \'həsh-,həsh\ *adj* : SECRET 1a, CONFIDENTIAL

¹husk \'həsk\ *n* **1** : a usually thin dry outer covering of a seed or fruit **2** : an outer layer : SHELL [Middle English]

²husk *vt* : to strip the husk from — **husk·er** *n*

husk·ing *n* : a gathering of farm families to husk corn — called also *husking bee*

¹husky \'həs-kē\ *adj* **husk·i·er; -est** : resembling, containing, or full of husks

²husky *adj* **husk·i·er; -est** : hoarse with or as if with emotion [probably from obsolete *husk* "to have a dry cough"] — **husk·i·ly** \'həs-kə-lē\ *adv* — **husk·i·ness** \-kē-nəs\ *n*

³husky *adj* **husk·i·er; -est** : BURLY, ROBUST [probably from ¹*husk*]

⁴husky *n, pl* **husk·ies** : one that is husky

⁵hus·ky \'həs-kē\ *n, pl* **hus·kies** : a heavy-coated working dog especially of the New World arctic region [probably alteration of *Eskimo*]

hus·sar \hə-'zär, ,hə-, -'sär\ *n* : a member of any of various European military units originally of light cavalry [Hungarian *huszár* "highwayman, hussar", from

Serbian *husar* "pirate", from Medieval Latin *cursarius* "corsair"]

Huss·ite \'həs-ˌīt, 'hús-\ *n* : a member of the Bohemian religious and nationalist movement originating with John Huss — **Hussite** *adj*

hus·sy \'həz-ē, 'həs-\ *n, pl* **hus·sies** **1** : a lewd or brazen woman **2** : a pert or mischievous girl [alteration of *housewife*]

hus·tings \'həs-tingz\ *n pl* : a place where political campaign speeches are made; *also* : the proceedings in an election campaign [Old English *hūsting* "local court", from Old Norse *hūsthing,* from *hūs* "house" + *thing* "assembly"]

hus·tle \'həs-əl\ *vb* **hus·tled; hus·tling** \'həs-ling, -ə-ling\ **1** : to push, crowd, or force forward roughly ⟨*hustled* the prisoner to jail⟩ **2 a** : to move or work with energetic activity **b** : to sell something to or obtain something from by energetic and especially underhanded activity [Dutch *husselen* "to shake"] — **hustle** *n* — **hus·tler** \'həs-lər, -ə-lər\ *n*

hut \'hət\ *n* : an often small and temporary dwelling or shelter : SHACK [Middle French *hutte,* of Germanic origin] — **hut** *vb*

hutch \'həch\ *n* **1 a** : a chest or compartment for storage **b** : a low cupboard usually surmounted by open shelves **2** : a pen or coop for an animal **3** : SHANTY, SHACK [Old French *huche*]

hut·ment \'hət-mənt\ *n* **1** : a camp of huts **2** : HUT

huz·zah *or* **huz·za** \hə-'zä, hə-\ *interj* — used to express joy or approbation [origin unknown]

hy·a·cinth \'hī-ə-ˌsinth, -ˌsintth\ *n* **1** : a red or brownish gem zircon or garnet **2** : any of a genus of bulbous herbs of the lily family; *esp* : a common garden plant widely grown for its showy fragrant bell-shaped 6-lobed flowers **3** : a light violet to moderate purple [Latin *hyacinthus,* a precious stone, a flowering plant, from Greek *hyakinthos*] — **hy·a·cin·thine** \ˌhī-ə-'sinthən, -'sint-\ *adj*

Hy·a·des \'hī-ə-ˌdēz\ *n pl* : a V-shaped cluster of stars in the head of the constellation Taurus held by the ancients to indicate rainy weather when they rise with the sun [Latin, from Greek]

hy·ae·na *variant of* HYENA

hy·a·line \'hī-ə-lən, -ˌlīn\ *adj* : transparent or nearly so and usually homogeneous ⟨a *hyaline* membrane⟩ [derived from Greek *hyalos* "glass"]

hy·a·lite \'hī-ə-ˌlīt\ *n* : a colorless opal that is clear or translucent or whitish [German *hyalit,* from Greek *hyalos* "glass"]

hy·brid \'hī-brəd\ *n* **1** : an offspring of genetically different parents especially of different races, breeds, varieties, species, or genera **2** : something of mixed origin or composition [Latin *hybrida*] — **hybrid** *adj* — **hy·brid·ism** \'hī-brə-ˌdiz-əm\ *n* — **hy·brid·i·ty** \hī-'brid-ət-ē\ *n*

hybrid corn *n* : the grain of Indian corn developed by hybridizing two or more inbred strains; *also* : the plant grown from hybrid corn

hy·brid·ize \'hī-brə-ˌdīz\ *vb* : to produce or cause to produce hybrids : INTERBREED — **hy·brid·iza·tion** \ˌhī-brəd-ə-'zā-shən\ *n* — **hy·brid·iz·er** \'hī-brə-ˌdī-zər\ *n*

hybrid vigor *n* : HETEROSIS

hy·da·tid \'hīd-ə-təd, -ˌtid\ *n* : a larval tapeworm that occurs in the host's tissues as a fluid-filled sac containing daughter cysts and scolices [Greek *hydatid-, hydatis* "watery cyst", from *hydat-, hydōr* "water"]

hydr- *or* **hydro-** *combining form* **1** : water ⟨*hydro*electric⟩ ⟨*hydr*ous⟩ **2** : hydrogen ⟨*hydro*carbon⟩ [Greek, from *hydōr*]

Hy·dra \'hī-drə\ *n* **1** : a many-headed serpent or monster of Greek mythology slain by Hercules **2** : a southern constellation of great length **3** *not cap* : any of numerous small tubular freshwater animals related to the jellyfishes and having a mouth surrounded by tentacles at one end [Latin, from Greek]

hy·dran·gea \hī-'drān-jə\ *n* : any of a genus of shrubby plants of the saxifrage family with showy clusters of usually sterile white or tinted flowers [*hydr-* + Greek *angeion* "vessel"]

hy·drant \'hī-drənt\ *n* : a discharge pipe with a valve and spout at which water may be drawn from a main

¹hy·drate \'hī-ˌdrāt\ *n* : a compound formed by the union of water with some other substance ⟨a *hydrate* of copper sulfate⟩

²hydrate *vt* : to cause to take up or combine with water or the elements of water — **hy·dra·tion** \hī-'drā-shən\ *n*

hy·drau·lic \hī-'drò-lik\ *adj* **1** : operated, moved, or effected by means of water **2** : of or relating to hydraulics ⟨*hydraulic* engineer⟩ **3** : operated by the resistance offered or the pressure transmitted when a quantity of liquid is forced through a comparatively small orifice or through a tube ⟨*hydraulic* brakes⟩ **4** : hardening or setting under water ⟨*hydraulic* cement⟩ [Latin *hydraulicus,* from Greek *hydraulikos,* from *hydraulis* "hydraulic organ", from *hydr-* + *aulos* "reed instrument"] — **hy·drau·li·cal·ly** \-li-kə-lē, -klē\ *adv*

hydraulic ram *n* : a pump that forces running water to a higher level by utilizing the kinetic energy of flow

hy·drau·lics \-liks\ *n* : science that deals with practical applications of liquid (as water) in motion

hy·dra·zine \'hī-drə-ˌzēn\ *n* : a colorless fuming corrosive liquid N_2H_4 used especially in fuels for rocket engines [*hydr-* + *az-* (from French *azote* "nitrogen", from Greek *a-* + *zōē* "life") + *-ine*]

hy·dride \'hī-ˌdrīd\ *n* : a compound of hydrogen usually with a more electropositive element or radical

hy·dro \'hī-drō\ *adj* : HYDROELECTRIC ⟨*hydro* power⟩

hy·dro·bro·mic acid \ˌhī-drə-'brō-mik-\ *n* : a strong acid that is a solution of the bromide of hydrogen in water

hy·dro·car·bon \ˌhī-drə-'kär-bən\ *n* : an organic compound (as acetylene) containing only carbon and hydrogen

hy·dro·ceph·a·lus \ˌhī-drō-'sef-ə-ləs\ *also* **hy·dro·ceph·a·ly** \-lē\ *n* : an abnormal state in which increased cerebrospinal fluid results in expansion of the cerebral ventricles, enlargement of the skull, and wasting away of the brain [derived from Greek *hydr-* + *kephalē* "head"] — **hy·dro·ce·phal·ic** \-sə-'fal-ik\ *adj or n*

hy·dro·chlo·ric acid \ˌhī-drə-'klōr-ik-, -'klòr-\ *n* : an aqueous solution of hydrogen chloride HCl that is a strong corrosive liquid acid, is normally present in dilute form in gastric juice, and is widely used in industry and in the laboratory

hy·dro·chlo·ride \-'klōr-ˌīd, -'klòr-\ *n* : a compound of hydrochloric acid

hy·dro·cor·ti·sone \-'kòrt-ə-ˌsōn, -ˌzōn\ *n* : CORTISOL

hy·dro·cy·an·ic acid \ˌhī-drō-sī-'an-ik-\ *n* : an aqueous solution of hydrogen cyanide HCN that is a weak poisonous acid and is used in fumigating

hy·dro·dy·nam·ics \ˌhī-drō-dī-'nam-iks\ *n* : a science that deals with the motion of fluids and the forces acting on solid bodies immersed in fluids and in motion relative to them — **hy·dro·dy·nam·ic** \-ik\ *adj*

hy·dro·elec·tric \ˌhī-drō-i-'lek-trik\ *adj* : of or relating to production of electricity by waterpower — **hy·dro·elec·tric·i·ty** \-ˌlek-'tris-ət-ē, -'tris-tē\ *n*

hy·dro·flu·or·ic acid \ˌhī-drō-flu̇-'òr-ik, -'är-\ *n* : an aqueous solution of hydrogen fluoride HF that is a weak poisonous acid and is used especially in finishing and etching glass

hy·dro·foil \'hī-drə-ˌfòil\ *n* : a body similar to an airfoil but designed for action in or on the water

hy·dro·gen \'hī-drə-jən\ *n* : a univalent chemical element that is the simplest and lightest of the elements and is a colorless odorless highly flammable diatomic gas — compare DEUTERIUM, TRITIUM; see ELEMENT table [French *hydrogène,* from *hydr-* "hydr-" + *-gène*

hyacinth 2

\ə\ abut   \ng\ sing
\ər\ further \ō\ bone
\a\ mat   \ò\ saw
\ā\ take   \òi\ coin
\ä\ cot, cart \th\ thin
\au̇\ out   \th\ this
\ch\ chin   \ü\ food
\e\ pet   \u̇\ foot
\ē\ easy   \y\ yet
\g\ go   \yü\ few
\i\ tip   \yu̇\ cure
\ī\ life   \zh\ vision
\j\ job

"-gen"; from the fact that water is generated by its combustion] — **hy·drog·e·nous** \hī-'dräj-ə-nəs\ *adj*

hy·dro·ge·nate \'hī-drə-jə-ˌnāt, hī-'dräj-ə-\ *vt* : to combine or treat with hydrogen; *esp* : to add hydrogen to the molecule of ⟨*hydrogenate* a vegetable oil to form a fat⟩ — **hy·dro·ge·na·tion** \ˌhī-drə-jə-'nā-shən, hī-ˌdräj-ə-\ *n*

hydrogen bomb *n* : a bomb whose violent explosive power is due to the sudden release of atomic energy resulting from the union of light nuclei (as of hydrogen atoms)

hydrogen chloride *n* : a colorless pungent poisonous gas HCl that fumes in moist air and yields hydrochloric acid when dissolved in water

hydrogen fluoride *n* : a colorless corrosive fuming poisonous liquid or gas HF that yields hydrofluoric acid when dissolved in water

hydrogen ion *n* **1** : the cation H^+ of acids consisting of a hydrogen atom whose electron has been transferred to the anion of the acid **2** : HYDRONIUM

hydrogen peroxide *n* : an unstable liquid compound H_2O_2 used especially as an oxidizing and bleaching agent, an antiseptic, and a propellant

hydrogen sulfide *n* : a flammable poisonous gas H_2S of disagreeable odor found especially in many mineral waters and in decomposing matter

hy·drog·ra·phy \hī-'dräg-rə-fē\ *n* **1** : the study of bodies of water (as seas, lakes, rivers) especially with reference to their use by man **2** : the mapping of bodies of water — **hy·drog·ra·pher** \-fər\ *n* — **hy·dro·graph·ic** \ˌhī-drə-'graf-ik\ *adj*

¹hy·droid \'hī-ˌdrȯid\ *adj* : of or relating to the hydrozoans; *esp* : resembling a typical hydra

²hydroid *n* : HYDROZOAN; *esp* : a hydrozoan polyp as distinguished from a hydrozoan jellyfish

hy·drol·o·gy \hī-'dräl-ə-jē\ *n* : a science dealing with the properties, distribution, and circulation of water on and below the surface of the land and in the atmosphere — **hy·dro·log·ic** \ˌhī-drə-'läj-ik\ *adj* — **hy·drol·o·gist** \hī-'dräl-ə-jəst\ *n*

hy·drol·y·sis \hī-'dräl-ə-səs\ *n* : a chemical process of decomposition involving splitting of a bond and addition of the elements of water — **hy·dro·lyt·ic** \ˌhī-drə-'lit-ik\ *adj*

hy·dro·lyze \'hī-drə-ˌlīz\ *vb* : to subject to or undergo hydrolysis

hy·drom·e·ter \hī-'dräm-ət-ər\ *n* : an instrument for determining specific gravities of liquids and hence the strength (as of alcoholic liquors or battery acids) — **hy·dro·met·ric** \ˌhī-drə-'me-trik\ *adj* — **hy·drom·e·try** \hī-'dräm-ə-trē\ *n*

hy·dro·ni·um \hī-'drō-nē-əm\ *n* : a hydrated hydrogen ion H_3O^+ [*hydr-* + *-onium* (as in ammonium)]

hy·dro·phil·ic \ˌhī-drə-'fil-ik\ *adj* : of, relating to, or having a strong affinity for water

hy·dro·pho·bia \ˌhī-drə-'fō-bē-ə\ *n* **1** : a morbid dread of water **2** : RABIES

hy·dro·pho·bic \-'fō-bik, -'fäb-ik\ *adj* **1** : of, relating to, or suffering from rabies **2** : lacking affinity for water — **hy·dro·pho·bic·i·ty** \-fō-'bis-ət-ē\ *n*

hy·dro·phone \'hī-drə-ˌfōn\ *n* : an instrument for listening to sound transmitted through water

hy·dro·phyte \-ˌfīt\ *n* : a plant growing in water or in waterlogged soil — **hy·dro·phyt·ic** \ˌhī-drə-'fit-ik\ *adj*

¹hy·dro·plane \'hī-drə-ˌplān\ *n* **1** : a speedboat with fins or a bottom so designed that the hull is raised wholly or partly out of the water **2** : SEAPLANE

²hydroplane *vi* **1** : to skim over the water with the hull more or less clear of the surface **2** : to drive or ride in a hydroplane

hy·dro·pon·ics \ˌhī-drə-'pän-iks\ *n* : the growing of plants in nutrient solutions [*hydr-* + *-ponics* (as in *geoponics* "agriculture", from Greek *geōponein* "to plow", from *geō-* "ge-" + *ponein* "to toil")] — **hy-**

dro·pon·ic \-ik\ *adj* — **hy·dro·pon·i·cal·ly** \-'pän-i-kə-lē, -klē\ *adv*

hy·dro·qui·none \ˌhī-drō-kwin-'ōn, -'kwin-ˌōn\ *n* : a white crystalline compound used as a photographic developer and as an antioxidant and stabilizer [derived from *hydr-* + *quinine*]

hy·dro·sphere \'hī-drə-ˌsfiər\ *n* **1** : the water vapor that surrounds the earth as part of the atmosphere **2** : the surface waters of the earth and the water vapor in the atmosphere

hy·dro·stat·ic \ˌhī-drə-'stat-ik\ *adj* : of or relating to liquids at rest or to the pressures they exert or transmit

hy·dro·stat·ics \-iks\ *n* : a branch of physics that deals with the characteristics of liquids at rest and especially with the pressure in a liquid or exerted by a liquid on an immersed body

hy·dro·ther·a·py \-'ther-ə-pē\ *n* : the use of water in the treatment of disease

hy·drot·ro·pism \hī-'drä-trə-ˌpiz-əm\ *n* : a tropism (as in plant roots) in which water or water vapor is the orienting factor — **hy·dro·tro·pic** \ˌhī-drə-'trō-pik, -'träp-ik\ *adj*

hy·drous \'hī-drəs\ *adj* : containing water usually chemically combined

hy·drox·ide \hī-'dräk-ˌsīd\ *n* : a negatively charged ion consisting of one atom of oxygen and one atom of hydrogen

hy·drox·yl \hī-'dräk-səl\ *n* : a chemical group that consists of one atom of oxygen and one atom of hydrogen and is neutral or positively charged

hy·dro·zo·an \ˌhī-drə-'zō-ən\ *n* : any of a class (Hydrozoa) of coelenterates including the hydras and various polyps and jellyfishes — **hydrozoan** *adj*

hy·e·na *also* **hy·ae·na** \hī-'ē-nə\ *n* : any of several large strong nocturnal flesh-eating Old World mammals [Latin *hyaena,* from Greek *hyaina,* from *hys* "hog"]

hy·giene \'hī-ˌjēn\ *n* **1** : a science dealing with the establishment and maintenance of health **2** : conditions or practices (as of cleanliness) tending to promote or aid health [French *hygiène,* from Greek *hygienos* "healthful", from *hygiēs* "healthy"] — **hy·gien·ic** \ˌhī-jē-'en-ik, hī-'jen-, hī-'jēn-\ *adj* — **hy·gien·i·cal·ly** \-i-kə-lē, -klē\ *adv* — **hy·gien·ist** \hī-'jēn-əst, -'jen-, 'hī-ˌ\ *n*

hygr- *or* **hygro-** *combining form* : humidity : moisture ⟨*hygro*graph⟩ [Greek *hygros* "wet"]

hy·gro·graph \'hī-grə-ˌgraf\ *n* : an instrument for automatic recording of variations in atmospheric humidity

hy·grom·e·ter \hī-'gräm-ət-ər\ *n* : any of several instruments for measuring the humidity of the atmosphere — **hy·gro·met·ric** \ˌhī-grə-'me-trik\ *adj* — **hy·grom·e·try** \hī-'gräm-ə-trē\ *n*

hy·gro·scop·ic \ˌhī-grə-'skäp-ik\ *adj* **1** : readily taking up and retaining moisture ⟨salt is somewhat *hygroscopic*⟩ **2** : taken up and retained ⟨*hygroscopic* moisture⟩

hying *present participle of* HIE

Hyk·sos \'hik-ˌsōs\ *n* : a Semitic dynasty ruling Egypt from about 1750 to 1580 B.C. [Greek *Hyksōs,* from Egyptian *ḥq̣,š,sw* "ruler of the countries of the nomads"]

hy·la \'hī-lə\ *n* : any of a genus of tree frogs [Greek *hylē* "wood"]

hy·men \'hī-mən\ *n* : a fold of mucous membrane partly closing the opening of the vagina — called also *maidenhead* [Late Latin, from Greek *hymēn* "membrane"] — **hy·men·al** \'hī-mən-l\ *adj*

hy·me·nop·ter·on \ˌhī-mə-'näp-tə-ˌrän, -rən\ *n, pl* **-tera** \-rə\ : any of an order (Hymenoptera) of highly specialized and often colonial insects (as bees, wasps, and ants) that have usually four membranous wings and the abdomen on a slender stalk [derived from Greek *hymēn* "membrane" + *pteron* "wing"] — **hy·me·nop·ter·an** \-rən\ *adj or n* — **hy·me·nop·ter·ous** \-rəs\ *adj*

hyena

hymn \'him\ *n* **1** : a song of praise especially to God **2** : a religous song [Old French *ymne*, from Latin *hymnus*, from Greek *hymnos*]

hym·nal \'him-nəl\ *n* : a book of hymns

hymn·book \'him-,bùk\ *n* : HYMNAL

hym·no·dy \'him-nəd-ē\ *n* **1** : hymn singing **2** : hymn writing **3** : the hymns of a time, place, or church [Late Latin *hymnodia*, from Greek *hymnōidia*, from *hymnos* "hymn" + *aeidein* "to sing"]

hy·oid bone \'hī-,óid-\ *n* : a bone or complex of bones supporting the tongue and its muscles [Greek *hyoeidēs* "shaped like the letter upsilon (υ)", from *hy* "upsilon"] — **hy·oid** \'hī-,óid\ *adj or n*

hyp- — see HYPO-

hyper- *prefix* **1** : above : beyond : SUPER- ⟨*hyper*sonic⟩ **2 a** : excessively ⟨*hyper*critical⟩ **b** : excessive ⟨*hyper*xemia⟩ [Greek *hyper*]

See *hyper-* and 2d element

hyperacuity	hyperexcitement	hyperreactive
hyperacute	hyperfastidious	hyperreactivity
hyperaggressive	hyperintellectual	hyperreactor
hyperalert	hyperintelligent	hyperresponsive
hyperaware	hyperintense	hyper-romantic
hyperawareness	hypermasculine	hypersaline
hypercautious	hypermodern	hypersalinity
hypercivilized	hypermodernist	hyperstimulation
hyperconcentration	hypernationalistic	hypersusceptibility
hyperconscious	hyperpigmented	hypersusceptible
hyperconsciousness	hyperproducer	hypertense
hyperdevelopment	hyperproduction	hypertypical
hyperemotional	hyperpure	hypervigilance
hyperenergetic	hyperrational	hypervigilant
hyperexcitability	hyperrationality	hypervirulent
hyperexcitable		

hy·per·acid·i·ty \,hī-pə-rə-'sid-ət-ē\ *n* : the condition of containing more than the normal amount of acid — **hy·per·acid** \,-pə-'ras-əd\ *adj*

hy·per·ac·tive \-'rak-tiv\ *adj* : excessively or abnormally active — **hy·per·ac·tiv·i·ty** \-,rak-'tiv-ət-ē\ *n*

hy·per·bo·la \hī-'pər-bə-lə\ *n, pl* **-las** *or* **-lae** \-,lē\ : a plane curve generated by a point moving so that the difference of the distances from two fixed points is a constant : a curve formed by the intersection of a double right circular cone with a plane that cuts both halves of the cone [Greek *hyperbolē*]

hy·per·bo·le \hī-'pər-bə-lē\ *n* : extravagant exaggeration [Latin, from Greek *hyperbolē* "excess, hyperbole, hyperbola", from *hyperballein* "to exceed", from *hyper* "beyond" + *ballein* "to throw"]

hy·per·bol·ic \,hī-pər-'bäl-ik\ *adj* **1** : of, characterized by, or given to hyperbole **2** : of or relating to a hyperbola — **hy·per·bol·i·cal·ly** \-i-kə-lē, -klē\ *adv*

Hy·per·bo·re·an \,hī-pər-'bōr-ē-ən, -'bór-; -bə-'rē-ən\ *n* **1** : a member of a people held by the ancient Greeks to live beyond the north wind in a region of perpetual sunshine **2** *often not cap* : an inhabitant of a remote northern region [Latin *Hyperborei*, pl., from Greek *Hyperboreoi*, from *hyper* "beyond" + *Boreas* "north wind"]

hy·per·cor·rec·tion \,hī-pər-kə-'rek-shən\ *n* : a mistaken word or form (as *widely* used for *wide* in "open widely") used especially to avoid what one believes to be a grammatical error but is not — **hy·per·cor·rect** \-'rekt\ *adj* — **hy·per·cor·rect·ly** *adv* — **hy·per·cor·rect·ness** \-'rek-nəs, -'rekt-\ *n*

hy·per·crit·i·cal \,hī-pər-'krit-i-kəl\ *adj* : excessively critical — **hy·per·crit·i·cal·ly** \-kə-lē, -klē\ *adv*

hy·per·emia \,hī-pə-'rē-mē-ə\ *n* : excess of blood in a body part : CONGESTION — **hy·per·emic** \-mik\ *adj*

hy·per·gly·ce·mia \,hī-pər-glī-'sē-mē-ə\ *n* : excess of sugar in the blood [Greek *glykys* "sweet"] — **hy·per·gly·ce·mic** \-mik\ *adv*

hy·per·in·fla·tion \,hī-pər-in-'flā-shən\ *n* : inflation growing at a very high rate in a very short time

hy·per·opia \,hī-pə-'rō-pē-ə\ *n* : a condition in which visual images come to a focus behind the retina and the eye is farsighted

hy·per·pla·sia \,hī-pər-'plā-zhə, -zhē-ə\ *n* : an abnormal or unusual increase in the elements (as tissue cells) composing a bodily part — **hy·per·plas·tic** \-'plas-tik\ *adj*

hy·per·re·al·ism \,hī-pər-'ri-ə-,liz-əm, -'rē\ *n* : realism in painting showing real life in an unusual or striking way — **hy·per·re·al·ist** \-list\ *adj* — **hy·per·re·al·is·tic** \-,ri-ə-'lis-tik, -,rē-\ *adj*

hy·per·sen·si·tive \-'sen-sət-iv, -'sen-stiv\ *adj* **1** : excessively or abnormally sensitive **2** : abnormally susceptible to a drug, antigen, or other agent — **hy·per·sen·si·tive·ness** *n* — **hy·per·sen·si·tiv·i·ty** \-,sen-sə-'tiv-ət-ē\ *n*

hy·per·sex·u·al \-'seksh-wəl, -ə-wəl; -'sek-shəl\ *adj* : showing excessive concern with or indulgence in sexual activity — **hy·per·sex·u·al·i·ty** \,sek-shə-,wa-lə-tē\ *n*

hy·per·son·ic \-'sän-ik\ *adj* **1** : of or relating to speed five or more times that of sound in air — compare SONIC **2** : moving, capable of moving, or utilizing air currents that move at hypersonic speed ⟨a *hypersonic* wind tunnel⟩

hy·per·ten·sion \,hī-pər-'ten-chən\ *n* : HIGH BLOOD PRESSURE — **hy·per·ten·sive** \-'ten-siv\ *adj or n*

hy·per·thy·roid·ism \-'thī-,róid,iz-əm, -rəd-\ *n* : excessive activity of the thyroid gland; *also* : the resulting abnormal state of health — compare GOITER — **hy·per·thy·roid** \-,róid\ *adj*

hy·per·ton·ic \-'tän-ik\ *adj* : having a higher osmotic pressure than a fluid under comparison — **hy·per·to·nic·i·ty** \-tə-'nis-ət-ē\ *n*

hy·per·tro·phy \hī-'pər-trə-fē\ *n, pl* **-phies** : excessive development of a bodily part; *esp* : increase in bulk (as by thickening of muscle fibers) without multiplication of constituent units — **hy·per·tro·phic** \hī-'pər-trə-fik, ,hī-pər-'träf-ik\ *adj* — **hypertrophy** *vb*

hy·pha \'hī-fə\ *n, pl* **hy·phae** \-fē\ : one of the threads that make up the mycelium of a fungus [Greek *hyphē* "web"] — **hy·phal** \-fəl\ *adj*

¹hy·phen \'hī-fən\ *n* : a punctuation mark - used to divide or to compound words or word elements [Greek, from *hyph' hen* "under one"]

²hyphen *vt* : HYPHENATE

hy·phen·ate \'hī-fə-,nāt\ *vt* : to connect or mark with a hyphen — **hy·phen·ation** \,hī-fə-'nā-shən\ *n*

hyp·no·sis \hip-'nō-səs\ *n, pl* **-no·ses** \-'nō-,sēz\ : an induced state which resembles sleep but in which the subject is very responsive to suggestions of the hypnotizer [derived from Greek *hypnos* "sleep"]

hyp·no·ther·a·py \,hip-nō-'ther-ə-pē\ *n* : the use of hypnotism in medical or psychiatric practice

¹hyp·not·ic \hip-'nät-ik\ *adj* **1** : tending to induce sleep : SOPORIFIC **2** : of or relating to hypnosis or hypnotism [Late Latin *hypnoticus*, from Greek *hypnōtikos*, from *hypnoun* "to put to sleep", from *hypnos* "sleep"] — **hyp·not·i·cal·ly** \-i-kə-lē, -klē\ *adv*

²hypnotic *n* : a sleep-inducing agent : SOPORIFIC

hyp·no·tism \'hip-nə-,tiz-əm\ *n* **1** : the study of or act of inducing hypnosis **2** : HYPNOSIS — **hyp·no·tist** \-təst\ *n*

hyp·no·tize \-,tīz\ *vt* **1** : to induce hypnosis in **2** : to deaden (judgment or resistance) by or as if by hypnotic suggestion — **hyp·no·tiz·able** \-,tī-zə-bəl\ *adj* — **hyp·no·ti·za·tion** \,hip-nət-ə-'zā-shən\ *n* — **hyp·no·tiz·er** \'hip-nə-,tī-zər\ *n*

¹hy·po \'hī-pō\ *n* : sodium thiosulfate used in photography as a fixing agent [short for *hyposulfite*]

²hypo *n, pl* **hypos** : a hypodermic syringe or injection

hypo- *or* **hyp-** *prefix* **1** : under : beneath : down ⟨*hypo*dermic⟩ **2** : less than normal or normally ⟨*hypo*tension⟩ **3** : in a lower state of oxidation : in a

\ə\	abut	\ng\	si**ng**
\ər\	further	\ō\	bone
\a\	mat	\ó\	saw
\ā\	take	\ói\	coin
\ä\	cot, cart	\th\	thin
\aù\	out	\th\	this
\ch\	chin	\ü\	food
\e\	pet	\ù\	foot
\ē\	easy	\y\	yet
\g\	go	\yü\	few
\i\	tip	\yù\	cure
\ī\	life	\zh\	vision
\j\	job		

low and usually the lowest position in a series of compounds ⟨*hypo*chlorous acid⟩ [Greek *hypo*]

hy·po·chlo·rite \,hī-pə-'klōr-,īt, -'klȯr-\ *n* : a salt or ester of hypochlorous acid

hy·po·chlo·rous acid \,hī-pə-'klōr-əs-, -'klȯr-\ *n* : an unstable weak acid HClO used especially in the form of salts as an oxidizing agent, bleaching agent, and disinfectant

hy·po·chon·dria \,hī-pə-'kän-drē-ə\ *n* : severe depression of mind or spirits often centered on imaginary physical ailments [Late Latin, pl., "upper abdomen" (formerly regarded as the seat of hypochondria), from Greek, literally, "the parts under the cartilage (of the breastbone)", from *hypo* "under" + *chondros* "cartilage"] — **hy·po·chon·dri·ac** \-drē-,ak\ *adj or n* — **hy·po·chon·dri·a·cal** \-kən-'drī-ə-kəl, -,kän-\ *adj* — **hy·po·chon·dri·a·cal·ly** \-'drī-ə-kə-lē, -klē\ *adv* □ ORIGIN Many ancient theories of disease have been discarded. That dire humor, black bile (or melancholy), was said to be a secretion of the spleen or kidneys and was believed to produce a morbid state of depression. This disease was named for the region below the breastbone in which it had its origin, the *hypochondria*. This Late Latin word is a derivative of Greek *hypo*, "under", and *chondros*, "cartilage of the breastbone".

hy·po·cot·yl \'hī-pə-,kät-l\ *n* : the part of the main stem of a plant embryo or seedling below the cotyledons

hy·poc·ri·sy \hip-'äk-rə-sē\ *n, pl* **-sies** : a pretending to be what one is not or to believe what one does not; *esp* : a pretending to be more virtuous or religious than one really is

hyp·o·crite \'hip-ə-,krit\ *n* : a person who affects virtues or qualities he does not have : DISSEMBLER [Old French *ypocrite*, from Late Latin *hypocrita*, from Greek *hypokritēs* "actor, hypocrite", from *hypokrinesthai* "to answer, act on the stage"] — **hyp·o·crit·i·cal** \,hip-ə-'krit-i-kəl\ *adj* — **hyp·o·crit·i·cal·ly** \-i-kə-lē, -klē\ *adv*

¹hy·po·der·mic \,hī-pə-'dər-mik\ *adj* : of, relating to, or injected into the parts beneath the skin — **hy·po·der·mi·cal·ly** \-mi-kə-lē, -klē\ *adv*

²hypodermic *n* **1** : HYPODERMIC INJECTION **2** : HYPODERMIC SYRINGE

hypodermic injection *n* : an injection made into the tissues beneath the skin

hypodermic needle *n* **1** : NEEDLE 1c **2** : a hypodermic syringe complete with needle

hypodermic syringe *n* : a small syringe used with a hollow needle for injection of material into or beneath the skin

hy·po·der·mis \,hī-pə-'dər-məs\ *n* : a layer of tissue immediately beneath an outermost layer; *esp* : a layer just beneath the epidermis of a plant and often modified to serve as a supporting and protecting layer

hy·po·glos·sal nerve \,hī-pə-'gläs-əl-\ *n* : either of the 12th and final pair of cranial nerves that are motor nerves arising from the medulla oblongata and supply muscles of the tongue in higher vertebrates [Greek *glōssa* "tongue"]

hy·po·gly·ce·mia \,hī-pə-,glī-'sē-mē-ə\ *n* : abnormal decrease of sugar in the blood [Greek *glykys* "sweet"] — **hy·po·gly·ce·mic** \-mik\ *adj*

hy·poph·y·sis \hī-'päf-ə-səs\ *n, pl* **-y·ses** \-ə-,sēz\ : PITUITARY GLAND [Greek, "attachment beneath", from *hypophyein* "to grow beneath", from *hypo* "under" + *phyein* "to grow"] — **hy·poph·y·se·al** \hī-,päf-ə-'sē-əl\ *adj*

hy·po·style \'hī-pə-,stīl\ *adj* : having the roof resting on rows of columns [Greek *hypostylos*, from *hypo* "under" + *stylos* "pillar"]

hy·po·sul·fite \,hī-pō-'səl-,fīt\ *n* : ¹HYPO

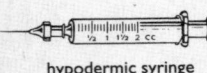

hypodermic syringe

A
B   C

AC hypotenuse

hy·po·ten·sion \,hī-pō-'ten-chən\ *n* : LOW BLOOD PRESSURE — **hy·po·ten·sive** \-'ten-siv\ *adj or n*

hy·pot·e·nuse \hī-'pät-n-,üs, -,üz, -,yüs, -,yüz\ *n* : the side of a right triangle that is opposite the right angle [Latin *hypotenusa*, from Greek *hypoteinousa*, from *hypoteinein* "to subtend", from *hypo* "under" + *teinein* "to stretch"]

hy·po·thal·a·mus \,hī-pō-'thal-ə-məs\ *n* : a part of the brain that lies beneath the thalamus, produces hormones which pass to the front part of the pituitary gland, and is important in the regulation of the activities of the autonomic nervous system — **hy·po·thal·am·ic** \-thə-'lam-ik\ *adj*

hy·po·ther·mia \,hī-pō-'thər-mē-ə\ *n* : reduction of the body temperature to an abnormally low level

hy·poth·e·sis \hī-'päth-ə-səs\ *n, pl* **-e·ses** \-ə-,sēz\ **1** : something not proved but assumed to be true for purposes of argument or further study or investigation **2** : the conditional clause in a conditional statement [Greek, "supposition", from *hypotithenai* "to put under, suppose", from *hypo* "under", + *tithenai* "to put"] □ SYN HYPOTHESIS, THEORY, LAW mean a formula derived by inference from scientific data that explains a principle operating in nature. HYPOTHESIS implies insufficient evidence to provide more than a tentative explanation; THEORY implies a greater range of evidence and greater likelihood of truth; LAW applies to a statement of order and relation in nature that has been found to be invariable under the same conditions.

hy·poth·e·size \hī-'päth-ə-,sīz\ *vb* **1** : to make a hypothesis **2** : to adopt as a hypothesis

hy·po·thet·i·cal \,hī-pə-'thet-i-kəl\ *adj* : being or involving a hypothesis ⟨a *hypothetical* situation⟩ : CONJECTURAL — **hy·po·thet·i·cal·ly** \-i-kə-lē, -klē\ *adv*

hy·po·thy·roid·ism \,hī-pō-'thī-,ròid-,iz-əm\ *n* : deficient activity of the thyroid gland; *also* : the resultant condition marked especially by lowered metabolic rate and loss of vigor — compare GOITER — **hy·po·thy·roid** \-,ròid\ *adj*

hy·po·ton·ic \,hī-pə-'tän-ik\ *adj* : having a lower osmotic pressure than a fluid under comparison — **hy·po·to·nic·i·ty** \-tə-'nis-ət-ē\ *n*

hyp·ox·ia \hip-'äk-sē-ə, hī-'päk-\ *n* : a deficiency of oxygen reaching the tissues of the body — **hyp·ox·ic** \-sik\ *adj*

hyp·som·e·ter \hip-'säm-ət-ər\ *n* : any of various instruments for determining the height of trees by triangulation [Greek *hypsos* "height"]

hy·rax \'hī-,raks\ *n, pl* **hy·rax·es** *also* **hy·ra·ces** \'hī-rə-,sēz\ : any of several small thickset Old World mammals (order Hyracoidea) with short ears, legs, and tail and feet with soft pads and broad nails [Greek, "shrew"]

hys·sop \'his-əp\ *n* **1** : a plant used in purificatory sprinkling rites by the ancient Hebrews **2** : a woody European mint with pungent aromatic leaves sometimes used in folk medicine for bruises [Old English *ysope*, from Latin *hyssopus*, from Greek *hyssōpos*, of Semitic origin]

hys·te·ria \his-'ter-ē-ə, -'tir-\ *n* **1** : a neurosis marked by emotional excitability and a tendency to develop sensory and physical disturbances with no apparent organic basis **2** : unmanageable fear or emotional excess [derived from Greek *hystera* "womb"; from the former notion that hysterical women were suffering from disturbances of the womb] — **hys·ter·ic** \-'ter-ik\ *n*

hys·ter·i·cal \-'ter-i-kəl\ *also* **hys·ter·ic** \-'ter-ik\ *adj* : of, relating to, or exhibiting hysteria or emotional excess — **hys·ter·i·cal·ly** \-i-kə-lē, -klē\ *adv*

hys·ter·ics \his-'ter-iks\ *n sing or pl* : a fit of uncontrollable laughter or crying : HYSTERIA

Ii

i \'ī\ *n, pl* **i's** *or* **is** \'īz\ *often cap* **1** : the 9th letter of the English alphabet **2** : one in Roman numerals **3** : a grade rating a student's work as incomplete

I \ī, 'ī, ə\ *pron* : the one who is speaking or writing ⟨*I* feel fine⟩ ⟨it wasn't *I*⟩ — compare ME, MINE, MY, WE [Old English *ic*]

-i- — used as a connective vowel to join word elements especially of Latin origin ⟨pest*i*cide⟩ [Latin, stem vowel of most nouns and adjectives in combination]

-ia *n suffix* **1** : pathological condition ⟨hyster*ia*⟩ **2** : genus of plants or animals ⟨Fuchs*ia*⟩ **3** : territory : world : society ⟨suburb*ia*⟩ [New Latin, from Latin and Greek, suffix forming feminine nouns]

-ial *adj suffix* : ¹-AL ⟨manor*ial*⟩ [Latin *-ialis,* from *-i-* + *-alis* "-al"]

iamb \'ī-,am, -,amb\ *or* **iam·bus** \ī-'am-bəs\ *n, pl* **iambs** \'ī-,amz\ *or* **iam·bus·es** : a metrical foot consisting of one unaccented syllable followed by one accented syllable (as in away) [Latin *iambus* "metrical foot of one short syllable followed by one long syllable", from Greek *iambos*] — **iam·bic** \ī-'am-bik\ *adj*

-ian — see -AN

-iana — see -ANA

-i·a·sis \'ī-ə-səs\ *n suffix, pl* **-i·a·ses** \-,sēz\ : disease having characteristics of or produced by ⟨something specified⟩ ⟨ameb*iasis*⟩ [New Latin, from Greek, suffix of action]

iat·ro·gen·ic \ī-,a-trə-'jen-ik\ *adj* : caused by the physician ⟨*iatrogenic* illness⟩ [Greek *iatros* "physician"]

-i·a·try \'ī-ə-trē, *in a few words* ē-,a-trē\ *n combining form* : medical treatment : healing ⟨psych*iatry*⟩ [Greek *iatreia* "art of healing", from *iatros* "physician"]

Ibe·ri·an \ī-'bir-ē-ən\ *n* **1** : a member of one or more Caucasoid peoples anciently inhabiting the peninsula comprising Spain and Portugal **2** : a native or inhabitant of Spain or Portugal [*Iberia,* peninsula in Europe] — **Iberian** *adj*

ibex \'ī-,beks\ *n, pl* **ibex** *or* **ibex·es** : any of several wild goats living chiefly in high mountain areas of the Old World and having large recurved horns transversely ridged in front [Latin]

ibi·dem \'ib-ə-,dem, ib-'īd-əm\ *adv* : in the same place [Latin]

-ibil·i·ty — see -ABILITY

ibis \'ī-bəs\ *n, pl* **ibis** *or* **ibis·es** : any of several wading birds related to the herons but distinguished by a long slender downward curving bill [Latin, from Greek, from Egyptian *hby*]

-ible — see -ABLE

IC \ī-'sē, 'ī-,\ *n* : INTEGRATED CIRCUIT

¹-ic \ik\ *adj suffix* **1** : having the character or form of : being : consisting of ⟨panoram*ic*⟩ ⟨run*ic*⟩ **2 a** : of or relating to ⟨alderman*ic*⟩ **b** : related to, derived from, or containing ⟨alcohol*ic*⟩ ⟨ole*ic*⟩ **3** : in the manner of : like that of : characteristic of ⟨Byron*ic*⟩ **4** : associated or dealing with : utilizing ⟨electron*ic*⟩ **5** : characterized by : exhibiting ⟨nostalg*ic*⟩ : affected with ⟨para-

pleg*ic*⟩ **6** : caused by ⟨amoeb*ic*⟩ **7** : tending to produce ⟨analges*ic*⟩ **8** : having a valence higher than in compounds or ions named with an adjective ending in -ous ⟨ferr*ic* iron⟩ [Latin *-icus*]

²-ic *n suffix* : one having the character or nature of : one belonging to or associated with : one exhibiting or affected by ⟨alcohol*ic*⟩ : one that produces [Latin *-icus,* from *-icus,* adj. suffix]

-i·cal \i-kəl\ *adj suffix* : -IC ⟨geolog*ical*⟩ ⟨symmetr*ical*⟩ — sometimes differing from *-ic* in that adjectives formed with *-ical* have a wider range of meaning than corresponding adjectives in *-ic* [Late Latin *-icalis,* from nouns in *-icus* + Latin *-alis* "-al"]

¹ice \'īs\ *n* **1 a** : frozen water **b** : an expanse of frozen water **2** : a state of coldness (as from formality or reserve) **3** : a substance resembling ice **4** : a frozen dessert; *esp* : one containing no milk or cream [Old English *īs*] — **on ice 1** : with every likelihood of being won or accomplished **2** : in reserve or safekeeping

²ice *vb* **1 a** : to coat or become coated with ice : change into ice **b** : to chill with ice **c** : to supply with ice **2** : to cover with or as if with icing

ice age *n* **1** : a time of widespread glaciation **2** *cap I & A* : the Pleistocene glacial epoch

ice bag *n* : a waterproof bag to hold ice for local application of cold to the body

ice·berg \'īs-,bərg\ *n* : a large floating mass of ice detached from a glacier [probably from Danish or Norwegian *isberg,* from *is* "ice" + *berg* "mountain"]

ice·boat \-,bōt\ *n* : a skeleton boat or frame on runners propelled on ice usually by sails

ice·bound \-,baund\ *adj* : surrounded or obstructed by ice

ice·box \-,bäks\ *n* : REFRIGERATOR

ice·break·er \-,brā-kər\ *n* **1** : a ship equipped to make and maintain a channel through ice **2** : something that breaks the ice (as at a social occasion)

ice cap *n* : a glacier forming on an extensive area of relatively level land and flowing outward from its center

ice–cold \'ī-'skōld\ *adj* : extremely cold

ice cream \'ī-'skrēm, ī-', 'ī-,\ *n* : a flavored and sweetened frozen food containing cream or butterfat and usually eggs

ice field *n* **1** : an extensive sheet of sea ice **2** : ICE CAP

ice floe *n* : a flat free mass of floating sea ice

ice hockey *n* : a game played on an ice rink between two teams of six players in which the players move a puck along the ice with sticks and try to shoot it past the opposing goalkeeper into the goal

ice·house \'īs-,haùs\ *n* : a building for storing ice

¹Ice·lan·dic \ī-'slan-dik\ *adj* : of, relating to, or characteristic of Iceland, the Icelanders, or Icelandic

²Icelandic *n* : the Germanic language of the Icelandic people

Ice·land moss \,ī-slənd-, -slən-, -,sland-, -,slan-\ *n* : an arctic lichen sometimes used medicinally or as food

Iceland spar *n* : a pure transparent variety of calcite

ice·man \'ī-,sman\ *n* : one who sells or delivers ice

ibex

iceboat

\ə\ abut	\ng\ sing
\ər\ further	\ō\ bone
\a\ mat	\ò\ saw
\ā\ take	\òi\ coin
\ä\ cot, cart	\th\ thin
\aù\ out	\t̲h̲\ this
\ch\ chin	\ü\ food
\e\ pet	\ù\ foot
\ē\ easy	\y\ yet
\g\ go	\yü\ few
\i\ tip	\yù\ cure
\ī\ life	\zh\ vision
\j\ job	

ice pack *n* : an expanse of pack ice

ice pick *n* : a hand tool ending in a spike for chipping ice

ice sheet *n* : ICE CAP

ice-skate \'īs-ˌskāt, 'ī-\ *vi* : to skate on ice — **ice skater** *n*

ice skate *n* : a metal runner usually attached to the bottom of a boot that is used for skating on ice

ice storm *n* : a storm in which falling rain freezes as it lands

ice water *n* : chilled or iced water especially for drinking

ich·neu·mon \ik-'nü-mən, -'nyü-\ *n* **1** : MONGOOSE **2** : ICHNEUMON FLY [Latin, from Greek *ichneumōn*, literally, "tracker", from *ichneuein* "to track", from *ichnos* "track, trail"] □ ORIGIN The ancient Egyptians thought very highly of the African mongoose (a close relative of the mongoose of India) because they believed that it sought out and devoured the eggs of crocodiles. The Greeks, hearing this story, named the beast *ichneumōn,* which means "tracker". In English we call any mongoose, including the Indian, *ichneumon.* The Greek word *ichneumōn* was also used for a certain kind of small wasp that hunts spiders. We use *ichneumon* today for an insect rather distantly related to the Greek *ichneumōn.*

ichneumon fly *n* : any of numerous small insects which are related to the wasps and whose larvae are usually internal parasites of other insect larvae

ichor \'īk-ˌór, 'īk-ər, 'ik-\ *n* : an ethereal fluid taking the place of blood in the veins of the ancient Greek gods [Greek *ichōr*] — **ichor·ous** \-ə-rəs\ *adj*

ichthy- *or* **ichthyo-** *combining form* : fish ⟨*ichthyo*logy⟩ [Greek *ichthys*]

ich·thy·ol·o·gy \ˌik-thē-'äl-ə-jē\ *n* : a branch of zoology that deals with fishes — **ich·thy·o·log·i·cal** \ˌik-thē-ə-'läj-i-kəl\ *adj* — **ich·thy·ol·o·gist** \ˌik-thē-'äl-ə-jəst\ *n*

ich·thyo·saur \'ik-thē-ə-ˌsór\ *n* : any of an order (Ichthyosauria) of extinct marine reptiles with a fish-shaped body and long snout [Greek *sauros* "lizard"] — **ich·thyo·sau·ri·an** \ˌik-thē-ə-'sór-ē-ən\ *adj or n*

-i·cian \'ish-ən\ *n suffix* : specialist : practitioner ⟨beaut*ician*⟩ [Old French *-icien*, from Latin *-ica* "-ic, -ics" + Old French *-ien* "-ian"]

ici·cle \'ī-ˌsik-əl\ *n* : a hanging mass of ice formed by the freezing of dripping water [Middle English *isikel,* from *is* "ice" + *ikel* "icicle", from Old English *gicel*] □ ORIGIN Old English *gicel,* "icicle", became Middle English *ikyl* or *ikel* and later modern English *ickle,* which still survives as a dialect word in Yorkshire, England. The word for ice in Old English is *īs,* and in a manuscript of about the year 1000 we find Latin *stiria,* "icicle", glossed somewhat redundantly as *īses gicel,* that is, "an icicle of ice". Some three hundred years later in Middle English this became the compound we know today as *icicle,* which means precisely what it did a thousand years ago.

¹ic·ing \'ī-siŋ\ *n* : a sweet and usually creamy mixture used to coat baked goods — called also *frosting*

²icing *n* : the shooting of a hockey puck the length of the rink

icon \'ī-ˌkän\ *n* **1** : a usually pictorial representation **2** *also* **ikon** : a conventional religious image typically painted on a small wooden panel and used in the devotions of Eastern Christians [Latin, from Greek *eikōn,* from *eikenai* "to resemble"] — **icon·ic** \ī-'kän-ik\ *adj* — **icon·i·cal·ly** \-'kän-i-kə-lē, -klē\ *adv*

icon·o·clasm \ī-'kän-ə-ˌklaz-əm\ *n* : the doctrine, practice, or attitude of an iconoclast

icon·o·clast \-ˌklast\ *n* **1** : one who destroys religious images or opposes their veneration **2** : one who attacks established beliefs or institutions [Medieval Latin *iconoclastes,* from Middle Greek *eikonoklastēs,* from Greek *eikōn* "image" + *klan* "to break"] — **icon·o·clas·tic** \ī-ˌkän-ə-'klas-tik\ *adj* — **icon·o·clas·ti·cal·ly** \-ti-kə-lē, -klē\ *adv*

ico·sa·he·dron \ī-ˌkō-sə-'hē-drən, -ˌkäs-ə-\ *n, pl* **-drons** *or* **-dra** \-drə\ : a polyhedron having 20 faces [Greek *eikosaedron,* from *eikosi* "twenty" + *-edron* "-hedron"]

-ics \iks, ˌiks\ *n sing or pl suffix* **1** : study : knowledge : skill : practice ⟨linguist*ics*⟩ **2** : characteristic actions or activities ⟨acrobat*ics*⟩ **3** : characteristic qualities, operations, or phenomena ⟨acoust*ics*⟩

ic·ter·us \'ik-tə-rəs\ *n* : JAUNDICE 1 [Greek *ikteros*] — **ic·ter·ic** \ik-'ter-ik\ *adj*

ic·tus \'ik-təs\ *n* : the recurring stress or beat in a rhythmic or metrical series of sounds [Latin *ictus,* from *icere* "to strike"]

icy \'ī-sē\ *adj* **ic·i·er; -est** **1 a** : covered with, full of, or consisting of ice ⟨*icy* roads⟩ **b** : intensely cold ⟨*icy* weather⟩ **2** : characterized by coldness : FRIGID ⟨an *icy* stare⟩ — **ic·i·ly** \-sə-lē\ *adv* — **ic·i·ness** \-sē-nəs\ *n*

id \'id\ *n* : the one of the three divisions of the psyche in psychoanalytic theory that is completely unconscious and is the source of psychic energy derived from instinctual needs and drives — compare EGO, SUPEREGO [Latin, "it"]

I'd \īd, ˌīd\ : I had : I should : I would

-ide \ˌīd\ *also* **-id** \əd, id, ˌid\ *n suffix* **1** : binary chemical compound ⟨hydrogen sulf*ide*⟩ ⟨cyan*ide*⟩ **2** : chemical compound derived from or related to another (usually specified) compound ⟨anhydr*ide*⟩ ⟨glucos*ide*⟩ [French *-ide* (as in *oxide*)]

idea \ī-'dē-ə, 'īd-ē-ə, *especially Southern* 'īd-ē-\ *n* **1** : a plan of action : INTENTION ⟨my *idea* is to study law⟩ **2** : something imagined or pictured in the mind : NOTION ⟨form an *idea* of a foreign country from reading⟩ **3** : a central meaning or purpose ⟨the *idea* of the game is to keep from getting caught⟩ [Latin, "form, notion", from Greek, from *idein* "to see"] — **idea·less** \ī-'dē-ə-ləs\ *adj* □ SYN CONCEPT, CONCEPTION: IDEA may apply to a mental image of something seen, known, or imagined or to an abstraction or to something assumed or vaguely sensed ⟨the *idea* of interplanetary travel⟩ ⟨a new *idea* for redecorating a room⟩ ⟨*ideas* about the nature of democracy⟩ CONCEPT may apply to the idea formed after knowing many instances of a type or to an idea of what a thing ought to be ⟨the *concepts* of modern architecture⟩ ⟨the *concept* of the role of a citizen in a democracy⟩ CONCEPTION is often interchangeable with CONCEPT, but it may stress the act of imagining or formulating rather than the result ⟨the primitive *conception* of all nature as animate⟩

¹ide·al \ī-'dē-əl, -'dēl\ *adj* **1** : existing only in the mind : not real **2** : embodying or symbolizing an ideal : PERFECT ⟨an *ideal* place for a picnic⟩ ⟨*ideal* weather⟩

²ideal *n* **1** : a standard of perfection, beauty, or excellence **2** : a perfect type : a model for imitation **3** : an ultimate object or aim of endeavor : GOAL — **ide·al·less** \ī-'dē-əl-ləs, -'dēl-\ *adj*

ide·al·ism \ī-'dē-ə-ˌliz-əm, -'dē-ˌliz-\ *n* **1 a** : a theory that ultimate reality lies in a realm transcending phenomena **b** : a theory that reality lies essentially in consciousness or reason **2** : the practice of forming ideals or living under their influence **3** : literary or artistic theory or practice that affirms the value of imagination over the representation of objective reality — compare REALISM

ide·al·ist \ī-'dē-ə-ləst, -'dē-ləst\ *n* **1 a** : an adherent of a philosophical theory of idealism **b** : an artist or author who advocates or practices idealism in art or writing **2** : one guided by ideals; *esp* : one that places ideals before practical considerations — **ide·al·is·tic** \-ˌdē-ə-'lis-tik, -ˌdē-'lis-\ *adj* — **ide·al·is·ti·cal·ly** \-ti-kə-lē, -klē\ *adv*

ide·al·ize \ī-'dē-ə-ˌlīz, -'dē-ˌlīz\ *vt* : to think of or represent as ideal ⟨*idealize* life on a farm⟩ — **ide·al·i·za·tion** \ī-ˌdē-ə-lə-'zā-shən, -ˌdē-lə-\ *n* — **ide·al·iz·er** *n*

ide·al·ly \ī-'dē-ə-lē, -'dē-lē\ *adv* **1** : in idea or imagination : MENTALLY ⟨it's possible only *ideally*, not in fact⟩ **2** : conformably to an ideal : PERFECTLY ⟨*ideally* suited to the position⟩

ide·ation \ˌīd-ē-'ā-shən\ *n* : the capacity for or the act of forming or entertaining ideas — **ide·ate** \'īd-ē-ˌāt\ *vb* — **ide·ation·al** \ˌīd-ē-'ā-shnəl, -shən-l\ *adj*

idem \'īd-ˌem, 'ēd-, 'id-\ *pron* : something previously mentioned : SAME [Latin, "same"]

iden·ti·cal \ī-'dent-i-kəl, ə-\ *adj* **1** : being the same ⟨the *identical* place we stopped before⟩ **2** : being essentially the same or exactly alike ⟨*identical* hats⟩ — **iden·ti·cal·ly** \-i-kə-lē, -klē\ *adv* — **iden·ti·cal·ness** \-kəl-nəs\ *n*

identical twin *n* : either member of a pair of twins that are produced from a single fertilized egg cell, carry the same genes, and are physically similar

iden·ti·fi·ca·tion \ī-ˌdent-ə-fə-'kā-shən, ə-\ *n* **1** : an act of identifying : the state of being identified **2** : evidence of identity ⟨carry *identification*⟩

iden·ti·fy \ī-'dent-ə-ˌfī, ə-\ *vt* **-fied; -fy·ing 1 a** : to regard as identical ⟨*identifies* democracy with capitalism⟩ **b** : to think of as united (as in principle) ⟨groups that are *identified* with conservation⟩ **2** : to establish the identity of ⟨*identified* the dog as my lost pet⟩ — **iden·ti·fi·able** \-ˌfī-ə-bəl\ *adj* — **iden·ti·fi·ably** \-blē\ *adv* — **iden·ti·fi·er** \-ˌfī-ər, -ˌfīr\ *n*

iden·ti·ty \ī-'dent-ət-ē, ə-\ *n, pl* **-ties 1** : the fact or condition of being exactly alike : SAMENESS ⟨an *identity* of interests⟩ **2** : distinguishing character or personality : INDIVIDUALITY **3** : the fact of being the same as something described or known to exist ⟨establish the *identity* of stolen goods⟩ **4 a** : an equation that is true for all values substituted for the variables **b** : IDENTITY ELEMENT [Middle French *identité*, from Late Latin *identitas*, from Latin *idem* "same", from *is* "that"]

identity element *n* : an element (as 0 in the set of all integers under addition) of a set that leaves any element of the set to which it belongs unchanged when combined with it by a specified operation

ideo·gram \'īd-ē-ə-ˌgram, 'id-\ *n* **1** : a picture or symbol used in a system of writing to represent a thing or an idea but not a particular word or phrase for it **2** : a character or symbol used in a system of writing to represent an entire word

ideo·graph \-ˌgraf\ *n* : IDEOGRAM — **ideo·graph·ic** \ˌīd-ē-ə-'graf-ik, ˌid-\ *adj* — **ideo·graph·i·cal·ly** \-'graf-i-kə-lē, -klē\ *adv*

ide·ol·o·gy \ˌīd-ē-'äl-ə-jē, ˌid-\ *n, pl* **-gies 1** : a systematic body of concepts especially about human life or culture **2** : a manner or the content of thinking characteristic of an individual, group, or culture **3** : the integrated assertions, theories, and aims that constitute a political, social and economic program [French *idéologie*, from Greek *idea* "form, notion, idea"] — **ideo·log·i·cal** \-ē-ə-'läj-i-kəl\ *adj* — **ideo·log·i·cal·ly** \-i-kə-lē, -klē\ *adv* — **ide·ol·o·gist** \-ē-'äl-ə-jəst\ *n*

ides \'īdz\ *n pl* : the 15th day of March, May, July, or October or the 13th day of any other month in the ancient Roman calendar [Middle French, from Latin *idus*]

idio- *combining form* : one's own : personal : separate : distinct ⟨*idio*lect⟩ [Greek *idios* "one's own, private"]

id·i·o·cy \'id-ē-ə-sē\ *n, pl* **-cies 1** : extreme mental deficiency commonly due to a brain defect **2** : something notably stupid or foolish

id·io·lect \'id-ē-ə-ˌlekt\ *n* : the speech pattern of one individual [*idio-* + *-lect* (as in *dialect*)]

id·i·om \'id-ē-əm\ *n* **1** : the language peculiar to a group ⟨doctors speaking in their professional *idiom*⟩ **2** : the characteristic form of expression of a language ⟨know the vocabulary of a foreign language but not its *idiom*⟩ **3** : an expression that cannot be understood from the meanings of its separate words but must be

learned as a whole ⟨the expression *give way*, meaning "retreat", is an *idiom*⟩ [Late Latin *idioma* "individual peculiarity of language", from Greek *idiōmat-*, *idiōma*, from *idios* "one's own"] — **id·i·om·at·ic** \ˌid-ē-ə-'mat-ik\ *adj* — **id·i·om·at·i·cal·ly** \-'mat-i-kə-lē, -klē\ *adv* — **id·i·om·at·ic·ness** \-'mat-ik-nəs\ *n*

id·io·syn·cra·sy \ˌid-ē-ə-'sing-krə-sē\ *n, pl* **-sies** : characteristic peculiarity of habit or structure [Greek *idiosynkrasia*, from *idios* "one's own" + *synkerannynai* "to blend", from *syn-* + *kerannynai* "to mix"] SYN see ECCENTRICITY — **id·io·syn·crat·ic** \ˌid-ē-ō-sin-'krat-ik\ *adj* — **id·io·syn·crat·i·cal·ly** \-'krat-i-kə-lē, -klē\ *adv*

id·i·ot \'id-ē-ət\ *n* **1** : a person affected with idiocy; *esp* : a mentally retarded person having a mental age not exceeding three years and requiring complete custodial care **2** : a silly or foolish person [Latin *idiota* "ignorant person", from Greek *idiōtēs* "one in a private station, layman, ignorant person", from *idios* "one's own, private"] — **idiot** *adj* □ ORIGIN The Greek adjective *idios* means "one's own" or "private". The derivative noun *idiōtēs* means "private person". A Greek *idiōtēs* was a person who was not in the public eye, who held no public office. From this sense came the sense "common man", and later "ignorant person" — a natural extension, for the common people of ancient Greece were not, in general, particularly learned. English *idiot* originally meant "ignorant person", but this mild meaning is now obsolete. By carrying ignorance to extremes, we have arrived at the *idiot* who is mentally deficient. □ SYN IDIOT, IMBECILE, MORON mean one who is mentally defective and technically designate three grades of mental deficiency. An IDIOT is incapable of coherent speech and of avoiding ordinary hazards and therefore requires constant care; an IMBECILE is incapable of earning a living but can be taught to attend to his basic wants and to avoid ordinary dangers; a MORON can learn a simple trade but requires constant supervision in work and play.

id·i·ot·ic \ˌid-ē-ə-'ät-ik\ *adj* **1** : characterized by idiocy **2** : showing complete lack of thought : FOOLISH — **id·i·ot·i·cal·ly** \-'ät-i-kə-lē, -klē\ *adv*

¹idle \'īd-l\ *adj* **idler** \'īd-lər, -l-ər\; **idlest** \'īd-ləst, -l-əst\ **1** : lacking worth or basis ⟨*idle* rumor⟩ **2** : not employed : doing nothing ⟨*idle* workers⟩ ⟨*idle* machines⟩ **3** : disliking work : LAZY [Old English *īdel*] SYN see INACTIVE — **idle·ness** \'īd-l-nəs\ *n* — **idly** \'īd-lē\ *adv*

²idle *vb* **idled; idling** \'īd-ling, -l-ing\ **1 a** : to spend time in idleness **b** : to move idly **2** : to run disengaged so that power is not used for useful work ⟨the engine is *idling*⟩ **3** : to pass in idleness : WASTE — **idler** \'īd-lər, -l-ər\ *n*

idol \'īd-l\ *n* **1** : an image of a god made or used as an object of worship **2** : one that is very greatly or excessively loved and admired [Old French *idole*, from Late Latin *idolum*, from Greek *eidōlon* "phantom, idol"]

idol·a·ter \ī-'däl-ət-ər\ *n* **1** : a worshiper of idols **2** : a person that admires or loves intensely and often blindly [Middle French *idolatre*, from Late Latin *idolatres*, from Greek *eidōlatrēs*, from *eidōlon* "idol" + *-latrēs* "worshiper"]

idol·a·tress \ī-'däl-ə-trəs\ *n* : a female idolater

idol·a·trous \ī-'däl-ə-trəs\ *adj* **1** : of or relating to idolatry **2** : having the character of idolatry **3** : given to idolatry — **idol·a·trous·ly** *adv* — **idol·a·trous·ness** *n*

idol·a·try \-trē\ *n, pl* **-tries 1** : the worship of a physical object as a god **2** : excessive attachment or devotion to something

idol·ize \'īd-l-ˌīz\ *vb* **1** : to worship idolatrously **2** : to love or admire to excess — **idol·iza·tion** \ˌīd-l-ə-'zā-shən\ *n* — **idol·iz·er** \'īd-l-ˌī-zər\ *n*

idyll *or* **idyl** \'īd-l\ *n* **1 a** : a simple poetic or prose work descriptive of peaceful rustic life or pastoral scenes

\ə\	abut	\ng\	sing
\ər\	further	\ō\	bone
\a\	mat	\ȯ\	saw
\ā\	take	\ȯi\	coin
\ä\	cot, cart	\th\	thin
\au̇\	out	\t͟h\	this
\ch\	chin	\ü\	food
\e\	pet	\u̇\	foot
\ē\	easy	\y\	yet
\g\	go	\yü\	few
\i\	tip	\yu̇\	cure
\ī\	life	\zh\	vision
\j\	job		

b : a romantic narrative poem **2** : a fit subject for an idyll [Latin *idyllium,* from Greek *eidyllion,* from *eidos* "form"] — **idyl·lic** \ī-'dil-ik\ *adj* — **idyl·li·cal·ly** \-'dil-i-kə-lē, -klē\ *adv*

-ie *also* **-y** \ē\ *n suffix, pl* **-ies 1** : little one : dear little one (lass*ie*) (sonn*y*) — sometimes used in names of articles of clothing (night*ie*) **2** : one belonging to : one having to do with (cabb*y*) **3** : one of (such) a kind or quality (good*y*) (smart*y*) [Middle English]

-ier — see **-ER**

¹if \if, əf, ,if\ *conj* **1** : in the event that (come *if* you can) **2** : WHETHER (asked *if* the mail had come) **3** — used as a function word to introduce an exclamation expressing a wish (*if* it would only rain) **4** : even though (an interesting *if* untenable argument) [Old English *gif*]

²if \'if\ *n* **1** : CONDITION 3, STIPULATION **2** : SUPPOSITION (a theory full of *ifs*)

-if·er·ous \'if-rəs, -ə-rəs\ *adj combining form* : -FER·OUS

if·fy \'if-ē\ *adj* : full of contingencies or unknown qualities or conditions

-i·form \ə-,fȯrm\ *adj combining form* : -FORM

-i·fy \ə-,fī\ *vb suffix* **-i·fied; -i·fy·ing** : -FY

ig·loo \'ig-lü\ *n, pl* **igloos 1** : an Eskimo house often made of snow blocks and in the shape of a dome **2** : a structure shaped like a dome [Eskimo *iglu* "house"]

igloo 1

ig·ne·ous \'ig-nē-əs\ *adj* **1** : of, relating to, or resembling fire : FIERY **2** : formed by solidification of magma (*igneous* rock) [Latin *igneus,* from *ignis* "fire"]

ig·nis fatuus \,ig-nəs-'fach-ə-wəs\ *n, pl* **ig·nes fat·ui** \-,nēz-'fach-ə-,wī\ **1** : a light that sometimes appears in the night over marshy ground and is often attributable to the combustion of gas from decomposed organic matter **2** : WILL-O'-THE-WISP 2 [Medieval Latin, literally, "foolish fire"]

ig·nite \ig-'nīt\ *vb* **1 a** : to set afire (*ignite* a piece of paper); *also* : KINDLE (*ignite* a fire) **b** : to cause (a fuel mixture) to burn **2** : to catch fire (dry wood *ignites* quickly) [Latin *ignire,* from *ignis* "fire"] — **ig·nit·able** \-'nīt-ə-bəl\ *adj* — **ig·nit·er** *or* **ig·ni·tor** \-'nīt-ər\ *n*

ig·ni·tion \ig-'nish-ən\ *n* **1** : the act or action of igniting : KINDLING **2** : the process or means (as an electric spark) of igniting a fuel mixture

ig·no·ble \ig-'nō-bəl\ *adj* **1** : of low birth : PLEBEIAN **2** : characterized by baseness or meanness (*ignoble* conduct) [Latin *ignobilis,* from *in-* + *gnobilis, nobilis* "noble"] — **ig·no·ble·ness** *n* — **ig·no·bly** \-blē\ *adv*

ig·no·min·i·ous \,ig-nə-'min-ē-əs\ *adj* **1** : marked by disgrace or shame : DISHONORABLE **2** : deserving of shame : DESPICABLE **3** : SHAMEFUL, DEGRADING (an *ignominious* defeat) — **ig·no·min·i·ous·ly** *adv* — **ig·no·min·i·ous·ness** *n*

ig·no·mi·ny \'ig-nə-,min-ē, ig-'näm-ə-nē\ *n, pl* **-nies 1** : deep personal humiliation and disgrace **2** : disgraceful conduct, quality, or action [Latin *ignominia,* from *ig-* (as in *ignorare* "to be ignorant of, ignore") + *nomen* "name, repute"]

ig·no·ra·mus \,ig-nə-'rā-məs\ *n, pl* **-mus·es** : an utterly ignorant person : DUNCE [from *Ignoramus,* an ignorant lawyer in *Ignoramus* (1615), a play by George Ruggle]

ig·no·rance \'ig-nə-rəns\ *n* : the state of being ignorant

ig·no·rant \-rənt\ *adj* **1 a** : lacking knowledge or education **b** : resulting from or showing lack of knowledge (an *ignorant* mistake) **2** : not knowing : UNAWARE (*ignorant* of the true facts) — **ig·no·rant·ly** *adv* — **ig·no·rant·ness** *n* □ SYN ILLITERATE: IGNORANT indicates a lack of knowledge in general or of a particular thing; ILLITERATE implies inability to read or write or complete unfamiliarity with the world of learning (the vast problem of teaching the *illiterate* millions of this world)

ig·nore \ig-'nōr, -'nȯr\ *vt* : to refuse to take notice of (*ignore* an interruption) [French *ignorer* "to be ignorant of", from Latin *ignorare* "to be ignorant of, ig-

nore", from *ignarus* "ignorant, unknown", from *in-* + *gnoscere, noscere* "to know"] — **ig·nor·er** *n*

igua·na \i-'gwän-ə\ *n* : any of various large plant-eating tropical American lizards with a serrated crest on the back that are locally important as human food [Spanish, of American Indian origin]

IHS \,ī-,ā-'ches\ — used as a Christian symbol and monogram for Jesus [Late Latin, part transliteration of Greek ΙΗΣ, abbreviation for ΙΗΣΟΨΣ *Iēsous* "Jesus"]

ikon *variant of* ICON

il- — see IN-

-ile \əl, ᵊl, ,īl, il\ *adj suffix* : of, relating to, or capable of (contract*ile*) [Latin *-ilis*]

il·e·i·tis \,il-ē-'īt-əs\ *n* : inflammation of the ileum

il·e·um \'il-ē-əm\ *n, pl* **il·ea** \-ē-ə\ : the part of the small intestine between the jejunum and the large intestine [Latin, "groin, viscera"] — **il·e·al** \-ē-əl\ *adj*

ilex \'ī-,leks\ *n* : HOLLY [Latin, a kind of oak]

il·i·um \'il-ē-əm\ *n, pl* **il·ia** \-ē-ə\ : the broad expanded upper one of the three bones composing either lateral half of the pelvis [Latin *ilium, ileum* "groin"] — **il·i·ac** \-ē-,ak\ *adj*

ilk \'ilk\ *n* : SORT 1, FAMILY — used chiefly in the phrase *of that ilk* [Old English *ilca* "same"]

¹ill \'il\ *adj* **worse** \'wərs\; **worst** \'wərst\ **1** : showing or implying evil intention (*ill* deeds) **2 a** : causing suffering or distress : DISAGREEABLE (*ill* weather) **b** : not normal or sound : FAILING (*ill* health) **c** : not in good health (an *ill* person) **d** : NAUSEATED (felt *ill*) **3** : UNFORTUNATE, UNLUCKY (an *ill* omen) **4** : UNKIND, UNFRIENDLY (*ill* feelings) **5** : not right or proper (an *ill* use of power) [Old Norse *illr* "evil"] SYN see SICK

²ill *adv* **worse; worst 1 a** : with displeasure (the remark was *ill* received) **b** : HARSHLY (*ill* treated) **2** : in a reprehensible manner (an *ill*-spent youth) **3** : SCARCELY (can *ill* afford it) **4** : BADLY, POORLY (*ill* equipped)

³ill *n* **1** : EVIL, MISFORTUNE (for good or *ill*) **2** : SICKNESS (childhood *ills*) **3** : TROUBLE, AFFLICTION (the *ills* of society) **4** : something that reflects unfavorably (spoke no *ill* of them)

I'll \īl, ,īl\ : I shall : I will

ill–ad·vised \,il-əd-'vīzd\ *adj* : showing lack of wise and sufficient advice or consideration : UNWISE — **ill–ad·vis·ed·ly** \-'vī-zəd-lē\ *adv*

ill–bred \'il-'bred\ *adj* : badly brought up : IMPOLITE

il·le·gal \il-'lē-gəl, -'ē-\ *adj* : not lawful — **il·le·gal·i·ty** \,il-ē-'gal-ət-ē\ *n* — **il·le·gal·ly** \il-'lē-gə-lē, -'ē-\ *adv*

il·leg·ible \il-'lej-ə-bəl, -'ej-\ *adj* : impossible or very hard to read (*illegible* handwriting) SYN see UNREADABLE — **il·leg·ibil·i·ty** \il-,ej-ə-'bil-ət-ē\ *n* — **il·leg·ibly** \il-'lej-ə-blē, -'ej-\ *adv*

il·le·git·i·mate \,il-i-'jit-ə-mət\ *adj* **1** : born of a father and mother who are not married **2** : not correctly deduced or reasoned (an *illegitimate* conclusion) **3** : not lawful or proper — **il·le·git·i·ma·cy** \-'jit-ə-mə-sē\ *n* — **il·le·git·i·mate·ly** *adv*

ill–fat·ed \'il-'fāt-əd\ *adj* : doomed to failure or disaster (an *ill-fated* expedition)

ill–fa·vored \-'fā-vərd\ *adj* : unattractive in physical appearance; *esp* : having an ugly face

ill–got·ten \-'gät-n\ *adj* : acquired by evil means

ill–hu·mored \'il-'hyü-mərd, -'yü-\ *adj* : SURLY, IRRITABLE (became *ill-humored* when tired) — **ill–hu·mored·ly** *adv*

il·lib·er·al \il-'lib-rəl, -'ib-, -ə-rəl\ *adj* : not broad-minded : BIGOTED — **il·lib·er·al·i·ty** \il-,ib-ə-'ral-ət-ē\ *n* — **il·lib·er·al·ly** \-'lib-rə-lē, -'ib-, -ə-rə-\ *adv* — **il·lib·er·al·ness** *n*

il·lic·it \il-'lis-ət, -'is-\ *adj* : not permitted : UNLAWFUL — **il·lic·it·ly** *adv*

il·lim·it·able \il-'lim-ət-ə-bəl, -'im-\ *adj* : incapable of being limited : BOUNDLESS — **il·lim·it·abil·i·ty** \-,lim-ət-ə-'bil-ət-ē, -,im-\ *n* — **il·lim·it·able·ness** \-'lim-ət-ə-bəl-nəs, -'im-\ *n* — **il·lim·it·ably** \-blē\ *adv*

iguana

il·lit·er·a·cy \il-ˈlit-ə-rə-sē, -ˈit-; -ˈli-trə-sē, -ˈi-trə-\ *n, pl* **-cies** **1** : the quality or state of being illiterate; *esp* : inability to read or write **2** : a mistake or crudity made by one who is illiterate

il·lit·er·ate \il-ˈlit-ə-rət, -ˈit-; -ˈli-trət, -ˈi-trət\ *adj* **1** : having little or no education; *esp* : unable to read or write **2 a** : showing or marked by a lack of familiarity with language and literature **b** : showing ignorance of the fundamentals of a particular field of knowledge SYN see IGNORANT — **illiterate** *n* — **il·lit·er·ate·ly** *adv* — **il·lit·er·ate·ness** *n*

ill–man·nered \ˈil-ˈman-ərd\ *adj* : marked by bad manners : RUDE

ill–na·tured \-ˈnā-chərd\ *adj* : having a bad disposition — **ill–na·tured·ly** *adv*

ill·ness \ˈil-nəs\ *n* : an unhealthy condition of body or mind : SICKNESS

il·log·i·cal \il-ˈläj-i-kəl, -ˈäj-\ *adj* : not observing the principles of logic or good reasoning — **il·log·i·cal·ly** \-i-kə-lē, -klē\ *adv* — **il·log·i·cal·ness** \-kəl-nəs\ *n*

ill–starred \ˈil-ˈstärd\ *adj* : ILL-FATED ⟨*ill-starred* lovers⟩

ill–tem·pered \-ˈtem-pərd\ *adj* : ILL-NATURED, QUARREL-SOME — **ill–tem·pered·ly** *adv*

ill–treat \-ˈtrēt\ *vt* : to treat cruelly or improperly : MALTREAT — **ill–treat·ment** \-mənt\ *n*

il·lu·mi·nant \il-ˈü-mə-nənt\ *n* : an illuminating device (as an electric lamp) or substance (as natural gas)

il·lu·mi·nate \-ˌnāt\ *vt* **1 a** : to supply or brighten with light : light up ⟨*illuminate* a building⟩ **b** : ENLIGHTEN **2** : to make clear : EXPLAIN **3** : to decorate with designs or pictures in gold or colors ⟨*illuminate* a manuscript⟩ [Latin *illuminare*, from *in-* + *luminare* "to light up", from *lumen* "light"] — **il·lu·mi·na·tive** \-ˌnāt-iv\ *adj* — **il·lu·mi·na·tor** \-ˌnāt-ər\ *n*

illuminating gas *n* : a gas that is burned for illumination

il·lu·mi·na·tion \il-ˌü-mə-ˈnā-shən\ *n* **1** : the action of illuminating or state of being illuminated: as **a** : spiritual or intellectual enlightenment **b** : decorative lighting or lighting effects **c** : decoration by the art of illuminating **2** : the quantity of light or the luminous flux per unit area on an intercepting surface at any given point

il·lu·mine \il-ˈü-mən\ *vt* : ILLUMINATE

ill–us·age \ˈil-ˈyü-sij, -ˈyü-zij\ *n* : harsh or abusive treatment

ill–use \-ˈyüz\ *vt* : to use badly : MALTREAT, ABUSE

il·lu·sion \il-ˈü-zhən\ *n* **1 a** : a misleading image (as a hallucination) presented to the vision **b** : perception of something actually existing so as to misinterpret its real nature **c** : a figure or pattern capable of being perceived in several ways — called also *optical illusion* **2** : the state or fact of being led to accept as true something unreal or imagined **3** : a misleading or inaccurate idea or impression of reality [Middle French, from Latin *illusio* "action of mocking", from *illudere* "to mock at", from *in-* + *ludere* "to play, mock"] SYN see DELUSION — **il·lu·sion·ary** \-zhə-ner-ē\ *adj*

il·lu·sion·ist \il-ˈüzh-nəst, -ə-nəst\ *n* : one that produces illusions; *esp* : a ventriloquist or sleight-of-hand performer

il·lu·sive \il-ˈü-siv, -ˈü-ziv\ *adj* : ILLUSORY — **il·lu·sive·ly** *adv* — **il·lu·sive·ness** *n*

il·lu·so·ry \il-ˈüs-rē, -ˈüz-, -ə-rē\ *adj* : based on or producing illusion : DECEPTIVE — **il·lu·so·ri·ly** \-rə-lē\ *adv* — **il·lu·so·ri·ness** \-rē-nəs\ *n*

il·lus·trate \ˈil-ə-ˌstrāt\ *vt* **1** : to make clear especially by serving as or giving an example or instance ⟨*illustrate* a point from one's own experience⟩ **2 a** : to provide with pictures or figures intended to explain or decorate ⟨*illustrate* a book⟩ **b** : to serve to explain or decorate ⟨*illustrates* the operation of a computer⟩ [Latin *illustrare*, from *in-* + *lustrare* "to purify, make bright"] — **il·lus·tra·tor** \-ˌstrāt-ər\ *n*

il·lus·tra·tion \ˌil-ə-ˈstrā-shən\ *n* **1** : the action of illustrating : the condition of being illustrated **2 a** : an example or instance intended to make something clear **b** : a picture or diagram intended to explain or decorate

il·lus·tra·tive \il-ˈəs-trət-iv\ *adj* : serving, tending, or designed to illustrate ⟨an *illustrative* diagram⟩ — **il·lus·tra·tive·ly** *adv*

il·lus·tri·ous \il-ˈəs-trē-əs\ *adj* : notably outstanding because of rank or achievement : EMINENT — **il·lus·tri·ous·ly** *adv* — **il·lus·tri·ous·ness** *n*

ill will *n* : unfriendly feeling : MALICE

ill–wish·er \ˈil-ˈwish-ər\ *n* : one that wishes ill to another

il·ly \ˈil-lē, ˈil-ē\ *adv* : BADLY, ILL ⟨*illy* chosen⟩

il·men·ite \ˈil-mə-ˌnīt\ *n* : a metallic-black mineral composed of iron, titanium, and oxygen that is an ore of titanium [*Ilmen* range, Ural Mountains, Russia and Kazakhstan]

im- — see IN-

I'm \ˈīm, ˌīm\ : I am

¹im·age \ˈim-ij\ *n* **1** : a reproduction or imitation of the form of a person or thing; *esp* : STATUE **2 a** : a picture of an object produced by a lens, a mirror, or an electronic system **b** : a likeness of an object produced on a photographic material **3** : a mental picture of something not actually present : IMPRESSION **4** : a vivid or graphic representation or description **5** : FIGURE OF SPEECH **6** : a person strikingly like another person ⟨the child is the *image* of the father⟩ **7** : a set of values of a mathematical function that corresponds to a particular subset of the domain [Old French, from Latin *imago*]

²image *vt* **1** : to describe or portray in language especially vividly **2** : to call up a mental picture of : IMAGINE **3 a** : REFLECT, MIRROR ⟨a face *imaged* in a mirror⟩ **b** : to make appear : PROJECT ⟨a film *imaged* on a screen⟩

imag·ery \ˈim-ij-rē, -ə-rē\ *n, pl* **-er·ies** **1** : the product of image makers : IMAGES; *also* : the art of making images **2** : figurative language ⟨*imagery* of a poem⟩ **3** : mental images; *esp* : the products of imagination

imag·in·able \im-ˈaj-nə-bəl, -ə-nə-\ *adj* : capable of being imagined : CONCEIVABLE — **imag·in·ably** \-blē\ *adv*

imag·i·nary \im-ˈaj-ə-ˌner-ē\ *adj* **1** : existing only in imagination : FANCIED **2** : of, relating to, or being an imaginary number — **imag·i·nar·i·ly** \-ˌaj-ə-ˈner-ə-lē\ *adv* — **imag·i·nar·i·ness** \-ˈaj-ə-ˌner-ē-nəs\ *n*

imaginary number *n* : a complex number in which the part (as $3\sqrt{-1}$ in $2+3\sqrt{-1}$) containing the positive square root of minus 1 is not equal to zero — called also *imaginary*

imag·i·na·tion \im-ˌaj-ə-ˈnā-shən\ *n* **1** : the act or power of forming a mental image of something not present to the senses or never before wholly perceived in reality **2 a** : creative ability **b** : ability to confront and deal with a problem : RESOURCEFULNESS **3 a** : a creation of the mind; *esp* : an idealized or poetic creation **b** : fanciful or empty assumption

imag·i·na·tive \im-ˈaj-nət-iv, -ə-nət-, -ˈaj-ə-ˌnāt-\ *adj* **1** : of, relating to, or characterized by imagination **2** : given to imagining : having a lively imagination **3** : of or relating to images; *esp* : showing a command of imagery — **imag·i·na·tive·ly** *adv* — **imag·i·na·tive·ness** *n*

imag·ine \im-ˈaj-ən\ *vb* **imag·ined; imag·in·ing** \-ˈaj-ning, -ə-ning\ **1** : to form a mental image of something not present : use the imagination **2** : SUPPOSE, GUESS ⟨I *imagine* it will rain⟩ [Middle French *imaginer*, from Latin *imaginari*, from *imagin-, imago* "image"]

im·ag·ing \ˈim-ij-ing\ *n* : the action or process of producing an image especially by means (as ultrasound) other than visible light

im·ag·ism \ˈim-ij-ˌiz-əm\ *n* : a movement in poetry advocating free verse and the expression of ideas and

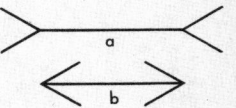

illusion 1c: a equals b in length

\ə\ abut		\ng\ sing	
\ər\ further		\ō\ bone	
\a\ mat		\ȯ\ saw	
\ā\ take		\ȯi\ coin	
\ä\ cot, cart		\th\ thin	
\aů\ out		\th\ this	
\ch\ chin		\ü\ food	
\e\ pet		\ů\ foot	
\ē\ easy		\y\ yet	
\g\ go		\yü\ few	
\i\ tip		\yů\ cure	
\ī\ life		\zh\ vision	
\j\ job			

emotions through clear precise images — **im·ag·ist** \'ij-əst\ *n* — **imagist** *or* **im·ag·is·tic** \,im-ij-'is-tik\ *adj* — **im·ag·is·ti·cal·ly** \,im-ij-'is-ti-kə-lē, -klē\ *adv*

ima·go \im-'ā-gō, -'äg-ō\ *n, pl* **imagoes** *or* **ima·gi·nes** \-'ā-gə-,nēz, -'äg-ə-\ : an insect in its final adult, sexually mature, and usually winged state [Latin, "image"] — **ima·gi·nal** \-'ā-gən-l, -'äg-ən-\ *adj*

imam \i-'mäm, -'mam\ *n* **1** : the prayer leader of a mosque **2** *cap* : a Muslim leader held to be a divinely appointed successor of Muhammad **3** : any of various Muslim rulers that claim descent from Muhammad [Arabic *imām*] — **imam·ate** \-,āt\ *n, often cap*

im·bal·ance \im-'bal-əns, 'im-\ *n* : lack of balance : the state of being out of equilibrium or out of proportion

im·be·cile \'im-bə-səl, -,sil\ *n* **1** : a mentally deficient person; *esp* : a mentally retarded person having a mental age of three to seven years and requiring supervision in the performance of routine daily tasks of personal care **2** : FOOL 1, SIMPLETON [French *imbécile*, from *imbécile* "weak, weak-minded", from Latin *imbecillus*] SYN see IDIOT — **imbecile** *or* **im·be·cil·ic** \,im-bə-'sil-ik\ *adj* — **im·be·cile·ly** \'im-bə-səl-lē, -sə-lē, -,sil-lē\ *adv*

im·be·cil·i·ty \,im-bə-'sil-ət-ē\ *n, pl* **-ties 1** : the quality or state of being imbecile or an imbecile **2 a** : utter foolishness; *also* : FUTILITY **b** : something foolish or nonsensical

imbed *variant of* EMBED

im·bibe \im-'bīb\ *vb* **1** : to receive into the mind and retain ⟨*imbibe* knowledge⟩ **2 a** : DRINK 1a **b** : to take in or up : ABSORB ⟨sponges *imbibe* moisture⟩ [Latin *imbibere* "to drink in", from *in-* + *bibere* "to drink"] — **im·bib·er** *n*

im·bri·cate \'im-brə-,kāt\ *vb* : OVERLAP ⟨*imbricated* shingles⟩ [Late Latin *imbricare* "to cover with tiles", from Latin *imbrex* "roofing tile", from *imber* "rain"] — **im·bri·ca·tion** \,im-brə-'kā-shən\ *n*

im·bro·glio \im-'brōl-yō\ *n, pl* **-glios 1** : a confused mass ⟨an *imbroglio* of papers and books⟩ **2 a** : an intricate or complicated situation (as in a novel) **b** : a painful or embarrassing misunderstanding : EMBROILMENT ⟨an *imbroglio* between foreign ministers⟩ [Italian, from *imbrogliare* "to embroil", from French *embrouiller*]

im·bue \im-'byü\ *vt* **1** : to tinge or dye deeply **2** : to cause to become penetrated : PERMEATE ⟨*imbued* with a deep sense of loyalty⟩ [Latin *imbuere*]

im·i·ta·ble \'im-ət-ə-bəl\ *adj* : capable or worthy of being imitated or copied

im·i·tate \'im-ə-,tāt\ *vt* **1** : to follow as a pattern, model, or example **2** : to be or appear similar to : RESEMBLE **3** : to copy exactly ⟨*imitated* a dog's bark⟩ [Latin *imitari*] — **im·i·ta·tor** \-,tāt-ər\ *n* □ SYN MIMIC, APE, MOCK: IMITATE suggests following a model or a pattern but may allow for some variation ⟨*imitate* a poet's style⟩ MIMIC implies a close copying as of voice or mannerism often for fun, ridicule, or lifelike imitation ⟨*mimicked* the bird's notes⟩ ⟨children *mimicking* adults⟩ APE may suggest presumptuous, slavish, or inept imitating of a superior original ⟨peasants *aping* their feudal lords⟩ MOCK usually implies imitation with derision ⟨*mocking* a crippled beggar⟩

¹im·i·ta·tion \,im-ə-'tā-shən\ *n* **1** : an act of imitating **2** : something produced as a copy **3** : the repetition in a voice part of the melodic theme, phrase, or motive previously found in another part — **im·i·ta·tion·al** \-shnəl, -shən-l\ *adv*

²imitation *adj* : resembling something else especially of greater worth : not real ⟨*imitation* leather⟩

im·i·ta·tive \'im-ə-,tāt-iv\ *adj* **1 a** : marked by imitation **b** : reproducing or representing a natural sound ⟨*hiss* is an *imitative* word⟩ **2** : inclined to imitate **3** : imitating something superior — **im·i·ta·tive·ly** *adv* — **im·i·ta·tive·ness** *n*

im·mac·u·late \im-'ak-yə-lət\ *adj* **1** : having no stain or blemish : PURE ⟨an *immaculate* heart⟩ **2** : containing no flaw or error **3** : spotlessly clean ⟨*immaculate* linen⟩ [Latin *immaculatus*, from *in-* + *maculare* "to stain", from *macula* "spot, stain"] — **im·mac·u·late·ly** *adv* — **im·mac·u·late·ness** *n*

im·ma·te·ri·al \,im-ə-'tir-ē-əl\ *adj* **1** : not consisting of matter **2** : of no consequence : UNIMPORTANT — **im·ma·te·ri·al·i·ty** \-,tir-ē-'al-ət-ē\ *n* — **im·ma·te·ri·al·ly** \-'tir-ē-ə-lē\ *adv* — **im·ma·te·ri·al·ness** *n*

im·ma·ture \,im-ə-'tūr, -'tyūr\ *adj* : not mature or fully developed : YOUNG, UNRIPE — **immature** *n* — **im·ma·ture·ly** *adv* — **im·ma·ture·ness** *n* — **im·ma·tu·ri·ty** \-'tūr-ət-ē, -'tyūr-\ *n*

im·mea·sur·able \im-'ezh-rə-bəl, -'ezh-ə-rə-, -'ezh-ər-bəl, -'āzh-, 'im-\ *adj* : incapable of being measured : indefinitely extensive ⟨the *immeasurable* sea⟩ — **im·mea·sur·able·ness** *n* — **im·mea·sur·ably** \-blē\ *adv*

im·me·di·a·cy \im-'ēd-ē-ə-sē\ *n, pl* **-cies 1** : the quality or state of being immediate **2** : something that is of immediate importance — usually used in pl.

im·me·di·ate \im-'ēd-ē-ət\ *adj* **1** : next in line or relationship ⟨the monarch's *immediate* heir⟩ **2** : closest in importance ⟨our *immediate* interest⟩ **3** : acting directly and alone without anything intervening ⟨an *immediate* cause of disease⟩ **4** : not distant or separated : NEXT ⟨their *immediate* neighbors⟩ **5** : close in time ⟨the *immediate* past⟩ **6** : made or done at once ⟨ask for an *immediate* reply⟩ [Late Latin *immediatus*, derived from Latin *in-* "¹in-" + *medius* "middle"] — **im·me·di·ate·ness** *n*

im·me·di·ate·ly *adv* **1** : with nothing between : DIRECTLY ⟨the house *immediately* beyond this one⟩ **2** : without delay : STRAIGHTWAY ⟨do it *immediately*⟩

im·me·mo·ri·al \,im-ə-'mōr-ē-əl, -'mor-\ *adj* : extending beyond the reach of memory, record, or tradition ⟨since time *immemorial*⟩ — **im·me·mo·ri·al·ly** \-ē-ə-lē\ *adv*

im·mense \im-'ens\ *adj* **1** : very great in size or degree : HUGE **2** : supremely good : EXCELLENT [Middle French, from Latin *immensus* "immeasurable", from *in-* + *mensus*, past participle of *metiri* "to measure"] SYN see ENORMOUS — **im·mense·ly** *adv* — **im·mense·ness** *n*

im·men·si·ty \im-'en-sət-ē\ *n, pl* **-ties 1** : the quality or state of being immense **2** : something immense

im·merse \im-'ərs\ *vt* **1** : to plunge into something that surrounds or covers; *esp* : to plunge or dip into a fluid **2** : to baptize by submerging in water **3** : ENGROSS, ABSORB ⟨completely *immersed* in my work⟩ [Latin *immersus*, past participle of *immergere* "to immerse", from *in-* + *mergere* "to dip"]

im·mer·sion \im-'ər-zhən, -shən\ *n* : an act of immersing : a state of being immersed

im·mi·grant \'im-i-grənt\ *n* : one that immigrates: **a** : a person who comes to a country to become a permanent resident **b** : a plant or animal that becomes established in an area where it was previously unknown SYN see EMIGRANT — **immigrant** *adv*

im·mi·grate \'im-ə-,grāt\ *vi* : to enter and usually become established; *esp* : to come into a country of which one is not a native to take up permanent residence — **im·mi·gra·tion** \,im-ə-'grā-shən\ *n*

im·mi·nence \'im-ə-nəns\ *n* **1** *also* **im·mi·nen·cy** \-nən-sē\ : the quality or state of being imminent **2** : something imminent; *esp* : impending evil or danger

im·mi·nent \-nənt\ *adj* : ready to take place; *esp* : hanging threateningly over one's head [Latin *imminens*, present participle of *imminēre* "to project, threaten"] SYN see IMPENDING — **im·mi·nent·ly** *adv* — **im·mi·nent·ness** *n*

im·mis·ci·ble \im-'is-ə-bəl, 'im-\ *adj* : incapable of mixing ⟨ether and water are *immiscible*⟩ — **im·mis·ci·bil·i·ty** \im-,is-ə-'bil-ət-ē\ *n*

im·mo·bile \im-'ō-bəl, -ˌbēl, -ˌbīl, 'im-\ *adj* : incapable of being moved : FIXED — **im·mo·bil·i·ty** \ˌim-ō-'bil-ət-ē\ *n*

im·mo·bi·lize \im-'ō-bə-ˌlīz\ *vt* : to make immobile; *esp* : to prevent freedom of movement or effective use of — **im·mo·bi·li·za·tion** \im-ˌō-bə-lə-'zā-shən\ *n* — **im·mo·bi·liz·er** \im-'ō-bə-ˌlī-zər\ *n*

im·mod·er·ate \im-'äd-rət, 'im-, -ə-rət\ *adj* : lacking in moderation : EXCESSIVE — **im·mod·er·a·cy** \-'äd-rə-sē, -ə-rə-\ *n* — **im·mod·er·ate·ly** *adv* — **im·mod·er·ate·ness** *n* — **im·mod·er·a·tion** \ˌim-ˌäd-ə-'rā-shən\ *n*

im·mod·est \im-'äd-əst, 'im-\ *adj* : not modest; *esp* : INDECENT ⟨*immodest* clothing⟩ — **im·mod·est·ly** *adv* — **im·mod·es·ty** \-ə-stē\ *n*

im·mo·late \'im-ə-ˌlāt\ *vt* **1** : to offer in sacrifice; *esp* : to kill as a sacrificial victim **2** : KILL 1, DESTROY [Latin *immolare*, from *in-* + *mola* "meal"; from the custom of sprinkling victims with sacrificial meal] — **im·mo·la·tion** \ˌim-ə-'lā-shən\ *n* — **im·mo·la·tor** \'im-ə-ˌlāt-ər\ *n*

im·mor·al \im-'ór-əl, 'im-, -'är-\ *adj* : not moral — **im·mor·al·ly** \-ə-lē\ *adv*

im·mor·al·ist \-ə-ləst\ *n* : an advocate of immorality

im·mo·ral·i·ty \ˌim-ˌó-'ral-ət-ē, ˌim-ə-'ral-\ *n, pl* **-ties** **1** : the quality or state of being immoral; *esp* : UNCHASTITY **2** : an immoral act or practice

¹im·mor·tal \im-'órt-l, 'im-\ *adj* **1** : not subject to death ⟨*immortal* gods⟩ **2** : connected with or relating to immortality ⟨*immortal* longings⟩ **3** : lasting forever ⟨*immortal* fame⟩ — **im·mor·tal·ly** \-l-ē\ *adv*

²immortal *n* **1 a** : one exempt from death **b** *pl, often cap* : the gods of the Greek and Roman pantheon **2** : a person whose fame is lasting ⟨one of the *immortals* of baseball⟩

im·mor·tal·i·ty \ˌim-ˌór-'tal-ət-ē\ *n* : the quality or state of being immortal: **a** : unending existence **b** : lasting fame

im·mor·tal·ize \im-'órt-l-ˌīz\ *vt* : to make immortal — **im·mor·tal·iza·tion** \-ˌórt-l-ə-'zā-shən\ *n* — **im·mor·tal·iz·er** \-'órt-l-ī-zər\ *n*

im·mor·telle \ˌim-ˌór-'tel\ *n* : EVERLASTING 3 [French, from *immortel* "immortal"]

im·mov·able \im-'ü-və-bəl, 'im-\ *adj* **1 a** : incapable of being moved ⟨*immovable* mountains⟩ **b** : STATIONARY 1 **2 a** : STEADFAST, UNYIELDING ⟨an *immovable* purpose⟩ **b** : not capable of being moved emotionally — **im·mov·abil·i·ty** \ˌim-ˌü-və-'bil-ət-ē\ *n* — **im·mov·able·ness** \im-'ü-və-bəl-nəs, 'im-\ *n* — **im·mov·ably** \-blē\ *adv*

im·mune \im-'yün\ *adj* **1** : FREE, EXEMPT ⟨*immune* from punishment⟩ **2** : not susceptible or responsive ⟨*immune* to fatigue⟩ ⟨*immune* to persuasion⟩; *esp* : having a high degree of resistance to a disease ⟨*immune* to diphtheria⟩ **3 a** : containing or producing antibodies ⟨an *immune* serum⟩ **b** : produced by or concerned with immunity or an immune response [Latin *immunis*, from *in-* "¹in-" + *munia* "services, obligations"] — **immune** *n*

immune response *n* : a bodily response to a foreign substance, cell, or tissue that involves the formation of antibodies and cells capable of reacting with it and rendering it harmless — called also *immune reaction*

immune system *n* : the bodily system that protects the body from foreign substances, cells, and tissues by producing the immune response and that includes especially the thymus, spleen, lymph nodes, lymphocytes including the B cells and T cells, and antibodies

im·mu·ni·ty \im-'yü-nət-ē\ *n, pl* **-ties** : the quality or state of being immune; *esp* : bodily power to resist an infectious disease usually by preventing development of the causative microorganism or by neutralizing its poisons

im·mu·nize \'im-yə-ˌnīz\ *vt* : to make immune — **im·mu·ni·za·tion** \ˌim-yə-nə-'zā-shən\ *n*

immuno- *comb form* : physiological immunity ⟨*immuno*logy⟩

im·mu·no·de·fi·cien·cy \-di-'fish-ən-sē\ *n* : inability to produce a normal number of antibodies or immunologically sensitized cells in an immune response to a foreign substance, cell, or tissue

im·mu·no·gen·ic \ˌim-yə-nō-'jen-ik\ *adj* : producing immunity — **im·mu·no·gen·i·cal·ly** \-'jen-i-kə-lē, -klē\ *adv* — **im·mu·no·ge·nic·i·ty** \-jə-'nis-ət-ē\ *n*

im·mu·nol·o·gy \ˌim-yə-'näl-ə-jē\ *n* : a science that deals with the processes and causes of immunity — **im·mu·no·log·ic** \-yən-l-'äj-ik\ *or* **im·mu·no·log·i·cal** \-i-kəl\ *adj* — **im·mu·no·log·i·cal·ly** \-i-kə-lē, -klē\ *adv* — **im·mu·nol·o·gist** \ˌim-yə-'näl-ə-jəst\ *n*

im·mu·no·sup·pres·sion \ˌim-yə-nō-sə-'presh-ən\ *n* : suppression (as by drugs) of natural immune responses — **im·mu·no·sup·pres·sant** \-'pres-nt\ *n or adj* — **im·mu·no·sup·pres·sive** \-'pres-iv\ *adj*

im·mure \im-'yùr\ *vt* **1 a** : to enclose within or as if within walls **b** : to shut up : IMPRISON **2** : to build into a wall; *esp* : to entomb in a wall [Medieval Latin *immurare*, from Latin *in-* + *murus* "wall"] — **im·mure·ment** \-mənt\ *n*

im·mu·ta·ble \im-'yüt-ə-bəl, 'im-\ *adj* : not capable of change — **im·mu·ta·bil·i·ty** \im-ˌyüt-ə-'bil-ət-ē\ *n* — **im·mu·ta·ble·ness** \im-'yüt-ə-bəl-nəs, 'im-\ *n* — **im·mu·ta·bly** \-blē\ *adv*

imp \'imp\ *n* **1** : a small demon **2** : a mischievous child [Old English *impa* "bud, shoot, scion"]

¹im·pact \im-'pakt\ *vt* **1 a** : to fix firmly by or as if by packing or wedging **b** : to press together **2** : to impinge upon [Latin *impactus*, past participle of *impingere* "to push against, impinge"]

²im·pact \'im-ˌpakt\ *n* **1 a** : an impinging or striking (as of one body against another) **b** : a forceful contact, collision, or onset; *also* : the impetus communicated in or as if in a collision **2** : the force of impression or operation of one thing on another : EFFECT ⟨the *impact* of technology on society⟩

im·pact·ed \im-'pak-təd\ *adj* : wedged between the jawbone and another tooth

im·pac·tion \im-'pak-shən\ *n* : the act of becoming or the state of being impacted; *also* : accumulation and packing of something (as feces) in a body passage or cavity

impact printer *n* : a printing device in which a printing element directly strikes a surface (as in a typewriter)

im·pair \im-'paər, -'peər\ *vt* : to diminish in quantity, value, excellence, strength, or efficiency : DAMAGE [Middle French *empeirer*, derived from Latin *in-* "²in-" + *pejor* "worse"] — **im·pair·er** *n* — **im·pair·ment** \-mənt\ *n*

im·pa·la \im-'pal-ə, -'päl-\ *n* : a large brownish African antelope that in the male has slender curving horns [Zulu]

im·pale \im-'pāl\ *vt* : to pierce with or as if with something pointed; *esp* : to torture or kill by fixing on a sharp stake [Medieval Latin *impalare*, from Latin *in-* + *palus* "stake"] — **im·pale·ment** \-mənt\ *n*

im·pal·pa·ble \im-'pal-pə-bəl, 'im-\ *adj* **1** : incapable of being felt by the touch : INTANGIBLE **2** : not readily discerned or understood — **im·pal·pa·bil·i·ty** \im-ˌpal-pə-'bil-ət-ē\ *n* — **im·pal·pa·bly** \im-'pal-pə-blē, 'im-\ *adv*

im·pan·el \im-'pan-l\ *vt* **-eled** *or* **-elled; -el·ing** *or* **-el·ling** : to enter in or on a panel or list : ENROLL

im·pa·ra·dise \im-'par-ə-ˌdīs, -ˌdīz\ *vt* : ENRAPTURE

im·par·i·ty \im-'par-ət-ē, 'im-\ *n, pl* **-ties** : INEQUALITY 1, DISPARITY

im·part \im-'pärt\ *vt* **1** : to give from or as if from one's store or abundance ⟨the sun *imparts* warmth⟩ **2** : to communicate the knowledge of : DISCLOSE ⟨*imparted* their plans⟩ [Latin *impartire*, from *in-* + *partire* "to divide, part"] — **im·part·able** \-ə-bəl\ *adj* — **im·par-**

impala

\ə\ abut   \ng\ sing
\ər\ further   \ō\ bone
\a\ mat   \ó\ saw
\ā\ take   \ói\ coin
\ä\ cot, cart   \th\ thin
\aú\ out   \th\ this
\ch\ chin   \ü\ food
\e\ pet   \ú\ foot
\ē\ easy   \y\ yet
\g\ go   \yü\ few
\i\ tip   \yú\ cure
\ī\ life   \zh\ vision
\j\ job

ta·tion \im-,pär-'tā-shən\ n — im·part·ment \im-'part-mənt\ n

im·par·tial \im-'pär-shəl, 'im-\ adj : not partial : UNBIASED SYN see FAIR — im·par·ti·al·i·ty \,im-,pär-shē-'al-ət-ē, -,pär-'shal-\ n — im·par·tial·ly \im-'pärsh-lē, 'im-, -ə-lē\ adv

im·pass·able \im-'pas-ə-bəl, 'im-\ adj : incapable of being passed, traveled, crossed, or climbed — im·pass·abil·i·ty \,im-,pas-ə-'bil-ət-ē\ n — im·pass·able·ness \im-'pas-ə-bəl-nəs, 'im-\ n — im·pass·ably \-blē\ adv

im·passe \'im-,pas, im-'\ n 1 : an impassable road or way 2 a : a predicament from which there is no obvious escape b : DEADLOCK [French, from in- "¹in-" + passer "to pass"]

im·pas·si·ble \im-'pas-ə-bəl, 'im-\ adj 1 a : incapable of experiencing pain b : incapable of being harmed 2 : incapable of feeling : IMPASSIVE [Late Latin impassibilis, derived from Latin in- + passus, past participle of pati "to suffer"] — im·pas·si·bil·i·ty \,im-,pas-ə-'bil-ət-ē\ n — im·pas·si·bly \im-'pas-ə-blē, 'im-\ adv

im·pas·sioned \im-'pash-ənd\ adj : filled with passion or zeal : showing great warmth or intensity of feeling ⟨impassioned plea for justice⟩ □ SYN IMPASSIONED, PASSIONATE mean showing intense feeling. IMPASSIONED implies warmth and intensity without violence and suggests a fluent verbal expression; PASSIONATE implies great vehemence and often violence and wasteful diffusion of emotion.

im·pas·sive \im-'pas-iv, 'im-\ adj : not feeling or not showing any emotion ⟨an impassive stare⟩ — im·pas·sive·ly adv — im·pas·sive·ness n — im·pas·siv·i·ty \,im-,pas-'iv-ət-ē\ n □ SYN IMPASSIVE, APATHETIC, STOLID, PHLEGMATIC mean unresponsive to something that might normally excite interest or emotion. IMPASSIVE stresses the absence of any external sign of emotion in action or facial expression; APATHETIC may imply a puzzling or deplorable indifference or inertness ⟨people apathetic to the evils of gambling⟩ STOLID implies an habitual absence of interest, responsiveness, or curiosity; PHLEGMATIC implies a temperament hard to arouse.

im·pas·to \im-'pas-tō, -'päs-\ n : the thick application of a pigment to a canvas or panel in painting; also : the body of pigment so applied [Italian, derived from in- "in" + pasta "paste", from Late Latin]

im·pa·tience \im-'pā-shəns, 'im-\ n : the quality or state of being impatient

im·pa·tiens \im-'pā-shənz, -shəns\ n : any of a large genus of juicy annual herbs with often showy irregular flowers [Latin, "impatient"]

im·pa·tient \im-'pā-shənt, 'im-\ adj 1 a : not patient : restless or short of temper especially under irritation, delay, or opposition ⟨an impatient disposition⟩ b : INTOLERANT ⟨impatient of delay⟩ 2 : prompted or marked by impatience ⟨an impatient answer⟩ 3 : eagerly desirous : ANXIOUS — im·pa·tient·ly adv

im·peach \im-'pēch\ vt 1 : to charge (a public official) formally with misconduct in office 2 : to cast doubt on; esp : to challenge the credibility or validity of ⟨impeach the testimony of a witness⟩ [Middle French empeechier "to hinder", from Late Latin impedicare "to fetter", from Latin in- + pedica "fetter", from ped-, pes "foot"] — im·peach·able \-'pē-chə-bəl\ adj — im·peach·ment \-'pēch-mənt\ n

im·pearl \im-'pərl\ vt : to form into pearls; also : to form of or adorn with pearls

im·pec·ca·ble \im-'pek-ə-bəl, 'im-\ adj 1 : not capable of sinning or liable to sin 2 : free from fault or blame : FLAWLESS ⟨a person of impeccable character⟩ [Latin impeccabilis, from in- + peccare "to sin"] — im·pec·ca·bil·i·ty \,im-,pek-ə-'bil-ət-ē\ n — im·pec·ca·bly \im-'pek-ə-blē, 'im-\ adv

im·pe·cu·nious \,im-pi-'kyü-nyəs, -nē-əs\ adj : having very little or no money usually habitually : PENNILESS [derived from Latin pecunia "money"] — im·pe·cu·ni·os·i·ty \-,kyü-nē-'äs-ət-ē\ n — im·pe·cu·ni·ous·ly adv — im·pe·cu·ni·ous·ness n

im·ped·ance \im-'pēd-ns\ n : the apparent opposition in an electrical circuit to the flow of an alternating current as a result of a combination of resistance and reactance

im·pede \im-'pēd\ vt : to interfere with the progress of : BLOCK, HINDER ⟨traffic impeded by heavy rain⟩ [Latin impedire, from in- "²in-" + ped-, pes "foot"] — im·ped·er n

im·ped·i·ment \im-'ped-ə-mənt\ n 1 : something that impedes 2 : a defect in speech

im·ped·i·men·ta \im-,ped-ə-'ment-ə\ n pl : things (as baggage or supplies) that impede progress or movement [Latin, "impediments"]

im·pel \im-'pel\ vt im·pelled; im·pel·ling 1 : to urge or drive forward or into action ⟨felt impelled to speak up in their defense⟩ 2 : to impart motion to : PROPEL ⟨impel water through a pipe⟩ [Latin impellere, from in- + pellere "to drive"] SYN see MOVE — im·pel·ler also im·pel·lor \-'pel-ər\ n

im·pend \im-'pend\ vi 1 : to hover threateningly : MENACE ⟨warning of a danger that impends⟩ 2 : to be about to occur [Latin impendēre, from in- + pendēre "to hang"]

im·pend·ing adj : threatening to occur soon : APPROACHING □ SYN IMPENDING, IMMINENT mean threatening to occur very soon. IMPENDING implies signs that keep one in suspense ⟨an impending thunderstorm kept us from going on a picnic⟩ IMMINENT emphasizes the shortness of time before happening ⟨execution of the death sentence was now imminent⟩

im·pen·e·tra·bil·i·ty \im-,pen-ə-trə-'bil-ət-ē\ n : the quality or state of being impenetrable

im·pen·e·tra·ble \im-'pen-ə-trə-bəl, 'im-\ adj 1 a : incapable of being penetrated or pierced ⟨impenetrable rock⟩ ⟨impenetrable jungle⟩ b : inaccessible to knowledge, reason, or sympathy : IMPERVIOUS 2 : incapable of being comprehended : INSCRUTABLE ⟨impenetrable mystery⟩ — im·pen·e·tra·ble·ness n — im·pen·e·tra·bly \-blē\ adv

im·pen·i·tent \im-'pen-ə-tənt, 'im-\ adj : not penitent : not sorry for having done wrong — im·pen·i·tent·ly adv

¹im·per·a·tive \im-'per-ət-iv\ adj 1 a : of, relating to, or constituting the grammatical mood that expresses a command, request, or strong encouragement b : expressive of a command, entreaty, or exhortation ⟨an imperative gesture⟩ 2 : not to be avoided or evaded : URGENT ⟨imperative business⟩ [Late Latin imperativus, from Latin imperare "to command"] — im·per·a·tive·ly adv — im·per·a·tive·ness n

²imperative n 1 : the imperative mood or a verb form expressing it 2 : something that is imperative: a : COMMAND 2, ORDER b : an obligatory act or duty

im·pe·ra·tor \,im-pə-'rät-ər, -'rä,tòr\ n : a supreme leader of the ancient Romans : EMPEROR [Latin] — im·per·a·to·ri·al \,im-,per-ə-'tōr-ē-əl, -'tòr-\ adj

im·per·cep·ti·ble \,im-pər-'sep-tə-bəl\ adj 1 : not perceptible by a sense or by the mind 2 : extremely slight, gradual, or subtle — im·per·cep·ti·bil·i·ty \-,sep-tə-'bil-ət-ē\ n — im·per·cep·ti·bly \-'sep-tə-blē\ adv

im·per·cep·tive \,im-pər-'sep-tiv\ adj : not perceptive — im·per·cep·tive·ness n

im·per·cip·i·ent \,im-pər-'sip-ē-ənt\ adj : not percipient : UNPERCEPTIVE

¹im·per·fect \im-'pər-fikt, 'im-\ adj 1 : not perfect : DEFECTIVE 2 : of, relating to, or constituting a verb tense used to designate a continuing state or an incomplete action especially in the past — im·per·fect·ly \-fik-lē, -tlē\ adv — im·per·fect·ness \-fik-nəs, -fikt-\ n

²imperfect *n* : the imperfect tense of a verb; *also* : a verb in this tense

imperfect flower *n* : a flower with stamens or pistils but not both

imperfect fungus *n* : any of an order (Fungi Imperfecti) of fungi of which only the asexual stage is known

im·per·fec·tion \,im-pər-'fek-shən\ *n* : the quality or state of being imperfect; *also* : BLEMISH, FAULT

im·per·fo·rate \im-'pər-fə-rət, 'im-, -,frāt, -fə-,rāt\ *adj* : lacking perforations or rouletting ⟨*imperforate* postage stamps⟩ — **imperforate** *n*

¹im·pe·ri·al \im-'pir-ē-əl\ *adj* **1 a** : of, relating to, or befitting an empire or an emperor ⟨by *imperial* decree⟩ **b** : of or relating to the British Commonwealth or Empire **2 a** : SUPREME 2 **b** : REGAL 1, IMPERIOUS **3** : of superior or unusual size or excellence **4** : belonging to a British series of weights and measures ⟨an *imperial* gallon⟩ [Middle French, from Late Latin *imperialis,* from Latin *imperium* "command, empire"] — **im·pe·ri·al·ly** \-ē-ə-lē\ *adv*

²imperial *n* : a pointed beard growing below the lower lip [from the beard worn by Napoleon III]

im·pe·ri·al·ism \im-'pir-ē-ə-,liz-əm\ *n* **1** : imperial government, authority, or system **2** : the policy or practice of extending the power and dominion of one nation by direct territorial acquisitions or by indirect control over the political or economic life of other areas — **im·pe·ri·al·ist** \-ləst\ *n* — **imperialist** *or* **im·pe·ri·al·is·tic** \im-,pir-ē-ə-'lis-tik\ *adj* — **im·pe·ri·al·is·ti·cal·ly** \-ti-kə-lē, -klē\ *adv*

im·per·il \im-'per-əl\ *vt* **-iled** *or* **-illed; -il·ing** *or* **-il·ling** : to bring into peril : ENDANGER — **im·per·il·ment** \-əl-mənt\ *n*

im·pe·ri·ous \im-'pir-ē-əs\ *adj* **1** : befitting or characteristic of one of eminent rank or attainments **2** : marked by arrogant assurance : DOMINEERING **3** : IMPERATIVE, URGENT ⟨*imperious* problems⟩ [Latin *imperiosus,* from *imperium* "command, empire"] SYN see MASTERFUL — **im·pe·ri·ous·ly** *adv* — **im·pe·ri·ous·ness** *n*

im·per·ish·able \im-'per-ish-ə-bəl, 'im-\ *adj* : not perishable or subject to decay : INDESTRUCTIBLE ⟨*imperishable* fame⟩ — **im·per·ish·abil·i·ty** \,im-,per-ish-ə-'bil-ət-ē\ *n* — **im·per·ish·able·ness** \im-'per-ish-ə-bəl-nəs, 'im-\ *n* — **im·per·ish·a·bly** \-blē\ *adv*

im·pe·ri·um \im-'pir-ē-əm\ *n* **1 a** : supreme power or dominion **b** : the right to supreme power : SOVEREIGN·TY **2** : EMPIRE 1a(2) [Latin]

im·per·ma·nent \im-'pər-mə-nənt, 'im-\ *adj* : not permanent : TRANSIENT — **im·per·ma·nence** \-nəns\ *n* — **im·per·ma·nent·ly** *adv*

im·per·me·able \im-'pər-mē-ə-bəl, 'im-\ *adj* : not permitting passage (as of a fluid) through its substance : IMPERVIOUS — **im·per·me·abil·i·ty** \,im-,pər-mē-ə-'bil-ət-ē\ *n* — **im·per·me·able·ness** \im-'pər-mē-ə-bəl-nəs, 'im-\ *n* — **im·per·me·a·bly** *adv*

im·per·mis·si·ble \,im-pər-'mis-ə-bəl\ *adj* : not permissible — **im·per·mis·si·bil·i·ty** \-,mis-ə-'bil-ət-ē\ *n* — **im·per·mis·si·bly** \-'mis-ə-blē\ *adv*

im·per·son·al \im-'pərs-nəl, 'im-, -n-əl\ *adj* **1** : of, relating to, or being a verb used with no expressed subject or with a merely formal subject ⟨*methinks* in "methinks you are wrong" and *rained* in "it rained" are *impersonal* verbs⟩ **2 a** : having no personal reference or connection ⟨*impersonal* criticism⟩ **b** : not engaging the human personality or emotions ⟨the *impersonal* attitude of a doctor⟩ **c** : not existing as a person ⟨an *impersonal* deity⟩ — **im·per·son·al·i·ty** \,im-,pərs-n-'al-ət-ē\ *n* — **im·per·son·al·ize** \im-'pərs-nə-,līz, 'im-, -n-ə-,līz\ *vt* — **im·per·son·al·ly** \-nə-lē, -n-ə-lē\ *adv*

im·per·son·ate \im-'pərs-n-,āt\ *vt* : to act the part of or pretend to be (some other person) ⟨*impersonate* a circus barker⟩ — **im·per·son·ation** \-,pərs-n-'ā-shən\ *n* — **im·per·son·ator** \-'pərs-n-,āt-ər\ *n*

im·per·ti·nence \im-'pərt-n-əns, 'im-\ *also* **im·per·ti·nen·cy** \-ən-sē\ *n, pl* **-nences** *also* **-nencies** **1** : the quality or state of being impertinent **2** : something impertinent

im·per·ti·nent \-ənt\ *adj* **1** : not pertinent : IRRELEVANT **2** : not restrained within due or proper bounds : RUDE, INSOLENT — **im·per·ti·nent·ly** *adv*

im·per·turb·able \,im-pər-'tər-bə-bəl\ *adj* : marked by extreme calm, impassivity, and steadiness : SERENE — **im·per·turb·abil·i·ty** \-,tər-bə-'bil-ət-ē\ *n* — **im·per·turb·ably** \-'tər-bə-blē\ *adv*

im·per·vi·ous \im-'pər-vē-əs, 'im-\ *adj* **1** : not allowing entrance or passage : IMPENETRABLE ⟨a coat *impervious* to rain⟩ **2** : not capable of being affected or disturbed ⟨*impervious* to criticism⟩ — **im·per·vi·ous·ly** *adv* — **im·per·vi·ous·ness** *n*

im·pe·ti·go \,im-pə-'tē-gō, -'tī-\ *n* : an acute contagious skin disease characterized by small pus-filled blisters and yellowish crusts [Latin, from *impetere* "to attack"] — **im·pe·tig·i·nous** \-'tij-ə-nəs\ *adj*

im·pet·u·os·i·ty \im-,pech-ə-'wäs-ət-ē\ *n, pl* **-ties** **1** : the quality or state of being impetuous **2** : an impetuous action or impulse

im·pet·u·ous \im-'pech-wəs, -ə-wəs\ *adj* **1** : marked by force and violence **2** : marked by impulsive vehemence [Middle French *impetueux,* from Late Latin *impetuosus,* from Latin *impetus*] — **im·pet·u·ous·ly** *adv* — **im·pet·u·ous·ness** *n*

im·pe·tus \'im-pət-əs\ *n* **1 a** : a driving force : IMPULSE **b** : INCENTIVE, STIMULUS **2** : MOMENTUM 1 ⟨the *impetus* of a bullet⟩ [Latin, "assault, impetus", from *impetere* "to attack", from *in-* + *petere* "to go to, seek"]

im·pi·e·ty \im-'pī-ət-ē, 'im-\ *n, pl* **-ties** **1** : the quality or state of being impious : IRREVERENCE **2** : an impious act

im·pinge \im-'pinj\ *vi* **1** : to strike or dash especially with a sharp collision ⟨sound waves *impinge* upon the eardrums⟩ **2** : to come into close contact **3** : ENCROACH, INFRINGE ⟨*impinge* on another person's rights⟩ [Latin *impingere,* from *in-* + *pangere* "to fasten, drive in"] — **im·pinge·ment** \-mənt\ *n*

im·pi·ous \'im-pē-əs; im-'pī-, 'im-\ *adj* : lacking in reverence or proper respect — **im·pi·ous·ly** *adv*

imp·ish \'im-pish\ *adj* : of, relating to, or befitting an imp; *esp* : MISCHIEVOUS — **imp·ish·ly** *adv* — **imp·ish·ness** *n*

im·pla·ca·ble \im-'plak-ə-bəl, 'im-, -'plā-kə-\ *adj* : not placable : not capable of being appeased, pacified, or mitigated ⟨an *implacable* enemy⟩ — **im·pla·ca·bil·i·ty** \,im-,plak-ə-'bil-ət-ē, -,plā-kə-\ *n* — **im·plac·a·ble·ness** \im-'plak-ə-bəl-nəs, 'im-, -'plā-kə-\ *n* — **im·pla·ca·bly** \-blē\ *adv*

im·plant \im-'plant\ *vt* **1 a** : to fix or set securely or deeply **b** : to set permanently in the consciousness or habit patterns ⟨*implant* patriotism in children⟩ **2** : to insert in a living site ⟨*implant* a graft of tissue⟩ — **implant** *n* — **im·plan·ta·tion** \,im-,plan-'tā-shən\ *n* — **im·plant·er** *n*

im·plau·si·ble \im-'plò-zə-bəl, 'im-\ *adj* : not plausible — **im·plau·si·bil·i·ty** \,im-,plò-zə-'bil-ət-ē\ *n* — **im·plau·si·bly** \im-'plò-zə-blē, 'im-\ *adv*

¹im·ple·ment \'im-plə-mənt\ *n* **1** : a piece of equipment : TOOL **2** : one that serves as an instrument or tool [Late Latin *implementum* "action of filling up", from Latin *implēre* "to fill up", from *in-* + *plēre* "to fill"] □ SYN IMPLEMENT, TOOL, UTENSIL, INSTRUMENT apply to a device for performing work. IMPLEMENT may apply to anything necessary to bring about an end or perform a task ⟨propaganda as an *implement* of peace and war⟩ ⟨agricultural and garden *implements*⟩ TOOL suggests an implement adapted for a specific task and implies the need of skill in its use ⟨carpenter's *tools*⟩ UTENSIL suggests a device useful for domestic tasks ⟨kitchen *utensils*⟩ or some routine unskilled activity;

²imperial

\ə\ abut	\ng\ sing
\ər\ further	\ō\ bone
\a\ mat	\ò\ saw
\ā\ take	\òi\ coin
\ä\ cot, cart	\th\ thin
\au̇\ out	\th\ this
\ch\ chin	\ü\ food
\e\ pet	\u̇\ foot
\ē\ easy	\y\ yet
\g\ go	\yü\ few
\i\ tip	\yu̇\ cure
\ī\ life	\zh\ vision
\j\ job	

INSTRUMENT suggests a device capable of delicate or precise work ⟨a surgeon's *instruments*⟩

²**im·ple·ment** \-,ment\ *vt* **I** : CARRY OUT, FULFILL; *esp* : to give practical effect to by positive action ⟨*implement* the provisions of a treaty⟩ **2** : to provide implements for — **im·ple·men·ta·tion** \,im-plə-mən-'tā-shən, -men-\ *n*

im·pli·cate \'im-plə-,kāt\ *vt* : to bring into connection : INVOLVE ⟨the confession *implicated* several others in the crime⟩ [Latin *implicare*, literally, "to enfold", from *in-* + *plicare* "to fold"]

im·pli·ca·tion \,im-plə-'kā-shən\ *n* **I a** : the act of implicating : the state of being implicated **b** : an incriminating involvement **2 a** : the act of implying : the state of being implied **b** : something implied **3** : a sentence which is composed of two parts beginning with "if" and "then" and for which the "then" part is true whenever the "if" part is true ⟨"If P then Q" is an *implication*⟩ — called also *conditional* — **im·pli·ca·tive** \'im-plə-,kāt-iv\ *adj* — **im·pli·ca·tive·ly** *adv* — **im·pli·ca·tive·ness** *n*

im·plic·it \im-'plis-ət\ *adj* **I** : understood though not directly stated ⟨an *implicit* agreement⟩ **2** : being without reserve : COMPLETE, UNQUESTIONING ⟨*implicit* trust⟩ — compare EXPLICIT [Latin *implicitus,* past participle of *implicare* "to enfold, implicate"] — **im·plic·it·ly** *adv* — **im·plic·it·ness** *n*

im·plode \im-'plōd\ *vi* : to burst inward [*in-* + *-plode* (as in *explode*)] — **im·plo·sion** \-'plō-zhən\ *n* — **im·plo·sive** \-'plō-siv, -ziv\ *adj*

im·plore \im-'plōr, -'plȯr\ *vt* **I** : to call upon in supplication : BESEECH **2** : to call or pray for earnestly [Latin *implorare,* from *in-* + *plorare* "to cry out"] SYN see BEG

im·ply \im-'plī\ *vt* **im·plied; im·ply·ing I a** : to include or involve as a natural or necessary though not definitely stated part or effect ⟨the rights of citizenship *imply* certain obligations⟩ **b** : to involve as a necessary consequence or condition ⟨"If A then B" means that A *implies* B⟩ **2** : to express indirectly : suggest rather than say plainly ⟨remarks that *implied* consent⟩ [Middle French *emplier* "to enfold", from Latin *implicare* "to enfold, implicate"] □ SYN INFER: INFER is sometimes used for IMPLY but to most users the two words are complementary rather than synonymous. IMPLY means conveying or drawing attention to a fact or relationship by suggestion or hint rather than by direct statement ⟨their silence *implied* disapproval⟩ INFER means to arrive at a conclusion by reasoning from evidence and if the evidence is slight, comes close to *surmise* ⟨I *inferred* their disapproval from their silence⟩ ⟨a future rise in the number of college students may be *inferred* from the present population statistics⟩

im·po·lite \,im-pə-'līt\ *adj* : not polite : RUDE — **im·po·lite·ly** *adv* — **im·po·lite·ness** *n*

im·pol·i·tic \im-'päl-ə-,tik, 'im-\ *adj* : not politic : UNWISE — **im·pol·i·tic·ly** *adv*

im·pon·der·able \im-'pän-də-rə-bəl, 'im-, -drə-bəl\ *adj* : not capable of being weighed or evaluated with exactness — **im·pon·der·abil·i·ty** \im-,pän-də-rə-'bil-ət-ē, -drə-'bil-\ *n* — **imponderable** *n* — **im·pon·der·able·ness** \im-'pän-də-rə-bəl-nəs, 'im-, -drə-bəl-\ *n* — **im·pon·der·ably** \-blē\ *adv*

¹**im·port** \im-'pōrt, -'pȯrt, 'im-,\ *vb* **I a** : MEAN ⟨their words *imported* a need for change⟩ **b** : to be of importance : MATTER **2** : to bring in or introduce from a foreign country; *esp* : to bring in (goods) to be resold ⟨*import* coffee⟩ [Latin *importare* "to bring in", from *in-* + *portare* "to carry"] — **im·port·able** \-ə-bəl\ *adj* — **im·port·er** *n*

²**im·port** \'im-,pōrt, -,pȯrt\ *n* **I** : MEANING **2** : IMPORTANCE **3 a** : something imported **b** : IMPORTATION 1

im·por·tance \im-'pȯrt-ns, -əns\ *n* **I** : the quality or state of being important **2** : an important aspect or bearing

im·por·tant \im-'pȯrt-nt, -ənt\ *adj* **I** : having great meaning or influence ⟨an *important* change in printing methods⟩ **2** : having considerable power or authority ⟨an *important* official⟩ **3** : showing a feeling of personal importance — **im·por·tant·ly** *adv*

im·por·ta·tion \,im-,pōr-'tā-shən, -,pȯr-, -pər-\ *n* **I** : the act or practice of importing **2** : IMPORT 3a

im·por·tu·nate \im-'pȯrch-nət, -ə-nət\ *adj* **I** : BURDENSOME, TROUBLESOME **2** : overly persistent in request or demand — **im·por·tu·nate·ly** *adv* — **im·por·tu·nate·ness** *n*

¹**im·por·tune** \,im-pər-'tün, -'tyün; im-'pȯr-chən\ *adj* : IMPORTUNATE [Latin *importunus,* from *in-* + *-portunus* (as in *opportunus* "opportune")] — **im·por·tune·ly** *adv*

²**importune** *vb* **I** : to press, beg, or urge with troublesome persistence **2** : ANNOY, TROUBLE — **im·por·tun·er** *n*

im·por·tu·ni·ty \,im-pər-'tü-nət-ē, -'tyü-\ *n, pl* **-ties I** : the quality or state of being importunate **2** *pl* : importunate requests or demands

im·pose \im-'pōz\ *vb* **I a** : to establish or apply as a charge or penalty : LEVY ⟨*impose* a fine⟩ ⟨*impose* a tax⟩ **b** : to establish by force **2** : to use trickery or deception to get what one wants ⟨*impose* on an ignorant person⟩ **3** : to arrange (as type or printing plates) in proper order for printing **4** : to take unwarranted advantage of something ⟨*impose* upon a friend's good nature⟩ [Middle French *imposer,* from Latin *imponere,* literally, "to put upon", from *in-* + *ponere* "to put"] — **im·pos·er** *n*

im·pos·ing \im-'pō-zing\ *adj* : impressive because of size, bearing, dignity, or grandeur ⟨an *imposing* building⟩ — **im·pos·ing·ly** \-zing-lē\ *adv*

im·po·si·tion \,im-pə-'zish-ən\ *n* **I** : the act of imposing **2** : something imposed: as **a** : LEVY 1, TAX **b** : an overly burdensome requirement or demand **3** : TRICK 1a, DECEPTION

im·pos·si·bil·i·ty \im-,päs-ə-'bil-ət-ē\ *n, pl* **-ties I** : the quality or state of being impossible **2** : something impossible

im·pos·si·ble \im-'päs-ə-bəl, 'im-\ *adj* **I a** : not capable of being or of occurring **b** : very difficult to accomplish or deal with ⟨an *impossible* situation⟩ **2 a** : extremely undesirable : OBJECTIONABLE, UNACCEPTABLE ⟨living in *impossible* conditions⟩ — **im·pos·si·bly** \-blē\ *adv*

¹**im·post** \'im-,pōst\ *n* : TAX; *esp* : a customs duty [Middle French, from Medieval Latin *impositum,* from Latin *imponere* "to impose"]

²**impost** *n* : a block, capital, or molding (as of a pillar or pier) from which an arch extends

im·pos·tor \im-'päs-tər\ *n* : one that practices deceit; *esp* : a person who fraudulently pretends to be someone else [Late Latin, from Latin *impositus, impostus,* past participle of *imponere* "to impose"]

im·pos·ture \im-'päs-chər\ *n* : the act or conduct of an impostor

im·po·tence \'im-pət-əns\ *n* : the quality or state of being impotent

im·po·tent \'im-pət-ənt\ *adj* **I** : not potent : lacking in power, strength, or vigor : HELPLESS **2** : unable to copulate; *also* : STERILE 1 — usually used of males — **impotent** *n* — **im·po·tent·ly** *adv*

im·pound \im-'paund\ *vt* **I** : to shut up in or as if in a pound : CONFINE **2** : to seize and hold in legal custody ⟨*impound* funds pending decision of a case⟩ **3** : to collect (water) in a reservoir

im·pound·ment \im-'paund-mənt, -'paun-\ *n* **I** : the act of impounding : the state of being impounded **2** : a body of water formed by impounding

im·pov·er·ish \im-'päv-rish, -ə-rish\ *vt* **I** : to make poor **2** : to use up the strength, richness, or fertility of [Middle French *empovriss-,* stem of *empovrir,* from

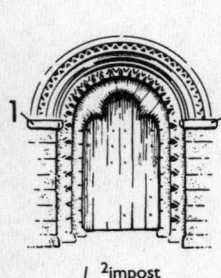

I ²impost

en- + *povre* "poor", from Latin *pauper*] — **im·pov·er·ish·er** *n* — **im·pov·er·ish·ment** \-mənt\ *n*

im·prac·ti·ca·ble \im-'prak-ti-kə-bəl, 'im-\ *adj* **1** : not practicable : not capable of being put into practice or use ⟨an *impracticable* plan⟩ **2** : IMPASSABLE ⟨an *impracticable* road⟩ — **im·prac·ti·ca·bil·i·ty** \im-ˌprak-ti-kə-'bil-ət-ē\ *n* — **im·prac·ti·ca·ble·ness** \im-'prak-ti-kə-bəl-nəs, 'im-\ *n* — **im·prac·ti·ca·bly** \-blē\ *adv*

im·prac·ti·cal \im-'prak-ti-kəl, 'im-\ *adj* : not practical: as **a** : not wise to put into or keep in practice or effect **b** : THEORETICAL 1, IDEALISTIC **c** : not capable of dealing sensibly with practical matters **d** : IMPRACTICABLE 1 — **im·prac·ti·cal·i·ty** \im-ˌprak-ti-'kal-ət-ē\ *n* — **im·prac·ti·cal·ness** \im-'prak-ti-kəl-nəs, 'im-\ *n*

im·pre·cate \'im-pri-ˌkāt\ *vb* : to invoke evil upon : CURSE [Latin *imprecari*, from *in-* "²in-" + *precari* "to pray"] — **im·pre·ca·tion** \ˌim-pri-'kā-shən\ *n* — **im·pre·ca·to·ry** \'im-pri-kə-ˌtōr-ē, im-'prek-ə-, -ˌtȯr-\ *adj*

im·pre·cise \ˌim-pri-'sīs\ *adj* : not precise — **im·pre·cise·ly** *adv* — **im·pre·cise·ness** *n* — **im·pre·ci·sion** \-'sizh-ən\ *n*

im·preg·na·ble \im-'preg-nə-bəl\ *adj* : not capable of being taken by assault : able to resist any attack [Middle French *imprenable*, from *in-* "not" + *prenable* "vulnerable to capture", from *prendre* "to take", from Latin *prehendere*] — **im·preg·na·bil·i·ty** \-ˌpreg-nə-'bil-ət-ē\ *n* — **im·preg·na·ble·ness** \-'preg-nə-bəl-nəs\ *n* — **im·preg·na·bly** \-blē\ *adv*

im·preg·nate \im-'preg-ˌnāt\ *vt* **1 a** (1) : to make pregnant (2) : to introduce sperm cells into **b** : to make fertile or fruitful **2** : to cause ⟨a material or substance⟩ to be filled, permeated, or saturated ⟨*impregnate* wood with a preservative⟩ [Late Latin *impraegnare*, from Latin *in-* + *praegnas* "pregnant"] — **im·preg·na·tion** \ˌim-ˌpreg-'nā-shən\ *n* — **im·preg·na·tor** \im-'preg-ˌnāt-ər\ *n*

im·pre·sa·rio \ˌim-prə-'sär-ē-ˌō, -'sar-, -'ser-\ *n, pl* **-rios** **1** : the manager or conductor of an opera or concert company **2** : one who puts on an entertainment **3** : PRODUCER 2, MANAGER [Italian, from *impresa* "undertaking"]

¹im·press \im-'pres\ *vt* **1 a** : to apply with pressure so as to imprint **b** : to produce ⟨as a mark⟩ by pressure **c** : to mark by or as if by pressure or stamping **2 a** : to produce a vivid impression of **b** : to affect especially forcibly or deeply : INFLUENCE [Latin *impressus*, past participle of *imprimere* "to press into, imprint", from *in-* + *premere* "to press"]

²im·press \'im-ˌpres\ *n* **1** : the act of impressing **2 a** : a mark made by pressure **b** : an image of something formed by or as if by pressure; *esp* : SEAL **c** : a product of pressure or influence **3** : a characteristic or distinctive mark : STAMP **4** : EFFECT 4, IMPRESSION

³im·press \im-'pres\ *vt* **1** : to seize for public service; *esp* : to force into naval service **2** : to enlist the aid or services of by strong argument or appeal [*in-* + *press*]

⁴im·press \'im-ˌpres\ *n* : IMPRESSMENT

im·press·ible \im-'pres-ə-bəl\ *adj* : capable of being impressed : SENSITIVE — **im·press·ibil·i·ty** \-ˌpres-ə-'bil-ət-ē\ *n* — **im·press·ibly** \-'pres-ə-ble\ *adv*

im·pres·sion \im-'presh-ən\ *n* **1** : the act or process of impressing **2** : the effect produced by impressing: as **a** : a stamp, form, or figure resulting from physical contact **b** : an especially marked influence or effect on feeling, sense, or mind **3 a** : a characteristic trait or feature resulting from influence **b** : an effect of change or improvement **c** : a telling image impressed on the senses or the mind **4 a** : one instance of the meeting of a printing surface and the material being printed; *also* : a single print or copy so made **b** : all the copies of a publication ⟨as a book⟩ printed at one time **5** : a usually indistinct or imprecise notion or remembrance **6** : an imitation of outstanding features in an artistic or theatrical medium; *esp* : an imitation in caricature of a noted personality as a form of theatri-

cal entertainment — **im·pres·sion·al** \-'presh-nəl, -ən-l\ *adj*

im·pres·sion·able \im-'presh-nə-bəl, -ə-nə-\ *adj* : capable of being easily impressed : easily molded or influenced : PLASTIC — **im·pres·sion·abil·i·ty** \-ˌpresh-nə-'bil-ət-ē, -ə-nə-\ *n* — **im·pres·sion·able·ness** \-'presh-nə-bəl-nəs, -ə-nə-\ *n* — **im·pres·sion·ably** \-blē\ *adv*

im·pres·sion·ism \im-'presh-ə-ˌniz-əm\ *n* **1** *often cap* : a theory or practice in painting especially among French painters of about 1870 of representing the effect of light on objects by means of broken strokes of unmixed pigment that blend together when viewed from a distance **2 a** : the depiction of scene, emotion, or character by details evoking impressions rather than by recreating reality **b** : a style of musical composition designed to create moods through rich and varied harmonies **3** : a practice of presenting and elaborating one's reactions to a work of art — **im·pres·sion·ist** \-'presh-nəst, -ə-nəst\ *n or adj* — **im·pres·sion·is·tic** \-ˌpresh-ə-'nis-tik\ *adj* — **im·pres·sion·is·ti·cal·ly** \-ti-kə-lē, -klē\ *adv*

im·pres·sive \im-'pres-iv\ *adj* : making or tending to make a marked impression : stirring deep feeling especially of awe or admiration ⟨an *impressive* speech⟩ — **im·pres·sive·ly** *adv* — **im·pres·sive·ness** *n*

im·press·ment \im-'pres-mənt\ *n* : the act of seizing for public use or of impressing into public service

im·pri·ma·tur \ˌim-prə-'mät-ər\ *n* **1 a** : a license to print or publish **b** : official approval of a publication by a censor **2** : APPROVAL 1 [New Latin, "let it be printed", from *imprimere* "to print", from Latin, "to impress, imprint"]

¹im·print \im-'print, 'im-\ *vt* **1** : to mark by or as if by pressure : STAMP, IMPRESS **2** : to fix firmly ⟨as in the memory⟩

²im·print \'im-ˌprint\ *n* : something imprinted or printed: as **a** : ²IMPRESS 2 **b** : a publisher's name often with address and date of publication printed at the foot of a title page **c** : an indelible distinguishing effect or influence

im·print·ing \'im-ˌprint-ing, im-'\ *n* : a behavior pattern that is firmly established during a susceptible period early in the life of a social animal and involves especially the recognition of and attraction to characters of its own kind or a substitute

im·pris·on \im-'priz-n\ *vt* **-pris·oned; -pris·on·ing** \-'priz-ning, -n-ing\ : to confine in or as if in prison — **im·pris·on·ment** \-'priz-n-mənt\ *n*

im·prob·able \im-'präb-ə-bəl, 'im-\ *adj* : unlikely to be true or to occur — **im·prob·a·bil·i·ty** \im-ˌpräb-ə-'bil-ət-ē\ *n* — **im·prob·a·ble·ness** \im-'präb-ə-bəl-nəs, 'im-\ *n* — **im·prob·a·bly** \-'präb-ə-blē\ *adv*

im·pro·bi·ty \im-'prō-bət-ē, 'im-, -'präb-ət-\ *n* : DISHONESTY

im·promp·tu \im-'präm-tü, -'prämp-, -tyü\ *adj* **1** : made or done on or as if on the spur of the moment **2** : produced without previous study or preparation ⟨an *impromptu* speech⟩ [French, from *impromptu* "extemporaneously", from Latin *in promptu* "in readiness"] — **impromptu** *adv or n*

im·prop·er \im-'präp-ər, 'im-\ *adj* **1** : not proper, fit, or suitable ⟨*improper* dress for the occasion⟩ **2** : INCORRECT, INACCURATE ⟨an *improper* deduction⟩ **3** : not in accordance with good taste or good manners ⟨*improper* language⟩ SYN see INDECOROUS — **im·prop·er·ly** *adv* — **im·prop·er·ness** *n*

improper fraction *n* : a fraction whose numerator is equal to or larger than the denominator

improper subset *n* : a set which contains the same elements as another set ⟨every set is an *improper subset* of itself⟩

im·pro·pri·ety \ˌim-prə-'prī-ət-ē\ *n, pl* **-ties** **1** : the quality or state of being improper **2** : an improper act or remark; *esp* : an unacceptable use of a word or of language

im·prove \im-'prüv\ *vb* **1** : to make greater in amount or degree : INCREASE **2 a** : to increase in value or quality : make or grow better **b** : to increase the value of (real estate) by betterment (as by cultivation or the erection of buildings) **c** : to grade and drain (a road) and apply surfacing material other than pavement **3** : to make good use of ⟨*improved* their time by studying⟩ **4** : to make improvements ⟨*improve* on the carburetor⟩ [Anglo-French *emprouer* "to invest profitably", from Old French *en-* + *prou* "advantage", from Late Latin *prode,* from Latin *prodesse* "to be advantageous"] — **im·prov·able** \-'prü-və-bəl\ *adj* — **im·prov·er** *n*

im·prove·ment \im-'prüv-mənt\ *n* **1** : the act or process of improving **2 a** : the state of being improved; *esp* : increased value or excellence **b** : an instance or result of improvement **3** : something that increases value especially of real estate ⟨make *improvements* in an old house⟩

im·prov·i·dent \im-'präv-əd-ənt, 'im-, -ə-,dent\ *adj* : not providing for the future : THRIFTLESS — **im·prov·i·dence** \-əd-əns, -ə-,dens\ *n* — **im·prov·i·dent·ly** *adv*

im·prov·i·sa·tion \im-,präv-ə-'zā-shən, ,im-prə-və-\ *n* **1** : the act or art of improvising **2** : something that is improvised — **im·prov·i·sa·tion·al** \-shnəl, -shən-l\ *adj*

im·prov·i·sa·tor \im-'präv-ə-,zāt-ər\ *n* : IMPROVISER — **im·prov·i·sa·to·ri·al** \-,präv-ə-zə-'tōr-ē-əl, -'tór-\ *or* **im·prov·i·sa·to·ry** \-'präv-ə-zə-,tōr-ē, -,tór-\ *adj*

im·pro·vise \'im-prə-,vīz\ *vb* **1** : to compose, recite, or sing on the spur of the moment **2** : to make, invent, or arrange offhand [French *improviser,* from Italian *improvvisare,* from Latin *improvisus* "sudden, unforeseen", from *in-* + *providēre* "to see ahead, provide"] — **im·pro·vis·er** *n*

im·pru·dent \im-'prüd-nt, 'im-\ *adj* : not prudent : RASH, UNWISE — **im·pru·dence** \-ns\ *n* — **im·pru·dent·ly** *adv*

im·pu·dent \'im-pyəd-ənt\ *adj* : showing contempt for or disregard of others : INSOLENT, DISRESPECTFUL [Latin *impudens* "shameless, impudent", from *in-* + *pudēre* "to feel shame"] — **im·pu·dence** \-əns\ *n* — **im·pu·dent·ly** *adv*

im·pugn \im-'pyün\ *vt* : to oppose or attack as false : cast doubt on [Middle French *impugner,* from Latin *impugnare,* from *in-* + *pugnare* "to fight"] — **im·pugn·er** *n*

im·puis·sance \im-'pwis-ns, 'im-, -'pyü-ə-səns\ *n* : WEAKNESS 1, POWERLESSNESS

im·pulse \'im-,pəls\ *n* **1 a** : a force that starts a body into motion : IMPULSION **b** : the motion produced by such an impulsion **2** : a sudden spontaneous arousing of the mind and spirit to do something : an inclination to act ⟨an *impulse* to run away⟩ ⟨acts on *impulse*⟩ **3** : NERVE IMPULSE **4** : the product of the average value of a force and the time during which it acts [Latin *impulsus,* from *impellere* "to impel"] SYN see MOTIVE

im·pul·sion \im-'pəl-shən\ *n* **1 a** : the action of impelling : the state of being impelled **b** : an impelling force **c** : IMPETUS 1 **2** : IMPULSE 2 **3** : COMPULSION 2

im·pul·sive \im-'pəl-siv\ *adj* : acting or liable to act on impulse : moved or caused by an impulse SYN see SPONTANEOUS — **im·pul·sive·ly** *adv* — **im·pul·sive·ness** *n*

im·pu·ni·ty \im-'pyü-nət-ē\ *n* : immunity or freedom from punishment, harm, or loss [Latin *impunitas,* from *impune* "without punishment", from *in-* + *poena* "pain, penalty"]

im·pure \im-'pyûr, 'im-\ *adj* : not pure: as **a** : UNCHASTE, OBSCENE ⟨*impure* language⟩ **b** : containing something unclean : FOUL ⟨*impure* water⟩ **c** : ritually unclean **d** : marked by an intermixture of foreign elements or by substandard, incongruous, or objectionable locutions **e** : mixed with some other substance

and especially some inferior substance ⟨an *impure* chemical⟩ **f** : MIXED, BASTARD ⟨an *impure* style of ornamentation⟩ — **im·pure·ly** *adv* — **im·pure·ness** *n*

im·pu·ri·ty \im-'pyûr-ət-ē, 'im-\ *n, pl* **-ties** **1** : the quality or state of being impure **2** : something that is impure or that makes something else impure ⟨*impurities* in water⟩

im·pute \im-'pyüt\ *vt* **1** : to place the responsibility or blame for : CHARGE **2** : to credit to a person or a cause : ATTRIBUTE [Latin *imputare,* from *in-* "²in-" + *putare* "to reckon"] SYN see ASCRIBE — **im·put·able** \-'pyüt-ə-bəl\ *adj* — **im·put·ably** \-blē\ *adv* — **im·pu·ta·tion** \,im-pyə-'tā-shən\ *n* — **im·pu·ta·tive** \im-'pyüt-ət-iv\ *adj* — **im·pu·ta·tive·ly** *adv*

¹in \in, 'in, ən, ᵊn\ *prep* **1 a** — used as a function word to indicate inclusion, location, or position within limits ⟨*in* the lake⟩ ⟨*in* the summer⟩ **b** : INTO 1a ⟨went *in* the house⟩ **2** : by means of : WITH ⟨written *in* pencil⟩ **3 a** — used as a function word to indicate manner, state, or situation ⟨alike *in* some respects⟩ ⟨left *in* a hurry⟩ **b** : INTO 2a ⟨broke *in* pieces⟩ **4** — used as a function word to indicate purpose ⟨said *in* reply⟩ [Old English]

²in \'in\ *adv* **1 a** : to or toward the inside ⟨went *in* and closed the door⟩ **b** : to or toward some particular place ⟨flew *in* on the first plane⟩ **c** : at close quarters : NEAR ⟨play close *in*⟩ **d** : into the midst of something ⟨mix *in* the flour⟩ **e** : to or at its proper place ⟨fit a piece *in*⟩ **f** : into line ⟨fell *in* with our plans⟩ **2 a** : within a particular place; *esp* : within the customary place of residence or business ⟨tell them I'm not *in*⟩ **b** : in the position of insider ⟨*in* on the scheme⟩ **c** : on good terms **d** : in a position of assured success; *also* : in style or season **e** : at hand or on hand ⟨the evidence is all *in*⟩ ⟨harvests are *in*⟩

³in \'in\ *adj* **1 a** : being inside or within ⟨the *in* part⟩ **b** : being in position, operation, or power ⟨the *in* party⟩ **2** : directed or bound inward : INCOMING ⟨the *in* train⟩ **3** : keenly aware of and responsive to what is new and smart ⟨the *in* crowd⟩ **4** : extremely fashionable ⟨the *in* thing to do⟩

⁴in \'in\ *n* **1** : one who is in office or power or on the inside **2** : INFLUENCE, PULL ⟨had an *in* with the boss⟩

¹in- *or* **il-** *or* **im-** *or* **ir-** *prefix* : not : NON- : UN- — usually *il-* before *l* ⟨*il*logical⟩, *im-* before *b, m,* or *p* ⟨*im*balance⟩ ⟨*im*moral⟩ ⟨*im*practical⟩, *ir-* before *r* ⟨*ir*reducible⟩, and *in-* before other sounds ⟨*in*conclusive⟩ [Latin]

²in- *or* **il-** *or* **im-** *or* **ir-** *prefix* **1** : in : within : into : toward : on **2** : ¹EN- ⟨*im*plant⟩ — in both senses usually *il-* before *l, im-* before *b, m,* or *p, ir-* before *r,* and *in-* before other sounds [Latin, from *in* "in, into"]

¹-in \ən, ᵊn, ,in\ *n suffix* : chemical compound ⟨*in*sulin⟩ [French *-ine,* from Latin *-ina,* feminine of *-inus* "¹-ine"]

²-in \-,in\ *n combining form* **1** : organized public protest by means of or in favor of : demonstration ⟨teach-*in*⟩ ⟨love-*in*⟩ **2** : public group activity ⟨sing-*in*⟩ [*in* (as in *sit-in*)]

in·abil·i·ty \,in-ə-'bil-ət-ē\ *n* : the condition of being unable : lack of ability, power, or means □ SYN INABILITY, DISABILITY both denote lack of ability to perform a given act or to pursue a specific trade or profession. INABILITY implies lack of power to perform and suggests lack of means, health, training, or temperamental fitness ⟨*inability* to see⟩ ⟨*inability* to understand⟩ DISABILITY implies the loss of power to perform due to accident, illness, or disqualification and applies both to the resulting inability and to the cause of it ⟨because of *disabilities* many veterans failed to return to their former occupations⟩

in absentia \,in-ab-'sen-chə, -chē-ə\ *adv* : in one's absence : while absent ⟨was awarded the degree *in absentia*⟩ [Latin, "in absence"]

in·ac·ces·si·ble \,in-ak-'ses-ə-bəl, -ik-\ *adj* : not accessible — **in·ac·ces·si·bil·i·ty** \-,ses-ə-'bil-ət-ē\ *n* — **in·ac·ces·si·bly** \-'ses-ə-blē\ *adv*

in·ac·cu·ra·cy \in-'ak-yə-rə-sē, 'in-\ *n, pl* **-cies** **1** : the quality or state of being inaccurate **2** : MISTAKE, ERROR

in·ac·cu·rate \-rət\ *adj* : not accurate : FAULTY — **in·ac·cu·rate·ly** *adv*

in·ac·tion \in-'ak-shən, 'in-\ *n* : lack of action or activity

in·ac·ti·vate \in-'ak-tə-,vāt, 'in-\ *vt* : to make inactive — **in·ac·ti·va·tion** \in-,ak-tə-'vā-shən\ *n*

in·ac·tive \in-'ak-tiv, 'in-\ *adj* : not active: as **a** : INDOLENT **2**, SLUGGISH **b** : being out of use or activity **c** : relating to members of the armed forces who are not performing or available for military duties **d** : chemically inert — **in·ac·tive·ly** *adv* — **in·ac·tiv·i·ty** \,in-ak-'tiv-ət-ē\ *n* □ SYN INERT, IDLE: INACTIVE applies to anyone or anything not in action or in operation or at work ⟨an *inactive* mine⟩ ⟨an *inactive* seasonal worker⟩ INERT as applied to a thing implies being powerless to move itself or to affect other things ⟨an *inert* gas⟩ ⟨*inert* drugs no longer effective⟩ and applied to a person suggests an inherent or habitual indisposition to activity ⟨politically *inert* citizens⟩ IDLE applies to people who are not busy or occupied or to their powers or implements ⟨*idle* laborers hoping for work⟩

in·ad·e·qua·cy \in-'ad-i-kwə-sē, 'in-\ *n, pl* **-cies** **1** : the quality or state of being inadequate **2 a** : an inadequate amount **b** : failure to come up to expectations ⟨feelings of *inadequacy*⟩

in·ad·e·quate \-kwət\ *adj* : not adequate : not enough or not good enough — **in·ad·e·quate·ly** *adv* — **in·ad·e·quate·ness** *n*

in·ad·mis·si·ble \,in-əd-'mis-ə-bəl\ *adj* : not admissible — **in·ad·mis·si·bil·i·ty** \-,mis-ə-'bil-ət-ē\ *n*

in·ad·ver·tence \,in-əd-'vərt-ns\ *n* : INATTENTION; *also* : a result of inattention [Medieval Latin *inadvertentia*, from Latin *in-* + *advertere* "to notice"] — **in·ad·ver·ten·cy** \-n-sē\ *n*

in·ad·ver·tent \-nt\ *adj* **1** : INATTENTIVE **2** : UNINTENTIONAL — **in·ad·ver·tent·ly** *adv*

in·ad·vis·able \,in-əd-'vī-zə-bəl\ *adj* : not wise to do : not advisable — **in·ad·vis·abil·i·ty** \-,vī-zə-'bil-ət-ē\ *n*

in·alien·able \in-'āl-yə-nə-bəl, 'in-, -'ā-lē-ə-nə-\ *adj* : not capable of being taken away, given up, or transferred ⟨*inalienable* rights⟩ — **in·alien·abil·i·ty** \in-,āl-yə-nə-'bil-ət-ē, -,ā-lē-ə-nə-\ *n* — **in·alien·ably** \in-'āl-yə-nə-blē, 'in-, -'ā-lē-ə-nə-\ *adv*

in·al·ter·a·ble \in-'ól-tə-rə-bəl, 'in-, -trə-\ *adj* : UNALTERABLE — **in·al·ter·abil·i·ty** \in-,ól-tə-rə-'bil-ət-ē, -trə-\ *n* — **in·al·ter·able·ness** \in-'ól-tə-rə-bəl-nəs, -trə-\ *n* — **in·al·ter·ably** \in-'ól-tə-rə-blē\ *adv*

in·amo·ra·ta \in-,am-ə-'rät-ə\ *n* : a woman with whom one is in love [Italian *innamorata,* from *innamorare* "to inspire with love", from *in-* "²in-" + *amore* "love", from Latin *amor*]

inane \in-'ān\ *adj* : lacking significance, meaning, or point : SILLY [Latin *inanis*] SYN see INSIPID — **inane·ly** *adv* — **inane·ness** \-'ān-nəs\ *n*

in·an·i·mate \in-'an-ə-mət, 'in-\ *adj* **1** : not animate: **a** : not endowed with life or spirit **b** : lacking consciousness or power of motion **2** : not animated or lively : DULL — **in·an·i·mate·ly** *adv* — **in·an·i·mate·ness** *n*

in·a·ni·tion \,in-ə-'nish-ən\ *n* : a weakened condition resulting from or as if from lack of food and water [Medieval Latin *inanitio,* from Latin *inanire* "to empty", from *inanis* "empty, inane"]

inan·i·ty \in-'an-ət-ē\ *n, pl* **-ties** **1** : the quality or state of being inane; *esp* : foolish or trivial character **2** : something that is inane; *esp* : a senseless or foolish remark

in·ap·peas·able \,in-ə-'pē-zə-bəl\ *adj* : UNAPPEASABLE

in·ap·pe·tence \in-'ap-ət-əns\ *n* : lack of appetite

in·ap·pli·ca·ble \in-'ap-li-kə-bəl, 'in-; ,in-ə-'plik-ə-\ *adj* : not applicable : UNSUITABLE, IRRELEVANT — **in·ap·pli·ca·bil·i·ty** \in-,ap-li-kə-'bil-ət-ē, ,in-ə-,plik-ə-\ *n* — **in·ap·pli·ca·bly** \in-'ap-li-kə-blē, 'in-; ,in-ə-'plik-ə-\ *adv*

in·ap·pre·cia·ble \,in-ə-'prē-shə-bəl\ *adj* : too small to be perceived : very slight — **in·ap·pre·cia·bly** \-blē\ *adv*

in·ap·pro·pri·ate \,in-ə-'prō-prē-ət\ *adj* : not appropriate : UNSUITABLE — **in·ap·pro·pri·ate·ly** *adv* — **in·ap·pro·pri·ate·ness** *n*

in·apt \in-'apt, 'in-\ *adj* **1** : not suitable **2** : INEPT **1** — **in·apt·ly** *adv* — **in·apt·ness** \-'apt-nəs, -'ap-\ *n*

in·ap·ti·tude \-'ap-tə-,tüd, -,tyüd\ *n* : lack of aptitude

in·ar·tic·u·late \,in-är-'tik-yə-lət\ *adj* **1 a** : not understandable as spoken words ⟨*inarticulate* cries⟩ **b** : incapable of speech especially under emotional stress : MUTE **c** : incapable of being expressed by speech ⟨*inarticulate* longings⟩ **d** : not voiced or expressed **2** : incapable of giving coherent, clear, or effective expression to one's ideas or feelings — **in·ar·tic·u·late·ly** *adv* — **in·ar·tic·u·late·ness** *n*

in·ar·tis·tic \,in-är-'tis-tik\ *adj* **1** : not conforming to the principles of art **2** : not appreciative of art — **in·ar·tis·ti·cal·ly** \-'tis-ti-kə-lē, -klē\ *adv*

in·as·much as \,in-əz-,məch-əz\ *conj* **1** : to the extent that **2** : in view of the fact that : SINCE

in·at·ten·tion \,in-ə-'ten-chən\ *n* : failure to pay attention

in·at·ten·tive \-'tent-iv\ *adj* : marked by inattention — **in·at·ten·tive·ly** *adv* — **in·at·ten·tive·ness** *n*

¹in·au·gu·ral \in-'ó-gyə-rəl, -gə-rəl, -grəl\ *adj* **1** : of or relating to an inauguration ⟨*inaugural* address⟩ **2** : marking a beginning : first in a projected series ⟨*inaugural* run of a new luxury liner⟩

²inaugural *n* **1** : an inaugural address **2** : INAUGURATION

in·au·gu·rate \in-'ó-gyə-,rāt, -gə-\ *vt* **1** : to introduce into office with suitable ceremonies : INSTALL ⟨*inaugurate* a president⟩ **2** : to celebrate or mark the opening of ⟨*inaugurate* the new athletic field⟩ **3** : to commence or enter upon : BEGIN ⟨*inaugurate* a reform⟩ [Latin *inaugurare* "to practice augury, inaugurate", from *in-* + *augur* "augur"; from the consulting of omens at inaugurations] — **in·au·gu·ra·tor** \-,rāt-ər\ *n*

in·au·gu·ra·tion \in-,ó-gyə-'rā-shən, -gə-\ *n* : an act of inaugurating; *esp* : a ceremonial introduction into office

in·aus·pi·cious \,in-ó-'spish-əs\ *adj* : not auspicious : UNPROMISING — **in·aus·pi·cious·ly** *adv* — **in·aus·pi·cious·ness** *n*

¹in between *adv* : BETWEEN ⟨were neither young nor old but fell somewhere *in between*⟩

²in between *prep* : BETWEEN ⟨a meadow lies *in between* the house and the woods⟩

in·board \'in-,bōrd, -,bórd\ *adv* **1** : inside the line of a ship's bulwarks or hull : toward the center line of a ship **2** : in a position closer or closest to the longitudinal axis of an aircraft — **inboard** *adj*

in·born \'in-'bórn\ *adj* **1** : born in or with one : not acquired by training or experience : NATURAL **2** : HEREDITARY **1**, INHERITED SYN see INNATE

in·bound \'in-'baùnd\ *adj* : inward bound ⟨*inbound* traffic⟩

in·breathe \'in-'brēth\ *vt* : INHALE **2**

in·bred \'in-'bred\ *adj* **1 a** : present from birth **b** : planted in by early teaching or training : INCULCATED **2** : subjected to or produced by inbreeding SYN see INNATE

in·breed \'in-'brēd\ *vb* **-bred** \-'bred\; **-breed·ing** : to produce by or subject to inbreeding

in·breed·ing \'in-,brēd-ing\ *n* **1** : the interbreeding of closely related individuals especially to preserve and fix desirable characters of and to eliminate unfavorable characters from a stock **2** : confinement to a narrow range or a local or limited field of choice

\ə\ abut		\ng\ sing	
\ər\ further		\ō\ bone	
\a\ mat		\ó\ saw	
\ā\ take		\ói\ coin	
\ä\ cot, cart		\th\ thin	
\aù\ out		\th\ this	
\ch\ chin		\ü\ food	
\e\ pet		\ù\ foot	
\ē\ easy		\y\ yet	
\g\ go		\yü\ few	
\i\ tip		\yù\ cure	
\ī\ life		\zh\ vision	
\j\ job			

In·ca \'ing-kə\ *n* **1** : a noble or a member of the Quechuan peoples of Peru maintaining an empire until the Spanish conquest **2** : a member of any people under Inca influence [Spanish, from Quechua *inka* "king, prince"] — **In·can** \-kən\ *adj*

in·cal·cu·la·ble \in-'kal-kyə-lə-bəl, 'in-\ *adj* **1** : not capable of being calculated; *esp* : too large or numerous to be calculated **2** : not capable of being known in advance : UNCERTAIN — **in·cal·cu·la·bil·i·ty** \in-,kal-kyə-lə-'bil-ət-ē\ *n* — **in·cal·cu·la·bly** \-blē\ *adv*

in·can·des·cence \,in-kən-'des-ns\ *n* : a glowing condition of a body due to its high temperature

in·can·des·cent \-nt\ *adj* **1 a** : white or glowing with intense heat **b** : strikingly bright, radiant, or clear **c** : BRILLIANT ⟨*incandescent* wit⟩ **2 a** : of, relating to, or being light produced by incandescence **b** : producing light by incandescence [derived from Latin *incandescere* "to become hot", from *in-* + *candēre* "to glow"] — **in·can·des·cent·ly** *adv*

incandescent lamp *n* : a lamp whose light is produced by the glow of a filament heated by an electric current

in·can·ta·tion \,in-,kan-'tā-shən\ *n* : a use of spells or charms spoken or sung as part of a ritual of magic; *also* : a formula of words so used [Middle French, from Late Latin *incantatio*, from Latin *incantare* "to enchant"] — **in·can·ta·tion·al** \-shnəl, -shən-l\ *adj* — **in·can·ta·to·ry** \in-'kant-ə-,tōr-ē, -,tȯr-\ *adj*

in·ca·pa·ble \in-'kā-pə-bəl, 'in-\ *adj* : not capable : lacking capacity, ability, or qualification for the purpose or end in view: as **a** : not in a state or of a kind to admit : INSUSCEPTIBLE ⟨*incapable* of precise measurement⟩ **b** : not able or fit : UNQUALIFIED, INCOMPETENT — **in·ca·pa·bil·i·ty** \in-,kā-pə-'bil-ət-ē\ *n* — **in·ca·pa·ble·ness** \in-'kā-pə-bəl-nəs, 'in-\ *n* — **in·ca·pa·bly** \-blē\ *adv*

in·ca·pac·i·tate \,in-kə-'pas-ə-,tāt\ *vt* **1** : to deprive of natural capacity or power : DISABLE **2** : to make legally incapable or ineligible — **in·ca·pac·i·ta·tion** \-,pas-ə-'tā-shən\ *n*

in·ca·pac·i·ty \,in-kə-'pas-ət-ē, -'pas-tē\ *n, pl* **-ties** : lack of ability or power ⟨a seeming *incapacity* for telling the truth⟩

in·car·cer·ate \in-'kär-sə-,rāt\ *vt* : IMPRISON, CONFINE [Latin *incarcerare*, from *in-* + *carcer* "prison" — see CANCEL *origin*] — **in·car·cer·a·tion** \in-,kär-sə-'rā-shən\ *n*

¹in·car·na·dine \in-'kär-nə-,dīn, -,dēn\ *adj* : RED 1a; *esp* : BLOODRED [Middle French *incarnadin*, from Italian *incarnadino*, from *incarnato* "flesh-colored", from Late Latin *incarnare* "to incarnate"]

²incarnadine *vt* : to make incarnadine : REDDEN

¹in·car·nate \in-'kär-nət, -,nāt\ *adj* **1** : invested with bodily and especially human nature and form **2** : EMBODIED, PERSONIFIED ⟨a fiend *incarnate*⟩ [Late Latin *incarnatus*, past participle of *incarnare* "to incarnate", from Latin *in-* + *carn-, caro* "flesh"]

²in·car·nate \-,nāt\ *vt* : to make incarnate

in·car·na·tion \,in-,kär-'nā-shən\ *n* **1** : the act of incarnating : the state of being incarnate **2 a** : the embodiment of a deity or spirit in an earthly form; *esp, cap* : the union of divinity with humanity in Jesus Christ **b** : a concrete example of a quality or concept; *esp* : a person showing a trait or typical character to a marked degree

incase *variant of* ENCASE

in·cau·tious \in-'kȯ-shəs, 'in-\ *adj* : lacking in caution : CARELESS — **in·cau·tious·ly** *adv* — **in·cau·tious·ness** *n*

in·cen·di·a·rism \in-'sen-dē-ə-,riz-əm\ *n* : incendiary action or behavior

¹in·cen·di·ary \in-'sen-dē-,er-ē\ *n, pl* **-ar·ies** **1 a** : a person who unlawfully sets fire to property **b** : an incendiary agent (as a bomb) **2** : a person who excites quarrels : AGITATOR [Latin *incendiarius*, from *incendium* "conflagration", from *incendere* "to set on fire"]

²incendiary *adj* **1** : of, relating to, or involving unlawful burning of property **2** : tending to excite or inflame quarrels : INFLAMMATORY **3 a** : igniting combustible materials spontaneously **b** : relating to or being a missile containing chemicals that ignite on bursting or on contact

¹in·cense \'in-,sens\ *n* **1** : material used to produce a fragrant odor when burned **2 a** : the perfume given off by some spices and gums when burned **b** : a pleasing scent [Old French *encens*, from Late Latin *incensum*, from Latin *incendere* "to set on fire"]

²in·cense \in-'sens\ *vt* : to inflame with anger or indignation ⟨*incensed* by their bad behavior⟩ [Middle French *encenser*, from Latin *incendere*, literally, "to set on fire"]

in·cen·ter \'in-,sent-ər\ *n* : the point of intersection of the bisectors of the angles of a triangle

in·cen·tive \in-'sent-iv\ *n* : something that arouses or spurs one on to action or effort : STIMULUS [Late Latin *incentivum*, from Latin *incentivus* "setting the tune", from *incinere* "to set the tune", from *in-* + *canere* "to sing"] — **incentive** *adj*

in·cep·tion \in-'sep-shən\ *n* : an act, process, or instance of beginning : COMMENCEMENT ⟨the program has been a success since its *inception*⟩ [Latin *inceptio*, from *incipere* "to begin", from *in-* + *capere* "to take"] SYN see ORIGIN

in·cep·tive \in-'sep-tiv\ *adj* : of or relating to a beginning — **in·cep·tive·ly** *adv*

in·cer·ti·tude \in-'sərt-ə-,tüd, 'in-, -,tyüd\ *n* : UNCERTAINTY: **a** : absence of assurance : DOUBT, INDECISION **b** : INSTABILITY, INSECURITY

in·ces·sant \in-'ses-nt, 'in-\ *adj* : continuing without interruption : UNCEASING ⟨*incessant* rains⟩ [Late Latin *incessans*, from Latin *in-* + *cessare* "to delay"] SYN see CONTINUAL — **in·ces·sant·ly** *adv*

in·cest \'in-,sest\ *n* : sexual intercourse between persons so closely related that they are forbidden by law to marry; *also* : the statutory crime of such a relationship [Latin *incestum*, from *incestus* "impure", from *in-* + *castus* "pure"]

in·ces·tu·ous \in-'ses-chə-wəs\ *adj* **1** : constituting or involving incest **2** : guilty of incest — **in·ces·tu·ous·ly** *adv* — **in·ces·tu·ous·ness** *n*

¹inch \'inch\ *n* **1** : a unit of length equal to ¹/₃₆ yard (2.54 centimeters) — see MEASURE table **2** : a small amount, distance, or degree ⟨wouldn't move an *inch*⟩ **3** *pl* : STATURE 1, HEIGHT [Old English *ynce*, from Latin *uncia* "12th part, inch, ounce"]

²inch *vb* : to move by small degrees

³inch *n, chiefly Scottish* : ISLAND 1 [Scottish Gaelic *innis*]

inch·meal \'inch-,mēl\ *adv* : little by little : GRADUALLY

in·cho·ate \in-'kō-ət, 'in-kə-,wāt\ *adj* : being recently begun or only partly in existence or operation; *esp* : imperfectly formed ⟨*inchoate* suspicions⟩ [Latin *inchoatus*, past participle of *inchoare* "to begin"] — **in·cho·ate·ly** *adv* — **in·cho·ate·ness** *n*

inch·worm \'inch-,wərm\ *n* : LOOPER 1

in·ci·dence \'in-səd-əns, -sə-,dens\ *n* **1 a** : an act or fact of affecting : OCCURRENCE **b** : rate of occurrence or influence ⟨a high *incidence* of crime⟩ **2 a** : the arrival of something (as a projectile or a ray of light) at a surface **b** : ANGLE OF INCIDENCE

¹in·ci·dent \'in-səd-ənt, -sə-,dent\ *n* **1 a** : an occurrence that is a separate item of experience : HAPPENING **b** : an accompanying minor occurrence **2** : an action likely to lead to grave consequences especially in diplomatic matters **3** : something dependent on or subordinate to something else of greater importance [Middle French, from Medieval Latin *incidens*, from Latin *incidere* "to fall into, occur", from *in-* + *cadere* "to fall"] SYN see OCCURRENCE

filament

incandescent lamp

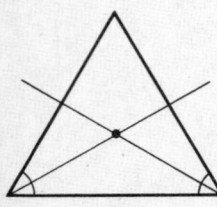

incenter

²incident *adj* **1** : occurring or likely to occur as a minor consequence or accompaniment ⟨a question *incident* to the main topic⟩ **2** : dependent on or relating to another thing **3** : falling or striking on something ⟨*incident* light rays⟩

¹in·ci·den·tal \ˌin-sə-'dent-l\ *adj* **1** : occurring merely by chance or without intention **2** : being likely to happen as a chance or minor consequence ⟨*incidental* expenses of a trip⟩ — **in·ci·den·tal·ly** \-'dent-lē, -l-ē\ *adv*

²incidental *n* **1** : something incidental **2** *pl* : minor items (as of expense) that are not listed individually

in·cin·er·ate \in-'sin-ə-ˌrāt\ *vt* : to burn to ashes [Medieval Latin *incinerare*, from Latin *in-* + *ciner-, cinis* "ashes"] — **in·cin·er·a·tion** \in-ˌsin-ə-'rā-shən\ *n*

in·cin·er·a·tor \in-'sin-ə-ˌrāt-ər\ *n* : one that incinerates; *esp* : a furnace or a container for incinerating waste materials

in·cip·i·ent \in-'sip-ē-ənt\ *adj* : beginning to come into existence or become apparent [Latin *incipiens*, present participle of *incipere* "to begin", from *in-* + *capere* "to take"] — **in·cip·i·en·cy** \-ən-sē\ *also* **in·cip·i·ence** \-əns\ *n* — **in·cip·i·ent·ly** *adv*

in·cise \in-'sīz\ *vt* **1** : to cut into **2** : ENGRAVE 1a [Latin *incisus*, past participle of *incidere* "to cut into", from *in-* + *caedere* "to cut"]

in·cised \-'sīzd\ *adj* : cut in; *esp* : decorated with incised figures

in·ci·sion \in-'sizh-ən\ *n* **1** : CUT, GASH; *esp* : an incised wound made surgically in the body **2** : an act of incising **3** : incisive quality

in·ci·sive \in-'sī-siv\ *adj* : impressively direct and decisive ⟨an *incisive* writing style⟩ ⟨an *incisive* and convincing argument⟩ — **in·ci·sive·ly** *adv* — **in·ci·sive·ness** *n* □ SYN INCISIVE, TRENCHANT, CUTTING, BITING mean having or manifesting a keen mind. INCISIVE implies a power to impress the mind by keen penetration, directness, and decisiveness ⟨no one could ignore that *incisive* command⟩ TRENCHANT implies an energetic cutting or deep probing so as to reveal distinctions or get to the heart of the matter ⟨a *trenchant* critic of political pretensions⟩ CUTTING suggests sarcasm or penetrating accuracy that wounds the feelings ⟨makes the most *cutting* remarks with that quiet voice⟩ BITING adds a greater implication of harsh vehemence or ironic force ⟨a *biting* commentary on the election⟩

in·ci·sor \in-'sī-zər\ *n* : a tooth adapted for cutting; *esp* : one of the cutting teeth in front of the canines of a mammal — **incisor** *adj*

in·ci·ta·tion \ˌin-ˌsī-'tā-shən, in-sə-\ *n* : INCITEMENT

in·cite \in-'sīt\ *vt* : to move to action : stir up : urge on [Middle French *inciter*, from Latin *incitare* "to put in motion, rouse, cite"] — **in·cite·ment** \-'sīt-mənt\ *n* — **in·cit·er** *n* □ SYN INSTIGATE, ABET, FOMENT: INCITE stresses a stirring up and urging on and may or may not imply initiative ⟨propaganda *inciting* war⟩ INSTIGATE implies responsibility for initiating another's action and often connotes dubious or evil intention ⟨pamphleteers whose writings *instigated* rebellion⟩ ABET implies both assisting and encouraging ⟨traitors *abetting* the enemy⟩ FOMENT stresses persistence in goading ⟨hawks incessantly *fomented* war⟩

in·ci·vil·i·ty \ˌin-sə-'vil-ət-ē\ *n, pl* **-ties** **1** : the quality or state of being uncivil **2** : a rude or discourteous act

in·clem·ent \in-'klem-ənt, 'in-\ *adj* : physically severe : STORMY, ROUGH ⟨*inclement* weather⟩; *also* : marked by such weather ⟨an *inclement* day⟩ — **in·clem·en·cy** \-ən-sē\ *n* — **in·clem·ent·ly** *adv*

in·clin·able \in-'klī-nə-bəl\ *adj* **1** : having a tendency or inclination : DISPOSED ⟨*inclinable* to idleness⟩ **2** : favorably disposed ⟨*inclinable* to their request⟩

in·cli·na·tion \ˌin-klə-'nā-shən, ˌing-\ *n* **1** : an act or the action of bending or inclining: as **a** : ²BOW, NOD **b** : a tilting of something **2** : a particular disposition of mind or character; *esp* : LIKING **3 a** : a departure from

the true vertical or horizontal : SLANT ⟨the *inclination* of the earth's axis⟩; *also* : the degree of such departure **b** : an inclined surface : SLOPE **4** : a tendency to a particular state, character, or action ⟨the weather showed some *inclination* to snow⟩ — **in·cli·na·tion·al** \-shnəl, -shən-l\ *adj*

¹in·cline \in-'klīn\ *vb* **1** : to bend the head or body forward : BOW **2** : to lean in one's mind : be favorable ⟨as toward a person, an opinion, or a course of action⟩ : TEND ⟨*incline* toward the second of two proposals⟩ **3** : to deviate from a line, direction, or course : SLOPE, SLANT; *esp* : to deviate from the vertical or horizontal **4** : to cause to bend, bow, slope, or slant **5** : to have influence on (as in direction, course of action, or opinion) [Middle French *incliner*, from Latin *inclinare*, from *in-* + *clinare* "to lean"] — **in·clin·er** *n*

²in·cline \'in-ˌklīn\ *n* : an inclined plane : GRADE, SLOPE

in·clined \in-'klīnd, 2 also 'in-,\ *adj* **1** : having an inclination, disposition, or tendency **2 a** : having a slant or slope **b** : making an angle with a line or plane

inclined plane *n* : a plane surface that makes an oblique angle with the plane of the horizon

inclose, inclosure *variant of* ENCLOSE, ENCLOSURE

in·clude \in-'klüd\ *vt* **1** : to shut up : ENCLOSE **2** : to take in or comprise as a part of a whole **3** : to contain between ⟨two sides and the *included* angle⟩ [Latin *includere*, from *in-* + *claudere* "to close"] — **in·clud·able** *or* **in·clud·ible** \-'klüd-ə-bəl\ *adj* □ SYN INCLUDE, COMPREHEND, INVOLVE mean to contain within as a part of the whole. INCLUDE suggests containing something as a constituent or subordinate part of a larger whole ⟨most oaks are *included* in the genus *Quercus*⟩ COMPREHEND implies that something comes within the range or scope of a statement or definition ⟨in some cases the term commerce does not *comprehend* navigation⟩ INVOLVE suggests an intimate entangling or mingling a thing with a whole, often as an inevitable result or an essential antecedent ⟨surrender *involves* submission⟩ ⟨freedom *involves* responsibility⟩ SYN see in addition COMPRISE

in·clu·sion \in-'klü-zhən\ *n* **1** : the act of including : the state of being included **2** : something that is included; *esp* : a passive product of cell activity (as a starch grain) within the protoplasm [Latin *inclusio*, from *includere* "to include"]

in·clu·sive \in-'klü-siv, -ziv\ *adj* **1** : including the specified limits and everything in between ⟨March to June *inclusive*⟩ **2** : broad or complete in orientation, scope, or coverage ⟨an *inclusive* insurance policy⟩ — **in·clu·sive·ly** *adv* — **in·clu·sive·ness** *n*

inclusive of *prep* : taking into account ⟨the cost of building *inclusive of* materials⟩

in·co·erc·ible \ˌin-kō-'ər-sə-bəl\ *adj* : incapable of being controlled, checked, or confined

¹in·cog·ni·to \ˌin-ˌkäg-'nēt-ō, in-'käg-nə-ˌtō\ *adv or adj* : with one's identity concealed [Italian, from Latin *incognitus* "unknown", from *in-* + *cognoscere* "to know"]

²incognito *n, pl* **-tos** **1** : one appearing or living incognito **2** : the state or disguise of an incognito

in·co·her·ence \ˌin-kō-'hir-əns, -'her-\ *n* **1** : the quality or state of being incoherent **2** : an incoherent utterance

in·co·her·ent \-ənt\ *adj* : not coherent: as **a** : not sticking closely or compactly together : LOOSE **b** : not clearly or logically connected ⟨an *incoherent* story⟩ — **in·co·her·ent·ly** *adv*

in·com·bus·ti·ble \ˌin-kəm-'bəs-tə-bəl\ *adj* : not combustible : incapable of being burned

in·come \'in-ˌkəm\ *n* : a gain usually measured in money that comes from capital or labor; *also* : the amount of such gain received by an individual in a given period of time

income tax \ˌin-kəm-\ *n* : a tax on the net income of an individual or business concern

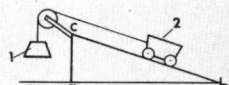

inclined plane: *ab* base, *ac* height, *cb* inclined plane, *l* force, *2* resistance

\ə\ abut   \ng\ si**ng**
\ər\ **further**   \ō\ b**o**ne
\a\ m**a**t   \o\ s**a**w
\ā\ t**a**ke   \oi\ c**oi**n
\ä\ c**o**t, c**a**rt   \th\ **th**in
\au\ **ou**t   \t**h**\ **th**is
\ch\ **ch**in   \ü\ f**oo**d
\e\ p**e**t   \u\ f**oo**t
\ē\ **e**asy   \y\ **y**et
\g\ **g**o   \yü\ f**ew**
\i\ t**i**p   \yu\ c**u**re
\ī\ l**i**fe   \zh\ vi**si**on
\j\ **j**ob

¹in·com·ing \'in-ˌkəm-ing\ *n* : the act of coming in : ARRIVAL

²incoming *adj* : coming in: as **a** : taking a place or position formerly held by another ⟨the *incoming* president⟩ **b** : arriving at a usual or designated destination ⟨*incoming* mail⟩ **c** : just starting or beginning ⟨the *incoming* class⟩

in·com·men·su·rate \ˌin-kə-'mens-rət, -'mench-rət, -ə-rət\ *adj* : not commensurate; *esp* : not enough to satisfy ⟨funds *incommensurate* with need⟩

in·com·mode \ˌin-kə-'mōd\ *vt* : to give inconvenience or trouble to [Middle French *incommoder,* from Latin *incommodare,* from *incommodus* "inconvenient", from *in-* + *commodus* "convenient"]

in·com·mod·i·ty \-'mäd-ət-ē\ *n* : INCONVENIENCE 2, DISADVANTAGE

in·com·mu·ni·ca·ble \ˌin-kə-'myü-ni-kə-bəl\ *adj* : not capable of being communicated or imparted — **in·com·mu·ni·ca·bil·i·ty** \-ˌmyü-ni-kə-'bil-ət-ē\ *n* — **in·com·mu·ni·ca·bly** \-'myü-ni-kə-blē\ *adv*

in·com·mu·ni·ca·do \ˌin-kə-ˌmyü-nə-'käd-ō\ *adv or adj* : without means of communication with others ⟨a prisoner held *incommunicado*⟩ [Spanish *incomunicado,* from *incomunicar* "to deprive of communication"]

in·com·mu·ni·ca·tive \ˌin-kə-'myü-nə-ˌkāt-iv, -ni-kət-\ *adj* : UNCOMMUNICATIVE

in·com·pa·ra·ble \in-'käm-pə-rə-bəl, -prə-bəl\ *adj* **1** : having no equal (as in quality or worth) : MATCHLESS **2** : not suitable for comparison — **in·com·pa·ra·bil·i·ty** \in-ˌkäm-pə-rə-'bil-ət-ē, -prə-\ — **in·com·pa·ra·bly** \in-'käm-pə-rə-blē, -prə-\ *adv*

in·com·pat·i·bil·i·ty \ˌin-kəm-ˌpat-ə-'bil-ət-ē\ *n, pl* **-ties** **1** : the quality or state of being incompatible **2** *pl* : mutually antagonistic things or qualities

in·com·pat·i·ble \ˌin-kəm-'pat-ə-bəl\ *adj* : incapable of or unsuitable for association ⟨were temperamentally *incompatible*⟩: as **a** : lacking harmony or congruity : DISCORDANT ⟨*incompatible* colors⟩ ⟨conduct *incompatible* with honor⟩ **b** : unsuitable for use together because of undesirable chemical or bodily effects ⟨*incompatible* blood types⟩ **c** : infertile in a particular genetic cross ⟨*incompatible* plants⟩ — **in·com·pat·i·bly** \-blē\ *adv*

in·com·pe·tence \in-'käm-pət-əns, 'in-\ *also* **in·com·pe·ten·cy** \-ən-sē\ *n, pl* **-tenc·es** *also* **-tencies** : the quality, state, or fact of being incompetent

¹in·com·pe·tent \in-'käm-pət-ənt, 'in-\ *adj* **1** : lacking the qualities (as knowledge, skill, or ability) necessary for effective independent action **2** : not legally qualified **3** : inadequate to or unsuitable for the purpose ⟨an *incompetent* heart valve⟩ ⟨an *incompetent* system of government⟩ — **in·com·pe·tent·ly** *adv*

²incompetent *n* : an incompetent person

in·com·plete \ˌin-kəm-'plēt\ *adj* : not complete : lacking some part : UNFINISHED, IMPERFECT — **in·com·plete·ly** *adv* — **in·com·plete·ness** *n*

in·com·pre·hen·si·ble \in-ˌkäm-pri-'hen-sə-bəl\ *adj* : incapable of being understood — **in·com·pre·hen·si·bil·i·ty** \-ˌhen-sə-'bil-ət-ē\ *n* — **in·com·pre·hen·si·ble·ness** \-'hen-sə-bəl-nəs\ *n* — **in·com·pre·hen·si·bly** \-blē\ *adv*

in·com·pre·hen·sion \in-ˌkäm-pri-'hen-chən\ *n* : lack of understanding

in·com·press·ible \ˌin-kəm-'pres-ə-bəl\ *adj* : incapable of or resistant to compression — **in·com·press·ibil·i·ty** \-ˌpres-ə-'bil-ət-ē\ *n* — **in·com·press·ibly** \-'pres-ə-blē\ *adv*

in·com·put·able \ˌin-kəm-'pyüt-ə-bəl\ *adj* : greater than can be computed or counted — **in·com·put·ably** \-blē\ *adv*

in·con·ceiv·able \ˌin-kən-'sē-və-bəl\ *adj* : impossible to imagine or conceive — **in·con·ceiv·abil·i·ty** \-ˌsē-və-'bil-ət-ē\ *n* — **in·con·ceiv·able·ness** \-'sē-və-bəl-nəs\ *n* — **in·con·ceiv·ably** \-blē\ *adv*

in·con·clu·sive \ˌin-kən-'klü-siv, -ziv\ *adj* : leading to no conclusion or definite result — **in·con·clu·sive·ly** *adv* — **in·con·clu·sive·ness** *n*

in·con·for·mi·ty \ˌin-kən-'for-mət-ē\ *n* : NONCONFORMITY 2

in·con·gru·ence \ˌin-kən-'grü-əns; in-'käng-grə-wəns, 'in-\ *n* : INCONGRUITY

in·con·gru·ent \ˌin-kən-'grü-ənt; in-'käng-grə-wənt, 'in-\ *adj* : marked by incongruity — **in·con·gru·ent·ly** *adv*

in·con·gru·i·ty \ˌin-kən-'grü-ət-ē, -ˌkän-\ *n, pl* **-ties** **1** : the quality or state of being incongruous **2** : something that is incongruous

in·con·gru·ous \in-'käng-grə-wəs, 'in-\ *adj* : not consistent with or suitable to the surroundings or associations : not harmonious, appropriate, or proper ⟨*incongruous* colors⟩ ⟨an act *incongruous* with their duty⟩ — **in·con·gru·ous·ly** *adv* — **in·con·gru·ous·ness** *n*

in·con·se·quence \in-'kän-sə-ˌkwens, -si-kwəns, 'in-\ *n* : the quality or state of being inconsequent

in·con·se·quent \-ˌkwent, -ˌkwent\ *adj* **1 a** : lacking reasonable sequence : ILLOGICAL **b** : not consecutive **2** : IRRELEVANT **3** : INCONSEQUENTIAL 2 — **in·con·se·quent·ly** \-ˌkwent-lē, -kwənt-\ *adv*

in·con·se·quen·tial \in-ˌkän-sə-'kwen-chəl\ *adj* **1 a** : ILLOGICAL **b** : IRRELEVANT **2** : of no significance : UNIMPORTANT — **in·con·se·quen·ti·al·i·ty** \-ˌkwen-chē-'al-ət-ē\ *n* — **in·con·se·quen·tial·ly** \-'kwench-lē, -ə-lē\ *adv*

in·con·sid·er·able \ˌin-kən-'sid-ər-bəl, -'sid-ər-ə-bəl, -'sid-rə-bəl\ *adj* : not worth considering : SLIGHT, TRIVIAL — **in·con·sid·er·able·ness** *n* — **in·con·sid·er·ably** \-blē\ *adv*

in·con·sid·er·ate \ˌin-kən-'sid-rət, -ə-rət\ *adj* **1** : acting or tending to act without due thought **2** : careless of the rights or feelings of others — **in·con·sid·er·ate·ly** *adv* — **in·con·sid·er·ate·ness** *n*

in·con·sis·ten·cy \ˌin-kən-'sis-tən-sē\ *n, pl* **-cies** **1** : the quality or state of being inconsistent **2** : an instance of being inconsistent

in·con·sis·tent \ˌin-kən-'sis-tənt\ *adj* **1 a** : not being in agreement or harmony : INCOMPATIBLE ⟨an explanation *inconsistent* with the facts⟩ **b** : containing incompatible elements ⟨an *inconsistent* argument⟩ **2** : not logical in thought or actions : CHANGEABLE ⟨a very *inconsistent* person⟩ — **in·con·sis·tent·ly** *adv*

in·con·sol·able \ˌin-kən-'sō-lə-bəl\ *adj* : incapable of being consoled : DISCONSOLATE — **in·con·sol·able·ness** *n* — **in·con·sol·ably** \-blē\ *adv*

in·con·so·nance \in-'kän-sə-nəns, 'in-, -snəns\ *n* : lack of consonance or harmony : DISAGREEMENT

in·con·so·nant \-sə-nənt, -snənt\ *adj* : DISCORDANT

in·con·spic·u·ous \ˌin-kən-'spik-yə-wəs\ *adj* : not readily noticeable — **in·con·spic·u·ous·ly** *adv* — **in·con·spic·u·ous·ness** *n*

in·con·stan·cy \in-'kän-stən-sē, 'in-\ *n, pl* **-cies** : the quality or state of being inconstant

in·con·stant \-stənt\ *adj* : given to changing frequently without apparent reason : CHANGEABLE — **in·con·stant·ly** *adv*

in·con·test·able \ˌin-kən-'tes-tə-bəl\ *adj* : not open to doubt or contest : INDISPUTABLE, UNQUESTIONABLE — **in·con·test·abil·i·ty** \-ˌtes-tə-'bil-ət-ē\ *n* — **in·con·test·ably** \-'tes-tə-blē\ *adv*

in·con·ti·nent \in-'känt-n-ənt, 'in-\ *adj* **1** : lacking in self-restraint especially in the gratification of sensuous desires **2** : unable to retain a bodily discharge (as urine) voluntarily — **in·con·ti·nence** \-əns\ *n* — **in·con·ti·nent·ly** *adv*

in·con·trol·la·ble \ˌin-kən-'trō-lə-bəl\ *adj* : UNCONTROLLABLE

in·con·tro·vert·ible \in-ˌkän-trə-'vərt-ə-bəl\ *adj* : not open to question : INDISPUTABLE ⟨*incontrovertible* evidence⟩ — **in·con·tro·vert·ibly** \-blē\ *adv*

¹in·con·ve·nience \,in-kən-'vē-nyəns\ *n* **1** : the quality or state of being inconvenient; *esp* : lack of suitability for personal ease or comfort **2** : something inconvenient

²inconvenience *vt* : to cause inconvenience to

in·con·ve·nient \-nyənt\ *adj* : not convenient : causing difficulty, discomfort, or annoyance — **in·con·ve·nient·ly** *adv*

in·con·vert·ible \,in-kən-'vərt-ə-bəl\ *adj* : not convertible into something else; *esp* : not exchangeable for a foreign currency or into specie — **in·con·vert·ibil·i·ty** \-,vərt-ə-'bil-ət-ē\ *n* — **in·con·vert·ibly** \-'vərt-ə-blē\ *adv*

in·con·vinc·ible \,in-kən-'vin-sə-bəl\ *adj* : incapable of being convinced

in·co·or·di·na·tion \,in-kō-,ȯrd-n-'ā-shən\ *n* : lack of coordination especially of muscular movement

¹in·cor·po·rate \in-'kȯr-pə-,rāt\ *vb* **1** : to unite with or work into something already existent **2** : to unite or combine to form a single body or a consistent whole **3** : to give material form to : EMBODY **4** : to form, form into, or become a corporation 〈*incorporate* a firm〉 〈an *incorporated* town〉 [Late Latin *incorporare*, from Latin *in-* + *corpor-*, *corpus* "body"] — **in·cor·po·ra·tion** \in-,kȯr-pə-'rā-shən\ *n* — **in·cor·po·ra·tive** \in-'kȯr-pə-,rāt-iv, -pə-rət-, -prət-\ *adj* — **in·cor·po·ra·tor** \-pə-,rāt-ər\ *n*

²in·cor·po·rate \in-'kȯr-pə-rət, -prət\ *adj* : INCORPORATED

in·cor·po·rat·ed \-pə-,rāt-əd\ *adj* : united in one body; *esp* : formed into a legal corporation

in·cor·po·re·al \,in-kȯr-'pōr-ē-əl, -'pȯr-\ *adj* : having no material body or form : IMMATERIAL — **in·cor·po·re·al·ly** \-ə-lē\ *adv*

in·cor·po·re·i·ty \,in-,kȯr-pə-'rē-ət-ē\ *n* : the quality or state of being incorporeal : IMMATERIALITY

in·cor·rect \,in-kə-'rekt\ *adj* **1 a** : INACCURATE, FAULTY 〈an *incorrect* copy〉 **b** : not true : WRONG 〈an *incorrect* answer〉 **2** : UNBECOMING, IMPROPER 〈*incorrect* behavior〉 — **in·cor·rect·ly** *adv* — **in·cor·rect·ness** \-'rekt-nəs, -'rek-nəs\ *n*

¹in·cor·ri·gi·ble \in-'kȯr-ə-jə-bəl, 'in-, -'kär-\ *adj* : not to be corrected or improved: as **a** : incapable of being reformed 〈an *incorrigible* gambler〉 **b** : UNRULY, UNMANAGEABLE 〈*incorrigible* hair〉 — **in·cor·ri·gi·bil·i·ty** \in-,kȯr-ə-jə-'bil-ət-ē, -,kär-\ *n* — **in·cor·ri·gi·ble·ness** \in-'kȯr-ə-jə-bəl-nəs, 'in-, -'kär-\ *n* — **in·cor·ri·gi·bly** \-blē\ *adv*

²incorrigible *n* : an incorrigible person

in·cor·rupt·ible \,in-kə-'rəp-tə-bəl\ *adj* : not to be corrupted: as **a** : not subject to decay **b** : incapable of being bribed or morally corrupted — **in·cor·rupt·ibil·i·ty** \-,rəp-tə-'bil-ət-ē\ *n* — **in·cor·rupt·ibly** \-'rəp-tə-blē\ *adv*

¹in·crease \in-'krēs, 'in-,\ *vb* **1** : to make or become greater (as in size, number, value, or power) 〈*increase* speed〉 〈skill *increases* with practice〉 **2** : to multiply by the production of young [Middle French *encreistre*, from Latin *increscere*, from *in-* + *crescere* "to grow"] — **in·creas·able** \-'krē-sə-bəl, -,krē-\ *adj* — **in·creas·er** *n*

²in·crease \'in-,krēs, in-'\ *n* **1** : the act of increasing : addition or enlargement in size, extent, or quantity **2** : something (as offspring, produce, or profit) added to an original stock by enlargement or growth

in·creas·ing·ly \in-'krē-siŋ-lē, 'in-,\ *adv* : to an increasing degree : more and more

in·cred·i·ble \in-'kred-ə-bəl, 'in-,\ *adj* : too extraordinary and improbable to be believed; *also* : hard to believe — **in·cred·i·bil·i·ty** \in-,kred-ə-'bil-ət-ē\ *n* — **in·cred·i·bly** \in-'kred-ə-blē, 'in-,\ *adv*

in·cre·du·li·ty \,in-kri-'dü-lət-ē, -'dyü-\ *n* : the quality or state of being incredulous : DISBELIEF SYN see UNBELIEF

in·cred·u·lous \in-'krej-ə-ləs, 'in-\ *adj* **1** : tending to disbelieve : SKEPTICAL **2** : indicating or caused by disbelief 〈an *incredulous* stare〉 — **in·cred·u·lous·ly** *adv*

in·cre·ment \'iŋ-krə-mənt, 'in-\ *n* **1** : an increasing or growth especially in quantity or value : ENLARGEMENT, INCREASE; *also* : QUANTITY **2 a** : something gained or added **b** : one of a series of regular consecutive additions **c** : a minute increase in quantity [Latin *incrementum*, from *increscere* "to increase"] — **in·cre·men·tal** \,iŋ-krə-'ment-l, ,in-\ *adj*

in·crim·i·nate \in-'krim-ə-,nāt\ *vt* : to charge with or involve in a crime or fault : ACCUSE [Late Latin *incriminare*, from Latin *in-* + *crimen* "crime, accusation"] — **in·crim·i·na·tion** \in-,krim-ə-'nā-shən\ *n* — **in·crim·i·na·to·ry** \in-'krim-nə-,tōr-ē, -ə-nə-, -,tȯr-\ *adj*

incrust *variant of* ENCRUST

in·crus·ta·tion \,in-,krəs-'tā-shən\ *or* **en·crus·ta·tion** \,in-, ,en-\ *n* **1** : the act of encrusting : the state of being encrusted **2** : a hard coating : CRUST **3 a** : OVERLAY **b** : INLAY 1

in·cu·bate \'iŋ-kyə-,bāt, 'in-\ *vb* **1** : to sit upon (eggs) to hatch by warmth **2** : to maintain (as bacteria or a chemically active system) under conditions favorable for development or reaction **3** : to undergo incubation [Latin *incubare*, from *in-* + *cubare* "to lie"]

in·cu·ba·tion \,iŋ-kyə-'bā-shən, ,in-\ *n* **1** : the act or process of incubating **2** : the period between infection and the manifestation of a disease

in·cu·ba·tor \'iŋ-kyə-,bāt-ər, 'in-\ *n* : one that incubates; *esp* : an apparatus providing suitable conditions (as of warmth and moisture) for incubating something 〈an *incubator* for premature babies〉

in·cu·bus \'iŋ-kyə-bəs, 'in-\ *n, pl* **-bi** \-,bī, -,bē\ *also* **-bus·es** **1** : an evil spirit held to lie upon persons in their sleep **2** : NIGHTMARE 1 **3** : one that oppresses or burdens like a nightmare [Late Latin, from Latin *incubare* "to lie on, incubate"]

in·cul·cate \in-'kəl-,kāt, 'in-,kəl-\ *vt* : to impress on the mind by frequent repetition 〈*inculcated* high ideals in their children〉 [Latin *inculcare*, literally, "to tread on", from *in-* + *calcare* "to trample", from *calx* "heel"] — **in·cul·ca·tion** \,in-,kəl-'kā-shən\ *n* — **in·cul·ca·tor** \in-'kəl-,kāt-ər, 'in-,kəl-\ *n*

in·cul·pa·ble \in-'kəl-pə-bəl, 'in-\ *adj* : free from guilt : BLAMELESS

in·cul·pate \in-'kəl-,pāt, 'in-,kəl-\ *vt* : INCRIMINATE [derived from Latin *in-* "²in-" + *culpa* "blame, fault"] — **in·cul·pa·tion** \,in-,kəl-'pā-shən\ *n*

in·cum·ben·cy \in-'kəm-bən-sē\ *n, pl* **-cies** **1** : the quality or state of being incumbent **2** : the office or period of office of an incumbent

¹in·cum·bent \-bənt\ *n* : the holder of an office or position [Latin *incumbere* "to lie down on"]

²incumbent *adj* **1** : lying or resting on something else **2** : imposed as a duty : OBLIGATORY

incumber, incumbrance *variant of* ENCUMBER, ENCUMBRANCE

in·cu·nab·u·lum \,in-kyə-'nab-yə-ləm, ,iŋ-\ *n, pl* **-la** \-lə\ : a book printed before 1501; *also* : a work of art or industry of an early period [New Latin, from Latin *incunabula* "swaddling clothes, cradle", from *in-* + *cunae* "cradle"]

in·cur \in-'kər\ *vt* **in·curred; in·cur·ring** : to become liable or subject to : bring down upon oneself 〈*incur* punishment〉 〈*incur* expenses〉 [Latin *incurrere*, literally, "to run into", from *in-* + *currere* "to run"] — **in·cur·rence** \in-'kər-əns, -'kə-rəns\ *n*

¹in·cur·able \in-'kyùr-ə-bəl, 'in-\ *adj* : not capable of being cured — **in·cur·abil·i·ty** \in-,kyùr-ə-'bil-ət-ē\ *n* — **in·cur·ably** \-blē\ *adv*

²incurable *n* : a person suffering from a disease that is beyond cure

in·cu·ri·ous \in-'kyùr-ē-əs, 'in-\ *adj* : showing no interest or concern : INDIFFERENT — **in·cu·ri·ous·ly** *adv* — **in·cu·ri·ous·ness** *n*

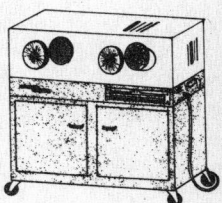

incubator

\ə\ abut	\ng\ sing
\ər\ further	\ō\ bone
\a\ mat	\ȯ\ saw
\ā\ take	\òi\ coin
\ä\ cot, cart	\th\ thin
\aù\ out	\th\ this
\ch\ chin	\ü\ food
\e\ pet	\ù\ foot
\ē\ easy	\y\ yet
\g\ go	\yü\ few
\i\ tip	\yù\ cure
\ī\ life	\zh\ vision
\j\ job	

in·cur·rent \in-'kər-ənt, -'kə-rənt\ *adj* : characterized by a current that flows inward ⟨*incurrent* canals of a sponge⟩

in·cur·sion \in-'kər-zhən\ *n* : a sudden usually temporary invasion : RAID [Latin *incursio*, from *incurrere* "to run into"]

in·cur·vate \'in-,kər-,vāt, in-'\ *vt* : to cause to curve inward : BEND — **in·cur·vate** \'in-,kər-,vāt, in-'kər-vət\ *adj* — **in·cur·va·tion** \,in-,kər-'vā-shən\ *n* — **in·cur·va·ture** \in-'kər-və-,chùr, 'in-, -chər\ *n*

in·curve \in-'kərv, 'in-\ *vb* : to bend so as to curve inward

in·cus \'ing-kəs\ *n, pl* **in·cu·des** \ing-'kyüd-ēz, 'ing-kyə-,dēz\ : the middle of a chain of three small bones in the ear of a mammal — called also *anvil;* compare MALLEUS, STAPES [Latin, "anvil"]

Ind- *or* **Indo-** *combining form* **1** : India or the East Indies **2** : Indo-European

in·debt·ed \in-'det-əd\ *adj* : owing something (as money, gratitude, or recognition)

in·debt·ed·ness *n* **1** : the condition of being indebted **2** : something owed

in·de·cen·cy \in-'dēs-n-sē, 'in-\ *n* **1** : lack of decency **2** : an indecent act or word

in·de·cent \-nt\ *adj* **1** : UNSEEMLY, UNBECOMING ⟨remarried in *indecent* haste⟩ **2** : morally offensive — **in·de·cent·ly** *adv*

in·de·ci·sion \,in-di-'sizh-ən\ *n* : slowness or hesitation in making up one's mind

in·de·ci·sive \-'sī-siv\ *adj* **1** : not decisive ⟨an *indecisive* battle⟩ **2** : characterized by indecision : UNCERTAIN ⟨an *indecisive* person⟩ — **in·de·ci·sive·ly** *adv* — **in·de·ci·sive·ness** *n*

in·de·clin·able \,in-di-'klī-nə-bəl\ *adj* : having no grammatical inflections

in·dec·o·rous \in-'dek-ə-rəs, 'in-; ,in-di-'kōr-əs, -'kòr-\ *adj* : not decorous : UNBECOMING — **in·dec·o·rous·ly** *adv* — **in·dec·o·rous·ness** *n* ☐ SYN IMPROPER, UNSEEMLY, UNBECOMING: INDECOROUS suggests a violation of accepted standards of good manners ⟨talking in church is *indecorous*⟩ IMPROPER applies to a broader range of violation of rules not only of social behavior but also of ethical practice or logical procedure ⟨inferred an *improper* conclusion from the premises⟩ ⟨telling *improper* jokes⟩ UNSEEMLY adds a suggestion of an offensiveness to good taste ⟨they married with *unseemly* haste⟩ UNBECOMING suggests behavior or language that does not suit one's character or status ⟨conduct *unbecoming* an officer⟩

in·de·co·rum \,in-di-'kōr-əm, -'kòr-\ *n* : lack of decorum

in·deed \in-'dēd\ *adv* **1** : without any question : TRULY — often used interjectionally to express disbelief or surprise **2** : in reality **3** : as a matter of fact : all things considered

in·de·fat·i·ga·ble \,in-di-'fat-i-gə-bəl\ *adj* : capable of working a long time without tiring : TIRELESS [Middle French, from Latin *indefatigabilis*, from *in-* + *defatigare* "to fatigue", from *de-* + *fatigare* "to fatigue"] — **in·de·fat·i·ga·bil·i·ty** \-,fat-i-gə-'bil-ət-ē\ *n* — **in·de·fat·i·ga·ble·ness** \-'fat-i-gə-bəl-nəs\ *n* — **in·de·fat·i·ga·bly** \-blē\ *adv*

in·de·fea·si·ble \,in-di-'fē-zə-bəl\ *adj* : not capable of being abolished or annulled ⟨*indefeasible* rights⟩ [*in-* + earlier *defeasible* "capable of being annulled", from Anglo-French *defaisible*, from Old French *deffaire* "to undo, destroy", from Medieval Latin *disfacere*, from Latin *dis-* + *facere* "to do"] — **in·de·fea·si·bil·i·ty** \-,fē-zə-'bil-ət-ē\ *n* — **in·de·fea·si·bly** \-'fē-zə-blē\ *adv*

in·de·fec·ti·ble \,in-di-'fek-tə-bəl\ *adj* **1** : not subject to failure or decay : LASTING **2** : free of faults : FLAWLESS — **in·de·fec·ti·bil·i·ty** \-,fek-tə-'bil-ət-ē\ *n* — **in·de·fec·ti·bly** \-'fek-tə-blē\ *adv*

in·de·fen·si·ble \,in-di-'fen-sə-bəl\ *adj* : not capable of being defended or justified ⟨an *indefensible* position⟩ — **in·de·fen·si·bil·i·ty** \-,fen-sə-'bil-ət-ē\ *n* — **in·de·fen·si·bly** \-'fen-sə-blē\ *adv*

in·de·fin·able \,in-di-'fī-nə-bəl\ *adj* : incapable of being precisely described or analyzed — **in·de·fin·abil·i·ty** \-,fī-nə-'bil-ət-ē\ *n* — **in·de·fin·able·ness** \-'fī-nə-bəl-nəs\ *n* — **in·de·fin·ably** \-blē\ *adv*

in·def·i·nite \in-'def-nət, 'in-, -ə-nət\ *adj* **1** : typically designating an unidentified or not immediately identifiable person or thing ⟨the *indefinite* articles *a* and *an*⟩ **2** : not precise in meaning or details : VAGUE ⟨an *indefinite* answer⟩ **3** : not fixed or limited (as in amount or length) ⟨an *indefinite* period⟩ — **in·def·i·nite·ly** *adv* — **in·def·i·nite·ness** *n*

in·de·his·cent \,in-di-'his-nt\ *adj* : remaining closed at maturity ⟨*indehiscent* fruits⟩ — **in·de·his·cence** \-ns\ *n*

in·del·i·ble \in-'del-ə-bəl\ *adj* **1** : not capable of being erased, removed, or blotted out ⟨an *indelible* impression⟩ **2** : making marks not easily erased ⟨an *indelible* pencil⟩ [Latin *indelebilis*, from *in-* + *delēre* "to delete"] — **in·del·i·bil·i·ty** \in-,del-ə-'bil-ət-ē\ *n* — **in·del·i·bly** \in-'del-ə-blē\ *adv*

in·del·i·ca·cy \in-'del-i-kə-sē, 'in-\ *n* **1** : the quality or state of being indelicate **2** : something that is indelicate

in·del·i·cate \-kət\ *adj* : offensive to good manners or taste : IMMODEST, COARSE — **in·del·i·cate·ly** *adv* — **in·del·i·cate·ness** *n*

in·dem·ni·fy \in-'dem-nə-,fī\ *vt* **-fied; -fy·ing 1** : to insure or protect against loss, damage, or injury **2** : to compensate for loss, damage, or injury ⟨*indemnify* victims of a disaster⟩ **3** : to make compensation for : make good ⟨have their losses *indemnified*⟩ [Latin *indemnis* "unharmed", from *in-* + *damnum* "damage"] — **in·dem·ni·fi·ca·tion** \-,dem-nə-fə-'kā-shən\ *n* — **in·dem·ni·fi·er** \-'dem-nə-,fī-ər, -,fīr\ *n*

in·dem·ni·ty \in-'dem-nət-ē\ *n, pl* **-ties 1** : protection from loss, damage, or injury : INSURANCE **2** : freedom from penalty for past offenses **3** : compensation for loss, damage, or injury

¹in·dent \in-'dent\ *vt* **1 a** : to notch the edge of : make jagged **b** : to cut into for the purpose of mortising or dovetailing **2** : to set in from the margin ⟨*indent* the first line of a paragraph⟩ [Middle French *endenter*, from *en-* + *dent* "tooth", from Latin *dent-, dens*] — **in·dent·er** *n*

²indent *vt* **1** : to force inward so as to form a depression **2** : to form a dent in — **in·dent·er** *n*

³indent *n* **1** : INDENTATION 1b **2** : DENT 1

in·den·ta·tion \,in-,den-'tā-shən\ *n* **1 a** : an angular cut in an edge **b** : a recess in a surface **2 a** : the action of indenting : the state of being indented **b** : INDENTION 2 **3** : DENT 1

in·den·tion \in-'den-chən\ *n* **1** : INDENTATION 2a **2** : the space left by indentation

¹in·den·ture \in-'den-chər\ *n* **1** : a written agreement : CONTRACT **2** : a contract that binds a person to serve another for a specified period — usually used in pl. [Middle French *endenture* "document carrying two or more copies and divided by an irregular notched cut so that the sections might be proved to belong to the same document by matching the divided edges", from *endenter* "to indent, notch"]

²indenture *vt* : to bind (as an apprentice) by indentures

in·de·pen·dence \,in-də-'pen-dəns\ *n* : the quality or state of being independent : freedom from outside control

Independence Day *n* : July 4 observed as a legal holiday in commemoration of the adoption of the Declaration of Independence in 1776

in·de·pen·den·cy \,in-də-'pen-dən-sē\ *n* : FREEDOM 1b, INDEPENDENCE

¹in·de·pen·dent \,in-də-'pen-dənt\ *adj* **1** : not subject to control or rule by another : SELF-GOVERNING, FREE ⟨an *independent* nation⟩ **2** : not having connections with another : SEPARATE ⟨*independent* conclusions⟩ **3** : not supported by or relying on another : having or providing enough money to live on ⟨a person of *independent* means⟩ **4** : not easily influenced : showing self-reliance ⟨an *independent* person⟩ **5** : having full meaning in itself and capable of standing alone as a simple sentence : MAIN ⟨an *independent* clause⟩ **6** : not committed to a political party **7** : having probabilities such that the occurrence or nonoccurrence of one event does not influence the outcome of another ⟨the outcomes of the tossing of two dice are *independent*⟩ SYN see FREE — **in·de·pend·ent·ly** *adv*

²independent *n* : one that is independent; *esp, often cap* : one not committed to a political party

independent assortment *n* : formation of random combinations of chromosomes and genes in meiosis with one of each pair of homologous chromosomes passing into each gamete independently of each other pair

in·de·scrib·able \,in-di-'skrī-bə-bəl\ *adj* : incapable of being described : being beyond description ⟨*indescribable* beauty⟩ — **in·de·scrib·able·ness** *n* — **in·de·scrib·ably** \-bə-blē\ *adv*

in·de·struc·ti·ble \,in-di-'strək-tə-bəl\ *adj* : impossible to destroy — **in·de·struc·ti·bil·i·ty** \-,strək-tə-bil-ət-ē\ *n*

in·de·ter·min·able \,in-di-'tərm-nə-bəl, -ə-nə-\ *adj* : incapable of being definitely decided or ascertained — **in·de·ter·min·able·ness** *n* — **in·de·ter·min·ably** \-blē\ *adv*

in·de·ter·mi·nate \,in-di-'tərm-nət, -ə-nət\ *adj* **1 a** : not definitely or precisely determined : VAGUE ⟨*indeterminate* plans⟩ **b** : not leading to a definite end or result **2** : having the capacity for growing in length indefinitely; *esp* : having or being an inflorescence in which the main stem continues to grow without forming a terminal flower and the lower flowers on the stem bloom first — **in·de·ter·mi·na·cy** \-nə-sē\ *n* — **in·de·ter·mi·nate·ly** *adv* — **in·de·ter·mi·nate·ness** *n*

in·de·ter·mi·na·tion \-,tər-mə-'nā-shən\ *n* : a state of mental indecision

¹in·dex \'in-,deks\ *n, pl* **in·dex·es** *or* **in·di·ces** \-də-,sēz\ **1** : a guide (as a table or file) for facilitating reference; *esp* : an alphabetical list of items treated in a printed work that gives with each item the page number where it may be found **2** : POINTER, INDICATOR ⟨the *index* on a scale⟩ **3** : SIGN, INDICATION ⟨an *index* of your mood⟩ **4** *pl usually* **indices** : a mathematical figure, letter, or expression associated with another to indicate a mathematical operation to be performed or to indicate use or position in an arrangement ⟨2 is the *index* in $\sqrt[2]{5}$ to specify a square root of 5⟩ **5** : a character ☞ used to direct attention — called also *fist* **6** : a number derived from a series of observations and used as an indicator or measure; *esp* : INDEX NUMBER [Latin *indic-, index,* from *indicare* "to indicate"] — **in·dex·i·cal** \in-'dek-si-kəl\ *adj*

²index *vt* **1 a** : to provide with an index **b** : to list in an index **2** : to serve as an index of — **in·dex·er** *n*

index finger *n* : the finger next to the thumb

index fossil *n* : a fossil that is found over a relatively short span of geological time and can be used in dating formations in which it is found

index number *n* : a number used to indicate change in magnitude (as of cost or price) as compared with the magnitude at some specified time usually taken as 100

index of refraction : the ratio of the speed of light in the first of two media to its speed in the second as it passes from one into the other

in·dia ink \,in-dē-ə-\ *n, often cap 1st I* **1** : a solid black pigment (as lampblack) used in drawing and lettering **2** : a fluid consisting of a fine suspension of india ink in a liquid

In·dia·man \'in-dē-ə-mən\ *n* : a large sailing ship formerly used in trade with India

In·di·an \'in-dē-ən\ *n* **1** : a native or inhabitant of the subcontinent of India or the East Indies **2 a** : AMERICAN INDIAN **b** : one of the native languages of American Indians [sense 2 from Columbus's belief that the lands he discovered were part of Asia] — **Indian** *adj*

Indian club *n* : a wooden club that resembles a tenpin and is swung for exercise

Indian corn *n* **1** : a tall widely cultivated American cereal grass bearing seeds on elongated ears **2** : the ears of Indian corn; *also* : its edible seeds

Indian giver *n* : one that gives something to another and then takes it back or expects an equivalent in return — **Indian giving** *n*

Indian meal *n* : CORNMEAL

Indian paintbrush *n* **1** : any of a large genus of American and northeast Asian herbs that have dense spikes of hooded flowers with brightly colored bracts **2** : ORANGE HAWKWEED

Indian pipe *n* : a waxy white leafless saprophytic herb with a solitary nodding bell-shaped flower

Indian pudding *n* : a pudding made chiefly of cornmeal, milk, and molasses

Indian summer *n* : a period of mild weather in late autumn or early winter

Indian tobacco *n* : any of several plants resembling or used in place of tobacco; *esp* : an American wild lobelia with small blue flowers

Indian wrestling *n* : any of various contests of strength or of strength and balance in which two individuals try to overcome each other using only one arm or one leg; *esp* : ARM WRESTLING

India paper *n* : a thin tough opaque printing paper

india rubber *n, often cap I* : RUBBER 2a

In·dic \'in-dik\ *adj* **1** : of or relating to the subcontinent of India : INDIAN **2** : of, relating to, or constituting the Indian branch of the Indo-European languages — **Indic** *n*

in·di·cate \'in-də-,kāt\ *vt* **1 a** : to point out or point to **b** : to be a sign, symptom, or index of **2** : to state or express briefly : SUGGEST [Latin *indicare,* from *in-* + *dicare* "to proclaim"]

in·di·ca·tion \,in-də-'kā-shən\ *n* **1** : the action of indicating **2** : something that indicates : SIGN **3** : the degree or amount indicated on a graduated instrument

¹in·dic·a·tive \in-'dik-ət-iv\ *adj* **1** : of, relating to, or constituting the grammatical mood that represents the denoted act or state as an objective fact **2** : indicating something not visible or obvious : SUGGESTIVE ⟨remarks *indicative* of anger⟩ — **in·dic·a·tive·ly** *adv*

²indicative *n* : the indicative mood of a verb or a verb in this mood

in·di·ca·tor \'in-də-,kāt-ər\ *n* **1** : one that indicates: as **a** : a pointer on an instrument (as a dial) **b** : a pressure gauge **2** : a substance used to show visually (as by change of color) the condition of a solution with respect to the presence of free acid, alkali, or other substance — **in·dic·a·to·ry** \in-'dik-ə-,tōr-ē, -,tor-\ *adj*

indices *pl of* INDEX

in·di·cia \in-'dish-ə, -'dish-ē-ə\ *n pl* **1** : distinctive marks : INDICATIONS **2** : postal markings often imprinted on mail or on labels to be affixed to mail [Latin, pl. of *indicium* "sign", from *indicare* "to indicate"]

in·dict \in-'dīt\ *vt* : ACCUSE; *esp* : to charge with a crime by the finding of a grand jury [Anglo-French *enditer,* from Old French, "to write down, indite"] — **in·dict·able** \-ə-bəl\ *adj* — **in·dict·er** *n*

in·dict·ment \in-'dīt-mənt\ *n* **1** : the act or process of indicting **2** : a formal statement charging a person with an offense that is drawn up by a prosecuting attorney and reported by a grand jury after an inquiry

in·dif·fer·ence \in-'dif-ərns, -'dif-rəns, -'dif-ə-rəns\ *n* **1** : lack of feeling for or against something **2** : lack of importance ⟨a matter of *indifference* to them⟩ □ SYN

\ə\ abut	\ng\ sing	
\ər\ further	\ō\ bone	
\a\ mat	\o\ saw	
\ā\ take	\oi\ coin	
\ä\ cot, cart	\th\ thin	
\au\ out	\th\ this	
\ch\ chin	\ü\ food	
\e\ pet	\u\ foot	
\ē\ easy	\y\ yet	
\g\ go	\yü\ few	
\i\ tip	\yu\ cure	
\ī\ life	\zh\ vision	
\j\ job		

UNCONCERN: INDIFFERENCE implies neutrality of feeling from lack of inclination, preference, or prejudice; UNCONCERN suggests a lack of sensitivity or regard for others' needs or troubles.

in·dif·fer·ent \in-'dif-ərnt, -'dif-rənt, -'dif-ə-rənt\ *adj* **1** : having no preference : not interested or concerned ⟨*indifferent* to the troubles of others⟩ **2** : showing neither liking nor dislike ⟨an *indifferent* audience⟩ **3** : neither good nor bad : MEDIOCRE ⟨*indifferent* health⟩ **4** : of no special influence or value : UNIMPORTANT **5** : capable of development in more than one direction — **in·dif·fer·ent·ly** *adv*

in·di·gence \'in-di-jəns\ *n* : POVERTY 1, NEEDINESS

in·dig·e·nous \in-'dij-ə-nəs\ *adj* : originating in or produced, growing, or living naturally in a particular region or environment [Late Latin *indigenus,* from Latin *indigena,* n., "native", derived from *gignere* "to beget"] SYN see NATIVE — **in·dig·e·nous·ly** *adv* — **in·dig·e·nous·ness** *n*

in·di·gent \'in-di-jənt\ *adj* : POOR 1, NEEDY [Middle French, from Latin *indigēre* "to need"]

in·di·gest·ible \,in-dī-'jes-tə-bəl, -də-\ *adj* : not digestible : hard to digest — **in·di·gest·ibil·i·ty** \-,jes-tə-'bil-ət-ē\ *n*

in·di·ges·tion \-'jes-chən\ *n* **1** : inability to digest or difficulty in digesting something **2** : a case or attack of indigestion — **in·di·ges·tive** \-'jes-tiv\ *adj*

in·dig·nant \in-'dig-nənt\ *adj* : filled with or marked by indignation [Latin *indignari* "to be indignant", from *indignus* "unworthy", from *in-* + *dignus* "worthy"] — **in·dig·nant·ly** *adv*

in·dig·na·tion \,in-dig-'nā-shən\ *n* : anger aroused by something unjust, unworthy, or mean

in·dig·ni·ty \in-'dig-nət-ē\ *n, pl* **-ties** **1** : an act that offends against a person's dignity or self-respect : INSULT **2** : humiliating treatment SYN see AFFRONT

in·di·go \'in-di-,gō\ *n, pl* **-gos** *or* **-goes** **1** : a blue dye made artificially and formerly obtained from indigo plants **2** : a dark grayish blue [Italian dialect, from Latin *indicum,* from Greek *indikon,* from *indikos* "Indian", from *Indos* "India"]

indigo plant *n* : any of various mostly leguminous plants that yield indigo

indigo snake *n* : a large harmless blue-black snake of the southern United States

in·di·rect \,in-də-'rekt, -dī-\ *adj* **1** : not straight : not the shortest ⟨an *indirect* route⟩ **2** : not straightforward : ROUNDABOUT ⟨*indirect* methods⟩ **3** : not having a plainly seen connection ⟨an *indirect* cause⟩ **4** : not straight to the point ⟨an *indirect* answer⟩ **5** : stating what an original speaker said with changes in wording that adapt the statement grammatically to the rest of the sentence ⟨*they would come* in "they said that they would come" is in *indirect* discourse⟩ — **in·di·rect·ly** *adv* — **in·di·rect·ness** \-'rekt-nəs, -'rek-\ *n*

in·di·rec·tion \-'rek-shən\ *n* **1** : lack of straightforwardness and openness : DECEITFULNESS **2** : lack of direction : AIMLESSNESS

indirect lighting *n* : lighting in which the light emitted by a source is diffusely reflected (as by the ceiling)

indirect object *n* : a grammatical object representing the secondary goal of the action of its verb ⟨*me* in "gave me the book" is an *indirect object*⟩

indirect tax *n* : a tax exacted from a person other than the one on whom the ultimate burden of the tax is expected to fall

in·dis·cern·ible \,in-dis-'ər-nə-bəl, -diz-\ *adj* : incapable of being discerned

in·dis·creet \,in-dis-'krēt\ *adj* : not discreet : IMPRUDENT — **in·dis·creet·ly** *adv* — **in·dis·creet·ness** *n*

in·dis·crete \,in-dis-'krēt; in-'dis-,, 'in-\ *adj* : not separated into distinct parts ⟨an *indiscrete* mass⟩

in·dis·cre·tion \,in-dis-'kresh-ən\ *n* **1** : lack of discretion : IMPRUDENCE **2** : an indiscreet act or remark

in·dis·crim·i·nate \,in-dis-'krim-nət, -ə-nət\ *adj* : showing lack of discrimination : not making careful distinctions ⟨an *indiscriminate* reader⟩ ⟨*indiscriminate* criticism⟩ — **in·dis·crim·i·nate·ly** *adv* — **in·dis·crim·i·nate·ness** *n*

in·dis·crim·i·na·tion \-,krim-ə-'nā-shən\ *n* : lack of discrimination

in·dis·pens·able \,in-dis-'pen-sə-bəl\ *adj* : absolutely necessary ⟨an *indispensable* employee⟩ — **in·dis·pens·abil·i·ty** \-,pen-sə-'bil-ət-ē\ *n* — **indispensable** *n* — **in·dis·pens·able·ness** \-'pen-sə-bəl-nəs\ *n* — **in·dis·pens·ably** \-blē\ *adv*

in·dis·pose \,in-dis-'pōz\ *vt* **1** : to make unfit : DISQUALIFY **2** : to make averse : DISINCLINE

in·dis·posed \-'pōzd\ *adj* **1** : slightly ill **2** : UNWILLING, AVERSE

in·dis·po·si·tion \,in-,dis-pə-'zish-ən\ *n* **1** : a slight illness **2** : AVERSION 1, RELUCTANCE

in·dis·put·able \,in-dis-'pyüt-ə-bəl; in-'dis-pyət-, 'in-\ *adj* : not disputable : UNQUESTIONABLE ⟨*indisputable* proof⟩ — **in·dis·put·able·ness** *n* — **in·dis·put·ably** \-blē\ *adv*

in·dis·sol·u·ble \,in-dis-'äl-yə-bəl\ *adj* : not capable of being dissolved, undone, broken up, or decomposed ⟨an *indissoluble* contract⟩ — **in·dis·sol·u·bil·i·ty** \-,äl-yə-'bil-ət-ē\ *n* — **in·dis·sol·u·ble·ness** \-'äl-yə-bəl-nəs\ *n* — **in·dis·sol·u·bly** \-blē\ *adv*

in·dis·tinct \,in-dis-'tingt, -'tingkt\ *adj* : not distinct: as **a** : BLURRED ⟨*indistinct* figures in the fog⟩ **b** : FAINT 4, DIM **c** : not clearly recognizable or understandable : UNCERTAIN — **in·dis·tinct·ly** *adv* — **in·dis·tinct·ness** *n*

in·dis·tinc·tive \-'ting-tiv, -'tingk-\ *adj* : lacking distinctive qualities

in·dis·tin·guish·able \,in-dis-'ting-gwish-ə-bəl\ *adj* : not capable of being clearly distinguished — **in·dis·tin·guish·able·ness** *n* — **in·dis·tin·guish·ably** \-blē\ *adv*

in·dite \in-'dīt\ *vt* **1** : MAKE UP, COMPOSE ⟨*indite* a poem⟩ **2** : to put down in writing ⟨*indite* a message⟩ [Old French *enditer* "to write down, proclaim", from Latin *indictus,* past participle of *indicere* "to proclaim", from *in-* + *dicere* "to say"] — **in·dit·er** *n*

in·di·um \'in-dē-əm\ *n* : a malleable fusible silvery metallic chemical element — see ELEMENT table [New Latin, from Latin *indicum* "indigo"; from the indigo lines in its spectrum]

¹in·di·vid·u·al \,in-də-'vij-ə-wəl, -'vij-əl\ *adj* **1 a** : of or relating to an individual ⟨*individual* traits⟩ **b** : intended for one person ⟨*individual* servings⟩ **2** : PARTICULAR, SEPARATE ⟨*individual* copies⟩ **3** : having marked individuality ⟨an *individual* style⟩ [Medieval Latin *individualis* "inseparable, individual", from Latin *individuus* "indivisible", from *in-* + *dividere* "to divide"] SYN see CHARACTERISTIC — **in·di·vid·u·al·ly** \-ē\ *adv*

²individual *n* **1** : a particular being or thing as distinguished from a class, species, or collection **2** : a particular person ⟨an odd *individual*⟩

in·di·vid·u·al·ism \-'vij-ə-wə-,liz-əm, -'vij-ə-,liz-\ *n* **1** : a doctrine that the interests of the individual are primary **2** : a doctrine that the individual has certain political or economic rights with which the state must not interfere **3** : INDIVIDUALITY 1

in·di·vid·u·al·ist \-ləst\ *n* **1** : a person showing marked individuality or independence in thought or behavior **2** : a supporter of individualism — **in·di·vid·u·al·is·tic** \-,vij-ə-wə-'lis-tik, -,vij-ə-'lis-\ *adj* — **in·di·vid·u·al·is·ti·cal·ly** \-ti-kə-lē, -klē\ *adv*

in·di·vid·u·al·i·ty \,in-də-,vij-ə-'wal-ət-ē\ *n, pl* **-ties** **1** : the qualities that distinguish one person or thing from all others **2** : the condition of having separate existence

in·di·vid·u·al·ize \-'vij-ə-wə-,līz, -'vij-ə-,līz\ *vt* **1** : to make individual in character **2** : to treat or notice individually **3** : to adapt to the needs of an individual —

in·di·vid·u·al·iza·tion \-,vij-ə-wə-lə-'zā-shən, -,vij-ə-lə-\ *n*

in·di·vis·i·ble \,in-də-'viz-ə-bəl\ *adj* : not capable of being divided or separated — **in·di·vis·i·bil·i·ty** \-,viz-ə-'bil-ət-ē\ *n* — **in·di·vis·i·ble·ness** \-'viz-ə-bəl-nəs\ *n* — **in·di·vis·i·bly** \-blē\ *adv*

Indo- — see IND-

In·do–Ar·y·an \,in-dō-'ar-ē-ən, -'er-; -'är-yən\ *n* **1** : a member of one of the peoples of India of Aryan speech and physique **2** : one of the early Indo-European invaders of Persia, Afghanistan, and India — **Indo–Aryan** *adj*

in·doc·ile \in-'däs-əl, 'in-\ *adj* : unwilling to be taught or disciplined : INTRACTABLE — **in·do·cil·i·ty** \,in-dä-'sil-ət-ē, -dō-\ *n*

in·doc·tri·nate \in-'däk-trə-,nāt\ *vt* **1** : to instruct especially in fundamentals **2** : to teach the beliefs or doctrines of a particular group — **in·doc·tri·na·tion** \in-,däk-trə-'nā-shən\ *n* — **in·doc·tri·na·tor** \in-'däk-trə-,nāt-ər\ *n*

¹In·do–Eu·ro·pe·an \,in-dō-,yur-ə-'pē-ən\ *adj* : of, relating to, or constituting a family of languages comprising those spoken in most of Europe and in the parts of the world colonized by Europeans since 1500 and also in some parts of Asia (as Iran and the subcontinent of India)

²Indo–European *n* **1** : the Indo-European languages **2** : a member of a people whose original tongue is one of the Indo-European languages

in·dole·ace·tic acid \,in-,dōl-ə-,sēt-ik-\ *n* : a crystalline plant hormone that promotes growth and rooting of plants [*indole*, a crystalline compound, derived from Latin *indicum* "indigo"]

in·dole·bu·tyr·ic acid \-byü-,tir-ik-\ *n* : a crystalline acid similar to indoleacetic acid in its effects on plants

in·do·lent \'in-də-lənt\ *adj* **1** : slow to develop or heal **2** : averse to exertion : LAZY ⟨felt *indolent* every spring⟩ [Late Latin *indolens* "insensitive to pain", from Latin *in-* + *dolēre* "to feel pain"] — **in·do·lence** \-ləns\ *n* — **in·do·lent·ly** *adv*

in·dom·i·ta·ble \in-'däm-ət-ə-bəl\ *adj* : incapable of being subdued : UNCONQUERABLE [Late Latin *indomitabilis*, from Latin *in-* + *domitare* "to tame, daunt"] — **in·dom·i·ta·bil·i·ty** \-,däm-ət-ə-'bil-ət-ē\ *n* — **in·dom·i·ta·ble·ness** \-'däm-ət-ə-bəl-nəs\ *n* — **in·dom·i·ta·bly** \-blē\ *adv* □ **SYN INVINCIBLE**: INDOMITABLE stresses courage or determination that cannot be overcome or subdued; INVINCIBLE more often applies to a person and implies having strength and ability superior to all enemies.

In·do·ne·sian \,in-də-'nē-zhən, -shən\ *n* **1** : a native or inhabitant of the Malay archipelago **2 a** : a native or inhabitant of the Republic of Indonesia **b** : the language based on Malay that is the national language of the Republic of Indonesia — **Indonesian** *adj*

in·door \'in-,dōr, -,dȯr\ *adj* **1** : of or relating to the interior of a building **2** : done, living, or belonging within a building

in·doors \in-'dōrz, 'in-, -'dȯrz\ *adv* : in or into a building

indorse, indorsement *variant of* ENDORSE, ENDORSEMENT

in·du·bi·ta·ble \in-'dü-bət-ə-bəl, 'in-, -'dyü-\ *adj* : too evident to be doubted : UNQUESTIONABLE — **in·du·bi·ta·ble·ness** *n* — **in·du·bi·ta·bly** \-blē\ *adv*

in·duce \in-'düs, -'dyüs\ *vt* **1** : to lead on to do something : PERSUADE **2** : BRING ABOUT, CAUSE ⟨an illness *induced* by overwork⟩ **3** : to conclude or infer by reasoning from particular instances **4** : to produce (as an electric current) by induction [Latin *inducere*, from *in-* + *ducere* "to lead"] — **in·duc·er** *n* — **in·duc·ible** \-'dü-sə-bəl, -'dyü-\ *adj*

in·duce·ment \in-'düs-mənt, -'dyüs-\ *n* **1** : the act of inducing **2** : something that induces ⟨advertising gimmicks that are mere *inducements* to buy⟩

in·duct \in-'dəkt\ *vt* **1** : to place formally in office : INSTALL **2** : to enroll into military service [Latin *inductus*, past participle of *inducere* "to lead in, induce"] — **in·duct·ee** \in-,dək-'tē\ *n*

in·duc·tance \in-'dək-təns\ *n* : a property of an electric circuit by which an electromotive force is induced in it by a variation of current either in the circuit itself or in a neighboring circuit

in·duc·tion \in-'dək-shən\ *n* **1 a** : the act or process of inducting (as into office) **b** : an initial experience : INITIATION **c** : the procedure by which a civilian is inducted into military service **2 a** : reasoning from particular instances to a general conclusion; *also* : the conclusion so reached **b** : mathematical demonstration of the validity of a law concerning all the positive integers by proving that it holds for the integer 1 and that if it holds for all the integers preceding a given integer it must hold for the next following integer **3 a** : the act of causing or bringing on or about **b** : the process by which an electrical conductor becomes electrified when near a charged body, by which a body becomes magnetized when in a magnetic field or in the flux set up by a magnetizing force, or by which an electromotive force is produced in a circuit by varying the magnetic field linked with the circuit **c** : the way in which one embryonic tissue or structure influences the development and differentiation of another

induction coil *n* : an apparatus for obtaining intermittent high voltage consisting of a primary coil through which the direct current flows, an interrupter, and a secondary coil of a larger number of turns in which the high voltage is induced

induction heating *n* : the heating of material by means of an electric current that is caused to flow through the material or its container by electromagnetic induction

in·duc·tive \in-'dək-tiv\ *adj* : relating to, employing, or based on induction — **in·duc·tive·ly** *adv* — **in·duc·tive·ness** *n*

in·duc·tor \in-'dək-tər\ *n* **1** : one that inducts **2** : a part of an electrical apparatus that acts upon another or is itself acted upon by induction **3** : ORGANIZER 2

indue *variant of* ENDUE

in·dulge \in-'dəlj\ *vb* **1** : to be tolerant toward : HUMOR ⟨*indulge* a child⟩ **2** : to allow oneself to use, do, or have ⟨refused to *indulge* in liquor⟩ [Latin *indulgēre*] — **in·dulg·er** *n*

in·dul·gence \in-'dəl-jəns\ *n* **1** : a release from punishment in this world or in purgatory gained by performing pious acts authorized by the Roman Catholic Church **2 a** : the act of indulging : the state of being indulgent **b** : an indulgent act **c** : something indulged in

in·dul·gent \-jənt\ *adj* : disinclined to be severe or rigorous : LENIENT — **in·dul·gent·ly** *adv*

in·dult \'in-,dəlt, in-'\ *n* : a special often temporary privilege granted in the Roman Catholic Church [Medieval Latin *indultum*, from Latin *indultus*, past participle of *indulgēre* "to indulge"]

¹in·du·rate \'in-də-rət, -dyə-; in-'dur-ət, -'dyur-\ *adj* : physically or morally hardened

²in·du·rate \'in-də-,rāt, -dyə-\ *vb* **1** : to make unfeeling, stubborn, or obdurate **2** : to make hardy : INURE **3** : to make fibrous or hard ⟨great heat *indurates* clay⟩ ⟨*indurated* tissue⟩ **4** : to grow hard : HARDEN [Latin *indurare*, from *in-* + *durare* "to harden", from *durus* "hard"] — **in·du·ra·tion** \,in-də-'rā-shən, -dyə-\ *n* — **in·du·ra·tive** \'in-də-,rāt-iv, -dyə-; in-'dur-ət-, -'dyur-\ *adj*

in·dus·tri·al \in-'dəs-trē-əl\ *adj* **1** : of, relating to, or engaged in industry **2** : characterized by highly developed industries ⟨an *industrial* nation⟩ **3** : derived from human industry **4** : used in industry ⟨*industrial* diamonds⟩ — **in·dus·tri·al·ly** \-trē-ə-lē\ *adv*

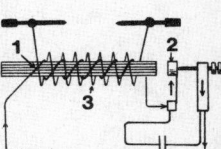

induction coil: *1* primary coil, *2* interrupter, *3* secondary coil

\ə\ abut	\ng\ sing
\ər\ further	\ō\ bone
\a\ mat	\ȯ\ saw
\ā\ take	\ȯi\ coin
\ä\ cot, cart	\th\ thin
\au̇\ out	\th\ this
\ch\ chin	\ü\ food
\e\ pet	\u̇\ foot
\ē\ easy	\y\ yet
\g\ go	\yü\ few
\i\ tip	\yu̇\ cure
\ī\ life	\zh\ vision
\j\ job	

industrial arts *n sing or pl* : a subject taught in elementary and secondary schools that aims at developing manual skill and familiarity with tools and machines

in·dus·tri·al·ism \in-'dəs-trē-ə-,liz-əm\ *n* : social organization in which large-scale industries are dominant

in·dus·tri·al·ist \-ləst\ *n* : one owning or engaged in the management of an industry : MANUFACTURER

in·dus·tri·al·ize \in-'dəs-trē-ə-,līz\ *vb* : to make or become industrial ⟨*industrialize* an agricultural region⟩ — **in·dus·tri·al·iza·tion** \-,dəs-trē-ə-lə-'zā-shən\ *n*

industrial revolution *n* : a rapid major change in an economy (as in England in the late 18th century) marked by the general introduction of power-driven machinery or by an important change in the prevailing types and methods of use of such machines

industrial school *n* : a school specializing in the teaching of the industrial arts

industrial union *n* : a labor union that admits to membership workers in an industry irrespective of their occupation or craft — compare TRADE UNION

in·dus·tri·ous \in-'dəs-trē-əs\ *adj* : constantly, regularly, or habitually occupied : DILIGENT — **in·dus·tri·ous·ly** *adv* — **in·dus·tri·ous·ness** *n*

in·dus·try \'in-dəs-trē, -,dəs-\ *n, pl* **-tries** **1** : diligence in an employment or pursuit **2 a** : systematic labor ⟨live by one's own *industry*⟩ **b** : a department or branch of a craft or art or of business or manufacturing; *esp* : one that employs a large number of persons and considerable capital usually in manufacturing **c** : a distinct group of productive or profit-making enterprises ⟨the steel *industry*⟩ ⟨the tourist *industry*⟩ **d** : manufacturing activity as a whole ⟨commerce and *industry*⟩ [Middle French *industrie* "skill", from Latin *industria* "diligence"] SYN see BUSINESS

¹-ine \,īn, ən, in, ,in, ēn\ *adj suffix* **1** : of or relating to ⟨alkal*ine*⟩ **2** : made of : like ⟨opal*ine*⟩ [sense 1 from Latin *-īnus*; sense 2 from Latin *-inus,* from Greek *-inos*]

²-ine \,ēn, 'ēn, ən, in, ,in\ *n suffix* **1** : chemical substance: as **a** : halogen element ⟨chlor*ine*⟩ **b** : basic or base-containing carbon compound that contains nitrogen ⟨cyst*ine*⟩ **c** : mixture of compounds (as of hydrocarbons) ⟨gasol*ine*⟩ **d** : hydride ⟨ars*ine*⟩ **2** : neutral chemical compound [Latin *-ina,* from *-inus,* adj. suffix]

ine·bri·ate \in-'ē-brē-,āt\ *vt* : to make drunk : INTOXICATE [Latin *inebriare,* from *in-* + *ebrius* "drunk"] — **ine·bri·ate** \-brē-ət\ *adj or n* — **ine·bri·a·tion** \in-,ē-brē-'ā-shən\ *n*

ine·bri·at·ed *adj* : exhilarated or confused by or as if by alcohol : INTOXICATED

in·e·bri·e·ty \,in-i-'brī-ət-ē\ *n* : the state of being inebriated : DRUNKENNESS

in·ed·i·ble \in-'ed-ə-bəl, 'in-\ *adj* : not fit or safe for food ⟨*inedible* mushrooms⟩

in·ef·fa·ble \-'ef-ə-bəl\ *adj* : INEXPRESSIBLE, UNUTTERABLE ⟨*ineffable* bliss⟩ [Middle French, from Latin *ineffabilis,* from *in-* + *effari* "to utter", from *ex-* + *fari* "to speak"] — **in·ef·fa·bil·i·ty** \in-,ef-ə-'bil-ət-ē\ *n* — **in·ef·fa·ble·ness** \in-'ef-ə-bəl-nəs, 'in-\ *n* — **in·ef·fa·bly** \-blē\ *adv*

in·ef·fec·tive \,in-ə-'fek-tiv\ *adj* **1** : not effective : INEFFECTUAL ⟨an *ineffective* law⟩ **2** : not efficient : INCAPABLE ⟨an *ineffective* leader⟩ — **in·ef·fec·tive·ly** *adv* — **in·ef·fec·tive·ness** *n*

in·ef·fec·tu·al \,in-ə-'fek-chə-wəl, -'fek-chəl, -'feksh-wəl\ *adj* : not producing the proper or usual effect : FUTILE — **in·ef·fec·tu·al·ly** \-ē\ *adv* — **in·ef·fec·tu·al·ness** *n*

in·ef·fi·ca·cious \,in-,ef-ə-'kā-shəs\ *adj* : lacking the power to produce a desired effect : INADEQUATE — **in·ef·fi·ca·cious·ly** *adv* — **in·ef·fi·ca·cious·ness** *n* — **in·ef·fi·ca·cy** \-'ef-ə-kə-sē\ *n*

in·ef·fi·cient \,in-ə-'fish-ənt\ *adj* **1** : not producing the intended or desired effect : INEFFICACIOUS **2** : INCAPA-

BLE b, INCOMPETENT ⟨*inefficient* management⟩ — **in·ef·fi·cien·cy** \-'fish-ən-sē\ *n* — **in·ef·fi·cient·ly** *adv*

in·elas·tic \,in-ə-'las-tik\ *adj* **1** : not elastic **2** : slow to respond to changing conditions — **in·elas·tic·i·ty** \,in-i-,las-'tis-ət-ē\ *n*

in·el·e·gance \in-'el-i-gəns, 'in-\ *n* : lack of elegance

in·el·e·gant \in-'el-i-gənt, 'in-\ *adj* : lacking in refinement, grace, or good taste — **in·el·e·gant·ly** *adv*

in·el·i·gi·ble \in-'el-ə-jə-bəl, 'in-\ *adj* : not qualified or worthy to be chosen — **in·el·i·gi·bil·i·ty** \,in-,el-ə-jə-'bil-ət-ē\ *n* — **ineligible** *n*

in·eluc·ta·ble \,in-i-'lək-tə-bəl\ *adj* : not to be avoided, changed, or resisted : INEVITABLE [Latin *ineluctabilis,* from *in-* + *eluctari* "to struggle out", from *ex-* + *luctari* "to struggle"] — **in·eluc·ta·bil·i·ty** \-,lək-tə-'bil-ət-ē\ *n* — **in·eluc·ta·bly** \-'lək-tə-blē\ *adv*

in·ept \in-'ept\ *adj* **1** : lacking in fitness or aptitude : UNFIT **2** : not suited to the occasion : INAPPROPRIATE **3** : lacking sense or reason : FOOLISH **4** : generally incompetent : BUNGLING [French *inepte,* from Latin *ineptus,* from *in-* + *aptus* "apt"] SYN see AWKWARD — **in·ep·ti·tude** \-'ep-tə-,tüd, -,tyüd\ *n* — **in·ept·ly** *adv* — **in·ept·ness** \-'ep-nəs, -'ep-nəs\ *n*

in·equal·i·ty \,in-i-'kwäl-ət-ē\ *n* **1** : the quality of being unequal or uneven **2** : an instance of being unequal (as an irregularity in a surface) **3** : a formal logical or mathematical statement that two quantities are unequal

in·eq·ui·ta·ble \in-'ek-wət-ə-bəl, 'in-\ *adj* : not equitable : UNFAIR, UNJUST — **in·eq·ui·ta·bly** \-blē\ *adv*

in·eq·ui·ty \-wət-ē\ *n* **1** : INJUSTICE 1, UNFAIRNESS **2** : an instance of injustice or unfairness

in·ert \in-'ərt\ *adj* **1** : not having the power to move itself **2** : deficient in active properties; *esp* : lacking a usual or anticipated chemical or biological action **3** : very slow to move or act : SLUGGISH [Latin *inert-, iners* "unskilled, idle", from *in-* + *art-, ars* "skill, art"] SYN see INACTIVE — **in·ert·ly** *adv* — **in·ert·ness** *n*

in·er·tia \in-'ər-shə, -shē-ə\ *n* **1** : a property of matter by which it remains at rest or in uniform motion in the same straight line unless acted upon by some external force; *also* : an analogous property of other physical quantities (as electricity) **2** : a disposition not to move, change, or exert oneself : INERTNESS [Latin, "lack of skill", from *iners* "unskilled"] — **in·er·tial** \-shəl\ *adj*

inertial guidance *n* : guidance (as of a spacecraft) by means of self-contained automatically controlling devices that respond to changes in velocity or direction

in·es·cap·able \,in-ə-'skā-pə-bəl\ *adj* : incapable of being escaped : INEVITABLE — **in·es·cap·ably** \-blē\ *adv*

in·es·ti·ma·ble \in-'es-tə-mə-bəl, 'in-\ *adj* **1** : incapable of being estimated or computed ⟨the storm caused *inestimable* damage⟩ **2** : too valuable or excellent to be measured or appreciated — **in·es·ti·ma·bly** \-blē\ *adv*

in·ev·i·ta·ble \in-'ev-ət-ə-bəl\ *adj* : bound to happen : CERTAIN [Latin *inevitabilis,* from *in-* + *evitare* "to avoid", from *ex-* + *vitare* "to shun"] — **in·ev·i·ta·bil·i·ty** \in-,ev-ət-ə-'bil-ət-ē\ *n* — **in·ev·i·ta·ble·ness** \in-'ev-ət-ə-bəl-nəs, 'in-\ *n* — **in·ev·i·ta·bly** \-blē\ *adv*

in·ex·act \,in-ig-'zakt\ *adj* : not precisely correct or true : INACCURATE — **in·ex·ac·ti·tude** \-'zak-tə-,tüd, -,tyüd\ *n* — **in·ex·act·ly** \-'zak-tlē, -lē\ *adv* — **in·ex·act·ness** \-'zakt-nəs, -'zak-\ *n*

in·ex·cus·able \,in-ik-'skyü-zə-bəl\ *adj* : not to be excused : not justifiable ⟨*inexcusable* rudeness⟩ — **in·ex·cus·able·ness** *n* — **in·ex·cus·ably** \-blē\ *adv*

in·ex·haust·ible \,in-ig-'zȯ-stə-bəl\ *adj* **1** : plentiful enough not to give out or be used up : UNFAILING ⟨an *inexhaustible* supply⟩ **2** : not subject to fatigue or wear — **in·ex·haust·ibil·i·ty** \-,zȯ-stə-'bil-ət-ē\ *n* — **in·ex·haust·ibly** \-'zȯ-stə-blē\ *adv*

in·ex·o·ra·ble \in-'eks-rə-bəl, 'in-, -ə-rə-\ *adj* : not to be persuaded or moved by entreaty : RELENTLESS [Latin

inexorabilis, from *in-* + *exorabilis* "pliant", from *ex- orare* "to prevail upon", from *ex-* + *orare* "to speak"]
— **in·ex·o·ra·bil·i·ty** \,in-,eks-rə-'bil-ət-ē, -ə-rə-\ *n* —
in·ex·o·ra·ble·ness \in-'eks-rə-bəl-nəs, -ə-rə-\ *n* — **in-ex·o·ra·bly** \-blē\ *adv*

in·ex·pe·di·ent \,in-ik-'spēd-ē-ənt\ *adj* : not suited to bring about a desired result : UNWISE — **in·ex·pe·di·en-cy** \-ən-sē\ *n* — **in·ex·pe·di·ent·ly** *adv*

in·ex·pen·sive \,in-ik-'spen-siv\ *adj* : reasonable in price : CHEAP — **in·ex·pen·sive·ly** *adv* — **in·ex·pen-sive·ness** *n*

in·ex·pe·ri·ence \,in-ik-'spir-ē-əns\ *n* : lack of experience or of knowledge or skill gained by experience — **in·ex·pe·ri·enced** \-ənst\ *adj*

in·ex·pert \in-'ek-,spərt, ,in-ik-'\ *adj* : not expert : UN-SKILLED — **in·ex·pert·ly** *adv* — **in·ex·pert·ness** *n*

in·ex·pli·ca·ble \,in-ik-'splik-ə-bəl; in-'ek-splik-, 'in-\ *adj* : incapable of being explained, interpreted, or accounted for — **in·ex·plic·abil·i·ty** \,in-ik-,splik-ə-'bil-ət-ē, in-,ek-splik-ə-'bil-\ *n* — **in·ex·plic·able·ness** \,in-ik-'splik-ə-bəl-nəs; in-'ek-splik-, 'in-\ *n* — **in·ex-plic·ably** \-blē\ *adv*

in·ex·press·ible \,in-ik-'spres-ə-bəl\ *adj* : being beyond one's power to express : INDESCRIBABLE ⟨*inex-pressible* joy⟩ — **in·ex·press·ibil·i·ty** \-,spres-ə-'bil-ət-ē\ *n* — **in·ex·press·ible·ness** \-'spres-ə-bəl-nəs\ *n* — **in·ex·press·ibly** \-blē\ *adv*

in·ex·pres·sive \-'spres-iv\ *adj* : lacking expression or meaning ⟨an *inexpressive* face⟩ — **in·ex·pres·sive·ly** *adv* — **in·ex·pres·sive·ness** *n*

in ex·tre·mis \,in-ik-'strā-məs, -,mēs\ *adv* : in extreme circumstances; *esp* : at the point of death [Latin]

in·ex·tric·able \,in-ik-'strik-ə-bəl; in-'ek-strik-, 'in-\ *adj* 1 : forming a tangle from which one cannot free one-self 2 : not capable of being disentangled ⟨an *inextric-able* knot⟩ — **in·ex·tric·ably** \-blē\ *adv*

in·fal·li·ble \in-'fal-ə-bəl, 'in-\ *adj* 1 : not capable of being wrong ⟨an *infallible* memory⟩ 2 : not liable to fail, deceive, or disappoint : CERTAIN ⟨an *infallible* remedy⟩ — **in·fal·li·bil·i·ty** \in-,fal-ə-'bil-ət-ē\ *n* — **in-fal·li·bly** \in-'fal-ə-blē, 'in-\ *adv*

in·fa·mous \'in-fə-məs\ *adj* 1 : having an evil reputa-tion ⟨an *infamous* person⟩ 2 : DETESTABLE, DISGRACE-FUL ⟨an *infamous* crime⟩ [Latin *infamis,* from *in-* + *fama* "fame, reputation"] — **in·fa·mous·ly** *adv*

in·fa·my \-mē\ *n, pl* **-mies** 1 : evil reputation brought about by something grossly criminal, shocking, or bru-tal 2 **a** : an infamous act **b** : the state of being infa-mous

in·fan·cy \'in-fən-sē\ *n, pl* **-cies** 1 : early childhood 2 : a beginning or early period of existence 3 : the legal status of a minor

¹**in·fant** \'in-fənt\ *n* 1 : a child in the first period of life 2 : MINOR 1 [Middle French *enfant,* from Latin *infans,* from *infans* "incapable of speech, young", from *in-* + *fari* "to speak"] □ ORIGIN Latin *infans* means literally "not speaking, incapable of speech". In classical Latin the noun *infans* designated a very young child who had not yet learned to talk. But later *infans* became the most common word for any child, however talk-ative. In the Romance languages, too, the descendants of Latin *infans* are words that mean "child". In En-glish the word *infant,* which was borrowed from the French, was originally used for any child. But the word usually is used now in the earlier Latin sense "a very young child, a baby".

²**infant** *adj* : of, relating to, or being in infancy

in·fan·ti·cide \in-'fant-ə-,sīd\ *n* 1 : the killing of an in-fant 2 : one who deliberately kills an infant

in·fan·tile \'in-fən-,tīl, -təl, -,tēl\ *adj* 1 : of, relating to, or resembling infants or infancy : CHILDISH 2 : being in a very early stage of development following an up-lift or equivalent change ⟨an *infantile* river⟩ — **in·fan-til·i·ty** \,in-fən-'til-ət-ē\ *n*

infantile paralysis *n* : POLIOMYELITIS

in·fan·til·ism \'in-fən-,tīl-,iz-əm, -təl-, -,tēl-\ *n* : reten-tion of childish qualities in adult life; *esp* : failure to attain sexual maturity

in·fan·try \'in-fən-trē\ *n, pl* **-tries** 1 : soldiers trained, armed, and equipped to fight on foot 2 : a branch of an army composed of infantry [Middle French *infan-terie,* from Italian *infanteria,* from *infante* "infant, boy, foot soldier", from Latin *infans* "infant"] — **in-fan·try·man** \-mən\ *n* □ ORIGIN In the Middle Ages in France, a young soldier of good family who had not yet been made a knight was called *enfant,* which means literally "child". Similarly, in Italy one of the soldiers who followed a mounted knight on foot was an *in-fante.* Soon foot soldiers collectively became *infante-ria,* which was borrowed into French as *infanterie* and into English as *infantry.*

in·farct \'in-,färkt\ *n* : an area of dead tissue (as of the heart wall) caused by blockage of local blood circula-tion [Latin *infarctus,* past participle of *infarcire* "to stuff in", from *in-* + *farcire* "to stuff"] — **in·farc·tion** \in-'färk-shən\ *n*

in·fat·u·ate \in-'fach-ə-,wāt\ *vt* : to fill with a foolish or extravagant love or admiration [Latin *infatuare,* from *in-* + *fatuus* "fatuous"] — **in·fat·u·a·tion** \in-,fach-ə-'wā-shən\ *n*

in·fect \in-'fekt\ *vt* 1 : to contaminate with a disease-producing substance or organism ⟨*infected* bedding⟩ 2 **a** : to communicate a germ or disease to ⟨coughing people who *infect* others⟩ **b** : to enter and cause dis-ease in ⟨bacteria that *infect* wounds⟩ 3 : to cause to share one's feelings ⟨*infected* everyone with their en-thusiasm⟩ [Latin *infectus,* past participle of *inficere* "to infect", from *in-* "³in-" + *facere* "to make, do"] — **in·fec·tor** \-'fek-tər\ *n*

in·fec·tion \in-'fek-shən\ *n* 1 : an act or process of in-fecting 2 **a** : the state produced by the establishment of a germ in or on a suitable host **b** : a disease result-ing from infection 3 : an infective agent or material contaminated with an infective agent 4 : the commu-nication of emotions or qualities through example or contact

in·fec·tious \in-'fek-shəs\ *adj* 1 **a** : capable of causing infection **b** : communicable by infection 2 : spreading or capable of spreading rapidly to others ⟨their enthu-siasm was *infectious*⟩ — **in·fec·tious·ly** *adv* — **in·fec-tious·ness** *n*

infectious mononucleosis *n* : an acute infectious dis-ease characterized by fever, swelling of the lymph glands, and an abnormal increase in the number of lymphocytes in the blood

in·fec·tive \in-'fek-tiv\ *adj* : producing or able to pro-duce infection — **in·fec·tiv·i·ty** \in-,fek-'tiv-ət-ē\ *n*

in·fe·lic·i·tous \,in-fi-'lis-ət-əs\ *adj* : not apt : not suit-ably chosen for the occasion ⟨an *infelicitous* remark⟩ — **in·fe·lic·i·tous·ly** *adv*

in·fe·lic·i·ty \-ət-ē\ *n, pl* **-ties** 1 : a lack of suitability or aptness 2 : an unsuitable or inappropriate act or utter-ance

in·fer \in-'fər\ *vt* **in·ferred; in·fer·ring** 1 : to derive as a conclusion from facts or premises : GUESS 1, SURMISE 3 : HINT, SUGGEST [Latin *inferre,* literally, "to carry in-to", from *in-* + *ferre* "to carry"] SYN see IMPLY — **in-fer·able** *or* **in·fer·ri·ble** \-'fər-ə-bəl\ *adj* — **in·fer·rer** \-'fər-ər\ *n*

in·fer·ence \'in-fə-rəns, -frəns\ *n* 1 : the act or process of inferring 2 : something inferred; *esp* : a proposition arrived at by inference

in·fe·ri·or \in-'fir-ē-ər\ *adj* 1 **a** : situated lower down **b** : situated below another usually similar part of the upright body ⟨*inferior* vena cava⟩ 2 : of low or lower degree or rank 3 : of little or less importance, value, or merit [Latin, comparative of *inferus* "low, situated beneath"] — **inferior** *n* — **in·fe·ri·or·i·ty** \in-,fir-ē-'or-ət-ē, -'är-\ *n* — **in·fe·ri·or·ly** \in-'fir-ē-ər-lē\ *adv*

\ə\ abut	\ng\ sing
\ər\ further	\ō\ bone
\a\ mat	\o'\ saw
\ā\ take	\oi\ coin
\ä\ cot, cart	\th\ thin
\au̇\ out	\th\ this
\ch\ chin	\ü\ food
\e\ pet	\u̇\ foot
\ē\ easy	\y\ yet
\g\ go	\yü\ few
\i\ tip	\yu̇\ cure
\ī\ life	\zh\ vision
\j\ job	

inferiority complex *n* : an acute sense of personal inferiority resulting either in timidity or in exaggerated aggressiveness

inferior vena cava *n* : a branch of the vena cava that returns blood to the heart from the lower parts of the body including the viscera below the lungs and the lower limbs

in·fer·nal \in-'fərn-l\ *adj* 1 : of or relating to a netherworld of the dead 2 a : of or relating to hell b : suggestive of or appropriate to hell : FIENDISH 3 : DAMNABLE 2, DAMNED [Old French, from Late Latin *infernus* "hell", from Latin, "lower"] — **in·fer·nal·ly** \-l-ē\ *adv*

infernal machine *n* : an apparatus designed to explode and destroy life or property

in·fer·no \in-'fər-nō\ *n, pl* **-nos** : a place or a state that resembles or suggests hell especially in intense heat or raging fire [Italian, "hell", from Late Latin *infernus*]

in·fer·tile \in-'fərt-l, 'in-\ *adj* : not fertile or productive : BARREN — **in·fer·til·i·ty** \,in-fər-'til-ət-ē\ *n*

in·fest \in-'fest\ *vt* 1 : to spread or swarm in or over in a troublesome manner 2 : to live in or on as a parasite [Middle French *infester*, from Latin *infestare*, from *infestus* "hostile"] — **in·fes·ta·tion** \,in-,fes-'tā-shən\ *n* — **in·fest·er** \in-'fes-tər\ *n*

in·fi·del \'in-fəd-l, -fə-,del\ *n* : a person who does not believe in a particular religion [Middle French *infidele*, from Latin *infidelis* "unfaithful", from *in-* + *fidelis* "faithful", from *fides* "faith"] — **infidel** *adj*

in·fi·del·i·ty \,in-fə-'del-ət-ē, -fī-\ *n, pl* **-ties** 1 : lack of faith in a religion 2 : unfaithfulness especially to one's spouse

in·field \'in-,fēld\ *n* 1 : the part of a baseball field enclosed by the three bases and home plate 2 : the area enclosed by a racetrack or running track — **in·field·er** \-,fēl-dər\ *n*

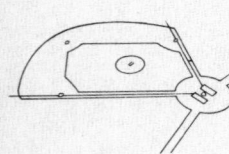

infield 1

in·fight·ing \'in-,fīt-ing\ *n* 1 : fighting or boxing at close quarters 2 : prolonged and often bitter disagreement among members of a group — **in·fight·er** *n*

in·fil·trate \in-'fil-,trāt, 'in-fil-\ *vb* 1 : to pass into or through by filtering or permeating 2 : to enter or become established gradually or inconspicuously — **in·fil·tra·tion** \,in-fil-'trā-shən\ *n* — **in·fil·tra·tor** \'in-fil-,trāt-ər, in-'fil-\ *n*

in·fi·nite \'in-fə-nət\ *adj* 1 : being without limits of any kind : ENDLESS ⟨*infinite* space⟩ 2 : seeming to be without limits : VAST, INEXHAUSTIBLE ⟨*infinite* patience⟩ ⟨*infinite* wealth⟩ 3 a : extending, lying, or being beyond any preassigned value however large b : having an infinite number of elements or terms — **infinite** *n* — **in·fi·nite·ly** *adv* — **in·fi·nite·ness** *n*

in·fin·i·tes·i·mal \in-,fin-ə-'tes-ə-məl\ *adj* : immeasurably or incalculably small — **in·fin·i·tes·i·mal·ly** \-mə-lē\ *adv*

in·fin·i·tive \in-'fin-ət-iv\ *n* : an uninflected verb form serving as a noun or as a modifier and yet showing certain characteristics of a verb (as association with objects and adverbial modifiers) ⟨*have* in "let me have it" and *to run* in "able to run fast" are *infinitives*⟩ — **infinitive** *adj*

in·fin·i·tude \in-'fin-ə-,tüd, -,tyüd\ *n* 1 : INFINITY 1a 2 : something infinite especially in extent 3 : an infinite number or quantity

in·fin·i·ty \in-'fin-ət-ē\ *n, pl* **-ties** 1 a : the quality of being infinite b : unlimited extent of time, space, or quantity 2 : INFINITUDE 3 3 : a distance so great that the rays of light from a point source at that distance may be regarded as parallel ⟨a camera focused at *infinity*⟩

in·firm \in-'fərm\ *adj* 1 : poor or weakened in vitality; *esp* : feeble from age 2 : not solid or stable : INSECURE — **in·firm·ly** *adv*

in·fir·ma·ry \in-'fərmı-rē, -ə-rē\ *n, pl* **-ries** : a place (as in a school or factory) where the infirm, sick, or hurt are lodged for care and treatment

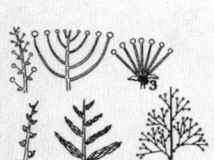

inflorescence 1a

in·fir·mi·ty \in-'fər-mət-ē\ *n, pl* **-ties** 1 : the quality or state of being infirm : FEEBLENESS, FRAILTY 2 a : DISEASE, AILMENT b : a personal failing : FOIBLE

in·flame \in-'flām\ *vb* 1 : to set on fire : KINDLE 2 a : to excite to excess or unnatural action or feeling b : to make more heated or violent : INTENSIFY 3 : to cause to redden or grow hot from anger or excitement 4 : to cause inflammation in (bodily tissue) 5 : to become affected with inflammation — **in·flam·er** *n*

in·flam·ma·ble \in-'flam-ə-bəl\ *adj* 1 : FLAMMABLE 2 : easily inflamed : EXCITABLE — **in·flam·ma·bil·i·ty** \-,flam-ə-'bil-ət-ē\ *n* — **inflammable** *n* — **in·flam·ma·ble·ness** \-'flam-ə-bəl-nəs\ *n* — **in·flam·ma·bly** \-blē\ *adv*

in·flam·ma·tion \,in-flə-'mā-shən\ *n* 1 : the act of inflaming : the state of being inflamed 2 : a local bodily response to injury in which an affected area becomes red, hot, painful, and congested with blood

in·flam·ma·to·ry \in-'flam-ə-,tōr-ē, -,tòr-\ *adj* 1 : tending to excite anger, disorder, or tumult 2 : causing or accompanied by inflammation ⟨*inflammatory* diseases⟩

in·flate \in-'flāt\ *vb* 1 : to swell with air or gas ⟨*inflate* a balloon⟩ 2 : to puff up : ELATE ⟨*inflated* with pride⟩ 3 : to increase abnormally ⟨*inflated* prices⟩ ⟨*inflated* currency⟩ [Latin *inflare*, from *in-* + *flare* "to blow"] SYN see EXPAND — **in·flat·able** \in-'flāt-ə-bəl\ *adj* — **in·fla·tor** \-'flāt-ər\ *n*

in·fla·tion \in-'flā-shən\ *n* 1 : an act of inflating : the state of being inflated 2 : an increase in the volume of money and credit relative to available goods resulting in a substantial and continuing rise in prices

in·fla·tion·ary \-shə-,ner-ē\ *adj* : of, relating to, or tending to cause inflation

in·flect \in-'flekt\ *vb* 1 : to turn from a direct line or course : CURVE 2 : to vary a word by inflection 3 : to vary the pitch of the voice [Latin *inflectere*, from *in-* + *flectere* "to bend"]

in·flec·tion \in-'flek-shən\ *n* 1 : the act or result of curving or bending 2 : a change in the pitch of a person's voice 3 : the change in the form of a word showing its case, gender, number, person, tense, mood, voice, or comparison — **in·flec·tion·al** \-shnəl, -shən-l\ *adj* — **in·flec·tion·al·ly** \-ē\ *adv*

in·flex·ible \in-'flek-sə-bəl, 'in-\ *adj* 1 : not easily bent or twisted : RIGID, STIFF 2 : not easily influenced or persuaded : FIRM ⟨an *inflexible* judge⟩ 3 : incapable of change ⟨*inflexible* laws⟩ — **in·flex·ibil·i·ty** \in-,flek-sə-'bil-ət-ē\ *n* — **in·flex·ibly** \in-'flek-sə-blē, 'in-\ *adv*

in·flict \in-'flikt\ *vt* 1 : to give by striking ⟨*inflict* a wound⟩ 2 : to cause (something damaging or painful) to be endured : IMPOSE ⟨*inflict* punishment⟩ [Latin *inflictus*, past participle of *infligere* "to inflict", from *in-* + *fligere* "to strike"] — **in·flic·tion** \in-'flik-shən\ *n* — **in·flic·tive** \-'flik-tiv\ *adj*

in·flo·res·cence \,in-flə-'res-ns\ *n* 1 a : the mode of development and arrangement of flowers on a stem b : a flowering stem with all its parts; *also* : a flower cluster or sometimes a solitary flower 2 : the forming and unfolding of blossoms [Late Latin *inflorescere* "to begin to bloom", from Latin *in-* + *florescere* "to begin to bloom", from *florēre* "to blossom, flourish"] — **in·flo·res·cent** \-nt\ *adj*

in·flow \'in-,flō\ *n* 1 : the act of flowing in 2 : something that flows in

¹**in·flu·ence** \'in-,flü-əns\ *n* 1 : the act or power of producing an effect without apparent exertion of force or direct exercise of command 2 : corrupt interference with authority for personal gain 3 : a person or thing that exerts influence [Middle French, from Medieval Latin *influentia* "ethereal fluid thought to flow from the stars and affect people's actions", from Latin *influere* "to flow in", from *in-* + *fluere* "to flow"]

²**influence** *vt* 1 : to affect or alter (as behavior) by indirect or intangible means 2 : to have an effect on the

condition or development of : MODIFY — **in·flu·enc·er** *n* □ SYN AFFECT, SWAY: INFLUENCE is used of a force that brings about a change or determines a course of action or behavior ⟨traditions that *influenced* resistance to change⟩ AFFECT implies a stimulus strong enough to bring about a reaction or modification without a total change ⟨rainfall *affects* the growth of plants⟩ ⟨the new law *affects* only some aspects of commerce⟩ SWAY suggests that the forces either are not resisted or are irresistible and bring about a change ⟨advertising that *sways* public taste⟩

in·flu·en·tial \ˌin-flü-'en-chəl\ *adj* : having or exerting influence — **in·flu·en·tial·ly** \-'ench-lē, -ə-lē\ *adv*

in·flu·en·za \ˌin-flü-'en-zə\ *n* **1** : an acute and very contagious virus disease with sudden onset, fever, exhaustion, severe aches and pains, and inflammation of the respiratory tract **2** : any of various feverish usually virus diseases of humans or domestic animals typically with respiratory symptoms and inflammation and often affecting the body as a whole [Italian, literally, "influence", from Medieval Latin *influentia*] □ ORIGIN Italian *influenza* has the same meaning as its English cognate *influence*. But in the 15th century sudden epidemics whose earthly causes were not apparent were blamed on the influence of the stars, so in Italy epidemic diseases were given the name *influenza*. The report of a Roman epidemic which spread through much of Europe in 1743 brought the word to England.

in·flux \'in-ˌfləks\ *n* : a flowing in : INFLOW [Late Latin *influxus*, from Latin *influere* "to flow in"]

in·fold *vb* **1** \in-'fōld\ : ENFOLD **2** \'in-ˌfōld\ : to fold inward or toward one another

in·form \in-'fórm\ *vb* **1** : to let a person know something : TELL **2** : to give information so as to accuse or cast suspicion ⟨*inform* against someone to the police⟩ [Middle French *enformer* "to give form to, inform", from Latin *informare*, from *in-* + *forma* "form"]

in·for·mal \in-'fór-məl, 'in-\ *adj* **1** : conducted or carried out without formality or ceremony **2** : appropriate for ordinary or casual use ⟨*informal* clothes⟩ — **in·for·mal·i·ty** \ˌin-fór-'mal-ət-ē, -fər-\ *n* — **in·for·mal·ly** \in-'fór-mə-lē, 'in-\ *adv*

in·for·mant \in-'fór-mənt\ *n* : INFORMER

in·for·ma·tion \ˌin-fər-'mā-shən\ *n* **1** : the communication or reception of knowledge or intelligence **2 a** : knowledge obtained from investigation, study, or instruction **b** : knowledge of a particular event or situation : NEWS **c** : FACT **3**, DATA **d** : a signal or mark put into or put out by a computing machine — **in·for·ma·tion·al** \-shnəl, -shən-l\ *adj*

information theory *n* : a mathematical and statistical theory that deals with information, its measurement, and the efficiency of processes of communication between men and machines

in·for·ma·tive \in-'fór-mət-iv\ *adj* : imparting knowledge : INSTRUCTIVE — **in·for·ma·tive·ly** *adv* — **in·for·ma·tive·ness** *n*

in·formed \in-'fórmd\ *adj* **1** : having information ⟨*informed* sources⟩ **2** : EDUCATED, KNOWLEDGEABLE ⟨what an *informed* person should know about psychology⟩

in·form·er \in-'fór-mər\ *n* : one that informs; *esp* : a person who informs against someone else

infra- *prefix* **1** : below ⟨*infra*human⟩ ⟨*infra*sonic⟩ **2** : below in a scale or series ⟨*infra*red⟩ [Latin *infra*]

in·frac·tion \in-'frak-shən\ *n* : the act of infringing : VIOLATION [Latin *infractio*, from *infractus*, past participle of *infringere* "to infringe"]

in·fra·hu·man \ˌin-frə-'hyü-mən, -'yü-\ *adj* : less or lower than human ⟨*infrahuman* primates⟩ — **infrahuman** *n*

in·fra·red \ˌin-frə-'red, -frā-\ *adj* **1** : lying outside the visible spectrum at its red end — used of heat radiation of wavelengths longer than those of visible light **2** : relating to, producing, or employing infrared radiation — **infrared** *n*

in·fra·son·ic \-'sän-ik\ *adj* **1** : having a frequency below the audibility range of the human ear **2** : utilizing or produced by infrasonic waves or vibrations

in·fre·quent \in-'frē-kwənt, 'in-\ *adj* **1** : seldom happening or occurring : RARE **2** : placed or occurring at considerable distances or intervals — **in·fre·quen·cy** \-kwən-sē\ *n* — **in·fre·quent·ly** *adv* □ SYN SPORADIC, SCATTERED: INFREQUENT applies to that which occurs at wide intervals in time or space ⟨*infrequent* church attendance⟩ ⟨*infrequent* stands of pine alongside the highway⟩ SPORADIC applies to that which occurs in scattered instances without continuity or continuous existence ⟨*sporadic* cases of food poisoning⟩ ⟨*sporadic* border fighting⟩ SCATTERED more often applies to wide intervals in space and implies haphazard irregular distribution ⟨*scattered* showers⟩ ⟨*scattered* misspellings in the report⟩

in·fringe \in-'frinj\ *vb* **1** : VIOLATE, TRANSGRESS ⟨*infringe* a treaty⟩ ⟨*infringe* a patent⟩ **2** : ENCROACH 1 ⟨*infringe* upon a person's rights⟩ [Latin *infringere*, literally, "to break off", from *in-* "²in-" + *frangere* "to break"] — **infringement** *n* — **in·fring·er** *n*

in·fun·dib·u·lum \ˌin-fən-'dib-yə-ləm\ *n, pl* **-la** \-lə\ : a conical or dilated body part: as **a** : the stalk by which the pituitary body is continuous with the brain **b** : the abdominal opening of a fallopian tube [Latin, "funnel", from *infundere* "to pour in", from *in-* + *fundere* "to pour"] — **in·fun·dib·u·lar** \-lər\ *adj*

in·fu·ri·ate \in-'fyùr-ē-ˌāt\ *vt* : to make furious : ENRAGE — **in·fu·ri·at·ing·ly** \-ˌāt-ing-lē\ *adv* — **in·fu·ri·a·tion** \-ˌfyùr-ē-'ā-shən\ *n*

in·fuse \in-'fyüz\ *vt* **1** : to put in as if by pouring ⟨*infused* courage into their followers⟩ **2** : to make full ⟨*infused* with a desire to help⟩ **3** : to steep (as tea) without boiling [Latin *infusus*, past participle of *infundere* "to pour in", from *in-* + *fundere* "to pour"] — **in·fus·er** *n*

in·fus·ible \in-'fyü-zə-bəl, 'in-\ *adj* : difficult or impossible to fuse ⟨*infusible* clays⟩ — **in·fus·ibil·i·ty** \in-ˌfyü-zə-'bil-ət-ē\ *n* — **in·fus·ible·ness** \in-'fyü-zə-bəl-nəs, 'in-\ *n*

in·fu·sion \in-'fyü-zhən\ *n* **1** : the act or process of infusing **2** : a substance extracted especially from a plant material by infusing

in·fu·so·ri·an \ˌin-fyü-'zōr-ē-ən, -'zór-\ *n* : any of a heterogeneous group of minute organisms found especially in decomposing infusions of organic matter; *esp* : a ciliated protozoan — **in·fu·so·ri·al** \-ē-əl\ *or* **infusorian** *adj*

¹-ing \ing; *in some dialects usually, in other dialects informally,* ən, in, ən; *(after certain consonants)* ᵊn, ᵊm, ᵊng\ *vb suffix or adj suffix* — used to form the present participle ⟨sail*ing*⟩ and sometimes to form an adjective resembling a present participle but not derived from a verb ⟨swashbuckl*ing*⟩ [Middle English, alteration of *-ende*, from Old English]

²-ing *n suffix* : one of a (specified) kind ⟨sweet*ing*⟩ [Old English]

³-ing *n suffix* **1** : action or process ⟨runn*ing*⟩ ⟨sleep*ing*⟩ : instance of an action or process ⟨a meet*ing*⟩ **2 a** : product or result of an action or process ⟨an engrav*ing*⟩ — often in pl. ⟨earn*ings*⟩ **b** : something used in an action or process ⟨a bed cover*ing*⟩ **3** : action or process connected with ⟨a specified thing⟩ **4** : something connected with, consisting of, or used in making ⟨a specified thing⟩ ⟨roof*ing*⟩ **5** : something related to ⟨a specified concept⟩ ⟨off*ing*⟩ [Old English, suffix forming nouns from verbs]

in·gath·er·ing \'in-ˌgath-ring, -ə-ring\ *n* **1** : COLLECTION 1, HARVEST **2** : ASSEMBLY 3

in·ge·nious \in-'jē-nyəs\ *adj* : marked by ingenuity ⟨*ingenious* planning⟩ ⟨an *ingenious* device⟩ [Middle French *ingenieux*, from Latin *ingeniosus*, from Latin *ingenium* "natural capacity", from *in-* + *gignere* "to beget"] — **in·ge·nious·ly** *adv* — **in·ge·nious·ness** *n*

\ə\ abut	\ng\ sing
\ər\ further	\ō\ bone
\a\ mat	\ò\ saw
\ā\ take	\ói\ coin
\ä\ cot, cart	\th\ thin
\aú\ out	\th\ this
\ch\ chin	\ü\ food
\e\ pet	\ú\ foot
\ē\ easy	\y\ yet
\g\ go	\yü\ few
\i\ tip	\yú\ cure
\ī\ life	\zh\ vision
\j\ job	

□ **SYN** INGENIOUS, INGENUOUS are not synonymous but they are readily confused. INGENIOUS implies having inborn inventiveness and cleverness; INGENUOUS implies keeping a childlike innocence, frankness, or lack of sophistication.

in·ge·nue *or* **in·gé·nue** \'an-jə-ˌnü, 'än-; 'aⁿ-zhə-, 'äⁿ-\ *n* : a naive girl or young woman; *also* : an actress representing such a person [French *ingénue*, from *ingénu* "ingenuous", from Latin *ingenuus*]

in·ge·nu·i·ty \ˌin-jə-'nü-ət-ē, -'nyü-\ *n, pl* **-ties 1 a** : skill or cleverness in devising or combining : INVENTIVENESS **b** : cleverness or aptness of design or contrivance **2** : an ingenious device or contrivance [obsolete *ingenuity* "ingenuousness"]

in·gen·u·ous \in-'jen-yə-wəs\ *adj* **1** : FRANK 1 **2** : showing innocent or childlike simplicity : NAIVE [Latin *ingenuus* "native, freeborn, ingenuous", from *in-* + *gignere* "to beget"] **SYN** see INGENIOUS — **in·gen·u·ous·ly** *adv* — **in·gen·u·ous·ness** *n*

in·gest \in-'jest\ *vt* : to take in for or as if for digestion [Latin *ingestus,* past participle of *ingerere* "to carry in", from *in-* + *gerere* "to carry"] — **in·gest·ible** \-'jes-tə-bəl\ *adj* — **in·ges·tion** \-'jes-chən\ *n* — **in·ges·tive** \-'jes-tiv\ *adj*

in·ges·ta \in-'jes-tə\ *n pl* : material taken into the body by way of the mouth [New Latin]

in·gle \'ing-gəl, -əl\ *n* **1** : a fire in a fireplace **2** : an indoor fireplace [Scottish Gaelic *aingeal*]

in·gle·nook \-ˌnúk\ *n* **1** : a corner by the fire or chimney **2** : a high-backed wooden bench placed close to a fireplace

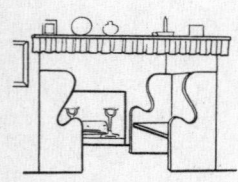

inglenook 2

in·glo·ri·ous \in-'glōr-ē-əs, 'in-, -'glȯr-\ *adj* **1** : not glorious : lacking fame or honor **2** : bringing disgrace : SHAMEFUL ⟨*inglorious* defeat⟩ — **in·glo·ri·ous·ly** *adv* — **in·glo·ri·ous·ness** *n*

in·got \'ing-gət\ *n* : a mass of metal cast into a convenient shape for storage or transportation [Middle English]

¹in·grain \in-'grān, 'in-\ *vt* : to work indelibly into the natural texture or mental or moral constitution : IMBUE

²in·grain \'in-ˌgrān\ *adj* **1 a** : made of fiber that is dyed before being spun into yarn **b** : made of yarn that is dyed before being woven or knitted ⟨*ingrain* carpet⟩ **2** : thoroughly worked in : INNATE — **ingrain** *n*

in·grained \'in-ˌgrānd, in-', 'in-'\ *adj* : worked into the grain or fiber : DEEP-SEATED ⟨*ingrained* prejudice⟩ — **in·grain·ed·ly** \-ˌgrā-nəd-lē, -'grā-\ *adv*

in·grate \'in-ˌgrāt\ *n* : an ungrateful person [Latin *ingratus* "ungrateful", from *in-* + *gratus* "grateful"]

in·gra·ti·ate \in-'grā-shē-ˌāt\ *vt* : to gain favor or favorable acceptance for by deliberate effort ⟨*ingratiate* oneself with a new boss⟩ [²*in-* + Latin *gratia* "grace"] — **in·gra·ti·a·tion** \-ˌgrā-shē-'ā-shən\ *n* — **in·gra·tia·to·ry** \-'grā-shə-ˌtōr-ē, -shē-ə-, -ˌtȯr-\ *adj*

in·gra·ti·at·ing *adj* **1** : capable of winning favor : PLEASING ⟨an *ingratiating* smile⟩ **2** : intended or adopted in order to gain favor ⟨*ingratiating* manners⟩ — **in·gra·ti·at·ing·ly** \-ˌāt-ing-lē\ *adv*

in·grat·i·tude \in-'grat-ə-ˌtüd, 'in-, -ˌtyüd\ *n* : forgetfulness of or poor return for kindness received

in·gre·di·ent \in-'grēd-ē-ənt\ *n* : one of the substances that make up a mixture ⟨*ingredients* of a cake⟩ [Latin *ingrediens,* present participle of *ingredi* "to go into", from *in-* + *gradi* "to go"] **SYN** see ELEMENT — **ingredient** *adj*

in·gress \'in-ˌgres\ *n* **1** : the act of entering : ENTRANCE **2** : the power or liberty of entrance or access ⟨free *ingress* to the circus grounds⟩ [Latin *ingressus,* from *ingredi* "to go into"]

in·grow·ing \'in-ˌgrō-ing\ *adj* : growing or tending inward

in·grown \-ˌgrōn\ *adj* : grown in; *esp* : having the free tip or edge embedded in the flesh ⟨an *ingrown* toenail⟩ — **in·grown·ness** \-ˌgrōn-nəs\ *n*

in·growth \'in-ˌgrōth\ *n* **1** : a growing inward (as to fill a void) **2** : something that grows in or into a space

in·gui·nal \'ing-gwən-l\ *adj* : of, relating to, or located in the region of the groin [Latin *inguinalis,* from *inguen* "groin"]

in·gur·gi·tate \in-'gər-jə-ˌtāt\ *vt* : to swallow greedily or in large quantity [Latin *ingurgitare,* from *in-* + *gurges* "whirlpool"] — **in·gur·gi·ta·tion** \-ˌgər-jə-'tā-shən\ *n*

in·hab·it \in-'hab-ət\ *vt* : to live or dwell in [Latin *inhabitare,* from *in-* + *habitare* "to dwell", from *habēre* "to have"] — **in·hab·it·able** \-ə-bəl\ *adj* — **in·hab·i·ta·tion** \-ˌhab-ə-'tā-shən\ *n* — **in·hab·it·er** \-'hab-ət-ər\ *n*

in·hab·it·an·cy \-ən-sē\ *n* : OCCUPANCY

in·hab·it·ant \in-'hab-ət-ənt\ *n* : one that lives permanently in a place

¹in·hal·ant \in-'hā-lənt\ *n* : something (as an allergen or medicated spray) that is inhaled

²inhalant *adj* **1** : of or relating to an inhalant **2** : bearing in or inward ⟨an *inhalant* siphon of a clam⟩

in·ha·la·tion \ˌin-hə-'lā-shən, ˌin-ə-'lā-, ˌin-l-'ā-\ *n* : the act or an instance of inhaling — **in·ha·la·tion·al** \-shnəl, -shən-l\ *adj*

in·ha·la·tor \'in-hə-ˌlāt-ər, ˌin-ə-ˌlāt-, 'in-l-ˌāt-\ *n* : an apparatus used in inhaling something (as a mixture of oxygen and carbon dioxide)

in·hale \in-'hāl\ *vb* **1** : to draw in by breathing **2** : to breathe in [²*in-* + *-hale* (as in *exhale*)]

in·hal·er \in-'hā-lər\ *n* **1** : one that inhales **2** : INHALATOR

in·har·mon·ic \ˌin-här-'män-ik\ *adj* : not harmonic : DISCORDANT

in·har·mo·ni·ous \-'mō-nē-əs\ *adj* **1** : not harmonious : DISCORDANT **2** : not fitting or congenial ⟨*inharmonious* ideas⟩ — **in·har·mo·ni·ous·ly** *adv* — **in·har·mo·ni·ous·ness** *n*

in·har·mo·ny \in-'här-mə-nē, 'in-\ *n* : DISCORD

in·here \in-'hiər\ *vi* : to be inherent : BELONG ⟨power to make laws *inheres* in the state⟩ [*inhaerēre,* from *in-* + *haerēre* "to stick, adhere"]

in·her·ent \in-'hir-ənt, -'her-\ *adj* : belonging to or being a part of the nature of a person or thing : INTRINSIC ⟨an *inherent* sense of fair play⟩ ⟨fluidity is an *inherent* quality of gas⟩ — **in·her·ence** \-əns\ *n* — **in·her·ent·ly** *adv*

in·her·it \in-'her-ət\ *vt* **1** : to come into possession of : RECEIVE **2** : to receive by legal right from a person at the person's death **3 a** : to receive by genetic transmission ⟨*inherit* a strong constitution⟩ **b** : to have handed on to one by a predecessor ⟨the president *inherited* the problem of unemployment⟩ [Middle French *inheriter* "to make heir", from Latin *in-* + *hereditas* "inheritance", from *hered-, heres* "heir"] — **in·her·i·tor** \-ət-ər\ *n* — **in·her·i·tress** \-ə-trəs\ *or* **in·her·i·trix** \-ə-ˌtriks\ *n*

in·her·it·able \in-'her-ət-ə-bəl\ *adj* : capable of being inherited — **in·her·it·able·ness** *n*

in·her·it·ance \in-'her-ət-əns\ *n* **1** : the act of inheriting **2** : something that is or may be inherited **SYN** see HERITAGE

in·hib·it \in-'hib-ət\ *vt* **1** : to prohibit from doing something **2 a** : to hold in check : RESTRAIN **b** : to discourage from free or spontaneous activity : REPRESS [Latin *inhibitus,* past participle of *inhibēre* "to inhibit", from *in-* + *habēre* "to have, hold"] **SYN** see FORBID — **in·hib·i·tive** \-ət-iv\ *adj* — **in·hib·i·to·ry** \-ə-ˌtōr-ē, -ˌtȯr-\ *adj*

in·hi·bi·tion \ˌin-ə-'bish-ən, ˌin-hə-\ *n* **1 a** : the act of inhibiting : the state of being inhibited **b** : something that forbids **2** : an inner force that interferes with free activity, expression, or functioning

in·hib·i·tor *or* **in·hib·it·er** \in-'hib-ət-ər\ *n* : one that inhibits; *esp* : an agent that slows or interferes with a chemical action ⟨rust *inhibitor*⟩

in·hos·pi·ta·ble \,in-,häs-'pit-ə-bəl; in-'häs-pit-, 'in-\ *adj* **1** : not showing hospitality **2** : providing no shelter or food : BARREN ⟨miles of *inhospitable* desert⟩ — **in·hos·pi·ta·ble·ness** *n* — **in·hos·pi·ta·bly** \-blē\ *adv*

in·hos·pi·tal·i·ty \in-,häs-pə-'tal-ət-ē\ *n* : the quality or state of being inhospitable

in·hu·man \in-'hyü-mən, in-'yü-, 'in-\ *adj* **1 a** : lacking pity or kindness : SAVAGE **b** : lacking human warmth : IMPERSONAL **c** : not fit, adequate, or worthy to meet human needs ⟨living in *inhuman* conditions⟩ **2** : of or suggesting a nonhuman class of beings — **in·hu·man·ly** *adv*

in·hu·mane \,in-hyü-'mān, -yü-\ *adj* : INHUMAN 1 — **in·hu·mane·ly** *adv*

in·hu·man·i·ty \-'man-ət-ē\ *n, pl* **-ties 1** : the quality or state of being cruel or barbarous **2** : a cruel or barbarous act

in·hume \in-'hyüm\ *vt* : BURY 1, INTER [derived from Latin *inhumare,* from *in-* + *humus* "earth"]

in·im·i·cal \in-'im-i-kəl\ *adj* **1 a** : having the disposition of an enemy : HOSTILE **b** : reflecting or indicating hostility : UNFRIENDLY ⟨*inimical* stares⟩ **2** : HARMFUL, ADVERSE ⟨habits *inimical* to health⟩ [Late Latin *inimicalis,* from Latin *inimicus* "enemy"] — **in·im·i·cal·ly** \-'im-i-kə-lē, -klē\ *adv*

in·im·i·ta·ble \in-'im-ət-ə-bəl, 'in-\ *adj* : not capable of being imitated : MATCHLESS — **in·im·i·ta·bil·i·ty** \in-,im-ət-ə-'bil-ət-ē\ *n* — **in·im·i·ta·ble·ness** \in-'im-ət-ə-bəl-nəs, 'in-\ *n* — **in·im·i·ta·bly** \-blē\ *adv*

in·iq·ui·tous \in-'ik-wət-əs\ *adj* : characterized by iniquity : WICKED — **in·iq·ui·tous·ly** *adv* — **in·iq·ui·tous·ness** *n*

in·iq·ui·ty \in-'ik-wət-ē\ *n, pl* **-ties 1** : shameful injustice : WICKEDNESS **2** : an unjust or wicked act or thing [Middle French *iniquité,* from Latin *iniquitas,* from *iniquus* "uneven, unfair", from *in-* + *aequus* "equal, fair"]

¹ini·tial \in-'ish-əl\ *adj* **1** : of, relating to, or existing at the beginning : INCIPIENT ⟨*initial* stages of a disease⟩ **2** : placed or standing at the beginning : FIRST ⟨*initial* letter of a word⟩ [Latin *initialis,* from *initium* "beginning", from *inire* "to go in", from *in-* + *ire* "to go"]

²initial *n* **1** : the first letter of a name **2** : a large letter beginning a text or a division or paragraph

³initial *vt* **ini·tialed** *or* **ini·tialled; ini·tial·ing** *or* **ini·tial·ling** \-'ish-ling, -ə-ling\ : to affix initials or an initial to : mark with an initial ⟨*initial* a memorandum⟩

ini·tial·ly \in-'ish-lē, -ə-lē\ *adv* : in the first place : at the beginning

initial side *n* : a straight line containing a point about which another line rotates to generate an angle

¹ini·ti·ate \in-'ish-ē-,āt\ *vt* **1** : to set going : BEGIN ⟨*initiate* a new policy⟩ **2** : to instruct in the basics or principles of something : INTRODUCE ⟨*initiate* tourists to the local customs⟩ **3** : to admit into membership by or as if by special ceremonies — **ini·ti·a·tor** \-,āt-ər\ *n*

²ini·tiate \in-'ish-ət, -ē-ət\ *adj* : INITIATED

³ini·tiate \in-'ish-ət, -ē-ət\ *n* **1** : a person who is undergoing or has passed an initiation **2** : an expert in a special field

ini·ti·a·tion \in-,ish-ē-'ā-shən\ *n* **1** : the act of initiating : the process of being initiated **2** : the ceremonies by which a person is made a member of a society or club

ini·tia·tive \in-'ish-ət-iv\ *n* **1** : a first step or movement ⟨take the *initiative* in making friends⟩ **2** : energy or ability displayed in initiating something : ENTERPRISE ⟨has the desire to win but lacks *initiative*⟩ **3 a** : the right to initiate legislative action **b** : a procedure enabling a specified number of voters to propose a law for approval of the electorate or the legislature — compare REFERENDUM

ini·tia·to·ry \in-'ish-ə-,tōr-ē, -'ish-ə-, -,tór-\ *adj* **1** : constituting a beginning : INTRODUCTORY ⟨*initiatory* remarks⟩ **2** : serving to initiate ⟨*initiatory* ceremonies⟩

in·ject \in-'jekt\ *vt* **1 a** : to throw, drive, or force into something ⟨*inject* fuel into an engine⟩ **b** : to force a fluid into especially for medical purposes **2** : to introduce as an additional element ⟨*injected* humor into the speech⟩ [Latin *injectus,* past participle of *inicere* "to inject", from *in-* + *jacere* "to throw"] — **in·ject·able** \-'jek-tə-bəl\ *adj* — **in·jec·tor** \-tər\ *n*

in·jec·tion \in-'jek-shən\ *n* **1** : an act or instance of injecting (as by a syringe or pump) **2** : something (as a medication) that is injected

injection molding *n* : a method of forming articles (as of plastic) by heating the molding material until it can flow and injecting it into a mold — **injection–molded** *adj*

in·ju·di·cious \,in-jù-'dish-əs\ *adj* : not judicious : INDISCREET, UNWISE — **in·ju·di·cious·ly** *adv* — **in·ju·di·cious·ness** *n*

in·junc·tion \in-'jəng-shən, -'jəngk-\ *n* **1** : the act or an instance of enjoining : ORDER **2** : a court order requiring a party to do or refrain from doing a specified act ⟨sought an *injunction* against the strike⟩ [Late Latin *injunctio,* from Latin *injungere* "to enjoin"] — **in·junc·tive** \-'jəng-tiv, -'jəngk-\ *adj*

in·jure \'in-jər\ *vt* **in·jured; in·jur·ing** \'inj-ring, -ə-ring\ **1 a** : to do an injustice to : WRONG **b** : to harm, impair, or tarnish the standing of **c** : to give pain to ⟨*injure* one's pride⟩ **2 a** : to inflict bodily hurt on **b** : to impair the soundness of **c** : to inflict material damage or loss on [back-formation from *injury*]

in·ju·ri·ous \in-'jùr-ē-əs\ *adj* : causing injury : HARMFUL — **in·ju·ri·ous·ly** *adv* — **in·ju·ri·ous·ness** *n*

in·ju·ry \'inj-rē, -ə-rē\ *n, pl* **-ries 1** : an act that damages or hurts : WRONG **2** : hurt, damage, or loss sustained [Latin *injuria,* from *in-* + *jur-, jus* "justice, right"] □ SYN DAMAGE, HARM: INJURY implies an act or result detrimental to one's rights, well-being, freedom, property, or success ⟨the accident resulted in both physical and emotional *injuries*⟩ DAMAGE applies to injury involving loss ⟨the pest did considerable *damage* to the crop⟩ ⟨scandal that resulted in *damage* to the company's prestige⟩ HARM applies to any evil that injures and often suggests suffering, pain, or annoyance ⟨assured there would be no bodily *harm*⟩

in·jus·tice \in-'jəs-təs, 'in-\ *n* **1** : violation of the rights of another : UNFAIRNESS **2** : an unjust act

¹ink \'ingk\ *n* **1** : a usually liquid and colored material for writing and printing **2** : the black protective secretion of a cephalopod [Old French *enke,* from Late Latin *encaustum,* from Latin *encaustus* "burned in", from Greek *enkaustos,* from *enkaiein* "to burn in", from *en-* + *kaiein* "to burn"]

²ink *vt* : to put ink on — **ink·er** *n*

ink·ber·ry \'ingk-,ber-ē\ *n* **1** : a black-berried American holly **2** : POKEWEED **3** : the fruit of an inkberry

ink·blot test \'ingk-,blät-\ *n* : any of several psychological tests based on the interpretation of irregular figures (as blots of ink)

¹ink·horn \'ingk-,hórn\ *n* : a small portable bottle (as of horn) for holding ink

²inkhorn *adj* : ostentatiously learned : PEDANTIC ⟨*inkhorn* terms⟩

ink·jet \'ingk-'jet\ *adj* : of, relating to, or being a dot matrix printer in which electrically charged droplets of ink are projected onto the paper

in·kling \'ing-kling\ *n* **1** : a slight suggestion : HINT **2** : a slight knowledge or vague notion ⟨didn't have an *inkling* of what it all meant⟩ [Middle English *yngkiling*]

ink·stand \'ingk-,stand\ *n* : INKWELL; *also* : a pen and inkwell

ink·well \'ing-,kwel\ *n* : a container for ink

inky \'ing-kē\ *adj* **ink·i·er; -est 1** : consisting of or using ink ⟨an *inky* blot⟩ **2** : suggestive of ink: as **a** : very dark or black ⟨an *inky* cloud⟩ **b** : dark with dirt ⟨*inky* fingernails⟩ — **ink·i·ness** *n*

initial side

\ə\ abut	\ng\ sing
\ər\ further	\ō\ bone
\a\ mat	\ò\ saw
\ā\ take	\òi\ coin
\ä\ cot, cart	\th\ thin
\aù\ out	\th\ this
\ch\ chin	\ü\ food
\e\ pet	\ù\ foot
\ē\ easy	\y\ yet
\g\ go	\yü\ few
\i\ tip	\yù\ cure
\ī\ life	\zh\ vision
\j\ job	

inky cap *n* : a small mushroom whose cap dissolves into an inky fluid after the spores mature

in·laid \'in-'lād\ *adj* **1** : set into a surface in a decorative design **2** : decorated with a design or material set into a surface ⟨a table with an *inlaid* top⟩ **3** : having a design that goes all the way through to the backing ⟨*inlaid* linoleum⟩

in·land \'in-,land, -lənd\ *n* : the land away from the coast or boundaries : INTERIOR — **inland** *adj or adv* — **in·land·er** \'in-,lan-dər, -lən-\ *n*

in·law \'in-,lȯ\ *n* : a relative by marriage [back-formation from *mother-in-law,* etc.]

¹in·lay \in-'lā, 'in-,\ *vt* **in·laid; in·lay·ing** : to set into a surface or ground material for decoration or reinforcement — **in·lay·er** *n*

²in·lay \'in-,lā\ *n* **1** : inlaid work or material used in inlaying **2** : a tooth filling shaped to fit a cavity and then cemented into place

in·let \'in-,let, -lət\ *n* **1** : a small or narrow indentation into the land formed by a body of water **2** : an opening for intake

in–line \'in-'līn, ,in-\ *adj or adv* : having the parts or units arranged in a straight line; *also* : being so arranged

in·mate \'in-,māt\ *n* : one of a group occupying a single residence; *esp* : a person confined to an institution (as a hospital or prison)

in me·di·as res \in-,med-ē-əs-'rās, -,med-ē-əs-'rēz\ *adv* : in or into the middle of a narrative or plot [Latin, literally, "into the midst of things"]

in me·mo·ri·am \,in-mə-'mōr-ē-əm, -'mȯr-\ *prep* : in memory of — used especially in epitaphs [Latin]

in·most \'in-,mōst\ *adj* : INNERMOST [Old English *in-nemest,* superlative of *inne* "in, within", from *in*]

inn \'in\ *n* **1** : a public house that provides lodging and food for travelers : HOTEL **2** : TAVERN 1 [Old English]

in·nards \'in-ərdz\ *n pl* **1** : the internal organs of a human being or animal; *esp* : VISCERA **2** : the internal parts of a structure or mechanism [alteration of *in-wards*]

in·nate \in-'āt, 'in-,\ *adj* **1** : existing in or belonging to an individual from birth : NATIVE **2** : belonging to the essential nature of something : INHERENT [Latin *inna-tus,* past participle of *innasci* "to be born in", from *in-* + *nasci* "to be born"] — **in·nate·ly** *adv* — **in·nate·ness** *n* □ SYN INNATE, INBORN, INBRED, CONGENITAL mean not acquired after birth. INNATE applies to qualities or characteristics that are part of the essential nature of a person or thing ⟨develop the *innate* talent of the young⟩ ⟨the *innate* defect of the scheme⟩ INBORN suggests a quality or tendency either present at birth or so deep-seated as to seem so ⟨an *inborn* ability to act⟩ INBRED suggests something deeply rooted and acquired from parents by heredity or early nurture ⟨an *inbred* hatred of injustice⟩ CONGENITAL applies to something acquired during fetal development ⟨*congenital* heart defects⟩

in·ner \'in-ər\ *adj* **1 a** : situated farther in ⟨an *inner* room⟩ **b** : being near a center especially of influence ⟨the *inner* circle of party leaders⟩ **2** : of or relating to the mind or spirit ⟨valued a rich *inner* life⟩ — **in·ner·ly** *adv*

inner city *n* : the usually older and more densely populated central section of a city — **inner–city** *adj*

inner ear *n* : a cavity in the temporal bone that encloses a complex membranous labyrinth containing sense organs of hearing and of awareness of position in space

inner light *n, often cap I&L* : a divine presence held (as in Quaker doctrine) to enlighten and guide the soul

in·ner·most \'in-ər-,mōst\ *adj* **1** : situated farthest inward **2** : most intimate : DEEPEST ⟨one's *innermost* feelings⟩

in·ner·sole \,in-ər-'sōl\ *n* : INSOLE

inner tube *n* : an airtight tube of rubber placed inside the casing of a pneumatic tire to hold air under pressure

in·ner·vate \in-'ər-,vāt, 'in-,ər-, 'in-,ər-\ *vt* : to supply with nerves — **in·ner·va·tion** \,in-,ər-'vā-shən, ,in-,ər-\ *n* — **in·ner·va·tion·al** \-shnəl, -shən-l\ *adj*

in·ning \'in-ing\ *n* **1** : a baseball team's turn at bat ending with the 3d out; *also* : a division of a baseball game consisting of a turn at bat for each team **2** : a chance or turn for action or accomplishment ⟨time for the opposition to have its *innings*⟩ [²*in*]

inn·keep·er \'in-,kē-pər\ *n* : the landlord of an inn

in·no·cence \'in-ə-səns\ *n* **1** : the quality or state of being innocent **2** : BLUET

in·no·cent \-sənt\ *adj* **1** : free from sin : PURE **2** : free from guilt or blame : GUILTLESS ⟨*innocent* of the crime⟩ **3** : free from evil influence or effect : HARMLESS ⟨*innocent* fun⟩ **4** : lacking or reflecting a lack of sophistication, guile, or self-consciousness [Middle French, from Latin *innocens,* from *in-* + *nocens* "wicked", from *nocēre* "to harm"] — **innocent** *n* — **in·no·cent·ly** *adv*

in·noc·u·ous \in-'äk-yə-wəs\ *adj* **1** : causing no injury : HARMLESS **2 a** : not likely to give offense : INOFFENSIVE ⟨an *innocuous* joke⟩ **b** : INSIPID 2, DULL ⟨*innocuous* poems⟩ [Latin *innocuus,* from *in-* + *nocēre* "to harm"] — **in·noc·u·ous·ly** *adv* — **in·noc·u·ous·ness** *n*

in·nom·i·nate \in-'äm-ə-nət\ *adj* : having no name; *also* : ANONYMOUS [Late Latin *innominatus,* from Latin *in-* + *nominare* "to name, nominate"]

innominate artery *n* : a short artery arising from the arched first part of the aorta and dividing into the carotid and subclavian arteries of the right side

innominate bone *n* : HIPBONE

innominate vein *n* : either of a pair of veins that receive blood from the head and upper limbs and fuse to form the superior vena cava

in·no·vate \'in-ə-,vāt\ *vb* **1** : to introduce as or as if new **2** : to make changes [Latin *innovare,* from *in-* + *novus* "new"] — **in·no·va·tive** \-,vāt-iv\ *adj* — **in·no·va·tor** \-,vāt-ər\ *n*

in·no·va·tion \,in-ə-'vā-shən\ *n* **1** : the introduction of something new **2** : a new idea, method, or device

in·nu·en·do \,in-yə-'wen-dō\ *n, pl* **-dos** *or* **-does** : a subtle or indirect suggestion; *esp* : an unfavorable insinuation [Latin, "by hinting", from *innuere* "to hint", from *in-* + *nuere* "to nod"]

in·nu·mer·a·ble \in-'üm-rə-bəl, -'yüm-, -ə-rə-\ *adj* : too many to be numbered : COUNTLESS — **in·nu·mer·a·ble·ness** *n* — **in·nu·mer·a·bly** \-blē\ *adv*

in·nu·mer·ous \in-'üm-rəs, -'yüm-, -ə-rəs\ *adj* : INNUMERABLE

in·ob·ser·vance \,in-əb-'zər-vəns\ *n* **1** : lack of attention : HEEDLESSNESS **2** : failure to fulfill : NONOBSERVANCE — **in·ob·ser·vant** \-vənt\ *adj*

in·oc·u·late \in-'äk-yə-,lāt\ *vt* **1 a** : to introduce a microorganism into ⟨beans *inoculated* with nitrogen-fixing bacteria⟩ **b** : to introduce (a microorganism) into a suitable situation for growth **c** : to introduce a serum, antibody, or antigen into in order to treat or prevent a disease **2** : to introduce something into the mind of [Latin *inoculare* "to insert a bud in a plant", from *in-* + *oculus* "eye, bud"] — **in·oc·u·la·tive** \-,lāt-iv\ *adj* — **in·oc·u·la·tor** \-,lāt-ər\ *n* □ ORIGIN We often give to inanimate objects the names of parts of the body. We speak, for example, of the foot of a mountain, the leg of a table, the lip of a pitcher. And an undeveloped bud on a potato is an eye. In Latin, any bud of a plant may be called *oculus* "eye". And the verb *inoculare* means "to insert or graft a bud from one plant into another". When *inoculate* was first borrowed into English it had the same meaning as the Latin verb. Later, by extension, *inoculate* came to mean "to introduce a microorganism or serum into".

in·oc·u·la·tion \in-ˌäk-yə-'lā-shən\ *n* **1** : the act or process or an instance of inoculating **2** : INOCULUM

in·oc·u·lum \in-'äk-yə-ləm\ *n, pl* **-la** \-lə\ : material used for inoculation [New Latin]

in·of·fen·sive \ˌin-ə-'fen-siv\ *adj* : not offensive : HARMLESS — **in·of·fen·sive·ly** *adv* — **in·of·fen·sive·ness** *n*

in·op·er·a·ble \in-'äp-rə-bəl, 'in-, -ə-rə-\ *adj* **1** : not suitable for surgery **2** : not being in working order

in·op·er·a·tive \-'äp-rət-iv, -ə-rət-; -'äp-ə-ˌrāt-\ *adj* : not operative: as **a** : not functioning ⟨an *inoperative* clock⟩ **b** : having no effect or force ⟨an *inoperative* law⟩ — **in·op·er·a·tive·ness** *n*

in·oper·cu·late \ˌin-ō-'pər-kyə-lət\ *adj* : lacking an operculum ⟨*inoperculate* snails⟩

in·op·por·tune \in-ˌäp-ər-'tün, ˌin-, -'tyün\ *adj* : INCONVENIENT ⟨happened at an *inopportune* time⟩ — **in·op·por·tune·ly** *adv* — **in·op·por·tune·ness** \-'tün-nəs, -'tyün-\ *n*

in order that *conj* : THAT

in·or·di·nate \in-'órd-n-ət, -'órd-nət\ *adj* : exceeding reasonable limits : IMMODERATE ⟨an *inordinate* curiosity⟩ [Latin *inordinatus* "disordered", from *in-* + *ordinare* "to arrange", from *ordin-, ordo* "order"] SYN see EXCESSIVE — **in·or·di·nate·ly** *adv* — **in·or·di·nate·ness** *n*

in·or·gan·ic \ˌin-ór-'gan-ik\ *adj* **1** : being or composed of matter of other than plant or animal origin : MINERAL **2** : of or relating to a branch of chemistry concerned with substances not usually classed as organic — **in·or·gan·i·cal·ly** \-'gan-i-kə-lē, -klē\ *adv*

in·pa·tient \'in-ˌpā-shənt\ *n* : a hospital patient who receives lodging and food as well as treatment — compare OUTPATIENT

¹in·put \'in-ˌpùt\ *n* **1** : something that is put in: as **a** : power or energy put into a machine or system **b** : information fed into a computer **2** : a point at which an input (as power, an electronic signal, or data) is made **3** : the act or process of putting in

²input *vt* **in·put·ted** *or* **input; in·put·ting** : to enter (data) into a computer

in·quest \'in-ˌkwest\ *n* **1** : a judicial or official inquiry or investigation especially before a jury **2** : a body of persons assembled to conduct an inquest **3** : the finding of an inquest [Old French *enqueste,* derived from Latin *inquirere* "to inquire"]

in·qui·line \'in-kwə-ˌlīn, 'ing-, -lən\ *n* : an animal that habitually lives in the nest or den of another kind of animal [Latin *inquilinus* "tenant, lodger", from *in-* + *colere* "to cultivate, dwell"] — **in·qui·lin·ism** \-ˌiz-əm\ *n* — **in·qui·li·nous** \ˌin-kwə-'lī-nəs, ˌing-\ *adj*

in·quire *also* **en·quire** \in-'kwīr\ *vb* **1** : to ask about **2** : to make an investigation or inquiry : INVESTIGATE **3** : to seek information by questioning [Old French *enquerre,* from Latin *inquirere,* from *in-* + *quaerere* "to seek"] — **in·quir·er** *n* — **in·quir·ing·ly** \-ing-lē\ *adv* — **inquire after** : to ask about the health of

in·qui·ry *also* **en·qui·ry** \'in-ˌkwīr-ē, in-'; 'in-kwə-rē, 'ing-\ *n, pl* **-ries** **1 a** : the act of inquiring ⟨learn by *inquiry*⟩ **b** : a request for information **2** : a search for truth or knowledge **3** : a systematic examination : INVESTIGATION

in·qui·si·tion \ˌin-kwə-'zish-ən\ *n* **1** : the act of inquiring **2** : a judicial or official inquiry **3 a** *cap* : a former Roman Catholic tribunal for the discovery and punishment of heresy **b** : an investigation conducted with little regard for individual rights **c** : a severe questioning [Middle French, from Latin *inquisitio,* from *inquirere* "to inquire"] — **in·qui·si·tion·al** \-'zish-nəl, -ən-l\ *adj*

in·quis·i·tive \in-'kwiz-ət-iv\ *adj* **1** : given to examination or investigation **2** : given to asking questions; *esp* : too curious about other people's affairs SYN see CURIOUS — **in·quis·i·tive·ly** *adv* — **in·quis·i·tive·ness** *n*

in·quis·i·tor \in-'kwiz-ət-ər\ *n* : one that inquires; *esp* : one that conducts an inquisition — **in·quis·i·to·ri·al** \-ˌkwiz-ə-ˌtōr-ē-əl, -ˌtór-\ *adj* — **in·quis·i·to·ri·al·ly** \-ē-ə-lē\ *adv*

in re \in-'rē, -'rā\ *prep* : in the matter of : CONCERNING, RE [Latin]

in·road \'in-ˌrōd\ *n* **1** : a sudden hostile entry : RAID **2** : a serious encroachment

in·rush \'in-ˌrəsh\ *n* : a crowding or flooding in : INFLUX

in·sa·lu·bri·ous \ˌin-sə-'lü-brē-əs\ *adj* : UNWHOLESOME, NOXIOUS — **in·sa·lu·bri·ty** \-brət-ē\ *n*

in·sane \in-'sān, 'in-\ *adj* **1** : not sane : unsound in mind **2** : showing evidence of an unsound mind ⟨an *insane* look⟩ **3** : used by or for the insane ⟨an *insane* asylum⟩ **4** : utterly foolish or unreasonable — **in·sane·ly** *adv* — **in·sane·ness** \-'sān-nəs\ *n* □ SYN MAD, CRAZY: INSANE technically means such unsoundness of mind that one is not responsible for one's actions; in general use it implies utter folly or irrationality ⟨an *insane* scheme⟩ MAD carries implications of wildness or rashness or lack of restraint ⟨*mad* pursuit of fortunes⟩ CRAZY suggests a distraught state of mind induced by intense emotion ⟨*crazy* with anxiety⟩

in·san·i·tary \in-'san-ə-ˌter-ē, 'in-\ *adj* : unclean enough to endanger health : CONTAMINATED

in·san·i·ty \in-'san-ət-ē\ *n, pl* **-ties** **1 a** : unsoundness or disorder of the mind **b** : a mental illness **2** : such unsoundness of mind as excuses one from criminal or civil responsibility **3 a** : extreme folly or unreasonableness **b** : something utterly foolish or unreasonable □ SYN INSANITY, LUNACY, MANIA denote serious mental disorder. INSANITY implies unfitness to manage one's own affairs or to behave safely in a state of freedom; LUNACY may imply alternating periods of madness and lucidity and commonly stresses wildness of thought and behavior; MANIA is often used specifically of one of the spells of intense excitement characteristic of some mental disorders.

in·sa·tia·ble \in-'sā-shə-bəl, 'in-\ *adj* : incapable of being satisfied ⟨*insatiable* thirst⟩ ⟨an *insatiable* desire for knowledge⟩ — **in·sa·tia·bil·i·ty** \in-ˌsā-shə-'bil-ət-ē\ *n* — **in·sa·tia·ble·ness** \in-'sā-shə-bəl-nəs, 'in-\ *n* — **in·sa·tia·bly** \-blē\ *adv*

in·sa·tiate \in-'sā-shət, -shē-ət\ *adj* : not satiated or satisfied; *also* : INSATIABLE ⟨*insatiate* desires⟩ — **in·sa·tiate·ly** *adv* — **in·sa·tiate·ness** *n*

in·scribe \in-'skrīb\ *vt* **1 a** : to write, engrave, or print as a lasting record **b** : to enter on a list : ENROLL **2 a** : to write, engrave, or print characters on **b** : to autograph or address as a gift **3** : to dedicate (as a poem) to someone **4** : to draw within a figure so as to touch in as many places as possible [Latin *inscribere,* from *in-* + *scribere* "to write"] — **in·scrib·er** *n*

in·scrip·tion \in-'skrip-shən\ *n* **1** : something that is inscribed **2** : the wording on a coin, medal, or seal : LEGEND **3** : the dedication of a book or work of art **4** : the act of inscribing [Latin *inscriptio,* from *inscribere* "to inscribe"] — **in·scrip·tion·al** \-shnəl, -shən-l\ *adj*

in·scru·ta·ble \in-'skrüt-ə-bəl\ *adj* : not readily understood : ENIGMATIC ⟨an *inscrutable* mystery⟩ [Late Latin *inscrutabilis,* from Latin *in-* + *scrutari* "to search"] — **in·scru·ta·bil·i·ty** \-ˌskrüt-ə-'bil-ət-ē\ *n* — **in·scru·ta·ble·ness** \-'skrüt-ə-bəl-nəs\ *n* — **in·scru·ta·bly** \-blē\ *adv*

in·seam \'in-ˌsēm\ *n* : the seam on the inside of the leg of a pair of pants; *also* : the length of this seam

in·sect \'in-ˌsekt\ *n* **1** : any of numerous small animals that are usually more or less obviously segmented **2** : any of a class (Insecta) of arthropods (as bugs or bees) with well-defined head, thorax, and abdomen, three pairs of jointed legs, and typically one or two pairs of wings [Latin *insectum,* from *insecare* "to cut into", from *in-* + *secare* "to cut"] □ ORIGIN The bodies of insects are segmented. This makes them look as if

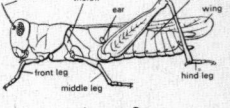

insect 2

\ə\ abut   \ng\ sing
\ər\ further   \ō\ bone
\a\ mat   \ó\ saw
\ā\ take   \oi\ coin
\ä\ cot, cart   \th\ thin
\aù\ out   \th\ this
\ch\ chin   \ü\ food
\e\ pet   \ù\ foot
\ē\ easy   \y\ yet
\g\ go   \yü\ few
\i\ tip   \yù\ cure
\ī\ life   \zh\ vision
\j\ job

notches have been cut into them at intervals. For this reason the Greek philosopher Aristotle gave insects the name *entomon*, "a thing cut into", derived from the prefix *en-*, "in", and the verb *temnein*, "to cut". (From this Greek word we derive our name for the study of insects, *entomology*.) Later, when the Romans wanted a word for this kind of creature, they did not simply borrow the Greek word but translated it *insectum*, from the verb *insecare* "to cut into". The Latin word was borrowed into English.

in·sec·ta·ry \'in-,sek-tə-rē\ *also* **in·sec·tar·i·um** \,in-,sek-'ter-ē-əm\ *n, pl* **-taries** \-tə-rēz\ *also* **-tar·ia** \-'ter-ē-ə\ : a place for rearing or keeping live insects

in·sec·ti·cide \in-'sek-tə-,sīd\ *n* : an agent that destroys insects — **in·sec·ti·cid·al** \-,sek-tə-'sīd-l\ *adj*

in·sec·ti·vore \in-'sek-tə-,vōr, -,vȯr\ *n* **1** : any of an order (Insectivora) of mammals comprising forms (as the moles, shrews, hedgehogs) that are mostly small, insectivorous, and nocturnal **2** : an insectivorous plant or animal [derived from Latin *insectum* "insect" + *vorare* "to devour"]

in·sec·tiv·o·rous \,in-,sek-'tiv-rəs, -ə-rəs\ *adj* : depending on insects as food

in·se·cure \,in-si-'kyu̇r\ *adj* **1** : not confident or sure **2** : not well protected **3** : not firmly fastened **4** : not stable or well-adjusted — **in·se·cure·ly** *adv* — **in·se·cure·ness** *n* — **in·se·cu·ri·ty** \-'kyu̇r-ət-ē\ *n*

in·sem·i·nate \in-'sem-ə-,nāt\ *vt* : to introduce semen into the genital tract of (a female) — **in·sem·i·na·tion** \-,sem-ə-'nā-shən\ *n*

in·sen·sate \in-'sen-,sāt, 'in-\ *adj* **1** : lacking awareness or sensation : INANIMATE **2** : lacking sense or understanding; *also* : FOOLISH **3** : lacking humane feeling : BRUTAL (*insensate* hatred) — **in·sen·sate·ly** *adv* — **in·sen·sate·ness** *n*

in·sen·si·ble \in-'sen-sə-bəl, 'in-\ *adj* **1** : incapable or deprived of feeling or sensation: as **a** : INANIMATE 1a, INSENTIENT (*insensible* earth) **b** : UNCONSCIOUS 2b **c** : lacking or deprived of sensory perception : INSENSITIVE (*insensible* to pain) **2 a** : IMPERCEPTIBLE 1 **b** : SLIGHT, GRADUAL (*insensible* motion) **3** : APATHETIC, INDIFFERENT (*insensible* to fear); *also* : UNAWARE (*insensible* of their danger) **4** : not intelligible : MEANINGLESS **5** : lacking delicacy or refinement — **in·sen·si·bil·i·ty** \in-,sen-sə-'bil-ət-ē\ *n* — **in·sen·si·ble·ness** \in-'sen-sə-bəl-nəs, 'in-\ *n* — **in·sen·si·bly** \-blē\ *adv*

in·sen·si·tive \in-'sen-sət-iv, 'in-, -'sen-stiv\ *adj* : not sensitive; *esp* : lacking feeling — **in·sen·si·tive·ly** *adv* — **in·sen·si·tive·ness** *n* — **in·sen·si·tiv·i·ty** \in-,sen-sə-'tiv-ət-ē\ *n*

in·sen·tient \in-'sen-chənt, 'in-, -chē-ənt\ *adj* : lacking perception, consciousness, or animation — **in·sen·tience** \-chəns, -chē-əns\ *n*

in·sep·a·ra·ble \in-'sep-rə-bəl, 'in-, -ə-rə-\ *adj* : incapable of being separated (*inseparable* friends) — **in·sep·a·ra·bil·i·ty** \in-,sep-rə-'bil-ət-ē, -ə-rə-\ *n* — **in·sep·a·ra·ble·ness** \in-'sep-rə-bəl-nəs, 'in-, -ə-rə-\ *n* — **in·sep·a·ra·bly** \-blē\ *adv*

¹in·sert \in-'sərt\ *vb* **1** : to put or place in (*inserted* the key in the lock) **2** : to introduce into the body of something : INTERPOLATE (*insert* an explanation into a text) **3** : to set in and make fast **4** : to be in attachment to the part to be moved (a muscle which *inserts* on the humerus) [Latin *insertus*, past participle of *inserere* "to insert", from *in-* + *serere* "to join"] SYN see INTRODUCE — **in·sert·er** *n*

²in·sert \'in-,sərt\ *n* : something that is inserted or is for insertion

in·ser·tion \in-'sər-shən\ *n* **1** : the act or process of inserting **2** : something that is inserted: as **a** : the part of a muscle that inserts on a part to be moved **b** : the mode or place of attachment of an organ or part **c** : embroidery or needlework inserted as ornament between two pieces of fabric — **in·ser·tion·al** \-shnəl, -shən-l\ *adj*

in·ses·so·ri·al \,in-,se-'sōr-ē-əl, -'sȯr-\ *adj* : adapted for perching : PERCHING (*insessorial* birds) [Latin *insessus*, past participle of *insidēre* "to sit on", from *in-* + *sedēre* "to sit"]

¹in·set \'in-,set\ *n* : something that is inset: as **a** : a small graphic representation (as a map or picture) set within the compass of a larger one **b** : a piece of cloth set into a garment for decoration

²in·set \'in-,set, in-'\ *vt* **inset** *or* **in·set·ted**; **in·set·ting** : to set in : insert as an inset

¹in·shore \'in-'shōr, -'shȯr\ *adj* **1** : situated or carried on near shore (*inshore* fishing) **2** : moving toward shore (an *inshore* wind)

²inshore *adv* : to or toward shore (debris drifting *inshore*)

¹in·side \in-'sīd, 'in-,\ *n* **1** : an inner side or surface **2 a** : an interior or internal part **b** : inward nature, thoughts, or feeling **c** : VISCERA, ENTRAILS — usually used in pl.

²inside *adv* **1** : on the inner side (cleaned the car *inside* and out) **2** : in or into the interior (went *inside*)

³inside *adj* **1** : of, relating to, or being on or near the inside (an *inside* wall) **2** : relating or known to a special group of people (*inside* information)

⁴inside *prep* **1 a** : in or into the interior of (went *inside* the house) **b** : on the inner side of (put the dot *inside* the curve) **2** : before the end of : WITHIN (*inside* an hour)

inside of *prep* : INSIDE

in·sid·er \in-'sīd-ər, 'in-\ *n* : a person who has access to confidential information

inside track *n* : an advantageous competitive position [from the fact that the inner side of a curved racetrack is shorter than the outer]

in·sid·i·ous \in-'sid-ē-əs\ *adj* **1 a** : awaiting a chance to entrap : TREACHEROUS **b** : harmful but attractive **2** : having a gradual and cumulative effect (an *insidious* disease) [Latin *insidiosus*, from *insidiae* "ambush", from *insidēre* "to sit in, sit on", from *in-* + *sedēre* "to sit"] — **in·sid·i·ous·ly** *adv* — **in·sid·i·ous·ness** *n*

in·sight \'in-,sīt\ *n* **1** : the power or act of seeing into a situation **2** : the act of understanding the inner nature of things or of seeing intuitively

in·sig·nia \in-'sig-nē-ə\ *or* **in·sig·ne** \-nē\ *n, pl* **-nia** *or* **-ni·as** : a distinguishing mark especially of authority, office, or honor : BADGE, EMBLEM [Latin *insignia*, pl. of *insigne* "mark, badge", from *in-* + *signum* "mark, sign"]

in·sig·nif·i·cant \,in-sig-'nif-i-kənt\ *adj* : not significant: as **a** : lacking meaning or importance : INCONSEQUENTIAL (*insignificant* details) **b** : lacking weight, position, or influence : CONTEMPTIBLE (an *insignificant* hanger-on) **c** : LITTLE, TRIVIAL (an *insignificant* amount) — **in·sig·nif·i·cance** \-kəns\ *n* — **in·sig·nif·i·cant·ly** *adv*

in·sin·cere \,in-sin-'siər\ *adj* : lacking in sincerity — **in·sin·cere·ly** *adv* — **in·sin·cer·i·ty** \-'ser-ət-ē, -'sir-\ *n*

in·sin·u·ate \in-'sin-yə-,wāt\ *vt* **1** : to introduce gradually or in a subtle, indirect, or artful way **2** : to imply in a subtle or devious way [Latin *insinuare*, from *in-* + *sinuare* "to bend, curve", from *sinus* "curve"] — **in·sin·u·a·tor** \-,wāt-ər\ *n*

in·sin·u·at·ing *adj* **1** : tending gradually to cause doubt, distrust, or change of outlook (*insinuating* remarks) **2** : intended to win favor and confidence by subtle or artful means (an *insinuating* voice) — **in·sin·u·at·ing·ly** \-,wāt-ing-lē\ *adv*

in·sin·u·a·tion \in-,sin-yə-'wā-shən\ *n* **1** : a subtle suggestion : INNUENDO **2** : the artful pursuit of favor : INGRATIATION

in·sip·id \in-'sip-əd\ *adj* **1** : lacking taste or savor : TASTELESS **2** : lacking in interest, stimulation, or challenge : DULL, FLAT (*insipid* fiction) [Late Latin *insipidus*, from Latin *in-* + *sapidus* "savory", from *sapere* "to taste"] — **in·si·pid·i·ty** \,in-sə-'pid-ət-ē\ *n* — **in-**

sip·id·ly \in-'sip-əd-lē\ *adv* □ SYN VAPID, BANAL, INANE: INSIPID implies a lack of sufficient taste or savor to please or interest ⟨over-cooked *insipid* cabbage⟩ ⟨*insipid* art and dull prose⟩ VAPID suggests lack of liveliness, force, or spirit ⟨exchange of *vapid* remarks⟩ BANAL stresses the complete absence of freshness, novelty, or immediacy ⟨a *banal* tale of unrequited love⟩ INANE implies lacking any significant or convincing quality ⟨a purposeless *inane* life⟩ ⟨*inane* criticism⟩

in·sist \in-'sist\ *vb* 1 : to place special emphasis or great importance ⟨*insists* on punctuality⟩ 2 : to request urgently ⟨*insisted* that I come⟩ 3 : to maintain in a persistent or positive manner ⟨*insisted* that their rights had been violated⟩ [Latin *insistere* "to stand upon, insist", from *in-* + *sistere* "to stand"]

in·sis·tence \in-'sis-təns\ *n* 1 : the act of insisting 2 : the quality or state of being insistent : URGENCY ⟨the *insistence* of a need⟩

in·sis·tent \-tənt\ *adj* : compelling attention : PERSISTENT ⟨*insistent* demands⟩ — **in·sist·ent·ly** *adv*

in situ \in-'sī-tü *also* -'si-\ *adv or adj* : in the natural or original position [Latin, "in position"]

in·so·far as \'in-sə-,fär-əz\ *conj* : to the extent or degree that

in·so·la·tion \,in-,sō-'lā-shən\ *n* 1 : solar radiation that has been received 2 : the rate of delivery of all direct solar energy per unit of horizontal surface [Latin *insolatio* "exposure to the sun", from *insolare* "to expose to the sun", from *in-* + *sol* "sun"]

in·sole \'in-,sōl\ *n* 1 : an inside sole of a shoe 2 : a loose thin strip placed inside a shoe for warmth or comfort

in·so·lent \'in-sə-lənt\ *adj* 1 : arrogant or rude in speech or conduct ⟨an *insolent* child⟩ 2 : exhibiting boldness or rudeness ⟨an *insolent* act⟩ [Latin *insolens*] — **in·so·lence** \-ləns\ *n* — **in·so·lent·ly** *adv*

in·sol·u·ble \in-'säl-yə-bəl, 'in-\ *adj* : not soluble: as **a** : incapable of being solved or explained **b** : incapable of being dissolved in a liquid or soluble only with difficulty or to a slight degree — **in·sol·u·bil·i·ty** \in-,säl-yə-'bil-ət-ē\ *n* — **insoluble** *n* — **in·sol·u·ble·ness** \in-'säl-yə-bəl-nəs, 'in-\ *n* — **in·sol·u·bly** \-blē\ *adv*

in·sol·vent \in-'säl-vənt, 'in-\ *adj* 1 : unable or having ceased to pay debts 2 : insufficient to pay all debts ⟨an *insolvent* estate⟩ — **in·sol·ven·cy** \-vən-sē\ *n* — **insolvent** *n*

in·som·nia \in-'säm-nē-ə\ *n* : prolonged and usually abnormal inability to get enough sleep [Latin, from *insomnis* "sleepless", from *in-* + *somnus* "sleep"] — **in·som·ni·ac** \-nē-,ak\ *adj or n*

in·so·much as \,in-sə-,məch-əz\ *conj* : inasmuch as

insomuch that \-,thət\ *conj* : to such a degree that : so that

in·sou·ci·ance \in-'sü-sē-əns\ *n* : a lighthearted unconcern : NONCHALANCE [French] — **in·sou·ci·ant** \-ənt\ *adj* — **in·sou·ci·ant·ly** *adv*

in·spect \in-'spekt\ *vb* 1 : to examine closely (as for judging quality or condition) ⟨*inspect* foodstuffs⟩ 2 : to view and examine (as troops) officially 3 : to make an examination [Latin *inspectus*, past participle of *inspicere* "to inspect", from *in-* + *specere* "to look"] — **in·spec·tive** \-'spek-tiv\ *adj*

in·spec·tion \in-'spek-shən\ *n* **1 a** : the act of inspecting : EXAMINATION **b** : recognition of a familiar pattern leading to immediate solution of a mathematical problem ⟨solve an equation by *inspection*⟩ 2 : a checking or testing of an individual against established standards

in·spec·tor \in-'spek-tər\ *n* 1 : a person employed to make inspections ⟨meat *inspector*⟩ 2 : a police officer ranking next below a superintendent or deputy superintendent — **in·spec·tor·ate** \-tə-rət, -trət\ *n* — **in·spec·tor·ship** \-tər-,ship\ *n*

in·spi·ra·tion \,in-spə-'rā-shən\ *n* 1 : a divine influence on a person 2 : the drawing of air into the lungs in breathing : INHALATION 3 : the act or power of stimulating the intellect or emotions ⟨the *inspiration* of music⟩ **4 a** : the quality or state of being inspired ⟨the artist's *inspiration* came from many sources⟩ **b** : something that is inspired ⟨a scheme that was an *inspiration*⟩ 5 : one that inspires — **in·spi·ra·tion·al** \-shnəl, -shən-l\ *adj* — **in·spi·ra·tion·al·ly** \-ē\ *adv*

in·spire \in-'spīr\ *vb* **1 a** (1) : to move or guide by divine or supernatural influence ⟨prophets *inspired* by God⟩ (2) : to exert an animating, enlivening, or exalting influence on ⟨*inspired* by their mother⟩ **b** : to give inspiration **c** : to affect with a particular thought or feeling ⟨a childhood that *inspired* them with a desire for education⟩ 2 : INHALE **3 a** : to communicate to an agent supernaturally ⟨words *inspired* by God⟩ **b** : to infuse or introduce into the mind : AROUSE ⟨*inspire* trust in listeners⟩ 4 : to bring about : OCCASION ⟨studies that *inspired* several inventions⟩ [Latin *inspirare*, literally, "to breathe into", from *in-* + *spirare* "to breathe"] — **in·spir·er** *n*

in·spir·it \in-'spir-ət\ *vt* : to fill with spirit, courage, or energy

in·sta·bil·i·ty \,in-stə-'bil-ət-ē\ *n* : the quality or state of being unstable

in·stall *or* **in·stal** \in-'stol\ *vt* **in·stalled; in·stall·ing** 1 : to induct into an office, rank, or order 2 : to put in an indicated place, condition, or status ⟨*install* oneself in the best chair⟩ 3 : to set up for use or service ⟨*install* a furnace⟩ [Middle French *installer*, from Medieval Latin *installare*, from *in-* "in" + *stallum* "stall", from Old High German *stal*] — **in·stall·er** *n*

in·stal·la·tion \,in-stə-'lā-shən\ *n* 1 : the act of installing : the state of being installed 2 : something that is installed for use 3 : a military camp, fort, or base

¹**in·stall·ment** *or* **in·stal·ment** \in-'stol-mənt\ *n* : INSTALLATION 1

²**installment** *also* **instalment** *n* 1 : one of the parts into which a debt is divided when payment is made at intervals 2 : one of several parts (as of a publication) presented at intervals [earlier *estallment* "payment by parts", derived from Old French *estaler* "to place, fix", from *estal* "place", of Germanic origin] — **installment** *adj*

installment plan *n* : a system of paying for something in installments

¹**in·stance** \'in-stəns\ *n* 1 : SUGGESTION, REQUEST ⟨entered a contest at the *instance* of his teacher⟩ 2 : an individual illustrative of a category ⟨an *instance* of rare courage⟩ 3 : OCCASION, CASE ⟨in the first *instance*⟩ — **for instance** \fər-'in-stəns, 'frin-stəns\ : as an example □ SYN INSTANCE, CASE, EXAMPLE mean something that exhibits the distinguishing characteristics of its category. INSTANCE applies to any individual person, act, or thing that may be offered to illustrate or explain ⟨a good *instance* of the power of suggestion⟩ CASE is used to direct attention to a real or assumed occurrence or situation that is to be considered, studied, or dealt with ⟨reported isolated *cases* of typhoid⟩ EXAMPLE applies to a typical or illustrative instance or case ⟨a fine *example* of Georgian architecture⟩

²**instance** *vt* 1 : to illustrate or demonstrate by an instance 2 : to mention as a case or example : CITE

¹**in·stant** \'in-stənt\ *n* : a very short period of time : MOMENT [Medieval Latin *instans*, from Latin, "present, urgent", from *instare* "to stand on, impend, urge", from *in-* + *stare* "to stand"]

²**instant** *adj* 1 : PRESSING 1, URGENT ⟨in *instant* need⟩ 2 : IMMEDIATE, DIRECT ⟨an *instant* response⟩ **3 a** : partially prepared by the manufacturer to make final preparation easy ⟨*instant* mashed potatoes⟩ **b** : immediately soluble in water ⟨*instant* coffee⟩ [Latin *instans*, from *instare* "to urge"] — **in·stant·ness** *n*

in·stan·ta·neous \,in-stən-'tā-nē-əs, -nyəs\ *adj* 1 : done, occurring, or acting in an instant ⟨death was *instantaneous*⟩ 2 : done without delay 3 : occurring or

\ə\ abut	\ng\ sing
\ər\ further	\ō\ bone
\a\ mat	\ȯ\ saw
\ā\ take	\ȯi\ coin
\ä\ cot, cart	\th\ thin
\aù\ out	\th\ this
\ch\ chin	\ü\ food
\e\ pet	\ù\ foot
\ē\ easy	\y\ yet
\g\ go	\yü\ few
\i\ tip	\yù\ cure
\ī\ life	\zh\ vision
\j\ job	

present at a particular instant ⟨*instantaneous* velocity⟩ [Medieval Latin *instantaneus,* from *instans* "instant"] — **in·stan·ta·neous·ly** *adv* — **in·stan·ta·neous·ness** *n*

in·stan·ter \in-'stant-ər\ *adv* : at once : **INSTANTLY** [Medieval Latin, from *instans* "instant"]

in·stant·ly \'in-stənt-lē\ *adv* **1** : **IMPORTUNATELY, URGENTLY 2** : without the least delay : **IMMEDIATELY**

in·star \'in-ˌstär\ *n* : a stage in the life of an insect between two successive molts [Latin, "equivalent, figure"]

in·stead \in-'sted\ *adv* : as a substitute or alternative ⟨was going to write but called *instead*⟩

instead of \in-ˌsted-əv, -ˌsted-ə, -ˌstid-\ *prep* : as a substitute for or alternative to ⟨called *instead of* writing⟩

in·step \'in-ˌstep\ *n* **1** : the arched middle part of the human foot **2** : the part of a shoe or stocking over the instep

in·sti·gate \'in-stə-ˌgāt\ *vt* : to goad or urge forward [Latin *instigare*] **SYN** see **INCITE** — **in·sti·ga·tion** \ˌin-stə-'gā-shən\ *n* — **in·sti·ga·tive** \'in-stə-ˌgāt-iv\ *adj* — **in·sti·ga·tor** \-ˌgāt-ər\ *n*

in·still *also* **in·stil** \in-'stil\ *vt* **in·stilled; in·still·ing 1** : to cause to enter drop by drop **2** : to impart gradually ⟨*instill* a love of music⟩ [Latin *instillare,* from *in-* + *stillare* "to drip"] — **in·stil·la·tion** \ˌin-stə-'lā-shən\ *n* — **in·still·er** \in-'stil-ər\ *n* — **in·still·ment** \-'stil-mənt\ *n*

¹in·stinct \'in-ˌstingt, -ˌstingkt\ *n* **1** : a natural aptitude, impulse, or capacity **2 a** : a complex pattern of response by an organism to environmental stimuli that is largely inborn and unalterable **b** : behavior based on reactions below the conscious level [Latin *instinctus* "impulse", from *instinguere* "to incite"] — **in·stinc·tu·al** \in-'sting-chə-wəl, -chəl\ *adj*

²in·stinct \in-'stingt, -'stingkt, 'in-,\ *adj* : entirely filled ⟨a heart *instinct* with faith⟩

in·stinc·tive \in-'sting-tiv, -'stingk-\ *adj* : of, relating to, or prompted by instinct **SYN** see **SPONTANEOUS** — **in·stinc·tive·ly** *adv*

¹in·sti·tute \'in-stə-ˌtüt, -ˌtyüt\ *vt* **1** : to set up : **ESTABLISH, FOUND** ⟨*institute* a society⟩ **2** : to set going : **BEGIN** ⟨*institute* an investigation⟩ [Latin *institutus,* past participle of *instituere* "to institute", from *in-* + *statuere* "to set up", from *status* "condition, state"] — **in·sti·tut·er** *or* **in·sti·tu·tor** \-ˌtüt-ər, -ˌtyüt-\ *n*

²institute *n* **1** : something that is instituted **2 a** : an organization for the promotion of a cause : **ASSOCIATION** ⟨an *institute* for mental health⟩ **b** : an educational institution **3** : a brief course of instruction ⟨teachers' *institute*⟩

in·sti·tu·tion \ˌin-stə-'tü-shən, -'tyü-\ *n* **1** : the act of instituting : **ESTABLISHMENT 2** : an established custom, practice, or law ⟨the turkey dinner is a Thanksgiving *institution*⟩ **3 a** : an established society or corporation; *esp* : a public one ⟨educational *institutions*⟩ **b** : the building used by such an organization — **in·sti·tu·tion·al** \-shnəl, -shən-l\ *adj* — **in·sti·tu·tion·al·ly** \-ē\ *adv*

in·sti·tu·tion·al·ize \-'tü-shnə-ˌlīz, -'tyü-, -shən-l-ˌīz\ *vt* **1** : to make into or treat like an institution **2** : to put in the care of an institution — **in·sti·tu·tion·al·iza·tion** \-ˌtü-shnəl-ə-'zā-shən, -ˌtyü-, -shən-l-\ *n*

in·struct \in-'strəkt\ *vt* **1** : to impart knowledge to : **TEACH 2** : to give information to : **INFORM 3** : to give directions or commands to [Latin *instructus,* past participle of *instruere* "to construct, instruct", from *in-* + *struere* "to build"] **SYN** see **TEACH**

in·struc·tion \in-'strək-shən\ *n* **1 a** : **LESSON b** : **COMMAND 2, ORDER c** *pl* : an outline or manual of procedure to be followed : **DIRECTIONS d** : a code that tells a computer to perform a particular operation **2** : the action or practice of an instructor or teacher — **in·struc·tion·al** \-shnəl, -shən-l\ *adj*

in·struc·tive \in-'strək-tiv\ *adj* : giving knowledge : serving to instruct or inform ⟨an *instructive* experience⟩ — **in·struc·tive·ly** *adv* — **in·struc·tive·ness** *n*

in·struc·tor \-tər\ *n* : one that instructs : **TEACHER;** *esp* : a college teacher below professorial rank — **in·struc·tor·ship** \-ˌship\ *n*

in·struc·tress \-'strək-trəs\ *n* : a woman who is an instructor

in·stru·ment \'in-strə-mənt\ *n* **1** : a means whereby something is done **2 a** : **IMPLEMENT;** *esp* : one designed for precision work ⟨a surgical *instrument*⟩ **b** : a device used to produce music **3** : a formal legal document (as a deed, bond, or agreement) **4 a** : a measuring device for determining the present value of a quantity under observation **b** : an electrical or mechanical device used in navigating an airplane; *esp* : such a device used as the sole means of navigating [Latin *instrumentum,* from *instruere* "to construct, instruct"] **SYN** see **IMPLEMENT**

in·stru·men·tal \ˌin-strə-'ment-l\ *adj* **1** : acting as an instrument or means ⟨*instrumental* in sending a thief to jail⟩ **2** : designed for or performed with or on an instrument and especially a musical instrument ⟨an unusual *instrumental* arrangement⟩ — **in·stru·men·tal·ly** \-l-ē\ *adv*

in·stru·men·tal·ist \-l-əst\ *n* : a player of a musical instrument

in·stru·men·tal·i·ty \ˌin-strə-mən-'tal-ət-ē, -ˌmen-\ *n, pl* **-ties 1** : the quality or state of being instrumental **2** : **AGENCY 2, MEANS**

in·stru·men·ta·tion \ˌin-strə-mən-'tā-shən, -ˌmen-\ *n* **1** : the use or application of instruments for observation, measurement, or control **2** : the arrangement or composition of music for instruments **3** : instruments for a particular purpose

instrument flying *n* : navigation of an airplane by instruments only

instrument landing *n* : a landing made with little or no external visibility by means of instruments within an airplane and by ground radio devices

instrument panel *n* : a panel on which instruments are mounted; *esp* : **DASHBOARD 2**

in·sub·or·di·nate \ˌin-sə-'bȯrd-n-ət, -'bȯrd-nət\ *adj* : unwilling to submit to authority : **DISOBEDIENT** — **in·sub·or·di·nate·ly** *adv* — **in·sub·or·di·na·tion** \ˌin-sə-ˌbȯrd-n-'ā-shən\ *n*

in·sub·stan·tial \ˌin-səb-'stan-chəl\ *adj* **1** : lacking substance or reality : **IMAGINARY 2** : lacking firmness or solidity — **in·sub·stan·ti·al·i·ty** \-ˌstan-chē-'al-ət-ē\ *n*

in·suf·fer·able \in-'səf-rə-bəl, 'in-, -ə-rə-\ *adj* : incapable of being endured : **INTOLERABLE** ⟨an *insufferable* bore⟩ ⟨*insufferable* wrongs⟩ — **in·suf·fer·able·ness** *n* — **in·suf·fer·ably** \-blē\ *adv*

in·suf·fi·cien·cy \ˌin-sə-'fish-ən-sē\ *n, pl* **-cies 1** : the quality or state of being insufficient: as **a** : lack of mental or moral fitness **b** : lack of adequate supply **c** : lack of physical or functional adequacy ⟨cardiac *insufficiency*⟩ **2** : something insufficient ⟨aware of their own *insufficiencies*⟩

in·suf·fi·cient \-'fish-ənt\ *adj* : not sufficient : **INADEQUATE;** *also* : **INCOMPETENT** — **in·suf·fi·cient·ly** *adv*

in·su·lar \'ins-ə-lər, -yə-; 'in-shə-lər\ *adj* **1** : of, relating to, or forming an island **2** : **ISOLATED, DETACHED** ⟨an *insular* building⟩ **3** : being isolated and illiberal : **NARROW** [Late Latin *insularis,* from Latin *insula* "island"] — **in·su·lar·ism** \-lə-ˌriz-əm\ *n* — **in·su·lar·i·ty** \ˌins-ə-'lar-ət-ē, -yə-; ˌin-shə-'lar-\ *n* — **in·su·lar·ly** *adv*

in·su·late \'in-sə-ˌlāt\ *vt* : to place in a detached situation : **ISOLATE;** *esp* : to separate from conducting bodies by means of nonconductors so as to prevent transfer of electricity, heat, or sound [Latin *insula* "island"]

in·su·la·tion \ˌin-sə-'lā-shən\ *n* **1** : the act of insulating : the state of being insulated **2** : material used in insulating

in·su·la·tor \'in-sə-ˌlāt-ər\ *n* : one that insulates; *esp* : a material that is a poor conductor of heat or electricity or a device made of such material

in·su·lin \'in-sə-lən, -slən\ *n* : a pancreatic hormone needed especially for the normal utilization of sugar by the body and used in the treatment and control of diabetes [New Latin *insula* "islet of Langerhans", from Latin, "island"]

insulin shock *n* : a condition of deficient blood sugar associated with excessive insulin in the system and marked by progressive development of coma

¹in·sult \in-'səlt\ *vt* **1** : to treat with insolence, indignity, or contempt : AFFRONT **2** : to make little of : BELITTLE [Latin *insultare*, literally, "to spring upon", from *in-* + *saltare* "to leap"] SYN see OFFEND — **in·sult·er** *n*

²in·sult \'in-ˌsəlt\ *n* **1** : an act or speech showing disrespect or contempt **2** : damage to the body or one of its parts; *also* : a cause of this ⟨thermal *insult*⟩ SYN see AFFRONT

in·su·per·a·ble \in-'sü-pə-rə-bəl, 'in-, -prə-bəl\ *adj* : incapable of being surmounted or overcome ⟨*insuperable* difficulties⟩ [Latin *insuperabilis*, from *in-* + *superare* "to surmount", from *super* "over"] — **in·su·per·a·bly** \-blē\ *adv*

in·sup·port·able \ˌin-sə-'pȯrt-ə-bəl, -'pȯrt-\ *adj* : not supportable: **a** : UNENDURABLE ⟨an *insupportable* burden⟩ **b** : UNJUSTIFIABLE ⟨*insupportable* charges⟩ — **in·sup·port·able·ness** *n* — **in·sup·port·ably** \-blē\ *adv*

in·sup·press·ible \ˌin-sə-'pres-ə-bəl\ *adj* : not suppressible — **in·sup·press·ibly** \-blē\ *adv*

in·sur·able \in-'shu̇r-ə-bəl\ *adj* : capable of being insured — **in·sur·abil·i·ty** \in-ˌshu̇r-ə-'bil-ət-ē\ *n*

in·sur·ance \in-'shu̇r-əns\ *n* **1** : the act of insuring : the state of being insured **2 a** : the business of insuring persons or property **b** : coverage by contract whereby one party undertakes to guarantee another against loss by a specified event or peril **c** : the sum for which something is insured

in·sure \in-'shu̇r\ *vt* **1** : to give or procure insurance on or for **2** : to make certain : ENSURE

in·sured *n* : a person whose life or property is insured

in·sur·er \in-'shu̇r-ər\ *n* : one that insures

in·sur·gence \in-'sər-jəns\ *n* : UPRISING

in·sur·gen·cy \-jən-sē\ *n, pl* **-cies** **1** : the quality or state of being insurgent; *esp* : a state of revolt against a government that is less than an organized revolution **2** : UPRISING

¹in·sur·gent \in-'sər-jənt\ *n* : a person who revolts; *esp* : a rebel not recognized as a belligerent [Latin *insurgere* "to rise up", from *in-* + *surgere* "to rise"]

²insurgent *adj* : rising in opposition to authority : REBELLIOUS — **in·sur·gent·ly** *adv*

in·sur·mount·able \ˌin-sər-'mau̇nt-ə-bəl\ *adj* : incapable of being surmounted

in·sur·rec·tion \ˌin-sə-'rek-shən\ *n* : an act or instance of revolting against civil authority or an established government [Middle French, from Late Latin *insurrectio*, from Latin *insurgere* "to rise up"] — **in·sur·rec·tion·ary** \-shə-ˌner-ē\ *adj or n* — **in·sur·rec·tion·ist** \-shə-nəst\ *n*

in·tact \in-'takt\ *adj* : untouched especially by anything that harms or diminishes : ENTIRE, UNINJURED [Latin *intactus*, from *in-* + *tangere* "to touch"] — **in·tact·ness** \-'takt-nəs, -'tak-nəs\ *n*

in·ta·glio \in-'tal-yō, -'tag-lē-ˌō\ *n, pl* **-glios** **1 a** : an engraving or incised figure in a hard material (as stone) depressed below the surface of the material **b** : the process of making intaglios **c** : printing (as in photogravure) done from a plate in which the image is sunk below the surface **2** : something (as a gem) carved in intaglio [Italian, from *intagliare* "to engrave", from Medieval Latin *intaliare*, from Latin *in-* + Late Latin *taliare* "to cut"]

in·take \'in-ˌtāk\ *n* **1** : a place where liquid or air is taken into something (as a pump) **2** : the act of taking in **3** : something taken in ⟨food *intake*⟩

¹in·tan·gi·ble \in-'tan-jə-bəl, 'in-\ *adj* : not tangible: as **a** : incapable of being touched ⟨light is *intangible*⟩ **b** :

incapable of being thought of as matter or substance : ABSTRACT ⟨goodwill is an *intangible* asset⟩ — **in·tan·gi·bil·i·ty** \in-ˌtan-jə-'bil-ət-ē\ *n* — **in·tan·gi·ble·ness** \in-'tan-jə-bəl-nəs, 'in-\ *n* — **in·tan·gi·bly** \-blē\ *adv*

²intangible *n* : something intangible; *esp* : an asset (as goodwill) that is not corporeal

in·te·ger \'int-i-jər\ *n* **1** : a number that is a natural number (as 1, 2, or 3), the negative of a natural number, or 0 — called also *whole number* **2** : a complete entity [Latin, "whole, entire"]

in·te·gral \'int-i-grəl (*usually so in mathematics*); in-'teg-rəl, -'tēg-\ *adj* **1 a** : essential to completeness : CONSTITUENT ⟨an *integral* part of the plan⟩ **b** : of, relating to, or being a mathematical integer ⟨9 is an *integral* factor of 72⟩ **c** : formed as a unit with another part **2** : composed of integral parts : INTEGRATED **3** : lacking nothing essential : ENTIRE — **in·te·gral·i·ty** \ˌint-ə-'gral-ət-ē\ *n* — **in·te·gral·ly** \'int-i-grə-lē; in-'teg-rə-, -'tēg-\ *adv*

integral calculus *n* : a branch of mathematics applying special advanced techniques especially to the determination of lengths, areas, and volumes — compare DIFFERENTIAL CALCULUS

in·te·grate \'int-ə-ˌgrāt\ *vb* **1** : to form into a whole : UNITE ⟨*integrate* the countries' economies⟩ **2 a** : to unite with something else ⟨free enterprise *integrated* with some government controls⟩ **b** : to incorporate into a larger unit ⟨*integrate* migrant workers into the organized labor movement⟩ **3 a** : to end the segregation of and bring into common and equal membership in society or an organization **b** : DESEGREGATE ⟨*integrate* school districts⟩ **4** : to become integrated [Latin *integrare*, from *integer* "whole, entire"]

integrated circuit *n* : a tiny complex of electronic components and their connections that is produced in or on a small slice of material (as silicon) — **integrated circuitry** *n*

in·te·gra·tion \ˌint-ə-'grā-shən\ *n* : the act, the process, or an instance of integrating; *esp* : incorporation as equals into society or an organization of persons from different groups (as races)

in·te·gra·tion·ist \-shə-nəst, -shnəst\ *n* : a person who believes in, advocates, or practices social integration

in·teg·ri·ty \in-'teg-rət-ē\ *n* **1** : an unimpaired condition : SOUNDNESS **2** : adherence to a code of especially moral or artistic values **3** : the quality or state of being complete or undivided : COMPLETENESS

in·teg·u·ment \in-'teg-yə-mənt\ *n* : something that covers or encloses; *esp* : an enclosing layer (as a skin, membrane, or husk) of an organism or one of its parts [Latin *integumentum*, from *integere* "to cover", from *in-* + *tegere* "to cover"] — **in·teg·u·men·tal** \in-ˌteg-yə-'ment-l\ *adj* — **in·teg·u·men·ta·ry** \-'ment-ə-rē, -'men-trē\ *adj*

in·tel·lect \'int-l-ˌekt\ *n* **1 a** : the power of knowing **b** : the capacity for thought especially when highly developed **2** : a person of superior intellect [Latin *intellectus*, from *intellegere* "to understand"]

in·tel·lec·tion \ˌint-l-'ek-shən\ *n* **1** : exercise of the intellect : REASONING **2** : a specific act of the intellect : THOUGHT — **in·tel·lec·tive** \-'ek-tiv\ *adj* — **in·tel·lec·tive·ly** *adv*

¹in·tel·lec·tu·al \ˌint-l-'ek-chə-wəl, -chəl\ *adj* **1 a** : having to do with the intellect or understanding **b** : originating in or chiefly guided by intellect rather than by emotion or experience **c** : performed by the intellect ⟨*intellectual* processes⟩ **2** : having intellect to a high degree : engaged in or given to learning and thinking ⟨an *intellectual* person⟩ **3** : requiring study and thought ⟨*intellectual* work⟩ SYN see INTELLIGENT, MENTAL — **in·tel·lec·tu·al·i·ty** \-ˌek-chə-'wal-ət-ē\ *n* — **in·tel·lec·tu·al·ly** \-'ek-chə-wə-lē, -chə-lē\ *adv* — **in·tel·lec·tu·al·ness** \-chə-wəl-nəs, -chəl-\ *n*

²intellectual *n* : an intellectual person

intaglio

in·tel·lec·tu·al·ism \,int-l-'ek-chə-wə-,liz-əm, -chə-,liz-\ *n* : devotion to the exercise of intellect or to intellectual pursuits — **in·tel·lec·tu·al·ist** \-ləst\ *n* — **in·tel·lec·tu·al·is·tic** \-,ek-chə-wə-'lis-tik, -chə-'lis-\ *adj*

in·tel·lec·tu·al·ize \,int-l-'ek-chə-wə-,līz, -chə-,līz\ *vt* : to give rational form or content to

in·tel·li·gence \in-'tel-ə-jəns\ *n* **I a** : the ability to learn and understand or to deal with new or challenging situations : REASON, INTELLECT **b** : mental acuteness : SHREWDNESS **2** : an intelligent being **3** : the act of understanding : COMPREHENSION **3 a** : information communicated : NEWS **b** : information concerning an enemy or possible enemy; *also* : a group or agency gathering such intelligence

intelligence quotient *n* : a number held to express the relative intelligence of a person and determined by dividing his mental age by his chronological age and multiplying by 100

intelligence test *n* : a test designed to measure the relative mental capacity of a person

in·tel·li·gent \in-'tel-ə-jənt\ *adj* : having or indicating a high or satisfactory degree of intelligence [Latin *intelligens,* from *intelligere, intellegere* "to understand", from *inter-* + *legere* "to select"] — **in·tel·li·gent·ly** *adv* □ SYN INTELLECTUAL: INTELLIGENT implies having quickness of perception and understanding of any sort; INTELLECTUAL suggests having greater than average interest in things of the mind or in thinking abstractly and often implies a contrast with practical activity or capacity for simple emotional response to experience. SYN see in addition CLEVER

in·tel·li·gen·tsia \in-,tel-ə-'jen-sē-ə, -'gen-\ *n* : intellectuals as a group [Russian *intelligentsiya,* from Latin *intelligentia* "intelligence"]

in·tel·li·gi·ble \in-'tel-ə-jə-bəl\ *adj* : capable of being understood : COMPREHENSIBLE — **in·tel·li·gi·bil·i·ty** \-,tel-ə-jə-'bil-ət-ē\ *n* — **in·tel·li·gi·ble·ness** \-'tel-ə-jə-bəl-nəs\ *n* — **in·tel·li·gi·bly** \-blē\ *adv*

in·tem·per·ance \in-'tem-pə-rəns, 'in-, -prəns\ *n* : lack of moderation; *esp* : habitual or excessive use of intoxicants

in·tem·per·ate \-pə-rət, -prət\ *adj* : not temperate: as **a** : not moderate or mild : EXTREME, SEVERE ⟨*intemperate* weather⟩ **b** : lacking or showing lack of restraint or self-control **c** : given to excessive use of intoxicants — **in·tem·per·ate·ly** *adv* — **in·tem·per·ate·ness** *n*

in·tend \in-'tend\ *vt* : to have in mind as a purpose or aim : PLAN [Middle French *entendre,* from Latin *intendere* "to stretch out, intend", from *in-* + *tendere* "to stretch"]

in·ten·dant \in-'ten-dənt\ *n* : an administrative official (as a governor) especially under the French, Spanish, or Portuguese monarchies [French, from Latin *intendere* "to intend, give attention to"]

¹in·tend·ed \in-'ten-dəd\ *adj* **I** : planned for the future ⟨one's *intended* career⟩ **2** : INTENTIONAL ⟨an *intended* insult⟩

²intended *n* : an affianced person : BETROTHED

in·tense \in-'tens\ *adj* **I a** : existing in an extreme degree ⟨an *intense* light⟩ **b** : having or showing a characteristic trait in extreme degree ⟨an *intense* sun shone down⟩ **c** : very large ⟨*intense* amounts of radiation⟩ **2** : most energetic or concentrated ⟨*intense* study⟩ **3 a** : feeling deeply especially by nature or temperament ⟨an *intense* person⟩ **b** : deeply felt ⟨*intense* convictions⟩ [Middle French, from Latin *intensus,* from *intendere* "to stretch out, intend"] — **in·tense·ly** *adv* — **in·tense·ness** *n*

in·ten·si·fy \in-'ten-sə-,fī\ *vb* -**fied;** -**fy·ing** **I** : to make or become intense or more intensive : STRENGTHEN **2** : to make or become more acute : SHARPEN — **in·ten·si·fi·ca·tion** \-,ten-sə-fə-'kā-shən\ *n* — **in·ten·si·fi·er** \-'ten-sə-,fī-ər, -,fīr\ *n* □ SYN INTENSIFY, HEIGHTEN, AGGRAVATE, ENHANCE mean to increase markedly in measure or degree. INTENSIFY implies a deepening or

strengthening of a thing or its characteristics ⟨*intensify* efforts for peace⟩ ⟨colors were *intensified* by the clear atmosphere⟩ HEIGHTEN suggests a lifting above the ordinary or accustomed ⟨tried to *heighten* awareness of possible danger⟩ AGGRAVATE stresses the worsening of something already bad ⟨inflation *aggravated* the economic depression⟩ ENHANCE suggests a raising above normal in desirability or attractiveness ⟨shrubbery *enhances* a lawn⟩

in·ten·si·ty \in-'ten-sət-ē\ *n, pl* -**ties** **I** : the quality or state of being intense; *esp* : extreme degree of strength, force, or energy **2 a** : the degree or amount of a quality or condition **b** : the magnitude of force or energy per unit (as of surface, charge, or mass) ⟨the *intensity* of an electric or magnetic field⟩ **3** : SATURATION 2

¹in·ten·sive \in-'ten-siv\ *adj* **I** : involving or marked by special effort : THOROUGH, EXHAUSTIVE ⟨an *intensive* campaign⟩ ⟨*intensive* agriculture⟩ **2** : serving to give emphasis ⟨the *intensive* pronoun *myself* in the sentence "I myself was present"⟩ — **in·ten·sive·ly** *adv* — **in·ten·sive·ness** *n*

²intensive *n* : an intensive word

¹in·tent \in-'tent\ *n* **I** : the act, fact, or state of mind of intending ⟨with *intent* to kill⟩ **2** : MEANING, SIGNIFICANCE ⟨understand the *intent* of the message⟩ [Old French *entent,* from Late Latin *intentus,* from Latin *intendere* "to intend"]

²intent *adj* **I** : directed with strained or eager attention ⟨an *intent* gaze⟩ **2 a** : closely occupied ⟨*intent* upon their plans⟩ **b** : set on some end or purpose ⟨*intent* on going⟩ — **in·tent·ly** *adv* — **in·tent·ness** *n*

in·ten·tion \in-'ten-chən\ *n* **I** : a determination to act in a certain way ⟨done without *intention*⟩ **2** : an intended object : PURPOSE, END ⟨carry out one's *intention*⟩ **3** : IMPORT, SIGNIFICANCE ⟨grasp the *intention* of a speaker⟩ □ SYN PURPOSE, DESIGN, AIM: INTENTION applies to what one has in mind to do or bring about; PURPOSE suggests a more settled determination; DESIGN implies a carefully calculated plan; AIM adds implications of definite purpose and effort to attain or accomplish an end.

in·ten·tion·al \in-'tench-nəl, -'ten-chən-l\ *adj* : done by intention or design : DELIBERATE ⟨*intentional* damage⟩ SYN see VOLUNTARY — **in·ten·tion·al·i·ty** \-,ten-chə-'nal-ət-ē\ *n* — **in·ten·tion·al·ly** \in-'tench-nə-lē, -'ten-chən-l-ē\ *adv*

in·ter \in-'tər\ *vt* **in·terred; in·ter·ring** : to deposit (a dead body) in the earth or in a tomb [Old French *enterrer,* from Latin *in-* + *terra* "earth"]

inter- *prefix* **I** : between : among : in the midst ⟨*inter*penetrate⟩ ⟨*inter*stellar⟩ **2** : reciprocal : reciprocally ⟨*inter*marry⟩ **3** : located between ⟨*inter*face⟩ **4** : carried on between ⟨*inter*national⟩ **5** : occurring between : intervening ⟨*inter*glacial⟩ **6** : shared by or derived from two or more ⟨*inter*faith⟩ [Latin, from *inter*]

See *inter-* and 2d element

interagency	interdenominational	interlayer
interatomic	interdepartmental	interlibrary
interbank	interdepartmentally	intermolecular
interborough	interdialectal	intermolecularly
interbranch	interdivisional	intermountain
intercampus	interelectronic	internuclear
intercellular	interethnic	interoceanic
interchannel	interfaculty	interoffice
interchurch	interfamily	interparish
intercity	interfiber	interparty
interclan	interfraternity	interplanetary
interclass	intergang	interpopulation
interclub	intergenerational	interprofessional
intercoastal	intergeneric	interprovincial
intercolonial	intergroup	interregional
intercommunal	interhemispheric	interreligious
intercommunity	interindustry	interrow
intercompany	interinstitutional	interschool
intercultural	interisland	intersectional

intersegmental   intertroop   intervalley
intersocietal   interunion   intervillage
interterminal   interunit   interwar
interterritorial   interuniversity   interzonal
intertribal   interurban   interzone

in·ter·act \,int-ə-'rakt\ *vi* : to act upon one another

in·ter·ac·tion \,int-ə-'rak-shən\ *n* : the action or influence of people, groups, or things on one another — **in·ter·ac·tion·al** \-shnəl, -shə-nəl\ *adj*

in·ter·ac·tive \-'rak-tiv\ *adj* 1 : active between people, groups, or things 2 : of, relating to, or allowing two-way electronic communications (as between a person and a computer) — **in·ter·ac·tive·ly** *adv*

in·ter alia \,int-ə-'rā-lē-ə, -'rä-\ *adv* : among other things [Latin]

in·ter·breed \,int-ər-'brēd\ *vb* **-bred** \-'bred\; **-breeding** : to breed or cause to breed together; *esp* : CROSSBREED

in·ter·ca·lary \in-'tər-kə-,ler-ē, ,int-ər-'kal-ə-rē\ *adj* : inserted between other things or parts

in·ter·ca·late \in-'tər-kə-,lāt\ *vt* 1 : to insert (as a day) in a calendar 2 : to insert between or among existing elements or layers [Latin *intercalare,* from *inter-* + *calare* "to call, summon"] — **in·ter·ca·la·tion** \-,tər-kə-'lā-shən\ *n*

in·ter·cede \,int-ər-'sēd\ *vi* 1 : to act as a go-between between unfriendly parties 2 : to beg or plead in behalf of another ⟨*intercede* for a friend⟩ [Latin *intercedere,* from *inter-* + *cedere* "to go"] SYN see INTERPOSE

¹in·ter·cept \,int-ər-'sept\ *vt* 1 : to stop or seize on the way to or before arrival at a destination ⟨*intercept* a letter⟩ ⟨*intercept* a pass in football⟩ 2 : to include part of (a curve, surface, or solid) between two points, curves, or surfaces [Latin *interceptus,* past participle of *intercipere* "to intercept", from *inter-* + *capere* "to take, seize"]

²in·ter·cept \'int-ər-,sept\ *n* : the distance from the origin to a point where a graph crosses a coordinate axis

in·ter·cep·tion \,int-ər-'sep-shən\ *n* : the act of intercepting : the state of being intercepted

in·ter·cep·tor *or* **in·ter·cep·ter** \,int-ər-'sep-tər\ *n* : one that intercepts; *esp* : a light high-speed fast-climbing fighter plane designed for defense against raiding bombers

in·ter·ces·sion \,int-ər-'sesh-ən\ *n* : the act of interceding : MEDIATION [Latin *intercessio,* from *intercedere* "to intercede"] — **in·ter·ces·sion·al** \-'sesh-nəl, -ən-l\ *adj* — **in·ter·ces·sor** \-'ses-ər\ *n* — **in·ter·ces·so·ry** \-'ses-rē, -ə-rē\ *adj*

¹in·ter·change \,int-ər-'chānj\ *vb* 1 : to put each of (two things) in the place of the other ⟨*interchange* two tires⟩ 2 : EXCHANGE ⟨*interchange* ideas⟩ 3 : to change places mutually — **in·ter·chang·er** *n*

²in·ter·change \'int-ər-,chānj\ *n* 1 : the act, the process, or an instance of interchanging 2 : a joining of two or more highways by a system of separate levels that permit traffic to pass from one to another without the crossing of traffic streams

in·ter·change·able \,int-ər-'chān-jə-bəl\ *adj* : capable of being interchanged; *esp* : permitting mutual substitution ⟨*interchangeable* parts⟩ — **in·ter·change·abil·i·ty** \-,chān-jə-'bil-ət-ē\ *n* — **in·ter·change·able·ness** \-'chān-je-bəl-nəs\ *n* — **in·ter·change·ably** \-blē\ *adv*

in·ter·col·le·giate \,int-ər-kə-'lē-jət, -jē-ət\ *adj* : existing or carried on between colleges ⟨*intercollegiate* athletics⟩

in·ter·com \'int-ər-,käm\ *n* : INTERCOMMUNICATION SYSTEM

in·ter·com·mu·ni·cate \,int-ər-kə-'myü-nə-,kāt\ *vi* 1 : to exchange communication with one another 2 : to afford passage from one to another ⟨the rooms *intercommunicate*⟩ — **in·ter·com·mu·ni·ca·tion** \-,myü-nə-'kā-shən\ *n*

intercommunication system *n* : a two-way communication system with microphone and loudspeaker at each station for localized use

in·ter·com·mu·nion \,int-ər-kə-'myü-nyən\ *n* : interdenominational participation in communion

in·ter·con·nect \,int-ər-kə-'nekt\ *vb* : to connect with one another ⟨the rooms *interconnect*⟩ ⟨*interconnect-ed* switches⟩ — **in·ter·con·nec·tion** \-'nek-shən\ *n*

in·ter·con·ti·nen·tal \,int-ər-,känt-n-'ent-l\ *adj* 1 : extending among or carried on between continents ⟨*intercontinental* trade⟩ 2 : capable of traveling between continents ⟨an *intercontinental* missile⟩

in·ter·con·ver·sion \,int-ər-kən-'vər-zhən, -shən\ *n* : mutual conversion ⟨*interconversion* of chemical compounds⟩ — **in·ter·con·vert** \-'vərt\ *vt* — **in·ter·con·vert·ible** \-'vərt-ə-bəl\ *adj*

in·ter·cool·er \,int-ər-'kü-lər\ *n* : a device for cooling a fluid between successive heat-generating processes

in·ter·cos·tal \,int-ər-'käs-tl\ *adj* : situated between the ribs; *also* : of or relating to an intercostal part [Latin *costa* "rib"] — **intercostal** *n* — **in·ter·cos·tal·ly** \-'käs-tə-lē\ *adv*

in·ter·course \'int-ər-,kōrs, -,kȯrs\ *n* 1 : connection or relations between persons or groups : COMMUNICATION ⟨social *intercourse*⟩ 2 : physical sexual contact between individuals that involves the genitalia of at least one person; *esp* : SEXUAL INTERCOURSE [derived from Latin *intercursus* "act of running between", from *intercurrere* "to run between", from *inter-* + *currere* "to run"]

in·ter·crop \,int-ər-'kräp\ *vb* : to grow two or more crops at one time on the same piece of land ⟨*intercrop* corn and pumpkins⟩

in·ter·cross \'int-ər-,krȯs\ *n* : an instance or a product of crossbreeding — **in·ter·cross** \,int-ər-'krȯs\ *vb*

in·ter·de·pend \,int-ər-di-'pend\ *vi* : to depend upon one another — **in·ter·de·pen·dence** \-'pen-dəns\ *n* — **in·ter·de·pen·den·cy** \-dən-sē\ *n* — **in·ter·de·pen·dent** \-dənt\ *adj* — **in·ter·de·pen·dent·ly** *adv*

¹in·ter·dict \'int-ər-,dikt\ *n* 1 : a Roman Catholic church censure withdrawing most sacraments and Christian burial from a person or district 2 : PROHIBITION 2 [Old French *entredit,* from Latin *interdictum* "official prohibition", from *interdicere* "to interpose, forbid", from *inter-* + *dicere* "to say"]

²in·ter·dict \,int-ər-'dikt\ *vt* : to prohibit or forbid especially by an interdict — **in·ter·dic·tion** \,int-ər-'dik-shən\ *n* — **in·ter·dic·tor** \-'dik-tər\ *n* — **in·ter·dic·to·ry** \-'dik-tə-rē, -trē\ *adj*

in·ter·dig·i·tate \-'dij-ə-,tāt\ *vi* : to interlock like the fingers of folded hands [Latin *digitus* "finger"] — **in·ter·dig·i·ta·tion** \-,dij-ə-'tā-shən\ *n*

in·ter·dis·ci·pli·nary \,int-ər-'dis-ə-plə-,ner-ē\ *adj* : involving two or more academic disciplines

¹in·ter·est \'in-trəst; 'int-ə-,rest, -ə-rəst, -ərst; 'in-,trest\ *n* 1 : a right, title, or legal share in something 2 : WELFARE, BENEFIT; *esp* : SELF-INTEREST 3 a : a charge for borrowed money that is generally a percentage of the amount borrowed b : the return received by capital on its investments 4 : a group financially interested in an industry or enterprise ⟨mining *interests*⟩ 5 a : readiness to be concerned with or moved by something b : the quality in a thing that arouses interest ⟨your plans are of great *interest* to me⟩ [derived from Latin *interesse* "to make a difference, concern", from *inter-* + *esse* "to be"]

²interest *vt* 1 : to engage (oneself) in advancing something ⟨*interest* oneself in a friend's welfare⟩ 2 : to persuade to participate or take part 3 : to arouse the interest of

in·ter·est·ed *adj* 1 : having the attention occupied ⟨*interested* listeners⟩ 2 : being involved ⟨*interested* parties⟩ — **in·ter·est·ed·ly** *adv*

interest group *n* : a group of persons having a common interest that often provides a basis for action

\ə\ abut	\ng\ sing
\ər\ further	\ō\ bone
\a\ mat	\ȯ\ saw
\ā\ take	\ȯi\ coin
\ä\ cot, cart	\th\ thin
\au̇\ out	\th\ this
\ch\ chin	\ü\ food
\e\ pet	\u̇\ foot
\ē\ easy	\y\ yet
\g\ go	\yü\ few
\i\ tip	\yu̇\ cure
\ī\ life	\zh\ vision
\j\ job	

in·ter·est·ing *adj* : holding the attention : arousing interest — **in·ter·est·ing·ly** \-ing-lē\ *adv*

¹in·ter·face \'int-ər-ˌfās\ *n* **1** : a surface forming a common boundary of two bodies, spaces, or phases ⟨an *interface* between oil and water⟩ **2** : a place at which two independent systems meet and act on or communicate with each other; *also* : a means of communication at an interface — **in·ter·fa·cial** \ˌint-ər-'fā-shəl\ *adj*

²interface *vb* **1** : to connect or become connected through an interface **2** : to serve as an interface for

in·ter·faith \ˌint-ər-ˌfāth\ *adj* : involving persons of different religious faiths ⟨*interfaith* conference⟩

in·ter·fere \ˌint-ər-'fiər, ˌint-ə-'fiər\ *vi* **1** : to strike one foot against the opposite foot or ankle in walking or running **2** : to come in collision or be in opposition : CLASH ⟨our neighbor's arrival *interfered* with our plan⟩ **3** : to meddle in the affairs of others ⟨don't *interfere* with my business⟩ **4** : to act so as to augment, diminish, or otherwise affect one another ⟨*interfering* light waves⟩ **5** : to hinder illegally an attempt of a player to receive a pass or to play a ball or puck [Middle French *s'entreferir* "to strike one another", from Old French *entre-* "inter-" + *ferir* "to strike", from Latin *ferire*] SYN see INTERPOSE — **in·ter·fer·er** *n*

in·ter·fer·ence \ˌint-ər-'fir-əns, ˌint-ə-'fir-\ *n* **1 a** : the act or process of interfering **b** : something that interferes : OBSTRUCTION **2** : the mutual effect on meeting of two waves (as of light or sound) whereby the resulting neutralization at some points and reinforcement at others produces in the case of light waves alternate light and dark bands or colored bands **3 a** : the legal blocking of an opponent in football **b** : the illegal hindering of an opponent (as in baseball) **4 a** : confusion of received radio signals due to undesired signals or electrical effects **b** : an electrical effect that produces such confusion — **in·ter·fer·en·tial** \-fə-'ren-chəl, -ˌfir-'en-\ *adj*

in·ter·fer·tile \ˌint-ər-'fərt-l\ *adj* : capable of interbreeding — **in·ter·fer·til·i·ty** \-fər-'til-ət-ē\ *n*

in·ter·fuse \ˌint-ər-'fyüz\ *vb* **1** : to combine by or as if by fusing **2** : PERVADE, PERMEATE — **in·ter·fu·sion** \-'fyü-zhən\ *n*

in·ter·ga·lac·tic \ˌint-ər-gə-'lak-tik\ *adj* : situated or occurring in the spaces between galaxies

in·ter·gla·cial \ˌint-ər-'glā-shəl\ *adj* : occurring or relating to the time between successive glaciations

in·ter·gov·ern·men·tal \-ˌgəv-ərn-'ment-l, -ər-\ *adj* : existing or occurring between two or more governments or levels of government

in·ter·grade \ˌint-ər-'grād\ *vi* : to merge gradually one with another through a continuous series of intermediates — **in·ter·gra·da·tion** \-grā-'dā-shən, -grə-\ *n* — **in·ter·gra·da·tion·al** \-shnəl, -shən-l\ *adj*

in·ter·im \'int-ə-rəm\ *n* : an intervening time : INTERVAL [Latin, adv., "meanwhile", from *inter* "between"] — **interim** *adj*

¹in·te·ri·or \in-'tir-ē-ər\ *adj* **1** : being or acting within a limiting boundary **2** : remote from the border or shore : INLAND [Latin] — **in·te·ri·or·ly** *adv*

²interior *n* **1** : the internal part of something ⟨the *interior* of the body⟩ **2** : the inland part (as of a country) **3** : inner nature : CHARACTER **4** : the internal affairs of a state or nation — **in·te·ri·or·i·ty** \in-ˌtir-ē-'ȯr-ət-ē, -'är-\ *n*

interior angle *n* **1** : the inner of the two angles formed where two sides of a polygon come together **2** : any of the four angles formed in the area between a pair of parallel lines when a third line cuts them

interior decoration *n* : INTERIOR DESIGN

interior design *n* : the art of planning the layout and furnishings of the interior of a building

in·ter·ject \ˌint-ər-'jekt\ *vt* : to throw in between or among other things : INSERT ⟨*interject* a remark⟩ [Latin *interjectus*, past participle of *intericere* "to inter-

ject", from *inter-* + *jacere* "to throw"] SYN see INTRODUCE — **in·ter·jec·tor** \-'jek-tər\ *n* — **in·ter·jec·to·ry** \-tə-rē, -ˌtrē\ *adj*

in·ter·jec·tion \ˌint-ər-'jek-shən\ *n* **1** : an interjecting of something **2** : something interjected ⟨the speaker was interrupted by *interjections* from the audience⟩ **3** : a word or cry expressing sudden or strong feeling and usually lacking grammatical connection — **in·ter·jec·tion·al** \-shnəl, -shən-l\ *adj* — **in·ter·jec·tion·al·ly** \-ē\ *adv*

in·ter·lace \ˌint-ər-'lās\ *vb* **1** : to unite by or as if by lacing together ⟨*interlaced* fibers⟩ **2** : to vary by alternating : INTERSPERSE **3** : to cross one another as if woven together ⟨*interlacing* boughs⟩ — **in·ter·lace·ment** \-'lā-smənt\ *n*

in·ter·lard \ˌint-ər-'lärd\ *vt* : to insert or introduce at intervals : INTERSPERSE ⟨a speech *interlarded* with quotations⟩

in·ter·leave \ˌint-ər-'lēv\ *vt* **-leaved; -leaving** **1** : to equip with an interleaf **2** : to arrange in or as if in alternating layers

in·ter·leu·kin \ˌin-tər-'lü-kən\ *n* : any of several compounds that are produced by lymphocytes, macrophages, and monocytes and that function especially in regulation of the immune system [*inter-* + *leuk-* + *¹-in*]

¹in·ter·line \ˌint-ər-'līn\ *vt* : to insert between lines already written or printed — **in·ter·lin·ea·tion** \-ˌlin-ē-'ā-shən\ *n*

²interline *vt* : to provide (a garment) with an interlining

in·ter·lin·ear \ˌint-ər-'lin-ē-ər\ *adj* **1** : inserted between lines already written or printed **2** : written or printed in different languages or texts in alternate lines — **in·ter·lin·ear·ly** *adv*

in·ter·lin·ing \'int-ər-ˌlī-ning\ *n* : a lining (as of a coat) between the ordinary lining and the outside fabric

in·ter·link \ˌint-ər-'lingk\ *vt* : to link together

in·ter·lock \ˌint-ər-'läk\ *vb* : to lock together : UNITE ⟨*interlocked* fingers⟩ ⟨a series of rings *interlocking* to form a chain⟩ — **in·ter·lock** \'int-ər-ˌläk\ *n* — **in·ter·lock·er** \ˌint-ər-'läk-ər\ *n*

in·ter·loc·u·tor \ˌint-ər-'läk-yət-ər\ *n* **1** : one who takes part in dialogue or conversation **2** : a man in a minstrel show who questions the end men

in·ter·lop·er \ˌint-ər-'lō-pər, 'int-ər-ˌ\ *n* : a person who intrudes or interferes wrongly : INTRUDER [probably derived from Dutch *loper* "runner", from *lopen* "to run"]

in·ter·lude \'int-ər-ˌlüd\ *n* **1** : a performance or entertainment between the acts of a play **2** : an intervening period, space, or event : INTERVAL ⟨an *interlude* of peace between wars⟩ **3** : a musical composition inserted between the parts of a longer composition, a drama, or a religious service [Medieval Latin *interludium*, from Latin *inter-* + *ludus* "play"]

in·ter·mar·riage \ˌint-ər-'mar-ij\ *n* : marriage between members of different racial, social, or religious groups

in·ter·mar·ry \-'mar-ē\ *vi* **1** : to marry each other **2** : to become connected by intermarriage

in·ter·med·dle \ˌint-ər-'med-l\ *vi* : to meddle officiously — **in·ter·med·dler** \-'med-lər, -l-ər\ *n*

¹in·ter·me·di·ary \ˌint-ər-'mēd-ē-ˌer-ē\ *adj* **1** : INTERMEDIATE ⟨an *intermediary* stage⟩ **2** : acting as a mediator ⟨an *intermediary* agent⟩

²intermediary *n*, *pl* **-ar·ies** : MEDIATOR 1, GO-BETWEEN ⟨acting as *intermediary* between the warring factions⟩

¹in·ter·me·di·ate \ˌint-ər-'mēd-ē-ət\ *adj* : being or occurring at the middle place or degree or between extremes [Medieval Latin *intermediatus*, from Latin *intermedius*, from *inter-* + *medius* "middle"] — **in·ter·me·di·ate·ly** *adv* — **in·ter·me·di·ate·ness** *n*

²intermediate *n* **1** : an intermediate term, thing, or class **2** : MEDIATOR 1, GO-BETWEEN

in·ter·ment \in-'tər-mənt\ *n* : FUNERAL 1, BURIAL

in·ter·mez·zo \,int-ər-'met-sō, -'med-zō\ *n, pl* **-zi** \-sē, -zē\ *or* **-zos 1 :** a short light piece between the acts of a serious drama or opera **2 a :** a movement coming between the major sections of an extended musical work (as a symphony) **b :** a short independent instrumental composition [Italian, derived from Latin *intermedius* "intermediate"]

in·ter·mi·na·ble \in-'tərm-nə-bəl, 'in-, -ə-nə-\ *adj* : ENDLESS; *esp* : wearisomely dragged out ⟨an *interminable* speech⟩ — **in·ter·mi·na·ble·ness** *n* — **in·ter·mi·na·bly** \-blē\ *adv*

in·ter·min·gle \,int-ər-'ming-gəl\ *vb* : INTERMIX

in·ter·mis·sion \,int-ər-'mish-ən\ *n* **1 :** INTERRUPTION ⟨continuing without *intermission*⟩ **2 :** a pause or interval especially between the acts of a play [Latin *intermissio,* from *intermittere* "to intermit"]

in·ter·mit \-'mit\ *vb* **-mit·ted; -mit·ting :** to stop for a time or at intervals [Latin *intermittere,* from *inter-* + *mittere* "to send"] — **in·ter·mit·ter** *n*

in·ter·mit·tent \-'mit-nt\ *adj* : coming and going at intervals : not continuous ⟨*intermittent* rain⟩ — **in·ter·mit·tence** \-'mit-ns\ *n* — **in·ter·mit·tent·ly** *adv*

in·ter·mix \,int-ər-'miks\ *vb* : to mix together — **in·ter·mix·ture** \-'miks-chər\ *n*

¹in·tern \'in-,tərn, in-'\ *vt* : to confine or impound especially during a war ⟨*intern* enemy aliens⟩ [French *interner,* from Latin *internus* "internal"]

²in·tern *or* **in·terne** \'in-,tərn\ *n* : an advanced student or graduate especially in medicine gaining supervised practical experience (as in a hospital) [French *interne,* from *interne* "internal", from Latin *internus*] — **in·tern·ship** \-,ship\ *n*

³in·tern \'in-,tərn\ *vi* : to act as an intern

in·ter·nal \in-'tərn-l\ *adj* **1 a :** existing or situated within the limits or surface of something ⟨*internal* structure⟩ **b :** having to do with or situated in the inside of the body ⟨*internal* organs⟩ ⟨*internal* pain⟩ **2 :** relating or belonging to or existing within the mind **3 :** INTRINSIC, INHERENT ⟨*internal* evidence⟩ **4 :** of or relating to the domestic affairs of a state ⟨*internal* revenue⟩ [Latin *internus*] — **in·ter·nal·i·ty** \,in-,tər-'nal-ət-ē\ *n* — **in·ter·nal·ly** \in-'tərn-l-ē\ *adv*

internal–combustion engine *n* : an engine run by a fuel mixture ignited within the engine cylinder

internal medicine *n* : a branch of medicine that deals with nonsurgical diseases

internal respiration *n* : exchange of gases between the cells of the body and the blood — compare EXTERNAL RESPIRATION

internal rhyme *n* : rhyme between a word within a line and another at the end of the same line or within another line

internal secretion *n* : HORMONE

¹in·ter·na·tion·al \,int-ər-'nash-nəl, -ən-l\ *adj* **1 :** involving or affecting two or more nations ⟨*international* trade⟩ **2 :** of, relating to, or constituting a group having members in two or more nations ⟨an *international* union⟩ — **in·ter·na·tion·al·i·ty** \-,nash-ə-'nal-ət-ē\ *n* — **in·ter·na·tion·al·ly** \-'nash-nə-lē, -ən-l-ē\ *adv*

²in·ter·na·tion·al \-'nash-nəl, -ən-l, *in sense 1 often* -,nash-ə-'nal, -'näl\ *n* **1 :** one of several socialist or communist organizations of international scope **2 :** a labor union having locals in more than one country

international date line *n* : DATE LINE

in·ter·na·tion·al·ism \,int-ər-'nash-nəl-,iz-əm, -'nash-ən-l-\ *n* **1 :** international character or outlook **2 a :** a policy of political and economic cooperation among nations **b :** an attitude favoring such a policy — **in·ter·na·tion·al·ist** \-əst\ *n or adj*

in·ter·na·tion·al·ize \-'nash-nəl-,īz, -'nash-ən-l-\ *vt* : to make international; *esp* : to place under international control — **in·ter·na·tion·al·iza·tion** \-,nash-nəl-ə-'zā-shən, -,nash-ən-l-\ *n*

international law *n* : a body of rules that control or affect the rights of nations in their relations with each other

International System *n* : METRIC SYSTEM

international unit *n* : a quantity (as of a vitamin) that barely produces a particular biological effect agreed upon as an international standard of activity

in·ter·nec·ine \,int-ər-'nes-,ēn, -'nē-,sīn; in-'tər-nə-,sēn\ *adj* **1 :** marked by slaughter : DEADLY **2 :** of, relating to, or involving conflict within a group ⟨bitter *internecine* feuds⟩ [Latin *internecinus,* from *internecare* "to slay", from *inter-* + *necare* "to kill", from *nex* "violent death"]

in·tern·ee \,in-,tər-'nē\ *n* : an interned person

in·ter·neu·ron \,int-ər-'nü-,rän, -'nyü-; -'nur-,än, -'nyur-\ *n* : a nerve cell that carries an impulse from one nerve cell to another

in·tern·ist \in-'tər-nəst\ *n* : a specialist in internal medicine [*internal* medicine]

in·tern·ment \in-'tərn-mənt\ *n* : the act of interning : the state of being interned

in·ter·node \'int-ər-,nōd\ *n* : a space or part between two nodes (as of a stem) : SEGMENT

in·ter·nun·ci·al \,int-ər-'nən-sē-əl, -'nùn-\ *adj* **1 :** of or relating to an internuncio **2 :** serving to link sensory and motor neurons — **in·ter·nun·ci·al·ly** \-sē-ə-lē\ *adv*

in·ter·nun·cio \-sē-,ō\ *n* : a papal legate of lower rank than a nuncio [Italian *internunzio,* literally, "messenger between two parties", from Latin *internuntius,* from *inter-* + *nuntius* "messenger"]

in·tero·cep·tive \,int-ə-rō-'sep-tiv\ *adj* : of, relating to, or being stimuli arising within the body and especially the viscera [*inter-* (as in *interior*) + *-o-* + *-ceptive* (as in *receptive*)] — **in·tero·cep·tor** \-'sep-tər\ *n*

in·ter·pen·e·trate \,int-ər-'pen-ə-,trāt\ *vb* **1 :** to penetrate between, within, or throughout : PERMEATE **2 :** to penetrate mutually — **in·ter·pen·e·tra·tion** \-,pen-ə-'trā-shən\ *n*

in·ter·per·son·al \-'pərs-nəl, -n-əl\ *adj* : being, relating to, or involving relations between persons — **in·ter·per·son·al·ly** *adv*

in·ter·phase \'int-ər-,fāz\ *n* : the period between the end of one mitotic division and the beginning of the next

in·ter·plant \,int-ər-'plant\ *vt* : to plant (a crop) between plants of another kind

in·ter·play \'int-ər-,plā\ *n* : mutual action or influence : INTERACTION — **in·ter·play** \,int-ər-'plā\ *vi*

in·ter·po·late \in-'tər-pə-,lāt\ *vb* **1 a :** to alter or corrupt (as a text) by inserting new matter **b :** to insert (words) into a text or into a conversation **2 :** to insert between other things or parts **3 :** to estimate values of (as a logarithm) between two known values **4 :** to make insertions [Latin *interpolare*] SYN see INTRODUCE — **in·ter·po·la·tion** \-,tər-pə-'lā-shən\ *n* — **in·ter·po·la·tive** \-'tər-pə-,lāt-iv\ *adj* — **in·ter·po·la·tor** \-,lāt-ər\ *n*

in·ter·pose \,int-ər-'pōz\ *vb* **1 a :** to place in an intervening position **b :** to put (oneself) between : INTRUDE **2 :** to introduce or throw in between the parts of a conversation or argument **3 :** to be or come between; *esp* : to step in between opposing parties [Middle French *interposer,* from Latin *interponere,* from *inter-* + *ponere* "to put"] — **in·ter·pos·er** *n* — **in·ter·po·si·tion** \-pə-'zish-ən\ *n* □ SYN INTERPOSE, INTERFERE, INTERVENE, INTERCEDE mean to come or go between. INTERPOSE implies no more than this ⟨*interposed* in the argument⟩ INTERFERE implies a getting in the way or otherwise hindering ⟨strikes *interfere* with production plans⟩ INTERVENE may imply an occurring in space or time between two things or a stepping in to halt or settle a dispute ⟨years *intervening* between graduation and marriage⟩ INTERCEDE implies acting in behalf of an offender or between two parties needing reconciliation ⟨the United Nations *intercedes* in international disputes⟩

\ə\ abut	\ng\ sing
\ər\ further	\ō\ bone
\a\ mat	\ȯ\ saw
\ā\ take	\ȯi\ coin
\ä\ cot, cart	\th\ thin
\au̇\ out	\th\ this
\ch\ chin	\ü\ food
\e\ pet	\u̇\ foot
\ē\ easy	\y\ yet
\g\ go	\yü\ few
\i\ tip	\yu̇\ cure
\ī\ life	\zh\ vision
\j\ job	

in·ter·pret \in-'tər-prət\ *vb* 1 : to explain or tell the meaning of ⟨*interpret* a dream⟩ 2 : to understand according to one's own belief, judgment, or interest ⟨*interpret* an action as unfriendly⟩ 3 : to bring out the meaning of by performing ⟨an actor *interprets* a role⟩ 4 : to translate orally for others [Latin *interpretari,* from *interpres* "agent, interpreter"] SYN see EXPLAIN — **in·ter·pret·able** \-prət-ə-bəl\ *adj*

in·ter·pre·ta·tion \in-ˌtər-prə-'tā-shən\ *n* 1 : the act or the result of interpreting : EXPLANATION 2 : an instance of artistic interpretation in performance — **in·ter·pre·ta·tion·al** \-shnəl, -shən-l\ *adj* — **in·ter·pre·ta·tive** \-'tər-prə-ˌtāt-iv\ *adj* — **in·ter·pre·ta·tive·ly** *adv* — **in·ter·pre·tive** \-'tər-prət-iv\ *adj* — **in·ter·pre·tive·ly** *adv*

in·ter·pret·er \in-'tər-prət-ər\ *n* 1 : one that interprets; *esp* : a person who translates orally for people speaking different languages 2 : a computer program that translates an instruction into machine language and executes it before going to the next instruction

in·ter·ra·cial \ˌint-ər-'rā-shəl, ˌint-ə-'rā-\ *adj* : of, involving, or designed for members of different races

in·ter·reg·num \ˌint-ə-'reg-nəm\ *n, pl* **-nums** *or* **-na** \-nə\ 1 : a period between two successive reigns or regimes 2 : a lapse or pause in a continuous series [Latin, from *inter-* + *regnum* "reign"]

in·ter·re·late \ˌint-ər-ri-'lāt, ˌint-ə-ri-\ *vb* : to bring into or have a mutual relationship — **in·ter·re·la·tion** \-'lā-shən\ *n* — **in·ter·re·la·tion·ship** \-ˌship\ *n*

in·ter·ro·gate \in-'ter-ə-ˌgāt\ *vt* : to question usually formally and systematically ⟨*interrogate* a prisoner of war⟩ [Latin *interrogare,* from *inter-* + *rogare* "to ask"] — **in·ter·ro·ga·tion** \-ˌter-ə-'gā-shən\ *n* — **in·ter·ro·ga·tion·al** \-shnəl, -shən-l\ *adj* — **in·ter·ro·ga·tor** \-'ter-ə-ˌgāt-ər\ *n*

interrogation point *n* : QUESTION MARK

¹**in·ter·rog·a·tive** \ˌint-ə-'räg-ət-iv\ *adj* 1 : having the form or force of a question 2 : used in a question ⟨an *interrogative* pronoun⟩ — **in·ter·rog·a·tive·ly** *adv*

²**interrogative** *n* : a word (as *who, what, which*) used in asking questions

in·ter·rog·a·to·ry \ˌint-ə-'räg-ə-ˌtōr-ē, -ˌtȯr-\ *adj* : containing, expressing, or implying a question

in·ter·rupt \ˌint-ə-'rəpt\ *vb* 1 : to stop or hinder by breaking in ⟨*interrupt* a conversation⟩ 2 : to break the uniformity or continuity of ⟨*interrupt* a sequence⟩ 3 : to break in upon an action; *esp* : to break in with questions or remarks while another is speaking [Latin *interruptus,* past participle of *interrumpere* "to interrupt", from *inter-* + *rumpere* "to break"] — **in·ter·rupt·ible** \-'rəp-tə-bəl\ *adj* — **in·ter·rup·tion** \-'rəp-shən\ *n* — **in·ter·rup·tive** \-'rəp-tiv\ *adj*

in·ter·rupt·er \ˌint-ə-'rəp-tər\ *n* : one that interrupts; *esp* : a device for periodically and automatically interrupting an electric current

in·ter·scho·las·tic \ˌint-ər-skə-'las-tik\ *adj* : existing or carried on between schools ⟨*interscholastic* athletics⟩

in·ter se \ˌint-ər-'sā, -'sē\ *adv or adj* : among or between themselves [Latin]

in·ter·sect \ˌint-ər-'sekt\ *vb* 1 : to pierce or divide by passing through or across : CROSS ⟨a line *intersects* a plane in a point⟩ 2 : to meet and cross at a point ⟨the streets *intersect* at right angles⟩ [Latin *intersectus,* past participle of *intersecare* "to intersect", from *inter-* + *secare* "to cut"]

in·ter·sec·tion \ˌint-ər-'sek-shən\ *n* 1 : the act or process of intersecting 2 : the place or point where two or more things and especially streets intersect ⟨a busy *intersection*⟩ 3 : the set of elements common to two sets; *esp* : the set of points common to two geometric figures

in·ter·sex \'int-ər-ˌseks\ *n* : an intersexual individual

in·ter·sex·u·al \ˌint-ər-'sek-shə-wəl, -shəl\ *adj* 1 : existing between sexes ⟨*intersexual* hostility⟩ 2 : intermediate in sexual characters between a typical male and a typical female — **in·ter·sex·u·al·i·ty** \-ˌsek-shə-'wal-ət-ē\ *n* — **in·ter·sex·u·al·ly** \-'seksh-wə-lē, -ə-wə-; -'seksh-lē, -ə-lē\ *adv*

¹**in·ter·space** \'int-ər-ˌspās\ *n* : an intervening space : INTERVAL

²**in·ter·space** \ˌint-ər-'spās\ *vt* : to separate by spaces

in·ter·spe·cif·ic \ˌint-ər-spi-'sif-ik\ *or* **in·ter·spe·cies** \-'spē-shēz, -sēz\ *adj* : existing or arising between species ⟨*interspecific* hybrids⟩

in·ter·sperse \ˌint-ər-'spərs\ *vt* 1 : to place here and there among others ⟨*intersperse* pictures in a book⟩ 2 : to vary with things inserted here and there ⟨a serious talk *interspersed* with jokes⟩ [Latin *interspersus* "interspersed", from *inter-* + *sparsus,* past participle of *spargere* "to scatter"] — **in·ter·sper·sion** \-'spər-zhən\ *n*

in·ter·state \ˌint-ər-'stāt\ *adj* : of, connecting, or existing between two or more states especially of the United States

in·ter·stel·lar \-'stel-ər\ *adj* : located or taking place among the stars ⟨*interstellar* space⟩

in·ter·stice \in-'tər-stəs\ *n, pl* **in·ter·stic·es** \-stə-ˌsēz, -stə-səz\ : a little space between two things : CHINK, CREVICE [French, from Late Latin *interstitium,* from Latin *intersistere* "to stand in the middle", from *inter-* + *sistere* "to stand"]

in·ter·sti·tial \ˌint-ər-'stish-əl\ *adj* 1 : relating to or situated in the interstices 2 : situated within organs or tissues ⟨*interstitial* connective tissue⟩; *also* : affecting the interstitial tissues of a body part — **in·ter·sti·tial·ly** \-'stish-ə-lē\ *adv*

in·ter·tid·al \-'tīd-l\ *adj* : of, relating to, or being the area that is above low-tide mark but exposed to tidal flooding

in·ter·twine \-'twīn\ *vb* : to twine or cause to twine about one another : INTERLACE — **in·ter·twine·ment** \-mənt\ *n*

in·ter·twist \-'twist\ *vb* : INTERTWINE — **intertwist** *n*

in·ter·val \'int-ər-vəl\ *n* 1 : a space of time between events or states ⟨the *interval* between elections⟩ ⟨an *interval* of three months⟩ 2 a : a space between things ⟨the *interval* between two desks⟩ b : difference in pitch between tones 3 : a set of numbers between two numbers either including or excluding one or both of them; *also* : the set of real numbers greater or less than and including or excluding a real number [Middle French *intervalle,* from Latin *intervallum* "space between ramparts, interval", from *inter-* + *vallum* "rampart"]

in·ter·vene \ˌint-ər-'vēn\ *vi* 1 : to happen as an unrelated event ⟨rain *intervened* and we postponed the match⟩ 2 : to come between events or points of time ⟨a second *intervened* between the flash and the report⟩ 3 : to interpose in order to stop, settle, or change something ⟨*intervene* in a quarrel⟩ 4 : to be or lie between ⟨*intervening* hills⟩ [Latin *intervenire* "to come between", from *inter-* + *venire* "to come"] SYN see INTERPOSE — **in·ter·ve·nor** \-'vē-nər, -ˌnȯr\ *also* **in·ter·ven·er** \-'vē-nər\ *n* — **in·ter·ven·tion** \-'ven-chən\ *n*

in·ter·ven·tion·ism \-'ven-chə-ˌniz-əm\ *n* : the theory or practice of intervening; *esp* : interference by one country in the political affairs of another — **in·ter·ven·tion·ist** \-'vench-nəst, -ə-nəst\ *n or adj*

in·ter·ver·te·bral \-'vərt-ə-brəl\ *adj* : situated between adjacent vertebrae ⟨*intervertebral* disks⟩

in·ter·view \'int-ər-ˌvyü\ *n* 1 : a face-to-face meeting especially for the purpose of talking or consulting 2 : a meeting at which information is obtained (as by a journalist) from a person; *also* : an account of such a meeting — **interview** *vt* — **in·ter·view·er** *n*

in·ter·vo·cal·ic \ˌint-ər-vō-'kal-ik\ *adj* : immediately preceded and immediately followed by a vowel

in·ter·weave \ˌint-ər-'wēv\ *vb* **-wove** \-'wōv\ *also* **-weaved; -wo·ven** \-'wō-vən\ *also* **-weaved; -weav·ing**

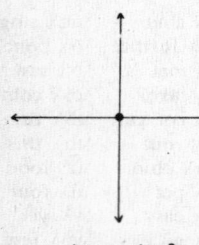

intersection 3

1 : to weave together **2** : to blend or cause to blend together

¹in·tes·tate \in-'tes-ˌtāt, -'tes-tət\ *adj* **1** : not having made a will ⟨died *intestate*⟩ **2** : not disposed of by will — **in·tes·ta·cy** \-'tes-tə-sē\ *n*

²intestate *n* : one who dies intestate

in·tes·ti·nal \in-'tes-tən-l\ *adj* **1** : of or relating to the intestine **2** : affecting or occurring in the intestine — **in·tes·ti·nal·ly** \-l-ē\ *adv*

intestinal fortitude *n* : COURAGE, GRIT [euphemism for *guts*]

in·tes·tine \in-'tes-tən\ *n* : the tubular part of the alimentary canal that extends from the stomach to the anus [Middle French *intestin,* from Latin *intestinum,* from *intestinus* "internal", from *intus* "within"]

in·ti·ma·cy \'int-ə-mə-sē\ *n* : the state of being intimate

¹in·ti·mate \'int-ə-ˌmāt\ *vt* **1** : to announce formally : DECLARE **2** : to communicate indirectly : HINT [Late Latin *intimare* "to put in, announce", from Latin *intimus* "innermost"] SYN see SUGGEST — **in·ti·mat·er** *n* — **in·ti·ma·tion** \ˌint-ə-'mā-shən\ *n*

²in·ti·mate \'int-ə-mət\ *adj* **1** : belonging to or characterizing one's deepest nature ⟨*intimate* reflections⟩ **2** : marked by very close association or contact **3 a** : marked by a warm friendship developing through long association ⟨on *intimate* terms with a neighbor⟩ **b** : suggesting informal warmth or privacy ⟨*intimate* clubs⟩ **4** : of a very personal or private nature ⟨*intimate* family matters⟩ [derived from Latin *intimus* "innermost"] — **in·ti·mate·ly** *adv* — **in·ti·mate·ness** *n*

³in·ti·mate \'int-ə-mət\ *n* : an intimate friend : CONFIDANT

in·tim·i·date \in-'tim-ə-ˌdāt\ *vt* : to make timid or fearful; *esp* : to compel or deter by or as if by threats — **in·tim·i·da·tion** \-ˌtim-ə-'dā-shən\ *n* — **in·tim·i·da·tor** \-'tim-ə-ˌdāt-ər\ *n*

in·to \'in-tə, -tü\ *prep* **1 a** : to the inside of ⟨came *into* the room⟩ **b** — used as a function word to indicate entry, introduction, or inclusion ⟨enter *into* an alliance⟩ **2 a** : to the state, condition, or form of ⟨got *into* trouble⟩ **b** : to the occupation, action, or possession of ⟨go *into* farming⟩ **c** : involved with ⟨wasn't *into* drugs anymore⟩ **3** : to a position of contact with : AGAINST ⟨ran *into* a wall⟩

in·tol·er·able \in-'täl-rə-bəl, -'täl-ə-rə-bəl, -'täl-ər-bəl, 'in-\ *adj* **1** : not tolerable : UNBEARABLE **2** : EXTREME 1c, EXCESSIVE — **in·tol·er·abil·i·ty** \in-ˌtäl-rə-'bil-ət-ē, -ə-rə-\ *n* — **in·tol·er·able·ness** *n* — **in·tol·er·ably** \-blē\ *adv*

in·tol·er·ance \in-'täl-ə-rəns, 'in-\ *n* **1** : the quality or state of being intolerant **2** : exceptional sensitivity (as to a drug or food)

in·tol·er·ant \-rənt\ *adj* **1** : unable or unwilling to endure **2 a** : unwilling to grant equality or freedom especially in religious matters **b** : unwilling to grant or share social, political, or professional advantages — **in·tol·er·ant·ly** *adv*

in·to·nate \'in-tə-ˌnāt\ *vt* : UTTER 1, INTONE

in·to·na·tion \ˌin-tə-'nā-shən\ *n* **1** : the act of intoning; *also* : something intoned **2** : the act of singing or playing music in tune **3** : the rise and fall in pitch of the voice in speech — **in·to·na·tion·al** \-shnəl, -shən-l\ *adj*

in·tone \in-'tōn\ *vb* : to utter in musical or prolonged tones : CHANT — **in·ton·er** *n*

in to·to \in-'tōt-ō\ *adv* : TOTALLY, ENTIRELY ⟨accepted the plan *in toto*⟩ [Latin, "on the whole"]

in·tox·i·cant \in-'täk-si-kənt\ *n* : something (as alcohol) that intoxicates — **intoxicant** *adj*

in·tox·i·cate \in-'täk-sə-ˌkāt\ *vt* **1 a** : POISON 1a **b** : to affect by alcohol or a drug especially to the point where physical and mental control is greatly diminished **2** : to excite or elate to the point of enthusiasm or frenzy ⟨*intoxicated* with joy⟩

in·tox·i·ca·tion \in-ˌtäk-sə-'kā-shən\ *n* **1 a** : an abnormal state that is essentially a poisoning ⟨intestinal *intoxication*⟩ **b** : the condition of being drunk : INEBRIATION **2** : a strong excitement or elation

in·tra- \ˌ,in-trə, -trä, -ˌträ\ *prefix* **1** : within ⟨*intra*cellular⟩ **2** : in : into ⟨*intra*venous⟩ [Latin *intra*]

in·tra·cel·lu·lar \ˌin-trə-'sel-yə-lər\ *adj* : being or occurring within a protoplasmic cell — **in·tra·cel·lu·lar·ly** *adv*

in·trac·ta·ble \in-'trak-tə-bəl, 'in-\ *adj* **1** : not easily managed or controlled ⟨an *intractable* child⟩ **2** : not easily relieved or cured ⟨*intractable* pain⟩ — **in·trac·ta·bil·i·ty** \in-ˌtrak-tə-'bil-ət-ē\ *n* — **in·trac·ta·ble·ness** \in-'trak-tə-bəl-nəs, 'in-\ *n* — **in·trac·ta·bly** \-blē\ *adv*

in·tra·cu·ta·ne·ous \ˌin-trə-kyù-'tā-nē-əs\ *adj* : INTRADERMAL

in·tra·der·mal \-'dər-məl\ *adj* : situated or done within or between the layers of the skin — **in·tra·der·mal·ly** \-mə-lē\ *adv*

in·tra·dos \'in-trə-ˌdäs, -ˌdō; in-'trā-ˌdäs\ *n, pl* **-dos** \-ˌdōz, -ˌdäs\ *or* **-dos·es** \-ˌdäs-əz\ : the interior curve of an arch [French, from Latin *intra* "within" + French *dos* "back", from Latin *dorsum*]

in·tra·mu·ral \ˌin-trə-'myùr-əl\ *adj* : being, occurring, or undertaken within the limits usually of a school ⟨*intramural* sports⟩ — **in·tra·mu·ral·ly** \-'myùr-ə-lē\ *adv*

in·tran·si·geance \in-'trans-ə-jəns, -'tranz-\ *n* : INTRANSIGENCE — **in·tran·si·geant** \-jənt\ *adj or n* — **in·tran·si·geant·ly** *adv*

in·tran·si·gence \-jəns\ *n* : the quality or state of being intransigent

in·tran·si·gent \-jənt\ *adj* **1 a** : refusing to compromise or to give up an extreme position or attitude : UNCOMPROMISING **b** : IRRECONCILABLE ⟨*intransigent* enemies⟩ **2** : characteristic of one that is uncompromising [Spanish *intransigente,* from *in-* + *transigir* "to compromise", from Latin *transigere* "to transact"] — **intransigent** *n* — **in·tran·si·gent·ly** *adv*

in·tran·si·tive \in-'trans-ət-iv, -'tranz-, -'in-\ *adj* : not transitive; *esp* : characterized by not having or containing a direct object ⟨an *intransitive* verb⟩ — **in·tran·si·tive·ly** *adv* — **in·tran·si·tive·ness** *n*

in·tra·spe·cif·ic \ˌin-trə-spi-'sif-ik\ *also* **in·tra·spe·cies** \-'spē-shēz, -sēz\ *adj* : occurring within a species or involving members of one species ⟨*intraspecific* variation⟩

in·tra·state \ˌin-trə-'stāt\ *adj* : existing or occurring within a state

in·tra·uter·ine \-'yüt-ə-rən, -ˌrīn\ *adj* : being or occurring within the uterus ⟨*intrauterine* growth⟩

in·tra·ve·nous \ˌin-trə-'vē-nəs\ *adj* : being within or entering by way of the veins ⟨*intravenous* feeding⟩ — **in·tra·ve·nous·ly** *adv*

in·tra·vi·tam \-'vī-ˌtam, -'wē-ˌtäm\ *adj* : done, acting on, or found in a living subject [New Latin *intra vitam* "during life"]

in·tra·zon·al \ˌin-trə-'zōn-l\ *adj* : of, relating to, or being a soil or a major soil group having relatively well-developed characteristics — compare AZONAL, ZONAL

intrench *variant of* ENTRENCH

in·trep·id \in-'trep-əd\ *adj* : resolutely firm and fearless [Latin *intrepidus,* from *in-* + *trepidus* "alarmed"] — **in·tre·pid·i·ty** \ˌin-trə-'pid-ət-ē\ *n* — **in·trep·id·ly** \in-'trep-əd-lē\ *adv* — **in·trep·id·ness** *n*

in·tri·ca·cy \'in-tri-kə-sē\ *n, pl* **-cies 1** : the quality or state of being intricate **2** : something intricate

in·tri·cate \'in-tri-kət\ *adj* : difficult to follow, understand, or analyze : COMPLICATED ⟨an *intricate* machine⟩ ⟨*intricate* problems⟩ [Latin *intricatus,* past participle of *intricare* "to entangle", from *in-* + *tricae* "trifles, impediments"] SYN see COMPLEX — **in·tri·cate·ly** *adv* — **in·tri·cate·ness** *n*

1 intrados

¹in·trigue \in-'trēg\ *vb* **I** : to make or accomplish by intrigue ⟨*intrigued* their way into power⟩ **2** : PLOT 3, SCHEME **3** : to arouse the interest or curiosity of ⟨was *intrigued* by the tale⟩ [French *intriguer,* from Italian *intrigare,* from Latin *intricare* "to entangle, perplex"] — **in·trigu·er** *n*

²in·trigue \'in-ˌtrēg, in-'\ *n* **I** : a secret and involved scheme : PLOT **2** : a secret love affair SYN see PLOT

in·trin·sic \in-'trin-zik, -'trin-sik\ *adj* : belonging to the essential nature or makeup of a thing : REAL [Middle French *intrinsèque* "internal", from Latin *intrinsicus* "inwardly"] — **in·trin·si·cal** \-zi-kəl, -si-\ *adj* — **in·trin·si·cal·ly** \-kə-lē, -klē\ *adv* — **in·trin·si·cal·ness** \-kəl-nəs\ *n*

intro- *prefix* **I** : in : into **2** : inward ⟨*intro*vert⟩ [Latin, from *intro* "inside, to the inside"]

in·tro·duce \ˌin-trə-'düs, -'dyüs\ *vt* **I** : to lead or bring in especially for the first time **2** : to bring into practice or use ⟨*introduce* a new fashion⟩ **3 a** : to cause to be acquainted ⟨*introduce* two strangers⟩ **b** : to present formally ⟨*introduce* a speaker to a group⟩ **4** : to present or bring forward for discussion ⟨*introduce* a topic⟩ **5** : to put in : INSERT ⟨*introduce* a probe into a cavity⟩ [Latin *introducere,* from *intro-* + *ducere* "to lead"] — **in·tro·duc·er** *n* □ SYN INTRODUCE, INSERT, INTERPOLATE, INTERJECT mean to put among or between others. INTRODUCE is the general term for bringing or putting a thing or person into a body or thing already in existence; INSERT implies putting into an open, fixed, or prepared space between or among things; INTERPOLATE applies especially to the inserting of something extraneous or spurious; INTERJECT strongly implies an abrupt or forced introduction.

in·tro·duc·tion \ˌin-trə-'dək-shən\ *n* **I a** : the action of introducing **b** : something introduced **2** : the part of a book that leads up to and explains what will be found in the main part : PREFACE **3** : a book for beginners in a subject ⟨an *introduction* to chemistry⟩

in·tro·duc·to·ry \ˌin-trə-'dək-tə-rē, -trē\ *adj* : serving to introduce : PRELIMINARY — **in·tro·duc·to·ri·ly** \-tə-rə-lē, -trə-\ *adv*

in·troit \'in-ˌtrō-ət, -ˌtroit, in-'\ *n* **I** *often cap* : the first part of the proper of the Mass consisting of an antiphon, verse from a psalm, and the Gloria Patri **2** : a piece of music sung or played at the beginning of a worship service [Middle French *introite,* from Latin *introitus* "entrance", from *introire* "to go in", from *intro-* + *ire* "to go"]

in·tro·spec·tion \ˌin-trə-'spek-shən\ *n* : a reflective examination of one's own thoughts or feelings [Latin *introspectus,* past participle of *introspicere* "to look into", from *intro-* + *specere* "to look"] — **in·tro·spect** \-'spekt\ *vb* — **in·tro·spec·tion·al** \-'spek-shnəl, -shən-l\ *adj* — **in·tro·spec·tive** \-'spek-tiv\ *adj* — **in·tro·spec·tive·ly** *adv*

in·tro·ver·sion \ˌin-trə-'vər-zhən, -shən\ *n* : the state of an introvert

¹in·tro·vert \'in-trə-ˌvərt\ *n* : a person whose attention and interests are directed wholly or predominantly toward what is within the self [earlier *introvert* "to turn inward", from *intro-* + *-vert* (as in *divert*)]

²introvert *adj* : turning in upon itself; *esp* : INTROVERTED

in·tro·vert·ed \'in-trə-ˌvərt-əd\ *adj* : characteristic of or having the characteristics of an introvert ⟨an *introverted* voice⟩ ⟨*introverted* people⟩

in·trude \in-'trüd\ *vb* **I** : to bring or force in unasked ⟨*intrude* one's views into a discussion⟩ **2** : to come or go in without invitation : TRESPASS ⟨*intrude* on another's property⟩ **3** : to enter or cause to enter as if by force [Latin *intrudere* "to thrust in", from *in-* + *trudere* "to thrust"] — **in·trud·er** *n* □ SYN INTRUDE, OBTRUDE mean to thrust oneself or something in without invitation or authorization. INTRUDE implies rudeness, officiousness, or encroachment ⟨no wish to *intrude* on

your privacy⟩ OBTRUDE suggests more strongly the impropriety, boldness, futility, or disagreeableness of an intrusion ⟨*obtrude* personal matters in a serious discussion⟩

in·tru·sion \in-'trü-zhən\ *n* **I** : the act of intruding : the state of being intruded **2** : the forcible entry of magma into or between other rock formations; *also* : the intruded magma [Middle French, from Medieval Latin *intrusio,* from Latin *intrudere* "to thrust in"]

in·tru·sive \in-'trü-siv, -ziv\ *adj* **I** : characterized by intrusion; *esp* : intruding where one is not welcome or invited **2** : having been forced while in a molten state into cavities or between layers ⟨*intrusive* rock⟩ — **intrusive** *n* — **in·tru·sive·ly** *adv* — **in·tru·sive·ness** *n*

intrust *variant of* ENTRUST

in·tu·i·tion \ˌin-tü-'ish-ən, -tyü-\ *n* **I** : the power of knowing immediately and without conscious reasoning **2** : something known or understood at once and without an effort of the mind ⟨act upon an *intuition*⟩ [Late Latin *intuitio* "act of contemplating", from Latin *intueri* "to contemplate", from *in-* + *tueri* "to look at"] — **in·tu·i·tion·al** \-'ish-nəl, -ən-l\ *adj*

in·tu·i·tive \in-'tü-ət-iv, -'tyü-\ *adj* **I** : knowing or understanding by intuition ⟨an *intuitive* person⟩ **2** : having or characterized by intuition ⟨an *intuitive* mind⟩ **3** : known or understood by intuition ⟨*intuitive* knowledge⟩ — **in·tu·i·tive·ly** *adv* — **in·tu·i·tive·ness** *n*

in·u·lin \'in-yə-lən\ *n* : a white polysaccharide that consists of fructose molecules and occurs as a storage carbohydrate especially in the roots or tubers of plants of the composite family [derived from Latin *inula,* a kind of composite plant]

in·un·date \'in-ən-ˌdāt\ *vt* **I** : to cover with a flood : OVERFLOW **2** : DELUGE 2 [Latin *inundare,* from *in-* + *unda* "wave"] — **in·un·da·tion** \ˌin-ən-'dā-shən\ *n* — **in·un·da·tor** \ˌin-ən-ˌdāt-ər\ *n* — **in·un·da·to·ry** \in-'ən-də-ˌtōr-ē, -ˌtór-\ *adj*

Inu·pi·at \in-'ü-pē-ˌät, in-'yü-\ *also* **Inu·pi·aq** \-ˌäk\ *n* **I** *pl* **Inupiat** *or* **Inupiats** *also* **Inupiaq** *or* **Inupiaqs** : a member of the Eskimo people of northern Alaska **2** : the language of the Inupiat people

in·ure \in-'ùr, -'yùr\ *vb* **I** : to make less sensitive : HARDEN ⟨*inured* to cold⟩ **2** : to become advantageous ⟨profits that *inure* from education⟩ [Middle English *enuren,* from *en-* + *ure* "use, custom", from Middle French *uevre* "work", from Latin *opera*] — **in·ure·ment** \-mənt\ *n*

in vac·uo \in-'vak-yə-ˌwō\ *adv* : in a vacuum [New Latin]

in·vade \in-'vād\ *vt* **I** : to enter for conquest or plunder ⟨*invade* a country⟩ **2** : to encroach upon : INFRINGE ⟨*invaded* their privacy⟩ **3** : to spread progressively over or into and usually affect injuriously ⟨bacteria *invading* tissue⟩ ⟨stores *invading* a residential section⟩ [Latin *invadere,* from *in-* + *vadere* "to go"] — **in·vad·er** *n*

in·vag·i·nate \in-'vaj-ə-ˌnāt\ *vb* : to fold or cause to fold in so that an outer becomes an inner surface [Medieval Latin *invaginare* "to enclose, sheathe", from Latin *in-* + *vagina* "sheath"] — **in·vag·i·na·tion** \-ˌvaj-ə-'na-shən\ *n*

¹in·val·id \in-'val-əd, 'in-\ *adj* : having no force or effect : not valid ⟨an *invalid* license⟩ [Latin *invalidus* "weak", from *in-* + *validus* "strong"] — **in·va·lid·i·ty** \ˌin-və-'lid-ət-ē\ *n* — **in·val·id·ly** \in-'val-əd-lē, 'in-\ *adv* — **in·val·id·ness** *n*

²in·va·lid \'in-və-ləd\ *adj* **I** : suffering from disease or disability : SICKLY **2** : of, relating to, or suited to one that is sick [French *invalide,* from Latin *invalidus* "weak"]

³invalid \like ²\ *n* : one that is ill, sickly, or disabled — **in·va·lid·ism** \-ˌiz-əm\ *n*

⁴in·va·lid \'in-və-ləd, -ˌlid\ *vt* **I** : to make an invalid of ⟨*invalided* by heart disease⟩ **2** : to remove from active duty by reason of sickness or disability ⟨*invalided* home after the battle⟩

in·val·i·date \in-'val-ə-ˌdāt, 'in-\ *vt* : to make invalid ⟨a petition *invalidated* by false signatures⟩; *esp* : to weaken or destroy the effect of SYN see NULLIFY — **in·val·i·da·tion** \in-ˌval-ə-'dā-shən\ *n* — **in·val·i·da·tor** \in-'val-ə-ˌdāt-ər\ *n*

in·valu·able \in-'val-yə-wə-bəl, -yə-bəl\ *adj* : having value too great to be estimated : PRICELESS — **in·valu·able·ness** *n* — **in·valu·ably** \-blē\ *adv*

in·vari·able \in-'ver-ē-ə-bəl, -'var-, 'in-\ *adj* : not changing or capable of change : CONSTANT ⟨an *invariable* daily routine⟩ — **in·vari·abil·i·ty** \in-ˌver-ē-ə-'bil-ət-ē, -ˌvar-\ *n* — **invariable** *n* — **in·vari·able·ness** *n* — **in·vari·ably** \in-'ver-ē-ə-blē, -'var-, 'in-\ *adv*

in·vari·ant \in-'ver-ē-ənt, -'var-, 'in-\ *adj* : CONSTANT, UNCHANGING ⟨an *invariant* factor⟩ — **in·vari·ance** \-əns\ *n* — **invariant** *n*

in·va·sion \in-'vā-zhən\ *n* 1 : an act of invading; *esp* : entrance of an army into a country for conquest 2 : the entry or spread of some usually harmful thing ⟨bacterial *invasion* of tissue⟩ [Middle French, from Late Latin *invasio,* from Latin *invadere* "to invade"] — **in·va·sive** \-'vā-siv, -ziv\ *adj* — **in·va·sive·ness** *n*

in·vec·tive \in-'vek-tiv\ *n* : condemnation expressed in a harsh or bitter tone ⟨attack the opposing candidate with *invective*⟩ [Middle French *invectif* "condemnatory", from Latin *invectivus,* from *invehere* "to carry in"] SYN see ABUSE

in·veigh \in-'vā\ *vi* : to protest or complain bitterly : RAIL ⟨*inveigh* against high taxes⟩ [Latin *invehi* "to attack, inveigh", from *invehere* "to carry in", from *in-* + *vehere* "to carry"] — **in·veigh·er** *n*

in·vei·gle \in-'vā-gəl, -'vē-\ *vt* **in·vei·gled; in·vei·gling** \-gə-ling, -gling\ 1 : to bring or lead by flattery : ENTICE ⟨was *inveigled* into marriage⟩ 2 : to acquire by ingenuity or flattery ⟨*inveigled* a loan⟩ [Middle French *aveugler* "to blind, hoodwink", from Old French *avogle* "blind", from Medieval Latin *ab oculis,* literally, "lacking eyes"] — **in·vei·gle·ment** \-gəl-mənt\ *n* — **in·vei·gler** \-gə-lər, -glər\ *n* □ ORIGIN When we permit ourselves to be *inveigled* we are blinded, figuratively speaking, by flattery. The ancestor of our word *inveigle* is a Medieval Latin phrase meaning "blind". Literally, *ab oculis* is "lacking (or away from) eyes" — the Latin preposition *ab* expresses separation. From *ab oculis* are derived the French adjective *aveugle* "blind" and the verb *aveugler* "to blind". French *aveugler,* like its English equivalent, *blind,* is often used figuratively. When English borrowed the French verb in the late Middle Ages, only the figurative use was taken. English *inveigle* originally meant "to blind or delude in judgment". This sense is now obsolete, but the present meaning is not far removed.

in·vent \in-'vent\ *vt* 1 : to think up : make up 2 : to create or produce for the first time [Latin *inventus,* past participle of *invenire* "to come upon, find", from *in-* + *venire* "to come"] SYN see DISCOVER — **in·ven·tor** \-'vent-ər\ *n*

in·ven·tion \in-'ven-chən\ *n* 1 : something invented: as **a** : an original device or process **b** : a product of the imagination; *esp* : FALSEHOOD 2 : the act, process, or power of inventing

in·ven·tive \in-'vent-iv\ *adj* : gifted with the skill and imagination to invent — **in·ven·tive·ly** *adv* — **in·ven·tive·ness** *n*

in·ven·to·ry \'in-vən-ˌtōr-ē, -ˌtor-\ *n, pl* **-ries** 1 : an itemized list of assets or goods on hand 2 : the stock of goods on hand 3 : the making of an inventory — **in·ven·to·ri·al** \ˌin-vən-'tōr-ē-əl, -'tor-\ *adj* — **in·ven·to·ri·al·ly** \-ē-ə-lē\ *adv*

inventory *vt* **-ried; -ry·ing** : to make an inventory of

in·ver·ness \ˌin-vər-'nes\ *n* : a loose belted coat having a cape with a close round collar [*Inverness,* Scotland]

in·verse \in-'vərs, 'in-, 'in-ˌ\ *adj* 1 : opposite in order, nature, or effect 2 : so relating two numbers that their product is a constant ⟨an *inverse* proportion⟩ ⟨*inverse* variation⟩ [Latin *inversus,* from *invertere* "to invert"] — **in·verse·ly** *adv*

inverse \'in-ˌvərs, in-'vərs\ *n* : something inverse or resulting in or from inversion: as **a** : a statement formed by contradicting the hypothesis of a given statement but keeping the conclusion unchanged **b** : an inverse function or operation in mathematics

inverse function *n* : a function that is derived from a given function by interchanging the two variables

inversely proportional *adj* : having their products constant — used of two variables one of which varies directly as the reciprocal of the other

inverse square law *n* : a statement in physics: a physical quantity (as illumination) varies with the distance from the source inversely as the square of the distance

in·ver·sion \in-'vər-zhən, -shən\ *n* 1 : the act or process of inverting 2 : a reversal of position, order, or relationship 3 : an increase in the temperature of the air with increasing altitude

in·ver·sive \in-'vər-siv, -ziv\ *adj* : marked by inversion

in·vert \in-'vərt\ *vt* 1 : to reverse the position, order, or relationship of 2 **a** : to turn inside out or upside down **b** : to turn inward [Latin *invertere,* from *in-* + *vertere* "to turn"] SYN see REVERSE — **in·vert·ible** \-ə-bəl\ *adj*

in·ver·tase \in-'vərt-ˌās, -ˌāz; 'in-vər-ˌtās, -ˌtāz\ *n* : an enzyme that splits sucrose into glucose and fructose

in·ver·te·brate \in-'vərt-ə-brət, -ˌbrāt, 'in-\ *adj* : lacking a spinal column; *also* : of or relating to invertebrate animals — **invertebrate** *n*

in·vert·er \in-'vərt-ər\ *n* : a device for converting direct current into alternating current

invert sugar \ˌin-ˌvərt-\ *n* : a mixture of dextrose and levulose found in fruits or produced artificially from sucrose

in·vest \in-'vest\ *vt* 1 **a** : INSTALL 1 **b** : to furnish with power or authority 2 : to cover completely : ENVELOP 3 : to surround with troops or ships : BESIEGE 4 : to endow with a quality or characteristic ⟨*invest* an incident with mystery⟩ [Latin *investire* "to clothe, surround", from *in-* + *vestis* "garment"]

invest *vb* 1 : to lay out money in order to earn a financial return 2 : to expend for future benefits or advantages ⟨*invest* time and effort in a project⟩ [Italian *investire* "to clothe, invest money", from Latin, "to clothe"] — **in·vest·able** \-'ves-tə-bəl\ *adj* — **in·ves·tor** \-tər\ *n*

in·ves·ti·gate \in-'ves-tə-ˌgāt\ *vb* : to observe or study by close and systematic examination [Latin *investigare* "to track, investigate", from *in-* + *vestigium* "footprint"] — **in·ves·ti·ga·tion** \-ˌves-tə-'gā-shən\ *n* — **in·ves·ti·ga·tive** \-'ves-tə-ˌgāt-iv\ *adj* — **in·ves·ti·ga·tor** \-ˌgāt-ər\ *n* — **in·ves·ti·ga·to·ry** \-'ves-ti-gə-ˌtōr-ē, -ˌtor-\ *adj*

in·ves·ti·ture \in-'ves-tə-ˌchùr, -chər\ *n* : the action of investing a person especially with the robes of office [Medieval Latin *investitura,* from Latin *investire* "to clothe"]

in·vest·ment \in-'vest-mənt, -'ves-\ *n* 1 : an outer layer of any kind : ENVELOPE, COATING 2 : INVESTITURE 3 : SIEGE 1, BLOCKADE

investment *n* : an outlay of money for income or profit; *also* : the sum invested or the property purchased

in·vet·er·ate \in-'vet-ə-rət, -'ve-trət\ *adj* 1 : firmly established by age or by being long continued 2 : HABITUAL ⟨an *inveterate* smoker⟩ [Latin *inveteratus,* from *inveterare* "to age", from *in-* + *veter-, vetus* "old"] — **in·vet·er·a·cy** \-'vet-ə-rə-sē, -'ve-trə-sē\ *n* — **in·vet·er·ate·ly** *adv*

in·vi·a·ble \in-'vī-ə-bəl, 'in-\ *adj* : incapable of surviving — **in·vi·a·bil·i·ty** \in-ˌvī-ə-'bil-ət-ē\ *n*

\ə\ abut		\ng\ sing	
\ər\ further		\ō\ bone	
\a\ mat		\ó\ saw	
\ā\ take		\oi\ coin	
\ä\ cot, cart		\th\ thin	
\aù\ out		\th\ this	
\ch\ chin		\ü\ food	
\e\ pet		\ù\ foot	
\ē\ easy		\y\ yet	
\g\ go		\yü\ few	
\i\ tip		\yú\ cure	
\ī\ life		\zh\ vision	
\j\ job			

in·vid·i·ous \in-'vid-ē-əs\ *adj* : tending to cause dislike, ill will, or envy ⟨*invidious* criticism⟩ [Latin *invidiosus* "envious, invidious", from *invidia* "envy"] — **in·vid·i·ous·ly** *adv* — **in·vid·i·ous·ness** *n*

in·vig·o·rate \in-'vig-ə-ˌrāt\ *vt* : to give life and energy to : ANIMATE — **in·vig·o·ra·tion** \-ˌvig-ə-'rā-shən\ *n* — **in·vig·o·ra·tor** \-'vig-ə-ˌrāt-ər\ *n*

in·vin·ci·ble \in-'vin-sə-bəl, 'in-\ *adj* : incapable of being defeated, overcome, or subdued ⟨an *invincible* army⟩ [Middle French, from Late Latin *invincibilis,* from Latin *in-* + *vincere* "to conquer"] SYN see INDOMITABLE — **in·vin·ci·bil·i·ty** \in-ˌvin-sə-'bil-ət-ē\ *n* — **in·vin·ci·ble·ness** *n* — **in·vin·ci·bly** \in-'vin-sə-blē, 'in-\ *adv*

in·vi·o·la·ble \in-'vī-ə-lə-bəl, 'in-\ *adj* **1** : too sacred to be violated ⟨an *inviolable* oath⟩ **2** : incapable of being assaulted or destroyed — **in·vi·o·la·bil·i·ty** \in-ˌvī-ə-lə-'bil-ət-ē\ *n* — **in·vi·o·la·bly** \in-'vī-ə-lə-blē, 'in-\ *adv*

in·vi·o·late \in-'vī-ə-lət, 'in-\ *adj* **1** : not violated or profaned; *esp* : PURE **2** : INVIOLABLE 2 — **in·vi·o·late·ly** *adv* — **in·vi·o·late·ness** *n*

in·vis·i·ble \in-'viz-ə-bəl\ *adj* **1 a** : incapable of being seen ⟨sound is *invisible*⟩ **b** : inaccessible to view : HIDDEN ⟨the sun is *invisible* on a cloudy day⟩ **2** : IMPERCEPTIBLE, INCONSPICUOUS ⟨an *invisible* hair net⟩ — **in·vis·i·bil·i·ty** \in-ˌviz-ə-'bil-ət-ē\ *n* — **in·vis·i·ble·ness** *n* — **in·vis·i·bly** \in-'viz-ə-blē, 'in-\ *adv*

in·vi·ta·tion \ˌin-və-'tā-shən\ *n* **1** : the act of inviting **2** : the written, printed, or spoken expression by which a person is invited — **in·vi·ta·tion·al** \-shnəl, -shən-l\ *adj*

¹in·vite \in-'vīt\ *vt* **1** : to increase the likelihood of : INDUCE ⟨*invite* disaster by speeding⟩ **2 a** : to request the presence or participation of **b** : to request formally or politely : ENCOURAGE ⟨*invite* suggestions⟩ [Latin *invitare*] — **in·vit·er** *n*

²in·vite \'in-ˌvīt\ *n, chiefly dialect* : INVITATION

in·vit·ing \in-'vīt-ing\ *adj* : ATTRACTIVE, TEMPTING ⟨a very *inviting* dinner⟩ — **in·vit·ing·ly** \-ing-lē\ *adv*

in vi·tro \in-'vē-ˌtrō\ *adv or adj* : outside the living body and in an artificial environment [New Latin, literally, "in glass"]

in vi·vo \in-'vē-vō\ *adv or adj* : in the living body of a plant or animal [New Latin, literally, "in the living"]

in·vo·ca·tion \ˌin-və-'kā-shən\ *n* **1** : the act or process of invoking **2** : a prayer for blessing or guidance especially at the beginning of a religious service **3** : a formula for conjuring : INCANTATION **4** : an act of legal or moral enforcement ⟨*invocation* of the law⟩ — **in·vo·ca·tion·al** \-shnəl, -shən-l\ *adj*

¹in·voice \'in-ˌvȯis\ *n* : an itemized statement given to a buyer by a seller and usually specifying the price of goods or services and the terms of sale; *also* : a shipment of goods sent with such a statement [Middle French *envois,* pl. of *envoi* "message", from *envoier* "to send on one's way", from Latin *in* "in, on" + *via* "way"]

²invoice *vt* : to submit an invoice for : BILL

in·voke \in-'vōk\ *vt* **1 a** : to call on for aid or protection (as in prayer) ⟨*invoke* God's blessing⟩ **b** : to appeal to as an authority or for support ⟨*invoke* a law⟩ **2** : to call forth by magic : CONJURE ⟨*invoke* spirits⟩ [Middle French *invoquer,* from Latin *invocare,* from *in-* + *vocare* "to call"] — **in·vok·er** *n*

in·vo·lu·cre \'in-və-ˌlü-kər\ *n* : one or more whorls of bracts immediately below a flower, flower cluster, or fruit [French, from Latin *involucrum* "sheath", from *involvere* "to wrap, involve"] — **in·vo·lu·cral** \ˌin-və-'lü-krəl\ *adj*

in·vol·un·tary \in-'väl-ən-ˌter-ē, 'in-\ *adj* **1** : not made or done willingly or from choice **2** : COMPULSORY ⟨*involuntary* servitude⟩ **3** : not subject to direct control by the will : REFLEX — **in·vol·un·tar·i·ly** \in-ˌväl-ən-'ter-ə-lē\ *adv*

involuntary muscle *n* : SMOOTH MUSCLE

involucre

in·vo·lu·tion \ˌin-və-'lü-shən\ *n* **1 a** : the act or an instance of enfolding or entangling : INVOLVEMENT **b** : INTRICACY 1, COMPLEXITY **2** : the act or process of raising a quantity to any power **3** : an inward curving or penetration **4 a** : a shrinking or return to a former size **b** : the regressive changes that accompany aging and are marked by a decrease of bodily vigor [Latin *involutio,* from *involvere* "to wrap, involve"] — **in·vo·lu·tion·al** \-shnəl, -shən-l\ *adj* — **in·vo·lu·tion·ary** \-shə-ˌner-ē\ *adj*

in·volve \in-'välv, -'vȯlv\ *vt* **1 a** : to draw in as a participant : ENGAGE ⟨many workers are *involved* in the job⟩ **b** : to oblige to take part ⟨was *involved* in a lawsuit⟩ **c** : to occupy (as oneself) absorbingly ⟨was *involved* in the hero's fate⟩ **2 a** : to have within or as part of itself : INCLUDE ⟨one problem *involves* others⟩ **b** : to require as a necessary accompaniment ⟨the road job *involved* building 10 bridges⟩ **c** : to have an effect on ⟨breathing *involves* the whole organism⟩ [Latin *involvere* "to roll up, wrap, involve", from *in-* + *volvere* "to roll"] SYN see INCLUDE — **in·volve·ment** \-mənt\ *n* — **in·volv·er** *n*

in·volved \-'välvd, -'vȯlvd\ *adj* **1** : INTRICATE 1 ⟨an *involved* plot⟩ **2** : difficult to deal with because of confusion or disorder : TANGLED SYN see COMPLEX — **in·volv·ed·ly** \-'väl-vəd-lē, -'vȯl-\ *adv*

in·vul·ner·a·ble \in-'vəln-rə-bəl, -ə-rə-; -'vəl-nər-bəl\ *adj* **1** : incapable of being wounded, injured, or damaged **2** : immune to or secure against attack : IMPREGNABLE — **in·vul·ner·a·bil·i·ty** \in-ˌvəln-rə-'bil-ət-ē, -ə-rə\ *n* — **in·vul·ner·a·ble·ness** \in-'vəln-rə-bəl-nəs, -ə-rə-; -'vəl-nər-bəl-\ *n* — **in·vul·ner·a·bly** \-blē\ *adv*

¹in·ward \'in-wərd\ *adj* **1** : located on the inside : INNER **2** : of or relating to the mind or spirit **3** : directed toward the interior ⟨an *inward* flow⟩

²inward *or* **in·wards** \-wərdz\ *adv* **1** : toward the inside, center, or interior ⟨slope *inward*⟩ **2** : toward the inner being ⟨turned their thoughts *inward*⟩

³inward *n* : something that is inward

in·ward·ly \'in-wərd-lē\ *adv* **1** : in the mind or spirit **2 a** : on the inside ⟨bled *inwardly*⟩ **b** : to oneself : PRIVATELY ⟨cursed *inwardly*⟩

in·ward·ness *n* **1** : fundamental nature : ESSENCE **2** : absorption in one's own mental or spiritual life

in·weave \in-'wēv, 'in-\ *vt* **-wove** \-'wōv\ *also* **-weaved; -wo·ven** \-'wō-vən\ *also* **-weaved; -weav·ing** : to weave in or together : INTERLACE

in·wrought \in-'rȯt, 'in-\ *adj* : having or being a decorative element worked or woven in

in–your–face \ˌin-yər-ˌfās\ *adj* : characterized by bold and often arrogant aggressiveness ⟨*in-your-face* basketball⟩

iod- *or* **iodo-** *combining form* : iodine ⟨*iod*ize⟩ ⟨*iodo*form⟩ [French *iode*]

io·dide \'ī-ə-ˌdīd\ *n* : a compound of iodine with another element or radical

io·dine \'ī-ə-ˌdīn, -əd-n, -ə-ˌdēn\ *n* **1** : a nonmetallic usually univalent chemical element that occurs in seawater, seaweeds, and underground brines, is obtained usually as heavy shining blackish gray crystals, and is used especially in medicine, photography, and analysis — see ELEMENT table **2** : a solution of iodine in alcohol used as an antiseptic [French *iode,* from Greek *ioeidēs* "violet colored", from *ion* "violet"]

io·dize \'ī-ə-ˌdīz\ *vt* : to treat with iodine or an iodide ⟨*iodized* salt⟩

io·do·form \ī-'ōd-ə-ˌfȯrm, -'äd-\ *n* : a yellow crystalline volatile iodine compound that is used as an antiseptic dressing [*iod-* + *-form* (as in *chloroform*)]

io·dop·sin \ˌī-ə-'däp-sən\ *n* : a violet light-sensitive pigment in the retinal cones that is formed from vitamin A and is important in daylight vision — compare RHODOPSIN [Greek *ioeidēs* "violet colored" + *opsis* "sight, vision"]

io moth \ˌī-ō-\ *n* : a large yellowish American moth with a large spot on each hind wing [Latin *Io,* a mythical maiden loved by Zeus, from Greek *Īō*]

ion \ˈī-ən, ˈī-ˌän\ *n* : an atom or group of atoms that carries a positive or negative electric charge as a result of having lost or gained one or more electrons [Greek *ïon,* present participle of *ienai* "to go"]

-ion *n suffix* **1 a** : act or process ⟨validat*ion*⟩ **b** : result of an act or process ⟨regulat*ion*⟩ **2** : state or condition ⟨deflat*ion*⟩ [Latin *-ion-, -io*]

Io·ni·an \ī-ˈō-nē-ən\ *n* **1** : one of an ancient Greek people who settled in Attica, on the islands of the Aegean sea, and on the shore of Asia Minor **2** : a native or inhabitant of Ionia — **Ionian** *adj*

ion·ic \ī-ˈän-ik\ *adj* : of, relating to, or existing in the form of ions

Ion·ic \ī-ˈän-ik\ *adj* **1** : of or relating to Ionia or the Ionians **2** : belonging to or resembling the Ionic order of architecture characterized especially by the spiral volutes of its capital

ionic bond *n* : a chemical bond formed between ions of opposite charge

io·ni·um \ī-ˈō-nē-əm\ *n* : a natural radioactive isotope of thorium having a mass number of 230 [*ion;* from its ionizing action]

ion·ize \ˈī-ə-ˌnīz\ *vb* : to convert or become converted wholly or partly into ions — **ion·iza·tion** \ˌī-ə-nə-ˈzā-shən\ *n* — **ion·iz·er** \ˈī-ə-ˌnī-zər\ *n*

iono·sphere \ī-ˈän-ə-ˌsfiər\ *n* : the part of the earth's atmosphere beginning at an altitude of about 40 kilometers and extending outward 400 kilometers or more and containing free electrically charged particles by means of which radio waves are transmitted to great distances around the earth — **iono·spher·ic** \ī-ˌän-ə-ˈsfiər-ik, -ˈsfer-\ *adj*

io·ta \ī-ˈōt-ə\ *n* **1** : the 9th letter of the Greek alphabet — I or ι **2** : a tiny amount : JOT ⟨not one *iota* of truth⟩

IOU \ˌī-ō-ˈyü\ *n* : a paper that has on it the letters IOU, a stated sum, and a signature and that is given as an acknowledgment of debt [from the pronunciation of *I owe you*]

-ious *adj suffix* : -OUS ⟨capac*ious*⟩ [partly from Latin *-iosus,* from *-i-* + *-osus* "-ous"; partly from Latin *-ius,* adj. suffix]

IPA \ˌī-ˌpē-ˈā\ *n* : an alphabet designed to represent each human speech sound with a different character [*I*nternational *P*honetic *A*lphabet]

ip·e·cac \ˈip-i-ˌkak\ *or* **ipe·ca·cu·a·nha** \ē-ˌpek-ə-kù-ˈän-yə\ *n* : a South American creeping plant of the madder family; *also* : its dried rhizome and roots or an extract of these used especially formerly as an emetic and purgative [Portuguese *ipecacuanha,* from Tupi *ipekaaguéne*]

ip·se dixit \ˌip-sē-ˈdik-sət\ *n* : an assertion made but not proved : DICTUM [Latin, "he himself said it"]

ip·so facto \ˌip-sō-ˈfak-tō\ *adv* : by the very nature of the case [New Latin, literally, "by the fact itself"]

IQ \ˈī-ˈkyü\ *n* : INTELLIGENCE QUOTIENT

ir- — see IN-

Ira·ni·an \ir-ˈā-nē-ən\ *n* **1** : a native or inhabitant of Iran **2** : a branch of the Indo-European family of languages that includes Persian — **Iranian** *adj*

iras·ci·ble \ir-ˈas-ə-bəl, ī-ˈras-\ *adj* : marked by hot temper and easily aroused anger [Middle French, from Late Latin *irascibilis,* from Latin *irasci* "to become angry", from *ira* "ire"] — **iras·ci·bil·i·ty** \ir-ˌas-ə-ˈbil-ət-ē, ī-ˌras-\ *n* — **iras·ci·ble·ness** \ir-ˈas-ə-bəl-nəs, ī-ˈras-\ *n* — **iras·ci·bly** \-blē\ *adv* □ SYN IRASCIBLE, CHOLERIC, TESTY, TOUCHY mean easily angered. IRASCIBLE implies a tendency to be fiery tempered; CHOLERIC may suggest impatient excitability and unreasonable irritability; TESTY implies a quick temper irritated by trivial annoyances; TOUCHY suggests oversensitive readiness to take offense or flare up at slight or implied criticism.

irate \ī-ˈrāt\ *adj* : ANGRY 1a, b ⟨*irate* taxpayers⟩ — **irate·ly** *adv* — **irate·ness** *n*

ire \ˈīr\ *n* : WRATH 1, ANGER [Old French, from Latin *ira*] — **ire** *vt* — **ire·ful** \-fəl\ *adj* — **ire·ful·ly** \-fə-lē\ *adv*

iren·ic \ī-ˈren-ik\ *adj* : PACIFIC 1 [Greek *eirēnikos,* from *eirēnē* "peace"] — **iren·i·cal·ly** \-ˈren-i-kə-lē, -klē\ *adv*

ir·i·des·cence \ˌir-ə-ˈdes-ns\ *n* : a play of colors producing rainbow effects (as in a soap bubble) [derived from Latin *irid-, iris* "rainbow"] — **ir·i·des·cent** \-nt\ *adj* — **ir·i·des·cent·ly** *adv*

irid·i·um \ir-ˈid-ē-əm\ *n* : a silver-white hard brittle very heavy metallic chemical element — see ELEMENT table [New Latin, from Latin *irid-, iris* "rainbow"; from the colors produced by its dissolving in hydrochloric acid]

iris \ˈī-rəs\ *n, pl* **iris·es** *or* **iri·des** \ˈī-rə-ˌdēz, ˈir-ə-\ **1** : the colored part of the eye that surrounds the pupil and alters in size to control the amount of light entering the eye **2** : any of a large genus of perennial herbaceous plants with sword-shaped basal leaves and large showy flowers [Latin, "rainbow, iris plant", from Greek, "rainbow, iris plant, iris of the eye"]

iris diaphragm *n* : an adjustable diaphragm of thin opaque plates used for changing the diameter of a central opening to control the amount of light passing (as into a microscope or camera)

Irish \ˈīr-ish\ *n* **1** *pl in construction* : the natives or inhabitants of Ireland or their descendants **2** : the Celtic language of Ireland — **Irish** *adj* — **Irish·man** \-mən\ *n* — **Irish·wom·an** \-ˌwùm-ən\ *n*

Irish Gaelic *n* : the Celtic language of Ireland especially as used since the end of the medieval period

Irish·ism \ˈī-rish-ˌiz-əm\ *n* : a word, phrase, or expression characteristic of the Irish

Irish moss *n* : either of two red algae; *also* : the dried and bleached plants of these used especially in cooking and pharmacy

Irish potato *n* : POTATO 2b

Irish setter *n* : any of a breed of bird dogs similar to English setters but with a chestnut-brown or mahogany-red coat

irk \ˈərk\ *vt* : to make weary, irritated, or bored : ANNOY [Middle English *irken*]

irk·some \ˈərk-səm\ *adj* : tending to irk : TEDIOUS — **irk·some·ly** *adv* — **irk·some·ness** *n*

¹iron \ˈī-ərn, ˈīrn\ *n* **1** : a heavy malleable ductile magnetic silver-white metallic chemical element that readily rusts in moist air, occurs in meteorites and combined in rocks, and is vital to biological processes — see ELEMENT table **2 a** : something (as handcuffs or chains) used to bind or restrain — usually used in pl. **b** : a heated metal implement used for branding **c** : FLATIRON **d** : one of a set of golf clubs with flat metal heads **3** : great strength or hardness [Old English *īsern, īren*]

²iron *adj* **1** : of, relating to, or made of iron **2** : resembling iron (as in hardness or strength) **3 a** : being strong and healthy : ROBUST ⟨an *iron* constitution⟩ **b** : INFLEXIBLE, UNRELENTING ⟨*iron* determination⟩

³iron *vb* **1** : to furnish or cover with iron **2** : to smooth or press with a heated flatiron ⟨*iron* a shirt⟩ **3** : to iron clothes ⟨spent all day *ironing*⟩

Iron Age *n* : the period of human culture characterized by the first smelting and use of iron and beginning somewhat before 1000 B.C. in western Asia and Egypt

¹iron·clad \-ˈklad\ *adj* **1** : sheathed in iron armor **2** : RIGOROUS, EXACTING ⟨*ironclad* laws⟩

²iron·clad \-ˌklad\ *n* : an armored naval vessel

iron curtain *n* : a political, military, and ideological barrier that cuts off and isolates an area; *esp* : one between an area under Soviet control and other areas

iron hand *n* : stern or rigorous control ⟨rule with an *iron hand*⟩

iris 2

\ə\ abut	\ng\ sing
\ər\ further	\ō\ bone
\a\ mat	\ȯ\ saw
\ā\ take	\ȯi\ coin
\ä\ cot, cart	\th\ thin
\aú\ out	\th\ this
\ch\ chin	\ü\ foot
\e\ pet	\ù\ foot
\ē\ easy	\y\ yet
\g\ go	\yü\ few
\i\ tip	\yù\ cure
\ī\ life	\zh\ vision
\j\ job	

iron horse *n* : a locomotive engine

iron·ic \ī-'rän-ik\ *adj* **1** : relating to, containing, or constituting irony ⟨an *ironic* turn of events⟩ **2** : given to irony — **iron·i·cal** \-i-kəl\ *adj* — **iron·i·cal·ly** \-i-kə-lē, -klē\ *adv*

iron lung *n* : a device for artificial respiration in which rhythmic alternations in the air pressure in a chamber surrounding a patient's chest force air into and out of the lungs

iron oxide *n* **1** : FERRIC OXIDE **2** : FERROUS OXIDE **3** : a black magnetic oxide of iron Fe_3O_4 used as a pigment and polishing material

iron pyrites *n* : PYRITE — called also *iron pyrite*

iron·stone \'ī-ərn-ˌstōn, 'īrn-\ *n* **1** : a hard sedimentary rock rich in iron **2** : a hard white pottery first made in England during the 18th century — called also *ironstone china*

iron sulfide *n* : a compound (as a pyrite) of iron and sulfur

iron·ware \-ˌwaər, -ˌweər\ *n* : articles made of iron

iron·wood \-ˌwu̇d\ *n* **1** : any of numerous trees and shrubs with exceptionally tough or hard wood **2** : the wood of an ironwood

iron·work \-ˌwərk\ *n* **1** : work in iron **2** *pl* : a mill or building where iron or steel is smelted or heavy iron or steel products are made — **iron·work·er** \-ˌwər-kər\ *n*

iro·ny \'ī-rə-nē\ *n, pl* **-nies** **1 a** : the humorous or sardonic use of words to express the opposite of what one really means (as when words of praise are given but blame is intended) **b** : an ironic expression or utterance **2 a** : inconsistency between an actual and an expected result **b** : a result marked by such inconsistency [Latin *ironia,* from Greek *eirōnia,* from *eirōn* "dissembler"]

Ir·o·quoi·an \ˌir-ə-'kwȯi-ən\ *n* **1** : a stock of Indian languages spoken from the St. Lawrence valley to the southern Appalachian mountains **2** : a member of the Indian peoples speaking Iroquoian languages — **Iroquoian** *adj*

Ir·o·quois \'ir-ə-ˌkwȯi\ *n, pl* **Iroquois** \-ˌkwȯi, -ˌkwȯiz\ : a member of an Indian confederacy consisting originally of the Cayugas, Mohawks, Oneidas, Onondagas, and Senecas and later including the Tuscaroras [French, of American Indian origin]

ir·ra·di·ant \ir-'ād-ē-ənt\ *adj* : emitting rays of light — **ir·ra·di·an·cy** \-ən-sē\ *n*

ir·ra·di·ate \ir-'ād-ē-ˌāt\ *vt* **1 a** : to cast rays of light on : ILLUMINATE **b** : to affect or treat by exposure to radiations (as of ultraviolet light, X rays, or gamma rays) **2** : to emit like rays of light : RADIATE — **ir·ra·di·a·tion** \-ˌād-ē-'ā-shən\ *n* — **ir·ra·di·a·tive** \-'ād-ē-ˌāt-iv\ *adj*

ir·ra·tio·nal \ir-'ash-nəl, 'ir-, -ən-l\ *adj* **1 a** : incapable of reasoning ⟨*irrational* beasts⟩ **b** : not governed by or according to reason ⟨an *irrational* hatred of strangers⟩ **2** : of, relating to, or being an irrational number — **ir·ra·tio·nal·i·ty** \ir-ˌash-ə-'nal-ət-ē\ *n* — **ir·ra·tio·nal·ly** \ir-'ash-nə-lē, 'ir-, -'ash-ən-l-ē\ *adv* — **ir·ra·tio·nal·ness** \-nəl-nəs, -ən-l-nəs\ *n* □ SYN IRRATIONAL, UNREASONABLE mean not guided by reason. IRRATIONAL may imply mental derangement but oftener suggests lack of control or guidance by reason ⟨*irrational* fears⟩ UNREASONABLE suggests control by some force other than reason (as greed or rage) which makes for a deficiency in good sense ⟨*unreasonable* demands⟩

irrational number *n* : a real number (as $\sqrt{2}$) that is not expressible as the quotient of two integers — called also *irrational*

ir·re·claim·able \ˌir-i-'klā-mə-bəl\ *adj* : incapable of being reclaimed — **ir·re·claim·ably** \-blē\ *adv*

ir·rec·on·cil·able \ir-ˌek-ən-'sī-lə-bəl; ir-'ek-ən-, 'ir-\ *adj* : impossible to reconcile, adjust, or harmonize ⟨*irreconcilable* enemies⟩ — **ir·rec·on·cil·abil·i·ty** \ir-ˌek-ən-ˌsī-lə-'bil-ət-ē\ *n* — **ir·rec·on·cil·ably** \ir-ˌek-ən-'sī-lə-blē; ir-'ek-ən-ˌ, 'ir-\ *adv*

ir·re·cov·er·able \ˌir-i-'kəv-rə-bəl, -ə-rə-\ *adj* : not capable of being recovered ⟨an *irrecoverable* debt⟩ — **ir·re·cov·er·ably** \-blē\ *adv*

ir·re·deem·able \ˌir-i-'dē-mə-bəl\ *adj* **1** : not redeemable; *esp* : not convertible into gold or silver at the will of the holder **2** : being beyond remedy : HOPELESS ⟨*irredeemable* mistakes⟩ — **ir·re·deem·ably** \-blē\ *adv*

ir·re·duc·ible \ˌir-i-'dü-sə-bəl, -'dyü-\ *adj* : not reducible — **ir·re·duc·ibil·i·ty** \-ˌdü-sə-'bil-ət-ē, -ˌdyü-\ *n* — **ir·re·duc·ibly** \-'dü-sə-blē, -'dyü-\ *adv*

ir·re·fut·able \ˌir-i-'fyüt-ə-bəl; ir-'ef-yət-, 'ir-\ *adj* : not capable of being proved wrong : INDISPUTABLE — **ir·re·fut·abil·i·ty** \ˌir-i-ˌfyüt-ə-'bil-ət-ē, ir-ˌef-yət-ə-'bil-\ *n* — **ir·re·fut·ably** \ˌir-i-'fyüt-ə-blē; ir-'ef-yət-, 'ir-\ *adv*

¹ir·reg·u·lar \ir-'eg-yə-lər, 'ir-\ *adj* **1 a** : not conforming to established laws, customs, or moral principles **b** : not belonging to a recognized or organized body ⟨*irregular* troops⟩ ⟨*irregular* Democrats⟩ **2** : not conforming to the normal or usual manner of inflection ⟨the *irregular* verbs *sell* and *cast*⟩; *esp* : STRONG 13 ⟨the *irregular* verb *write*⟩ **3** : lacking perfect symmetry or evenness **4** : lacking continuity or regularity of occurrence ⟨*irregular* intervals⟩ ⟨*irregular* payments⟩ — **ir·reg·u·lar·ly** *adv*

²irregular *n* : a soldier (as a guerrilla) who is not a member of a regular military force

ir·reg·u·lar·i·ty \ir-ˌeg-yə-'lar-ət-ē\ *n, pl* **-ties** **1** : the quality or state of being irregular **2** : something (as dishonest conduct) that is irregular

ir·rel·e·vant \ir-'el-ə-vənt, 'ir-\ *adj* : not relevant : not applicable or pertinent — **ir·rel·e·vance** \-vəns\ *or* **ir·rel·e·van·cy** \-vən-sē\ *n* — **ir·rel·e·vant·ly** *adv*

ir·re·li·gious \-'lij-əs\ *adj* **1** : lacking religious emotions, doctrines, or practices **2** : indicating lack of religion ⟨*irreligious* talk⟩ — **ir·re·li·gious·ly** *adv*

ir·re·me·di·a·ble \ˌir-i-'mēd-ē-ə-bəl\ *adj* : not remediable — **ir·re·me·di·a·ble·ness** *n* — **ir·re·me·di·a·bly** \-blē\ *adv*

ir·re·mov·able \ˌir-i-'mü-və-bəl\ *adj* : not removable — **ir·re·mov·abil·i·ty** \-ˌmü-və-'bil-ət-ē\ *n* — **ir·re·mov·ably** \-'mü-və-blē\ *adv*

ir·rep·a·ra·ble \ir-'ep-rə-bəl, 'ir-, -ə-rə-\ *adj* : not capable of being repaired or made good ⟨an *irreparable* loss⟩ — **ir·rep·a·ra·ble·ness** *n* — **ir·rep·a·ra·bly** \-blē\ *adv*

ir·re·place·able \ˌir-i-'plā-sə-bəl\ *adj* : not replaceable

ir·re·press·ible \ˌir-i-'pres-ə-bəl\ *adj* : not capable of being checked or held back ⟨*irrepressible* laughter⟩ — **ir·re·press·ibil·i·ty** \-ˌpres-ə-'bil-ət-ē\ *n* — **ir·re·press·ibly** \-'pres-ə-blē\ *adv*

ir·re·proach·able \-'prō-chə-bəl\ *adj* : not reproachable : BLAMELESS — **ir·re·proach·able·ness** *n* — **ir·re·proach·ably** \-blē\ *adv*

ir·re·sist·ible \-'zis-tə-bəl\ *adj* : impossible to successfully resist or oppose ⟨an *irresistible* attraction⟩ — **ir·re·sist·ibil·i·ty** \-ˌzis-tə-'bil-ət-ē\ *adj* — **ir·re·sist·ible·ness** \-'zis-tə-bəl-nəs\ *n* — **ir·re·sist·ibly** \-blē\ *adv*

ir·res·o·lute \ir-'ez-ə-ˌlüt, 'ir-, -lət\ *adj* : uncertain how to act or proceed : HESITANT — **ir·res·o·lute·ly** *adv* — **ir·res·o·lute·ness** *n* — **ir·res·o·lu·tion** \ir-ˌez-ə-'lü-shən\ *n*

irrespective of *prep* : without regard to : regardless of

ir·re·spon·si·ble \ˌir-i-'spän-sə-bəl\ *adj* : not responsible: as **a** : not answerable to higher authority **b** : said or done with no sense of responsibility ⟨*irresponsible* charges⟩ **c** : lacking a sense of responsibility **d** : unable especially mentally or financially to bear responsibility — **ir·re·spon·si·bil·i·ty** \-ˌspän-sə-'bil-ət-ē\ *n* — **ir·re·spon·si·bly** \-'spän-sə-blē\ *adv*

ir·re·triev·able \ˌir-i-'trē-və-bəl\ *adj* : not capable of being regained or remedied ⟨an *irretrievable* mistake⟩ — **ir·re·triev·ably** \-blē\ *adv*

ir·rev·er·ence \ir-'ev-rəns, 'ir-, -'ev-ə-rəns, -'ev-ərns\ *n* **1** : lack of reverence **2** : an irreverent act or utterance

ir·rev·er·ent \-'ev-rənt, -'ev-ə-rənt, -'ev-ərnt\ *adj* : showing lack of reverence : DISRESPECTFUL — **ir·rev·er·ent·ly** *adv*

ir·re·vers·ible \,ir-i-'vər-sə-bəl\ *adj* : incapable of being reversed — **ir·re·vers·ibil·i·ty** \-,vər-sə-'bil-ət-ē\ *n* — **ir·re·vers·ibly** \-'vər-sə-blē\ *adv*

ir·rev·o·ca·ble \ir-'ev-ə-kə-bəl, 'ir-\ *adj* : not capable of being revoked ⟨an *irrevocable* decision⟩ — **ir·rev·o·ca·bil·i·ty** \ir-,ev-ə-kə-'bil-ət-ē\ *n* — **ir·rev·o·ca·bly** \ir-'ev-ə-kə-blē, 'ir-\ *adv*

ir·ri·gate \'ir-ə-,gāt\ *vb* **1** : WET, MOISTEN: as **a** : to supply (as land) with water by artificial means **b** : to flush with a liquid ⟨*irrigate* a wound⟩ **2** : to practice irrigation [Latin *irrigare,* from *in-* + *rigare* "to water"] — **ir·ri·ga·tion** \,ir-ə-'gā-shən\ *n* — **ir·ri·ga·tor** \'ir-ə-,gāt-ər\ *n*

ir·ri·ta·bil·i·ty \,ir-ət-ə-'bil-ət-ē\ *n, pl* **-ties** : the quality or state of being irritable: as **a** : quick excitability to annoyance, impatience, or anger **b** : the property of protoplasm and of living organisms that permits them to react to stimuli

ir·ri·ta·ble \'ir-ət-ə-bəl\ *adj* : capable of being irritated; *esp* : readily or easily irritated — **ir·ri·ta·ble·ness** *n* — **ir·ri·ta·bly** \-blē\ *adv*

ir·ri·tant \'ir-ə-tənt\ *adj* : IRRITATING; *esp* : tending to produce physical irritation — **irritant** *n*

ir·ri·tate \'ir-ə-,tāt\ *vb* **1** : to excite impatience, anger, or displeasure in : ANNOY **2** : to make sore or inflamed [Latin *irritare*] — **ir·ri·ta·tive** \-,tāt-iv\ *adj* □ SYN AGGRAVATE, EXASPERATE, PROVOKE: IRRITATE implies arousing feelings that may range from impatience to rage; AGGRAVATE may apply to repeated action that intensifies anger or irritation; EXASPERATE suggests intense annoyance or patience strained beyond endurance; PROVOKE implies an often deliberate arousing of strong annoyance or vexation that may excite to action.

ir·ri·ta·tion \,ir-ə-'tā-shən\ *n* **1** : the act of irritating **2** : something that irritates **3** : the state of being irritated

ir·rupt \ir-'əpt, 'ir-\ *vi* **1** : to rush in forcibly or violently **2** : to increase suddenly in numbers ⟨rabbits *irrupt* in cycles⟩ [Latin *irruptus,* past participle of *irrumpere* "to break in, irrupt", from *in-* + *rumpere* "to break"] — **ir·rup·tion** \ir-'əp-shən, 'ir-\ *n* — **ir·rup·tive** \-'əp-tiv\ *adj* — **ir·rup·tive·ly** \-'əp-tiv-lē\ *adv*

is *present 3d sing of* BE [Old English]

is- *or* **iso-** *combining form* **1** : equal : uniform ⟨*iso*bar⟩ **2** : isomeric ⟨*iso*leucine⟩ [Greek *isos*]

Isa·iah \ī-'zā-ə\ *n* — see BIBLE table

isch·emia \is-'kē-mē-ə\ *n* : local deficiency of blood due to decreased arterial inflow [Greek *ischaimos* "styptic", from *ischein* "to restrain" + *haima* "blood"] — **isch·emic** \-mik\ *adj*

is·chi·um \'is-kē-əm\ *n, pl* **-chia** \-kē-ə\ : the dorsal and posterior of the three principal bones composing either half of the pelvis [Latin, "hip joint", from Greek *ischion*] — **is·chi·al** \-kē-əl\ *adj*

-ise \,īz\ *vb suffix, chiefly British* : -IZE

-ish \ish\ *adj suffix* **1** : of, relating to, or being ⟨Finn*ish*⟩ **2 a** : characteristic of ⟨girl*ish*⟩ : having the undesirable qualities of ⟨mul*ish*⟩ **b** : inclined or liable to ⟨book*ish*⟩ ⟨qualm*ish*⟩ **c** (1) : somewhat ⟨small*ish*⟩ (2) : having the approximate age of ⟨forty*ish*⟩ (3) : being or occurring at the approximate time of ⟨eight*ish*⟩ [Old English *-isc*]

Ish·ma·el \'ish-mā-əl, -mē-\ *n* : a social outcast [*Ishmael,* outcast son of Abraham and Hagar]

Ish·ma·el·ite \'ish-mā-ə-,līt, -mē-\ *n* : a member of an ancient Semitic people of the deserts of southwestern Asia held to be descended from Ishmael and sometimes held to be ancestral to the modern Arabs

isin·glass \'īz-n-,glas, 'ī-zing-\ *n* **1** : a very pure gelatin prepared from the air bladders of fishes **2** : mica in thin sheets [probably by folk etymology from Dutch *huizenblas,* from *huus* "sturgeon" + *blase* "bladder"]

Is·lam \is-'läm, iz-, -'lam, 'is-,, 'iz-,\ *n* **1** : a religion dominant in much of Asia and northern Africa since the 7th century A.D. that is marked by belief in Allah as the sole deity, in Muhammad as his prophet, and in the Koran **2 a** : the civilization erected upon Islamic faith **b** : the group of modern nations in which Islam is the dominant religion [Arabic *islām* "submission (to the will of Allah)"] — **Is·lam·ic** \is-'läm-ik, iz-, -'lam-\ *adj* — **Is·lam·ize** \'iz-lə-,mīz\ *vt*

is·land \'ī-lənd\ *n* **1** : an area of land surrounded by water and smaller than a continent **2** : something suggestive of an island in its isolation [Middle English *iland,* from Old English *īgland*] □ ORIGIN The words *island* and *isle* are etymologically distinct. *Island* can be traced back to Old English *īgland,* composed of two elements *īg* and *land. Land,* as we might expect, means "land", but *īg* is also found in Old English as a word meaning "island". In a sense, then, *īgland* is "island-land". English *isle,* on the other hand, is derived through Old French from Latin *insula.* In the 16th century, under the influence of *isle,* the letter *s* was added to *iland,* the earlier form of *island.*

is·land·er \'ī-lən-dər\ *n* : a native or inhabitant of an island

island universe *n* : a galaxy other than the Milky Way

isle \'īl\ *n* : ISLAND 1; *esp* : a small island [Old French, from Latin *insula* — see ISLAND *origin*]

is·let \'ī-lət\ *n* : a little island

islet of Lang·er·hans \-'läng-ər-,häns, -,hänz\ : any of the groups of small granular endocrine cells that form interlacing strands in the pancreas and secrete insulin [Paul *Langerhans,* died 1888, German physician]

ism \'iz-əm\ *n* : a distinctive doctrine, cause, or theory [*-ism*]

-ism \,iz-əm\ *n suffix* **1 a** : act : practice : process ⟨plagiar*ism*⟩ **b** : manner of action or behavior characteristic of a (specified) person or thing ⟨animal*ism*⟩ **2 a** : state : condition : property ⟨barbarian*ism*⟩ **b** : abnormal state or condition resulting from excess of a (specified) thing ⟨alcohol*ism*⟩ or marked by resemblance to (such) a person or thing ⟨mongol*ism*⟩ **3 a** : doctrine : theory : cult ⟨Buddh*ism*⟩ **b** : adherence to a system or a class of principles ⟨stoic*ism*⟩ **4** : characteristic or peculiar feature or trait ⟨colloquial*ism*⟩ [Greek *-isma* and *-ismos,* from verbs in *-izein* "-ize"]

isn't \'iz-nt\ : is not

iso·bar \'ī-sə-,bär\ *n* : a line drawn on a map connecting places having the same atmospheric pressure at a given time or for a given period [*is-* + Greek *baros* "weight"] — **iso·bar·ic** \,ī-sə-'bär-ik, -'bar-\ *adj*

iso·ga·mete \,ī-sō-gə-'mēt, -'gam-,ēt\ *n* : a gamete indistinguishable from another gamete with which it can unite to form a zygote — **iso·ga·met·ic** \-gə-'met-ik\ *adj*

iso·gon·ic line \,ī-sə-,gän-ik-\ *n* : a line on a map joining points on the earth's surface at which the magnetic declination is the same [Greek *gōnia* "angle"]

iso·late \'ī-sə-,lāt *also* 'is-ə-\ *vb* **1** : to set apart from others; *also* : QUARANTINE **2** : to select from among others; *esp* : to separate from other substances so as to obtain pure or in a free state [back-formation from *isolated* "set apart", from French *isolé,* from Italian *isolato,* from *isola* "island", from Latin *insula*]

iso·la·tion \,ī-sə-'lā-shən, ,is-ə-\ *n* : the act of isolating : the condition of being isolated

iso·la·tion·ism \-shə-,niz-əm\ *n* : a national policy of avoiding international political and economic relations (as alliances) — **iso·la·tion·ist** \-shə-nəst, -shnəst\ *n or adj*

iso·leu·cine \,ī-sō-'lü-,sēn\ *n* : a crystalline essential amino acid isomeric with leucine

iso·mer \'ī-sə-mər\ *n* : a compound, radical, ion, or nuclide exhibiting isomerism with one or more others

\ə\ abut · \ng\ sing
\ər\ further · \ō\ bone
\a\ mat · \ò\ saw
\ā\ take · \òi\ coin
\ä\ cot, cart · \th\ thin
\aù\ out · \th\ this
\ch\ chin · \ü\ food
\e\ pet · \ù\ foot
\ē\ easy · \y\ yet
\g\ go · \yü\ few
\i\ tip · \yù\ cure
\ī\ life · \zh\ vision
\j\ job

[back-formation from *isomeric,* from Greek *isomerēs* "equally divided", from *isos* "equal" + *meros* "part"]

isom·er·ism \ī-'säm-ə-,riz-əm\ *n* **1** : the relation of two or more chemical compounds, radicals, or ions that contain the same numbers of atoms of the same elements but differ in structural arrangement and properties **2** : the relation of two or more nuclides with the same mass numbers and atomic numbers but different energy states and rates of radioactive decay — **iso·mer·ic** \,ī-sə-'mer-ik\ *adj*

iso·met·ric \,ī-sə-'me-trik\ *adj* **1** : of, relating to, or characterized by equality of measure **2** : relating to or being a crystallographic system characterized by three equal axes at right angles — **iso·met·ri·cal·ly** \-tri-kə-lē, -klē\ *adv*

iso·met·rics \,ī-sə-'me-triks\ *n sing or pl* : a form of exercise in which the muscles strain against an unmoving resistance (as a wall or door frame)

iso·pod \'ī-sə-,päd\ *n* : any of a large order (Isopoda) of small sessile-eyed crustaceans with seven free thoracic segments each bearing a pair of legs — **isop·o·dan** \ī-'säp-əd-ən\ *adj or n*

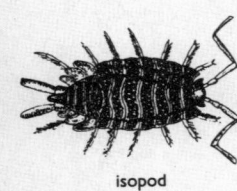
isopod

iso·pro·pyl alcohol \,ī-sə-'prō-pəl-\ *n* : a volatile flammable alcohol C_3H_8O used especially as a solvent and rubbing alcohol [*isopropyl* from *is-* + *prop-* (derived from *propionic acid*) + *-yl*]

isos·ce·les \ī-'säs-,lēz, -ə-,lēz\ *adj* **1** : being a triangle with two equal sides **2** : being a trapezoid whose two nonparallel sides are equal [Late Latin, from Greek *isoskelēs,* from *isos* "equal" + *skelos* "leg"]

isos·ta·sy \ī-'säs-tə-sē\ *n* : general equilibrium in vertical movement between segments of the earth's crust maintained by a yielding flow of rock material beneath the surface under the force of gravity [Greek *-stasia* "condition of standing", from *histanai* "to cause to stand"] — **iso·stat·ic** \,ī-sə-'stat-ik\ *adj*

iso·therm \'ī-sə-,thərm\ *n* : a line on a map connecting points having the same temperature at a given time or the same mean temperature for a given period [French *isotherme* "isothermal", from Greek *isos* "equal" + *thermē* "heat"]

iso·ther·mal \,ī-sə-'thər-məl\ *adj* : of, relating to, or marked by equality of temperature

iso·ton·ic \,ī-sə-'tän-ik\ *adj* : having the same or equal osmotic pressure ⟨a salt solution *isotonic* with red blood cells⟩ [Greek *tonos* "tension, tone"] — **iso·ton·i·cal·ly** \-'tän-i-kə-lē, -klē\ *adj* — **iso·to·nic·i·ty** \-tō-'nis-ət-ē\ *n*

iso·tope \'ī-sə-,tōp\ *n* : any of two or more species of atoms of a chemical element with the same atomic number and position in the periodic table and nearly identical chemical behavior but with differing atomic mass or mass number and different physical properties [Greek *topos* "place"] — **iso·top·ic** \,ī-sə-'täp-ik, -'tō-pik\ *adj* — **iso·top·i·cal·ly** \-'täp-i-kə-lē, -'tō-pi-, -klē\ *adv*

Is·ra·el \'iz-rē-əl\ *n* **1** : the Jewish people **2** : a group of people held to be God's elect [derived from Hebrew *Yiśrā'ēl*] — **Israel** *adj*

Is·rae·li \iz-'rā-lē\ *adj* of, relating to, or characteristic of the republic of Israel or its people — **Israeli** *n*

Is·ra·el·ite \'iz-rē-ə-,līt\ *n* : a descendant of the Hebrew patriarch Jacob; *esp* : a native or inhabitant of the ancient northern kingdom of Israel — **Israelite** *or* **Is·ra·el·it·ish** \-,līt-ish\ *adj*

is·su·ance \'ish-ə-wəns\ *n* : the act of issuing especially officially

¹is·sue \'ish-ü\ *n* **1** : the action of going, coming, or flowing out **2** : a means or place of going out : EXIT, OUTLET **3** : PROGENY 1 **4** : final outcome : RESULT **5 a** : a matter in dispute : a point of debate or controversy **b** : a final result or conclusion : DECISION **6** : something issued or issuing; *esp* : the copies of a periodical published at one time ⟨the latest *issue* of a magazine⟩

[Middle French, from *issir* "to come out, go out", from Latin *exire,* from *ex-* + *ire* "to go"]

²issue *vb* **1** : to go, come, or flow out : DISCHARGE ⟨water *issuing* from a pipe⟩ **2 a** : to cause to come forth : EMIT **b** : to distribute officially ⟨*issue* a new stamp⟩ **c** : to send out for sale or circulation : PUBLISH **3** : to come as an effect : RESULT — **is·su·er** *n*

¹-ist \əst\ *n suffix* **1 a** : one that performs a (specified) action ⟨cycl*ist*⟩ : one that makes or produces ⟨novel*ist*⟩ **b** : one that plays a (specified) musical instrument ⟨harp*ist*⟩ **c** : one that operates a (specified) mechanical instrument or contrivance ⟨automobil*ist*⟩ **2** : one that specializes in a (specified) art or science or skill ⟨geolog*ist*⟩ ⟨ventriloqu*ist*⟩ **3** : one that adheres to or advocates a (specified) doctrine or system or code of behavior ⟨royal*ist*⟩ ⟨social*ist*⟩ or that of a (specified) individual ⟨Calvin*ist*⟩ ⟨Darwin*ist*⟩ [Greek *-istēs,* from verbs in *-izein* "-ize"]

²-ist *adj suffix* : -ISTIC

¹isth·mi·an \'is-mē-ən\ *n* : a native or inhabitant of an isthmus

²isthmian *adj* : of, relating to, or situated in or near an isthmus: as **a** *often cap* : of or relating to the Isthmus of Corinth in Greece or the games anciently held there **b** *often cap* : of or relating to the Isthmus of Panama

isth·mus \'is-məs\ *n* **1** : a narrow strip of land connecting two larger land areas **2** : a narrow anatomical part or passage connecting two larger structures or cavities [Latin, from Greek *isthmos*]

-is·tic \'is-tik\ *also* **-is·ti·cal** \'is-ti-kəl\ *adj suffix* : of, relating to, or characteristic of ⟨altru*istic*⟩ [Greek *-istikos,* from *-istēs* "-ist" + *-ikos* "-ic"]

is·tle \'ist-lē\ *n* : a strong fiber (as for cordage or basketry) from tropical American plants [American Spanish *ixtle,* from Nahuatl *ichtli*]

¹it \it, 'it, ət\ *pron* **1** : that one — used usually in reference to a lifeless thing ⟨caught the ball and threw *it* back⟩, a plant, a person or animal whose sex is unknown or disregarded ⟨don't know who *it* is⟩, a group of individuals or things, or an abstract entity; compare HE, ITS, SHE, THEY **2** — used as subject of a verb that expresses a condition or action without reference to an agent ⟨*it* is raining⟩ **3 a** — used to mark the logical place of a noun, phrase, or clause that has been shifted to a later place in a sentence ⟨*it* is necessary to repeat the whole thing⟩; often used to shift emphasis to a part of a statement other than the subject ⟨*it* was in this city that the treaty was signed⟩ **b** — used with many verbs as a direct object with little or no meaning ⟨footed *it* back to camp⟩ **4** : the general state of affairs or circumstances ⟨how is *it* going⟩ [Old English *hit*]

²it \'it\ *n* : the player in a game who performs the principal action of the game (as trying to catch others in a game of tag)

Ital·ian \ə-'tal-yən, i-\ *n* **1 a** : a native or inhabitant of Italy **b** : a person of Italian descent **2** : the Romance language of the Italians — **Italian** *adj*

Italian sonnet *n* : a sonnet consisting of an octave rhyming *abba abba* and a sestet rhyming in any of several patterns (as *cde cde* or *cdc dcd*)

¹ital·ic \ə-'tal-ik, i-, ī-\ *adj* **1** *cap* : of or relating to ancient Italy, its peoples, or their Indo-European languages **2** : of or relating to a type style with characters that slant upward to the right (as in *"these words are italic"*)

²italic *n* : an italic character or type

ital·i·cize \ə-'tal-ə-,sīz, i-, ī-\ *vt* **1** : to print in italics **2** : to underscore with a single line

¹itch \'ich\ *vb* **1** : to have or produce an itch **2** : to cause to itch **3** : to have a strong persistent desire ⟨*itching* to get a new car⟩ [Middle English *icchen,* from Old English *giccan*]

²itch *n* **1 a** : an uneasy irritating sensation in the skin usually held to result from mild stimulation of pain receptors **b** : a skin disorder accompanied by an itch;

esp : a contagious eruption caused by a mite **2** : a constant restless desire ⟨an *itch* to travel⟩ — **itch·i·ness** \'ich-ē-nəs\ *n* — **itchy** \-ē\ *adj*

it'd \ˌit-əd\ : it had : it would

¹-ite \ˌīt\ *n suffix* **1 a** : native : resident ⟨Brooklyn*ite*⟩ **b** : descendant ⟨Ishmael*ite*⟩ **c** : adherent : follower ⟨Jacob*ite*⟩ **2** : product ⟨metabol*ite*⟩ **3** : fossil ⟨ammon*ite*⟩ **4** : mineral ⟨hal*ite*⟩ : rock ⟨quartz*ite*⟩ **5** : segment or constituent part ⟨som*ite*⟩ [Greek *-itēs*]

²-ite *n suffix* : salt or ester of an acid with a name ending in *-ous* ⟨nitr*ite*⟩ [French, alteration of *-ate* "¹-ate"]

item \'īt-əm\ *n* **1** : a separate thing in a list, account, group, or series : ARTICLE ⟨check each *item* before you pack it⟩ **2** : a separate piece of news or information : a short news paragraph ⟨column of local *items*⟩ [Latin *item* "also", from *ita* "thus"]

item·ize \'īt-ə-ˌmīz\ *vt* : to set down in detail : LIST ⟨*itemize* expenditures⟩ — **item·iza·tion** \ˌīt-ə-mə-'zā-shən\ *n*

it·er·ate \'it-ə-ˌrāt\ *vt* : REITERATE, REPEAT [Latin *iterare*, from *iterum* "again"] — **it·er·a·tive** \'it-ə-ˌrāt-iv, -rət-\ *adj*

it·er·a·tion \ˌit-ə-'rā-shən\ *n* : REPETITION; *esp* : a computational process in which a series of operations is repeated a number of times

itin·er·ant \ī-'tin-ə-rənt, ə-'tin-\ *adj* : traveling from place to place ⟨*itinerant* preachers⟩ [Late Latin *itinerari* "to journey", from Latin *itiner-, iter* "journey", from *ire* "to go"] — **itinerant** *n* — **itin·er·ant·ly** *adv*

itin·er·ary \ī-'tin-ə-ˌrer-ē, ə-\ *n, pl* **-ar·ies** **1** : the route of a journey **2** : a travel diary **3** : a traveler's guidebook — **itinerary** *adj*

-i·tis \'īt-əs\ *n suffix, pl* **-i·tis·es** *also* **-it·i·des** \'it-ə-ˌdēz\ *or* **-i·tes** \'īt-ēz\ **1** : disease or inflammation ⟨bronch*itis*⟩ **2** : heated or excessive response to [Greek]

it'll \ˌit-l\ : it shall : it will

its \its, ˌits, əts\ *adj* : of or relating to it or itself especially as possessor, agent, or object of an action ⟨going to *its* kennel⟩ ⟨a child proud of *its* first drawings⟩ ⟨*its* final enactment into law⟩

it's \its, ˌits, əts\ : it is : it has

it·self \it-'self, ət-\ *pron* **1** : that identical one — used reflexively or for emphasis ⟨watched the cat giving *it-self* a bath⟩ ⟨the letter *itself* was missing⟩; compare IT 1 **2** : its normal, healthy, or sane condition or self

-ity \ət-ē\ *n suffix, pl* **-ities** : quality : state : degree ⟨asinin*ity*⟩ [Old French or Latin; Old French *-ité*, from Latin *-itat-, -itas*]

-ium *n suffix* **1** : chemical element ⟨europ*ium*⟩ **2** : chemical radical ⟨ammon*ium*⟩ [Latin, ending of some neuter nouns]

-ive \iv\ *adj suffix* : that performs or tends toward an (indicated) action ⟨regress*ive*⟩ [Latin *-ivus*]

I've \īv, ˌīv\ : I have

ivied \'ī-vēd\ *adj* : overgrown with ivy

ivo·ry \'īv-rē, -ə-rē\ *n, pl* **-ries** **1** : the hard creamy-white modified dentine that composes the tusks of a tusked mammal (as an elephant) **2** : a pale yellow **3** : something (as piano keys) made of ivory or of a similar substance [Old French *ivoire*, from Latin *eboreus* "of ivory", from *ebur* "ivory", from Egyptian ; *b* "elephant, ivory"]

ivory black *n* : a fine black pigment made by calcining ivory

ivory tower *n* **1** : a lack of concern with practical matters or urgent problems **2** : a secluded place for meditation : RETREAT

ivy \'ī-vē\ *n, pl* **ivies** **1** : a climbing woody vine with glossy evergreen leaves, small yellowish flowers, and black berries **2** : any of several plants resembling ivy [Old English *īfig*]

Ivy League *adj* : of, relating to, or characteristic of a group of long-established eastern United States colleges widely regarded as high in scholastic and social prestige [from the prevalence of ivy-covered buildings on the campuses of the older United States colleges]

-iza·tion \ə-'zā-shən *also especially when an unstressed syllable precedes* ī-'zā-\ *n suffix* : action, process, or result of making ⟨social*ization*⟩ ⟨union*ization*⟩ ⟨special*ization*⟩

-ize \ˌīz\ *vb suffix* **1 a** (1) : cause to be or conform to or resemble ⟨american*ize*⟩ : cause to be formed into ⟨union*ize*⟩ (2) : subject to a (specified) action ⟨satir*ize*⟩ (3) : impregnate or treat or combine with ⟨macadam*ize*⟩ **b** : treat like ⟨idol*ize*⟩ **2 a** : become : become like ⟨crystall*ize*⟩ **b** : be productive in or of ⟨hypothes*ize*⟩ : engage in a (specified) activity ⟨botan*ize*⟩ [Greek *-izein*]

ivy 1

\ə\ abut	\ng\ sing
\ər\ further	\ō\ bone
\a\ mat	\o̅\ saw
\ā\ take	\oi\ coin
\ä\ cot, cart	\th\ thin
\au̇\ out	\th\ this
\ch\ chin	\ü\ food
\e\ pet	\u̇\ foot
\ē\ easy	\y\ yet
\g\ go	\yü\ few
\i\ tip	\yu̇\ cure
\ī\ life	\zh\ vision
\j\ job	

Jj

j \'jā\ *n, pl* **j's** *or* **js** \,jāz\ *often cap* : the 10th letter of the English alphabet

jab \'jab\ *vb* **jabbed; jab·bing** : to thrust quickly or abruptly with or as if with something sharp : POKE [Middle English *jobben*] — **jab** *n*

jab·ber \'jab-ər\ *vb* **jab·bered; jab·ber·ing** \'jab-ring, -ə-ring\ : to utter or speak rapidly, indistinctly, or unintelligibly [Middle English *jaberen*] — **jabber** *n* — **jab·ber·er** \'jab-ər-ər\ *n*

jab·ber·wocky \'jab-ər-,wäk-ē\ *n* : meaningless speech or writing [*Jabberwocky*, nonsense poem by Lewis Carroll]

ja·bot \zha-'bō, 'jab-,ō\ *n* : a ruffle of cloth or lace that falls from the collar down the front of a dress or shirt [French]

jac·a·ran·da \,jak-ə-'ran-də\ *n* : a tropical American tree often grown for its showy panicles of blue flowers [Portuguese]

ja·cinth \'jās-nth, 'jas-; zhā-'sant\ *n* : HYACINTH 1 [Old French *jacinthe*, from Latin *hyacinthus*, a flowering plant]

¹jack \'jak\ *n* **1** *often cap* : SAILOR 1a **2 a** : a device for turning a spit (as in roasting meat) **b** : any of various portable mechanisms for exerting pressure or lifting a heavy body a short distance **3** : any of various animals: as **a** : a male ass **b** : JACKRABBIT **4 a** : a small target ball in lawn bowling **b** : a small national flag flown by a ship **c** (1) : a small 6-pointed metal object used in a game (2) *pl* : a game played with jacks **5** : a playing card bearing the stylized figure of a man **6** *slang* : MONEY 1 **7** : a socket in an electric circuit used with a plug to make a connection with another circuit [*Jack*, nickname for *John*]

²jack *vb* **1** : to hunt or fish for game at night with a jacklight **2** : to move or lift by or as if by a jack **3** : to raise the level or quality of ⟨*jack* up prices⟩ — **jack·er** *n*

jack·al \'jak-əl, -,ól\ *n* **1** : any of several Old World wild dogs smaller than the related wolves **2** : a person who performs routine or menial tasks for another [Turkish *çakal*, from Persian *shagāl*, from Sanskrit *śṛgāla*]

jack·a·napes \'jak-ə-,nāps\ *n* **1** : MONKEY 1, APE **2** : an impudent or conceited person [Middle English *Jack Napis*, nickname for William de la Pole, died 1450, duke of Suffolk]

jack·ass \'jak-,as\ *n* **1** : a male ass; *also* : DONKEY **2** : ASS 2

jackrabbit

jack·boot \'jak-,büt\ *n* **1** : a heavy military boot reaching above the knee and worn especially in the 17th and 18th centuries **2** : a laceless military boot reaching to the calf

jack·daw \'jak-,dó\ *n* : a common black and gray Eurasian bird smaller than the related common crow

jack·et \'jak-ət\ *n* **1** : a short coat usually having a front opening, collar, and sleeves **2** : an outer covering or casing: as **a** : a tough metal covering on a bullet or projectile **b** : a coating or covering of a nonconducting material used to prevent heat radiation **c** : a detachable outer paper wrapper on a bound book [Middle French *jaquet*, from *jaque* "short jacket", from *jaques* "peasant", from the name *Jaques* "James"] — **jack·et·ed** \-ət-əd\ *adj*

Jack Frost *n* : frost or frosty weather personified

jack·ham·mer \'jak-,ham-ər\ *n* : a pneumatic percussive tool for drilling or breaking up hard substances (as rock or pavement)

jack–in–the–box \'jak-ən-thə-,bäks\ *n, pl* **jack–in–the–box·es** *or* **jacks–in–the–box** : a small box out of which a figure (as of a clown's head) springs when the lid is raised

jack–in–the–pul·pit \,jak-ən-thə-'púl-,pit\ *n, pl* **jack–in–the–pulpits** *or* **jacks–in–the–pulpit** : an American spring-flowering woodland herb with an upright club-shaped flower cluster arched over by a green and purple spathe

¹jack·knife \'jak-,nīf\ *n* **1** : a large strong pocketknife **2** : a dive in which the diver bends from the waist and touches the ankles before straightening out

²jackknife *vi* **1** : to double up like a jackknife **2** : to turn or rise and form an angle of 90 degrees or less with each other — used especially of a pair of connected vehicles

jack·leg \'jak-,leg\ *adj* **1** : lacking skill or training : AMATEUR ⟨a *jackleg* carpenter⟩ **2** : designed as a temporary expedient : MAKESHIFT

jack·light \'jak-,līt\ *n* : a light used especially in hunting or fishing at night

jack–of–all–trades \,jak-ə-'vòl-,trādz\ *n, pl* **jacks–of–all–trades** : a person who can do a satisfactory job at varied kinds of work : a versatile person

jack–o'–lan·tern \'jak-ə-,lant-ərn\ *n* **1** : IGNIS FATUUS **2** : a lantern made of a pumpkin cut to look like a human face

jack pine *n* : a North American pine with paired twisted needles that is used for pulp and box lumber

jack·pot \'jak-,pät\ *n* **1 a** : a large pot (as in poker) formed by the accumulation of stakes from previous play **b** (1) : a combination on a slot machine that wins a top prize or all the coins in the machine (2) : the sum so won **2** : an impressive often unexpected success or reward

jack·rab·bit \-,rab-ət\ *n* : any of several large hares of western North America with long ears and long hind legs [*jack*ass + *rabbit*; from its long ears]

jack·screw \-,skrü\ *n* : a screw-operated jack for lifting or for exerting pressure

Jack·so·ni·an \jak-'sō-nē-ən\ *adj* : of, relating to, or characteristic of Andrew Jackson or his political principles or policies — **Jacksonian** *n*

jack·stone \'jak-,stōn\ *n* **1** : JACK 4c(1) **2** *pl* : JACK 4c(2)

jack·straw \-,stró\ *n* **1** : one of the pieces used in the game jackstraws **2** *pl* : a game in which a set of straws or thin strips are dropped in a heap with each player in turn trying to remove one at a time without disturbing the rest

jack–tar \-'tär\ *n, often cap* : SAILOR 1a

Jac·o·be·an \,jak-ə-'bē-ən\ *adj* : of, relating to, or characteristic of James I of England or his age [New Latin *Jacobus* "James"] — **Jacobean** *n*

Jac·o·bin \'jak-ə-bən\ *n* : a member of a radical political group advocating egalitarian democracy and engaging in terrorist activities during the French Revolution of 1789 [French, from *Jacobin* "Dominican" (from Late Latin *Jacobus* "James"; from the location of the first Dominican convent in Paris in the street of Saint James—*Rue Saint Jacques*); from the group's having been founded in a former Dominican convent] — **Jac·o·bin·ism** \-bə-,niz-əm\ *n*

Jac·o·bite \'jak-ə-,bīt\ *n* : a partisan of James II of England or of the Stuarts after the revolution of 1688 — **Jac·o·bit·i·cal** \,jak-ə-'bit-i-kəl\ *adj* — **Jac·o·bit·ism** \'jak-ə-,bīt,iz-əm\ *n*

Jacob's ladder *n* : a ship's ladder of rope or chain with wooden or iron steps [from the ladder seen in a dream by Jacob in Genesis 28:12]

jac·quard \'jak-,ärd\ *n, often cap* : a fabric of intricate variegated weave or pattern [Joseph *Jacquard*, died 1834, French inventor]

¹jade \'jād\ *n* **1** : a broken-down, vicious, or worthless horse **2** : a disreputable woman [Middle English]
□ **ORIGIN** The English word *jade* that is used for a horse or a woman is not related to the name of the green stone jade. The origin of the earlier *jade* is uncertain. It was first used in Middle English to mean "a broken-down horse". Later the word for a worthless horse was often applied to a woman (or, very rarely, to a man) considered worthless. Now a *jade* is more often a disreputable woman than a broken-down horse.
Jaded, meaning "worn out", is also derived from the equine *jade.* Originally, to *jade* a horse was to make a *jade* of it, to wear it out or break it down by overwork or abuse. It was not long before people, too, could be called *jaded.*

²jade *vb* **1 a** : to wear out by overwork or abuse **b** : to tire by tedious tasks **2** : to become weary

³jade *n* : a tough dense usually green gemstone that takes a high polish [French, from obsolete Spanish (*piedra de la*) *ijada,* literally, "loin stone"] □ **ORIGIN** Gemstones were once believed to have magical and medicinal properties. Jade was supposed to be especially effective in combating kidney disorders. The 16th century Spanish, who brought jade home with them from the New World, named the powerful green stone *piedra de la ijada,* "loin stone". Not only in Spain but throughout western Europe jade became popular both as an ornament and as a cure or preventive for internal problems. In England jade was formerly called *spleen stone,* but this term has not survived. Our modern word *jade* was borrowed from the French, who had so transformed Spanish *ijada.*

jad·ed *adj* **1** : very fatigued **2** : dulled by overindulgence — **jad·ed·ly** *adv* — **jad·ed·ness** *n*

jade green *n* : a light bluish green

jae·ger \'yā-gər\ *n* : any of several large dark-colored birds of northern seas that harass weaker birds and steal their prey [German *jäger* "hunter"]

¹jag \'jag\ *vb* **jagged** \'jagd\; **jag·ging** : to make ragged : NOTCH [Middle English *jaggen*]

²jag *n* : a sharp projecting part : BARB

³jag *n* **1** : a small load (as of hay) **2** : SPREE ⟨a crying *jag*⟩ ⟨drinking *jags*⟩ [origin unknown]

jag·ged \'jag-əd\ *adj* : sharply notched : ROUGH ⟨a *jagged* edge⟩ — **jag·ged·ly** *adv* — **jag·ged·ness** *n*

jag·uar \'jag-,wär, 'jag-yə-,wär\ *n* : a large cat of tropical America that is larger and stockier than the leopard and is brownish yellow or buff with black spots [Spanish *yaguar* and Portuguese *jaguar,* from Tupi *jaguara*]

jag·ua·run·di \,zhag-wə-'rən-dē\ *n* : a slender long-tailed short-legged grayish wildcat of Central and South America [American Spanish and Portuguese, from Tupi]

jai alai \'hı¢ovba [Spanish, from Basque, from *jai* "festival" + *alai* "merry"]

¹jail \'jāl\ *n* : PRISON; *esp* : a building for the temporary custody of prisoners [Old French *jaiole,* from Late Latin *caveola* "little cage", from Latin *cavea* "cage"]
□ **ORIGIN** *Jail* and *cage,* similar in meaning but quite different in form, are actually etymologically related. Both are descendants of Latin *cavea,* which means "cavity" or "cage". In medieval France the direct descendant of Latin *cavea* appeared in a variety of forms. Among these variants were *gave, gage, cage,* and *jaie.* It was *cage* that survived into modern French, and it was *cage* that was borrowed into English. During the Late Latin period a diminutive of Latin *cavea* was formed. This diminutive, *caveola,* developed into Old French *jaole, jaiole,* and *geole.* This Old French word is the source of our British and American English variants *gaol* and *jail.*

²jail *vt* : to confine in or as if in a jail

jail·bird \'jāl-,bərd\ *n* : a person confined in jail; *esp* : an habitual criminal

jail·break \-,brāk\ *n* : an escape from jail

jail·er *or* **jail·or** \'jā-lər\ *n* : the keeper of a jail

Jain \'jīn\ *or* **Jai·na** \'jī-nə\ *n* : an adherent of Jainism [Hindi *Jain,* from Sanskrit *jaina*]

Jain·ism \'jī-,niz-əm\ *n* : a religion of India originating in the 6th century B.C. and teaching liberation of the soul by right knowledge, right faith, and right conduct

jal·ap \'jal-əp, 'jäl-\ *n* : a purgative tuberous root obtained especially from a Mexican plant related to the morning glory; *also* : a drug prepared from this [French, from Spanish *jalapa,* from *Jalapa,* Mexico]

ja·lopy \jə-'läp-ē\ *n, pl* **-lop·ies** : a dilapidated old automobile or airplane [origin unknown]

jal·ou·sie \'jal-ə-sē\ *n* **1** : a blind with adjustable horizontal slats for admitting light and air while excluding sun and rain **2** : a window made of adjustable glass louvers that control ventilation [French, literally, "jealousy"]

¹jam \'jam\ *vb* **jammed; jam·ming** **1 a** : to press into a close or tight position ⟨*jam* a hat on⟩ **b** : to cause to be wedged so as to be unworkable ⟨*jam* the typewriter keys⟩ **c** : to block passage of : OBSTRUCT **d** : to fill full or to excess : PACK **2** : to push forcibly; *esp* : to apply the brakes suddenly with full force **3** : to squeeze or crush painfully ⟨*jammed* a finger⟩ **4** : to make unintelligible by sending out interfering signals or messages ⟨*jam* a radio program⟩ **5** : to become unworkable through the jamming of a movable part ⟨the gun *jammed*⟩ **6** : to force one's way into a restricted space [perhaps imitative] — **jam·mer** *n*

²jam *n* **1 a** : an act or instance of jamming **b** : a crowded mass that impedes or blocks ⟨a traffic *jam*⟩ **2** : a difficult state of affairs

³jam *n* : a spread made by boiling fruit and sugar to a thick consistency [probably from ¹*jam*]

jamb \'jam\ *n* : an upright piece forming the side of an opening (as of a door) [Middle French *jambe,* literally, "leg", from Late Latin *gamba*]

jam·ba·laya \,jəm-bə-'lī-ə\ *n* : rice cooked with ham, sausage, chicken, shrimp, or oysters and seasoned with herbs [Louisiana French, from Provençal *jambalaia* "stew of rice and fowl"]

jam·bo·ree \,jam-bə-'rē\ *n* **1** : a large festive gathering **2** : a national or international camping assembly of boy scouts [origin unknown]

James \'jāmz\ *n* — see BIBLE table

jam session *n* : an informal performance by jazz musicians characterized by group improvisation [²*jam*]

¹jan·gle \'jang-gəl\ *vb* **jan·gled; jan·gling** \-gə-ling, -gling\ **1** : to quarrel verbally **2** : to make or cause to make a harsh or discordant sound [Old French *jangler,* of Germanic origin] — **jan·gler** \-gə-lər, -glər\ *n*

jaguar

²**jangle** *n* **1** : noisy quarreling **2** : discordant sound

jan·is·sary *or* **jan·i·zary** \'jan-ə-ˌser-ē, -ˌzer-\ *n*, *pl* **-sar·ies** *or* **-zar·ies** *often cap* : a soldier of a select corps of Turkish troops organized in the 14th century and abolished in 1826 [Italian *gianizzero,* from Turkish *yeni̇çeri̇*]

jan·i·tor \'jan-ət-ər\ *n* **1** : DOORKEEPER **2** : a person who has the care of a building [Latin, from *janua* "door", from *janus* "arch, gate"] — **jan·i·to·ri·al** \ˌjan-ə-'tōr-ē-əl, -'tȯr-\ *adj*

Jan·u·ary \'jan-yə-ˌwer-ē\ *n* : the 1st month of the year [Latin *Januarius,* from *Janus,* a Roman god]

¹**ja·pan** \jə-'pan\ *n* **1** : a varnish giving a hard brilliant surface coating **2** : work varnished and figured in the Japanese manner [*Japan,* country of Asia]

²**japan** *vt* **ja·panned; ja·pan·ning** : to cover with or as if with a coat of japan

Jap·a·nese \ˌjap-ə-'nēz, -'nēs\ *n*, *pl* **Japanese 1 a** : a native or inhabitant of Japan **b** : a person of Japanese descent **2** : the language of the Japanese — **Japanese** *adj*

Japanese beetle *n* : a small metallic green and brown scarab beetle introduced into America from Japan that as a grub feeds on roots and decaying vegetation and as an adult consumes foliage and fruits

Japanese beetle

Japanese iris *n* : any of various beardless garden irises with very large showy flowers

Japanese persimmon *n* : an Asian persimmon widely grown for its large edible fruits

Japanese quince *n* : a hardy Chinese ornamental shrub of the rose family with scarlet flowers

¹**jape** \'jāp\ *vt* : to make mocking fun of [Middle English *japen*] — **jap·er** \'jā-pər\ *n* — **jap·ery** \'jā-pə-rē, -prē\ *n*

²**jape** *n* : JEST 2, GIBE

ja·pon·i·ca \jə-'pän-i-kə\ *n* : JAPANESE QUINCE [New Latin, from *Japonicus* "Japanese", from *Japonia* "Japan"]

¹**jar** \'jär\ *vb* **jarred; jar·ring 1 a** : to make a harsh or discordant sound **b** : to affect disagreeably **c** : to be out of harmony; *esp* : BICKER **d** : to have a harsh or disagreeable effect **2** : to undergo severe vibration **3** : to make unstable : SHAKE [probably imitative]

²**jar** *n* **1** : a harsh grating sound **2** : CONFLICT 2, DISCORD **3** : JOLT 1 **4** : an unsettling shock

³**jar** *n* **1** : a widemouthed container usually of earthenware or glass **2** : the quantity that a jar will hold [Middle French *jarre,* from Provençal *jarra,* from Arabic *jarrah* "earthen water vessel"] — **jar·ful** \-ˌfu̇l\ *n*

jar·di·niere \ˌjärd-n-'iər\ *n* : an ornamental stand or receptacle for potted plants or flowers [French *jardinière,* literally, "female gardener"]

jar·gon \'jär-gən, -ˌgän\ *n* **1 a** : confused unintelligible language : GIBBERISH **b** : a hybrid language or dialect used for communication between peoples of different speech **2** : the technical or specialized vocabulary of a particular profession or group **3** : obscure and often pretentiously wordy language [Middle French] SYN see DIALECT

jas·mine \'jaz-mən\ *or* **jes·sa·mine** \'jes-mən, -ə-mən\ *n* : any of numerous often climbing shrubs of the olive family with extremely fragrant flowers; *also* : any of various plants noted for sweet-scented flowers — compare YELLOW JESSAMINE [French *jasmin,* from Arabic *yāsamīn,* from Persian]

jas·per \'jas-pər\ *n* : an opaque fine-grained usually red, yellow, or brown quartz; *esp* : green chalcedony [Middle French *jaspre,* from Latin *jaspis,* from Greek *iaspis,* of Semitic origin] — **jas·pery** \-pə-rē\ *adj*

jaun·dice \'jȯn-dəs, 'jän-\ *n* **1** : yellowish discoloration of the skin, tissues, and body fluids caused by the deposition of bile pigments; *also* : a disease or abnormal condition marked by jaundice **2** : a state or attitude marked by satiety, distaste, or hostility [Middle French *jaunisse,* from *jaune* "yellow", derived from Latin *galbus*]

jaun·diced \-dəst\ *adj* **1** : affected with or as if with jaundice **2** : showing or influenced by envy, distaste, or hostility

jaunt \'jȯnt, 'jänt\ *n* : a short trip taken for pleasure [origin unknown] — **jaunt** *vi*

jaun·ty \'jȯnt-ē, 'jänt-\ *adj* **jaun·ti·er; -est** : sprightly in manner or appearance : LIVELY [French *gentil* "genteel"] — **jaun·ti·ly** \'jȯnt-l-ē, 'jänt-\ *adv* — **jaun·ti·ness** \'jȯnt-ē-nəs, 'jänt-\ *n*

Ja·va man \ˌjäv-ə-, ˌjav-\ *n* : an extinct human being of the Pleistocene that is known from fragments of skeletons found in Java and is classified with the pithecanthropines

Ja·va·nese \ˌjav-ə-'nēz, ˌjäv-, -'nēs\ *n* **1** : a member of an Indonesian people inhabiting the island of Java **2** : an Austronesian language of the Javanese people — **Javanese** *adj*

jav·e·lin \'jav-lən, -ə-lən\ *n* **1** : a light spear **2** : a slender usually metal shaft thrown for distance in an athletic field event [Middle French *javeline,* of Celtic origin]

¹**jaw** \'jȯ\ *n* **1 a** : either of two cartilaginous or bony structures that support the soft parts enclosing the mouth and usually bear teeth on their oral margin — compare MANDIBLE 1a, MAXILLA 1 **b** : the structures including the jaws and soft parts that make up the walls of the mouth and that serve to open and close it — usually used in pl. **c** : any of various organs of invertebrates that perform the function of the vertebrate jaws **2** : something resembling the jaw of an animal in form or action ⟨the *jaws* of a mountain pass⟩; *esp* : one of a set of opposing parts that open and close for holding or crushing something between them ⟨the *jaws* of a vise⟩ [Middle English] — **jawed** \'jȯd\ *adj*

²**jaw** *vi* : to talk in a scolding or boring way

jaw·bone \'jȯ-ˌbōn, -ˌbȯn\ *n* : one of the bones of an animal's jaw; *esp* : MANDIBLE 1a

jaw·break·er \-ˌbrā-kər\ *n* **1** : a word difficult to pronounce **2** : a round hard candy

jaw·less fish \ˌjȯ-ləs-\ *n* : CYCLOSTOME

jaw·line \'jȯ-ˌlīn\ *n* : the outline of the lower jaw

jay \'jā\ *n* : any of several noisy birds of the crow family that are smaller and usually more brightly colored than a crow [Middle French *jai,* from Latin *gaius*]

jay·cee \'jā-'sē\ *n* : a member of a major national and international civic organization [from the initials of *J*unior *C*itizens, former name of the organization]

jay·vee \'jā-'vē\ *n* **1** : JUNIOR VARSITY **2** : a member of a junior varsity team [*j*unior *v*arsity]

jay·walk \'jā-ˌwȯk\ *vi* : to cross a street carelessly without heeding traffic regulations and signals — **jay·walk·er** *n*

¹**jazz** \'jaz\ *vt* **1** : ENLIVEN — usually used with *up* **2** : to play in the manner of jazz [origin unknown]

²**jazz** *n* **1** : music of American origin developed mainly from blues and ragtime and marked especially by solo instrumental improvisation **2** : empty talk : HUMBUG **3** : STUFF 3b

jazzy \'jaz-ē\ *adj* **jazz·i·er; -est 1** : having the characteristics of jazz **2** : marked by unrestraint, animation, or flashiness — **jazz·i·ly** \'jaz-ə-lē\ *adv* — **jazz·i·ness** \'jaz-ē-nəs\ *n*

jeal·ous \'jel-əs\ *adj* **1 a** : intolerant of rivalry or unfaithfulness **b** : suspicious that a person one loves is not faithful **2** : hostile toward a rival or one believed to enjoy an advantage : ENVIOUS **3** : careful in guarding a right or possession ⟨their *jealous* love of freedom⟩ [Old French *jelous,* from Late Latin *zelus* "zeal"] SYN see ENVIOUS — **jeal·ous·ly** *adv*

jeal·ou·sy \'jel-ə-sē\ *n*, *pl* **-sies 1** : a jealous disposition, attitude, or feeling **2** : zealous vigilance

jean \'jēn\ *n* **1** : a durable twilled cotton cloth used especially for sportswear and work clothes **2** *pl* : close-fitting pants made of jean, denim, or corduroy

[short for *jean fustian,* from Middle English *Gene, Jene* "Genoa, Italy" + *fustian*]

jeep \\'jēp\\ *n* : a small general-purpose motor vehicle with ¼-ton capacity and four-wheel drive used by the United States Army in World War II [alteration of *gee pee,* from *g*eneral-*p*urpose] □ ORIGIN In 1937 work was begun by several American manufacturers to develop an all-purpose vehicle for military use. When the vehicle was ready, it was apparently designated *g.p.* for *general purpose.* The pronunciation of the letters *g.p.* became shortened to one syllable and the spelling *jeep* was adopted. For a similar alteration, compare the spelling and pronunciation of *veep,* from *v.p.,* an abbreviation of *vice-president.*

jeep *trademark* — used for a civilian automotive vehicle

jee·pers \\'jē-pərz\\ *interj* — used as a mild oath or to express surprise [euphemism for *Jesus*]

¹**jeer** \\'jiər\\ *vb* I : to speak or cry out in derision or mockery 2 : DERIDE, MOCK [origin unknown] SYN see SCOFF — **jeer·er** \\'jir-ər\\ *n* — **jeer·ing·ly** \\-ing-lē\\ *adv*

²**jeer** *n* : a jeering remark or sound : TAUNT

jef·fer·so·ni·an \\,jef-ər-'sō-nē-ən\\ *adj* : of, relating to, or characteristic of Thomas Jefferson or his political principles — **Jeffersonian** *n*

je·had *variant of* JIHAD

je·ho·vah \\ji-'hō-və\\ *n* : GOD 1 [New Latin, from Hebrew *Yahweh*]

Jehovah's Witness *n* : a member of a group that by distributing literature and by personal evangelism witness to beliefs in the theocratic rule of God, the sinfulness of organized religions and governments, and an approaching millennium

je·june \\ji-'jün\\ *adj* I : lacking nutritive value ⟨*jejune* diets⟩ 2 : lacking interest or significance : DULL 3 : lacking maturity : CHILDISH ⟨*jejune* remarks⟩ [Latin *jejunus*] — **je·june·ly** *adv* — **je·june·ness** \\-'jün-nəs\\ *n*

je·ju·num \\ji-'jü-nəm\\ *n* : the section of the small intestine between the duodenum and the ileum [Latin, from *jejunus* "jejune"] — **je·ju·nal** \\-'jün-l\\ *adj*

jell \\'jel\\ *vb* I : to make or become jelly 2 : to take shape ⟨an idea began to *jell* in my mind⟩ [back-formation from *jelly*]

Jell-O \\'jel-ō\\ *trademark* — used for a fruit-flavored gelatin dessert

¹**jel·ly** \\'jel-ē\\ *n, pl* **jellies** I : a food with a soft elastic consistency due usually to gelatin or pectin; *esp* : a fruit product made by boiling sugar and the juice of fruit 2 : a substance resembling jelly in consistency [Middle French *gelee,* from *geler* "to freeze, congeal" from Latin *gelare*] — **jel·ly·like** \\-ē-,līk\\ *adj*

²**jelly** *vb* **jel·lied; jel·ly·ing** I : JELL 1 2 : to set in jelly ⟨*jellied* salmon⟩

jelly bean *n* : a sugar-glazed bean-shaped candy

jel·ly·fish \\'jel-ē-,fish\\ *n* I : a free-swimming sexually-reproducing coelenterate animal with a gelatinous, disk-shaped, and usually nearly transparent body; *also* : any of various somewhat similar sea animals (as a ctenophore) 2 : a weak spineless person

jelly roll *n* : a thin sheet of sponge cake spread with jelly and rolled up

jen·net \\'jen-ət\\ *n* I : a small Spanish horse 2 : a female donkey [Middle French *genet,* from Catalan]

jen·ny \\'jen-ē\\ *n, pl* **jennies** I a : a female bird ⟨*jenny* wren⟩ b : a female donkey 2 : SPINNING JENNY [from the name *Jenny*]

jeop·ar·dize \\'jep-ər-,dīz\\ *vt* : to expose to danger : IMPERIL

jeop·ar·dy \\'jep-ərd-ē\\ *n* I : exposure to death, loss, or injury : DANGER 2 : the danger of conviction and punishment that an accused person is subjected to when on trial for a criminal offense [Old French *jeu parti* "alternative", literally, "divided game"] □ ORIGIN In French *jeu parti* means literally "divided game". In Old French, the major criterion for a *jeu parti* was the involvement of alternative possibilities or opposed viewpoints. A *jeu parti* could be a poem in dialogue form representing the discussion of problems. Or it could be a situation in a game like chess in which the relative worth of alternative plays is uncertain. The word was borrowed into English in this sense. Any position that provides equal chances of success and of failure can be described in terms of a similar position in chess and called a *jeopardy.* But the word was early used in its present extended sense, "risk or danger, with a greater probability of losing than of winning"

jer·boa \\jər-'bō-ə\\ *n* : any of several social nocturnal Old World jumping rodents with long hind legs and long tail [Arabic *yarbū*ʿ]

jer·e·mi·ah \\,jer-ə-'mī-ə\\ *n* — see BIBLE table

¹**jerk** \\'jərk\\ *vb* I : to give a sharp quick push, pull, or twist to 2 a : to make or move in jerks : move with a jerk 3 : to mix and dispense (as sodas) [probably from Middle English *yerken* "to bind tightly"] — **jerk·er** *n*

²**jerk** *n* I a : a single quick motion b : a jolting, bouncing, or thrusting motion 2 a : an involuntary muscular movement or spasm due to reflex action b *pl* : involuntary twitchings due to nervous excitement 3 : an annoyingly stupid or foolish person

³**jerk** *vt* : to cut (meat) into long strips and dry in the sun [back-formation from ²*jerky*]

jer·kin \\'jər-kən\\ *n* : a close-fitting hip-length sleeveless jacket [origin unknown]

jerk·wa·ter \\'jər-,kwót-ər, -,kwät-\\ *adj* : being small and remote ⟨*jerkwater* towns⟩ [earlier *jerkwater* "rural train"] □ ORIGIN In the early days of the steam locomotive many rural railroad lines were not so well-provided with water tanks as were the main lines. It was sometimes necessary for trains on the rural lines to stop at streams while the crew went to fetch (or *jerk*) water in buckets. For this reason rural trains were given the name *jerkwater.* Eventually the term came to be applied to anything small or insignificant.

¹**jerky** \\'jər-kē\\ *adj* **jerk·i·er; -est** I : moving by sudden starts and stops 2 : FOOLISH ⟨a *jerky* idea⟩ — **jerk·i·ly** \\-kə-lē\\ *adv* — **jerk·i·ness** \\-kē-nəs\\ *n*

²**jerky** *n* : jerked meat [Spanish *charqui*]

jer·ry–build \\'jer-ē-,bild\\ *vt* **–built** \\-,bilt\\; **–build·ing** : to build cheaply and flimsily [back-formation from *jerry-built* "flimsily built", of unknown origin] — **jer·ry–build·er** *n*

jer·sey \\'jər-zē\\ *n, pl* **jerseys** I : a plain knitted fabric of wool, cotton, nylon, rayon, or silk 2 : any of various close-fitting knitted garments for the upper body 3 : any of a breed of small usually fawn-colored dairy cattle noted for their rich milk [*Jersey,* one of the Channel islands]

Je·ru·sa·lem artichoke \\jə-,rü-sə-ləm-, -sləm-; -,rüz-ləm-, -ə-ləm-\\ *n* : a perennial American sunflower grown for its tubers that are eaten as a vegetable [*Jerusalem* by folk etymology from Italian *girasole*]

Jerusalem cherry *n* : a plant of the potato family grown as a houseplant for its showy orange or red berries [*Jerusalem,* Israel]

jess \\'jes\\ *n* : a strap placed on a leg of a falcon or hawk for attachment of a leash [Middle French *gies,* derived from *jeter* "to throw"]

jessamine *variant of* JASMINE

¹**jest** \\'jest\\ *n* I a : an act intended to cause laughter : PRANK b : a comic incident 2 : a witty remark 3 a : a frivolous mood or manner (spoken in *jest*) b : a state of gaiety and merriment 4 : ³BUTT 2, LAUGHINGSTOCK [Old French *geste* "exploit, tale", from Latin *gesta* "exploits", from *gerere* "to carry, perform"] □ SYN JEST, JOKE, QUIP, WISECRACK mean something said for the purpose of evoking laughter. JEST applies to an utterance not seriously intended whether sarcastic, ironic, witty, or merely playful; JOKE may apply to an act as well as an utterance and suggests no intent to hurt feelings; QUIP suggests a quick, light, neatly phrased

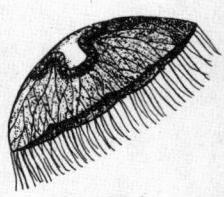

jellyfish I

jeroba

\\ə\\ abut	\\ng\\ sing
\\ər\\ further	\\ō\\ bone
\\a\\ mat	\\ȯ\\ saw
\\ā\\ take	\\ȯi\\ coin
\\ä\\ cot, cart	\\th\\ thin
\\aů\\ out	\\th\\ this
\\ch\\ chin	\\ü\\ food
\\e\\ pet	\\ů\\ foot
\\ē\\ easy	\\y\\ yet
\\g\\ go	\\yü\\ few
\\i\\ tip	\\yů\\ cure
\\ī\\ life	\\zh\\ vision
\\j\\ job	

remark; **WISECRACK** stresses cleverness of phrasing and may suggest unfeeling flippancy.

²**jest** *vi* **1** : to utter taunts : **GIBE 2** : to speak or act without seriousness **3** : **JOKE** 1

jest·er \'jes-tər\ *n* **1** : **FOOL** 2a ⟨court *jester*⟩ **2** : one given to jests

Je·su·it \'jezh-wət, -ə-wət, 'jez-\ *n* : a member of the Roman Catholic Society of Jesus founded by Saint Ignatius of Loyola in 1534 and devoted to missionary and educational work — **je·su·it·ic** \,jezh-ə-'wit-ik, ,jez-\ *adj, often cap* — **je·su·it·i·cal·ly** \-i-kə-lē, -klē\ *adv, often cap*

Je·sus \'jē-zəs, -zəz\ *n* : the founder of the Christian religion — called also *Jesus Christ* [Late Latin, from Greek *Iēsous*, from Hebrew *Yēshūa'*]

¹**jet** \'jet\ *n* **1** : a dense velvet-black coal that takes a good polish and is often used for jewelry **2** : an intense black [Middle French *jaiet*, from Latin *gagates*, from Greek *gagatēs*, from *Gagas*, town and river in Asia Minor]

²**jet** *vb* **jet·ted**; **jet·ting** : to spout or emit in a stream : **SPURT** [Middle French *jeter*, literally, "to throw", from Latin *jactare*, from *jactus*, past participle of *jacere* "to throw"]

³**jet** *n* **1 a** : a forceful rush of liquid, gas, or vapor through a narrow opening or a nozzle **b** : a nozzle for a jet of fluid (as gas or water) **2 a** : **JET ENGINE b** : **JET AIRPLANE**

⁴**jet** *vi* **jet·ted**; **jet·ting** : to travel by jet airplane

jet airplane *n* : an airplane powered by one or more jet engines — called also *jet plane*

jet engine *n* : an airplane engine that uses atmospheric oxygen to burn fuel and produces a rearward discharge of heated air and exhaust gases

jet–pro·pelled \,jet-prə-'peld\ *adj* **1** : propelled by a jet engine **2** : suggestive of the speed and force of a jet airplane

jet propulsion *n* : propulsion of a body in a forward direction as a result of the rearward discharge of a jet of fluid; *esp* : propulsion of an airplane by jet engines

jet·sam \'jet-səm\ *n* : goods thrown overboard to lighten a ship in distress [alteration of *jettison*]

jet set *n* : an international social group of wealthy people who frequent fashionable resorts — **jet–set·ter** \'jet-,set-ər\ *n*

jet stream *n* : a long narrow meandering current of high-speed winds blowing from a generally westerly direction several miles above the earth's surface

¹**jet·ti·son** \'jet-ə-sən\ *n* : a voluntary sacrifice of cargo to lighten a ship's load in time of distress [Old French *getaison* "act of throwing", from Latin *jactatio*, from *jactare* "to throw"]

²**jettison** *vt* **1 a** : to throw (goods) overboard to lighten a ship in distress **b** : to drop from an airplane or spacecraft in flight **2** : to cast away or aside : **DISCARD** — **jet·ti·son·able** \-sə-nə-bəl\ *adj*

jet·ty \'jet-ē\ *n, pl* **jetties 1** : a pier built out into the water to influence the current or to protect a harbor **2** : a landing wharf [Middle French *jetee*, from *jeter* "to throw"]

Jew \'jü\ *n* **1 a** : a member of the tribe of Judah **b** : **ISRAELITE 2** : a member of a nation existing in Palestine from the 6th century B.C. to the 1st century A.D. **3 a** : a person of Jewish descent **b** : one whose religion is Judaism [Old French *gyu*, from Latin *Judaeus*, from Greek *Ioudaios*, from Hebrew *Yĕhūdī*, from *Yĕhūdāh*, "Judah, Jewish kingdom"]

¹**jew·el** \'jü-əl\ *n* **1** : an ornament of precious metal set with stones or finished with enamel and worn as an accessory of dress **2** : one that is highly esteemed **3** : a precious stone : **GEM 4** : a bearing for a pivot in a watch made of a crystal, precious stone, or glass [Old French *juel*, from *jeu* "game, play", from Latin *jocus* "joke, game"]

²**jewel** *vt* **-eled** *or* **-elled**; **-el·ing** *or* **-el·ling** : to adorn or equip with jewels

jew·el·er *or* **jew·el·ler** \'jü-ə-lər\ *n* : a maker or repairer of or dealer in jewelry

jew·el·ry \'jü-əl-rē\ *n* : **JEWELS**; *esp* : objects of precious metal set with gems and worn for personal adornment

jew·el·weed \'jü-əl-,wēd\ *n* : **IMPATIENS**

jew·fish \'jü-,fish\ *n* : any of various large groupers that are usually dusky green or blackish, thickheaded, and rough-scaled

jew·ish \'jü-ish\ *adj* : of, relating to, or characteristic of the Jews — **jew·ish·ly** *adv* — **jew·ish·ness** *n*

Jewish calendar *n* : a calendar in use among Jewish peoples that is reckoned from the year 3761 B.C. and dates in its present form from about A.D. 360

jew·ry \'jùr-ē, 'jü-rē\ *n* **1** *pl* **jewries** : a community of Jews **2** : the Jewish people

Jew's harp *or* **Jews' harp** \'jüz-,härp\ *n* : a small lyre-shaped instrument that when placed between the teeth gives tones from a metal tongue struck by the finger

¹**jib** \'jib\ *n* : a triangular sail set on a stay forward of the mast or foremast [origin unknown]

²**jib** *vb* **jibbed**; **jib·bing 1** : to shift or swing from one side of a ship to the other **2** : to cause (a sail) to jib

³**jib** *n* **1** : the projecting arm of a crane **2** : a derrick boom [probably from *gibbet*]

jib·boom \'jib-'büm, -'üm\ *n* : a spar that serves as an extension of the bowsprit

¹**jibe** *or* **gybe** \'jīb\ *vb* **1** : to shift suddenly from one side to the other **2** : to change the course of a ship when sailing with the wind aft so that the sail jibes **3** : to cause (a sail) to jibe [perhaps from Dutch *gijben*]

²**jibe** *variant of* **GIBE**

³**jibe** *vi* : to be in accord : **AGREE** [origin unknown]

jif·fy \'jif-ē\ *n* : **MOMENT** 1, **INSTANT** ⟨in a *jiffy*⟩ [origin unknown]

¹**jig** \'jig\ *n* **1** : a lively springy dance in triple rhythm **2** : **TRICK**, **GAMBIT** ⟨the *jig* is up⟩ **3 a** : any of several fishing lures that are jerked up and down and drawn through the water **b** : a device used to maintain mechanically the correct position of a piece of work and a tool or of parts of work during assembly [probably from Middle French *giguer* "to dance", from *gigue* "fiddle", of Germanic origin]

²**jig** *vb* **jigged**; **jig·ging 1** : to dance a jig **2** : to jerk up and down or to and fro **3** : to fish or catch with a jig **4** : to machine by means of a jig-controlled tool operation

¹**jig·ger** \'jig-ər\ *n* **1** : one that jigs or operates a jig **2** : **JIG** 3a **3** : the mast nearest the stern of a 4-masted ship **4 a** : a mechanical device; *esp* : one operating with a jerky reciprocating motion **b** : **CONTRIVANCE** 2, **GADGET 5** : a measure used in mixing drinks that usually holds 1½ ounces (about 44 milliliters)

²**jigger** *n* : **CHIGGER** [of African origin]

jig·gle \'jig-əl\ *vb* **jig·gled**; **jig·gling** \'jig-ling, -ə-ling\ : to move or cause to move with quick little jerks [derived from ²*jig*] — **jiggle** *n*

jig·saw \'jig-,sȯ\ *n* **1** : a machine saw with a narrow blade that moves up and down for cutting curved and irregular lines or openwork patterns **2** : **SCROLL SAW**

jigsaw puzzle *n* : a puzzle consisting of small irregular pieces fitted together to form a picture

ji·had \ji-'häd, -'had\ *n* **1** : a holy war waged on behalf of Islam as a religious duty **2** : a crusade for a principle or belief [Arabic *jihād*]

¹**jilt** \'jilt\ *n* : a person who jilts a lover [from earlier *jillet* "flirtatious girl", from the name *Jill*]

²**jilt** *vt* : to drop (one's lover) capriciously or unfeelingly

jim crow \'jim-'krō\ *n, often cap J & C* : ethnic discrimination especially against blacks by legal enforcement or traditional sanctions [from *Jim Crow*, stereotype

jet engine: *1* air intake, 2 compressor, 3 fuel injection, 4 drive shaft, 5 turbine, 6 exhaust

Negro in a 19th century song-and-dance act] — **jim-crow·ism** \-,iz-əm\ *n, often cap J & C*

jim–dan·dy \'jim-'dan-dē\ *n* : something excellent of its kind

¹jim·my \'jim-ē\ *n, pl* **jimmies** : a short crowbar [from *Jimmy*, nickname for *James*]

²jimmy *vt* **jim·mied; jim·my·ing** : to force open with or as if with a jimmy ⟨*jimmy* a window⟩

jim·son·weed \'jim-sən-,wēd, 'jimp-\ *n, often cap* : a poisonous coarse annual weed of the potato family with rank-smelling foliage and large white or violet trumpet-shaped flowers [alteration of *Jamestown weed,* from *Jamestown,* Virginia]

¹jin·gle \'jing-gəl\ *vb* **jin·gled; jin·gling** \-gə-ling, -gling\ **1** : to make or cause to make a light clinking sound **2** : to rhyme or sound in a catchy repetitious manner [Middle English *ginglen*] — **jin·gler** \-gə-lər, -glər\ *n*

²jingle *n* **1** : a light clinking sound **2 a** : a catchy repetition of sounds in a poem **b** : a short verse or song with such repetition — **jin·gly** \-gə-lē, -glē\ *adj*

¹jin·go \'jing-gō\ *interj* — used as a mild oath usually in the phrase *by jingo* [probably euphemism for *Jesus*]

²jingo *n, pl* **jingoes** : one characterized by jingoism [from the fact that the phrase *by jingo* appeared in the refrain of a chauvinistic song] — **jin·go·ish** \-ish\ *adj*

jin·go·ism \'jing-gō-,iz-əm\ *n* : extreme chauvinism or nationalism marked especially by a belligerent foreign policy — **jin·go·ist** \-əst\ *n* — **jin·go·is·tic** \,jing-gō-'is-tik\ *adj* — **jin·go·is·ti·cal·ly** \-'is-ti-kə-lē, -klē\ *adv*

jin·ni \jə-'nē, 'jin-ē\ *or* **jinn** \'jin\ *n, pl* **jinn** *or* **jinns** : one of a class of spirits held by the Muslims to inhabit the earth, to assume various forms, and to exercise supernatural power [Arabic *jinnīy* "demon"]

jin·rik·i·sha \jin-'rik-,shó\ *n* : **RICKSHA** [Japanese, from *jin* "man" + *-riki* "strength" + *sha* "vehicle"]

¹jinx \'jings, 'jingks\ *n* **1** : one that brings bad luck **2** : the state or spell of bad luck brought on by a jinx [probably from *jynx,* a kind of woodpecker; from the use of woodpeckers in witchcraft]

²jinx *vt* : to bring bad luck to

jit·ney \'jit-nē\ *n, pl* **jitneys** **1** *slang* : **NICKEL** 2a **2** : **BUS** 1a; *esp* : a small bus that carries passengers over a regular route according to a flexible schedule [origin unknown; sense 2 from the original 5-cent fare]

jit·ter·bug \'jit-ər-,bəg\ *n* **1** : a dance in which couples swing, balance, and twirl in standardized patterns often with vigorous acrobatics **2** : one who dances the jitterbug [from earlier *jitter* "to be nervous", of unknown origin] — **jitterbug** *vi*

jit·ters \'jit-ərz\ *n pl* : extreme nervousness — **jit·tery** \-ə-rē\ *adj*

jiujitsu *or* **jiujutsu** *variant of* **JUJITSU**

¹jive \'jīv\ *n* **1** : swing music or dancing performed to it **2 a** : glib, deceptive, or silly talk **b** : the jargon of hipsters **c** : a special jargon of difficult or slang terms [origin unknown]

²jive *vb* **1** : **KID** 1 **2** : to dance to or play jive

¹job \'jäb\ *n* **1 a** : a piece of work; *esp* : one undertaken at a stated rate **b** : something produced by or as if by work **2 a** : something done for private advantage **b** : a criminal act; *esp* : **ROBBERY** **3 a** : **TASK, DUTY** ⟨your *job* is to mow the lawn⟩ **b** : a position at which one regularly works for pay ⟨lost their *jobs*⟩ [perhaps from obsolete *job* "lump"] **SYN** see **TASK** — **job·less** \-ləs\ *adj* — **job·less·ness** *n*

²job *vb* **jobbed; job·bing** **1** : to do occasional pieces of work for hire **2** : to hire or let by the job

Job \'jōb\ *n* — see **BIBLE** table

job action *n* : a temporary action (as a slowdown) by workers as a protest and means of enforcing demands

job·ber \'jäb-ər\ *n* **1** : one that buys goods and sells them to other dealers (as retailers) : **MIDDLEMAN** **2** : one that works by the job

job·hold·er \'jäb-,hōl-dər\ *n* : one having a regular job

job lot *n* **1** : a miscellaneous collection of goods for sale as a lot usually to a retailer **2** : a miscellaneous and often inferior collection or group

Job's tears \'jōbz-\ *n* : an Asian grass with large hard pearly white seeds often used as beads

¹jock \'jäk\ *n* **1** : **JOCKEY** 1 **2** : **DISC JOCKEY**

²jock *n* **1** : **ATHLETIC SUPPORTER** **2** : **ATHLETE** [short for earlier *jockstrap*]

¹jock·ey \'jäk-ē\ *n, pl* **jockeys** **1** : one who rides a horse especially as a professional in a race **2** : **OPERATOR** 1a [*Jockey,* Scottish nickname for *John*]

²jockey *vb* **jock·eyed; jock·ey·ing** **1** : to ride (a horse) as a jockey **2** : to move or maneuver skillfully ⟨*jockey* a truck into a lot⟩ ⟨*jockey* for power⟩ **3** : **FINESSE** 2a, **OUTWIT**

jo·cose \jō-'kōs\ *adj* **1** : given to joking : **MERRY** **2** : characterized by joking : **HUMOROUS** [Latin *jocosus,* from *jocus* "joke, sport"] — **jo·cose·ly** *adv* — **jo·cose·ness** *n*

joc·u·lar \'jäk-yə-lər\ *adj* **1** : **JOCOSE** 1 **2** : said or done in jest [Latin *jocularis,* from *joculus* "little jest", from *jocus* "joke"] — **joc·u·lar·i·ty** \,jäk-yə-'lar-ət-ē\ *n* — **joc·u·lar·ly** *adv*

joc·und \'jäk-ənd *also* 'jōk-ənd\ *adj* : **GAY** 1, **MERRY** [Late Latin *jocundus* "pleasant, agreeable", from Latin *jucundus,* from *juvare* "to help"] — **joc·und·ly** *adv*

jodh·pur \'jäd-pər\ *n* **1** *pl* : riding breeches cut full through the hips and close-fitting from knee to ankle **2** : an ankle-high boot fastened with a strap that is buckled at the side [*Jodhpur,* India]

Jo·el \'jō-əl\ *n* — see **BIBLE** table

¹jog \'jäg\ *vb* **jogged; jog·ging** **1** : to give a slight shake or push to : **NUDGE** **2** : **STIR** 5 ⟨*jog* one's memory⟩ **3** : to move up and down or about with a short heavy motion **4 a** : to go or cause to go at a jog **b** : to run at a slow pace especially for exercise **c** : to go at a slow or monotonous pace : **TRUDGE** [probably from Middle English *shoggen*] — **jog·ger** *n*

²jog *n* **1** : a slight shake : **PUSH** **2 a** : a jogging movement, pace, or trip **b** : a horse's slow gait with marked beats

³jog *n* **1** : a projecting or retreating part (as of a line or surface) **2** : a brief abrupt change in direction [probably alteration of *²jag*]

¹jog·gle \'jäg-əl\ *vb* **jog·gled; jog·gling** \'jäg-ling, -ə-ling\ **1** : to shake slightly **2** : to move shakily or jerkily [derived from *¹jog*] — **jog·gler** \'jäg-lər, -ə-lər\ *n*

²joggle *n* : **²JOG** 2a

John \'jän\ *n* — see **BIBLE** table

john·boat \'jän-,bōt\ *n* : a narrow flat-bottomed square-ended boat propelled by a pole or paddle and used on inland waterways [from the name *John*]

John Bull \'jän-'bül\ *n* **1** : the English nation personified : the English people **2** : a typical Englishman [*John Bull,* character typifying the English nation in *The History of John Bull* (1712) by John Arbuthnot, died 1735, Scottish physician and writer]

John Doe \-'dō\ *n* **1** : a party to legal proceedings whose true name is unknown **2** : **MAN IN THE STREET**

John Do·ry \-'dōr-ē, -'dór-\ *n, pl* **John Dories** : a yellow to olive marine food fish with a dark spot on each side [earlier *dory,* from Middle French *doree,* literally, "gilded one"]

John Han·cock \-'han-,käk\ *n* : an autograph signature [from the prominence of John Hancock's signature on the Declaration of Independence]

john·ny \'jän-ē\ *n, pl* **johnnies** : a short gown opening in the back that is used by hospital bed patients [from *Johnny,* nickname for *John*]

john·ny·cake \'jän-ē-,kāk\ *n* : a bread made with cornmeal

john·ny–come–late·ly \,jän-ē-kəm-'lāt-lē\ *n, pl* **Johnny-come-latelies** *or* **Johnnies-come-lately** **1** : a late or recent arrival **2** : **UPSTART**

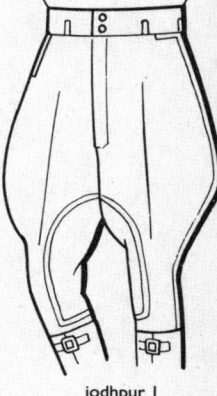

jodhpur 1

\ə\ abut	\ng\ sing
\ər\ further	\ō\ bone
\a\ mat	\ó\ saw
\ā\ take	\ói\ coin
\ä\ cot, cart	\th\ thin
\aù\ out	\th\ this
\ch\ chin	\ü\ food
\e\ pet	\ú\ foot
\ē\ easy	\y\ yet
\g\ go	\yü\ few
\i\ tip	\yú\ cure
\ī\ life	\zh\ vision
\j\ job	

john·ny–jump–up \ˌjän-ē-ˈjəm-ˌpəp\ *n* : **WILD PANSY**; *also* : any of various other small-flowered pansies or violets

john·ny–on–the–spot \ˌjän-ē-ˌȯn-<u>th</u>ə-ˈspät, -ē-ˌän-\ *n* : one that is on hand and ready to act whenever needed

Johnny Reb \-ˈreb\ *n* : a Confederate soldier [*reb*, short for *rebel*]

John·so·ni·an \jän-ˈsō-nē-ən\ *adj* : of, relating to, or characteristic of Samuel Johnson or his writings

joie de vi·vre \ˌzhwäd-ə-ˈvēvr̩\ *n* : keen enjoyment of life [French, literally, "joy of living"]

¹join \ˈjȯin\ *vb* **1 a** : to bring or fasten together in close physical contact ⟨*join* hands⟩ **b** : to connect (as points) by a line **2** : to come or bring into close associaton ⟨*join* a club⟩ ⟨*joined* them in marriage⟩ **3** : to come into the company of ⟨*join* friends for lunch⟩ **4 a** : to come together so as to be connected ⟨nouns *join* to form compounds⟩ **b** : **ADJOIN** ⟨the two estates *join*⟩ **5** : to take part in a collective activity ⟨*join* in singing⟩ [Old French *joindre*, from Latin *jungere*] — **join·able** \-ə-bəl\ *adj* □ **SYN JOIN, COMBINE, UNITE, CONNECT** mean to bring or come together in some kind of union. **JOIN** suggests a physical contact or conjunction between two or more things ⟨*join* the ends with glue⟩ ⟨*joined* forces in a common purpose to win⟩ **COMBINE** implies some merging or mingling with corresponding loss of identity of each unit; **UNITE** implies a greater loss of separate identity; **CONNECT** suggests a loose or external attachment with little or no loss of separate identity.

²join *n* : a point of joining : **JOINT**

join·er \ˈjȯi-nər\ *n* : one that joins: as **a** : a person whose craft is to construct articles by joining pieces of wood **b** : a gregarious person who joins many organizations

join·ery \ˈjȯin-rē, -ə-rē\ *n* **1** : the craft or trade of a joiner **2** : articles made by a joiner

¹joint \ˈjȯint\ *n* **1 a** (1) : the point of contact between elements of an animal skeleton together with the parts that surround and support it (2) : a node of a plant stem **b** : a part or space included between two animal or plant joints **c** : a large piece of meat for roasting **2 a** : a place where two things or parts are joined ⟨a *joint* in a pipe⟩ **b** : a space between the adjacent surfaces of two bodies joined and held together by an adhesive material (as cement or mortar) ⟨a thin *joint*⟩ **c** : a fracture or crack in rock **3 a** : a shabby or disreputable place of entertainment **b** : **PLACE** 2b, **ESTABLISHMENT** **4** : a marijuana cigarette [Old French *jointe*, from *joindre* "to join"] — **joint·ed** \-əd\ *adj*

²joint *adj* **1** : **UNITED** 1 ⟨the *joint* effect of study and play⟩ **2** : common to two or more: as **a** : done or shared by two or more ⟨a *joint* report⟩ ⟨*joint* efforts⟩ **b** : sharing in something (as a right or duty ⟨*joint* owners⟩

³joint *vb* **1 a** : to unite by a joint **b** : to provide with a joint **2** : to separate the joints of — **joint·er** *n*

joint·ly *adv* : **TOGETHER** ⟨owned *jointly*⟩

joint–stock company *n* : a form of business organization intermediate in many respects between a partnership and a corporation

joist \ˈjȯist\ *n* : any of the small timbers or metal beams placed parallel from wall to wall in a building to support the floor or ceiling [Middle French *giste*, derived from Latin *jacēre* "to lie"]

joist

Joshua tree

¹joke \ˈjōk\ *n* **1 a** : something said or done to provoke laughter; *esp* : a brief oral narrative with a climactic humorous twist **b** (1) : the humorous or ridiculous element in something (2) : **RAILLERY, KIDDING** ⟨can't take a *joke*⟩ **c** : **PRACTICAL JOKE** **d** : **LAUGHINGSTOCK 2 a** : something not to be taken seriously **b** : something presenting no difficulty [Latin *jocus*] **SYN** see **JEST**

²joke *vb* **1** : to make jokes : **JEST** **2** : to make the object of a joke : **KID** — **jok·ing·ly** \ˈjō-king-lē\ *adv*

jok·er \ˈjō-kər\ *n* **1** : a person who jokes **2** : an extra card used in some card games **3** : a part (as of an agreement) meaning something quite different from what it seems to mean and changing the apparent intention of the whole

jol·li·fi·ca·tion \ˌjäl-i-fə-ˈkā-shən\ *n* : **MERRYMAKING** 1

jol·li·ty \ˈjäl-ət-ē\ *n, pl* **-ties** : the quality or state of being jolly **SYN** see **MIRTH**

¹jol·ly \ˈjäl-ē\ *adj* **jol·li·er; -est 1 a** (1) : full of high spirits : **JOYOUS** (2) : given to conviviality : **JOVIAL b** : expressing, suggesting, or inspiring gaiety : **CHEERFUL 2** : extremely pleasant or agreeable : **SPLENDID** [Old French *joli*] **SYN** see **MERRY**

²jolly *adv* : **VERY** ⟨had a *jolly* good time⟩

³jolly *vb* **jol·lied; jol·ly·ing 1** : to engage in good-natured banter **2** : to put in good humor especially in order to gain an end

jol·ly boat \ˈjäl-ē-\ *n* : a medium-sized ship's boat used for general rough or small work [origin unknown]

Jol·ly Rog·er \ˌjäl-ē-ˈräj-ər\ *n* : a black flag with a white skull and crossbones

¹jolt \ˈjōlt\ *vb* **1** : to move or cause to move with a sudden jerky motion **2** : to give a knock or blow to : **JAR 3** : to disturb the composure of **4** : to interfere with roughly, abruptly, and disconcertingly [probably blend of obsolete *joll* "to strike" and *jot* "to bump"] — **jolt·er** *n*

²jolt *n* **1** : an abrupt sharp jerky blow or movement **2** : a sudden shock, surprise, or disappointment

Jo·nah \ˈjō-nə\ *n* **1** — see **BIBLE** table **2** : **JINX** 1 [sense 2 from the fact that by disobeying God's command Jonah caused a storm to endanger the ship he was traveling in]

jon·gleur \zhōⁿ-ˈglər\ *n* : a wandering medieval minstrel [French, from Old French *jogleour*, derived from Latin *jocus* "joke"]

jon·quil \ˈjän-kwəl, ˈjäng-\ *n* : a Mediterranean perennial bulbous herb with long grassy leaves that is widely grown for its yellow or white fragrant short-tubed clustered flowers — compare **DAFFODIL** [French *jonquille*, from Spanish *junguillo*, from *junco* "reed", from Latin *juncus*]

jor·dan almond \ˌjȯrd-n-\ *n* **1** : an almond imported from Málaga **2** : an almond coated with sugar [Middle English *jardin almande*, from Middle French *jardin* "garden" + Middle English *almande* "almond"]

jo·seph \ˈjō-zəf\ *n* : a long cloak worn especially by women in the 18th century [probably from *Joseph*, Old Testament patriarch; from his coat of many colors (Genesis 37:3)]

josh \ˈjäsh\ *vb* : to make fun of : **TEASE, JOKE** [origin unknown] — **josh·er** *n*

Josh·ua \ˈjäsh-wə, -ə-wə\ *n* — see **BIBLE** table

Joshua tree *n* : a tall branched yucca of the southwestern United States with short leaves and clustered greenish white flowers

joss \ˈjäs, ˈjȯs\ *n* : a Chinese idol or cult image [Pidgin English, from Portuguese *deus* "god," from Latin]

joss house *n* : a Chinese temple or shrine

¹jos·tle \ˈjäs-əl\ *vb* **jos·tled; jos·tling** \ˈjäs-ling, -ə-ling\ **1** : to move against so as to jar : push roughly ⟨*jostled* by a crowd⟩ **2** : to make one's way by pushing and shoving : **ELBOW** [earlier *justle*, derived from *joust*]

²jostle *n* **1** : a jostling encounter or experience **2** : the state of being jostled together

¹jot \ˈjät\ *n* : the least bit : **IOTA** [Latin *iota, jota* "iota"] □ **ORIGIN** "Till heaven and earth pass, one jot or one tittle shall in no wise pass from the law, till all be fulfilled." This is Christ's assurance (Matthew 5:18) that He was not "come to destroy the law or the prophets." Not the smallest letter, not a single stroke of a letter, we are told, will be lost. *Jot* is an anglicized form of Latin *jota* (or *iota*), itself simply a transliteration of the Greek name of the ninth letter of the Greek alphabet. The original Aramaic version must have referred to *yōdh,* the smallest letter in the Hebrew alphabet. The transfer across language boundaries was easily made because the Greek equivalent *tōta* was also the smallest letter in its alphabet. A *jot* now simply means "a very small part".

²jot *vt* **jot·ted; jot·ting** : to write briefly or hurriedly : set down in the form of a note ⟨*jot* this down⟩

jot·ting \'jät-ing\ *n* : a brief note : MEMORANDUM

joule \'jül\ *n* : the mks unit of work equal to the work done by a force of one newton acting through a distance of one meter [James P. *Joule,* died 1889, English physicist]

jounce \'jaùns\ *vb* : to move or cause to move in an up-and-down manner [Middle English *jouncen*] — **jounce** *n*

jour·nal \'jərn-l\ *n* **1 a** : a brief account of daily events **b** : a record of experiences, ideas, or reflections kept for private use **c** : a record of transactions kept by a deliberative or legislative body **2 a** : a daily newspaper **b** : a periodical that deals with current events [Middle French, "service book containing the day hours", from *journal* "daily", from Latin *diurnalis,* from *diurnus* "of the day", from *dies* "day"]

jour·nal·ese \,jərn-l-'ēz, -'ēs\ *n* : a style of writing held to be characteristic of newspapers

jour·nal·ism \'jərn-l-,iz-əm\ *n* **1** : the collection and editing of material of current interest for presentation through news media (as newspapers or television) **2** : writing designed for or characteristic of newspapers or popular magazines

jour·nal·ist \-l-əst\ *n* : a person engaged in journalism

jour·nal·is·tic \,jərn-l-'is-tik\ *adj* : of, relating to, or characteristic of journalism or journalists — **jour·nal·is·ti·cal·ly** \-ti-kə-lē, -klē\ *adv*

jour·nal·ize \'jərn-l-,īz\ *vt* : to record in a journal — **jour·nal·iz·er** *n*

¹jour·ney \'jər-nē\ *n, pl* **journeys** : travel or passage from one place to another [Old French *journee* "day's journey", from *jour* "day", from Late Latin *diurnum,* from Latin *diurnus* "of a day", from *dies* "day"]

²journey *vb* **jour·neyed; jour·ney·ing** **1** : to go on a journey : TRAVEL **2** : to travel over or through : TRAVERSE — **jour·ney·er** *n*

jour·ney·man \'jər-nē-mən\ *n* **1** : a worker who has learned a trade and usually works for wages **2** : an experienced and reliable but not brilliant worker or performer [Middle English *journey* "journey, day's labor"]

¹joust \'jaùst\ *vi* : to engage in a joust : TILT [Old French *juster,* derived from Latin *juxta* "near"] — **joust·er** *n*

²joust *n* : a combat on horseback between two knights with lances especially as part of a tournament

jo·vi·al \'jō-vē-əl\ *adj* : markedly good-humored especially as shown by jollity and good-fellowship [Late Latin *jovialis* "of the god Jupiter", from Latin *Jov-, Juppiter* "Jupiter"; from the belief that those born under the astrological influence of the planet Jupiter are jolly] SYN see MERRY — **jo·vi·al·i·ty** \,jō-vē-'al-ət-ē\ *n* — **jo·vi·al·ly** \'jō-vē-ə-lē\ *adv*

¹jowl \'jaùl\ *n* **1** : JAW; *esp* : the lower jaw **2** : CHEEK 1 [Old English *ceafl*]

²jowl *n* : loose flesh (as a wattle) hanging from the lower jaw or throat [Middle English *cholle*] — **jowly** \-ē\ *adj*

¹joy \'jòi\ *n* **1** : a feeling of great pleasure or happiness that comes from success, good fortune, or a sense of well-being : GLADNESS **2** : something that gives great pleasure or happiness ⟨a *joy* to behold⟩ [Old French *joie,* from Latin *gaudium,* from *gaudēre* "to rejoice"]

²joy *vi* : to experience great pleasure or delight : REJOICE

joy·ful \'jòi-fəl\ *adj* : experiencing, causing, or showing joy : HAPPY — **joy·ful·ly** \-fə-lē\ *adv* — **joy·ful·ness** *n*

joy·less \'jòi-ləs\ *adj* : not feeling or causing joy : CHEERLESS — **joy·less·ly** *adv* — **joy·less·ness** *n*

joy·ous \'jòi-əs\ *adj* : JOYFUL — **joy·ous·ly** *adv* — **joy·ous·ness** *n*

joy·ride \'jòi-,rīd\ *n* : a ride taken for pleasure and often marked by reckless driving — **joy·rid·er** *n* — **joy·rid·ing** *n*

joy·stick \-,stik\ *n* : a control lever for a device (as a computer display) that allows motion in two or more directions

ju·bi·lant \'jü-bə-lənt\ *adj* : feeling or expressing great joy : EXULTANT [Latin *jubilare* "to rejoice"] — **ju·bi·lant·ly** *adv*

ju·bi·la·tion \,jü-bə-'lā-shən\ *n* **1** : an act of rejoicing : the state of being jubilant **2** : an expression of great joy

ju·bi·lee \'jü-bə-,lē, ,jü-bə-'lē\ *n* **1 a** : a special anniversary; *esp* : a 50th anniversary **b** : a celebration of such an anniversary **2 a** : a period of time proclaimed by the Roman Catholic pope ordinarily every 25 years as a time of special solemnity **b** : a special plenary indulgence granted during a year of jubilee to Roman Catholics who perform specified works of repentance and piety [Late Latin *jubilaeus* "year of emancipation and restoration provided by ancient Hebrew law", from Late Greek *iōbēlaios,* from Hebrew *yōbhēl,* literally, "ram's horn"] □ ORIGIN Ancient Hebrew law established every 50th year as a year of emancipation and restoration. All Hebrew slaves were freed; lands were restored to their former owners; fields were left uncultivated. This year took its name, *yōbbēl,* from the ram's horn trumpets used to proclaim its coming. When the Old Testament was translated into Greek and later into Latin, the translators borrowed the Hebrew name. The Greek form *iōbēlaios* was borrowed into Latin as *jubilaeus.* Since *jubilee* came into English with the translation of the Bible from Latin, it has acquired new meanings.

Ju·da·ic \jü-'dā-ik\ *adj* : of, relating to, or characteristic of Jews or Judaism [Latin *judaicus,* from Greek *ioudaikos,* from *Ioudaios* "Jew"] — **Ju·da·ical** \-'dā-ə-kəl\ *adj*

Ju·da·ism \'jüd-ə-,iz-əm, 'jüd-ē-\ *n* **1** : a religion developed among the ancient Hebrews and marked by belief in one God who is creator, ruler, and redeemer of the universe and by the moral and ceremonial laws of the Old Testament and the rabbinic tradition **2** : conformity to Jewish rites, ceremonies, and practices **3** : the cultural, social, and religious beliefs and practices of the Jews **4** : the whole body of Jews — **Ju·da·ist** \-ə-əst, -ē-əst\ *n* — **Ju·da·is·tic** \,jüd-ə-'is-tik, ,jüd-ē-\ *adj*

Ju·da·ize \'jüd-ə-,īz, 'jüd-ē-\ *vb* **1** : to adopt the customs, beliefs, or character of a Jew **2** : to make Jewish — **Ju·da·iza·tion** \,jüd-ə-ə-'zā-shən, ,jüd-ē-ə-\ *n* — **Ju·da·iz·er** *n*

Ju·das \'jüd-əs\ *n* : TRAITOR [*Judas* Iscariot, apostle who betrayed Jesus]

Judas tree *n* : a leguminous tree often grown for its showy usually rosy flowers borne before the leaves appear [from the belief that Judas Iscariot hanged himself from a tree of this kind]

Jude \'jüd\ *n* — see BIBLE table

¹judge \'jəj\ *vb* **1** : to form an authoritative opinion **2** : to decide as a judge : TRY **3** : to determine or pronounce after inquiry and deliberation : CONSIDER **4** : GOVERN, RULE — used of a Hebrew tribal leader **5** : to form an estimate, conclusion, or evaluation about something : THINK [Old French *jugier,* from Latin *judicare,* from *judic-, judex* "judge", from *jus* "right, law" + *dicere* "to say"] — **judg·er** *n*

²judge *n* **1** : a public official authorized to decide questions brought before a court **2** *often cap* : a tribal hero exercising authority over the Hebrews after the death of Joshua **3** : one who decides in a contest or competition : UMPIRE **4** : one who gives an authoritative opinion : CRITIC — **judge·ship** \-,ship\ *n*

\ə\ abut	\ng\ sing
\ər\ further	\ō\ bone
\a\ mat	\ò\ saw
\ā\ take	\òi\ coin
\ä\ cot, cart	\th\ thin
\aù\ out	\th\ this
\ch\ chin	\ü\ food
\e\ pet	\ù\ foot
\ē\ easy	\y\ yet
\g\ go	\yü\ few
\i\ tip	\yù\ cure
\ī\ life	\zh\ vision
\j\ job	

judg·es \'jəj-əz\ *n* — see BIBLE table

judg·ment *or* **judge·ment** \'jəj-mənt\ *n* **1 a** : the act of judging **b** : a decision or opinion formed or given after judging **2 a** : a formal decision given by a court **b** : a court decree that a defendant has an obligation to the plaintiff for a specified amount **3** *cap* : the final judging of mankind by God **4** : the process of forming an opinion by discerning and comparing **5** : the capacity for judging — **judg·men·tal** \,jəj-'ment-l\ *adj*

Judgment Day *n* : the day of the Last Judgment

ju·di·ca·ture \'jüd-i-kə-,chur\ *n* **1** : the administration of justice **2** : JUDICIARY 1 [Middle French, from Medieval Latin *judicatura,* from Latin *judicare* "to judge"]

ju·di·cial \jù-'dish-əl\ *adj* **1** : of or relating to a judgment, the function of judging, the administration of justice, or the judiciary **2** : pronounced, ordered, or enforced by a court ⟨a *judicial* decision⟩ **3** : of, characterized by, or expressing judgment : CRITICAL [Latin *judicialis,* from *judicium* "judgment", from *judex* "judge"] — **ju·di·cial·ly** \-'dish-lē, -ə-lē\ *adv*

ju·di·cia·ry \jù-'dish-ē-,er-ē, -'dish-ə-rē\ *n, pl* **-ries 1 a** : a system of law courts **b** : the judges of these courts **2** : a branch of government in which judicial power is vested — **judiciary** *adj*

ju·di·cious \jù-'dish-əs\ *adj* : having, exercising, or characterized by sound judgment : DISCREET — **ju·di·cious·ly** *adv* — **ju·di·cious·ness** *n*

Ju·dith \'jüd-əth\ *n* — see BIBLE table

ju·do \'jüd-ō\ *n, pl* **judos** : a form of wrestling developed in Japan from jujitsu [Japanese *jūdō,* from *jū* "weakness, gentleness" + *dō* "art"]

¹jug \'jəg\ *n* **1 a** : a large deep earthenware, glass, or plastic container with a narrow mouth and a handle **b** : JUGFUL **2** : JAIL [perhaps from *jug,* nickname for *Joan*]

²jug *vt* **jugged; jug·ging** : IMPRISON

jug·ful \'jəg-,fùl\ *n, pl* **jugfuls** \-,fùlz\ *or* **jugs·ful** \'jəgz-,fùl\ : the quantity held by a jug

jug·ger·naut \'jəg-ər-,nòt\ *n* : a massive inexorable force or object that crushes whatever is in its path [Hindi *Jagannāth,* title of Vishnu, literally, "lord of the world"] ☐ ORIGIN One of the titles of the Hindu god Vishnu is *Jagannāth,* which means "lord of the world". Every year the image of *Jagannāth* is taken from his temple at Puri, India, placed on an enormous car or carriage, and drawn through the streets in procession. In earlier times, some of the worshipers of *Jagannāth* would allow themselves to be crushed beneath the wheels of the car in sacrifice to their god. The English form of the god's name, *Juggernaut,* came to be used in the sense of a massive inexorable force or object that crushes everything in its path.

¹jug·gle \'jəg-əl\ *vb* **jug·gled; jug·gling** \'jəg-ling, -ə-ling\ **1** : to keep several objects in motion in the air at the same time **2** : to manipulate especially in order to achieve a desired and often fraudulent end ⟨*juggle* an account to hide a loss⟩ **3** : to hold or balance insecurely [Middle French *jogler* "to joke, sing", from Latin *joculari* "to joke", from *joculus* "little joke", from *jocus* "joke"] — **jug·gler** \'jəg-lər, -ə-lər\ *n*

²juggle *n* : an act or instance of juggling

jug·glery \'jəg-lə-rē\ *n, pl* **-gler·ies 1** : the art or practice of a juggler **2** : TRICKERY

¹jug·u·lar \'jəg-yə-lər\ *adj* **1** : of, relating to, or situated in or on the throat or neck **2** : of or relating to the jugular vein [Late Latin *jugularis,* from Latin *jugulum* "collarbone, throat"]

²jugular *n* : JUGULAR VEIN

jugular vein *n* : any of several veins of each side of the neck that return blood from the head

juice \'jüs\ *n* **1** : the fluid contents that can be separated from cells or tissues **2 a** : the natural fluids (as blood and lymph) of an animal body; *esp* : any of several chiefly digestive secretions **b** : the liquid or moisture contained in something **3** : a medium (as electric-

ity or gasoline) that supplies power [Old French *jus* "broth, juice", from Latin] — **juiced** \'jüst\ *adj* — **juice·less** \'jüs-ləs\ *adj*

juic·er \'jü-sər\ *n* : an appliance for extracting juice from fruit or vegetables

juice up *vt* : to give life, energy, or spirit to

juicy \'jü-sē\ *adj* **juic·i·er; -est 1** : having much juice : SUCCULENT **2 a** : rich in interest : COLORFUL **b** : agreeably interesting or titillating ⟨a *juicy* scandal⟩ — **juic·i·ly** \-sə-lē\ *adv* — **juic·i·ness** \-sē-nəs\ *n*

ju·jit·su *or* **ju·jut·su** *or* **jiu·jit·su** *or* **jiu·jut·su** \jü-'jit-sü\ *n* : the Japanese art of unarmed fighting employing holds, throws, and paralyzing blows [Japanese *jūjutsu,* from *jū* "weakness" + *jutsu* "art, skill"]

ju·jube \'jü-,jüb, *2 is often* 'jü-jù-,bē\ *n* **1** : the edible fruit of a tree of the buckthorn family; *also* : this tree **2** : a fruit-flavored gumdrop or lozenge [Medieval Latin *jujuba,* from Latin *ziziphum,* from Greek *zizyphon*]

juke·box \'jük-,bäks\ *n* : a coin-operated phonograph that automatically plays records selected from its list [*juke* brothel, probably of African origin]

juke joint *n* : a small inexpensive establishment for eating, drinking, or dancing to the music of a jukebox

ju·lep \'jü-ləp\ *n* : a drink of alcoholic liquor and sugar poured over crushed ice and garnished with mint — called also *mint julep* [Middle French, a drink made from syrup, from Arabic *julāb,* from Persian *gulāb,* from *gul* "rose" + *āb* "water"]

Ju·lian calendar \,jül-yən-\ *n* : a calendar introduced in Rome in 46 B.C. establishing the 12-month year of 365 days with each 4th year having 366 days and the months each having 31 or 30 days except for February which has 28 or in leap years 29 days — compare GREGORIAN CALENDAR [Gaius *Julius* Caesar, who introduced it]

Ju·ly \jù-'lī\ *n* : the 7th month of the year [Old English *Julius,* from Latin, from Gaius *Julius* Caesar]

¹jum·ble \'jəm-bəl\ *vb* **jum·bled; jum·bling** \-bə-ling, -bling\ : to move or mix in a confused mass [perhaps imitative]

²jumble *n* : a disorderly mass or pile

jum·bo \'jəm-bō\ *n, pl* **jumbos** : a very large specimen of its kind [*Jumbo,* a huge elephant exhibited by P.T. Barnum] — **jumbo** *adj*

¹jump \'jəmp\ *vb* **1 a** : to spring or cause to spring into the air : LEAP ⟨*jump* up⟩ ⟨*jump* a horse over a ditch⟩ **b** : to give a sudden movement : START **c** : to move over a position occupied by an opponent's piece in a board game **d** : SKIP ⟨this typewriter *jumps*⟩ **e** : to begin a forward movement — used with *off* **2 a** : to rise or cause to rise suddenly in rank or status **b** : to undergo or cause to undergo a sudden sharp increase ⟨prices *jumped*⟩ **3** : to pounce suddenly or unexpectedly : ATTACK **4** : to bustle with activity **5 a** : to leap over ⟨*jump* a hurdle⟩ **b** : BYPASS ⟨*jump* electrical connections⟩ **c** : ANTICIPATE ⟨*jump* the gun in starting the race⟩ **d** : to escape from usually in a hasty or furtive manner ⟨*jump* town without paying their bills⟩ **e** : to abscond while at liberty under (bail) **f** : to depart from (a normal course) ⟨*jump* the track⟩ **g** : to get aboard by jumping ⟨*jump* a train⟩ **h** : to occupy illegally ⟨*jump* a mining claim⟩ [probably related to Low German *gumpen* "to jump"]

²jump *n* **1 a** (1) : an act of jumping : LEAP (2) : a sports competition featuring a leap, spring, or bound (3) : a distance covered by a leap **b** : a sudden involuntary movement **c** : a move made in a board game by jumping **2 a** : a sharp sudden increase **b** : one in a series of moves **3** : an advantage at the start

jump ball *n* : a method of putting a basketball into play in which the referee tosses the ball up between two opposing players who jump and try to tap it to a teammate

¹jump·er \'jəm-pər\ *n* **1** : one that jumps **2** : any of various devices operating with a jumping motion **3** : a wire used to close a break or cut out part of a circuit

²jumper *n* **I** : a loose blouse or jacket worn by workmen **2** : a sleeveless one-piece dress worn usually with a blouse **3** *pl* : a child's coverall [probably from English dialect *jump* "jumper"]

jumping bean *n* : a seed of any of several Mexican shrubs of the spurge family that tumbles about because of the movements of the larva of a small moth inside it

jumping jack *n* : a toy figure of a man jointed and made to jump or dance by means of strings or a sliding stick

jumping mouse *n* : any of several small hibernating North American rodents with long hind legs and tail and no cheek pouches

jump·ing–off place \,jəm-ping-'ȯf-\ *n* **I** : a remote or isolated place **2** : a place from which an enterprise is launched

jump seat *n* **I** : a movable carriage seat **2** : a folding seat between the front and rear seats of a passenger automobile

jump shot *n* : a shot made by a basketball player at the peak of a jump

jumpy \'jəm-pē\ *adj* **jump·i·er; -est** : very nervous : JITTERY — **jump·i·ness** *n*

jun·co \'jəng-kō\ *n, pl* **juncos** *or* **juncoes** : any of a genus of small American finches usually with a pink bill, ashy gray head and back, and conspicuous white lateral tail feathers [Spanish, "reed", from Latin *juncus*]

junc·tion \'jəng-shən, 'jəngk-\ *n* **I** : an act of joining : the state of being joined **2** : a place or point of meeting ⟨a railroad *junction*⟩ **3** : something that joins [Latin *junctio*, from *jungere* "to join"] — **junc·tion·al** \-shnəl, -shən-l\ *adj*

junc·ture \'jəng-chər, 'jəngk-\ *n* **I** : an instance of joining : UNION **2 a** : JOINT 2a, CONNECTION **b** : the manner of transition between two consecutive sounds in speech **3** : a point of time; *esp* : one made critical by a concurrence of circumstances — **junc·tur·al** \-chə-rəl, -shrəl\ *adj* □ SYN JUNCTURE, EMERGENCY, CRISIS mean a critical or crucial time or state of affairs. JUNCTURE stresses the significant convergence of events or developments; EMERGENCY emphasizes the sudden unforeseen nature of a situation and the need for quick action; CRISIS applies to a juncture whose outcome will make a decisive difference.

June \'jün\ *n* : the 6th month of the year [Latin *Junius*]

june beetle *n, often cap J* : any of various large leaf-eating beetles that fly chiefly in late spring and have as larvae white grubs that live in soil and feed on roots — called also *june bug*

June·ber·ry \'jün-,ber-ē\ *n* : SERVICEBERRY 2

jun·gle \'jəng-gəl\ *n* **I a** : a thick tangled mass of tropical vegetation **b** : a tract overgrown with jungle or other rank vegetation **2** : a hobo camp **3** : a place of ruthless struggle for survival [Hindi *jaṅgal*] — **jun·gly** \-gə-lē, -glē\ *adj*

jungle fowl *n* : any of several Asian wild birds related to the pheasants; *esp* : one from which domestic fowls are held to have descended

jungle gym *n* : a structure of vertical and horizontal bars for use of children at play

¹ju·nior \'jün-yər\ *n* **I** : a person who is younger or of lower rank than another **2** : a student in the next-to-last year before graduating from an educational institution of secondary or higher level [Latin, from *junior*, comparative of *juvenis* "young"]

²junior *adj* **I a** : YOUNGER — used chiefly to distinguish a son with the same given name or names as his father and usually placed in its abbreviated form after a surname (John M. Doe, *Jr.*) **b** : of more recent date **2** : lower in standing or rank ⟨*junior* partner⟩ **3** : of or relating to juniors in a school or college

ju·nior·ate \'jün-yə-,rāt, -rət\ *n* **I** : a course of high school or college study for candidates for the priesthood, brotherhood, or sisterhood; *esp* : one preparatory to the course in philosophy **2** : a seminary for the juniorate

junior college *n* : an educational institution that offers two years of studies corresponding to the first two years of a four-year college

junior high school *n* : a school usually including the 7th, 8th, and 9th grades

junior varsity *n* : a team composed of players lacking the experience or qualifications for the varsity

ju·ni·per \'jü-nə-pər\ *n* **I** : any of a genus of evergreen shrubs and trees of the pine family; *esp* : one of prostrate or shrubby habit **2** : any of various coniferous trees resembling true junipers [Latin *juniperus*]

¹junk \'jəngk\ *n* **I** : hard salted beef for use on shipboard **2 a** (1) : waste (as iron or glass) that may be used again in some form (2) : articles discarded as worthless **b** : a shoddy product : TRASH [Middle English *jonke* "piece of old rope or cable"] — **junk·man** \-,man\ *n* — **junky** *adj*

²junk *vt* : to get rid of as worthless : SCRAP

³junk *n* : a flat-bottomed sailing vessel of Chinese waters having an overhanging bow, high stern, high masts with lugsails, and a deep rudder [Portuguese *junco*, of Austronesian origin]

jun·ker \'yu̇ng-kər\ *n* : a member of the Prussian landed aristocracy [German, from Old High German *junchērro*, literally, "young lord"]

¹jun·ket \'jəng-kət\ *n* **I** : a dessert of sweetened flavored milk with a jellylike consistency **2 a** : a festive social affair **b** : JOURNEY, TRIP; *esp* : a trip made by an official at public expense [probably from Italian *giuncata* "cream cheese", from Latin *juncus* "reed, rush"] □ ORIGIN Long ago a type of cream cheese was prepared in baskets made of reeds or rushes. In Italy in the Middle Ages this cream cheese was called *giuncata*, a derivative of Latin *juncus,* which means "reed" or "rush". It was probably from this Italian source that English borrowed *junket. Junket* was first used for cream cheese and later for a dessert made of sweetened curdled milk. In the early modern period, indeed, *junket* was a popular term for any sweet dish. From this sense of *junket* developed the extended sense "a feast or banquet". *Junket* came to be used for large picnics and later for any pleasure outing or trip.

²junket *vi* **I** : BANQUET, FEAST **2** : to go on a junket

junk food *n* : food that is high in calories but low in nutritional content

junk·ie *or* **junky** \'jəng-kē\ *n, pl* **junk·ies** *slang* : a narcotics peddler or addict [English slang *junk* "narcotics", from ¹*junk*]

jun·ta \'hu̇n-tə, 'jənt-ə, 'hən-tə\ *n* **I** : a council or committee for political or governmental purposes; *esp* : a group of persons controlling a government after a revolutionary seizure of power **2** : JUNTO [Spanish, from *junto* "joined", from Latin *jungere* "to join"]

jun·to \'jənt-ō\ *n, pl* **juntos** : a group of persons joined for a common purpose [probably alteration of *junta*]

Ju·pi·ter \'jü-pət-ər\ *n* : the largest of the planets and 5th in order of distance from the sun — see PLANET table [Latin *Jupiter*, chief Roman god]

Ju·ras·sic \ju̇-'ras-ik\ *n* : the period of the Mesozoic era between the Triassic and Cretaceous marked by the presence of dinosaurs and the first appearance of birds; *also* : the corresponding system of rocks — see GEOLOGIC TIME table [French *jurassique*, from *Jura* mountain range] — **jurassic** *adj*

ju·rid·i·cal \ju̇-'rid-i-kəl\ *adj* **I** : of or relating to the administration of justice or the office of a judge **2** : of or relating to law or jurisprudence : LEGAL [Latin *juridicus*, from *jur-, jus* "right, law" + *dicere* "to say"] — **ju·rid·i·cal·ly** \-kə-lē, -klē\ *adv*

ju·ris·dic·tion \,ju̇r-əs-'dik-shən\ *n* **I** : the power, right, or authority to interpret and apply the law **2** : the authority of a sovereign power to govern or legislate **3** : the limits or territory within which authority

jumping bean

³junk

\ə\ abut	\ng\ sing
\ər\ further	\ō\ bone
\a\ mat	\ȯ\ saw
\ā\ take	\ȯi\ coin
\ä\ cot, cart	\th\ thin
\au̇\ out	\th̄\ this
\ch\ chin	\ü\ food
\e\ pet	\u̇\ foot
\ē\ easy	\y\ yet
\g\ go	\yü\ few
\i\ tip	\yu̇\ cure
\ī\ life	\zh\ vision
\j\ job	

may be exercised [Latin *jurisdictio*, from *jur-, jus* "right, law" + *dictio* "act of saying", from *dicere* "to say"] — **ju·ris·dic·tion·al** \-shnəl, -shən-l\ *adj* — **ju·ris·dic·tion·al·ly** \-ē\ *adv*

ju·ris·pru·dence \ˌjùr-ə-'sprüd-ns\ *n* **1** : a system of laws **2** : the science or philosophy of law **3** : a department of law ⟨medical *jurisprudence*⟩ [Late Latin *jurisprudentia*, from *jur-, jus* "right, law" + *prudens* "skilled, prudent"] — **ju·ris·pru·den·tial** \-sprü-'den-chəl\ *adj* — **ju·ris·pru·den·tial·ly** \-'dench-lē, -ə-lē\ *adv*

ju·rist \'jùr-əst\ *n* : one having a thorough knowledge of law [Middle French *juriste*, from Latin *jur-, jus* "law, right"]

ju·ris·tic \jù-'ris-tik\ *adj* **1** : of or relating to a jurist or jurisprudence **2** : of, relating to, or recognized in law — **ju·ris·ti·cal·ly** \-ti-kə-lē, -klē\ *adv*

ju·ror \'jùr-ər, 'jùr-ȯr\ *n* : a member of or a person summoned to serve on a jury

¹ju·ry \'jùr-ē\ *n, pl* **juries** **1** : a body of persons sworn to hear evidence on a matter submitted to them and to give their verdict according to the evidence presented **2** : a committee that judges and awards prizes at an exhibition or contest [Anglo-French *juree*, from Old French *jurer* "to swear", from Latin *jurare*, from *jur-, jus* "law"] — **ju·ry·man** \-mən\ *n* — **ju·ry·wom·an** \-ˌwù-mən\ *n*

²jury *adj* : improvised for temporary use especially in an emergency : MAKESHIFT ⟨a *jury* mast⟩ [origin unknown]

¹just \'jəst\ *adj* **1 a** : having a basis in or conforming to fact or reason : REASONABLE ⟨a *just* comment⟩ **b** *archaic* : faithful to an original **c** : conforming to a standard of correctness : PROPER ⟨*just* proportions⟩ **2 a** (1) : morally right or good : RIGHTEOUS ⟨a *just* war⟩ (2) : MERITED, DESERVED ⟨*just* punishment⟩ **b** : legally right ⟨a *just* title⟩ [Latin *justus*, from *jus* "right, law"] — **just·ly** *adv* — **just·ness** \'jəst-nəs, 'jəs-\ *n*

²just \jəst, jəst, jist, ˌjist, jest, ˌjest\ *adv* **1 a** : EXACTLY, PRECISELY ⟨*just* right⟩ **b** : very recently ⟨the bell *just* rang⟩ **2 a** : by a very small margin : BARELY ⟨*just* over the line⟩ **b** : only a little ⟨*just* west of here⟩ **3 a** : no more than : MERELY ⟨*just* a note⟩ **b** : QUITE, VERY ⟨*just* wonderful⟩

jus·tice \'jəs-təs\ *n* **1 a** : the maintenance or administration of what is just **b** : JUDGE 1 **c** : the administration of law **2 a** : the quality of being just, impartial, or fair **b** : RIGHTEOUSNESS ⟨defend the *justice* of their cause⟩ **c** : the quality of conforming to law [Old French, from Latin *justitia*, from *justus* "just"] — **do**

justice **1 a** : to act justly **b** : to treat fairly or properly **c** : to consume in a manner showing due appreciation **2** : to conduct in a way worthy of one's capabilities

justice of the peace : a local magistrate empowered chiefly to try minor cases, to administer oaths, and to perform marriages

jus·ti·fi·able \'jəs-tə-ˌfī-ə-bəl\ *adj* : capable of being justified : EXCUSABLE — **jus·ti·fi·ably** \-blē\ *adv*

jus·ti·fi·ca·tion \ˌjəs-tə-fə-'kā-shən\ *n* **1** : the act, process, or state of being justified by God **2 a** : the act or an instance of justifying : VINDICATION **b** : something that justifies : DEFENSE

jus·ti·fy \'jəs-tə-ˌfī\ *vb* **-fied; -fy·ing** **1 a** : to prove or show to be just, right, or reasonable : VINDICATE **b** : to show a sufficient lawful reason for an act done **2** : to release from the guilt of sin and accept as righteous **3** : to adjust or arrange exactly; *esp* : to cause (as lines of typewritten text) to come out even at the right margin SYN see MAINTAIN — **jus·ti·fi·er** \-ˌfī-ər, -ˌfīr\ *n*

¹jut \'jət\ *vb* **jut·ted; jut·ting** : to shoot or cause to shoot out, up, or forward : PROJECT [perhaps from Middle English *jutteyen*]

²jut *n* : something that juts : PROJECTION

jute \'jüt\ *n* : a glossy fiber from either of two East Indian plants that is used chiefly for sacking and twine [Hindi and Bengali *jūṭ*]

Jute \'jüt\ *n* : a member of a Germanic people invading England from Jutland and settling in Kent in the 5th century A.D. — compare ANGLO-SAXON [Medieval Latin *Jutae* "Jutes"] — **Jut·ish** \'jüt-ish\ *adj*

¹ju·ve·nile \'jü-və-ˌnīl, -vən-l\ *adj* **1 a** : showing incomplete development : IMMATURE **b** : CHILDISH **2** ⟨*juvenile* conduct⟩ **2** : derived from sources within the earth and coming to the surface for the first time ⟨*juvenile* water⟩ **3** : of, relating to, or characteristic of children or young people [Latin *juvenilis*, from *juvenis* "young person", from *juvenis* "young"] — **ju·ve·nil·i·ty** \ˌjü-və-'nil-ət-ē\ *n*

²juvenile *n* **1 a** : a young person **b** : a book for young people **2 a** : a fledged bird not yet in adult plumage **b** : a 2-year-old racehorse **3** : an actor or actress who plays youthful parts

juvenile delinquency *n* : violation of the law or antisocial behavior by a juvenile — **juvenile delinquent** *n*

jux·ta·pose \'jək-stə-ˌpōz\ *vt* : to place side by side [probably back-formation from *juxtaposition*]

jux·ta·po·si·tion \ˌjək-stə-pə-'zish-ən\ *n* : a placing or being placed side by side [Latin *juxta* "near" + English *position*] — **jux·ta·po·si·tion·al** \-'zish-nəl, -ən-l\ *adj*

Kk

k \'kā\ *n, pl* **k's** *or* **ks** \'kāz\ *often cap* : the 11th letter of the English alphabet

Ko·a·ba \'käb-ə\ *n* : a small stone building in the court of the Great Mosque at Mecca that contains a sacred black stone and is the point toward which Muslims turn in praying [Arabic *ka'bah,* literally, "square building"]

kabbala *or* **kabbalah** *or* **kabala** *variant of* CABALA

ka·bob *or* **ke·bab** *also* **ke·bob** \'kā-,bäb, kə-'\ *n* : cubes of meat cooked with vegetables usually on a skewer [Arabic *kabāb,* from Turkish *kebap*]

Ka·bu·ki \kə-'bü-kē, 'käb-ù-,kē\ *n* : traditional Japanese popular drama with singing and dancing performed in a stylized manner [Japanese, literally, "art of singing and dancing"]

kad·dish \'käd-ish\ *n, often cap* : a Jewish prayer recited in the daily ritual of the synagogue and by mourners at public services after the death of a close relative [Aramaic *qaddīsh* "holy"]

kaf·fee·klatsch \'kȯf-ē-,kläch, 'käf-, -,klach, -,kläch\ *n, often cap* : an informal social gathering for coffee and talk [German, from *kaffee* "coffee" + *klatsch* "gossip"]

Kaf·fir *or* **Kaf·ir** \'kaf-ər\ *n* : a member of a group of southern African Bantu-speaking peoples [Arabic *kāfir* "infidel"]

kaf·ir \'kaf-ər\ *n* : a stocky grain sorghum with erect heads

kaftan *variant of* CAFTAN

kai·ser \'kī-zər\ *n* : EMPEROR; *esp* : the ruler of Germany from 1871 to 1918 [Old Norse *keisari* and German *kaiser;* both from Latin *Caesar,* cognomen of the Emperor Augustus] — **kai·ser·dom** \-zərd-əm\ *n* — **kai·ser·ism** \-zə-,riz-əm\ *n* □ ORIGIN Although Julius Caesar was never emperor, his name became synonymous with the office of emperor of the Roman empire. Caesar adopted his grandnephew Gaius Octavius, who, upon his adoption, took the name Gaius Julius Caesar Octavianus. This man, after the death of Julius Caesar, gained control in Italy and became the first Roman emperor, with the title *Augustus,* "exalted, august". Later Roman emperors adopted his name, Caesar, to indicate their right to the imperial title. Subsequently other European languages borrowed this name from Latin as a word for emperor.

ka·ka \'käk-ə\ *n* : a brownish New Zealand parrot with gray and red markings that is a good mimic and talker [Maori]

kal·an·choe \,kal-ən-'kō-ē, kə-'lang-kə-wē\ *n* : any of a genus of succulent tropical Old World plants including several grown as ornamentals [New Latin, genus name, probably of Chinese origin]

kale \'kāl\ *n* : a hardy cabbage with curled often finely cut leaves that do not form a dense head [Scottish, from Old English *cāl*]

ka·lei·do·scope \kə-'līd-ə-,skōp\ *n* **1** : an instrument containing loose bits of colored glass between two flat plates and two plane mirrors so placed that changes of position of the bits of glass are reflected in an endless variety of symmetrical patterns **2** : a changing pattern or scene [Greek *kalos* "beautiful" + *eidos* "shape, form" + English -scope] — **ka·lei·do·scop·ic** \-,līd-ə-'skäp-ik\ *adj* — **ka·lei·do·scop·i·cal·ly** \-'skäp-i-kə-lē, -klē\ *adv*

kalends *variant of* CALENDS

Kal·muck *or* **Kal·muk** \'kal-,mək, kal-'\ *n* **1** : a member of a Buddhist Mongol people originally of northern Sinkiang, China **2** : the language of the Kalmucks [Russian *Kalmyk*]

kal·so·mine *variant of* CALCIMINE

ka·ma·ai·na \,käm-ə-'ī-nə\ *n* : one who has lived in Hawaii for a long time [Hawaiian *kama'āina,* from *kama* "child" + *'āina* "land"]

kame \'kām\ *n* : a short ridge or mound of material deposited by water from a melting glacier [Scottish, literally, "comb", from Old English *camb*]

ka·mi·ka·ze \,käm-i-'käz-ē\ *n* : a member of a corps of Japanese pilots in World War II assigned to make a crash on a target; *also* : an airplane flown in such an attack [Japanese, literally, "divine wind"] □ ORIGIN In 1281 Kublai Khan sent an immense fleet against Japan. Although Japan was prepared, the Mongol horde was not easy to resist. But after some weeks of fighting, a great and sudden storm arose and destroyed the Mongol fleet. To the Japanese this salvation was *kamikaze,* "divine wind". In the Second World War Japan sent out pilots willing to give up their lives to help save their country by destroying American ships. These were the members of a special corps named *kamikaze* after the storm that had saved Japan seven centuries earlier.

kan·ga·roo \,kang-gə-'rü\ *n, pl* **-roos** : any of various plant-eating leaping marsupial mammals of Australia, New Guinea, and adjacent islands with a small head, long powerful hind legs, and a long thick tail used as a support and in balancing [probably native name in Australia]

kangaroo

kangaroo court *n* **1** : a court whose status or procedures are irresponsible or irregular **2** : judgment or punishment given outside of legal procedure

kangaroo rat *n* : a pouched burrowing rodent of dry regions of the western United States

Kant·ian \'kant-ē-ən, 'känt-\ *adj* : of, relating to, or characteristic of Kant or his philosophy

ka·o·lin *also* **ka·o·line** \'kā-ə-lən\ *n* : a fine usually white clay that is used in ceramics and refractories and as an adsorbent [French *kaolin,* from *Kao-ling,* hill in China]

ka·pok \'kā-,päk\ *n* : a mass of silky fibers that clothe the seeds of the ceiba tree and are used as a filling for mattresses, life preservers, and sleeping bags and as insulation [Malay]

Ka·po·si's sarcoma \'kap-ə-sēz-, kə-'pō, -shēz-\ *n* : a neoplastic disease especially of the skin and mucous membranes that is associated especially with AIDS and is characterized usually by the formation of colored blotches on the skin [Mortiz *Kaposi,* died 1902, Hungarian dermatologist]

\ə\ abut		\ng\ sing	
\ər\ further		\ō\ bone	
\a\ mat		\ȯ\ saw	
\ā\ take		\ȯi\ coin	
\ä\ cot, cart		\th\ thin	
\aú\ out		\th\ this	
\ch\ chin		\ü\ food	
\e\ pet		\ú\ foot	
\ē\ easy		\y\ yet	
\g\ go		\yü\ few	
\i\ tip		\yú\ cure	
\ī\ life		\zh\ vision	
\j\ job			

kap·pa \'kap-ə\ *n* : the 10th letter of the Greek alphabet — K or κ

ka·put \kä-'pùt, kə-, -'püt\ *adj* **1** : utterly defeated or destroyed **2** : made useless or unable to function **3** : hopelessly outmoded [German, from French *capot* "not having made a trick at piquet"] □ ORIGIN To win all the tricks in the card game piquet is *faire capot,* "to make *capot*", in French, while *être capot,* "to be *capot*", is to have lost all the tricks in a game. In German *capot* was transliterated as *kaput,* and from the sense of having lost a game German *kaput* developed the senses "broken", "finished", "utterly destroyed". *Kaput* was borrowed into English from German early in the 20th century.

kar·a·kul \'kar-ə-kəl\ *n* **1** : any of a breed of hardy fat-tailed Asian sheep with coarse wiry brown fur **2** : the tightly curled glossy black coat of the newborn lamb of a karakul valued as fur [*Karakul,* village in Soviet Central Asia]

kar·a·o·ke \,kar-ē-'ō-kē, kə-'rō-kē\ *n* : a device that plays music to which the user sings along and that records the user's singing with the music [Japanese]

kar·at *or* **car·at** \'kar-ət\ *n* : a unit of fineness for gold equal to ¹⁄₂₄ part of pure gold in an alloy [probably from Middle French *carat,* from Medieval Latin *carratus* "²carat"]

ka·ra·te \kə-'rät-ē\ *n* : an oriental system of self-defense in which an attacker is disabled with kicks and punches [Japanese, literally, "empty hand"]

kar·ma \'kär-mə, 'kər-\ *n, often cap* **1** : the force generated by one's actions that is held in Hinduism and Buddhism to sustain the cycle of deaths and rebirths and to determine destiny in one's next existence **2** : a distinctive spirit or atmosphere that can be sensed [Sanskrit *karman,* literally, "work"] — **kar·mic** \-mik\ *adj, often cap*

kar·roo *or* **ka·roo** \kə-'rü\ *n* : a dry tableland of southern Africa [Afrikaans *karo*]

karst \'kärst\ *n* : an irregular limestone region with sinks, underground streams, and caverns [German]

kart·ing \'kärt-ing\ *n* : the sport of racing miniature automobiles [probably from *GoKart,* a trademark]

kary- *or* **karyo-** *combining form* : nucleus of a cell ⟨*karyo*kinesis⟩ [Greek *karyon* "nut"]

karyo·ki·ne·sis \,kar-ē-ō-kə-'nē-səs, -kī-'nē-\ *n* : MITOSIS — **karyo·ki·net·ic** \-'net-ik\ *adj*

¹karyo·type \'kar-ē-ə-,tīp\ *n* : the set of characteristics that distinguish the chromosomes of a particular cell or group — **karyo·typ·ic** \,kar-ē-ə-'tip-ik\ *adj* — **ka·ryo·typ·i·cal·ly** \-i-kə-lē, -klē\ *adv*

²karyotype *vt* : to determine the karyotype of

Kash·mir goat \,kash-,miər-, ,kazh-\ *n* : an Indian goat whose soft woolly undercoat forms cashmere wool [*Kashmir,* region in India]

kash·ruth *or* **kash·rut** \kä-'shrüt, -'shrüth\ *n* **1** : the state of being kosher **2** : the Jewish dietary laws [Hebrew *kashrūth,* literally, "fitness"]

Kas·site \'kas-,īt\ *n* : a member of a people from the Iranian plateau ruling Babylon between 1600 and 1200 B.C.

ka·ty·did \'kāt-ē-,did\ *n* : any of several large green American long-horned grasshoppers with stridulating organs on the fore wings of the males that produce a loud shrill sound [imitative]

kau·ri \'kaùr-ē\ *n* **1 a** : any of several trees of the pine family; *esp* : a tall New Zealand timber tree **b** : the tough white straight-grained wood of a kauri **2** : a recent or fossil resin from New Zealand kauris used especially in varnish and linoleum [Maori *kawri*]

kay·ak \'kī-,ak\ *n* **1** : an Eskimo canoe made of a frame entirely covered with skins except for a small opening in the center where one or two paddlers sit **2** : a covered canoe resembling a kayak [Eskimo *qajaq*]

ka·zoo \kə-'zü\ *n, pl* **kazoos** : a toy musical instrument containing a membrane which produces a buzzing

tone when one hums or sings into the mouth hole [imitative]

kea \'kē-ə\ *n* : a New Zealand parrot that is normally insectivorous but sometimes attacks and kills sheep for their flesh [Maori]

ke·bab *or* **ke·bob** *variant of* KABOB

¹kedge \'kej\ *vt* : to move (a ship) by hauling on a line attached to a small anchor dropped at the distance and in the direction desired [Middle English *caggen*]

²kedge *n* : a small anchor used especially in kedging

¹keel \'kēl\ *n* **1 a** : a timber or plate running lengthwise along the center of the bottom of a ship and usually projecting from the bottom **b** : SHIP **2 a** : something (as the breastbone of a bird) like a ship's keel in form or use; *esp* : a ridged part **b** : the lower two petals of a pea flower [Old Norse *kjölr*]

²keel *vb* **1 a** : to turn over **b** : to fall in or as if in a faint — usually used with *over* **2** : to provide with a keel

keel·boat \'kēl-,bōt\ *n* : a shallow covered riverboat with a keel that is usually rowed, poled, or towed and that is used for freight — **keel·boat·man** \-mən\ *n*

keel·haul \-,hòl\ *vt* **1** : to haul under the keel of a ship as punishment or torture **2** : to rebuke severely

¹keen \'kēn\ *adj* **1** : having a fine edge or point : SHARP ⟨a *keen* knife⟩ **2** : CUTTING 2, STINGING ⟨a *keen* wind⟩ **3** : EAGER, ENTHUSIASTIC ⟨*keen* about baseball⟩ **4 a** : very alert and perceptive ⟨a *keen* mind⟩ **b** : unusually sensitive ⟨*keen* eyesight⟩ [Old English *cēne* "brave, fierce"] SYN see SHARP — **keen·ly** *adv* — **keen·ness** \'kēn-nəs\ *n*

²keen *vb* : to lament with a keen [Irish Gaelic *caoinim* "I lament"] — **keen·er** *n*

³keen *n* : a loud wailing lament for the dead

¹keep \'kēp\ *vb* **kept** \'kept\; **keep·ing** **1 a** : to perform as a duty : FULFILL ⟨*keep* a promise⟩ **b** : to observe in a fitting or customary manner : not neglect ⟨*keep* a holiday⟩ **2 a** : GUARD ⟨*keep* us from harm⟩ **b** : to take care of ⟨*keep* a war orphan⟩ ⟨*keep* house⟩ **3** : to continue doing something : MAINTAIN ⟨*keep* silence⟩ ⟨*keep* on working⟩ **4** : HOLD, DETAIN ⟨*keep* a prisoner in jail⟩ **5 a** : to cause to remain in a given place, situation, or condition ⟨*keep* someone waiting⟩ **b** : to remain unspoiled ⟨milk may not *keep* in hot weather⟩ **6** : to hold back : WITHHOLD ⟨*keep* a secret⟩ **7** : to possess permanently ⟨*keep* what you have earned⟩ **8** : REFRAIN ⟨unable to *keep* from talking⟩ **9** : to have in one's service or at one's disposal ⟨*keep* servants⟩ ⟨*keep* a car⟩ **10** : to preserve a record in ⟨*keep* a diary⟩ **11** : STAY, REMAIN ⟨*keep* off the grass⟩ **12** : to have on hand regularly for sale ⟨*keep* neckties⟩ [Old English *cēpan*] □ SYN KEEP, OBSERVE, CELEBRATE, COMMEMORATE mean to notice or honor a day, occasion, or deed. KEEP stresses the idea of not neglecting or violating ⟨*keep* the Sabbath⟩ OBSERVE is likely to imply marking by ceremonious performance ⟨not all holidays are *observed* nationally⟩ CELEBRATE suggests acknowledging an occasion by festivity ⟨*celebrate* Christmas by giving gifts⟩ COMMEMORATE implies remembrance and suggests observances that tend to call to mind what the occasion stands for ⟨*commemorate* Memorial Day with the laying of wreaths⟩ — **keep one's end up** : to do one's share or duty

²keep *n* **1** : FORTRESS; *esp* : the strongest part of a medieval castle **2** : the means by which one is kept; *esp* : one's food and lodging ⟨earned their *keep*⟩ — **for**

keeps **1 a** : with the provision that one keep one's winnings ⟨play marbles for *keeps*⟩ **b** : with deadly seriousness **2** : PERMANENTLY ⟨came home for *keeps*⟩

keep·er \'kē-pər\ *n* : a person who watches, guards, maintains, or takes care of something ⟨the *keeper* of a bar⟩

keep·ing \'kē-ping\ *n* **1** : OBSERVANCE ⟨the *keeping* of a holiday⟩ **2** : CUSTODY 1, CARE **3** : AGREEMENT, HARMONY ⟨in *keeping* with good taste⟩

kayak 1

keep·sake \'kēp-,sāk\ *n* : something kept or given to be kept as a memento [*keep* + *-sake* (as in *namesake*)]

keep up *vb* **1** : MAINTAIN, SUSTAIN ⟨*keep* standards *up*⟩ **2** : to keep informed ⟨*keep up* on politics⟩ **3** : to continue without interruption ⟨rain *kept up* all night⟩ **4** : to stay even with others (as in a race)

keet \'kēt\ *n* : a young guinea fowl [imitative]

keg \'keg, 'kag, 'kāg\ *n* **1** : a small cask or barrel holding about 114 liters or less **2** : the contents of a keg [Middle English *kag*, of Scandinavian origin]

kelp \'kelp\ *n* **1** : any of various large brown seaweeds; *also* : a mass of these **2** : the ashes of seaweed used as a fertilizer and a source of iodine [Middle English *culp*]

kel·pie \'kel-pē\ *n* : an Australian sheep dog of a breed developed by crossing the dingo with British sheep dogs [*Kelpie,* the name of an early dog of this breed]

Kelt, Kelt·ic *variant of* CELT, CELTIC

kel·vin \'kel-vən\ *n* : a unit of temperature equal to ¹/₂₇₃.₁₆ of the Kelvin scale temperature of the triple point of water

Kel·vin \'kel-vən\ *adj* : relating to, conforming to, or having a temperature scale on which the unit of measurement is the same size as the Celsius degree and according to which absolute zero is 0° or the equivalent of −273.15°C — abbreviation *K* [William Thomson, Lord *Kelvin*]

¹ken \'ken\ *vb* **kenned; ken·ning** *chiefly Scottish* : KNOW [Old Norse *kenna* "to perceive"]

²ken *n* **1** : range of vision **2** : range of understanding

ke·naf \kə-'naf\ *n* : an East Indian hibiscus that yields a strong cordage fiber; *also* : its fiber [Persian]

ken·do \'ken-dō\ *n* : a traditional Japanese sport of fencing with bamboo staves [Japanese *kendō,* from *ken* "sword" + *dō* "art"]

¹ken·nel \'ken-l\ *n* **1** : a shelter for a dog **2** : an establishment for the breeding or boarding of dogs [derived from Latin *canis* "dog"]

²kennel *vb* **-neled** *or* **-nelled; -nel·ing** *or* **-nel·ling** : to put, keep, or take shelter in or as if in a kennel

Ken·tucky coffee tree \kən-,tək-ē-\ *n* : a tall North American leguminous tree with large woody pods whose seeds have been used as a substitute for coffee

ke·pi \'kā-pē, 'kep-ē\ *n* : a military cap with a round flat top sloping toward the front and a visor [French *képi*]

ker·a·tin \'ker-ət-n\ *n* : any of various sulfur-containing fibrous proteins that form the chemical basis of hair and horny tissues [Greek *kerat-, keras* "horn"] — **ke·ra·ti·nous** \kə-'rat-n-əs, ,ker-ə-'tī-nəs\ *adj*

kerb \'kərb\ *n, British* : CURB 4

ker·chief \'kər-chəf, -,chēf\ *n, pl* **kerchiefs** \-chəfs, -,chēfs\ *also* **kerchieves** \-,chēvz\ **1** : a square of cloth worn especially by women as a head covering or around the neck **2** : HANDKERCHIEF 1 [Old French *cuevrechief,* from *covrir* "to cover" + *chief* "head", from Latin *caput*]

kerf \'kərf\ *n* : a slit or notch made by a saw or cutting torch [Old English *cyrf* "action of cutting"]

ker·mes \'kər-mēz\ *n* : the dried bodies of the females of various scale insects used as a red dyestuff [French *kermès,* from Arabic *qirmiz*]

ker·mis *or* **ker·mess** \'kər-məs\ *n* : an outdoor festival of the Low Countries [Dutch *kermis*]

kern *or* **kerne** \'kərn, 'keərn\ *n* : a foot soldier of medieval Ireland or Scotland [Irish *cethern* "band of soldiers"]

ker·nel \'kərn-l\ *n* **1 a** : the inner softer part of a seed, fruit stone, or nut **b** : a whole seed of a cereal **2** : a central or essential part : CORE [Old English *cyrnel,* from *corn* "grain"]

kern·ite \'kər-,nīt\ *n* : a mineral $Na_2B_4O_7 \cdot 4H_2O$ that consists of sodium, boron, and water and is an important source of borax [*Kern* county, California]

ker·o·sene *or* **ker·o·sine** \'ker-ə-,sēn, ,ker-ə-', 'kar-, ,kar-\ *n* : a thin oil consisting of a mixture of hydrocarbons usually obtained by distillation of petroleum and used for a fuel and as a solvent [Greek *kēros* "wax"]

ker·ria \'ker-ē-ə\ *n* : any of a genus of yellow-flowered shrubs related to the roses [William *Kerr,* died 1814, English gardener]

Ker·ry blue terrier \,ker-ē-\ *n* : any of an Irish breed of medium-sized terriers with a long head, deep chest, and silky bluish coat [County *Kerry,* Ireland]

ker·sey \'kər-zē\ *n* : a coarse ribbed woolen cloth for hose and work clothes [*Kersey,* England]

kes·trel \'kes-trəl\ *n* : a small European falcon that hovers in the air against a wind [Middle French *crecerelle*]

ketch \'kech\ *n* : a 2-masted fore-and-aft-rigged sailing vessel with the mizzenmast forward of the rudder [Middle English *cache*]

ketch·up *variant of* CATSUP

ke·tone \'kē-,tōn\ *n* : an organic compound with a carbonyl group attached to two carbon atoms [German *keton*] — **ke·ton·ic** \kē-'tän-ik\ *adj*

ket·tle \'ket-l\ *n* **1** : a metallic vessel for boiling liquids; *esp* : TEAKETTLE **2** : a steep-sided hollow without surface drainage formed especially by the melting of a glacier [Old Norse *ketill,* from Latin *catillus* "small bowl", from *catinus* "bowl"]

ket·tle·drum \-,drəm\ *n* : a kettle-shaped drum whose head can be tuned to different pitches by changing its tension

¹key \'kē\ *n, pl* **keys** **1 a** : a usually metal instrument by which the bolt of a lock is turned **b** : a device having the form or function of a key ⟨a *key* for winding a clock⟩ **2 a** : a means of gaining or preventing entrance, possession, or control **b** : an instrumental or deciding factor **3 a** : something that gives an explanation or solution **b** : a list of words or phrases giving an explanation of symbols or abbreviations **c** : an arrangement of usually opposed characteristics of a group of plants or animals used for identification **d** : a map legend **4** : a small piece of wood or metal used as a wedge or for preventing motion between parts **5** : one of the levers with a flat surface that is pressed by a finger in operating or playing an instrument (as a typewriter, piano, or clarinet) **6** : SAMARA **7** : a system of seven tones based on their relationship to a tonic; *esp* : the tonality of a scale **8 a** : characteristic style or tone **b** : the tone or pitch of a voice **9** : a small switch for opening or closing an electric circuit [Old English *cǣg*]

²key *vb* **keyed** \'kēd\; **key·ing** **1** : to lock or secure with a key **2** : to regulate the musical pitch of **3** : to make appropriate : ATTUNE **4** : to make nervous or tense — usually used with *up* **5** : to use a key **6** : ²KEYBOARD

³key *adj* : of basic importance : FUNDAMENTAL

⁴key *n* : a low island or reef; *esp* : one of the coral islets off the southern coast of Florida [Spanish *cayo,* of American Indian origin]

¹key·board \'kē-,bōrd, -,bȯrd\ *n* **1** : a bank of keys on a musical instrument (as a piano) **2** : an arrangement of keys by which a machine (as a typewriter) is operated **3** : a small usually portable musical instrument that is played by means of a keyboard like that on a piano and that produces a variety of sounds electronically

²keyboard *vb* **1** : to operate a machine with a keyboard **2** : to capture or set (as data or text) by means of a machine with a keyboard — **key·board·er** *n*

key·hole \'kē-,hōl\ *n* : a hole for receiving a key

keyhole saw *n* : a narrow pointed fine-toothed saw used for cutting tight curves

¹key·note \-,nōt\ *n* **1** : the first and fundamental tone of a scale **2** : the fundamental or central fact, idea, or mood

²keynote *vt* **1** : to set the keynote of **2** : to deliver the keynote address at — **key·not·er** *n*

kelpie

ketch

\ə\ abut		\ng\ sing	
\ər\ further		\ō\ bone	
\a\ mat		\ȯ\ saw	
\ā\ take		\ȯi\ coin	
\ä\ cot, cart		\th\ thin	
\au̇\ out		\th\ this	
\ch\ chin		\ü\ food	
\e\ pet		\u̇\ foot	
\ē\ easy		\y\ yet	
\g\ go		\yü\ few	
\i\ tip		\yu̇\ cure	
\ī\ life		\zh\ vision	
\j\ job			

| keystone |

keynote address *n* : an address designed to present the issues of primary interest to a gathering and often to arouse unity and enthusiasm — called also *keynote speech*

key·pad \'kē-,pad\ *n* : a small keyboard (as on a calculator)

key·punch \'kē-,pənch\ *n* : a machine with a keyboard used to cut holes or notches in punch cards — **keypunch** *vt* — **key·punch·er** *n*

key signature *n* : the sharps or flats placed after a clef in music to indicate the key

key·stone \'kē-,stōn\ *n* **1** : the wedge-shaped piece at the crown of an arch that locks the other pieces in place **2** : something on which associated things depend for support

key·stroke \-,strōk\ *n* : the act or an instance of pushing down a key on a keyboard — **keystroke** *vb*

kha·ki \'kak-ē, 'käk-, *Canadian often* 'kärk-\ **1** : a light yellowish brown **2 a** : a khaki-colored cloth made usually of cotton or wool **b** : a military uniform of this cloth — usually used in pl. [Hindi *khākī* "dust-colored", from *khāk* "dust", from Persian]

Khal·kha \'kal-kə\ *n* **1** : a member of a Mongol people of Outer Mongolia **2** : the language of the Khalkha people used as the official language of the Mongolian People's Republic

¹khan \'kän, 'kan\ *n* **1** : a medieval sovereign of China and ruler over the Turkish, Tatar, and Mongol tribes **2** : a local chieftain or man of rank in some countries of central Asia [Middle French *caan*, of Turkic origin] — **khan·ate** \-,āt\ *n*

²khan *n* : an inn or rest house in some Asian countries : CARAVANSARY [Arabic *khān*]

khe·dive \kə-'dēv\ *n* : a Turkish governor of Egypt from 1867 to 1914 [French *khédive*, from Turkish *hidiv*]

Khmer \kə-'meər\ *n* **1** : a member of an aboriginal people of Cambodia **2** : the official language of Cambodia — **Khmer·ian** \-'mer-ē-ən\ *adj*

kib·butz \kib-'úts, -'üts\ *n, pl* **kib·but·zim** \-,út-'sēm, -,üt-\ : a collective farm or settlement in Israel [Modern Hebrew *qibbūs*]

kibe \'kīb\ *n* : CHILBLAIN [Middle English]

kib·itz·er \'kib-ət-sər\ *n* : one who looks on and often offers unwanted advice or comment especially at a card game [Yiddish *kibetsn* "to kibitz"] — **kib·itz** \-əts\ *vb*

ki·bosh \'kī-,bäsh\ *n* : something that serves as a check or stop ⟨put the *kibosh* on⟩

¹kick \'kik\ *vb* **1** : to strike out (as in defense or at a ball in games) with the foot or feet **2** : to strike, thrust, or hit violently with the foot **3** : to object strongly : PROTEST ⟨*kick* because prices were raised⟩ **4** : to recoil when fired **5** : to score by kicking a ball ⟨*kick* a goal⟩ **6** : to be full of pep and energy ⟨still alive and *kicking*⟩ [Middle English *kiken*] — **kick·er** *n*

²kick *n* **1 a** (1) : a blow with the foot (2) : a propelling of a ball with the foot **b** : the power to kick **c** : a motion of the legs in swimming **2** : a forceful jolt or thrust; *esp* : the recoil of a gun **3 a** : a feeling or expression of opposition **b** : the grounds for objection **4** : a stimulating effect especially of pleasure

kick around *vt* **1** : to treat in an inconsiderate or high-handed way **2** : to consider, examine, or discuss from various angles

kick·back \'kik-,bak\ *n* **1** : a sharp violent reaction **2** : a secret return of a part of a sum received

kick in *vb* : CONTRIBUTE 1

kick·off \'kik-,óf\ *n* **1** : a kick that puts the ball into play in a football or soccer game **2** : COMMENCEMENT 1

kick off \kik-'óf, 'kik-\ *vb* **1** : to start or resume play in football or soccer by a placekick **2** : to begin or begin something : COMMENCE ⟨*kicked* the campaign *off* with a dinner⟩

kick out *vt* : to throw out ⟨*kicked* them *out* of the club⟩

¹kid \'kid\ *n* **1** : the young of a goat or of a related animal **2 a** : the flesh, fur, or skin of a kid **b** : something (as leather) made of kid **3** : CHILD 2a, YOUNGSTER [Middle English *kide*, of Scandinavian origin] — **kid·dish** \'kid-ish\ *adj*

²kid *vb* **kid·ded; kid·ding** **1** : to deceive as a joke : FOOL **2** : to make fun of : TEASE [probably from ¹*kid*] — **kid·der** *n* — **kid·ding·ly** \'kid-ing-lē\ *adv*

kid glove *n* : a dress glove made of kidskin — **kid·gloved** \'kid-'gləvd\ *adj* — **with kid gloves** : with special consideration

kid·nap \'kid-,nap\ *vb* **kid·napped** *or* **kid·naped** \-,napt\; **kid·nap·ping** *or* **kid·nap·ing** \-,nap-ing\ : to carry away a person by unlawful force or by fraud and against his or her will [probably back-formation from *kidnapper*, from ¹*kid* + obsolete *napper* "thief"] — **kid·nap·per** *or* **kid·nap·er** \-,nap-ər\ *n*

kid·ney \'kid-nē\ *n, pl* **kidneys** **1** : either of a pair of oval to bean-shaped organs situated in the body cavity near the spinal column that excrete waste in the form of urine **2** : an excretory organ of an invertebrate animal [Middle English]

kidney bean *n* : a common garden bean grown especially for its nutritious seeds; *also* : a rather large dark red bean seed

kid·skin \'kid-,skin\ *n* : the skin of a young goat or leather made from or resembling this

kie·sel·guhr *or* **kie·sel·gur** \'kē-zəl-,gùr\ *n* : loose or porous diatomite [German *kieselgur*]

¹kill \'kil\ *vb* **1** : to deprive of life : put to death **2** : DESTROY, RUIN ⟨*kill* all chance of success⟩ **3** : to use up ⟨*kill* time⟩ **4** : DEFEAT ⟨*kill* a proposed law⟩ **5** : to mark for omission ⟨*kill* a news story⟩ **6** : to hit so hard that a return is impossible [Middle English *killen*] □ SYN KILL, SLAY, MURDER, ASSASSINATE mean to deprive of life. KILL simply states the fact of death by any agency in any manner; SLAY, chiefly literary, implies deliberateness and violence but not necessarily motive; MURDER implies motive and premeditation and usually secrecy and stresses full moral responsibility; ASSASSINATE applies to open or secret killing often for political motives.

²kill *n* **1** : an act of killing **2 a** : an animal killed in a hunt, season, or particular period of time **b** : an enemy airplane, submarine, or ship destroyed by military action

kill·deer \'kil-,diər\ *n, pl* **killdeers** *or* **killdeer** : a North American plover with a plaintive penetrating cry [imitative]

¹kill·er \'kil-ər\ *n* **1** : one that kills **2** : KILLER WHALE

²killer *adj* **1** : strikingly impressive or effective ⟨a *killer* smile⟩ **2** : extremely difficult to deal with ⟨a *killer* exam⟩; *also* : causing death or devastation ⟨a *killer* tornado⟩

killer cell *n* : a T cell that functions in an immune response by destroying a cell (as a tumor cell) having a specific antigenic molecule on its surface—called also *killer T cell*

killer whale *n* : a gregarious largely black flesh-eating whale 5 to 10 meters long

kil·li·fish \'kil-ē-,fish\ *n* : any of numerous small fishes including some used as bait, in mosquito control, and as aquarium fishes [earlier *killie*, from Dutch *kil* "river, stream"]

kill·ing \'kil-ing\ *n* **1** : the act of one that kills **2** : a quick profit

kill·joy \'kil-,jól\ *n* : a person who spoils others' fun

kiln \'kiln, 'kil\ *n* : an oven, furnace, or heated enclosure for processing a substance by burning, firing, or drying [Old English *cyln*, from Latin *culina* "kitchen"] — **kiln** *vt*

ki·lo \'kē-lō\ *n, pl* **kilos** : KILOGRAM

kilo- *combining form* : thousand [French, from Greek *chilioi*]

killer whale

ki·lo·cal·o·rie \'kē-lə-ˌkal-rē, 'kil-ə-, -ə-rē\ *n* : CALORIE 1b

kilo·cy·cle \'kil-ə-ˌsī-kəl\ *n* : 1000 cycles; *esp* : KILO-HERTZ

ki·lo·gram \'kē-lə-ˌgram, 'kil-ə-\ *n* **1** : the base unit of mass in the metric system that has been agreed upon by international convention and is nearly equal to the mass of 1000 cubic centimeters of water at its maximum density — see METRIC SYSTEM table **2** : the weight of a kilogram mass that is under a gravitational acceleration equal to that of the earth

ki·lo·hertz \'kil-ə-ˌhərts, 'kē-lə-, -ˌheərts\ *n* : 1000 hertz

kilo·joule \'kil-ə-ˌjül\ *n* : 1000 joules

kilo·li·ter \'kil-ə-ˌlēt-ər\ *n* — see METRIC SYSTEM table

ki·lo·me·ter \kil-'äm-ət-ər, 'kil-ə-ˌmēt-\ *n* — see MET-RIC SYSTEM table

ki·lo·pas·cal \ˌkil-ə-pas-ˈkal\ *n* : 1000 pascals

ki·lo·ton \'kil-ə-ˌtən, 'kē-lə- *also* -ˌtän\ *n* **1** : 1000 tons **2** : an explosive force equivalent to that of 1000 tons of TNT

ki·lo·volt \-ˌvōlt\ *n* : 1000 volts

kilo·watt \'kil-ə-ˌwät\ *n* : 1000 watts

kilowatt–hour *n* : a unit of work or energy (as electrical energy) equal to that expended in one hour at a rate of one kilowatt or to 3.6 million joules

kilt \'kilt\ *n* **1** : a knee-length pleated skirt usually of tartan worn by men in Scotland **2** : a garment that resembles a Scottish kilt [Middle English *kilten* "to gather up (a skirt)", of Scandinavian origin] — **kilt·ed** \'kil-təd\ *adj*

kil·ter \'kil-tər\ *n* : proper condition : ORDER (out of *kilter*) [origin unknown]

ki·mo·no \kə-'mō-nə\ *n, pl* **-nos** **1** : a loose robe with wide sleeves and a broad sash traditionally worn as an outer garment by the Japanese **2** : a loose dressing gown worn chiefly by women [Japanese, "clothes"]

¹kin \'kin\ *n* **1** : a person's relatives : KINDRED **2** : KINS-MAN [Old English *cyn*]

²kin *adj* : KINDRED, RELATED

-kin \kən\ *also* **-kins** \kənz\ *n suffix* : little ⟨nap*kin*⟩ [Dutch *-kin*]

¹kind \'kīnd\ *n* **1 a** : a natural group : VARIETY ⟨different *kinds* of sharks⟩ **b** : a group united by common qualities, traits, or interests : CATEGORY **c** : a doubtful or barely admissible member of a category ⟨a *kind* of gray⟩ **2** : essential quality or character ⟨punishment different in *kind* rather than degree⟩ **3 a** : goods or commodities as distinguished from money **b** : the equivalent of what has been offered or received [Old English *cynd* "birth, nature"] □ SYN SORT, TYPE: KIND and SORT are close synonyms and usually imply a group with less specific resemblances than TYPE; KIND may suggest natural or logical grouping; SORT sometimes suggests disparagement ⟨the flashier *sort* of holiday resorts⟩ TYPE may suggest clearly marked similarity throughout the items included so that each is typical of the group; TYPE, KIND, and SORT are usually interchangeable and are used most of the time without attention to special connotations.

²kind *adj* **1** : having the will to do good and to bring happiness to others **2** : showing or growing out of gentleness or goodness of heart ⟨a *kind* act⟩

kin·der·gar·ten \'kin-dər-ˌgärt-n, -də-, -ˌgärd-\ *n* : a school or class for children usually from four to six years old [German, from *kinder* "children" + *garten* "garden"]

kin·der·gart·ner \-ˌgärt-nər, -ˌgärd-\ *n* **1** : a kindergarten pupil **2** : a kindergarten teacher

kind·heart·ed \'kīnd-'härt-əd\ *adj* : having or showing a kind and sympathetic nature — **kind·heart·ed·ly** *adv* — **kind·heart·ed·ness** *n*

kin·dle \'kin-dl\ *vb* **kin·dled; kin·dling** \-dling, -dl-ing\ **1** : to set on fire or catch fire : start burning ⟨*kindle* a fire⟩ **2** : to stir up : AROUSE ⟨*kindle* anger⟩ **3** : to light

up as if with flame : GLOW ⟨with *kindling* eyes⟩ [Old Norse *kynda*] — **kin·dler** \-dlər, -dl-ər\ *n*

kin·dling \'kin-dling\ *n* : material that burns easily for starting a fire

¹kind·ly \'kīn-dlē\ *adj* **kind·li·er; -est** **1** : of an agreeable or beneficial nature : PLEASANT ⟨*kindly* climate⟩ **2** : of a sympathetic or generous nature : FRIENDLY ⟨*kindly* people⟩ — **kind·li·ness** *n*

²kindly *adv* **1** : READILY ⟨does not take *kindly* to criticism⟩ **2 a** : in a kind manner **b** : as a gesture of goodwill **c** : in a gracious manner : COURTEOUSLY **d** : as a matter of courtesy : PLEASE ⟨would you *kindly* be seated⟩

kind·ness \'kīnd-nəs, 'kīn-\ *n* **1** : a kind deed : FAVOR **2** : the quality or state of being kind

kind of \ˌkīn-dəv, -də\ *adv* : to a moderate degree : SOMEWHAT ⟨it's *kind* of cold in here⟩

¹kin·dred \'kin-drəd\ *n* **1** : a group of related individuals **2** : a person's relatives [Middle English, from *kin* + Old English *rǣden* "condition", from *rǣdan* "to advise, read"]

²kindred *adj* : of like nature or character

kine \'kīn\ *archaic pl of* COW

ki·ne·sics \kə-'nē-siks, kī-, -ziks\ *n* : the study of body motions (as blushes, shrugs, or eye movement) that communicate [Greek *kinēsis* "motion" + *-ics*]

ki·ne·si·ol·o·gy \kə-ˌnē-sē-'äl-ə-jē, kī-, -ˌnē-zē-\ *n* : the study of the mechanical and anatomical relations involved in human movement

-ki·ne·sis \kə-'nē-səs, kī-, ˌkī-\ *n combining form, pl* **-ki·ne·ses** \-ˌsēz\ : division ⟨karyo*kinesis*⟩ [Greek *kinēsis* "motion", from *kinein* "to move"]

kin·es·the·sia \ˌkin-əs-'thē-zhə, -zhē-ə\ *or* **kin·es·the·sis** \-'thē-səs\ *n, pl* **-the·sias** *or* **-the·ses** \-'thē-ˌsēz\ : the sensation of bodily position, movement, or effort arising from receptors in the joints, tendons, and muscles; *also* : the sense involved [Greek *kinein* "to move" + *aisthēsis* "perception"] — **kin·es·thet·ic** \-'thet-ik\ *adj* — **kin·es·thet·i·cal·ly** \-'thet-i-kə-lē, -klē\ *adv*

ki·net·ic \kə-'net-ik, kī-\ *adj* : of or relating to the motion of material bodies and the forces and energy associated with them [Greek *kinētikos*, from *kinein* "to move"]

kinetic energy *n* : energy associated with motion

ki·net·ics \kə-'net-iks, kī-\ *n sing or pl* **1** : a science that deals with the effects of forces upon the motions of material bodies or with changes in a physical or chemical system **2** : the means by which a physical or chemical change is effected

kinetic theory *n* : a theory that states that all matter is composed of particles in motion and that the rate of motion varies directly with the temperature

kin·folk \'kin-ˌfōk\ *n* : a person's relatives

king \'king\ *n* **1** : a male ruler of a country; *esp* : one whose position is hereditary and who rules for life **2** *cap* (1) : GOD 1 (2) : CHRIST **3** : one that holds a dominant position; *esp* : a chief among competitors **4** : the principal piece in a set of chessmen that can move ordinarily one square in any direction and has the power to capture but may never enter or remain in check **5** : a playing card bearing the stylized figure of a king **6** : a checker that has been crowned [Old English *cyning*]

king·bird \-ˌbərd\ *n* : an American tyrant flycatcher

king crab *n* **1** : HORSESHOE CRAB **2** : any of several large edible crabs

king·dom \'king-dəm\ *n* **1** : a country whose ruler is a king or queen **2** : a sphere in which something or someone is dominant **3 a** : one of the three primary divisions into which natural objects are classified — compare ANIMAL KINGDOM, MINERAL KINGDOM, PLANT KINGDOM **b** : a major category (as Plantae) in biological taxonomy that ranks above the phylum and is the highest and most encompassing group

kimono 1

kingfisher

kiwi

kingdom come *n* : the next world (as heaven) ⟨blew it to *kingdom come*⟩

king·fish \'king-ˌfish\ *n* : any of various sea fishes; *esp* : a large sport and food fish of the warm western Atlantic resembling the related Spanish mackerel

king·fish·er \-ˌfish-ər\ *n* : any of a family of usually crested and bright-colored birds with a short tail and a long stout sharp bill

king·let \'king-lət\ *n* : any of several small birds that resemble warblers but have some of the habits of titmice

king·ly \'king-lē\ *adj* **1** : having royal rank **2** : of, relating to, or befitting a king — **king·li·ness** *n* — **kingly** *adv*

king·pin \'king-ˌpin\ *n* **1** : the number 5 bowling pin **2** : the chief person in a group or undertaking

king post *n* : a vertical member connecting the apex of a triangular truss with the base

Kings \'kingz\ *n* — see BIBLE table

King's English *n* : standard or correct English speech or usage

king·ship \'king-ˌship\ *n* **1** : the position, office, or dignity of a king **2** : the personality of a king : MAJESTY **3** : government by a king

king–size \'king-ˌsīz\ *or* **king–sized** \-ˌsīzd\ *adj* : longer or larger than the usual or standard size

king snake *n* : any of numerous harmless brightly marked snakes of the southern and central United States that feed on rodents

king's ransom *n* : a very large sum of money

¹kink \'kingk\ *n* **1** : a short tight twist or curl **2** : a mental or physical peculiarity : QUIRK **3** : a cramp or stiffness in some part of the body : CRICK **4** : an imperfection (as in design) likely to cause difficulties in operation [Dutch] — **kinky** \'king-kē\ *adj*

²kink *vb* : to form a kink : make a kink in

kin·ka·jou \'king-kə-ˌjü\ *n* : a slender long-tailed mammal of Central and South America related to the raccoon [French, of American Indian origin]

-kins — see -KIN

kins·folk \'kinz-ˌfōk\ *n* : a person's relatives

kin·ship \'kin-ˌship\ *n* : the quality or state of being kin

kins·man \'kinz-mən\ *n* : RELATIVE 3; *esp* : a male relative

kins·wom·an \'kinz-ˌwu̇m-ən\ *n* : a female relative

ki·osk \'kē-ˌäsk, kē-'\ *n* **1** : an open summerhouse or pavilion **2** : a small light structure with one or more open sides used especially as a newsstand or a telephone booth [Turkish *köşk,* from Persian *kūshk* "portico"]

¹kip·per \'kip-ər\ *n* : a kippered herring or salmon [Old English *cypera* "spawning salmon"]

²kipper *vt* **kip·pered; kip·per·ing** \'kip-ring, -ə-ring\ : to cure by salting and smoking

Kir·ghiz \kiər-'gēz\ *n* : a member of a Mongolian people with some Caucasian intermixture inhabiting chiefly the Kirghiz Republic

kirk \'kiərk, 'kərk\ *n* **1** *chiefly Scottish* : CHURCH 1 **2** *cap* : the national church of Scotland as distinguished from the Church of England or the Anglican Church in Scotland [Old Norse *kirkja,* from Old English *cirice*]

kir·tle \'kərt-l\ *n* **1** : a tunic or coat worn by men in the Middle Ages **2** : a long gown or dress worn by a woman [Old English *cyrtel*]

¹kiss \'kis\ *vb* **1** : to touch with the lips as a mark of affection or greeting **2** : to touch gently or lightly ⟨a soft wind *kissing* the trees⟩ [Old English *cyssan*] — **kiss·able** \-ə-bəl\ *adj*

²kiss *n* **1** : a caress with the lips **2** : a gentle touch or contact **3 a** : a small cookie made of meringue **b** : a bite-size candy

kiss·er \'kis-ər\ *n* **1** : one that kisses **2** *slang* : MOUTH 1a; *also* : FACE 1

¹kit \'kit\ *n* **1 a** : a collection of articles for personal use ⟨a shaving *kit*⟩ **b** : a set of tools or supplies ⟨a first-aid *kit*⟩ **c** : a set of parts to be assembled ⟨model-airplane *kit*⟩ **d** : a packaged collection of related material ⟨convention *kit*⟩ **2** : a container (as a bag or case) for a kit **3** : a group of persons or things — used in the phrase the whole kit and caboodle [Middle English, "wooden tub"]

²kit *n* **1** : KITTEN **2** : a young or undersized fur-bearing animal; *also* : its pelt

³kit *n* : a small narrow violin [origin unknown]

kitch·en \'kich-ən\ *n* : a place (as a room) with cooking facilities [Old English *cycene,* from Late Latin *coquina,* from Latin *coquere* "to cook"]

kitchen cabinet *n* **1** : a cupboard with drawers and shelves for use in a kitchen **2** : an informal group of advisers to the head of a government

kitch·en·ette \ˌkich-ə-'net\ *n* : a small kitchen or an alcove containing cooking facilities

kitchen garden *n* : a plot in which vegetables are grown for domestic use

kitchen midden *n* : a refuse heap; *esp* : a mound marking the site of a primitive human habitation

kitchen police *n* : KP

kitch·en·ware \'kich-ən-ˌwaər, -ˌweər\ *n* : utensils and appliances for use in a kitchen

kite \'kīt\ *n* **1** : any of various hawks with long narrow wings, a deeply forked tail, and feet adapted for taking insects and small reptiles as prey **2** : a light frame covered with paper or cloth, often provided with a balancing tail, and designed to be flown in the air at the end of a long string [Old English *cȳta*]

kith \'kith\ *n* : familiar friends, neighbors, or relatives ⟨*kith* and kin⟩ [Old English *cȳththth,* from *cūth* "known"]

kitsch \'kich\ *n* : something that appeals to popular or lowbrow taste and is often of poor quality [German]

kit·ten \'kit-n\ *n* : the young of a small mammal and especially of a cat [Middle English *kitoun,* derived from Late Latin *cattus* "cat"]

kit·ten·ish \'kit-nish, -n-ish\ *adj* : resembling a kitten; *esp* : PLAYFUL — **kit·ten·ish·ly** *adv* — **kit·ten·ish·ness** *n*

kit·ti·wake \'kit-ē-ˌwāk\ *n* : any of various gulls having the hind toe short and the wing tips black [imitative]

¹kit·ty \'kit-ē\ *n, pl* **kitties** : CAT 1a; *esp* : KITTEN

²kitty *n, pl* **kitties** **1** : a fund in a poker game made up of contributions from each pot **2** : a sum of money or a collection of goods made up of small contributions : POOL [¹*kit*]

kit·ty–cor·ner *or* **kit·ty–cor·nered** *variant of* CATERCORNER

ki·va \'kē-və\ *n* : a Pueblo Indian ceremonial structure that is usually round and partly underground [Hopi]

Ki·wa·ni·an \kə-'wän-ē-ən\ *n* : a member of one of the major service clubs

ki·wi \'kē-ˌwē\ *n* : a flightless New Zealand bird with rudimentary wings, stout legs, a long bill, and grayish brown hairlike plumage [Maori]

Klan \'klan\ *n* : an organization of Ku Kluxers; *also* : a subordinate unit of such an organization — **Klans·man** \'klanz-mən\ *n*

Klee·nex \'klē-ˌneks\ *trademark* — used for a cleansing tissue

klep·to·ma·nia \ˌklep-tə-'mā-nē-ə, -nyə\ *n* : a persistent neurotic impulse to steal especially without economic motive [Greek *kleptein* "to steal"] — **klep·to·ma·ni·ac** \-nē-ˌak\ *adj or n*

klez·mer \'klez-mər\ *n, pl* **klez·mo·rim** \klez-'mór-əm\ **1** : a Jewish instrumentalist especially of traditional eastern European music **2** : the music played by klezmorim [Yiddish, from Hebrew *kēlēy zemer* musical instruments]

klieg light *or* **kleig light** \'klēg-ˌlīt\ *n* : an arc lamp used in taking motion pictures [John H. *Kliegl,* died 1959, and Anton T. *Kliegl,* died 1927, German-born American lighting experts]

knack \'nak\ *n* **1** : a clever way of doing something : TRICK **2** : a natural ability : TALENT [Middle English *knak*]

knack·er \'nak-ər\ *n, British* : a buyer of worn-out animals or their carcasses especially for use as animal feed and fertilizer [probably from English dialect *knacker* "saddle maker"]

knap·sack \'nap-,sak\ *n* : a case strapped on the back to carry supplies while on a march or hike [Low German *knappsack*, from *knappen* "to eat" + *sack* "bag"]

knap·weed \'nap-,wēd\ *n* : any of several weedy plants related to the cornflower [Middle English *knopwed*, from *knop* "knob" + *wed* "weed"]

knave \'nāv\ *n* **1** *archaic* **a** : a male servant **b** : a person of humble birth or position **2** : a tricky deceitful person : ROGUE **3** : JACK 5 [Old English *cnafa* "boy, servant"]

knav·ery \'nāv-rē, -ə-rē\ *n, pl* **-er·ies** **1** : the practices of a knave : RASCALITY **2** : a roguish or mischievous act

knav·ish \'nā-vish\ *adj* : of, relating to, or characteristic of a knave; *esp* : DISHONEST — **knav·ish·ly** *adv*

knead \'nēd\ *vt* **1** : to work and press into a mass with or as if with the hands **2** : to form or shape as if by kneading [Old English *cnedan*] — **knead·er** *n*

¹knee \'nē\ *n* **1** : the joint or middle part of the human leg in which the femur, tibia, and kneecap come together; *also* : a corresponding part of a four-footed animal **2** : something resembling the human knee **3** : the part of a garment covering the knee [Old English *cnēow*] — **kneed** \'nēd\ *adj* — **to one's knees** : into a state of submission or defeat

²knee *vt* **kneed; knee·ing** : to strike with the knee

knee·cap \'nē-,kap\ *n* : a thick flat triangular bone that forms the front part of the knee and protects the front of the joint — called also *patella*

knee–deep \-'dēp\ *adj* : sunk to the knees ⟨*knee-deep* in mud⟩

knee–high \-'hī\ *adj* : rising or reaching upward to the knees

knee·hole \-,hōl\ *n* : a space (as under a desk) for the knees

knee jerk *n* : an involuntary forward kick produced by a light blow on the tendon below the kneecap

kneel \'nēl\ *vi* **knelt** \'nelt\ *or* **kneeled** \'nēld\; **kneeling** : to bend the knee : fall or rest on the knees [Old English *cnēowlian*] — **kneel·er** *n*

¹knell \'nel\ *vb* **1** : to ring especially for a death, funeral, or disaster : TOLL **2** : to sound as a knell **3** : to summon or announce by or as if by a knell [Old English *cnyllan*]

²knell *n* **1** : a stroke or sound of a bell especially when rung slowly for a death, funeral, or disaster **2** : DEATH KNELL

knew *past of* KNOW

knick·er·bock·er \'nik-ər-,bäk-ər, 'nik-ə-,\ *n* **1** *cap* : a native or resident of the city or state of New York; *esp* : a descendant of the early Dutch settlers of New York **2** *pl* : KNICKERS [Diedrich *Knickerbocker*, fictitious author of *History of New York* (1809) by Washington Irving]

knick·ers \'nik-ərz\ *n pl* : loose-fitting short pants gathered just below the knee [short for *knickerbockers*]

knick·knack *or* **nick·nack** \'nik-,nak\ *n* : a small article intended for ornament [reduplication of *knack*]

¹knife \'nīf\ *n, pl* **knives** \'nīvz\ **1 a** : a cutting instrument consisting of a sharp blade fastened to a handle **b** : a weapon resembling a knife **2** : a sharp cutting blade or tool in a machine [Old English *cnīf*]

²knife *vb* **1** : to stab, slash, or wound with a knife **2** : to move like a knife ⟨*knifed* through the water⟩

knife–edge \'nī-,fej\ *n* : a sharp wedge usually of steel used as a fulcrum for a lever beam in a precision instrument (as a balance)

knife pleat *n* : one of a series of narrow sharply pressed pleats all turned in one direction

¹knight \'nīt\ *n* **1 a** : a mounted warrior of feudal times serving a superior (as a king); *esp* : one who after a period of early service has been awarded a special military rank and has sworn to obey certain rules of conduct **b** : a man honored by a sovereign for merit and in Great Britain ranking below a baronet **c** : a person of another age or area resembling a medieval knight in rank or way of life **d** : a member of any of various orders or societies **e** : a man devoted to the service of a lady as her attendant or champion **2** : a chess piece that has an L-shaped move of two squares in any row and one square in a perpendicular row over squares that may be occupied [Old English *cniht* "boy, warrior"]

²knight *vt* : to make a knight of

knight bachelor *n, pl* **knights bachelor** : a knight of the most ancient and lowest order of English knights

knight–er·rant \'nīt-'er-ənt\ *n, pl* **knights–errant** : a knight traveling in search of adventures in which to exhibit his military skill and generosity — **knight–er·rant·ry** \'nīt-'er-ən-trē\ *n*

knight·hood \'nīt-,hùd\ *n* **1** : the rank, dignity, or profession of a knight **2** : the qualities befitting a knight **3** : knights as a class or body

knight·ly \'nīt-lē\ *adj* **1** : of, relating to, or characteristic of a knight **2** : made up of knights — **knight·li·ness** *n* — **knightly** *adv*

Knight of Co·lum·bus \-kə-'ləm-bəs\ *n, pl* **Knights of Columbus** : a member of a fraternal and benevolent society of Roman Catholic men [Christopher *Columbus*]

Knight Templar *n, pl* **Knights Templars** *or* **Knights Templar** **1** : TEMPLAR 1 **2** : a member of an order of Freemasonry

knish \kə-'nish\ *n* : a small round or square piece of dough stuffed with a filling (as potato) and baked or fried [Yiddish, from Polish *knysz*]

¹knit \'nit\ *vb* **knit** *or* **knit·ted; knit·ting** **1** : to form a fabric or garment by interlacing yarn or thread in connected loops with needles ⟨*knit* a sweater⟩ **2** : to draw or come together closely as if knitted : unite firmly ⟨wait for a broken bone to *knit*⟩ **3** : WRINKLE ⟨*knit* one's brows⟩ **4** : to bind by some tie ⟨*knit* by common interests⟩ [Old English *cnyttan*] — **knit·ter** *n*

²knit *n* : KNIT STITCH; *also* : a knit fabric

knit stitch *n* : a basic knitting stitch usually made with the yarn at the back of the work by inserting the right needle into the front part of a loop on the left needle from the left side, catching the yarn with the point of the right needle, and bringing it through the first loop to form a new loop — compare PURL STITCH

knit·ting *n* **1** : the action or method of one that knits **2** : work done or being done by one that knits

knitting needle *n* : a slender rod (as of plastic or metal) with one or both ends pointed used for hand knitting

knit·wear \'nit-,waər, -,weər\ *n* : knitted clothing

knob \'näb\ *n* **1 a** : a rounded bulge : LUMP **b** : a small rounded ornament or handle **2** : a rounded usually isolated hill or mountain [Middle English *knobbe*] — **knobbed** \'näbd\ *adj* — **knob·by** \'näb-ē\ *adj*

¹knock \'näk\ *vb* **1 a** : to strike something with a sharp blow **b** : to drive, force, or make by so striking **2** : to collide with something **3 a** : BUSTLE ⟨*knocked* around in the kitchen most of the afternoon⟩ **b** : WANDER ⟨*knocked* about the world for years⟩ **4** : to make a pounding noise especially as a result of abnormal ignition ⟨an automobile engine that *knocks*⟩ **5** : to find fault with [Old English *cnocian*] — **knock together** : to make or assemble especially hurriedly or in a makeshift way

²knock *n* **1 a** : a sharp blow **b** : a severe misfortune or hardship **2 a** : a pounding noise **b** : a sharp metallic noise in an automobile engine caused by abnormal ignition

¹knock·about \'näk-ə-,baùt\ *adj* **1** : suitable for rough use **2** : being noisy and rough ⟨*knockabout* games⟩

\ə\ abut		\ng\ sing	
\ər\ further		\ō\ bone	
\a\ mat		\ȯ\ saw	
\ā\ take		\ȯi\ coin	
\ä\ cot, cart		\th\ thin	
\aù\ out		\th\ this	
\ch\ chin		\ü\ food	
\e\ pet		\ù\ foot	
\ē\ easy		\y\ yet	
\g\ go		\yü\ few	
\i\ tip		\yù\ cure	
\ī\ life		\zh\ vision	
\j\ job			

²**knockabout** *n* : a sloop with a simple rig and no bow-sprit and topmast

¹**knock·down** \'näk-,daun\ *n* **I** : a knocking down of something or someone (as a boxer) **2** : something that strikes down or overwhelms **3** : something easily assembled or disassembled

²**knockdown** *adj* **I** : having such force as to strike down or overwhelm **2** : that can easily be assembled or disassembled

knock down \näk-'daun, 'näk-\ *vt* **I** : to dispose of to a bidder at an auction sale **2** : to take apart : DISASSEMBLE

knock·er \'näk-ər\ *n* : one that knocks; *esp* : a device hinged to a door for use in knocking

knock-knee \'näk-'nē, -,nē\ *n* : a condition in which the legs curve inward at the knees — **knock-kneed** \-'nēd\ *adj*

knock off *vb* : to discontinue doing something : STOP

knock·out \'näk-,aut\ *n* **I a** : the act of knocking out : the condition of being knocked out **b** : a blow that knocks out an opponent **2** : something or someone sensationally striking or attractive — **knockout** *adj*

knock out \näk-'aut, 'näk-\ *vt* **I** : to knock (a boxing opponent) unconscious **2** : to make inoperative, useless, or unconscious

knock over *vt* **STEAL: a** : HIJACK 1 **b** : ROB 1

knock·wurst \'näk-wərst, -,wərst\ *n* : a short thick sausage [German knackwurst, from *knacken* "to crackle (when being fried)" + *wurst* "sausage"]

knoll \'nōl\ *n* : a small round hill : MOUND [Old English *cnoll*]

¹**knot** \'nät\ *n* **I** : an interlacing (as of string or ribbon) that forms a lump or knob **2** : something hard to solve : PROBLEM **3** : a bond of union; *esp* : the marriage bond **4 a** : a projecting lump or swelling in tissue **b** : the base of a woody branch enclosed in the stem from which it arises; *also* : its section in lumber **5** : a cluster of persons or things : GROUP **6** : one nautical mile per hour [Old English *cnotta*]

²**knot** *vb* **knot·ted; knot·ting** **I** : to tie in or with a knot : form knots in **2** : to unite closely or intricately : ENTANGLE

³**knot** *n* : any of several sandpipers that breed in the Arctic and winter in temperate or warm regions [Middle English *knott*]

knot·grass \'nät-,gras\ *n* : a weed related to buckwheat with bluish gray grassy leaves and tiny flowers

knot·hole \-,hōl\ *n* : a hole in a board or tree trunk where a knot has come out

knot·ted *adj* **I** : tied in or with a knot **2** : full of knots : GNARLED **3** : KNOTTY 2 **4** : ornamented with knots or knobs

knot·ty \'nät-ē\ *adj* **knot·ti·er; -est** **I** : marked by or full of knots **2** : puzzling because of intricacy : COMPLEX

knout \'naut, 'nüt\ *n* : a whip for flogging criminals [Russian *knut*, of Scandinavian origin]

¹**know** \'nō\ *vb* **knew** \'nü, 'nyü\; **known** \'nōn\; **know·ing** **I a** (1) : to perceive directly : have direct awareness of (2) : to have understanding of ⟨*know* yourself⟩ **b** (1) : to perceive and remember the identity of : RECOGNIZE (2) : to be acquainted or familiar with **2 a** : to be able to declare truthfully ⟨*know* them to be honest⟩ **b** : to have a practical understanding of ⟨*knows* how to write⟩ **3** : to have knowledge **4** : to be or become aware ⟨*knew* about us⟩ [Old English *cnāwan*] — **know·able** \'nō-ə-bəl\ *adj* — **know·er** \'nō-ər, 'nōr\ *n*

²**know** *n* : KNOWLEDGE — **in the know** : having confidential or exclusive information

know-how \'nō-,hau\ *n* : knowledge of how to do something smoothly and efficiently

¹**know·ing** \'nō-ing\ *n* : ACQUAINTANCE 1, COGNIZANCE

²**knowing** *adj* **I** : having or reflecting knowledge, information, or intelligence ⟨a *knowing* glance⟩ **2** :

shrewdly and keenly alert **3** : INTENTIONAL — **know·ing·ly** \-ing-lē\ *adv*

know-it-all \'nō-ət-,ål\ *n* : a person who claims to know everything and needs no advice

knowl·edge \'näl-ij\ *n* **I** : understanding gained by actual experience ⟨a *knowledge* of carpentry⟩ **2 a** : the state of being aware of something or of having information **b** : range of information or awareness ⟨to the best of my *knowledge*⟩ **3** : the act of understanding : clear perception of truth **4** : something learned and kept in the mind : LEARNING [Middle English *knowlege* "acknowledgment, cognizance", from *knowlechen* "to acknowledge", from *knowen* "to know"]

knowl·edge·able \'näl-i-jə-bəl\ *adj* : having or exhibiting knowledge or intelligence : WISE — **knowl·edge·able·ness** *n* — **knowl·edge·ably** \-blē\ *adv*

knowledge engineering *n* : a branch of artificial intelligence that emphasizes the development and use of expert systems — **knowledge engineer** *n*

know-noth·ing \'nō-,nəth-ing\ *n* **I** : IGNORAMUS **2** *cap* *K&N* : a member of a 19th-century secret American political organization hostile to the political influence of recent immigrants and Roman Catholics

¹**knuck·le** \'nək-əl\ *n* **I** : the rounded lump formed by the ends of two bones where they come together in a joint; *esp* : such a lump at a finger joint **2** : a cut of meat consisting of a tarsal or carpal joint with the adjoining flesh **3** *pl* : a set of joined metal finger rings worn over the front of the fist for use as a weapon — called also *brass knuckles* [Middle English *knokel*]

²**knuckle** *vi* **knuck·led; knuck·ling** \'nək-ling, -ə-ling\ : to place the knuckles on the ground in shooting a marble

knuck·le·bone \,nək-əl-'bōn, 'nək-əl-,\ *n* : a bone of a knuckle joint

knuckle down *vi* : to apply oneself earnestly

knuckle under *vi* : to give in : SUBMIT

knurl \'nərl\ *n* **I** : a small protuberance or knob; *also* : a gnarl or twisted knot of wood **2** : one of a series of small ridges or beads on a metal surface (as of a thumbscrew) to aid in gripping [probably blend of *knur* "gnarl" (from Middle English *knorre*) and *gnarl*] — **knurled** \'nərld\ *adj* — **knurly** \'nər-lē\ *adj*

¹**KO** \kā-'ō, 'kā-ō\ *n, pl* **KO's** : a knockout in boxing [*kn*ock *o*ut]

²**KO** *vt* **KO'd; KO'·ing** : to knock out in boxing

ko·ala \kō-'äl-ə, kə-'wäl-ə\ *n* : an Australian marsupial that has large hairy ears, gray fur, and no tail and lives in eucalyptus trees where it feeds on the leaves [native name in Australia]

ko·bold \'kō-,bōld\ *n* **I** : a gnome that in German folklore inhabits underground places **2** : an often mischievous spirit of German folklore [German]

Koch's postulates \'kóks-\ *n pl* : a statement of the steps required to identify a microorganism as the cause of a disease [Robert *Koch*, died 1910, German bacteriologist]

kohl \'kōl\ *n* : a preparation used especially in Arabia and Egypt to darken the edges of the eyelids [Arabic *kuḥl*]

kohl·ra·bi \kōl-'räb-ē, -'rab-\ *n, pl* **-bies** : a cabbage that forms no head but has a swollen fleshy edible stem [German, from Italian *cavolo rapa*, from *cavolo* "cabbage" + *rapa* "turnip"]

ko·la nut \'kō-lə-\ *n* : the bitter seed of an African tree containing much caffeine and used in beverages and medicine for its stimulant effect [of African origin]

ko·lin·sky *or* **ko·lin·ski** \kə-'lin-skē\ *n, pl* **-skies** **I** : any of several Asian minks **2** : the fur or pelt of a kolinsky [Russian *kolinskii* "of Kola", from *Kola*, town and peninsula in the Soviet Union]

kol·khoz \käl-'kóz, -'kós\ *n, pl* **kol·kho·zy** \-'kó-zē\ *or* **kol·khoz·es** : a collective farm of the Soviet Union — compare SOVKHOZ [Russian, from *kol*lektivnoe *khoz*yaĭstvo "collective farm"]

knot: *I* granny, 2 half hitch, 3 square, 4 overhand, 5 slipknot

koala

Kol Nidre \kōl-'nid-rā\ *n* : an Aramaic prayer chanted in the synagogue on the eve of Yom Kippur [Aramaic *kol nidhrē* "all the vows"; from its opening phrase]

kook \'kük\ *n* : a person whose ideas or actions are eccentric or crazy [from *cuckoo*] — **kooky** \'kü-kē\ *adj*

kook·a·bur·ra \'kük-ə-ˌbər-ə, 'kük-, -ˌbə-rə\ *n* : an Australian kingfisher that is about the size of a crow and has a call resembling loud laughter [native name in Australia]

ko·peck *or* **ko·pek** \'kō-ˌpek\ *n* 1 : a monetary unit equal to 1/100 ruble 2 : a coin representing one kopeck [Russian *kopeïka*]

Ko·ran \kə-'ran, -'rän; 'kōr-ˌan, 'kȯr-\ *n* : the book composed of writings accepted by Muslims as revelations made to Muhammad by Allah [Arabic *qur'ān*] — **Ko·ran·ic** \kə-'ran-ik\ *adj*

Ko·re·an \kə-'rē-ən\ *n* 1 : a native or inhabitant of Korea 2 : the language of the Korean people — **Korean** *adj*

ko·ru·na \'kȯr-ə-ˌnä, 'kär-\ *n, pl* **ko·ru·ny** \-ə-nē\ *or* **korunas** 1 : the basic monetary unit of Czechoslovakia 2 : a coin or note representing one koruna [Czech, literally, "crown", from Latin *corona*]

¹**ko·sher** \'kō-shər\ *adj* 1 a : accepted by Jewish law; *esp* : ritually fit for use b : selling or serving food ritually fit according to Jewish law 2 : PROPER 1 [Yiddish, from Hebrew *kāshēr* "fit, proper"]

²**kosher** *vt* **ko·shered; ko·sher·ing** \-shə-ring, -shring\ : to make kosher

kou·miss *or* **ku·miss** \kü-'mis, 'kü-məs\ *n* : a fermented milk beverage made originally by the nomadic peoples of central Asia from mare's milk [Russian *kumys*]

¹**kow·tow** \kau-'tau, 'kau-,\ *n* : an act of kowtowing [Chinese (Pekingese dialect) *k'o¹ t'ou²*, from *k'o¹* "to bump" + *t'ou²* "head"]

²**kowtow** *vi* 1 : to kneel and touch the forehead to the ground to show honor, worship, or deep respect 2 : to show slavish respect

KP \'kā-'pē\ *n, pl* **KPs** 1 : the military duty of helping to prepare, serve, and clean up after meals 2 : a person assigned to KP [*k*itchen *p*olice]

¹**kraal** \'krȯl, 'kräl\ *n* 1 : a village of southern African natives 2 : an enclosure for domestic animals in southern Africa [Afrikaans, from Portuguese *curral* "enclosure, corral"]

²**kraal** *vt* : to pen in a kraal

kraft \'kraft\ *n* : a strong paper or board used especially for paper bags and corrugated boxes [German, literally, "strength"]

krait \'krīt\ *n* : any of several brightly banded extremely venomous mostly Asian snakes [Hindi *karait*]

K ration \'kā-\ *n* : a lightweight packaged ration of emergency foods developed for the United States armed forces in World War II [A. B. *Keys*, born 1904, American physiologist]

kraut \'kraut\ *n* : SAUERKRAUT

Krebs cycle \'krebz-\ *n* : a sequence of reactions in the living organism in which oxidation of acetyl groups to carbon dioxide provides energy stored in ATP [H. A. *Krebs*, died 1900, German-born British biochemist]

krem·lin \'krem-lən\ *n* 1 : the citadel of a Russian city 2 *cap* : the government of the Soviet Union [derived from Russian *kreml'*; sense 2 from the *Kremlin*, citadel of Moscow and governing center of the Soviet Union]

kreu·zer \'krȯit-sər\ *n* : a small coin formerly used in Austria, Germany, and Hungary [German]

krill \'kril\ *n* : small planktonic organisms (as crustaceans and larvae) that form a major food of whales [Norwegian *kril* "recently hatched fishes"]

krim·mer \'krim-ər\ *n* : a gray fur made from the pelts of young lambs of the Crimean peninsula region [German, from *Krim* "Crimea"]

kris \'krēs\ *n* : a Malay or Indonesian dagger with a ridged and twisting blade [Malay *kĕris*]

¹**kro·na** \'krō-nə\ *n, pl* **kro·nur** \-nər\ 1 : the basic monetary unit of Iceland 2 : a coin representing one krona [Icelandic *krōna*, literally, "crown"]

²**kro·na** \'krō-nə, 'krü-\ *n, pl* **kro·nor** \-ˌnȯr, -nər\ 1 : the basic monetary unit of Sweden 2 : a coin representing one krona [Swedish, literally, "crown"]

¹**kro·ne** \'krō-nə\ *n, pl* **kro·nen** \-nən\ 1 : the basic monetary unit of Austria from 1892 to 1925 2 : a coin representing one krone [German, literally, "crown"]

²**kro·ne** \'krō-nə\ *n, pl* **kro·ner** \-nər\ 1 : the basic monetary unit of Denmark and Norway 2 : a coin representing one krone [Danish, literally, "crown"]

kryp·ton \'krip-ˌtän\ *n* : a colorless inert gaseous chemical element found in air and used especially in electric lamps — see ELEMENT table [Greek *kryptos* "hidden", from *kryptein* "to hide"]

ku·do \'kyüd-ō, 'küd-\ *n, pl* **kudos** : AWARD, HONOR [back-formation from *kudos* (taken as a pl.)]

ku·dos \'kyü-ˌdäs, 'kü-, -ˌdōs\ *n* : FAME, GLORY [Greek *kydos*]

ku·du *or* **koo·doo** \'küd-ü\ *n* : a large grayish brown African antelope with long ringed spirally twisted horns [Afrikaans *koedoe*]

kud·zu \'kud-zü\ *n* : a trailing Asian leguminous vine used widely for hay and forage and for erosion control [Japanese *kuzu*]

Ku Klux·er \'kü-ˌkləks-sər, 'kyü-\ *n* : a member of the Ku Klux Klan — **Ku Klux·ism** \-ˌkləks-ˌsiz-əm\ *n*

Ku Klux Klan \-ˌkü-ˌkləks-'klan, ˌkyü-, *also* ˌklü-\ *n* 1 : a post-Civil War secret society favoring white supremacy 2 : a 20th-century secret fraternal group held to confine its membership to American-born Protestant whites

ku·lak \kü-'lak, kyü-\ *n* : a prosperous peasant farmer in Czarist and early Soviet Russia [Russian, literally, "fist"]

kul·tur \kul-'tur\ *n, often cap* : German culture held to be superior especially by militant Nazi and Hohenzollern expansionists [German, "culture", from Latin *cultura*]

kum·quat \'kəm-ˌkwät\ *n* 1 : a small citrus fruit with sweet spongy rind and somewhat acid pulp used especially for preserves 2 : a tree or shrub that bears kumquats [Chinese (Cantonese dialect) *kam kwat*, from *kam* "gold" + *kwat* "orange"]

kung fu \ˌkəng-'fü, ˌkung-\ *n* : a Chinese system of self-defense that resembles karate [Chinese dialect; related to Chinese (Pekingese dialect) *ch'üan² fa³*, literally, "boxing principles"]

Kurd \'kurd, 'kərd\ *n* : a member of a nomadic herding and agricultural people inhabiting a plateau region in bordering parts of Turkey, Iran, Iraq, Syria, and Soviet Armenia and Azerbaidzhan — **Kurd·ish** \-ish\ *adj*

Kurd·ish \'kurd-ish, 'kərd-\ *n* : the Iranian language of the Kurds

kwash·i·or·kor \ˌkwäsh-ē-'ȯr-kər\ *n* : a disease of young children resulting from inadequate intake of protein [native name in Ghana, literally, "red boy"]

ky·pho·sis \kī-'fō-səs\ *n* : abnormal backward curvature of the spine — compare LORDOSIS, SCOLIOSIS [Greek *kyphōsis*, from *kyphos* "humpbacked"] — **ky·phot·ic** \-'fät-ik\ *adj*

ky·rie \'kir-ē-ˌā\ *n, often cap* : a short liturgical prayer that begins with or consists of the words "Lord have mercy" [Late Latin *kyrie eleison*, transliteration of Greek *kyrie eleēson* "Lord, have mercy"]

ky·rie elei·son \ˌkir-ē-ˌā-ə-'lā-ə-ˌsän, -ə-sən\ *n, often cap* K&E : KYRIE

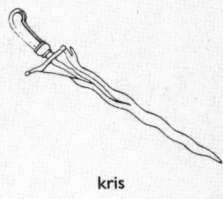

kris

\ə\ abut	\ng\ sing
\ər\ further	\ō\ bone
\a\ mat	\ȯ\ saw
\ā\ take	\ȯi\ coin
\ä\ cot, cart	\th\ thin
\au\ out	\th\ this
\ch\ chin	\ü\ food
\e\ pet	\u\ foot
\ē\ easy	\y\ yet
\g\ go	\yü\ few
\i\ tip	\yu\ cure
\ī\ life	\zh\ vision
\j\ job	

Ll

l \'el\ *n, pl* **l's** *or* **ls** \'elz\ *often cap* **1** : the 12th letter of the English alphabet **2** : fifty in Roman numerals

la \'lä\ *n* : the 6th note of the diatonic scale [Medieval Latin]

lab \'lab\ *n* : LABORATORY

¹la·bel \'lā-bəl\ *n* **1** : a slip (as of paper or cloth) with writing on it that is attached to something for identification or description **2** : a descriptive or identifying word or phrase : EPITHET [Middle French, "strip of cloth, ribbon"]

²label *vt* **la·beled** *or* **la·belled; la·bel·ing** *or* **la·bel·ling** \'lā-bə-ling, -bling\ **1 a** : to affix a label to ⟨*label* a medicine bottle⟩ **b** : to describe as : CALL ⟨*labeled* their opponents cheats⟩ **2** : to make (a chemical element) traceable (as through the steps of a biochemical process) by substitution of a detectable isotope — **la·bel·er** \-bə-lər, -blər\ *n*

la·bel·lum \lə-'bel-əm\ *n, pl* **-bel·la** \-'bel-ə\ : the median and often spurred petal of the corolla of an orchid [Latin, "little lip", from *labrum* "lip"] — **la·bel·late** \lə-'bel-ət\ *adj*

¹la·bi·al \'lā-bē-əl\ *adj* **1** : of or relating to the lips or labia **2** : uttered with the participation of one or both lips ⟨the *labial* sounds \f\, \p\, and \ü\⟩ [Latin *labium* "lip"] — **la·bi·al·ly** \-ə-lē\ *adv*

²labial *n* : a labial consonant

¹la·bi·ate \'lā-bē-ət, -bē-,āt\ *adj* **1** : LIPPED; *esp* : having a tubular corolla or calyx divided into two unequal parts projecting one over the other like lips **2** : of or relating to the mint family

²labiate *n* : a plant of the mint family

la·bile \'lā-,bīl, -bəl\ *adj* **1** : readily open to change : ADAPTABLE **2** : readily or continually undergoing chemical or physical change : UNSTABLE ⟨a *labile* mineral⟩ [French, from Late Latin *labilis* "fleeting, transient", from Latin *labi* "to slip"] — **la·bil·i·ty** \lā-'bil-ət-ē\ *n*

labio- *combining form* : labial and ⟨*labio*dental⟩

la·bio·den·tal \,lā-bē-ō-'dent-l\ *adj* : uttered with the participation of lip and teeth ⟨the *labiodental* sounds \f\ and \v\⟩ — **labiodental** *n*

la·bi·um \'lā-bē-əm\ *n, pl* **-bia** \-bē-ə\ **1** : any of the folds at the margin of the vulva **2** : the lower lip of a labiate corolla **3 a** : the lower lip of an insect **b** : a liplike part of various invertebrates [Latin, "lip"]

¹la·bor \'lā-bər\ *n* **1 a** : expenditure of physical or mental effort especially when difficult or compulsory **b** (1) : human activity that provides the goods or services in an economy (2) : the services performed by workers for wages as distinguished from those rendered by entrepreneurs for profits **c** (1) : the physical activities involved in childbirth (2) : the period of such labor **2** : TASK **3** : a product of labor **4 a** : those who do manual labor or work for wages **b** : labor unions or their officials **5** *usually* **La·bour** \-bər\ : the Labour party of the United Kingdom or of another nation of the Commonwealth [Old French, from Latin]

²labor *vb* **la·bored; la·bor·ing** \-bə-ring, -bring\ **1 a** : to exert one's body or mind : WORK **b** : to work for wages usually in actual production of goods **2** : to move with great effort **3** : to suffer from some disadvantage or distress ⟨*labor* under a delusion⟩ **4** : to pitch or roll heavily ⟨the ship *labored* in a rough sea⟩ **5** : to treat or work out in elaborate detail ⟨*labor* the obvious⟩ — **la·bor·er** \-bər-ər\ *n*

³labor *adj* **1** : of or relating to labor **2** *or* **Labour** *cap* : of, relating to, or constituting a political party held to represent the interests of workers or characterized by a membership in which organized labor groups predominate

lab·o·ra·to·ry \'lab-rə-,tōr-ē, -ə-rə-, -,tòr-\ *n, pl* **-ries** : a place equipped for experimental study in a science or for testing and analysis; *also* : a place providing opportunity for experimentation, observation, or practice in a field of study [Medieval Latin *laboratorium*, from Latin *laborare* "to labor", from *labor* "labor"] — **laboratory** *adj*

labor camp *n* **1** : a penal colony where forced labor is performed **2** : a camp for migratory laborers

Labor Day *n* : the 1st Monday in September observed in the United States and Canada as a legal holiday in recognition of the worker

la·bored *adj* **1** : produced or performed with labor; *esp* : not freely or easily done ⟨*labored* breathing⟩ **2** : lacking ease of expression ⟨a *labored* speech⟩

la·bo·ri·ous \lə-'bōr-ē-əs, -'bór-\ *adj* **1** : INDUSTRIOUS **2** : requiring or characterized by hard or toilsome effort : LABORED — **la·bo·ri·ous·ly** *adv* — **la·bo·ri·ous·ness** *n*

La·bor·ite \'lā-bə-,rīt\ *n* **1** : a member of a political party devoted chiefly to the interests of labor **2** *usually* **La·bour·ite** \-bə-,rīt\ : a member of the British Labour party

la·bor·sav·ing \'lā-bər-,sā-ving\ *adj* : adapted to replace or decrease human labor and especially manual labor

labor union *n* : an organization of workers formed to advance its members' interests in respect to wages and working conditions

la·bour \'lā-bər\ *chiefly British variant of* LABOR

lab·ra·dor·ite \'lab-rə-,dòr-,īt\ *n* : a feldspar showing a play of several colors [*Labrador* peninsula, Canada]

Labrador retriever *n* : a retriever developed from stock originating in Newfoundland and characterized by a short dense usually black coat and broad head and chest [*Labrador*, Newfoundland]

la·brum \'lā-brəm\ *n* : the upper lip of an arthropod in front of or above the mandibles [Latin, "lip"]

la·bur·num \lə-'bər-nəm\ *n* : any of several poisonous Eurasian shrubs and trees of the pea family with pendulous racemes of bright yellow flowers [Latin]

lab·y·rinth \'lab-ə-,rinth, -,rintth\ *n* **1** : a place constructed of or full of passageways and blind alleys : MAZE **2** : something extremely complex or tortuous **3** : a tortuous anatomical structure; *esp* : the internal ear or its bony or membranous part [Latin *labyrinthus*, from Greek *labyrinthos*] — **lab·y·rin·thine** \,lab-ə-'rin-thən, -'rint-\ *adj*

lac \'lak\ *n* : a resinous substance secreted by a scale insect and used in the manufacture of shellac, lacquers, and sealing wax [Persian *lak* and Hindi *lākh,* from Sanskrit *lākṣā*]

¹lace \'lās\ *n* **1** : a cord or string used for drawing together two edges (as of a garment or a shoe) **2** : an ornamental braid for trimming coats or uniforms **3** : a fine openwork usually figured fabric made of thread and used chiefly for household coverings or for ornament of dress [Old French *laz,* from Latin *laqueus* "noose, snare"] — **laced** \'lāst\ *adj* — **lace·less** \'lā-sləs\ *adj* — **lace·like** \'lā-ˌslīk\ *adj*

²lace *vb* **1** : to draw together the edges of with or as if with a lace passed through eyelets **2 a** : to adorn with or as if with lace **b** : INTERTWINE **3** : BEAT 1a, b **4 a** : to add a dash especially of an alcoholic liquor to **b** : to give savor or zest to — **lac·er** *n*

¹lac·er·ate \'las-ə-rət\ *adj* : having the edges deeply and irregularly cut ⟨a flower with *lacerate* petals⟩

²lac·er·ate \'las-ə-ˌrāt\ *vt* **1** : to tear roughly : injure by tearing ⟨a *lacerated* knee⟩ **2** : to cause sharp mental or emotional pain to : DISTRESS [Latin *lacerare*] — **lac·er·a·tive** \-ˌrāt-iv\ *adj*

lac·er·a·tion \ˌlas-ə-'rā-shən\ *n* **1** : an act or instance of lacerating **2** : a torn and ragged wound

lac·er·til·i·an \ˌlas-ər-'til-ē-ən\ *adj* : of or relating to the lizards [derived from Latin *lacerta* "lizard"] — **lacertilian** *n*

lace·wing \'lā-ˌswing\ *n* : any of various neuropteran insects with delicate lacy wings, long antennae, and brilliant eyes

lach·ry·mal *or* **lac·ri·mal** \'lak-ər-məl\ *adj* : of, relating to, or being the glands that produce tears [Latin *lacrima* "tear"]

lach·ry·mose \'lak-rə-ˌmōs\ *adj* **1** : given to tears or weeping : TEARFUL **2** : tending to cause tears : MOURNFUL ⟨*lacrymose* ballads⟩ — **lach·ry·mose·ly** *adv*

lac·ing \'lā-sing\ *n* **1** : the action of one that laces **2** : something that laces : LACE

la·cin·i·ate \lə-'sin-ē-ət, -ˌāt\ *adj* : bordered with a fringe [Latin *lacinia* "flap"] — **la·cin·i·a·tion** \lə-ˌsin-ē-'ā-shən\ *n*

¹lack \'lak\ *vb* **1** : to be missing ⟨the will to win is *lacking*⟩ **2** : to need, want, or be deficient in ⟨*lack* financial support⟩ [Dutch *laken*]

²lack *n* **1** : the fact or state of being in short supply ⟨a *lack* of good manners⟩ **2** : something that is lacking or is needed ⟨money is the club's biggest *lack*⟩

lack·a·dai·si·cal \ˌlak-ə-'dā-zi-kəl\ *adj* : lacking life, spirit, or zest : LANGUID [derived from *lackaday,* interj. used to express regret, from *alack the day*] — **lack·a·dai·si·cal·ly** \-kə-lē, -klē\ *adv*

lack·ey \'lak-ē\ *n, pl* **lackeys** **1** : a liveried retainer : FOOTMAN **2** : a servile follower [Middle French *laquais*]

lack·lus·ter \'lak-ˌləs-tər\ *adj* : lacking in sheen, radiance, or vitality : DULL — **lackluster** *n*

la·con·ic \lə-'kän-ik\ *adj* : sparing of words : TERSE [Latin *laconicus* "Spartan", from Greek *lakōnikos;* from the Spartan reputation for terseness of speech] — **la·con·i·cal·ly** \-'kän-i-kə-lē, -klē\ *adv*

lac·quer \'lak-ər\ *n* **1** : any of various durable natural varnishes; *esp* : one from an Asian sumac **2** : any of various clear or colored synthetic organic coatings that typically dry to form a film by evaporation of the solvent; *esp* : a solution of a cellulose derivative (as nitrocellulose) [Portuguese *lacré* "sealing wax", from *laca* "lac", from Arabic *lakk,* from Persian *lak*] — **lacquer** *vt*

lac·ri·ma·tion \ˌlak-rə-'mā-shən\ *n* : the secretion of tears especially when abnormal or excessive [Latin *lacrimatio,* from *lacrimare* "to weep", from *lacrima* "tear"]

lac·ri·ma·tor *or* **lach·ry·ma·tor** \'lak-rə-ˌmāt-ər\ *n* : TEAR GAS

la·crosse \lə-'krós\ *n* : a game played on a field in which the players use a long-handled stick with a triangular head to catch, carry, or throw the ball [Canadian French *la crosse,* literally, "the crosier"]

lact- *or* **lacti-** *or* **lacto-** *combining form* **1** : milk ⟨*lacto*genic⟩ **2 a** : lactic acid ⟨*lact*ate⟩ **b** : lactose ⟨*lact*ase⟩ [Latin *lact-, lac*]

lac·tase \'lak-ˌtās\ *n* : an enzyme that breaks down lactose and related compounds and occurs especially in the intestines of young mammals and in yeasts

¹lac·tate \'lak-ˌtāt\ *n* : a salt or ester of lactic acid

²lactate *vi* : to secrete milk — **lac·ta·tion** \lak-'tā-shən\ *adj* — **lac·ta·tion·al** \-shnəl, -shən-l\ *adj* — **lac·ta·tion·al·ly** \-ē\ *adv*

¹lac·te·al \'lak-tē-əl\ *adj* **1** : consisting of, producing, or resembling milk **2 a** : conveying or containing a milky fluid **b** : of or relating to the lacteals [Latin *lacteus* "of milk", from *lact-, lac* "milk"]

²lacteal *n* : one of the lymphatic vessels beginning in the villi of the small intestine and carrying chyle to the thoracic duct

lac·tic \'lak-tik\ *adj* : relating to or producing lactic acid ⟨*lactic* fermentation⟩

lactic acid *n* : an organic acid $C_3H_6O_3$ present in cells and especially muscle, produced from carbohydrate usually by bacterial fermentation, and used mostly in food and medicine

lac·tif·er·ous \lak-'tif-rəs, -ə-rəs\ *adj* **1** : secreting or conveying milk **2** : yielding or containing a milky juice — **lac·tif·er·ous·ness** *n*

lac·to·ba·cil·lus \ˌlak-tō-bə-'sil-əs\ *n* : any of a genus of lactic-acid-forming bacteria

lac·to·gen·ic \ˌlak-tə-'jen-ik\ *adj* : inducing the secretion of milk

lac·tose \'lak-ˌtōs\ *n* : a sugar $C_{12}H_{22}O_{11}$ present in milk that breaks down into glucose and galactose and on fermentation yields especially lactic acid

la·cu·na \lə-'kü-nə, -'kyü-\ *n, pl* **-cu·nae** \-'kyü-nē, -'kü-ˌnī\ *or* **-cu·nas** \-'kü-nəz,-'kyü-\ **1** : a blank space or a missing part : GAP **2** : a small cavity or pit in an anatomical structure [Latin, "pool, pit, gap", from *lacus* "lake"] — **la·cu·nal** \-'kün-l, -'kyün-\ *adj* — **la·cu·nar** \-'kü-nər, -'kyü-\ *adj* — **la·cu·nate** \-nət\ *adj*

la·cus·trine \lə-'kəs-trən\ *adj* : of, relating to, or growing in lakes [derived from Latin *lacus* "lake"]

lacy \'lā-sē\ *adj* **lac·i·er; -est** : resembling or consisting of lace

lad \'lad\ *n* **1** : BOY 1, YOUTH **2** : FELLOW, CHAP [Middle English *ladde*]

lad·der \'lad-ər\ *n* **1** : a structure for climbing that consists of two long parallel sidepieces joined at intervals by crosspieces on which one may step **2** : something that suggests a ladder in form or use **3** : a series of usually ascending steps or stages : SCALE [Old English *hlǣder*]

lad·die \'lad-ē\ *n* : a young lad

lade \'lād\ *vb* **lad·ed; lad·ed** *or* **lad·en** \'lād-n\; **lad·ing** **1 a** : to put a load or burden on or in : LOAD ⟨*lade* a vessel⟩ **b** : SHIP 1a, STOW ⟨*lading* a rich cargo⟩ **2** : to burden heavily : OPPRESS **3** : LADLE [Old English *hladan*]

la–di–da \ˌläd-ē-'dä\ *adj* : affectedly refined or polished [perhaps from earlier *lardy-dardy* "foppish"]

ladies' man *n* : a man who shows a marked liking for the company of women

lad·ing \'lād-ing\ *n* **1** : the act of one that lades **2** : CARGO, FREIGHT

la·di·no \lə-'dī-nō, -nə\ *n, pl* **-nos** : a large rapidly growing white clover widely planted for hay or silage [perhaps from *Lodi,* Italy]

¹la·dle \'lād-l\ *n* : a deep-bowled long-handled spoon or dipper used especially for dipping up and moving liquids [Old English *hlædel,* from *hladan* "to lade"]

²ladle *vt* **la·dled; la·dling** \'lād-ling, -l-ing\ : to take up and move in or as if in a ladle ⟨*ladle* soup⟩

lacewing

\ə\ abut	\ng\ sing
\ər\ further	\ō\ bone
\a\ mat	\ò\ saw
\ā\ take	\òi\ coin
\ä\ cot, cart	\th\ thin
\aù\ out	\th\ this
\ch\ chin	\ü\ food
\e\ pet	\ù\ foot
\ē\ easy	\y\ yet
\g\ go	\yü\ few
\i\ tip	\yù\ cure
\ī\ life	\zh\ vision
\j\ job	

la·dy \'lād-ē\ *n, pl* **ladies** **1 a** : a woman of property, rank, or authority; *esp* : one having a standing equivalent to that of a lord **b** : a woman receiving the homage or devotion of a knight or lover **2 a** : a woman of superior social position **b** : a woman of refinement and manners **c** : WOMAN — often used in a courteous reference (show the *lady* to her seat) **3** : WIFE 2 **4a** *cap* — used as a title of a woman of rank in Great Britain **b** : a woman who is a member of an order of knighthood — compare DAME 1c [Old English *hlǣfdīge*, from *hlāf* "loaf of bread" + *-dīge* "one that kneads"] □ ORIGIN Over the centuries the meaning of *lady* has become more and more generalized, and it is now widely used as a courteous term for a woman. *Lady* was formerly used to refer primarily to women of superior social standing. The Old English form, *hlǣfdīge,* was originally used to mean "female head of a household" or "mistress of servants". This sense reflects something of the ultimate etymology, for *hlǣfdīge* is composed of Old English *hlāf,* "loaf", and *-dīge,* "kneader of bread", which is related to our modern English *dough.*

la·dy·bug \-ˌbəg\ *n* : any of numerous small, nearly hemispherical, and often brightly colored beetles that mostly feed both as larvae and adults on other insects [Our *Lady,* the Virgin Mary]

lady chapel *n, often cap L&C* : a chapel dedicated to the Virgin Mary

Lady Day *n* : the feast of the Annunciation

la·dy·fin·ger \'lād-ē-ˌfing-gər\ *n* : a small finger-shaped sponge cake

la·dy·fish \-ˌfish\ *n* : a large silvery food and sport fish that resembles a herring but is related to the tarpon — called also *bonefish, tenpounder*

la·dy-in-wait·ing \ˌlād-ē-in-ˈwāt-ing\ *n, pl* **ladies-in-waiting** : a lady appointed to attend a queen or princess

la·dy·like \'lād-ē-ˌlīk\ *adj* **1** : resembling a lady in appearance or manners **2** : suitable to a lady (*ladylike* behavior)

la·dy·love \ˌlād-ē-ˌləv, ˌlād-ē-'\ *n* : a beloved woman

la·dy·ship \'lād-ē-ˌship\ *n* **1** : the condition of being a lady **2** *often cap* : the rank or dignity of a lady — used as a form of address (her *Ladyship*) (your *Ladyship*) (their *Ladyships*)

lady's slipper *or* **lady slipper** \'lād-ēz-ˌslip-ər, -ē-ˌslip-\ *n* : any of several North American temperate-zone orchids with flowers whose shape suggests a slipper

¹lag \'lag\ *vi* **lagged; lag·ging** **1** : to stay or fall behind: as **a** : to hang back : LINGER (*lagged* behind the other hikers) **b** : to move, function, or develop with comparative slowness (*lagged* behind the production schedule) **2** : to slacken little by little : FLAG (interest never *lagged* during the play) **3** : to pitch or shoot something (as a marble) at a mark [probably of Scandinavian origin] — **lag·ger** *n*

²lag *n* **1 a** : the action or condition of lagging **b** : comparative slowness or retardation **2 a** : an amount of lagging or the time during which lagging continues **b** : INTERVAL 1

la·ger \'läg-ər\ *n* : a beer brewed by slow fermentation and stored in refrigerated cellars for maturing [German *lagerbier,* from *lager* "storehouse" + *bier* "beer"]

lag·gard \'lag-ərd\ *adj* : lagging or tending to lag : DILATORY — **laggard** *n* — **lag·gard·ly** *adv or adj* — **lag·gard·ness** *n*

la·gniappe \'lan-ˌyap, lan-'\ *n* : something given free or by way of good measure [American French, from American Spanish *la ñapa* "the lagniappe"]

lago·morph \'lag-ə-ˌmȯrf\ *n* : any of an order (Lagomorpha) of gnawing mammals having two pairs of upper incisors one behind the other and comprising the rabbits, hares, and pikas — compare RODENT [derived from Greek *lagōs* "hare" + *morphē* "form"] — **lago-**

mor·phic \ˌlag-ə-'mȯr-fik\ *adj* — **lago·mor·phous** \-fəs\ *adj*

la·goon \lə-'gün\ *n* : a shallow sound, channel, or pond near or connected with a larger body of water [French *lagune,* from Italian *laguna,* from Latin *lacuna* "pit, pool", from *lacus* "lake"]

la·ical \'lā-ə-kəl\ *or* **la·ic** \'lā-ik\ *adj* : of or relating to the laity : SECULAR — **laic** *n* — **la·ical·ly** \'lā-ə-kə-lē, -klē\ *adv*

la·icism \'lā-ə-ˌsiz-əm\ *n* : a political system characterized by the exclusion of church control and influence

la·icize \'lā-ə-ˌsīz\ *vt* **1** : to reduce to lay status **2** : to put under the direction of or throw open to the laity — **la·ici·za·tion** \ˌlā-ə-sə-'zā-shən\ *n*

laid *past of* LAY

lain *past participle of* LIE

lair \'laər, 'leər\ *n* **1** : the resting or living place of a wild animal : DEN **2** : REFUGE 1, HIDEAWAY [Old English *leger*]

laird \'laərd, 'leərd\ *n, Scottish* : a landed proprietor [Middle English *lard, lord,* "lord"]

lais·sez–faire \ˌle-ˌsā-'faər, ˌlā-, -ˌzā-, -'feər\ *n* : a doctrine opposing governmental interference in economic affairs beyond the minimum necessary for the maintenance of peace and property rights [French *laissez faire,* imperative of *laisser faire* "to let (people) do (as they choose)"] — **laissez–faire** *adj*

la·ity \'lā-ət-ē\ *n, pl* **-ities** **1** : the people of a religious faith as distinguished from its clergy **2** : the mass of the people as distinguished from those of a particular profession or skill [⁵*lay*]

¹lake \'lāk\ *n* : a large inland body of standing water; *also* : a pool of liquid (as lava, oil, or pitch) [Old French *lac,* from Latin *lacus*]

²lake *n* **1** : any of numerous bright pigments composed of a soluble dye adsorbed on or combined with an inorganic substance **2** : a vivid red [French *laque* "lac", from Provençal *laca,* from Arabic *lakk,* from Persian *lak*]

lake dwelling *n* : a dwelling built on piles in a lake; *esp* : one built in prehistoric times — **lake dweller** *n*

lake herring *n* : any of several lake fish of commercial importance in the northern United States and Canada

lake trout *n* : any of several lake fishes: as **a** : BROWN TROUT **b** : a large dark American char that is an important sport and commerical fish in northern lakes

la·ma \'läm-ə\ *n* : a Lamaist monk [Tibetan *blama*]

La·ma·ism \'läm-ə-ˌiz-əm\ *n* : the form of Buddhism of Tibet and Mongolia marked by a dominant hierarchy of monks — **La·ma·ist** \'läm-ə-əst\ *n or adj* — **La·ma·is·tic** \ˌläm-ə-'is-tik\ *adj*

La·marck·ism \lə-'mär-ˌkiz-əm\ *n* : a theory of organic evolution asserting that environmental changes cause structural changes in animals and plants which are transmitted to offspring [J.B. de Monet *Lamarck*] — **La·marck·i·an** \-'mär-kē-ən\ *adj or n*

la·ma·sery \'läm-ə-ˌser-ē\ *n, pl* **-ser·ies** : a monastery of lamas [French *lamaserie,* from *lama* "lama + Persian *sarāi* "palace"]

¹lamb \'lam\ *n* **1 a** : a young sheep; *esp* : one less than a year old or without permanent teeth **b** : the young of various animals (as the smaller antelopes) **2** : an innocent, weak, or gentle person **3** : the flesh of a lamb used as food [Old English]

²lamb *vb* **1** : to bring forth a lamb **2** : to tend (ewes) at lambing time — **lamb·er** \'lam-ər\ *n*

lam·baste *or* **lam·bast** \lam-'bāst, -'bast\ *vt* **1** : to assault violently : BEAT **2** : to attack verbally [probably of Scandinavian origin]

lamb·da \'lam-də\ *n* : the 11th letter of the Greek alphabet — Λ or λ

lam·bent \'lam-bənt\ *adj* **1** : playing lightly over a surface : FLICKERING (a *lambent* flame) **2** : softly radiant (*lambent* eyes) **3** : marked by lightness or brilliance ⟨*lambent* humor⟩ [Latin *lambens*, present participle of *lambere* "to lick"] — **lam·ben·cy** \-bən-sē\ *n*

lam·bre·quin \'lam-bər-kən, -bri-kən\ *n* : a short decorative drapery for a shelf edge or for the top of a window casing : VALANCE [French]

lamb·skin \'lam-ˌskin\ *n* : a lamb's skin or a small fine-grade sheepskin or the leather made from either

lamb's–quar·ters \'lamz-ˌkwȯrt-ərz, -ˌkwȯt-\ *n sing or pl* : a goosefoot with glaucous foliage that is sometimes used as a potherb

¹**lame** \'lām\ *adj* **1 a** : physically disabled **b** (1) : having a part and especially a limb so disabled as to impair freedom of movement (2) : halting in movement : LIMPING **2** : lacking substance : WEAK ⟨a *lame* excuse⟩ [Old English *lama*] — **lame·ly** *adv* — **lame·ness** *n*

²**lame** *vt* **1** : to make lame : CRIPPLE **2** : to make weak or ineffective

la·mé \lä-'mā, la-\ *n* : a brocaded fabric woven with metallic filling threads often of gold or silver [French]

lame duck *n* : an elected official continuing to hold political office after being defeated and before a successor is inaugurated

la·mel·la \lə-'mel-ə\ *n, pl* **-mel·lae** \-'mel-ē, -ˌī\ *also* **-mellas** : a thin flat scale or part [Latin, "little plate", from *lamina* "thin plate"] — **la·mel·lar** \lə-'mel-ər\ *adj* — **la·mel·late** \-'mel-ət\ *adj* — **la·mel·late·ly** *adv*

lam·el·la·tion \ˌlam-ə-'lā-shən\ *n* **1** : formation or division into lamellae **2** : LAMELLA

la·mel·li·branch \lə-'mel-ə-ˌbrangk\ *n, pl* **-branchs** : any of a class (Lamellibranchia) of mollusks (as clams, oysters, or mussels) with a shell made up of right and left parts joined by a hinge [*lamella* + Latin *branchia* "gill"] — **lamellibranch** *adj* — **la·mel·li·bran·chi·ate** \lə-ˌmel-ə-'brang-kē-ət\ *adj or n*

¹**la·ment** \lə-'ment\ *vb* **1** : to mourn aloud : WAIL **2** : to feel or express sorrow for : BEWAIL [Latin *lamentari*, from *lamentum* "lament"] — **lam·en·ta·tion** \ˌlam-ən-'tā-shən\ *n*

²**lament** *n* **1** : a crying out in grief : WAILING **2** : a mournful song or poem

lam·en·ta·ble \'lam-ən-tə-bəl, lə-'ment-ə-\ *adj* **1** : that is to be regretted : DEPLORABLE ⟨a *lamentable* error⟩ **2** : expressing grief : MOURNFUL — **lam·en·ta·ble·ness** *n* — **lam·en·ta·bly** \-blē\ *adv*

Lam·en·ta·tions \ˌlam-ən-'tā-shənz\ *n* — see BIBLE table

la·mia \'lā-mē-ə\ *n* : a man-eating she-demon [Latin, from Greek]

lam·i·na \'lam-ə-nə\ *n, pl* **-nae** \-ˌnē, -ˌnī\ *or* **-nas** **1** : a thin plate or scale **2** : BLADE 1b [Latin] — **lam·i·nar** \-nər\ *adj*

lam·i·nar·ia \ˌlam-ə-'ner-ē-ə, -'nar-\ *n* : any of various large kelps with an unbranched cylindrical or flattened stalk and a smooth or convoluted blade [derived from Latin *lamina* "lamina"] — **lam·i·nar·i·an** \-ē-ən\ *adj or n*

¹**lam·i·nate** \'lam-ə-ˌnāt\ *vt* **1** : to roll or compress into a thin plate **2** : to make by uniting superposed layers of one or more materials — **lam·i·na·tor** \-ˌnāt-ər\ *n*

²**lam·i·nate** \-nət, -ˌnāt\ *adj* : consisting of laminae **2** : bearing or covered with laminae

³**lam·i·nate** \-nət, -ˌnāt\ *n* : a product made by laminating

lam·i·nat·ed \-ˌnāt-əd\ *adj* : composed of layers of firmly united material; *esp* : made by bonding or impregnating superposed layers of paper, wood, or fabric with resin and compressing under heat

lam·i·na·tion \ˌlam-ə-'nā-shən\ *n* **1** : the process of laminating **2** : a laminate structure **3** : LAMINA

Lam·mas \'lam-əs\ *n* : August 1 originally celebrated in England as a harvest festival [Old English *hlāfmæsse*, from *hlāf*, "loaf" + *mæsse* "mass"]

lam·mer·gei·er *or* **lam·mer·gey·er** \'lam-ər-ˌgī-ər, -ˌgīr\ *n* : the largest Eurasian bird of prey found chiefly in mountainous regions [German *lämmergeier*, from *lämmer* "lambs" + *geier* "vulture"]

lamp \'lamp\ *n* : a device for producing light or heat: as **a** : a vessel with a wick for burning an inflammable liquid (as oil) **b** : an incandescent or fluorescent bulb together with its housing [Old French *lampe*, from Latin *lampas*, from Greek, from *lampein* "to shine"]

lamp·black \-ˌblak\ *n* : a finely powdered deep black soot made by incomplete burning of carbon-containing material and used chiefly as a pigment (as in paints and ink)

lamp·light·er \'lam-ˌplīt-ər\ *n* : one that lights a lamp; *esp* : a person employed to light gas street lights

¹**lam·poon** \lam-'pün\ *n* **1** : a harsh satire usually aimed at an individual **2** : a light mocking satire [French *lampon*]

²**lampoon** *vt* : to make the subject of a lampoon : RIDICULE — **lam·poon·er** *n* — **lam·poon·ery** \-'pün-rē, -ə-rē\ *n*

lam·prey \'lam-prē\ *n, pl* **lampreys** : any of an order (Hyperoartia) of aquatic vertebrates that resemble eels but have a large sucking mouth with no jaws [Old French *lampreie*, from Medieval Latin *lampreda*]

lamp·shell \'lamp-ˌshel\ *n* : BRACHIOPOD

la·nai \lə-'nī, lä-\ *n* : a roofed patio used as a living room [Hawaiian]

la·nate \'lā-ˌnāt, 'lan-ˌāt\ *adj* : covered with fine hair or filaments : WOOLLY [Latin *lanatus*, from *lana* "wool"]

Lan·cas·tri·an \lan-'kas-trē-ən, lang-\ *adj* : of or relating to the English royal house that ruled from 1399 to 1461 — compare YORKIST [John of Gaunt, duke of *Lancaster*, died 1399] — **Lancastrian** *n*

¹**lance** \'lans\ *n* **1** : a weapon consisting of a long shaft with a sharp head and carried by knights or light cavalry **2** : a sharp object suggestive of a lance; *esp* : LANCET **3** : LANCER 1b [Old French, from Latin *lancea*]

²**lance** *vt* **1** : to pierce with or as if with a lance **2** : to open with or as if with a lancet ⟨*lance* a boil⟩

lance corporal *n* : an enlisted rank in the Marine Corps above private first class and below corporal [*lance* (as in obsolete *lancepesade* "lance corporal", from Middle French *lancepessade*)]

lance·let \'lan-slət\ *n* : AMPHIOXUS

lan·ce·o·late \'lan-sē-ə-ˌlāt\ *also* **lan·ce·o·lat·ed** \-ˌlāt-əd\ *adj* : shaped like a lance head; *esp* : being narrow and tapering to a point at the tip ⟨*lanceolate* leaves⟩ [Late Latin *lanceolatus*, from Latin *lanceola* "small lance", from *lancea* "lance"]

lanc·er \'lan-sər\ *n* **1 a** : one that carries a lance **b** : a light cavalryman armed with a lance **2** *pl but sing in construction* **a** : a set of five quadrilles each in a different meter **b** : the music for such dances

lan·cet \'lan-sət\ *n* : a sharp-pointed and usually 2-edged surgical instrument

lancet arch *n* : an acutely pointed arch

¹**land** \'land\ *n* **1** : the solid part of the surface of the earth **2** : a portion of the earth's solid surface distinguished by ownership boundaries: as **a** : COUNTRY 2 **b** : privately or publically owned territory ⟨buy some *land*⟩ **3** : REALM, DOMAIN ⟨in the *land* of dreams⟩ **4** : the people of a country : NATION [Old English] — **land·less** \'lan-dləs\ *adj*

²**land** *vb* **1 a** : to set or go ashore from a ship : DISEMBARK ⟨*land* troops⟩ ⟨troops *landed*⟩ **b** : to stop at or near a place on shore ⟨the boat *landed* at the dock⟩ **2** : to alight or cause to alight on a surface ⟨the plane *landed*⟩ ⟨*landed* the plane in a corn field⟩ **3** : to bring to or arrive at a specified destination, position, or condition ⟨*landed* downtown⟩ ⟨never *landed* a punch⟩ ⟨carelessness *landed* them in trouble⟩ **4 a** : to catch with a hook and bring in ⟨*land* a fish⟩ **b** : GAIN, SECURE ⟨*land* a job⟩

lan·dau \'lan-ˌdaů, -ˌdȯ\ *n* **1** : a four-wheeled carriage with a top divided into two sections that can be lowered, thrown back, or removed **2** : a closed automo-

lammergeier

lamprey

landau 1

\ə\ abut		\ng\ sing	
\ər\ further		\ō\ bone	
\a\ mat		\ȯ\ saw	
\ā\ take		\ȯi\ coin	
\ä\ cot, cart		\th\ thin	
\aů\ out		\tẖ\ this	
\ch\ chin		\ü\ foot	
\e\ pet		\ů\ foot	
\ē\ easy		\y\ yet	
\g\ go		\yü\ few	
\i\ tip		\yů\ cure	
\ī\ life		\zh\ vision	
\j\ job			

bile body with a folding top over the rear passenger compartment [*Landau,* Bavaria, Germany]

land·ed \'lan-dəd\ *adj* **1** : owning land ⟨*landed* proprietors⟩ **2** : consisting of real estate ⟨*landed* property⟩

land·fall \'land-ˌfȯl, 'lan-\ *n* : a sighting or reaching of land after a voyage or flight; *also* : the land first sighted

land·fill \-ˌfil\ *n* **1** : a system of trash and garbage disposal in which the waste is buried between layers of earth to build up low-lying land — called also *sanitary landfill* **2** : an area built up by landfill

land·form \-ˌfȯrm\ *n* : a natural feature of a land surface

land grant *n* : a grant of land by a government especially for roads, railroads, or agricultural colleges

land·hold·er \'land-ˌhōl-dər\ *n* : one that holds or owns land — **land·hold·ing** \-diŋ\ *n*

land·ing \'lan-diŋ\ *n* **1** : the action of one that lands **2** : a place for discharging or taking on passengers and cargo **3** : a level part of a staircase (as at the end of a flight of stairs)

landing craft *n* : any of various naval craft designed for putting troops and equipment ashore

landing field *n* : a field where aircraft may land and take off

landing gear *n* : the part that supports an aircraft or spacecraft when on the ground

landing strip *n* : AIRSTRIP

land·la·dy \'land-ˌlād-ē, 'lan-\ *n* : a female landlord

land·locked \-ˌläkt\ *adj* **1** : enclosed or nearly enclosed by land ⟨a *landlocked* country⟩ **2** : confined to fresh water by some barrier ⟨*landlocked* salmon⟩

land·lord \-ˌlȯrd\ *n* **1** : the owner of real estate which is leased or rented to another **2** : a person who runs an inn or rooming house : INNKEEPER

land·lub·ber \'lan-ˌdləb-ər, -ˌləb-\ *n* **1** : one whose life is spent on land **2** : one who is unacquainted with the sea or seamanship — **land·lub·ber·ly** *adj*

land·mark \'land-ˌmärk, 'lan-\ *n* **1** : an object (as a stone or tree) that marks the boundary of land **2 a** : a conspicuous object on land that directs toward or identifies a place **b** : an anatomical structure used as a point of orientation in locating other structures **3** : an event or development that marks a turning point or a stage ⟨the album was a musical *landmark*⟩ **4** : a structure of unusual historic interest

land·mass \-ˌmas\ *n* : a large area of land

land–office business *n* : extensive and rapid business [from the fact that government land offices were swamped with would-be homesteaders when public lands were opened for homesteading]

land·own·er \'lan-ˌdō-nər\ *n* : an owner of land — **land·own·ing** \-niŋ\ *adj*

land–poor \'land-ˌpu̇r, 'lan-\ *adj* : owning so much unprofitable or encumbered land as to lack funds to develop it or pay the charges due on it

land reform *n* : usually legislative measures intended to achieve a fairer distribution of agricultural land

¹land·scape \'land-ˌskāp, 'lan-\ *n* **1** : a picture of natural inland scenery **2** : a portion of land that the eye can see in one glance [Dutch *landschap,* from *land* + *-schap* "-ship"]

²landscape *vt* : to modify or improve (a tract of land) by grading, clearing, or gardening

landscape gardener *n* : one skilled in the development and decorative planting of gardens and grounds

land·slide \'land-ˌslīd, 'lan-\ *n* **1** : the slipping down of a mass of rocks or earth on a steep slope; *also* : the mass of material that slides **2** : an overwhelming victory especially in an election

lands·man \'landz-mən, 'lanz-\ *n* : LANDLUBBER

¹land·ward \'lan-dwərd\ *also* **land·wards** \-dwərdz\ *adv* : to or toward the land

²landward *adj* : lying or being toward the land or on the side toward the land

langur

lane \'lān\ *n* **1** : a narrow way between fences, hedges, or buildings **2** : a relatively narrow way: as **a** : an ocean route for ships; *also* : AIR LANE **b** : a strip of roadway for a single line of vehicles **c** : a long hardwood surface with pins at one end for use in bowling [Old English *lanu*]

Lan·go·bard \'laŋ-gə-ˌbärd\ *n* : LOMBARD [Latin *Langobardus*]

lan·gouste \län-'gu̇st\ *n* : SPINY LOBSTER [French]

lang syne \laŋ-'zīn\ *n, chiefly Scottish* : times past [Middle English, from *lang* "long" + *syne* "since"] — **lang syne** *adv or adj, chiefly Scottish*

lan·guage \'laŋ-gwij\ *n* **1 a** : the words, their pronunciation, and the methods of combining them used and understood by a large group of people **b** (1) : audible, articulate, and meaningful sound as produced by the action of the vocal organs (2) : a systematic means of communicating ideas by signs or marks with understood meanings ⟨sign *language*⟩ **2 a** : form or manner of verbal expression; *esp* : STYLE ⟨forceful *language*⟩ **b** : the words and expressions of a particular group or field ⟨the *language* of medicine⟩ **3** : the study of language especially as a school subject [Old French, from *langue* "tongue, language", from Latin *lingua*]

lan·guid \'laŋ-gwəd\ *adj* **1** : drooping or flagging from or as if from exhaustion **2** : sluggish in character or disposition : LISTLESS **3** : lacking force or quickness of movement : LAZY [Middle French *languide,* from Latin *languidus,* from *languēre* "to languish"] — **lan·guid·ly** *adv* — **lan·guid·ness** *n*

lan·guish \'laŋ-gwish\ *vi* **1 a** : to be or become languid **b** : to lose strength or force : DECLINE **2** : to become depressed : PINE ⟨*languished* in prison⟩ **3** : to assume a weary or sad look appealing for sympathy [Middle French *languiss-,* stem of *languir* "to languish", from Latin *languēre*] — **lan·guish·er** *n* — **lan·guish·ing** *adj* — **lan·guish·ing·ly** \-iŋ-lē\ *adv* — **lan·guish·ment** \-gwish-mənt\ *n*

lan·guor \'laŋ-gər, -ər\ *n* **1** : weakness or weariness of body or mind **2** : a state of dreamy inactivity [Old French, from Latin, from *languēre* "to languish"] SYN see LETHARGY — **lan·guor·ous** \-gə-rəs, -ə-rəs\ *adj* — **lan·guor·ous·ly** *adv*

lan·gur \läŋ-'gu̇r\ *n* : any of various slender long-tailed Asian monkeys [Hindi *lāgūr*]

lank \'laŋk\ *adj* **1** : not well filled out : THIN ⟨*lank* cattle⟩ **2** : hanging straight and limp without spring or curl ⟨*lank* hair⟩ [Old English *hlanc*] — **lank·ly** *adv* — **lank·ness** *n* □ SYN LANKY, GAUNT, RAWBONED: LANK implies tallness as well as leanness of figure; LANKY suggests awkwardness and loose-jointedness as well as thinness; GAUNT implies marked thinness as from overwork, suffering, or undernourishment; RAWBONED suggests a large ungainly build without implying undernourishment.

lanky \'laŋ-kē\ *adj* **lank·i·er; -est** : being tall, thin, and usually loose-jointed SYN see LANK — **lank·i·ly** \-kə-lē\ *adv* — **lank·i·ness** \-kē-nəs\ *n*

lan·ner \'lan-ər\ *n* : a widely distributed Old World falcon [Middle French *lanier*]

lan·o·lin \'lan-l-ən\ *n* : the fatty coating of sheep's wool especially when refined for use in ointments and cosmetics [derived from Latin *lana* "wool" + *oleum* "oil"]

lan·ta·na \lan-'tän-ə\ *n* : any of a genus of tropical shrubs that are related to vervains and have showy heads of small bright flowers [Italian dialect, "viburnum"]

lan·tern \'lant-ərn\ *n* **1** : a usually portable light that has a protective transparent or translucent covering **2 a** : the chamber in a lighthouse containing the light **b** : a structure with glazed or open sides above an opening in a roof for light, ventilation, or decoration **3** : PROJECTOR 2b [Middle French *lanterne,* from Latin *lanterna,* from Greek *lamptēr,* from *lampein* "to shine"]

lantern fly *n* : any of several large brightly marked insects that are related to the cicadas and aphids and have the front of the head lengthened into a hollow structure

lantern jaw *n* : a long thin jaw — **lan·tern–jawed** \,lant-ərn-'jòd\ *adj*

lan·tha·nide series \'lan-thə-,nīd-, 'lant-\ *n* : a group of chemical elements consisting of the rare earth elements

lan·tha·num \'lan-thə-nəm, 'lant-\ *n* : a white soft malleable metallic chemical element — see ELEMENT table [New Latin, from Greek *lanthanein* "to escape notice"]

lan·yard \'lan-yərd\ *n* **1** : a piece of rope or line for fastening something in ships **2 a** : a cord worn around the neck to hold a knife or a whistle **b** : a cord worn on a uniform as a symbol of a military citation **3** : a strong cord with a hook at one end used in firing cannon [Middle French *laniere* "thong, strap"]

Lao \'laù\ *or* **Lao·tian** \lā-'ō-shən, 'laù-shən\ *n* **1** : a member of a Buddhist people living in Laos and northeastern Thailand **2** : the Thai language of the Lao people — **Lao** *or* **Laotian** *adj*

¹lap \'lap\ *n* **1** : a loose panel in a garment : FLAP **2 a** : the clothing that lies on the knees and thighs of a seated person **b** : the front part of the lower trunk and thighs of a seated person **3** : responsible custody : CONTROL ⟨dropped the problem into my *lap*⟩ [Old English *læppa*] — **lap·ful** \'lap-,fùl\ *n* — **the lap of luxury** : an environment of great comfort and wealth

²lap *vb* **lapped; lap·ping 1** : ⁴WIND 6b, WRAP ⟨*lap* a bandage around the wrist⟩ **2** : ENVELOP, SWATHE ⟨*lap* the child in a blanket⟩ **3 a** : to place or lay so that one covers part of another ⟨*lap* shingles on a roof⟩ **b** : to project or spread beyond a certain point **4** : to smooth or polish (as a metal surface) to a fine finish or accurate fit — **lap·per** *n*

³lap *n* **1 a** : the amount by which one object overlaps or projects beyond another **b** : the part of an object that overlaps another **2** : a smoothing and polishing tool **3 a** : one circuit around a racecourse **b** : one segment of a journey **c** : one complete turn

⁴lap *vb* **lapped; lap·ping 1** : to take in food or drink with the tongue; *also* : DEVOUR — usually used with *up* **2** : to wash or splash gently [Old English *lapian*] — **lap·per** *n*

⁵lap *n* **1 a** : an act or instance of lapping **b** : the amount that can be carried to the mouth by one lick or scoop of the tongue **2** : a gentle splashing sound

lap·board \'lap-,bōrd, -,bòrd\ *n* : a board used on the lap as a table or desk

lap·dog \-,dòg\ *n* : a small dog that may be held in the lap

la·pel \lə-'pel\ *n* : the part of the front of a garment that is turned back and is usually a continuation of the collar [derived from ¹*lap*]

¹lap·i·dary \'lap-ə-,der-ē\ *n, pl* **-dar·ies** : a person who cuts, polishes, and engraves precious stones [Latin *lapidarius,* from *lapid-, lapis* "stone"]

²lapidary *adj* **1** : of or relating to precious stones or the art of cutting them **2** : of, relating to, or suitable for engraved inscriptions

lap·in \'lap-ən\ *n* : rabbit fur usually sheared and dyed [French, "rabbit"]

la·pis la·zu·li \,lap-əs-'lazh-ə-lē, -'laz-\ *n* : a deep blue semiprecious stone that is essentially a complex silicate often with spangles of iron pyrites [Medieval Latin, from Latin *lapis* "stone" + Medieval Latin *lazulum* "lapis lazuli", from Arabic *lāzaward*]

lap joint *n* : a joint made by overlapping two ends or edges and fastening them together — **lap–jointed** \'lap-'jòint-əd\ *adj*

Lapp \'lap\ *n* : a member of a people of northern Scandinavia, Finland, and the Kola peninsula of Russia [Swedish]

lap·pet \'lap-ət\ *n* **1** : a fold or flap on a garment or headdress **2** : a flat overlapping or hanging piece

¹lapse \'laps\ *n* **1 a** : a slight error ⟨a *lapse* in manners⟩ **b** : a temporary deviation or fall especially from a higher to a lower state ⟨a *lapse* from grace⟩ **2** : a becoming less : DECLINE **3 a** : the ending of a right or privilege by neglect to exercise it or failure to meet requirements **b** : DISUSE, DISCONTINUANCE ⟨*lapse* of a custom⟩ **4** : a passage of time; *also* : INTERVAL [Latin *lapsus,* from *labi* "to slip"]

²lapse *vi* **1 a** : to fall from a better or higher state into a poorer or lower one ⟨*lapsed* into carelessness⟩ **b** : to sink or slip gradually ⟨*lapse* into silence⟩ **2** : to fall into disuse **3** : to come to an end : CEASE **4** : to let something (as insurance or a legacy) come to an end or to pass to another by omission or negligence — **laps·er** *n*

lapse rate *n* : the rate of decrease in temperature of an air mass with increase in altitude

lap·top \'lap-,täp\ *adj* : of a size and design that makes use on one's lap convenient ⟨a *laptop* personal computer⟩ — **laptop** *n*

lap·wing \'lap-,wing\ *n* : a crested Old World plover with a slow irregular flapping flight and a shrill wailing cry [Old English *hlēapewince*]

lar·board \'lär-bərd\ *n* : ³PORT [Middle English *ladeborde*] — **larboard** *adj*

lar·ce·ny \'lärs-nē, -n-ē\ *n, pl* **-nies** : the unlawful taking and carrying away of personal property with intent to deprive the owner of it permanently : THEFT [Middle French *larcin* "theft", from Latin *latrocinium* "robbery", from *latro* "mercenary soldier"] — **lar·ce·nous** \'lärs-nəs, -n-əs\ *adj*

larch \'lärch\ *n* **1** : any of a genus of trees of the pine family with short deciduous needles; *also* : any of several related trees **2** : the wood of a larch [probably from German *lärche,* from Latin *larix*]

¹lard \'lärd\ *vt* **1** : to insert strips of pork fat or bacon into (meat) before cooking **2** : to smear with lard, fat, or grease **3** : to add to; *esp* : ENRICH ⟨a book *larded* with illustrations⟩

²lard *n* : a soft white fat obtained from fatty tissue of the hog by heating [Old French, from Latin *lardum*] — **lardy** \'lärd-ē\ *adj*

lar·der \'lärd-ər\ *n* : a place where foods are kept [Middle French *lardier,* from *lard,* "lard"]

large \'lärj\ *adj* : exceeding most other things of like kind especially in quantity or size : BIG [Old French, "abundant, generous, broad", from Latin *largus* "abundant, generous"] — **large·ness** *n* □ SYN LARGE, BIG, GREAT mean above average in magnitude. LARGE is likely to be chosen when the dimensions, extent, capacity, or quantity are being considered ⟨a *large* sum of money⟩ BIG suggests emphasis on bulk, weight, or volume ⟨*big* boxes⟩ GREAT may imply physical magnitude usually with connotations of wonder or awe but more often implies degree of intensity ⟨*great* kindness⟩ ⟨*great* fear⟩ LARGE figuratively implies breadth, comprehensiveness, or generosity; BIG suggests impressiveness often at the expense of solidity; GREAT implies eminence, distinction, or supremacy. — **at large 1** : at liberty : FREE ⟨an escaped prisoner still *at large*⟩ **2** : as a whole : in general ⟨society *at large*⟩ **3** : representing a whole area rather than one of its subdivisions — used in combination with a preceding noun ⟨a delagate-*at-large*⟩

large calorie *n* : CALORIE 1b

large-heart·ed \'lärj-'härt-əd\ *adj* : GENEROUS 1, LIBERAL

large intestine *n* : the posterior division of the vertebrate intestine consisting of the cecum, colon, and rectum and functioning especially in the removal of water from digestive residues to form feces

\ə\ abut	\ng\ sing
\ər\ further	\ō\ bone
\a\ mat	\ò\ saw
\ā\ take	\òi\ coin
\ä\ cot, cart	\th\ thin
\aù\ out	\th\ this
\ch\ chin	\ü\ food
\e\ pet	\ù\ foot
\ē\ easy	\y\ yet
\g\ go	\yü\ few
\i\ tip	\yù\ cure
\ī\ life	\zh\ vision
\j\ job	

large·ly \'lärj-lē\ *adv* : for the most part : CHIEFLY, MOSTLY

large–mind·ed \'lärj-'mīn-dəd\ *adj* : generous or comprehensive in outlook, range, or capacity — **large–mind·ed·ly** *adv* — **large–mind·ed·ness** *n*

large·mouth bass \,lärj-,maúth-\ *n* : a large bass of sluggish warm waters that is blackish green above and lighter below — called also *largemouth black bass*

large–scale \'lärj-'skāl\ *adj* : larger than others of its kind

large–scale integration *n* : the process of placing a large number of circuits on a small chip

lar·gess *or* **lar·gesse** \lär-'zhes, lär-'jes\ *n* 1 : liberal giving 2 : a generous gift [Old French *largesse,* from *large* "generous"]

¹lar·ghet·to \lär-'get-ō\ *adv or adj* : slower than andante but not so slow as largo — used as a direction in music [Italian, "somewhat slow", from *largo* "slow"]

²larghetto *n, pl* **-tos** : a larghetto movement

¹lar·go \'lär-gō\ *adv or adj* : in a very slow and broad manner — used as a direction in music [Italian, "slow, broad", from Latin *largus* "abundant"]

²largo *n, pl* **largos** : a largo movement

lar·i·at \'lar-ē-ət, 'ler-\ *n* : a long light rope used to catch livestock or to picket grazing animals [American Spanish *la reata* "the lasso"]

¹lark \'lärk\ *n* 1 : any of numerous Old World singing birds; *esp* : SKYLARK 2 : any of various usually dull-colored ground-living birds (as the meadowlark) [Old English *lāwerce*]

²lark *n* : something done solely for fun or adventure [probably derived from Old Norse *leika* "to play, deceive, dance"] — **lark** *vi*

lark·spur \'lärk-,spər\ *n* : DELPHINIUM; *esp* : a cultivated annual delphinium grown for its flowers

lar·rup \'lar-əp\ *vt, dialect* : WHIP 2a, 4 [perhaps imitative]

lar·va \'lär-və\ *n, pl* **lar·vae** \-,vē, -,vī\ *also* **larvas** 1 : the immature, wingless, and often wormlike form that hatches from the egg of many insects 2 : the early form of any animal that at birth or hatching is fundamentally unlike its parent ⟨the tadpole is the *larva* of the frog⟩ [Latin, "specter, mask"] — **lar·val** \-vel\ *adj*
□ ORIGIN Many insects hatch from their eggs looking very different from their eventual adult forms. The caterpillar, although it is a young butterfly, seems to have very little in common with that winged creature. The immature insect appears to be in disguise, to be masked. Linnaeus, the great 18th-century Swedish naturalist, was struck by this and gave the immature insect form the name *larva,* from a Latin word that means "mask".

lar·vi·cide \'lär-və-,sīd\ *n* : an agent for killing larval pests — **lar·vi·cid·al** \,lär-və-sīd-l\ *adj*

¹la·ryn·geal \lə-'rin-jəl, -jē-əl, ,lar-ən-'jē-əl\ *adj* : of, relating to, or used on the larynx [derived from Greek *laryng-, larynx* "larynx"] — **la·ryn·geal·ly** \-ē\ *adv*

²laryngeal *n* : a laryngeal part

lar·yn·gi·tis \,lar-ən-'jīt-əs\ *n* : inflammation of the larynx — **lar·yn·git·ic** \-'jit-ik\ *adj*

lar·ynx \'lar-ings, -ingks\ *n, pl* **la·ryn·ges** \lə-'rin-,jēz\ *or* **lar·ynx·es** : the modified upper part of the trachea that in humans and most mammals contains the vocal cords [Greek *laryng-, larynx*]

la·sa·gna \lə-'zän-yə\ *n* : broad flat noodles baked with a sauce usually of tomatoes, cheese, and meat [Italian *lasagna,* from Latin *lasanum* "cooking pot", from Greek *lasanon* "chamber pot"]

las·civ·i·ous \lə-'siv-ē-əs\ *adj* : sexually loose : LEWD [Latin *lascivia* "wantonness", from *lascivus* "wanton"] — **las·civ·i·ous·ly** *adv* — **las·civ·i·ous·ness** *n*

la·ser \'lā-zər\ *n* : a device that utilizes the natural oscillations of atoms or molecules between energy levels for generating electromagnetic waves with a narrow frequency range [*l*ight *a*mplification by *s*timulated *e*mission of *r*adiation]

¹lash \'lash\ *vb* 1 : to move violently or suddenly ⟨a cat *lashing* its tail⟩ 2 : to strike with or as if with a whip ⟨rain *lashing* the window⟩ 3 : to attack or retort verbally — usually used with *out* [Middle English *lashen*] — **lash·er** *n*

²lash *n* 1 a (1) : a stroke with or as if with a whip (2) : the flexible part of a whip; *also* : WHIP b : a sudden swinging blow 2 : a verbal attack 3 : EYELASH

³lash *vt* : to bind with a rope, cord, or chain [Middle French *lacier* "to lace"] — **lash·er** *n*

lash·ing *n* : something used for binding, wrapping, or fastening

lass \'las\ *n* 1 : young woman : GIRL 2 : SWEETHEART 2 [Middle English *las*]

lass·ie \'las-ē\ *n* : LASS 1, GIRL

las·si·tude \'las-ə-,tüd, -,tyüd\ *n* 1 : FATIGUE 1a, WEARINESS 2 : LANGUOR 2, LISTLESSNESS [Middle French, from Latin *lassitudo,* from *lassus* "weary"]

las·so \'las-ō, la-'sü\ *n, pl* **lassos** *or* **lassoes** : a rope or long thong of leather with a running noose that is used especially for catching livestock [Spanish *lazo,* from Latin *laqueus* "noose, snare"] — **lasso** *vt*

¹last \'last\ *vb* 1 : to continue in being or operation : go on ⟨the meeting *lasted* three hours⟩ 2 a : to remain valid or important : ENDURE ⟨a book that will *last*⟩ b : to manage to continue ⟨won't *last* on that job⟩ 3 : to be enough for the needs of ⟨supplies to *last* you for a week⟩ [Old English *lǣstan* "to last, follow"] — **last·er** *n* □ ORIGIN English *last* has several homonyms. The verb *last* means "to continue" or "to endure". In Old English, *lǣstan* was used like its modern decendant to mean "to continue", but it also meant "to follow". The original meaning was probably "to follow a track". Old English *lǣstan* is related to the Old English noun *lāst,* which means "footprint" or "track". This noun is the ancestor of the shoemaker's *last,* a form in the shape of a foot. The very common adjective and adverb *last,* which mean "after the others", are not related to this verb and noun. They come from Old English *latost,* superlative of *lǣt,* "late, slow."

²last *adj* 1 a : following all the rest ⟨*last* on the list⟩ b : being the only remaining ⟨my *last* dollar⟩ 2 a : belonging to the final stage ⟨the four *last* things⟩ b : administered to the dying ⟨*last* rites⟩ 3 a : next before the present ⟨*last* week⟩ b : most up-to-date : LATEST 4 : least likely ⟨the *last* thing they'd want⟩ 5 a : CONCLUSIVE, ULTIMATE ⟨no *last* answer to that problem⟩ b : highest in degree : SUPREME [Old English *latost,* superlative of *lǣt* "late"] — **last·ly** *adv* □ SYN FINAL, ULTIMATE: LAST applies to something that comes at the end of a series but does not always imply that the series is completed or stopped ⟨the *last* stop on the bus line⟩ ⟨the *last* news bulletin I heard⟩ FINAL stresses a definite closing of a series, process, or stage of progress ⟨*final* exams⟩ ULTIMATE implies the last degree or stage of a long process beyond which further progress or change is impossible ⟨*ultimate* collapse of civilization⟩

³last *adv* 1 : after all others : at the end ⟨ran *last* in the race⟩ 2 : most lately ⟨saw them *last* in New York⟩ 3 : in conclusion ⟨and *last,* I'd like to talk about money⟩

⁴last *n* : something that is last

⁵last *n* : a wooden or metal form which is shaped like the human foot and on which a shoe is shaped or repaired [Old English *lǣste,* from *lāst* "footprint"]

⁶last *vt* : to shape with a last — **last·er** *n*

last·ing *adj* : existing or continuing a long while : ENDURING — **last·ing·ly** \'las-ting-lē\ *adv* — **last·ing·ness** *n* □ SYN LASTING, PERMANENT, DURABLE mean enduring for so long as to seem fixed or established. LASTING implies a capacity to continue indefinitely ⟨*lasting* friendships⟩ PERMANENT may add the implication of being designed to stand or continue indefinitely ⟨a *permanent* arrangement⟩ ⟨*permanent* buildings⟩

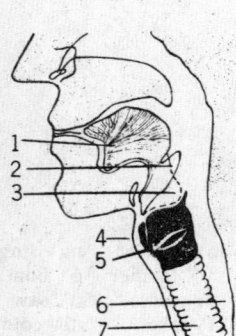

larynx: *1* tongue, *2* epiglottis opening larynx, *3* epiglottis closing larynx, *4* Adam's apple, *5* vocal cords, *6* esophagus, *7* trachea

DURABLE implies power to resist destructive agencies ⟨*durable* fabrics⟩

Last Judgment *n* : JUDGMENT 3

Last Supper *n* : the supper eaten by Jesus and his disciples on the night of his betrayal

last straw *n* : the last of a series that brings one beyond the point of endurance [from the fable of the last straw that broke the camel's back when added to his burden]

last word *n* **1** : the final remark in a verbal exchange **2** : the power of final decision **3** : the most advanced, up-to-date, or fashionable one of its kind ⟨the *last word* in cars⟩

¹latch \'lach\ *vi* **1** : to catch or get hold ⟨*latch* onto a pass⟩ **2** : to attach oneself [Old English *læccan*]

²latch *n* : a device that holds something in place by entering a notch or cavity; *esp* : a catch that holds a door or gate closed and that sometimes is operated by a key on one side and a knob on the other

³latch *vb* : to make fast with or as if with a latch : SHUT 1

latch·string \-,string\ *n* : a string for raising a latch so as to release it

¹late \'lāt\ *adj* **1 a** : coming or remaining after the due, usual, or proper time ⟨a *late* spring⟩ **b** : of or relating to an advanced stage in time or development ⟨the *late* Middle Ages⟩; *esp* : far advanced toward the close of the day or night ⟨*late* hours⟩ **2 a** : living comparatively recently ⟨the *late* president⟩ **b** : being something or holding a position or relationship recently but not now ⟨the *late* belligerents⟩ **c** : made, appearing, or happening in times close to the present ⟨a *late* discovery⟩ [Old English *læt*] SYN see RECENT — **late·ness** *n*

²late *adv* **1 a** : after the usual or proper time **b** : at or to an advanced point of time ⟨stayed *late* at the party⟩ — often used with on ⟨see me *later* on⟩ **2** : not long ago : RECENTLY ⟨a person *late* of Chicago⟩ — **of late** : LATELY, RECENTLY

late·com·er \'lāt-,kəm-ər\ *n* : one that arrives late; *also* : a recent arrival

¹la·teen \lə-'tēn\ *adj* : of, relating to, or being a sailing rig characterized by a triangular sail extended by a long spar crossing a low mast at an angle of about 45 degrees [French *voile latine* "lateen sail", derived from Latin *Latinus* "Latin"]

²lateen *n* **1** *also* **la·teen·er** \-'tē-nər\ : a lateen-rigged ship **2** : a lateen sail

Late Greek *n* : the Greek language used in the 3d to 6th centuries

Late Latin *n* : the Latin language used by writers in the 3d to 6th centuries

late·ly \'lāt-lē\ *adv* : in recent time ⟨what have you done for me *lately*⟩

lat·en \'lāt-n\ *vb* : to grow or cause to grow late

la·ten·cy \'lāt-n-sē\ *n, pl* **-cies** : the quality or state of being latent : DORMANCY

la·tent \'lāt-nt\ *adj* : present but not visible or active ⟨*latent* abilities⟩ ⟨*latent* infection⟩ [Latin *latens*, from *latēre* "to lie hidden"] — **la·tent·ly** *adv* ☐ SYN LATENT, DORMANT, QUIESCENT mean not now showing its presence or existence. LATENT applies to a power or quality that has not yet come forth but may emerge and develop ⟨talents which were *latent* in childhood⟩ DORMANT suggests inactivity as though sleeping ⟨a *dormant* volcano⟩ QUIESCENT suggests a temporary cessation of activity ⟨*quiescent* lung disease⟩

latent heat *n* : heat energy absorbed or evolved in a process (as fusion or vaporization)

latent period *n* : the interval (as the incubation period of a disease) between the introduction of a cause and the occurrence of its effect

lat·er·ad \'lat-ə-,rad\ *adv* : toward the side [Latin *later-*, *latus* "side"]

¹lat·er·al \'lat-ə-rəl, 'la-trəl\ *adj* **1** : of or relating to the side : situated on, directed toward, or coming from the side ⟨the *lateral* branches of a tree⟩ **2** : being a part of the outside of a geometric solid that is not a base or completely included in a base ⟨a *lateral* edge⟩ ⟨a *lateral* face⟩ [Latin *lateralis*, from *later-*, *latus* "side"] — **lat·er·al·ly** \-ē\ *adv*

²lateral *n* **1** : a lateral part or branch **2** : a pass in football thrown to the side or to the rear

lateral line *n* : a sense organ of the skin of most fishes that is sensitive to low vibrations and extends along each side of the body

lat·er·ite \'lat-ə-,rīt\ *n* : a residual product of rock decay that is red in color and rich in the oxides of iron and hydroxide of aluminum [Latin *later* "brick"] — **lat·er·it·ic** \,lat-ə-'rit-ik\ *adj*

lat·est \'lāt-əst\ *n* : the most recent style or development ⟨have you heard the *latest*?⟩

la·tex \'lā-,teks\ *n, pl* **la·ti·ces** \'lāt-ə-,sēz, 'lat-\ *or* **la·tex·es** **1** : a milky juice produced by plants especially of the milkweed family ⟨rubber is produced from a *latex*⟩ **2** : a water emulsion of a synthetic rubber or plastic used especially in paints and adhesives [Latin, "fluid"] — **lat·i·cif·er·ous** \,lāt-ə-'sif-rəs, ,lat-, -ə-rəs\ *adj*

lath \'lath *also* 'lath\ *n, pl* **laths** : a thin narrow strip of wood used especially as a base for plaster [Old English *lætt*] — **lath** *vt*

lathe \'lāth\ *n* : a machine in which a piece of material is held and turned while being shaped by a tool [probably from Middle English *lath* "supporting stand"]

¹lath·er \'lath-ər\ *n* **1 a** : a thick foam or froth formed when a detergent is agitated in water **b** : foam or froth from profuse sweating (as on a horse) **2** : an overwrought state : DITHER [Old English *lēathor*] — **lathery**, \'lath-rē-ə-rē\ *adj*

²lather *vb* **lath·ered; lath·er·ing** \'lath-ring, -ə-ring\ **1 a** : to spread lather over ⟨to *lather* one's face for shaving⟩ **b** : to form a lather or a froth like lather ⟨this soap *lathers* well⟩ **2** : to beat severely : FLOG — **lath·er·er** \'lath-ər-ər\ *n*

lath·ing \'lath-ing, 'lath-\ *n* **1** : the action or process of placing laths **2** : a quantity or an installation of laths

lat·i·me·ria \,lat-ə-'mir-ē-ə\ *n* : any of a genus of living coelacanth fishes of deep seas off southern Africa — compare LOBE-FIN [Marjorie E. D. Courtenay-*Latimer*, born 1907, South African museum director]

¹Lat·in \'lat-n\ *adj* **1 a** : of, relating to, or composed in Latin ⟨*Latin* grammar⟩ **b** : ROMANCE ⟨*Latin* languages⟩ **2** : of or relating to the part of the Catholic Church that until recently used a Latin rite **3** : of or relating to the peoples or countries using Romance languages; *esp* : of or relating to the peoples or countries of Latin America [Old English, from Latin *Latinus*, from *Latium*, ancient country of Italy]

²Latin *n* **1** : the Italic language of ancient Rome and until modern times the dominant language of school, church, and state in western Europe **2** : a Catholic of the Latin rite **3** : a member of one of the peoples speaking Romance languages; *esp* : a native or inhabitant of Latin America

Latin alphabet *n* : an alphabet that was used for writing Latin and that has been modified for writing many modern languages (as English)

Lat·in·ate \'lat-n-,āt\ *adj* : of, relating to, resembling, or derived from Latin

Latin cross *n* : a cross having a long upright shaft and a shorter crossbar above the middle

Lat·in·ism \'lat-n-,iz-əm\ *n* **1** : a word, idiom, or mode of speech derived from or modeled on Latin **2** : Latin quality, character, or mode of thought

Lat·in·ist \-n-əst\ *n* : a specialist in the Latin language or Roman culture

la·tin·i·ty \la-'tin-ət-e, lə-\ *n, often cap* **1** : a way of speaking or writing Latin **2** : LATINISM 2

lat·in·ize \'lat-n-,īz\ *vt, often cap* : to give Latin characteristics or forms to — **lat·in·i·za·tion** \,lat-n-ə-'zā-shən\ *n*

lat·ish \'lāt-ish\ *adj* : somewhat late

²lateen 1

\ə\ abut \ng\ sing
\ər\ further \ō\ bone
\a\ mat \ȯ\ saw
\ā\ take \ȯi\ coin
\ä\ cot, cart \th\ thin
\au̇\ out \th\ this
\ch\ chin \ü\ food
\e\ pet \u̇\ foot
\ē\ easy \y\ yet
\g\ go \yü\ few
\i\ tip \yu̇\ cure
\ī\ life \zh\ vision
\j\ job

latitude 1a

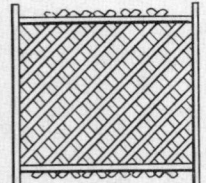

lattice 1a

lat·i·tude \'lat-ə-,tüd, -,tyüd\ *n* **1 a** : angular distance north or south from the earth's equator measured in degrees **b** : angular distance of a celestial body from the ecliptic **c** : a region or locality as marked by its latitude **2** : the range of exposures within which a film or plate will produce a negative or positive of satisfactory quality **3** : freedom from narrow restrictions ⟨were allowed great *latitude* in their editorials⟩ [Latin *latitudin-, latitudo* "width", from *latus* "wide"] — **lat·i·tu·di·nal** \,lat-ə-'tüd-nəl, -'tyüd-, -n-əl\ *adj* — **lat·i·tu·di·nal·ly** \-ē-\ *adv*

lat·i·tu·di·nar·i·an \,lat-ə-,tüd-n-'er-ē-ən, -,tyüd-\ *n* : a person who is broad and liberal in standards of religious belief and conduct — **latitudinarian** *adj* — **lat·i·tu·di·nar·i·an·ism** \-ē-ə-,niz-əm\ *n*

la·trine \lə-'trēn\ *n* **1** : a receptacle (as a pit in the earth) for use as a toilet **2** : BATHROOM [French, from Latin *latrina* "bath, toilet", derived from *lavere* "to wash"]

lat·ter \'lat-ər\ *adj* **1 a** : more recent : LATER **b** : of or relating to the end : FINAL **2** : of, relating to, or being the second of two things referred to [Old English *lætra,* comparative of *læt* "late"]

lat·ter–day \,lat-ər-,dā\ *adj* **1** : of a later or subsequent time **2** : of present or recent times

Latter–day Saint *n* : a member of a religious body founded by Joseph Smith in 1830 and accepting the Book of Mormon as divine revelation : MORMON

lat·ter·ly \'lat-ər-lē\ *adv* : LATELY, RECENTLY

lat·tice \'lat-əs\ *n* **1 a** : a framework or structure of crossed wood or metal strips **b** : a window, door, or gate having a lattice **2** : a regular geometrical arrangement of points or objects over an area or in space ⟨the *lattice* of atoms in a crystal⟩ [Middle French *lattis*] — **lattice** *vt* — **lat·ticed** \-əst\ *adj*

lat·tice·work \'lat-ə-,swərk\ *n* : a lattice or work made of lattices

¹Lat·vi·an \'lat-vē-ən\ *adj* : of, relating to, or characteristic of Latvia, the Latvians, or Latvian

²Latvian *n* **1** : a native or inhabitant of Latvia **2** : the Baltic language of the Latvian people

¹laud \'lod\ *n* **1** *pl* : an office of solemn praise to God forming with matins the first of the canonical hours **2** : PRAISE 1, ACCLAIM [derived from Latin *laud-, laus* "praise"]

²laud *vt* : PRAISE 2, EXTOL

laud·able \'lod-ə-bəl\ *adj* : worthy of praise : COMMENDABLE — **laud·abil·i·ty** \,lod-ə-'bil-ət-ē\ *n* — **laud·able·ness** \'lod-ə-bəl-nəs\ *n* — **laud·ably** \-blē\ *adv*

lau·da·num \'lod-nəm, -n-əm\ *n* **1** : a formerly used preparation of opium **2** : a tincture of opium [New Latin]

lau·da·tion \lo-'dā-shən\ *n* : the act of praising : EULOGY

lau·da·to·ry \'lod-ə-,tōr-ē, -,tor-\ *adj* : of, relating to, or expressing praise

¹laugh \'laf, 'laf\ *vb* **1 a** : to show mirth, joy, or scorn with a smile and chuckle or explosive sound **b** : to become amused or derisive ⟨*laughed* at their early efforts⟩ **2** : to produce the sound or appearance of laughter **3** : to utter with a laugh ⟨to *laugh* one's consent⟩ [Old English *hliehhan, hlæhan*] — **laugh·er** *n*

²laugh *n* **1** : the act or sound of laughing **2** : a cause for derision or merriment

laugh·able \'laf-ə-bəl, 'laf-\ *adj* : of a kind to provoke laughter or derision : RIDICULOUS — **laugh·able·ness** *n* — **laugh·ably** \-blē\ *adv* □ SYN LAUGHABLE, RISIBLE, LUDICROUS, RIDICULOUS mean provoking laughter or mirth. LAUGHABLE and RISIBLE may apply to anything that arouses laughter; LUDICROUS suggests obvious absurdity or preposterousness that excites both laughter and scorn or sometimes pity; RIDICULOUS implies extreme absurdity, foolishness, or ineptness.

laugh·ing *adj* : fit to be treated or accompanied with laughter : LAUGHABLE ⟨this is no *laughing* matter⟩

laughing gas *n* : NITROUS OXIDE

laughing jackass *n* : KOOKABURRA

laugh·ing·ly \'laf-ing-lē, 'laf-\ *adv* : with laughter

laugh·ing·stock \'laf-ing-,stäk, 'laf-\ *n* : an object of ridicule

laugh·ter \'laf-tər, 'laf-\ *n* : the action or sound of laughing [Old English *hleahtor*]

¹launch \'lonch, 'länch\ *vb* **1 a** : to throw forward : HURL ⟨*launch* a spear⟩ **b** : to send off (a self-propelled object) ⟨*launch* a rocket⟩ **2** : to set (a ship) afloat **3 a** : to put in operation : BEGIN ⟨*launch* an attack⟩ **b** : to give (a person) a start ⟨*launched* their children in the family business⟩ **4 a** : to make a start (as on a course of action) ⟨had *launched* on a difficult course of study⟩ **b** : to throw oneself energetically : PLUNGE ⟨*launched* into a dreary monologue⟩ [Old North French *lancher,* from Late Latin *lanceare* "to wield a lance", from Latin *lancea* "lance"]

²launch *n* : an act of launching

³launch *n* : a small motorboat that is open or that has the forepart of the hull covered [Portuguese *lancha*]

launch·er \'lon-chər, 'län-\ *n* : one that launches: as **a** : a device for firing a grenade from a rifle **b** : a device for launching a rocket or rocket shell **c** : CATAPULT

launch pad *or* **launching pad** *n* : a nonflammable platform from which a rocket can be launched

laun·der \'lon-dər, 'län-\ *vb* **laun·dered; laun·der·ing** \-də-ring, -dring\ **1** : to wash (as clothes) in water; *also* : to wash and iron ⟨a freshly *laundered* shirt⟩ **2** : to wash or wash and iron clothing or household linens **3** : to undergo washing and ironing ⟨fabrics guaranteed to *launder* well⟩ [Middle English *launder* "launderer", from Middle French *lavandier,* from Medieval Latin *lavandarius,* from Latin *lavare* "to wash"] — **laun·der·er** \-dər-ər\ *n* — **laun·dress** \-drəs\ *n*

Laun·dro·mat \'lon-drə-,mat, 'län-\ *trademark* — used for a self-service laundry

laun·dry \'lon-drē, 'län-\ *n, pl* **-dries** **1** : clothes or linens that have been or are to be laundered **2** : a place where laundering is done

lau·re·ate \'lor-ē-ət, 'lar-\ *n* : a recipient of honor for achievement in an art or science; *esp* : POET LAUREATE [Latin *laureatus* "crowned with laurel", from *laurea* "laurel wreath", from *laurus* "laurel"] — **laureate** *adj* — **lau·re·ate·ship** \-,ship\ *n*

lau·rel \'lor-əl, 'lar-\ *n* **1** : any of a genus of trees or shrubs related to the sassafras and cinnamon; *esp* : a small evergreen tree of southern Europe with foliage used by the ancient Greeks to crown victors in various contests **2** : a tree or shrub (as a mountain laurel) like the true laurel **3** : a crown of laurel : HONOR [derived from Latin *laurus*]

la·va \'läv-ə, 'lav-\ *n* : molten rock coming from a volcano; *also* : such rock that has cooled and hardened [Italian, from Latin *labes* "fall"]

la·va·bo \lə-'väb-ō\ *n, often cap* : a ceremony at Mass in which the celebrant after offering the oblations washes his hands and says Psalm 25:6–12 [Latin, "I shall wash", from *lavare* "to wash"]

la·vage \lə-'väzh\ *n* : a washing out (as of a wound or hollow organ) for medicinal reasons [French, from *laver* "to wash", from Latin *lavare*]

la·va·liere *or* **la·val·liere** \,läv-ə-'liər, ,lav-\ *n* : a pendant on a fine chain that is worn as a necklace [French *lavallière* "necktie with a large bow"]

lav·a·to·ry \'lav-ə-,tōr-ē, -,tor-\ *n, pl* **-ries** **1** : a vessel for washing; *esp* : a fixed bowl or basin with running water and drainpipe **2** : a room with conveniences for washing and usually with one or more toilets **3** : WATER CLOSET [Medieval Latin *lavatorium,* from Latin *lavare* "to wash"]

lave \'lāv\ *vb* **1 a** : WASH 1 **b** *archaic* : to wash oneself : BATHE **2** : to flow along or against ⟨water *laving* the shore⟩ [Old English *lafian,* from Latin *lavare*]

lav·en·der \'lav-ən-dər\ **1** : a Mediterranean mint widely cultivated for its narrow aromatic leaves and spikes of lilac-purple flowers which are dried and used in sachets; *also* : any of several related plants used similarly **2** : a pale purple [Anglo-French *lavendre,* from Medieval Latin *lavandula*]

¹la·ver \'lā-vər\ *n* : a large basin used for ceremonial ablutions in ancient Judaism [Middle French *lavoir,* derived from Latin *lavare* "to wash"]

²la·ver \'lā-vər, 'lä-\ *n* : any of several mostly edible seaweeds [Latin, a water plant]

¹lav·ish \'lav-ish\ *adj* **1** : spending or giving more than is necessary : EXTRAVAGANT ⟨*lavish* with money⟩ ⟨*lavish* of praise⟩ **2** : produced or given freely or in abundance ⟨*lavish* hospitality⟩ [Middle English *lavas* "abundance", from Middle French *lavasse* "downpour of rain", from *laver* "to wash", from Latin *lavare*] — **lav·ish·ly** *adv* — **lav·ish·ness** *n*

²lavish *vt* : to spend or give freely ⟨*lavish* affection on them⟩

law \'lȯ\ *n* **1 a** : a rule of conduct or action established by custom or laid down by the supreme governing authority of a community, state, or nation **b** : a body of such rules and customs **2 a** : the state of order brought about by observance and enforcement of laws ⟨preserve *law* and order⟩ **b** : an agent or agency for enforcing laws ⟨an officer of the *law*⟩ **c** : the action of laws and especially court action as a means of achieving justice or redressing wrongs **3** *cap* **a** : the revelation of the divine will set forth in the Old Testament **b** : the first part of the Jewish scriptures — compare HAGIOGRAPHA, PROPHETS **4 a** : the legal profession **b** : law as an area of knowledge ⟨study *law*⟩ **5** : a rule of construction or procedure (as in an art, craft, or game) **6** : something that has the force of authority and must be obeyed ⟨in the classroom the teacher's word is *law*⟩ **7** : a rule or principle stating something that always works in the same way under the same conditions ⟨the *law* of gravity⟩ [Old English *lagu,* of Scandinavian origin] □ SYN LAW, REGULATION, STATUTE, ORDINANCE mean a principle that governs action or procedure. LAW implies imposition by a sovereign authority and obligation of obedience by all; REGULATION carries an implication of authority exercised in order to control an organization or system; STATUTE implies a law enacted by a legislative body often as distinguished from the common or unwritten law; ORDINANCE applies to an order governing some detail or procedure enforced by a limited authority such as a municipality ⟨city *ordinances* for traffic regulation⟩ SYN see in addition HYPOTHESIS

law–abid·ing \'lȯ-ə-,bīd-ing\ *adj* : obedient to the law

law·break·er \'lȯ-,brā-kər\ *n* : a person who breaks the law — **law·break·ing** \-king\ *adj or n*

law·ful \'lȯ-fəl\ *adj* **1** : permitted or not prohibited by law ⟨conduct a demonstration in a *lawful* manner⟩ **2** : established or recognized by law : RIGHTFUL ⟨the *lawful* owner⟩ — **law·ful·ly** \-'fə-lē, -flē\ *adv* — **law·ful·ness** \-fəl-nəs\ *n* □ SYN LAWFUL, LEGAL, LEGITIMATE, LICIT mean being in accordance with law. LAWFUL stresses conformity to law of any kind; LEGAL implies reference to the law of courts; LEGITIMATE implies a legal right or one supported by tradition, custom, or accepted standards of authenticity ⟨the *legitimate* heir to the throne⟩ LICIT emphasizes strict conformity to law specifically regulating the way something is performed or carried on.

law·giv·er \'lȯ-,giv-ər\ *n* **1** : one who gives a code of laws to a people **2** : LEGISLATOR

law·less \'lȯ-ləs\ *adj* **1** : having no laws : not based on or regulated by law ⟨the *lawless* frontier⟩ **2** : not controlled by law : UNRULY, DISORDERLY ⟨a *lawless* mob⟩ — **law·less·ly** *adv* — **law·less·ness** *n*

law·mak·er \'lȯ-,mā-kər\ *n* : a person who has a part in framing laws : LEGISLATOR — **law·mak·ing** *adj or n*

¹lawn \'lȯn, 'län\ *n* : a fine sheer linen or cotton fabric of plain weave that is thinner than cambric [*Laon,* France] — **lawny** \-ē\ *adj*

²lawn *n* : ground (as around a house) covered with grass that is kept mowed [Middle English *launde* "glade, pasture", from Middle French *lande* "heath", of Celtic origin]

lawn bowling *n* : a bowling game played on a green with wooden balls which are rolled at a jack

lawn mower *n* : a machine for cutting grass on lawns

lawn tennis *n* : TENNIS

law of cosines : a theorem in trigonometry : the square of a side of a plane triangle equals the sum of the squares of the remaining sides minus twice the product of those sides and the cosine of the angle included between them

law of definite proportions : a statement in chemistry : every definite compound always contains the same elements in the same proportions by mass

law of dominance : MENDEL'S LAW 3

law of independent assortment : MENDEL'S LAW 2

law of Mo·ses \-'mō-zəz, -zəs\ : PENTATEUCH

law of segregation : MENDEL'S LAW 1

law of sines : a theorem in trigonometry : the ratio of the length of each side of a plane triangle to the sine of the opposite angle is the same for all three sides and angles

law·ren·ci·um \lȯ-'ren-sē-əm\ *n* : a short-lived radioactive element produced from californium — see ELEMENT table [New Latin, from Ernest O. *Lawrence,* died 1958, American physicist]

law·suit \'lȯ-,süt\ *n* : ACTION 1, SUIT

law·yer \'lȯ-yər, 'lȯi-ər\ *n* : one whose profession is to practice law and to advise clients on legal matters and represent them in court

lax \'laks\ *adj* **1** : lacking in restraint or the power to restrain ⟨*lax* bowels⟩ ⟨*lax* morals⟩ **2** : not strict or stringent ⟨*lax* discipline⟩ **3 a** : not firm or rigid **b** : having an open or loose texture ⟨a *lax* flower cluster⟩ **4** : produced with the speech muscles in a relatively relaxed state ⟨the *lax* vowels \i\ and \u̇\⟩ — compare TENSE [Latin *laxus* "loose"] — **lax·ly** \'lak-slē\ *adv* — **lax·ness** *n*

¹lax·a·tive \'lak-sət-iv\ *adj* : having a tendency to loosen or relax; *esp* : relieving constipation — **lax·a·tive·ly** *adv* — **lax·a·tive·ness** *n*

²laxative *n* : a usually mild laxative drug — compare PURGATIVE

lax·i·ty \'lak-sət-ē\ *n* : the quality or state of being lax ⟨*laxity* in discipline⟩

¹lay \'lā\ *vb* **laid** \'lād\; **lay·ing** **1** : to beat or strike down ⟨wheat *laid* flat by a hailstorm⟩ **2 a** : to put or set on or against something ⟨*lay* the book on the table⟩ ⟨*lay* a watch to one's ear⟩ **b** : to place or put down in an orderly sequence ⟨*lay* a sewer⟩ **c** : to set in order for a meal ⟨*lay* the table⟩ ⟨three places were *laid*⟩ **3** : BURY 1 **4** : to produce and deposit eggs ⟨the hens won't *lay*⟩ **5 a** : to put forward for consideration : SUBMIT ⟨*laid* their case before the committee⟩ **b** : ASSERT, ALLEGE ⟨*lay* claim to the estate⟩ **c** : to place (as emphasis or importance) on something ⟨*lay* great stress on neatness⟩ **6** : SET, IMPOSE ⟨*lay* a tax on liquor⟩ **7 a** : CONTRIVE, DEVISE ⟨*lay* plans⟩ **b** : to make ready or put in operation ⟨*laid* a trap⟩ **8 a** : BET 1 ⟨*lay* $10 on the race⟩ **b** : BET 2 ⟨*lay* you ten to one⟩ **9** : to cause to settle or subside ⟨a shower *laid* the dust⟩; *also* : CALM, ALLAY ⟨*laid* their fears⟩ **10** : to assign as a burden of reproach ⟨*laid* the theft to the chauffeur⟩ **11** : to bring to a specified condition ⟨*lay* waste the land⟩ **12** : to place (as the action or a scene of a story) in a particular location ⟨the scene was *laid* in wartime London⟩ [Old English *lecgan*] — **lay aside 1** : DISCARD, ABANDON ⟨*lay aside* prejudices⟩ **2** : to put away for future or special use ⟨*lay* a few dollars *aside* each week⟩ — **lay bare** : to expose or make known : REVEAL — **lay eyes on** : to

\ə\ abut	\ng\ sing
\ər\ further	\ō\ bone
\a\ mat	\ȯ\ saw
\ā\ take	\ȯi\ coin
\ä\ cot, cart	\th\ thin
\au̇\ out	\th\ this
\ch\ chin	\ü\ food
\e\ pet	\u̇\ foot
\ē\ easy	\y\ yet
\g\ go	\yü\ few
\i\ tip	\yu̇\ cure
\ī\ life	\zh\ vision
\j\ job	

catch sight of : SEE — **lay for** : to lie in wait to attack — **lay hold of** : GRASP, SEIZE ⟨*lay hold of* a rope⟩ — **lay into** : ATTACK — **lay one's finger on** : to discover and point out accurately

²lay *n* **1** : the way in which a thing lies or is laid in relation to something else ⟨*lay* of the land⟩ **2** : an egg-laying condition

³lay *past of* LIE

⁴lay *n* **1** : a simple narrative poem : BALLAD **2** : MELODY 2, SONG [Old French *lai*]

⁵lay *adj* **1** : of or relating to the laity : not ecclesiastical **2** : of or relating to members of a religious house occupied with domestic or manual work ⟨a *lay* brother⟩ **3** : not of or from a particular profession : UNPROFESSIONAL ⟨the *lay* public⟩ [Old French *lai*, from Late Latin *laicus*, from Greek *laikos* "of the people", from *laos* "people"]

lay away *vt* : to put aside for future use or delivery

lay by *vt* : to store for future use : SAVE

lay down *vt* **1** : to give up : SURRENDER ⟨*lay down* your arms⟩ **2 a** : ESTABLISH, PRESCRIBE ⟨*lays down* standards⟩ **b** : to assert or command dogmatically ⟨*lay down* the law⟩

¹lay·er \'lā-ər, 'le-ər, 'ler\ *n* **1** : one that lays ⟨the hens were poor *layers*⟩ **2** : one thickness, course, or fold laid or lying over or under another ⟨a *layer* of rock⟩ **3 a** : a branch or shoot of a plant that roots while still attached to the parent plant **b** : a plant developed by layering — **lay·ered** \'lā-ərd, 'le-ərd, 'lerd\ *adj*

²layer *vt* : to propagate (a plant) by means of layers

lay·er·age \'lā-ə-rij, 'le-ə-\ *n* : the practice, art, or process of rooting plants by layering

lay·ette \lā-'et\ *n* : a complete outfit of clothing and equipment for a newborn infant [French, from Middle French *laye* "box", from Dutch *lade*]

lay figure \'lā-\ *n* **1** : a jointed model of the human body used by artists to show the disposition of drapery **2** : a person of no importance or individuality : DUMMY, PUPPET [obsolete *layman* "lay figure", from Dutch *ledeman, leeman*, from *lid* "limb" + *man* "man"]

lay in *vt* : to store up : lay by ⟨*lay in* a supply of groceries⟩

lay·man \'lā-mən\ *n* **1** : a person who is not a member of the clergy **2** : a person who is not a member of a particular profession

lay·off \'lā-,óf\ *n* **1** : the act of laying off an employee or a work force **2** : a period of inactivity or idleness

lay off \lā-'óf, 'lā-\ *vb* **1** : to mark or measure off **2** : to cease to employ (a worker) usually temporarily **3 a** : to leave undisturbed ⟨*lay off* me, will you⟩ **b** : AVOID, QUIT ⟨*lay off* smoking⟩ **4** : to stop or rest from work

lay on *vi* : ATTACK ⟨grabbed clubs and *laid on* for all they were worth⟩

lay·out \'lā-,aút\ *n* **1** : ARRANGEMENT, PLAN ⟨the *layout* of a house⟩ **2** : something that is laid out ⟨a model train *layout*⟩ **3** : the way in which a piece of printed matter is arranged ⟨the *layout* of a page⟩; *also* : DUMMY 6 **4** : a set or outfit especially of tools

lay out \lā-'aút, 'lā-\ *vt* **1** : to prepare (a corpse) for burial **2** : to plan in detail ⟨*lay out* a campaign⟩ **3** : ARRANGE 1, DESIGN **4** : SPEND 1

lay·over \'lā-,ō-vər\ *n* : STOPOVER 1

lay over \lā-'ō-vər, 'lā-\ *vi* : to make a temporary halt or stop ⟨*laid over* in New York for three days before flying back⟩

lay reader *n* **1** : an Anglican layman licensed to read sermons and conduct some religious services **2** : LECTOR

lay to \lā-'tü, 'lā-\ *vb* **1** : to bring (a ship) into the wind and hold stationary : lie to **2** : to apply or exert oneself

lay-up \'lā-,əp\ *n* **1** : the action of laying up or the condition of being laid up **2** : a jumping one-hand shot in basketball made from close under the basket by laying the ball over the rim or bouncing it off the backboard

lay up \lā-'əp, 'lā-\ *vt* **1** : to store up : lay by **2** : to disable or confine with illness or injury **3** : to take out of active service

lay·wom·an \-,wùm-ən\ *n* : a woman who is a member of the laity

la·zar \'laz-ər, 'lā-zər\ *n* : a person afflicted with a repulsive disease; *esp* : LEPER [Medieval Latin *lazarus*, from Late Latin *Lazarus*, beggar in parable in Luke 16:20–31]

laz·a·ret·to \,laz-ə-'ret-ō\ *or* **laz·a·ret** \-'ret, -'rēt\ *n, pl* **-rettos** *or* **-rets** **1** *usually* **lazaretto** : a hospital for contagious diseases **2** : a building or a ship used for detention in quarantine **3** *usually* **lazaret** : a space in a ship between decks used as a storeroom [Italian dialect *lazareto*, alteration of *nazareto*, from *Santa Maria di Nazaret*, church in Venice that maintained a hospital]

laze \'lāz\ *vb* : to pass time in idleness or relaxation : IDLE [back-formation from *lazy*]

la·zy \'lā-zē\ *adj* **la·zi·er; -est** **1** : not willing to act or work : IDLE, INDOLENT **2** : SLOW, SLUGGISH ⟨a *lazy* stream⟩ [perhaps from Low German *lasich* "feeble"] — **la·zi·ly** \-zə-lē\ *adv* — **la·zi·ness** \-zē-nəs\ *n* — **la·zy·ish** \-zē-ish\ *adj*

la·zy·bones \'lā-zē-,bōnz\ *n sing or pl* : a lazy person

lazy Su·san \,lā-zē-'süz-n\ *n* : a revolving tray placed on a dining table for serving food, condiments, or relishes

lea *or* **ley** \'lē, 'lā\ *n* **1** : GRASSLAND, PASTURE **2** *usually* **ley** : arable land used temporarily for hay or grazing [Old English *lēah*]

leach \'lēch\ *vt* : to pass a liquid and especially water through to carry off the soluble components; *also* : to dissolve out by such means ⟨*leach* alkali from ashes⟩ [probably derived from Old English *leccan* "to wet, moisten"]

¹lead \'lēd\ *vb* **led** \'led\; **lead·ing** \'lēd-ing\ **1** : to force to go with one ⟨police *led* the prisoner to jail⟩ **2 a** : to guide on the way : show the way ⟨you *lead* and we will follow⟩ **b** : to serve as a route or passage ⟨this road *leads* straight into town⟩ **c** : to be an entrance or connection ⟨that door *leads* to the kitchen⟩ **3** : to serve as a channel for ⟨a pipe *leads* water to the house⟩ **4** : to pass one's days in : LIVE ⟨*lead* an active life⟩ **5 a** : to march or go at the head of ⟨*lead* a parade⟩ **b** : to have first place in ⟨*leads* the world in coffee exports⟩; *also* : to serve as an example — often used in the phrase *lead the way* ⟨*lead* the way on political reform⟩ **c** : to have a margin over ⟨*leading* by 20 points at halftime⟩ **d** : to direct the operations, activity, or performance of ⟨*lead* an orchestra⟩ ⟨*leads* a Bible-study group⟩ **e** : to serve as guide for by performing one's own part ⟨*led* the choir in singing⟩ **6 a** : to influence to come to a conclusion ⟨you *led* me to believe you loved me⟩ **b** : to tempt or talk into going ⟨*led* them all astray⟩ **7 a** : to play as the first card or suit in a round ⟨*lead* trumps⟩ **b** : to be the first player of a round at cards ⟨*led* with an ace⟩ **8** : to begin a series of blows in boxing ⟨*leading* with a right⟩ **9** : to have as a definite aim or result ⟨study that *leads* to a degree⟩ [Old English *lǣdan*]

²lead *n* **1 a** (1) : position at the front : VANGUARD (2) : INITIATIVE 1 (3) : the act or privilege of leading in cards; *also* : the card or suit led **b** : EXAMPLE, PRECEDENT ⟨follow their *lead*⟩ **c** : a margin or measure of advantage or superiority or position in advance ⟨has a 2-length *lead*⟩ **2** : one that leads: as **a** : INDICATION 2, CLUE **b** : a principal role in a dramatic production; *also* : one who plays such a role **c** : LEASH 1 **d** : an introductory section of a news story; *also* : a news story of chief importance **e** : the first in a series or exchange of blows in boxing **3** : an insulated electrical conductor **4** : a position taken by a base runner off a base toward the next

³lead *adj* : acting or serving as a lead or leader ⟨the *lead* article in this month's issue⟩

⁴lead \'led\ *n* **1** : a heavy soft malleable bluish white metallic chemical element that is found mostly in combination and is used in pipes, cable sheaths, solder, and type metal — see ELEMENT table **2 a** : a mass of lead used on a line for finding the depth of water (as in the ocean) **b** *pl* : lead framing for panes in windows **c** : a thin strip of metal used to separate lines of type in printing **3 a** : a thin stick of marking substance (as graphite) in or for a pencil **b** : WHITE LEAD **4** : bullets in quantity **5** : TETRAETHYL LEAD [Old English *lēad*] — **lead·less** \-ləs\ *adj*

⁵lead \'led\ *vt* **1** : to cover, line, or weight with lead **2** : to fix (glass) in position with lead **3** : to place lead or other spacing material between the lines of (type matter) **4** : to treat or mix with lead or a lead compound ⟨*leaded* gasoline⟩

lead acetate *n* : a poisonous soluble salt of lead $PbC_4H_6O_4 \cdot 3H_2O$ used in dyeing and printing

lead arsenate *n* : an acid salt of lead $PbHAsO_4$ used as an insecticide

lead dioxide *n* : a poisonous compound PbO_2 that is used as an oxidizing agent and as an electrode in batteries — called also *lead peroxide*

lead·en \'led-n\ *adj* **1 a** : made of lead **b** : of the color of lead : dull gray **2** : low in quality : POOR **3 a** : oppressively heavy **b** : SLUGGISH **c** : lacking spirit or animation : DULL ⟨*leaden* spirits⟩ — **lead·en·ly** *adv* — **lead·en·ness** \-n-nəs, -n-əs\ *n*

lead·er \'led-ər\ *n* **1** : one that leads: as **a** : one that goes along to guide and show the way **b** : one that directs or has authority over others : (1) : COMMANDER 1 (2) : FOREMAN, STRAW BOSS **c** : one that is foremost or that sets an example ⟨a *leader* in fashion⟩ **d** : CONDUCTOR **b e** : an animal placed at the head of a team **f** *pl* : dots or hyphens used (as in an index) to lead the eye horizontally across the page; *also* : ELLIPSIS **2 a** : a main shoot of a plant **b** : TENDON, SINEW **3** : a short length of material for attaching a lure or hook to the end of a fishing line — **lead·er·less** \-ləs\ *adj* — **lead·er·ship** \-,ship\ *n*

lead-in \'led-,in\ *n* : something that leads in; *esp* : the part of a radio antenna that runs to the transmitting or receiving set — **lead-in** *adj*

lead·ing \'led-ing\ *adj* **1** : coming or ranking first or among the first : FOREMOST **2** : exercising leadership **3** : serving to guide or direct ⟨a *leading* question⟩ **4** : given most prominent display

leading lady *n* : an actress who plays the leading feminine role in a play or movie

leading man *n* : an actor who plays the leading male role in a play or movie

leading tone *n* : the seventh musical degree of a major or minor scale — called also *subtonic* [from its leading harmonically to the tonic]

lead monoxide \'led-\ *n* : a yellow to brownish red poisonous compound PbO used in rubber manufacture and glassmaking

lead-off \'led-,ȯf\ *n* : a beginning or leading action — **lead-off** *adj*

lead off \led-'ȯf, 'led-\ *vt* : to make a start on : BEGIN

lead on *vt* : to entice or induce to proceed in a course especially when unwise or mistaken ⟨*led on* by the promise of wealth⟩

lead pencil \'led-\ *n* : a pencil using graphite as the marking material

lead poisoning *n* : chronic intoxication produced by absorption of lead into the system and characterized by severe colicky pains, a dark line along the gums, and local muscular paralysis

lead up \led-'əp, 'led-\ *vi* **1** : to prepare the way — used with *to* ⟨events *leading up* to the war⟩ **2** : to make a gradual or indirect approach to a topic — used with *to*

¹leaf \'lēf\ *n, pl* **leaves** \'lēvz\ **1 a** : a usually flat lateral outgrowth from a plant stem that functions primarily in food manufacture by photosynthesis **b** : FOLIAGE **2** : something suggestive of a leaf: as **a** : a part of a book or folded sheet containing a page on each side **b** : a part (as of window shutters, folding doors, or gates) that slides or is hinged **c** : a movable or removable part of a table top **d** : a thin sheet (as of metal) : LAMINA **e** : one of the plates of a leaf spring [Old English *lēaf*] — **leaf·less** \'lē-fləs\ *adj* — **leaf·like** \'lē-,flīk\ *adj*

²leaf *vi* **1** : to produce leaves **2** : to turn the pages of a book

leaf·age \'lē-fij\ *n* : FOLIAGE

leaf bud *n* : a bud that develops into a leafy shoot and does not produce flowers

leaf fat *n* : the fat that lines the abdominal cavity and encloses the kidneys; *esp* : such hog fat used in the manufacture of lard

leaf·hop·per \'lēf-,häp-ər\ *n* : any of numerous small leaping insects that are related to the cicadas and suck the juices of plants

leaf lard *n* : high quality lard made from leaf fat

leaf·let \'lē-flət\ *n* **1 a** : one of the divisions of a compound leaf **b** : a small or young foliage leaf **2 a** : a single printed sheet of paper unfolded or folded but not trimmed at the fold **b** : a sheet of small pages folded but not stitched

leaf miner *n* : any of various small insects that as larvae burrow in and eat the tissue of leaves

leaf mold *n* : a compost or layer composed chiefly of decayed vegetable matter

leaf spring *n* : a usually crescent-shaped spring made of several strips of metal of unequal length stacked and fastened together and arranged in length from longest to shortest

leaf·stalk \'lēf-,stȯk\ *n* : PETIOLE 1

leafy \'lē-fē\ *adj* **leaf·i·er; -est** **1** : having or abounding in leaves ⟨*leafy* woodlands⟩ **2** : consisting mostly of leaves ⟨*leafy* vegetables⟩

¹league \'lēg\ *n* : any of various units of distance from about 2.4 to 4.6 statute miles (3.9 to 7.4 kilometers) [Late Latin *leuga*, of Gaulish origin]

²league *n* **1 a** : an association or alliance of nations for a common purpose **b** : an association of persons or groups united for common interests or goals; *esp* : an association of athletic teams **2** : CLASS, CATEGORY ⟨a bit out of your *league*⟩ [Middle French *ligue*, from Italian *liga*, from *ligare* "to bind", from Latin] — **league** *vb*

leagu·er \'lē-gər\ *n* : a member of a league

¹leak \'lēk\ *vb* **1** : to enter or escape or permit to enter or escape through an opening usually by a fault or mistake ⟨fumes *leak* in⟩ **2** : to become known despite efforts at concealment ⟨the secret *leaked* out⟩ **3** : to give out (information) secretly ⟨*leaked* the story to the press⟩ [Old Norse *leka*]

²leak *n* **1 a** : a hole, crack, or flaw that lets something enter or escape **b** : a person who leaks information **2** : LEAKAGE 1a — **leak·proof** \-,prüf\ *adj*

leak·age \'lē-kij\ *n* **1 a** : the act, process, or an instance of leaking **b** : loss of electricity due especially to faulty insulation **2** : something or the amount that leaks in or out

leaky \'lē-kē\ *adj* **leak·i·er; -est** : permitting fluid to leak in or out — **leak·i·ness** *n*

¹lean \'lēn\ *vb* **leaned** \'lēnd, *chiefly British* 'lent\; **lean·ing** \'lē-ning\ **1 a** : to incline, deviate, or bend from a vertical position **b** : to shift one's weight to one side for support : rest against something ⟨*lean* on me⟩ **2** : to rely for support or inspiration ⟨children who *lean* on their parents⟩ **3** : to incline in opinion, taste, or desire ⟨*lean* toward simplicity⟩ [Old English *hleonian*]

²lean *n* : the act or an instance of leaning : INCLINATION

³lean *adj* **1 a** : lacking or deficient in flesh ⟨*lean* cattle⟩ **b** : containing little or no fat ⟨*lean* meat⟩ **2** : lacking

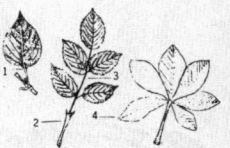

¹leaf 1a: *1* petiole,
2 stipule, 3 rachis,
4 leaflet

\ə\ abut   \ng\ sing
\ər\ further   \ō\ bone
\a\ mat   \ȯ\ saw
\ā\ take   \ȯi\ coin
\ä\ cot, cart   \th\ thin
\aú\ out   \th\ this
\ch\ chin   \ü\ food
\e\ pet   \ú\ foot
\ē\ easy   \y\ yet
\g\ go   \yü\ few
\i\ tip   \yú\ cure
\ī\ life   \zh\ vision
\j\ job

leatherback

richness, sufficiency, or productiveness **3** : character-ized by economy of style or expression ⟨*lean,* compact writing⟩ [Old English *hlǣne*] — **lean·ness** \'lēn-nəs\ *n*

⁴lean *n* : the part of meat that consists principally of fat-free muscle

lean·ing \'lē-niŋ\ *n* : INCLINATION 2, TENDENCY

leant \'lent\ *chiefly British past of* LEAN

¹lean-to \'lēn-,tü\ *n, pl* **lean-tos** **1** : a wing or exten-sion of a building having a lean-to roof **2** : a rough shed or shelter with a lean-to roof

²lean-to *adj* : having only one slope or pitch ⟨a *lean-to* roof⟩

¹leap \'lēp\ *vb* **leaped** *or* **leapt** \'lēpt, 'lept\; **leap·ing** \'lē-piŋ\ **1** : to spring or cause to spring free from or as if from the ground : JUMP ⟨*leap* over a fence⟩ ⟨*leap* a horse over a ditch⟩ **2 a** : to pass abruptly from one state or topic to another **b** : to act precipitately ⟨*leaped* at the chance⟩ [Old English *hlēapan*] — **leap·er** \'lē-pər\

²leap *n* **1 a** : an act of leaping : SPRING, BOUND **b** (1) : a place leaped over or from (2) : the distance covered by a leap **2** : a sudden transition — **by leaps and bounds** : very rapidly ⟨improved *by leaps and bounds*⟩

leap·frog \'lēp-,frȯg, -,fräg\ *n* : a game in which one player vaults over another who has bent down

leap year *n* : a year in the Gregorian calendar contain-ing 366 days with February 29 as the extra day

learn \'lərn\ *vb* **learned** \'lərnd, 'lərnt\ *also* **learnt** \'lərnt\; **learn·ing** **1 a** : to gain knowledge or under-standing of or skill in by study, instruction, or experi-ence **b** : MEMORIZE ⟨*learn* the lines of a play⟩ **c** : to come to realize ⟨*learned* that honesty paid⟩ **2** *substan-dard* : to cause to learn : TEACH **3** : to find out : ASCER-TAIN **4** : to acquire knowledge ⟨never too late to *learn*⟩ [Old English *leornian*] — **learn·able** \'lər-nə-bəl\ *adj* — **learn·er** *n* □ SYN LEARN and TEACH are not synonyms; though LEARN has been used for TEACH this is not accepted usage. LEARN implies acquiring knowl-edge; TEACH implies imparting it.

learned *adj* **1** \'lər-nəd\ : characterized by or associat-ed with learning ⟨*learned* professors⟩ **2** \'lərnd, 'lərnt\ : acquired by learning ⟨*learned* responses⟩ — **learn·ed·ly** \'lər-nəd-lē\ *adv* — **learn·ed·ness** \'lər-nəd-nəs\ *n*

learn·ing *n* **1** : the act or experience of one that learns **2** : knowledge or skill acquired by instruction or study

learning disabled *adj* : having difficulty in learning a basic scholastic skill because of a disorder (as dyslex-ia) that interferes with the learning process — **learn-ing disability** *n*

¹lease \'lēs\ *n* **1** : a contract by which one party grants the use of property or facilities to another for a fixed or open period of time usually for a specified rent; *also* : the act of making such a grant or the term for which it is made **2** : a piece of land or property that is leased [Anglo-French *les,* from Old French *laissier* "to let go", from Latin *laxare* "to loosen", from *laxus* "loose"]

²lease *vt* **1** : to grant by lease : LET **2** : to hold or use under a lease SYN see HIRE

lease·hold \'lēs-,hōld\ *n* **1** : a tenure by lease **2** : land held by lease — **lease·hold·er** \-,hōl-dər\ *n*

leash \'lēsh\ *n* **1** : a line for leading or restraining an animal **2** : a set of three animals (as dogs) [Old French *laisse,* from *laissier* "to let go", from Latin *laxare* "to loosen", from *laxus* "loose"] — **leash** *vt*

¹least \'lēst\ *adj* **1** : lowest in importance or position **2 a** : smallest in size or degree **b** : smallest possible : SLIGHTEST [Old English *lǣst,* superlative of *lǣssa* "less"]

²least *n* : one that is least (as in value, importance, or scope) ⟨I don't care in the *least*⟩ ⟨the *least* that can be said⟩ — **at least** **1** : at the minimum **2** : in any case

³least *adv* : in the smallest or lowest degree

least common denominator *n* : the lowest common multiple of the denominators of two or more fractions

least common multiple *n* : the smallest common multi-ple of two or more numbers

least·wise \'lēst-,wīz\ *adv* : at least

¹leath·er \'leth-ər\ *n* **1** : animal skin dressed for use **2** : something wholly or partly made of leather [Old En-glish *lether-*] — **leather** *adj*

²leather *vt* **leath·ered; leath·er·ing** \'leth-riŋ, -ə-riŋ\ **1** : to cover with leather **2** : to beat with a strap : THRASH

leath·er·back \'leth-ər-,bak\ *n* : a very large sea turtle with a flexible carapace

Leath·er·ette \,leth-ə-'ret\ *trademark* — used for a product colored, finished, and embossed in imitation of leather grains

leath·ern \'leth-ərn\ *adj* : made of, consisting of, or re-sembling leather

leath·er·neck \'leth-ər-,nek\ *n* : a United States marine [from the leather collar formerly part of the uniform]

leath·ery \'leth-rē, -ə-rē\ *adj* : resembling leather in appearance or texture : TOUGH

¹leave \'lēv\ *vb* **left** \'left\; **leav·ing** **1** : to allow or cause to remain behind ⟨*leave* your books at home⟩ **2** : DELIVER ⟨*leave* a book at the library⟩ **3** : to have re-maining (as after death or subtraction) ⟨*leave* a widow and two children⟩ ⟨taking 7 from 10 *leaves* 3⟩ **4** : to give by will : BEQUEATH **5** : to let stay without interfer-ence ⟨*leave* someone alone⟩ **6** : to go away : depart from ⟨*leave* the house⟩ [Old English *lǣfan*]

²leave *n* **1 a** : PERMISSION **2 b** : authorized absence from duty or employment **2** : an act of leaving : DEPARTURE [Old English *lēaf*]

³leave *vi* **leaved; leav·ing** : LEAF 1

leaved \'lēvd\ *adj* : having such or so many leaves ⟨broad-*leaved*⟩

¹leav·en \'lev-ən\ *n* **1 a** : a substance (as yeast) used to produce gaseous fermentation (as in dough) **b** : a ma-terial (as baking powder) used to produce a gas that lightens dough or batter **2** : something that modifies or lightens a mass or whole ⟨a *leaven* of common sense⟩ [Middle French *levain,* derived from Latin *le-vare* "to raise"]

²leaven *vt* **leav·ened; leav·en·ing** \'lev-niŋ, -ə-niŋ\ **1** : to raise (dough) with a leaven **2** : to lighten or im-prove with a leaven ⟨a speech *leavened* with wit⟩

leav·en·ing *n* : a leavening agent : LEAVEN

leave off *vb* : STOP 6, CEASE

leaves *pl of* LEAF

leave–tak·ing \'lēv-,tā-kiŋ\ *n* : DEPARTURE 1a, FARE-WELL

leav·ings \'lē-viŋz\ *n pl* : RESIDUE; *esp* : food leftovers

lech·ery \'lech-rē, -ə-rē\ *n, pl* **-er·ies** : excessive con-cern with or indulgence in sexual activity [Old French *lecherie* "gluttony, lechery", from *lechier* "to lick", of Germanic origin] — **lecher** *n* — **lech·er·ous** \-rəs\ *adj* — **lech·er·ous·ly** *adv* — **lech·er·ous·ness** *n*

lec·i·thin \'les-ə-thən\ *n* : any of several waxy phosphorus-containing substances that are common in animals and plants, form colloidal solutions in water, and have emulsifying, wetting, and antioxidant prop-erties [Greek *lekithos* "egg yolk"]

lec·tern \'lek-tərn\ *n* : READING DESK; *esp* : one from which scripture lessons are read in a church service [Middle French *letrun,* from Medieval Latin *lectori-num,* from Latin *lector* "reader"]

lec·tor \'lek-tər\ *n* : one whose chief duty is to read the lessons in a church service [Latin, "reader", from *lec-tus,* past participle of *legere* "to read"]

¹lec·ture \'lek-chər, -shər\ *n* **1** : a discourse given be-fore an audience especially for instruction **2** : a dress-ing down : REPRIMAND [Late Latin *lectura* "act of read-ing", from Latin *legere* "to gather, read"]

²lecture *vb* **lec·tured; lec·tur·ing** \'lek-chə-riŋ, 'lek-shriŋ\ **1** : to give a lecture or a course of lectures **2** :

to instruct by lectures **3** : to dress down : REPRIMAND
— **lec·tur·er** \-chər-ər, -shrər\ *n*

led *past of* LEAD

le·der·ho·sen \'läd-ər-ˌhōz-n\ *n pl* : knee-length leather
trousers worn especially in Bavaria [German, literally,
"leather trousers"]

ledge \'lej\ *n* **1** : a projecting ridge or raised edge along
a surface : SHELF **2** : an underwater ridge or reef especially near the shore **3** : a narrow flat surface or shelf;
esp : one that projects (as from a wall of rock) **4** :
LODE, VEIN [Middle English *legge* "bar of a gate"]

led·ger \'lej-ər\ *n* : a book containing accounts to
which debits and credits are posted in final form [Mid-
dle English *legger*]

ledger line *n* : a short line added above or below a musical staff for notes that are too high or too low to be
placed on the staff

¹lee \'lē\ *n* **1** : protecting shelter **2** : the side (as of a
ship) that is sheltered from the wind [Old English
hlēo]

²lee *adj* : of or relating to the lee — compare WEATHER

¹leech \'lēch\ *n* **1** *archaic* : PHYSICIAN, SURGEON **2** : any
of numerous flesh-eating or bloodsucking segmented
usually flattened freshwater worms (class Hirudinea)
having a sucker at each end **3** : a hanger-on who seeks
advantage or gain : PARASITE [Old English *lǣce*; sense 2
from the worm's former use by physicians for bleeding
patients]

²leech *vb* **1** : to drain the substance of : EXHAUST **2** : to
attach oneself to a person as a leech

³leech *n* **1** : either vertical edge of a square sail **2** : the
after edge of a fore-and-aft sail [Low German *līk* "rope
stitched to the edges of a sail"]

leek \'lēk\ *n* : a garden herb closely related to the onion and grown for its mildly pungent leaves and thick
stalk [Old English *lēac*]

¹leer \'liər\ *vi* : to cast a sidelong glance; *esp* : to give a
suggestive, knowing, or malicious look [probably from
obsolete *leer* "cheek", from Old English *hlēor*]

²leer *n* : suggestive, knowing, or malicious look

leery \'liər-ē\ *adj* : SUSPICIOUS 2, WARY

lees \'lēz\ *n pl* : the settlings of liquor during fermentation and aging : DREGS [Middle French *lie*, from Medieval Latin *lia*]

lee shore *n* : a shore lying off a ship's leeward side and
toward which a ship could be driven by storm winds

¹lee·ward \'lē-wərd, *especially nautical* 'lü-ərd\ *adj* :
situated away from the wind : DOWNWIND — compare
WINDWARD — **leeward** *adv*

²leeward *n* : the lee side

lee·way \'lē-ˌwā\ *n* **1** : off-course lateral movement of a
ship to leeward when under way **2** : an allowable margin of freedom or variation : TOLERANCE ⟨enough *lee-
way* to arrive on time⟩

¹left \'left\ *adj* **1** : of, relating to, or being a bodily part
on the side of the body in which the heart is mostly
located **2** : located nearer to the left side of the body
than to the right ⟨the *left* arm of my chair⟩; *also* : lying
in the direction that an observer's left hand would naturally extend ⟨the *left* fork of the road⟩ **3** *often cap* :
of, adhering to, or constituted by the political Left
[Old English, "weak"; from the left hand's being the
weaker in most people] — **left** *adv*

²left *n* **1 a** : the left hand **b** : the location or direction of
or part on the left side **2** *often cap* **a** : the part of a
legislative chamber located to the left of the presiding
officer **b** : the members of a continental European legislative body occupying the left and holding more radical political views than other members **3** *cap* **a** :
those professing views usually characterized by desire
to reform or overthrow the established order especially in politics and usually advocating greater freedom
or well-being of the common man **b** : a liberal as distinguished from a conservative position

³left *past of* LEAVE

left field *n* **1** : the part of the baseball outfield to the
left looking out from the plate **2** : the position of the
player defending left field — **left fielder** *n*

left–hand \ˌ,left-'hand\ *adj* **1** : situated on the left **2** :
LEFT-HANDED 1, 2

left–hand·ed \'left-'han-dəd\ *adj* **1** : using the left
hand habitually or more easily than the right **2** : relating to, designed for, or done with the left hand **3 a** :
CLUMSY 1a, AWKWARD **b** : INSINCERE, DUBIOUS ⟨a *left-
handed* compliment⟩ **4 a** : COUNTERCLOCKWISE **b** : having a structure involving a counterclockwise direction
— **left–handed** *adv* — **left–hand·ed·ly** *adv* — **left–
hand·ed·ness** *n* — **left–hand·er** \-'han-dər\ *n*

left·ist \'lef-təst\ *n* : a liberal or radical in politics —
leftist *adj*

left·over \'left-ˌō-vər\ *n* : an unused or unconsumed
residue; *esp* : food left over from one meal and served
at another — **leftover** *adj*

left·ward \'left-wərd\ *also* **left·wards** \-wərdz\ *adv* :
toward or on the left — **leftward** *adj*

left wing *n* **1** : the leftist division of a group **2** : LEFT 3a
— **left–wing** *adj* — **left–wing·er** \'left-ˌwing-ər\ *n*

¹leg \'leg\ *n* **1** : a limb of an animal used especially for
supporting the body and for walking; *also* : the part of
the vertebrate limb between the knee and foot **2** :
something resembling an animal leg in shape or use
⟨the *legs* of a table⟩ **3** : the part of an article of clothing
that covers the leg **4** : a side of a right triangle that is
not the hypotenuse; *also* : a side of an isosceles triangle that is not the base **5** : BOOST 1, 3 — called also
leg up **6 a** : the course and distance sailed by a boat
on a single tack **b** : a portion of a trip : STAGE **c** : one
section of a relay race **7** : a branch or part of an object
or system ⟨the *legs* of a pair of compasses⟩ [Old Norse
leggr]

²leg *vi* **legged; leg·ging** : to use the legs in walking or
especially in running

leg·a·cy \'leg-ə-sē\ *n, pl* **-cies** **1** : something left to a
person by will : INHERITANCE, BEQUEST **2** : something
that has come from an ancestor or predecessor or the
past ⟨a *legacy* of ill will⟩ [Medieval Latin *legatia* "office of a legate", from Latin *legatus* "legate"]

le·gal \'lē-gəl\ *adj* **1** : of or relating to law or lawyers **2**
a : deriving authority from or founded on law : de jure
b : established by law; *esp* : STATUTORY **3** : conforming
to or permitted by law or established rules **4** : recognized or made effective at law rather than in equity
[Middle French, from Latin *legalis*, from *leg-, lex*
"law"] SYN see LAWFUL — **le·gal·ly** \-gə-lē\ *adv*

legal age *n* : the age at which a person enters into full
adult legal rights and responsibilities (as of making
contracts or wills)

legal holiday *n* : a holiday established by legal authority
and characterized by legal restrictions on work and
transaction of official business

le·gal·ism \'lē-gə-ˌliz-əm\ *n* : strict, literal, or excessive
conformity to the law or to a religious or moral code
— **le·gal·ist** \-gə-ləst\ *n* — **le·gal·is·tic** \ˌlē-gə-'lis-
tik\ *adj* — **le·gal·is·ti·cal·ly** \-ti-kə-lē, -klē\ *adv*

le·gal·i·ty \li-'gal-ət-ē\ *n, pl* **-ties** : the quality or state
of being legal

le·gal·ize \'lē-gə-ˌlīz\ *vt* : to make legal; *esp* : to give
legal validity to — **le·gal·iza·tion** \ˌlē-gə-lə-'zā-shən\
n

legal tender *n* : money that the law authorizes a debtor
to pay with and requires a creditor to accept

leg·ate \'leg-ət\ *n* : an official representative (as an ambassador or envoy) [Latin *legatus* "deputy, emissary",
from *legare* "to depute, bequeath", from *leg-, lex*
"law"]

leg·a·tee \ˌleg-ə-'tē\ *n* : one to whom a legacy is bequeathed

le·ga·tion \li-'gā-shən\ *n* **1** : a diplomatic mission;
esp : one headed by a minister **2** : the official residence and office of a diplomatic minister

¹leech 2

\ə\ abut	\ng\ sing
\ər\ further	\ō\ bone
\a\ mat	\o\ saw
\ā\ take	\oi\ coin
\ä\ cot, cart	\th\ thin
\au̇\ out	\t̲h̲\ this
\ch\ chin	\ü\ food
\e\ pet	\u̇\ foot
\ē\ easy	\y\ yet
\g\ go	\yü\ few
\i\ tip	\yu̇\ cure
\ī\ life	\zh\ vision
\j\ job	

le·ga·to \li-'gät-ō\ *adv or adj* : in a manner that is smooth and connected between successive tones — used as a direction in music [Italian, literally, "tied", from *legare* "to tie", from Latin *ligare*]

leg·end \'lej-ənd\ *n* **1 a** : a story coming down from the past whose truth is popularly accepted but cannot be checked **b** : a popular myth of recent origin **c** : a person or thing that inspires legends **2 a** : an inscription or title on an object (as a coin) **b** : CAPTION 2 **c** : an explanatory list of the symbols on a map or chart [Medieval Latin *legenda*, from Latin *legere* "to gather, read"] SYN SEE MYTH ☐ ORIGIN The Latin verb *legere* originally meant "to gather". In the course of time the verb came to be used in a figurative sense, "to gather with the eye, see", which led to the sense "to read". In Medieval Latin the word *legenda,* meaning literally "a thing to be read", was used specifically to mean "the story of the life of a saint". Many saints' lives that were written in the Middle Ages incorporated a generous measure of fanciful material along with solid fact. This accounts for the use of English *legend* to mean "a traditional story popularly believed to be historical though not entirely verifiable". We owe other senses of *legend,* "inscription", "caption", "explanatory list", to the literal meaning of Latin *legenda,* "a thing to be read".

leg·end·ary \'lej-ən,der-ē\ *adj* **1** : of or resembling a legend (*legendary* heroes) **2** : consisting of legends (*legendary* writings) SYN SEE FABULOUS

leg·er·de·main \,lej-ərd-ə-'mān\ *n* **1** : SLEIGHT OF HAND, MAGIC **2** : a display of skill or adroitness [Middle French *leger de main* "light of hand"]

legged \'leg-əd, 'legd\ *adj* : having (such or so many) legs (four-*legged*)

leg·ging *or* **leg·gin** \'leg-ən, 'leg-ing\ *n* : a covering for the leg

leg·gy \'leg-ē\ *adj* **leg·gi·er; -est 1** : having disproportionately long legs **2** : having attractive legs **3** : SPINDLY (a *leggy* plant)

leg·horn \'leg-,hȯrn, -,ȯrn, 'leg-ərn\ *n* **1 a** : a fine plaited straw made from an Italian wheat **b** : a hat of this straw **2** : any of a Mediterranean breed of small hardy fowls noted for their large production of white eggs [*Leghorn,* Italy]

leg·i·ble \'lej-ə-bəl\ *adj* : capable of being read : PLAIN [Late Latin *legibilis,* from Latin *legere* "to read"] — **leg·i·bil·i·ty** \,lej-ə-'bil-ət-ē\ *n* — **leg·i·bly** \'lej-ə-blē\ *adv*

le·gion \'lē-jən\ *n* **1** : the principal unit of the Roman army comprising 3000 to 6000 foot soldiers with cavalry **2** : ARMY 1a **3** : a very large number : MULTITUDE [Old French, from Latin *legio,* from *legere* "to gather, read"]

¹le·gion·ary \'lē-jə-,ner-ē\ *adj* : of, relating to, or constituting a legion

²legionary *n, pl* **-ar·ies** : LEGIONNAIRE

le·gion·naire \,lē-jə-'naər, -'neər\ *n* : a member of a legion [French *légionnaire*]

leg·is·late \'lej-ə-,slāt\ *vb* **1** : to make or enact laws **2** : to bring about by legislation [back-formation from *legislator*]

leg·is·la·tion \,lej-ə-'slā-shən\ *n* **1** : the action of making laws **2** : the laws made by a legislator or legislative body

leg·is·la·tive \'lej-ə-,slāt-iv\ *adj* **1** : having the power or performing the function of legislating **2** : of or relating to a legislature or legislation — **leg·is·la·tive·ly** *adv*

legislative assembly *n, often cap L&A* **1** : a bicameral legislature in an American state; *also* : its lower house **2** : a unicameral legislature especially in a Canadian province

legislative council *n, often cap L&C* : a permanent committee from both houses of a state legislature that

meets between sessions to study state problems and plan a legislative program

leg·is·la·tor \'lej-ə-,slāt-ər\ *n* : a person who makes laws for a state or community; *esp* : a member of a legislature [Latin *legis later,* literally, "proposer of a law"]

leg·is·la·ture \'lej-ə-,slā-chər\ *n* : an organized body of persons with authority to make laws for a political unit

le·git \li-'jit\ *adj, slang* : LEGITIMATE 2, 3

¹le·git·i·mate \li-'jit-ə-mət\ *adj* **1** : born of parents who are married to each other (*legitimate* children) **2** : being in accordance with law or established requirements : LAWFUL (a *legitimate* claim) **3** : being in keeping with what is right or in accordance with accepted standards (a *legitimate* excuse for absence) **4** : relating to acted plays not including burlesque, revues, or some forms of musical comedy (*legitimate* theater) SYN SEE LAWFUL — **le·git·i·ma·cy** \-mə-sē\ *n* — **le·git·i·mate·ly** *adv*

²le·git·i·mate \-,māt\ *vt* : to make lawful or legal [Medieval Latin *legitimare,* from Latin *legitimus* "lawful", from *leg-, lex* "law"] — **le·git·i·ma·tion** \li-,jit-ə-'mā-shən\ *n*

le·git·i·ma·tize \li-'jit-ə-mə-,tīz\ *vt* : LEGITIMIZE

le·git·i·mize \li-'jit-ə-,mīz\ *vt* : LEGITIMIZE

leg·less \'leg-ləs\ *adj* : having no legs (a *legless* insect)

leg·man \'leg-,man\ *n* **1** : a newspaper employee assigned usually to gather information **2** : an assistant who gathers information and runs errands

leg-of-mut·ton \,leg-əv-'mət-n, -ə-\ *adj* : having the sharply tapering shape or outline of a leg of mutton (*leg-of-mutton* sleeves)

leg·ume \'leg-,yüm, li-'gyüm\ *n* **1 a** : any of a large family of herbs, shrubs, and trees that have fruits developing into dry single-celled pods and splitting into two valves when ripe, that bear nodules on the roots containing nitrogen-fixing bacteria, and that include important food and forage plants (as peas, beans, or clovers) **b** : the part (as seeds or pods) of a legume used as food; *also* : VEGETABLE 1b **2** : the pod characteristic of a legume [French *légume,* from Latin *legumen,* from *legere* "to gather"] — **le·gu·mi·nous** \li-'gyü-mə-nəs, le-\ *adj*

leg·work \'leg-,wərk, 'lāg-\ *n* : work (as gathering data) that involves physical activity and is the basis of more creative activity (as writing a book)

le·hua \lā-'hü-ə\ *n* : a showy tree of the myrtle family with bright red flowers and a hard wood; *also* : its flower [Hawaiian]

lei \'lā, 'lā-ē\ *n* : a wreath usually of flowers [Hawaiian]

lei·sure \'lēzh-ər, 'lezh-, 'lāzh-\ *n* **1** : freedom provided by the stopping of activities; *esp* : time free from work or duties **2** : apparent effortlessness : EASE [Old French *leisir,* from *leisir* "to be permitted", from Latin *licēre*] — **leisure** *adj* — **at leisure** : in one's leisure time : at one's convenience

lei·sure·ly \-lē\ *adj* : characterized by leisure : UNHURRIED (a *leisurely* pace) — **lei·sure·li·ness** *n* — **leisurely** *adv*

leit·mo·tiv *or* **leit·mo·tif** \'līt-mō-,tēf\ *n* : a dominant recurring theme (as in a musical or literary work) [German *leitmotiv,* from *leiten* "to lead" + *motiv* "motive"]

lem·ma \'lem-ə\ *n* : the lower of the two bracts enclosing the flower in the spikelet of grasses [Greek, "husk"]

lem·ming \'lem-ing\ *n* : any of several small short-tailed northern rodents with furry feet and small ears [Norwegian]

¹lem·on \'lem-ən\ *n* **1 a** : an acid citrus fruit that is botanically a many-seeded pale yellow nearly oval berry **b** : the stout thorny tree that bears this fruit **2** : DUD, FAILURE (the new car proved to be a *lemon*) [Middle

lemming

French *limon,* from Medieval Latin *limo,* from Arabic *laymūn*]

²**lemon** *adj* **1 a :** containing lemon **b :** having the flavor or scent of lemon **2 :** of the color lemon yellow

lem·on·ade \,lem-ə-'nād\ *n* **:** a drink made of lemon juice, sugar, and water

lemon balm *n* **:** a perennial Old World mint often grown for its fragrant lemon-flavored leaves

lemon law *n* **:** a law offering car buyers relief (as by repair or refund) for defects detected during a specified period after purchase

lemon shark *n* **:** a dangerous medium-sized shark of the warm Atlantic that is yellowish brown to gray above with yellow or greenish sides

lemon yellow *n* **:** a brilliant greenish yellow

lem·pi·ra \lem-'pir-ə\ *n* **1 :** the basic monetary unit of Honduras **2 :** a coin or note representing one lempira [American Spanish, from *Lempira,* 16th century Indian chief]

le·mur \'lē-mər\ *n* **:** any of numerous arboreal and mostly nocturnal mammals that are related to the monkeys and usually have a muzzle like a fox, large eyes, very soft woolly fur, and a long furry tail [Latin *lemures* "ghosts"] □ **ORIGIN** The ancient Romans believed that if the dead were not buried their spirits would return by night to haunt the living. In Latin such ghosts were called *lemures.* In none of the Latin writings that have survived does the singular of this word appear, but the normal singular form would be *lemur.* In the trees of Madagascar lives a kind of small nocturnal mammal. Its large-eyed face, glimpsed through the trees at night, must look quite ghostly. 18th century naturalists, struck by the nocturnal habits and strange appearance of the creature, named it *lemur,* after the ancient Roman ghosts.

lend \'lend\ *vb* **lent** \'lent\; **lend·ing 1 :** to give or hand over as a loan ⟨*lend* a book⟩ ⟨*lend* money⟩ **2 :** to give temporarily ⟨*lend* assistance⟩ **3 :** to have the quality or nature that makes suitable ⟨a voice that *lends* itself to singing in opera⟩ [Old English *lǣnan,* from *lǣn* "loan"] — **lend·er** *n*

lending library *n* **:** RENTAL LIBRARY

lend–lease \'len-'dlēs\ *n* **:** the transfer of goods and services to an ally to aid in a common cause with payment being made by a return of the original items or their use in the common cause or by a similar transfer of other goods and services [United States *Lend-Lease* Act (1941)] — **lend–lease** *vt*

length \'length, 'lengkth, 'lenth\ *n* **1 a :** the longer or longest dimension of an object **b :** a measured distance or dimension ⟨a 2-meter *length*⟩ — see MEASURE table, METRIC SYSTEM table **c :** the quality or state of being long ⟨criticized the *length* of the story⟩ **2 a :** duration or extent in time ⟨the *length* of an interview⟩ **b :** relative duration or stress of a sound **3 :** the length of something taken as a unit of measure ⟨that horse led by a *length*⟩ **4 :** a piece constituting or usable as part of a whole or of a connected series : SECTION ⟨a *length* of pipe⟩ **5 :** a vertical dimension of an article of clothing [Old English *lengthu,* from *lang* "long"] — **at length 1 :** in full : FULLY **2 :** at last : FINALLY

length·en \'leng-thən, 'lengk-, 'len-\ *vb* **length·ened; length·en·ing** \'length-ning, 'lengkth-, 'lenth-, -ə-ning\ **:** to make or become longer SYN see EXTEND — **length·en·er** \-nər\ *n*

length·ways \'length-,wāz, 'lengkth-, 'lenth-\ *adv* **:** LENGTHWISE

length·wise \-,wīz\ *adv* **:** in the direction of the length : LONGITUDINALLY — **lengthwise** *adj*

lengthy \'leng-thē, 'lengk-, 'len-\ *adj* **length·i·er; -est 1 :** excessively drawn out : OVERLONG ⟨a *lengthy* speech⟩ **2 :** LONG 1 ⟨a *lengthy* journey⟩ — **length·i·ly** \-thə-lē\ *adv* — **length·i·ness** \-thē-nəs\ *n*

le·ni·en·cy \'lē-nē-ən-sē\ *or* **le·ni·ence** \-əns\ *n* **:** the quality or state of being lenient SYN see MERCY

le·ni·ent \'lē-nē-ənt\ *adj* **:** of mild and tolerant disposition or effect; *esp* **:** INDULGENT ⟨was *lenient* with the naughty child⟩ [Latin *leniens,* present participle of *lenire* "to soothe", from *lenis* "soft, mild"] — **le·ni·ent·ly** *adv*

Len·in·ism \'len-ə-,niz-əm\ *n* **:** the political, economic, and social principles and policies advocated by Lenin; *esp* **:** the theory of communism developed by or associated with Lenin — **Len·in·ist** \-nəst\ *n or adj*

len·i·tive \'len-ət-iv\ *adj* **:** easing pain or acrimony : MITIGATING [Middle French *lenitif,* from Medieval Latin *lenitivus,* from Latin *lenire* "to soothe", from *lenis* "mild"] — **lenitive** *n*

lens \'lenz\ *n* **1 a :** a piece of transparent substance (as glass) that has two opposite surfaces either both curved or one curved and the other plane and that is used either singly or combined in an optical instrument for forming an image by focusing rays of light **b :** a piece of glass or plastic used (as in safety goggles or sunglasses) to protect the eye from dust or glare **2 :** a device for directing or focusing radiation (as sound waves or electrons) other than light **3 :** something (as a geologic deposit) shaped like an optical lens **4 :** a transparent biconvex lens-shaped or nearly spherical body in the eye that focuses light rays (as upon the retina) [Latin, "lentil"; from its shape]

lens 1: *left* convex, *right* concave

Lent \'lent\ *n* **:** a period of penitence and fasting observed on the 40 weekdays from Ash Wednesday to Easter by many churches [Old English *lengten* "springtime"]

Lent·en \'lent-n\ *adj* **:** of, relating to, or suitable to Lent; *esp* **:** MEAGER ⟨*Lenten* fare⟩

len·ti·cel \'lent-ə-,sel\ *n* **:** a pore in a stem of a woody plant through which gases are exchanged between the atmosphere and the stem tissues [derived from Latin *lent-, lens* "lentil"]

len·tic·u·lar \len-'tik-yə-lər\ *adj* **:** shaped like a biconvex lens [Latin *lenticularis* "lentil-shaped", from *lenticula* "small lentil", from *lens* "lentil"]

len·til \'lent-l\ *n* **:** a Eurasian annual legume widely grown for its flattened edible seeds and leafy stalks used as fodder; *also* **:** its seed [Old French *lentille,* from Latin *lenticula,* from *lent-, lens*]

len·to \'len-,tō\ *adv or adj* **:** in a slow manner — used as a direction in music [Italian, from *lento,* adj., "slow", from Latin *lentus* "pliant, sluggish, slow"]

Leo \'lē-ō\ *n* **1 :** a zodiacal northern constellation east of Cancer **2 :** the 5th sign of the zodiac; *also* **:** one born under this sign [Latin, literally, "lion"]

le·o·nine \'lē-ə-,nīn\ *adj* **:** of, relating to, or resembling a lion [Latin *leoninus,* from *leo* "lion"]

leop·ard \'lep-ərd\ *n* **:** a large strong cat of southern Asia and Africa that is usually tawny or buff with black spots arranged in broken rings or rosettes — called also *panther* [Old French *leupart,* from Late Latin *leopardus,* from Greek *leopardos,* from *leōn* "lion" + *pardos* "leopard"] — **leop·ard·ess** \-əs\ *n*

leopard

leopard frog *n* **:** the common spotted frog of the eastern United States

le·o·tard \'lē-ə-,tärd\ *n* **:** a stretchable close-fitting one-piece garment typically covering the torso that is worn for practice or performance by dancers, acrobats, and aerialists [Jules Léotard, 19th century French aerial gymnast]

lep·er \'lep-ər\ *n* **1 :** a person affected with leprosy **2 :** PARIAH 2, OUTCAST [Old French *lepre* "leprosy", from Late Latin *lepra*]

lep·i·dop·tera \,lep-ə-'däp-tə-rə\ *n pl* **:** insects that are lepidopterans [New Latin, from Greek *lepid-, lepis* "scale" + *pteron* "wing"]

lep·i·dop·ter·an \,lep-ə-'däp-tə-rən\ *n* **:** any of a large order (Lepidoptera) of insects that comprise the butterflies and moths, as adults have four wings usually covered with minute overlapping often brightly col-

ored scales, and as larvae are caterpillars —
lepidopteran *adj* — **lep·i·dop·ter·ous** \-tə-rəs\ *adj*
lep·re·chaun \'lep-rə-ˌkän, -ˌkȯn\ *n* : a mischievous elf
of Irish folklore usually believed to reveal the hiding
place of treasure if caught [Irish Gaelic *leipreachān*]
lep·ro·sy \'lep-rə-sē\ *n* : a chronic bacterial disease
marked by slow-growing spreading swellings accompanied by loss of sensation, wasting, and deformities
— called also *Hansen's disease* [*leprous* + -*y*] — **lep-
rot·ic** \le-'prät-ik\ *adj*
lep·rous \'lep-rəs\ *adj* : infected with, relating to, or
resembling leprosy [Late Latin *leprosus,* from *lepra*
"leprosy", from Greek, from *lepein* "to peel"] — **lep-
rous·ly** *adv* — **lep·rous·ness** *n*
lep·to·ceph·a·lus \ˌlep-tə-'sef-ə-ləs\ *n, pl* **-li** \-ˌlī\ : the
slender transparent first larva of an eel [New Latin,
from Greek *leptos* "peeled, slender, small" + *kephalē*
"head"]
les·bi·an \'lez-bē-ən\ *n, often cap* : a woman who is a
homosexual [*Lesbos,* Greek island; from the reputed
homosexual band associated with Sappho of Lesbos]
— **lesbian** *adj, often cap* — **les·bi·an·ism** \-bē-ə-ˌniz-
əm\ *n*
lese maj·es·ty *or* **lèse ma·jes·té** \'lēz-'maj-ə-stē\ *n* I **a** :
a crime committed against a sovereign power **b** : an
offense violating the dignity of a ruler **2** : a detraction
from or affront to dignity or importance [Middle
French *lese majesté,* from Latin *laesa majestas,* literally, "injured majesty"]
le·sion \'lē-zhən\ *n* : an abnormal structural change in
an organ or part due to injury or disease [Middle
French, "injury", from Latin *laesio,* from *laedere* "to
injure"]
les·pe·de·za \ˌles-pə-'dē-zə\ *n* : any of a genus of herbaceous or shrubby plants of the pea family including
some widely used for forage, soil improvement, and
especially hay [derived from V. M. de *Zespedes,* 18th
century Spanish governor of East Florida]
¹**less** \'les\ *adj* I : of a smaller number : FEWER ⟨*less*
than three⟩ **2** : of lower rank, degree, or importance
⟨no *less* a person than the principal⟩ **3 a** : of reduced
size or extent **b** : more limited in quantity ⟨in *less*
time⟩ [Old English *lǣs,* adv. and n., and *lǣssa,* adj.] SYN
SEE FEWER
²**less** *adv* : to a lesser extent or degree ⟨*less* difficult⟩
³**less** *prep* : diminished by ⟨full price *less* the discount⟩
⁴**less** *n, pl* **less** I : a smaller portion or quantity ⟨spent
less than usual⟩ **2** : something of less importance
⟨could have killed them for *less*⟩
-less \-ləs\ *adj suffix* I : destitute of : not having
⟨wit*less*⟩ **2** : unable to be acted on or to act (in a specified way) ⟨daunt*less*⟩ ⟨fade*less*⟩ [Old English *-lēas,*
from *lēas* "devoid, false"]
les·see \le-'sē\ *n* : a tenant under a lease [Anglo-French,
from *lesser* "to lease"]
less·en \'les-n\ *vb* **less·ened; less·en·ing** \'les-ning, -n-
ing\ : to make or become less SYN SEE DECREASE
¹**less·er** \'les-ər\ *adj* : of less size, quality, or importance ⟨subtract the *lesser* number⟩ ⟨the *lesser* nobility⟩
²**lesser** *adv* : LESS ⟨*lesser*-known⟩
lesser celandine *n* : CELANDINE 2
¹**les·son** \'les-n\ *n* I : a passage from sacred writings
read in a worship service **2** : a piece of instruction ⟨the
story carries a *lesson*⟩; *esp* : a reading or exercise to be
studied by a pupil ⟨master each *lesson*⟩ **3 a** : something learned by study or experience ⟨the *lessons* of
life⟩ **b** : a rebuke or punishment meant to forestall the
repetition of an offense ⟨gave the naughty child a *lesson*⟩ [Old French *leçon,* from Latin *lectio* "act of reading", from *legere* "to read"]
²**lesson** *vt* **les·soned; les·son·ing** \'les-ning, -n-ing\ I :
to give a lesson to **2** : REBUKE
les·sor \'les-ˌȯr, le-'sȯr\ *n* : one that grants a lease [An-
glo-French *lessour,* from *lesser* "to lease"]

lest \lest, ˌlest\ *conj* : for fear that ⟨worried *lest* they be
late⟩ [derived from Old English *lǣs* "less"]
¹**let** \'let\ *vt* **let·ted; letted** *or* **let; let·ting** *archaic* : HIN-
DER, PREVENT [Old English *lettan*]
²**let** \'let\ *n* I : something that impedes : OBSTRUCTION
⟨talk without *let* or hindrance⟩ **2** : a shot or rally (as in
tennis) that is not counted and that must be played
over because of interference with the play [Old English *lettan* "to delay, hinder"]
³**let** *vb* **let; let·ting** I : to cause to : MAKE ⟨*let* it be
known⟩ **2 a** : to offer or grant for rent or lease ⟨*let*
rooms⟩ **b** : to assign or award especially after bids ⟨*let* a
contract⟩ **3 a** : to allow to ⟨live and *let* live⟩ ⟨*let* me go⟩
b : to allow to go or pass ⟨*let* them through⟩ **4** — used
imperatively to introduce a request or proposal ⟨*let* us
pray⟩ ⟨*let* x be any number⟩ **5** : to allow (sound) to
issue or be uttered : RELEASE — used with out ⟨*let* out
a whoop⟩ [Old English *lǣtan*] □ SYN LET, ALLOW, PER-
MIT mean not to forbid or prevent. LET may imply a
positive giving of permission but more often implies
failure to prevent either through inadvertence and
negligence or through lack of power or effective authority; ALLOW simply suggests a forbearing to prohibit; PERMIT implies willingness or acquiescence. SYN see
in addition HIRE
-let \lət\ *n suffix* I : small one ⟨book*let*⟩ **2** : article
worn on ⟨wrist*let*⟩ [Middle French *-elet,* from *-el,* diminutive suffix (from Latin *-ellus*) + *-et*]
let alone *prep* : to say nothing of ⟨lacked the courage,
let alone the skill⟩
let·down \'let-ˌdau̇n\ *n* I : DISAPPOINTMENT 2 **2** : a
slackening of effort : RELAXATION
let down \let-'dau̇n, 'let-\ *vb* I : to fail to support : DES-
ERT ⟨*let down* a friend in a crisis⟩ **2** : DISAPPOINT ⟨the
end of the story *lets* the reader *down*⟩ **3** : to slacken
effort : RELAX
¹**le·thal** \'lē-thəl\ *adj* I : of, relating to, or causing
death **2 a** : capable of causing death **b** : being or involving a gene that in some genetic conditions may
prevent development or cause the death of an organism or its germ cells ⟨a *lethal* mutation⟩ [Latin *letalis,
lethalis,* from *letum* "death"] SYN see DEADLY — **le-
thal·i·ty** \lē-'thal-ət-ē\ *n* — **le·thal·ly** \'lē-thə-lē\ *adv*
²**lethal** *n* : a lethal gene
le·thar·gic \li-'thär-jik, le-\ *adj* I : of, relating to, or
characterized by lethargy : SLUGGISH **2** : APATHETIC —
le·thar·gi·cal·ly \-ji-kə-lē, -klē\ *adv*
leth·ar·gy \'leth-ər-jē\ *n* I : abnormal drowsiness **2** :
the quality or state of being lazy or indifferent [Late
Latin *lethargia,* from Greek *lēthargia,* from *lēthargos*
"forgetful, lethargic", from *lēthē* "forgetfulness" +
argos "lazy", from *a-* + *ergon* "work"] □ SYN LETH-
ARGY, LANGUOR, STUPOR, TORPOR mean physical or
mental inertness. LETHARGY implies drowsiness or apathy induced by disease, injury, or drugs; LANGUOR suggests inertia induced by enervating climate, illness, or
amorous emotion; STUPOR implies a deadening of the
mind and senses by shock, narcotics, or intoxicants;
TORPOR implies a state of suspended animation or extreme sluggishness.
Le·the \'lē-thē\ *n* : OBLIVION, FORGETFULNESS ⟨the *Lethe*
of sleep⟩ [Greek *Lēthē,* river of Hades whose water
causes those who drink it to forget their past, from
lēthē "forgetfulness"] — **Le·the·an** \'lē-thē-ən\ *adj*
let on *vb* I : ADMIT ⟨know more than they *let on*⟩ **2** : to
make known ⟨don't *let on* that I told you⟩ **3** : PRETEND
⟨not so surprised as I *let on*⟩
let's \lets, ˌlets, les, ˌles\ : let us
Lett \'let\ *n* : a member of a people closely related to
the Lithuanians and mainly inhabiting Latvia [German
Lette, from Latvian *Latvi*]
¹**let·ter** \'let-ər\ *n* I : a symbol in writing or print that
stands for a speech sound and constitutes a unit of an
alphabet **2** : a written or printed message addressed to
a person or organization **3** *pl* **a** : LITERATURE 2a **b** :

LEARNING 2 4 : the strict meaning (the *letter* of the law) 5 a : a single piece of type b : a style of type [Old French *lettre*, from Latin *littera* "letter of the alphabet" and *litterae*, pl., "epistle, literature"]

²letter *vt* 1 : to set down in letters : PRINT 2 : to mark with letters — let·ter·er \-ər-ər\ *n*

letter carrier *n* : a person who delivers mail

let·tered \'let-ərd\ *adj* 1 a : LEARNED, EDUCATED (a *lettered* person) b : of or relating to learning (a *lettered* environment) 2 : marked with or as if with letters (a *lettered* sign)

let·ter·head \'let-ər-,hed\ *n* : stationery having a printed or engraved heading; *also* : the heading itself

let·ter·ing *n* : letters used in an inscription

let·ter–per·fect \,let-ər-'pər-fikt\ *adj* : correct in every detail; *esp* : VERBATIM

let·ter·press \'let-ər-,pres\ *n* : printing done directly by impressing the paper on an inked raised surface

letters of marque \-'märk\ : written authority granted to a private person by a government to seize the subjects of a foreign state or their goods; *esp* : a license granted to a private person to fit out an armed ship to plunder the enemy [obsolete *marque* "reprisal", from Middle French, from Provençal *marca*, from *marcar* "to mark, seize as pledge", of Germanic origin]

letters pat·ent \-'pat-nt\ *n pl* : a writing (as from a sovereign) that confers on a person a grant in a form open for public inspection

¹Lett·ish \'let-ish\ *adj* : of or relating to the Letts or the Latvian language

²Lettish *n* : LATVIAN 2

let·tuce \'let-əs\ *n* : a common garden vegetable of the daisy family that has succulent leaves used especially in salads [Old French *laitues*, pl. of *laitue* "lettuce", from Latin *lactuca*, from *lac* "milk"] □ ORIGIN Many types of lettuce have a milky white juice, and it is this property that accounts for the name of the vegetable. The English singular form, *lettuce*, comes from Old French *laitues*, the plural of *laitue*. The Old French word is derived in turn from Latin *lactuca*, which is still used as the scientific name of the lettuce. The root of *lactuca* is Latin *lac*, which means "milk".

let-up \'let-,əp\ *n* : a lessening of effort

let up \let-'əp, 'let-\ *vi* 1 : to lessen in force or intensity : ABATE 2 : STOP 6, CEASE 3 : to become less severe — used with *on* (hope the principal *lets up* on me)

leu·cine \'lü-,sēn\ *n* : an essential amino acid obtained by the hydrolysis of most dietary proteins

leu·co·plast \'lü-kə-,plast\ *n* : a colorless plastid of a plant cell usually concerned with starch formation and storage [*leuk-* + *-plast* "granule", from Greek *plastos* "formed, molded"]

leuk- *or* leuko- *or* leuc- *or* leuco- *combining form* 1 : white : colorless : weakly colored (*leuko*cyte) 2 : leukocyte (*leuk*emia) [Greek *leukos*]

leu·ke·mia \lü-'kē-mē-ə\ *n* : a cancerous disease of warm-blooded animals (as human beings) in which leukocytes increase abnormally in the tissues and often in the blood — leu·ke·mic \-mik\ *adj*

leu·ko·cyte *also* leu·co·cyte \'lü-kə-,sīt\ *n* : any of the white or colorless cells (as a lymphocyte) having a nucleus and occurring in the blood — leu·ko·cyt·ic \,lü-kə-'sit-ik\ *adj*

leu·ko·cy·to·sis \,lü-kə-,sī-'tō-səs\ *n, pl* -to·ses \-'tō-,sēz\ : an increase in the number of leukocytes in the circulating blood — leu·ko·cy·tot·ic \-'tät-ik\ *adj*

leu·ko·pe·nia \,lü-kə-'pē-ne-ə\ *n* : a condition in which the number of leukocytes circulating in the blood is abnormally low [Greek *penia* "poverty, lack"] — leu·ko·pe·nic \-'nik\ *adj*

leu·ko·sis \lü-'kō-səs\ *n, pl* -ko·ses \-,sēz\ : LEUKEMIA — leu·kot·ic \-'kät-ik\ *adj*

lev- *or* levo- *combining form* : turning the plane of polarization of light to the left (*levo*ulose) [Latin *laevus* "left"]

le·va·tor \li-'vāt-ər\ *n, pl* lev·a·to·res \,lev-ə-'tōr-ēz\ *or* le·va·tors \li-'vāt-ərz\ : a muscle that serves to raise a body part — compare DEPRESSOR [derived from Latin *levare* "to raise"]

¹lev·ee \'lev-ē; lə-'vē, -'vā\ *n* 1 : a reception held by a distinguished person originally on rising from bed 2 : a reception usually in honor of a particular person [French *lever*, literally, "act of arising", from *se lever* "to raise oneself, rise"]

²levee \'lev-ē\ *n* 1 : an embankment or dike to prevent flooding 2 : a river landing place : PIER [French *levée*, from Old French, "act of raising", from *lever* "to raise", from Latin *levare*]

¹lev·el \'lev-əl\ *n* 1 : a device for establishing a horizontal line or plane (a carpenter's *level*) (a surveyor's *level*) 2 : horizontal condition; *esp* : a condition of liquids marked by a horizontal surface of even altitude 3 : a horizontal position, line, or surface often taken as an index of altitude (placed at eye *level*); *also* : a flat surface (easier to walk on the *level*) 4 : a position in a scale or rank (students at the same learning *level*) 5 : the concentration of a constituent especially of a body fluid (as blood) [Middle French *livel*, from Latin *libella*, from *libra* "pound, balance"] — on the level : bona fide : HONEST

²level *vb* lev·eled *or* lev·elled; lev·el·ing *or* lev·el·ling \'lev-ling, -ə-ling\ 1 : to make (a line or surface) horizontal : make flat or level (*leveled* the ground for a road) 2 : DIRECT 3, AIM (*leveled* a charge of fraud at them) 3 : to bring to a common level or plane : EQUALIZE 4 : to lay level with the ground : RAZE (the cyclone *leveled* the village) 5 : to attain or come to a level (the jet *leveled* off at 10,000 meters) — lev·el·er *or* lev·el·ler \'lev-lər, -ə-lər\ *n*

³level *adj* 1 : having no part higher than another 2 : being on a line with the horizon : HORIZONTAL 3 a : of the same height or rank : being on a line : EVEN (stood in water *level* with my shoulders) b (1) : STEADY, UNWAVERING (a *level* stare) (2) : CALM, UNEXCITED (spoke in *level* tones) — lev·el·ly \'lev-əl-lē, 'lev-ə-lē\ *adv* — lev·el·ness \-əl-nəs\ *n* — level best : very best

lev·el·head·ed \,lev-əl-'hed-əd\ *adj* : having good judgment : SENSIBLE — lev·el·head·ed·ness *n*

¹le·ver \'lev-ər, 'lē-vər\ *n* 1 a : a bar used for prying or dislodging something b : an instrument or means used to achieve a purpose : TOOL (used food distribution as a *lever* to gain votes) 2 a : a rigid bar that pivots on a fulcrum and that is used to exert a pressure or sustain a weight at one point of its length by the application of a force at a second b : a projecting piece by which a mechanism is operated or adjusted [Old French *levier*, from *lever* "to raise", from Latin *levare*]

²lever *vt* le·vered; le·ver·ing \'lev-ring, 'lēv-, -ə-ring\ : to pry, raise, or move with or as if with a lever

le·ver·age \'lev-rij, 'lēv-, -ə-rij\ *n* 1 : the action of a lever or the mechanical advantage gained by it 2 : power to influence or dominate (the strike threat gave the union bargaining *leverage*)

lev·er·et \'lev-rət, -ə-rət\ *n* : a hare in its first year [Middle French *levre* "hare", from Latin *lepor-, lepus*]

le·vi·a·than \li-'vī-ə-thən\ *n* 1 a *often cap* : a sea monster often symbolizing evil in the Old Testament and Christian literature b : a large sea animal 2 : GIANT 3 [Late Latin, from Hebrew *liwyāthān*] — leviathan *adj*

Le·vi's \'lē-,vīz\ *trademark* — used for jeans

lev·i·tate \'lev-ə-,tāt\ *vb* : to rise or cause to rise in the air in seeming defiance of gravity [*levity*] — lev·i·ta·tion \,lev-ə-'tā-shən\ *n*

Le·vite \'lē-,vīt\ *n* 1 : a member of the Hebrew tribe of Levi 2 : a descendant of Levi assigned to assist the priests in the care of the temple — Le·vit·i·cal \li-'vit-i-kəl\ *adj*

Le·vit·i·cus \li-'vit-i-kəs\ *n* — see BIBLE table

lev·i·ty \'lev-ət-ē\ *n, pl* -ties : an often inappropriate lack of seriousness : FRIVOLITY [Latin *levitas*, from *levis* "light in weight"]

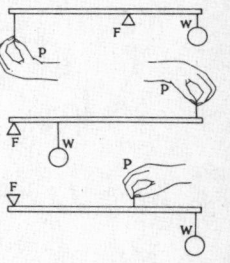

¹lever 2a: P power, F fulcrum, W weight

\ə\ abut	\ng\ sing
\ər\ further	\ō\ bone
\a\ mat	\o͝\ saw
\ā\ take	\oi\ coin
\ä\ cot, cart	\th\ thin
\au̇\ out	\t͟h\ this
\ch\ chin	\ü\ food
\e\ pet	\u̇\ foot
\ē\ easy	\y\ yet
\g\ go	\yü\ few
\i\ tip	\yu̇\ cure
\ī\ life	\zh\ vision
\j\ job	

lev·u·lose \\'lev-yə-ˌlōs\ *n* : FRUCTOSE [derived from *lev-* + *-ose*]

¹levy \\'lev-ē\ *n, pl* **lev·ies 1 a** : the imposition or collection of an assessment **b** : an amount levied **2 a** : the raising of men for military service **b** : troops raised by levy [Middle French *levee,* from Old French, "act of raising", from *lever* "to raise", from Latin *levare*]

²levy *vb* **lev·ied; lev·y·ing 1 a** : to impose or collect by legal authority ⟨*levy* a tax⟩ **b** : to require (as a service) by authority **2** : to enlist or conscript for military service **3** : to carry on (war) : WAGE **4** : to seize property to satisfy a legal claim — **lev·i·er** *n*

lewd \\'lüd\ *adj* **1** : lacking in sexual restraint : LICENTIOUS **2** : OBSCENE 2, SALACIOUS [Middle English *lewed* "vulgar", from Old English *lǣwede* "laical, ignorant"] — **lewd·ly** *adv* — **lewd·ness** *n*

lex·i·cal \\'lek-si-kəl\ *adj* **1** : of or relating to the vocabulary of a language **2** : of or relating to a lexicon or to lexicography — **lex·i·cal·ly** \-si-kə-lē, -klē\ *adv*

lex·i·cog·ra·pher \ˌlek-sə-'käg-rə-fər\ *n* : a specialist in lexicography

lex·i·cog·ra·phy \-fē\ *n* **1** : the editing or making of a dictionary **2** : the principles and practices of dictionary making — **lex·i·co·graph·i·cal** \ˌlek-sə-kō-'graf-i-kəl\ *or* **lex·i·co·graph·ic** \-ik\ *adj* — **lex·i·co·graph·i·cal·ly** \-i-kə-lē, -klē\ *adv*

lex·i·con \\'lek-sə-ˌkän, -si-kən\ *n, pl* **lex·i·ca** \-si-kə\ *or* **lexicons 1** : DICTIONARY 1 **2** : the vocabulary of a language, an individual speaker, or a subject [Late Greek *lexikon,* from *lexikos* "of words", from Greek *lexis* "speech, word", from *legein* "to say"]

ley *variant of* LEA

Ley·den jar \ˌlīd-n-\ *n* : an electrical condenser consisting of a glass jar coated inside and outside with metal foil and having the inner coating connected to a conducting rod passed through the insulating stopper [*Leiden, Leyden,* Netherlands]

li·a·bil·i·ty \ˌlī-ə-'bil-ət-ē\ *n, pl* **-ties 1** : the state of being liable ⟨*liability* for one's actions⟩ ⟨*liability* to disease⟩ **2** *pl* : that for which a person is liable : DEBTS **3** : something that is a disadvantage : DRAWBACK

li·a·ble \\'lī-ə-bəl, *especially in sense 2b also* 'lī-bəl\ *adj* **1** : bound by law : RESPONSIBLE ⟨*liable* for damages⟩ **2 a** : SUSCEPTIBLE ⟨*liable* to disease⟩ **b** : exposed to or likely to experience something usually undesirable ⟨*liable* to get hurt⟩ [Old French *lier* "to bind", from Latin *ligare*] SYN see APT

li·aise \lē-'āz\ *vi* **1** : to establish liaison **2** : to act as a liaison officer [back-formation from *liaison*]

li·ai·son \\'lē-ə-ˌzän, lē-'ā-\ *n* **1 a** : a connecting link; *esp* : a linking or coordinating of activities **b** : AFFAIR 3a **2** : the pronunciation of an otherwise absent consonant sound at the end of a word when immediately followed by a word beginning with a vowel sound **3** : communication especially between parts of an armed force [French, from *lier* "to bind", from Latin *ligare*]

li·a·na \lē-'än-ə, -'an-ə\ *n* : any of various usually woody vines especially of tropical rain forests that root in the ground [French *liane*]

li·ar \\'lī-ər, 'līr\ *n* : one that tells lies

li·ba·tion \lī-'bā-shən\ *n* **1** : the act of pouring a liquid (as wine) in honor of a god; *also* : the liquid poured out **2** : a drink usually of an alcoholic beverage [Latin *libatio,* from *libare* "to pour as an offering"] — **li·ba·tion·ary** \-shə-ˌner-ē\ *adj*

¹li·bel \\'lī-bəl\ *n* **1** : a written or spoken statement or a representation that gives an unjustly unfavorable impression of a person or thing **2** : the act or crime of injuring a person's reputation by way of something printed or written or by a visible representation (as a picture) — compare SLANDER [Middle French, "written declaration", from Latin *libellus,* from *liber* "book"] — **li·bel·ous** \-bə-ləs\ *adj*

²libel *vt* **li·beled** *or* **li·belled; li·bel·ing** *or* **li·bel·ling** \-bə-ling, -bling\ : to make or publish a libel against — **li·bel·er** \-bə-lər\ *n* — **li·bel·ist** \-bə-list\ *n*

¹lib·er·al \\'lib-rəl, -ə-rəl\ *adj* **1** : of, relating to, or based on the liberal arts ⟨a *liberal* education⟩ **2 a** : GENEROUS 1 ⟨a *liberal* giver⟩ **b** : AMPLE, BOUNTIFUL ⟨a *liberal* serving⟩ **3** : not literal : LOOSE ⟨a *liberal* translation⟩ **4** : BROAD-MINDED, TOLERANT; *esp* : not bound by orthodox or traditional forms or beliefs **5 a** : of, favoring, or based on the principles of liberalism **b** *cap* : of or making up a political party (as in the United Kingdom) advocating or associated with the principles of political liberalism [Middle French, from Latin *liberalis* "suitable for a freeman, generous", from *liber* "free"] — **lib·er·al·ly** \-rə-lē\ *adv* □ SYN RADICAL: LIBERAL suggests an independence of mind, a freedom from conventionality, tradition, or dogma, a practical tolerant recognition of changing conditions and the need to adapt to them, and readiness to experiment; RADICAL usually suggests extremeness in breaking with established order and in a political desire to uproot and destroy.

²liberal *n* : one who is liberal: as **a** : one who is open-minded or not strict in the observance of orthodox or traditional forms **b** *cap* : a member or supporter of a Liberal party **c** : an advocate of liberalism especially in individual rights

liberal arts *n pl* : the studies (as language, philosophy, history, literature, or abstract science) in a college or university intended to provide chiefly general knowledge and to develop the general intellectual capacities

lib·er·al·ism \\'lib-rə-ˌliz-əm, -ə-rə-\ *n* **1** : the quality or state of being liberal **2 a** *often cap* : a movement in modern Protestantism emphasizing intellectual liberty and the spiritual and ethical content of Christianity **b** : a theory in economics emphasizing individual freedom from restraint and usually based on free competition, the self-regulating market, and the gold standard **c** : a political philosophy based on belief in progress, the essential goodness of man, and the autonomy of the individual and standing for the protection of political and civil liberties **d** *cap* : the principles or policies of a Liberal party — **lib·er·al·ist** \-rə-ləst\ *n or adj* — **lib·er·al·is·tic** \ˌlib-rə-'lis-tik, -ə-rə-\ *adj*

lib·er·al·i·ty \ˌlib-ə-'ral-ət-ē\ *n, pl* **-ties** : the quality or state of being liberal; *also* : an instance of being liberal

lib·er·al·ize \\'lib-rə-ˌlīz, -ə-rə-\ *vb* : to make or become liberal — **lib·er·al·iza·tion** \ˌlib-rə-lə-'zā-shən, -ə-rə-\ *n* — **lib·er·al·iz·er** \\'lib-rə-ˌlī-zər, -ə-rə-\ *n*

lib·er·ate \\'lib-ə-ˌrāt\ *vt* **1** : to free from bondage or restraint : set at liberty **2** : to free (as a gas) from combination [Latin *liberare,* from *liber* "free"] SYN see FREE — **lib·er·a·tion** \ˌlib-ə-'rā-shən\ *n* — **lib·er·a·tor** \\'lib-ə-ˌrāt-ər\ *n*

liberation theology *n* : a Christian movement especially in Latin America that combines political philosophy with a theology of salvation as liberation from injustice — **liberation theologian** *n*

lib·er·tar·i·an \ˌlib-ər-'ter-ē-ən\ *n* **1** : an advocate of the doctrine of free will **2** : one who upholds liberty of thought and action — **libertarian** *adj* — **lib·er·tar·i·an·ism** \-ē-ə-ˌniz-əm\ *n*

lib·er·tine \\'lib-ər-ˌtēn\ *n* : a person who is unrestrained by convention or morality; *esp* : one leading a dissolute life [Latin *libertinus* "freedman", derived from *liber* "free"] — **libertine** *adj* — **lib·er·tin·ism** \-ˌtē-ˌniz-əm\ *n*

lib·er·ty \\'lib-ərt-ē\ *n, pl* **-ties 1** : the condition of being free and independent : FREEDOM **2** : power to do what one pleases : freedom from restraint **3 a** : FAMILIARITY **4 b** : an imprudent action : RISK ⟨don't take foolish *liberties* with your health⟩ **4** : a short authorized absence from naval duty [Middle French *liberté,* from Latin *libertas,* from *liber* "free"] SYN see FREEDOM — **at liberty 1** : FREE 1a **2** : at leisure : UNOCCUPIED

liberty cap *n* : a close-fitting conical cap used as a symbol of liberty by the French revolutionists and in the United States especially before 1800

li·bid·i·nous \lə-'bid-n-əs\ *adj* **1** : having or marked by lustful desires : LASCIVIOUS **2** : of or relating to the libido — **li·bid·i·nous·ly** *adv* — **li·bid·i·nous·ness** *n*

li·bi·do \lə-'bēd-ō, -'bīd-\ *n, pl* **-dos 1** : emotion or psychic energy that in psychoanalytic theory is derived from primitive biological urges **2** : sexual drive [Latin *libidin-, libido* "desire, lust"] — **li·bid·i·nal** \-'bid-n-əl, -'bid-nəl\ *adj* — **li·bid·i·nal·ly** \-ē\ *adv*

Li·bra \'lī-brə, 'lē-\ *n* **1** : a southern zodiacal constellation between Virgo and Scorpio **2** : the 7th sign of the zodiac; *also* : one born under this sign [Latin, literally, "scales, pound"]

li·brar·i·an \lī-'brer-ē-ən\ *n* : a specialist in the care or management of a library — **li·brar·i·an·ship** \-,ship\ *n*

li·brary \'lī-,brer-ē\ *n, pl* **-brar·ies 1** : a place in which literary, reference, and artistic materials (as books, recordings, films) are kept for use but not for sale **2** : a collection of literary or artistic materials (as books or prints) [Medieval Latin *librarium,* from Latin *liber* "book"]

library paste *n* : a thick white adhesive made from starch

li·bret·tist \lə-'bret-əst\ *n* : the writer of a libretto

li·bret·to \lə-'bret-ō\ *n, pl* **-tos** *or* **-ti** \-ē\ : the text of an opera or a musical; *also* : a book containing such a text [Italian, from *libro* "book", from Latin *liber*]

Lib·ri·um \'lib-rē-əm\ *trademark* — used for a tranquilizer containing chlordiazepoxide

lice *pl of* LOUSE

¹li·cense *or* **li·cence** \'līs-ns\ *n* **1 a** : permission to act **b** : freedom of action **2 a** : permission granted by competent authority to engage in a business, occupation, or activity otherwise unlawful **b** : a document, plate, or tag showing that a license has been granted **3 a** : freedom that is used irresponsibly **b** : licentious conduct **4** : deviation from fact, form, or rule by an artist or writer for the sake of effect [Middle French *licence,* from Latin *licentia,* from *licēre* "to be permitted"] SYN SEE FREEDOM

²license *also* **licence** *vt* **1** : to issue a license to **2** : to permit or authorize especially by formal license — **li·cens·able** \-ə-bəl\ *adj*

licensed practical nurse *n* : a trained person authorized by license (as from a state) to provide routine care for the sick

licensed vocational nurse *n* : a licensed practical nurse authorized by license to practice in the states of California or Texas

li·cens·ee \,līs-n-'sē\ *n* : one that is licensed

li·cen·tious \lī-'sen-chəs\ *adj* : loose and lawless in behavior; *esp* : LEWD, LASCIVIOUS — **li·cen·tious·ly** *adv* — **li·cen·tious·ness** *n*

lichee *variant of* LITCHI

li·chen \'lī-kən\ *n* : any of numerous complex plants (group Lichenes) that are thallophytes and are made up of an alga and a fungus growing in symbiotic association on a solid surface (as a tree, a rock, or the ground) [Latin, from Greek *leichēn, lichēn*] — **li·chen·ous** \-kə-nəs\ *adj*

lic·it \'lis-ət\ *adj* : conforming to the requirements of the law : PERMISSIBLE [Middle French *licite,* from Latin *licitus,* from *licēre* "to be permitted"] — **lic·it·ly** *adv* SYN SEE LAWFUL

¹lick \'lik\ *vb* **1 a** : to draw the tongue over **b** : to dart or dart at or over like a tongue (flames *licked* the ceiling) **2** : to lap up **3 a** : to strike repeatedly : THRASH **b** : DEFEAT **2** [Old English *liccian*] — **lick into shape** : to put into proper form or condition

²lick *n* **1 a** : an act or instance of licking **b** : a small amount : BIT (not a *lick* of work) **2** : a sharp hit : BLOW **3** : a place (as a spring) having a deposit of salt that

animals regularly lick — **lick and a promise** : a careless performance of a task

lick·e·ty-split \,lik-ət-ē-'split\ *adv* : at great speed : very fast [probably derived from ¹*lick* + *split*]

lick·ing \'lik-ing\ *n* **1** : a sound thrashing **2** : a severe setback : DEFEAT

lick·spit·tle \'lik-,spit-l\ *n* : a fawning or abject subordinate : TOADY

lic·o·rice \'lik-rish, -ə-rish, -rəs\ *n* **1** : a European plant of the pea family with spikes of blue flowers **2** : the dried root of licorice; *also* : an extract from it used especially in brewing, confectionery, and medicine [Old French, from Late Latin *liquiritia,* from Latin *glycyrrhiza,* from Greek *glykyrrhiza,* from *glykys* "sweet" + *rhiza* "root"]

lic·tor \'lik-tər\ *n* : a Roman officer carrying the fasces as the insignia of his office with duties that included attending the chief magistrates in public appearances [Latin]

lid \'lid\ *n* **1** : a movable cover (the *lid* of a box) **2** : EYELID **3** *slang* : CAP 1, HAT **4** : RESTRAINT 2 (put a *lid* on all news coverage) [Old English *hlid*] — **lid·ded** \'lid-əd\ *adj* — **lid·less** \'lid-ləs\ *adj*

li·do \'lēd-ō\ *n, pl* **lidos** : a fashionable beach resort [*Lido,* Italy]

¹lie \'lī\ *vi* **lay** \'lā\; **lain** \'lān\; **ly·ing** \'lī-ing\ **1 a** : to be in, stay in, or take up a horizontal position (decided to *lie* on the bed) (*lie* asleep) **b** *archaic* : to have sexual intercourse — used with *with* **c** : to stay quietly (as in hiding) **2** : to be in a helpless or defenseless state (*lay* at the mercy of the invaders) **3** : to have direction : EXTEND (the route *lay* to the west) **4 a** : to occupy a specified relative place or position (hills *lie* behind us) **b** : to have an effect by mere presence, weight, or relative position (guilt *lay* heavily on them) **5** : to have a place : EXIST (the choice *lies* here) **6** : REMAIN (machinery *lying* idle) [Old English *licgan*] — **lie low 1** : to stay in hiding **2** : to bide one's time but remain ready for action

²lie *n* **1** : the position in which something lies **2** : *chiefly British* : ²LAY 1 **3** : the haunt of an animal : COVERT

³lie *vi* **lied; ly·ing** \'lī-ing\ **1** : to make an untrue statement with intent to deceive (*lie* about one's age) **2** : to create a false impression (statistics sometimes *lie*) [Old English *lēogan*]

⁴lie *n* **1** : a deliberate telling of an untruth **2** : something that misleads or deceives (your show of innocence was a *lie*)

lie detector *n* : an apparatus for detecting bodily changes considered to accompany lying

lie down *vi* **1** : to submit meekly to defeat, disappointment, or insult (refused to take the setback *lying down*) **2** : to fail to do one's part (*lying down* on the job)

lief \'lēv, 'lēf\ *adv* : SOON, GLADLY (I'd as *lief* go as not) [Old English *lēof* "dear, agreeable"]

¹liege \'lēj\ *adj* **1** : having the right to receive service and allegiance (*liege* lord) **2** : owing or giving service to a lord (a *liege* subject) [Old French, from Late Latin *laeticus,* from *laetus* "serf", of Germanic origin]

²liege *n* **1** : VASSAL 1 **2** : a feudal superior

liege man *n* **1** : VASSAL 1 **2** : a devoted follower

lien \'lēn, 'lē-ən\ *n* : a legal claim on the property of a person until he or she has met a certain obligation (as a debt) [Middle French, "tie, band", from Latin *ligamen,* from *ligare* "to bind"]

lie to \lī-'tü, 'lī-\ *vi* : to stay stationary with head to windward

lieu \'lü\ *n, archaic* : PLACE, STEAD [Middle French, from Latin *locus*] — **in lieu of** : in the place of : instead of

lieu·ten·an·cy \lü-'ten-ən-sē\ *n, pl* **-cies** : the office, rank, or commission of a lieutenant

lieu·ten·ant \lü-'ten-ənt\ *n* **1 a** : an officer empowered to act for a higher official **b** : a representative of an-

life preserver

other in the performance of duty **2 a** (1) : FIRST LIEU-TENANT (2) : SECOND LIEUTENANT **b** : an officer rank in the Navy and Coast Guard above lieutenant junior grade and below lieutenant commander **c** : a fire or police department officer ranking below a captain [Middle French, from *lieu* "place" + *tenant* "holding"]

lieutenant colonel *n* : an officer rank in the Army, Marine Corps, and Air Force above major and below colonel

lieutenant commander *n* : an officer rank in the Navy and Coast Guard above lieutenant and below commander

lieutenant general *n* : an officer rank in the Army, Marine Corps, and Air Force above major general and below general

lieutenant governor *n* **1** : an elected official serving as deputy to the governor of an American state **2** : the formal head of the government of a Canadian province appointed to represent the crown

lieutenant junior grade *n, pl* **lieutenants junior grade** : an officer rank in the Navy and Coast Guard above ensign and below lieutenant

¹**life** \'līf\ *n, pl* **lives** \'līvz\ **1 a** : the quality that distinguishes a vital and functional being from a dead body or inanimate matter **b** : a state of an organism characterized especially by capacity for metabolism, growth, reaction to stimuli, and reproduction **2** : the sequence of physical and mental experiences that make up the existence of an individual **3** : BIOGRAPHY 1 **4 a** : the period during which an organism lives **b** : a specific phase or aspect of such a life ⟨adult *life*⟩ ⟨sex *life*⟩ **5 a** : a way or manner of living **6** : a vital or living being; *esp* : PERSON ⟨saving *lives*⟩ **7** : ANIMATION, SPIRIT ⟨eyes full of *life*⟩ **8** : the period of utility, duration, or existence of something ⟨*life* of a car⟩ **9** : living beings ⟨forest *life*⟩ **10 a** : human activities **b** : animate activity and movement ⟨stirrings of *life*⟩ **11** : one providing interest and vigor ⟨the *life* of the party⟩ [Old English *līf*]

²**life** *adj* **1** : of or relating to animate being ⟨the *life* force⟩ **2** : LIFELONG ⟨*life* tenure⟩ **3** : using a living model ⟨a *life* class⟩

life-and-death *adj* : ending in life or death : deciding which will survive

life belt *n* : a life preserver in the form of a buoyant belt

life·blood \'līf-'bləd\ *n* : something that gives strength and energy : the vital force or essence

life·boat \-,bōt\ *n* **1** : a strong buoyant boat especially designed for use in saving lives at sea **2** : a boat carried by a ship for use in an emergency

life buoy *n* : a ring-shaped life preserver

life cycle *n* **1** : the series of stages through which an organism passes from a particular first stage (as the egg) to the corresponding stage of its offspring **2** : LIFE HISTORY 1a

life expectancy *n* : an expected number of years of life based on statistical probability

life·guard \'līf-,gärd\ *n* : a usually expert swimmer employed to safeguard other swimmers

life history *n* **1 a** : a history of the changes through which an organism passes in its development from its first stage to its natural death **b** : LIFE CYCLE 1 **2** : the history of an individual's development in a social environment

life insurance *n* : insurance providing for payment of a fixed sum to a specified individual upon death of the insured

life jacket *n* : a life preserver in the form of a sleeveless jacket or a collar which extends down the chest — called also *life vest*

life·less \'līf-ləs\ *adj* : having no life : **a** : DEAD 1 **b** : INANIMATE ⟨*lifeless* as marble⟩ **c** : lacking qualities expressive of life and vigor : DULL ⟨*lifeless* voice⟩ **d** : destitute of living beings ⟨a *lifeless* desert⟩ — **life·less·ly** *adv* — **life·less·ness** *n*

life·like \'līf-,līk\ *adj* : accurately representing or imitating real life ⟨a *lifelike* portrait⟩ — **life·like·ness** *n*

life·line \'līf-,līn\ *n* **1 a** : a line to which persons may cling to save or protect their lives **b** : a line attached to a diver's helmet by which he is lowered and raised **c** : a rope line for lowering a person to safety **2** : an important land, sea, or air route

life·long \'līf-,lông\ *adj* : continuing through life ⟨a *lifelong* friendship⟩

life plant *n* : BRYOPHYLLUM

life preserver *n* : a device designed to save a person from drowning by buoying up the body while in the water

lif·er \'lī-fər\ *n* : a person sentenced to life imprisonment

life raft *n* : a raft usually made of wood or an inflatable material and designed for rescue use in an emergency at sea

life·sav·ing \'līf-,sā-ving\ *n* : the skill or practice of saving or protecting lives especially of drowning persons — **life·sav·er** \-vər\ *n* — **lifesaving** *adj*

life science *n* : a branch of science (as biology, medicine, anthropology, or sociology) that deals with living organisms and life processes — **life scientist** *n*

life-size \'līf-'sīz\ *or* **life-sized** \-'sīzd\ *adj* : of natural size : of the size of the original ⟨a *life-size* statue⟩

life span *n* **1** : the duration of existence of an individual **2** : the average length of life of a kind of organism or of an object

life·style \'līf-'stīl\ *n* : the usual way of life of a person, group, or society

life-support system *n* : a system that supplies some or all of the items necessary for maintaining life or health

life·time \-,tīm\ *n* : the duration of an individual's existence

life vest *n* : LIFE JACKET

life·work \'līf-'wərk\ *n* : the entire or principal work of one's lifetime; *also* : a work extending over a lifetime

¹**lift** \'lift\ *vb* **1** : to raise from a lower to a higher position, rate, or amount : ELEVATE **2** : REVOKE, REPEAL ⟨*lift* an embargo⟩ **3 a** : STEAL ⟨had their wallets *lifted*⟩ **b** : PLAGIARIZE **4** : to move from one place to another : TRANSPORT **5** : RISE, ASCEND ⟨the jet *lifted* from the airport⟩ **6** : to disperse upward ⟨until the fog *lifts*⟩ [Old Norse *lypta*] — **lift·er** *n* □ SYN LIFT, RAISE, HOIST, BOOST mean to move from a lower to a higher place or position. LIFT implies effort exerted to bring up from and especially clear of the ground and may apply to immaterial as well as material things; RAISE often suggests bringing something to a vertical or high position for which it is suited or intended; HOIST implies lifting something very heavy by mechanical means; BOOST suggests assisting to climb or advance by a push.

²**lift** *n* **1** : the amount that may be lifted at one time : LOAD **2** : the action or an instance of lifting **3 a** : ASSISTANCE, HELP **b** : a ride along one's way **4** : the distance or extent to which something rises ⟨the *lift* of a canal lock⟩ **5 a** *chiefly British* : ELEVATOR 1b **b** : an apparatus for raising an automobile (as for repair) **c** : a conveyor for carrying people up or down a mountain slope **6 a** : an elevating influence **b** : an elevation of the spirits **7** : the part of the total aerodynamic force acting on an airplane or airfoil that is upward and opposes the pull of gravity

lift·off \'lift-,óf\ *n* : a vertical takeoff by an aircraft, rocket, or missile

lig·a·ment \'lig-ə-mənt\ *n* : a tough band of tissue that holds bones together or keeps an organ in place in the body [Latin *ligamentum* "band, tie", from *ligare* "to bind"] — **lig·a·men·tous** \,lig-ə-'ment-əs\ *adj*

li·gate \'lī-,gāt, lī-'\ *vt* : to tie with a ligature — **li·ga·tion** \lī-'gā-shən\ *n*

lig·a·ture \'lig-ə-,chúr, -chər\ *n* **1** : a binding or tying of something **2** : something that binds or connects : BOND **3** : a thread or filament used in surgery especially for tying blood vessels **4** : a printed or written character consisting of two or more letters or characters united ⟨the *ligature* æ⟩ [Middle French, from Late Latin *ligatura*, from Latin *ligare* "to bind"]

¹light \'līt\ *n* **1 a** : something that makes vision possible **b** : the sensation aroused by stimulation of the visual receptors **c** : an electromagnetic radiation in the wavelength range including infrared, visible, ultraviolet, and X rays and traveling in a vacuum with a speed of about 299,726 kilometers per second; *esp* : the part of this range that is visible to the human eye **2 a** : DAYLIGHT 1 **b** : DAWN 1 **3** : a source of light: as **a** : a celestial body **b** : CANDLE 1 **c** : an electric lamp ⟨turned on all the *lights*⟩ **4 a** : mental or spiritual insight **b** : TRUTH ⟨see the *light*⟩ **5 a** : public knowledge ⟨facts brought to *light*⟩ **b** : a particular aspect presented to view ⟨saw the matter in a false *light*⟩ **6** : a particular illumination ⟨by the *light* of the moon⟩ **7 a** : WINDOW 1 **b** : SKYLIGHT **8** *pl* : way of thinking : BELIEFS ⟨worship according to one's *lights*⟩ **9** : a noteworthy person : LUMINARY **10** : a particular expression of the eye **11** : LIGHTHOUSE, BEACON **b** : TRAFFIC SIGNAL **12** : a source of heat for lighting something [Old English *lēoht*] — **light·less** \-ləs\ *adj*

²light *adj* **1** : having light : BRIGHT ⟨a *light* room⟩ **2 a** : not dark or swarthy in color ⟨a *light* skin⟩ **b** : medium in saturation and high in lightness ⟨*light* blue⟩

³light *vb* **light·ed** *or* **lit** \'lit\; **light·ing** **1** : to make or become light : BRIGHTEN **2** : to burn or cause to burn : IGNITE **3 a** : to conduct with a light ⟨*light* them to their room⟩ **b** : ILLUMINATE ⟨rockets *lit* up the sky⟩

⁴light *adj* **1 a** : having little weight : not heavy ⟨*light* as a feather⟩ **b** : designed to carry a comparatively small load ⟨a *light* truck⟩ **c** : having relatively little weight in proportion to bulk ⟨aluminum is a *light* metal⟩ **2 a** : not important or serious : TRIVIAL **b** : not abundant : SCANTY ⟨*light* rain⟩ ⟨a *light* breakfast⟩ **3 a** : easily disturbed ⟨a *light* sleeper⟩ **b** : exerting little force or pressure : GENTLE ⟨a *light* touch⟩ **4** : requiring little effort ⟨*light* exercise⟩ **5** : capable of moving swiftly or nimbly ⟨the dancers were *light* on their feet⟩ **6** : FRIVOLOUS ⟨*light* conduct⟩ **7** : free from care : CHEERFUL **8** : intended chiefly to entertain ⟨*light* reading⟩ **9** : having a comparatively low alcoholic content ⟨*light* wines⟩ **10** : lightly armed or equipped ⟨*light* cavalry⟩ **11** : being coarse and sandy : easily reduced to dust ⟨*light* soil⟩ **12** : producing goods for direct consumption by the consumer ⟨*light* industry⟩ **13** : UNACCENTED ⟨*light* syllables⟩ **14** : having a clear soft quality ⟨a *light* voice⟩ [Old English *lēoht*]

⁵light *adv* **1** : LIGHTLY **2** : with little baggage ⟨travels *light*⟩

⁶light *vi* **light·ed** *or* **lit** \'lit\; **light·ing** **1** : SETTLE, ALIGHT ⟨birds *lit* on the lawn⟩ **2 a** : to strike or fall unexpectedly ⟨bad luck *lighted* on the party⟩ **b** : to arrive by chance : HAPPEN ⟨*lit* upon a solution⟩ [Old English *līhtan* "to dismount, alight"]

light adaptation *n* : the process by which the eye adapts to seeing in strong light — **light-adapt·ed** \'līt-ə-,dap-təd\ *adj*

light bulb *n* : INCANDESCENT LAMP

¹light·en \'līt-n\ *vb* **light·ened; light·en·ing** \'līt-ning, -n-ing\ **1** : to make or grow light or clear : BRIGHTEN **2** : to make or become lighter — **light·en·er** \'līt-nər, -n-ər\ *n*

²lighten *vb* **light·ened; light·en·ing** \'līt-ning, -n-ing\ **1** : to relieve of a burden in whole or in part ⟨*lighten* the plane⟩ ⟨*lighten* their duties⟩ **2** : GLADDEN **3** : to become lighter SYN see RELIEVE — **light·en·er** \'līt-nər, -n-ər\ *n*

¹ligh·ter \'līt-ər\ *n* : a large usually flat-bottomed barge used especially in unloading or loading ships [Dutch *lichten* "to unload"]

²lighter *vt* : to convey by a lighter

³light·er \'līt-ər\ *n* : one that lights; *esp* : a device for lighting

lighter-than-air *adj* : of less weight than the air displaced

light·face \'līt-,fās\ *n* : a typeface having thin light lines — **light-faced** \-'fāst\ *adj*

light-fast \-'fast\ *adj* : resistant to light and especially to sunlight; *esp* : colorfast to light — **light·fast·ness** \-,fast-nəs, -,fas-\ *n*

light-fin·gered \-'fing-gərd\ *adj* **1** : adroit in stealing especially by picking pockets **2** : having a light and dexterous touch : NIMBLE — **light-fin·gered·ness** *n*

light-foot·ed \-'fut-əd\ *adj* : having a light and springy step or movement

light-head·ed \-'hed-əd\ *adj* **1** : mentally disoriented : DIZZY **2** : lacking in maturity or seriousness : FRIVOLOUS — **light-head·ed·ly** *adv* — **light-head·ed·ness** *n*

light-heart·ed \-'härt-əd\ *adj* : free from care or anxiety : MERRY — **light-heart·ed·ly** *adv* — **light-heart·ed·ness** *n*

light heavyweight *n* : a boxer in a weight division having the approximate range of 75 to 81 kilograms

light·house \'līt-,haus\ *n* : a structure (as a tower) with a powerful light signal for guiding navigators at night

light·ing \'līt-ing\ *n* **1 a** : ILLUMINATION 2 **b** : IGNITION 1 **2** : an artificial supply of light or the apparatus providing it

light·ly \'līt-lē\ *adv* **1** : with little weight or force : GENTLY **2** : in a small degree or amount ⟨sprinkle *lightly*⟩ **3** : with little difficulty : EASILY ⟨was let off *lightly* with a warning⟩ **4** : in an agile manner : NIMBLY **5** : with indifference or carelessness ⟨took the rebuff *lightly*⟩

light meter *n* **1** : a small portable device for measuring illumination **2** : a device for indicating correct photographic exposure under varying conditions of illumination

light microscope *n* : MICROSCOPE 1

light-mind·ed \'līt-'mīn-dəd\ *adj* : lacking in seriousness : FRIVOLOUS — **light·mind·ed·ly** *adv*

¹light·ness \'līt-nəs\ *n* **1** : the quality or state of being light or lighted : ILLUMINATION **2** : the degree to which the achromatic element of a color is nearer white than black ⟨pink is high in *lightness*⟩

²lightness *n* **1** : the quality or state of being light in weight **2** : LEVITY **3 a** : physical agility **b** : cheery ease of style or manner **4** : DELICACY ⟨*lightness* of touch⟩

¹light·ning \'līt-ning\ *n* : the flashing of light produced by a discharge of atmospheric electricity from one cloud to another or between a cloud and the earth; *also* : the discharge itself [Middle English, from *lightenen* "to lighten"]

²lightning *adj* : moving or accomplished with or as if with the speed of lightning ⟨a *lightning* attack⟩

lightning arrester *n* : a device for protecting an electrical apparatus from damage by lightning

lightning bug *n* : FIREFLY

lightning rod *n* : a metal rod set up on a building or a ship and connected with the earth or water below to decrease the chances of damage from lightning

light opera *n* : OPERETTA

light out *vi* : to leave in a hurry ⟨*lit out* for home⟩

light pen *n* : a pen-shaped device for immediate handling of information on the display screen of a computer

light·plane \'līt-'plān\ *n* : a small and comparatively lightweight airplane; *esp* : a privately owned passenger airplane

light·proof \'līt-'prüf\ *adj* : impenetrable by light

lights \'līts\ *n pl* : the lungs especially of a slaughtered animal [Middle English *lightes*, from *⁴light*]

light·ship \'līt-,ship\ *n* : a ship equipped with a powerful light signal and moored at a place dangerous to navigation

lighthouse

\ə\ abut	\ng\ sing
\ər\ further	\ō\ bone
\a\ mat	\ȯ\ saw
\ā\ take	\ȯi\ coin
\ä\ cot, cart	\th\ thin
\au̇\ out	\th\ this
\ch\ chin	\ü\ food
\e\ pet	\u̇\ foot
\ē\ easy	\y\ yet
\g\ go	\yü\ few
\i\ tip	\yu̇\ cure
\ī\ life	\zh\ vision
\j\ job	

light·some \'līt-səm\ *adj* 1 : AIRY 3, NIMBLE 2 : free from care : CHEERFUL — **light·some·ly** *adv* — **light·some·ness** *n*

light-tight \'līt-,tīt\ *adj* : LIGHTPROOF

light trap *n* : a device for collecting or destroying insects by attracting them to a light and trapping or killing them

¹light·weight \'līt-,wāt\ *n* 1 : one of less than average weight; *esp* : a boxer in a weight division having the approximate range of 57 to 60 kilograms 2 : one of little consequence

²lightweight *adj* 1 : of, relating to, or characteristic of a lightweight 2 : having less than average weight 3 : of no significance : UNIMPORTANT

light–year \'līt-,yiər\ *n* : a unit of length in astronomy equal to the distance that light travels in one year or 9,460,000,000,000 kilometers

lign- *or* **ligni-** *or* **ligno-** *combining form* : wood ⟨*lign*in⟩ [Latin *lignum*]

lig·ne·ous \'lig-nē-əs\ *adj* : of or resembling wood : WOODY [Latin *ligneus,* from *lignum* "firewood, wood", from *legere* "to gather"]

lig·ni·fy \'lig-nə-,fī\ *vb* -**fied;** -**fy·ing** : to convert into or become wood or woody tissue — **lig·ni·fi·ca·tion** \,lig-nə-fə-'kā-shən\ *n*

lig·nin \'lig-nən\ *n* : a substance related to cellulose that occurs in the woody cell walls of plants and in the cementing material between them

lig·nite \'lig-,nīt\ *n* : a usually brownish black coal intermediate between peat and bituminous coal; *esp* : one in which the texture of the original wood is distinct

lig·num vi·tae \,lig-nəm-'vīt-ē\ *n, pl* **lignum vitaes** : any of several tropical American trees or their very hard heavy wood [New Latin, literally, "wood of life"]

lig·u·late \'lig-yə-lət, -,lāt\ *also* **lig·u·lat·ed** \-,lāt-əd\ *adj* 1 : shaped like a strap ⟨*ligulate* ray flowers⟩ 2 : having ligules

lig·ule \'lig-yül\ *n* : an elongated flattened projection especially on a plant: as **a** : an appendage of a leaf and especially of the sheath of a blade of grass **b** : the limb of a ray flower [Latin *ligula* "small tongue, strap"]

lik·able *or* **like·able** \'lī-kə-bəl\ *adj* : easily liked : PLEASANT, AGREEABLE — **lik·able·ness** *n*

¹like \'līk\ *vb* 1 : to feel attraction toward or take pleasure in : ENJOY ⟨*likes* baseball⟩ 2 : to feel toward : REGARD ⟨how do you *like* this plan⟩ 3 : to wish to have : WANT ⟨would *like* a vacation⟩ 4 : to feel inclined : CHOOSE ⟨allowed to do as they *liked*⟩ [Old English *līcian* "to be suitable, be pleasing"]

²like *n* : LIKING, PREFERENCE ⟨*likes* and dislikes⟩

³like *adj* 1 : the same or nearly the same ⟨as in appearance, character, or quantity⟩ ⟨suits of *like* design⟩ **2 a** : LIKELY 1 3 : having the same unknowns raised to the same powers ⟨9xy⁴ and 6xy⁴ are *like* terms⟩ [Old English *gelīc,* from *līc* "body"]

⁴like *prep* **1 a** : similar to ⟨their house is *like* a barn⟩ **b** : typical of ⟨was *like* them to do that⟩ 2 : in the manner of : similarly to ⟨acts *like* a fool⟩ 3 : inclined to ⟨looks *like* rain⟩ 4 : such as ⟨a subject *like* physics⟩

⁵like *n* : one that is like another : COUNTERPART ⟨may never see its *like* again⟩

⁶like *adv* 1 : LIKELY, PROBABLY ⟨*like* enough, you will⟩ 2 : to some extent : SEEMINGLY ⟨came in nonchalantly *like*⟩ 3 : close to ⟨the rate is more *like* 12 percent⟩

⁷like *conj* 1 : in the same way that : AS 2 : as if ⟨acted *like* they were scared⟩

-like *adj combining form* : resembling or characteristic of ⟨bell-*like*⟩ ⟨lady*like*⟩

like·li·hood \'lī-klē-,hùd\ *n* : PROBABILITY

¹like·ly \'lī-klē\ *adj* **like·li·er;** -**est** 1 : being such as to make a certain happening or result probable ⟨the stronger team is *likely* to win⟩ 2 : seeming like the truth : BELIEVABLE ⟨a *likely* story⟩ 3 : PROMISING ⟨a *likely* place to fish⟩ [Old Norse *glīkligr,* from *glīkr* "like"]

²likely *adv* : in all probability : PROBABLY

like-mind·ed \'līk-'mīn-dəd\ *adj* : of the same mind or habit of thought — **like-mind·ed·ly** *adv* — **like-mind·ed·ness** *n*

lik·en \'lī-kən\ *vt* **lik·ened; lik·en·ing** \'līk-ning, -ə-ning\ : to represent as like something : COMPARE

like·ness \'līk-nəs\ *n* 1 : the quality or state of being like : RESEMBLANCE 2 : APPEARANCE, SEMBLANCE ⟨in the *likeness* of a clown⟩ 3 : COPY, PORTRAIT □ SYN LIKENESS, SIMILARITY, RESEMBLANCE mean agreement or correspondence in details. LIKENESS implies a closer correspondence than SIMILARITY, which often implies that things are only somewhat alike; RESEMBLANCE implies similarity chiefly in appearance or external qualities.

like·wise \'līk-,wīz\ *adv* 1 : in like manner : SIMILARLY 2 : in addition : ALSO

lik·ing \'lī-king\ *n* : favorable regard : FONDNESS, TASTE

li·lac \'lī-lək, -,lak, -,läk\ *n* 1 : any of a genus of shrubs and trees of the olive family; *esp* : a European shrub widely grown for its showy clusters of fragrant pink, purple, or white flowers 2 : a moderate purple [obsolete French, from Arabic *līlak,* from Persian *nīlak* "bluish", from *nīl* "blue", from Sanskrit *nīla* "dark blue"]

lil·i·a·ceous \,lil-ē-'ā-shəs\ *adj* : of or relating to lilies

lil·li·pu·tian \,lil-ə-'pyü-shən\ *adj, often cap* 1 : extremely small : MINIATURE 2 : SMALL-MINDED, PETTY [*Lilliput,* island in Swift's *Gulliver's Travels* (1726) inhabited by people six inches high]

¹lilt \'lilt\ *vt* 1 : to sing or speak rhythmically and with varying pitch 2 : to move in a lively springy manner [Middle English *lulten*] — **lilt·ing·ly** \'lil-ting-lē\ *adv*

²lilt *n* 1 : a lively and usually happy song or tune 2 : a rhythmical swing, flow, or cadence

¹lily \'lil-ē\ *n, pl* **lil·ies** 1 : any of a genus of erect perennial leafy-stemmed bulbous herbs widely grown for their showy funnel-shaped flowers; *also* : any of various related plants 2 : any of various plants ⟨as a water lily or a calla⟩ with showy flowers [Old English *lilie,* from Latin *lilium*]

²lily *adj* : of, relating to, or resembling a lily

lily–liv·ered \,lil-ē-'liv-ərd\ *adj* : lacking courage : COWARDLY □ ORIGIN White, the lily's color, is a color associated with fear. A badly frightened person may turn pale—"white as a sheet". But the sudden fright that drains the blood from one's face is quite different from the habitual cowardice of one who is *lily-livered.* Although the liver does not turn pale with fear, it was once believed that a deficiency of choler or yellow bile—the humor that governed anger, spirit, and courage—would leave the liver colorless. A person deficient in choler, and so white-livered, or *lily-livered,* would be spiritless and a coward.

lily of the valley : a low perennial herb of the lily family with usually two large oblong leaves and a stalk of fragrant nodding bell-shaped flowers

lily pad *n* : a floating leaf of a water lily

lily–white \,lil-ē-'hwīt, -'wīt\ *adj* 1 : white as a lily 2 : FAULTLESS, PURE

li·ma bean \,lī-mə-\ *n* : any of various bush or tall-growing beans widely grown for their flat edible usually pale green or whitish seeds; *also* : this seed [*Lima,* Peru]

¹limb \'lim\ *n* 1 : one of the projecting paired appendages ⟨as wings⟩ of an animal body used especially for movement and grasping; *esp* : a leg or arm of a human being 2 : a large primary branch of a tree [Old English *lim*] — **limbed** \'limd\ *adj*

²limb *vt* : to cut off the limbs of ⟨a felled tree⟩

³limb *n* 1 : the outer edge of the apparent disk of a celestial body ⟨the eastern *limb* of the sun⟩ 2 : the expanded portion of a bodily organ; *esp* : the spreading upper portion of a calyx or corolla that is not made up of separate parts [Latin *limbus* "border"]

¹lim·ber \\'lim-bər\\ *adj* : bending easily : SUPPLE ⟨a *limber* willow twig⟩ ⟨a *limber* gymnast⟩ [origin unknown] — **lim·ber·ly** *adv* — **lim·ber·ness** *n*

²limber *vb* **lim·bered; lim·ber·ing** \\'lim-bə-ring, -bring\\ : to become or cause to become limber ⟨*limbered* up with calisthenics⟩

limbic system \\,lim-bik-\\ *n* : a group of structures below the cortex of the brain that are concerned especially with emotion and motivation [Latin *limbus* "border"]

limb·less \\'lim-ləs\\ *adj* : having no limbs

lim·bo \\'lim-bō\\ *n, pl* **limbos** **1** *often cap* : an abode of souls (as of unbaptized infants) barred from heaven through no fault of their own **2 a** : a place or state of restraint, confinement, or oblivion **b** : an intermediate or transitional place or state [Medieval Latin in *limbo* "on the border", from Latin *limbus* "border"]

Lim·burg·er \\'lim-bər-gər\\ *n* : a creamy semisoft surface-ripened cheese with a pungent rind [*Limburg,* Belgium]

¹lime \\'līm\\ *n* **1** : BIRDLIME **2 a** : a caustic highly infusible solid that consists of an oxide of calcium often together with magnesia, is obtained by calcining forms of calcium carbonate (as limestone or shells), and is used in mortar and plaster and in agriculture — called also *quicklime* **b** : a dry white powder consisting essentially of an hydroxide of calcium that is made by treating lime with water **c** : CALCIUM ⟨carbonate of *lime*⟩ [Old English *līm*]

²lime *vt* : to treat or cover with lime

³lime *adj* : of, relating to, or containing lime or limestone

⁴lime *n* : a European linden tree [Old English *lind*]

⁵lime *n* : a citrus fruit like the lemon but smaller and with greenish yellow rind; *also* : the tree that bears it [French, from Provençal *limo,* from Arabic *līm*]

lime·ade \\,līm-'ād, 'lī-,mād\\ *n* : a drink made of lime juice, sugar, and water

lime·kiln \\'līm-,kiln, -,kil\\ *n* : a furnace for reducing limestone or shells to lime by burning

lime·light \\-,līt\\ *n* **1** : a device formerly used for lighting of the stage producing light by means of a flame directed on a cylinder of lime; *also* : the light produced by this device **2** : the center of public attention

lim·er·ick \\'lim-rik, -ə-rik\\ *n* : a light or humorous verse form of 5 lines of which the 1st, 2d, and 5th follow one rhyme and the 3d and 4th follow another [*Limerick,* Ireland]

lime·stone \\'līm-,stōn\\ *n* : a rock that is formed chiefly by accumulation of organic remains (as shells or coral), consists mainly of calcium carbonate, is extensively used in building, and yields lime when burned

lime·wa·ter \\'līm-,wȯt-ər, -,wät-\\ *n* : an alkaline water solution of calcium hydroxide often used in medicine as an antacid

¹lim·it \\'lim-ət\\ *n* **1 a** : a geographical or political boundary **b** *pl* : ²BOUND **3** **2 a** : something that bounds, restrains, or confines ⟨cooperate within *limits*⟩ **b** : the utmost extent ⟨reach the *limit* of one's tolerance⟩ **3** : LIMITATION 2 **4** : a prescribed maximum or minimum amount, quantity, or number **5** : a fixed number that is related to a variable in such a way that the difference between them as the variable approaches the number becomes and remains less than any positive value no matter how close to zero **6** : one that is exasperating or intolerable [Middle French *limite,* from Latin *limit-, limes* "boundary"]

²limit *vt* **1** : to set limits to **2** : to reduce in quantity or extent — **lim·it·able** \\'lim-ət-ə-bəl\\ *adj* — **lim·it·er** *n*

lim·i·ta·tion \\,lim-ə-'tā-shən\\ *n* **1** : an act or instance of limiting **2** : the quality or state of being limited **3** : something that limits : RESTRAINT — **lim·i·ta·tion·al** \\-shnəl, -shən-l\\ *adj*

lim·it·ed *adj* **1 a** : confined within limits : RESTRICTED **b** : having a limited number of passengers and offering

superior and faster service and transportation ⟨a *limited* train⟩ **2** : relating to or being a government in which constitutional limitations are placed on the powers of one or more of its branches ⟨a *limited* monarchy⟩ — **lim·it·ed·ly** *adv* — **lim·it·ed·ness** *n*

limited war *n* : a war with an objective less than the total defeat of the enemy

lim·it·ing *adj* **1** : functioning as a limit : RESTRICTIVE ⟨*limiting* value⟩ **2** : serving to limit population size of organisms in an environment ⟨food is a *limiting* factor⟩

lim·it·less \\'lim-ət-ləs\\ *adj* : having no limits — **lim·it·less·ly** *adv* — **lim·it·less·ness** *n*

limn \\'lim\\ *vt* **limned; limn·ing** \\'lim-ing, -ning\\ **1** : to draw or paint on a surface **2 a** : to outline in clear sharp detail **b** : to describe or portray in symbols (as words or musical notes) [Middle English *luminen, limnen* "to illuminate", derived from Latin *illuminare*] — **limn·er** \\'lim-ər, -nər\\ *n*

lim·nol·o·gy \\lim-'näl-ə-jē\\ *n* : the scientific study of fresh waters [Greek *limnē* "pool"] — **lim·no·log·i·cal** \\,lim-nə-'läj-i-kəl\\ *adj* — **lim·nol·o·gist** \\lim-'näl-ə-jəst\\ *n*

li·mo·nite \\'lī-mə-,nīt\\ *n* : an ore of iron consisting of a hydrous ferric oxide or a mixture of oxides [German *limonit,* from Greek *leimōn* "meadow"] — **li·mo·nit·ic** \\,lī-mə-'nit-ik\\ *adj*

lim·ou·sine \\'lim-ə-,zēn, ,lim-ə-'\\ *n* **1** : a large luxurious often chauffeur-driven sedan **2** : a small bus with doors along the sides ⟨an airport *limousine*⟩ [French, literally, "cloak", from *Limousin,* France]

¹limp \\'limp\\ *vi* **1** : to walk lamely **2** : to proceed slowly or with difficulty ⟨the ship *limped* into port⟩ [probably from Middle English *lympen* "to fall short"] — **limp·er** *n*

²limp *n* : a limping movement or gait ⟨walked with a *limp*⟩

³limp *adj* **1** : lacking firm texture, substance, or structure ⟨*limp* curtains⟩ ⟨a *limp* bookbinding⟩ **2 a** : WEARY 1, EXHAUSTED **b** : lacking strength or firmness : SPIRITLESS [related to ¹*limp*] — **limp·ly** *adv* — **limp·ness** *n*
□ SYN LIMP, FLACCID, FLABBY mean lacking in firmness in texture or substance; LIMP implies a lack or loss of stiffness and a tendency to droop ⟨arms *limp* from exhaustion⟩ FLACCID implies a loss of power to keep or return to shape ⟨*flaccid* muscles⟩ FLABBY implies hanging or sagging by its own weight as through loss of muscular tone ⟨*flabby* cheeks⟩

lim·pa \\'lim-pə\\ *n* : rye bread made with molasses or brown sugar [Swedish]

lim·pet \\'lim-pət\\ *n* : any of numerous marine gastropod mollusks that have a low conical shell, browse over rocks or timbers, and cling very tightly when disturbed [Old English *lempedu,* from Medieval Latin *lampreda*]

lim·pid \\'lim-pəd\\ *adj* **1** : completely free from cloudiness or other obstacles to the passage of light ⟨a *limpid* pool of water⟩ **2** : clear and simple in style ⟨*limpid* prose⟩ [Latin *limpidus,* from *lympha, limpa* "water"] — **lim·pid·i·ty** \\lim-'pid-ət-ē\\ *n* — **lim·pid·ly** \\'lim-pəd-lē\\ *adv* — **lim·pid·ness** *n* □ SYN LIMPID, LUCID, PELLUCID mean clear and untroubled. LIMPID stresses freedom from murkiness or agitation and suggests the soft transparency of pure quiet water; LUCID, chiefly literary in this use, implies being both clear and full of light; PELLUCID suggests unusual transparency or shining clearness as of crystal.

limp·kin \\'lim-kən, 'limp-\\ *n* : a large brown wading bird resembling a bittern but having longer bill, neck, and legs and white stripes on head and neck [¹*limp*]

lim·u·lus \\'lim-yə-ləs\\ *n, pl* **-li** \\-,lī, -,lē\\ : HORSESHOE CRAB [derived from Latin *limus* "sidelong"]

limy \\'lī-mē\\ *adj* **lim·i·er; -est** : containing lime or limestone

lin·age \\'lī-nij\\ *n* **1** : the number of lines of printed or written matter **2** : payment for literary matter based on the number of lines

limpet

\\ə\\ abut	\\ng\\ sing
\\ər\\ further	\\ō\\ bone
\\a\\ mat	\\o\\ saw
\\ā\\ take	\\oi\\ coin
\\ä\\ cot, cart	\\th\\ thin
\\au̇\\ out	\\th\\ this
\\ch\\ chin	\\ü\\ food
\\e\\ pet	\\u̇\\ foot
\\ē\\ easy	\\y\\ yet
\\g\\ go	\\yü\\ few
\\i\\ tip	\\yu̇\\ cure
\\ī\\ life	\\zh\\ vision
\\j\\ job	

linch·pin \'linch-ˌpin\ *n* : a locking pin inserted crosswise (as through the end of an axle or shaft) [Old English *lynis* "linch pin"]

lin·dane \'lin-ˌdān\ *n* : an insecticide consisting of not less than 99 percent of an isomer of a chloride of benzene [T. van der *Linden,* 20th-century Dutch chemist]

lin·den \'lin-dən\ *n* **1** : any of a genus of trees with large heart-shaped leaves and clustered yellowish flowers rich in nectar **2** : the light fine-grained white wood of a linden; *esp* : BASSWOOD [Old English, "made of linden wood", from *lind* "linden tree"]

¹line \'līn\ *n* **1** : THREAD, STRING, CORD, ROPE; *esp* : a comparatively strong slender cord (a fishing *line*) **2** : a cord, wire, or tape used in measuring and leveling **3 a** : piping for conveying a fluid (as steam or oil) **b** : wire connecting one telegraph or telephone station with another or a whole system of such wires **c** : the principal circuits of an electric power system (a power *line*) **4 a** : a row of words, letters, numbers, or symbols that are written, printed, or displayed (as on a page or TV screen); *also* : space for such a line **b** : a structural unit of something written (as a poem or computer program) **c** : a short letter : NOTE (drop me a *line*) **d** : the words making up a part in a drama — usually used in pl. (forgot my *lines*) **5 a** : something (as a ridge, seam, or wrinkle) that is distinct, elongated, and narrow **b** : the course or direction of something in motion : ROUTE (the *line* of flight of a bullet) **c** : a boundary of an area (the state *line*) **d** : the track and roadbed of a railway **6** : a state of agreement (bring ideas into *line*) **7 a** : a course of conduct, action, or thought; *esp* : a publicly proclaimed policy (a political *line*) **b** : a field of activity or interest (out of my *line*) **c** : a glib persuasive way of talking **8 a** : LIMIT, RESTRAINT (overstep the *line* of good taste) **b** *archaic* : position in life : LOT **9** : any of various things arranged in or as if in a row or sequence: as **a** : LINEAGE (a noble *line*) **b** : a strain produced and maintained by selective breeding (a high-fat *line* of cattle) **c** (1) : the position of military forces in actual combat with the enemy at the front (2) : a military formation in which the different elements are abreast of each other (3) : naval ships arranged in a regular order (4) : fighting forces as distinguished from staff and supply personnel (5) : the force of a regular navy **d** : a set of objects of one general kind (a *line* of merchandise) **e** (1) : a group of public conveyances plying regularly under one management over a route (2) : a system of transportation; *also* : the company owning or operating it **f** : an arrangement of manufacturing processes in which each step is carried out separately and in proper order **g** : the football players who line up on or within one foot of the line of scrimmage **10** : a long narrow mark: as **a** : a circle of latitude or longitude on a map **b** : EQUATOR **2** **c** : any of the horizontal parallel strokes on a music staff **d** : LINE OF SCRIMMAGE **11** : a geometric element that is generated by a moving point and that has length but no width or thickness; *esp* : a straight line **12 a** : a defining outline : CONTOUR (a ship's *lines*) **b** : a general plan (thinking along these *lines*) **13** : a source of information : INSIGHT (got a *line* on their plans) **14** : a complete game of 10 frames in bowling — called also *string* [partly from Old French *ligne,* from Latin *linea,* from *linum* "flax"; partly from Old English *līne*] — **between the lines 1** : in an indirect way **2** : by inference — **down the line** : all the way : FULLY — **in line for** : due or in a position to receive — **in the line of duty** : while on duty — **on the line 1** : in full view and at great risk **2** : on the border between two categories **3** : at once : IMMEDIATELY — **out of line** : beyond what is reasonable to put up with (these prices are way *out of line*) (your behavior is getting *out of line*)

²line *vb* **1** : to mark or cover with a line **2** : to depict by lines : DRAW **3** : to place or form a line along

³line *vt* **1** : to cover the inner surface of (*line* a box with paper) **2** : to put something in the inside of : FILL **3** : to serve as the lining of (tapestries *lined* the walls) [Middle English *linen,* from *line* "flax, linen", from Old English *līn*]

lin·e·age \'lin-ē-ij\ *n* **1** : lineal descent from a common progenitor **2** : a group of persons tracing descent from a common ancestor

lin·e·al \'lin-ē-əl\ *adj* **1** : LINEAR (*lineal* measure) **2 a** : consisting of or being in a direct line of ancestry or descent (*lineal* descendants) **b** : HEREDITARY **4** — **lin·e·al·ly** \-ē-ə-lē\ *adv*

lin·e·a·ment \'lin-ē-ə-mənt\ *n* : a feature or contour of a body or figure and especially of the face [Latin *lineamentum,* from *linea* "line"]

lin·ear \'lin-ē-ər\ *adj* **1 a** : relating to, consisting of, or resembling a line : STRAIGHT (a direct *linear* approach) **b** : involving a single dimension **c** : characterized by an emphasis on line (*linear* art) **d** (1) : containing variables and terms of the first degree only (*linear* factors such as $x - 1$ and $x - 2$) (2) : based on, involving, or expressed by linear functions or linear equations **2** : long and uniformly narrow (the *linear* leaves of grasses) — **lin·ear·i·ty** \ˌlin-ē-'ar-ət-ē\ *n* — **lin·ear·ly** \'lin-ē-ər-lē\ *adv*

linear accelerator *n* : a device in which charged particles are accelerated in a straight line by successive impulses from a series of electric fields

linear combination *n* : a mathematical entity (as $4x + 5y + 6z$) composed of sums and differences of elements (as variables or equations) each multiplied by a constant coefficient

linear equation *n* : an equation in which each term is a monomial of degree one or a constant

linear function *n* : a polynomial function (as $f(x) = 2x - 3$) of degree one

linear interpolation *n* : estimation of a function (as a logarithm) by assuming that it is a straight line between known values

linear measure *n* **1** : a measure of length **2** : a system of measures of length

linear programming *n* : mathematical planning of industrial or military operations in terms of maximum or minimum values of linear functions in two or more variables subject to specific restrictions

line·back·er \'līn-ˌbak-ər\ *n* : a defensive football player who lines up immediately behind the line of scrimmage

line·breed·ing \'līn-'brēd-ing\ *n* : the interbreeding of individuals within a particular line of descent usually to fix desirable characters — **line·breed** *vb*

line drawing *n* : a drawing made in solid lines

line drive *n* : a batted baseball hit in a nearly straight line not far off the ground — called also *liner*

line engraving *n* : a metal plate for use in intaglio printing made by hand-engraving lines of different widths and closeness; *also* : a process involving such plates or a print made with them

line graph *n* : a graph consisting of connected segments of straight lines which join points representing specific values

line·man \'līn-mən\ *n* **1** : one who sets up or repairs electric wire communication or power lines — called also *linesman* **2** : a player in the line in football

lin·en \'lin-ən\ *n* **1 a** : cloth made of flax and noted for its strength, coolness, and luster **b** : thread or yarn spun from flax **2** : clothing or household articles made of linen cloth or a similar fabric **3** : paper made from linen fibers or with a linen finish [Old English *līnen* "of flax", from *līn* "flax, linen", from Latin *linum*] — **linen** *adj*

line of force : an imaginary line serving as a convenience in indicating the direction in space in which a force (as from an electric, magnetic, or gravitational field) acts

line of scrimmage : an imaginary line in football parallel to the goal lines that marks the position of the ball at the start of each down

line of sight **1** : a line from an observer's eye to a distant point toward which he is looking **2** : the straight path between a radio transmitting antenna and receiving antenna when unobstructed by the horizon — **line–of–sight** *adj*

line out *vb* **1** : to indicate with or as if with lines : OUTLINE ⟨*line out* a route⟩ **2** : to arrange in an extended line **3** : to move rapidly ⟨*lined out* for home⟩

line printer *n* : a very fast printing machine for a computer that prints a whole line at one time instead of one character at a time

¹lin·er \'lī-nər\ *n* **1** : one that makes, draws, or uses lines **2** : something with which lines are made **3 a** : a ship belonging to a regular line of ships **b** : an airplane belonging to an airline **4** : LINE DRIVE

²liner *n* : one that lines or is used to line or back something

line segment *n* : SEGMENT 2b

lines·man \'līnz-mən\ *n* **1** : LINEMAN 1 **2** : an official who assists a referee by determining whether a puck or ball or a player is beyond a boundary line

line·up \'lī-,nəp\ *n* **1** : a line of persons arranged especially for inspection or for identification by police **2 a** : a list of players taking part in a game (as of baseball); *also* : the players on such a list **b** : an alignment of persons or things having a common purpose or interest

line up \lī-'nəp, 'lī-\ *vb* **1 a** : to assume an orderly linear arrangement ⟨*line up* for inspection⟩ **b** : to take one's position in a formation **2** : to put into alignment **3** : to organize and make available ⟨*line up* supporters⟩

¹ling \'ling\ *n* **1** : any of various fishes (as a hake or burbot) of the cod family [Middle English]

²ling *n* : a heath plant; *esp* : a common Old World heather [Old Norse *lyng*]

¹-ling \ling\ *n suffix* **1** : one connected with or having the quality of ⟨hire*ling*⟩ **2** : young, small, or inferior one ⟨duck*ling*⟩ [Old English]

²-ling \ling\ *or* **-lings** \lingz\ *adv suffix* : in (such) a direction or manner ⟨side*ling*⟩ [Middle English *-ling, -linges*]

ling·cod \'ling-,käd\ *n* : a large greenish-fleshed food fish of the Pacific coast of North America related to the greenlings

lin·ger \'ling-gər\ *vi* **lin·gered; lin·ger·ing** \-gə-ring, -gring\ **1** : to be slow in leaving a place or activity ⟨*lingered* in bed⟩ **2** : to remain alive although close to dying **3** : to be slow to act [Middle English *lengeren* "to dwell", from Old English *lengan* "to prolong"] SYN see STAY — **lin·ger·er** \-gər-ər\ *n* — **lin·ger·ing·ly** \-gə-ring-lē, -gring-\ *adv*

lin·ge·rie \,län-jə-'rā, ,laⁿ-zhə-, -'rē\ *n* : women's intimate apparel [French, from *linge* "linen", from Latin *lineus* "made of linen", from *linum* "flax, linen"]

lin·go \'ling-gō\ *n, pl* **lingoes** **1** : strange or incomprehensible language or speech; *esp* : a foreign language **2** : JARGON 2 **3** : language characteristic of an individual [probably from Provençal, "tongue", from Latin *lingua*] SYN see DIALECT

lin·gua fran·ca \,ling-gwə-'frang-kə\ *n, pl* **lingua francas** *or* **lin·guae fran·cae** \-,gwī-'frang-,kī\ **1** : a language that consists of Italian mixed with French, Spanish, Greek, and Arabic and is spoken in Mediterranean ports **2** : any of various languages used for mutual understanding by speakers of different languages [Italian, literally, "Frankish language"]

lin·gual \'ling-gwəl, -gyə-wəl\ *adj* **1 a** : of, relating to, or resembling a tongue **b** : lying near or next to the tongue; *esp* : relating to or being the surface of a tooth next to the tongue **2** : produced by the tongue ⟨*lingual* sounds such as \t\ or \l\⟩ [Medieval Latin *lingua-*

lis, from Latin *lingua* "tongue, language"] — **lin·gual·ly** \-ē\ *adv*

lin·guist \'ling-gwəst\ *n* **1** : a person skilled in languages **2** : one who specializes in linguistics

lin·guis·tic \ling-'gwis-tik\ *adj* : of or relating to language or linguistics — **lin·guis·ti·cal·ly** \-ti-kə-lē, -klē\ *adv*

linguistic form *n* : a meaningful unit of speech (as a morpheme, word, or sentence)

lin·guis·tics \ling-'gwis-tiks\ *n* : the study of human speech including the units, nature, structure, and modification of language

lin·i·ment \'lin-ə-mənt\ *n* : a preparation that is thinner in consistency than an ointment and is used on the skin especially to relieve pain [Late Latin *linimentum,* from Latin *linere* "to smear"]

lin·ing \'lī-ning\ *n* : material used to line something (as a garment)

¹link \'lingk\ *n* **1** : a connecting structure: as **a** : a single ring or division of a chain **b** : a division of a surveyor's chain that is 7.92 inches (about 20.12 centimeters) long and is used as a measure of length **c** : a usually ornamental device for fastening a cuff **d** : BOND 3b **e** : an intermediate rod or piece for transmitting force or motion **2** : something resembling a link of chain: as **a** : a segment of sausage in a chain **b** : a connecting element ⟨a *link* with the past⟩ [of Scandinavian origin]

²link *vb* : to join by or as if by a link : UNITE — **link·er** *n*

link·age \'ling-kij\ *n* **1** : the manner or style of being united: as **a** : the manner in which atoms or radicals are linked in a molecule **b** : BOND 3b **2** : the quality or state of being linked; *esp* : the occurrence of genes on the same chromosome so that they tend to be inherited and expressed together **3** : a system of links; *esp* : a system of links or bars jointed together by means of which lines or curves may be traced

linked \'lingt, 'lingkt\ *adj* : marked by linkage and especially genetic linkage

linking verb *n* : a verb that connects the subject of a sentence with a word or phrase that tells how, what, or where the subject is ⟨the *feel* of "I feel bad," *seems* of "it seems a reasonable request" and *am* of "I am upstairs" are *linking verbs*⟩

links \'lings, 'lingks\ *n pl* : a golf course [Old English *hlinc* "ridge, hill"]

link·up \'ling-,kəp\ *n* **1** : establishment of contact : MEETING **2** : something that serves as a linking device or factor

Lin·nae·an *or* **Lin·ne·an** \lə-'nē-ən, -'nā-; 'lin-ē-\ *adj* : of, relating to, or following the method of the Swedish botanist Linnaeus who established the system of binomial nomenclature [Carolus *Linnaeus* (Carl von Linné)]

lin·net \'lin-ət\ *n* : a common small Old World finch with variable plumage [Middle French *linette,* from *lin* "flax", from Latin *linum*]

lin·ole·ic acid \,lin-ə-,lē-ik-, -,lā-\ *n* : a liquid unsaturated fatty acid found in various oils and held to be essential in animal nutrition [Greek *linon* "flax" + English *oleic acid*]

lin·ole·nic acid \-,lē-nik-, -,lā-\ *n* : a liquid unsaturated fatty acid found especially in drying oils and held to be essential in animal nutrition [derived from *linoleic acid*]

li·no·le·um \lə-'nō-lē-əm, -'nōl-yəm\ *n* : a floor covering with a canvas back and a surface of hardened linseed oil and a filler (as cork dust) [Latin *linum* "flax" + *oleum* "oil"]

Li·no·type \'lī-nə-,tīp\ *trademark* — used for a keyboard-operated typesetting machine that uses circulating matrices and produces each line of type in the form of a solid metal slug

lin·seed \'lin-,sēd\ *n* : FLAXSEED [Old English *līnsǣd,* from *līn* "flax" + *sǣd* "seed"]

\ə\ abut		\ng\ sing	
\ər\ further		\ō\ bone	
\a\ mat		\o'\ saw	
\ā\ take		\oi\ coin	
\ä\ cot, cart		\th\ thin	
\aù\ out		\th\ this	
\ch\ chin		\ü\ food	
\e\ pet		\ù\ foot	
\ē\ easy		\y\ yet	
\g\ go		\yü\ few	
\i\ tip		\yù\ cure	
\ī\ life		\zh\ vision	
\j\ job			

l lintel

linseed oil *n* : a yellowish drying oil obtained from flax-seed and used especially in paint, varnish, printing ink, and linoleum

lin·sey–wool·sey \ˌlin-zē-ˈwùl-zē\ *n* : a coarse sturdy fabric of wool and linen or cotton [Middle English *lynsy wolsye*]

lint \ˈlint\ *n* **1 a** : a soft fleecy material made from linen usually by scraping **b** : fuzz consisting of short fibers from yarn and fabric **2** : fibers forming a close thick coating about cotton seeds and constituting the staple of cotton [Middle English] — **linty** \-ē\ *adj*

lin·tel \ˈlint-l\ *n* : a horizontal piece across the top of an opening (as of a door) that carries the weight of the structure above it [Middle French, from Late Latin *limitaris* "threshold", from Latin *limit-, limes* "boundary"]

lint·er \ˈlint-ər\ *n* **1** : a machine for removing linters **2** *pl* : the fuzz of short fibers that adheres to cottonseed after ginning

li·on \ˈlī-ən\ *n, pl* **lion** *or* **lions** **1 a** : a large tawny flesh-eating chiefly nocturnal cat of open or rocky areas of Africa and especially formerly southern Asia with a tufted tail and a shaggy mane in the male **b** : any of several large wildcats; *esp* : COUGAR **2 a** : a person held to resemble a lion (as in courage or ferocity) **b** : a person of outstanding interest or importance ⟨a literary *lion*⟩ **3** *cap* : a member of one of the major service clubs [Old French, from Latin *leo*, from Greek *leōn*] — **li·on·ess** \ˈlī-ə-nəs\ *n* — **li·on·like** \ˈlī-ən-ˌlīk\ *adj*

li·on·heart·ed \ˌlī-ən-ˈhärt-əd\ *adj* : BOLD 1, COURAGEOUS

li·on·ize \ˈlī-ə-ˌnīz\ *vt* : to treat as an object of great interest or importance — **li·on·iza·tion** \ˌlī-ə-nə-ˈzā-shən\ *n*

lion's share *n* : the largest portion

¹lip \ˈlip\ *n* **1** : either of the two fleshy folds that surround the mouth **2** *slang* : BACK TALK **3 a** : a fleshy edge or margin ⟨*lips* of a wound⟩ **b** : LABIUM 2; *also* : the protruding part of an irregular corolla (as of an orchid) **4 a** : the edge of a hollow vessel especially where it flares slightly **b** : a projecting edge ⟨the *lip* of a cliff⟩ **c** : a short open spout (as on a pitcher) **5** : EMBOUCHURE 1 [Old English *lippa*] — **lip·less** \-ləs\ *adj* — **lip·like** \-ˌlīk\ *adj*

²lip *adj* **1** : spoken with the lips only : INSINCERE ⟨*lip* praise⟩ **2** : produced with the lips : LABIAL ⟨*lip* consonants⟩

³lip *vt* **lipped; lip·ping** **1** : to touch with the lips; *esp* : KISS **2** : to speak usually softly

lip- *or* **lipo-** *combining form* : fat : fatty tissue : fatty ⟨*lip*oma⟩ [Greek *lipos*]

li·pase \ˈlī-ˌpās, -ˌpāz\ *n* : an enzyme that functions especially in the breakdown or digestion of fats

lip·id \ˈlip-əd\ *n* : any of various substances including fats, waxes, and phosphatides that with proteins and carbohydrates constitute the principal structural components of living cells

li·poid \ˈlī-ˌpóid, ˈlip-ˌóid\ *n* : LIPID — **lipoid** *or* **li·poi·dal** \lī-ˈpóid-l, lip-ˈóid-\ *adj*

li·po·ma \lī-ˈpō-mə, lip-ˈō-\ *n, pl* **-mas** *or* **-ma·ta** \-mət-ə\ : a tumor of fatty tissue — **li·po·ma·tous** \-mət-əs\ *adj*

li·po·pro·tein \ˌlī-pō-ˈprō-ˌtēn, ˌlip-ō-, -ˈprōt-ē-ən\ *n* : a protein containing a lipid group

lipped \ˈlipt\ *adj* : having lips or a lip : having such or so many lips ⟨tight-*lipped*⟩ ⟨a 2-*lipped* corolla⟩

lip·py \ˈlip-ē\ *adj* **lip·pi·er; -est** : given to back talk

lip·read·ing \ˈlip-ˌrēd-ing\ *n* : interpretation of speech by watching the speaker's lip and facial movements — **lip–read** *vb* — **lip–read·er** *n*

lip service *n* : a declaration of allegiance not matched by action

lip·stick \ˈlip-ˌstik\ *n* : a waxy solid usually colored cosmetic in stick form for the lips; *also* : this cosmetic with its case

liq·ue·fac·tion \ˌlik-wə-ˈfak-shən\ *n* **1** : the process of making or becoming liquid **2** : the state of being liquid [Late Latin *liquefactio*, from Latin *liquefacere* "to liquefy"]

liquefied petroleum gas *n* : a compressed gas consisting of flammable light hydrocarbons and used especially as fuel or as raw material for chemical synthesis

liq·ue·fy *also* **liq·ui·fy** \ˈlik-wə-ˌfī\ *vb* **-fied; -fy·ing** : to make or become liquid [Middle French *liquefier*, from Latin *liquefacere*, from *liquēre* "to be fluid" + *facere* "to make"] — **liq·ue·fi·able** \-ˌfī-ə-bəl\ *adj* — **liq·ue·fi·er** \-ˌfī-ər, -ˌfīr\ *n*

li·queur \li-ˈkər, -ˈkyùr, -ˈkùr\ *n* : an alcoholic beverage flavored with aromatic substances and usually sweetened [French, literally, "liquor, liquid", from Latin *liquor*]

¹liq·uid \ˈlik-wəd\ *adj* **1** : flowing freely like water **2** : neither solid nor gaseous : characterized by free movement of the constituent molecules among themselves but without the tendency to separate that characterizes gases ⟨*liquid* mercury⟩ **3 a** : shining clear ⟨large *liquid* eyes⟩ **b** : being musical and free of harshness in sound **c** : smooth and unconstrained in movement **d** : pronounced without friction and capable of being prolonged like a vowel ⟨the *liquid* consonant \l\⟩ **4** : consisting of or capable of ready conversion into cash ⟨*liquid* assets⟩ [Middle French *liquide*, from Latin *liquidus*, from *liquēre* "to be fluid"] — **li·quid·i·ty** \lik-ˈwid-ət-ē\ *n* — **liq·uid·ly** \ˈlik-wəd-lē\ *adv* — **liq·uid·ness** *n*

²liquid *n* **1** : a liquid substance **2** : a liquid consonant

liquid air *n* : air in the liquid state prepared by subjecting it to great pressure and then cooling it by its own expansion and used chiefly as a refrigerant

liq·ui·date \ˈlik-wə-ˌdāt\ *vt* **1** : to pay off ⟨*liquidate* a debt⟩ **2** : to bring (as a business) to an end by selling off assets, paying debts, and dividing any remainder among the owners **3** : to do away with [Late Latin *liquidare* "to melt", from Latin *liquidus* "liquid"] — **liq·ui·da·tion** \ˌlik-wə-ˈdā-shən\ *n* — **liq·ui·da·tor** \ˈlik-wə-ˌdāt-ər\ *n*

liquid measure *n* **1** : a unit or series of units for measuring liquid capacity — see MEASURE table, METRIC SYSTEM table **2** : a measure for liquids

¹li·quor \ˈlik-ər\ *n* : a liquid substance; *esp* : a distilled alcoholic beverage [Old French *licour*, from Latin *liquor*, from *liquēre* "to be fluid"]

²liquor *vb* **li·quored; li·quor·ing** \ˈlik-ring, -ə-ring\ : to make or become drunk with alcoholic liquor — usually used with *up*

li·quo·rice *chiefly British variant of* LICORICE

li·ra \ˈlir-ə, ˈlē-rə\ **1** *pl* **li·re** \ˈlē-rā\ *also* **liras** : the basic monetary unit of Italy **2** *pl* **liras** *also* **lire** : the basic monetary unit of Turkey **3** : a coin or note representing one lira [Italian, from Latin *libra* "pound"]

lisle \ˈlīl\ *n* : a smooth tightly twisted thread usually made of long-staple cotton [*Lisle* "Lille, France"]

¹lisp \ˈlisp\ *vb* **1** : to pronounce \s\ and \z\ imperfectly especially by giving them the sound of \th\ and \t͟h\ **2** : to speak falteringly, childishly, or with a lisp [Old English *-wlyspian*] — **lisp·er** *n*

²lisp *n* **1** : a speech defect or mannerism marked by lisping **2** : a sound resembling a lisp

lis·some *also* **lis·som** \ˈlis-əm\ *adj* **1** : LITHE 1 **2** : NIMBLE 1 [alteration of *lithesome*] — **lis·some·ly** *adv* — **lis·some·ness** *n*

¹list \ˈlist\ *vb* **1** : LISTEN **2** : to listen to : HEAR [Old English *hlystan*, from *hlyst* "hearing", from *hlysnan* "to listen"]

²list *n* **1** : a band or strip of material; *esp* : SELVAGE **2** *pl* **a** : an arena for jousting **b** : an arena for combat ⟨entered the *lists*⟩ **c** : a field of competition or controversy [Old English *līste* "border"]

³list *n* : a roll, record, or catalog of names or objects ⟨guest *list*⟩ [French *liste*, from Italian *lista*, of Germanic origin]

⁴list *vb* **1 a :** to make a list of : ENUMERATE **b :** to include on a list : REGISTER ⟨securities *listed* on the exchange⟩ **2 a :** to place (oneself) in a specified category **b :** to have a list price

⁵list *vb* **:** to lean or cause to lean to one side : TILT ⟨a ship *listing* to port⟩ [origin unknown]

⁶list *n* **:** a deviation from the vertical : TILT

lis·ten \'lis-n\ *vi* **lis·tened; lis·ten·ing** \'lis-ning, -n-ing\ **1 :** to pay attention in order to hear ⟨*listen* for a signal⟩ ⟨*listen* to a record⟩ **2 :** to give heed : follow advice ⟨*listen* to a warning⟩ [Old English *hlysnan* "to hear"] SYN see HEAR — **lis·ten·er** \'lis-nər, -n-ər\ *n*

listen in *vi* **1 :** to tune in to or monitor a broadcast **2 :** to listen to a conversation without participating in it; *esp* : EAVESDROP — **lis·ten·er-in** \,lis-nər-'in, -n-ər-\ *n*

list·er \'lis-tər\ *n* **:** a double-moldboard plow that throws up ridges of earth on both sides of the furrow [derived from Old English *līste* "border"]

list·ing \'lis-ting\ *n* **1 :** an act or instance of making or including in a list **2 :** something listed

list·less \'list-ləs\ *adj* **:** marked by lack of energy or willingness to exert oneself : LANGUID [Middle English *list* "desire, inclination"] — **list·less·ly** *adv* — **list·less·ness** *n*

list price *n* **:** a price of an item published (as in a catalog or advertisement) but subject to discounts

lit *past of* LIGHT

lit·a·ny \'lit-n-ē\ *n, pl* **-nies 1 :** a prayer consisting of a series of supplications and responses said alternately by a leader and a group **2 a :** a resonant or repetitive chant ⟨*litany* of cheers⟩ **b :** a long list ⟨*litany* of complaints⟩ [Old French *letanie*, from Late Latin *litania*, from Greek *litaneia* "entreaty"]

li·tchi *also* **li·chee** \'lē-chē, 'lē-\ *n* **:** the oval fruit of an Asian tree having a hard outer covering and a seed surrounded by sweetish edible flesh that when dried is firm and black; *also* : the tree itself [Chinese (Pekingese dialect) *li⁴ chih¹*]

-lite \,līt\ *n combining form* **:** mineral : rock : fossil ⟨cryo*lite*⟩ [French, from Greek *lithos* "stone"]

li·ter *or* **li·tre** \'lēt-ər\ *n* **:** a metric unit of capacity equal to one cubic decimeter — see METRIC SYSTEM table [French *litre*, from Medieval Latin *litra*, a measure, from Greek, a weight]

lit·er·a·cy \'lit-ə-rə-sē, 'li-trə-sē\ *n* **:** the quality or state of being literate

lit·er·al \'lit-ə-rəl, 'li-trəl\ *adj* **1 a :** according with the letter of the scriptures **b :** following the ordinary or usual meaning of a term or expression **c :** FACTUAL 2, ACCURATE **d :** concerned mainly with facts : PROSAIC ⟨a very *literal* person⟩ **e :** UNVARNISHED 1, PLAIN **2 :** of, relating to, or expressed in letters **3 :** reproduced word for word ⟨a *literal* translation⟩ [Middle French, from Latin *litteralis* "of a letter", from *littera* "letter"] — **lit·er·al·ness** *n*

lit·er·al·ism \'lit-ə-rə-,liz-əm, 'li-trə-\ *n* **1 :** adherence to the exact meaning of an idea or expression **2 :** fidelity to fact : REALISM — **lit·er·al·ist** \-ləst\ *n* — **lit·er·al·is·tic** \,lit-ə-rə-'lis-tik, ,li-trə-\ *adj*

lit·er·al·ly \'lit-ər-ə-lē, -ər-lē, 'li-trə-lē\ *adv* **1 :** in a literal sense or manner : ACTUALLY ⟨the flying machine *literally* never got off the ground⟩ ⟨took the remark *literally*⟩ **2 :** in effect : VIRTUALLY ⟨*literally* poured out new ideas⟩

lit·er·ary \'lit-ə-,rer-ē\ *adj* **1 a :** of, relating to, or having the characteristics of literature or humane learning **b :** BOOKISH 2 **2 a :** LITERATE 2a, WELL-READ **b :** of or relating to writers or writing as a profession — **lit·er·ar·i·ly** \,lit-ə-'rer-ə-lē\ *adv* — **lit·er·ar·i·ness** \'lit-ə-,rer-ē-nəs\ *n*

lit·er·ate \'lit-ə-rət, 'li-trət\ *adj* **1 a :** characterized by education and culture **b :** able to read and write **2 a :** versed in literature or creative writing **b :** having knowledge or competence ⟨computer-*literate*⟩ — **literate** *n* — **lit·er·ate·ly** *adv*

li·te·ra·ti \,lit-ə-'rät-ē\ *n pl* **1 :** INTELLIGENTSIA **2 :** persons interested in literature or the arts [obsolete Italian *litterati*, from Latin *litteratus* "literate", from *littera* "letter"]

lit·er·a·tim \,lit-ə-'rät-əm, -'rät-\ *adv or adj* **:** letter for letter [Medieval Latin, from Latin *littera* "letter"]

lit·er·a·ture \'lit-ə-rə-,chùr, 'li-trə-, -chər\ *n* **1 :** the writing of literary work especially as an occupation **2 a :** writings in prose or verse; *esp* : writings that are excellent in form or expression and that set forth ideas of permanent or universal interest **b :** the body of writings on a particular subject ⟨medical *literature*⟩ **c :** printed matter (as leaflets or circulars) **3 :** a whole body of musical compositions

lith- *or* **litho-** *combining form* **:** stone ⟨*litho*logy⟩ [Greek *lithos*]

-lith \,lith\ *n combining form* **1 :** structure or implement of stone ⟨mega*lith*⟩ **2 :** calculus ⟨oto*lith*⟩ **3 :** -LITE ⟨rego*lith*⟩ [Greek *lithos* "stone"]

li·tharge \'lith-,ärj, lith-'\ *n* **:** LEAD MONOXIDE [Middle French, from Latin *lithargyrus*, from Greek *lithargyros*, from *lithos* "stone" + *argyros* "silver"]

lithe \'līth, 'līth\ *adj* **1 :** easily bent : FLEXIBLE ⟨long *lithe* stems⟩ **2 :** gracefully limber : SUPPLE ⟨*lithe* dancers⟩ [Old English *līthe* "gentle"] — **lithe·ly** *adv* — **lithe·ness** *n*

lithe·some \'līth-səm, 'līth-\ *adj* **:** LITHE 2

lith·ia \'lith-ē-ə\ *n* **:** an oxide of lithium occurring as a white crystalline substance [New Latin, from Greek *lithos* "stone"]

lith·ic \'lith-ik\ *adj* **1 :** of, relating to, or made of stone **2 :** of or relating to lithium — **lith·i·cal·ly** \'lith-i-kə-lē, -klē\ *adv*

-lithic \'lith-ik\ *adj combining form* **:** relating to or characteristic of a (specified) stage in the use of stone as a cultural tool by humans ⟨Neo*lithic*⟩

lith·i·um \'lith-ē-əm\ *n* **:** a soft silver-white univalent chemical element that is the lightest metal known and is used especially in nuclear reactions and metallurgy — see ELEMENT table [New Latin, from *lithia*]

¹litho·graph \'lith-ə-,graf\ *vt* **:** to produce, copy, or portray by lithography — **li·thog·ra·pher** \lith-'äg-rə-fər, 'lith-ə-,graf-ər\ *n*

²lithograph *n* **:** a print made by lithography — **litho·graph·ic** \,lith-ə-'graf-ik\ *adj* — **litho·graph·i·cal·ly** \-'graf-i-kə-lē, -klē\ *adv*

li·thog·ra·phy \lith-'äg-rə-fē\ *n* **1 :** the process of printing from a flat surface (as a smooth stone or metal plate) on which the image to be printed is ink-receptive and the blank area ink-repellent **2 :** PLANOGRAPHY

lith·o·pone \'lith-ə-,pōn\ *n* **:** a white pigment consisting essentially of zinc sulfide and barium sulfate [*lith*- + Greek *ponos* "work, artifact"]

litho·sphere \-,sfiər\ *n* **:** the outer part of the solid earth

Lith·u·a·ni·an \,lith-ə-'wā-nē-ən, -yə-'wā-, -nyən\ *n* **1 :** a native or inhabitant of Lithuania **2 :** the Baltic language of the Lithuanian people — **Lithuanian** *adj*

lit·i·gant \'lit-i-gənt\ *n* **:** a party to a lawsuit

lit·i·gate \'lit-ə-,gāt\ *vb* **1 :** to carry on a legal contest by judicial process **2 :** to contest in law [Latin *litigare*, from *lit-, lis* "lawsuit" + *agere* "to drive, act, do"] — **lit·i·ga·tion** \,lit-ə-'gā-shən\ *n*

li·ti·gious \lə-'tij-əs\ *adj* **1 a :** CONTROVERSIAL **2 :** ARGUMENTATIVE **b :** inclined to engage in lawsuits **2 :** of or relating to lawsuits — **li·ti·gious·ly** *adv* — **li·ti·gious·ness** *n*

lit·mus \'lit-məs\ *n* **:** a coloring matter from lichens that turns red in acid solutions and blue in alkaline solutions and is used as an acid-base indicator [of Scandinavian origin]

litmus paper *n* **:** paper impregnated with litmus and used as a pH indicator

li·to·tes \'līt-ə-,tēz, lī-'tōt-,ēz\ *n, pl* **litotes :** understatement in which an affirmative is expressed by the nega-

\ə\ abut		\ng\ **sing**	
\ər\ **further**		\ō\ **bone**	
\a\ **mat**		\ò\ **saw**	
\ā\ **take**		\ȯi\ **coin**	
\ä\ **cot, cart**		\th\ **thin**	
\aủ\ **out**		\th̬\ **this**	
\ch\ **chin**		\ü\ **food**	
\e\ **pet**		\ủ\ **foot**	
\ē\ **easy**		\y\ **yet**	
\g\ **go**		\yü\ **few**	
\i\ **tip**		\yủ\ **cure**	
\ī\ **life**		\zh\ **vision**	
\j\ **job**			

tive of the contrary (as in "not a bad singer") [Greek *litotēs,* from *litos* "simple"]

litre *variant of* LITER

¹**lit·ter** \'lit-ər\ *n* **1 a** : a covered and curtained couch having shafts that is used for carrying a single passenger **b** : a device (as a stretcher) for carrying a sick or injured person **2 a** : material spread in areas where farm animals (as cows or chickens) are kept especially to absorb their urine and feces **b** : the uppermost layer of organic debris on the forest floor **3** : the offspring of an animal at one birth **4 a** : trash, wastepaper, or garbage lying about ⟨roadside *litter*⟩ **b** : an untidy accumulation of objects [Old French *litiere,* from *lit* "bed", from Latin *lectus*] □ ORIGIN Latin *lectus,* "bed", is the ancestor of English *litter.* From *lectus* comes the French *lit,* "bed". *Litiere,* an Old French derivative of *lit,* was used not only for a bed but also for that type of vehicle we call a *litter.* English *litter,* borrowed from the French, originally meant "bed" or "litter (vehicle)". The first sense, "bed", did not survive, but before it became obsolete it gave rise to other senses of litter. The straw, hay, or like material laid down or strewn about to serve as bedding was called *litter.* So were the offspring of an animal born, or "bedded", at one time. Once *litter* had been applied to straw laid down for bedding, it was not farfetched to use the word for any odds and ends of rubbish lying scattered about.

²**litter** *vb* **1** : to give birth to young **2 a** : to strew with litter **b** : to scatter about in disorder **c** : to lie about in disorder

lit·ter·a·teur \ˌlit-ə-rə-'tər, ˌli-trə-\ *n* : a literary person; *esp* : a professional writer [French *littérateur*]

lit·ter·bag \'lit-ər-ˌbag\ *n* : a bag used (as in an automobile) for temporary disposal of refuse

lit·ter·bug \'lit-ər-ˌbəg\ *n* : one who litters a public area

¹**lit·tle** \'lit-l\ *adj* **lit·tler** \'lit-l-ər, 'lit-lər\ *or* **less** \'les\ *or* **less·er** \'les-ər\; **lit·tlest** \'lit-l-əst, 'lit-ləst\ *or* **least** \'lēst\ **1 a** : small in size or extent : TINY **b** : small in comparison with related forms ⟨*little* blue heron⟩ **c** : small in number **d** : small in condition, distinction, or scope **e** : NARROW, MEAN ⟨the pettiness of *little* minds⟩ **f** : pleasingly small ⟨a cute *little* thing⟩ **g** : being younger ⟨my *little* brother⟩ **2 a** : small in quantity or degree : not much ⟨have *little* money⟩ **b** : short in duration : BRIEF **3** : small in importance or interest : TRIVIAL [Old English *lȳtel*] SYN see SMALL — **lit·tle·ness** \'lit-l-nəs\ *n*

²**little** *adv* **less** \'les\ *or* **les·ser** \'les-ər\; **least** \'lēst\ **1 a** : in only a small quantity or degree : SLIGHTLY ⟨*little* known facts⟩ **b** : not at all ⟨cared *little* for them⟩ **2** : INFREQUENTLY, RARELY ⟨saw them very *little*⟩

³**little** *n* **1** : a small amount or quantity **2** : a short time or distance — **a little** : ²SOMEWHAT, RATHER — **in little** : on a small scale; *esp* : in miniature

Little Bear *n* : URSA MINOR

Little Dipper *n* : DIPPER 2b

Little Hours *n pl* : the offices of prime, terce, sext, and none forming part of the canonical hours

Little League *n* : a commercially sponsored baseball league for children from 8 to 12 years old — **Little Leaguer** *n*

little slam *n* : the winning of all tricks except one in bridge

little theater *n* : a small theater for low-cost dramatic productions designed for fairly limited audiences

¹**lit·to·ral** \'lit-ə-rəl; ˌlit-ə-'ral, -'räl\ *adj* : of, relating to, or situated or growing on or near a shore especially of the sea [Latin *litoralis,* from *litor-, litus* "seashore"]

²**littoral** *n* : a coastal region

li·tur·gi·cal \lə-'tər-ji-kəl\ *adj* **1** : of, relating to, or having the characteristics of liturgy **2** : using or favoring the use of liturgy — **li·tur·gi·cal·ly** \-kə-lē, -klē\ *adv*

lit·ur·gist \'lit-ər-jəst\ *n* : one who adheres to, compiles, or leads a liturgy

lit·ur·gy \'lit-ər-jē\ *n, pl* **-gies 1** *often cap* : a communion rite **2** : a rite or body of rites prescribed for public worship [Late Latin *liturgia,* from Greek *leitourgia* "public service, divine service"]

liv·abil·i·ty \ˌliv-ə-'bil-ət-ē\ *n* **1** : survival expectancy : VIABILITY **2** : suitability for human living

liv·able *also* **live·able** \'liv-ə-bəl\ *adj* **1** : suitable for living in or with **2** : ENDURABLE — **liv·able·ness** *n*

¹**live** \'liv\ *vb* **1** : to be or continue alive : have life **2** : to maintain oneself : SUBSIST ⟨*live* on fruits⟩ **3** : to conduct or pass one's life ⟨*lived* up to their principles⟩ **4** : to occupy a home : RESIDE **5** : to attain eternal life **6** : to remain in human memory or record **7** : to have a life rich in experience **8** : COHABIT **9** : to pass through or spend the duration of **10** : PRACTICE **11** : to exhibit vigor, gusto, or enthusiasm in [Old English *libban*]

²**live** \'līv\ *adj* **1** : having life : LIVING **2** : abounding with life : VIVID **3** : exerting force or containing energy: as **a** : AFIRE, GLOWING ⟨*live* coals⟩ **b** : carrying an electric current ⟨a *live* wire⟩ **c** : charged with explosives and containing shot or a bullet ⟨*live* ammunition⟩; *also* : UNEXPLODED ⟨*live* bomb⟩ **d** : rotating or imparting motion ⟨a *live* spindle⟩ **e** : power-driven ⟨a *live* axle⟩ **4** : of continuing or current interest : UNCLOSED ⟨*live* issue⟩ **5** : being in the native uncut state ⟨*live* rock⟩ **6** : of bright vivid color **7** : being in play ⟨a *live* ball⟩ **8 a** : of or involving the actual presence of real people ⟨*live* audience⟩ **b** : broadcast directly at the time of production instead of from recorded or filmed material ⟨*live* television⟩ [short for *alive*]

live–bear·er \'līv-ˌbar-ər, -ˌber-\ *n* : a fish that brings forth living young rather than eggs; *esp* : any of a family of numerous small surface-feeding fishes

live–bear·ing \'līv-ˌbaər-ing, -'beər-\ *adj* : VIVIPAROUS

-lived \'līvd, 'livd\ *adj combining form* : having a life of a specified kind or length ⟨long-*lived*⟩

live down *vt* : to live so as to wipe out the memory or effects of

live–for·ev·er \'liv-fə-ˌrev-ər\ *n* : SEDUM

live·li·hood \'līv-lē-ˌhùd\ *n* : means of support or subsistence ⟨an honest *livelihood*⟩ [Old English *līflād* "course of life", from *līf* "life" + *lād* "course"]

live·long \ˌliv-'lóng\ *adj* : WHOLE, ENTIRE ⟨the *livelong* day⟩ [Middle English *lef long,* from *lef* "dear" + *long* "long"]

live·ly \'līv-lē\ *adj* **live·li·er; -est 1** : full of life or vigor : ACTIVE, ALERT **2** : KEEN, INTENSE ⟨a *lively* interest in sports⟩ **3** : SPIRITED, BRILLIANT ⟨a *lively* wit⟩ **4** : quick to rebound : RESILIENT — **live·li·ly** \'līv-lə-lē\ *adv* — **live·li·ness** \'līv-lē-nəs\ *n* — **lively** *adv* □ SYN LIVELY, ANIMATED, VIVACIOUS mean being keenly alive. LIVELY suggests briskness, alertness, or energy; ANIMATED applies to what is spirited, active, or vigorous ⟨an *animated* conversation⟩ VIVACIOUS suggests attractive gaiety and quickness of gesture and wit.

liv·en \'lī-vən\ *vb* **liv·ened; liv·en·ing** \'līv-ning, -ə-ning\ : to make or become lively

live oak \'līv-ˌōk\ *n* : any of several American evergreen oaks

¹**liv·er** \'liv-ər\ *n* **1 a** : a large vascular glandular organ of vertebrates that secretes bile and regulates the concentration of various blood substances (as by converting sugars into glycogen) **b** : any of various large probably digestive glands of invertebrate animals **2** : the tissue of the liver (as of a calf or pig) eaten as food [Old English *lifer*]

²**liv·er** \'liv-ər\ *n* : one that lives in a specified way

-liv·ered \'liv-ərd\ *adj combining form* : expressing courage or spirit that suggests a person having (such) a liver ⟨lily-*livered*⟩ ⟨chicken-*livered*⟩

liver fluke *n* : any of various flatworms that invade the liver of mammals

liv·er·ied \'liv-rēd, -ə-rēd\ *adj* : wearing a livery

liv·er·ish \'liv-rish, -ə-rish\ *adj* **1** : suffering from liver disorder : BILIOUS **2** : CROSS **3**, MELANCHOLY — **liv·er·ish·ness** *n*

liv·er·wort \'liv-ər-,wərt, -,wort\ *n* : any of a class (Hepaticae) of bryophytes resembling the related mosses but differing especially in reproduction and development

liv·er·wurst \'liv-ər-,wərst, 'liv-ə-, -,wůrst, -,wůst, -,wůsht\ *n* : sausage consisting chiefly of liver [German *leberwurst,* from *leber* "liver" + *wurst* "sausage"]

liv·ery \'liv-rē, -ə-rē\ *n, pl* **-er·ies** **1** : a special uniform worn by the servants of a wealthy household ⟨a footman in *livery*⟩ **2** : distinctive dress ⟨the *livery* of a school⟩ **3 a** : the feeding, care, and stabling of horses for pay; *also* : the keeping of horses and vehicles for hire **b** : LIVERY STABLE [Old French *livree* "delivery, allotment of provisions to servants", from *livrer* "to deliver", from Latin *liberare* "to liberate"]

liv·ery·man \-mən\ *n* : the keeper of a livery stable

livery stable *n* : a stable where horses and vehicles are kept for hire and where stabling is provided

lives *pl of* LIFE

live steam *n* : steam direct from a boiler and under full pressure

live·stock \'līv-,stäk\ *n* : animals kept or raised for use or pleasure; *esp* : farm animals kept for use and profit

live wire *n* : an alert, active, and aggressive person

liv·id \'liv-əd\ *adj* **1** : discolored by bruising : BLACK-AND-BLUE **2** : ASHEN, PALLID ⟨*livid* with fear⟩ **3** : very angry [French *livide,* from Latin *lividus,* from *livēre* "to be blue"] — **li·vid·i·ty** \liv-'id-ət-ē\ *n* — **liv·id·ly** \'liv-əd-lē\ *adv* — **liv·id·ness** *n*

¹liv·ing \'liv-ing\ *adj* **1 a** : having life **b** : ACTIVE ⟨a *living* language⟩ **2** : exhibiting the life or motion of nature : NATURAL **3 a** : full of life or vigor ⟨made mathematics a *living* subject⟩ **b** : true to life : VIVID **4** : VERY — used as an intensive

²living *n* **1** : the condition of being alive **2** : conduct or manner of life **3** : means of subsistence : LIVELIHOOD

living fossil *n* : an animal or plant (as the horseshoe crab or ginkgo tree) that has remained almost unchanged from earlier geologic times and whose near relatives are nearly all extinct

living room *n* : a room in a residence used for the common social activities of the occupants

living wage *n* : a wage sufficient to provide the necessities and comforts held to comprise an acceptable standard of living

liz·ard \'liz-ərd\ *n* : any of a group (Lacertilia) of reptiles distinguished from the related snakes by a fused inseparable lower jaw, external ears, eyes with movable lids, and usually two pairs of functional limbs [Middle French *laisarde,* from Latin *lacerta*]

'll \l, əl, əl\ *vb* : WILL ⟨it *'ll* do for now⟩ : SHALL ⟨I *'ll* be there⟩

lla·ma \'läm-ə\ *n* : any of several wild and domesticated South American cud-chewing mammals related to the camels but smaller and without a hump; *esp* : one domesticated in the Andes and used as a beast of burden and a source of food [Spanish, from Quechua]

lla·no \'län-ō, 'lan-\ *n, pl* **llanos** : an open grassy plain especially of Spanish America [Spanish, "plain", from Latin *planum*]

lo \'lō\ *interj* — used to call attention or to express wonder or surprise [Old English *lā*]

loach \'lōch\ *n* : any of a family of small Old World freshwater fishes related to the carps [Middle French *loche*]

¹load \'lōd\ *n* **1 a** : whatever is put on a person or pack animal to be carried : PACK **b** : whatever is put in a ship or vehicle or airplane for conveyance : CARGO; *esp* : a quantity of material assembled or packed as a shipping unit **c** : the quantity that can be carried at one time by a specified means — often used in combination ⟨a boat*load* of tourists⟩ **2** : a mass or weight supported by something **3 a** : something that weighs down the mind or spirits ⟨a *load* of care⟩ **b** : a burdensome or laborious responsibility **4** : a large quantity : LOT — usually used in pl. **5 a** : a charge for a firearm **b** : the quantity of material loaded into a device at one time **6** : external resistance overcome by a machine **7 a** : power output (as of a power plant) **b** : a device to which power is delivered **8 a** : the amount of work that a person, department, or machine performs or is expected to perform **b** : the demand upon the operating resources of a system (as a telephone exchange or a refrigerating apparatus) **9** *slang* : EYEFUL ⟨get a *load* of that⟩ [Old English *lād* "way, course, act of carrying"]

²load *vb* **1 a** : to put a load in or on; *also* : to receive a load **b** : to place in or on a means of conveyance or in a container ⟨*load* freight⟩ ⟨*load* film in a camera⟩ **2 a** : to encumber or oppress with something heavy, laborious, or disheartening : BURDEN **b** : to place as a burden or obligation ⟨*load* more work on us⟩ **3 a** : to increase the weight of by adding something heavy **b** : BIAS ⟨*loaded* questions⟩ **c** : to weight (as a test) with factors influencing validity or outcome **4** : to supply in abundance or excess : HEAP **5** : to alter by adding an adulterant or drug — **load·er** *n*

load·ed *adj* **1** *slang* : DRUNK **2** : having a large amount of money

load line *n* : the line on a ship indicating the depth to which it sinks in the water when properly loaded

load·star *variant of* LODESTAR

load·stone *variant of* LODESTONE

¹loaf \'lōf\ *n, pl* **loaves** \'lōvz\ **1** : a shaped or molded mass of bread **2** : a regularly molded often rectangular mass: as **a** : a conical mass of sugar **b** : a dish (as of meat or fish) baked in the form of a loaf [Old English *hlāf*]

²loaf *vb* **1** : to spend time in idleness : LOUNGE **2** : to pass idly ⟨*loaf* the time away⟩ [probably back-formation from *loafer*]

loaf·er \'lō-fər\ *n* : one that loafs : IDLER [perhaps from German *landläufer* "tramp", from *land* "land" + *läufer* "runner"]

Loaf·er \'lō-fər\ *trademark* — used for a low step-in shoe

loam \'lōm, 'lüm\ *n* : SOIL; *esp* : a soil consisting of a crumbly mixture of varying proportions of clay, silt, and sand [Old English *lām*] — **loamy** \'lō-mē, 'lü-\ *adj*

¹loan \'lōn\ *n* **1 a** : money let out at interest **b** : something loaned for the borrower's temporary use **2** : the grant of temporary use [Old Norse *lān*]

²loan *vt* : to give for temporary possession or use

loan shark *n* : a person who lends money at excessive rates of interest

loan·word \'lōn-,wərd\ *n* : a word taken from another language and at least partly naturalized

loath *or* **loth** \'lōth, 'lōth\ *adj* : very unwilling or reluctant ⟨was *loath* to run for office again⟩ [Old English *lāth* "hateful, hostile"]

loathe \'lōth\ *vt* : to dislike greatly and often with disgust or intolerance : DETEST ⟨*loathe* the smell of burning rubber⟩ [Old English *lāthian,* from *lāth* "hateful"] SYN SEE HATE

loath·ing \'lō-thing\ *n* : extreme disgust : DETESTATION

¹loath·ly \'lōth-lē, 'lōth-\ *adj* : LOATHSOME, REPULSIVE

²loath·ly \'lōth-lē, 'lōth-\ *adv* : not willingly

loath·some \'lōth-səm, 'lōth-\ *adj* : utterly disgusting — **loath·some·ly** *adv* — **loath·some·ness** *n*

¹lob \'läb\ *vb* **lobbed; lob·bing** **1 a** : to throw, hit, or propel in a high arc **b** : to propel a ball gently especially in a high arc **2** : to move slowly and heavily [probably of Low German origin]

²lob *n* : a ball that is lobbed

llama

¹lob·by \'läb-ē\ *n, pl* **lobbies** **1** : a corridor or hall connected with a larger room or series of rooms and used as a passageway or waiting room: as **a** : an anteroom of a legislative chamber **b** : a large hall serving as a foyer (as of a hotel or theater) **2** : a group of persons engaged in lobbying especially as representatives of a particular interest group [Medieval Latin *lobium* "gallery", of Germanic origin]

²lobby *vb* **lob·bied; lob·by·ing** **1** : to try to influence public officials and especially members of a legislative body **2** : to promote or secure the passage of by influencing public officials — **lob·by·ist** \'läb-ē-əst\ *n*

lobe \'lōb\ *n* : a curved or rounded projection or division; *esp* : such a subdivision of a bodily organ or part [Middle French, from Late Latin *lobus*, from Greek *lobos*] — **lo·bar** \'lō-bər, -,bär\ *adj* — **lo·bate** \-,bāt\ *adj* — **lobed** \'lōbd\ *adj*

lobe–fin \'lōb-,fin\ *n* : any of a large group (Crossopterygii) of mostly extinct fishes that have paired fins suggesting limbs and may be ancestral to the land-dwelling vertebrates — compare LATIMERIA — **lobe–finned** \-'find\ *adj*

lo·be·lia \lō-'bēl-yə\ *n* : any of a genus of widely distributed herbs often grown for their terminal clusters of showy lipped flowers [Matthias de *Lobel,* died 1616, Flemish botanist]

lob·lol·ly pine \,läb-,läl-ē-\ *n* : a pine of the southern United States with thick flaky bark, long needles in threes, and spiny-tipped cones; *also* : its coarse-grained wood — called also *loblolly* [English dialect *loblolly* "gruel, mire"]

lo·bot·o·my \lō-'bät-ə-mē\ *n, pl* **-mies** : surgical cutting of nerve fibers especially in the frontal lobes of the brain for the relief of some mental disorders

lob·ster \'läb-stər\ *n* : any of several large edible marine crustaceans with stalked eyes, a pair of large claws, and a long abdomen; *also* : SPINY LOBSTER [Old English *loppestre,* from *loppe* "spider"]

lobster pot *n* : a trap for catching lobsters

lob·ule \'läb-yül\ *n* : a small lobe; *also* : a subdivision of a lobe — **lob·u·lar** \'läb-yə-lər\ *adj* — **lob·u·late** \-,lāt\ *adj* — **lob·u·la·tion** \,läb-yə-'lā-shən\ *n*

¹lo·cal \'lō-kəl\ *adj* **1** : characterized by or relating to position in space **2** : characterized by, relating to, being from, or occupying a particular place ⟨*local* news⟩ **3** : not broad or general; *esp* : involving or affecting only a small part of the body ⟨a *local* infection⟩ **4 a** : primarily serving the needs of a particular limited district ⟨*local* government⟩ **b** : making all the stops on a run ⟨a *local* train⟩ [Middle French, from Late Latin *localis,* from Latin *locus* "place"] — **lo·cal·ly** \-kə-lē\ *adv*

²local *n* : a local person or thing: as **a** : a local train or other public conveyance **b** : a local branch, lodge, or chapter (as of a labor union)

local color *n* : features and peculiarities used in a story or play that suggest a particular locality and its inhabitants

lo·cale \lō-'kal\ *n* **1** : a place or locality that is the setting for a particular event or characteristic **2** : SITE, SCENE ⟨the *locale* of a story⟩ [French *local,* from *local,* adj., "local"]

lo·cal·ism \'lō-kə-,liz-əm\ *n* **1** : often undue partiality for one's own locality : SECTIONALISM **2** : a local idiom or peculiarity of speech

lo·cal·i·ty \lō-'kal-ət-ē\ *n, pl* **-ties** : a particular spot, situation, or location

lo·cal·ize \'lō-kə-,līz\ *vb* : to make or become local : fix in or assign or confine to a definite place or locality ⟨pain *localized* in a joint⟩ — **lo·cal·iza·tion** \,lō-kə-lə-'zā-shən\ *n*

local option *n* : the power granted by a legislature to a political subdivision to determine by popular vote whether a particular law is to apply locally

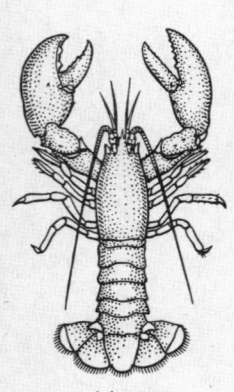

lobster

lo·cate \'lō-,kāt, lō-'\ *vb* **1** : to establish oneself or one's business : set or establish in a particular spot **2 a** : to seek out and find the location of **b** : to find the position of (a point) by means of coordinates **3** : to find or fix the place of in a sequence [Latin *locare* "to place", from *locus* "place"] — **lo·cat·er** *n*

lo·ca·tion \lō-'kā-shən\ *n* **1** : the process of locating **2** : SITUATION, PLACE; *esp* : a locality of or for a building **3** : a tract of land (as a mining claim) whose boundaries and purpose have been designated **4** : a place outside a studio where a motion picture is filmed ⟨on *location* in the desert⟩ — **lo·ca·tion·al** \-shnəl, -shən-l\ *adj* — **lo·ca·tion·al·ly** \-ē\ *adv*

loc·a·tive \'läk-ət-iv\ *adj* : of or being a grammatical case that denotes place — **locative** *n*

loch \'läk, 'läk\ *n* **1** *Scottish* : LAKE **2** *Scottish* : a bay or arm of the sea especially when nearly landlocked [Scottish Gaelic]

loci *pl of* LOCUS

¹lock \'läk\ *n* : a strand or ringlet of hair; *also* : a lump of fibers (as of wool) [Old English *locc*]

²lock *n* **1 a** : a fastening (as for a door) in which a bolt is operated (as by a key) **b** : the mechanism for exploding the charge or cartridge of a firearm **2 a** : an enclosure (as in a canal) with gates at each end used in raising or lowering boats as they pass from level to level **b** : AIR LOCK **3** : a hold in wrestling that prevents movement of a part of the body ⟨a leg *lock*⟩ [Old English *loc*]

³lock *vb* **1 a** : to fasten the lock of **b** : to make or be made fast with or as if with a lock ⟨*lock* up the house⟩ **2 a** : to shut or keep or make secure or inaccessible by means of locks **b** : to hold fast or inactive : FIX **3 a** : to make fast by the interlacing or interlocking of parts **b** : to hold in a close embrace **c** : to grapple in conflict **4** : to move by raising or lowering in a lock : go or pass by means of a lock (as in a canal)

lock·er \'läk-ər\ *n* **1 a** : a drawer, cabinet, compartment, or chest usually with a lock **b** : a storage chest or compartment on shipboard **2** : an insulated compartment for storing frozen food at a low temperature **3** : one that locks

locker room *n* : a room containing lockers for personal effects (as clothing); *esp* : one for use by sports players

lock·et \'läk-ət\ *n* : a small case usually of precious metal that has space for a memento and that is usually worn suspended from a neck chain [Middle French *loquet* "latch", from Dutch *loke*]

lock·jaw \'läk-,jö\ *n* : a symptom of tetanus characterized by spasm of the jaw muscles and inability to open the jaws; *also* : TETANUS 1

lock·nut \'läk-,nət\ *n* **1** : a nut screwed down tightly on another to prevent it from loosening **2** : a nut constructed to remain fast when tightly screwed down

lock·out \'läk-,aut\ *n* : the suspension of work or closing of a plant by an employer during a labor dispute in order to make the employees accept terms

lock out \läk-'aut, 'läk-\ *vt* : to subject (a body of employees) to a lockout

lock·smith \'läk-,smith\ *n* : one who makes, repairs, or installs locks

lock·step \'läk-,step\ *n* : a way of marching in step in which a body of marchers go one after another as closely as possible

lock·stitch \'läk-,stich\ *n* : a sewing machine stitch formed by the looping together of two threads one on each side of the material being sewn

lock, stock, and barrel *adv* : WHOLLY 1 ⟨sold out *lock, stock, and barrel*⟩ [from the principal parts of a flintlock]

lock·up \'läk-,əp\ *n* : JAIL; *esp* : one where persons are detained prior to court hearing

¹lo·co \'lō-kō\ *n, pl* **locos** *or* **locoes** **1** : LOCOWEED **2** : LOCOISM [Mexican Spanish, from Spanish, "crazy"]

²loco *adj, slang* : out of one's mind : CRAZY [Spanish]

lo·co·ism \'lō-kō-,iz-əm\ *n* : a nervous disease of horses, cattle, and sheep caused by chronic poisoning with locoweeds

lo·co·mo·tion \,lō-kə-'mō-shən\ *n* : the act or power of moving from place to place [Latin *locus* "place" + English *motion*]

¹lo·co·mo·tive \,lō-kə-'mōt-iv\ *adj* **1 a** : of, relating to, or functioning in locomotion **b** : having the ability to move independently from place to place **2** : of or relating to travel **3** : of, relating to, or being a machine that moves under its own power

²locomotive *n* : an engine that moves under its own power; *esp* : one that hauls cars on a railroad

lo·co·mo·tor \,lō-kə-'mōt-ər\ *adj* **1** : LOCOMOTIVE 1 **2** : affecting or involving the locomotive organs

locomotor ataxia *n* : a syphilitic disorder of the nervous system marked especially by disturbances of gait and difficulty in coordinating voluntary movements

lo·co·weed \'lō-kō-,wēd\ *n* : any of several plants of the pea family that are found in western North America and cause locoism in livestock

loc·ule \'läk-yül\ *n* : LOCULUS; *esp* : any of the cells of a compound ovary of a plant — **loc·uled** \-yüld\ *adj*

loc·u·lus \'läk-yə-ləs\ *n, pl* **-li** \-,lī, -,lē\ : a small chamber or cavity especially in a plant or animal body — compare LOCULE [Latin, "little place", from *locus* "place"]

lo·cum te·nens \,lō-kəm-'tē-,nenz\ *n, pl* **locum te·nen·tes** \-tə-'nen-,tēz\ : a person (as a doctor or clergyman) filling an office for a time or temporarily taking the place of another [Medieval Latin, literally, "one holding a place"]

lo·cus \'lō-kəs\ *n, pl* **lo·ci** \'lō-,sī, -,kī, -,kē\ **1** : PLACE 1b, LOCALITY **2** : the set of all points whose location is determined by stated conditions **3** : the position in a chromosome of a particular gene or allele [Latin]

lo·cus clas·si·cus \,lō-kəs-'klas-i-kəs\ *n, pl* **lo·ci clas·si·ci** \-,sī-'klas-ə-,sī, -,kī-'klas-ə-,kī, -,kē-'klas-ə-,kē\ : a standard passage important for the explanation of a word or subject [New Latin]

lo·cust \'lō-kəst\ *n* **1 a** : SHORT-HORNED GRASSHOPPER; *esp* : a migratory grasshopper often traveling in vast swarms and stripping the areas passed of vegetation **b** : CICADA — compare SEVENTEEN-YEAR LOCUST **2 a** : any of various hard-wooded trees of the pea family **b** : the wood of a locust [Latin *locusta*]

lo·cu·tion \lō-'kyü-shən\ *n* **1** : a particular form of expression or phrasing (involved *locutions*) **2** : style of discourse : PHRASEOLOGY [Latin *locutio*, from *loqui* "to speak"]

lode \'lōd\ *n* : an ore deposit [Old English *lād* "way, course, support"]

lode·star *or* **load·star** \-,stär\ *n* **1** : a star that leads or guides; *esp* : NORTH STAR **2** : one that is a guide or a focus of attention

lode·stone *or* **load·stone** \-,stōn\ *n* **1** : magnetite having magnetic properties **2** : something that strongly attracts

¹lodge \'läj\ *vb* **1 a** : to provide temporary quarters for **b** : to establish or settle oneself in a place **c** : to rent lodgings to **2** : to serve as a receptacle for **3** : to bring or come to a rest and remain (the bone *lodged* in the throat) **4** : to lay (as a complaint) before a proper authority **5** : to fall or become beaten down (the tall grass *lodged* in the storm)

²lodge *n* **1 a** : a house set apart for residence in a special season (a hunting *lodge*) **b** : a resort hotel **c** : a house for an employee on an estate (a gamekeeper's *lodge*) **2** : a den or lair especially of a group of gregarious animals **3** : the meeting place of a branch (as of a fraternal organization); *also* : the members of such a branch **4 a** : WIGWAM **b** : a family of North American Indians [Old French *loge* "hut, cabin", of Germanic origin]

lodge·pole pine \,läj-,pōl-\ *n* : either of two western North American pines with paired needles and short rough cones

lodg·er \'läj-ər\ *n* : one that lodges; *esp* : one that occupies a rented room in another's house

lodg·ing \'läj-ing\ *n* **1** : DWELLING; *esp* : a temporary dwelling or sleeping place **2** : a room in the house of another person rented as a dwelling place — usually used in pl.

lodging house *n* : ROOMING HOUSE

loess \'les, 'lús, 'lərs, 'lō-əs\ *n* : a usually yellowish brown loamy deposit believed to be deposited chiefly by the wind [German *löss*] — **loess·ial** \-ē-əl\ *adj*

¹loft \'lóft\ *n* **1** : a room or floor above another : ATTIC **2 a** : a gallery in a church or hall (an organ *loft*) **b** : an upper floor of a warehouse or business building especially when not partitioned **c** : HAYLOFT **3 a** : the backward slant of the face of a golf-club head **b** : HEIGHT (the ball had too much *loft* to reach the green) [Old Norse *lopt* "air, sky, loft"]

²loft *vb* **1** : to place, house, or store in a loft **2** : to strike or throw a ball high into the air (*lofted* a high fly to center field)

lofty \'lóf-tē\ *adj* **loft·i·er; -est** **1** : marked by a haughty overbearing manner (a *lofty* air) **2 a** : elevated in character and spirit (*lofty* ideals) **b** : elevated in position : SUPERIOR **3** : rising high in the air : TOWERING (a *lofty* oak) — **loft·i·ly** \-tə-lē\ *adv* — **loft·i·ness** \-tē-nəs\ *n*

¹log \'lóg, 'läg\ *n* **1** : a bulky piece of unshaped timber; *esp* : a long piece of a tree trunk trimmed and ready for sawing **2** : an apparatus for measuring the rate of a ship's motion through the water that consists of a block fastened to a line and run out from a reel **3 a** : the daily record of a ship's speed and progress **b** : the full record of a ship's voyage or of an aircraft's flight **4** : a record of performance, events, or day-to-day activities (a computer *log*) [Middle English *logge*] — **log** *adj*

²log *vb* **logged; log·ging** **1** : to cut trees for lumber or clear (land) of trees in lumbering **2** : to enter details of or about in a log **3 a** : to move (an indicated distance) or attain (an indicated speed) as noted in a log **b** (1) : to sail a ship or fly an airplane for (an indicated distance or an indicated period of time) (2) : to have (an indicated record) to one's credit

³log *n* : LOGARITHM

lo·gan·ber·ry \'lō-gən-,ber-ē\ *n* : a red-fruited upright-growing shrub related to the raspberry; *also* : its berry [James H. *Logan,* died 1928, American lawyer]

log·a·rithm \'lóg-ə-,rith-əm, 'läg-\ *n* : the exponent that indicates the power to which a number and especially 10 is raised to produce a given number (the *logarithm* of 100 to the base 10 is 2) [Greek *logos* "word, reckoning" + *arithmos* "number"]

log·a·rith·mic \,lóg-ə-'rith-mik, ,läg-\ *adj* : relating to, based on, or characteristic of logarithms (a *logarithmic* table)

log·book \'lóg-,búk, 'läg-\ *n* : a book in which a log is kept; *also* : the log itself

loge \'lōzh\ *n* **1 a** : a small compartment : BOOTH **b** : a box in a theater **2 a** : a small partitioned area **b** : the forward section of a theater mezzanine [French, "hut, lodge, loge"]

log·ger \'lóg-ər, 'läg-\ *n* : one engaged in logging

log·ger·head \'lóg-ər-,hed, 'läg-\ *n* : any of various very large turtles; *esp* : a flesh-eating sea turtle of the warmer parts of the western Atlantic

log·gia \'läj-ē-ə, 'lō-jä\ *n* : a roofed gallery open on at least one side [Italian, from French *loge* "lodge, hut"]

log·ic \'läj-ik\ *n* **1** : a science that deals with the rules and tests of sound thinking and proof by reasoning **2** : REASONING; *esp* : sound reasoning (no *logic* in that remark) **3** : connection (as of facts or events) in a way that seems reasonable (the *logic* of a situation) **4** : the arrangement of circuit elements (as in a computer)

1 loggia

\ə\ abut	\ng\ sing
\ər\ further	\ō\ bone
\a\ mat	\ó\ saw
\ā\ take	\ói\ coin
\ä\ cot, cart	\th\ thin
\aú\ out	\th\ this
\ch\ chin	\ü\ food
\e\ pet	\ú\ foot
\ē\ easy	\y\ yet
\g\ go	\yü\ few
\i\ tip	\yú\ cure
\ī\ life	\zh\ vision
\j\ job	

needed for computation [Middle French *logique,* from Latin *logica,* from Greek *logikē,* from *logos* "reason"] — **lo·gi·cian** \lō-'jish-ən\ *n*

log·i·cal \'läj-i-kəl\ *adj* **1** : of or relating to logic : used in logic **2** : conforming to or consistent with the rules of logic ⟨a *logical* argument⟩ **3** : skilled in logic ⟨a *logical* thinker⟩ **4** : being in agreement with what may be reasonably expected ⟨a *logical* result of an action⟩ — **log·i·cal·ly** \-kə-lē, -klē\ *adv* — **log·i·cal·ness** \-kəl-nəs\ *n*

lo·gis·tics \lō-'jis-tiks\ *n sing or pl* **1** : a branch of military science that deals with the transportation, quartering, and supplying of troops in military operations **2** : the handling of the details of an operation [French, literally, "art of calculating", from Greek *logistikē,* from *logizein* "to calculate", from *logos* "reason"] — **lo·gis·tic** \-tik\ *or* **lo·gis·ti·cal** \-ti-kəl\ *adj* — **lo·gis·ti·cal·ly** \-ti-kə-lē, -klē\ *adv*

log·jam \'lóg-,jam, 'läg-\ *n* **1** : a jumble of logs jammed together in a watercourse **2** : IMPASSE 2

LO·GO *or* **lo·go** \'lō-gō\ *n* : a simplified language for programming and communicating with a computer that uses drawing on a display screen as a tool for teaching programming principles [probably derived from Greek *logos* "word, speech, reason"]

Lo·gos \'lō-,gäs, -,gōs\ *n* : the divine wisdom manifest in the creation, government, and redemption of the world and often identified with the second person of the Trinity [Greek, "speech, word, reason"]

log·roll·ing \'lóg-,rō-ling, 'läg-\ *n* **1** : the trading of votes by legislators to secure favorable action on projects of interest to each one **2** : the rolling of logs in water by treading; *also* : a sport in which individuals treading logs try to dislodge one another — **log·roll·er** \-,rō-lər\ *n*

-logue *or* **-log** \,lóg, ,läg\ *n combining form* **1** : discourse : talk ⟨duo*logue*⟩ **2** : student : specialist [Middle English *-logue,* derived from Greek *-logos,* from *legein* "to speak"]

log·wood \'lóg-,wud, 'läg-\ *n* : a Central American and West Indian tree of the pea family; *also* : its hard brown or brownish red heartwood used in dyeing or an extract of this

lo·gy \'lō-gē\ *adj* **lo·gi·er; -est** : marked by sluggishness and lack of vitality [perhaps from Dutch *log* "heavy"] — **lo·gi·ly** \-gə-lē\ *adv* — **lo·gi·ness** \-gē-nəs\ *n*

-l·o·gy \l-ə-jē\ *n combining form* **1** : oral or written expression ⟨phrase*ology*⟩ **2** : doctrine : theory : science ⟨ethn*ology*⟩ [Greek *-logia,* from *logos* "word, speech, reason"]

loin \'lóin\ *n* **1 a** : the part of the body on each side of the spinal column and between the hip and the lower ribs **b** : a cut of meat comprising this part of one or both sides of a carcass with the adjoining half of the vertebrae included but without the flank **2** *pl* **a** : the pubic region **b** : the organs of reproduction [Middle French *loigne,* derived from Latin *lumbus*]

loin·cloth \-,klóth\ *n* : a cloth worn about the loins often as the sole article of clothing in warm climates

loi·ter \'lóit-ər\ *vi* **1** : to interrupt or delay an activity with aimless idle stops and pauses **2 a** : to hang around idly **b** : to lag behind [Middle English *loiteren*] — **loi·ter·er** \-ər-ər\ *n*

loll \'läl\ *vb* **1** : to hang or let hang loosely : DROOP **2** : to act or move in a lax, lazy, or indolent manner : LOUNGE ⟨*loll* around in the sun⟩ [Middle English *lollen*]

lol·li·pop *or* **lol·ly·pop** \'läl-ē-,päp\ *n* : a lump of hard candy on the end of a stick [probably from *loll* + *-i-* + *pop*]

Lom·bard \'läm-,bärd, -bərd\ *n* **1** : a member of a Teutonic people invading Italy in A. D. 568 and establishing a kingdom in the Po valley **2** : a native of Lombardy or of the Kingdom of the Lombards [Middle French, from Italian *Lombardo,* from Latin *Langobardus*]

Lom·bar·dy poplar \,läm-,bärd-ē, -bərd-\ *n* : a tall slender poplar of European origin that tapers at the top and has strongly ascending upright branches [*Lombardy,* Italy]

lo·ment \'lō-,ment, -mənt\ *n* : a fruit resembling a pod but breaking transversely into segments at maturity [Latin *lomentum* "wash made from bean meal", derived from *lavare* "to wash"]

lone \'lōn\ *adj* **1 a** : having no company : SOLITARY ⟨a *lone* traveler⟩ **b** : preferring solitude **2** : ONLY, SOLE ⟨the *lone* theater in town⟩ **3** : situated by itself : ISOLATED [Middle English, short for *alone*] — **lone·ness** \'lōn-nəs\ *n*

lone·ly \'lōn-lē\ *adj* **lone·li·er; -est** **1** : being without company : LONE ⟨a *lonely* hiker⟩ **2** : UNFREQUENTED, DESOLATE ⟨a *lonely* spot⟩ **3** : LONESOME SYN see ALONE — **lone·li·ness** *n*

lone·some \'lōn-səm\ *adj* **1** : sad from lack of companionship or separation from others **2 a** : REMOTE, UNFREQUENTED ⟨a *lonesome* stretch of highway⟩ **b** : LONE SYN see ALONE — **lone·some·ly** *adv* — **lone·some·ness** *n*

¹long \'lóng\ *adj* **long·er** \'lóng-gər\; **long·est** \'lóng-gəst\ **1** : of great or greater than usual extent from end to end **2 a** : having a specified length **b** : forming the chief linear dimension ⟨the *long* side⟩ **3** : lasting for a considerable or a specified time **4 a** : containing many items in a series **b** : having a specified number of units ⟨300 pages *long*⟩ **5 a** : being a syllable or speech sound of relatively great duration **b** : being the member of a pair of similarly spelled vowel or vowel-containing sounds that is descended from a vowel long in duration ⟨*long a* in fate⟩ ⟨*long i* in sign⟩ **6** : having the capacity to reach or extend a considerable distance **7** : larger or longer than the standard **8 a** : extending far into the future **b** : extending beyond what is known **9** : strong in or well furnished with something **10** : of an unusual degree of difference between the amounts wagered on each side ⟨*long* odds⟩ [Old English *long, lang*] — **at long last** : after a long wait : FINALLY

²long *adv* **1** : for or during a long time **2** : for the duration of a specified period **3** : at a distant point of time ⟨*long* before we arrived⟩ — **so long** : GOOD-BYE

³long *vi* **longed; long·ing** \'lóng-ing\ : to feel a strong desire or wish : YEARN [Old English *langian*] □ SYN LONG, YEARN, HANKER, PINE mean to have a strong desire for something. LONG implies wishing with one's whole heart and often striving to attain; YEARN suggests an eager, restless, or painful longing ⟨*yearned* to be understood⟩ HANKER suggests somewhat disparagingly an uneasiness due to an unsatisfied and often unreasonable appetite or desire ⟨*hankered* for complete approval⟩ PINE implies a languishing or fruitless longing.

long·boat \'lóng-,bōt\ *n* : a large boat carried on a ship

long bone *n* : one of the bones supporting a vertebrate limb and consisting of a long nearly cylinder-shaped shaft that contains marrow and ends in enlarged heads that each form a joint with another bone

long·bow \'lóng-,bō\ *n* : a wooden bow about 1¾ meters long that is drawn by hand

long–day *adj* : flowering or developing to maturity only in response to alternating long light and short dark periods — compare DAY-NEUTRAL, SHORT-DAY

¹long–dis·tance \-'dis-təns\ *adj* : of or relating to telephone communication with a distant point

²long–distance *adv* : by long-distance telephone

long distance *n* **1** : communication by long-distance telephone **2** : a telephone operator or exchange that gives long-distance connections

long division *n* : arithmetical division in which the several steps corresponding to the division of parts of the dividend by the divisor are indicated in detail

lon·gev·i·ty \län-'jev-ət-ē, lón-\ *n* **1** : a long duration of individual life **2** : length of life [Late Latin *longaevi-*

tas, from Latin *longaevus* "long-lived", from *longus* "long" + *aevum* "age"]

long·hair \'lóng-,haər, -,heər\ *n* **1** : a person of artistic gifts or interests; *esp* : a lover of classical music **2** : an impractical intellectual **3 a** : a person having long hair **b** : HIPPIE — **long-hair** *or* **long-haired** \-'haərd, -'heərd\ *adj*

long·hand \'lóng-,hand\ *n* : the characters used in ordinary writing : HANDWRITING

long·head·ed \-'hed-əd\ *adj* **1** : having unusual foresight or wisdom **2** : having a head relatively long from front to back but narrow from side to side — **long·head·ed·ness** *n*

long·horn \'lóng-,hórn\ *n* : any of the long-horned cattle of Spanish derivation formerly common in the southwestern United States

long–horned \-'hórnd\ *adj* : having long horns or antennae

long·house \-,haús\ *n* : a communal dwelling of the Iroquois

long hundredweight *n, British* : HUNDREDWEIGHT 2

lon·gi·corn \'län-jə-,kórn\ *adj* : of, relating to, or being beetles with long antennae [Latin *longus* "long" + *cornu* "horn"]

long·ing \'lóng-ing\ *n* : an eager desire often for the unattainable : CRAVING — **long·ing·ly** \-ing-lē\ *adv*

long·ish \'lóng-ish\ *adj* : somewhat long

lon·gi·tude \'län-jə-,tüd, -,tyüd\ *n* : distance measured by degrees or time east or west from the prime meridian ⟨the *longitude* of New York is 74 degrees or about five hours west of Greenwich⟩ [Latin *longitudin-, longitudo* "length", from *longus* "long"]

lon·gi·tu·di·nal \,län-jə-'tüd-nəl, -'tyüd-, -n-əl\ *adj* **1** : of or relating to length or the lengthwise dimension **2** : placed or running lengthwise — **lon·gi·tu·di·nal·ly** \-ē\ *adv*

long jump *n* : a jump for distance in track-and-field sports — **long jumper** *n*

long–leaf pine \,lóng-,lēf-\ *n* : a large pine of the southern United States that has long thin clustered needles and long cones and is a major timber tree; *also* : its tough coarse-grained durable wood

long–leaved pine \,lóng-,lēvd-\ *n* : LONGLEAF PINE

long–lived \'lóng-'līvd, -'livd\ *adj* : living or lasting a long time — **long–lived·ness** \-'līvd-nəs, -'liv-, -'livd-, -'liv-\ *n*

long–play·ing \'lóng-'plā-ing\ *adj* : of, relating to, or being a phonograph record designed to be played at 33⅓ revolutions per minute

long–range \-'rānj\ *adj* **1** : relating to or fit for long distances ⟨a *long-range* gun⟩ **2** : lasting over or taking into account a long period : LONG-TERM

long·shore·man \'lóng-'shōr-mən, -'shór-\ *n* : a laborer who loads and unloads ships at a seaport [*longshore* "existing along the seacoast", short for *alongshore*]

long shot \'lóng-,shät\ *n* **1** : an entry (as in a horse race) given little chance of winning **2** : a bet in which the chances of winning are slight but the possible winnings great **3** : a venture involving great risk but promising a great reward if successful — **by a long shot** : at all : ANYWAY ⟨give up? Not *by a long shot*⟩

long·sight·ed \-'sīt-əd\ *adj* : FARSIGHTED — **long·sight·ed·ness** *n*

long–suf·fer·ing \-'səf-ring, -ə-ring\ *n* : long and patient endurance — **long-suffering** *adj* — **long·suf·fer·ing·ly** \-ring-lē\ *adv*

long suit *n* **1** : a suit containing the most cards in a hand **2** : the activity or quality in which a person excels

long–term \'lóng-'tərm\ *adj* **1** : extending over or involving a long period of time **2** : constituting a financial obligation based on a term usually of more than 10 years ⟨a *long-term* mortgage⟩

long–wind·ed \'lóng-'win-dəd\ *adj* **1** : not easily subject to loss of breath **2** : tediously long in speaking or

writing — **long–wind·ed·ly** *adv* — **long–wind·ed·ness** *n*

loo \'lü\ *n* **1** : an old card game **2** : money staked at loo [short for obsolete *lanterloo,* from French *lanturelu* "piffle"]

¹look \'lük\ *vb* **1** : to exercise the power of vision upon : EXAMINE, SEE **2** : EXPECT ⟨we *look* to see you soon⟩ **3** : to express by the eyes or facial expression **4** : to have an appearance that suits or agrees with ⟨*look* my age⟩ **5** : to have the appearance of being : SEEM **6** : to direct one's attention or eyes ⟨*look* in the mirror⟩ **7** : to have a specified outlook : POINT ⟨the house *looks* east⟩ **8** : to gaze in wonder or surprise : STARE [Old English *lōcian*] — **look after** : to take care of : attend to — **look for 1** : to await with hope or anticipation : EXPECT **2** : to search for : SEEK — **look on** *or* **look upon** : CONSIDER, REGARD ⟨*looked upon* them as friends⟩

²look *n* **1 a** : the action of looking **b** : GLANCE 3b **2 a** : the expression of the face **b** : physical appearance; *esp* : attractive physical appearance — usually used in pl. **3** : the state or form in which something appears : ASPECT

look·er–on \,lük-ər-'ón, -'än\ *n, pl* **lookers–on** : ONLOOKER, SPECTATOR

looking glass *n* : MIRROR 1

look·out \'lük-,aút\ *n* **1** : a person engaged in watching; *esp* : one assigned to watch (as on a ship) **2** : an elevated place or structure offering a wide view for observation **3** : a careful looking or watching **4** : a probability for the future : OUTLOOK **5** : a matter of care or concern

¹loom \'lüm\ *n* : a frame or machine for weaving together threads or yarns into cloth [Old English *gelōma* "tool"]

²loom *vi* **1** : to come into sight in an unnaturally large, indistinct, or distorted form ⟨*loomed* out of the fog⟩ **2** : to be about to happen ⟨trouble was *looming*⟩ [origin unknown]

loon \'lün\ *n* **1** : any of several fish-eating diving birds with webbed feet, black head, and white-spotted black back **2** : a person of dull or disordered mind : LUNATIC [of Scandinavian origin; sense 2 from the popular phrase *crazy as a loon*]

loo·ny *or* **loo·ney** \'lü-nē\ *adj* **loo·ni·er; -est** : CRAZY 2, FOOLISH [derived from *lunatic*] — **loony** *n*

¹loop \'lüp\ *n* **1** : a fold or doubling of a line leaving an opening between the parts through which another line can be passed or into which a hook may be hooked **2** : a loop-shaped figure, bend, or course ⟨a *loop* in a river⟩ **3** : a circular airplane maneuver involving flying upside down **4 a** : the portion of a vibrating body between two nodes **b** : the middle point of such a portion **5** : a complete electric circuit **6** : a series of instructions for a computer that is repeated until a terminating condition is reached [Middle English *loupe*] — **for a loop** : into a state of amazement, confusion, or distress ⟨the news knocked us *for a loop*⟩

²loop *vb* **1** : to make or form a loop **2 a** : to make a loop in, on, or about **b** : to fasten with a loop **3** : to execute a loop in an airplane

loop·er \'lü-pər\ *n* **1** : any of numerous small hairless moth larvae that move with a looping movement **2** : one that loops

loop·hole \'lüp-,hōl\ *n* **1** : a small opening in a wall through which small firearms may be discharged **2** : a means of escape; *esp* : an ambiguity or omission (as in the wording of a law or contract) that makes evasion of one's obligation possible

loop of Hen·le \-'hen-lē\ : a part of the vertebrate nephron that lies in the midst of the convoluted portion and plays a part in water resorption [F. G. J. *Henle,* died 1885, German pathologist]

¹loose \'lüs\ *adj* **1 a** : not rigidly fastened or securely attached **b** : having worked partly free from attachments **c** : not tight-fitting **2 a** : free from confinement,

longhouse

longitude

loon 1

\ə\ abut		\ng\ sing	
\ər\ further		\ō\ bone	
\a\ mat		\ó\ saw	
\ā\ take		\ói\ coin	
\ä\ cot, cart		\th\ thin	
\aú\ out		\th\ this	
\ch\ chin		\ü\ food	
\e\ pet		\ú\ foot	
\ē\ easy		\y\ yet	
\g\ go		\yü\ few	
\i\ tip		\yú\ cure	
\ī\ life		\zh\ vision	
\j\ job			

restraint, or obligation **b** : not brought together in a bundle, container, or binding **3** : not dense or compact in structure or arrangement ⟨*loose* soil⟩ **4** : lacking in restraint or power of restraint ⟨*loose* conduct⟩ **5 a** : not tightly drawn or stretched : SLACK **b** : having a flexible or relaxed character **6 a** : lacking in precision, exactness, or care **b** : permitting freedom of interpretation [Old Norse *lauss*] — **loose·ly** *adv* — **loose·ness** *n*

²**loose** *vb* **1 a** : to let loose : RELEASE **b** : to free from restraint **2** : to make loose : UNTIE ⟨*loose* a knot⟩ **3** : to let fly : DISCHARGE **4** : to make less rigid, tight, or strict : RELAX

loose constructionist *n* : one favoring a liberal interpretation of the United States Constitution as granting broad implied powers to the federal government

loose end *n* **1** : something left hanging loose **2** : a fragment of unfinished business

loose-joint·ed \'lüs-'jóint-əd\ *adj* : having a flexibility or lack of rigidity suggesting the absence of rigid joints; *esp* : moving with unusual freedom or ease — **loose-joint·ed·ness** *n*

loose-leaf \'lüs-'lēf\ *adj* **1** : having leaves secured in book form in a cover whose backbone contains a locking device that may be opened for adding, arranging, or removing leaves ⟨a *loose-leaf* notebook⟩ **2** : of, relating to, or used with a loose-leaf binding ⟨*loose-leaf* paper⟩

loos·en \'lüs-n\ *vb* **loos·ened; loos·en·ing** \'lüs-ning, -n-ing\ **1** : to release from restraint **2** : to make or become loose or looser **3** : to cause or permit to become less strict

loose·strife \'lüs-,strīf, 'lü-\ *n* **1** : any of a genus of plants of the primrose family with leafy stems and yellow or white flowers **2** : any of a genus of herbs including some with showy spikes of purple flowers [intended as translation of Greek *lysimacheios* "loose-strife" (as if from *lysis* "act of loosing" + *machesthai* "to fight"), from *Lysimachos*, 5th or 4th century B.C. Greek physician]

¹**loot** \'lüt\ *n* **1** : goods taken in war : SPOIL **2** : something stolen or taken by force or violence **3** : the action of looting [Hindi *lūt*, from Sanskrit *luṇṭati* "he robs"]

²**loot** *vb* **1** : to plunder or sack in war **2** : to rob or steal especially on a large scale and by violence or corruption **3** : to seize and carry away by force especially in war — **loot·er** *n*

lop \'läp\ *vt* **lopped; lop·ping 1 a** : to cut branches or twigs from : TRIM ⟨*lop* a tree⟩ **b** : to cut or shear from a woody plant ⟨*lop* dead branches⟩ **c** : to cut (as a portion or part) from something **2** : to remove unnecessary or undesirable parts from — usually used with *off* [Middle English *loppe* "small branches and twigs cut from a tree"] — **lop·per** *n*

¹**lope** \'lōp\ *n* **1** : an easy natural gait of a horse resembling a canter **2** : an easy bounding gait capable of being sustained for a long time [Old Norse *hlaup* "leap"]

²**lope** *vi* : to go, move, or ride at a lope — **lop·er** *n*

lop-eared \'läp-'iərd\ *adj* : having ears that droop [earlier *lop* "to droop"]

loph·o·phore \'läf-ə-,fōr, -,fòr\ *n* : a circular or horseshoe-shaped organ about the mouth of a brachiopod or bryozoan that bears tentacles and functions especially in food-getting [Greek *lophos* "crest"]

lop-sid·ed \'läp-'sīd-əd\ *adj* **1** : leaning to one side **2** : lacking in balance, symmetry, or proportion — **lop-sid·ed·ly** *adv* — **lop-sid·ed·ness** *n*

lo·qua·cious \lō-'kwā-shəs\ *adj* : given to too much talking [Latin *loquac-, loquax*, from *loqui* "to speak"] — **lo·qua·cious·ly** *adv* — **lo·qua·cious·ness** *n* — **lo·quac·i·ty** \-'kwas-ət-ē\ *n*

lo·quat \'lō-,kwät\ *n* : a small Asian evergreen tree bearing a yellow plumlike fruit; *also* : its fruit used especially in preserves [Chinese (Cantonese dialect) *lō-kwat*]

¹**lord** \'lòrd\ *n* **1** : one having power and authority over others : **a** : a ruler to whom service and obedience are due **b** : a person from whom a feudal fee or estate is held : HUSBAND **2** *cap* **a** : GOD 1 **b** : JESUS **3** : a man of rank or high position: as **a** : a feudal tenant whose right or title comes directly from the king **b** *often cap* : a British nobleman or a bishop in the Church of England entitled to sit in the House of Lords — used as a title **4** *pl, cap* : HOUSE OF LORDS [Old English *blāford*, from *blāf* "loaf" + *weard* "keeper, ward"]

□ ORIGIN *Lord* is etymologically similar to *lady*. A lady is, etymologically, a kneader of bread and a lord a keeper of bread. Old English *blāford* is formed from *blāf*, "loaf, bread", and *weard*, "keeper, guard", the Old English form of modern *ward*. The earliest known instances of *blāford* show the sense of "head of household". Apparently the *blāf-* element was to be taken no more literally than is the first element of the modern term *breadwinner*.

²**lord** *vi* : to act in an arrogant or domineering manner — used with *it*

lord chancellor *n, pl* **lords chancellor** : a British officer of state who presides over the House of Lords, serves as the head of the British judiciary, and is usually a leading member of the cabinet

lord·ly \'lòrd-lē\ *adj* **lord·li·er; -est 1 a** : of, relating to, or having the characteristics of a lord **b** : fit for a lord ⟨a *lordly* estate⟩ **2** : haughtily proud or superior — **lord·li·ness** *n* — **lordly** *adv*

lor·do·sis \lòr-'dō-səs\ *n* : abnormal forward curvature of the spine — compare KYPHOSIS, SCOLIOSIS [Greek *lordōsis*, from *lordos* "curving forward"] — **lor·dot·ic** \-'dät-ik\ *adj*

Lord's day *n, often cap D* : SUNDAY

lord·ship \'lòrd-,ship\ *n* **1** *often cap* : the rank or dignity of a lord — used as a title ⟨his *Lordship* is not at home⟩ **2** : the authority, power, or territory of a lord

Lord's Prayer *n* : the prayer in Matthew 6:9–13 that Christ taught his disciples

Lord's Supper *n* : COMMUNION 1a

lore \'lōr, 'lòr\ *n* : KNOWLEDGE 4; *esp* : a particular body of knowledge or tradition ⟨forest *lore*⟩ [Old English *lār* "teaching"]

lor·gnette \lòrn-'yet\ *n* : a pair of eyeglasses or opera glasses with a handle [French, from *lorgner* "to take a sidelong look at", from *lorgne* "cross-eyed"]

lo·ri·ca \lə-'rī-kə\ *n, pl* **-cae** \-,kē, -,sē\ *or* **-cas** \-kəz\ **1** : a Roman cuirass of leather or metal **2** : a hard protective case or shell (as of a rotifer) [Latin, from *lorum* "thong, rein"]

lor·i·keet \'lòr-ə-,kēt, 'lär-\ *n* : any of numerous small arboreal parrots of Australasia that feed chiefly on nectar [*lory*, a kind of parrot (from Malay *nuri, luri*) + *-keet* (as in *parakeet*)]

lo·ris \'lōr-əs, 'lòr-\ *n* : either of two small nocturnal slow-moving lemurs [French]

lorn \'lòrn\ *adj* : left alone : DESOLATE [Middle English, from *loren*, past participle of *lesen* "to lose", from Old English *lēosan*] — **lorn·ness** \'lòrn-nəs\ *n*

lor·ry \'lòr-ē, 'lär-\ *n, pl* **lorries 1** : a large low horse-drawn wagon without sides **2** *British* : a motor truck especially if open [origin unknown]

lose \'lüz\ *vb* **lost** \'lòst\; **los·ing** \'lü-zing\ **1** : to bring to destruction ⟨the ship was *lost* on the reef⟩ **2** : to be unable to find or have at hand ⟨*lose* a billfold⟩ **3** : to become deprived of especially accidentally or by death ⟨*lose* one's eyesight⟩ ⟨*lost* a child in the war⟩ **4** : to fail to keep control of or allegiance of ⟨*lose* votes⟩ **5 a** : to fail to use : let slip by : WASTE **b** (1) : to fail to win, gain, or obtain ⟨*lose* a prize⟩ ⟨*lose* a contest⟩ (2) : to undergo defeat ⟨*lose* with good grace⟩ **c** : to fail to catch with the senses or the mind ⟨*lost* part of what they said⟩ **6** : to cause the loss of ⟨one careless statement *lost* the election⟩ **7** : to fail to keep, sustain, or maintain ⟨*lose* one's balance⟩ **8 a** : to cause to miss one's way or bearings ⟨*lost* myself in the maze of streets⟩ **b** : to make (oneself) withdrawn from immediate reality ⟨*lost* myself in daydreaming⟩ **9 a** : to wander or go astray from ⟨*lost* my way⟩ **b** : to go faster than : shake off ⟨*lost* their pursuers⟩ **10** : to fail to keep in sight or in mind **11** : to free oneself from : get rid of ⟨dieting to *lose* some weight⟩ [Old English *losian* "to perish, lose", from *los* "destruction"] — **lose ground** : to suffer loss or disadvantage : fail to advance or improve — **lose one's heart** : to fall in love

lose out *vi* : to fail to win in competition : fail to receive an expected reward or gain

los·er \'lü-zər\ *n* **1** : one that loses **2** : one that does poorly : FAILURE

loss \'lós\ *n* **1 a** : the act of losing **b** : the harm or privation resulting from losing ⟨their death was a *loss* to the community⟩ **c** : an instance of losing **2 a** : a person or thing or an amount that is lost **b** *pl* : killed, wounded, or captured soldiers **3 a** : failure to gain, win, obtain, or utilize **b** : an amount by which the cost of an article or service exceeds the selling price **4** : decrease in amount, magnitude, or degree **5** : DESTRUCTION 2, RUIN [Middle English *loss*] — **at a loss** : unable to determine : PUZZLED, UNCERTAIN — **for a loss** : into a state of distress

loss leader *n* : an article sold at a loss in order to draw customers

lost \'lóst\ *adj* **1** : not made use of, won, or claimed **2 a** : unable to find the way **b** : no longer visible **c** : lacking assurance or self-confidence **3** : ruined or destroyed physically or morally **4 a** : no longer possessed **b** : no longer known **5 a** : taken away or beyond reach or attainment ⟨regions *lost* to the faith⟩ **b** : become callous : INSENSIBLE ⟨*lost* to shame⟩ **6** : ABSORBED, RAPT ⟨*lost* in revery⟩ [past participle of *lose*] — **lost·ness** \'lóst-nəs, 'lós-\ *n*

¹lot \'lät\ *n* **1** : an object used as a counter in determining a question by chance **2** : the use of lots as a means of deciding something ⟨choose by *lot*⟩; *also* : the resulting choice **3 a** : something that comes to one by or as if by lot : SHARE **b** : one's way of life or worldly fate : FORTUNE **4 a** : a portion of land ⟨a building *lot*⟩ **b** : a motion-picture studio and its adjoining property **5** : a number of units of an article or a parcel of articles offered as one item (as in an auction sale) **6** : a number of associated persons : SET **7** : a considerable quantity ⟨*lots* of money⟩ [Old English *hlot*] SYN see FATE

²lot *vb* **lot·ted; lot·ting 1** : to form or divide into lots **2** : ALLOT

loth \'lóth, 'lóth\ *variant of* LOATH

lo·thar·io \lō-'thar-ē-,ō, -'ther-, -'thär-\ *n, pl* **-ios** *often cap* : SEDUCER [*Lothario*, seducer in the play *The Fair Penitent* (1703) by Nicholas Rowe]

lo·tion \'lō-shən\ *n* : a liquid preparation for cosmetic and medicinal use on the skin [Latin *lotio* "act of washing", from *lotus*, past participle of *lavare, lavere* "to wash"]

lots \'läts\ *adv* : MUCH 1a ⟨feeling *lots* better⟩ [pl. of *¹lot*]

lot·tery \'lät-ə-rē, 'lä-trē\ *n, pl* **-ter·ies** : a drawing of lots in which prizes are given to holders of the winning tickets

lot·to \'lät-ō\ *n* : a game of chance similar to bingo [Italian, "lottery, lotto", from French *lot* "lot", of Germanic origin]

lo·tus \'lōt-əs\ *n* **1** *also* **lo·tos** \'lōt-əs\ : a fruit held in Greek legend to cause indolence and forgetfulness; *also* : a tree bearing this fruit **2** : any of various water lilies including several represented in ancient Egyptian and Hindu art and religious symbolism **3** : any of various erect plants of the pea family including some used for hay and pasture [Latin, from Greek *lōtos*, from Hebrew *lōt* "myrrh"]

lotus–eater \'lōt-ə-,sēt-ər\ *n* **1** : one of a people in classical mythology who subsist on the lotus and live in its induced dreamy indolence **2** : DREAMER 2a, IDLER

loud \'laud\ *adj* **1 a** : marked by intensity or volume of sound **b** : producing a loud sound **2** : CLAMOROUS, NOISY **3** : obtrusive or offensive in color or pattern ⟨a *loud* suit⟩ [Old English *hlūd*] — **loud** *adv* — **loud·ly** *adv* — **loud·ness** *n*

loud·en \'laud-n\ *vb* **loud·ened; loud·en·ing** \'laud-ning, -n-ing\ : to make or become loud or louder

loud·mouth \'laud-,mauth\ *n* : a person given to loud offensive talk — **loud·mouthed** \-'mauthd, -,ma"\overline{u}"tht\ *adj*

loud·speak·er \'laud-'spē-kər\ *n* : a device similar to a telephone receiver in operation but amplifying sound

lou·is d'or \,lü-ē-'dór\ *n, pl* **louis d'or 1** : a French gold coin first struck in 1640 and issued up to the Revolution **2** : the French 20-franc gold piece issued after the Revolution [French, from *Louis* XIII of France + *d'or* "of gold"]

Lou·is Qua·torze \,lü-ē-kə-'tórz\ *adj* : of, relating to, or characteristic of the architecture or furniture of the reign of Louis XIV of France [French, "Louis XIV"]

Louis Quinze \-'ka[n]z\ *adj* : of, relating to, or characteristic of the architecture or furniture of the reign of Louis XV of France [French, "Louis XV"]

Louis Seize \-'sāz, -'sez\ *adj* : of, relating to, or characteristic of the architecture or furniture of the reign of Louis XVI of France [French, "Louis XVI"]

Louis Treize \-'trāz, -'trez\ *adj* : of, relating to, or characteristic of the architecture or furniture of the reign of Louis XIII of France [French, "Louis XIII"]

¹lounge \'launj\ *vb* **1** : to move or act idly or lazily : LOAF **2** : to stand, sit, or lie in a relaxed manner **3** : to pass (time) idly ⟨*lounged* away the day⟩ [origin unknown] — **loung·er** *n*

²lounge *n* **1** : a place for lounging: as **a** : LIVING ROOM **b** : LOBBY **c** : a room in a public building or vehicle often combining lounging, smoking, and toilet facilities **2** : a long couch

lounge car *n* : a railroad passenger car with seats for lounging and facilities for serving refreshments

loup–ga·rou \,lü-gə-'rü\ *n, pl* **loups-garous** \,lü-gə-'rü, -'rüz\ : WEREWOLF [Middle French]

lour \'lau̇-ər, 'lau̇r\, **lour·ing, loury** \'lau̇-rē, -ə-rē\ *variant of* LOWER, LOWERING, LOWERY

louse \'lau̇s\ *n* **1** *pl* **lice** \'līs\ **a** : any of various small wingless usually flat insects (orders Anoplura and Mallophaga) parasitic on warm-blooded animals **b** : any of several other small arthropods **2** *pl* **lous·es** \'lau̇-səz\ : a contemptible person [Old English *lūs*]

louse up *vb* : to make a mess of something : BUNGLE

lousy \'lau̇-zē\ *adj* **lous·i·er; -est 1** : infested with lice **2 a** : totally repulsive : CONTEMPTIBLE **b** : miserably poor or inferior **c** : amply supplied ⟨*lousy* with money⟩ — **lous·i·ly** \-zə-lē\ *adv* — **lous·i·ness** \-zē-nəs\ *n*

lout \'lau̇t\ *n* : a clownish awkward fellow [perhaps from Old Norse *lūtr* "bent down"] — **lout·ish** \-ish\ *adj* — **lout·ish·ly** *adv* — **lout·ish·ness** *n*

lou·ver *or* **lou·vre** \'lü-vər\ *n* **1** : an opening provided with one or more slanted fixed or movable strips (as of metal or wood) to allow flow of air but to exclude rain or sun or to provide privacy; *also* : a similar device with movable strips for controlling the passage of air or light **2** : one of the slanted strips of a louver [Middle French *lovier* "dormer window"] — **lou·vered** \-vərd\ *adj*

lov·able *also* **love·able** \'ləv-ə-bəl\ *adj* : having qualities that win affection — **lov·able·ness** *n* — **lov·ably** \-blē\ *adv*

lov·age \'ləv-ij\ *n* : any of several aromatic perennial herbs of the carrot family [Anglo-French *lovache*]

¹love \'ləv\ *n* **1 a** : strong affection for another based on kinship ties ⟨maternal *love* for a child⟩ **b** : attraction based on sexual desire **c** : affection based on ad-

lotus 2

louver 1

\ə\	abut	\ng\	sing
\ər\	further	\ō\	bone
\a\	mat	\ó\	saw
\ā\	take	\ói\	coin
\ä\	cot, cart	\th\	thin
\au̇\	out	\th\	this
\ch\	chin	\ü\	food
\e\	pet	\ú\	foot
\ē\	easy	\y\	yet
\g\	go	\yü\	few
\i\	tip	\yu̇\	cure
\ī\	life	\zh\	vision
\j\	job		

lowboy

miration or benevolence **2** : warm attachment, enthusiasm, or devotion ⟨*love* of the sea⟩ **3 a** : the object of attachment or devotion **b** : a beloved person : DARLING **4 a** : unselfish loyal concern for the good of another : (1) : the fatherly concern of God for man (2) : brotherly concern for others **b** : a person's adoration of God **5** : an amorous episode **6** : a score of zero in tennis [Old English *lufu*] — **in love** : feeling love for and devotion toward someone

²**love** *vb* **1** : to hold dear : CHERISH **2 a** : to feel a lover's passion, devotion, or tenderness for **b** : CARESS **3** : to like or desire actively : take pleasure in ⟨*loved* to play the violin⟩ **4** : to thrive in ⟨the rose *loves* sunlight⟩ **5** : to feel affection : experience desire

love·bird \'ləv-ˌbərd\ *n* : any of various small usually gray or green parrots that actively court their mates

love feast *n* **1** : a meal eaten in common by a Christian congregation in token of brotherly love **2** : a banquet or celebration held to reconcile differences or show someone honor

love-in-a-mist \ˈləv-ə-nə-ˌmist\ *n* : a European garden plant of the buttercup family that has flowers enveloped in finely dissected bracts

love knot *n* : a stylized knot sometimes used as an emblem of love

love·less \'ləv-ləs\ *adj* **1** : marked by the absence of love ⟨a *loveless* marriage⟩ **2** : not feeling or showing love **3** : not loved — **love·less·ly** *adv* — **love·less·ness** *n*

love·lorn \'ləv-ˌlȯrn\ *adj* : deserted by one's love — **love·lorn·ness** \-ˌlȯrn-nəs\ *n*

love·ly \'ləv-lē\ *adj* **love·li·er; -est 1** : beautiful in moral or spiritual character : GRACIOUS **2** : delicately beautiful ⟨a *lovely* dress⟩ **3** : highly pleasing : FINE ⟨a *lovely* view⟩ SYN see BEAUTIFUL — **love·li·ness** *n*

love·mak·ing \'ləv-ˌmā-king\ *n* **1** : COURTSHIP **2** : sexual activity

lov·er \'ləv-ər\ *n* **1 a** : a person in love; *esp* : a man in love **b** *pl* : two persons in love with each other **2** : DEVOTEE **3 a** : PARAMOUR **b** : a person with whom one has sexual relations

lov·er·ly \-lē\ *adj* : befitting a lover

love seat *n* : a double chair, sofa, or settee for two persons

love·sick \'ləv-ˌsik\ *adj* **1** : languishing with love : YEARNING **2** : expressing a lover's longing — **love·sick·ness** *n*

lov·ing \'ləv-ing\ *adj* : feeling or showing love : AFFECTIONATE — **lov·ing·ly** \-ing-lē\ *adv*

loving cup *n* : a large ornamental drinking vessel with two or more handles; *esp* : one given as a prize or trophy

lov·ing–kind·ness \ˌləv-ing-'kīnd-nəs, -ˈkīn-\ *n* : tender and benevolent affection

¹**low** \'lō\ *vi* : to utter a low or a similar sound [Old English *blōwan*]

²**low** *n* : the characteristic deep sustained sound of a cow

³**low** \'lō\ *adj* **low·er** \'lō-ər, 'lȯr\; **low·est** \'lō-əst\ **1 a** : not high or tall ⟨a *low* wall⟩ ⟨a *low* bridge⟩ **b** : having a low-cut neckline **2 a** : situated or passing below the normal level, surface, or base of measurement ⟨*low* ground⟩ **b** : marking a bottom ⟨the *low* point of a career⟩ **3** : PROSTRATE ⟨laid *low* by the flu⟩ **4** : not loud : SOFT; *also* : FLAT 10a **5 a** : being near the equator ⟨*low* latitudes⟩ **b** : being near the horizon ⟨the sun is *low*⟩ **6** : humble in status ⟨*low* birth⟩ **7 a** : lacking strength, health, or vitality **b** : lacking spirit or vivacity : DEPRESSED **8 a** : of lesser degree, size, or amount than average or ordinary ⟨*low* pressure⟩ **b** : less than usual in number, amount, or value ⟨a *low* price⟩ **9** : falling short of some standard : as **a** : lacking dignity or elevation ⟨a *low* style of writing⟩ **b** : morally reprehensible : BASE ⟨a *low* trick⟩ **c** : COARSE, VULGAR ⟨*low* language⟩ **10** : not advanced in complexity, develop-

ment, or elaboration ⟨*low* organisms⟩ **11** : UNFAVORABLE a, DISPARAGING ⟨had a *low* opinion of it⟩ **12** : pronounced with a wide opening between the relatively flat tongue and the palate ⟨the *low* vowel \ä\⟩ [Old Norse *lāgr*] — **low** *adv* — **low·ness** *n*

⁴**low** *n* **1** : something that is low; *esp* : a region of low barometric pressure **2** : the arrangement of gears (as of an automobile) in a position to transmit the greatest power from the engine to the propeller shaft

low beam *n* : the point of aim of a vehicle headlight for short distances

low blood pressure *n* : blood pressure that is abnormally low especially in the arteries

low·born \'lō-'bȯrn\ *adj* : born in a low condition or rank

low·boy \'lō-ˌbȯi\ *n* : a chest of drawers about a meter high with long legs

low·bred \'lō-'bred\ *adj* : RUDE 2, VULGAR

low·brow \'lō-ˌbrau̇\ *n* : an uncultivated person — **lowbrow** *adj*

Low Church *adj* : tending especially in Anglican worship to minimize the priesthood, sacraments, and formal rites and often to emphasize evangelical principles — compare HIGH CHURCH

low·down \-ˌdau̇n\ *n* : basic and usually private data

low–down \'lō-ˈdau̇n\ *adj* **1** : CONTEMPTIBLE, DESPICABLE **2** : deeply emotional ⟨*low-down* blues⟩

¹**low·er** *or* **lour** \'lau̇-ər, 'lau̇r\ *vi* **1** : to look sullen : FROWN **2** : to become dark, gloomy, and threatening [Middle English *louren*]

²**lower** *or* **lour** *n* : a lowering look : FROWN

³**low·er** \'lō-ər, 'lȯr\ *adj* **1** : relatively low in position, rank, or order ⟨*lower* court⟩ **2** : less advanced in the scale of evolutionary development ⟨*lower* animals⟩ **3** : constituting the popular and more representative branch of a bicameral legislative body **4 a** : situated or held to be situated beneath the earth's surface **b** *cap* : of, relating to, or constituting an earlier geologic period or formation **5** : SOUTHERN 2 ⟨*lower* New York State⟩

⁴**low·er** \'lō-ər, 'lȯr\ *vb* **1** : to move down : DROP; *also* : DIMINISH **2 a** : to let descend by its own weight **b** : to make the aim lower **c** : to reduce the height of **3 a** : to reduce in value or amount ⟨*lower* the price⟩ **b** (1) : to bring down : DEGRADE (2) : ABASE, HUMBLE **c** : to reduce the objective of — **lower the boom** : to crack down

low·er·case \ˌlō-ər-'kās, ˌlȯr-\ *adj* : being a letter that belongs to or conforms to the series a, b, c, etc. rather than A, B, C, etc. [from the printer's practice of keeping such letters in the lower of a pair of type cases] — **lowercase** *n*

lower class *n* : a social class occupying a position below the middle class and having the lowest status in a society

low·er·ing *also* **lour·ing** \'lau̇-ring, -ə-ring\ *adj* : dark and threatening : GLOOMY

low·er·most \'lō-ər-ˌmōst, 'lȯr-\ *adj* : LOWEST

low·ery *also* **loury** \'lau̇-rē, -ə-rē\ *adj* : GLOOMY, LOWERING ⟨a *lowery* sky⟩

lowest common denominator *n* : LEAST COMMON DENOMINATOR

lowest terms *n pl* : the form of a fraction in which the numerator and denominator have no factor in common

low frequency *n* : a radio frequency in the range between 30 and 300 kilohertz — abbreviation LF

Low German *n* **1** : the German dialects of northern Germany especially since the end of the medieval period **2** : the West Germanic languages other than High German

low–grade \'lō-'grād\ *adj* **1** : of inferior grade or quality **2** : being near that extreme of a specified range which is lowest, least intense, or least favorable ⟨a *low-grade* fever⟩

low–key \'lō-ˌkē\ *also* **low–keyed** \-'kēd\ *adj* : of low intensity : RESTRAINED

low·land \'lō-lənd, -ˌland\ *n* : low and usually level country — **lowland** *adj*

low·land·er \-lən-dər, -ˌlan-\ *n* **1** : a native or inhabitant of a lowland region **2** *cap* : an inhabitant of the Lowlands of Scotland

¹low·ly \'lō-lē\ *adv* **1** : in a humble way **2** : in a low position, manner, or degree **3** : not loudly

²lowly *adj* **low·li·er; -est** **1** : HUMBLE 1, MEEK **2** : of or relating to a low social or economic rank **3** : LOW 10 ⟨*lowly* organisms like the amoeba⟩ **4** : ranking low in some hierarchy — **low·li·ness** *n*

low–ly·ing \'lō-'lī-ng\ *adj* : having little upward extension or elevation

low mass *n, often cap L&M* : a mass that is said in the simplest ceremonial form — compare HIGH MASS

low–mind·ed \'lō-'mīn-dəd\ *adj* : inclined mentally to low or unworthy things — **low–mind·ed·ly** *adv* — **low–mind·ed·ness** *n*

low–pres·sure \'lō-'presh-ər\ *adj* **1 a** : having, exerting, or operating under a relatively small pressure **b** : having or resulting from a low atmospheric pressure **2** : EASYGOING

low relief *n* : BAS-RELIEF

low–spir·it·ed \'lō-'spir-ət-əd\ *adj* : DEJECTED, DEPRESSED — **low–spir·it·ed·ly** *adv* — **low–spir·it·ed·ness** *n*

low tide *n* : the tide when the water is at its farthest ebb

¹lox \'läks\ *n* : liquid oxygen [*liquid ox*ygen]

²lox *n, pl* **lox** *or* **lox·es** : smoked salmon [Yiddish *laks,* from Middle High German *lahs* "salmon"]

loy·al \'lȯi-əl, 'lȯil\ *adj* **1 a** : faithful in allegiance to one's lawful government **b** : faithful to a private person to whom fidelity is due **2** : faithful to a cause or ideal [Middle French, from Old French *leial,* from Latin *legalis* "legal"] SYN *see* FAITHFUL — **loy·al·ly** \'lȯi-ə-lē\ *adv*

loy·al·ist \'lȯi-ə-ləst\ *n* : one who is loyal to a political cause, party, government, or sovereign; *esp* : TORY 2

loy·al·ty \'lȯi-əl-tē, 'lȯil-\ *n, pl* **-ties** : the quality or state of being loyal SYN *see* FIDELITY

loz·enge \'läz-nj\ *n* **1 a** : a diamond-shaped figure **b** : something shaped like a lozenge **2** : a small often medicated candy [Middle French *losange*]

LP \'el-'pē\ *trademark* — used for a long-playing phonograph record

LSD \ˌel-ˌes-'dē\ *n* : an organic compound that induces psychotic symptoms similar to those of schizophrenia [*lys*ergic acid *d*iethylamide]

lu·au \'lü-ˌau\ *n* : an Hawaiian feast [Hawaiian *lu'au*]

lub·ber \'ləb-ər\ *n* **1** : a big clumsy fellow **2** : an unskilled seaman [Middle English *lobur*] — **lub·ber·li·ness** \-lē-nəs\ *n* — **lub·ber·ly** \-lē\ *adj or adv*

lube \'lüb\ *n* : LUBRICANT

lu·bri·cant \'lü-bri-kənt\ *n* : something (as a grease or oil) capable of reducing friction when applied between moving parts — **lubricant** *adj*

lu·bri·cate \'lü-brə-ˌkāt\ *vb* **1** : to make smooth or slippery **2** : to apply a lubricant to ⟨*lubricate* a car⟩ **3** : to act as a lubricant [Latin *lubricare,* from *lubricus* "slippery"] — **lu·bri·ca·tion** \ˌlü-brə-'kā-shən\ *n* — **lu·bri·ca·tive** \'lü-brə-ˌkāt-iv\ *adj* — **lu·bri·ca·tor** \-ˌkāt-ər\ *n*

lu·bri·cious \lü-'brish-əs\ *or* **lu·bri·cous** \'lü-bri-kəs\ *adj* **1** : LECHEROUS; *also* : SALACIOUS 1 **2** : smooth or slippery in texture ⟨a *lubricious* skin⟩ [Latin *lubricus* "slippery, easily led astray"] — **lu·bri·cious·ly** *adv* — **lu·bric·i·ty** \lü-'bris-ət-ē\ *n*

lu·cent \'lüs-nt\ *adj* **1** : glowing with light : LUMINOUS **2** : marked by clearness or translucence [Latin *lucens,* present participle of *lucēre* "to shine"] — **lu·cent·ly** *adv*

lu·cerne *also* **lu·cern** \lü-'sərn\ *n, chiefly British* : ALFALFA [French *luzerne,* from Provençal *luserno*]

lu·cid \'lü-səd\ *adj* **1 a** : suffused with light : LUMINOUS **b** : penetrated with light : TRANSLUCENT **2** : having full use of one's faculties : clear in mind **3** : clear to the understanding : PLAIN [Latin *lucidus*] SYN *see* LIMPID — **lu·cid·i·ty** \lü-'sid-ət-ē\ *n* — **lu·cid·ly** *adv* — **lu·cid·ness** *n*

Lu·ci·fer \'lü-sə-fər\ *n* : DEVIL 1 [Old English, the morning star, a fallen angel, the Devil, from Latin, the morning star, from *lucifer* "light-bearing", from *luc-, lux* "light" + *-fer* "-ferous"] □ ORIGIN *Lucifer,* "bearer of light", is a strange name for the Devil. Latin *Lucifer* (from *lux,* "light", and *ferre,* "to carry") was the name of the chief morning star (the planet Venus), which heralds, if it does not exactly carry in, the dawn. In telling about the fall of Babylon, the Prophet Isaiah compares the king of Babylon to the morning star: "How art thou fallen from Heaven, O Lucifer, son of the morning!" (Isaiah 14:12). Later, Christians interpreted Isaiah's description of the downfall of Babylon as an allegory for the fall from heaven of the rebel archangel Satan. *Lucifer,* they concluded, must have been the Devil's original name.

lu·cif·er·ase \lü-'sif-ə-ˌrās\ *n* : an enzyme that catalyzes the oxidation of luciferin

lu·cif·er·in \lü-'sif-ə-rən\ *n* : a component of luminescent organisms that furnishes practically heatless light in undergoing oxidation [Latin *lucifer* "light-bearing"]

Lu·cite \'lü-ˌsīt\ *trademark* — used for an acrylic resin or plastic consisting essentially of methacrylate

luck \'lək\ *n* **1** : whatever happens to a person apparently by chance : FORTUNE ⟨we had a run of good *luck*⟩ **2** : the accidental way events occur ⟨happening by pure *luck*⟩ **3** : good fortune : SUCCESS ⟨out of *luck*⟩ [Dutch *luc*] — **luck·less** \'lək-ləs\ *adj*

lucky \'lək-ē\ *adj* **luck·i·er; -est** **1** : favored by luck : FORTUNATE **2** : producing or resulting in good by chance ⟨a *lucky* hit⟩ **3** : seeming to bring good luck ⟨a *lucky* coin⟩ — **luck·i·ly** \'lək-ə-lē\ *adv* — **luck·i·ness** \'lək-ē-nəs\ *n* □ SYN LUCKY, FORTUNATE mean meeting with unforeseen or unpredictable success. LUCKY stresses the operation of pure chance in producing a favorable result; FORTUNATE suggests being rewarded beyond what one strictly deserves or succeeding beyond reasonable expectation.

lu·cra·tive \'lü-krət-iv\ *adj* : producing wealth : PROFITABLE ⟨invested in a *lucrative* business⟩ — **lu·cra·tive·ly** *adv* — **lu·cra·tive·ness** *n*

lu·cre \'lü-kər\ *n* : monetary gain : PROFIT; *also* : MONEY 1 [Latin *lucrum*]

lu·cu·bra·tion \ˌlü-kyə-'brā-shən, -kə-\ *n* **1** : laborious study : MEDITATION **2** : studied or pretentious expression in speech or writing [Latin *lucubratio* "study by night", from *lucubrare* "to work by lamplight"]

lu·di·crous \'lüd-ə-krəs\ *adj* **1** : amusing or laughable through obvious absurdity or incongruity **2** : deserving scorn as absurdly inept, false, or foolish [Latin *ludicrus,* from *ludus* "play, sport"] SYN *see* LAUGHABLE — **lu·di·crous·ly** *adv* — **lu·di·crous·ness** *n*

lu·es \'lü-ˌēz\ *n, pl* **lues** : SYPHILIS [Latin, "plague"] — **lu·et·ic** \lü-'et-ik\ *adj*

¹luff \'ləf\ *n* **1** : the act of turning a sailing vessel's head into the wind **2** : the forward edge of a fore-and-aft sail [Middle French *lof* "weather side of a ship"]

²luff *vi* : to turn the head of a sailing vessel into the wind

¹lug \'ləg\ *vb* **lugged; lug·ging** **1** : DRAG 1a, PULL **2** : to carry laboriously **3** : to introduce in a forced manner ⟨*lug* a story into the conversation⟩ [Middle English *luggen*]

²lug *n* **1** : a part (as a handle) that projects like an ear **2** : a big loutish person [Middle English *lugge*]

lug·gage \'ləg-ij\ *n* **1** : a traveler's belongings : BAGGAGE **2** : containers (as suitcases) for carrying belongings

\ə\ abut		\ng\ sing	
\ər\ further		\ō\ bone	
\a\ mat		\ȯ\ saw	
\ā\ take		\ȯi\ coin	
\ä\ cot, cart		\th\ thin	
\au\ out		\th\ this	
\ch\ chin		\ü\ food	
\e\ pet		\u̇\ foot	
\ē\ easy		\y\ yet	
\g\ go		\yü\ few	
\i\ tip		\yu̇\ cure	
\ī\ life		\zh\ vision	
\j\ job			

lugger

luna moth

lug·ger \'ləg-ər\ *n* : a boat that carries one or more lug-sails

Lu·gol's solution \'lü-ˌgȯlz-, -ˌgälz-\ *n* : any of several deep brown solutions of iodine and potassium iodide in water or alcohol that are used in medicine and as microscopic stains — called also *Lugol's iodine solution* [J.G.A. *Lugol*, died 1851, French physician]

lug·sail \'ləg-ˌsāl, -səl\ *n* : a 4-sided sail fastened at the top to a yard that crosses the mast obliquely [perhaps from ²*lug*]

lu·gu·bri·ous \lu̇-'gü-brē-əs, -'gyü-\ *adj* : MOURNFUL; *esp* : overly or affectedly mournful [Latin *lugubris*, from *lugēre* "to mourn"] — **lu·gu·bri·ous·ly** *adv* — **lu·gu·bri·ous·ness** *n*

lug·worm \'ləg-ˌwərm\ *n* : any of a genus of marine annelid worms that have a row of tufted gills along each side of the back and are used for bait [origin unknown]

Luke \'lük\ *n* — see BIBLE table

luke·warm \'lü-'kwȯrm\ *adj* 1 : neither hot nor cold : TEPID ⟨a *lukewarm* bath⟩ 2 : not enthusiastic : HALF-HEARTED ⟨received a *lukewarm* reception⟩ [Middle English, from *luke* "lukewarm" + *warm*] — **luke·warm·ly** *adv* — **luke·warm·ness** *n*

¹lull \'ləl\ *vt* 1 : to cause to sleep or rest : SOOTHE 2 : to cause to relax vigilance [Middle English *lullen*]

²lull *n* 1 : a temporary calm before or during a storm 2 : a temporary drop in activity

lul·la·by \'ləl-ə-ˌbī\ *n, pl* **-bies** : a song to quiet children or lull them to sleep [Middle English *lulla*, interj. used to lull a child + *by*, interj. used to lull a child]

lum·ba·go \ˌləm-'bā-gō\ *n* : usually painful muscular rheumatism involving the lumbar region [Latin, from *lumbus* "loin"]

lum·bar \'ləm-bər, -ˌbär\ *adj* : of, relating to, or adjacent to the loins or the vertebrae between the thoracic vertebrae and sacrum ⟨*lumbar* region⟩ [Latin *lumbus* "loin"]

¹lum·ber \'ləm-bər\ *vi* **lum·bered; lum·ber·ing** \-bə-ring, -bring\ 1 : to move heavily or clumsily 2 : RUMBLE 1 [Middle English *lomeren*]

²lumber *n* 1 : surplus or disused articles (as furniture) that are stored away 2 : timber or logs especially when sawed up for use [perhaps from earlier *Lombard* "moneylender" (from the prominence of Lombards as moneylenders); from the use of pawnshops as storehouses of disused property] — **lumber** *adj*

³lumber *vb* **lum·bered; lum·ber·ing** \-bə-ring, -bring\ 1 : to clutter with or as if with lumber : ENCUMBER 2 : to heap together in disorder 3 : to cut timber or saw logs into lumber — **lum·ber·er** \-bər-ər\ *n*

lum·ber·jack \'ləm-bər-ˌjak\ *n* : LOGGER

lum·ber·man \-mən\ *n* : one engaged in lumbering

lum·ber·yard \-ˌyärd\ *n* : a place where a stock of lumber is kept for sale

lu·men \'lü-mən\ *n, pl* **lu·mi·na** \-mə-nə\ *or* **lumens** 1 : the cavity or bore of a tube or tubular organ ⟨*lumen* of a blood vessel⟩ ⟨*lumen* of a catheter⟩ 2 : a unit of luminous flux equal to the light on a unit surface all points of which are at a unit distance from a uniform point source of one candle [Latin, "light, air shaft, opening"] — **lu·mi·nal** \'lü-mən-l\ *adj*

lumin- *or* **lumini-** *or* **lumino-** *combining form* : light ⟨*lumin*iferous⟩ [Latin *lumin-*, *lumen*]

lu·mi·naire \ˌlü-mə-'naər, -'neər\ *n* : a complete lighting unit (as for a streetlight) [French, "lamp, lighting"]

lu·mi·nance \'lü-mə-nəns\ *n* : luminous intensity (as of a surface)

lu·mi·nary \'lü-mə-ˌner-ē\ *n, pl* **-nar·ies** 1 : a source of light; *esp* : one of the celestial bodies 2 : a very famous and distinguished person — **luminary** *adj*

lu·mi·nes·cence \ˌlü-mə-'nes-ns\ *n* : emission of light at low temperatures as a by-product of a physiological,

chemical, or electrical process; *also* : such light — **lu·mi·nesce** \-'nes\ *vi*

lu·mi·nes·cent \-'nes-nt\ *adj* : relating to, exhibiting, or adapted for the production of luminescence ⟨*luminescent* animals⟩

lu·mi·nif·er·ous \ˌlü-mə-'nif-rəs, -ə-rəs\ *adj* : transmitting, producing, or yielding light

lu·mi·nos·i·ty \ˌlü-mə-'näs-ət-ē\ *n, pl* **-ties** 1 : the quality or state of being luminous : BRIGHTNESS 2 : something luminous

lu·mi·nous \'lü-mə-nəs\ *adj* 1 : emitting light : SHINING 2 : bathed in or exposed to steady light ⟨a plaza *luminous* with sunlight⟩ 3 : CLEAR 3c, INTELLIGIBLE — **lu·mi·nous·ly** *adv* — **lu·mi·nous·ness** *n*

luminous flux *n* : radiant flux in the visible-wavelength range

lum·mox \'ləm-əks\ *n* : a clumsy person [origin unknown]

¹lump \'ləmp\ *n* 1 : a piece or mass of indefinite size or shape 2 : AGGREGATE, TOTALITY ⟨taken in the *lump*⟩ 3 : an abnormal swelling or growth 4 : a thickset heavy person; *esp* : one who is stupid or dull 5 *pl* : DEFEAT, LOSS [Middle English]

²lump *vb* 1 : to group without discrimination 2 : to make into lumps 3 : to become formed into lumps

³lump *adj* : not divided into parts : ENTIRE ⟨a *lump* sum⟩

⁴lump *vt* : to put up with ⟨like it or *lump* it⟩ [origin unknown]

lump·ish \'ləm-pish\ *adj* 1 : DULL 3, SLUGGISH 2 : CLUMSY 1a, UNGAINLY — **lump·ish·ly** *adv* — **lump·ish·ness** *n*

lumpy \'ləm-pē\ *adj* **lump·i·er; -est** 1 : filled or covered with lumps 2 : having a thickset clumsy appearance — **lump·i·ly** \-pə-lē\ *adv* — **lump·i·ness** \-pē-nəs\ *n*

lu·na·cy \'lü-nə-sē\ *n, pl* **-cies** 1 : unsoundness of mind interrupted by lucid intervals 2 : wild foolishness : extreme folly [*lunatic*] SYN see INSANITY

lu·na moth \ˌlü-nə-\ *n* : a large mostly pale green North American moth with long tails on the hind wings [Latin *luna* "moon"]

lu·nar \'lü-nər\ *adj* 1 : of or relating to the moon 2 : measured by the moon's revolution ⟨*lunar* month⟩ [Latin *lunaris*, from *luna* "moon"]

lunar caustic *n* : silver nitrate molded into sticks for use as a caustic

lunar eclipse *n* : an eclipse in which the moon passes partially or wholly through the umbra of the earth's shadow

lunar module *n* : a space vehicle module designed to carry astronauts from the command module to the surface of the moon and back — called also *lunar excursion module*

lu·nate \'lü-ˌnāt\ *adj* : shaped like a crescent

lu·na·tic \'lü-nə-ˌtik\ *adj* 1 **a** : affected with lunacy : INSANE **b** : designed for insane persons ⟨*lunatic* asylum⟩ 2 : wildly foolish or reckless [Late Latin *lunaticus*, from Latin *luna* "moon"; from the belief that lunacy fluctuated with the phases of the moon] — **lunatic** *n*

lunatic fringe *n* : the members of a political or social movement advocating eccentric or fanatical views

lunch \'lənch\ *n* 1 : a light meal; *esp* : one eaten in the middle of the day 2 : the food prepared for a lunch [probably short for *luncheon*] — **lunch** *vb* — **lunch·er** *n*

lun·cheon \'lən-chən\ *n* : a light meal at midday; *esp* : a formal lunch [perhaps alteration of *nuncheon* "light snack", from Middle English *noneschench*, literally, "noon drink", from *none* "noon" + *schench* "drink, cup"]

lun·cheon·ette \ˌlən-chə-'net\ *n* : a place where light lunches are sold

lunch·room \'lənch-ˌrüm, -ˌru̇m\ *n* 1 : LUNCHEONETTE 2 : a room (as in a school) where lunches supplied on the premises or brought from home may be eaten

lune \'lün\ *n* : a crescent-shaped figure on a plane surface or a sphere formed by two intersecting arcs of circles [Latin *luna* "moon"]

lung \'ləng\ *n* **1 a** : one of the usually paired thoracic organs that form the special breathing apparatus of air-breathing vertebrates **b** : any of various other respiratory organs **2** : a device (as an iron lung) to promote and facilitate breathing [Old English *lungen*]

¹lunge \'lənj\ *vb* **1 a** : to stride forward and make a thrust with a sword **b** : to drive or thrust with or as if with a lunge **2** : to make a sudden forceful forward movement : RUSH [obsolete *allonge*, from French *allonger* "to extend (an arm), make long", derived from Latin *ad-* + *longus* "long"]

²lunge *n* **1** : a sudden stretching thrust or pass (as with a sword) **2** : the act of striding or leaping suddenly forward

¹lung·er \'lən-jər\ *n* : one that lunges

²lung·er \'ləng-ər\ *n* : one suffering from a chronic disease of the lungs; *esp* : a tubercular person

lung·fish \'ləng-,fish\ *n* : any of various fishes (order Dipneusti or Cladistia) that breathe by a modified air bladder as well as gills

lung·wort \'ləng-,wərt, -,wȯrt\ *n* : a European herb that is related to the forget-me-not, has bristly leaves and bluish flowers, and was formerly used in the treatment of respiratory diseases

lunk·head \'ləngk-,hed\ *n* : a dull-witted person : DOLT [*lunk*, probably alteration of *lump*] — **lunk·head·ed** \-'hed-əd\ *adj*

lu·nule \'lü-nyül\ *n* : a crescent-shaped body part or marking; *esp* : the whitish mark at the base of a fingernail [Latin *lunula* "crescent-shaped ornament", from *luna* "moon"]

Lu·per·ca·lia \,lü-pər-'kā-lē-ə\ *n* : an ancient Roman festival celebrated February 15 to ensure fertility for the people, fields, and flocks [Latin, from *Lupercus*, god of flocks] — **Lu·per·ca·li·an** \-lē-ən\ *adj*

¹lu·pine \'lü-pən\ *n* : any of a genus of usually blue- or purple-flowered herbs of the pea family some of which are poisonous and others grown for green manure, fodder, or their edible seeds [Latin *lupinum*, from *lupinus* "of wolves", from *lupus* "wolf"]

²lu·pine \'lü-,pīn\ *adj* : of, relating to, or befitting or characteristic of wolves

lu·pus \'lü-pəs\ *n* : any of several diseases marked by skin lesions [Medieval Latin, from Latin, "wolf"]

¹lurch \'lərch\ *n* : a decisive defeat (as in cribbage) in which an opponent wins a game by more than double the defeated player's score [Middle French *lourche* "defeated by a lurch, deceived"] — **in the lurch** : in a helpless or unsupported position ⟨left them *in the lurch*⟩

²lurch *n* : a sudden swaying or tipping movement ⟨the car gave a *lurch*⟩; *also* : a staggering gait [origin unknown]

³lurch *vi* : to roll or tip abruptly : PITCH; *also* : STAGGER

lurch·er \'lər-chər\ *n, British* : a mongrel dog; *esp* : one used by poachers [Middle English *lorchen* "to prowl, steal"]

¹lure \'lu̇r\ *n* **1 a** : an inducement to pleasure or gain : ENTICEMENT **b** : APPEAL 3, ATTRACTION **2** : a decoy for attracting animals to capture; *esp* : an artificial bait used for catching fish [Middle French *loire*, a device used by a falconer to recall a hawk, of Germanic origin]

²lure *vt* : to tempt with a promise of pleasure or gain : ENTICE — **lur·er** *n*

lu·rid \'lu̇r-əd\ *adj* **1** : ghastly pale : WAN, LIVID **2** : shining with the red glow of fire seen through smoke **3 a** : causing horror or revulsion : GRUESOME ⟨*lurid* tales of murder⟩ **b** : SENSATIONAL 2 [Latin *luridus* "pale yellow, sallow"] SYN see GHASTLY — **lu·rid·ly** *adv* — **lu·rid·ness** *n*

lurk \'lərk\ *vi* **1 a** : to lie in ambush **b** : to move furtively or inconspicuously : SNEAK **c** : to persist in staying **2** : to be present but unseen or unrecognized ⟨a *lurking* danger⟩ [Middle English *lurken*] — **lurk·er** *n*

lus·cious \'ləsh-əs\ *adj* **1** : having a delicious taste or smell ⟨*luscious* berries⟩ **2** : having sensual appeal : SEDUCTIVE **3** : richly luxurious or appealing to the senses; *also* : overly ornate [Middle English *lucius*] — **lus·cious·ly** *adv* — **lus·cious·ness** *n*

¹lush \'ləsh\ *adj* **1** : producing or covered with luxuriant growth ⟨*lush* grass⟩ ⟨*lush* pastures⟩ **2 a** : doing well : VIGOROUS **b** : characterized by abundance : PLENTIFUL **3 a** : DELECTABLE 1, DELIGHTFUL **b** : LUXURIOUS 3, OPULENT [Middle English *lusch* "soft, tender"] — **lush·ly** *adv* — **lush·ness** *n*

²lush *n* **1** *slang* : intoxicating liquor : DRINK **2** : an habitual heavy drinker : DRUNKARD [origin unknown]

¹lust \'ləst\ *n* **1** : usually intense sexual desire **2** : an intense longing : CRAVING [Old English, "pleasure, delight, lust"]

²lust *vi* : to have an intense desire or need : CRAVE; *esp* : to have sexual desire

lus·ter *or* **lus·tre** \'ləs-tər\ *n* **1** : a shine or sheen especially from reflected light : GLOSS; *esp* : the appearance of the surface of a mineral with respect to its reflecting qualities ⟨a pearly *luster*⟩ **2** : inner beauty : RADIANCE **3** : GLORY 1a, SPLENDOR ⟨the *luster* of a famous name⟩ [Middle French *lustre*, from Italian *lustro*, from *lustrare* "to brighten", from Latin] — **lus·ter·less** \-tər-ləs\ *adj*

lus·ter·ware \-,waȧr, -,weȧr\ *n* : pottery decorated by applying to the glaze metallic compounds which become iridescent metallic films in the process of firing

lust·ful \'ləst-fəl\ *adj* : excited by lust; *esp* : LECHEROUS — **lust·ful·ly** \-fə-lē\ *adv* — **lust·ful·ness** *n*

lus·trous \'ləs-trəs\ *adj* **1** : having a high gloss or shine **2** : radiant in character or reputation : ILLUSTRIOUS — **lus·trous·ly** *adv* — **lus·trous·ness** *n*

lus·trum \'ləs-trəm\ *n, pl* **lustrums** *or* **lus·tra** \-trə\ **1 a** : a purification of the ancient Roman people made after the census every five years **b** : the Roman census **2** : a period of five years [Latin]

lusty \'ləs-tē\ *adj* **lust·i·er; -est** : full of vitality : VIGOROUS — **lust·i·ly** \-tə-lē\ *adv* — **lust·i·ness** \-tē-nəs\ *n*

¹lute \'lüt\ *n* : a stringed instrument with a large pear-shaped body, a neck with a fretted fingerboard, and a head with pegs for tuning [Middle French *lut*, from Provençal *laut*, from Arabic *al-'ūd*, literally, "the wood"]

²lute *n* : material (as cement or clay) for packing a joint or coating a porous surface to make it impervious to fluid [Latin *lutum* "mud"]

³lute *vt* : to seal or cover with lute ⟨*lute* a joint⟩

lu·te·al \'lüt-ē-əl\ *adj* : of, relating to, or involving the corpus luteum

lu·tein·iz·ing hormone \'lüt-ē-ə-,nīz-ing-, 'lü-,tēn-,īz-\ *n* : a hormone of the pituitary gland that in the female stimulates especially the development of the corpora lutea

lu·te·nist *or* **lu·ta·nist** \'lüt-n-əst, 'lüt-nəst\ *n* : one who plays the lute [Medieval Latin *lutanista*, from *lutana* "lute", probably from Middle French *lut*]

lu·teo·tro·phic hormone \,lüt-ē-ə-,trō-fik-, -,traf-ik-\ *or* **lu·teo·tro·pic hormone** \-,trō-pik-, -,träp-ik-\ *n* : PROLACTIN [*lute-* (as in *corpus luteum*) + Greek *trophē* "nourishment"]

lu·te·tium *or* **lu·te·cium** \lü-'tē-shē-əm, -shəm\ *n* : a soft ductile metallic chemical element — see ELEMENT table [New Latin, from Latin *Lutetia*, ancient name of Paris]

¹Lu·ther·an \'lü-thə-rən, -thrən\ *n* : a member of a Lutheran church

²Lutheran *adj* **1** : of or relating to Martin Luther or his religious doctrines **2** : of or relating to the Protestant

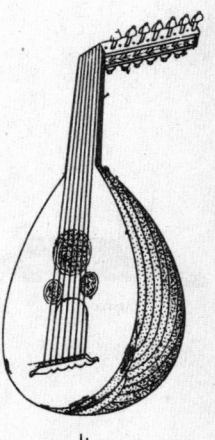

¹lute

\ə\ abut	\ng\ sing
\ər\ further	\ō\ bone
\a\ mat	\ȯ\ saw
\ā\ take	\ȯi\ coin
\ä\ cot, cart	\th\ thin
\au̇\ out	\t͟h\ this
\ch\ chin	\ü\ food
\e\ pet	\u̇\ foot
\ē\ easy	\y\ yet
\g\ go	\yü\ few
\i\ tip	\yu̇\ cure
\ī\ life	\zh\ vision
\j\ job	

churches adhering to Lutheran doctrines, liturgy, or polity — **Lu·ther·an·ism** \-,iz-əm\ *n*

lux \'ləks\ *n, pl* **lux** *or* **lux·es** : a unit of illumination equal to one lumen per square meter [Latin, "light"]

lux·u·ri·ant \ləg-'zhùr-ē-ənt, ,ləg-; lək-'shùr-, ,lək-\ *adj* **1 a** : yielding abundantly : PRODUCTIVE **b** : characterized by abundant growth : LUSH **2 a** : exuberantly rich and varied : PROFUSE **b** : excessively elaborate : FLORID **3** : LUXURIOUS 3 — **lux·u·ri·ance** \-əns\ *n* — **lux·u·ri·ant·ly** *adv* □ SYN LUXURIOUS: LUXURIANT implies profuseness and rich abundance and suggests splendor of display ⟨a *luxuriant* bed of peonies⟩ ⟨a style decked with *luxuriant* imagery⟩ LUXURIOUS applies to what is choice and costly and suggests the satisfactions of sensuous comforts and pleasures ⟨a *luxurious* apartment⟩

lux·u·ri·ate \-ē-,āt\ *vi* **1** : to grow profusely : PROLIFERATE **2** : to indulge oneself luxuriously : REVEL

lux·u·ri·ous \ləg-'zhùr-ē-əs, ,ləg-; lək-'shùr-, ,lək-\ *adj* **1** : of or relating to unrestrained gratification of the senses : VOLUPTUOUS **2** : fond of luxury or self-indulgence **3 a** : characterized by opulence or rich abundance **b** : excessively ornate SYN see LUXURIANT — **lux·u·ri·ous·ly** *adv* — **lux·u·ri·ous·ness** *n*

lux·u·ry \'ləksh-rē, 'ləgzh-, -ə-rē\ *n, pl* **-ries 1** : sumptuous living or equipment : great ease or comfort : rich surroundings ⟨live in *luxury*⟩ **2 a** : something desirable but costly or hard to get ⟨a *luxury* few can afford⟩ **b** : something adding to pleasure but not absolutely necessary : FRILL [Middle French *luxurie,* from Latin *luxuria* "rankness, luxury, excess"] — **luxury** *adj*

¹-ly \lē\ *adj suffix* **1** : like in appearance, manner, or nature : having the characteristics of ⟨king*ly*⟩ ⟨sister*ly*⟩ **2** : characterized by regular recurrence in (specified) units of time : every ⟨year*ly*⟩ [Old English *-līc, -lic,* from *līc* "body"]

²-ly *adv suffix* **1** : in a (specified) manner ⟨easi*ly*⟩ **2** : from a (specified) point of view ⟨theological*ly*⟩ **3** : with respect to ⟨part*ly*⟩ [Old English *-līce, -lice,* from *-līc,* adj. suffix]

ly·cée \lē-'sā\ *n* : a French public secondary school that prepares students for the university [French, from Middle French *lyceum,* from Latin *Lyceum*]

ly·ce·um \lī-'sē-əm, 'lī-sē-\ *n* **1** : a hall for public lectures or discussions **2** : an association providing public lectures, concerts, and entertainments [Latin *Lyceum,* gymnasium near Athens where Aristotle taught, from Greek *Lykeion,* from *lykeios,* epithet of Apollo]

lych–gate \'lich-,gāt\ *n* : a roofed gate in a churchyard under which a bier rests during the first part of a burial service [Middle English *lich, lych* "body, corpse", from Old English *līc*]

lych·nis \'lik-nəs\ *n* : any of a genus of often sticky-stemmed herbs of the pink family with usually red or white flowers [Latin, a kind of red flower, from Greek]

ly·co·pod \'lī-kə-,päd\ *n* : CLUB MOSS; *esp* : LYCOPODIUM 1

ly·co·po·di·um \,lī-kə-'pōd-ē-əm\ *n* **1** : any of a large genus of erect or creeping club mosses with evergreen leaves in four to many ranks **2** : a fine yellowish flammable powder of lycopodium spores used especially in pharmacy and in fireworks [Greek *lykos* "wolf" + *podion* "little foot", from *pod-, pous* "foot"]

Lyd·i·an \'lid-ē-ən\ *n* **1** : a native or inhabitant of Lydia **2** : an extinct Indo-European language of ancient Anatolia — **Lydian** *adj*

lye \'lī\ *n* **1** : a strong alkaline liquor rich in potassium carbonate leached from wood ashes and used especially in making soap and in washing **2** : any of various strong alkaline solutions; *also* : SODIUM HYDROXIDE **3** : a solid caustic [Old English *lēag*]

ly·gus bug \'lī-gəs-\ *n* : any of several small sucking bugs some of which transmit virus diseases to plants [New Latin *Lygus,* genus name]

ly·ing \'lī-ing\ *adj* : FALSE 2a, UNTRUTHFUL [present participle of ³*lie*]

lynx c

ly·ing–in \,lī-ing-'in\ *n, pl* **lyings–in** *or* **lying–ins** : the state during and immediately after childbirth — **lying-in** *adj*

Lyme disease \'līm-\ *n* : an acute inflammatory disease that is caused by a spirochete transmitted by ticks, that is often characterized at first by a round spreading red patch on the skin at the place of infection, and that may result in joint pain, arthritis, and disorders of the heart and nervous system [*Lyme,* Connecticut, where it was first reported]

lymph \'limf, 'limpf\ *n, pl* **lymphs** \'limfs, 'limpfs, 'lims, 'limps\ : a pale coagulable fluid that resembles blood plasma, contains white blood cells, circulates in lymphatic vessels, and bathes the cells of the body [Latin *lympha* "water goddess, water", from Greek *nymphē* "nymph"] — **lymph** *adj*

lymph·ad·e·ni·tis \,lim-,fad-n-'īt-əs\ *n* : inflammation of the lymph glands [Greek *adēn* "gland"]

¹lym·phat·ic \lim-'fat-ik\ *adj* **1 a** : of, relating to, or produced by lymph, lymphoid tissue, or lymphocytes **b** : conveying lymph **2** : lacking physical or mental energy — **lym·phat·i·cal·ly** \-'fat-i-kə-lē, -klē\ *adv*

²lymphatic *n* : a vessel that contains or conveys lymph — called also *lymph vessel*

lymph node *n* : one of the masses of tissue occurring in association with the lymphatic vessels and giving rise to the lymphocytes — called also *lymph gland*

lym·pho·cyte \'lim-fə-,sīt, 'limp-\ *n* : a colorless weakly motile cell that is produced in lymphoid tissue, is the typical cellular element of lymph, and constitutes 20 to 30 percent of the leukocytes of normal human blood — **lym·pho·cyt·ic** \,lim-fə-'sit-ik, ,limp-\ *adj*

lym·phoid \'lim-,fóid\ *adj* **1** : of, relating to, or resembling lymph **2** : of, relating to, or constituting the tissue characteristic of the lymph nodes

lym·pho·ma \lim-'fō-mə\ *n, pl* **-mas** *or* **-ma·ta** \-mət-ə\ : a tumor of lymphoid tissue

lynch \'linch\ *vt* : to put to death by mob action without due process of law [*lynch law*] — **lynch·er** *n*

lynch law *n* : the punishment of presumed crimes or offenses usually by death without due process of law [probably from Charles *Lynch,* died 1796, American justice of the peace; from his presiding over an irregular court to suppress Tory activity]

lynx \'lings, 'lingks\ *n, pl* **lynx** *or* **lynx·es** : any of several wildcats with relatively long legs, a short stubby tail, mottled coat, and often tufted ears: as **a** : the common large wildcat of northern Europe and Asia **b** : BOBCAT **c** : a North American cat distinguished from the bobcat by its larger size, longer tufted ears, large padded paws, and wholly black tail tip — called also *Canadian lynx* [Latin, from Greek]

lynx–eyed \'lings-'īd, 'lingks-\ *adj* : having keen sight

ly·on·naise \,lī-ə-'nāz\ *adj* : prepared with onions ⟨*lyonnaise* potatoes⟩ [French *à la lyonnaise* "in the manner of Lyons", from *Lyon* "Lyons, France"]

Ly·ra \'lī-rə\ *n* : a northern constellation containing Vega [Latin, literally, "lyre"]

lyre \'līr\ *n* : a stringed instrument of the harp class used by the ancient Greeks [Old French *lire,* from Latin *lyra,* from Greek]

lyre·bird \'līr-,bərd\ *n* : either of two Australian birds of which the males have very long tail feathers that are arranged during courtship in a way resembling a lyre

¹lyr·ic \'lir-ik\ *adj* **1** : of or relating to a lyre **2 a** : resembling a song in form, feeling, or literary quality **b** : expressing a poet's own feeling **3** : having a light flexible voice ⟨a *lyric* soprano⟩

²lyric *n* **1** : a lyric poem or song **2** *pl* : the words of a song

lyr·i·cal \'lir-i-kəl\ *adj* **1** : resembling a song in mood or expression **2** : unrestrained in expressing enthusiasm, delight, or praise — **lyr·i·cal·ly** \-kə-lē, -klē\ *adv*

lyr·i·cism \'lir-ə-,siz-əm\ *n* **1** : the quality or state of being lyric **2** : an intense personal style or quality in an art (as poetry)

lyr·i·cist \'lir-ə-səst\ *n* : a writer of lyrics

lyr·ist \'līr-əst\ *n* : a lyre player

ly·ser·gic ac·id di·eth·yl·am·ide \lə-,sər-jik-'as-əd-,dī-,eth-ə-'lam-,īd, lī-\ *n* : LSD [*lysergic* from *lysis* + *ergot*]

ly·sin \'līs-n\ *n* : a substance capable of causing lysis; *esp* : an antibody capable of causing disintegration of red blood cells or microorganisms

ly·sine \'lī-,sēn\ *n* : a crystalline basic amino acid that is essential to animal nutrition

ly·sis \'lī-səs\ *n, pl* **ly·ses** \'lī-,sēz\ : a process of disintegration or dissolution; *esp* : disintegration of a bacterium following invasion by a bacteriophage [Greek, "act of loosening, breaking down", from *lyein* "to loosen"] — **lyt·ic** \'lit-ik\ *adj*

-ly·sis \l-ə-səs, 'lī-səs\ *n combining form, pl* **-ly·ses** \-l-ə-,sēz\ : decomposition ⟨electro*lysis*⟩ — **-lyt·ic** \'lit-ik\ *adj combining form*

ly·so·some \'lī-sə-,sōm\ *n* : a saclike cellular organelle that contains hydrolytic enzymes

ly·so·zyme \'lī-sə-,zīm\ *n* : any of various enzymes that destroy the capsules of certain bacteria and include some found in egg white and saliva

-lyze \,līz\ *vb combining form* : produce or undergo lytic disintegration or dissolution ⟨electro*lyze*⟩ [probably derived from *-lysis*]

Mm

m \'em\ *n, pl* **m's** *or* **ms** \'emz\ 1 : the 13th letter of the English alphabet 2 : one thousand in Roman numerals

'm \m\ *vb* : AM ⟨I'*m* going⟩

ma \'mä, 'mȯ\ *n, pl* **mas** : MOTHER [short for *mama*]

ma'am \'mam, *after* "yes" *often* əm\ *n* : MADAM

ma·ca·bre \mə-'käb, -'käb-rə, -'käb-ər, -'käbr\ *adj* 1 : having death as a subject : including a representation of death personified 2 **a** : dwelling on the gruesome **b** : tending to produce horror in a beholder ⟨a *macabre* procession of starving peasants⟩ [French, from *danse macabre* "dance of death", from Middle French *danse de Macabré*]

mac·ad·am \mə-'kad-əm\ *n* : macadamized roadway or pavement especially with a bituminous binder [John L. *McAdam,* died 1836, British engineer]

mac·a·da·mia nut \,mak-ə-'dā-mē-ə-\ *n* : a hard-shelled nut produced by an Australian evergreen tree [John *McAdam,* died 1865, Australian chemist]

mac·ad·am·ize \mə-'kad-ə-,mīz\ *vt* : to construct or surface (as a road) by packing a layer of small broken stone on a well-drained earth roadbed and using a binder for the mass

ma·caque \mə-'kak, -'käk\ *n* : any of several short-tailed monkeys of Asia and the East Indies; *esp* : RHESUS MONKEY [French, from Portuguese *macaco*]

mac·a·ro·ni \,mak-ə-'rō-nē\ *n, pl* **-nis** *or* **-nies** : a food made chiefly of semolina paste dried in the form of slender tubes [Italian *maccheroni,* pl. of *maccherone,* from Italian dialect *maccarone* "dumpling, macaroni"]

mac·a·roon \,mak-ə-'rün\ *n* : a cookie usually made of egg whites, sugar, and ground almonds or coconut [French *macaron,* from Italian dialect *maccarone* "dumpling, small cake, macaroni"]

ma·caw \mə-'kȯ\ *n* : any of numerous parrots of South and Central America including some of the largest and showiest [Portuguese *macau*]

Mac·ca·bees \'mak-ə-,bēz\ *n pl* 1 : a priestly family who led a Jewish revolt against Hellenism and Syrian rule and governed Palestine from 142 B.C. to 63 B.C. 2 — see BIBLE table — **Mac·ca·be·an** \,mak-ə-'bē-ən\ *adj*

Mc·Coy \mə-'kȯi\ *n* : something genuine ⟨the real *Mc-Coy*⟩ [alteration of *Mackay* (in the phrase *the real Mackay,* of unknown origin)]

'mace \'mās\ *n* 1 : a heavy spiked club used as a weapon in the Middle Ages 2 : an ornamental staff borne as a symbol of authority [Middle French]

²mace *n* : a spice consisting of the dried outer fibrous covering of the nutmeg [Middle French *macis,* from Latin *macir,* a kind of spice, from Greek *makir*]

mac·er·ate \'mas-ə-,rāt\ *vb* 1 : to waste away or cause to waste away 2 : to cause to become soft or separated into constituent elements by or as if by steeping [Latin *macerare,* "to soften, steep"] — **mac·er·a·tion** \,mas-ə-'rā-shən\ *n*

Mach \'mäk\ *n* : MACH NUMBER

ma·chete \mə-'shet-ē, -'chet-ē; -'shet\ *n* : a large heavy knife used for cutting sugarcane and underbrush [Spanish]

Ma·chi·a·vel·lian \,mak-ē-ə-'vel-ē-ən, -'vel-yən\ *adj* 1 : of or relating to Niccolò Machiavelli or Machiavellianism 2 : characterized by cunning, deceitfulness, or bad faith — **Machiavellian** *n*

Ma·chi·a·vel·lian·ism \-,iz-əm\ *n* : the political theory of Machiavelli; *esp* : the view that any means however unscrupulous can justifiably be used in achieving political power

mach·i·nate \'mak-ə-,nāt, 'mash-ə-\ *vb* : CONTRIVE, PLOT; *esp* : to plot or scheme to do harm [Latin *machinari,* from *machina* "machine, contrivance"] — **mach·i·na·tor** \-,nāt-ər\ *n*

mach·i·na·tion \,mak-ə-'nā-shən, ,mash-ə-\ *n* : a crafty scheme or plot usually intended to accomplish some evil end — usually used in pl.

'ma·chine \mə-'shēn\ *n* 1 **a** : VEHICLE, CONVEYANCE; *esp* : AUTOMOBILE **b** : a combination of parts that transmit forces, motion, and energy in a way that accomplishes some desired work ⟨a sewing *machine*⟩ **c** : an instrument (as a lever or pulley) designed to transmit or modify the application of power, force, or motion 2 **a** : a person or organization that acts like a machine **b** : a combination of persons acting together for a common end together with the means they use; *esp* : a highly organized political group under the leadership of a boss or a small clique [Middle French, "structure, contrivance", from Latin *machina,* from Greek *mēchanē,* from *mēchos* "means, expedient"] — **ma·chine·like** \-,līk\ *adj*

macaw

\ə\ abut	\ng\ sing
\ər\ further	\ō\ bone
\a\ mat	\ȯ\ saw
\ā\ take	\ȯi\ coin
\ä\ cot, cart	\th\ thin
\aú\ out	\th\ this
\ch\ chin	\ü\ food
\e\ pet	\ú\ foot
\ē\ easy	\y\ yet
\g\ go	\yü\ few
\i\ tip	\yú\ cure
\ī\ life	\zh\ vision
\j\ job	

²**machine** vt : to shape or finish by machine-operated tools — **ma·chin·able** also **ma·chine·able** \-'shē-nə-bəl\ adj

machine gun n : an automatic gun capable of continuous firing — **ma·chine–gun** \mə-'shēn-ˌgən\ vb — **machine gunner** n

machine language n **1** : the set of symbolic instruction codes used to represent operations and data in a machine (as a computer) usually in binary form **2** : ASSEMBLY LANGUAGE

ma·chin·ery \mə-'shēn-rē, -ə-rē\ n **1** : MACHINES ⟨factory machinery⟩ **2** : the working parts of a machine or instrument having moving parts ⟨the machinery of a watch⟩ **3** : the organization or system by which something is done or carried on ⟨the machinery of government⟩

machine–readable adj : directly usable by a computer ⟨machine-readable text⟩

machine shop n : a workshop in which metal articles are machined and assembled

machine tool n : a machine (as a lathe or drill) that is operated by power and is partly or wholly automatic

ma·chin·ist \mə-'shē-nəst\ n : a person who makes or works on machines and engines

ma·chis·mo \mä-'chēz-mō, mə-, -'kēz-, -'kiz-, -'chiz-\ n : a strong sense of masculine pride : an exaggerated awareness and assertion of masculinity [Mexican Spanish, from Spanish macho "male"]

Mach number \'mäk-\ n : a number representing the ratio of the speed of a body to the speed of sound in the surrounding atmosphere ⟨a Mach number of 2 indicates a speed that is twice the speed of sound⟩ [Ernst Mach, died 1916, Austrian physicist]

¹**ma·cho** \'mä-ˌchō\ adj : aggressively virile [Spanish, "male", from Latin masculus]

²**macho** n, pl **machos 1** : MACHISMO **2** : one who exhibits machismo

mack·er·el \'mak-rəl, -ə-rəl\ n, pl **-el** or **-els** : a North Atlantic food fish that is green with blue bars above and silvery below; also : any of various usually small or medium-sized related fishes [Old French makerel]

mackerel

mackerel sky n : a sky covered with rows of clouds resembling the patterns on a mackerel's back

mack·i·naw \'mak-ə-ˌnȯ\ n **1** : a flat-bottomed boat with pointed prow and square stern formerly much used on the upper Great Lakes **2** : a short heavy coat reaching to about mid-thigh [Mackinaw City, Michigan, formerly an Indian trading post]

mack·in·tosh or **mac·in·tosh** \'mak-ən-ˌtäsh\ n, chiefly British : RAINCOAT [Charles Macintosh, died 1843, Scottish chemist and inventor]

Mac·Pher·son strut \mək-'firs-n-, -'fərs-\ n : a component of an automobile suspension consisting of a shock absorber mounted within a coil spring [Earle S. MacPherson, died 1960, American engineer]

macr- or **macro-** combining form : large ⟨macronucleus⟩ [Greek makros "long"]

mac·ro·ceph·a·lous \ˌmak-rō-'sef-ə-ləs\ or **mac·ro·ce·phal·ic** \-sə-'fal-ik\ adj : having or being an exceptionally large head or cranium ⟨a macrocephalic idiot⟩ — **mac·ro·ceph·a·ly** \-'sef-ə-lē\ n

mac·ro·cosm \'mak-rə-ˌkäz-əm\ n : the great world : UNIVERSE [French macrocosme, from Medieval Latin macrocosmos, from Greek makros "long, large" + kosmos "order, universe"] — **mac·ro·cos·mic** \ˌmak-rə-'käz-mik\ adj — **mac·ro·cos·mi·cal·ly** \-mi-kə-lē, -klē\ adv

mac·ro·eco·nom·ics \ˌmak-rō-ek-ə-'näm-iks, -ē-kə-\ n : a study of economics in terms of whole systems especially with reference to general levels of output and income and to the interrelations among sectors of the economy — compare MICROECONOMICS — **mac·ro·eco·nom·ic** \-ik\ adj

mac·ro·ga·mete \ˌmak-rō-gə-'mēt, -'gam-ˌēt\ n : the larger and usually female gamete of an organism with two kinds of gametes — compare MICROGAMETE

mac·ro lens \'mak-ˌrō-\ n : a camera lens designed to focus at very short distances with up to life-size magnification of the image [macr-, from the fact that the focal length is greater than normal]

mac·ro·mol·e·cule \ˌmak-rō-'mäl-i-ˌkyül\ n : a large molecule built up from smaller chemical structures — **mac·ro·mo·lec·u·lar** \ˌmak-rō-mə-'lek-yə-lər\ adj

ma·cron \'māk-ˌrän, 'mak-, -rən\ n : a mark ‾ placed over a vowel (as in \māk\) to show that the vowel is long [Greek makron, from makros "long"]

mac·ro·nu·cle·us \ˌmak-rō-'nü-klē-əs, -'nyü-\ n : a large densely staining nucleus held to exert a major influence over the nutritional activities of most ciliated protozoans

mac·ro·phage \'mak-rə-ˌfāj, -ˌfäzh\ n : a large phagocyte — **mac·ro·phag·ic** \ˌmak-rə-'faj-ik\ adj

mac·ro·scop·ic \ˌmak-rə-'skäp-ik\ adj **1** : large enough to be observed by the naked eye **2** : considered in terms of large units or elements [macr- + -scopic (as in microscopic)] — **mac·ro·scop·i·cal·ly** \-i-kə-lē, -klē\ adv

mac·u·la \'mak-yə-lə\ n, pl **-lae** \-ˌlē, -ˌlī\ also **-las** : an anatomical structure (as the macula lutea) having the form of a spot differentiated from surrounding tissues [Latin, "spot, stain"] — **mac·u·lar** \-lər\ adj

mac·u·la lu·tea \ˌmak-yə-lə-'lüt-ē-ə\ n, pl **mac·u·lae lu·te·ae** \-lē-'lüt-ē-ˌē, -lī-'lüt-ē-ˌī\ : a small yellowish area lying slightly lateral to the center of the retina that constitutes the region of most acute vision — called also yellow spot [New Latin, literally, "yellow spot"]

mac·u·la·tion \ˌmak-yə-'lā-shən\ n : the arrangement of spots and markings on an animal or plant

mac·ule \'mak-ˌyül\ n : a patch of skin altered in color but usually not elevated that is a characteristic feature of various diseases (as smallpox)

mad \'mad\ adj **mad·der; mad·dest 1** : disordered in mind : INSANE **2** : being rash and foolish ⟨a mad promise⟩ **3** : FURIOUS, ENRAGED ⟨a mad bull⟩ **4** : FRANTIC ⟨mad with pain⟩ **5** : carried away by enthusiasm ⟨mad about dancing⟩ **6** : wildly merry ⟨a mad party⟩ **7** : affected with rabies : RABID ⟨a mad dog⟩ [Old English gemǣd] SYN see INSANE — **mad·ly** adv

mad·am \'mad-əm\ n, pl **madams 1** pl **mes·dames** \mā-'däm, -'dam\ — used as a form of respectful address to a high-ranking woman **2** cap — used as a title before the surname of a high-ranking woman and especially before a designation of her rank or office ⟨Madam President⟩ **3** : a woman who runs a brothel [Old French ma dame, literally, "my lady"]

ma·dame \mə-'dam, ma-', before a surname also, ˌmad-əm\ n, pl **mes·dames** \mā-'däm, -'dam\ — used as a courtesy title equivalent to Mrs. for a married woman not of English-speaking nationality [French, from Old French ma dame "my lady"]

mad·cap \'mad-ˌkap\ adj : being impulsive and rash ⟨a madcap scheme⟩ — **madcap** n

mad·den \'mad-n\ vt : to make mad

mad·den·ing \'mad-ning, -n-ing\ adj : that irritates or infuriates ⟨a maddening habit⟩ — **mad·den·ing·ly** \-ning-lē, -n-ing-lē\ adv

mad·der \'mad-ər\ n **1** : a Eurasian herb with spear-shaped leaves, small yellowish flowers followed by berries, and red fleshy roots used to make a dye; also : any of several related plants **2** : madder root or a dye prepared from it [Old English mædere]

mad·ding \'mad-ing\ adj **1** : acting as if mad : FRENZIED ⟨the madding crowd⟩ **2** : MADDENING

made past of MAKE

Ma·dei·ra \mə-'dir-ə, -'der-\ n : an amber-colored dessert wine of the Madeira islands; also : a similar wine made elsewhere

ma·de·moi·selle \ˌmad-mə-'zel, -ə-mə-, -mwə-'zel; mam-'zel\ n, pl **ma·de·moi·selles** \-'zelz\ or **mes·de·moi·selles** \ˌmād-mə-'zel, -ə-mə-, -mwə-'zel\ — used by or to French-speaking people as a courtesy title equivalent to Miss [French, from Old French *ma da-moisele* "my young lady"]

made-up \'mād-əp\ *adj* **1** : marked by the use of make-up ⟨*made-up* eyelids⟩ **2** : fancifully conceived or falsely devised ⟨a *made-up* story⟩ **3** : fully manufactured

mad·house \'mad-ˌhaùs\ *n* **1** : a place where insane persons are detained and treated **2** : a place of uproar or confusion

mad·man \'mad-ˌman, -mən\ *n* : a man who is or acts as if insane

mad·ness \'mad-nəs\ *n* **1** : the quality or state of being mad: as **a** : INSANITY **b** : extreme folly **c** : FURY 1, RAGE **2** : any of several disorders of animals marked by frenzied behavior; *esp* : RABIES

Ma·don·na lily \mə-ˌdän-ə-\ *n* : a white-flowered lily often forced for spring bloom [*Madonna*, the Virgin Mary, from Italian *ma donna* "my lady"]

ma·dras \'mad-rəs; mə-'dras, -'dräs\ *n* : a fine usually corded or striped cotton fabric [*Madras*, India]

mad·ri·gal \'mad-ri-gəl\ *n* **1 a** : a short love poem suitable for a musical setting **b** : a musical setting for a madrigal **2** : a complex 16th century part-song [Italian *madrigale*] — **mad·ri·gal·ist** \-gə-ləst\ *n*

ma·dro·na \mə-'drō-nə\ *n* : an evergreen heath of western North America with shiny leaves and edible red berries [Spanish *madroño*]

mad·wom·an \'mad-ˌwùm-ən\ *n* : a woman who is or acts as if insane

Mae·ce·nas \mi-'sē-nəs\ *n* : a generous patron especially of literature or art [Latin, from Gaius *Maecenas*, died 8 B.C., Roman statesman and patron of literature]

mael·strom \'māl-strəm\ *n* **1** : a whirlpool of great force and violence **2** : something resembling a whirlpool especially in whirling confusion ⟨a *maelstrom* of emotions⟩ [obsolete Dutch, from *malen* "to grind" + *strom* "stream"]

mae·nad \'mē-ˌnad\ *n* **1** : BACCHANTE **2** : an excessively excited or distraught woman [Latin *maenad-, maenas*, from Greek *mained-, mainas*, from *mainesthai* "to be mad"] — **mae·nad·ic** \mē-'nad-ik\ *adj*

mae·sto·so \mī-'stō-sō, -zō\ *adv or adj* : so as to be majestic and stately — used as a direction in music [Italian, from Latin *majestosus*, from *majestas* "majesty"]

mae·stro \'mī-strō\ *n, pl* **mae·stros** \-strōz\ *or* **mae·stri** \-ˌstrē\ : a master in an art; *esp* : an eminent composer, conductor, or teacher of music [Italian, literally, "master", from Latin *magister*]

Mae West \'mā-'west\ *n* : an inflatable life jacket in the form of a collar extending down the chest that was worn by fliers in World War II [*Mae West*, born 1892, American actress noted for her full figure]

Ma·fia \'mäf-ē-ə, 'maf-\ *n* **1** : a secret terrorist society **2** : a secret criminal organization held to control illicit activities (as racketeering) throughout the world [*Mafia, Maffia*, a Sicilian secret criminal society, from Italian]

ma·fi·o·so \ˌmäf-ē-'ō-sō, ˌmaf-, -zō\ *n, pl* **-si** \-sē, -zē\ : a member of a Mafia [Italian, from *Mafia*]

mag·a·zine \'mag-ə-ˌzēn, ˌmag-ə-'\ *n* **1** : STOREHOUSE 1, WAREHOUSE **2** : a place for keeping gunpowder in a fort or ship **3** : a periodical containing miscellaneous stories, articles, or poems **4** : a supply chamber: as **a** : a chamber in a gun for holding cartridges **b** : a chamber for film on a camera or motion-picture projector [Middle French *magazin*, from Provençal, from Arabic *makhāzin*, pl. of *makhzan* "storehouse"]

ma·gen·ta \mə-'jent-ə\ *n* **1** : FUCHSINE **2** : a deep purplish red [*Magenta*, Italy]

mag·got \'mag-ət\ *n* **1** : a soft-bodied legless grub that is the larva of a two-winged fly (as the housefly) **2** : an odd or fantastic idea : WHIM [of Scandinavian origin; sense 2 from the suggestion that a whim might be the

result of a maggot in the brain] — **mag·goty** \-ət-ē\ *adj*

ma·gi \'mā-ˌjī\ *n pl, often cap* : the three wise men from the East who paid homage to the infant Jesus [Latin, pl. of *magus* "Persian wise man, magician", from Greek *magos*]

¹mag·ic \'maj-ik\ *n* **1** : the art of persons who claim to be able to do things by the help of supernatural creatures or by their own knowledge of nature's secrets **2 a** : something that charms ⟨the *magic* of your smile⟩ **b** : seemingly hidden or secret power ⟨the *magic* of a great name⟩ **3** : SLEIGHT OF HAND 1 [Middle French *magique*, from Latin *magice*, from Greek *magikos* "magical", from *magos* "Persian wise man, magician, sorcerer", of Iranian origin]

²magic *adj* **1** : of or relating to magic **2 a** : having seemingly supernatural qualities or powers **b** : ENCHANTING — **mag·i·cal** \'maj-i-kəl\ *adj* — **mag·i·cal·ly** \-kə-lē, -klē\ *adv*

magic bullet *n* : a substance or therapy capable of destroying pathogenic agents (as cancer cells) without harmful side effects

ma·gi·cian \mə-'jish-ən\ *n* **1** : a person skilled in magic; *esp* : SORCERER **2** : a performer of sleight of hand

magic lantern *n* : an early type of slide projector

magic square *n* : a square containing a number of integers so arranged that the sum of the numbers in each row, column, and diagonal is always the same

mag·is·te·ri·al \ˌmaj-ə-'stir-ē-əl\ *adj* **1** : AUTHORITATIVE 3 **2** : of or relating to a magistrate or magistracy [Late Latin *magisterialis* "of authority", derived from Latin *magister* "master"] — **mag·is·te·ri·al·ly** \-ē-ə-lē\ *adv*

mag·is·tra·cy \'maj-ə-strə-sē\ *n, pl* **-cies** **1** : the state of being a magistrate **2** : the office, power, or dignity of a magistrate **3** : a body of magistrates

ma·gis·tral \'maj-ə-strəl, mə-'jis-trəl\ *adj* : MAGISTERIAL 1 — **ma·gis·tral·ly** \-ē\ *adv*

mag·is·trate \'maj-ə-ˌstrāt, -strət\ *n* : an official entrusted with administration of the laws: as **a** : a principal official exercising executive powers over a major political unit **b** : a local official exercising administrative and often judicial functions **c** : a local judiciary official having jurisdiction in some criminal cases [Latin *magistratus* "magistracy, magistrate", from *magister* "master"]

mag·ma \'mag-mə\ *n* : molten rock material within the earth from which an igneous rock results by cooling [Latin *magmat-, magma* "dregs, sediment", from Greek, "pasty substance", from *massein* "to knead"] — **mag·mat·ic** \mag-'mat-ik\ *adj*

Mag·na Char·ta *or* **Mag·na Car·ta** \ˌmag-nə-'kärt-ə\ *n* **1** : a charter of civil liberties to which the English barons forced King John to give his assent in June 1215 at Runnymede **2** : a document constituting a fundamental guarantee of rights and privileges [Medieval Latin, literally, "great charter"]

mag·na cum lau·de \ˌmäg-nə-ˌkùm-'laùd-ə, -'laùd-ē; ˌmag-nə-ˌkəm-'lòd-ē\ *adv or adj* : with great academic distinction ⟨graduated *magna cum laude*⟩ [Latin, "with great praise"]

mag·na·nim·i·ty \ˌmag-nə-'nim-ət-ē\ *n, pl* **-ties** **1 a** : nobility of character : HIGH-MINDEDNESS **b** : GENEROSITY 1 **2** : a magnanimous act

mag·nan·i·mous \mag-'nan-ə-məs\ *adj* **1** : showing or suggesting a lofty and courageous spirit : NOBLE **2** : free of all meanness or pettiness [Latin *magnanimus*, from *magnus* "great" + *animus* "spirit"] — **mag·nan·i·mous·ly** *adv* — **mag·nan·i·mous·ness** *n*

mag·nate \'mag-ˌnāt, -nət\ *n* : a person of rank, power, influence, or distinction (as in an industry) [Late Latin *magnates*, pl., from Latin *magnus* "great"]

mag·ne·sia \mag-'nē-shə, -'nē-zhə\ *n* **1** : a white highly infusible earthy solid MgO that consists of magnesium and oxygen and is used in refractories, fertilizers, and rubber and as an antacid and mild laxative **2** :

magic square

\ə\ abut   \ng\ sing
\ər\ further   \ō\ bone
\a\ mat   \ȯ\ saw
\ā\ take   \ȯi\ coin
\ä\ cot, cart   \th\ thin
\aù\ out   \t̷h\ this
\ch\ chin   \ü\ food
\e\ pet   \ù\ foot
\ē\ easy   \y\ yet
\g\ go   \yü\ few
\i\ tip   \yù\ cure
\ī\ life   \zh\ vision
\j\ job

MAGNESIUM [New Latin, from *magnes carneus*, a white earth, literally, "flesh magnet"] — **mag·ne·sian** \-shən, -zhən\ *adj*

mag·ne·sium \mag-'nē-zē-əm, -zhəm\ *n* : a silver-white metallic element that is lighter than aluminum, is easily worked, burns with a dazzling light, and is used in making lightweight alloys — see ELEMENT table [New Latin, from *magnesia*]

magnesium chloride *n* : a bitter salt $MgCl_2$ found in seawater and used in producing magnesium metal

magnesium hydroxide *n* : a weakly alkaline compound used especially as a laxative and an antacid

magnesium sulfate *n* : any of several sulfates of magnesium; *esp* : EPSOM SALT

mag·net \'mag-nət\ *n* 1 : a piece of some material (as the mineral iron oxide) that is able to attract iron; *esp* : a mass of iron or steel so treated that it has this property 2 : something that attracts ⟨the *magnet* of fame⟩ [Middle French *magnete*, from Latin *magnes*, from Greek *magnēs lithos*, literally, "stone of Magnesia (ancient city in Asia Minor)"]

magnet- *or* **magneto-** *combining form* : magnetism : magnetic ⟨*magneto*electric⟩

mag·net·ic \mag-'net-ik\ *adj* 1 : of or relating to a magnet or magnetism 2 : of or relating to the earth's magnetism ⟨the *magnetic* meridian⟩ 3 : capable of being magnetized 4 : working by magnetic attraction 5 : gifted with great power to attract ⟨a *magnetic* personality⟩ — **mag·net·i·cal·ly** \-'net-i-kə-lē, -klē\ *adv*

magnetic bubble *n* : a tiny movable magnetized cylindrical volume in a thin amorphous or cystalline magnetic material that along with other like volumes can be used to represent a bit of information (as in a computer)

magnetic disk *n* : ¹DISK 3c

magnetic field *n* : the portion of space near a magnetic body or a body carrying an electric current within which magnetic forces due to the body or current can be detected

magnetic needle *n* : a narrow strip of magnetized steel that is free to swing horizontally or vertically to show the direction of the earth's magnetism and that is the essential part of a compass

magnetic north *n* : the northerly direction in the earth's magnetic field indicated by the north-seeking pole of a horizontal magnetic needle

magnetic pole *n* 1 : either of the poles of a magnet 2 : either of two small regions which are located respectively in the polar areas of the northern and southern hemispheres and toward which a compass needle points

magnetic resonance *n* : the response of electrons, atoms, molecules, or nuclei to various discrete radiation frequencies as a result of space quantization in a magnetic field

magnetic resonance imaging *n* : a diagnostic technique that produces computerized images of internal body tissues and is based on nuclear magnetic resonance of atoms within the body induced by the application of radio waves

magnetic storm *n* : a marked temporary disturbance of the earth's magnetic field held to be related to sunspots

magnetic tape *n* : a thin ribbon (as of plastic) coated with a magnetic material on which information (as sound or television images) may be stored

mag·ne·tism \'mag-nə-ˌtiz-əm\ *n* 1 a : the property of attracting certain metals or producing a magnetic field as shown by a magnet, a magnetized material, or a conductor carrying an electric current b : the science that deals with magnetic occurrences or conditions 2 : the power to attract or charm others

mag·ne·tite \'mag-nə-ˌtīt\ *n* : a black mineral Fe_3O_4 that is an oxide of iron, is strongly attracted by a magnet, and is an important iron ore

mag·ne·tize \'mag-nə-ˌtīz\ *vt* 1 : to attract like a magnet : CHARM 2 : to give magnetic properties to — **mag·ne·tiz·able** \-ˌtī-zə-bəl\ *adj* — **mag·ne·ti·za·tion** \ˌmag-nət-ə-'zā-shən\ *n* — **mag·ne·tiz·er** \'mag-nə-ˌtī-zər\ *n*

mag·ne·to \mag-'nēt-ō\ *n, pl* **-tos** : a small electric generator using permanent magnets; *esp* : one used to produce sparks in an internal-combustion engine [short for *magnetoelectric machine*]

mag·ne·to·elec·tric \mag-ˌnēt-ō-ə-'lek-trik\ *adj* : relating to electromotive forces developed by magnetic means ⟨*magnetoelectric* induction⟩

mag·ne·tom·e·ter \ˌmag-nə-'täm-ət-ər\ *n* : an instrument for measuring magnetic intensity especially of the earth's magnetic field

mag·ne·to·sphere \mag-'nēt-ə-ˌsfiər, -'net-\ *n* : a region of the upper atmosphere that extends out for thousands of kilometers and is dominated by the earth's magnetic field so that charged particles are trapped in it; *also* : a region surrounding a celestial body that is comparable to the earth's magnetosphere

mag·ne·to·stric·tion \mag-ˌnēt-ō-'strik-shən, -ˌnet-\ *n* : the change in the dimensions of various magnetic bodies caused by a change in their state of magnetization [*magnet-* + *-striction* (as in *constriction*)] — **mag·ne·to·stric·tive** \-'strik-tiv\ *adj*

magnet school *n* : a school with superior facilities and staff designed to attract pupils from all segments of the community

Mag·nif·i·cat \mag-'nif-i-ˌkat, -ˌkät; män-'yif-i-ˌkät\ *n* : the canticle of the Virgin Mary in Luke 1:46-55 [Latin, "magnifies", its first word]

mag·ni·fi·ca·tion \ˌmag-nə-fə-'kā-shən\ *n* 1 : the act of magnifying : the state of being magnified 2 : the apparent enlargement of an object by an optical instrument

mag·nif·i·cence \mag-'nif-ə-səns\ *n* : the quality or state of being magnificent : SPLENDOR, GRANDEUR [Middle French, from Latin *magnificentia*, from *magnificus* "noble, magnificent", from *magnus* "great" + *-ficus* "-fic"]

mag·nif·i·cent \-sənt\ *adj* 1 : having grandeur and beauty : SPLENDID ⟨*magnificent* palaces⟩ ⟨a *magnificent* view⟩ 2 : NOBLE 5 SYN see GRAND — **mag·nif·i·cent·ly** *adv*

mag·nif·i·co \mag-'nif-i-ˌkō\ *n, pl* **-coes** *or* **-cos** 1 : a nobleman of Venice 2 : a person of high position [Italian, from *magnifico* "magnificent", from Latin *magnificus*]

mag·ni·fy \'mag-nə-ˌfī\ *vb* **-fied; -fy·ing** 1 : EXTOL, LAUD 2 : to enlarge in fact or appearance ⟨a microscope *magnifies* an object seen through it⟩ 3 : to exaggerate in importance ⟨*magnify* a fault⟩ [Middle French *magnifier*, from Latin *magnificare*, from *magnificus* "great, magnificent"] — **mag·ni·fi·er** \-ˌfī-ər, -ˌfīr\ *n*

mag·ni·fy·ing glass *n* : a lens that magnifies an object seen through it

mag·ni·tude \'mag-nə-ˌtüd, -ˌtyüd\ *n* 1 a : greatness especially in size or extent b : spatial quality : SIZE 2 : greatness in influence or effect 3 : degree of brightness; *esp* : a number representing the relative brightness of a star on a scale on which the lowest number represents the brightest star [Latin *magnitudo*, from *magnus* "large"]

mag·no·lia \mag-'nōl-yə\ *n* : any of a genus of North American and Asian shrubs and trees with usually showy white, yellow, rose, or purple flowers appearing in early spring [Pierre *Magnol*, died 1715, French botanist]

mag·num opus \ˌmag-nə-'mō-pəs\ *n* : a great work; *esp* : a literary or artistic masterpiece [Latin]

mag·pie \'mag-ˌpī\ *n* 1 : any of numerous noisy birds related to the jays but having a long tapered tail and black-and-white plumage 2 : a person who chatters constantly [*Mag* (nickname for *Margaret*) + ¹*pie*]

magnolia

ma·guey \mə-'gā\ *n, pl* **magueys** 1 : any of various fleshy-leaved agaves or closely related fiber-yielding plants 2 : any of several hard fibers derived from magueys [Spanish, of American Indian origin]

Mag·yar \'mag-ˌyär, 'mäg-; 'mäj-ˌär\ *n* 1 : a member of the dominant people of Hungary 2 : the language of the Magyars — called also *Hungarian* [Hungarian] — **Magyar** *adj*

ma·ha·ra·ja *or* **ma·ha·ra·jah** \ˌmä-hə-'räj-ə, -'räzh-ə\ *n* : a Hindu prince ranking above a raja [Sanskrit *mahārāja*, from *mahat* "great" + *rājan* "raja"]

ma·ha·ra·ni *or* **ma·ha·ra·nee** \-'rän-ē\ *n* 1 : the wife of a maharaja 2 : a Hindu princess ranking above a rani [Hindi *mahārānī*, from *mahā* "great" (from Sanskrit *mahat*) + *rānī* "rani"]

ma·hat·ma \mə-'hät-mə, -'hat-\ *n* : a person revered for high-mindedness, wisdom, and selflessness — used as a title of honor especially by Hindus [Sanskrit *mahātman*, from *mahat* "great" + *ātman* "soul"]

Ma·hi·can *variant of* MOHICAN

mah-jongg \mäzh-'äng, mäj-, -'òng\ *n* : a game of Chinese origin for 4 players that is played with usually 144 tiles [from *Mah-Jongg*, a former trademark]

ma·hog·a·ny \mə-'häg-ə-nē\ *n, pl* **-nies** 1 : the wood of any of various chiefly tropical trees: as **a** : the durable usually reddish brown and moderately hard and heavy wood of a West Indian tree that is widely used for cabinetwork **b** : any of several African woods that vary in color from pinkish to deep reddish brown 2 : any of various woods resembling or substituted for true mahogany 3 : a tree that yields mahogany 4 : a moderate reddish brown [origin unknown]

ma·ho·nia \mə-'hō-nē-ə\ *n* : any of a genus of shrubs of the barberry family including one grown for its showy evergreen leaves that resemble holly [Bernard *McMahon*, died 1816, American botanist]

ma·hout \mə-'haut\ *n* : a keeper and driver of an elephant [Hindi *mahāut*]

maid \'mād\ *n* 1 : an unmarried girl or woman; *esp* : MAIDEN 2 : a female servant [Middle English *maide*, short for *maiden*]

¹maid·en \'mād-n\ *n* : a young unmarried girl or woman [Old English *mægden, mēden*] — **maid·en·hood** \-ˌhud\ *n* — **maid·en·li·ness** \-lē-nəs\ *n* — **maid·en·ly** \-lē\ *adj*

²maiden *adj* 1 **a** : not married ⟨my *maiden* aunt⟩ **b** : VIRGIN 1 2 : of, relating to, or befitting a maiden 3 : FIRST, EARLIEST ⟨the ship's *maiden* voyage⟩ 4 : INTACT, FRESH

maid·en·hair \'mād-n-ˌhaər, -ˌheər\ *n* : any of a genus of ferns with slender stems and delicate much-divided often feathery leaves — called also *maidenhair fern*

maidenhair tree *n* : GINKGO

maid·en·head \'mād-n-ˌhed\ *n* : HYMEN [Middle English *maidenhed* "maidenhood, virginity", from *maiden* + *-hed* "-hood"]

maiden name *n* : the surname of a woman before she is married

maid of honor 1 : an unmarried woman usually of noble birth who attends a queen or princess 2 : a bride's principal unmarried wedding attendant

maid·ser·vant \'mād-ˌsər-vənt\ *n* : a female servant

¹mail \'māl\ *n* 1 : matter (as letters or parcels) sent under public authority from one person to another through the post office 2 : the whole system used in the public sending and delivery of letters and parcels ⟨do business by *mail*⟩ 3 : something that comes in the mail; *esp* : the contents of a single delivery 4 : a conveyance that transports mail [Middle English *male* "bag", from Old French, of Germanic origin]

²mail *vt* : to send by mail : POST — **mail·able** \'mā-lə-bəl\ *adj* — **mail·er** *n*

³mail *n* : a flexible network of small metal rings linked together for use as armor ⟨a coat of *mail*⟩ [Middle French *maille*, from Latin *macula* "spot, mesh"] — **mailed** \'māld\ *adj*

mail·box \'māl-ˌbäks\ *n* 1 : a public box for the collection of mail 2 : a private box for the delivery of mail

mail carrier *n* : LETTER CARRIER

mail·man \'māl-ˌman\ *n* : LETTER CARRIER

mail order *n* : an order for goods that is received and filled by mail — **mail-order** \'māl-ˌòrd-ər\ *adj*

mail-order house *n* : a retail establishment whose business is conducted by mail

maim \'mām\ *vt* : to mutilate, disfigure, or wound seriously : CRIPPLE [Old French *maynier*] — **maim·er** *n*

¹main \'mān\ *n* 1 : physical strength : FORCE — used in the phrase *with might and main* 2 **a** : MAINLAND **b** : HIGH SEAS 3 : a principal pipe, duct, or circuit of a utility system ⟨gas *main*⟩ 4 **a** : MAINMAST **b** : MAINSAIL [Old English *mægen*] — **in the main** : for the most part

²main *adj* 1 : CHIEF 2, PRINCIPAL 2 : fully exerted : SHEER ⟨by *main* force⟩ 3 : connected with or located near the mainmast or mainsail 4 : being a clause that is capable of standing alone as a simple sentence but actually is part of a larger sentence that includes also a subordinate clause or another main clause

main·frame \'mān-ˌfräm\ *n* : a large fast computer that can do many jobs at once

main·land \'mān-ˌland, -lənd\ *n* : a continent or the main part of a continent as distinguished from an off-shore island or sometimes from a cape or a peninsula — **main·land·er** \-ər\ *n*

main·line \'mān-'līn\ *vi, slang* : to inject a narcotic drug (as heroin) into a principal vein

main·ly \'mān-lē\ *adv* : forthe most part : CHIEFLY

main·mast \'mān-ˌmast, -məst\ *n* : the principal mast of a sailing ship

main·sail \'mān-ˌsāl, 'mān-səl\ *n* : the principal sail on the mainmast

main·spring \-ˌspring\ *n* 1 : the principal spring in a mechanism especially of a watch or clock 2 : the chief motive, cause, or force underlying or causing an action

main·stay \-ˌstā\ *n* 1 : a forward stay which helps support the mainmast of a ship 2 : a chief support

main·stream \'mān-ˌstrēm\ *n* : a general movement or direction of activity or influence

main·tain \mān-'tān, mən-\ *vt* 1 : to keep in an existing state; *esp* : to keep in good condition ⟨*maintain* one's health⟩ ⟨*maintain* machinery⟩ 2 : to uphold and defend against opposition or danger ⟨*maintain* a position⟩ 3 : to continue in : keep up ⟨*maintain* one's balance⟩ ⟨*maintain* one's composure⟩ 4 **a** : to provide for : SUPPORT ⟨*maintain* their family by working⟩ **b** : SUSTAIN ⟨enough food to *maintain* life⟩ 5 : to affirm in or as if in argument : ASSERT ⟨*maintained* that the earth is flat⟩ [Old French *maintenir*, from Latin *manu tenēre* "to hold in the hand"] — **main·tain·able** \-'tā-nə-bəl\ *adj* — **main·tain·er** *n* □ SYN MAINTAIN, ASSERT, VINDICATE, JUSTIFY mean to uphold as true, right, or just. MAINTAIN stresses firmness of conviction; ASSERT suggests vigor of statement and determination to make others accept one's claim; VINDICATE implies successfully defending what was under question or attack; JUSTIFY implies showing to be true or valid especially by appeal to a standard or to precedent.

main·te·nance \'mānt-nəns, -n-əns\ *n* 1 : the act of maintaining : the state of being maintained 2 : something that maintains or supports; *esp* : a supply of necessities and conveniences 3 : the upkeep of property or machinery ⟨workers in charge of *maintenance*⟩

maî·tre d'hô·tel \ˌmā-trə-dō-'tel\ *n, pl* **maîtres d'hôtel** *same*\ 1 : MAJORDOMO 2 : HEADWAITER [French, literally, "master of house"]

maize \'māz\ *n* : INDIAN CORN [Spanish *maíz*, of American Indian origin]

ma·jes·tic \mə-'jes-tik\ *adj* : being stately and dignified : NOBLE SYN see GRAND — **ma·jes·ti·cal·ly** \-ti-kə-lē, -klē\ *adv*

\ə\ abut		\ng\ sing	
\ər\ further		\ō\ bone	
\a\ mat		\ò\ saw	
\ā\ take		\òi\ coin	
\ä\ cot, cart		\th\ thin	
\au\ out		\th\ this	
\ch\ chin		\ü\ food	
\e\ pet		\u\ foot	
\ē\ easy		\y\ yet	
\g\ go		\yü\ few	
\i\ tip		\yu\ cure	
\ī\ life		\zh\ vision	
\j\ job			

maj·es·ty \'maj-ə-stē\ *n, pl* **-ties** **1 a** : sovereign power, authority, or dignity **b** *cap* — used as a form of address for reigning sovereigns and their consorts ⟨His *Majesty* King George⟩ ⟨Her *Majesty* Queen Elizabeth⟩ **2 a** : royal bearing or quality : GRANDEUR **b** : greatness of quality or character [Old French *majesté*, from Latin *majestas*]

¹ma·jor \'mā-jər\ *adj* **1 a** : greater in dignity, rank, or importance ⟨a *major* poet⟩ **b** : greater in number, quantity, or extent ⟨the *major* part of the blame⟩ **2** : having attained majority **3** : involving risk to life : SERIOUS ⟨a *major* illness⟩ **4** : of or relating to an academic major **5 a** : having half steps between the 3d and 4th and the 7th and 8th degrees ⟨a *major* scale⟩ **b** : based on a major scale ⟨a *major* key⟩ ⟨a *major* chord⟩ [Latin, comparative of *magnus* "great, large"]

²major *n* **1** : a major musical interval, scale, key, or mode **2** : an officer rank in the Army, Marine Corps, and Air Force above captain and below lieutenant colonel **3** : an academic subject chosen by a student as a field of specialization

³major *vi* **ma·jored; ma·jor·ing** \'māj-ring, -ə-ring\ : to pursue an academic major

ma·jor·do·mo \,mā-jər-'dō-mō\ *n, pl* **-mos** : a man in charge of a great household and especially of a royal establishment [Spanish *mayordomo* or obsolete Italian *maiordomo*, from Medieval Latin *major domus*, literally, "chief of the house"]

ma·jor·ette \,mā-jə-'ret\ *n* : DRUM MAJORETTE

major general *n* : an officer rank in the Army, Marine Corps, and Air Force above brigadier general and below lieutenant general

ma·jor·i·ty \mə-'jȯr-ət-ē, -'jär-\ *n, pl* **-ties** **1 a** : the age at which one is given full civil rights **b** : the status of one who has attained this age **2 a** : a number greater than half of a total **b** : the amount by which such a greater number exceeds the smaller number ⟨won by a *majority* of seven⟩ **c** : the greater part or share ⟨the *majority* of our fuel is imported⟩ **3** : the group or party that makes up the greater part of a whole body of persons **4** : the military office or rank of a major ☐ SYN MAJORITY, PLURALITY mean a winning margin of votes. MAJORITY specifically refers to the number in excess of half of all the votes cast ⟨270 votes gave the winner a *majority* of 20 out of the total of 500 votes⟩ PLURALITY refers to the number that is in excess of those of the nearest rival but may not be more than half of the total votes cast.

majority rule *n* : a political principle providing that a majority of an organized group shall have the power to make decisions binding upon the whole group

major league *n* : a league in the highest class of United States professional baseball; *also* : a league of major importance in another sport (as hockey)

major order *n* **1** : the order of priest or deacon in the Roman Catholic Church **2** : the order of bishop, priest, or deacon in the Eastern or Anglican Church

major penalty *n* : a 5-minute suspension of a player in ice hockey

major suit *n* : hearts or spades in bridge

¹make \'māk\ *vb* **made** \'mād\; **mak·ing** **1 a** : to seem to begin an action ⟨*made* as if to go⟩ **b** : to act so as to appear ⟨*make* merry⟩ **2 a** : to cause to exist or occur : CREATE ⟨*make* a disturbance⟩ ⟨*made* trouble for us⟩ **b** : to create for some purpose or goal ⟨they were *made* for each other⟩ **3 a** : to form or shape out of material or parts : FASHION, BUILD ⟨*make* a dress⟩ ⟨*make* a table⟩ **b** : to comprise or become combined into a whole : CONSTITUTE ⟨a house *made* of stone⟩ **4** : to frame or formulate in the mind ⟨*make* plans⟩ **5 a** : ESTIMATE 1, COMPUTE ⟨I *make* it an even $5⟩ **b** : UNDERSTAND ⟨unable to *make* anything of the story⟩ **6** : to set in order : PREPARE ⟨*make* a bed⟩ **7** : to cut and spread for drying ⟨*make* hay⟩ **8** : to cause to be or become ⟨*make* oneself useful⟩ **9 a** : ENACT, ESTABLISH ⟨*make* laws⟩ **b** : to

execute in an appropriate manner ⟨*make* a will⟩ **c** : SET, NAME ⟨*make* clubs trump⟩ **10** : to complete an electric circuit **11 a** : to carry out a specific action ⟨*make* war⟩ ⟨*make* a curtsy⟩ **b** : FOLLOW, TRAVERSE ⟨*make* one's rounds⟩ **12** : to produce by action or effort spent on something ⟨*made* a mess of the job⟩ **13** : to cause to act in some manner : COMPEL ⟨*made* them return home⟩ **14** : to cause or assure the success of ⟨the first case *makes* or breaks a lawyer⟩ **15** : to amount to in significance ⟨it *makes* a great difference⟩ **16** : REACH, ATTAIN ⟨the ship *makes* port tonight⟩ **17 a** : to gain by or as if by working ⟨*makes* good money at the foundry⟩ **b** : to acquire by effort ⟨*makes* friends easily⟩ **c** : to score in a game or sport ⟨*make* a point after a touchdown⟩ **18 a** : CATCH ⟨*make* the train⟩ **b** : to set out in pursuit ⟨*made* after the fox⟩ [Old English *macian* "to form, construct, do, act"] — **make a mountain out of a molehill** : to treat something unimportant as a matter of great importance — **make away with** : to carry off — **make believe** : FEIGN, PRETEND — **make do** : to get along with the means at hand — **make fun of** : to make an object of amusement or laughter — **make good** **1** : to make complete : FULFILL ⟨*make good* a promise⟩ **2** : to make up for a deficiency ⟨*make good* the loss⟩ **3** : SUCCEED ⟨*made good* as a photographer⟩ — **make it** : to be successful ⟨trying to *make it* as an actor⟩ — **make time** **1** : to travel fast **2** : to gain time — **make way** **1** : to open or give room for passing or entering ⟨the crowd *made way* for the police⟩ **2** : to make progress

²make *n* **1** : the way in which a thing is made : manner of construction ⟨the *make* was so poor the chair fell apart⟩ **2** : the type or process of making or manufacturing ⟨the latest *make* of car⟩

¹make–be·lieve \'māk-bə-,lēv\ *n* : a pretending to believe (as in the play of children) : PRETENSE

²make–believe *adj* : PRETENDED, IMAGINARY ⟨a *make-believe* playmate⟩

make out *vb* **1** : to draw up in writing ⟨*make out* a shopping list⟩ **2** : to find or grasp the meaning of : UNDERSTAND ⟨couldn't *make out* what was going on⟩ **3** : to represent as being ⟨*made* them *out* to be heroes⟩ **4** : to see and identify with difficulty or effort ⟨*make out* a form in the fog⟩ **5** : SUCCEED, PROSPER ⟨*make out* well in business⟩ **6** : to engage in kissing and petting

make over *vt* **1** : to transfer the title of : CONVEY **2** : REMAKE, REMODEL

mak·er \'mā-kər\ *n* : one that makes: as **a** *cap* : GOD **1** **b** : a person who makes a promissory note **c** : MANUFACTURER

make·ready \'mā-,kred-ē\ *n* : final preparation (as of a form on a printing press) for running

make·shift \'māk-,shift\ *n* : a temporary replacement : SUBSTITUTE — **makeshift** *adj*

make·up \'mā-,kəp\ *n* **1** : the way the parts or elements of somthing are put together : COMPOSITION ⟨last-minute changes in the *makeup* of the book⟩ **2** : materials (as wigs or cosmetics) used in making up ⟨put on *makeup* for a play⟩

make up \mā-'kəp, 'mā-\ *vb* **1 a** : INVENT, CONCOCT ⟨*make up* a story⟩ **b** : to combine to produce a whole : COMPRISE ⟨nine players *make up* a team⟩ **2** : to form by fitting together or assembling **3** : to compensate for a deficiency **4** : to become reconciled ⟨they quarreled and *made up*⟩ **5** : SETTLE, DECIDE ⟨*made up* their minds to sell the house⟩ **6 a** : to put on costumes or makeup (as for a play) **b** : to apply cosmetics

mak·ing \'mā-king\ *n* **1** : the action of one that makes **2** : a process or means of advancement or success ⟨misfortune is sometimes the *making* of a person⟩ **3** : material from which something can be developed ⟨there is the *making* of a racehorse in this colt⟩ **4** *for cigarette materials usually* 'mā-kənz\ *pl* : the materials from which something can be made ⟨roll a cigarette from the *makings*⟩

mal- *combining form* **1** : bad : badly ⟨*mal*odorous⟩ ⟨*mal*practice⟩ **2** : abnormal : abnormally ⟨*mal*formation⟩ [Middle French, from *mal* "bad", from Latin *malus*]

See *mal-* and 2d element

malabsorption	maladaptive	malapportionment
maladaptation	maladminister	maldistribution
maladapted	maladministration	malposition

Mal·a·chi \'mal-ə-ˌkī\ *n* — see BIBLE table

mal·a·chite \'mal-ə-ˌkīt\ *n* : a green mineral $Cu_2CO_3(OH)_2$ that consists of copper, carbon, oxygen, and hydrogen and is used as an ore of copper and for ornamental objects [Latin *molochites*, from Greek *molochītēs*, from *molochē* "mallow"]

mal·a·col·o·gy \ˌmal-ə-'käl-ə-jē\ *n* : a branch of zoology dealing with mollusks [French *malacologie*, derived from Greek *malakos* "soft"] — **mal·a·col·o·gist** \-jəst\ *n*

mal·ad·just·ed \ˌmal-ə-'jəs-təd\ *adj* : poorly or inadequately adjusted; *esp* : lacking harmony with one's environment — **mal·ad·just·ment** \-'jəst-mənt, -'jəs-\ *n*

mal·adroit \ˌmal-ə-'drȯit\ *adj* : not adroit : AWKWARD, CLUMSY — **mal·adroit·ly** *adv* — **mal·adroit·ness** *n*

mal·a·dy \'mal-əd-ē\ *n, pl* **-dies** : a disease or disorder of the body or mind : AILMENT [Old French *maladie*, from *malade* "sick", from Latin *male habitus* "in bad condition"]

Mal·a·gasy \ˌmal-ə-'gas-ē\ *n* **1** : a native or inhabitant of Madagascar or the Malagasy Republic **2** : the language of the Malagasy people — **Malagasy** *adj*

mal·aise \mə-'lāz, ma-; ma-'lez\ *n* : a vague feeling of bodily or mental disorder [French, from *mal-* + *aise* "ease, comfort"]

mal·a·mute *or* **mal·e·mute** \'mal-ə-ˌmyüt\ *n* : a sled dog of northern North America; *esp* : ALASKAN MALAMUTE [*Malemute*, an Alaskan Eskimo people]

mal·a·pert \ˌmal-ə-'pərt\ *adj* : impudently bold : SAUCY [Middle French, "unskillful", from *mal-* + *apert* "skillful", from Latin *expertus* "expert"] — **mal·a·pert·ly** *adv* — **mal·a·pert·ness** *n*

mal·a·prop·ism \'mal-ə-ˌpräp-ˌiz-əm\ *n* **1** : a usually humorous misuse of a word especially for one of similar sound by someone unaware of the error **2** : an example of malapropism [Mrs. *Malaprop*, character in Sheridan's *The Rivals* (1775) given to misusing words] — **mal·a·prop** \-ˌpräp\ *or* **mal·a·prop·ian** \ˌmal-ə-'präp-ē-ən\ *adj*

mal·ap·ro·pos \ˌmal-ˌap-rə-'pō\ *adv* : in an inappropriate or inopportune way [French *mal à propos*] — **mal·apropos** *adj*

ma·lar \'mā-lər, -ˌlär\ *adj* : of or relating to the cheek or the side of the head [Latin *mala* "jawbone, cheek"]

ma·lar·ia \mə-'ler-ē-ə\ *n* : a disease caused by protozoan parasites in the red blood cells, transmitted by the bite of mosquitoes, and characterized by periodic attacks of chills and fever [Italian, from *mala aria* "bad air"] — **ma·lar·i·al** \-ē-əl\ *adj* — **ma·lar·i·ous** \-ē-əs\ *adj*

ma·lar·key \mə-'lär-kē\ *n* : insincere or foolish talk [origin unknown]

mal·a·thi·on \ˌmal-ə-'thī-ən, -ˌän\ *n* : a pesticide $C_{10}H_{19}O_6PS_2$ that is less toxic to mammals than parathion and is used against insects and mites [from *Malathion*, a former trademark]

Ma·lay \mə-'lā, 'mā-ˌlā\ *n* **1** : a member of a people of the Malay peninsula and adjacent islands **2** : the language of the Malay people [obsolete Dutch *Malayo*, from Malay *Mĕlayu*] — **Malay** *adj* — **Ma·lay·an** \mə-'lā-ən, 'mā-ˌlā\ *adj or n*

mal·con·tent \ˌmal-kən-'tent\ *adj* : dissatisfied with the existing state of affairs — **malcontent** *n*

mal de mer \ˌmal-də-'meər\ *n* : SEASICKNESS [French]

¹male \'māl\ *adj* **1 a** : of, relating to, or being the sex that fathers young **b** : STAMINATE; *esp* : having only staminate flowers and not producing fruit or seeds ⟨a *male* holly⟩ **2 a** : of, relating to, or characteristic of the male sex ⟨a deep *male* voice⟩ **b** : made up of males ⟨a *male* choir⟩ **3** : designed for fitting into a corresponding hollow part [Middle French, from Latin *masculus*, from *mas* "male"] — **male·ness** *n*

²male *n* : a male plant or animal

mal·e·dic·tion \ˌmal-ə-'dik-shən\ *n* : a prayer for harm to befall someone : CURSE [Late Latin *maledictio*, from *maledicere* "to curse", from Latin, "to speak evil of", from *male* "badly" + *dicere* "to say"] — **mal·e·dic·to·ry** \-'dik-tə-rē, -ˌtrē\ *adj*

male·fac·tion \-'fak-shən\ *n* : an evil deed : CRIME

male·fac·tor \'mal-ə-ˌfak-tər\ *n* **1** : one guilty of a crime or offense **2** : EVILDOER [Latin, from *malefacere* "to do evil", from *male* "badly" + *facere* "to do"]

male fern *n* : a fern that yields a resinous substance used as a worm remedy

ma·lef·i·cent \mə-'lef-ə-sənt\ *adj* : doing or producing harm or evil : HARMFUL [back-formation from *maleficence*, from Italian *maleficenza*, from Latin *maleficentia*, from *maleficus* "baleful, harmful", from *male* "badly" + *-ficus* "-fic"] — **ma·lef·i·cence** \-səns\ *n*

ma·lev·o·lent \mə-'lev-ə-lənt\ *adj* : having or showing intense often vicious ill will toward others [Latin *malevolens*, from *male* "badly" + *volens*, present participle of *velle* "to wish"] SYN see MALICE — **ma·lev·o·lence** \-'lev-ə-ləns\ *n* — **ma·lev·o·lent·ly** *adv*

mal·fea·sance \mal-'fēz-ns, 'mal-\ *n* : wrongful conduct especially by a public official [*mal-* + obsolete *feasance* "doing", from Middle French *faisance*, from *faire* "to make, do"]

mal·for·ma·tion \ˌmal-fȯr-'mā-shən, -fər-\ *n* : an irregular or defective formation or structure

mal·formed \mal-'fȯrmd, 'mal-\ *adj* : marked by malformation

mal·func·tion \mal-'fəng-shən, 'mal-, -'fəngk-\ *vi* : to fail to operate in the normal or usual manner — **malfunction** *n*

ma·lic acid \ˌmal-ik-, ˌmā-lik-\ *n* : an acid $C_4H_6O_5$ found especially in various plant juices [French *acide malique*, from Latin *malum* "apple", from Greek *mēlon, malon*]

mal·ice \'mal-əs\ *n* : ILL WILL; *esp* : the deliberate intention of doing unjustified harm for the satisfaction of doing it [Old French, from Latin *malitia*, from *malus* "bad"] □ SYN MALEVOLENCE, MALIGNITY: MALICE may range from a passing mischievous impulse to a deep-seated unreasoning dislike and desire to cause harm and suffering; MALEVOLENCE stresses evil intent or influence that is likely to lead to malicious action; MALIGNITY stresses the intensity and driving force of malevolence and suggests a quality that is part of one's nature.

ma·li·cious \mə-'lish-əs\ *adj* **1** : feeling strong ill will : being mean and spiteful **2** : done or carried on with malice or caused by malice ⟨*malicious* gossip⟩ — **ma·li·cious·ly** *adv* — **ma·li·cious·ness** *n*

¹ma·lign \mə-'līn\ *adj* **1** : operating so as to injure or hurt ⟨hindered by *malign* influences⟩ **2** : moved by ill will toward others : MALEVOLENT [Middle French *maligne*, from Latin *malignus*, from *male* "bad" + *gignere* "to beget"]

²malign *vt* : to utter injurious or false reports about : speak evil of : DEFAME SYN see SLANDER

ma·lig·nan·cy \mə-'lig-nən-sē\ *n, pl* **-cies** **1** : the quality or state of being malignant **2** : a malignant tumor

ma·lig·nant \-nənt\ *adj* **1 a** : evil in influence or effect : INJURIOUS **b** : passionately and relentlessly malevolent **2** : tending or likely to produce death especially through being dispersed and growing throughout the body ⟨*malignant* tumor⟩ — **ma·lig·nant·ly** *adv*

ma·lig·ni·ty \mə-'lig-nət-ē\ *n, pl* **-ties** **1** : the quality or state of being malignant : MALIGNANCY **2** : something (as an act or an event) that is malignant SYN see MALICE

\ə\ abut		\ng\ sing	
\ər\ further		\ō\ bone	
\a\ mat		\ȯ\ saw	
\ā\ take		\ȯi\ coin	
\ä\ cot, cart		\th\ thin	
\au̇\ out		\th\ this	
\ch\ chin		\ü\ food	
\e\ pet		\u̇\ foot	
\ē\ easy		\y\ yet	
\g\ go		\yü\ few	
\i\ tip		\yu̇\ cure	
\ī\ life		\zh\ vision	
\j\ job			

ma·li·hi·ni \,mäl-i-'hē-nē\ *n* : a newcomer to Hawaii [Hawaiian]

ma·lin·ger \mə-'ling-gər\ *vi* **ma·lin·gered; ma·lin·ger·ing** \-gə-ring, -gring\ : to pretend incapacity (as illness) so as to avoid duty or work [French *malingre* "sickly"] — **ma·lin·ger·er** \-gər-ər\ *n*

mall \'mȯl\ *n* **1** : a shaded walk : PROMENADE **2** : a grassy strip between two roadways **3** : a group of stores and shops with associated passageways and parking space [The *Mall,* promenade in London, England]

mal·lard \'mal-ərd\ *n, pl* **mallard** *or* **mallards** : a common and widely distributed wild duck of the northern hemisphere that is the source of the domestic ducks [Middle French *mallart*]

mal·lea·ble \'mal-ē-ə-bəl, 'mal-yə-bəl, 'mal-ə-bəl\ *adj* **1** : capable of being beaten out, extended, or shaped by hammer blows or by the pressure of rollers ⟨a *malleable* metal⟩ **2** : ADAPTABLE, PLIABLE [Medieval Latin *malleabilis,* from *malleare* "to hammer", from Latin *malleus* "hammer"] — **mal·le·abil·i·ty** \,mal-ē-ə-'bil-ət-ē, ,mal-yə-'bil-, ,mal-ə-'\ *n*

mal·lee \'mal-ē\ *n* : a dense growth of shrubby eucalypts; *also* : Australian land covered with mallee [native name in Australia]

mal·let \'mal-ət\ *n* **1** : a hammer usually having a barrel-shaped head of wood; *esp* : a tool with a short handle and a large head used for driving another tool (as a chisel) **2** : a long-handled club with a cylindrical head used in playing croquet **3** : a polo stick [Middle French *maillet,* from *mail* "hammer", from Latin *malleus*]

mal·le·us \'mal-ē-əs\ *n, pl* **mal·lei** \-ē-,ī, -ē-,ē\ : the outermost of the three small bones of the mammalian ear — compare INCUS, STAPES [Latin, "hammer"]

mal·low \'mal-ō\ *n* : any of a genus of herbs with lobed or dissected leaves, usually showy flowers, and a disk-shaped fruit [Old English *mealwe,* from Latin *malva*]

malm·sey \'mäm-zē, 'mälm-\ *n, pl* **malmseys** *often cap* : a sweet aromatic wine originally produced in Greece [Medieval Latin *Malmasia* "Monemvasia", village in Greece]

mal·nour·ished \mal-'nər-isht, 'mal-, -'nə-risht\ *adj* : marked by or affected with malnutrition

mal·nu·tri·tion \,mal-nù-'trish-ən, -nyù-\ *n* : faulty and especially inadequate nutrition — **mal·nu·tri·tion·al** \-'trish-nəl, -ən-l\ *adj*

mal·oc·clu·sion \,mal-ə-'klü-zhən\ *n* : faulty coming together of teeth in the upper and lower jaws when biting

mal·odor·ous \mal-'ōd-ə-rəs, 'mal-\ *adj* : bad-smelling — **mal·odor·ous·ly** *adv* — **mal·odor·ous·ness** *n*

Mal·pigh·i·an corpuscle \mal-,pig-ē-ən-, -,pē-gē-\ *n* : a kidney glomerulus with its membrane — called also *Malpighian body* [Marcello *Malpighi,* died 1694, Italian anatomist]

Malpighian tubule *n* : any of a group of long blind vessels opening into the intestine in various arthropods and functioning in excretion

mal·prac·tice \mal-'prak-təs, 'mal-\ *n* **1** : violation of professional standards especially by negligence or improper conduct **2** : an injurious, negligent, or improper practice — **mal·prac·ti·tion·er** \,mal-,prak-'tish-(ə-)nər\ *n*

¹malt \'mȯlt\ *n* **1** : grain and especially barley softened in water, allowed to germinate, and used chiefly in brewing and distilling **2** : MALTED MILK 2 [Old English *mealt*] — **malt** *adj* — **malty** \'mȯl-tē\ *adj*

²malt *vb* **1** : to convert into malt **2** : to make or treat with malt or malt extract **3** : to become malt

malt·ase \'mȯl-,tās\ *n* : an enzyme that accelerates the hydrolysis of maltose to glucose

malted milk *n* **1** : a soluble powder prepared from dried milk and malted cereals **2** : a beverage made by dissolving malted milk in a liquid (as milk)

Mal·tese \mȯl-'tēz\ *n, pl* **Maltese** **1** : a native or inhabitant of Malta **2** : the Semitic language of the Maltese people — **Maltese** *adj*

Maltese cat *n* : a bluish gray domestic short-haired cat

Maltese cross *n* : a cross with four arms of equal size that increase in width toward the outward ends

Mal·thu·sian \mal-'thü-zhən, mȯl-, -'thyü-\ *adj* : of or relating to Malthus or to his theory that population unless checked (as by war or disease) tends to increase at a faster rate than its means of subsistence — **Malthusian** *n* — **Mal·thu·sian·ism** \-zhə-,niz-əm\ *n*

malt·ose \'mȯl-,tōs\ *n* : a sugar formed especially from starch by the action of enzymes and used in brewing and distilling — called also *malt sugar*

mal·treat \mal-'trēt, 'mal-\ *vt* : to treat unkindly or roughly : ABUSE ⟨*maltreat* animals⟩ — **mal·treat·ment** \-mənt\ *n*

ma·ma *or* **mam·ma** \'mäm-ə\ *n* : MOTHER [baby talk]

mam·ba \'mäm-bə, 'mam-\ *n* : any of several African venomous snakes related to the cobras but lacking a hood [Zulu *im-amba*]

mam·bo \'mäm-bō\ *n, pl* **mambos** : a dance of Haitian origin related to the rumba [American Spanish] — **mambo** *vi*

mam·ma \'mam-ə\ *n, pl* **mam·mae** \'mam-,ē, -,ī\ : a mammary gland and its accessory parts [Latin, "mother, breast"] — **mam·mate** \'mam-,āt\ *adj*

mam·mal \'mam-əl\ *n* : any of a class (Mammalia) of higher vertebrates comprising man and all other animals that nourish their young with milk secreted by mammary glands and have the skin usually more or less covered with hair — **mam·ma·li·an** \mə-'mā-lē-ən, ma-'māl-\ *adj or n*

mam·mal·o·gy \mə-'mal-ə-jē, ma-'mal-\ *n* : a branch of zoology dealing with mammals — **mam·mal·o·gist** \-jəst\ *n*

mam·ma·ry \'mam-ə-rē\ *adj* : of, relating to, lying near, or affecting the mammae

mammary gland *n* : one of the large compound sebaceous glands that in female mammals are modified to secrete milk and in males are usually rudimentary, are situated in pairs on the abdominal side of the organism, and usually end in a nipple

mam·mil·la·ry \'mam-ə-,ler-ē, ma-'mil-ə-rē\ *adj* **1** : of, relating to, or resembling a breast **2** : studded with breast-shaped protuberances [Latin *mammilla* "breast, nipple", from *mamma* "mother, breast"]

mam·mil·lat·ed \'mam-ə-,lāt-əd\ *adj* : having or being small bluntly rounded protuberances

mam·mon \'mam-ən\ *n, often cap* : an often personified devotion to material possessions; *also* : WEALTH [Late Latin *mammona,* from Greek *mamōna,* from Aramaic *māmōnā* "riches"]

¹mam·moth \'mam-əth\ *n* **1** : any of numerous large hairy extinct elephants with very long upward-curving tusks **2** : something immense of its kind : GIANT [Russian *mamont, mamot*]

²mammoth *adj* : of very great size : GIGANTIC

mam·my \'mam-ē\ *n, pl* **mammies** **1** : MAMA **2** : a black woman serving as a nurse to white children especially formerly in the American South

¹man \'man\ *n, pl* **men** \'men\ **1 a** : HUMAN BEING; *esp* : an adult male human **b** : the human race : MANKIND **c** : any member of the natural family to which human beings belong including both human beings and extinct related forms known only from fossils **d** : one possessing in high degree the qualities considered distinctive of manhood **2 a** : VASSAL 1 **b** : an adult male servant **c** *pl* : the working force as distinguished from the employer **3** : any person ⟨a *man* could easily be killed there⟩ **4** : one of the pieces with which various games (as chess) are played [Old English]

²man *vt* **manned; man·ning** **1** : to supply with personnel (as for management or operation) ⟨*man* a business⟩ **2** :

to station members of a ship's crew at ⟨*man* the pumps⟩

man–about–town \ˌman-ə-ˌbau̇t-ˈtau̇n\ *n, pl* **men–about–town** : a worldly and socially active man

¹**man·a·cle** \ˈman-i-kəl\ *n* **1** : a shackle for the hand or wrist : HANDCUFF **2** : something that restrains or restricts [Middle French *manicle,* from Latin *manicula* "little hand", from *manus* "hand"]

²**manacle** *vt* **-cled; -cling** \-kə-ling, -kling\ **1** : to put manacles on **2** : SHACKLE 2 SYN see HAMPER

man·age \ˈman-ij\ *vb* **1** : to oversee and make decisions about : DIRECT ⟨*manage* a factory⟩ **2** : to make and keep compliant ⟨skill in *managing* problem children⟩ **3** : to treat with care : use to best advantage ⟨there's enough food if it's *managed* well⟩ **4** : to succeed in one's purpose ⟨*managed* to escape⟩ [Italian *maneggiare* "to handle", from *mano* "hand", from Latin *manus*] SYN see CONDUCT

man·age·able \ˈman-ij-ə-bəl\ *adj* : capable of being managed — **man·age·abil·i·ty** \ˌman-ij-ə-ˈbil-ət-ē\ *n* — **man·age·able·ness** \ˈman-ij-ə-bəl-nəs\ *n* — **man·age·ably** \-blē\ *adv*

man·age·ment \ˈman-ij-mənt\ *n* **1** : the act or art of managing : CONTROL, DIRECTION **2** : skillfulness in managing **3** : those who manage an enterprise

man·ag·er \ˈman-ij-ər\ *n* : one that manages: as **a** : a person who conducts business or household affairs **b** : a person whose work or profession is management **c** : a person who directs a team or an athlete — **man·a·ge·ri·al** \ˌman-ə-ˈjir-ē-əl\ *adj* — **man·a·ge·ri·al·ly** \-ē-ə-lē\ *adv* — **man·ag·er·ship** \ˈman-ij-ər-ˌship\ *n*

ma·ña·na \mən-ˈyän-ə\ *n* : an indefinite time in the future [Spanish, literally, "tomorrow"] — **mañana** *adv*

man–at–arms \ˌman-at-ˈärmz\ *n, pl* **men–at–arms** : SOLDIER; *esp* : a heavily armed mounted soldier

man·a·tee \ˈman-ə-ˌtē\ *n* : any of several chiefly tropical plant-eating aquatic mammals that differ from the related dugong especially in having the tail broad and rounded [Spanish *manatí*]

man·chi·neel \ˌman-chə-ˈnēl\ *n* : a tropical American tree with a blistering milky juice and poisonous apple-shaped fruits [French *mancenille,* from Spanish *manzanilla,* from *manzana* "apple"]

Man·chu \ˈman-chü, man-ˈ\ *n* **1** : a member of the native Mongolian race of Manchuria that conquered China and established a dynasty there in 1644 **2** : the language of the Manchu people — **Manchu** *adj*

man·ci·ple \ˈman-sə-pəl\ *n* : a person responsible for procuring and distributing food especially for a college or monastery [Medieval Latin *mancipium* "office of steward", from Latin *manceps* "purchaser", from *manus* "hand" + *capere* "to take"]

-man·cy \ˌman-sē\ *n combining form, pl* **-mancies** : divination [Greek *manteia,* from *mantis* "diviner, prophet"]

man·da·mus \man-ˈdā-məs\ *n* : a writ issued by a superior court commanding that a specified official act or duty be performed [Latin, "we enjoin", its first word]

¹**man·da·rin** \ˈman-də-rən, -drən\ *n* **1** : a public official under the Chinese Empire of any of nine superior grades **2** *cap* **a** : the primarily northern dialect of China used by the court and the official classes under the Empire **b** : the chief dialect of China that is spoken in about four fifths of the country and has a standard variety centering about Peking **3** : a small spiny Chinese orange tree with yellow to reddish orange loose-skinned fruits; *also* : its fruit — compare TANGERINE [Portuguese *mandarim,* from Malay *měntěri,* from Sanskrit *mantrin* "counselor"] — **man·da·rin·ate** \-ˌāt\ *n*

²**mandarin** *adj* : of, relating to, or typical of a mandarin

mandarin orange *n* : MANDARIN 3

man·da·tary \ˈman-də-ˌter-ē\ *n, pl* **-tar·ies** : MANDATORY

man·date \ˈman-ˌdāt\ *n* **1** : a formal order from a superior court or official to an inferior one **2 a** : an authoritative command, instruction, or direction **b** : authorization or approval given to a representative **3 a** : a commission granted by the former League of Nations to a member nation to administer a conquered territory as guardian on behalf of the League **b** : a mandated territory [Latin *mandatum* "command", from *mandare* "to entrust, enjoin"] — **mandate** *vt*

¹**man·da·to·ry** \ˈman-də-ˌtōr-ē, -ˌtȯr-\ *adj* **1** : containing or constituting a command ⟨*mandatory* tasks⟩ **2** : of, relating to, or holding a League of Nations mandate ⟨a *mandatory* power⟩

²**mandatory** *n, pl* **-ries** : one given a mandate

man·di·ble \ˈman-də-bəl\ *n* **1 a** : a single bone or completely fused bones forming the lower jaw **b** : either the upper or lower segment of the bill of a bird **2** : an invertebrate mouthpart that holds or bites food; *esp* : either of the front pair of mouth appendages of an arthropod often forming strong biting jaws [Middle French, from Late Latin *mandibula,* from Latin *mandere* "to chew"] — **man·dib·u·lar** \man-ˈdib-yə-lər\ *adj*

man·do·lin \ˌman-də-ˈlin, ˈman-dl-ən\ *also* **man·do·line** \ˌman-də-ˈlēn, ˈman-dl-ən\ *n* : a musical instrument of the lute family that has a pear-shaped body and fretted neck and four to six pairs of strings [Italian *mandolino*] — **man·do·lin·ist** \ˌman-də-ˈlin-əst\ *n*

man·drag·o·ra \man-ˈdrag-ə-rə\ *n* : MANDRAKE 1

man·drake \ˈman-ˌdrāk\ *n* **1** : a Mediterranean herb of the potato family with a large forked root superstitiously credited with human and medicinal attributes **2** : MAYAPPLE [Old English *mandragora,* from Latin *mandragoras,* from Greek]

man·drel \ˈman-drəl\ *n* **1** : an axle or spindle inserted into a hole in a piece of work to support it during machining **2** : a metal bar used as a core around which material may be cast, shaped, or molded [probably from French *mandrin*]

man·drill \ˈman-drəl\ *n* : a large gregarious baboon of western Africa with a red rump and in the male with blue ridges on each side of the red-bridged nose [probably from ¹*man* + ³*drill*]

mane \ˈmān\ *n* **1** : long heavy hair growing about the neck of some mammals (as a horse) **2** : long heavy hair on a person's head [Old English *manu*] — **maned** \ˈmānd\ *adj*

man–eat·er \ˈman-ˌēt-ər\ *n* : one (as a cannibal, shark, or tiger) that has or is thought to have an appetite for human flesh — **man–eat·ing** \-ˌēt-ing\ *adj*

ma·nege *also* **ma·nège** \ma-ˈnezh\ *n* **1** : a school for teaching horsemanship **2** : the art of horsemanship or of training horses [French *manège,* from Italian *maneggio* "training of a horse", from *maneggiare* "to handle, manage"]

ma·nes \ˈmän-ˌās, ˈmā-ˌnēz\ *n pl, often cap* : the deified spirits of the ancient Roman dead [Latin]

¹**ma·neu·ver** *also* **ma·noeu·vre** *or* **ma·noeu·ver** \mə-ˈnü-vər, -ˈnyü-\ *n* **1 a** : a planned movement of military forces **b** : an armed forces training exercise; *esp* : an extensive exercise involving large-scale deployment of military forces **2 a** : a physical movement or procedure ⟨avoided a collision by a quick *maneuver*⟩ **b** : a variation from the straight and level flight path of an airplane **3** : a clever often evasive move or action : a shift of position to gain a tactical end ⟨tried by various *maneuvers* to win support from both sides⟩ [French *manœuvre,* from Medieval Latin *manuopera* "work done by hand", from Latin *manu operare* "to work by hand"] □ ORIGIN We owe both *manure* and *maneuver* to the same source, Latin *manu operare* "to do work by hand". This Latin phrase is the ancestor of the Middle French verb *manouvrer.* The French verb originally meant "to work by hand" but later developed the more specific sense "to cultivate (land)". In

mandolin

mandrake 1

\ə\ abut	\ng\ sing
\ər\ further	\ō\ bone
\a\ mat	\ȯ\ saw
\ā\ take	\ȯi\ coin
\ä\ cot, cart	\th\ thin
\au̇\ out	\th\ this
\ch\ chin	\ü\ food
\e\ pet	\u̇\ foot
\ē\ easy	\y\ yet
\g\ go	\yü\ few
\i\ tip	\yu̇\ cure
\ī\ life	\zh\ vision
\j\ job	

the late Middle Ages the English borrowed the word as *manouren,* "to cultivate". From this verb we get the noun *manure* for the dung used to fertilize the land. Latin *manu operare* is also the source of French *manœuvre,* "maneuver". The original meaning of the French noun was "work done by hand", but the older sense gave way to a more general sense, "work". Still later the noun developed a new specific meaning, "military operation".

²**maneuver** *also* **manoeuvre** *or* **manoeuver** *vb* **1** : to move (as troops or ships) in a maneuver **2** : to perform a maneuver **3** : to guide with adroitness and design : HANDLE, MANIPULATE **4** : to use stratagems : SCHEME — **ma·neu·ver·abil·i·ty** \-,nüv-rə-'bil-ət-ē, -,nyüv-, -ə-rə-\ *n* — **ma·neu·ver·able** \-'nüv-rə-bəl, -'nyüv-, -ə-rə-\ *adj*

man Fri·day \'man-'frīd-ē\ *n* : a valued efficient helper or employee [*Friday,* native servant in *Robinson Crusoe* (1719), novel by Daniel Defoe]

man·ful \'man-fəl\ *adj* : showing courage and resolution — **man·ful·ly** \-fə-lē\ *adv* — **man·ful·ness** *n*

man·ga·nese \'mang-gə-,nēz, -,nēs\ *n* : a grayish white usually hard and brittle metallic element that resembles iron but is not magnetic — see ELEMENT table [French *manganèse,* from Italian *manganese* "magnesia, manganese", from Medieval Latin *magnesia* "magnesia"]

manganese dioxide *n* : a brown or gray-black insoluble compound MnO_2 that consists of manganese and oxygen and is used as an oxidizing agent, in making glass, and in ceramics

man·gan·ic \man-'gan-ik, mang-\ *or* **man·ga·nous** \'mang-gə-nəs\ *adj* : of, relating to, or derived from manganese

mange \'mānj\ *n* : any of several persistent contagious skin diseases marked especially by itching and loss of hair in domestic animals and sometimes humans; *esp* : one caused by a minute parasitic mite [Middle French *mangene* "itching", from *mangier* "to eat"]

man·ger \'mān-jər\ *n* : a trough or open box for livestock feed or fodder [Middle French *maingeure,* from *mangier* "to eat", from Latin *manducare* "to chew, devour", from *manducus* "glutton", from *mandere* "to chew"]

¹**man·gle** \'mang-gəl\ *vt* **man·gled; man·gling** \-gə-ling, -gling\ **1** : to cut, bruise, or hack with repeated blows or strokes **2** : to spoil or injure in making or performing : BOTCH [Anglo-French *mangler,* from Old French *maynier* "to maim"] — **man·gler** \-gə-lər, -glər\ *n*

²**mangle** *n* : a machine for ironing laundry by passing it between heated rollers [Dutch *mangel*]

³**mangle** *vt* **man·gled; man·gling** \-gə-ling, -gling\ : to press or smooth with a mangle — **man·gler** \-gə-lər, -glər\ *n*

man·go \'mang-gō\ *n, pl* **mangoes** *or* **mangos** : a yellowish red tropical fruit with a firm skin, hard central stone, and juicy aromatic mildly acid pulp; *also* : the evergreen tree of the sumac family that bears this fruit [Portuguese *manga,* from Tamil *mān-kāy*]

man·go·steen \'mang-gə-,stēn\ *n* : a dark reddish brown fruit with thick rind and juicy flesh having a flavor suggestive of both peach and pineapple; *also* : an East Indian tree that bears this fruit [Malay *mangustan*]

man·grove \'man-,grōv, 'mang-\ *n* : any of various tropical trees or shrubs that throw out many prop roots and form dense masses in brackish marshes or shallow salt water [probably from Portuguese *mangue,* from Spanish *mangle,* of American Indian origin]

mangy \'mān-jē\ *adj* **mang·i·er; -est** **1** : affected with or resulting from mange **2** : SHABBY 1, SEEDY — **mang·i·ness** \'mān-jē-nəs\ *n*

man·han·dle \'man-,han-dl\ *vt* **1** : to move or manage by human force **2** : to handle roughly

man·hat·tan \man-'hat-n, mən-\ *n, often cap* : a cocktail consisting of vermouth and whiskey [*Manhattan,* borough of New York City]

man·hole \'man-,hōl\ *n* : a hole through which a person may go especially to gain access to an underground or enclosed structure

man·hood \'man-,hůd\ *n* **1** : qualities generally associated with a man **2** : the condition of being an adult male **3** : adult males : MEN ⟨the nation's *manhood*⟩

man·hour \'man-'au̇-ər, -'au̇r\ *n* : a unit of one hour's work by one person used especially as a basis for wages and in accounting

man·hunt \'man-,hənt\ *n* : an organized hunt for a person and especially for one charged with a crime

ma·nia \'mā-nē-ə, -nyə\ *n* **1** : MADNESS 1; *esp* : insanity characterized by uncontrollable emotion or excitement **2** : excessive or unreasonable enthusiasm : CRAZE [Late Latin, from Greek, from *mainesthai* "to be mad"] SYN SEE INSANITY

¹**ma·ni·ac** \'mā-nē-,ak\ *adj* : affected with or suggestive of madness — **ma·ni·a·cal** \mə-'nī-ə-kəl\ *adj* — **ma·ni·a·cal·ly** \-kə-lē, -klē\ *adv*

²**maniac** *n* **1** : MADMAN, LUNATIC **2** : a person wildly enthusiastic about something : FAN

man·ic \'man-ik\ *adj* : affected with, relating to, or resembling mania — **manic** *n*

man·ic-de·pres·sive \,man-ik-di-'pres-iv\ *adj* : characterized by alternating mania and depression — **manic-depressive** *n*

¹**man·i·cure** \'man-ə-,kyur\ *n* **1** : MANICURIST **2** : a treatment for the care of the hands and nails [French, from Latin *manus* "hand" + French *-icure* (as in *pédicure* "pedicure")]

²**manicure** *vt* **1** : to give a manicure to **2** : to trim closely and evenly ⟨*manicure* the lawn⟩

man·i·cur·ist \-,kyur-əst\ *n* : a person who gives manicures

¹**man·i·fest** \'man-ə-,fest\ *adj* : clear to the senses or mind : OBVIOUS ⟨heard the verdict with *manifest* relief⟩ [Latin *manifestus,* literally, "hit by the hand"] — **man·i·fest·ly** *adv*

²**manifest** *vt* : to show plainly : make evident : DISPLAY

³**manifest** *n* : a list (as of cargo or passengers) especially for a ship or plane

man·i·fes·ta·tion \,man-ə-fə-'stā-shən, -,fes-'tā-\ *n* **1 a** : the act, process, or an instance of manifesting **b** : an outward or visible expression **2** : a public demonstration of power and purpose ⟨rallies, parades, and other *manifestations*⟩

manifest destiny *n, often cap M&D* : a future event accepted as inevitable ⟨in the 19th century expansion to the Pacific was regarded as the *manifest destiny* of the United States⟩

man·i·fes·to \,man-ə-'fes-tō\ *n, pl* **-tos** *or* **-toes** : a public declaration of policy, purpose, or views [Italian, derived from Latin *manifestus* "manifest"]

¹**man·i·fold** \'man-ə-,fōld\ *adj* **1** : of many and various kinds ⟨*manifold* excuses⟩ **2** : including or uniting various features ⟨a *manifold* personality⟩ — **man·i·fold·ly** *adv* — **man·i·fold·ness** \-,fōld-nəs, -,fōl-\ *n*

²**manifold** *n* : something that is manifold: as **a** : a whole consisting of many different elements **b** : a pipe fitting having several outlets for connecting one pipe with others **c** : a fitting on an internal-combustion engine that either receives exhaust gases or directs a fuel charge

³**manifold** *vb* **1** : to make many or several copies ⟨*manifold* a manuscript⟩ **2** : to make manifold

man·i·kin *or* **man·ni·kin** \'man-i-kən\ *n* **1** : MANNEQUIN **2** : a little man : DWARF, PYGMY

ma·nila *also* **ma·nil·la** \mə-'nil-ə\ *adj* : made of manila paper or from Manila hemp

Manila hemp *n* : a strong fiber obtained from the leafstalk of a Philippine banana — called also *abaca* [*Manila,* Philippine islands]

manila paper *n, often cap M* : a tough brownish paper made originally from Manila hemp and used especially for wrapping

man in the street : a typical or ordinary person

man·i·oc \'man-ē-ˌäk\ *also* **man·i·o·ca** \ˌman-ē-'ō-kə\ *n* : CASSAVA [French *manioc* and Spanish and Portuguese *mandioca,* of American Indian origin]

man·i·ple \'man-ə-pəl\ *n* **1** : a long narrow band worn at mass over the left arm by clerics of or above the order of subdeacon **2** : a subdivision of a Roman legion consisting of either 120 or 60 men [Latin *manipulus* "handful", from *manus* "hand"]

ma·nip·u·late \mə-'nip-yə-ˌlāt\ *vt* **1** : to treat or operate with the hands or by mechanical means especially with skill ⟨*manipulate* the TV dials⟩ **2 a** : to manage or utilize skillfully ⟨*manipulate* masses of statistics⟩ **b** : to manage artfully, unfairly, or fraudulently ⟨*manipulate* accounts⟩ ⟨*manipulate* public opinion⟩ **c** : to influence (as prices) by artificial means [back-formation from *manipulation,* from French, derived from Latin *manipulus* "handful"] — **ma·nip·u·la·tion** \-ˌnip-yə-'lā-shən\ *n* — **ma·nip·u·la·tor** \-'nip-yə-ˌlāt-ər\ *n*

man·i·tou *or* **man·i·tu** \'man-ə-ˌtü\ *also* **man·i·to** \-ˌtō\ *n* : one of the Algonquian deities or spirits dominating the forces of nature [of American Indian origin]

man·kind *n* **1** \'man-'kīnd, -ˌkīnd\ : the human race : the totality of human beings **2** \-ˌkīnd\ : men especially as distinguished from women

man·like \'man-ˌlīk\ *adj* **1** : resembling human beings ⟨*manlike* apes⟩ **2** : befitting or belonging to a man : MANLY

man·ly \'man-lē\ *adj* **man·li·er; -est** **1** : having desirable qualities held to be appropriate to a man **2** : befitting a man ⟨*manly* sports⟩ — **man·li·ness** *n*

man–made \'man-'mād\ *adj* : made by humans rather than nature ⟨*man-made* systems⟩; *also* : SYNTHETIC ⟨*man-made* fibers⟩

man·na \'man-ə\ *n* **1** : food miraculously supplied to the Israelites in the wilderness **2** : something much needed and joyfully received [Old English, from Late Latin, from Greek, from Hebrew *mān*]

manned \'mand\ *adj* : carrying or performed by a person ⟨*manned* spaceflight⟩

man·ne·quin \'man-i-kən\ *n* **1** : an artist's, tailor's, or dressmaker's jointed figure of the human body; *also* : a form representing the human figure used especially for displaying clothes **2** : a woman who models clothing : MODEL [French, from Dutch *mannekijn* "little man", from *man* "man"]

man·ner \'man-ər\ *n* **1 a** : KIND ⟨what *manner* of person are you⟩ **b** : SORTS ⟨all *manner* of information⟩ **2 a** : a way of acting or proceeding ⟨worked in a brisk *manner*⟩ **b** : HABIT, CUSTOM ⟨spoke bluntly as is my *manner*⟩ **c** : STYLE ⟨painted in the artist's early *manner*⟩ **3** *pl* **a** : social conduct or rules of conduct as shown in prevalent customs **b** : characteristic or habitual deportment : BEHAVIOR ⟨mind your *manners*⟩ **c** : pleasing or socially acceptable deportment ⟨teach children *manners*⟩ [Old French *maniere* "way of acting", from Latin *manuarius* "of the hand", from *manus* "hand"]

man·nered \'man-ərd\ *adj* **1** : having manners of a specified kind ⟨well-*mannered*⟩ **2** : having an artificial character ⟨a highly *mannered* style⟩

man·ner·ism \'man-ə-ˌriz-əm\ *n* : an often affected peculiarity of action, bearing, or treatment ⟨the *mannerism* of constantly smoothing one's hair⟩ SYN see AFFECTATION

man·ner·ly \'man-ər-lē\ *adj* : showing good manners : POLITE — **man·ner·li·ness** \-lē-nəs\ *n* — **mannerly** *adv*

man·nish \'man-ish\ *adj* : resembling or suggesting, suitable to, or characteristic of a man rather than a woman ⟨a *mannish* voice⟩ ⟨often wore *mannish* clothes⟩ — **man·nish·ly** *adv* — **man·nish·ness** *n*

man·ni·tol \'man-ə-ˌtól, -ˌtōl\ *n* : a slightly sweet crystalline alcohol $C_6H_8(OH)_6$ found in many plants [derived from *manna*]

manoeuvre, manoeuver *variant of* MANEUVER

man–of–war \ˌman-əv-'wór, -ə-\ *n, pl* **men–of–war** \ˌmen-\ : WARSHIP

ma·nom·e·ter \mə-'näm-ət-ər\ *n* : an instrument for measuring pressure (as of gases and vapors) [derived from Greek *manos* "sparse, loose, rare"]

man·or \'man-ər\ *n* : a usually large landed estate; *esp* : one granted by a sovereign to a feudal lord [Old French *manoir* "residence", from *manoir* "to dwell", from Latin *manēre* "to stay"] — **ma·no·ri·al** \mə-'nōr-ē-əl, -'nór-\ *adj* — **ma·no·ri·al·ism** \-ē-ə-ˌliz-əm\ *n*

manor house *n* : the house of the lord of a manor

man–o'–war bird \ˌman-ə-'wór-ˌbərd\ *n* : FRIGATE BIRD

man power *n* **1** : power available from or supplied by the physical effort of humans **2** *usually* **man·pow·er** \'man-ˌpaù-ər, -ˌpaúr\ : the total supply of persons available and fitted for service (as in the armed forces or industry)

man·qué \män-'kā\ *adj* : UNSUCCESSFUL — used after the word modified ⟨a poet *manqué*⟩ [French, from *manquer* "to lack, fall short"]

man·sard \'man-ˌsärd, -sard\ *n* : a roof having two slopes on all sides with the lower slope much steeper than the upper [French *mansarde,* from François *Mansart,* died 1666, French architect]

manse \'mans\ *n* : the residence of a member of the clergy; *esp* : the house of a Presbyterian minister [Medieval Latin *mansa* "residence", from Latin *manēre* "to stay, dwell"]

man·ser·vant \'man-ˌsər-vənt\ *n, pl* **men·ser·vants** \'men-ˌsər-vəns\ : a male servant

man·sion \'man-chən\ *n* : a large imposing residence [Middle French, literally, "act of staying, lodging", from Latin *mansio,* from *manēre* "to stay"]

man–size \'man-ˌsīz\ *or* **man–sized** \-ˌsīzd\ *adj* **1** : suitable for or felt to require a man ⟨a *man-size* job⟩ **2** : LARGE-SCALE ⟨a *man-size* model⟩

man·slaugh·ter \'man-ˌslòt-ər\ *n* : the unlawful killing of a person without intent to do so

man·slay·er \-ˌslā-ər\ *n* : one that slays a person

man·sue·tude \'man-swi-ˌtüd, man-'sü-ə-ˌtüd, -ˌtyüd\ *n* : the quality or state of being gentle : MEEKNESS, TAMENESS [Latin *mansuetudo,* from *mansuetus* "tame, mild", from *mansuescere* "to tame", from *manus* "hand" + *suescere* "to accustom"]

man·ta \'mant-ə\ *n* **1** : a square piece of cloth or blanket used in southwestern United States and Latin America as a cloak or shawl **2** : DEVILFISH 1 [Spanish; sense 2 from its being caught in traps resembling blankets]

man·teau \man-'tō\ *n* : a loose cloak, coat, or robe [French, from Old French *mantel*]

man·tel \'mant-l\ *n* **1** : the beam, stone, arch, or shelf above a fireplace **2** : the finish covering the chimney around a fireplace [Middle French, from Old French, "mantle"]

man·telet \'mant-lət\ *n* : a very short cape or cloak

man·tel·piece \'mant-l-ˌpēs\ *n* **1** : a mantel with its side elements **2** : the shelf of a mantel

man·ti·core \'mant-i-ˌkōr, -ˌkór\ *n* : a legendary animal with the head of a man, the body of a lion, and the tail of a dragon or scorpion [Latin *mantichora,* from Greek *mantichōras*]

man·til·la \man-'tē-ə, -'tē-yə, -'til-ə\ *n* **1** : a light scarf worn over the head and shoulders especially by Spanish and Latin American women **2** : a short light cape or cloak [Spanish, from *manta* "manta"]

man·tis \'mant-əs\ *n, pl* **man·tis·es** *or* **man·tes** \'man-ˌtēz\ : any of various insects related to the grasshoppers and roaches that feed upon insects and hold their prey in forelimbs raised as if in prayer [Greek, literally, "diviner, prophet"]

mantis

\ə\ abut		\ng\ sing	
\ər\ further		\ō\ bone	
\a\ mat		\ó\ saw	
\ā\ take		\ói\ coin	
\ä\ cot, cart		\th\ thin	
\aú\ out		\th\ this	
\ch\ chin		\ü\ food	
\e\ pet		\ú\ foot	
\ē\ easy		\y\ yet	
\g\ go		\yü\ few	
\i\ tip		\yú\ cure	
\ī\ life		\zh\ vision	
\j\ job			

man·tis·sa \man-'tis-ə\ *n* : the decimal part of a logarithm [Latin *mantisa, mantissa* "something used to make up weight", from Etruscan]

¹man·tle \'mant-l\ *n* **1** : a loose sleeveless outer garment : CLOAK **2 a** : something that covers or envelops **b** : a fold or lobe or pair of lobes of the body wall of a mollusk or brachiopod lining and secreting the shell in shell-bearing forms **3** : a lacy sheath that gives light by incandescence when placed over a flame [Old French *mantel,* from Latin *mantellum*]

²mantle *vt* **man·tled; man·tling** \'mant-ling, -l-ing\ : to cover or envelop with or as if with a mantle

man·tle·rock \'mant-l-,räk\ *n* : unconsolidated material that overlies the earth's solid rock

man·trap \'man-,trap\ *n* : a trap for catching men : SNARE

man·tua \'manch-wə, -ə-wə\ *n* : a usually loose-fitting gown worn especially in the 17th and 18th centuries [French *manteau*]

¹man·u·al \'man-yə-wəl, -yəl\ *adj* **1 a** : of, relating to, or involving the hands ⟨*manual* dexterity⟩ **b** : worked by hand ⟨a *manual* choke⟩ **2** : requiring or using physical skill and energy ⟨*manual* labor⟩ ⟨*manual* workers⟩ [Middle French *manuel,* from Latin *manualis,* from *manus* "hand"] — **man·u·al·ly** \-ē\ *adv*

²manual *n* **1** : a small book; *esp* : HANDBOOK **2** : the set movements in the handling of a weapon during a military drill or ceremony

manual alphabet *n* : an alphabet for the deaf in which the letters are represented by finger positions

manual training *n* : a course of training to develop skill in using the hands (as in woodworking)

ma·nu·bri·um \mə-'nü-brē-əm, -'nyü-\ *n, pl* **-bria** \-brē-ə\ *also* **-briums** : an anatomical part (as the upper end of the sternum) suggesting a handle [Latin, "handle", from *manus* "hand"]

man·u·fac·to·ry \,man-yə-'fak-tə-rē, ,man-ə-, -trē\ *n, pl* **-ries** : FACTORY

¹man·u·fac·ture \,man-yə-'fak-chər, ,man-ə-\ *n* **1** : something made from raw materials **2** : the process of making wares by hand or by machinery especially when carried on systematically with division of labor **3** : the act or process of producing something ⟨the *manufacture* of blood by the body⟩ [Middle French, from Latin *manu factus* "made by hand"]

²manufacture *vt* **-fac·tured; -fac·tur·ing** \-'fak-chə-ring, -'fak-shring\ **1** : to make into a product suitable for use **2** : to make from raw materials by hand or by machinery especially systematically and with division of labor **3** : FABRICATE 2, INVENT — **man·u·fac·tur·ing** *n*

man·u·fac·tur·er \-'fak-chər-ər, -'fak-shrər\ *n* : one that manufactures; *esp* : an employer of workers in manufacturing

man·u·mis·sion \,man-yə-'mish-ən\ *n* : emancipation from slavery [Middle French, from Latin *manumissio,* from *manumittere* "to manumit"]

man·u·mit \,man-yə-'mit\ *vt* **-mit·ted; -mit·ting** : to set free; *esp* : to release from slavery [Middle French *manumitter,* from Latin *manumittere,* from *manus* "hand" + *mittere* "to let go, send"]

¹ma·nure \mə-'nür, -'nyür\ *vt* : to enrich (land) by the application of manure [Middle English *manouren* "to cultivate", from Middle French *manouvrer,* literally, "to work by hand", from Latin *manu operare*] — see MANEUVER origin

²manure *n* : material that fertilizes land; *esp* : refuse of stables and barnyards consisting of bodily waste of livestock with or without litter — **ma·nu·ri·al** \mə-'nür-ē-əl, -'nyür-\ *adj*

¹man·u·script \'man-yə-,skript\ *adj* : written by hand or typed [Latin *manu scriptus* "written by hand"]

²manuscript *n* **1** : a written or typewritten composition or document **2** : writing as opposed to print

Manx \'mangks, 'mangks\ *n, pl* **Manx** **1** *pl* : the people of the Isle of Man **2** : the Celtic language of the Manx

people almost completely displaced by English — **Manx** *adj* — **Manx·man** \-mən\ *n*

Manx cat *n* : a short-haired domestic cat having no external tail

¹many \'men-ē\ *adj* **more** \'mōr, 'mòr\; **most** \'mōst\ **1** : consisting of or amounting to a large but indefinite number ⟨worked for *many* years⟩ **2** : being one of a large but indefinite number ⟨*many* a person⟩ [Old English *manig*] — **as many** : the same in number ⟨saw three plays in *as many* days⟩ □ **SYN NUMEROUS, COUNTLESS:** MANY implies a relatively large number usually of like things in contrast with a few or several or with an exact number; NUMEROUS implies very many and often suggests crowding, thronging, or clustering; COUNTLESS may imply a number too great to count or apparently without limit.

²many *pron, pl in construction* : a large number of persons or things ⟨*many* of them⟩

³many *n, pl in construction* : a large but indefinite number ⟨a good *many* went⟩

many·fold \,men-ē-'fōld\ *adv* : by many times

many-sid·ed \,men-ē-'sid-əd\ *adj* **1** : having many sides or aspects **2** : having many interests or aptitudes : VERSATILE — **many·sid·ed·ness** *n*

man·za·ni·ta \,man-zə-'nēt-ə\ *n* : any of various western North American evergreen shrubs of the heath family [American Spanish, from Spanish *manzana* "apple"]

Mao·ism \'maù-,iz-əm\ *n* : the theory and practice of Marxism-Leninism developed in China chiefly by Mao Tse-tung — **Mao·ist** \'maù-əst\ *n or adj*

Mao·ri \'maù-rē\ *n, pl* **Maori** *or* **Maoris** **1** : a member of a Polynesian people native to New Zealand **2** : the language of the Maori people — **Maori** *adj*

¹map \'map\ *n* **1 a** : a drawing or picture showing features of an area (as the surface of the earth) **b** : a drawing or picture of the sky showing the position of stars and planets **2** : the arrangement of genes on a chromosome as deduced from genetic experiments [Medieval Latin *mappa,* from Latin, "napkin"]

²map *vt* **mapped; map·ping** **1 a** : to make a map of ⟨*map* the surface of the moon⟩ **b** : to assign (a set or element) in mathematical correspondence ⟨*map* the set of integers onto itself⟩ **2** : to plan in detail ⟨*map* out a campaign⟩ — **map·per** *n*

ma·ple \'mā-pəl\ *n* : any of a genus of trees or shrubs with opposite leaves and a 2-winged dry fruit; *also* : the hard light-colored close-grained wood of a maple [Old English *mapul-*]

maple sugar *n* : a brown sugar made by boiling maple syrup

maple syrup *n* : syrup made by concentrating the sap of maples and especially the sugar maple

map·ping \'map-ing\ *n* **1** : the act or process of making a map **2** : FUNCTION 5a ⟨a one-to-one *mapping* of the positive integers onto their squares⟩

ma·quette \ma-'ket\ *n* : a usually small preliminary model (as of a sculpture) [French]

ma·quis \ma-'kē, mä-\ *n, pl* **ma·quis** \-'kē, -'kēz\ *often cap* : a guerrilla fighter in the French underground during World War II [French, literally, "underbrush"]

mar \'mär\ *vt* **marred; mar·ring** **1** : to make a blemish on : DAMAGE, SPOIL **2** *archaic* **a** : ¹MANGLE 1, MUTILATE **b** : DESTROY 1 [Old English *mierran* "to waste"]

mar·a·bou *or* **mar·a·bout** \'mar-ə-,bü\ *n* **1 a** : a large Old World stork **b** : the long soft feathers from under the tail and wings of this bird used especially formerly in millinery **2 a** : a thrown raw silk **b** : a fabric (as a feathery trimming material) made of this silk [French *marabout,* literally, "marabout"]

mar·a·bout \'mar-ə-,bü, -,büt\ *n, often cap* : a dervish in Muslim Africa held to have supernatural power [French, from Portuguese *marabuto,* from Arabic *murābit*]

marabou 1a

ma·ra·ca \mə-'räk-ə, -'rak-\ *n* : a dried gourd or a rattle like a gourd that contains dried seeds or pebbles and is used as a percussion instrument [Portuguese *maracá*]

mar·a·schi·no \,mar-ə-'skē-nō, -'shē-\ *n, often cap* **1** : a sweet liqueur distilled from the fermented juice of a bitter wild cherry **2** : a usually large cherry preserved in true or imitation maraschino [Italian, from *marasca* "bitter wild cherry"]

ma·ras·mus \mə-'raz-məs\ *n* : a progressive wasting away usually associated with faulty nutrition [Late Latin, from Greek *marasmos,* from *marainein* "to waste away"]

Ma·ra·thi \mə-'rät-ē\ *n* : the chief Indic language of the state of Maharashtra in India [Marathi *marāṭhī*]

mar·a·thon \'mar-ə-,thän\ *n* **1** : a long-distance race; *esp* : a footrace run on an open course of 26 miles 385 yards (about 42 kilometers) **2** : an unusually long and exhausting contest or activity [*Marathon,* Greece, site of a victory of Greeks over Persians in 490 B. C., the news of which was carried to Athens by a long-distance runner] — **marathon** *adj*

ma·raud \mə-'ród\ *vb* : to roam about and raid in search of plunder [French *marauder*] — **ma·raud·er** *n*

¹mar·ble \'mär-bəl\ *n* **1 a** : a usually crystalline metamorphosed limestone that is capable of taking a high polish and is used in architecture and sculpture **b** : something made from marble; *esp* : a piece of sculpture **2 a** : a little ball (as of glass) used in various games **b** *pl* : a children's game played with these little balls [Old French *marbre,* from Latin *marmor,* from Greek *marmaros*]

²marble *vt* **mar·bled; mar·bling** \'mar-bə-ling, -bling\ : to give a mottled appearance to ⟨*marble* the edges of a book⟩

³marble *adj* : made of, resembling, or suggestive of marble

mar·ble·ize \'mär-bə-,līz\ *vt* : MARBLE

mar·bling \'mär-bə-ling, -bling\ *n* **1** : coloration or markings resembling or suggestive of marble **2** : an intermixture of fat through the lean of a cut of meat

mar·bly \'mär-bə-lē, -blē\ *adj* : MARBLE

mar·ca·site \'mär-kə-,sīt, -,zīt; ,mär-kə-'zēt\ *n* : a mineral FeS₂ consisting of iron and sulfur and having a metallic luster [Medieval Latin *marcasita,* from Arabic *marqashītā*]

¹mar·cel \mär-'sel\ *n* : a deep soft wave made in the hair by the use of a heated curling iron [*Marcel* Grateau, died 1936, French hairdresser]

²marcel *vt* **mar·celled; mar·cel·ling** : to make a marcel in

¹march \'märch\ *n* : a border region : FRONTIER; *esp* : a district originally set up to defend a boundary ⟨the Welsh *marches*⟩ [Old French *marche,* of Germanic origin]

²march *vi* : to have common borders or frontiers

³march \'märch, *imperatively often* härch *in the military*\ *vb* **1** : to move along usually with a steady regular stride in step with others **2 a** : to move in a direct purposeful manner : PROCEED **b** : to make steady progress : ADVANCE [Middle French *marchier*] — **march·er** *n*

⁴march \'märch\ *n* **1 a** : the action of marching **b** : the distance covered within a specific period of time by marching **c** : a regular even step used in marching **2** : forward movement **3** : a musical composition in duple rhythm (as ⁴/₄ time) with a strongly accentuated beat suitable to accompany marching

March \'märch\ *n* : the 3d month of the year [Old French, from Latin *Martius,* from *Mart-, Mars,* the god Mars]

mär·chen \'meər-kən\ *n, pl* **märchen** : TALE 1; *esp* : FOLKTALE [German]

mar·chio·ness \'mär-shə-nəs, -shnəs\ *n* **1** : the wife or widow of a marquess **2** : a woman who holds the rank of marquess in her own right [Medieval Latin *mar-*

chionissa, from *marchio* "marquess", from *marca* "border region", of Germanic origin]

march·pane \'märch-,pān\ *n* : MARZIPAN [Italian *marzapane*]

march–past \'märch-,past\ *n* : a marching by especially of troops in review

Mar·di Gras \,märd-ē-'grä\ *n* : Shrove Tuesday often observed with parades and festivities [French, literally, "fat Tuesday"]

¹mare \'maər, 'meər\ *n* : the female of a member of the horse family [Old English *mere*]

²ma·re \'mär-ā\ *n, pl* **ma·ria** \'mär-ē-ə\ : one of several large dark areas on the surface of the moon or Mars [Latin, "sea"]

ma·re clau·sum \,mär-ā-'klau-səm, -'klò-\ *n* : a navigable body of water (as a sea) under the jurisdiction of one nation and closed to other nations [New Latin, literally, "closed sea"]

mare's nest *n, pl* **mare's nests** *or* **mares' nests** **1** : a false discovery or a deliberate hoax **2** : a situation or condition of great confusion

mare's tail *n* : a cirrus cloud that has a long slender flowing appearance

mar·ga·rine \'märj-rən, -ə-rən, -ə-,rēn\ *n* : a food product made usually from vegetable oils and skim milk often with vitamins A and D added and used as a spread and a cooking fat [French, from Greek *margaron* "pearl"]

mar·gay \'mär-,gā\ *n* : a small American spotted wildcat [French, from Tupi *maracaja*]

marge \'märj\ *n* : MARGIN 2

¹mar·gin \'mär-jən\ *n* **1** : the part of a page outside the main body of printed or written matter **2** : the outside limit and adjoining area of something **3 a** : an allowance (as of time or money) to meet unexpected demands **b** : the point (as of rising costs or shortage of raw material) at which an economic activity becomes impracticable **4 a** : the difference between cost and selling price **b** : cash or collateral deposited to secure a broker from loss on a contract **c** : an allowance above or below a certain figure within which a purchase or sale is to be made **5** : measure or degree of difference ⟨won by a single vote *margin*⟩ [Latin *margin-, margo* "border"] SYN see BORDER — **mar·gined** \-jənd\ *adj*

²margin *vt* **1** : to provide with an edging or border **2** : BORDER 2

mar·gin·al \'märj-nəl, -ən-l\ *adj* **1** : written or printed in the margin of a page or sheet ⟨*marginal* notes⟩ **2** : of, relating to, or situated at a margin or border **3 a** : close to the lower limit of qualification or acceptability ⟨*marginal* students⟩ **b** : yielding a supply of goods which when marketed at existing price levels will barely cover the cost of production ⟨*marginal* land⟩; *also* : relating to or derived from goods produced and marketed and with such result ⟨*marginal* profits⟩ — **mar·gin·al·i·ty** \,mär-jə-'nal-ət-ē\ *n* — **mar·gin·al·ly** \'märj-nə-lē, -ən-l-ē\ *adv*

mar·gi·na·lia \,mär-jə-'nā-lē-ə\ *n pl* : marginal notes

marginalize \'märj-nəl-,īz, -ən-l-\ *vt* **-ized; -iz·ing** : to relegate to a marginal position within a society or group — **mar·gin·al·i·zation** \,märj-nəl-ə-'zā-shən, -ən-l-\ *n*

marginal utility *n* : the amount of additional utility to a consumer provided by an additional unit of an economic good or service

mar·grave \'mär-,grāv\ *n* **1** : the military governor especially of a medieval German border province **2** : a member of the German nobility corresponding in rank to a British marquess [Dutch *markgraaf*] — **mar·gra·vate** \-grə-,vāt\ *or* **mar·gra·vi·ate** \mär-'grā-vē-ət\ *n* — **mar·gra·vi·al** \-vē-əl\ *adj*

mar·gra·vine \'mär-grə-,vēn, ,mär-grə-'\ *n* : the wife of a margrave

mar·gue·rite \,mär-gyə-'rēt, -gə-\ *n* **1** : DAISY 1a **2** : any of various single-flowered chrysanthemums **3** : any of

\ə\ abut	\ng\ sing
\ər\ further	\ō\ bone
\a\ mat	\ó\ saw
\ā\ take	\oi\ coin
\ä\ cot, cart	\th\ thin
\aù\ out	\th\ this
\ch\ chin	\ü\ food
\e\ pet	\ù\ foot
\ē\ easy	\y\ yet
\g\ go	\yü\ few
\i\ tip	\yù\ cure
\ī\ life	\zh\ vision
\j\ job	

several cultivated chamomiles [French, derived from Greek *margaron* "pearl"]

maria *pl of* [2]*MARE*

Mar·i·an \'mer-ē-ən, 'mar-ē-, 'mā-rē-\ *adj* **1** : of or relating to Mary Tudor or her reign (1553-58) **2** : of or relating to the Virgin Mary

Mar·i·an·ist \-ē-ə-nəst\ *n* : a member of the Roman Catholic Society of Mary of Paris devoted especially to education

mari·gold \'mar-ə-ˌgōld, 'mer-\ *n* **1** : POT MARIGOLD **2** : any of a genus of tropical American herbs of the daisy family that are grown for their showy variously colored yellow, orange, or maroon flower heads [Middle English, from *Mary,* mother of Jesus + *gold*]

mar·i·jua·na *or* **mar·i·hua·na** \ˌmar-ə-'wän-ə *also* -'hwän-\ *n* **1** : HEMP **2** : the dried leaves and flowering tops of the female hemp plant that are sometimes smoked for their intoxicating effect — compare BHANG, CANNABIS, HASHISH [Mexican Spanish *mariguana, marihuana*]

ma·rim·ba \mə-'rim-bə\ *n* : a primitive xylophone with resonators beneath each bar; *also* : a modern form of this instrument [of African origin]

marimba

ma·ri·na \mə-'rē-nə\ *n* : a dock or basin providing secure moorings for boats and yachts [Italian and Spanish, "seashore", from *marino,* adj., "marine", from Latin *marinus*]

[1]mar·i·nade \ˌmar-ə-'nād\ *vt* : MARINATE

[2]marinade *n* : a savory usually acid sauce in which food (as meat) is soaked to enrich its flavor

mar·i·nate \'mar-ə-ˌnāt\ *vt* : to soak in a marinade [probably from Italian *marinare,* from *marino* "marine"]

[1]ma·rine \mə-'rēn\ *adj* **1 a** : of or relating to the sea ⟨*marine* life⟩ **b** : of or relating to the navigation of the sea : NAUTICAL ⟨a *marine* chart⟩ **c** : of or relating to the commerce of the sea ⟨*marine* insurance⟩ **2** : of or relating to marines ⟨*marine* barracks⟩ [Latin *marinus,* from *mare* "sea"]

[2]marine *n* **1** : the mercantile and naval shipping of a country **2** : one of a class of soldiers serving on shipboard or in close association with a naval force; *esp* : a member of the United States Marine Corps

mar·i·ner \'mar-ə-nər\ *n* : one who navigates or assists in navigating a ship : SAILOR

Mar·i·ol·a·try \ˌmer-ē-'äl-ə-trē, ˌmar-\ *n* : excessive veneration of the Virgin Mary [*Mary* + Greek *latreia* "worship"]

mar·i·o·nette \ˌmar-ē-ə-'net, ˌmer-\ *n* : a small usually wooden figure with jointed limbs moved by strings or wires [French *marionnette,* from the name *Marion*]

Mar·i·po·sa lily \ˌmar-ə-ˌpō-zə-, -sə-\ *n* : any of a genus of western North American plants of the lily family with showily blotched flowers [probably from American Spanish *mariposa,* from Spanish, "butterfly"]

Mar·ist \'mar-əst, 'mer-\ *n* : a member of the Roman Catholic Society of Mary devoted to education

mar·i·tal \'mar-ət-l\ *adj* **1** : of or relating to marriage **2** : of or relating to a husband [Latin *maritalis,* from *maritus* "married"] SYN see MATRIMONIAL — **mar·i·tal·ly** \-l-ē\ *adv*

mar·i·time \'mar-ə-ˌtīm\ *adj* **1** : of or relating to navigation or commerce on the sea ⟨*maritime* law⟩ **2** : of, relating to, or bordering on the sea ⟨a *maritime* province⟩ **3** : having characteristics controlled primarily by oceanic winds and air masses ⟨a *maritime* climate⟩ [Latin *maritimus,* from *mare* "sea"]

mar·jo·ram \'märj-rəm, -ə-rəm\ *n* : any of various usually fragrant and aromatic mints sometimes used in cookery [Middle French *marjorane,* from Medieval Latin *marjorana*]

[1]mark \'märk\ *n* **1** : [1]MARCH **2 a** (1) : a conspicuous object serving as a guide for travelers (2) : something (as a line, notch, or fixed object) designed to record position ⟨high-water *mark*⟩ **b** : something aimed at :

TARGET **c** : the starting line or position **d** (1) : an object of ridicule or abuse : BUTT (2) : the point under discussion ⟨a comment beside the *mark*⟩ **e** : a standard of performance, quality, or condition : NORM **3 a** (1) : SIGN, INDICATION ⟨gave the necklace as a *mark* of esteem⟩ (2) : an impression (as a scratch, scar, or stain) made on something (3) : a distinguishing trait or quality : CHARACTERISTIC ⟨the *marks* of an educated person⟩ **b** : a symbol used for identification or indication of ownership **c** : a cross made in place of a signature **d** : a written or printed symbol (as a comma or colon) **e** : a symbol (as a number or letter) representing an estimation of the quality of work or conduct; *esp* : GRADE 5 **4 a** : ATTENTION, NOTICE ⟨nothing worthy of *mark*⟩ **b** : IMPORTANCE, DISTINCTION ⟨a person of *mark*⟩ **c** : a lasting or strong impression ⟨make one's *mark* in the world⟩ [Old English *mearc* "boundary, march, sign"]

[2]mark *vt* **1 a** (1) : to fix or trace out the bounds of (2) : to plot the course of : CHART **b** : to set apart by a line or boundary ⟨*mark* off a mining claim⟩ **2 a** : to designate as if by a mark ⟨*marked* for greatness⟩ **b** : to make a mark on **c** : to furnish with natural marks ⟨wings *marked* with white⟩ **d** : to label so as to indicate price or quality **e** : to make note of in writing : JOT **f** : to indicate by a mark or symbol; *also* : RECORD **g** : to determine the quality or value of by means of marks or symbols : GRADE **h** : CHARACTERIZE, DISTINGUISH ⟨the flamboyance that *marks* their stage performance⟩ **3** : to take notice of : OBSERVE ⟨*mark* my words⟩ — **mark time 1** : to keep the time of a marching step by moving the feet alternately without advancing **2** : to function or operate without making progress

[3]mark *n* **1 a** : the basic monetary unit of East Germany **b** : a coin representing one mark **2** : DEUTSCHE MARK [German]

Mark \'märk\ *n* — see BIBLE table

mark·down \'märk-ˌdaun\ *n* **1** : a lowering of price **2** : the amount by which an original selling price is reduced

mark down \märk-'daun, 'märk-\ *vt* : to put a lower price on

marked \'märkt\ *adj* **1** : having marks ⟨a *marked* card⟩ **2** : having a distinctive character : NOTICEABLE **3 a** : having fame or notoriety **b** : being an object of attack, suspicion, or vengeance — **mark·ed·ly** \'mär-kəd-lē\ *adv*

mark·er \'mär-kər\ *n* **1** : one that marks **2** : something used for marking

[1]mar·ket \'mär-kət\ *n* **1 a** : a meeting together of people to buy and sell; *also* : the people at such a meeting **b** : a public place where a market is held; *esp* : a place where provisions are sold at wholesale **c** : a retail establishment usually of a specified kind ⟨a meat *market*⟩ **2 a** : a geographical area of demand for commodities ⟨our foreign *markets*⟩ **b** : the course of commercial activity by which the exchange of commodities is effected ⟨the *market* is dull⟩ **c** : an opportunity for selling ⟨a good *market* for used cars⟩ **3** : the area of economic activity in which buyers and sellers come together and the forces of supply and demand affect prices [Old North French, from Latin *mercatus* "trade, marketplace", from *mercari* "to trade", from *merx* "merchandise"] — **in the market** : interested in buying ⟨in the *market* for a house⟩

[2]market *vb* **1** : to deal in a market **2** : to offer for sale in a market : SELL — **mar·ke·teer** \ˌmär-kə-'tiər\ *or* **mar·ket·er** \'mär-kət-ər\ *n* — **mar·ket·ing** \'mär-kət-ing\ *n*

mar·ket·able \'mär-kət-ə-bəl\ *adj* **1** : fit for sale **2** : wanted by purchasers : SALABLE — **mar·ket·abil·i·ty** \ˌmär-kət-ə-'bil-ət-ē\ *n*

market garden *n* : a plot in which vegetables are raised for market — **market gardener** *n* — **market gardening** *n*

mar·ket·place \'mär-kət-ˌplās\ *n* **1** : an open square or place in a town where markets or public sales are held **2** : the world of trade or economic activity

market price *n* : a price actually given in current market dealings

market research *n* : the gathering of factual information as to consumer preferences for goods and services

market value *n* : a price at which both buyers and sellers are willing to do business

mark·ing \'mär-king\ *n* **1** : the act, process, or an instance of making or giving a mark **2 a** : a mark made **b** : arrangement, pattern, or disposition of marks (as on the coat of a mammal)

mark·ka \'mär-ˌkä\ *n, pl* **mark·kaa** \'mär-ˌkä\ *or* **mark·kas** \-ˌkäz\ **1** : the basic monetary unit of Finland **2** : a coin representing one markka [Finnish, from Swedish *mark*, a unit of value]

marks·man \'märk-smən\ *n* : a person skilled in shooting at a mark or target — **marks·man·ship** \-ˌship\ *n*

mark·up \'mär-ˌkəp\ *n* : an amount added to the cost price of an article to determine the selling price

mark up \mär-ˈkəp, ˈmär-\ *vt* : to put a higher price on

¹marl \'märl\ *n* : a loose or crumbling earthy deposit that contains a substantial amount of calcium carbonate [Middle French *marle*, from Medieval Latin *margila*, from Latin *marga*, from Gaulish] — **marly** \'mär-lē\ *adj*

²marl *vt* : to dress (land) with marl

mar·lin \'mär-lən\ *n* : any of several large oceanic sport fishes related to sailfishes [short for *marlinespike*; from the appearance of its beak]

mar·line \'mär-lən\ *also* **mar·lin** *n* : a small loosely twisted line of two strands used for seizing and as a covering for wire rope [Dutch *marlijn*]

mar·line·spike *also* **mar·lin·spike** \'mär-lən-ˌspīk\ *n* : a pointed iron tool used to separate strands of rope or wire (as in splicing)

mar·ma·lade \'mär-mə-ˌlād\ *n* : a clear jelly in which pieces of fruit and fruit rind are suspended [Portuguese *marmelada* "quince conserve", from *marmelo* "quince", from Latin *melimelum*, a kind of sweet apple, from Greek *melimēlon*, from *meli* "honey" + *mēlon* "apple"]

mar·mo·re·al \mär-ˈmōr-ē-əl, mär-ˈmȯr-\ *also* **mar·mo·re·an** \-ē-ən\ *adj* : of, relating to, or resembling marble or a marble statue [Latin *marmoreus*, from *marmor* "marble"] — **mar·mo·re·al·ly** \-ē-ə-lē\ *adv*

mar·mo·set \'mär-mə-ˌset, -mə-ˌzet\ *n* : any of numerous soft-furred bushy-tailed South and Central American monkeys with claws instead of nails except on the great toe [Middle French, "grotesque figure", from *marmouser* "to mumble"]

mar·mot \'mär-mət\ *n* : a stout-bodied short-legged burrowing rodent with coarse fur, a short bushy tail, and very small ears — compare WOODCHUCK [French *marmotte*]

¹ma·roon \mə-ˈrün\ *vt* **1** : to put ashore and abandon on a desolate island or coast **2** : to leave isolated and helpless [American Spanish *cimarrón* "fugitive Negro slave", from *cimarrón* "wild, savage"]

²maroon *n* : a dark red [French *marron* "Spanish chestnut"]

mar·quee \mär-ˈkē\ *n* **1** : a large tent set up for an outdoor party, reception, or exhibition **2** : a canopy usually of metal and glass projecting over an entrance (a theater *marquee*) [French *marquise*, literally, "marchioness"]

mar·quess \'mär-kwəs\ *or* **mar·quis** \'mär-kwəs, mär-ˈkē\ *n, pl* **mar·quess·es** *or* **mar·quis·es** \-kwə-səz\ *or* **mar·quis** \-ˈkē, -ˈkēz\ **1** : a nobleman of hereditary rank in Europe and Japan **2** : a member of the British peerage ranking below a duke and above an earl [Middle French *marquis*, alteration of *marchis*, from *marche* "border region, march"] — **mar·quess·ate** \'mär-kwə-sət\ *or* **mar·quis·ate** \'mär-kwə-zət, -sət\ *n*

mar·que·try \'mär-kə-trē\ *n, pl* **-tries** : decoration in which elaborate patterns are formed by the insertion of pieces of wood, shell, or ivory into a wood veneer that is then applied to a piece of furniture [Middle French *marqueterie*, from *marqueter* "to checker, inlay", from *marque* "mark"]

mar·quise \mär-ˈkēz\ *n, pl* **mar·quises** \-ˈkēz, -ˈkēz-əz\ : MARCHIONESS [French, from *marquis* "marquess"]

mar·qui·sette \ˌmär-kwə-ˈzet, -kə-\ *n* : a sheer meshed fabric used for clothing, curtains, and mosquito nets

mar·riage \'mar-ij\ *n* **1 a** : the state of being married **b** : the mutual relation of husband and wife : WEDLOCK **c** : the institution whereby a man and a woman are joined in a special social and legal relationship for the purpose of making a home and raising a family **2 a** : an act of marrying **b** : WEDDING 1 **3** : an intimate or close union (a *marriage* of music and verse) — **mar·riage·able** \-ə-bəl\ *adj*

marriage of convenience : a marriage contracted for social, political, or economic advantage

¹mar·ried \'mar-ēd\ *adj* **1** : united in marriage : WEDDED (a *married* couple) **2** : of or relating to marriage

²married *n, pl* **marrieds** *or* **married** : a married person

mar·ron \ma-ˈrōⁿ\ *n* **1** : a Mediterranean chestnut or its large sweet nut **2** *pl* : chestnuts preserved in vanilla-flavored syrup [French]

mar·row \'mar-ō\ *n* **1 a** : a soft vascular tissue that fills the cavities of most bones **b** : the substance of the spinal cord **2** : HEART 5b, CORE [Old English *mearg*] — **mar·row·less** \-ō-ləs\ *adj* — **mar·rowy** \'mar-ə-wē\ *adj*

mar·row·bone \'mar-ə-ˌbōn\ *n* **1** : a bone (as a shinbone) rich in marrow **2** *pl* : a person's knees

mar·row·fat \'mar-ō-ˌfat\ *n* : any of several wrinkled-seeded garden peas

¹mar·ry \'mar-ē\ *vb* **mar·ried; mar·ry·ing** **1 a** : to join as husband and wife according to law or custom (were *married* yesterday) **b** : to give in marriage (*married* their daughter to a lawyer) **c** : to take as husband or wife (*married* my neighbor) **d** : to take a spouse : WED **2** : to unite in a close and usually permanent relation [Old French *marier*, from Latin *maritare*, from *maritus* "married"]

²marry *interj, archaic* — used to express amused or surprised agreement [Middle English *marie*, from *Marie*, the virgin Mary]

Mars \'märz\ *n* : the planet 4th in order from the sun conspicuous for the redness of its light — see PLANET table [Latin, from *Mars*, god of war]

marsh \'märsh\ *n* : an area of soft wet land usually overgrown by grasses and sedges — compare SWAMP [Old English *mersc*]

¹mar·shal \'mär-shəl\ *n* **1 a** : a high official in a medieval royal household **b** : a person who arranges and directs ceremonies **2** : an officer of the highest rank in some military forces **3** : a federal official having duties similar to those of a sheriff; *also* : a city official having similar duties [Old French *mareschal*, of Germanic origin] — **mar·shal·cy** \-sē\ *n* — **mar·shal·ship** \-ˌship\ *n* ☐ **ORIGIN** The Old French word *mareschal* was borrowed from a Germanic language. A *mareschal* is, etymologically, a "horse-servant"; the compound is related to Old English *mere* (modern English *mare*) and *scealc*, "servant". In addition to its original sense of "a groom or keeper of horses", Old French *mareschal* became the title of a high official in a royal court. In the Middle English period, the English borrowed French *mareschal*, "high official". The earlier sense, "keeper of horses", was borrowed a little later but is now obsolete.

²marshal *vt* **mar·shaled** *or* **mar·shalled; mar·shal·ing** *or* **mar·shal·ling** \'märsh-ling, -ə-ling\ **1** : to arrange in proper position or order **2** : to lead ceremoniously or solicitously : USHER

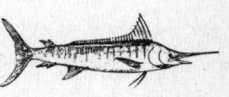

marlin

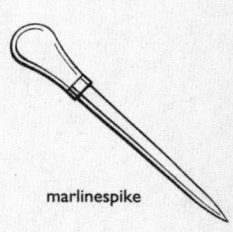

marlinespike

\ə\ abut		\ng\ sing	
\ər\ further		\ō\ bone	
\a\ mat		\ȯ\ saw	
\ā\ take		\ȯi\ coin	
\ä\ cot, cart		\th\ thin	
\au̇\ out		\th\ this	
\ch\ chin		\ü\ food	
\e\ pet		\u̇\ foot	
\ē\ easy		\y\ yet	
\g\ go		\yü\ few	
\i\ tip		\yu̇\ cure	
\ī\ life		\zh\ vision	
\j\ job			

marsh gas *n* : METHANE

marsh hawk *n* : a common North American hawk with a conspicuous white patch on the rump

marsh·mal·low \'märsh-,mel-ō, -,mal-\ *n* **1** : a pink-flowered perennial herb of the mallow family that has a root sometimes used in confectionery and in medicine **2** : a confection made from the root of the marshmallow or from corn syrup, sugar, albumen, and gelatin

marsh marigold *n* : a swamp herb having bright yellow flowers resembling those of the related buttercups — called also *cowslip*

marshy \'mär-shē\ *adj* **marsh·i·er; -est 1** : resembling or constituting marsh **2** : of or relating to marshes — **marsh·i·ness** \-shē-nəs\ *n*

¹mar·su·pi·al \mär-'sü-pē-əl\ *adj* : of, relating to, or being a marsupial

²marsupial *n* : any of an order (Marsupialia) of lowly mammals (as a kangaroo or opossum) that have a pouch on the abdomen of the female containing the teats and serving to carry the young

mar·su·pi·um \-pē-əm\ *n, pl* **-pia** \-pē-ə\ **1** : the pouch of a female marsupial **2** : a structure analogous to the marsupium in which an invertebrate animal carries eggs or young [Latin, "purse, pouch", from Greek *marsypion*]

mart \'märt\ *n* : MARKET 1b [Dutch *marct, mart,* probably from Old North French *market*]

mar·ten \'märt-n\ *n, pl* **marten** *or* **martens** : a slim flesh-eating mammal larger than the related weasels; *also* : its soft gray or brown fur [Middle French *martrine* "marten fur", from *martre* "marten", of Germanic origin]

mar·tial \'mär-shəl\ *adj* **1** : of, relating to, or suited for war or a warrior ⟨a *martial* stride⟩ **2** : of or relating to an army or to military life [Latin *martialis* "of Mars", from *Mart-, Mars* "Mars"] — **mar·tial·ly** \-shə-lē\ *adv* □ SYN MARTIAL, WARLIKE, MILITARY mean relating to or characteristic of war. MARTIAL suggests especially the pomp and ceremony of war and preparation for war ⟨*martial* music⟩ WARLIKE implies the feeling or temper that leads to or accompanies war ⟨*warlike* mountain tribes⟩ MILITARY applies to anything pertaining to the art or conduct of organized warfare especially on land ⟨*military* campaigns⟩

martial law *n* : the law applied (as by military or police forces) in occupied territory or in an emergency

Mar·tian \'mär-shən\ *adj* : of or relating to the planet Mars or its hypothetical inhabitants — **Martian** *n*

mar·tin \'märt-n\ *n* : a small European swallow with a forked tail, bluish black head and back, and white rump and underparts; *also* : any of various other swallows and flycatchers [Middle French, from Saint *Martin*]

mar·ti·net \,märt-n-'et\ *n* : a strict disciplinarian [Jean *Martinet,* 17th century French army officer]

mar·tin·gale \'märt-n-,gāl\ *n* : a strap connecting a horse's girth to the bit or reins so as to hold down its head [Middle French]

mar·ti·ni \mär-'tē-nē\ *n* : a cocktail consisting of gin or vodka and dry vermouth [probably from the name *Martini*]

Mar·tin·mas \'märt-n-məs, -,mas\ *n* : November 11 celebrated as the feast of Saint Martin [Middle English *martinmasse,* from Saint *Martin* + *masse* "mass"]

¹mar·tyr \'märt-ər\ *n* **1** : a person who suffers death rather than give up his or her religion **2** : one who sacrifices his or her life or something of great value for a principle or a cause **3** : a great or constant sufferer [Old English, from Late Latin, from Greek *martys,* literally, "witness"] — **mar·tyr·iza·tion** \,märt-ə-rə-'zā-shən\ *n* — **mar·tyr·ize** \'märt-ə-,rīz\ *vb*

²martyr *vt* **1** : to put to death for adhering to a belief **2** : TORTURE 1, 2

mar·tyr·dom \'märt-ər-dəm\ *n* **1** : the sufferings and death of a martyr **2** : TORMENT 1, 2, TORTURE

¹mar·vel \'mär-vəl\ *n* : something that causes wonder or astonishment [Old French *merveille,* from Late Latin *mirabilia* "marvels", from Latin *mirabilis* "wonderful", from *mirari* "to wonder"]

²marvel *vb* **mar·veled** *or* **mar·velled; mar·vel·ing** *or* **mar·vel·ling** \'marv-ling, -ə-ling\ : to become filled with surprise or astonishment ⟨*marveled* at the acrobat's feats⟩

mar·vel·ous *or* **mar·vel·lous** \'märv-ləs, -ə-ləs\ *adj* **1** : causing wonder : ASTONISHING **2** : MIRACULOUS 1 **3** : of the highest quality : SPLENDID ⟨a *marvelous* party⟩ — **mar·vel·ous·ly** *adv* — **mar·vel·ous·ness** *n*

Marx·ian \'märk-sē-ən, 'märk-shən\ *adj* : of, developed by, or influenced by the doctrines of Karl Marx ⟨*Marxian* socialism⟩

Marx·ism \'märk-,siz-əm\ *n* : the political, economic, and social doctrines developed by Karl Marx that provide the basis for Marxian socialism and much of modern Communism — **Marx·ist** \'märk-səst\ *n or adj*

Marx·ism-Len·in·ism \-'len-ə-,niz-əm\ *n* : a theory and practice of Communism developed by Lenin from Marxism primarily to fit Russian conditions — **Marx·ist-Len·in·ist** \-'len-ə-nəst\ *n or adj*

Mary Jane \'meər-ē-,jān, 'maər-ē-, 'mā-rē-\ *n, slang* : MARIJUANA [by folk etymology]

Mary·knoll·er \-,nō-lər\ : a member of the Catholic Foreign Mission Society of America founded at Maryknoll, N. Y., in 1911

mar·zi·pan \'märt-sə-,pän, -,pan; 'märz-ə-,pan\ *n* : a confection of almond paste, sugar, and egg white that is often shaped into forms [German, from Italian *marzapane,* a medieval coin, marzipan, from Arabic *mawthabān,* a medieval coin]

mas·cara \ma-'skar-ə\ *n* : a cosmetic for coloring the eyelashes and eyebrows [Italian *maschera* "mask"]

mas·con \'mas-,kän\ *n* : any of the large dense concentrations of mass under the surface of the maria of the moon [*mass* + concentration]

mas·cot \'mas-,kät also -kət\ *n* : a person, animal, or object adopted by a group as a symbol and supposed to bring good luck [French *mascotte,* from Provençal *mascoto* "charm, sorcery", from *masco* "witch", from Medieval Latin *masca*] □ ORIGIN The Medieval Latin word *masca,* meaning "witch", was borrowed as *masco* into the Provençal language of southern France. *Mascoto,* a diminutive form of *masco,* was used to mean "charm" or "sorcery". This word was borrowed into French as *mascotte* and was popularized by the operetta *La Mascotte,* composed by Edmond Audran in 1880. In this operetta *"la mascotte"* is the beautiful maiden Bettina, whose influence brings victories to the army of the prince of Pisa. *Mascot* appeared in English soon afterward, used to mean "a person or thing held to bring good luck".

¹mas·cu·line \'mas-kyə-lən\ *adj* **1** : of the male sex **2** : characteristic of or belonging to men : MANLY **3** : of, relating to, or constituting the class of words that ordinarily includes most of those referring to males ⟨a *masculine* noun⟩ ⟨*masculine* gender⟩ **4** : having or occurring in a stressed final syllable ⟨*masculine* rhyme⟩ [Middle French *masculin,* from Latin *masculinus,* from *masculus* "male", from *mas* "male"] — **mas·cu·line·ly** *adv* — **mas·cu·line·ness** \-lən-nəs\ *n* — **mas·cu·lin·i·ty** \,mas-kyə-'lin-ət-ē\ *n*

²masculine *n* **1** : a word or form of the masculine gender **2** : the masculine gender

ma·ser \'mā-zər\ *n* : a device that utilizes the natural oscillations of atoms or molecules between energy levels for generating monochromatic microwave radiation [*m*icrowave *a*mplification by *s*timulated *e*mission of *r*adiation]

¹mash \'mash\ *n* **1** : crushed malt or grain meal steeped and stirred in hot water to ferment (as in making whiskey) **2 :** a mixture of ground feeds for livestock **3 :** a soft pulpy mass [Old English *māx-*]

²mash *vt* **1 :** to reduce to a soft pulpy state by beating or pressure **2 :** to subject (as crushed malt) to the action of water with heating and stirring — **mash·er** *n*

¹mask \'mask\ *n* **1 :** a cover for the face used for disguise or protection ⟨a Halloween *mask*⟩ ⟨a baseball catcher's *mask*⟩ **2 :** a device usually covering the mouth and nose either to aid in or prevent the inhaling of something (as a gas or spray) **3 :** a covering (as of gauze) for the mouth and nose to prevent infective droplets from being blown into the air **4 :** something that disguises or conceals : CLOAK, PRETENSE **5 :** one that wears a mask : MASKER **6 :** a sculptured face made by a mold in plaster or wax ⟨a death *mask*⟩ **7 :** the face of a mammal (as a fox or dog) **8 :** MASQUE 2 [Middle French *masque,* from Italian *maschera*] SYN see DISGUISE

²mask *vb* **1 :** to take part in a masquerade **2 :** to put on or wear a mask **3 :** CONCEAL, DISGUISE ⟨*mask* one's real purpose⟩ **4 :** to cover for protection ⟨*mask* the glass before painting the windows⟩

masked \'maskt\ *adj* **:** marked by the use of masks ⟨a *masked* ball⟩

mask·er \'mas-kər\ *n* **:** one that wears a mask; *esp* **:** a participant in a masquerade

mas·och·ism \'mas-ə-ˌkiz-əm, 'maz-\ *n* **1 :** a sexual perversion characterized by pleasure in being abused especially by a loved one **2 :** a taste for suffering [Leopold von Sacher-*Masoch,* died 1895, German novelist]

ma·son \'mās-n\ *n* **1 :** a skilled worker who builds with stone, brick, or cement **2** *cap* **:** FREEMASON [Old French *maçon*]

Ma·son·ic \mə-'sän-ik\ *adj* **:** of, relating to, or characteristic of Freemasons or Freemasonry

Ma·son·ite \'mās-n-ˌīt\ *trademark* — used for a fiberboard made from steam-treated wood fiber

ma·son jar \ˌmās-n-\ *n* **:** a widemouthed jar used for home canning [John L. *Mason,* 19th century American inventor]

ma·son·ry \'mās-n-rē\ *n, pl* **-ries 1 a :** something built of materials used by masons **b :** the art, trade, or occupation of a mason **c :** work done by a mason **2** *cap* **:** FREEMASONRY 1

mason wasp *n* **:** a solitary wasp that constructs nests of hardened mud

masque \'mask\ *n* **1 :** MASQUERADE 1 **2 :** a short allegorical dramatic entertainment of the 16th and 17th centuries performed by masked actors [Middle French]

masqu·er \'mas-kər\ *n* **:** MASKER

¹mas·quer·ade \ˌmas-kə-'rād\ *n* **1 a :** a social gathering of persons wearing masks and often costumes **b :** a costume for wear at such a gathering **2 :** an action or appearance that is mere disguise or outward show [Middle French, from Italian dialect *mascarada,* from Italian *maschera* "mask"]

²masquerade *vi* **1 a :** to disguise oneself or go about disguised **b :** to take part in a masquerade **2 :** to assume the appearance of something one is not : POSE — **mas·quer·ad·er** *n*

¹mass \'mas\ *n* **1** *cap* **:** a sequence of prayers and ceremonies forming the eucharistic service especially of the Roman Catholic Church **2** *often cap* **:** a celebration of the Eucharist **3 :** a musical setting for parts of the Mass [Old English *mæsse,* from Late Latin *missa* "dismissal after a religious service, mass", from Latin *mittere* "to send, let go"]

²mass *n* **1 a :** a quantity of matter or the form of matter that holds or clings together in one body ⟨a *mass* of metal⟩ **b :** greatness of size : BULK **c :** the principal part : main body **2 :** the property of a body that is a measure of its inertia and is commonly taken as a measure of the quantity of matter it contains **3 :** a large quantity, amount, or number **4 a :** a large body of persons in a compact group **b** *pl* **:** the body of common

people as contrasted with the elite [Middle French *masse,* from Latin *massa,* from Greek *maza*] SYN see BULK

³mass *vb* **:** to form or collect into a mass

⁴mass *adj* **1 a :** of, relating to, or designed for the mass of the people ⟨a *mass* market⟩ ⟨*mass* education⟩ **b :** participated in by or affecting a large number of individuals ⟨*mass* demonstrations⟩ **c :** occurring on a large scale ⟨*mass* production⟩ **2 :** viewed as a whole : TOTAL ⟨the *mass* effect of a design⟩

¹mas·sa·cre \'mas-i-kər\ *vt* **-cred; -cring** \-kə-riŋ, -kriŋ\ **:** to kill by massacre : SLAUGHTER — **mas·sa·crer** \-kər-ər, -i-krər\ *n*

²massacre *n* **1 :** the violent, cruel, and indiscriminate killing of a number of people **2 :** a slaughter of animals in large numbers [Middle French]

¹mas·sage \mə-'säzh, -'säj\ *n* **:** manipulation of bodily tissues (as by rubbing, stroking, kneading, or tapping) for relaxation or treatment especially with the hand or an instrument [French, from *masser* "to massage", from Arabic *massa* "to stroke"]

²massage *vt* **:** to subject to massage — **mas·sag·er** *n*

mas·sa·sau·ga \ˌmas-ə-'sȯ-gə\ *n* **:** any of several small rattlesnakes [*Missisauga* river, Ontario, Canada]

mass driver *n* **:** a large electromagnetic catapult designed to hurl material (as from an asteroid) into space

mass–energy equation *n* **:** an equation for the conversion of mass and energy into one another : $E = mc^2$ where E is energy in ergs, m is mass in grams, and c is the velocity of light in centimeters per second

mas·se·ter \mə-'sēt-ər, ma-\ *n* **:** a large muscle that raises the lower jaw and assists in chewing [Greek *masētēr,* from *masasthai* "to chew"] — **mas·se·ter·ic** \ˌmas-ə-'ter-ik\ *adj*

mas·seur \ma-'sər, mə-\ *n* **:** a man who practices massage [French, from *masser* "to massage"]

mas·seuse \-'süz, -'sərz, -'süz\ *n* **:** a woman who practices massage [French, feminine of *masseur*]

mas·sif \ma-'sēf\ *n* **:** a principal mountain mass [French, from *massif* "massive"]

mas·sive \'mas-iv\ *adj* **1 :** forming or consisting of a large mass **a :** WEIGHTY, HEAVY ⟨*massive* walls⟩ **b :** exceedingly large : GIGANTIC **c :** having no regular form but not necessarily lacking crystalline structure ⟨*massive* sandstone⟩ **2 a :** large, solid, or heavy in structure ⟨*massive* jaws⟩ **b :** large in scope or degree ⟨a *massive* effort⟩ ⟨*massive* retaliation⟩ — **mas·sive·ly** *adv* — **mas·sive·ness** *n*

mass medium *n, pl* **mass media :** a communications medium (as newspapers, radio, or television) that is designed to reach mass audiences — usually used in pl.

mass number *n* **:** an integer that expresses the mass of an isotope and designates the number of nucleons in the nucleus

mass–pro·duce \ˌmas-prə-'düs, -'dyüs\ *vt* **:** to produce in quantity usually by machinery — **mass production** *n*

mass spectrograph *n* **:** an apparatus that separates a stream of charged particles into a spectrum according to their masses and records the data photographically

mass spectrometer *n* **:** an instrument similar to a mass spectrograph but usually adapted for the electrical measurement of the data

massy \'mas-ē\ *adj* **mass·i·er; -est :** MASSIVE 1a, b

¹mast \'mast\ *n* **1 :** a long pole or spar that rises from the keel or deck of a ship or boat and supports the sails and rigging **2 :** a vertical or nearly vertical tall pole (as a post on a lifting crane) [Old English *mæst*] — **mast·ed** \'mas-təd\ *adj* — **before the mast :** as a common sailor

²mast *vt* **:** to furnish with a mast

³mast *n* **:** nuts accumulated on the forest floor and often serving as food for animals (as hogs) [Old English *mæst*]

¹mask 1

mas·tec·to·my \ma-'stek-tə-mē\ *n, pl* **-mies** : surgical removal of a breast [Greek *mastos* "breast"]

¹mas·ter \'mas-tər\ *n* **1 a** : a male teacher **b** : a person holding an academic degree higher than a bachelor's but lower than a doctor's **c** *often cap* : a revered religious leader **d** : an independent worker qualified to teach apprentices **e** : an artist or performer of great skill **2 a** : one having authority : RULER **b** : one that conquers or masters : SUPERIOR **c** : a person licensed to command a merchant ship **d** : an owner especially of a slave or animal **e** : the male head of a household **3 a** *archaic* : MISTER **b** *often cap* — used as a courtesy title before the name of a boy too young to be called mister **4** : a presiding officer in an institution or society [Old English *magister* and Old French *maistre*, both from Latin *magister*]

²master *vt* **mas·tered; mas·ter·ing** \'mas-tə-riŋ, -triŋ\ **1** : to get the better of : OVERCOME **2** : to become skilled or proficient in or in the use of ⟨*master* arithmetic⟩

³master *adj* **1** : being a master ⟨a *master* carpenter⟩ **2** : being the chief or guiding one ⟨a *master* plan⟩ **3** : controlling the operation of other mechanisms ⟨a *master* cylinder⟩ **4** : establishing a standard (as of dimension or weight) for reference ⟨a *master* gauge⟩

mas·ter–at–arms \,mas-tər-ət-'ärmz\ *n, pl* **masters–at–arms** : a petty officer charged with maintaining discipline aboard ship

master chief petty officer *n* : an enlisted rank in the Navy and Coast Guard above senior chief petty officer

mas·ter·ful \'mas-tər-fəl\ *adj* **1** : inclined to take control or dominate **2** : having or showing the power and skill of a master — **mas·ter·ful·ly** \-fə-lē\ *adv* — **mas·ter·ful·ness** *n* □ SYN DOMINEERING, IMPERIOUS: MASTERFUL implies a strong forceful personality andthe ability to deal authoritatively with people and affairs; DOMINEERING suggests an overbearing or tyrannical manner and an obstinate attempt to enforce one's will; IMPERIOUS applies to one who by position or nature is fitted to command and it often suggests arrogant assurance.

master gunnery sergeant *n* : an enlisted rank in the Marine Corps above master sergeant

master key *n* : a key designed to open several different locks

mas·ter·ly \'mas-tər-lē\ *adj* : suitable to or resembling a master; *esp* : showing superior knowledge or skill — **mas·ter·li·ness** *n* — **masterly** *adv*

mas·ter·mind \-,mīnd\ *n* : a person who invents or directs a project — **mastermind** *vt*

master of ceremonies **1** : a person who determines the forms to be observed on a public occasion **2** : a person who acts as host at a formal event **3** : a person who acts as host for an entertainment program (as on television)

mas·ter·piece \'mas-tər-,pēs\ *n* **1** : a piece of work presented to amedieval guild as evidence of qualification for the rank of master **2** : a work done with great skill; *esp* : a supreme intellectual or artistic achievement

master race *n* : a people held to be racially preeminent and hence fitted to rule or enslave other peoples

master sergeant *n* : an enlisted rank in the Army above sergeant first class and below staff sergeant major, in the Marine Corps above gunnery sergeant and below sergeant major, and in the Air Force above technical sergeant and below senior master sergeant

mas·ter·ship \'mas-tər-,ship\ *n* **1** : the authority or control of a master **2** : the office or position of a master **3** : the skill or ability of a master

mas·ter·stroke \-,strōk\ *n* : a masterly performance or move

mas·ter·work \-,wərk\ *n* : MASTERPIECE 2

mas·tery \'mas-tə-rē, -trē\ *n, pl* **-ter·ies** **1** : the position or authority of a master **2** : the upper hand in a contest or competition **3** : skill or knowledge that makes one master of something : COMMAND ⟨a *mastery* of French⟩

mast·head \'mast-,hed\ *n* **1** : the top of a mast **2 a** : the printed matter in a newspaper or periodical that gives the title and pertinent details of ownership, advertising rates, and subscription rates **b** : the name of a newspaper displayed on the top of the first page

mas·tic \'mas-tik\ *n* **1** : a yellowish to greenish resin of a small southern European tree used in varnish **2** : a pasty material (as a preparation of asphalt) used as protective coating or cement [Latin *mastiche*, from Greek *mastichē*]

mas·ti·cate \'mas-tə-,kāt\ *vb* **1** : to grind or crush with or as if with the teeth in preparation for swallowing : CHEW **2** : to soften or reduce to pulp by crushing or kneading [Late Latin *masticare*, from Greek *masti·chan* "to gnash the teeth"] — **mas·ti·ca·tion** \,mas-tə-'kā-shən\ *n* — **mas·ti·ca·tor** \'mas-tə-,kāt-ər\ *n* — **mas·ti·ca·to·ry** \'mas-ti-kə-,tōr-ē, -,tor-\ *adj*

mas·ti·ca·to·ry \'mas-ti-kə-,tōr-ē, -,tor-\ *n, pl* **-ries** : a substance chewed to increase saliva

mas·tiff \'mas-təf\ *n* : a large powerful smooth-coated dog used chiefly as a watchdog and guard dog [Middle French *mastin*, derived from Latin *mansuetus* "tame"]

mas·ti·tis \mas-'tīt-əs\ *n, pl* **-tit·i·des** \-'tit-ə-,dēz\ : inflammation of the breast or udder usually caused by infection [Greek *mastos* "breast"]

mas·to·don \'mas-tə-,dän, -dən\ *also* **mas·to·dont** \'mas-tə-,dänt\ *n* : any of numerous huge extinct mammals related to the mammoths and existing elephants [Greek *mastos* "breast" + *odōn, odous* "tooth"] — **mas·to·don·ic** \,mas-tə-'dän-ik\ *adj*

¹mas·toid \'mas-,tȯid\ *adj* : of, relating to, or occurring in the region of a somewhat conical process of the temporal bone behind the ear [Greek *mastoeidēs*, literally, "breast-shaped", from *mastos* "breast"]

²mastoid *n* **1** : a mastoid bone or process **2 a** : MASTOIDITIS **b** : an operation for the relief of mastoiditis

mas·toid·itis \,mas-,tȯid-'īt-əs\ *n* : inflammation of the mastoid process

mas·tur·ba·tion \,mas-tər-'bā-shən\ *n* : erotic stimulation of the genital organs apart from sexual intercourse and especially by use of the hand [Latin *masturbatus*, past participle of *masturbari* "to masturbate"] — **mas·tur·bate** \'mas-tər-,bāt\ *vb*

¹mat \'mat\ *n* **1 a** : a piece of coarse fabric made of rushes, straw, or wool **b** : a piece of material in front of a door to wipe the shoes on **c** : a piece of material used under a dish or vase or as an ornament **d** : a paid or cushion for gynmastics or wrestling **2** : something made up of many intertwined or tangled strands ⟨a thick *mat* of vegetation⟩ [Old English *meatte*, from Late Latin *matta*, of Semitic origin]

²mat *vb* **mat·ted; mat·ting** **1** : to provide with a mat or matting **2** : to form into a tangled mass

³mat *or* **matt** *or* **matte** \'mat\ *vt* **mat·ted; mat·ting** **1** : to give a dull effect to **2** : to provide (a picture) with a mat

⁴mat *or* **matt** *or* **matte** *adj* : lacking luster or gloss [French *mat*, from Old French, "defeated", from Latin *mattus* "drunk"]

⁵mat *or* **matt** *or* **matte** *n* **1** : a border going around a picture between picture and frame or serving as the frame **2** : a dull finish or a roughened surface (as of gilt or paint) [French *mat* "dull color", from *mat* "mat, lacking luster"]

mat·a·dor \'mat-ə-,dȯr\ *n* : a bullfighter who has the principal role in the bullfight [Spanish, literally, "killer", from *matar* "to kill"]

¹match \'mach\ *n* **1 a** : a person or thing equal or similar to another **b** : one able to cope with another ⟨a *match* for the enemy⟩ **c** : an exact counterpart **2 a** : a pair that go well together ⟨curtains and carpet are a *match*⟩ **3** : a contest between two or more parties ⟨a tennis *match*⟩ **4 a** : a marriage union **b** : a prospective marriage partner [Old English *mæcca*]

mastiff

²match *vb* **1** : to meet successfully as a competitor **2 a** : to place in competition with or opposition to : PIT **b** : to provide with a worthy competitor **3** : to join or give in marriage **4 a** : to make or find the equal or the like of **b** : to cause to correspond **c** : to be the same as or suitable to one another ⟨these colors *match*⟩ **5 a** : to flip or toss (coins) and compare exposed faces **b** : to toss coins with — **match·er** *n*

³match *n* **1** : an evenly burning wick or cord formerly used for igniting a charge of powder **2** : a short slender piece of material (as wood) tipped with a mixture that ignites when subjected to friction [Middle French *meiche*]

match·board \'mach-,bōrd, -,bȯrd\ *n* : a board with a groove cut along one edge and a tongue along the other so as to fit snugly with the edges of similarly cut boards

match·book \'mach-,bu̇k\ *n* : a small folder containing rows of paper matches

match·less \'mach-ləs\ *adj* : having no equal : PEERLESS — **match·less·ly** *adv*

match·lock \'mach-,läk\ *n* : an old form of gunlock in which the charge was lighted by a cord match; *also* : a gun equipped with such a lock

match·mak·er \-,mā-kər\ *n* : one that arranges a match and especially a marriage — **match·mak·ing** \-king\ *n*

match point *n* : the last point needed to win a match

match·wood \'mach-,wu̇d\ *n* : small bits of wood

¹mate \'māt\ *vt* : CHECKMATE 2

²mate *n* : CHECKMATE 1

³mate *n* **1 a** : ASSOCIATE 1, COLLEAGUE **b** : an assistant to a more skilled worker : HELPER (plumber's *mate*) **2** : a deck officer on a merchant ship ranking below the captain **3** : one of a pair: as **a** : either member of a married couple **b** : either member of a breeding pair of animals ⟨a dove and its *mate*⟩ **c** : either of two matched objects ⟨a *mate* to a glove⟩ [Middle English]

⁴mate *vb* **1** : to join or fit together **2 a** : to bring together as mates **b** : to provide a mate for **3** : COPULATE

ma·té *or* **ma·te** \'mä-,tā\ *n* : an aromatic beverage made from the leaves and shoots of a South American holly; *also* : these leaves and shoots [American Spanish *mate*, from Quechua]

¹ma·te·ri·al \mə-'tir-ē-əl\ *adj* **1** : relating to, derived from, or consisting of matter; *esp* : PHYSICAL ⟨the *material* world⟩ ⟨*material* comforts⟩ **2** : having importance, relevance, or consequence ⟨facts *material* to the study⟩ **3** : relating to or concerned with physical rather than spiritual or intellectual things ⟨*material* progress⟩ **4** : of or relating to the production and distribution of economic goods and the social relationships of owners and laborers [Late Latin *materialis*, from Latin *materia* "matter"] — **ma·te·ri·al·i·ty** \-,tir-ē-'al-ət-ē\ *n* — **ma·te·ri·al·ly** \-'tir-ē-ə-lē\ *adv* — **ma·te·ri·al·ness** *n* □ SYN MATERIAL, PHYSICAL, CORPOREAL mean of or belonging to actuality. MATERIAL implies formation out of tangible matter; used in contrast with spiritual or ideal it suggests what is mundane, ignoble, or grasping; PHYSICAL applies to whatever is perceived by the senses and may contrast with mental, spiritual, or imaginary; CORPOREAL stresses having such tangible qualities of a body as fixed shape and size and resistance to force.

²material *n* **1** : the elements, constituents, or substance of which something is composed or can be made ⟨building *materials*⟩ **2 a** : apparatus needed for doing or making something ⟨writing *materials*⟩ **b** : EQUIPMENT 2a(1)

ma·te·ri·al·ism \mə-'tir-ē-ə-,liz-əm\ *n* **1 a** : a theory that everything can be explained as being or coming from matter **b** : a doctrine that the only or the highest values lie in material well-being and material progress **c** : a doctrine that economic or social change is caused by material factors **2** : a preoccupation with material rather than intellectual or spiritual things — **ma·te·ri-**

al·ist \-ē-ə-ləst\ *n or adj* — **ma·te·ri·al·is·tic** \-,tir-ē-ə-'lis-tik\ *adj* — **ma·te·ri·al·is·ti·cal·ly** \-'lis-ti-kə-lē, -klē\ *adv*

ma·te·ri·al·ize \mə-'tir-ē-ə-,līz\ *vb* **1 a** : to give form and substance to ⟨*materialize* an idea in words⟩ **b** : to appear or cause to appear in bodily form ⟨*materialize* a spirit⟩ **2 a** : to come into existence **b** : to put in an appearance; *esp* : to appear suddenly — **ma·te·ri·al·iza·tion** \-,tir-ē-ə-lə-'zā-shən\ *n* — **ma·te·ri·al·iz·er** \-'tir-ē-ə-,lī-zər\ *n*

ma·te·ria med·i·ca \mə-,tir-ē-ə-'med-i-kə\ *n* **1** : material or substances used in medical remedies **2** : a branch of medical science that deals with the sources, nature, properties, and preparation of drugs [New Latin, literally, "medical matter"]

ma·té·ri·el *or* **ma·te·ri·el** \mə-,tir-ē-'el\ *n* : equipment, apparatus, and supplies used by an organization or institution [French *matériel* "material"]

ma·ter·nal \mə-'tərn-l\ *adj* **1** : of, relating to, or characteristic of a mother : MOTHERLY **2 a** : related through a mother ⟨*maternal* grandparents⟩ **b** : derived or received from a mother [Middle French *maternel*, from Latin *maternus*, from *mater* "mother"] — **ma·ter·nal·ly** \-l-ē\ *adv*

ma·ter·ni·ty \mə-'tər-nət-ē\ *n, pl* **-ties** **1** : the state of being a mother : MOTHERHOOD **2** : the qualities of a mother : MOTHERLINESS

math \'math\ *n* : MATHEMATICS

math·e·mat·i·cal \,math-ə-'mat-i-kəl, math-'mat-\ *adj* **1** : of, relating to, or according with mathematics **2** : very exact : PRECISE ⟨*mathematical* accuracy⟩ **3** : possible but highly improbable ⟨only a *mathematical* chance⟩ [Latin *mathematicus*, from Greek *mathēmatikos*, from *mathēma* "mathematics", from *manthanein* "to learn"] — **math·e·mat·i·cal·ly** \-i-kə-lē, -klē\ *adv*

mathematical induction *n* : INDUCTION 2b

math·e·ma·ti·cian \,math-mə-'tish-ən, -ə-mə-\ *n* : a specialist or expert in mathematics

math·e·mat·ics \,math-ə-'mat-iks, math-'mat-\ *n* : the science of numbers and sets and their operations, relations, and combinations and of space configurations and their structure, measurement, and transformations

mat·i·nee *or* **mat·i·née** \,mat-n-'ā\ *n* : a musical or dramatic performance held in the daytime and especially in the afternoon [French *matinée*, literally, "morning", from *matin* "morning", from Latin *matutinum*, from *matutinus* "of the morning", from *Matuta*, goddess of morning]

mat·ins \'mat-nz\ *n pl, often cap* **1** : the office of prayer forming with lauds the first of the canonical hours **2** : MORNING PRAYER [Old French *matines*, from Late Latin *matutinae*, from Latin *matutinus* "of the morning"]

matr- *or* **matri-** *or* **matro-** *combining form* : mother ⟨*matri*lineal⟩ [Latin *matr-, mater*]

ma·tri·arch \'mā-trē-,ärk\ *n* : a woman who rules a group or state; *esp* : a mother who is the head of her family and descendants [*matr-* + Greek *archein* "to rule"] — **ma·tri·ar·chal** \,mā-trē-'är-kəl\ *adj*

ma·tri·ar·chate \'mā-trē-,är-kət, -,kāt\ *n* : MATRIARCHY 1

ma·tri·ar·chy \'mā-trē-,är-kē\ *n, pl* **-chies** **1** : a family, group, or state governed or headed by a matriarch **2** : a system of social organization in which descent and inheritance are traced through the female line

ma·tri·cide \'ma-trə-,sīd, 'mā-\ *n* **1** : murder of a mother by her child **2** : one who murders his or her own mother — **ma·tri·cid·al** \,ma-trə-'sīd-l, ,mā-\ *adj*

ma·tric·u·late \mə-'trik-yə-,lāt\ *vb* : to enroll as a member of a body and especially of a college or university [Medieval Latin *matriculare*, from Late Latin *matricula* "public roll", from *matrix* "list", from Latin, "womb"] — **ma·tric·u·la·tion** \-,trik-yə-'lā-shən\ *n*

\ə\ abut		\ng\ sing	
\ər\ further		\ō\ bone	
\a\ mat		\ȯ\ saw	
\ā\ take		\ȯi\ coin	
\ä\ cot, cart		\th\ thin	
\au̇\ out		\th\ this	
\ch\ chin		\ü\ food	
\e\ pet		\u̇\ foot	
\ē\ easy		\y\ yet	
\g\ go		\yü\ few	
\i\ tip		\yu̇\ cure	
\ī\ life		\zh\ vision	
\j\ job			

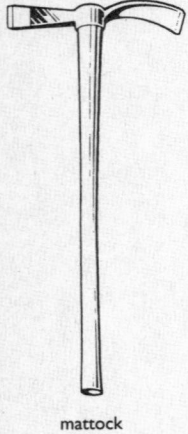

mattock

ma·tri·lin·eal \ˌma-trə-ˈlin-ē-əl, ˌmā-\ *adj* : relating to, based on, or tracing descent through the maternal line ⟨a *matrilineal* society⟩ — **ma·tri·lin·eal·ly** \-ē-ə-lē\ *adv*

mat·ri·mo·ni·al \ˌma-trə-ˈmō-nē-əl, -nyəl\ *adj* : of or relating to matrimony — **mat·ri·mo·ni·al·ly** \-ē\ *adv* □ SYN MARITAL, CONJUGAL, NUPTIAL: MATRIMONIAL may apply to whatever has to do with the married state or married persons; MARITAL may refer specifically to the husband's part in marriage but more often equals MATRIMONIAL; CONJUGAL refers especially to the relations and behavior of persons who are married; NUPTIAL applies to wedding rites and ceremonies.

mat·ri·mo·ny \ˈma-trə-ˌmō-nē\ *n, pl* **-nies** : the union of man and woman as husband and wife : MARRIAGE [Middle French *matremoine,* from Latin *matrimonium,* from *mater* "mother, married woman"]

matrimony vine *n* : a shrub or vine of the potato family with often showy flowers and bright berries

ma·trix \ˈmā-triks\ *n, pl* **ma·tri·ces** \ˈmā-trə-ˌsēz, ˈma-\ *or* **ma·trix·es** \ˈmā-trik-səz\ **1 a** : intercellular substance (as of cartilage) **b** : the thickened tissue at the base of a fingernail or toenail from which the nail grows **2** : a place or a surrounding or enclosing substance (as a rock) within which something (as a mineral) originates or develops **3** : something (as a mold) that gives form, foundation, or origin to something else (as molten metal) enclosed in it **4** : a rectangular array of mathematical elements that is subject to a special form of addition and multiplication [Latin, "womb", from *mater* "mother"]

ma·tron \ˈmā-trən\ *n* **1** : a usually mature and dignified or socially distinguished married woman **2 a** : a woman in charge of the household affairs of an institution **b** : a woman who supervises children or women (as in a school or a police station) [Middle French *matrone,* from Latin *matrona,* from *mater* "mother, married woman"]

ma·tron·ly \-lē\ *adj* : of, resembling, or suitable for a matron

matron of honor : a bride's principal married wedding attendant

matt *or* **matte** *variant of* MAT

¹mat·ter \ˈmat-ər\ *n* **1 a** : a subject of interest or concern ⟨a *matter* of dispute⟩ **b** : something to be dealt with : AFFAIR, CONCERN ⟨a few personal *matters* to take care of⟩ **c** : a condition affecting a person or thing unfavorably ⟨what's the *matter* with me⟩ **2** : the material of thought or discourse especially as contrasted with its form **3 a** : the substance of which a physical object is composed : something that occupies space and has weight **b** : material substance of a particular kind or function ⟨coloring *matter*⟩ ⟨the gray *matter* of the brain⟩ **c** : PUS **4** : a more or less definite amount or quantity ⟨a *matter* of 10 years or so⟩ **5** : something written or printed **6** : MAIL ⟨first-class *matter*⟩ [Old French *matere,* from Latin *materia* "physical substance, matter", from *mater* "mother"] — **for that matter** : so far as that is concerned — **no matter** : without regard to ⟨could remain cool *no matter* what the provocation⟩

²matter *vi* **1** : to be of importance : SIGNIFY **2** : to form or discharge pus : SUPPURATE ⟨a *mattering* wound⟩

matter of course : something that is to be expected as a natural or logical result of something else — **mat·ter-of-course** \ˌmat-ər-əv-ˈkōrs, -ər-ə-, -ˈkórs\ *adj*

mat·ter-of-fact \ˌmat-ər-ə-ˈfakt\ *adj* : sticking to or concerned with facts; *esp* : not fanciful or imaginative — **mat·ter-of-fact·ly** *adv* — **mat·ter-of-fact·ness** \-ˈfakt-nəs, -ˈfak-\ *n*

mat·tery \ˈmat-ə-rē\ *adj* : producing or containing pus or material resembling pus

Mat·thew \ˈmath-yü\ *n* — see BIBLE table — **Mat·the·an** *or* **Mat·thae·an** \ma-ˈthē-ən, mə-\ *adj*

mat·ting \ˈmat-ing\ *n* : material for mats; *also* : mats or stock of mats

mat·tock \ˈmat-ək\ *n* : an implement for digging consisting of a long wooden handle and a steel head one end of which comes to a blade and the other end to either a point or a cutting edge [Old English *mattuc*]

mat·tress \ˈma-trəs\ *n* **1** : a fabric case filled with springy material used either as a bed or on a bedstead **2** : an inflatable sack for use as a mattress — called also *air mattress* [Old French *materas,* from Arabic *maṭraḥ* "place where something is thrown"]

mat·u·ra·tion \ˌmach-ə-ˈrā-shən\ *n* **1** : the process of becoming mature **2** : the process by which diploid cells are transformed into haploid gametes — **mat·u·ra·tion·al** \-shnəl, -shən-l\ *adj*

¹ma·ture \mə-ˈtūr, -ˈtyūr\ *adj* **1** : based on slow careful consideration ⟨a *mature* judgment⟩ **2 a** : fully grown and developed : ADULT, RIPE ⟨*mature* fruit⟩ ⟨a youth physically but not yet emotionally *mature*⟩ **b** : having attained a final or desired state ⟨*mature* wine⟩ **3** : characteristic of or suitable to a mature individual ⟨a *mature* outlook⟩ **4** : due for payment ⟨the note becomes *mature* in 90 days⟩ [Latin *maturus* "ripe"] — **ma·ture·ly** *adv* — **ma·ture·ness** *n*

²mature *vb* **1** : to bring to maturity or completion **2** : to become fully developed or ripe **3** : to become due ⟨when a bond *matures*⟩

ma·tu·ri·ty \mə-ˈtūr-ət-ē, -ˈtyūr-\ *n* **1** : the quality or state of being mature; *esp* : full development **2** : the date when an obligation (as a bond or note) becomes due

mat·zo \ˈmät-sə, -ˌsō\ *n, pl* **mat·zoth** \-ˌsōth, -ˌsōt, -ˌsōs\ *or* **mat·zos** \-ˌsəz, -ˌsəs, -ˌsōz\ **1** : unleavened bread eaten at the Passover **2** : a wafer of matzo [Yiddish *matse,* from Hebrew *maṣṣāh*]

maud·lin \ˈmód-lən\ *adj* **1** : weakly and excessively sentimental **2** : drunk enough to be emotionally silly [Mary *Magdalene;* from the practice of depicting her as a weeping, penitent sinner] □ ORIGIN *Maudlin* is an alteration of *Magdalene,* the appellation of Mary, the woman mentioned in the Gospel of Luke (8.2): ". . . Mary, called Magdalene, out of whom went seven devils." Medieval representations of Mary Magdalene customarily showed her weeping, and by the 17th century *maudlin* had come to mean "tearful, weeping". Soon *maudlin* began to be used more generally to mean "tearfully or weakly emotional" and was used especially of anyone drunk enough to be emotionally silly, fuddled, or sentimental.

¹maul \ˈmól\ *n* : a heavy hammer often with a wooden head used especially for driving wedges or posts [Old French *mail,* from Latin *malleus*]

²maul *vt* **1 a** : to beat severely **b** : to injure by beating : MANGLE **2** : to handle roughly — **maul·er** *n*

maun·der \ˈmón-dər, ˈmän-\ *vi* **maun·dered; maun·der·ing** \-də-ring, -dring\ **1** : WANDER 1 **2** : to speak in an incoherent rambling way [British dialect *maunder* "to grumble"] — **maun·der·er** \-dər-ər\ *n*

Maun·dy Thursday \ˌmón-dē-, ˌmän-\ *n* : the Thursday before Easter [Old French *mandé,* ceremony of washing the feet of the poor on Maundy Thursday, from Latin *mandatum* "command"]

mau·so·le·um \ˌmó-sə-ˈlē-əm, ˌmó-zə-\ *n, pl* **-le·ums** *or* **-lea** \-ˈlē-ə\ : a large tomb; *esp* : a usually stone building for entombing the dead above ground [Latin, from Greek *Mausōleion,* tomb of Mausolus, died 353 B.C., ruler of Caria]

mauve \ˈmōv, ˈmóv\ *n* : a moderate purple, violet, or lilac color [French, "mallow", from Latin *malva*]

mav·er·ick \ˈmav-rik, -ə-rik\ *n* **1** : an unbranded range animal; *esp* : a motherless calf **2** : an independent individual who refuses to conform with the group [Samuel A. *Maverick,* died 1870, American pioneer who did not brand his calves] □ ORIGIN In south Texas in the middle of the 19th century lived a lawyer, Samuel

A. *Maverick*. A client once gave him 400 head of cattle instead of cash to settle a $1200 debt. Maverick had no use for the cattle, and so left them in the care of one of his men. The cattle were never branded and were left to roam at will. Eventually the term *maverick* came to be used to designate any unbranded cattle. Later *maverick* was applied to a member of a group who refused to accept one or more of the policies of that group or who refused to be "branded" with restrictive labels.

ma·vis \'mā-vəs\ *n* **1 :** SONGTHRUSH **2 :** a European thrush with spotted underparts [Middle French *mauvis*]

maw \'mo\ *n* **1 :** a receptacle (as a stomach or crop) into which food is taken by swallowing **2 :** the throat, gullet, or jaws especially of a carnivore [Old English *maga*]

mawk·ish \'mo-kish\ *adj* **1 :** having an insipid often unpleasant taste **2 :** sickly sentimental [Middle English *mawke* "maggot", from Old Norse *mathkr*] — **mawk·ish·ly** *adv* — **mawk·ish·ness** *n*

maxi- *combining form* **:** extra-long : extra-large [*maximum*]

max·il·la \mak-'sil-ə\ *n, pl* **max·il·lae** \-'sil-ē, -'sil-ī\ *or* **max·il·las** **1 a :** an upper jaw especially of a mammal **b :** either of two bones of the upper jaw that bear the upper teeth **2 :** one of the first or second pair of mouth appendages posterior to the mandibles in various arthropods [Latin] — **max·il·lary** \'mak-sə-,ler-ē\ *adj or n*

max·il·li·ped \mak-'sil-ə-,ped\ *n* **:** any of three pairs of appendages situated next behind the maxillae in a crustacean

max·im \'mak-səm\ *n* **1 :** a general truth, fundamental principle, or rule of conduct **2 :** a proverbial saying [Middle French *maxime*, from Medieval Latin *maxima*, from Latin *maximus*, superlative of *magnus* "great"]

max·i·mal \'mak-sə-məl, -sməl\ *adj* **:** MAXIMUM ⟨*maximal* growth⟩ ⟨a *maximal* dose⟩ — **max·i·mal·ly** \-ē\ *adv*

max·i·mize \'mak-sə-,mīz\ *vb* **1 :** to increase to a maximum ⟨*maximize* profits⟩ **2 :** to assign maximum importance to **3 :** to find a maximum value of **4 :** to interpret something in the broadest sense — **max·i·miz·er** *n*

max·i·mum \'mak-sə-məm, -sməm\ *n, pl* **max·i·ma** \-sə-mə\ *or* **max·i·mums** **1 a :** the greatest quantity or value attainable or attained **b :** the period of highest, greatest, or utmost development **2 :** an upper limit allowed (as by a legal authority) [Latin, neuter of *maximus*, superlative of *magnus* "great"] — **maximum** *adj*

may \mā, 'mā\ *auxiliary verb, past* **might** \mīt, 'mīt\; *present sing & pl* **may 1 a :** have permission to ⟨you *may* go now⟩ **b :** be in some degree likely to ⟨you *may* be right⟩ **2** — used to express a wish or desire ⟨long *may* you reign⟩ **3** — used to express purpose ⟨I laughed that I *might* not weep⟩, contingency ⟨I'll do my duty come what *may*⟩, or concession ⟨you *may* be slow but you are thorough⟩ [Old English *mæg* "can, may"] SYN SEE CAN

May \'mā\ *n* **:** the 5th month of the year [Latin *Maius*, from *Maia*, a Roman goddess]

Ma·ya \'mī-ə\ *n, pl* **Maya** *or* **Mayas :** a member of a group of Indian peoples of the Yucatán peninsula and adjacent areas [Spanish] — **Ma·yan** \'mī-ən\ *adj*

Ma·yan \'mī-ən\ *n* **1 :** an extensive language stock of Central America and Mexico **2 :** a member of any of the peoples speaking Mayan languages

may·ap·ple \'mā-,ap-əl\ *n* **:** a North American woodland herb of the barberry family that has a poisonous rootstock, leaves up to one foot in diameter, and a single large waxy white flower followed by a yellow egg-shaped edible berry; *also* **:** its fruit

may·be \'mā-bē, 'meb-ē\ *adv* **:** PERHAPS

May·day \'mā-'dā, 'mā-,\ — an international radio telephone signal word used as a distress call [French *m'aider* "help me"]

May Day \'mā-,dā\ *n* **:** May 1 celebrated as a springtime festival and in some countries as Labor Day

may·est *or* **mayst** \'mā-əst, māst, 'māst\ *archaic present 2d sing of* MAY

may·flow·er \'mā-,flau-ər, -,flaur\ *n* **:** any of various spring-blooming plants (as the trailing arbutus, hepatica, or several North American anemones)

may·fly \-,flī\ *n* **:** any of an order (Plectophora) of insects with an aquatic nymph and a short-lived fragile adult having membranous wings

may·hap \'mā-,hap, mā-'\ *adv* **:** PERHAPS

may·hem \'mā-,hem, 'mā-əm\ *n* **1 :** willful and permanent crippling, mutilation, or disfigurement of any part of the body **2 :** needless or willful damage or violence [Anglo-French *mahaim*, from Old French *maynier* "to maim"]

may·ing \'mā-ing\ *n, often cap* **:** the celebrating of May Day

mayn't \'mā-ənt, mānt, 'mānt\ **:** may not

may·on·naise \'mā-ə-,nāz, ,mā-ə-'\ *n* **:** a dressing (as for salads) consisting chiefly of yolk of egg, vegetable oil, and vinegar or lemon juice [French]

may·or \'mā-ər, 'me-ər, 'meər\ *n* **:** an official elected to act as chief executive or nominal head of a city or borough [Old French *maire*, from Latin *major*, comparative of *magnus* "great"] — **may·or·al** \'mā-ə-rəl, 'me-ə-\ *adj*

may·or·al·ty \'mā-ə-rəl-tē, 'me-; 'mer-əl-\ *n, pl* **-ties :** the office or the term of office of a mayor

mayor–council *adj* **:** of, relating to, or being a method of municipal government in which a usually elective mayor and council exercise both policy-making and administrative powers

may·pole \'mā-,pōl\ *n, often cap* **:** a tall flower-wreathed pole forming a center for May Day sports and dances

may·pop \'mā-,päp\ *n* **:** a climbing perennial passionflower of the southern United States; *also* **:** its ovoid yellow edible fruit [of American Indian origin]

May queen *n* **:** a girl chosen queen of a May Day festival

May·tide \'mā-,tīd\ *or* **May·time** \-,tīm\ *n* **:** the month of May

maze \'māz\ *n* **1 :** a confusingly intricate network of passages **2** *chiefly dialect* **:** a state of confusion or bewilderment [Middle English, from *mazen* "to confuse"]

ma·zur·ka \mə-'zər-kə, -'zùr-\ *n* **1 :** a Polish dance in moderate triple measure **2 :** music for the mazurka usually in moderate ¾ or ⅜ time [Polish *mazurek*]

mazy \'mā-zē\ *adj* **maz·i·er; -est :** resembling a maze

maz·zard \'maz-ərd\ *n* **:** SWEET CHERRY; *esp* **:** wild or seedling sweet cherry used as a rootstock for grafting [origin unknown]

MC \em-'sē, 'em-'sē\ *n* **:** MASTER OF CEREMONIES

me \mē, 'mē\ *pron, objective case of* I [Old English *mē*]

mead \'mēd\ *n* **:** a fermented drink made of water, honey, malt, and yeast [Old English *medu*]

mead·ow \'med-ō\ *n* **:** land in or mainly in grass; *esp* **:** a tract of moist low-lying usually level grassland [Middle English *medwe*, from Old English *mǣd*] — **mead·ow·land** \-,land\ *n*

meadow beauty *n* **:** any of a genus of low perennial American herbs with showy flowers

meadow fescue *n* **:** a tall vigorous perennial fescue with broad flat leaves cultivated for pasture and hay

mead·ow·lark \'med-ō-,lärk\ *n* **:** any of several North American songbirds largely brown and buff above with a yellow breast bearing a black crescent

meadow mushroom *n* **:** a common edible fungus that is the chief mushroom of commerce

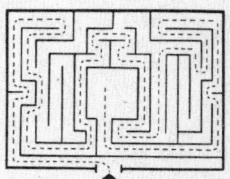

maze 1

\ə\ abut	\ng\ sing
\ər\ further	\ō\ bone
\a\ mat	\o\ saw
\ā\ take	\oi\ coin
\ä\ cot, cart	\th\ thin
\au\ out	\th\ this
\ch\ chin	\ü\ food
\e\ pet	\u\ foot
\ē\ easy	\y\ yet
\g\ go	\yü\ few
\i\ tip	\yu\ cure
\ī\ life	\zh\ vision
\j\ job	

meadow saffron *n* : a bulbous autumn-flowering herb of the lily family that bears white, lavender and white, or purple flowers and is a source of colchicine — called also *autumn crocus*

mead·ow·sweet \'med-ō-ˌswēt\ *n* : any of several North American native or naturalized spireas with pink or white fragrant flowers

mea·ger *or* **mea·gre** \'mē-gər\ *adj* 1 : having little flesh : THIN 2 : deficient in quality or quantity ⟨a *meager* serving of meat⟩ [Middle French *maigre,* from Latin *macer*] — **mea·ger·ly** *adv* — **mea·ger·ness** *n* ☐ SYN MEAGER, SCANTY, SPARSE mean falling short of what is normal, necessary, or desirable. MEAGER implies lack of fullness, richness, or plenty ⟨*meager* diets⟩ SCANTY stresses insufficiency in quantity, degree, or extent ⟨a *scanty* supply of fuel⟩ SPARSE implies a thin scattering of units ⟨a *sparse* population⟩

¹**meal** \'mēl\ *n* 1 : the food eaten or prepared for eating at one time 2 : the time or occasion of eating a meal [Old English *mǣl* "appointed time, meal"]

²**meal** *n* 1 : usually coarsely ground seeds of a cereal grass or pulse; *esp* : CORNMEAL 2 : something like meal especially in texture [Old English *melu*] SYN see FLOUR

meal·time \'mēl-ˌtīm\ *n* : the usual time at which a meal is served

meal·worm \-ˌwərm\ *n* : a small brownish worm that is the larva of various beetles and that lives in grain products and is often raised as food for insect-eating animals

mealy \'mē-lē\ *adj* **meal·i·er; -est** 1 : being soft, dry, and crumbly 2 : containing meal 3 : covered with fine granules or with flecks (as of color) 4 : MEALY-MOUTHED

mealy·bug \'mē-lē-ˌbəg\ *n* : any of numerous destructive scale insects with a white powdery covering

mealy·mouthed \ˌmē-lē-'maủthd, -'maủtht\ *adj* : not plain or straightforward in speech : DEVIOUS ⟨a *mealy-mouthed* politician⟩

¹**mean** \'mēn\ *adj* 1 : of low birth or station : HUMBLE 2 : ORDINARY 2a, COMMONPLACE ⟨a person of no *mean* ability⟩ 3 : POOR, SHABBY ⟨live in *mean* surroundings⟩ 4 : not honorable or worthy : UNKIND ⟨it is *mean* to take advantage of another's misfortunes⟩ 5 : STINGY 1, MISERLY 6 : SPITEFUL, MALICIOUS ⟨a *mean* remark⟩ 7 : of a vicious or troublesome disposition ⟨a *mean* horse⟩ 8 : UNWELL 1, INDISPOSED ⟨wake up feeling *mean*⟩ [Middle English *imene, mene,* from Old English *gemǣne*]

²**mean** \'mēn\ *vb* **meant** \'ment\; **mean·ing** \'mē-ning\ 1 a : to have as a purpose : INTEND ⟨I *mean* to go⟩ b : to intend for a particular purpose, use, or destination ⟨a book *meant* for children⟩ 2 : to serve to convey, show, or indicate : SIGNIFY ⟨what do these words *mean*⟩ ⟨those clouds *mean* rain⟩ 3 : to be of a specified degree of importance ⟨health *means* everything to me⟩ [Old English *mǣnan*] — **mean business** : to be in earnest

³**mean** *n* 1 : a middle point between extremes 2 a : a value that lies within a range of values and is computed according to a prescribed rule; *esp* : ARITHMETIC MEAN b : the arithmetic mean of the two extremes of a range of values c : either of the middle two terms of a proportion 3 *pl* : something by the use or help of which a desired end is accomplished or furthered ⟨*means* of production⟩ ⟨ready to use any *means* at their disposal⟩ 4 *pl* : resources available for disposal; *esp* : WEALTH ⟨a person of *means*⟩ [Middle French *meien,* from *meien,* adj., "mean, median"] SYN see AVERAGE — **by all means** : without fail : CERTAINLY — **by means of** : through the use of — **by no means** : not at all : certainly not

⁴**mean** *adj* 1 : holding a middle position : INTERMEDIATE 2 : occupying a position about midway between extremes: as a : being near the average b : being the mean of a set of values ⟨*mean* temperature⟩ [Middle French *meien,* from Latin *medianus* "median"]

¹**me·an·der** \mē-'an-dər\ *n* 1 : a turn or winding of a stream 2 : a winding path or course [Latin *maeander,* from Greek *maiandros,* from *Maiandros* (now *Menderes*), river in Asia Minor]

²**meander** *vi* **-dered; -der·ing** \-dəring, -dring\ 1 : to follow a winding or intricate course 2 : to wander aimlessly : RAMBLE

¹**mean·ing** \'mē-ning\ *n* 1 a : the sense one intends to convey especially by language : PURPORT ⟨do not mistake my *meaning*⟩ b : the sense that is conveyed ⟨the *meaning* of the poem is clear⟩ 2 : INTENT 1, PURPOSE 3 : intent to convey information : SIGNIFICANCE 1 ⟨a glance full of *meaning*⟩ ☐ SYN MEANING, SENSE, SIGNIFICATION, SIGNIFICANCE denote the idea conveyed to the mind by a word, sign, or symbol. MEANING is the general term used of anything (as a word, poem, action) requiring or allowing interpretation; SENSE applies especially to words or utterances and may denote one out of several meanings of any one word ⟨the word *charge* has many distinct *senses*⟩ SIGNIFICATION denotes the established meaning of a word, symbol, or written character; SIGNIFICANCE applies specifically to an underlying as distinguished from a surface meaning.

²**meaning** *adj* : SIGNIFICANT, EXPRESSIVE ⟨a *meaning* look⟩ — **mean·ing·ly** \-ning-lē\ *adv*

mean·ing·ful \-fəl\ *adj* : having a meaning or purpose; *esp* : SIGNIFICANT ⟨a *meaningful* experience⟩ — **mean·ing·ful·ly** \-fə-lē\ *adv* — **mean·ing·ful·ness** *n*

mean·ing·less \'mē-ning-ləs\ *adj* 1 : lacking sense or significance 2 : lacking motive — **mean·ing·less·ly** *adv* — **mean·ing·less·ness** *n*

mean·ly \'mēn-lē\ *adv* 1 : in a poor, humble, or shabby manner ⟨*meanly* dressed⟩ 2 : in an ungenerous or ignoble manner

mean·ness \'mēn-nəs\ *n* 1 : the quality or state of being low in station or ignoble in conduct 2 : a mean act

mean proportional *n* 1 : GEOMETRIC MEAN 1 2 : MEAN 2c

means test \'mēnz-\ *n* : an examination of a person's financial state to determine his eligibility to receive public assistance

meant *past of* MEAN

¹**mean·time** \'mēn-ˌtīm\ *n* : the intervening time

²**meantime** *adv* : MEANWHILE

¹**mean·while** \'mēn-ˌhwīl, -ˌwīl\ *n* : MEANTIME

²**meanwhile** *adv* : during the intervening time

mea·sle \'mē-zəl\ *n* 1 : infestation with or disease caused by larval tapeworms in the muscles and tissues 2 : a tapeworm larva in the muscles of a domesticated mammal [Old French *mesel* "leprous, infested with tapeworms", from Medieval Latin *misellus* "leper", from Latin, "wretch", from *miser* "miserable"] — **mea·sled** \-zəld\ *adj*

mea·sles \'mē-zəlz\ *n sing or pl* : an acute contagious virus disease marked by fever and red spots on the skin; *also* : any of several similar diseases (as German measles) [Middle English *meseles,* pl. of *mesel* "measles, spot characteristic of measles"]

mea·sly \'mēz-lē, -ə-lē\ *adj* **mea·sli·er; -est** 1 : infected or infested with measles or with trichina worms 2 : contemptibly small ⟨left a *measly* dime for a tip⟩

mea·sur·able \'mezh-rə-bəl, -ə-rə-; 'mezh-ər-bəl; 'māzh-\ *adj* : capable of being measured — **mea·sur·abil·i·ty** \ˌmezh-rə-'bil-ət-ē, -ə-rə-, ˌmāzh-\ *n* — **mea·sur·able·ness** *n* — **mea·sur·ably** *adv*

¹**mea·sure** \'mezh-ər, 'māzh-\ *n* 1 a : an adequate, fixed, or suitable limit or amount ⟨angry beyond *measure*⟩ ⟨all received their *measure* of praise or blame⟩ b : AMOUNT, EXTENT, DEGREE ⟨won themselves a *measure* of freedom⟩ 2 a : the dimensions, capacity, or quantity of something as fixed by measuring ⟨give full *measure*⟩ b : something (as a yardstick or cup) used in measuring c : a unit used in measuring ⟨the foot is a *measure* of length⟩ d : a system of measuring ⟨metric *measure*⟩ 3 : the act or process of measuring 4 a :

DANCE; *esp* : a stately dance **b** : rhythmic structure or movement in music or poetry : METER, CADENCE **c** : the part of a musical staff between two adjacent bars; *also* : the group or grouping of beats between these bars **5** : a basis or standard of comparison : CRITERION **6** : an action planned or taken as a means to an end; *esp* : a legislative bill or act [Old French *mesure*, from Latin *mensura*, from *mensus*, past participle of *metiri* "to measure"]
SEE MEASURES AND WEIGHTS TABLE NEXT PAGE

²**measure** *vb* **mea·sured; mea·sur·ing** \'mezh-ring, 'māzh-, -ə-ring\ **1** : to select or regulate with caution : GOVERN ⟨*measure* one's acts⟩ **2 a** : to mark or fix in multiples of a specific unit ⟨*measure* off three centimeters⟩ **b** : to allot or apportion in measured amounts ⟨*measure* out two liters⟩ **3** : to determine the dimensions, extent, or amount of ⟨*measure* the walk of the house⟩ **4 a** : ESTIMATE ⟨*measure* the distance by eye⟩ **b** : to bring into comparison ⟨*measure* one's skill against a rival⟩ **5** : to serve as a measure of ⟨a thermometer *measures* temperature⟩ **6** : to turn out to be of a certain measurement (as in length or breadth) ⟨the cloth *measures* 3 meters⟩ — **mea·sur·er** \-ər-ər\ *n*

mea·sured \-ərd\ *adj* **1 a** : marked by due proportion **b** : being slow and steady : EVEN ⟨a *measured* gait⟩ **2** : DELIBERATE, CALCULATED ⟨a *measured* response⟩ **3** : METRICAL 1, RHYTHMICAL

mea·sure·less \-ər-ləs\ *adj* : being without measure : IMMEASURABLE

mea·sure·ment \'mezh-ər-mənt, 'māzh-\ *n* **1** : the act or process of measuring **2** : a figure, extent, or amount obtained by measuring : DIMENSION **3** : a system of measures

measure up *vi* **1** : to have necessary or fitting qualifications **2** : to be the equal (as in ability) — used with *to*

measuring worm *n* : LOOPER 1

meat \'mēt\ *n* **1 a** : FOOD; *esp* : solid food as distinguished from drink **b** : the edible part of something as distinguished from the covering (as a shell or husk) **2** : animal and especially mammal tissue used as food [Old English *mete*]

meat·ball \-,bȯl\ *n* : a small ball of chopped or ground meat ⟨spaghetti and *meatballs*⟩

meat·man \-,man\ *n* : BUTCHER

me·a·tus \mē-'āt-əs\ *n, pl* **me·a·tus·es** *or* **me·a·tus** \-'āt-əs, -'ā-,tüs\ : a natural body passage [Late Latin, from Latin *meare* "to go, pass"]

meaty \'mēt-ē\ *adj* **meat·i·er; -est** **1** : full of meat : FLESHY **2** : rich in matter for thought : SUBSTANTIAL ⟨a *meaty* book⟩ — **meat·i·ness** \'mēt-ē-nəs\ *n*

mec·ca \'mek-ə\ *n, often cap* : a place considered extremely desirable especially by a particular group of people ⟨the university is a *mecca* for chemistry students⟩ [*Mecca*, Saudi Arabia, birthplace of Muhammad and holy city of Islam]

¹**me·chan·ic** \mi-'kan-ik\ *adj* : of or relating to manual work or skill ⟨*mechanic* arts⟩ [derived from Greek *mēchanikos*, from *mēchanē* "machine"]

²**mechanic** *n* **1** : a manual worker : ARTISAN **2** : a repairer of machines

me·chan·i·cal \mi-'kan-i-kəl\ *adj* **1 a** : of or relating to machinery ⟨*mechanical* engineering⟩ **b** : made or operated by a machine or tool ⟨a *mechanical* concrete mixer⟩ ⟨a *mechanical* toy⟩ **2** : of or relating to mechanics or artisans **3** : done as if by machine : IMPERSONAL ⟨gave a *mechanical* reply⟩ **4** : relating to or in accordance with the principles of mechanics **5** : relating to a process that involves a purely physical change — **me·chan·i·cal·ly** \-i-kə-lē, -klē\ *adv*

mechanical advantage *n* : the ratio of the force that performs the useful work of a machine to the force that is applied to the machine

mechanical drawing *n* : a method of drawing that makes use of such instruments as compasses, squares, and tri-

angles in order to insure mathematical precision; *also* : a drawing made by this method

me·chan·ics \mi-'kan-iks\ *n sing or pl* **1** : a branch of physical science that deals with energy and forces and their effect on bodies **2** : the practical application of mechanics to the making or operation of machines **3** : mechanical or functional details ⟨the *mechanics* of running⟩ ⟨the *mechanics* of writing plays⟩

mech·a·nism \'mek-ə-,niz-əm\ *n* **1** : a machine or mechanical device **2 a** : the parts by which a machine operates as a mechanical unit ⟨the *mechanism* of a watch⟩ **b** : the parts or steps that make up a process or activity ⟨the *mechanism* of democratic government⟩ **3** : the doctrine that natural processes (as of life) are orderly and wholly subject to natural law — compare VITALISM **4** : the fundamental physical or chemical processes involved in or responsible for a natural phenomenon (as an action or reaction) — **mech·a·nist** \-nəst\ *n*

mech·a·nis·tic \,mek-ə-'nis-tik\ *adj* **1** : mechanically determined ⟨*mechanistic* universe⟩ **2** : of or relating to the doctrine of mechanism — **mech·a·nis·ti·cal·ly** \-ti-kə-lē, -klē\ *adv*

mech·a·nize \'mek-ə-,nīz\ *vt* **1** : to make mechanical; *esp* : to make automatic **2 a** : to equip with machinery especially to replace human or animal labor **b** : to equip (a military force) with armed and armored motor-driven vehicles — **mech·a·ni·za·tion** \,mek-ə-nə-'zā-shən\ *n* — **mech·a·niz·er** \'mek-ə-,nī-zər\ *n*

me·co·ni·um \mi-'kō-nē-əm\ *n* : dark greenish matter in the bowel at birth [Latin, literally, "poppy juice", from Greek *mēkōnion*, from *mēkōn* "poppy"]

med·al \'med-l\ *n* **1** : a metal disk bearing a religious emblem or picture **2** : a piece of metal often in the form of a coin issued to commemorate a person or event or as an award [Middle French *medaille*, from Italian *medaglia* "coin worth half a denarius, medal", from Late Latin *medialis* "medial"]

med·al·ist *or* **med·al·list** \-l-əst\ *n* **1** : a designer or maker of medals **2** : a recipient of a medal

me·dal·lion \mə-'dal-yən\ *n* **1** : a large medal **2** : something resembling a large medal; *esp* : a tablet or panel (as in a wall) bearing a figure in relief [French *médaillon*, from Italian *medaglione*, from *medaglia* "medal"]

med·dle \'med-l\ *vi* **med·dled** \-ld\; **med·dling** \'med-ling, -l-ing\ : to interest oneself in what is not one's concern ⟨*meddle* in another's business⟩ [Old French *mesler, medler* "to mix, meddle", derived from Latin *miscēre* "to mix"] — **med·dler** \'med-lər, -l-ər\ *n*

med·dle·some \'med-l-səm\ *adj* : given to meddling : INTRUSIVE — **med·dle·some·ness** *n*

Mede \'mēd\ *n* : a native or inhabitant of ancient Media in northwestern Iran

medi- *or* **medio-** *combining form* : middle ⟨*medi*eval⟩ [Latin, from *medius*]

media *pl of* MEDIUM

me·di·ae·val *variant of* MEDIEVAL

me·di·al \'mēd-ē-əl\ *adj* **1 a** : MEDIAN 1 **b** : extending toward the middle **2** : situated between the beginning and the end of a word **3** : ORDINARY 2a, AVERAGE [Late Latin *medialis*, from Latin *medius* "middle"] — **medial** *n* — **me·di·al·ly** \-ə-lē\ *adv*

¹**me·di·an** \'mēd-ē-ən\ *n* **1** : a median part **2** : a value in a series below and above which there are an equal number of values or which is the average of the two middle values if there is no one middle number **3 a** : a line from a vertex of a triangle to the midpoint of the opposite side **b** : a line joining the midpoints of the nonparallel sides of a trapezoid SYN see AVERAGE

²**median** *adj* **1** : being in the middle or in an intermediate position **2** : relating to or constituting a median

median strip *n* : a paved or planted strip separating the opposing lanes of a highway

median strip

\ə\ abut	\ng\ sing
\ər\ further	\ō\ bone
\a\ mat	\ȯ\ saw
\ā\ take	\ȯi\ coin
\ä\ cot, cart	\th\ thin
\au̇\ out	\th\ this
\ch\ chin	\ü\ food
\e\ pet	\u̇\ foot
\ē\ easy	\y\ yet
\g\ go	\yü\ few
\i\ tip	\yu̇\ cure
\ī\ life	\zh\ vision
\j\ job	

MEASURES AND WEIGHTS[1]

UNIT	ABBREVIATION OR SYMBOL	EQUIVALENTS IN OTHER UNITS OF SAME SYSTEM	APPROXIMATE METRIC EQUIVALENT
LENGTH			
mile	mi	5280 feet, 320 rods, 1760 yards	1.609 kilometers
rod	rd	5.5 yards, 16.5 feet	5.029 meters
yard	yd	3 feet, 36 inches	0.914 meter
foot	ft *or* '	12 inches, 0.333 yard	30.480 centimeters
inch	in *or* "	0.0833 foot, 0.0278 yard	2.540 centimeters
AREA			
square mile	sq mi *or* mi^2	640 acres, 102,400 square rods	2.590 square kilometers
acre		4840 square yards, 43,560 square feet	4047 square meters
square rod	sq rd *or* rd^2	30.25 square yards, 0.00625 acre	25.293 square meters
square yard	sq yd *or* yd^2	1296 square inches, 9 square feet	0.836 square meter
square foot	sq ft *or* ft^2	144 square inches, 0.111 square yard	0.0929 square meter
square inch	sq in *or* in^2	0.00694 square foot, 0.000772 square yard	6.452 square centimeters
VOLUME			
cubic yard	cu yd *or* yd^3	27 cubic feet, 46,656 cubic inches	0.765 cubic meter
cubic foot	cu ft *or* ft^3	1728 cubic inches, 0.037 cubic yard	0.0283 cubic meter
cubic inch	cu in *or* in^3	0.000579 cubic foot, 0.0000214 cubic yard	16.387 cubic centimeters
WEIGHT			
AVOIRDUPOIS			
ton			
short ton		20 short hundredweight, 2000 pounds	0.907 metric ton
long ton		20 long hundredweight, 2240 pounds	1.016 metric tons
hundredweight	cwt		
short hundred-weight		100 pounds, 0.05 short ton	45.359 kilograms
long hundred-weight		112 pounds, 0.05 long ton	50.802 kilograms
pound	lb *or* lb av *also* #	16 ounces, 7000 grains	0.454 kilogram
ounce	oz *or* oz av	16 drams, 437.5 grains	28.350 grams
dram	dr *or* dr av	27.343 grains, 0.0625 ounce	1.772 grams
grain	gr	0.0366 dram, 0.00229 ounce	0.0648 grams
TROY			
pound	lb t	12 ounces, 240 pennyweight, 5760 grains	0.373 kilogram
ounce	oz t	20 pennyweight, 480 grains	31.103 grams
pennyweight	dwt *also* pwt	24 grains, 0.05 ounce	1.555 grams
grain	gr	0.0417 pennyweight, 0.00208 ounce	0.0648 gram
APOTHECARIES'			
pound	lb ap	12 ounces, 5760 grains	0.373 kilogram
ounce	oz ap *or* ℥	8 drams, 480 grains	31.103 grams
dram	dr ap *or* ℨ	3 scruples, 60 grains	3.888 grams
scruple	s ap *or* ℈	20 grains, 0.333 dram	1.296 grams
grain	gr	0.05 scruple, 0.00208 ounce, 0.0166 dram	0.0648 grams
CAPACITY			
UNITED STATES LIQUID MEASURE			
gallon	gal	4 quarts (231 cubic inches)	3.785 liters
quart	qt	2 pints (57.75 cubic inches)	0.946 liters
pint	pt	4 gills (28.875 cubic inches)	0.473 liter
gill	gi	4 fluid ounces (7.218 cubic inches)	.118 liter
fluid ounce	fl oz *or* f ℥	8 fluid drams (1.804 cubic inches)	29.574 milliliters
fluid dram	fl dr *or* f ℨ	60 minims (0.225 cubic inch)	3.696 milliliters
minim	minim *or* ♏	$\frac{1}{60}$ fluid dram (0.00376 cubic inch)	0.0616 milliliter
UNITED STATES DRY MEASURE			
bushel	bu	4 pecks (2150.42 cubic inches)	35.239 liters
peck	pk	8 quarts (537.605 cubic inches)	8.810 liters
quart	qt	2 pints (67.2 cubic inches)	1.101 liters
pint	pt	½ quart (33.6 cubic inches)	0.551 liter

[1]For United States equivalents of metric units see Metric System table

me·di·ant \ˈmēd-ē-ənt\ *n* : the third tone above the tonic [Italian *mediante,* from Late Latin *mediare* "to be in the middle"]

me·di·as·ti·num \ˌmēd-ē-ə-ˈstī-nəm\ *n, pl* **-na** \-nə\ : an irregular median partition that divides the chest cavity into right and left halves, is formed of the opposing medial walls of the pleura, and encloses between these walls all the viscera of the chest except the lungs [New Latin, from Latin *mediastinus* "medial", from *medius* "middle"] — **me·di·as·ti·nal** \-'stīn-l\ *adj*

¹me·di·ate \'mēd-ē-ət\ *adj* : acting through an intermediate agent or agency : not direct or immediate [Late Latin *mediatus* "intermediate", from *mediare* "to be in the middle", from Latin *medius* "middle"] — **me·di·ate·ly** *adv*

²me·di·ate \'mēd-ē-ˌāt\ *vb* **1** : to intervene between conflicting parties or viewpoints to promote reconciliation, settlement, or compromise **2 a** : to bring about by mediation ⟨*mediate* a settlement⟩ **b** : to bring accord out of by mediation ⟨*mediate* a dispute⟩ **3** : to transmit or act as an intermediate mechanism

me·di·a·tion \ˌmēd-ē-'ā-shən\ *n* : the act or process of mediating; *esp* : intervention by a third party in a dispute to promote reconciliation, settlement, or compromise between the conflicting parties

me·di·a·tor \'mēd-ē-ˌāt-ər\ *n* **1** : one that mediates; *esp* : an impartial third party (as a person, group, or country) that acts as a go-between in a dispute in order to arrange a peaceful settlement **2** : a mediating agent in a chemical or biological process — **me·di·a·to·ry** \'mēd-ē-ə-ˌtōr-ē, -ˌtȯr-\ *adj*

¹med·ic \'med-ik\ *n* : any of a genus of herbs of the pea family resembling clovers and important for hay and forage [Latin *medica*, from Greek *mēdikē*, from *mēdikos* "of Media"]

²medic *n* : one (as a physician, a medical student, or a soldier or sailor assigned to the medical services) engaged in medical work [Latin *medicus* "physician"]

med·i·ca·ble \'med-i-kə-bəl\ *adj* : CURABLE, REMEDIABLE — **med·i·ca·bly** \-blē\ *adv*

med·ic·aid \'med-i-ˌkād\ *n* : a program of medical aid designed for those unable to afford regular medical service and financed jointly by the state and federal governments

med·i·cal \'med-i-kəl\ *adj* : of or relating to the science or practice of medicine or the treatment of disease [Late Latin *medicalis*, from Latin *medicus* "physician", from *mederi* "to heal"] — **med·i·cal·ly** \-kə-lē, -klē\ *adv*

med·i·ca·ment \mi-'dik-ə-mənt\ *n* : a medicine or healing application

medi·care \'med-i-ˌkeər, -ˌkaər\ *n* : a government program of medical care especially for the aged

med·i·cate \'med-ə-ˌkāt\ *vt* **1** : to treat with medicine **2** : to add a medicinal substance to ⟨*medicate* a soap⟩

med·i·ca·tion \ˌmed-ə-'kā-shən\ *n* **1** : the act or process of medicating **2** : a medicinal substance : MEDICAMENT

me·dic·i·nal \mə-'dis-nəl, -n-əl\ *adj* : tending or used to relieve or cure disease or pain — **me·dic·i·nal·ly** \-ē\ *adv*

medicinal leech *n* : a large European freshwater leech formerly used by physicians for bleeding patients

med·i·cine \'med-ə-sən\ *n* **1** : a substance or preparation used in treating disease **2 a** : the science and art dealing with the maintenance of health and the prevention, easing, and cure of disease **b** : the branch of medicine concerned with the nonsurgical treatment of disease **3** : an object held to give control over natural or magical forces; *also* : a magical power or rite [Old French, from Latin *medicina*, from *medicus* "physician", from *mederi* "to heal"]

medicine ball *n* : a large stuffed leather-covered ball used for conditioning exercises

medicine dropper *n* : DROPPER 2

medicine man *n* : a person among primitive peoples believed to be able to cure diseases by potions and charms

medicine show *n* : a traveling show using entertainers to attract a crowd that may buy remedies or nostrums

med·i·co \'med-i-ˌkō\ *n*, *pl* **-cos** : a medical practitioner : PHYSICIAN; *also* : a medical student [Italian *medico* or Spanish *médico*, both from Latin *medicus*]

me·di·eval *or* **me·di·ae·val** \ˌmēd-ē-'ē-vəl, ˌmed-, ˌmid-; mē-'dē-vəl, med-'ē-, mid-'ē-\ *adj* : of, relating to, or characteristic of the Middle Ages [*medi-* + Latin *aevum* "age"] — **me·di·eval·ly** \-və-lē\ *adv*

me·di·eval·ism \-və-ˌliz-əm\ *n* **1** : medieval quality, character, or state **2** : devotion to the institutions, arts, and practices of the Middle Ages — **me·di·eval·ist** \-ləst\ *n*

Medieval Latin *n* : the Latin used especially for liturgical and literary purposes from the 7th to the 15th centuries inclusive

medio- — see MEDI-

me·di·o·cre \ˌmēd-ē-'ō-kər\ *adj* : of moderate or low quality : ORDINARY [Middle French, from Latin *mediocris*, literally, "halfway up a mountain", from *medi-* + *ocris* "stony mountain"]

me·di·oc·ri·ty \ˌmēd-ē-'äk-rət-ē\ *n*, *pl* **-ties** **1** : the quality or state of being mediocre **2** : a mediocre person

med·i·tate \'med-ə-ˌtāt\ *vb* **1 a** : to reflect on or muse over : CONTEMPLATE **b** : to engage in contemplation or reflection **2** : INTEND, PURPOSE [Latin *meditari*] — **med·i·ta·tor** \-ˌtāt-ər\ *n*

med·i·ta·tion \ˌmed-ə-'tā-shən\ *n* : the act or process of meditating : serious contemplation or reflection

med·i·ta·tive \'med-ə-ˌtāt-iv\ *adj* : given to meditation — **med·i·ta·tive·ly** *adv* — **med·i·ta·tive·ness** *n*

Med·i·ter·ra·nean \ˌmed-ə-tə-'rā-nē-ən, -'rā-nyən\ *adj* : of or relating to the Mediterranean sea or to the lands or peoples around it

Mediterranean fruit fly *n* : a widely distributed two-winged fly with black-and-white markings and a larva destructive to ripening fruit

¹me·di·um \'mēd-ē-əm\ *n*, *pl* **me·di·ums** *or* **me·dia** \'mēd-ē-ə\ **1** : something that is between or in the middle; *also* : a middle condition or degree **2** : a means of effecting or conveying something; *esp* : a substance through which a force acts or through which something is transmitted ⟨air is the common *medium* of sound⟩ **3** *pl usually* **media** : a channel (as newspapers, radio, or television) of communication **4 a** : GO-BETWEEN, INTERMEDIARY **b** *pl* **mediums** : a person through whom others seek to communicate with the spirits of the dead **5 a** : a surrounding substance **b** : a condition in which something may function or flourish ⟨slums are a good *medium* for delinquency⟩ **6** : a nutrient system for the artificial cultivation of organisms (as bacteria) or cells [Latin, from *medius* "middle"]

²medium *adj* : intermediate in amount, quality, position, or degree

medium frequency *n* : a radio frequency in the range between 300 and 3000 kilohertz — abbreviation *MF*

medium of exchange : something commonly accepted in exchange for goods and services and recognized as representing a standard of value

med·lar \'med-lər\ *n* : a small hairy-leaved Eurasian tree related to the apples; *also* : its fruit that resembles a crab apple and is used especially in preserves [Middle French *medlier*, from *medle* "medlar fruit", from Latin *mespilum*, from Greek *mespilon*]

med·ley \'med-lē\ *n*, *pl* **medleys** **1** : MIXTURE 2; *esp* : a confused mixture **2** : a musical composition made up of a series of songs or short musical pieces [Middle French *medlee*, from *mesler*, *medler* "to mix, meddle"]

me·dul·la \mə-'dəl-ə\ *n*, *pl* **-dul·las** *or* **-dul·lae** \-ˌē, -ˌī\ **1 a** : MARROW 1 **b** : MEDULLA OBLONGATA **2** : the inner or deep part of an animal or plant structure (as the adrenal gland or the kidney) [Latin] — **med·ul·lary** \'med-l-ˌer-ē, 'mej-ə-ˌler-\ *adj*

\ə\	abut	\ng\	sing
\ər\	further	\ō\	bone
\a\	mat	\ȯ\	saw
\ā\	take	\ȯi\	coin
\ä\	cot, cart	\th\	thin
\au̇\	out	\th\	this
\ch\	chin	\ü\	food
\e\	pet	\u̇\	foot
\ē\	easy	\y\	yet
\g\	go	\yü\	few
\i\	tip	\yu̇\	cure
\ī\	life	\zh\	vision
\j\	job		

megaphone

medulla ob·lon·ga·ta \-,äb-,lȯng-'gät-ə\ *n* : the somewhat pyramid-shaped hind part of the vertebrate brain that is continuous with the spinal cord [New Latin, literally, "oblong medulla"]

medullary sheath *n* : a layer of myelin about a nerve fiber

med·ul·lat·ed \'med-l-,āt-əd, 'mej-ə-,lāt-\ *adj* : having a medullary sheath ⟨*medullated* nerve fibers⟩

me·du·sa \mi-'dü-sə, -'dyü-, -zə\ *n, pl* **-sae** \-,sē, -,zē\ *or* **-sas** : JELLYFISH [*Medusa*, one of the three Gorgons] — **me·du·san** \-'düs-n, 'düz-, -'dyüs-, -'dyüz-\ *adj or n*

meed \'mēd\ *n* : something deserved or earned : REWARD ⟨receive one's *meed* of praise⟩ [Old English *mēd*]

meek \'mēk\ *adj* **1** : enduring injury with patience and without resentment **2** : lacking self-assurance : HUMBLE ⟨they became *meek* when confronted with the evidence against them⟩ [of Scandinavian origin] — **meek·ly** *adv* — **meek·ness** *n*

meer·schaum \'miər-shəm, -,shȯm\ *n* **1** : a soft white lightweight mineral resembling a very fine clay used especially for tobacco pipes **2** : a tobacco pipe made of meerschaum [German, from *meer* "sea" + *schaum* "foam"]

¹meet \'mēt\ *vb* **met** \'met\; **meet·ing** **1** : to come upon or across or into the presence of ⟨*met* an old friend by chance⟩ **2** : to come close together or into contact and join or cross ⟨a fork where two roads *meet*⟩ **3 a** : to get together with : JOIN ⟨agreed to *meet* them at school⟩ **b** : to become acquainted ⟨the couple *met* at a dance⟩ **c** : to make the acquaintance of ⟨*met* interesting people there⟩ **4 a** : to come together as opponents ⟨the teams *met* in the finals⟩ **b** : to struggle against : OPPOSE ⟨was chosen to *meet* the champion⟩ **c** : to cope with : MATCH ⟨tries to *meet* the competitor's price⟩ **d** : ENDURE 2b, BEAR ⟨learned to *meet* defeat bravely⟩ **5** : to come together for a common purpose : ASSEMBLE ⟨*meet* weekly for discussion⟩ **6** : to become one : UNITE ⟨all the virtues *meet* in the child⟩ **7** : to become noticed by ⟨sounds of revelry *meet* the ear⟩ **8 a** : to conform to or comply with : SATISFY ⟨*meets* all requirements⟩ **b** : to pay fully ⟨*meet* a financial obligation⟩ [Old English *mētan*]

²meet *n* : an assembly or meeting especially to engage in a competitive sport ⟨a track *meet*⟩

³meet *adj* : SUITABLE 2, PROPER [Old English *gemǣte*] — **meet·ly** *adv*

meet·ing \'mēt-ing\ *n* **1** : the act of persons or things that meet ⟨a chance *meeting* with a friend⟩ **2** : a coming together of a number of persons usually at a stated time and place and for a known purpose : ASSEMBLY, GATHERING ⟨the monthly club *meeting*⟩ **3** : an assembly for religious worship ⟨a Quaker *meeting*⟩ **4** : the place where two things come together : JUNCTION

meet·ing·house \-,haús\ *n* : a building used for public assembly and especially for Protestant worship

mega- *or* **meg-** *combining form* **1** : great : large ⟨*mega*spore⟩ **2** : million : multiplied by one million ⟨*mega*cycle⟩ ⟨*meg*ohm⟩ [Greek *megas* "large"]

mega·bit \'meg-ə-,bit\ *n* : one million bits

mega·byte \-,bīt\ *n* : one million bytes

mega·cycle \-,sī-kəl\ *n* : one million cycles; *esp* : MEGAHERTZ

mega·dose \-,dōs\ *n* : a large dose (as of a vitamin)

mega·hertz \-,hərts, -,heərts\ *n* : one million hertz

mega·hit \-,hit\ *n* : something (as a motion picture) that is extremely successful

mega·lith \'meg-ə-,lith\ *n* : one of the huge stones used in various prehistoric monuments — **mega·lith·ic** \,meg-ə-'lith-ik\ *adj*

meg·a·lo·ma·nia \,meg-ə-lō-'mā-nē-ə, -nyə\ *n* : a disorder of mind marked by feelings of great personal power and importance [Greek *megal-, megas* "large"] — **meg·a·lo·ma·ni·ac** \-'mā-nē-,ak\ *adj or n* — **meg·a·lo·ma·ni·a·cal** \-mə-'nī-ə-kəl\ *adj*

meg·a·lop·o·lis \,meg-ə-'läp-ə-ləs\ *n* **1** : a very large city **2** : a thickly populated region centering in a metropolis or embracing several metropolises [Greek *megal-, megas* "large" + *polis* "city"] — **meg·a·lo·pol·i·tan** \,meg-ə-lō-'päl-ət-n\ *n or adj* — **meg·a·lo·pol·i·tan·ism** \-n-,iz-əm\ *n*

mega·phone \'meg-ə-,fōn\ *n* : a cone-shaped device used to intensify or direct the voice — **mega·phon·ic** \,meg-ə-'fän-ik\ *adj*

mega·spore \'meg-ə-,spōr, -,spȯr\ *n* : a plant spore that produces a female gametophyte

mega·ton \'meg-ə-,tən\ *n* : an explosive force equal to that of one million tons of TNT

mega·watt \-,wät\ *n* : one million watts

meg·ohm \'meg-,ōm\ *n* : one million ohms

me·grim \'mē-grəm\ *n* **1** : a dizzy disordered state; *esp* : MIGRAINE **2 a** : WHIM, FANCY **b** *pl* : low spirits : mental depression [Middle French *migraine*]

mei·o·sis \mī-'ō-səs\ *n, pl* **-o·ses** \-'ō-,sēz\ : a cellular process that includes two cell divisions but only one duplication of chromosomes and that results in the number of chromosomes in gamete-producing cells being reduced to one half [Greek *meiōsis* "diminution", from *meioun* "to diminish", from *meiōn* "less"] — **mei·ot·ic** \mī-'ät-ik\ *adj* — **mei·ot·i·cal·ly** \-'ät-i-kə-lē, -klē\ *adv*

Mei·ster·sing·er \'mī-stər-,sing-ər, -stər-,zing-\ *n, pl* **-sing·er** *or* **-sing·ers** : a member of any of various German guilds formed chiefly in the 15th and 16th centuries for the cultivation of poetry and music [German, literally, "master singer"]

mel·a·mine \'mel-ə-,mēn\ *n* : a synthetic resin composed of carbon, hydrogen, and nitrogen and used in molded products, adhesives, and coatings [German *melamin*]

mel·an·cho·lia \,mel-ən-'kō-lē-ə\ *n* : a morbid mental state characterized especially by depression [Late Latin, "melancholy"] — **mel·an·cho·li·ac** \-lē-,ak\ *n*

mel·an·chol·ic \,mel-ən-'käl-ik\ *adj* **1** : inclined to or affected with melancholy **2** : affected with or relating to melancholia **3** : tending to depress the spirits — **mel·an·chol·i·cal·ly** \-'käl-i-kə-lē, -klē\ *adv*

¹mel·an·choly \'mel-ən-,käl-ē\ *n, pl* **-chol·ies** : depression of spirits : DEJECTION, SADNESS [Middle French *melancolie*, from Late Latin *melancholia*, from Greek, from *melan-, melas* "black" + *cholē* "bile"; from the former belief that the condition was caused by an excess of black bile, a fluid once believed to be secreted by the spleen or kidneys] □ SYN SADNESS, DEPRESSION, DEJECTION: MELANCHOLY suggests a sad and serious pensiveness often without evident cause; SADNESS usually suggests a mood of regret, longing, or disappointment without bitterness or anger; DEPRESSION suggests a condition in which one feels let down, disheartened, or enervated; DEJECTION implies a usually passing mood of discouragement or hopelessness.

²melancholy *adj* **1 a** : depressed in spirits : DEJECTED, SAD **b** : PENSIVE 2 **2 a** : suggestive or expressive of melancholy ⟨a *melancholy* voice⟩ **b** : causing sadness : DISMAL ⟨the *melancholy* conclusion that we were neither needed nor wanted⟩

Mel·a·ne·sian \,mel-ə-'nē-zhən, -shən\ *n* : a member of the dominant native group of Melanesia — **Melanesian** *adj*

mé·lange \mā-'läⁿzh, -'länj\ *n* : a mixture often of incongruous elements ⟨a *mélange* of styles from all over the world⟩ [French, from Middle French *mesler, meler* "to mix"]

mel·a·nin \'mel-ə-nən\ *n* : a dark brown or black animal or plant pigment that in man makes some skins darker than others [Greek *melan-, melas* "black"]

mel·a·nism \'mel-ə-,niz-əm\ *n* : an exceptionally dark pigmentation (as of skin, feathers, or hair) of an individual or kind of organism — **mel·a·nis·tic** \,mel-ə-'nis-tik\ *adj*

mel·a·no·ma \ˌmel-ə-ˈnō-mə\ *n, pl* **-no·mas** *also* **-no·ma·ta** \-ˈnō-mət-ə\ : a usually malignant tumor containing dark pigment

mel·a·not·ic \-ˈnät-ik\ *adj* : having or characterized by black pigmentation ⟨*melanotic* tumors⟩

mel·ba toast \ˌmel-bə-\ *n* : very thin bread toasted till crisp [Nellie *Melba*, died 1931, Australian soprano]

Mel·chiz·e·dek \mel-ˈkiz-ə-ˌdek\ *adj* : of or relating to the higher order of the Mormon priesthood [*Melchizedek*, biblical priest-king]

¹meld \ˈmeld\ *vb* : to show or lay down a combination of cards in a card game [German *melden* "to announce"]

²meld *n* : a card or combination of cards that is or can be melded

me·lee \ˈmā-ˌlā, mā-ˈlā\ *n* : a confused fight or struggle especially among several people [French *mêlée*, from Old French *meslee*, from *mesler* "to mix"]

me·lio·rate \ˈmēl-yə-ˌrāt, ˈmē-lē-ə-\ *vb* : to make or become better : IMPROVE [Late Latin *meliorare*, from Latin *melior* "better"] — **me·lio·ra·tion** \ˌmēl-yə-ˈrā-shən, ˌmē-lē-ə-\ *n* — **me·lio·ra·tive** \ˈmēl-yə-ˌrāt-iv, ˈmē-lē-ə-\ *adj* — **me·lio·ra·tor** \-ˌrāt-ər\ *n*

mel·lif·lu·ous \me-ˈlif-lə-wəs, mə-\ *adj* : smoothly or sweetly flowing ⟨*mellifluous* speech⟩ [Late Latin *mellifluus*, from Latin *mel* "honey" + *fluere* "to flow"] — **mel·lif·lu·ous·ly** *adv* — **mel·lif·lu·ous·ness** *n*

mel·lo·phone \ˈmel-ə-ˌfōn\ *n* : an althorn in circular form sometimes used as a substitute for the French horn [*mellow* + *-phone*]

¹mel·low \ˈmel-ō\ *adj* **1 a** : tender and sweet because of ripeness ⟨*mellow* peaches⟩ **b** : well aged and pleasingly mild ⟨a *mellow* wine⟩ **2** : made gentle by age or experience **3** : of soft and loamy consistency ⟨*mellow* soil⟩ **4** : being clear, full, and pure ⟨spoke in *mellow* tones⟩ [Middle English *melowe*] — **mel·low·ly** *adv* — **mel·low·ness** *n*

²mellow *vb* : to make or become mellow

me·lo·de·on \mə-ˈlōd-ē-ən\ *n* : a small reed organ in which a suction bellows draws air inward through the reeds [German *melodion*, from *melodie* "melody", from Old French]

me·lod·ic \mə-ˈläd-ik\ *adj* : of or relating to melody : MELODIOUS — **me·lod·i·cal·ly** \-ˈläd-i-kə-lē, -klē\ *adv*

me·lo·di·ous \mə-ˈlōd-ē-əs\ *adj* **1** : pleasing to the ear because of a succession of sweet sounds **2** : of, relating to, or producing melody ⟨*melodious* birds⟩ — **me·lo·di·ous·ly** *adv* — **me·lo·di·ous·ness** *n*

mel·o·dist \ˈmel-əd-əst\ *n* : a composer or singer of melodies

melo·dra·ma \ˈmel-ə-ˌdräm-ə, -ˌdram-\ *n* **1 a** : an extravagantly theatrical play in which action and plot predominate over characterization **b** : a dramatic category constituted by such plays **2** : melodramatic events or behavior [French *mélodrame*, from Greek *melos* "song" + *drama* "drama"] — **melo·dram·a·tist** \ˈdram-ət-əst, -ˈdräm-\ *n*

melo·dra·mat·ic \-drə-ˈmat-ik\ *adj* **1** : of or relating to melodrama ⟨*melodramatic* elements of suspense and surprise⟩ **2** : resembling or suitable for melodrama : SENSATIONAL ⟨made a *melodramatic* announcement of the discovery⟩ SYN see DRAMATIC — **melo·dra·mat·i·cal·ly** \-i-kə-lē, -klē\ *adv*

melo·dra·mat·ics \-ˈmat-iks\ *n sing or pl* : melodramatic conduct

mel·o·dy \ˈmel-əd-ē\ *n, pl* **-dies** **1** : pleasing succession of sounds : TUNEFULNESS **2** : a rhythmical series of musical tones of a given key so arranged as to make a pleasing effect **3** : the leading part in a harmonic composition [Old French *melodie*, from Late Latin *melodia*, from Greek *melōidia* "chanting, music", from *melos* "song, tune" + *aidein* "to sing"]

mel·on \ˈmel-ən\ *n* : any of several soft-fleshed sweet-flavored fruits (as a muskmelon or a watermelon) of the gourd family usually eaten raw [Middle French,

from Late Latin *melo*, from Latin *melopepo*, from Greek *mēlopepōn*, from *mēlon* "apple" + *pepōn*, a kind of gourd]

¹melt \ˈmelt\ *vb* **1** : to change from a solid to a liquid state usually through the application of heat ⟨*melt* sugar⟩ ⟨snow *melts*⟩ **2** : DISSOLVE ⟨sugar *melts* in the mouth⟩ **3** : to grow less : disappear as if by dissolving ⟨their fears *melted*⟩ **4** : to make or become gentle : SOFTEN ⟨a warm smile *melts* the heart⟩ **5** : to lose distinct outline or shape : BLEND, MERGE ⟨sky *melting* into sea⟩ [Old English *meltan*] — **melt·abil·i·ty** \ˌmel-tə-ˈbil-ət-ē\ *n* — **melt·able** \ˈmel-tə-bəl\ *adj* — **melt·er** *n*

²melt *n* : a melted substance

³melt *n* : SPLEEN 1 [Old English *milte*]

melt·down \ˈmelt-ˌdaùn\ *n* **1** : the accidental melting of the core of a nuclear reactor **2** : a rapid or disastrous decline or collapse

melting point *n* : the temperature at which a solid melts

melting pot *n* **1** : a container for melting something : CRUCIBLE **2 a** : a place (as a city or country) in which various nationalities or races live together and gradually blend into one community **b** : the population of such a place

mel·ton \ˈmelt-n\ *n* : a smooth heavy woolen cloth with a short nap used for overcoats [*Melton* Mowbray, England]

melt·wa·ter \ˈmelt-ˌwȯt-ər, -ˌwät-\ *n* : water derived from the melting of ice and snow

mem·ber \ˈmem-bər\ *n* **1** : a part (as an arm, leg, leaf, or branch) of the body of a person, lower animal, or plant **2** : one of the individuals or units belonging to or forming part of a group or organization ⟨a club *member*⟩ ⟨UN *members*⟩ **3** : a part of a whole: as **a** : a part of a structure (as a building) ⟨a horizontal *member* in a bridge⟩ **b** : an element of a mathematical set **c** : the whole expression on one side or the other of a mathematical equation or inequality [Old French *membre*, from Latin *membrum*]

mem·ber·ship \-ˌship\ *n* **1** : the state or status of being a member **2** : all the members of an organization

mem·brane \ˈmem-ˌbrān\ *n* : a thin soft pliable sheet or layer especially of animal or plant origin [Latin *membrana* "skin, parchment", from *membrum* "member"] — **mem·bra·na·ceous** \ˌmem-brə-ˈnā-shəs\ — **mem·bra·nous** \ˈmem-brə-nəs\ *adj*

me·men·to \mi-ˈment-ō\ *n, pl* **-tos** *or* **-toes** : something that serves as a reminder : SOUVENIR ⟨*mementos* of a trip⟩ [Latin, "remember", from *meminisse* "to remember"]

me·men·to mo·ri \mi-ˌment-ō-ˈmȯr-ē, -ˈmȯr-ē\ *n, pl* **memento mori** : a reminder (as a death's-head) of mortality [Latin, "remember that you must die"]

memo \ˈmem-ō\ *n, pl* **mem·os** : MEMORANDUM

mem·oir \ˈmem-ˌwär, -ˌwȯr\ *n* **1 a** : a story of a personal experience **b** : AUTOBIOGRAPHY — usually used in pl. **c** : BIOGRAPHY 1 **2 a** : REPORT **2 b** *pl* : the proceedings of a learned society [French *mémoire*, literally, "memory", from Latin *memoria*]

mem·o·ra·bil·ia \ˌmem-ə-rə-ˈbil-ē-ə, -ˈbil-yə\ *n pl* : things worthy of remembrance; *also* : a record of such things [Latin, from *memorabilis* "memorable"]

mem·o·ra·ble \ˈmem-rə-bəl, -ə-rə-\ *adj* : worth remembering : NOTABLE [Latin *memorabilis*, from *memorare* "to remind", from *memor* "mindful"] — **mem·o·ra·ble·ness** *n* — **mem·o·ra·bly** \-blē\ *adv*

mem·o·ran·dum \ˌmem-ə-ˈran-dəm\ *n, pl* **-dums** *or* **-da** \-də\ **1 a** : an informal record or communication **b** : a written reminder **2** : an informal written note of a transaction or proposed legal instrument [Latin, neuter of *memorandus* "to be remembered", from *memorare* "to remind"]

¹me·mo·ri·al \mə-ˈmȯr-ē-əl, -ˈmȯr-\ *adj* : serving to preserve the memory of a person or an event ⟨a *memorial* service⟩ — **me·mo·ri·al·ly** \-ē-ə-lē\ *adv*

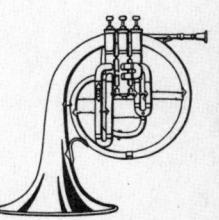

mellophone

\ə\ abut	\ng\ sing
\ər\ further	\ō\ bone
\a\ mat	\ȯ\ saw
\ā\ take	\ȯi\ coin
\ä\ cot, cart	\th\ thin
\aù\ out	\t̷h\ this
\ch\ chin	\ü\ food
\e\ pet	\ù\ foot
\ē\ easy	\y\ yet
\g\ go	\yü\ few
\i\ tip	\yù\ cure
\ī\ life	\zh\ vision
\j\ job	

²memorial *n* **1** : something that keeps alive the memory of a person or event; *esp* : MONUMENT **2 a** : RECORD 2 **b** : a statement of facts accompanying a petition to a government official

Memorial Day *n* **1** : May 30 formerly observed as a legal holiday in most states of the United States in remembrance of war dead **2** : the last Monday in May observed as a legal holiday in most states of the United States

me·mo·ri·al·ize \mə-'mōr-ē-ə-ˌlīz, -'mȯr-\ *vt* **1** : to address or petition (as a government official) by a memorial **2** : COMMEMORATE 1

mem·o·rize \'mem-ə-ˌrīz\ *vt* : to commit to memory : learn by heart — **mem·o·ri·za·tion** \ˌmem-rə-'zā-shən, -ə-rə-\ *n* — **mem·o·riz·er** \'mem-ə-ˌrī-zər\ *n*

mem·o·ry \'mem-rē, -ə-rē\ *n, pl* **-ries 1 a** : the power or process of recalling what has been learned and retained **b** : the store of things learned and retained (recite from *memory*) **2** : commemorative remembrance (a monument in *memory* of war dead) **3 a** : something remembered (has pleasant *memories* of the trip) **b** : the time within which past events can be or are remembered **4** : a device (as in a computer) in which information can be inserted and stored and from which it can be extracted when wanted [Middle French *memoire*, from Latin *memoria* from *memor* "mindful"] □ SYN REMEMBRANCE, RECOLLECTION, REMINISCENCE: MEMORY applies both to the ability to recall mentally and to what is recalled; REMEMBRANCE stresses the act of remembering or the state of being remembered; RECOLLECTION adds an implication of deliberately recalling often with some effort; REMINISCENCE suggests the recalling of things, actions, and especially of people from one's remote past.

mem·sa·hib \'mem-ˌsä-ˌhib, -ˌib, -ˌsäb\ *n* : a white foreign woman of some social status living in India; *esp* : the wife of a British official — compare SAHIB [Hindi *memṣāhib,* from English *ma'am* + Hindi *ṣāhib* "sahib"]

men *pl of* MAN

¹men·ace \'men-əs\ *n* **1** : a show of intention to inflict harm : THREAT **2 a** : someone or something that represents a threat : DANGER **b** : an annoying person : NUISANCE [Middle French, from Latin *minacia,* from *minax* "threatening", from *minari* "to threaten"]

²menace *vb* **1** : to make a show of intention to harm (*menaced* them with upraised arms) **2** : to appear likely to cause harm : ENDANGER SYN see THREATEN — **men·ac·ing·ly** \'men-ə-sing-lē\ *adv*

mé·nage \mā-'näzh\ *n* : HOUSEHOLD [French, from Old French *mesnage* "dwelling", from Latin *mansio,* from *manēre* "to stay"]

me·nag·er·ie \mə-'naj-ə-rē\ *n* **1** : a place where animals are kept and trained especially for exhibition **2** : a collection of wild or foreign animals kept especially for exhibition [French *ménagerie,* from *ménage* "household"]

¹mend \'mend\ *vb* **1 a** : to improve in manners or morals : REFORM **b** : to put into good shape or working order again : REPAIR **2** : to become corrected or improved **3** : to improve in health; *also* : HEAL [Middle English *menden,* short for *amenden* "to amend"] — **mend·er** *n*

²mend *n* **1** : an act of mending : REPAIR **2** : a mended place — **on the mend** : getting better (as in health)

men·da·cious \men-'dā-shəs\ *adj* : given to or characterized by deception or falsehood [Latin *mendac-, mendax*] — **men·da·cious·ly** *adv* — **men·da·cious·ness** *n*

men·dac·i·ty \men-'das-ət-ē\ *n, pl* **-ties** : the quality or state of being mendacious; *also* : ⁴LIE 1

men·de·le·vi·um \ˌmen-də-'lē-vē-əm\ *n* : a radioactive element artificially produced — see ELEMENT table [New Latin, from Dmitri *Mendeleev*]

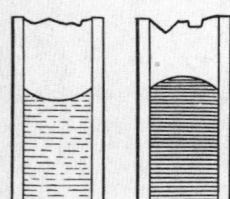

meniscus 3

Men·de·lian \men-'dē-lē-ən, -'dēl-yən\ *adj* : of, relating to, or according with Mendel's laws or Mendelism — **Mendelian** *n*

Men·del·ism \'men-dl-ˌiz-əm\ *n* : the principles or the operations of Mendel's laws

Men·del's law \ˌmen-dlz-\ *n* **1** : a principle in genetics : genes occur in pairs that separate during gamete formation so that every gamete receives but one member of a pair — called also *law of segregation* **2** : a principle in genetics : pairs of genes on different chromosomes are distributed to the gametes independently of each other, the gametes combine to form a zygote at random, and gene pairs on different chromosomes combine in the zygote in all their various possible combinations according to the laws of chance — called also *law of independent assortment* **3** : a principle of genetics subject to many limitations and exceptions : because one of each pair of genes dominates the other in expression, characters are inherited alternatively on an all or nothing basis — called also *law of dominance* [Gregor *Mendel*]

men·di·can·cy \'men-di-kən-sē\ *n* **1** : the condition of being a beggar **2** : the act or practice of begging

men·di·cant \-kənt\ *n* **1** : one who lives by begging **2** : a member of a religious order (as the Franciscans) combining monastic life and outside religious activity and originally owning neither personal nor community property : FRIAR [Latin *mendicare* "to beg", from *mendicus* "beggar"] — **mendicant** *adj*

men·dic·i·ty \men-'dis-ət-ē\ *n* : MENDICANCY

men·folk \'men-ˌfōk\ *or* **men·folks** \-ˌfōks\ *n pl* **1** : men in general **2** : the men of a family or community

men·ha·den \men-'hād-n, mən-\ *n, pl* **-den** *also* **-dens** : a fish of the herring family found along the Atlantic coast of the United States and used for bait or converted into oil and fertilizer [of American Indian origin]

men·hir \'men-ˌhiər\ *n* : an upright monolith usually of prehistoric origin [French, from Breton, from *men* "stone" + *hir* "long"]

¹me·nial \'mē-nē-əl, -nyəl\ *adj* **1** : of, relating to, or suitable for servants **2** : HUMBLE 2 [Middle English *meynie* "household, retinue", from Old French *mesnie,* from Latin *mansio* "dwelling"] — **me·nial·ly** \-ē\ *adv*

²menial *n* : a domestic servant

men·in·geal \ˌmen-ən-'jē-əl\ *adj* : of, relating to, or affecting the meninges

men·in·gi·tis \ˌmen-ən-'jīt-əs\ *n, pl* **-git·i·des** \-'jit-ə-ˌdēz\ : inflammation of the meninges; *also* : a usually bacterial disease in which this occurs — **men·in·git·ic** \-'jit-ik\ *adj*

me·ninx \'mē-nings, -ningks; 'men-ings, -ingks\ *n, pl* **me·nin·ges** \mə-'nin-ˌjēz\ : any of the three membranes that envelop the brain and spinal cord [Greek *mēninx* "membrane"]

me·nis·cus \mə-'nis-kəs\ *n, pl* **me·nis·ci** \-'nis-ˌkī, -ˌī, -ˌkē\ *also* **me·nis·cus·es 1** : a crescent-shaped body : CRESCENT **2** : a lens that is convex on one side and concave on the other **3** : the curved upper surface of a liquid column that is concave when the containing walls are wetted by the liquid and convex when not [Greek *mēniskos,* from *mēnē* "moon, crescent"]

Men·no·nite \'men-ə-ˌnīt\ *n* : a member of one of the Protestant groups derived from the Anabaptist movement in Holland and noted for simplicity of life and rejection of oaths, public office, and military service [German *Mennonit,* from *Menno* Simons, died 1561, Frisian religious reformer]

me·no mos·so \ˌmā-nō-'mȯ·sō, -'mȯs-\ *adv* : less rapidly — used as a direction in music [Italian]

meno·pause \'men-ə-ˌpȯz\ *n* : the period when menstruation naturally stops permanently usually between the ages of 45 and 50 [French *ménopause,* from *méno-* "menstruation" (from Greek *mēn* "month") + *pause* "pause"] — **meno·paus·al** \ˌmen-ə-'pȯ·zel\ *adj*

me·no·rah \mə-'nōr-ə, -'nȯr-\ *n* : a candelabrum used in Jewish worship [Hebrew *měnōrāh* "candlestick"]

menservants *pl of* MANSERVANT

men·ses \'men-,sēz\ *n sing or pl* : the menstrual flow [Latin, from pl. of *mensis* "month"]

Men·she·vik \'men-chə-,vik, -,vēk\ *n, pl* **Men·she·viks** *or* **Men·she·vi·ki** \,men-chə-'vik-ē, -'vē-kē\ : a member of a wing of the Russian Social Democratic party before and during the Russian Revolution believing in the gradual achievement of socialism by parliamentary methods in opposition to the Bolsheviks [Russian *men'shevik,* from *men'she* "less"; from their forming the minority group of the party] — **Men·she·vism** \'men-chə-,viz-əm\ *n* — **Men·she·vist** \-vest\ *n or adj*

men·stru·al \'men-strə-wəl, -strəl\ *adj* : of or relating to menstruation

menstrual cycle *n* : the whole cycle of physiological changes from the beginning of one menstrual period to the beginning of the next

men·stru·ate \'men-strə-,wāt, 'men-,strāt\ *vi* : to undergo menstruation [Late Latin *menstruari,* from Latin *menstrua* "menses", from *menstruus* "monthly", from *mensis* "month"]

men·stru·a·tion \,men-strə-'wā-shən, men-'strā-shən\ *n* : a discharging of blood, secretions, and tissue debris from the uterus that recurs at approximately monthly intervals in breeding-age primate females that are not pregnant; *also* : PERIOD 5c

men·stru·um \'men-strə-wəm\ *n, pl* **men·stru·ums** *or* **men·strua** \-strə-wə\ : a substance that dissolves a solid or holds it in suspension : SOLVENT [Medieval Latin, literally, "menses", from Latin *menstrua*]

men·su·ra·ble \'men-sə-rə-bəl, 'men-chə-\ *adj* : MEASURABLE [Late Latin *mensurabilis,* from *mensurare* "to measure", from Latin *mensura* "measure"] — **men·su·ra·bil·i·ty** \,men-sə-rə-'bil-ət-ē, ,men-chə-\ *n*

men·su·ra·tion \,men-sə-'rā-shən, ,men-chə-\ *n* 1 : the process or art of measuring 2 : the branch of mathematics that deals with the measurement of lengths, areas, and volumes

mens·wear \'menz-,waər, -,weər\ *n* : clothing for men

-ment \mənt; *homographic verbs are* ,ment *also* mənt\ *n suffix* 1 : result, object, or means of a (specified) action ⟨embank*ment*⟩ ⟨entertain*ment*⟩ 2 a : action : process ⟨develop*ment*⟩ b : place of a (specified) action ⟨encamp*ment*⟩ 3 : state : condition ⟨amaze*ment*⟩ [Latin *-mentum*]

men·tal \'ment-l\ *adj* 1 a : of or relating to the mind ⟨*mental* powers⟩ b : carried on or experienced in the mind ⟨*mental* arithmetic⟩ c : relating to spirit or idea as opposed to matter 2 a : of, relating to, or affected by a disorder of the mind ⟨a *mental* patient⟩ b : intended for the care or treatment of persons affected by mental disorders [Middle French, from Latin *ment-, mens* "mind"] — **men·tal·ly** \-l-ē\ *adv* □ SYN INTELLECTUAL: MENTAL implies a contrast with what is physically or materially caused, expressed, or performed ⟨make a *mental* note⟩ ⟨form a *mental* picture⟩ INTELLECTUAL applies to the higher mental powers (as of generalizing or discriminating abstractions) and often implies a contrast with *moral, emotional,* or *practical* ⟨*intellectual* appreciation of music⟩ ⟨the *intellectual* value of scientific study⟩

mental age *n* : a measure used in psychological testing that expresses an individual's mental attainment in terms of the number of years it takes an average child to reach the same level

men·tal·i·ty \men-'tal-ət-ē\ *n, pl* **-ties** 1 : mental power or capacity : INTELLIGENCE 2 : way of thinking

men·thol \'men-,thȯl, -,thōl\ *n* : a white crystalline alcohol $C_{10}H_{20}O$ that occurs especially in mint oils and has the odor and cooling properties of peppermint [German, derived from Latin *mentha* "mint"]

men·tho·lat·ed \'men-thə-,lāt-əd\ *adj* : treated with or containing menthol

¹men·tion \'men-chən\ *n* : a brief reference to something : a passing remark [Old French, from Latin *mentio,* from *ment-, mens* "mind"]

²mention *vt* **men·tioned; men·tion·ing** \'mench-ning, -ə-ning\ : to discuss or speak about briefly — **men·tion·able** \'mench-nə-bəl, -ə-nə-\ *adj* — **men·tion·er** \'mench-nər, -ə-nər\ — **not to mention** *n* : as well as

¹men·tor \'men-,tȯr, 'ment-ər\ *n* : a wise and faithful adviser or teacher [*Mentor,* adviser of Telemachus in Homer's *Odyssey*]

²mentor *vt* : to serve as a mentor

menu \'men-yū, 'mān-\ *n* 1 : a list of dishes served at a meal or available to order (as in a restaurant) 2 : the dishes making up a meal [French, from *menu* "small, detailed", from Latin *minutus* "minute" (adj.)]
□ ORIGIN The French word *menu,* which means "a list of foods", comes from the adjective *menu,* which means "small", "slender", or "detailed". Presumably the last sense is the one that gave us the noun, since a *menu* is a detailed list. The French adjective *menu* is derived from the Latin *minutus,* "small", which is also the source of the English adjective *minute.*

¹me·ow \mē-'au̇\ *n* : the characteristic cry of a cat [imitative]

²meow *vi* : to utter a meow or similar sound

me·phit·ic \mə-'fit-ik\ *adj* : foul-smelling [Latin *mephitis* "foul odor"]

mep·ro·bam·ate \,mep-rō-'bam-,āt\ *n* : a bitter drug $C_9H_{18}N_2O_4$ used as a tranquilizer [*me*thyl + *prop*- (derived from *propionic acid*) + *carbamate,* a type of chemical, from *carb*- + *am*ide + -*ate*]

mer·can·tile \'mər-kən-,tēl, -,tīl\ *adj* 1 : of or relating to merchants or trade 2 : of, relating to, or having the characteristics of mercantilism ⟨*mercantile* system⟩ [French, from Italian, from *mercante* "merchant", from Latin *mercans,* from *mercari* "to trade", from *merc-, merx* "merchandise"]

mer·can·til·ism \-,tēl-,iz-əm, -,tīl-\ *n* : an economic system developing during the 17th and 18th centuries to unify and increase the power and wealth of a nation by strict governmental regulation of the economy usually through policies designed to secure an accumulation of bullion, a favorable balance of trade, the development of agriculture and manufactures, and the establishment of foreign trading monopolies — **mer·can·til·ist** \-əst\ *n or adj* — **mer·can·til·is·tic** \,mər-kən-,tē-'lis-tik, -,tī-\ *adj*

Mer·ca·tor projection \mər-,kāt-ər-\ *n* : a map projection in which the meridians and parallels cross each other at right angles as they do on the globe and provide accurate directional relations but cause increasing distortion of shape and size with increasing distance from the equator [Gerhardus *Mercator*]

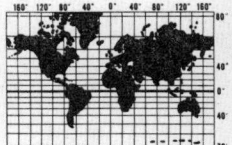

Mercator projection

¹mer·ce·nary \'mərs-n-,er-ē\ *n, pl* **-nar·ies** : one that serves merely for wages; *esp* : a soldier hired by a foreign country to serve in its army [Latin *mercenarius,* from *merces* "wages", from *merc-, merx,* "merchandise"]

²mercenary *adj* 1 : serving only for pay or reward 2 : greedy for money — **mer·ce·nari·ly** \,mərs-n-'er-ə-lē\ *adv* — **mer·ce·nari·ness** \'mərs-n-,er-ē-nəs\ *n*

mer·cer \'mər-sər\ *n, British* : a dealer in textile fabrics [Old French *mercier* "merchant", from *mers* "merchandise", from Latin *merx*]

mer·cer·ize \'mər-sə-,rīz\ *vt* : to treat (cotton yarn or fabric) with a chemical so that the fibers are strengthened, take dyes better, and often acquire a sheen [John *Mercer,* died 1866, English calico printer]

¹mer·chan·dise \'mər-chən-,dīz, -,dīs\ *n* : the goods that are bought and sold in trade [Old French *marcheandise,* from *marcheant* "merchant"]

²merchandise \-,dīz\ *vb* : to buy and sell : TRADE; *esp* : to try to further the sale of goods or use of services by

\ə\ abut
\ər\ further
\a\ mat
\ā\ take
\ä\ cot, cart
\au̇\ out
\ch\ chin
\e\ pet
\ē\ easy
\g\ go
\i\ tip
\ī\ life
\j\ job
\ng\ sing
\ō\ bone
\ȯ\ saw
\oi\ coin
\th\ thin
\th\ this
\ü\ food
\u̇\ foot
\y\ yet
\yü\ few
\yu̇\ cure
\zh\ vision

merganser

attractive presentation and publicity — **mer·chan·dis·er** *n*

¹mer·chant \'mər-chənt\ *n* **1** : a buyer and seller of goods for profit; *esp* : one who carries on trade on a large scale or with foreign countries **2** : the operator of a retail business : STOREKEEPER [Old French *marcheant,* derived from Latin *mercari* "to trade", from *merc-, merx* "merchandise"]

²merchant *adj* **1** : of, relating to, or used in trade ⟨a *merchant* ship⟩ **2** : of or relating to a merchant marine

mer·chant·able \-ə-bəl\ *adj* : of commercial quality : SALABLE ⟨*merchantable* goods⟩

mer·chant·man \-mən\ *n* : a ship used in commerce

merchant marine *n* **1** : the commercial ships of a nation **2** : the personnel of a merchant marine

mer·ci·ful \'mər-si-fəl\ *adj* : having, showing, or disposed to mercy : COMPASSIONATE — **mer·ci·ful·ly** \-fə-lē, -flē\ *adv* — **mer·ci·ful·ness** \-fəl-nəs\ *n*

mer·ci·less \'mər-si-ləs\ *adj* : having no mercy : PITILESS — **mer·ci·less·ly** *adv* — **mer·ci·less·ness** *n*

¹mer·cu·ri·al \mər-'kyur-ē-əl\ *adj* **1** : of or relating to the planet Mercury **2** : having qualities of eloquence, ingenuity, or thievishness **3** : marked by rapid and unpredictable change of mood ⟨a *mercurial* temperament⟩ **4** : of, relating to, or containing the element mercury ⟨*mercurial* medical preparations⟩ ⟨a *mercurial* thermometer⟩ — **mer·cu·ri·al·ly** \-ē-ə-lē\ *adv* — **mer·cu·ri·al·ness** *n*

²mercurial *n* : a drug or chemical containing mercury

mer·cu·ric \mər-'kyur-ik\ *adj* : of, relating to, or containing mercury; *esp* : containing mercury that has a valence of two

mercuric chloride *n* : a heavy poisonous substance $HgCl_2$ used as a disinfectant and fungicide and in photography

Mer·cu·ro·chrome \mər-'kyur-ə-ˌkrōm\ *trademark* — used for a red germicidal and antiseptic solution

mer·cu·rous \mər-'kyur-əs, 'mər-kyə-rəs\ *adj* : of, relating to, or containing mercury; *esp* : containing mercury that has a valence of one

mercurous chloride *n* : CALOMEL

mer·cu·ry \'mər-kyə-rē, -kə-rē, -krē\ *n,* **1 a** : a heavy silver-white metallic element that is liquid at ordinary temperatures — called also *quicksilver;* see ELEMENT table **b** : the column of mercury in a thermometer or barometer **2** *cap* : the planet nearest the sun — see PLANET table [Medieval Latin *mercurius,* from Latin *Mercurius* "Mercury (Roman god)"]

mer·cy \'mər-sē\ *n, pl* **mercies** **1** : compassion or forbearance shown to one (as an offender) having no claim to kindness **2** : a fortunate circumstance ⟨a *mercy* the weather cooled off⟩ **3** : compassion shown to victims of misfortune [Old French *merci,* from Medieval Latin *merces* "favor, mercy", from Latin, "price paid, wages", from *merc-, merx* "merchandise"]

□ ORIGIN *Mercy* is not something that can be bought or sold, but the word *mercy* is derived from Latin *merces,* which means "the price paid for something", "wages", "reward", or "recompense". The roots of what is now the primary sense of mercy are to be found in the Latin of Christian writers of the 6th century, who began to use *merces* for the spiritual reward that comes from kindness to those who do not necessarily have a claim to such mercy and from whom no recompense is to be expected. □ SYN CLEMENCY, LENIENCY: MERCY implies kindness and compassion that withholds punishment even when justice demands it; CLEMENCY implies a mild or merciful disposition in one having the power or duty of punishing; LENIENCY suggests an easy or indulgent treatment of faults or misbehavior.

mercy killing *n* : the act or practice of killing (as an incurable invalid) for reasons of mercy — called also *euthanasia*

¹mere \'miər\ *n* : a sheet of standing water : POOL [Old English]

²mere *adj, superlative* **mer·est** : being only this and nothing else : nothing more than ⟨a *mere* whisper⟩ ⟨a *mere* child⟩ [Latin *merus* "pure, unmixed"] — **mere·ly** *adv*

-mere \ˌmiər\ *n combining form* : part : segment ⟨meta*mere*⟩ [Greek *meros*]

mer·e·tri·cious \ˌmer-ə-'trish-əs\ *adj* : falsely attractive [Latin *meretricius* "of a prostitute", from *meretrix* "prostitute", from *merēre* "to earn"] — **mer·e·tri·cious·ly** *adv* — **mer·e·tri·cious·ness** *n*

mer·gan·ser \mər-'gan-sər\ *n, pl* **-sers** *or* **-ser** : any of various wild ducks with a slender hooked beak and a usually crested head [Latin *mergus,* a kind of waterfowl + *anser* "goose"]

merge \'mərj\ *vb* **1** : to be or cause to be swallowed up or absorbed in or within something else : MINGLE, BLEND ⟨*merging* traffic⟩ **2** : COMBINE, UNITE; *esp* : to undergo or cause to undergo a business merger [Latin *mergere* "to plunge"]

merg·er \'mər-jər\ *n* : the action or result of merging; *esp* : the combination of two or more business firms into one

me·rid·i·an \mə-'rid-ē-ən\ *n* **1** : the highest point attained **2 a** : an imaginary great circle on the earth's surface passing through the north and south poles and any given place between **b** : the half of such a circle included between the poles **c** : a representation of such a circle or half circle numbered for longitude on a globe or map [Middle French *meridien* "noon", from Latin *meridianus* "of noon", from *meridies* "noon", from *medius* "mid" + *dies* "day"] — **meridian** *adj*

me·rid·i·o·nal \mə-'rid-ē-ən-l\ *adj* **1** : of, relating to, or situated in the south : SOUTHERN **2** : of, relating to, or characteristic of people living in the south especially of France **3** : of or relating to a meridian [Middle French *meridionel,* derived from Latin *meridies* "noon, south"] — **me·rid·i·o·nal·ly** \-l-ē\ *adv*

me·ringue \mə-'rang\ *n* **1** : a mixture of beaten egg white and sugar put on pies or cakes and browned **2** : a shell of baked meringue filled with fruit or ice cream [French]

me·ri·no \mə-'rē-nō\ *n, pl* **-nos** **1** : any of a breed of fine-wooled white sheep producing a heavy fleece of exceptional quality **2** : a soft wool or wool and cotton fabric resembling cashmere **3** : a fine wooland cotton yarn [Spanish] — **merino** *adj*

mer·i·stem \'mer-ə-ˌstem\ *n* : a plant tissue made up of unspecialized cells capable of dividing indefinitely and of producing cells that differentiate into tissues and organs [Greek *meristos* "divided" + English -*em* (as in *system*)] — **mer·i·ste·mat·ic** \ˌmer-ə-stə-'mat-ik\ *adj*

¹mer·it \'mer-ət\ *n* **1** : the condition or fact of deserving well or ill **2** : a praiseworthy quality : VIRTUE ⟨an answer having the *merit* of honesty⟩ **3** : WORTH, EXCELLENCE ⟨an idea of great *merit*⟩ [Old French *merite,* from Latin *meritum,* from *merēre* "to deserve, earn"]

²merit *vb* : to earn by service or performance : DESERVE

mer·i·to·ri·ous \ˌmer-ə-'tōr-ē-əs, -'tör-\ *adj* : deserving reward or honor : PRAISEWORTHY — **mer·i·to·ri·ous·ly** *adv* — **mer·i·to·ri·ous·ness** *n*

merit system *n* : a system by which appointments and promotions in the civil service are based on competence rather than political favoritism

mer·lin \'mər-lən\ *n* : a small European falcon [Anglo-French *merilun*]

mer·maid \'mər-ˌmād\ *n* : an imaginary sea creature usually represented with a woman's body and a fish's tail [Old English *mere* "sea, mere"]

mer·man \-ˌman, -mən\ *n, pl* **mer·men** \-ˌmen, -mən\ : an imaginary sea creature usually represented with a man's body and a fish's tail

-m·er·ous \m-ə-rəs\ *adj combining form* : having (such or so many) parts ⟨penta*merous*⟩ [Greek *meros* "part"]

mer·ri·ment \'mer-i-mənt\ *n* : MERRYMAKING 1, FUN

mer·ry \'mer-ē\ *adj* **mer·ri·er; -est 1** : full of good humor and good spirits : MIRTHFUL **2** : marked by gaiety or festivity ⟨a *merry* Christmas⟩ [Old English *myrge, merge*] — **mer·ri·ly** \'mer-ə-lē\ *adv* — **mer·ri·ness** \'mer-ē-nəs\ *n* □ SYN BLITHE, JOVIAL, JOLLY: MERRY suggests high spirits and unrestrained enjoyment of frolic or festivity; BLITHE implies lightheartedness and carefree gaiety; JOVIAL suggests behavior that stimulates conviviality and good-fellowship; JOLLY suggests often habitual good spirits expressed in laughing, bantering, and jesting.

mer·ry-an·drew \,mer-ē-'an-drü\ *n, often cap M&A* : one that clowns publicly : BUFFOON [from the name *Andrew*]

mer·ry-go-round \'mer-ē-gō-raund, -gə-\ *n* **1** : a circular revolving platform fitted with seats and figures of animals on which people sit for a ride **2** : a rapid round of activities : WHIRL ⟨a *merry-go-round* of parties⟩

mer·ry·mak·ing \-,mā-king\ *n* **1** : merry activity **2** : a merry occasion or party — **mer·ry·mak·er** \-kər\ *n*

mes- *or* **meso-** *combining form* **1** : mid : in the middle ⟨*meso*carp⟩ **2** : intermediate (as in size or type) ⟨*mes*on⟩ [Greek, from *mesos*]

me·sa \'mā-sə\ *n* : a flat-topped hill or small plateau with steep sides [Spanish, literally, "table", from Latin *mensa*]

més·al·liance \,mā-,zal-'yäⁿs, ,mā-zə-'lī-əns\ *n, pl* **-li·ances** \-'yäⁿs, -'yäⁿs-əz\ '-lī-ən-səz\ : a marriage with a person of inferior social position [French, from *més-* "mis-" + *alliance* "alliance"]

mes·cal \me-'skal, mə-\ *n* **1** : a small cactus with rounded stems covered with jointed tubercles that are used as a stimulant and intoxicant especially among the Mexican Indians **2 a** : a usually colorless Mexican liquor distilled especially from the central leaves on maguey plants **b** : a plant from which mescal is produced [Spanish, from Nahuatl *mexcalli* "mescal liquor"]

mescal button *n* : one of the dried discoid tops of the mescal cactus

mes·ca·line \'mes-kə-lən, -,lēn\ *n* : a hallucination-inducing alkaloid $C_{11}H_{17}NO_3$ found in mescal buttons

mesdames *pl of* MADAM *or of* MADAME *or of* MRS.

mesdemoiselles *pl of* MADEMOISELLE

me·seems \mi-'sēmz\ *vb impersonal, past* **me·seemed** \-'sēmd\ *archaic* : it seems to me

mes·en·ceph·a·lon \,mez-,en-'sef-ə-,län, ,mez-n-, ,mēz-\ *n* : the middle division of the brain : MIDBRAIN — **mes·en·ce·phal·ic** \-,en-sə-'fal-ik, -n-sə-\ *adj*

mes·en·chyme \'mez-n-,kīm, 'mēz-\ *n* : a loosely organized mesodermal tissue that produces connective tissues, blood, lymphatics, bone, and cartilage [German *mesenchym*] — **mes·en·chy·mal** \mə-'zeng-kə-məl, -'seng-; ,mez-n-'kī-məl, ,mēz-\ *adj*

mes·en·tery \'mez-n-,ter-ē, 'mes-\ *n, pl* **-ter·ies** : a membranous tissue or one of the membranes that envelop and support visceral organs (as the intestines) [Greek *mesenterion*, from *mes-* + *enteron* "intestine"] — **mes·en·ter·ic** \,mez-n-'ter-ik, ,mes-\ *adj*

¹mesh \'mesh\ *n* **1** : one of the open spaces formed by the threads of a net or the wires of a sieve or screen **2 a** : a fabric of open texture with evenly spaced small holes **b** : NET 1a, NETWORK **3** : SNARE 2 — usually used in pl. ⟨caught in their own *meshes*⟩ **4** : the coming or fitting together of the teeth of two gears [probably from Dutch *maesche*] — **meshed** \'mesht\ *adj*

²mesh *vb* **1** : to catch in or as if in a mesh **2** : to fit together : INTERLOCK ⟨gears that *mesh*⟩

me·si·al \'mē-zē-əl, -sē-\ *adj* : of, relating to, or being the surface of a tooth that is next to the tooth in front of it or that is closest to the middle of the front of the jaw — **me·si·al·ly** \-ə-lē\ *adv*

mes·mer·ism \'mez-mə-,riz-əm\ *n* : HYPNOTISM [F. A. Mesmer, died 1815, Austrian physician] — **mes·mer·ic** \mez-'mer-ik\ *adj* — **mes·mer·ist** \'mez-mə-rəst\ *n*

mes·mer·ize \'mez-mə-,rīz\ *vt* **1** : HYPNOTIZE **2** : FASCINATE 1, SPELLBIND — **mes·mer·iz·er** *n*

me·so·carp \'mez-ə-,kärp, 'mēz-, 'mēs-, 'mes-\ *n* : the often fleshy middle layer of the pericarp of a fruit — compare ENDOCARP, EPICARP

me·so·derm \-,dərm\ *n* : the middle of the three primary germ layers of an embryo from which most of the muscular, skeletal, and connective tissues develop; *also* : tissue derived from this layer — **me·so·der·mal** \,mez-ə-'dər-məl, ,mēz-, ,mēs-, ,mes-\ *adj*

me·so·glea *or* **me·so·gloea** \,mez-ə-'glē-ə, ,mēz-, ,mēs-, ,mes-\ *n* : a jellylike substance between the endoderm and ectoderm of sponges or coelenterates [*mes-* + Late Greek *gloia, glia* "glue"]

Me·so·lith·ic \,mez-ə-'lith-ik, ,mēz-, ,mes-, ,mēs-\ *adj* : of or relating to a period of the Stone Age that is transitional between the Paleolithic and the Neolithic

me·so·mor·phic \,mez-ə-'mòr-fik, ,mēz-, ,mēs-, ,mes-\ *adj* : of a muscular or athletic type of body-build — **me·so·morph** \'mez-ə-,mòrf, 'mēz-, 'mēs-, 'mes-\ *n*

me·son \'mez-,än, 'mes-; 'mā-,zän, 'mē-, -,sän\ *n* : any of a group of elementary particles that have a mass between that of the electron and the proton and are either positively or negatively charged or neutral [*mes-* + *-on*]

me·so·pause \'mez-ə-,pòz, 'mēz-, 'mēs-, 'mes-\ *n* : the upper boundary of the mesosphere where the temperature of the atmosphere reaches its lowest point

me·so·phyll \-,fil\ *n* : the tissue of a foliage leaf consisting of photosynthetic and storage cells that lie between the surface layers

me·so·phyte \-,fīt\ *n* : a plant that grows under medium conditions of moisture — **me·so·phyt·ic** \,mez-ə-'fit-ik, ,mēz-, ,mēs-, ,mes-\ *adj*

me·so·sphere \'mez-ə-,sfiər, 'mēz-, 'mēs-, 'mes-\ *n* : a layer of the atmosphere extending from the top of the stratosphere to an altitude of about 90 kilometers

me·so·the·li·um \,mez-ə-'thē-lē-əm, ,mēz-, ,mēs-, ,mes-\ *n, pl* **-lia** \-lē-ə\ : epithelium derived from mesoderm — **me·so·the·li·al** \-lē-əl\ *adj*

me·so·tho·rax \-'thōr-,aks, -'thòr-\ *n* : the middle of the three segments of the thorax of an insect

Me·so·zo·ic \-'zō-ik\ *n* **1** : the 3rd of the four eras of geological history marked by the existence of dinosaurs, marine and flying reptiles, and evergreen trees — called also *Age of Reptiles*; see GEOLOGIC TIME table **2** : the system of rocks corresponding to the Mesozoic — **Mesozoic** *adj*

mes·quite \mə-'skēt, me-\ *n* : a spiny deep-rooted tree or shrub of the pea family that grows in the southwestern United States and in Mexico and bears pods rich in sugar and important as a livestock feed [Spanish, from Nahuatl *mizquitl*]

¹mess \'mes\ *n* **1 a** : a quantity of food **b** : a dish of soft food ⟨a *mess* of porridge⟩ **2 a** : a group of people who regularly eat together; *also* : the meal they eat **b** : a place where meals are regularly served to a group ⟨an officers' *mess*⟩ **3 a** : a confused heap **b** : a state of confusion or disorder ⟨left things in a *mess*⟩ [Old French *mes*, from Late Latin *missus* "course at a meal", from *mittere* "to put", from Latin, "to send"]

²mess *vb* **1 a** : to supply with meals **b** : to take meals with a mess **2 a** : to make dirty or untidy **b** : BUNGLE ⟨*messed* up the job⟩ **3** : to interfere with **4** : PUTTER ⟨likes to *mess* around the garden⟩

mes·sage \'mes-ij\ *n* **1** : a communication in writing, in speech, or by signals **2** : a messenger's errand or function **3** : an underlying theme or idea [Old French,

mescal 1

mesquite: flowering branch and pod

\ə\ abut	\ng\ sing
\ər\ further	\ō\ bone
\a\ mat	\ȯ\ saw
\ā\ take	\ȯi\ coin
\ä\ cot, cart	\th\ thin
\au̇\ out	\th\ this
\ch\ chin	\ü\ food
\e\ pet	\u̇\ foot
\ē\ easy	\y\ yet
\g\ go	\yü\ few
\i\ tip	\yu̇\ cure
\ī\ life	\zh\ vision
\j\ job	

from Medieval Latin *missaticum,* from Latin *missus,* past participle of *mittere* "to send"]

messeigneurs *pl of* MONSEIGNEUR

mes·sen·ger \'mes-n-jər\ *n* : one that bears a message or does an errand [Old French *messagier,* from *message* "message"]

messenger RNA *n* : an RNA that carries the code for a particular protein from the nuclear DNA to the ribosome and acts as a template for the formation of that protein — compare TRANSFER RNA

mes·si·ah \mə-'sī-ə\ *n* **1** *cap* **a** : the expected king and deliverer of the Jews **b** : JESUS **2** : a professed or accepted leader of some hope or cause [Hebrew *māshīaḥ* and Aramaic *mĕshīḥā,* literally, "anointed"] — **mes·si·ah·ship** \-,ship\ *n* — **mes·si·an·ic** \,mes-ē-'an-ik\ *adj* — **mes·si·a·nism** \'mes-ē-ə-,niz-əm, mə-'sī-ə-\ *n*

Mes·si·as \mə-'sī-əs\ *n* : MESSIAH 1 [Late Latin, from Greek, from Aramaic *mĕshīḥā*]

messieurs *pl of* MONSIEUR

mess jacket *n* : a man's short tight jacket

mess kit *n* : a kit consisting of cooking and eating utensils that fit together in a compact unit

mess·mate \'mes-,māt\ *n* : a member of a mess (as on a ship)

Messrs. \,mes-ərz\ *pl of* MR.

messy \'mes-ē\ *adj* **mess·i·er; -est** : marked by confusion, disorder, or dirt : UNTIDY — **mess·i·ly** \'mes-ə-lē\ *adv* — **mess·i·ness** \'mes-ē-nəs\ *n*

mes·ti·za \me-'stē-zə\ *n* : a woman who is a mestizo [Spanish, feminine of *mestizo*]

mes·ti·zo \-zō\ *n, pl* **-zos** : a person of mixed blood; *esp* : one of mixed European and American Indian ancestry [Spanish, from *mestizo* "mixed", derived from Latin *miscēre* "to mix"]

met *past of* MEET

meta- *or* **met-** *combining form* **1 a** : occurring after **b** : situated behind or beyond ⟨*met*encephalon⟩ **2** : change : transformation [Greek, from *meta* "among, with, after"]

me·tab·o·lism \mə-'tab-ə-,liz-əm\ *n* **1 a** : the sum of the processes in the building up and destruction of protoplasm; *esp* : the chemical changes in living cells by which energy is provided for vital processes and activities and new material is assimilated **b** : the sum of the processes by which a particular substance is handled in the living body **2** : METAMORPHOSIS **3** [Greek *metabolē* "change", from *metaballein* "to change", from *meta-* + *ballein* "to throw"] — **met·a·bol·ic** \,met-ə-'bäl-ik\ *adj* — **me·tab·o·lize** \me-'tab-ə-,līz\ *vb*

me·tab·o·lite \-,līt\ *n* **1** : a product of metabolism **2** : a substance essential to a metabolic process

meta·car·pal \,met-ə-'kär-pəl\ *n* : a bone of the metacarpus

meta·car·pus \-pəs\ *n* : the part of the hand between the wrist and fingers or of the forefoot between the ankle and toes — **meta·car·pal** \-pəl\ *adj*

meta·gal·axy \,met-ə-'gal-ək-sē\ *n* : the entire system of galaxies : UNIVERSE — **meta·ga·lac·tic** \-gə-'lak-tik\ *adj*

¹met·al \'met-l\ *n* **1** : any of various substances (as gold, tin, copper, or bronze) that have a more or less shiny appearance, are good conductors of electricity and heat, are opaque, can be melted, and are usually capable of being drawn into a wire or hammered into a thin sheet **2** : any of the chemical elements that exhibit the properties of a metal, typically are crystalline solids, and have atoms that readily lose electrons **3 a** : METTLE 2a **b** : the material or substance out of which a person or thing is made [Old French, from Latin *metallum* "mine, metal", from Greek *metallon*] — **metal** *adj*

²metal *vt* **-aled** *or* **-alled; -al·ing** *or* **-al·ling** : to cover or furnish with metal

me·tal·lic \mə-'tal-ik\ *adj* **1** : of, relating to, or being a metal **2** : containing or made of metal **3** : having iridescent and reflective properties **4** : STRIDENT, HARSH ⟨a *metallic* voice⟩ — **me·tal·li·cal·ly** \-'tal-i-kə-lē, -klē\ *adv*

met·al·lif·er·ous \,met-l-'if-rəs, -ə-rəs\ *adj* : yielding or containing metal

met·al·lize \'met-l-,īz\ *vt* : to treat or combine with a metal

met·al·log·ra·phy \,met-l-'äg-rə-fē\ *n* : a study of the structure of metals especially with the microscope — **met·al·log·ra·pher** \-fər\ *n* — **me·tal·lo·graph·ic** \mə-,tal-ə-'graf-ik\ *adj*

met·al·loid \'met-l-,öid\ *n* : a chemical element intermediate in properties between the typical metals and other elements

met·al·lur·gy \'met-l-,ər-jē\ *n* : the science and technology of metals [Greek *metallon* "metal" + *ergon* "work"] — **met·al·lur·gi·cal** \,met-l-'ər-ji-kəl\ *adj* — **met·al·lur·gist** \'met-l-,ər-jəst\ *n*

met·al·ware \'met-l-,waər, -,weər\ *n* : metal utensils for household use

met·al·work \'met-l-,wərk\ *n* **1** : the process or occupation of making things from metal **2** : work and especially artistic work made of metal — **met·al·work·er** \-,wər-kər\ *n* — **met·al·work·ing** \-,king\ *n*

meta·mere \'met-ə-,miər\ *n* : any of the series of segments into which the body of a higher invertebrate or vertebrate is divisible — **me·tam·er·ism** \mə-'tam-ə-,riz-əm\ *n* — **meta·mer·ic** \,met-ə-'mer-ik, -'mir-\ *adj*

meta·mor·phic \,met-ə-'mòr-fik\ *adj* : changed into a more compact form by the action of pressure, heat, and water ⟨a *metamorphic* rock⟩

meta·mor·phose \-,fōz, -,fōs\ *vb* **1** : to change or cause to change in form : undergo metamorphosis **2** : to cause (a rock) to undergo metamorphism SYN see TRANSFORM

meta·mor·pho·sis \,met-ə-'mòr-fə-səs\ *n, pl* **-pho·ses** \-fə-,sēz\ *n* **1 a** : a change of form, structure, or substance especially by witchcraft or magic **b** : a striking alteration in appearance, character, or circumstances **2** : a fundamental and usually rather abrupt change (as of an insect larva into an adult or a tadpole into a frog) in the form and often the habits of an animal [Latin, from Greek *metamorphōsis,* from *metamorphoun* "to transform", from *meta-* + *morphē* "form"]

meta·phase \'met-ə-,fāz\ *n* : the stage of mitosis and meiosis during which the chromosomes become arranged in the plane of the equator of the spindle

metaphase plate *n* : the plane at the equator of the spindle of a dividing cell in metaphase with the chromosomes arranged upon it — called also *equatorial plate*

met·a·phor \'met-ə-,fòr *also* -fər\ *n* : a figure of speech in which a word or phrase denoting one kind of object or idea is used in place of another to suggest a similarity between them (as in the ship plows the sea) — compare SIMILE [Latin *metaphora,* from Greek, from *metapherein* "to transfer", from *meta-* + *pherein* "to carry"] — **met·a·phor·ic** \,met-ə-'fòr-ik, -'fär-\ *or* **met·a·phor·i·cal** \-i-kəl\ *adj* — **met·a·phor·i·cal·ly** \-i-kə-lē, -klē\ *adv*

meta·phys·i·cal \,met-ə-'fiz-i-kəl\ *adj* **1** : of or relating to metaphysics **2** : SUPERNATURAL 1 **3** : highly abstract or difficult to understand **4** *often cap* : of or relating to poetry especially of the early 17th century that is marked by subtle and elaborate metaphors — **meta·phys·i·cal·ly** \-'fiz-i-kə-lē, -klē\ *adv*

meta·phy·si·cian \,met-ə-fə-'zish-ən\ *n* : a student of or specialist in metaphysics

meta·phys·ics \,met-ə-'fiz-iks\ *n* : the part of philosophy concerned with the ultimate causes and the underlying nature of things [Medieval Latin *Metaphysica,* title of Aristotle's treatise on the subject, from Greek (ta) meta (ta) physika "the (works) after the physical (works)"; from its position in his collected works]

meta·se·quoia \,met-ə-si-'kwòi-ə\ *n* : any of a genus of fossil and living deciduous cone-bearing trees of the pine family

meta·sta·ble \,met-ə-'stā-bəl\ *adj* : marked by only a slight margin of stability ⟨a *metastable* chemical⟩

me·tas·ta·sis \mə-'tas-tə-səs\ *n, pl* **-ta·ses** \-,sēz\ : transfer of a disease-producing agency from its original site to another part of the body; *also* : a secondary growth of a malignant tumor [Late Latin, "transition", from Greek, from *methistanai* "to change", from *meta-* + *histanai* "to stand"] — **met·a·stat·ic** \,met-ə-'stat-ik\ *adj* — **met·a·stat·i·cal·ly** \-'stat-i-kə-lē, -klē\ *adv*

me·tas·ta·size \mə-'tas-tə-,sīz\ *vi* : to spread by metastasis

meta·tar·sal \,met-ə-'tär-səl\ *n* : a bone of the metatarsus

meta·tar·sus \-səs\ *n* : the part of the foot in a human being or of the hind foot in a four-footed animal between the toes and the joint between the foot and the leg — **meta·tar·sal** \-səl\ *adj*

me·tath·e·sis \mə-'tath-ə-səs\ *n, pl* **-e·ses** \-,sēz\ : a change of place or condition; *esp* : transposition of two sounds or letters in a word (as in Modern English *bird* from Old English *bridd*) [Greek, from *metatithenai* "to transpose", from *meta-* + *tithenai* "to place"]

meta·tho·rax \,met-ə-'thōr-,aks, -'thòr-\ *n* : the hindmost of the three segments of the thorax of an insect

meta·zoa \,met-ə-'zō-ə\ *n pl* : animals that are metazoans

meta·zo·an \-'zō-ən\ *n* : any of a group (Metazoa) including all animals with a body composed of cells differentiated into tissues and organs — **metazoan** *adj*

mete \'mēt\ *vt* : to assign by measure ⟨*mete* out punishment⟩ [Old English *metan* "to measure"]

me·tem·psy·cho·sis \mə-,tem-si-'kō-səs, -,temp-; ,met-əm-,sī-\ *n* : the passing of the soul at death into another body either human or animal [Greek *metempsychōsis*, dervied from *meta-* + *en-* + *psychē* "soul"]

met·en·ceph·a·lon \,met-,en-'sef-ə-,län\ *n* : the anterior segment of the rhombencephalon

me·te·or \'mēt-ē-ər, -ē-,òr\ *n* : one of the small bodies of matter in the solar system observable when it falls into the earth's atmosphere where the heat of friction may cause it to glow brightly for a short time; *also* : the streak of light produced by the passage of a meteor [Middle French *meteore*, from Medieval Latin *meteorum*, from Greek *meteōron* "phenomenon in the sky", from *meteōros* "high in the air"]

me·te·or·ic \,mēt-ē-'òr-ik, -'är-\ *adj* **1** : of or relating to a meteor ⟨a *meteoric* shower⟩ **2** : resembling a meteor in speed or in sudden and temporary brilliance ⟨a *meteoric* rise to fame⟩ — **me·te·or·i·cal·ly** \-i-kə-lē, -klē\ *adv*

me·te·or·ite \'mēt-ē-ə-,rīt\ *n* : a meteor that reaches the surface of the earth

me·te·or·oid \-,ròid\ *n* : a meteor in interplanetary space

me·te·o·rol·o·gy \,mēt-ē-ə-'räl-ə-jē\ *n* : a science that deals with the atmosphere and its phenomena and especially with weather and weather forecasting — **me·te·o·ro·log·ic** \-rə-'läj-ik\ *or* **me·te·o·ro·log·i·cal** \-i-kəl\ *adj* — **me·te·o·rol·o·gist** \-'räl-ə-jəst\ *n*

¹**me·ter** *or* **me·tre** \'mēt-ər\ *n* : a systematic rhythm in verse and in music [Old English *mēter*, from Latin *metrum*, from Greek *metron* "measure, meter"]

²**meter** *n* : the basic metric unit of length — see METRIC SYSTEM table [French *mètre*, from Greek *metron* "measure"]

³**meter** *n* : an instrument for measuring and sometimes recording the amount of something ⟨a gas *meter*⟩

⁴**meter** *vt* **1** : to measure by means of a meter **2** : to supply in a measured or regulated amount

-me·ter \m-ət-ər, in some words, ,mēt-ər\ *n combining form* : instrument or means for measuring ⟨baro*meter*⟩

meter–kilogram–second *adj* : of, relating to, or being a system of units based on the meter as the unit of length, the kilogram as the unit of mass, and the second as the unit of time — abbreviation *mks*

me·ter·stick \'mēt-ər-,stik\ *n* : a measuring stick one meter long that is marked off in centimeters and usually millimeters

meth·ac·ry·late \meth-'ak-rə-,lāt\ *n* : a light strong acrylic resin used as a substitute for glass [*meth*yl + *acryl*ic + *-ate*]

meth·a·done \'meth-ə-,dōn\ *or* **meth·a·don** \-,dän\ *n* : a synthetic addictive narcotic drug used especially to replace heroin in the treatment of heroin addiction [derived from *methyl*]

meth·am·phet·amine \,meth-am-'fet-ə-,mēn, -əm-, -mən\ *n* : a derivative of amphetamine $C_{10}H_{15}N$ used as a stimulant of the central nervous system and in the treatment of obesity [*methyl* + *amphetamine*]

meth·ane \'meth-,ān\ *n* : an odorless flammable gas CH_4 consisting of carbon and hydrogen produced by decomposition of organic matter [*methyl* + *-ane*]

meth·a·nol \'meth-ə-,nòl, -,nōl\ *n* : a volatile flammable poisonous liquid CH_4O that consists of carbon, hydrogen, and oxygen and is used especially as a solvent and antifreeze

me·thinks \mi-'things, -'thingks\ *vb impersonal, past* **me·thought** \-'thòt\ *archaic* : it seems to me

me·thi·o·nine \mə-'thī-ə-,nēn\ *n* : a crystalline sulfur-containing essential amino acid $C_5H_{11}NO_2S$ [*methyl* + *thion-* (from Greek *theion* "sulfur") + *-ine*]

meth·od \'meth-əd\ *n* **1** : a regular systematic plan for or way of doing something **2 a** : orderly arrangement **b** : habitual regularity and orderliness [Latin *methodus*, from Greek *methodos*, from *meta-* + *hodos* "way"]

me·thod·i·cal \mə-'thäd-i-kəl\ *adj* **1** : arranged, characterized by, or performed with method or order **2** : habitually following a method : SYSTEMATIC — **me·thod·i·cal·ly** \-i-kə-lē, -klē\ *adv* — **me·thod·i·cal·ness** \-kəl-nəs\ *n*

Meth·od·ist \'meth-əd-əst\ *n* : a member of one of the denominations deriving from the Wesleyan revival, accepting the possibility of salvation for all and often a modified episcopal government, and stressing personal and social morality — **Meth·od·ism** \-ə-,diz-əm\ *n* — **Methodist** *adj*

meth·od·ize \'meth-ə-,dīz\ *vt* : to reduce to method : SYSTEMATIZE

meth·od·ol·o·gy \,meth-ə-'däl-ə-jē\ *n, pl* **-gies** **1** : a body of methods and rules followed in a science or discipline **2** : the study of the principles or procedures of inquiry in a particular field — **meth·od·olog·i·cal** \,meth-əd-l-'äj-i-kəl\ *adj* — **meth·od·ol·o·gist** \,meth-ə-däl-ə-jəst\ *n*

meth·yl \'meth-əl\ *n* : a chemical radical CH_3 consisting of carbon and hydrogen [back-formation from *methylene* "the radical CH_2" from French *méthylène*, from Greek *methy* "wine" + *hylē* "wood"]

methyl alcohol *n* : METHANOL

meth·y·lene blue \,meth-ə-,lēn\ *n* : a basic dye used as a biological stain and as an antidote in cyanide poisoning

methyl orange *n* : a basic dye used as a chemical indicator that in dilute solution is yellow when neutral and pink when acid

me·tic·u·lous \mə-'tik-yə-ləs\ *adj* : extremely or excessively careful in small details [Latin *meticulosus* "timid", from *metus* "fear"] SYN see CAREFUL — **me·tic·u·lous·ly** *adv* — **me·tic·u·lous·ness** *n*

mé·tier \mā-'tyā\ *n* **1** : TRADE 2a **2** : an area of activity in which one is expert or successful : FORTE [French,

\ə\ abut		\ng\ sing	
\ər\ further		\ō\ bone	
\a\ mat		\ò\ saw	
\ā\ take		\òi\ coin	
\ä\ cot, cart		\th\ thin	
\aù\ out		\th\ this	
\ch\ chin		\ü\ food	
\e\ pet		\ u̇\ foot	
\ē\ easy		\y\ yet	
\g\ go		\yü\ few	
\i\ tip		\yu̇\ cure	
\ī\ life		\zh\ vision	
\j\ job			

METRIC SYSTEM

LENGTH

UNIT	ABBREVIATION	NUMBER OF METERS	APPROXIMATE UNITED STATES EQUIVALENT
kilometer	km	1,000	0.621 mile
hectometer	hm	100	109.361 yards
dekameter	dam	10	32.808 feet
meter	m	1	39.370 inches
decimeter	dm	0.1	3.937 inches
centimeter	cm	0.01	0.394 inch
millimeter	mm	0.001	0.039 inch

AREA

UNIT	ABBREVIATION	NUMBER OF SQUARE METERS	APPROXIMATE UNITED STATES EQUIVALENT
square kilometer	sq km or km^2	1,000,000	0.386 square mile
hectare	ha	10,000	2.471 acres
are	a	100	119.599 square yards
square centimeter	sq cm or cm^2	0.0001	0.155 square inch

CAPACITY

UNIT	ABBREVIATION	NUMBER OF LITERS	CUBIC	DRY	LIQUID
			APPROXIMATE UNITED STATES EQUIVALENT		
kiloliter	kl	1,000	1.308 cubic yards		
hectoliter	hl	100	3.532 cubic feet	2.838 bushels	
dekaliter	dal	10	0.353 cubic foot	1.135 pecks	2.642 gallons
liter	l	1	61.024 cubic inches	0.908 quart	1.057 quarts
cubic decimeter	dm^3	1	61.024 cubic inches	0.908 quart	1.507 quarts
deciliter	dl	0.10	6.102 cubic inches	0.182 pint	0.211 pint
centiliter	cl	0.01	0.610 cubic inch		0.338 fluid ounce
milliliter	ml	0.001	0.061 cubic inch		0.271 fluid dram

MASS AND WEIGHT

UNIT	ABBREVIATION	NUMBER OF GRAMS	APPROXIMATE UNITED STATES EQUIVALENT
metric ton	MT or t	1,000,000	1.102 tons
kilogram	kg	1,000	2.205 pounds
hectogram	hg	100	3.527 ounces
dekagram	dag	10	0.353 ounce
gram	g or gm	1	0.035 ounce
decigram	dg	0.10	1.543 grains
centigram	cg	0.01	0.154 grain
milligram	mg	0.001	0.015 grain

derived from Latin *ministerium* "work, service", from Latin *minister* "servant"]

mé·tis \mā-'tē, -'tēs\ *n, pl* **métis** \-'tē, -'tēs, -'tēz\ : one of mixed blood; *esp* : the offspring of an American Indian and a white person [French, derived from Latin *miscēre* "to mix"]

me·ton·y·my \mə-'tän-ə-mē\ *n, pl* **-mies** : a figure of speech in which the name of one thing is used for the name of another associated with or related to it (as in "lands belonging to the crown") [Latin *metonymia*, from Greek *metōnymia*, from *meta-* + *onyma* "name"] — **met·onym** \'met-ə-,nim\ *n* — **met·onym·ic** \,met-ə-'nim-ik\ *adj*

me–too \'mē-'tü\ *adj* : similar to or accepting successful or persuasive policies or practices of a political rival ⟨a *me-too* policy⟩ — **me–too·ism** \-,iz-əm\ *n*

metre *variant of* METER

met·ric \'me-trik\ *adj* **1** : based on the meter as a standard of measurement ⟨the *metric* system⟩ **2** : METRICAL 1

-met·ric \'me-trik\ *or* **-met·ri·cal** \-tri-kəl\ *adj combining form* **1** : of, employing, or obtained by (such) a meter ⟨baro*metric*⟩ **2** : of or relating to (such) an art, process, or science of measuring ⟨titri*metric*⟩

met·ri·cal \'me-tri-kəl\ *adj* **1 a** : of or relating to meter (as in poetry or music) **b** : arranged in meter ⟨*metrical* verse⟩ **2** : of or relating to measurement — **met·ri·cal·ly** \-kə-lē, -klē\ *adv*

met·rics \'me-triks\ *n pl* : a part of prosody that deals with metrical structure

metric system *n* : a decimal system of weights and measures based on the meter as the unit of length and the kilogram as the unit of weight
SEE METRIC SYSTEM TABLE ABOVE

metric ton *n* — see METRIC SYSTEM table

met·ro \'me-tro\ *n, pl* **metros** : SUBWAY [French *métro*, short for *chemin de fer métropolitain* "metropolitan railroad"]

me·trol·o·gy \me-'träl-ə-jē\ *n* : the science of weights and measures or of measurements — **met·ro·log·i·cal** \,me-trə-'läj-i-kəl\ *adj*

met·ro·nome \'me-trə-,nōm\ *n* : an instrument designed to mark exact musical time by a regularly repeated tick [Greek *metron* "meter" + *-nomos* "controlling", from *nomos* "law"] — **met·ro·nom·ic** \,me-trə-'näm-ik\ *adj* — **met·ro·nom·i·cal·ly** \-'näm-i-kə-lē, -klē\ *adv*

me·trop·o·lis \mə-'träp-ləs, -ə-ləs\ *n* **1** : the mother city or state of a colony (as of ancient Greece) **2** : the chief or capital city of a country, state, or region **3 a** : a principal seat or center of an activity **b** : a large important city [Late Latin, from Greek *mētropolis*, from *mētēr* "mother" + *polis* "city"]

¹met·ro·pol·i·tan \,me-trə-'päl-ət-n\ *n* **1** : the head of an ecclesiastical see **2** : one who lives in a metropolis or who exhibits metropolitan manners or customs

²metropolitan *adj* **1** : of or constituting a metropolitan or his see **2** : of, relating to, or characteristic of a metropolis

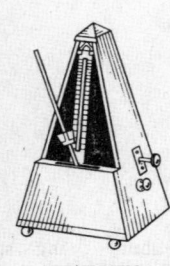

metronome

-me·try \m-ə-trē\ *n combining form, pl* **-metries** : art, process, or science of measuring (something specified) ⟨photo*metry*⟩

met·tle \'met-l\ *n* **1** : quality of temperament or disposition **2 a** : vigor and strength of spirit : ARDOR **b** : staying quality : STAMINA [alteration of *metal*] — **on one's mettle** : eager and ready to do one's best

met·tle·some \-l-səm\ *adj* : full of mettle : SPIRITED

¹mew \'myü\ *n* : GULL; *esp* : the common European gull [Old English *mǣw*]

²mew *vi* : MEOW [Middle English *mewen*] — **mew** *n*

³mew *n* **1** *archaic* : a cage for hawks **2** *pl, chiefly British* **a** : stables usually with living quarters built around a court **b** : a back street : ALLEY [Middle French *mue*, from *muer* "to molt", from Latin *mutare* "to change"]

⁴mew *vt* : to shut up : CONFINE — often used with *up*

mewl \'myül\ *vi* : to cry weakly : WHIMPER [imitative]

Mex·i·can \'mek-si-kən\ *n* **1** : a native or inhabitant of Mexico **2** : a person of Mexican descent — **Mexican** *adj*

Mexican bean beetle *n* : a spotted ladybug that is a garden pest feeding on bean plants

me·zu·zah *or* **me·zu·za** \mə-'zùz-ə\ *n* : a small parchment scroll inscribed with Deuteronomy 6:4–9 and 11:13–21 and the name Shaddai (the Almighty) and placed in a case fixed to the doorpost of some Jewish families as a sign and reminder of their faith [Hebrew *mĕzūzāh* "doorpost"]

mez·za·nine \'mez-n-ˌēn, ˌmez-n-'\ **1** : a low story between two main stories of a building often projecting as a balcony **2** : the lowest balcony in a theater or its first few rows [French, from Italian *mezzanino*, from *mezzano* "middle", from Latin *medianus* "middle, median"]

mez·zo for·te \ˌmet-sō-'fòr-ˌtā, ˌmed-zò-, -'fòrt-ē\ *adj or adv* : moderately loud — used as a direction in music [Italian, from *mezzo* "half, medium, middle"]

mez·zo–so·pra·no \-sə-'pran-ō, -'prän-\ *n* : a woman's voice of a full deep quality between that of the soprano and contralto; *also* : a singer having such a voice

mez·zo·tint \'met-sō-ˌtint, 'med-zō-\ *n* : a process of engraving on copper or steel by scraping or burnishing a roughened surface to produce light and shade; *also* : an engraving produced by this process [Italian *mezzatinta*, from *mezza* (feminine of *mezzo* "medium") + *tinta* "tint"]

mho \'mō\ *n, pl* **mhos** : the unit of conductance equal to the reciprocal of the ohm [backward spelling of *ohm*]

mi \'mē\ *n* : the 3d note of the diatonic scale [Medieval Latin]

mi·as·ma \mī-'az-mə, mē-\ *n, pl* **-mas** *or* **-ma·ta** \-mət-ə\ **1** : a vapor (as from a swamp) formerly believed to cause disease **2** : an unhealthy or harmful influence or atmosphere ⟨the *miasma* of poverty⟩ [Greek, "defilement", from *miainein* "to pollute"] — **mi·as·mal** \-məl\ *adj* — **mi·as·mat·ic** \ˌmī-əz-'mat-ik\ *or* **mi·as·mic** \mī-'az-mik, mē-\ *adj*

mi·ca \'mī-kə\ *n* : any of various silicon-containing minerals that may be separated easily into thin transparent sheets [Latin, "grain, crumb"] — **mi·ca·ceous** \mī-'kā-shəs\ *adj*

Mi·cah \'mī-kə\ *n* — see BIBLE table

mice *pl of* MOUSE

mi·celle \mī-'sel\ *n* **1** : an ordered region or structural unit in a fiber (as of cellulose) **2** : a molecular aggregate that constitutes a colloidal particle [New Latin *micella*, from Latin *mica* "crumb"] — **mi·cel·lar** \-'sel-ər\ *adj*

Mich·ael·mas \'mik-əl-məs\ *n* : September 29 celebrated as the feast of St. Michael the Archangel [Old English *Michaeles mæsse* "Michael's mass"]

Michaelmas daisy *n* : a wild aster; *esp* : one blooming about Michaelmas

Mick·ey Finn \ˌmik-ē-'fin\ *n* : a drink of liquor doctored with a drug [probably from the name *Mickey Finn*]

Mickey Mouse \-'maùs\ *adj* : lacking importance : PETTY [*Mickey Mouse*, cartoon character created by Walt Disney]

Mic·mac \'mik-ˌmak\ *n, pl* **Micmac** *or* **Micmacs** **1** : a member of an Algonquian people of eastern Canada **2** : the language of the Micmac people [Micmac *Migmac*, literally, "allies"]

micr- *or* **micro-** *combining form* **1 a** : small : minute ⟨*micro*film⟩ **b** : used for or involving minute quantities or variations ⟨*micro*scope⟩ **2** : millionth ⟨*micro*second⟩ **3** : using or used in microscopy ⟨*micro*projector⟩ [Greek *mikros*]

mi·cro \'mī-krō\ *adj* : MICROSCOPIC

mi·cro·am·pere \ˌmī-krō-'am-ˌpiər\ *n* : one millionth of an ampere

mi·crobe \'mī-ˌkrōb\ *n* : MICROORGANISM, GERM [*micr-* + Greek *bios* "life"] — **mi·cro·bi·al** \mī-'krō-bē-əl\ *adj*

mi·cro·bi·ol·o·gy \ˌmī-krō-bī-'äl-ə-jē\ *n* : a branch of biology dealing especially with microscopic forms of life — **mi·cro·bi·o·log·i·cal** \-ˌbī-ə-'läj-i-kəl\ *adj* — **mi·cro·bi·o·log·i·cal·ly** \-i-kə-lē, -klē\ *adv* — **mi·cro·bi·ol·o·gist** \-bī-'äl-ə-jəst\ *n*

mi·cro·cap·sule \'mī-krō-ˌkap-səl, -ˌsül\ *n* : a tiny capsule containing material (as a medicine) that is released when the capsule is broken, melted, or dissolved

mi·cro·cas·sette \ˌmī-krō-kə-'set\ *n* : a small casette of magnetic tape that is used especially for dictation

mi·cro·chip \'mī-krō-ˌchip\ *n* : INTEGRATED CIRCUIT

mi·cro·cline \'mī-krō-ˌklīn\ *n* : a white to pale yellow, red, or green mineral $KAISi_3O_8$ that is like orthoclase in composition [German *mikroklin*, from *mikr-* "micr-" + Greek *klinein* "to lean"]

mi·cro·coc·cus \ˌmī-krō-'käk-əs\ *n, pl* **-coc·ci** \-'käk-ˌsī, -ˌī\ : a small spherical bacterium

mi·cro·com·put·er \'mī-krō-kəm-ˌpyüt-ər\ *n* : a very small computer that uses a microprocessor to handle information

mi·cro·copy \'mī-krō-ˌkäp-ē\ *n* : a photographic copy in which graphic matter is greatly reduced in size — **microcopy** *vb*

mi·cro·cosm \'mī-krə-ˌkäz-əm\ *n* : a little world; *esp* : an individual or a community that is a miniature universe or a world in itself [Medieval Latin *microcosmus*, from Greek *mikros kosmos*] — **mi·cro·cos·mic** \ˌmī-krə-'käz-mik\ *adj*

mi·cro·eco·nom·ics \ˌmī-krō-ˌek-ə-'näm-iks, -ˌē-kə-\ *n* : study of economics in terms of individual areas of activity (as a firm or a household)

mi·cro·el·e·ment \ˌmī-krō-'el-ə-mənt\ *n* : TRACE ELEMENT

mi·cro·en·cap·su·lat·ed \-in-'kap-sə-ˌlāt-əd\ *adj* : enclosed in a microcapsule ⟨*microencapsulated* aspirin⟩ — **mi·cro·en·cap·su·la·tion** \-in-ˌkap-sə-'lā-shən\ *n*

mi·cro·far·ad \ˌmī-krō-'far-ˌad, -'far-əd\ *n* : one millionth of a farad

mi·cro·fiche \'mī-krō-ˌfēsh, -ˌfish\ *n, pl* **-fiche** *or* **-fiches** \-ˌfēsh, -ˌfēsh-əz, -ˌfish, -ˌfish-əz\ : a sheet of microfilm containing rows of images [French, from *micr-* "micr-" + *fiche* "peg, tag, slide", from *ficher* "to stick in"]

mi·cro·film \'mī-krə-ˌfilm\ *n* : a film bearing a photographic record on a greatly reduced scale of graphic matter (as printing) — **microfilm** *vb*

mi·cro·ga·mete \ˌmī-krō-gə-'mēt, -'gam-ˌēt\ *n* : the smaller and usually male gamete of an organism with two kinds of gametes — compare MACROGAMETE

mi·cro·gram \'mī-krə-ˌgram\ *n* : one millionth of a gram

mi·cro·graph \-ˌgraf\ *n* : a reproduction of the image of an object formed by a microscope

\ə\	abut	\ng\	sing
\ər\	further	\ō\	bone
\a\	mat	\ò\	saw
\ā\	take	\òi\	coin
\ä\	cot, cart	\th\	thin
\aù\	out	\th\	this
\ch\	chin	\ü\	food
\e\	pet	\ù\	foot
\ē\	easy	\y\	yet
\g\	go	\yü\	few
\i\	tip	\yù\	cure
\ī\	life	\zh\	vision
\j\	job		

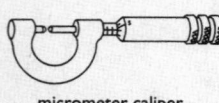

micrometer caliper

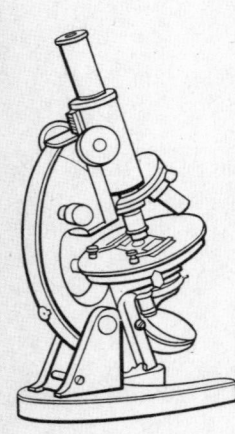

microscope 1

mi·cro·groove \'mī-krō-ˌgrüv\ *n* : a minute closely spaced V-shaped groove used on long-playing phonograph records

¹mi·crom·e·ter \mī-'kräm-ət-ər\ *n* **1** : an instrument used with a telescope or microscope for measuring very small distances **2** : MICROMETER CALIPER — **mi·crom·e·try** \-ə-trē\ *n*

²mi·cro·me·ter \'mī-krō-ˌmēt-ər\ *n* : a unit of length equal to one millionth of a meter

mi·crom·e·ter caliper \mī-'kräm-ət-ər-\ *n* : a caliper having a spindle moved by a finely threaded screw for making precise measurements

mi·cro·mi·cron \ˌmī-krō-'mī-ˌkrän\ *n* : one millionth of a micrometer

mi·cron \'mī-ˌkrän\ *n* : ² MICROMETER [Greek *mikron,* neuter of *mikros* "small"]

Mi·cro·ne·sian \ˌmī-krə-'nē-zhən, -shən\ *n* **1** : a native or inhabitant of Micronesia **2** : a group of Austronesian languages spoken in the Micronesian islands — **Micronesian** *adj*

mi·cro·nu·cle·us \ˌmī-krō-'nü-klē-əs, -'nyü-\ *n* : a minute nucleus held to be primarily concerned with reproductive and genetic functions in most ciliated protozoans

mi·cro·nu·tri·ent \-'nü-trē-ənt, -'nyü-\ *n* **1** : TRACE ELEMENT **2** : an organic compound (as a vitamin) essential in minute amounts to the growth and welfare of an animal

mi·cro·or·gan·ism \-'òr-gə-ˌniz-əm\ *n* : an organism (as a bacterium) of microscopic or less than microscopic size

mi·cro·phone \'mī-krə-ˌfōn\ *n* : an instrument used to amplify, record, or transmit sounds

mi·cro·pho·to·graph \ˌmī-krə-'fōt-ə-ˌgraf\ *n* **1** : a small photograph that is normally magnified for viewing **2** : PHOTOMICROGRAPH

mi·cro·print \'mī-krə-ˌprint\ *n* : a photographic copy of printed or drawn matter in reduced size — **microprint** *vb*

mi·cro·pro·ces·sor \'mī-krō-ˌpräs-ˌes-ər, -ˌprōs-\ *n* : a computer processor contained on an integrated-circuit chip

mi·cro·pro·jec·tor \ˌmī-krō-prə-'jek-tər\ *n* : a projector using a compound microscope to throw a greatly enlarged image of a microscopic object on a screen

mi·cro·pyle \'mī-krə-ˌpīl\ *n* : a tiny opening in an ovule of a seed plant through which the pollen tube penetrates to the embryo sac [*micr-* + Greek *pylē* "gate"] — **mi·cro·py·lar** \ˌmī-krə-'pī-lər\ *adj*

mi·cro·scope \'mī-krə-ˌskōp\ *n* **1** : an optical instrument consisting of a lens or a combination of lenses for making enlarged images of minute objects — called also *light microscope* **2** : an instrument using radiations other than light for making enlarged images of minute objects

mi·cro·scop·ic \ˌmī-krə-'skäp-ik\ *or* **mi·cro·scop·i·cal** \-i-kəl\ *adj* **1** : of, relating to, or conducted with the microscope or microscopy ⟨a *microscopic* examination⟩ **2** : resembling a microscope especially in being able to see very tiny objects ⟨some insects have *microscopic* vision⟩ **3** : able to be seen only through a microscope : very small ⟨a *microscopic* plant⟩ — **mi·cro·scop·i·cal·ly** \-'skäp-i-kə-lē, -klē\ *adv*

mi·cros·co·py \mī-'kräs-kə-pē\ *n* : the use of the microscope : investigation with the microscope — **mi·cros·co·pist** \-pəst\ *n*

mi·cro·sec·ond \ˌmī-krō-'sek-ənd, -ənt\ *n* : one millionth of a second

mi·cro·some \'mī-krə-ˌsōm\ *n* : a cellular particle that is obtained by centrifuging broken cells and that consists of various amounts of ribosomes, fragmented endoplasmic reticulum, and parts of mitochondria — **mi·cro·som·al** \ˌmī-krə-'sō-məl\ *adj*

mi·cro·sphere \'mī-krə-ˌsfiər\ *n* : a minute sphere ⟨a glass *microsphere* 30 micrometers in diameter⟩

mi·cro·spore \-ˌspōr, -ˌspór\ *n* : a plant spore that produces a male gametophyte

mi·cro·struc·ture \'mī-krō-ˌstrək-chər\ *n* : the microscopic structure of a material

mi·cro·sur·gery \ˌmī-krō-'sərj-rē, -ə-rē\ *n* : minute dissection or manipulation of living structures (as cells) for surgical or experimental purposes

mi·cro·tome \'mī-krə-ˌtōm\ *n* : an instrument for cutting sections (as of plant or animal tissues) for microscopic examination [*micr-* + Greek *tomos* "section", from *temnein* "to cut"]

¹mi·cro·wave \-ˌwāv\ *n* **1** : a radio wave between 1 millimeter and 1 meter in wavelength **2** : MICROWAVE OVEN

²microwave *vt* : to cook or heat in a microwave oven — **mi·cro·wav·able** *or* **mi·cro·wave·able** \ˌmī-krə-'wā-və-bəl\ *adj*

microwave oven *n* : an oven in which food is cooked by the heat produced as a result of penetration of the food by microwaves

mic·tu·rate \'mik-chə-ˌrāt, 'mik-tə-\ *vi* : URINATE [Latin *micturire*] — **mic·tu·ri·tion** \ˌmik-chə-'rish-ən, ˌmik-tə-\ *n*

¹mid \'mid\ *adj* **1** : being the part in the middle or midst ⟨in *mid* ocean⟩ ⟨*mid*-August⟩ **2** : occupying a middle position ⟨the *mid* finger⟩ **3** : uttered with the tongue midway between its highest and its lowest elevation ⟨the *mid* vowel \e\ in pet⟩ [Old English *midde*]

²mid \'mid, mid\ *prep* : AMID

mid·brain \'mid-ˌbrān\ *n* : the middle division of the embryonic vertebrate brain containing especially the optic lobes; *also* : the parts developed from it

mid·day \'mid-ˌdā, -'dā\ *n* : the middle part of the day : NOON — **midday** *adj*

mid·den \'mid-n\ *n* : a refuse heap; *esp* : KITCHEN MIDDEN [of Scandinavian origin]

¹mid·dle \'mid-l\ *adj* **1** : equally distant from the extremes : CENTRAL ⟨the *middle* house in the row⟩ **2** : being at neither extreme : INTERMEDIATE ⟨of *middle* size⟩ **3** *cap* : constituting an intermediate division or period ⟨*Middle* Paleozoic⟩ ⟨*Middle* Dutch⟩ [Old English *middel*]

²middle *n* **1** : a middle part, point, or position **2** : WAIST 1a **3** : the position of being in the midst of something ⟨in the *middle* of the battle⟩

middle age *n* : the period of life from about 40 to about 60 — **mid·dle-aged** \ˌmid-l-'ājd\ *adj*

Middle Ages *n pl* : the period of European history from about A. D. 500 to about 1500

mid·dle·brow \'mid-l-ˌbrau\ *n* : a person who is moderately but not highly cultivated — **middlebrow** *adj*

middle C *n* : the note designated by the first ledger line below the treble staff and the first above the bass staff

middle–class *adj* : of or relating to the middle class; *esp* : characterized by a fairly high material standard of living, sexual morality, and respect for property

middle class *n* : a social class occupying a position between the upper class and the lower class; *esp* : a fluid grouping composed principally of business and professional people, bureaucrats, and some farmers and skilled workers sharing common social characteristics and values

middle distance *n* : a part of a picture or scene between the foreground and the background

middle ear *n* : a small membrane-lined cavity that is separated from the outer ear by the eardrum and that transmits sound waves from the eardrum to the partition between the middle and inner ears through a chain of tiny bones

Middle English *n* : the English language of the 12th to 15th centuries

middle finger *n* : the third digit of the hand

Middle French *n* : the French language of the 14th to 16th centuries

Middle Greek *n* : the Greek language used in the 7th to 15th centuries

Middle High German *n* : the High German in use from about 1100 to 1500

middle lamella *n* : a layer of sticky material between adjacent plant cells that helps to hold them together

mid·dle·man \'mid-l-,man\ *n* : an agent between two parties; *esp* : a dealer or agent intermediate between the producer of goods and the retailer or the consumer

mid·dle–of–the–road \,mid-l-əv-thə-'rōd, -ə-thə-\ *adj* : standing for or following a course of action midway between extremes; *esp* : being neither liberal nor conservative in politics — **mid·dle–of–the–road·er** \-'rōd-ər\ *n*

middle school *n* : a school usually including grades 5–8 or 6–8

mid·dle·weight \'mid-l-,wāt\ *n* : one of average weight; *esp* : a boxer in a weight division having the approximate range of 67 to 75 kilograms

¹**mid·dling** \'mid-ling, -lən\ *adj* 1 : of middle, medium, or moderate size, degree, or quality 2 : MEDIOCRE — **middling** *adv*

²**middling** *n* 1 : any of various commodities of medium quality or size 2 *pl* : a granular product of grain milling; *esp* : a wheat milling by-product used in animal feeds

mid·dy \'mid-ē\ *n, pl* **mid·dies** 1 : MIDSHIPMAN 2 : a loosely fitting blouse especially for children with a collar that is wide and square at the back

midge \'mij\ *n* : a very small fly : GNAT [Old English *mycg*]

midg·et \'mij-ət\ *n* : one that is much smaller than the usual or typical [*midge*] — **midget** *adj*

mid·gut \'mid-,gət\ *n* : the middle part of an alimentary canal

mid·land \'mid-lənd, -,land\ *n* 1 : the interior or central region of a country 2 *cap* : the dialect of English spoken in parts of New Jersey and Delaware, northern Maryland, central and southern Pennsylvania, Ohio, Indiana, Illinois, the Appalachian Mountain area, West Virginia, Kentucky, and most of Tennessee — **midland** *adj, often cap*

mid·line \-,līn\ *n* : a median line or plane

mid·most \'mid-,mōst\ *adj or adv* : in the exact middle — **midmost** *n*

mid·night \-,nīt\ *n* : the middle of the night; *esp* : 12 o'clock at night — **midnight** *adj* — **mid·night·ly** \-lē\ *adv or adj*

midnight sun *n* : the sun above the horizon at midnight in the arctic or antarctic summer

mid·point \'mid-,point\ *n* : a point at or near the center or middle

mid·rib \-,rib\ *n* : the central vein of a leaf

mid·riff \-,rif\ *n* 1 : DIAPHRAGM 1 2 : the middle region of the human torso [Old English *midhrif*, from *midde* "mid" + *hrif* "belly"]

mid·ship·man \'mid-,ship-mən, mid-'ship-\ *n* : one in training for a naval commission : a student naval officer

mid·ships \'mid-,ships\ *adv* : AMIDSHIPS

¹**midst** \'midst\ *n* 1 : the interior or central part or point : MIDDLE ⟨in the *midst* of the forest⟩ 2 : a position among the members of a group ⟨a visitor in our *midst*⟩ 3 : the condition of being surrounded or beset ⟨in the *midst* of troubles⟩ [Middle English *middest*, alteration of *middes*, from *amiddes* "amid"]

²**midst** \'midst, ,midst\ *prep* : AMID

mid·stream \'mid-'strēm\ *n* : the middle of a stream

mid·sum·mer \'mid-'səm-ər\ *n* 1 : the middle of summer 2 : the summer solstice

¹**mid·way** \'mid-,wā, -'wā\ *adv or adj* : in the middle of the way or distance : HALFWAY

²**mid·way** \-,wā\ *n* : an avenue at a fair, carnival, or amusement park for concessions and light amusements

[*Midway (Plaisance)*, Chicago, site of the amusement section of the Columbian Exposition of 1893]

mid·week \'mid-,wēk\ *n* : the middle of the week — **midweek** *adj* — **mid·week·ly** \-lē\ *adj or adv*

mid·wife \'mid-,wīf\ *n* : a woman who helps other women in childbirth [Middle English *midwif*, from *mid* "with" (from Old English) + *wif* "woman, wife"] — **mid·wife·ry** \mid-'wif-rē, -ə-re; 'mid-,wīf-\ *n*

mid·win·ter \'mid-'wint-ər\ *n* 1 : the middle of winter 2 : the winter solstice

mid·year \-,yiər\ *n* 1 : the middle of an academic or a calendar year 2 : a midyear examination — **midyear** *adj*

mien \'mēn\ *n* : look, appearance, or bearing especially as showing mood or personality ⟨a kindly *mien*⟩ [derived from ¹*demean*]

¹**miff** \'mif\ *n* 1 : a fit of ill humor 2 : a trivial quarrel [origin unknown]

²**miff** *vt* : to put into an ill humor : OFFEND ⟨was *miffed* by their behavior⟩

¹**might** \mīt, 'mīt\ *past of* MAY — used as an auxiliary verb to express permission ⟨asked if they *might* leave⟩, probability ⟨I *might* go, if urged⟩, possibility in the past ⟨thought you *might* try⟩, or a present condition contrary to fact ⟨if you were older, you *might* understand⟩ [Old English *meahte, mihte*]

²**might** \'mīt\ *n* : power to do something : FORCE ⟨the nation's *might*⟩ [Old English *miht*]

might·i·ly \'mīt-l-ē\ *adv* 1 : in a mighty manner : VIGOROUSLY 2 : very much

mightn't \'mīt-nt\ : might not

¹**mighty** \'mīt-ē\ *adj* **might·i·er; -est** 1 : having might : POWERFUL, STRONG ⟨a *mighty* army⟩ 2 : done by might : showing great power ⟨*mighty* deeds⟩ 3 : great or imposing in size or extent ⟨a *mighty* famine⟩ — **might·i·ness** *n*

²**mighty** *adv* : VERY, EXTREMELY ⟨a *mighty* strong smell⟩

mi·gnon·ette \,min-yə-'net\ *n* : a garden plant with long spikes of small fragrant greenish white flowers [French]

mi·graine \'mī-,grān\ *n* : a condition marked by recurrent severe headache often with nausea and vomiting [French, from Late Latin *hemicrania* "pain on one side of the head", from Greek *hēmikrania*, from *hēmi-* "hemi-" + *kranion* "cranium"] — **mi·grain·ous** \-,grā-nəs\ *adj*

mi·grant \'mī-grənt\ *n* : a person, animal, or plant that migrates — **migrant** *adj*

mi·grate \'mī-,grāt\ *vi* 1 : to move from one country, place, or locality to another 2 : to pass usually periodically from one region or climate to another for feeding or breeding 3 : to change position in an organism or substance [Latin *migrare*] — **mi·gra·tion** \mī-'grā-shən\ *n* — **mi·gra·tion·al** \-shnəl, -shən-l\ *adj*

mi·gra·to·ry \'mī-grə-,tōr-ē, -,tȯr-\ *adj* : of, relating to, or characterized by migration ⟨*migratory* birds⟩

mi·ka·do \mə-'käd-ō\ *n, pl* **-dos** : an emperor of Japan [Japanese]

mike \'mīk\ *n* : MICROPHONE [by shortening and alteration]

mil \'mil\ *n* : a unit of length equal to ¹/₁₀₀₀ inch (about .025 millimeter) used especially for the diameter of wire [Latin *mille* "thousand"]

mi·lady \mil-'ād-ē, in the United States also mī-'lād-\ *n* 1 : an Englishwoman of noble or gentle birth 2 : a woman of fashion [French, from English *my lady*]

milch \'milk, 'milch, 'milks\ *adj* : giving milk : kept for milk production ⟨a *milch* cow⟩ [Old English *-milce*]

mild \'mīld\ *adj* 1 : gentle in nature or behavior 2 : moderate in action or effect : not strong ⟨a *mild* drug⟩ 3 : TEMPERATE ⟨*mild* weather⟩ [Old English *milde*] — **mild·ly** \'mīld-lē, 'mīl-\ *adv* — **mild·ness** \'mīld-nəs, 'mīl-\ *n*

¹**mil·dew** \'mil-,dü, -,dyü\ *n* : a superficial usually whitish growth produced on organic matter or living

milkweed

plants by fungi; *also* : a fungus producing mildew [Old English *meledēaw* "honeydew"] — **mil·dewy** \-ē\ *adj*

²**mildew** *vb* : to affect with or become affected with mildew

mile \'mīl\ *n* **1** : a unit of measure equal to 5280 feet (about 1609 meters) — called also *statute mile*; see MEASURE table **2** : NAUTICAL MILE [Old English *mīl*, from Latin *milia* "miles", from *milia passuum*, literally, "thousands of paces"]

mile·age \'mī-lij\ *n* **1** : an allowance for traveling expenses at a set rate per mile **2** : distance or length in miles **3 a** : the number of miles that something (as a car or tire) will travel before wearing out **b** : the average number of miles a car will travel on a gallon of gas **4** : USEFULNESS, PROFIT ⟨gets a lot of *mileage* out of that old joke⟩

mile·post \'mīl-,pōst\ *n* : a post indicating the distance in miles from or to a stated place

mil·er \'mī-lər\ *n* : a person or a horse that competes in mile races

mile·stone \'mīl-,stōn\ *n* **1** : a stone serving as a milepost **2** : an important point in progress or development

mil·foil \'mil-,fòil\ *n* : YARROW [Old French, from Latin *millefolium*, from *mille* "thousand" + *folium* "leaf"]

mi·lieu \mēl-'yər, 'mēl-,yü; mē-'lyœ̄\ *n, pl* **milieus** *or* **milieux** *same or* -'yərz, -,yüz, -'lyœ̄z\ : ENVIRONMENT 1 [French]

mil·i·tant \'mil-ə-tənt\ *adj* **1** : engaged in warfare **2** : aggressively active especially in a cause ⟨a *militant* conservationist⟩ — **mil·i·tan·cy** \-tən-sē\ *n* — **militant** *n* — **mil·i·tant·ly** *adv* — **mil·i·tant·ness** *n*

mil·i·ta·rism \'mil-ə-tə-,riz-əm\ *n* **1 a** : control or domination by a military class **b** : glorification of military virtues and ideals **2** : a policy of aggressive military preparedness — **mil·i·ta·rist** \-rəst\ *n* — **mil·i·ta·ris·tic** \,mil-ə-tə-'ris-tik\ *adj* — **mil·i·ta·ris·ti·cal·ly** \-'ris-ti-kə-lē,-klē\ *adv*

mil·i·ta·rize \'mil-ə-tə-,rīz\ *vt* **1** : to equip with military forces and defenses **2** : to give a military character to — **mil·i·ta·ri·za·tion** \,mil-ə-tə-rə-'zā-shən, -trə-'zā-\ *n*

¹**mil·i·tary** \'mil-ə-,ter-ē\ *adj* **1** : of, relating to, or characteristic of soldiers, arms, or war ⟨*military* drill⟩ **2** : carried on or supported by armed force ⟨*military* dictatorship⟩ **3** : of or relating to the army ⟨*military* and naval affairs⟩ [Middle French *militaire*, from Latin *militaris*, from *milit-, miles* "soldier"] SYN see MARTIAL — **mil·i·tar·i·ly** \,mil-ə-'ter-ə-lē\ *adv*

²**military** *n, pl* **military** **1** : ARMED FORCES **2** : military persons; *esp* : army officers

military police *n* : a branch of an army that performs guard and police functions

mil·i·tate \'mil-ə-,tāt\ *vi* : to have an influence or effect ⟨factors *militating* against the success of an enterprise⟩ [Latin *militare* "to engage in warfare", from *milit-, miles* "soldier"]

mi·li·tia \mə-'lish-ə\ *n* : a body of citizens with military training who are called to active duty only in an emergency [Latin, "military service", from *milit-, miles* "soldier"] — **mi·li·tia·man** \-mən\ *n*

¹**milk** \'milk\ *n* **1** : a fluid secreted by the mammary glands of females for the nourishment of their young **2** : a liquid (as a plant juice) resembling milk [Old English *meolc, milc*]

²**milk** *vb* **1** : to draw milk from the breasts or udder of **2** : to draw or yield milk **3** : to draw something from as if by milking; *esp* : to draw unreasonable or excessive profit or advantage from ⟨*milk* a business⟩ — **milk·er** *n*

milk–liv·ered \'mil-'kliv-ərd\ *adj, archaic* : COWARDLY 1

milk·maid \'milk-,mād\ *n* : DAIRYMAID

milk·man \-,man, -mən\ *n* : a person who sells or delivers milk

milk of magnesia : a milk-white liquid preparation of magnesium in water used as a laxative and as a medicine to counteract acidity

milk shake *n* : a drink made of milk, a flavoring syrup, and often ice cream shaken or mixed thoroughly

milk snake *n* : a common harmless gray or tan snake with black-bordered blotches and an arrow-shaped spot on the head

milk·sop \'milk-,säp\ *n* : a timid unmanly man or boy

milk sugar *n* : LACTOSE

milk tooth *n* : one of the first temporary teeth of a young mammal that in human beings number 20

milk·weed \'mil-,kwēd\ *n* : any of a group of herbs and shrubs with milky juice and flowers usually in dense clusters

milky \'mil-kē\ *adj* **milk·i·er; -est** **1** : resembling milk in color or consistency **2** : TAME 3, TIMID **3** : consisting of, containing, or full of milk — **milk·i·ness** *n*

milky disease *n* : a destructive bacterial disease of some beetle larvae used especially in the control of Japanese beetles

Milky Way *n* **1** : a broad luminous irregular band of light that stretches across the sky and is caused by the light of a vast multitude of faint stars **2** : MILKY WAY GALAXY **3** : GALAXY 1b

Milky Way galaxy *n* : the galaxy of which the sun and the solar system are a part and which contains the myriads of stars that comprise the Milky Way

¹**mill** \'mil\ *n* **1** : a building with machinery for grinding grain into flour **2** : a machine used in treating (as by grinding, crushing, stamping, cutting, or finishing) raw material **3** : a building or group of buildings with machinery for manufacturing [Old English *mylen*, from Late Latin *molina*, from Latin *mola* "millstone, mill"] — **through the mill** : through a difficult experience

²**mill** *vb* **1** : to subject to an operation or process in a mill: as **a** : to grind into flour, meal, or powder **b** : to shape or dress by means of a rotary cutter **c** : to mix and condition (as rubber) by passing between rotating rolls **2** : to give a raised rim or a corrugated edge to (a coin) **3** : to hit out hard with the fists **4** : to move about in a disorderly mass ⟨rioters *milling* in the streets⟩ **5** : to undergo milling

³**mill** *n* : one tenth of a cent [Latin *mille* "thousand"]

mill·dam \'mil-,dam\ *n* : a dam to make a millpond; *also* : MILLPOND

mil·le·nar·i·an \,mil-ə-'ner-ē-ən\ *adj* **1** : of or relating to 1000 years **2** : of or relating to belief in the millennium — **millenarian** *n* — **mil·le·nar·i·an·ism** \-ē-ə-,niz-əm\ *n*

mil·le·nary \'mil-ə-,ner-ē, mə-'len-ə-rē\ *n, pl* **-nar·ies** **1** : a thousand units or things **2** : 1000 years : MILLENNIUM [Late Latin *millenarium*, derived from Latin *mille* "thousand"] — **millenary** *adj*

mil·len·ni·um \mə-'len-ē-əm\ *n, pl* **-nia** \-ē-ə\ *or* **-niums** **1 a** : a period of 1000 years **b** : a 1000th anniversary or its celebration **2 a** : the thousand years mentioned in Revelation 20 during which holiness is to prevail and Christ is to reign on earth **b** : a period of great happiness or of perfection in human existence [Latin *mille* "thousand" + *-ennium* (as in *biennium*)] — **mil·len·ni·al** \-ē-əl\ *adj*

mill·er \'mil-ər\ *n* **1** : one that operates a mill; *esp* : one that grinds grain into flour **2** : a moth whose wings are covered with powdery dust

mil·let \'mil-ət\ *n* **1** : any of several small-seeded annual cereal and forage grasses; *esp* : one with small shiny whitish seeds **2** : the seed of a millet [Middle French *milet*, from *mil* "millet", from Latin *milium*]

milli- *combining form* : thousandth ⟨*milli*ampere⟩ [Latin *mille* "thousand"]

mil·li·am·pere \,mil-ē-'am-,piər\ *n* : one thousandth of an ampere

mil·liard \'mil-,yärd, 'mil-ē-,ärd\ *n, British* : a thousand millions — see NUMBER table [French, derived from Latin *mille* "thousand"]

mil·li·bar \'mil-ə-,bär\ *n* : a unit used in measuring atmospheric pressure equal to a force of 1000 dynes per square centimeter [*bar*, unit of pressure equal to one million dynes per square centimeter, derived from Greek *baros* "weight"]

mil·li·gram \'mil-ə-,gram\ *n* — see METRIC SYSTEM table

mil·li·ter \'mil-ə-,lēt-ər\ *n* — see METRIC SYSTEM table

mil·li·me·ter \'mil-ə-,mēt-ər\ *n* — see METRIC SYSTEM table

mil·li·mi·cron \,mil-ə-'mī-,krän\ *n* : a unit of length equal to 1/1000 micrometer

mil·li·ner \'mil-ə-nər\ *n* : a person who makes or sells women's hats [derived from *Milan*, Italy; from the importation of women's finery into England from Italy in the 16th century]

mil·li·nery \'mil-ə-,ner-ē\ *n* 1 : women's hats 2 : the business or work of a milliner

mill·ing \'mil-ing\ *n* : a corrugated edge on a coin

milling machine *n* : a machine tool on which work usually of metal is secured to a carriage and shaped by being fed against rotating cutters

mil·lion \'mil-yən, 'mi-yən\ *n, pl* **millions** *or* **million** 1 : one thousand times one thousand; *also* : a symbol representing this — see NUMBER table 2 : a very large or indefinitely great number ⟨*millions* of mosquitoes⟩ [Middle French *milion*, from Italian *milione*, from *mille* "thousand", from Latin] — **million** *adj* — **mil·lionth** \-yənth, -yəntth\ *adj or n*

mil·lion·aire \,mil-yə-'naər, -'neər, 'mil-yə-,, ,mi-yə-', 'mi-yə-,\ *n* : one whose wealth is estimated at a million or more (as of dollars) [French *millionnaire*, from *million* "million", from Middle French *milion*]

mil·li·pede *or* **mil·le·pede** \'mil-ə-,pēd\ *n* : any of a class (Diplopoda) of arthropods having a long segmented body with a hard covering, two pairs of legs on most apparent segments, and no poison fangs — compare CENTIPEDE [Latin *millipeda*, a small crawling animal, from *mille* "thousand" + *ped-, pes* "foot"]

mil·li·sec·ond \'mil-ə-,sek-ənd\ *n* : one thousandth of a second

mil·li·volt \-,vōlt\ *n* : one thousandth of a volt

mill·pond \'mil-,pänd\ *n* : a pond produced by damming a stream to produce a head of water for operating a mill

mill·race \-,rās\ *n* : a canal in which water flows to and from a mill wheel; *also* : the current that drives the wheel

mill·stone \-,stōn\ *n* 1 : either of two circular stones used for grinding a substance (as grain) 2 a : something that grinds or crushes b : a heavy burden

mill·stream \-,strēm\ *n* 1 : a stream whose flow is utilized to run a mill 2 : the stream in a millrace

mill wheel *n* : a waterwheel that drives a mill

mill·wright \'mil-,rīt\ *n* : one whose occupation is planning and building mills or setting up their machinery

mi·lo \'mī-lō\ *n* : a small usually early and drought-resistant grain sorghum [of Bantu origin]

mi·lord \mil-'òr, -'òrd\ *n* : an Englishman of noble or gentle birth [French, from English *my lord*]

milt \'milt\ *n* : the sperm-containing fluid of fishes [probably from Dutch *milte*]

Mil·ton·ic \mil-'tän-ik\ *or* **Mil·to·ni·an** \mil-'tō-nē-ən\ *adj* : of, relating to, or characteristic of John Milton or his work

¹mime \'mīm *also* 'mēm\ *n* 1 a : an actor of mime b : MIMIC 2 2 : an ancient play or skit representing scenes from life usually in a ridiculous manner 3 : the art of portraying a character or of narration by body movement : PANTOMIME [Latin *mimus*, from Greek *mimos*]

²mime *vb* 1 : to act as a mime : play a part with gesture and action usually without words 2 : to imitate closely : MIMIC 3 : to act out in the manner of a mime

mim·eo·graph \'mim-ē-ə-,graf\ *n* : a machine for making copies of typewritten or written matter by means of a stencil [from *Mimeograph*, a former trademark] — **mimeograph** *vb*

mi·me·sis \mə-'mē-səs, mī-\ *n* : IMITATION 1, MIMICRY [Late Latin, from Greek *mimēsis*, from *mimeisthai* "to imitate"]

mi·met·ic \-'met-ik\ *adj* 1 : IMITATIVE 2 2 : relating to, characterized by, or exhibiting mimicry ⟨*mimetic* coloring of a butterfly⟩ [Late Latin *mimeticus*, from Greek *mimētikos*, from *mimeisthai* "to imitate"] — **mi·met·i·cal·ly** \-'met-i-kə-lē, -klē\ *adv*

¹mim·ic \'mim-ik\ *n* 1 : MIME 1a 2 : one that mimics

²mimic *adj* 1 a : IMITATIVE 2 b : IMITATION, MOCK ⟨*mimic* battle⟩ 2 : of or relating to mime or mimicry [Latin *mimicus*, from Greek *mimikos*, from *mimos* "mime"]

³mimic *vt* **mim·icked** \'mim-ikt\; **mim·ick·ing** 1 : to imitate closely : APE 2 : to ridicule by imitation 3 : SIMULATE 4 : to resemble by biological mimicry SYN see IMITATE

mim·ic·ry \'mim-i-krē\ *n, pl* **-ries** 1 : the action, art, or an instance of mimicking 2 : a superficial resemblance of one organism to another or to natural objects among which it lives that secures it a selective advantage (as protection from predators)

mi·mo·sa \mə-'mō-sə, mī-, -zə\ *n* : any of a genus of trees, shrubs, and herbs of the pea family that produce small white or pink flowers in ball-shaped heads [derived from Latin *mimus* "mime"]

mi·na \'mī-nə\ *n* : an ancient unit of weight and value equal to 1/60 talent (varying around 400 and 800 grams) [Latin, from Greek *mna*, of Semitic origin]

min·a·ret \,min-ə-'ret, 'min-ə-,\ *n* : a tall slender tower of a mosque from a balcony of which the people are called to prayer [French, from Turkish *minare*, from Arabic *manārah* "lighthouse"]

mi·na·to·ry \'min-ə-,tōr-ē, 'mī-nə-, -,tòr-\ *adj* : having a menacing quality : THREATENING [Late Latin *minatorius*, from Latin *minari* "to threaten"]

¹mince \'mins\ *vb* 1 : to cut into very small pieces 2 : to utter with affectation 3 : to avoid being plainspoken in the use of (words) ⟨don't *mince* words with me⟩ 4 : to walk with short steps in a prim affected manner [Middle French *mincer*, from Latin *minutia* "smallness", from *minutus* "minute"] — **minc·er** *n*

²mince *n* : small bits into which something is chopped; *esp* : MINCEMEAT

mince·meat \'min-,smēt\ *n* 1 : minced meat 2 : a finely chopped mixture of ingredients (as raisins, apples, or spices) with or without meat

minc·ing \'min-sing\ *adj* : affectedly dainty or delicate — **minc·ing·ly** \-sing-lē\ *adv*

¹mind \'mīnd\ *n* 1 : MEMORY, RECOLLECTION ⟨keep it in *mind*⟩ 2 a : the element or complex of elements in an individual that feels, perceives, thinks, wills, and especially reasons b : mental ability ⟨has the *mind* of a 5-year-old⟩ 3 a : INTENTION, DESIRE ⟨that is not what I had in *mind*⟩ ⟨makeup your *mind*⟩ b : OPINION, VIEW ⟨speak your *mind*⟩ c : CHOICE, LIKING ⟨to my *mind* it is satisfactory⟩ d : ATTENTION ⟨keep your *mind* on your work⟩ 4 : the normal or healthy condition of the mental faculties ⟨lose one's *mind*⟩ 5 : way of thinking or feeling : MOOD, DISPOSITION ⟨keep an open *mind* on the issue⟩ 6 : a person embodying mental qualities especially of a specified kind ⟨one of the greatest *minds* of the century⟩ 7 : IMAGINATION ⟨it's all in your *mind*⟩ 8 *dialect* : ATTENTION, HEED ⟨don't pay them any *mind*⟩ [Old English *gemynd*]

²mind *vb* 1 *chiefly dialect* : REMIND 2 *chiefly dialect* : REMEMBER 1 3 : to attend to ⟨*mind* your own business⟩ 4 : to take notice of 5 : to give heed to ⟨*mind* your

millipede

1 minaret

\ə\ abut	\ng\ sing
\ər\ further	\ō\ bone
\a\ mat	\ò\ saw
\ā\ take	\òi\ coin
\ä\ cot, cart	\th\ thin
\aú\ out	\th\ this
\ch\ chin	\ü\ food
\e\ pet	\ú\ foot
\ē\ easy	\y\ yet
\g\ go	\yü\ few
\i\ tip	\yú\ cure
\ī\ life	\zh\ vision
\j\ job	

manners); *also* : OBEY ⟨*mind* your parents⟩ **6 a** : to be concerned or troubled over ⟨never *mind* your mistake⟩ **b** : to have an objection : object to ⟨I don't *mind* if you go⟩ **7 a** : to be careful : make sure ⟨*mind* you finish it⟩ **b** : to be cautious of : watch out for ⟨*mind* the broken glass⟩ **8** : to have charge of : TEND ⟨*mind* the store⟩

mind·ed \'mīn-dəd\ *adj* **1** : having a specified kind of mind — usually used in combination ⟨narrow-*minded*⟩ **2** : INCLINED 1, DISPOSED ⟨was *minded* to help⟩

mind–ex·pand·ing \'mīn-dik-,span-ding\ *adj* : PSYCHE-DELIC 1a

mind·ful \'mīnd-fəl, 'mīn-\ *adj* : bearing in mind : AWARE ⟨*mindful* of the needs of others⟩ — **mind·ful·ly** \-fə-lē\ *adv* — **mind·ful·ness** *n*

mind·less \'mīn-dləs, -ləs\ *adj* **1 a** : lacking the ability to think, feel, or respond ⟨a *mindless* killer⟩ **b** : showing no use of the intelligence ⟨*mindless* violence⟩ **2** : not mindful : HEEDLESS ⟨*mindless* of danger⟩ — **mind·less·ly** *adv* — **mind·less·ness** *n*

mind reader *n* : one who professes or is held to be able to perceive another's thought by telepathy — **mind reading** *n*

mind's eye *n* : the mental faculty of creating images or of recalling scenes previously seen

¹**mine** \mīn, 'mīn\ *adj, archaic* : MY — used before a word beginning with a vowel or *h* ⟨*mine* eyes⟩ ⟨*mine* host⟩ or sometimes as a modifier of a preceding noun ⟨mother *mine*⟩ [Old English *mīn*]

²**mine** \'mīn\ *pron, sing or pl in construction* : that which belongs to me : those which belong to me — used without a following noun as an equivalent in meaning to the adjective *my*

³**mine** \'mīn\ *n* **1** : a pit or tunnel from which mineral substances (as coal or gold) are taken **2** : a deposit of ore **3** : a subterranean passage under an enemy position **4 a** : a charge buried in the ground and set to explode when disturbed (as by an enemy) **b** : an explosive device placed underwater to sink enemy ships **5** : a rich source of supply ⟨a *mine* of information⟩ [Middle French]

⁴**mine** \'mīn\ *vb* **1** : to dig a mine **2** : to obtain from a mine ⟨*mine* coal⟩ **3** : to work in a mine **4 a** : to burrow in the earth : dig or form mines under a place **b** : to lay military mines in or under ⟨*mine* a harbor⟩

mine·lay·er \'mīn-,lā-ər\ *n* : a naval vessel for placing underwater mines

min·er \'mī-nər\ *n* : one that mines; *esp* : a person who works in a mine

¹**min·er·al** \'min-rəl, -ə-rəl\ *n* **1** : a naturally occurring crystalline element or compound (as diamond or quartz) that has a definite chemical composition and results from processes other than those of plants and animals ⟨most rocks are composed of more than one *mineral*⟩ **2** : any of various naturally occurring substances (as ore, coal, salt, sand, stone, petroleum, natural gas, or water) obtained for human use usually from the ground **3 a** : a natural substance that is neither plant nor animal **b** : an inorganic substance [Medieval Latin *minerale*, from *mineralis*, "of a mine", from *minera* "mine, ore", from Old French *miniere*, from *mine* "mine"]

²**mineral** *adj* **1** : of, relating to, or having the characteristics of a mineral : INORGANIC **2** : containing mineral salts or gases

min·er·al·ize \'min-rə-,līz, -ə-rə-\ *vb* **1** : to transform a metal into an ore **2** : PETRIFY ⟨*mineralized* bones⟩ **3 a** : to impregnate or supply with minerals **b** : to change into mineral form — **min·er·al·iza·tion** \,min-rə-lə-'zā-shən, -ə-rə-\ *n*

mineral kingdom *n* : a basic group of natural objects that includes inorganic objects — compare ANIMAL KINGDOM, PLANT KINGDOM

min·er·al·o·gy \,min-ə-'räl-ə-jē, -'ral-\ *n* : a science dealing with the properties and classification of min-erals — **min·er·al·og·i·cal** \,min-rə-'läj-i-kəl, -ə-rə-\ *adj* — **min·er·al·o·gist** \,min-ə-'räl-ə-jəst, -'ral-\ *n*

mineral oil *n* **1** : an oil (as petroleum) of mineral origin **2** : a refined petroleum oil having no color, odor, or taste that is used as a laxative

mineral water *n* : water naturally or artificially impregnated with mineral salts or gases

mineral wool *n* : any of various lightweight materials that resemble wool in texture, are made from slag, rock, or glass, and are used especially in heat and sound insulation

min·e·stro·ne \,min-ə-'strō-nē, -'strōn\ *n* : a rich thick vegetable soup usually made with dried beans and pasta (as macaroni) [Italian, from *minestrare* "to serve", from Latin *ministrare*, from *minister* "servant"]

mine·sweep·er \'mīn-,swē-pər\ *n* : a warship designed for removing or neutralizing mines

Ming \'ming\ *n* : a Chinese dynasty dated 1368–1644 and noted for restoration of earlier traditions and in the arts for perfection of established techniques [Chinese (Pekingese dialect) *ming*² "luminous"]

min·gle \'ming-gəl\ *vb* **min·gled; min·gling** \-gə-ling, -gling\ **1 a** : to bring or mix together or with something else usually without fundamental loss of identity **b** : to become mingled **2** : to come in contact : ASSOCIATE ⟨*mingles* with all sorts of people⟩ [Middle English *menglen*, from *mengen* "to mix", from Old English *mengan*] SYN see MIX

ming tree \'ming-\ *n* : a dwarfed usually evergreen tree grown in a pot; *also* : an artificial ming tree made from plant materials [perhaps from *Ming*]

mini- *combining form* : miniature : of small dimensions ⟨*mini*bike⟩ [*miniature*]

See *mini-* and 2d element

minibus	mini-course	mini-series
minicar	minipark	ministate
minicomputer	minischool	minivan

¹**min·ia·ture** \'min-ē-ə-,chur, 'min-i-,chur, 'min-yə-, -chər\ *n* **1** : something much smaller than the usual size; *esp* : a copy on a much reduced scale **2** : a painting in an illuminated book or manuscript **3** : the art of painting miniatures **4** : a very small portrait or painting (as on ivory or metal) [Italian *miniatura* "art of illuminating a manuscript", from Medieval Latin, from Latin *miniare* "to color with red lead", from *minium* "red lead"] — **min·ia·tur·ist** \-,chur-əst, -chər-\ *n*

☐ ORIGIN Before printing was introduced in Europe, books were written by hand; and titles and initials were often written in red to contrast with the black ink of the text. The red coloring often used for this purpose and for decorative drawings was called, in Latin, *minium*. The Italian word *miniatura*, derived from Latin *minium*, was used for the art of illuminating a manuscript and for a picture in a manuscript. Because manuscript illustrations are relatively small, the word *miniature*, borrowed into English from Italian, came to be used for anything very small.

²**miniature** *adj* : very small : represented on a small scale

miniature golf *n* : a novelty golf game played on a miniature course having such obstacles as bridges, tunnels, and windmills

min·ia·tur·ize \-,chur-,īz, -chər-\ *vt* : to design or construct in small size — **min·ia·tur·iza·tion** \,min-ē-ə-,chur-ə-'zā-shən, ,min-i-,chur-, ,min-yə-, -chər-\ *n*

mini·bike \'min-i-,bīk\ *n* : a small one-passenger motorcycle having a low frame and elevated handlebars — **mini·bik·er** *n*

mini·com·put·er \'min-i-kəm-,pyüt-ər\ *n* : a small computer that is between a mainframe and a microcomputer in size and speed

min·i·fy \'min-ə-,fī\ *vt* **-fied; -fy·ing** : to make small or smaller : LESSEN [Latin *minimus* "smallest" + English *-fy*]

min·im \'min-əm\ *n* **1** : something very tiny **2** : a unit of liquid capacity equal to ¹⁄₆₀ fluid dram (about .06 milliliter) — see MEASURE table [Latin *minimus* "least, smallest"]

min·i·mal \'min-ə-məl\ *adj* : relating to or being a minimum : LEAST — **min·i·mal·ly** \-mə-lē\ *adv*

min·i·mize \'min-ə-,mīz\ *vt* **1** : to make as small as possible : reduce to a minimum ⟨*minimize* the chance of error⟩ **2** : to place a low estimate or value on

min·i·mum \'min-ə-məm\ *n, pl* **-i·ma** \-ə-mə\ *or* **-i·mums 1 a** : the least quantity or value possible or permissible **b** : the least of a set of numbers; *esp* : the smallest value assumed by a function over a closed interval where its graph is an uninterrupted line or curve **2** : the lowest degree or amount reached or recorded [Latin, neuter of *minimus* "smallest"] — **minimum** *adj*

minimum wage *n* : a wage fixed by legal authority or by contract as the least that may be paid either to employed persons generally or to a specific group of workers

min·ing \'mī-ning\ *n* : the process or business of working mines

min·ion \'min-yən\ *n* **1** : a servile dependent **2** : FAVORITE 1, IDOL **3** : a subordinate official [Middle French *mignon* "darling"]

min·is·cule \'min-əs-,kyül\ *variant of* MINUSCULE

mini·skirt \'min-i-,skərt\ *n* : a woman's very short skirt — **mini·skirt·ed** \-əd\ *adj*

¹min·is·ter \'min-ə-stər\ *n* **1** : AGENT 3 **2 a** : one officiating or assisting at the administration of a sacrament **b** : a Protestant clergyman **c** : a person exercising the functions of a clergyman **3** : a high government official entrusted with the management of a division of governmental activities **4 a** : a diplomatic representative (as an ambassador) sent to the seat of government of a foreign state **b** : a diplomatic representative ranking below an ambassador and usually sent to states of less importance [Old French *ministre*, from Latin *minister* "servant"]

²minister *vi* **min·is·tered; min·is·ter·ing** \-stə-ring, -string\ : to give aid or service ⟨*minister* to the sick⟩

min·is·te·ri·al \,min-ə-'stir-ē-əl\ *adj* **1** : of or relating to a minister or ministry **2 a** : prescribed by law as part of the duties of an administrative office **b** : done in obedience to a legal order without exercise of personal judgment or discretion — **min·is·te·ri·al·ly** \-ē-ə-lē\ *adv*

min·is·tra·tion \,min-ə-'strā-shən\ *n* : the act or process of ministering

min·is·try \'min-ə-strē\ *n, pl* **-tries 1** : MINISTRATION **2** : the office, duties, or functions of a minister ⟨study for the *ministry*⟩ **3** : the body of ministers of religion : CLERGY **4** : AGENCY 2, INSTRUMENTALITY **5** : the period of service or office of a minister or ministry **6** *often cap* **a** : the body of ministers governing a nation or state from which a smaller cabinet is sometimes selected **b** : the group of ministers constituting a cabinet **7 a** : a government department presided over by a minister ⟨*ministry* of foreign affairs⟩ **b** : the building in which the business of a ministry is transacted

min·i·ver \'min-ə-vər\ *n* : a white fur worn by medieval nobles [Old French *menu vair* "small fur"]

mink \'mingk\ *n, pl* **mink** *or* **minks** \'mings, 'mingks\ : any of several slender-bodied mammals resembling the related weasels, having partially webbed feet and a somewhat bushy tail, and living near water; *also* : the soft typically dark brown fur of a mink [Middle English]

min·ne·sing·er \'min-i-,sing-ər, 'min-ə-,zing-\ *n* : one of a class of German lyric poets and musicians of the 12th to the 14th centuries [German, from *minne* "love" + *singer* "singer"]

min·now \'min-ō\ *n, pl* **minnows** *also* **minnow** : any of various small freshwater bottom-feeding fish (as the

dace or shiner) related to the carps; *also* : any of various similar small fishes [Middle English *menawe*]

¹Mi·no·an \mə-'nō-ən, mī-\ *adj* : of or relating to a Bronze Age culture centered in Crete (3000 B. C.– 1100 B. C.) [Latin *minous* "of Minos (a legendary king of Crete)", from Greek *minōios*, from *Minōs* "Minos"]

²Minoan *n* : a native or inhabitant of ancient Crete

¹mi·nor \'mī-nər\ *adj* **1 a** : inferior in dignity, rank, or importance ⟨a *minor* poet⟩ **b** : relatively small in number, quantity, or extent ⟨received a *minor* share of the blame⟩ **2** : not having attained legal age **3 a** : having the 3d, 6th, and sometimes the 7th degrees lowered a half step ⟨a *minor* scale⟩ **b** : based on a minor scale ⟨*minor* keys⟩ **c** : less by a half step than the corresponding major interval ⟨*minor* third⟩ **4** : not involving risk to life : not serious ⟨*minor* illness⟩ **5** : of or relating to an academic minor [Latin, "smaller, inferior"]

²minor *n* **1** : a person who has not attained legal age **2** : a minor musical interval, scale, key, or mode **3** : an academic subject chosen by a student as a secondary field of specialization

³minor *vi* : to pursue an academic minor

mi·nor·i·ty \mə-'nòr-ət-ē, mī-, -'när-\ *n, pl* **-ties 1 a** : the period before attainment of legal age **b** : the state of being a legal minor **2** : the smaller in number of two groups constituting a whole; *esp* : a group (as in a legislature) having less than the number of votes necessary for control **3** : a part of a population differing from others (as in race) and often treated differently

minority leader *n* : the leader of the minority party in a legislative body

minor league *n* : a league of professional clubs in a sport (as baseball) other than the recognized major leagues

minor order *n* : one of the Roman Catholic or Eastern clerical orders that are lower in rank than major orders and involve minor liturgical duties — normally used in pl.

minor party *n* : a political party whose strength in elections is so small as to prevent its gaining control of a government except in rare and exceptional circumstances

minor penalty *n* : a two-minute suspension of a player in ice hockey

minor seminary *n* : a Roman Catholic seminary giving all or part of high school and junior college training

minor suit *n* : clubs or diamonds in bridge

min·ster \'min-stər\ *n* **1** : a church attached or once attached to a monastery **2** : a large or important church [Old English *mynster* "monastery, minster", from Late Latin *monasterium* "monastery"]

min·strel \'min-strəl\ *n* **1** : a medieval musical entertainer; *esp* : a singer of verses to the accompaniment of a harp **2 a** : MUSICIAN **b** : POET 1 **3 a** : one of a troupe of performers typically giving a program of Negro melodies and jokes and usually blacked in imitation of Negroes **b** : a performance by a troupe of minstrels [Old French *menestrel* "servant, minstrel", derived from Latin *minister* "servant"]

min·strel·sy \-sē\ *n, pl* **-sies 1** : the singing and playing of a minstrel **2** : a body of minstrels **3** : a group of songs or verse [Middle French *menestralsie*, from *menestrel* "minstrel"]

¹mint \'mint\ *n* **1** : a place where coins, medals, or tokens are made **2** : a huge amount ⟨caused a *mint* of trouble⟩ [Old English *mynet* "coin, money", from Latin *moneta* "mint, coin", from *Moneta*, epithet of the goddess Juno; from the fact that the Romans coined money in the temple of Juno Moneta]

²mint *vt* **1** : to make (as coins) out of metal **2** : CREATE 1, COIN — **mint·er** *n*

³mint *adj* : unmarred as if fresh from a mint ⟨*mint* coins⟩

mink

\ə\ abut		\ng\ sing	
\ər\ further		\ō\ bone	
\a\ mat		\ò\ saw	
\ā\ take		\òi\ coin	
\ä\ cot, cart		\th\ thin	
\aú\ out		\th\ this	
\ch\ chin		\ü\ food	
\e\ pet		\ú\ foot	
\ē\ easy		\y\ yet	
\g\ go		\yü\ few	
\i\ tip		\yú\ cure	
\ī\ life		\zh\ vision	
\j\ job			

⁴mint *n* **1** : any of a family of herbs and shrubs (as basil and salvia) with square stems, opposite aromatic leaves, and commonly 2-lipped flowers; *esp* : one (as peppermint or spearmint) that is fragrant and yields a flavoring oil **2** : a piece of candy flavored with mint [Old English *minte,* from Latin *mentha*]

mint·age \'mint-ij\ *n* **1** : the action or process of minting coins **2** : coins produced by minting

mint julep *n* : JULEP

min·u·end \'min-yə-,wend\ *n* : a number from which another number is to be subtracted — compare SUBTRAHEND [Latin *minuendus* "to be lessened", from *minuere* "to lessen"]

min·u·et \,min-yə-'wet\ *n* **1** : a slow graceful dance consisting of forward balancing, bowing, and toe pointing **2** : music for or in the rhythm of a minuet [French *menuet,* from Old French *menu* "small", from Latin *minutus*]

¹mi·nus \'mī-nəs\ *prep* **1** : diminished by ⟨seven *minus* four is three⟩ **2** : deprived of : WITHOUT [Latin, "less", from *minor* "smaller"]

²minus *n* **1** : a negative quantity **2** : DEFECT, DEFICIENCY

³minus *adj* **1** : mathematically negative ⟨a *minus* quantity⟩ **2** : falling low in a specified range ⟨a grade of C *minus*⟩ **3** : relating to or being a particular one of the two mating types that are required for successful fertilization in sexual reproduction in some lower plants (as a fungus)

mi·nus·cule \'min-əs-,kyül, min-'əs-, 'min-yəs-, mī-'nəs-\ *or* **min·is·cule** \'min-əs-,kyül\ *adj* : very small [French *minuscule* "lowercase letter", from Latin *minusculus* "rather small", from *minor* "smaller"]

¹min·ute \'min-ət\ *n* **1** : the 60th part of an hour of time or of a degree : 60 seconds **2** : the distance one can cover comfortably in a minute ⟨10 *minutes* from home to office⟩ **3** : MOMENT 1 **4 a** : a brief note of instructions or recommendations written on a document **b** : an official memorandum authorizing or recommending some action **5** *pl* : a series of brief notes taken to provide a record of the proceedings of a meeting [Middle French, from Late Latin *minuta,* from Latin *minutus* "small, minute"]

²minute *vt* **min·ut·ed; min·ut·ing** : to make notes or a brief summary of ⟨*minute* a meeting⟩

³mi·nute \mī-'nüt, mə-, -'nyüt\ *adj* **1** : very small : INFINITESIMAL **2** : of small importance : TRIFLING **3** : marked by close attention to details ⟨*minute* description⟩ [Latin *minutus,* from *minuere* "to lessen, make small"] SYN see CIRCUMSTANTIAL — **mi·nute·ness** *n*

mi·nute·ly \-lē\ *adv* **1** : into very small pieces **2** : in a minute manner or degree

min·ute·man \'min-ət-,man\ *n* : a member of a militia ready to take up arms at a minute's notice during and immediately before the American Revolution

mi·nu·tia \mə-'nü-shē-ə, mī-, -'nyü-, -shə\ *n, pl* **-ti·ae** \-shē-,ē, -shē-,ī\ : a minute or minor detail — usually used in pl. [Latin, from *minutus* "minute"]

minx \'mings, 'mingks\ *n* **1** : a pert girl **2** *obsolete* : a wanton woman [origin unknown]

Mio·cene \'mī-ə-,sēn\ *n* : the epoch of the Tertiary between the Oligocene and Pliocene; *also* : the corresponding system of rocks [Greek *meiōn* "less"] — **Miocene** *adj*

mir \'miər\ *n* : a village community common in czarist Russia in which the land was owned jointly by the peasants and cultivable land was redistributed among the individual families at regular intervals [Russian]

mi·ra·cid·i·um \,mir-ə-'sid-ē-əm, ,mī-rə-\ *n, pl* **-cid·ia** \-ē-ə\ : the free-swimming ciliated first larva that is characteristic of a group (Digenea) of trematode worms and that seeks out and penetrates a suitable snail intermediate host [New Latin, from Greek *meirax* "youth, stripling"]

mir·a·cle \'mir-i-kəl\ *n* **1** : an extraordinary event believed to manifest a supernatural work of God **2** : an extremely outstanding or unusual event, thing, or accomplishment [Old French, from Latin *miraculum,* from *mirari* "to wonder at"]

miracle play *n* **1** : MYSTERY PLAY **2** : a medieval play based on the life of a saint or martyr

mi·rac·u·lous \mə-'rak-yə-ləs\ *adj* **1** : of the nature of a miracle : SUPERNATURAL **2** : resembling a miracle : MARVELOUS **3** : working or able to work miracles — **mi·rac·u·lous·ly** *adv* — **mi·rac·u·lous·ness** *n*

mi·rage \mə-'räzh\ *n* **1** : an optical effect that is sometimes seen at sea, in the desert, or over a hot pavement, that may have the appearance of a pool of water or a mirror in which distant objects are seen inverted, and that is caused by the bending or reflection of rays of light by a layer of heated air of varying density **2** : something only seemingly real [French, from *mirer* "to look at", from Latin *mirari* "to wonder at"]

Mi·ran·da \mə-'ran-də\ *adj* : of, relating to, or being the legal rights of an arrested person to have an attorney and to remain silent so as to avoid self-incrimination [from *Miranda v. Arizona,* the United States Supreme Court ruling establishing such rights]

¹mire \'mīr\ *n* **1** : MARSH, BOG **2** : heavy often deep mud, slush, or dirt [Old Norse *mȳrr*]

²mire *vb* **1 a** : to sink or stick fast in mire **b** : ENTANGLE, INVOLVE ⟨*mired* in detail⟩ **2** : to soil with mud, slush, or dirt

mirk, mirky *variant of* MURK, MURKY

¹mir·ror \'mir-ər\ *n* **1** : a glass backed with a reflecting substance (as silver) **2** : a smooth or polished surface that reflects an image **3** : something that reflects a true likeness or gives a true description [Old French *mirour,* from *mirer* "to look at", from Latin *mirari* "to wonder at"]

²mirror *vt* : to reflect in or as if in a mirror

mirth \'mərth\ *n* : gladness or gaiety as shown by or accompanied with laughter [Old English *myrgth,* from *myrge* "merry"] □ SYN GLEE, JOLLITY, HILARITY: MIRTH implies generally lightness of heart and love of gaiety and specifically denotes laughter ⟨tried to suppress their *mirth*⟩ GLEE suggests an exulting sometimes malicious delight expressed in laughter or cries of joy; JOLLITY suggests exuberance or lack of restraint in mirth or glee; HILARITY implies loud or irrepressible laughter or boisterousness.

mirth·ful \-fəl\ *adj* : full of, expressing, or producing mirth — **mirth·ful·ly** \-fə-lē\ *adv* — **mirth·ful·ness** *n*

miry \'mīr-ē\ *adj* **mir·i·er; -est 1** : MARSHY 1 **2** : very muddy or slushy

mis- *prefix* **1 a** : badly : wrongly ⟨*mis*judge⟩ **b** : unfavorably **c** : in a suspicious manner ⟨*mis*doubt⟩ **2** : bad : wrong ⟨*mis*deed⟩ **3** : opposite or lack of ⟨*mis*trust⟩ **4** : not ⟨*mis*fire⟩ [Old English]

See *mis-* and 2d element

misaddress	mischoice	misemphasis
misadjust	miscitation	misemphasize
misadministration	misclassification	misemploy
misadvise	misclassify	misemployment
misaim	miscomputation	misestimate
misalign	miscompute	misestimation
misalignment	misconnect	misevaluate
misallocate	misconnection	misevaluation
misallocation	miscopy	misfocus
misanalysis	miscorrelation	misfunction
misapplication	miscount	misgauge
misapply	miscut	misgrade
misarticulate	misdate	mishit
misassemble	misdefine	misidentification
misassumption	misdescribe	misidentify
misattribute	misdescription	misimpression
misattribution	misdevelop	miskick
miscaption	misdiagnose	mislabel
miscatalog	misdiagnosis	mislearn
mischannel	misdial	mislocate
mischaracterization	miseducate	mislocation
mischaracterize	miseducation	misperceive

misperception
misplan
misposition
misquotation
misquote
misreckon
misregister

misregistration
misremember
misreport
misroute
missort
misthrow
mistime

mistitle
mistranslate
mistranslation
mistune
misutilization
miswrite

mis·ad·ven·ture \,mis-əd-'ven-chər\ *n* : an unlucky adventure : MISHAP

mis·al·li·ance \,mis-ə-'lī-əns\ *n* : an improper or unsuitable alliance especially in marriage

mis·an·thrope \'mis-n-,thrōp\ *n* : a person who dislikes and distrusts other people [Greek *misanthrōpos* "hating mankind", from *misein* "to hate" + *anthrōpos* "man"]

mis·an·thro·py \mis-'an-thrə-pē, -'ant-\ *n* : a dislike or hatred of other people — **mis·an·throp·ic** \,mis-n-'thräp-ik\ *adj* — **mis·an·throp·i·cal·ly** \-'thräp-i-kə-lē, -klē\ *adv*

mis·ap·pre·hend \,mis-,ap-ri-'hend\ *vt* : MISUNDERSTAND — **mis·ap·pre·hen·sion** \-'hen-chən\ *n*

mis·ap·pro·pri·ate \,mis-ə-'prō-prē-,āt\ *vt* : to appropriate wrongly; *esp* : to take dishonestly for one's own use — **mis·ap·pro·pri·a·tion** \-,prō-prē-'ā-shən\ *n*

mis·be·come \,mis-bi-'kəm\ *vt* : to be inappropriate or unbecoming to

mis·be·got·ten \,mis-bi-'gät-n\ *adj* **1** : ILLEGITIMATE 1 **2** : having or suggesting a disreputable or improper origin ⟨a *misbegotten* scheme⟩

mis·be·have \,mis-bi-'hāv\ *vi* : to behave in a wrong or improper manner — **mis·be·hav·ior** \-'hā-vyər\ *n*

mis·be·lief \,mis-bə-'lēf\ *n* : a mistaken or false belief

mis·be·liev·er \-'lē-vər\ *n* : one who is held to have false beliefs especially in religion

mis·brand \mis-'brand, 'mis-\ *vt* : to brand falsely or in a misleading way

mis·cal·cu·late \-'kal-kyə-,lāt\ *vb* : to calculate wrongly : make a mistake in calculation — **mis·cal·cu·la·tion** \,mis-,kal-kyə-'lā-shən\ *n*

mis·call \mis-'kol, 'mis-\ *vt* : to call by a wrong name

mis·car·riage \mis-'kar-ij\ *n* **1** : a going astray: as **a** : a failure or blunder resulting usually from mismanagement ⟨a *miscarriage* of justice⟩ **b** : a failure (as of a letter) to arrive **c** : a failure of a purpose or plan **2** : the accidental separation and loss of an unborn child from the body of its mother before it is capable of living independently — compare ABORTION

mis·car·ry \mis-'kar-ē\ *vi* **1** : to have a miscarriage : give birth prematurely **2** : to fail of the intended purpose : go wrong ⟨the plan *miscarried*⟩

mis·cast \mis-'kast, 'mis-\ *vt* : to cast in an unsuitable role

mis·ceg·e·na·tion \mis-,ej-ə-'nā-shən, ,mis-i-jə-'nā-\ *n* : a mixture of races; *esp* : marriage or cohabitation between a white person and a member of another race [Latin *miscēre* "to mix" + *genus* "kind, race"]

mis·cel·la·ne·ous \,mis-ə-'lā-nē-əs\ *adj* **1** : consisting of numerous things of different sorts **2 a** : marked by an interest in unrelated topics or subjects **b** : having the characteristics of a patchwork [Latin *miscellaneus*, from *miscellus* "mixed"] — **mis·cel·la·ne·ous·ly** *adv* — **mis·cel·la·ne·ous·ness** *n*

mis·cel·la·nist \'mis-ə-,lā-nəst\ *n* : a writer of miscellanies

mis·cel·la·ny \-nē\ *n, pl* **-nies** **1** : a mixture of various things **2** *pl* : a collection of writings : ANTHOLOGY

mis·chance \mis-'chans, 'mis-\ *n* **1** : bad luck **2** : a piece of bad luck SYN see MISFORTUNE

mis·chief \'mis-chəf, 'mish-\ *n* **1** : injury or damage caused by a human agency **2** : a source of mischief; *esp* : a person who causes mischief **3 a** : action that annoys ⟨that child always gets into *mischief*⟩ **b** : mischievous quality [Old French *meschief* "calamity", from *mes-* "mis-" (of Germanic origin) + *chief* "head, end", from Latin *caput*]

mis·chie·vous \'mis-chə-vəs, 'mish-\ *adj* **1** : causing mischief : intended to do harm ⟨*mischievous* gossip⟩ **2 a** : causing or tending to cause petty injury or annoyance **b** : irresponsibly playful **3** : showing a spirit of mischief — **mis·chie·vous·ly** *adv* — **mis·chie·vous·ness** *n*

mis·ci·ble \'mis-ə-bəl\ *adj* : capable of being mixed; *esp* : soluble in each other ⟨alcohol and water are *miscible*⟩ [Medieval Latin *miscibilis*, from Latin *miscēre* "to mix"] — **mis·ci·bil·i·ty** \,mis-ə-'bil-ət-ē\ *n*

mis·con·ceive \,mis-kən-'sēv\ *vt* : to interpret incorrectly : MISJUDGE — **mis·con·ceiv·er** *n* — **mis·con·cep·tion** \-'sep-shən\ *n*

¹mis·con·duct \mis-'kän-dəkt, 'mis-, -,dəkt\ *n* **1** : bad management **2** : improper or unlawful behavior

²mis·con·duct \,mis-kən-'dəkt\ *vt* **1** : MISMANAGE **2** : to behave (oneself) badly

mis·con·struc·tion \,mis-kən-'strək-shən\ *n* : the act, the process, or an instance of misconstruing

mis·con·strue \,mis-kən-'strü\ *vt* : to construe wrongly : MISINTERPRET

mis·count \mis-'kaunt, 'mis-\ *vb* : to count incorrectly — **mis·count** *n*

mis·cre·ant \'mis-krē-ənt\ *n* : one that behaves badly : RASCAL [Middle English *miscreaunt* "infidel", from Middle French *mescreant*, present participle of *mescroire* "to disbelieve", from *mes-* "mis-" (of Germanic origin) + *croire* "to believe", from Latin *credere*] — **miscreant** *adj*

¹mis·cue \mis-'kyü, 'mis-\ *n* **1** : a faulty stroke (as in billiards) **2** : MISTAKE 2, SLIP

²miscue *vi* **1** : to make a miscue **2 a** : to miss a stage cue **b** : to answer a wrong cue

mis·deal \mis-'dēl, 'mis-\ *vb* **-dealt** \-'delt\; **-deal·ing** \-'dē-ling\ : to deal wrongly ⟨*misdeal* cards⟩ — **misdeal** *n*

mis·deed \mis-'dēd, 'mis-\ *n* : a wrong deed; *esp* : an immoral or criminal action

mis·de·mean·or \,mis-di-'mē-nər\ *n* **1** : a crime less serious than a felony **2** : MISDEED

mis·di·rect \,mis-də-'rekt, -dī-\ *vt* : to direct incorrectly — **mis·di·rec·tion** \-'rek-shən\ *n*

mis·do \mis-'dü, 'mis-\ *vt* **-did** \-'did\; **-done** \-'dən\; **-do·ing** \-'dü-ing\; **-does** \-'dəz\ : to do wrongly or improperly — **mis·do·er** \-'dü-ər\ *n*

mis·do·ing \mis-'dü-ing, 'mis-\ *n* **1** : wrong or improper behavior or action **2** : MISDEED

mis·doubt \mis-'daut, 'mis-\ *vt* **1** : to doubt the reality or truth of **2** : SUSPECT 1, FEAR — **misdoubt** *n*

mise–en–scène \,mē-,zän-'sen\ *n, pl* **mise–en–scènes** \-'sen, -'senz\ **1** : the setting of a play **2** : physical setting : ENVIRONMENT [French *mise en scène* "putting onto the stage"]

mi·ser \'mī-zər\ *n* : a mean grasping person; *esp* : one who lives miserably in order to hoard wealth [Latin, "wretched, miserable"]

mis·er·a·ble \'miz-ər-bəl, 'miz-rə-bəl, -ə-rə-\ *adj* **1 a** : wholly inadequate or scanty ⟨a *miserable* shanty⟩ **b** : causing great discomfort or unhappiness ⟨a *miserable* cold⟩ **2** : extremely poor or unhappy **3** : arousing pity **4** : SHAMEFUL ⟨played a *miserable* trick⟩ [Middle French, from Latin *miserabilis* "pitiable, wretched", from *miserari* "to pity", from *miser* "wretched"] — **miserable** *n* — **mis·er·a·ble·ness** *n* — **mis·er·a·bly** \-blē\ *adv*

Mi·se·re·re \,miz-ə-'riər-ē, -'rer-ē, ,mē-zə-'rā-rā\ *n* : the 50th Psalm in the Vulgate [Latin, "be merciful" (the first word of the Psalm), from *misereri* "to be merciful", from *miser* "wretched"]

mi·ser·ly \'mī-zər-lē\ *adj* : of, relating to, or characteristic of a miser SYN see STINGY — **mi·ser·li·ness** *n*

mis·ery \'miz-rē, -ə-rē\ *n, pl* **-er·ies** **1** : a state of great suffering and want due to poverty or distress **2** : a source of suffering or discomfort ⟨the *miseries* of life

\ə\ abut   \ng\ sing
\ər\ further   \ō\ bone
\a\ mat   \ȯ\ saw
\ā\ take   \ȯi\ coin
\ä\ cot, cart   \th\ thin
\au\ out   \th\ this
\ch\ chin   \ü\ food
\e\ pet   \u̇\ foot
\ē\ easy   \y\ yet
\g\ go   \yü\ few
\i\ tip   \yu̇\ cure
\ī\ life   \zh\ vision
\j\ job

in prison⟩ **3** : a state of great unhappiness and emotional distress SYN see DISTRESS

mis·fea·sance \mis-ˈfēz-ns\ n : the performance of a lawful action in an illegal or improper manner [Middle French *mesfaisance,* from *mesfaire* "to do wrong", from *mes-* "mis-" (of Germanic origin) + *faire* "to do", from Latin *facere*]

mis·file \mis-ˈfīl, ˈmis-\ vt : to file in an inappropriate place

mis·fire \mis-ˈfīr, ˈmis-\ vi **1** : to have the explosive or propulsive charge fail to ignite at the proper time ⟨the engine *misfired*⟩ **2** : to fail to fire ⟨the gun *misfired*⟩ **3** : to miss an intended effect — **misfire** n

mis·fit \ˈmis-ˌfit, ˈmis-ˈfit\ n **1** : something that fits badly **2** : a person poorly adjusted to his or her environment

mis·for·tune \mis-ˈfȯr-chən\ n **1** : bad fortune : ill luck **2** : an unfortunate condition or event : DISASTER □ SYN MISFORTUNE, MISCHANCE, MISHAP mean adverse fortune or an instance of this. MISFORTUNE is a general term for bad luck; applied to a single instance it implies resulting distress usually of some considerable duration; MISCHANCE emphasizes the immediate practical inconvenience or disruption of plans resulting from a chance happening or fall of circumstances; MISHAP implies a trivial instance of bad luck.

mis·give \mis-ˈgiv, ˈmis-\ vb **-gave** \-ˈgāv\; **-giv·en** \-ˈgiv-ən\; **-giv·ing** **1** : to suggest doubt or fear to **2** : to be fearful

mis·giv·ing \-ˈgiv-ing\ n : a feeling of doubt or suspicion especially concerning a future event

mis·gov·ern \-ˈgəv-ərn\ vt : to rule or govern badly — **mis·gov·ern·ment** \-ərn-mənt, -ər-mənt\ n

mis·guide \mis-ˈgīd, ˈmis-\ vt : to lead astray : MISDIRECT ⟨we have been *misguided* in our planning⟩ — **mis·guid·ance** \-ˈgīd-ns\ n — **mis·guid·er** n

mis·guid·ed \-ˈgīd-əd\ adj : marked or directed by mistaken ideas, principles, or motives ⟨*misguided* philanthropists⟩ — **mis·guid·ed·ly** adv — **mis·guid·ed·ness** n

mis·han·dle \mis-ˈhan-dl, ˈmis-\ vt **1** : to treat roughly : MALTREAT **2** : to manage wrongly

mis·hap \ˈmis-ˌhap, mis-ˈ\ n **1** *archaic* : bad luck : MISFORTUNE **2** : an unfortunate accident SYN see MISFORTUNE

mis·hear \mis-ˈhiər, ˈmis-\ vb **1** : to hear wrongly **2** : to misunderstand what is heard

mish·mash \ˈmish-ˌmash, -ˌmäsh\ n : a disorderly mixture : JUMBLE [Middle High German *misch-masch,* reduplication of *mischen* "to mix"]

Mish·nah or **Mish·na** \ˈmish-nə\ n : the collection of Jewish halakic traditions compiled about A. D. 200 and made the basic half of the Talmud [Hebrew *mishnāh* "instruction"]

mis·in·form \ˌmis-n-ˈfȯrm\ vt : to give false or misleading information to — **mis·in·for·ma·tion** \ˌmis-ˌin-fər-ˈmā-shən\ n

mis·in·ter·pret \ˌmis-n-ˈtər-prət, *rapid* -pət\ vt : to understand or explain wrongly — **mis·in·ter·pre·ta·tion** \-ˌtər-prə-ˈtā-shən, *rapid* -pə-ˈtā-\ n

mis·judge \mis-ˈjəj, ˈmis-\ vb : to judge wrongly or unjustly — **mis·judg·ment** \-ˈjəj-mənt\ n

mis·lay \mis-ˈlā, ˈmis-\ vt **-laid** \-ˈlād\; **-lay·ing** : to put in a place later forgotten : LOSE

mis·lead \-ˈlēd\ vt **-led** \-ˈled\; **-lead·ing** : to lead in a wrong direction or into a mistaken action or belief SYN see DECEIVE — **misleading** adj

mis·like \-ˈlīk\ vt : DISLIKE — **mislike** n

mis·man·age \mis-ˈman-ij, ˈmis-\ vt : to manage badly or improperly — **mis·man·age·ment** \-mənt\ n

mis·match \mis-ˈmach, ˈmis-\ vt : to match (as in marriage) unsuitably or badly — **mismatch** n

mis·mate \-ˈmāt\ vt : to mate unsuitably

mis·name \-ˈnām\ vt : to name incorrectly : MISCALL

mis·no·mer \mis-ˈnō-mər, ˈmis-\ n : a wrong or unsuitable name [Middle French *mesnommer* "to mis-

name", from *mes-* "mis-" (of Germanic origin) + *nommer* "to name", from Latin *nominare*]

mi·sog·a·mist \mə-ˈsäg-ə-məst\ n : one who hates marriage [derived from Greek *misein* "to hate" + *gamos* "marriage"] — **mi·sog·a·my** \-ˈsäg-ə-mē\ n

mi·sog·y·nist \mə-ˈsäj-ə-nəst\ n : one who hates or distrusts women [from *mysogyny,* from Greek *misogynia,* from *misein* "to hate" and *gynē* "woman"] — **mis·o·gyn·ic** \ˌmis-ə-ˈjin-ik, -ə-ˈgī-nik\ adj — **mi·sog·y·ny** \mə-ˈsäj-ə-nē\ n

mis·place \mis-ˈplās, ˈmis-\ vt **1** : to put in a wrong place **2** : MISLAY — **mis·place·ment** \-mənt\ n

mis·play \ˈplā\ n : a wrong or unskillful play (as in a game or sport) — **misplay** vt

mis·print \mis-ˈprint, ˈmis-\ vt : to print incorrectly — **misprint** \ˈmis-ˌprint, mis-ˈ, ˈmis-ˈ\ n

mis·prize \mis-ˈprīz, ˈmis-\ vt **1** : SCORN 1 **2** : UNDERVALUE 1

mis·pro·nounce \ˌmis-prə-ˈnaùns\ vt : to pronounce incorrectly or in a way regarded as incorrect — **mis·pro·nun·ci·a·tion** \-ˌnən-sē-ˈā-shən\ n

mis·read \mis-ˈrēd, ˈmis-\ vt **-read** \-ˈred\; **-read·ing** \-ˈrēd-ing\ **1** : to read incorrectly **2** : to misinterpret in reading

mis·rep·re·sent \ˌmis-ˌrep-ri-ˈzent\ vt : to give a false or misleading representation of — **mis·rep·re·sen·ta·tion** \mis-ˌrep-ri-ˌzen-ˈtā-shən\ n

¹**mis·rule** \mis-ˈrül, ˈmis-\ vt : to rule or govern badly

²**misrule** n **1** : the action of misruling : the state of being misruled **2** : public disorder : ANARCHY

¹**miss** \ˈmis\ vb **1** : to fail to hit, catch, reach, or get ⟨*miss* a target⟩ **2** : ESCAPE, AVOID ⟨just *missed* being hurt⟩ **3** : to leave out : OMIT **4** : to discover or feel the absence of ⟨*miss* an absent friend⟩ **5** : to fail to understand, sense, or experience ⟨*missed* the point⟩ **6** : MISFIRE ⟨the engine *missed*⟩ [Old English *missan*] — **miss out on** : to lose a good opportunity for — **miss the boat** : to fail to take advantage of an opportunity

²**miss** n **1** : a failure to reach a desired goal or result **2** : an instance of misfiring

³**miss** n **1** *cap* **a** — used as a courtesy title before the name of an unmarried woman **b** — used before the name of a place, an activity, or an epithet to form a title for a woman representing the thing indicated ⟨*Miss* America⟩ **2** : a woman whose marital status is unknown — used without a name as a conventional term of address [short for *mistress*]

mis·sal \ˈmis-əl\ n : a book containing the prayers to be said or sung in the Mass during the year [Medieval Latin *missale,* from Late Latin *missa* "mass"]

mis·send \mis-ˈsend, ˈmis-\ vt **-sent** \-ˈsent\; **-send·ing** : to send (as mail) to a wrong address

mis·shape \mis-ˈshāp, mish-, ˈmis-, ˈmish-\ vt : to shape badly : DEFORM — **mis·shap·en** \-ˈshā-pən\ adj

mis·sile \ˈmis-əl\ n : an object (as a stone, arrow, artillery shell, bullet, or rocket) that is thrown or projected usually so as to strike something at a distance; *esp* : GUIDED MISSILE [Latin, from *missilis* "capable of being thrown", from *mittere* "to let go, send"]

mis·sile·man \-mən\ n : one who helps to design, build, or operate guided missiles

mis·sile·ry \-rē\ n **1** : MISSILES; *esp* : GUIDED MISSILES **2** : the science dealing with the design, manufacture, and use of guided missiles

miss·ing \ˈmis-ing\ adj : ABSENT; *also* : LOST ⟨*missing* in action⟩

missing link n **1** : an absent member needed to complete a series **2** : a hypothetical intermediate form between human beings and apes that has not been found as a fossil

mis·sion \ˈmish-ən\ n **1 a** : a ministry commisioned by a religious organization to spread its faith or carry on humanitarian work **b** : assignment to or work in missionary enterprise **c** (1) : a mission establishment (2) : a local church or parish dependent on a larger religious organization for direction or financial support **d** *pl* : organized missionary work **e** : a course of sermons and services given to convert to or quicken Christian faith **2** : a group of persons sent to perform a service or carry on an activity: as **a** : a group sent to a foreign country to conduct negotiations **b** : a permanent embassy or legation **c** : a team of military or technical specialists or cultural leaders sent to a foreign country **3** : a task or function assigned or undertaken; *esp* : an official assignment ⟨my *mission* is to recover the stolen plans⟩ [Latin *missio* "act of sending", from *missus*, past participle of *mittere* "to send"] — **mission** *adj*

¹mis·sion·ary \'mish-ə-ˌner-ē\ *adj* **1** : relating to, engaged in, or devoted to missions **2** : characteristic of a missionary

²missionary *n*, *pl* **-ar·ies** : one sent to spread a religious faith among unbelievers

mis·sion·er \'mish-ə-nər\ *n* : MISSIONARY

Mis·sis·sip·pi·an \ˌmis-ə-'sip-ē-ən\ *adj* **1** : of or relating to Mississippi, its people, or the Mississippi river **2** : of, relating to, or being the period of the Paleozoic era between the Devonian and Pennsylvanian or the corresponding system of rocks — see GEOLOGIC TIME table — **Mississippian** *n*

mis·sive \'mis-iv\ *n* : a written communication : LETTER [Middle French *lettre missive*, literally, "letter intended to be sent"]

mis·spell \mis-'spel, 'mis-\ *vt* : to spell incorrectly
mis·spell·ing \-'spel-ing\ *n* : an incorrect spelling
mis·spend \mis-'spend, 'mis-\ *vt* **-spent** \-'spent\; **-spend·ing** : to spend unwisely ⟨a *misspent* youth⟩
mis·state \mis-'stāt, 'mis-\ *vt* : to give a false or inaccurate account of — **mis·state·ment** \-mənt\ *n*
mis·step \-'step\ *n* **1** : a wrong step **2** : a mistake in judgment or action : BLUNDER
missy \'mis-ē\ *n* : a young girl

¹mist \'mist\ *n* **1** : water in the form of particles floating in the air or falling as fine rain **2** : something (as a haze or film) that blurs or hinders vision **3** : a cloud of small particles or objects resembling a mist [Old English] — **mist·like** \-ˌlīk\ *adj*

²mist *vb* **1** : to be or become misty **2** : to become dim or blurred **3** : to cover with mist

mis·tak·able \mə-'stā-kə-bəl\ *adj* : capable of being misunderstood or mistaken

¹mis·take \mə-'stāk\ *vb* **mis·took** \-'stuk\; **mis·tak·en** \-'stā-kən\; **mis·tak·ing** **1** : to choose wrongly **2 a** : to understand wrongly : MISINTERPRET **b** : to estimate incorrectly ⟨*mistook* the strength of the enemy⟩ **3** : to identify wrongly — **mis·tak·en·ly** *adv* — **mis·tak·er** *n*

²mistake *n* **1** : a wrong judgment : MISUNDERSTANDING **2** : a wrong action or statement : BLUNDER **SYN** see ERROR

mis·ter \'mis-tər, *for sense 1* ˌmis-tər\ *n* **1** *cap* **a** — used sometimes in writing instead of the usual Mr. before the name of a man **b** — used before the name of a place, an activity, or an epithet to form a title for a man representing the thing indicated ⟨*Mister* Conservative⟩ **2** : SIR — used without a name as a term of address for a man who is a stranger ⟨hey, *mister*, do you want to buy a paper?⟩ [alteration of *master*]

mis·tle·toe \'mis-əl-ˌtō\ *n* : a green plant with yellowish flowers and waxy white berries that grows on the branches and trunks of trees [Old English *misteltān*, from *mistel* "mistletoe" + *tān* "twig"]

mis·tral \'mis-trəl, mi-'sträl\ *n* : a strong cold dry northerly wind of the northwest Mediterranean [French, from Provençal, from *mistral* "masterful", from Latin *magistralis*, from *magister* "master"]

mis·treat \mis-'trēt, 'mis-\ *vt* : to treat badly : ABUSE — **mis·treat·ment** \-mənt\ *n*

mis·tress \'mis-trəs\ *n* **1** : a woman (as the head of a household or school) who has power, authority, or ownership **2** : something personified as female that

rules or directs **3 a** : a woman other than his wife with whom a married man has a continuing sexual relationship **b** *archaic* : SWEETHEART **4** *cap* — used formerly as a courtesy title before the name of a woman [Middle French *maistresse*, feminine of *maistre* "master", from Latin *magister*]

mis·tri·al \mis-'trī-əl, 'mis-, -'trīl\ *n* : a trial that is legally void because of some error in the proceedings

¹mis·trust \mis-'trəst, 'mis-\ *n* : a lack of confidence : DISTRUST — **mis·trust·ful** \-fəl\ *adj* — **mis·trust·ful·ly** \-fə-lē\ *adv* — **mis·trust·ful·ness** *n*

²mistrust *vt* **1** : SUSPECT ⟨I *mistrust* their motives⟩ **2** : to lack confidence in ⟨*mistrust* one's own ability⟩

misty \'mis-tē\ *adj* **mist·i·er; -est** **1** : full of mist ⟨a *misty* valley⟩ **2** : blurred by or as if by mist ⟨*misty* eyes⟩ **3** : VAGUE, INDISTINCT ⟨a *misty* memory⟩ — **mist·i·ly** \-tə-lē\ *adv* — **mist·i·ness** \-tē-nəs\ *n*

mis·un·der·stand \mis-ˌən-dər-'stand, ˌmis-\ *vb* **-stood** \-'stud\; **-stand·ing** **1** : to fail to understand **2** : to interpret incorrectly

mis·un·der·stand·ing \-'stan-ding\ *n* **1** : a failure to understand **2** : QUARREL 2

mis·us·age \mish-'ü-sij, mish-'yü-, mis-'yü-, -zij\ *n* **1** : bad treatment : ABUSE **2** : wrong or improper use

¹mis·use \mish-'üz, mish-'yüz, mis-'yüz\ *vt* **1** : to use incorrectly : MISAPPLY ⟨*misuse* words⟩ **2** : ABUSE 2, MISTREAT

²mis·use \mish-'üs, mish-'yüs, mis-'yüs\ *n* : incorrect or improper use : MISAPPLICATION ⟨*misuse* of public funds⟩

mite \'mīt\ *n* **1** : any of various tiny animals that are related to the ticks and spiders, often live on plants, animals, and stored foods, and include important carriers of disease **2** : a very small coin or sum of money **3** : a very small object or creature [Old English *mīte*]

¹mi·ter *or* **mi·tre** \'mīt-ər\ *n* **1** : a high pointed headdress worn by a bishop or abbot in church ceremonies **2 a** : the beveled surface of a piece where a miter joint is made **b** : MITER JOINT [Middle French *mitre*, from Latin *mitra* "headband, turban", from Greek]

²miter *or* **mitre** *vt* **mi·tered** *or* **mi·tred**; **mi·ter·ing** *or* **mi·tring** \'mīt-ə-ring\ **1** : to match or fit together in a miter joint **2** : to bevel the ends of for making a miter joint

miter box *n* : a device for guiding a handsaw at the proper angle in cutting wood for a miter joint

miter joint *n* : the joint or corner made by cutting the square edges of two boards at an angle and fitting them together

mit·i·gate \'mit-ə-ˌgāt\ *vt* : to make less severe ⟨*mitigate* a punishment⟩ ⟨*mitigate* pain⟩ [Latin *mitigare* "to soften", from *mitis* "soft"] — **mit·i·ga·tion** \ˌmit-ə-'gā-shən\ *n* — **mit·i·ga·tive** \'mit-ə-ˌgāt-iv\ *adj* — **mit·i·ga·tor** \-ˌgāt-ər\ *n* — **mit·i·ga·to·ry** \'mit-i-gə-ˌtōr-ē, -ˌtȯr-\ *adj*

mi·to·chon·dri·on \ˌmīt-ə-'kän-drē-ən\ *n*, *pl* **-dria** \-drē-ə\ : any of various round or long cellular organelles that are located outside the nucleus, produce energy for the cell through cellular respiration, and are rich in fats, proteins, and enzymes [Greek *mitos* "thread" + *chondrion* "granule", from *chondros* "grain"] — **mi·to·chon·dri·al** \-drē-əl\ *adj*

mi·to·sis \mī-'tō-səs\ *n*, *pl* **-to·ses** \-ˌsēz\ **1** : a process that takes place in the nucleus of a dividing cell and results in the formation of two new nuclei each having the same number of chromosomes as the parent nucleus **2** : a cell division in which mitosis occurs [New Latin, from Greek *mitos* "thread"] — **mi·tot·ic** \-'tät-ik\ *adj* — **mi·tot·i·cal·ly** \-'tät-i-kə-lē, -klē\ *adv*

mi·tral valve \ˌmī-trəl-\ *n* : BICUSPID VALVE [from its resemblance in shape to a miter]

mitt \'mit\ *n* **1 a** : a woman's glove that leaves the fingers uncovered **b** : MITTEN **c** : a baseball catcher's or first baseman's glove in the style of a mitten **2** *slang* : HAND 1a [short for *mitten*]

mistletoe

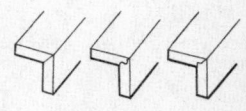

miter joint

\ə\ abut	\ng\ sing
\ər\ further	\ō\ bone
\a\ mat	\ȯ\ saw
\ā\ take	\ȯi\ coin
\ä\ cot, cart	\th\ thin
\au̇\ out	\th\ this
\ch\ chin	\ü\ food
\e\ pet	\u̇\ foot
\ē\ easy	\y\ yet
\g\ go	\yü\ few
\i\ tip	\yu̇\ cure
\ī\ life	\zh\ vision
\j\ job	

moa

mit·ten \'mit-n\ *n* : a covering for the hand and wrist having a separate section for the thumb only [Middle French *mitaine*]

mitz·vah \'mits-və\ *n, pl* **mitz·voth** \-,vōth, -,vōt, -,vōs\ *or* **mitz·vahs** 1 : a commandment of the Jewish law 2 : a praiseworthy act [Hebrew *miṣwāh*]

¹mix \'miks\ *vb* 1 : to combine or blend into one mass 2 : to make by blending different things ⟨*mix* a salad dressing⟩ 3 : to become one mass through blending ⟨oil will not *mix* with water⟩ 4 : to associate with others on friendly terms ⟨*mixes* well in any company⟩ 5 : CONFUSE ⟨*mix* up facts⟩ [Middle English *mixen*, back-formation from *mixte* "mixed", from Middle French, from Latin *mixtus*, past participle of *miscēre* "to mix"] □ SYN MIX, MINGLE, BLEND, COALESCE mean to put or come together into a more or less uniform whole. MIX may or may not imply loss of each element's separate identity; MINGLE suggests that the elements are still somewhat distinguishable or separately active; BLEND implies that the elements lose some or all of their individuality; COALESCE stresses the action or process of like things growing into an organic unity.

²mix *n* : MIXTURE; *esp* : a commercially prepared mixture of food ingredients

mixed \'mikst\ *adj* 1 : combining features of more than one kind; *esp* : combining features of different systems ⟨a *mixed* economy⟩ 2 : involving individuals or items of more than one kind: as **a** : involving persons differing in race, national origin, or religion ⟨a *mixed* marriage⟩ **b** : involving individuals of both sexes ⟨*mixed* company⟩ **c** : containing two or more kinds of organisms in abundance ⟨a *mixed* forest⟩ 3 : including or accompanied by inconsistent or incompatible elements ⟨*mixed* emotions⟩ 4 : deriving from two or more races or breeds ⟨a stallion of *mixed* blood⟩

mixed bud *n* : a plant that produces a branch and leaves as well as flowers

mixed nerve *n* : a nerve containing both sensory and motor fibers

mixed number *n* : a number (as 5⅔) composed of an integer other than zero and a proper fraction — called also *mixed numeral*

mix·er \'mik-sər\ *n* 1 : one that mixes: as **a** : something used in mixing **b** : ICEBREAKER 2 2 **a** : a sociable person **b** : a nonalcoholic beverage used in preparing an alcoholic drink

mix·ture \'miks-chər\ *n* 1 : the act, the process, or an instance of mixing 2 **a** : something mixed or being mixed ⟨add eggs to the *mixture*⟩ **b** : cloth made of thread of different colors **c** : a preparation consisting of two or more ingredients or kinds ⟨a smoking *mixture*⟩ 3 : the relative proportion of the elements in a mixture ⟨the choke controls the *mixture* of fuel and air in the carburetor⟩ 4 : two or more substances mixed together but not chemically united and not necessarily present in definite proportions ⟨sand mixed with sugar forms a *mixture*⟩ [Middle French, from Latin *mixtura*, from *miscēre* "to mix"]

mix-up \'mik-,səp\ *n* 1 : a state or an instance of confusion ⟨a *mix-up* in plans⟩ 2 : FIGHT 1a, MELEE

¹miz·zen *or* **miz·en** \'miz-n\ *n* 1 : a fore-and-aft sail set on the mizzenmast 2 : MIZZENMAST [Middle English *meson*, probably from Middle French *misaine*, derived from Arabic *mazzān* "mast"]

²mizzen *or* **mizen** *adj* : of or relating to the mizzenmast ⟨*mizzen* shrouds⟩

miz·zen·mast \-,mast, -məst\ *n* : the mast just behind the mainmast in a ship

mks system \,em-,kā-,es-\ *n* : a system of metric measure based on the meter, kilogram, and second as fundamental units

mne·mon·ic \ni-'män-ik\ *adj* 1 : assisting or intended to assist memory ⟨*mnemonic* devices⟩ 2 : of or relating to memory [Greek *mnēmonikos*, from *mnēmōn*

"mindful", from *mimnēskesthai* "to remember"] — **mne·mon·i·cal·ly** \-'män-i-kə-lē, -klē\ *adv*

moa \'mō-ə\ *n* : any of various extinct flightless birds of New Zealand [Maori]

Mo·ab·ite \'mō-ə-,bīt\ *n* : a member of an ancient Semitic people related to the Hebrews [*Moab*, ancient kingdom in Syria] — **Moabite** *or* **Mo·ab·it·ish** \-,bīt-ish\ *adj*

¹moan \'mōn\ *n* 1 : COMPLAINT 1, LAMENTATION 2 : a low drawn-out sound usually indicative of pain or grief [Middle English *mone*]

²moan *vb* 1 : LAMENT 1 2 : to utter with a moan or moans 3 : COMPLAIN 1

moat \'mōt\ *n* : a deep wide trench around the walls of a castle or fortress usually filled with water [Middle English *mote*]

¹mob \'mäb\ *n* 1 : the lower classes of a community : RABBLE 2 : a large disorderly crowd often tending to violent or destructive actions 3 : an organized criminal group : GANG [Latin *mobile vulgus* "vacillating crowd"] SYN SEE MULTITUDE

²mob *vt* **mobbed; mob·bing** 1 : to crowd about and attack or annoy 2 : to crowd to capacity ⟨customers *mobbed* the store⟩

¹mo·bile \'mō-bəl, -,bēl, -,bīl\ *adj* 1 : MOVABLE 1 2 : changing quickly in expression ⟨a *mobile* face⟩ 3 : readily moved ⟨*mobile* troops⟩ 4 : characterized by movement from one class or group to another ⟨a *mobile* society⟩ [Middle French, from Latin *mobilis*, from *movēre* "to move"] — **mo·bil·i·ty** \mō-'bil-ət-ē\ *n*

²mo·bile \'mō-,bēl\ *n* : an artistic structure (as of sheet metal) with parts that can be moved by air currents especially when suspended

mo·bi·lize \'mō-bə-,līz\ *vb* 1 : to put into movement or circulation 2 : to assemble and make ready for action ⟨*mobilize* army reserves⟩ — **mo·bi·li·za·tion** \,mō-bə-lə-'zā-shən, -blə-'zā-\

Mö·bi·us strip \,mœb-ē-əs, ,mərb-, ,mōb-\ *n* : a continuous one-sided surface that is constructed from a rectangle by holding one end fixed, rotating the opposite end through 180 degrees, and applying it to the first end [August F. *Möbius*, died 1868, German mathematician]

mob·oc·ra·cy \mä-'bäk-rə-sē\ *n* 1 : mob rule 2 : the mob as a ruling class — **mob·o·crat** \'mäb-ə-,krat\ *n* — **mob·o·crat·ic** \,mäb-ə-'krat-ik\ *adj*

mob·ster \'mäb-stər\ *n* : a member of a criminal gang

moc·ca·sin \'mäk-ə-sən\ *n* 1 : a soft leather shoe without a heel and with the sole and sides made of one piece joined on top by a seam to a U-shaped piece across the front; *also* : a shoe resembling a true moccasin 2 : WATER MOCCASIN [of American Indian origin]

moccasin flower *n* : any of several lady's slippers; *esp* : a woodland orchid of eastern North America with usually pink flowers

mo·cha \'mō-kə\ *n* 1 **a** : choice coffee grown in Arabia **b** : a flavoring made by mixing chocolate and coffee 2 : a pliable suede-finished glove leather from African sheepskins [*Mocha*, seaport in Arabia]

¹mock \'mäk, 'mók\ *vt* 1 : to laugh at scornfully : RIDICULE 2 : to mimic in sport or derision [Middle French *mocquer*] SYN SEE IMITATE, RIDICULE — **mock·er** *n* — **mock·ing·ly** \-iŋ-lē\ *adv*

²mock *n* 1 : an act of mocking : JEER 2 : an object of ridicule

³mock *adj* : not real : SHAM ⟨*mock* grief⟩ ⟨a *mock* diamond⟩

⁴mock *adv* : in an insincere or sham manner — usually used in combination ⟨*mock*-serious⟩

mock·ery \'mäk-rē, 'mók-, -ə-rē\ *n, pl* **-er·ies** 1 : insulting or contemptuous action or speech 2 : one that is laughed at 3 : an insincere or a poor imitation ⟨the trial was a *mockery* of justice⟩ 4 : something ridiculously unsuitable

mock–he·ro·ic \\,mäk-hi-'rō-ik, ,mȯk-\\ *adj* : ridiculing or burlesquing heroic style, character, or action

mock·ing·bird \\'mäk-ing-,bərd, 'mȯk-\\ *n* : a songbird of the southern United States that is related to the catbirds and thrashers and is noted for the sweetness of its song and for its imitations of the notes of other birds

mock orange *n* : a hardy white-flowered shrub; *esp* : PHILADELPHUS

mock turtle soup *n* : a soup made with meat (as calf's head or veal) in imitation of green turtle soup

mock–up \\'mäk-,əp, 'mȯk-\\ *n* : a full-sized structural model built accurately to scale chiefly for study, testing, or display

mod \\'mäd\\ *adj* : MODERN; *esp* : bold and free in style, behavior, or dress

mod·acryl·ic fiber \\,mäd-ə-,kril-ik-\\ *n* : a synthetic fiber used for clothing that dries quickly and resists burning [*mod*ified *acrylic*]

mod·al \\'mōd-l\\ *adj* 1 : of or relating to a mode or to form as opposed to substance 2 : relating to or being a modal auxiliary — **mo·dal·i·ty** \\mō-'dal-ət-ē\\ *n* — **mo·dal·ly** \\'mōd-l-ē\\ *adv*

modal auxiliary *n* : a verb (as *can, must, might, should*) that is typically used with another verb to indicate that the state or action expressed is something other than a simple fact (as a possibility or a necessity) ⟨in "we may go tomorrow" *may* is a *modal auxiliary*⟩

¹**mode** \\'mōd\\ *n* 1 : an arrangement of the eight tones of an octave according to one of several fixed schemes of their intervals 2 : ²MOOD 3 a : a particular form or variety of something b : a form or manner of expression : STYLE c : a manner of doing something ⟨*mode* of travel⟩ 4 : the most frequent value of a set of data [Latin *modus* "measure, manner, musical mode"]

²**mode** *n* : a prevailing fashion or style (as of dress or behavior) SYN see FASHION [French, "manner", from Latin *modus*]

¹**mod·el** \\'mäd-l\\ *n* 1 a : a small but exact copy of something ⟨a ship *model*⟩ b : a pattern or figure of something to be made ⟨clay *models* for a statue⟩ 2 : person who sets a good example ⟨a *model* of politeness⟩ 3 a : a person or thing that serves as an artist's pattern; *esp* : a person who poses for an artist b : a person employed to display garments or other merchandise; *esp* : MANNEQUIN 4 : a type of design of product (as a car or airplane) 5 a : a description or analogy used to help visualize something (as an atom) that cannot be directly observed b : a system of assumptions, data, and inferences used to describe mathematically an object or state of affairs 6 : a theoretical projection of a possible or imaginary system [Middle French *modelle*, from Italian *modello*, from Latin *modulus* "small measure", from *modus* "measure, mode"]

²**model** *vb* **mod·eled** *or* **mod·elled; mod·el·ing** *or* **mod·el·ling** \\'mäd-ling, -l-ing\\ 1 : to plan or shape after a pattern ⟨a sports car *modeled* on a racing car⟩ 2 : to make a model : MOLD ⟨*model* a dog in clay⟩ 3 : to act or serve as a model ⟨*model* for an artist⟩ — **mod·el·er** *or* **mod·el·ler** \\'mäd-lər, -l-ər\\ *n*

³**model** *adj* 1 : serving as or worthy of being a pattern ⟨a *model* student⟩ 2 : being a miniature representation of something ⟨a *model* airplane⟩

mo·dem \\'mō-,dem\\ *n* : a device that changes signals from one form to another that can be used by a different kind of equipment ⟨a *modem* for sending computer data over telephone lines⟩

¹**mod·er·ate** \\'mäd-rət, -ə-rət\\ *adj* 1 a : avoiding extremes (as of behavior) ⟨a *moderate* smoker⟩ b : CALM, TEMPERATE ⟨were *moderate* in your protests⟩ 2 : tending toward the average ⟨a *moderate* rain⟩ b : neither very good nor very bad : MEDIOCRE ⟨*moderate* success⟩ 3 : avoiding extreme political or social measures ⟨a *moderate* candidate⟩ 4 : reasonable in price ⟨*moderate* rates⟩ 5 : of medium lightness and medium chro-

ma ⟨a *moderate* blue⟩ [Latin *moderatus,* from *moderare* "to moderate"] — **mod·er·ate·ly** *adv* — **mod·er·ate·ness** *n* □ SYN MODERATE, TEMPERATE mean being neither very much nor very little. MODERATE implies absence or avoidance of excess ⟨*moderate* prices⟩ ⟨a *moderate* appetite⟩ TEMPERATE suggests the exercise of restraint ⟨*temperate* use of alcohol⟩

²**mod·er·ate** \\'mäd-ə-,rāt\\ *vb* 1 : to make or become less violent, severe, or intense 2 : to preside over a meeting

³**mod·er·ate** \\'mäd-rət, -ə-rət\\ *n* : one holding moderate views or belonging to a moderate group (as in politics)

mod·er·a·tion \\,mäd-ə-'rā-shən\\ *n* 1 : the action of moderating 2 : the quality or state of being moderate : an avoidance of extremes ⟨do everything in *moderation*⟩

mo·der·a·to \\,mäd-ə-'rät-ō\\ *adv or adj* : MODERATE 1a — used as a direction in music to indicate tempo [Italian, from Latin *moderatus*]

mod·er·a·tor \\'mäd-ə-,rät-ər\\ *n* 1 : one that moderates 2 : a presiding officer (as of a town meeting or a discussion group) 3 : a substance (as graphite) used for slowing down neutrons in a nuclear reactor — **mod·er·a·tor·ship** \\-,ship\\ *n*

¹**mod·ern** \\'mäd-ərn\\ *adj* 1 : of or relating to the period from about 1500 to the present ⟨*modern* history⟩ 2 : of, relating to, or characteristic of the present or the immediate past : CONTEMPORARY 3 : involving recent techniques, methods, and ideas : UP-TO-DATE [Late Latin *modernus,* from Latin *modo* "just now", from *modus* "measure, mode"] SYN see RECENT — **mo·der·ni·ty** \\mə-'dər-nət-ē, mä-\\ *n* — **mod·ern·ly** \\'mäd-ərn-lē\\ *adv* — **mod·ern·ness** \\-ərn-nəs\\ *n*

²**modern** *n* : a modern person

Modern Greek *n* : Greek as used by the Greeks since the end of the Medieval period

Modern Hebrew *n* : Hebrew as used in present-day Israel

mod·ern·ism \\'mäd-ər-,niz-əm\\ *n* 1 : a practice, usage, or expression peculiar to modern times 2 *often cap* : a movement to adapt religion to modern thought and especially to lessen traditional supernatural elements 3 : the theory and practices of modern art; *esp* : an intentional break with the past and a search for new forms of expression — **mod·ern·ist** \\-nəst\\ *n or adj* — **mod·ern·is·tic** \\,mäd-ər-'nis-tik\\ *adj*

mod·ern·ize \\'mäd-ər-,nīz\\ *vb* : to make or become modern; *esp* : to adapt to present usage, style, or taste ⟨*modernize* an old house⟩ — **mod·ern·iza·tion** \\,mäd-ər-nə-'zā-shən\\ *n* — **mod·ern·iz·er** \\'mäd-ər-,nī-zər\\ *n*

mod·est \\'mäd-əst\\ *adj* 1 : having a moderate opinion of one's own good qualities and abilities : not boastful 2 : showing moderation : not excessive ⟨a *modest* request⟩ 3 : pure in thought, conduct, and dress : DECENT [Latin *modestus* "moderate"] SYN see CHASTE, SHY — **mod·est·ly** *adv*

mod·es·ty \\'mäd-ə-stē\\ *n* : the quality of being modest; *esp* : freedom from conceit or impropriety

mo·di·cum \\'mäd-i-kəm, 'mōd-\\ *n* : a limited quantity : a small amount ⟨a *modicum* of intelligence⟩ [Latin, neuter of *modicus* "moderate", from *modus* "measure, mode"]

mod·i·fi·ca·tion \\,mäd-ə-fə-'kā-shən\\ *n* 1 : a limiting of the meaning or application (as of a statement) 2 : partial alteration

mod·i·fi·er \\'mäd-ə-,fī-ər, -,fīr\\ *n* : a word (as an adjective or adverb) or group of words (as a phrase or clause) used with another word or group of words to limit or qualify its meaning

mod·i·fy \\'mäd-ə-,fī\\ *vb* **-fied; -fy·ing** 1 a : to make changes in : ALTER ⟨*modify* a plan⟩ b : to become modified 2 : to lower or reduce in extent or degree : MODERATE ⟨*modify* a punishment⟩ 3 : to limit in meaning :

\\ə\\ abut	\\ng\\ sing
\\ər\\ further	\\ō\\ bone
\\a\\ mat	\\ȯ\\ saw
\\ā\\ take	\\ȯi\\ coin
\\ä\\ cot, cart	\\th\\ thin
\\au̇\\ out	\\th\\ this
\\ch\\ chin	\\ü\\ food
\\e\\ pet	\\u̇\\ foot
\\ē\\ easy	\\y\\ yet
\\g\\ go	\\yü\\ few
\\i\\ tip	\\yu̇\\ cure
\\ī\\ life	\\zh\\ vision
\\j\\ job	

QUALIFY ⟨in the phrase "green gloves" "green" *modifies* "gloves"⟩ [Middle French *modifier,* from Latin *modificare* "to measure, moderate", from *modus* "measure"] SYN see CHANGE — **mod·i·fi·able** \-,fī-ə-bəl\ *adj* — **mod·i·fi·able·ness** *n*

mod·ish \'mōd-ish\ *adj* : FASHIONABLE 1, STYLISH ⟨was a *modish* dresser⟩ — **mod·ish·ly** *adv* — **mod·ish·ness** *n*

mod·u·lar \'mäj-ə-lər\ *adj* 1 : of, relating to, or based on a module or a modulus 2 : made in similar sizes or with similar units for flexibility and variety in use

modular arithmetic *n* : arithmetic that deals with whole numbers where the numbers are replaced by their remainders after division by a fixed number ⟨5 hours after 10 o'clock is 3 o'clock because clocks follow a *modular arithmetic* with modulus 12⟩

mod·u·late \'mäj-ə-,lāt\ *vb* 1 : to tune to a key or pitch 2 : to adjust or regulate to a certain proportion ⟨*modulated* the voice⟩ 3 : to vary the frequency, amplitude, or phase of (a carrier wave or signal) in radio, television, telephony, or telegraphy 4 : to pass from one musical key to another usually in a gradual movement [Latin *modulari* "to play, sing", from *modulus* "small measure, rhythm", from *modus* "measure, mode"] — **mod·u·la·tor** \-,lāt-ər\ *n* — **mod·u·la·to·ry** \-lə-,tōr-ē, -,tȯr-\ *adj*

mod·u·la·tion \,mäj-ə-'lā-shən\ *n* 1 : an action of modulating 2 : the extent or degree by which something is modulated 3 : variation of some quality (as the frequency or amplitude) of the carrier wave in radio, television, telephony, or telegraphy in accordance with the signal that is to be transmitted

mod·ule \'mäj-ül\ *n* 1 : a standard or unit of measurement 2 a : any of a series of units intended for use together b : a usually packaged functional subassembly of parts (as for an electronic device) 3 : an independent unit that is a part of the total structure of a space vehicle [Latin *modulus* "small measure", from *modus* "measure, mode"]

mod·u·lo \'mäj-ə-,lō\ *prep* : with respect to a modulus of [New Latin, from *modulus*]

mod·u·lus \'mäj-ə-ləs\ *n, pl* **-li** \-,lī, -,lē\ 1 : a number that expresses the degree in which a property (as elasticity) is possessed by a substance or body 2 a : ABSOLUTE VALUE 2 b : an integer that when divided into the difference of two numbers leaves no remainder c : the number of different numbers used in a system of modular arithmetic [New Latin, from Latin, "small measure"]

mo·dus ope·ran·di \,mōd-ə-,säp-ə-'ran-dē, -,dī\ *n, pl* **mo·di operandi** \,mō-,dē-,äp-, 'mō-,dī-\ : a method of procedure [New Latin]

mo·dus vi·ven·di \,mō-dəs-vi-'ven-dē, -,dī\ *n, pl* **mo·di vivendi** \'mō-,dē-vi-, 'mō-,dī-\ 1 : a feasible arrangement or practical compromise 2 : a way of life [New Latin, "manner of living"]

¹mo·gul \'mō-gəl, 'mō-,gəl, mō-'gəl\ *n* 1 *or* **mo·ghul** *often cap* : an Indian Muslim of or descended from one of several conquering groups of Mongol, Turkish, and Persian origin 2 : a great personage : MAGNATE [Persian *Mughul,* from Mongolian *Moġol* "Mongol"] — **mogul** *adj, often cap*

²mogul \'mō-gəl\ *n* : a bump on a ski slope [probably of Scandinavian origin]

mo·hair \'mō-,haər, -,heər\ *n* : a fabric or yarn made of or with the long silky hair of the Angora goat; *also* : hair of this goat [obsolete Italian *mocaiarro,* from Arabic *mukhayyar,* literally, "choice"]

Mo·ham·med·an *variant of* MUHAMMADAN

Mo·hawk \'mō-,hȯk\ *pl* **Mohawk** *or* **Mohawks** : a member of an Iroquoian people of northeastern and east central New York

Mo·hi·can \mō-'hē-kən, mə-\ *or* **Ma·hi·can** \mə-\ *n, pl* **Mohican** *or* **Mohicans** *or* **Mahican** *or* **Mahicans** 1 : a member of an Algonquian people of the upper Hud-

son river valley 2 : the language of the Mohican people

Mo·ho \'mō-,hō\ *n* : the transition zone between the earth's crust and mantle [short for *Mohorovicic discontinuity,* from Andrija *Mohorovičic,* died 1936, Yugoslav geologist]

Mo·ho·ro·vi·cic discontinuity \,mō-hə-'rō-və-,chich-\ *n* : MOHO

Mohs' scale \'mōz-, 'mōs-, ,mō-səz-\ *n* : a scale of hardness for minerals ranging from 1 for the softest to 10 for the hardest in which 1 represents the hardness of talc; 2, gypsum; 3, calcite; 4, fluorite; 5, apatite; 6, orthoclase; 7, quartz; 8, topaz; 9, corundum; and 10, diamond [Friedrich *Mohs,* died 1839, German mineralogist]

moi·ety \'mȯi-ət-ē\ *n, pl* **-ties** : one of two equal or approximately equal parts : HALF [Middle French *moité,* from Late Latin *medietas,* from Latin *medius* "middle"]

¹moil \'mȯil\ *vi* : to work hard : DRUDGE [Middle English *moillen* "to wet, dirty", from Middle French *moillier* "to wet", derived from Latin *mollis* "soft"] — **moil·er** *n*

²moil *n* 1 : hard work : DRUDGERY 2 : CONFUSION 1

moi·ré \mȯ-'rā, mwä-\ *or* **moire** *same, or* 'mȯir, 'mȯr, 'mwär\ *n* : a fabric with a shimmering watery look; *also* : an appearance suggesting this [French *moiré,* from *moire* "watered mohair", from English *mohair*] — **moiré** *adj*

moist \'mȯist\ *adj* : slightly wet : not completely dry : DAMP ⟨*moist* earth⟩ [Middle French *moiste,* derived from Latin *mucidus* "slimy", from *mucus* "mucus"] — **moist·ly** *adv* — **moist·ness** \'mȯist-nəs, 'mȯis-\ *n*

moist·en \'mȯis-n\ *vb* **moist·ened; moist·en·ing** \-n-ing, 'mȯis-ning\ : to make or become moist — **moist·en·er** \'mȯis-n-ər, 'mȯis-nər\ *n*

mois·ture \'mȯis-chər\ *n* : the small amount of liquid that causes moistness : DAMPNESS

mois·tur·ize \-chə-,rīz\ *vt* : to add moisture to

mo·jo \'mō-jō\ *n, pl* **mojoes** *or* **mojos** : a magic spell, hex, or charm; *also* : magical power [probably of African origin]

mol·al \'mō-ləl\ *adj* : of, relating to, or containing one mole of solute per 1000 grams of solvent — **mo·lal·i·ty** \mō-'lal-ət-ē\ *n*

¹mo·lar \'mō-lər\ *n* : a tooth with a rounded or flattened surface adapted for grinding; *esp* : a grinding tooth of a mammal that is situated behind the premolars [Latin *molaris,* from *mola* "millstone"]

²molar *adj* 1 : able or fitted to grind 2 : of or relating to a molar

³molar *adj* 1 : of or relating to a molecule or mole 2 : of, relating to, or containing one mole of solute per liter of solution — **mo·lar·i·ty** \mō-'lar-ət-ē\ *n*

mo·las·ses \mə-'las-əz\ *n* : a thick brown syrup that is separated from raw sugar in sugar manufacture [Portuguese *melaço,* from Late Latin *mellaceum* "grape juice", from Latin *mel* "honey"]

¹mold *or* **mould** \'mōld\ *n* : light rich crumbly earth containing decayed organic matter [Old English *molde*]

²mold *or* **mould** 1 : distinctive nature or character : TYPE ⟨a person of austere *mold*⟩ 2 : the frame on or around which an object is constructed 3 a : a cavity in which something is shaped ⟨a *mold* for metal type⟩ b : something shaped in a mold ⟨a *mold* of ice cream⟩ [Old French *modle,* from Latin *modulus* "small measure", from *modus* "measure, mode"]

³mold *or* **mould** *vb* 1 : to knead into shape ⟨*mold* loaves of bread⟩ 2 : to form or become formed in or as if in a mold ⟨*mold* butter⟩ — **mold·able** \'mōl-də-bəl\ *adj* — **mold·er** *n*

⁴mold *also* **mould** *n* : an often woolly surface growth of fungus especially on damp or decaying organic matter;

also : a fungus that produces mold [Middle English *mowlde*]

⁵**mold** *also* **mould** *vi* : to become moldy

mold·board \'mōld-,bōrd, 'mōl-, -,bȯrd\ *n* : a curved iron plate attached above the plowshare of a plow to lift and turn the soil

mol·der \'mōl-dər\ *vi* **mol·dered; mol·der·ing** \-də-ring, -dring\ : to crumble into particles [derived from ⁵*mold*]

mold·ing \'mōl-ding\ *n* **1** : the act or work of a person who molds **2** : an object produced by molding **3** : a strip of material having a shaped surface and used (as on a wall or the edge of a table) as a decoration or finish

moldy \'mōl-dē\ *adj* **mold·i·er; -est** **1** : of, resembling, or covered with a mold **2 a** : being old and moldering **b** : OUTMODED — **mold·i·ness** *n*

¹**mole** \'mōl\ *n* : a small usually brown and sometimes protruding permanent spot on the skin [Old English *māl*]

²**mole** *n* : any of numerous burrowing insectivores with tiny eyes, concealed ears, and soft fur [Middle English]

³**mole** *n* **1** : a heavy masonry structure built in the sea as a breakwater or pier **2** : the harbor formed by a mole [Middle French, from Italian *molo*, from Late Greek *mōlos*, from Latin *moles*, literally, "mass"]

⁴**mole** *also* **mol** \'mōl\ *n* : the quantity of a chemical substance that has a weight in mass units (as grams) numerically equal to its molecular weight [German *mol*, short for *molekulargewicht* "molecular weight"]

mo·lec·u·lar \mə-'lek-yə-lər\ *adj* : of, relating to, or produced by molecules

molecular biology *n* : a branch of biology dealing with the ultimate physical and chemical organization of living matter and with the molecular basis of inheritance and protein synthesis — **molecular biologist** *n*

molecular formula *n* : a chemical formula that gives the total number of atoms of each element present in a molecule

molecular mass *n* : the mass of a molecule equal to the sum of the masses of all the atoms contained in it

molecular weight *n* : the weight of a molecule equal to the sum of the weights of the atoms contained in it

mol·e·cule \'mäl-i-,kyül\ *n* **1** : the smallest portion of a substance that retains all the properties of the substance and is composed of one or more atoms **2** : a very small bit : PARTICLE [French *molécule*, derived from Latin *moles* "mass"]

mole·hill \'mōl-,hil\ *n* : a ridge of earth pushed up by a mole

mole·skin \-,skin\ *n* **1** : the skin of the mole used as fur **2 a** : a heavy cotton fabric with a velvety nap on one side **b** *pl* : trousers of this fabric

mo·lest \mə-'lest\ *vt* **1** : to annoy, disturb, or persecute especially with hostile or injurious effect **2** : to make annoying sexual advances to [Middle French *molester*, from Latin *molestare*, from *molestus* "burdensome", from *moles* "mass, burden"] — **mo·les·ta·tion** \,mōl-,es-'tā-shən, ,mōl-əs-, mäl-\ *n* — **mo·lest·er** \mə-'les-tər\ *n*

moll \'mäl\ *n* : a gangster's girl friend [probably from *Moll*, nickname for *Mary*]

mol·lie \'mäl-ē\ *n* : any of several brightly colored topminnows often kept in a tropical aquarium [François N. *Mollien*, died 1850, French statesman]

mol·li·fy \'mäl-ə-,fī\ *vt* **-fied; -fy·ing** **1** : CALM 2, QUIET **2** : to soothe in temper or disposition [Middle French *mollifier*, from Late Latin *mollificare*, from Latin *mollis* "soft"] SYN SEE PACIFY — **mol·li·fi·ca·tion** \,mäl-ə-fə-'kā-shən\ *n*

mol·lusk *or* **mol·lusc** \'mäl-əsk\ *n* : any of a large phylum (Mollusca) of invertebrate animals (as snails or clams) with a soft body lacking segments and usually enclosed in a calcareous shell [French *mollusque*, de-

rived from Latin *molluscus* "soft", from *mollis*] — **mol·lus·can** \mə-'ləs-kən, mä-\ *adj*

¹**mol·ly·cod·dle** \'mäl-ē-,käd-l\ *n* : a person who is used to being coddled or petted; *esp* : a pampered man or boy [from *Molly*, nickname for *Mary*]

²**mollycoddle** *vt* **-cod·dled; -cod·dling** \-,käd-ling, -l-ing\ : CODDLE 2, PAMPER — **mol·ly·cod·dler** \-,käd-lər, -l-ər\ *n*

Mo·lo·tov cocktail \,mäl-ə-,tȯf-, ,mȯl-, ,mōl-, -,tȯv-\ *n* : a crude incendiary device made of a bottle filled with a flammable liquid (as gasoline) and fitted with a wick or saturated rag that is ignited at the moment of hurling [Vyacheslav M. *Molotov*]

¹**molt** *or* **moult** \'mōlt\ *vb* : to shed hair, feathers, outer skin, or horns periodically with the cast-off parts being replaced by a new growth [Middle English *mouten*, derived from Latin *mutare* "to change"] — **molt·er** *n*

²**molt** *or* **moult** *n* : the act or process of molting

mol·ten \'mōlt-n\ *adj* **1** *obs* : made by melting and casting **2** : melted especially by intense heat ⟨*molten* rock⟩ [Middle English, from past participle of *melten* "to melt"]

mol·to \'mōl-tō, 'mȯl-\ *adv* : MUCH, VERY — used in music directions ⟨*molto* adagio⟩ [Italian, from Latin *multum*, from *multus*, adj., "much"]

mo·ly \'mō-lē\ *n* : a mythical herb with black root, white flowers, and magic powers [Latin, from Greek *mōly*]

mo·lyb·de·nite \mə-'lib-də-,nīt\ *n* : a soft bluish gray mineral MoS_2 consisting of molybdenum and sulfur and constituting a source of molybdenum

mo·lyb·de·num \-də-nəm\ *n* : a gray metallic element used in steel alloys to give greater strength and hardness — see ELEMENT table [New Latin, from Latin *molybdaena* "galena", from Greek *molybdaina*, from *molybdos* "lead"]

mom \'mäm, 'məm\ *n* : MOTHER 1a [short for *momma*]

mo·ment \'mō-mənt\ *n* **1** : a minute portion or point of time : INSTANT **2 a** : present time **b** : a time of importance or conspicuousness ⟨we have our *moments*⟩ **3** : IMPORTANCE, CONSEQUENCE ⟨a matter of great *moment*⟩ [Middle French, from Latin *momentum* "movement, particle sufficient to turn the scales, moment", from *movēre* "to move"]

mo·men·tar·i·ly \,mō-mən-'ter-ə-lē\ *adv* **1** : for a moment ⟨the pain eased *momentarily*⟩ **2** *archaic* : INSTANTLY **3** : at any moment ⟨we expect them *momentarily*⟩

mo·men·tary \'mō-mən-,ter-ē\ *adj* : lasting only a moment : SHORT-LIVED, TRANSITORY — **mo·men·tar·i·ness** *n*

mo·ment·ly \'mō-mənt-lē\ *adv* **1** : from moment to moment **2** : MOMENTARILY 1, 3

mo·men·tous \mō-'ment-əs\ *adj* : very important : CONSEQUENTIAL ⟨a *momentous* decision⟩ — **mo·men·tous·ly** *adv* — **mo·men·tous·ness** *n*

mo·men·tum \mō-'ment-əm\ *n*, *pl* **-men·ta** \-'ment-ə\ *or* **-men·tums** \-'ment-əmz\ **1** : property of a moving body that determines the length of time required to bring it to rest when under the action of a constant force or moment : the product of the mass of a body and its velocity **2** : IMPETUS 1 [Latin, "movement, moment"]

mom·ma \'mäm-ə, 'məm-\ *variant of* MAMA

mon- *or* **mono-** *combining form* **1** : one : single : alone ⟨*mono*mania⟩ ⟨*mono*plane⟩ **2** : containing one (usually specified) atom or group ⟨*mono*xide⟩ [Greek, from *monos* "alone, single"]

mo·nad·nock \mə-'nad-,näk\ *n* : a hill or mountain of resistant rock surmounting a peneplain [Mount *Monadnock*, New Hampshire]

mon·arch \'män-ərk, -,ärk\ *n* **1** : a person who reigns over a kingdom or empire : **a** : a sovereign ruler ⟨an absolute *monarch*⟩ **b** : one acting primarily as chief of state and exercising only limited powers ⟨a constitutional *monarch*⟩ — compare CZAR, EMPEROR, KAISER,

²mole

\ə\ abut	\ng\ sing
\ər\ further	\ō\ bone
\a\ mat	\ȯ\ saw
\ā\ take	\ȯi\ coin
\ä\ cot, cart	\th\ thin
\aú\ out	\th\ this
\ch\ chin	\ü\ food
\e\ pet	\ú\ foot
\ē\ easy	\y\ yet
\g\ go	\yü\ few
\i\ tip	\yú\ cure
\ī\ life	\zh\ vision
\j\ job	

mongoose

KING, QUEEN **2** : one holding preeminent position or power **3** : a large orange and black migratory American butterfly — called also *monarch butterfly* [Late Latin *monarcha,* from Greek *monarchos,* from *mon- + archein* "to rule"] — **mo·nar·chal** \mə-'när-kəl, mä-\ *or* **mo·nar·chi·al** \-kē-əl\ *adj*

mo·nar·chi·cal \mə-'när-ki-kəl, mä-\ *or* **mo·nar·chic** \-'när-kik\ *adj* : of, relating to, or characteristic of a monarch or monarchy — **mo·nar·chi·cal·ly** \-ki-kə-lē, -klē\ *adv*

mon·ar·chism \'män-ər-,kiz-əm\ *n* : monarchical government or principles — **mon·ar·chist** \-kəst\ *n*

mon·ar·chy \'män-ər-kē\ *n, pl* **-chies** **1** : undivided or absolute rule by one person **2** : a nation or country having a monarch as chief of state **3** : a government having a hereditary chief of state with life tenure and powers varying from nominal to absolute

mon·as·tery \'män-ə-,ster-ē\ *n, pl* **-ter·ies** : an establishment in which members of a religious community (as of monks) live and carry on their work [Late Latin *monasterium,* from Late Greek *monastērion,* from Greek, "hermit's cell", from *monazein* "to live alone", from *monos* "alone"]

mo·nas·tic \mə-'nas-tik\ *adj* **1** : of or relating to monks or monasteries **2** : separated from worldly affairs ⟨a *monastic* life⟩ — **monastic** *n* — **mo·nas·ti·cal·ly** \-ti-kə-lē, -klē\ — **mo·nas·ti·cism** \-tə-,siz-əm\ *n*

mon·atom·ic \,män-ə-'täm-ik\ *adj* : consisting of one atom; *esp* : having one atom in the molecule

mon·au·ral \mä-'nȯr-əl, 'mä-\ *adj* : MONOPHONIC 2 — **monau·ral·ly** \-rə-lē\ *adv*

Mon·day \'mən-dē\ *n* : the 2d day of the week [Old English *mōnandæg,* derived from a translation of Latin *dies Lunae* "day of the moon", translation of Greek *hēmera Selēnēs*]

mon·e·tary \'män-ə-,ter-ē, 'mən-\ *adj* : of or relating to money SYN see FINANCIAL [Late Latin *monetarius,* from Latin *moneta* "mint, money"]

monetary unit *n* : the standard unit of value of a currency

mon·e·tize \'män-ə-,tīz, 'mən-\ *vt* : to coin into money; *also* : to establish as legal tender — **mon·e·ti·za·tion** \,män-ət-ə-'zā-shən, ,mən-\ *n*

mon·ey \'mən-ē\ *n, pl* **mon·eys** *or* **mon·ies** \-ēz\ **1** : something generally accepted as a medium of exchange, a measure of value, or a means of payment: as **a** : officially coined or stamped metal currency **b** : PAPER MONEY **c** : an amount or a sum of money **2** : wealth reckoned in terms of money **3** : a form or denomination of coin or paper money **4** : the 1st, 2d, and 3d place in a horse or dog race ⟨finished in the *money*⟩ **5** : persons or interests possessing or controlling great wealth [Middle French *moneie,* from Latin *moneta* "mint, money"]

money changer *n* : one whose business is the exchanging of kinds or denominations of currency

mon·eyed *or* **mon·ied** \'mən-ēd\ *adj* **1** : having money : WEALTHY **2** : consisting of or derived from money

mon·ey·lend·er \'mən-ē-,len-dər\ *n* : one whose business is lending money

mon·ey–mak·er \'mən-ē-,mā-kər\ *n* **1** : one who accumulates wealth **2** : a plan or product that produces profit — **mon·ey–mak·ing** \-king\ *adj or n*

money order *n* : an order for the payment of a specified amount of money to a named payee that can be purchased and cashed at issuing offices (as post offices or banks)

mon·ger \'mən-gər, 'mäng-\ *n* **1** : a dealer in some commodity — usually used in combination ⟨fish*monger*⟩ **2** : one dealing in or promoting something petty or discreditable — usually used in combination ⟨hate*monger*⟩ [Old English *mangere,* from Latin *mango,* of Greek origin]

Mon·gol \'mäng-gəl, 'män-,gōl\ *n* **1** : a member of one of the chiefly pastoral Mongoloid peoples of Mongolia **2** : MONGOLIAN 2 [Mongolian *Mongol*]

Mon·go·lian \män-'gōl-yən, mäng-\ *n* **1** : a native or inhabitant of Mongolia **2** : the Mongolic language of the Mongol people — **Mongolian** *adj*

Mon·gol·ic \män-'gäl-ik, mäng-\ *n* : a subfamily of Altaic languages including Mongolian and Kalmuck — **Mongolic** *adj*

mon·gol·ism \'mäng-gə-,liz-əm\ *n* : DOWN'S SYNDROME

mon·gol·oid \'mäng-gə-,lȯid\ *adj* **1** *cap* : of or relating to a major racial stock native to Asia and considered to comprise peoples of northern and eastern Asia, Malaysians, Eskimos, and often American Indians **2** : affected with Down's syndrome — **mongoloid** *n, often cap*

mon·goose \'män-,güs, 'mäng\ *n, pl* **mon·goos·es** : an agile Indian mammal that is related to the civets, is about the size of a ferret, and feeds on snakes and rodents; *also* : any of several related mammals [Hindi *māgūs*]

mon·grel \'mäng-grəl, 'mäng-\ *n* **1** : the offspring of parents of different breeds (as of dogs); *esp* : one of uncertain ancestry **2** : a person or thing of mixed origin [probably from Middle English *mong* "mixture"] — **mongrel** *adj* — **mon·grel·iza·tion** \,mäng-grə-lə-'zā-shən, ,mäng-\ *n* — **mon·grel·ize** \'mäng-grə-,līz, 'mäng-\ *vt*

mon·i·ker *or* **mon·ick·er** \'män-i-kər\ *n, slang* : NAME 1, NICKNAME [origin unknown]

mo·nism \'mō-,niz-əm, 'män-,iz-\ *n* : a view that a complex entity (as the universe) is basically one — **mo·nist** \'mō-nəst, 'män-əst\ *n* — **mo·nis·tic** \mō-'nis-tik, mä-\ *or* **mo·nis·ti·cal** \-ti-kəl\ *adj*

¹mon·i·tor \'män-ət-ər\ *n* **1 a** : a student appointed to assist a teacher **b** : one that warns or instructs **c** : one that monitors or is used in monitoring; *esp* : a screen used for display (as of television pictures or computer information) **2** : any of various large tropical Old World lizards closely related to the iguanas [Latin, "one that warns, overseer", from *monēre* "to warn"] — **mon·i·to·ri·al** \,män-ə-'tōr-ē-əl, -'tȯr-\ *adj* — **mon·i·tor·ship** \'män-ət-ər-,ship\ *n*

²monitor *vt* **mon·i·tored; mon·i·tor·ing** \'män-ət-ə-ring, 'män-ə-tring\ : to watch, observe, or check especially for a special purpose: as **a** : to check (a radio or television signal or program) by means of a receiver for quality of transmission **b** : to watch, listen to, or intercept often secretly ⟨*monitor* enemy communications⟩ **c** : to test for intensity of radioactivity

mon·i·to·ry \'män-ə-,tōr-ē, -,tȯr-\ *adj* : giving admonition : WARNING

monk \'məngk\ *n* : a member of a religious community of men; *esp* : one of a religious order of men taking vows of poverty, chastity, and obedience and living in community under a rule [Old English *munuc,* from Late Latin *monachus,* from Late Greek *monachos,* from Greek *monos* "alone"] — **monk·hood** \-,hùd\ *n*

¹mon·key \'məng-kē\ *n, pl* **monkeys** **1** : a primate mammal other than human beings or usually the lemurs and tarsiers; *esp* : any of the smaller longer-tailed primates as contrasted with the apes **2** : a ludicrous figure : DUPE [probably of Low German origin] — **mon·key·ish** \-kē-ish\ *adj*

²monkey *vi* **mon·keyed; mon·key·ing** **1** : to act in a grotesque or mischievous manner **2** : FOOL 1b, TRIFLE

monkey business *n* : mischievous activity or behavior

mon·key·shine \'məng-kē-,shīn\ *n* : a mischievous trick

monkey wrench *n* **1** : an adjustable wrench having jaws at right angles to a straight handle **2** : something that disrupts ⟨the storm threw a *monkey wrench* into our plans⟩

monk·ish \'məng-kish\ *adj* **1** : of or relating to monks **2** : resembling that of a monk ⟨lived in *monkish* retirement⟩ — **monk·ish·ly** *adv* — **monk·ish·ness** *n*

monks·hood \'məngs-,hùd, 'məngks-\ *n* : a poisonous Eurasian herb related to the buttercups and often cultivated for its showy hood-shaped white or purplish flowers

mono- — see MON-

mono·ba·sic \,män-ə-'bā-sik\ *adj* : having only one hydrogen atom replaceable by an atom or radical ⟨*mono·basic* acid⟩

mono·chrome \'män-ə-,krōm\ *n* : a painting, drawing, or photograph in a single hue — **monochrome** *adj*

mon·o·cle \'män-i-kəl\ *n* : an eyeglass for one eye [French, from Late Latin *monoculus* "one-eyed", from Latin *mon-* "mon-" + *oculus* "eye"] — **mon·o·cled** \-kəld\ *adj*

mono·clin·ic \,män-ə-'klin-ik\ *adj* : being a crystal in which the three axes are of unequal length with two of them at right angles to each other and the third perpendicular to only one of the other two

mono·cli·nous \-'klī-nəs\ *adj* : having both stamens and pistils in the same flower — compare DICLINOUS [*mon-* + Greek *klinē* "bed", from *klinein* "to lean, recline"]

mon·o·cot \'män-ə-,kät\ *n* : MONOCOTYLEDON — **monocot** *adj*

mono·cot·y·le·don \,män-ə-,kät-l-'ēd-n\ *n* : any of a group (Monocotyledoneae) of seed plants having an embryo with a single cotyledon and usually parallel=veined leaves and flower parts in groups of three — **mono·cot·y·le·don·ous** \-n-əs\ *adj*

mon·oc·u·lar \mä-'näk-yə-lər, mə-\ *adj* : of, relating to, or suitable for use with only one eye

mono·cul·ture \'män-ə-,kəl-chər\ *n* : the cultivation of a single crop to the exclusion of other uses of land

mono·cyte \'män-ə-,sīt\ *n* : a large phagocytic white blood cell — **mono·cyt·ic** \,män-ə-'sit-ik\ *adj*

mon·o·dy \'män-əd-ē\ *n, pl* **-dies** **1** : ELEGY **2** : a style of musical composition in which one voice part carries the melody; *also* : a composition in this style [Medieval Latin *monodia* "lyric sung by one voice", from Greek *monōidia,* from *mon-* + *aidein* "to sing"] — **mo·nod·ic** \mə-'näd-ik\ *adj* — **mon·o·dist** \'män-əd-əst\ *n*

mon·oe·cious \mə-'nē-shəs, män-ē-\ *adj* : having pistils and stamens in different flowers on the same plant [derived from Greek *mon-* + *oikos* "house"] — **mon·oe·cism** \mə-'nē-,siz-əm, män-ē-\ *n*

mo·nog·a·mous \mə-'näg-ə-məs\ *adj* : of, relating to, or practicing monogamy — **mo·nog·a·mous·ly** *adv* — **mo·nog·a·mous·ness** *n*

mo·nog·a·my \mə-'näg-ə-mē\ *n* : marriage with only one person at a time — **mo·nog·a·mist** \-'näg-ə-məst\ *n*

mono·gram \'män-ə-,gram\ *n* : an identifying symbol or character usually made up of two or more letters — **monogram** *vt* — **mono·grammed** \-,gramd\ *adj*

mono·graph \'män-ə-,graf\ *n* : a learned treatise on a particular subject; *esp* : a scholarly or scientific paper printed in a journal or as a pamphlet

mono·hy·brid \,män-ə-'hī-brəd\ *adj* : heterozygous in respect to a single gene pair — **monohybrid** *n*

mono·lay·er \'män-ə-,lā-ər, -,le-ər, -,ler\ *n* : a layer or film one cell or molecule in thickness

mono·lin·gual \,män-ə-'ling-gwəl\ *adj* : expressed in or knowing or using only one language

mon·o·lith \'män-l-,ith\ *n* **1** : a single great stone often in the form of a monument or column **2** : something (as a political organization) held to be a single massive whole exhibiting solid uniformity — **mon·o·lith·ic** \,män-l-'ith-ik\ *adj*

mon·o·logue *or* **mon·o·log** \'män-l-,óg, -,äg\ *n* **1** : a dramatic scene in which one person speaks alone **2** : a drama performed by one actor **3** : a literary composition (as a poem) in the form of a soliloquy **4** : a long speech monopolizing a conversation [French *monologue,* from *mon-* "mon-" + *-logue* (as in dialogue)] — **mon·o·logu·ist** \'män-l-,óg-əst, -,äg-\ *or* **mo·no·lo·gist** *same or* mə-'näl-ə-jest\ *n*

mono·ma·nia \,män-ə-'mā-nē-ə, -'mā-nyə\ *n* : excessive concentration on a single object or idea — **mono·ma·ni·ac** \-'mā-nē-,ak\ *n or adj*

mon·o·mer \'män-ə-mər\ *n* : one of the molecular units of a polymer [*mon-* + *-mer* (as in *polymer*)] — **mon·o·mer·ic** \,män-ə-'mer-ik\ *adj*

mo·nom·e·ter \mə-'näm-ət-ər, mä-\ *n* : a line of verse consisting of one metrical foot

mo·no·mi·al \mä-'nō-mē-əl, mə-'nō-\ *n* : a mathematical expression consisting of a single term [blend of *mon-* and *-nomial* (as in *binomial*)] — **monomial** *adj*

mono·mo·lec·u·lar \,män-ō-mə-'lek-yə-lər\ *adj* : being only one molecule thick ⟨a *monomolecular* film⟩ — **mono·mo·lec·u·lar·ly** *adv*

mono·nu·cle·o·sis \,män-ə-,nü-klē-'ō-səs, -,nyü-\ *n* : an abnormal increase in the blood of leukocytes lacking cytoplasmic granules; *esp* : INFECTIOUS MONONUCLEOSIS

mono·phon·ic \,män-ə-'fän-ik\ *adj* **1** : having a single melodic line with little or no accompaniment **2** : of or relating to sound transmission, recording, or reproduction involving a single transmission path — compare STEREOPHONIC

mon·oph·thong \'män-əf-,thóng, 'män-ə-,\ *n* : a vowel sound that throughout its duration has a single constant articulatory position [Late Greek *monophthongos* "single vowel", from Greek *mon-* + *phthongos* "sound"] — **mon·oph·thon·gal** \,män-əf-'thong-əl, ,män-ə-', -gəl\ *adj*

mono·plane \'män-ə-,plān\ *n* : an airplane with only one pair of wings

mono·ploid \'män-ə-,plóid\ *adj* : having or being a chromosome set comprising a single genome [*mon-* + *-ploid* (as in *diploid*)] — **monoploid** *n*

mo·nop·o·list \mə-'näp-ə-ləst\ *n* : one who has a monopoly or favors monopoly — **mo·nop·o·lis·tic** \mə-,näp-ə-'lis-tik\ — **mo·nop·o·lis·ti·cal·ly** \-'lis-ti-kə-lē, -klē\ *adv*

mo·nop·o·lize \mə-'näp-ə,līz\ *vt* : to get or have a monopoly of — **mo·nop·o·li·za·tion** \-,näp-ə-lə-'zā-shən\ *n* — **mo·nop·o·liz·er** \-'näp-ə-,lī-zər\ *n*

mo·nop·o·ly \mə-'näp-lē, -ə-lē\ *n, pl* **-lies** **1 a** : exclusive ownership or control through legal privilege, command of supply, or group action **b** : exclusive possession **2** : an instance of monopoly **3** : a commodity controlled by one party **4** : a person or group having a monopoly [Latin *monopolium,* from Greek *monopōlion,* from *mon-* + *pōlein* "to sell"] □ SYN TRUST, SYNDICATE, CARTEL: MONOPOLY implies exclusive power to buy or sell in a specified market; TRUST applies specifically to a merger of corporations by which control is given to trustees and the individual owners are compensated by shares of stock; SYNDICATE applies to a group organized to carry out an enterprise or purchase a property requiring large capital outlay; CARTEL commonly implies an international combination of firms for controlling production and control of products in one field or division of industry.

mono·rail \'män-ə-,rāl\ *n* : a single rail serving as a track for cars that are balanced upon it or suspended from it; *also* : a vehicle or system using such a track

mono·sac·cha·ride \,män-ə-'sak-ə-,rīd\ *n* : a sugar (as glucose) not decomposable to simpler sugars by hydrolysis

mono·so·mic \,män-ə-'sō-mik\ *adj* : having one less than the diploid number of chromosomes — **monosomic** *n* — **mono·so·my** \'män-ə-,sō-mē\ *n*

mono·syl·la·ble \'män-ə-,sil-ə-bəl, ,män-ə-'\ *n* : a word of one syllable — **mono·syl·lab·ic** \,män-ə-sə-'lab-ik\ *adj* — **mono·syl·lab·i·cal·ly** \-'lab-i-kə-lē, -klē\ *adv*

mono·the·ism \'män-ə-,thē-,iz-əm\ *n* : a doctrine or belief that there is only one deity — **mono·the·ist** \-,thē-əst\ *n* — **mono·the·is·tic** \-,thē-'is-tik-ik\ *adj*

mono·tone \'män-ə-,tōn\ *n* **1** : a succession of syllables, words, or sentences in one unvaried key or pitch ⟨speak in a *monotone*⟩ **2** : a single unvaried musical

monocle

\ə\ abut	\ng\ sing
\ər\ further	\ō\ bone
\a\ mat	\ó\ saw
\ā\ take	\ói\ coin
\ä\ cot, cart	\th\ thin
\aú\ out	\th\ this
\ch\ chin	\ü\ food
\e\ pet	\ú\ foot
\ē\ easy	\y\ yet
\g\ go	\yü\ few
\i\ tip	\yú\ cure
\ī\ life	\zh\ vision
\j\ job	

tone **3** : tedious sameness or repetition ⟨a *monotone* of yellow fields⟩ **4** : a person unable to produce or distinguish between musical intervals — **monotone** *adj* — **mono·ton·ic** \ˌmän-ə-'tän-ik\ *adj* — **mono·ton·i·cal·ly** \-'tän-i-kə-lē, -klē\ *adv*

mo·not·o·nous \mə-'nät-n-əs, -'nät-nəs\ *adj* **1** : uttered or sounded in one unvarying tone **2** : tediously uniform or unvarying ⟨*monotonous* scenery⟩ — **mo·not·o·nous·ly** *adv* — **mo·not·o·nous·ness** *n*

mo·not·o·ny \mə-'nät-n-ē, -'nät-nē\ *n, pl* **-nies 1** : sameness of tone or sound **2** : lack of variety; *esp* : tiresome sameness ⟨the *monotony* of the empty landscape⟩

mono·treme \'män-ə-ˌtrēm\ *n* : any of an order (Monotremata) of primitive mammals (as the echidna) that lay eggs [derived from Greek *mon-* + *trēma* "hole"]

mono·un·sat·u·rat·ed \ˌmän-ō-ˌən-'sach-ə-ˌrāt-əd\ *adj* : containing one double or triple bond per molecule — used especially of an oil or fatty acid

mono·va·lent \ˌmän-ə-'vā-lənt\ *adj* : UNIVALENT

mon·ovu·lar \män-'ō-vyə-lər, 'män-\ *adj* : MONOZYGOTIC

mon·ox·ide \mə-'näk-ˌsīd\ *n* : an oxide containing only one oxygen atom in the molecule

mono·zy·got·ic \ˌmän-ə-zī-'gät-ik\ *adj* : derived from a single egg ⟨*monozygotic* twins⟩

Mon·roe Doctrine \mən-ˌrō-\ *n* : a statement of United States foreign policy proclaimed in 1823 by President James Monroe expressing opposition to extension of European control or influence in the western hemisphere

mon·sei·gneur \ˌmōn-ˌsän-'yər\ *n, pl* **mes·sei·gneurs** \ˌmā-ˌsän-'yər, -'yərz\ : a French dignitary — used as a title before another title of office or rank ⟨*Monseigneur* the Archbishop⟩ [French, literally, "my lord"]

mon·sieur \məs-'yə, məsh-; mə-'siər\ *n, pl* **mes·sieurs** \məs-'yə, -'yəz, məsh-, mās-; mə-'siər, -'siərz\ : used by or to French-speaking people as a courtesy title equivalent to *Mr.* [Middle French, literally, "my lord"]

mon·si·gnor \män-'sē-nyər, mən-\ *n, pl* **mon·si·gnors** *or* **mon·si·gno·ri** \ˌmän-ˌsēn-'yōr-ē, -'yȯr-\ : a Roman Catholic prelate — used as a title before the surname or before the given name and the surname ⟨*Monsignor* Smith⟩ ⟨*Monsignor* John Smith⟩ [Italian *monsignore*, from French *monseigneur*] — **mon·si·gno·ri·al** \ˌmän-ˌsēn-'yōr-ē-əl, -'yȯr\ *adj*

mon·soon \män-'sün\ *n* **1** : a wind in the Indian ocean and southern Asia that blows from the southwest from April to October and from the northeast from October to April **2** : the rainy season that accompanies the southwest monsoon in India and adjacent areas [obsolete Dutch *monssoen,* from Portuguese *monção,* from Arabic *mawsim* "time, season"]

¹mon·ster \'män-stər\ *n* **1** : an animal or plant of abnormal form or structure **2** : a creature of strange or horrible form **3** : one unusually large for its kind **4** : an extremely wicked or cruel person [Middle French *monstre,* from Latin *monstrum* "omen, monster"]

²monster *adj* : very large : ENORMOUS

mon·strance \'män-strəns\ *n* : a vessel used for showing the Blessed Sacrament [Middle French, from Medieval Latin *monstrantia,* from Latin *monstrare* "to show"]

mon·stros·i·ty \män-'sträs-ət-ē\ *n, pl* **-ties 1** : the condition of being monstrous **2** : something monstrous : MONSTER

mon·strous \'män-strəs\ *adj* **1** : being great or overwhelming in size : GIGANTIC **2** : having the qualities or appearance of a monster **3 a** : very ugly or vicious : HORRIBLE **b** : shockingly wrong or ridiculous **4** : very different from the usual, natural, or expected — **monstrous·ly** *adv* — **mon·strous·ness** *n* □ **SYN** MONSTROUS, PRODIGIOUS, TREMENDOUS, STUPENDOUS mean extremely impressive especially in size. MON-

STROUS further implies ugliness or abnormality; PRODIGIOUS suggests a marvelousness that strains belief; TREMENDOUS implies an awe-inspiring or terrifying effect; STUPENDOUS suggests a power to stun or astound.

mon·tage \män-'täzh, mōⁿ-, -'tazh\ *n* **1** : an artistic composition made up of several different kinds of items (as strips of newspaper or bits of wood) arranged together **2** : PHOTOMONTAGE [French, from *monter* "to mount"]

mon·tane \män-'tān, 'män-\ *adj* : of, relating to, growing in, or being the relatively moist cool upland slopes below timberline characterized by large evergreen trees as the dominant form of life [Latin *montanus* "of a mountain", from *mont-, mons* "mountain"]

month \'mənth, 'məntth\ *n, pl* **months** \'məns, 'mənths, 'məntths\ : one of the 12 portions into which the year is divided [Old English *mōnath*]

¹month·ly \'mənth-lē, 'məntth-\ *adj* **1** : occurring, done, produced, or issued every month **2** : computed in terms of one month **3** : lasting a month — **monthly** *adv*

²monthly *n, pl* **monthlies** : a monthly periodical

mon·u·ment \'män-yə-mənt\ *n* **1** : something that serves as a memorial; *esp* : a building, pillar, stone, or statue erected in memory of a person or event **2** : a work, saying, or deed that lasts or that is worth preserving **3** : a boundary marker (as a stone) **4** : a natural feature or historic site set aside and maintained by the government as public property [Latin *monumentum,* from *monēre* "to remind, warn"]

mon·u·men·tal \ˌmän-yə-'ment-l\ *adj* **1** : serving as a monument **2** : OUTSTANDING ⟨a *monumental* achievement⟩ **3** : of, relating to, or suitable for a monument **4** : very great : COLOSSAL ⟨*monumental* stupidity⟩ — **mon·u·men·tal·ly** \-l-ē\ *adv*

moo \'mü\ *vi* : to make the natural throat noise of a cow : LOW [imitative] — **moo** *n*

mooch \'müch\ *vb* **1** : to wander about **2** : BEG, SPONGE [probably from French dialect *muchier* "to hide"] — **mooch·er** *n*

¹mood \'müd\ *n* : a state or frame of mind : HUMOR ⟨in a good *mood*⟩ [Old English *mōd* "mind, mood"] □ **SYN** MOOD, HUMOR, TEMPER mean a state of mind in which one emotion or desire temporarily has control. MOOD implies a pervasiveness and compelling quality of the emotion ⟨you can really write when you are in the *mood*⟩ HUMOR implies a mood resulting from one's special temperament or present physical condition ⟨a good dinner put us in a better *humor*⟩ TEMPER suggests the domination of a single strong emotion such as anger ⟨was in a foul *temper* that night⟩

²mood *n* : a set of inflectional forms of a verb that show whether the action or state expressed is to be thought of as a fact, a command, or a wish or possibility — compare IMPERATIVE, INDICATIVE, SUBJUNCTIVE [alteration of ¹*mode*]

moody \'müd-ē\ *adj* **mood·i·er; -est 1** : given to moods; *esp* : subject to fits of depression or temper **2** : showing a moody state of mind ⟨a *moody* face⟩ — **mood·i·ly** \'müd-l-ē\ *adv* — **mood·i·ness** \'müd-ē-nəs\ *n*

¹moon \'mün\ *n* **1 a** : the earth's natural satellite shining by the sun's reflected light, revolving about the earth from west to east in about 29½ days, and having a diameter of 3475 kilometers, a mean distance from the earth of about 384,321 kilometers, and a volume about one forty-ninth that of the earth **b** : SATELLITE 2 **2** : the average period of revolution of the moon about the earth **3** : MOONLIGHT [Old English *mōna*] — **moon·less** \-ləs\ *adj* — **moon·like** \-ˌlīk\ *adj*

²moon *vb* : to spend time in idle thought : DREAM

moon·beam \'mün-ˌbēm\ *n* : a ray of light from the moon

moon blindness *n* : a recurrent eye disorder of the horse — **moon–blind** \-ˌblīnd\ *adj*

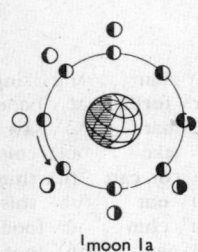

¹moon 1a

moon·calf \-,kaf, -,káf\ *n* : a foolish or absentminded person

moon·fish \-,fish\ *n* : any of various compressed often short deep-bodied silvery or yellowish marine fishes; *also* : PLATY

moon·flow·er \-,flaů-ər, -,flaůr\ *n* : a tropical American morning glory with fragrant night-blooming flowers; *also* : any of several related plants

moon·let \'mün-lət\ *n* : a small natural or artificial satellite

¹moon·light \-,līt\ *n* : the light of the moon

²moonlight *vi* **-light·ed; -light·ing** : to hold a second usually nighttime job in addition to a regular one — **moon·light·er** *n*

moon·lit \'mün-,lit\ *adj* : lighted by the moon ⟨a *moon-lit* night⟩

moon·scape \-,skāp\ *n* : the surface of the moon as seen or as pictured

moon·shine \-,shīn\ **1** : MOONLIGHT **2** : empty talk : NONSENSE **3** : intoxicating liquor; *esp* : illegally distilled corn whiskey — **moon·shin·er** \-,shī-nər\ *n*

moon·stone \-,stōn\ *n* : a transparent or translucent mineral with a pearly greenish or bluish luster that is a variety of feldspar and is used in jewelry

moon·struck \-,strək\ *adj* **1** : mentally unbalanced **2** : romantically sentimental

¹moor \'můr\ *n* **1** *chiefly British* : an expanse of open rolling infertile land **2** : a boggy peaty area dominated by grasses and sedges [Old English *mōr*]

²moor *vb* : to secure (as a boat) with cables, lines, or anchors [Middle English *moren*] — **moor·age** \-ij\ *n*

Moor \'můr\ *n* : one of a North African people of mixed Arab and Berber ancestry conquering Spain in the 8th century and ruling until 1492 [Middle French *More*, from Latin *Maurus* "inhabitant of Mauretania"] — **Moor·ish** \-ish\ *adj*

moor·hen \'můr-,hen\ *n* : GALLINULE

moor·ing \'můr-ing\ *n* **1 a** : a place where or an object to which a craft can be made fast **b** : a device (as a chain or line) by which an object is moored **2** : moral or spiritual resources — usually used in pl.

moor·land \'můr-lənd, -,land\ *n* : land consisting of moors

moose \'müs\ *n, pl* **moose 1** : a large ruminant mammal of the forested parts of Canada and the northern United States that has huge antlers in the male and is related to the typical deers **2** : ELK 1a [of American Indian origin]

¹moot \'müt\ *vt* **1** : to bring up for discussion **2** : DISCUSS 1 [obsolete *moot* "discussion", from Old English *mōt* "assembly"]

²moot *adj* **1** : subject to argument or discussion : DEBATABLE ⟨a *moot* question⟩ **2** : ACADEMIC 4

moot court *n* : a mock court in which students of law argue hypothetical cases for practice

¹mop \'mäp\ *n* **1** : an implement for cleaning made of a bundle of cloth or yarn or a sponge fastened to a handle **2** : something resembling a mop ⟨a *mop* of hair⟩ [Middle English *mappe*]

²mop *vb* **mopped; mop·ping** : to wipe or clean with or as if with a mop ⟨*mop* one's brow⟩ — **mop·per** *n*

¹mope \'mōp\ *vi* **1** : to be in a dull and dispirited state **2** : to move slowly or aimlessly : DAWDLE [probably from obsolete *mop, mope* "fool"] — **mop·er** *n*

²mope *n* **1** : a dull listless person **2** *pl* : low spirits : BLUES ⟨a fit of the *mopes*⟩

mo·ped \'mō-,ped\ *n* : a lightweight low-powered motorbike that can be pedaled [Swedish, from *motor* "motor" + *pedal* "pedal"]

mop·pet \'mäp-ət\ *n* : a young child [obsolete *mop* "fool, child"]

mop–up \'mäp-,əp\ *n* : a final clearance or disposal : a concluding action

mop up \'mäp-'əp, 'mäp-\ *vb* **1** : to clean up by or as if by mopping ⟨*mop up* spilt milk⟩ **2** : to eliminate re-

maining resistance ⟨*mop up* enemy forces⟩ **3** : to finish a task

mo·raine \mə-'rān\ *n* : an accumulation of earth and stones deposited by a glacier [French] — **mo·rain·al** \-'rān-l\ *adj* — **mo·rain·ic** \-'rā-nik\ *adj*

¹mor·al \'mȯr-əl, 'mär-\ *adj* **1 a** : of or relating to principles of right and wrong in behavior : ETHICAL **b** : expressing or teaching a conception of right behavior ⟨a *moral* poem⟩ **c** : conforming to a standard of right behavior : VIRTUOUS, GOOD ⟨a *moral* life⟩ **d** : capable of right and wrong action **2** : probable but not proved : VIRTUAL ⟨a *moral* certainty⟩ [Middle French, from Latin *moralis*, from *mor-, mos* "custom"] — **mor·al·ly** \-ə-lē\ *adv* ☐ SYN ETHICAL: MORAL and ETHICAL are both concerned with rightness or wrongness of actions and conduct, but MORAL is more often applied to the practice or acts of individuals, often specifically in sexual relations, ETHICAL more often to theoretical or general questions of rightness, fairness, or equity.

²moral *n* **1** : the moral significance or practical lesson (as of a story) **2** *pl* : moral conduct **3** *pl* : moral teachings or principles

mo·rale \mə-'ral\ *n* : the mental and emotional condition (as of enthusiasm, spirit, loyalty) of an individual or a group with regard to the function or tasks at hand [French *moral*, from *moral*, adj., "moral"]

mor·al·ist \'mȯr-ə-ləst, 'mär-\ *n* **1** : one who leads a moral life **2** : one who moralizes; *esp* : a person who teaches, studies, or points out morals

mor·al·is·tic \,mȯr-ə-'lis-tik, ,mär-\ *adj* **1** : teaching or pointing out morals ⟨a *moralistic* story⟩ **2** : narrowly conventional in morals ⟨*moralistic* attitudes⟩ — **mor·al·is·ti·cal·ly** \-'lis-ti-kə-lē, -klē\ *adv*

mo·ral·i·ty \mə-'ral-ət-ē\ *n, pl* **-ties 1** : moral quality or character : VIRTUE ⟨judge the *morality* of an action⟩ **2** : moral conduct ⟨standards of *morality*⟩ **3** : a system of morals : principles of conduct

morality play *n* : an allegorical play especially of the 15th and 16th centuries in which the characters personify moral qualities or abstractions (as beauty or death)

mor·al·ize \'mȯr-ə-,līz, 'mär-\ *vb* **1** : to explain in moral terms **2** : to make moral or morally better **3** : to talk or write in a moralistic way — **mor·al·iza·tion** \,mȯr-ə-lə-'zā-shən, ,mär-\ *n* — **mor·al·iz·er** \'mȯr-ə-,lī-zər, 'mär-\ *n*

mo·rass \mə-'ras\ *n* : MARSH, SWAMP [Dutch *moeras*]

mor·a·to·ri·um \,mȯr-ə-'tōr-ē-əm, ,mär-, -'tȯr-\ *n, pl* **-ri·ums** *or* **-ria** \-ē-ə\ **1** : a legally authorized period of delay in the performance of an obligation (as the payment of a debt) ⟨a *moratorium* on war debt payments⟩ **2** : a temporary ban or suspension ⟨a *moratorium* on atomic testing⟩ [New Latin, derived from Latin *morari* "to delay", from *mora* "delay"]

Mo·ra·vi·an \mə-'rā-vē-ən\ *n* **1** : a member of a Christian denomination that traces its history back through the evangelical movement in Moravia and Bohemia to the doctrines of reformer John Huss **2 a** : a native or inhabitant of Moravia **b** : the group of Czech dialects spoken by the Moravian people — **Moravian** *adj*

mo·ray \mə-'rā, 'mȯr-,ā\ *n* : any of numerous often brightly colored eels of warm seas that have sharp teeth capable of inflicting severe bites and that include a Mediterranean eel valued for food [Portuguese *moréia*, from Latin *muraena*, from Greek *myraina*]

mor·bid \'mȯr-bəd\ *adj* **1 a** : of, relating to, or characteristic of disease ⟨*morbid* anatomy⟩ **b** : not healthful : DISEASED ⟨*morbid* conditions⟩ **2** : characterized by gloomy or unwholesome ideas or feelings ⟨takes a *morbid* interest in funerals⟩ [Latin *morbidus* "diseased", from *morbus* "disease"] — **mor·bid·ly** *adv* — **mor·bid·ness** *n*

mor·bid·i·ty \mȯr-'bid-ət-ē\ *n, pl* **-ties 1** : the quality or state of being morbid **2** : the relative incidence of disease

morel

¹mor·dant \'mȯrd-ᵊnt\ *adj* : biting and caustic in thought, manner, or style : INCISIVE ⟨*mordant* criticism⟩ [Middle French, present participle of *mordre* "to bite", from Latin *mordēre*] — **mor·dan·cy** \-n-sē\ *n* — **mor·dant·ly** *adv*

²mordant *n* **1** : a chemical that fixes a dye in or on a substance by combining with the dye to form an insoluble compound **2** : a corroding substance used in etching

³mordant *vt* : to treat with a mordant

mor·dent \'mȯrd-ᵊnt, mȯr-'dent\ *n* : a musical ornament made by a quick alternation of a principal tone with the tone below [Italian *mordente*, from Latin *mordēre* "to bite"]

¹more \'mōr, 'mȯr\ *adj* **1** : greater in amount or degree ⟨felt *more* pain⟩ **2** : ADDITIONAL, FURTHER ⟨bought *more* apples⟩ [Old English *māra*]

²more *adv* **1 a** : in addition **b** : MOREOVER **2** : to a greater or higher degree — often used with an adjective or adverb to form the comparative ⟨*more* active⟩ ⟨*more* actively⟩

³more *n* **1** : a greater amount or number ⟨got *more* than we expected⟩ **2 a** : an additional amount ⟨too full to eat *more*⟩ **b** : additional persons or things ⟨the *more* the merrier⟩

mo·rel \mə-'rel, mȯ-\ *n* : any of several large pitted edible fungi [French *morille*, of Germanic origin]

mo·rel·lo \mə-'rel-ō\ *n* : a cultivated sour cherry with dark red fruit [probably from Flemish *amarelle, marelle*]

more·over \mōr-'ō-vər, mȯr-\ *adv* : in addition to what has been said : BESIDES

mo·res \'mȯr-ˌāz, 'mōr-, -ˌēz\ *n, pl* **1** : the fixed morally binding customs of a particular group **2** : habitual behavior [Latin, pl. of *mor-, mos* "custom"]

Mor·gan \'mȯr-gən\ *n* : any of an American breed of light horses originated in Vermont and noted for stamina, docility, beauty, courage, and especially longevity [Justin *Morgan*, died 1798, American teacher]

mor·ga·nat·ic marriage \ˌmȯr-gə-ˌnat-ik-\ *n* : a marriage between a person of royal or noble rank and a commoner who does not assume the superior partner's rank and whose children do not succeed to the title or inheritance of the parent of superior rank [New Latin *matrimonium ad morganaticum*, literally, "marriage with morning gift (given by the husband to the wife on the morning after consummation of the marriage)"]

morgue \'mȯrg\ *n* **1** : a place where the bodies of persons found dead are kept until claimed by relatives or released for burial **2** : a department of a newspaper where reference material is filed [French]

mor·i·bund \'mȯr-ə-ˌbənd, 'mär-, -bənd\ *adj* : being in a dying state [Latin *moribundus*, from *mori* "to die"] — **mor·i·bun·di·ty** \ˌmȯr-ə-'bən-dət-ē, ˌmär-\ *n*

Mor·mon \'mȯr-mən\ *n* : LATTER-DAY SAINT; *esp* : a member of the Church of Jesus Christ of Latter-Day Saints [*Mormon*, ancient compiler of the Book of Mormon presented as divine revelation by Joseph Smith] — **Mormon** *adj* — **Mor·mon·ism** \'mȯr-mə-ˌniz-əm\ *n*

morn \'mȯrn\ *n* : MORNING [Old English *morgen*]

morn·ing \'mȯr-ning\ *n* **1 a** : DAWN 1 **b** : the time from sunrise to noon **c** : the time from midnight to noon **2** : the first or early part ⟨the *morning* of life⟩ [Middle English, from *morn* + *-ing* (as in *evening*)]

morning glory *n* : any of various usually twining plants with showy trumpet-shaped flowers that usually close by noon; *also* : any of various related plants including herbs, vines, shrubs, or trees with alternate leaves and regular usually funnel-shaped flowers

Morning Prayer *n* : a morning service of the Anglican communion

morn·ings \'mȯr-ningz\ *adv* : in the morning repeatedly ⟨we work *mornings*⟩

morning glory

morning sickness *n* : nausea on arising usually associated with early pregnancy

morning star *n* : a bright planet (as Venus) seen in the eastern sky before sunrise

mo·roc·co \mə-'räk-ō\ *n* : a fine leather made of goat skins tanned with sumac [*Morocco*, Africa]

mo·ron \'mōr-ˌän, 'mȯr-\ *n* **1** : a feebleminded person having a potential mental age of between 8 and 12 years and being capable of doing routine work under supervision **2** : a very stupid person [Greek *mōros* "foolish, stupid"] SYN see IDIOT — **mo·ron·ic** \mə-'rän-ik, mȯ-\ *adj* — **mo·ron·i·cal·ly** \-'rän-i-kə-lē, -klē\ *adv*

mo·rose \mə-'rōs, mȯ-\ *adj* **1** : having a sullen and gloomy disposition **2** : marked by or expressive of gloom [Latin *morosus*, literally, "capricious", from *mor-, mos* "custom, will"] — **mo·rose·ly** *adv* — **mo·rose·ness** *n*

mor·pheme \'mȯr-ˌfēm\ *n* : a word or part of a word (as an affix or a base) that contains no smaller meaningful parts [French *morphème*, from Greek *morphē* "form"]

mor·phia \'mȯr-fē-ə\ *n* : MORPHINE

-mor·phic \'mȯr-fik\ *adj combining form* : having (such) a form ⟨endo*morphic*⟩ [Greek *morphē* "form"]

mor·phine \'mȯr-ˌfēn\ *n* : a bitter white crystalline habit-forming drug made from opium and used to deaden pain and to induce sleep [French, from *Morpheus*, Greek god of dreams]

mor·phol·o·gy \mȯr-'fäl-ə-jē\ *n* **1 a** : a branch of biology that deals with the form and structure of animals and plants **b** : the form and structure of an organism or any of its parts **2** : the part of grammar dealing with word formation and including inflection, derivation, and the formation of compounds **3** : STRUCTURE, FORM ⟨the *morphology* of rocks⟩ [German *morphologie*, from Greek *morphē* "form"] — **mor·pho·log·i·cal** \ˌmȯr-fə-'läj-i-kəl\ *adj* — **mor·pho·log·i·cal·ly** \-i-kə-lē, -klē\ *adv* — **mor·phol·o·gist** \mȯr-'fäl-ə-jəst\ *n*

-mor·phous \'mȯr-fəs\ *adj combining form* : having (such) a form [Greek *-morphos*, from *morphē* "form"]

mor·ris \'mȯr-əs, 'mär-\ *n* : a vigorous English dance traditionally performed by men wearing costumes and bells [Middle English *moreys* "Moorish"]

mor·ris chair \'mȯr-əs-, 'mär-\ *n* : an easy chair with adjustable back and removable cushions [William *Morris*, died 1896, English poet and artist]

mor·row \'mär-ō, 'mȯr-\ *n* **1** *archaic* : MORNING **2** : the next day [Middle English *morn, morwen*, from Old English *morgen*]

Morse code \'mȯrs-\ *n* : either of two codes consisting of dots and dashes or long and short sounds used for transmitting messages by audible or visual signals [Samuel F. B. *Morse*]

INTERNATIONAL MORSE CODE[1]

A	·—	N	—·	Á	·——·—	8	———··
B	—···	O	———	Ä	·—·—	9	————·
C	—·—·	P	·——·	É	··—··	0	—————
D	—··	Q	——·—	Ñ	——·——	, (comma)	——··——
E	·	R	·—·	Ö	———·	.	·—·—·—
F	··—·	S	···	Ü	··——	?	··——··
G	——·	T	—	1	·————	;	—·—·—·
H	····	U	··—	2	··———	:	———···
I	··	V	···—	3	···——	' (apostrophe)	·————·
J	·———	W	·——	4	····—	- (hyphen)	—····—
K	—·—	X	—··—	5	·····	/	—··—·
L	·—··	Y	—·——	6	—····	parenthesis	—·——·—
M	——	Z	——··	7	——···	underline	··——·—

[1]Often called the continental code; a modification of this code, with dots only, is used on ocean cables

mor·sel \\'mȯr-səl\\ *n* **1** : a small piece of food : BITE **2** : a small quantity or piece [Old French, from *mors* "bite", from Latin *morsus,* from *mordēre* "to bite"]

¹mor·tal \\'mȯrt-l\\ *adj* **1** : capable of causing death : FATAL ⟨a *mortal* wound⟩ **2** : subject to death ⟨*mortal* man⟩ **3** : extremely hostile ⟨a *mortal* enemy⟩ **4 a** : too grave or wicked to leave room for forgiveness : UNPARDONABLE ⟨a *mortal* sin⟩ **b** : very great, intense, or severe ⟨in *mortal* fear⟩ **5** : HUMAN ⟨*mortal* limitations⟩ **6** : of, relating to, or connected with death ⟨*mortal* agony⟩ [Middle French, from Latin *mortalis,* from *mort-, mors* "death"] SYN see DEADLY — **mor·tal·ly** \\-l-ē\\ *adv*

²mortal *n* : a human being

mor·tal·i·ty \\mȯr-'tal-ət-ē\\ *n, pl* **-ties 1** : the quality or state of being mortal **2** : the death of large numbers **3** : the human race : MANKIND **4 a** : the number of deaths in a given time or place **b** : the ratio of deaths to total population

mortality table *n* : a table of mortality statistics over a number of years used chiefly by insurance companies in computing premiums

¹mor·tar \\'mȯrt-ər\\ *n* **1** : a strong bowl-shaped container in which substances are pounded or rubbed with a pestle **2** : a muzzle-loading cannon that has a tube short in relation to its caliber and is used to throw projectiles at high angles [Middle French *mortier,* from Latin *mortarium*]

²mortar *n* : a building material (as one made of lime and cement mixed with sand and water) that hardens and is spread between bricks or stones to hold them together — **mortar** *vt*

mor·tar·board \\'mȯrt-ər-ˌbōrd, -ˌbȯrd\\ *n* **1** : a board for holding mortar while it is being applied **2** : an academic cap with a broad projecting square top

¹mort·gage \\'mȯr-gij\\ *n* **1** : a transfer of rights to a piece of property usually as security for the payment of a loan or debt that becomes void when the debt is paid **2** : the formal document by which a mortgage is made [Middle French, from *mort* "dead" + *gage* "pledge, gage"]

²mortgage *vt* : to subject to or as if to a mortgage

mort·gag·ee \\ˌmȯr-gi-'jē\\ *n* : a person to whom property is mortgaged

mort·ga·gor \\ˌmȯr-gi-'jȯr\\ *also* **mort·gag·er** \\'mȯr-gi-jər\\ *n* : a person who mortgages property

mor·ti·cian \\mȯr-'tish-ən\\ *n* : UNDERTAKER [Latin *mort-, mors* "death"]

mor·ti·fy \\'mȯrt-ə-ˌfī\\ *vb* **-fied; -fy·ing 1** : to subdue bodily appetites through penance and self-denial **2** : to subject to humiliation or shame **3** : to become necrotic or gangrenous [Middle French *mortifier* "to mortify, put to death", from Late Latin *mortificare* "to put to death", from Latin *mort-, mors* "death"] — **mor·ti·fi·ca·tion** \\ˌmȯrt-ə-fə-'kā-shən\\ *n*

¹mor·tise *also* **mor·tice** \\'mȯrt-əs\\ *n* : a hole cut in a piece of wood or other material into which a tenon fits so as to form a joint [Middle French *mortaise*]

²mortise *also* **mortice** *vt* **1** : to join or fasten securely especially by a tenon and mortise **2** : to cut a mortise in — **mor·tised** \\-əst\\ *adj*

¹mor·tu·ary \\'mȯr-chə-ˌwer-ē\\ *n, pl* **-ar·ies** : a place in which dead bodies are kept until burial; *esp* : FUNERAL HOME [Medieval Latin *mortuarium,* from Latin *mortuus* "dead", from *mori* "to die"]

²mortuary *adj* : of or relating to death or the burial of the dead

mor·u·la \\'mȯr-ə-lə, 'mär-, -yə-lə\\ *n, pl* **-lae** \\-ˌlē, -ˌlī\\ *or* **-las** : an early embryo that is a solid mass of cells and typically precedes the blastula [New Latin, from Latin *morum* "mulberry"]

mo·sa·ic \\mō-'zā-ik\\ *n* **1** : a surface decoration made by inlaying small pieces of variously colored material to form pictures or patterns; *also* : the process of making it **2** : a picture or design made in mosaic **3** : something resembling a mosaic; *esp* : a virus disease of plants characterized by mottling of the foliage **4** : the part of a television camera tube consisting of many minute particles that convert light to an electric charge [Middle French *mosaique,* from Italian *mosaico,* from Medieval Latin *musaicum,* derived from Latin *Musa* "Muse"] — **mosaic** *adj* — **mo·sa·i·cal·ly** \\-'zā-i-kə-lē, -klē\\ *adv*

Mos·lem \\'mäz-ləm *also* 'mäs-\\ *variant of* MUSLIM

mosque \\'mäsk\\ *n* : a Muslim place of worship [Middle French *mosquee,* from Italian *moschea,* from Spanish *mezquita,* from Arabic *masjid,* from *sajada* "to prostrate oneself"]

mos·qui·to \\mə-'skēt-ō\\ *n, pl* **-toes** *also* **-tos** : any of numerous two-winged flies having females with a needlelike proboscis adapted to puncture the skin of animals and suck their blood [Spanish, from *mosca* "fly", from Latin *musca*] — **mos·qui·to·ey** \\-'skēt-ə-wē\\ *adj*

mosquito net *n* : a net for keeping out mosquitoes

moss \\'mȯs\\ *n* **1** : any of a class (Musci) of plants without flowers but with small leafy often tufted stems growing in patches and bearing sex organs at the tip **2** : any of various plants (as lichens) resembling mosses [Old English *mōs* "bog, swamp"] — **moss·like** \\-ˌlīk\\ *adj*

moss animal *n* : BRYOZOAN

moss pink *n* : a low tufted perennial phlox widely cultivated for its abundant usually pink or white flowers

mossy \\'mȯ-sē\\ *adj* **moss·i·er; -est 1** : covered with moss or something like moss ⟨a *mossy* grave⟩ **2** : resembling moss

mossy zinc *n* : a granulated form of zinc made by pouring melted zinc into water

¹most \\'mōst\\ *adj* **1** : the majority of ⟨*most* people⟩ **2** : greatest in quantity, extent, or degree ⟨the *most* ability⟩ [Old English *mǣst*]

²most *adv* **1** : to the greatest or highest degree — often used with an adjective or adverb to form the superlative **2** : to a very great degree ⟨a *most* careful driver⟩

³most *n* : the greatest amount, number, or part — **at most** *or* **at the most** : as an extreme limit ⟨takes an hour at *most*⟩

⁴most *adv* : ALMOST

-most \\ˌmōst\\ *adj suffix* : most ⟨inner*most*⟩ : most toward ⟨head*most*⟩ [Middle English, alteration of Old English *-mest* (as in *formest* "foremost")]

most·ly \\'mōst-lē\\ *adv* : for the greatest part : MAINLY

Most Reverend — used as a title for an archbishop or a Roman Catholic bishop

mot \\'mō\\ *n, pl* **mots** \\'mō, 'mōz\\ : a pithy or witty saying [French, "word, saying", from Latin *muttum* "grunt", from *muttire* "to mutter"]

mote \\'mōt\\ *n* : a small particle : SPECK [Old English *mot*]

mo·tel \\mō-'tel\\ *n* : a building or group of buildings used as a hotel in which the rooms are directly accessible from an outdoor parking area for automobiles [blend of *motor* and *hotel*]

mo·tet \\mō-'tet\\ *n* : a polyphonic choral composition on a sacred text usually without accompaniment [Middle French, from *mot* "word"]

moth \\'mȯth\\ *n, pl* **moths** \\'mȯthz, 'mȯths\\ **1** : CLOTHES MOTH **2** : a usually night-flying insect (order Lepidoptera) often with a stouter body, duller coloring, and proportionately smaller wings than the related butterflies [Old English *moththe*]

moth·ball \\'mȯth-ˌbȯl\\ *n* **1** : a ball (as of naphthalene) used to keep moths out of clothing **2** *pl* : protective storage

moth-eat·en \\'mȯth-ˌēt-n\\ *adj* **1** : eaten into by moth larvae **2 a** : RUN-DOWN 1 **b** : OLD-FASHIONED 1

¹moth·er \\'məth-ər\\ *n* **1 a** : a female parent **b** : a woman in authority; *esp* : the superior of a religious order — often used as a title **2** : an old or elderly woman **3** : SOURCE, ORIGIN ⟨necessity is the *mother* of invention⟩

¹mortar 1

mosquito

\\ə\\ abut	\\ng\\ sing
\\ər\\ further	\\ō\\ bone
\\a\\ mat	\\ȯ\\ saw
\\ā\\ take	\\ȯi\\ coin
\\ä\\ cot, cart	\\th\\ thin
\\aù\\ out	\\th\\ this
\\ch\\ chin	\\ü\\ food
\\e\\ pet	\\ù\\ foot
\\ē\\ easy	\\y\\ yet
\\g\\ go	\\yü\\ few
\\i\\ tip	\\yù\\ cure
\\ī\\ life	\\zh\\ vision
\\j\\ job	

[Old English *mōdor*] — **moth·er·hood** \-,hùd\ *n* —
moth·er·less \-ləs\ *adj* — **moth·er·less·ness** *n*

²**mother** *adj* **1 a :** of, relating to, or being a mother **b :**
being in the relation of a mother to others ⟨a *mother*
church⟩ ⟨a *mother* country⟩ **2 :** derived from or as if
from one's mother

³**mother** *vt* **moth·ered; moth·er·ing** \'məth-ring, -ə-
ring\ **:** to be or act as mother to

⁴**mother** *n* **:** a slimy mass of yeast cells and bacteria that
forms on the surface of fermenting alcoholic liquids
and is added to wine or cider to produce vinegar [re-
lated to Low German *mudde* "mud"]

moth·er·board \'məth-ər-,bōrd, -,bórd\ *n* **:** the main
circuit board especially of a micro-computer

Mother Car·ey's chicken \,məth-ər-,kar-ēz, -,ker-\ *n* **:**
any of several small petrels; *esp* **:** STORM PETREL [origin
unknown]

mother cell *n* **:** a cell that gives rise to other cells usually of a different sort

moth·er·house \'məth-ər-,haùs\ *n* **1 :** the convent in
which the superior of a religious community resides
2 : the original convent of a religious community

Mother Hubbard \,məth-ər-'həb-ərd\ *n* **:** a loose usually
shapeless dress [probably from *Mother Hubbard*,
character in a nursery rhyme]

moth·er–in–law \'məth-ər-ən-,lò, 'məth-ərn-,lò\ *n, pl*
mothers–in–law \-ər-zən-,lò\ **:** the mother of one's
husband or wife

moth·er·land \'məth-ər-,land\ *n* **1 :** the land of origin
of something **2 :** FATHERLAND

moth·er·ly \'məth-ər-lē\ *adj* **1 :** of, relating to, or characteristic of a mother ⟨*motherly* affection⟩ **2 :** resembling a mother **:** MATERNAL — **moth·er·li·ness** \-lē-
nəs\ *n*

moth·er–of–pearl \,məth-ər-əv-'pərl, -ər-ə-'pərl\ *n* **:**
the hard pearly iridescent substance forming the inner
layer of a mollusk shell

Mother's Day *n* **:** the 2d Sunday in May appointed for
the honoring of mothers

mother tongue *n* **1 :** one's native language **2 :** a language from which another language derives

mo·tif \mō-'tēf\ *n* **1 :** a recurring idea or theme **2 :** a
feature in a decoration or design ⟨a flower *motif* in
wallpaper⟩ [French, "motive, motif"]

mo·tile \'mōt-l, 'mō-,tīl\ *adj* **:** exhibiting or being capable of movement [Latin *motus*, past participle of
movēre "to move"] — **mo·til·i·ty** \mō-'til-ət-ē\ *n*

¹**mo·tion** \'mō-shən\ *n* **1 :** a formal proposal for action
made in a deliberative assembly ⟨a *motion* to adjourn⟩
2 : an act, process, or instance of changing place **:**
MOVEMENT [Middle French, from Latin *motio* "movement", from *movēre* "to move"] — **mo·tion·less**
\-ləs\ *adj* — **mo·tion·less·ly** *adv* — **mo·tion·less·ness**
n

²**motion** *vb* **mo·tioned; mo·tion·ing** \'mō-shə-ning,
'mōsh-ning\ **:** to direct or signal by a movement or
gesture

motion picture *n* **1 :** a series of pictures projected on a
screen in rapid succession so as to produce the optical
effect of a continuous picture in which the objects
move **2 :** MOVIE 2

motion sickness *n* **:** sickness induced by motion (as in
travel by air, car, or ship) and characterized by nausea

mo·ti·vate \'mōt-ə-,vāt\ *vt* **:** to provide with a motive **:**
INDUCE — **mo·ti·va·tion** \,mōt-ə-'vā-shən\ *n* — **mo·ti-
va·tion·al** \-shnəl, -shən-l\ *adv* — **mo·ti·va·tive**
\'mōt-ə-,vāt-iv\ *adj*

¹**mo·tive** \'mōt-iv, 2 is *also* mō-'tēv\ *n* **1 :** something
(as a need or desire) that causes a person to act ⟨their
motive in running away was to avoid trouble⟩ **2 :** MO-
TIF 1 [Middle French *motif*, from *motif*, adj., "moving", derived from Latin *movēre* "to move"] — **mo-
tive·less** \-ləs\ *adj* □ SYN MOTIVE, IMPULSE mean a
stimulus to action. MOTIVE implies a desire or emotion
causing the will to act; IMPULSE suggests a driving pow-

er arising from personal temperament often without
explainable cause

²**motive** *adj* **:** of or relating to motion or the causing of
motion ⟨*motive* power⟩

¹**mot·ley** \'mät-lē\ *adj* **1 :** having various colors **2 :** of
various mixed kinds or parts ⟨a *motley* crowd⟩ [Middle
English]

²**motley** *n* **1 :** an old English woolen fabric of mixed
colors **2 a :** a garment of motley constituting the characteristic dress of a court jester **b :** FOOL 2a, JESTER **3 :**
a mixture of diverse elements

mo·to·cross \'mōt-ō-,krós\ *n* **:** a motorcycle race on a
course laid out over natural terrain

mo·to·neu·ron \,mōt-ə-'nü-,rän, -'nyü-; -'nùr-,än,
-'nyùr-\ *n* **:** a nerve cell with its processes that conducts an impulse to a muscle or gland — called also
motor neuron

¹**mo·tor** \'mōt-ər\ *n* **1 :** a small compact engine **2 :** IN-
TERNAL-COMBUSTION ENGINE; *esp* **:** a gasoline engine **3 :**
MOTOR VEHICLE; *esp* **:** AUTOMOBILE **4 :** a rotating machine that transforms electrical energy into mechanical energy [Latin, "one that moves", from *motus*, past
participle of *movēre* "to move"]

²**motor** *adj* **1 :** causing or imparting motion ⟨*motor*
power⟩ **2 a :** of, relating to, or being a nerve or nerve
fiber that conducts an impulse to a muscle or gland
which results in functional activity **b :** concerned with
or involving muscular movement ⟨*motor* areas of the
brain⟩ ⟨a *motor* reaction⟩ **3 a :** equipped with or driv-
en by a motor **b :** of or relating to an automobile **c :**
designed for motor vehicles or motorists

³**motor** *vi* **:** to travel by automobile

mo·tor·bike \'mōt-ər-,bīk\ *n* **:** a small usually lightweight motorcycle

mo·tor·boat \'mōt-ər-,bōt\ *n* **:** a boat propelled by a
motor

motor bus *n* **:** BUS 1a

mo·tor·cade \'mōt-ər-,kād\ *n* **:** a procession of motor
vehicles [*motor*+ *-cade* (as in *cavalcade*)]

mo·tor·car \-,kär\ *n* **:** AUTOMOBILE

motor court *n* **:** MOTEL

mo·tor·cy·cle \'mōt-ər-,sī-kəl\ *n* **:** a 2-wheeled motor
vehicle having one or two saddles — **motorcycle** *vi* —
mo·tor·cy·clist \-,sī-kə-ləst, -kləst\ *n*

motor home *n* **:** an automotive vehicle built on a truck
or bus chassis and equipped as a self-contained traveling home

motor inn *n* **:** a usually multistory urban motel —
called also *motor hotel*

mo·tor·ist \'mōt-ə-rəst\ *n* **:** a person who travels by automobile; *esp* **:** one who drives an automobile

mo·tor·ize \'mōt-ə-,rīz\ *vt* **1 :** to equip with a motor
2 : to equip with motor-driven vehicles for transportation ⟨*motorized* troops⟩ — **mo·tor·iza·tion** \,mōt-ə-rə-
'zā-shən\ *n*

mo·tor·man \'mōt-ər-mən\ *n* **:** an operator of a motor=
driven vehicle (as a streetcar or a subway train)

motor pool *n* **:** a group of motor vehicles centrally controlled (as by a government agency) and dispatched
for use as needed

motor scooter *n* **:** a low 2- or 3-wheeled automotive
vehicle resembling a child's scooter but having a seat

motor torpedo boat *n* **:** PT BOAT

mo·tor·truck \'mōt-ər-,trək\ *n* **:** an automotive truck
for transporting freight

motor vehicle *n* **:** an automotive vehicle not operated
on rails; *esp* **:** one for use on highways

mot·tle \'mät-l\ *n* **1 :** a colored spot **2 :** a pattern of
colored spots or blotches [probably back-formation
from ¹*motley*] — **mottle** *vt* — **mot·tled** \-ld\ *adj* —
mot·tler \'mät-lər, -l-ər\ *n*

mottled enamel *n* **:** spotted tooth enamel caused by
drinking water containing excessive fluorides during
the time calcium salts are being deposited in the teeth

mot·to \'mät-ō\ *n, pl* **mottoes** *also* **mottos** 1 : a sentence, phrase, or word inscribed on something as suitable to its character or use ⟨a *motto* on a sundial⟩ 2 : a short expression of a guiding principle [Italian, from Latin *muttum* "grunt", from *muttire* "to mutter"]

moue \'mü\ *n* : a little grimace : POUT [French, of Germanic origin]

mou·flon *or* **mouf·flon** \mü-'flōⁿ\ *n* : a wild sheep of the mountains of Sardinia and Corsica with large curling horns in the male; *also* : a wild sheep with large horns [French *mouflon*, from Italian dialect *movrone*, from Late Latin *mufro*]

mou·jik \mü-'zhĕk, -'zhik\ *variant of* MUZHIK

mould *variant of* MOLD

moult *variant of* MOLT

¹mound \'maùnd\ *vt* : to form into a mound [origin unknown]

²mound *n* 1 : a small hill or heap of dirt 2 : the slightly elevated ground on which a baseball pitcher stands [origin unknown]

Mound Builder *n* : a member of a prehistoric Amerindian people whose extensive earthworks are found from the Great Lakes down the Mississippi valley to the Gulf of Mexico

¹mount \'maùnt\ *n* : a high hill : MOUNTAIN — used especially before a proper name ⟨*Mount* Everest⟩ [Old English *munt* and Old French *mont*; both from Latin *mont-, mons*]

²mount *vb* 1 **a** : RISE 7a, ASCEND **b** : to go up : CLIMB ⟨*mount* a ladder⟩ 2 **a** : to get up onto ⟨*mount* a platform⟩ **b** : to get astride a horse 3 : to furnish with riding animals or vehicles ⟨*mounted* police⟩ 4 : to increase rapidly in amount ⟨debts *mounting*⟩ 5 **a** : to prepare for use or display by fastening in proper position on a support ⟨*mount* a picture on cardboard⟩ ⟨*mount* an engine⟩ **b** : to prepare (a specimen) for examination or display 6 : to furnish with scenery, properties, and costumes ⟨*mount* a play⟩ 7 : to post as a means of defense or observation ⟨*mount* guard⟩ 8 : to place (as artillery) in position SYN see ASCEND — **mount·er** *n*

³mount *n* 1 : something on which a thing is mounted: as **a** : a jewelry setting **b** : a microscope slide with its accessories (as a cover glass) on which objects are placed for examination 2 : a means of conveyance; *esp* : SADDLE HORSE — **mount·able** \'maùnt-ə-bəl\ *adj*

moun·tain \'maùnt-n\ *n* 1 : a land mass that is higher than a hill 2 : a great quantity or amount ⟨a *mountain* of mail⟩ [Old French *montaigne*, derived from Latin *mont-, mons*]

mountain ash *n* : any of various trees of the rose family with red fruits and compound leaves having numerous leaflets

moun·tain·eer \,maùnt-n-'iər\ *n* 1 : a person who lives in the mountains 2 : a mountain climber — **mountaineer** *vi*

mountain goat *n* : an antelope of the mountains of western North America that has a thick white hairy coat and slightly curved black horns and closely resembles a goat

mountain laurel *n* : a North American evergreen shrub of the heath family with glossy leaves and pink or white cup-shaped flowers

mountain lion *n* : COUGAR

moun·tain·ous \'maùnt-n-əs, 'maùnt-nəs\ *adj* 1 : having many mountains ⟨*mountainous* country⟩ 2 : resembling a mountain especially in size : HUGE ⟨*mountainous* waves⟩ — **moun·tain·ous·ly** *adv* — **moun·tain·ous·ness** *n*

mountain range *n* : a series of mountains or mountain ridges closely related in direction and position

mountain sheep *n* : any of various wild sheep (as a bighorn) inhabiting high mountains

moun·tain·side \'maùnt-n-,sīd\ *n* : the side of a mountain

Mountain time *n* : the time of the 7th time zone west of Greenwich that includes the west central United States

moun·tain·top \'maùnt-n-,täp\ *n* : the summit of a mountain

moun·te·bank \'maùnt-i-,bangk\ *n* 1 : a person who sells quack medicines : QUACK 2 : an unscrupulous impostor : SWINDLER [Italian *montimbanco*] — **moun·te·bank·ery** \-,bang-kə-rē, -krē\ *n*

Mount·ie \'maùnt-ē\ *n* : a member of the Royal Canadian Mounted Police

mount·ing \'maùnt-ing\ *n* 1 : the act of one that mounts 2 : something that serves as a mount : SUPPORT ⟨an engine *mounting*⟩ ⟨a *mounting* for a diamond⟩

mourn \'mōrn, 'mòrn\ *vb* : to feel or show grief or sorrow; *esp* : to grieve over someone's death [Old English *murnan*] — **mourn·er** *n* — **mourn·ing·ly** \-ing-lē\ *adv*

mourn·ful \'mōrn-fəl, 'mòrn-\ *adj* 1 : full of sorrow : SAD ⟨a *mournful* face⟩ 2 : causing sorrow : SADDENING ⟨*mournful* news⟩ 3 : of a melancholy nature ⟨took a *mournful* view of the future⟩ — **mourn·ful·ly** \-fə-lē\ *adv* — **mourn·ful·ness** *n*

mourn·ing \'mōr-ning, 'mòr-\ *n* 1 : an act of grieving 2 : an outward sign (as black clothes or a veil) of grief for a person's death ⟨wear *mourning*⟩ 3 : a period of time during which signs of grief are shown

mourning cloak *n* : a blackish brown butterfly of North America, Europe, and parts of Asia having a broad yellow border on the wings

mourning dove *n* : a wild dove of the United States with a mournful cry

¹mouse \'maùs\ *n, pl* **mice** \'mīs\ 1 : any of numerous small rodents with a pointed snout, rather small ears, an elongated body, and a slender tail 2 : a timid or spiritless person 3 : a dark-colored swelling caused by a blow; *esp* : BLACK EYE [Old English *mūs*]

²mouse \'maùz, 'maùs\ *vb* 1 : to hunt for mice 2 : to search or move stealthily or slowly 3 : to discover by careful searching ⟨*mouse* out a scandal⟩

mous·er \'maù-zər, -sər\ *n* : a catcher of mice and rats; *esp* : a cat proficient at mousing

mouse·trap \'maù-,strap\ *n* : a trap for mice

¹mousse \'müs\ *n* 1 : a light spongy food; *esp* : a molded chilled dessert of sweetened and flavored whipped cream or egg whites and gelatin 2 : a foamy preparation used in styling hair [French, *literally,* "froth", from Late Latin *mulsa* "mixture of honey and water"]

²mousse *vt* **moussed; mouss·ing** : to style (hair) with mousse

mous·tache *variant of* MUSTACHE

mous·ta·chio *variant of* MUSTACHIO

mousy *or* **mous·ey** \'maù-sē, -zē\ *adj* **mous·i·er; -est** : of, relating to, or resembling a mouse: as **a** : TIMID **b** : making no noise **c** : DRAB 1

¹mouth \'maùth\ *n, pl* **mouths** \'maù(th)z, 'maùths\ 1 **a** : the opening through which food passes into the body of an animal **b** : the cavity that encloses in the typical vertebrate the tongue, gums, and teeth 2 : GRIMACE ⟨make a *mouth*⟩ 3 : something that resembles a mouth especially in affording entrance or exit ⟨the *mouth* of a cave⟩ 4 : the place where a stream enters a larger body of water [Old English *mūth*] — **mouthed** \'maùthd, 'maùtht\ *adj* — **mouth·like** \'maùth-,līk\ *adj* — **down in the mouth** : DEPRESSED 1

²mouth \'maùth\ *vb* 1 **a** : UTTER 2, PRONOUNCE **b** : to utter loudly or pompously **c** : to repeat without understanding or sincerity ⟨*mouth* platitudes⟩ 2 : to take into the mouth; *esp* : EAT — **mouth·er** \'maù-thər\ *n*

mouth·breed·er \'maùth-,brēd-ər\ *n* : a fish that carries its eggs and young in its mouth

mouth·ful \'maùth-,fùl\ *n* 1 : as much as the mouth will hold; *also* : the amount put into the mouth at one time 2 : a word or phrase that is very long or difficult to say

mouflon

mountain goat

\ə\ abut	\ng\ sing
\ər\ further	\ō\ bone
\a\ mat	\ò\ saw
\ā\ take	\òi\ coin
\ä\ cot, cart	\th\ thin
\aù\ out	\th\ this
\ch\ chin	\ü\ food
\e\ pet	\ù\ foot
\ē\ easy	\y\ yet
\g\ go	\yü\ few
\i\ tip	\yù\ cure
\ī\ life	\zh\ vision
\j\ job	

mouth hook *n* : one of a pair of clawlike structures that occur on either side of the mouth opening of some fly larvae and function as jaws

mouth organ *n* : HARMONICA

mouth·part \'maùth-ˌpärt\ *n* : a structure or appendage near the mouth

mouth·piece \-ˌpēs\ *n* **1** : something placed at or held in the mouth **2** : a part (as of an instrument) to which the mouth is held ⟨a telephone *mouthpiece*⟩ **3 a** : one that expresses another's views : SPOKESPERSON **b** *slang* : a criminal lawyer

mouth-to-mouth *adj* : of, relating to, or being a method of artificial respiration in which the rescuer's mouth is placed tightly over the victim's mouth in order to force air into the lungs by blowing forcefully enough every few seconds to inflate them

mouth·wash \-ˌwȯsh, -ˌwäsh\ *n* : a usually antiseptic liquid preparation for cleaning the mouth and teeth or freshening the breath

mouthy \'maù-thē, -thē\ *adj* **mouth·i·er; -est** **1** : excessively talkative **2** : given to or marked by bombast

mou·ton \'mü-ˌtän\ *n* : processed sheepskin that has been sheared and dyed to resemble beaver or seal [French, "sheep, mutton"]

¹**mov·able** *or* **move·able** \'mü-və-bəl\ *adj* **1** : capable of being moved ⟨*movable* property⟩ **2** : changing date from year to year ⟨Easter is a *movable* holiday⟩ — **mov·abil·i·ty** \ˌmü-və-'bil-ət-ē\ *n* — **mov·able·ness** *n* — **mov·ably** \'mü-və-blē\ *adv*

²**movable** *or* **moveable** *n* : a piece of property (as an article of furniture) that can be moved

¹**move** \'müv\ *vb* **1** : to change the place or position of : SHIFT ⟨*move* the chair closer⟩ **2** : to go from one place to another ⟨*move* into the shade⟩ **3** : to proceed in a given direction or toward a given condition ⟨*moved* ahead in business⟩ **4** : to set in motion ⟨*moved* their feet⟩ **5 a** : to cause a person to act or decide : PERSUADE ⟨*moved* me to change my mind⟩ **b** : to take action : ACT **6** : to affect the feelings of ⟨the sad story *moved* them to tears⟩ **7 a** : to propose something formally in a deliberative assembly ⟨*move* that the meeting adjourn⟩ **b** : to present a motion or make an appeal **8** : to change hands or cause to change hands through sale or rental ⟨the store's stock must be *moved*⟩ **9 a** : to change residence ⟨*move* to Iowa⟩ **b** : to change position or posture : STIR ⟨don't *move*⟩ **10** : to cause to operate or function : ACTUATE ⟨*move* the handle to increase pressure⟩ **11** : to live one's life in a specified environment ⟨*moves* in high circles⟩ **12** : to go away : DEPART ⟨made the crowd *move* on⟩ **13** : to transfer a piece in a game (as chess or checkers) from one place to another **14** : to evacuate or cause to evacuate ⟨the medicine *moves* the bowels⟩ [Middle French *movoir*, from Latin *movēre*] □ SYN MOVE, ACTUATE, DRIVE, IMPEL mean to set or keep in motion. MOVE is very general and implies no more than the fact of changing position; ACTUATE stresses the transmission of power so as to work or set in motion; DRIVE implies imparting continuous forward motion and often stresses the effect rather than the impetus; IMPEL implies a greater impetus producing more headlong action.

²**move** *n* **1 a** : the act of moving a piece in a game **b** : the turn of a player to move **2 a** : a step taken to gain an objective : MANEUVER **b** : the action of moving : MOVEMENT **c** : a change of residence or location — **on the move** **1** : in a state of moving from one place to another **2** : in a state of making progress

move·less \'müv-ləs\ *adj* : not moving — **move·less·ly** *adv* — **move·less·ness** *n*

move·ment \'müv-mənt\ *n* **1 a** : the act or process of moving **b** : an instance or manner of moving ⟨observe the *movement* of a star⟩ **c** : ACTION, ACTIVITY ⟨a lot of *movement* in the crowd⟩ **2** : TENDENCY, TREND ⟨a *movement* toward fairer pricing⟩ **3 a** : a series of actions taken by a group to achieve an objective ⟨a *move-*

ment for reform⟩ **b** : the group taking part in such a series ⟨joined the *movement*⟩ **4** : a mechanical arrangement (as of wheels) for causing a particular motion (as in a clock or watch) **5 a** : RHYTHM 2 **b** : CADENCE 1a, TEMPO **c** : a section of a longer piece of music ⟨a *movement* in a symphony⟩ **6** : an emptying of the bowels or the matter emptied

mov·er \'mü-vər\ *n* : one that moves or sets in motion; *esp* : a person or company that moves the belongings of others from one home or place of business to another

mov·ie \'mü-vē\ *n* **1** : MOTION PICTURE 1 **2 a** : a representation of a story or other subject matter by means of motion pictures **b** : a showing of a motion picture — often used in pl. with the **3** *pl* : the motion-picture industry [*moving picture*]

mov·ing \'mü-ving\ *adj* **1 a** : marked by or capable of moving ⟨a machine with *moving* parts⟩ **b** : of or relating to a change of residence ⟨a *moving* van⟩ **2** : causing motion or action **3** : having the power to affect feelings or sympathies — **mov·ing·ly** \-ving-lē\ *adv*

moving picture *n* : MOTION PICTURE 1

¹**mow** \'maù\ *n* **1** : a stack of hay or straw especially in a barn **2** : the part of a barn where hay or straw is stored [Old English *mūga* "heap, stack"]

²**mow** \'mō\ *vb* **mowed; mowed** *or* **mown** \'mōn\; **mowing** **1** : to cut down with a scythe or machine ⟨*mow* hay⟩ **2** : to cut the standing herbage from ⟨*mow* a lawn⟩ **3** : to kill or destroy in great numbers ⟨machine guns *mowed* down the attackers⟩ **4** : to overcome decisively [Old English *māwan*] — **mow·er** \'mō-ər, 'mȯr\ *n*

mowing machine *n* : an implement with blades for cutting standing grass or grain

mox·ie \'mäk-sē\ *n* **1** : ENERGY 1, PEP **2** : BRAVERY 2, COURAGE [from *Moxie*, a trademark for a soft drink]

moz·za·rel·la \ˌmät-sə-'rel-ə\ *n* : a moist white cheese with a mild flavor and smooth texture [Italian]

Mr. \ˌmis-tər\ *n, pl* **Messrs.** \ˌmes-ərz\ **1** — used as a courtesy title before the name of a man **2** — used as a form of respectful address to a high-ranking man and followed by a designation of his rank or office ⟨*Mr.* President⟩ **3** — used before the name of a place, an activity, or an epithet to form a title for a man representing the thing indicated ⟨*Mr.* Baseball⟩ [*Mr.* from Middle English, abbreviation of *maister* "master"; *Messrs.* abbreviation of *Messieurs*, from French, pl. of *Monsieur*]

Mrs. \ˌmis-əz, -əs; *especially South* ˌmiz-əz, -əs, (for sense 1) miz, ˌmis, before given names mis, ˌmis\ *n, pl* **Mes·dames** \mā-'däm, -'dam\ **1** — used as a courtesy title before the name of a married woman **2** — used before the name of a place, an activity, or an epithet to form a title for a married woman representing the thing indicated ⟨*Mrs.* America⟩ [*Mrs.* from abbreviation of *mistress*; *Mesdames* from French, pl. of *Madame*]

Ms. \ˌmiz, 'miz\ *n* — used instead of *Miss* or *Mrs.* as a courtesy title for a woman whose marital status is unknown or irrelevant ⟨*Ms.* Mary Smith⟩ [probably blend of *Miss* and *Mrs.*]

mu \'myü, 'mü\ *n* : the 12th letter of the Greek alphabet — M or μ

¹**much** \'məch\ *adj* **more** \'mȯr, 'mȯr\; **most** \'mōst\ : great in quantity, amount, extent, or degree ⟨has *much* money⟩ ⟨takes too *much* time⟩ [Middle English *michel, muchel, muche* "large, much", from Old English *micel, mycel*]

²**much** *adv* **more; most** **1 a** : to a great degree or extent : CONSIDERABLY ⟨*much* happier⟩ **b** (1) : many times : OFTEN (2) : LONG 1 **2** : just about : NEARLY ⟨*much* the same⟩

³**much** *n* **1** : a great quantity, amount, extent, or degree **2** : something considerable or impressive

mu·ci·lage \'myü-sə-lij, -slij\ *n* **1** : a gelatinous substance especially from seaweeds that contains protein and carbohydrates and is similar to plant gums **2** : an aqueous solution of a gum or similar substance used especially as an adhesive [Late Latin *mucilagin-*, *mucilago* "musty juice, mucus", from Latin *mucus*]

mu·ci·lag·i·nous \,myü-sə-'laj-ə-nəs\ *adj* **1** : STICKY 1a, VISCID **2** : producing or full of mucilage — **mu·ci·lag·i·nous·ly** *adv*

mu·cin \'myüs-n\ *n* : any of various complex proteins found as viscid solutions in animal secretions and tissues [*mucus*] — **mu·cin·ous** \-əs\ *adj*

muck \'mək\ *n* **1** : soft moist barnyard manure **2** : DIRT 1a, FILTH **3 a** : dark highly organic soil **b** : MIRE 2, MUD [Middle English *muk*] — **mucky** \'mək-ē\ *adj*

muck·rake \'mək-,rāk\ *vi* : to search out and expose publicly real or seeming misconduct of prominent people [obsolete *muckrake*, n., "rake for dung"] — **muck·rak·er** *n*

mu·co·sa \myü-'kō-zə\ *n, pl* **-sae** \-,zē, -,zī\ *or* **-sas** : MUCOUS MEMBRANE [New Latin, from Latin *mucosus* "mucous"] — **mu·co·sal** \-zəl\ *adj*

mu·cous \'myü-kəs\ *adj* **1** : of, relating to, or resembling mucus ⟨*mucous* discharges⟩ **2** : secreting or containing mucus ⟨a *mucous* gland⟩ [Latin *mucosus*, from *mucus* "mucus"]

mucous membrane *n* : a membrane rich in mucous glands; *esp* : one that lines body passages and cavities which communicate directly or indirectly with the exterior

mu·cro \'myü-,krō\ *n, pl* **mu·cro·nes** \myü-'krō-,nēz\ : an abrupt sharp terminal point (as of a leaf) [Latin *mucron-*, *mucro* "point, edge"] — **mu·cro·nate** \'myü-krə-,nāt\ *adj*

mu·cus \'myü-kəs\ *n* : a slippery animal secretion produced especially by mucous membranes which it moistens and protects [Latin, "nasal mucus"] — **mu·coid** \-,kȯid\ *adj*

mud \'məd\ *n* : soft wet earth [Middle English *mudde*, probably from Low German]

mud dauber *n* : any of various wasps that construct mud cells in which the female places an egg with spiders or insects paralyzed by a sting to serve as food for the larva

¹mud·dle \'məd-l\ *vb* **mud·dled; mud·dling** \'məd-ling, -l-ing\ **1** : CONFUSE 1b, BEFUDDLE ⟨*muddled* by too much advice⟩ **2** : to throw into disorder ⟨*muddle* the household accounts⟩ **3** : to think or act in a confused aimless way ⟨*muddle* through a task⟩ [probably from obsolete Dutch *moddelen*, from *modde* "mud"] — **mud·dler** \'məd-lər, -l-ər\ *n*

²muddle *n* **1** : a state of confusion **2** : a confused mess

mud·dle·head·ed \,məd-l-'hed-əd\ *adj* **1** : mentally confused **2** : INEPT 4, BUNGLING — **mud·dle·head·ed·ness** *n*

¹mud·dy \'məd-ē\ *adj* **mud·di·er; -est** **1** : filled or covered with mud **2** : resembling or suggesting mud ⟨a *muddy* color⟩ ⟨a *muddy* flavor⟩ **3** : not clear or bright : DULL, CLOUDY ⟨a *muddy* complexion⟩ **4** : CONFUSED, MUDDLED ⟨*muddy* thinking⟩ — **mud·di·ly** \'məd-l-ē\ *adv* — **mud·di·ness** \'məd-ē-nəs\ *n*

²muddy *vt* **mud·died; mud·dy·ing** **1** : to soil or stain with or as if with mud **2** : to make turbid **3** : to make cloudy or dull **4** : CONFUSE 2

mud·guard \'məd-,gärd\ *n* **1** : FENDER d **2** : SPLASH GUARD

mud puppy *n* : any of several large American salamanders; *esp* : HELLBENDER

mud·sling·er \'məd-,sling-ər\ *n* : one that uses abusive tactics (as invective or slander) especially against a political opponent — **mud·sling·ing** \-,sling-ing\ *n*

mud·stone \'məd-,stōn\ *n* : a hardened shale produced by the consolidation of mud

mud turtle *n* : a bottom-dwelling freshwater turtle (as a musk turtle)

Muen·ster \'mən-stər, 'mün-, 'myün-, 'mun-\ *n* : a semisoft cheese whose flavor may be bland or sharp [*Münster, Munster*, France]

mu·ez·zin \mü-'ez-n, myü-\ *n* : a Muslim crier who calls the hours of daily prayers [Arabic *mu'adhdhin*]

¹muff \'məf\ *n* : a warm tube-shaped cover for the hands [Dutch *mof*, from Middle French *moufle* "mitten", from Medieval Latin *muffula*]

²muff *n* : a bungling performance; *esp* : a failure to hold a ball in attempting a catch — **muff** *vb*

muf·fin \'məf-ən\ *n* : a bread made of egg batter and baked in individual servings [probably from Low German *muffen*, pl. of *muffe* "cake"]

muf·fle \'məf-əl\ *vt* **muf·fled; muf·fling** \'məf-ling, -ə-ling\ **1** : to wrap up so as to conceal or protect **2** : to deaden the sound of **3** : to keep down : SUPPRESS ⟨*muffled* the opposition⟩ [Middle English *muflen*]

muf·fler \'məf-lər\ *n* **1** : a scarf for the neck **2** : a device that deadens noises; *esp* : one forming part of the exhaust system of an automotive vehicle

¹muf·ti \'məf-tē\ *n* : a professional jurist who interprets Muslim law [Arabic *muftī*]

²mufti *n* : civilian clothes

¹mug \'məg\ *n* **1** : a usually large cylindrical drinking cup **2** : the face or mouth of a person **3** : a stupid or criminal person [origin unknown]

²mug *vb* **mugged; mug·ging** **1** : to make faces especially to attract attention **2** : PHOTOGRAPH; *esp* : to take a police photograph of

³mug *vt* **mugged; mug·ging** : to assault with intent to rob [back-formation from *²mugger*]

¹mug·ger \'məg-ər\ *n* : a common usually harmless freshwater crocodile of southeastern Asia [Hindi *magar*, from Sanskrit *makara* "water monster"]

²mugger *n* : one that attacks with intent to rob [probably from obsolete *mug* "to punch in the face"]

mug·gy \'məg-ē\ *adj* **mug·gi·er; -est** : being warm, damp, and stifling [English dialect *mug* "drizzle"] — **mug·gi·ly** \'məg-ə-lē\ *adv* — **mug·gi·ness** \'məg-ē-nəs\ *n*

mu·gho pine \,mü-gō-, myü-\ *n* : a shrubby spreading pine widely grown as an ornamental [probably from French *mugho* "mugho pine", from Italian *mugo*]

mug·wump \'məg-,wəmp\ *n* **1** : a bolter from the Republican party in 1884 **2** : a person who is undecided or neutral in politics [obsolete slang, "chief, kingpin", from Natick (an American Indian language of Massachusetts) *mugwomp* "captain"] □ ORIGIN When James G. Blaine received the Republican Party's nomination for the presidency in 1884, many Republicans refused to have anything to do with his candidacy, supporting instead the Democratic candidate, Grover Cleveland. Those Republicans who remained loyal to their party accused the bolters of a lofty and supercilious attitude and nicknamed them *mugwumps*. The word had previously been used as a jesting term for someone who considered himself a great man. *Mugwump* originally came from *mugwomp*, a word meaning "captain" in the American Indian language Natick.

Mu·ham·mad·an *or* **Mo·ham·med·an** \mō-'ham-əd-ən, mü-\ *n* : MUSLIM — **Muhammadan** *adj* — **Mu·ham·mad·an·ism** \-əd-ə-,niz-əm\ *n*

mu·ja·hid·een *or* **mu·ja·hed·in** *also* **mu·ja·hed·een** \mü-,ja-hid-'ēn, mu-, -,jä-\ *n pl* : Islamic guerrilla fighters especially in the Middle East [Arabic *mujāhid*, literally, person who wages religious war]

muk·luk \'mək-,lək\ *n* **1** : an Eskimo boot of sealskin or reindeer skin **2** : a boot with a soft leather sole often worn over several pairs of socks [Eskimo *muklok* "large seal"]

mu·lat·to \mu-'lat-ō, myü-\ *n, pl* **-toes** *or* **-tos** **1** : a person with one Negro and one white parent **2** : a person of mixed white and Negro descent [Spanish *mulato*, from *mulo* "mule", from Latin *mulus*]

mud turtle

\ə\	abut	\ng\	sing
\ər\	further	\ō\	bone
\a\	mat	\ȯ\	saw
\ā\	take	\ȯi\	coin
\ä\	cot, cart	\th\	thin
\au̇\	out	\t͟h\	this
\ch\	chin	\ü\	food
\e\	pet	\u̇\	foot
\ē\	easy	\y\	yet
\g\	go	\yü\	few
\i\	tip	\yu̇\	cure
\ī\	life	\zh\	vision
\j\	job		

¹mule 1a

mul·ber·ry \'məl-ˌber-ē\ *n* **1** : any of a genus of trees with edible usually purple fruits; *also* : this fruit **2** : a dark purple or purplish black [Middle English *murberie, mulberie*, from Old French *moure* "mulberry", from Latin *morum*, from Greek *moron*]

mulch \'məlch\ *n* : a protective covering (as of straw, compost, or paper) used on the ground especially to reduce evaporation, prevent erosion, control weeds, or enrich the soil; *also* : the material used [perhaps from English dialect *melch* "soft, mild"] — **mulch** *vt*

¹**mulct** \'məlkt\ *n* : a fine imposed as a punishment [Latin *multa, mulcta*]

²**mulct** *vt* **1** : to punish by a fine **2 a** : to defraud especially of money : SWINDLE **b** : to obtain (as money) by fraud, duress, or theft

¹**mule** \'myül\ *n* **1 a** : a hybrid between a horse and a donkey; *esp* : the offspring of a male donkey and a mare **b** : a usually sterile hybrid plant or animal **2** : a very stubborn person **3** : a machine for drawing and twisting fiber into yarn or thread and winding it onto spindles [Old French *mul*, from Latin *mulus*]

²**mule** *n* : a slipper whose upper does not extend around the heel of the foot [Middle French, a kind of slipper, from Latin *mulleus* "shoe worn by magistrates"]

mule deer *n* : a long-eared deer of western North America that is larger and more heavily built than the common white-tailed deer

mule skinner *n* : a driver of mules

mu·le·teer \ˌmyü-lə-'tiər\ *n* : a driver of mules [French *muletier*, from *mulet* "mule", from Old French *mul*]

mu·ley *also* **mul·ley** \'myü-lē, 'mül-ē\ *adj* : having no horns; *esp* : naturally hornless ⟨a *muley* cow⟩ [of Celtic origin]

mul·ish \'myü-lish\ *adj* : STUBBORN 1a, OBSTINATE — **mul·ish·ly** *adv* — **mul·ish·ness** *n*

¹**mull** \'məl\ *vb* : to consider at length : PONDER ⟨*mull* over an idea⟩ [Middle English *mullen* "to grind, pulverize", from *mul* "dust"]

²**mull** *vt* : to sweeten, spice, and heat ⟨*mulled* wine⟩ [origin unknown]

³**mull** *n* : granular forest humus with a layer of mixed organic matter and mineral soil merging gradually into the mineral soil beneath [German, from Danish *muld*, from Old Norse *mold* "dust, soil"]

mul·lah \'məl-ə, 'mül-ə\ *n* : a Muslim of a class trained in traditional law and doctrine; *esp* : one who is head of a mosque [Hindi *mulla*, from Arabic *mawlā*]

mul·lein *also* **mul·len** \'məl-ən\ *n* : a tall herb having coarse woolly leaves and spikes of usually yellow flowers [Anglo-French *moleine*]

mul·let \'məl-ət\ *n, pl* **mullet** *or* **mullets** **1** : any of a family of largely gray food fishes **2** : any of a family of moderate-sized usually red or golden fishes with two barbels on the chin [Middle French *mulet*, from Latin *mullos* "red mullet", from Greek *myllos*]

mul·li·gan \'məl-i-gən\ *n* : a stew basically of vegetables and meat or fish [probably from the name *Mulligan*]

mul·li·ga·taw·ny \ˌməl-i-gə-'tȯ-nē, -'tän-ē\ *n* : a soup usually of chicken stock seasoned with curry [Tamil *miḷakutaṇṇi*, a strongly seasoned soup, from *miḷaku* "pepper" + *taṇṇi* "water"]

mul·lion \'məl-yən\ *n* : a slender vertical bar between units of windows, doors, or screens [probably from earlier *monial* "mullion", from Middle French *moinel*] — **mullion** *vt*

multi- *combining form* **1 a** : many : multiple : much ⟨*multi*valent⟩ **b** : more than two ⟨*multi*lateral⟩ **c** : more than one ⟨*multi*stage⟩ **2** : many times over ⟨*multi*millionaire⟩ [Latin, from *multus* "much, many"]

See *multi-* and 2d element

multiage	multiarmed	multibarreled
multiagency	multiaxial	multibillion

multibillionaire	multifocal	multipolar
multibladed	multifunction	multipole
multibranched	multifunctional	multipotential
multibuilding	multigenerational	multipower
multicampus	multigenic	multiproblem
multicar	multigrade	multiproduct
multicausal	multihandicapped	multipronged
multicelled	multiheaded	multipurpose
multicenter	multihospital	multiroom
multichambered	multihued	multiservice
multichannel	multiindustry	multisided
multicharacter	multiinstitutional	multisite
multicity	multilane	multisize
multicolor	multilayered	multiskilled
multicolumn	multilevel	multisource
multicomponent	multilobed	multispeed
multicounty	multimanned	multistep
multicurrency	multimember	multistory
multidialectal	multimetallic	multisyllabic
multidimensional	multimillennial	multisystem
multidirectional	multimillion	multitalented
multidisciplinary	multimodal	multitiered
multidiscipline	multimolecular	multitone
multidivisional	multinational	multitowered
multielement	multiparameter	multitrack
multiengine	multipart	multiunion
multiethnic	multipartite	multiunit
multifaceted	multiparty	multiuse
multifamily	multiphasic	multiwarhead
multifilament	multiplant	multiyear

mul·ti·cel·lu·lar \ˌməl-ti-'sel-yə-lər, -ˌtī-\ *adj* : having or consisting of many cells — **mul·ti·cel·lu·lar·i·ty** \-ˌsel-yə-'lar-ət-ē\ *n*

mul·ti·col·ored \ˌməl-ti-'kəl-ərd\ *adj* : having or including many colors

mul·ti·cul·tur·al *adj* : of, relating to, reflecting, or adapted to diverse cultures ⟨a *multicultural* society⟩ — **mul·ti·cul·tur·al·ism** \-rə-ˌliz-schwam\ *n*

mul·ti·far·i·ous \ˌməl-tə-'far-ē-əs, -'fer-\ *adj* : of various kinds : being many and varied ⟨the *multifarious* complexities of language⟩ [Latin *multifarius*] — **mul·ti·far·i·ous·ly** *adv* — **mul·ti·far·i·ous·ness** *n*

mul·ti·flo·ra rose \ˌməl-tə-ˌflōr-ə-, -ˌflȯr-\ *n* : a vigorous thorny rose that produces clusters of small flowers and is used for hedges

mul·ti·fold \'məl-ti-ˌfōld\ *adj* : MANIFOLD 1

mul·ti·form \'məl-ti-ˌfȯrm\ *adj* : having many forms, shapes, or appearances

mul·ti·lat·er·al \ˌməl-ti-'lat-ə-rəl, -ˌtī-, -'la-trəl\ *adj* **1** : having many sides **2** : involving more than two nations or parties ⟨a *multilateral* treaty⟩ — **mul·ti·lat·er·al·ly** \-ē\ *adv*

mul·ti·mil·lion·aire \-ˌmil-yə-'naər, -'neər, -'mil-yə-,\ *n* : a person whose wealth amounts to many millions (as of dollars)

mul·ti·nu·cle·ate \-'nü-klē-ət, -'nyü-\ *adj* : having more than two nuclei

mul·ti·par·tite \ˌməl-ti-'pär-ˌtīt\ *adj* : having numerous members or signatories ⟨a *multipartite* treaty⟩

¹**mul·ti·ple** \'məl-tə-pəl\ *adj* : containing, involving, or consisting of more than one ⟨*multiple* copies⟩ [French, from Latin *multiplex*, from *multi-* + *-plex* "-fold"]

²**multiple** *n* : the product of a quantity by an integer ⟨35 is a *multiple* of 7⟩

multiple allele *n* : any of a group of more than two different alleles any two of which can make up a particular gene pair on homologous chromosomes

multiple–choice *adj* : having several answers given from which the correct one is to be chosen ⟨a *multiple-choice* question⟩

multiple fruit *n* : a fruit (as a mulberry) formed from a cluster of flowers

multiple sclerosis *n* : a disease marked by patches of hardened tissue in the brain or spinal cord resulting in partial or complete paralysis and muscular twitching

¹**mul·ti·plex** \'məl-tə-ˌpleks\ *adj* **1** : MULTIPLE **2** : being or relating to a system of transmitting several messages simultaneously on the same circuit or channel [Latin]

²**mutiplex** *n* : a complex that houses several movie the-aters

mul·ti·pli·cand \,məl-tə-pli-'kand\ *n* : the number that is to be multiplied by another [Latin *multiplicandus* "to be multiplied", from *multiplicare* "to multiply"]

mul·ti·pli·ca·tion \,məl-tə-plə-'kā-shən\ *n* **1** : the act or process of multiplying **2 a** : a mathematical opera-tion that at its simplest is an abbreviated process of adding an integer to itself a specified number of times and that is extended to other numbers in accordance with laws that are valid for integers **b** : a similar math-ematical operation defined for sets of mathematical el-ements (as matrices or complex numbers) other than the real numbers — **mul·ti·pli·ca·tive** \,məl-tə-'plik-ət-iv, 'məl-tə-plə-,kāt-\ *adj* — **mul·ti·pli·ca·tive·ly** *adv*

multiplicative identity *n* : an identity element in a set that when multiplied by any element of the set leaves the element unchanged ⟨the integer 1 is a *multiplica-tive identity* element in the set of all real numbers⟩

multiplicative inverse *n* : an element of a mathematical set that when multiplied by a given element gives the identity element

mul·ti·plic·i·ty \,məl-tə-'plis-ət-ē\ *n, pl* **-ties 1** : the quality or state of being multiple or various **2** : a great number ⟨a *multiplicity* of ideas⟩

mul·ti·pli·er \'məl-tə-,plī-ər, -,plīr\ *n* : one that multi-plies: as **a** : a number by which another is multiplied **b** : a device for multiplying or for intensifying some effect

mul·ti·ply \'məl-tə-,plī\ *vb* **-plied; -ply·ing 1 a** : to in-crease in number : make or become more numerous **b** : to produce offspring : BREED, PROPAGATE **2 a** : to find the product of by multiplication ⟨*multiply* 7 and 8⟩ **b** : to perform the operation of multiplication [Old French *multiplier*, from Latin *multiplicare*, from *multiplex* "multiple"]

mul·ti·ra·cial \,məl-ti-'rā-shəl, -,tī-\ *adj* : composed of, relating to, or representing various races

mul·ti·stage \-,stāj\ *adj* : operating in or involving two or more steps or stages ⟨a *multistage* rocket⟩

mul·ti·tude \'məl-tə-,tüd, -,tyüd\ *n* : a very great num-ber of things or people : HOST [Latin *multitudin-, mul-titudo*, from *multus* "much"] □ SYN CROWD, THRONG, MOB: MULTITUDE implies great numbers ⟨a *multitude* of stars⟩ CROWD stresses packing together and loss of indi-viduality ⟨a *crowd* of onlookers⟩ THRONG suggests a crowd in motion ⟨people came to the fair in *throngs*⟩ MOB implies disorganization and agitation and in spe-cific use the intent of violence ⟨police dispersed the *mob*⟩

mul·ti·tu·di·nous \,məl-tə-'tüd-nəs, -'tyüd-, -n-əs\ *adj* : consisting of a multitude ⟨a *multitudinous* gathering⟩ — **mul·ti·tu·di·nous·ly** *adv* — **mul·ti·tu·di·nous·ness** *n*

mul·ti·va·lent \,məl-ti-'vā-lənt, -,tī-\ *adj* : POLYVALENT

mul·ti·vi·ta·min \-'vīt-ə-mən\ *adj* : containing several vitamins and especially all known to be essential to health ⟨a *multivitamin* formula⟩

mul·ti·vol·ume \-'väl-yəm, -,yüm\ *or* **mul·ti·vol·umed** \-,yəmd, -,yümd\ *adj* : composed of several volumes

¹**mum** \'məm\ *adj* : SILENT ⟨keep *mum*⟩ [probably imi-tative of a sound made with closed lips]

²**mum** *n* : CHRYSANTHEMUM

mum·ble \'məm-bəl\ *vb* **mum·bled; mum·bling** \-bə-ling, -bling\ **1** : to speak indistinctly usually with lips partly closed ⟨*mumble* one's words⟩ **2** : to chew or bite with or as if with toothless gums ⟨a baby *mum-bling* its food⟩ [Middle English *momelen*] — **mumble** *n* — **mum·bler** \-bə-lər, -blər\ *n* — **mum·bling·ly** \-bling-lē\ *adv*

mum·ble·ty-peg \'məm-bəl-tē-,peg, -bəl-,peg\ *n* : a game in which the players try to flip a knife from vari-ous positions so that the blade will stick into the ground [from the phrase *mumble the peg*; from the

loser's originally having to pull out with his teeth a peg driven into the ground]

mum·bo jum·bo \,məm-bō-'jəm-bō\ *n* **1** : an object of superstitious homage and fear **2 a** : a complicated ritu-al with elaborate trappings **b** : complicated activity or language that obscures and confuses [*Mumbo Jumbo*, an idol or deity held to have been worshiped in Africa]

mum·mer \'məm-ər\ *n* **1** : an actor especially in a pan-tomime **2** : one who goes merrymaking in disguise during festivals [Middle French *momeur*, from *mom-er* "to go masked"]

mum·mery \'məm-ə-rē\ *n, pl* **-mer·ies 1** : a perfor-mance by mummers **2** : a ridiculous or pompous cere-mony

mum·mi·fy \'məm-i-,fī\ *vb* **-fied; -fy·ing 1** : to embalm and dry as a mummy **2** : to dry up like the skin of a mummy : SHRIVEL — **mum·mi·fi·ca·tion** \,məm-i-fə-'kā-shən\ *n*

mum·my \'məm-ē\ *n, pl* **mummies 1** : a body em-balmed for burial in the manner of the ancient Egyptians **2** : an unusually well-preserved body [Mid-dle French *momie* "powdered parts of a mummy used as a drug", from Medieval Latin *mumia* "mummy, powdered mummy", from Arabic *mūmiyah* "bitu-men, mummy", from Persian *mūm* "wax"]

mumps \'məmps\ *n sing or pl* : an acute contagious virus disease marked by fever and by swelling espe-cially of salivary glands [obsolete *mump* "grimace"]

munch \'mənch\ *vb* : to chew with a crunching sound ⟨*munch* on celery⟩ [Middle English *monchen*] — **munch·er** *n*

mun·dane \,mən-'dān, 'mən-, *adj* **1** : of or relating to the world : WORLDLY **2** : concerned with the practical, immediate, andordinary ⟨*mundane* problems of every-day life⟩ [Middle French *mondain*, from Late Latin *mondanus*, from Latin *mundus* "world"] SYN see EARTHLY — **mun·dane·ly** *adv*

mu·nic·i·pal \myü-'nis-ə-pəl\ *adj* **1** : of or relating to the internal affairs of a nation **2** : of or relating to a municipality ⟨*municipal* government⟩ [Latin *munici-palis* "of a municipality", from *municeps* "inhabitant of a municipality", from *munus* "duty" + *capere* "to take"] — **mu·nic·i·pal·ly** \-pə-lē, -plē\ *adv*

mu·nic·i·pal·i·ty \myù-,nis-ə-'pal-ət-ē\ *n, pl* **-ties** : a primarily urban political unit (as a city or town) hav-ing corporate status and usually powers of self-govern-ment

mu·nif·i·cent \myù-'nif-ə-sənt\ *adj* : extremely liberal in giving : very generous [derived from Latin *munifi-cus* "generous", from *munus* "service, gift" + *-ficus* "-fic"] SYN see GENEROUS — **mu·nif·i·cence** \-səns\ *n* — **mu·nif·i·cent·ly** *adv*

mu·ni·tions \myù-'nish-ənz\ *n pl* : military supplies, equipment, or provisions; *esp* : AMMUNITION [Middle French *munition* "rampart, defense", from Latin *mu-nitio*, from *munire* "to fortify", from *moenia* "walls"] — **mu·ni·tion** \-'nish-ən\ *vt*

mun·tin \'mənt-n\ *n* : a strip separating panes of glass in a sash [French *montant* "vertical dividing bar", from *monter* "to rise", derived from Latin *mont-, mons* "mount"]

¹**mu·ral** \'myùr-əl\ *adj* **1** : of or relating to a wall **2** : applied to and made a part of a wall surface ⟨a *mural* painting⟩ [Latin *muralis*, from *murus* "wall"]

²**mural** *n* : a mural painting — **mu·ral·ist** \-ə-ləst\ *n*

¹**mur·der** \'mərd-ər\ *n* : the crime of unlawfully killing a person especially with deliberate intent or design [partly from Old English *morthor*; partly from Old French *murdre*, of Germanic origin]

²**murder** *vb* **mur·dered; mur·der·ing** \'mərd-ring, -ə-ring\ **1** : to kill a human being unlawfully and espe-cially with deliberate intent or design : commit mur-der **2** : to spoil by performing in a wretched manner ⟨*murder* a song⟩ SYN see KILL — **mur·der·er** \'mərd-ər-ər\ *n* — **mur·der·ess** \'mərd-ə-rəs\ *n*

\ə\ abut	\ng\ sing
\ər\ further	\ō\ bone
\a\ mat	\o\ saw
\ā\ take	\oi\ coin
\ä\ cot, cart	\th\ thin
\au\ out	\th\ this
\ch\ chin	\ü\ food
\e\ pet	\u\ foot
\ē\ easy	\y\ yet
\g\ go	\yü\ few
\i\ tip	\yu\ cure
\ī\ life	\zh\ vision
\j\ job	

Muscovy duck

¹mushroom I

mur·der·ous \'mərd-rəs, -ə-rəs\ *adj* I **a** : characterized by or causing murder or bloodshed ⟨*murderous* machine-gun fire⟩ ⟨a *murderous* act⟩ **b** : having or appearing to have the purpose of murder ⟨with *murderous* intent⟩ ⟨a *murderous* glance⟩ **2** : dangerously severe ⟨the desert's *murderous* heat⟩ — **mur·der·ous·ly** *adv* — **mur·der·ous·ness** *n*

mu·rex \'myùr-,eks\ *n, pl* **mu·ri·ces** \'myùr-ə-,sēz\ *or* **mu·rex·es** : any of a genus of sea snails that yield a purple dye [Latin, a kind of mollusk]

mu·ri·ate \'myùr-ē-,āt\ *n* : CHLORIDE [French, from (*acide*) *muriatique* "muriatic acid"]

mu·ri·at·ic acid \,myùr-ē-,at-ik-\ *n* : HYDROCHLORIC ACID [French *muriatique*, derived from Latin *muria* "brine"]

mu·rine \'myùr-,īn\ *adj* : of or relating to the common house mouse or closely related rodents ⟨*murine* typhus⟩ [derived from Latin *mur-, mus* "mouse"]

murk *also* **mirk** \'mərk\ *n* : intense darkness or gloom; *also* : FOG [Middle English *mirke*] — **murk·i·ly** \-kə-lē\ *adv* — **murk·i·ness** \-kē-nəs\ *n* — **murky** \'mər-kē\ *adj*

mur·mur \'mər-mər\ *n* I : a muttered complaint : GRUMBLE **2** : a low indistinct sound ⟨the *murmur* of the wind⟩ **3** : an abnormal heart sound occurring when the heart is disordered in function or structure [Middle French *murmure*, from Latin *murmur* "murmur, roar"] — **murmur** *vb* — **mur·mur·er** \'mər-mər-ər\ *n*

mur·mur·ous \'mərm-rəs, -ə-rəs\ *adj* : filled with or characterized by murmurs — **mur·mur·ous·ly** *adv*

mur·rain \'mər-ən, 'mə-rən\ *n* : a pestilence or plague especially of domestic animals [Middle French *morine*, from *morir* "to die", from Latin *mori*]

murre \'mər\ *n* : any of several guillemots [origin unknown]

mus·ca·dine \'məs-kə-,dīn\ *n* : a grape of the southern United States with musky fruits in small clusters [probably alteration of *muscatel*]

mus·cat \'məs-,kat, -kət\ *n* : any of several cultivated grapes used in making wine and raisins [French, from Provençal, from *muscat* "musky", from *musc* "musk", from Latin *muscus*]

mus·ca·tel \,məs-kə-'tel\ *n* : a sweet wine made from muscat grapes [Middle French *muscadel*, from Provençal, from *muscat* "muscat"]

¹mus·cle \'məs-əl\ *n* I **a** : a body tissue consisting of long cells that contract when stimulated and produce motion **b** : an organ that is essentially a mass of muscle tissue attached at either end to a fixed point and that by contracting moves or checks the movement of a body part **2 a** : muscular strength : BRAWN **b** : effective strength : POWER [Middle French, from Latin *musculus* "muscle, little mouse", from *mus* "mouse"] □ ORIGIN Diminutives like Latin *musculus*, "little mouse", are used not only to name small things but often to express such diverse feelings as endearment and ridicule as well. Some muscles, especially the major muscles of the arm and leg, look a little like stylized mice, their tendons playing the part of a mouse's tail. This fancied resemblance, which ignores the fact that muscles are often much larger than mice, accounts for the Latin word *musculus*, the ultimate source of English *muscle*.

²muscle *vi* **mus·cled; mus·cling** \'məs-ling, -ə-ling\ : to force one's way ⟨*muscle* in on a business⟩

mus·cle-bound \'məs-əl-,baùnd\ *adj* : having some of the muscles abnormally enlarged and lacking in elasticity (as from excessive athletic exercise)

mus·co·vite \'məs-kə-,vīt\ *n* I *cap* **a** : a native or resident of the ancient principality of Moscow or of the city of Moscow **b** : RUSSIAN 1 **2** : a mineral that consists of a colorless to pale brown potassium-containing mica [Medieval Latin *Muscovia* "Moscow"] — **Muscovite** *adj*

Mus·co·vy duck \,məs-,kō-vē-\ *n* : a large crested tropical American duck widely kept in domestication [*Muscovy*, principality of Moscow, Russia]

mus·cu·lar \'məs-kyə-lər\ *adj* I **a** : of, relating to, or constituting muscle **b** : performed by the muscles **2 a** : having well-developed muscles **b** : of or relating to physical strength : STRONG — **mus·cu·lar·i·ty** \,məs-kyə-'lar-ət-ē\ *n* — **mus·cu·lar·ly** \'məs-kyə-lər-lē\ *adv*

muscular dystrophy *n* : a disease characterized by progressive wasting of muscles

mus·cu·la·ture \'məs-kyə-lə-,chùr\ *n* : the muscles of the body or of one of its parts

¹muse \'myüz\ *vb* : to consider carefully : PONDER, MEDITATE [Middle French *muser* "to gape, muse", from *muse* "mouth of an animal"] — **mus·er** *n*

²muse *n* I *cap* : any of nine sister goddesses in Greek mythology presiding over song and poetry and the arts and sciences **2** : a source of inspiration [Middle French, from Latin *Musa*, from Greek *Mousa*]

mu·sette \myù-'zet\ *n* : a small knapsack with a shoulder strap used especially by soldiers — called also *musette bag* [French, literally, "small bagpipe", derived from Middle French *muser* "to muse, play the bagpipe"]

mu·se·um \myù-'zē-əm\ *n* : a building or part of a building in which are displayed objects of permanent interest in one or more of the arts or sciences [Latin, "place for learned occupation", from Greek *Mouseion*, from *Mousa* "Muse"]

¹mush \'məsh\ *n* I : cornmeal boiled in water **2** : something soft and spongy or shapeless **3** : insipid sentimentality or courting [probably alteration of *mash*]

²mush *vi* : to travel over snow with a sled drawn by dogs — sometimes used as a command to a dog team [probably from American French *moucher* "to go fast", from French *mouche* "fly", from Latin *musca*] — **mush·er** *n*

³mush *n* : a hike across snow with a dog team

¹mush·room \'məsh-,rüm, -,rùm\ *n* I : a fleshy aerial fruiting body of a fungus that consists typically of a stem bearing a flattened cap; *esp* : one that is edible **2** : FUNGUS 1 [Middle French *mousseron*, from Medieval Latin *mussirio*]

²mushroom *adj* I : springing up suddenly or multiplying rapidly ⟨*mushroom* growth of new agencies⟩ **2** : having the shape of a mushroom

³mushroom *vi* : to spring up suddenly or multiply rapidly

mushy \'məsh-ē\ *adj* **mush·i·er; -est** I : soft like mush **2** : weakly sentimental — **mush·i·ly** \'məsh-ə-lē\ *adv* — **mush·i·ness** \'məsh-ē-nəs\ *n*

mu·sic \'myü-zik\ *n* I **a** : the art of combining tones so that they are pleasing, expressive, or intelligible **b** : compositions made according to the rules of music **c** : the score of music compositions set down on paper ⟨did you bring your *music* with you⟩ **2** : sounds that have rhythm, harmony, and melody; *also* : an agreeable sound ⟨the *music* of a brook⟩ **3** : punishment for a misdeed ⟨must face the *music*⟩ [Old French *musique*, from Latin *musica*, from Greek *mousikē* "art presided over by the Muses", from *Mousa* "Muse"]

¹mu·si·cal \'myü-zi-kəl\ *adj* I **a** : of or relating to music ⟨*musical* instruments⟩ **b** : having the pleasing harmonious qualities of music : MELODIOUS ⟨a *musical* voice⟩ **2** : having an interest in or talent for music ⟨a *musical* family⟩ **3** : set to or accompanied by music **4** : of or relating to musicians or music lovers — **mu·si·cal·i·ty** \,myü-zi-'kal-ət-ē\ *n* — **mu·si·cal·ly** \'myü-zi-kə-lē, -klē\ *adv*

²musical *n* : a film or theatrical production consisting of musical numbers and dialogue that develop a plot — called also *musical comedy*; compare REVUE

musical chairs *n pl* : a children's game in which players march to music around a group of chairs numbering one less than the number of players and scramble for a seat when the music stops

mu·si·cale \‚myü-zi-'kal\ *n* : a usually private social gathering featuring a concert of music [French *soirée musicale*, literally, "musical evening"]

music box *n* : a box or case enclosing an apparatus that reproduces music mechanically when activated by clockwork

music hall *n* : a vaudeville theater

mu·si·cian \myü-'zish-ən\ *n* : one skilled in music; *esp* : a composer or professional performer of music — **mu·si·cian·ly** \-lē\ *adj* — **mu·si·cian·ship** \-‚ship\ *n*

mu·si·col·o·gy \‚myü-zi-'käl-ə-jē\ *n* : a study of music as a branch of knowledge or field of research — **mu·si·co·log·i·cal** \-zi-kə-'läj-i-kəl\ *adj* — **mu·si·col·o·gist** \-zi-'käl-ə-jəst\ *n*

mus·ing \'myü-zing\ *n* : MEDITATION ⟨considered it in their *musings*⟩ — **musing** *adj* — **mus·ing·ly** \-zing-lē\ *adv*

musk \'məsk\ *n* **1 a** : a substance of penetrating persistent odor obtained usually from the male musk deer and used in perfume **b** : a substance (as from a skunk) of comparable odor **2** : the odor of a musk [Middle French *musc*, from Late Latin *muscus*, from Greek *moschos*, from Persian *mushk*, from Sanskrit *muṣka* "testicle", from *mūṣ* "mouse"]

musk deer *n* : a small hornless deer about one meter long and ½ meter tall that lives in the high regions of central Asia

mus·keg \'məs-‚keg\ *n* : BOG; *esp* : a dense sphagnum bog of northern North America [of American Indian origin]

mus·kel·lunge \'məs-kə-‚lənj\ *n, pl* **muskellunge** : a large North American pike that may weigh 30 to 35 kilograms and is a valuable sport fish [of American Indian origin]

mus·ket \'məs-kət\ *n* : a large-caliber usually muzzle-loading military shoulder firearm with a smooth bore [Middle French *mousquet*, from Italian *moschetto* "arrow for a crossbow, musket", from *mosca* "fly", from Latin *musca*] □ ORIGIN The *musket* was originally a Spanish weapon, first used by the Spanish army in the 16th century. The musket was introduced to France through her conflict with Spain, which was fought in Italy. Although the French borrowed the new weapon from their enemy, they took the name *mousquet* from the Italians. Italian *moschetto*, diminutive of *mosca*, "fly", was the word for the arrow of a crossbow. When the new weapon was introduced, the name of the old one was taken over for it. French *mousquet* was borrowed into English (as *musket*) late in the 16th century.

mus·ke·teer \‚məs-kə-'tiər\ *n* : a soldier armed with a musket

mus·ket·ry \'məs-kə-trē\ *n, pl* **-ries** : small-arms fire

musk·mel·on \'məsk-‚mel-ən\ *n* : a small round to oval and sometimes ridged melon that has usually sweet edible green or orange flesh; *also* : a vine bearing muskmelons — compare CANTALOUPE

Mus·ko·gee \məs-'kō-gē, ‚məs-\ *n* : a member of an Indian people of what is now Georgia, South Carolina, and eastern Alabama

musk–ox \'məs-‚käks\ *n* : a heavy-set shaggy-coated wild ox that is confined to Greenland and to the barren lands of northern North America

musk·rat \'məs-‚krat\ *n, pl* **muskrat** *or* **muskrats** : a North American aquatic rodent with a long scaly tail, webbed hind feet, and dark glossy brown fur; *also* : its fur or pelt [probably by folk etymology from a word of American Indian origin]

musk turtle *n* : any of several small American freshwater turtles with a strong musky odor

musky \'məs-kē\ *adj* **musk·i·er; -est** : having an odor of or resembling musk — **musk·i·ness** *n*

Mus·lim \'məz-ləm, 'mùs-, 'mùz-\ *or* **Mos·lem** \'mäz-ləm *also* 'mäs-\ *n* : an adherent of Islam [Arabic *muslim*, literally, "one who surrenders (to God)"] — **Muslim** *adj*

mus·lin \'məz-lən\ *n* : a cotton fabric of plain weave [French *mousseline*, from Italian *mussolina*, from Arabic *mawṣilīy* "of Mosul", from *al-Mawṣil* "Mosul, Iraq"]

mus·quash \'məs-‚kwäsh, -‚kwȯsh\ *n* : MUSKRAT [of American Indian origin]

¹muss \'məs\ *n* : a state of disorder : MESS [origin unknown]

²muss *vt* : to make untidy : RUMPLE ⟨*mussed* my hair⟩

mus·sel \'məs-əl\ *n* **1** : an edible saltwater 2-valved mollusk with a long dark shell **2** : any of numerous 2-valved freshwater mollusks especially of the central United States having shells with pearly inner linings [Old English *muscelle*, derived from Latin *musculus* "muscle, mussel"]

mussy \'məs-ē\ *adj* **muss·i·er; -est** : MESSY, UNTIDY — **muss·i·ly** \'məs-ə-lē\ *adv* — **muss·i·ness** \'məs-ē-nəs\ *n*

¹must \məst, məs, 'məst\ *auxiliary verb, present & past all persons* **must 1 a** : be commanded or requested to ⟨the train *must* stop⟩ **b** : be urged to ⟨you *must* read that book⟩ **2 a** : be compelled, required, or obliged to ⟨one *must* eat to live⟩ ⟨we *must* be quiet⟩ **b** : be determined to ⟨if you *must* go⟩ **3** : be logically inferred or supposed to ⟨it *must* be time⟩ **4** : be reasonably certain to ⟨I *must* have lost it⟩ [Old English *mōste* "was allowed to, had to", past of *mōtan* "to be allowed to, have to"]

²must \'məst\ *n* : something necessary, required, or indispensable ⟨new shoes are a *must*⟩

³must *n* : the juice of fruit (as grapes) before and during fermentation [Old English, from Latin *mustum*]

mus·tache *or* **mous·tache** \'məs-‚tash, məs-'-\ *n* **1** : the hair growing on the human upper lip **2** : hair or bristles about the mouth of a lower animal [Middle French *moustache*, from Italian *mustaccio*, derived from Greek *mystax* "upper lip, mustache"]

mus·ta·chio *or* **mous·ta·chio** \məs-'tash-ō, -'täsh-, -ē-‚ō\ *n, pl* **-chios** : MUSTACHE; *esp* : a large mustache [Italian *mustaccio*] — **mus·ta·chioed** \-ōd, -ē-‚ōd\ *adj*

mus·tang \'məs-‚tang\ *n* : the small hardy naturalized horse of the western plains directly descended from horses brought in by the Spaniards; *also* : BRONCO [American Spanish *mestengo*, from Spanish, "stray", from *mesta* "annual roundup of stray cattle", from Medieval Latin (*animalia*) *mixta* "mixed animals"]

mus·tard \'məs-tərd\ *n* **1** : a pungent yellow powder of the seeds of a common mustard used as a seasoning or in medicine **2** : any of several yellow-flowered herbs related to the turnips and cabbages [Old French *mostarde*, from *moust* "must", from Latin *mustum*]

mustard gas *n* : a poisonous oily liquid $C_4H_8Cl_2S$ consisting of carbon, hydrogen, chlorine, and sulfur and having violent irritating and especially blistering effects

mustard plaster *n* : a counterirritant medicinal plaster containing powdered mustard

¹mus·ter \'məs-tər\ *vb* **mus·tered; mus·ter·ing** \-tə-ring, -tring\ **1** : to enlist or enroll a person in military service **2 a** : to assemble (as troops or a ship's company) for roll call or inspection **b** : CONGREGATE, ASSEMBLE **3** : to collect and display ⟨all the strength I could *muster*⟩ [Middle English *mustren* "to show, muster", from Old French *monstrer* "to show", from Latin *monstrare*, from *monstrum* "sign, portent, monster"]

²muster *n* **1 a** : an act of assembling; *esp* : a formal military inspection **b** : critical examination ⟨slipshod

musk deer

musk-ox

\ə\ abut		\ng\ sing	
\ər\ further		\ō\ bone	
\a\ mat		\ȯ\ saw	
\ā\ take		\ȯi\ coin	
\ä\ cot, cart		\th\ thin	
\aù\ out		\t͟h\ this	
\ch\ chin		\ü\ food	
\e\ pet		\ù\ foot	
\ē\ easy		\y\ yet	
\g\ go		\yü\ few	
\i\ tip		\yù\ cure	
\ī\ life		\zh\ vision	
\j\ job			

work that would never pass *muster*⟩ **2** : an assembled group

muster out *vt* : to discharge from service

mustn't \'məs-nt\ : must not

musty \'məs-tē\ *adj* **must·i·er; -est** **1 a** : impaired by damp or mildew : MOLDY **b** : tasting or smelling of damp and decay **2 a** : TRITE, STALE ⟨a *musty* proverb⟩ **b** : OUTMODED **2** ⟨*musty* laws⟩ [earlier *must* "musk, mold", from Middle French, "musk", from *musc*] — **must·i·ly** \-tə-lē\ *adv* — **must·i·ness** \-tē-nəs\ *n*

mu·ta·ble \'myüt-ə-bəl\ *adj* **1** : prone to change : IN-CONSTANT **2 a** : capable of change in form or nature **b** : capable of or liable to mutation ⟨*mutable* vowels⟩ ⟨a *mutable* bacterium⟩ [Latin *mutabilis*, from *mutare* "to change"] — **mu·ta·bil·i·ty** \,myüt-ə-'bil-ət-ē\ *n*

mu·ta·gen \'myüt-ə-jən, -,jen\ *n* : an agent inducing mutation — **mu·ta·gen·ic** \,myüt-ə-'jen-ik\ *adj* — **mu·ta·ge·nic·i·ty** \-jə-'nis-ət-ē\ *n*

mu·tant \'myüt-nt\ *adj* : of, relating to, or produced by mutation — **mutant** *n*

mu·tate \'myü-,tāt\ *vb* : to undergo or cause to undergo mutation [Latin *mutare* "to change"]

mu·ta·tion \myü-'tā-shən\ *n* **1** : a basic alteration : CHANGE **2 a** : a relatively permanent change in heredi-tary material involving either a change in the position of the genes on the chromosomes or a fundamental change in the chemical structure of the genes them-selves **b** : an individual or strain resulting from muta-tion — **mu·ta·tion·al** \-shnəl, -shən-l\ *adj* — **mu·ta·tive** \'myü-,tāt-iv, 'myüt-ət-iv\ *adj*

mu·ta·tis mu·tan·dis \mü-,tät-ə-smü-'tän-dəs\ *adv* : with the necessary changes having been made [New Latin]

¹**muzzle** 1

¹**mute** \'myüt\ *adj* **1** : unable to speak : DUMB **2** : marked by absence of speech ⟨a *mute* appeal for help⟩ **3** : not pronounced : SILENT ⟨the *mute* *b* in *thumb*⟩ [Middle French *muet*, from Latin *mutus*] SYN see DUMB — **mute·ly** *adv* — **mute·ness** *n* — **mut·ism** \'myüt-,iz-əm\ *n*

²**mute** *n* **1 a** : a person who cannot or does not speak **b** : a professional mourner formerly hired to take part in a funeral **2** : a device on a musical instrument that deadens, softens, or muffles its tone **3** : STOP 8

³**mute** *vt* **1** : to muffle or reduce the sound of **2** : to tone down ⟨*muted* their criticism⟩ ⟨*muted* the colors⟩

mu·ti·late \'myüt-l-,āt\ *vt* **1 a** : to deprive of an essen-tial part ⟨*mutilated* refugees⟩ **b** : to cut off or perma-nently destroy the use of (as a limb) **2** : to make im-perfect by cutting or alteration ⟨*multilate* a document⟩ [Latin *mutilare*] — **mu·ti·la·tion** \,myüt-l-'ā-shən\ *n* — **mu·ti·la·tor** \'myüt-l-,āt-ər\ *n*

mu·ti·neer \,myüt-n-'iər\ *n* : one that mutinies

mu·ti·nous \'myüt-n-əs, 'myüt-nəs\ *adj* **1** : disposed to or engaged in mutiny : REBELLIOUS ⟨a *mutinous* crew⟩ **2** : of, relating to, or constituting mutiny ⟨*mutinous* acts⟩ — **mu·ti·nous·ly** *adv* — **mu·ti·nous·ness** *n*

mu·ti·ny \'myüt-n-ē, 'myüt-nē\ *n, pl* **-nies** **1** : willful refusal to obey constituted authority; *esp* : revolt by a military group against a superior officer **2** : an act or instance of mutiny [obsolete *mutine* "to rebel", from Middle French *se mutiner*, from *meute* "revolt", de-rived from Latin *movēre* "to move"] — **mutiny** *vi*

mutt \'mət\ *n* : MONGREL 1, CUR [earlier *mutt* "fool", short for *muttonhead*]

mut·ter \'mət-ər\ *vb* **1** : MUMBLE 1 **2** : to murmur com-plainingly or angrily : GRUMBLE [Middle English *muter-en*] — **mutter** *n* — **mut·ter·er** \'mət-ər-ər\ *n*

mut·ton \'mət-n\ *n* : the flesh of a mature sheep [Old French *moton* "sheep", of Celtic origin] — **mut·tony** \-ē\ *adj*

mut·ton·chops \-,chäps\ *n pl* : side-whiskers that are narrow at the temple and broad and round by the low-er jaws — called also *muttonchop whiskers*

mu·tu·al \'myüch-wəl, -ə-wəl, 'myü-chəl\ *adj* **1 a** : giv-en and received in equal amount ⟨*mutual* favors⟩ **b** :

having the same feelings one for the other ⟨*mutual* enemies⟩ **2** : participated in, shared, or enjoyed by two or more at the same time : JOINT ⟨our *mutual* friend⟩ ⟨*mutual* defense⟩ **3** : organized so that the members share in the profits, benefits, expenses, and liabilities ⟨*mutual* savings bank⟩ ⟨*mutual* life insurance compa-ny⟩ [Middle French *mutuel*, from Latin *mutuus*] SYN see RECIPROCAL — **mu·tu·al·i·ty** \,myü-chə-'wal-ət-ē\ *n* — **mu·tu·al·ly** \'myü-chə-wə-lē, -chə-lē\ *adv*

mutual fund *n* : an investment company that invests money of its shareholders in a usually diversified group of securities

mu·tu·al·ism \'myüch-wə-,liz-əm, -ə-wə-, 'myü-chə-,liz-\ *n* : mutually beneficial association between dif-ferent kinds of organisms — **mu·tu·al·is·tic** \,myü-chə-wə-'lis-tik, -chə-'lis-\ *adj*

muu·muu \'mü-mü\ *n* : a loose dress of Hawaiian origin for informal wear [Hawaiian *mu'umu'u*]

mu·zhik *or* **mou·jik** \mü-'zhēk, -'zhik\ *n* : a Russian peasant [Russian]

¹**muz·zle** \'məz-əl\ *n* **1** : the projecting jaws and nose of an animal : SNOUT **2** : a fastening or covering for the mouth of an animal used to prevent eating or biting **3** : the open end of a weapon from which the missile is discharged [Middle French *musel*, from *muse* "mouth of an animal"]

²**muzzle** *vt* **muz·zled; muz·zling** \'məz-ling, -ə-ling\ **1** : to fit with a muzzle **2** : to prevent free or normal ex-pression by : GAG ⟨*muzzle* the press⟩ — **muz·zler** \'məz-lər, -ə-lər\ *n*

muz·zle–load·er \,məz-əl-'lōd-ər, -ə-'\ *n* : a gun that is loaded through the muzzle — **muz·zle–load·ing** \-'lōd-ing\ *adj*

muz·zy \'məz-ē\ *adj* **muz·zi·er; -est** **1** : muddled or confused in mind **2 a** : not clear ⟨a *muzzy* photograph⟩ ⟨*muzzy* ideas⟩ **b** : DULL, GLOOMY ⟨a *muz-zy* day⟩ [perhaps blend of *muddled* and *fuzzy*] — **muz·zi·ly** \'məz-ə-lē\ *adv* — **muz·zi·ness** \'məz-ē-nəs\ *n*

my \mī, 'mī, mə\ *adj* **1** : of or relating to me or myself especially as possessor, agent, or object of an action ⟨*my* car⟩ ⟨*my* promise⟩ ⟨*my* injuries⟩ **2** — used inter-jectionally to express surprise ⟨oh *my*⟩ [Old English *mīn*]

my- *or* **myo-** *combining form* : muscle ⟨*myo*fibril⟩ : muscle and ⟨*myo*neural⟩ [Greek *mys* "mouse, mus-cle"]

my·as·the·nia gra·vis \,mī-əs-,thē-nē-ə-'grav-əs, -'gräv-\ *n* : a disease of the muscular system characterized by fatigue and weakness and progressive paralysis with-out wasting or sensory disturbance [New Latin *myasthenia* "muscular debility" (from *my-* + Greek *asthenia* "asthenia") + Latin *gravis* "grave"]

myc- *or* **myco-** *combining form* : fungus ⟨*myco*logy⟩ [Greek *mykēs*]

my·ce·li·um \mī-'sē-lē-əm\ *n, pl* **-lia** \-lē-ə\ *also* **-li·ums** : the vegetative part of the body of a fungus typi-cally consisting of a mass of interwoven hyphae and often being submerged in another body (as of soil, or-ganic matter, or the tissues of a plant or animal host) [derived from Greek *mykēs* "fungus" + *hēlos* "nail, wart, callus"] — **my·ce·li·al** \-lē-əl\ *adj*

My·ce·nae·an \,mī-sə-'nē-ən\ *adj* : of or relating to the Bronze Age culture of the eastern Mediterranean area centering in Mycenae especially from 1600 to 1100 B. C.

my·co·bac·te·ri·um \,mī-kō-bak-'tir-ē-əm\ *n* : any of a genus of bacteria that includes the causative agents of tuberculosis and of leprosy as well as harmless sapro-phytes

my·col·o·gy \mī-'käl-ə-jē\ *n* **1** : a branch of botany dealing with fungi **2** : fungal life — **my·co·log·i·cal** \,mī-kə-'läj-i-kəl\ *adj* — **my·col·o·gist** \mī-'käl-ə-jəst\ *n*

my·co·plas·ma \,mī-kō-'plaz-mə\ *n, pl* **-mas** *or* **-ma·ta** \-mət-ə\ : any of a genus of minute microorganisms without cell walls that are intermediate in some respects between viruses and bacteria and are parasitic usually in mammals

my·cor·rhi·za \ˌmī-kə-ˈrī-zə\ *n, pl* **-zae** \-ˌzē\ *or* **-zas** : a symbiotic association of the mycelium of a fungus with the roots of a seed plant [*myc-* + Greek *rhiza* "root"] — **my·cor·rhi·zal** \-zəl\ *adj*

my·co·sis \mī-ˈkō-səs\ *n, pl* **-co·ses** \-ˌsez\ : infection with or disease caused by a fungus — **my·cot·ic** \-ˈkät-ik\ *adj*

my·e·lin \ˈmī-ə-lən\ *n* : a soft white somewhat fatty material that forms a thick sheath about certain nerve fibers [derived from Greek *myelos* "marrow", from *mys* "mouse, muscle"] — **my·e·lin·at·ed** \-lə-ˌnāt-əd\ *adj*

my·i·a·sis \mī-ˈī-ə-səs, mē-\ *n, pl* **-a·ses** \-ə-ˌsēz\ : infestation (as of tissue) with fly maggots [Greek *myia* "fly"]

my·na *or* **my·nah** \ˈmī-nə\ *n* : any of various Asian starlings; *esp* : a dark brown slightly crested bird of southeastern Asia with a white tail tip and wing markings and bright yellow bill and feet [Hindi *mainā,* from Sanskrit *madana*]

myn·heer \mə-ˈner\ *n* : a man from the Netherlands — used as a title equivalent to *Mr.* [Dutch *mijnheer,* from *mijn* "my" + *heer* "master, sir"]

myo- — see MY-

myo·car·di·um \ˌmī-ə-ˈkärd-ē-əm\ *n* : the middle muscular layer of the heart wall [New Latin, from *my-* + Greek *kardia* "heart"] — **myo·car·di·al** \-ē-əl\ *adj*

myo·fi·bril \ˌmī-ō-ˈfīb-rəl, -ˈfib-\ *n* : one of the long thin protein filaments of a muscle cell that are the contractile elements of muscle

myo·glo·bin \ˌmī-ə-ˈglō-bən, ˈmī-ə-ˌ\ *n* : a red iron-containing protein pigment in muscles that is similar to hemoglobin

myo·neu·ral junction \ˌmī-ə-ˌnûr-əl-, -ˌnyûr-\ *n* : the region of contact between a motor neuron and a muscle fiber

my·o·pia \mī-ˈō-pē-ə\ *n* : the condition of being nearsighted [Greek *myōpia,* from *myein* "to be closed" + *ōps* "eye, face"] — **my·o·pic** \-ˈōp-ik, -ˈäp-\ *adj* — **my·o·pi·cal·ly** \-i-kə-lē, -klē\ *adv*

my·o·sin \ˈmī-ə-sən\ *n* : a protein of muscle that with actin is active in muscular contraction [derived from Greek *mys* "mouse, muscle"]

¹myr·i·ad \ˈmir-ē-əd\ *n* **1** : ten thousand **2** : an indefinitely large number ⟨the *myriads* of stars⟩ [Greek *myriad-, myrias,* from *myrioi* "countless, ten thousand"]

²myriad *adj* : consisting of a very great but indefinite number ⟨the *myriad* grains of sand on a beach⟩

myr·io·pod *or* **myr·ia·pod** \ˈmir-ē-ə-ˌpäd\ *n* : any of a group (Myriopoda) of arthropods including the millipedes and centipedes [derived from Greek *myrioi* "countless, ten thousand" + *pod-, pous* "foot"] — **myriopod** *adj*

myr·mi·don \ˈmər-mə-ˌdän, ˈmər-məd-ən\ *n* **1** *cap* : any of a legendary Thessalian people following Achilles to the Trojan war **2 a** : a loyal follower or retainer **b** : a subordinate who executes orders without question or scruple [Greek *Myrmidōn*]

myrrh \ˈmər\ *n* : a brown slightly bitter aromatic gum resin obtained from African and Arabian trees and used especially in perfumes or formerly in incense [Old English *myrre,* from Latin *myrrha,* from Greek, of Semitic origin]

myr·tle \ˈmərt-l\ *n* **1** : a common evergreen bushy shrub of southern Europe with oval to lance-shaped shining leaves, fragrant white or rosy flowers, and black berries **2 a** : any of the family of chiefly tropical shrubs or trees to which the common myrtle of Europe belongs: **¹ PERIWINKLE** [Middle French *mirtille,* from Medieval Latin *myrtillus,* from Latin *myrtos,* from Greek *myrtos*]

my·self \mī-ˈself, mə-\ *pron* **1** : that identical one that is I — used reflexively or for emphasis ⟨I'm going to

get *myself* a new suit⟩ ⟨I *myself* will go⟩ **2** : my normal, healthy, or sane condition or self ⟨didn't feel *myself* yesterday⟩

mys·te·ri·ous \mis-ˈtir-ē-əs\ *adj* : containing, suggesting, or implying a mystery ⟨the *mysterious* ways of nature⟩ — **mys·te·ri·ous·ly** *adv* — **mys·te·ri·ous·ness** *n*

mys·tery \ˈmis-tə-rē, -trē\ *n, pl* **-ter·ies** **1 a** : a religious truth that man can know by revelation alone and cannot fully understand **b** : any of the 15 events (as the Nativity, the Crucifixion, or the Assumption) serving as a subject for meditation during the saying of the rosary **2 a** : something that has not been or cannot be explained ⟨where they went is a *mystery*⟩ **b** : a deep secret ⟨kept our plans a *mystery*⟩ **3** : a piece of fiction dealing with a mysterious crime **4** : mysterious quality or character ⟨the *mystery* of that smile⟩ [Latin *mysterium,* from Greek *mystērion,* from *myein* "to be closed (of eyes or lips)"] □ SYN ENIGMA, RIDDLE: MYSTERY applies to what is not or cannot be fully understood or explained ⟨the disappearance of the money remained a *mystery*⟩ ENIGMA applies to words or actions very difficult to interpret correctly; RIDDLE suggests especially a problem or enigma involving paradox or apparent contradiction.

mystery play *n* : a medieval play based on scriptural incidents (as the life, death, and resurrection of Christ)

¹mys·tic \ˈmis-tik\ *adj* **1** : MYSTICAL 1 **2** : of or relating to mysteries or magical rites : OCCULT **3** : of or relating to mysticism or mystics **4 a** : MYSTERIOUS **b** : AWESOME **2 c** : MAGICAL [Latin *mysticus* "of mysteries", from Greek *mystikos,* from *myein* "to be closed"]

²mystic *n* : a person who seeks direct knowledge of God through contemplation and prayer

mys·ti·cal \ˈmis-ti-kəl\ *adj* **1** : having a spiritual meaning or reality that is neither apparent to the senses nor obvious to the intelligence **2** : of, relating to, or resulting from direct communion with God or ultimate reality **3** : MYSTIC 2 — **mys·ti·cal·ly** \-ti-kə-lē, -klē\ *adv*

mys·ti·cism \ˈmis-tə-ˌsiz-əm\ *n* **1** : the experience of mystical union or direct communion with ultimate reality **2** : the belief that direct knowledge of God or of spiritual truth can be achieved by personal insight and inspiration **3** : vague guessing or speculation

mys·ti·fy \ˈmis-tə-ˌfī\ *vb* **-fied; -fy·ing** **1** : to make obscure or difficult to understand **2** : to baffle and disturb the mind of : PERPLEX ⟨strange actions that *mystified* everyone⟩ SYN see PUZZLE — **mys·ti·fi·ca·tion** \ˌmis-tə-fə-ˈkā-shən\ *n*

mys·tique \mi-ˈstēk\ *n* : a set of beliefs and attitudes developing around an object or associated with a particular group : CULT ⟨the *mystique* of mountain climbing⟩ [French, from *mystique* "mystic", from Latin *mysticus*]

myth \ˈmith\ *n* **1** : a usually legendary narrative that presents part of the beliefs of a people or explains a practice, belief, or natural phenomenon **2** : PARABLE, ALLEGORY **3 a** : a person or thing having only an imaginary existence ⟨the dragon is a *myth*⟩ **b** : a false or unsupported belief [Greek *mythos*] □ SYN LEGEND, FABLE: in specific use a MYTH is a story dealing with gods or imaginary beings representing natural phenomena; a LEGEND may include supernatural incidents but deals with human beings or particular places; a FABLE is an invented story in which talking animals or things illustrate human follies and weaknesses.

myth·i·cal \ˈmith-i-kəl\ *also* **myth·ic** \-ik\ *adj* **1** : based on, described in, or being a myth ⟨Hercules is a *mythical* hero⟩ **2** : IMAGINARY, INVENTED ⟨the novelist created a *mythical* town⟩ SYN see FABULOUS — **myth·i·cal·ly** \-i-kə-lē, -klē\ *adv*

my·thol·o·gy \mith-ˈäl-ə-jē\ *n, pl* **-gies** **1** : a body of myths; *esp* : the myths dealing with the gods and

myna

\ə\ abut   \ng\ sing
\ər\ further   \ō\ bone
\a\ mat   \ȯ\ saw
\ā\ take   \ȯi\ coin
\ä\ cot, čart   \th\ thin
\au̇\ out   \t͟h\ this
\ch\ chin   \ü\ food
\e\ pet   \u̇\ foot
\ē\ easy   \y\ yet
\g\ go   \yü\ few
\i\ tip   \yu̇\ cure
\ī\ life   \zh\ vision
\j\ job

heroes of a people ⟨Greek *mythology*⟩ **2** : a branch of knowledge that deals with myth — **myth·o·log·i·cal** \,mith-ə-'läj-i-kəl\ *adj* — **myth·o·log·i·cal·ly** \-kə-lē, -klē\ *adv* — **my·thol·o·gist** \mith-'äl-ə-jəst\ *n*
myth·os \'mith-,ōs, -,äs\ *n, pl* **myth·oi** \-,ȯi\ : a pattern of beliefs expressing often symbolically the characteristic or prevalent attitudes in a group or culture [Greek, "myth"]

myx·ede·ma \,mik-sə-'dē-mə\ *n* : a disorder caused by deficient thyroid secretion and marked by puffy swelling, dry skin and hair, and loss of mental and physical vigor [Greek *myxa* "lamp wick, nasal mucus" + New Latin *edema* "edema"] — **myx·ede·ma·tous** \-'dem-ət-əs, -'dē-mət-\ *adj*
myxo·my·cete \,mik-sō-'mī-,sēt, -mī-'sēt\ *n* : SLIME MOLD [derived from Greek *myxa* "mucus" + *mykēt-, mykēs* "fungus"]

Nn

n \'en\ *n, pl* **n's** *or* **ns** \'enz\ *often cap* **1** : the 14th letter of the English alphabet **2** : an unspecified quantity ⟨sum the integers from one to *n*⟩ **3** : the haploid number of chromosomes
-n — see -EN
nab \'nab\ *vt* **nabbed; nab·bing 1** : to seize and take into custody : ARREST **2** : to seize suddenly [perhaps from English dialect *nap* "to grab, nab"]
na·bob \'nā-,bäb\ *n* **1** : a provincial governor of the Mogul empire in India **2** : a man of great wealth or prominence [Hindi *nawwāb*, from Arabic *nuwwāb*, pl. of *nā'ib* "governor"]
na·celle \nə-'sel\ *n* : an enclosed shelter on an aircraft for an engine or sometimes for crew [French, literally, "small boat", from Late Latin *navicella*, from Latin *navis* "ship"]
na·cre \'nā-kər\ *n* : MOTHER-OF-PEARL [Middle French, from Italian *naccara* "drum, nacre", from Arabic *naggārah* "drum"] — **na·cre·ous** \-krē-əs, -kə-rəs, -krəs\ *adj*
NAD \,en-,ā-'dē\ *n* : a coenzyme $C_{21}H_{27}N_7O_{14}P_2$ of numerous dehydrogenases that occurs in most cells and plays an important role in respiration and photosynthesis as an oxidizing agent or when in the reduced form as a reducing agent — called also *nicotinamide-adenine dinucleotide*
na·dir \'nā-,diər, 'nād-ər\ *n* **1** : the point of the celestial sphere that is directly opposite the zenith and vertically downward from the observer **2** : the lowest point ⟨our hopes had reached their *nadir*⟩ [Middle French, from Arabic *nazīr* "opposite"]
NADP \,en-,ā-,dē-'pē\ *n* : a coenzyme $C_{21}H_{27}N_7O_{14}P_2$ of numerous dehydrogenases that plays a role in respiration and photosynthesis similar to NAD — called also *nicotinamide-adenine diphosphate*
¹nag \'nag\ *n* : HORSE; *esp* : one that is old or in poor condition [Middle English *nagge*]
²nag *vb* **nagged; nag·ging 1** : to find fault incessantly : COMPLAIN **2** : to irritate by constant scolding or urging **3** : to be a continuing source of annoyance ⟨a *nagging* toothache⟩ [probably of Scandinavian origin] — **nag·ger** *n*
Na·hua·tl \'nä-,wät-l\ *n* **1** : a group of peoples of southern Mexico and Central America **2** : the language of the Nahuatl people [Spanish, from Nahuatl] — **Na·huat·lan** \-,wät-lən\ *adj or n*
Na·hum \'nā-əm, -həm\ *n* — see BIBLE table
na·iad \'nā-əd, 'nī-, -,ad\ *n, pl* **na·iads** *or* **na·ia·des** \-ə-,dēz\ **1** : one of the nymphs in classical mythology living in and giving life to lakes, rivers, springs, and

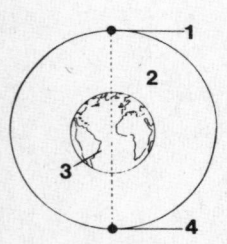
nadir 1: *1* zenith, 2 celestial sphere, 3 earth, 4 nadir

fountains **2** : the aquatic young of a mayfly, dragonfly, damselfly, or stone fly [Latin *naiad-, naias,* from Greek, from *nan* "to flow"]
¹nail \'nāl\ *n* **1 a** : a horny sheath protecting the end of each finger and toe in man and most other primates **b** : a corresponding structure (as a claw) terminating a digit in other vertebrates **2** : a slender pointed piece of metal driven into or through something for fastening [Old English *nægl*]
²nail *vt* **1** : to fasten with or as if with a nail **2** : CATCH, TRAP ⟨*nail* a thief⟩ — **nail·er** *n*
nail·brush \'nāl-,brəsh\ *n* : a small firm-bristled brush for cleaning the hands and fingernails
nail down *vt* : to settle or establish clearly and unmistakably
na·ive *or* **na·ïve** \nä-'ēv\ *adj* **1** : marked by unaffected simplicity **2** : showing lack of informed judgment [French *naïve*, feminine of *naïf*, from Old French, "inborn, natural", from Latin *nativus* "native"] — **na·ive·ly** *adv* — **na·ive·ness** *n*
na·ive·té *or* **na·ïve·té** *or* **na·ive·te** \nä-,ē-və-'tā, nä-'ē-və-,\ *n* **1** : the quality or state of being naive **2** : a naive remark or action [French *naïveté*, from *naïf* "naive"]
na·ive·ty *also* **na·ïve·ty** \nä-'ē-vət-ē, -'ēv-tē\ *n* : NAIVETÉ
na·ked \'nā-kəd, *especially South* 'nek-əd\ *adj* **1** : having no clothes on : NUDE **2 a** : lacking a usual or natural covering (as of foliage or feathers) ⟨*naked* hills⟩ **b** : not sheathed ⟨a *naked* sword⟩ **c** : lacking protective enveloping parts (as membranes, scales, or shells) ⟨a *naked* seed⟩ ⟨slugs and other *naked* mollusks⟩ **3** : lacking embellishment of any kind : PLAIN ⟨the *naked* truth⟩ **4** : not aided by artificial means ⟨seen by the *naked* eye⟩ [Old English *nacod*] — **na·ked·ly** *adv* — **na·ked·ness** *n*
nam·by–pam·by \,nam-bē-'pam-bē\ *adj* **1** : lacking in character or substance : INSIPID **2** : WEAK 1c, INDECISIVE [*Namby Pamby*, nickname given to Ambrose Phillips, died 1749, English poet, to ridicule his poetic style] — **namby–pamby** *n*
¹name \'nām\ *n* **1** : a word or combination of words by which a person or thing is regularly known **2** : a descriptive often disparaging term ⟨call someone *names*⟩ **3** : REPUTATION; *esp* : a distinguished reputation ⟨make a *name* for oneself⟩ **4** : FAMILY, CLAN ⟨was a disgrace to the *name*⟩ **5** : appearance as opposed to fact ⟨a friend in *name* only⟩ [Old English *nama*]
²name *vt* **1** : to give a name to : CALL **2 a** : to mention or identify by name **b** : to accuse by name **3** : to nominate for office **4** : to decide on **5** : to speak about

⟨*name* a price⟩ — **name·able** *also* **nam·able** \'nā-mə-bəl\ *adj* — **nam·er** *n*

³name *adj* **I** : of, relating to, or bearing a name ⟨a *name* tag⟩ **2** : having an established reputation ⟨*name* brands⟩

name·less \'nām-ləs\ *adj* **I** : having no name **2** : not marked with a name ⟨a *nameless* grave⟩ **3** : not known by name : ANONYMOUS ⟨a *nameless* author⟩ **4** : not to be described ⟨*nameless* fears⟩ — **name·less·ly** *adv* — **name·less·ness** *n*

name·ly \'nām-lē\ *adv* : that is to say ⟨the cat family, *namely,* lions, tigers, and related animals⟩

name·plate \-,plāt\ *n* : a plate or plaque bearing a name

name·sake \'nām-,sāk\ *n* : one that has the same name as another; *esp* : one named after another

nan·keen \nan-'kēn, 'nan-\ *also* **nan·kin** \-'kēn, -'kin\ *n* : a durable brownish yellow cotton fabric originally woven by hand in China [*Nanking,* China]

nan·ny goat \'nan-ē-\ *n* : a female domestic goat [*Nanny,* nickname for *Anne*]

nano- \'nan-ō, -ə\ *combining form* : billionth [Greek *nanos* "dwarf"]

nano·sec·ond \'nan-ə-,sek-ənd, -ənt\ *n* : one billionth of a second

¹nap \'nap\ *vi* **napped; nap·ping** **I** : to sleep briefly especially during the day : DOZE **2** : to be off guard ⟨was caught *napping*⟩ [Old English *hnappian*]

²nap *n* : a short sleep especially during the day : SNOOZE

³nap *n* : a hairy or downy surface (as on cloth) [Dutch *noppe* "tuft of wool, nap"] — **nap·less** \'nap-ləs\ *adj* — **napped** \'napt\ *adj* — **nap·py** \'nap-ē\ *adj*

⁴nap *vt* **napped; nap·ping** : to raise a nap on (as cloth)

na·palm \'nā-,päm, -,pälm\ *n* **I** : a thickener used in jelling gasoline (as for incendiary bombs) **2** : fuel jelled with napalm [derived from *naphtha* + *palmitic acid*]

nape \'nāp, 'nap\ *n* : the back of the neck [Middle English]

naph·tha \'naf-thə, 'nap-\ *n* **I** : PETROLEUM **2** : any of various volatile often flammable liquid hydrocarbon mixtures used chiefly as solvents and diluting agents [Latin, from Greek, of Iranian origin]

naph·tha·lene \-,lēn\ *n* : a crystalline hydrocarbon $C_{10}H_8$ usually obtained by distillation of coal tar and used in chemical manufacture and as a moth repellent [derived from *naphtha*] — **naph·tha·le·nic** \,naf-thə-'lēn-ik, ,nap-, -'len-\ *adj*

naph·thol \'naf-,thȯl, 'nap-, -,thōl\ *n* : either of two derivatives of naphthalene found in coal tar or made synthetically and used as antiseptics and in the manufacture of dyes

Na·pier·ian logarithm \nə-,pir-ē-ən-, nā-\ *n* : NATURAL LOGARITHM [John *Napier,* died 1617, Scottish mathematician]

nap·kin \'nap-kən\ *n* **I** : a piece of material (as cloth or paper) used during a meal to wipe the lips or fingers and protect the clothes **2** : a small cloth or towel [Middle English *nappekin,* from *nappe* "tablecloth", from Middle French, from Latin *mappa* "napkin"]

na·po·leon \nə-'pōl-yən, -'pō-lē-ən\ *n* **I** : a French 20-franc gold coin **2** : an oblong pastry consisting of layers of puff paste with a filling of cream, custard, or jelly [French *napoléon,* from *Napoléon* "Napoleon I"]

nappe \'nap\ *n* : one of the two similar parts of a conical surface on either side of the vertex [French, "tablecloth, sheet", from Latin *mappa* "napkin"]

narc *or* **nark** \'närk\ *n* : a person (as a government agent) who investigates narcotics violations

nar·cis·sism \'när-sə-,siz-əm\ *n* : undue dwelling on one's own self or attainments : SELF-LOVE [German *narzissismus,* from *Narziss* "Narcissus (mythological character)" — see NARCISSUS origin] — **nar·cis·sist** \'när-sə-səst\ *n or adj* — **nar·cis·sis·tic** \,när-sə-'sis-tik\ *adj*

nar·cis·sus \när-'sis-əs\ *n, pl* **-cissus** *or* **-cis·sus·es** \-'sis-ə-səz\ *or* **-cis·si** \-'sis-,ī, -,ē\ : DAFFODIL; *esp* : one whose flowers have a short corona and are usually borne separately [*Narcissus,* Greek mythological character, from Latin, from Greek *Narkissos*] □ ORIGIN Narcissus, according to Greek mythology, was an unusually beautiful young man. The nymph Echo loved him but was rebuffed and wasted away. To punish Narcissus for his indifference, the gods made him fall in love with his own image, which he saw reflected in a fountain. He sat admiring himself day after day and finally pined away and was transformed into the flower that we call *narcissus.* From the youth Narcissus we also get a word for self-love, *narcissism.*

nar·co·sis \när-'kō-səs\ *n, pl* **-co·ses** \-'kō-,sēz\ : a state of stupor, unconsciousness, or arrested activity produced by the influence of chemicals (as narcotics)

¹nar·cot·ic \när-'kät-ik\ *n* **I a** : a drug (as opium) that in moderate doses dulls the senses, relieves pain, and induces sleep but in excessive doses causes stupor, coma, or convulsions **b** : a drug (as marijuana or LSD) subject to restriction similar to that of addictive narcotics whether in fact physiologically addictive and narcotic or not **2** : something that soothes, relieves, or lulls [Middle French *narcotique,* from *narcotique,* adj., from Medieval Latin *narcoticus,* from Greek *narkōtikos,* from *narkoun* "to benumb", from *narkē* "numbness"]

²narcotic *adj* **I** : having the properties of or yielding a narcotic **2** : of or relating to narcotics, to their use, or to addicts — **nar·cot·i·cal·ly** \-'kät-i-kə-lē, -klē\ *adv*

nar·co·tize \'när-kə-,tīz\ *vt* **I a** : to treat with or subject to a narcotic **b** : to put into a state of narcosis **2** : to soothe to unconsciousness or unawareness

nard \'närd\ *n* : SPIKENARD 1b [Latin *nardus,* from Greek *nardos,* of Semitic origin]

na·ris \'nar-əs, 'ner-\ *n, pl* **na·res** \'naər-,ēz, 'neər-\ : any of the internal or external openings of the nose or nasal cavity of a vertebrate [Latin]

nar·rate \'nar-,āt, na-'rāt\ *vt* : to recite the details of (as a story) : RELATE, TELL [Latin *narrare,* from *gnarus* "knowing"] — **nar·ra·tor** \'nar-,āt-ər; na-'rāt-, nə-; 'nar-ət-\ *n*

nar·ra·tion \na-'rā-shən, nə-\ *n* **I** : the act or process or an instance of narrating **2** : NARRATIVE 1, STORY — **nar·ra·tion·al** \-shnəl, -shən-l\ *adj*

nar·ra·tive \'nar-ət-iv\ *n* **I** : something (as a story) that is narrated **2** : the art or practice of narration — **narrative** *adj* — **nar·ra·tive·ly** *adv*

¹nar·row \'nar-ō\ *adj* **I a** : of slender width **b** : of less than standard width **2** : limited in size or scope : RESTRICTED **3 a** : not liberal in views : PREJUDICED **b** : interpreted or interpreting strictly ⟨a *narrow* view⟩ **4** : barely sufficient : CLOSE ⟨a *narrow* escape⟩ ⟨won by a *narrow* margin⟩ [Old English *nearu*] — **nar·row·ly** *adv* — **nar·row·ness** *n*

²narrow *n* : a narrow part or passage; *esp* : a strait connecting two bodies of water — usually used in pl.

³narrow *vb* : to lessen in width or extent : CONTRACT

nar·row–mind·ed \,nar-ō-'mīn-dəd\ *adj* : lacking in tolerance or breadth of vision — **nar·row–mind·ed·ly** *adv* — **nar·row–mind·ed·ness** *n*

nar·thex \'när-,theks\ *n* **I** : the portico of an ancient church **2** : a vestibule leading to the nave of a church [Late Greek *narthēx,* from Greek, "giant fennel, cane, casket"]

nar·whal \'när-,hwäl, -,wäl, -,hwȯl, -,hwōl, -,wȯl, -,hwāl, -,wāl, -wəl\ *n* : an arctic sea animal about 6 meters long that is related to the dolphin and in the male has a long twisted ivory tusk [Norwegian and Danish *narhval* and Swedish *narval,* derived from Old Norse *nāhvalr,* from *nār* "corpse" + *hvalr* "whale"]

nary \'naər-ē, 'neər-\ *adj, dialect* : not one [alteration of *ne'er a*]

narcissus

narwhal

\ə\	abut	\ng\	sing
\ər\	further	\ō\	bone
\a\	mat	\ȯ\	saw
\ā\	take	\ȯi\	coin
\ä\	cot, cart	\th\	thin
\aü\	out	\th\	this
\ch\	chin	\ü\	food
\e\	pet	\u̇\	foot
\ē\	easy	\y\	yet
\g\	go	\yü\	few
\i\	tip	\yu̇\	cure
\ī\	life	\zh\	vision
\j\	job		

¹na·sal \'nā-zəl\ *n* **1** : a nasal part **2** : a nasal consonant or vowel [derived from Latin *nasus* "nose"]

²nasal *adj* **1** : of or relating to the nose **2 a** : uttered with the mouth passage closed and the nose passage open ⟨the *nasal* consonants \m\, \n\, and \ng\⟩ **b** : uttered with the nose passage as well as the mouth passage open ⟨the *nasal* vowels in French⟩ **c** : characterized by resonance produced through the nose ⟨speaking in a *nasal* tone⟩ — **na·sal·i·ty** \nā-'zal-ət-ē\ *n* — **na·sal·ly** \'nā-zə-lē\ *adv*

nasal cavity *n* : an incompletely divided chamber that lies between the floor of the skull and the roof of the mouth and functions in the warming and filtering of inhaled air and in the sensing of odors

nas·cent \'nas-nt, 'nās-\ *adj* : coming into existence : beginning to develop [Latin *nascens*, from *nasci* "to be born"] — **nas·cence** \-ns\ *n*

na·so·phar·ynx \ˌnā-zō-'far-ings, -ingks\ *n* : the upper part of the pharynx continuous with the nasal passages — **na·so·pha·ryn·geal** \ˌnā-zō-fə-'rin-jəl, -ˌfar-ən-'jē-əl\ *adj*

nas·tic \'nas-tik\ *adj* : of, relating to, or being a movement of a plant part caused by disproportionate growth or increase of turgor in one surface [Greek *nastos* "close-pressed", from *nassein* "to press"]

nas·tur·tium \nə-'stər-shəm, na-\ *n* : any of a genus of watery-stemmed herbs with showy spurred flowers and pungent 3-seeded fruits [Latin, a kind of cress]

nas·ty \'nas-tē\ *adj* **nas·ti·er; -est 1** : very dirty or foul : FILTHY **2** : morally offensive : VILE **3** : DISAGREEABLE ⟨*nasty* weather⟩ **4** : MEAN, ILL-NATURED ⟨a *nasty* temper⟩ **5** : DISHONORABLE ⟨a *nasty* trick⟩ **6** : HARMFUL, DANGEROUS ⟨a *nasty* fall on the ice⟩ [Middle English] SYN see DIRTY — **nas·ti·ly** \-tə-lē\ *adv* — **nas·ti·ness** \-tē-nəs\ *n*

na·tal \'nāt-l\ *adj* **1** : NATIVE **2** : of, relating to, or present at birth [Latin *natalis*, from *natus*, past participle of *nasci* "to be born"]

na·tal·i·ty \nā-'tal-ət-ē, nə-\ *n, pl* **-ties** : BIRTHRATE

na·ta·tion \nā-'tā-shən, na-\ *n* : the action or art of swimming [Latin *natatio*, from *natare* "to swim"]

na·ta·to·ri·al \ˌnāt-ə-'tōr-ē-əl, ˌnat-, -'tȯr-\ *or* **na·ta·to·ry** \'nāt-ə-ˌtōr-ē, 'nat-, -ˌtȯr-\ *adj* : of or relating to swimming

na·ta·to·ri·um \ˌnāt-ə-'tōr-ē-əm, ˌnat-, -'tȯr-\ *n* : an indoor swimming pool [Late Latin, from Latin *natare* "to swim"]

Natch·ez \'nach-əz\ *n* : a member of an Indian people of the region along the Mississippi river in what is now central Mississippi and Louisiana [French, of American Indian origin]

na·tion \'nā-shən\ *n* **1 a** : NATIONALITY 3a **b** : a community of people composed of one or more nationalities with its own territory and government **c** : the territory of a nation **2** : a tribe or federation of tribes (as of American Indians) [Middle French, from Latin *natio* "birth, race, nation", from *nasci* "to be born"]

¹na·tion·al \'nash-nəl, -ən-l\ *adj* **1** : of or relating to a nation **2** : comprising or characteristic of a nationality **3** : FEDERAL 1c — **na·tion·al·ly** \-ē\ *adv*

²national *n* : one who is under the protection of a nation without regard to the more formal status of citizen or subject SYN see CITIZEN

national anthem *n* : a song or hymn officially adopted and played or sung on formal occasions as a mark of loyalty to the nation

national bank *n* : a commercial bank organized under laws passed by Congress and chartered and supervised by the national government

National Guard *n* : a militia force recruited by each state, equipped by the federal government, and subject to the call of either

national income *n* : the total earnings from a nation's current production including wages of employees, interest, rental income, and business profits after taxes

na·tion·al·ism \'nash-nəl-iz-əm, -ən-l-\ *n* : loyalty and devotion to a nation especially as expressed by praise of one nation above all others and intense concern with promotion of its culture and interests

na·tion·al·ist \-nəl-əst, -ən-l-əst\ *n* **1** : an advocate of nationalism **2** *cap* : a member of a political party or group advocating national independence or strong national government — **nationalist** *adj, often cap* — **na·tion·al·is·tic** \ˌnash-nəl-'is-tik, -ən-l-'is-\ *adj*

na·tion·al·i·ty \ˌnash-'nal-ət-ē, -ə-'nal-\ *n, pl* **-ties 1** : the fact or state of belonging to a nation ⟨a person of French *nationality*⟩ **2** : political independence or existence as a separate nation **3 a** : a people having a common origin, tradition, and language and capable of forming or actually constituting a state **b** : an ethnic group within a larger unit (as a nation)

na·tion·al·ize \'nash-nəl-ˌīz, -ən-l-\ *vt* **1** : to make national : make a nation of **2** : to remove from private ownership and place under government control ⟨*nationalize* railroads⟩ — **na·tion·al·iza·tion** \ˌnash-nəl-ə-'zā-shən, ˌnash-ən-l-\ *n* — **na·tion·al·iz·er** *n*

national park *n* : an area of special scenic, historical, or scientific importance set aside and maintained by a national government especially for recreation or study

national socialism *n* : NAZISM — **national socialist** *adj*

na·tion·hood \'nā-shən-ˌhu̇d\ *n* : the quality or state of being a nation

na·tion·wide \ˌnā-shən-'wīd\ *adj* : extending throughout a nation

¹na·tive \'nāt-iv\ *adj* **1** : INBORN, NATURAL ⟨*native* shrewdness⟩ **2** : born in a particular place or country ⟨*native* Americans⟩ **3** : belonging to a person because of the place or circumstances of birth ⟨one's *native* language⟩ **4** : grown, produced, or having its origin in a particular region ⟨*native* art⟩ **5** : occurring in nature : not artificially prepared ⟨*native* salt⟩ [Middle French *natif*, from Latin *nativus*, from *nasci* "to be born"] — **na·tive·ly** *adv* — **na·tive·ness** *n* □ SYN NATIVE, INDIGENOUS, ENDEMIC, ABORIGINAL mean belonging to a locality. NATIVE implies birth or origin in a place or region and may suggest special compatibility with it; INDIGENOUS applies to species or races and adds an implication of not having been introduced from elsewhere; ENDEMIC stresses the notion that something is peculiar to a place; ABORIGINAL implies having no known predecessor in occupying a region.

²native *n* **1** : one born or reared in a particular place **2 a** : an original inhabitant **b** : something (as an animal or plant) native to a particular locality **3** : a local or lifelong resident

Native American *n* : AMERICAN INDIAN — **Native American** *adj*

na·tiv·i·ty \nə-'tiv-ət-ē, nā-\ *n, pl* **-ties 1** *cap* : the birth of Christ **2** *cap* : CHRISTMAS 1 **3** : the process or circumstances of being born : BIRTH

nat·ty \'nat-ē\ *adj* **nat·ti·er; -est** : trimly neat and tidy : SMART [perhaps from obsolete *net* "neat, clean"] — **nat·ti·ly** \'nat-l-ē\ *adv* — **nat·ti·ness** \'nat-ē-nəs\ *n*

¹nat·u·ral \'nach-rəl, -ə-rəl\ *adj* **1** : born in or with one : INNATE ⟨*natural* ability⟩ **2** : being such by nature : BORN ⟨a *natural* fool⟩ **3** : born of unmarried parents : ILLEGITIMATE ⟨a *natural* child⟩ **4** : existing or used in or produced by nature ⟨the *natural* woodland flora⟩ ⟨meat is the *natural* food of dogs⟩ **5** : having or showing qualities held to be part of human nature ⟨it is not *natural* to hate your children⟩ **6 a** : of or relating to nature as an object of study and research **b** : conforming to the laws of nature or of the physical world ⟨*natural* causes⟩ ⟨*natural* history⟩ **7** : not made or altered by humans ⟨a *natural* complexion⟩ **8** : marked by simplicity and sincerity ⟨*natural* manners⟩ **9** : closely resembling the object imitated : LIFELIKE ⟨the people in the picture look *natural*⟩ **10** : having neither sharps nor flats in the key signature or having a

sharp or a flat changed in pitch by a natural sign —
nat·u·ral·ness *n*
²**natural** *n* **1** : IDIOT **2 a** : a sign ♮ placed on a line or
space of the musical staff to nullify the effect of a preceding sharp or flat **b** : a note or tone affected by the
natural sign **3 a** : one having natural skills, talents, or
abilities **b** : one obviously suitable for a specific purpose **4** : AFRO
natural gas *n* : gas issuing from the earth's crust
through natural openings or bored wells; *esp* : a combustible mixture of methane and higher hydrocarbons
used chiefly as a fuel and raw material
natural history *n* : the study of natural objects especially in the field from an amateur or popular point of
view
natural immunity *n* : inherent genetically determined
immunity as distinguished from that acquired by vaccination or having a disease
nat·u·ral·ism \'nach-rə-ˌliz-əm, -ə-rə-\ *n* **1** : a theory
denying a supernatural explanation of the origin and
development of the universe and holding that scientific laws account for everything in nature **2** : realism in
art or literature; *esp* : a theory in literature emphasizing realistic observation of life without idealization or
the avoidance of the ugly
nat·u·ral·ist \-ləst\ *n* **1** : one that advocates or practices naturalism **2** : a student of natural history; *esp* : a
field biologist — **naturalist** *adj*
nat·u·ral·is·tic \ˌnach-rə-'lis-tik, -ə-rə-\ *adj* : of, characterized by, or according with naturalism — **nat·u·ral-
is·ti·cal·ly** \-ti-kə-lē, -klē\ *adv*
nat·u·ral·ize \'nach-rə-ˌlīz, -ə-rə-\ *vb* **1** : to introduce
into common use ⟨*naturalize* a foreign word⟩ **2** : to
become or cause to become established as if native
⟨*naturalized* weeds⟩ **3** : to make less artificial or conventional **4** : to confer the rights and privileges of citizenship on (an alien) — **nat·u·ral·iza·tion** \ˌnach-rə-
lə-'zā-shən, -ə-rə-\ *n*
natural law *n* : a body of law or a specific principle
held to be derived from nature and binding on human
society in the absence of or in addition to positive law
natural logarithm *n* : a logarithm in a system that uses
as a base the transcendental number *e* whose value is
approximately 2.71828
nat·u·ral·ly \'nach-rə-lē, -ə-rə-; 'nach-ər-lē\ *adv* **1** : by
natural character or ability ⟨*naturally* timid⟩ **2** : according to the usual course of things ⟨we *naturally*
dislike being hurt⟩ **3 a** : without artificial aid ⟨hair that
curls *naturally*⟩ **b** : without affectation ⟨speak *naturally*⟩ **4** : in a lifelike manner ⟨paints flowers *naturally*⟩
natural number *n* : the number 1 or any number (as 3,
12, or 432) obtained by repeatedly adding 1 to this
number
natural philosophy *n* : NATURAL SCIENCE; *esp* : PHYSICAL
SCIENCE
natural resource *n* : something (as a mineral, waterpower source, forest, or kind of animal) that occurs in
nature and is of value to human life
natural science *n* : a science (as physics, chemistry, or
biology) that deals with matter, energy, and their interrelations and transformations or with objectively
measurable phenomena — **natural scientist** *n*
natural selection *n* : a natural process that results in
the survival of individuals or groups best adapted to
the conditions under which they live and in the per-
petuation of adaptive genetic traits and the elimination of those that are not adaptive
na·ture \'nā-chər\ *n* **1** : the basic quality, character, or
constitution of a person or thing ⟨the *nature* of steel⟩
2 : general character : KIND ⟨and things of that *nature*⟩
3 : DISPOSITION, TEMPERAMENT ⟨behavior contrary to
one's *nature*⟩ **4** *often cap* : a power or set of forces
thought of as controlling the universe ⟨Mother
Nature⟩ **5** : natural feeling especially as shown in

one's attitude toward others **6** : humanity's native
state : primitive life ⟨return to *nature*⟩ **7** : the whole
physical universe ⟨the study of *nature*⟩ **8** : the physical workings or drives of an organism ⟨sex is a part of
nature⟩ **9** : natural scenery ⟨the beauties of *nature*⟩
[Middle French, from Latin *natura*, from *nasci* "to be
born"]
¹**naught** *or* **nought** \'nȯt, 'nät\ *pron* : NOTHING [Old English *nāwiht*, from *nā* "no" + *wiht* "creature, thing"]
²**naught** *or* **nought** *n* **1 a** : NOTHING **b** : the quality or
state of being nothing **2** : ZERO 1 — see NUMBER table
³**naught** *or* **nought** *adj* : of no importance : INSIGNIFI-
CANT
naugh·ty \'nȯt-ē, 'nät-\ *adj* **naugh·ti·er; -est 1** : guilty
of disobedience or misbehavior **2** : not moral or proper [²*naught*] — **naugh·ti·ly** \'nȯt-l-ē, 'nät-\ *adv* —
naugh·ti·ness \'nȯt-ē-nəs, 'nät-\ *n*
nau·pli·us \'nȯ-plē-əs\ *n, pl* **-plii** \-plē-ˌī, -ˌē\ : an early
crustacean larva with three pairs of appendages and a
median eye [Latin, a kind of shellfish, from Greek *nau-
plios*]
nau·sea \'nȯ-zē-ə, -sē-ə; 'nȯ-zhə, -shə\ *n* **1** : a stomach
distress with distaste for food and an urge to vomit **2** :
extreme disgust [Latin, "seasickness, nausea", from
Greek *nautia, nausia,* from *nautēs* "sailor", from
naus "ship"] □ ORIGIN Nausea, stomach distress accompanied by an urge to vomit, is one of the most
unpleasant symptoms of seasickness. Latin *nausea* and
its Greek source *nausia* or *nautia* have the same
meaning as English *nausea*. But these Greek and Latin
words also have the specific sense of "seasickness".
The Greek name for the illness is derived from the
word *naus,* which means "ship".
nau·se·ate \'nȯ-zē-ˌāt, -sē-, -zhē-, -shē-\ *vb* : to affect or
become affected with nausea — **nau·se·at·ing** \-ˌāt-
ing\ *adj* — **nau·se·at·ing·ly** \-ing-lē\ *adv*
nau·seous \'nȯ-shəs, 'nȯ-zē-əs\ *adj* **1** : causing nausea
⟨*nauseous* odors⟩ **2** : affected with nausea ⟨feel *nauseous*⟩ — **nau·seous·ly** *adv* — **nau·seous·ness** *n*
nau·ti·cal \'nȯt-i-kəl\ *adj* : of or relating to seamen,
ships, or navigation on water [Latin *nauticus,* from
Greek *nautikos,* from *nautēs* "sailor", from *naus*
"ship"] — **nau·ti·cal·ly** \-kə-lē, -klē\ *adv*
nautical mile *n* : a unit of distance used for sea and air
navigation equal to about 6076 feet (1852 meters)
nau·ti·loid \'nȯt-l-ˌȯid\ *n* : any of an ancient group
(Nautiloidea) of cephalopods represented in the recent fauna by the nautiluses — **nautiloid** *adj*
nau·ti·lus \'nȯt-l-əs\ *n, pl* **-lus·es** *or* **-li** \-l-ˌī, -ˌē\ **1** : any
of a genus of cephalopod mollusks of the South Pacific
and Indian oceans having a spiral chambered shell that
is pearly on the inside **2** : PAPER NAUTILUS [Latin, "paper nautilus", from Greek *nautilos,* literally, "sailor",
from *naus* "ship"]

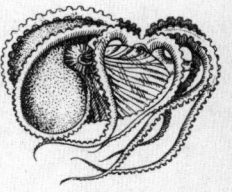

nautilus 1

Na·va·jo *also* **Na·va·ho** \'nav-ə-ˌhō, 'näv-\ *n, pl* **Navajo**
or **Navajos** *also* **Navaho** *or* **Navahos 1** : a member of an
Amerindian people of what is now northwestern New
Mexico and the adjacent part of Arizona **2** : the language of the Navaho people [Spanish *Apache de Navajó,* literally, "Apache of Navajó", from *Navajó,* a pu-
eblo]
na·val \'nā-vəl\ *adj* **1** : of or relating to a navy or warships ⟨*naval* shipyards⟩ **2** : possessing a navy ⟨a *naval*
power⟩
naval stores *n pl* : products (as pitch, turpentine, or
rosin) obtained from resinous conifers (as pines)
[from their former use in the construction and maintenance of wooden sailing vessels]
¹**nave** \'nāv\ *n* : the hub of a wheel [Old English *nafu*
— see AUGER *origin*]
²**nave** *n* : the main body of a church interior; *esp* : the
long central hall in a cruciform church that rises higher than the aisles flanking it to form a clerestory [Medi-
eval Latin *navis,* from Latin, "ship"]

\ə\	abut	\ng\	sing
\ər\	further	\ō\	bone
\a\	mat	\ȯ\	saw
\ā\	take	\ȯi\	coin
\ä\	cot, cart	\th\	thin
\au̇\	out	\th\	this
\ch\	chin	\ü\	food
\e\	pet	\u̇\	foot
\ē\	easy	\y\	yet
\g\	go	\yü\	few
\i\	tip	\yu̇\	cure
\ī\	life	\zh\	vision
\j\	job		

na·vel \'nā-vəl\ *n* **1** : a depression in the middle of the abdomen marking the point of attachment of the umbilical cord or yolk stalk **2** : the central point : MIDDLE [Old English *nafela*] — see AUGER origin

navel orange *n* : a seedless orange having a pit at the apex where the fruit encloses a small secondary fruit

nav·i·ga·ble \'nav-i-gə-bəl\ *adj* **1** : deep enough and wide enough to afford passage to ships **2** : capable of being steered ⟨a *navigable* balloon⟩ — **nav·i·ga·bil·i·ty** \,nav-i-gə-'bil-ət-ē\ *n* — **nav·i·ga·ble·ness** \'nav-i-gə-bəl-nəs\ *n* — **nav·i·ga·bly** \-blē\ *adv*

nav·i·gate \'nav-ə-,gāt\ *vb* **1 a** : to travel by water **b** : to sail over, on, or through **2 a** : to direct one's course in a ship or aircraft **b** : to steer, direct, or control the course of (as a boat or aircraft) **3 a** : to get about; *esp* : WALK **b** : to make one's way over or through [Latin *navigare*, derived from *navis* "ship"]

nav·i·ga·tion \,nav-ə-'gā-shən\ *n* **1** : the act or practice of navigating **2** : the science of getting ships or airplanes from place to place; *esp* : the method of determining position, course, and distance traveled **3** : ship traffic or commerce — **nav·i·ga·tion·al** \-shnəl, -shən-l\ *adj* — **nav·i·ga·tion·al·ly** \-ē\ *adv*

nav·i·ga·tor \'nav-ə-,gāt-ər\ *n* : a person who navigates or is qualified to navigate: as **a** : an officer on a ship or airplane responsible for its navigation **b** : a person who explores by ship

nav·vy \'nav-ē\ *n, pl* **navvies** *British* : an unskilled laborer [from *navigator* "construction worker on a canal, navvy"]

na·vy \'nā-vē\ *n, pl* **navies** **1** : a group of ships : FLEET **2** : a nation's warships **3** *often cap* : a nation's complete naval establishment including yards, stations, ships, and personnel **4** : a dark blue [Middle French *navie*, from Latin *navigia* "ships", from *navigare* "to navigate"]

navy bean *n* : a kidney bean grown especially for its small white nutritious seeds

navy yard *n* : a yard where naval vessels are built or repaired

na·wab \nə-'wäb\ *n* **1** : NABOB 1 **2** : a Muslim prince of India [Hindi *nawwāb*]

¹nay \'nā\ *adv* **1** : NO 3 **2** : not merely this but also : not only so but ⟨the letter made me happy, *nay*, ecstatic⟩ [Old Norse *nei*, from *ne* "not" + *ei* "ever"]

²nay *n* **1** : REFUSAL 1, DENIAL **2 a** : a negative reply or vote **b** : one who votes no

Naz·a·rene \,naz-ə-'rēn\ *n* **1** : a native or resident of Nazareth **2** : a member of the Church of the Nazarene which adheres to Wesleyan doctrine and church government — **Nazarene** *adj*

na·zi \'nät-sē, 'nat-\ *n* **1** *often cap* : a member of a German fascist party controlling Germany from 1933 to 1945 under Adolf Hitler **2** *often cap* : one held to resemble a German Nazi [German, from *Nationalsozialist* "national socialist"] — **nazi** *adj, often cap* — **na·zi·fi·ca·tion** \,nät-si-fə-'kā-shən, ,nat-\ *n, often cap* — **na·zi·fy** \'nät-si-,fī, 'nat-\ *vt, often cap* — **Na·zism** \'nät-,siz-əm, 'nat-\ *or* **Na·zi·ism** \-sē-,iz-əm\ *n*

NC–17 \'en-,sē-,sev-ən-'tēn, -'sev-ən-\ *trademark* — used to certify that a motion picture is of such as nature that no one under the age of 17 can be admitted; compare G, PG, PG-13, R

-nd *symbol* — used after the figure 2 to indicate that the number is an ordinal ⟨2*nd*⟩ ⟨32*nd*⟩

ne- *or* **neo-** *combining form* : new : recent ⟨*neo*-impressionism⟩ [Greek, from *neos* "new"]

Ne·an·der·thal \nē-'an-dər-,thȯl, -,tȯl; nā-'än-dər-,täl\ *adj* **1** : being, relating to, or resembling Neanderthal man **2** : suggesting a caveman in appearance or behavior — **Neanderthal** *or* **Ne·an·der·thal·er** \-ər\ *n*

Neanderthal man *n* : a prehistoric man known from skeletal remains and artifacts and intermediate in some respects between modern man and pithecanthropus

[*Neanderthal,* valley in western Germany] — **Ne·an·der·thal·oid** \-,ȯid\ *adj or n*

neap \'nēp\ *adj* : of, relating to, or constituting a neap tide [Old English *nēp* "being at the stage of neap tide"]

Ne·a·pol·i·tan ice cream \,nē-ə-,päl-ət-n-\ *n* : a brick of from two to four layers of ice cream of different flavors [*Neapolitan* "of Naples, Italy", derived from Greek *Neapolis* "Naples"]

neap tide *n* : a tide of minimum range occurring at the first and the third quarters of the moon

¹near \'niər\ *adv* **1** : at, within, or to a short distance or time **2** : ALMOST, NEARLY ⟨*near* dead⟩ **3** : CLOSELY ⟨*near* related⟩ [partly from Old English *nēar* "nearer", comparative of *nēah* "nigh"; partly from Old Norse *nær* "nearer, near", from comparative of *nā-* "nigh"]

²near *prep* : close to ⟨standing *near* the door⟩

³near *adj* **1** : closely related or associated **2 a** : being little apart in time, place, value, or degree ⟨the *near* future⟩ **b** : barely avoided ⟨a *near* disaster⟩ **c** : failing or missing by very little ⟨a *near* miss⟩ **3 a** : being the closer of two ⟨the *near* side⟩ **b** : being the left-hand one of a pair ⟨the *near* wheel of a cart⟩ **4** : DIRECT, SHORT ⟨the *nearest* route⟩ **5** : STINGY 1 **6 a** : closely resembling a prototype **b** : approximating the genuine ⟨*near* silk⟩ — **near·ness** *n* □ SYN NEAR, CLOSE mean not distant or not much removed in space, time, or resemblance. NEAR implies that the space, interval, or degree of difference though small is none the less distinct and real; CLOSE implies virtual or approximate contact, coincidence, or identity.

⁴near *vb* : to draw near : APPROACH

near·by \niər-'bī, 'niər-,\ *adv or adj* : close at hand

near·ly \'niər-lē\ *adv* : ALMOST ⟨we *nearly* got hit⟩

near·sight·ed \'niər-'sīt-əd\ *adj* : able to see near things more clearly than distant ones : MYOPIC — **near·sight·ed·ly** *adv* — **near·sight·ed·ness** *n*

¹neat \'nēt\ *n, pl* **neat** : the common domestic bovine (as a cow, bull, or ox) [Old English *nēat*]

²neat *adj* **1** : not mixed or diluted ⟨*neat* brandy⟩ **2** : marked by tasteful simplicity **3 a** : PRECISE, SYSTEMATIC ⟨*neat* plans⟩ **b** : marked by skill or ingenuity : ADROIT **4** : being orderly and clean : TIDY **5** : CLEAR, NET ⟨a *neat* profit⟩ **6** *slang* : TERRIFIC 3 [Middle French *net,* from Latin *nitidus* "bright, neat", from *nitēre* "to shine"] — **neat·ly** *adv* — **neat·ness** *n*

neat's–foot oil \'nēts-,fut-\ *n* : a pale yellow fatty oil made especially from the bones of cattle and used chiefly to condition leather

neb \'neb\ *n* **1 a** : the beak of a bird or tortoise : BILL **b** : NOSE 1, 3, 4; *also* : SNOUT **2** : NIB 2b, 3 [Old English]

neb·u·la \'neb-yə-lə\ *n, pl* **-las** *or* **-lae** \-,lē, -,lī\ **1** : any of many immense bodies of highly rarefied gas or dust in interstellar space **2** : GALAXY 1b [Latin, "mist, cloud"] — **neb·u·lar** \-lər\ *adj*

nebular hypothesis *n* : a hypothesis in astronomy : the solar system has evolved from a hot gaseous nebula

neb·u·lize \'neb-yə-,līz\ *vt* : to reduce to a fine spray — **neb·u·li·za·tion** \,neb-yə-lə-'zā-shən\ *n* — **neb·u·liz·er** \'neb-yə-,lī-zər\ *n*

neb·u·los·i·ty \,neb-yə-'läs-ət-ē\ *n, pl* **-ties** **1** : the quality or state of being nebulous **2** : nebulous matter : NEBULA

neb·u·lous \'neb-yə-ləs\ *adj* **1** : VAGUE ⟨*nebulous* concepts⟩ **2** : of, relating to, or resembling a nebula : NEBULAR — **neb·u·lous·ly** *adv* — **neb·u·lous·ness** *n*

¹nec·es·sary \'nes-ə-,ser-ē\ *n, pl* **-sar·ies** : an indispensable item : ESSENTIAL ⟨*necessaries* of life⟩

²necessary *adj* **1 a** : bound to happen : INEVITABLE **b** (1) : being the only possible result of an argument (2) : logically required for a particular result **c** : COMPULSORY 1 **2** : absolutely needed : INDISPENSABLE [Latin *necessarius,* from *necesse* "necessary", from *ne-* "not" + *cedere* "to withdraw"] — **nec·es·sar·i·ly**

\,nes-ə-'ser-ə-lē\ *adv* □ SYN REQUISITE, ESSENTIAL: NECESSARY applies to what cannot be done without or avoided and may stress lack of choice or uselessness of wishing or resisting; REQUISITE implies being needful especially for fulfillment or attainment of a set purpose or standard; ESSENTIAL implies being absolutely or urgently necessary.

ne·ces·si·tate \ni-'ses-ə-ˌtāt\ *vt* : to make necessary or unavoidable : REQUIRE, COMPEL ⟨the attack *necessitated* a troop withdrawal⟩ — **ne·ces·si·ta·tion** \-ˌses-ə-'tā-shən\ *n*

ne·ces·si·tous \ni-'ses-ət-əs\ *adj* **1** : hard up : NEEDY **2** : forced by necessity : NECESSARY ⟨*necessitous* bargaining⟩ — **ne·ces·si·tous·ly** *adv* — **ne·ces·si·tous·ness** *n*

ne·ces·si·ty \ni-'ses-ət-ē, -'ses-tē\ *n, pl* **-ties 1** : very great need especially of help or relief **2** : conditions that cannot be changed ⟨compelled by *necessity*⟩ **3** : lack of necessary things : WANT, POVERTY **4** : something badly needed ⟨daily *necessities*⟩ SYN see NEED

¹neck \'nek\ *n* **1** : the part of the body connecting the head and the trunk **2** : the part of a garment covering or nearest to the neck **3** : something like a neck in shape or position ⟨the *neck* of a bottle⟩ ⟨a *neck* of land⟩ **4** : a narrow margin ⟨won by a *neck*⟩ [Old English *hnecca*] — **necked** \'nekt\ *adj*

²neck *vb* : to kiss and caress amorously

neck·er·chief \'nek-ər-chəf, -ˌchif, -ˌchēf\ *n, pl* **-chiefs** *also* **-chieves** \see HANDKERCHIEF pl \ : a kerchief for the neck

neck·lace \'nek-ləs\ *n* : an ornament for the neck

neck·line \-ˌlīn\ *n* : the line formed by the neck opening of a garment

neck·tie \-ˌtī\ *n* : a band or strip of material worn about the neck and tied in front; *esp* : FOUR-IN-HAND

necr- *or* **necro-** *combining form* **1** : those that are dead ⟨*necro*logy⟩ **2** : dead body ⟨*necr*opsy⟩ [Greek *nekros* "dead body"]

ne·crol·o·gy \nə-'kräl-ə-jē, ne-\ *n, pl* **-gies 1** : a list of the recently dead **2** : OBITUARY — **nec·ro·log·i·cal** \ˌnek-rə-'läj-i-kəl\ *adj* — **ne·crol·o·gist** \nə-'kräl-ə-jəst, ne-\ *n*

nec·ro·man·cy \'nek-rə-ˌman-sē\ *n* **1** : the practice of conjuring up the spirits of the dead for purposes of magically revealing the future or influencing the course of events **2** : MAGIC 1, SORCERY — **nec·ro·man·cer** \-sər\ *n* — **nec·ro·man·tic** \ˌnek-rə-'mant-ik\ *adj* — **nec·ro·man·ti·cal·ly** \-'mant-i-kə-lē, -klē\ *adv*

ne·crop·o·lis \nə-'kräp-ə-ləs, ne-\ *n, pl* **-lis·es** *or* **-les** \-ˌlēz\ : CEMETERY; *esp* : a large elaborate cemetery of an ancient city [Late Latin, "city of the dead", from Greek *nekropolis*, from *nekros* "dead body" + *polis* "city"]

nec·rop·sy \'nek-ˌräp-sē\ *n, pl* **-sies** : POSTMORTEM EXAMINATION

ne·cro·sis \nə-'krō-səs, ne-\ *n, pl* **-cro·ses** \-'krō-ˌsēz\ : usually local death of body tissue — **ne·crot·ic** \-'krät-ik\ *adj*

nec·tar \'nek-tər\ *n* **1 a** : the drink of the Greek and Roman gods **b** : a delicious drink **2** : a sweet liquid secreted by plants that is the chief raw material of honey [Latin, from Greek *nektar*]

nec·tar·ine \ˌnek-tə-'rēn\ *n* : a smooth-skinned peach; *also* : a tree producing this fruit

nec·tary \'nek-tə-rē, -trē\ *n, pl* **-tar·ies** : a plant gland that secretes nectar

née *or* **nee** \'nā\ *adj* : BORN — used to identify a woman by her maiden family name [French *née*, feminine of *né* "born", from *naître* "to be born", from Latin *nasci*]

¹need \'nēd\ *n* **1** : necessary duty ⟨no *need* to go⟩ **2 a** : a lack of something necessary, desirable, or useful **b** : REQUIREMENT ⟨my *needs* are few and simple⟩ **3** : a condition requiring supply or relief **4** : POVERTY 1 [Old English *nīed, nēd*] □ SYN NEED, NECESSITY, EXIGENCY

mean a pressing lack of something essential. NEED implies urgency and may suggest distress ⟨a critical *need* for medical supplies⟩ NECESSITY stresses imperative demand or compelling cause ⟨the great *necessity* for a new investigation⟩ EXIGENCY implies unusual or special difficulty ⟨the *exigencies* of war⟩

²need *vb* **1** : to be in want **2** : to have cause or occasion for ⟨they *need* advice⟩ **3** : to be obligated to — used as an auxiliary verb ⟨you *need* not answer⟩

need·ful \'nēd-fəl\ *adj* : NECESSARY 2, REQUISITE — **need·ful·ly** \-fə-lē\ *adv* — **need·ful·ness** *n*

¹nee·dle \'nēd-l\ *n* **1 a** : a slender usually steel instrument having an eye for thread and used for sewing **b** : a device for carrying thread and making stitches (as in suturing a wound) **c** : a slender hollow instrument for introducing material into or removing material from the body **2** : a slender usually sharp-pointed indicator on a dial; *esp* : MAGNETIC NEEDLE **3 a** : a slender pointed object resembling a needle (as a pointed crystal) **b** : OBELISK **c** : a needle-shaped leaf (as of a pine) **d** : a slender piece of jewel, steel, wood, or fiber used in a phonograph to transmit vibrations from the record **e** : a slender pointed rod controlling a fine inlet or outlet (as in a valve) [Old English *nǣdl*] — **nee·dle·like** \'nēd-l-ˌlīk, -ˌīk\ *adj*

²needle *vb* **nee·dled; nee·dling** \'nēd-ling, -l-ing\ **1** : to sew or pierce with or as if with a needle **2 a** : TEASE 2a, HARASS **b** : to incite to action by repeated gibes ⟨*needled* us into a fight⟩ — **nee·dler** \'nēd-lər, -l-ər\ *n* — **nee·dling** *n*

nee·dle·leaf \'nēd-l-ˌlēf, -ˌēf\ *adj* : populated with trees having leaves that are needles ⟨*needleleaf* forests⟩; *also* : having leaves that are needles ⟨*needleleaf* trees⟩

nee·dle·point \'nēd-l-ˌpȯint\ *n* **1** : lace worked with a needle in buttonhole stitch over a paper pattern **2** : embroidery done on canvas usually in simple even stitches across counted threads — **needlepoint** *adj*

need·less \'nēd-ləs\ *adj* : UNNECESSARY ⟨*needless* expenses⟩ — **need·less·ly** *adv* — **need·less·ness** *n*

nee·dle·wom·an \'nēd-l-ˌwùm-ən\ *n* : a woman who does needlework; *esp* : SEAMSTRESS

nee·dle·work \-ˌwərk\ *n* : work done with a needle; *esp* : work (as embroidery) other than plain sewing — **nee·dle·work·er** *n*

needn't \'nēd-nt\ : need not

needs \'nēdz\ *adv* : of necessity : NECESSARILY ⟨must *needs* be recognized⟩ [Old English *nēdes*, from genitive of *nēd* "need"]

needy \'nēd-ē\ *adj* **need·i·er; -est** : being in want : very poor — **need·i·ness** *n*

ne'er \neər, 'neər, naər, 'naər\ *adv* : NEVER

ne'er-do-well \'neər-dù-ˌwel, 'naər-\ *n* : an idle worthless person — **ne'er-do-well** *adj*

ne·far·i·ous \ni-'far-ē-əs, -'fer-\ *adj* : flagrantly wicked or impious : EVIL [Latin *nefarius*, from *nefas* "crime", from *ne-* "not" + *fas* "right, divine law"] — **ne·far·i·ous·ly** *adv* — **ne·far·i·ous·ness** *n*

ne·gate \ni-'gāt\ *vt* **1** : to deny the existence or truth of **2** : to cause to be ineffective or invalid [Latin *negare* "to say no, deny"] SYN see NULLIFY — **ne·ga·tor** \-'gāt-ər\ *n*

ne·ga·tion \ni-'gā-shən\ *n* **1 a** : the action of negating : DENIAL **b** : a negative statement; *esp* : NEGATIVE 1a **2** : something considered the opposite of something positive — **ne·ga·tion·al** \-shnəl, -shən-l\ *adj*

¹neg·a·tive \'neg-ət-iv\ *adj* **1** : marked by denial, prohibition, or refusal ⟨a *negative* reply⟩ **2** : not positive or constructive ⟨a *negative* attitude⟩ **3 a** : less than zero and opposite in sign to a positive number of like absolute value **b** : taken in a direction opposite to one chosen as positive ⟨a *negative* angle⟩ **4 a** : of, being, or relating to electricity of a kind of which the electron is the elementary unit ⟨a *negative* charge⟩ **b** : being the part toward which the electric current flows from the external circuit ⟨the *negative* pole of a discharging storage battery⟩ **c** : electron-emitting — used of an electrode in an electron tube **5 a** : not affirming the presence of what is sought or suspected ⟨a *negative* TB test⟩ **b** : directed or moving away from a source of stimulation ⟨a *negative* tropism⟩ **6** : having the light and dark parts in approximately inverse order to those of the original photographic subject ⟨a *negative* photographic image⟩ — **neg·a·tive·ly** *adv* — **neg·a·tive·ness** *n* — **neg·a·tiv·i·ty** \ˌneg-ə-ˈtiv-ət-ē\ *n*

²negative *n* **I a** : a proposition by which something is denied or contradicted **b** : a reply that indicates the withholding of assent : REFUSAL **2** : NEGATION 2 **3 a** : an expression (as the word *no*) of negation or denial **b** : a negative number; *also* : ADDITIVE INVERSE **4** : the side that argues or votes against something in a debate **5** : a negative photographic image on transparent material used for printing positive pictures; *also* : the material that carries such an image

³negative *vt* **I** : to refuse to accept or approve : VETO **2** : DENY 4 **3** : NEGATE 2

neg·a·tiv·ism \ˈneg-ət-iv-ˌiz-əm\ *n* : an attitude of skepticism about nearly everything affirmed or suggested by others — **neg·a·tiv·ist** \-iv-əst\ *n* — **neg·a·tiv·is·tic** \ˌneg-ət-iv-ˈis-tik\ *adj*

¹ne·glect \ni-ˈglekt\ *vt* **I** : to give little attention, respect, or care to ⟨*neglect*ed their children⟩ **2** : to leave undone or unattended to especially through carelessness ⟨*neglect* one's duty⟩ **3** : FAIL ⟨*neglect*ed to mention a previous conviction⟩ [Latin *neglectus,* past participle of *neglegere* "to neglect", from *neg-* "not" + *legere* "to gather"] — **ne·glect·er** *n*

²neglect *n* **I** : an act or instance of neglecting **2** : the condition of being neglected

ne·glect·ful \ni-ˈglekt-fəl, -ˈglek-\ *adj* : given to neglecting : CARELESS SYN see NEGLIGENT — **ne·glect·ful·ly** \-fə-lē\ *adv* — **ne·glect·ful·ness** *n*

neg·li·gee *also* **neg·li·gé** \ˌneg-lə-ˈzhā\ *n* **I** : a woman's long flowing dressing gown **2** : carelessly informal or incomplete attire [French *négligé,* from *négliger* "to neglect", from Latin *neglegere*]

neg·li·gence \ˈneg-li-jəns\ *n* **I a** : the quality or state of being negligent **b** : failure to use the care that a prudent person exercises **2** : an act or instance of negligence

neg·li·gent \-jənt\ *adj* **I** : marked by or given to neglect **2** : marked by a carelessly easy manner [Latin *neglegens,* present participle of *neglegere* "to neglect"] — **neg·li·gent·ly** *adv* □ SYN NEGLECTFUL, REMISS: NEGLIGENT implies inattention to one's duty or business; NEGLECTFUL adds a stronger implication of laziness or callousness; REMISS implies blameworthy carelessness or forgetfulness in performance of duty.

neg·li·gi·ble \ˈneg-li-jə-bəl\ *adj* : deserving neglect : TRIVIAL — **neg·li·gi·bil·i·ty** \ˌneg-li-jə-ˈbil-ət-ē\ *n* — **neg·li·gi·bly** \ˈneg-li-jə-blē\ *adv*

ne·go·tia·ble \ni-ˈgō-shə-bəl, -shē-ə-bəl\ *adj* : capable of being negotiated: as **a** : transferable from one person to another by being delivered with or without endorsement so that the title passes to the recipient ⟨*negotiable* bonds⟩ **b** : that can be traversed or accomplished ⟨a *negotiable* road⟩ **c** : that can be discussed or changed ⟨*negotiable* demands⟩ — **ne·go·tia·bil·i·ty** \-ˌgō-shə-ˈbil-ət-ē, -shē-ə-\ *n*

ne·go·tiant \ni-ˈgō-shē-ənt, -shənt\ *n* : one that negotiates

ne·go·ti·ate \ni-ˈgō-shē-ˌāt\ *vb* **I** : to discuss with another so as to arrive at a settlement or agreement; *also* : to arrange for or bring about by such conference ⟨*negotiate* a treaty⟩ **2** : to transfer to another in return for something of equal value ⟨*negotiate* a check⟩ **3** : to get through, around, or over successfully ⟨*negotiate* a turn⟩ [Latin *negotiari* "to transact business", from *negotium* "business", from *neg-* "not" + *otium* "leisure"] — **ne·go·ti·a·tion** \-ˌgō-shē-ˈā-shən, -sē-ˈā-\

n — **ne·go·ti·a·tor** \-ˈgō-shē-ˌāt-ər\ *n* — **ne·go·tia·to·ry** \-shə-ˌtōr-ē, -shē-ə-, -ˌtȯr-\ *adj*

Ne·gril·lo \ni-ˈgril-ō; -ˈgrē-ō, -yō\ *n, pl* **-los** *or* **-loes** : a member of a people (as the Pygmies) belonging to a group of African negroid peoples of small stature [Spanish, from *negro* "Negro"]

Ne·gri·to \nə-ˈgrēt-ō\ *n, pl* **-tos** *or* **-toes** : a member of a people (as the Andamanese) belonging to a group of negroid peoples of small stature that live in Oceania and southeastern Asia [Spanish, from *negro* "Negro"]

ne·gri·tude \ˈneg-rə-ˌtüd, ˈnē-grə-, -ˌtyüd\ *n* : a consciousness of and pride in black culture and history [French *négritude,* from *nègre* "Negro"]

Ne·gro \ˈnē-grō\ *n, pl* **Negroes** **I** : a member of the black race of mankind distinguished from members of other races by classification according to physical features but without regard to language or culture; *esp* : a member of a black people of Africa **2** : a person of Negro ancestry [Spanish or Portuguese, from *negro,* adj., "black", from Latin *niger*] — **Negro** *adj* — **ne·groid** \ˈnē-ˌgrȯid\ *n or adj, often cap*

Ne·he·mi·ah \ˌnē-ə-ˈmī-ə, ˌnē-hə-\ *n* — see BIBLE table

neigh \ˈnā\ *vi* : to utter the characteristic loud prolonged cry of a horse or a similar sound [Old English *hnǣgan*] — **neigh** *n*

¹neigh·bor \ˈnā-bər\ *n* **I** : one living or located near another **2** : a fellow being [Old English *nēahgebūr,* from *nēah* "near" + *gebūr* "dweller"]

²neighbor *vt* **neigh·bored; neigh·bor·ing** \-bə-ring, -bring\ : to be next to or near to

neigh·bor·hood \ˈnā-bər-ˌhu̇d\ *n* **I** : the quality or state of being neighbors : NEARNESS **2 a** : a place or region near : VICINITY **b** : an approximate amount, extent, or degree ⟨cost in the *neighborhood* of $10⟩ **3 a** : the people living near one another **b** : a section lived in by neighbors and usually having distinguishing characteristics ⟨an older *neighborhood*⟩

neigh·bor·ly \ˈnā-bər-lē\ *adj* : of, relating to, or characteristic of neighbors; *esp* : FRIENDLY — **neigh·bor·li·ness** *n*

¹nei·ther \ˈnē-ᵺər *also* ˈnī-\ *pron* : not the one and not the other ⟨*neither* of the two⟩ [Middle English, alteration of *nauther,* from Old English *nāhwæther,* from *nā* "not" + *hwæther* "which of two, whether"]

²neither *conj* **I** : not either ⟨*neither* black nor white⟩ **2** : also not ⟨*neither* did I⟩

³neither *adj* : not either ⟨*neither* hand⟩

nek·ton \ˈnek-tən, -ˌtän\ *n* : free-swimming aquatic animals whose distribution is essentially independent of wave and current action — compare PLANKTON [German, from Greek *nēktos* "swimming", from *nēchein* "to swim"] — **nek·ton·ic** \nek-ˈtän-ik\ *adj*

nel·son \ˈnel-sən\ *n* : a wrestling hold in which leverage is exerted against an opponent's arm, neck, and head [probably from the name *Nelson*]

ne·ma \ˈnē-mə\ *n* : NEMATODE

ne·ma·to·cide \ˈnem-ət-ə-ˌsīd, ni-ˈmat-ə-\ *n* : a substance or preparation used to destroy nematodes

ne·ma·to·cyst \ˈnem-ət-ə-ˌsist, nə-ˈmat-ə-\ *n* : one of the minute stinging organs of various coelenterates [Greek *nēmat-, nēma* "thread"]

nem·a·tode \ˈnem-ə-ˌtōd\ *n* : any of a class or phylum (Nematoda) of elongated cylindrical worms parasitic in animals or plants or free-living in soil or water [derived from Greek *nēmat-, nēma* "thread"] — **nematode** *adj*

Nem·bu·tal \ˈnem-byə-ˌtȯl\ *trademark* — used for the sodium salt of pentobarbital

ne·mer·te·an \ni-ˈmərt-ē-ən\ *n* : any of a class (Nemertea) of often vividly colored marine worms most of which burrow in the mud or sand along seacoasts [derived from Greek *Nēmertēs* "Nemertes (a sea nymph)"] — **nemertean** *adj* — **nem·er·tine** \ˈnem-ər-ˌtīn\ *adj or n*

nem·e·sis \'nem-ə-səs\ *n, pl* **-e·ses** \-ə-ˌsēz\ **1 a** : one that inflicts retribution or vengeance **b** : a formidable and usually victorious rival or opponent **2 a** : an act or instance of just punishment **b** : BANE 2 [*Nemesis,* Greek goddess of fate and punisher of pride]

ne·moph·i·la \ni-ˈmäf-ə-lə\ *n* : any of a genus of American herbs widely grown for their showy blue or white usually spotted flowers [Greek *nemos* "wooded pasture" + *philos* "loving"]

neo- — see NE-

neo·clas·sic \ˌnē-ō-ˈklas-ik\ *adj* : of or relating to a revival or adaptation of the classical style especially in literature, art, architecture, or music — **neo·clas·si·cal** \-ˈklas-i-kəl\ *adj* — **neo·clas·si·cism** \-ˈklas-ə-ˌsiz-əm\ *n*

neo–Dar·win·ism \-ˈdär-wə-ˌniz-əm\ *n* : a theory that explains evolution in terms of natural selection and the genetics of populations and specifically denies the possibility of inheriting acquired characters — **neo–Dar·win·i·an** \-där-ˈwin-ē-ən\ *adj* — **neo–Dar·win·ist** \-ˈdär-wə-nəst\ *n*

neo·dym·i·um \ˌnē-ō-ˈdim-ē-əm\ *n* : a yellow metallic chemical element — see ELEMENT table [*ne-* + *-dymium* (from *didymium,* a mixture of rare-earth elements, from Greek *didymos* "double", from *dyo* "two")]

neo–im·pres·sion·ism \-im-ˈpresh-ə-ˌniz-əm\ *n, often cap N&I* : a late 19th century French art theory and practice marked by an attempt to make impressionism more precise in form and the use of a pointillist painting technique — **neo–im·pres·sion·ist** \-ˈpresh-nəst, -ə-nəst\ *adj or n, often cap N&I*

Ne·o·lith·ic \ˌnē-ə-ˈlith-ik\ *adj* : of or relating to the latest period of the Stone Age characterized by polished stone implements — compare EOLITHIC, PALEOLITHIC

ne·ol·o·gism \nē-ˈäl-ə-ˌjiz-əm\ *n* : a new word or expression — **ne·ol·o·gist** \-jəst\ *n* — **ne·ol·o·gis·tic** \-ˌäl-ə-ˈjis-tik\ *adj*

ne·ol·o·gy \-jē\ *n, pl* **-gies** : the use of a new word or expression or of an established word in a new or different sense

neo·my·cin \ˌnē-ə-ˈmīs-n\ *n* : a broad-spectrum antibiotic or mixture of antibiotics produced by a soil actinomycete

ne·on \'nē-ˌän\ *n* **1** : a colorless odorless inert gaseous chemical element found in minute amounts in air and used in electric lamps — see ELEMENT table **2 a** : a discharge lamp in which the gas contains a large amount of neon **b** : a sign composed of such lamps [Greek, neuter of *neos* "new"]

neo·na·tal \ˌnē-ō-ˈnāt-l\ *adj* : of, relating to, or affecting the newborn — **neo·na·tal·ly** \-l-ē\ *adv* — **neo·nate** \'nē-ə-ˌnāt\ *n*

neo·or·tho·dox \ˌnē-ō-ˈȯr-thə-ˌdäks\ *adj* : of or relating to a 20th century Protestant theological movement characterized by a reaction against liberalism and emphasis on Reformation doctrines — **neo·or·tho·doxy** \-ˌdäk-sē\ *n*

neo·phyte \'nē-ə-ˌfīt\ *n* **1** : a new convert **2** : NOVICE 2 [Late Latin *neophytus,* from Greek *neophytos,* from *neophytos* "newly planted", from *neos* "new" + *phyein* "to bring forth"]

neo·plasm \'nē-ə-ˌplaz-əm\ *n* : a new growth of tissue serving no physiologic function : TUMOR — **neo·plas·tic** \ˌnē-ə-ˈplas-tik\ *adj*

neo·prene \'nē-ə-ˌprēn\ *n* : a synthetic rubber that is resistant to deterioration caused by oil, gasoline, oxygen, and ozone [*ne-* + *-prene* (as in *isoprene,* a flammable liquid used in synthetic rubber, probably from *is-* + *propyl* + *-ene*)]

ne·o·te·ny \nē-ˈät-n-ē\ *n* : attainment of sexual maturity during the larval stage; *also* : retention of immature characters in adulthood [*ne-* + Greek *teinein* "to stretch"] — **ne·o·ten·ic** \ˌnē-ə-ˈten-ik\ *adj*

ne·pen·the \nə-ˈpen-thē, -ˈpent-\ *n* **1** : a potion used by the ancients to dull pain and sorrow **2** : something capable of making one forget grief or suffering [Latin *nepenthes,* from Greek *nēpenthēs* "banishing pain and sorrow", from *nē-* "not" + *penthos* "sorrow"] — **ne·pen·the·an** \-thē-ən\ *adj*

neph·e·line \'nef-ə-ˌlēn\ *also* **neph·e·lite** \-ˌlīt\ *n* : a usually glassy silicate mineral common in igneous rocks [French *néphéline,* from Greek *nephelē* "cloud"]

neph·ew \'nef-yü\ *n* : a son of one's brother, sister, brother-in-law, or sister-in-law [Old Fench *neveu,* from Latin *nepos* "grandson, nephew"]

nepho·scope \'nef-ə-ˌskōp\ *n* : an instrument for observing the direction and velocity of cloud motion [Greek *nephos* "cloud"]

neph·ric \'nef-rik\ *adj* : RENAL

ne·phrid·i·um \ni-ˈfrid-ē-əm\ *n, pl* **-ia** \-ē-ə\ : a tubular excretory organ of various invertebrates (as an earthworm) [New Latin, from Greek *nephros* "kidney"] — **ne·phrid·i·al** \-ē-əl\ *adj*

ne·phri·tis \ni-ˈfrīt-əs\ *n, pl* **ne·phrit·i·des** \-ˈfrit-ə-ˌdēz\ : inflammation of the kidneys — **ne·phrit·ic** \-ˈfrit-ik\ *adj*

neph·ron \'nef-ˌrän\ *n* : a single excretory unit especially of the vertebrate kidney [German, from Greek *nephros* "kidney"]

ne plus ul·tra \ˌnā-ˌpləs-ˈəl-trə, ˌnē-\ *n* : the highest point capable of being attained : ACME ⟨that hotel is the *ne plus ultra* of elegance⟩ [New Latin, "no more beyond"]

nep·o·tism \'nep-ə-ˌtiz-əm\ *n* : favoritism shown to a relative (as by giving an appointive job) [French *népotisme,* from Italian *nepotismo,* from *nepote* "nephew", from Latin *nepot-, nepos* "grandson, nephew"]

Nep·tune \'nep-ˌtün, -ˌtyün\ *n* : the planet 8th in order from the sun — see PLANET table [Latin *Neptunus,* Roman god of the sea] — **Nep·tu·ni·an** \nep-ˈtü-nē-ən, -ˈtyü-\ *adj*

nep·tu·ni·um \nep-ˈtü-nē-əm, -ˈtyü-\ *n* : a radioactive metallic chemical element that is similar to uranium and is obtained in nuclear reactors as a by-product in the production of plutonium — see ELEMENT table [New Latin, from *Neptunus,* the planet Neptune]

nerd \'nərd\ *n* **1** : an unstylish, unattractive, or socially inept person **2** : a person slavishly devoted to intellectual or academic pursuits [perhaps from *nerd,* a creature in the children's book *If I Ran the Zoo* by Dr. Seuss (Theodor Geisel)] — **nerd·ish** \'nərd-ish\ *adj* — **nerdy** \-dē\ *adj*

ne·re·is \'nir-ē-əs\ *n, pl* **ne·re·ides** \nə-ˈrē-ə-ˌdēz\ : any of a genus of usually large greenish marine annelid worms [Latin, a sea nymph]

ne·rit·ic \nə-ˈrit-ik\ *adj* : of, relating to, or being the shallow water adjoining the seacoast [perhaps from New Latin *Nerita,* a genus of marine snails]

¹nerve \'nərv\ *n* **1** : SINEW 1, TENDON ⟨strain every *nerve*⟩ **2** : one of the filamentous bands of nervous tissue connecting parts of the nervous system with the other organs and conducting nervous impulses **3 a** : power of endurance or control **b** (1) : venturesome boldness (2) : BRASS 3, GALL **4 a** : a sore or sensitive point **b** *pl* : nervous disorganization or collapse : HYSTERIA **5** : VEIN 2b, 2c **6** : the sensitive pulp of a tooth [Latin *nervus* "sinew, nerve"] — **nerve** *adj* — **nerved** \'nərvd\ *adj*

²nerve *vt* : to give strength or courage to

nerve cell *n* : NEURON; *also* : a nerve cell body exclusive of its processes

nerve center *n* **1** : CENTER 2b **2** : a source of leadership, control, or energy

nerve cord *n* **1** : the pair of closely united ventral longitudinal nerves with their segmental ganglia that is characteristic of many elongate invertebrates **2** : the

\ə\ abut	\ng\ sing
\ər\ further	\ō\ bone
\a\ mat	\ȯ\ saw
\ā\ take	\ȯi\ coin
\ä\ cot, cart	\th\ thin
\aü\ out	\th\ this
\ch\ chin	\ü\ food
\e\ pet	\u̇\ foot
\ē\ easy	\y\ yet
\g\ go	\yü\ few
\i\ tip	\yu̇\ cure
\ī\ life	\zh\ vision
\j\ job	

dorsal tubular cord of nervous tissue that develops into the central nervous system in chordates

nerve ending *n* : a structure forming an end of a nerve axon that is distant from the cell body

nerve fiber *n* : AXON, DENDRITE

nerve gas *n* : a war gas damaging especially to the nervous and respiratory systems

nerve impulse *n* : the progressive alteration along a nerve fiber that follows stimulation and serves to transmit a record of sensation from a receptor or an instruction to act to an effector — called also *nervous impulse*

nerve·less \'nərv-ləs\ *adj* **1** : lacking strength or courage : FEEBLE **2** : showing control or balance : POISED, COOL — **nerve·less·ly** *adv* — **nerve·less·ness** *n*

nerve net *n* : a network of nerve cells apparently continuous one with another and conducting impulses in all directions; *also* : a nervous system (as in a jellyfish) consisting of such a network

nerve–rack·ing *or* **nerve–wrack·ing** \'nərv-,rak-ing\ *adj* : extremely trying on the nerves

nerve tube *n* : NERVE CORD 2

nerv·ous \'nər-vəs\ *adj* **1** : marked by vigor of thought, feeling, or style : SPIRITED **2 a** : of, relating to, or composed of neurons **b** : of or relating to the nerves; *also* : originating in or affected by the nerves **3 a** : easily excited or irritated : JUMPY **b** : TIMID, APPREHENSIVE ⟨a *nervous* smile⟩ **4** : tending to cause nervousness or agitation : TRYING ⟨a *nervous* situation⟩ — **nerv·ous·ly** *adv* — **nerv·ous·ness** *n*

nervous breakdown *n* : a serious mental or emotional disorder; *esp* : one that incapacitates or requires hospital care

nervous system *n* : the bodily system that receives and interprets stimuli and transmits impulses to the effector organs and that in vertebrates is made up of brain and spinal cord, nerves, ganglia, and parts of the receptor organs

nervy \'nər-vē\ *adj* **nerv·i·er; -est 1 a** : showing calm courage : BOLD **b** : marked by impudence or presumption : BRASH ⟨a *nervy* salesperson⟩ **2** : NERVOUS 3a — **nerv·i·ness** *n*

ne·science \'nesh-əns, 'nēsh-, -ē-əns\ *n* : lack of knowledge or awareness : IGNORANCE [Late Latin *nescientia,* from Latin *nescire* "not to know", from *ne-* "not" + *scire* "to know"] — **ne·scient** \-ənt\ *adj*

ness \'nes\ *n* : ¹CAPE, PROMONTORY [Old English *næss*]

-ness \nəs\ *n suffix* : state : condition : quality : degree ⟨hard*ness*⟩ [Old English]

Nes·sel·rode \'nes-əl-,rōd\ *n* : a mixture of candied fruits, nuts, and maraschino used in puddings, pies, and ice cream [Count Karl R. *Nesselrode,* died 1862, Russian statesman]

¹nest \'nest\ *n* **1 a** : a bed or shelter prepared by a bird for its eggs and young **b** : a place where eggs are laid and hatched **2 a** : a place of rest, retreat, or lodging **b** : DEN 2a, HANGOUT **3** : the occupants or frequenters of a nest **4 a** : a group of similar things : AGGREGATION **b** : HOTBED 2 **5** : a group of objects made to fit close together or one within another ⟨a *nest* of tables⟩ [Old English]

¹nest 5

²nest *vb* **1** : to build or occupy a nest ⟨robins *nested* in the underbrush⟩ **2** : to fit compactly together or within one another

nest egg *n* **1** : a natural or artificial egg left in a nest to induce a fowl to continue to lay there **2** : a fund of money set aside as a reserve

nest·er \'nes-tər\ *n* **1** : one that nests **2** *West* : a homesteader or squatter who takes up open range for a farm

nes·tle \'nes-əl\ *vb* **nes·tled; nes·tling** \'nes-ling, -ə-ling\ **1** : to settle snugly or comfortably **2 a** : to settle, shelter, or house as if in a nest **b** : to press closely and affectionately : CUDDLE [Old English *nestlian* "to make a nest", from *nest*] — **nes·tler** \-lər\ *n*

nest·ling \'nest-ling\ *n* : a young bird not yet able to leave the nest

¹net \'net\ *n* **1 a** : a meshed fabric twisted, knotted, or woven together at regular intervals **b** : something made of net: as (1) : a device for catching fish, birds, or insects (2) : a fabric barricade which divides a court in half (as for tennis) and over which a ball or shuttlecock must be hit in play **2** : an entrapping situation ⟨in a *net* of suspicion⟩ **3** : a network of lines, fibers, or figures [Old English *nett*] — **net·like** \-,līk\ *adj* — **net·ty** \'net-ē\ *adj*

²net *vt* **net·ted; net·ting 1** : to cover with or as if with a net **2** : to catch in or as if in a net — **net·ter** *n*

³net *adj* **1** : free from all charges or deductions ⟨a *net* profit⟩ ⟨*net* weight⟩ — compare GROSS 3b **2** : FINAL ⟨the *net* result⟩ [Middle French, "clean, neat"]

⁴net *vt* **net·ted; net·ting** : to gain or produce as profit : CLEAR

⁵net *n* : a net amount, profit, or price

neth·er \'neth-ər\ *adj* **1** : situated down or below : LOWER **2** : situated beneath the earth's surface ⟨the *nether* regions⟩ [Old English *nithera,* from *nither* "down"]

neth·er·most \-,mōst\ *adj* : farthest down : LOWEST

neth·er·world \-,wərld\ *n* **1** : the world of the dead **2** : UNDERWORLD 2, 3

net·ting \'net-ing\ *n* **1** : NETWORK 1 **2** : the act or process of making a net or network

¹net·tle \'net-l\ *n* : any of various coarse herbs with stinging hairs [Old English *netel*]

²nettle *vt* **net·tled; net·tling** \'net-ling, -l-ing\ **1** : to strike or sting with or as if with nettles **2** : IRRITATE 1, PROVOKE

net·tle·some \'net-l-səm\ *adj* : causing annoyance

net–veined \'net-'vānd\ *adj* : having veins that branch and interlace to form a network ⟨dicotyledons have *net-veined* leaves⟩ — compare PARALLEL-VEINED

net·work \'net-,wərk\ *n* **1** : a fabric or structure of cords or wires that cross at regular intervals and are knotted or secured at the crossings **2** : a system of elements (as lines or channels) resembling a network **3 a** : an interconnected or interrelated chain, group, or system; *esp* : a group of radio or television stations linked by wire or radio relay **b** : a television or radio company that broadcasts over such a network

neur- *or* **neuro-** *combining form* : nerve ⟨*neur*al⟩ ⟨*neuro*logy⟩ [Greek *neuron* "sinew, nerve"]

neu·ral \'nur-əl, 'nyur-\ *adj* **1** : of, relating to, or involving a nerve or the nervous system **2** : situated in the region of or on the same side of the body as the brain and spinal cord — **neu·ral·ly** \-ə-lē\ *adv*

neu·ral·gia \nu-'ral-jə, nyu-\ *n* : a condition marked by acute pain that follows the course of a nerve — **neu·ral·gic** \-jik\ *adj*

neural net *n* : a computer design in which a number of processors are interconnected in a manner suggestive of the connections between neurons in a human brain and which is able to learn by a process of trial and error — called also *neural network*

neural tube *n* : a hollow longitudinal tube produced from dorsal ectodermal folds and giving rise to the central nervous system of a vertebrate embryo

neu·ri·lem·ma \,nur-ə-'lem-ə, ,nyur-\ *n* : the outer sheath of a nerve fiber [*neur-* + Greek *eilēma* "covering, coil", from *eilein* "to wind"] — **neu·ri·lem·mal** \-'lem-əl\ *adj*

neu·ri·tis \nu-'rīt-əs, nyu-\ *n, pl* **-ri·tis·es** *or* **-rit·i·des** \-'rit-ə-,dēz\ : inflammation of a nerve — **neu·rit·ic** \-'rit-ik\ *adj or n*

neu·ro·fi·bril \,nur-ō-'fīb-rəl, ,nyur-, -'fib-\ *n* : a filament (as in a protozoan or a neuron) believed to be a conducting element

neu·rog·lia \nu-'räg-lē-ə, nyu-; ,nur-ə-'glē-ə, ,nyur-, -'glī-\ *n* : supporting tissue of the brain, spinal cord, and ganglia [*neur.* + Middle Greek *glia* "glue"] — **neu·rog·li·al** \-əl\ *adj*

neu·ro·hor·mone \ˌnūr-ō-ˈhȯr-ˌmōn, ˌnyūr-\ *n* : a hormone (as acetylcholine or norepinephrine) produced by or acting on nervous tissue

neu·ro·hu·mor \ˌnūr-ō-ˈhyü-mər, ˌnyūr-, -ˈyü-\ *n* : a substance released at a nerve ending that plays a part in transmitting a nerve impulse — **neu·ro·hu·mor·al** \-ˈhyüm-rəl, -ˈyüm-, -ə-rəl\ *adj*

neu·rol·o·gy \nū-ˈräl-ə-jē, nyū-\ *n* : the scientific study of the structure, functions, and disorders of the nervous system — **neu·ro·log·i·cal** \ˌnūr-ə-ˈläj-i-kəl, ˌnyūr-\ *or* **neu·ro·log·ic** \-ˈläj-ik\ *adj* — **neu·rol·o·gist** \nū-ˈräl-ə-jəst, nyū-\ *n*

neu·ro·mo·tor \ˌnūr-ə-ˈmōt-ər, ˌnyūr-\ *adj* : relating to efferent nervous impulses

neu·ro·mus·cu·lar \ˌnūr-ō-ˈməs-kyə-lər, ˌnyūr-\ *adj* : of or relating to nerves and muscles; *esp* : jointly involving nervous and muscular elements ⟨a *neuromuscular* junction⟩

neu·ron \ˈnū-ˌrän, ˈnyü-; ˈnūr-ˌän, ˈnyūr-\ *also* **neu·rone** \-ˌrōn, -ˌōn\ *n* : a cell with specialized processes that is the fundamental functional unit of nervous tissue [Greek *neuron* "nerve, sinew"] — **neu·ro·nal** \ˈnūr-ən-l, ˈnyūr-; nū-ˈrōn-l, nyū-\ *adj*

neu·rop·ter·an \nū-ˈräp-tə-rən, nyū-\ *n* : any of a family (order Neuroptera) of insects (as an ant lion) with a fine network of wing veins [derived from Greek *neuron* "sinew, nerve" + *pteron* "wing"] — **neuropteran** *adj*

neu·ro·sis \nū-ˈrō-səs, nyū-\ *n, pl* **-ro·ses** \-ˈrō-ˌsēz\ : a nervous disorder marked by anxiety and the use of defense mechanisms to escape from it and by the absence of obvious physical cause

neu·ros·po·ra \nū-ˈräs-pə-rə, nyū-\ *n* : any of a genus of often pink-spored ascomycetous fungi that are destructive in bakeries but important objects of genetic research [New Latin, from *neur-* + *spora* "spore"]

¹**neu·rot·ic** \nū-ˈrät-ik, nyū-\ *adj* : of, relating to, constituting, or affected with neurosis — **neu·rot·i·cal·ly** \-ˈrät-i-kə-lē, -klē\ *adv*

²**neurotic** *n* : an emotionally unstable person or one affected with a neurosis

neu·ro·tox·ic \ˌnūr-ə-ˈtäk-sik, ˌnyūr-\ *adj* : poisonous to nervous tissue

neu·ro·tox·in \-ˈtäk-sən\ *n* : a poisonous protein that acts on the nervous system

¹**neu·ter** \ˈnüt-ər, ˈnyüt-\ *adj* **1** : of, relating to, or constituting the class of words that ordinarily includes most of those referring to things that are neither male nor female ⟨a *neuter* noun⟩ ⟨the *neuter* gender⟩ **2** : lacking sex organs; *also* : having imperfectly developed sex organs [Latin, literally, "neither", from *ne-* "not" + *uter* "which of two"]

²**neuter** *n* **1 a** : a word or form of the neuter gender **b** : the neuter gender **2** : one that is neutral **3 a** : WORKER 2 **b** : a spayed or castrated animal

³**neuter** *vt* : ALTER 2, CASTRATE

¹**neu·tral** \ˈnü-trəl, ˈnyü-\ *adj* **1** : not favoring either side in a quarrel, contest, or war **2** : of or relating to a neutral state or power **3 a** : neither one thing nor the other : INDIFFERENT **b** : ACHROMATIC **c** : neither acid nor basic **d** : not electrically charged **4** : produced with the tongue in the position it has when at rest ⟨the *neutral* vowels of \ə-ˈbəv\ above⟩ [Middle French, from Latin *neutralis* "of neuter gender", from *neuter* "neuter, neither"] — **neu·tral·ly** \-trə-lē\ *adv* — **neu·tral·ness** *n*

²**neutral** *n* **1** : one that is neutral **2** : a neutral color **3** : a position of disengagement (as of gears)

neu·tral·ism \ˈnü-trə-ˌliz-əm, ˈnyü-\ *n* : a policy or the advocacy of neutrality especially in international affairs — **neu·tral·ist** \-ləst\ *n* — **neu·tral·is·tic** \ˌnü-trə-ˈlis-tik, ˌnyü-\ *adj*

neu·tral·i·ty \nü-ˈtral-ət-ē, nyü-\ *n* **1** : the quality or state of being neutral **2** : immunity from invasion or from use by belligerents

neu·tral·ize \ˈnü-trə-ˌlīz, ˈnyü-\ *vt* **1** : to make chemically neutral **2** : to destroy the effectiveness of : NULLIFY ⟨*neutralize* an opponent's move⟩ **3** : to make electrically inert by combining equal positive and negative quantities **4** : to provide for the neutrality of under international law ⟨*neutralize* a country⟩ — **neu·tral·i·za·tion** \ˌnü-trə-lə-ˈzā-shən, ˌnyü-\ *n* — **neu·tral·iz·er** \ˈnü-trə-ˌlī-zər, ˈnyü-\ *n*

neutral spirits *n pl* : ethyl alcohol of 190 or higher proof used especially for blending alcoholic liquors

neu·tri·no \nü-ˈtrē-nō, nyü-\ *n, pl* **-nos** : an uncharged elementary particle having a mass less than ¹/₁₀ that of the electron [Italian, from *neutrone* "neutron"]

neu·tron \ˈnü-ˌträn, ˈnyü-\ *n* : an uncharged elementary particle that has a mass nearly equal to that of the proton and is present in all known atomic nuclei except the hydrogen nucleus [probably from *neutral* + *-on*]

neutron star *n* : any of various hypothetical dense celestial objects that consist of closely packed nuclear particles and result from the collapse of a much larger star [from the hypothesis that the cores of such stars are composed entirely of neutrons]

neu·tro·phil \ˈnü-trə-ˌfil, ˈnyü-\ *n* : a finely granular cell that is the chief phagocytic white blood cell [Latin *neuter* "neither"; from its staining to the same degree with acid or basic dyes]

né·vé \nā-ˈvā\ *n* : the partially compacted granular snow that forms the surface part of the upper end of a glacier; *also* : a field of granular snow [French (Swiss dialect), from Latin *niv-, nix* "snow"]

nev·er \ˈnev-ər\ *adv* **1** : not ever : at no time ⟨*never* saw them before⟩ **2** : not in any degree, way, or condition ⟨*never* fear, we'll win⟩ [Old English *nǣfre*, from *ne* "not" + *ǣfre* "ever"]

nev·er·more \ˌnev-ər-ˈmōr, -ˈmȯr\ *adv* : never again

nev·er–nev·er land \ˌnev-ər-ˈnev-ər-\ *n* : an ideal or imaginary place

nev·er·the·less \ˌnev-ər-thə-ˈles\ *adv* : in spite of that : HOWEVER

ne·vus \ˈnē-vəs\ *n, pl* **ne·vi** \-ˌvī\ : a congenital pigmented area on the skin : BIRTHMARK [Latin *naevus*]

¹**new** \ˈnü, ˈnyü\ *adj* **1** : not old : RECENT, MODERN **2** : not the same as the former : taking the place of one that came before ⟨a *new* teacher⟩ **3** : recently discovered, recognized, or learned about ⟨*new* lands⟩ **4** : not formerly known or experienced ⟨*new* feelings⟩ **5** : not accustomed ⟨*new* to her work⟩ **6** : beginning as a repetition of some previous act or thing ⟨a *new* year⟩ ⟨make a *new* start⟩ **7** : renewed in strength and vigor **8** : being in a position or place for the first time ⟨a *new* member⟩ **9** *cap* : having been in use after medieval times : MODERN ⟨*New* Latin⟩ [Old English *nīwe*] — **new·ness** *n* □ SYN NEW, NOVEL, FRESH mean having recently come into existence or use. NEW may apply to what is freshly made and unused ⟨*new* bricks⟩ or has not been known before ⟨a *new* design⟩ or not experienced before ⟨start on a *new* job⟩ NOVEL applies to what is not only new but strange and unprecedented ⟨*novel* hair styles⟩ FRESH applies to what has not yet had time to grow dim, soiled, or stale ⟨put on a *fresh* shirt⟩ ⟨offering *fresh* ideas⟩

²**new** *adv* : NEWLY, RECENTLY ⟨*new*-mown hay⟩

New Age *adj* **1** : of, relating to, or being a late 20th century social movement that draws on ancient Eastern and American Indian traditions and incorporates themes of spirituality, harmony, and metaphysics **2** : of, relating to, or being a soothing form of instrumental music

new·born \ˈnü-ˈbȯrn, ˈnyü-\ *adj* **1** : recently born **2** : born again

new·com·er \ˈnü-ˌkəm-ər, ˈnyü-\ *n* **1** : one recently arrived **2** : NOVICE 2, BEGINNER

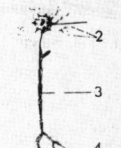

neuron: *1* cell body,
2 dendrite, *3* axon,
4 nerve ending

\ə\ abut	\ng\ sing
\ər\ **further**	\ō\ bone
\a\ mat	\ȯ\ saw
\ā\ take	\ȯi\ coin
\ä\ cot, cart	\th\ thin
\au̇\ out	\t͟h\ this
\ch\ chin	\ü\ food
\e\ pet	\u̇\ foot
\ē\ easy	\y\ yet
\g\ go	\yü\ few
\i\ tip	\yu̇\ cure
\ī\ life	\zh\ vision
\j\ job	

New Deal *n* **1** : the legislative and administrative program of President Franklin D. Roosevelt designed to promote economic recovery and social reform during the 1930s **2** : the period of the New Deal — **New Deal-er** \-'dē-lər\ *n*

new·el \'nü-əl, 'nyü-\ *n* **1** : an upright post about which the steps of a circular staircase wind **2** : a post at the foot of a straight stairway or one at a landing [Middle French *nouel* "stone of a fruit", from Late Latin *nucalis* "like a nut", from Latin *nuc-, nux* "nut"]

new·fan·gled \'nü-'fang-gəld, 'nyü-\ *adj* : of the newest style : NOVEL ⟨*newfangled* ideas⟩ [Middle English, from *newefangel,* from *new* + Old English *fangen,* past participle of *fōn* "to take, seize"]

new–fash·ioned \-'fash-ənd\ *adj* **1** : made in a new fashion or form **2** : UP-TO-DATE 2

new·found \-'faùnd\ *adj* : newly found ⟨a *newfound* friend⟩

newt

New·found·land \'nü-fən-dlənd, 'nyü-, -lənd, -,dland, -,land; nü-'faùn-dlənd, nyü-, -lənd\ *n* : any of a breed of very large usually black dogs developed in Newfoundland

New Hamp·shire \nù-'ham-shər, nyù-, -'hamp-, -,shiər\ *n* : any of a breed of single-combed domestic fowls developed chiefly in New Hampshire and noted for heavy winter egg production

new·ish \'nü-ish, 'nyü-\ *adj* : rather new

New Latin *n* : Latin as used since the end of the medieval period especially in scientific description and classification

New Left *n* : a political movement beginning in the United States during the 1960s that is composed chiefly of students and extremist groups and advocates (as by demonstrations) radical changes in political, social, and educational practices — **New Leftist** *adj or n*

new·ly \'nü-lē, 'nyü-\ *adv* **1** : LATELY, RECENTLY ⟨*newly* married⟩ **2** : ANEW, AFRESH ⟨a *newly* furnished house⟩

new·ly·wed \-,wed\ *n* : one recently married

new math *n* : mathematics that is based on set theory especially as taught in elementary and secondary school — called also *new mathematics*

new moon *n* **1** : the moon's phase when it is in conjunction with the sun so that its dark side is toward the earth; *also* : the thin crescent moon seen shortly after sunset a few days after the actual occurrence of the new moon phase **2** : the 1st day of the Jewish month

new penny *n* : a British monetary unit equal to ¹/₁₀₀ pound; *also* : a coin representing this unit

news \'nüz, 'nyüz\ *n* **1** : a report of recent events ⟨brought us the office *news*⟩ **2 a** : material reported in a newspaper or news periodical or on a newscast **b** : matter that is newsworthy

news agency *n* : an organization that supplies news to subscribing newspapers, periodicals, and newscasters — called also *news service*

news·boy \'nüz-,bòi, 'nyüz-\ *n* : a person who delivers or sells newspapers

news·cast \-,kast\ *n* : a radio or television news broadcast [*news* + broad*cast*] — **news·cast·er** \-,kas-tər\ *n*

news conference *n* : PRESS CONFERENCE

news·girl \'nüz-,gərl, 'nyüz-\ *n* : a girl or woman who delivers or sells newspapers

news·let·ter \'nüz-,let-ər, 'nyüz-\ *n* : a newspaper containing news or information of interest chiefly to a special group

news·man \-mən, -,man\ *n* : one (as a reporter or correspondent) who gathers, reports, or comments on the news

news·mon·ger \-,məng-gər, -,mäng-\ *n* : GOSSIP 1

news·pa·per \'nüz-,pā-pər, 'nyüz-, 'nüs-, 'nyüs-\ *n* **1** : a paper that is printed and distributed usually daily or weekly and contains news, articles of opinion, features, and advertising **2** : an organization publishing a newspaper **3** : the paper making up a newspaper

news·pa·per·man \-,man\ *n* : one who owns or is employed by a newspaper; *esp* : one who writes or edits copy for a newspaper

news·print \'nüz-,print, 'nyüz-\ *n* : a relatively cheap paper made from wood pulp and used mostly for newspapers

news·reel \-,rēl\ *n* : a short motion picture dealing with current events

news·stand \'nüz-,stand, 'nyüz-\ *n* : a place where newspapers and periodicals are sold

New Style *adj* : using or according to the Gregorian calendar

news·wom·an \'nüz-,wùm-ən, 'nyüz-\ *n* : a woman who works as a newsman

news·wor·thy \'nüz-,wər-thē, 'nyüz-\ *adj* : sufficiently interesting to the general public to warrant reporting

newsy \'nü-zē, 'nyü-\ *adj* **news·i·er; -est** : filled with news; *esp* : CHATTY ⟨a *newsy* letter⟩

newt \'nüt, 'nyüt\ *n* : any of various small salamanders that live mostly in water [Middle English *newte,* the phrase *an ewte* (from Old English *efete* "eft") being understood as a *newte*]

New Testament *n* : the second of the two chief divisions of the Christian Bible consisting of the books dealing with Christ's life and death and the work done by his apostles after his death — see BIBLE table

new·ton \'nüt-n, 'nyüt-n\ *n* : a unit of force in the mks system of such size that under its influence a body whose mass is one kilogram would experience an acceleration of one meter per second per second [Sir Isaac *Newton*]

New·to·ni·an \nü-'tō-nē-ən, nyü-\ *adj* : of, relating to, or characteristic of Sir Isaac Newton, his discoveries, or his doctrines

New World *n* : the western hemisphere; *esp* : the continental landmass of North and South America

New Year \'nü-,yiər, 'nyü-\ *n* **1** : NEW YEAR'S DAY; *also* : the first days of the year **2** : ROSH HASHANAH

New Year's Day *n* : January 1 observed as a legal holiday

¹next \'nekst\ *adj* : immediately preceding or following : NEAREST ⟨the *next* page⟩ ⟨the *next* house was empty⟩ [Old English *nīehst,* superlative of *nēah* "nigh"]

²next *adv* **1** : in the time, place, or order nearest or immediately succeeding ⟨open this package *next*⟩ **2** : on the first occasion to come ⟨when *next* we meet⟩

³next *prep* : next to

next of kin : a person's nearest relation or relations

¹next to *prep* : immediately following : adjacent to ⟨*next to* the head of the class⟩

²next to *adv* : very nearly : ALMOST ⟨*next to* impossible⟩

nex·us \'nek-səs\ *n, pl* **nex·us·es** \-sə-səz\ *or* **nex·us** \-səs, -,süs\ : CONNECTION 2, LINK [Latin, from *nectere* "to bind"]

Nez Percé \'nez-'pərs, 'nes-'pеərs, *French* nā-per-sā\ *n* : a member of an Indian people of what is now central Idaho and adjacent parts of Washington and Oregon [French, literally, "pierced nose"]

ni·a·cin \'nī-ə-sən\ *n* : NICOTINIC ACID [*ni*cotinic *ac*id + -*in*]

ni·a·cin·amide \,nī-ə-'sín-ə-,mīd\ *n* : a compound of the vitamin B complex found especially as a constituent of coenzymes and used similarly to nicotinic acid

Ni·ag·a·ra \nī-'ag-rə, -ə-rə\ *n* : an overwhelming flood : TORRENT ⟨a *Niagara* of protests⟩ [*Niagara* Falls, waterfall of the Niagara river]

nib \'nib\ *n* **1** : BEAK 1, BILL **2 a** : the sharpened point of a quill pen **b** : a pen point **3** : a small pointed or projecting part [probably alteration of *neb*]

¹nib·ble \'nib-əl\ *vb* **nib·bled; nib·bling** \'nib-ling, -ə-ling\ **1 a** : to bite or chew gently or bit by bit **b** : to take away gradually ⟨*nibbling* our freedom⟩ **2** : to deal with something cautiously [origin unknown] — **nib·bler** \'nib-lər, -ə-lər\ *n*

²nibble *n* **1** : an act of nibbling; *esp* : a small bite or cautious approach **2 a** : a very small quantity **b** : a dainty morsel

Ni·be·lung \'nē-bə-,lùng\ *n* **I** : a member of a race of dwarfs in Germanic legend from whom a hoard and ring were taken by Siegfried **2** : any of the followers of Siegfried **3** : any of the Burgundian kings in the medieval German epic *Nibelungenlied* [German]

nibs \'nibz\ *n* : an important or self-important person — used chiefly in the phrase *his* (or *her*) *nibs* [origin unknown]

nice \'nīs\ *adj* **I** : showing fastidious or finicky tastes **2** : marked by or demanding delicate discrimination or treatment ⟨a *nice* distinction⟩ **3 a** : PLEASING, AGREEABLE ⟨a *nice* time⟩ ⟨a *nice* person⟩ **b** : well-executed : GOOD ⟨a *nice* shot⟩ **4 a** : socially acceptable : WELL=BRED ⟨offensive to *nice* people⟩ **b** : VIRTUOUS, RESPECTABLE [Middle English, "foolish, wanton", from Old French, from Latin *nescius* "ignorant", from *nescire* "not to know", from *ne-* "not" + *scire* "to know"] — **nice·ly** *adv* — **nice·ness** *n* □ ORIGIN While it is difficult to trace the precise development of the many senses of this word in English, a brief look at its history reveals that *nice* has come to have a number of meanings that are almost opposite to its earliest senses. *Nice* is derived from Latin *nescius*, "ignorant". It was earliest used in English, in the 13th and 14th centuries, to mean "foolish" or "stupid". Also in its early history in English *nice* had the sense of "wanton" or "dissolute". From these senses *nice* began in the 16th century to develop the meaning "coy" or "reserved", and then "fastidious" or "finicky". Not until the 18th century did *nice* come to be used in the variety of senses generally meaning "pleasurable" or "agreeable".

Ni·cene Creed \,nī-,sēn-\ *n* : a Christian creed issued by the first Council of Nicaea in A. D. 325 and later expanded that begins "I believe in one God" [Late Latin *nicaenus* "of Nicaea"]

nice–nel·ly \'nīs-'nel-ē\ *adj, often cap 2d N* **I** : PRUDISH **2** : EUPHEMISTIC [from the name *Nelly*] — **nice nelly** *n, often cap 2d N* — **nice·nel·ly·ism** \-,iz-əm\ *n, often cap 2d N*

ni·ce·ty \'nī-sət-ē, -stē\ *n, pl* **-ties** **I** : a dainty, delicate, or elegant thing ⟨the *niceties* of life⟩ **2** : a small point : a fine detail ⟨the *niceties* of manners⟩ **3** : careful attention to details ⟨the greatest *nicety* is needed in making watches⟩ **4** : the point at which a thing is at its best ⟨roasted to a *nicety*⟩

¹niche \'nich\ *n* **I a** : a recess in a wall especially for a statue **b** : something that resembles a niche **2** : a place, use, or work for which a person is best fitted **3** : the ecological role of an organism in a community [French, from Middle French *nicher* "to nest", from Latin *nidus* "nest"]

²niche *vt* : to place in a niche

¹nick \'nik\ *n* **I** : a small groove, notch, or cut **2** : CHIP ⟨a *nick* in a cup⟩ **3** : the final critical moment ⟨in the *nick* of time⟩ [Middle English *nyke*]

²nick *vb* **I a** : to make a nick in : NOTCH, CHIP **b** : to wound or cut slightly ⟨a bullet *nicked* my leg⟩ **2** : to make petty attacks : SNIPE **3** : to complement one another genetically and produce superior offspring

¹nick·el \'nik-əl\ *n* **I** : a silver-white hard malleable ductile metallic chemical element that is capable of a high polish, resistant to corrosion, and used chiefly in alloys and as a catalyst — see ELEMENT table **2 a** *also* **nick·le** : the United States 5-cent piece made of nickel and copper **b** : five cents [derived from German *kupfernickel* "a compound of nickel and arsenic", probably from *kupfer* "copper" + *nickel* "goblin"; from the deceptive copper color of the ore]

²nick·el *vb* **-eled** *or* **-elled; -el·ing** *or* **-el·ling** \'nik-ling, -ə-ling\ : to plate with nickel

nic·kel·ic \nik-'el-ik\ *adj* : of, relating to, or containing nickel especially with a higher valence than two

nick·el·if·er·ous \,nik-ə-'lif-rəs, -ə-rəs\ *adj* : containing nickel

nick·el·ode·on \,nik-ə-'lōd-ē-ən\ *n* **I** : a theater presenting entertainment for an admission price of five cents **2** : JUKEBOX [probably from *nickel* + *-odeon* (as in archaic *melodeon* "music hall")]

nick·el·ous \'nik-ə-ləs\ *adj* : of, relating to, or containing nickel especially with a valence of two

nickel silver *n* : a silver-white alloy of copper, zinc, and nickel

nick·er \'nik-ər\ *vi* **nick·ered; nick·er·ing** \'nik-ring, -ə-ring\ : to neigh gently : WHINNY [perhaps alteration of *neigh*] — **nicker** *n*

nick·nack *variant of* KNICKKNACK

¹nick·name \'nik-,nām\ *n* **I** : a usually descriptive name given instead of or in addition to the one belonging to an individual **2** : a familiar form of a proper name [Middle English *nekename* "additional name", the phrase an *ekename* (from *eke* "addition" + *name*) being understood as a *nekename*] □ ORIGIN *Nickname* was earliest used for a descriptive name given to a person, or even a place, in addition to the proper name. Today it can also mean "a shortened or familiar form of a proper name". In Middle English the word expressed the first of these senses very explicitly. The noun *eke*, meaning "an addition or extension", was combined with *name*, and an *ekename* was an additional name. By the 15th century an *ekename* began to be a *nekename*, in modern spelling a *nickname*. The Middle English noun *eke* is related to the verb *eke*, as in "eke out a living".

²nickname *vt* **I** : MISCALL **2** : to give a nickname to — **nick·nam·er** *n*

ni·co·ti·ana \nik-,ō-shē-'an-ə, -'än-ə, -'ā-nə\ *n* : any of several tobaccos grown for their showy flowers [Jean *Nicot,* died 1600, French diplomat and scholar who introduced tobacco into France]

nic·o·tin·amide–ad·e·nine di·nu·cle·o·tide \,nik-ə-'tēn-ə-,mīd,ad-n-,ēn-dī-'nü-klē-ə-,tīd, -'nyü-\ *n* : NAD

nicotinamide–adenine dinucleotide phos·phate \-'fäs-,fāt\ *n* : NADP

nic·o·tine \'nik-ə-,tēn\ *n* : a poisonous alkaloid that is the chief active principle of tobacco and is used as an insecticide

nic·o·tin·ic \,nik-ə-'tē-nik, -'tin-ik\ *adj* : of or relating to nicotine or nicotinic acid

nicotinic acid *n* : an organic acid of the vitamin B complex found widely in animals and plants and used especially against pellagra — called also *niacin*

nic·ti·tat·ing membrane \,nik-tə-,tāt-ing-\ *n* : a thin membrane found in many animals at the inner angle or beneath the lower lid of the eye and capable of extending across the eyeball [derived from Latin *nictare* "to wink"]

niece \'nēs\ *n* : a daughter of one's brother, sister, brother-in-law, or sister-in-law [Old French, "granddaughter, niece", from Late Latin *neptia,* from Latin *neptis*]

nif·ty \'nif-tē\ *adj* **nif·ti·er; -est** : FINE, SWELL ⟨*nifty* new clothes⟩ [origin unknown] — **nifty** *n*

nig·gard \'nig-ərd\ *n* : a meanly covetous and stingy person [of Scandinavian origin] — **niggard** *adj*

nig·gard·ly \-lē\ *adj* **I** : grudgingly reluctant to spend or grant : STINGY **2** : provided in meanly limited supply : SCANTY — **nig·gard·li·ness** *n* — **niggardly** *adv*

nig·gling \'nig-ling, -ə-ling\ *adj* **I** : PETTY **2** : demanding meticulous care [from earlier *niggle* "to carp", of unknown origin] — **niggling** *n* — **nig·gling·ly** \-lē\ *adv*

¹nigh \'nī\ *adv* **I** : near in place, time, or relationship **2** : NEARLY, ALMOST [Old English *nēah*]

²nigh *adj* **I** : not far : NEAR **2** : being on the left side ⟨the *nigh* horse⟩

³nigh *prep* : NEAR

⁴nigh *vb* : to draw near : APPROACH

night \'nīt\ *n* **I** : the time between dusk and dawn when there is no sunlight **2** : the beginning of dark-

\ə\	abut	\ng\	sing
\ər\	further	\ō\	bone
\a\	mat	\ó\	saw
\ā\	take	\ói\	coin
\ä\	cot, cart	\th\	thin
\aù\	out	\th\	this
\ch\	chin	\ü\	food
\e\	pet	\ù\	foot
\ē\	easy	\y\	yet
\g\	go	\yü\	few
\i\	tip	\yù\	cure
\ī\	life	\zh\	vision
\j\	job		

ness : NIGHTFALL **3** : the darkness of night [Old English *niht*]

night blindness *n* : subnormal vision in faint light (as at night) — **night–blind** \'nīt-,blīnd\ *adj*

night–blooming cereus *n* : any of several night-blooming cacti; *esp* : a slender sprawling or climbing cactus often grown for its large show y fragrant white flowers

night·cap \'nīt-,kap\ *n* **1** : a cloth cap worn with nightclothes **2** : a usually alcoholic drink taken at bedtime **3** : the final race or contest of a day's sports; *esp* : the final game of a baseball doubleheader

night·clothes \-,klōz, -,klōthz\ *n pl* : clothing worn in bed

night·club \-,kləb\ *n* : a place of entertainment open at night that usually serves food and liquor, has a floor show, and provides music and space for dancing

night crawler *n* : EARTHWORM; *esp* : a large earthworm that often occurs on the soil surface at night

night·dress \'nīt-,dres\ *n* **1** : NIGHTGOWN **2** : NIGHTCLOTHES

night·fall \-,fȯl\ *n* : the coming of night

night·gown \-,gaün\ *n* : a loose garment worn in bed

night·hawk \-,hȯk\ *n* **1** : any of several goatsuckers that resemble the related whippoorwill **2** : NIGHT OWL

night·ie \'nīt-ē\ *n* : a nightgown for a woman or a child [*night*gown + *-ie*]

nightingale

night·in·gale \'nīt-n-,gāl\ *n* : any of several Old World thrushes noted for the sweet usually nocturnal song of the male [Old English *nihtegale*, from *niht* "night" + *galan* "to sing"]

night·jar \'nīt-,jär\ *n* : a common grayish brown European goatsucker; *also* : GOATSUCKER [from its harsh sound]

night latch *n* : a door lock having a spring bolt operated from the outside by a key and from the inside by a knob

night letter *n* : a telegram sent at night at a reduced rate for delivery the following morning — compare DAY LETTER

nimbus 2

¹night·long \'nīt-,lȯng\ *adj* : lasting the whole night

²night·long \-'lȯng\ *adv* : through the whole night

night·ly \'nīt-lē\ *adj* **1** : of or relating to the night or every night **2** : happening, done, or produced by night or every night — **nightly** *adv*

night·mare \-,maər, -,meər\ *n* **1** : a horribly frightening dream **2** : an experience, situation, or object having the monstrous character of a nightmare or producing a feeling of anxiety or terror [Middle English "evil spirit thought to oppress people during sleep", from *night* + *mare* "incubus", from Old English] — **night·mar·ish** \-ish\ *adj*

night owl *n* : a person who habitually stays up late

night rider *n* : a member of a secret band who ride masked at night doing acts of violence for the purpose of punishing or terrorizing

night–robe \'nīt-,rōb\ *n* : NIGHTGOWN

nights \'nīts\ *adv* : in the nighttime repeatedly (getting a degree by going to school *nights*)

night·shade \'nīt-,shād\ *n* **1** : any of a genus of herbs, shrubs, and trees having alternate leaves, cymes of usually white, yellow, or purple flowers, and fruits that are berries and including many poisonous forms and important food plants (as the potato, tomato, and eggplant) **2** : BELLADONNA 1

night·shirt \-,shərt\ *n* : a nightgown resembling a shirt

night·stick \-,stik\ *n* : a police officer's club : BILLY

night·tide \'nīt-,tīd\ *n* : NIGHTTIME

night·time \'nīt-,tīm\ *n* : the time from dusk to dawn

night·walk·er \-,wȯ-kər\ *n* : a person who roves about at night especially with criminal or immoral intent

ni·gri·tude \'nī-grə-,tüd, 'nig-rə-, -,tyüd\ *n* : intense darkness : BLACKNESS [Latin *nigritudo*, from *niger* "black"]

ni·hil·ism \'nī-ə-,liz-əm, 'nē-\ *n* : a doctrine or belief that conditions in the social organization are so bad as

to make destruction desirable for its own sake independent of any constructive program [German *nihilismus*, from Latin *nihil* "nothing"] — **ni·hil·ist** \-ə-ləst\ *n* — nihilist *or* **ni·hil·is·tic** \,nī-ə-'lis-tik, ,nē-\ *adj*

ni·hil·i·ty \nī-'hil-ət-ē, nē-\ *n* : NOTHINGNESS

ni·hil ob·stat \,nī-,hil-'äb-,stät, ,nē-,hil-, ,nik-,il-, -,stat\ *n* : authoritative or official approval (as of a censor) [Latin, "nothing hinders"]

-nik \nik\ *n suffix* : one connected with or characterized by being ⟨beat*nik*⟩ [Yiddish, from Russian and Polish]

nil \'nil\ *n* : nothing at all : ZERO [Latin, "nothing", contraction of *nihil*] — **nil** *adj*

nile green \'nīl-\ *n, often cap N* : a pale yellow green [*Nile* river, Africa]

Ni·lot·ic \nī-'lät-ik\ *adj* : of or relating to the Nile or the peoples of the Nile basin

nim·ble \'nim-bəl\ *adj* **nim·bler** \-bə-lər, -blər\; **-blest** \-bə-ləst, -bləst\ **1** : quick and light in motion : AGILE ⟨a *nimble* dancer⟩ **2** : quick in understanding and learning : CLEVER ⟨a *nimble* mind⟩ [Old English *numol* "holding much", from *niman* "to take"] — **nim·ble·ness** \-bəl-nəs\ *n* — **nim·bly** \-blē\ *adv*

nim·bo·stra·tus \,nim-bō-'strāt-əs, -'strat-\ *n* : a low dark gray cloud layer that usually produces precipitation

nim·bus \'nim-bəs\ *n, pl* **nim·bi** \-,bī, -,bē\ *or* **nim·bus·es** **1** : a luminous vapor, cloud, or atmosphere about a god or goddess when on earth **2** : an indication (as a circle) of radiant light or glory about the head of a drawn or sculptured divinity, saint, or sovereign **3** : a rain cloud that is of uniform grayness and extends over the entire sky [Latin, "rainstorm, cloud"]

nim·rod \'nim-,räd\ *n, often cap* : HUNTER 1a [*Nimrod*, grandson of Noah]

nin·com·poop \'nin-kəm-,püp, 'ning-\ *n* : SIMPLETON, BOOBY [origin unknown]

nine \'nīn\ *n* **1** : one more than eight; *also* : a symbol representing this — see NUMBER table **2** : the ninth in a set or series **3** : something having nine units or members [Old English *nigon*] — **nine** *adj or pron*

nine days' wonder *n* : something that creates a short-lived sensation

nine·pin \'nīn-,pin\ *n* **1** : a pin used in ninepins **2** *pl* : a bowling game resembling tenpins played with nine pins in a diamond arrangement

nine·teen \nīn-'tēn, nīnt-, 'nīn-, 'nīnt-\ *n* : one more than 18; *also* : a symbol representing this — see NUMBER table [Old English *nigontēne*] — **nineteen** *adj or pron* — **nine·teenth** \-'tēnth, -'tēntth\ *adj or n*

nine·ty \'nīnt-ē\ *n, pl* **nineties** : ten more than 80; *also* : a symbol representing this — see NUMBER table [Old English *nigontig*] — **ninety** *adj or pron* — **nine·ti·eth** \-ē-əth\ *adj or n*

nin·ja \'nin-jə, -,jä\ *n, pl* **ninja** *also* **ninjas** : a person trained in ancient Japanese martial arts and employed especially for espionage and assassinations [Japanese]

nin·ny \'nin-ē\ *n, pl* **ninnies** : FOOL 1, SIMPLETON [perhaps from *an innocent*]

nin·ny·ham·mer \'nin-ē-,ham-ər\ *n* : NINNY

ninth \'nīnth, 'nīntth\ *n, pl* **ninths** \'nīns, 'nīnts, 'nīnths, 'nīntths\ **1** : number nine in a countable series — see NUMBER table **2 a** : a musical interval embracing an octave and a second **b** : a chord containing a ninth — **ninth** *adj or adv*

ni·o·bi·um \nī-'ō-bē-əm\ *n* : a lustrous platinum-gray ductile metallic chemical element that is used in alloys — see ELEMENT table [New Latin, from *Niobe*, a daughter of Tantalus; from its occurrence in ores with tantalum]

¹nip \'nip\ *vb* **nipped; nip·ping** **1** : to catch hold of and squeeze tightly between two surfaces, edges, or points ⟨the dog *nipped* my ankle⟩ **2 a** : to sever by or as if by pinching sharply **b** : to destroy the growth, progress, maturing, or fulfillment of ⟨*nipped* the rumor in the bud) **3** : to injure or make numb with cold : CHILL **4** : STEAL ⟨*nipped* the dessert⟩ **5** *chiefly British* : to move briskly, nimbly, or quickly [Middle English *nippen*]

²nip *n* **1** : something that nips: as **a** : a sharp stinging cold **b** : a biting or pungent flavor : TANG **2** : the act of nipping : PINCH, BITE **3** : a small portion : BIT

³nip *n* : a small quantity of liquor ⟨takes a *nip* now and then⟩ [probably from *nipperkin*, a liquor container, of unknown origin]

⁴nip *vi* **nipped; nip·ping** : to take liquor in nips : TIPPLE

ni·pa \'nē-pə\ *n* **1** : an alcoholic drink made from the juice of an Australasian creeping palm; *also* : this palm **2** : thatch made of nipa leaves [probably from Italian, from Malay *nipah* "nipa palm"]

nip and tuck \,nip-ən-'tək\ *adj or adv* : so close that the lead or advantage shifts rapidly from one contestant to another

nip·per \'nip-ər\ *n* **1** : a device (as pincers) for nipping — usually used in pl. **2** : CHELA **3** *chiefly British* : CHILD; *esp* : a small boy

nip·ple \'nip-əl\ *n* **1** : the protuberance of a mammary gland upon which the ducts open and from which milk is drawn **2** : something resembling a nipple; *esp* : the mouthpiece of a baby's nursing bottle [earlier *neble, nible,* probably from *neb, nib*]

Nip·pon·ese \,nip-ə-'nēz, -'nēs\ *adj* : JAPANESE 1 [*Nippon* (Japan)] — **Nipponese** *n*

nip·py \'nip-ē\ *adj* **nip·pi·er; -est** **1** : brisk, quick, or nimble in movement **2** : CHILLY, CHILLING ⟨a *nippy* day⟩

nir·va·na \niər-'vän-ə, nər-\ *n, often cap* **1** : the final beatitude that transcends suffering, karma, and samsara and is sought in Hinduism and Buddhism through the extinction of desire and individual consciousness **2** : a place or state of oblivion to care, pain, or external reality [Sanskrit *nirvāna,* literally, "act of extinguishing"]

ni·sei \nē-'sā, 'nē-\ *n, pl* **nisei** *also* **niseis** : a son or daughter of immigrant Japanese parents who is born and educated in America [Japanese, literally, "second generation"]

Nis·sen hut \,nis-n-\ *n* : a prefabricated shelter built of a semicircular arching roof of corrugated iron and a cement floor [Peter N. *Nissen,* died 1930, British mining engineer]

nit \'nit\ *n* : the egg of a louse or other parasitic insect; *also* : the insect itself when young [Old English *hnitu*]

ni·ter *also* **ni·tre** \'nīt-ər\ *n* **1** : POTASSIUM NITRATE **2** : SODIUM NITRATE [Middle French *nitre* "sodium carbonate", from Latin *nitrum,* from Greek *nitron,* from Egyptian *nt̠ry*]

nit·pick \'nit-ˌpik\ *vi* : to engage in nit-picking — **nit·pick·er** *n*

nit–pick·ing \'nit-ˌpik-ing\ *n* : minute and usually unjustified criticism

nitr- *or* **nitro-** *combining form* **1** : niter : nitrate **2 a** : nitrogen ⟨*nitr*ide⟩ **b** *usually* **nitro-** : containing the univalent group –NO₂ composed of one nitrogen and two oxygen atoms ⟨*nitro*benzene⟩

¹ni·trate \'nī-ˌtrāt, -trət\ *n* **1** : a salt or ester of nitric acid **2** : sodium nitrate or potassium nitrate used as a fertilizer

²ni·trate \-ˌtrāt\ *vt* : to treat or combine with nitric acid or a nitrate — **ni·tra·tion** \nī-'trā-shən\ *n* — **ni·tra·tor** \'nī-ˌtrāt-ər\ *n*

ni·tric \'nī-trik\ *adj* : of, relating to, or containing nitrogen especially with a higher valence than in corresponding nitrous compounds

nitric acid *n* : a corrosive liquid acid HNO_3 used especially as an oxidizing agent, in nitrations, and in making fertilizers, explosives, and dyes

nitric oxide *n* : a colorless poisonous gas NO obtained by oxidation of nitrogen or ammonia

ni·tride \'nī-ˌtrīd\ *n* : a compound of nitrogen with a more electropositive element

ni·tri·fi·ca·tion \,nī-trə-fə-'kā-shən\ *n* : the process of combining or impregnating with nitrogen or a nitrogen compound; *esp* : the oxidation (as by bacteria) of ammonium salts to nitrites and the further oxidation of nitrites to nitrates

ni·tri·fi·er \'nī-trə-ˌfī-ər, -ˌfīr\ *n* : any of various soil organisms capable of nitrification

ni·tri·fy·ing \-ˌfī-ing\ *adj* : active in nitrification

nitrifying bacteria *n pl* : bacteria of a family commonly found in the soil and obtaining energy through the process of nitrification

ni·trite \'nī-ˌtrīt\ *n* : a salt or ester of nitrous acid

ni·tro \'nī-trō\ *n* : any of various nitrated products; *esp* : NITROGLYCERIN

ni·tro·ben·zene \,nī-trō-'ben-ˌzēn, -ˌben-'-\ *n* : a poisonous insoluble oil made by nitration of benzene and used as a solvent, oxidizing agent, and source of aniline

ni·tro·cel·lu·lose \-'sel-yə-ˌlōs\ *n* : CELLULOSE NITRATE

ni·tro·gen \'nī-trə-jən\ *n* : a colorless tasteless odorless gaseous chemical element that constitutes 78 percent of the atmosphere by volume and is a constituent of all living tissues — see ELEMENT table [French *nitrogène,* from *nitre* "niter" + *-gène* "-gen"] — **ni·trog·e·nous** \nī-'träj-ə-nəs\ *adj*

nitrogen balance *n* : the ratio between nitrogen intake and nitrogen loss of the body or the soil

nitrogen cycle *n* : a continuous series of natural processes by which nitrogen passes successively from air to soil to organisms and back involving principally nitrogen fixation, nitrification, decay, and denitrification

nitrogen dioxide *n* : a brownish to yellowish poisonous gas NO_2 that is used especially in making nitric acid and in nitration and is an air pollutant formed in the oxidation of automobile exhausts

nitrogen fixation *n* : the conversion of free nitrogen into combined forms especially by microorganisms in soil and root nodules and its subsequent release in a form fit for plant use

nitrogen–fixing *adj* : capable of nitrogen fixation ⟨*nitrogen-fixing* bacteria⟩ — **nitrogen–fixer** *n*

nitrogen mustard *n* : any of various toxic blistering compounds that are analogous to mustard gas but with nitrogen replacing sulfur

ni·tro·glyc·er·in *or* **ni·tro·glyc·er·ine** \,nī-trō-'glis-rən, -ə-rən\ *n* : a heavy oily explosive poisonous liquid obtained by nitrating glycerol and used chiefly in making dynamites and in medicine to expand blood vessels

ni·trous \'nī-trəs\ *adj* **1** : of, relating to, or containing niter **2** : of, relating to, or containing nitrogen especially with a lower valence than in corresponding nitric compounds

nitrous acid *n* : an unstable acid HNO_2 known only in solution or in the form of its salts

nitrous oxide *n* : a colorless gas N_2O that when inhaled produces loss of sensibility to pain preceded by exhilaration and sometimes laughter and is often used as an anesthetic in dentistry — called also *laughing gas*

nit·ty–grit·ty \'nit-ē-ˌgrit-ē, ,nit-ē-'grit-ē\ *n* : what is essential and basic : specific practical details [origin unknown] — **nitty–gritty** *adj*

nit·wit \'nit-ˌwit\ *n* : a scatterbrained or stupid person [probably from German dialect *nit* "not" + English *wit*]

¹nix \'niks\ *n* : a water sprite of Germanic folklore [German]

²nix *adv* : NO — used to express disagreement or the withholding of permission [German *nichts* "nothing"]

³nix *vt* : VETO, FORBID ⟨the court *nixed* the merger⟩

nix·ie \'nik-sē\ *n* : NIX [German *nixe* "female nix"]

ni·zam \ni-'zäm, 'nī-ˌzam, nī-'-\ *n* : one of a line of sovereigns of Hyderabad from 1713 to 1950 [Hindi *nizām* "order, governor", from Arabic *nizām*] — **ni·zam·ate** \-ˌāt\ *n*

\ə\ abut		\ng\ sing	
\ər\ further		\ō\ bone	
\a\ mat		\ȯ\ saw	
\ā\ take		\oi\ coin	
\ä\ cot, cart		\th\ thin	
\au̇\ out		\th\ this	
\ch\ chin		\ü\ food	
\e\ pet		\u̇\ foot	
\ē\ easy		\y\ yet	
\g\ go		\yü\ few	
\i\ tip		\yu̇\ cure	
\ī\ life		\zh\ vision	
\j\ job			

¹no \nō, ˈnō\ *adv* **1 a** : chiefly Scottish : NOT **b** — used to express the negative of an alternative choice or possibility ⟨shall we continue or *no*⟩ **2** : in no respect or degree — used in comparisons ⟨they are *no* better than they should be⟩ **3** : not so — used to express negation, dissent, denial, or refusal ⟨*no*, I'm not hungry⟩ **4** — used with a following adjective to imply a meaning expressed by the opposite positive statement ⟨*no* uncertain terms⟩ **5** — used to introduce a word that is stronger or more emphatic than the preceding one ⟨has the right, *no*, the duty to continue⟩ **6** — used as an interjection to express surprise, doubt, or incredulity ⟨*no* — you don't say⟩ [Old English *nā*, from *ne* "not" + *ā* "always"]

²no *adj* **1 a** : not any ⟨I've *no* money⟩ **b** : hardly any : very little ⟨finished in *no* time⟩ **2** : not a ⟨I'm *no* expert⟩

³no \ˈnō\ *n, pl* **noes** *or* **nos** \ˈnōz\ **1** : an act or instance of refusing or denying by the use of the word no **2 a** : a negative vote or decision **b** *pl* : persons voting in the negative

nob \ˈnäb\ *n, chiefly British* : one in a superior position in life [perhaps from earlier *nob* "head", probably from *knob*]

nob·by \ˈnäb-ē\ *adj* **nob·bi·er; -est** : CHIC, SMART

no·bel·i·um \nō-ˈbel-ē-əm\ *n* : a radioactive chemical element produced artificially — see ELEMENT table [Alfred B. *Nobel*]

No·bel prize \nō-ˌbel-\ *n* : any of various annual prizes (as in peace, literature, medicine) established by the will of Alfred Nobel for the encouragement of persons who work for the interests of humanity

no·bil·i·ty \nō-ˈbil-ət-ē\ *n, pl* **-ties** **1** : the quality or state of being noble ⟨*nobility* of character⟩ **2** : noble rank ⟨confer *nobility* on a person⟩ **3** : a class or group of nobles ⟨the British *nobility*⟩ [Middle French *nobilité*, from Latin *nobilitas*, from *nobilis* "noble"]

¹no·ble \ˈnō-bəl\ *adj* **no·bler** \-bə-lər, -blər\; **no·blest** \-bə-ləst, -bləst\ **1 a** : having outstanding qualities : ILLUSTRIOUS ⟨a *noble* warrior⟩ **b** : FAMOUS, NOTABLE ⟨*noble* deeds⟩ **2** : of high birth or exalted rank : ARISTOCRATIC **3** : having fine qualities ⟨a *noble* hawk⟩ **4** : grand or impressive especially in appearance : IMPOSING ⟨a *noble* edifice⟩ **5** : having or characterized by superiority of mind or character : LOFTY ⟨*noble* aims⟩ **6** : chemically inert or inactive especially toward oxygen ⟨a *noble* metal⟩ [Old French, from Latin *nobilis* "knowable, well known, noble", from *noscere* "to come to know"] — **no·ble·ness** \-bəl-nəs\ *n* — **no·bly** \-blē\ *adv*

²noble *n* : a person of noble rank or birth

no·ble·man \ˈnō-bəl-mən\ *n* : a man of the nobility

no·blesse oblige \nō-ˌbles-ə-ˈblēzh\ *n* : the obligation to behave honorably that is associated with high rank or birth [French, literally, "nobility obligates"]

no·ble·wom·an \ˈnō-bəl-ˌwûm-ən\ *n* : a woman of the nobility

¹no·body \ˈnō-ˌbäd-ē, -bəd-ē\ *pron* : no person : not anybody

²nobody *n, pl* **no·bod·ies** : a person of no influence or importance

¹nock \ˈnäk\ *n* : a notch on the end of a bow or in an arrow in which the bowstring fits [Middle English *nocke* "notch on the end of a bow"]

²nock *vt* **1** : to make a nock in (a bow or an arrow) **2** : to fit (an arrow) against the bowstring for shooting

noc·tur·nal \näk-ˈtərn-l\ *adj* **1** : of, relating to, or occurring in the night ⟨a *nocturnal* journey⟩ **2** : active at night ⟨*nocturnal* insects⟩ [Late Latin *nocturnalis*, from Latin *nocturnus*, from noct-, *nox* "night"] — **noc·tur·nal·ly** \-l-ē\ *adv*

noc·turne \ˈnäk-ˌtərn\ *n* : a work of art dealing with night; *esp* : a dreamy pensive composition for the piano [French, "nocturnal", from Latin *nocturnus*]

noc·u·ous \ˈnäk-yə-wəs\ *adj* : likely to cause injury : HARMFUL [Latin *nocuus*, from *nocēre* "to harm"] — **noc·u·ous·ly** *adv*

¹nod \ˈnäd\ *vb* **nod·ded; nod·ding** **1** : to make a quick downward motion of the head (as in answering "yes" or in going to sleep); *also* : to cause (the head) to move in this way **2** : to move up and down ⟨the tulips *nodded* in the breeze⟩ **3** : to show by a nod of the head ⟨*nod* agreement⟩ **4** : to make a slip or an error in a moment of inattention [Middle English *nodden*] — **nod·der** *n*

²nod *n* : the action of nodding

nod·dle \ˈnäd-l\ *n* : HEAD 1 [Middle English *nodle* "back of the head or neck"]

nod·dy \ˈnäd-ē\ *n, pl* **noddies** **1** : a stupid person **2** : any of several stout-bodied terns of warm seas [probably from obsolete *noddypoll*]

node \ˈnōd\ *n* **1** : an entangling complication (as in a drama) **2 a** : a thickened or swollen enlargement (as of a rheumatic joint) **b** : a discrete mass of one kind of tissue enclosed in tissue of a different kind **3** : either of the two points where the orbit of a planet or comet intersects the ecliptic **4** : a point on a stem at which a leaf is attached **5** : a part of a vibrating body marked by absolute or relative freedom from vibratory motion [Latin *nodus* "knot, node"] — **nod·al** \ˈnōd-l\ *adj*

no·di·cal \ˈnōd-i-kəl, ˈnäd-\ *adj* : of or relating to astronomical nodes

nod·ule \ˈnäj-ül\ *n* : a small mass of rounded or irregular shape: as **a** : a small rounded lump of a mineral or mineral aggregate **b** : a swelling on the root of a legume that contains nitrogen-fixing bacteria — **nod·u·lar** \ˈnäj-ə-lər\ *adj*

no·el \nō-ˈel\ *n* **1** : a Christmas carol **2** *cap* : the Christmas season [French *noël* "Christmas, carol", from Latin *natalis* "birthday", from *natalis* "natal"]

noes *pl of* NO

nog \ˈnäg\ *n* **1** : a strong ale formerly brewed in Norfolk, England **2** : EGGNOG [origin unknown]

nog·gin \ˈnäg-ən\ *n* **1** : a small mug or cup **2** : a small quantity of drink usually equivalent to a gill (about .1 liter) **3** : HEAD 1 [origin unknown]

¹no-good \ˌnō-ˈgùd\ *adj* : having no worth, use, or chance of success

²no-good \ˈnō-ˌgùd\ *n* : a no-good person or thing

no·how \ˈnō-ˌhaù\ *adv* : in no manner or way ⟨*nohow* up to the job⟩

¹noise \ˈnòiz\ *n* **1** : loud, confused, or senseless shouting or outcry **2 a** : SOUND; *esp* : one that lacks agreeable musical quality or is noticeably unpleasant **b** : an unwanted signal in an electronic communication system [Old French, "strife, quarrel, noise", from Latin *nausea* "seasickness, nausea"] — **noise·less** \-ləs\ *adj* — **noise·less·ly** *adv* — **noise·less·ness** *n* □ ORIGIN
The commotion and complaints so often associated with sufferers of seasickness have given us the word *noise,* a derivative of Latin *nausea,* which means "seasickness" or "nausea". The form *noise* developed in Old French, with the meanings "noisy strife", "quarrel", and "noise". Today in English *noise* may be used of sound in general, but it most often denotes disagreeable or undesirable sound.

²noise *vt* : to spread by rumor or report

noise·mak·er \-ˌmā-kər\ *n* : one that makes noise; *esp* : a device used to make noise at parties

noise pollution *n* : environmental pollution consisting of annoying or harmful noise (as of jet planes) — called also *sound pollution*

noi·some \ˈnòi-səm\ *adj* **1** : UNHEALTHY 1, NOXIOUS **2** : offensive especially to the sense of smell [Middle English *noysome*, from *noy* "annoyance", from Old French *enui*, from *enuier* "to annoy"] — **noi·some·ly** *adv* — **noi·some·ness** *n*

noisy \ˈnòi-zē\ *adj* **nois·i·er; -est** **1** : making noise **2** : full of or characterized by noise — **nois·i·ly** \-zə-lē\ *adv* — **nois·i·ness** \-zē-nəs\ *n*

node

node 4

nol·le pro·se·qui \ˌnäl-ē-ˈpräs-ə-ˌkwī\ *n* : an entry on the record of a legal action that the prosecutor or plaintiff will proceed no further in an action or suit [Latin, "to be unwilling to pursue"]

no·lo con·ten·de·re \ˌnō-lō-kən-ˈten-də-rē\ *n* : a plea by the defendant in a criminal prosecution that without admitting guilt subjects him or her to conviction but does not preclude denial of the charges in another proceeding [Latin, "I do not wish to contend"]

nol–pros \ˈnäl-ˈpräs\ *vt* **nol–prossed; nol–pros·sing** : to discontinue by entering a nolle prosequi

no·mad \ˈnō-ˌmad\ *n* **1** : a member of a people that have no fixed residence but wander from place to place **2** : an individual who roams about aimlessly [Latin *nomad-, nomas* "member of a wandering pastoral people", from Greek, from *nemein* "to pasture"] — **no·mad·ic** \nō-ˈmad-ik\ *adj* — **no·mad·ism** \ˈnō-ˌmad-ˌiz-əm\ *n*

no–man's–land \ˈnō-ˌmanz-ˌland\ *n* **1** : an area of unowned, unclaimed, or uninhabited land **2** : an unoccupied area between opposing troops **3** : an area of indefinite or uncertain character

nom de guerre \ˌnäm-di-ˈgeər\ *n, pl* **noms de guerre** \ˌnäm-di-, ˌnämz-di-\ : PSEUDONYM [French, literally, "war name"]

nom de plume \ˌnäm-di-ˈplüm\ *n, pl* **noms de plume** \ˌnäm-di-, ˌnämz-di-\ : PEN NAME [French *nom* "name" + *de* "of" + *plume* "pen"]

no·men \ˈnō-mən\ *n, pl* **no·mi·na** \ˈnäm-ə-nə, ˈnō-mə-\ : the second of the usual three names of an ancient Roman [Latin, literally, "name"]

no·men·cla·ture \ˈnō-mən-ˌklā-chər\ *n* **1** : NAME 1, DESIGNATION **2** : a system of terms used in a particular science, discipline, or art; *esp* : the standardized New Latin names used in biology for kinds and groups of kinds of plants and animals [Latin *nomenclatura* "calling by name, list of names", from *nomen* "name" + *calare* "to call"] — **no·men·cla·tur·al** \ˌnō-mən-ˈklāch-rəl, -ə-rəl\ *adj*

¹nom·i·nal \ˈnäm-ən-l, ˈnäm-nəl\ *adj* **1** : of, relating to, or being a noun or a word or expression taking a noun construction **2** : of, relating to, or being a name **3 a** : existing or being something in name or form only 〈the *nominal* head of the party〉 **b** : very small : TRIFLING 〈a *nominal* price〉 [Latin *nominalis* "of a name", from Latin *nomen* "name"] — **nom·i·nal·ly** \-ē\ *adv*

²nominal *n* : a word or word group functioning as a noun

nom·i·nate \ˈnäm-ə-ˌnāt\ *vt* : to choose as a candidate for election, appointment, or honor; *esp* : to propose for office 〈was *nominated* for president〉 [Latin *nominare* "to name", from *nomen* "name"] — **nom·i·na·tor** \-ˌnāt-ər\ *n*

nom·i·na·tion \ˌnäm-ə-ˈnā-shən\ *n* **1** : the act, process, or an instance of nominating **2** : the state of being nominated 〈three names have been placed in *nomination*〉

nom·i·na·tive \ˈnäm-nət-iv, -ə-nət-\ *adj* : relating to or being a grammatical case marking typically the subject of a verb — **nominative** *n*

nom·i·nee \ˌnäm-ə-ˈnē\ *n* : a person who has been nominated

non- \ *before syllables with primary stress* ˈnän, ˈnän *also* ˌnän, ˈnən; *before syllables with secondary or weak stress* ˌnän *also* ˌnən\ *prefix* : not : reverse of : absence of 〈*non*calcareous〉 [Middle French, from Latin *non* "not"]

See *non-* and 2d element

nonabrasive	nonacademic	nonacidic
nonabrupt	nonacceptable	nonacquisitive
nonabsorbable	nonacceptance	nonactinic
nonabsorbent	nonaccessible	nonaction
nonabsorptive	nonaccountable	nonactive
nonabstemious	nonaccredited	nonadaptive
nonabstract	nonacid	nonaddicted

nonaddicting	nonclinical	noncultivation
nonaddictive	nonclotting	noncumulative
nonadditive	noncoagulable	noncurrent
nonadherence	noncoated	noncyclic
nonadherent	noncoercive	noncyclical
nonadhesion	noncognitive	nondeceptive
nonadhesive	noncoherent	nondecreasing
nonadjacent	noncohesive	nondeferrable
nonadjustable	noncollapsible	nondefining
nonadministrative	noncollectible	nondegenerate
nonadmission	noncollinear	nondegenerated
nonadolescent	noncolloid	nondegradable
nonaffiliated	noncombat	nondelinquent
nonaffluent	noncombining	nondelivery
nonaggression	noncombustible	nondemocratic
nonaggressive	noncommercial	nondepartmental
nonagreement	noncommunicable	nonderivative
nonagricultural	noncommunicant	nondestructive
nonalcoholic	noncommunication	nondeteriorative
nonallergenic	non-Communist	nondetonating
nonallergic	noncommutative	nondevelopable
nonalphabetic	noncommutativity	nondevelopment
nonanalytic	noncompensating	nondiabetic
nonanthropological	noncompetent	nondifferentiation
nonantigenic	noncompeting	nondiffusible
nonappearance	noncompetition	nondigestible
nonaquatic	noncompetitive	nondipolar
nonaqueous	noncomplementary	nondirectional
nonarbitrary	noncompliance	nondisclosure
nonaromatic	noncomplying	nondiscrimination
nonascetic	noncompound	nondiscriminatory
nonaspirated	noncomprehension	nondiscursive
nonassessable	noncompressible	nondisqualifying
nonassociative	nonconclusive	nondisruptive
nonathlete	nonconcurrent	nondistribution
nonathletic	noncondensable	nondivided
nonattendance	noncondensing	nondoctrinaire
nonattentive	nonconditioned	nondocumentary
nonattributive	nonconfidential	nondogmatic
nonauditory	nonconflicting	nondollar
nonauthoritative	nonconforming	nondomesticated
nonautomatic	noncongenital	nondramatic
nonautomotive	noncongruent	nondurable
nonbacterial	nonconjugated	nondynastic
nonbasic	nonconscious	nonecclesiastical
nonbearing	nonconsecutive	noneducational
nonbeing	nonconservation	noneffective
nonbeliever	nonconserved	noneffervescent
nonbelieving	nonconsolidated	nonelastic
nonbelligerency	nonconstitutional	nonelected
nonbelligerent	nonconstructive	nonelectric
nonbetting	nonconsumable	nonelectrical
nonbinding	noncontact	nonelectronic
nonbiodegradable	noncontagious	noneligible
nonbiological	noncontemporary	nonelite
nonbiologist	noncontentious	nonemergency
nonbiting	noncontiguous	nonemotional
nonbonded	noncontinuous	nonempirical
nonbonding	noncontraband	nonempty
nonbreakable	noncontradiction	nonencapsulated
nonburnable	noncontradictory	nonenforceable
noncaking	noncontributing	nonenforcement
noncancerous	noncontributory	nonentanglement
noncanonical	noncontrollable	nonequal
noncarbohydrate	noncontrolled	nonequilateral
noncarbonaceous	noncontrolling	nonequilibrium
noncarbonated	noncontroversial	nonequivalence
noncarnivorous	nonconventional	nonequivalent
noncash	nonconvertible	noneruptive
noncatalytic	noncoplanar	nonessential
noncellular	noncorporate	nonesterified
noncertified	noncorrectable	nonethical
nonchallenging	noncorrodible	nonexchangeable
nonchargeable	noncorroding	nonexclusive
nonchauvinist	noncorrosive	nonexempt
nonchosen	noncovalent	nonexistence
non-Christian	noncovered	nonexistent
nonchurchgoer	noncreative	nonexpendable
noncitizen	noncriminal	nonexperimental
nonclassical	noncritical	nonexpert
nonclassified	noncrystalline	nonexplosive
nonclerical	noncultivated	nonexposed

nonextant
nonfaculty
nonfading
nonfan
nonfarm
nonfarmer
nonfatal
nonfattening
nonfebrile
nonfederal
nonfederated
nonfeeding
nonferromagnetic
nonferrous
nonfilamentous
nonfilterable
nonfinancial
nonfissionable
nonflagellated
nonflammable
nonfluorescent
nonflying
nonforfeiture
nonfossiliferous
nonfraternal
nonfreezing
nonfulfillment
nonfunctional
nongaseous
nongeneric
nongenetic
nonghetto
nonglamorous
nongovernment
nongovernmental
nongraded
nongranular
nongregarious
nongrowing
nonhandicapped
nonhardy
nonharmonic
nonhazardous
nonhelical
nonhereditary
nonheritable
nonhistorical
nonhomogeneous
nonhormonal
nonhostile
nonideal
nonidentical
nonidentity
nonideological
nonimmigrant
nonimmune
nonimmunity
nonincreasing
nonindustrial
nonindustrialized
noninfectious
noninfective
noninfested
noninflammable
noninflammatory
noninflationary
noninflectional
noninformation
noninjurious
noninjury
noninsecticidal
noninstitutional
noninstitutionalized
noninstructional
nonintegral
nonintegrated
nonintellectual
noninterference
nonintersecting
nonintoxicant
nonintoxicating
noninvasive

noninvolvement
nonirradiated
nonirrigated
nonirritating
non-hermal
non-Jew
non-Jewish
nonleaded
nonlegal
nonleguminous
nonlethal
nonlexical
nonlife
nonlinguistic
nonliquid
nonliterary
nonliturgical
nonliving
nonlocal
nonlogical
nonluminous
nonmagnetic
nonmailable
nonmalicious
nonmalignant
nonmalleable
nonmammalian
nonmanagerial
nonmanufacturing
nonmarine
nonmarital
nonmarketable
nonmaterial
nonmaterialistic
nonmathematical
nonmathematician
nonmeaningful
nonmeasurable
nonmechanical
nonmechanistic
nonmedical
nonmember
nonmembership
nonmetered
nonmetric
nonmetrical
nonmetropolitan
nonmicrobial
nonmigratory
nonmilitary
nonmimetic
nonmolecular
nonmoney
nonmotile
nonmotility
nonmoving
nonmusical
nonmutant
nonnarcotic
nonnational
nonnative
nonnatural
nonnaturalism
nonnaturalist
nonnecessity
nonnegotiable
nonnitrogenous
nonnormative
nonnumerical
nonnutritious
nonnutritive
nonobese
nonobligatory
nonobscene
nonobservance
nonobvious
nonoccurrence
nonofficial
nonoily
nonopaque
nonoperating
nonoperational

nonorganic
nonoriented
nonoriginal
nonorthodox
nonorthogonal
nonoscillatory
nonoverlapping
nonpalatal
nonparallel
nonparalytic
nonparasitic
nonparticipant
nonparticipating
nonparticipation
nonparticipatory
nonparty
nonpathogenic
nonpaying
nonpayment
nonpeak
nonpecuniary
nonpenetrating
nonperformance
nonperishable
nonpermanent
nonpermissive
nonpersonal
nonphonemic
nonphonetic
nonphosphatic
nonphotosynthetic
nonphysical
nonphysiological
nonpigmented
nonplastic
nonplaying
nonpoisonous
nonpolarizable
nonpolitical
nonpolluting
nonpoor
nonporosity
nonporous
nonpossession
nonpractical
nonpredicative
nonpregnant
nonprinting
nonproducer
nonprofessional
nonprofessionally
nonprogressive
nonproportional
nonpropositional
nonproprietary
nonprotein
nonproven
nonpsychedelic
nonpublic
nonpungent
nonpunitive
nonquota
nonrabbinic
nonracial
nonracialism
nonracially
nonradiative
nonradical
nonradioactive
nonrandom
nonrandomness
nonrated
nonrational
nonreactive
nonreactivity
nonreactor
nonrealistic
nonreciprocal
nonrecognition
nonrecoverable
nonrecurrent
nonrecurring

nonreducing
nonredundant
nonrefillable
nonregistered
nonregulation
nonrelevant
nonreligious
nonremovable
nonrenewable
nonrepayable
nonrepresentative
nonresidential
nonresonant
nonrespondent
nonresponse
nonresponsive
nonrestraint
nonrestricted
nonretractile
nonretroactive
nonreusable
nonrevenue
nonreversible
nonrhetorical
nonrhombic
nonrioter
nonrioting
nonrotating
nonruminant
non-Russian
nonsalable
nonsaline
nonscientific
nonscientist
nonseasonal
nonsecret
nonsecretory
nonsecure
nonsegregated
nonsegregation
nonselected
nonselective
non-self-governing
nonsensitive
nonserious
nonsexist
nonsexual
nonshrinkable
nonsignificance

nonsignificant
nonsingular
nonsinkable
nonskier
nonslaveholding
nonsolar
nonsolid
nonspatial
nonspeaking
nonspecialist
nonspecialized
nonspecific
nonspecifically
nonspectacular
nonspectral
nonspeculative
nonspherical
nonspontaneous
nonstaining
nonstarchy
nonstationary
nonstatistical
nonstellar
nonstrategic
nonstriker
nonstriking
nonstructural
nonstructured
nonstudent
nonsubscriber
nonsuccess
nonsugar
nonsurfer
nonsurgical
nonsusceptible
nonsymbiotic
nonsymbolic
nonsymmetric
nonsymmetrical
nonsynchronous
nonsyntactical
nonsystemic
nontarnishable
nontaxable
nontechnical
nontechnological
nonteleological
nontemporal
nontenured

nonterritorial
nontheatrical
nontheistic
nonthermal
nonthreatening
nontidal
nontobacco
nontoxic
nontoxicity
nontraditional
nontransferable
nontransparency
nontransparent
nontransposing
nontreated
nontrivial
nontropical
nontrump
nontuberculous
nontypical
nonunanimous
nonunderstandable
nonuniform
nonuniformity
nonurban
nonurgent
nonuse
nonuser
nonutilitarian
nonvariable
nonvariant
nonvegetative
nonvenomous
nonvertical
nonvibratory
nonviewer
nonvintage
nonviral
nonviscous
nonvisual
nonvocal
nonvocational
nonvoluntary
nonvoter
nonvoting
nonwoody
nonworker
nonworking
nonyellowing

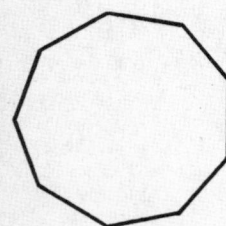

nonagon

non·age \'nän-ij, 'nō-nij\ *n* **1** : MINORITY 1 **2 a** : a period of youth **b** : lack of maturity [Middle French, from *non-* + *age* "age"]

no·na·ge·nar·i·an \,nō-nə-jə-'ner-ē-ən, ,nän-ə-\ *n* : a person who is 90 or more but less than 100 years old [Latin *nonagenarius* "containing ninety", derived from *nonaginta* "ninety"] — **nonagenarian** *adj*

no·na·gon \'nō-nə-,gän\ *n* : a polygon of nine angles and nine sides [Latin *nonus* "ninth"]

non·aligned \,nän-l-'īnd\ *adj* : not allied with other nations

non·al·le·lic \,nän-ə-'lē-lik, -'lel-ik\ *adj* : not behaving as alleles toward one another ⟨*nonallelic* genes⟩

non·cal·car·e·ous \,nän-kal-'kar-ē-əs, -'ker-\ *adj* : lacking or deficient in lime ⟨*noncalcareous* soils⟩

¹nonce \'näns\ *n* : the one, particular, or present occasion, purpose, or use ⟨for the *nonce*⟩ [Middle English *nanes,* from incorrect division of *then anes* in such phrases as *to then anes* "for the one purpose"]

²nonce *adj* : occurring, used, or made only once or for a special occasion ⟨a *nonce* word⟩

non·cha·lant \,nän-shə-'länt, 'nän-shə-,\ *adj* : giving an effect of easy unconcern or indifference ⟨face a crowd with *nonchalant* ease⟩ [French, from Old French *nonchaloir* "to disregard", from *non-* + *chaloir* "to concern", from Latin *calēre* "to be warm"] — **non·cha·lance** \-'läns, -,läns\ *n* — **non·cha·lant·ly** *adv*

non·com \'nän-,käm\ *n* : NONCOMMISSIONED OFFICER

non·com·bat·ant \,nän-kəm-'bat-nt; nän-'käm-bət-ənt, 'nän-\ *n* : a member (as a chaplain) of the armed forces whose duties exclude fighting; *also* : CIVILIAN — **non·com·bat·ant** *adj*

non·com·mis·sioned officer \ˌnän-kə-ˌmish-ənd-\ *n* : a subordinate officer (as a sergeant) in the armed forces appointed from enlisted personnel

non·com·mit·tal \ˌnän-kə-ˈmit-l\ *adj* : not telling or showing one's thoughts or decisions ⟨a *noncommittal* answer⟩ — **non·com·mit·tal·ly** \-l-ē\ *adv*

non com·pos men·tis \ˌnän-ˌkäm-pə-ˈsment-əs, -ˌnōn-\ *adj* : not of sound mind [Latin, literally, "not having control of one's mind"]

non·con·duc·tor \ˌnän-kən-ˈdək-tər\ *n* : a substance that conducts heat, electricity, or sound only in very small degree

non·con·fi·dence \ˌnän-ˈkän-fəd-əns, -fə-ˌdens\ *n* : lack of confidence especially of a parliamentary body in a government ⟨a vote of *nonconfidence*⟩

non·con·form·ist \ˌnän-kən-ˈfȯr-məst\ *n* **1** *often cap* : a person who does not conform to an established church and especially the Church of England **2** : a person who does not conform to a generally accepted pattern of thought or action — **nonconformist** *adj, often cap*

non·con·for·mi·ty \-ˈfȯr-mət-ē\ *n* **1 a** : failure or refusal to conform to an established church **b** *often cap* : the movement or principles of English Protestant dissent **c** *often cap* : the body of English Nonconformists **2** : refusal to conform to conventional rules or customs

non·co·op·er·a·tion \ˌnän-kō-ˌäp-ə-ˈrā-shən\ *n* : failure or refusal to cooperate especially with the government of a country — **non·co·op·er·a·tive** \-ˈäp-rət-iv, -ə-rət-, -ə-ˌrāt-\ *adj*

non·dairy \ˈnän-ˈder-ē\ *adj* : containing no milk or milk products ⟨*nondairy* whipped topping⟩

non·de·nom·i·na·tion·al \ˌnän-di-ˌnäm-ə-ˈnā-shnəl, -shən-l\ *adj* : not restricted to a single religious denomination

non·de·script \ˌnän-di-ˈskript\ *adj* : belonging or seeming to belong to no particular class or kind [*non-* + Latin *descriptus,* past participle of *describere* "to describe"] — **nondescript** *n*

non·dis·junc·tion \ˌnän-dis-ˈjəng-shən, -ˈjəngk-\ *n* : the failure of two homologous chromosomes to separate during meiosis so that one daughter cell has both and the other neither of the chromosomes — **non·dis·junc·tion·al** \-shnəl, -shən-l\ *adj*

¹none \ˈnən\ *pron, sing or pl in construction* **1** : not any ⟨*none* of them went⟩ ⟨*none* of it is needed⟩ **2** : not one ⟨*none* of the family⟩ **3** : not any such thing or person ⟨half a loaf is better than *none*⟩ [Old English *nān,* from *ne* "not" + *ān* "one"]

²none *adj, archaic* : not any : NO

³none *adv* **1** : by no means : not at all ⟨*none* too soon⟩ **2** : in no way : to no extent ⟨*none* the worse for wear⟩

⁴none \ˈnōn\ *n, often cap* : the fifth of the canonical hours [Late Latin *nona,* from Latin, "9th hour of the day (from sunrise)", from *nonus* "ninth"]

non·elec·tro·lyte \ˌnän-ə-ˈlek-trə-ˌlīt\ *n* : a substance (as sugar) that does not ionize in water and is therefore a poor conductor of electricity

non·en·ti·ty \nä-ˈnent-ət-ē, -ˈnen-ət-\ *n* **1** : something that does not exist or exists only in the imagination **2** : one of no consequence or significance

nones \ˈnōnz\ *n pl* : the 9th day before the ides according to ancient Roman reckoning [Latin *nonae,* from *nonus* "ninth"]

none·such \ˈnən-ˌsəch\ *or* **non·such** \ˈnən-ˌsəch *also* ˈnän-\ *n* : a person or thing without an equal — **nonesuch** *adj*

none·the·less \ˌnən-thə-ˈles\ *adv* : HOWEVER 2, NEVERTHELESS

non–eu·clid·e·an \ˌnän-yü-ˈklid-ē-ən\ *adj, often cap E* : not assuming or in accordance with all the postulates of Euclid's *Elements* ⟨*non-euclidean* geometry⟩

non·fat \ˈnän-ˈfat\ *adj* : having much or all of the fat removed ⟨*nonfat* milk⟩

non·fea·sance \nän-ˈfēz-ns, ˈnän-\ *n* : omission to do especially what ought to be done [*non-* + obsolete *feasance* "performance, doing", from Middle French *faisance* "act", from *faire* "to do", from Latin *facere*]

non·fic·tion \ˈnän-ˈfik-shən\ *n* : literature that is not fictional — **non·fic·tion·al** \ˌnän-ˈfik-shnəl, ˈnän-, -shən-l\ *adj*

non·flow·er·ing \ˌnän-ˈflaú-ring, ˈnän-, -ə-ring\ *adj* : lacking a flowering stage in the life cycle

non·green \ˈnän-ˈgrēn\ *adj* : lacking chlorophyll ⟨*nongreen* plants such as fungi⟩

non·ho·mol·o·gous \ˌnän-hō-ˈmäl-ə-gəs, -hə-\ *adj* : of unlike genic constitution ⟨*nonhomologous* chromosomes⟩

non·hu·man \nän-ˈhyü-mən, ˈnän-, -ˈyü-mən\ *adj* **1** : not belonging to the human race **2** : not befitting to, produced by, or involving human beings

no·nil·lion \nō-ˈnil-yən\ *n* — see NUMBER table [French, from Latin *nonus* "ninth" + French *-illion* (as in *million*)]

non·in·ter·ven·tion \ˌnän-ˌint-ər-ˈven-chən\ *n* : the state or habit of not intervening — **non·in·ter·ven·tion·ist** \-ˈvench-nəst, -ə-nəst\ *n or adj*

non·ju·ror \nän-ˈjúr-ər, ˈnän-\ *n* : a person refusing to take an oath (as of allegiance) — **non·jur·ing** \-ˈjúr-ing\ *adj*

non·lin·e·ar \nän-ˈlin-ē-ər, ˈnän-\ *adj* : not linear; *esp* : not representing or being a curve that can be graphed as a straight line ⟨*nonlinear* equations⟩

non·man·u·al \-ˈman-yə-wəl, -ˈman-yəl\ *adj* : not involving or occupied with manual labor

non·met·al \-ˈmet-l\ *n* : a chemical element (as carbon or nitrogen) that lacks metallic properties

non·me·tal·lic \ˌnän-mə-ˈtal-ik\ *adj* **1** : not metallic **2** : of, relating to, or being a nonmetal

non·neg·a·tive \nän-ˈneg-ət-iv, ˈnän-\ *adj* : being either positive or zero ⟨*nonnegative* real numbers⟩

no–no \ˈnō-ˌnō\ *n, pl* **no-no's** *or* **no-nos** : something unacceptable or forbidden

non·ob·jec·tive \ˌnän-əb-ˈjek-tiv\ *adj* : representing or intended to represent no natural or actual object, figure, or scene ⟨*nonobjective* art⟩

¹non·pa·reil \ˌnän-pə-ˈrel\ *adj* : having no equal [Middle French, from *non-* + *pareil* "equal", from Latin *par*]

²nonpareil *n* **1** : one of unequaled excellence : PARAGON **2 a** : a small flat chocolate disk covered with white sugar pellets **b** : small sugar pellets of various colors

non·par·ti·san \nän-ˈpärt-ə-zən, ˈnän-\ *adj* : not partisan; *esp* : free from party affiliation, bias, or designation ⟨*nonpartisan* ballot⟩ ⟨a *nonpartisan* board⟩ — **non·par·ti·san·ship** \-ˌship\ *n*

non·pas·ser·ine \nän-ˈpas-ə-ˌrīn, ˈnän-\ *adj* : not passerine; *esp* : belonging to the order (Coraciiformes) that includes the kingfishers and related birds

non·per·sis·tent \ˌnän-pər-ˈsis-tənt, -ˈzis-\ *adj* : not persistent; *esp* : decomposed rapidly by environmental action ⟨*nonpersistent* insecticides⟩

¹non·plus \nän-ˈpləs, ˈnän-\ *n* : a state of bafflement or perplexity : QUANDARY [Latin *non plus* "no more"]

²nonplus *vt* **non·plussed** *also* **non·plused; non·plus·sing** *also* **non·plus·ing** : to cause to be at a loss as to what to say, think, or do : PERPLEX

non·po·lar \nän-ˈpō-lər, ˈnän-\ *adj* **1** : lacking electrical poles ⟨a *nonpolar* molecule⟩ **2** : of or characterized by covalence ⟨a *nonpolar* liquid⟩

non·pos·i·tive \nän-ˈpäz-ət-iv, ˈnän-, -ˈpäz-tiv\ *adj* : being either negative or zero ⟨*nonpositive* real numbers⟩

non·pro·duc·tive \ˌnän-prə-ˈdək-tiv\ *adj* **1** : failing to produce or yield : UNPRODUCTIVE ⟨*nonproductive* land⟩ **2** : not directly concerned with production ⟨*nonproductive* labor⟩ — **non·pro·duc·tive·ness** *n*

\ə\ abut	\ng\ sing
\ər\ further	\ō\ bone
\a\ mat	\ò\ saw
\ā\ take	\òi\ coin
\ä\ cot, cart	\th\ thin
\aú\ out	\th\ this
\ch\ chin	\ü\ food
\e\ pet	\ú\ foot
\ē\ easy	\y\ yet
\g\ go	\yü\ few
\i\ tip	\yú\ cure
\ī\ life	\zh\ vision
\j\ job	

non·prof·it \nän-'präf-ət, 'nän-\ *adj* : not conducted or maintained for the purpose of profit ⟨a *nonprofit* organization⟩

non·re·peat·ing decimal \,nän-ri-'pēt-ing-\ *n* : a decimal that has an infinite number of digits but is not a repeating decimal

non·rep·re·sen·ta·tion·al \,nän-,rep-ri-,zən-'tā-shnəl, -shən-l\ *adj* : NONOBJECTIVE

non·res·i·dent \nän-'rez-əd-ənt, 'nän-, -'rez-dənt, -'rez-ə-,dent\ *adj* : not living in a specified or implied place — **non·res·i·dence** \-'rez-əd-əns, -'rez-dəns, -'rez-ə-,dens\ — **nonresident** *n*

non·re·sis·tance \,nän-ri-'zis-təns\ *n* : the principles or practice of passive submission to authority even when unjust or oppressive; *also* : the principle or practice of not resisting violence by force — **non·re·sis·tant** \-tənt\ *adj*

non·re·stric·tive \,nän-ri-'strik-tiv\ *adj* 1 : not restrictive 2 : not limiting the reference of a modified word or phrase ⟨a *nonrestrictive* clause⟩

non·rig·id \nän-'rij-əd, 'nän-\ *adj* : maintaining form by pressure of contained gas ⟨a *nonrigid* airship⟩

non·sched·uled \-'skej-üld, -əld\ *adj* : licensed to carry passengers or freight by air without a regular schedule ⟨*nonscheduled* airline⟩

non·sec·tar·i·an \,nän-sek-'ter-ē-ən\ *adj* : not having a sectarian character ⟨a *nonsectarian* school⟩

non·sense \'nän-,sens, 'nän-səns\ *n* 1 : foolish or meaningless words or actions 2 : things of no importance or value ⟨spent their money on *nonsense*⟩ — **non·sen·si·cal** \nän-'sen-si-kəl, 'nän-\ *adj* — **non·sen·si·cal·ly** \-kə-lē, -klē\ *adv* — **non·sen·si·cal·ness** \-kəl-nəs\ *n*

non se·qui·tur \nän-'sek-wət-ər, 'nän-\ *n* : a statement that does not follow logically from anything previously said [Latin, "it does not follow"]

non·sked \nän-'sked, 'nän-\ *n* : a nonscheduled airline or transport plane

non·skid \nän-'skid, 'nän-\ *adj* : designed or equipped to prevent skidding

non·smok·er \-'smō-kər\ *n* : a person who does not smoke tobacco — **non·smok·ing** \-'smō-king\ *n*

non·sport·ing \-'spōrt-ing, -'spórt-\ *adj* : lacking the qualities characteristic of a hunting dog

non·stan·dard \-'stan-dərd\ *adj* 1 : not standard 2 : not conforming in pronunciation, grammatical construction, idiom, or word choice to the usage generally characteristic of educated native speakers of the language

non·stick \nän-'stik, 'nän-\ *adj* : allowing easy removal of cooked food particles ⟨a *nonstick* coating on a pan⟩

non·stop \-'stäp\ *adj* : done or made without a stop ⟨a *nonstop* flight⟩ — **nonstop** *adv*

non·stri·at·ed muscle \nän-,strī-,āt-əd-\ *n* : SMOOTH MUSCLE

non·such *variant of* NONESUCH

non·suit \nän-'süt, 'nän-\ *n* : a judgment against a plaintiff for failure to prosecute the case or inability to establish a prima facie case [Anglo-French *nounsuyte,* from *noun-* "non-" + Old French *siute* "following, pursuit"] — **nonsuit** *vt*

non·sup·port \,nän-sə-'pōrt, -'pórt\ *n* : failure to support; *esp* : failure (as of a parent) to honor an obligation to provide financial support to a dependent

non·syl·lab·ic \,nän-sə-'lab-ik\ *adj* : not constituting a syllable or the nucleus of a syllable

non·tast·er \nän-'tā-stər, 'nän-\ *n* : a person unable to taste the chemical phenylthiocarbamide

non trop·po \nän-'trò-pō, 'nän-, 'nōn-\ *adv or adj* : not too much so : without excess — used as a direction in music [Italian, literally, "not too much"]

non·union \nän-'yün-yən, 'nän-\ *adj* 1 : not belonging to a trade union ⟨*nonunion* carpenters⟩ 2 : not recognizing or favoring trade unions or their members

non·vas·cu·lar plant \,nän-,vas-kyə-lər-\ *n* : a plant (as an alga or a fungus) that has no vascular tissue

non·ver·bal \nän-'vər-bəl, 'nän-\ *adj* 1 : being other than verbal ⟨*nonverbal* symbols⟩ 2 : involving little use of language ⟨*nonverbal* tests⟩ — **non·ver·bal·ly** \-bə-lē\ *adv*

non·vi·a·ble \nän-'vī-ə-bəl, 'nän-\ *adj* : not capable of living, growing, or developing and functioning successfully

non·vi·o·lence \-'vī-ə-ləns\ *n* 1 : abstention on principle from violence; *also* : the principle of such abstention 2 : nonviolent demonstrations to secure political ends — **non·vi·o·lent** \-lənt\ *adj*

non·vol·a·tile \nän-'väl-ət-l\ *adj* : not volatile : not volatilizing readily

non·ze·ro \nän-'zē-rō, -'ziər-ō\ *adj* : either positive or negative but not zero

¹**noo·dle** \'nüd-l\ *n* 1 : a stupid person : SIMPLETON 2 : HEAD 1 [perhaps alteration of *noddle*]

²**noodle** *n* : a food paste made with egg and shaped into long flat strips [German *nudel*]

nook \'nùk\ *n* 1 : an interior angle formed by two meeting walls : RECESS ⟨a chimney *nook*⟩ 2 : a secluded or sheltered place ⟨a shady *nook*⟩ [Middle English *noke, nok*]

noon \'nün\ *n* : the middle of the day : 12 o'clock in the daytime [Old English *nōn* "9th hour from sunrise", from Latin *nona,* from *nonus* "ninth"] — **noon** *adj* □ **ORIGIN** *Noon* has not always indicated that time of day at which the sun is most nearly overhead. According to the Roman method of reckoning time, the hours of the day were counted from sunrise to sunset. English *noon* is derived from Latin *nona,* from *nonus,* which means "ninth". *Noon,* then, was the ninth hour of the day, or about three p.m. A church service which was held daily at this time is called *none,* and perhaps in anticipation of this service or possibly of a mealtime, the time denoted by *none* or *noon* shifted to the hour of midday.

noon·day \-,dā\ *n* : MIDDAY

no one *pron* : NOBODY

noon·ing \'nü-ning, -nən\ *n, chiefly dialect* : a midday meal; *also* : a period at noon for eating or resting

noon·tide \'nün-,tīd\ *n* 1 : NOONTIME 2 : the highest or culminating point

noon·time \-,tīm\ *n* : the time of noon : MIDDAY

¹**noose** \'nüs\ *n* : a loop with a running knot that becomes tighter the more it is drawn [probably from Provençal *nous* "knot", from Latin *nodus*]

²**noose** *vt* : to catch or fasten with or as if with a noose

no–par *adj* : having no face value ⟨*no-par* stock⟩

nor \nər, nór, 'nór\ *conj* : and not ⟨the book is too long; *nor* is the style easy⟩ ⟨not for you *nor* for me⟩ — used especially to introduce and negate the second member and each later member of a series of items of which the first is preceded by neither ⟨neither here *nor* there⟩ [Middle English, contraction of *nother* "neither, nor"]

nor·adren·a·line \,nór-ə-'dren-l-ən\ *n* : NOREPINEPHRINE [*nor*mal + *adrenaline*]

¹**Nor·dic** \'nòrd-ik\ *adj* 1 : of or relating to the Germanic peoples of northern Europe and especially of Scandinavia 2 : of or relating to a physical type characterized by tall stature, long head, light skin and hair, and blue eyes [French *nordique,* from *nord* "north", from Old English *north*]

²**Nordic** *n* 1 : a native of northern Europe 2 : a person of Nordic physical type or of a hypothetical Nordic division of the Caucasian race 3 : a member of a Scandinavian people

nor·epi·neph·rine \'nór-,ep-ə-'nef-rən\ *n* : a compound that causes blood vessels to contract and assists in the transmission of nerve impulses in the sympathetic nervous system [*nor*mal + *epinephrine*]

norm \'nórm\ *n* 1 : an authoritative standard : MODEL 2 : AVERAGE; *esp* : a set standard of development or achievement usually derived from the average or median achievement of a large group [Latin *norma,* literally, "carpenter's square"]

¹nor·mal \'nȯr-məl\ *adj* **1** : forming a right angle; *esp* : perpendicular to a tangent at a point of tangency **2** : according with or constituting a norm, rule, or principle **3 a** : of, relating to, or characterized by average intelligence or development **b** : free from disorder of body or mind : SOUND **4 a** : having a concentration of one gram equivalent of solute per liter ⟨a *normal* salt solution⟩ **b** : containing neither basic hydroxyl nor acid hydrogen ⟨a *normal* salt⟩ **c** : having a straight-chain structure ⟨a *normal* alcohol⟩ [Latin *normalis,* from *norma* "carpenter's square"] SYN see REGULAR — **nor·mal·cy** \-sē\ *n* — **nor·mal·i·ty** \nȯr-'mal-ət-ē\ *n* — **nor·mal·ly** \'nȯr-mə-lē\ *adv* □ ORIGIN Latin *norma* means "rule" or "pattern" as well as "carpenter's square", for a square provides a standard or rule which ensures that a carpenter can make corners and edges that are straight and that form right angles. The Latin adjective *normalis,* formed from *norma,* originally meant "forming a right angle" or "according to a square", and it is from this Latin sense that we get the earliest sense of *normal* in English, "perpendicular". Latin *normalis* was also used in more extended senses, however, and by the Late Latin period its usual meaning was "according to rule". Most of the senses of our word *normal* are derived from this Late Latin usage.

²normal *n* **1** : one (as a line or person) that is normal **2** : a form or state regarded as the norm : STANDARD

nor·mal·ize \'nȯr-mə-ˌlīz\ *vt* : to bring or restore to a normal state

normal school *n* : a usually two-year school for training chiefly elementary teachers [translation of French *école normale*]

Nor·man \'nȯr-mən\ *n* **1** : any of the Scandinavians who conquered Normandy in the 10th century **2** : any of the people of mixed Norman and French blood who conquered England in 1066 **3** : a native or inhabitant of the province of Normandy [Old French *Normant,* from Old Norse *Northmathr* "Norseman", from *northr* "north" + *mathr* "man"] — **Norman** *adj*

Norman–French *n* : the French language of the Normans

nor·ma·tive \'nȯr-mət-iv\ *adj* : of, conforming to, or prescribing norms — **nor·ma·tive·ly** *adv* — **nor·mative·ness** *n*

Norse \'nȯrs\ *n, pl* **Norse 1** *pl* **a** : the Scandinavian people **b** : the Norwegian people **2 a** : NORWEGIAN 2 **b** : any of the western Scandinavian dialects or languages **c** : the Scandinavian group of Germanic languages [probably from obsolete Dutch *noorsch,* adj., "Norwegian, Scandinavian", from *noordsch* "northern", from *noord* "north"] — **Norse** *adj*

Norse·man \'nȯr-smən\ *n* : any of the ancient Scandinavians

¹north \'nȯrth\ *adv* : to, toward, or in the north [Old English]

²north *adj* **1** : situated toward or at the north **2** : coming from the north

³north *n* **1 a** : the direction to the left of one facing east **b** : the compass point directly opposite to south **2** *cap* : regions or countries north of a specified or implied point

north·bound \'nȯrth-ˌbau̇nd\ *adj* : headed north

¹north·east \nȯr-'thēst, *nautical* nȯ-'rēst\ *adv* : to, toward, or in the northeast

²northeast *n* **1 a** : the general direction between north and east **b** : the compass point midway between north and east : N 45° E **2** *cap* : regions or countries northeast of a specified or implied point

³northeast *adj* **1** : coming from the northeast **2** : situated toward or at the northeast

north·east·er \nȯr-'thē-stər, nȯ-'rē-\ *n* **1** : a strong northeast wind **2** : a storm with northeast winds

north·east·er·ly \nȯr-'thē-stər-lē\ *adv or adj* **1** : from the northeast **2** : toward the northeast

north·east·ern \-stərn\ *adj* **1** *often cap* : of, relating to, or characteristic of a region conventionally designated Northeast **2** : lying toward or coming from the northeast — **north·east·ern·most** \-stərn-ˌmōst\ *adj*

North·east·ern·er \-stər-nər, -stə-nər\ *n* : a native or inhabitant of a northeastern region (as of the United States)

¹north·east·ward \nȯr-'thēs-twərd\ *adv or adj* : toward the northeast — **north·east·wards** \-twərdz\ *adj*

²northeastward *n* : NORTHEAST

north·er \'nȯr-thər\ *n* **1** : a strong north wind **2** : a storm with north winds

¹north·er·ly \-lē\ *adv or adj* **1** : from the north **2** : toward the north

²northerly *n, pl* **-lies** : a wind from the north

north·ern \'nȯr-thərn, -thən\ *adj* **1** *often cap* : of, relating to, or characteristic of a region conventionally designated North **2** : lying toward or coming from the north [Old English *northerne*] — **north·ern·most** \-ˌmōst\ *adj*

Northern *n* : the dialect of English spoken in the part of the U.S. north of a line running northwest through central New Jersey, below the northern tier of counties in Pennsylvania, through northern Ohio, Indiana, and Illinois, across central Iowa, and through the northwest corner of South Dakota

Northern Cross *n* : a cross formed by six stars in Cygnus

Northern Crown *n* : CORONA BOREALIS

North·ern·er \'nȯr-thər-nər, -thə-nər\ *n* : a native or inhabitant of the North (as of the United States)

northern hemisphere *n* : the half of the earth that lies north of the equator

northern lights *n pl* : AURORA BOREALIS

north·ing \'nȯr-thing, -thing\ *n* **1** : difference in latitude to the north from the last preceding point of reckoning **2** : northerly progress

north·land \'nȯrth-ˌland, -lənd\ *n, often cap* : land in the north : the north of a country or region

North·man \-mən\ *n* : NORSEMAN

north–north·east \'nȯrth-ˌnȯr-'thēst, *nautical* -ˌnȯ-'rēst\ *n* : two points east of north : N 22° 30' E

north–north·west \'nȯrth-ˌnȯrth-'west, *nautical* -ˌnȯr-'west\ *n* : two points west of north : N 22° 30' W

north pole *n* **1** *often cap N&P* : the northernmost point of the earth : the northern end of the earth's axis **2** : the pole of a magnet that points toward the north

north–seeking pole *n* : NORTH POLE 2

North Star *n* : the star toward which the northern end of the earth's axis very nearly points — called also *polestar*

¹north·ward \'nȯrth-wərd\ *adv or adj* : toward the north — **north·wards** \-wərdz\ *adv*

²northward *n* : northward direction or part

¹north·west \nȯrth-'west, *nautical* nȯr-'west\ *adv* : to, toward, or in the northwest

²northwest *n* **1 a** : the general direction between north and west **b** : the compass point midway between north and west : N 45° W **2** *cap* : regions or countries northwest of a specified or implied point

³northwest *adj* **1** : coming from the northwest **2** : situated toward or at the northwest

north·west·er \nȯrth-'wes-tər, nȯr-'wes-\ *n* **1** : a strong northwest wind **2** : a storm with northwest winds

north·west·er·ly \nȯrth-'wes-tər-lē\ *adv or adj* **1** : from the northwest **2** : toward the northwest

north·west·ern \nȯrth-'wes-tərn\ *adj* **1** *often cap* : of, relating to, or characteristic of a region conventionally designated Northwest **2** : lying toward or coming from the northwest — **north·west·ern·most** \-tərn-ˌmōst\ *adj*

North·west·ern·er \-tər-nər, -tə-nər\ *n* : a native or inhabitant of a northwestern region (as of the United States)

¹**north·west·ward** \nȯrth-'wes-twərd\ *adv or adj* : toward the northwest — **north·west·wards** \-twərdz\ *adv*

²**northwestward** *n* : NORTHWEST

Nor·way maple \,nȯr-,wā-\ *n* : a European maple with dark green or often reddish leaves

Norway pine *n* : a North American pine with reddish bark and hard but not durable wood; *also* : its wood

Nor·we·gian \nȯr-'wē-jən\ *n* **1 a** : a native or inhabitant of Norway **b** : a person of Norwegian descent **2** : the Germanic language of the Norwegian people [Medieval Latin *Norwegia* "Norway"] — **Norwegian** *adj*

nos *pl of* NO

¹**nose** \'nōz\ *n* **1 a** : the part of the face or head that bears the nostrils and covers the front or outer part of the nasal cavity; *also* : this part together with the nasal cavity **b** : the front part of the head above or projecting beyond the jaws (the length of a whale from the tip of the *nose* to the notch between the flukes) **2** : the sense of smell : OLFACTION **3** : the vertebrate organ of smell **4** : something (as a point, edge, or projecting front part) that resembles a nose (the *nose* of a plane) **5 a** : the nose as a symbol of prying curiosity **b** : a knack for discovery or understanding (a good *nose* for news) [Old English *nosu*] — **nosed** \'nōzd\ *adj*

¹nose 4

²**nose** *vb* **1** : to detect by or as if by smell : SCENT **2 a** : to push or move with the nose **b** : to touch or rub with the nose **3** : to search impertinently : PRY **4** : to move ahead slowly or cautiously (the car *nosed* out into traffic)

nose·band \'nōz-,band\ *n* : the part of a bridle or halter that passes over a horse's nose

nose·bleed \-,blēd\ *n* : bleeding from the nose

nose cone *n* : a protective cone constituting the forward end of a rocket or missile

nose dive *n* **1** : the downward nose-first plunge of a flying object (as an airplane) **2** : a sudden extreme drop — **nose–dive** \'nōz-,dīv\ *vi*

nose·gay \'nōz-,gā\ *n* : a small bunch of flowers [*nose* + English dialect *gay* "ornament"]

nose·piece \-,pēs\ *n* **1** : a piece of armor for protecting the nose **2** : a fitting at the lower end of a microscope tube to which the objectives are attached

no–show \nō-'shō\ *n* : a person who reserves space especially on an airplane but neither uses nor cancels the reservation

nos·tal·gia \nä-'stal-jə, nə-\ *n* : a wistful sentimental yearning for something past or irrecoverable [New Latin, from Greek *nostos* "return home" + New Latin *-algia* "-algia"] — **nos·tal·gic** \-jik\ *adj* — **nos·tal·gi·cal·ly** \-ji-kə-lē, -klē\ *adv*

nos·toc \'näs-,täk\ *n* : any of a genus of blue-green algae able to use atmospheric nitrogen [New Latin, genus name]

nos·tril \'näs-trəl\ *n* : either of the outer openings of the nose with its adjoining passage; *also* : either fleshy lateral wall of the nose [Old English *nosthyrl*, from *nosu* "nose" + *thyrel* "hole"]

nos·trum \'näs-trəm\ *n* **1** : a medicine of secret composition recommended especially by its preparer **2** : a questionable remedy or scheme : PANACEA [Latin, neuter of *noster* "our, ours", from *nos* "we"]

nosy *or* **nos·ey** \'nō-zē\ *adj* **nos·i·er; -est** SNOOPY — **nos·i·ly** \-zə-lē\ *adv* — **nos·i·ness** \-zē-nəs\ *n*

not \nät, 'nät\ *adv* **1** — used to make negative a group of words or a word (the books are *not* here) **2** — used to stand for the negative of a preceding group of words (is sometimes hard to see and sometimes *not*) [Middle English, alteration of *nought* "naught"]

no·ta·bil·i·ty \,nōt-ə-'bil-ət-ē\ *n*, *pl* **-ties 1** : the quality or state of being notable **2** : NOTABLE

¹**no·ta·ble** \'nōt-ə-bəl\ *adj* **1** : worthy of note : REMARKABLE **2** : DISTINGUISHED 1, PROMINENT — **no·ta·bly** \-blē\ *adv*

²**notable** *n* : a person of note or of great reputation

no·ta·rize \'nōt-ə-,rīz\ *vt* : to make legally authentic through the use of the powers granted to a notary public — **no·ta·ri·za·tion** \,nōt-ə-rə-'zā-shən\ *n*

no·ta·ry public \,nōt-ə-rē-\ *n*, *pl* **notaries public** *or* **notary publics** : a public officer who attests or certifies writings (as deeds) as authentic and takes affidavits, depositions, and protests of negotiable paper — called also **notary** [Latin *notarius* "clerk, secretary", derived from *nota* "note"]

no·tate \'nō-,tāt\ *vt* : to put into notation

no·ta·tion \nō-'tā-shən\ *n* **1** : ANNOTATION, NOTE (make *notations* for corrections on the margin) **2** : the act, process, or method of representing data symbolically by marks, signs, figures, or characters; *also* : a system of symbols (as letters, numerals, or musical notes) used in such notation — **no·ta·tion·al** \-shnəl, -shən-l\ *adj*

¹**notch** \'näch\ *n* **1** : a V-shaped or rounded indentation **2** : a narrow pass between mountains : GAP **3** : DEGREE, STEP (the team moved up a *notch* in the standings) [perhaps derived from Middle French *oche* "notch"] — **notched** \'nächt\ *adj*

²**notch** *vt* **1** : to cut or make notches in **2 a** : to mark or record with a notch **b** : ACHIEVE 2, SCORE (*notched* another victory)

¹**note** \'nōt\ *vt* **1 a** : to notice or observe with care **b** : to record in writing **2** : to make special mention of : REMARK [Old French *noter*, from Latin *notare* "to mark, note", from *nota* "note"] — **not·er** *n*

²**note** *n* **1 a** : a musical sound **b** : an animal's cry, call, or sound (a bird's *note*) **c** : a special tone of voice (a *note* of fear) **2 a** : MEMORANDUM 1b **b** : a brief and informal record **c** : a written or printed comment or explanation (*notes* in the back of the book) **d** : a short informal letter **e** : a formal diplomatic or official communication **3 a** : a written promise to pay — called also **promissory note b** : a piece of paper money **4** : a character in music that by its shape shows the length of time a tone is to be held and by its place on the staff shows the pitch of a tone **5** : MOOD, QUALITY (a *note* of optimism) **6 a** : REPUTATION, DISTINCTION (a person of *note*) **b** : NOTICE, HEED (take *note* of the exact time) [Latin *nota* "mark, character, written note"]

note·book \'nōt-,bùk\ *n* : a book for notes or memoranda

note·case \-,kās\ *n*, *British* : BILLFOLD, WALLET

not·ed \'nōt-əd\ *adj* : widely and favorably known (a *noted* author) □ SYN NOTORIOUS: NOTED implies being singled out for public attention for excellence of achievement; NOTORIOUS stresses being widely known for usually questionable acts or qualities

note·wor·thy \'nōt-,wər-thē\ *adj* : worthy of note : REMARKABLE — **note·wor·thi·ly** \-thə-lē\ *adv* — **note·wor·thi·ness** \-thē-nəs\ *n*

¹**noth·ing** \'nəth-ing\ *pron* **1** : not anything (there's *nothing* in the box) **2** : one of no interest, value, or consequence [Old English *nān* thing, *nāthing*, from *nān* "no, none" + *thing*] — **nothing doing** : by no means : definitely no

²**nothing** *adv* : not at all : in no degree

³**nothing** *n* **1 a** : something that does not exist **b** : absence of magnitude : ZERO **2** : something of little or no worth or importance — **noth·ing·ness** *n*

¹**no·tice** \'nōt-əs\ *n* **1 a** : warning or indication of something : ANNOUNCEMENT **b** : notification of the ending of an agreement at a specified time **2** : ATTENTION, HEED (sit up and take *notice*) **3** : a written or printed announcement **4** : a short critical account [Middle French, "acquaintance", from Latin *notitia* "knowledge, acquaintance", from *notus* "known", from *noscere* to come to know"]

²**notice** *vt* **1** : to make mention of : remark on **2** : to take notice of : OBSERVE (*notice* even the smallest details)

no·tice·able \'nōt-ə-sə-bəl\ *adj* **1** : worthy of notice (*noticeable* for its fine quality) **2** : capable of being or likely to be noticed ⟨a *noticeable* improvement⟩ — **no·tice·ably** \-blē\ *adv*

no·ti·fi·ca·tion \ˌnōt-ə-fə-'kā-shən\ *n* **1** : the act or an instance of notifying **2** : written or printed matter that gives notice

no·ti·fy \'nōt-ə-ˌfī\ *vt* **-fied; -fy·ing 1** : to give notice of or report the occurrence of **2** : to give notice to [Middle French *notifier* "to make known", from Late Latin *notificare*, from Latin *notus* "known"] — **no·ti·fi·er** \-ˌfī-ər, -ˌfīr\ *n*

no·tion \'nō-shən\ *n* **1 a** : IDEA, CONCEPTION ⟨have a *notion* of a poem's meaning⟩ **b** : a belief held : OPINION **c** : WHIM, FANCY ⟨a sudden *notion* to go home⟩ **2** *pl* : small useful articles : SUNDRIES [Latin *notio*, from *noscere* "to come to know"]

no·tion·al \'nō-shnəl, -shən-l\ *adj* **1** : existing in idea only **2** : inclined to foolish or visionary fancies or moods

no·to·chord \'nōt-ə-ˌkord\ *n* : a longitudinal flexible rod of cells that in the lowest chordates (as amphioxi and the lampreys) and in the embryos of the higher vertebrates forms the supporting axis of the body [Greek *nōton* "back" + Latin *chorda* "cord"] — **no·to·chord·al** \ˌnōt-ə-'kord-l\ *adj*

no·to·ri·ety \ˌnōt-ə-'rī-ət-ē\ *n, pl* **-ties** : the quality or state of being notorious

no·to·ri·ous \nō-'tōr-ē-əs, -'tor-\ *adj* : generally known and talked of; *esp* : widely and unfavorably known [Medieval Latin *notorius*, derived from Latin *noscere* "to come to know"] SYN see NOTED — **no·to·ri·ous·ly** *adv* — **no·to·ri·ous·ness** *n*

no-trump \'nō-ˌtrəmp\ *adj* : being a bid, contract, or hand suitable to play (as in bridge) without any suit being trumps — **no-trump** *n*

¹not·with·stand·ing \ˌnät-with-'stan-ding, -with-\ *prep* : in spite of ⟨they succeeded *notwithstanding* many obstacles⟩

²notwithstanding *adv* : NEVERTHELESS, HOWEVER

³notwithstanding *conj* : ALTHOUGH

nou·gat \'nü-gət\ *n* : a candy of nuts or fruit pieces in a sugar paste [French, from Provençal, from *noga* "nut", from Latin *nuc-, nux*]

nought \'not, 'nät\ *variant of* NAUGHT

noun \'naun\ *n* : a word that is the name of something (as a person, animal, plant, place, thing, substance, quality, idea, action, or state) and that is typically used in a sentence as subject or object of a verb or as object of a preposition [Anglo-French, "name, noun", from Old French *nom*, from Latin *nomen*]

nour·ish \'nər-ish, 'nə-rish\ *vt* **1** : to promote the growth and development of **2** : to provide with food : FEED ⟨plants *nourished* by rain and soil⟩ **3** : SUPPORT, MAINTAIN ⟨a friendship *nourished* by trust⟩ [Old French *noriss-*, stem of *norrir* "to nourish", from Latin *nutrire*]

nour·ish·ing *adj* : giving nourishment ⟨*nourishing* food⟩

nour·ish·ment \'nər-ish-mənt, 'nə-rish-\ *n* **1** : something that nourishes : NUTRIMENT **2** : the act of nourishing : the state of being nourished

nou·veau riche \ˌnü-ˌvō-'rēsh\ *n, pl* **nou·veaux riches** \same\ : a person newly rich [French, literally, "new rich"]

no·va \'nō-və\ *n, pl* **novas** *or* **no·vae** \-ˌvē, -ˌvī\ : a star that suddenly increases greatly in brightness and then within a few months or years grows dim again [New Latin, from Latin *novus* "new"]

¹nov·el \'näv-əl\ *adj* : new or striking in conception, kind, or style : having no precedent [Middle French, "new", from Latin *novellus*, from *novus* "new"] SYN see NEW

²novel *n* : a prose narrative longer than a short story that usually portrays imaginary characters and events [Italian *novella*] — **nov·el·is·tic** \ˌnäv-ə-'lis-tik\ *adj*

nov·el·ette \ˌnäv-ə-'let\ *n* : a brief novel or long short story

nov·el·ist \'näv-ləst, -ə-ləst\ *n* : a writer of novels

nov·el·ize \'näv-ə-ˌlīz\ *vt* : to convert into the form of a novel — **nov·el·iza·tion** \ˌnäv-ə-lə-'zā-shən\ *n*

no·vel·la \nō-'vel-ə\ *n, pl* **no·vel·le** \-'vel-ē\ : a story with a compact and pointed plot [Italian, from *novello* "new", from Latin *novellus*]

nov·el·ty \'näv-əl-tē\ *n, pl* **-ties 1** : something new or unusual **2** : the quality or state of being novel **3** : a small manufactured article intended to amuse or for use as a plaything or an adornment — usually used in pl.

No·vem·ber \nō-'vem-bər\ *n* : the 11th month of the year [Old French *Novembre*, from Latin *November*, from *novem* "nine", from its having been originally the 9th month of the Roman calendar]

no·ve·na \nō-'vē-nə\ *n, pl* **-nas** *or* **-nae** \-ˌnē\ : a Roman Catholic devotion in which prayers are said for the same purpose on nine successive days [Medieval Latin, from Latin *novenus* "nine each", from *novem* "nine"]

nov·ice \'näv-əs\ *n* **1** : a new member of a religious order who is preparing to take the vows of religion **2** : one who has no previous training or experience in a specific field or activity : BEGINNER [Middle French, from Medieval Latin *novicius*, from Latin, "new, inexperienced", from *novus* "new"]

no·vi·tiate \nō-'vish-ət\ *n* **1** : the period or state of being a novice **2** : NOVICE 1 **3** : a house where novices are trained [French *noviciat*, from Medieval Latin *noviciatus*, from *novicius* "novice"]

No·vo·cain \'nō-və-ˌkān\ *trademark* — used for the hydrochloride of procaine

¹now \naù, 'naù\ *adv* **1 a** : at the present time or moment ⟨I am busy *now*⟩ **b** : in the time immediately before the present ⟨they left just *now*⟩ **c** : in the time immediately to follow : FORTHWITH ⟨we will leave *now*⟩ **2** — used with the sense of present time weakened or lost to express command, request, or reproach ⟨*now* hear this⟩ **3** : SOMETIMES ⟨*now* one and *now* another⟩ **4** : under the present circumstances ⟨*now* what can we do⟩ **5** : at the time referred to ⟨*now* the trouble began⟩ [Old English *nū*] — **now and then** : OCCASIONALLY ⟨we eat out *now* and *then*⟩

²now *conj* : in view of the fact that : SINCE — often followed by *that* ⟨*now* we are here⟩

³now \'naù\ *n* : the present time or moment ⟨up to *now*⟩

⁴now \'naù\ *adj* : of or relating to the present time : CURRENT ⟨the *now* president⟩

now·a·days \'naù-ə-ˌdāz, 'naù-ˌdāz\ *adv* : at the present time [Middle English *now a dayes*, from *now* + *a* *dayes* "during the day"]

no·way \'nō-ˌwā\ *or* **no·ways** \-ˌwāz\ *adv* : NOWISE

no·where \'nō-ˌhweər, -ˌweər, -ˌhwaər, -ˌwaər, -ˌhwər, -ˌwər\ *adv* **1** : not in or at any place **2** : to no place — **nowhere** *n*

nowhere near *adv* : not nearly

no·wise \'nō-ˌwīz\ *adv* : in no way : not at all

nox·ious \'näk-shəs\ *adj* : harmful or injurious especially to health or morals ⟨*noxious* fumes⟩ [Latin *noxius*, from *noxa* "harm"] — **nox·ious·ly** *adv* — **nox·ious·ness** *n*

noz·zle \'näz-əl\ *n* : a projecting part with an opening that usually serves as an outlet ⟨the *nozzle* of a bellows⟩; *esp* : a short tube with a taper or constriction used on a hose or pipe to direct or speed up a flow of fluid [derived from *nose*]

n't \ənt, nt, ənt\ *adv* : not — used in combination ⟨isn*'t*⟩ ⟨doesn*'t*⟩

nth \'enth, 'entth\ *adj* **1** : numbered with an indefinitely large or an unspecified ordinal number **2** : EXTREME, UTMOST ⟨to the *nth* degree⟩

nu \'nü, 'nyü\ *n* : the 13th letter of the Greek alphabet — N or ν

nozzle

\ə\ abut		\ng\ sing	
\ər\ further		\ō\ bone	
\a\ mat		\o\ saw	
\ā\ take		\oi\ coin	
\ä\ cot, cart		\th\ thin	
\aù\ out		\th\ this	
\ch\ chin		\ü\ food	
\e\ pet		\ù\ foot	
\ē\ easy		\y\ yet	
\g\ go		\yü\ few	
\i\ tip		\yù\ cure	
\ī\ life		\zh\ vision	
\j\ job			

nu·ance \\'nü-ˌäns, 'nyü-, -ˌäⁿs, nů-', nyů-'\\ *n* : a slight shade or degree of difference : a delicate gradation or variation (as in color, tone, or meaning) [French, from *nuer* "to make shades of color", from *nue* "cloud", from Latin *nubes*]

nub \\'nəb\\ *n* **1** : KNOB 1a, LUMP **2** : GIST, POINT ⟨the *nub* of the story⟩ [English dialect *knub*]

nub·bin \\'nəb-ən\\ *n* **1** : a small or imperfect ear of Indian corn; *also* : any small shriveled or undeveloped fruit **2** : a small projecting part [perhaps from *nub*]

nub·ble \\'nəb-əl\\ *n* : a small knob or lump [derived from *nub*] — **nub·bly** \\'nəb-lē, -ə-lē\\ *adj*

nu·bile \\'nü-bəl, 'nyü-, -ˌbīl\\ *adj* : of marriageable condition or age [French, from Latin *nubilis,* from *nubere* "to marry"] — **nu·bil·i·ty** \\nü-'bil-ət-ē, nyü-\\ *n*

nu·cel·lus \\nü-'sel-əs, nyü-\\ *n, pl* **-cel·li** \\-'sel-ˌī\\ : the central and chief part of a plant ovule containing the embryo sac [New Latin, from Latin *nucella* "small nut", from *nuc-, nux* "nut"] — **nu·cel·lar** \\-'sel-ər\\ *adj*

nu·chal \\'nü-kəl, 'nyü-\\ *adj* : of, relating to, or lying in the region of the nape [Medieval Latin *nucha* "nape", from Arabic *nukhā* "spinal cord"] — **nuchal** *n*

nucle- *or* **nucleo-** *combining form* **1** : nucleus ⟨*nucle*on⟩ **2** : nucleic acid ⟨*nucleo*protein⟩

nu·cle·ar \\'nü-klē-ər, 'nyü-\\ *adj* **1** : of, relating to, or being a nucleus (as of a cell) **2** : of, relating to, or utilizing the atomic nucleus, atomic energy, the atom bomb, or atomic power

nuclear energy *n* : ATOMIC ENERGY

nuclear family *n* : a family group that consists only of father, mother, and children

nuclear medicine *n* : a branch of medicine dealing with the use of radioactive materials in the diagnosis and treatment of disease

nuclear membrane *n* : the boundary of a cell nucleus

nuclear reactor *n* : REACTOR 2b

nuclear sap *n* : the part of a cell nucleus that is relatively fluid and does not include the chromatin and nucleoli

nu·cle·ase \\'nü-klē-ˌās, 'nyü-\\ *n* : an enzyme that promotes hydrolysis of nucleic acids

nu·cle·ate \\'nü-klē-ˌāt, 'nyü-\\ *vb* **1** : to gather about or into a center; *also* : to act as a nucleus for or provide with a nucleus **2** : to form, act as, or have a nucleus — **nu·cle·ation** \\ˌnü-klē-'ā-shən, nyü-\\ *n*

nu·cle·at·ed \\'nü-klē-ˌāt-əd, 'nyü-\\ *also* **nu·cle·ate** \\-klē-ət\\ *adj* : having a nucleus or nuclei ⟨*nucleated* cells⟩

nu·cle·ic acid \\nü-ˌklē-ik-, nyü-, -ˌklā-\\ *n* : any of various acids (as a DNA or an RNA) that are composed of a sugar or derivative of a sugar, phosphoric acid, and a base arranged in linked nucleotides and that are found especially in cell nuclei

nu·cle·o·lus \\nü-'klē-ə-ləs, nyü-\\ *n, pl* **-li** \\-ˌlī\\ : a spherical body in a cell nucleus that is associated with a specific part of a chromosome and contains much ribosomal RNA [New Latin, from Latin *nucleus* "kernel"] — **nu·cle·o·lar** \\-lər\\ *adj*

nu·cle·on \\'nü-klē-ˌän, 'nyü-\\ *n* : a proton or a neutron especially in the atomic nucleus

nu·cle·on·ics \\ˌnü-klē-'än-iks, ˌnyü-\\ *n* : a branch of physical science that deals with nucleons or with all phenomena of the atomic nucleus

nu·cleo·plasm \\'nü-klē-ə-ˌplaz-əm, 'nyü-\\ *n* : the protoplasm of a nucleus; *esp* : NUCLEAR SAP

nu·cleo·pro·tein \\ˌnü-klē-ō-'prō-ˌtēn, ˌnyü-, -'prōt-ē-ən\\ *n* : any of the proteins joined to nucleic acid that occur especially in the nuclei of living cells and are an essential constituent of genes and viruses

nu·cle·o·side \\'nü-klē-ə-ˌsīd, 'nyü-\\ *n* : a compound that is formed by partial hydrolysis of a nucleic acid or a nucleotide and contains a purine or pyrimidine base combined with deoxyribose or ribose [*nucle-* + *-ose* + *-ide*]

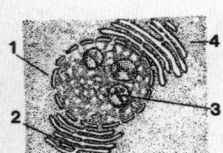

nucleus b: *1* nuclear membrane, *2* endoplasmic reticulum, *3* nucleolus, *4* cytoplasm

nu·cle·o·tide \\-ˌtīd\\ *n* : any of several compounds that consist of a ribose or deoxyribose sugar joined to a purine or pyrimidine base and to a phosphate group and that are the basic structural groups of RNA and DNA [derived from *nucle-* + *-ide*]

nu·cle·us \\'nü-klē-əs, 'nyü-\\ *n, pl* **-clei** \\-klē-ˌī\\ *also* **-cle·us·es** : a central point, group, or mass of something: as **a** : the small, brighter, and denser part of a galaxy or of the head of a comet **b** : a part of the cell that controls many cell functions (as reproduction and protein synthesis), contains the chromosomes, and is bounded by a nuclear membrane **c** : a mass of gray matter or group of nerve cells in the central nervous system **d** : a characteristic and stable complex of atoms or groups in a molecule **e** : the positively charged central part of an atom that comprises nearly all of the atomic mass and that consists of protons and neutrons except in hydrogen in which it consists of one proton only [Latin, "kernel", from *nuc-, nux* "nut"]

nu·clide \\'nü-ˌklīd, 'nyü-\\ *n* : a species of atom characterized by the constitution of its nucleus [*nucleus* + Greek *eidos* "form, species"] — **nu·clid·ic** \\nü-'klid-ik, nyü-\\ *adj*

¹nude \\'nüd, 'nyüd\\ *adj* : NAKED, BARE; *esp* : having no clothes on [Latin *nudus*] — **nude·ly** *adv* — **nude·ness** *n* — **nu·di·ty** \\'nüd-ət-ē, 'nyüd-\\ *n*

²nude *n* **1** : a nude human figure especially as depicted in art **2** : the condition of being nude ⟨in the *nude*⟩

nudge \\'nəj\\ *vt* : to touch or push gently; *esp* : to seek the attention of by a push with the elbow [perhaps of Scandinavian origin] — **nudge** *n* — **nudg·er** *n*

nu·di·branch \\'nüd-ə-ˌbrangk, 'nyüd-\\ *n, pl* **-branchs** : any of a group (Nudibranchia) of marine mollusks without a shell as adults and without true gills [derived from Latin *nudus* "nude" + *branchia* "gill"] — **nudibranch** *adj*

nud·ism \\'nü-ˌdiz-əm, 'nyü-\\ *n* : the practice of going nude especially in groups and during periods of time spent in secluded places — **nud·ist** \\'nüd-əst, 'nyüd-\\ *n*

nug·get \\'nəg-ət\\ *n* : a solid lump usually of precious metal [origin unknown]

nui·sance \\'nüs-ns, 'nyüs-\\ *n* : one that is annoying, unpleasant, or obnoxious [Anglo-French *nusaunce* "harm, injury", from Old French *nuisir* "to harm", from Latin *nocēre*]

¹null \\'nəl\\ *adj* **1** : having no legal or binding force : INVALID **2** : amounting to nothing : NIL **3** : having no value **4** : containing no elements ⟨*null* set⟩ [Middle French *nul,* literally, "not any", from Latin *nullus,* from *ne-* "not" + *ullus* "any"]

²null *n* : ZERO 2a

null and void *adj* : having no force, binding power, or validity

nul·li·fi·ca·tion \\ˌnəl-ə-fə-'kā-shən\\ *n* **1** : the act of nullifying : the state of being nullified **2** : the action of a state obstructing or attempting to prevent the operation and enforcement within its territory of a law of the United States — **nul·li·fi·ca·tion·ist** \\-shə-nəst, -shnəst\\ *n*

nul·li·fy \\'nəl-ə-ˌfī\\ *vt* **-fied; -fy·ing** **1** : to make null : VOID **2** : to make of no value or consequence □ SYN NULLIFY, NEGATE, ANNUL, INVALIDATE mean to deprive of effective or continued existence. NULLIFY implies counteracting completely the force, effectiveness, or value of something ⟨all our work *nullified* by one act of carelessness⟩ NEGATE implies the destruction or canceling out of each of two things by the other ⟨slavery *negates* freedom⟩ ANNUL suggests making ineffective by legal or official action ⟨the treaty *annuls* all previous agreements⟩ INVALIDATE implies a legal or moral flaw that makes something not acceptable or not valid ⟨the absence of a signature *invalidated* the will⟩

numb \\'nəm\\ *adj* **1** : lacking in sensation especially as a result of cold or anesthesia **2** : lacking in emotion :

INDIFFERENT [Middle English *nomen,* from *nimen* "to take, seize", from Old English *niman*] — **numb** *vt* — **numb·ly** *adv* — **numb·ness** *n*

¹**num·ber** \'nəm-bər\ *n* **1 a** : the total of individual items taken together ⟨the *number* of people in the room⟩ **b** : an indefinite usually large total ⟨a *number* of accidents occur on wet roads⟩ **2 a** : the possibility of being counted ⟨mosquitoes in swarms beyond *number*⟩ **b** : the property involved in seeing things as units subject to separating ⟨observing the difference between few and many and calling it *number*⟩ **3 a** : a unit (as an integer or irrational number) belonging to a mathematical system and subject to its laws **b** *pl* : ARITHMETIC 1 **4** : a distinction of word form to denote reference to one or more than one ⟨a verb agrees in *number* with its subject⟩; *also* : a form or group of forms so distinguished — compare **PLURAL, SINGULAR** **5 a** : a symbol (as a character, letter, or word) used to represent a mathematical number; *esp* : NUMERAL 1 **b** : a number used to identify or designate ⟨*number* one on the list⟩ ⟨a phone number⟩ **6** *pl* : regular count especially of syllables in poetry : METER; *also* : metrical verse **7** : a member of a sequence or series ⟨the best *number* on the program⟩ ⟨lost the last *number* of the magazine⟩ **8** *pl* : a form of lottery in which bets are placed on numbers regularly published [Old French *nombre,* from Latin *numerus*] — **by the numbers 1** : in unison to a specific count or cadence **2** : in a systematic, routine, or mechanical manner
SEE NUMBER CHART NEXT PAGE

²**number** *vb* **num·bered; num·ber·ing** \-bə-ring, -bring\ **1** : COUNT 1, ENUMERATE **2** : to claim as part of a total : INCLUDE **3** : to restrict to a definite number ⟨their days are *numbered*⟩ **4** : to assign a number to **5** : to comprise in number ⟨our group *numbered* 10 in all⟩ **6** : comprise a total number ⟨their fans *number* in the millions⟩ — **num·ber·able** \'nəm-bə-rə-bəl, -brə-bəl\ *adj* — **num·ber·er** \-bər-ər\ *n*

number crunch·er \-,krən-chər\ *n* **1** : a computer that performs fast numerical calculations especially on large amounts of data **2** : a person concerned with complex numerical data — **number crunching** *n*

num·ber·less \'nəm-bər-ləs\ *adj* : too many to count

number line *n* : an infinite line whose points correspond to the real numbers according to their distance in a positive or negative direction from a point arbitrarily labeled zero

Num·bers \'nəm-bərz\ *n* — see BIBLE table

number theory *n* : the study of the properties of integers

numb·ing \'nəm-ing\ *adj* : causing numbness — **numb·ing·ly** \-ing-lē\ *adv*

numb·skull *variant of* NUMSKULL

nu·mer·a·ble \'nüm-rə-bəl, 'nyüm-, -ə-rə-\ *adj* : that can be counted

nu·mer·al \'nüm-rəl, 'nyüm-, -ə-rəl\ *n* **1** : a symbol representing a number **2** *pl* : numbers designating by year a school or college class that are awarded for distinction especially in sports [Middle French, "of numbers", from Late Latin *numeralis,* from Latin *numerus* "number"]

nu·mer·ate \'nü-mə-,rāt, 'nyü-\ *vt* : ENUMERATE [Latin *numerare* "to count", from *numerus* "number"]

nu·mer·a·tion \,nü-mə-'rā-shən, ,nyü-\ *n* : the act or process or a system or instance of enumeration

nu·mer·a·tor \'nü-mə-,rāt-ər, 'nyü-\ *n* **1** : the part of a fraction written above or to the left of the line that signifies the number of parts of the denominator taken **2** : one that counts

nu·mer·i·cal \nu̇-'mer-i-kəl, nyu̇-\ *adj* : of, relating to, being, or given in numbers — **nu·mer·i·cal·ly** \-kə-lē, -klē\ *adv*

nu·mer·ol·o·gy \,nü-mə-'räl-ə-jē, ,nyü-\ *n* : the study of the occult significance of numbers — **nu·mer·ol·o·gist** \-jəst\ *n*

nu·mer·ous \'nüm-rəs, 'nyüm-, -ə-rəs\ *adj* : consisting of great numbers of units or individuals ⟨*numerous* occasions⟩ SYN see MANY — **nu·mer·ous·ly** *adv* — **nu·mer·ous·ness** *n*

nu·mis·mat·ic \,nü-məz-'mat-ik, ,nyü-, -məs-\ *adj* **1** : of or relating to numismatics **2** : of or relating to coins [French *numismatique,* from Latin *nomisma* "coin", from Greek, "custom, coin"] — **nu·mis·mat·i·cal·ly** \-'mat-i-kə-lē, -klē\ *adv*

nu·mis·mat·ics \-iks\ *n* : the study or collection of coins, tokens, medals, or paper money — **nu·mis·ma·tist** \nü-'miz-mət-əst, nyü-\ *n*

num·skull *or* **numb·skull** \'nəm-,skəl\ *n* : a stupid person

nun \'nən\ *n* : a woman belonging to a religious order; *esp* : one under solemn vows of poverty, chastity, and obedience [Old English *nunne,* from Late Latin *nonna*]

Nunc Di·mit·tis \,nəngk-də-'mit-əs\ *n* : the prayer of Simeon in Luke 2:29–32 used as a canticle [Latin, "now lettest thou depart"; from the first words of the canticle]

nun·ci·a·ture \'nən-sē-ə-,chur, 'nün-, -chər\ *n* **1** : the office or period of office of a nuncio **2** : a papal delegation headed by a nuncio [Italian *nunciatura,* from *nuncio* "nuncio"]

nun·cio \'nən-sē-,ō, 'nün-\ *n, pl* **-ci·os** : a papal representative of the highest rank permanently accredited to a civil government [Italian, from Latin *nuntius* "messenger, message"]

nun·cu·pa·tive \'nən-kyu̇-,pāt-iv, nən-'kyü-pət-\ *adj* : not written : ORAL ⟨a *nuncupative* will⟩ [Medieval Latin *nuncupativus,* from Late Latin, "so-called", from Latin *nuncupare* "to name, call", from *nomen* "name" + *capere* "to take"]

nun·nery \'nən-rē, -ə-rē\ *n, pl* **-ner·ies** : a convent of nuns

¹**nup·tial** \'nəp-shəl, -chəl\ *adj* **1** : of or relating to marriage or the marriage ceremony **2** : characteristic of mating or the breeding season [Latin *nuptialis,* from *nuptiae* "wedding", from *nubere* "to marry"] SYN see MATRIMONIAL

²**nuptial** *n* : WEDDING 1 — usually used in pl.

¹**nurse** \'nərs\ *n* **1** : a woman who has the care of a young child **2** : one skilled or trained in caring for the sick or infirm especially under the supervision of a physician **3** : a worker of a social insect that cares for the young [Old French *nurice,* from Late Latin *nutricia,* from Latin *nutricius* "nourishing, nutritious"]

²**nurse** *vb* **1** : to feed at the breast : SUCKLE **2** : REAR 3b, EDUCATE **3** : to manage with care or economy ⟨*nurse* one's funds⟩ **4** : to care for as a nurse ⟨*nursed* them back to health⟩ **5** : to hold in one's memory or consideration ⟨*nurse* a grudge⟩ **6** : to treat with special care ⟨*nurse* a car over a rough road⟩ **7** : to act or serve as a nurse [Middle English *nurshen* "to nourish", from *nurishen*] — **nurs·er** *n*

nurse·maid \'nər-,smād\ *n* : a girl or woman employed to look after children

nurs·ery \'nərs-rē, -ə-rē\ *n, pl* **-er·ies** **1 a** : a room or suite set apart in a house for the children **b** : a place where children are temporarily cared for in their parents' absence **c** : DAY NURSERY **2** : a place where plants (as trees or shrubs) are grown for transplanting, for use as stocks in grafting, or for sale

nurs·ery·maid \-,mād\ *n* : NURSEMAID

nurs·ery·man \-mən\ *n* : a person whose occupation is the growing of plants (as trees and shrubs) especially for sale

nursery rhyme *n* : a short rhyme for children that often tells a story

nursery school *n* : a school for children usually under five years of age

nurse's aid *n* : a worker who assists trained nurses in a hospital

\ə\	abut	\ng\	sing
\ər\	further	\ō\	bone
\a\	mat	\ȯ\	saw
\ā\	take	\ȯi\	coin
\ä\	cot, cart	\th\	thin
\au̇\	out	\th\	this
\ch\	chin	\ü\	food
\e\	pet	\u̇\	foot
\ē\	easy	\y\	yet
\g\	go	\yü\	few
\i\	tip	\yu̇\	cure
\ī\	life	\zh\	vision
\j\	job		

TABLE OF NUMBERS

CARDINAL NUMBERS[1]			ORDINAL NUMBERS[4]	
NAME[2]	SYMBOL		NAME[5]	SYMBOL[6]
	ARABIC	ROMAN[3]		
zero or naught or cipher	0		first	1st
one	1	I	second	2d or 2nd
two	2	II	third	3d or 3rd
three	3	III	fourth	4th
four	4	IV	fifth	5th
five	5	V	sixth	6th
six	6	VI	seventh	7th
seven	7	VII	eighth	8th
eight	8	VIII	ninth	9th
nine	9	IX	tenth	10th
ten	10	X	eleventh	11th
eleven	11	XI	twelfth	12th
twelve	12	XII	thirteenth	13th
thirteen	13	XIII	fourteenth	14th
fourteen	14	XIV	fifteenth	15th
fifteen	15	XV	sixteenth	16th
sixteen	16	XVI	seventeenth	17th
seventeen	17	XVII	eighteenth	18th
eighteen	18	XVIII	nineteenth	19th
nineteen	19	XIX	twentieth	20th
twenty	20	XX	twenth-first	21st
twenty-one	21	XXI	twenty-second	22d or 22nd
twenty-two	22	XXII	twenty-third	23d or 23rd
twenty-three	23	XXIII	twenty-fourth	24th
twenty-four	24	XXIV	twenty-fifth	25th
twenty-five	25	XXV	twenty-sixth	26th
twenty-six	26	XXVI	twenty-seventh	27th
twenty-seven	27	XXVII	twenty-eighth	28th
twenty-eight	28	XXVIII	twenty-ninth	29th
twenty-nine	29	XXIX	thirtieth	30th
thirty	30	XXX	thirty-first etc	31st
thirty-one etc	31	XXXI	fortieth	40th
forty	40	XL	fiftieth	50th
fifty	50	L	sixtieth	60th
sixty	60	LX	seventieth	70th
seventy		LXX	eightieth	80th
eighty	80	LXXX	ninetieth	90th
ninety	90	XC	hundredth or one hundredth	100th
one hundred	100	C	hundred and first or	
one hundred and one or	101	CI	one hundred and first etc	101st
one hundred one etc			two hundredth	200th
two hundred	200	CC	three hundredth	300th
three hundred	300	CCC	four hundredth	400th
four hundred	400	CD	five hundredth	500th
five hundred	500	D	six hundredth	600th
six hundred	600	DC	seven hundredth	700th
seven hundred	700	DCC	eight hundredth	800th
eight hundred	800	DCCC	nine hundredth	900th
nine hundred	900	CM	thousandth or one thousandth	1,000th
one thousand or ten	1,000	M	two thousandth etc	2,000th
hundred etc			five thousandth	5,000th
two thousand etc	2,000	MM	ten thousandth	10,000th
five thousand	5,000	$\bar{V}$	hundred thousandth or	100,000th
ten thousand	10,000	$\bar{X}$	one hundred thousandth	
one hundred thousand	100,000	$\bar{C}$	millionth or one millionth	1,000,000th
one million	1,000,000	$\bar{M}$		

(continued on next page)

[1]The cardinal numbers are used in simple counting or in answer to "how many?" The words for these numbers may be used as nouns (I counted to *twelve*), as pronouns (*twelve* were found), or as adjectives (*twelve* cows).
[2]In formal contexts the numbers one to one hundred and in less formal contexts the numbers one to nine are commonly written out, while larger numbers are given in numerals. In nearly all contexts a number occuring at the beginning of a sentence is usually written out. Except in very formal contexts numerals are invariably used for dates. Arabic numerals from 1,000 to 9,999 are often written without commas (1000; 9999). Year numbers are always written without commas (1783).
[3]The Roman numerals are written either in capitals or in lowercase letters.

TABLE OF NUMBERS (*CONTINUED*)

[4]The ordinal numbers are used to show the order of succession in which items such as names, objects, and periods of time are considered (the *twelfth* month; the *fourth* row of seats; the *18th* century).

[5]Each of the terms for the ordinal numbers excepting *first* and *second* is used in designating one of a number of parts into which a whole may be divided (a *fourth;* a *sixth;* a *tenth*) and used as the denominator in fractions designating the number of such parts constituting a certain portion of a whole (*one fourth; three fifths*). When used as nouns the fractions are usually written as two words, although they are regularly hyphenated as adjectives (a *two-thirds* majority). When fractions are written in numerals, the cardinal symbols are used (¼, ⅗, ⅚).

[6]The Arabic symbols for the cardinal numbers may be read as ordinals in certain contexts (January 1 = January first; 2 Samuel = Second Samuel). The Roman numerals are sometimes read as ordinals (Henry IV = Henry the Fourth); sometimes they are written with the ordinal suffixes (XIXth Dynasty).

DENOMINATIONS ABOVE ONE MILLION

AMERICAN SYSTEM[1]

NAME	VALUE IN POWERS OF TEN	NUMBER OF ZEROS[2]	NUMBER OF GROUPS OF THREE 0'S AFTER 1,000
billion	10^9	9	2
trillion	10^{12}	12	3
quadrillion	10^{15}	15	4
quintillion	10^{18}	18	5
sextillion	10^{21}	21	6
septillion	10^{24}	24	7
octillion	10^{27}	27	8
nonillion	10^{30}	30	9
decillion	10^{33}	33	10

BRITISH SYSTEM[1]

NAME	VALUE IN POWERS OF TEN	NUMBER OF ZEROS[2]	POWERS OF 1,000,000
milliard	10^9	9	—
billion	10^{12}	12	2
trillion	10^{18}	18	3
quadrillion	10^{24}	24	4
quintillion	10^{30}	30	5
sextillion	10^{36}	36	6
septillion	10^{42}	42	7
octillion	10^{48}	48	8
nonillion	10^{54}	54	9
decillion	10^{60}	60	10

[1]The American system of numeration for denominations above one million was modeled on the French system but more recently the French system has been changed to correspond to the British and German systems. In the American system each of the denominations above 1,000 millions (the American *billion*) is 1,000 times the one preceding (one trillion = 1,000 billions; one quadrillion = 1,000 trillions). In the British system the first denomination above 1,000 millions (the British *milliard*) is 1,000 times the preceding one, but each of the denominations above 1,000 milliards (the British *billion*) is 1,000,000 times the preceding one (one trillion = 1,000,000 billions; one quadrillion = 1,000,000 trillions).

[2]For convenience in reading large numerals the thousands, millions, etc., are usually separated by commas (21,530; 1,155,465) or by half spaces (1 155 465). Serial numbers (as a social security number or the engine number of a car) are often written with hyphens (583-695-20).

nursing bottle *n* : a bottle with a nipple used for feeding a baby

nursing home *n* : a privately operated establishment where nursing care is provided for persons (as the aged) who are unable to care for themselves

nurs·ling \'nərs-ling\ *n* **1** : one tended with special care **2** : a nursing child

[1]**nur·ture** \'nər-chər\ *n* **1** : TRAINING 1, UPBRINGING **2** : something that nourishes : FOOD **3** : the influences that modify the expression of the genes of an organism [Middle French *norriture,* from Late Latin *nutritura* "act of nursing", from Latin *nutrire* 'to nourish, nurse'']

[2]**nurture** *vt* **nur·tured; nur·tur·ing** \'nərch-ring, -ə-ring\ **1** : to supply with nourishment **2** : EDUCATE 2 **3** : to further the development of : FOSTER — **nur·tur·er** \'nər-chər-ər\ *n*

[1]**nut** \'nət\ *n* **1 a** : a hard-shelled dry fruit or seed with a separable rind or shell and an inner kernel; *also* : this kernel **b** : a dry one-seeded fruit that has a woody outer layer and that does not split open when ripe **2** : a small block usually of metal with a hole in it that has an internal screw thread and is used on a bolt or screw for tightening or holding something **3** : the ridge in a stringed musical instrument over which the strings pass on the upper end of the fingerboard **4 a** : a foolish, eccentric, or crazy person **b** : ENTHUSIAST, FAN [Old English *hnutu*] — **nut·like** \-,līk\ *adj*

[2]**nut** *vi* **nut·ted; nut·ting** : to gather or seek nuts

nut·crack·er \'nət-,krak-ər\ *n* **1** : an instrument for cracking the shells of nuts **2** : a bird related to the crows that lives largely on seeds from the cones of the pine tree

nut·hatch \'nət-,hach\ *n* : any of various small birds intermediate in appearance and habits between the tit-

mice and creepers [Middle English *notebache,* from *note* "nut" + *hache* "ax", from Old French, "battle-ax"]

nut·let \'nət-lət\ *n* : a small fruit similar to a nut

nut·meg \'nət-,meg\ *n* **1** : the aromatic seed of a tree grown in the East and West Indies and Brazil; *also* : this tree **2** : a spice consisting of ground nutmeg seeds [Middle English *notemuge,* derived from Provençal *noz muscada,* from *noz* "nut" (from Latin *nux*) + *muscada,* feminine of *muscat* "musky"]

nut·pick \-,pik\ *n* : a small sharp-pointed table implement for extracting the kernels from nuts

nu·tria \'nü-trē-ə, 'nyü-\ *n* **1** : COYPU 1 **2** : the durable usually light brown fur of the coypu [Spanish, "otter", from Latin *lutra*]

[1]**nu·tri·ent** \'nü-trē-ənt, 'nyü-\ *adj* : furnishing nourishment [Latin *nutriens,* present participle of *nutrire* "to nourish"]

[2]**nutrient** *n* : a nutritive substance or ingredient

nu·tri·ment \'nü-trə-mənt, 'nyü-\ *n* : something that nourishes

nu·tri·tion \nù-'trish-ən, nyù-\ *n* : the act or process of nourishing or being nourished; *esp* : the processes by which an animal or plant takes in and utilizes food substances [Middle French, from Late Latin *nutritio,* from Latin *nutrire* "to nourish"] — **nu·tri·tion·al** \-'trish-nəl, -ən-l\ *adj* — **nu·tri·tion·al·ly** \-ē\ *adv*

nu·tri·tion·ist \-'trish-nəst, -ə-nəst\ *n* : a specialist in the study of nutrition

nu·tri·tious \nù-'trish-əs, nyù-\ *adj* : NOURISHING [Latin *nutricius,* from *nutrix* "nurse"] — **nu·tri·tious·ly** *adv* — **nu·tri·tious·ness** *n*

nu·tri·tive \'nü-trət-iv, 'nyü-\ *adj* **1** : of or relating to nutrition **2** : NOURISHING — **nu·tri·tive·ly** *adv*

nuts \'nəts\ *adj* **1** : ENTHUSIASTIC, KEEN **2** : CRAZY 2a

nuthatch

\ə\ abut	\ng\ sing
\ər\ further	\ō\ bone
\a\ mat	\ȯ\ saw
\ā\ take	\ȯi\ coin
\ä\ cot, cart	\th\ thin
\au̇\ out	\t̲h̲\ this
\ch\ chin	\ü\ food
\e\ pet	\u̇\ foot
\ē\ easy	\y\ yet
\g\ go	\yü\ few
\i\ tip	\yu̇\ cure
\ī\ life	\zh\ vision
\j\ job	

nut·shell \'nət-ˌshel\ *n* : the shell of a nut — **in a nutshell** : in a small space : in brief

nut·ty \'nət-ē\ *adj* **nut·tier; -est** 1 : containing or suggesting nuts (as in flavor) 2 : ECCENTRIC 2 ⟨a *nutty* idea⟩; *also* : mentally unbalanced — **nut·ti·ness** *n*

nux vom·i·ca \'nəks-'väm-i-kə\ *n, pl* **nux vomica** : the poisonous seed of an Asian tree that contains strychnine; *also* : this tree [New Latin, literally, "emetic nut"]

nuz·zle \'nəz-əl\ *vb* **nuz·zled; nuz·zling** \'nəz-ling, -ə-ling\ 1 : to push or rub with the nose 2 : to lie close [Middle English *noselen* "to bring the nose toward the ground", from nose]

ny·lon \'nī-ˌlän\ *n* 1 : any of numerous strong tough elastic synthetic materials used especially in textiles and plastics 2 *pl* : stockings made of nylon [coined word] — **nylon** *adj*

nymph \'nimf, 'nimpf\ *n, pl* **nymphs** \'nimfs, 'nimpfs, 'nims, 'nimps\ 1 : one of the minor divinities of nature in ancient mythology represented as beautiful maidens dwelling in the mountains, forests, meadows, and waters 2 : an immature insect (as a dragonfly or grasshopper) that differs from the adult especially in size and in its incompletely developed wings and sex organs [Middle French *nimphe,* from Latin *nympha* "bride, nymph", from Greek *nymphē*] — **nymph·al** \'nim-fəl, 'nimp-\ *adj*

nys·tag·mus \nis-'tag-məs\ *n* : a rapid involuntary oscillation (as from dizziness) of the eyeballs [Greek *nystagmos* "drowsiness", from *nystazein* "to doze"]

Oo

o \'ō\ *n, pl* o's *or* os \'ōz\ *often cap* **1** : the 15th letter of the English alphabet **2** : ZERO

O *variant of* OH

o- *or* oo- *combining form* : egg : ovum ⟨*oo*cyte⟩ [Greek *ōion* "egg"]

-o- — used as a connective vowel originally to join word elements of Greek origin and now also to join word elements of Latin or other origin ⟨speed*o*meter⟩ [Greek, stem vowel of many nouns and adjectives in combination]

o' *also* o \ə\ *prep* **1** *chiefly dialect* : ON **2** : OF ⟨one o'clock⟩

oaf \'ōf\ *n* : a stupid or awkward person [obsolete *oaf* "changeling", of Scandinavian origin] — oaf·ish \'ō-fish\ *adj* — oaf·ish·ly *adv* — oaf·ish·ness *n* □ ORIGIN The elves, like the fairies, were believed to steal human children, leaving in their stead elf children, changelings. Such a changeling was called an *oaf*; the word is related to *elf*. The word *oaf* in its strictest sense should have been applied only to genuine changelings, but it was soon used for any deformed or retarded child. From the sense "idiot child" it was a short and easy step to the present meaning, "a stupid or awkward person".

oak \'ōk\ *n, pl* oaks *or* oak **1** : any of various trees or shrubs closely related to the beech and chestnut and having a rounded one-seeded thin-shelled nut **2** : the usually tough hard durable wood of the oak much used for furniture and flooring [Old English *āc*] — oak *adj* — oak·en \'ō-kən\ *adj*

oak apple *n* : a large round gall produced on oak leaves by a small wasp

oa·kum \'ō-kəm\ *n* : hemp or jute fiber impregnated with tar or a tar derivative and used in caulking seams and packing joints [Old English *ācumba*]

oar \'ōr, 'ȯr\ *n* **1** : a long pole with a broad blade at one end used for propelling or steering a boat **2** : OARSMAN [Old English *ār*] — oared \'ōrd, 'ȯrd\ *adj*

oar·lock \'ōr-ˌläk, 'ȯr-\ *n* : a U-shaped device for holding an oar in place

oars·man \'ōrz-mən, 'ȯrz-\ *n* : a person who rows especially in a racing crew

oa·sis \ō-'ā-səs\ *n, pl* oa·ses \-'ā-ˌsēz\ **1** : a fertile or green area in an arid region **2** : something providing relief [Late Latin, from Greek]

oat \'ōt\ *n* **1** : a cereal grass with long spikelets in loose clusters that is widely grown for its seed which is used for human food and livestock feed **2** *pl* : a crop or plot of the oat; *also* : oat seed [Old English *āte*]

oat·en \'ōt-n\ *adj* : of or relating to oats, oat straw, or oatmeal

oath \'ōth\ *n, pl* oaths \'ōthz, 'ōths\ **1** : a solemn appeal to God or to some revered person or thing to bear witness to the truth of one's word or the sacredness of a promise **2** : a careless or profane use of a sacred name [Old English *āth*]

oat·meal \'ōt-ˌmēl, ōt-'\ *n* : oats husked and crushed into coarse meal or flattened into flakes; *also* : porridge made from such meal or flakes

oak 1

\ə\ abut	\ng\ sing	
\ər\ further	\ō\ bone	
\a\ mat	\ȯ\ saw	
\ā\ take	\ȯi\ coin	
\ä\ cot, cart	\th\ thin	
\au̇\ out	\th\ this	
\ch\ chin	\ü\ food	
\e\ pet	\u̇\ foot	
\ē\ easy	\y\ yet	
\g\ go	\yü\ few	
\i\ tip	\yu̇\ cure	
\ī\ life	\zh\ vision	
\j\ job		

ob- *prefix* : inversely ⟨*ob*ovate⟩ [Latin, "in the way, against, toward", from *ob* "in the way of, on account of"]

Oba·di·ah \ˌō-bə-'dī-ə\ *n* — see BIBLE table

¹ob·bli·ga·to \ˌäb-lə-'gät-ō\ *adj* : not to be omitted — used as a direction in music [Italian, "obligatory", from *obbligare* "to oblige", from Latin *obligare*]

²obbligato *n, pl* **-gatos** *also* **-ga·ti** \-'gät-ē\ : a prominent accompanying part usually played by a solo instrument ⟨a violin *obbligato*⟩; *also* : any accompanying part

ob·du·ra·cy \'äb-də-rə-sē, -dyə-; äb-'duṙ-ə-, -'dyuṙ-\ *n, pl* **-cies** : the quality or state or an instance of being obdurate

ob·du·rate \'äb-də-rət, -dyə-; äb-'duṙ-ət, -'dyuṙ-\ *adj* **1 a** : hardened in feelings **b** : stubbornly persistent in wrongdoing **2** : resisting change : UNYIELDING [Latin *obduratus*, past participle of *obdurare* "to harden", from *ob-* "against" + *durus* "hard"] — **ob·du·rate·ly** *adv* — **ob·du·rate·ness** *n*

obe·di·ence \ō-'bēd-ē-əns, ə-\ *n* **1** : an act or instance of obeying **2** : the quality or state of being obedient

obe·di·ent \-ənt\ *adj* : willing or inclined to obey [Old French, from Latin *oboediens*, from *oboedire* "to obey"] — **obe·di·ent·ly** *adv*

obei·sance \ō-'bās-ns, -'bēs-\ *n* **1** : a movement of the body made as a sign of respect : BOW **2** : DEFERENCE, HOMAGE [Middle French *obeissance* "obedience, obeisance", from *obeir* "to obey"] — **obei·sant** \-nt\ *adj*

obe·lia \ō-'bēl-yə\ *n* : any of a genus of small colonial marine hydroids that branch like trees [New Latin, genus name]

ob·e·lisk \'äb-ə-ˌlisk\ *n* : a 4-sided pillar that tapers toward the top and ends in a pyramid [Middle French *obelisque*, from Latin *obeliscus*, from Greek *obeliskos*, from *obelos* "spit, pointed pillar"]

obese \ō-'bēs\ *adj* : excessively fat [Latin *obesus*, from *obedere* "to eat up", from *ob-* "against" + *edere* "to eat"] — **obe·si·ty** \ō-'bē-sət-ē\ *n*

obey \ō-'bā, ə-\ *vb* **obeyed; obey·ing 1** : to follow the commands or guidance of **2** : to comply with : EXECUTE ⟨*obey* an order⟩ **3** : to behave obediently [Old French *obeir*, from Latin *oboedire*] — **obey·er** *n*

ob·fus·cate \'äb-fə-ˌskāt, äb-'fəs-ˌkāt\ *vt* **1** : to make dark or obscure **2** : CONFUSE [Late Latin *obfuscare*, from Latin *ob-* "in the way" + *fuscus* "dark brown"] — **ob·fus·ca·tion** \ˌäb-fəs-'kā-shən\ *n* — **ob·fus·ca·to·ry** \äb-'fəs-kə-ˌtōr-ē, -ˌtȯr-\ *adj*

obi \'ō-bē\ *n* : a broad sash worn with a Japanese kimono [Japanese]

obit \ō-'bit, 'ō-bət\ *n* : OBITUARY

obit·u·ary \ə-'bich-ə-ˌwer-ē\ *n, pl* **-ar·ies** : a notice of a person's death usually with a short biographical account [Medieval Latin *obituarium*, from Latin *obitus* "decease", from *obire* "to go to meet, die", from *ob-* "toward, against" + *ire* "to go"] — **obituary** *adj*

¹ob·ject \'äb-jikt\ *n* **1 a** : something that may be seen or felt ⟨tables and chairs are *objects*⟩ **b** : something that may be thought about ⟨an *object* of study⟩ **2** : something that arouses an emotional response (as of affection, hatred, or pity) ⟨an *object* of envy⟩ **3** : AIM, PURPOSE ⟨the *object* is to raise money⟩ **4 a** : a word or phrase denoting someone or something that the action of a verb is directed toward **b** : the word or words in a prepositional phrase other than the preposition [Medieval Latin *objectum*, from Latin *obicere* "to throw in the way, present, hinder, object", from *ob-* "in the way" + *jacere* "to throw"] — **ob·ject·less** \'äb-jikt-ləs\ *adj*

²ob·ject \əb-'jekt\ *vb* **1** : to offer or cite as an objection ⟨*objected* that the price was too high⟩ **2 a** : to state one's opposition ⟨*objected* to the plan⟩ **b** : to be opposed ⟨I *object* to paying high prices for junk⟩ [Latin *objectus*, past participle of *obicere* "to throw in the way, object"] — **ob·jec·tor** \-'jek-tər\ *n*

object ball \'äb-jikt-, -jik-\ *n* : the ball struck by the cue ball in billiards and pool

ob·jec·tion \əb-'jek-shən\ *n* **1** : an act of objecting **2** : a reason for or feeling of disapproval

ob·jec·tion·able \-shə-nə-bəl, -shnə-bəl\ *adj* : DISPLEASING, OFFENSIVE ⟨was written in *objectionable* language⟩ — **ob·jec·tion·able·ness** *n* — **ob·jec·tion·ably** \-blē\ *adv*

¹ob·jec·tive \əb-'jek-tiv\ *adj* **1** : existing outside and independent of the mind ⟨*objective* reality⟩ — compare SUBJECTIVE 2 **2** : relating to, characteristic of, or constituting the grammatical case marking typically the object of a verb or preposition — compare ACCUSATIVE 3 **3** : expressing or dealing with facts or conditions as perceived without distortion by personal feelings, prejudices, or interpretations ⟨an *objective* history of the war⟩ — **ob·jec·tive·ly** *adv* — **ob·jec·tive·ness** *n* — **ob·jec·tiv·i·ty** \ˌäb-ˌjek-'tiv-ət-ē, əb-\ *n*

²objective *n* **1** : a lens or system of lenses (as in a microscope) that forms an image of an object **2** : something toward which effort is directed : an aim, goal, or end of action

objective complement *n* : a noun, adjective, or pronoun used in the predicate as complement to a verb and as qualifier of its direct object ⟨green in "paint the wall green" is an *objective complement*⟩

object lesson \'äb-jikt-\ *n* : a lesson taught by means of illustrative objects or concrete examples; *also* : something that teaches by a concrete example

ob·jet d'art \ˌōb-ˌzhā-'där\ *n, pl* **ob·jets d'art** \same\ : an article of artistic value [French, literally, "art object"]

¹ob·late \äb-'lāt, 'äb-\ *adj* : flattened or depressed at the poles ⟨the *oblate* shape of the earth⟩ [New Latin *oblatus*, from *ob-* "ob-" + *-latus* (as in *prolatus* "elongated in the direction of the poles", from Latin, past participle of *proferre* "to extend", from *pro-* + *ferre* "to carry")]

²ob·late \'äb-ˌlāt\ *n* **1** : a layman living in a monastery under a modified rule and without vows **2** *cap* : a member of one of several Roman Catholic communities of men or women [Medieval Latin *oblatus*, literally, "one offered up", from Latin, past participle of *offerre* "to offer"]

ob·la·tion \ə-'blā-shən, ō-\ *n* : a religious offering [Middle French, from Late Latin *oblatio*, from Latin *offerre* "to offer"]

¹ob·li·gate \'äb-li-gət, -lə-ˌgāt\ *adj* : restricted to one particular mode of life ⟨an *obligate* parasite⟩ — **ob·li·gate·ly** *adv*

²ob·li·gate \'äb-lə-ˌgāt\ *vt* : to bring under obligation : bind legally or morally ⟨*obligated* to pay taxes⟩ [Latin *obligare*, from *ob-* "toward" + *ligare* "to bind"]

ob·li·ga·tion \ˌäb-lə-'gā-shən\ *n* **1** : an act of making oneself responsible for doing something **2 a** : something (as a promise or contract) that requires one to do something **b** : something one must do : DUTY **3** : indebtedness for an act of kindness

oblig·a·to·ry \ə-'blig-ə-ˌtōr-ē, ä-, -ˌtȯr-\ *adj* : legally or morally binding : REQUIRED ⟨attendance was *obligatory*⟩

oblige \ə-'blīj\ *vb* **1** : FORCE, COMPEL ⟨laws *oblige* citizens to pay taxes⟩ **2 a** : to bind by a favor ⟨*oblige* an acquaintance with a loan⟩ **b** : to do something as a favor ⟨a person always willing to *oblige*⟩ [Old French *obliger*, from Latin *obligare* "to obligate"] — **oblig·er** *n*

oblig·ing \ə-'blī-jing\ *adj* : willing to do favors : ACCOMMODATING — **oblig·ing·ly** \-jing-lē\ *adv* — **oblig·ing·ness** *n*

¹oblique \ō-'blēk, ə-, -'blīk\ *adj* **1 a** : neither perpendicular nor parallel : INCLINED **b** : having an axis or lateral edges that are not perpendicular to the plane of the base ⟨an *oblique* circular cone⟩ ⟨an *oblique* prism⟩ **2** : not straightforward : INDIRECT ⟨*oblique* accusations⟩

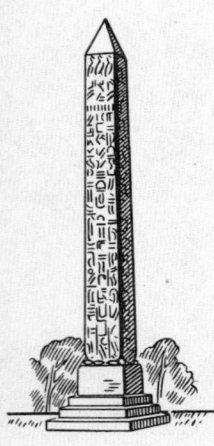

obelisk

[Latin *obliquus*] — **oblique·ly** *adv* — **oblique·ness** *n* — **obliq·ui·ty** \ō-'blik-wət-ē, ə-\ *n*

²**oblique** *n* **1** : something that is oblique **2** : any of several obliquely placed muscles; *esp* : one of the thin flat diagonal muscles of the abdominal wall

oblique angle *n* : an acute or obtuse angle

oblit·er·ate \ə-'blit-ə-,rāt, ō-\ *vt* : to remove or destroy completely : wipe out (wind *obliterated* the tracks) [Latin *oblitterare,* from *ob* "in the way of" + *littera* "letter"] SYN see ERASE — **oblit·er·a·tion** \-,blit-ə-'rā-shən\ *n* — **oblit·er·a·tive** \-'blit-ə-,rāt-iv\ *adj*

obliv·i·on \ə-'bliv-ē-ən, ō-, ä-\ *n* **1** : the state of forgetting or having forgotten or of being unaware or unconscious **2** : the state of being forgotten [Middle French, from Latin *oblivio,* from *oblivisci* "to forget"]

obliv·i·ous \-ē-əs\ *adj* **1** : lacking memory or mindful attention : FORGETFUL **2** : lacking active conscious knowledge : UNAWARE (*oblivious* to the risk of swimming alone) — **obliv·i·ous·ly** *adv* — **obliv·i·ous·ness** *n*

ob·long \'äb-,lóng\ *adj* : longer in one direction than in the other with opposite sides parallel : RECTANGULAR [Latin *oblongus,* from *ob-* "toward" + *longus* "long"] — **oblong** *n*

ob·lo·quy \'äb-lə-kwē\ *n, pl* **-quies** **1** : strongly condemnatory utterance or language **2** : bad repute : DISGRACE [Late Latin *obloquium,* from *obloqui* "to speak against", from *ob-* "against" + *loqui* "to speak"]

ob·nox·ious \äb-'näk-shəs, əb-\ *adj* : extremely disagreeable : OFFENSIVE [Latin *obnoxius,* from *ob* "in the way of, exposed to" + *noxa* "harm"] — **ob·nox·ious·ly** *adv* — **ob·nox·ious·ness** *n*

oboe \'ō-bō\ *n* : a slender conical woodwind musical instrument with holes and keys that is played by blowing into a reed mouthpiece [Italian, from French *hautbois,* from *haut* "high" + *bois* "wood"] — **obo·ist** \'ō-,bō-əst\ *n*

obol \'äb-əl, 'ō-bəl\ *n* : an ancient Greek coin or weight equal to ⅙ drachma (about .6 gram) [Latin *obolus,* from Greek *obolos*]

ob·ovate \äb-'ō-,vāt, 'äb-\ *adj* : ovate with the base narrower (an *obovate* leaf)

ob·scene \äb-'sēn, əb-\ *adj* **1** : disgusting to the senses : REPULSIVE **2** : deeply offensive to morality or decency; *esp* : designed to incite to lust or depravity [Middle French "repulsive, disgusting", from Latin *obscenus*] SYN see COARSE — **ob·scene·ly** *adv*

ob·scen·i·ty \-'sen-ət-ē\ *n, pl* **-ties** **1** : the quality or state of being obscene **2** : something that is obscene

¹**ob·scure** \äb-'skyúr, əb-\ *adj* **1** : lacking or inadequately supplied with light : DIM, GLOOMY **2 a** : withdrawn from the centers of human activity : REMOTE (an *obscure* country village) **b** : not readily understood or not clearly expressed **c** : lacking showiness or prominence : HUMBLE (an *obscure* poet) **d** : not distinct : FAINT **3** : constituting the unstressed vowel \ə\ or having unstressed \ə\ as its value [Middle French *obscur,* from Latin *obscurus*] — **ob·scure·ly** *adv* — **ob·scure·ness** *n* — **ob·scu·ri·ty** \äb-'skyúr-ət-ē, əb-\ *n* □ SYN OBSCURE, DARK, VAGUE, CRYPTIC mean not clearly understandable. OBSCURE implies a veiling of meaning through defective expression or a withholding of full knowledge. DARK implies an imperfect revelation often with ominous or sinister suggestion (*dark* prophecies) VAGUE implies lacking clarity because imperfectly conceived, grasped, or thought out; CRYPTIC implies a purposely concealed meaning (made *cryptic* remarks about future plans)

²**obscure** *vt* **1** : to make dark, dim, or indistinct **2** : to conceal or hide by or as if by covering **3** : to use the unstressed vowel \ə\ as the sound of

ob·se·qui·ous \əb-'sē-kwē-əs, äb-\ *adj* : humbly or excessively attentive (as to a person in authority) : FAWNING, SERVILE [Latin *obsequiosus* "compliant", from *obsequi* "to comply", from *ob-* "toward" + *sequi* "to

follow"] — **ob·se·qui·ous·ly** *adv* — **ob·se·qui·ous·ness** *n*

ob·se·quy \'äb-sə-kwē\ *n, pl* **-quies** : a funeral or burial rite — usually used in pl. [Middle French *obsequie,* from Medieval Latin *obsequiae,* pl., alteration of Latin *exsequiae,* from *exsequi* "to follow, perform", from *ex-* + *sequi* "to follow"]

ob·serv·ance \əb-'zər-vəns\ *n* **1** : a customary practice or ceremony **2** : an act or instance of following a custom, rule, or law **3** : an act or instance of noticing : OBSERVATION

ob·serv·ant \-vənt\ *adj* **1** : paying strict attention : WATCHFUL **2** : careful in observing : MINDFUL **3** : quick to observe : KEEN — **ob·serv·ant·ly** *adv*

ob·ser·va·tion \,äb-sər-'vā-shən, -zər-\ *n* **1** : an act or the power of observing with the eyes or mind **2** : the gathering of information (as for scientific studies) by noting facts or occurrences (weather *observations*) **3 a** : a conclusion drawn from observing : VIEW **b** : REMARK 3, COMMENT **4** : the state of being observed — **ob·ser·va·tion·al** \-shnəl, -shən-l\ *adj*

ob·ser·va·to·ry \əb-'zər-və-,tōr-ē, -,tór-\ *n, pl* **-ries** **1** : a place or institution given over to or equipped for observation of natural phenomena (as in astronomy) **2** : a place or structure commanding a wide view

ob·serve \əb-'zərv\ *vb* **1** : to conform one's action or practice to (*observe* rules) **2** : to celebrate or solemnize (as an occasion) in a customary or accepted way **3** : to pay attention to : WATCH **4** : to discover by the senses or by considering mentally : NOTICE **5** : to utter as a remark **6** : to make a scientific observation of [Middle French *observer,* from Latin *observare* "to guard, watch, observe", from *ob-* "in the way, toward" + *servare* "to keep"] SYN see KEEP — **ob·serv·able** \-'zər-və-bəl\ *adj* — **ob·serv·ably** \-'zər-və-blē\ *adv*

ob·serv·er \əb-'zər-vər\ *n* : one that observes; *esp* : a representative sent to observe but not participate officially

ob·sess \əb-'ses, äb-\ *vt* : to occupy the mind of intensely or abnormally : HAUNT (*obsessed* by fear) [Latin *obsessus,* past participle of *obsidēre* "to besiege", from *ob-* "against" + *sedēre* "to sit"]

ob·ses·sion \äb-'sesh-ən, əb-\ *n* : a prolonged and disturbed concern with a thought, emotion, or impulse even when it is seen as unreasonable; *also* : such a thought, emotion, or impulse — **ob·ses·sive** \-'ses-iv\ *adj* — **ob·ses·sive·ly** \-'ses-iv-lē\ *adv*

ob·sid·i·an \əb-'sid-ē-ən\ *n* : a dark natural glass formed by the cooling of molten lava [Latin *obsidianus lapis,* mistaken manuscript reading for *obsianus lapis,* literally, "stone of Obsius (its supposed discoverer)"]

ob·so·les·cent \,äb-sə-'les-nt\ *adj* : going out of use : becoming obsolete [Latin *obsolescens,* present participle of *obsolescere* "to grow old, become disused"] — **ob·so·lesce** \-'les\ *vi* — **ob·so·les·cence** \-'les-ns\ *n* — **ob·so·les·cent·ly** *adv*

ob·so·lete \,äb-sə-'lēt, 'äb-sə-,\ *adj* **1** : no longer in use (an *obsolete* word) **2** : OUTMODED (*obsolete* machinery) [Latin *obsoletus,* from past participle of *obsolescere* "to grow old, become disused"] — **ob·so·lete·ly** *adv* — **ob·so·lete·ness** *n*

ob·sta·cle \'äb-sti-kəl\ *n* : something that stands in the way or opposes : OBSTRUCTION [Middle French, from Latin *obstaculum,* from *obstare* "to stand in the way", from *ob-* "in the way" + *stare* "to stand"]

ob·stet·ric \əb-'ste-trik, äb-\ *or* **ob·stet·ri·cal** \-tri-kəl\ *adj* : of or relating to childbirth or obstetrics [derived from Latin *obstetric-, obstetrix* "midwife", from *obstare* "to stand in the way"] — **ob·stet·ri·cal·ly** \-tri-kə-lē, -klē\ *adv*

ob·ste·tri·cian \,äb-stə-'trish-ən\ *n* : a physician specializing in obstetrics

oboe

ob·stet·rics \əb-'ste-triks, äb-\ *n* : a branch of medical science that deals with childbirth and with the care of women before, during, and after this

ob·sti·na·cy \'äb-stə-nə-sē\ *n, pl* **-cies** 1 : the quality or state of being obstinate 2 : an instance of being obstinate

ob·sti·nate \'äb-stə-nət\ *adj* 1 : clinging to an opinion, purpose, or course in spite of reason, arguments, or persuasion 2 : not easily subdued, remedied, or removed ⟨an *obstinate* fever⟩ [Latin *obstinatus,* past participle of *obstinare* "to be firm"] — **ob·sti·nate·ly** *adv* — **ob·sti·nate·ness** *n* □ SYN OBSTINATE, DOGGED, STUBBORN, PERTINACIOUS mean fixed and unyielding in course or purpose. OBSTINATE implies a persistent adherence and suggests unreasonableness and perversity ⟨too *obstinate* to take advice⟩ DOGGED suggests a tenacious sometimes sullen persistence ⟨shoveled with a *dogged* regularity⟩ STUBBORN implies sturdiness in resisting attempts to change or abandon a course or opinion ⟨met persuasion with *stubborn* resistance⟩ PERTINACIOUS suggests an annoying persistence ⟨a *pertinacious* beggar⟩

ob·strep·er·ous \əb-'strep-rəs, äb-, -ə-rəs\ *adj* 1 : uncontrollably noisy 2 : stubbornly defiant : UNRULY [Latin *obstreperus,* from *obstrepere* "to clamor against", from *ob-* "against" + *strepere* "to make a noise"] — **ob·strep·er·ous·ly** *adv* — **ob·strep·er·ous·ness** *n*

ob·struct \əb-'strəkt, äb-\ *vt* 1 : to block or close up by an obstacle 2 : to hinder from passage, action, or operation : IMPEDE 3 : to cut off from sight ⟨a wall *obstructing* the view⟩ [Latin *obstructus,* past participle of *obstruere* "to obstruct", from *ob-* "in the way" + *struere* "to build"] — **ob·struc·tive** \-'strək-tiv\ *adj or n* — **ob·struc·tor** \-tər\ *n*

ob·struc·tion \əb-'strək-shən, äb-\ *n* 1 : an act of obstructing : the state of being obstructed 2 : something that obstructs : HINDRANCE

ob·struc·tion·ist \-shə-nəst, -shnəst\ *n* : a person who hinders progress especially in a legislative body — **ob·struc·tion·ism** \-shə-,niz-əm\ *n* — **ob·struc·tion·is·tic** \-,strək-shə-'nis-tik\ *adj*

ob·tain \əb-'tān, äb-\ *vb* 1 : to gain, find, or attain usually by planning, calculation, or effort 2 : to be generally recognized or established : PREVAIL [Middle French *obtenir,* from *obtinēre* "to hold on to, possess, obtain", from *ob-* "in the way" + *tenēre* to hold"] — **ob·tain·able** \-'tā-nə-bəl\ *adj* — **ob·tain·er** *n* — **ob·tain·ment** \-'tān-mənt\ *n*

ob·trude \əb-'trüd, äb-\ *vb* 1 : to thrust out 2 : to thrust forward or call to notice without warrant or request 3 : to thrust oneself upon attention [Latin *obtrudere* "to thrust out", from *ob-* "in the way" + *trudere* "to thrust"] SYN see INTRUDE — **ob·trud·er** *n* — **ob·tru·sion** \-'trü-zhən\ *n*

ob·tru·sive \əb-'trü-siv, äb-, -ziv\ *adj* : inclined to obtrude : FORWARD, PUSHING [Latin *obtrusus,* past participle of *obtrudere* "to thrust at"] — **ob·tru·sive·ly** *adv* — **ob·tru·sive·ness** *n*

ob·tuse \äb-'tüs, -'tyüs\ *adj* 1 : lacking sharpness or quickness of wit : DULL, INSENSITIVE 2 **a** (1) : exceeding 90 degrees but less than 180 degrees ⟨*obtuse* angle⟩ (2) : having an obtuse angle ⟨an *obtuse* triangle⟩ **b** : not pointed or acute : BLUNT ⟨an *obtuse* leaf⟩ [Latin *obtusus* "blunt, dull", from *obtundere* "to beat against, blunt", from *ob-* "against" + *tundere* "to beat"] SYN see BLUNT — **ob·tuse·ly** *adv* — **ob·tuse·ness** *n*

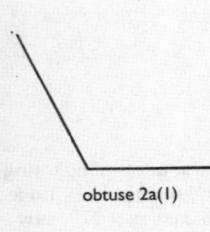

obtuse 2a(1)

¹ob·verse \äb-'vərs, 'äb-,\ *adj* 1 : facing the observer or opponent 2 : being a counterpart or complement [Latin *obversus,* from *obvertere* "to turn toward", from *ob-* "toward" + *vertere* "to turn"] — **ob·verse·ly** *adv*

²ob·verse \'äb-,vərs, äb-\ *n* 1 : the side of something (as a coin or medal) bearing the principal design or lettering 2 : a front or principal surface 3 : COUNTERPART 2

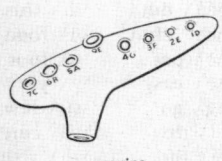

ocarina

ob·vi·ate \'äb-vē-,āt\ *vt* : to anticipate and dispose of beforehand : make unnecessary ⟨*obviate* an objection⟩ [Late Latin *obviare* "to meet, withstand", from Latin *obviam* "in the way"] — **ob·vi·a·tion** \,äb-vē-'ā-shən\ *n*

ob·vi·ous \'äb-vē-əs\ *adj* : easily discovered, seen, or understood : PLAIN ⟨an *obvious* mistake⟩ [Latin *obvius* "being in the way", from *obviam* "in the way", from *ob* "in the way of" + *via* "way"] — **ob·vi·ous·ly** *adv* — **ob·vi·ous·ness** *n*

oc·a·ri·na \,äk-ə-'rē-nə\ *n* : a wind instrument having an oval body with finger holes and giving soft flutelike tones — called also *sweet potato* [Italian, from *oca* "goose", from Late Latin *auca,* derived from Latin *avis* "bird"]

¹oc·ca·sion \ə-'kā-zhən\ *n* 1 : a favorable opportunity or circumstance 2 : a state of affairs that provides a ground or reason 3 : an occurrence or condition that brings something about; *esp* : the immediate inciting circumstance as distinguished from fundamental cause 4 : a time at which something happens 5 : a need arising from a particular circumstance : EXIGENCY 6 *pl* : AFFAIR 1a, BUSINESS 7 : a special event or ceremony : CELEBRATION [Latin *occasio,* from *occidere* "to fall, fall down", from *ob-* "toward" + *cadere* "to fall"] SYN see CAUSE

²occasion *vt* **oc·ca·sioned; oc·ca·sion·ing** \-'kāzh-ning, -ə-ning\ : to give occasion to : CAUSE

oc·ca·sion·al \ə-'kāzh-nəl, -ən-l\ *adj* 1 : happening or met with now and then ⟨made *occasional* references to the war⟩ 2 : used or meant for a special occasion ⟨*occasional* verse⟩ — **oc·ca·sion·al·ly** \-ē\ *adv*

Oc·ci·dent \'äk-səd-ənt, -sə-,dent\ *n* : WEST 2 [Middle French, from Latin *occidens,* from *occidere* "to fall, set (of the sun)", from *ob-* "toward" + *cadere* "to fall"]

oc·ci·den·tal \,äk-sə-'dent-l\ *adj, often cap* 1 : of, relating to, or situated in the Occident : WESTERN 2 : of or relating to Occidentals — **oc·ci·den·tal·ly** \-l-ē\ *adv*

Occidental *n* : a member of one of the occidental peoples; *esp* : a person of European ancestry

oc·cip·i·tal \äk-'sip-ət-l\ *adj* : of or relating to the occiput or the occipital bone — **occipital** *n* — **oc·cip·i·tal·ly** \-l-ē\ *adv*

occipital bone *n* : a compound bone that forms the back part of the skull and articulates with the atlas

occipital lobe *n* : the back part of the cerebral hemisphere that contains the visual areas of the brain

oc·ci·put \'äk-sə-pət, -,pət\ *n, pl* **occiputs** *or* **oc·cip·i·ta** \äk-'sip-ət-ə\ : the back part of the head or skull [Latin *occipit-, occiput,* from *ob-* "against" + *capit-, caput* "head"]

oc·clude \ə-'klüd, ä-\ *vb* 1 : to stop up : OBSTRUCT 2 : to shut in or out 3 : to take up and hold by absorption or adsorption 4 : to come together with opposing surfaces in contact ⟨the teeth do not *occlude* properly⟩ [Latin *occludere* (past participle *occlusus*), from *ob-* "in the way" + *claudere* "to shut, close"] — **oc·clu·sive** \-'klü-siv, -ziv\ *adj*

occluded front *n* : OCCLUSION 2

oc·clu·sal \ə-'klü-səl, ä-, -zəl\ *adj* : of, relating to, or being the surface of a molar or premolar tooth that is used for crushing and grinding [Latin *occlusus,* past participle of *occludere* "to occlude"] — **oc·clu·sal·ly** \-ē\ *adv*

oc·clu·sion \ə-'klü-zhən\ *n* 1 : the act of occluding : the state of being occluded 2 : the front formed by a cold front overtaking a warm front and lifting the warm air over the cold air

¹oc·cult \ə-'kəlt, ä-\ *vb* : to shut off from view : COVER, ECLIPSE

²occult *adj* 1 : not revealed : SECRET, HIDDEN 2 : ABSTRUSE, MYSTERIOUS 3 : of or relating to supernatural agencies, their effects, or knowledge of them [Latin *occultus,* from *occulere* "to cover up, hide"] — **oc·cult·ly** *adv*

oc·cul·ta·tion \ˌäk-əl-'tā-shən, ˌäk-ˌəl-\ *n* **1** : the state of being hidden from view or lost to notice **2** : the shutting out of the light of one celestial body by the intervention of another; *esp* : an eclipse of a star or planet by the moon

oc·cult·ism \ə-'kəl-ˌtiz-əm, ä-\ *n* : a belief in or study of supernatural powers — **oc·cult·ist** \-təst\ *n*

oc·cu·pan·cy \'äk-yə-pən-sē\ *n, pl* **-cies** : the act of occupying : the state of being occupied

oc·cu·pant \'äk-yə-pənt\ *n* : one that occupies something or takes or has possession of it

oc·cu·pa·tion \ˌäk-yə-'pā-shən\ *n* **1** : an activity in which one engages; *esp* : one's business or vocation **2 a** : the taking possession of property : OCCUPANCY **b** : the taking possession or holding and controlling of an area by a foreign military force; *also* : such a military force — **oc·cu·pa·tion·al** \-shnəl, -shən-l\ *adj* — **oc·cu·pa·tion·al·ly** \-ē\ *adv*

occupational therapy *n* : therapy by means of activity; *esp* : creative activity prescribed for its effect in promoting recovery or rehabilitation — **occupational therapist** *n*

oc·cu·py \'äk-yə-ˌpī\ *vt* **-pied; -py·ing** **1 a** : to engage the attention or energies of ⟨*occupy* oneself with reading⟩ **b** : to fill up (an extent in space or time) ⟨sports *occupied* their spare time⟩ ⟨a liter of water *occupies* 1000 cubic centimeters of space⟩ **2** : to take or hold possession of **3** : to reside in as an owner or tenant [Middle French *occuper* "to take possession of", from Latin *occupare*] — **oc·cu·pi·er** \-ˌpī-ər, -ˌpīr\ *n*

oc·cur \ə-'kər\ *vi* **oc·curred; oc·cur·ring** \-'kər-ing\ **1** : to be found or met with : APPEAR **2** : to take place **3** : to come to mind : suggest itself [Latin *occurrere,* from *ob-* "in the way" + *currere* "to run"] **SYN** see **HAPPEN**

oc·cur·rence \ə-'kər-əns, -'kə-rəns\ *n* **1** : something that takes place; *esp* : something that happens unexpectedly **2** : the action or process of taking place □ **SYN** OCCURRENCE, EVENT, INCIDENT, EPISODE mean something that happens or takes place. OCCURRENCE suggests a happening without plan, intent, or volition; EVENT usually implies a significant occurrence and frequently one resulting from or giving rise to another ⟨Columbus' voyage was one of the great *events* of history⟩ INCIDENT suggests an occurrence of brief duration or secondary importance ⟨the plot of the play is strung with amusing *incidents*⟩ or a minor but unusual happening of consequence ⟨the death of the little-known general was one of those *incidents* that pass unnoticed⟩ EPISODE stresses the distinctiveness or apartness of an incident ⟨a memorable *episode* in their lives was their trip to Africa⟩

ocean \'ō-shən\ *n* **1** : the whole body of salt water that covers nearly three fourths of the surface of the earth **2** : one of the large bodies of water into which the great ocean is divided **3** : an immense space or quantity [Latin *oceanus,* from Greek *ōkeanos*] — **oce·an·ic** \ˌō-shē-'an-ik\ *adj*

ocean·ar·i·um \ˌō-shə-'nar-ē-əm, -'ner-\ *n, pl* **-i·ums** *also* **-ia** \-ē-ə\ : a large marine aquarium

ocean·go·ing \'ō-shən-ˌgō-ing\ *adj* : of, relating to, or suitable for travel on the ocean

Oce·a·nid \ō-'sē-ə-nəd\ *n* : any of the ocean nymphs in Greek mythology

ocean·og·ra·phy \ˌō-shə-'näg-rə-fē\ *n* : a science that deals with the ocean and its phenomena — **ocean·og·ra·pher** \-fər\ *n* — **ocean·o·graph·ic** \ˌō-shə-nə-'graf-ik\ *adj* — **ocean·o·graph·i·cal·ly** \-'graf-i-kə-lē, -klē\ *adv*

ocel·lus \ō-'sel-əs\ *n, pl* **ocel·li** \-'sel-ˌī, -ˌē\ **1** : a tiny simple eye or eyespot of an invertebrate **2** : a spot of color encircled by a band of another color [Latin, "little eye", from *oculus* "eye"] — **ocel·lat·ed** \'ō-sə-ˌlāt-əd\ *adj*

oc·e·lot \'äs-ə-ˌlät, 'ō-sə-\ *n* : a medium-sized American wildcat ranging from Texas to Patagonia and having a tawny yellow or grayish coat marked with black [French, from Nahuatl *ocelotl* "jaguar"]

ocher *or* **ochre** \'ō-kər\ *n* **1** : an earthy usually red or yellow and often impure iron ore used as a pigment **2** : the color of yellow ocher [Middle French *ocre,* from Latin *ochra,* from Greek *ōchra,* from *ōchros* "yellow"] — **ocher·ous** \'ō-kə-rəs, -krəs\ *or* **ochre·ous** \'ō-kə-rəs, -krəs, -krē-əs\ *adj*

-ock \ək, ik, äk\ *n suffix* : small one ⟨hill*ock*⟩ [Old English *-oc*]

o'·clock \ə-'kläk\ *adv* **1** : according to the clock ⟨the time is three *o'clock*⟩ **2** — used for indicating position or direction as if on a clock dial ⟨an airplane approaching at eleven *o'clock*⟩ [contraction of *of the clock*]

oco·ti·llo \ˌō-kə-'tē-yō, -'tē-ō\ *n, pl* **-llos** : a thorny scarlet-flowered shrub of the southwestern United States and Mexico [Mexican Spanish]

octa- *or* **octo-** *also* **oct-** *combining form* : eight [Greek *oktō* and Latin *octo*]

oc·ta·gon \'äk-tə-ˌgän\ *n* : a polygon of eight angles and eight sides — **oc·tag·o·nal** \äk-'tag-ən-l\ *adj* — **oc·tag·o·nal·ly** \-l-ē\ *adv*

oc·ta·he·dron \ˌäk-tə-'hē-drən\ *n, pl* **-drons** *or* **-dra** \-drə\ : a solid bounded by eight plane faces — **oc·ta·he·dral** \-drəl\ *adj*

oc·tal \'äk-tl\ *adj* : of, relating to, or being a number system with a base of 8

oc·tam·e·ter \äk-'tam-ət-ər\ *n* : a line of verse consisting of eight metrical feet [Late Latin, "having eight feet", derived from Greek *oktō* "eight" + *metron* "measure"]

oc·tane \'äk-ˌtān\ *n* **1** : any of several isomeric liquid hydrocarbons C_8H_{18} **2** : OCTANE NUMBER

octane number *n* : a number that is used to measure or indicate the antiknock properties of a liquid motor fuel and that increases as the likelihood of knocking decreases — called also *octane rating*

oc·tant \'äk-tənt\ *n* **1** : an instrument for observing altitudes of a celestial body from a moving ship or aircraft **2** : any group of eight similar units or parts ⟨an *octant* of spores⟩ [Latin *octans* "eighth of a circle", from *octo* "eight"]

oc·tave \'äk-tiv, -təv, -ˌtāv\ *n* **1** : an 8-day period of observances beginning with the festival day **2** : a stanza or poem of eight lines; *esp* : the first eight lines of an Italian sonnet — compare **SESTET** **3 a** : a musical interval embracing eight degrees **b** : a tone or note at this interval **c** : the whole series of notes, tones, or keys within this interval **4** : a group of eight [Medieval Latin *octava,* from Latin *octavus* "eighth", from *octo* "eight"]

oc·ta·vo \äk-'tā-vō, -'tāv-ō\ *n, pl* **-vos** : a book made of sheets of paper each folded 3 times to make 8 leaves or 16 pages [Latin, ablative of *octavus* "eighth"]

oc·tet \äk-'tet\ *n* **1** : a musical composition for eight voices or eight instruments; *also* : the performers of such a composition **2** : a group or set of eight

oc·til·lion \äk-'til-yən\ *n* — see NUMBER table [French, from *oct-* "octa-" + *-illion* (as in *million*)]

Oc·to·ber \äk-'tō-bər\ *n* : the 10th month of the year [Old French *Octobre,* from Latin *October,* from *octo* "eight"; from its having been originally the 8th month of the Roman calendar]

oc·to·ge·nar·i·an \ˌäk-tə-jə-'ner-ē-ən\ *n* : a person who is 80 or more but less than 90 years old [Latin *octogenarius* "containing 80", from *octogeni* "80 each", from *octoginta* "eighty", from *octo* "eight"]

oc·to·pus \'äk-tə-pəs\ *n, pl* **-pus·es** *or* **-pi** \-ˌpī, -ˌpē\ **1** : any of various cephalopod sea mollusks having eight muscular arms with two rows of suckers **2** : something suggestive of an octopus; *esp* : a powerful grasping or-

ocelot

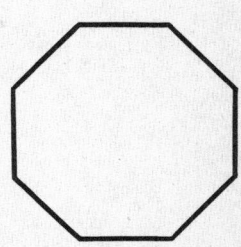
octagon

octopus 1

\ə\ abut	\ng\ sing
\ər\ further	\ō\ bone
\a\ mat	\ȯ\ saw
\ā\ take	\ȯi\ coin
\ä\ cot, cart	\th\ thin
\au̇\ out	\th\ this
\ch\ chin	\ü\ food
\e\ pet	\u̇\ foot
\ē\ easy	\y\ yet
\g\ go	\yü\ few
\i\ tip	\yu̇\ cure
\ī\ life	\zh\ vision
\j\ job	

ganization with many branches [Greek *oktōpous* "having 8 feet", from *oktō* "eight" + *pous* "foot"]

oc·to·roon \,äk-tə-'rün\ *n* : a person of one-eighth Negro ancestry [*octa-* + *-roon* (as in *quadroon*)]

oc·to·syl·lab·ic \,äk-tə-sə-'lab-ik\ *adj* : having eight syllables : composed of verses of eight syllables — **octosyllabic** *n*

¹oc·u·lar \'äk-yə-lər\ *adj* **1** : of or relating to the eye or the eyesight **2** : obtained or perceived by the sight : VISUAL ⟨*ocular* proof⟩ [Late Latin *ocularis* "of eyes", from Latin *oculus* "eye"]

²ocular *n* : EYEPIECE

oc·u·list \'äk-yə-ləst\ *n* **1** : OPHTHALMOLOGIST **2** : OPTOMETRIST

oc·u·lo·mo·tor \,äk-yə-lə-'mōt-ər\ *adj* **1** : moving or acting to move the eyeball **2** : of or relating to the oculomotor nerve

oculomotor nerve *n* : either of the 3d pair of cranial nerves that arise from the midbrain and supply most muscles of the eye — called also *oculomotor*

odd \'äd\ *adj* **1** : being only one of a pair or set ⟨an *odd* shoe⟩ ⟨an *odd* chair⟩ **2 a** : being one of the sequence of natural numbers beginning with one and counting by twos that are not divisible by two ⟨1, 3, 5, and 7 are *odd* numbers⟩ **b** : numbered with an odd number ⟨an *odd* year⟩ **c** : somewhat more than the number mentioned ⟨fifty *odd* years ago⟩ **3** : additional to or apart from what is usual, planned on, or taken into account : RANDOM, CASUAL, OCCASIONAL ⟨*odd* jobs⟩ ⟨done at *odd* moments⟩ ⟨*odd* bits of material⟩ **4** : not usual or conventional : STRANGE ⟨an *odd* way of behaving⟩ ⟨what an *odd* place to keep cereal⟩ [Old Norse *oddi* "point of land, triangle, odd number"] — **odd·ly** *adv* — **odd·ness** *n* □ ORIGIN Although a triangle is a 3-angled figure, it is possible, by concentrating attention on the apex, to look at it as a point. An arrowhead, after all, is basically a triangle, and likewise a point of land reaching out into a body of water is roughly triangular in shape. The Old Norse word *oddi* was used both for a point of land and for a triangle. *Oddi* also developed the meaning "odd number", since the apex of a triangle is the unpaired angle and an odd number is a sum of pairs and one unpaired unit. English never called a triangle *odd*, but it did borrow the *odd* number from Old Norse *oddi*. Later anything singular or different came to be called *odd*.

odd·ball \'äd-,bȯl\ *n* : one whose behavior is eccentric

Odd Fellow *n* : a member of one of the major benevolent and fraternal orders [Independent Order of *Odd Fellows*]

odd·i·ty \'äd-ət-ē\ *n, pl* **-ties** **1** : an odd person, thing, event, or trait **2** : the quality or state of being odd ⟨the *oddity* of your behavior⟩

odd·ment \'äd-mənt\ *n* : something left over : REMNANT

odds \'ädz\ *n pl* **1** *archaic* : unequal things or conditions **2** : DIFFERENCE ⟨made little *odds* whether they stayed⟩; *esp* : a difference by which one thing is favored over another ⟨the *odds* are in favor of our side⟩ **3 a** : the advantage of an unequal wager granted to a bettor believed to have a less than even chance of winning **b** : the ratio between the amount to be won and the amount wagered on a bet **4** : DISAGREEMENT, QUARRELING — used with *at* ⟨the children were at *odds*⟩

odds and ends *n pl* : miscellaneous things or matters

odds–on \'äd-'zȯn, -'zän\ *adj* : having or viewed as having a better than even chance to win

ode \'ōd\ *n* : a lyric poem characterized usually by elevated feeling and style, varied length of line, and complex stanza forms [Late Latin, from Greek *ōidē*, literally, "song", from *aidein* "to sing"]

-ode \,ōd\ *n combining form* **1** : way : path ⟨electr*ode*⟩ **2** : electrode ⟨di*ode*⟩ [Greek *hodos*]

odi·ous \'ōd-ē-əs\ *adj* : causing or deserving hatred or repugnance — **odi·ous·ly** *adv* — **odi·ous·ness** *n*

odi·um \'ōd-ē-əm\ *n* **1** : the condition of being generally hated and condemned usually for shameful conduct : merited loathing **2** : the disgrace or shame attached to something considered hateful or low [Latin, "hatred", from *odisse* "to hate"]

odom·e·ter \ō-'däm-ət-ər\ *n* : an instrument for measuring the distance traveled (as by a vehicle) [French *odomètre*, from Greek *hodometron*, from *hodos* "way, road" + *metron* "measure"]

odon·tol·o·gy \,ō-,dän-'täl-ə-jē\ *n* : a science dealing with the teeth, their structure and development, and their diseases [French *odontologie*, from Greek *odont-, odous* "tooth"] — **odon·tol·o·gist** \-jest\ *n*

odor \'ōd-ər\ *n* **1** : something that stimulates the sense of smell : SCENT; *also* : the resulting sensation : SMELL **2 a** : a predominant quality : FLAVOR ⟨*odor* of sanctity⟩ **b** : REPUTE, ESTIMATION ⟨in bad *odor*⟩ [Old French *odour*, from Latin *odor*] SYN see SMELL — **odored** \-ərd\ *adj* — **odor·less** \-ər-ləs\ *adj*

odor·ant \'ōd-ə-rənt\ *n* : an odorous substance

odor·if·er·ous \,ōd-ə-'rif-rəs, -ə-rəs\ *adj* **1** : ODOROUS **2** : morally offensive — **odor·if·er·ous·ly** *adv* — **odor·if·er·ous·ness** *n*

odor·ous \'ōd-ə-rəs\ *adj* : having an odor — **odor·ous·ly** *adv* — **odor·ous·ness** *n*

odour \'ōd-ər\ *chiefly British variant of* ODOR

od·ys·sey \'äd-ə-sē\ *n, pl* **-seys** : a long wandering usually marked by many changes of fortune [the *Odyssey*, epic poem attributed to Homer recounting the long wanderings of Odysseus]

Oe·di·pus complex \'ed-ə-pəs, 'ēd-\ *n* : a sexual attraction of a child toward the parent of the opposite sex that may be a source of adult personality disorder if left unresolved [*Oedipus*, hero of ancient Greek legend who killed his father and married his mother] — **oe·di·pal** \'ed-ə-pəl, 'ēd-\ *adj*

oe·do·go·ni·um \,ēd-ə-'gō-nē-əm\ *n* : any of a genus of threadlike green algae [New Latin, from Greek *oidos* "swelling" + *gonos* "offspring, seed"]

¹o'er \'ōr, 'ȯr\ *adv* : OVER

²o'er \ōr, ȯr, 'ōr, 'ȯr\ *prep* : OVER

oer·sted \'ər-stəd\ *n* : a unit of magnetic intensity equal to the intensity of a magnetic field in a vacuum in which a unit magnetic pole experiences a mechanical force of one dyne in the direction of the field [Hans Christian *Oersted*, died 1851, Danish physicist]

oe·soph·a·gus *variant of* ESOPHAGUS

oestr- *or* **oestro-** — see ESTR-

of \əv, 'əv, 'äv\ *prep* **1** : from as a point of reckoning ⟨north *of* the lake⟩ **2 a** : from by origin or derivation ⟨a person *of* noble birth⟩ **b** : from as a consequence ⟨died *of* flu⟩ **c** : by as author or doer ⟨plays *of* Shakespeare⟩ **d** : as experienced or performed by ⟨love *of* parents for their children⟩ **3** : having as its material, parts, or contents ⟨a throne *of* gold⟩ ⟨cups *of* water⟩ **4** — used as a function word to indicate the whole that includes the part denoted by the preceding word ⟨most *of* the army⟩ **5 a** : CONCERNING ⟨stories *of* their travels⟩ **b** : in respect to ⟨slow *of* speech⟩ **6** : possessed by : belonging to ⟨courage *of* the pioneers⟩ ⟨4 is the square *of* 2⟩ **7** — used as a function word to indicate something that is removed ⟨cured *of* a cold⟩ ⟨eased *of* pain⟩ **8** : specified as : which is or are : BEING ⟨month *of* August⟩ ⟨crime *of* murder⟩ ⟨the city *of* Rome⟩ **9** : having as its object ⟨love *of* nature⟩ **10** : having as a distinctive quality or possession ⟨a person *of* courage⟩ [Old English, "off, of"]

¹off \'ȯf\ *adv* **1 a** (1) : from a place or position ⟨march *off*⟩ (2) : away from land ⟨the ship stood *off* to sea⟩ **b** : so as to prevent close approach ⟨drove the dogs *off*⟩ **c** (1) : from a course : ASIDE ⟨turned *off* into a bypath⟩ (2) : away from the wind **2** : into an unconscious state ⟨dozed *off*⟩ **3 a** : so as not to be supported ⟨rolled to the edge of the table and *off*⟩ or covering or enclosing ⟨blew the lid *off*⟩ or attached ⟨the handle came *off*⟩ **b** :

so as to be divided ⟨surface marked *off* into squares⟩ **4** : to a state of discontinuance ⟨shut *off* an engine⟩ or exhaustion ⟨drink *off* a glass⟩ or completion ⟨paint to finish it *off*⟩ **5** : in absence from or suspension of regular work or service ⟨take time *off* for lunch⟩ [Old English *of*]

²off \'òf, 'óf\ *prep* **1** : away from; *esp* : from a place or situation on ⟨take it *off* the table⟩ **2** : at the expense of ⟨lived *off* friends⟩ **3** : to seaward of ⟨two miles *off* the coast⟩ **4 a** : not now engaged in ⟨*off* duty⟩ **b** : below the usual standard or level of ⟨*off* my game⟩ ⟨a dollar *off* the list price⟩ **5 a** : diverging or opening from ⟨a path *off* the main walk⟩ **b** : being or occurring away or apart from ⟨a shop just *off* the main street⟩

³off \'òf, 'óf\ *adj* **1 a** : more removed or distant ⟨the *off* side of the building⟩ **b** : SEAWARD **c** : RIGHT ⟨*off* horse in a team⟩ **2 a** : started on the way ⟨*off* on a spree⟩ **b** : CANCELED ⟨the picnic's *off*⟩ **c** : not operating ⟨current is *off*⟩ **d** : not placed so as to permit operation ⟨the switch is *off*⟩ **3 a** : not corresponding to fact : INCORRECT ⟨*off* in their reckoning⟩ **b** : not being at one's best : SUBNORMAL **c** : not entirely sane : ECCENTRIC **d** : REMOTE, SLIGHT ⟨an *off* chance⟩ **4 a** : spent off duty ⟨reading on our *off* days⟩ **b** : SLACK ⟨*off* season⟩ **5 a** : OFF-COLOR **b** : INFERIOR ⟨*off* grade of oil⟩ **c** : DOWN 1c ⟨stocks were *off*⟩ **6** : CIRCUMSTANCED ⟨comfortably *off*⟩

of·fal \'ò-fəl, 'äf-əl\ *n* **1** : the waste or by-product of a process: as **a** : trimmings of a hide **b** : the by-products of milling used especially for stock feeds **c** : the viscera and trimmings of a butchered animal removed in dressing **2** : RUBBISH [Middle English, from *of* "off" + *fall*]

¹off·beat \'òf-,bēt\ *n* : the unaccented part of a musical measure

²offbeat *adj* : ECCENTRIC, UNCONVENTIONAL ⟨an *offbeat* style⟩

off–col·or \'òf-'kəl-ər\ *or* **off–col·ored** \-ərd\ *adj* **1** : not having the right or standard color **2** : of doubtful propriety : RISQUÉ

of·fend \ə-'fend\ *vb* **1 a** : to transgress the moral or divine law : SIN **b** : to break a law or rule : do wrong **2 a** : to cause difficulty, discomfort, or injury **b** : to cause dislike, anger, or vexation **3** : to cause pain to **4** : to cause to feel vexed or resentful usually by hurting pride or self-respect [Middle French *offendre*, from Latin *offendere* "to strike against, offend"] — **of·fend·er** *n* □ SYN OFFEND, OUTRAGE, INSULT, AFFRONT mean to cause hurt feelings or deep resentment. OFFEND may also suggest a violating of ideas of what is right or proper without implying intent ⟨such candor *offended* the diplomats⟩ OUTRAGE implies offending beyond endurance and calling forth extreme feelings ⟨*outraged* by the vandalism⟩ INSULT suggests deliberately and insolently causing humiliation, hurt pride, or shame; AFFRONT implies treating with deliberate rudeness or contempt ⟨*affronted* by such arrogant neglect⟩

of·fense *or* **of·fence** \ə-'fens; *especially for 2* 'äf-,ens, 'òf-\ *n* **1** : something that outrages the moral or physical senses **2 a** : the act of attacking : ASSAULT **b** : the side that is attacking in a contest or battle **3 a** : the act of displeasing or affronting **b** : the state of being insulted or morally outraged **4 a** : a breach of moral or divine law **b** : an infraction of law : CRIME [Middle French, from Latin *offensa*, from *offendere* "to offend"] — **offense·less** \-ləs\ *adj*

¹of·fen·sive \ə-'fen-siv\ *adj* **1 a** : of, relating to, or designed for attack ⟨*offensive* weapons⟩ **b** : being on the offense ⟨the *offensive* team⟩ **2** : giving unpleasant sensations ⟨*offensive* smells⟩ **3** : causing displeasure or resentment : INSULTING ⟨an *offensive* word⟩ — **of·fen·sive·ly** *adv* — **of·fen·sive·ness** *n*

²offensive *n* **1** : the act of an attacking party ⟨on the *offensive*⟩ **2** : ATTACK ⟨launch an *offensive*⟩

¹of·fer \'òf-ər, 'äf-\ *vb* **of·fered; of·fer·ing** \'òf-ring, 'äf-, -ə-ring\ **1** : to present as an act of worship : SACRIFICE **2** : to present for acceptance or rejection ⟨was *offered* a job⟩ **3 a** : PROPOSE, SUGGEST ⟨*offer* a solution to the problem⟩ **b** : to declare one's readiness or willingness ⟨*offered* to help me⟩ **4 a** : to put up ⟨*offered* stubborn resistance⟩ **b** : THREATEN ⟨*offered* to strike me with a cane⟩ **5** : to place (merchandise) on sale [derived from Latin *offerre* "to present, offer", from *ob-* "toward" + *ferre* "to carry"]

²offer *n* **1 a** : PROPOSAL **b** : an agreement to do or give something on condition that the party to whom the proposal is made do or give something specified in return **2** : a price named by one proposing to buy **3** : an action or movement indicating a purpose or intention

of·fer·ing *n* **1 a** : the act of one who offers **b** : something offered; *esp* : a sacrifice ceremonially offered as a part of worship **c** : a contribution to the support of a church **2** : something offered for sale

of·fer·to·ry \'òf-ər-,tōr-ē, 'òf-ə-,, 'äf-, -,tòr-\ *n, pl* **-ries** **1** *often cap* **a** : the offering of the sacramental bread and wine to God before they are consecrated at Communion **b** : a verse from a psalm said or sung at the beginning of the offertory **2 a** : the presentation of the offerings of the congregation at public worship **b** : the music played or sung during an offertory [Medieval Latin *offertorium*, derived from Latin *offerre* "to offer"]

off·hand \'òf-'hand\ *adv or adj* : without previous thought or preparation ⟨couldn't give the figures *offhand*⟩

off·hand·ed \-'han-dəd\ *adj* : OFFHAND — **off·hand·ed·ly** *adv* — **off·hand·ed·ness** *n*

of·fice \'òf-əs, 'äf-\ *n* **1 a** : a special duty, charge, or position; *esp* : a position of authority in government ⟨hold public *office*⟩ **b** : a position of responsibility or some degree of executive authority ⟨the *office* of president⟩ **2** : a prescribed form or service of worship; *esp, cap* : DIVINE OFFICE **3** : RITE 1a, 2 **4 a** : an assigned or assumed duty, task, or role **b** : FUNCTION 2 **c** : something done for another : SERVICE **5** : a place where a business is transacted or a service is supplied ⟨ticket *office*⟩: as **a** : a place in which record keeping and clerical work are performed **b** : the directing headquarters of an enterprise or organization **c** : the place in which a professional person (as a physician) conducts business **6 a** : a major administrative unit in some governments ⟨British Foreign *Office*⟩ **b** : a subdivision of some government departments ⟨Patent *Office*⟩ [Old French, from Latin *officium* "service, duty, office", from *opus* "work" + *facere* "to do"]

office boy *n* : a boy employed for odd jobs in a business office

of·fice·hold·er \-,hōl-dər\ *n* : one holding a public office

¹of·fi·cer \'òf-ə-sər, 'äf-\ *n* **1** : POLICE OFFICER **2** : one who holds an office of trust, authority, or command **3 a** : one who holds a commission in the armed forces **b** : the master or a mate of a merchant or passenger ship

²officer *vt* **1** : to furnish with officers **2** : to command or direct as an officer

¹of·fi·cial \ə-'fish-əl\ *n* **1** : one who holds an office : OFFICER **2** : REFEREE 2, UMPIRE

²official *adj* **1** : of or relating to an office, position, or trust ⟨*official* duties⟩ **2** : holding an office ⟨an *official* referee⟩ **3 a** : AUTHORITATIVE 1 ⟨*official* statement⟩ **b** : prescribed or recognized as authorized **4** : befitting or characteristic of a person in office : FORMAL ⟨an *official* greeting⟩ — **of·fi·cial·ly** \-'fish-lē, -ə-lē\ *adv*

of·fi·cial·dom \ə-'fish-əl-dəm\ *n* : officials as a class

of·fi·cial·ism \-'fish-ə-,liz-əm\ *n* : lack of flexibility and initiative combined with excessive adherence to regulations (as in the behavior of government officials)

of·fi·ci·ant \ə-'fish-ē-ənt\ *n* : an officiating clergyman

\ə\ abut		\ng\ sing	
\ər\ further		\ō\ bone	
\a\ mat		\ò\ saw	
\ā\ take		\òi\ coin	
\ä\ cot, cart		\th\ thin	
\au̇\ out		\th\ this	
\ch\ chin		\ü\ food	
\e\ pet		\u̇\ foot	
\ē\ easy		\y\ yet	
\g\ go		\yü\ few	
\i\ tip		\yu̇\ cure	
\ī\ life		\zh\ vision	
\j\ job			

of·fi·ci·ate \ə-'fish-ē-ˌāt\ *vi* **1** : to perform a ceremony, function, or duty **2** : to act in an official capacity; *esp* : to serve as an officer or official — **of·fi·ci·a·tion** \-ˌfish-ē-'ā-shən\ *n*

of·fi·cious \ə-'fish-əs\ *adj* : offering one's services where they are neither asked nor needed : MEDDLESOME [Latin *officiosus* "obliging, helpful", from *officium* "service, office"] — **of·fi·cious·ly** *adv* — **of·fi·cious·ness** *n*

off·ing \'ȯf-ing, 'äf-\ *n* **1** : the part of the deep sea seen from the shore **2** : the near or foreseeable future ⟨sees trouble in the *offing*⟩

off·ish \'ȯf-ish\ *adj* : inclined to be aloof — **off·ish·ly** *adv* — **off·ish·ness** *n*

off–line \-'līn\ *adj* : not connected to or served by a system and especially a computer or telecommunications system; *also* : done independently of a system ⟨*off-line* computer storage⟩ — **off–line** *adv*

off·print \'ȯf-ˌprint\ *n* : a separately printed excerpt (as from a magazine)

off–road \'ȯf-'rōd\ *adj* : of, relating to, done with, or being a vehicle designed especially to operate away from public roads

¹off·set \'ȯf-ˌset\ *n* **1 a** : a short prostrate shoot arising from the base of a plant **b** : OFFSHOOT 2b **2** : a horizontal ledge on the face of a wall formed by a decrease in its thickness above **3** : an abrupt bend in an object by which one part is turned aside out of line **4** : something that serves to counterbalance or to compensate for something else **5 a** : unintentional transfer of ink (as on a freshly printed sheet) **b** : a printing process in which an inked impression is first made on a rubber-blanketed cylinder and then transferred to the paper being printed

²off·set \'ȯf-ˌset, *1 is also* ȯf-'\ *vb* -**set**; -**set·ting 1 a** : BALANCE ⟨credits *offset* debits⟩ **b** : to compensate for **2** : to form an offset in ⟨*offset* a wall⟩ SYN see COMPENSATE

off·shoot \'ȯf-ˌshüt\ *n* **1** : a branch of a main stem especially of a plant **2 a** : a lateral branch (as of a mountain range) **b** : a collateral branch, descendant, or member

¹off·shore \'ȯf-'shōr, -'shȯr\ *adv* : from the shore : at a distance from the shore

²off·shore \'ȯf-ˌ\ *adj* **1** : coming or moving away from the shore ⟨an *offshore* breeze⟩ **2 a** : situated off the shore but within waters under a country's control ⟨*offshore* fisheries⟩ **b** : distant from the shore

off·side \'ȯf-'sīd\ *adv or adj* : illegally in advance of the ball or puck

off·spring \'ȯf-ˌspring\ *n, pl* **offspring** *also* **offsprings** : the progeny of an animal or plant : YOUNG [Old English *ofspring*, from *of* "off" + *springan* "to spring"]

off·stage \'ȯf-'stāj, -ˌstāj\ *adv or adj* : off or away from the stage

off–the–record *adj* : given or made in confidence and not for publication ⟨*off-the-record* remarks⟩

off–the–wall *adj* : highly unusual : BIZARRE ⟨an *off-the-wall* sense of humor⟩

off–white \'ȯf-'hwīt, -'wīt\ *n* : a yellowish or grayish white

off year *n* **1** : a year in which no major election is held **2** : a year of diminished activity or production

oft \'ȯft\ *adv* : OFTEN ⟨an *oft* neglected factor⟩ [Old English]

of·ten \'ȯ-fən, 'ȯf-tən\ *adv* : many times : FREQUENTLY [Middle English, from *oft,* from Old English]

of·ten·times \-ˌtīmz\ *or* **oft·times** \'ȯf-ˌtīmz, 'ȯft-\ *adv* : OFTEN

ogee *also* **OG** \'ō-ˌjē\ *n* **1** : a molding with an S-shaped profile **2** : a pointed arch having on each side a reversed curve near the apex [obsolete *ogee,* a kind of arch, from French *ogive*]

¹ogle \'ō-gəl\ *vb* **ogled**; **ogling** \-gə-ling, -gling\ : to glance in a flirtatious way : eye amorously [probably

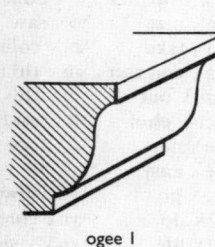

ogee 1

from Low German *oegeln,* from *oog* "eye"] — **ogler** \-gə-lər, -glər\ *n*

²ogle *n* : a flirtatious glance

ogre \'ō-gər\ *n* **1** : a hideous man-eating giant of fairy tales and folklore **2** : a dreaded person or object [French] — **ogre·ish** \'ō-gə-rish, -grish\ *adj*

¹oh *or* **O** \ō, 'ō\ *interj* **1** — used to express an emotion (as astonishment, pain, or desire) **2** — used in direct address ⟨*oh* sir, you forgot your change⟩ **3** — used to express acknowledgment or understanding of a statement or explanation ⟨*oh,* that's how you do it⟩ [Middle English *o*]

²oh \'ō\ *n* : ZERO [*o;* from the similarity of the symbol for zero (0) to the letter O]

ohm \'ōm\ *n* : the mks unit of electric resistance equal to the resistance of a circuit in which a potential difference of one volt produces a current of one ampere [Georg Simon *Ohm*, died 1854, German physicist] — **ohm·age** \'ō-mij\ *n* — **ohm·ic** \'ō-mik\ *adj*

ohm·me·ter \'ōm-ˌmēt-ər, 'ō-\ *n* : an instrument for indicating resistance in ohms directly

Ohm's law *n* : a law in electricity that states that the current in a circuit is equal to the potential difference divided by the resistance of the circuit

¹-oid \ˌȯid\ *n suffix* : something resembling a (specified) object or having a (specified) quality ⟨planet*oid*⟩ [Latin *-oīdes,* from *-oīdes,* adj. suffix]

²-oid *adj suffix* : resembling : having the form or appearance of [Latin *-oīdes,* from Greek *-oeidēs,* from *-o-* + *eidos* "appearance, form"]

¹oil \'ȯil\ *n* **1 a** : any of numerous greasy combustible and usually liquid substances from plant, animal, or mineral sources that are soluble in ether but not in water **b** : PETROLEUM **2** : a substance of oily consistency **3 a** : an oil color used by an artist **b** : a painting done in oil colors [Old French *oile,* from Latin *oleum* "olive oil", from Greek *elaion,* from *elaia* "olive"] — **oil** *adj*

²oil *vt* : to treat, furnish, or lubricate with oil

oil·cloth \'ȯil-ˌklȯth\ *n* : cloth treated with oil or paint and used for table and shelf coverings

oil color *n* : a pigment used for oil paint

oil·er \'ȯi-lər\ *n* : one that oils; *esp* : a receptacle or device for applying oil

oil field *n* : a region rich in petroleum deposits

oil gland *n* : a gland that produces an oily secretion

oil–im·mer·sion \ˌȯil-im-ˌər-zhən, -shən\ *adj* : being an objective lens of short focal distance designed to work with a drop of oil connecting the lens and the cover glass of the slide

oil of vitriol : concentrated sulfuric acid

oil of wintergreen : the methyl ester of salicylic acid used as a flavoring

oil paint *n* : paint in which a drying oil is the vehicle

oil painting *n* **1** : the act or art of painting in oil colors **2** : a picture painted in oils

oil·seed \'ȯil-ˌsēd\ *n* : a seed or crop (as flaxseed) grown largely for oil

oil shale *n* : a rock and especially shale from which oil can be recovered

oil·skin \-ˌskin\ *n* **1** : an oiled waterproof cloth **2** : an oilskin raincoat **3** *pl* : an oilskin suit of coat and trousers

oil slick *n* : a film of oil floating on water

oil·stone \'ȯil-ˌstōn\ *n* : a whetstone for use with oil

oil well *n* : a well from which petroleum is obtained

oily \'ȯi-lē\ *adj* **oil·i·er; -est 1** : of, relating to, or consisting of oil **2** : covered or impregnated with oil : GREASY **3** : excessively smooth or suave in manner : UNCTUOUS — **oil·i·ness** *n*

oint·ment \'ȯint-mənt\ *n* : a semisolid usually greasy and medicated preparation for application to the skin [Old French *oignement,* from Latin *unguentum,* from *unguere* "to anoint"]

Ojib·wa or **Ojib·way** \ō-'jib-wā\ n : a member of an Algonquian people of the region around western Lake Superior [Ojibwa *ojib-ubway,* a kind of moccasin]

¹OK or **okay** \ō-'kā\ adv or adj : all right [abbreviation of *oll korrect,* alteration of *all correct*] □ ORIGIN In the late 1830s Boston newspapers were full of abbreviations. Apparently there was simply a fashion for abbreviation, and any expression might be abbreviated. The craze went so far as to produce abbreviations of intentional misspellings. Such popular expressions as *N.G.* (no go) and *A.R.* (all right) gave way to *K.G.* (know go) and *O.W.* (oll wright). *O.K.* (oll korrect) followed quite naturally. Several of these abbreviated misspellings gained some currency, but *OK* alone became widespread and survived.

²OK or **okay** vt **OK'd** or **okayed; OK'·ing** or **okay·ing** : APPROVE, AUTHORIZE

³OK or **okay** n : APPROVAL 1, ENDORSEMENT

oka·pi \ō-'käp-ē\ n : an African mammal closely related to the giraffe but lacking the long neck [native name in Africa]

okra \'ō-krə\ n : a tall annual plant related to the hollyhocks and grown for its edible green pods which are used especially in soups and stews; *also* : these pods [of African origin]

-ol \,ȯl, ,ōl\ n suffix : chemical compound (as an alcohol or phenol) containing hydroxyl (glycer*ol*) [*alcohol*]

¹old \'ōld\ adj **1 a** : dating from the remote past : ANCIENT (*old* traditions) **b** : persisting from an earlier time : of long standing (an *old* friend) **2** cap : belonging to an early period in the development of a language (*Old* Irish) **3** : having existed for a specified period of time (a child three years *old*) **4** : of, relating to, or originating in a past era (*old* chronicles record the event) **5 a** : advanced in years or age (an *old* person) **b** : showing the characteristics of age (looked *old* at 20) **6** : FORMER (my *old* students) **7 a** : showing the effects of time or use (*old* shoes) **b** : no longer in use **8** : long familiar (the same *old* story) [Old English *eald*]
□ SYN ANCIENT, ANTIQUE, ARCHAIC: OLD may imply actual or relative length of existence (*old* castles) (*old* dogs) ANCIENT implies occurrence, existence, or use in the distant past (*ancient* history) ANTIQUE is a close synonym of ANCIENT, though it suggests something old-fashioned that has acquired value through rarity and sentimental associations (a collector of *antique* clocks) ARCHAIC implies having the characteristics of an earlier period (an *archaic* chivalry) (*methinks* is an *archaic* construction)

²old n : old or earlier time (days of *old*)

Old Church Slavonic n : the Slavic language used in the Bible translation of Cyril and Methodius and as the liturgical language of several Eastern churches — called also *Old Church Slavic*

old country n : an emigrant's country of origin

old·en \'ōl-dən\ adj : of or relating to a bygone era

Old English n **1** : the language of the English people from the time of the earliest documents in the 7th century to about 1100 **2** : English of any period before Modern English

old–fash·ioned \'ōld-'fash-ənd, 'ōl-\ adj **1** : of, relating to, or characteristic of a past era **2** : adhering to customs of a past era : CONSERVATIVE **3** : OUTMODED

Old French n : the French language from the 9th to the 16th century; *esp* : French from the 9th to the 13th century

Old Glory n : the flag of the United States

old guard n, often cap O&G : the conservative or reactionary members especially of a political party

old hand n : VETERAN 1

Old High German n : High German exemplified in documents prior to the 12th century

old·ish \'ōl-dish\ adj : somewhat old : ELDERLY

old–line \'ōl-'dlīn, -'līn\ adj **1** : having an established reputation **2** : adhering to traditional policies or practices

old maid n **1** : SPINSTER 2 **2** : a prim fussy person **3** : a simple card game in which players lay down matched pairs with the player holding the odd queen at the end being the loser — **old–maid·ish** \'ōld-'mād-ish, 'ōl-\ adj

old man n **1 a** : HUSBAND **b** : FATHER 1a **2** cap : one in authority; *esp* : COMMANDING OFFICER

old master n **1** : a superior artist or craftsman of established reputation; *esp* : a distinguished painter of the 16th, 17th, or early 18th century **2** : a work by an old master

Old Nick \'ōld-'nik, 'ōl-\ n : DEVIL 1

Old Norse n : the Germanic language of the Scandinavian peoples prior to about 1350

Old North French n : the northern dialects of Old French including especially those of Normandy and Picardy

old school n : adherents to traditional policies and practices

old–squaw \'ōld-'skwȯ, 'ōl-\ n : a common sea duck of the more northern parts of the northern hemisphere

old·ster \'ōld-stər, 'ōl-\ n : an old or elderly person

Old Style n : a style of reckoning time used before the adoption of the Gregorian calendar

Old Testament n : the first of the two chief divisions of the Bible consisting of the books dealing with the history of the Hebrews before the time of Christ — see BIBLE table

old–time \'ōld-,tīm, 'ōl-\ adj : of, relating to, or characteristic of an earlier period

old–tim·er \-'tī-mər\ n **1 a** : VETERAN 1 **b** : OLDSTER **2** : something that is old-fashioned : ANTIQUE

old wives' tale n : an often traditional belief that is not based on fact : SUPERSTITION

old–world \'ōl-'dwərld, -'wərld\ adj : of, relating to, or having the qualities of the Old World; *esp* : PICTURESQUE

Old World n : EASTERN HEMISPHERE; *esp* : Europe

ole·ag·i·nous \,ō-lē-'aj-ə-nəs\ adj **1** : resembling or having the properties of oil; *also* : containing or producing oil **2** : UNCTUOUS 2 [Middle French *oleagineux,* from Latin *oleagineus* "of an olive tree", from *olea* "olive tree", from Greek *elaia*] — **ole·ag·i·nous·ly** adv — **ole·ag·i·nous·ness** n

ole·an·der \'ō-lē-,an-dər\ n : a poisonous evergreen shrub of the dogbane family often grown for its showy fragrant white to red or purple flowers [Medieval Latin]

ole·as·ter \-,as-tər\ n : any of a genus of trees and shrubs with usually silvery foliage and fruits suggesting small olives [Latin, from *olea* "olive tree"]

ole·cra·non \,ō-lə-'krā-,nän\ n : a process of the ulna that projects behind the elbow joint [Greek *ōlekranon,* from *ōlenē* "elbow" + *kranion* "skull"]

ole·fin \'ō-lə-fən\ n : a chemical compound made up of carbon and hydrogen atoms that contains at least one double bond; *esp* : any of various long-chain synthetic polymers (as of ethylene) used especially as textile fibers [French (*gaz*) *oléfiant* "ethylene", from Latin *oleum* "oil"]

ole·ic \ō-'lē-ik\ adj **1** : relating to, derived from, or contained in oil **2** : of or relating to oleic acid [Latin *oleum* "oil"]

oleic acid n : an unsaturated fatty acid $C_{18}H_{34}O_2$ found as glycerides in natural fats and oils

oleo \'ō-lē-,ō\ n, pl **ole·os** : MARGARINE

oleo·mar·ga·rine \,ō-lē-ō-'märj-rən, -'märj-ə-rən, -'märj-ə-,rēn\ n : MARGARINE [French *oléomargarine,* from Latin *oleum* "oil" + French *margarine*]

oleo·res·in \-'rez-n\ n : a plant product (as a turpentine) containing chiefly essential oil and resin — **oleo·res·in·ous** \-'rez-n-əs, -'rez-nəs\ adj

okapi

ole·um \'ō-lē-əm\ *n, pl* **oleums** : a heavy oily fuming strongly corrosive solution of sulfur trioxide in anhydrous sulfuric acid [Latin, "oil"]

ol·fac·tion \al-'fak-shən, ōl-\ *n* : the sense of smell : the act or process of smelling

ol·fac·to·ry \al-'fak-tə-rē, ōl-, -trē\ *adj* : of or relating to the sense of smell [Latin *olfactorius,* from *olfacere* "to smell", from *olēre* "to have odor" + *facere* "to make, do"]

olfactory bulb *n* : a bulbous projection at the front of each olfactory lobe that is the place where the olfactory nerves terminate and is especially well developed in lower vertebrates (as fishes)

olfactory lobe *n* : a projection at the front of each cerebral hemisphere that is continuous with the olfactory nerve

olfactory nerve *n* : either of the 1st pair of cranial nerves that arise in the sensory membranes of the nose and conduct smell stimuli to the brain

ol·i·garch \'äl-ə-,gärk, 'ō-lə-\ *n* : a member of an oligarchy [Greek *oligarchēs,* from *oligos* "few" + *archein* "to rule"]

ol·i·gar·chy \-'gär-kē\ *n, pl* **-chies** **1** : government by a few persons **2** : a government in which a small group exercises control usually for selfish purposes; *also* : the group of persons having such power — **ol·i·gar·chic** \,äl-ə-'gär-kik\ *or* **ol·i·gar·chi·cal** \-ki-kəl\ *adj*

Oli·go·cene \'äl-i-gō-,sēn, 'ō-li-, ə-'lig-ə-\ *n* : the epoch of the Tertiary between the Eocene and Miocene; *also* : the corresponding system of rocks [Greek *oligos* "few, little"] — **Oligocene** *adj*

oli·go·chaete \-,kēt\ *n* : any of a class or order (Oligochaeta) of annelid worms lacking a specialized head and including the earthworms [derived from Greek *oligos* "few, little" + *chaitē* "long hair"] — **oligochaete** *adj*

olio \'ō-lē-,ō\ *n, pl* **oli·os** : JUMBLE, MEDLEY [Spanish *olla,* a kind of stew, literally, "pot", from Latin]

¹ol·ive \'äl-iv, -əv\ *n* **1** : an Old World evergreen tree grown for its fruit that is an important food and source of oil; *also* : this fruit **2** : a yellow to yellowish green color [Old French, from Latin *oliva,* from Greek *elaia*]

²olive *adj* **1** : of the color olive or olive green **2** : approaching olive in color or complexion

olive branch *n* **1** : a branch of the olive tree especially when used as a symbol of peace **2** : an offer or gesture of conciliation or goodwill

olive drab *n* **1** : a grayish olive color **2 a** : a wool or cotton fabric of an olive drab color **b** : a uniform of this fabric

olive green *n* : a color greener, lighter, and stronger than average olive color

olive oil *n* : a pale yellow to yellowish green oil obtained from the pulp of olives and used especially as a salad oil, in cooking, and in soaps

ol·iv·ine \'äl-i-,vēn\ *n* : a usually green mineral $(Mg,Fe)_2SiO_4$ that is a complex silicate of magnesium and iron [German *olivin,* from Latin *oliva* "olive"]

ol·la po·dri·da \,äl-ə-pə-'drēd-ə\ *n, pl* **olla podridas** \-'drēd-əz\ *also* **ollas podridas** \,äl-əz-pə-drēd-əz, ,äl-ə-pə-\ : OLIO [Spanish, a kind of stew, literally, "rotten pot"]

olym·pi·ad \ə-'lim-pē-,ad, ō-\ *n, often cap* **1** : one of the 4-year intervals between Olympic Games by which time was reckoned in ancient Greece **2** : a celebration of the modern Olympic Games [Middle French *Olympiade,* from Latin *Olympias,* from Greek, from *Olympia,* site of ancient Olympic Games]

¹Olym·pi·an \-pē-ən\ *adj* **1** : of or relating to the ancient Greek region of Olympia **2** : of, relating to, or constituting the Olympic Games

²Olympian *n* : a participant in Olympic Games

³Olympian *adj* **1** : of or relating to Mount Olympus in Thessaly **2** : befitting or characteristic of the gods of Olympus : LOFTY

⁴Olympian *n* **1** : one of the 12 major gods in Greek mythology dwelling on Mount Olympus **2** : a being of lofty detachment or superior attainment

Olym·pic \ə-'lim-pik, ō-\ *adj* : ³OLYMPIAN

Olympic Games *n pl* **1** : an ancient Panhellenic festival held at Olympia every 4th year and made up of contests in sports, music, and literature with the victor's prize being a crown of wild olive **2** : a modern revival of the Olympic Games held once every four years and made up of international athletic contests — called also *Olympics*

-o·ma \'ō-mə\ *n suffix, pl* **-o·mas** \-məz\ *or* **-o·ma·ta** \-mət-ə\ : tumor ⟨lip*oma*⟩ [Greek *-ōmat-, -ōma,* ending of nouns denoting result formed from verbs in *-oun*]

Oma·ha \'ō-mə-,hȯ, -,hä\ *n* : a member of a Siouan people of what is now northeastern Nebraska [Omaha, literally, "those going upstream or against the wind"]

oma·sum \ō-'mā-səm\ *n, pl* **-sa** \-sə\ : the division between the reticulum and the abomasum in the stomach of a ruminant [Latin, "tripe of a bullock"]

om·buds·man \'äm-,bu̇dz-mən, 'ȯm-, -bədz-; äm-'bu̇dz-, ȯm-\ *n* **1** : a government appointee who receives and investigates complaints made by individuals against public officials **2** : one that investigates and helps settle reported complaints [Swedish, literally, "representative", from Old Norse *umbothsmathr,* from *umboth* "commission" + *mathr* "man"]

ome·ga \ō-'meg-ə, -'mē-gə, -'mā-gə\ *n* **1** : the 24th and last letter of the Greek alphabet — Ω or ω **2** : END

om·elet *also* **om·elette** \'äm-lət, -ə-lət\ *n* : eggs beaten with milk or water, cooked usually without stirring until set, and folded over [French *omelette,* from Middle French *alumette,* alteration of *alumelle,* literally, "knife blade", from Latin *lamella* "small metal plate", from *lamina* "thin plate"] □ ORIGIN The word *omelet* bears little resemblance to the Latin word *lamina,* but the shape of an omelet is rather like a thin plate, which is what *lamina,* the ancestor of *omelet,* means. The Romans used *lamella,* a diminutive of *lamina,* to mean "a small metal plate". This became Middle French *alumelle,* which meant "knife blade". The word acquired the additional meaning "eggs beaten and cooked without stirring", because such a dish resembled a thin plate or blade. *Alumelle,* under the influence of the common suffix *-ette,* was altered to *alumette,* which became *omelette* in modern French.

omen \'ō-mən\ *n* : an event or phenomenon believed to be a sign or warning of some future occurrence : PORTENT [Latin *omin-, omen*]

omen·tum \ō-'ment-əm\ *n, pl* **-ta** \-ə\ *or* **-tums** : a free fold of peritoneum or one connecting or supporting abdominal structures (as the viscera) [Latin] — **omen·tal** \-'ment-l\ *adj*

omer \'ō-mər\ *n* **1** : an ancient Hebrew unit of dry capacity equal to ¹⁄₁₀ ephah (about 3.5 liters) **2** *often cap* : a 7-week period in the Jewish year between Passover and Shabuoth [Hebrew *'ōmer*]

omi·cron \'äm-ə-,krän, 'ōm-\ *n* : the 15th letter of the Greek alphabet — O or o

om·i·nous \'äm-ə-nəs\ *adj* : being or showing an omen; *esp* : foretelling evil ⟨*ominous* events leading to war⟩ — **om·i·nous·ly** *adv* — **om·i·nous·ness** *n*

omis·si·ble \ō-'mis-ə-bəl, ə-\ *adj* : that may be omitted

omis·sion \ō-'mish-ən, ə-\ *n* **1** : something neglected or left undone **2** : the act of omitting : the state of being omitted [Late Latin *omissio,* from Latin *omissus,* past participle of *omittere* "to omit"]

omit \ō-'mit, ə-\ *vt* **omit·ted; omit·ting** **1** : to leave out or leave unmentioned ⟨*omitted* their names from the list⟩ **2** : to fail to perform : leave undone : NEGLECT [Latin *omittere,* from *ob-* "toward" + *mittere* "to let go, send"]

om·ma·tid·i·um \,äm-ə-'tid-ē-əm\ *n, pl* **-ia** \-ē-ə\ : one of the elements corresponding to a small simple eye

¹olive 1

that make up the compound eye of an arthropod [New Latin, from Greek *omma* "eye"] — **om·ma·tid·i·al** \-ē-əl\ *adj*

omni- *combining form* : all : universally ⟨*omni*directional⟩ [Latin, from *omnis*]

¹**om·ni·bus** \'äm-ni-,bəs, -bəs\ *n* **1** : a usually automotive public vehicle designed to carry a comparatively large number of passengers : BUS **2** : a book containing reprints of a number of works [French, from Latin, "for all", from *omnis* "all"]

²**omnibus** *adj* : of, relating to, or providing for many things or classes at once ⟨an *omnibus* legislative bill⟩

om·ni·di·rec·tion·al \,äm-ni-də-'rek-shnəl, -dī-, -shən-l\ *adj* : receiving or sending radiations in all directions ⟨an *omnidirectional* antenna⟩

om·ni·far·i·ous \,äm-nə-'far-ē-əs, -'fer-\ *adj* : of all varieties, forms, or kinds [Late Latin *omnifarius,* from Latin *omni-* + *-farius* (as in *multifarius* "having great diversity")]

om·nip·o·tence \äm-'nip-ət-əns\ *n* : the quality or state of being omnipotent

om·nip·o·tent \-ət-ənt\ *adj* **1** *often cap* : ALMIGHTY **2** : having virtually unlimited authority or influence [Middle French, from Latin *omnipotens,* from *omni-* + *potens* "powerful, potent"] — **omnipotent** *n* — **om·nip·o·tent·ly** *adv*

om·ni·pres·ent \,äm-ni-'prez-nt\ *adj* : present in all places at all times — **om·ni·pres·ence** \-ns\ *n*

om·ni·range \'äm-ni-,rānj\ *n* : a system of radio navigation in which any bearing relative to a special radio transmitter on the ground may be chosen and flown by an airplane pilot

om·ni·scient \äm-'nish-ənt\ *adj* **1** : having infinite awareness, understanding, and insight **2** : possessed of universal or complete knowledge [derived from Medieval Latin *omniscientia* "omniscience", from Latin *omni-* + *scientia* "knowledge, science"] — **om·ni·science** \-əns\ *n,* — **om·ni·scient·ly** *adv*

om·ni·um–gath·er·um \,äm-nē-əm-'gath-ə-rəm\ *n* : a miscellaneous collection of a variety of things or persons : HODGEPODGE [Latin *omnium* "of all" (from *omnis* "all") + English *gather* + Latin *-um,* n. ending]

om·ni·vore \'äm-ni-,vōr, -,vȯr\ *n* : one that is omnivorous

om·niv·o·rous \äm-'niv-rəs, -ə-rəs\ *adj* **1** : feeding on both animal and vegetable substances **2** : avidly taking in everything as if devouring or consuming [Latin *omnivorus,* from *omni-* + *vorare* "to devour"] — **om·niv·o·rous·ly** *adv* — **om·niv·o·rous·ness** *n*

¹**on** \ȯn, 'ȯn, än, 'än\ *prep* **1 a** (1) : over and in contact with or supported by ⟨the book *on* the table⟩ ⟨stand *on* one foot⟩ (2) : in contact or side by side with ⟨a fly *on* on the wall⟩ ⟨a town *on* the river⟩ (3) : in the area of ⟨*on* the right⟩ **b** (1) : to a position over and in contact with : ONTO ⟨jumped *on* the horse⟩ (2) : into contact with ⟨put my hand *on* her shoulder⟩ **2** — used as a function word to indicate someone or something that action or feeling is directed against or toward ⟨crept up *on* them⟩ ⟨keen *on* sports⟩ **3** — used as a function word to indicate the basis or source (as of an action, opinion, or computation) ⟨know it *on* good authority⟩ ⟨ten cents *on* the dollar⟩ **4** : with respect to ⟨agreed *on* a price⟩ **5 a** : in connection, association, or activity with or with regard to ⟨*on* a committee⟩ ⟨*on* tour⟩ **b** : in a state or process of ⟨*on* fire⟩ ⟨*on* the increase⟩ **6** : during or at a specified time ⟨every hour *on* the hour⟩ ⟨cash *on* delivery⟩ **7** : through the means or agency of ⟨talking *on* the phone⟩ **8** : following in series : AFTER ⟨loss *on* loss⟩ [Old English *an, on*]

²**on** \'ȯn, 'än\ *adv* **1 a** : on a supporting surface ⟨put the plates *on*⟩ **b** : on one's person ⟨has new shoes *on*⟩ **2 a** : forward in space, time, or action : ONWARD ⟨let's go *on*⟩ ⟨went *on* home⟩ **b** : in continuance or succession ⟨and so *on*⟩ **3** : into operation or a position permitting operation ⟨turn the light *on*⟩

³**on** \'ȯn, 'än\ *adj* **1** : engaged in an activity or function (as a dramatic role) **2 a** : being in operation ⟨the radio is *on*⟩ **b** : placed so as to permit operation ⟨the switch is *on*⟩ **3** : taking place or planned to take place ⟨the game is *on*⟩ ⟨has nothing *on* for tonight⟩

-on \,än\ *n suffix* **1** : elementary particle ⟨nucle*on*⟩ **2 a** : unit : quantum ⟨phot*on*⟩ **b** : basic hereditary component ⟨oper*on*⟩ [*ion*]

on·a·ger \'än-i-jər\ *n* **1** : an Asian wild ass **2** : an ancient and medieval heavy catapult [Latin, "wild ass", from Greek *onagros,* from *onos* "ass" + *agros* "field"]

¹**once** \'wəns\ *adv* **1** : one time and no more ⟨will repeat the question *once*⟩ **2** : at any time : under any circumstances : EVER ⟨if you *once* hesitate, you are lost⟩ **3** : at some indefinite time in the past : FORMERLY ⟨*once* lived in luxury⟩ **4** : by one degree of relationship ⟨a cousin *once* removed⟩ [Middle English *ones,* from genitive of *on* "one"]

²**once** *n* : one single time : one time at least ⟨just this *once*⟩ — **at once 1** : at the same time : SIMULTANEOUSLY **2** : IMMEDIATELY

³**once** *conj* : at the moment when : as soon as ⟨*once* that's done, we can leave⟩

once–over \'wəns-,ō-vər\ *n* : a swift examination or survey

on·co·gene \'äng-kō-,jēn\ *n* : a gene having the potential to cause a normal cell to become cancerous [Greek *onkos* "mass"]

on·col·o·gy \än-'käl-ə-jē, äng-\ *n* : the study of tumors

on·com·ing \'ȯn-,kəm-ing, 'än-\ *adj* : coming on : APPROACHING ⟨*oncoming* traffic⟩ ⟨*oncoming* generations⟩

¹**one** \'wən, ,wən\ *adj* **1** : being a single unit or thing ⟨*one* person left⟩ **2 a** : being one in particular ⟨early *one* morning⟩ **b** : being notably what is indicated ⟨*one* fine person⟩ **3 a** : being the same in kind or quality ⟨both of *one* race⟩ **b** : not divided : UNITED **4** : existing or occurring as something not definitely fixed or placed ⟨will see you again *one* day⟩ **5** : being the only individual of a stated or implied kind ⟨the *one* person they wanted to see⟩ [Middle English *on,* from Old English *ān*]

²**one** *pron* **1 a** : a single member or specimen of a usually specified class or group ⟨saw *one* of my friends⟩ **b** : a person in general : SOMEBODY ⟨*one* never knows⟩ **2** — used for *I* or *we* ⟨*one* hopes to see you there⟩

³**one** \'wən\ *n* **1** : the number denoting unity; *also* : a symbol representing this — see NUMBER table **2** : the first in a set or series **3** : a single person or thing ⟨caught five big *ones*⟩

one another *pron* : EACH OTHER

one–horse *adj* **1** : drawn or operated by one horse **2** : small in scope or importance ⟨a *one-horse* town⟩

Onei·da \ō-'nīd-ə\ *n* : a member of an Iroquoian people originally of what is now central New York [Iroquois *Onĕyóde',* literally, "standing rock"]

onei·ric \ō-'nīr-ik\ *adj* : of or relating to dreams : DREAMY [Greek *oneiros* "dream"]

one·ness \'wən-nəs\ *n* **1** : the quality, state, or fact of being one (as in thought, spirit, or purpose) **2** : IDENTITY 1

oner·ous \'än-ə-rəs, 'ō-nə-\ *adj* : being difficult or burdensome [Middle French *onereus,* from Latin *onerosus,* from *oner-, onus* "burden"] — **oner·ous·ly** *adv* — **oner·ous·ness** *n*

ones digit *n* : UNITS DIGIT

one·self \wən-'self, ,wən-\ *also* **one's self** \wən-, ,wən-, ,wənz-\ *pron* **1** : a person's self : one's own self — used reflexively as object of a preposition or verb or for emphasis in various constructions **2** : one's normal, healthy, or sane condition or self

one–sid·ed \'wən-'sīd-əd\ *adj* **1** : lacking in objectivity : BIASED ⟨take a *one-sided* view of a problem⟩ **2** : decided or differing by a wide margin ⟨a *one-sided* game⟩

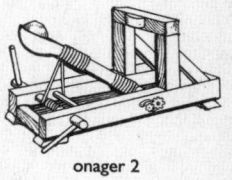

onager 2

\ə\	abut	\ng\	sing
\ər\	further	\ō\	bone
\a\	mat	\ȯ\	saw
\ā\	take	\ȯi\	coin
\ä\	cot, cart	\th\	thin
\au̇\	out	\th\	this
\ch\	chin	\ü\	food
\e\	pet	\u̇\	foot
\ē\	easy	\y\	yet
\g\	go	\yü\	few
\i\	tip	\yu̇\	cure
\ī\	life	\zh\	vision
\j\	job		

ones place *n* : UNITS PLACE

one–step \'wən-,step\ *n* : a ballroom dance marked by quick walking steps backward and forward in 2/4 time — **one–step** *vi*

one·time \'wən-,tīm\ *adj* : FORMER ⟨a *onetime* teacher⟩

one–to–one \,wən-tə-'wən, -də-\ *adj* : pairing each element of a set with one and only one element of another set

one–track *adj* : obsessed or seemingly obsessed with one thing or one idea

one–way *adj* : that moves in, allows movement in, or functions in only one direction ⟨*one-way* traffic⟩ ⟨a *one-way* ticket⟩

on·go·ing \'ȯn-,gō-ing, 'än-\ *adj* **1** : being in process **2** : making progress

on·ion \'ən-yən\ *n* : a widely grown Asian herb of the lily family with pungent edible bulbs; *also* : its bulb [Middle French *oignon*, from Latin *unio*]

on·ion·skin \-,skin\ *n* : a thin strong translucent paper of very light weight

on–line *adj or adv* : connected to, served by, or available through a system and especially a computer or telecommunications system ⟨an *on-line* database⟩; *also* : done while connected to a system ⟨*on-line* computer storage⟩

on·look·er \'ȯn-,lùk-ər, 'än-\ *n* : SPECTATOR — **on·look·ing** \-,lùk-ing\ *adj*

¹on·ly \'ōn-lē\ *adj* **1** : unquestionably best : PEERLESS ⟨the *only* dog for me⟩ **2** : alone in its class or kind : SOLE ⟨the *only* survivor⟩ [Old English *ānlīc*, from *ān* "one" + *-līc* "-ly"]

²only *adv* **1 a** : JUST, MERELY ⟨worked *only* in the morning⟩ **b** : EXCLUSIVELY, SOLELY ⟨known *only* to me⟩ **2** : at the very least ⟨it was *only* too true⟩ **3 a** : in the final outcome ⟨will *only* make you sick⟩ **b** : with nevertheless the final result being ⟨won the battles, *only* to lose the war⟩ **4 a** : as recently as ⟨*only* last week⟩ **b** : in the immediate past ⟨*only* just talked to them⟩

³only *conj* **1** : with this sole restriction ⟨you may go, *only* come back early⟩ **2** : were it not that ⟨I'd go, *only* I'm too tired⟩

on·o·mas·tics \,än-ə-'mas-tiks\ *n sing or pl* : the study of the proper names of people and places [derived from Greek *onoma* "name"]

on·o·mat·o·poe·ia \,än-ə-,mat-ə-'pē-ə, -'pē-yə\ *n* **1** : formation of words in imitation of natural sounds (as *buzz* or *hiss*) **2** : the use of words whose sound suggests the sense [Late Latin, from Greek *onomatopoiia*, from *onoma* "name" + *poiein* "to make"] — **on·o·mat·o·poe·ic** \-'pē-ik\ *or* **on·o·mat·o·po·et·ic** \-pō-'et-ik\ *adj* — **on·o·mat·o·poe·i·cal·ly** \-'pē-ə-kə-lē, -klē\ *or* **on·o·mat·o·po·et·i·cal·ly** \-pō-'et-i-kə-lē, -klē\ *adv*

On·on·da·ga \,än-ən-'dȯ-gə, ,än-ə-'dȯ-\ *n* : a member of an Iroquoian people of what is now central New York [Iroquois *Onŏtáge'*, a village of the Onondaga people]

on·rush \'ȯn-,rəsh, 'än-\ *n* **1** : a rushing forward or onward **2** : ONSET ⟨the first *onrush* of grief⟩

on·set \-,set\ *n* **1** : ATTACK 1 **2** : BEGINNING 4a

on·shore \'ȯn-,shōr, 'än-, -,shȯr\ *adj* : moving toward the shore ⟨*onshore* winds⟩ — **on·shore** \'ȯn-', 'än-'\ *adv*

on side *adv or adj* : in a position legally to play the ball or puck

on·slaught \'än-,slȯt, 'ȯn-\ *n* : an especially fierce attack [Dutch *aanslag* "act of striking"]

on·to \,ȯn-tə, ,än-; 'ȯn-tü, 'än-\ *prep* **1** : to a position or point on ⟨climbed *onto* the roof⟩ **2** : in or into awareness of

on·tog·e·ny \än-'täj-ə-nē\ *n, pl* **-nies** : the development or course of development of an individual organism — compare PHYLOGENY [Greek *ont-, ōn*, present participle of *einai* "to be"] — **on·to·ge·net·ic** \,än-tə-jə-'net-ik\ *adj* — **on·to·ge·net·i·cal·ly** \-'net-i-kə-lē, -klē\ *adv*

onus \'ō-nəs\ *n* **1 a** : something (as a duty) that is burdensome or trying **b** : an obligation (as to do something) that is disagreeable **2** : BLAME 2 [Latin]

¹on·ward \'ȯn-wərd, 'än-\ *also* **on·wards** \-wərdz\ *adv* : toward or at a point lying ahead in space or time : FORWARD ⟨kept moving *onward*⟩

²onward *adj* : directed or moving onward : FORWARD ⟨the *onward* march of time⟩

on·y·choph·o·ran \,än-i-'käf-ə-rən\ *n* : PERIPATUS [derived from Greek *onych-, onyx* "claw" + *-phoros* "-phore"] — **onychophoran** *adj*

on·yx \'än-iks\ *n* : chalcedony with straight parallel layers of different colors [Latin *onych-, onyx*, from Greek, literally, "claw, nail"]

oo- — see O-

oo·cyte \'ō-ə-,sīt\ *n* : an immature ovum

oo·dles \'üd-lz\ *n pl* : a great quantity [perhaps from ²*huddle*]

oog·a·mous \ō-'äg-ə-məs\ *adj* : reproducing by egg and sperm : HETEROGAMETIC — **oog·a·my** \-mē\ *n*

oo·gen·e·sis \,ō-ə-'jen-ə-səs\ *n, pl* **-gen·e·ses** \-,sēz\ : formation and maturation of the egg — **oo·ge·net·ic** \-jə-'net-ik\ *adj*

oo·go·ni·um \,ō-ə-'gō-nē-əm\ *n, pl* **-nia** \-nē-ə\ **1** : a female sexual organ in various algae and fungi **2** : a cell that gives rise to oocytes [derived from Greek *ōion* "egg" + *gonos* "procreation, seed"] — **oo·go·ni·al** \-nē-əl\ *adj*

ooh \'ü\ *interj* — used to express amazement, joy, or surprise [imitative]

oo·lite \'ō-ə-,līt\ *n* : a rock consisting of small round grains usually of calcium carbonate cemented together — **oo·lit·ic** \,ō-ə-'lit-ik\ *adj*

oo·mi·ak *variant of* UMIAK

oomph \'ùmf, 'ümpf\ *n* **1** : personal charm or magnetism : GLAMOUR **2** : SEX APPEAL **3** : VITALITY 2b, ENTHUSIASM

oops \'ùps, 'wùps\ *interj* — used to express mild apology, surprise, or dismay [imitative]

oo·spore \'ō-ə-,spōr, -,spȯr\ *n* : ZYGOTE; *esp* : a spore that is produced by union of a large female cell with a small male cell and that yields a sporophyte — compare ZYGOSPORE

oo·tid \'ō-ə-,tid\ *n* : an egg cell after meiosis [derived from Greek *ōion* "egg"]

¹ooze \'üz\ *n* **1** : a soft deposit (as of mud, slime, or shells) especially on the bottom of a body of water **2** : soft wet ground : MUD [Old English *wāse* "mire"]

²ooze *n* **1** : the action of oozing **2** : something that oozes [Middle English *wose* "sap, juice", from Old English *wōs*]

³ooze *vb* **1** : to pass or flow slowly through or as if through small openings ⟨sap *oozed* from the tree⟩ **2** : to move slowly or imperceptibly **3** : to give off : EXUDE ⟨*oozing* confidence⟩

oozy \'ü-zē\ *adj* **ooz·i·er; -est** **1** : containing or composed of ooze **2** : exuding moisture : SLIMY

opac·i·ty \ō-'pas-ət-ē\ *n, pl* **-ties** **1** : the quality or state of being opaque to radiant energy (as light) **2** : obscurity of meaning **3** : mental dullness **4** : an opaque spot on an otherwise or normally transparent structure (as the lens of the eye) [French *opacité* "shadiness", from Latin *opacitas*, from *opacus* "shaded, dark"]

opal \'ō-pəl\ *n* : a mineral that is a hydrated amorphous silica softer and less dense than quartz and typically with an irridescent play of colors [Latin *opalus*, from Sanskrit *upala* "stone, jewel"]

opal·es·cent \,ō-pə-'les-nt\ *adj* : having a play of colors like an opal — **opal·esce** \-'les\ *vi* — **opal·es·cence** \-'les-ns\

opal·ine \'ō-pə-,līn, -,lēn\ *adj* : resembling opal : OPALESCENT

¹opaque \ō-'pāk\ *adj* **1** : exhibiting opacity : not transmitting radiant energy (as light) **2 a** : not easily understood : OBSCURE **b** : DULL 1, STUPID, OBTUSE [Latin *opa-*

cus "shaded, dark"] — **opaque·ly** *adv* — **opaque·ness** *n*

²opaque *n* : something that is opaque

ope \'ōp\ *vb, archaic* : OPEN

¹open \'ō-pən, 'ōp-m\ *adj* **1 a** : free or far from boundaries or restrictions ⟨*open* sea⟩ ⟨*open* range⟩ **b** : permitting passage or access : not shut or shut up : not stopped or clogged ⟨an *open* door⟩ ⟨*open* books⟩ ⟨*open* pores⟩ **c** : having openings or spaces ⟨an *open* soil⟩ ⟨*open* type⟩ **2 a** : not enclosed or covered : BARE ⟨an *open* boat⟩ ⟨an *open* fire⟩ ⟨*open* wounds⟩ **b** : not protected against something : LIABLE ⟨*open* to challenge⟩ ⟨*open* to infection⟩ **c** (1) : not secret : exposed to general knowledge : PUBLIC ⟨*open* dislike⟩ (2) : candidly and often artlessly frank ⟨*open* about their plans⟩ **3 a** : free to the use, entry, or participation of all ⟨an *open* meeting⟩ ⟨*open* classes⟩ **b** : easy to enter, get through, or see ⟨*open* country⟩ ⟨an *open* woodland⟩; *also* : free from hampering restraints or controls ⟨an *open* economy⟩ ⟨*open* gambling⟩ **c** : available or ready for use or operation ⟨keep an hour *open* for our meeting⟩ ⟨the store was still *open*⟩ **4** : not snowy or stormy ⟨an *open* winter⟩ **5** : not drawn together : not folded or contracted : spread out ⟨an *open* flower⟩ ⟨*open* umbrellas⟩ **6 a** : not finally decided or settled ⟨an *open* question⟩ **b** : receptive to appeals or ideas : RESPONSIVE ⟨an *open* mind⟩ ⟨*open* to suggestion⟩ **7** : not made up of a continuous closed system of vessels ⟨the insect circulatory system is *open*⟩ **8** : not containing endpoints or boundary points ⟨an *open* interval⟩ **9** : not allowing the flow of electricity : being an incomplete electrical circuit ⟨an *open* switch⟩ [Old English] SYN *see* FRANK — **open·ly** \'ō-pən-lē\ *adv* — **open·ness** \'ō-pən-nəs\ *n*

²open *vb* **opened** \'ō-pənd, 'ōp-md\; **open·ing** \'ōp-ning, -ə-ning\ **1 a** : to change or move from a shut condition : UNFASTEN, UNCLOSE ⟨*open* a book⟩ ⟨*open* a switch⟩ ⟨the door *opened* slowly⟩ **b** : to make or become open by or as if by clearing away obstacles ⟨*open* a road blocked with snow⟩ ⟨the clouds *opened*⟩ **c** : to make an opening or openings in ⟨*open* a boil⟩ **d** : to spread out : UNFOLD ⟨an *opening* flower⟩ ⟨*open* a napkin⟩ **2** : to make or become functional ⟨*open* a new store⟩ ⟨the office *opens* early⟩ **3** : to give access ⟨the rooms *open* onto a hall⟩ **4** : to enter upon : BEGIN, START ⟨*open* fire⟩ ⟨*open* talks⟩ **5** : to speak out — **open·able** \'ōp-nə-bəl, -ə-nə-\ *adj* — **open·er** \'ōp-nər, -ə-nər\ *n*

³open *n* **1 a** : open and unobstructed space or water **b** : OUTDOORS **2** : an open contest, competition, or tournament

open–air *adj* : OUTDOOR ⟨*open-air* theaters⟩

open air *n* : space where air is unconfined; *esp* : OUT-OF-DOORS

open–and–shut \,ōp-nən-'shət, -ə-nən-\ *adj* : perfectly simple : OBVIOUS

open door *n* : a policy giving opportunity for commercial relations with a country to all nations on equal terms — **open–door** *adj*

open–end *adj* : organized or formulated to allow for contingencies ⟨an *open-end* mortgage⟩

open–eyed \,ō-pə-'nīd\ *adj* **1** : having the eyes open **2 a** : WATCHFUL **b** : DISCERNING

open–hand·ed \,ō-pən-'han-dəd\ *adj* : generous in giving — **open–hand·ed·ly** *adv* — **open–hand·ed·ness** *n*

open–heart·ed \-'härt-əd\ *adj* **1** : FRANK 1 **2** : GENEROUS 1 — **open–heart·ed·ly** *adv* — **open–heart·ed·ness** *n*

open–hearth *adj* : being or relating to a process of making steel from pig iron in a furnace that reflects heat from the roof onto the material

open house *n* : ready and usually informal hospitality or entertainment for all comers

open·ing \'ōp-ning, -ə-ning\ *n* **1** : an act or instance of making or becoming open **2** : an open place or span : HOLE **3** : something that constitutes a beginning: as **a** : a planned series of moves made at the start of a game

of chess or checkers **b** : a first performance **4 a** : OCCASION 1, CHANCE **b** : an opportunity for employment

open letter *n* : a letter of protest or appeal intended for the general public and printed in a newspaper or periodical

open–mind·ed \,ō-pən-'mīn-dəd\ *adj* : willing to listen to arguments or ideas : not prejudiced — **open–mind·ed·ly** *adv* — **open–mind·ed·ness** *n*

open·mouthed \,ō-pən-'maůthd, -'maůtht\ *adj* **1** : having the mouth wide open **2** : struck with amazement or wonder — **open·mouthed·ly** \-'maů-thəd-lē, -'maůth-tlē\ *adv* — **open·mouthed·ness** \-'maů-thəd-nəs, -'maůtht-nəs, -'maůth-nəs\ *n*

open–pol·li·nat·ed \,ō-pən-'päl-ə-,nāt-əd\ *adj* : pollinated by natural agencies without human interference

open secret *n* : something supposedly secret but in fact generally known

open sentence *n* : an equation or inequality that contains one or more unknown quantities and in itself is neither true nor false

open sesame \,ōpən-'ses-ə-mē\ *n* : something that unfailingly brings about a desired end [from *open sesame*, the magical command used by Ali Baba to open the door of the robbers' den in the story *Ali Baba and the Forty Thieves* in the *Arabian Nights' Entertainments*]

open shop *n* : an establishment that employs both members and nonmembers of a labor union

open·work \'ō-pən-,wərk\ *n* : work constructed so as to show openings through its substance — **openwork** *or* **open–worked** \,ō-pən-'wərkt\ *adj*

¹opera *pl of* OPUS

²op·era \'äp-rə, -ə-rə\ *n* **1** : a drama set to music and made up of vocal pieces with orchestral accompaniment and orchestral overtures and interludes **2** : a performance of an opera; *also* : a building where operas are performed [Italian, "work, opera", from Latin "work, pains"] — **op·er·at·ic** \,äp-ə-'rat-ik\ *adj* — **op·er·at·i·cal·ly** \-i-kə-lē, -,klē\ *adv*

op·er·a·ble \'äp-rə-bəl, -ə-rə-\ *adj* **1** : fit, possible, or desirable to use **2** : suitable for surgical treatment

opé·ra bouffe \,äp-rə-'büf, -ə-rə-\ *n* : farcical comic opera [French, from Italian *opera buffa*]

opé·ra co·mique \,äp-rə-käm-'ēk, -ə-rə-, -kō-'mēk\ *n* : COMIC OPERA [French]

opera glasses *n pl* : small low-power binoculars or field glasses for use in a theater

opera hat *n* : a collapsible top hat consisting usually of a dull silky fabric stretched over a steel frame

op·er·ate \'äp-,rāt, -ə-,rāt\ *vb* **1** : to perform or cause to perform an appointed function ⟨learn to *operate* a car safely⟩ **2** : to produce an effect ⟨a drug that *operates* quickly⟩ **3** : to carry on the activities of ⟨*operate* a farm⟩; *esp* : MANAGE ⟨*operate* a business⟩ **4** : to perform surgery ⟨*operate* on a tumor⟩ [Latin *operari* "to work", from *oper-*, *opus* "work"]

operating system *n* : a program or series of programs that controls the operation of a computer and directs the processing of the user's programs

op·er·a·tion \,äp-ə-'rā-shən\ *n* **1** : a doing of a practical work **2** : the quality or state of being functional or operative **3** : a surgical procedure carried out on the living body **4** : a process (as addition or multiplication) of deriving one mathematical expression from others according to a rule **5 a** : a usually military action, mission, or maneuver including its planning and execution **b** *pl* : the office of an airfield which controls flying from the field — **op·er·a·tion·al** \-shnəl, -shən-l\ *adj* — **op·er·a·tion·al·ly** \-ē-\ *adv*

¹op·er·a·tive \'äp-rət-iv, -ə-rət-; 'äp-ə-,rāt-\ *adj* **1** : producing an appropriate or intended effect **2** : exerting force or influence : OPERATING ⟨an *operative* motive⟩ **3 a** : having to do with physical operations ⟨*operative* costs⟩ **b** : engaged in work ⟨an *operative* craftsman⟩ **4** :

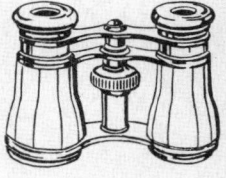

opera glasses

\ə\ abut	\ng\ sing
\ər\ further	\ō\ bone
\a\ mat	\ȯ\ saw
\ā\ take	\ȯi\ coin
\ä\ cot, cart	\th\ thin
\aů\ out	\th\ this
\ch\ chin	\ü\ food
\e\ pet	\ů\ foot
\ē\ easy	\y\ yet
\g\ go	\yü\ few
\i\ tip	\yů\ cure
\ī\ life	\zh\ vision
\j\ job	

opossum

based on or consisting of operation ⟨*operative* dentistry⟩ — **op·er·a·tive·ly** *adv* — **op·er·a·tive·ness** *n*

²**operative** *n* : OPERATOR: as **a** : ARTISAN, MECHANIC **b** (1) : a secret agent (2) : DETECTIVE

op·er·a·tor \'äp-ˌrāt-ər, -ə-ˌrāt-\ *n* **1** : one that operates: as **a** : one that operates a machine or device (telephone *operator*) **b** : one that operates a business **c** : one that deals in stocks or commodities **2** : a shrewd person who knows how to get around restrictions or difficulties **3** : a part of a chromosome that starts the formation of messenger RNA by one or more nearby structural genes and is itself subject to inhibition by a genetic repressor — called also *operator gene;* compare OPERON

oper·cu·lum \ō-'pər-kyə-ləm\ *n, pl* **-la** \-lə\ *also* **-lums** **1** : a lid or covering flap (as of a moss capsule) **2** : a body part that suggests a lid: as **a** : a plate on the foot of a gastropod mollusk that closes the shell **b** : the covering of the gills of a fish [Latin, "cover", from *operire* "to shut, cover"] — **oper·cu·lar** \-lər\ *adj* — **oper·cu·late** \-lət\ *adj*

op·er·et·ta \ˌäp-ə-'ret-ə\ *n* : a usually romantic comic opera that includes songs and dancing [Italian, from *opera* "opera"] — **op·er·et·tist** \-'ret-əst\ *n*

op·er·on \'äp-ə-ˌrän\ *n* : the combination of an operator and the structural genes it regulates [*operator* + *-on*]

ophid·i·an \ō-'fid-ē-ən\ *adj* : of, relating to, or resembling snakes [derived from Greek *ophis* "snake"] — **ophidian** *n*

oph·thal·mia \äf-'thal-mē-ə, äp-\ *n* : inflammation of the conjunctiva or eyeball [Late Latin, from Greek, from *ophthalmos* "eye"]

oph·thal·mic \-mik\ *adj* : of, relating to, or situated near the eye : OCULAR

oph·thal·mol·o·gist \ˌäf-thə-'mäl-ə-jəst, äp-, -thəl-, -ˌthal-\ *n* : a physician specializing in ophthalmology — compare OPTICIAN, OPTOMETRIST

oph·thal·mol·o·gy \-jē\ *n* : a branch of medical science dealing with the structure, functions, and diseases of the eye — **oph·thal·mo·log·i·cal·ly** \ˌäf-thə-mə-'läj-i-kə-lē, äp-, -thəl-, -ˌthal-, -klē\ *adv*

oph·thal·mo·scope \äf-'thal-mə-ˌskōp, äp-\ *n* : an instrument for use in viewing the interior of the eye and especially the retina

-opia \'ō-pē-ə\ *n combining form* : condition of having (such) vision ⟨hyper*opia*⟩ [Greek *ōps* "eye"]

¹**opi·ate** \'ō-pē-ət, -ˌāt\ *adj* **1** : containing or mixed with opium **2 a** : inducing sleep : NARCOTIC **b** : causing dullness or inaction

²**opiate** *n* **1** : a preparation or derivative of opium; *also* : NARCOTIC 1 **2** : something that induces rest or inaction or quiets uneasiness

opine \ō-'pīn\ *vb* **1** : to state as an opinion **2** : to express opinions [Middle French *opiner,* from Latin *opinari* "to have an opinion"]

opin·ion \ə-'pin-yən\ *n* **1** : a judgment about a person or thing ⟨has a high *opinion* of the doctor⟩ **2** : a belief stronger than an impression but less strong than positive knowledge **3** : a formal statement by an expert after careful study [Middle French, from Latin *opinio*] □ SYN OPINION, BELIEF, CONVICTION mean a judgment one holds as true. OPINION implies a conclusion still open to dispute ⟨differing *opinions* on the safety of nuclear power⟩ BELIEF implies deliberate acceptance and intellectual assent ⟨a basic *belief* in a supreme being⟩ CONVICTION applies to a firm, unshakable belief ⟨a *conviction* that all life is sacred⟩

opin·ion·at·ed \-yə-ˌnāt-əd\ *adj* : adhering unduly to one's own opinions or preconceived notions — **opin·ion·at·ed·ly** *adv* — **opin·ion·at·ed·ness** *n*

opin·ion·ative \-ˌnāt-iv\ *adj* **1** : of, relating to, or consisting of opinion **2** : OPINIONATED

opi·um \'ō-pē-əm\ *n* **1** : a bitter brownish addictive narcotic drug consisting of the dried juice from the unripe seed capsules of the opium poppy **2** : something having an effect like that of opium [Latin, from Greek *opion,* from *opos* "sap"]

opium poppy *n* : an annual Eurasian poppy grown since antiquity for opium, for its edible oily seeds, and for its showy flowers

opos·sum \ə-'päs-əm, 'päs-əm\ *n, pl* **-sums** *also* **-sum** : any of various American marsupials; *esp* : a common largely nocturnal and arboreal mammal of the eastern United States [of American Indian origin]

¹**op·po·nent** \ə-'pō-nənt\ *n* **1** : a person or thing that opposes another person or thing **2** : a muscle that counteracts and resists the action of another [Latin *opponens,* present participle of *opponere* "to oppose"] □ SYN ANTAGONIST, ADVERSARY: OPPONENT implies a position on the other side as in a debate, election, or conflict; ANTAGONIST implies sharper opposition in a struggle for supremacy; ADVERSARY suggests active hostility.

²**opponent** *adj* **1** : ANTAGONISTIC **2** : OPPOSITE 1

op·por·tune \ˌäp-ər-'tün, -'tyün\ *adj* : SUITABLE, TIMELY ⟨an *opportune* moment to act⟩ [Middle French *opportun,* from Latin *opportunus,* from *ob* "toward" + *portus* "port, harbor"] — **op·por·tune·ly** *adv* — **op·por·tune·ness** \-'tün-nəs, -'tyün-\ *n*

op·por·tun·ism \-'tü-ˌniz-əm, -'tyü-\ *n* : the art, policy, or practice of taking advantage of opportunities or circumstances especially with little regard for principles or ultimate consequences — **op·por·tun·ist** \-nəst\ *n or adj* — **op·por·tu·nis·tic** \-tü-'nis-tik, -tyü-\ *adj*

op·por·tu·ni·ty \ˌäp-ər-'tü-nət-ē, -'tyü-\ *n, pl* **-ties** **1** : a favorable juncture of circumstances, time, and place **2** : a good chance for advancement or progress

op·pos·able \ə-'pō-zə-bəl\ *adj* **1** : capable of being resisted **2** : capable of being placed opposite something else ⟨the thumb is *opposable* to the forefinger⟩ — **op·pos·abil·i·ty** \ə-ˌpō-zə-'bil-ət-ē\ *n*

op·pose \ə-'pōz\ *vt* **1** : to place over against something for resistance, counterbalance, or contrast **2** : to offer resistance to [French *opposer,* from Latin *opponere,* from *ob-* "against" + *ponere* "to put, place"] — **op·pos·er** *n* □ SYN RESIST, WITHSTAND: OPPOSE may apply to an act or attitude ranging from mild objection to bitter hostility or warfare; RESIST implies a recognition of a hostile or threatening force and a positive effort to counteract it ⟨*resist* temptation⟩ WITHSTAND usually suggests a successful resistance.

¹**op·po·site** \'äp-ə-zət, 'äp-sət\ *adj* **1 a** : set over against something that is at the other end or side ⟨*opposite* ends of a diameter⟩ **b** : attached to a stem or axis in exactly opposite pairs ⟨*opposite* leaves⟩ — compare ALTERNATE **2 a** : occupying an opposing and often hostile position ⟨*opposite* sides of the question⟩ **b** : as different as possible : CONTRADICTORY ⟨*opposite* meanings⟩ **3** : contrarily turned or moving ⟨go in *opposite* directions⟩ **4** : being the other of a matching or contrasting pair ⟨a member of the *opposite* sex⟩ [Middle French, from Latin *oppositus,* past participle of *opponere* "to oppose"] SYN see CONTRARY — **op·po·site·ly** *adv* — **op·po·site·ness** *n*

²**opposite** *n* **1** : something that is opposed or contrary **2** : ANTONYM **3** : ADDITIVE INVERSE; *esp* : the additive inverse of a real number

³**opposite** *adv* : on or to an opposite side

⁴**opposite** *prep* : across from and usually facing

op·po·si·tion \ˌäp-ə-'zish-ən\ *n* **1** : a setting opposite or being set opposite; *also* : a configuration in which the difference in celestial longitude of two heavenly bodies is 180° **2** : resistant or contrary action or condition ⟨offer *opposition* to a plan⟩ ⟨the *opposition* of two forces⟩ **3 a** : something that opposes; *esp* : a body of persons opposing something **b** *often cap* : a political party opposing and prepared to replace the party in power — **op·po·si·tion·al** \-'zish-nəl, -ən-l\ *adj*

op·press \ə-'pres\ *vt* **1** : to crush or burden by harsh rule ⟨a country *oppressed* by a dictator's rule⟩ **2** : to burden in spirit as if with weight ⟨*oppressed* by debts⟩ [Middle French *oppresser*, from Latin *oppressus*, past participle of *opprimere* "to oppress", from *ob-* "against" + *premere* "to press"] **syn** see **depress** — **op·pres·sor** \-'pres-ər\ *n*

op·pres·sion \ə-'presh-ən\ *n* **1 a** : unjust or cruel exercise of authority or power **b** : something that oppresses cruelly or unjustly **2** : a sense of being weighed down in body or mind : **depression**

op·pres·sive \ə-'pres-iv\ *adj* **1** : unreasonably burdensome or severe ⟨*oppressive* laws⟩ **2** : **tyrannical** ⟨*oppressive* rulers⟩ **3** : overpowering or depressing to the spirit or senses ⟨*oppressive* heat⟩ — **op·pres·sive·ly** *adv* — **op·pres·sive·ness** *n*

op·pro·bri·ous \ə-'prō-brē-əs\ *adj* : expressing contemptuous distaste and usually reproach ⟨*opprobrious* language⟩ — **op·pro·bri·ous·ly** *adv* — **op·pro·bri·ous·ness** *n*

op·pro·bri·um \-brē-əm\ *n* **1** : public disgrace or bad reputation that follows from conduct considered grossly wrong or vicious **2** : very strong disapproval ⟨a term of *opprobrium*⟩ [Latin, from *opprobrare* "to reproach", from *ob* "in the way of" + *probrum* "reproach"]

op·so·nin \'äp-sə-nən\ *n* : a constituent of blood serum that makes foreign cells more susceptible to the action of the phagocytes [Latin *opsonium* "relish", from Greek *opsōnion* "victuals", from *opsōnein* "to purchase victuals"] — **op·son·ic** \äp-'sän-ik\ *adj*

-op·sy \,äp-sē, əp-\ *n combining form, pl* **-opsies** : examination ⟨necr*opsy*⟩ [Greek *opsis* "appearance"]

opt \'äpt\ *vi* : to make a choice : **decide** [French *opter*, from Latin *optare*]

op·tic \'äp-tik\ *adj* : of or relating to vision or the eye [Middle French *optique*, from Medieval Latin *opticus*, from Greek *optikos*, from *opsesthai* "to be going to see"]

op·ti·cal \'äp-ti-kəl\ *adj* **1** : relating to optics **2** : **optic** **3** : of, relating to, or using light ⟨an *optical* telescope⟩ — **op·ti·cal·ly** \-kə-lē, -klē\ *adv*

optical disk *n* : a disk with a plastic coating on which information (as music or visual images) is recorded digitally (as in the form of tiny pits) and which is read by using a laser

optical illusion *n* : **illusion 1c**

op·ti·cian \äp-'tish-ən\ *n* **1** : a maker of or dealer in optical items and instruments **2** : one that grinds eyeglass lenses to prescription and sells glasses — compare **ophthalmologist**, **optometrist**

optic lobe *n* : either of two prominences of the midbrain concerned with vision

optic nerve *n* : either of the 2d pair of cranial nerves that arise from the bottom part of the diencephalon, supply the eye, and conduct visual nerve impulses to the brain

op·tics \'äp-tiks\ *n* : a science that deals with the nature and properties of light and the effects that it undergoes and produces

op·ti·mal \'äp-tə-məl\ *adj* : most desirable or satisfactory : **optimum** — **op·ti·mal·ly** \-mə-lē\ *adv*

op·ti·mism \'äp-tə-,miz-əm\ *n* **1** : a doctrine that this world is the best possible world **2** : an inclination to put the most favorable construction upon actions and events or to anticipate the best possible outcome [French *optimisme*, from Latin *optimus* "best"] — **op·ti·mist** \-məst\ *n or adj* — **op·ti·mis·tic** \,äp-tə-'mis-tik\ *or* **op·ti·mis·ti·cal** \-ti-kəl\ *adj* — **op·ti·mis·ti·cal·ly** \-ti-kə-lē, -klē\ *adv*

op·ti·mum \'äp-tə-məm\ *n, pl* **-ma** \-mə\ *also* **-mums** **1** : the amount or degree of something that is most favorable to some end **2** : greatest degree attained under implied or specified conditions [Latin, from *optimus* "best"] — **optimum** *adj*

op·tion \'äp-shən\ *n* **1 a** : the power or right to choose **b** : a right to buy or sell something at a specified price during a specified period **c** : a right of an insured person to choose the form in which payments due him or her are to be made **2** : something offered for choice [French, from Latin *optio*] **syn** see **choice**

op·tion·al \'äp-shnəl, -shən-l\ *adj* : permitting a choice : not compulsory — **op·tion·al·ly** \-ē\ *adv*

op·tom·e·trist \äp-'täm-ə-trəst\ *n* : a specialist in optometry — compare **optician**, **ophthalmologist**

op·tom·e·try \-trē\ *n* : the art or profession of examining the eye for defects of vision and prescribing correctional glasses or exercises but not drugs or surgery [derived from Greek *opsesthai* "to be going to see"] — **op·to·met·ric** \,äp-tə-'me-trik\ *adj*

op·u·lence \'äp-yə-ləns\ *n* **1** : **wealth 1**, **riches** **2** : **abundance**, **profusion**

op·u·lent \-lənt\ *adj* : marked by opulence: as **a** : **wealthy 1** **b** : amply provided or fashioned ⟨living in *opulent* comfort⟩ [Latin *opulentus*, from *ops* "power, wealth, help"] — **op·u·lent·ly** *adv*

opun·tia \ō-'pən-chə, -chē-ə\ *n* : **prickly pear** [Latin, a kind of plant, derived from *Opus*, ancient city in Greece]

opus \'ō-pəs\ *n, pl* **opera** \'ō-pə-rə, 'äp-ə-\ *also* **opus·es** \'ō-pə-səz\ : **work 6**; *esp* : a musical composition or set of compositions [Latin, "work"]

¹**or** \ər, ȯr, ,ȯr\ *conj* — used as a function word to indicate an alternative ⟨coffee *or* tea⟩ ⟨sink *or* swim⟩ [Middle English *other, or*, from Old English *oththe*]

²**or** *prep, archaic* : **before** [Old Norse *ār*, adv., "early, before"]

³**or** *conj, archaic* : **before**

⁴**or** \'ȯr\ *n* : the heraldic color gold or yellow [Middle French, "gold", from Latin *aurum*]

-or \ər, ,ȯr, 'ȯr\ *n suffix* : one that does a (specified) thing ⟨elevat*or*⟩ [Latin]

or·a·cle \'ȯr-ə-kəl, 'är-\ *n* **1 a** : a person (as a priestess of ancient Greece) through whom a deity is held to speak **b** : a shrine in which a deity so reveals hidden knowledge or the divine purpose **c** : an answer or revelation given by an oracle **2 a** : a person giving wise or authoritative decisions or opinions **b** : an authoritative or wise expression or answer [Middle French, from Latin *oraculum*, from *orare* "to speak"]

orac·u·lar \ȯ-'rak-yə-lər, ə-\ *adj* **1** : of, relating to, or being an oracle **2** : resembling an oracle in wisdom, solemnity, or obscurity — **orac·u·lar·i·ty** \-,rak-yə-'lar-ət-ē\ *n* — **orac·u·lar·ly** \-'rak-yə-lər-lē\ *adv*

oral \'ōr-əl, 'ȯr-, 'är-\ *adj* **1 a** : uttered by the mouth or in words : **spoken** ⟨an *oral* agreement⟩ **b** : using speech or the lips ⟨*oral* reading⟩ **2** : of, relating to, given through, or situated near the mouth ⟨*oral* hygiene⟩ ⟨the *oral* surface of a starfish⟩ [Latin *or-, os* "mouth"] — **oral·ly** \-ə-lē\ *adv* □ **syn verbal: oral** applies to what is spoken rather than written ⟨an *oral* report⟩ **verbal** applies to words whether oral or written and stresses the use of words in contrast to other forms of communication or expression ⟨*verbal* communication was supplemented by signs and gestures⟩

or·ange \'ȯr-inj, 'är-, -ənj\ *n* **1 a** : a roundish citrus fruit with a reddish yellow rind and a sweet edible pulp **b** : any of various rather small evergreen citrus trees that bear oranges **2** : a color between red and yellow [Middle French, from Provençal *auranja*, from Arabic *nāranj*, from Persian *nārang*, from Sanskrit *nāraṅga*, of Dravidian origin] — **orange** *adj*

or·ange·ade \,ȯr-in-'jād, ,är-, -ən-\ *n* : a drink made of orange juice, sugar, and water

orange hawkweed *n* : a European plant of the daisy family that has bright orange-red flower heads and is a weed in northeastern North America — called also *Indian paintbrush*

Or·ange·man \'ȯr-inj-mən, 'är-\ *n* **1** : a member of a secret society organized in the north of Ireland in

\ə\ abut	\ng\ sing
\ər\ **further**	\ō\ bone
\a\ mat	\ȯ\ saw
\ā\ take	\ȯi\ coin
\ä\ cot, cart	\th\ thin
\au̇\ out	\th\ **this**
\ch\ chin	\ü\ food
\e\ pet	\u̇\ foot
\ē\ easy	\y\ yet
\g\ go	\yü\ few
\i\ tip	\yu̇\ cure
\ī\ life	\zh\ vision
\j\ job	

orangutan

1795 to defend the British sovereign and to support the Protestant religion **2** : a Protestant Irishman especially of Ulster [William III of England, prince of *Orange*]

or·ange·ry \'òr-inj-rē, 'är-, -ənj-, -ə-rē\ *n, pl* **-ries** : a protected place (as a greenhouse) for raising oranges in cool climates

or·ange·wood \-,wùd\ *n* : the wood of the orange tree used especially in turnery and carving

orang·u·tan *or* **orang·ou·tan** \ə-'rang-ə-,tang, -,tan\ *n* : a largely plant-eating and tree-dwelling anthropoid ape of Borneo and Sumatra about two thirds as large as the gorilla [Malay *orang hutan*, literally, "man of the forest"]

orate \ò-'rāt\ *vi* : to speak in an elevated and often pompous manner [back-formation from *oration*]

ora·tion \ə-'rā-shən, ò-\ *n* : an elaborate discourse delivered in a formal and dignified manner [Latin *oratio*, from *orare* "to speak, pray"]

or·a·tor \'òr-ət-ər, 'är-\ *n* **1** : one that delivers an oration **2** : one noted for skill and power in public speaking

Or·a·to·ri·an \,òr-ə-'tōr-ē-ən, 'är-, -'tòr-\ *n* : a member of the Congregation of the Oratory of St. Philip Neri founded in Rome in 1575 and comprising independent communities of secular priests under obedience but without vows — **Oratorian** *adj*

or·a·tor·i·cal \,òr-ə-'tòr-i-kəl, 'är-ə-'tär-\ *adj* : of, relating to, or characteristic of an orator or oratory — **or·a·tor·i·cal·ly** \-kə-lē, -klē\ *adv*

or·a·to·rio \,òr-ə-'tōr-ē-,ō, 'är-, -'tòr-\ *n, pl* **-ri·os** : a choral work usually on a scriptural subject consisting chiefly of recitatives, arias, and choruses without action or scenery [Italian, from the *Oratorio* di San Filippo Neri (Oratory of Saint Philip Neri) in Rome]

¹or·a·to·ry \'òr-ə-,tōr-ē, 'är-, -,tòr-\ *n, pl* **-ries** : a place of prayer; *esp* : a private or institutional chapel [Late Latin *oratorium*, from Latin *orare* "to speak, pray"]

²oratory *n* **1** : the art of speaking in public effectively **2** : public speaking that uses oratory [Latin *oratoria*, from *oratorius* "oratorical", from *orare* "to speak, pray"]

¹orb \'òrb\ *n* : a spherical body: as **a** : a heavenly body (as a planet) **b** : EYE 1a **c** : a sphere surmounted by a cross symbolizing kingly power and justice [Middle French *orbe*, from Latin *orbis* "circle, disk, orbit"]

²orb *vt* **1** : to form into a disk or circle **2** *archaic* : ENCIRCLE 1, ENCLOSE

or·bic·u·lar \òr-'bik-yə-lər\ *adj* : SPHERICAL, CIRCULAR [Late Latin *orbicularis*, derived from Latin *orbis* "circle, disk"] — **or·bic·u·lar·i·ty** \-,bik-yə-'lar-ət-ē\ *n* — **or·bic·u·lar·ly** \-'bik-yə-lər-lē\ *adv*

¹or·bit \'òr-bət\ *n* **1** : the bony socket of the eye **2** : a path described by one body in its revolution about another (the earth's *orbit* about the sun) **3** : range or sphere of activity or influence [Latin *orbita* "wheel track, orbit"] — **or·bit·al** \-l\ *adj*

²orbit *vb* **1** : to revolve in an orbit around : CIRCLE **2** : to send up and make revolve in an orbit (*orbit* a satellite) **3** : to travel in circles — **or·bit·er** *n*

orb weaver *n* : any of a group of spiders that spin a large web with a spiral thread suspended on radial threads diverging from the center of the web

or·chard \'òr-chərd\ *n* : a planting of fruit trees or nut trees; *also* : the trees of such a planting [Old English *ortgeard*, from Latin *hortus* "garden" + Old English *geard* "yard"] — **or·chard·ist** \-əst\ *n* — **or·chard·man** \-mən, -,man\ *n*

or·ches·tra \'òr-kə-strə, -,kes-trə\ *n* **1** : a group of instrumentalists including especially string players organized to perform ensemble music **2** : a front part of a theater: as **a** : the space in front of the stage in a modern theater that is used by an orchestra **b** : the forward section of seats on the main floor of a theater [Latin, "space occupied by the chorus in a Greek theater", from Greek *orchēstra*, from *orcheisthai* "to dance"]

or·ches·tral \òr-'kes-trəl\ *adj* **1** : of, relating to, or composed for an orchestra **2** : suggestive of an orchestra or its musical qualities — **or·ches·tral·ly** \-trə-lē\ *adv*

or·ches·trate \'òr-kə-,strāt\ *vt* **1** : to compose or arrange (music) for an orchestra; *also* : to provide (as a ballet) with such music **2** : to organize and manage skillfully (*orchestrate* a political campaign) — **or·ches·tra·tion** \,òr-kə-'strā-shən\ *n* — **or·ches·tra·tor** *also* **or·ches·trat·er** \-,strāt-ər\ *n*

or·chid \'òr-kəd\ *n* **1** : any of a large family of perennial plants that have usually showy 3-petaled flowers with the middle petal enlarged into a lip and differing from the others in shape and color; *also* : this flower **2** : a light purple [derived from Latin *orchis*]

or·chis \'òr-kəs\ *n* : ORCHID; *esp* : a woodland plant having fleshy roots and flowers with the lip spurred [Latin, "orchid", from Greek, "testicle, orchid"]

or·dain \òr-'dān\ *vb* **1** : to admit to the Christian ministry or priesthood by the ritual of a church : confer holy orders upon **2 a** : to establish or order by appointment, decree, or law **b** : PREDESTINE, DESTINE [Old French *ordener*, from Latin *ordinare* "to put in order, appoint", from *ordin-, ordo* "order"] — **or·dain·er** *n* — **or·dain·ment** \-'dān-mənt\ *n*

or·deal \òr-'dēl\ *n* **1** : a primitive method of deciding guilt or innocence by submitting the accused to dangerous or painful tests believed to be under supernatural control (*ordeal* by fire) **2** : a severe trial or experience [Old English *ordāl*]

¹or·der \'òrd-ər\ *n* **1 a** : a group of people formally united in some way (as by living under the same religious rules, by having won the same distinction, or by loyalty to common interests and obligations) (an *order* of monks) (an *order* of knighthood) **b** : the badge or insignia of such an order **c** : a military decoration **2 a** : any of the several grades of the Christian ministry **b** *pl* : Christian ordination **3 a** : a rank, class, or special group in a community or society **b** : a class grouped according to quality, value, or natural characteristics; *esp* : a category of taxonomic classification ranking above the family and below the class **4 a** : RANK, KIND (an artist of the first *order*) (emergencies of this *order*) **b** : the arrangement or sequence of objects in position or of events in time **c** : the number of columns or rows in a matrix with the same number of rows and columns **d** : the prevailing mode or arrangement of things (the old *order*) **e** : regular or harmonious arrangement (the *order* of nature); *also* : a condition characterized by such an arrangement **5 a** : a customary or prescribed mode of procedure (as in debate or religious ritual) **b** : the rule of law or proper authority (*order* was restored) **c** : a specific rule, regulation, or authoritative direction **6 a** : a style of building **b** : an architectural column with its related structures forming the unit of a style **7** : proper condition (out of *order*) **8 a** : a written direction to pay money to someone **b** : a commission to purchase, sell, or supply goods or to perform work **c** : goods or items bought or sold [Middle French *ordre*, from Latin *ordo* "arrangement, group, class, order"] — **in order to** : for the purpose of

²order *vb* **1** : to put in or bring about order **2 a** : to direct or command with an order (*order* them to stop) **b** : to give an order for (*order* breakfast) **3** : to place an order — **or·der·er** *n*

or·dered \'òrd-ərd\ *adj* : having elements any two of which are related in such a way that one is greater than or less than the other (the set of real numbers is *ordered*)

ordered pair *n* : a set with two elements in which one element is identified as the first and the other as the second

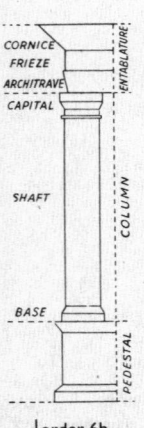

CORNICE
FRIEZE
ARCHITRAVE
ENTABLATURE
CAPITAL
SHAFT
COLUMN
BASE
PEDESTAL

¹order 6b

¹or·der·ly \'ord-ər-lē\ *adj* **I a** : arranged or disposed according to some order or pattern : REGULAR **b** : not marked by disorder : TIDY; *also* : METHODICAL **c** : governed by law or system ⟨an *orderly* universe⟩ **2** : well behaved : PEACEFUL ⟨an *orderly* crowd⟩ — **or·der·li·ness** *n* — **orderly** *adv*

²orderly *n, pl* **-lies** **I** : a soldier who attends a superior officer to carry messages and perform services **2** : a hospital attendant who does general work

¹or·di·nal \'ord-nəl, -n-əl\ *n* **I** *cap* : a collection of forms to be used in ordination **2** : ORDINAL NUMBER [derived from Latin *ordin-, ordo* "order"]

²ordinal *adj* : of a specified order or rank (as sixth) in a series

ordinal number *n* : a number designating the place (as first, second, third) occupied by an item in an ordered sequence — see NUMBER table; compare CARDINAL NUMBER

or·di·nance \'ord-nəns, 'ord-n-əns\ *n* **I** : an authoritative decree or direction : ORDER **2** : a law enacted by governmental authority; *esp* : a municipal regulation **3** : a prescribed usage, practice, or ceremony [Middle French *ordenance*, literally, "art of arranging", from Medieval Latin *ordinantia*, from Latin *ordinare* "to put in order"] SYN see LAW

or·di·nand \,ord-n-'and\ *n* : a person being ordained especially into holy orders [derived from Late Latin *ordinare* "to ordain", from Latin, "to put in order"]

or·di·nari·ly \,ord-n-'er-ə-lē\ *adv* **I** : USUALLY ⟨would *ordinarily* be here by now⟩ **2** : in an ordinary or commonplace way or manner

¹or·di·nary \'ord-n-,er-ē\ *n, pl* **-nar·ies** **I** : a prelate (as the bishop of a diocese) exercising jurisdiction over a territory or group by virtue of the office **2** *often cap* : the parts of the Mass that do not vary from day to day **3** : regular or customary condition or course of things ⟨nothing out of the *ordinary*⟩ **4 a** *British* : a meal served at a fixed price **b** *chiefly British* : a tavern or eating house serving regular meals [Medieval Latin *ordinarius*, from Latin *ordinarius*, adj., "ordinary"]

²ordinary *adj* **I** : of a kind to be expected : ROUTINE, NORMAL **2 a** : of common quality, rank, or ability ⟨*ordinary* people⟩ **b** : POOR 4, INFERIOR [Latin *ordinarius*, from *ordin-, ordo* "order"] — **or·di·nar·i·ness** \'ord-n-,er-ē-nəs\ *n*

ordinary seaman *n* : a seaman with less experience than an able seaman

or·di·nate \'ord-nət, -n-ət, -n-,āt\ *n* : the vertical coordinate of a point in a plane Cartesian coordinate system obtained by measuring parallel to the y-axis — called also *y-coordinate*; compare ABSCISSA [New Latin *linea ordinate applicata*, literally, "line applied in an orderly manner"]

or·di·na·tion \,ord-n-'ā-shən\ *n* : the act of ordaining : the state of being ordained

ord·nance \'ord-nəns\ *n* **I a** : military supplies including weapons, ammunition, vehicles, and equipment **b** : a service of the army in charge of ordnance **2** : ARTILLERY 1, CANNON [Middle French *ordenance*, literally, "act of arranging"]

Or·do·vi·cian \,ord-ə-'vish-ən\ *n* : the period of the Paleozoic era between the Cambrian and Silurian; *also* : the corresponding system of rocks — see GEOLOGIC TIME table [Latin *Ordovices*, ancient people in northern Wales] — **Ordovician** *adj*

or·dure \'or-jər\ *n* **I** : EXCREMENT **2** : something morally degrading or depraving [Middle French, from *ord* "filthy", from Latin *horridus* "horrid"]

ore \'ōr, 'or\ *n* : a mineral containing a constituent for which it is mined and worked ⟨get iron from its *ore*⟩ [Old English *ār* "brass, copper, ore"]

öre \'ər-ə\ *n, pl* **öre** **I** : a monetary unit equal to ¹/₁₀₀ krona or ¹/₁₀₀ krone **2** : a coin representing one öre [Swedish *öre* and Danish and Norwegian *øre*]

ore·ad \'ōr-ē-,ad, 'or-, -ē-əd\ *n* : any of the nymphs of mountains and hills [Latin *oread-, oreas,* from Greek *oreiad-, oreias,* derived from *oros* "mountain"]

oreg·a·no \ə-'reg-ə-,nō\ *n, pl* **-nos** : a bushy perennial mint used as a seasoning and a source of aromatic oil — called also *wild marjoram* [Spanish *orégano,* from Latin *origanum*]

Or·e·gon grape \,or-i-gən-, -,ar-, -,gän-\ *n* : a yellow-flowered mahonia of the northwestern United States sometimes grown as an ornamental [*Oregon,* United States]

or·gan \'or-gən\ *n* **I a** : a wind instrument that consists of sets of pipes sounding by compressed air, controlled by keyboards, and producing a variety of musical effects — called also *pipe organ* **b** : REED ORGAN **c** : an instrument in which the sounds of the pipe organ are approximated by means of electronic devices **d** : any of various similar cruder instruments **2** : a differentiated animal or plant structure (as a kidney or leaf) consisting of cells and tissues and performing some specific function — compare SYSTEM 1b(2) **3** : a means of performing some function or accomplishing some end ⟨the courts and other *organs* of government⟩ **4** : a publication (as a newspaper) expressing the opinions or serving the interests of a special group [Old English *organa* and Old French *organe,* both from Latin *organum,* from Greek *organon,* literally, "tool, instrument"]

organ- *or* **organo-** *combining form* **I** : organ **2** : organic

or·gan·dy *also* **or·gan·die** \'or-gən-dē\ *n, pl* **-dies** : a very fine transparent muslin with a stiff finish [French *organdi*]

or·gan·elle \,or-gə-'nel\ *n* : a specialized part (as a mitochondrion) of a cell analogous to an organ [New Latin *organella,* from Latin *organum* "organ"]

organ–grind·er \'or-gən-,grīn-dər\ *n* : one that cranks a hand organ; *esp* : an itinerant street musician who grinds a barrel organ

or·gan·ic \or-'gan-ik\ *adj* **I a** : of, relating to, or arising in a bodily organ **b** : affecting the structure of the organism — compare FUNCTIONAL 1b **2 a** (1) : of, relating to, or derived from living organisms (2) : relating to or produced with the use of fertilizer of plant or animal origin and without chemically formulated fertilizers or pesticides ⟨*organic* foods⟩ **b** (1) : of, relating to, or containing carbon compounds (2) : of, relating to, or dealt with by a branch of chemistry concerned with carbon compounds **3 a** : forming an integral element of a whole **b** : having systematic coordination of parts : ORGANIZED ⟨an *organic* whole⟩ **c** : developing in the manner of a living plant or animal ⟨society is *organic*⟩ — **or·gan·i·cal·ly** \-i-kə-lē, -klē\ *adv*

or·gan·ism \'or-gə-,niz-əm\ *n* **I** : an individual constituted to carry on the activities of life by means of organs separate in function but mutually dependent : a living person, plant, or animal **2** : a complex structure (as society) like a living organism in having many interdependent parts — **or·gan·is·mic** \-mik\ *adj* — **or·gan·is·mi·cal·ly** \-mi-kə-lē, -klē\ *adv*

or·gan·ist \'or-gə-nəst\ *n* : one who plays an organ

or·ga·ni·za·tion \,org-nə-'zā-shən, -ə-nə-\ *n* **I** : the act or process of organizing or of being organized **2** : the condition or manner of being organized **3 a** : ASSOCIATION 2 **b** : an administrative body or its personnel **c** : an administrative and functional unit (as a business or a political party) — **or·ga·ni·za·tion·al** \-shnəl, -shən-l\ *adj* — **or·ga·ni·za·tion·al·ly** \-ē-\ *adv*

or·ga·nize \'or-gə-,nīz\ *vb* **I** : to develop an organic structure : undergo or cause to undergo organization **2** : to arrange or form into a complete and functioning whole **3 a** : to set up an administrative structure for ⟨*organize* a business⟩ **b** : to enroll or associate in an organization (as a union) **4** : to arrange by systematic planning and united effort ⟨*organize* a prom⟩

\ə\ abut		\ng\ sing	
\ər\ further		\ō\ bone	
\a\ mat		\o\ saw	
\ā\ take		\oi\ coin	
\ä\ cot, cart		\th\ thin	
\au\ out		\th\ this	
\ch\ chin		\ü\ food	
\e\ pet		\u\ foot	
\ē\ easy		\y\ yet	
\g\ go		\yü\ few	
\i\ tip		\yu\ cure	
\ī\ life		\zh\ vision	
\j\ job			

or·ga·niz·er \-,nī-zər\ *n* **1** : one that organizes **2** : something (as a kind of tissue) able to cause a specific type of development in undifferentiated tissue — called also *inductor*

or·gano·chlo·rine \,òr-,gan-ə-'klōr-,ēn, -'klòr-, -ən\ *adj* : of, relating to, or belonging to the chlorinated hydrocarbon pesticides (as DDT) — **organochlorine** *n*

or·gano·phos·phate \-'fäs-,fāt\ *n* : an organophosphorus pesticide — **organophosphate** *adj*

or·gano·phos·pho·rus \-'fäs-fə-rəs, -frəs\ *adj* : of, relating to, or being a phosphorus-containing organic compound and especially a pesticide (as malathion) that acts by inhibiting cholinesterase — **organophosphorus** *n*

or·gan·za \òr-'gan-zə\ *n* : a sheer dress fabric resembling organdy and usually made of silk, rayon, or nylon [probably from *Lorganza*, a trademark]

or·gasm \'òr-,gaz-əm\ *n* : the climax of sexual excitement in coitus [Greek *orgasmos*, from *organ* "to grow ripe, be lustful"] — **or·gas·mic** \òr-'gaz-mik\ *or* **or·gas·tic** \-'gas-tik\ *adj*

or·gi·as·tic \,òr-jē-'as-tik\ *adj* : of, relating to, or marked by orgies [Greek *orgiastikos*, from *orgiazein* "to celebrate *orgies*", from *orgia* "orgy"] — **or·gi·as·ti·cal·ly** \-ti-kə-lē, -klē\ *adv*

or·gu·lous \'òr-gyə-ləs\ *adj* : PROUD 1a, HAUGHTY [Old French *orgueilleus*, from *orgueil* "pride", of Germanic origin]

or·gy \'òr-jē\ *n, pl* **orgies** **1** : secret ceremonial rites held in honor of an ancient Greek or Roman deity and usually characterized by ecstatic singing and dancing **2** : drunken revelry **3** : any excessive indulgence (an *orgy* of reading) (the riot was an *orgy* of senseless violence) [Middle French *orgie*, from Latin *orgia*, pl., from Greek]

ori·el \'ōr-ē-əl, 'òr-\ *n* : a large bay window projecting from a wall and supported by a corbel or bracket [Middle English, "porch, oriel", from Middle French *oriol* "porch"]

¹ori·ent \'ōr-ē-ənt, 'òr-, -ē-,ent\ *adj* **1** *archaic* : ORIENTAL **2** : being lustrous and sparkling (*orient* gems) **3** *archaic* : RISING

²ori·ent \-,ent\ *vt* **1 a** : to cause to face or point toward the east; *esp* : to build (as a church) with the longitudinal axis pointing east and the chief altar at the eastern end **b** : to set or arrange in a definite position especially in relation to the points of the compass **2 a** : to set right by adjusting to facts or principles **b** : to acquaint with an existing situation or environment

Ori·ent \'ōr-ē-ənt, 'òr-, -ē-,ent\ *n* : EAST 2; *esp* : the countries of eastern Asia [Middle French, from Latin *oriens*, from *oriri* "to rise"] □ ORIGIN The noun *orient* is derived from the Latin adjective *oriens*, which comes from the present participle of the verb *oriri*, "to rise or come forth". The earliest English sense of *orient* is "the place on the horizon where the sun rises when it is near one of the equinoxes", that is, the east. *Orient* has come to be used today to refer to the Asian countries to the east of Europe. With the spread of Christianity into Europe it became customary to build churches with their longitudinal axes pointing eastward toward Jerusalem. This practice gave rise to the use of *orient* as a verb meaning "to cause to face or point to the east". This sense became generalized to yield the sense "to set or arrange in any determinate position, especially in relation to the points of the compass".

ori·en·tal \,ōr-ē-'ent-l, 'òr-\ *adj, often cap* : of or relating to the Orient — **ori·en·tal·ly** \-lē\ *adv*

Oriental *n* : a member of one of the indigenous peoples of the Orient

ori·en·tal·ism \-l-,iz-əm\ *n, often cap* **1** : a trait, custom, or habit of expression characteristic of oriental peoples **2** : learning in oriental subjects — **ori·en·tal·ist** \-l-əst\ *n, often cap*

ori·en·tal·ize \-l-,īz\ *vb* : to make or become oriental

Oriental poppy *n* : an Asian perennial poppy widely grown for its very large showy flowers

Oriental rug *n* : a handwoven or hand-knotted rug or carpet made in the Orient

ori·en·tate \'ōr-ē-ən-,tāt, 'òr-, -,en-\ *vb* **1** : ORIENT 1b **2** : to face east

ori·en·ta·tion \,ōr-ē-ən-'tā-shən, 'òr-, -,en-\ *n* **1** : the act or process of orienting : the state of being oriented **2** : change of position by a cell, organelle, organ, or organism in response to external stimulus — **ori·en·ta·tion·al** \-shnəl, -shən-l\ *adj*

ori·en·teer·ing \,ōr-ē-ən-'tiər-ing, 'òr-, -,en-\ *n* : cross-country racing in which participants must find their way over an unfamiliar course using a map and compass [Swedish *orientering*, from *orientera* "to orient"]

or·i·fice \'òr-ə-fəs, 'är-\ *n* : an opening (as a vent, mouth, hole, or aperture) through which something may pass [Middle French, from Late Latin *orificium*, from Latin *or-, os* "mouth"] — **or·i·fi·cial** \,òr-ə-'fish-əl, ,är-\ *adj*

ori·flamme \'òr-ə-,flam, 'är-\ *n* : a banner, symbol, or ideal inspiring devotion or courage [Middle French *oriflamble*, from Medieval Latin *aurea flamma*, literally, "golden flame"]

ori·ga·mi \,òr-ə-'gäm-ē\ *n* : the art or process of Japanese paper folding [Japanese]

orig·a·num \ə-'rig-ə-nəm\ *n* : any of various fragrant aromatic plants of the mint or vervain families used as seasonings; *esp* : OREGANO [Latin, "wild marjoram", from Greek *origanon*]

or·i·gin \'òr-ə-jən, 'är-\ *n* **1** : ANCESTRY, PARENTAGE **2 a** : rise, beginning, or derivation from a source **b** : primary source or cause **3** : the more fixed, more central, or larger attachment of a muscle **4** : the intersection of the axes in a coordinate system [derived from Latin *origin-, origo*, from *oriri* "to rise"] □ SYN ORIGIN, SOURCE, INCEPTION, ROOT mean the point at which something begins its course or existence. ORIGIN applies to the things or persons from which something is ultimately derived and often to the causes operating before the thing itself comes into being; SOURCE stresses the point from which something springs into being (an insect bite was the *source* of the infection) INCEPTION stresses the beginning point without implying causes (a member from the *inception* of the club) ROOT suggests a first, ultimate, or fundamental source not always discernible (their quarrel had *roots* deep in the past)

¹orig·i·nal \ə-'rij-ən-l, -'rij-nəl\ *n* **1** *archaic* : the source or cause from which something arises **2 a** : that from which a copy, reproduction, or translation is made **b** : a work composed firsthand **3 a** : a person who is original in thought or action **b** *archaic* : an eccentric person

²original *adj* **1** : of or relating to a beginning : existing from the start : FIRST (the *original* part of an old house) (*original* inhabitants) **2 a** : not copied, reproduced, or translated (*original* paintings) (an *original* idea) **b** : being the one from which a copy, reproduction, or translation is made **3** : independent and creative in thought or action : INVENTIVE — **orig·i·nal·ly** \-ē\ *adv*

orig·i·nal·i·ty \ə-,rij-ə-'nal-ət-ē\ *n* **1** : the quality or state of being original : FRESHNESS, NOVELTY **2** : the power or ability to think, to act, or to do something in ways that are new (an artist of great *originality*)

original sin *n* : the state of sin that according to Christian theology humans are born in as a result of the sin of Adam and Eve

orig·i·nate \ə-'rij-ə-,nāt\ *vb* **1** : to bring into existence : give rise to (*originate* a plan) **2** : to take or have origin : come into existence — **orig·i·na·tion** \ə-,rij-ə-'nā-shən\ *n* — **orig·i·na·tor** \ə-'rij-ə-,nāt-ər\ *n*

orig·i·na·tive \ə-'rij-ə-,nāt-iv\ *adj* : having ability to originate : CREATIVE — **orig·i·na·tive·ly** *adv*

oriel

ori·ole \'ōr-ē-,ōl, 'ȯr-, -ē-əl\ *n* **1** : any of a family of usually brightly colored Old World passerine birds related to the crows **2** : any of a family of New World passerine birds of which the males are usually black and yellow or orange and the females chiefly greenish or yellowish [French *oriol*, from Latin *aureolus* "golden", from *aureus* "golden", from *aurum* "gold"]

Ori·on \ə-'rī-ən, ȯ-\ *n* : a constellation on the equator east of Taurus [Latin, a hunter of Greek mythology, from Greek *Ōriōn*]

or·i·son \'ȯr-ə-sən, 'är-, -zən\ *n* : PRAYER [Old French, from Late Latin *oratio*, from Latin *orare* "to speak, pray"]

Or·lean·ist \'ȯr-lē-ə-nəst; ȯr-'lē-nəst, -ə-nəst\ *n* : a supporter of the Orleans family in its claim to the throne of France by descent from a younger brother of Louis XIV

Or·lon \'ȯr-,län\ *trademark* — used for acrylic fiber

or·mo·lu \'ȯr-mə-,lü\ *n* : a brass made to imitate gold and used for decorative purposes [French *or moulu*, literally, "ground gold"]

¹or·na·ment \'ȯr-nə-mənt\ *n* **1** : something that adorns or adds beauty : DECORATION, EMBELLISHMENT **2** : the act of adorning : addition or inclusion of something that beautifies **3** : an embellishing note in music that does not belong to the essential harmony or melody [Old French *ornement*, from Latin *ornamentum*, from *ornare* "to adorn"]

²or·na·ment \-,ment\ *vt* : to provide with ornament

¹or·na·men·tal \,ȯr-nə-'ment-l\ *adj* : of, relating to, or serving as ornament — **or·na·men·tal·ly** \-l-ē\ *adv*

²ornamental *n* : a decorative object; *esp* : a plant cultivated for its beauty rather than for use

or·na·men·ta·tion \,ȯr-nə-mən-'tā-shən, -,men-\ *n* **1** : the act or process of ornamenting : the state of being ornamented **2 a** : a decorative device **b** : the ornaments of something

or·nate \ȯr-'nāt\ *adj* **1** : marked by elaborate rhetoric or florid style **2** : elaborately or excessively decorated [Latin *ornatus*, past participle of *ornare* "to furnish, adorn"] — **or·nate·ly** *adv* — **or·nate·ness** *n*

or·nery \'ȯrn-rē, 'än-, -ə-rē\ *adj* **or·ner·i·er**; **-est** : having a touchy and self-willed disposition [alteration of *ordinary*] — **or·ner·i·ness** *n*

ornith- *or* **ornitho-** *combining form* : bird ⟨*ornitho*logy⟩ [Greek *ornith-, ornis*]

or·ni·thine \'ȯr-nə-,thēn\ *n* : a crystalline amino acid $C_5H_{12}N_2O_2$ that functions in the body especially in urea production [*ornith*uric acid (an acid of which it is a component, found in the urine of birds) + -*ine*]

or·ni·thol·o·gy \,ȯr-nə-'thäl-ə-jē\ *n* : a branch of zoology dealing with birds — **or·ni·tho·log·i·cal** \,ȯr-,nith-ə-'läj-i-kəl\ *adj* — **or·ni·tho·log·i·cal·ly** \-i-kə-lē, -klē\ *adv* — **or·ni·thol·o·gist** \,ȯr-nə-'thäl-ə-jəst\ *n*

orog·e·ny \ȯ-'räj-ə-nē\ *n, pl* **-nies** : the process of mountain formation [Greek *oros* "mountain"] — **oro·gen·ic** \,ȯr-ə-'jen-ik, ,ȯr-\ *adj*

¹or·phan \'ȯr-fən\ *n* **1** : a child whose parents are dead **2** : a motherless young animal [Late Latin *orphanus*, from Greek *orphanos*] — **or·phan·hood** \-,hùd\ *n*

²orphan *vt* **or·phaned**; **or·phan·ing** \'ȯrf-ning, -ə-ning\ : to cause to become an orphan

or·phan·age \'ȯrf-nij, -ə-nij\ *n* : an institution for the care of orphans

or·pi·ment \'ȯr-pə-mənt\ *n* : a yellow to orange sulfide of arsenic used as a pigment [Middle French, from Latin *auripigmentum*, from *aurum* "gold" + *pigmentum* "pigment"]

or·pine \'ȯr-pən\ *n* : a pink- or purple-flowered sedum formerly used in folk medicine [Middle French *orpin*, from *orpiment* "orpiment"]

or·ris \'ȯr-əs, 'är-\ *n* : a European iris with a fragrant rhizome used especially in perfume and sachet powder; *also* : its rootstock [probably derived from Latin *iris*]

or·ris·root \-,rüt, -,rùt\ *n* : the rootstock of an orris

orth- *or* **ortho-** *combining form* **1** : straight : upright : vertical **2** : perpendicular ⟨*ortho*rhombic⟩ **3** : correct : corrective ⟨*ortho*dontics⟩ [Greek *orthos* "straight, right"]

or·tho·cen·ter \'ȯr-thə-,sent-ər\ *n* : the common point of intersection of the altitudes of a triangle

or·tho·chro·mat·ic \,ȯr-thə-krō-'mat-ik\ *adj* : sensitive to all colors except red ⟨an *orthochromatic* film⟩

or·tho·clase \'ȯr-thə-,klās\ *n* : a mineral $KAlSi_3O_8$ consisting of common potassium feldspar often with sodium in place of some of the potassium [German *orthoklas*, from *orth-* "orth-" + Greek *klasis* "breaking", from *klan* "to break"]

orth·odon·tia \,ȯr-thə-'dän-chē-ə, -chə\ *n* : ORTHODONTICS

orth·odon·tics \-'dänt-iks\ *n* : a branch of dentistry dealing with irregularities of the teeth and their correction [*orth-* + Greek *odont-, odous* "tooth"] — **orth·odon·tic** \-'dänt-ik\ *adj* — **orth·odon·tist** \-'dänt-əst\ *n*

or·tho·dox \'ȯr-thə-,däks\ *adj* **1** : holding established beliefs especially in religion ⟨an *orthodox* Christian⟩ **2** : approved as measuring up to some standard : CONVENTIONAL ⟨*orthodox* dress for a church wedding⟩ **3** *cap* **a** : EASTERN ORTHODOX **b** : of or relating to Orthodox Judaism [Late Latin *orthodoxus*, from Late Greek *orthodoxos*, from Greek *orthos* "right" + *doxa* "opinion"]

Orthodox Judaism *n* : Judaism that adheres to biblical law as interpreted in the authoritative rabbinic tradition and seeks to observe all the practices commanded in it

or·tho·doxy \'ȯr-thə-,däk-sē\ *n, pl* **-dox·ies** **1** : the quality or state of being orthodox **2** : an orthodox belief or practice

or·thog·o·nal \ȯr-'thäg-ən-l\ *adj* : mutually perpendicular [Middle French, from Latin *orthogonius*, from Greek *orthogōnios*, from *orthos* "straight, upright" + *gōnia* "angle"] — **or·thog·o·nal·ly** \ȯr-'thäg-nə-lē, -ən-l-ē\ *adv*

or·thog·ra·phy \ȯr-'thäg-rə-fē\ *n, pl* **-phies** **1 a** : the writing of words with the proper letters according to standard usage **b** : a manner of representing the sounds of a language by written or printed symbols ⟨17th century *orthography*⟩ **2** : a part of language study that deals with letters and spelling — **or·tho·graph·ic** \,ȯr-thə-'graf-ik\ *adj* — **or·tho·graph·i·cal·ly** \-'graf-ik-ə-lē, -ik-lē\ *adv*

or·tho·pe·dic \,ȯr-thə-'pēd-ik\ *adj* **1** : of or relating to orthopedics **2** : marked by deformities or crippling [French *orthopédique*, from *orthopédie* "orthopedics", from *orth-* "orth-" + Greek *paid-, pais* "child"] — **or·tho·pe·di·cal·ly** \-'pēd-i-kə-lē, -klē\ *adv*

or·tho·pe·dics \-'pēd-iks\ *n* : a medical specialty concerned with preserving and restoring the form and function of the skeletal system and associated structures (as tendons, muscles, and ligaments)

or·tho·pe·dist \,ȯr-thə-'pēd-əst\ *n* : one who specializes in orthopedics

or·thop·ter·an \ȯr-'thäp-tə-rən\ *n* : any of an order (Orthoptera) comprising insects with biting mouthparts, two pairs of wings or none, and an incomplete metamorphosis and usually including the grasshoppers, mantises, and crickets [Greek *pteron* "wing"] — **orthopteran** *adj*

or·tho·rhom·bic \,ȯr-thə-'räm-bik\ *adj* : of, relating to, or constituting a system of crystallization characterized by three unequal axes at right angles to each other

¹-o·ry \,ōr-ē, ȯr-ē, ə-rē, rē\ *n suffix, pl* **-ories** **1** : place of or for ⟨observa*tory*⟩ **2** : something that serves for ⟨crema*tory*⟩ [Latin *-orium*, from neuter of *-orius*, adj. suffix]

\ə\ abut   \ng\ sing
\ər\ further   \ō\ bone
\a\ mat   \ȯ\ saw
\ā\ take   \ȯi\ coin
\ä\ cot, cart   \th\ thin
\aù\ out   \t̲h̲\ this
\ch\ chin   \ü\ food
\e\ pet   \ù\ foot
\ē\ easy   \y\ yet
\g\ go   \yü\ few
\i\ tip   \yù\ cure
\ī\ life   \zh\ vision
\j\ job

osprey

²-ory *adj suffix* **1** : of, relating to, or characterized by ⟨gustat*ory*⟩ **2** : serving for, producing, or maintaining ⟨classificat*ory*⟩ [Latin *-orius*]

oryx \'ōr-iks, 'ōr-, 'är-\ *n, pl* **oryx·es** *or* **oryx** : a large straight-horned African antelope [Latin, a kind of gazelle, from Greek "pickax, antelope", from *oryssein* "to dig"]

os \'äs\ *n, pl* **os·sa** \'äs-ə\ : BONE [Latin]

Osage \ō-'sāj, 'ō-,\ *n* : a member of a Siouan people of the area between the Missouri and Arkansas rivers in what is now Missouri and parts of Arkansas, Oklahoma, and Kansas

Osage orange *n* : an ornamental American tree of the mulberry family with shiny ovate leaves and hard bright orange wood; *also* : its yellowish fruit

Os·car \'äs-kər\ *trademark* — used especially for any of a number of golden statuettes awarded annually by a professional organization for notable achievement in motion pictures

os·cil·late \'äs-ə-,lāt\ *vi* **1 a** : to swing backward and forward like a pendulum : VIBRATE **b** : to move or travel back and forth between two points **2** : to vary between opposing beliefs, feelings, or theories **3** : to vary above and below a mean value **4** : to exhibit or cause electrical oscillation [Latin *oscillare* "to swing", from *oscillum* "swing"] SYN see SWAY — **os·cil·la·to·ry** \ə-'sil-ə-,tōr-ē, -,tór-\ *adj*

os·cil·la·tion \,äs-ə-'lā-shən\ *n* **1** : the act or fact of oscillating : VIBRATION **2** : VARIATION 1, FLUCTUATION **3** : a flow of electricity changing periodically from a maximum to a minimum; *esp* : a flow periodically changing direction **4** : a single swing or change (as of an oscillating body) from one extreme limit to the other — **os·cil·la·tion·al** \-shnəl, -shən-l\ *adj*

os·cil·la·tor \'äs-ə-,lāt-ər\ *n* **1** : one that oscillates **2** : a device for producing alternating current; *esp* : a radiofrequency or audio-frequency generator

os·cil·la·to·ria \ə-,sil-ə-'tōr-ē-ə, -'tór-\ *n* : any of a genus of blue-green algae growing in soil or water as filaments which have a gentle oscillatory movement

os·cil·lo·scope \ə-'sil-ə-,skōp, ə-\ *n* : an instrument in which the variations in a fluctuating electrical quantity appear temporarily as a visible wave form on the fluorescent screen of a cathode-ray tube

os·cu·lum \'äs-kyə-ləm\ *n, pl* **-la** \-lə\ : an opening of a sponge for the outflow of water [Latin, "little mouth, kiss", from *os* "mouth"]

¹-ose \,ōs, 'ōs *sometimes* ,ōz, 'ōz\ *adj suffix* : full of : having : possessing the qualities of ⟨cym*ose*⟩ [Latin *-osus*]

²-ose \,ōs, ,ōz\ *n suffix* **1** : carbohydrate; *esp* : sugar ⟨pent*ose*⟩ **2** : primary hydrolysis product ⟨prote*ose*⟩ [French, from *glucose*]

Osee \'ō-,zē, ō-'zā-ə\ *n* — see BIBLE table

osier \'ō-zhər\ *n* **1** : any of various willows with pliable twigs used for furniture and basketry **2** : a willow rod used in making baskets **3** : any of several American dogwoods [Middle French, from Medieval Latin *auseria* "osier bed"]

-o·sis \'ō-səs\ *n suffix, pl* **-o·ses** \-,sēz\ *or* **-o·sis·es** **1** : action : process : condition ⟨hypn*osis*⟩ **2** : abnormal or diseased condition ⟨leuk*osis*⟩ [Greek *-ōsis*]

os·mi·um \'äz-mē-əm\ *n* : a hard brittle blue-gray or blue-black metallic element with a high melting point that is the heaviest metal known and that is used especially as a catalyst and in hard alloys — see ELEMENT table [New Latin, from Greek *osmē* "odor"]

os·mom·e·ter \äz-'mäm-ət-ər, äs-\ *n* : an apparatus for measuring the pressure produced by osmosis

os·mose \'äz-,mōs, 'äs-\ *vi* : to diffuse by osmosis [back-formation from *osmosis*]

os·mo·sis \äz-'mō-səs, äs-\ *n* : a diffusion through a semipermeable membrane typically separating a solvent and a solution that tends to equalize their concentrations; *esp* : the passage of solvent in distinction

from the passage of solute [derived from Greek *ōsmos* "act of pushing", from *ōthein* "to push"] — **os·mot·ic** \-'mät-ik\ *adj* — **os·mot·i·cal·ly** \-'mät-i-kə-lē, -klē\ *adv*

osmotic shock *n* : a rapid change in osmotic pressure (as by transfer to a medium of different concentration) affecting a living system

os·prey \'äs-prē, -,prā\ *n, pl* **ospreys** : a large fish-eating brown and white hawk [derived from Latin *ossifraga* "sea eagle", literally, "bone breaker"]

ossa *pl of* **os**

os·se·ous \'äs-ē-əs\ *adj* : BONY 1 [Latin *osseus,* from *os* "bone"]

os·si·cle \'äs-i-kəl\ *n* : a small bone or bony structure (as the malleus, incus, or stapes) [Latin *ossiculum* "small bone", from *os* "bone"]

os·si·fi·ca·tion \,äs-ə-fə-'kā-shən\ *n* **1** : formation of or conversion into bone or a bony substance **2** : an area of ossified tissue

os·si·fy \'äs-ə-,fī\ *vb* **-fied; -fy·ing** **1** : to become or change into bone or bony tissue **2** : to become or make callous or set in one's ways

oste- *or* **osteo-** *combining form* : bone ⟨*osteo*pathy⟩ [Greek *osteon*]

os·ten·si·ble \ä-'sten-sə-bəl\ *adj* : shown outwardly : PROFESSED ⟨her *ostensible* motive⟩ [French, from Latin *ostendere* "to show", from *obs-* "in front of" + *tendere* "to stretch"]

os·ten·si·bly \ä-'sten-sə-blē\ *adv* : to all outward appearances ⟨was *ostensibly* frank, but deceitful in actuality⟩

os·ten·ta·tion \,äs-tən-'tā-shən\ *n* : showy or excessive display [Middle French, from Latin *ostentatio,* limit from *ostentare* "to show off", from *ostendere* "to show"]

os·ten·ta·tious \-shəs\ *adj* : marked by or fond of conspicuous and sometimes pretentious display — **os·ten·ta·tious·ly** *adv* — **os·ten·ta·tious·ness** *n*

os·teo·ar·thri·tis \,äs-tē-ō-,är-'thrīt-əs\ *n* : an arthritis marked by degeneration of the cartilage and bone of joints

os·teo·my·eli·tis \,äs-tē-ō-,mī-ə-'līt-əs\ *n* : an infectious inflammatory disease of bone marked by local death and separation of nonliving from living tissue [*oste-* + Greek *myelos* "marrow" + English *-itis*]

os·teo·path \'äs-tē-ə-,path\ *n* : a practitioner of osteopathy

os·te·op·a·thy \,äs-tē-'äp-ə-thē\ *n* : a system of treating diseases that places emphasis on manipulation especially of bones but does not exclude other treatment (as the use of medicine and surgery) — **os·teo·path·ic** \,äs-tē-ə-'path-ik\ *adj* — **os·teo·path·i·cal·ly** \-'path-i-kə-lē, -klē\ *adv*

os·ti·ole \'äs-tē-,ōl\ *n* : a small opening [Latin *ostiolum* "little door", from *ostium* "door"]

os·ti·um \'äs-tē-əm\ *n, pl* **os·tia** \-tē-ə\ : an anatomical opening (as in the heart of a crayfish) [Latin, "door, mouth of a river"]

ostler *variant of* HOSTLER

os·tra·cism \'äs-trə-,siz-əm\ *n* **1** : a method of temporary banishment by popular vote without trial or special accusation practiced in ancient Greece **2** : exclusion by general consent from common privileges or social acceptance

os·tra·cize \'äs-trə-,sīz\ *vt* **1** : to exile by ostracism **2** : to exclude from a group by common consent [Greek *ostrakizein* "to banish by voting with potsherds", from *ostrakon* "shell, potsherd"] □ ORIGIN Greek *ostrakon* is a word for a shell or for an earthen vessel or a broken fragment of such a vessel. Such potsherds served ancient Athens as ballots in a particular kind of popular vote. Once a year the citizens would gather in the agora or marketplace of Athens to decide who, if anyone, should be banished temporarily for the good of the city. Each voter wrote a name on his *ostrakon.* If at least 6000 votes were cast and if a majority of them named one man, then that man was banished, or ostracized.

os·tra·cod \'äs-trə-ˌkäd\ *also* **os·tra·code** \-ˌkōd\ *n* : any of a group (Ostracoda) of small mostly freshwater crustaceans [derived from Greek *ostrakon* "shell"]

os·tra·co·derm \'äs-trə-kō-ˌdərm, äs-'trak-ə-\ *n* : any of an order (Ostracodermi) of primitive fossil armored fishes [derived from Greek *ostrakon* "shell" + *derma* "skin"]

os·trich \'äs-trich, 'ós-\ *n* **1** : a swift-footed 2-toed flightless bird of Africa and Arabia with valuable wing and tail plumes that is the largest of existing birds **2** : one that attempts to avoid danger by refusing to face it [Old French *ostrusce*, from Latin *avis* "bird" + Late Latin *struthio* "ostrich", from Greek *strouthos* "sparrow, ostrich"]

Os·tro·goth \'äs-trə-ˌgäth\ *n* : a member of the eastern division of the Goths — called also *East Goth*; compare VISIGOTH [Late Latin *Ostrogothi* "Ostrogoths"]

Os·we·go tea \ä-ˌswē-gō-\ *n* : a North American mint with showy bright scarlet irregular flowers [*Oswego* river, New York]

ot- *or* **oto-** *combining form* : ear ⟨*ot*itis⟩ [Greek *ōt-, ous*]

¹oth·er \'əth-ər\ *adj* **1 a** : being the one (as of two or more) left ⟨held my *other* arm straight⟩ **b** : being the ones distinct from those first mentioned ⟨thought the *other* members dull⟩ **c** : SECOND ⟨every *other* day⟩ **2** : not the same : DIFFERENT ⟨*other* times and customs⟩ **3** : ADDITIONAL ⟨some *other* guests are coming⟩ **4** : recently past ⟨the *other* evening⟩ [Old English *ōther*]

²other *n* **1 a** : one that remains of two or more ⟨lift one foot and then the *other*⟩ **b** : a thing opposite to or excluded by something else ⟨from one side to the *other*⟩ **2** : a different or additional one ⟨the *others* came later⟩

³other *pron, sometimes pl in construction* : a different or additional one ⟨something or *other* happened⟩

⁴other *adv* : OTHERWISE

oth·er·wise \'əth-ər-ˌwīz\ *adv* **1** : in a different way : DIFFERENTLY ⟨could not do *otherwise*⟩ **2** : in different circumstances ⟨*otherwise* we might have won⟩ **3** : in other respects ⟨the *otherwise* busy street⟩ [Old English *on ōthre wīsan* "in another manner"] — **otherwise** *adj*

oth·er·world \'əth-ər-ˌwərld\ *n* : a world beyond death or beyond present reality — **oth·er·world·li·ness** \-ˌwərl-dlē-nəs, -lē-\ *n* — **oth·er·world·ly** \-ˌwərl-dlē, -lē\ *adj*

otic \'ōt-ik\ *adj* : of, relating to, or located near the ear

-ot·ic \'ät-ik\ *adj suffix* **1** : of, relating to, or characterized by a (specified) action, process, or condition ⟨symbi*otic*⟩ **2** : having an abnormal or diseased condition of a (specified) kind ⟨leuk*otic*⟩ [Greek *-ōtikos*]

oti·tis \ō-'tīt-əs\ *n* : inflammation of the ear

oto·lar·yn·gol·o·gy \ˌōt-ō-ˌlar-ən-'gäl-ə-jē\ *n* : a branch of medicine dealing with the ear, nose, and throat

oto·lith \'ōt-l-ˌith\ *n* : a calcium-containing stony mass in the inner ear — **oto·lith·ic** \ˌōt-l-'ith-ik\ *adj*

Ot·ta·wa \'ät-ə-wə, -ˌwä, -ˌwó\ *n* : a member of an Algonquian people of what is now southern Ontario

ot·ter \'ät-ər\ *n, pl* **otters** *also* **otter** **1** : any of several aquatic fish-eating mammals that are related to the weasels and minks and that have webbed and clawed feet and dark brown fur **2** : the fur or pelt of an otter [Old English *otor*]

ot·to·man \'ät-ə-mən\ *n, pl* **-mans** **1** *cap* : TURK **2** — called also *Ottoman Turk* **2 a** : an upholstered often overstuffed seat or couch usually without a back **b** : an overstuffed footstool [French, derived from Arabic *'othmānī*, from *'Othmān* "Othman (founder of the Ottoman Empire)"] — **Ottoman** *adj*

ouch \'aúch\ *interj* — used to express sudden pain [probably imitative]

ought \'ót\ *auxiliary verb* — used to express obligation ⟨*ought* to pay our debts⟩, advisability ⟨*ought* to

take care of yourself⟩, natural expectation ⟨*ought* to be here by now⟩, or logical consequence ⟨the result *ought* to be infinity⟩ [Middle English *oughte*, past of *owen* "to owe"]

oughtn't \'ót-nt\ : ought not

¹ounce \'aúns\ *n* **1 a** : a unit of weight equal to ¹⁄₁₂ troy pound (about 31.1 grams) — see MEASURE table **b** : a unit of weight equal to ¹⁄₁₆ avoirdupois pound (about 28.3 grams) **c** : a small portion or quantity **2** : FLUID OUNCE [Middle French *unce*, from Latin *uncia* "twelfth part, ounce", from *unus* "one"] □ ORIGIN The ancient Romans used a system of weights and measures based on units that were divided into 12 parts. The Latin *uncia*, meaning "a 12th part", was used for the 12th part of a *pes* or "foot". From this is derived Old English *ince* or *ynce*, which became modern English *inch*. The Roman pound, called *libra* in Latin, was also divided into 12 parts similarly designated by the word *uncia*. In this sense *uncia* followed a different path. It became Middle French *unce*, which was borrowed into Middle English as *unce* or *ounce*.

²ounce *n* : SNOW LEOPARD [Old French *once* "wildcat", from *lonce* (understood as *l'once* "the ounce"), from Latin *lynx* "lynx"]

our \är, aúr, 'aúr\ *adj* : of or relating to us or ourselves or ourself especially as possessors or possessor, agents or agent, or objects or object of an action ⟨*our* throne⟩ ⟨*our* actions⟩ ⟨*our* being chosen⟩ [Old English *ūre*]

Our Father *n* : LORD'S PRAYER

ours \aúrz, 'aúrz, ärz\ *pron, sing or pl in construction* : our one or our ones — used without a following noun as an equivalent in meaning to the adjective *our*

our·self \är-'self, aúr-\ *pron* : MYSELF — used (as by a sovereign or writer) to refer to the single-person subject when *we* is used instead of *I*

our·selves \-'selvz\ *pron pl* **1** : those identical ones that are we — used reflexively or for emphasis ⟨we're doing it solely for *ourselves*⟩ ⟨we *ourselves* will never go⟩; compare WE 1 **2** : our normal, healthy, or sane condition or selves ⟨we weren't feeling *ourselves* that day⟩

-ous \əs\ *adj suffix* **1** : full of : having : possessing the qualities of ⟨clamor*ous*⟩ ⟨poison*ous*⟩ **2** : having a valence lower than in compounds or ions named with an adjective ending in *-ic* ⟨mercur*ous*⟩ [partly from Old French *-ous, -eus, -eux*, from Latin *-osus*; partly from Latin *-us*, nominative sing. masculine ending of many adjectives]

oust \'aúst\ *vt* : to force or drive out (as from office or from possession of something) : EXPEL ⟨*oust* a corrupt official⟩ [Anglo-French *ouster*, from Old French *oster*, from Latin *obstare* "to stand against", from *ob-* "against" + *stare* "to stand"] SYN see EJECT

oust·er \'aús-tər\ *n* : the act or an instance of ousting or being ousted : EXPULSION [Anglo-French, "to oust"]

¹out \'aút\ *adv* **1 a** : in a direction away from the inside or the center ⟨look *out* of a window⟩ **b** : from among others ⟨picked *out* a hat⟩ **2** : away from home, business, or the usual or proper place ⟨*out* to lunch⟩ ⟨left a word *out*⟩ **3** : into a state of loss or deprivation ⟨vote the party *out* of office⟩ **4** : beyond control, possession, or occupation ⟨let a secret *out*⟩ ⟨lent *out* money⟩ **5** : into a state of disagreement ⟨friends fall *out*⟩ **6 a** : beyond the limits of existence, continuance, or supply ⟨the food ran *out*⟩ **b** : to extinction, exhaustion, or completion ⟨burn *out*⟩ **7 a** : in or into the open ⟨the sun came *out*⟩ **b** : ALOUD ⟨cried *out*⟩ **8** — used as an intensive with numerous verbs ⟨sketch *out* the plans⟩ **9 a** : so as to put out a batter or base runner ⟨the catcher threw *out* the runner trying to steal second base⟩ **b** : so as to be put out ⟨grounded *out* to the shortstop⟩ [Old English *ūt*]

²out *vi* : to become known ⟨the truth will *out*⟩

ostrich 1

otter 1

\ə\ abut		\ng\ sing	
\ər\ **further**		\ō\ bone	
\a\ mat		\ò\ saw	
\ā\ take		\òi\ coin	
\ä\ cot, cart		\th\ thin	
\aú\ out		\th\ this	
\ch\ chin		\ü\ food	
\e\ pet		\ù\ foot	
\ē\ easy		\y\ yet	
\g\ go		\yü\ few	
\i\ tip		\yù\ cure	
\ī\ life		\zh\ vision	
\j\ **job**			

³out *adj* **1** : situated outside : EXTERNAL ⟨the *out* edge⟩ **2** : situated at a distance : OUTLYING ⟨the *out* islands⟩ **3 a** : not being in power ⟨the *out* party⟩ **b** : not successful in reaching base ⟨the batter was *out*⟩ **4** : directed outward or serving to direct something outward : OUTGOING ⟨put the letter in the *out* basket⟩ **5** : ABSENT ⟨a basket with its bottom *out*⟩ **6** : no longer in fashion

⁴out \ aùt, 'aùt \ *prep* **1** : out through ⟨ran *out* the door⟩ **2** : outward along or on ⟨drive *out* the old road⟩

⁵out \ 'aùt \ *n* **1** : one who is out of power **2 a** : the putting out of a batter or base runner in baseball **b** : a player put out **3** : a ball hit out of bounds in tennis or squash **4** : an item that is out of stock **5** : a way of escaping from an embarrassing situation or a difficulty

out- *prefix* : in a manner that goes beyond, surpasses, or excels ⟨*out*maneuver⟩ [¹*out*]

See *out-* and 2d element

outachieve	outfish	outproduce
outact	outfox	outrace
outbluff	outfumble	outride
outbox	outglitter	outscheme
outbrawl	outgross	outscore
outcatch	outhit	outshout
outclimb	outhunt	outsing
outcoach	outhustle	outsparkle
outcompete	outjump	outspeed
outdance	outkick	outspend
outdazzle	outleap	outsprint
outdebate	outlearn	outstride
outdesign	outmarch	outswear
outdress	outmatch	outswim
outdrink	outperform	outthink
outdrive	outplay	outthrow
outearn	outpoll	outwait
outeat	outpopulate	outwalk
outfight	outpray	outwrite

out-and-out \ ,aùt-n-'aùt, -'daùt \ *adj* : being wholly what is stated ⟨an *out-and-out* crook⟩

out·bal·ance \ aùt-'bal-əns, 'aùt- \ *vt* : OUTWEIGH

out·bid \ -'bid \ *vt* **-bid; -bid·ding** : to make a higher bid than

¹out·board \ 'aùt-,bōrd, -,bórd \ *adj* **1** : situated outboard **2** : having or using an outboard motor

²outboard *adv* **1** : outside the line of a ship's bulwarks or hull : away from the center line of a ship **2** : in a position closer or closest to either of the wing tips of an airplane or of the sides of an automobile

outboard motor *n* : a small internal-combustion engine with propeller attached for mounting at the stern of a small boat

out·bound \ 'aùt-,baùnd \ *adj* : outward bound ⟨*outbound* traffic⟩

out·brave \ aùt-'brāv, 'aùt- \ *vt* **1** : to face or resist defiantly **2** : to exceed in courage

out·break \ 'aùt-,brāk \ *n* **1** : a sudden or violent breaking out : a sudden increase of activity or currency ⟨the *outbreak* of war⟩ **2** : something that breaks out : as **a** : EPIDEMIC ⟨an *outbreak* of measles⟩ **b** : INSURRECTION, REVOLT

out·breed *vt* **-bred** \ -,bred, -'bred \; **-breed·ing 1** \ 'aùt-,brēd \ : to subject to outbreeding **2** \ aùt-', aùt-'\ : to breed faster than

out·breed·ing \ 'aùt-,brēd-ing \ *n* : the interbreeding of relatively unrelated individuals

out·build·ing \ 'aùt-,bil-ding \ *n* : a building separate from and smaller than the main one

out·burst \ -,bərst \ *n* **1** : a violent expression of feeling **2** : a surge of activity or growth ⟨a new *outburst* of creative power⟩

out·cast \ -,kast \ *n* : a person cast out by society : PARIAH — **outcast** *adj*

out·caste \ -,kast \ *n* : one who has no caste

out·class \ aùt-'klas, 'aùt- \ *vt* : to excel or surpass so decisively as to appear of a higher class

out·come \ 'aùt-,kəm \ *n* : something that follows as a result

¹out·crop \ 'aùt-,kräp \ *n* : exposed bedrock or an unconsolidated deposit at the surface of the ground

²out·crop \ 'aùt-'kräp \ *vi* : to come to the surface : APPEAR

out·crop·ping \ -'kräp-ing \ *n* : ¹OUTCROP

out·cross \ 'aùt-,krós \ *n* : a cross between relatively unrelated individuals or strains — **outcross** *vt*

out·cry \ 'aùt-,krī \ *n* **1** : a loud cry : CLAMOR **2** : a strong protest

out·dat·ed \ aùt-'dāt-əd, 'aùt- \ *adj* : OUTMODED

out·dis·tance \ aùt-'dis-təns, 'aùt- \ *vt* : to go far ahead of ⟨as in a race⟩ : OUTSTRIP

out·do \ aùt-'dü, 'aùt- \ *vt* **-did** \ -'did \; **-done** \ -'dən \; **-do·ing** \ -'dü-ing \ : to go beyond in action or performance : SURPASS

out·door \ ,aùt-,dōr, -,dór *also* **out·doors** \ -,dōrz, -,dórz \ *adj* **1** : of or relating to the outdoors ⟨an *outdoor* setting⟩ **2** : done outdoors ⟨*outdoor* games⟩ **3** : not roofed or enclosed ⟨an *outdoor* theater⟩ [*out (of) door, out (of) doors*]

¹out·doors \ aùt-'dōrz, 'aùt-, -'dórz \ *adv* : outside a building : in or into the open air

²outdoors *n* **1** : the open air **2** : the world away from human dwellings

out·draw \ aùt-'dró, 'aùt- \ *vt* : to attract a larger audience or following than

out·er \ 'aùt-ər \ *adj* **1** : EXTERNAL 1 ⟨*outer* appearance⟩ **2 a** : situated farther out ⟨the *outer* wall⟩ **b** : being away from a center ⟨the *outer* solar planets⟩

outer ear *n* : the outer visible portion of the ear that collects and directs sound waves toward the eardrum by way of a canal which extends inward through the temporal bone

out·er·most \ 'aùt-ər-,mōst \ *adj* : farthest out

outer space *n* : SPACE 5; *esp* : the region beyond the solar system

out·face \ aùt-'fās, 'aùt- \ *vt* **1** : to stare down **2** : to confront without fear or weakening : DEFY

out·fall \ 'aùt-,fól \ *n* : the outlet of a river, stream, lake, drain, or sewer

out·field \ -,fēld \ *n* : the part of a baseball field beyond the infield and between the foul lines — **out·field·er** \ -,fēl-dər \ *n*

¹out·fit \ 'aùt-,fit \ *n* **1** : the equipment or apparel for some purpose or occasion ⟨a camping *outfit*⟩ ⟨a sports *outfit*⟩ **2** : a group of persons working together or associated in the same undertaking ⟨soldiers belonging to the same *outfit*⟩

²outfit *vt* **1** : to furnish with an outfit : EQUIP ⟨*outfit* an expedition⟩ **2** : SUPPLY 3 — **out·fit·ter** *n*

out·flank \ aùt-'flangk, 'aùt- \ *vt* : to get around the flank of ⟨an opposing force⟩

out·flow \ 'aùt-,flō \ *n* **1** : a flowing out **2** : something that flows out

out·foot \ aùt-'fùt, 'aùt- \ *vt* : to outdo in speed : OUTSTRIP

out·gen·er·al \ -'jen-rəl, -ə-rəl \ *vt* **-gen·er·aled** *or* **-gen·er·alled; -gen·er·al·ing** *or* **-gen·er·al·ling** : to surpass in generalship : OUTMANEUVER

out·go \ 'aùt-,gō \ *n, pl* **outgoes** : something ⟨as goods or money⟩ that goes out

out·go·ing \ 'aùt-,gō-ing \ *adj* **1 a** : going out ⟨the *outgoing* tide⟩ **b** : retiring from a place or position ⟨the *outgoing* governor⟩ **2** : FRIENDLY, RESPONSIVE ⟨an *outgoing* person⟩

out·grow \ aùt-'grō, 'aùt- \ *vt* **-grew** \ -'grü \; **-grown** \ -'grōn \; **-grow·ing 1** : to grow faster than **2** : to grow too large or too mature for ⟨*outgrow* one's clothes⟩ ⟨*outgrew* childish fancies⟩

out·growth \ 'aùt-,grōth \ *n* **1** : a product of growing out ⟨an *outgrowth* of hair⟩ **2** : CONSEQUENCE, BY-PRODUCT ⟨crime is often an *outgrowth* of poverty⟩

out·guess \ aùt-'ges, 'aùt- \ *vt* : to anticipate the intentions, plans, or actions of

out·house \ 'aùt-,haùs \ *n* : OUTBUILDING; *esp* : PRIVY

out·ing \'aut-ing\ *n* **1** : an excursion usually with a picnic (the club *outing* at the seashore) **2** : a brief stay or trip in the open (took the baby for an *outing*)

outing flannel *n* : a flannelette sometimes containing some wool

out·land·er \'aut-,lan-dər\ *n* : a person belonging to another culture or region

out·land·ish \aut-'lan-dish, 'aut-\ *adj* **1** : of or relating to another country **2 a** : of foreign or unfamiliar appearance or quality (*outlandish* language) **b** : strikingly out of the ordinary : BIZARRE **3** : remote from civilization (lived in *outlandish* places) SYN see STRANGE — **out·land·ish·ly** *adv* — **out·land·ish·ness** *n*

out·last \aut-'last, 'aut-\ *vt* : to last longer than

¹out·law \'aut-,lo\ *n* **1** : a person excluded from the benefit or protection of the law **2 a** : a lawless person or a fugitive from the law **b** : one (as a person or organization) under a ban [Old English *ūtlaga*, from Old Norse *ūtlagi*, from *ūt* "out" + *lag-*, *lög* "law"] — **outlaw** *adj*

²outlaw *vt* **1 a** : to deprive of the benefit and protection of law **b** : to make illegal **2** : to place under a ban — **out·law·ry** \'aut-,lo-rē\ *n*

out·lay \'aut-,lā\ *n* **1** : the act of expending **2** : EXPENDITURE 2

out·let \'aut-,let, -lət\ *n* **1** : a place or opening through which something is let out **2** : a means of release or satisfaction for an emotion or impulse **3** : a place (as in a wall) at which an electrical device can be plugged into the wiring system **4 a** : a market for a commodity **b** : a retail store or distributor

¹out·line \'aut-,līn\ *n* **1** : a line that traces or forms the outer limits of an object or figure and shows its shape **2 a** : a drawing or picture giving only the outlines of something **b** : this method of drawing **3 a** : a brief summary often in numbered divisions **b** : a preliminary account of a project **4** : a brief treatment of a subject : DIGEST

²outline *vt* **1** : to draw the outline of **2** : to indicate the main features or parts of

out·live \aut-'liv, 'aut-\ *vt* : to live longer than : OUTLAST

out·look \'aut-,luk\ *n* **1 a** : a place offering a view **b** : a view from a particular place **2** : POINT OF VIEW **3** : the prospect for the future

out·ly·ing \'aut-,lī-ing\ *adj* : far from a center or main body (an *outlying* suburb)

out·ma·neu·ver \,aut-mə-'nü-vər, -'nyü-\ *vt* **1** : to get the better of by more skillful maneuvering **2** : to be more maneuverable than

out·mod·ed \aut-'mōd-əd, 'aut-\ *adj* **1** : no longer in style (an *outmoded* dress) **2** : no longer acceptable or usable (*outmoded* beliefs) (*outmoded* equipment)

out·most \'aut-,mōst\ *adj* : farthest out : OUTERMOST

out·num·ber \aut-'nəm-bər, 'aut-\ *vt* : to be greater in number than (girls *outnumber* boys in the class)

out of *prep* **1 a** (1) : from within to the outside of (walked *out of* the room) (2) — used as a function word to indicate a change in quality, state, or form (woke up *out of* a deep sleep) **b** (1) : beyond the range or limits of (*out of* sight) (2) : from among (one *out of* four survived) **2** : in or into a state of not having (all *out of* milk) (*out of* a job) **3** : because of : FROM (came *out of* curiosity) **4** — used as a function word to indicate the constituent material, basis, or source (built *out of* old lumber)

out-of-bounds \,aut-əv-'baunz, -ə-\ *adv or adj* : outside the prescribed area of play

out-of-date \,aut-əv-'dāt, -ə-\ *adj* : OUTMODED (*out-of-date* ideas)

out-of-door \,aut-əv-'dōr, -ə-, -'dor\ *or* **out-of-doors** \-'dōrz, -'dorz\ *adj* : OUTDOOR

out-of-doors *n* : OUTDOORS

out-of-the-way \,aut-əv-thə-'wā, -ə-\ *adj* **1** : not centrally or conveniently located (an *out-of-the-way* restaurant) **2** : not commonly found or met : UNUSUAL

out·pa·tient \'aut-,pā-shənt\ *n* : a person who receives diagnosis or treatment in a clinic or dispensary of a hospital — compare INPATIENT — **outpatient** *adj*

out·post \'aut-,pōst\ *n* **1 a** : a guard stationed at a distance from a military post **b** : the position occupied by an outpost **2 a** : an outlying settlement **b** : an outer limit : FRONTIER

out·pour \aut-'pōr, -'por\ *vt* : to pour out — **out·pour** \'aut-,\ *n*

out·pour·ing \'aut-,pōr-ing, -,por-\ *n* **1** : the act of pouring out **2 a** : something that pours out or is poured out : OUTFLOW **b** : an outburst of emotion

¹out·put \-,put\ *n* **1** : the amount produced or able to be produced usually in a stated time by a man, machine, factory, or industry **2 a** : power or energy delivered by a machine or system **b** : a point at which something (as power, an electronic signal, or data) comes out

²output *vt* **out·put·ted** *or* **output**; **out·put·ting** : to produce as output

¹out·rage \'aut-,rāj\ *n* **1** : a violent or brutal act **2** : INJURY 1, INSULT **3** : the resentment aroused by injury or insult [Old French, "excess, outrage", from *outre* "beyond, in excess" (from Latin *ultra*) + *-age*] □ ORIGIN The English word *outrage* is related neither to *out* nor to *rage*. It is ultimately derived from Latin *ultra*, "beyond". Latin *ultra* became *outre* in Old French. *Outre* was combined with the common suffix *-age* to produce the word *outrage*, which meant "excess, outrage", and the Old French word was borrowed into English in the Middle English period. Old French *outre* is also the ancestor of French *outré*, which was borrowed into English in modern times.

²outrage *vt* **1 a** : RAPE **2 b** : to subject to violent injury or abuse **2** : to arouse anger or great resentment in SYN see OFFEND

out·ra·geous \aut-'rā-jəs\ *adj* : being beyond all bounds of decency or justice : extremely offensive, insulting, or shameful : SHOCKING — **out·ra·geous·ly** *adv* — **out·ra·geous·ness** *n* □ SYN OUTRAGEOUS, ATROCIOUS, HEINOUS mean exceedingly bad or horrible. OUTRAGEOUS implies exceeding the limits of what is tolerable or decent (*outrageous* manners) ATROCIOUS implies merciless cruelty, savagery, or contempt of ordinary values (*atrocious* killings by the invaders) HEINOUS implies being so flagrantly evil as to induce hatred or horror (the *heinous* torturing of prisoners)

out·rank \aut-'rangk, 'aut-\ *vt* : to rank higher than : be more important than

ou·tré \ü-'trā\ *adj* : going beyond what is usual or proper : BIZARRE [French, from *outrer* "to carry to excess", from Old French *outre* "beyond" — see OUTRAGE *origin*]

out·reach \aut-'rēch, 'aut-\ *vb* **1 a** : to be greater in reach than **b** : to go beyond : EXCEED (the demand *outreaches* the supply) **2** : to get the better of by trickery : OVERREACH **3** : to go too far

out·rid·er \'aut-,rīd-ər\ *n* **1** : a mounted attendant **2** : FORERUNNER 1, HARBINGER

out·rig·ger \'aut-,rig-ər\ *n* **1 a** : a projecting frame on a float attached to the side of a canoe or boat to prevent upsetting **b** : a projecting beam run out from a ship's side to help secure the masts or from a mast to extend a rope or sail **c** : a craft fitted with an outrigger **2** : a projecting frame to support the elevator or tail planes of an airplane or the rotor of a helicopter

¹out·right \aut-'rīt, 'aut-\ *adv* **1 a** : with nothing kept back : COMPLETELY (repeal a law *outright*) **b** : without restraint (laughed *outright*) **2** : at once : INSTANTANEOUSLY (killed *outright*)

²out·right \'aut-,rīt\ *adj* **1** : being exactly what is stated (*outright* persecution) **2** : given without reservation (an *outright* gift)

out·run \aut-'rən, 'aut-\ *vt* **-ran** \-'ran\; **-run**; **-run·ning** : to run faster than; *also* : EXCEED (their needs *outran* their funds)

outrigger 1c

\ə\ abut	\ng\ sing
\ər\ further	\ō\ bone
\a\ mat	\o\ saw
\ā\ take	\oi\ coin
\ä\ cot, cart	\th\ thin
\au\ out	\th\ this
\ch\ chin	\ü\ food
\e\ pet	\u\ foot
\ē\ easy	\y\ yet
\g\ go	\yü\ few
\i\ tip	\yu\ cure
\ī\ life	\zh\ vision
\j\ job	

out·sell \-'sel\ *vt* **-sold** \-'sōld\; **-sell·ing** 1 : to exceed in sales ⟨cigarettes far *outsold* cigars⟩ 2 : to surpass in selling

out·set \'auṫ-ˌset\ *n* : BEGINNING 1, START

out·shine \auṫ-'shīn, 'auṫ-\ *vt* **-shone** \-'shōn\; **-shin·ing** 1 a : to shine brighter than b : to exceed in splendor or showiness 2 : SURPASS ⟨*outshone* most of the competitors⟩

out·shoot \-'shüt\ *vt* **-shot** \-'shät\; **-shoot·ing** : to go beyond : SURPASS ⟨*outshoot* one's competitors⟩

¹out·side \auṫ-'sīd, 'auṫ-,\ *n* 1 : a place or region beyond an enclosure or boundary 2 : an outer side or surface 3 : the utmost limit or extent ⟨would sell 500 copies at the *outside*⟩

²outside *adj* 1 : of, relating to, or being on or toward the outside ⟨the *outside* edge⟩ 2 a : situated or performed outside a particular place ⟨*outside* noises⟩ b : giving access to the outside ⟨the *outside* door⟩ 3 : MAXIMUM ⟨cost more than our *outside* estimate⟩ 4 a : not included or originating in a particular group or organization ⟨*outside* influences⟩ b : not part of one's regular routine or duties ⟨*outside* activities⟩ ⟨*outside* reading⟩ 5 : barely possible : REMOTE ⟨an *outside* chance⟩

³outside *adv* : on or to the outside : OUTDOORS

⁴outside *prep* 1 : on or to the outside of ⟨*outside* the house⟩ 2 : beyond the limits of ⟨*outside* the law⟩ 3 : EXCEPT 1 ⟨nobody *outside* a few close friends⟩

outside of *prep* : OUTSIDE 2, 3

out·sid·er \auṫ-'sīd-ər, 'auṫ-\ *n* 1 : a person who does not belong to a particular group 2 : a contender not expected to win

out·sit \-'sit\ *vt* **-sat** \-'sat\; **-sit·ting** : to remain sitting or in session longer than or beyond the time of

¹out·size \'auṫ-ˌsīz\ *n* : an unusual size; *esp* : a size larger than the standard

²outsize *also* **out·sized** \-ˌsīzd\ *adj* : unusually large or heavy

out·skirts \'auṫ-ˌskərts\ *n pl* : the outlying parts of a place or town

out·smart \auṫ-'smärt, 'auṫ-\ *vt* : to get the better of; *esp* : OUTWIT

out·soar \-'sōr, -'sȯr\ *vt* : to soar beyond or above

out·sole \'auṫ-ˌsōl\ *n* : the outside sole of a boot or shoe

out·spo·ken \auṫ-'spō-kən\ *adj* : direct and open in speech or expression : FRANK ⟨an *outspoken* person⟩ ⟨*outspoken* criticism⟩ — **out·spo·ken·ness** \-kən-nəs\ *n*

out·spread \auṫ-'spred\ *vt* **-spread**; **-spread·ing** : to spread out : EXTEND — **out·spread** \'auṫ-ˌspred\ *adj*

out·stand·ing \auṫ-'stan-diŋ\ *adj* 1 : standing out or projecting 2 a : not paid ⟨*outstanding* bills⟩ b : remaining in existence ⟨among problems still *outstanding*⟩ c : publicly issued and sold ⟨20,000 shares *outstanding*⟩ 3 a : standing out from a group : CONSPICUOUS ⟨*outstanding* talent⟩ b : DISTINGUISHED 1, EMINENT ⟨*outstanding* scholars⟩ — **out·stand·ing·ly** \auṫ-'stan-diŋ-lē\ *adv*

out·stay \auṫ-'stā, 'auṫ-\ *vt* 1 : to stay beyond or longer than ⟨*outstay* one's welcome⟩ 2 : to surpass in staying power ⟨*outstayed* the early leaders to win at the finish⟩

out·stretch \auṫ-'strech\ *vt* : to stretch out or beyond

out·strip \auṫ-'strip\ *vt* 1 : to go faster or farther than ⟨*outstripped* the other runners⟩ 2 a : EXCEL ⟨*outstripped* all rivals⟩ b : EXCEED ⟨demand *outstrips* supply⟩ [*out-* + obsolete *strip* "to move fast"]

¹out·ward \'auṫ-wərd\ *adj* 1 : moving or directed toward the outside or away from a center ⟨an *outward* flow⟩ 2 : exposed to view or notice : not private or inward ⟨*outward* optimism⟩

²outward *or* **out·wards** \-wərdz\ *adv* 1 : toward the outside ⟨the city stretches *outward* for miles⟩ ⟨fold it *outward*⟩ 2 *obs* : EXTERNALLY

out·ward·ly \'auṫ-wərd-lē\ *adv* : on the outside : in outward appearance ⟨*outwardly* calm⟩

out·wear \auṫ-'waar, 'auṫ-, -'wear\ *vt* **-wore** \-'wōr, -'wȯr\; **-worn** \-'wōrn, -'wȯrn\; **-wear·ing** : to wear or last longer than ⟨a fabric that *outwears* most others⟩

out·weigh \-'wā\ *vt* : to exceed in weight, value, or importance

out·wit \auṫ-'wit\ *vt* : to get the better of by superior cleverness : OUTSMART

¹out·work \auṫ-'wərk, 'auṫ-\ *vt* : to outdo in working

²outwork \'auṫ-ˌwərk\ *n* : a minor defensive position constructed outside a fortified area

out·worn \auṫ-'wōrn, 'auṫ-, -'wȯrn\ *adj* : no longer useful or accepted : OUT-OF-DATE ⟨an *outworn* system⟩

ou·zel \'ü-zəl\ *n* 1 : a European blackbird or a related bird 2 : WATER OUZEL [Old English ōsle]

ov- *or* **ovi-** *or* **ovo-** *combining form* : egg ⟨*ovi*cidal⟩ [Latin *ovum*]

ova *pl of* OVUM

¹oval \'ō-vəl\ *adj* : having the shape of an egg; *also* : broadly elliptical

²oval *n* : an oval figure or object

²oval

ova·ry \'ōv-rē, -ə-rē\ *n, pl* **-ries** 1 : the typically paired female reproductive organ that produces eggs and in vertebrates female sex hormones 2 : the enlarged rounded part at the base of the pistil of a flowering plant in which seeds are produced [New Latin *ovarium*, from Latin *ovum* "egg"] — **ovar·i·an** \ō-'var-ē-ən, -'ver-\ *adj*

ovate \'ō-ˌvāt\ *adj* : shaped like an egg especially with the basal end broader ⟨*ovate* leaves⟩

ova·tion \ō-'vā-shən\ *n* 1 : a ceremony honoring a Roman general who had won a victory less important than one for which a triumph was granted 2 : a public expression of praise : enthusiastic applause ⟨a standing *ovation*⟩ [Latin *ovatio*, from *ovare* "to exult"]

ov·en \'əv-ən\ *n* : a chamber used for baking, heating, or drying [Old English *ofen*]

ov·en·bird \-ˌbərd\ *n* : an American warbler that builds a dome-shaped nest on the ground [from the shape of its nest]

ovenbird

¹over \'ō-vər\ *adv* 1 a : across a barrier or intervening space ⟨fly *over* to London⟩ b : down or forward and down ⟨went too near the edge and fell *over*⟩ c : across the brim ⟨the soup boiled *over*⟩ d : so as to bring the underside up ⟨turned the cards *over*⟩ e : from a vertical to a prone or inclined position ⟨tripped and fell *over*⟩ ⟨knocked it *over*⟩ f : from one person or side to another ⟨hand it *over*⟩ 2 a : ACROSS ⟨got their point *over*⟩ b : to agreement or concord ⟨won them *over*⟩ 3 : beyond a quantity, limit, or norm often by a specified amount or to a specified degree ⟨the show ran a minute *over*⟩; *also* : in or to excess 4 : so as to cover the whole surface ⟨windows boarded *over*⟩ 5 a : at an end ⟨the day is *over*⟩ b — used on a two-way radio circuit to indicate that a message is complete and a reply is expected 6 a (1) : THROUGH ⟨read it *over*⟩ (2) : in an intensive or comprehensive way b : once more ⟨do it *over*⟩ [Old English *ofer*]

²over *prep* 1 : higher than : ABOVE ⟨flew *over* the city⟩ 2 a : having authority, power, or jurisdiction in regard to ⟨respected those *over* me⟩ b : having superiority, advantage, or preference in comparison to ⟨a big lead *over* the others⟩ 3 : more than ⟨cost *over* $5⟩ 4 a : on or down on especially so as to cover ⟨laid a blanket *over* the child⟩ b : all through or throughout the area of ⟨went *over* my notes⟩ ⟨showed me *over* the house⟩ c : by or through the medium of ⟨heard it *over* TV⟩ 5 a : moving above and across ⟨jump *over* a stream⟩ b : on the other side of ⟨lives *over* the way⟩ 6 : THROUGHOUT, DURING ⟨*over* the past 25 years⟩ 7 — used to indicate an object of solicitude or interest ⟨the Lord watches *over* his own⟩, an activity ⟨spent an hour *over* cards⟩, or concern ⟨trouble *over* money⟩ 8 : for values of the unknown from ⟨find the solution set of the equation *over* the real numbers) — **over one's head** : beyond one's comprehension or control

³**over** *adj* **1** : being outside or above **2 a** : EXCESSIVE ⟨*over* imagination⟩ **b** : having or showing an excess or surplus ⟨the cash is $3 *over* in your books⟩

over- *prefix* **1** : so as to exceed or surpass **2** : excessive **3** : excessively

See *over-* and 2d element

overabstract	overemphatic	overoptimistic
overaccentuate	overenergetic	overorganize
overadvertise	overenthusiasm	overornamented
overambitious	overenthusiastic	overparticular
overambitiousness	overexaggerate	overpay
overanalysis	overexaggeration	overpayment
overanalyze	overexcite	overplan
overanxiety	overexercise	overpraise
overanxious	overexert	overprecise
overapplication	overexertion	overprescribe
overarousal	overexpand	overprescription
overarticulate	overexpansion	overpressure
overassert	overexpectation	overprivileged
overassertion	overexplain	overproduce
overassertive	overexploit	overproduction
overassessment	overexploitation	overpromise
overattention	overextravagant	overpromote
overbake	overexuberant	overpump
overbill	overfamiliar	overqualified
overbleach	overfamiliarity	overreact
overboil	overfastidious	overreaction
overbold	overfat	overreactive
overbright	overfeed	overrefined
overbroad	overfertilization	overregulate
overbrowse	overfertilize	overreliance
overbusy	overfond	overreport
overcareful	overfussy	overrepresented
overcaution	overgeneralization	overrepresentation
overcautious	overgeneralize	overrespond
overcentralization	overgenerosity	overrich
overcentralize	overgenerous	oversanguine
overcivilized	overglamorize	oversaturate
overclean	overharvest	oversaturation
overcommercialization	overhasty	overscrupulous
overcommercialize	overhunt	oversensitive
overcommunicate	overidealize	oversensitivity
overcommunication	overimaginative	overserious
overcomplex	overimpress	overseriously
overcomplicate	overindebtedness	oversimplification
overcompress	overindulge	oversimplify
overconcentration	overindulgence	oversolicitous
overconcern	overindulgent	oversophisticated
overconfidence	overindustrialize	overspecialization
overconfident	overinflate	overspecialize
overconfidently	overinflation	overspeculate
overconscious	overinform	overstaff
overconservative	overingenious	overstimulate
overconsume	overinsistent	overstimulation
overconsumption	overintellectualize	overstrain
overcontrol	overintense	overstress
overcook	overintensity	overstretch
overcorrect	overinvestment	oversuspicious
overcritical	overlabor	overtalkative
overdecorate	overladen	overtax
overdependence	overlarge	overthin
overdependent	overlavish	overtighten
overdramatic	overliteral	overtip
overdramatize	overlong	overtired
overdrink	overloud	overtrain
overeager	overlush	overtreat
overeagerness	overmature	overtreatment
overearnest	overmedicate	overutilization
overeat	overmedication	overutilize
overedit	overmodest	overvaluation
overeducate	overmodestly	overvalue
overelaborate	overmuscled	overviolent
overelaboration	overnice	overvivid
overemotional	overnourish	overwithhold
overemphasis	overobvious	overzealous
overemphasize	overoptimism	overzealousness

over·abun·dance \ˌō-və-rə-'bən-dəns\ *n* : EXCESS 1, SURFEIT — **over·abun·dant** \-dənt\ *adj*

---

over·achiev·er \ˌō-və-rə-'chē-vər\ *n* : one that achieves success above the standard level — **over·achieve·ment** \-'chēv-mənt\ *n*

over·act \ˌō-və-'rakt\ *vb* : to exaggerate or overdo in acting — **over·ac·tion** \-'rak-shən\ *n*

over·ac·tive \-'rak-tiv\ *adj* : excessively or abnormally active ⟨an *overactive* thyroid⟩ — **over·ac·tiv·i·ty** \-rak-'tiv-ət-ē\ *n*

over against *prep* : as opposed to : in contrast with

¹**over·age** \ˌō-və-'rāj\ *adj* : older than is normal for one's position, function, or grade ⟨*overage* students⟩ [²*over* + *age*]

²**over·age** \'ōv-rij, -ə-rij\ *n* : EXCESS 1, SURPLUS [³*over* + *-age*]

¹**over·all** \ˌō-və-'rȯl\ *adv* : as a whole : GENERALLY ⟨we find your work satisfactory, *overall*⟩

²**over·all** \ˌō-və-'rȯl, 'ō-və-ˌ\ *adj* **1** : including everything ⟨*overall* expenses⟩ **2** : viewed as a whole : GENERAL

over·alls \'ō-və-ˌrȯlz\ *n pl* : trousers of strong material usually with a bib and shoulder straps

over and above *prep* : ¹BESIDES

over and over *adv* : many times : OFTEN

over·arm \'ō-və-ˌrärm\ *adj* : done with the arm raised above the shoulder ⟨swim with an *overarm* stroke⟩

over·awe \ˌō-və-'rȯ\ *vt* : to restrain or subdue by awe

over·bal·ance \ˌō-vər-'bal-əns\ *vb* **1** : to have greater weight or importance than ⟨their good qualities more than *overbalanced* their shortcomings⟩ **2** : to lose or cause to lose balance ⟨a boat *overbalanced* by shifting cargo⟩

over·bear \ˌō-vər-'baər, -'beər\ *vt* **-bore** \-'bōr, -'bȯr\; **-borne** \-'bōrn, -'bȯrn\ *also* **-born** \-'bȯrn\; **-bear·ing** **1** : to bear or carry down (as by too much weight) : OVERBURDEN **2** : to domineer over

over·bear·ing \-'baər-ing, -'beər-\ *adj* : haughtily arrogant — **over·bear·ing·ly** \-ing-lē\ *adv*

over·bid \ˌō-vər-'bid\ *vb* **-bid**; **-bid·ding** : to bid too high; *esp* : to bid more than the value of (as one's hand at cards) — **over·bid** \'ō-vər-ˌbid\ *n*

¹**over·blown** \ˌō-vər-'blōn\ *adj* **1** : excessively large in girth : FAT **2** : PRETENTIOUS ⟨*overblown* oratory⟩ [¹*blow*]

²**overblown** *adj* : past the prime of bloom ⟨*overblown* roses⟩ [³*blow*]

over·board \'ō-vər-ˌbōrd, -ˌbȯrd\ *adv* **1** : over the side of a ship into the water **2** : to extremes of enthusiasm ⟨go *overboard* for a new fad⟩ **3** : into discard : ASIDE ⟨threw the rules *overboard*⟩

over·build \ˌō-vər-'bild\ *vb* **-built** \-'bilt\; **-build·ing** : to build beyond need or demand

¹**over·bur·den** \ˌō-vər-'bərd-n\ *vt* : to burden too heavily

²**over·bur·den** \'ō-vər-ˌbərd-n\ *n* : material overlying a deposit of useful geological materials

over·buy \ˌō-vər-'bī\ *vb* **-bought** \-'bȯt\; **-buy·ing** : to buy beyond need or ability to pay

over·call \ˌō-vər-'kȯl\ *vb* **1** : to make a higher bridge bid than (the previous bid or player) **2** : to bid over an opponent's bid in bridge when one's partner has not bid or doubled — **over·call** \'ō-vər-ˌkȯl\ *n*

over·cap·i·tal·ize \ˌō-vər-'kap-ət-l-ˌīz\ *vt* : to assign a value to (the capital of a business) greater than justified by assets or prospects — **over·cap·i·tal·iza·tion** \-ˌkap-ət-l-ə-'zā-shən\ *n*

¹**over·cast** *vt* **-cast**; **-cast·ing** **1** \ˌō-vər-'kast, 'ō-vər-ˌ\ : DARKEN 1, OVERSHADOW **2** \'ō-vər-ˌ\ : to sew (raw edges of a seam) with long slanting widely spaced stitches to prevent raveling

²**over·cast** \'ō-vər-ˌkast, ˌō-vər-'\ *adj* : clouded over : GLOOMY ⟨an *overcast* night⟩

³**over·cast** \'ō-vər-ˌkast\ *n* : COVERING; *esp* : a covering of clouds over the sky

over·charge \ˌō-vər-'chärj\ *vb* **1** : to charge too much **2** : to load too full ⟨*overcharge* an old cannon⟩ **3** : EXAGGERATE 1 — **over·charge** \'ō-vər-ˌchärj\ *n*

\ə\ abut		\ng\ sing
\ər\ further		\ō\ bone
\a\ mat		\ȯ\ saw
\ā\ take		\ȯi\ coin
\ä\ cot, cart		\th\ thin
\au̇\ out		\th\ this
\ch\ chin		\ü\ food
\e\ pet		\u̇\ foot
\ē\ easy		\y\ yet
\g\ go		\yü\ few
\i\ tip		\yu̇\ cure
\ī\ life		\zh\ vision
\j\ job		

over·cloud \ˌō-vər-'klaud\ *vt* : to overspread with clouds

over·coat \'ō-vər-ˌkōt\ *n* : a warm coat worn over indoor clothing

over·come \ˌō-vər-'kəm\ *vb* **-came** \-'kām\; **-come; -com-ing** 1 : to get the better of : CONQUER ⟨*overcome* an enemy⟩ ⟨*overcome* temptation⟩ 2 : to make helpless or exhausted ⟨*overcome* by gas⟩ 3 : to gain superiority : WIN ⟨we shall *overcome*⟩

over·com·pen·sa·tion \-ˌkäm-pən-'sā-shən, -ˌpen-\ *n* : excessive compensation; *esp* : excessive reaction to a feeling of inferiority, guilt, or inadequacy — **over·com-pen·sate** \-'käm-pən-ˌsāt\ *vb* — **over·com·pen·sa·to-ry** \-kəm-'pen-sə-ˌtōr-ē, -ˌtȯr-\ *adj*

over·crowd \ˌō-vər-'kraud\ *vb* : to be or cause to be too crowded

over·de·vel·op \ˌō-vər-di-'vel-əp\ *vt* : to develop excessively; *esp* : to subject (an exposed photographic plate or film) too long to the developing process — **over·de-vel·op·ment** \-mənt\ *n*

over·do \ˌō-vər-'dü\ *vb* **-did** \-'did\; **-done** \-'dən\; **-do-ing** \-'dü-ing\ 1 : to do too much 2 : EXAGGERATE 1 3 : to cook too long 4 : to tire oneself

¹**over·dose** \'ō-vər-ˌdōs\ *n* : too great a dose — **over-dos·age** \ˌō-vər-'dō-sij\ *n*

²**over·dose** \ˌō-vər-'dōs\ *vt* : to give an overdose or too many doses to

over·draft \'ō-vər-ˌdraft, -ˌdraft\ *n* : an overdrawing of a bank account; *also* : the amount overdrawn

over·draw \ˌō-vər-'drȯ\ *vb* **-drew** \-'drü\; **-drawn** \-'drȯn\; **-draw·ing** 1 a : to draw checks on (a bank account) for more than the balance b : to make an overdraft 2 : EXAGGERATE, OVERSTATE ⟨*overdrew* the dangers in the task⟩

¹**over·dress** \ˌō-vər-'dres\ *vb* : to dress too formally for an occasion

²**over·dress** \'ō-vər-ˌdres\ *n* : a dress worn over another

over·drive \'ō-vər-ˌdrīv\ *n* : an automotive gear mechanism so arranged as to provide a higher car speed for a specific engine speed than that provided by ordinary high gear

over·due \ˌō-vər-'dü, -'dyü\ *adj* 1 a : unpaid when due ⟨*overdue* bills⟩ b : delayed beyond an appointed time ⟨an *overdue* train⟩ ⟨the flight is two hours *overdue*⟩ 2 : more than ready ⟨a country *overdue* for reform⟩

over·es·ti·mate \ˌō-və-'res-tə-ˌmāt\ *vt* : to estimate too highly — **over·es·ti·mate** \-mət\ *n* — **over·es·ti·ma-tion** \-ˌres-tə-'mā-shən\ *n*

over·ex·pose \ˌō-və-rik-'spōz\ *vt* : to expose excessively; *esp* : to expose (photographic material) for a longer time than is needed — **over·ex·po·sure** \-'spō-zhər\ *n*

over·ex·tend \-'stend\ *vt* : to extend or expand beyond a safe or reasonable point ⟨*overextend* credit⟩

over·fill \ˌō-vər-'fil\ *vb* : to fill to overflowing

over·fish \-'fish\ *vt* : to fish to the depletion of (a kind of fish) or to the detriment of (a fishing ground)

over·flight \'ō-vər-ˌflīt\ *n* : a passage over an area in an airplane

¹**over·flow** \ˌō-vər-'flō\ *vb* 1 : to cover with or as if with water : INUNDATE 2 : to flow over the top or edge of ⟨the stream *overflowed* its banks⟩ 3 : to flow over bounds ⟨the stream *overflows* every spring⟩ 4 : to fill a space to capacity and spread beyond its limits ⟨the crowd *overflowed* into the street⟩

²**over·flow** \'ō-vər-ˌflō\ *n* 1 : a flowing over : FLOOD 2 : SURPLUS, EXCESS 3 : an outlet or receptacle for surplus liquid

over·fly \ˌō-vər-'flī\ *vt* **-flew** \-flü\; **-flown** \-flōn\; **-fly-ing** : to fly over especially in an airplane

over·gar·ment \'ō-vər-ˌgär-mənt\ *n* : an outer garment

over·glaze \-ˌglāz\ *adj* : applied or suitable for use over a fired glaze ⟨*overglaze* decoration on china⟩ — **overglaze** *n*

over·graze \ˌō-vər-'grāz\ *vt* : to allow animals to graze (land) to the point of damaging the vegetation

over·grow \ˌō-vər-'grō\ *vb* **-grew** \-'grü\; **-grown** \-'grōn\; **-grow·ing** 1 : to grow over so as to cover 2 : to grow beyond or rise above : OUTGROW 3 : to grow excessively 4 : to become grown over — **over·growth** \'ō-vər-ˌgrōth\ *n*

over·grown \ˌō-vər-'grōn\ *adj* : grown unusually or too big ⟨*overgrown* boys⟩ ⟨*overgrown* cities⟩

¹**over·hand** \'ō-vər-ˌhand\ *adj* : made with the hand brought down from above ⟨an *overhand* tennis stroke⟩ — **overhand** *adv* — **over·hand·ed** \ˌō-vər-'han-dəd\ *adv*

²**overhand** *n* : an overhand stroke (as in tennis)

overhand knot \ˌō-vər-ˌhand-, -ˌhan-\ *n* : a small knot often used to prevent the end of a cord from fraying

¹**over·hang** \'ō-vər-ˌhang, ˌō-vər-'\ *vb* **-hung** \-ˌhəng, -'həng\; **-hang·ing** \-ˌhang-ing, -'hang-\ 1 : to jut, project, or be suspended over 2 : to loom over threateningly

²**over·hang** \'ō-vər-ˌhang\ *n* : a part that overhangs ⟨the *overhang* of a roof⟩

over·haul \ˌō-vər-'hȯl\ *vt* 1 : to make a thorough examination of and the necessary repairs and adjustments on ⟨*overhaul* an engine⟩ 2 : OVERTAKE 1 — **over·haul** \'ō-vər-ˌhȯl\ *n*

¹**over·head** \ˌō-vər-'hed\ *adv* : above one's head : ALOFT

²**over·head** \'ō-vər-ˌhed\ *adj* 1 : operating or lying above ⟨an *overhead* door⟩ 2 : of or relating to business overhead

³**over·head** \'ō-vər-ˌhed\ *n* 1 : general business expenses (as rent or heating) 2 : a stroke (as in tennis) made above head height : SMASH

over·hear \ˌō-vər-'hiər\ *vb* **-heard** \-'hərd\; **-hear·ing** \-'hiər-ing\ : to hear without the speaker's knowledge or intention

over·heat \ˌō-vər-'hēt\ *vb* : to heat too much : become too hot

over·joy \ˌō-vər-'jȯi\ *vt* : to fill with great joy

¹**over·kill** \ˌō-vər-'kil\ *vt* : to obliterate (a target) with more nuclear force than required

²**over·kill** \'ō-vər-ˌkil\ *n* 1 : the capability of destroying a target with more nuclear force than required 2 : EXCESS 1 ⟨advertising *overkill*⟩

over·land \'ō-vər-ˌland, -lənd\ *adv or adj* : by, on, or across land

over·lap \ˌō-vər-'lap\ *vb* 1 : to lap over 2 : to have something in common or in common with — **over·lap** \'ō-vər-ˌlap\ *n*

¹**over·lay** \ˌō-vər-'lā\ *vt* **-laid** \-'lād\; **-lay·ing** 1 : to lay or spread over or across : SUPERIMPOSE ⟨*overlay* silver on gold⟩ 2 : OVERLIE 1 ⟨silver *overlaying* gold⟩

²**over·lay** \'ō-vər-ˌlā\ *n* : something (as a veneer on wood) that is overlaid

over·leap \ˌō-vər-'lēp\ *vt* 1 : to leap over or across ⟨*overleap* a ditch⟩ 2 : to defeat (oneself) by going too far

over·lie \ˌō-vər-'lī\ *vt* **-lay** \-'lā\; **-lain** \-'lān\; **-ly·ing** \-'lī-ing\ 1 : to lie over or on 2 : to kill by lying on

over·load \ˌō-vər-'lōd\ *vt* : to load to excess — **over-load** \'ō-vər-ˌlōd\ *n*

over·look \ˌō-vər-'lúk\ *vt* 1 : to look over : INSPECT 2 a : to look down on from above b : to provide a view of from above ⟨the hill *overlooks* a lake⟩ 3 a : to fail to see : MISS b : to pass over : IGNORE c : EXCUSE ⟨*overlook* a beginner's mistakes⟩ 4 : to watch over : SUPERVISE

over·lord \'ō-vər-ˌlȯrd\ *n* 1 : a lord who has supremacy over other lords 2 : an absolute ruler — **over·lord·ship** \-ˌship\ *n*

over·ly \'ō-vər-lē\ *adv* : to an excessive degree

over·man \ˌō-vər-'man\ *vt* : to have or get too many workers for the needs of ⟨*overman* a ship⟩

over·mas·ter \ˌō-vər-'mas-tər\ *vt* : SUBDUE 1

over·match \ˌō-vər-'mach\ *vt* 1 : to be more than a match for : DEFEAT 2 : to match with a superior opponent ⟨a boxer who was badly *overmatched*⟩

¹over·much \ˌō-vər-'məch\ *adj or adv* : too much

²over·much \'ō-vər-ˌməch, ˌō-vər-'\ *n* : too great an amount

¹over·night \ˌō-vər-'nīt\ *adv* **1** : on or during the evening or night ⟨stayed away *overnight*⟩ **2** : SUDDENLY ⟨became famous *overnight*⟩

²overnight *adj* **1** : of, lasting, or staying the night ⟨an *overnight* trip⟩ ⟨*overnight* guests⟩ **2** : SUDDEN ⟨an *overnight* success⟩

¹over·pass \ˌō-vər-'pas\ *vt* **1** : SURPASS 1 **2** : to pass across, over, or beyond : CROSS ⟨*overpass* the bounds of politeness⟩ **3** : OVERLOOK 3b

²over·pass \'ō-vər-ˌpas\ *n* : a crossing (as by means of a bridge) of two highways or of a highway and pedestrian path or railroad at different levels; *also* : the upper level of such a crossing

over·per·suade \ˌō-vər-pər-'swād\ *vt* : to persuade to act contrary to conviction or preference — **over·per·sua·sion** \-'swā-zhən\ *n*

over·play \ˌō-vər-'plā\ *vt* **1 a** : to present (as a dramatic role) extravagantly **b** : to give undue emphasis **2** : to rely too much on the strength of ⟨*overplayed* your hand⟩

over·plus \'ō-vər-ˌpləs\ *n* : EXCESS 1, SURPLUS

over·pop·u·la·tion \ˌō-vər-ˌpäp-yə-'lā-shən\ *n* : the condition of having a population so dense as to cause environmental deterioration, a reduced quality of life, or a population crash — **over·pop·u·late** \-'päp-yə-ˌlāt\ *vt*

over·pow·er \ˌō-vər-'paů-ər, -'paůr\ *vt* **1** : to overcome by superior force : DEFEAT **2** : OVERWHELM ⟨*overpowered* by hunger⟩

over·pow·er·ing \ˌō-vər-'paůr-ing\ *adj* : having great power or influence ⟨*overpowering* beauty⟩ — **over·pow·er·ing·ly** *adv*

¹over·print \ˌō-vər-'print\ *vt* : to print over with something additional

²over·print \'ō-vər-ˌprint\ *n* : something added by overprinting; *esp* : a printed marking added to a postage or revenue stamp (as to commemorate a special event) — **over·print** \'ō-vər-ˌprint\ *n*

over·pro·por·tion \ˌō-vər-prə-'pōr-shən, -'pȯr-\ *vt* : to make disproportionately large — **overproportion** *n* — **over·pro·por·tion·ate** \-shə-nət, -shnət\ *adj* — **over·pro·por·tionate·ly** *adv*

over·pro·tect \ˌō-vər-prə-'tekt\ *vt* : to protect beyond what is wholesome or desirable ⟨*overprotected* children⟩ — **over·pro·tec·tion** \-'tek-shən\ *n* — **over·pro·tec·tive** \-'tek-tiv\ *adj*

over·rate \ˌō-vər-'rāt, -və-\ *vt* : to rate too highly

over·reach \-'rēch\ *vb* **1** : to reach above or beyond **2** : to defeat (oneself) by seeking to do or gain too much **3** : to get the better of : OUTWIT **4** : to go to excess — **over·reach·er** *n*

over·ride \-'rīd\ *vt* **-rode** \-'rōd\; **-rid·den** \-'rid-n\; **-rid·ing** \-'rīd-ing\ **1** : to ride over or across : TRAMPLE **2** : to ride (as a horse) too much or too hard **3 a** : to prevail over : DOMINATE **b** : to set aside : ANNUL ⟨Congress *overrode* the president's veto⟩ **4** : to extend or pass over; *esp* : OVERLAP

over·ripe \-'rīp\ *adj* : passed beyond maturity or ripeness toward decay

over·rule \-'rül\ *vt* **1** : to rule against ⟨the judge *overruled* the objection⟩ **2** : to set aside : REVERSE ⟨a higher court *overruled* the judge's action⟩

¹over·run \-'rən\ *vt* **-ran** \-'ran\; **-run; -run·ning 1 a** : to defeat and occupy the positions of (the enemy *overran* the outpost⟩ **b** : to spread or swarm over : INFEST ⟨a ship *overrun* with rats⟩ **2 a** : to run or go beyond ⟨the plane *overran* the runway⟩ **b** : EXCEED ⟨*overran* my allotted time⟩ **3** : to flow over

²over·run \'ō-vər-ˌrən, -və-\ *n* : an act or instance of overrunning ⟨a cost *overrun*⟩; *also* : the amount by which something overruns

over·sea \ˌō-vər-'sē, 'ō-vər-ˌ\ *adj or adv* : OVERSEAS

over·seas \-'sēz, -ˌsēz\ *adv or adj* : beyond or across the sea

over·see \ˌō-vər-'sē\ *vt* **-saw** \-'sȯ\; **-seen** \-'sēn\; **-see·ing 1** : to look down upon **2 a** : to look over : EXAMINE **b** : SUPERINTEND ⟨*oversee* a road crew⟩

over·seer \'ō-vər-ˌsiər, -ˌsē-ər, ˌō-vər-', -və-\ *n* : one that oversees : SUPERINTENDENT

over·sell \ˌō-vər-'sel\ *vt* **-sold** \-'sōld\; **-sell·ing 1 a** : to sell too much to **b** : to sell too much of **2** : to make excessive claims or claims for

over·set \ˌō-vər-'set\ *vt* **-set; -set·ting** : to turn or tip over : OVERTURN — **over·set** \'ō-vər-ˌset\ *n*

over·sexed \ˌō-vər-'sekst\ *adj* : exhibiting an excessive sexual drive or interest

over·shad·ow \ˌō-vər-'shad-ō\ *vt* **1** : to cast a shadow over : DARKEN **2** : to exceed in importance : OUTWEIGH

over·shoe \'ō-vər-ˌshü\ *n* : an outer shoe; *esp* : GALOSH

over·shoot \ˌō-vər-'shüt\ *vt* **-shot** \-'shät\; **-shoot·ing** : to pass swiftly beyond ⟨the train *overshot* the platform⟩; *also* : to miss by going beyond ⟨the plane *overshot* the runway⟩

over·shot \'ō-vər-ˌshät\ *adj* **1** : having the upper jaw extending beyond the lower **2** : moved by water passing over and flowing from above ⟨an *overshot* waterwheel⟩

over·sight \'ō-vər-ˌsīt\ *n* **1** : the act or duty of overseeing : SUPERVISION **2** : an unintentional omission or error

over·size \ˌō-vər-'sīz\ *or* **over·sized** \-'sīzd\ *adj* : being of more than ordinary size

over·skirt \'ō-vər-ˌskərt\ *n* : a skirt worn over another skirt

over·sleep \ˌō-vər-'slēp\ *vi* **-slept** \-'slept\; **-sleep·ing** : to sleep beyond the time for waking

over·spend \-'spend\ *vb* **-spent** \-'spent\; **-spend·ing 1** : to spend more than **2** : to spend beyond one's means or to excess

over·spread \ˌō-vər-'spred\ *vt* **-spread; -spread·ing** : to spread over or above ⟨branches *overspreading* a garden path⟩ — **over·spread** \'ō-vər-ˌspred\ *n*

over·state \ˌō-vər-'stāt\ *vt* : to state in too strong terms : EXAGGERATE — **over·state·ment** \-mənt\ *n*

over·stay \ˌō-vər-'stā\ *vt* : to stay beyond the time or the limits of ⟨*overstay* one's welcome⟩

over·step \-'step\ *vt* : to step over or go beyond : EXCEED ⟨*overstepped* their authority⟩

over·stock \ˌō-vər-'stäk\ *vb* : to stock beyond requirements or facilities — **over·stock** \'ō-vər-ˌstäk\ *n*

over·strew \ˌō-vər-'strü\ *vt* **-strewed; -strewed** *or* **-strewn** \-'strün\; **-strew·ing 1** : to scatter about **2** : to cover here and there

over·strung \ˌō-vər-'strəng\ *adj* : too highly strung : too sensitive

over·stuffed \ˌō-vər-'stəft\ *adj* **1** : stuffed too full **2** : covered completely and deeply with upholstery ⟨an *overstuffed* chair⟩

over·sub·scribe \ˌō-vər-səb-'skrīb\ *vt* : to subscribe for more of than is available, asked for, or offered for sale — **over·sub·scrip·tion** \-'skrip-shən\ *n*

over·sub·tle \ˌō-vər-'sət-l\ *adj* : excessively or impracticably subtle

over·sup·ply \ˌō-vər-sə-'plī\ *n* : SURPLUS — **oversupply** *vt*

overt \ō-'vərt, 'ō-ˌvərt, 'ō-vərt\ *adj* : open to view : MANIFEST [Middle French *ouvert, overt*, from *ouvrir* "to open", derived from Latin *aperire*] — **overt·ly** *adv*

over·take \ˌō-vər-'tāk\ *vt* **-took** \-'tůk\; **-tak·en** \-'tā-kən\; **-tak·ing 1 a** : to catch up with **b** : to catch up with and pass by **2** : to come upon suddenly ⟨a blizzard *overtook* the hunting party⟩

over–the–count·er *adj* **1** : not traded on an organized securities exchange **2** : sold lawfully without prescription

over·throw \ˌō-vər-'thrō\ *vt* **-threw** \-'thrü\; **-thrown** \-'thrōn\; **-throw·ing 1** : OVERTURN 1, UPSET **2** : to

\ə\ abut \ng\ sing
\ər\ further \ō\ bone
\a\ mat \ȯ\ saw
\ā\ take \ȯi\ coin
\ä\ cot, cart \th\ thin
\aů\ out \t̄h\ this
\ch\ chin \ü\ food
\e\ pet \ů\ foot
\ē\ easy \y\ yet
\g\ go \yü\ few
\i\ tip \yů\ cure
\ī\ life \zh\ vision
\j\ job

bring down : DEFEAT ⟨a government *overthrown* by rebels⟩ — **over·throw** \'ō-vər-ˌthrō\ *n*

over·time \'ō-vər-ˌtīm\ *n* **1** : time exceeding a set limit; *esp* : working time exceeding a standard day or week **2** : the wage paid for overtime work — **overtime** *adv or adj*

over·tone \'ō-vər-ˌtōn\ *n* **1** : one of the higher tones that with the fundamental comprise a musical tone : HARMONIC 1a **2** : a secondary effect, quality, or meaning : SUGGESTION ⟨the words carried an unfriendly *overtone*⟩

over·top \ˌō-vər-'täp\ *vt* **1** : to rise above the top of : surpass in height ⟨*overtopped* my cousin by 6 centimeters⟩ **2** : to stand above : OVERRIDE **3** : OVERSHADOW

over·trick \'ō-vər-ˌtrik\ *n* : a card trick won in excess of the number bid

over·trump \ˌō-vər-'trəmp\ *vb* : to trump with a higher trump card than the highest previously played to the same trick

over·ture \'ō-vər-ˌchùr, -və-, -chər\ *n* **1** : an opening offer : a first proposal ⟨made *overtures* for peace⟩ **2** : an orchestral introduction to an oratorio, opera, or dramatic work; *also* : a composition in this style for concert performance [Middle English, literally, "opening", from Middle French *ouverture,* derived from Latin *apertura* "aperture"]

over·turn \ˌō-vər-'tərn\ *vb* **1** : to turn over : UPSET **2** : OVERTHROW 2, DESTROY — **over·turn** \'ō-vər-ˌtərn\ *n*

over·use \ˌō-vər-'yüs\ *n* : excessive use — **over·use** \-'yüz\ *vt*

over·view \'ō-vər-ˌvyü\ *n* : a general view : SURVEY

over·watch \ˌō-vər-'wäch\ *vt* : to watch over

over·ween·ing \ˌō-vər-'wē-ning\ *adj* **1** : unduly confident : PRESUMPTUOUS **2** : EXCESSIVE, IMMODERATE ⟨*overweening* greed⟩ [Middle English *overwening,* present participle of *overwenen* "to be arrogant", from *over* + *wenen* "to ween"] — **over·ween·ing·ly** \-ning-lē\ *adv*

over·weigh \ˌō-vər-'wā\ *vt* **1** : OUTWEIGH **2** : to weigh down : OPPRESS

¹**over·weight** \'ō-vər-ˌwāt, *2 is usually* ˌō-vər-'\ *n* **1** : weight above what is required or allowed **2** : excessive or burdensome weight; *esp* : bodily weight in excess of what is normal to one's age, height, and build — **over·weight** \ˌō-vər-'\ *adj*

²**over·weight** \ˌō-vər-'wāt\ *vt* **1** : to give too much weight or consideration to ⟨you *overweight* their opinion⟩ **2** : to weight excessively ⟨*overweighted* prose⟩ **3** : OUTWEIGH

over·whelm \-'hwelm, -'welm\ *vt* **1** : to cover completely : SUBMERGE ⟨a wave *overwhelmed* the boat⟩ **2** : WHIP 4 **3** : to overpower in thought or feeling : PROSTRATE ⟨*overwhelmed* by grief⟩ [Middle English *overwhelmen,* from *over* + *whelmen* "to turn over, cover up"] — **over·whelm·ing·ly** \-'hwel-ming-lē, -'wel-\ *adv*

over·wind \ˌō-vər-'wīnd\ *vt* **-wound** \-'waùnd\; **-winding** : to wind too much

over·win·ter \ˌō-vər-'wint-ər\ *vi* : to survive the winter

over·work \ˌō-vər-'wərk\ *vb* **1** : to work or cause to work too hard, too long, or to exhaustion **2** : to decorate all over ⟨a tombstone *overworked* with designs⟩ **3 a** : to work too much on : OVERDO **b** : to make excessive use of ⟨*overworked* phrases⟩ — **overwork** *n*

over·write \ˌō-vər-'rīt, -və-\ *vb* **-wrote** \-'rōt\; **-writ·ten** \-'rit-n\; **-writ·ing** \-'rīt-ing\ **1** : to write over the surface of **2** : to write in a too elaborate or pretentious style ⟨*overwritten* accounts of simple events⟩ **3** : to write too much

over·wrought \ˌō-vər-'rȯt, -və-\ *adj* **1** : extremely excited **2** : decorated to excess [past participle of *overwork*]

ovi- *or* **ovo-** — see OV-

ovi·cid·al \ˌō-və-'sīd-l\ *adj* : capable of killing eggs — **ovi·cide** \'ō-və-ˌsīd\ *n*

ovi·duct \'ō-və-ˌdəkt\ *n* : a tube for the passage of eggs from the ovary of an animal

ovine \'ō-ˌvīn\ *adj* : of or relating to sheep [Late Latin *ovinus,* from Latin *ovis* "sheep"] — **ovine** *n*

ovip·a·rous \ō-'vip-rəs, -ə-rəs\ *adj* : producing eggs that develop and hatch outside the maternal body [Latin *oviparus,* from *ovum* "egg" + *parere* "to produce"] — **ovip·a·rous·ly** *adv*

ovi·pos·it \'ō-və-ˌpäz-ət\ *vi* : to lay eggs — used especially of insects [probably back-formation from *ovipositor*] — **ovi·po·si·tion** \ˌō-və-pə-'zish-ən\ *n*

ovi·pos·i·tor \'ō-və-ˌpäz-ət-ər\ *n* : a specialized organ (as of an insect) for depositing eggs [Latin *ovum* "egg" + *positor* "one that places", from *ponere* "to place"]

ovoid \'ō-ˌvȯid\ *also* **ovoi·dal** \ō-'vȯid-l\ *adj* : shaped like an egg : OVATE — **ovoid** *n*

ovo·vi·vip·a·rous \ˌō-vō-ˌvī-'vip-rəs, -ə-rəs\ *adj* : producing eggs that develop within the maternal body and hatch within or immediately after leaving the parent — **ovo·vi·vip·a·rous·ly** *adv*

ovu·late \'äv-yə-ˌlāt, 'ōv-\ *vi* : to produce eggs or discharge them from an ovary — **ovu·la·tion** \ˌäv-yə-'lā-shən, ˌōv-\ *n*

ovule \'äv-ˌyül, 'ōv-\ *n* **1** : an outgrowth of the ovary of a seed plant that after fertilization develops into a seed **2** : a small egg; *esp* : one in an early stage of growth [New Latin *ovulum,* from Latin *ovum* "egg"] — **ovu·lar** \-yə-lər\ *adj*

ovum \'ō-vəm\ *n, pl* **ova** \-və\ : a female gamete : MACROGAMETE — called also *egg, egg cell* [Latin, "egg"]

ow \'aù, 'ü\ *interj* — used to express sudden pain

owe \'ō\ *vb* **1** : to have (an emotion or attitude) to someone or something ⟨*owes* the seller a grudge⟩ **2 a** (1) : to be under obligation to pay or repay ⟨*owes* me $5⟩ (2) : to be obligated to render (as duty or a service) **b** : to be indebted to ⟨*owes* the grocer for supplies⟩ **c** : to be in debt ⟨*owes* for the house⟩ [Old English *āgan* "to possess, own, owe"]

ow·ing \'ō-ing\ *adj* : due to be paid

owing to *prep* : because of ⟨delayed *owing to* traffic⟩

owl \'aùl\ *n* : any of an order (Strigiformes) of birds of prey with large head and eyes, short hooked bill, strong talons, and more or less nocturnal habits [Old English *ūle*]

owl·et \'aù-lət\ *n* : a young or small owl

owl·ish \'aù-lish\ *adj* : resembling or suggesting an owl — **owl·ish·ly** *adv* — **owl·ish·ness** *n*

¹**own** \'ōn\ *adj* : belonging to oneself or itself — usually used following a possessive case or possessive adjective ⟨wanted my *own* room⟩ [Old English *āgen*]

²**own** *vb* **1 a** : POSSESS 2a **b** : to have legal title to **2** : ACKNOWLEDGE, ADMIT ⟨*own* a debt⟩ **3** : CONFESS — used with *to* or *up* ⟨*owned* to being scared⟩ ⟨if you broke the window, *own* up⟩ — **own·er** \'ō-nər\ *n* — **own·er·ship** \-ˌship\ *n*

³**own** *pron, sing or pl in construction* : one or ones belonging to oneself — used after a possessive and without a following noun as a pronoun equivalent in meaning to the adjective *own* ⟨want rooms of their *own*⟩ — **on one's own** : for or by oneself

ox \'äks\ *n, pl* **ox·en** \'äk-sən\ *also* **ox** **1** : a common large domestic bovine mammal kept for milk, draft, and meat; *esp* : an adult castrated male **2** : any of the larger hollow-horned cud-chewing mammals (as a buffalo) [Old English *oxa*]

ox- *or* **oxo-** *combining form* : oxygen [French, from *oxygène*]

ox·a·late \'äk-sə-ˌlāt\ *n* : a salt or ester of oxalic acid

ox·al·ic acid \äk-ˌsal-ik-\ *n* : a poisonous strong acid $C_2H_2O_4$ that occurs in various plants as oxalates and is used especially as a bleaching or cleaning agent and in making dyes [French *acide oxalique,* from Latin *oxalis* "wood sorrel"]

ox·al·is \ˈäk-ˈsal-əs\ *n* : **WOOD SORREL** [Latin, from Greek, from *oxys* "sharp"]

ox·blood \ˈäks-ˌbləd\ *n* : a moderate reddish brown

ox·bow \ˈäks-ˌbō\ *n* **1** : a U-shaped collar worn by a draft ox **2 a** : a U-shaped bend in a river **b** : a U-shaped lake formed when such a bend becomes isolated when bypassed by the river channel — called also *oxbow lake* — **oxbow** *adj*

ox·eye \ˈäk-ˌsī\ *n* : any of several composite plants having heads with both disk and ray flowers; *esp* : **DAISY** 1b

oxeye daisy *n* : **DAISY** 1b

ox·ford \ˈäks-fərd\ *n* : a low shoe laced or tied over the instep [*Oxford*, England]

ox·heart \ˈäks-ˌhärt\ *n* : any of various large sweet cherries

ox·i·dant \ˈäk-səd-ənt\ *n* : **OXIDIZING AGENT**

ox·i·dase \ˈäk-sə-ˌdās, -ˌdāz\ *n* : any of various enzymes that catalyze oxidations

ox·i·da·tion \ˌäk-sə-ˈdā-shən\ *n* **1** : the process of oxidizing **2** : the state or result of being oxidized — **ox·i·da·tive** \ˈäk-sə-ˌdāt-iv\ *adj*

oxidation number *n* : a positive or negative number that represents the effective charge of an atom or element and indicates the extent of or possibility for oxidation of the atom or element 〈the usual *oxidation number* of sodium is +1 and of oxygen −2〉 — called also *oxidation state*

oxidation–reduction *n* : a chemical reaction in which one or more electrons are transferred from one atom or molecule to another

ox·ide \ˈäk-ˌsīd\ *n* : a compound of oxygen with an element or radical [French, from *ox-* + *-ide* (from *acide* "acid")]

ox·i·dize \ˈäk-sə-ˌdīz\ *vb* **1** : to combine with oxygen **2** : to dehydrogenate especially by the action of oxygen **3** : to remove one or more electrons from (an atom, ion, or molecule) **4** : to become oxidized — **ox·i·diz·er** *n*

oxidizing agent *n* : a substance (as oxygen or nitric acid) that oxidizes by taking up electrons

Ox·o·ni·an \äk-ˈsō-nē-ən\ *n* : a student or graduate of Oxford University [Medieval Latin *Oxonia* "Oxford"] — **Oxonian** *adj*

ox·tail \ˈäk-ˌstāl\ *n* : the tail of cattle; *esp* : the skinned tail for use as food

oxy \ˈäk-sē\ *adj* : **OXYGENIC**; *esp* : containing oxygen or additional oxygen — often used in combination 〈*oxy*hemoglobin〉 〈*oxy*hydrogen〉 [French, from *oxygène* "oxygen"]

oxy·acet·y·lene \ˌäk-sē-ə-ˈset-l-ən, -l-ˌēn\ *adj* : of, relating to, or utilizing a mixture of oxygen and acetylene 〈*oxyacetylene* torch〉

ox·y·gen \ˈäk-si-jən\ *n* : a chemical element that is found free as a colorless tasteless odorless gas in the atmosphere of which it forms about 21 percent or combined in water, that is capable of combining with all elements except the inert gases, that is active in physiological processes, and that is involved in combustion processes — see **ELEMENT** table [French *oxygène*, from Greek *oxys* "sharp, acid" + French *-gène* "-gen"] — **ox·y·gen·ic** \ˌäk-si-ˈjen-ik\ *adj*

ox·y·gen·ate \ˈäk-si-jə-ˌnāt, äk-ˈsij-ə-\ *vt* : to impregnate, combine, or supply (as blood) with oxygen — **ox·y·gen·ation** \ˌäk-si-jə-ˈnā-shən, äk-ˌsij-ə-\ *n*

oxygen debt *n* : a cumulative oxygen deficit that develops during periods of intense bodily activity and must be made good when the body returns to rest

oxygen mask *n* : a device worn over the nose and mouth through which oxygen is supplied from a storage tank

oxygen tent *n* : a canopy which can be placed over a bedridden person and within which a flow of oxygen can be maintained

oxy·he·mo·glo·bin \ˌäk-si-ˈhē-mə-ˌglō-bən\ *n* : a compound of hemoglobin with oxygen that is the chief means of transportation of oxygen from the air (as in the lungs) by way of the blood to the tissues

oxy·hy·dro·gen \ˌäk-si-ˈhī-drə-jən\ *adj* : of, relating to, or utilizing a mixture of oxygen and hydrogen 〈*oxyhydrogen* torch〉

oxy·mo·ron \ˌäk-si-ˈmōr-ˌän, -ˈmȯr-\ *n, pl* **-mo·ra** \-ˈmōr-ə, -ˈmȯr-ə\ : a combination of contradictory or incongruous words (as *cruel kindness*) [Late Greek *oxymōron*, from *oxymōros* "pointedly foolish", from Greek *oxys* "sharp, keen" + *mōros* "foolish"]

oxy·to·cin \ˌäk-si-ˈtōs-n\ *n* : a pituitary hormone that helps to regulate blood pressure and stimulates the contraction of smooth muscle in the uterus [derived from Greek *oxys* "sharp, quick" + *tokos* "childbirth", from *tiktein* "to bear"]

oyez \ō-ˈyā, -ˈyes\ *imperative verb* — used by a court or public crier to gain attention before a proclamation [Anglo-French, "hear ye", from *oir* "to hear", from Latin *audire*]

oys·ter \ˈȯi-stər\ *n* : any of various marine bivalve mollusks having a rough irregular shell and including important edible shellfish [Middle French *oistre*, from Latin *ostrea*, from Greek *ostreon*]

oyster bed *n* : a place where oysters grow or are cultivated

oyster catcher *n* : any of a genus of wading birds with stout legs, a heavy wedge-shaped bill, and often black and white plumage

oyster cracker *n* : a small salted cracker

oys·ter·man \ˈȯi-stər-mən\ *n* : a gatherer, opener, breeder, or seller of oysters

oyster plant *n* : **SALSIFY**

ozone \ˈō-ˌzōn\ *n* **1** : a form O_3 of oxygen that has three atoms in the molecule, is a faintly blue irritating gas with a pungent odor, is generated usually in dilute form by a silent electric discharge in oxygen or air, and is used especially in disinfection and deodorization and in oxidation and bleaching **2** : pure and refreshing air [German *ozon*, from Greek *ozōn*, present participle of *ozein* "to smell"] — **ozo·nic** \ō-ˈzō-nik\ *adj* — **ozo·nif·er·ous** \ˌō-ˌzō-ˈnif-rəs, -ə-rəs\ *adj*

ozone hole *n* : an area of the ozone layer (as near the south pole) that is seasonally depleted of ozone

ozone layer *n* : an atmospheric layer at heights of about 20 to 30 miles (32 to 48 kilometers) that is normally characterized by high ozone content which blocks most solar ultraviolet radiation from entry into the lower atmosphere

ozo·no·sphere \ō-ˈzō-nə-ˌsfiər\ *n* : **OZONE LAYER**

oyster catcher

\ə\	abut	\ng\	sing
\ər\	further	\ō\	bone
\a\	mat	\ȯ\	saw
\ā\	take	\ȯi\	coin
\ä\	cot, cart	\th\	thin
\au̇\	out	\th\	this
\ch\	chin	\ü\	food
\e\	pet	\u̇\	foot
\ē\	easy	\y\	yet
\g\	go	\yü\	few
\i\	tip	\yu̇\	cure
\ī\	life	\zh\	vision
\j\	job		

Pp

p \'pē\ *n, pl* **p's** *or* **ps** \'pēz\ *often cap* : the 16th letter of the English alphabet

pa \'pä, 'pȯ\ *n* : FATHER 1a [short for *papa*]

PABA \'pab-ə, ‚pē-‚ā-'bē-‚ā\ *n* : PARA-AMINOBENZOIC ACID [*para-a*mino*b*enzoic *a*cid]

pab·u·lum \'pab-yə-ləm\ *n* : FOOD; *esp* : a suspension or solution of nutrients suitable for absorption [Latin, "food, fodder"]

pa·ca \'päk-ə, 'pak-\ *n* : any of a genus of large South and Central American rodents [Portuguese and Spanish, from Tupi *páca*]

¹pace \'pās\ *n* **1** : rate of moving or progressing especially on foot **2 a** : a manner of walking : TREAD **b** : GAIT; *esp* : a fast 2-beat gait of a horse in which the legs on the same side move in pairs and support the animal alternately on the right and left **3** : a single step or a measure based on the length of a human step [Old French *pas* "step", from Latin *passus,* from *pandere* "to spread"]

²pace *vb* **1 a** : to walk with slow measured steps **b** : to move along : PROCEED **2** : to go or cover at a pace — used of a horse **3** : to measure by paces — often used with *off* **4 a** : to set or regulate the pace of **b** : PRECEDE 2, LEAD — **pac·er** *n*

pace·mak·er \'pā-‚smā-kər\ *n* **1** : one that sets the pace for another **2 a** : a bodily part (as of the heart) that serves to establish and maintain a rhythmic activity **b** : an electrical device for steadying or establishing the heartbeat

pa·chi·si \pə-'chē-zē\ *n* : an ancient board game played with dice and counters [Hindi *pacīsī*]

pachy·derm \'pak-i-‚dərm\ *n* : any of various thick-skinned hoofed mammals (as an elephant or a rhinoceros) [French *pachyderme,* from Greek *pachydermos* "thick-skinned", from *pachys* "thick" + *derma* "skin"] — **pachy·der·ma·tous** \‚pak-i-'dər-mət-əs\ *adj*

pach·ys·an·dra \‚pak-ə-'san-drə\ *n* : any of a genus of evergreen woody trailing plants of the box family often used as a ground cover [derived from Greek *pachys* "thick" + *andr-, anēr* "man"]

pa·cif·ic \pə-'sif-ik\ *adj* **1** : making or promoting peace ⟨a *pacific* policy⟩ **2** : having a mild and calm nature : PEACEABLE ⟨a quiet *pacific* people⟩ [Latin *pacificus,* from *pac-, pax* "peace"] — **pa·cif·i·cal·ly** \-'sif-i-kə-lē, -klē\ *adv*

pac·i·fi·ca·tion \‚pas-ə-fə-'kā-shən\ *n* : the act or process of pacifying : the state of being pacified

Pacific time *n* : the time of the 8th time zone west of Greenwich that includes the Pacific coastal region of the United States

pac·i·fi·er \'pas-ə-‚fī-ər, -‚fīr-\ *n* **1** : one that pacifies **2** : a usually nipple-shaped device for babies to suck on

pac·i·fism \'pas-ə-‚fiz-əm\ *n* : opposition to war or violence as a means of settling disputes; *esp* : refusal to bear arms on moral or religious grounds — **pac·i·fist** \-fəst\ *n* — **pacifist** *or* **pac·i·fis·tic** \‚pas-ə-'fis-tik\ *adj*

pac·i·fy \'pas-ə-‚fī\ *vt* **-fied; -fy·ing 1** : to ease the anger or agitation of : SOOTHE ⟨*pacify* a crying child⟩ **2** : to

restore to a peaceful state : SUBDUE ⟨*pacify* a country⟩ [Latin *pacificare,* from *pac-, pax* "peace"] — **pac·i·fi·able** \-‚fī-ə-bəl\ *adj* □ SYN APPEASE, PLACATE, MOLLIFY: PACIFY may imply a soothing or calming of anger or agitation or the forceful quelling of insurrection; APPEASE implies quieting anger or averting threats by making concessions to insistent demands; PLACATE suggests changing resentment or bitterness to goodwill; MOLLIFY stresses a soothing of feelings by concession or flattery.

¹pack \'pak\ *n* **1 a** : a bundle arranged for carrying especially on the back **b** : a group or pile of related objects ⟨a *pack* of cards⟩ **2** : a large amount or number : HEAP **3** : an act, an instance, or a method of packing; *also* : arrangement in a pack **4 a** : a group of often predatory animals of the same kind **b** : a group of persons with a common interest ⟨a *pack* of thieves⟩ **c** : an organized troop (as of cub scouts) **5** : a concentrated mass **6** : absorbent material used medically (as for checking bleeding or applying medication or moisture) **7 a** : a cosmetic paste for the face **b** : an application or treatment of oils or creams for conditioning the scalp and hair [Middle English, of Low German or Dutch origin]

²pack *vb* **1 a** : to make into a compact bundle ⟨*pack* papers into an envelope⟩ **b** : to stow one's personal belongings in luggage ⟨I'll go home and *pack*⟩ **c** : to fill completely ⟨the stadium was *packed*⟩ **d** : to arrange closely and securely in a protective container ⟨glasses *packed* for shipment⟩ **2 a** : to crowd together so as to fill full : CRAM ⟨the crowd was *packed* into the hall⟩ **b** : to increase the density of : COMPRESS **3** : to fill or cover so as to prevent passage (as of air or steam) ⟨*pack* a joint in a pipe⟩ **4** : to send or go away without ceremony ⟨*pack* the children off to school⟩ **5 a** : to transport on foot or on the back of an animal ⟨*pack* water from a spring⟩ **b** : to be supplied or equipped with : POSSESS ⟨*pack* a gun⟩ **6** : to assemble in a group : CONGREGATE — **pack·abil·i·ty** \‚pak-ə-'bil-ət-ē\ *n* — **pack·able** \‚pak-ə-bəl\ *adj*

³pack *vt* : to influence the makeup of (as a jury) improperly to gain a desired result [obsolete *pack* "to make a secret agreement"]

¹pack·age \'pak-ij\ *n* **1 a** : a small or moderate-sized pack : PARCEL **b** : a unit of a product uniformly wrapped or sealed **2** : a covering wrapper or container **3** : something that suggests a package of merchandise; *esp* : PACKAGE DEAL

²package *vt* : to make into or enclose in a package — **pack·ag·er** *n*

package deal *n* : an offer or agreement involving more than one item or making acceptance of one item dependent on the acceptance of another

package store *n* : a store that sells alcoholic beverages only in containers that may not lawfully be opened on the premises

pack animal *n* : an animal used for carrying packs

pack·er \'pak-ər\ *n* : one that packs: as **a** : a dealer who prepares and packs foods for the market ⟨a meat *pack-*

er) **b** : ²PORTER 1 **c** : one that conveys goods on pack animals

pack·et \'pak-ət\ *n* **1** : a small bundle or parcel **2** : a passenger boat carrying mail and cargo on a regular schedule [Middle French *pacquet*, of Germanic origin]

pack·horse \'pak-,hȯrs\ *n* : a horse used as a pack animal

pack ice *n* : sea ice formed into a mass by the crushing together of chunks and sheets of ice

pack·ing \'pak-ing\ *n* : material used to pack or caulk something

pack·ing·house \'pak-ing-,hau̇s\ *n* : an establishment for processing and packing foodstuffs and especially meat and its by-products — called also *packing plant*

pack rat *n* **1** : WOOD RAT; *esp* : a large bushy-tailed rodent of the Rocky Mountain area that hoards food and miscellaneous objects **2** : a person who hoards trivial or unneeded items

pack·sack \'pak-,sak\ *n* : a case used to carry gear on the back when traveling on foot : BACKPACK

pack·sad·dle \'pak-,sad-l\ *n* : a saddle that supports the load on the back of a pack animal

pack·thread \-,thred\ *n* : strong thread or small twine used for sewing or tying packs or parcels

pact \'pakt\ *n* : ⁴COMPACT; *esp* : an international treaty [Middle French, from Latin *pactum*, from *pacisci* "to agree, contract"]

¹pad \'pad\ *n* **1 a** : a cushioned part or thing : CUSHION **b** : a piece of material that holds ink for inking the surface of a rubber stamp **2 a** : the foot of some mammals **b** : the cushioned bottom of the toes of some mammals **3** : a floating leaf of a water plant **4** : TABLET 1b **5** : LAUNCH PAD [origin unknown]

²pad *vt* **pad·ded; pad·ding 1** : to furnish with a pad or padding **2** : to expand with useless or trivial matter

³pad *vb* **pad·ded; pad·ding 1** : to go on foot **2** : to move along with a muffled step [perhaps from Dutch *paden* "to follow a path", from *pad* "path"]

⁴pad *n* : a soft muffled or slapping sound [imitative]

pad·ding \'pad-ing\ *n* : material used to pad something

¹pad·dle \'pad-l\ *vi* **pad·dled; pad·dling** \'pad-ling, -l-ing\ **1** : to move the hands or feet about in shallow water **2** : TODDLE ⟨the small child *paddled* over to them⟩ [origin unknown]

²paddle *n* **1 a** : an implement with a flat blade to propel and steer a small craft (as a canoe) **b** : something (as the flipper of a seal) suggesting a paddle in appearance or action **2 a** : an implement used for stirring, mixing, or beating **b** : a short bat with a broad flat blade used to hit the ball in various games (as table tennis) **c** : a small hand-held device with a dial used to control movement of an object along a line on a computer display screen **3** : one of the broad boards at the circumference of a paddle wheel or waterwheel [Middle English *padell*]

³paddle *vb* **pad·dled; pad·dling** \'pad-ling, -l-ing\ **1** : to go, propel, or carry by or as if by means of a paddle or paddle wheel **2 a** : to beat or stir with or as if with a paddle **b** : to punish with or as if with a paddle — **pad·dler** \'pad-lər, -l-ər\ *n*

pad·dle·fish \'pad-l-,fish\ *n* : a fish of the Mississippi valley about a meter long with a paddle-shaped snout

paddle wheel *n* : a wheel with paddles, floats, or boards around its circumference used to propel a vessel

pad·dock \'pad-ək, -ik\ *n* : a usually enclosed area used especially for pasturing or exercising animals; *esp* : an enclosure where racehorses are saddled and paraded before a race [alteration of Middle English *parrok*, from Old English *pearroc*]

pad·dy \'pad-ē\ *n, pl* **paddies 1** : RICE; *esp* : threshed unmilled rice **2** : wet land in which rice is grown [Malay *padi*]

pad·dy wagon \'pad-ē-\ *n* : PATROL WAGON [probably from English slang *Paddy* "Irishman, policeman", from *Paddy*, nickname for *Patrick*]

pad·lock \'pad-,läk\ *n* : a removable lock with a hinged bow-shaped piece attached at one end so that the other end can be passed into a catch in the lock [Middle English *padlok*] — **padlock** *vt*

pa·dre \'päd-rā, -rē\ *n* **1** : a Christian clergyman; *esp* : PRIEST **2** : a military chaplain [Spanish or Italian or Portuguese, literally, "father", from Latin *pater*]

pae·an \'pē-ən\ *n* : a joyous song of praise, tribute, thanksgiving, or triumph [Latin, "hymn of thanksgiving especially to Apollo", from Greek *paian*, from *Paian*, epithet of Apollo]

paed- *or* **paedo-** *or* **ped-** *or* **pedo-** *combining form* : child ⟨*ped*iatrics⟩ [Greek *paid-*, *pais* "child, boy"]

pa·gan \'pā-gən\ *n* **1** : HEATHEN 1 **2** : an irreligious person [Late Latin *paganus*, from Latin, "country dweller", from *pagus* "country district"] — **pagan** *adj* — **pa·gan·ish** \-gə-nish\ *adj* — **pa·gan·ism** \-gə-,niz-əm\ *n* — **pa·gan·ize** \-gə-,nīz\ *vt*

¹page \'pāj\ *n* **1** : a medieval youth being trained for knighthood in the service of a knight; *also* : a youth attending a person of rank **2** : one employed to deliver messages, assist patrons, or serve as a guide [Old French, from Italian *paggio*]

²page *vt* **1** : to serve in the capacity of a page **2** : to summon by calling out the name

³page *n* **1 a** : one side of a printed or written leaf; *also* : the entire leaf **b** : the matter printed or written on a page ⟨set several *pages* of type⟩ **2 a** : a written record ⟨the *pages* of history⟩ **b** : an event or circumstance worth recording ⟨an exciting *page* in one's life⟩ [Middle French, from Latin *pagina*]

⁴page *vt* : to number or mark the pages of

pag·eant \'paj-ənt\ *n* **1 a** : a mere show : PRETENSE **b** : a showy display **2** : a usually elaborate entertainment consisting of scenes based on history or legend ⟨a Christmas *pageant*⟩ [Middle English *padgeant*, literally, "scene of a play", from Medieval Latin *pagina*, from Latin, "page"]

pag·eant·ry \'paj-ən-trē\ *n, pl* **-ries 1** : pageants and the presentation of pageants **2** : colorful, rich, or splendid display

page boy *n* **1** : a boy serving as a page **2** *usually* **page·boy** \'pāj-,bȯi\ : a woman's often shoulder-length haircut with the ends turned under in a smooth roll

pag·er \'pā-jər\ *n* : one that pages; *esp* : BEEPER

pag·i·nate \'paj-ə-,nāt\ *vt* : ⁴PAGE

pag·i·na·tion \,paj-ə-'nā-shən\ *n* **1** : the paging of written or printed matter **2** : the number and arrangement of pages (as of a book) or an indication of these

pa·go·da \pə-'gōd-ə\ *n* : a Far Eastern temple or memorial in the form of a tower usually with roofs curving upward at the division of each of several stories [Portuguese *pagode* "oriental idol, temple", derived from Sanskrit *bhagavatī*, epithet of Hindu goddesses, feminine of *bhagavat* "blessed"]

paid *past of* PAY

pail \'pāl\ *n* : a usually cylindrical vessel that is open at the top and has a handle : BUCKET [Middle English *payle, paille*] — **pail·ful** \-,fu̇l\ *n*

¹pain \'pān\ *n* **1** *pl* : PUNISHMENT ⟨prescribed *pains* and penalties⟩ **2 a** (1) : physical suffering associated with disease, injury, or other bodily disorder ⟨a *pain* in the back⟩ ⟨in constant *pain*⟩ (2) : a basic bodily sensation induced by a harmful stimulus, characterized by physical discomfort (as pricking, throbbing, or aching), and typically leading to attempts to escape its cause **b** : acute mental or emotional distress : GRIEF **3** *pl* : the throes of childbirth **4** *pl* : care or effort taken in accomplishing something ⟨took *pains* with their work⟩ **5** : someone or something that annoys or is troublesome ⟨studying can be a real *pain*⟩ [Old French *peine*, from Latin *poena*, from Greek *poinē* "payment, penalty"] SYN see EFFORT — **pain** *adj* — **pain·less** \-ləs\ *adj* — **pain·less·ly** *adv* — **pain·less·ness** *n* — **on pain of**

pack rat 1

pagoda

\ə\ abut	\ng\ sing
\ər\ further	\ō\ bone
\a\ mat	\ȯ\ saw
\ā\ take	\ȯi\ coin
\ä\ cot, cart	\th\ thin
\au̇\ out	\th\ this
\ch\ chin	\ü\ food
\e\ pet	\u̇\ foot
\ē\ easy	\y\ yet
\g\ go	\yü\ few
\i\ tip	\yu̇\ cure
\ī\ life	\zh\ vision
\j\ job	

or **under pain of** : subject to penalty or punishment by — **pain in the neck** : a source of annoyance : NUISANCE

²**pain** *vb* **1** : to cause pain in or to : HURT **2** : to give or experience pain

pain·ful \'pān-fəl\ *adj* **1 a** : feeling or giving pain **b** : that troubles or distresses ⟨a *painful* interview⟩ **2** : requiring effort or care — **pain·ful·ly** \-fə-lē\ *adv* — **pain·ful·ness** *n*

pain·kill·er \'pān-,kil-ər\ *n* : something (as a drug) that relieves pain — **pain·kill·ing** \-ing\ *adj*

pains·tak·ing \'pān-,stā-king\ *adj* : marked by diligent care and effort — **pains·tak·ing·ly** \-king-lē\ *adv*

¹**paint** \'pānt\ *vb* **1** : to apply paint or a comparable covering or coloring substance to ⟨*paint* a wall⟩ ⟨*paint* the wound with iodine⟩ **2 a** : to represent in lines and colors on a surface by applying pigments ⟨*paint* a picture⟩ **b** : to produce or evoke as if by painting ⟨*paints* glowing pictures of their vacation⟩ **3** : to practice the art of painting **4** : to use cosmetics [Old French *peint* "painted", from *peindre* "to paint", from Latin *pingere*]

²**paint** *n* **1** : MAKEUP; *esp* : a cosmetic to add color **2 a** : a mixture of a pigment and a suitable liquid to form a closely adherent coating when spread on a surface in a thin coat **b** : an applied coating of paint ⟨scrape old *paint* from woodwork⟩

paint·brush \'pānt-,brəsh\ *n* **1** : a brush for applying paint **2 a** : INDIAN PAINTBRUSH 1 **b** : ORANGE HAWKWEED

painted bunting *n* : a brightly colored finch of the southern United States

painted turtle *n* : any of several common freshwater turtles that are found chiefly in the eastern United States and have a greenish black upper shell with yellow bands and red markings and a yellow lower shell

¹**paint·er** \'pānt-ər\ *n* : one that paints: as **a** : an artist who paints **b** : a worker who applies paint as an occupation — **paint·er·ly** \-lē\ *adj*

²**pain·ter** \'pānt-ər\ *n* : a line used for securing or towing a boat [Middle English *paynter*, probably from Middle French *pendoir, pentoir* "line for hanging clothes to dry", from *pendre* "to hang"]

paint·ing \'pānt-ing\ *n* **1** : a product of painting; *esp* : a painted work of art **2** : the art or occupation of painting

¹**pair** \'paər, 'peər\ *n, pl* **pairs** *also* **pair** **1** : two corresponding things either naturally matched or intended to be used together ⟨a *pair* of hands⟩ ⟨a *pair* of gloves⟩ **2** : a single unit made up of two corresponding pieces ⟨a *pair* of scissors⟩ **3** : a set of two: as **a** : two mated animals **b** : a couple in love, engaged, or married **c** : two members of a deliberative body who hold opposing views and agree not to vote on a specific issue **4** *chiefly dialect* : a set or series of small objects (as beads) [Old French *paire*, from Latin *paria* "equal things", from *par* "equal"]

²**pair** *vb* : to join in a pair or in pairs ⟨*paired* the guests⟩

pair of compasses : COMPASS 2c

pais·ley \'pāz-lē\ *adj, often cap* **1** : made typically of soft wool with colorful curved abstract figures **2** : having a pattern like that of a paisley fabric [*Paisley*, Scotland] — **paisley** *n*

Pai·ute \'pī-,üt, -,yüt\ *n* : a member of a group of Indian peoples of the Great Basin having an Aztec-related language

pa·ja·mas \pə-'jäm-əz, -'jam-\ *n pl* : a loose usually 2-piece lightweight suit designed especially for sleeping [Hindi *pājāma* "lightweight trousers", from Persian *pā* "leg" + *jāma* "garment"]

¹**pal** \'pal\ *n* : a close friend [Romany *phral, phal* "brother, friend", from Sanskrit *bhrātr* "brother"]

²**pal** *vi* **palled; pal·ling** : to be or associate as pals

pal·ace \'pal-əs\ *n* **1 a** : the official residence of a sovereign **b** *chiefly British* : the official residence of an archbishop or bishop **2 a** : a large stately house **b** : a large public building **c** : a gaudy place for public amusement or refreshment ⟨a movie *palace*⟩ [Old French *palais*, from Latin *palatium*, from *Palatium*, hill in Rome where the emperors' residences were built]

pal·a·din \'pal-əd-ən\ *n* **1** : a knightly hero or champion **2** : a strong supporter of a cause [French, from Italian *paladino*, from Medieval Latin *palatinus* "courtier", from Latin, "palatine"]

pa·laes·tra \pə-'les-trə\ *n, pl* **-trae** \-,trē\ **1** : a school in ancient Greece or Rome for sports (as wrestling) **2** : GYMNASIUM 1 [Latin, from Greek *palaistra*, from *palaiein* "to wrestle"]

pal·at·able \'pal-ət-ə-bəl\ *adj* **1** : agreeable to the taste : SAVORY **2** : agreeable to the mind : ACCEPTABLE — **pal·at·abil·i·ty** \,pal-ət-ə-'bil-ət-ē\ *n* — **pal·at·able·ness** \'pal-ət-ə-bəl-nəs\ *n* — **pal·at·ably** \-blē\ *adv*

pal·a·tal \'pal-ət-l\ *adj* **1** : of or relating to the palate **2** : pronounced with the front or blade of the tongue near or touching the hard palate ⟨the \y\ in *yeast* and the \sh\ in *she* are *palatal* sounds⟩ — **palatal** *n* — **pal·a·tal·ly** \-l-ē\ *adv*

pal·a·tal·ize \'pal-ət-l-,īz\ *vt* : to pronounce as or change into a palatal sound — **pal·a·tal·iza·tion** \,pal-ət-l-ə-'zā-shən\ *n*

pal·ate \'pal-ət\ *n* **1** : the roof of the mouth separating the mouth from the nasal cavity **2 a** : intellectual relish or taste **b** : the sense of taste [Latin *palatum*]

pa·la·tial \pə-'lā-shəl\ *adj* **1** : of, relating to, or being a palace **2** : suitable to a palace : MAGNIFICENT — **pa·la·tial·ly** \-shə-lē\ *adv* — **pa·la·tial·ness** *n*

pa·lat·i·nate \pə-'lat-n-ət\ *n* : the territory of a palatine

¹**pal·a·tine** \'pal-ə-,tīn\ *adj* **1 a** : of or relating to a palace especially of a Roman or Holy Roman emperor **b** : PALATIAL **2 a** : possessing royal privileges **b** : of or relating to a palatine or a palatinate [Latin *palatinus*, from *palatium* "palace"]

²**palatine** *n* **1 a** : a high officer of an imperial palace **b** : a feudal lord having sovereign power within his domains **2** *cap* : a native or inhabitant of the Palatinate

³**palatine** *adj* : of, relating to, or lying near the palate

⁴**palatine** *n* : a palatine bone

¹**pa·lav·er** \pə-'lav-ər, -'läv-\ *n* **1** : a long parley usually between persons of different cultural levels **2 a** : idle talk **b** : misleading or beguiling speech [Portuguese *palavra* "word, speech", from Late Latin *parabola* "parable, speech"]

²**palaver** *vi* : to talk at length or idly

¹**pale** \'pāl\ *adj* **1 a** : lacking color or intensity of color **b** : not vivid in hue or luster; *esp* : low in saturation and high in lightness ⟨a *pale* pink⟩ **c** : not having the warm skin color of a person in good health **2** : not bright or brilliant : DIM ⟨a *pale* moon⟩ [Middle French, from Latin *pallidus* "pallid"] — **pale·ly** \'pāl-lē\ *adv* — **pale·ness** \'pāl-nəs\ *n* — **pal·ish** \'pā-lish\ *adj*

²**pale** *vb* : to make or become pale

³**pale** *vt* : to enclose with pales : FENCE [Middle French *paler*, from *pal* "stake", from Latin *palus*]

⁴**pale** *n* **1** : a stake or picket of a fence or palisade **2 a** : an enclosed place **b** : a territory within specified bounds or under a particular jurisdiction **3** : limits within which one is protected or privileged ⟨conduct beyond the *pale* of decency⟩

pale- *or* **paleo-** *or* **palae-** *or* **palaeo-** *combining form* **1** : involving or dealing with ancient forms or conditions ⟨*paleo*botany⟩ **2** : early : primitive : archaic ⟨*Paleo*lithic⟩ [Greek *palaios* "ancient", from *palai* "long ago"]

pa·lea \'pā-lē-ə\ *n, pl* **-le·as** *or* **-le·ae** \-lē-,ē\ : the upper bract of the flower of a grass [Latin, "chaff"]

pa·leo·bot·a·ny \,pā-lē-ō-'bät-n-ē, -'bät-nē\ *n* : a branch of botany dealing with fossil plants — **pa·leo·bot·a·nist** \-'bät-n-əst, -'bät-nəst\ *n*

Pa·leo·cene \'pā-lē-ə-,sēn\ *n* : the earliest epoch of the Tertiary; *also* : its system of rocks — **Paleocene** *adj*

pa·le·og·ra·phy \,pā-lē-'äg-rə-fē\ *n* **1 a** : an ancient manner of writing **b** : ancient writings **2** : the study of ancient writings and inscriptions — **pa·le·og·ra·pher** \-fər\ *n* — **pa·leo·graph·ic** \,pā-lē-ə-'graf-ik\ *adj* — **pa·leo·graph·i·cal·ly** \-'graf-i-kə-lē, -klē\ *adv*

pa·leo·lith \'pā-lē-ə-,lith\ *n* : a Paleolithic stone implement

Pa·leo·lith·ic \,pā-lē-ə-'lith-ik\ *adj* : of, relating to, or being the 2d period of the Stone Age which is characterized by rough or crudely chipped stone implements — compare EOLITHIC, NEOLITHIC

pa·le·on·tol·o·gy \,pā-lē-än-'täl-ə-jē\ *n* : a science dealing with the life of past geological periods as known especially from fossil remains [French *paléontologie*, from Greek *palaios* "ancient" + *onta* "existing things", from *ont-, ōn*, present participle of *einai* "to be" + French *-logie* "-logy"] — **pa·le·on·to·log·i·cal** \-,änt-l-'äj-i-kəl\ *or* **pa·le·on·to·log·ic** \-'äj-ik\ *adj* — **pa·le·on·tol·o·gist** \-än-'täl-ə-jəst\ *n*

Pa·le·o·zo·ic \,pā-lē-ə-'zō-ik\ *n* : the second earliest era of geological history which is the period of greatest development of nearly all classes of invertebrates except the insects and in the later epochs of which seed-bearing plants, amphibians, and reptiles first appeared; *also* : the corresponding system of rocks — see GEOLOGIC TIME table — **Paleozoic** *adj*

pal·ette \'pal-ət\ *n* **1** : a thin board or tablet on which a painter mixes pigments **2 a** : the set of colors put on the palette **b** : a particular range, quality, or use of color [French, from Middle French *pale* "spade, shovel", from Latin *pala*]

palette knife *n* : a knife with a flexible steel blade and no cutting edge used to mix or to apply colors

pal·frey \'pol-frē\ *n, pl* **palfreys** *archaic* : a saddle horse; *esp* : one suitable for a woman [Old French *palefrei*, from Medieval Latin *palafredus*, from Late Latin *paraveredus* "post-horse for secondary roads", from Greek *para-* "beside, subsidiary" + Latin *veredus* "post-horse", of Gaulish origin]

pal·imp·sest \'pal-əm-,sest, -əmp-\ *n* : writing material (as a parchment) used again after earlier writing has been erased [Latin *palimpsestus*, from Greek *palimpsēstos* "scraped again", from *palin* "back, again" + *psēn* "to scrape"]

pal·in·drome \'pal-ən-,drōm\ *n* : a word, verse, or sentence (as "Able was I ere I saw Elba") or a number (as 1881) that reads the same backward or forward [Greek *palindromos* "running back again", from *palin* "back, again" + *dramein* "to run"]

¹pal·ing \'pā-liŋ\ *n* **1** : ⁴PALE 1, PICKET **2 a** : material for pales **b** : a fence of pales

pal·in·ode \'pal-ə-,nōd\ *n* **1** : an ode or song recanting or retracting something in an earlier poem **2** : a formal retraction [Greek *palinōidia*, from *palin* "back" + *aeidein* "to sing"]

¹pal·i·sade \,pal-ə-'sād\ *n* **1 a** : a fence of stakes especially for defense **b** : a long strong stake pointed at the top and set close with others as a defense **2** : a line of steep cliffs [French *palissade*, derived from Latin *palus* "stake"]

²palisade *vt* : to surround or fortify with palisades

palisade cell *n* : a cell of the palisade layer

palisade layer *n* : a layer of columnar or cylindrical chlorophyll-rich cells just under the upper epidermis of a leaf — called also *palisade parenchyma*; compare SPONGY PARENCHYMA

¹pall \'pol\ *n* **1** : a chalice cover made of a square piece of stiffened linen **2** : a heavy cloth draped over a coffin **3** : something that covers, darkens, or produces a gloomy effect ⟨a *pall* of smoke⟩ [Old English *pæll* "cloak, mantle", from Latin *pallium*]

²pall *vi* : to become dull or uninteresting : lose the ability to give pleasure [Middle English *pallen*, from *appallen* "to become pale, make pale"]

¹pal·la·di·um \pə-'lād-ē-əm\ *n, pl* **-dia** \-ē-ə\ : something that protects or defends : SAFEGUARD [Latin, a statue of Pallas Athene which was held to ensure the safety of Troy, from Greek *palladion*, from *Pallad-, Pallas* "Pallas"]

²palladium *n* : a silver-white ductile malleable metallic chemical element that is used especially as a catalyst and in alloys — see ELEMENT table [New Latin, from *Pallad-, Pallas*, an asteroid, from Latin, "Pallas, goddess of wisdom", from Greek]

pall·bear·er \'pol-,bar-ər, -,ber-\ *n* : a person who carries or escorts the coffin at a funeral

¹pal·let \'pal-ət\ *n* **1** : a straw-filled tick or mattress **2** : a small, hard, or temporary bed [Middle English *pailet*, from Middle French *paille* "straw", from Latin *palea* "chaff, straw"]

²pallet *n* **1** : a flat-bladed tool for forming, beating, or rounding clay or glass **2** : PALETTE 1 **3** : a lever or surface in a timepiece that receives an impulse from the escapement wheel and imparts motion to a balance or pendulum [Middle French *palette* "small shovel", from *pale* "spade, shovel", from Latin *pala*]

pal·li·ate \'pal-ē-,āt\ *vt* **1** : to make (as a disease) less intense or severe **2** : to cover by excuses and apologies [Late Latin *palliare* "to cloak, conceal", from Latin *pallium* "cloak"] — **pal·li·a·tion** \,pal-ē-'ā-shən\ *n* — **pal·li·a·tor** \'pal-ē-,āt-ər\ *n*

pal·li·a·tive \'pal-ē-,āt-iv, 'pal-yət-\ *adj* : serving to palliate — **palliative** *n* — **pal·li·a·tive·ly** *adv*

pal·lid \'pal-əd\ *adj* : lacking color : WAN [Latin *pallidus*, from *pallēre* "to be pale"] — **pal·lid·i·ty** \pa-'lid-ət-ē\ *n* — **pal·lid·ly** \'pal-əd-lē\ *adv* — **pal·lid·ness** *n*

pal·li·um \'pal-ē-əm\ *n, pl* **-lia** \-ē-ə\ *or* **-li·ums** **1 a** : a draped rectangular cloak worn by men of ancient Greece and Rome **b** : a white woolen band with pendants in front and back worn over the chasuble by a pope or archbishop [Latin]

pal·lor \'pal-ər\ *n* : lack of color especially of the face : PALENESS [Latin, from *pallēre* "to be pale"]

pal·ly \'pal-ē\ *adj* : sharing the relationship of pals : INTIMATE

¹palm \'päm, 'pälm\ *n* **1** : any of a family of mostly tropical or subtropical trees, shrubs, or vines usually with a simple but often tall stem topped by a crown of huge feathery or fan-shaped leaves **2 a** : a palm leaf especially when carried as a symbol of victory or rejoicing **b** : a symbol of success; *also* : VICTORY, TRIUMPH [Old English, from Latin *palma*, literally, "palm of the hand"; from the resemblance of the tree's leaves to an outstretched hand] — **palm·like** \-,līk\ *adj*

²palm *n* **1** : the under part of the hand between the fingers and the wrist **2** : a unit of length based on the width or length of the hand [Middle French *paume*, from Latin *palma*]

³palm *vt* **1** : to conceal in or pick up stealthily with the hand ⟨*palm* a card⟩ **2** : to pass off by fraud ⟨*palm* off shoddy goods⟩

pal·mar \'pal-mər, 'päm-ər, 'päl-mər\ *adj* : of, relating to, situated in, or involving the palm of the hand

pal·mate \'pal-,māt, 'päm-,āt, 'päl-,māt\ *adj* : resembling a hand with the fingers spread : **a** : having lobes or veins radiating from a common point ⟨a *palmate* leaf⟩ **b** : having the distal portion broad, flat, and lobed ⟨a *palmate* antler⟩ — **pal·mate·ly** *adv*

palm·er \'päm-ər, 'päl-mər\ *n* : a person wearing two crossed palm leaves as a sign of a pilgrimage to the Holy Land

pal·met·to \pal-'met-ō\ *n, pl* **-tos** *or* **-toes** : any of several usually low-growing palms with fan-shaped leaves [Spanish *palmito*, from *palma* "palm", from Latin]

palm·ist·ry \'päm-ə-strē, 'päl-mə-\ *n* : the art or practice of reading a person's character or future from markings on the palms [Middle English *pawmestry*, probably from *paume* "palm" + *maistrie* "mastery"] — **palm·ist** \'päm-əst, 'päl-məst\ *n*

¹palm 1

pal·mit·ic acid \pal-'mit-ik-, pä-, päl-\ *n* : a waxy fatty acid occurring free or especially in the form of glycerides in most fats and fatty oils

pal·mi·tin \'pal-mət-ən, 'päm-ət-, 'päl-mət-\ *n* : an ester of glycerol and palmitic acid [French *palmitine*, derived from Latin *palma* "palm"]

palm oil *n* : an edible fat obtained from the fruit of several palms and used especially in soap, candles, and lubricating greases

Palm Sunday *n* : the Sunday before Easter celebrated in commemoration of Christ's triumphal entry into Jerusalem [from the palm branches strewn in Christ's way]

palmy \'päm-ē, 'päl-mē\ *adj* **palm·i·er; -est** **1** : abounding in or bearing palms **2** : marked by prosperity : FLOURISHING

pal·o·mi·no \,pal-ə-'mē-nō\ *n, pl* **-nos** : a slender-legged short-bodied horse of a light tan or cream color with lighter mane and tail [American Spanish, from Spanish, "like a dove", from Latin *palumbinus*, from *palumbes*, a kind of pigeon]

palp \'palp\ *n* : PALPUS — **pal·pal** \'pal-pəl\ *adj*

pal·pa·ble \'pal-pə-bəl\ *adj* **1** : that can be touched or felt : TANGIBLE **2** : easily perceptible : NOTICEABLE **3** : easily understood : MANIFEST [Late Latin *palpabilis*, from Latin *palpare* "to stroke"] — **pal·pa·bil·i·ty** \,pal-pə-'bil-ət-ē\ *n* — **pal·pa·bly** \'pal-pə-blē\ *adv*

pal·pate \'pal-,pāt\ *vt* : to examine by touch especially medically [derived from Latin *palpare* "to stroke"] — **pal·pa·tion** \pal-'pā-shən\ *n*

pal·pi·tate \'pal-pə-,tāt\ *vi* : to beat rapidly and strongly : THROB, QUIVER (*palpitating* with excitement) [Latin *palpitare*, derived from *palpare* "to stroke"] — **pal·pi·tant** \'pal-pət-ənt\ *adj* — **pal·pi·ta·tion** \,pal-pə-'tā-shən\ *n*

pal·pus \'pal-pəs\ *n, pl* **pal·pi** \-,pī, -pē\ : a segmented sense organ on an arthropod mouthpart [Latin, "caress, soft palm of the hand"] — **pal·pate** \'pal-,pāt\ *adj*

pal·sy \'pol-zē\ *n, pl* **palsies** **1** : PARALYSIS 1 **2** : a condition marked by uncontrollable tremor of the body or a part [Middle French *paralisie*, from Latin *paralysis*] — **palsy** *vt*

pal·ter \'pol-tər\ *vi* **pal·tered; pal·ter·ing** \-tə-riŋ, -triŋ\ **1** : to act insincerely : EQUIVOCATE **2** : HAGGLE 2, BARGAIN [origin unknown] — **pal·ter·er** \-tər-ər\ *n*

pal·try \'pol-trē\ *adj* **pal·tri·er; -est** **1** : CHEAP 2, SHODDY **2** : contemptibly limited : MEAN, LITTLE (*paltry* minds) **3** : PETTY 2, TRIVIAL [obsolete *paltry* "trash"] — **pal·tri·ness** *n*

pal·y·nol·o·gy \,pal-ə-'näl-ə-jē\ *n* : a branch of science dealing with pollen and spores [Greek *palynein* "to sprinkle", from *pale* "fine meal"] — **pal·y·no·log·i·cal** \-nə-'läj-i-kəl\ *adj* — **pal·y·nol·o·gist** \-'näl-ə-jəst\ *n*

pam·pa \'pam-pə, 'päm-\ *n, pl* **pampas** \-pəz, -pəs\ : an extensive generally grass-covered plain of South America [American Spanish, from Quechua] — **pam·pe·an** \'pam-pē-ən, 'päm-, pam-', päm-'\ *adj*

pam·per \'pam-pər\ *vt* **pam·pered; pam·per·ing** \'pam-pə-riŋ, -priŋ\ : to treat with extreme or excessive care and attention [Middle English *pamperen*] — **pam·per·er** \-pər-ər\ *n*

pam·phlet \'pam-flət, 'pamp-\ *n* : an unbound printed publication with no cover or a paper cover [Middle English *pamflet* "unbound booklet", from *Pamphilus, seu De Amore* "Pamphilus, or About Love", popular Latin poem of the 12th century] □ ORIGIN *Pamphilus, seu De Amore* ("Pamphilus, or About Love"), written in the late 12th century by an author now unknown, is a poem detailing a series of amusing amorous adventures. This poem was very popular in its day. In the late Middle Ages the names of short literary works were often given diminutive forms. *Pamphilus* became *Pamphilet* (at least in French—the name, although probably used, is not attested in English). And Middle English *pamflet* was soon the word for any written work too short to be called a book.

panda 2

¹pam·phle·teer \,pam-flə-'tiər, ,pamp-\ *n* : a writer of pamphlets attacking something or urging a cause

²pamphleteer *vi* : to write and publish pamphlets

¹pan \'pan\ *n* **1 a** : a usually broad, shallow, and open container for household use **b** : a broad shallow open vessel: as (1) : either of the receptacles of a pair of scales (2) : a round shallow metal container used to wash waste from metal (as gold) **2** : a basin or depression in the earth (a salt *pan*) **3** : HARDPAN 1 [Old English *panne*, from Latin *patina*, from Greek *patanē*]

²pan *vb* **panned; pan·ning** **1** : to wash earthy material in a pan to concentrate bits of native metal; *also* : to separate (metal) from debris by panning **2** : to yield precious metal in panning **3** : to criticize severely

pan- *combining form* **1** : all : completely (*pan*chromatic) **2** : involving all of a (specified) group (*Pan*-American) **3** : total : general (*pan*leucopenia) [Greek, from *pan*, neuter of *pas* "all, every"]

pan·a·cea \,pan-ə-'sē-ə\ *n* : a remedy for all ills or difficulties : CURE-ALL [Latin, from Greek *panakeia*, from *pan-* + *akeisthai* "to heal", from *akos* "remedy"] — **pan·a·ce·an** \-'sē-ən\ *adj*

pa·nache \pə-'nash, -'näsh\ *n* **1** : an ornamental tuft (as of feathers) especially on a helmet **2** : dash or colorfulness in style and action : VERVE [Middle French *pennache*, from Italian *pennachio*, from Latin *pinnaculum* "small wing", from *pinna* "feather, wing", alteration of *penna*]

pan·a·ma \'pan-ə-,mä, -,mò\ *n, often cap* : a lightweight hat made of narrow strips from the young leaves of a tropical American tree [American Spanish *panamá*, from *Panama*, Central America]

Pan–Amer·i·can \,pan-ə-'mer-ə-kən\ *adj* : of, relating to, or involving the independent republics of North America and South America

Pan–Amer·i·can·ism \-kə-,niz-əm\ *n* : a movement for greater cooperation among the Pan-American nations

¹pan·cake \'pan-,kāk\ *n* : a flat cake made of thin batter and cooked on both sides (as on a griddle)

²pancake *vb* : to make or cause to make a pancake landing

pancake landing *n* : a landing in which an airplane is leveled off higher than for a normal landing causing it to stall and drop in an approximately horizontal position with little forward motion

pan·chro·mat·ic \,pan-krō-'mat-ik\ *adj* : sensitive to light of all colors in the visible spectrum (*panchromatic* film)

pan·cre·as \'paŋ-krē-əs, 'pan-\ *n* : a large compound gland of vertebrates that lies near the stomach and secretes digestive enzymes and the hormone insulin [Greek *pankreat-, pankreas*, from *pan-* + *kreas* "flesh, meat"] — **pan·cre·at·ic** \,paŋ-krē-'at-ik, ,pan-\ *adj*

pancreatic duct *n* : the duct leading from the pancreas and opening into the duodenum

pancreatic juice *n* : a clear alkaline secretion of pancreatic enzymes that is poured into the duodenum and acts on food already partly digested by the gastric juice and saliva

pan·da \'pan-də\ *n* **1** : a long-tailed flesh-eating reddish mammal of the Himalayas that resembles a raccoon **2** : a large black-and-white mammal of western China and Tibet that suggests a bear but is related to the raccoon — called also *giant panda* [French, from native name in Nepal]

pan·da·nus \pan-'dā-nəs, -'dan-əs\ *n* : SCREW PINE [Malay *pandan*]

pan·dem·ic \pan-'dem-ik\ *n* : an outbreak of disease occurring over a wide area and affecting many people (an influenza *pandemic*) [derived from Greek *pan-* + *dēmos* "people"] — **pandemic** *adj*

pan·de·mo·ni·um \,pan-də-'mō-nē-əm\ *n* : a wild uproar : TUMULT [*Pandemonium*, capital of Hell, from pan- + Late Latin *daemonium* "evil spirit", from Greek *daimonion*, from *daimōn* "spirit, deity"]

¹pan·der \'pan-dər\ *n* **1 a** : a go-between in love intrigues **b** : one who solicits clients for a prostitute **2** : one who caters to or exploits the weaknesses of others [*Pandarus*]

²pander *vi* **pan·dered; pan·der·ing** \-də-riŋ, -driŋ\ : to act as a pander — **pan·der·er** \-dər-ər\ *n*

Pan·do·ra's box \pan-,dōr-əz-, -,dȯr-\ *n* : a source of many usually unforeseen troubles [from the box containing all the ills of mankind opened by the mythical Pandora against the command of Zeus]

pan·dow·dy \pan-'daȯd-ē\ *n, pl* **-dies** : a deep-dish apple dessert spiced, sweetened, and covered with a rich crust [origin unknown]

pane \'pān\ *n* **1 a** : a section or side of something (as a facet of a gem) **b** : one of the sections into which a sheet of postage stamps is cut for distribution **2** : a framed sheet of glass in a window or door [Middle French *pan* "strip of cloth, pane", from Latin *pannus* "cloth, rag"]

pan·e·gy·ric \,pan-ə-'jir-ik, -'jī-rik\ *n* : a formal speech or writing eulogizing someone or something; *also* : formal or elaborate praise [Latin *panegyricus*, from Greek *panēgyrikos*, from *panēgyrikos* "for a festival", from *panēgyris* "festival assembly", from *pan-* + *agyris* "assembly"] — **pan·e·gy·ri·cal** \-'jir-i-kəl, -'jī-ri-\ *adj* — **pan·e·gy·ri·cal·ly** \-kə-lē, -klē\ *adv* — **pan·e·gy·rist** \,pan-ə-'jir-əst, -'jī-rəst\ *n*

¹pan·el \'pan-l\ *n* **1 a** : a schedule containing names of persons summoned as jurors; *also* : JURY 1 **b** : a group of persons who discuss a topic before an audience **c** : a group of entertainers or guests engaged as players in a quiz or guessing game on a radio or television program **2** : a separate or distinct part of a surface: as **a** : a usually rectangular and sunken or raised section of a surface (as of a door, wall, or ceiling) set off by a margin **b** : a unit of construction material (as plywood) made to form part of a surface (as of a wall or an airplane wing) **c** : a vertical section (as a gore) of cloth **d** : a section of a switchboard; *also* : a mount for controls (as of an electrical device) **3** : a thin flat piece of wood on which a picture is painted; *also* : a painting on such a surface [Middle English, "piece of cloth, slip of parchment, jury schedule", from Middle French, "piece of cloth", derived from Latin *pannus* "cloth"]

²panel *vt* **-eled** *or* **-elled; -el·ing** *or* **-el·ling** : to furnish or decorate with panels

pan·el·ing \'pan-l-iŋ\ *n* : panels joined in a continuous surface; *esp* : decorative wood panels so combined

pan·el·ist \'pan-l-əst\ *n* : a member of a panel for discussion or entertainment

panel truck *n* : a small light motortruck with a fully enclosed body

pan·fish \'pan-,fish\ *n* : a small food fish (as a sunfish) usually caught with hook and line and not sold commercially

pang \'paŋ\ *n* : a sudden sharp attack or spasm (as of pain or emotional distress) (hunger *pangs*) [origin unknown]

pan·go·lin \'paŋ-gə-lən; pan-'gō-lən, paŋ-\ *n* : any of several Asian and African mammals having the body covered with large overlapping horny scales [Malay *pĕngguling*]

¹pan·han·dle \'pan-,han-dl\ *n* : a narrow projection of a larger territory (as a state)

²panhandle *vb* **-dled; -dling** \-dliŋ, -dl-iŋ\ : to beg for money or food on the street — **pan·han·dler** \-dlər\ *n*

Pan·hel·len·ic \,pan-hə-'len-ik\ *adj* **1** : of or relating to all Greece or all the Greeks **2** : of or relating to the Greek-letter sororities or fraternities in American colleges and universities or to an association representing them

pan·ic \'pan-ik\ *n* **1** : a sudden overpowering fright; *esp* : a sudden unreasoning terror often causing mass flight **2** : a sudden widespread fright concerning financial affairs that causes hurried selling and a sharp fall in prices **3** *slang* : something very funny [*panic, adj.*, from French *panique*, from Greek *panikos*, literally, "of Pan", from *Pan* "Pan"] **SYN** see **FEAR** — **panic** *adj* — **pan·icky** \'pan-i-kē\ *adj* □ **ORIGIN** The Greek god Pan is often represented playing the panpipes, which he was believed to have invented. According to the story, Pan was once chasing a nymph named Syrinx. Unable to escape across a river, Syrinx asked the river nymphs for help, and they changed her into a bed of reeds. Pan cut pieces of those reeds and made a panpipe. Pan was also believed to have given a great shout which instilled fear into the giants in their battle against the gods. And in Athens Pan was worshiped because the citizens believed that it was he who had caused the Persians to flee in fear from the battle of Marathon. From this more awesome aspect of Pan's nature comes the word *panic*.

²panic *vb* **pan·icked** \-ikt\; **pan·ick·ing** **1** : to affect or be affected with panic **2** : to produce demonstrative appreciation on the part of (*panic* an audience with a gag)

pan·i·cle \'pan-i-kəl\ *n* : a branched flower cluster (as of a lilac or some grasses) in which each branch from the main axis bears more than one flower [Latin *panicula*, from *panus* "swelling"] — **pan·i·cled** \-kəld\ *adj* — **pa·nic·u·late** \pə-'nik-yə-lət\ *adj*

pan·ic–strick·en \'pan-ik-,strik-ən\ *adj* : overcome with panic

Pan·ja·bi \,pən-'jäb-ē, -'jab-\ *n* **1** : an Indic language of the Punjab region of the Indian subcontinent **2** : **PUNJABI 1** [Hindi *pañjābī*, from *pañjābī* "of Punjab"]

pan·jan·drum \pan-'jan-drəm\ *n* : a powerful personage or pretentious official [Grand *panjandrum*, title of an imaginary personage in nonsense lines by Samuel Foote, died 1777, English playwright]

pan·leu·co·pe·nia \,pan-,lü-kə-'pē-nē-ə\ *n* : an acute usually fatal viral disease of cats characterized by fever, diarrhea and dehydration, and extensive destruction of white blood cells

pan·nier \'pan-yər, 'pan-ē-ər\ *n* **1** : a large basket; *esp* : one of wicker carried on the back of an animal or the shoulder of a person **2 a** : either of a pair of hoops formerly used by women to expand their skirts at the hips **b** : an overskirt draped and puffed out at the sides [Middle French *panier*, from Latin *panarium*, from *panis* "bread"]

pan·ni·kin \'pan-i-kən\ *n, chiefly British* : a small pan or cup

pan·o·ply \'pan-ə-plē\ *n, pl* **-plies** **1 a** : a full suit of armor **b** : ceremonial attire **2** : something that covers or hides protectively **3** : a magnificently impressive array or display [Greek *panoplia*, from *pan-* + *hopla* "arms, armor"] — **pan·o·plied** \-plēd\ *adj*

pan·ora·ma \,pan-ə-'ram-ə, -'räm-\ *n* **1 a** : **CYCLORAMA** **b** : a picture exhibited a part at a time by being unrolled before the spectator **2 a** : a full and unobstructed view in every direction **b** : a comprehensive presentation of a subject **3** : a mental picture of a series of images or events [*pan-* + Greek *horama* "sight", from *horan* "to see"] — **pan·oram·ic** \-'ram-ik\ *adj*

pan out *vi* : to turn out; *esp* : **SUCCEED** [²*pan*]

pan·pipe \'pan-,pīp\ *n* : a primitive wind instrument consisting of a graduated series of short vertical pipes bound together with the mouthpieces in an even row — often used in pl. [*Pan*, its traditional inventor] — see **PANIC** origin

pan·sy \'pan-zē\ *n, pl* **pansies** : a garden plant originated by hybridization of various violets and violas; *also* : its showy velvety 5-petaled flower [Middle French *pensée*, from *pensée* "thought", from *penser* "to think", from Latin *pensare* "to ponder"]

panicle

<ə\ abut | \ŋ\ sing
<ər\ further | \ō\ bone
\a\ mat | \ȯ\ saw
\ā\ take | \ȯi\ coin
\ä\ cot, cart | \th\ thin
\aȯ\ out | \th\ this
\ch\ chin | \ü\ food
\e\ pet | \u̇\ foot
\ē\ easy | \y\ yet
\g\ go | \yü\ few
\i\ tip | \yu̇\ cure
\ī\ life | \zh\ vision
\j\ job

¹pant \'pant\ *vb* **1 a** : to take short rapid breaths **b** : to make a puffing sound **c** : to progress with panting ⟨the car *panted* up the hill⟩ **2** : to long eagerly : YEARN **3** : to utter with panting ⟨ran up and *panted* out the message⟩ [Middle English *panten*, from Middle French *pantaisier*, from Greek *phantasioun* "to have hallucinations", from *phantasia* "imagination"]

²pant *n* **1** : a panting breath **2** : a puffing sound

pan·ta·lets *or* **pan·ta·lettes** \ˌpant-l-'ets\ *n pl* : long drawers with a ruffle at the bottom of each leg

pan·ta·loons \ˌpant-l-'ünz\ *n pl* : close-fitting trousers usually with straps passing under the insteps [Italian *Pantaleone, Pantalone*, character in old Italian comedies]

pan·the·ism \'pan-thē-ˌiz-əm, 'pant-\ *n* : a doctrine that equates God with the forces and laws of the universe — **pan·the·ist** \-thē-əst\ *n* — **pan·the·is·tic** \ˌpan-thē-'is-tik, ˌpant-\ *adj* — **pan·the·is·ti·cal** \-ti-kəl\ *adj* — **pan·the·is·ti·cal·ly** \-kə-lē, -klē\ *adv*

pan·the·on \'pan-thē-ˌän, 'pant-\ *n* **1** : a temple dedicated to all the gods **2** : a building serving as the burial place of or containing memorials to famous dead **3** : the gods of a people; *esp* : the gods officially recognized [Latin, from Greek *pantheion*, from *pan-* + *theos* "god"]

pan·ther \'pan-thər, 'pant-\ *n, pl* **panthers** *also* **panther** **1** : LEOPARD **2** : COUGAR **3** : JAGUAR [Old French *pantere*, from Latin *panthera*, from Greek *panthēr*]

pant·ies \'pant-ēz\ *n pl* : a woman's or child's undergarment covering the lower trunk

pan·to·graph \'pant-ə-ˌgraf\ *n* : an instrument for manually copying a figure (as a map or plan) to scale [French *pantographe*, from Greek *pant-, pas* "all" + French *-graphe* "-graph"] — **pan·to·graph·ic** \ˌpant-ə-'graf-ik\ *adj*

pan·to·mime \'pant-ə-ˌmīm\ *n* **1** : PANTOMIMIST **2** : a dramatic or dancing performance in which a story is told primarily by expressive bodily or facial movements of the performers **3** : conveyance of information by bodily or facial movements [Latin *pantomimus*, from Greek *pant-, pas* "all" + Latin *mimus* "mime"] — **pantomime** *vb* — **pan·to·mim·ic** \ˌpant-ə-'mim-ik\ *adj*

pan·to·mim·ist \'pant-ə-ˌmim-əst, -ˌmīm-\ *n* : an actor or dancer in or a composer of pantomimes

pan·to·then·ic acid \ˌpant-ə-ˌthen-ik-\ *n* : a viscous oily acid of the vitamin B complex found in all living tissues and necessary for growth [Greek *pantothen* "from all sides", from *pant-, pas* "all"]

pan·trop·ic \pan-'träp-ik, 'pan-\ *or* **pan·trop·i·cal** \-'träp-i-kəl\ *adj* : occurring or growing throughout the tropics

pan·try \'pan-trē\ *n, pl* **pantries** : a small room in which food and dishes are kept or from which food is brought to the table [Middle French *paneterie*, from *panetier* "servant in charge of the pantry", from *pan* "bread", from Latin *panis*]

pants \'pans\ *n pl* **1** : an outer garment extending from the waist to the ankle and covering each leg separately **2** : UNDERPANTS; *esp* : PANTIES [short for *pantaloons*]

panty hose *n pl* : a one-piece undergarment for women that consists of hosiery combined with panties

panty·waist \'pant-ē-ˌwāst\ *n* **1** : a child's garment consisting of short pants buttoned to a waist **2** : SISSY

pan·zer \'pan-zər, 'pänt-sər\ *adj* : of or relating to a panzer division or similar armored unit [German *panzer* "coat of mail, armor", from Old French *panciere*, from *pance* "belly, paunch", from Latin *pantex*]

panzer division *n* : a German armored division

¹pap \'pap\ *n* **1** *chiefly dialect* : NIPPLE 1, TEAT **2** : something shaped like a nipple [Middle English *pappe*]

²pap *n* : soft or bland food for infants or invalids [Middle English]

pa·pa \'päp-ə\ *n* : FATHER 1a [French (baby talk)]

pa·pa·cy \'pā-pə-sē\ *n, pl* **-cies** **1** : the office of pope **2** : a line of popes **3** : the term of a pope's reign **4** *cap* : the government of the Roman Catholic Church [Medieval Latin *papatia*, from Late Latin *papa* "pope"]

pa·pa·in \pə-'pā-ən, -'pī-ən\ *n* : a proteinase in papaya juice used especially as a meat tenderizer and in medicine

pa·pal \'pā-pəl\ *adj* : of or relating to the pope or the papacy [Middle French, from Medieval Latin *papalis*, from Late Latin *papa* "pope"] — **pa·pal·ly** \-pə-lē\ *adv*

pa·paw *or* **paw·paw** *n* **1** \pə-'pó\ : PAPAYA **2** \'päp-ó, 'póp-\ : a North American tree of the custard-apple family with purple flowers and a yellow edible fruit; *also* : its fruit [probably from Spanish *papaya*]

pa·pa·ya \pə-'pī-ə\ *n* : a tropical American tree with large lobed leaves and oblong yellow black-seeded edible fruit; *also* : its fruit [Spanish, of American Indian origin]

¹pa·per \'pā-pər\ *n* **1 a** : a felted sheet of usually vegetable fibers laid down on a fine screen from a water suspension **b** : a sheet or piece of paper **2 a** : a piece of paper containing a written or printed statement; *esp* : a document of identification or authorization **b** : a written composition (as a piece of schoolwork) **3** : a paper container or wrapper **4** : NEWSPAPER **5** : WALLPAPER [Middle French *papier*, from Latin *papyrus* "papyrus, paper"]

²paper *vb* **pa·pered; pa·per·ing** \'pā-pə-ring, -pring\ **1** : to cover or line with paper; *esp* : to apply wallpaper to **2** : to hang wallpaper — **pa·per·er** \-pər-ər\ *n*

³paper *adj* **1 a** : of, relating to, or made of paper or a related composition **b** : resembling paper : PAPERY **2** : NOMINAL **3a** ⟨a *paper* blockade⟩

pa·per·back \'pā-pər-ˌbak\ *n* : a book with a flexible paper binding — **paperback** *adj*

pa·per·board \-ˌbōrd, -ˌbórd\ *n* : a material made from cellulose fiber (as wood pulp) like paper but usually thicker : CARDBOARD

paper boy *n* : NEWSBOY

paper cutter *n* : a machine or device for cutting or trimming sheets of paper

pa·per·hang·er \-ˌhang-ər\ *n* : one that applies wallpaper — **pa·per·hang·ing** \-ˌhang-ing\ *n*

paper money *n* : money consisting of government notes and bank notes

paper mulberry *n* : an Asian tree of the mulberry family widely grown as a shade tree

paper nautilus *n* : an 8-armed mollusk related to the octopus that in the female has two of the arms expanded at the tips to clasp the thin fragile shell — called *also* **nautilus**

paper profit *n* : a profit that can be realized only by selling something that has gone up in value

paper trail *n* : documents (as financial records or published materials) from which a person's actions may be traced or opinions learned

pa·per·weight \'pā-pər-ˌwāt\ *n* : an object used to hold down loose papers by its weight

paper work *n* : routine clerical or record-keeping work often incidental to a more important task

pa·pery \'pā-pə-rē, -prē\ *adj* : resembling paper in thinness or consistency — **pa·per·i·ness** *n*

pa·pier–mâ·ché \ˌpā-pər-mə-'shā, ˌpap-ˌyā-mə-, -ma-\ *n* : a light strong molding material of wastepaper pulped with glue and other additives [French, literally, "chewed paper"] — **papier-mâché** *adj*

pa·pil·la \pə-'pil-ə\ *n, pl* **-pil·lae** \-'pil-ē, -ˌī\ : a small projecting bodily structure (as one of those on the surface of the tongue) that suggests a nipple [Latin, "nipple"] — **pap·il·lary** \'pap-ə-ˌler-ē, pə-'pil-ə-rē\ *adj* — **pap·il·late** \'pap-ə-ˌlāt, pə-'pil-ət\ *adj*

pap·il·lo·ma \ˌpap-ə-'lō-mə\ *n, pl* **-mas** *or* **-ma·ta** \-mət-ə\ : a usually benign epithelial tumor

pa·pist \'pā-pəst\ *n, often cap* : ROMAN CATHOLIC — usually used disparagingly [Middle French *papiste*, from *pape* "pope", from Late Latin *papa*] — **papist** *adj* — **pa·pist·ry** \-pə-strē\ *n*

pa·poose \pa-'püs, pə-\ *n* : a North American Indian infant [of American Indian origin]

pap·pus \'pap-əs\ *n, pl* **pap·pi** \'pap-ˌī, -ē\ : a downy or bristly appendage or tuft of appendages crowning the seed or fruit of some seed plants and functioning in its dispersal [Latin, from Greek *pappos*]

pa·pri·ka \pə-'prē-kə, pa-\ *n* : a mild red seasoning consisting of the dried finely ground pods of various cultivated sweet peppers; *also* : a sweet pepper used for making paprika [Hungarian, from Serbian, from *papar* "pepper", from Greek *peperi*]

Pap smear \'pap-\ *also* **Pap test** *n* : a method for the early detection of cancer using a special cell-staining technique to identify diseased tissue [George N. *Papanicolaou*, died 1962, American medical scientist]

pa·py·rus \pə-'pī-rəs\ *n, pl* **rus·es** *or* **·ri** \-rē, -ˌrī\ 1 : a tall sedge of the Nile valley 2 : the pith of the papyrus plant especially when cut in strips and pressed to make a material to write on 3 : a writing on or written scroll of papyrus [Latin, from Greek *papyros*]

par \'pär\ *n* 1 **a** : the established value of the monetary unit of one country expressed in terms of the monetary unit of another country using the same metal as the standard of value **b** : the face value of a security ⟨stocks that sell near *par*⟩ 2 : common level : EQUALITY ⟨their abilities are about on a *par*⟩ 3 : an accepted standard (as of health) ⟨not feeling up to *par*⟩ 4 : the score standard set for each hole of a golf course [Latin, "one that is equal", from *par* "equal"] — **par** *adj*

¹**para-** \ˌpar-ə, 'par-ə\ *or* **par-** *prefix* 1 **a** : beside : alongside ⟨*para*thyroid⟩ **b** : beyond : outside of 2 **a** : closely related to or resembling ⟨*para*typhoid⟩ **b** : associated in a subsidiary or accessory capacity ⟨*para*professional⟩ 3 : faulty : abnormal [Greek, from *para*]

²**para-** \'par-ə\ *combining form* : parachute ⟨*para*troops⟩ [*parachute*]

para–ami·no·ben·zo·ic acid \ˌpar-ə-ə-ˌmē-nō-ben-ˌzō-ik-, 'par-ə-ˌam-ə-ˌnō-\ *n* : a colorless organic acid that is a derivative of benzoic acid and is a growth factor of the vitamin B complex

par·a·ble \'par-ə-bəl\ *n* : a short simple story illustrating a moral or spiritual truth [Middle French, from Late Latin *parabola*, from Greek *parabolē*, from *paraballein* to compare", from *para-* + *ballein* "to throw"]

pa·rab·o·la \pə-'rab-ə-lə\ *n* 1 : the curve formed by the intersection of a cone with a plane parallel to a straight line in its surface : a plane curve generated by a point moving so that its distance from a fixed point is equal to its distance from a fixed line 2 : something bowl-shaped [Greek *parabolē* "comparison, parable, parabola"] — **par·a·bol·ic** \ˌpar-ə-'bäl-ik\ *adj* — **par·a·bol·i·cal·ly** \-'bäl-i-kə-lē, -klē\ *adv*

¹**para·chute** \'par-ə-ˌshüt\ *n* 1 : a folding umbrella-shaped device of light fabric used especially for making a safe descent after jumping from an airplane 2 : something (as the tuft of hairs on a dandelion seed) suggestive of a parachute in form, use, or operation [French, from *para-* (as in *parasol*) + *chute* "fall"]

²**parachute** *vb* : to convey or descend by means of a parachute

para·chut·ist \'par-ə-ˌshüt-əst\ *n* : one that descends by parachute

Par·a·clete \'par-ə-ˌklēt\ *n* : HOLY SPIRIT [Middle French *Paraclet*, from Late Latin *Paracletus*, from Greek *Paraklētos*, literally, "advocate, intercessor", from *parakalein* "to invoke", from *para-* + *kalein* "to call"]

¹**pa·rade** \pə-'rād\ *n* 1 : pompous show or display 2 : a ceremonial formation of a body of troops before a superior officer 3 : a public procession (as of military units and bands) 4 : a place of promenade; *also* : those who promenade [French, from *parer* "to prepare", from Latin *parare*]

²**parade** *vb* 1 **a** : to cause to maneuver or march **b** : to march in a procession 2 : PROMENADE 3 : to exhibit ostentatiously : show off — **pa·rad·er** *n*

para·di·chlo·ro·ben·zene \ˌpar-ə-dī-ˌklōr-ə-'ben-ˌzēn, -ˌklȯr-, -ˌben-\ *n* : a white crystalline chlorinated benzene used chiefly in mothballs

par·a·digm \'par-ə-ˌdīm, -ˌdim\ *n* 1 : MODEL, PATTERN ⟨an essay that is a *paradigm* of clear writing⟩ 2 : an example of a conjugation or declension showing a word in all its inflectional forms [Late Latin *paradigma*, from Greek *paradeigma*, from *paradeiknynai* "to show side by side", from *para-* + *deiknynai* "to show"] — **par·a·dig·mat·ic** \ˌpar-ə-dig-'mat-ik\ *adj*

par·a·dise \'par-ə-ˌdīs, -ˌdīz\ *n* 1 : the garden of Eden 2 : HEAVEN 2a 3 : a place or state of bliss [Old French *paradis*, from Late Latin *paradisus*, from Greek *paradeisos*, literally, "enclosed park", of Iranian origin]

par·a·di·si·a·cal \ˌpar-ə-də-'sī-ə-kəl, ˌ-dī-, -'zī-\ *or* **par·a·dis·i·ac** \-'diz-ē-ˌak\ *adj* : of, relating to, or resembling paradise [Late Latin *paradisiacus*, from *paradisus* "paradise"] — **par·a·di·si·a·cal·ly** \-də-'sī-ə-kə-lē, -klē\ *adv*

par·a·dox \'par-ə-ˌdäks\ *n* 1 **a** : a statement that seems to contradict common sense and yet is perhaps true **b** : a self-contradictory statement that at first seems true 2 : something (as a person, condition, or act) with seemingly contradictory qualities or phases [Latin *paradoxum*, from Greek *paradoxon*, from *paradoxos* "contrary to expectation", from *para-* + *dokein* "to think"] — **par·a·dox·i·cal** \ˌpar-ə-'däk-si-kəl\ *adj* — **par·a·dox·i·cal·ly** \-kə-lē, -klē\ *adv* — **par·a·dox·i·cal·ness** \-kəl-nəs\ *n*

¹**par·af·fin** \'par-ə-fən\ *n* 1 : a flammable waxy crystalline mixture of hydrocarbons obtained especially from distillates of wood, coal, or petroleum and used chiefly in coating and sealing, in candles, and in drugs and cosmetics 2 : a hydrocarbon of the methane series 3 *chiefly British* : KEROSENE [German, from Latin *parum* "too little" + *affinis* "bordering on, associated with"; from the small affinity it has for other bodies] — **par·af·fin·ic** \ˌpar-ə-'fin-ik\ *adj*

²**paraffin** *vt* : to coat or saturate with paraffin

par·a·gon \'par-ə-ˌgän, -gən\ *n* : a model of excellence or perfection [Middle French, from Italian *paragone*, literally, "touchstone", from *paragonare* "to test on a touchstone", from Greek *parakonan* "to sharpen", from *para-* + *akonē* "whetstone", from *akē* "point"]

¹**para·graph** \'par-ə-ˌgraf\ *n* 1 **a** : a subdivision of a piece of writing or a speech that consists of one or more sentences and develops in an organized manner one point of a subject or gives the words of one speaker **b** : a short written article (as in a newspaper) that is complete in one undivided section 2 : a character ¶. used as a reference mark or to indicate the beginning of a paragraph [Medieval Latin *paragraphus* "sign marking a paragraph", from Greek *paragraphos* "marginal sign used to mark change of speakers in a dialogue", from *para-* + *graphein* "to write"] — **para·graph·ic** \ˌpar-ə-'graf-ik\ *adj*

²**paragraph** *vb* 1 : to divide into paragraphs 2 : to write paragraphs

par·a·keet *or* **par·ra·keet** \'par-ə-ˌkēt\ *n* : any of numerous small slender parrots with a long pointed tail [Spanish *periquito*, from Middle French *perroquet* "parrot"]

par·al·de·hyde \pa-'ral-də-ˌhīd, pə-\ *n* : a liquid derivative of acetaldehyde used as a hypnotic

Par·a·li·pom·e·non \ˌpar-ə-lə-'päm-ə-ˌnän, -lī-\ *n* — see BIBLE table [Late Latin, from Greek *Paraleipomenōn*, genitive of *Paraleipomena*, literally, "things left out", from *paraleipein* "to leave out", from *para-* +

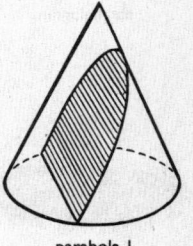

parabola 1

\ə\ abut	\ng\ sing
\ər\ further	\ō\ bone
\a\ mat	\ȯ\ saw
\ā\ take	\ȯi\ coin
\ä\ cot, cart	\th\ thin
\au̇\ out	\t͟h\ this
\ch\ chin	\ü\ food
\e\ pet	\u̇\ foot
\ē\ easy	\y\ yet
\g\ go	\yü\ few
\i\ tip	\yu̇\ cure
\ī\ life	\zh\ vision
\j\ job	

leipein "to leave"; from its forming a supplement to Samuel and Kings]

par·al·lax \'par-ə-ˌlaks\ *n* : the apparent displacement or the difference in apparent direction of an object as seen from two different points not on a straight line with the object; *esp* : the difference in direction of a celestial body as measured from two points on the earth or from opposite points on the earth's orbit [Middle French *parallaxe,* from Greek *parallaxis,* from *parallassein* "to change", from *para-* + *allassein* "to change", from *allos* "other"] — **par·al·lac·tic** \ˌpar-ə-'lak-tik\ *adj*

¹**par·al·lel** \'par-ə-ˌlel\ *adj* **1 a** : extending in the same direction, everywhere equidistant, and not meeting ⟨*parallel* rows of trees⟩ **b** : everywhere equally distant ⟨concentric spheres are *parallel*⟩ **2 a** : relating to or being an electrical circuit having a number of conductors in parallel **b** : relating to or being a connection in a computer system in which the bits of a byte are transmitted over separate wires at the same time **3 a** : marked by likeness or correspondence : SIMILAR, ANALOGOUS ⟨*parallel* situations⟩ **b** : having corresponding syntactical elements ⟨*parallel* clauses⟩ [Latin *parallelus,* from Greek *parallēlos,* from *para* "beside" + *allēlōn* "of one another", from *allos* "other"] SYN see SIMILAR

²**parallel** *n* **1 a** : a parallel line, curve, or surface **b** (1) : one of the imaginary circles on the surface of the earth paralleling the equator and marking the latitude (2) : the corresponding line on a globe or map **c** : a character ‖ used as a reference mark **2 a** : something equal or similar in all essential particulars : COUNTERPART **b** : SIMILARITY 2, ANALOGUE **3** : a tracing of similarity ⟨draw a *parallel* between two eras⟩ **4 a** : the state of being physically parallel : PARALLELISM **b** : an arrangement of electrical devices in a circuit in which the same potential difference is applied to two or more resistances with each resistance on a parallel branch of the circuit

³**parallel** *vt* **1** : to indicate similarity or analogy of : COMPARE **2 a** : to show something equal to : MATCH **b** : to correspond to **3** : to place so as to be parallel in direction with something **4** : to extend, run, or move in a direction parallel to

⁴**parallel** *adv* : in a parallel manner

parallel bars *n pl* : a pair of bars that are parallel to each other on an adjustable support and are used for swinging and balancing exercises in gymnastics

par·al·lel·epi·ped \ˌpar-ə-ˌlel-ə-'pī-pəd, -'pip-əd\ *n* : a 6-faced polyhedron all of whose faces are parallelograms lying in pairs of parallel planes [Greek *parallēlepipedon,* from *parallēlos* "parallel" + *epipedon* "plane surface", from *epipedos* "flat", from *epi-* + *pedon* "ground"]

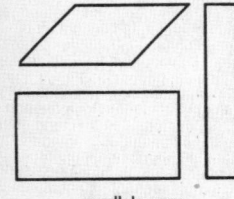
parallelogram

parallel evolution *n* : CONVERGENT EVOLUTION

par·al·lel·ism \'par-ə-ˌlel-ˌiz-əm\ *n* **1** : the quality or state of being parallel **2** : RESEMBLANCE 1, CORRESPONDENCE **3** : similarity of syntactical construction of adjacent word groups especially for rhetorical effect or rhythm

par·al·lel·o·gram \ˌpar-ə-'lel-ə-ˌgram\ *n* : a quadrilateral whose opposite sides are parallel and equal [Greek *parallēlogrammon,* derived from *parallēlos* "parallel" + *grammē* "line", from *graphein* "to write"]

par·al·lel-veined \ˌpar-ə-ˌlel-'vānd, -ləl-\ *adj* : having linear veins that do not branch and interlace ⟨monocotyledons have *parallel-veined* leaves⟩ — compare NET-VEINED

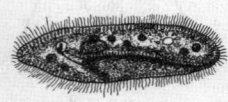
paramecium

pa·ral·y·sis \pə-'ral-ə-səs\ *n, pl* **-y·ses** \-ə-ˌsēz\ **1** : complete or partial loss of function especially when involving motion or sensation in a part of the body **2** : loss of the ability to move or act ⟨*paralysis* of highway traffic⟩ [Latin, from Greek, from *paralyein* "to loosen, disable", from *para-* + *lyein* "to loosen"] — **par·a·lyt·ic** \ˌpar-ə-'lit-ik\ *adj or n*

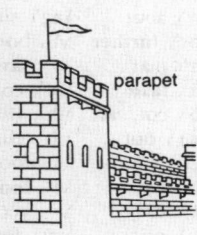
parapet 1

par·a·lyze \'par-ə-ˌlīz\ *vt* **1** : to affect with paralysis **2** : to make powerless, ineffective, or unable to act or function ⟨a labor dispute that *paralyzed* the industry⟩ [French *paralyser,* back-formation from *paralysie* "paralysis", from Latin *paralysis*] — **par·a·ly·za·tion** \ˌpar-ə-lə-'zā-shən\ *n*

para·mag·net·ic \ˌpar-ə-mag-'net-ik\ *adj* : being or relating to a slightly magnetizable substance (as aluminum) — **para·mag·ne·tism** \-'mag-nə-ˌtiz-əm\ *n*

par·a·me·cium \ˌpar-ə-'mē-sē-əm, -shē-əm, -shəm\ *n, pl* **-cia** \-sē-ə, -shē-ə, -shə\ *also* **-ciums** : any of a genus of somewhat slipper-shaped protozoans that move by cilia [Greek *paramēkēs* "oblong", from *para-* + *mēkos* "length"]

para·med·ic \ˌpar-ə-'med-ik\ *n* : one who assists a physician (as by giving injections and taking X rays)

pa·ram·e·ter \pə-'ram-ət-ər\ *n* **1** : an arbitrary constant each of whose values characterizes a member of a system (as a family of curves) **2** : any set of physical properties whose values determine the characteristics or behavior of something **3** : a characteristic element : CHARACTERISTIC, FACTOR ⟨political dissent as a *parameter* of modern life⟩ [*para-* + Greek *metron* "measure"] — **para·met·ric** \ˌpar-ə-'me-trik\ *adj*

par·a·mount \'par-ə-ˌmaúnt\ *adj* : superior to all others : SUPREME [Anglo-French *paramont,* from Old French *par* "by" (from Latin *per*) + *amont* "above", from *a* "to" (from Latin *ad*) + *mont* "mountain"]

par·amour \'par-ə-ˌmúr\ *n* : an illicit lover [Old French *par amour* "by way of love"]

par·a·noia \ˌpar-ə-'nói-ə\ *n* **1** : a serious mental disorder marked by feelings of persecution or distorted ideas of one's own importance usually without hallucinations **2** : a tendency toward excessive or unreasonable feelings of suspicion or distrust of others [Greek, "madness", from *paranous* "demented", from *para-* + *nous* "mind"] — **par·a·noi·ac** \-'nói-ˌak, -'nói-ik\ *adj or n*

par·a·noid \'par-ə-ˌnóid\ *adj* **1** : resembling paranoia **2** : characterized by suspiciousness, feelings of persecution, or an exaggerated sense of one's own importance — **paranoid** *n*

par·a·pet \'par-ə-pət, -ˌpet\ *n* **1** : a wall of earth or stone to protect soldiers **2** : a low wall or railing to protect the edge of a platform, roof, or bridge [Italian *parapetto,* from *parare* "to shield" (from Latin, "to prepare") + *petto* "breast, chest", from Latin *pectus*]

par·a·pher·na·lia \ˌpar-ə-fər-'nāl-yə, -fə-'nāl-\ *n sing or pl* **1** : personal belongings **2** : articles of equipment [Medieval Latin, derived from Greek *parapherna* "goods a bride brings over and above the dowry", from *para-* + *phernē* "dowry", from *pherein* "to bear"]

¹**para·phrase** \'par-ə-ˌfrāz\ *n* : a restatement of a text, passage, or work giving the meaning in another form

²**paraphrase** *vb* : to make a paraphrase of : give the meaning of something in different words — **para·phras·er** *n*

para·ple·gia \ˌpar-ə-'plē-jə, -jē-ə\ *n* : paralysis of the lower half of the body including both legs [Greek *paraplēgiē* "paralysis of one side of the body", from *para-* + *-plēgia* "paralysis", from *plēssein* "to strike"] — **para·ple·gic** \-jik\ *adj or n*

para·po·di·um \ˌpar-ə-'pōd-ē-əm\ *n, pl* **-dia** \-ē-ə\ : either of a pair of fleshy lateral processes borne by most segments of a polychaete worm [derived from Greek *para-* + *podion* "small foot", from *pod-, pous* "foot"]

para·pro·fes·sion·al \ˌpar-ə-prə-'fesh-nəl, -ən-l\ *n* : a trained aide who assists a professional person

para·psy·chol·o·gy \ˌpar-ə-sī-'käl-ə-jē\ *n* : a branch of study involving the investigation of telepathy, clairvoyance, and related psychological phenomena

par·a·site \'par-ə-ˌsīt\ *n* **1** : a person who lives at the expense of another **2** : an organism living in or on another organism in parasitism **3** : something that resembles a biological parasite in dependence on something else for existence or support without making a useful or adequate return [Middle French, "one habitually dining at the tables of others, sycophant", from Latin *parasitus,* from Greek *parasitos,* from *para-* + *sitos* "grain, food"] — **par·a·sit·ic** \ˌpar-ə-ˈsit-ik\ *also* **par·a·sit·i·cal** \-ˈsit-i-kəl\ *adj* — **par·a·sit·i·cal·ly** \-i-kə-lē, -klē\ *adv*

par·a·sit·ism \ˈpar-ə-ˌsīt-ˌiz-əm\ *n* : an intimate association between organisms of two or more kinds in which a parasite obtains benefits from a host which it usually injures

par·a·sit·ize \ˈpar-ə-sə-ˌtīz, -ˌsīt-ˌīz\ *vt* : to infest or live on or with as a parasite

par·a·si·tol·o·gy \ˌpar-ə-sə-ˈtäl-ə-jē, -ˌsīt-ˈäl-\ *n* : a branch of biology dealing with parasites and parasitism especially among animals — **par·a·si·tol·o·gist** \-jəst\ *n*

para·sol \ˈpar-ə-ˌsȯl\ *n* : a lightweight umbrella used as a sunshade [French, from Italian *parasole,* from *parare* "to shield" (from Latin, "to prepare") + *sole* "sun", from Latin *sol*]

para·sym·pa·thet·ic \ˌpar-ə-ˌsim-pə-ˈthet-ik\ *adj* : of, relating to, being, or acting on the parasympathetic nervous system — **parasympathetic** *n*

parasympathetic nervous system *n* : the part of the autonomic nervous system that tends to induce secretion, increase the tone of smooth muscle, and cause the dilatation of blood vessels — compare SYMPATHETIC NERVOUS SYSTEM

para·thi·on \ˌpar-ə-ˈthī-ən, -ˌän\ *n* : an extremely toxic insecticide that is a derivative of a sulfur-containing phosphoric acid [derived from *para-* + *thi-*]

par·a·thor·mone \ˌpar-ə-ˈthȯr-ˌmōn\ *n* : a hormone produced by the parathyroid glands and concerned with control of the use of calcium in the body

para·thy·roid \-ˈthī-ˌrȯid\ *adj* : of, relating to, or produced by the parathyroid glands — **parathyroid** *n*

parathyroid gland *n* : any of usually four small endocrine glands adjacent to or embedded in the thyroid gland that produce parathormone

para·troops \ˈpar-ə-ˌtrüps\ *n pl* : troops trained and equipped to parachute from an airplane — **para·troop** \-ˌtrüp\ *adj* — **para·troop·er** \-ˌtrü-pər\ *n*

¹**para·ty·phoid** \ˌpar-ə-ˈtī-ˌfȯid, -tī-ˈ\ *adj* 1 : resembling typhoid fever 2 : of or relating to paratyphoid or its causative organisms ⟨*paratyphoid* infection⟩

²**paratyphoid** *n* : a disease caused by bacteria that resembles typhoid fever and occurs as a food poisoning

par·boil \ˈpär-ˌbȯil\ *vt* : to boil briefly usually before cooking in another manner [Middle French *parbouillir* "to boil thoroughly", from Late Latin *perbullire,* from Latin *per-* + *bullire* "to boil"]

¹**par·cel** \ˈpär-səl\ *n* 1 : a part of a whole 2 : a plot of land 3 : a group or collection of persons or things ⟨told a *parcel* of lies⟩ 4 : a wrapped bundle : PACKAGE [Middle French, derived from Latin *particula* "small part, particle"]

²**parcel** *vt* **par·celed** *or* **par·celled**; **par·cel·ing** *or* **par·cel·ling** \ˈpär-sə-ling, -sling\ 1 : to divide into parts : DISTRIBUTE 2 : to make up into a parcel

parcel post *n* 1 : a mail service handling parcels 2 : packages handled by parcel post

parch \ˈpärch\ *vb* 1 : to toast under dry heat 2 : to dry up : shrivel with heat [Middle English *parchen*]

parch·ment \ˈpärch-mənt\ *n* 1 : the skin of a sheep or goat prepared for use as a writing material 2 : a paper made to resemble parchment 3 : something (as a diploma) written on parchment [Old French *parchemin,* from Latin *pergamena,* from Greek *pergamēnē,* from *Pergamēnos* "of Pergamum", from *Pergamon* "Pergamum"]

¹**pard** \ˈpärd\ *n, archaic* : LEOPARD [Old French *parde,* from Latin *pardus,* from Greek *pardos*]

²**pard** *n, chiefly dialect* : CHUM [short for *pardner,* alteration of *partner*]

¹**par·don** \ˈpärd-n\ *n* 1 **a** : the excusing of an offense without a penalty **b** : a release from the legal penalties of an offense 2 : excuse for a fault or discourtesy [Old French, from *pardonner* "to pardon", from Late Latin *perdonare* "to grant freely", from Latin *per-* + *donare* "to give"] — **par·don·able** \ˈpärd-nə-bəl, -n-ə-bəl\ *adj* — **par·don·ably** \-blē\ *adv*

²**pardon** *vt* **par·doned**; **par·don·ing** \ˈpärd-ning, -n-ing\ 1 : to free from penalty 2 : to allow (an offense) to pass without punishment : FORGIVE SYN *see* EXCUSE

pare \ˈpaər, ˈpeər\ *vt* 1 : to cut or shave off the outside or the ends of ⟨*pare* an apple⟩ 2 : to reduce as if by paring ⟨*pare* expenses⟩ [Middle French *parer* "to prepare, trim", from Latin *parare* "to prepare, acquire"]

par·e·go·ric \ˌpar-ə-ˈgȯr-ik, -ˈgȯr-, -ˈgär-\ *n* : a solution of opium and camphor in alcohol used especially to relieve pain [French *parégorique* "alleviating pain", from Latin *paregoricus,* from Greek *parēgorikos,* from *parēgorein* 'to talk over, soothe", from *para-* + *agora* "assembly"]

pa·ren·chy·ma \pə-ˈreng-kə-mə\ *n* 1 : a tissue of higher plants consisting of thin-walled living cells that remain capable of cell division even when mature, are agents of photosynthesis and storage, and make up much of the substance of leaves and roots and the pulp of fruits as well as parts of stems and supporting structures 2 : the distinctive functional tissue of an animal organ (as a gland) as distinguished from its supporting tissue or framework [Greek, "tissue of the viscera", from *parenchein* "to pour in beside", from *para-* + *en-* + *chein* "to pour"] — **par·en·chy·ma·tous** \ˌpar-ən-ˈkim-ət-əs, -ˈkīm-\ *also* **pa·ren·chy·mal** \pə-ˈreng-kə-məl\ *adj*

par·ent \ˈpar-ənt, ˈper-\ *n* 1 **a** : a person who is a father or mother **b** : an animal or plant that produces offspring 2 : the source or originator of something [Middle French, from Latin *parens,* from *parere* "to give birth to"] — **parent** *adj*

par·ent·age \-ənt-ij\ *n* : descent from parents or ancestors : LINEAGE ⟨a person of noble *parentage*⟩

pa·ren·tal \pə-ˈrent-l\ *adj* : of, typical of, or being parents ⟨*parental* affection⟩ — **pa·ren·tal·ly** \-l-ē\ *adv*

pa·ren·the·sis \pə-ˈren-thə-səs\ *n, pl* **-the·ses** \-thə-ˌsēz\ 1 **a** : a word, phrase, or sentence inserted in a passage to explain or comment on it **b** : DIGRESSION 2 : one of a pair of marks ( ) used to enclose a parenthesis or to group a symbolic unit in a mathematical expression [Late Latin, from Greek, literally, "act of inserting", from *parentithenai* "to insert", from *para-* + *en-* + *tithenai* "to place"] — **par·en·thet·ic** \ˌpar-ən-ˈthet-ik\ *or* **par·en·thet·i·cal** \-ˈthet-i-kəl\ *adj* — **par·en·thet·i·cal·ly** \-i-kə-lē, -klē\ *adv*

pa·ren·the·size \pə-ˈren-thə-ˌsīz, -ˈrent-\ *vt* : to make a parenthesis of

par·ent·hood \ˈpar-ənt-ˌhud, ˈper-\ *n* : the position, function, or standing of a parent

pa·re·sis \pə-ˈrē-səs, ˈpar-ə-\ *n, pl* **-re·ses** \-ˌsēz\ : GENERAL PARESIS [Greek, "paralysis, neglect", from *parienai* "to let fall", from *para-* + *hienai* "to let go, send"] — **pa·ret·ic** \pə-ˈret-ik\ *adj or n*

par excellence \ˌpär-ˌek-sə-ˈläⁿs\ *adv or adj* : in the highest degree [French, literally, "by excellence"]

par·fait \pär-ˈfā\ *n* 1 : a flavored custard containing whipped cream and syrup frozen without stirring 2 : a cold dessert made of layers of fruit, syrup, ice cream, and whipped cream [French, from *parfait* "perfect", from Latin *perfectus*]

par·he·lion \pär-ˈhēl-yən\ *n, pl* **-lia** \-yə\ : any one of several bright spots often tinged with color that often appear on both sides of the sun and at the same altitude as the sun [Latin *parelion,* from Greek *parēlion,* from *para-* + *hēlios* "sun"]

\ə\ abut	\ng\ sing	
\ər\ further	\ō\ bone	
\a\ mat	\ȯ\ saw	
\ā\ take	\ȯi\ coin	
\ä\ cot, cart	\th\ thin	
\au\ out	\th\ this	
\ch\ chin	\ü\ food	
\e\ pet	\u\ foot	
\ē\ easy	\y\ yet	
\g\ go	\yü\ few	
\i\ tip	\yu\ cure	
\ī\ life	\zh\ vision	
\j\ job		

pa·ri·ah \pə-'rī-ə\ *n* **1** : a member of a former low caste of southern India and Burma **2** : a person despised or rejected by society : OUTCAST [Tamil *paraiyan,* literally, "drummer"]

pa·ri·e·tal \pə-'rī-ət-l\ *adj* : of, relating to, or forming the walls of a part or cavity and especially the upper back wall of the head [Middle French, from Latin *pariet-, paries* "wall"]

parietal bone *n* : either of a pair of bones of the roof of the skull between the frontal bones and the occipital bones

pari–mu·tu·el \,par-i-'myü-chə-wəl, -chəl\ *n* : a system of betting (as on a race) in which those who bet on the competitors finishing in the first three places share the total amount bet minus a percentage for the management [French *pari mutuel,* literally, "mutual stake"]

par·ing \'paər-ing, 'peər-\ *n* **1** : the act of cutting away an edge or surface **2** : something pared off ⟨apple *parings*⟩

par·ish \'par-ish\ *n* **1 a** : a section of a diocese in the charge of a priest or minister **b** : the persons who live in such a section and attend the parish church **2** : the members of any church **3** : a civil division of the state of Louisiana corresponding to a county in other states [Middle French *parroche,* from Late Latin *parochia,* from Late Greek *paroikia,* from *paroikos* "Christian", from Greek, "stranger", from *para-* + *oikos* "house"]

pa·rish·io·ner \pə-'rish-nər, -ə-nər\ *n* : a member or resident of a parish

par·i·ty \'par-ət-ē\ *n, pl* **-ties** : the quality or state of being equal or equivalent [Latin *paritas,* from *par* "equal"]

¹park \'pärk\ *n* **1** : a tract of land attached to a country house and used for recreation **2 a** : a piece of ground in or near a city or town kept as a place of beauty and recreation **b** : an area maintained in its natural state as a public property **3 a** : a space occupied by military animals, vehicles, or materials **b** : PARKING LOT **4** : an enclosed arena or stadium used especially for ball games [Old French *parc* "enclosure"]

²park *vb* **1 a** : to leave a vehicle temporarily on a public way or in a parking lot or garage **b** : to land or leave an airplane **2** : to set and leave temporarily

par·ka \'pär-kə\ *n* : a winter jacket with a hood [Aleut, "skin, outer garment", from Russian, "pelt", of Uralic origin]

parka

parking lot *n* : an outdoor area for the parking of motor vehicles

park·way \'pär-,kwā\ *n* : a broad landscaped thoroughfare

par·lance \'pär-ləns\ *n* : choice of words : IDIOM [Middle French, from *parler* "to speak"]

par·lay \'pär-,lā, -lē\ *n* : a series of bets in which the original stake plus its winnings are risked on the successive wagers [French *paroli,* from Italian dialect, from *paro* "equal", from Latin *par*] — **parlay** *vt*

par·ley \'pär-lē\ *vi* **par·leyed; par·ley·ing** : to speak with another : CONFER; *esp* : to discuss terms with an enemy [Middle French *parler* "to speak", from Medieval Latin *parabolare,* from Late Latin *parabola* "speech, parable"] — **parley** *n*

par·lia·ment \'pär-lə-mənt *also* 'pärl-yə-\ *n* **1** : a formal conference on public affairs; *esp* : a council of state in early medieval England **2 a** : an assemblage of the nobility, clergy, and commons called together by the British sovereign as the supreme legislative body in the United Kingdom **b** : a similar assemblage in another nation or state **3 a** : the supreme legislative body of a political unit comprising a series of successive parliaments **b** : the British House of Commons [Old French *parliament,* from *parler* "to speak"]

parrot fish

par·lia·men·tar·i·an \,pär-lə-,men-'ter-ē-ən, -mən- *also* ,pärl-yə-\ *n* : an expert in parliamentary procedure

par·lia·men·ta·ry \-'ment-ə-rē, -'men-trē\ *adj* **1** : of, relating to, or enacted by a parliament **2** : of or relating to government by a cabinet whose members belong to and are responsible to the legislature **3** : being in accordance with the rules and customs of a parliament or other deliberative body

par·lor \'pär-lər\ *n* **1** : a room in a home, hotel, or club used for conversation or the reception of guests **2** : any of various business places ⟨funeral *parlor*⟩ ⟨beauty *parlor*⟩ [Old French *parlour,* from *parler* "to speak"]

parlor car *n* : an extra-fare railroad passenger car equipped with individual chairs and formerly used for day travel

par·lous \'pär-ləs\ *adj* : full of uncertainty or risk ⟨*parlous* times⟩ [Middle English, alteration of *perilous*] — **par·lous·ly** *adv*

pa·ro·chi·al \pə-'rō-kē-əl\ *adj* **1** : of or relating to a parish **2** : limited in range or scope : NARROW ⟨a *parochial* attitude⟩ [Middle French, from Late Latin *parochialis,* from *parochia* "parish"] — **pa·ro·chi·al·ism** \-kē-ə-,liz-əm\ *n* — **pa·ro·chi·al·ly** \-kē-ə-lē\ *adv*

parochial school *n* : a school maintained by a religious body

par·o·dy \'par-əd-ē\ *n, pl* **-dies** **1** : a literary or musical work in which the style of an author or work is closely imitated for comic effect or in ridicule **2** : a feeble or ridiculous imitation [Latin *parodia,* from Greek *parōidia,* from *para-* + *aidein* "to sing"] SYN see CARICATURE — **par·o·dist** \-əd-əst\ *n* — **parody** *vt*

¹pa·role \pə-'rōl\ *n* **1** : a promise confirmed by a pledge; *esp* : the promise of a prisoner of war to fulfill stated conditions in return for release **2** : a conditional release of a prisoner before the sentence has expired [French, "speech, parole", from Late Latin *parabola* "speech, parable"]

²parole *vt* : to release (a prisoner) on parole — **pa·rol·ee** \pə-,rō-'lē, ,par-ə-'lē\ *n*

pa·rot·id \pə-'rät-əd\ *adj* : of or relating to the parotid gland [New Latin *parotis* "parotid gland", from Latin, "tumor near the ear", from Greek *parōtis,* from *para-* + *ōt-, ous* "ear"]

parotid gland *n* : either of a pair of large salivary glands situated below and in front of the ear

par·ox·ysm \'par-ək-,siz-əm\ *n* **1** : a fit, attack, or sudden increase of violence of a disease that occurs at intervals ⟨a *paroxysm* of coughing⟩ **2** : a sudden violent emotion or action ⟨*paroxysms* of rage⟩ [Medieval Latin *paroxysmus,* from Greek *paroxysmos,* from *paroxynein* "to stimulate", from *para-* + *oxynein* "to provoke", from *oxys* "sharp"] — **par·ox·ys·mal** \,par-ək-'siz-məl\ *adj*

par·quet \'pär-,kā, pär-'\ *n* **1** : a flooring of parquetry **2** : the lower floor of a theater especially in front of the balcony [French, literally, "small enclosure", from *parc* "park"]

par·que·try \'pär-kə-trē\ *n, pl* **-tries** : a patterned wood inlay used especially for floors

parr \'pär\ *n, pl* **parr** *also* **parrs** : a young salmon actively feeding in fresh water [origin unknown]

par·ra·keet *variant of* PARAKEET

par·ri·cide \'par-ə-,sīd\ *n* **1** : one who murders one's father or mother or a close relative **2** : the act of a parricide [Latin *parricida* "killer of a close relative"] — **par·ri·cid·al** \,par-ə-'sīd-l\ *adj*

¹par·rot \'par-ət\ *n* **1** : a bright-colored tropical bird of a family characterized by a strong hooked bill, by toes arranged in pairs with two in front and two behind, and often by the ability to mimic speech **2** : a person who repeats words mechanically and without understanding [probably from Middle French *perroquet*]

²parrot *vt* : to repeat mechanically

parrot fever *n* : an infectious disease of birds caused by a rickettsia, marked by diarrhea and wasting, and communicable to man — called also *psittacosis*

parrot fish *n* : any of various sea fishes related to the perches that have the teeth fused into a cutting plate resembling a beak

par·ry \'par-ē\ *vb* **par·ried; par·ry·ing** 1 : to ward off a weapon or blow : turn aside skillfully 2 : to evade especially by a clever answer ⟨*parry* an embarrassing question⟩ [probably from French *parer*, from Provençal *parar*, from Latin *parare* "to prepare"] — **par·ry** *n*

parse \'pärs, 'pärz\ *vb* 1 : to analyze a sentence by naming its parts and their relations to each other 2 : to give the part of speech of a word and explain its relation to other words in a sentence [Latin *pars orationis* "part of speech"]

par·sec \'pär-,sek\ *n* : a unit of measure for interstellar space equal to 19.2 trillion miles (about 30.8 trillion kilometers) [*par*allax + *sec*ond]

Par·si *also* **Par·see** \'pär-,sē\ *n* : a Zoroastrian descended from Persian refugees settled principally at Bombay [Persian *pārsi*, from *Pārs* "Persia"]

par·si·mo·ny \'pär-sə-,mō-nē\ *n* : extreme frugality : STINGINESS [Latin *parsimonia*, from *parcere* "to spare"] — **par·si·mo·ni·ous** \,pär-sə-'mō-nē-əs\ *adj* — **par·si·mo·ni·ous·ly** *adv*

pars·ley \'pär-slē\ *n, pl* **parsleys** : a southern European herb of the carrot family widely grown for its finely divided leaves which are used as a flavoring or garnish [Old English *petersilie*, from Latin *petroselinum*, from Greek *petroselinon*, from *petros* "stone" + *selinon* "celery"]

pars·nip \'pär-snəp\ *n* : a European biennial herb of the carrot family grown for its long white root used as a vegetable; *also* : this root [Middle English *pasnepe*, from Middle French *pasnaie*, from Latin *pastinaca*]

par·son \'pärs-n\ *n* 1 : RECTOR 1 2 : CLERGYMAN; *esp* : a Protestant pastor [Old French *persone*, from Medieval Latin *persona*, literally, "person", from Latin]

par·son·age \'pär-snij, 'pärs-n-ij\ *n* : the house provided by a church for its pastor

¹**part** \'pärt\ *n* 1 **a** : one of the portions into which something is divisible and which together constitute the whole **b** : one of several or many equal units of which something is composed ⟨a fifth *part* for each⟩ **c** : a portion of a plant or animal body : MEMBER, ORGAN ⟨wash the injured *part*⟩ **d** : a vocal or instrumental line or melody in music written in harmony; *also* : the score for it **e** : a constituent member of a machine or apparatus; *also* : a spare piece or member 2 : something falling to one in a division or apportionment : SHARE 3 : one's shared or allotted task ⟨one must do one's *part*⟩ 4 : one of the sides in a conflict ⟨take someone's *part* in a quarrel⟩ 5 : a portion of an unspecified territorial area — usually used in pl. ⟨took off for *parts* unknown⟩ 6 : a function or course of action performed 7 **a** : an actor's lines in a play **b** : the role of a character in a play 8 : a constituent of character or capacity : TALENT ⟨a person of many *parts*⟩ 9 : the line where the hair is divided in combing [Old French and Old English, both from Latin *part-, pars*] □ SYN PART, PORTION, PIECE, SEGMENT mean something less than the whole. PART is the general term and is interchangeable with any of the others; PORTION suggests an assigned or allotted part ⟨a minor *portion* of the voting population⟩ ⟨each child received a *portion* of the cake⟩ PIECE applies to a separate or detached part ⟨a *piece* of pie⟩ SEGMENT applies to a part separated or marked out by natural lines of cleavage ⟨*segments* of an orange⟩ — **for the most part** : in general — **in part** : in some degree — **on the part of** : with regard to the one specified

²**part** *vb* 1 **a** : to leave someone — used with *from* or *with* **b** : to take leave of one another ⟨the friends had to *part*⟩ 2 : to become separated into parts 3 : to go away : DEPART 4 : to give up possession or control ⟨wouldn't *part* with the old car⟩ 5 **a** : to divide into parts **b** : to separate by combing on each side of a line 6 **a** : to keep separate ⟨the channel that *parts* England and France⟩ **b** : to hold (as fighters) apart [Old French

partir, from Latin *partire* "to divide", from *part-, pars* "part"]

³**part** *adv* : in a measure : PARTLY ⟨was only *part* right⟩

par·take \pär-'tāk, pər-\ *vi* **par·took** \-'tùk\; **par·tak·en** \-'tā-kən\; **par·tak·ing** 1 **a** : to take a share ⟨*partake* of a meal⟩ **b** : PARTICIPATE ⟨all may *partake* in the ceremony⟩ 2 : to have some of the qualities or attributes of something ⟨their actions *partook* of rebellion⟩ [back-formation from *partaker*, from *part taker*] — **par·tak·er** *n*

part·ed \'pärt-əd\ *adj* : divided into parts

par·terre \pär-'teər\ *n* 1 : an ornamental garden with paths between the beds 2 : the part of the floor of a theater behind the orchestra [French, from *par terre* "on the ground"]

par·the·no·car·py \'pär-thə-nō-,kär-pē\ *n* : the production of fruits without fertilization [Greek *parthenos* "virgin" + *karpos* "fruit"] — **par·the·no·car·pic** \,pär-thə-nō-'kär-pik\ *adj*

par·the·no·gen·e·sis \,pär-thə-nō-'jen-ə-səs\ *n, pl* **-gen·e·ses** \-ə-,sēz\ : reproduction especially among lower plants and invertebrate animals in which an unfertilized gamete develops into a new individual [Greek *parthenos* "virgin"] — **par·the·no·ge·net·ic** \-jə-'net-ik\ *adj* — **par·the·no·ge·net·i·cal·ly** \-'net-i-kə-lē, -klē\ *adv*

par·tial \'pär-shəl\ *adj* 1 : inclined to favor one side or party over another ⟨the judge was *partial*⟩ 2 : markedly or overly fond of someone or something ⟨*partial* to milk shakes⟩ 3 : of, relating to, or being a part rather than the whole ⟨a *partial* eclipse⟩ [Middle French, from Medieval Latin *partialis*, from Late Latin, "of a part", from Latin *part-, pars* "part"] — **par·tial·ly** \'pärsh-lē, -ə-lē\ *adv*

partial denture *n* : an often removable artificial replacement for one or more teeth

par·ti·al·i·ty \,pär-shē-'al-ət-ē, pär-'shal-\ *n, pl* **-ties** 1 : the quality or state of being partial : BIAS 2 : a special taste or liking

partial product *n* : one of the products obtained by multiplying successively the multiplicand by each digit of the multiplier

par·ti·ble \'pärt-ə-bəl\ *adj* : DIVISIBLE

par·tic·i·pant \pər-'tis-ə-pənt, pär-\ *n* : one that participates

par·tic·i·pate \pər-'tis-ə-,pāt, pär-\ *vi* : to engage or have a share in something in common with others [Latin *participare*, from *particeps* "participant", from *part-, pars* "part" + *capere* "to take"] — **par·tic·i·pa·tion** \-,tis-ə-'pā-shən\ *n* — **par·tic·i·pa·tor** \-'tis-ə-,pāt-ər\ *n* — **par·tic·i·pa·to·ry** \-'tis-ə-pə-,tōr-ē, -,tòr-\ *adj*

par·ti·cip·i·al \,pärt-ə-'sip-ē-əl\ *adj* : of, relating to, or formed with or from a participle ⟨*participial* phrase⟩ — **par·ti·cip·i·al·ly** \-ē-ə-lē\ *adv*

par·ti·ci·ple \'pärt-ə-,sip-əl\ *n* : a verb form that sometimes can also be used like an adjective ⟨"burning" and "collapsed" are *participles* in "the burning building had collapsed"⟩ [Middle French, from Latin *participium*, from *particeps* "participant"]

par·ti·cle \'pärt-i-kəl\ *n* 1 : one of the minute subdivisions of matter (as a molecule, atom, electron); *also* : ELEMENTARY PARTICLE 2 **a** : a tiny amount or fragment **b** : the smallest possible part 3 : a word (as an article, preposition, or conjunction) expressing a general meaning or a connective or limiting relation [Latin *particula*, from *part-, pars* "part"]

par·ti·col·ored \,pärt-ē-'kəl-ərd\ *adj* : showing different colors or tints [obsolete English *party* "parti-colored" (from Middle French *parti* "striped", from Old French *partir* "to divide, part") + English *colored*]

¹**par·tic·u·lar** \pər-'tik-yə-lər, pə-, -'tik-ə-lər, -'tik-lər\ *adj* 1 : of or relating to a single person or thing 2 : of or relating to details : MINUTE 3 : distinctive among others : SPECIAL 4 **a** : attentive to details : EXACT **b** :

hard to please : EXACTING [Middle French *particuler,* from Late Latin *particularis,* from Latin *particula* "small part, particle"] SYN see CIRCUMSTANTIAL

²**particular** *n* : an individual fact, detail, or item — **in particular** : in distinction from others : SPECIFICALLY

par·tic·u·lar·i·ty \-,tik-yə-'lar-ət-ē\ *n, pl* **-ties** **1 a** : a minute detail **b** : an individual characteristic : PECULIARITY **2** : attentiveness to detail : EXACTNESS, CARE

par·tic·u·lar·ize \-'tik-yə-lə-,rīz, -'tik-lə-\ *vb* : to go into details : state in detail : SPECIFY — **par·tic·u·lar·iza·tion** \-,tik-yə-lə-rə-'zā-shən, -,tik-lə-\ *n*

par·tic·u·lar·ly \pər-'tik-yə-lē, pə-, -yə-lər-lē, -'tik-lē, -'tik-ə-lē\ *adv* **1** : in detail **2** : to an unusual degree

par·tic·u·late \pər-'tik-yə-lət, pär-, -,lāt\ *adj* : relating to or existing as minute separate particles — **particulate** *n*

particulate inheritance *n* : inheritance of characters specifically transmitted by genes in accord with Mendel's laws

¹**part·ing** \'pärt-ing\ *n* **1** : FAREWELL 2 **2** : a place or point where a division or separation occurs — **parting of the ways** **1** : PARTING 2 **2** : a place or time at which a choice must be made

²**parting** *adj* : involving, given, taken, or performed at parting ⟨a *parting* kiss⟩

par·ti·san \'pärt-ə-zən\ *n* **1** : a person who supports the position of another; *esp* : a devoted adherent to the cause of another **2** : an irregular soldier who operates behind enemy lines [Middle French *partisan,* from Italian *partigiano,* from *parte* "part", from Latin *part-, pars*] — **partisan** *adj* — **par·ti·san·ship** \-,ship\ *n*

par·tite \'pär-,tīt\ *adj* : divided into a usually specified number of parts [Latin *partitus,* from *partire* "to divide", from *part-, pars* "part"]

par·ti·tion \pər-'tish-ən, pär-\ *n* **1 a** : the action of parting : DIVISION **b** : separation of a class or whole into components; *esp* : the division of a united territory among two or more governments **2** : an interior dividing wall **3** : PART 1a, SECTION — **partition** *vt* — **par·ti·tion·er** \-'tish-nər, -ə-nər\ *n*

par·ti·tive \'pärt-ət-iv\ *adj* **1** : of, relating to, or denoting a part ⟨a *partitive* construction⟩ **2** : serving to indicate the whole of which a part is specified ⟨*partitive* genitive⟩ — **partitive** *n* — **par·ti·tive·ly** *adv*

part·ly \'pärt-lē\ *adv* : in some measure or degree

¹**part·ner** \'pärt-nər\ *n* **1 a** : one associated in action with another : COLLEAGUE **b** : either of a couple who dance together **c** : one of usually two persons who play together in a game against an opposing side **d** : SPOUSE **2** : a member of a partnership [Middle English *partener* "sharer", alteration of *parcener,* from Old French *parçonier,* from *parçon* "division, share", from Latin *partitio,* from *partire* "to divide"]

²**partner** *vb* : to join as a partner : be or act as a partner

part·ner·ship \'pärt-nər-,ship\ *n* **1** : the state of being a partner **2** : a business organization owned by two or more persons who agree to share the profits and usually are liable individually for losses

part of speech : a traditional class of words distinguished according to the kind of idea denoted and the function performed in a sentence — compare ADJECTIVE, ADVERB, CONJUNCTION, INTERJECTION, NOUN, PREPOSITION, PRONOUN, VERB

partook *past of* PARTAKE

par·tridge \'pär-trij\ *n, pl* **partridge** *or* **par·tridg·es** : any of several stout-bodied Old World game birds related to the common domestic fowl; *also* : any of various similar and related North American birds (as a bobwhite or ruffed grouse) [Old French *perdris,* from Latin *perdix,* from Greek]

partridge

par·tridge·ber·ry \-,ber-ē\ *n* : an American trailing evergreen plant with small somewhat round leaves and scarlet berries

part–song \'pärt-,song\ *n* : a usually unaccompanied song of two or more voice parts with one part carrying the melody

part–time \'pärt-'tīm\ *adj* : involving or working less than customary or standard hours — **part–time** *adv*

par·tu·ri·ent \pär-'tur-ē-ənt, -'tyur-\ *adj* : bringing forth or about to bring forth young; *also* : of or relating to parturition [Latin *parturiens,* present participle of *parturire* "to be in labor", from *parere* "to bring forth"]

par·tu·ri·tion \,pärt-ə-'rish-ən, ,par-chə-\ *n* : the act or process of giving birth to offspring [Late Latin *parturitio,* from Latin *parturire* "to be in labor"]

¹**par·ty** \'pärt-ē\ *n, pl* **parties** **1** : a side in a dispute or contest ⟨the *parties* to a lawsuit⟩ **2** : a group of persons organized for the purpose of directing the policies of a government **3** : a person or group participating in an activity : PARTICIPANT ⟨a *party* to the transaction⟩ **4** : PERSON ⟨get the right *party* on the telephone⟩ **5** : a detail of soldiers **6** : a social gathering; *also* : the entertainment provided for it [Old French *partie* "part, party", from *partir* "to divide, part"] — **party** *adj*

²**party** *vi* **par·tied; par·ty·ing** : to give or attend parties

party line *n* **1** : a single telephone circuit connecting two or more subscribers with the exchange **2** : the principles or policies of an individual or organization; *esp* : the official policies of a Communist party — **par·ty·lin·er** \,pärt-ē-'lī-nər\ *n*

par·ve·nu \'pär-və-,nü, -,nyü\ *n* : one who has recently or suddenly risen to wealth or power and has not yet secured the social position appropriate to it : UPSTART [French, from *parvenir* "to arrive", from Latin *pervenire,* from *per-* "through" + *venire* "to come"] — **parvenu** *adj*

pas·cal \pas-'kal\ *n* **1** : a unit of pressure in the metric system equal to one newton per square meter **2** *cap P or all cap* : a computer programming language in which a problem is solved by a step-by-step process and each step is done by a separate part of a program [Blaise *Pascal*]

Pasch \'pask\ *n* **1** : PASSOVER **2** : EASTER [Old French *pasche,* from Late Latin *pascha,* from Greek, from Hebrew *pesaḥ*] — **pas·chal** \'pas-kəl\ *adj*

Paschal Lamb *n* : AGNUS DEI 2

pas de deux \,päd-ə-'dər, -'dü, -'dœ\ *n, pl* **pas de deux** \-'dər, -'dərz, -'dü, -'düz, -'dœ, -'dœz\ : a dance or figure for two performers [French, literally, "step for two"]

pas de trois \-'trwä, -trə-'wä\ *n, pl* **pas de trois** \-'trwä, -'trwäz, -trə-'wä, -trə-'wäz\ : a dance or figure for three performers [French, literally, "step for three"]

pa·sha \'päsh-ə, 'pash-ə, pə-'shä\ *n* : a high-ranking official (as in Turkey or northern Africa) [Turkish *paşa*]

Pash·to \'pəsh-tō\ *also* **Push·tu** \-tü\ *n* : the Iranian language of the Pathan people which is the chief vernacular of eastern Afghanistan and adjacent parts of Pakistan [Persian *pashtu,* from Pashto]

pasque·flow·er \'pask-,flaù-ər, -,flaùr\ *n* : any of several low perennial herbs of the buttercup family that have compound leaves arranged like a hand with fingers spread and large usually white or purple flowers in early spring [Middle French *passefleur,* from *passer* 'to pass' + *fleur* "flower", from Latin *flor-, flos*]

¹**pass** \'pas\ *vb* **1** : GO 1, PROCEED **2 a** : to go away : DEPART **b** : DIE 1 — often used with *on* or *away* **3** : to go by : move past **4 a** : to go or cause or let go across, over, or through **b** : to go unchallenged ⟨let that remark *pass*⟩ **5 a** : to change or transfer ownership **b** : to go from the control or possession of one person or group to that of another ⟨the throne *passed* to the heir⟩ **6 a** : HAPPEN 2, OCCUR **b** : to take place as a mutual exchange or transaction ⟨words *passed*⟩ **7 a** : to become approved by a legislative body **b** : to go through or let go through an inspection, test, or course of study successfully **8 a** : to serve as a medium of ex-

change **b** : to be held or regarded ⟨*passed* for an honest person⟩ **9** : to execute a pass in a game **10** : to decline to bid, bet, or draw an additional card in a card game **11** : to go beyond; *esp* : SURPASS ⟨*passes* all expectations⟩ **12** : to leave out in an account or narration **13 a** : to live through : UNDERGO **b** : to cause or permit to elapse : SPEND ⟨*pass* time⟩ **14** : to secure the approval of ⟨the bill *passed* the Senate⟩ **15 a** : to give official sanction or approval to ⟨*pass* a law⟩ **b** : OVERLOOK 3b **16 a** : to put in circulation ⟨*pass* bad checks⟩ **b** : to transfer from one person to another ⟨*pass* the salt⟩ **c** : to take a turn with (as a rope) around something **d** : to transfer (as a ball) to another player on the same team **17 a** : to pronounce judicially ⟨*pass* sentence⟩ **b** : UTTER 2 **18** : to cause to march or go by in order ⟨*pass* the troops in review⟩ **19** : to emit or discharge from the bowels [Old French *passer*, from Latin *passus* "step, pace"] — **pass·er** *n* — **pass muster** : to gain approval or acceptance — **pass the buck** : to shift a responsibility to someone else — **pass the hat** : to take up a collection of money

²pass *n* **1** : an opening or way for passing along or through **2** : a gap in a mountain range

³pass *n* **1** : the act or an instance of passing : PASSAGE **2** : REALIZATION ⟨brought their dreams to *pass*⟩ **3** : a usually difficult or disturbing state of affairs **4 a** : a written permission to enter or leave or to move about freely ⟨a soldier's 3-day *pass*⟩ **b** : a ticket allowing one free transportation or free admission **5 a** : a transference of objects by sleight of hand **b** : a moving of the hands over or along something **6** : a transfer of a ball or a puck from one player to another on the same team **7** : a refusal to bid, bet, or draw an additional card in a card game **8** : EFFORT, TRY; *esp* : a sexually inviting approach

pass·able \'pas-ə-bəl\ *adj* **1** : capable of being passed, crossed, or traveled on ⟨*passable* roads⟩ **2** : barely good enough ⟨a *passable* meal⟩ — **pass·ably** \-blē\ *adv*

pas·sage \'pas-ij\ *n* **1** : the action or process of passing from one place or condition to another **2 a** : a road, path, channel, or course by which something can pass ⟨nasal *passages*⟩ **b** : a corridor or lobby giving access to the different rooms or parts of a building or apartment **3 a** : a specific act of traveling especially by sea or air **b** : the right to travel as a passenger ⟨take *passage* on a freighter⟩ **4** : the passing of a legislative measure : ENACTMENT **5 a** : INCIDENT 1a **b** : something that takes place between two persons mutually ⟨a *passage* of wit⟩ **6 a** : a usually brief portion of a written work or speech that concerns a point under discussion or is noteworthy for content or style **b** : a phrase or short section of a musical composition

pas·sage·way \-,wā\ *n* : a way that allows passage

pass·book \'pas-,bùk\ *n* : BANKBOOK

pas·sé \pa-'sā\ *adj* **1** : no longer active or in use : OBSOLETE **2** : OLD-FASHIONED 1 [French, from *passer* "to pass"]

passed ball *n* : a pitched ball that passes the catcher when he should have stopped it and that allows a base runner to advance

pas·sel \'pas-əl\ *n* : a large number [alteration of *parcel*]

pas·sen·ger \'pas-n-jər\ *n* **1** : WAYFARER **2** : a traveler in a public or private conveyance [Middle French *passager*, from *passage* "act of passing", from *passer* "to pass"]

passenger pigeon *n* : an extinct but formerly abundant North American migratory pigeon

passe–par·tout \,pas-pər-'tü\ *n* **1** : something that passes or enables one to pass everywhere **2** : strong paper gummed on one side and used especially for mounting pictures [French, from *passe partout* "pass everywhere"]

pass·er·by \,pas-ər-'bī\ *n, pl* **pass·ers·by** \-ərz-\ : one that passes by

pas·ser·ine \'pas-ə-,rīn\ *adj* : of or relating to the largest order (Passeriformes) of birds including more than half of all living birds and consisting chiefly of songbirds of perching habits [Latin *passerinus* "of sparrows", from *passer* "sparrow"] — **passerine** *n*

pas seul \pä-'sərl, -'səl, -'sœl\ *n* : a solo dance or dance figure [French, literally, "solo step"]

pas·sim \'pas-əm, -,im\ *adv* : here and there — used to indicate that something (as a phrase) is to be found at many places in the same book or work [Latin, from *passus* "scattered", from *pandere* "to spread"]

¹pass·ing \'pas-ing\ *n* : the act of one that passes or causes to pass; *esp* : DEATH — **in passing** : by the way

²passing *adj* **1** : going by or past ⟨the *passing* crowd⟩ **2** : having a brief duration ⟨a *passing* whim⟩ **3** : marked by haste or inattention : SUPERFICIAL ⟨a *passing* glance⟩ **4** : given on satisfactory completion of an examination or course of study ⟨a *passing* grade⟩

³passing *adv* : to a surpassing degee : EXCEEDINGLY ⟨*passing* fair⟩

pas·sion \'pash-ən\ *n* **1** *often cap* : the sufferings of Christ between the night of the Last Supper and his death **2 a** *pl* : the emotions as distinguished from reason **b** : violent, intense, or overmastering feeling **c** : an outbreak of anger **3 a** : ardent affection : LOVE **b** : a strong liking ⟨a *passion* for cars⟩ **c** : sexual desire **d** : an object of desire or deep interest ⟨bowling is their *passion*⟩ [Old French, from Late Latin *passio* "suffering", from Latin *pati* "to suffer"] — **pas·sion·al** \-ən-l\ *adj* — **pas·sion·less** \-ən-ləs\ *adj* □ SYN PASSION, FERVOR, ARDOR mean intense emotion. PASSION implies an emotion that is deeply stirring or ungovernable ⟨stalked out of the room in a towering *passion*⟩ FERVOR implies a strong, steadily glowing emotion ⟨sang their hymns with deep *fervor*⟩ ARDOR suggests a warm excited feeling likely to be fitful or short-lived ⟨the cost of the project dampened their *ardor* for reform⟩ SYN see in addition FEELING

pas·sion·ate \'pash-nət, -ə-nət\ *adj* **1 a** : easily aroused to anger **b** : filled with anger : ANGRY **2** : capable of, affected by, or expressing intense feeling **3** : strongly affected with sexual desire SYN see IMPASSIONED — **pas·sion·ate·ly** *adv* — **pas·sion·ate·ness** *n*

pas·sion·flow·er \'pash-ən-,flaù-ər, -,flaùr\ *n* : any of a genus of chiefly tropical climbing vines or erect herbs having showy symmetrical flowers and pulpy often edible fruits [from the fancied resemblance of parts of the flower to the cross, nails, and crown of thorns used in Christ's crucifixion]

Pas·sion·ist \'pash-nəst, -ə-nəst\ *n* : a member of a Roman Catholic monastic order devoted chiefly to missionary work and retreats

passion play *n, often cap 1st P* : a play representing scenes connected with Christ's suffering and crucifixion

Passion Sunday *n* : the 5th Sunday in Lent

Pas·sion·tide \'pash-ən-,tīd\ *n* : the last two weeks of Lent

Passion Week *n* **1** : HOLY WEEK **2** : the 2d week before Easter

¹pas·sive \'pas-iv\ *adj* **1 a** : not active but acted on : receptive to or affected by outside force, agency, or influence ⟨*passive* spectators⟩ **b** : of, relating to, or being a verb form or voice indicating that the person or thing represented by the subject is subjected to the action represented by the verb ⟨"was bitten" in "I was bitten by a dog" is *passive*⟩ **2** : not involving expenditure of chemical energy ⟨*passive* transport across a cell membrane⟩ **3** : receiving or enduring without resistance : SUBMISSIVE ⟨*passive* surrender to fate⟩ [Latin *passivus*, from *pati* "to be acted upon, suffer"] — **pas·sive·ly** *adv* — **pas·sive·ness** *n* — **pas·siv·i·ty** \pa-'siv-ət-ē\ *n*

passenger pigeon

\ə\ abut		\ng\ sing	
\ər\ further		\ō\ bone	
\a\ mat		\ò\ saw	
\ā\ take		\òi\ coin	
\ä\ cot, cart		\th\ thin	
\aù\ out		\th\ this	
\ch\ chin		\ü\ food	
\e\ pet		\ù\ foot	
\ē\ easy		\y\ yet	
\g\ go		\yü\ few	
\i\ tip		\yù\ cure	
\ī\ life		\zh\ vision	
\j\ job			

²passive *n* **1** : a passive verb form **2** : the passive voice of a language

passive immunity *n* : immunity acquired by transfer (as by injection of serum from an individual with active immunity) of antibodies

passive resistance *n* : resistance especially to a government or an occupying power characterized mainly by noncooperation

passive smoking *n* : the involuntary inhalation of tobacco smoke (as from another's cigarette) especially by a nonsmoker

pass·key \'pas-,kē\ *n* **1** : MASTER KEY **2** : SKELETON KEY

pass off *vt* **1** : to make public or offer for sale with intent to deceive **2** : to give a false identity or character to

pass out *vi* **1** : to lose consciousness **2** : DIE 1

Pass·over \'pas-,ō-vər\ *n* : a Jewish holiday celebrated in March or April in commemoration of the liberation of the Hebrews from slavery in Egypt [from the exemption of the Israelites from the slaughter of the firstborn of Egypt (Exodus 12:23-27)]

pass·port \'pas-,pōrt, -,pȯrt\ *n* **1 a** : an official document issued to a person that is usually necessary for exit from and reentry into the country, that allows the person to travel in foreign countries, and that requests protection for the person in foreign countries **b** : an identification document required by law to be carried by persons living or traveling in a country **2** : something that secures admission or acceptance ⟨education as a *passport* to success⟩ [Middle French *passeport,* from *passer* "to pass" + *port* 'port']

pass up *vt* : DECLINE 4b, c, REJECT

pass·word \'pas-,wərd\ *n* **1** : a word or phrase that a person must utter before being allowed to pass a guard **2** : WATCHWORD 1

¹past \'past\ *adj* **1 a** : AGO ⟨10 years *past*⟩ **b** : just gone by ⟨for the *past* few days⟩ **2** : having existed or taken place in a period before the present : BYGONE ⟨*past* customs⟩ **3** : of, relating to, or being a verb tense that in English is usually formed by internal vowel change (as in *sang*) or by the addition of a suffix (as in *laughed*) and that expresses elapsed time **4** : no longer serving ⟨*past* president⟩ [Middle English, from past participle of *passen* "to pass"]

²past *prep* **1 a** : beyond the age for or of ⟨*past* playing with toys⟩ **b** : AFTER ⟨half *past* two⟩ **2 a** : at the farther side of : BEYOND **b** : in a course or direction going close to and then beyond ⟨drove *past* the house⟩ **3** : beyond the range, scope, or sphere of ⟨a situation *past* belief⟩

³past *n* **1 a** : time gone by **b** : something that happened or was done in the past **2 a** : PAST TENSE **b** : a verb form in the past tense **3** : a past life, history, or course of action; *esp* : a past life that is secret

⁴past *adv* : so as to reach and go beyond a point near at hand

pas·ta \'päs-tə\ *n* **1** : a wheaten paste in processed form (as spaghetti) or in the form of fresh dough (as ravioli) **2** : pasta prepared for eating [Italian, from Late Latin "paste, dough"]

¹paste \'pāst\ *n* **1 a** : a dough rich in fat used for pastry **b** : a candy made by evaporating fruit with sugar or by flavoring a gelatin, starch, or gum arabic preparation **c** : a smooth food product made by evaporation or grinding ⟨almond *paste*⟩ **d** : a shaped dough (as spaghetti or ravioli) prepared from wheat products (as semolina, farina, or flour) **2** : a soft plastic mixture or composition: as **a** : a preparation of flour and water or starch and water used for sticking things together **b** : a clay mixture prepared for shaping into pottery or porcelain **3** : a very brilliant glass used for the manufacture of artificial gems [Middle French, from Late Latin *pasta* "dough, paste"]

²paste *vt* **1** : to cause to adhere by paste : STICK **2** : to cover with or as if with something pasted on ⟨*paste* a wall with notices⟩

³paste *vt* : to hit hard [alteration of *baste*]

paste·board \'pāst-,bōrd, 'pās-, -,bȯrd\ *n* : paperboard with paper pasted to the outside to provide a smooth surface; *also* : CARDBOARD, PAPERBOARD

¹pas·tel \pas-'tel\ *n* **1 a** : a paste made of ground color and used for making crayons **b** : a crayon made of such paste **2** : a drawing in pastel **3** : any of various pale or light colors [French, from Italian *pastello,* from Late Latin *pastellus* "woad", from *pasta* "paste"]

²pastel *adj* **1 a** : of or relating to a pastel **b** : made with pastels **2** : pale and light in color

pas·tern \'pas-tərn\ *n* : the part of the foot of a horse between the fetlock and the joint at the hoof; *also* : the corresponding part of some other four-footed animals [Middle French *pasturon,* from *pasture* "pasture, tether attached to the foot of a horse at pasture"]

pas·teur·iza·tion \,pas-chə-rə-'zā-shən, ,pas-tə-\ *n* : partial sterilization of a substance and especially a fluid (as milk) at a temperature and period of exposure that destroys objectionable organisms without major chemical alteration of the substance [Louis *Pasteur*] — **pas·teur·ize** \'pas-chə-,rīz, 'pas-tə-\ *vt* — **pas·teur·iz·er** \-,rī-zər\ *n*

Pas·teur treatment \pas-'tər-\ *n* : a method of aborting rabies by stimulating antibody production through successive inoculations with attenuated virus of gradually increasing strength

pas·tiche \pas-'tēsh, päs-\ *n* : a composition (as in literature or music) made up of selections from different works : POTPOURRI [French, from Italian *pasticcio,* literally, "pasty", derived from Late Latin *pasta* "paste"]

pas·tille \pas-'tēl\ *n* **1** : a small mass of aromatic paste for fumigating or scenting the air of a room **2** : an aromatic or medicated lozenge : TROCHE [French *pastille,* from Latin *pastillus* "small loaf, lozenge"]

pas·time \'pas-,tīm\ *n* : something that helps to make time pass agreeably : DIVERSION

past master *n* **1** : one who has held the office of master (as in a guild, club, or lodge) **2** : one who is expert

pas·tor \'pas-tər\ *n* : a member of the clergy who is in charge of a church or parish [Old French *pastour,* from Latin *pastor* "herdsman", from *pascere* "to feed"] — **pas·tor·ship** \-,ship\ *n*

¹pas·to·ral \'pas-tə-rəl, -trəl\ *adj* **1 a** : of or relating to shepherds or rural life **b** : devoted to or based on livestock raising **c** : RURAL **d** : depicting rural life and people especially in an idealistic way ⟨*pastoral* poetry⟩ **2** : of or relating to the pastor of a church — **pas·to·ral·ly** \-tə-rə-lē, -trə-lē\ *adv* — **pas·to·ral·ness** *n*

²pas·to·ral \'pas-tə-rəl, -trəl; *sense 2d is often* ,pas-tə-'räl, -'ral\ *n* **1** : a letter of a spiritual overseer; *esp* : one written by a bishop to his diocese **2 a** : a literary work dealing with shepherds or rural life in a usually artificial manner **b** : pastoral poetry or drama **c** : a rural picture or scene **d** : PASTORALE

pas·to·rale \,pas-tə-'räl, -'ral\ *n* : an instrumental or vocal composition having a pastoral theme [Italian, from *pastorale* "pastoral"]

pas·tor·ate \'pas-tə-rət, -trət\ *n* **1** : the office, duties, or term of service of a pastor **2** : a body of pastors

past participle *n* : a participle that expresses completed action, that is traditionally one of the principal parts of the verb, and that is used in English in the formation of perfect tenses in the active voice and of all tenses in the passive voice ⟨*raised* in "Many hands were raised" and *thrown* in "The ball has been thrown" are *past participles*⟩

past perfect *adj* : of, relating to, or being a verb tense formed in English with *had* and expressing an action or state completed at or before a past time spoken of — **past perfect** *n*

pas·tra·mi *also* **pas·tromi** \pə-'sträm-ē\ *n* : a highly seasoned smoked beef prepared especially from shoulder cuts [Yiddish, from Rumanian *pastramă*]

past·ry \'pā-strē\ *n, pl* **pastries** 1 : sweet baked goods made of dough or having a crust made of enriched dough 2 : a piece of pastry [¹*paste*]

past tense *n* : a verb tense expressing action or state in the past

pas·tur·age \'pas-chə-rij\ *n* : PASTURE

¹pas·ture \'pas-chər\ *n* 1 : plants (as grass) for the feeding especially of grazing animals 2 : land or a plot of land used for grazing [Middle French, from Late Latin *pastura,* from Latin *pascere* "to feed"]

²pasture *vb* 1 : to feed on or put (as cattle) to feed on pasture : GRAZE 2 : to use as pasture

¹pas·ty \'pas-tē\ *n, pl* **pasties** : ²PIE 1; *esp* : a meat pie [Middle French *pasté,* from *paste* "dough, paste"]

²pasty \'pā-stē\ *adj* **past·i·er; -est** : resembling paste; *esp* : pallid and unhealthy in appearance — **past·i·ness** *n*

PA system \pē-'ā-\ *n* : PUBLIC-ADDRESS SYSTEM

¹pat \'pat\ *n* 1 : a light blow especially with the hand or a flat instrument 2 : a light tapping sound 3 : something (as butter) provided in a small flat portion [Middle English *patte*]

²pat *adv* : in a pat manner : APTLY, PERFECTLY

³pat *vb* **pat·ted; pat·ting** 1 : to strike lightly with the hand or a flat instrument 2 : to flatten, smooth, or shape with light blows ⟨*pat* one's hair into place⟩ 3 : to soothe or show approval by striking gently ⟨*pat* someone's hand⟩

⁴pat *adj* 1 **a** : exactly suited to the purpose or occasion : APT ⟨a *pat* answer⟩ **b** : suspiciously suitable ⟨*pat* excuses⟩ 2 : learned, mastered, or memorized exactly ⟨have a lesson down *pat*⟩

¹patch \'pach\ *n* 1 : a piece of material used to mend or cover a hole, a torn place, or a weak spot 2 : a tiny piece of black silk or court plaster formerly worn on the face especially by women to cover a defect or to heighten beauty 3 : a shield worn over the socket of an injured or missing eye 4 : a small piece : SCRAP 5 **a** : a small area or plot distinguished from its surroundings ⟨a *patch* of oats⟩ ⟨a *patch* of blistered skin⟩ **b** : a spot of color : BLOTCH ⟨a *patch* of white on a dog's head⟩ 6 : a piece of cloth attached to a garment as an ornament or insignia [Middle English *pacche*]

²patch *vt* 1 : to mend, cover, or fill up a hole or weak spot in 2 : to provide with a patch 3 **a** : to make out of patches **b** : to mend or put together especially hastily or clumsily — usually used with *up* ⟨*patched* up their differences⟩

pa·tchou·li *or* **pa·tchou·ly** \'pach-ə-lē, pə-'chü-lē\ *n, pl* **-lis** *or* **-lies** 1 : an East Indian shrubby mint that yields a fragrant essential oil 2 : a heavy perfume made from patchouli [Tamil *paccuḷi*]

patch pocket *n* : a flat pocket applied to the outside of a garment

patch test *n* : a test for determining allergy made by applying to the unbroken skin small pads soaked with the allergen in question

patch·work \'pach-,wərk\ *n* 1 : something made up of various different parts : HODGEPODGE 2 : pieces of cloth of various colors and shapes sewed together usually in a pattern — **patchwork** *adj*

patchy \'pach-ē\ *adj* **patch·i·er; -est** : consisting of or marked by patches; *also* : SPOTTY 2

pate \'pāt\ *n* : HEAD; *esp* : the crown of the head [Middle English]

pâ·té \pä-'tā, pa-\ *n* 1 : a meat or fish pie or patty 2 : a spread of finely mashed seasoned and spiced meat [French, from Old French *pasté,* from *paste* "dough, paste"]

pâ·té de foie gras \pä-,tād-ə-,fwä-'grä, pa-\ *n, pl* **pâtés de foie gras** \-,tād-ə-, -,tāz-də-\ : a rich pâté of fat goose liver and truffles [French]

pa·tel·la \pə-'tel-ə\ *n, pl* **-tel·lae** \-'tel-ē, -,ī\ *or* **-tellas** : KNEECAP [Latin, from *patina* "shallow dish, pan"] — **pa·tel·lar** \-'tel-ər\ *adj*

pat·en \'pat-n\ *n* 1 : a plate of precious metal for holding the eucharistic bread 2 : a shallow dish or plate 3 : a thin metal disk [Old French *patene,* from Latin *patina* "shallow dish, pan"]

¹pa·tent \ *1-4 are* 'pat-nt, *5 is* 'pāt-, *6 is* 'pāt-, 'pat-\ *adj* 1 : open to public inspection — used chiefly in the phrase *letters patent* 2 : protected by a patent ⟨*patent* locks⟩ 3 : marketed as a proprietary commodity ⟨*patent* drugs⟩ 4 : of, relating to, or concerned with the granting of patents especially for inventions ⟨a *patent* lawyer⟩ 5 : offering free passage : UNOBSTRUCTED ⟨a *patent* opening⟩ 6 : EVIDENT, OBVIOUS ⟨a *patent* lie⟩ [Middle French, from Latin *patens,* from *patēre* "to be open"] — **pa·ten·cy** \'pāt-n-sē\ *n* — **pa·tent·ly** \'pāt-n-tlē, 'pat-, -lē\ *adv*

²pat·ent \'pat-nt\ *n* 1 : an official document conferring a right or privilege 2 : a writing securing to an inventor for a term of years the exclusive right to make, use, or sell his or her invention; *also* : the right so granted 3 : something (as a privilege) resembling a patent

³patent *vt* 1 : to grant a privilege, right, or license to by patent 2 : to obtain or secure by patent; *esp* : to secure by letters patent exclusive right to make, use, or sell 3 : to obtain or grant a patent right to — **pat·ent·able** \'pat-n-tə-bəl\ *adj*

pat·en·tee \,pat-n-'tē\ *n* : one to whom a grant is made or a privilege secured by patent

pat·ent leather \,pat-n-, ,pat-nt-\ *n* : a leather with a hard smooth glossy surface

patent medicine *n* : a packaged medicine made from a secret formula, often protected by a trademark, and sold without a prescription with a label bearing the name of the medicine, the manufacturer's name, and directions for use

patent office *n* : a government office for examining claims to patents and granting patents

pat·en·tor \'pat-n-tər, ,pat-n-'tòr\ *n* : one that grants a patent

patent right *n* : a right granted by letters patent; *esp* : the exclusive right to an invention

pa·ter *n* 1 *often cap* \'pä-,teər\ : PATERNOSTER 1 2 \'pāt-ər\ *chiefly British* : FATHER 1a [sense 2 from Latin *pater* "father"]

pa·ter·fa·mil·i·as \,pāt-ər-fə-'mil-ē-əs\ *n* 1 : the male head of a household 2 : the father of a family [Latin, from *pater* "father" + *familia* "family"]

pa·ter·nal \pə-'tərn-l\ *adj* 1 : of or relating to a father : FATHERLY 2 : received or inherited from one's father 3 : related through the father ⟨a *paternal* grandfather⟩ [Latin *paternus,* from *pater* "father"] — **pa·ter·nal·ly** \-l-ē\ *adv*

pa·ter·nal·ism \-l-,iz-əm\ *n* : the principle or practice of governing or of exercising authority (as over employees) in a way suggesting that of a father over his children — **pa·ter·nal·ist** \-l-əst\ *adj or n* — **pa·ter·nal·is·tic** \-,tərn-l-'is-tik\ *adj*

pa·ter·ni·ty \pə-'tər-nət-ē\ *n* 1 : the quality or state of being a father 2 : origin or descent from a father

pat·er·nos·ter \,pät-ər-'näs-tər, 'pat-ər-,, 'pä-,teər-, -'näs-,teər\ *n* 1 *often cap* : LORD'S PRAYER 2 : a word formula repeated as a prayer or magical charm [Latin *pater noster* "our father"]

path \'path, 'påth\ *n, pl* **paths** \'pathz, 'paths, 'påthz, 'påths\ 1 : a course or way formed by or as if by repeated footsteps 2 : a track constructed for a particular use (as horseback riding) 3 **a** : the way traversed by something : COURSE, ROUTE **b** : a way of life, conduct, or thought [Old English *pæth*] — **path·less** *adj*

path- *or* **patho-** *combining form* : pathological state : disease ⟨*patho*gen⟩ [Greek *pathos,* literally, "suffering"]

-path \,path\ *n combining form* 1 : practitioner of a (specified) system of medicine that emphasizes one aspect of disease or its treatment ⟨osteo*path*⟩ 2 : one suffering from (such) an ailment ⟨psycho*path*⟩

patchwork 2

\ə\ abut	\ng\ sing
\ər\ **further**	\ō\ bone
\a\ **mat**	\ò\ **saw**
\ā\ **take**	\òi\ **coin**
\ä\ **cot, cart**	\th\ **thin**
\au̇\ **out**	\th̲\ **this**
\ch\ **chin**	\ü\ **food**
\e\ **pet**	\u̇\ **foot**
\ē\ **easy**	\y\ **yet**
\g\ **go**	\yü\ **few**
\i\ **tip**	\yu̇\ **cure**
\ī\ **life**	\zh\ **vision**
\j\ **job**	

Pa·than \pə-'tän\ *n* : a member of the principal ethnic group of Afghanistan [Hindi *Paṭhān*]

pa·thet·ic \pə-'thet-ik\ *adj* 1 : arousing tenderness, pity, or sorrow : PITIABLE 2 : marked by sorrow or melancholy : SAD ⟨a *pathetic* story⟩ [Late Latin *patheticus*, from Greek *pathētikos* "capable of feeling, pathetic", from *paschein* "to experience, suffer"] — **pa·thet·i·cal·ly** \-'thet-i-kə-lē, -klē\ *adv*

path·find·er \'path-ˌfīn-dər, 'path-\ *n* : one that discovers a way and especially a new route in unexplored regions

patho·gen \'path-ə-jən\ *n* : a specific cause (as a bacterium or virus) of disease — **patho·gen·ic** \ˌpath-ə-'jen-ik\ *adj* — **patho·gen·i·cal·ly** \-'jen-i-kə-lē, -klē\ *adv* — **patho·ge·nic·i·ty** \-jə-'nis-ət-ē\ *n*

pa·thol·o·gy \pə-'thäl-ə-jē, pa-\ *n, pl* **-gies** 1 : the study of diseases and especially of the bodily changes produced by them 2 : something abnormal; *esp* : the disorders in structure and function that constitute disease or characterize a particular disease — **patho·log·i·cal** \ˌpath-ə-'läj-i-kəl\ *or* **patho·log·ic** \-ik\ *adj* — **patho·log·i·cal·ly** \-i-kə-lē, -klē\ *adv* — **pa·thol·o·gist** \pə-'thäl-ə-jəst, pa-\ *n*

pa·thos \'pā-ˌthäs, -ˌthȯs\ *n* 1 : an element in experience or in artistic representation arousing pity or compassion 2 : an emotion of sympathetic pity [Greek, "suffering, experience, emotion", from *paschein* "to experience, suffer"]

path·way \'path-ˌwā, 'path-\ *n* : PATH 1, 3

-p·a·thy \p-ə-thē\ *n combining form, pl* **-pathies** 1 : feeling : suffering ⟨em*pathy*⟩ : being acted upon ⟨tele*pathy*⟩ 2 : disease of (such) a part or kind 3 : system of medicine based on (such) a factor ⟨osteo*pathy*⟩

pa·tience \'pā-shəns\ *n* : the capacity, habit, or fact of being patient

¹pa·tient \'pā-shənt\ *adj* 1 : bearing pains or trials calmly or without complaint 2 : being kindly and tolerant 3 : not hasty or impetuous 4 : steadfast despite opposition, difficulty, or adversity ⟨years of *patient* labor⟩ [Middle French *pacient*, from Latin *patiens*, from *pati* "to suffer"] — **pa·tient·ly** *adv*

²patient *n* : an individual awaiting or under medical care and treatment

pat·i·na \'pat-ə-nə, pə-'tē-nə\ *n, pl* **patinas** *or* **pat·i·nae** \'pat-ə-ˌnē, -ˌnī\ 1 : a usually green film formed on copper and bronze by long exposure or by chemicals and often valued aesthetically 2 : a surface appearance (as a coloring or mellowing) of something grown beautiful especially with age or use [Latin, "shallow dish, pan"]

pa·tio \'pat-ē-ˌō *also* 'pät-\ *n, pl* **pa·ti·os** 1 : COURTYARD; *esp* : an inner court open to the sky 2 : an often paved recreation area that adjoins a dwelling [Spanish]

pa·tois \'pa-ˌtwä, 'pä-\ *n, pl* **patois** \-ˌtwäz\ 1 a : a dialect other than the standard or literary dialect b : illiterate or provincial speech 2 : JARGON 2 [French]

patr- *or* **patri-** *or* **patro-** *combining form* : father ⟨*patr*istic⟩ [Latin *pater* and Greek *patēr*]

pa·tri·arch \'pā-trē-ˌärk\ *n* 1 a : one of the Old Testament fathers of the human race or of the Hebrew people b : a man who is father or founder c (1) : the oldest male member or representative of a group (2) : a venerable old man 2 a : a bishop of the leading ancient sees of Constantinople, Alexandria, Antioch, Jerusalem, and Rome b : the head of any of various Eastern churches c : a Roman Catholic bishop next in rank to the pope [Old French *patriarche*, from Late Latin *patriarcha*, from Greek *patriarchēs*, from *patria* "lineage" (from *patēr* "father") + *-archēs* "-arch"] — **pa·tri·ar·chal** \ˌpā-trē-'är-kəl\ *adj*

pa·tri·arch·ate \'pā-trē-ˌär-kət, -ˌkät\ *n* 1 a : the office, juris-diction, or time in office of a patriarch b : the residence or headquarters of a patriarch 2 : PATRIAR-CHY 2

pa·tri·ar·chy \-ˌär-kē\ *n, pl* **-chies** 1 : social organization marked by the supremacy of the father in the clan or family and the reckoning of descent and inheritance in the male line 2 : a society organized according to the principles of patriarchy

pa·tri·cian \pə-'trish-ən\ *n* 1 : a member of one of the original citizen families of ancient Rome 2 : a person of high birth and cultivation : ARISTOCRAT [Middle French *patricien*, from Latin *patricius*, from *patres* "senators", from pl. of *pater* "father"] — **patrician** *adj* — **pa·tri·ci·ate** \-'trish-ē-ət, -ē-ˌāt\ *n*

pat·ri·cide \'pa-trə-ˌsīd\ *n* 1 : one who murders his or her own father 2 : the murder of one's own father — **pat·ri·cid·al** \ˌpa-trə-'sīd-l\ *adj*

pat·ri·mo·ny \'pa-trə-ˌmō-nē\ *n, pl* **-nies** 1 a : an estate inherited from one's father or ancestors b : something derived from one's father or ancestors : HERITAGE 2 : an estate or endowment belonging by ancient right to a church [Middle French *patrimonie*, from Latin *patrimonium*, from *pater* "father"] — **pat·ri·mo·ni·al** \ˌpa-trə-'mō-nē-əl\ *adj*

pa·tri·ot \'pā-trē-ət, -trē-ˌät\ *n* : a person who loves his or her country and zealously supports it [Middle French *patriote* "compatriot", from Late Latin *patriota*, from Greek *patriōtēs*, from *patrios* "of one's father", from *patēr* "father"]

pa·tri·ot·ic \ˌpā-trē-'ät-ik\ *adj* 1 : inspired by patriotism 2 : suitable to or characteristic of a patriot — **pa·tri·ot·i·cal·ly** \-'ät-i-kə-lē, -klē\ *adv*

pa·tri·o·tism \'pā-trē-ə-ˌtiz-əm\ *n* : love for or devotion to one's country

pa·tris·tic \pə-'tris-tik\ *adj* : of or relating to the church fathers or their writings — **pa·tris·ti·cal** \-ti-kəl\ *adj*

¹pa·trol \pə-'trōl\ *n* 1 a : the action or duty of going the rounds of an area for observation or guarding b : the person or group performing such an action 2 : a detachment of persons employed for reconnaissance, security, or combat 3 : a subdivision of a Boy Scout or Girl Scout troop [French *patrouille*, from *patouiller* "to patrol", from Middle French, "to tramp around in the mud", from *patte* "paw"]

²patrol *vb* **pa·trolled; pa·trol·ling** : to be on patrol : carry out a patrol of — **pa·trol·ler** *n*

pa·trol·man \pə-'trōl-mən\ *n* : one who patrols; *esp* : a police officer assigned to a beat

patrol wagon *n* : an enclosed motor vehicle used by police to carry prisoners

pa·tron \'pā-trən\ *n* 1 : a person chosen as a special guardian or supporter ⟨a *patron* of poets⟩ 2 : one who gives generous support or approval ⟨a *patron* of the arts⟩ 3 : a regular client or customer [Middle French, from Latin *patronus* "defender", from *pater* "father"] — see PATTERN origin

pat·ron·age \'pa-trə-nij, 'pā-\ *n* 1 : the support or influence of a patron 2 : business or trade provided by customers 3 a : the power to distribute government jobs on a basis other than merit alone b : the distribution of jobs on this basis c : the jobs so distributed

pa·tron·ess \'pā-trə-nəs\ *n* : a woman who is a patron

pa·tron·ize \'pā-trə-ˌnīz, 'pa-\ *vt* 1 : to act as a patron to or of ⟨*patronize* the arts⟩ 2 : to treat with a superior air : be condescending toward 3 : to do business with ⟨*patronize* a neighborhood store⟩ — **pa·tron·iz·ing·ly** \-ˌnī-zing-lē\ *adv*

patron saint *n* : a saint to whose protection and intercession a person, a society, a church, or a place is dedicated

pat·ro·nym·ic \ˌpa-trə-'nim-ik\ *n* : a name derived from that of the father or a paternal ancestor [Late Latin *patronymicum*, derived from Greek *patronymia*, from *patēr* "father" + *onyma* "name"] — **patronymic** *adj*

pa·troon \pə-'trün\ *n* : the proprietor of a manorial estate granted by the Dutch especially in New York or

New Jersey [Dutch, literally, "boss, superior", from French *patron* "patron"]

pat·sy \'pat-sē\ *n, pl* **patsies** : one who is duped or victimized : SUCKER [perhaps from Italian *pazzo* "fool"]

¹**pat·ter** \'pat-ər\ *vb* **1** : to say or speak in a rapid or mechanical manner **2** : to talk glibly and volubly [Middle English *patren*, from *paternoster*] — **pat·ter·er** *n*

²**patter** *n* **1** : a specialized lingo : CANT; *esp* : the jargon of criminals (as thieves) **2** : the spiel of a street hawker or of a circus barker **3** : empty chatter **4 a** : the rapid-fire talk of a comedian **b** : the talk with which an entertainer accompanies a routine

³**patter** *vi* **1** : to strike or pat rapidly and repeatedly ⟨rain *pattering* on a roof⟩ **2** : to run with quick light-sounding steps [derived from ³*pat*]

⁴**patter** *n* : a quick succession of light sounds or pats ⟨the *patter* of little feet⟩

¹**pat·tern** \'pat-ərn\ *n* **1** : a form or model proposed for imitation : EXEMPLAR **2** : something designed or used as a model for making things ⟨a dress *pattern*⟩ **3** : a model for making a mold into which molten metal is poured to form a casting **4** : SPECIMEN 1, SAMPLE **5 a** : an artistic or mechanical design ⟨cloth with a small *pattern*⟩ **b** : form or style in literary or musical composition **6** : a natural or chance configuration ⟨frost *patterns*⟩ **7** : a complex of individual or group characteristics (as traits or behavior) ⟨behavior *patterns*⟩ ⟨the *pattern* of American industry⟩ [Middle English *patron*, from Middle French, "pattern, patron"] □ ORIGIN Latin *patronus* is derived from *pater*, "father", and the duties of a Roman *patronus* were comparable to those of a father. He was a protector of his city or province; a defender in a court of law was his client's *patronus;* the man who freed his slave became that slave's *patronus.* The use of *patronus* in Medieval Latin shifted to suit the new requirements of the Christian era. Such a father figure as a patron saint or the patron of a benefice was called a *patronus,* as was anyone who served like a father as a model or pattern to be emulated. Middle English *patron* (borrowed from Middle French) had a range of meaning similar to that of its Medieval Latin ancestor. During the 16th century another pronunciation of *patron* appeared, represented by such spellings as *pattern.* By the beginning of the 18th century the two forms, *patron* and *pattern,* were identified with separate senses and became two distinct words.

²**pattern** *vt* : to make or fashion according to a pattern

pat·ty *also* **pat·tie** \'pat-ē\ *n, pl* **patties** **1** : a little pie **2 a** : a small flat cake of chopped food ⟨a hamburg *patty*⟩ **b** : a small flat candy ⟨mint *patties*⟩ [French *pâté*]

pau·ci·ty \'pȯ-sət-ē\ *n* : smallness of number or quantity ⟨a *paucity* of tenor voices⟩ ⟨*paucity* of experience⟩ [Latin *paucitas*, from *paucus* "little"]

Paul·ist \'pȯ-ləst\ *n* : a member of the Roman Catholic Congregation of the Missionary Priests of St. Paul the Apostle founded in the United States in 1858

pau·low·nia \pȯ-'lō-nē-ə\ *n* : a Chinese tree widely grown in warm regions for its showy clusters of fragrant violet flowers [Anna *Paulovna*, died 1865, Russian princess]

paunch \'pȯnch, 'pänch\ *n* **1 a** : the belly together with its contents **b** : POTBELLY 1 **2** : RUMEN [Middle French *panche*, from Latin *pantex*]

paunchy \'pȯn-chē, 'pän-\ *adj* : having a potbelly — **paunch·i·ness** *n*

pau·per \'pȯ-pər\ *n* : a very poor person; *esp* : one supported by charity [Latin, "poor"] — **pau·per·ism** \-pə-ˌriz-əm\ *n* — **pau·per·ize** \-ˌrīz\ *vt*

¹**pause** \'pȯz\ *n* **1** : a temporary stop **2 a** : a break in a verse **b** : a brief suspension of the voice to indicate the limits and relations of sentences and their parts **3** : temporary inaction often because of doubt or uncertainty **4** : the sign denoting a musical hold **5** : a reason or cause for pausing ⟨it was a thought to give one

pause⟩ [Latin *pausa*, from Greek *pausis*, from *pauein* "to stop"]

²**pause** *vi* **1** : to stop temporarily **2** : to linger for a time ⟨*pause* on a high note⟩

pa·vane \pə-'vän, -'van\ *also* **pa·van** *same or* \'pav-ən\ *n* **1** : a stately court dance by couples that was introduced from southern Europe into England in the 16th century **2** : music for the pavane [Middle French *pavane*, from Spanish *pavana*, from Italian]

pave \'pāv\ *vt* **1** : to lay or cover with material (as stone or concrete) that makes a firm level surface for travel **2** : to cover firmly and solidly as if with paving material [Middle French *paver*, from Latin *pavire* "to strike, stamp"] — **pave the way** : to prepare a smooth easy way ⟨*pave the way* for those who come after⟩

pave·ment \'pāv-mənt\ *n* **1** : a paved surface **2** : the material with which something is paved

pa·vil·ion \pə-'vil-yən\ *n* **1** : a usually large luxurious tent **2** : a lightly constructed often ornamental building serving as a shelter in a park, garden, or athletic field **3** : a part of a building projecting from the main body of the structure **4** : a building either partly or completely detached from the main building or main group of buildings [Old French *paveillon*, from Latin *papilio* "butterfly"]

pav·ing \'pā-ving\ *n* : PAVEMENT

¹**paw** \'pȯ\ *n* **1** : the foot of a four-footed animal (as a lion or dog) that has claws; *also* : the foot of an animal **2** : a human hand especially when large or clumsy [Middle French *poue*]

²**paw** *vb* **1** : to feel or touch clumsily or rudely ⟨merchandise *pawed* by customers⟩ **2** : to touch, strike, or scrape with a paw or hoof **3** : to flail at or grab wildly ⟨hands *pawing* the air⟩

pawl \'pȯl\ *n* : a pivoted tongue or sliding bolt on one part of a machine that is adapted to fall into notches on another part (as a ratchet wheel) so as to permit motion in only one direction [perhaps from Dutch *pal*]

¹**pawn** \'pȯn, 'pän\ *n* **1** : something deposited with another as security for a loan : PLEDGE **2** : the state of being pledged ⟨the watch was in *pawn*⟩ [Middle French *pan*]

²**pawn** *vt* : to give temporarily as security ⟨*pawned* the silverware⟩ — **pawn·er** \'pȯ-nər, 'pän-ər\ *n*

³**pawn** *n* **1** : a piece in chess of least value that can move only one square forward at a time after its first move and can capture only diagonally forward **2** : one used or exploited to further the purposes of another [Middle French *poon*, from Medieval Latin *pedon-, pedo* "foot soldier", from Latin *ped-, pes* "foot"]

pawn·bro·ker \'pȯn-ˌbrō-kər, 'pän-\ *n* : one who lends money to customers who have pledged personal property as security — **pawn·bro·king** \-king\ *n*

Paw·nee \pȯ-'nē, pä-\ *n* : a member of an Amerindian people of what is now Nebraska and Kansas

pawn·shop \'pȯn-ˌshäp, 'pän-\ *n* : a pawnbroker's shop

paw·paw *variant of* PAPAW

¹**pay** \'pā\ *vb* **paid** \'pād\ *also in sense* **7** **payed; paid; pay·ing** **1** : to give money especially in return for services received or for something bought ⟨*pay* the taxi driver⟩ ⟨*pay* for a ticket⟩ **2** : to pay what is indicated or required by ⟨*pay* a bill⟩ ⟨*pay* a tax⟩ **3** : to get even with ⟨*pay* someone back for an injury⟩ **4** : to give or offer freely ⟨*pay* a compliment⟩ ⟨*pay* attention⟩ **5** : to return as profit ⟨an investment *paying* 5 percent⟩ **6** : to make or secure suitable return for expense or trouble : be worth the effort or pains required ⟨it *pays* to drive carefully⟩ **7** : to make (as a rope) slack and allow to run out — usually used with *out* [Old French *paier*, from Latin *pacare* "to pacify", from *pac-, pax* "peace"] □ ORIGIN Etymologically, to *pay* is "to pacify". The Latin verb *pacare*, "to pacify", is derived from *pax*, "peace". In the Middle Ages, *pacare* was used specifically to mean "to pacify a creditor by paying a debt" and eventually, more generally, "to pay".

Old French *paier* had both the original sense "to pacify or appease" and the later, "to pay". Middle English *payen*, too, borrowed from the French in the late 12th or early 13th century, was used in both senses. But the original sense of *pay* is now long obsolete. □ SYN PAY, COMPENSATE, REMUNERATE mean to give money or its equivalent in return for something. PAY implies the discharge of an obligation incurred ⟨*pay* the worker's wages⟩ COMPENSATE implies making up for services rendered or help given or loss suffered ⟨gave $10 more to *compensate* us for our trouble⟩ REMUNERATE suggests paying for services rendered rather than for material goods.

²**pay** *n* **1 a** : the act or fact of paying or being paid : PAYMENT **b** : the status of being paid by an employer : EMPLOY **2** : something paid; *esp* : WAGES, SALARY

³**pay** *adj* **1** : containing or leading to something precious or valuable (as gold or oil) ⟨*pay* rock⟩ **2** : equipped with a coin slot for receiving a fee for use ⟨a *pay* phone⟩ **3** : requiring payment ⟨*pay* TV⟩

pay·able \'pā-ə-bəl\ *adj* : that may, can, or must be paid; *esp* : DUE ⟨accounts *payable*⟩

pay·check \'pā-,chek\ *n* **1** : a check in payment of wages or salary **2** : WAGES, SALARY

pay dirt *n* **1** : earth or ore that yields a profit to a miner **2** : a useful or remunerative discovery or object ⟨really hit *pay dirt* with that invention⟩

pay·ee \pā-'ē\ *n* : one to whom money is or is to be paid

pay·er \'pā-ər\ *also* **pay·or** \'pā-ər, pā-'ór\ *n* : one that pays

pay·load \'pā-,lōd\ *n* : something (as cargo, passengers, instruments, or explosives) carried by a vehicle, missile, rocket, or spacecraft in addition to what is necessary for its operation

pay·mas·ter \-,mas-tər\ *n* : an officer or agent of an employer whose duty it is to pay salaries or wages

pay·ment \'pā-mənt\ *n* **1** : the act of paying **2** : money given to pay for something ⟨*payments* on a car⟩ ⟨*payment* for a day's work⟩

pay·off \'pā-,óf\ *n* **1** : payment at the outcome of an enterprise ⟨a big *payoff* from an investment⟩ **2** : the climax of an incident or enterprise ⟨the *payoff* of a story⟩

pay off \pā-'óf, 'pā-\ *vt* **1** : to pay in full often through small payments made at intervals ⟨*pay off* a mortgage⟩ **2** : to take revenge on ⟨*pay off* an enemy⟩

pay·ola \pā-'ō-lə\ *n* : secret or indirect payment for a commercial favor [probably alteration of *payoff*]

pay·roll \'pā-,rōl\ *n* : a list of persons entitled to receive pay with the amounts due to each; *also* : the amount of money necessary to pay those on such a list

pay station *n* : a pay telephone or a booth containing a pay telephone

pay up *vb* : to pay (as an overdue debt) in full

PCB \,pē-,sē-'bē\ *n* : POLYCHLORINATED BIPHENYL

PDQ \,pē-,dē-'kyü\ *adv, often not cap* : IMMEDIATELY **2** [abbreviation of *pretty damned quick*]

pea \'pē\ *n, pl* **peas** *also* **pease** \'pēz\ **1 a** : a variable annual leguminous vine grown for its rounded smooth or wrinkled edible protein-rich seeds **b** : the seed of the pea **c** *pl* : the immature pods of the pea with their included seeds **2** : any of various plants of the same family as the pea [back-formation from Middle English *pease* (taken as a pl.), from Old English *pise*, from Late Latin *pisa*, pl. of *pisum*, from Greek *pison*]

peace \'pēs\ *n* **1** : a state of tranquillity or quiet: as **a** : freedom from civil disturbance or foreign war **b** : a state of security or order within a community protected by law or custom ⟨breach of the *peace*⟩ **2** : freedom from disquieting or oppressive thoughts or emotions **3** : harmony in personal relations **4 a** : a state or period of agreement between governments **b** : a pact or agreement between combatants to end hostilities [Old French *pais*, from Latin *pax*]

¹peacock 1

peace·able \'pē-sə-bəl\ *adj* **1** : inclined toward peace : not quarrelsome **2** : free from strife or disorder — **peace·ably** \-blē\ *adv*

peace·ful \'pēs-fəl\ *adj* **1** : PEACEABLE 1 ⟨a *peaceful* person⟩ **2** : untroubled by conflict, agitation, or commotion : QUIET, TRANQUIL ⟨a *peaceful* countryside⟩ **3** : free from violence or force ⟨settled the conflict by *peaceful* means⟩ — **peace·ful·ly** \-fə-lē\ *adv* — **peace·ful·ness** *n*

peace·mak·er \'pē-,smā-kər\ *n* : a person who arranges a peace : one who settles an argument or stops a fight — **peace·mak·ing** \-king\ *n or adj*

peace offering *n* : a gift or service to procure peace or reconciliation

peace officer *n* : a civil officer (as a policeman or sheriff) whose duty it is to preserve the public peace

peace pipe *n* : an ornamented ceremonial pipe of the Amerindians — compare CALUMET

peace·time \'pē-,stīm\ *n* : a time when a nation is not at war

¹**peach** \'pēch\ *n* **1** : a low spreading Chinese tree related to the plums and cherries that is grown in most temperate areas for its sweet juicy fruit with pulpy white or yellow flesh, thin downy skin, and single rough hard stone; *also* : its fruit **2** : a moderate yellowish pink **3** : one likened to a peach (as in beauty, or excellence) [Middle French *peche* "peach fruit", from Late Latin *persica*, from Latin *persicum*, from *persicus* "Persian", from *Persia*]

²**peach** *vi* : to turn informer : BLAB [Middle English *pechen*, short for *apechen* "to accuse, impeach", derived from Late Latin *impedicare* "to entangle"]

peachy \'pē-chē\ *adj* **peach·i·er; -est** **1** : resembling a peach **2** : unusually fine : DANDY

¹**pea·cock** \'pē-,käk\ *n* **1** : a male peafowl distinguished by a small upright tuft on the head and by greatly elongated feathers in the tail mostly tipped with eyelike spots and erected and spread at will in a fan shimmering with iridescent color; *also* : PEAFOWL **2** : one showing off personal attributes or possessions (as clothing) [Middle English *pecok*, from *pe-* (from Old English *pēa* "peafowl", from Latin *pavo* "peacock") + *cok* "cock"]

²**peacock** *vi* : to make a proud self-important display

peacock blue *n* : a moderate greenish blue

pea·fowl \'pē-,faúl\ *n* : a very large pheasant of southeastern Asia and the East Indies that is often kept in captivity for its beauty [*pea-* (as in *peacock*) + *fowl*]

pea green *n* : a moderate yellow-green

pea·hen \'pē-,hen, -'hen\ *n* : a female peafowl

pea jacket \'pē-\ *n* : a heavy woolen double-breasted jacket worn chiefly by sailors [by folk etymology from Dutch *pijjekker*, from *pij*, a kind of cloth + *jekker* "jacket"]

¹**peak** \'pēk\ *n* **1** : a pointed or projecting part; *esp* : the visor of a cap or hat **2** : PROMONTORY **3** : a sharp or pointed ridge or end ⟨the *peak* of a roof⟩ **4 a** : the top of a hill or mountain ending in a point **b** : a whole hill or mountain especially when isolated **5** : the narrow part of a ship's bow or stern **6** : the highest level or value or greatest degree of development ⟨the *peak* of perfection⟩ [perhaps alteration of *pike*] SYN SEE SUMMIT

²**peak** *vb* : to come or cause to come to a peak, point, or maximum

³**peak** *adj* : being at or reaching the maximum ⟨an athlete in *peak* condition⟩ ⟨a *peak* year for sales⟩

¹**peaked** *adj* \'pēkt, 'pē-kəd\ : having a peak : POINTED — **peaked·ness** \'pēkt-nəs, 'pēk-nəs, 'pē-kəd-nəs\ *n*

²**peak·ed** \'pē-kəd\ *adj* : being pale and wan : SICKLY [from *peak* "to look sickly", of unknown origin]

¹**peal** \'pēl\ *n* **1** : a loud ringing of bells **2** : a loud sound or succession of sounds ⟨a *peal* of laughter⟩ ⟨a *peal* of thunder⟩ [Middle English, "appeal, summons to church", short for *appel* "appeal", from *appelen* "to appeal"]

²peal *vb* : to sound in peals ⟨bells *pealing* in the distance⟩

pea·like \'pē-ˌlīk\ *adj* **1** : resembling a garden pea (as in firmness or shape) **2** : being showy and resembling a butterfly in shape ⟨*pealike* flowers⟩

pea·nut \'pē-nət, -ˌnət\ *n* **1** : a low-branching widely cultivated annual herb of the pea family with showy yellow flowers and pods that ripen underground; *also* : this pod or one of the oily edible seeds it contains **2** : an insignificant or tiny person **3** *pl* : a trifling amount

peanut butter *n* : a paste made by grinding roasted skinned peanuts

peanut oil *n* : a colorless to yellow fatty oil from peanuts that is used chiefly as a salad oil, in margarine, in soap, and as an inert medium in medicinal preparations and cosmetics

pear \'paər, 'peər\ *n* : a fleshy pome fruit that usually tapers toward the stem end; *also* : a tree that bears pears and is related to the apple [Old English *peru*, from Latin *pirum*]

¹pearl \'pərl\ *n* **1 a** : a dense usually lustrous body formed of layers of nacre as an abnormal growth within the shell of some mollusks and used as a gem **b** : MOTHER-OF-PEARL **2** : something resembling a pearl (as in shape, color, or value) **3** : a slightly bluish medium gray [Middle French *perle*, derived from Latin *perna* "mussel"]

²pearl *vb* **1** : to set or adorn with pearls **2** : to sprinkle or bead with pearly drops **3** : to form into drops or beads like pearls or into small round grains **4** : to give a pearly color or luster to **5** : to fish or search for pearls — **pearl·er** *n*

³pearl *adj* **1 a** : of, relating to, or resembling pearl **b** : made of or adorned with pearls **2** : having grains of medium size ⟨*pearl* barley⟩

pearl gray *n* **1** : a yellowish to light gray **2** : a pale blue

pearly \'pər-lē\ *adj* **pearl·i·er; -est** : resembling, containing, or adorned with pearls or mother-of-pearl

peart \'piərt\ *adj, chiefly South & Midland* : in good spirits : LIVELY [alteration of *pert*]

peas·ant \'pez-nt\ *n* **1** : a European small farmer or farm laborer; *also* : one of similar agricultural status elsewhere **2** : an uncouth person or one of low social status [Middle French *paisant*, from *païs* "country", from Late Latin *pagensis* "inhabitant of a district", from Latin *pagus* "district"]

peas·ant·ry \'pez-n-trē\ *n* : peasants as a group ⟨a nation's *peasantry*⟩ ⟨the local *peasantry*⟩

pease *pl of* PEA

pea·shoot·er \'pē-ˈshüt-ər\ *n* : a toy blowgun for shooting peas

pea soup *n* **1** : a thick soup made of dried peas **2** : a heavy fog

peat \'pēt\ *n* **1** : TURF 2b **2** : a dark brown or black vegetable substance formed when some plants (as sphagnum moss) partly decay under water [Medieval Latin *peta*] — **peaty** \'pēt-ē\ *adj*

peat moss *n* : SPHAGNUM

pea·vey *or* **pea·vy** \'pē-vē\ *n, pl* **peaveys** *or* **peavies** : a lever like a cant hook but with the end armed with a strong sharp spike used in handling logs [probably from the name *Peavey*]

¹peb·ble \'peb-əl\ *n* **1** : a small usually round stone especially when worn by the action of water **2** : an irregular, crinkled, or grainy surface [Middle English *pobble*, from Old English *papolstān*] — **peb·bly** \'peb-lē, -ə-lē\ *adj*

²pebble *vt* **peb·bled; peb·bling** \'peb-ling, -ə-ling\ : to treat (as leather) so as to produce a rough and irregularly indented surface

pe·can \pi-ˈkän, -ˈkan\ *n* : a large hickory of the south central United States; *also* : its edible oblong nut [of American Indian origin]

pec·ca·dil·lo \ˌpek-ə-ˈdil-ō\ *n, pl* **-loes** *or* **-los** : a slight offense or fault [Spanish *pecadillo*, from *pecado* "sin", from Latin *peccatum*, from *peccare* "to sin"]

pec·ca·ry \'pek-ə-rē\ *n, pl* **-ries** : either of two American chiefly tropical mammals resembling but smaller than the related pigs [of American Indian origin]

¹peck \'pek\ *n* **1** — see MEASURE table **2** : a large quantity : great deal ⟨a *peck* of trouble⟩ [Old French *pek*]

²peck *vb* **1 a** (1) : to strike, pick up, or move with a pointed bill or tool ⟨chickens *pecking* corn⟩ (2) : to make by pecking ⟨*peck* a hole⟩ **b** : to strike at or pick up something with or as if with a bill **2** : to eat daintily : NIBBLE, PICK [Middle English *pecken*, from *piken* "to pierce, pick"] — **peck·er** *n*

³peck *n* **1** : an impression or hole made by pecking **2** : a quick sharp stroke

pecking order *or* **peck order** *n* **1** : a basic pattern of social organization within a flock of poultry in which each bird pecks another lower in the scale without being pecked in return and submits to pecking by one of higher rank **2** : a social order with ranks or classes

pec·ten \'pek-tən\ *n* : SCALLOP 1a [Latin, "comb, scallop"]

pec·tin \'pek-tən\ *n* : any of various water-soluble substances in plant tissues that yield a gel which is the basis of fruit jellies; *also* : a commercial product rich in pectins [French *pectine*, derived from Greek *pēktikos* "coagulating", from *pēgnynai* "to fix, coagulate"] — **pec·tin·ous** \-tə-nəs\ *adj*

pec·ti·nate \'pek-tə-ˌnāt\ *adj* : having narrow parallel projections or divisions resembling the teeth of a comb [Latin *pectinatus*, from *pecten* "comb"] — **pec·ti·na·tion** \ˌpek-tə-ˈnā-shən\ *n*

¹pec·to·ral \'pek-tə-rəl, -trəl\ *adj* **1** : of, relating to, or situated in, near, or on the chest **2** : coming from the breast or heart as the seat of emotion : SUBJECTIVE [Latin *pectoralis*, from *pector-*, *pectus* "breast"]

²pectoral *n* **1** : PECTORAL FIN **2** : PECTORAL MUSCLE

pectoral cross *n* : a cross worn on the breast especially by a prelate

pectoral fin *n* : either of a pair of fins that correspond in a fish to the forelimbs of a four-footed animal — compare PELVIC FIN

pectoral girdle *n* : an arch of bone or cartilage supporting the forelimbs of a vertebrate

pectoral muscle *n* : one of the muscles which connect the ventral walls of the chest with the bones of the upper arm and shoulder and of which there are two on each side in humans

pec·u·late \'pek-yə-ˌlāt\ *vt* : EMBEZZLE [Latin *peculari*, from *peculium* "private property"] — **pec·u·la·tion** \ˌpek-yə-ˈlā-shən\ *n* — **pec·u·la·tor** \'pek-yə-ˌlāt-ər\ *n*

pe·cu·liar \pi-ˈkyül-yər\ *adj* **1** : characteristic of only one person, group, or thing : DISTINCTIVE **2** : different from the usual or normal : **a** : SPECIAL 1a, PARTICULAR **b** : distinctly odd or eccentric [Latin *peculiaris* "of private property, special", from *peculium* "private property", from *pecu* "cattle"] SYN see STRANGE, CHARACTERISTIC — **pe·cu·liar·ly** *adv*

pe·cu·liar·i·ty \pi-ˌkyül-ˈyar-ət-ē, -ˌkyü-lē-ˈar-\ *n, pl* **-ties** **1** : the quality or state of being peculiar **2** : a distinguishing characteristic **3** : an odd trait or habit : QUIRK

pe·cu·ni·ary \pi-ˈkyü-nē-ˌer-ē\ *adj* : of, relating to, or consisting of money ⟨*pecuniary* aid⟩ ⟨*pecuniary* policies⟩ [Latin *pecuniarius*, from *pecunia* "money"] SYN see FINANCIAL

ped- — see PAED-

-ped \ˌped *also* pəd\ *or* **-pede** \ˌpēd\ *n combining form* : foot ⟨maxilli*ped*⟩ [Latin *ped-*, *pes*]

ped·a·gog·ics \ˌped-ə-ˈgäj-iks, -ˈgōj-\ *n* : PEDAGOGY

ped·a·gogue *also* **ped·a·gog** \'ped-ə-ˌgäg\ *n* **1** : TEACHER, SCHOOLMASTER; *esp* : a dull, formal, and pedantic teacher [Middle French *pedagoge*, from Latin *paedagogus*, from Greek *paidagōgos*, slave who escorted

peanut 1

\ə\ abut	\ng\ sing
\ər\ further	\ō\ bone
\a\ mat	\ó\ saw
\ā\ take	\ói\ coin
\ä\ cot, cart	\th\ thin
\aú\ out	\th\ this
\ch\ chin	\ü\ food
\e\ pet	\ú\ foot
\ē\ easy	\y\ yet
\g\ go	\yü\ few
\i\ tip	\yú\ cure
\ī\ life	\zh\ vision
\j\ job	

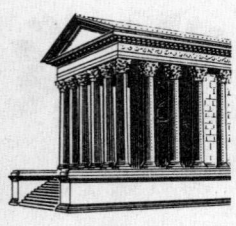

pediment

children to school, from *paid-* "paed-" + *agōgos* 'leader'', from *agein* "to lead"]

ped·a·go·gy \'ped-ə-₁gō-jē *also* -₁gäj-ē\ *n* : the art, science, or profession of teaching; *esp* : EDUCATION 2 — **ped·a·gog·ic** \₁ped-ə-'gäj-ik\ *or* **ped·a·gog·i·cal** \-'gäj-i-kəl\ *adj* — **ped·a·gog·i·cal·ly** \-i-kə-lē, -klē\ *adv*

¹ped·al \'ped-l\ *n* **1** : a lever acted on by the foot in the playing of musical instruments **2** : a foot lever or treadle by which a part is activated in a mechanism

²pedal *adj* : of or relating to the foot [Latin *pedalis*, from *ped-*, *pes* "foot"]

³pedal *vb* **ped·aled** *also* **ped·alled; ped·al·ing** *also* **ped·al·ling** \'ped-l-ing, 'ped-ling\ **1 a** : to use or work the pedals of something **b** : to work the pedals of ⟨*pedal* a bike⟩ **2** : to ride a bicycle ⟨*pedal* down the street⟩

pedal point *n* : a single tone that is normally sustained in the bass and sounds against changing harmonies in the other parts

pedal pushers *n pl* : women's and girls' calf-length pants

ped·ant \'ped-nt\ *n* **1** : a person who shows off his or her learning **2** : a dull formal teacher who emphasizes petty details [Middle French, from Italian *pedante*] — **pe·dan·tic** \pə-'dant-ik\ *adj* — **pe·dan·ti·cal·ly** \-'dant-i-kə-lē, -klē\ *adv*

ped·ant·ry \'ped-n-trē\ *n, pl* **-ries** **1** : pedantic presentation or application of knowledge or learning **2** : an instance of pedantry

ped·dle \'ped-l\ *vb* **ped·dled; ped·dling** \'ped-ling, -l-ing\ **1** : to travel about especially from house to house with wares for sale **2** : to sell or offer for sale from place to place usually in small quantities : HAWK [back-formation from *peddler*, from Middle English *pedlere*] — **ped·dler** *or* **ped·lar** \'ped-lər\ *n*

ped·es·tal \'ped-əst-l\ *n* **1** : the support or foot of a column; *also* : the base of any upright structure (as a vase, lamp, or statue) **2** : a position of high regard or esteem ⟨placed on a *pedestal* by one's children⟩ [Middle French *piedestal*, from Italian *piedestallo*, from *pie di stallo* "foot of a stall"]

¹pe·des·tri·an \pə-'des-trē-ən\ *adj* **1** : lacking imagination or originality : COMMONPLACE ⟨*pedestrian* writing⟩ **2 a** : going or performed on foot **b** : of or relating to walking **3** : of or designed for pedestrians [Latin *pedester*, literally, "going on foot", derived from *ped-*, *pes* "foot"]

²pedestrian *n* : a person going on foot

pe·des·tri·an·ism \-₁iz-əm\ *n* **1 a** : the practice of walking **b** : fondness for walking **2** : the quality or state of being unimaginative or commonplace

pe·di·a·tri·cian \₁pēd-ē-ə-'trish-ən\ *n* : a specialist in pediatrics

pe·di·at·rics \₁pēd-ē-'a-triks\ *n* : a branch of medicine dealing with the development, care, and diseases of children [*paed-* + Greek *iatros* "physician"] — **pe·di·at·ric** \-trik\ *adj*

pedi·cab \'ped-i-₁kab\ *n* : a small 3-wheeled hooded passenger vehicle that is pedaled [Latin *ped-*, *pes* "foot" + English *cab*]

ped·i·cel \'ped-ə-₁sel\ *n* : a slender basal part of an organism; *esp* : a stalk that supports a single flower — compare PEDUNCLE [New Latin *pedicellus*, from Latin *pediculus* "little foot, pedicel", from *ped-*, *pes* "foot"]

pe·dic·u·lo·sis \pi-₁dik-yə-'lō-səs\ *n* : infestation with lice [Latin *pediculus* "louse", from *pedis* "louse"] — **pe·dic·u·lous** \-'dik-yə-ləs\ *adj*

ped·i·cure \'ped-i-₁kyùr\ *n* **1** : a specialist in chiropody **2 a** : care of the feet, toes, and toenails **b** : a single treatment of these parts [French *pédicure*, from Latin *ped-*, *pes* "foot" + *curare* "to take care", from *cura* "care"] — **ped·i·cur·ist** \-₁kyùr-əst\ *n*

ped·i·gree \'ped-ə-₁grē\ *n* **1** : a table or list showing the line of ancestors of an animal or person **2 a** : an ancestral line : LINEAGE **b** : the origin and history of

something (as a document or a collector's coin or stamp) **3 a** : distinguished ancestry **b** : purity of a breed of an individual or strain recorded by a pedigree [Middle English *pedegru*, from Middle French *pie de grue* "crane's foot"; from the shape made by the lines of a genealogical chart] — **ped·i·greed** \-₁grēd\ *adj*

ped·i·ment \'ped-ə-mənt\ *n* : a triangular space forming the gable of a 2-pitched roof in classic architecture; *also* : a similar form used as a decoration (as over a door or a window) [obsolete *periment*, probably alteration of *pyramid*] — **ped·i·men·tal** \₁ped-ə-'ment-l\ *adj*

pedi·palp \'ped-ə-₁palp\ *n* : either of the second pair of head appendages of an arachnid (as a spider) borne near the mouth and often modified for a special (as sensory) function [New Latin *pedipalpus*, from *ped-*, *pes* "foot" + *palpus* "palpus"]

pedo- — SEE PAED-

pe·dom·e·ter \pi-'däm-ət-ər\ *n* : an instrument that measures the distance a walker covers by responding to body motion at each step [French *pédomètre*, from Latin *ped-*, *pes* "foot" + French *-mètre* "-meter"]

pe·dun·cle \'pē-₁dəng-kəl, pi-'\ *n* : a narrow part by which some larger part or the body of an organism is attached; *esp* : a stalk that supports a flower cluster — compare PEDICEL [New Latin *pedunculus*, from Latin *ped-*, *pes* "foot"] — **pe·dun·cu·late** \pi-'dəng-kyə-lət\ *or* **pe·dun·cu·lat·ed** \-₁lāt-əd\ *adj*

¹peek \'pēk\ *vi* **1 a** : to look slyly or stealthily **b** : to peer through a crack or hole or from a place of concealment **2** : to take a brief look : GLANCE [Middle English *piken*]

²peek *n* : a brief or stealthy look

¹peel \'pēl\ *vb* **1** : to strip off the skin, bark, or rind of ⟨*peel* an apple⟩ **2** : to remove as if by stripping or tearing ⟨*peeled* off my coat⟩ **3 a** : to come off in strips or patches ⟨the paint is *peeling*⟩ **b** : to lose the skin, bark, or rind ⟨your face is *peeling*⟩ [Middle French *peler*, from Latin *pilare* "to remove the hair from", from *pilus* "hair"] — **peel·er** *n*

²peel *n* : a skin or rind especially of a fruit

³peel *n* : a usually long-handled spade-shaped utensil used chiefly by bakers for getting something into or out of an oven [Middle French *pele*, from Latin *pala*]

peel·ing \'pē-ling\ *n* : a peeled-off piece or strip (as of skin)

peel off *vi* : to veer away from an airplane formation especially for diving or landing

peen \'pēn\ *n* : the usually hemispherical or wedge-shaped end of the head of some hammers opposite the face that is used for cutting and shaping [probably of Scandinavian origin]

¹peep \'pēp\ *vi* **1** : to utter the characteristic feeble shrill cry of a newly hatched bird or a similar sound **2** : to utter the slightest sound [Middle English *pepen*, of imitative origin]

²peep *n* **1** : a feeble shrill sound **2** : a slight utterance especially of complaint or protest ⟨not another *peep* out of you⟩

³peep *vb* **1 a** : to peer through a crevice **b** : to look cautiously or slyly **2** : to begin to emerge from concealment : show slightly **3** : to cause (as the head of one peeping) to protrude slightly [Middle English *pepen*, perhaps alteration of *piken* "to peek"]

⁴peep *n* **1** : the first glimpse or faint appearance ⟨at the *peep* of dawn⟩ **2** : a brief or furtive look

¹peep·er \'pē-pər\ *n* : any of various small tailless amphibians (as a spring peeper) that peep shrilly in spring

²peeper *n* **1** : one that peeps; *esp* : PEEPING TOM **2** : EYE 1a

peep·hole \'pēp-₁hōl\ *n* : a hole or crevice to peep through

peeping tom \-'täm\ *n, often cap* : a person who spies into the windows of private dwellings : one who furtively watches others [*Peeping Tom,* legendary 11th century tailor of Coventry supposed to have been struck blind for peeping at Lady Godiva]

peep show *n* : a display of objects or pictures viewed through a small hole usually fitted with a lens

peep sight *n* : a rear sight for a gun having an adjustable metal piece pierced with a small hole to look through in aiming

¹**peer** \'piər\ *n* **1** : one that is of equal standing with another : EQUAL **2** *archaic* : COMPANION, FELLOW **3 a** : a member (as a duke, marquess, earl, viscount, or baron) of one of the five ranks of the British peerage **b** : NOBLE [Old French *per,* from *per,* adj., "equal", from Latin *par*]

²**peer** *vi* **1** : to look narrowly or curiously; *esp* : to look searchingly at something difficult to discern **2** : to come slightly into view [perhaps from *appear*]

peer·age \'piər-ij\ *n* **1** : the body of peers **2** : the rank or dignity of a peer **3** : a book containing a list of peers

peer·ess \'pir-əs\ *n* **1** : the wife or widow of a peer **2** : a woman who holds the rank of a peer in her own right

peer·less \'piər-ləs\ *adj* : having no equal : MATCHLESS, INCOMPARABLE — **peer·less·ly** *adv* — **peer·less·ness** *n*

¹**peeve** \'pēv\ *vt* : to make peevish or resentful : ANNOY, IRRITATE [back-formation from *peevish*]

²**peeve** *n* **1** : a peevish mood : a feeling of resentment **2** : a particular grievance : GRUDGE

pee·vish \'pē-vish\ *adj* **1** : cross and complaining in temperament or mood **2** : unreasonably stubborn : OBSTINATE **3** : marked by ill temper [Middle English *pevish* "spiteful"] — **pee·vish·ly** *adv* — **pee·vish·ness** *n*

pee·wee \'pē-,wē\ *n* : something or someone diminutive or tiny [earlier *peewee* "pewee", of imitative origin] — **peewee** *adj*

pee·wit \'pē-,wit, 'pyü-ət\ *n* : any of several birds: as **a** : LAPWING **b** : a small black-headed European gull **c** : PEWEE [imitative]

¹**peg** \'peg\ *n* **1** : a small usually cylindrical pointed or tapered piece (as of wood) used especially to pin down or fasten things or to fit into or close holes ⟨a tent *peg*⟩ **2** : a projecting piece used as a support or boundary marker **3 a** : any of the pins of a stringed musical instrument that are turned to regulate the pitch of the strings **b** : a step or degree especially in estimation ⟨took you down a *peg*⟩ **4** : a pointed prong or claw for catching or tearing **5** *British* : a small drink (as of whiskey) **6** : a hard throw in baseball ⟨a quick *peg* to first base⟩ [Middle English *pegge*]

²**peg** *vb* **pegged; peg·ging** **1 a** : to fasten or mark with pegs **b** : to pin down : RESTRICT **c** : to fix or hold (as prices) at a planned level **d** : to place in a definite category **2** : THROW 2 **3** : to work steadily and diligently **4** : to move along vigorously or hastily : HUSTLE

Peg·a·sus \'peg-ə-səs\ *n* : a northern constellation near the vernal equinoctial point [*Pegasus,* winged horse in Greek mythology]

Peg-Board \'peg-,bōrd, -,bȯrd\ *trademark* — used for material (as fiberboard) with evenly spaced holes into which hooks may be inserted for the storage and display of articles

peg leg *n* : an artificial leg; *esp* : one fitted at the knee

peg·ma·tite \'peg-mə-,tīt\ *n* : a coarse variety of granite occurring in dikes or veins [French, from Greek *pēgma* "something fastened together", from *pēgnynai* "to fasten together"]

peg-top \'peg-,täp\ *or* **peg-topped** \-,täpt\ *adj* : wide at the top and narrow at the bottom ⟨*peg-top* trousers⟩

peg top *n* **1** : a pear-shaped top with a sharp metal peg spun by a string as it is thrown from the hand **2** *pl* : peg-top trousers

pei·gnoir \pān-'wär, pen-\ *n* : a woman's loose negligee or dressing gown [French, from *peigner* "to comb the hair", from Latin *pectinare,* from *pecten* "comb"]

pe·jor·a·tive \pi-'jȯr-ət-iv, -'jär-; 'pej-rət-, -ə-rət-\ *adj* : tending to disparage or belittle : DEPRECIATORY ⟨*pejorative* language⟩ [Late Latin *pejoratus,* past participle of *pejorare* "to make or become worse", from Latin *pejor* "worse"] — **pe·jor·a·tive·ly** *adv*

Pe·kin \pi-'kin, 'pē-,\ *n* : any of a breed of large white ducks of Chinese origin used for meat production [*Peking, Pekin,* China]

Pe·king·ese *or* **Pe·kin·ese** \,pē-kən-'ēz, -king-, -'ēs\ *n, pl* **Pekingese** *or* **Pekinese** **1 a** : a native or resident of Peking **b** : the Chinese dialect of Peking **2** : any of a Chinese breed of small short-legged dogs with a broad flat face and a profuse long soft coat

Pe·king man \,pē-king-\ *n* : an extinct Pleistocene human being known from skeletal and cultural remains found in cave deposits in northeastern China and now classified with the pithecanthropines

pel·age \'pel-ij\ *n* : the hairy covering of a mammal [French, from *poil* "hair", from Latin *pilus*]

pe·lag·ic \pə-'laj-ik\ *adj* : of, relating to, living, or occurring in the open sea : OCEANIC [Latin *pelagicus,* from Greek *pelagikos,* from *pelagos* "sea"]

pel·ar·go·ni·um \,pel-är-'gō-nē-əm, ,pel-ər-\ *n* : any of a genus of southern African herbs of the geranium family that includes the garden geraniums [derived from Greek *pelargos* "stork"]

Pe·las·gian \pə-'laz-jē-ən, -jən; -'laz-gē-ən\ *n* : any of an ancient people mentioned by classical writers as early inhabitants of Greece and the eastern islands of the Mediterranean [Greek *Pelasgoi* "Pelasgians"] — **Pelasgian** *adj*

pe·lecy·pod \pə-'les-ə-,päd\ *adj or n* : LAMELLIBRANCH [derived from Greek *pelekys* "ax" + *pod-, pous* "foot"]

pelf \'pelf\ *n* : MONEY 2, RICHES [Middle French *pelfre* "booty"]

pel·i·can \'pel-i-kən\ *n* : any of a genus of large webfooted birds with a very large pouched bill in which fish are caught [Old English *pellican,* from Late Latin *pelecanus,* from Greek *pelekan*]

pel·la·gra \pə-'lag-rə, -'läg-, -'läg-\ *n* : a disease associated with a diet deficient in niacin and protein and marked by skin rash, digestive disorders, and nervous and mental symptoms [Italian, derived from Latin *pellis* "skin" + *agra* "hunt, catch"] — **pel·la·grous** \-rəs\ *adj*

¹**pel·let** \'pel-ət\ *n* **1** : a little ball (as of food, medicine, or debris) **2 a** : a usually stone ball used as a missile in medieval times **b** : BULLET 1 **c** : a piece of small shot [Middle French *pelote,* derived from Latin *pila* "ball"]

²**pellet** *vt* **1** : to form into pellets **2** : to strike with pellets

pel·let·ize \'pel-ət-,īz\ *vt* **-ized; -iz·ing** : to make or compact into pellets ⟨*pelletize* ore⟩ — **pel·let·iza·tion** \,pel-ət-ə-'zā-shən\ *n* — **pel·let·iz·er** \'pel-ət-,ī-zər\ *n*

pel·li·cle \'pel-i-kəl\ *n* : a thin skin or film [Middle French *pellicule,* from Medieval Latin *pellicula,* from Latin *pellis* "skin"] — **pel·lic·u·lar** \pə-'lik-yə-lər\ *adj*

pell-mell \'pel-'mel\ *adv* **1** : in confusion or disorder **2** : in confused or headlong haste [Middle French *pelemele*] — **pell-mell** *adj or n*

pel·lu·cid \pə-'lü-səd\ *adj* **1** : extremely clear or transparent **2** : reflecting light evenly from all surfaces **3** : very easy to understand [Latin *pellucidus,* from *per* "through" + *lucidus* "lucid"] SYN see LIMPID — **pel·lu·cid·i·ty** \,pel-yü-'sid-ət-ē\ *n* — **pel·lu·cid·ly** \pə-'lü-səd-lē\ *adv* — **pel·lu·cid·ness** *n*

pe·lo·rus \pə-'lōr-əs, -'lȯr-\ *n* : a navigational instrument having a disk marked in degrees and two sights by which bearings are taken [origin unknown]

¹**pelt** \'pelt\ *n* : a usually undressed skin with its hair, wool, or fur [Middle English]

pelican

\ə\ abut	\ng\ sing
\ər\ further	\ō\ bone
\a\ mat	\ȯ\ saw
\ā\ take	\ȯi\ coin
\ä\ cot, cart	\th\ thin
\aů\ out	\th\ this
\ch\ chin	\ü\ food
\e\ pet	\ů\ foot
\ē\ easy	\y\ yet
\g\ go	\yü\ few
\i\ tip	\yů\ cure
\ī\ life	\zh\ vision
\j\ job	

²**pelt** *vb* **1 a :** to strike with or deliver a succession of blows or missiles ⟨*pelted* them with snowballs⟩ **b :** BOMBARD **2** ⟨was *pelted* with questions by the reporters⟩ **2 :** HURL, THROW **3 :** to beat or dash repeatedly ⟨hail *pelting* the roof⟩ **4 :** to move rapidly and vigorously or with pounding blows or thuds ⟨turned and *pelted* for home⟩ [Middle English *pelten*] — **pelt·er** *n*

³**pelt** *n* : BLOW, WHACK

pelt·ry \'pel-trē\ *n, pl* **peltries :** animal pelts; *esp* : raw undressed skins

pel·vic \'pel-vik\ *adj* : of, relating to, or located in or near the pelvis — **pelvic** *n*

pelvic fin *n* : either of a pair of fins that correspond in a fish to the hind limbs of a four-footed animal — compare PECTORAL FIN

pelvic girdle *n* : an arch of bone or cartilage that supports the hind limbs of a vertebrate

pel·vis \'pel-vəs\ *n, pl* **pel·vis·es** *or* **pel·ves** \'pel-ˌvēz\ **1 :** a basin-shaped structure in the skeleton of many vertebrates formed by the pelvic girdle and adjoining bones of the spine; *also* : its cavity **2 :** the funnel-shaped cavity of the kidney into which urine is discharged [Latin, "basin"]

pel·y·co·saur \'pel-i-kə-ˌsȯər\ *n* : any of an order (Pelycosauria) of primitive Permian reptiles that resemble mammals and often have the back processes on the vertebrae greatly developed [derived from Greek *pelyx* "wooden bowl" + *sauros* "lizard"]

Pem·broke Welsh corgi \'pem-ˌbrōk-, -ˌbrùk-\ *n* : a Welsh corgi of a variety characterized by pointed ears, straight legs, and short tail [*Pembroke*, Wales] — called also *Pembroke*

pem·mi·can \'pem-i-kən\ *n* : dried lean meat pounded fine and mixed with melted fat and used for food especially by North American Indians [Cree *pimikân*]

¹**pen** \'pen\ *n* **1 :** a small enclosure for animals; *also* : a small group of animals handled as a unit **2 :** a small place of confinement or storage [Old English *penn*]

²**pen** *vt* **penned; pen·ning :** to shut in a pen

³**pen** *n* **1 :** an implement for writing or drawing with ink or a similar fluid: as **a :** QUILL **b :** a small thin convex metal device tapering to a split point and fitting into a holder **c :** a penholder containing a pen **d :** FOUNTAIN PEN **e :** BALLPOINT **2 a :** a writing instrument regarded as a means of expression **b :** WRITER **3 :** the internal horny feather-shaped shell of a squid [Middle French *penne* "feather, pen", from Latin *penna, pinna* "feather"]

⁴**pen** *vt* **penned; pen·ning :** to write especially with a pen

⁵**pen** *n* : a female swan [origin unknown]

⁶**pen** *n, slang* : PENITENTIARY

pe·nal \'pēn-l\ *adj* : of, relating to, or involving punishment, penalties, or punitive institutions ⟨*penal* laws⟩ ⟨a *penal* colony⟩ [Middle French, from Latin *poenalis,* from *poena* "punishment", from Greek *poinē* "payment, penalty"] — **pe·nal·ly** \-l-ē\ *adv*

penal code *n* : a code of laws concerning crimes and offenses and their punishment

pe·nal·ize \'pēn-l-ˌīz, 'pen-\ *vt* **1 :** to subject to a penalty ⟨*penalize* an athlete for a foul⟩ **2 :** to place at a disadvantage : HANDICAP ⟨the system *penalized* slow learners⟩ — **pe·nal·iza·tion** \ˌpēn-l-ə-'zā-shən, ˌpen-\ *n*

pen·al·ty \'pen-l-tē\ *n, pl* **-ties 1 :** punishment for a crime or offense **2 :** something forfeited when a person fails to do what he agreed to do **3 :** disadvantage, loss, or hardship due to some action or condition **4 :** a punishment or handicap imposed for breaking a rule in a sport or game

pen·ance \'pen-əns\ *n* **1 :** an act of self-abasement, mortification, or devotion performed to show sorrow or repentance for sin **2 :** a sacrament in the Roman Catholic and Eastern churches consisting in sorrow for sin, confession to a priest, a penance imposed by the

confessor, and absolution [Old French, from Medieval Latin *poenitentia* "penitence"]

pence \'pens\ *pl of* PENNY

pen·chant \'pen-chənt\ *n* : a strong leaning : LIKING [French, from *pencher* "to lean, incline", derived from Latin *pendere* "to weigh"] □ SYN FLAIR: PENCHANT may imply a decided taste and strong inclination for ⟨a *penchant* for gardening⟩ FLAIR implies instinctive ability or perception and acumen ⟨a real *flair* for cooking⟩

¹**pen·cil** \'pen-səl\ *n* **1 a :** an implement for writing, drawing, or marking consisting of or containing a slender cylinder or strip of a solid marking substance **b :** a small medicated or cosmetic roll or stick **2 :** an aggregate of rays of light especially when diverging from or converging to a point **3 :** something long and thin like a pencil [Middle French *pincel* "artist's brush", from Latin *penicillus,* literally, "little tail", from *penis* "tail, penis"]

²**pencil** *vt* **-ciled** *or* **-cilled; -cil·ing** *or* **-cil·ling** \-sə-ling, -sling\ : to mark, draw, or write with or as if with a pencil — **pen·cil·er** \-sə-lər, -slər\ *n*

pen·dant *also* **pen·dent** \'pen-dənt\ *n* : something that hangs down especially as an ornament [Middle French *pendant,* from *pendre* "to hang", from Latin *pendēre*]

pen·den·cy \'pen-dən-sē\ *n* : the state of being pending

pen·dent *or* **pen·dant** \'pen-dənt\ *adj* **1 :** supported from above : SUSPENDED **2 :** jutting or leaning over : OVERHANGING **3 :** remaining undetermined : PENDING — **pen·dent·ly** *adv*

¹**pend·ing** \'pen-ding\ *prep* **1 :** DURING **2 :** while awaiting ⟨*pending* a reply⟩ [French *pendant,* from *pendre* "to hang"]

²**pending** *adj* : not yet decided ⟨court cases *pending*⟩

pen·du·lar \'pen-jə-lər, -dyə-lər, -dl-ər\ *adj* : being or resembling the movement of a pendulum

pen·du·lous \'pen-jə-ləs\ *adj* **1 :** suspended so as to swing freely ⟨*pendulous* vines⟩ **2 :** inclined or hanging downward ⟨flabby *pendulous* jowls⟩ [Latin *pendulus,* from *pendēre* "to hang"] — **pen·du·lous·ly** *adv*

pen·du·lum \'pen-jə-ləm, -dyə-ləm, -dl-əm\ *n* : a body suspended from a fixed point so as to swing freely to and fro under the action of gravity ⟨the *pendulum* of a clock⟩ [Latin, neuter of *pendulus* "pendulous"]

pe·ne·plain *also* **pe·ne·plane** \'pēn-i-ˌplān, 'pen-\ *n* : a land surface of considerable area and slight relief shaped by erosion [Latin *paene, pene* "almost" + English *plain* or *plane*]

pen·e·tra·ble \'pen-ə-trə-bəl\ *adj* : capable of being penetrated — **pen·e·tra·bil·i·ty** \ˌpen-ə-trə-'bil-ət-ē\ *n* — **pen·e·tra·ble·ness** \'pen-ə-trə-bəl-nəs\ *n* — **pen·e·tra·bly** \-blē\ *adv*

pen·e·trate \'pen-ə-ˌtrāt\ *vb* **1 a :** to pass into or through **b :** to enter by overcoming resistance : PIERCE **2 :** to come to understand **3 :** to move deeply **4 :** to seep through : PERMEATE [Latin *penetrare*] SYN see ENTER

pen·e·trat·ing *adj* **1 :** SHARP, BITING ⟨*penetrating* cold⟩ **2 :** ACUTE, DISCERNING ⟨a *penetrating* mind⟩ — **pen·e·trat·ing·ly** \-ˌtrāt-ing-lē\ *adv*

pen·e·tra·tion \ˌpen-ə-'trā-shən\ *n* **1 :** the act or process of penetrating **2 a :** the depth to which something penetrates **b :** the power to penetrate; *esp* : the ability to discern deeply and acutely

pen·e·tra·tive \'pen-ə-ˌtrāt-iv\ *adj* : tending or able to penetrate — **pen·e·tra·tive·ly** *adv* — **pen·e·tra·tive·ness** *n*

pen·guin \'pen-gwən, 'peng-\ *n* : any of various erect short-legged flightless aquatic birds of the southern hemisphere with the wings reduced to flippers and used in swimming [origin unknown]

pen·hold·er \'pen-ˌhōl-dər\ *n* : a holder or handle for a pen

pen·i·cil·lin \ˌpen-ə-'sil-ən\ *n* : any of several antibiotics or a mixture of these produced by penicillia or synthetically and used especially against cocci

penguin

pen·i·cil·lin·ase \-'sil-ə-,nās, -,nāz\ *n* : an enzyme that inactivates the penicillins by hydrolyzing them and that is found especially in bacteria

pen·i·cil·li·um \-'sil-ē-əm\ *n, pl* -**lia** \-ē-ə\ : any of a genus of fungi comprising mostly blue molds found chiefly on moist nonliving organic matter — compare PENICILLIN [New Latin, from Latin *penicillus* "brush, little tail"]

pen·in·su·la \pə-'nin-sə-lə, -'nin-slə, -'nin-chə-lə\ *n* : a portion of land nearly surrounded by water; *also* : a piece of land jutting out into the water [Latin *paeninsula,* from *paene* "almost" + *insula* "island"] — **pen·in·su·lar** \-lər\ *adj*

pe·nis \'pē-nəs\ *n, pl* **pe·nes** \'pē-,nēz\ *or* **pe·nis·es** : a male organ of copulation [Latin, "penis, tail"] — **pe·nile** \-,nīl\ *adj*

pen·i·tence \'pen-ə-təns\ *n* : sorrow for one's sins or faults : REPENTANCE □ SYN PENITENCE, REPENTANCE, CONTRITION mean regret for sin or wrongdoing. PENITENCE implies humble realization of and regret for one's faults; REPENTANCE emphasizes the change of mind of one who not only regrets errors but abandons them for a new standard; CONTRITION suggests penitence shown by signs of grief or pain.

¹**pen·i·tent** \-tənt\ *adj* : feeling or expressing pain or sorrow for sins or offenses : REPENTANT [Middle French, from Latin *paenitens,* from *paenitēre* "to be sorry"] — **pen·i·tent·ly** *adv*

²**penitent** *n* **1** : a person who repents of sin **2** : a person under church censure but admitted to penance especially under the direction of a confessor

pen·i·ten·tial \,pen-ə-'ten-chəl\ *adj* : of or relating to penitence or penance — **pen·i·ten·tial·ly** \-'tench-lē, -ə-lē\ *adv*

¹**pen·i·ten·tia·ry** \,pen-ə-'tench-rē, -ə-rē\ *n, pl* -**ries** : a public institution in which criminals are confined; *esp* : a state or federal prison in the United States

²**penitentiary** *adj* : of, relating to, or incurring confinement in a penitentiary

pen·knife \'pen-,nīf\ *n* : a small pocketknife [from its original use for mending quill pens]

pen·man \'pen-mən\ *n* **1 a** : COPYIST 1, SCRIBE **b** : one who is expert in penmanship **2** : AUTHOR 1

pen·man·ship \'pen-mən-,ship\ *n* **1** : the art or practice of writing with the pen **2** : quality or style of handwriting

pen name *n* : an author's pseudonym

pen·nant \'pen-ənt\ *n* **1 a** : a nautical flag tapering to a point or swallowtail and used for identification or signaling **b** : a long narrow flag or banner that tapers to a point **2** : a flag emblematic of championship [alteration of *pendant*]

pen·ni·less \'pen-i-ləs, 'pen-l-əs\ *adj* : having no money at all : very poor

pen·non \'pen-ən\ *n* **1** : a long usually triangular or swallow-tailed streamer typically attached to the head of a lance as an ensign **2** : PENNANT 1a [Middle French *penon,* from *penne* "feather, pen"]

Penn·syl·va·nia Dutch \,pen-səl-,vā-nyə-\ *n* **1** : a people living mostly in eastern Pennsylvania whose characteristic cultural traditions go back to the German migrations of the 18th century **2** : a German dialect spoken by the Pennsylvania Dutch — **Pennsylvania Dutchman** *n*

Penn·syl·va·nian \-'vā-nyən\ *adj* **1** : of or relating to Pennsylvania or its people **2** : of, relating to, or being the period of the Paleozoic era between the Mississippian and Permian or the corresponding system of rocks — see GEOLOGIC TIME table — **Pennsylvanian** *n*

pen·ny \'pen-ē\ *n, pl* **pen·nies** \-ēz\ *or* **pence** \'pens\ **1 a** : a former British monetary unit equal to ¹/₂₄₀ pound or ¹/₁₂ shilling **b** : a similar monetary unit of any of various other countries in or formerly in the British Commonwealth **c** : a coin representing this unit **d** : NEW PENNY **2** : DENARIUS **3** *pl* pennies : a cent of the United States or Canada **4** : a piece or sum of money ⟨earn an honest *penny*⟩ [Old English *penning*]

penny ante *n* : poker played for very low stakes

penny arcade *n* : an amusement center where each device for entertainment may be operated for a small sum and originally for a penny

penny dreadful *n* : a novel of violent adventure or crime originally costing one penny

pen·ny pinch·er \'pen-ē-,pin-chər\ *n* : a stingy person — **pen·ny–pinch·ing** \-ching\ *adj or n*

pen·ny·roy·al \,pen-ē-'rói-əl, -'róil; 'pen-i-,rīl\ *n* : a European perennial mint with small aromatic leaves; *also* : a similar American mint that yields an oil used in folk medicine and as a mosquito repellent [probably by folk etymology from Middle French *poullieul,* from Latin *pulegium*]

pen·ny·weight \'pen-ē-,wāt\ *n* — see MEASURE table

pen·ny–wise \-,wīz\ *adj* : wise or prudent only in small matters

pen·ny·worth \'pen-ē-,wərth\ *n, pl* -**worth** *or* -**worths** : a penny's worth : as much as a penny will buy

Pe·nob·scot \pə-'näb-skət, -,skät\ *n, pl* **Penobscot** *or* **Penobscots** : a member of an Algonquian people of the Penobscot river valley and the Penobscot Bay region

pe·nol·o·gy \pi-'näl-ə-jē\ *n* : a branch of criminology dealing with prison management and the treatment of offenders [Greek *poinē* "penalty"] — **pe·no·log·i·cal** \,pēn-l-'äj-i-kəl\ *adj* — **pe·nol·o·gist** \pi-'näl-ə-jəst\ *n*

pen pal *n* : a friend made and kept through correspondence often without any face-to-face acquaintance

pen·sile \'pen-,sīl\ *adj* : suspended from above [Latin *pensilis,* from *pensus,* past participle of *pendēre* "to hang"]

¹**pen·sion** *n* **1** \'pen-chən\ : a fixed sum paid regularly to a person; *esp* : one paid to a person following retirement or to surviving dependents **2** \päⁿs-yōⁿ\ : a boardinghouse especially in continental Europe [Middle French, from Latin *pensio,* from *pensus,* past participle of *pendere* "to weigh, pay"] — **pen·sion·less** \'pen-chən-ləs\ *adj*

²**pen·sion** \'pen-chən\ *vt* **pen·sioned; pen·sion·ing** \'pench-ning, -ə-ning\ : to grant or pay a pension to

pen·sion·er \'pench-nər, -ə-nər\ *n* **1** : a person who receives or lives on a pension **2** : a mercenary dependent : HIRELING

pen·sive \'pen-siv\ *adj* **1** : musingly or dreamily thoughtful **2** : suggestive of sad thoughtfulness : MELANCHOLY [Middle French *pensif,* from *penser* "to think", from Latin *pensare* "to ponder", from *pendere* "to weigh"] — **pen·sive·ly** *adv* — **pen·sive·ness** *n*

pen·stock \'pen-,stäk\ *n* **1** : a sluice or gate for regulating a flow (as of water) **2** : a conduit or pipe for conducting water

pent \'pent\ *adj* : shut up : held back ⟨*pent*-up feelings⟩ [probably from past participle of obsolete *pend* "to confine"]

penta- *or* **pent-** *combining form* : five ⟨*pent*ode⟩ [Greek, from *pente*]

pen·ta·gon \'pent-i-,gän\ *n* : a polygon of five angles and five sides

Pentagon *n* : the American military establishment [the *Pentagon* building, headquarters of the United States Department of Defense]

pen·tag·o·nal \pen-'tag-ən-l\ *adj* **1** : having five sides and five angles **2** : having a pentagon as a cross section or as a base ⟨a *pentagonal* pyramid⟩

pen·tam·e·ter \pen-'tam-ət-ər\ *n* : a line consisting of five metrical feet [Latin, derived from Greek *penta-* + *metron* "measure"]

pen·tane \'pen-,tān\ *n* : any of three isomeric hydrocarbons C_5H_{12} occurring in petroleum and natural gas

Pen·ta·teuch \'pent-ə-,tük, -,tyük\ *n* : the first five books of the Old Testament [Late Latin *Pentateuchus,*

pentagon

\ə\ abut		\ng\ sing
\ər\ further		\ō\ bone
\a\ mat		\ȯ\ saw
\ā\ take		\ȯi\ coin
\ä\ cot, cart		\th\ thin
\aȯ\ out		\th\ this
\ch\ chin		\ü\ food
\e\ pet		\u̇\ foot
\ē\ easy		\y\ yet
\g\ go		\yü\ few
\i\ tip		\yu̇\ cure
\ī\ life		\zh\ vision
\j\ job		

from Greek *Pentateuchos,* from *penta-* + *teuchos* "tool, vessel, book"]

pen·tath·lon \pen-'tath-lən, -,län\ *n* : an athletic contest in which each contestant participates in five different events [Greek, from *penta-* + *athlon* "contest"]

Pen·te·cost \'pent-i-,kòst, -,käst\ *n* **1** : SHABUOTH **2** : the 7th Sunday after Easter observed as a church festival in commemoration of the descent of the Holy Spirit on the apostles [Old English *pentecosten,* from Late Latin *pentecoste,* from Greek *pentēkostē,* literally, "50th (day)", from *pentēkonta* "fifty"]

Pen·te·cos·tal \,pent-i-'käs-tl, -'kòs-\ *adj* **1** : of, relating to, or suggesting Pentecost **2** : of, relating to, or constituting any of various usually fundamentalist sects that stress religious revivals — **Pentecostal** *n* — **Pen·te·cos·tal·ism** \-tə-,liz-əm\ *n*

pent·house \'pent-,haùs\ *n* **1** : a roof or a shed attached to and sloping from a wall or building **2** : a structure (as an apartment) built on the roof of a building [Middle English *pentis,* from Middle French *appentis,* probably from Medieval Latin *appenticium* "appendage", from Latin *appendix*] □ ORIGIN In Middle English *pentis* meant primarily "a shed or roof attached to a wall or building". *Pentis,* borrowed from Middle French *appentis,* is probably derived from Latin *appendix,* which means "appendage" or "supplement" (A direct borrowing from Latin gives English *appendix* in its various senses.) A *pentis,* then, was a smaller building or structure attached to a larger one. It was widely though mistakenly believed that *pentis* was related to Middle French *pente* "slope", and this belief was likely encouraged by the fact that many such structures did have sloping roofs. The second syllable of the word was altered by folk etymology to *-house.*

pent·land·ite \'pent-lən-,dīt\ *n* : a bronzy yellow mineral (Fe,Ni)₉S₈ that is a nickel iron sulfide and the principal ore of nickel [Joseph *Pentland,* died 1873, Irish scientist]

pen·to·bar·bi·tal \,pent-ə-'bär-bə-,tòl\ *n* : a barbiturate used especially in the form of its sodium or calcium salt chiefly as a sedative and hypnotic [*penta-* + *-o-* + *barbital*]

pen·tode \'pen-,tōd\ *n* : a vacuum tube with five electrodes

pen·tom·ic \pen-'täm-ik\ *adj* **1** : made up of five battle groups ⟨a *pentomic* division⟩ **2** : organized into pentomic divisions ⟨*pentomic* armies⟩ [blend of *penta-* and *atomic*]

pen·tose \'pen-,tōs\ *n* : any of various sugars C₅H₁₀O₅ containing five carbon atoms in the molecule

Pen·to·thal \'pent-ə-,thòl\ *trademark* — used for a substance that is used as an intravenous anesthetic of short duration and as a hypnotic

pent·ox·ide \pent-'äk-,sīd\ *n* : an oxide containing five atoms of oxygen in the molecule

¹pepper 1b

pent·ste·mon *or* **pen·ste·mon** \pen-'stē-mən, 'pen-stə-\ *n* : any of a genus of chiefly American herbs of the snapdragon family with showy blue, purple, red, yellow, or white flowers [derived from Greek *penta-* + *stēmōn* "thread"]

pe·nu·che \pə-'nü-chē\ *n* : fudge made usually of brown sugar, butter, cream or milk, and nuts [Mexican Spanish *panocha* "raw sugar", from Spanish *pan* "bread", from Latin *panis*]

pe·nult \'pē-,nəlt, pi-'\ *n* : the next to the last syllable of a word [Latin *paenultima,* from *paenultimus* "almost last", from *paene* "almost" + *ultimus* "last"]

pen·ul·ti·mate \pi-'nəl-tə-mət\ *adj* **1** : next to the last **2** : of or relating to a penult — **penultimate** *n* — **pen·ul·ti·mate·ly** *adv*

pen·um·bra \pə-'nəm-brə\ *n, pl* **-brae** \-,brē, -,brī\ *or* **-bras** **1** : the partial shadow surrounding a perfect shadow (as in an eclipse) **2** : the shaded region around the dark central portion of a sunspot [Latin

paene "almost" + *umbra* "shadow"] — **pen·um·bral** \-'brəl\ *adj*

pe·nu·ri·ous \pə-'nùr-ē-əs, -'nyùr-\ *adj* **1** : marked by or suffering from penury **2** : given to or marked by extreme frugality SYN see STINGY — **pe·nu·ri·ous·ly** *adv* — **pe·nu·ri·ous·ness** *n*

pen·u·ry \'pen-yə-rē\ *n* **1** : extreme poverty : PRIVATION **2** : absence of resources : SCANTINESS [Latin *penuria* "want"]

pe·on \'pē-,än, -ən\ *n* **1** : a member of the landless laboring class in Spanish America **2** : a person held in compulsory servitude to work out an indebtedness **3** : DRUDGE, MENIAL [Portuguese *peão* and French *pion,* both from Medieval Latin *pedo* "foot soldier", from Latin *ped-, pes* "foot"]

pe·on·age \'pē-ə-nij\ *n* **1** : the condition of a peon **2** : the use of laborers bound in servitude because of debt

pe·o·ny \'pē-ə-nē\ *n, pl* **-nies** : any of a genus of perennial plants of the buttercup family widely grown for their large usually double flowers of red, pink, or white [Middle French *pioine,* from Latin *paeonia,* from Greek *paiōnia,* from *Paiōn* "Paeon (physician of the gods)"]

¹peo·ple \'pē-pəl\ *n, pl* **people** **1** *pl* : HUMAN BEINGS, PERSONS — often used in compounds instead of persons ⟨sales*people*⟩ **2** *pl* : the members of a family : KINDRED; *also* : ANCESTORS **3** *pl* : the mass of a community as distinguished from a special class **4** *pl* **peoples** : a body of persons united by a common culture, tradition, or sense of kinship, typically having common language, institutions, and beliefs, and often politically organized ⟨English-speaking *peoples*⟩ **5** : a body of enfranchised citizens : ELECTORATE [Old French *peuple* "body of citizens, populace", from Latin *populus*]

²people *vt* **peo·pled; peo·pling** \'pē-pə-ling, -pling\ **1** : to supply or fill with people **2** : to dwell in : INHABIT

¹pep \'pep\ *n* : brisk energy or initiative and high spirits : LIVELINESS [short for *pepper*]

²pep *vt* **pepped; pep·ping** : to inject pep into : STIMULATE ⟨*pep* them up⟩

pep·lum \'pep-ləm\ *n* : a short section attached to the waistline of a blouse, jacket, or dress [Latin, a kind of upper garment for women, from Greek *peplos*]

pe·po \'pē-pō\ *n* : a fleshy many-seeded fruit (as a pumpkin, squash, melon, or cucumber) of the gourd family that has a hard rind and is technically classed as a berry [Latin, a kind of melon]

¹pep·per \'pep-ər\ *n* **1 a** : either of two pungent products from the fruit of an East Indian vine used as seasoning and in medicine : (1) : BLACK PEPPER (2) : WHITE PEPPER **b** : a woody vine with rounded leaves and flowers arranged in a spike that is widely cultivated in the tropics for its red berries from which pepper is prepared **c** : any of several somewhat similar products obtained from other plants **2** : CAPSICUM; *esp* : a New World capsicum whose fruits are hot peppers or sweet peppers [Old English *pipor,* from Latin *piper,* from Greek *peperi*] — **pepper** *adj*

²pepper *vt* **pep·pered; pep·per·ing** \'pep-ring, -ə-ring\ **1 a** : to sprinkle or season with or as if with pepper **b** : to shower with missiles (as shot) **2** : to hit with rapid repeated blows **3** : to sprinkle as pepper is sprinkled

pep·per-and-salt \,pep-ər-ən-'sòlt, ,pep-ərn-'sòlt\ *adj* : having black and white or dark and light color intermingled in small flecks ⟨a *pepper-and-salt* overcoat⟩

pep·per·corn \'pep-ər-,kòrn\ *n* : a dried berry of the East Indian pepper

peppered moth *n* : a European moth that typically has white wings with small black specks but often has black wings in areas with heavy air pollution

pep·per·grass \'pep-ər-,gras\ *n* : any of a genus of herbs of the mustard family having a rounded fruit with a notch or depression at the top

pepper mill *n* : a hand mill for grinding peppercorns

pep·per·mint \-,mint, -mənt\ *n* **1** : a pungent and aromatic mint with dark green leaves and whorls of small purple or white flowers in spikes **2** : candy flavored with peppermint

pep·per·o·ni \,pep-ə-'rō-nē\ *n* : a highly seasoned beef and pork sausage [Italian *peperoni* "chilies", pl. of *peperone* "chili", from *pepe* "pepper", from Latin *piper*]

pep·per·pot \'pep-ər-,pät\ *n* **1** : PEPPER SHAKER **2** : a thick highly seasoned soup of tripe, meat, dumplings, and vegetables

pepper shaker *n* : a container with a perforated top for sprinkling pepper on food

pep·pery \'pep-rē, -ə-rē\ *adj* **1** : of, relating to, or having the qualities of pepper : HOT, PUNGENT **2** : having a hot temper : TOUCHY **3** : FIERY, STINGING ⟨*peppery* words⟩

pep pill *n* : any of various stimulant drugs (as an amphetamine) in pill or tablet form

pep·py \'pep-ē\ *adj* **pep·pi·er; -est** : full of pep — **pep·pi·ness** *n*

pep·sin \'pep-sən\ *n* **1** : a proteinase of the stomach that begins the digestion of most proteins **2** : a preparation of pepsin obtained especially from the stomach of the hog and used medicinally [German, from Greek *pepsis* "digestion", from *pessein* "to cook, digest"]

pep·sin·o·gen \pep-'sin-ə-jən\ *n* : a product of the gastric glands that is converted into pepsin in the acid medium of the stomach

pep talk *n* : a usually brief, high-pressure, and emotional utterance designed to influence or encourage an audience

pep·tic \'pep-tik\ *adj* **1** : relating to or promoting digestion **2** : of, relating to, producing, or caused by pepsin ⟨*peptic* digestion⟩ **3** : resulting from the action of digestive juices ⟨a *peptic* ulcer⟩ [Latin *pepticus*, from Greek *peptikos*, from *peptos* "cooked", from *peptein, pessein* "to cook, digest"]

pep·ti·dase \'pep-tə-,dās, -,dāz\ *n* : an enzyme that hydrolyzes simple peptides or their derivatives

pep·tide \'pep-,tīd\ *n* : any of various amides derived from two or more amino acids by combination of the amino group of one acid with the carboxyl group of another and usually obtained by partial hydrolysis of proteins [*pept*one + *-ide*]

peptide bond *n* : the chemical bond between carbon and nitrogen in the CO-NH group that unites the amino acid residues in a peptide

pep·tone \'pep-,tōn\ *n* : any of various water-soluble products of partial hydrolysis of proteins [German *pepton*, from Greek *peptos* "cooked", from *pessein* "to cook, digest"]

Pe·quot \'pē-,kwät\ *n* : a member of an Algonquian people of what is now southeastern Connecticut

per \pər, 'pər\ *prep* **1** : by the means or agency of ⟨*per* bearer⟩ **2** : to or for each ⟨$10 *per* day⟩ **3** : as indicated by : according to ⟨*per* list price⟩ [Latin, "through, by"]

per- *prefix* **1** : throughout : thoroughly **2 a** : containing the largest possible or a relatively large proportion of a (specified) chemical element ⟨*per*oxide⟩ **b** : containing an element in its highest or a high oxidation state ⟨*per*chloric acid⟩ [Latin, "through, throughout, thoroughly, to destruction", from *per*]

¹per·ad·ven·ture \'pər-əd-,ven-chər, 'pər-; ,pər-əd-', ,per-\ *adv, archaic* : PERHAPS, POSSIBLY [Old French *per aventure* "by chance"]

²peradventure *n* : a possibility of error or uncertainty

per·am·bu·late \pə-'ram-byə-,lāt\ *vb* **1** : to travel over or through especially on foot : TRAVERSE **2** : STROLL, RAMBLE [Latin *perambulare*, from *per-* + *ambulare* "to walk"] — **per·am·bu·la·tion** \-,ram-byə-'lā-shən\ *n*

per·am·bu·la·tor \pə-'ram-byə-,lāt-ər\ *n* **1** : one that perambulates **2** *chiefly British* : a baby carriage — **per·am·bu·la·to·ry** \-lə-,tōr-ē, -,tòr-\ *adj*

per an·num \,pər-'an-əm\ *adv* : in or for each year : ANNUALLY [Medieval Latin]

per·cale \pər-'kāl, ,pər-, -'kal\ *n* : a fine closely woven cotton cloth [Persian *pargālah*]

per cap·i·ta \,pər-'kap-ət-ə\ *adv or adj* : per unit of population : by or for each person ⟨*per capita* income⟩ [Medieval Latin, "by heads"]

per·ceiv·able \pər-'sē-və-bəl\ *adj* : that can be perceived — **per·ceiv·ably** \-blē\ *adv*

per·ceive \pər-'sēv\ *vt* **1** : to attain awareness or understanding of **2** : to become aware of through the senses and especially through sight [Old French *perceivre*, from Latin *percipere*, from *per-* "thoroughly" + *capere* "to take"] — **per·ceiv·er** *n*

¹per·cent \pər-'sent\ *adv* : in the hundred : of each hundred [*per* + Latin *centum* "hundred"]

²percent *n, pl* **percent** **1** : one part in a hundred : HUNDREDTH **2** : PERCENTAGE

³percent *adj* **1** : reckoned on the basis of a whole divided into one hundred parts **2** : paying interest at a specified percent ⟨a 7 *percent* bond⟩

per·cent·age \pər-'sent-ij\ *n* **1 a** : a part of a whole expressed in hundredths **b** : the result obtained by multiplying a number by a percent **2 a** : a share of winnings or profits ⟨my agent collects a *percentage*⟩ **b** : ADVANTAGE, PROFIT ⟨no *percentage* in going it alone⟩ **3** : an indeterminate part : PROPORTION **4 a** : PROBABILITY **3** ⟨a gambler who plays the *percentages*⟩ **b** : favorable odds

per·cen·tile \pər-'sen-,tīl\ *n* : a measure widely used in educational testing that expresses the standing of a score or grade in terms of the percentage of scores or grades falling with or below it ⟨a person in the 75th *percentile* has done as well as or better than 75 percent of the people with whom he or she is being compared⟩

per cen·tum \pər-'sent-əm\ *n* : PERCENT

per·cep·ti·ble \pər-'sep-tə-bəl\ *adj* : capable of being perceived ⟨a *perceptible* change⟩ — **per·cep·ti·bil·i·ty** \-,sep-tə-'bil-ət-ē\ *n* — **per·cep·ti·bly** \-'sep-tə-blē\ *adv*

per·cep·tion \pər-'sep-shən\ *n* **1 a** : a result of perceiving : OBSERVATION, DISCERNMENT **b** : a mental image : CONCEPT **2** : awareness of the elements of environment through physical sensation ⟨color *perception*⟩ **3 a** : INSIGHT **2 b** : a capacity for comprehension [Latin *perceptio* "act of perceiving", from *percipere* "to perceive"] — **per·cep·tion·al** \-shnəl, -shən-l\ *adj*

per·cep·tive \pər-'sep-tiv\ *adj* **1** : responsive to sensory stimulus : DISCERNING **2 a** : capable of or exhibiting keen perception : OBSERVANT **b** : characterized by sympathetic understanding or insight — **per·cep·tive·ly** *adv* — **per·cep·tive·ness** *n* — **per·cep·tiv·i·ty** \,pər-,sep-'tiv-ət-ē\ *n*

per·cep·tu·al \pər-'sep-chə-wəl\ *adj* : of, relating to, or involving stimulation of the senses as opposed to abstract concept — **per·cep·tu·al·ly** \-wə-lē\ *adv*

¹perch \'pərch\ *n* **1** : a bar or peg on which something is hung **2 a** : a roost for a bird **b** : a resting place or vantage point : SEAT **c** : a prominent position **3** *chiefly British* : ROD **2** [Old French *perche*, from Latin *pertica* "pole"]

²perch *vb* **1** : to place on a perch, a height, or precarious spot ⟨*perched* itself on the table⟩ **2** : to alight, settle, or rest on or as if on a perch

³perch *n, pl* **perch** *or* **perch·es** **1** : a small largely olive-green and yellow European freshwater spiny-finned fish; *also* : YELLOW PERCH **2** : any of numerous fishes related to or resembling the true perches [Middle French *perche*, from Latin *perca*, from Greek *perkē*]

per·chance \pər-'chans\ *adv* : PERHAPS, POSSIBLY

Per·che·ron \'pər-chə-,rän, -shə-\ *n* : any of a breed of powerful rugged draft horses that originated in France [French, from *Perche*, region in northern France]

\ə\ abut	\ng\ sing	
\ər\ further	\ō\ bone	
\a\ mat	\ò\ saw	
\ā\ take	\òi\ coin	
\ä\ cot, cart	\th\ thin	
\aú\ out	\th\ this	
\ch\ chin	\ü\ food	
\e\ pet	\ú\ foot	
\ē\ easy	\y\ yet	
\g\ go	\yü\ few	
\i\ tip	\yú\ cure	
\ī\ life	\zh\ vision	
\j\ job		

per·chlo·rate \pər-'klōr-ˌāt, ˌpər-, -'klȯr-\ *n* : a salt or ester of perchloric acid

per·chlo·ric acid \pər-ˌklōr-ik-, ˌpər-, -ˌklȯr-\ *n* : a fuming corrosive strong acid $HClO_4$ that is a powerful oxidizing agent when heated

per·cip·i·ent \pər-'sip-ē-ənt\ *adj* : capable of or characterized by perception : DISCERNING [Latin *percipiens,* present participle of *percipiens* "to perceive"] — **per·cip·i·ence** \-ē-əns\ *n* — **percipient** *n*

per·coid \'pər-ˌkȯid\ *adj* : of or relating to a very large suborder (Percoidea) of spiny-finned fishes including the true perches, sunfishes, sea basses, and sea breams [derived from Latin *perca* "perch"] — **percoid** *n*

per·co·late \'pər-kə-ˌlāt\ *vb* **1 a** : to pass or cause to pass through a permeable substance (as a powdered drug) especially for extracting a soluble constituent : FILTER, SEEP **b** : to prepare (coffee) in a percolator **2** : to be or become diffused through : PENETRATE **3 a** : to become percolated **b** : to become lively or effervescent [Latin *percolare,* from *per-* "through" + *colare* "to sieve"] — **per·co·la·tion** \ˌpər-kə-'lā-shən\ *n*

per·co·la·tor \'pər-kə-ˌlāt-ər\ *n* : one that percolates; *esp* : a coffeepot in which boiling water rising through a tube is repeatedly deflected downward through a perforated basket containing the ground coffee beans

per·cuss \pər-'kəs\ *vt* : to tap sharply; *esp* : to practice percussion on

per·cus·sion \pər-'kəsh-ən\ *n* **1** : the act of tapping sharply: as **a** : the striking of a percussion cap so as to set off the charge in a firearm **b** : the beating or striking of a musical instrument **c** : the act or technique of tapping the surface of a body part to learn the condition of the parts beneath by the resultant sound **2** : the striking of sound sharply on the ear **3** : percussion instruments especially as forming a section of a band or orchestra [Latin *percussio,* from *percussus,* past participle of *percutere* "to beat", from *per-* "thoroughly" + *quatere* "to shake"] — **percussion** *adj*

percussion cap *n* : CAP 4

percussion instrument *n* : a musical instrument (as a drum) sounded by striking

per·cus·sion·ist \pər-'kəsh-nəst, -ə-nəst\ *n* : one skilled in the playing of percussion instruments

per·cus·sive \pər-'kəs-iv\ *adj* : of or relating to percussion; *esp* : operative or operated by striking — **per·cus·sive·ly** *adv* — **per·cus·sive·ness** *n*

per·cu·ta·ne·ous \ˌpər-kyù-'tā-nē-əs\ *adj* : effected or performed through the skin — **per·cu·ta·ne·ous·ly** *adv*

¹per di·em \ˌpər-'dē-əm, -'dī-\ *adv* : by the day : for each day [Medieval Latin] — **per diem** *adj*

²per diem *n* **1** : a daily allowance (as for traveling expenses) **2** : a daily fee

per·di·tion \pər-'dish-ən\ *n* **1** *archaic* : utter destruction **2 a** : eternal damnation **b** : HELL [Late Latin *perditio,* from Latin *perdere* "to destroy", from *per-* "to destruction" + *dare* "to give"]

per·du·ra·ble \pər-'dùr-ə-bəl, -'dyùr-\ *adj* : very durable — **per·du·ra·bly** \-blē\ *adv*

per·e·gri·nate \'per-ə-grə-ˌnāt\ *vb* : to travel especially on foot : WALK, TRAVERSE — **per·e·gri·na·tion** \ˌper-ə-grə-'nā-shən\ *n*

per·e·grine \'per-ə-grən, -ˌgrēn\ *adj* : having a tendency to wander [Latin *peregrinus* "foreign"]

peregrine falcon *n* : a swift nearly cosmopolitan falcon much used in falconry — called also *peregrine*

pe·remp·to·ry \pə-'rem-tə-rē, -'remp-, -ˌtrē\ *adj* **1 a** : putting an end to or making impossible a right of action, debate, or delay **b** : not contradictable **2** : expressive of urgency or command : IMPERATIVE ⟨*peremptory* tone⟩ **3 a** : marked by self-assurance : POSITIVE **b** : HAUGHTY, DICTATORIAL [Latin *peremptorius* "destructive", from *perimere* "to take entirely, destroy", from *per-* + *emere* "to take"] — **pe·remp·to·ri-**ly \-tə-rə-lē, -trə-lē\ *adv* — **pe·remp·to·ri·ness** \-tə-rē-nəs, -trē-nəs\ *n*

pe·ren·ni·al \pə-'ren-ē-əl\ *adj* **1** : present at all seasons of the year **2** : persisting for several years usually with new herbaceous growth from a basal crown ⟨*perennial* asters⟩ **3 a** : lasting indefinitely **b** : continuing without interruption : CONSTANT **c** : regularly repeated : RECURRENT [Latin *perennis,* from *per-* "throughout" + *annus* "year"] — **perennial** *n* — **pe·ren·ni·al·ly** \-ē-ə-lē\ *adv*

¹per·fect \'pər-fikt\ *adj* **1 a** : being entirely without fault or defect **b** : satisfying all requirements **c** : corresponding to an ideal standard **2** : faithfully reproducing the original **3 a** : being exactly as stated ⟨*perfect* stillness⟩ **b** : lacking in no essential detail : COMPLETE **c** : of an extreme kind ⟨a *perfect* fool⟩ **4** : of, relating to, or constituting a verb form or verbal that expresses an action or state completed at the time of speaking or at a time spoken of **5** : belonging to the musical consonances unison, fourth, fifth, and octave **6** : MONOCLINOUS ⟨a *perfect* flower⟩ [Old French *parfit,* from Latin *perfectus,* from *perficere* "to carry out, perfect", from *per-* "thoroughly" + *facere* "to make, do"] SYN see WHOLE — **per·fect·ness** \-fikt-nəs, -fik-nəs\ *n*

²per·fect \pər-'fekt, *also* 'pər-fikt\ *vt* **1** : to make perfect : IMPROVE, REFINE **2** : to bring to final form — **perfect·er** *n*

³per·fect \'pər-fikt\ *n* : the perfect tense of a language; *also* : a verb form in the perfect tense

per·fect·ible \pər-'fek-tə-bəl, *also* 'pər-fik-\ *adj* : capable of improvement or perfection — **per·fect·ibil·i·ty** \pər-ˌfek-tə-'bil-ət-ē *also* ˌpər-fik-\ *n*

per·fec·tion \pər-'fek-shən\ *n* **1** : the quality or state of being perfect: as **a** : freedom from fault or defect : FLAWLESSNESS **b** : MATURITY 1 **c** : saintly quality or state **2 a** : an exemplification of supreme excellence **b** : an unsurpassable degree of accuracy or excellence **3** : the act or process of perfecting

per·fec·tion·ist \pər-'fek-shə-nəst, -shnəst\ *n* : a person who will not accept or be content with anything less than perfection — **perfectionist** *adj*

per·fect·ly \'pər-fik-tlē, -fik-lē\ *adv* **1** : in a perfect manner ⟨understand *perfectly*⟩ **2** : to an adequate extent : QUITE ⟨*perfectly* willing to go⟩

perfect number *n* : an integer that is equal to the sum of all its divisors except itself ⟨28 is a *perfect number* because it is the sum of $1 + 2 + 4 + 7 + 14$⟩

perfect participle *n* : PAST PARTICIPLE

perfect square *n* : an integer whose square root is an integer ⟨9 is a *perfect square* because it is the square of 3⟩

per·fer·vid \ˌpər-'fər-vəd\ *adj* : extremely fervent

per·fid·i·ous \pər-'fid-ē-əs\ *adj* : of, relating to, or characterized by perfidy SYN see FAITHLESS — **per·fid·i·ous·ly** *adv* — **per·fid·i·ous·ness** *n*

per·fi·dy \'pər-fəd-ē\ *n* : the quality or state of being faithless or disloyal : TREACHERY [Latin *perfidia,* from *perfidus* "faithless", from *per fidem decipere* "to betray", literally, "to deceive by trust"]

per·fo·rate \'pər-fə-ˌrāt\ *vb* **1** : to make a hole through or through something; *esp* : to make perforations in (as sheets of postage stamps) **2** : to pass through or into by or as if by making a hole [Latin *perforare* "to bore through", from *per-* "through" + *forare* "to bore"] — **per·fo·rate** \'pər-fə-rət, -frət, -fə-ˌrāt\ *adj* — **per·fo·ra·tor** \-fə-ˌrāt-ər\ *n*

per·fo·ra·tion \ˌpər-fə-'rā-shən\ *n* **1** : the act or process of perforating **2 a** : a hole or pattern made by or as if by piercing or boring **b** : any of the series of holes made between rows of postage stamps in a sheet

per·force \pər-'fōrs, -'fȯrs\ *adv* : by force of circumstances ⟨we went *perforce*⟩ [Middle French *par force* "by force"]

peregrine falcon

per·form \pər-'fòrm\ *vb* **1** : to stick to the terms of : FULFILL ⟨*perform* a contract⟩ **2 a** : to carry out : DO ⟨*perform* miracles⟩ **b** : ACT, FUNCTION ⟨the car *performed* well⟩ **3 a** : to do in a formal manner or according to prescribed ritual **b** : to give a performance of : PRESENT ⟨the first time they had *performed* Hamlet⟩ [Anglo-French *performer,* from Old French *perfournir,* from *per-* "thoroughly" + *fournir* "to complete"] — **per·form·able** \-'fòr-mə-bəl\ *adj* — **per·form·er** *n*

per·for·mance \pər-'fòr-məns\ *n* **1 a** : the execution of an action **b** : something accomplished : DEED, FEAT **2** : the fulfillment of a claim, promise, or request **3 a** : the action of representing a character in a play **b** : a public presentation or exhibition ⟨a benefit *performance*⟩ **4 a** : the ability to perform : EFFICIENCY **b** : the manner in which a mechanism performs — **per·for·ma·to·ry** \-mə-,tōr-ē, -,tòr-\ *adj*

per·form·ing *adj* : of, relating to, or constituting an art (as drama) that involves public performance

¹per·fume \'pər-,fyüm, pər-'\ *n* **1** : the scent of something sweet-smelling **2** : a substance that emits a pleasant odor; *esp* : a fluid preparation of floral essences or synthetics and a fixative used for scenting [Middle French *perfum*]

²per·fume \pər-'fyüm, ,pər-', 'pər-,\ *vt* : to fill with an odor (as of something pleasant) ⟨a kitchen *perfumed* with spices⟩

per·fum·er \pər-'fyü-mər, pə-'fyü-\ *n* : one that makes or sells perfumes

per·fum·ery \pər-'fyüm-rē, pə-'fyüm-, -ə-rē\ *n, pl* **-er·ies 1** : the art or process of making perfume **2** : the products made by a perfumer

per·func·to·ry \pər-'fəng-tə-rē, -'fəngk-, -trē\ *adj* **1** : characterized by routine or superficiality : MECHANICAL **2** : lacking in interest or enthusiasm : INDIFFERENT [Late Latin *perfunctorius,* from Latin *perfungi* "to accomplish, get through with", from *per-* "through" + *fungi* "to perform"] — **per·func·to·ri·ly** \-tə-rə-lē, -trə-lē\ *adv* — **per·func·to·ri·ness** \-tə-rē-nəs, -trē-nəs\ *n*

per·fuse \pər-'fyüz\ *vt* **1** : SUFFUSE **2 a** : to cause to flow or spread : DIFFUSE **b** : to force a fluid through (an organ or tissue) especially by way of the blood vessels [Latin *perfusus,* past participle of *perfundere* "to pour over", from *per-* "through" + *fundere* "to pour"] — **per·fu·sion** \-'fyü-zhən\ *n*

per·go·la \'pər-gə-lə, pər-'gō-\ *n* : a structure consisting of posts supporting an open roof in the form of a trellis [Italian, from Latin *pergula* "projecting roof"]

per·haps \pər-'haps, pər-'aps, 'praps\ *adv* : possibly but not certainly : MAYBE [*per* + *hap*]

pe·ri \'piər-ē\ *n, pl* **peris** : a supernatural being in Persian folklore descended from fallen angels and excluded from paradise until penance is accomplished [Persian *perī*]

peri- *prefix* **1** : all around : about ⟨*peri*scope⟩ **2** : near ⟨*peri*helion⟩ **3** : enclosing : surrounding ⟨*peri*odontal⟩ [Greek, "around, in excess", from *peri* "around"]

peri·anth \'per-ē-,anth, -,anth\ *n* : the outer part of a flower especially when consisting of a combined calyx and corolla [*peri-* + Greek *anthos* "flower"]

peri·car·di·um \,per-ə-'kärd-ē-əm\ *n, pl* **-dia** \-ē-ə\ : the cone-shaped sac of membrane that encloses the heart and the roots of the great blood vessels of vertebrates [New Latin, from Greek *perikardios* "around the heart", from *peri-* + *kardia* "heart"] — **peri·car·di·al** \-ē-əl\ *adj*

peri·carp \'per-ə-,kärp\ *n* : the ripened and variously modified walls of a plant ovary that form the substance of a fruit and enclose the seeds — compare ENDOCARP, EPICARP, MESOCARP

peri·cy·cle \'per-ə-,sī-kəl\ *n* : a thin layer of cells at the outer edge of a vascular cylinder in vascular plants [French *péricycle,* from Greek *perikyklos* "spherical", from *peri-* + *kyklos* "circle"]

peri·derm \'per-ə-,dərm\ *n* : an outer layer of tissue; *esp* : a cortical protective layer of many roots and stems — **peri·der·mal** \,per-ə-'dər-məl\ *adj*

peri·gee \'per-ə-,jē\ *n* : the point nearest the center of a celestial body (as the earth or moon) reached by an object (as a satellite) orbiting it — compare APOGEE [Greek *gē* "earth"]

pe·rig·y·nous \pə-'rij-ə-nəs\ *adj* **1** : growing from a ring or cup of the receptacle surrounding a pistil ⟨*perigynous* petals⟩ **2** : having perigynous flower parts — **pe·rig·y·ny** \-nē\ *n*

per·i·he·lion \,per-ə-'hēl-yən\ *n, pl* **-he·lia** \-'hēl-yə-\ : the point in the path of a celestial body (as a planet) that is nearest to the sun — compare APHELION [New Latin, from *peri-* + Greek *hēlios* "sun"]

¹per·il \'per-əl\ *n* **1** : exposure to the risk of being injured, destroyed, or lost ⟨fire put the city in *peril*⟩ **2** : something that imperils : RISK ⟨*perils* of the highway⟩ [Old French, from Latin *periculum*] SYN see DANGER

²peril *vt* **-iled** *also* **-illed; -il·ing** *also* **-il·ling** : to expose to danger : HAZARD, RISK

per·il·ous \'per-ə-ləs\ *adj* : full of or involving peril : HAZARDOUS — **per·il·ous·ly** *adv* — **per·il·ous·ness** *n*

pe·rim·e·ter \pə-'rim-ət-ər\ *n* **1** : the boundary of a closed plane figure; *also* : the length of this boundary **2** : a line or strip bounding or protecting an area **3** : outer limits [French *périmètre,* from Latin *perimetros,* from Greek, from *peri-* + *metron* "measure"]

per·i·ne·um \,per-ə-'nē-əm\ *n, pl* **-nea** \-'nē-ə\ : an area between the thighs which marks the approximate lower boundary of the pelvis and through which the urinary and genital ducts and rectum pass [Late Latin *perinaion,* from Greek, from *peri-* + *inein* "to empty out"] — **per·i·ne·al** \-'nē-əl\ *adj*

¹pe·ri·od \'pir-ē-əd\ *n* **1 a** : an utterance from one full stop to another : SENTENCE **b** : PERIODIC SENTENCE **2 a** : the full pause with which a sentence closes **b** : END 2a, STOP **3** : a punctuation mark . used chiefly to mark the end of a declarative sentence or an abbreviation **4** : the completion of a cycle, a series of events, or a single action : CONCLUSION **5 a** : a portion of time determined by some recurring phenomenon **b** : the interval of time required for a motion or phenomenon to complete a cycle and begin to repeat itself ⟨the *period* of a pendulum⟩ **c** : a single cyclic occurrence of menstruation **6 a** : a chronological division : STAGE **b** : a division of geologic time longer than an epoch and shorter than an era **c** : a stage of culture having a definable place in time and space ⟨the colonial *period*⟩ **7 a** : one of the divisions of the academic day **b** : one of the divisions of the playing time of a game **8** : the length of the shortest interval required on the x-axis for a periodic function to repeat itself **9** : a series of elements of increasing atomic number as listed in horizontal rows in the periodic table [Middle French *periode,* from Greek *periodos* "circuit, period of time, rhetorical period", from *peri-* + *hodos* "way"] □ SYN PERIOD, EPOCH, ERA, AGE mean a division of time. PERIOD may designate any extent of time; EPOCH applies to a period begun by some striking or significant event ⟨the steam engine marked a new *epoch* in industry⟩ ERA suggests a period in history marked by a new or distinct order ⟨the *era* of exploration⟩ AGE is applied to a fairly definite period strongly dominated by a central figure ⟨the *age* of Jackson⟩ or by a prominent feature ⟨the nuclear *age*⟩

²period *adj* : of, relating to, or representing a particular historical period ⟨*period* furniture⟩

pe·ri·od·ic \,pir-ē-'äd-ik\ *adj* **1** : occurring or recurring at regular intervals **2** : consisting of or containing stages or values repeated at equal intervals : CYCLIC ⟨*periodic* vibrations⟩ ⟨the sine is a *periodic* function⟩ **3** : of or relating to a period — **pe·ri·od·ic·i·ty** \,pir-ē-ə-'dis-ət-ē\ *n*

\ə\ abut		\ng\ sing	
\ər\ further		\ō\ bone	
\a\ mat		\ò\ saw	
\ā\ take		\òi\ coin	
\ä\ cot, cart		\th\ thin	
\au̇\ out		\th\ this	
\ch\ chin		\ü\ food	
\e\ pet		\u̇\ foot	
\ē\ easy		\y\ yet	
\g\ go		\yü\ few	
\i\ tip		\yu̇\ cure	
\ī\ life		\zh\ vision	
\j\ job			

¹pe·ri·od·i·cal \,pir-ē-'äd-i-kəl\ *adj* **1** : PERIODIC 1 **2 a** : published with a fixed interval between the issues or numbers **b** : published in, characteristic of, or connected with a periodical — **pe·ri·od·i·cal·ly** \-kə-lē, -klē\ *adv*

²periodical *n* : a periodical publication

periodical decimal *n* : REPEATING DECIMAL

periodic law *n* : a law in chemistry : the elements when arranged in the order of their atomic numbers show a periodic variation in most of their properties

periodic sentence *n* : a usually complex sentence that has no subordinate or trailing elements following its principal clause (as in "yesterday, while I was walking down the street, I saw them")

periodic table *n* : an arrangement of chemical elements based on the periodic law

peri·odon·tal \,per-ē-ō-'dänt-l\ *adj* **1** : surrounding or occurring about the teeth **2** : affecting periodontal tissues ⟨*periodontal* disease⟩ [*peri-* + Greek *odont-*, *odous* "tooth"]

periodontal membrane *n* : the fibrous connective-tissue layer covering the cement layer of a tooth

peri·os·te·um \,per-ē-'äs-tē-əm\ *n, pl* **-tea** \-tē-ə\ : the membrane of connective tissue that covers all bones except at the surfaces in a joint [Late Latin *periosteon*, from Greek *periosteos* "around the bone", from *peri-* + *osteon* "bone"] — **peri·os·te·al** \-tē-əl\ *adj*

peri·pa·tet·ic \,per-ə-pə-'tet-ik\ *adj* : moving about from place to place : ITINERANT ⟨a *peripatetic* preacher⟩ [Latin *peripateticus*, from Greek *peripatētikos*, from *peripatein* "to walk about", from *peri-* + *patein* "to walk"] — **peri·pa·tet·i·cal·ly** \-'tet-i-kə-lē, -klē\ *adv*

pe·rip·a·tus \pə-'rip-ət-əs\ *n* : any of a class (Onychophora) of primitive tropical arthropods in some respects intermediate between annelid worms and typical arthropods [Greek *peripatos* "act of walking", from *peri-* + *patein* "to walk"]

¹pe·riph·er·al \pə-'rif-rəl, -ə-rəl\ *adj* **1** : of, relating to, located in, or forming a periphery ⟨*peripheral* vision⟩ **2** : of, relating to, or being part of the peripheral nervous system **3** : having an auxiliary function — **pe·riph·er·al·ly** \-ē\ *adv*

²peripheral *n* : a device connected to a computer to provide communication (as input and output) or extra storage capacity

peripheral nervous system *n* : the part of the nervous system that is outside the central nervous system and consists of the cranial nerves excepting the optic nerve, the spinal nerves, and the autonomic nervous system

pe·riph·ery \pə-'rif-rē, -ə-rē\ *n, pl* **-er·ies** **1** : the perimeter of a closed curve; *also* : the perimeter of a polygon **2** : the external boundary or surface of a body **3 a** : the outward bounds of something as distinguished from its more internal regions or center **b** : an area lying beyond the strict limits of a thing [Middle French *peripherie*, from Late Latin *peripheria*, from Greek *periphereia*, from *peripherein* "to carry around", from *peri-* + *pherein* "to carry"]

pe·riph·ra·sis \pə-'rif-rə-səs\ *n, pl* **-ra·ses** \-rə-,sēz\ : use of a longer phrasing in place of a possible shorter and usually plainer form of expression : CIRCUMLOCUTION [Latin, from Greek, from *periphrazein* "to express periphrastically", from *peri-* + *phrazein* "to point out"]

per·i·phras·tic \,per-ə-'fras-tik\ *adj* **1** : of, relating to, or characterized by periphrasis **2** : formed by the use of function words or auxiliaries instead of by inflection ⟨*more fair* is a *periphrastic* comparative⟩ — **per·i·phras·ti·cal·ly** \-ti-kə-lē, -klē\ *adv*

peri·scope \'per-ə-,skōp\ *n* : a tubular optical instrument containing lenses and mirrors by which an observer (as on a submerged submarine) obtains an oth-

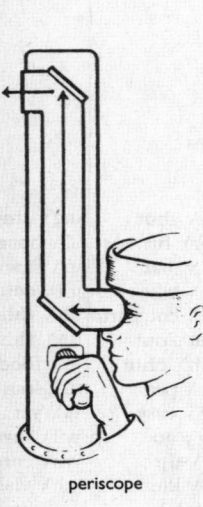

periscope

erwise obstructed field of view — **peri·scop·ic** \,per-ə-'skäp-ik\ *adj*

per·ish \'per-ish\ *vt* : to pass away completely : become destroyed or ruined : DIE [Old French *periss-*, stem of *perir* "to perish", from Latin *perire*, from *per-* "to destruction" + *ire* "to go"]

per·ish·able \'per-ish-ə-bəl\ *adj* : liable to spoil or decay ⟨*perishable* products such as fruit⟩ — **per·ish·abil·i·ty** \,per-ish-ə-'bil-ət-ē\ *n* — **perishable** *n*

pe·ris·so·dac·tyl \pə-,ris-ə-'dak-tl\ *n* : any of an order (Perissodactyla) of hoofed mammals (as the horse or rhinoceros) with an odd number of functional toes on each foot [Greek *perissos* "excessive, odd" + *daktylos* "finger, toe"] — **perissodactyl** *adj*

peri·stal·sis \,per-ə-'stol-səs, -'stäl-, -'stal-\ *n, pl* **-stal·ses** \-,sēz\ : successive waves of involuntary contraction passing along the walls of a hollow muscular structure (as the intestine) and forcing the contents onward [derived from Greek *peristellein* "to wrap around", from *peri-* + *stellein* "to place"] — **peri·stal·tic** \-'stol-tik, -'stal-\ *adj* — **peri·stal·ti·cal·ly** \-ti-kə-lē, -klē\ *adv*

peri·style \'per-ə-,stīl\ *n* **1** : a colonnade surrounding a building or court **2** : an open space enclosed by a row of columns [French *péristyle*, from Latin *peristylum*, from Greek *peristylon*, derived from *peri-* + *stylos* "pillar"]

peri·to·ne·um \,per-ət-n-'ē-əm\ *n, pl* **-ne·ums** *or* **-nea** \-'ē-ə\ : the smooth transparent membrane that lines the cavity of the abdomen and encloses the abdominal and pelvic viscera [Late Latin, from Greek *peritonaios* "stretched around", from *peri-* + *teinein* "to stretch"] — **peri·to·ne·al** \-'ē-əl\ *adj*

peri·to·ni·tis \,per-ət-n-'īt-əs\ *n* : inflammation of the peritoneum

peri·wig \'per-i-,wig\ *n* : WIG [French *perruque*]

¹peri·win·kle \'per-i-,wing-kəl\ *n* : a European creeper widely grown as a ground cover and for its blue or white flowers [Old English *perwince*, from Latin *pervinca*]

²periwinkle *n* : any of numerous small edible marine snails of coastal regions; *also* : the shell of a periwinkle [Old English *pīnewincle*]

per·jure \'pər-jər\ *vt* **per·jured; per·jur·ing** \'pərj-ring, -ə-ring\ : to make (oneself) guilty of perjury [Middle French *perjurer*, from Latin *perjurare*, from *per-* "destruction, to the bad" + *jurare* "to swear"]

per·jur·er \'pər-jər-ər\ *n* : a person guilty of perjury

per·ju·ri·ous \pər-'jùr-ē-əs\ *adj* : marked by perjury — **per·ju·ri·ous·ly** *adv*

per·ju·ry \'pərj-rē, -ə-rē\ *n, pl* **-ries** : violation of an oath by knowingly swearing to what is untrue : false swearing

perk \'pərk\ *vb* **1** : to stick up or out jauntily ⟨a dog *perking* its ears⟩ **2** : to regain vigor or cheerfulness ⟨*perked* up as the cold got better⟩ **3** : to smarten the appearance of ⟨*perked* the room up with new curtains⟩ [Middle English *perken* "to be jaunty"]

perky \'pər-kē\ *adj* **perk·i·er; -est** : JAUNTY, LIVELY — **perk·i·ly** \-kə-lē\ *adv* — **perk·i·ness** \-kē-nəs\ *n*

per·lite \'pər-,līt\ *n* : glassy cooled volcanic lava of shelly structure that when expanded by heat forms a lightweight water-absorbent material [French, from *perle* "pearl"]

per·ma·frost \'pər-mə-,frost\ *n* : a permanently frozen layer at variable depth below the earth's surface in frigid regions [*perma*nent *frost*]

per·ma·nence \'pər-mə-nəns\ *n* : the quality or state of being permanent

per·ma·nen·cy \-nən-sē\ *n, pl* **-cies** : PERMANENCE

¹per·ma·nent \'pər-mə-nənt\ *adj* : lasting or intended to last for a very long time without fundamental or marked change [Middle French, from Latin *permanēre*, from *per-* "throughout" + *manēre* "to remain"] SYN see LASTING — **per·ma·nent·ly** *adv* — **per·ma·nent·ness** *n*

²**permanent** *n* : a long-lasting hair wave produced by mechanical and chemical means

permanent magnet *n* : a magnet that retains its magnetism after removal of the magnetizing force

permanent press *adj* : of, relating to, or made from a fabric chemically treated to resist wrinkling

permanent tooth *n* : one of the second set of teeth of a mammal that follow the milk teeth, typically persist into old age, and in humans are 32 in number

per·man·ga·nate \pər-'mang-gə-ˌnāt\ *n* : POTASSIUM PERMANGANATE

per·me·abil·i·ty \ˌpər-mē-ə-'bil-ət-ē\ *n, pl* **-ties** 1 : the quality or state of being permeable 2 : the property of a substance that determines the degree to which it is magnetizable

per·me·able \'pər-mē-ə-bəl\ *adj* : having pores or openings that permit liquids or gases to pass through ⟨a *permeable* membrane⟩ ⟨*permeable* limestone⟩ — **per·me·able·ness** *n* — **per·me·ably** \-blē\ *adv*

per·me·ate \'pər-mē-ˌāt\ *vb* 1 : to pass through the pores or small openings of ⟨water *permeates* sand⟩ 2 : to spread throughout : PERVADE ⟨a room *permeated* with the odor of tobacco⟩ [Latin *permeare*, from *per-* "through" + *meare* "to go, pass"] — **per·me·a·tion** \ˌpər-mē-'ā-shən\ *n* — **per·me·a·tive** \'pər-mē-ˌāt-iv\ *adj*

Perm·ian \'pər-mē-ən\ *n* : the most recent period of the Paleozoic era; *also* : the corresponding system of rocks — see GEOLOGIC TIME table [*Perm*, region in eastern Russia] — **Permian** *adj*

per·mis·si·ble \pər-'mis-ə-bəl\ *adj* : that may be permitted : ALLOWABLE — **per·mis·si·bil·i·ty** \-ˌmis-ə-'bil-ət-ē\ *n* — **per·mis·si·ble·ness** \-'mis-ə-bəl-nəs\ *n* — **per·mis·si·bly** \-blē\ *adv*

per·mis·sion \pər-'mish-ən\ *n* 1 : the act of permitting 2 : the consent of a person in authority : AUTHORIZATION [Middle French, from Latin *permissio*, from *permissus*, past participle of *permittere* "to permit"]

per·mis·sive \pər-'mis-iv\ *adj* 1 a : granting or tending to grant permission b : allowing freedom (as of choice or behavior) ⟨*permissive* parents⟩ 2 : not forbidden : ALLOWABLE — **per·mis·sive·ly** *adv* — **per·mis·sive·ness** *n*

¹**per·mit** \pər-'mit\ *vb* **per·mit·ted; per·mit·ting** 1 : to consent to expressly or formally : give permission 2 : to make possible : give an opportunity : ALLOW ⟨if time *permits*⟩ [Latin *permittere* "to let through, permit", from *per-* "through" + *mittere* "to let go, send"] SYN see LET — **per·mit·ter** *n*

²**per·mit** \'pər-ˌmit, pər-'\ *n* : a written statement of permission given by one having authority ⟨a *permit* to learn to drive⟩

per·mu·ta·tion \ˌpər-myù-'tā-shən\ *n* 1 : a thorough change in character or condition : TRANSFORMATION 2 a : the act or process of changing the order of a set of objects b : an ordered arrangement of a set of objects — **per·mu·ta·tion·al** \-shnəl, -shən-l\ *adj*

per·mute \pər-'myüt\ *vt* : to change the order or arrangement of; *esp* : to arrange in all possible ways [Latin *permutare*, from *per-* + *mutare* "to change"]

per·ni·cious \pər-'nish-əs\ *adj* : very destructive or injurious ⟨a *pernicious* disease⟩ ⟨a *pernicious* habit⟩ [Middle French *pernicieux*, from Latin *perniciosus*, from *pernicies* "destruction", from *per-* + *nec-, nex* "violent death"] — **per·ni·cious·ly** *adv* — **per·ni·cious·ness** *n*

pernicious anemia *n* : a severe anemia in which the red blood cells progressively decrease in number and increase in size and which is associated with a deficiency of vitamin B₁₂

per·nick·e·ty \pər-'nik-ət-ē\ *adj* : PERSNICKETY [perhaps alteration of *particular*]

per·o·ra·tion \ˌper-ər-'ā-shən, 'pər-\ *n* 1 : the concluding part of a speech and especially an oration 2 : a very rhetorical speech — **per·o·rate** \'per-ər-ˌāt\ *vi* — **per·o·ra·tion·al** \ˌper-ər-'ā-shnəl, ˌpər-, -shən-l\ *adj*

¹**per·ox·ide** \pə-'räk-ˌsīd\ *n* 1 : an oxide containing a high proportion of oxygen; *esp* : a compound (as hydrogen peroxide) in which oxygen is joined to oxygen 2 : HYDROGEN PEROXIDE

²**peroxide** *vt* : to bleach (hair) with hydrogen peroxide

¹**per·pen·dic·u·lar** \ˌpər-pən-'dik-yə-lər\ *adj* 1 a : exactly vertical or upright b : being at right angles to a given line or plane 2 : extremely steep : PRECIPITOUS [Middle French *perpendiculer*, from Latin *perpendicularis*, from *perpendiculum* "plumb line", from *per-* + *pendēre* "to hang"] SYN see VERTICAL — **per·pen·dic·u·lar·i·ty** \-ˌdik-yə-'lar-ət-ē\ *n* — **per·pen·dic·u·lar·ly** \-'dik-yə-lər-lē\ *adv*

²**perpendicular** *n* : a line at right angles to the plane of the horizon or to another line or surface

per·pe·trate \'pər-pə-ˌtrāt\ *vt* : to be guilty of doing or performing : COMMIT ⟨*perpetrate* a crime⟩ [Latin *perpetrare*, from *per-* + *patrare* "to accomplish"] — **per·pe·tra·tion** \ˌpər-pə-'trā-shən\ *n* — **per·pe·tra·tor** \'pər-pə-ˌtrāt-ər\ *n*

per·pet·u·al \pər-'pech-ə-wəl, -'pech-əl\ *adj* 1 a : continuing forever : EVERLASTING b (1) : valid for all time ⟨a *perpetual* right-of-way⟩ (2) : holding (as an office) for life or for an unlimited time 2 : going on and on without interruption : CONSTANT 3 : blooming continuously throughout the season [Middle French *perpetuel*, from Latin *perpetuus*, from *per-* + *petere* "to go to"] — **per·pet·u·al·ly** \-ē\ *adv*

perpetual calendar *n* : a table for finding the day of the week for any one of a wide range of dates

per·pet·u·ate \pər-'pech-ə-ˌwāt\ *vt* : to make perpetual or cause to last indefinitely ⟨*perpetuate* a tradition⟩ — **per·pet·u·a·tion** \-ˌpech-ə-'wā-shən\ *n* — **per·pet·u·a·tor** \-'pech-ə-ˌwāt-ər\ *n*

per·pe·tu·i·ty \ˌpər-pə-'tü-ət-ē, -'tyü-\ *n, pl* **-ties** 1 : perpetual existence or duration ⟨the *perpetuity* of their fame⟩ 2 : endless time : ETERNITY

per·plex \pər-'pleks\ *vt* 1 : to make mentally uncertain : BEWILDER, NONPLUS 2 : to make intricate or involved : COMPLICATE [Latin *perplexus* "involved, perplexed", from *per-* "thoroughly" + *plexus* "involved", from *plectere* "to braid, twine"] SYN see PUZZLE

per·plexed \-'plekst\ *adj* 1 : filled with uncertainty 2 : full of difficulty : COMPLICATED — **per·plexed·ly** \-'plek-səd-lē, -'pleks-tlē\ *adv*

per·plex·i·ty \pər-'plek-sət-ē\ *n, pl* **-ties** 1 : the state of being perplexed : BEWILDERMENT 2 : something that perplexes

per·qui·site \'pər-kwə-zət\ *n* 1 : a profit made from one's employment in addition to one's regular pay; *esp* : such a profit when expected or promised 2 : ⁸TIP [Medieval Latin *perquisitum* "property acquired by other means than inheritance", from *perquirere* "to purchase, acquire", from Latin, "to search out", from *per-* + *quaerere* "to seek"]

per·ry \'per-ē\ *n* : pear cider [Middle French *peré*, from Latin *pirum* "pear"]

per se \ˌpər-'sā\ *adv* : by, of, or in itself or oneself or themselves : as such : INTRINSICALLY [Latin]

per second per second *adv* : per second every second — used of acceleration

per·se·cute \'pər-si-ˌkyüt\ *vt* 1 : to harass in a manner to injure, grieve, or afflict; *esp* : to cause to suffer because of belief 2 : to annoy with persistent or urgent approaches : PESTER [Middle French *persecuter*, derived from Late Latin *persequi*, from Latin, "to pursue", from *per-* "through" + *sequi* "to follow"] — **per·se·cu·tor** \-ˌkyüt-ər\ *n* — **per·se·cu·to·ry** \-kyü-ˌtōr-ē, -ˌtòr-\ *adj*

²perpindicular

per·se·cu·tion \ˌpər-si-'kyü-shən\ *n* **1** : the act or practice of persecuting especially those who differ in origin, religion, or social outlook **2** : the condition of being persecuted, harassed, or annoyed

Per·seus \'pər-ˌsüs, -sē-əs\ *n* : a northern constellation between Taurus and Cassiopeia [Latin *Perseus,* son of Zeus, from Greek]

per·se·ver·ance \ˌpər-sə-'vir-əns\ *n* : the action, condition, or an instance of persevering : STEADFASTNESS

per·se·vere \ˌpər-sə-'viər\ *vi* : to keep at something in spite of difficulties, opposition, or discouragement [Middle French *perseverer,* from Latin *perseverare,* from *per-* "through" + *severus* "severe"]

per·se·ver·ing \-'viər-ing\ *adj* : showing perseverance : PERSISTENT — **per·se·ver·ing·ly** \-ing-lē\ *adv*

Per·sian \'pər-zhən\ *n* **1** : one of the people of Persia: as **a** : one of the ancient Iranian Caucasians who under Cyrus and his successors dominated western Asia **b** : a member of one of the peoples forming the modern Iranian nation **2 a** : any of several Iranian languages dominant in Persia at different periods **b** : the modern language of Iran and western Afghanistan **3** : a thin soft silk formerly used especially for linings — **Persian** *adj*

Persian cat *n* : a stocky round-headed domestic cat with long silky fur

Persian lamb *n* : a pelt obtained from karakul lambs older than those yielding broadtail and characterized by very silky tightly curled fur

per·si·flage \'pər-sə-ˌfläzh, 'per-\ *n* : frivolous or lightly jesting talk : BANTER [French, from *persifler* "to banter", from *per-* "thoroughly" + *siffler* "to whistle, hiss, boo", from Latin *sibilare*]

per·sim·mon \pər-'sim-ən\ *n* **1** : any of a genus of trees with hard fine wood, oblong leaves, and small bell-shaped white flowers **2** : the usually orange several-seeded fruit of a persimmon that resembles a plum, is edible when fully ripe, and is technically a berry [of American Indian origin]

per·sist \pər-'sist, -'zist\ *vi* **1** : to go on resolutely in spite of opposition, warnings, or pleas : PERSEVERE **2** : to last on and on : continue to exist ⟨rain *persisting* for days⟩ [Middle French *persister,* from Latin *persistere,* from *per-* + *sistere* "to take a stand, stand firm"] — **per·sist·er** *n*

per·sis·tence \pər-'sis-təns, -'zis-\ *n* **1** : the act or fact of persisting **2** : the quality or state of being persistent; *esp* : PERSEVERANCE

per·sis·ten·cy \-tən-sē\ *n* : PERSISTENCE 2

per·sis·tent \-tənt\ *adj* **1** : continuing, existing, or acting for a long or longer than usual time ⟨a *persistent* cough⟩ ⟨*persistent* gills⟩ **2** : DOGGED, TENACIOUS ⟨a *persistent* salesman⟩ [Latin *persistens,* present participle of *persistere* "to persist"] — **per·sis·tent·ly** *adv*

per·snick·e·ty \pər-'snik-ət-ē\ *adj* : fussy about small details : FASTIDIOUS [alteration of *pernickety*]

per·son \'pərs-n\ *n* **1** : HUMAN BEING, INDIVIDUAL — used in combination especially by those who prefer to avoid *man* in compounds applicable to both sexes ⟨chair*person*⟩ **2** : a character or part in or as if in a play : GUISE **3 a** : bodily appearance **b** : the body of a human being **4 a** : the individual personality of a human being : SELF **b** : bodily presence ⟨appear in *person*⟩ **5** : an entity (as a human being or corporation) recognized by law as having rights and duties **6** : reference to the speaker, to one spoken to, or to one spoken of as indicated especially by means of certain pronouns [Old French *persone,* from Latin *persona* "actor's mask, character in a play, person"]

per·son·able \'pərs-nə-bəl, -n-ə-bəl\ *adj* : attractive in looks and manner : PLEASING — **per·son·able·ness** *n*

per·son·age \'pərs-nij, -n-ij\ *n* **1** : a person of rank or distinction **2** : a character in a book or play

¹per·son·al \'pərs-nəl, -n-əl\ *adj* **1** : of, relating to, or belonging to a person : PRIVATE **2 a** : done in person or

proceeding from a single person **b** : carried on between individuals directly **3** : relating to the person or body ⟨*personal* hygiene⟩ **4** : closely related to an individual : INTIMATE **5** : denoting grammatical person

²personal *n* : a short newspaper paragraph relating to a person or group or to personal matters

personal computer *n* : MICROCOMPUTER

personal effects *n pl* : personal property (as clothing and toilet articles) normally worn or carried on the person

personal equation *n* : variation (as in scientific observation) due to the personal peculiarities of an individual; *also* : a correction or allowance made for such variation

personal foul *n* : a foul (as in basketball or lacrosse) which involves unnecessary roughness or illegal obstruction of an opponent

per·son·al·i·ty \ˌpərs-n-'al-ət-ē, ˌpər-'snal-\ *n, pl* **-ties** **1** : the state of being a person **2** : the emotional and behavioral characteristics of a person : INDIVIDUALITY **3** : pleasing qualities of character ⟨lack *personality*⟩ **4** : a person who has strongly marked qualities ⟨a great stage *personality*⟩ **5** : a personal remark : a slighting reference to a person ⟨use *personalities* in an argument⟩

per·son·al·ize \'pərs-nə-ˌlīz, -n-ə-\ *vt* **1** : PERSONIFY **2** : to make personal or individual; *esp* : to mark as belonging to a particular person ⟨*personalized* stationery⟩

per·son·al·ly \'pərs-nə-lē, -n-ə-\ *adv* **1** : in person ⟨attend to the matter *personally*⟩ **2** : as a person : in personality ⟨*personally* attractive but not very trustworthy⟩ **3** : for oneself : as far as oneself is concerned ⟨*personally,* I am against it⟩

personal pronoun *n* : a pronoun (as I, *you,* or *they*) expressing a distinction of person

personal property *n* : movable property (as money, clothing, or furnishings) : CHATTELS — compare REAL PROPERTY

per·son·al·ty \'pərs-nəl-tē, -n-əl-\ *n, pl* **-ties** : PERSONAL PROPERTY

per·so·na non gra·ta \pər-ˌsō-nə-ˌnän-'grat-ə, -'grät-\ *adj* : personally unacceptable or unwelcome [New Latin, "person not acceptable"]

per·son·ate \'pərs-n-āt\ *vt* **1** : IMPERSONATE, REPRESENT **2** : to invest with personality or personal characteristics — **per·son·ation** \ˌpərs-n-'ā-shən\ *n* — **per·son·ative** \'pərs-n-ˌāt-iv\ *adj* — **per·son·ator** \-ˌāt-ər\ *n*

per·son·i·fi·ca·tion \pər-ˌsän-ə-fə-'kā-shən\ *n* **1** : the act of personifying **2** : an imaginary being thought of as representing a thing or an idea **3** : EMBODIMENT 1, INCARNATION ⟨you are the *personification* of generosity⟩ **4** : a figure of speech in which a lifeless object or abstract quality is spoken of as if alive

per·son·i·fy \pər-'sän-ə-ˌfī\ *vt* **-fied; -fy·ing** **1** : to think of or represent as a person ⟨*personify* the forces of nature⟩ **2** : to represent in a physical form ⟨the law was *personified* in the sheriff⟩ **3** : to serve as the perfect type or example of — **per·son·i·fi·er** \-ˌfī-ər, -ˌfīr\ *n*

per·son·nel \ˌpərs-n-'el\ *n* : a group of persons employed (as in a public service, a factory, or an office) [French]

¹per·spec·tive \pər-'spek-tiv\ *n* **1** : the art or technique of painting or drawing a scene so that objects in it have apparent depth and distance **2** : the power to see or think of things in their true relationship to each other ⟨lose one's *perspective*⟩ **3** : the true relationship of objects or events to one another ⟨view events in proper *perspective*⟩ **4 a** : a visible scene; *esp* : one giving a definite impression of distance **b** : a mental view or prospect **5** : the appearance to the eye of objects in respect to their relative distance and positions [Middle French, probably from Italian *prospettiva,* from *prospetto* "view, prospect", from Latin *prospectus*]

Persian cat

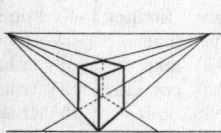

¹perspective 1

²perspective *adj* : of, relating to, or seen in perspective — **per·spec·tive·ly** *adv*

per·spi·ca·cious \ˌpər-spə-'kā-shəs\ *adj* : having or showing keen understanding or discernment [Latin *perspicax,* from *perspicere* "to look through, see clearly", from *per-* "through" + *specere* "to look"] — **per·spi·ca·cious·ly** *adv* — **per·spi·ca·cious·ness** *n*

per·spi·cac·i·ty \ˌpər-spə-'kas-ət-ē\ *n* : the quality or state of being perspicacious

per·spic·u·ous \pər-'spik-yə-wəs\ *adj* : plain to the understanding : CLEAR [Latin *perspicuus* "transparent, perspicuous", from *perspicere* "to look through"] — **per·spi·cu·ity** \ˌpər-spə-'kyü-ət-ē\ *n* — **per·spic·u·ous·ly** \pər-'spik-yə-wə-slē\ *adv* — **per·spic·u·ous·ness** *n*

per·spi·ra·tion \ˌpər-spə-'rā-shən\ *n* **1** : the act or process of perspiring **2** : a saline fluid secreted by the sweat glands : SWEAT

per·spire \pər-'spīr\ *vi* : to secrete and emit perspiration : SWEAT [French *perspirer,* from Latin *per-* "through" + *spirare* "to blow, breathe"]

per·suad·able \pər-'swād-ə-bəl\ *adj* : capable of being persuaded

per·suade \pər-'swād\ *vt* : to win over to a belief or to a course of action by argument or earnest request : induce to do or believe something [Latin *persuadēre,* from *per-* "thoroughly" + *suadēre* "to advise, urge"] — **per·suad·er** *n*

per·sua·si·ble \pər-'swā-zə-bəl, -'swā-sə-\ *adj* : PERSUADABLE

per·sua·sion \pər-'swā-zhən\ *n* **1** : the act of persuading **2** : the power or ability to persuade : persuasive quality **3** : the state of being persuaded **4** : a way of believing : BELIEF; *esp* : a system of religious beliefs **5** : a group having the same religious beliefs [Latin *persuasio,* from *persuadēre* "to persuade"]

per·sua·sive \pər-'swā-siv, -ziv\ *adj* : tending to persuade : having the power or effect of persuading ⟨a *persuasive* speech⟩ — **per·sua·sive·ly** *adv* — **per·sua·sive·ness** *n*

pert \'pərt\ *adj* **1 a** : saucily free and forward : IMPUDENT **b** : being trim and chic : JAUNTY **c** : piquantly stimulating **2** : VIVACIOUS, LIVELY [Middle English, "open, bold, pert", from Old French *apert,* from Latin *apertus* "open", from *aperire* "to open"] — **pert·ly** *adv* — **pert·ness** *n*

per·tain \pər-'tān\ *vi* **1** : to belong as a part, quality, or function ⟨duties that *pertain* to an office⟩ **2** : to have reference ⟨books *pertaining* to birds⟩ [Middle French *partenir,* from Latin *pertinēre* "to hold out, reach to, pertain", from *per-* "through" + *tenēre* "to hold"]

per·ti·na·cious \ˌpərt-n-'ā-shəs\ *adj* **1** : holding strongly to an opinion, purpose, or course of action **2** : stubbornly or annoyingly persistent [Latin *pertinax,* from *per-* "thoroughly" + *tenax* "tenacious"] SYN see OBSTINATE — **per·ti·na·cious·ly** *adv* — **per·ti·na·cious·ness** *n* — **per·ti·nac·i·ty** \ˌpərt-n-'as-ət-ē\ *n*

per·ti·nent \'pərt-n-ənt\ *adj* : having to do with the subject or matter that is being considered : being to the point ⟨a *pertinent* suggestion⟩ [Middle French, from Latin *pertinēre* "to pertain"] — **per·ti·nence** \-n-əns\ *or* **per·ti·nen·cy** \-n-ən-sē\ *n* — **per·ti·nent·ly** *adv*

per·turb \pər-'tərb\ *vt* **1** : to disturb greatly in mind : DISQUIET **2** : to throw into confusion : AGITATE [Middle French *perturber,* from Latin *perturbare* "to throw into confusion", from *per-* + *turbare* "to disturb"] SYN see DISTURB — **per·turb·able** \-'tər-bə-bəl\ *adj*

per·tur·ba·tion \ˌpərt-ər-'bā-shən, ˌpər-tər-\ *n* **1** : the action of perturbing : the state of being perturbed **2** : a disturbance of the regular motion of a celestial body produced by some force additional to that which causes its regular motion — **per·tur·ba·tion·al** \-shnəl, -shən-l\ *adj*

per·tus·sis \pər-'təs-əs\ *n* : WHOOPING COUGH [Latin *per-* + *tussis* "cough"]

pe·ruke \pə-'rük\ *n* : WIG [Middle French *perruque,* from Italian *parrucca*]

pe·ruse \pə-'rüz\ *vt* **1** : to examine or study attentively and in detail **2** : READ 1a (1) [Middle English *perusen*] — **pe·rus·al** \-'rü-zəl\ *n* — **pe·rus·er** *n*

per·vade \pər-'vād\ *vt* : to spread or become diffused throughout every part of [Latin *pervadere* (past participle *pervasus*) "to go through, pervade", from *per-* "through" + *vadere* "to go"] — **per·va·sion** \-'vā-zhən\ *n* — **per·va·sive** \-'vā-siv, -ziv\ *adj* — **per·va·sive·ly** *adv* — **per·va·sive·ness** *n*

per·verse \pər-'vərs, 'pər-,\ *adj* **1** : turned away from what is right or good : CORRUPT **2 a** : obstinate in opposing what is right, reasonable, or accepted : WRONGHEADED **b** : arising from or showing stubbornness or obstinacy **3** : marked by peevishness or petulance : CRANKY [Latin *perversus,* from *pervertere* "to pervert"] — **per·verse·ly** *adv* — **per·verse·ness** *n* — **per·ver·si·ty** \pər-'vər-sət-ē, -stē\ *n*

per·ver·sion \pər-'vər-zhən\ *n* **1** : the action of perverting : the condition of being perverted **2** : a perverted form of something; *esp* : atypical sexual behavior

¹per·vert \pər-'vərt\ *vt* **1 a** : to cause to turn aside or away from what is good or true or morally right : CORRUPT **b** : to cause to turn aside or away from what is generally done or accepted : MISDIRECT **2 a** : to divert to a wrong end or purpose : MISUSE **b** : to twist the meaning or sense of : MISINTERPRET [Middle French *pervertir,* from Latin *pervertere* "to overturn, corrupt, pervert", from *per-* + *vertere* "to turn"] — **per·ver·sive** \-'vər-siv, -ziv\ *adj* — **per·vert·er** *n*

²per·vert \'pər-,vərt\ *n* : one that is perverted; *esp* : one given to some form of sexual perversion

per·vert·ed \pər-'vərt-əd\ *adj* **1** : CORRUPT 1, TWISTED **2** : marked by perversion — **per·vert·ed·ly** *adv* — **per·vert·ed·ness** *n*

per·vi·ous \'pər-vē-əs\ *adj* : allowing entrance or passage : PERMEABLE ⟨*pervious* rock⟩ [Latin *pervius,* from *per-* "through" + *via* "way"] — **per·vi·ous·ness** *n*

Pe·sach \'pā-,säk\ *n* : PASSOVER [Hebrew *pesah*]

pe·se·ta \pə-'sāt-ə\ *n* **1** : the basic monetary unit of Spain **2** : a coin or note representing one peseta [Spanish, from *peso* "peso"]

pes·ky \'pes-kē\ *adj* **pes·ki·er; -est** : TROUBLESOME, VEXATIOUS [probably derived from *pest*] — **pes·ki·ly** \-kə-lē\ *adv* — **pes·ki·ness** \-kē-nəs\ *n*

pe·so \'pā-sō\ *n, pl* **pesos 1** : an old silver coin of Spain and Spanish America equal to eight reals **2 a** : the basic monetary unit of Bolivia, Colombia, Cuba, Dominican Republic, Mexico, Philippines, and Uruguay **b** : a coin or note representing one peso [Spanish, literally, "weight", from Latin *pensum,* from *pendere* "to weigh"]

pes·si·mism \'pes-ə-,miz-əm\ *n* **1** : an inclination to emphasize bad, disagreeable, or unpleasant aspects, conditions, and possibilities or to expect the worst **2** : a belief that evil is more common or powerful than good [French *pessimisme,* from Latin *pessimus* "worst"] — **pes·si·mist** \-məst\ *n*

pes·si·mis·tic \ˌpes-ə-'mis-tik\ *adj* : marked by, given to, or exhibiting pessimism ⟨a *pessimistic* report on the economy⟩ ⟨*pessimistic* about our chances of winning⟩ — **pes·si·mis·ti·cal·ly** \-ti-kə-lē, -klē\ *adv*

pest \'pest\ *n* **1** : an epidemic disease with a high mortality; *esp* : PLAGUE **2** : something resembling a pest in destructiveness; *esp* : a plant or animal harmful to humans **3** : one that pesters or annoys : NUISANCE [Middle French *peste,* from Latin *pestis*]

pes·ter \'pes-tər\ *vt* **pes·tered; pes·ter·ing** \-tə-ring, -tring\ : ANNOY, BOTHER [Middle French *empestrer* "to hobble (a horse), embarrass", derived from Latin *pastor* "herdsman"]

pest·hole \'pest-,hōl\ *n* : a place in which pestilences are common

\ə\ abut	\ng\ sing
\ər\ further	\ō\ bone
\a\ mat	\o'\ saw
\ā\ take	\oi\ coin
\ä\ cot, cart	\th\ thin
\au\ out	\th\ this
\ch\ chin	\ü\ food
\e\ pet	\u'\ foot
\ē\ easy	\y\ yet
\g\ go	\yü\ few
\i\ tip	\yu'\ cure
\ī\ life	\zh\ vision
\j\ job	

pest·house \-,haús\ *n* : a shelter or hospital for those infected with a contagious or epidemic disease

pes·ti·cide \'pes-tə-,sīd\ *n* : an agent used to destroy pests — **pes·ti·cid·al** \,pes-tə-'sīd-l\ *adj*

pes·tif·er·ous \pe-'stif-rəs, -ə-rəs\ *adj* 1 : dangerous to society : PERNICIOUS 2 : carrying or causing infection 3 : causing annoyance : TROUBLESOME — **pes·tif·er·ous·ly** *adv* — **pes·tif·er·ous·ness** *n*

pes·ti·lence \'pes-tə-ləns\ *n* : a contagious or infectious epidemic disease that spreads quickly and has devastating effects; *esp* : BUBONIC PLAGUE

pes·ti·lent \-lənt\ *adj* 1 : dangerous or destructive to life : DEADLY ⟨a *pestilent* drug⟩; *also* : being or conveying a pestilence ⟨a *pestilent* disease⟩ ⟨*pestilent* infections⟩ 2 : harmful or dangerous to society : PERNICIOUS ⟨the *pestilent* influence of the slums⟩ 3 : that is a pest ⟨a *pestilent* child⟩ [Latin *pestilens* "pestilential", from *pestis* "plague"] — **pes·ti·lent·ly** *adv*

pes·ti·len·tial \,pes-tə-'len-chəl\ *adj* : causing or likely to cause pestilence : PESTILENT — **pes·ti·len·tial·ly** \-lench-lē, -ə-lē\ *adv*

pes·tle \'pes-əl, 'pes-tl\ *n* : a usually club-shaped implement for pounding or grinding substances in a mortar [Middle French *pestel*, from Latin *pistillum*] — **pestle** *vb*

¹**pet** \'pet\ *n* 1 : a domesticated animal kept for pleasure rather than utility 2 **a** : a pampered and usually spoiled child **b** : a person who is treated with unusual kindness or consideration : DARLING [perhaps from Middle English *pety* "small"]

²**pet** *adj* 1 : kept or treated as a pet ⟨a *pet* dog⟩ 2 : expressing fondness or endearment ⟨a *pet* name⟩ 3 : FAVORITE ⟨a *pet* project⟩ ⟨my *pet* peeve⟩

³**pet** *vb* **pet·ted; pet·ting** 1 : to stroke in a gentle or loving manner 2 : to treat with unusual kindness and consideration : PAMPER 3 : to engage in amorous embracing, caressing, and kissing — **pet·ter** *n*

⁴**pet** *n* : a fit of peevishness, sulkiness, or anger [origin unknown]

pet·al \'pet-l\ *n* : one of the often brightly colored modified leaves making up the corolla of a flower [Greek *petalon*] — **pet·aled** *or* **pet·alled** \-ld\ *adj* — **pet·al·like** \-l-,līk, -l-,īk\ *adj*

pe·tard \pə-'tärd, -'tär\ *n* : a case containing an explosive to break down a door or gate or breach a wall [Middle French, from *peter* "to break wind", from *pet* "expulsion of intestinal gas", from Latin *peditum*, from *pedere* "to break wind"]

pet·cock \'pet-,käk\ *n* : a small cock, faucet, or valve for letting out air, releasing compression, or draining [*pet-* (perhaps from *petty*) + *cock*]

pe·ter \'pēt-ər\ *vi* : to diminish gradually and come to an end : give out ⟨the stream *peters* out⟩ [origin unknown]

Pe·ter \'pēt-ər\ *n* — see BIBLE table

Pe·ter's pence *n* 1 : an annual tribute of a penny formerly paid by each householder in England to the papal see 2 : a voluntary annual contribution made by Roman Catholics to the pope [from the tradition that Saint Peter founded the papal see]

pet·i·ole \'pet-ē-,ōl\ *n* 1 : the stem of a leaf 2 : STALK; *esp* : a narrow segment joining the abdomen and thorax in some insects (as wasps) [Latin *petiolus* "small foot, fruit stalk", derived from *pes* "foot"] — **pet·i·o·late** \'pet-ē-ə-,lāt, ,pet-ē-'ō-lət\ *adj* — **pet·i·oled** \'pet-ē-,ōld\ *adj*

pet·it \'pet-ē, 'pet-ət\ *adj* : PETTY 1 — chiefly in legal compounds [Middle French, "small"]

pe·tite \pə-'tēt\ *adj* : having a small trim figure — usually used of a woman [French, feminine of *petit* "small"] — **pe·tite·ness** *n*

pe·tit four \,pet-ē-'fòr, -'fòr\ *n, pl* **petits fours** *or* **petit fours** \-ē-'fòrz, -'fòrz\ : a small frosted and ornamented cake cut from pound or sponge cake [French, literally, "small oven"]

¹**pe·ti·tion** \pə-'tish-ən\ *n* 1 : an earnest request : ENTREATY 2 : a formal written request made to a superior or authority 3 : something asked or requested [Middle French, from Latin *petitio*, from *petere* "to seek, request"] — **pe·ti·tion·ary** \-'tish-ə-,ner-ē\ *adj*

²**petition** *vb* **pe·ti·tioned; pe·ti·tion·ing** \-'tish-ning, -ə-ning\ : to make a request to or for : SOLICIT; *esp* : to make a formal written request — **pe·ti·tion·er** \-'tish-nər, -ə-nər\ *n*

pet·it jury \'pet-ē-\ *n* : a jury of 12 persons who listen to the testimony in a trial and try to determine which side is in the right

pe·tit mal \pə-,tē-'mal, -'mäl\ *n* : a mild form of epilepsy [French, literally, "small illness"]

pet·it point \'pet-ē-,pòint\ *n* : TENT STITCH; *also* : embroidery made with this stitch [French, literally, "small point"]

petr- *or* **petri-** *or* **petro-** *combining form* : stone : rock ⟨*petro*logy⟩ [Greek *petros* "stone" and *petra* "rock"]

pe·trel \'pe-trəl, 'pē-\ *n* : any of various small long-winged seabirds (as the storm petrel) that fly far from land [alteration of earlier *pitteral*]

Pe·tri dish \,pē-trē-\ *n* : a small shallow dish of thin glass with a loose cover used especially for cultures in bacteriology [Julius R. *Petri*, died 1921, German bacteriologist]

pet·ri·fac·tion \,pe-trə-'fak-shən\ *n* 1 : the process of petrifying or state of being petrified 2 : something that is petrified — **pet·ri·fac·tive** \-'fak-tiv\ *adj*

pet·ri·fi·ca·tion \,pe-trə-fə-'kā-shən\ *n* : PETRIFACTION

pet·ri·fy \'pe-trə-,fī\ *vb* **-fied; -fy·ing** 1 : to convert (an organic object) into stony material 2 : to make or become rigid or inert like stone : **a** : to make lifeless or inactive : DEADEN **b** : to confound with fear, amazement, or awe : PARALYZE

Pe·trine \'pē-,trīn\ *adj* : of, relating to, or characteristic of the apostle Peter or the doctrines associated with his name [Late Latin *Petrus* "Peter"]

pet·ro·chem·i·cal \,pe-trō-'kem-i-kəl\ *n* : a chemical isolated or derived from petroleum or natural gas

pe·trog·ra·phy \pə-'träg-rə-fē\ *n* : the description and systematic classification of rocks — compare PETROLOGY — **pe·trog·ra·pher** \-fər\ *n* — **pet·ro·graph·ic** \,pe-trə-'graf-ik\ *or* **pet·ro·graph·i·cal** \-'graf-i-kəl\ *adj*

pet·rol \'pe-trəl, -,träl\ *n, British* : GASOLINE [French *essence de pétrole*, literally, "essence of petroleum"]

pet·ro·la·tum \,pe-trə-'lāt-əm\ *n* : a tasteless, odorless, and oily or greasy substance from petroleum that is used especially in ointments and dressings [New Latin, from Medieval Latin *petroleum*]

pe·tro·leum \pə-'trō-lē-əm, -'trōl-yəm\ *n* : an oily flammable liquid widely distributed in the upper strata of the earth that is a complex mixture mostly of hydrocarbons and is the source of gasoline and lubricants and a major industrial raw material [Medieval Latin, from Latin *petr-* "petr-" + *oleum* "oil"]

petroleum jelly *n* : PETROLATUM

pe·trol·o·gy \pə-'träl-ə-jē\ *n* : a science that deals with the origin, history, occurrence, structure, chemical composition, and classification of rocks — compare PETROGRAPHY — **pet·ro·log·ic** \,pe-trə-'läj-ik\ *or* **pet·ro·log·i·cal** \-'läj-i-kəl\ *adj* — **pet·ro·log·i·cal·ly** \-i-kə-lē, -klē\ *adv* — **pe·trol·o·gist** \pə-'träl-ə-jəst\ *n*

¹**pet·ti·coat** \'pet-ē-,kōt\ *n* 1 **a** : an outer skirt formerly worn by women and small children **b** : a skirt worn under a dress or outer skirt 2 : something (as a valance) resembling a petticoat [Middle English *petycote* "short tunic, petticoat", from *pety* "small" + *cote* "coat"]

²**petticoat** *adj* : exercised by women ⟨*petticoat* rule⟩

pet·ti·fog \'pet-ē-,fòg, -,fäg\ *vi* **-fogged; -fog·ging** 1 : to engage in legal trickery 2 : to quibble over insignificant details : CAVIL [back-formation from *pettifogger*, probably from *petty* + obsolete *fogger* "pettifogger"]

— **pet·ti·fog·ger** *n* — **pet·ti·fog·gery** \-,fȯg-rē, -,fäg-, -ə-rē\ *n*

petting zoo *n* : a collection of farm animals or gentle exotic animals for children to pet and feed

pet·tish \'pet-ish\ *adj* : FRETFUL 1, PEEVISH — **pet·tish·ly** *adv* — **pet·tish·ness** *n*

pet·ty \'pet-ē\ *adj* **pet·ti·er; -est** 1 : having secondary rank or importance : MINOR, SUBORDINATE ⟨a *petty* prince⟩ 2 : having little or no importance or significance 3 : marked by or reflective of narrow interests and sympathies [Middle English *pety* "small, minor", from Middle French *petit* "small"] — **pet·ti·ly** \'pet-l-ē\ *adv* — **pet·ti·ness** \'pet-ē-nəs\ *n*

petty cash *n* : cash kept on hand for payment of minor items

petty officer *n* : an officer in the Navy or Coast Guard appointed from among the enlisted ranks that is comparable to a noncommissioned officer in the Army

petty officer first class *n* : an enlisted rank in the Navy and Coast Guard above petty officer second class and below chief petty officer

petty officer second class *n* : an enlisted rank in the Navy and Coast Guard above petty officer third class and below petty officer first class

petty officer third class *n* : an enlisted rank in the Navy and Coast Guard above seaman and below petty officer second class

pet·u·lant \'pech-ə-lənt\ *adj* : characterized by temporary or capricious ill humor : PEEVISH [Latin *petulans*] — **pet·u·lance** \-ləns\ *n* — **pet·u·lant·ly** *adv*

pe·tu·nia \pə-'tü-nyə, -'tyü-\ *n* : any of a genus of tropical American herbs of the potato family widely grown for their showy funnel-shaped flowers [obsolete French *petun* "tobacco", from Tupi *petyn*]

pew \'pyü\ *n* 1 : a compartment in the auditorium of a church providing seats for several persons 2 : one of the benches with backs and sometimes doors fixed in rows in a church [Middle French *puie* "balustrade", from Latin *podium* "parapet, podium"]

pe·wee \'pē-wē, -,wē\ *n* : any of various small olive green flycatchers [imitative]

pew·ter \'pyüt-ər\ *n* 1 : any of various tin-based alloys; *esp* : a dull alloy with lead formerly used for domestic utensils 2 : wares (as table utensils) of pewter [Middle French *peutre*] — **pewter** *adj*

pew·ter·er \'pyüt-ər-ər\ *n* : one that makes pewter wares

pey·o·te \pā-'ōt-ē\ *also* **pey·otl** \-'ōt-l\ *n* : any of a genus of American cacti including the mescal; *also* : a drug obtained from mescal tops [Mexican Spanish *peyote*, from Nahuatl *peyotl*]

pfen·nig \'fen-ig, -ik\ *n, pl* **pfennigs** *or* **pfen·ni·ge** \'fen-i-gə\ 1 : a monetary unit equal to ¹⁄₁₀₀ mark 2 : a coin representing one pfennig [German]

PG \'pē-'jē\ *trademark* — used to certify that a motion picture is of such a nature that all ages may be allowed admission but parental guidance is suggested

PG-13 \-,thər-'tēn, -,thərt-\ *trademark* — used to certify that a motion picture is of such a nature that persons of all ages may be admitted but parental guidance is suggested especially for children under 13

pH \pē-'āch, 'pē-\ *n* : a number used in expressing acidity or alkalinity that is the negative logarithm of the effective hydrogen-ion concentration on a scale whose values run from 0 to 14 with 7 representing neutrality, numbers less than 7 increasing acidity, and numbers greater than 7 increasing alkalinity; *also* : the condition with respect to acidity or alkalinity □ ORIGIN In 1909 the Danish chemist Søren Peter Lauritz Sørensen developed the concept of pH. He suggested that the concentration of hydrogen ions in a solution should be expressed in terms of the negative logarithm (the power to which 10 is raised). Sørensen's *p* stood for *Potenz,* the German word for "power", and his *H* for *hydrogen.*

phage \'fāj *also* 'fāzh\ *n* : BACTERIOPHAGE

-phage \,fāj *also* ,fāzh\ *n combining form* : one that eats ⟨bacterio*phage*⟩ [Greek *phagein* "to eat"]

phago·cyte \'fag-ə-,sīt\ *n* : a cell (as a white blood cell) that takes in and consumes debris and foreign bodies [Greek *phagein* "to eat"] — **phago·cyt·ic** \,fag-ə-'sit-ik\ *adj*

phago·cy·to·sis \,fag-ə-sī-'tō-səs\ *n* : the taking and usually the destruction of particulate matter by phagocytes — **phago·cy·tot·ic** \-'tät-ik\ *adj*

-ph·a·gous \f-ə-gəs\ *adj combining form* : eating [Greek *phagein* "to eat"]

pha·lan·ger \fə-'lan-jər\ *n* : any of various marsupial mammals of the Australian region ranging in size from a mouse to a large cat [derived from Greek *phalanx* "log, line of battle, bone of the finger or toe"]

pha·lanx \'fā-,langs, -,langks\ *n, pl* **pha·lanx·es** *or* **pha·lan·ges** \fə-'lan-,jēz, fā-\ 1 : a body of heavily armed infantry formed in close deep ranks and files; *also* : a body of troops in close array 2 *pl phalanges* : one of the bones of a finger or toe 3 *pl usu phalanxes* **a** : a massed arrangement of persons, animals, or things **b** : an organized body of persons [Latin, from Greek, literally, "log"] — **pha·lan·ge·al** \fə-'lan-jē-əl, -jəl\ *adj*

phal·a·rope \'fal-ə-,rōp\ *n* : any of various small shorebirds that resemble sandpipers but have lobed toes and are good swimmers [French, derived from Greek *phalaris* "coot" + *pod-, pous* "foot"]

phal·lus \'fal-əs\ *n, pl* **phal·li** \'fal-,ī, -,ē\ *or* **phal·lus·es** 1 : a symbol or representation of the human penis 2 : PENIS [Latin, from Greek *phallos*] — **phal·lic** \'fal-ik\ *adj*

Phan·er·o·zo·ic \,fan-ə-rə-'zō-ik\ *adj* : of, relating to, or being an eon of geologic history that comprises the Paleozoic, Mesozoic, and Cenozoic or the corresponding system of rocks — see GEOLOGIC TIME table [Greek *phaneros* visible] — **Phanerozoic** *n*

phan·tasm \'fan-,taz-əm\ *n* : a product of fantasy: as **a** : delusive appearance : ILLUSION **b** : GHOST 2, SPECTER **c** : a figment of the imagination : FANTASY 2 : a deceptive or illusory appearance of a thing [Old French *fantasme,* from Latin *phantasma,* from Greek, from *phantazein* "to present to the mind", from *phainein* "to show"] — **phan·tas·mal** \fan-'taz-məl\ *adj* — **phan·tas·mic** \-'taz-mik\ *adj*

phan·tas·ma·go·ria \fan-,taz-mə-'gōr-ē-ə, -'gȯr-\ *n* 1 : an optical effect by which figures on a screen appear to dwindle into the distance or to rush toward the observer with enormous increase of size 2 **a** : a constantly shifting complex succession of things seen or imagined **b** : a scene that constantly changes or fluctuates [French *phantasmagorie,* derived from *phantasme* "phantasm", from Old French *fantasme*] — **phan·tas·ma·go·ric** \-'gōr-ik, -'gȯr-, -'gär-\ *adj*

phantasy *variant of* FANTASY

¹phan·tom \'fant-əm\ *n* 1 **a** : something (as a specter) apparent to sense but with no substantial existence **b** : something elusive or visionary : WILL-O'-THE-WISP **c** : an object of continual dread or abhorrence : BUGBEAR 2 : something existing in appearance only 3 : a representation of something abstract, ideal, or incorporeal [Middle French *fantosme,* from Latin *phantasma* "phantasm"]

²phantom *adj* 1 : of the nature of, suggesting, or being a phantom 2 : FICTITIOUS, DUMMY ⟨*phantom* voters⟩

phar·aoh \'fear-ō, 'faar-ō, 'fā-rō\ *n, often cap* : a ruler of ancient Egypt [Late Latin *pharaon-, pharao,* from Greek *pharaō,* from Hebrew *parʿōh,* from Egyptian pr-ʿ;] — **phar·a·on·ic** \,fer-ā-'än-ik, ,far-\ *adj, often cap*

phar·i·sa·ic \,far-ə-'sā-ik\ *adj* 1 *cap* : of or relating to the Pharisees 2 : PHARISAICAL

phar·i·sa·i·cal \-'sā-ə-kəl\ *adj* : marked by hypocritical censorious self-righteousness — **phar·i·sa·i·cal·ly** \-kə-lē, -klē\ *adv* — **phar·i·sa·i·cal·ness** \-kəl-nəs\ *n*

petunia

\ə\ abut		\ng\ sing	
\ər\ further		\ō\ bone	
\a\ mat		\ȯ\ saw	
\ā\ take		\ȯi\ coin	
\ä\ cot, cart		\th\ thin	
\au̇\ out		\th\ this	
\ch\ chin		\ü\ food	
\e\ pet		\u̇\ foot	
\ē\ easy		\y\ yet	
\g\ go		\yü\ few	
\i\ tip		\yu̇\ cure	
\ī\ life		\zh\ vision	
\j\ job			

phar·i·sa·ism \'far-ə-sā-,iz-əm, -,sā-\ *n* **1** *cap* : the doctrines or practices of the Pharisees **2** *often cap* : pharisaical character, spirit, or attitude

phar·i·see \'far-ə-,sē\ *n* **1** *cap* : a member of a Jewish sect of New Testament times noted for strict observance of rites and ceremonies of the written law and for insistence on the validity of the oral tradition **2** : a pharisaical person [Old French *farise*, from Late Latin *pharisaeus*, from Greek *pharisaios*, from Aramaic *pĕrīshayyā*, pl. of *pĕrīshā*, literally, "separated"]

¹phar·ma·ceu·ti·cal \,fär-mə-'süt-i-kəl\ *or* **phar·ma·ceu·tic** \-'süt-ik\ *adj* : of or relating to pharmacy or pharmacists [Late Latin *pharmaceuticus*, from Greek *pharmakeutikos*, from *pharmakeuein* "to administer drugs"] — **phar·ma·ceu·ti·cal·ly** \-i-kə-lē, -klē\ *adv*

²pharmaceutical *n* : a medicinal drug

phar·ma·cist \'fär-mə-səst\ *n* : a specialist in pharmacy

pharmaco- *combining form* : medicine : drug (*pharmaco*logy) [Greek *pharmakon*]

phar·ma·col·o·gy \,fär-mə-'käl-ə-jē\ *n* **1** : the science of drugs especially as related to their use in medicine **2** : the properties and reactions of drugs especially with relation to their medicinal value — **phar·ma·co·log·i·cal** \-kə-'läj-i-kəl\ *or* **phar·ma·co·log·ic** \-'läj-ik\ *adj* — **phar·ma·co·log·i·cal·ly** \-i-kə-lē, -klē\ *adv* — **phar·ma·col·o·gist** \-'käl-ə-jəst\ *n*

phar·ma·co·poe·ia *also* **phar·ma·co·pe·ia** \,fär-mə-kə-'pē-ə\ *n* **1** : a book describing drugs, chemicals, and medicinal preparations **2** : a collection or stock of drugs [Late Greek *pharmakopoiia* "preparation of drugs", from Greek *pharmakon* "drug" + *poiein* "to make"] — **phar·ma·co·poe·ial** \-əl\ *adj*

phar·ma·cy \'fär-mə-sē\ *n, pl* **-cies** **1** : the art, practice, or profession of preparing, preserving, compounding, and dispensing drugs; *esp* : the profession of mixing drugs according to a doctor's prescription **2 a** : a place where medicines are compounded or dispensed **b** : DRUGSTORE **3** : PHARMACOPOEIA 2 [Late Latin *pharmacia* "administration of drugs", from Greek *pharmakeia*, from *pharmakeuein* "to administer drugs", from *pharmakon* "magic charm, poison, drug"]

phar·yn·gi·tis \,far-ən-'jīt-əs\ *n* : inflammation of the pharynx

phar·ynx \'far-ings, -ingks\ *n, pl* **pha·ryn·ges** \fə-'rin-,jēz\ *also* **phar·ynx·es** : the space in a vertebrate just behind the cavity of the mouth into which the nostrils, eustachian tubes, esophagus, and trachea open; *also* : a corresponding part of an invertebrate [Greek, "throat, pharynx"] — **pha·ryn·geal** \fə-'rin-jē-əl, -jəl; ,far-ən-'jē-əl\ *adj*

¹phase \'fāz\ *n* **1** : the apparent shape of the moon or a planet at any time in its series of changes with respect to illumination (the new moon and the full moon are *phases* of the moon) **2 a** : a stage or interval in a development or cycle **b** : an aspect or part under consideration **3** : the stage of progress in a regularly recurring motion or a cyclic process (as a wave or vibration) in relation to a reference point **4 a** : a homogeneous physically distinct portion of matter present in a nonhomogeneous system **b** : one of the fundamental states of matter usually considered to include the solid, liquid, and gaseous forms [Greek *phasis* "appearance of a star, phase of the moon", from *phainein* "to show"] — **pha·sic** \'fā-zik\ *adj*

²phase *vb* **phased; phas·ing** **1** : to do in steps according to a plan (successfully *phased* orphaned animals back to the wild) **2** : to introduce in stages — often used with *in* (*phase* in new models)

phase microscope *n* : a microscope that translates differences in phase of the light transmitted through or reflected by the object into differences of intensity in the image — called also *phase-contrast microscope*

pheas·ant \'fez-nt\ *n, pl* **pheasant** *or* **pheasants** : any of numerous large long-tailed brilliantly colored Old World birds related to the domestic fowl many of

which are reared as ornamental or game birds [Old French *fesan*, from Latin *phasianus*, from Greek *phasianos*, from *Phasis*, river in Colchis]

phel·lem \'fel-,em\ *n* : CORK 1b [Greek *phellos* "cork" + English *-em* (as in *phloem*)]

phel·lo·gen \'fel-ə-jən\ *n* : an outer layer of meristem that produces cells inwardly and outwardly in many roots and stems [Greek *phellos* "cork"]

phen- *or* **pheno-** *combining form* : related to or derived from benzene (*phen*ol) : containing phenyl (*pheno*barbital) [French *phène* "benzene", from Greek *phainein* "to show"; from its occurrence in illuminating gas]

phe·no·bar·bi·tal \,fē-nō-'bär-bə-,tól\ *n* : a crystalline barbiturate drug used as a hypnotic and sedative

phe·nol \'fē-,nól, -,nól, fi-'\ *n* **1** : a caustic poisonous crystalline acidic compound C_6H_5OH present in coal tar and wood tar that in dilute solution is used as a disinfectant **2** : any of various acidic compounds analogous to phenol and regarded as hydroxyl derivatives of aromatic hydrocarbons — **phe·no·lic** \fi-'nō-lik, -'näl-ik\ *adj*

phe·no·lic \fi-'nō-lik, -'näl-ik\ *n* : a resin or plastic made by condensation of a phenol with an aldehyde and used especially for molding and electrical insulation and in coatings and adhesives

phe·nol·phtha·lein \,fē-,nól-'thal-ē-ən, -'thal-,ēn, -'thāl-\ *n* : a white or yellowish white crystalline compound used as a laxative and as an acid-base indicator because its solution is red in alkalies and is decolorized by acids [*phenol* + *phthalein*, a kind of dye, from *phthalic acid*, an acid, short for obsolete *naphthalic acid*, from *naphthalene*]

phe·nom·e·nal \fi-'näm-ən-l\ *adj* **1** : of, relating to, or being a phenomenon **2** : EXTRAORDINARY 1, REMARKABLE (a *phenomenal* memory) — **phe·nom·e·nal·ly** \-l-ē\ *adv*

phe·nom·e·non \fi-'näm-ə-,nän, -nən\ *n, pl* **-na** \-nə, -,nä\ *or* **-nons** **1** : an observable fact or event **2** : a fact or event that can be scientifically described and explained **3 a** : a rare or significant fact or event **b** *pl* **phenomenons** : an exceptional person, thing, or event : PRODIGY [Late Latin *phaenomenon*, from Greek *phainomenon*, from *phainesthai* "to appear", from *phainein* "to show"]

phe·no·thi·azine \,fē-nō-'thī-ə-,zēn\ *n* : any of various tranquilizing drugs (as chlorpromazine) used especially in the treatment of schizophrenia [*phen-* + *thi-* + *azine*, a type of nitrogen compound, derived from French *azote* "nitrogen", derived from Greek *a-* + *zōē* "life"]

phe·no·type \'fē-nə-,tīp\ *n* : the visible characters of an organism resulting from the interaction of genotype and environment [German *phänotypus*, from Greek *phainein* "to show" + *typos* "type"] — **phe·no·typ·ic** \,fē-nə-'tip-ik\ *adj* — **phe·no·typ·i·cal·ly** \-i-kə-lē, -klē\ *adv*

phe·nyl \'fen-l, 'fēn-\ *n* : a univalent radical C_6H_5 derived from benzene by removal of one hydrogen atom — **phe·nyl·ic** \fi-'nil-ik\ *adj*

phe·nyl·al·a·nine \,fen-l-'al-ə-,nēn, ,fēn-\ *n* : an essential amino acid $C_9H_{11}NO_2$ obtained by the hydrolysis of proteins

phe·nyl·ke·ton·uria \-,kēt-n-'ùr-ē-ə, -'yùr-\ *n* : an inherited disorder of metabolism that is characterized by inability to oxidize a metabolic product of phenylalanine and by severe mental deficiency [*phenyl* + *ketone* + *-uria* (from Greek *ouron* "urine")]

phen·yl·thio·car·ba·mide \,fen-l-,thī-ō-'kär-bə-,mīd\ *n* : a crystalline compound $C_7H_8N_2S$ that is extremely bitter or tasteless depending on the presence or absence of a single dominant gene in the taster

pher·o·mone \'fer-ə-,mōn\ *n* : a chemical substance (as a scent) that is produced by an animal and serves to stimulate behavior of other individuals of the same

pheasant

species [*phero-* (from Greek *pherein* "to carry") + *-mone* (as in *hormone*)]

phi \'fī\ *n* : the 21st letter of the Greek alphabet — Φ or φ

phi·al \'fī-əl, 'fīl\ *n* : VIAL [Latin *phiala*, from Greek *phialē*]

phil- *or* **philo-** *combining form* : loving : having an affinity for [Greek, from *philos* "dear, friendly"]

¹-phil \,fil\ *or* **-phile** \,fīl\ *n combining form* : lover : one having an affinity for ⟨Franco*phile*⟩ [Greek *philos*]

²-phil *or* **-phile** *adj combining form* : being strongly attracted to

phil·a·del·phus \,fil-ə-'del-fəs\ *n* : any of a genus of shrubs of the saxifrage family including several widely grown for their showy white flowers — called also *mock orange, syringa* [Greek *philadelphos* "brotherly", from *phil-* + *adelphos* "brother"]

phi·lan·der \fə-'lan-dər\ *vi* **phi·lan·dered; phi·lan·der·ing** \-də-riŋ, -driŋ\ : to make love without serious intent [from obsolete *philander* "lover, philanderer", probably from the name *Philander*] — **phi·lan·der·er** \-dər-ər\ *n*

phil·an·throp·ic \,fil-ən-'thräp-ik\ *also* **phil·an·throp·i·cal** \-'thräp-i-kəl\ *adj* : of, relating to, or characterized by philanthropy : BENEVOLENT, CHARITABLE — **phil·an·throp·i·cal·ly** \-i-kə-lē, -klē\ *adv*

phi·lan·thro·pist \fə-'lan-thrə-pəst, -'lant-\ *n* : one who practices philanthropy

phi·lan·thro·py \-pē\ *n, pl* **-pies** **1** : goodwill to all people; *esp* : active effort to promote human welfare **2 a** : a philanthropic act or gift **b** : an organization distributing or supported by philanthropic funds

phi·lat·e·ly \fə-'lat-l-ē\ *n* : the collection and study of postage and imprinted stamps [French *philatélie*, from Greek *phil-* + *atelia* "tax exemption", derived from *a-* + *telos* "tax"; from the fact that a stamped letter frees the recipient from paying the mailing charges] — **phil·a·tel·ic** \,fil-ə-'tel-ik\ *adj* — **phi·lat·e·list** \fə-'lat-l-əst\ *n*

Phi·le·mon \fə-'lē-mən, fī-\ *n* — see BIBLE table

Phi·lip·pi·ans \fə-'lip-ē-ənz\ *n* — see BIBLE table

phi·lip·pic \fə-'lip-ik\ *n* : TIRADE [Middle French *philippique*, from Greek *philippikoi logoi*, speeches of Demosthenes against Philip II of Macedon, literally, "speeches relating to Philip"]

Phil·ip·pine mahogany \,fil-ə-,pēn-\ *n* : any of several Philippine timber trees with wood resembling that of the true mahoganies; *also* : this wood

phi·lis·tine \'fil-ə-,stēn; fə-'lis-tən, -,tēn\ *n* **1** *cap* : a native or inhabitant of ancient Philistia **2** *often cap* **a** : an individual guided by material rather than intellectual or artistic values **b** : one uninformed in a special area of knowledge — **philistine** *adj, often cap* — **phi·lis·tin·ism** \-,stē-,niz-əm; -tə-,niz-, -,tē-\ *n, often cap*

phil·o·den·dron \,fil-ə-'den-drən\ *n, pl* **-drons** *or* **-dra** \-drə\ : any of various arums grown for their showy often variegated foliage [Greek *philodendros* "loving trees", from *phil-* + *dendron* "tree"]

phi·lol·o·gy \fə-'läl-ə-jē\ *n* **1** : the study of literature and of relevant fields **2** : LINGUISTICS; *esp* : historical and comparative linguistics [French *philologie*, from Latin *philologia* "love of learning and literature", from Greek, from *phil-* + *logos* "word, speech"] — **phil·o·log·i·cal** \,fil-ə-'läj-i-kəl\ *adj* — **phil·o·log·i·cal·ly** \-'läj-i-kə-lē, -klē\ *adv* — **phi·lol·o·gist** \fə-'läl-ə-jəst\ *n*

phi·los·o·pher \fə-'läs-ə-fər\ *n* **1 a** : one that seeks wisdom or enlightenment **b** : a student of philosophy **2** : a person who takes misfortunes with wisdom, calmness, and courage

philosophers' stone *n* : an imaginary stone, substance, or chemical preparation believed to have the power of transmuting base metals into gold and sought for by alchemists

phil·o·soph·ic \,fil-ə-'säf-ik\ *or* **phil·o·soph·i·cal** \-i-kəl\ *adj* **1** : of, relating to, or based on philosophy **2** : characterized by the attitude of a philosopher; *esp* : calm in the face of trouble — **phil·o·soph·i·cal·ly** \-i-kə-lē, -klē\ *adv*

phi·los·o·phize \fə-'läs-ə-,fīz\ *vi* **1** : to reason in the manner of a philosopher **2** : to expound a philosophy : MORALIZE — **phi·los·o·phiz·er** *n*

phi·los·o·phy \fə-'läs-ə-fē\ *n, pl* **-phies** **1** : the study of the nature of knowledge and existence and the principles of moral and esthetic value **2** : the philosophical teachings or principles of a person or group ⟨Greek *philosophy*⟩ **3** : the general principles of a field of study ⟨*philosophy* of history⟩ **4** : the most general beliefs, concepts, and attitudes of an individual or group [Old French *philosophie*, from Latin *philosophia*, from Greek, from *philosophos* "philosopher", from *phil-* + *sophia* "wisdom", from *sophos* "wise"]

phil·ter *or* **phil·tre** \'fil-tər\ *n* **1** : a potion, drug, or charm held to have the power to excite sexual passion **2** : a magic potion [Middle French *philtre*, from Latin *philtrum*, from Greek *philtron*]

phle·bi·tis \fli-'bīt-əs\ *n* : inflammation of a vein [Greek *phleb-, phleps* "vein"]

phlegm \'flem\ *n* **1** : viscid mucus secreted in abnormal quantity in the respiratory passages **2 a** : dull or apathetic coldness or indifference **b** : intrepid coolness : CALMNESS [Middle French *fleume*, from Late Latin *phlegmat-, phlegma*, from Greek, "flame, inflammation, phlegm", from *phlegein* "to burn"] — **phlegmy** \'flem-ē\ *adj*

phleg·mat·ic \fleg-'mat-ik\ *adj* : having or showing a slow and stolid temperament SYN see IMPASSIVE — **phleg·mat·i·cal·ly** \-i-kə-lē, -klē\ *adv*

phlo·em \'flō-,em\ *n* : a vascular tissue of higher plants that transports dissolved food material, contains sieve tubes, and lies mostly external to the cambium — compare XYLEM [German, from Greek *phloios* "bark"]

phloem ray *n* : a vascular ray or part of a vascular ray that is located in phloem — compare XYLEM RAY

phlo·gis·ton \flō-'jis-tən\ *n* : the hypothetical principle of fire regarded formerly as a material substance [Greek *phlogistos* "inflammable", from *phlogizein* "to set on fire", from *phlog-, phlox* "flame", from *phlegein* "to burn"]

phlox \'fläks\ *n, pl* **phlox** *or* **phlox·es** : any of a genus of American annual or perennial herbs with showy red, purple, white, or variegated flowers [Greek, "flame, wallflower"]

-phobe \,fōb\ *n combining form* : one fearing or averse to (something specified) ⟨anglo*phobe*⟩ [Greek *phobos* "fear"] — **-pho·bic** \'fō-bik\ *adj combining form*

pho·bia \'fō-bē-ə\ *n* : an unreasonable persistent fear of a particular thing [Greek *-phobia*, from *phobos* "fear"] — **pho·bic** \'fō-bik\ *adj*

phoe·be \'fē-bē\ *n* : any of several American flycatchers; *esp* : one of the eastern United States that has a slight crest and is plain grayish brown above and yellowish white below [alteration of *pewee*]

Phoe·ni·cian \fi-'nēsh-ən\ *n* **1** : a native or inhabitant of ancient Phoenicia **2** : the Semitic language of ancient Phoenicia — **Phoenician** *adj*

phoe·nix \'fē-niks\ *n* : a legendary bird that according to one account lived 500 years, burned itself to death, and rose youthfully alive from its own ashes [Old English *fenix*, from Latin *phoenix*, from Greek *phoinix*]

phon- *or* **phono-** *combining form* : sound : voice : speech ⟨*phon*ation⟩ ⟨*phono*graph⟩ [Greek *phōnē* "voice, sound"]

pho·na·tion \fō-'nā-shən\ *n* : the act or process of producing speech sounds ⟨organs of *phonation*⟩ — **pho·nate** \'fō-,nāt\ *vi*

¹phone \'fōn\ *n* **1** : EARPHONE **2** : TELEPHONE

²phone *vb* : TELEPHONE

phoebe

\ə\ abut	\ng\ sing
\ər\ further	\ō\ bone
\a\ mat	\ȯ\ saw
\ā\ take	\ȯi\ coin
\ä\ cot, cart	\th\ thin
\au̇\ out	\t̲h̲\ this
\ch\ chin	\ü\ food
\e\ pet	\u̇\ foot
\ē\ easy	\y\ yet
\g\ go	\yü\ few
\i\ tip	\yu̇\ cure
\ī\ life	\zh\ vision
\j\ job	

³phone *n* : a speech sound considered as a physical event without regard to its status in the structure of a language [Greek *phōnē*]

-phone \ˌfōn\ *n combining form* : sound ⟨homo*phone*⟩ — often in names of musical instruments and sound-transmitting and sound-receiving devices ⟨tele*phone*⟩ ⟨xylo*phone*⟩ [Greek *phōnē* "voice, sound"]

pho·neme \ˈfō-ˌnēm\ *n* : a member of the set of the smallest units of speech that serve to distinguish one utterance from another in a language or dialect ⟨\n\ and \t\ in *pin* and *pit* are different *phonemes*⟩ — compare ALLOPHONE [French *phonème,* from Greek *phōnēma* "speech sound", from *phōnein* "to sound"]

pho·ne·mic \fə-ˈnē-mik\ *adj* **1** : of, relating to, or having the characteristics of a phoneme **2** : being different phonemes (in English \n\ and \ng\ are *phonemic*) — **pho·ne·mi·cal·ly** \-mi-kə-lē, -klē\ *adv*

pho·net·ic \fə-ˈnet-ik\ *adj* **1 a** : of or relating to spoken language or speech sounds **b** : of or relating to phonetics **2** : representing speech sounds [Greek *phōnētikos,* from *phōnein* "to sound", from *phōnē* "voice"] — **pho·net·i·cal·ly** \-i-kə-lē, -klē\ *adv*

phonetic alphabet *n* : a set of symbols used for phonetic transcription

pho·ne·ti·cian \ˌfō-nə-ˈtish-ən\ *n* : a specialist in phonetics

pho·net·ics \fə-ˈnet-iks\ *n* **1** : the study and classification of speech sounds **2** : the system of speech sounds of a language or group of languages

phon·ic \ˈfän-ik\ *adj* **1** : of, relating to, or producing sound **2** : of or relating to the sounds of speech or to phonics — **phon·i·cal·ly** \-i-kə-lē, -klē\ *adv*

phon·ics \ˈfän-iks\ *n* : a method of teaching beginners to read and pronounce words by learning the phonetic value of letters, letter groups, and especially syllables

pho·no·gram \ˈfō-nə-ˌgram\ *n* : a character or symbol used to represent a word, syllable, or phoneme

pho·no·graph \ˈfō-nə-ˌgraf\ *n* : an instrument for reproducing sounds by means of the vibration of a needle following a spiral groove on a revolving disc

pho·no·graph·ic \ˌfō-nə-ˈgraf-ik\ *adj* **1** : of or relating to phonography **2** : of or relating to a phonograph — **pho·no·graph·i·cal·ly** \-i-kə-lē, -klē\ *adv*

pho·nog·ra·phy \fō-ˈnäg-rə-fē\ *n* : spelling based on pronunciation

pho·nol·o·gy \fə-ˈnäl-ə-jē, fō-\ *n* : the science of speech sounds including especially the history and theory of sound changes in a language or in two or more related languages — **pho·no·log·i·cal** \ˌfōn-l-ˈäj-i-kəl *also* ˌfän-l-\ *adj* — **pho·no·log·i·cal·ly** \-kə-lē, -klē\ *adv* — **pho·nol·o·gist** \fə-ˈnäl-ə-jəst, fō-\ *n*

¹pho·ny *or* **pho·ney** \ˈfō-nē\ *adj* **pho·ni·er; -est** : not genuine or real: as **a** : COUNTERFEIT ⟨a *phony* $10 bill⟩ **b** : probably dishonest ⟨a *phony* alibi⟩ **c** : FICTITIOUS ⟨*phony* publicity stories⟩ **d** : FALSE ⟨*phony* pearls⟩ [origin unknown] — **pho·ni·ly** \ˈfōn-l-ē\ *adv* — **pho·ni·ness** \ˈfō-nē-nəs\ *n*

²phony *or* **phoney** *n, pl* **phonies** *or* **phoneys** : one that is phony

phoo·ey \ˈfü-ē\ *interj* — used to express repudiation or disgust

-phore \ˌfōr, ˌfor\ *n combining form* : carrier ⟨sema*phore*⟩ [Greek *-phoros,* from *pherein* "to carry"]

phos·gene \ˈfäz-ˌjēn\ *n* : a colorless gas of unpleasant odor that is a severe irritant of the respiratory system and is used as a war gas [Greek *phōs* "light"; from its originally having been obtained by the action of sunlight]

phosph- *or* **phospho-** *combining form* : phosphorus ⟨*phosph*ide⟩ ⟨*phospho*lipid⟩

phos·pha·tase \ˈfäs-fə-ˌtās, -ˌtāz\ *n* : any of various enzymes that accelerate the hydrolysis and synthesis of organic phosphates or the transfer of phosphate groups

phos·phate \ˈfäs-ˌfāt\ *n* **1** : a salt or ester of a phosphoric acid **2** : an effervescent drink of carbonated water with a small amount of phosphoric acid or an acid phosphate flavored with fruit syrup **3** : a phosphatic material used for fertilizers

phos·phat·ic \fäs-ˈfat-ik, -ˈfāt-\ *adj* : of, relating to, or containing phosphoric acid or phosphates

phos·pha·tide \ˈfäs-fə-ˌtīd\ *n* : PHOSPHOLIPID — **phos·pha·tid·ic** \ˌfäs-fə-ˈtid-ik\ *adj*

phos·phide \ˈfäs-ˌfīd\ *n* : a compound of phosphorus usually with a more electropositive element or radical

phos·phite \-ˌfīt\ *n* : a salt or ester of phosphorous acid

phos·pho·glyc·er·al·de·hyde \ˈfäs-fō-ˌglis-ə-ˈral-də-ˌhīd\ *n* : a phosphate of glyceraldehyde $C_3H_7PO_6$ formed especially in the anaerobic metabolism of carbohydrates by the splitting of a phosphate of fructose containing two phosphate groups

phos·pho·gly·cer·ic acid \-glis-ˌer-ik-\ *n* : either of two isomeric phosphates $C_3H_7PO_7$ of glyceric acid that are formed as intermediates in photosynthesis and in carbohydrate metabolism

phos·pho·lip·id \ˌfäs-fō-ˈlip-əd\ *n* : a complex phosphoric ester lipid found in all living cells in association with stored fats — called also *phosphatide*

phos·phor \ˈfäs-fər, -ˌfor\ *n* : a phosphorescent substance; *esp* : one that emits light when excited by radiation [derived from Greek *phōsphoros* "light-bearing", from *phōs* "light" + *pherein* "to carry, bring"]

phosphor bronze *n* : a bronze of great hardness, elasticity, and toughness that contains a small amount of phosphorous

phos·pho·res·cence \ˌfäs-fə-ˈres-ns\ *n* **1** : the property of emitting light without easily perceptible heat shown by phosphorus or living organisms (as various bacteria and fungi); *also* : the light so produced **2** : luminescence caused by the absorption of radiations (as X rays or ultraviolet light) and continuing for a noticeable time after these radiations have stopped — **phos·pho·resce** \ˌfäs-fə-ˈres\ *vi* — **phos·pho·res·cent** \-nt\ *adj*

phos·phor·ic \fäs-ˈfor-ik, -ˈfär-\ *adj* : of, relating to, or containing phosphorus especially with a valence higher than in phosphorous compounds

phosphoric acid *n* : an oxygen-containing acid of phosphorus; *esp* : a syrupy or crystalline acid H_3PO_4 used in making fertilizers and as a flavoring in soft drinks

phos·pho·rous \ˈfäs-fə-rəs, -frəs; fäs-ˈfor-əs, -ˈfor-\ *adj* : of, relating to, or containing phosphorus especially with a valence lower than in phosphoric compounds

phosphorous acid *n* : a deliquescent crystalline acid H_3PO_3 used especially as a reducing agent and in making phosphites

phos·pho·rus \ˈfäs-fə-rəs, -frəs\ *n* **1** : a phosphorescent substance; *esp* : one that glows in the dark **2** : a poisonous active chemical element usually obtained in the form of waxy crystals that glow in moist air — see ELEMENT table [New Latin, from Greek *phōsphoros* "light-bearing", from *phōs* "light" + *pherein* "to carry"] — **phosphorus** *adj*

phos·phor·y·late \ˈfäs-ˈfor-ə-ˌlāt\ *vt* : to cause (an organic compound) to take up or combine with phosphoric acid or a phosphorus-containing group — **phos·phor·y·la·tion** \ˌfäs-ˌfor-ə-ˈlā-shən\ *n* — **phos·phor·y·la·tive** \fäs-ˈfor-ə-ˌlāt-iv\ *adj*

phot- *or* **photo-** *combining form* **1** : light ⟨*photo*graph⟩ ⟨*photo*n⟩ **2** : photograph : photographic ⟨*photo*engraving⟩ **3** : photoelectric ⟨*photo*cell⟩ [Greek *phōt-, phōs*]

pho·tic \ˈfōt-ik\ *adj* **1** : of, relating to, or involving light especially in relation to organisms ⟨a *photic* response⟩ **2** : penetrated by light especially of the sun ⟨*photic* layers of the sea⟩

pho·to \ˈfōt-ō\ *n, pl* **photos** : PHOTOGRAPH — **photo** *vb* — **photo** *adj*

pho·to·cell \'fōt-ə-ˌsel\ *n* : PHOTOELECTRIC CELL
pho·to·chem·is·try \ˌfōt-ō-'kem-ə-strē\ *n* **1** : a branch of chemistry that deals with the effect of radiant energy in producing chemical changes **2** : photochemical properties or processes — **pho·to·chem·i·cal** \-'kem-i-kəl\ *adj*
pho·to·com·pose \-kəm-'pōz\ *vt* : to set (as reading matter) by photocomposition — **pho·to·com·pos·er** *n*
pho·to·com·po·si·tion \-ˌkäm-pə-'zish-ən\ *n* : composition of reading matter directly on film or photosensitive paper for reproduction
pho·to·copy \'fōt-ə-ˌkäp-ē\ *n* : a photographic reproduction of graphic matter — **photocopy** *vb*
pho·to·du·pli·cate \ˌfōt-ō-'dü-plə-ˌkāt, -'dyü-\ *vb* : PHOTOCOPY — **pho·to·du·pli·cate** \-pli-kət\ *n*
pho·to·elec·tric \ˌfōt-ō-i-'lek-trik\ *adj* : relating to or utilizing electrical effects due to the interaction of light with matter — **pho·to·elec·tri·cal·ly** \-tri-kə-lē,-klē\ *adv*
photoelectric cell *n* : a cell in which variations of light are converted into corresponding variations in an electric current
photoelectric effect *n* : the emission of free electrons from a metal surface when light strikes it
pho·to·elec·tron \ˌfōt-ō-i-'lek-ˌträn\ *n* : an electron released in the photoelectric effect
pho·to·emis·sive \-i-'mis-iv\ *adj* : emitting electrons when exposed to radiation (as light)
pho·to·en·grave \-in-'grāv\ *vt* : to make a photoengraving of — **pho·to·en·grav·er** *n*
pho·to·en·grav·ing \-'grā-ving\ *n* **1** : a process for making linecuts and halftone cuts by photographing an image on a metal plate and then etching **2 a** : a plate made by photoengraving **b** : a print made from such a plate
photo finish *n* **1** : a race finish in which contestants are so close that a photograph of them as they cross the finish line has to be examined to determine the winner **2** : a close contest
pho·to·flash \'fōt-ə-ˌflash\ *n* : FLASHBULB
pho·to·flood \-ˌfləd\ *n* : a high-intensity electric lamp used in taking photographs
pho·to·gen·ic \ˌfōt-ə-'jen-ik, -'jēn-\ *adj* : suitable for being photographed : likely to photograph well (a *photogenic* child) — **pho·to·ge·ni·cal·ly** \-i-kə-lē, -klē\ *adv*
pho·to·gram·me·try \ˌfōt-ə-'gram-ə-trē\ *n* : the science of making reliable measurements by the use of usually aerial photographs in surveying and map making
¹**pho·to·graph** \'fōt-ə-ˌgraf\ *n* : a picture or likeness obtained by photography
²**photograph** *vb* **1** : to take a photograph of **2** : to take photographs **3** : to be photographed
pho·tog·ra·pher \fə-'täg-rə-fər\ *n* : one that practices or is skilled in photography; *esp* : one who takes photographs as a business
pho·to·graph·ic \ˌfōt-ə-'graf-ik\ *adj* **1** : relating to, obtained by, or used in photography (*photographic* supplies) **2** : representing nature and humans with the exactness of a photograph **3** : capable of retaining vivid impressions (a *photographic* mind) — **pho·to·graph·i·cal·ly** \-i-kə-lē, -klē\ *adv*
pho·tog·ra·phy \fə-'täg-rə-fē\ *n* : the art or process of producing images on a sensitized surface (as a film or plate) by the action of light or other radiant energy
pho·to·gra·vure \ˌfōt-ə-grə-'vyůr\ *n* : a process for making prints from an engraved plate prepared by photographic methods; *also* : a print produced by photogravure — **photogravure** *vt*
pho·to·li·thog·ra·phy \ˌfōt-ō-lith-'äg-rə-fē\ *n* : lithography in which photographically prepared plates are used — **pho·to·litho·graph·ic** \-ˌlith-ə-'graf-ik\ *adj*
pho·tol·y·sis \fō-'täl-ə-səs\ *n* : chemical decomposition by the action of radiant energy and especially light

pho·to·me·chan·i·cal \ˌfōt-ō-mi-'kan-i-kəl\ *adj* : relating to or involving any of various processes for producing printed matter from photographically prepared plates
pho·tom·e·ter \fō-'täm-ət-ər\ *n* : an instrument for measuring luminous intensity, illumination, or brightness
pho·to·met·ric \ˌfōt-ə-'me-trik\ *adj* : of or relating to photometry or the photometer — **pho·to·met·ri·cal·ly** \-tri-kə-lē, -klē\ *adv*
pho·tom·e·try \fō-'täm-ə-trē\ *n* : a branch of science that deals with measurement of the intensity of light
pho·to·mi·cro·graph \ˌfōt-ə-'mī-krə-ˌgraf\ *n* : a photograph of a magnified image of a small object — **pho·to·mi·cro·graph·ic** \-ˌmī-krə-'graf-ik\ *adj* — **pho·to·mi·crog·ra·phy** \-mī-'kräg-rə-fē\ *n*
pho·to·mon·tage \-män-'täzh, -mōⁿ-, -'tazh\ *n* : montage using photographic images; *also* : a picture made by photomontage
pho·to·mu·ral \ˌfōt-ō-'myůr-əl\ *n* : a greatly enlarged photograph used on walls especially as decoration
pho·ton \'fō-ˌtän\ *n* : a quantum of radiant energy
pho·to–off·set \ˌfōt-ō-'óf-ˌset\ *n* : offset printing from photolithographic printing plates
photo opportunity *n* : a situation or event that lends itself to and is often arranged expressly for the taking of pictures that favorably publicize the individuals photographed
pho·to·pe·ri·od \ˌfōt-ə-'pir-ē-əd\ *n* : the relative lengths of alternating periods of lightness and darkness as they affect the growth and maturity of an organism — **pho·to·pe·ri·od·ic** \-ˌpir-ē-'äd-ik\ *adj* — **pho·to·pe·ri·od·i·cal·ly** \-i-kə-lē, -klē\ *adv* — **pho·to·pe·ri·od·ism** \-'pir-ē-ə-ˌdiz-əm\ *n*
pho·to·phos·phor·y·la·tion \'fōt-ō-ˌfäs-ˌfór-ə-'lā-shən\ *n* : the formation of ATP in photosynthesis using radiant energy
pho·to·play \'fōt-ō-ˌplā\ *n* : MOVIE 2
pho·to·poly·mer \ˌfōt-ō-'päl-ə-mər\ *n* : a photosensitive plastic used to make printing plates
pho·to·re·cep·tor \ˌfōt-ō-ri-'sep-tər\ *n* : a receptor for light stimuli — **pho·to·re·cep·tion** \-'sep-shən\ *n* — **pho·to·re·cep·tive** \-'sep-tiv\ *adj*
pho·to·sen·si·tive \-'sen-sət-iv, -'sen-stiv\ *adj* : sensitive or sensitized to the action of radiant energy and especially light — **pho·to·sen·si·tiv·i·ty** \-ˌsen-sə-'tiv-ət-ē\ *n* — **pho·to·sen·si·ti·za·tion** \-ˌsen-sət-ə-'zā-shən\ *n* — **pho·to·sen·si·tize** \-'sen-sə-ˌtīz\ *vt*
pho·to·sphere \'fōt-ə-ˌsfiər\ *n* : the luminous surface of the sun or a star — **pho·to·spher·ic** \ˌfōt-ə-'sfiər-ik, -'sfer-\ *adj*
pho·to·stat \'fōt-ə-ˌstat\ *vb* : to copy by a Photostat device — **pho·to·stat·ic** \ˌfōt-ə-'stat-ik\ *adj*
Pho·to·stat \'fōt-ə-ˌstat\ *trademark* — used for a device for making a photographic copy of graphic matter
pho·to·syn·the·sis \ˌfōt-ə-'sin-thə-səs, -'sint-\ *n* : synthesis of chemical compounds with the aid of radiant energy; *esp* : formation of carbohydrates from carbon dioxide and water by the chlorophyll-containing tissues of plants exposed to light — **pho·to·syn·the·size** \-ˌsīz\ *vb* — **pho·to·syn·thet·ic** \-sin-'thet-ik\ *adj* — **pho·to·syn·thet·i·cal·ly** \-'thet-i-kə-lē, -klē\ *adv*
pho·to·tax·is \ˌfōt-ə-'tak-səs\ *n* : a taxis in which light is the directive factor — **pho·to·tac·tic** \-'tak-tik\ *adj*
pho·tot·ro·pism \fō-'tä-trə-ˌpiz-əm\ *n* : a tropism in which light is the orienting stimulus — **pho·to·trop·ic** \ˌfōt-ə-'träp-ik\ *adj*
phras·al \'frā-zəl\ *adj* : of, relating to, or consisting of a phrase (*phrasal* prepositions) — **phras·al·ly** \-zə-lē\ *adv*
¹**phrase** \'frāz\ *n* **1** : a manner of expression : DICTION **2** : a brief expression; *esp* : one commonly used **3** : a musical unit typically two tofour measures long and closing with a cadence **4** : a group of two or more words that form a sense unit but that do not by them-

photometer

\ə\	abut	\ng\	sing
\ər\	further	\ō\	bone
\a\	mat	\ó\	saw
\ā\	take	\ói\	coin
\ä\	cot, cart	\th\	thin
\aů\	out	\th̷\	this
\ch\	chin	\ü\	food
\e\	pet	\ů\	foot
\ē\	easy	\y\	yet
\g\	go	\yü\	few
\i\	tip	\yů\	cure
\ī\	life	\zh\	vision
\j\	job		

selves make up a complete sentence 〈"over the fence" in "hit it over the fence" is an adverbial *phrase*〉 [Latin *phrasis,* from Greek, from *phrazein* "to point out, explain, tell"]

²**phrase** *vt* **1 a** : to express in words : WORD 〈*phrase* a reply〉 **b** : to designate by a descriptive word or phrase : TERM **2** : to divide into melodic phrases

phrase·ol·o·gy \ˌfrā-zē-'äl-ə-jē\ *n* **1** : manner of organizing words and phrases into longer elements : STYLE **2** : choice of words

phras·ing \'frā-zing\ *n* **1** : PHRASEOLOGY 1 **2** : the act, method, or result of grouping notes into musical phrases

phre·net·ic \fri-'net-ik\ *adj* : FRENETIC [Latin *phreneticus*]

phre·nol·o·gy \fri-'näl-ə-jē\ *n* : the study of the conformation of the skull as indicative of mental faculties and character [Greek *phrēn* "diaphragm, mind"] — **phre·no·log·i·cal** \ˌfren-l-'äj-i-kəl, ˌfrēn-\ *adj* — **phre·nol·o·gist** \fri-'näl-ə-jəst\ *n*

phy·co·cy·a·nin \ˌfī-kō-'sī-ə-nən\ *n* : any of the bluish green protein pigments of blue-green algae [Greek *phykos* "seaweed"]

phy·co·er·y·thrin \-'er-ə-thrən\ *n* : any of the red protein pigments of red algae [derived from Greek *phykos* "seaweed" + *erythros* "red"]

phy·co·my·cete \-'mī-ˌsēt, -mī-'sēt\ *n* : any of a large class (Phycomycetes) of highly variable lower fungi in many respects similar to algae [derived from Greek *phykos* "seaweed" + *mykēs* "fungus"] — **phy·co·my·ce·tous** \-mī-'sēt-əs\ *adj*

phyl- *or* **phylo-** *combining form* : tribe : race : phylum 〈*phylo*geny〉 [Greek *phylē, phylon* "race, tribe"]

phy·lac·tery \fə-'lak-tə-rē, -trē\ *n, pl* **-ter·ies 1** : one of two small square leather boxes containing slips inscribed with scripture passages and worn by Jewish men during morning weekday prayers **2** : CHARM 2, AMULET [derived from Greek *phylaktērion* "amulet, phylactery", from *phylassein* "to guard", from *phylax* "guard"]

phy·let·ic \fī-'let-ik\ *adj* : of or relating to the course of evolutionary or phylogenetic development [derived from *phyl-*] — **phy·let·i·cal·ly** \-'let-i-kə-lē, -klē\ *adv*

-phyll \ˌfil\ *n combining form* : leaf 〈sporo*phyll*〉 [Greek *phyllon* "leaf"]

phyl·lo·taxy \'fil-ə-ˌtak-sē\ *also* **phyl·lo·tax·is** \ˌfil-ə-'tak-səs\ *n* : the arrangement of leaves on a stem and in relation to one another [*phyll-* + Greek *taxis* "arrangement, order", from *tassein* "to arrange"]

phyl·lox·e·ra \ˌfil-ˌäk-'sir-ə, fə-'läk-sə-rə\ *n* : any of various wholly oviparous plant lice; *esp* : one destructive to grapevines [derived from Greek *phyllon* "leaf" + *xēros* "dry"] — **phyl·lox·e·ran** \-'sir-ən, -sə-rən\ *adj or n*

phy·log·e·ny \fī-'läj-ə-nē\ *n, pl* **-nies** : the evolutionary development of a group as distinguished from the individual development of an organism — compare ONTOGENY — **phy·lo·ge·net·ic** \ˌfī-lə-jə-'net-ik\ *adj* — **phy·lo·ge·net·i·cal·ly** \-i-kə-lē, -klē\ *adv*

phy·lum \'fī-ləm\ *n, pl* **phy·la** \-lə\ : a group of animals or in some classifications plants sharing one or more fundamental characteristics that set them apart from all other animals and plants and forming a primary division of the animal or plant kingdom [New Latin, from Greek *phylon* "tribe, race"]

physi- *or* **physio-** *combining form* **1** : nature 〈*physio*graphy〉 **2** : physical 〈*physio*therapy〉 [Greek *physis*]

¹**phys·ic** \'fiz-ik\ *n* **1** : the practice or profession of medicine **2** : a medicinal agent or preparation; *esp* : PURGATIVE

²**physic** *vt* **phys·icked** \-ikt\; **phys·ick·ing** \-i-king\; **phys·ics** *or* **phys·icks** : to treat with or administer medicine to; *esp* : PURGE

phys·i·cal \'fiz-i-kəl\ *adj* **1** : of or relating to nature or the laws of nature **2** : of or relating to material things : not mental or spiritual **3** : of or relating to natural science **4** : of or relating to physics **5** : of or relating to the body : BODILY; *also* : preoccupied with the body or its needs SYN see MATERIAL — **phys·i·cal·ly** \-kə-lē, -klē\ *adv*

physical education *n* : instruction in the care and development of the body including training in hygiene, exercises, and athletic games

physical examination *n* : an examination of the bodily functions and condition of a person

physical geography *n* : a branch of geography that deals with the physical features and changes of the earth

physical science *n* : any of the natural sciences (as mineralogy or astronomy) that deal primarily with nonliving materials

physical therapy *n* : the treatment of disease by physical and mechanical means (as massage, exercise, water, or heat) — called also *physiotherapy* — **physical therapist** *n*

phy·si·cian \fə-'zish-ən\ *n* : a person skilled in the art of healing; *esp* : a doctor of medicine

phys·i·cist \'fiz-ə-səst\ *n* : a specialist in the science of physics

phys·ics \'fiz-iks\ *n* **1** : a science that deals with matter and energy and their interactions in the fields of mechanics, heat, light, electricity, sound, and nuclear phenomena **2** : physical composition, properties, or processes 〈the *physics* of sound〉 [Latin *physica,* pl., "natural science", from Greek *physika,* from *physikos* "of nature", from *physis* "growth, nature", from *phyein* "to bring forth"]

phys·i·og·no·my \ˌfiz-ē-'äg-nə-mē, -'än-ə-\ *n, pl* **-mies 1** : the art of discovering temperament and character from outward appearance **2** : the facial features held to show qualities of mind or character **3** : external aspect; *also* : inner character or quality revealed outwardly [Middle French *physiognomie,* from Late Latin *physiognomonia, physiognomia,* from Greek *physiognōmonia,* derived from *physis* "nature, physique, appearance" + *gnōmōn* "interpreter", from *gignōskein* "to know"] — **phys·i·og·nom·ic** \-ē-əg-'näm-ik, -ə-'näm-\ *adj* — **phys·i·og·nom·i·cal·ly** \-i-kə-lē, -klē\ *adv*

phys·i·og·ra·phy \ˌfiz-ē-'äg-rə-fē\ *n* : the study of landforms : PHYSICAL GEOGRAPHY — **phys·i·og·ra·pher** \-rə-fər\ *n* — **phys·io·graph·ic** \ˌfiz-ē-ə-'graf-ik\ *adj*

physiological saline *n* : a solution of a salt or salts with essentially the same concentration of ions as tissue fluids or blood

phys·i·ol·o·gy \ˌfiz-ē-'äl-ə-jē\ *n* **1** : a branch of biology dealing with the functions and activities of life or of living matter — compare ANATOMY **2** : the organic functions and activities of an organism or any of its parts or of a particular bodily process — **phys·i·o·log·i·cal** \ˌfiz-ē-ə-'läj-i-kəl\ *or* **phys·i·o·log·ic** \-'läj-ik\ *adj* — **phys·i·o·log·i·cal·ly** \-i-kə-lē, -klē\ *adv* — **phys·i·ol·o·gist** \ˌfiz-ē-'äl-ə-jəst\ *n*

phys·io·ther·a·py \ˌfiz-ē-ō-'ther-ə-pē\ *n* : PHYSICAL THERAPY

phy·sique \fə-'zēk\ *n* : the build of a person's body : physical constitution [French, from *physique* "physical"]

phyt- *or* **phyto-** *combining form* : plant 〈*phyto*plankton〉 [Greek *phyton,* from *phyein* "to bring forth"]

-phyte \ˌfīt\ *n combining form* **1** : plant having a (specified) characteristic or habitat 〈xero*phyte*〉 **2** : pathological growth

phy·to·plank·ton \ˌfīt-ō-'plang-tən, -'plangk-, -ˌtän\ *n* : planktonic plant life — **phy·to·plank·ton·ic** \-plang-'tän-ik, -plangk-\ *adj*

¹**pi** \'pī\ *n, pl* **pis** \'pīz\ **1** : the 16th letter of the Greek alphabet — Π or π **2 a** : the symbol π denoting the ratio of the circumference of a circle to its diameter

b : the ratio itself having a value to eight decimal places of 3.14159265

²pi *vb* **pied; pi·ing** **1** : to spill or throw (type or type matter) into disorder **2** : to become pied [origin unknown]

pia ma·ter \'pī-ə-ˌmät-ər, 'pē-ə-ˌmät-\ *n* : the innermost and thin vascular membrane investing the brain and spinal cord [Latin, "tender mother"] — **pi·al** \'pī-əl\ *adj*

pi·a·nis·si·mo \ˌpē-ə-'nis-ə-ˌmō\ *adv or adj* : very softly — used as a direction in music [Italian, from *piano* "softly"]

pi·an·ist \pē-'an-əst,'pē-ə-nəst\ *n* : a person who plays the piano

¹pi·a·no \pē-'än-ō\ *adv or adj* : in a soft or quiet manner — used as a direction in music [Italian, from Late Latin *planus* "smooth", from Latin, "level"]

²pi·ano \pē-'an-ō\ *n, pl* **-an·os** : a stringed percussion instrument having steel-wire strings that sound when struck by felt-covered hammers operated from a keyboard [Italian, short for *pianoforte*, from *piano e forte* "soft and loud"; from the fact that its tones could be varied in loudness] □ **ORIGIN** A harpsichord is played by means of a mechanism that plucks the strings, so it is not possible to achieve fine gradations of loudness. Feeling the need to overcome this drawback in the harpsichord, a Florentine named Bartolommeo Cristofori around the year 1709 invented a mechanism by means of which the strings of the instrument are struck by felt-covered hammers. This device allows the player more control over the loudness of his playing. Cristofori called his new instrument a *gravicembalo col piano e forte*, that is "a harpsichord with soft and loud". The instrument came to be designated by the term *piano e forte* or by contraction *pianoforte*, which was subsequently shortened to *piano*.

pi·ano·forte \pē-'an-ə-ˌfōrt, -ˌfort, -ˌfort-ē\ *n* : **PIANO** [Italian]

pi·as·ter *or* **pi·as·tre** \pē-'as-tər, -'äs-\ *n* **1** : **PIECE OF EIGHT 2 a** : a monetary unit of Egypt, Lebanon, Sudan, and Syria equal to ¹/₁₀₀ pound **b** : a coin representing one piaster [French *piastre*]

pi·az·za \pē-'az-ə, *1 is usually* -'at-sə, -'ät-\ *n, pl* **piazzas** *or* **pi·az·ze** \-'at-sā, -'ät-\ **1** : an open square especially in an Italian town **2 a** : an arcaded and roofed gallery **b** *dialect* : **VERANDA, PORCH** [Italian, from Latin *platea* "broad street", from Greek *plateia*, from *platys* "broad, flat"]

pi·broch \'pē-ˌbräk, -ˌbräk\ *n* : a set of martial or mournful variations for the Scottish bagpipe [Scottish Gaelic *piobaireachd* "pipe music"]

pi·ca \'pī-kə\ *n* **1** : 12-point type **2** : a unit of about ⅙ inch (about 4.2 millimeters) used in measuring typographical material **3** : a typewriter type providing 10 characters to the inch [probably from Medieval Latin, "collection of church rules"]

pic·a·dor \'pik-ə-ˌdor, ˌpik-ə-'\ *n, pl* **picadors** \-ˌdorz, -'dorz\ *or* **pic·a·do·res** \ˌpik-ə-'dor-ēz, -'dor-\ : a horseman in a bullfight who prods the bull with a lance to weaken its neck and shoulder muscles [Spanish, from *picar* "to prick", derived from Latin *picus* "woodpecker"]

pi·ca·resque \ˌpik-ə-'resk, ˌpē-kə-\ *adj* : of or relating to rogues or rascals; *also* : of or relating to a type of fiction of Spanish origin dealing with rogues and vagabonds [Spanish *picaresco*, from *pícaro* "rogue"]

¹pic·a·yune \ˌpik-ē-'ün, -'yün\ *n* **1** : a small coin of Spanish origin formerly circulated in the southern United States **2** : something trivial [French *picaillon* "halfpenny", from Provençal *picaion*, from *picaio* "money", from *pica* "to strike, prick, jingle", derived from Latin *picus* "woodpecker"] □ **ORIGIN** The eating habits of the woodpecker, which drills holes in trees in its search for insects, are responsible for the derivation from *picus*, its Latin name, of a verb meaning "to

pierce or prick". The Provençal verb *pica* developed a wide range of senses including "to jingle" as well as "to prick". Before the widespread use of paper currency, *picaio* was an appropriate name for money, which was likely to jingle. A small copper coin came to be called *picaioun*, and this was borrowed into French as *picaillon*. In 19th century Louisiana the French name, respelled in English as *picayune*, was transferred to a Spanish coin then in common use in some states of the American South. The picayune went the way of other small sums of money, and the word came to be used for anything trivial or of little value.

²picayune *adj* : of little value : **PALTRY**; *also* : **PETTY 3**

pic·ca·lil·li \ˌpik-ə-'lil-ē\ *n* : a pungent relish of chopped vegetables and spices [probably alteration of *pickle*]

pic·co·lo \'pik-ə-ˌlō\ *n, pl* **-los** : a small shrill flute pitched an octave higher than an ordinary flute [Italian, short for *piccolo flauto* "small flute"] — **pic·co·lo·ist** \-əst\ *n*

¹pick \'pik\ *vb* **1** : to pierce, penetrate, or break up with a pointed tool **2 a** : to clear or free from something by or as if by plucking ⟨*pick* meat from a bone⟩ **b** : to gather by plucking ⟨*pick* berries⟩ **c** : to play by plucking ⟨*pick* a guitar⟩ ⟨*pick* a tune on the banjo⟩ **3** : **CHOOSE, SELECT** ⟨*pick* out a suit⟩ ⟨*pick* a book⟩ **4** : to steal or pilfer from ⟨*pick* pockets⟩ **5** : **PROVOKE** ⟨*pick* a quarrel⟩ **6** : to eat sparingly or in a finicky manner **7** : to unlock without a key ⟨*pick* a lock⟩ [Middle French *piquer* "to prick", derived from Latin *picus* "woodpecker"] — **pick·er** *n* — **pick and choose** : to select carefully and deliberately — **pick on 1** : **TEASE, HARASS** ⟨*pick on* a smaller child⟩ **2** : to single out for a special purpose or for particular attention

²pick *n* **1** : a blow or stroke with a pointed instrument **2 a** : the act or privilege of choosing or selecting ⟨take your *pick*⟩ **b** : the best or choicest one ⟨the *pick* of the crop⟩

³pick *n* **1** : **PICKAX 2** : any of several slender pointed implements for picking or chipping **3** : a small thin piece (as of plastic or metal) used to pluck a stringed instrument [Middle English *pik*, probably alteration of *¹pike*]

pick·a·back \'pig-ē-ˌbak, 'pik-ə-\ *variant of* **PIGGYBACK**

pick·a·nin·ny *or* **pic·a·nin·ny** \'pik-ə-ˌnin-ē, ˌpik-ə-'\ *n, pl* **-nies** : a Negro child — often taken to be offensive [probably from Portuguese *pequenino* "very little"]

pick·ax \'pik-ˌaks\ *n* : a heavy tool with a wooden handle and a curved or straight blade pointed at one or both ends that is used especially in loosening or breaking up soil or rock [Old French *picois*, from *pic* "pick", from Latin *picus* "woodpecker"]

pick·er·el \'pik-rəl, -ə-ral\ *n, pl* **pickerel** *or* **pickerels 1** : any of several comparatively small pikes or related fishes **2** : **WALLEYE 2** [Middle English *pikerel*, from *pike*]

pick·er·el·weed \-ˌwēd\ *n* : any of various aquatic plants; *esp* : a blue-flowered American shallow-water herb

¹pick·et \'pik-ət\ *n* **1** : a pointed stake or post (as for a fence) **2** : a soldier or a detachment of soldiers posted as a guard against surprise attack **3 a** : a striker or strike sympathizer who protests or demonstrates at the struck work site **b** : a person posted for a demonstration or protest [French *piquet*, from *piquer* "to prick"]

²picket *vb* **1** : to enclose, fence, or fortify with pickets **2** : to guard with or post as a picket **3** : **TETHER 4 a** : to post pickets or act as a picket at ⟨*picket* a factory⟩ **b** : to serve as a picket — **pick·et·er** *n*

picket line *n* : a line of persons picketing a business, organization, or institution

pick·ings \'pik-iŋz, -ənz\ *n pl* **1** : something available or left over; *esp* : eatable remains **2** : yield or return for effort expended

²piano

\ə\ abut	\ng\ sing
\ər\ further	\ō\ bone
\a\ mat	\o\ saw
\ā\ take	\oi\ coin
\ä\ cot, cart	\th\ thin
\aú\ out	\th\ this
\ch\ chin	\ü\ food
\e\ pet	\ú\ foot
\ē\ easy	\y\ yet
\g\ go	\yü\ few
\i\ tip	\yú\ cure
\ī\ life	\zh\ vision
\j\ job	

¹pick·le \'pik-əl\ *n* **1** : a bath for preserving or cleaning; *esp* : a brine or vinegar solution in which foods are preserved **2** : a difficult situation : PLIGHT **3** : a food item (as a cucumber) preserved in brine or vinegar [Middle English *pekille*]

²pickle *vt* **pick·led; pick·ling** \'pik-ling, -ə-ling\ : to treat, preserve, or clean in or with a pickle

pick·lock \'pik-,läk\ *n* **1** : a tool for picking locks **2** : BURGLAR

pick off *vt* **1** : to shoot or bring down one by one **2** : to catch (a base runner) off base with a quick throw by the pitcher or catcher

pick out *vt* **1** : to make out : DISTINGUISH **2** : to play the notes of by ear or one by one

pick over *vt* : to examine in order to select the best or remove the unwanted

pick·pock·et \'pik-,päk-ət\ *n* : a person who steals from pockets

pick·up \'pik-,əp\ *n* **1 a** : a revival of activity ⟨a business *pickup*⟩ **b** : ACCELERATION **2** : a temporary chance acquaintance **3** : the conversion of mechanical movements into electrical impulses in the reproduction of sound; *also* : a device (as on a phonograph) for making such conversion **4 a** : the reception of sound or an image into a radio or television transmitting apparatus for conversion into electrical signals **b** : a device (as a microphone or a television camera) for converting sound or the image of a scene into electrical signals **c** : the place where a broadcast originates **5** : a light truck having an open body with low sides

pick up \pik-'əp, 'pik-\ *vb* **1 a** : to take hold of and lift ⟨*pick up* sticks⟩ **b** : to clean up : TIDY **2** : to take into a vehicle ⟨the bus *picked up* passengers⟩ **3 a** : to acquire casually, irregularly, or at a bargain ⟨*pick up* a bad habit⟩ ⟨*picked up* two shirts at the sale⟩ **b** : to strike up a casual acquaintance with (a previously unknown person) **4** : to take into custody ⟨was *picked up* by the police⟩ **5** : to bring within range of sight or hearing **6** : to recover speed, vigor, or activity ⟨business is *picking up*⟩

picky \'pik-ē\ *adj* **pick·i·er; -est** : FUSSY 2b, FINICKY

¹pic·nic \'pik-nik, -,nik\ *n* **1** : an excursion or outing with food usually taken along and eaten in the open **2** : something pleasant or easy **3** : a shoulder of pork that is often smoked and boned — **pic·nic·ky** \-ē\ *adj* [French *pique-nique*]

²picnic *vi* **pic·nicked; pic·nick·ing** : to go on a picnic : eat in picnic fashion — **pic·nick·er** *n*

pi·co- \'pē-kō, -kə\ *combining form* : one trillionth part of [perhaps from Italian *piccolo* "small"]

¹pi·cot \'pē-kō, pē-'\ *n* : one of a series of small ornamental loops forming an edging on ribbon or lace [French, literally, "small point", from Middle French *pic* "prick", from *piquer* "to prick"]

²picot *vt* **pi·cot·ed** \-kōd, -'kōd\; **pi·cot·ing** \-kō-ing, -'kō-\ : to finish with a picot

pic·ric acid \,pik-rik-\ *n* : a bitter toxic explosive yellow crystalline strong acid used especially in high explosives, as a dye, or in medicine [Greek *pikros* "bitter"]

Pict \'pikt\ *n* : any of a possibly non-Celtic people who once occupied Great Britain, were in many places displaced by the Britons, carried on continual border wars with the Romans, and in the mid-8th century amalgamated with the Scots [Late Latin *Picti* "Picts"] — **Pict·ish** \'pik-tish\ *adj or n*

pic·to·gram \'pik-tə-,gram\ *n* : PICTOGRAPH

pic·to·graph \-,graf\ *n* **1** : an ancient or prehistoric drawing or painting on a rock wall **2** : one of the symbols belonging to a system of picture writing **3** : a diagram representing statistical data by pictorial forms [Latin *pictus*, past participle of *pingere* "to paint" + English *-o-* + *-graph*] — **pic·to·graph·ic** \,pik-tə-'graf-ik\ *adj*

pic·tog·ra·phy \pik-'täg-rə-fē\ *n* : PICTURE WRITING 1

pictograph 1

pic·to·ri·al \pik-'tōr-ē-əl, -'tor-\ *adj* **1** : of or relating to painting or drawing ⟨*pictorial* art⟩ **2 a** : consisting of pictures ⟨*pictorial* records⟩ **b** : illustrated by pictures ⟨*pictorial* magazines⟩ **3** : having the qualities of a picture ⟨*pictorial* reporting⟩ [Late Latin *pictorius*, from Latin *pictor* "painter", from *pingere* "to paint"] — **pic·to·ri·al·ly** \-ē-ə-lē\ *adv*

¹pic·ture \'pik-chər\ *n* **1** : a representation made on a surface (as by painting, drawing, or photography) **2** : a very vivid description **3 a** : an exact likeness : COPY **b** : a tangible or visible representation : EMBODIMENT ⟨the *picture* of health⟩ **4 a** : a transitory visible image (as on a television screen) **b** : MOTION PICTURE 1 **5** : a state of affairs : SITUATION ⟨the bleak economic *picture*⟩ [Latin *pictura*, from *pictus*, past participle of *pingere* "to paint"]

²picture *vt* **pic·tured; pic·tur·ing** \'pik-chə-ring, 'pik-shring\ **1** : to make a picture of (as by drawing) : DEPICT **2** : to describe vividly **3** : to form a mental image of : IMAGINE

picture hat *n* : a woman's dressy hat with a broad brim

pic·tur·esque \,pik-chə-'resk\ *adj* **1** : resembling a picture : suggesting a painted scene **2** : CHARMING, QUAINT ⟨a *picturesque* village⟩ **3** : evoking striking mental images SYN see GRAPHIC — **pic·tur·esque·ly** *adv* — **pic·tur·esque·ness** *n*

picture tube *n* : a cathode-ray tube on which the picture appears in a television receiver

picture window *n* : an outsize window designed to frame a desirable exterior view

picture writing *n* **1** : the recording of events or messages by pictures representing actions or facts **2** : the record or message represented by picture writing

pid·dle \'pid-l\ *vi* **pid·dled; pid·dling** \'pid-ling, -l-ing\ : DAWDLE 1 [origin unknown]

pid·dling \'pid-lən, -l-ən, -ling, -l-ing\ *adj* : TRIVIAL 2, PALTRY

pid·dock \'pid-ək\ *n* : a marine bivalve mollusk that bores in stone, wood, or clay [origin unknown]

pid·gin \'pij-ən\ *n* : a simplified speech used for communication between people with different languages; *esp* : an English-based pidgin used in the Orient [short for *Pidgin English*, an English-based pidgin, from Pidgin English *pidgin* "business", from English *business*]

¹pie \'pī\ *n* : MAGPIE [Old French, from Latin *pica*]

²pie *n* **1** : a dish consisting of a pastry crust and a filling (as of fruit or meat) **2** : a layer cake with a thick filling (as of custard) [Middle English]

¹pie·bald \'pī-,bóld\ *adj* : of two colors; *esp* : spotted or blotched with black and white ⟨a *piebald* horse⟩ [¹*pie* + *bald*]

²piebald *n* : a piebald animal (as a horse)

¹piece \'pēs\ *n* **1** : a usually separated part of a whole ⟨a *piece* of the pie⟩ **2** : one of a group, set, or class of things ⟨a 3-*piece* suite of furniture⟩ ⟨a chess *piece*⟩ ⟨a *piece* of mail⟩ **3** : a portion marked off ⟨a *piece* of land⟩ **4** : a single item, example, instance, or unit ⟨a *piece* of news⟩ ⟨buy lumber by the *piece*⟩ **5** : a literary, artistic, or musical composition **6** : FIREARM **7** : COIN ⟨a gold *piece*⟩ [Old French, of Gaulish origin] SYN see PART — **of a piece** : of the same sort : ALIKE

²piece *vt* **1** : to repair, renew, or complete by adding pieces : PATCH **2** : to join into a whole ⟨*pieced* their stories together⟩ — **piec·er** *n*

pièce de ré·sis·tance \pē-,es-də-rə-,zē-'stäns\ *n, pl* **pièces de ré·sis·tance** \same\ **1** : the chief dish of a meal **2** : an outstanding item [French, literally, "piece of resistance"]

piece goods *n pl* : cloth fabrics sold from the bolt at retail in lengths specified by the customer

¹piece·meal \'pē-,smēl\ *adv* **1** : one piece at a time : GRADUALLY **2** : in pieces or fragments : APART [Middle English *pece·mele*, from *pece* "piece" + *-mele* (from Old English *mǣl* "appointed time")]

²piecemeal *adj* : done, made, or accomplished piece by piece or in a fragmentary way : GRADUAL

piece of eight : an old Spanish peso of eight reals

piece·work \'pē-ˌswərk\ *n* : work done by the piece and paid for at a set rate per unit — **piece·work·er** \-ˌswər-kər\ *n*

pie chart *n* : a circular chart that illustrates quantities or frequencies by wedge-shaped segments

pied \'pīd\ *adj* : of two or more colors in blotches [¹*pie*]

pied–à–terre \pē-ˌād-ə-'teər\ *n, pl* **pieds–à–terre** \same\ : a temporary or second lodging [French, literally, "foot to the ground"]

pied·mont \'pēd-ˌmänt\ *adj* : lying or formed at the base of mountains [*Piedmont,* region of Italy] — **piedmont** *n*

pie·plant \'pī-ˌplant\ *n* : garden rhubarb

pier \'piər\ *n* **1** : a support for a bridge span **2** : a structure built out into the water for use as a landing place or walk or to protect or form a harbor **3** : a single pillar or a structure used to support something **4** : a mass of masonry (as a buttress) used to strengthen a wall [Old English *per,* from Medieval Latin *pera*]

pierce \'piərs\ *vb* **1** : to run into or through as a pointed weapon does : STAB **2** : to make a hole through : PERFORATE **3** : to force or make a way into or through something **4** : to penetrate with the eye or mind : DISCERN **5** : to penetrate so as to move or touch the emotions of [Old French *percer*] SYN see ENTER — **pierc·ing·ly** \'pir-sing-lē\ *adv*

pier glass *n* : a tall mirror; *esp* : one designed to occupy the wall space between windows

Pier·rot \'pē-ə-ˌrō\ *n* : a standard comic character of Old French pantomime usually with whitened face and loose white clothes

pier table *n* : a table to be placed under a pier glass

pies *pl of* PI *or of* PIE

pie·tà \ˌpē-ā-'tä, pyā-\ *n, often cap* : a representation of the Virgin Mary mourning over the dead body of Christ [Italian, literally, "pity", from Latin *pietas*]

pi·etism \'pī-ə-ˌtiz-əm\ *n* **1** : emphasis in religion on devotional experience and practices **2** : affected piety — **pi·etist** \'pī-ət-əst\ *n, often cap* — **pi·etis·tic** \ˌpī-ə-'tis-tik\ *adj* — **pi·etis·ti·cal·ly** \-'tis-ti-kə-lē, -klē\ *adv*

pi·ety \'pī-ət-ē\ *n, pl* **-eties** **1** : the quality or state of being pious: as **a** : loyalty to natural obligations (as to one's parents) **b** : dutifulness in religion : DEVOUTNESS **2** : an act inspired by piety [French *piété* "piety, pity", from Latin *pietas,* from *pius* "dutiful, pious"]

pi·ezo·elec·tric·i·ty \pē-ˌā-zō-ə-ˌlek-'tris-ət-ē, -ˌāt-sō-, -'tris-tē\ *n* : electricity or electric polarity resulting from the application of mechanical force to certain crystals (as quartz) [Greek *piezein* "to press"] — **pi·ezo·elec·tric** \-'lek-trik\ *adj* — **pi·ezo·elec·tri·cal·ly** \-'lek-tri-kə-lē, -klē\ *adv*

¹pif·fle \'pif-əl\ *vi* **pif·fled; pif·fling** \'pif-ling, -ə-ling\ : to talk or act in a trivial, inept, or ineffective way : TRIFLE [perhaps blend of *piddle* and *trifle*]

²piffle *n* : NONSENSE 1

¹pig \'pig\ *n* **1 a** : a young swine not yet sexually mature : a wild or domestic swine **2 a** : PORK **b** : the dressed carcass of a young swine weighing less than 130 pounds **c** : PIGSKIN **3** : one held to resemble a pig **4** : a crude casting of metal (as iron or lead) [Middle English *pigge*] — **pig** *adj*

²pig *vb* **pigged; pig·ging** **1** : FARROW **2** : to live like a pig ⟨*pig* it⟩

pi·geon \'pij-ən\ *n* **1** : any of numerous birds (order Columbiformes) with a stout body, usually short legs, and smooth and compact plumage; *esp* : a domesticated bird derived from the rock pigeon **2** : an easy mark : DUPE [Middle French *pijon,* from Late Latin *pipio* "young bird", from Latin *pipere* "to chirp"]

¹pi·geon·hole \'pij-ən-ˌhōl\ *n* **1** : a hole or small place for pigeons to nest **2** : a small open compartment (as in a desk) for keeping letters or papers

²pigeonhole *vt* : to place in or as if in the pigeonhole of a desk: as **a** : to lay aside : SHELVE **b** : to assign to a category : CLASSIFY

pi·geon–toed \ˌpij-ən-'tōd\ *adj* : having the toes turned in

pig·gery \'pig-rē, -ə-rē\ *n, pl* **-ger·ies** : a place where pigs are kept

pig·gish \'pig-ish\ *adj* : suggesting a pig (as in greed, dirtiness, or stubbornness) — **pig·gish·ly** *adv*

pig·gy·back \'pig-ē-ˌbak\ *or* **pick·a·back** \'pig-ē-, 'pik-ə-\ *adv or adj* **1** : on the back or shoulders **2** : on a railroad flatcar [alteration of earlier *a pick pack,* of unknown origin]

piggy bank *n* : a coin bank often in the shape of a pig

pig·head·ed \'pig-'hed-əd\ *adj* : STUBBORN 1a, OBSTINATE

pig iron *n* : iron that is the direct product of the blast furnace and is refined to produce steel, wrought iron, or ingot iron

pig latin *n, often cap L* : a jargon that is made by systematic mutilation of English (as "ipskay the ointjay" for "skip the joint")

¹pig·ment \'pig-mənt\ *n* **1** : a substance that imparts black or white or a color to other materials; *esp* : a powdered substance mixed with a liquid in which it is relatively insoluble to impart color **2** : a natural coloring matter in animals and plants; *also* : any of various related colorless substances [Latin *pigmentum,* from *pingere* "to paint"] — **pig·men·tary** \-mən-ˌter-ē\ *adj*

²pig·ment \-mənt, -ˌment\ *vt* : to color with or as if with pigment

pig·men·ta·tion \ˌpig-mən-'tā-shən, -ˌmen-\ *n* : coloration with or deposition of pigment; *esp* : excessive pigment in bodily cells or tissues

pigmy *variant of* PYGMY

pig·nut \'pig-ˌnət\ *n* : any of several bitter-flavored hickory nuts; *also* : a tree bearing these

pig·pen \-ˌpen\ *n* **1** : PIGSTY 1 **2** : a filthy or messy place

pig·skin \-ˌskin\ *n* : the skin of a swine or leather made of it

pig·sty \'pig-ˌstī\ *n* **1** : a pen for pigs **2** : PIGPEN 2

pig·tail \-ˌtāl\ *n* **1** : tobacco in small twisted strands or rolls **2** : a tight braid of hair

pig–tailed \-ˌtāld\ *adj* : wearing a pigtail or pigtails

pig·weed \-ˌwēd\ *n* : any of various weedy plants especially of the goosefoot or amaranth families

pi·ka \'pē-kə\ *n* : any of various small short-eared mammals of rocky areas in the mountains of Asia and western North America that are related to the rabbits — called also *coney* [Tungusic *piika*]

¹pike \'pīk\ *n* **1** : PIKESTAFF 1 **2** : a sharp point or spike; *also* : the tip of a spear [Old English *pīc* "pickax"] — **piked** \'pīkt\ *adj*

²pike *n, pl* **pike** *or* **pikes** : a large long-bodied and long-snouted freshwater fish valued for food and sport and widely distributed in cool northern waters; *also* : any of various related or similar fishes [Middle English, from ¹*pike*]

³pike *n* : a long wooden shaft with a pointed steel head formerly used as a weapon by infantry [Middle French *pique,* from *piquer* "to prick", derived from Latin *picus* "woodpecker"]

⁴pike *n* : TURNPIKE 2

⁵pike *n* : a body position (as in diving or gymnastics) in which the body is bent at the waist in the shape of a V [probably from ²*pike*]

pike perch *n* : a fish (as a walleye) of the perch group that resembles the pike

pik·er \'pī-kər\ *n* **1** : one who gambles or speculates with small amounts of money **2** : one who does things in a small way; *also* : TIGHTWAD, CHEAPSKATE [*Pike*

pigtail 2

²pike

\ə\ abut		\ng\ sing	
\ər\ further		\ō\ bone	
\a\ mat		\ȯ\ saw	
\ā\ take		\ȯi\ coin	
\ä\ cot, cart		\th\ thin	
\au̇\ out		\th\ this	
\ch\ chin		\ü\ food	
\e\ pet		\u̇\ foot	
\ē\ easy		\y\ yet	
\g\ go		\yü\ few	
\i\ tip		\yu̇\ cure	
\ī\ life		\zh\ vision	
\j\ job			

county, Missouri, once thought to be the home of many shiftless gamblers]

pike·staff \'pīk-,staf\ *n* **1** : a spiked staff for use on slippery ground **2** : the shaft of a soldier's pike

pi·laf *or* **pi·laff** \pi-'läf, 'pē-,\ *or* **pi·lau** \pi-'lō, -'lȯ, 'pē-,, *South often* 'pər-lü, -lō\ *n* : a dish made of seasoned rice and often meat [Persian and Turkish *pilāu*]

pi·las·ter \'pī-,las-tər\ *n* : a rectangular slightly projecting column that ornaments or helps to support a wall [Middle French *pilastre,* from Italian *pilastro*]

pil·chard \'pil-chərd\ *n* : a fish resembling the related herring and occurring in great schools along the coasts of Europe; *also* : any of several related fishes — compare SARDINE [origin unknown]

¹pile \'pīl\ *n* : a long slender column usually of timber, steel, or reinforced concrete driven into the ground to carry a vertical load [Old English *pīl* "dart, stake", from Latin *pilum* "javelin"]

²pile *vt* : to drive piles into

³pile *n* **1 a** : a quantity of things heaped together **b** : a heap of wood for burning a corpse or a sacrifice : PYRE **2** : a great amount (as of money) **3** : REACTOR 2b [Middle French, from Latin *pila* "pillar"]

⁴pile *vb* **1** : to lay or place in a pile : STACK **2** : to heap in abundance : LOAD **3** : to move or press forward in or as if in a mass : CROWD ⟨*pile* into the car⟩

⁵pile *n* **1** : a coat or surface of usually short close fine furry hairs **2** : a velvety surface produced on textile by an extra set of filling yarns that form raised loops which are cut and sheared [Latin *pilus* "hair"] — **piled** \'pīld\ *adj*

pi·le·at·ed woodpecker \,pī-lē-,āt-əd-\ *n* : a North American woodpecker that is black with a red crest and white on the wings and sides of the neck [derived from Latin *pileus, pileum* "felt cap"]

pile driver *n* : a machine for driving or hammering piles into place

piles \'pīlz\ *n pl* : HEMORRHOIDS; *also* : the condition of one affected with hemorrhoids [Latin *pila* "ball"]

pi·le·us \'pī-lē-əs\ *n, pl* **-lei** \-lē-,ī\ : CAP 3a [Latin, "felt cap"]

pil·fer \'pil-fər\ *vb* **pil·fered; pil·fer·ing** \-fə-ring, -fring\ : to steal articles of small value or in small amounts [Middle English *pelfrer,* from *pelfre* "booty"] — **pil·fer·age** \-fə-rij, 'frij\ *n* — **pil·fer·er** \-fər-ər\ *n*

pil·grim \'pil-grəm\ *n* **1** : one who travels in foreign lands : WANDERER **2** : one who travels to a shrine or holy place as a devotee **3** *cap* : one of the English colonists founding the first permanent settlement in New England at Plymouth in 1620 [Old French *peligrin,* from Late Latin *pelegrinus,* from Latin *peregrinus* "foreigner", from *pereger* "being abroad", from *per* "through" + *ager* "land"]

pil·grim·age \'pil-grə-mij\ *n* : a journey of a pilgrim — **pilgrimage** *vi*

pil·ing \'pī-ling\ *n* : a structure or collection of piles

Pi·li·pi·no \,pil-ə-'pē-nō, ,pēl-\ *n* : the Tagalog-based official language of the Republic of the Philippines [Pilipino, from Spanish *Filipino* "Philippine"]

pill \'pil\ *n* **1 a** : medicine in a small rounded mass to be swallowed whole **b** : an oral contraceptive — usually used with *the* **2** : something resembling a pill (as in distasteful quality or globular form) **3** : a disagreeably tiresome person [Latin *pilula,* from *pila* "ball"]

¹pil·lage \'pil-ij\ *n* **1** : the act of looting or plundering especially in war **2** : BOOTY 1 [Middle French, from *piller* "to plunder", from *peille* "rag", from Latin *pilleus, pileus* "felt cap"]

²pillage *vb* : to take booty : PLUNDER, LOOT — **pil·lag·er** *n*

pil·lar \'pil-ər\ *n* **1** : a comparatively slender upright support (as for a roof) **2** : a column or shaft standing alone (as for a monument) **3** : one that suggests a pillar : a main support ⟨a *pillar* of society⟩ [Old French *piler,* from Medieval Latin *pilare,* from Latin *pila* "pil-

lar"] — **pil·lared** \-ərd\ *adj* — **from pillar to post** : from one place or situation to another

pill·box \'pil-,bäks\ *n* **1** : a small usually shallow round box for pills **2** : a small low concrete emplacement for machine guns and antitank weapons **3** : a small round hat without a brim

pill bug *n* : WOOD LOUSE [from its rolling into a ball when disturbed]

¹pil·lion \'pil-yən\ *n* **1** : a cushion or pad placed behind a saddle for an extra rider **2** : a passenger's saddle (as on a motorcycle) [Scottish Gaelic *pillean* or Irish Gaelic *pillin*]

²pillion *adv* : on or as if on a pillion ⟨ride *pillion*⟩

pil·lo·ry \'pil-rē, -ə-rē\ *n, pl* **-ries** **1** : a device for publicly punishing offenders that consists of a wooden frame with holes in which the head and hands can be locked — compare STOCK **2** : a means for exposing to public scorn or ridicule [Old French *pilori*] — **pillory** *vt*

¹pil·low \'pil-ō\ *n* : a support for the head of a person that consists usually of a bag filled with resilient material (as feathers or sponge rubber) [Old English *pyle, pylu,* from Latin *pulvinus*]

²pillow *vt* **1** : to place on or as if on a pillow **2** : to serve as a pillow for

pil·low·case \-,kās\ *n* : a removable covering for a pillow — called also *pillow slip*

¹pi·lot \'pī-lət\ *n* **1 a** : one employed to steer a ship **b** : a person qualified and usually licensed to conduct a ship into and out of a port or in specified waters **2** : GUIDE 1a, d, LEADER **3** : COWCATCHER **4** : one who flies or is qualified to fly an airplane **5** : a piece that guides a tool or machine part **6** : a television show produced as a sample of a proposed series **7** : PILOT LIGHT 2 [Middle French *pilote,* from Italian *pilota,* alteration of *pedota,* derived from Greek *pēdon* "oar"] — **pi·lot·less** \-ləs\ *adj*

²pilot *vt* **1** : GUIDE 1, CONDUCT **2 a** : to direct the navigation of : STEER ⟨*pilot* the ship through the canal⟩ **b** : to act as pilot of : FLY ⟨*pilot* the plane to the west coast⟩

³pilot *adj* : serving as a guiding or tracing device, an activating or auxiliary unit, or a trial apparatus or operation ⟨a *pilot* study⟩ ⟨a *pilot* plant⟩

pi·lot·age \'pī-lət-ij\ *n* **1** : the act or business of piloting **2** : the compensation paid to a pilot

pilot balloon *n* : a small unmanned balloon sent up to show the direction and speed of the wind

pilot biscuit *n* : HARDTACK — called also *pilot bread*

pilot engine *n* : a locomotive going in advance of a train to make sure that the way is clear

pilot fish *n* : a spiny-finned fish with narrow body and widely forked tail that often accompanies a shark

pi·lot·house \'pī-lət-,haůs\ *n* : an enclosed area on the upper deck of a ship that contains the steering and navigating equipment

pilot light *n* **1** : a light indicating location (as of a switch) or operational state (as of a motor) **2** : a small permanent flame used to ignite gas at a burner

Pilt·down man \,pilt-,daůn-\ *n* : a supposedly very early primitive modern human based on skull fragments uncovered in a gravel pit at Piltdown, England, and used in combination with comparatively recent skeletal remains of various animals in the development of an elaborate fraud

Pi·ma \'pē-mə\ : a member of an Indian people of what is now southern Arizona having an Aztec-related language

Pi·ma cotton \,pē-mə-, ,pim-ə-\ *n* : an American cotton with fiber of exceptional strength and firmness derived from Egyptian cottons [*Pima* county, Arizona]

pi·men·to \pə-'ment-ō\ *n, pl* **-tos** *or* **-to** **1** : PIMIENTO **2** : ALLSPICE [Spanish *pimiento,* from *pimienta* "allspice, pepper", from Late Latin *pigmentum* "plant juice", from Latin, "pigment"]

pillar 1

pi·mien·to \pə-'ment-ō, pəm-'yent-\ *n, pl* **-tos** : any of various thick-fleshed sweet peppers of mild flavor used especially as a source of paprika [Spanish]

¹pimp \'pimp\ *n* : PANDER 1b, PROCURER [origin unknown]

²pimp *vi* : to act as a pimp

pim·per·nel \'pim-pər-,nel\ *n* : any of a genus of herbs of the primrose family; *esp* : SCARLET PIMPERNEL [Middle French *pimprenelle,* from Late Latin *pimpinella,* a medicinal herb]

pim·ple \'pim-pəl\ *n* : a small inflamed swelling of the skin often containing pus : PUSTULE [Middle English *pinple*] — **pim·pled** \-pəld\ *adj* — **pim·ply** \-pə-lē, -plē\ *adj*

¹pin \'pin\ *n* **1 a** : a piece of wood, metal, or plastic used especially for fastening separate articles together or for hanging one article from another **b** : one of the pieces constituting the target in various games (as bowling) **c** : the staff of the flag marking a hole on a golf course **d** : a peg for regulating the tension of the strings of a musical instrument **2 a** : a small pointed piece of wire with a head used especially for fastening cloth or paper **b** : an ornament or emblem fastened to clothing with a pin **c** : a device (as a hairpin or a safety pin) used for fastening **3** : LEG 1 **4** : something of small value : TRIFLE ⟨doesn't care a *pin* for it⟩ [Old English *pinn*]

²pin *vt* **pinned; pin·ning 1** : to fasten, join, or pierce with or as if with a pin **2 a** : ATTACH, HANG ⟨*pinned* their hopes on a miracle⟩ **b** : to assign the blame or responsibility for ⟨*pinned* the robbery on the butler⟩ **3** : to hold (a wrestling opponent) down on the mat in a required position for a required length of time to win a match

pin·a·fore \'pin-ə-,fōr, -,fȯr\ *n* : a low-necked sleeveless garment worn by women and girls [²*pin* + *afore*]

pi·ña·ta *or* **pi·na·ta** \pēn-'yät-ə\ *n* : a decorated pottery jar filled with candies, fruits, and gifts and hung from the ceiling to be broken as part of Mexican Christmas festivities [Spanish, literally, "pot"]

pin·ball machine \'pin-,bȯl-\ *n* : an amusement device in which a ball propelled by a plunger scores points as it rolls down a slanting surface among pins and targets

pince–nez \paⁿ-'snā, pan-\ *n, pl* **pince–nez** \-'snā, -'snāz\ : eyeglasses clipped to the nose by a spring [French, from *pincer* "to pinch" + *nez* "nose"]

pin·cer \'pin-chər, 'pin-sər\ *n* **1 a** *pl* : an instrument with two short handles and two pivoting jaws that is used for gripping things **b** : CHELA **2** : one of two attacking forces advancing one on each side of an enemy position so as to surround it [Middle English *pinceour*] — **pin·cer·like** \-,līk\ *adj*

¹pinch \'pinch\ *vb* **1 a** : to squeeze between the finger and thumb or between the jaws of an instrument **b** : to squeeze painfully **c** : to cause to appear thin or shrunken ⟨a face *pinched* with hunger⟩ **2 a** : to subject to or practice strict economy **b** : to confine or limit narrowly **3 a** : STEAL 2a **b** : ARREST 2 [Middle English *pinchen*]

²pinch *n* **1 a** : a critical point : EMERGENCY **b** : a hurtful pressure or stress : HARDSHIP ⟨the *pinch* of hunger⟩ **2 a** : an act of pinching **b** : as much as may be taken between the finger and thumb ⟨a *pinch* of snuff⟩ **3 a** : the act of stealing : THEFT **b** : a police raid; *also* : ARREST

pinch bar *n* : a lever with a wedge-shaped end

pinch·beck \'pinch-,bek\ *n* **1** : an alloy of copper and zinc used especially to imitate gold in cheap jewelry **2** : something counterfeit or unauthentic [Christopher *Pinchbeck,* died 1732, English watchmaker] — **pinchbeck** *adj*

pinch·er \'pin-chər\ *n* **1** : one that pinches **2** : PINCER 1 — usually used in pl.

pinch hitter *n* **1** : a baseball player sent in to bat for another **2** : a person called on to do another's work in an emergency — **pinch–hit** \'pinch-'hit\ *vi*

pin curl *n* : a curl made usually by dampening a strand of hair, coiling it, and securing it with a hairpin or clip

pin·cush·ion \'pin-,kùsh-ən\ *n* : a small cushion in which pins may be stuck

Pin·dar·ic \pin-'dar-ik\ *adj* : of, relating to, or written in a manner or style characteristic of the poet Pindar

¹pine \'pīn\ *vi* **1** : to lose vigor, health, or weight through grief, worry, or distress ⟨*pine* away⟩ **2** : to have a continuing fruitless desire : YEARN ⟨*pine* for home⟩ [Old English *pīnian,* derived from Latin *poena* "punishment, pain"] SYN see LONG

²pine *n* **1** : any of a genus of cone-bearing evergreen trees having slender elongated needles and including valuable timber trees as well as many ornamentals **2** : the straight-grained white or yellow usually durable and resinous wood of a pine **3** : any of various Australian cone-bearing trees [Old English *pīn,* from Latin *pinus*] — **piny** *or* **pin·ey** \'pī-nē\ *adj*

pi·ne·al \'pin-ē-əl, 'pī-nē-\ *adj* : of, relating to, or being the pineal body [French *pinéal,* from Latin *pinea* "pine cone", from *pinus* "pine"]

pineal body *n* : a small usually conical appendage of the brain of most vertebrates that has an eyelike structure in reptiles and functions in time measurement in some birds

pine·ap·ple \'pī-,nap-əl\ *n* : a tropical plant with stiff spiny sword-shaped leaves and a short flowering stalk that develops into a fleshy edible fruit; *also* : this fruit

pine nut *n* : the edible seed of any of several chiefly western North American pines

pine tar *n* : tar obtained by distillation of pinewood and used especially in roofing and soaps and in the treatment of skin diseases

pine·wood \'pīn-,wùd\ *n* **1** : a wood or growth of pines **2** : PINE 2

pin·feath·er \'pin-,feth-ər\ *n* : an incompletely developed feather just breaking through the skin — **pin·feath·ered** \-ərd\ *adj* — **pin·feath·ery** \-,feth-rē, -ə-rē\ *adj*

ping \'ping\ *n* **1** : a sharp sound like that of a bullet striking **2** : ignition knock ⟨kept hearing a *ping* in the car engine⟩ [imitative] — **ping** *vi*

Ping–Pong \'ping-,päng, -,pȯng\ *trademark* — used for table tennis

pin·head·ed \'pin-'hed-əd\ *adj* : lacking intelligence or understanding : STUPID — **pin·head·ed·ness** *n*

pin·hole \-,hōl\ *n* : a small hole made by, for, or as if by a pin

¹pin·ion \'pin-yən\ *n* **1** : the end part of a bird's wing; *also* : a bird's wing **2** : a feather of a bird's pinion [Middle French *pignon*] — **pinioned** \-yənd\ *adj*

²pinion *vt* **1** : to restrain (a bird) from flight especially by cutting off the pinion of one wing **2 a** : to disable or restrain by binding the arms **b** : to bind fast : SHACKLE

³pinion *n* **1** : a gear with a small number of teeth designed to mesh with a larger wheel or rack **2** : the smallest of a train or set of gear wheels [French *pignon,* from Middle French *peignon,* from *peigne* "comb", from Latin *pecten*]

¹pink \'pingk\ *vt* **1** : PIERCE 1, STAB **2 a** : to perforate in an ornamental pattern **b** : to cut a saw-toothed edge on [Middle English *pinken*]

²pink *n* **1** : any of a genus of annual or perennial herbs that have stems with thick nodes and are often grown for their showy flowers borne singly or in clusters **2** : the highest degree ⟨the *pink* of condition⟩ [origin unknown] — **in the pink** : in the best of health

³pink *adj* **1** : of the color pink **2** : holding moderately radical and usually socialistic political or economic views [²*pink*] — **pink·ly** *adv* — **pink·ness** *n*

⁴pink *n* **1** : a pale red **2 a** : the scarlet color of a fox hunter's coat; *also* : a coat of this color **b** *pl* : light-colored trousers formerly worn by army officers **3** : a person who holds moderately radical political or eco-

pincer 1a

pineapple

\ə\ abut	\ng\ sing
\ər\ further	\ō\ bone
\a\ mat	\ȯ\ saw
\ā\ take	\ȯi\ coin
\ä\ cot, cart	\th\ thin
\au̇\ out	\t͟h\ this
\ch\ chin	\ü\ food
\e\ pet	\ù\ foot
\ē\ easy	\y\ yet
\g\ go	\yü\ few
\i\ tip	\yù\ cure
\ī\ life	\zh\ vision
\j\ job	

nomic views [sense 3 from the viewing of pink as a weak form of red]

pink·eye \'piṅ-,kī\ *n* : a painful and infectious disease in which the inner surface of the eyelid and part of the eyeball become pinkish and sore

pin·kie *or* **pin·ky** \'piṅ-kē\ *n, pl* **pinkies** : a little finger [probably from Dutch *pinkje*, from *pink* "little finger"]

pinking shears *n pl* : shears with a saw-toothed inner edge on the blades for making a zigzag cut

pink·ish \'piṅ-kish\ *adj* : somewhat pink; *esp* : tending to be pink in politics — **pink·ish·ness** *n*

pinko \'piṅ-kō\ *n, pl* **pink·os** *or* **pink·oes** : ⁴PINK 3

pin money *n* : money for incidental expenses

pin·na \'pin-ə\ *n, pl* **pin·nae** \'pin-,ē, -,ī\ *or* **pinnas** 1 : a primary division of a pinnate leaf or frond 2 : the largely cartilaginous projecting portion of the external ear [Latin, "feather, wing"]

pin·nace \'pin-əs\ *n* 1 : a light sailing ship used largely as a tender 2 : any of various ship's boats [Middle French *pinace*]

pin·na·cle \'pin-i-kəl\ *n* 1 : an upright structure (as on a tower) generally ending in a small spire 2 : a lofty peak 3 : the highest point of achievement or development [Middle French *pinacle*, from Late Latin *pinnaculum* "gable", from Latin *pinna* "wing, battlement"] SYN see SUMMIT

pin·nate \'pin-,āt\ *adj* : resembling a feather especially in having similar parts arranged on opposite sides of an axis ⟨a *pinnate* leaf⟩ [Latin *pinnatus* "feathered", from *pinna* "feather"] — **pin·nate·ly** *adv* — **pin·na·tion** \pin-'ā-shən\ *n*

pi·noch·le \'pē-,nək-əl\ *n* : a card game played with a 48-card pack containing two of each suit of A, K, Q, J, 10, 9; *also* : the combination of queen of spades and jack of diamonds which scores 40 points in this game [probably from German dialect *binokel*, a card game, from French dialect *binocle*]

pi·no·cy·to·sis \,pin-ə-sə-'tō-səs, ,pīn-, -,sī-\ *n, pl* **-to·ses** \-,sēz\ : the uptake of fluid by a cell by infolding and pinching off of the cell membrane [Greek *pinein* "to drink"]

pi·ñon *or* **pin·yon** \'pin-yōn, -,yän, -yən; pin-'yōn\ *n, pl* **piñons** *or* **pi·ño·nes** \pin-'yō-nēz\ *or* **pin·yons** : any of various low-growing pines of western North America with seeds that are pine nuts — called also *piñon pine* [American Spanish *piñón*, from Spanish, "pine nut", from *piña* "pine cone", from Latin *pinea*, from *pinus* "pine"]

¹pin·point \'pin-,point\ *vt* 1 : to locate or determine with precision 2 : to cause to stand out clearly : HIGHLIGHT

²pinpoint *adj* 1 : extremely fine or precise 2 : located, fixed, or directed with extreme precision

pin·prick \'pin-,prik\ *n* 1 : a small puncture made by or as if by a pin 2 : a petty irritation or annoyance — **pinprick** *vb*

pins and needles *n pl* : a pricking tingling sensation in a limb recovering from numbness — **on pins and needles** : in a nervous or jumpy state of anticipation

pin·set·ter \'pin-,set-ər\ *n* : one that sets up pins in a bowling alley

pin·spot·ter \-,spät-ər\ *n* : PINSETTER

pin·stripe \-,strīp\ *n* : a very narrow stripe on a fabric — **pin–striped** \-,strīpt\ *adj*

pint \'pīnt\ *n* 1 : a unit of capacity equal to ½ quart (about .47 liter) — see MEASURE table 2 : a pint vessel [Middle French *pinte*, from Medieval Latin *pincta*, derived from Latin *pingere* "to paint"]

pin·tail \'pin-,tāl\ *n, pl* **pintail** *or* **pintails** : a bird (as a duck or grouse) with long central tail feathers

pin·tailed \-,tāld\ *adj* 1 : having a tapered tail with the middle feathers longest 2 : having the tail feathers spiny

¹pin·to \'pin-tō\ *n, pl* **pintos** *also* **pintoes** : a spotted horse or pony [American Spanish, from obsolete Spanish *pinto* "spotted", derived from Latin *pingere* "to paint"]

²pinto *adj* : PIED, MOTTLED

pinto bean *also* **pinto** *n* : a kidney bean grown extensively in Colorado and the southwestern United States where its mottled seed is used for food and its herbage for forage

pint–size \'pīnt-,sīz\ *or* **pint–sized** \-,sīzd\ *adj* : DIMINUTIVE 2

pin–up \'pin-,əp\ *n* : an accessory (as a lamp) attached to a wall

pin·wale \'pin-,wāl\ *adj* : made with narrow wales ⟨*pinwale* corduroy⟩

pin·wheel \-,hwēl, -,wēl\ *n* 1 : a toy consisting of lightweight vanes that revolve at the end of a stick 2 : a fireworks device in the form of a revolving wheel of colored fire

pin·worm \-,wərm\ *n* : any of numerous small nematode worms that infest the intestines and usually the cecum of various vertebrates; *esp* : one parasitic in humans

pin·yin \'pin-'yin\ *n, often cap* : a system for writing Chinese using the Latin alphabet in which tones are indicated by diacritics, the letters *p, t,* and *k* are restricted to aspirates resembling English \p, t, k\, and *b, d,* and *g* are used to represent corresponding sounds without aspiration

pinyon *variant of* PIÑON

¹pi·o·neer \,pī-ə-'niər\ *n* 1 : a person who goes before opening up new ways (as of thought or activity) ⟨*pioneers* of American medicine⟩ 2 : one of the first to settle in an area : COLONIST 3 : a plant or animal capable of establishing itself in a bare or barren area [Middle French *pionier* "member of a unit of military engineers, pioneer", from Old French *peonier* "foot soldier", from *peon* "foot soldier", from Medieval Latin *pedo*, from Latin *ped-, pes* "foot"] — **pioneer** *adj*

☐ ORIGIN The pioneers Americans are most familiar with are people like Daniel Boone who opened up the American West. But a pioneer was originally a foot soldier. Old French *peonier* (derived from Latin *pes,* "foot") was used at first for any foot soldier, but by the Middle French period the word (now spelled *pionier*) had come to designate a particular type of foot soldier, a member of a unit that marched ahead of the army preparing the way by excavation and construction. Because of the pionier's position in advance of the main body of the army, anyone who helps to develop something new, to prepare a way for others to follow, came to be called a *pionier.*

²pioneer *vb* 1 : to act as a pioneer 2 : to open or prepare for others to follow; *esp* : SETTLE 3 : to originate or take part in the development of

pi·ous \'pī-əs\ *adj* 1 : having or showing reverence to God : DEVOUT 2 : marked by sham or hypocrisy ⟨a *pious* fraud⟩ [Latin *pius*] SYN see DEVOUT — **pi·ous·ly** *adv* — **pi·ous·ness** *n*

¹pip \'pip\ *n* : a disorder of a bird marked by formation of a scale or crust on the tongue; *also* : this scale or crust [Dutch *pippe*, derived from Latin *pituita* "phlegm, pip"]

²pip *n* : a dot or spot (as on dice or playing cards) to indicate numerical value [origin unknown]

³pip *n* 1 : a small fruit seed ⟨orange *pips*⟩ 2 *slang* : something very good of its kind [short for *pippin*]

⁴pip *vi* **pipped; pip·ping** 1 : ¹PEEP 1 2 **a** : to break the shell of the egg in hatching **b** : to be broken by a pipping bird ⟨eggs starting to *pip*⟩ [imitative]

⁵pip *n* : a short high-pitched tone ⟨broadcast six *pips* as a time signal⟩ [imitative]

¹pipe \'pīp\ *n* 1 **a** : a musical instrument consisting of a tube of reed, wood, or metal that is played by blowing **b** : a tube producing a musical sound ⟨an organ *pipe*⟩

c : BAGPIPE — usually used in pl. **d** : the whistle, call, or note especially of a bird or an insect **2 a** : a long tube or hollow body used especially to conduct a substance (as water, steam, or gas) **b** : a cylindrical object, part, or passage **3 a** : a tube with a small bowl at one end used for smoking tobacco **b** : a toy pipe for blowing bubbles **4 a** : a large cask used especially for wine and oil **b** : any of various units of liquid capacity based on the size of a pipe; *esp* : a unit of liquid capacity equal to 2 hogsheads (about 477 liters) [Old English *pīpa*, derived from Latin *pipare* "to peep"] — **pipe·less** \'pī-pləs\ *adj*

²**pipe** *vb* **1 a** : to play on a pipe **b** : to convey orders or direct by signals on a boatswain's whistle **2** : to speak in or have a high shrill tone **3** : to furnish or trim with piping **4** : to convey by or as if by pipes — **pip·er** *n*

pipe cleaner *n* : a piece of flexible wire in which tufted fabric is twisted and which is used to clean the stem of a tobacco pipe

pipe down *vi* : to become quiet : stop talking

pipe dream *n* : an unreal or fantastic plan, hope, or story [from the fantasies brought about by the smoking of opium]

pipe·fish \'pīp-ˌfish\ *n* : any of various long slender fishes that are related to the sea horses and have a tube-shaped snout and an angular body covered with bony plates

pipe fitter *n* : one who installs and repairs piping

pipe fitting *n* **1** : a piece (as a coupling or elbow) used to connect pipe or as accessory to a pipe **2** : the work of a pipe fitter

pipe·ful \'pīp-ˌfúl\ *n* : a quantity of tobacco smoked in a pipe at one time

pipe·line \'pī-ˌplīn\ *n* **1** : a line of pipe with pumps, valves, and control devices for conveying liquids, gases, or finely divided solids **2** : a direct channel for information or goods

pipe organ *n* : ORGAN 1a

pi·pette *or* **pi·pet** \pī-'pet\ *n* : a device for measuring and transferring small volumes of liquid that typically consists of a narrow glass tube into which the liquid is drawn by suction and retained by closing the upper end [French *pipette*, from *pipe* "pipe, cask"]

pipe up *vi* : to begin to play, sing, or speak

pip·ing \'pī-ping\ *n* **1 a** : the music of a pipe **b** : the producing of or a calling in shrill pipes (the *piping* of frogs) **2** : a quantity or system of pipes **3** : a narrow decorative fold stitched in seams or along edges (as of clothing or slipcovers)

piping hot *adj* : very hot

pip·it \'pip-ət\ *n* : any of various small singing birds resembling the lark [imitative]

pip·kin \'pip-kən\ *n* : a small earthenware or metal pot usually with a horizontal handle [perhaps from *pipe*]

pip·pin \'pip-ən\ *n* **1** : any of numerous apples with usually yellow or greenish yellow skins strongly flushed with red **2** : someone or something greatly admired [Old French *pepin*]

pip·sis·se·wa \pip-'sis-ə-ˌwó\ *n* : a low evergreen herb related to the wintergreens that has astringent leaves used medicinally [Cree *pipisisikweu*]

pip–squeak \'pip-ˌskwēk\ *n* : a small or insignificant person

pi·quant \'pē-kənt, -ˌkänt\ *adj* **1** : agreeably stimulating to the sense of taste **2** : pleasingly exciting (a *piquant* bit of gossip) **3** : having a lively roguish charm (a *piquant* face) [Middle French, from *piquer* "to prick"] — **pi·quan·cy** \-kən-sē\ *n* — **pi·quant·ly** *adv* — **pi·quant·ness** *n*

¹**pique** \'pēk\ *n* **1** : offense taken by one slighted **2** : a fit of resentment

²**pique** *vt* **1** : to arouse anger or resentment in : IRRITATE; *esp* : to offend by slighting **2** : EXCITE 1b, AROUSE (the package *piqued* my curiosity) [French *piquer*, literally, "to prick"]

pi·qué *or* **pi·que** \pi-'kā, 'pē-,\ *n* : a durable ribbed fabric [French *piqué*, from *piquer* "to prick, quilt"]

pi·quet \pi-'kā, pik-'et\ *n* : a two-handed card game played with 32 cards in which players score points for certain combinations and for winning tricks [French]

pi·ra·cy \'pī-rə-sē\ *n, pl* **-cies** **1** : robbery on the high seas **2** : the unauthorized use of another's production or invention especially in violation of a copyright

pi·ra·nha \pə-'ran-yə; -'rän-ə, -yə\ *n* : a small South American fish that often attacks and inflicts dangerous wounds upon men and large animals — called also *caribe* [Portuguese, from Tupi]

¹**pi·rate** \'pī-rət\ *n* : a person who commits or practices piracy [Latin *pirata*, from Greek *peiratēs*, from *peiran* "to attempt"] — **pi·rat·i·cal** \pə-'rat-i-kəl, pī-\ *adj* — **pi·rat·i·cal·ly** \-'rat-i-kə-lē, -klē\ *adv*

²**pirate** *vt* : to take or make use of by piracy (*pirate* an invention)

pi·rogue \'pē-ˌrōg\ *n* **1** : DUGOUT 1 **2** : a boat like a canoe [French, from Spanish *piragua*, of American Indian origin]

pir·ou·ette \ˌpir-ə-'wet\ *n* : a rapid whirling about of the body; *esp* : a full turn on the toe or ball of one foot in ballet [French] — **pirouette** *vi*

pis *pl of* PI

Pi·sces \'pī-ˌsēz, 'pis-ˌēz\ *n* **1** : a zodiacal constellation directly south of Andromeda **2** : the 12th sign of the zodiac; *also* : one born under this sign [Latin, from pl. of *piscis* "fish"]

pi·scine \'pī-ˌsēn; 'pis-ˌīn, -ˌkīn\ *adj* : of, relating to, or characteristic of fish [Latin *piscinus*, from *piscis* "fish"]

pis·mire \'pis-ˌmīr, 'piz-\ *n* : ANT [Middle English *pissemire*, from *pisse* "urine" + *mire* "ant", of Scandinavian origin]

pis·tach·io \pə-'stash-ē-ˌō, -'stash-ō, -'stäsh-\ *n, pl* **-chios** : a small tree of the sumac family whose fruit contains a greenish edible seed; *also* : its seed [Italian *pistacchio*, from Latin *pistacium* "pistachio nut", from Greek *pistakion*, from *pistakē* "pistachio tree", from Persian *pistah*]

pis·til \'pis-tl\ *n* : the seed-producing part and female reproductive organ of a flower consisting usually of stigma, style, and ovary [Latin *pistillum* "pestle"]

pis·til·late \'pis-tə-ˌlāt\ *adj* : having pistils; *esp* : having pistils but no stamens

pis·tol \'pis-tl\ *n* : a short firearm intended to be aimed and fired with one hand [Middle French *pistole*, from German, from Czech *pišťal*, literally, "pipe"] — **pistol** *vt*

pis·tol–whip \-ˌhwip, -ˌwip\ *vt* : to beat with a pistol

pis·ton \'pis-tən\ *n* **1** : a sliding piece moved by or moving against fluid pressure that usually consists of a short cylinder fitting within a cylindrical vessel along which it moves back and forth **2** : a sliding valve in a brass wind instrument serving when pressed down to lower its pitch [French, from Italian *pistone*, from *pistare* "to pound", from Medieval Latin, from Latin *pistus*, past participle of *pinsere* "to crush"]

piston ring *n* : a springy split metal ring around a piston for making a tight fit

piston rod *n* : a rod by which a piston is moved or by which it transmits motion

¹**pit** \'pit\ *n* **1** : a hole, shaft, or cavity in the ground (a gravel *pit*) **2** : an area set off from and often lower than adjacent areas: as **a** : an enclosure where animals (as cocks) are set to fight **b** : the space occupied by an orchestra in a theater **3 a** : a hollowed or indented area especially in the surface of the body **b** : an indented scar (as from a boil) **c** : a thin area in a plant cell wall through which dissolved materials can pass **4** : an area alongside an auto racetrack where cars are refueled and repaired during a race — often used in pl. with *the* [Old English *pytt*] — **pit·ted** *adj*

piranha

pistil

pistil

\ə\ abut	\ng\ sing
\ər\ further	\ō\ bone
\a\ mat	\ó\ saw
\ā\ take	\oi\ coin
\ä\ cot, cart	\th\ thin
\aú\ out	\th\ this
\ch\ chin	\ü\ food
\e\ pet	\ú\ foot
\ē\ easy	\y\ yet
\g\ go	\yü\ few
\i\ tip	\yú\ cure
\ī\ life	\zh\ vision
\j\ job	

²pit *vb* **pit·ted; pit·ting** **1 a** : to put into or store in a pit **b** : to make pits in; *esp* : to scar with pits **2** : to place in opposition or rivalry **3** : to become marked with pits

³pit *n* : the stone of a fruit (as the cherry) that is a drupe [Dutch] — **pit·less** \'pit-ləs\ *adj*

⁴pit *vt* **pit·ted; pit·ting** : to remove the pit from

pit-a-pat \,pit-i-'pat\ *n* : PITTER-PATTER [imitative] — **pit-a-pat** *adv or adj* — **pit-a-pat** *vi*

¹pitch \'pich\ *n* **1** : a dark sticky substance obtained as a residue in the distillation of organic materials (as tars) **2** : resin from various conifers [Old English *pic*, from Latin *pix*]

²pitch *vt* : to cover, smear, or treat with or as if with pitch

³pitch *vb* **1** : to erect and fix firmly in place ⟨*pitch* a tent⟩ **2** : THROW, TOSS ⟨*pitch* hay⟩; *also* : to deliver a baseball to a batter **3 a** : to cause to be at a particular pitch or level ⟨*pitch* a tune too high⟩ **b** : to incline or cause to incline at a particular angle **4 a** : to fall headlong **b** : to have the bow alternately plunge and rise abruptly ⟨a ship *pitching* in heavy seas⟩ **c** : BUCK 1a ⟨a *pitching* horse⟩ [Middle English *pichen*]

⁴pitch *n* **1** : the action or a manner of pitching; *esp* : an up and down movement **2 a** : SLOPE 2; *also* : degree of slope **b** (1) : distance between one point on a gear tooth and the corresponding point on the next tooth (2) : distance from any point on the thread of a screw to the corresponding point on an adjacent thread measured parallel to the axis **c** : the distance advanced by an aircraft with one revolution of its propeller **3** : a high point : ZENITH **4 a** : the property of a tone that is determined by the frequency of the sound waves producing it : highness or lowness of sound **b** : a standard frequency for tuning instruments **c** : the phonemic change of vibrational frequency in human speech **5** : a high-pressure sales talk **6 a** : the delivery of a baseball by a pitcher to a batter **b** : a baseball so thrown — **pitched** \'picht\ *adj*

pitch–black \'pich-'blak\ *adj* : extremely dark or black

pitch·blende \'pich-,blend\ *n* : a brown to black mineral that consists essentially of an oxide of uranium, often contains radium, and is a source of uranium [German *pechblende*, from *pech* "pitch" + *blende* "sphalerite"]

pitch–dark \-'därk\ *adj* : extremely dark

pitched battle \'picht-, 'pich-\ *n* : an intensely fought battle in which the opposing forces are locked in close combat

¹pitch·er \'pich-ər\ *n* : a container for holding and pouring liquids that usually has a lip or spout and a handle [Old French *pichier*, from Medieval Latin *bicarius* "goblet", from Greek *bikos* "earthen jug"]

²pitcher *n* : one (as a baseball player) that pitches

pitcher plant *n* : any of various plants with leaves modified into pitchers in which insects are trapped and digested by the plant

pitch·fork \'pich-,förk\ *n* : a usually long-handled fork used in pitching hay or straw [Middle English *pikfork*, from *pik* "pick" + *fork*] — **pitchfork** *vt*

pitch in *vi* **1** : to begin to work energetically **2** : to contribute to a common activity

pitch·out \'pich-,aut\ *n* **1** : a pitch in baseball deliberately out of reach of the batter to enable the catcher to check or put out a base runner **2** : a lateral pass in football between two backs behind the line of scrimmage

pitch pipe *n* : a small pipe blown to indicate musical pitch especially for singers or for tuning an instrument

pitchy \'pich-ē\ *adj* **1** : full of pitch : TARRY **2** : of, relating to, or having the qualities of pitch

pit·e·ous \'pit-ē-əs\ *adj* : PITIFUL 1 — **pit·e·ous·ly** *adv* — **pit·e·ous·ness** *n*

pit·fall \'pit-,föl\ *n* **1** : TRAP 1, SNARE; *esp* : a covered or camouflaged pit used to catch and hold an animal or

---

person **2** : a hidden or not easily recognized danger or difficulty

¹pith \'pith\ *n* **1 a** : a central strand of spongy tissue in the stems of most vascular plants that probably functions chiefly in storage **b** : any of various loose spongy internal tissues or parts **2** : the essential part : CORE [Old English *pitha*]

²pith *vt* : to destroy the spinal cord or central nervous system of (as a frog) by passing a wire or needle up and down the vertebral canal

pith·ec·an·thro·pine \,pith-i-'kan-thrə-,pīn, -'kant-\ *n* : any of a group of extinct human beings (as Java man) of the Pleistocene geologic epoch that had a smaller brain and larger canine and incisor teeth than human beings alive today and are now grouped as a single species of the same genus (*Homo*) as modern human beings

pith·e·can·thro·pus \,pith-i-'kan-thrə-pəs, -'kant-; -kan-'thrō-\ *n, pl* **-thro·pi** \-,pī, -,pē\ : PITHECANTHROPINE [New Latin, from Greek *pithēkos* "ape" + *anthrōpos* "human being"]

pithy \'pith-ē\ *adj* **pith·i·er; -est** **1** : consisting of or filled with pith **2** : being short and to the point ⟨a *pithy* comment⟩ — **pith·i·ly** \'pith-ə-lē\ *adv* — **pith·i·ness** \'pith-ē-nəs\ *n*

piti·able \'pit-ē-ə-bəl\ *adj* **1** : deserving or exciting pity : LAMENTABLE **2** : pitifully insignificant or scanty — **piti·able·ness** *n* — **piti·ably** \-blē\ *adv*

piti·ful \'pit-i-fəl\ *adj* **1** : arousing pity or sympathy ⟨a *pitiful* orphan⟩ **2** : deserving pitying contempt ⟨a *pitiful* excuse⟩ — **piti·ful·ly** \-fə-lē, -flē\ *adv*

piti·less \'pit-i-ləs, 'pit-l-əs\ *adj* : having no pity : MERCILESS — **piti·less·ly** *adv* — **piti·less·ness** *n*

pi·ton \'pē-,tän\ *n* : a spike, wedge, or peg that can be driven into a rock or ice surface as a support (as for a mountain climber) [French]

pit·tance \'pit-ns\ *n* : a small portion, amount, or allowance [Middle English *pitance* "piety, pity", from Old French, from Medieval Latin *pietantia*, from *pietare* "to be charitable", from Latin *pietas* "piety, pity"]

pit·ter–pat·ter \'pit-ər-,pat-ər, 'pit-ē-,pat-\ *n* : a rapid succession of light sounds or beats — **pit·ter-pat·ter** \,pit-ər-', ,pit-ē-'\ *adv or adj* — **pit·ter-pat·ter** \,pit-ər-', ,pit-ē-'\ *vi*

pi·tu·i·tary \pə-'tü-ə-,ter-ē, -'tyü-\ *adj* : of, relating to, or being the pituitary gland [Latin *pituita* "phlegm"; from the former belief that the pituitary gland secreted phlegm]

pituitary gland *n* : a small oval endocrine organ attached to the base of the brain that produces various internal secretions with a direct or indirect regulatory action on most basic body functions and especially on growth and reproduction — called also *pituitary, pituitary body*

pit viper *n* : any of a family of mostly New World venomous snakes with a sensory pit on each side of the head and hollow perforated fangs

¹pity \'pit-ē\ *n, pl* **pit·ies** **1** : sympathetic sorrow for one suffering, distressed, or unhappy : COMPASSION **2** : something to be regretted [Old French *pité*, from Latin *pietas* "piety, pity", from *pius* "pious"]

²pity *vb* **pit·ied; pity·ing** : to feel pity or pity for — **piti·er** *n*

pity·ing *adj* : expressing or feeling pity ⟨a *pitying* glance⟩ — **pity·ing·ly** \-ing-lē\ *adv*

¹piv·ot \'piv-ət\ *n* **1** : a shaft or pin on which something turns **2** : something upon which something else turns or depends : a central member, part, or point [French]

²pivot *vb* **1** : to turn on or as if on a pivot **2** : to provide with, mount on, or attach by a pivot **3** : to cause to pivot

piv·ot·al \'piv-ət-l\ *adj* **1** : of, relating to, or functioning as a pivot **2** : vitally important : CRUCIAL — **piv·ot·al·ly** \-l-ē\ *adv*

pivot joint *n* : an anatomical joint (as that of the head and spine) that consists of a bony pivot in a ring of bone and cartilage and that permits rotatory movement only

pix·ie *or* **pixy** \'pik-sē\ *n, pl* **pix·ies** : a mischievous sprite or fairy [origin unknown] — **pix·ie·ish** \-sē-ish\ *adj*

piz·za \'pēt-sə\ *n* : an open pie made typically of thinly rolled bread dough spread with a spiced mixture (as of tomatoes, cheese, and ground meat) and baked [Italian, derived from Latin *pix* "pitch"]

piz·ze·ria \,pēt-sə-'rē-ə\ *n* : an establishment where pizzas are made or sold [Italian, from *pizza*]

piz·zi·ca·to \,pit-si-'kät-ō\ *adv or adj* : by means of plucking by the fingers instead of bowing — used as a direction in music [Italian]

pla·ca·ble \'plak-ə-bəl, 'plā-kə-\ *adj* : easily placated — **pla·ca·bil·i·ty** \,plak-ə-'bil-ət-ē, ,plā-kə-\ *n* — **pla·ca·bly** \'plak-ə-blē, 'plā-kə-\ *adv*

¹plac·ard \'plak-ərd, -,ärd\ *n* : a notice posted or carried in a public place : POSTER [Middle French *placquart*, from *plaquier* "to plate, plaster"]

²plac·ard \'plak-,ärd, -ərd\ *vt* **1** : to post placards on or in **2** : to anounce by or as if by posting

pla·cate \'plāk-,āt, 'plak-\ *vt* : to calm the anger of especially by concessions : SOOTHE [Latin *placare*] SYN see PACIFY — **pla·ca·tion** \plā-'kā-shə\ *n* — **pla·ca·tive** \'plāk-,āt-iv, 'plak-\ *adj* — **pla·ca·to·ry** \'plāk-ə-,tōr-ē, 'plak-, -,tòr-\ *adj*

¹place \'plās\ *n* **1 a** : physical extension : SPACE (considerations of time and *place*) **b** : a particular but often unspecified location : LOCALITY (stopped several days at each *place*) **2 a** : DWELLING **b** : a building or locality used for a particular purpose (a *place* of resort) (a *place* of worship) **3** : a particular part of a surface or body : SPOT (a sore *place* on the shoulder) (lost my *place* in the book) **4 a** : position in an ordering (in the first *place*) **b** : the position next after the winner in a race or contest **c** : the position of a figure in a numeral (three *places* beyond the decimal point) **5 a** : suitable or assigned location or situation (not the *place* for an active person) **b** : an accommodation occupied by or available for one person (set 12 *places* at table) **c** : space or situation customarily or formerly occupied (paper towels taking the *place* of linen) **d** : JOB 3b, POSITION (lose one's *place* at the office) [Middle French, "open space", from Latin *platea* "broad street", from Greek *plateia*, from *platys* "broad"] — **place·less** \'plā-sləs\ *adj*

²place *vb* **1** : to distribute in an orderly manner : ARRANGE **2 a** : to put in or direct to a particular place **b** : to present for consideration (aquestion *placed* before the group) **c** : to put in a particular state **3 a** : to appoint to a position **b** : to find employment or a home for **4 a** : to assign to or hold a position in a series : RANK **b** : ESTIMATE (*placed* the value of the estate too high) **c** : to identify by association (could not *place* them although they looked familiar) **5** : to give an order for (*place* a bet) **6** : to come in second in a horse race — **place·able** \'plā-sə-bəl\ *adj*

pla·ce·bo \plə-'sē-bō\ *n, pl* **-bos** : an inert medication used for psychological reasons or as a control in an experiment [Latin, "I shall please", from *placēre* "to please"]

place·hold·er \'plās-,hōl-dər\ *n* : a symbol used in a mathematical or logical expression that may be replaced by the name of any element of a given set

place·kick \'plā-,skik\ *n* : the kicking of a ball placed or held in a stationary position on the ground — **placekick** *vb*

place·ment \'plā-smənt\ *n* : an act or instance of placing; *esp* : the assignment of a person to a suitable place (as a class in school or a job)

pla·cen·ta \plə-'sent-ə\ *n, pl* **-centas** *or* **-cen·tae** \-'sent-ē\ **1** : the vascular organ in most mammals by which the fetus is joined to the maternal uterus and nourished; *also* : an analogous organ in another animal **2** : a part of a plant ovary that bears ovules [Latin, "flat cake", from Greek *plakount-, plakous*, from *plak-, plax* "flat surface"] — **pla·cen·tal** \-'sent-l\ *adj or n* — **pla·cen·ta·tion** \,plas-n-'tā-shən, plə-,sen-\ *n*

plac·er \'plas-ər\ *n* : an alluvial or glacial deposit containing particles of valuable mineral (as gold) [Spanish, from Catalan, "submarine plain", from *plaza* "place", from Latin *platea* "broad street"]

place value *n* : the value of the location of a digit in a numeral (in 425 the location of the digit 2 has a *place value* of ten while the digit itself indicates that there are two tens)

plac·id \'plas-əd\ *adj* : peacefully free of interruption or disturbance : QUIET [Latin *placidus*, from *placēre* "to please"] SYN see CALM — **pla·cid·i·ty** \pla-'sid-ət-ē, plə-\ *n* — **plac·id·ly** \'plas-əd-lē\ *adv* — **plac·id·ness** *n*

plack·et \'plak-ət\ *n* : a slit or opening in a garment (as a skirt) often forming the closure [origin unknown]

plac·o·derm \'plak-ə-,dərm\ *n* : any of a class (Placodermi) of extinct Paleozoic armored and jawed fishes [Greek *plak-, plax* "flat surface"]

plac·oid \'plak-,òid\ *adj* : of, relating to, or being a fish scale (as of a shark) of dermal origin with an enamel-tipped spine [Greek *plak-, plax* "flat surface"]

pla·gia·rism \'plā-jə-,riz-əm\ *n* **1** : an act of plagiarizing **2** : something plagiarized [derived from Latin *plagiarius* "plunderer, plagiarist", from *plagium* "hunting net", from *plaga* "net"] — **pla·gia·rist** \-rəst\ *n* — **pla·gia·ris·tic** \,plā-jə-'ris-tik\ *adj*

pla·gia·rize \'plā-jə-,rīz\ *vb* : to steal and pass off as one's own (the ideas or work of another) : commit literary theft — **pla·gia·riz·er** *n*

pla·gio·clase \'plā-jē-ə-,klās, 'plā-jə-; 'plaj-ē-ə-, 'plaj-ə-; -,klāz\ *n* : a feldspar having calcium or sodium in its composition [Greek *plagios* "oblique" + *klasis* "breaking", from *klan* "to break"]

¹plague \'plāg\ *n* **1** : a disastrous evil or destructively numerous influx (a *plague* of locusts); *also* : a cause or occasion of annoyance **2 a** : an epidemic disease causing a high rate of mortality : PESTILENCE **b** : a virulent contagious disease that is caused by a bacterium, occurs or has occurred in several froms including bubonic plague, and is usually passed to human beings from rodents — called also *black death* [Middle French *plage*, from Late Latin *plaga*, from Latin, "blow"]

²plague *vt* **1** : to strike or afflict with or as if with disease, calamity, or natural evil **2** : TEASE 2a, TORMENT — **plagu·er** *n*

plagu·ey *or* **plaguy** \'plā-gē, 'pleg-ē\ *adj, chiefly dialect* : causing irritation or annoyance : TROUBLESOME — **plaguey** *adv* — **plagu·i·ly** \'plā-gə-lē, 'pleg-ə-\ *adv*

plaid \'plad\ *n* **1** : a rectangular length of tartan worn over the left shoulder by men and women as part of the Scottish national costume **2 a** : TARTAN 2 **b** : a fabric with a pattern of tartan or imitative of tartan **3 a** : TARTAN 1 **b** : a pattern of unevenly spaced repeated stripes crossing at right angles [Scottish Gaelic *plaide*] — **plaid** *adj* — **plaid·ed** \-əd\ *adj*

¹plain \'plān\ *n* : an extensive area of level or rolling treeless country; *also* : a broad unbroken expanse [Old French, from Latin *planum*, from *planus* "flat, level"]

²plain *adj* **1** : lacking ornament or pattern (the dress was *plain*) (*plain* fabrics) **2** : free of added or extraneous matter : PURE (a glass of *plain* water) **3** : free of impediments to view (in *plain* sight) **4 a** : clear to the mind or senses (the trouble was *plain* to the mechanic) **b** : marked by candor : BLUNT (*plain* speaking) **5 a** : of common or average attainments or status : neither notable nor lowly : ORDINARY (*plain* people) **b** : free from complexity : SIMPLE (a *plain* explanation); *also* : containing or using only simple wholesome ingredi-

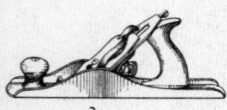

³plane

ents ⟨*plain* food⟩ ⟨*plain* cooking⟩ **c** : lacking beauty or ugliness : HOMELY [Middle French, "level", from Latin *planus*] SYN see FRANK — **plain·ly** *adv* — **plain·ness** \'plān-nəs\ *n*

³**plain** *adv* : in a plain manner ⟨if I may speak *plain*⟩

plain-clothes-man \'plān-'klōz-mən, -'klōthz-, -,man\ *n* : a police officer who does not wear a uniform while on duty : DETECTIVE

plain sailing *n* : easy progress over an unobstructed course

plains·man \'plānz-mən\ *n* : an inhabitant of plains

plain·song \'plān-,sȯng\ *n* : rhythmic but not metrical liturgical chant sung in unison in various Christian rites; *esp* : GREGORIAN CHANT

plain-spo·ken \'plān-'spō-kən\ *adj* : speaking or spoken plainly and especially bluntly ⟨a *plainspoken* teacher⟩ — **plain·spo·ken·ness** \-kən-nəs\ *n*

plaint \'plānt\ *n* **1** : LAMENTATION, WAIL **2** : PROTEST 3, COMPLAINT [Middle French, from Latin *planctus,* from *plangere* "to strike, beat one's breast, lament"]

plain·tiff \'plānt-əf\ *n* : a person who begins a lawsuit to enforce a claim — compare DEFENDANT [Middle French *plaintif,* from *plaintif* "complaining, plaintive"]

plain·tive \'plānt-iv\ *adj* : expressive of suffering or woe : MELANCHOLY [Middle French *plaintif,* from *plaint* "plaint"] — **plain·tive·ly** *adv* — **plain·tive·ness** *n*

plain weave *n* : a weave in which the threads interlace alternately — **plain-wo·ven** \,plān-'wō-vən\ *adj*

¹**plait** \'plāt, 'plat\ *n* **1** : PLEAT **2** : a braid of material (as hair or straw) [Middle French *pleit,* derived from Latin *plicare* "to fold"]

²**plait** *vt* **1** : PLEAT 1 **2 a** : to interweave the strands or locks of : BRAID **b** : to make by plaiting — **plait·er** *n*

¹**plan** \'plan\ *n* **1** : a drawing or diagram showing the parts or outline of something **2** : a method or scheme of acting, doing, or arranging ⟨a civil defense *plan*⟩ ⟨vacation *plans*⟩ **3** : INTENT 1, AIM ⟨the *plan* was to stop them at the bridge⟩ [French, "plane, foundation, ground plan"; partly from Latin *planum* "plain, plane"; partly from French *planter* "to plant, fix in place", from Late Latin *plantare*] — **plan·less** \-ləs\ *adj* — **plan·less·ly** *adv* — **plan·less·ness** *n* □ SYN PLAN, DESIGN, PLOT, SCHEME mean a method of making or doing something or achieving an end. PLAN implies mental formulation and often graphic representation ⟨studied the *plans* for the stage sets⟩ DESIGN suggests a pattern and a degree of order or harmony ⟨*designs* for three new gowns⟩ PLOT implies a laying out in clearly distinguished sections with attention to their relations and proportions ⟨outlined the *plot* of the new play⟩ SCHEME stresses systematic choice and ordering of detail for the end in view and may suggest a plan motivated by craftiness and self-seeking ⟨a *scheme* to swindle a neighbor⟩

²**plan** *vb* **planned; plan·ning 1** : to form a plan of or for : arrange the parts or details of in advance ⟨*plan* a party⟩ **2** : to have in mind : INTEND; *also* : to make plans — **plan·ner** *n*

plan- *or* **plano-** *combining form* : flat : flat and ⟨*plano*-convex⟩ [Latin *planus* "flat, level"]

pla·nar \'plā-nər, -,när\ *adj* : of, relating to, or lying in a plane

pla·nar·ia \plə-'nar-ē-ə, -'ner-\ *n* : PLANARIAN; *esp* : one of a common freshwater genus [derived from Late Latin *planarius* "lying on a plane", from Latin *planum* "plane"]

pla·nar·i·an \-ē-ən\ *n* : any of an order (Tricladida) of small soft-bodied ciliated mostly aquatic flatworms — **planarian** *adj*

¹**plane** \'plān\ *vt* : to make smooth or even especially with a plane; *also* : to remove by planing [Middle French *planer,* from Late Latin *planare,* from Latin *planus* "level"] — **plan·er** *n*

²**plane** *n* : PLANE TREE [Middle French, from Latin *platanus,* from Greek *platanos*]

³**plane** *n* : a tool for smoothing or shaping a wood surface

⁴**plane** *n* **1 a** : a surface such that any two of its points can be joined by a straight line lying wholly within the surface **b** : a flat or level material surface **2** : a level of existence, consciousness, or development **3 a** : one of the main supporting surfaces of an airplane **b** : AIRPLANE [Latin *planum,* from *planus* "level"]

⁵**plane** *adj* **1** : lacking elevations or depressions : FLAT, LEVEL **2** : of, relating to, or lying in a plane ⟨*plane* curves⟩ [Latin *planus*]

plane angle *n* : an angle formed by two intersecting lines each of which lies on a face of a dihedral angle and is perpendicular to the edge of the face

plane geometry *n* : a branch of elementary geometry that deals with plane figures — compare SOLID GEOMETRY

plan·et \'plan-ət\ *n* : a heavenly body other than a comet, asteroid, or satellite that revolves around the sun; *also* : such a body revolving around the sun of another solar system [Old French *planete,* from Late Latin *planeta,* from Greek *planēt-, planēs,* literally, "wanderer", from *planasthai* "to wander"] □ ORIGIN In studying the sky ancient astronomers observed that while most of the stars maintain fixed relative positions there are a few celestial bodies that quite obviously change their positions in relation to each other and to the greater number of fixed stars. The most notable of these, of course, were the sun and moon, but five others were also observed — Mercury, Venus, Mars, Jupiter, and Saturn. The Greek name for these was *planēs,* whose literal meaning is "wanderer". This is the ancestor of English *planet.* Since ancient times three more planets have been discovered, Uranus in the 18th century, Neptune in the 19th, and Pluto in the 20th.

PLANETS

SYMBOL	NAME	MEAN DISTANCE FROM THE SUN		PERIOD OF REVOLUTION IN DAYS OR YEARS	EQUATORIAL DIAMETER IN KILOMETERS
		ASTRONOMI-CAL UNITS	MILLION KILOMETERS		
☿	Mercury	0.387	57.9	87.97 d.	4878
♀	Venus	0.723	108.2	224.70 d.	12104
⊕	Earth	1.000	149.6	365.26 d.	12756
♂	Mars	1.524	228.0	686.98 d.	6787
♃	Jupiter	5.203	778.4	11.86 y.	142800
♄	Saturn	9.522	1426.7	29.46 y.	120000
♅	Uranus	19.201	2888.6	84.01 y.	50800
♆	Neptune	30.074	4530.5	164.79 y.	48600
♇	Pluto	39.725	5951.2	247.69 y.	3000

plan·e·tar·i·um \,plan-ə-'ter-ē-əm\ *n, pl* **-i·ums** *or* **-ia** \-ē-ə\ **1** : a model or representation of the solar system **2 a** : an optical device to project various celestial images and effects **b** : a building or room housing such a device

plan·e·tary \'plan-ə-,ter-ē\ *adj* **1 a** : of or relating to a planet **b** : having a motion like that of a planet ⟨*planetary* electrons of the atomic nucleus⟩ **2** : WORLDWIDE ⟨a matter of *planetary* concern⟩

plan·e·tes·i·mal \,plan-ə-'tes-ə-məl, -'tez-\ *n* : any of numerous small solid celestial bodies which may have existed at an early stage of the development of the solar system and from which the planets may have been formed [*planet* + *-esimal* (as in *infinitesimal*)]

plan·e·toid \'plan-ə-,tȯid\ *n* **1** : a body resembling a planet **2** : ASTEROID

plane tree *n* : any of a genus of trees (as the sycamore) with large lobed leaves and flowers in globe-shaped heads — called also *plane*

plan·gent \'plan-jənt\ *adj* **1** : having a loud reverberating sound **2** : having an expressive especially plaintive quality [Latin *plangens,* present participle of *plangere* "to strike, lament"] — **plan·gen·cy** *n* — **plan·gent·ly** *adv*

¹plank \'plangk\ *n* **1** : a heavy thick board usually 5 to 10 centimeters thick and at least 20 centimeters wide **2** : an article in the platform of a political party [Old North French *planke,* from Latin *planca*]

²plank *vt* **1** : to cover or floor with planks **2** : to set down forcefully ⟨*planked* the book onto the shelf⟩ **3** : to cook and serve on a board usually with an elaborate garnish

plank·ing *n* : a quantity or covering of planks ⟨deck *planking*⟩

plank·ter \'plang-tər, 'plangk-\ *n* : a planktonic organism [Greek *planktēr* "wanderer", from *plazesthai* "to wander"]

plank·ton \'plang-tən, 'plangk-, -ˌtän\ *n* : the passively floating or weakly swimming usually minute animal and plant life of a body of water — compare NEKTON [German, from Greek *planktos* "drifting", from *plazesthai* "to wander, drift"] — **plank·ton·ic** \plang-'tän-ik, plangk-\ *adj*

plano- — see PLAN-

pla·no-con·cave \ˌplā-nō-kän-'kāv, -'kän-,\ *adj* : flat on one side and concave on the other

pla·no-con·vex \-kän-'veks, -'kän-ˌ, -kən-'\ *adj* : flat on one side and convex on the other

pla·nog·ra·phy \plā-'näg-rə-fē, plə-\ *n* : a process (as lithography) for printing from a plane surface — **pla·no·graph·ic** \ˌplā-nə-'graf-ik\ *adj*

¹plant \'plant\ *vb* **1 a** : to put or set in the ground to grow ⟨*plant* seeds⟩ **b** : IMPLANT ⟨*plant* good habits⟩ **2 a** : to cause to become established ⟨*plant* colonies⟩ **b** : to stock, set, or sow with something usually to grow or increase ⟨*plant* fields to corn⟩ ⟨*plant* a stream with trout⟩ **3 a** : to place or fix in the ground ⟨*planted* stakes to hold the vines⟩ **b** : to place firmly or forcibly ⟨*planted* a hard blow on his chin⟩ **4** : to hide, place secretly, or prearrange with intent to mislead ⟨*planted* nuggets in a worthless mine⟩ ⟨*plant* a spy in an office⟩ ⟨*plant* a rumor⟩ **5** : to plant something [Old English *plantian,* from Late Latin *plantare* "to plant, fix in place", from Latin, "to plant", from *planta* "plant"] — **plant·able** \-ə-bəl\ *adj*

²plant *n* **1** : any of a kingdom (Plantae) of living beings typically lacking the ability to move from place to place under their own power, having no obvious nervous or sensory organs, and possessing cellulose cell walls and capacity for indefinite growth — compare ANIMAL **2 a** : land, buildings, and equipment of a business, institution, or organization ⟨the college *plant*⟩ **b** : a factory or workshop for the manufacture of a product ⟨an automobile *plant*⟩ **3** : something or someone planted ⟨the new clerk was a police *plant*⟩ [Old English *plante,* from Latin *planta*] — **plant·like** \-ˌlīk\ *adj*

Plan·tag·e·net \plan-'taj-nət, -ə-nət\ *adj* : of or relating to a royal house ruling England from 1154 to 1485 [*Plantagenet,* nickname of the family adopted as a surname] — **Plantagenet** *n*

¹plan·tain \'plant-n\ *n* : any of several common short-stemmed or stemless weedy herbs with parallel-veined leaves and a long spike of tiny greenish flowers [Old French, from Latin *plantago,* from *planta* "sole of the foot", from its broad leaves]

²plantain *n* : a banana plant with large greenish starchy fruit that is eaten cooked and is a staple food in the tropics; *also* : this fruit [Spanish *plántano* "plane tree, banana tree", from Medieval Latin *plantanus* "plane tree", from Latin *platanus*]

plantain lily *n* : a plant of the lily family with ribbed basal leaves and racemes of white or lilac flowers

plan·tar \'plant-ər, 'plan-ˌtär\ *adj* : of or relating to the sole of the foot [Latin *plantaris,* from *planta* "sole"]

plan·ta·tion \plan-'tā-shən\ *n* **1** : a usually large group of plants and especially trees under cultivation **2** : a settlement in a new country or region : COLONY **3** : a planted area; *esp* : an agricultural estate worked by resident labor

plant·er \'plant-ər\ *n* **1** : one that plants or cultivates ⟨a mechanical *planter*⟩; *esp* : an owner or operator of a plantation **2** : one who settles or founds a colony **3** : a container in which ornamental plants are grown

plant food *n* **1** : FOOD 1b **2** : soil fertilizer

plant hormone *n* : an organic substance that is not a nutrient, that in minute amounts modifies a plant physiological process, and that is active elsewhere than at the site of production

plan·ti·grade \'plant-ə-ˌgrād\ *adj* : walking on the sole with the heel touching the ground ⟨humans are *plantigrade* animals⟩ [French, from Latin *planta* "sole" + *gradi* "to step"] — **plantigrade** *n*

plant·ing *n* : an area where plants are grown for commercial or decorative purposes

plant kingdom *n* : the one of the three basic groups of natural objects that includes all living and extinct plants — compare ANIMAL KINGDOM, MINERAL KINGDOM

plant louse *n* : APHID; *also* : a related insect

plan·u·la \'plan-yə-lə\ *n, pl* **-lae** \-ˌlē, -ˌlī\ : the young usually flattened oval or oblong free-swimming ciliated larva of some coelenterates [New Latin, from Latin *planus* "level, flat"]

plaque \'plak\ *n* **1** : an ornamental brooch; *esp* : the badge of an honorary order **2** : a flat thin piece (as of metal) used for decoration; *also* : a commemorative or identifying inscribed tablet **3** : a film of mucus harboring bacteria on a tooth **4** : a clear area in a bacterial culture produced by destruction of cells by a virus [French, from Middle French, "metal sheet", from *plaquier* "to plate", from Dutch *placken* "to piece, patch"]

plash \'plash\ *n* : SPLASH [probably imitative] — **plash** *vb*

-pla·sia \'plā-zhə\ *n combining form* : development : formation ⟨hyper*plasia*⟩ [Greek *plasis* "molding", from *plassein* "to mold"]

-plasm \ˌplaz-əm\ *n combining form* : formative or formed material (as of a cell or tissue) ⟨endo*plasm*⟩ [Greek *plasma* "something molded", from *plassein* "to mold"]

plas·ma \'plaz-mə\ *n* **1** : the fluid part of blood, lymph, or milk as distinguished from suspended material; *esp* : BLOOD PLASMA **2** : a gas in a highly ionized condition [German, from Late Latin, "something molded", from Greek, from *plassein* "to mold"] — **plas·mat·ic** \plaz-'mat-ik\ *adj*

plas·ma·lem·ma \ˌplaz-mə-'lem-ə\ *n* : PLASMA MEMBRANE [*plasma* + Greek *lemma* "husk"]

plasma membrane *n* : a semipermeable outer covering of cell protoplasm that consists of a double layer of fat molecules sandwiched between an inner and outer layer of protein molecules

plas·mo·di·um \plaz-'mōd-ē-əm\ *n, pl* **-dia** \-ē-ə\ **1** : a motile mass of protoplasm that is the nonreproductive stage of a slime mold and contains many nuclei without dividing cell walls **2** : an individual malaria parasite [New Latin, from *plasma*] — **plas·mo·di·al** \-ē-əl\ *adj*

plas·mol·y·sis \plaz-'mäl-ə-səs\ *n* : shrinking of the cytoplasm away from the wall of a living cell — **plas·mo·lyt·ic** \ˌplaz-mə-'lit-ik\ *adj* — **plas·mo·lyze** \'plaz-mə-ˌlīz\ *vb*

¹plas·ter \'plas-tər\ *n* **1** : a medicated or protective dressing consisting of a film (as of cloth or plastic) spread with an often medicated substance ⟨adhesive

\ə\ abut		\ng\ sing	
\ər\ further		\ō\ bone	
\a\ mat		\ȯ\ saw	
\ā\ take		\ȯi\ coin	
\ä\ cot, cart		\th\ thin	
\au̇\ out		\th\ this	
\ch\ chin		\ü\ food	
\e\ pet		\u̇\ foot	
\ē\ easy		\y\ yet	
\g\ go		\yü\ few	
\i\ tip		\yu̇\ cure	
\ī\ life		\zh\ vision	
\j\ job			

plaster⟩ **2** : a pasty composition (as of lime, water, and sand) that hardens on drying and is used for coating walls, ceilings, and partitions [Old English, from Latin *emplastrum,* from Greek *emplastron,* from *em-plassein* "to plaster on", from *en-* + *plassein* "to mold, plaster"] — **plas·tery** \-tə-rē, -trē\ *adj*

²**plaster** *vb* **plas·tered; plas·ter·ing** \-tə-ring, -tring\ **1** : to apply plaster : overlay or cover with plaster **2** : to apply a plaster to **3** : to cover over or conceal as if with a coat of plaster **4** : to fasten or apply to another surface : stick tightly ⟨rain *plastered* the clothes to our backs⟩ **5** : to cover or alter the surface of in a way suggestive of plastering ⟨*plaster* a wall with signs⟩ — **plas·ter·er** \-tər-ər\ *n*

plas·ter·board \'plas-tər-,bōrd, -,bȯrd\ *n* : a board used in large sheets as a backing or as a substitute for plaster in walls and consisting of several plies of fiberboard, paper, or felt usually bonded to a hardened gypsum plaster core

plaster cast *n* : a rigid dressing of gauze impregnated with plaster of paris

plaster of par·is \-'par-əs\ *often cap 2d P* : a white powdery slightly hydrated calcium sulfate made by calcining gypsum and used chiefly for casts and molds in the form of a quick-setting paste with water [*Paris,* France]

¹**plas·tic** \'plas-tik\ *adj* **1** : FORMATIVE, CREATIVE ⟨*plastic* forces in nature⟩ **2 a** : capable of being molded or modeled ⟨*plastic* clay⟩ **b** : capable of adapting to varying conditions ⟨*plastic* species⟩ ⟨a *plastic* tissue⟩ **3** : SCULPTURAL **4** : made or consisting of a plastic **5** : capable of being deformed continuously and permanently in any direction without rupture **6** : of, relating to, or involving plastic surgery [Latin *plasticus* "of molding", from Greek *plastikos,* from *plassein* "to mold, form"] — **plas·ti·cal·ly** \-ti-kə-lē, -klē\ *adv* — **plas·tic·i·ty** \plas-'tis-ət-ē\ *n* □ SYN PLASTIC, PLIABLE, PLIANT mean subject to being modified in form or nature and are applied to materials or to persons perceived as workable material. PLASTIC applies to substances soft enough to mold into any desired form or to beings that readily adapt to circumstance; PLIABLE implies lack of resistance to bending, folding, or manipulating and when applied to persons suggests obedience to another's will; PLIANT may stress flexibility and springiness and so suggest ready responsiveness either in material or individuals.

²**plastic** *n* : a plastic substance; *esp* : any of numerous organic synthetic or processed materials that can be formed into objects, films, or filaments

plas·ti·ciz·er \'plas-tə-,sī-zər\ *n* : a chemical added to rubbers and resins to impart flexibility, workability, or stretchability

plastic surgery *n* : surgery concerned with the repair or restoration of lost, injured, or deformed parts of the body — **plastic surgeon** *n*

plas·tid \'plas-təd\ *n* : any of various cytoplasmic organelles of photosynthetic cells [German, from Greek *plastos* "molded"]

plas·tron \'plas-trən\ *n* **1** : a metal breastplate **2** : the ventral part of the shell of a turtle **3** : a trimming like a bib for a woman's dress [Middle French, from Italian *piastrone,* from *piastra,* "thin metal plate", from Latin *emplastra, emplastrum* "plaster"] — **plas·tral** \-trəl\ *adj*

-plas·ty \,plas-tē\ *n combining form , pl* **-plasties** : plastic surgery

¹**plat** \'plat\ *n* **1** : a small piece of ground : PLOT **2** : a plan or map of a piece of land (as a town) with lots and landmarks marked out [probably alteration of *plot*]

²**plat** *vt* **plat·ted; plat·ting** : to make a plat of

¹**plate** \'plāt\ *n* **1** : a flat, thin, and usually smooth piece of material ⟨mica splits easily into *plates*⟩: as **a** : metal in sheets usually thicker than about 6 millimeters ⟨steel *plate*⟩ **b** : a thin layer of one metal deposit-

ed on another usually by electrical means **c** : one of the broad metal pieces used in medieval armor; *also* : armor made of plates **d** : a usually flat bony or horny outgrowth forming part of a covering of an animal (as some fishes or reptiles) **e** : HOME PLATE **f** : the thin fatty underpart of a forequarter of beef or the back part of this cut **g** : any of the large movable segments into which the earth's crust is held to be divided **2** : precious metal; *esp* : silver bullion **3 a** : domestic hollow-ware usually of or plated with precious metal (as silver) **b** : a shallow usually circular dish **c** (1) : a main course served on a plate; *also* : food and service for one person ⟨ten dollars a *plate*⟩ (2) : PLATEFUL **d** : a dish or pouch used in taking a collection (as in a church) **e** : a flat glass dish used chiefly for culturing microorganisms **4 a** : a flat piece or surface on which something (as letters or a design) is or is to be embossed or incised ⟨license *plates*⟩ **b** : a sheet of material (as metal or plastic) with a specially prepared surface for printing **c** : a sheet of material (as glass) coated with a light-sensitive photographic emulsion **5** : a horizontal truss that supports the roof trusses or rafters of a building **6 a** : the electrode to which the electrons flow in an electron tube **b** : a metallic grid with its interstices filled with active material that forms one of the structural units of a storage cell or battery **7** : the part of a denture that bears the teeth and fits to the mouth; *also* : DENTURE 2 **8** : a full-page illustration often on special paper ⟨a book with color *plates*⟩ [Old French, from *plat* "flat"] — **platelike** \-,līk\ *adj*

²**plate** *vt* **1** : to cover or equip with plate: as **a** : to arm with armor plate **b** : to cover with an adherent layer (as of metal) ⟨had the teapot *plated* with silver⟩ **c** : to deposit (as a layer of metal) on a surface ⟨*plate* silver onto copper⟩ **2** : to make a printing surface from or for

pla·teau \pla-'tō, 'pla-,\ *n, pl* **plateaus** *or* **plateaux** \-'tōz, -,tōz\ **1** : a usually large relatively level land area raised above adjacent land on at least one side : TABLELAND **2** : a relatively stable level, period, or condition [French, from Middle French, "platter", from *plat* "flat"]

plate·ful \'plāt-,fúl\ *n, pl* **platefuls** \-,fúlz\ *also* **platesful** \'plāts-,fúl\ : the amount a plate will hold

plate glass *n* : fine rolled, ground, and polished sheet glass

plate·let \'plāt-lət\ *n* : BLOOD PLATELET

plat·en \'plat-n\ *n* **1** : a flat plate of metal that exerts or receives pressure; *esp* : one in some printing presses that presses the paper against the type **2** : the roller of a typewriter [Middle French *plateine,* from *plate* "plate"]

plat·er \'plāt-ər\ *n* : one that plates

plate tec·ton·ics \-tek-'tän-iks\ *n* **1** : a theory that the lithosphere of the earth is divided into a small number of movable plates whose movement causes seismic activity **2** : the process and dynamics of plate movement [*tectonics* "science or art of construction, branch of geology concerned with structure", derived from Greek *tektonikos* "of a builder", from *tektōn* "builder"]

plat·form \'plat-,form\ *n* **1** : a declaration of principles; *esp* : a declaration of principles and policies adopted by a political party or a candidate **2** : a horizontal flat surface usually higher than the adjoining area; *esp* : a raised flooring (as for speakers or performers) **3** : a thick layered sole for a shoe; *also* : a shoe with such a sole [Middle French *plate-forme* "diagram, map", literally, "flat form"]

platform rocker *n* : a chair that rocks on a stable platform

platform scale *n* : a weighing machine with a flat platform on which objects are weighed

platform tennis *n* : a variation of paddle tennis played on a wooden platform enclosed by a wire fence

plat·ing \'plāt-ing\ *n* **1** : the act or process of covering especially with metal plate **2** : a coating of metal plates or plate ⟨the *plating* of a ship⟩ ⟨the *plating* wore off the spoons⟩

pla·tin·ic \pla-'tin-ik\ *adj* : of, relating to, or containing platinum especially with a valence of four

plat·i·nous \'plat-nəs, -n-əs\ *adj* : of, relating to, or containing platinum especially with a valence of two

plat·i·num \'plat-nəm, -n-əm\ *n* : a heavy precious grayish white ductile malleable metallic element that is used especially in chemical ware and apparatus, as a catalyst, and in jewelry — see ELEMENT table [New Latin, from Spanish *platina,* from *plata* "silver"]

platinum blonde *n* : a pale silvery blonde color usually produced in human hair by bleach and a bluish rinse; *also* : a person with such hair

plat·i·tude \'plat-ə-,tüd, -,tyüd\ *n* **1** : the quality or state of being dull or trite **2** : a flat or trite remark [French, from *plat* "flat, dull"] — **plat·i·tu·di·nous** \,plat-ə-'tüd-nəs, -'tyüd-, -n-əs\ *adj*

pla·ton·ic \plə-'tän-ik, plā-\ *adj* **1** *cap* : of, relating to, or characteristic of Plato or Platonism **2** : of or relating to love freed from sexual desire [Latin, *platonicus* "of Plato", from Greek *platōnikos,* from *Platōn* "Plato"] — **pla·ton·i·cal·ly** \-'tän-i-kə-lē, klē\ *adv*

Pla·to·nism \'plāt-n-,iz-əm\ *n* : the philosophy of Plato stressing especially that actual things and ideas (as of truth or beauty) are only copies of transcendent ideas which are the objects of true knowledge — **Pla·to·nist** \-n-əst\ *n*

pla·toon \plə-'tün, pla-\ *n* : a subdivision of a military company normally consisting of a headquarters and two or more squads [French *peloton* "small detachment", literally, "ball", from *pelote* "little ball, pellet"]

platoon sergeant *n* : an enlisted rank in the Army above staff sergeant and below first sergeant

plat·ter \'plat-ər\ *n* **1** : a large plate used especially for serving meat **2** : a phonograph record [Anglo-French *plater,* from Middle French *plat* "plate, dish"]

platy \'plat-ē\ *n, pl* **platy** *or* **plat·ys** *or* **plat·ies** : either of two live-bearers that are popular for tropical aquariums and are noted for their varied and brilliant colors [New Latin *Platypoecilus,* genus name, from Greek *platys* "broad, flat" + *poikilos* "many-colored"]

plat·y·pus \'plat-i-pəs, -,pùs\ *n* : a small aquatic egg-laying mammal of southern and eastern Australia and Tasmania with a fleshy bill resembling that of a duck, webbed feet, and a broad flattened tail [Greek *platypous* "flat-footed", from *platys* "broad, flat" + *pous* "foot"]

plau·dit \'plȯd-ət\ *n* **1** : APPLAUSE **2** : enthusiastic approval [Latin, *plaudite* "applaud", pl. imperative of *plaudere* "to applaud"]

plau·si·bil·i·ty \,plȯ-zə-'bil-ət-ē\ *n, pl* **-ties** **1** : the quality or state of being plausible **2** : something plausible

plau·si·ble \'plȯ-zə-bəl\ *adj* **1** : apparently reasonable or worthy of belief ⟨a *plausible* explanation⟩ **2** : apparently trustworthy or fair ⟨a very *plausible* liar⟩ [Latin *plausibilis* "worthy of applause", from *plaudere* "to applaud"] — **plau·si·ble·ness** *n* — **plau·si·bly** \'plȯ-zə-blē\ *adv* □ SYN PLAUSIBLE, CREDIBLE, SPECIOUS mean outwardly acceptable as true or genuine. PLAUSIBLE implies reasonableness at first sight or hearing usually with a hint of a possibility of being deceived ⟨a *plausible* excuse⟩ CREDIBLE stresses worthiness of belief ⟨testimony given by a *credible* witness⟩ SPECIOUS stresses surface plausibility clearly with the implication of deceit or fraud ⟨*specious* reasoning⟩ ⟨*specious* claims for damage⟩

¹play \'plā\ *n* **1 a** : a brisk handling or using (as of a weapon) **b** : the conduct, course, or action of or a particular act or maneuver in a game; *also* : one's turn to participate in a game **2 a** : recreational activity; *esp* : the spontaneous activity of children **b** : JEST ⟨said it in *play*⟩ **c** : PUN ⟨a *play* on words⟩ **3 a** : a way or manner of acting or proceeding ⟨fair *play*⟩ **b** : OPERATION, ACTIVITY ⟨the normal *play* of economic pressures⟩ **c** : brisk, fitful, or light movement ⟨the light *play* of a breeze⟩ **d** : free or unhindered motion ⟨a jacket that gave *play* in the shoulders⟩ **e** : scope or opportunity for action ⟨the new job gave *play* to their talents⟩ **4 a** : the stage representation of an action or story **b** : a dramatic composition : DRAMA [Old English *plega*] — **in play** : in condition or position to be legitimately played

²play *vb* **1 a** : to move swiftly, aimlessly, or lightly ⟨shadows *playing* on the wall⟩ **b** : to move freely within limits **c** : to treat or behave frivolously or lightly ⟨*played* with the idea of getting a job⟩ ⟨*play* a person for a fool⟩ **d** : to make use of double meaning or of the similarity of sound of two words usually for humorous effect **2 a** : to take advantage ⟨were *playing* upon fears⟩ **b** : to finger or trifle with something ⟨*played* with the pencil⟩ **c** : to discharge in a stream ⟨hoses *playing* on the fire⟩ **3 a** : to engage in sport or recreation and especially in spontaneous activity for amusement **b** : to imitate in playing ⟨*play* house⟩ **c** : to take part or engage in (as a game) ⟨*play* cards⟩ ⟨*play* ball⟩ **d** : to compete against in a game ⟨Pittsburgh *plays* Chicago today⟩ **e** : to bet on : WAGER ⟨*play* the horses⟩ **4 a** : to perform on a musical instrument ⟨*play* the piano⟩ **b** : to produce music ⟨listen to an organ *playing*⟩ **5** : to be performed ⟨a new show *playing* for one week⟩ **6 a** : ACT, BEHAVE; *esp* : to conduct oneself in a particular way ⟨*play* safe⟩ **b** : to perform on or as if on the stage ⟨*play* a part⟩; *also* : to act the part of ⟨*play* the fool⟩ **c** : to put or keep in action ⟨*play* a card in a game⟩ **d** : to do for amusement or from mischief ⟨*play* a trick on someone⟩; *also* : to bring about : WREAK ⟨the wind *played* havoc with the garden⟩ — **play·able** \-ə-bəl\ *adj* — **play ball** : COOPERATE — **play second fiddle** : to take a subordinate position

pla·ya \'plī-ə\ *n* : the flat-floored bottom of an undrained desert basin that becomes at times a shallow lake [Spanish, literally, "beach"]

play·act·ing \'plā-,ak-ting\ *n* **1** : performance in theatrical productions **2** : insincere or artificial behavior

play·back \'plā-,bak\ *n* : an act of reproducing recorded sound or pictures often immediately after recording

play back \plā-'bak, 'plā-\ *vt* : to perform a playback of (a disc or tape)

play·bill \'plā-,bil\ *n* **1** : a poster advertising a play **2** : a theater program

play·boy \-,bȯi\ *n* : a man whose chief interest is the pursuit of pleasure

play–by–play \,plā-bə-,plā, -bī-\ *adj* **1** : being a running commentary on a sports event **2** : relating each event as it occurs

play down *vt* : to refrain from emphasizing

play·er \'plā-ər\ *n* : one that plays: as **a** : a person who plays a game **b** : MUSICIAN **c** : ACTOR 1b **d** : a mechanical device for producing or reproducing music ⟨a tape *player*⟩

player piano *n* : a piano containing a mechanical player

play·ful \-fəl\ *adj* **1** : full of play : SPORTIVE **2** : HUMOROUS, JOCULAR — **play·ful·ly** \-fə-lē\ *adv* — **play·ful·ness** *n*

play·girl \-,gərl\ *n* : a woman whose chief interest is the pursuit of pleasure

play·go·er \-,gō-ər, -,gȯr\ *n* : a person who frequently attends plays

play·ground \-,graund\ *n* : a piece of land used for games and recreation especially by children

play·house \-,haus\ *n* **1** : THEATER 1 **2** : a small house for children to play in

playing card *n* : one of a set of usually 32, 48, or 52 thin rectangular pieces of paperboard or plastic marked on one side to show rank and suit (as spades,

platypus

hearts, diamonds, or clubs) and used in playing various games

playing field *n* : a field for various games; *esp* : the part of a field officially marked off for play

play·let \'plā-lət\ *n* : a short play

play·mate \-,māt\ *n* : a companion in play

play–off \'plā-,óf\ *n* **1** : a final contest or series of contests to determine the winner between contestants or teams that have tied **2** : a series of contests played after the end of the regular season to determine a championship

play off \plā-'óf, 'plā-\ *vt* **1** : to complete the playing of (an interrupted contest) **2** : to break (a tie) by a play-off

play out *vb* **1** : to perform to the end **2 a** : to use up or become used up **b** : to become spent or exhausted **3** : UNREEL, UNFOLD

play·pen \'plā-,pen\ *n* : a portable enclosure in which a baby or young child may play

play·thing \-,thing\ *n* : TOY 2

play·time \-,tīm\ *n* : a time for play or diversion

play up *vt* : to give emphasis or prominence to — **play up to** \plā-'əp-tü\ : to support or flatter by eager agreement

play·wright \'plā-,rīt\ *n* : a person who writes plays [obsolete *wright* "maker", from Old English *wryhta*]

pla·za \'plaz-ə, 'pläz-\ *n* **1** : a public square in a city or town **2** : SHOPPING CENTER [Spanish, from Latin *platea* "broad street", from Greek *plateia*, from *platys* "broad"]

plea \'plē\ *n* **1** : a defendant's answer to a lawsuit or a criminal charge ⟨a *plea* of guilty⟩ **2** : something offered as an excuse **3** : an earnest request : APPEAL [Old French *plait, plaid* "lawsuit", from Medieval Latin *placitum*, from Latin, "decision, decree", from *placēre* "to please, be decided"]

plead \'plēd\ *vb* **plead·ed** \'plēd-əd\ *or* **pled** \'pled\; **plead·ing** **1** : to argue a case in a court of law **2** : to make a plea of a specified nature ⟨*plead* not guilty⟩ **3 a** : to argue for or against a claim **b** : to appeal earnestly : IMPLORE **4** : to offer in defense, apology, or excuse [Old French *plaidier*, from *plaid* "lawsuit"] — **plead·able** \'plēd-ə-bəl\ *adj* — **plead·er** *n*

pleas·ant \'plez-nt\ *adj* **1** : giving pleasure : AGREEABLE **2** : having or characterized by pleasing manners, behavior, or appearance — **pleas·ant·ly** *adv* — **pleas·ant·ness** *n*

pleas·ant·ry \-n-trē\ *n, pl* **-ries** **1** : agreeable playfulness especially in conversation **2** : a humorous act or speech : JEST

¹please \'plēz\ *vb* **1** : to give pleasure or satisfaction : GRATIFY **2** : to feel the desire or inclination : LIKE ⟨do as you *please*⟩ [Middle French *plaisir*, from Latin *placēre*]

²please *adv* **1** — used as a function word to express politeness or emphasis in a request ⟨*please* come in⟩ **2** — used as a function word to express polite affirmation ⟨Have some tea? *Please.*⟩

pleas·ing \'plē-zing\ *adj* : giving pleasure : AGREEABLE — **pleas·ing·ly** \-zing-lē\ *adv* — **pleas·ing·ness** *n*

plea·sur·able \'plezh-rə-bəl, 'plāzh-, -ə-rə-\ *adj* : PLEASANT 1, GRATIFYING — **plea·sur·able·ness** \'plezh-rə-bəl-nəs, 'plāzh-, -ə-rə-\ *n* — **plea·sur·ably** \-blē\ *adv*

plea·sure \'plezh-ər, 'plāzh-\ *n* **1** : DESIRE, INCLINATION ⟨what's your *pleasure*⟩ **2** : a state of gratification : ENJOYMENT **3** : a source of delight or joy

¹pleat \'plēt\ *vt* **1** : FOLD 1; *esp* : to arrange in pleats **2** : PLAIT 2 [Middle English *pleten*, from *plete, pleit* "plait"] — **pleat·er** *n*

²pleat *n* : a fold (as in cloth) made by doubling material over on itself — **pleat·ed** *adj*

plebe \'plēb\ *n* : a freshman at a military or naval academy [obsolete *plebe* "common people", from French *plèbe*, from Latin *plebs*]

¹ple·be·ian \pli-'bē-ən, -yən\ *n* **1** : a member of the Roman plebs **2** : one of the common people [Latin *plebeius* "of the common people", from *plebs* "common people"] — **ple·be·ian·ism** \-ə-,niz-əm, -yə-\ *n*

²plebeian *adj* **1** : of or relating to plebeians **2** : crude or coarse in manner or style : COMMON — **ple·be·ian·ly** *adv*

pleb·i·scite \'pleb-ə-,sīt, -sət\ *n* : a popular vote by which the people indicate their wishes on a measure officially submitted to them [Latin *plebis scitum* "decree of the common people"]

plebs \'plebz\ *n* **1** : the common people of ancient Rome **2** : the general populace [Latin]

plec·trum \'plek-trəm\ *n, pl* **plec·tra** \-trə\ *or* **plec·trums** : ³PICK 3 [Latin, from Greek *plēktron*, from *plēssein* "to strike"]

¹pledge \'plej\ *n* **1 a** : the handing over of a chattel to another as security for an obligation without transfer of title; *also* : the chattel so delivered **b** : the state of being held as a security ⟨given in *pledge*⟩ **2 a** : something given as security for the performance of an act **b** : a token, sign, or evidence of something else ⟨shake hands as a *pledge* of friendship⟩ **3 a** : TOAST 3 **b** : a binding promise or agreement **4 a** : a person pledged to join an organization (as a fraternity) **b** : a gift promised (as to a charity) [Middle French *plege* "security", from Late Latin *plebium*]

²pledge *vt* **1** : to deposit as a pledge **2** : to drink the health of : TOAST **3** : to bind by a pledge ⟨*pledge* oneself⟩ **4** : to promise by a pledge ⟨*pledge* money to charity⟩ — **pledg·ee** \ple-'jē\ *n* — **pledg·er** \'plej-ər\ *n* — **pled·gor** \'plej-ər, ple-'jór\ *n*

Ple·ia·des \'plē-ə-,dēz\ *n pl* : a conspicuous loose cluster of stars in the constellation Taurus consisting of six stars visible to the average eye [Latin, the seven daughters of Atlas, who were transformed into a group of stars, from Greek]

pleio·tro·pic \,plī-ə-'trōp-ik, -'träp-\ *adj* : affecting the phenotype in more than one way ⟨*pleiotropic* genes⟩ [Greek *pleiōn* "more" + *tropos* "turn, way"] — **pleio·trop·ism** \-'trōp-,iz-əm, -'träp-\ *n*

Pleis·to·cene \'plī-stə-,sēn\ *n* : the earlier epoch of the Quaternary; *also* : the corresponding system of rocks [Greek *pleistos* "most"] — **Pleistocene** *adj*

ple·na·ry \'plē-nə-rē, 'plen-ə-\ *adj* **1** : COMPLETE, FULL ⟨*plenary* powers⟩ **2** : including all entitled to attend ⟨a *plenary* session of an assembly⟩ [Late Latin *plenarius*, from Latin *plenus* "full"]

plen·i·po·ten·tia·ry \,plen-ə-pə-'tench-rē, -ə-rē; -'tench-ē-,er-ē\ *n, pl* **-ries** : a person and especially a diplomatic agent having full power to transact any business [Medieval Latin *plenipotentiarius*, derived from Latin *plenus* "full" + *potens* "powerful, potent"] — **plenipotentiary** *adj*

plen·i·tude \'plen-ə-,tüd, -,tyüd\ *or* **plent·i·tude** \'plen-ə-, 'plent-ə-\ *n* : the quality or state of being full or plentiful : ABUNDANCE [Latin *plenitudo*, from *plenus* "full"]

plen·te·ous \'plent-ē-əs\ *adj* : PLENTIFUL — **plen·te·ous·ly** *adv* — **plen·te·ous·ness** *n*

plen·ti·ful \'plent-i-fəl\ *adj* **1** : containing or yielding plenty : FRUITFUL **2** : characterized by, constituting, or existing in plenty — **plen·ti·ful·ly** \-fə-lē\ *adv* — **plen·ti·ful·ness** *n* □ **SYN** PLENTIFUL, AMPLE, ABUNDANT, COPIOUS mean more than sufficient yet not in excess. PLENTIFUL suggests a great or rich supply ⟨eggs are cheap when *plentiful*⟩ AMPLE implies a generous sufficiency to satisfy a particular requirement ⟨an income *ample* for one's needs⟩ ABUNDANT suggests an even greater or richer supply than does PLENTIFUL ⟨*abundant* harvests⟩ COPIOUS stresses largeness in quantity or number rather than fullness or richness ⟨shed *copious* tears⟩ ⟨took *copious* notes at the lecture⟩

¹plen·ty \'plent-ē\ *n* **1** : a full or abundant supply : a sufficient number or amount ⟨*plenty* to choose from⟩

⟨got there in *plenty* of time⟩ **2** : ABUNDANCE ⟨in times of *plenty*⟩ [Old French *plenté*, from Late Latin *plenitas*, from Latin, "fullness", from *plenus* "full"]

²plenty *adj* : PLENTIFUL, ABUNDANT ⟨had *plenty* help⟩

³plenty *adv* : ABUNDANTLY, QUITE ⟨a *plenty* exciting trip⟩

ple·num \'plen-əm, 'plēn-əm\ *n, pl* **-nums** *or* **-na** \-ə\ : a general assembly of all members of a public body [New Latin, from Latin *plenus* "full"]

ple·sio·saur \'plē-sē-ə-ˌsȯr, 'plē-zē-\ *n* : any of a group (Plesiosauria) of Mesozoic marine reptiles with flattened bodies and limbs modified into paddles [derived from Greek *plēsios* "close" + *sauros* "lizard"]

pleth·o·ra \'pleth-ə-rə\ *n* : an excessive quantity or fullness [Medieval Latin, from Greek *plēthōra*, from *plēthein* "to be full"] — **ple·tho·ric** \plə-'thȯr-ik, -'thär-; 'pleth-ə-rik\ *adj*

pleu·ra \'plu̇r-ə\ *n, pl* **pleu·rae** \'plu̇r-ˌē, -ˌī\ *or* **pleuras** : either of two separate membranous sacs each of which encloses a single lung of a mammal and consists of two layers of membrane with the outer layer lining half of the chest and the inner layer folded back over the surface of a lung [Greek, "rib, side"] — **pleu·ral** \'plu̇r-əl\ *adj*

pleu·ri·sy \'plu̇r-ə-sē\ *n* : inflammation of the pleura usually with fever, painful breathing, and coughing [Middle French *pleuresie*, derived from Greek *pleura* "side"] — **pleu·rit·ic** \plu̇-'rit-ik\ *adj*

pleu·ro·pneu·mo·nia \ˌplu̇r-ō-nu̇-'mō-nyə, -nyu̇-\ *n* : combined inflammation of the lungs and pleura; *also* : a disease (as of cattle) marked by this

Plexi·glas \'plek-si-ˌglas\ *trademark* — used for acrylic plastic sheets and molding powders

plex·us \'plek-səs\ *n* : an interlacing network especially of blood vessels or nerves [Latin, "braid, network", from *plectere* "to braid"]

pli·able \'plī-ə-bəl\ *adj* **1** : capable of being bent or folded without damage : FLEXIBLE **2** : easily influenced [Middle French, from *plier* "to bend, fold", from Latin *plicare* "to fold"] SYN see PLASTIC — **pli·abil·i·ty** \ˌplī-ə-'bil-ət-ē\ *n* — **pli·able·ness** \'plī-ə-bəl-nəs\ *n* — **pli·ably** \-blē\ *adv*

pli·an·cy \'plī-ən-sē\ *n* : the quality or state of being pliant

pli·ant \'plī-ənt\ *adj* **1** : readily yielding without breaking : FLEXIBLE ⟨*pliant* willow twigs⟩ **2** : PLIABLE 2 **3** : suitable for varied uses : ADAPTABLE SYN see PLASTIC — **pli·ant·ly** *adv*

pli·cate \'plī-ˌkāt\ *adj* : having lengthwise folds or ridges ⟨a *plicate* leaf⟩ [Latin *plicatus*, past participle of *plicare* "to fold"] — **pli·cate·ly** *adv*

pli·ers \'plī-ərz, 'plīrz\ *n pl* : a small pincers with long jaws for holding small objects or for bending and cutting wire

¹plight \'plīt\ *vt* : to put or give in pledge : ENGAGE [Old English *plihtan* "to endanger", from *pliht* "danger"] — **plight·er** *n*

²plight *n* : CONDITION 4a, STATE; *esp* : bad state or condition ⟨the *plight* of the unemployed⟩ [Anglo-French *plit*, derived from Latin *plicare* "to fold"]

Plim·soll mark \ˌplim-səl-, -plimp-, -ˌsȯl-\ *n* : a load line or a set of load-line markings on an oceangoing cargo ship — called also *Plimsoll line* [Samuel *Plimsoll*, died 1898, English shipping reformer]

plink \'plingk\ *vb* **1** : to make or cause to make a tinkling sound **2** : to shoot at especially in a casual manner [imitative] — **plink** *n*

plinth \'plinth, 'plintth\ *n* **1** : the lowest part of the base of an architectural column **2** : a block used as a base (as for a statue or vase) [Latin *plinthus*, from Greek *plinthos*]

Plio·cene \'plī-ə-ˌsēn\ *n* : the latest epoch of the Tertiary; *also* : the corresponding system of rocks [Greek *pleiōn* "more"] — **Pliocene** *adj*

Plio·film \'plī-ə-ˌfilm\ *trademark* — used for a glossy membrane used especially for raincoats and packaging material

plod \'pläd\ *vi* **plod·ded; plod·ding** **1** : to walk heavily or slowly : TRUDGE **2** : to work or study laboriously : DRUDGE [imitative] — **plod** *n* — **plod·der** *n* — **plod·ding·ly** \-ing-lē\ *adv*

ploi·dy \'plȯid-ē\ *n* : degree of repetition of the basic number of chromosomes [from such words as *diploidy, triploidy*]

plop \'pläp\ *vb* **plopped; plop·ping** **1** : to make or move with a sound like that of something dropping into water **2** : to allow the body to drop heavily **3** : to set, drop, or throw heavily [imitative] — **plop** *n*

¹plot \'plät\ *n* **1** : a small area of land : LOT **2** : GROUND PLAN 1 **3** : the main story of a literary work **4** : a secret plan for accomplishing a usually evil or unlawful end **5** : a graphic representation : CHART, DIAGRAM [Old English] □ SYN PLOT, INTRIGUE, CONSPIRACY mean a plan secretly devised to accomplish an evil purpose. PLOT implies careful foresight in planning positive action ⟨an elaborate kidnapping *plot*⟩ INTRIGUE suggests secret maneuvering ⟨the court thrived on *intrigues*⟩ CONSPIRACY implies a secret agreement among a number of persons not necessarily for positive action ⟨*conspiracy* in restraint of trade⟩ SYN see in addition PLAN

²plot *vb* **plot·ted; plot·ting** **1 a** : to make a plot, map, or plan of **b** : to mark or note on or as if on a map or chart **2 a** : to locate (a point) by means of coordinates **b** : to locate (a curve) by plotted points **3** : to plan or contrive especially secretly : CONSPIRE, SCHEME — **plot·ter** *n*

plo·ver \'pləv-ər, 'plō-vər\ *n, pl* **plover** *or* **plovers** : any of numerous shorebirds differing from the related sandpipers in having shorter and stouter bills [Middle French, derived from Latin *pluvia* "rain"]

¹plow *or* **plough** \'plau̇\ *n* **1** : an implement used to cut, lift, and turn over soil especially in preparing a seedbed **2** : any of various devices (as for spreading or opening something) that operate like a plow; *esp* : SNOWPLOW [Old English *plōh* "land a yoke of oxen could plow in one day"]

²plow *or* **plough** *vb* **1** : to open, break up, or work with a plow ⟨*plow* a straight furrow⟩ ⟨*plow* the soil⟩ ⟨*plow* a road out with a snowplow⟩ **2 a** : to move through like a plow cutting the soil ⟨a ship *plowing* the waves⟩ **b** : to proceed steadily and laboriously : PLOD ⟨*plow* through a report⟩ — **plow·able** \-ə-bəl\ *adj* — **plow·er** \'plau̇-ər, 'plau̇r\ *n*

plow back *vt* : to reinvest (profits) in a business

plow·boy \'plau̇-ˌbȯi\ *n* : a boy who guides a plow or leads the horse drawing it

plow·man \-mən\ *n* **1** : one that plows **2** : a farm laborer

plow·share \-ˌsheər, -ˌshaər\ *n* : the part of a plow that cuts the earth

plow sole *n* : a layer of earth at the bottom of the furrow compacted by repeated plowing at the same depth

ploy \'plȯi\ *n* : a tactic intended to embarrass or baffle an opponent [probably from *employ*]

¹pluck \'plək\ *vb* **1 a** : to pull or pick off or out ⟨*pluck* a flower⟩ **b** : to remove something and especially hair or feathers from by or as if by plucking ⟨*pluck* a fowl⟩ **2** : ROB 1, FLEECE **3** : to move or separate forcibly : TUG, SNATCH ⟨*plucked* the child from danger⟩ **4 a** : to pick, pull, or grasp at **b** : to play by sounding the strings with the fingers or a pick ⟨*pluck* a guitar⟩ **5** : to make a sharp pull or twitch ⟨a briar *plucked* at my sleeve⟩ [Old English *pluccian*] — **pluck·er** *n*

²pluck *n* **1** : a sharp pull : TUG **2** : the heart, liver, lungs, and windpipe of a slaughtered animal **3** : courageous readiness to fight or continue against odds : SPIRIT

plucky \'plək-ē\ *adj* **pluck·i·er; -est** : COURAGEOUS — **pluck·i·ly** \'plək-ə-lē\ *adv* — **pluck·i·ness** \'plək-ē-nəs\ *n*

¹plug \'pləg\ *n* **1 a** : a piece (as of wood or metal) used to stop or fill a hole : STOPPER **b** : an obtruding or obstructing mass of material (as in rock or tissue) resembling a stopper **2** : a worn-out horse **3 a** : FIREPLUG **b** : SPARK PLUG 1 **4** : a device for making an electrical connection by insertion into a receptacle **5** : a flat cake of tightly pressed tobacco leaves **6** : a fishing lure with two or more hooks **7** : a piece of favorable publicity usually placed in general material [Dutch]

²**plug** *vb* **plugged; plug·ging 1** : to stop, make tight, or secure with or as if with a plug **2** : to hit with a bullet **3** : to advertise or publicize insistently **4** : to become plugged — usually used with *up* — **plug·ger** *n*

plug hat *n* : a man's stiff hat (as a bowler or top hat)

plug in *vb* : to establish or connect to an electric circuit by inserting a plug

plug–ugly \'pləg-ˌəg-lē\ *n, pl* **-ug·lies** : THUG, TOUGH

¹**plum** \'pləm\ *n* **1 a** : any of numerous trees and shrubs related to the peach and cherries and having round to oval smooth-skinned fruits with oblong pits **b** : the edible fruit of a plum **2 a** : a raisin for use in cooking **b** : SUGARPLUM **3** : something excellent or superior; *esp* : something given as recompense for service **4** : a dark reddish purple [Old English *plūme,* from Latin *prunum* "plum fruit", from Greek *proumnon*] — **plum·like** \-ˌlīk\ *adj*

plum·age \'plü-mij\ *n* : the entire clothing of feathers of a bird

¹**plumb** \'pləm\ *n* : a weight often of lead used on a line especially to determine a vertical direction or distance [derived from Latin *plumbum* "lead"] — **out of plumb** *or* **off plumb** : out of vertical or true

²**plumb** *adv* **1** : straight down or up : VERTICALLY **2** chiefly dialect : WHOLLY 1, ABSOLUTELY

³**plumb** *vb* **1** : to sound, adjust, or test with a plumb ⟨*plumb* a wall⟩ ⟨*plumb* the depth of the well⟩ **2** : to examine and determine hidden aspects of ⟨*plumbed* their motives⟩ **3** : to supply with or install as plumbing; *also* : to work as a plumber

⁴**plumb** *also* **plum** *adj* **1** : exactly vertical or true **2** : ABSOLUTE 4, COMPLETE SYN see VERTICAL

plum·ba·go \ˌpləm-'bā-gō\ *n* : GRAPHITE [Latin, "galena", from *plumbum* "lead"]

plumb bob *n* : the metal bob of a plumb line

plumb·er \'pləm-ər\ *n* : one that installs, repairs, and maintains piping, fittings, and fixtures involved in the distribution and use of water in a building [derived from Latin *plumbum* "lead"]

plum·bic \'pləm-bik\ *adj* : of, relating to, or containing lead especially with a valence of four

plumb·ing \'pləm-ing\ *n* **1** : a plumber's occupation or trade **2** : the apparatus (as pipes and fixtures) concerned in the distribution and use of water in a building

plumb line *n* : a line or cord having at one end a weight (as a plumb bob) and serving especially to determine whether something is vertical or to measure depth

plum·bous \'pləm-bəs\ *adj* : of, relating to, or containing lead especially with a valence of two

¹**plume** \'plüm\ *n* **1** : a feather of a bird; *esp* : a large conspicuous or showy feather **2 a** : a feather, cluster of feathers, tuft of hair, or similar object worn as an ornament **b** : a token of honor or victory : PRIZE **3** : something (as a trail of smoke or a bushy tail of a dog) that resembles a plume [Middle French, from Latin *pluma* "small soft feather, down"] — **plumed** \'plümd\ *adj* — **plumy** \'plü-mē\ *adj*

²**plume** *vt* **1** : to provide or deck with plumes ⟨*plume* a hat⟩ **2** : to pride (oneself) on something **3** : PREEN 1 ⟨a bird *pluming* itself⟩

¹**plum·met** \'pləm-ət\ *n* : PLUMB BOB; *also* : PLUMB LINE [Middle French *plombet* "ball of lead", from *plomb* "lead", derived from Latin *plumbum*]

²**plummet** *vi* : to drop straight down or sharply and abruptly

plu·mose \'plü-ˌmōs\ *adj* : FEATHERY, FEATHERED

¹**plump** \'pləmp\ *vb* **1** : to drop, sink, or come in contact suddenly or heavily ⟨*plumped* down into the

¹plumb

chair⟩ **2** : to favor someone or something strongly — used with *for* [Middle English *plumpen*]

²**plump** *n* : a sudden plunge, fall, or blow; *also* : the sound accompanying such an act

³**plump** *adv* **1** : with a sudden or heavy drop **2** : STRAIGHT, DIRECTLY ⟨ran *plump* into the wall⟩

⁴**plump** *vb* : to make or become plump

⁵**plump** *adj* : having a full rounded usually pleasing form [Middle English, "dull, blunt"] — **plump·ness** *n*

plum pudding *n* : a boiled or steamed pudding containing fruits (as raisins) and usually rich in fat

plu·mule \'plü-myül\ *n* **1** : EPICOTYL **2** : a down feather [Latin *plumula* "small feather", from *pluma* "feather, down"]

¹**plun·der** \'plən-dər\ *vb* **plun·dered; plun·der·ing** \-də-ring, -dring\ : to rob especially openly and by force (as in a raid) [German *plündern*] — **plun·der·er** \-dər-ər\

²**plunder** *n* **1** : an act of plundering **2** : something taken by force or theft : LOOT

¹**plunge** \'plənj\ *vb* **1** : to thrust or force quickly and forcibly ⟨*plunging* a knife into the roast⟩ **2** : to thrust or cast oneself into or as if into water : DIVE **3 a** : to throw oneself or move suddenly and sharply forward and downward ⟨the horse reared and *plunged*⟩ **b** : to move rapidly or suddenly downward ⟨the market *plunged* after war was declared⟩ **4 a** : to rush or act with reckless haste ⟨*plunged* into debt⟩; *also* : to bring to a usually unpleasant state or course of action suddenly or unexpectedly ⟨the president's illness *plunged* the nation into gloom⟩ **b** : to speculate or gamble recklessly [Middle French *plonger,* derived from Latin *plumbum* "lead"]

²**plunge** *n* : a sudden dive, leap, or rush — **take the plunge** : to get married

plung·er \'plən-jər\ *n* **1** : a person (as a diver or a reckless gambler) that plunges **2 a** : a device (as a piston in a pump) that acts with a plunging motion **b** : a device consisting of a rubber suction cup on a handle used to free plumbing traps and waste outlets of obstructions

plunk \'pləngk\ *vb* **1** : to make or cause to make a hollow metallic sound ⟨*plunk* the strings of a banjo⟩ **2** : to drop heavily or suddenly ⟨*plunked* the money down⟩ **3** : to publicly favor someone or something — used with *for* [imitative] — **plunk** *n*

plu·per·fect \plü-'pər-fikt, 'plü-\ *adj* : PAST PERFECT [Late Latin *plusquamperfectus,* literally, "more than perfect"] — **pluperfect** *n*

plu·ral \'plür-əl\ *adj* **1** : belonging to a class of grammatical forms used to denote more than one ⟨a *plural* suffix⟩ **2** : relating to, consisting of, or containing more than one [Latin *pluralis,* from *plur-, plus* "more"] — **plural** *n* — **plu·ral·ly** \-ə-lē\ *adv*

plu·ral·ism \'plür-ə-ˌliz-əm\ : a state of society in which different (as ethnic or social) groups maintain their traditional cultures or special interests within the confines of a common civilization

plu·ral·i·ty \plù-'ral-ət-ē\ *n, pl* **-ties** **1** : the state of being plural or numerous **2** : the greater number or part ⟨a *plurality* of the nations want peace⟩ **3 a** : the fact of being chosen by the voters out of three or more candidates or measures when no one of them obtains more than half the total vote **b** : the excess of the number of votes received by one candidate over another; *esp* : that of the highest over the next highest SYN see MAJORITY

plu·ral·ize \'plür-ə-ˌlīz\ *vt* : to make plural or express in the plural form — **plu·ral·iza·tion** \ˌplür-ə-lə-'zā-shən\ *n*

¹**plus** \'pləs\ *adj* **1 a** : requiring addition ⟨the *plus* sign⟩ **b** : algebraically positive **2** : having, receiving, or being in addition **3 a** : falling high in a specified range ⟨a grade of C *plus*⟩ **b** : greater than that specified **4** : electrically positive **5** : relating to or being a particu-

lar one of the two mating types that are required for successful fertilization in sexual reproduction in some lower plants (as fungus)

²**plus** *n* **1** : an added quantity **2** : a positive quality : ADVANTAGE **3** : the amount that remains when use or need is satisfied

³**plus** *prep* **1** : increased by ⟨four *plus* five is nine⟩ ⟨the debt *plus* interest⟩ **2** : WITH 8a [Latin, "more"]

¹**plush** \'pləsh\ *n* : a fabric with pile longer and less dense than that of velvet [Middle French *peluche*] — **plushy** \-ē\ *adj*

²**plush** *adj* **1** : relating to, resembling, or made of plush **2** : very luxurious or satisfactory

Plu·to \'plüt-ō\ *n* : the planet farthest from the sun — see PLANET table [*Pluto*, Greek god of the dead]

plu·toc·ra·cy \plü-'täk-rə-sē\ *n, pl* **-cies 1** : government by the wealthy **2** : a controlling class of rich people [Greek *ploutokratia*, from *ploutos* "wealth"] — **plu·to·crat** \'plüt-ə-,krat\ *n* — **plu·to·crat·ic** \,plüt-ə-'krat-ik\ *adj* — **plu·to·crat·i·cal·ly** \-'krat-i-kə-lē, -klē\ *adv*

plu·ton·ic \plü-'tän-ik\ *adj* : formed by solidification of magma deep within the earth and crystalline throughout ⟨*plutonic* rock⟩ [Latin *Pluton-, Pluto*, god of the dead, from Greek *Ploutōn*]

plu·to·ni·um \plü-'tō-nē-əm\ *n* : a radioactive metallic chemical element that is formed by decay of neptunium and found in minute quantities in pitchblende and that is fissionable to yield atomic energy — see ELEMENT table [New Latin, from *Pluton-, Pluto*, the planet Pluto]

plu·vi·al \'plü-vē-əl\ *adj* **1** : of or relating to rain **2** : characterized by or resulting from the action of abundant rain ⟨a *pluvial* period⟩ [Latin *pluvialis*, from *pluvia* "rain", from *pluere* "to rain"]

¹**ply** \'plī\ *vt* **plied; ply·ing** : to twist together ⟨*ply* yarns⟩ [Middle French *plier* "to fold", from Latin *plicare*]

²**ply** *n, pl* **plies** : one of the folds, thicknesses, layers, or strands of which something (as yarn or plywood) is made up

³**ply** *vb* **plied; ply·ing 1 a** : to use or wield diligently ⟨*ply* an ax⟩ **b** : to practice or perform diligently ⟨*ply* a trade⟩ **2 a** : to keep supplying ⟨*ply* a guest with delicacies⟩ **b** : to press or harass with something ⟨*plied* them with questions⟩ **3** : to go or travel regularly [Middle English *plien*, short for *applien* "to apply"]

Plym·outh Rock \,plim-əth-\ *n* : a bird of an American breed of medium-sized single-combed domestic fowl raised for meat and eggs [from *Plymouth Rock*, on which the Pilgrims are supposed to have landed in 1620]

ply·wood \'plī-,wud\ *n* : a structural material consisting of thin sheets of wood glued or cemented together under heat and pressure with the grains of adjacent layers arranged at right angles or at a wide angle

pneu·mat·ic \nu-'mat-ik, nyu-\ *adj* **1** : of, relating to, or using air, wind, or other gas **2** : moved or worked by air pressure ⟨a *pneumatic* drill⟩ **3** : adapted for holding or inflated with compressed air ⟨*pneumatic* tires⟩ [Latin *pneumaticus*, from Greek *pneumatikos*, from *pneuma* "air, breath, spirit", from *pnein* "to breathe"] — **pneu·mat·i·cal·ly** \-'mat-i-kə-lē, -klē\ *adv*

pneu·mat·ics \nu-'mat-iks, nyu-\ *n* : a branch of physics that deals with the mechanical properties of gases

pneu·mo·coc·cus \,nü-mə-'käk-əs, ,nyü-\ *n, pl* **-coc·ci** \-'käk-,ī, -,sī, -,ē, -,sē\ : a bacterium that causes pneumonia [Greek *pneuma* "air, breath, spirit" + *kokkos* "grain, seed"] — **pneu·mo·coc·cal** \-'käk-əl\ *or* **pneu·mo·coc·cic** \-'käk-ik, -sik\ *adj*

pneu·mo·nia \nu-'mō-nyə, nyu-\ *n* : a disease of the lungs characterized by inflammation and congestion and caused especially by infection [Greek, from *pneumōn* "lung", alteration of *pleumōn*]

pneu·mon·ic \nu-'män-ik, nyu-\ *adj* **1** : of or relating to the lungs **2** : of, relating to, or affected with pneumonia

pneu·mo·tho·rax \,nü-mə-'thōr-,aks, ,nyü-, -'thor-\ *n* : a state in which gas is present in the pleural cavity and which may occur in disease or injury or be induced surgically to collapse a lung for therapeutic reasons [Greek *pneuma* "air, breath"]

¹**poach** \'pōch\ *vt* : to cook in simmering liquid ⟨*poach* an egg⟩ [Middle French *pocher*, literally, "to put into a bag", from *poche* "bag, pocket", of Germanic origin]

²**poach** *vb* : to hunt or fish unlawfully [Middle French *pocher* "to push, poke", of Germanic origin] — **poach·er** *n*

po·chard \'pō-chərd\ *n* : any of several large-bodied large-headed diving ducks [origin unknown]

pock \'päk\ *n* : a small swelling on the skin (as in chicken pox or smallpox) similar to a pimple; *also* : the scar it leaves [Old English *pocc*] — **pock** *vt* — **pocky** \-ē\ *adj*

¹**pock·et** \'päk-ət\ *n* **1 a** : a small bag carried by a person : PURSE **b** : a small bag open at the top or side inserted in a garment **2** : supply of money : MEANS ⟨out of *pocket*⟩ **3 a** : CONTAINER **b** : a hole at the corner or side of a billiard table **4** : a small isolated area or group : **a** : a cavity containing a deposit (as of gold or water) **b** : a small body of ore **c** : AIR POCKET [Old North French *pokete*, from *poke* "bag", of Germanic origin]

²**pocket** *vt* **1 a** : to put or enclose in or as if in one's pocket ⟨*pocketed* the change⟩ **b** : to take for one's own use especially dishonestly ⟨*pocket* the profits⟩ **2** : to put up with ⟨*pocket* an insult⟩ **3** : to set aside : forget about ⟨*pocket* one's pride⟩ **4 a** : to hem in **b** : to drive (a ball) into a pocket of a pool table **5** : to cover or supply with pockets

³**pocket** *adj* **1 a** : small enough to be carried in the pocket ⟨a *pocket* dictionary⟩ **b** : SMALL, MINIATURE ⟨a *pocket* submarine⟩ **2** : of or relating to money **3 a** : carried in one's pocket **b** : used for small cash outlays ⟨*pocket* money⟩

pocket billiards *n* : POOL 2

pock·et·book \'päk-ət-,buk\ *n* **1 a** : BILLFOLD, WALLET **b** : PURSE 1 **c** : HANDBAG 2 **2 a** : financial resources **b** : economic interests

pocket edition *n* : a miniature form of something

pock·et·ful \'päk-ət-,ful\ *n, pl* **pocketfuls** \-,fulz\ *or* **pock·ets·ful** \-əts-,ful\ : as much or as many as the pocket will contain

pocket gopher *n* : GOPHER 2a

pock·et·knife \'päk-ət-,nīf\ *n* : a knife with a folding blade to be carried in the pocket

pock·et·size \-,sīz\ *adj* : ³POCKET 1a, 1b

pocket veto *n* : an indirect veto of a legislative bill by an executive by failing to sign it before adjournment of the legislature

pock·mark \'päk-,märk\ *n* : the depressed scar left by a pock especially of smallpox — **pockmark** *vt*

po·co \,pō-kō, ,po-\ *adv* : SOMEWHAT — used to qualify an adverb used as a direction in music [Italian, "little", from Latin *paucus*]

po·co a po·co \,pō-kō-ä-'pō-kō, ,po-kō-ä-'po-kō\ *adv* : little by little : GRADUALLY — used as a direction in music [Italian]

po·co·sin \pə-'kōs-n\ *n* : an upland swamp of the coastal plain of the southeastern United States [Delaware *pâkwesen*]

pod \'päd\ *n* **1** : a fruit or seed vessel that splits open when ripe; *esp* : LEGUME **2** : any of various natural protective coverings or cases (as for grasshopper eggs) **3** : a streamlined compartment under the wings or fuselage of an airplane used as a container (as for fuel or a jet engine) **4** : a detachable compartment (as for instruments) on a spacecraft [probably alteration of *cod* "bag", from Old English *codd*]

\ə\ abut	\ng\ sing
\ər\ further	\ō\ bone
\a\ mat	\o\ saw
\ā\ take	\oi\ coin
\ä\ cot, cart	\th\ thin
\au\ out	\th\ this
\ch\ chin	\ü\ food
\e\ pet	\u\ foot
\ē\ easy	\y\ yet
\g\ go	\yü\ few
\i\ tip	\yu\ cure
\ī\ life	\zh\ vision
\j\ job	

poinsettia

-pod \,päd\ *n combining form* : foot : part resembling a foot ⟨uro*pod*⟩ [Greek *pod-, pous* "foot"]

podgy \'päj-ē\ *adj* **podg·i·er; -est** : PUDGY

po·di·a·try \pə-'dī-ə-trē\ *n* : the professional care and treatment of the human foot in health and disease — called also *chiropody* [Greek *pod-, pous* "foot" + English *-iatry*] — **po·di·a·trist** \-trəst\ *n*

po·di·um \'pōd-ē-əm\ *n, pl* **-di·ums** *or* **-dia** \-ē-ə\ **1** : a low wall serving as a foundation or terrace wall: as **a** : one around the arena of an ancient amphitheater serving as a base for the tiers of seats **b** : the masonry under the stylobate of a temple **2 a** : a dais especially for an orchestral conductor **b** : LECTERN [Latin, from Greek *podion* "base", from *pod-, pous* "foot"]

Po·dunk \'pō-,dəngk\ *n* : a small, unimportant, and isolated town [*Podunk*, village in Massachusetts or locality in Connecticut]

po·em \'pō-əm, -im, 'pōm also 'pō-,em\ *n* **1** : a composition in verse **2** : a creation, experience, or object likened to a poem [Middle French *poeme*, from Latin *poema*, from Greek *poiēma*, from *poiein* "to make, create"]

po·e·sy \'pō-ə-zē, -sē\ *n, pl* **-sies** **1 a** : a body of poems **b** : poetic form or composition **2** : poetic inspiration [Middle French *poesie*, from Latin *poesis*, from Greek *poiēsis*, literally, "creation", from *poiein* "to make, create"]

po·et \'pō-ət\ *n* **1** : a writer of poetry **2** : a creative artist of great imaginative and expressive gifts and special sensitivity to the medium [Old French *poete*, from Latin *poeta*, from Greek *poiētēs* "maker, poet", from *poiein* "to make, create"]

po·et·as·ter \'pō-ət-,as-tər\ *n* : an inferior poet [Latin *poeta* "poet" + *-aster*, suffix denoting partial resemblance]

po·et·ess \'pō-ət-əs\ *n* : a woman who is a poet

po·et·ic \pō-'et-ik\ *adj* **1 a** : of, relating to, or characteristic of poets or poetry ⟨*poetic* words⟩ **b** : given to writing poetry **2** : written in verse

po·et·i·cal \pō-'et-i-kəl\ *adj* **1** : POETIC **1 2** : highly and usually splendidly imaginative : IDEALIZED — **po·et·i·cal·ly** \-kə-lē, -klē\ *adv* — **po·et·i·cal·ness** \-kəl-nəs\ *n*

poetic justice *n* : an outcome in which vice is punished and virtue rewarded in a manner peculiarly or ironically appropriate

poetic license *n* : LICENSE 4

po·et·ics \pō-'et-iks\ *n sing or pl* **1 a** : a treatise on poetry or aesthetics **b** : poetic theory or practice **2** : poetic feelings or expression

poet laureate *n, pl* **poets laureate** *or* **poet laureates** **1** : a poet honored for achievement **2** : a poet appointed by a British sovereign as a member of the royal household to write poems for state occasions **3** : one regarded by a country or region as its most eminent or representative poet

po·et·ry \'pō-ə-trē\ *n* **1 a** : metrical writing : VERSE **b** : the productions of a poet : POEMS **2** : writing in language chosen and arranged to create a particular emotional response through meaning, sound, and rhythm **3 a** : a quality that stirs the imagination **b** : a quality of ease and grace

po·go stick \'pō-gō\ *n* : a pole with a strong spring at the bottom and two footrests on which a person stands and moves along the ground by jumping [from *Pogo*, a former trademark]

po·grom \'pō-grəm; pō-'gräm, pə-\ *n* : an organized slaughter of helpless people and especially of Jews [Yiddish, from Russian, literally, "devastation"]

po·gy \'pō-gē\ *n, pl* **pogies** : MENHADEN [of American Indian origin]

poi \'pòi\ *n, pl* **poi** *or* **pois** : a Hawaiian food made of cooked taro root pounded to a paste and often fermented [Hawaiian]

poi·gnant \'pòi-nyənt\ *adj* **1** : PUNGENT **2 a** (1) : painfully affecting the feelings : PIERCING ⟨*poignant* grief⟩ (2) : deeply affecting : TOUCHING **b** : SARCASTIC, INCISIVE ⟨*poignant* satire⟩ **3 a** : pleasurably exciting **b** : being to the point : APT ⟨*poignant* remarks⟩ [Middle French *poignant*, present participle of *poindre* "to prick, sting", from Latin *pungere*] — **poi·gnan·cy** \-nyən-sē\ *n* — **poi·gnant·ly** *adv*

poi·ki·lo·therm \'pòi-'kē-lə-,thərm, -'kil-ə-\ *n* : a cold-blooded organism [Greek *poikilos* "variegated" + *thermē* "heat"] — **poi·ki·lo·ther·mic** \,pòi-kə-lō-'thər-mik\ *adj* — **poi·ki·lo·ther·mism** \-'thər-,miz-əm\ *n*

poin·ci·ana \,pòin-sē-'an-ə, -,pwän-\ *n* : any of several showy tropical trees or shrubs of the pea family with bright orange or red flowers [De *Poinci*, 17th century governor of part of the French West Indies]

poin·set·tia \pòin-'set-ē-ə, -'set-ə\ *n* : a showy Mexican and South American plant of the spurge family with tapering scarlet bracts that grow like petals about its small yellow flowers [Joel R. *Poinsett*, died 1851, American diplomat]

¹point \'pòint\ *n* **1 a** (1) : an individual detail : ITEM ⟨interesting *points* in the proposal⟩ (2) : a distinguishing detail : CHARACTERISTIC ⟨tact isn't my strong *point*⟩ **b** : the most important essential in a discussion or matter ⟨the *point* of the joke⟩ **c** : FORCE 1e, COGENCY **2** : an end or object to be achieved : PURPOSE ⟨there's no *point* in continuing⟩ **3 a** (1) : a geometric element of which it is postulated that at least two exist and that two suffice to determine a line (2) : a geometric element determined by an ordered set of coordinates **b** (1) : a narrowly localized place having a precisely indicated position ⟨a *point* 50 feet north of the tree⟩ (2) : a particular place : LOCALITY ⟨visited many *points* of interest⟩ **c** (1) : an exact moment ⟨at this *point* in time⟩ (2) : a time interval immediately before something indicated : VERGE ⟨at the *point* of death⟩ **d** (1) : a particular step, stage, or degree in development ⟨at the *point* where I no longer cared⟩ (2) : a definite position in a scale **4 a** : the terminal usually sharp or narrowly rounded part of something (as a fin, sword, or pencil) : TIP **b** : a weapon or tool having such a part and used for stabbing or piercing **c** : either of two metal pieces in a distributor through which the circuit is made or broken **5 a** : a projecting usually tapering piece of land or a sharp prominence **b** (1) : the tip of a projecting body part (2) *pl* : terminal bodily projections or their markings especially when differing from the rest of the body in color **6** : a short musical phrase; *esp* : a phrase in contrapuntal music **7 a** : a very small mark **b** (1) : PUNCTUATION MARK; *esp* : PERIOD (2) : DECIMAL POINT **8 a** : one of the 32 pointed marks indicating direction on a mariner's compass **b** : the difference of 11¼ degrees between two such adjacent points **9 a** : NEEDLEPOINT 1 **b** : lace made with a bobbin **10** : one of 12 spaces marked off on each side of a backgammon board **11** : a unit in a scale of measurement: as **a** : a unit of counting in the scoring of a game or contest **b** : a unit of academic credit **c** : a unit of about ¹⁄₇₂ inch (about .35 millimeters) used to measure the size of printing type **12** : the action of pointing; *esp* : the action in dancing of extending one leg so that only the tips of the toes touch the floor [Old French, "puncture, small spot, point in time or space", from Latin *punctum*, from *pungere* "to prick"] — **in point** : RELEVANT, PERTINENT ⟨a case *in point*⟩ — **to the point** : RELEVANT, PERTINENT, APT ⟨a remark that was quite *to the point*⟩

²point *vb* **1 a** : to furnish with a point **b** : to give added force, emphasis, or piquancy to ⟨*point* up a remark⟩ **2** : to scratch out the old mortar from the joints of (as a brick wall) and fill in with new material **3 a** (1) : PUNCTUATE 1 (2) : to separate (a decimal fraction) from an integer by a decimal point ⟨*point* off three decimal places⟩ **b** : to mark the vowels in (as Hebrew words) **4 a** (1) : to indicate the existence of ⟨*point out a mistake*⟩ (2) : to indicate the location of ⟨*point a game bird*⟩ **b** : to indicate the route or direction ⟨*point the way home*⟩ **5 a** : to turn, face, or cause to be turned in a particular direction : AIM ⟨*point a gun*⟩ **b** : to extend (a leg) in executing a point in dancing **6** : to indicate the fact or probability of something specified ⟨the evidence *points* to murder⟩

point–blank \ˈpȯint-ˈblangk\ *adj* **1 a** : marked by no noticeable drop below initial horizontal line of flight **b** : so close to a target that a missile fired will travel in a straight line to the mark ⟨fired from *point-blank* range⟩ **2** : DIRECT, BLUNT ⟨a *point-blank* refusal⟩ — **point–blank** *adv*

pointe \ˈpwaⁿt, ˈpwaⁿnt\ *n* : a position of balance in ballet on the extreme tip of the toe [French, literally, "point"]

point·ed \ˈpȯint-əd\ *adj* **1 a** : having a point **b** : having a crown tapering to a point ⟨the *pointed* arch of Gothic architecture⟩ **2 a** : being to the point : TERSE **b** : aimed at a particular person or group ⟨*pointed* remarks⟩ **3** : CONSPICUOUS 1, MARKED ⟨*pointed* indifference⟩ — **point·ed·ly** *adv* — **point·ed·ness** *n*

point·er \ˈpȯint-ər\ *n* **1 a** : one that points out; *esp* : a rod used to direct attention **b pl, cap** : the two stars in Ursa Major a line through which points to the North Star **2** : a large strong slender smooth-haired hunting dog that hunts by scent and indicates the presence of game by pointing **3** : a useful suggestion or hint : TIP ⟨gave a few *pointers* on how to study⟩

poin·til·lism \ˈpwaⁿ-tē-ˌiz-əm, ˈpwaⁿn-\ *n* : the practice or technique of applying dots of color to a surface so that from a distance they blend together [French *pointillisme,* from *pointiller* "to stipple", from *point* "spot, point"] — **poin·til·list** \-tē-əst\ *n* — **poin·til·lis·tic** \ˌpwaⁿ-tē-ˈis-tik, ˌpwaⁿn-\ *adj*

point·less \ˈpȯint-ləs\ *adj* **1** : having no point **2** : lacking meaning ⟨a *pointless* remark⟩ **3** : INEFFECTIVE ⟨a *pointless* effort to help⟩ — **point·less·ly** *adv* — **point·less·ness** *n*

point of honor : a matter seriously affecting one's honor

point of view : a way of thinking about or looking at things : STANDPOINT

¹poise \ˈpȯiz\ *vb* **1 a** : BALANCE; *esp* : to hold or carry in equilibrium **b** : to hold or be supported or suspended without motion in a steady position ⟨a bird *poised* in the air⟩ **2** : to hold or carry (the head) in a particular way **3** : to put into readiness : BRACE ⟨*poised* for action⟩ [Middle French *pois-,* stem of *peser* "to ponder", from Latin *pensare,* from *pensus,* past participle of *pendere* "to weigh"]

²poise *n* **1** : BALANCE 4a, EQUILIBRIUM **2 a** (1) : self-possessed composure, assurance, and dignity (2) : peaceful state : CALM **b** : a particular way of carrying oneself : BEARING

poised \ˈpȯizd\ *adj* : showing an easy composure in bearing and manner

¹poi·son \ˈpȯiz-n\ *n* **1 a** : a substance that through its chemical action is able to kill, injure, or impair an organism **b** (1) : something destructive or harmful (2) : an object of aversion or abhorrence **2** : a substance that inhibits the activity of another substance or the course of a reaction or process ⟨a catalyst *poison*⟩ [Old French, "drink, poisonous drink, poison", from Latin *potio* "drink, potion"]

²poison *vb* **poi·soned; poi·son·ing** \ˈpȯiz-ning, -n-ing\ **1 a** : to injure or kill with poison **b** : to treat, taint, or impregnate with poison ⟨*poisoned* the air with its fumes⟩ **2** : to exert a baneful influence on : CORRUPT ⟨*poisoned* their minds⟩ **3** : to inhibit the activity, course, or occurrence of — **poi·son·er** \ˈpȯiz-nər, -n-ər\ *n*

³poison *adj* **1** : POISONOUS, VENOMOUS ⟨a *poison* plant⟩ ⟨a *poison* tongue⟩ **2** : impregnated with poison ⟨a *poison* arrow⟩

poison gas *n* : a poisonous gas or a liquid or a solid giving off poisonous vapors designed (as in chemical warfare) to kill, injure, or disable by inhalation or contact

poison hemlock *n* : a biennial poisonous herb of the carrot family with finely divided leaves and white flowers

poison ivy *n* **1** : a usually climbing plant of the sumac family mostly with three leaflets, greenish flowers and berries, and foliage and stems that when bruised and touched may cause an itching rash on the skin **2** : a rash caused by poison ivy

poison oak *n* : a slender woody plant of the sumac family closely resembling poison ivy and causing a similar rash but differing in not climbing or producing aerial roots

poi·son·ous \ˈpȯiz-nəs, -n-əs\ *adj* : having the properties or effects of poison : VENOMOUS — **poi·son·ous·ly** *adv*

poison sumac *n* : a swamp shrub of the sumac family that is related to poison ivy and causes a similar rash but has compound leaves with 7 to 13 leaflets

¹poke \ˈpōk\ *n, chiefly Midland* : BAG 1a, SACK [Old North French, of Germanic origin]

²poke *vb* **1 a** (1) : PROD, JAB ⟨*poked* me in the ribs⟩ (2) : to urge or stir by prodding or jabbing ⟨*poke* up the fire⟩ **b** (1) : PIERCE 1 (2) : to produce by piercing or jabbing ⟨*poke* a hole⟩ **c** : HIT 1a, PUNCH **2 a** : to cause to project ⟨*poked* its head out of the hole⟩ **b** (1) : to thrust forward so as to intrude or meddle ⟨don't *poke* your nose into our affairs⟩ (2) : MEDDLE ⟨*poking* about in other people's business⟩ **3** : to look about or through something without system : RUMMAGE **4** : to move or act slowly or aimlessly : DAWDLE ⟨*poke* along⟩ [Middle English *poken*] — **poke fun at** : RIDICULE, MOCK

³poke *n* **1 a** : a quick thrust : JAB **b** : a blow with the fist : PUNCH **2** : a projecting brim on the front of a woman's bonnet

poke·ber·ry \ˈpōk-ˌber-ē\ *n* : the berry of the pokeweed; *also* : POKEWEED

poke bonnet *n* : a woman's bonnet with a projecting brim at the front

¹pok·er \ˈpō-kər\ *n* : one that pokes; *esp* : a metal rod for stirring a fire

²po·ker \ˈpō-kər\ *n* : any of several card games in which players bet on the value of their hands [probably from French *poque,* a card game similar to poker]

poker face *n* : a face that does not reveal what a person thinks or feels [from the need of poker players to conceal the quality of their hands] — **po·ker–faced** \ˌpō-kər-ˈfāst\ *adj*

poke·weed \ˈpō-ˌkwēd\ *n* : an American perennial herb with spikes of white flowers, dark purple juicy berries, a poisonous root, and young shoots sometimes used as potherbs [*poke,* of American Indian origin]

poky *or* **pok·ey** \ˈpō-kē\ *adj* **pok·i·er; -est 1** : being small and cramped ⟨a *poky* room⟩ **2** : SHABBY, DULL ⟨a *poky* way of writing⟩ **3** : annoyingly slow ⟨a *poky* horse⟩ [²*poke*] — **pok·i·ly** \-kə-lē\ *adv* — **pok·i·ness** \-kē-nəs\ *n*

Po·land Chi·na \ˌpō-lənd-ˈchī-nə, -lən-\ *n* : any of a breed of large white-marked black swine adapted to converting feed into fat [*Poland,* Europe + *China,* Asia]

po·lar \ˈpō-lər\ *adj* **1** : of or relating to a geographical pole or the region around it; *also* : coming from or having the characteristics of such a region **2 a** : of or relating to one or more poles (as of a magnet) **b** : having a dipole or characterized by molecules having dipoles ⟨a *polar* molecule⟩ **3** : serving as a guide ⟨a *polar* idea⟩ **4** : diametrically opposite **5** : PIVOTAL 2, CRUCIAL ⟨*polar* events⟩

polar bear *n* : a large creamy-white bear of arctic regions

poison ivy 1

polar bear

\ə\ abut		\ng\ sing	
\ər\ further		\ō\ bone	
\a\ mat		\ȯ\ saw	
\ā\ take		\ȯi\ coin	
\ä\ cot, cart		\th\ thin	
\au̇\ out		\th\ this	
\ch\ chin		\ü\ food	
\e\ pet		\u̇\ foot	
\ē\ easy		\y\ yet	
\g\ go		\yü\ few	
\i\ tip		\yu̇\ cure	
\ī\ life		\zh\ vision	
\j\ job			

polar body *n* : a cell that separates from an oocyte during meiosis and that contains a nucleus produced in the first or second meiotic division but little cytoplasm

polar circle *n* : one of the two parallels of latitude each at a distance from a pole of the earth equal to about 23 degrees 27 minutes

polar coordinate *n* : either of two numbers that locate a point in a plane by its distance from a fixed point and the angle a line joining the two points makks with a fixed line

Po·lar·is \pə-'lar-əs, -'lär-\ *n* : NORTH STAR [New Latin, from *polaris* "polar"]

po·lari·scope \pō-'lar-ə-ˌskōp\ *n* : an instrument for studying the properties of substances in polarized light

po·lar·i·ty \pō-'lar-ət-ē, pə-\ *n, pl* **-ties** **1** : the quality or condition of being polar : having poles **2** : attraction toward a particular object or in a specific direction **3** : the particular state either positive or negative with reference to magnetic or electrical poles **4 a** : diametrical opposition **b** : an instance of diametrical opposition

po·lar·iza·tion \ˌpō-lə-rə-'zā-shən\ *n* **1** : the action of polarizing or state of being polarized: as **a** : the action of affecting radiation (as light) so that the vibrations of the wave assume a definite direction (as in one plane) **b** : the deposition of gas on one or both electrodes of an electrolytic cell increasing the resistance and setting up a counter electromotive force **c** : MAGNETIZATION **2 a** : division into two opposites ⟨*polarization* of views⟩ **b** : concentration about opposing extremes ⟨*polarization* of political factions⟩

po·lar·ize \'pō-lə-ˌrīz\ *vb* **1** : to cause to undergo polarization **2** : to give polarity to **3** : to become polarized — **po·lar·iz·able** \-ˌrī-zə-bəl\ *adj* — **po·lar·iz·er** *n*

polar nucleus *n* : either of the two nuclei of a seed plant embryo sac that are destined to form endosperm — compare DOUBLE FERTILIZATION

Po·lar·oid \'pō-lə-ˌròid\ *trademark* — used for a light-polarizing material used especially in eyeglasses to prevent glare

pol·der \'pōl-dər, 'päl-\ *n* : a tract of low land reclaimed from a body of water (as the sea) [Dutch]

¹pole \'pōl\ *n* **1** : a long slender usually cylindrical piece of material (as wood or metal) ⟨telephone *poles*⟩ **2 a** : a unit of length equal to 16½ feet (about 5 meters) **b** : a unit of area equal to a square rod (about 25.3 square meters) **3** : the inside position on a racetrack [Old English *pāl* "stake, pole", from Latin *palus* "stake"]

²pole *vb* **1** : to act upon, impel, or push with a pole **2 a** : to propel a boat with a pole **b** : to use ski poles to gain speed — **pol·er** *n*

³pole *n* **1** : either end of an axis of a sphere and especially of the earth's axis **2 a** : either of two related opposites **b** : a point of guidance or attraction **3 a** : one of the two terminals of an electric cell, battery, or dynamo **b** : one of two or more regions in a magnetized body at which the magnetism is concentrated **4** : either of the two specialized areas at opposite ends of an axis in an organism or cell ⟨chromosomes moving toward the *poles* of a dividing cell⟩ [Latin *polus*, from Greek *polos* "pivot, pole"]

Pole \'pōl\ *n* **1** : a native or inhabitant of Poland **2** : a person of Polish descent [German, of Slavic origin]

pole·ax \'pō-ˌlaks\ *n* : a battle-ax with a short handle and often with a hook or point opposite the blade [Middle English *pollax*, from *polle* "poll" + *ax*]

pole bean *n* : a cultivated bean having long internodes and twining stems and usually trained to grow upright on supports

pole·cat \'pōl-ˌkat\ *n, pl* **polecats** *or* **polecat** **1** : a European flesh-eating mammal of which the ferret is considered a domesticated variety **2** : SKUNK [Middle English *polcat*, probably from Middle French *poul, pol* "cock" + Middle English *cat*; probably from its preying on poultry]

po·lem·ic \pə-'lem-ik\ *n* **1 a** : an aggressive attack on or refutation of the opinions or principles of another **b** : the art or practice of disputation or controversy — usually used in pl. **2** : an aggressive controversialist : DISPUTANT **3** *pl* : the branch of Christian theology devoted to the refutation of errors [French *polémique*, derived from Greek *polemikos* "warlike, hostile", from *polemos* "war"] — **polemic** *or* **po·lem·i·cal** \-'lem-i-kəl\ *adj* — **po·lem·i·cal·ly** \-i-kə-lē, -klē\ *adv* — **po·lem·i·cist** \-'lem-ə-səst\ *n*

pole·star \'pōl-ˌstär\ *n* **1** : NORTH STAR **2 a** : a directing principle : GUIDE **b** : a center of attraction

pole vault *n* : a field event consisting of a vault for height over a crossbar with the aid of a pole — **pole-vault** \'pōl-ˌvòlt\ *vi* — **pole–vault·er** *n*

¹po·lice \pə-'lēs\ *vt* **1** : to control, regulate, or keep in order by use or as if by use of police **2** : to make clean and put in order : clean up ⟨*police* an area⟩ **3** : to supervise the operation, execution, or administration of

²police *n, pl* **police** **1** : the department of government the members of which constitute the police force **2** : POLICE FORCE **3** : a private organization resembling a police force ⟨railroad *police*⟩ [Middle French, "government", from Late Latin *politia*, from Greek *politeia*, from *politeuein* "to be a citizen, engage in political activity", from *politēs* "citizen", from *polis* "city, state"]

police action *n* : a military action undertaken without formal declaration of war by regular forces against persons held to be violators of international peace and order

police court *n* : a court having jurisdiction over various minor offenses and authority to send cases involving serious offenses to a superior court

police dog *n* **1** : a dog trained to assist police **2** : GERMAN SHEPHERD

police force *n* : a body of trained officers entrusted by a government with maintenance of public peace and order, enforcement of laws, and prevention and detection of crime

po·lice·man \pə-'lē-smən\ *n* : a male police officer

police officer *n* : a member of a police force

police power *n* : the inherent power of a government to exercise reasonable control over persons and property within its jurisdiction in the interest of the general security, health, safety, morals, and welfare

police reporter *n* : a reporter assigned to cover police news (as crimes, accidents, and arrests)

police state *n* : a state in which the social, economic, and political activities of the people are under the arbitrary power of the government often acting through a secret police force

police station *n* : the headquarters of the police for a particular locality

po·lice·wom·an \pə-'lē-ˌswùm-ən\ *n* : a female police officer

¹pol·i·cy \'päl-ə-sē\ *n, pl* **-cies** **1 a** : prudence or wisdom in the management of affairs : SAGACITY **b** : management or procedure based primarily on material interest **2** : a frame of reference or a set of principles or rules determining what and how things are done by a person or group ⟨it's our *policy* not to give refunds⟩ [Middle French *policie* "government, regulation", from Late Latin *politia*]

²policy *n, pl* **-cies** **1** : a writing embodying a contract of insurance **2 a** : a daily lottery in which participants bet that certain numbers will be drawn **b** : NUMBER 8 [Middle French *police* "certificate", from Italian *polizza*, from Medieval Latin *apodixa* "receipt", from Greek *apodeixis* "proof", from *apodeiknynai* "to demonstrate"]

pol·i·cy·hold·er \-ˌhōl-dər\ *n* : one granted an insurance policy

po·lio \'pō-lē-ˌō\ *n* : POLIOMYELITIS — **polio** *adj*

po·lio·my·e·li·tis \ˌpō-lē-ō-ˌmī-ə-'līt-əs\ *n* : an acute infectious virus disease marked by inflammation of nerve cells in the spinal cord accompanied by fever and often paralysis and wasting of muscles — called also *infantile paralysis* [Greek *polios* "gray" + *myelos* "marrow"] — **po·lio·my·e·lit·ic** \-'lit-ik\ *adj*

po·lio·vi·rus \'pō-lē-ō-ˌvī-rəs\ *n* : a virus that causes human poliomyelitis and occurs in several distinct forms

¹pol·ish \'päl-ish\ *vb* **1** : to make smooth and glossy usually by friction ⟨*polish* furniture⟩ **2** : to smooth or refine in manners or condition **3** : to bring to a highly developed, finished, or refined state ⟨*polish* a technique⟩ [Old French *poliss-*, stem of *polir* "to polish", from Latin *polire*] SYN see BURNISH — **pol·ish·er** *n*

²polish *n* **1 a** : a smooth glossy surface : LUSTER **b** : REFINEMENT 2, CULTURE **c** : a state of high development or refinement **2** : the action or process of polishing **3** : a preparation used in polishing

¹Pol·ish \'pō-lish\ *adj* : of, relating to, or characteristic of Poland, the Poles, or Polish

²Polish *n* : the Slavic language of the Poles

polish off *vt* : to dispose of rapidly or completely

po·lit·bu·ro \'päl-ət-ˌbyúr-ō, 'pō-lət-, pə-'lit-\ : the principal policy-making body of a Communist party [Russian *politbyuro*, from *politicheskoe byuro* "political bureau"]

po·lite \pə-'līt\ *adj* **1** : of, relating to, or having the characteristics of advanced culture ⟨customs of *polite* society⟩ **2 a** : showing or characterized by correct social usage ⟨*polite* forms of address⟩ **b** : marked by consideration, tact, deference, or courtesy : COURTEOUS [Latin *politus*, from *polire* "to polish"] SYN see CIVIL — **po·lite·ly** *adv* — **po·lite·ness** *n*

po·li·tesse \ˌpäl-ē-'tes, ˌpó-li-\ *n* : formal politeness [French]

pol·i·tic \'päl-ə-ˌtik\ *adj* **1** : characterized by shrewdness in managing, contriving, or dealing **2** : sagacious in promoting a policy **3** : shrewdly tactful ⟨a *politic* answer⟩ [Middle French *politique* "political", from Latin *politicus*, from Greek *politikos*, from *politēs* "citizen", from *polis* "citizen"] SYN see EXPEDIENT — **pol·i·tick·er** *n*

po·lit·i·cal \pə-'lit-i-kəl\ *adj* **1** : of or relating to government, a government, or the conduct of government **2** : of or relating to politics **3** : organized in governmental terms ⟨*political* units⟩ **4** : involving or concerned with acts against a government or political system ⟨*political* crimes⟩ ⟨*political* police⟩ — **po·lit·i·cal·ly** \-kə-lē, -klē\ *adv*

political action committee *n* : a group formed (as by an industry or an issue-oriented organization) to raise money for the campaigns of candidates likely to advance the group's interests

political economy *n* : a modern social science dealing with the interrelationship of political and economic processes — **political economist** *n*

politically correct *adj* : conforming to a belief that language and practices which could offend political sensibilities (as in matters of sex or race) should be eliminated

political science *n* : a social science concerned chiefly with the description and analysis of political institutions and processes — **political scientist** *n*

pol·i·ti·cian \ˌpäl-ə-'tish-ən\ *n* **1** : one experienced in the art or science of government; *esp* : one actively conducting governmental affairs **2** : one engaged in party politics as a profession

pol·i·tick \'päl-ə-ˌtik\ *vi* : to engage in political discussion or activity — **pol·i·tick·er** *n*

po·lit·i·co \pə-'lit-i-ˌkō\ *n, pl* **-cos** *also* **-coes** : POLITICIAN 2 [Italian *politico* or Spanish *político*, derived from Latin *politicus* "political"]

pol·i·tics \'päl-ə-ˌtiks\ *n sing or pl* **1 a** : the art or science of government **b** : the art or science of guiding or influencing governmental policy **c** : the art or science of winning and holding control over a government **2 a** : political affairs or business; *esp* : competition between groups or individuals for power and leadership **b** : political life especially as a profession **3** : political opinions

pol·i·ty \'päl-ət-ē\ *n, pl* **-ties 1** : political organization **2** : a form of political organization ⟨a republican *polity*⟩ **3** : a politically organized unit **4** : the form of government of a religious denomination

pol·ka \'pōl-kə\ *n* **1** : a vivacious couple dance of Bohemian origin with three steps and a hop in duple time **2** : a lively Bohemian dance tune in ²/₄ time [Czech, from Polish *Polka* "Polish woman"] — **polka** *vi*

pol·ka dot \'pō-kə-ˌdät\ *n* : a dot in a pattern of regularly distributed dots in textile design — **polka–dot** *or* **polka–dot·ted** \-ˌdät-əd\ *adj*

¹poll \'pōl\ *n* **1 a** : HEAD 1 **b** : the prominent hairy top or back of the head **c** : NAPE **2** : the broad or flat end of a hammer or similar tool **3 a** : a casting or recording of votes **b** : a place where votes are cast or recorded — usually used in pl. **4 a** : a questioning of persons to obtain information or opinions **b** : the information so obtained [Low German *polle*]

²poll *vb* **1 a** : to cut off or cut short the hair or wool of : CROP, SHEAR **b** : to cut off or cut short (as wool) **2 a** : to receive and record the votes of **b** : to request each member of to declare his or her vote individually ⟨*poll* a jury⟩ **3** : to receive (as votes) in an election **4** : to question or canvass in a poll **5** : to cast one's vote at a poll — **poll·ee** \pō-'lē\ *n* — **poll·er** \'pō-lər\ *n*

pol·lack *or* **pol·lock** \'päl-ək\ *n, pl* **pollack** *or* **pollock 1** : a commercially important north Atlantic food fish resembling the related cods but darker **2** : a commercially important food fish of the northern Pacific that is related to and resembles the pollack [Scottish *podlok*]

polled \'pōld\ *adj* : having no horns

pol·len \'päl-ən\ *n* : a mass of microspores in a seed plant that usually appears as a fine yellow dust — compare POLLEN GRAIN, POLLEN TUBE [Latin *pollin-, pollen* "fine flour"]

pollen basket *n* : a flat or hollow area bordered with stiff hairs on the hind leg of a bee in which it carries pollen

pollen grain *n* : one of the granular microspores in pollen that give rise to the male gametophyte of a seed plant

pol·len·iz·er \'päl-ə-ˌnī-zər\ *n* **1** : a plant that is a source of pollen **2** : POLLINATOR 1

pollen sac *n* : one of the pouches of a seed plant anther in which pollen is formed

pollen tube *n* : a tube formed by the pollen grain that passes down the style and conveys the sperm nuclei to the embryo sac of a flower

pol·lex \'päl-ˌeks\ *n, pl* **pol·li·ces** \'päl-ə-ˌsēz\ : THUMB 1 [Latin, "thumb, big toe"]

pol·li·nate \'päl-ə-ˌnāt\ *vt* : to place pollen on the stigma of — **pol·li·na·tion** \ˌpäl-ə-'nā-shən\ *n*

pol·li·na·tor \'päl-ə-ˌnāt-ər\ *n* **1** : an agent that pollinates flowers **2** : POLLENIZER 1

pol·li·no·sis *also* **pol·len·osis** \ˌpäl-ə-'nō-səs\ *n* : an acute recurrent allergic respiratory disorder caused by sensitivity to particular pollens

pol·li·wog *or* **pol·ly·wog** \'päl-ē-ˌwäg, -ˌwȯg\ *n* : TADPOLE [Middle English *polwygle*, probably from *pol* "poll" + *wiglen* "to wiggle"]

poll·ster \'pōl-stər\ *n* : one that conducts a poll or compiles data obtained by a poll

poll tax *n* : a tax of a fixed amount per person levied on adults

pol·lu·tant \pə-'lüt-nt\ *n* : something that pollutes

\ə\ abut	\ng\ sing
\ər\ further	\ō\ bone
\a\ mat	\ȯ\ saw
\ā\ take	\ȯi\ coin
\ä\ cot, cart	\th\ thin
\aú\ out	\th\ this
\ch\ chin	\ü\ food
\e\ pet	\ú\ foot
\ē\ easy	\y\ yet
\g\ go	\yü\ few
\i\ tip	\yú\ cure
\ī\ life	\zh\ vision
\j\ job	

pol·lute \pə-'lüt\ *vt* : to make impure; *esp* : to contaminate (as a natural resource) with man-made waste (industrial wastes *polluted* the river) [Latin *pollutus,* past participle of *polluere* "to pollute"] — **pol·lut·er** *n*

pol·lu·tion \pə-'lü-shən\ *n* : the action of polluting : the state of being polluted

Pol·lux \'päl-əks\ *n* : a first-magnitude star in the constellation Gemini [*Pollux,* twin of Castor]

Pol·ly·an·na \,päl-ē-'an-ə\ : one characterized by unshakable optimism and a tendency to find good in everything [*Pollyanna,* heroine of the novel *Pollyanna* (1913) by Eleanor Porter]

po·lo \'pō-lō\ *n* **1** : a game played by teams of players on horseback using mallets with long flexible handles to drive a wooden ball **2** : WATER POLO [of Tibetan origin] — **po·lo·ist** \'pō-lə-wəst\ *n*

polo coat *n* : a tailored casual overcoat made especially of camel's hair

po·lo·naise \,päl-ə-'nāz, ,pō-lə-\ *n* **1** : an elaborate 18th century overdress with short-sleeved fitted waist and draped cutaway overskirt **2 a** : a stately 19th century Polish processional dance **b** : music for this dance in moderate ¾ time [French, from *polonais* "Polish"]

po·lo·ni·um \pə-'lō-nē-əm\ *n* : a radioactive metallic chemical element that emits a helium nucleus to form an isotope of lead — see ELEMENT table [New Latin, from Medieval Latin *Polonia* "Poland"]

polo shirt *n* : a close-fitting knitted cotton pullover shirt with a turnover collar or round banded neck

pol·ter·geist \'pōl-tər-,gīst\ *n* : a noisy usually mischievous ghost held to be responsible for unexplained noises (as rappings) [German, from *poltern* "to knock" + *geist* "spirit"]

¹pol·troon \päl-'trün\ *n* : a spiritless coward : CRAVEN [Middle French *poultron,* from Italian *poltrone,* from *poltro* "colt", derived from Latin *pullus* "young of an animal"]

²poltroon *adj* : characterized by complete cowardice

poly- *combining form* **1 a** : many : several : much : MULTI- (*poly*gyny) **b** : excessive : HYPER- **2 a** : containing more than one of a (specified) substance (*poly*nucleotide) **b** : polymeric (*poly*ethylene) [Greek, from *polys*]

poly·an·dry \'päl-ē-,an-drē\ *n* : the practice of having more than one husband or male mate at one time — compare POLYGYNY [Greek *polyandros* "having many husbands", from *poly-* + *andr-, anēr* "man, husband"] — **poly·an·drous** \,päl-ē-'an-drəs\ *adj*

poly·chaete \'päl-i-,kēt\ *n* : any of a class (Polychaeta) of chiefly marine annelid worms that usually have paired segmental appendages [derived from Greek *polychaitēs* "having much hair", from *poly-* + *chaitē* "long hair"] — **polychaete** *adj*

poly·chlo·ri·nat·ed biphenyl \,päl-i-'klōr-ə-,nāt-əd-, -'klôr-\ *n* : any of several compounds that have various industrial applications and are poisonous environmental pollutants which tend to accumulate in animal tissues

poly·chro·mat·ic \,päl-i-krō-'mat-ik\ *adj* : showing a variety or a change of colors : MULTICOLORED

poly·chrome \'päl-i-,krōm\ *adj* : relating to, made with, or decorated in several colors (*polychrome* pottery)

poly·clin·ic \,päl-i-'klin-ik\ *n* : a clinic or hospital treating diseases of many sorts

poly·dac·ty·ly \,päl-i-'dak-tə-lē\ *n* : the condition of having several to many and especially abnormally many toes or fingers [*poly-* + Greek *daktylos* "finger, toe"] — **poly·dac·tyl** \-'dak-tl\ *adj or n* — **poly·dac·ty·lous** \-tə-ləs\ *adj*

poly·es·ter \'päl-ē-,es-tər\ *n* : a complex ester formed by polymerization or condensation and used especially in making fibers or plastics

poly·eth·yl·ene \,päl-ē-'eth-ə-,lēn\ *n* : one of various lightweight plastics resistant to chemicals and mois-

ture that are used especially in packaging and electrical insulation

po·lyg·a·mous \pə-'lig-ə-məs\ *adj* **1** : of, relating to, or being a marriage form in which a spouse of either sex has more than one mate at one time **2** : having more than one spouse or mate at one time — **po·lyg·a·mist** \-məst\ *n* — **po·lyg·a·mous·ly** *adv* — **po·lyg·a·my** \-mē\ *n*

poly·gene \'päl-i-,jēn\ *n* : any of a group of genes that collectively control or modify the expression of a particular character — **poly·gen·ic** \,päl-i-'jē-nik\ *adj*

poly·glot \'päl-i-,glät\ *adj* **1** : speaking or writing several languages **2** : containing matter in or derived from several languages [Greek *polyglōttos,* from *poly-* + *glōtta* "language"] — **polyglot** *n*

poly·gon \'päl-i-,gän\ *n* : a closed plane figure bounded by straight lines — **po·lyg·o·nal** \pə-'lig-ən-l\ *adj*

poly·graph \'päl-i-,graf\ *n* : an instrument for recording tracings of several different pulsations simultaneously; *also* : LIE DETECTOR — **poly·graph·ic** \,päl-i-'graf-ik\ *adj*

po·lyg·y·ny \pə-'lij-ə-nē\ *n* : the practice of having more than one wife or female mate at one time — compare POLYANDRY [*poly-* + Greek *gynē* "woman, wife"] — **po·lyg·y·nous** \-nəs\ *adj*

poly·he·dron \,päl-i-'hē-drən\ *n, pl* **-drons** *or* **-dra** \-drə\ : a solid formed by plane faces — **poly·he·dral** \-drəl\ *adj*

poly·math \'päl-i-,math\ *n* : one of encyclopedic learning [Greek *polymathēs* "very learned", from *poly-* + *manthanein* "to learn"]

poly·mer \'päl-ə-mər\ *n* : a chemical compound or mixture of compounds that is formed by polymerization and consists essentially of repeating structural units [back-formation from *polymeric,* from Greek *polymerēs* "having many parts", from *poly-* + *meros* "part"] — **poly·mer·ic** \,päl-ə-'mer-ik\ *adj*

po·ly·mer·iza·tion \pə-,lim-ə-rə-'zā-shən, ,päl-ə-mə-rə-\ *n* : a chemical reaction in which two or more small molecules combine to form larger molecules — **po·ly·mer·ize** \pə-'lim-ə-,rīz, 'päl-ə-mə-\ *vb*

poly·morph \'päl-i-,môrf\ *n* : a polymorphic organism; *also* : one of the several forms of such an organism

poly·mor·phic \,päl-i-'môr-fik\ *or* **poly·mor·phous** \-fəs\ *adj* : having, assuming, or occurring in various forms, characters, or styles (a *polymorphic* butterfly) — **poly·mor·phism** \-,fiz-əm\ *n*

poly·mor·pho·nu·cle·ar \-,môr-fə-'nü-klē-ər, -'nyü-\ *adj* : having the nucleus complexly lobed (*polymorphonuclear* leukocytes) — **polymorphonuclear** *n*

Poly·ne·sian \,päl-ə-'nē-zhən, -shən\ *n* **1** : a member of any of the native peoples of Polynesia **2** : a group of Austronesian languages spoken in Polynesia — **Polynesian** *adj*

poly·no·mi·al \,päl-i-'nō-mē-əl\ *n* : a sum of two or more algebraic terms each of which consists of a constant multiplied by one or more variables raised to a nonnegative integral power $(6 + 3x + 5x^2$ is a *polynomial*) [*poly-* + *-nomial* (as in *binomial*)] — **polynomial** *adj*

polynomial equation *n* : an equation in which one side is a polynomial and the other side is a constant, monomial, or polynomial

poly·nu·cle·o·tide \,päl-i-'nü-klē-ə-,tīd, -'nyü-\ *n* : a polymeric chain of nucleotides

pol·yp \'päl-əp\ *n* **1** : a coelenterate (as a sea anemone) having a hollow cylindrical body closed and attached at one end and opening at the other by a central mouth surrounded by tentacles armed with minute stinging organs **2** : a tumor that often has a stalk and occurs especially in the lower intestine [Middle French *polype* "octopus, nasal tumor", from Latin *polypus,* from Greek *polypous,* from *poly-* + *pous* "foot"] — **pol·yp·oid** \'päl-ə-,pôid\ *adj*

poly·pep·tide \,päl-i-'pep-,tīd\ *n* : a chain of amino acids that contributes to the structure of a protein

poly·phase \'päl-i-,fāz\ *or* **poly·pha·sic** \,päl-i-'fā-zik\ *adj* : having or producing two or more phases ⟨a *polyphase* machine⟩ ⟨a *polyphase* current⟩

po·lyph·o·ny \pə-'lif-ə-nē\ *n* : music consisting of two or more independent but harmonious melodies [Greek *polyphōnia* "variety of tones", derived from *poly-* + *phōnē* "voice"] — **poly·phon·ic** \,päl-i-'fän-ik\ *adj* — **poly·phon·i·cal·ly** \-i-kə-lē, -klē\ *adv*

poly·ploid \'päl-i-,ploid\ *adj* : having or being a chromosome number that is a multiple greater than two of the basic haploid chromosome number [*poly-* + *-ploid* (as in *diploid*)] — **polyploid** *n* — **poly·ploi·dy** \-,ploid-ē\ *n*

poly·po·dy \'päl-ə-,pōd-ē\ *n, pl* **-dies** : a widely distributed fern with creeping rhizomes and usually deeply cleft fronds [Latin *polypodium*, from Greek *polypodion*, from *poly-* + *pod-, pous* "foot"]

poly·sac·cha·ride \,päl-i-'sak-ə-,rīd\ *n* : a carbohydrate that can be decomposed by hydrolysis into two or more molecules of monosaccharides; *esp* : one of the more complex carbohydrates (as cellulose, starch, or glycogen)

poly·sty·rene \-'stīr-,ēn\ *n* : a clear rigid plastic of good physical and electrical insulating properties

poly·syl·lab·ic \,päl-i-sə-'lab-ik\ *adj* 1 : having more than three syllables 2 : using polysyllabic words — **poly·syl·lab·i·cal·ly** \-'lab-i-kə-lē, -klē\ *adv* — **poly·syl·la·ble** \'päl-i-,sil-ə-bəl, ,päl-i-'\ *n*

poly·syn·de·ton \,päl-i-'sin-də-,tän\ *n* : repetition of conjunctions in close succession (as in "paper and pencils and books") [Late Greek, neuter of *polysyndetos* "using many conjunctions", from Greek *poly-* + *syndetos* "bound together"]

poly·tech·nic \,päl-i-'tek-nik\ *adj* : relating to or devoted to instruction in many technical arts or applied sciences ⟨a *polytechnic* school⟩ [French *polytechnique*, from Greek *polytechnos* "skilled in many arts", from *poly-* + *technē* "art"] — **polytechnic** *n*

poly·the·ism \'päl-i-,thē-,iz-əm\ *n* : belief in or worship of more than one god — **poly·the·ist** \-,thē-əst\ *adj or n* — **poly·the·is·tic** \,päl-i-thē-'is-tik\ *adj*

poly·to·nal·i·ty \,päl-i-tō-'nal-ət-ē\ *n* : the simultaneous use of two or more musical keys — **poly·ton·al** \-'tōn-l\ *adj*

poly·un·sat·u·rat·ed \,päl-ē-,ən-'sach-ə-,rāt-əd\ *adj* : rich in unsaturated chemical bonds ⟨a *polyunsaturated* oil⟩ ⟨*polyunsaturated* fats⟩

poly·va·lent \,päl-i-'vā-lənt\ *adj* 1 a : having a valence greater usually than two b : having variable valence 2 : effective against or sensitive toward more than one exciting agent (as a toxin or antigen) — **poly·va·lence** \-ləns\ *n*

pom·ace \'pəm-əs, 'päm-\ *n* : the dry or pulpy residue of plant material (as apples, olives, or sugarcane) from which a liquid (as a juice) has been pressed or extracted [probably from Medieval Latin *pomacium* "cider", from Late Latin *pomum* "apple", from Latin, "fruit"]

po·made \pō-'mād, -'mäd\ *n* : a perfumed ointment especially for the hair or scalp [Middle French *pommade* "ointment formerly made from apples", from Italian *pomata*, from *pomo* "apple", from Late Latin *pomum*] — **pomade** *vt*

po·man·der \'pō-,man-dər, pō-'\ *n* : a mixture of aromatic substances enclosed in a perforated bag or box and formerly carried as a guard against infection [Middle French *pome d'ambre*, literally, "apple or ball of amber"]

pome \'pōm\ *n* : a fleshy fruit (as an apple) consisting of a central core with usually five seeds enclosed in a capsule and surrounded by a thick fleshy outer layer [Middle French *pome, pomme* "apple, pome, ball", from Late Latin *pomum* "apple", from Latin, "fruit"]

pome·gran·ate \'päm-,gran-ət, 'päm-ə-,gran-, 'pəm-,gran-\ *n* : a thick-skinned reddish fruit about the size of an orange having many seeds in a tangy crimson pulp; *also* : a tropical Old World tree bearing pomegranates [Middle French *pomme grenate*, literally, "seedy apple"]

Pom·er·a·nian \,päm-ə-'rā-nē-ən, -nyən\ *n* 1 : a native or inhabitant of Pomerania 2 : any of a breed of very small compact long-haired dogs — **Pomeranian** *adj*

¹**pom·mel** \'pəm-əl, 'päm-\ *n* 1 : the knob on the hilt of a sword or saber 2 : the projection at the front and top of a saddlebow 3 : either of a pair of rounded or U-shaped handles on a pommel horse [Middle French *pomel*, derived from Late Latin *pomum* "apple"]

²**pom·mel** \'pəm-əl\ *vt* **-meled** *or* **-melled; -mel·ing** *or* **-mel·ling** \'pəm-ling, -ə-ling\ : POUND 2a, PUMMEL [¹*pommel*]

pommel horse *n* : a leather-covered rectangular or cylindrical form with two pommels on the top that is used for swinging and balancing feats in gymnastics

pomp \'pämp\ *n* 1 : a show of magnificence : SPLENDOR ⟨the *pomp* of a coronation ceremony⟩ 2 : a showy display ⟨a person who loves *pomp*⟩ [Middle French *pompe*, from Latin *pompa* "procession, pomp", from Greek *pompē*]

pom·pa·dour \'päm-pə-,dōr, -,dȯr\ *n* : a style of dressing the hair high over the forehead; *also* : hair dressed in this style [Marquise de *Pompadour*]

pom·pa·no \'päm-pə-,nō, 'pəm-\ *n, pl* **-nos** : a spiny-finned food fish of the southern Atlantic and Gulf coasts having a narrow body and forked tail; *also* : any of several related or similar fishes [Spanish *pámpano*, a kind of fish]

¹**pom–pom** \'päm-,päm\ *n* : an automatic gun of 20 to 40 millimeters mounted on ships in pairs, fours, or eights [imitative]

²**pom–pom** *n* : an ornamental ball or tuft used on clothing, caps, and costumes [alteration of *pompon*]

pom·pon \'päm-,pän\ *n* 1 : ²POM-POM 2 : a chrysanthemum or dahlia with small rounded flower heads [French]

pom·pos·i·ty \päm-'päs-ət-ē\ *n, pl* **-ties** 1 : the quality or state of being pompous 2 : a pompous gesture or act

pomp·ous \'päm-pəs\ *adj* 1 : marked by stately show ⟨a *pompous* procession⟩ 2 : SELF-IMPORTANT ⟨a very *pompous* person⟩ 3 : too elevated or ornate ⟨*pompous* prose⟩ — **pomp·ous·ly** *adv* — **pomp·ous·ness** *n*

pon·cho \'pän-chō\ *n, pl* **ponchos** : a cloak resembling a blanket with a slit in the middle for the head; *also* : a waterproof garment of similar style worn chiefly as a raincoat [American Spanish, from Araucanian *pontho* "woolen fabric"]

pond \'pänd\ *n* : a body of standing water usually smaller than a lake [Middle English, "artificially confined body of water", alteration of *pounde* "enclosure"]

pon·der \'pän-dər\ *vb* **pon·dered; pon·der·ing** \'pän-dring, -də-ring\ : to consider carefully [Middle French *ponderer*, from Latin *ponderare* "to weigh, ponder", from *ponder-, pondus* "weight"] — **pon·der·er** \-dər-ər\ *n*

pon·der·a·ble \'pän-də-rə-bəl, -drə-bəl\ *adj* : capable of being weighed or appraised : APPRECIABLE [Late Latin *ponderabilis*, from Latin *ponderare* "to weigh, ponder"]

pon·der·o·sa pine \,pän-də-,rō-sə, -zə-\ *n* : a tall timber pine of western North America with long needles in bundles of 2 to 5; *also* : its strong straight-grained wood [Latin *ponderosa*, feminine of *ponderosus* "ponderous"]

pon·der·ous \'pän-də-rəs, -drəs\ *adj* 1 : very heavy 2 : UNWIELDY 3 : unpleasantly or oppressively dull ⟨*ponderous* prose⟩ [Middle French *pondereux*, from Latin *ponderosus*, from *ponder-, pondus* "weight"] — **pon·der·ous·ly** *adv* — **pon·der·ous·ness** *n*

pomegranate

\ə\ abut	\ng\ sing	
\ər\ further	\ō\ bone	
\a\ mat	\ȯ\ saw	
\ā\ take	\ȯi\ coin	
\ä\ cot, cart	\th\ thin	
\au̇\ out	\th̲\ this	
\ch\ chin	\ü\ food	
\e\ pet	\u̇\ foot	
\ē\ easy	\y\ yet	
\g\ go	\yü\ few	
\i\ tip	\yu̇\ cure	
\ī\ life	\zh\ vision	
\j\ job		

pond lily *n* : WATER LILY

pond scum *n* **1** : SPIROGYRA; *also* : any of various related algae **2** : a mass of tangled algal filaments in stagnant water

pond·weed \'pän-ˌdwēd\ *n* : any of several water plants with both submerged and floating leaves and spikes of greenish flowers

pone \'pōn\ *n, Southern & Midland* : CORN PONE [of American Indian origin]

pon·gee \pän-'jē, 'pän-ˌ\ *n* : a thin soft beige or tan fabric of Chinese origin woven from raw silk; *also* : an imitation of this fabric in cotton or rayon [Chinese (Pekingese dialect) *pen³ chi¹*, from *pen³* "own" + *chi¹* "loom"]

pon·gid \'pän-jəd, 'päng-gəd\ *n* : an anthropoid ape [derived from Kongo (a language of western Africa) *mpungu* "ape"] — **pongid** *adj*

¹pon·iard \'pän-yərd\ *n* : a slender dagger [Middle French *poignard*, from *poing* "fist", from Latin *pugnus*]

¹poniard

²poniard *vt* : to stab with a poniard

pons \'pänz\ *n, pl* **pon·tes** \'pän-ˌtēz\ : a broad mass of nerve fibers on the ventral surface of the brain at the anterior end of the medulla oblongata [New Latin *pons Varoli*, literally, "bridge of Varoli", from Costanzo Varoli, died 1575, Italian surgeon and anatomist]

pon·ti·fex \'pänt-ə-ˌfeks\ *n, pl* **pon·tif·i·ces** \pän-'tif-ə-ˌsēz\ : a member of the ancient Roman council of priests [Latin *pontific-, pontifex*, literally, "bridge maker", from *pont-, pons* "bridge" + *facere* "to make"]

pon·tiff \'pänt-əf\ *n* **1** : PONTIFEX **2** : BISHOP 1; *esp* : POPE [French *pontif*, from Latin *pontifex*]

¹pon·tif·i·cal \pän-'tif-i-kəl\ *adj* **1** : of or relating to a pontiff or pontifex **2** : celebrated by a prelate of episcopal rank with distinctive ceremonies ⟨a *pontifical* mass⟩ **3** : POMPOUS 2, 3 — **pon·tif·i·cal·ly** \-kə-lē, -klē\ *adv*

²pontifical *n* **1** : episcopal attire; *esp* : the insignia of the episcopal order worn by a prelate when celebrating a pontifical service — usually used in pl. **2** : a book containing the forms for sacraments and rites performed by a bishop

¹pon·tif·i·cate \pän-'tif-i-ket, -'tif-ə-ˌkāt\ *n* : the office or term of office of a pontiff

²pon·tif·i·cate \-'tif-ə-ˌkāt\ *vi* **1** : to officiate as a pontiff **2** : to speak pompously ⟨*pontificating* on the subject⟩ — **pon·tif·i·ca·tor** \-ˌkāt-ər\ *n*

pon·toon \pän-'tün\ *n* **1** : a flat-bottomed boat; *esp* : a flat-bottomed boat or portable float used in building a floating temporary bridge **2** : a float of a seaplane [French *ponton* "floating bridge, punt", from Latin *ponto*, from *pont-, pons* "bridge"]

pontoon bridge *n* : a bridge whose deck is supported on pontoons

po·ny \'pō-nē\ *n, pl* **ponies** **1** : a small horse; *esp* : one of any of several breeds of very small stocky animals **2** : a small glass for an alcoholic drink or the amount it will hold **3** : a literal translation of a foreign language text [probably from obsolete French *poulenet*, from French *poulain* "colt", derived from Latin *pullus* "young of an animal, foal"]

Pony Express *n* : a rapid postal and express system across the western United States in 1860-61 operating by relays of horses

po·ny·tail \'pō-nē-ˌtāl\ *n* : hair arranged to resemble the tail of a pony

po·ny up \ˌpō-nē-'əp\ *vb* : to pay especially in settlement of an account [origin unknown]

pooch \'püch\ *n* : DOG 1 [origin unknown]

poo·dle \'püd-l\ *n* : any of an old breed of lively intelligent heavy-coated solid-colored dogs [German *pudel*, short for *pudelhund*, from *pudeln* "to splash" (from *pudel* "puddle") + *hund* "dog"]

pooh \'pü, 'pu̇\ *interj* — used to express contempt or disapproval [imitative]

pooh–pooh \'pü-ˌpü, pü-'pü\ *also* **pooh** \'pü\ *vb* **1** : to express contempt or impatience **2** : to make fun of : SCORN ⟨*pooh-poohed* the idea that the house is haunted⟩

¹pool \'pül\ *n* **1** : a small and rather deep natural or artificial body of usually fresh water **2** : a small body of standing liquid : PUDDLE **3** : SWIMMING POOL [Old English *pōl*]

²pool *n* **1 a** : a stake to which each player of a game has contributed **b** : all the money bet by a number of persons on an event **2** : a game of billiards played with usually 15 object balls on a table having 6 pockets **3 a** : a common fund for buying or selling especially securities or commodities **b** : a combination between competing firms for the control of business by removing competition **4 a** : a group of people whose services or skills are available for use ⟨a typing *pool*⟩ ⟨a *pool* of talent⟩ **b** : a group whose members share or take turns providing a facility ⟨car *pool*⟩ [French *poule*, literally, "hen"]

³pool *vt* : to combine in a common fund, sample, or effort

pool·room \'pül-ˌrüm, -ˌru̇m\ *n* : a room for the playing of pool

¹poop \'püp\ *n* **1** *obsolete* : STERN 1 **2** : an enclosed superstructure at the stern of a ship above the main deck [Middle French *poupe* "stern", from Latin *puppis*]

²poop *vt* **1** : to break over the stern of **2** : to ship (a sea or wave) over the stern

³poop *vb* : to become or cause to become exhausted or worn out — often used with *out* [origin unknown]

poop deck *n* : a partial deck above the main deck at the stern of a ship

¹poor \'pu̇r, 'pōr\ *adj* **1** : lacking riches : NEEDY **2** : SCANTY, INSUFFICIENT ⟨a *poor* crop⟩ **3** : meriting pity ⟨the *poor* soul is lost⟩ **4** : not good of its kind ⟨*poor* workmanship⟩ ⟨in *poor* health⟩ **5** : lacking fertility ⟨*poor* land⟩ **6** : not good : UNFAVORABLE ⟨had a *poor* opinion of the child⟩ **7** : lacking in signs of wealth or good taste ⟨*poor* furnishings⟩ **8** : not efficient or capable ⟨a *poor* carpenter⟩ [Old French *povre*, from Latin *pauper*] — **poor·ly** *adv* — **poor·ness** *n*

²poor *n pl* : people who lack money or material riches

poor box *n* : a box for alms for the poor; *esp* : one placed near the door of a church

poor farm \'pu̇r-ˌfärm, 'pōr-\ *n* : a farm formerly maintained at public expense for the support and employment of needy or dependent persons

poor·house \-ˌhȧu̇s\ *n* : a place formerly maintained at public expense to house needy or dependent persons

poor·ly \-lē\ *adj* : somewhat ill : INDISPOSED

poor–spir·it·ed \-'spir-ət-əd\ *adj* : lacking confidence or courage — **poor–spir·it·ed·ly** *adv* — **poor–spir·it·ed·ness** *n*

¹pop \'päp\ *vb* **popped; pop·ping** **1** : to burst or cause to burst with a pop ⟨the balloon *popped*⟩ **2** : to go, come, push, or enter quickly or unexpectedly **3** : to shoot with a gun **4** : to stick out ⟨eyes *popping* with surprise⟩ **5** : to cause to burst open ⟨*pop* corn⟩ **6** : to hit a pop fly [Middle English *poppen*] — **pop the question** : to propose marriage

²pop *n* **1** : a sharp explosive sound **2** : a shot from a gun **3** : a flavored carbonated beverage

³pop *adv* : like or with a pop : SUDDENLY

⁴pop *adj* **1** : POPULAR ⟨*pop* music⟩ **2** : of or relating to pop music ⟨*pop* singer⟩ **3** : of or relating to pop art

pop art *n* : art in which commonplace objects are used as subject matter

pop·corn \'päp-ˌkȯrn\ *n* : an Indian corn with kernels that burst open to form a white starchy mass when heated; *also* : the popped kernels

pope \'pōp\ *n, often cap* : the head of the Roman Catholic Church [Old English *pāpa*, from Late Latin *papa*, from Greek *pappas*, title of bishops, literally, "papa"]

pop·ery \'pō-pə-rē, 'pō-prē\ *n* : ROMAN CATHOLICISM — usually used disparagingly

pop·eyed \'päp-'īd\ *adj* : having eyes that bulge (as from disease or excitement)

pop fly *n* : a short high fly in baseball

pop·gun \'päp-,gən\ *n* : a toy gun that usually shoots a cork and makes a popping sound

pop·in·jay \'päp-ən-,jā\ *n* : a vain talkative thoughtless person [Middle English *papejay* "parrot" from Middle French *papegai*, from Arabic *babghā*']

pop·ish \'pō-pish\ *adj* : Roman Catholic — often used disparagingly — **pop·ish·ly** *adv*

pop·lar \'päp-lər\ *n* 1 : any of a genus of slender quick growing trees (as an aspen or cottonwood) of the willow family 2 : the wood of a poplar [Middle French *pouplier*, from *pouple* "poplar", from Latin *populus*]

pop·lin \'päp-lən\ *n* : a strong ribbed fabric in plain weave [French *papeline*]

pop·over \'päp-,ō-vər\ *n* : a quick bread made from a thin batter of eggs, milk, and flour which bakes into a hollow shell

pop·per \'päp-ər\ *n* : one that pops; *esp* : a utensil for popping corn

pop·ple \'päp-əl\ *n, chiefly dialect* : POPLAR 1 [Old English *popul*, from Latin *populus*]

pop·py \'päp-ē\ *n, pl* **poppies** : any of a genus of chiefly annual or perennial herbs with milky juice, showy regular flowers, and capsular fruits including one that is the source of opium and several that are grown as ornamentals [Old English *popæg, popig*, from Latin *papaver*]

pop·py·cock \'päp-ē-,käk\ *n* : empty talk : NONSENSE [Dutch dialect *pappekak, literally,* "soft dung", from Dutch *pap* "pap" + *kak* "dung"]

pop·u·lace \'päp-yə-ləs\ *n* 1 : the common people 2 : POPULATION 1 [Middle French, from Italian *popolaccio* "rabble", from *popolo* "the people", from Latin *populus*]

pop·u·lar \'päp-yə-lər\ *adj* 1 : of, relating to, or coming from the whole body of people ⟨*popular* government⟩ 2 : suitable to the majority: as **a** : easy to understand ⟨*popular* science⟩ **b** : suited to the means of the majority : INEXPENSIVE ⟨*popular* prices⟩ 3 : generally current : PREVALENT ⟨*popular* opinion⟩ 4 : commonly liked or approved ⟨voted the most *popular* person in the class⟩ [Latin *popularis*, from *populus* "the people, a people"] — **pop·u·lar·ly** *adv*

pop·u·lar·i·ty \,päp-yə-'lar-ət-ē\ *n* : the quality or state of being popular

pop·u·lar·ize \'päp-yə-lə-,rīz\ *vt* : to make popular — **pop·u·lar·i·za·tion** \,päp-yə-lə-rə-'zā-shən\ *n* — **pop·u·lar·iz·er** \'päp-yə-lə-,rī-zər\ *n*

pop·u·late \'päp-yə-,lāt\ *vt* : to provide with inhabitants

pop·u·la·tion \,päp-yə-'lā-shən\ *n* 1 : the whole number of people or inhabitants in a country or region 2 : the act or process of populating 3 : the organisms inhabiting a particular area or habitat 4 : a group of persons or objects from which samples are taken for statistical measurement

population explosion *n* : the recent great increase in human numbers that is usually related to both increased survival and increased reproduction

pop·u·list \'päp-yə-ləst\ *n* 1 *cap* : a member of a United States political party formed in 1891 primarily to represent agrarian interests and to advocate the free coinage of silver and government control of monopolies 2 : a member of any of various popular or agrarian political parties — **pop·u·lism** \-,liz-əm\ *n, often cap* — **populist** *adj, often cap*

pop·u·lous \'päp-yə-ləs\ *adj* : densely populated — **pop·u·lous·ly** *adv* — **pop·u·lous·ness** *n*

pop–up \'päp-,əp\ *n* : POP FLY

por·bea·gle \'pȯr-,bē-gəl\ *n* : a small viviparous shark of northern seas with a pointed nose and crescent-shaped tail [Cornish *porgh-bugel*]

por·ce·lain \'pōr-sə-lən, 'pȯr-, -slən\ *n* : a hard, fine-grained, nonporous, and usually translucent and white ceramic ware that consists essentially of kaolin, quartz, and feldspar and is used for dishes and chemical utensils [Middle French *porcelaine* "cowrie shell, porcelain", from Italian *porcellana*, from *porcello* "little pig, vulva", from Latin *porcellus*, from *porcus* "pig, vulva"] — **por·ce·lain·like** \-,līk\ *adj*

porch \'pōrch, 'pȯrch\ *n* 1 : a covered entrance to a building usually with a separate roof 2 : VERANDA [Old French *porche*, from Latin *porticus* "portico", from *porta* "gate"]

por·cine \'pȯr-,sīn\ *adj* : of, relating to, or suggesting swine [Latin *porcinus*, from *porcus* "pig"]

por·cu·pine \'pȯr-kyə-,pīn\ *n* : any of various rather large rodents with stiff sharp quills mingled with the hair [Middle French *porc espin*, from Italian *porcospino*, from Latin *porcus* "pig" + *spina* "spine, prickle"]

porcupine

¹pore \'pōr, 'pȯr\ *vi* : to gaze, study, or think long or earnestly ⟨*pore* over a book⟩ [Middle English *pouren*]

²pore *n* : a tiny opening or space (as in the skin or the soil) often giving passage to a fluid [Middle French, from Latin *porus*, from Greek *poros* "passage, pore"] — **pored** \'pōrd, 'pȯrd\ *adj*

por·gy \'pȯr-gē\ *n, pl* **porgies** *also* **porgy** : a blue-spotted crimson food fish of the coasts of Europe and America; *also* : any of various other fishes [partly from earlier *pargo* "porgy", derived from Latin *pagarus*, a kind of fish, from Greek *phagros*; partly from earlier *scuppaug* "porgy", of American Indian origin]

pork \'pōrk, 'pȯrk\ *n* : the fresh or salted flesh of swine dressed for food [Old French *porc* "pig", from Latin *porcus*]

pork barrel *n* : a government project or appropriation yielding rich patronage benefits

pork·er \'pōr-kər, 'pȯr-\ *n* : a domestic swine and especially a young pig suitable for use as fresh pork

por·nog·ra·phy \pȯr-'näg-rə-fē\ *n* : pictures or writings describing erotic behavior and intended to cause sexual excitement [Greek *pornographos*, adj., "writing of harlots", from *pornē* "harlot" + *graphein* "to write"] — **por·nog·ra·pher** \-fər\ *n* — **por·no·graph·ic** \,pȯr-nə-'graf-ik\ *adj* — **por·no·graph·i·cal·ly** \-'graf-i-kə-lē, -klē\ *adv*

po·ros·i·ty \pə-'räs-ət-ē, pȯr-'äs-, pȯ-'räs-\ *n, pl* **-ties** 1 : the quality or state of being porous 2 : PORE

po·rous \'pōr-əs, 'pȯr-\ *adj* 1 : full of pores 2 : capable of absorbing liquids : permeable to fluids — **po·rous·ly** *adv* — **po·rous·ness** *n*

por·phy·ry \'pȯr-fə-rē, -frē\ *n, pl* **-ries** 1 : a rock consisting of feldspar crystals embedded in a compact dark red or purple groundmass 2 : an igneous rock having distinct crystals in a relatively fine-grained base [Medieval Latin *porphyrium*, from Latin *porphyrites*, from Greek *porphyrītēs lithos*, literally, "purple-colored stone", from *porphyra* "purple"] — **por·phy·rit·ic** \,pȯr-fə-'rit-ik\ *adj*

por·poise \'pȯr-pəs\ *n* 1 : any of several small blunt-snouted toothed whales that live and travel in groups 2 : DOLPHIN 1a [Middle French *porpois*, from Medieval Latin *porcopiscis*, from Latin *porcus* "pig" + *piscis* "fish"]

por·ridge \'pȯr-ij, 'pär-\ *n* : a soft food made by boiling meal in milk or water until thick [alteration of *pottage*]

por·rin·ger \'pȯr-ən-jər, 'pär-\ *n* : a low one-handled metal bowl or cup [alteration of Middle English *poteger, potinger*, from Middle French *potager* "of pottage", from *potage* "pottage"]

porpoise 1

¹**port** \'pōrt, 'pȯrt\ *n* **1** : a place where ships may ride secure from storms **2 a** : a harbor town or city where ships may take on or discharge cargo **b** : AIRPORT [Old English and Old French, both from Latin *portus* "house, door, port"]

²**port** *n* **1** : an opening (as in machinery) for intake or exhaust of a fluid **2** : PORTHOLE [Middle French *porte* "gate, door", from Latin *porta* "passage, gate"]

³**port** *n* : the left side of a ship or airplane looking forward — called also *larboard*; compare STARBOARD [probably from ¹*port* or ²*port*] — **port** *adj*

⁴**port** *vt* : to turn or put (the helm) to the left — used chiefly as a command

⁵**port** *n* : a rich sweet wine [*Oporto*, Portugal]

por·ta·ble \'pōrt-ə-bəl, 'pȯrt-\ *adj* : capable of being carried : easily moved from place to place [Middle French, from Late Latin *portabilis*, from Latin *portare* "to carry"] — **por·ta·bil·i·ty** \,pōrt-ə-'bil-ət-ē, ,pȯrt-\ *n*

¹**por·tage** \'pōrt-ij, 'pȯrt-, *2 is also* pȯr-'tāzh\ *n* **1** : the labor of carrying or transporting **2** : the carrying of boats or goods overland from one body of water to another; *also* : a regular route for such carrying [Middle French, from *porter* "to carry", from Latin *portare*]

²**por·tage** \'pōrt-ij, 'pȯrt-; pȯr-'tāzh\ *vb* **1** : to carry over a portage ⟨a canoe light enough to *portage*⟩ **2** : to move gear over a portage ⟨we *portaged* around the falls⟩

¹**por·tal** \'pōrt-l, 'pȯrt-\ *n* **1** : DOOR 1a, ENTRANCE; *esp* : a grand or imposing one **2** : the point at which something enters the body of an organism ⟨infection *portals*⟩ [Middle French, from Medieval Latin *portale* "city gate, porch", derived from Latin *porta* "gate"]

²**portal** *adj* : of, relating to, or being a portal vein [derived from Latin *porta* "gate"]

portal–to–portal *adj* : of or relating to the time spent by a worker in traveling from the entrance to the employer's property to the actual working place (as in a mine) and in returning after the work shift

portal vein *n* : a vein that collects blood from one part of the body and distributes it in another through capillaries; *esp* : one carrying blood from the digestive organs and spleen to the liver

por·ta·men·to \,pōrt-ə-'men-tō, ,pȯrt-\ *n, pl* -**ti** \-tē\ : a continuous glide effected by the voice, a trombone, or a bowed stringed musical instrument in passing from one tone to another [Italian, literally, "act of carrying", from *portare* "to carry", from Latin]

port·cul·lis \pōrt-'kəl-əs, pȯrt-\ *n* : a grating at the gateway of a castle or fortress that can be lowered to prevent entrance [Middle French *porte coleïce*, literally, "sliding door"]

porte co·chere \,pōrt-kō-'sheər, ,pȯrt-\ *n* : a roofed structure extending from the entrance to a building over an adjacent driveway and sheltering those getting in or out of vehicles [French *porte cochère*, literally, "coach door"]

por·tend \pȯr-'tend, pōr-\ *vt* : to give a sign or warning of beforehand ⟨the distant thunder *portended* a storm⟩ [Latin *portendere*, from *por-* "forward" + *tendere* "to stretch"]

por·tent \'pȯr-,tent, 'pōr-\ *n* : a sign or warning that foreshadows something usually evil : OMEN [Latin *portentum*, from *portendere* "to portend"]

por·ten·tous \pȯr-'tent-əs, pōr-\ *adj* **1** : being a portent : THREATENING ⟨*portentous* signs⟩ **2** : AMAZING, MARVELOUS ⟨will require a *portentous* effort⟩ **3** : self-consciously weighty : POMPOUS ⟨a solemn and *portentous* voice⟩ — **por·ten·tous·ly** *adv* — **por·ten·tous·ness** *n*

¹**por·ter** \'pōrt-ər, 'pȯrt-\ *n, chiefly British* : DOORKEEPER [Old French *portier*, from Late Latin *portarius*, from Latin *porta* "gate"]

²**porter** *n* **1** : one that carries burdens; *esp* : one employed to carry baggage for patrons at a hotel or transportation terminal **2** : a parlor-car or sleeping-car attendant **3** : a dark heavy ale [Middle French *porteour*, from Late Latin *portator*, from Latin *portare* "to carry"; sense 3 short for *porter's beer*]

por·ter·house \-,haüs\ *n* : a beefsteak with a large piece of tenderloin on a T-shaped bone [earlier *porterhouse* "house where porter is sold"]

port·fo·lio \pōrt-'fō-lē-,ō, pȯrt-\ *n, pl* -**lios** **1** : a case for carrying papers or drawings **2** : the office and functions of a minister of state or member of a cabinet **3** : the securities held by an investor or a financial house [Italian *portafoglio*, from *portare* "to carry" (from Latin) + *foglio* "leaf, sheet", from Latin *folium*; sense 2 from the use of such a case to carry documents of state]

port·hole \'pōrt-,hōl, 'pȯrt-\ *n* **1** : an opening (as a window) in the side of a ship or airplane **2** : an opening (as in a wall) to shoot through **3** : ²PORT 1

por·ti·co \'pōrt-i-,kō, 'pȯrt-\ *n, pl* -**coes** *or* -**cos** : a colonnade or covered walkway around or at the entrance of a building [Italian, from Latin *porticus*, from *porta* "gate"]

¹**por·tion** \'pōr-shən, 'pȯr-\ *n* **1** : an individual's share of something ⟨a *portion* of food⟩ **2** : one's lot, fate, or fortune **3** : an element, section, or division of a whole [Old French, from Latin *portio*] SYN see PART

²**portion** *vt* **por·tioned; por·tion·ing** \'pōr-shə-ning, 'pȯr-, -shning\ **1** : to divide into portions **2** : to give as a portion

port·land cement \,pōrt-lənd-, ,pȯrt-, -lən-\ *n* : a cement made by burning and grinding a mixture of clay and limestone or a mixture of similar materials [Isle of *Portland*, England; from its resemblance to a limestone found there]

port·ly \'pōrt-lē, 'pȯrt-\ *adj* **port·li·er; -est** : heavy of body : STOUT [derived from Latin *portare* "to carry"] — **port·li·ness** *n*

port·man·teau \pōrt-'man-tō, pȯrt-\ *n, pl* -**teaus** *or* -**teaux** \-tōz\ : a large traveling bag [Middle French *portemanteau*, from *porter* "to carry" + *manteau* "mantle", from Latin *mantellum*]

port of call : an intermediate port where ships customarily stop for supplies, repairs, or transferring of cargo

port of entry **1** : a place where foreign goods may be cleared through a customhouse **2** : a place where an alien may enter a country

por·trait \'pōr-trət, 'pȯr-, -,trāt\ *n* **1** : a pictorial representation (as a painting) of a person usually showing the face **2** : a portrayal in words [Middle French, from *portraire* "to portray"]

por·trait·ist \-əst\ *n* : a maker of portraits

por·trai·ture \'pōr-trə-,chu̇r, 'pȯr-, -chər\ *n* : the making of portraits : PORTRAYAL **2** : PORTRAIT

por·tray \pōr-'trā, pȯr-\ *vt* **1** : to make a picture of **2 a** : to describe in words **b** : to play the role of : ENACT [Middle French *portraire*, from Latin *protrahere* "to draw forth, reveal", from *pro-* "forth" + *trahere* "to draw, drag"] — **por·tray·er** *n*

por·tray·al \-'trā-əl, -'trāl\ *n* **1** : the act or process of portraying : REPRESENTATION **2** : PORTRAIT

Por·tu·guese \,pōr-chə-'gēz, ,pȯr-, -'gēs\ *n, pl* **Portuguese** **1 a** : a native or inhabitant of Portugal **b** : a person of Portuguese descent **2** : the Romance language of Portugal and Brazil — **Portuguese** *adj*

Portuguese man–of–war *n* : any of several large colonial coelenterates having a large crested bladder by means of which the colony floats at the surface of the sea

por·tu·la·ca \,pōr-chə-'lak-ə, ,pȯr-\ *n* : any of a genus of mostly tropical succulent herbs of the purslane family; *esp* : one cultivated for its showy flowers [Latin, "purslane", derived from *porta* "gate"; from the lid of its capsule]

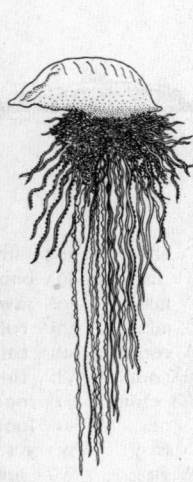

Portuguese man-of-war

¹pose \'pōz\ *vb* **1 a** : to hold or cause to hold a special posture ⟨*posed* for fashion photographers⟩ **b** : to pretend to be what one is not ⟨*pose* as a hero⟩ **2** : to put forth : PROPOUND ⟨*pose* a question⟩ [Middle French *poser* "to put, place", from Late Latin *pausare* "to stop, rest, pause", from Latin *pausa* "pause"]

²pose *n* **1** : a sustained posture; *esp* : one assumed for artistic effect **2** : an assumed attitude ⟨that wide-eyed innocence is just a *pose*⟩ SYN see AFFECTATION

¹po·ser \'pō-zər\ *n* : a puzzling or baffling question [from earlier *pose* "to puzzle", derived from Middle English *opposen* "to oppose"]

²pos·er \'pō-zər\ *n* : a person who poses

po·seur \pō-'zər\ *n* : an affected person insincere in bearing or actions [French, from *poser* "to put, pose"]

posh \'päsh\ *adj* : ELEGANT 1, FASHIONABLE [origin unknown]

pos·it \'päz-ət\ *vt* : to assume the existence of [Latin *positus*, past participle of *ponere* "to put, place, assume"]

¹po·si·tion \pə-'zish-ən\ *n* **1** : the manner in which something is placed or arranged **2** : the stand taken on a question **3** : the point or area occupied by something ⟨the *position* of the heart⟩ **4 a** : social or official rank or status **b** : EMPLOYMENT 2b, JOB **c** : a situation that confers advantage or preference ⟨jockeyed for *position* in the race⟩ [Middle French, from Latin *positio*, from *positus*, past participle of *ponere* "to lay down, put, place"] — **po·si·tion·al** \-'zish-nəl, -ən-l\ *adj*

²position *vt* **po·si·tioned; po·si·tion·ing** \-'zish-ning, -ə-ning\ : to put in proper position

positional notation *n* : a system of expressing numbers in which the digits are arranged in succession, the position of each digit has a place value, and the number is equal to the sum of the products of each digit by its place value

¹pos·i·tive \'päz-ət-iv, 'päz-tiv\ *adj* **1 a** : formally laid down or imposed ⟨*positive* laws⟩ **b** : clearly or definitely stated ⟨*positive* orders⟩ **c** : fully assured : CONFIDENT ⟨were *positive* they'd win⟩ **2 a** : of the degree of comparison expressed by the unmodified and uninflected form of an adjective or adverb **b** : definite, accurate, or certain in its action ⟨*positive* traction of a sprocket chain⟩ **c** : UNQUALIFIED 2 ⟨a *positive* disgrace⟩ **3 a** : not fictitious : REAL ⟨a *positive* influence for good⟩ **b** : active in the social or economic sphere ⟨a *positive* government⟩ **4 a** : having or expressing actual existence or quality as distinguished from deprivation or deficiency ⟨a *positive* change in temperature⟩ **b** : capable of being logically applied ⟨*positive* suggestions for improvement⟩ **c** : showing light and shade similar in tone to the tones of the original subject ⟨a *positive* photographic image⟩ **d** : being a real number numerically greater than zero ⟨+2 is a *positive* integer⟩ **e** (1) : reckoned or proceeding in a direction taken as that of increase or progression (2) : directed or moving toward a source of stimulation ⟨a *positive* taxis⟩ **5 a** : of, being, or relating to electricity of a kind that predominates in a glass rod after being rubbed with silk ⟨a *positive* charge⟩ **b** : charged with positive electricity : having a deficiency of electrons ⟨a *positive* particle⟩ **c** : being the part from which the current flows to the external circuit ⟨the *positive* pole of a discharging storage battery⟩ **d** : electron-collecting — used of an electrode in an electron tube **6 a** : marked by or indicating agreement or affirmation ⟨a *positive* response⟩ **b** : affirming the presence of what is sought or suspected to be present ⟨a *positive* test for blood⟩ [Old French *positif*, from Latin *positivus*, from *positus*, past participle of *ponere* "to lay down, put, place"] SYN see SURE — **pos·i·tive·ly** \-lē, *for emphasis often* ,päz-ə-'tiv-lē\ *adv* — **pos·i·tive·ness** *n*

²positive *n* : something positive: as **a** : the positive degree or a positive form in a language **b** : a positive photograph or a print from a negative

pos·i·tron \'päz-ə-,trän\ *n* : a positively charged particle having the same mass and magnitude of charge as the electron [*positive* + -*tron* (as in *electron*)]

pos·se \'päs-ē\ *n* **1** : a group of people called upon by a sheriff to aid in law enforcement ⟨a *posse* pursued the robber⟩ **2** : a number of people organized to make a search (as for a lost child) [Medieval Latin *posse comitatus*, literally, "power of the county"]

pos·sess \pə-'zes\ *vt* **1 a** : to make (as a person) the owner or holder (as of property or power) **b** : to have possession of **2 a** : to have and hold as property : OWN **b** : to have as an attribute, knowledge, or skill ⟨*possesses* a keen wit⟩ **3 a** : to make one's own **b** : to enter into and control firmly : DOMINATE ⟨what *possessed* you to do that⟩ [Middle French *possesser* "to have or take possession of", from Latin *possidēre*, from *potis* "able, in power" + *sedēre* "to sit"] — **pos·ses·sor** \-ər\ *n*

pos·ses·sion \pə-'zesh-ən\ *n* **1 a** : the act of possessing or holding as one's own : OWNERSHIP **b** : physical control of property without regard to ownership **2 a** : something held as one's own : PROPERTY **b** : an area under the control of but not formally part of a nation ⟨island *possessions* of the United States⟩ **3 a** : domination by something (as an evil spirit, an idea, or a passion) **b** : the fact or condition of being self-controlled — **pos·ses·sion·al** \-'zesh-nəl, -ən-l\ *adj*

¹pos·ses·sive \pə-'zes-iv\ *adj* **1** : of, relating to, or being a grammatical case that denotes ownership or a similar relation — compare GENITIVE **2** : showing the desire to possess or keep ⟨a *possessive* attitude⟩ — **pos·ses·sive·ly** *adv* — **pos·ses·sive·ness** *n*

²possessive *n* **1** : the possessive case **2** : a word in the possessive case

possessive adjective *n* : a pronominal adjective expressing possession

possessive pronoun *n* : a pronoun that derives from a personal pronoun and expresses possession

pos·set \'päs-ət\ *n* : a hot drink of sweetened and spiced milk curdled with ale or wine [Middle English *poshet, possot*]

pos·si·bil·i·ty \,päs-ə-'bil-ət-ē\ *n, pl* -**ties** **1** : the condition or fact of being possible **2** : something possible

pos·si·ble \'päs-ə-bəl\ *adj* **1** : being something that can be done or brought about **2** : being something that may or may not occur ⟨*possible* dangers⟩ **3** : able or fitted to be or to become ⟨a *possible* camp site⟩ [Middle French, from Latin *possibilis*, from *posse* "to be able", from *potis* "able" + *esse* "to be"] — **pos·si·bly** \-blē\ *adv* □ SYN POSSIBLE, PRACTICABLE, FEASIBLE mean capable of being realized. POSSIBLE implies that a thing may exist or occur given the proper conditions; PRACTICABLE implies that something may be easily or readily put into operation by current available means ⟨when television became *practicable*⟩ FEASIBLE applies to what is likely to work or be useful in attaining an end ⟨commercially *feasible* for mass production⟩ SYN see in addition PROBABLE

pos·sum \'päs-əm\ *n* : OPOSSUM

¹post \'pōst\ *n* **1** : a piece of timber or metal fixed firmly in an upright position especially as a stay or support : PILLAR, COLUMN **2** : a pole or stake set up to mark or indicate something ⟨starting *post*⟩ [Old English, from Latin *postis*]

²post *vt* **1** : to fasten to a place (as a wall) for public notices **2 a** : to publish or announce by or as if by a placard **b** : to enter on a public listing ⟨*post* all daily flights⟩ **3** : to forbid persons from entering or using by putting up warning notices ⟨*post* a trout stream⟩

³post *n* **1** *obsolete* : one that carries messages : COURIER **2** *archaic* : one of a series of stations for keeping horses for relays **3** *chiefly British* **a** : a nation's organization for handling mail; *also* : the mail handled **b** : a single dispatch of mail [Middle French *poste* "relay station, courier", from Italian *posta* "relay station",

\ə\ abut	\ng\ si**ng**
\ər\ fur**ther**	\ō\ b**o**ne
\a\ m**a**t	\ȯ\ s**a**w
\ā\ t**a**ke	\oi\ c**oi**n
\ä\ c**o**t, c**a**rt	\th\ **th**in
\au̇\ **ou**t	\t̶h̶\ **th**is
\ch\ **ch**in	\ü\ f**oo**d
\e\ p**e**t	\u̇\ f**oo**t
\ē\ **ea**sy	\y\ **y**et
\g\ **g**o	\yü\ f**ew**
\i\ t**i**p	\yu̇\ c**u**re
\ī\ l**i**fe	\zh\ vi**si**on
\j\ **j**ob	

from *posto,* past participle of *porre* "to place", from Latin *ponere*]

⁴post *vb* **1** : to ride or travel with haste : HURRY **2** : MAIL ⟨*post* a letter⟩ **3 a** : to transfer (a bookkeeping item) from a book of original entry to a ledger **b** : to make transfer entries in **4** : to make familiar with a subject : INFORM ⟨kept *posted* on the latest news⟩ [earlier *post* "to travel with post-horses"]

⁵post *adv* : with post-horses : EXPRESS

⁶post *n* **1 a** : the place at which a soldier is stationed; *esp* : a sentry's beat or station **b** : a station or task to which one is assigned **c** : a place to which troops are assigned **d** : a local subdivision of a veterans' organization **2** : an office or position to which a person is appointed **3** : TRADING POST; *also* : SETTLEMENT 3a ⟨sent supplies to the frontier *posts*⟩ [Middle French, from Italian *posto,* from *porre* "to place"]

⁷post *vt* **1 a** : to station in a given place ⟨*post* a guard⟩ **b** : to carry ceremoniously to a position ⟨*posting* the colors⟩ **2** : to put up as security ⟨*post* bond⟩

post- *prefix* **1 a** : after : subsequent : later ⟨*post*date⟩ **b** : behind : posterior : following after ⟨*post*consonantal⟩ **2 a** : subsequent to : later than ⟨*post*operative⟩ **b** : posterior to [Latin, from *post*]

See *post-* and 2d element

postaccident	postflight	postpuberty
postadolescence	postgame	postpubescent
postadolescent	postgraduation	postrecession
postattack	postharvest	postretirement
postbaccalaureate	posthospital	postrevolutionary
postbiblical	postimperial	postseason
postcollege	postinaugural	postsecondary
postcolonial	postindustrial	postsurgical
postdrug	postinjection	posttransfusion
postediting	postinoculation	posttreatment
postelection	postmarital	posttrial
postexercise	postnuptial	postvaccination
postexperimental	postoperative	postwar

post·age \'pō-stij\ *n* : the charge imposed for carrying an article by mail

postage meter *n* : a machine that prints postal markings on pieces of mail, records the amount of postage given in the markings, and subtracts it from a total amount which has been paid at the post office and for which the machine has been set

postage stamp *n* : a government stamp used on mail to show that postage has been paid

post·al \'pōst-l\ *adj* : of or relating to mail or to the post office

postal card *n* : POSTCARD; *esp* : one bearing a government imprinted stamp and sold by a post office

postal service *n* : POST OFFICE 1

postal union *n* : an association of governments setting up uniform regulations and practices for international mail

post·card \'pōst-,kärd, 'pōs-\ *n* : a card on which a message may be written for mailing without an envelope

post chaise *n* : a carriage usually having a closed body on four wheels and seating two or four persons [³*post*]

post·clas·si·cal \pōst-'klas-i-kəl, 'pōst-, pōs-, 'pōs-\ *adj* : of or relating to a period following the classical

post–com·mu·nion \,pōst-kə-'myü-nyən, pōs-\ *n, often cap P&C* : a prayer formerly following the communion at Mass

post·con·so·nan·tal \,pōst-,kän-sə-'nant-l, pōs-\ *adj* : immediately following a consonant

post·date \pōst-'dāt, 'pōst-, pōs-, 'pōs-\ *vt* **1** : to date with a date later than that of execution ⟨*postdate* a check⟩ **2** : to follow in time ⟨the text changes *postdated* the first printing⟩

post·doc·tor·al \-'däk-tə-rəl, -trəl\ *adj* : of, relating to, or engaged in advanced academic or professional work beyond a doctor's degree

post·er \'pō-stər\ *n* : a notice or advertisement to be posted in a public place

¹pos·te·ri·or \pō-'stir-ē-ər, pä-\ *adj* **1** : later in time : SUBSEQUENT **2** : situated behind : situated toward or on the back [Latin, comparative of *posterus* "coming after", from *post* "after"] — **pos·te·ri·or·ly** *adv*

²pos·te·ri·or \pä-'stir-ē-ər, pō-\ *n* : the hinder parts of the body; *esp* : BUTTOCKS

pos·ter·i·ty \pä-'ster-ət-ē\ *n* **1** : offspring to the furthest generation **2** : those who come after in time ⟨leave a record for *posterity*⟩ [Middle French *posterité,* from Latin *posteritas,* from *posterus* "coming after"]

pos·tern \'pōs-tərn, 'päs-\ *n* **1** : a back door or gate **2** : a private or side entrance or way [Old French *posterne,* alteration of *posterle,* from Late Latin *posterula,* from *postera* "back door", from Latin *posterus* "coming after"] — **postern** *adj*

post exchange *n* : a store at a military post that sells to military personnel and authorized civilians

post·gan·gli·on·ic \,pōst-,gang-glē-'än-ik, ,pōs-\ *adj* : distal to a ganglion; *also* : of, relating to, or being an axon arising from a cell body within an autonomic ganglion

post·gla·cial \pōst-'glā-shəl, 'pōst-, pōs-, 'pōs-\ *adj* : coming or occurring after a period of glaciation

¹post·grad·u·ate \-'graj-wət, -ə-wət, -ə-,wāt\ *adj* : GRADUATE 2

²postgraduate *n* : a student continuing his or her education after graduation from high school or college

post·haste \'pōst-'hāst\ *adv* : with all possible speed ⟨sent *posthaste* for the doctor⟩ [³*post*]

post·hole \'pōst-,hōl\ *n* : a hole for a post and especially a fence post

post–horse \-,hórs\ *n* : a horse for use especially by couriers or mail carriers [³*post*]

post·hu·mous \'päs-chə-məs\ *adj* **1** : born after the death of the father ⟨*posthumous* twins⟩ **2** : published after the death of the author ⟨a *posthumous* novel⟩ **3** : following or occurring after one's death ⟨a *posthumous* award⟩ [Latin *posthumus,* alteration of *postumus* "late-born, posthumous", from *posterus* "coming after"] — **post·hu·mous·ly** *adv*

post·hyp·not·ic \,pōst-hip-'nät-ik, ,pōst-ip-\ *adj* : of, relating to, or characteristic of the period following a hypnotic trance

pos·til·ion *or* **pos·til·lion** \pō-'stil-yən, pə-\ *n* : a person who rides as a guide on the left-hand horse of a pair drawing a coach [Middle French *postillon* "mail carrier using post-horses", from Italian *postiglione,* from *posta* "post"]

Post·im·pres·sion·ism \,pō-stim-'presh-ə-,niz-əm\ *n* : a theory or practice of art originating in France in the last quarter of the 19th century that in revolt against impressionism stresses variously volume, picture structure, or expressionism

post·lude \'pōst-,lüd\ *n* : a closing piece of music; *esp* : an organ voluntary at the end of a church service [*post-* + *-lude* (as in *prelude*)]

post·man \'pōst-mən, 'pōs-, -,man\ *n* : LETTER CARRIER

post·mark \-,märk\ *n* : an official postal marking on a piece of mail; *esp* : a cancellation of the postage stamp that gives the date and place of mailing — **postmark** *vt*

post·mas·ter \-,mas-tər\ *n* : an official in charge of a post office

postmaster general *n, pl* **postmasters general** : an official in charge of a national post office department

post me·ri·di·em \'pōst-mə-'rid-ē-əm, 'pōs-, -ē-,em\ *adj* : being after noon — abbreviation *p.m.* [Latin]

post·mis·tress \-,mis-trəs\ *n* : a woman in charge of a post office

post·mor·tem \pōst-'mórt-əm, pōs-\ *adj* **1 a** : occurring after death **b** : of or relating to a postmortem examination **2** : following the event ⟨a *postmortem* analysis of the game⟩ [Latin *post mortem* "after death"] — **postmortem** *n*

postmortem examination *n* : an examination of a dead body especially to determine the cause of death

post·na·sal drip \ˌpōst-ˈnā-zəl-, ˈpōst-, -pōs-, -ˈpōs-\ *n* : a flow of mucous secretion from the back of the nasal cavity onto the wall of the pharynx that occurs in some allergic states (as hay fever)

post·na·tal \-ˈnāt-l\ *adj* : subsequent to birth; *also* : of or relating to a newborn child ⟨*postnatal* care⟩ — **post·na·tal·ly** \-l-ē\ *adv*

post office *n* **1** : a government department handling the transmission of mail **2** : a local branch of a post office department handling the mail for a particular place **3** : a kissing game in which the one pretending to deliver a letter may demand a kiss as payment

post·op·er·a·tive \pōst-ˈäp-rət-iv, ˈpōst-, -ə-rət-, -ə-ˌrāt-\ *adj* : following a surgical operation ⟨*postoperative* care⟩ — **post·op·er·a·tive·ly** *adv*

post·paid \ˈpōst-ˈpād, ˈpōs-\ *adv* : with postage paid by the sender and not chargeable to the receiver [³*post*]

post·par·tum \pōst-ˈpärt-əm, pōs-\ *adj* : following parturition [New Latin *post partum* "after birth"]

post·pone \-ˈpōn\ *vt* : to hold back to a later time : put off [Latin *postponere* "to place after, postpone", from *post-* + *ponere* "to place"] SYN see DEFER — **post·pone·ment** \-mənt\ *n* — **post·pon·er** *n*

post·pran·di·al \-ˈpran-dē-əl\ *adj* : following a meal ⟨taking a *postprandial* nap⟩

post·script \ˈpōs-ˌskript, ˈpō-\ *n* : a note or series of notes added at the end of a letter, article, or book [Latin *postscriptus*, past participle of *postscribere* "to write after", from *post-* + *scribere* "to write"]

pos·tu·lant \ˈpäs-chə-lənt\ *n* **1** : a person admitted to a religious community as a probationary candidate for membership **2** : a person on probation before being admitted as a candidate for holy orders in the Episcopal Church [French, "petitioner, candidate, postulant", from *postuler* "to demand, solicit", from Latin *postulare*] — **pos·tu·lan·cy** \-lən-sē\ *n*

¹pos·tu·late \ˈpäs-chə-ˌlāt\ *vt* : to claim as true : assume as a postulate [Latin *postulare* "to demand", from *poscere* "to ask"] — **pos·tu·la·tion** \ˌpäs-chə-ˈlā-shən\ *n*

²pos·tu·late \ˈpäs-chə-lət, -ˌlāt\ *n* **1** : a hypothesis advanced as an essential basis of a system of thought or premise of a train of reasoning **2** : a statement (as in logic or mathematics) that often cannot be proved to be true or false but that is assumed to be true without proof; *also* : AXIOM 2a

¹pos·ture \ˈpäs-chər\ *n* **1** : the position or bearing of the body or of a body part ⟨an erect *posture*⟩ **2** : relative place or position : SITUATION **3** : a particular state with reference to something else ⟨a country's defense *posture*⟩ **4** : frame of mind : ATTITUDE ⟨a *posture* of arrogance⟩ [French, from Italian *postura*, from Latin *positura*, from *positus*, past participle of *ponere* "to place"] — **pos·tur·al** \-chə-rəl\ *adj*

²posture *vb* : to assume or cause to assume a given posture; *esp* : to strike a pose for effect — **pos·tur·er** *n*

post·vo·cal·ic \ˌpōst-vō-ˈkal-ik\ *adj* : immediately following a vowel

post·war \ˈpōst-ˈwȯr\ *adj* : of, relating to, or being a period after a war

po·sy \ˈpō-zē\ *n*, *pl* **posies 1** : a brief motto **2 a** : FLOWER 1c **b** : a bunch of flowers : BOUQUET [alteration of *poesy*]

¹pot \ˈpät\ *n* **1 a** : a rounded metal or earthen container used chiefly for domestic purposes **b** : the quantity held by a pot **2** : an enclosed framework for catching fish or lobsters **3 a** : a large quantity or sum **b** : the total of the bets at stake at one time **4** : RUIN 1, DETERIORATION ⟨their business went to *pot*⟩ **5** : MARIJUANA [Old English *pott*] — **pot·ful** *n*

²pot *vt* **pot·ted; pot·ting 1** : to preserve in a sealed pot, jar, or can ⟨*potted* chicken⟩ **2** : to plant or grow in a pot ⟨*potted* plants⟩ **3** : to shoot with a potshot ⟨*pot* a rabbit⟩

po·ta·ble \ˈpōt-ə-bəl\ *adj* : suitable for drinking [Late Latin *potabilis*, from Latin *potare* "to drink"] — **po·ta·bil·i·ty** \ˌpōt-ə-ˈbil-ət-ē\ *n* — **po·ta·ble·ness** \ˈpōt-ə-bəl-nəs\ *n*

po·tage \pō-ˈtäzh\ *n* : a thick soup [Middle French, from Old French, "pottage"]

pot·ash \ˈpät-ˌash\ *n* **1 a** : potassium carbonate especially from wood ashes **b** : POTASSIUM HYDROXIDE **2** : potassium or a potassium compound especially as used in agriculture or industry [¹*pot* + *ash*]

po·tas·si·um \pə-ˈtas-ē-əm\ *n* : a silver-white soft light low-melting univalent metallic chemical element that occurs abundantly in nature especially combined in minerals — see ELEMENT table [New Latin, from *potassa* "potash", from English *potash*]

potassium bromide *n* : a crystalline salt KBr with a saline taste used as a sedative and in photography

potassium carbonate *n* : a white salt K_2CO_3 that forms a strongly alkaline solution and is used in making glass and soap

potassium chlorate *n* : a crystalline salt $KClO_3$ that is used as an oxidizing agent in matches, fireworks, and explosives

potassium chloride *n* : a crystalline salt KCl that occurs as a mineral and in natural waters and is used as a fertilizer

potassium cyanide *n* : a very poisonous crystalline salt KCN used in electroplating

potassium dichromate *n* : a soluble salt $K_2Cr_2O_7$ forming large orange-red crystals used in dyeing, in photography, and as an oxidizing agent

potassium hydroxide *n* : a white deliquescent solid KOH that dissolves in water with much heat to form a strongly alkaline and caustic liquid and is used in making soap and as a reagent

potassium iodide *n* : a crystalline salt KI that is soluble in water and used in photographic emulsions and in medicine

potassium nitrate *n* : a crystalline salt KNO_3 that occurs as a product of nitrification in soil, is a strong oxidizer, and is used in making gunpowder, in preserving meat, and in medicine — called also *saltpeter*

potassium permanganate *n* : a dark purple salt $KMnO_4$ used as an oxidizer and disinfectant

po·ta·tion \pō-ˈtā-shən\ *n* **1** : a usually alcoholic drink or brew **2 a** : the act of drinking **b** : DRAFT 4a [Middle French, from Latin *potatio* "act of drinking", from *potare* "to drink"]

po·ta·to \pə-ˈtāt-ō, pət-ˈāt-\ *n*, *pl* **-toes 1** : SWEET POTATO **2 a** : an erect American herb of the nightshade family widely cultivated as a vegetable crop **b** : its edible starchy tuber — called also *white potato* [Spanish *batata*, of American Indian origin]

potato beetle *n* : COLORADO POTATO BEETLE

potato blight *n* : any of several destructive fungus diseases of the potato

potato bug *n* : COLORADO POTATO BEETLE

potato chip *n* : a thin slice of potato fried crisp and salted

pot·bel·ly \ˈpät-ˌbel-ē\ *n* **1** : an enlarged, swollen, or protruding abdomen **2** : a stove with a bulging body — called also *potbellied stove* — **pot·bel·lied** \-ēd\ *adj*

pot·boil·er \-ˌbȯi-lər\ *n* : a usually inferior work of art or literature produced only to earn money

pot cheese *n* : COTTAGE CHEESE

po·teen \pə-ˈtēn\ *n* : illicitly distilled whiskey of Ireland [Irish Gaelic *poitín*]

po·ten·cy \ˈpōt-n-sē\ *n*, *pl* **-cies** : the quality or condition of being potent; *esp* : power to bring about a given result

po·tent \ˈpōt-nt\ *adj* **1** : having or exercising force, authority, or influence : POWERFUL **2** : producing a given effect **3 a** : chemically or medicinally effective ⟨a *potent* vaccine⟩ **b** : rich in a constituent : STRONG ⟨*potent*

potbelly 2

potter's wheel

tea) **4** : able to copulate [Latin *potens,* derived from *potis, pote* "able"] — **po·tent·ly** *adv*

po·ten·tate \'pōt-n-,tāt\ *n* : one who exercises controlling power

¹po·ten·tial \pə-'ten-chəl\ *adj* : capable of becoming real : POSSIBLE ⟨the *potential* dangers in the scheme⟩ [Late Latin *potentialis,* from Latin *potentia* "power", from *potens* "potent"] — **po·ten·tial·ly** \-'tench-lē, -ə-lē\ *adv*

²potential *n* **1** : something that can develop or become actual : POSSIBILITY **2** : the degree of electrification with reference to a standard

potential difference *n* : the difference in electrical potential between two points that represents the work involved or the energy released in the transfer of a unit quantity of electricity from one point to the other

potential energy *n* : the amount of energy a thing (as a weight raised to a height or a coiled spring) has because of its position or because of the arrangement of its parts

po·ten·ti·al·i·ty \pə-,ten-chē-'al-ət-ē\ *n, pl* **-ties** **1** : the ability to develop or to come into existence **2** : POTENTIAL 1

po·ten·ti·ate \pə-'ten-chē-,āt\ *vt* : to make potent; *esp* : to increase ⟨the effect of a drug or treatment⟩ synergistically — **po·ten·ti·a·tion** \-,ten-chē-'ā-shən\ *n* — **po·ten·ti·a·tor** \-'ten-chē-,āt-ər\ *n*

po·ten·ti·om·e·ter \pə-,ten-chē-'äm-ət-ər\ *n* **1** : an instrument for measuring electromotive forces **2** : VOLTAGE DIVIDER [*potential* + *-o-* + *-meter*]

pot·head \'pät-,hed\ *n* : a person who smokes marijuana

¹poth·er \'päth-ər\ *n* **1 a** : COMMOTION **b** : FUSS **2 2** : a choking cloud of dust or smoke **3** : mental turmoil [origin unknown]

²pother *vb* **poth·ered; poth·er·ing** \'päth-ring, -ə-ring\ : to put into or be in a pother

pot·herb \'pät-,ərb, -,hərb\ *n* : an herb whose leaves or stems are cooked for use as greens; *also* : one (as mint) used to season food

pot·hole \-,hōl\ *n* : a large pit or hole (as in the bed of a river or in a road surface)

pot·hook \-,hůk\ *n* **1** : an S-shaped hook for hanging pots and kettles over an open fire **2** : an S-shaped stroke in writing

pot·hunt·er \-,hənt-ər\ *n* : one who hunts game for food — **pot–hunt·ing** \-,hənt-ing\ *n*

po·tion \'pō-shən\ *n* : a mixed drink (as of liquor) or dose (as of medicine) [Middle French, from Latin *potio* "drink, potion", from *potare* "to drink"]

pot·latch \'pät-,lach\ *n* **1** : a ceremonial feast of northwest coast Indians in which the host distributes gifts lavishly and the guests must reciprocate **2** *Northwest* : a social event or celebration [of American Indian origin]

pot liquor *n* : the liquid left in a pot after cooking

pot·luck \'pät-'lək\ *n* : the regular meal available to a guest for whom no special preparations have been made

pot marigold *n* : a variable hardy calendula widely grown especially for ornament

pot·pie \'pät-'pī\ *n* : a stew of meat or poultry usually with vegetables and served with a crust or dumplings

pot·pour·ri \,pō-pů-'rē\ *n* **1** : a jar of flower petals and spices used for scent **2** : a miscellaneous collection : MEDLEY [French *pot pourri,* literally, "rotten pot"]

pot roast *n* : a piece of beef cooked by braising usually on top of the stove

pot·sherd \'pät-,shərd\ *n* : a pottery fragment

pot·shot \-,shät\ *n* **1** : a shot taken in a casual manner or at an easy target **2** : a critical remark made in a random or sporadic way [from the sportsman's feeling that such shots were worthy only of pothunters] — **pot·shot** *vb*

pot·tage \'pät-ij\ *n* : a thick soup of vegetables or vegetables and meat [Old French *potage,* from *pot* "pot", of Germanic origin]

¹pot·ter \'pät-ər\ *n* : one that makes pottery

²potter *vi* : FIDDLE 2b, PUTTER [probably from English dialect *pote* "to poke"] — **pot·ter·er** *n*

potter's clay *n* : a plastic clay suitable for making pottery — called also *potter's earth*

potter's field *n* : a public burial place for paupers, unknown persons, and criminals [from the mention in Matthew 27:7 of the purchase of a potter's field for use as a graveyard]

potter's wheel *n* : a horizontal disk revolving on a spindle and carrying the clay being shaped by a potter

pot·tery \'pät-ə-rē\ *n, pl* **-ter·ies** **1** : a place where earthen vessels are made **2** : the art of the potter : CERAMICS **3** : ware made usually from clay that is shaped while moist and soft and hardened by heat; *esp* : coarser ware so made

pot·to \'pät-ō\ *n, pl* **pottos** : one of several African primates; *esp* : a West African primate that has a vestigial index finger and tail [of African origin]

¹pot·ty \'pät-ē\ *adj, chiefly British* : slightly crazy [probably from ¹*pot*]

²potty *n, pl* **potties** : a small child's pot for urinating or defecating

pot·ty–chair \-,cheər, -,chaər\ *n* : a child's chair having an open seat under which a pot is placed for toilet training

¹pouch \'pauch\ *n* **1** : a small drawstring bag carried on the person **2** : a bag of small or moderate size for storing or carrying goods; *esp* : a bag with a lock for first class mail or diplomatic dispatches **3** : an anatomical structure in the form of a bag or sac; *esp* : one for carrying the young on the abdomen of a female marsupial (as a kangaroo or opossum) [Middle French *pouche,* of Germanic origin] — **pouched** \'paucht\ *adj*

²pouch *vb* : to put or form into or as if into a pouch

pouchy \'pau-chē\ *adj* **pouch·i·er; -est** : having, tending to have, or resembling a pouch

poult \'pōlt\ *n* : a young fowl; *esp* : a young turkey [Middle English *polet, pulte* "young fowl, pullet"]

poul·ter·er \'pōl-tər-ər\ *n* : one that deals in poultry [Middle French *pouletier*]

poul·tice \'pōl-təs\ *n* : a soft usually heated and often medicated mass spread on cloth and applied to lesions (as sores) [Medieval Latin *pultes* "pap", from Latin *pult-, puls* "porridge"] — **poultice** *vt*

poul·try \'pōl-trē\ *n* : domesticated birds kept for eggs or meat [Middle French *pouleterie,* from *pouletier* "poulterer", from *poulet* "young fowl, pullet"]

poul·try·man \-mən\ *n* **1** : one that raises domestic fowls especially on a commercial scale **2** : a dealer in poultry or poultry products

¹pounce \'pauns\ *vi* **1** : to swoop upon and seize something with or as if with talons ⟨the cat *pounced*⟩ **2** : to make an abrupt assault or approach [Middle English *pounce* "talon"]

²pounce *n* : the act of pouncing

³pounce *vt* : to dust, rub, finish, or stencil with pounce

⁴pounce *n* **1** : a fine powder formerly used to prevent ink from spreading **2** : a fine powder for making stenciled patterns [French *ponce* "pumice", from Latin *pumex*]

¹pound \'paund\ *n, pl* **pounds** *also* **pound** **1** : any of various units of mass and weight; *esp* : a unit in general use among English-speaking peoples equal to 16 ounces (about 0.454 kilogram) — see MEASURE table **2 a** : the basic monetary unit of the United Kingdom — called also *pound sterling* **b** : the basic monetary unit of Cyprus, Egypt, Ireland, Israel, Lebanon, Malta, Sudan, and Syria **c** : a coin or note representing one pound [Old English *pund,* from Latin *pondo*]

²pound *n* **1** : an enclosure for animals; *esp* : a public enclosure for stray or unlicensed animals **2 a** : an enclosure within which fish or crustaceans (as lobsters) are kept or caught; *esp* : the inner compartment of a fish trap **b** : an establishment selling live lobsters [Middle English, "enclosure", from Old English *pund-*]

³**pound** *n* : an act or sound of pounding

⁴**pound** *vb* **1** : to reduce to powder or pulp by beating **2 a** : to strike heavily or repeatedly ⟨*pound* the piano⟩ **b** : to produce by means of repeated vigorous strokes ⟨*pound* out a story on the typewriter⟩ **c** : DRIVE 5b **3** : to move heavily or persistently ⟨the horses *pounded* along the lane⟩ [Old English *pūnian*]

pound·al \'paùn-dl\ *n* : a unit of force equal to the force that would give a free mass of one pound an acceleration of one foot per second per second that is equal to .138 newton [*pound* + *-al* (as in *quintal*)]

pound cake *n* : a rich butter cake made with a large amount of eggs and shortening [from the original recipe calling for a pound of each of the principal ingredients]

¹**pound·er** \'paùn-dər\ *n* : one that pounds

²**pounder** *n* **1** : one having a specified weight or value in pounds **2** : a gun throwing a projectile of a specified weight in pounds

pound–fool·ish \'paùnd-'fü-lish, 'paùn-\ *adj* : imprudent in dealing with large sums or weighty matters [from the phrase *penny-wise and pound-foolish*]

¹**pour** \'pōr, 'pòr\ *vb* **1** : to flow or to cause to flow in a stream ⟨*pour* the tea⟩ ⟨tears *pouring* down my cheeks⟩ **2** : to supply or produce copiously **3** : to rain hard [Middle English *pouren*] — **pour·able** \-ə-bəl\ *adj* — **pour·er** *n*

²**pour** *n* : the action of pouring; *esp* : a heavy rainfall

¹**pout** \'paùt\ *n, pl* **pout** *or* **pouts** : any of several large-headed fishes (as a bullhead) [Old English *-pūte*]

²**pout** *vb* **1 a** : to show displeasure by thrusting out the lips **b** : SULK **2** : to protrude or cause to protrude [Middle English *pouten*]

³**pout** *n* **1** : a thrusting out of the lips expressing displeasure **2** *pl* : a fit of bad humor

pout·er \'paùt-ər\ *n* **1** : one that pouts **2** : a domestic pigeon of erect carriage with an inflatable crop

pouty \'paùt-ē\ *adj* : SULKY 1

pov·er·ty \'päv-ərt-ē\ *n* **1** : the state of being poor : lack of money or material possessions : WANT **2** : an inadequate supply **3** : lack of fertility ⟨*poverty* of the soil⟩ [Old French *poverté*, from Latin *paupertas*, from *pauper* "poor"]

pov·er·ty–strick·en \-,strik-ən\ *adj* : very poor : DESTITUTE

¹**pow·der** \'paùd-ər\ *n* **1** : dry material made up of fine particles; *also* : a medicinal or cosmetic preparation in this form **2** : any of various solid explosives used chiefly in gunnery and blasting [Old French *poudre* "dust, powder", from Latin *pulver-*, *pulvis*]

²**powder** *vb* **1** : to sprinkle or cover with or as if with powder **2** : to reduce to or become powder — **pow·der·er** \-ər-ər\ *n*

powder blue *n* : a pale blue

powder horn *n* : a flask for carrying gunpowder; *esp* : one made of the horn of an ox or cow

powder keg *n* **1** : a small usually metal cask for holding gunpowder or blasting powder **2** : something (as an unstable political situation) liable to explode

powder puff *n* : a soft pad for applying cosmetic powder

powder room *n* : a rest room for women

pow·dery \'paùd-ə-rē\ *adj* **1 a** : resembling or consisting of powder **b** : easily reduced to powder : CRUMBLY **2** : covered with or as if with powder

powdery mildew *n* : a parasitic fungus producing abundant powdery conidia on the host; *also* : a plant disease caused by such a fungus

¹**pow·er** \'paù-ər, 'paùr\ *n* **1 a** : possession of control, authority, or influence over others **b** : one having such power; *esp* : a sovereign state **2 a** : ability to act or do ⟨lose the *power* of speech⟩ **b** : legal or official authority, capacity, or right **3 a** : physical might **b** : mental strength and effectiveness **4 a** : the number of times as indicated by an exponent a number or expression is to be multiplied by itself **b** : the product obtained by raising a number or expression to a power **5 a** : force or energy that is or can be applied to work; *esp* : mechanical or electrical force or energy **b** : the time rate at which work is done or energy emitted or transferred **6** : MAGNIFICATION 2 [Old French *poeir*, from *poeir* "to be able", derived from Latin *potis, pote* "able"] □ SYN POWER, FORCE, ENERGY, STRENGTH mean the ability to exert effort. POWER may imply latent or exerted physical, mental, or spiritual ability to act or be acted upon; FORCE implies the actual effective exercise of power ⟨pushed with enough *force* to overturn the chair⟩ ⟨a wind of intense *force*⟩ ENERGY applies to power expended or capable of being transformed into work ⟨a crusader of untiring *energy*⟩ STRENGTH applies to the quality or characteristic that enables one to exert force or withstand pressure or attack ⟨a mind of *strength* and decisiveness⟩

²**power** *adj* : relating to, supplying, or utilizing power; *esp* : utilizing mechanical or electrical energy ⟨a *power* drill⟩ ⟨*power* steering⟩

³**power** *vt* : to supply with power

pow·er·boat \-,bōt\ *n* : MOTORBOAT

power dive *n* : a dive of an airplane accelerated by the power of the engine — **power–dive** *vb*

pow·er·ful \'paù-ər-fəl, 'paùr-\ *adj* : having great power, strength, or influence — **pow·er·ful·ly** \-fə-lē, -flē\ *adv*

pow·er·house \-,haùs\ *n* **1 a** : POWER PLANT 1 **b** : a source of influence or inspiration **2** : one that has great power or unusual energy or strength

pow·er·less \-ləs\ *adj* **1** : lacking power, force, or energy : unable to produce an effect **2** : lacking authority to act — **pow·er·less·ly** *adv* — **pow·er·less·ness** *n*

power of attorney : a legal instrument authorizing a person to act as the attorney or agent of another

power pack *n* : a unit for converting a power supply to a voltage suitable for an electronic device

power plant *n* **1** : an electric utility generating station **2** : an engine and related parts supplying the motive power of a self-propelled vehicle

power play *n* : a situation in ice hockey in which the players on the ice for one team outnumber those for the other team because of a penalty

power politics *n sing or pl* : politics characterized by attempts to advance national interests through military and economic coercion

power shovel *n* : a power-operated excavating machine consisting of a boom or crane that supports a dipper handle with a dipper at the end of it

¹**pow·wow** \'paù-,waù\ *n* **1** : an American Indian medicine man **2 a** : an American Indian ceremony (as for victory in war) **b** : a conference of or with American Indians **3 a** : a noisy gathering **b** : a meeting for discussion [of American Indian origin]

²**powwow** *vi* : to hold a powwow

pox \'päks\ *n* : a disease (as smallpox, chicken pox, or syphilis) that causes a rash on the skin [alteration of *pocks*, pl. of *pock*]

prac·ti·ca·ble \'prak-ti-kə-bəl\ *adj* **1** : capable of being done, put into practice, or accomplished : FEASIBLE ⟨the idea was not *practicable*⟩ **2** : USABLE ⟨a *practicable* substitute⟩ — **prac·ti·ca·bil·i·ty** \,prak-ti-kə-'bil-ət-ē\ *n* — **prac·ti·ca·ble·ness** \'prak-ti-kə-bəl-nəs\ *n* — **prac·ti·ca·bly** \-blē\ *adv* □ SYN PRACTICABLE, PRACTICAL both mean relating to practice or use but they are not interchangeable. PRACTICABLE applies to what seems feasible but has not been tested in use; PRACTICAL applies to things and to persons and implies suc-

\ə\ abut		\ng\ sing	
\ər\ further		\ō\ bone	
\a\ mat		\ȯ\ saw	
\ā\ take		\ȯi\ coin	
\ä\ cot, cart		\th\ thin	
\aù\ out		\th\ this	
\ch\ chin		\ü\ food	
\e\ pet		\ù\ foot	
\ē\ easy		\y\ yet	
\g\ go		\yü\ few	
\i\ tip		\yù\ cure	
\ī\ life		\zh\ vision	
\j\ job			

cess in meeting the demands of actual use or living
SYN see in addition POSSIBLE

prac·ti·cal \'prak-ti-kəl\ *adj* 1 : actively engaged in an
action or occupation ⟨a *practical* farmer⟩ 2 a : of, relating to, or manifested in practice or action ⟨for *practical* purposes⟩ b : being such in practice or effect :
VIRTUAL ⟨a *practical* failure⟩ 3 : capable of being put
to use or account : USEFUL 4 a : inclined to action rather than planning or theorizing ⟨a *practical* person⟩ b
(1) : qualified by practice or practical training (2) :
designed to supplement theoretical training by experience [Latin *practicus*, from Greek *praktikos*, from
prassein "to pass over, act, do"] SYN see PRACTICABLE
— **prac·ti·cal·i·ty** \,prak-ti-'kal-ət-ē\ *n* — **prac·ti·cal·
ness** \'prak-ti-kəl-nəs\ *n*

practical joke *n* : a joke that depends on the tricking or
abuse of a person at a disadvantage — **practical joker**
n

prac·ti·cal·ly \'prak-ti-kə-lē, -klē\ *adv* 1 : in a practical
manner ⟨talked *practically* about the problem⟩ 2 :
NEARLY, ALMOST ⟨*practically* everyone was there⟩

practical nurse *n* : a nurse that cares for the sick professionally without having the training or experience required of a registered nurse; *esp* : LICENSED PRACTICAL
NURSE

prairie dog

¹**prac·tice** *or* **prac·tise** \'prak-təs\ *vb* 1 a : to perform
or work at repeatedly so as to become skilled ⟨*practiced* their act⟩ b : to train by repeated exercises ⟨*practice* pupils in writing⟩ 2 a : to carry out : APPLY ⟨*practice* what you preach⟩ b : to do or perform often, customarily, or habitually ⟨*practice* politeness⟩ c : to be
professionally engaged in ⟨*practice* law⟩ [Middle
French *practiser*, from *practique*, n., "practice", from
Late Latin *practice*, from Greek *praktikē*, from *practi-
kos* "practical"] — **prac·tic·er** *n*

²**practice** *also* **practise** *n* 1 a : actual performance or
application b : a repeated or customary action c : the
usual way of doing something ⟨local *practices*⟩ d : an
established manner of conducting legal proceedings 2
a : systematic exercise for gaining skill ⟨*practice*
makes perfect⟩ b *archaic* : skill acquired by practice
3 a : the exercise of a profession ⟨the *practice* of law⟩
b : a professional business SYN see HABIT — **in practice**
1 : in actual or accepted usage 2 : in good or superior
condition as a result of practice ⟨athletes must keep *in
practice*⟩

prac·ticed *or* **prac·tised** \'prak-təst\ *adj* 1 : EXPERI-
ENCED, SKILLED ⟨a *practiced* welder⟩ 2 : learned by
practice

prac·tice–teach \,prak-təs-'tēch\ *vi* : to engage in practice teaching — **practice teacher** *n*

practice teaching *n* : teaching in which a student practices educational skills and methods under the supervision of an experienced teacher in preparation for
professional teaching

prac·ti·tio·ner \prak-'tish-nər, -ə-nər\ *n* 1 : a person
who practices a profession and especially law or medicine 2 : a Christian Scientist who is an authorized
healer [from earlier *practician*, from Middle French
praticien, from *pratique, practique* "practice"]

prae·no·men \prē-'nō-mən\ *n, pl* -**nomens** *or* -**no·mi·na**
\-'näm-ə-nə, -'nō-mə-\ : the first of the usual three
names of an ancient Roman [Latin, from *prae-* "pre" +
nomen "name"]

prae·tor \'prēt-ər\ *n* : an ancient Roman magistrate
ranking below a consul and having chiefly judicial
duties [Latin]

prae·to·ri·an \prē-'tōr-ē-ən, -'tòr-\ *adj* 1 : of or relating to a praetor 2 *often cap* : of, forming, or resembling the Roman imperial bodyguard — **praetorian** *n,
often cap*

prag·mat·ic \prag-'mat-ik\ *also* **prag·mat·i·cal** \-'mat-i-
kəl\ *adj* 1 a : concerned with practical rather than
intellectual or artistic matters b : practical as opposed
to idealistic 2 : relating to or in accordance with prag-

matism [Latin *pragmaticus* "skilled in law or business", from Greek *pragmatikos*, from *pragma* "deed,
action", from *prassein* "to do"] — **prag·mat·i·cal·ly**
\-i-kə-lē, -klē\ *adv*

pragmatic sanction *n* : a solemn decree of a sovereign
on a matter of primary importance and with the force
of fundamental law

prag·ma·tism \'prag-mə-,tiz-əm\ *n* 1 : a practical approach to problems and affairs 2 : philosophical doctrine holding that the meaning of an idea is to be
sought in its practical bearings, that the function of
thought is to guide action, and that truth is to be tested by the practical consequences of belief — **prag·ma·
tist** \-mət-əst\ *adj or n* — **prag·ma·tis·tic** \,prag-mə-
'tis-tik\ *adj*

prai·rie \'preər-ē\ *n* : a tract of grassland; *esp* : a large
area of level or rolling land (as in the central United
States) with deep fertile soil, a cover of tall coarse
grasses, and few trees [French, derived from Latin *pra-
tum* "meadow"]

prairie chicken *n* : a grouse of the Mississippi valley
with a patch of bare inflatable skin on the neck

prairie dog *n* : a colonial buff or grayish American burrowing rodent related to the marmots

prairie schooner *n* : a covered wagon used by pioneers
in cross-country travel — called also *prairie wagon*

prairie wolf *n* : COYOTE

¹**praise** \'prāz\ *vb* 1 : to express approval : COMMEND
2 : to glorify especially in song : EXTOL [Middle French
preisier "to prize, praise", from Late Latin *pretiare*
"to prize", from Latin *pretium* "price"] — **prais·er** *n*

²**praise** *n* 1 : an act of praising : COMMENDATION 2 :
WORSHIP ⟨in *praise* of the Lord⟩

praise·wor·thy \-,wər-thē\ *adj* : worthy of praise :
LAUDABLE — **praise·wor·thi·ly** \-thə-lē\ *adv* — **praise-
wor·thi·ness** \-thē-nəs\ *n*

Pra·krit \'präk-,rit, -rət\ *n* 1 : any or all of the ancient
Indic languages or dialects other than Sanskrit 2 : any
of the modern Indic languages [Sanskrit *prākṛta*, from
prākṛta "natural, vulgar"]

pra·line \'prä-,lēn, 'prā-\ *n* : a candy of nut kernels embedded in boiled brown sugar or maple sugar [French,
from Count Plessy-*Praslin*, died 1675, French soldier]

pram \'pram\ *n, chiefly British* : a baby carriage [short
for *perambulator*]

prance \'prans\ *vi* 1 : to spring from the hind legs or
move by so doing 2 : to ride on a prancing horse 3 : to
move in a spirited manner : STRUT; *also* : CAPER [Mid-
dle English *prauncen*] — **prance** *n* — **pranc·er**
\'pran-sər\ *n* — **pranc·ing·ly** \-singlē\ *adv*

pran·di·al \'pran-dē-əl\ *adj* : of or relating to a meal
[Latin *prandium* "late breakfast, luncheon"]

¹**prank** \'prangk\ *n* : a playful or mischievous act: as a :
PRACTICAL JOKE ⟨Halloween *pranks*⟩ b : a ludicrous
act [obsolete *prank* "to play tricks"] — **prank·ish**
\'prang-kish\ *adj* — **prank·ish·ly** *adv* — **prank·ish-
ness** *n*

²**prank** *vt* : to dress or adorn (as oneself) gaily or showily [probably from Dutch *pranken* "to strut"]

prank·ster \'prang-stər, 'prangk-\ *n* : one that plays
pranks

pra·seo·dym·i·um \,prā-zē-ō-'dim-ē-əm\ *n* : a yellowish white metallic chemical element used chiefly in
the form of its salts as a coloring agent — see ELEMENT
table [derived from Greek *prasios* "light green" +
New Latin *didymium*, a mixture of rare earth elements, from Greek *didymos* "double"]

¹**prate** \'prāt\ *vb* : to talk long and idly or foolishly
[Dutch *praten*] — **prat·er** *n* — **prat·ing·ly** \'prāt-ing-
lē\ *adv*

²**prate** *n* : idle or foolish talk

prat·fall \'prat-,fȯl\ *n* 1 : a fall on the buttocks 2 : a
humiliating mishap or blunder [earlier *prat* "buttocks"]

pra·tique \pra-'tēk\ *n* : clearance given an incoming ship by the health authority of a port [French, literally, "practice"]

¹prat·tle \'prat-l\ *vb* **prat·tled; prat·tling** \'prat-ling, -l-ing\ **1** : PRATE **2** : to utter meaningless sounds suggestive of the chatter of children [Low German *pratelen*] — **prat·tler** \'prat-lər, -l-ər\ *n* — **prat·tling·ly** \'prat-ling-lē\ *adv*

²prattle *n* **1** : PRATE **2** : a sound that is meaningless, repetitive, and suggestive of the chatter of children

prau \'praù\ *n* : any of several usually undecked Indonesian boats propelled by sails, oars, or paddles [Malay *pĕrahu*]

prawn \'pròn, 'prän\ *n* : any of numerous widely distributed edible decapod crustaceans resembling shrimps with large compressed abdomens; *also* : SHRIMP [Middle English *prane*]

pray \'prā\ *vb* **1** : ENTREAT, IMPLORE ⟨*pray* tell me the time⟩ **2** : to get or bring by praying **3** : to make entreaty or supplication : PLEAD **4** : to address God with adoration, confession, supplication, or thanksgiving [Old French *preier*, from Latin *precari*, from *prec-*, *prex* "request, prayer"]

¹prayer \'praər, 'preər\ *n* **1** : the act or practice of praying to God ⟨a moment of silent *prayer*⟩ **2 a** : a supplication or expression addressed to God ⟨a *prayer* of thanksgiving⟩ **b** : an earnest request or wish : PLEA **3** : a religious service consisting chiefly of prayers ⟨had regular family *prayers*⟩ **4** : a set form of words used in praying ⟨a book of *prayers*⟩ [Old French *preiere*, from Medieval Latin *precaria*, from Latin *precarius* "obtained by entreaty", from *prec-*, *prex* "request, entreaty"]

²pray·er \'prā-ər\ *n* : one that prays : SUPPLIANT

prayer book *n* : a book containing prayers and often other forms and directions for worship

prayer·ful \'praər-fəl, 'preər-\ *adj* **1** : given to or characterized by prayer : DEVOUT **2** : EARNEST 1 — **prayer·ful·ly** \-fə-lē\ *adv* — **prayer·ful·ness** *n*

prayer meeting *n* : a Protestant Christian service of evangelical worship usually held regularly on a weeknight — called also *prayer service*

prayer plant *n* : a Brazilian plant with oval leaves folding upward at night as if in prayer that is widely grown as an ornamental foliage plant

praying mantis *n* : MANTIS

pre- *prefix* **1 a** (1) : earlier than : prior to : before ⟨*pre*historic⟩ (2) : preparatory or prerequisite to ⟨*pre*medical⟩ **b** : in advance : beforehand ⟨*pre*cancel⟩ **2 a** : in front of : anterior to ⟨*pre*molar⟩ **b** : front : anterior [Latin *prae-*, from *prae* "in front of, before"]

See **pre-** and 2d element

preadmission	predeparture	premoisten
preadult	predesignate	premold
preagricultural	predevelopment	prenoon
preannounce	prediscverge	prenotification
prearrange	prediscovery	prenotify
prearrangement	predrill	preopening
prebattle	preelection	peroperational
prebiblical	preelectric	preplan
prebreakfast	preemployment	preproduction
preclear	preestablish	preprogram
preclearance	prefight	prepublication
precode	prefile	prepunch
precollege	prefire	prepurchase
precolonial	pregame	prequalification
precombustion	preinaugural	prequalify
precommitment	preindustrial	prerace
precompute	preinterview	prerehearsal
preconvention	preinvasion	prerelease
precool	prelaunch	preretirement
precrash	prelife	prerevolutionary
predawn	premarriage	preriot
predefine	premigration	presale
predelinquent	premodern	preseason
predelivery	premodify	preselection

preset	pretape	preuniversity
prestamp	pretelevision	prewar
presterilize	pretournament	prewash
prestrike	pretreat	prewrap
presweeten	pretreatment	

preach \'prēch\ *vb* **1 a** : to deliver a sermon : utter publicly **b** : to set forth in a sermon ⟨*preach* the gospel⟩ **2** : to urge acceptance or abandonment of an idea or course of action : ADVOCATE ⟨*preach* patience⟩; *esp* : to exhort in an officious or tiresome manner **3** : to bring, put, or affect by preaching [Old French *prechier*, from Late Latin *praedicare*, from Latin, "to proclaim publicly", from *prae-* "pre-" + *dicare* "to proclaim"] — **preach·er** *n* — **preach·ing·ly** \'prē-ching-lē\ *adv*

preach·ify \'prē-chə-,fī\ *vi* **-fied; -fy·ing** : to preach ineptly or tediously

preach·ment \'prēch-mənt\ *n* **1** : the act or practice of preaching **2** : SERMON, EXHORTATION; *esp* : a tedious or unwelcome exhortation

preachy \'prē-chē\ *adj* **preach·i·er; -est** : marked by obvious moral exhortation — **preach·i·ly** \-chə-lē\ *adv* — **preach·i·ness** \-chē-nəs\ *n*

pre·ad·o·les·cence \,prē-,ad-l-'es-ns\ *n* : the period of human development just preceding adolescence — **pre·ad·o·les·cent** \-nt\ *adj or n*

pre·am·ble \'prē-am-bəl, prē-'\ *n* **1** : an introductory statement; *esp* : the usually explanatory introductory part of a constitution or statute **2** : an introductory fact or circumstance : PRELIMINARY; *esp* : one indicating what is to follow [Middle French *preambule*, from Medieval Latin *praeambulum*, from Late Latin *praeambulus* "walking in front", from Latin *prae-* "pre-" + *ambulare* "to walk"]

pre·as·signed \,prē-ə-'sīnd\ *adj* : assigned beforehand

preb·end \'preb-ənd\ *n* **1 a** : an endowment held by a cathedral or collegiate church for the maintenance of a prebendary **b** : the stipend paid from this endowment **2** : PREBENDARY [Middle French *prebende*, from Medieval Latin *praebenda*, from Late Latin, "subsistence allowance granted by the state", from Latin *praebēre* "to offer", from *prae-* "pre-" + *habēre* "to have, hold"]

preb·en·dary \'preb-ən-,der-ē\ *n, pl* **-dar·ies** **1** : a clergyman receiving a prebend for officiating at stated times in the church **2** : an honorary canon

Pre·cam·bri·an \prē-'kam-brē-ən, 'prē-\ *n* : the earliest era of geological history equivalent to the Archean and Proterozoic; *also* : the corresponding system of rocks — **Precambrian** *adj*

pre·can·cel \prē-'kan-səl, 'prē-\ *vt* : to cancel (a postage stamp) in advance of use — **pre·can·cel·la·tion** \,prē-,kan-sə-'lā-shən\ *n*

pre·can·cer·ous \prē-'kans-rəs, 'prē-, -ə-rəs\ *adj* : likely to become cancerous ⟨a *precancerous* lesion⟩

pre·car·i·ous \pri-'kar-ē-əs, -'ker-\ *adj* **1** : dependent upon uncertain premises ⟨*precarious* theories⟩ **2 a** : dependent on chance circumstances, unknown conditions, or uncertain developments **b** : characterized by a lack of security or stability that threatens with danger ⟨a *precarious* state of health⟩ [Latin *precarius* "obtained by entreaty, uncertain", from *prec-*, *prex* "request, entreaty"] — **pre·car·i·ous·ly** *adv* — **pre·car·i·ous·ness** *n*

pre·cau·tion \pri-'kò-shən\ *n* **1** : care taken in advance : FORESIGHT **2** : a measure taken beforehand to prevent harm or secure good : SAFEGUARD ⟨*precautions* against fire⟩ — **pre·cau·tion·ary** \-shə-,ner-ē\ *adj*

pre·cede \pri-'sēd\ *vb* **1** : to surpass in rank, dignity, or importance **2** : to be, go, or come before or in front of in position or time **3** : to cause to be preceded : PREFACE ⟨*preceded* the speech with a welcome to the visitors⟩ [Middle French *preceder*, from *praecedere*, from *prae-* "pre-" + *cedere* "to go"]

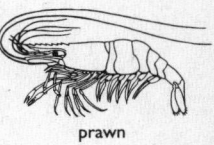

prawn

\ə\ abut	\ng\ sing
\ər\ further	\ō\ bone
\a\ mat	\ó\ saw
\ā\ take	\òi\ coin
\ä\ cot, cart	\th\ thin
\aù\ out	\th\ this
\ch\ chin	\ü\ food
\e\ pet	\ù\ foot
\ē\ easy	\y\ yet
\g\ go	\yü\ few
\i\ tip	\yù\ cure
\ī\ life	\zh\ vision
\j\ job	

pre·ce·dence \'pres-əd-əns, pri-'sēd-ns\ *n* **1** : the act or fact of preceding (as in time, importance, or position) **2** : PREFERENCE 1, PRIORITY

pre·ce·den·cy \-ən-sē, -n-sē\ *n* : PRECEDENCE

¹pre·ce·dent \pri-'sēd-nt, 'pres-əd-ənt\ *adj* : prior in time, order, arrangement, or significance [Middle French, from Latin *praecedens,* present participle of *praecedere* "to precede"]

²prec·e·dent \'pres-əd-ənt\ *n* **1** : an earlier occurrence of something similar **2** : something that may serve as an example or rule to authorize or justify a similar future act or statement (this decision will set a *precedent*)

pre·ced·ing \pri-'sēd-ing\ *adj* : going before in time or place □ SYN PRECEDING, ANTECEDENT, FOREGOING mean being before. PRECEDING implies being immediately before in time or place (on the *preceding* day) (the last line in the *preceding* stanza) ANTECEDENT applies to order in time and may suggest a causal relation (study the revolution and *antecedent* economic distress) FOREGOING applies to what has preceded especially in a discourse (the *foregoing* phrase)

pre·cen·tor \pri-'sent-ər\ *n* : a leader of the singing of a choir or congregation [Late Latin *praecentor,* from Latin *praecentus,* past participle of *praecinere* "to sing before", from *prae-* "pre-" + *canere* "to sing"] — **pre·cen·to·ri·al** \,prē-,sen-'tōr-ē-əl, -'tor-\ *adj* — **pre·cen·tor·ship** \pri-'sent-ər-,ship\ *n*

pre·cept \'prē-,sept\ *n* : a command or principle intended as a general rule of action [Latin *praeceptum,* from *praeceptus,* past participle of *praecipere* "to take beforehand, instruct", from *prae-* "pre-" + *capere* "to take"]

pre·cep·tor \pri-'sep-tər, 'prē-,\ *n* **1** : TEACHER, TUTOR **2** : the principal of a school — **pre·cep·to·ri·al** \pri-,sep-'tōr-ē-əl, ,prē-, -'tor-\ *adj* — **pre·cep·tor·ship** \pri-'sep-tər-,ship, 'prē-,\ *n*

pre·ces·sion \prē-'sesh-ən\ *n* : a comparatively slow circling of the rotation axis of a spinning body about another line intersecting the axis [Medieval Latin *praecessio* "act of preceding", from Latin *praecessus,* past participle of *praecedere* "to precede"]

pre·cinct \'prē-,singt, -,singkt\ *n* **1** : an administrative subdivision of a territory: as **a** : a subdivision of a county, town, city, or ward for election purposes **b** : a division of a city for police control **2** : the enclosure bounded by the walls or limits of a building or place (within the *precincts* of the college) **3** *pl* : the region immediately surrounding a place : ENVIRONS (the *precincts* of the city) [Medieval Latin *praecinctum* "bounded district", from Latin *praecinctus,* past participle of *praecingere* "to gird about", from *prae-* "pre-" + *cingere* "to gird"]

pre·ci·os·i·ty \,presh-ē-'äs-ət-ē, ,pres-\ *n, pl* **-ties** : often excessive fastidious refinement (as in language)

¹pre·cious \'presh-əs\ *adj* **1** : of great value or high price (diamonds, emeralds, and other *precious* stones) **2** : highly esteemed or cherished (*precious* memories) **3** : excessively refined : AFFECTED (*precious* language) **4** : THOROUGHGOING, UTTER (a *precious* scoundrel) [Old French *precios,* from Latin *pretiosus,* from *pretium* "price"] — **pre·cious·ly** *adv* — **pre·cious·ness** *n*

²precious *adv* : EXTREMELY, VERY (they had *precious* little to say)

prec·i·pice \'pres-ə-pəs\ *n* **1** : a very steep or overhanging place (as the face of a cliff) **2** : the brink of disaster [Middle French, from Latin *praecipitium,* from *praecipit-, praeceps* "headlong", from *prae-* "pre-" + *caput* "head"]

pre·cip·i·tance \pri-'sip-ət-əns\ *n* : rash haste

pre·cip·i·tan·cy \-ən-sē\ *n, pl* **-cies** : PRECIPITANCE

pre·cip·i·tant \-ənt\ *adj* : PRECIPITATE — **pre·cip·i·tant·ly** *adv* — **pre·cip·i·tant·ness** *n*

¹pre·cip·i·tate \pri-'sip-ə-,tāt\ *vb* **1 a** : to throw violently : HURL **b** : to fall headlong **c** : to fall or come suddenly into some condition **2 a** : to move, urge, or press on with haste or violence **b** : to bring on abruptly (the tactless remark *precipitated* a long, bitter quarrel) **3 a** : to separate or cause to separate from solution or suspension **b** : to condense from a vapor and fall as rain or snow [Latin *praecipitare,* from *praecipit-, praeceps* "headlong"] — **pre·cip·i·ta·tor** \-,tāt-ər\ *n*

²pre·cip·i·tate \pri-'sip-ət-ət, -ə-,tāt\ *n* : a usually solid substance separated from a solution or suspension by chemical or physical change

³pre·cip·i·tate \pri-'sip-ət-ət\ *adj* **1** : exhibiting violent or unwise speed (a *precipitate* attack) **2** : falling, flowing, or rushing with steep descent — **pre·cip·i·tate·ly** *adv* — **pre·cip·i·tate·ness** *n*

pre·cip·i·ta·tion \pri-,sip-ə-'tā-shən\ *n* **1** : the quality or state of being precipitate : HASTE **2** : the process of precipitating or of forming a precipitate **3 a** : a deposit on the earth of hail, mist, rain, sleet, or snow; *also* : the quantity of water deposited **b** : PRECIPITATE

pre·cip·i·tin \pri-'sip-ət-ən\ *n* : an antibody that forms an insoluble precipitate when it unites with its antigen

pre·cip·i·tous \pri-'sip-ət-əs\ *adj* **1 a** : very steep, perpendicular, or overhanging **b** : having precipices (a *precipitous* ledge) **2** : falling very quickly : very rapid (*precipitous* rush of water) **3** : SUDDEN 2, RASH (a *precipitous* act) SYN see STEEP — **pre·cip·i·tous·ly** *adv* — **pre·cip·i·tous·ness** *n*

pré·cis \prā-'sē, 'prā-,sē\ *n, pl* **pré·cis** \-'sēz, -,sēz\ : a concise summary of essential points, statements, or facts [French, from *précis* "precise"]

pre·cise \pri-'sīs\ *adj* **1** : free from vagueness or inaccuracy **2** : very exact : ACCURATE (*precise* scales) (*precise* time of arrival) **3** : clear and sharp in enunciation : DISTINCT (a low *precise* voice) **4** : strictly conforming to rule or convention (*precise* habits) **5** : distinguished from every other (at that *precise* moment) [Middle French *precis,* from Latin *praecisus,* past participle of *praecidere* "to cut off", from *prae-* "pre-" + *caedere* "to cut"] SYN see CORRECT — **pre·cise·ly** *adv* — **pre·cise·ness** *n*

pre·ci·sian \pri-'sizh-ən\ *n* : a person who stresses or practices scrupulous adherence to a strict standard especially of religious observance or morality

¹pre·ci·sion \pri-'sizh-ən\ *n* : the quality or state of being precise; *esp* : the degree of refinement with which an operation is performed or a measurement stated — **pre·ci·sion·ist** \-'sizh-nəst, -ə-nəst\ *n*

²precision *adj* **1** : adapted for extremely accurate measurement or operation (a *precision* gauge) **2** : marked by precision of execution (a *precision* drill team)

pre·clin·i·cal \prē-'klin-i-kəl, 'prē-\ *adj* : of or relating to the period preceding clinical manifestations (*preclinical* infection)

pre·clude \pri-'klüd\ *vt* : to prevent or make impossible by acting, existing, or occurring beforehand [Latin *praecludere* (past participle *praeclusus*), literally, "to shut out", from *prae-* "pre-" + *claudere* "to close"] — **pre·clu·sion** \-'klü-zhən\ *n* — **pre·clu·sive** \-'klü-siv, -ziv\ *adj* — **pre·clu·sive·ly** *adv*

pre·co·cial \pri-'kō-shəl\ *adj* : capable of a high degree of independent activity from birth (*precocial* birds) — compare ALTRICIAL

pre·co·cious \pri-'kō-shəs\ *adj* **1** : exceptionally early in development or occurrence (*precocious* behavior) **2** : exhibiting mature qualities at an unusually early age (a *precocious* child) [Latin *praecoc-, praecox* "early ripening, precocious", from *prae-* "pre-" + *coquere* "to cook"] — **pre·co·cious·ly** *adv* — **pre·co·cious·ness** *n* — **pre·coc·i·ty** \pri-'käs-ət-ē\ *n*

pre·cog·ni·tion \,prē-käg-'nish-ən\ *n* : clairvoyance concerning something not yet experienced

pre·con·ceive \,prē-kən-'sēv\ *vt* : to form an opinion of prior to knowledge or experience (*preconceived* ideas about foreigners) — **pre·con·cep·tion** \-'sep-shən\ *n*

pre·con·cert·ed \,prē-kən-'sərt-əd\ *adj* : arranged or agreed upon in advance ⟨a *preconcerted* plan of attack⟩

pre·con·di·tion \,prē-kən-'dish-ən\ *vt* : to put in proper or desired condition or frame of mind in advance

pre·con·scious \prē-'kän-chəs, 'prē-\ *adj* : not present in consciousness but capable of being readily recalled — **pre·con·scious·ly** *adv*

pre·cook \prē-'kůk, 'prē-\ *vt* : to cook partially or entirely in advance

pre·cur·sor \pri-'kər-sər, 'prē-,\ *n* **1 a** : one that precedes and indicates the approach of another : FORERUNNER **b** : PREDECESSOR 1 **2** : a substance from which another substance is formed [Latin *praecursor,* from *praecurrere* "to run before", from *prae-* "pre-" + *currere* "to run"]

pre·cur·so·ry \pri-'kərs-rē, -ə-rē\ *adj* : having the character of a precursor : PRELIMINARY, PREMONITORY ⟨*precursory* symptoms of a fever⟩

pre·da·ceous *or* **pre·da·cious** \pri-'dā-shəs\ *adj* : living by preying on others : PREDATORY — **pre·da·ceous·ness** *n* — **pre·dac·i·ty** \-'das-ət-ē\ *n*

pre·date \prē-'dāt, 'prē-\ *vt* : ANTEDATE

pre·da·tion \pri-'dā-shən\ *n* **1** : the act of preying or plundering : DEPREDATION **2** : a mode of life in which food is primarily obtained by killing and consuming animals [Latin *praedatio,* from *praedatus,* past participle of *praedari* "to prey upon", from *praeda* "prey"] — **pred·a·tor** \'pred-ət-ər\ *n*

pred·a·to·ry \'pred-ə-,tōr-ē, -,tor-\ *adj* **1** : of, relating to, or marked by plundering ⟨*predatory* raids⟩ **2** : living by predation : PREDACEOUS; *also* : adapted to predation — **pred·a·to·ri·ly** \,pred-ə-'tōr-ə-lē, -'tor-\ *adv*

pre·de·cease \,prēd-i-sēs\ *vb* : to die before another person

pre·de·ces·sor \'pred-ə-,ses-ər, 'prēd-\ *n* **1** : one that precedes; *esp* : a person who has held a position or office before another **2** *archaic* : ANCESTOR 1 [Middle French *predecesseur,* from Late Latin *praedecessor,* from Latin *prae-* "pre-" + *decessor* "retiring governor", from *decessus,* past participle of *decedere* "to depart, retire from office", from *de-* + *cedere* "to go"]

pre·des·ti·nate \prē-'des-tə-,nāt\ *vt* **1** : to foreordain to an earthly or eternal destiny by divine decree **2** *archaic* : PREDETERMINE 1b

pre·des·ti·na·tion \,prē-,des-tə-'nā-shən\ *n* : the act of predestinating : the state of being predestinated

pre·des·tine \prē-'des-tən, 'prē-\ *vt* : to destine, decree, determine, appoint, or settle beforehand; *esp* : PREDESTINATE 1

pre·de·ter·mine \,prēd-i-'tər-mən\ *vt* **1 a** : FOREORDAIN, PREDESTINE **b** : to determine or settle beforehand ⟨meet at a *predetermined* place⟩ **2** : to impose a direction or tendency on beforehand — **pre·de·ter·mi·na·tion** \-,tər-mə-'nā-shən\ *n*

pred·i·ca·ble \'pred-i-kə-bəl\ *adj* : capable of being predicated or affirmed

pre·dic·a·ment \pri-'dik-ə-mənt\ *n* : a difficult, perplexing, or trying situation : FIX [Late Latin *praedicamentum* "that which is predicated, category", from *praedicare* "to predicate"] □ SYN DILEMMA, QUANDARY: PREDICAMENT suggests a difficult situation offering no satisfactory solution ⟨increased population poses a *predicament* for our society⟩ DILEMMA implies the need to choose between two alternatives offering essentially equal advantages or disadvantages ⟨in a *dilemma* about a choice of careers⟩ QUANDARY stresses puzzlement and perplexity ⟨in a *quandary* as to what excuse to make⟩

¹pred·i·cate \'pred-i-kət\ *n* **1** : something that is affirmed or denied of the subject in a proposition in logic ⟨in "paper is white", whiteness is the *predicate*⟩ **2** : the part of a sentence or clause that expresses what is said of the subject and that usually consists of a verb with or without objects, complements, or adverbial modifiers [Late Latin *praedicatum,* from *praedicare* "to assert, predicate"] — **pred·i·ca·tive** \'pred-i-kət-iv, 'pred-ə-,kāt-\ *adj* — **pred·i·ca·tive·ly** *adv*

²predicate *adj* : belonging to the predicate; *esp* : completing the meaning of a linking verb ⟨*hot* in "the sun is hot" is a *predicate* adjective⟩ — compare ATTRIBUTIVE

³pred·i·cate \'pred-ə-,kāt\ *vt* **1** : AFFIRM 1b, DECLARE **2 a** : to assert as a predicate in a proposition **b** : to assert to be a quality or property ⟨*predicate* sweetness of sugar⟩ **3** : BASE, FOUND ⟨a proposal *predicated* upon the belief that sufficient support could be obtained⟩ [Late Latin *praedicare* "to assert, predicate, preach"]

predicate nominative *n* : a noun or pronoun in the nominative case completing the meaning of a linking verb

pred·i·ca·tion \,pred-ə-'kā-shən\ *n* : an act or instance of predicating; *esp* : the expression of action, state, or quality by a grammatical predicate

pre·dict \pri-'dikt\ *vt* : to declare in advance : foretell on the basis of observation, experience, or scientific reasoning [Latin *praedictus,* past participle of *praedicere* "to predict", from *prae-* "pre-" + *dicere* "to say"] SYN see FORETELL — **pre·dict·able** \-'dik-tə-bəl\ *adj* — **pre·dict·ably** \-blē\ *adv*

pre·dic·tion \pri-'dik-shən\ *n* **1** : an act of predicting **2** : something that is predicted : FORECAST — **pre·dic·tive** \-'dik-tiv\ *adj* — **pre·dic·tive·ly** *adv*

pre·di·gest \,prēd-ī-'jest, ,prēd-ə-\ *vt* : to subject to predigestion

pre·di·ges·tion \-'jes-chən, -'jesh-chən\ *n* : artificial partial digestion of food for use in illness or impaired digestion

pre·di·lec·tion \,pred-l-'ek-shən-, ,prēd-\ *n* : an inclination in favor of something : PREFERENCE, PARTIALITY [French *prédilection,* from Medieval Latin *praedilectus,* past participle of *praediligere* "to prefer", from Latin *prae-* "pre-" + *diligere* "to love", from *dis-* "apart" + *legere* "to pick, choose"]

pre·dis·pose \,prēd-is-'pōz\ *vt* : to dispose in advance : make susceptible : INCLINE ⟨an inherited weakness *predisposing* one to certain diseases⟩

pre·dis·po·si·tion \,prē-,dis-pə-'zish-ən\ *n* : a condition of being predisposed : INCLINATION

pre·dom·i·nance \pri-'däm-ə-nəns\ *also* **pre·dom·i·nan·cy** \-nən-sē\ *n* : the quality or state of being predominant

pre·dom·i·nant \-nənt\ *adj* : having superior strength, influence, or authority ⟨the *predominant* color in a painting⟩ — **pre·dom·i·nant·ly** *adv*

pre·dom·i·nate \pri-'däm-ə-,nāt\ *vb* **1** : to exert controlling power or influence : PREVAIL **2** : to hold advantage in numbers or quantity : PREPONDERATE — **pre·dom·i·na·tion** \-,däm-ə-'nā-shən\ *n*

pre·em·i·nence \prē-'em-ə-nəns\ *n* : the quality or state of being preeminent : SUPERIORITY

pre·em·i·nent \-nənt\ *adj* : of the highest rank, dignity, or importance : OUTSTANDING — **pre·em·i·nent·ly** *adv*

pre·empt \prē-'emt, -'empt\ *vt* **1** : to settle upon (as public land) with the right to purchase before others; *also* : to take by such a right **2** : to take before someone else can ⟨*preempt* a seat at the stadium⟩ [back-formation from *preemption,* from Medieval Latin *praeemptus,* past participle of *praeemere* "to buy before", from Latin *prae-* "pre-" + *emere* "to buy"] — **pre·emp·tion** \-'em-shən, -'emp-\ *n* — **pre·emp·tive** \-'em-tiv, -'emp-\ *adj* — **pre·emp·tive·ly** *adv* — **pre·emp·tor** \-tər\ *n*

preen \'prēn\ *vb* **1** : to trim or dress with the bill **2** : to dress or smooth oneself up : PRIMP **3** : to indulge oneself in pride : congratulate oneself : GLOAT [Middle English *preinen*] — **preen·er** *n*

pre·ex·ist \,prē-ig-'zist\ *vb* : to exist earlier or before something

\ə\	abut	\ng\	si**ng**
\ər\	f**ur**ther	\ō\	b**o**ne
\a\	m**a**t	\o\	s**aw**
\ā\	t**a**ke	\oi\	c**oi**n
\ä\	c**o**t, c**a**rt	\th\	**th**in
\aů\	**ou**t	\th\	**th**is
\ch\	**ch**in	\ü\	f**oo**d
\e\	p**e**t	\u\	f**oo**t
\ē\	**e**asy	\y\	**y**et
\g\	**g**o	\yü\	f**ew**
\i\	t**i**p	\yů\	c**u**re
\ī\	l**i**fe	\zh\	vi**s**ion
\j\	**j**ob		

pre·ex·ist·ence \-'zis·təns\ *n* : existence in a former state or previous to something else; *esp* : existence of the soul before its union with the body — **pre·ex·ist·ent** \-tənt\ *adj*

pre·fab \prē-'fab, 'prē-,\ *n* : a prefabricated structure — **prefab** *adj*

pre·fab·ri·cate \prē-'fab·ri-,kāt, 'prē-\ *vt* **1** : to make the parts of at a factory so that construction consists mainly of assembling and uniting standardized parts **2** : to give a synthetic or artificial quality to — **pre·fab·ri·ca·tion** \,prē-,fab·ri-'kā-shən\ *n*

¹pref·ace \'pref-əs\ *n* **1** *often cap* : a prayer introducing the central part of the eucharistic service **2** : the introductory remarks of a speaker or author : PROLOGUE [Middle French, from Latin *prefatio* "foreword", from *praefari* "to say beforehand", from *prae-* "pre-" + *fari* "to say"]

²preface *vb* **1** : to say or write as a preface ⟨a note *prefaced* to the manuscript⟩ **2** : PRECEDE 2, HERALD **3** : to introduce by or begin with a preface **4** : to locate in front of **5** : to be a preliminary to — **pref·ac·er** *n*

pref·a·to·ri·al \,pref-ə-'tōr-ē-əl, -'tòr-\ *adj* : PREFATORY — **pref·a·to·ri·al·ly** \-ē-ə-lē\ *adv*

pref·a·to·ry \'pref-ə-,tōr-ē, -,tòr-\ *adj* : of, relating to, or constituting a preface ⟨*prefatory* remarks⟩

pre·fect \'prē-,fekt\ *n* **1** : a high official or magistrate (as of ancient Rome or France) **2** : a presiding or chief officer or magistrate **3** : a student monitor in a private school [Middle French, from Latin *praefectus,* from *praeficere* "to place at the head of", from *prae-* "pre-" + *facere* "to make"]

prefect apostolic *n* : a Roman Catholic priest functioning like a bishop over a district of a missionary territory

pre·fec·ture \'prē-,fek-chər\ *n* **1** : the office or term of office of a prefect **2** : the district governed by a prefect — **pre·fec·tur·al** \prē-'fek-chə-rəl\ *adj*

pre·fer \pri-'fər\ *vt* **pre·ferred; pre·fer·ring** **1** : to choose or like above another ⟨*prefer* dark clothes⟩ **2** *archaic* : to put or set forward or before someone : RECOMMEND **3** : to present for action or consideration ⟨*prefer* charges against a person⟩ [Middle French *preferer,* from Latin *praeferre* "to put before, prefer", from *prae-* "pre-" + *ferre* "to carry"] — **pre·fer·rer** *n*

pref·er·a·ble \'pref-rə-bəl, -ə-rə-; 'pref-ər-bəl\ *adj* : worthy to be preferred : more desirable — **pref·er·a·bil·i·ty** \,pref-rə-'bil-ət-ē, -ə-rə-\ *n* — **pref·er·a·bleness** \'pref-rə-bəl-nəs, -ə-rə-; -ər-bəl-nəs\ *n* — **pref·er·a·bly** \-blē\ *adv*

pref·er·ence \'pref-ərns; 'pref-rəns, -ə-rəns\ *n* **1 a** : the act of preferring : the state of being preferred **b** : the power or opportunity of choosing ⟨gave us our *preference*⟩ **2** : one that is preferred : FAVORITE, CHOICE **3** : the act, fact, or principle of giving advantages to some over others ⟨show *preference*⟩ [French *préférence,* from Medieval Latin *praeferentia,* from Latin *praeferre* "to prefer"] SYN see CHOICE

pref·er·en·tial \,pref-ə-'ren-chəl\ *adj* **1** : showing preference ⟨*preferential* treatment⟩ **2** : creating or using preference ⟨a *preferential* tariff⟩ **3** : permitting the showing of preference or order of choice (as of candidates in an election) ⟨a *preferential* ballot⟩ **4** : giving preference in hiring to union members ⟨a *preferential* shop⟩ — **pref·er·en·tial·ly** \-'rench-lē, -ə-lē\ *adv*

pre·fer·ment \pri-'fər-mənt\ *n* **1 a** : advancement or promotion in dignity, office, or station **b** : a position or office of honor or profit **2** : the act of bringing forward (as charges)

preferred stock *n* : stock guaranteed priority by a corporation's charter over common stock in the payment of dividends and usually in the distribution of assets

pre·fig·ure \prē-'fig-yər, 'prē-, *especially British* -'fig-ər\ *vt* **1** : to show, suggest, or announce by an earlier type, image, or likeness : FORESHOW ⟨other religions *prefigured* the Christian Easter⟩ **2** : to picture or imagine beforehand : FORESEE ⟨*prefigure* the outcome of a ball game⟩ — **pre·fig·u·ra·tion** \prē-,fig-yə-'rā-shən, -,fig-ə-\ *n* — **pre·fig·u·ra·tive** \prē-'fig-yə-rət-iv, 'prē-, -'fig-ə-; -'fig-yərt-iv, -ərt-\ *adj* — **pre·fig·u·ra·tive·ly** *adv* — **pre·fig·u·ra·tive·ness** *n* — **pre·fig·ure·ment** \prē-'fig-yər-mənt, 'prē-, *especially British* -'fig-ər-\ *n*

¹pre·fix *vt* **1** \prē-'fiks, 'prē-\ *archaic* : to fix or appoint beforehand **2** \'prē-,, prē-'\ : to place in front : add as a prefix ⟨*prefix* a syllable to a word⟩

²pre·fix \'prē-,fiks\ *n* : a sound or sequence of sounds or a letter or sequence of letters occurring as a bound form attached to the beginning of a word and serving to produce a derivative word [New Latin *praefixum,* from Latin *praefixus,* past participle of *praefigere* "to fasten before", from *prae-* "pre-" + *figere* "to fasten"] — **pre·fix·al** \'prē-,fik-səl, prē-'\ *adj* — **pre·fix·al·ly** \-sə-lē\ *adv*

pre·flight \'prē-'flīt\ *adj* : preparing for or preliminary to flight ⟨*preflight* training⟩

pre·form \'prē-'fórm\ *vt* : to form or shape beforehand

pre·for·ma·tion \,prē-fòr-'mā-shən\ *n* **1** : previous formation **2** : a discredited biological theory holding that every germ cell contains the organism of its kind fully formed and that development consists merely in increase in size — **pre·for·ma·tion·ist** \-shə-nəst\ *n*

pre·fron·tal \prē-'frənt-l, 'prē-\ *adj* : anterior to or involving the anterior part of a frontal structure ⟨a *prefrontal* bone⟩

pre·gan·gli·on·ic \,prē-,gang-glē-'än-ik\ *adj* : situated proximal to or preceding a ganglion; *also* : of, relating to, or being an axon passing from the central nervous system into an autonomic ganglion

preg·na·ble \'preg-nə-bəl\ *adj* : capable of being taken or captured : VULNERABLE ⟨a *pregnable* fort⟩ [Middle French *prenable,* from *prendre* "to take", from Latin *prehendere*] — **preg·na·bil·i·ty** \,preg-nə-'bil-ət-ē\ *n*

preg·nan·cy \'preg-nən-sē\ *n, pl* **-cies** : the condition or quality of being pregnant : GESTATION

preg·nant \'preg-nənt\ *adj* **1 a** : containing unborn young within the uterus **b** : capable of producing **2** : abounding in fancy, wit, or resourcefulness : INVENTIVE ⟨a *pregnant* mind⟩ **3** : rich in significance or implication : MEANINGFUL ⟨*pregnant* ideas⟩ **4** : containing the germ or shape of future events ⟨*pregnant* years⟩ **5** : exhibiting fertility ⟨nature was *pregnant* with life⟩ [Latin *praegnans,* alteration of *praegnas*] — **preg·nant·ly** *adv*

pre·heat \prē-'hēt, 'prē-\ *vb* : to heat beforehand; *esp* : to heat (an oven) to a designated temperature before using for cooking — **pre·heat·er** *n*

pre·hen·sile \prē-'hen-səl\ *adj* : adapted for grasping especially by wrapping around ⟨a *prehensile* tail⟩ [French *préhensile,* from Latin *prehensus,* past participle of *prehendere* "to grasp, take"]

pre·hen·sion \-'hen-chən\ *n* : the act of taking hold, seizing, or grasping

pre–His·pan·ic \,prē-is-'pan-ik, -his-\ *adj* : of, relating to, or being the time prior to Spanish conquests in the western hemisphere

pre·his·tor·ic \,prē-is-'tòr-ik, -his-, -'tär-\ *adj* : of, relating to, or existing in times before written history — **pre·his·tor·i·cal** \-i-kəl\ *adj* — **pre·his·tor·i·cal·ly** \-i-kə-lē, -klē\ *adv*

pre·his·to·ry \prē-'his-tə-rē, 'prē-, -trē\ *n* **1** : the study of prehistoric man **2** : a history of what leads up to an event or situation — **pre·his·to·ri·an** \,prē-is-'tòr-ē-ən, -his-, -'tòr-\ *n*

pre·hu·man \'prē-'hyü-mən, -'yü-\ *adj* : being or relating to an animal in some respects like an ape but regarded as an ancestor of human beings — **prehuman** *n*

pre·judge \prē-'jəj, 'prē-\ *vt* : to judge before hearing or before full and sufficient examination — **pre·judgment** \-'jəj-mənt\ *n*

¹prej·u·dice \'prej-əd-əs\ *n* **1** : injury resulting from an unfair judgment or action of another; *esp* : an infringing of one's legal rights **2 a** (1) : a judgment or opinion formed before considering or without knowing the facts (2) : a favoring or dislike of something without grounds or before sufficient knowledge **b** : an irrational attitude of hostility directed against an individual, a group, or a race [Old French, from Latin *praejudicium* "previous judgment, damage", from *prae-* "pre-" + *judicium* "judgment"] □ SYN BIAS: PREJUDICE implies usually but not always an unfavorable view or fixed dislike and suggests a feeling rooted in suspicion, fear, or intolerance; BIAS implies partiality or distortion of individual judgments owing to a consistent mental leaning in favor of or against persons or things of a particular kind or class.

²**prejudice** *vt* **1** : to injure by an unfair judgment or action **2** : to cause to have predjudice : BIAS ⟨the incident *prejudiced* them against me⟩

prej·u·di·cial \ˌprej-ə-'dish-əl\ *adj* **1** : tending to injure or impair : DETRIMENTAL **2** : leading to premature judgment or unwarranted opinion — **prej·u·di·cial·ly** \-'dish-lē, -ə-lē\ *adv* — **prej·u·di·cial·ness** \-'dish-əl-nəs\ *n*

prej·u·di·cious \ˌprej-ə-'dish-əs\ *adj* : PREJUDICIAL — **prej·u·di·cious·ly** *adv*

prel·a·cy \'prel-ə-sē\ *n, pl* **-cies** **1** : the office or dignity of a prelate **2** : church government by prelates

prel·ate \'prel-ət\ *n* : a high-ranking clergyman (as a bishop) [Old French *prelat*, from Medieval Latin *praelatus*, literally, "one receiving preferment", from Latin, past participle of *praeferre* "to prefer"]

prelate nul·li·us \-nü-'lē-əs\ *n* : a Roman Catholic prelate usually a titular bishop with ordinary jurisdiction over a district independent of any diocese [*nullius* from New Latin *nullius dioecesis* "of no diocese"]

pre·lim \'prē-ˌlim, pri-'\ *n or adj* : PRELIMINARY

¹**pre·lim·i·nary** \pri-'lim-ə-ˌner-ē\ *n, pl* **-nar·ies** : something that precedes or is introductory or preparatory: as **a** : a preliminary scholastic examination ⟨pass the *preliminaries*⟩ **b** : a minor match preceding the main event [French *préliminaires*, pl., from Medieval Latin *praeliminaris*, adj., "preliminary", from Latin *prae-* "pre-" + *limin-, limen* "threshold"]

²**preliminary** *adj* : coming before the main part : INTRODUCTORY — **pre·lim·i·nar·i·ly** \-ˌlim-ə-'ner-ə-lē\ *adv*

pre·lit·er·ate \prē-'lit-ə-rət, ˌprē-, -'li-trət\ *adj* **1** : not yet using writing as a cultural medium **2** : lacking the use of writing

¹**pre·lude** \'prel-ˌyüd, 'prā-ˌlüd\ *n* **1** : an introductory performance, action, or event preceding and preparing for a principal matter : INTRODUCTION ⟨the wind was a *prelude* to the storm⟩ **2 a** : a musical movement introducing the chief subject (as of a fugue) or serving as an introduction to an opera or oratorio **b** : a short musical piece (as an organ solo) played at the beginning of a church service **c** : a separate concert piece usually for piano or orchestra and based entirely on a short motif [Middle French, from Medieval Latin *praeludium*, from Latin *praeludere* "to play beforehand", from *prae-* "pre-" + *ludere* "to play"]

²**prelude** *vb* **1** : to give, play, or serve as a prelude; *esp* : to play a musical introduction **2** : FORESHADOW ⟨the gray dawn *preluded* a gloomy day⟩ — **pre·lud·er** *n*

pre·man \'prē-ˌman\ *n* : a hypothetical ancient primate immediately ancestral to human beings

pre·ma·ture \ˌprē-mə-'tùr, -'tyùr, -'chùr\ *adj* : happening, arriving, existing, or performed before the proper or usual time; *esp* : born after a gestation period of less than 37 weeks ⟨*premature* babies⟩ — **premature** *n* — **pre·ma·ture·ly** *adv* — **pre·ma·tu·ri·ty** \-'tùr-ət-ē, -'tyùr-, -'chùr-\ *n*

¹**pre·med** \'prē-'med\ *adj* : PREMEDICAL

²**premed** *n* : a premedical student or course of study

pre·med·i·cal \prē-'med-i-kəl, 'prē-\ *adj* : preceding and preparing for the professional study of medicine

pre·med·i·tate \pri-'med-ə-ˌtāt, 'prē-\ *vt* : to think about and plan beforehand ⟨*premeditate* murder⟩ — **pre·med·i·tat·ed·ly** \-ˌtāt-əd-lē\ *adv* — **pre·med·i·ta·tion** \pri-ˌmed-ə-'tā-shən, ˌprē-\ *n*

pre·men·stru·al \prē-'men-strə-wəl, 'prē-, -strəl\ *adj* : of, relating to, occurring in, or being the time period just preceding menstruation ⟨*premenstrual* tension⟩ — **pre·men·stru·al·ly** *adv*

premenstrual syndrome *n* : a varying group of symptoms manifested by some women prior to menstruation that may include irritability, insomnia, fatigue, anxiety, depression, headache, edema, and abdominal pain — abbreviation *PMS*

¹**pre·mier** \pri-'miər, -'myiər; 'prē-mē-ər, 'prem-ē-\ *adj* **1** : first in position, rank, or importance : PRINCIPAL **2** : first in time : EARLIEST [Middle French, from Latin *primarius* "of the first rank", from *primus* "first"]

²**premier** *n* : the chief minister and head of government : PRIME MINISTER — **pre·mier·ship** \-ˌship\ *n*

¹**pre·miere** \pri-'myeər, -'miər\ *n* : a first performance or exhibition ⟨the *premiere* of a play⟩ [French *première*, from *premier* "first"]

²**premiere** *vb* : to present or appear in a first public performance

³**premiere** *adj* : most eminent ⟨the nation's *premiere* author⟩ [alteration of ¹*premier*]

¹**prem·ise** \'prem-əs\ *n* **1** : a proposition assumed as a basis of argument or inference; *esp* : either of the first two propositions of a syllogism from which the conclusion is drawn **2** *pl* : matters previously stated **3** *pl* **a** : a tract of land with the buildings thereon **b** : a building or part of a building usually with its grounds [Medieval Latin *praemissa*, from Latin *praemittere* "to place ahead", from *prae-* "pre-" + *mittere* "to send"; sense 3 from its being identified in the premises of the deed]

²**premise** *vt* **1** : to set forth beforehand as introductory or as postulated : POSTULATE **2** : to offer as a premise in an argument

¹**pre·mi·um** \'prē-mē-əm\ *n* **1 a** : a reward or recompense for a particular act **b** : a sum over and above a regular price or a face or par value **c** : something given free or at a reduced price with a purchase **2** : the amount paid for a contract of insurance **3** : a high value or a value in excess of that normally or usually expected ⟨put a *premium* on accuracy⟩ [Latin *praemium* "booty, profit, reward", from *prae-* "pre-" + *emere* "to take, buy"] — **at a premium** : usually valuable because of demand ⟨housing was *at a premium*⟩

²**premium** *adj* : of exceptional quality, value, or price

pre·mix \prē-'miks, 'prē-\ *vb* : to mix before use

pre·mo·lar \prē-'mō-lər, 'prē-\ *n* : any of the double-pointed grinding teeth which occur between the true molars and the canines and of which in humans there are two on each side of each jaw — **premolar** *adj*

pre·mo·ni·tion \ˌprē-mə-'nish-ən, ˌprem-ə-\ *n* **1** : previous warning or notice **2** : anticipation of an event without conscious reason : PRESENTIMENT [Middle French, from Late Latin *praemonitio*, from Latin *praemonēre* "to warn in advance", from *prae-* "pre-" + *monēre* "to warn"] — **pre·mon·i·to·ry** \prē-'män-ə-ˌtōr-ē, -ˌtòr-\ *adj*

pre·name \'prē-ˌnām\ *n* : FORENAME

pre·na·tal \prē-'nāt-l, 'prē-\ *adj* : occurring or existing before birth ⟨*prenatal* care⟩ — **pre·na·tal·ly** \-l-ē\ *adv*

pren·tice \'prent-əs\ *n* : APPRENTICE 1, LEARNER — **prentice** *adj*

pre·oc·cu·pied \prē-'äk-yə-ˌpīd\ *adj* **1** : lost in thought ⟨too much *preoccupied* to notice⟩ **2** : already occupied

pre·oc·cu·py *vt* **-pied; -py·ing** **1** \prē-'äk-yə-ˌpī\ : to engage or absorb the attention of beforehand **2** \ˌprē-, 'prē-\ : to take possession of or fill beforehand or be-

\ə\	abut	\ng\	sing
\ər\	further	\ō\	bone
\a\	mat	\ò\	saw
\ā\	take	\òi\	coin
\ä\	cot, cart	\th\	thin
\aù\	out	\th\	this
\ch\	chin	\ü\	food
\e\	pet	\ù\	foot
\ē\	easy	\y\	yet
\g\	go	\yü\	few
\i\	tip	\yù\	cure
\ī\	life	\zh\	vision
\j\	job		

fore another — **pre·oc·cu·pa·tion** \prē-ˌäk-yə-'pā-shən\ *n*

pre·op·er·a·tive \prē-'äp-rət-iv, 'prē-, -'äp-ə-rət-, -'äp-ə-ˌrāt-\ *adj* : occurring before a surgical operation — **pre·op·er·a·tive·ly** *adv*

pre·or·dain \ˌprē-ȯr-'dān\ *vt* : to decree in advance : FOREORDAIN — **pre·or·di·na·tion** \prē-ˌȯrd-n-'ā-shən\ *n*

¹prep \'prep\ *n* : PREPARATORY SCHOOL

²prep *vb* **prepped; prep·ping 1** : to engage in preparatory study or training **2** : to get ready : PREPARE ⟨*prepped* the patient for the operation⟩

prep·a·ra·tion \ˌprep-ə-'rā-shən\ *n* **1** : the action or process of getting something ready (as for use or service) or of getting ready for some occasion, test, or duty **2** : a state of being prepared **3** : a preparatory act or measure **4** : something that is prepared; *esp* : a medicinal material made ready for use

pre·par·a·to·ry \pri-'par-ə-ˌtōr-ē, -ˌtȯr-\ *adj* : preparing or serving to prepare for something : INTRODUCTORY — **pre·par·a·to·ri·ly** \-ˌpar-ə-'tōr-ə-lē, -'tȯr-\ *adv*

preparatory school *n* **1** : a usually private school preparing students primarily for college **2** *British* : a private elementary school preparing students primarily for public schools

pre·pare \pri-'paər, -'peər\ *vb* **1** : to make or get ready ⟨*prepared* them for the shocking news⟩ ⟨*prepare* for a test⟩ **2** : to put together : COMPOUND ⟨*prepare* a vaccine⟩ ⟨*prepare* a prescription⟩ [Middle French *preparer,* from Latin *praeparare,* from *prae-* "pre-" + *parare* "to procure, prepare"] — **pre·par·er** *n*

pre·par·ed·ness \pri-'par-əd-nəs, -'per-; -'paərd-nəs, -'peərd-\ *n* : the quality or state of being prepared

pre·pay \prē-'pā, 'prē-\ *vt* **pre·paid** \-'pād\ **pre·pay·ing** : to pay or pay for in advance — **pre·pay·ment** \-'pā-mənt\ *n*

pre·pon·der·ance \pri-'pän-də-rəns, -drəns\ *n* **1** : a superiority in weight or in power, importance, or strength ⟨the *preponderance* of the evidence⟩ **2** : a superiority or excess in number or quantity ⟨the *preponderance* of lawyers in the legislature⟩

pre·pon·der·ant \pri-'pän-də-rənt, -drənt\ *adj* **1** : outweighing others : PREDOMINANT **2** : having greater frequency or prevalence — **pre·pon·der·ant·ly** *adv*

pre·pon·der·ate \pri-'pän-də-ˌrāt\ *vi* **1** : to exceed in weight, power, or importance : PREDOMINATE **2** : to exceed in numbers [Latin *praeponderare,* literally, "to outweigh", from *prae-* "pre-" + *ponder-, pondus* "weight"] — **pre·pon·der·a·tion** \-ˌpän-də-'rā-shən\ *n*

prep·o·si·tion \ˌprep-ə-'zish-ən\ *n* : a linguistic form that combines with a noun, pronoun, or nominal to form a phrase that typically has an adverbial, adjectival, or substantival relation to some other word [Latin *praepositio,* from *praeponere* "to put in front", from *prae-* "pre-" + *ponere* "to put, place"] — **prep·o·si·tion·al** \-'zish-nəl, -ən-l\ *adj* — **prep·o·si·tion·al·ly** \-ē\ *adv*

pre·pos·sess \ˌprē-pə-'zes\ *vt* **1** : to cause to be preoccupied (as with an idea or belief) **2** : to influence beforehand; *esp* : to move to a favorable opinion beforehand

pre·pos·sess·ing *adj* : tending to create a favorable impression : ATTRACTIVE ⟨a *prepossessing* appearance⟩ — **pre·pos·sess·ing·ly** \-ing-lē\ *adv* — **pre·pos·sess·ing·ness** *n*

pre·pos·ses·sion \ˌprē-pə-'zesh-ən\ *n* **1** : an attitude, belief, or impression formed beforehand : PREJUDICE **2** : an exclusive concern with one idea or object

pre·pos·ter·ous \pri-'päs-tə-rəs, -trəs\ *adj* : contrary to nature, reason, or common sense : ABSURD [Latin *praeposterus,* literally, "with the back part in front", from *prae-* "pre-" + *posterus* "hinder, posterior"] — **pre·pos·ter·ous·ly** *adv* — **pre·pos·ter·ous·ness** *n*

pre·po·tent \prē-'pōt-nt, 'prē-\ *adj* : having an unusual ability to transmit characters to offspring ⟨a *prepotent* sire⟩ — **pre·po·ten·cy** \-n-sē\ *n*

pre·pu·ber·ty \-'pyü-bərt-ē\ *n* : the period immediately preceding puberty — **pre·pu·ber·tal** \-bərt-l\ *adj*

pre·puce \'prē-ˌpyüs\ *n* : FORESKIN; *also* : a similar fold investing the clitoris [Middle French, from Latin *praeputium*] — **pre·pu·tial** \'prē-'pyü-shəl\ *n*

pre·re·cord \ˌprē-ri-'kȯrd\ *vt* : to record (as a radio or television program) in advance of presentation or use

pre·reg·is·tra·tion \ˌprē-ˌrej-ə-'strā-shən\ *n* : a special registration (as for returning students) prior to an official registration period — **pre·reg·is·ter** *vb*

pre·req·ui·site \prē-'rek-wə-zət, 'prē-\ *n* : something that is required beforehand or is necessary as a preliminary to something else ⟨the course is a *prerequisite* for more advanced study⟩ — **prerequisite** *adj*

pre·rog·a·tive \pri-'räg-ət-iv\ *n* : a special privilege or advantage; *esp* : a right attached to an office, rank, or status ⟨a royal *prerogative*⟩ [Latin *praerogativa* "Roman century voting first in the assembly, privilege", from *praerogativus* "voting first", from *praerogare* "to ask for an opinion before another", from *prae-* "pre-" + *rogare* "to ask"]

¹pres·age \'pres-ij\ *n* **1** : something that foreshadows or portends a future event : OMEN **2** : FOREBODING, PRESENTIMENT [Latin *praesagium,* from *praesagire* "to forebode", from *prae-* "pre-" + *sagire* "to perceive keenly"] — **pre·sage·ful** \pri-'sāj-fəl\ *adj*

²pre·sage \'pres-ij, pri-'sāj\ *vt* **1** : to give an omen or warning of : FORESHADOW, PORTEND **2** : FORETELL, PREDICT

pre·sanc·ti·fied \prē-'sang-ti-ˌfīd, 'prē-, -'sangk-\ *adj* : consecrated at a previous service — used of eucharistic elements

pres·by·o·pia \ˌprez-bē-'ō-pē-ə, ˌpres-\ *n* : a visual condition of old age in which loss of elasticity of the lens of the eye causes defective accommodation and inability to focus sharply for near vision [Greek *presbys* "old man"] — **pres·by·opic** \-'ō-pik, -'äp-ik\ *adj or n*

pres·by·ter \'prez-bət-ər, 'pres-\ *n* **1** : a member of the governing body of an early Christian church **2** : a Christian priest [Late Latin, "elder, priest", from Greek *presbyteros,* from *presbys* "old man"] — **pres·byt·er·ate** \prez-'bit-ə-rət, pres-\ *n*

Pres·by·te·ri·an \ˌprez-bə-'tir-ē-ən, ˌpres-\ *adj* **1** *often not cap* : characterized by a system of representative governing councils of ministers and elders **2** : of, relating to, or constituting a Protestant Christian church that is presbyterian in government and traditionally Calvinistic in doctrine — **Presbyterian** *n* — **Pres·by·te·ri·an·ism** \-ē-ə-ˌniz-əm\ *n*

pres·by·tery \'prez-bə-ˌter-ē, 'pres-\ *n, pl* **-ter·ies 1** : the part of a church reserved for the officiating clergy **2** : a ruling body in presbyterian churches consisting of the ministers and representative elders from congregations within a district **3** : the territorial jurisdiction of a presbytery

pre·school \'prē-'skül\ *adj* : of, relating to, or being the period in a child's life from infancy to the age of five or six

pre·science \'prēsh-əns, 'presh-, -ē-əns\ : foreknowledge of events: **a** : omniscience with regard to the future **b** : FORESIGHT 1 [Late Latin *praescientia,* from Latin *praescire* "to know beforehand", from *prae-* "pre-" + *scire* "to know"] — **pre·scient** \-ənt\ *adj* — **pre·scient·ly** *adv*

pre·scribe \pri-'skrīb\ *vb* **1 a** : to lay down as a guide, direction, or rule of action : ORDAIN ⟨*prescribe* a way of life⟩ **b** : to specify with authority ⟨*prescribed* the courses for freshmen⟩ **2** : to order or direct the use of something as a remedy ⟨the doctor *prescribed* rest⟩ [Latin *praescribere* "to write at the beginning, dictate, order", from *prae-* "pre-" + *scribere* "to write"] — **pre·scrib·er** *n*

pre·script \'prē-ˌskript\ *n* : something prescribed — **prescript** *adj*

pre·scrip·tion \pri-'skrip-shən\ *n* **1 a** : the establishment of a claim of title to something usually by use and enjoyment for a fixed period **b** : the right or title acquired by possession **2** : the action of laying down authoritative rules or directions **3 a** : a written direction or order for the preparation and use of a medicine **b** : a medicine prescribed [Latin *praescriptio* "writing at the beginning, order", from *praescriptus,* past participle of *praescribere* "to write at the beginning, order"] — **pre·scrip·tive** \-'skrip-tiv\ *adj* — **pre·scrip·tive·ly** *adv*

pres·ence \'prez-ns\ *n* **1** : the fact or condition of being present ⟨no one noticed my *presence*⟩ **2 a** : the part of space within one's immediate vicinity ⟨felt awkward in their *presence*⟩ **b** : the neighborhood of one of superior and especially royal rank **3** : one that is present ⟨an influential *presence* in the group⟩ **4** : the bearing or air of a person; *esp* : stately or distinguished bearing **5** : something (as a spirit) felt to be present

presence chamber *n* : the room where a dignitary receives those entitled to come into his or her presence

presence of mind : self-control in an emergency such that one can say and do the right thing

¹pres·ent \'prez-nt\ *n* : something presented : GIFT [Old French, from *presenter* "to present"]

²pre·sent \pri-'zent\ *vt* **1 a** : to bring or introduce into the presence of someone; *esp* : to introduce socially **b** : to bring (as a play) before the public **2** : to make a gift to **3** : to give or bestow formally **4** : to lay (a charge) against a person **5** : to offer to view : DISPLAY, SHOW **6** : to aim, point, or direct (as a weapon) so as to face something or in a particular direction [Old French *presenter,* from Latin *praesentare,* from *praesens,* adj., "present"] SYN see GIVE — **pre·sent·er** *n*

³pres·ent \'prez-nt\ *adj* **1** : now existing or in progress **2 a** : being in view or at hand **b** : existing in something mentioned or under consideration **3** : of, relating to, or being a verb tense that expresses present time or the time of speaking [Old French, from Latin *praesens,* from *praeesse* "to be before one", from *prae-* "pre-" + *esse* "to be"]

⁴pres·ent \'prez-nt\ *n* **1** *pl* : the present words or statements; *also* : the document in which these words are used ⟨know all men by these *presents*⟩ **2 a** : PRESENT TENSE **b** : a verb form in the present tense **3** : the present time

pre·sent·able \pri-'zent-ə-bəl\ *adj* **1** : capable of being presented ⟨whipped the speech into *presentable* form⟩ **2** : being in condition to be seen or inspected especially by the critical ⟨made the room *presentable*⟩ — **pre·sent·abil·i·ty** \-,zent-ə-'bil-ət-ē\ *n* — **pre·sent·able·ness** \-'zent-ə-bəl-nəs\ *n* — **pre·sent·ably** \-blē\ *adv*

pre·sen·ta·tion \,prē-,zen-'tā-shən, ,prez-n-\ *n* **1** : the act of presenting **2** : something presented: as **a** : something offered or given : GIFT **b** : something set forth for one's attention **3** : the position in which the fetus lies in the uterus in labor with respect to the opening through which it passes in birth — **pre·sen·ta·tion·al** \-shnəl, -shən-l\ *adj*

pres·ent–day \,prez-nt-,dā\ *adj* : now existing or occurring

pre·sen·ti·ment \pri-'zent-ə-mənt\ *n* : a feeling that something will or is about to happen : PREMONITION [French *pressentiment,* from *pressentir* "to have a presentiment", from Latin *praesentire* "to feel beforehand", from *prae-* "pre-" + *sentire* "to feel"]

pres·ent·ly \'prez-nt-lē\ *adv* **1** *archaic* : at once **2** : before long : SOON ⟨*presently* they arrived⟩ **3** : at the present time : NOW ⟨*presently* we have none⟩

pre·sent·ment \pri-'zent-mənt\ *n* **1** : the act of presenting; *esp* : the act of offering a draft or a promissory note at the proper time and place to be paid by another **2 a** : the act of presenting to view or consciousness **b** : something set forth, presented, or exhibited

present participle *n* : a participle that expresses present action in relation to the time expressed by the finite verb in its clause and that in English is formed with the suffix *-ing* and is used in the formation of the progressive tenses

present perfect *adj* : of, relating to, or constituting a verb tense formed in English with *have* and expressing action or state completed at the time of speaking — **present perfect** *n*

present tense *n* : the tense of a verb that expresses action or state in the present time and is used of what occurs or is true at the time of speaking and of what is habitual or characteristic or is always or necessarily true, that is sometimes used to refer to action in the past (as in the historical present), and that is sometimes used for future events

¹pre·ser·va·tive \pri-'zər-vət-iv\ *adj* : having the power of preserving

²preservative *n* : something that preserves; *esp* : an additive used to protect against decay, discoloration, or spoilage

¹pre·serve \pri-'zərv\ *vt* **1** : to keep safe from harm or destruction : PROTECT ⟨*preserve* the republic⟩ **2 a** : to keep alive, intact, or free from decay ⟨*preserve* laboratory specimens⟩ **b** : to keep up : MAINTAIN **3 a** : to keep from decomposition **b** : to prepare (as by canning or pickling) for future use ⟨*preserve* beets⟩ [Middle French *preserver,* from Medieval Latin *praeservare,* from Latin *prae-* "pre-" + *servare* "to keep, guard"] — **pre·serv·able** \pri-'zər-və-bəl\ *adj* — **pres·er·va·tion** \,prez-ər-'vā-shən\ *n* — **pre·serv·er** *n*

²preserve *n* **1** : fruit canned or made into jams or jellies or cooked whole or in large pieces in a syrup so as to keep its shape — often used in pl. ⟨strawberry *preserves*⟩ **2** : an area restricted for the protection and preservation of natural resources (as animals and trees); *esp* : one used primarily for regulated hunting or fishing **3** : something regarded as reserved for certain persons

pre·shrink \'prē-'shringk\ *vt* **pre·shrank; pre·shrunk** : to shrink (as a fabric) before making into a garment so that the garment will not shrink much when washed

pre·side \pri-'zīd\ *vi* **1 a** : to occupy the place of authority : act as chairman **b** : to occupy a position similar to that of a president or chairman ⟨*preside* over a ceremony⟩ **2** : to exercise guidance or control ⟨*presided* over the destinies of the empire⟩ **3** : to occupy a position of featured instrumental performer [Latin *praesidēre,* literally, "to sit at the head of", from *prae-* "pre-" + *sedēre* "to sit"] — **pre·sid·er** *n*

pres·i·den·cy \'prez-əd-ən-sē, 'prez-dən-; 'prez-ə-,den-sē\ *n, pl* **-cies 1** : the office or term of a president **2** : an executive council in the Mormon Church

pres·i·dent \'prez-əd-ənt, 'prez-dənt, 'prez-ə-,dent\ *n* **1** : one who presides over a meeting or assembly **2** : an appointed governor of a subordinate political unit **3** : the chief officer of an organization (as a corporation) **4** : the presiding officer of a governmental body **5 a** : an elected official serving as both chief of state and chief political executive in a republic having a presidential government **b** : an elected official having the position of chief of state but usually only minimal political powers in a republic having a parliamentary government [Middle French, from Latin *praesidens,* from *praesidēre* "to preside"] — **pres·i·den·tial** \,prez-ə-'den-chəl\ *adj*

Presidents' Day *n* : WASHINGTON'S BIRTHDAY 2

pre·si·dio \pri-'sēd-ē-,ō, -'sid-, -'zēd-, -'zid-\ *n, pl* **-di·os** : a garrisoned place; *esp* : a military post or fortified settlement in areas currently or originally under Spanish control [Spanish, from Latin *praesidium*]

pre·sid·i·um \pri-'sid-ē-əm, -'zid-\ *n, pl* **-ia** \-ē-ə\ *or* **-i·ums** : a permanent executive committee selected especially in Communist countries to act for a larger body [Russian *prezidium,* from Latin *praesidium* "garri-

\ə\ abut	\ng\ sing
\ər\ further	\ō\ bone
\a\ mat	\ȯ\ saw
\ā\ take	\ȯi\ coin
\ä\ cot, cart	\th\ thin
\au̇\ out	\th\ this
\ch\ chin	\ü\ food
\e\ pet	\u̇\ foot
\ē\ easy	\y\ yet
\g\ go	\yü\ few
\i\ tip	\yu̇\ cure
\ī\ life	\zh\ vision
\j\ job	

son'', from *praesid-*, *praeses* ''guard, governor'', from *praesidēre* ''to guard, preside'']

¹pre·soak \prē-'sōk\ *vt* : to soak before washing

²pre·soak \'prē-ˌsōk\ *n* **1** : an instance of presoaking **2** : a product used for presoaking clothes

pre·sort \prē-'sórt\ *vb* : to sort (outgoing mail) by zip code usually before delivery to a post office

¹press \'pres\ *n* **1** : a crowd or a crowded condition **2** : an apparatus or machine for exerting pressure (as for shaping material, extracting liquid, drilling, or preventing something from warping) **3** : CLOSET 2 **4 a** : an act of pressing or pushing : PRESSURE **b** : an aggressive defense in basketball **5** : the properly smoothed and creased condition of a freshly pressed garment **6 a** : PRINTING PRESS **b** : the act or the process of printing **c** : a printing or publishing establishment **7 a** : the gathering and publishing of news : JOURNALISM **b** : newspapers, periodicals, and often radio and television news broadcasting **c** : comment or notice in newspapers and periodicals ⟨is getting good *press*⟩ [Old French *presse*, from *presser* ''to press'']

¹press 6a

²press *vb* **1** : to act upon through steady pushing or thrusting force exerted in contact : SQUEEZE **2 a** : ASSAIL **b** : OPPRESS 1 **3 a** : to squeeze out the juice or contents of ⟨*press* grapes⟩ **b** : to squeeze out ⟨*press* juice from grapes⟩ **4 a** : to shape by pressure (as with an apparatus) **b** : to smooth by pressure and especially by ironing **5** : to urge strongly or forcefully : CONSTRAIN ⟨*pressed* them to attend⟩ **6 a** : to present earnestly or insistently ⟨*press* a claim⟩ **b** : to follow through (a course of action) **7** : to clasp in affection or courtesy : EMBRACE **8 a** : to crowd closely : MASS ⟨reporters *pressed* around the celebrity⟩ **b** : to force or push one's way ⟨*pressed* forward through the throng⟩ **9** : to seek urgently : CONTEND ⟨*pressed* for higher salaries⟩ [Middle French *presser*, from Latin *pressare*, from *pressus*, past participle of *premere* ''to press''] — **press·er** *n*

³press *vt* : to force into service especially in an army or navy : IMPRESS [obsolete *prest* ''to enlist by giving pay in advance'', derived from Latin *praestare* ''to be responsible for, perform, pay'']

press agent *n* : an agent employed to establish and maintain good public relations through publicity

press box *n* : a space reserved for reporters (as at a baseball or football game)

press conference *n* : an interview given by a public figure to newsmen by appointment

press–gang \'pres-ˌgang\ *n* : a detachment of men formerly empowered to force men into military or naval service [³*press*]

press·ing *adj* **1** : urgently important : CRITICAL ⟨the *pressing* national interest⟩ **2** : EARNEST, WARM ⟨a *pressing* invitation⟩ — **press·ing·ly** \-ing-lē\ *adv*

press·man \'pres-mən, -ˌman\ *n* **1** : an operator of a press; *esp* : the operator of a printing press **2** *British* : NEWSPAPERMAN

pres·sor \'pres-ˌòr, -ər\ *adj* : raising or tending to raise blood pressure [Late Latin, ''one that presses'', from Latin *pressus*, past participle of *premere* ''to press'']

press release *n* : material given in advance to a newspaper for publication at a future date

press·room \'pres-ˌrüm, -ˌrùm\ *n* : a room in a printing plant containing the printing presses

press secretary *n* : a person officially in charge of press relations for a prominent public figure

¹pres·sure \'presh-ər\ *n* **1 a** : a painful feeling of weight or burden : OPPRESSION, DISTRESS **b** : a burdensome or restricting force or influence ⟨the *pressure* of taxes⟩ ⟨the constant *pressures* of modern life⟩ **2 a** : the action of pressing ⟨use steady *pressure*⟩ **b** : the condition of being pressed ⟨kept under *pressure*⟩ **3 a** : the action of a force against an opposing force **b** : the force exerted over a surface divided by its area **c** : ELECTROMOTIVE FORCE **4** : the stress of matters demand-

ing attention : URGENCY **5** : the force exerted by the weight of the atmosphere

²pressure *vt* **pres·sured; pres·sur·ing** \'presh-ring, -ə-ring\ **1** : to apply pressure to : CONSTRAIN **2** : PRESSURIZE **3** : to cook in a pressure cooker

pressure cooker *n* : an airtight utensil for quick cooking or preserving of foods by means of steam under pressure — **pressure–cook** \ˌpresh-ər-'kùk\ *vb*

pressure group *n* : an interest group that seeks to influence governmental policy but not to elect candidates to office

pressure point *n* : a point where a blood vessel runs near a bone and can be compressed (as to check bleeding) by pressure against the bone

pressure suit *n* : an inflatable suit for high-altitude or space flight to protect the body from low pressure

pres·sur·ize \'presh-ə-ˌrīz\ *vt* **1** : to maintain near-normal atmospheric pressure in (as an airplane cabin) during high-altitude or space flight **2** : to apply pressure to — **pres·sur·iza·tion** \ˌpresh-ə-rə-'zā-shən\ *n* — **pres·sur·iz·er** *n*

pres·ti·dig·i·ta·tion \ˌpres-tə-ˌdij-ə-'tā-shən\ *n* : SLEIGHT OF HAND 1, LEGERDEMAIN [French, from *presti-digitateur* ''prestidigitator'', from *preste* ''nimble, quick'', (from Italian *presto*) + Latin *digitus* ''finger''] — **pres·ti·dig·i·ta·tor** \-'dij-ə-ˌtāt-ər\ *n*

pres·tige \pre-'stēzh, -'stēj\ *n* : usually high standing or fine reputation based on past performance or merit [French, from Middle French, ''conjuror's trick, illusion'', from Latin *praestigiae*, pl., ''conjuror's tricks'', from *praestringere* ''to blindfold'', from *prae-* ''pre-'' + *stringere* ''to bind tight''] — **pres·ti·gious** \-'stij-əs\ *adj* — **pres·ti·gious·ly** *adv* — **pres·ti·gious·ness** *n*

pres·to \'pres-tō\ *adv or adj* **1** : suddenly as if by magic ⟨*presto*, it's gone⟩ **2** : at a rapid tempo — used as a direction in music [Italian, ''quick, quickly'', from Latin *praestus* ''ready'', from *praesto*, adv., ''on hand'']

pre·sume \pri-'züm\ *vb* **1** : to undertake without leave or clear justification : DARE ⟨*presume* to question the authority of a superior⟩ **2** : to expect or assume especially with confidence **3** : to suppose to be true without proof ⟨*presumed* innocent until proved guilty⟩ **4** : to act or behave boldly without reason [Late Latin *praesumere* ''to dare'', from Latin, ''to anticipate, assume'', from *prae-* ''pre-'' + *sumere* ''to take''] SYN see ASSUME — **pre·sum·able** \-'zü-mə-bəl\ *adj* — **pre·sum·er** *n*

pre·sum·ably \pri-'zü-mə-blē\ *adv* : one would presume : it seems likely : PROBABLY

pre·sum·ing *adj* : PRESUMPTUOUS — **pre·sum·ing·ly** \-'zü-ming-lē\ *adv*

pre·sump·tion \pri-'zəm-shən, -'zəmp-\ *n* **1** : presumptuous attitude or conduct : AUDACITY **2 a** : a conclusion reached on strong grounds of belief : something believed to be so but not proved **b** : the grounds or evidence leading one to believe something [Old French, from Latin *praesumptio* ''assumption'', from *praesumere* ''to assume'']

pre·sump·tive \-'zəm-tiv, -'zəmp-\ *adj* **1** : giving grounds for reasonable opinion or belief ⟨*presumptive* evidence⟩ **2** : based on probability or presumption ⟨the *presumptive* heir⟩ — **pre·sump·tive·ly** *adv*

pre·sump·tu·ous \pri-'zəm-chə-wəs, -'zəmp-, -chəs, -shəs\ *adj* : overstepping due bounds : taking liberties — **pre·sump·tu·ous·ly** *adv* — **pre·sump·tu·ous·ness** *n*

pre·sup·pose \ˌprē-sə-'pōz\ *vt* : to suppose beforehand ⟨a book that *presupposes* wide knowledge in its readers⟩ — **pre·sup·po·si·tion** \prē-ˌsəp-ə-'zish-ən\ *n*

pre·sweet·ened \'prē-'swēt-ənd\ *adj* : sweetened by the manufacturer ⟨*presweetened* cereal⟩

¹pre·teen \'prē-'tēn\ *n* : a boy or girl not yet 13 years old

²preteen *adj* **1** : relating to or produced for children especially in the 9 to 12 year-old age group ⟨*preteen* fashions⟩ **2** : being younger than 13

¹**pre·tend** \pri-'tend\ *vb* **1 :** to give a false appearance of being, possessing, or performing **: PROFESS 2 a :** to make believe **: FEIGN b :** to claim, represent, or assert falsely **3 :** to put in a claim (as to a throne or title) [Latin *praetendere* "to allege as an excuse", literally, "to stretch in front of like a curtain", from *prae-* "pre-" + *tendere* "to stretch"]

²**pretend** *adj* **: IMAGINARY, MAKE-BELIEVE**

pre·tend·ed *adj* **:** professed or avowed but not genuine ⟨*pretended* affection⟩ — **pre·tend·ed·ly** *adv*

pre·tend·er \pri-'ten-dər\ *n* **:** one that pretends; *esp* **:** a claimant to a throne who has no just title

pre·tense *or* **pre·tence** \'prē-,tens, pri-'\ *n* **1 :** a claim made or implied and usually not supported by fact **2 a :** mere show **: OSTENTATION b :** a pretentious act or assertion **3 :** an insincere attempt to attain a condition or quality **4 :** professed rather than real intention or purpose **: PRETEXT 5 : MAKE-BELIEVE, FICTION 6 :** false show **: SIMULATION** ⟨saw through your *pretense* of indifference⟩ [Middle French *pretensse,* derived from Latin *praetendere* "to allege as an excuse"]

pre·ten·sion \pri-'ten-chən\ *n* **1 : PRETEXT 2 :** an effort to establish a claim **3 :** a claim or right to attention or honor because of merit **4 : VANITY 2c** — **pre·ten·sion·less** \-ləs\ *adj*

pre·ten·tious \-chəs\ *adj* **1 :** making or having claims especially as to excellence or worth **: SHOWY** ⟨living in a *pretentious* style⟩ **2 :** making demands on one's skill, ability, or means **: AMBITIOUS** ⟨*pretentious* plans⟩ [French *prétentieux,* derived from Latin *praetendere* "to allege as an excuse"] — **pre·ten·tious·ly** *adv* — **pre·ten·tious·ness** *n*

pret·er·it *or* **pret·er·ite** \'pret-ə-rət\ *n* **: PAST TENSE** [Middle French *preterit,* from Latin *praeteritus,* from *praeterire* "to go by, pass", from *praeter* "beyond, past", + *ire* "to go"]

pre·ter·nat·u·ral \,prēt-ər-'nach-rəl, -ə-rəl\ *adj* **1 :** not conforming to what is natural or regular in nature **: ABNORMAL 2 :** inexplicable by ordinary means; *esp* **: PSYCHIC** [Medieval Latin *praeternaturalis,* from Latin *praeter naturam* "beyond nature"] — **pre·ter·nat·u·ral·ly** \-'nach-rə-lē, -ə-rə-; -'nach-ər-lē\ *adv* — **pre·ter·nat·u·ral·ness** \-'nach-rəl-nəs, -ə-rəl-\ *n*

pre·test \'prē-,test, prē-'\ *n* **:** a preliminary test serving for exploration rather than evaluation — **pretest** *vt*

pre·text \'prē-,tekst\ *n* **:** a purpose or motive put forward in order to conceal a real intention or state of affairs [Latin *praetextus,* from *praetexere* "to assign as a pretext", literally, "to weave in front", from *prae-* "pre-" + *texere* "to weave"]

pret·ti·fy \'prit-i-,fī, 'pûrt-\ *vt* **-fied; -fy·ing :** to make pretty — **pret·ti·fi·ca·tion** \,prit-i-fə-'kā-shən, ,pûrt-\ *n*

¹**pret·ty** \'prit-ē, 'pûrt-\ *adj* **pret·ti·er; -est 1 a : ARTFUL 1, CLEVER b : PAT 1a, APT 2 :** pleasing by delicacy or grace especially of appearance or sound **:** conventionally attractive but without elements of grandeur, stateliness, and excellence usually associated with true beauty ⟨a *pretty* face⟩ ⟨light *pretty* tunes⟩ ⟨a *pretty* manner⟩ **3 : MISERABLE** ⟨a *pretty* mess we're in⟩ **4 :** moderately large **: CONSIDERABLE** ⟨a very *pretty* profit⟩ [Old English *prættig* "tricky", from *prætt* "trick"] **SYN** *see* **BEAUTIFUL** — **pret·ti·ly** \'prit-l-ē, 'pûrt-\ *adv* — **pret·ti·ness** \'prit-ē-nəs, 'pûrt-\ *n* — **pret·ty·ish** \-ē-ish\ *adj*

²**pret·ty** \'prit-ē, pərt-ē\ *adv* **:** in some degree **: MODERATELY** ⟨*pretty* cold weather⟩

³**pretty** *like*¹\ *n, pl* **pretties 1 :** a pretty person or thing **2** *pl* **:** dainty clothes

pret·zel \'pret-səl\ *n* **:** a brittle glazed and salted cracker typically shaped like a loose knot [German *brezel,* derived from Latin *brachiatus* "having branches like arms", from *brachium* "arm"] □ **ORIGIN** Pretzels were most likely introduced into the United States during the 19th century by German immigrants. Our word *pretzel* comes from the German *brezel.* The familiar knot-shaped pretzel has been known, at least in Germanic countries, for centuries. Its name is derived from Latin *brachiatus,* which means "having branches like arms". Apparently the pretzel is so called because of the similarity between its knot shape and a pair of folded arms.

pre·vail \pri-'vāl\ *vi* **1 :** to gain ascendancy through strength or superiority **: TRIUMPH 2 :** to be or become effective or effectual **3 :** to urge successfully ⟨was *prevailed* upon to sing⟩ **4 :** to be frequent **: PREDOMINATE** ⟨the west winds that *prevail* in the mountains⟩ **5 :** to be or continue in use or fashion **: PERSIST** ⟨a custom that still *prevails*⟩ [Latin *praevalēre,* from *prae-* "pre-" + *valēre* "to be strong"]

pre·vail·ing *adj* **1 :** having superior force or influence **2 a :** most frequent ⟨*prevailing* winds⟩ **b :** generally current **: COMMON** — **pre·vail·ing·ly** \-'vā-ling-lē\ *adv* □ **SYN PREVAILING, PREVALENT, CURRENT** mean generally circulated, accepted, or used in a certain time or place. **PREVAILING** applies especially to something that is predominant ⟨*prevailing* opinion⟩ **PREVALENT** implies widespread frequency ⟨a *prevalent* custom⟩ ⟨a disease that is *prevalent* in many countries⟩ **CURRENT** applies to things subject to change and implies prevalence at the present time ⟨*current* fashions⟩ ⟨*current* scientific trends⟩

prev·a·lent \'prev-lənt, -ə-lənt\ *adj* **1** *archaic* **:** being in ascendancy **: DOMINANT 2 :** generally or widely accepted, practiced, or favored **: WIDESPREAD** [Latin *praevalens* "very powerful", from *praevalēre* "to prevail"] **SYN** *see* **PREVAILING** — **prev·a·lence** \-ləns\ *n* — **prev·a·lent·ly** *adv*

pre·var·i·cate \pri-'var-ə-,kāt\ *vi* **:** to avoid telling the truth [Latin *praevaricari* "to walk crookedly", from *prae-* "pre-" + *varicus* "having the feet spread apart", from *varus* "bent, knock-kneed"] — **pre·var·i·ca·tion** \-,var-ə-'kā-shən\ *n* — **pre·var·i·ca·tor** \-'var-ə-,kāt-ər\ *n*

pre·vent \pri-'vent\ *vt* **1 :** to keep from happening or existing ⟨steps to *prevent* war⟩ **2 :** to hold or keep back **: STOP, HINDER** ⟨there's nothing to *prevent* us from going⟩ [Latin *praeventus,* past participle of *praevenire* "to come before, anticipate, forestall", from *prae-* "pre-" + *venire* "to come"] — **pre·vent·able** *also* **pre·vent·ible** \-ə-bəl\ *adj* — **pre·vent·er** *n* □ **SYN PREVENT, AVERT, FORESTALL** mean to stop something from coming or occurring. **PREVENT** implies placing an insurmountable obstacle or impediment ⟨took measures to *prevent* an epidemic⟩ **AVERT** implies taking immediate or effective measures to force back, avoid, or counteract a threatening evil ⟨efforts to *avert* a revolution⟩ **FORESTALL** implies forehanded action to stop or interrupt something in its course ⟨radar helped *forestall* surprise attacks⟩

pre·ven·ta·tive \-'vent-ət-iv\ *adj or n* **: PREVENTIVE**

pre·ven·tion \pri-'ven-chən\ *n* **:** the act of preventing

¹**pre·ven·tive** \-'vent-iv\ *n* **:** something that prevents; *esp* **:** something used to prevent disease

²**preventive** *adj* **:** devoted to, concerned with, or undertaken for prevention — **pre·ven·tive·ly** *adv* — **pre·ven·tive·ness** *n*

¹**pre·view** \'prē-,vyü\ *vt* **:** to view or to show in advance

²**preview** *n* **1 :** an advance showing or performance **2** *also* **pre·vue** \-,vyü\ **:** a showing of snatches from a motion picture advertised for appearance in the near future **3 :** an advance statement, sample, or survey

pre·vi·ous \'prē-vē-əs\ *adj* **1 :** going before in time or order ⟨the *previous* lesson⟩ **2 :** acting too soon **: PREMATURE** ⟨was a bit *previous* with the answer⟩ [Latin *praevius* "leading the way", from *prae-* "pre-" + *via* "way"] — **pre·vi·ous·ly** *adv* — **pre·vi·ous·ness** *n*

previous question *n* **:** a parliamentary motion that the pending question be put to an immediate vote without further debate or amendment

previous to *prep* **:** prior to **: BEFORE**

\ə\ abut	\ng\ sing
\ər\ further	\ō\ bone
\a\ mat	\ȯ\ saw
\ā\ take	\ȯi\ coin
\ä\ cot, cart	\th\ thin
\au̇\ out	\t̲h̲\ this
\ch\ chin	\ü\ food
\e\ pet	\u̇\ foot
\ē\ easy	\y\ yet
\g\ go	\yü\ few
\i\ tip	\yu̇\ cure
\ī\ life	\zh\ vision
\j\ job	

¹pre·vi·sion \prē-'vizh-ən\ *n* **1** : FORESIGHT 1, PRE-SCIENCE **2** : FORECAST, PREDICTION — **pre·vi·sion·al** \-'vizh-nəl, -ən-l\ *adj* — **pre·vi·sion·ary** \-'vizh-ə-,ner-ē\ *adj*

²prevision *vt* : FORESEE

pre·vo·cal·ic \,prē-vō-'kal-ik\ *adj* : immediately preceding a vowel

pre·writ·ing \'prē-,rīt-ing\ *n* : planning and getting ideas in order before writing

¹prey \'prā\ *n* **1 a** : an animal taken by a predator as food **b** : one that is helpless or unable to resist attack : VICTIM **2** : the act or habit of preying [Old French *preie* "booty, prey", from Latin *praeda*]

²prey *vi* **1** : to raid for booty **2** : to seize and devour something as prey **3** : to have an injurious, destructive, or wasting effect ⟨fears that *prey* on the mind⟩ — **prey·er** *n*

¹price \'prīs\ *n* **1 a** : the quantity of one thing that is exchanged or sought in barter or sale for another **b** : the amount of money given or asked for a specified thing **2** : the terms for the sake of which something is done or undertaken: as **a** : an amount sufficient to bribe one **b** : a reward for the apprehension or death of a person **3** : the cost at which something is obtainable ⟨the *price* of freedom⟩ [Old French *pris*, from Latin *pretium* "price, money"] SYN see WORTH

²price *vt* **1** : to set a price on **2** : to ask the price of **3** : to drive by raising prices excessively — **pric·er** *n*

price–cut·ter \'prī-,skət-ər\ *n* : one that reduces prices especially to a level designed to cripple competition

price·less \'prī-sləs\ *adj* **1** : having a value beyond any price : INVALUABLE **2** : surprisingly amusing, odd, or absurd

price support *n* : artificial maintenance of prices of a commodity at a level usually fixed through government action

price tag *n* **1** : a tag on merchandise showing the price at which it is offered for sale **2** : PRICE 1b, COST

price war *n* : a period of commercial competition in which prices are repeatedly cut below those of competitors

¹prick \'prik\ *n* **1** : a mark or shallow hole made by a pointed instrument **2** : a pointed instrument or part **3** : an instance of pricking or the sensation of being pricked [Old English *prica*]

²prick *vb* **1 a** : to pierce slightly with a sharp point **b** : to have or cause a pricking sensation **2** : to cause to feel anguish, grief, or remorse ⟨if your conscience *pricks* you⟩ **3** : to urge a horse with spurs **4** : to mark or outline with or as if with pricks ⟨*prick* a design on paper⟩ **5** : to make or become erect ⟨the dog *pricked* its ears⟩ — **prick up one's ears** : to listen intently

prick·er \'prik-ər\ *n* **1** : one that pricks **2** : PRICKLE 1, THORN

¹prick·le \'prik-əl\ *n* **1** : a fine sharp projection; *esp* : a sharp pointed process of the epidermis or bark of a plant **2** : a prickling sensation [Old English *pricle*]

²prickle *vb* **prickled; prick·ling** \'prik-ling, -ə-ling\ **1** : to prick slightly **2** : TINGLE

prick·ly \'prik-lē\ *adj* **prick·li·er; -est** **1** : full of or covered with prickles ⟨*prickly* plants⟩ **2** : marked by prickling ⟨a *prickly* sensation⟩ — **prick·li·ness** *n*

prickly heat *n* : a skin eruption of red pimples with intense itching and tingling caused by inflammation around the sweat ducts

prickly pear *n* **1** : any of numerous flat-jointed often prickly cacti **2** : the pear-shaped edible pulpy fruit of a prickly pear

¹pride \'prīd\ *n* **1** : the quality or state of being proud: as **a** : excessive self-esteem : CONCEIT **b** : a reasonable or justifiable self-respect **c** : pleasure or satisfaction taken in some act, accomplishment, or possession **2** : proud or disdainful behavior or treatment : DISDAIN **3** : something that is or is fit to be a source of pride ⟨this

pup is the *pride* of the litter⟩ **4** : a company of lions [Old English *prȳde*, from *prūd* "proud"]

²pride *vt* : to indulge in pride : PLUME ⟨*pride* oneself on one's skill⟩

pride·ful \'prīd-fəl\ *adj* : full of pride: as **a** : HAUGHTY **b** : ELATED — **pride·ful·ly** \-fə-lē\ *adv* — **pride·ful·ness** *n*

prie–dieu \prēd-'yər, -'yù, -'yœ̄\ *n, pl* **prie–dieux** *same or* -'yərz, -'yùz, -'yœ̄z\ : a small kneeling bench designed for use by a person at prayer and fitted with a raised shelf on which the elbows or a book may be rested [French, literally, "pray God"]

priest \'prēst\ *n* : a person who has the authority to conduct religious rites [Old English *prēost*, from Late Latin *presbyter* "elder, priest", from Greek *presbyteros*, from *presbys* "old man"]

priest·ess \'prē-stəs\ *n* : a woman who is a priest ⟨ancient Roman *priestesses*⟩

priest·hood \'prēst-,hùd, 'prē-,stùd\ *n* **1** : the office, dignity, or status of a priest **2** : the whole group of priests

priest·ly \'prēst-lē\ *adj* **priest·li·er; -est** **1** : of or relating to a priest or the priesthood **2** : characteristic of or befitting a priest — **priest·li·ness** *n*

prig \'prig\ *n* : a person who annoys others by a too careful or rigid observance of niceties and proprieties (as of speech or manners) [from earlier *prig* "fellow, person", probably from *prig* "to steal"] — **prig·gery** \'prig-ə-rē\ *n* — **prig·gish** \'prig-ish\ *adj* — **prig·gish·ly** *adv* — **prig·gish·ness** *n*

prim \'prim\ *adj* **prim·mer; prim·mest** : very or excessively formal and precise (as in conduct or dress) ⟨a *prim* scholar⟩ ⟨*prim* remarks⟩ [from earlier *prim* "to give a prim expression to", of unknown origin] — **prim·ly** *adv* — **prim·ness** *n*

pri·ma ballerina \,prē-mə-\ *n* : the principal female dancer in a ballet company [Italian, "leading ballerina"]

pri·ma·cy \'prī-mə-sē\ *n* **1** : the condition of being first (as in time, place, or rank) **2** : the office, status, or dignity of a bishop of the highest rank

pri·ma don·na \,prim-ə-'dän-ə, ,prē-mə-\ *n, pl* **prima donnas** **1** : a principal female singer (as in an opera) **2** : an extremely sensitive, vain, or undisciplined person [Italian, literally, "first lady"]

¹pri·ma fa·cie \,prī-mə-'fā-shə, -shē, -sē\ *adv* : at first view : on the first appearance [Latin]

²prima facie *adj* **1** : APPARENT, SEEMING ⟨a *prima facie* solution to a problem⟩ **2** : adequate to legally establish a fact or case unless disproved ⟨*prima facie* evidence⟩

pri·mal \'prī-məl\ *adj* **1** : ORIGINAL 1, PRIMITIVE **2** : first in importance : CHIEF [Medieval Latin *primalis*, from Latin *primus* "first"]

pri·mar·i·ly \prī-'mer-ə-lē\ *adv* **1** : for the most part : CHIEFLY **2** : in the first place : ORIGINALLY

¹pri·mary \'prī-,mer-ē; 'prīm-rē, -ə-rē\ *adj* **1** : first in order of time or development : INITIAL, PRIMITIVE ⟨the *primary* stages of a process⟩ **2 a** : of first rank, importance, or value : CHIEF ⟨the *primary* elective officer is the president⟩ **b** : BASIC, FUNDAMENTAL ⟨our *primary* duty⟩ **c** : of, relating to, or being one of the principal quills of a bird's wing **d** : expressive of present or future time ⟨*primary* tense⟩ **e** : of, relating to, or constituting the strongest of the three or four degrees of stress ⟨the first syllable of *basketball* carries *primary* stress⟩ **3 a** : not derived from or dependent on something else ⟨a *primary* source of information⟩ **b** : not derivable from other colors, odors, or tastes **c** : coming before and usually preparatory to something else ⟨*primary* instruction⟩ **4** : of, relating to, or being the current or circuit that is connected to the source of electricity in an induction coil or transformer **5** : of, relating to, or being meristem **6** : of, relating to, or involved in the production of organic substances by

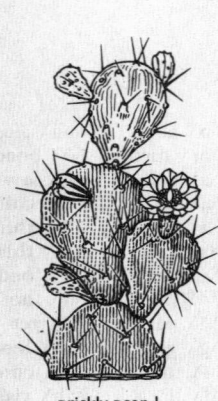

prickly pear 1

green plants [Late Latin *primarius* "basic, primary", from Latin, "principal", from *primus* "first"]

²**primary** *n, pl* **-mar·ies** **1** : something that is primary: as **a** : a planet as distinguished from its satellites **b** : a primary quill or feather **c** : any of a set of colors (as red, yellow, or blue) from which all other colors may be derived **2** : an election in which voters select party candidates for political office, choose party officials, or select delegates for a party convention **3** : the coil that is connected to the source of electricity in an induction coil or transformer — called also *primary coil*

primary cell *n* : a cell that converts chemical energy into electrical energy by irreversible chemical reactions

primary germ layer *n* : GERM LAYER

primary root *n* : the root of a plant that develops first

primary school *n* : ELEMENTARY SCHOOL

pri·mate \'prī-ˌmāt *or especially for 1* -mət\ *n* **1** : a bishop or archbishop governing or having highest status in a district, nation, or church **2** : any of an order (Primates) of mammals comprising especially human beings, apes, monkeys, lemurs, and tarsiers [Old French *primat,* from Medieval Latin *primat-, primas* "archbishop", from Latin, "leader", from *primus* "first"]

¹**prime** \'prīm\ *n* **1** *often cap* : the second of the canonical hours **2** : the first part : earliest stage **3** : the most active, thriving, or successful stage or period (as of one's life) **4** : the chief or best individual or part : PICK **5** : PRIME NUMBER **6** : the symbol ′ [Old English *prīm,* from Latin *prima hora* "first hour"]

²**prime** *adj* **1** : first in time : ORIGINAL **2 a** : of, relating to, or being a prime number **b** : having no polynomial factors other than itself and no monomial factors other than 1 ⟨a *prime* polynomial⟩ **c** : expressed as a product of prime factors (as prime numbers and prime polynomials) ⟨a *prime* factorization⟩ **3 a** : first in rank, authority, or significance : PRINCIPAL **b** : first in excellence, quality, or value **c** : of the highest grade regularly marketed ⟨*prime* rib of beef⟩ [Middle French, feminine of *prin* "first", from Latin *primus*] — **prime·ly** *adv* — **prime·ness** *n*

³**prime** *vt* **1** : to prepare for firing by supplying with priming or a primer **2** : to apply (as in painting) a first color, coating, or preparation to **3** : to put into working order by filling or charging with something ⟨*prime* a pump with water⟩ **4** : to instruct beforehand : COACH [probably from ¹*prime*]

prime meridian *n* : the meridian of 0° longitude which runs through the original site of the Royal Observatory at Greenwich, England, and from which other longitudes are reckoned east and west

prime minister *n* **1** : the chief minister of a ruler or state **2** : the head of a cabinet or ministry; *esp* : the chief executive of a parliamentary government — **prime ministry** *n*

prime number *n* : an integer other than 0 or ±1 that is not divisible without remainder by any other integers except ±1 and ± the integer itself

¹**prim·er** \'prim-ər, *especially British* 'prī-mər\ *n* **1** : a small book for teaching children to read **2** : a small introductory book on a subject [Medieval Latin *primarium,* from Late Latin *primarius* "primary"]

²**prim·er** \'prī-mər\ *n* **1** : a device (as a cap, tube, or wafer) containing a substance that ignites an explosive charge **2** : material used in priming a surface [³*prime*]

prime time *n* : the evening period during which television has its largest number of viewers

pri·me·val \prī-'mē-vəl\ *adj* : of or relating to the earliest ages : PRIMITIVE [Latin *primaevus,* from *primus* "first" + *aevum* "age"] — **pri·me·val·ly** \-və-lē\ *adv*

prim·ing *n* **1** : the explosive used in priming a charge **2** : ²PRIMER 2

¹**prim·i·tive** \'prim-ət-iv\ *adj* **1** : not derived : ORIGINAL, PRIMARY ⟨nature, the *primitive* source of art⟩ **2 a** : of or relating to the earliest age or period : PRIMEVAL ⟨*primitive* forests⟩ ⟨the *primitive* church⟩ **b** : little evolved and closely approximating an early ancestral type ⟨a *primitive* fish⟩ **3 a** : of or relating to a relatively simple people or culture ⟨*primitive* society⟩ **b** : marked by the style, simplicity, or crudity held to characterize simple people ⟨*primitive* building techniques⟩ **c** : lacking formal or technical training; *also* : produced by a self-taught artist [Latin *primitivus,* from *primitus* "originally", from *primus* "first"] — **prim·i·tive·ly** *adv* — **prim·i·tive·ness** *n*

²**primitive** *n* **1 a** : something primitive; *esp* : a primitive idea, term, or proposition **b** : a root word **2 a** (1) : an artist of an early period of a culture or artistic movement (2) : a later imitator or follower of such an artist **b** : a work of art produced by a primitive artist **3** : a member of a primitive people

pri·mo·gen·i·tor \ˌprī-mō-'jen-ət-ər\ *n* : ANCESTOR 1, FOREFATHER [Late Latin, from Latin *primus* "first" + *genitor* "begetter", from *genitus,* past participle of *gignere* "to beget"]

pri·mo·gen·i·ture \-'jen-ə-ˌchùr, -'jen-i-chər\ *n* **1** : the state of being the firstborn of the children of the same parents **2** : an exclusive right of inheritance belonging to the eldest son [Late Latin *primogenitura,* from Latin *primus* "first" + *genitura* "birth", from *genitus,* past participle of *gignere* "to beget"]

pri·mor·di·al \prī-'mòrd-ē-əl\ *adj* **1 a** : first created or developed : PRIMEVAL **b** : earliest formed in the growth of an individual or organ : PRIMITIVE ⟨*primordial* germ cells⟩ **2** : FUNDAMENTAL 1, PRIMARY [Late Latin *primordialis,* from Latin *primordium* "origin", from *primordius* "original", from *primus* "first" + *ordiri* "to begin"] — **pri·mor·di·al·ly** \-ē-ə-lē\ *adv*

pri·mor·di·um \-ē-əm\ *n, pl* **-dia** \-ē-ə\ : the first-formed rudiment of a part or organ [Latin, "origin"]

primp \'primp\ *vb* : to dress, adorn, or arrange in a careful or finicky manner [perhaps alteration of *prim* "to give a prim expression to, dress primly"]

prim·rose \'prim-ˌrōz\ *n* : any of a genus of perennial herbs with large tufted basal leaves and showy variously colored flowers borne in clusters on leafless stalks [Middle French *primerose*]

primrose path *n* : a path of ease or pleasure and especially sensual pleasure

primrose yellow *n* : a light to moderate yellow

prim·u·la \'prim-yə-lə\ *n* : PRIMROSE [Medieval Latin]

prince \'prins\ *n* **1 a** : MONARCH 1, SOVEREIGN **b** : the ruler of a principality or state **2** : a male member of a royal family; *esp* : a son of a king **3** : a nobleman of varying rank **4** : a person of high standing in a class or profession [Old French, from Latin *princeps,* literally, "one who takes the first part", from *primus* "first" + *capere* "to take"] — **prince·dom** \-dəm\ *n* — **prince·ship** \-ˌship\ *n*

Prince Al·bert \prin-'sal-bərt\ *n* : a long double-breasted frock coat [Prince *Albert* Edward (later Edward VII, king of England), died 1910]

prince charming *n* : a suitor who fulfills the dreams of his beloved; *also* : a man deceptively charming and attractive to women [*Prince Charming,* hero of the fairy tale *Cinderella* by Charles Perrault, died 1703, French writer]

prince consort *n, pl* **princes consort** : the husband of a reigning female sovereign

prince·ling \'prins-ling\ *n* : a petty or insignificant prince

prince·ly \'prins-lē\ *adj* **prince·li·er; -li·est** **1** : of or relating to a prince : ROYAL **2** : befitting a prince : REGAL, MAGNIFICENT ⟨*princely* manners⟩ ⟨a *princely* sum⟩ — **prince·li·ness** *n*

Prince of Wales \-'wālz\ : the male heir apparent to the British throne — used as a title only after it has been specifically conferred by the sovereign

primrose

prince's–feath·er \'prin-səz-ˌfeth-ər\ *n* : a showy annual amaranth often grown for its dense usually red
spikes of bloom

¹**prin·cess** \'prin-səs, 'prin-ˌses, prin-'ses\ *n* **1** *archaic* :
a woman having sovereign power **2** : a female member
of a royal family; *esp* : a daughter or granddaughter of
a sovereign **3** : the wife of a prince **4** : a woman of
outstanding merit

²**princess** *like* ¹\ *or* **prin·cesse** \prin-'ses\ *adj* : close=
fitting and usually with gores from neck to flaring
hemline ⟨a *princess* gown⟩

princess royal *n, pl* **princesses royal** : the eldest daughter of a sovereign

¹**prin·ci·pal** \'prin-sə-pəl, -sə-bəl\ *adj* **1** : most important or influential : CHIEF **2** : of, relating to, or being
principal or a principal [Old French, from Latin *prin-
cipalis,* from *princip-, princeps* "one who takes the
first part"] — **prin·ci·pal·ly** \-ē, 'prin-splē\ *adv*

²**principal** *n* **1 a** : a person (as a ruler or employer) who
exercises authority : HEAD, CHIEF **b** : the chief executive officer of a school **c** : one who engages another to
act as his or her agent **d** : an actual participant in a
crime **e** : the person primarily liable on a legal obligation **f** : a leading performer : STAR **2 a** : a capital sum
placed at interest, due as a debt, or used as a fund **b** :
the main body of an estate or bequest left by will —
prin·ci·pal·ship \-ˌship\ *n*

prin·ci·pal·i·ty \ˌprin-sə-'pal-ət-ē\ *n, pl* **-ties 1** : the office or position of a prince or principal **2** : the territory or jurisdiction of a prince

principal parts *n pl* : a series of verb forms from which
all the other forms of a verb can be derived including
in English the present infinitive, the past tense, the
past participle, and sometimes the present participle

prin·ci·ple \'prin-sə-pəl, -sə-bəl\ *n* **1 a** : a fundamental
law or doctrine **b** : a rule or code of conduct **c** : devotion to right principles **d** : the laws or facts of nature
underlying the working of an artificial device ⟨trying
to grasp the *principles* of radar⟩ **2 a** : a primary
source : ORIGIN **b** : an underlying faculty or endowment ⟨such *principles* of human nature as greed and
curiosity⟩ **3** : a constituent that exhibits or imparts a
characteristic quality ⟨quinine is the active *principle*
of cinchona bark⟩ [Middle French *principe,* from Latin
principium "beginning", from *princip-, princeps*
"one taking the first part"]

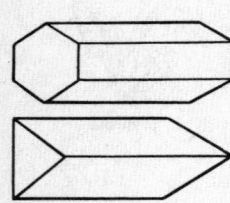

prism 1

prin·ci·pled \-sə-pəld, -sə-bəld, -spəld\ *adj* : exhibiting, based on, or characterized by principle
⟨high-*principled*⟩

prink \'pringk\ *vb* : PRIMP [probably alteration of
²*prank*] — **prink·er** *n*

¹**print** \'print\ *n* **1 a** : a mark made by pressure : IMPRES-
SION **b** : something impressed with a print or formed
in a mold **2** : a device or instrument for impressing or
forming a print **3 a** : printed state or form ⟨put a manuscript into *print*⟩ **b** : printed matter **c** : printed letters : TYPE **4 a** : a copy made by printing ⟨as from a
photographic negative⟩ **b** : cloth with a pattern applied by printing; *also* : an article of such cloth [Old
French *preinte,* from *preindre* "to press", from Latin
premere] — **in print** : available from the publisher —
out of print : not available from the publisher

²**print** *vb* **1 a** : to make an impression in or on **b** : to
cause (as a mark) to be stamped **2 a** : to make a copy
of especially by pressing paper against an inked
surface **b** : to impress (a surface) with a design by
pressure ⟨*print* wallpaper⟩ **c** : to publish in printed
form **d** : to write on a surface (as a computer display
screen) for viewing **3** : to write in unconnected letters
like those made by a printing press **4** : to make (a positive picture) on a sensitized photographic surface

print·able \'print-ə-bəl\ *adj* **1** : capable of being printed or of being printed from **2** : worthy or fit to be
published — **print·abil·i·ty** \ˌprint-ə-'bil-ət-ē\ *n*

printed circuit *n* : a circuit for electronic apparatus
made by depositing conductive material on an insulating surface

printed matter *n* : matter mechanically printed that is
eligible for mailing at a special rate

print·er \'print-ər\ *n* : one that prints: as **a** : a person
whose business or occupation is printing **b** : a device
used for printing

printer's devil *n* : an apprentice in a printing office

print·ery \'print-ə-rē\ *n, pl* **-er·ies** : an establishment
where printing is done

print·ing *n* **1** : reproduction in printed form **2** : the art,
practice, or business of a printer **3** : IMPRESSION 4b

printing press *n* : a machine that produces printed copies

print·mak·er \'print-ˌmā-kər\ *n* : an artist who makes
prints

print·out \'print-ˌaut\ *n* : a printed record produced by
a computer

¹**pri·or** \'prī-ər, 'prīr\ *n* **1** : the deputy head of an abbey
2 : the head of a monastic house, province, or order
[Old English and Middle French, both from Medieval
Latin, from Latin, "former, superior"] — **pri·or·ate**
\'prī-ə-rət\ *n* — **pri·or·ship** \'prī-ər-ˌship\ *n*

²**prior** *adj* **1** : earlier in time or order **2** : taking precedence logically or in importance or value ⟨a *prior* re-
sponsibility⟩ [Latin, "former, superior"] — **pri·or·ly**
adv

pri·or·ess \'prī-ə-rəs\ *n* : a nun who is the head of a
religious house or order

pri·or·i·ty \prī-'òr-ət-ē, -'är-\ *n, pl* **-ties 1** : the quality
or state of coming before another in time or impor-
tance: as **a** : superiority in rank, position, or privilege
b : order of preference based on urgency, importance,
or merit **2** : something deserving or requiring attention before others of its kind ⟨it's high on our list of
priorities⟩

prior to *prep* : in advance of : BEFORE

pri·o·ry \'prī-rē, -ə-rē\ *n, pl* **-ries** : a religious house under a prioress or prior

prise \'prīz\ *chiefly British variant of* ⁵PRIZE

prism \'priz-əm\ *n* **1** : a solid whose ends are similar,
equal, and parallel polygons and whose faces are parallelograms **2 a** : a transparent body bounded in part
by two plane faces that are not parallel used to deviate
or disperse a beam of light **b** : a prism-shaped decorative glass pendant [Late Latin *prismat-, prisma,* literally, "anything sawn", from *priein* "to saw"]

pris·mat·ic \priz-'mat-ik\ *adj* **1** : relating to, resembling, or being a prism **2** : formed by refraction of
light through a transparent prism ⟨*prismatic* colors⟩
3 : highly colored : BRILLIANT — **pris·mat·i·cal·ly**
\-'mat-i-kə-lē, -klē\ *adv*

pris·ma·toid \'priz-mə-ˌtòid\ *n* : a polyhedron in
which every vertex lies in one or the other of two parallel planes

pris·on \'priz-n\ *n* **1** : a state of confinement for criminals ⟨sentenced to *prison*⟩ **2** : a place in which persons are locked up while awaiting or on trial or as
punishment after conviction; *esp* : PENITENTIARY [Old
French, from Latin *prehension-, prehensio* "act of
seizing", from *prehensus,* past participle of *prehendere* "to seize"]

pris·on·er \'priz-nər, -n-ər\ *n* : a person kept under involuntary restraint, confinement, or custody; *esp* : one
in prison

prisoner of war : a person captured in war; *esp* : a member of the armed forces of a nation taken by the enemy
during combat

prisoner's base *n* : a children's game in which players
of one team seek to tag and imprison players of the
other team who have ventured out of their home territory

pris·sy \'pris-ē\ *adj* **pris·si·er; -est** : being prim and finicky [probably blend of *prim* and *sissy*] — **pris·si·ly**
\'pris-ə-lē\ *adv* — **pris·si·ness** \'pris-ē-nəs\ *n*

pris·tine \'pris-ˌtēn\ *adj* : of or relating to the earliest period or condition : ORIGINAL, PRIMITIVE; *esp* : having the purity or freshness of an original state [Latin *pristinus*] — **pris·tine·ly** *adv*

prith·ee \'priṯh-ē, 'priṯh-\ *interj, archaic* — used to express a wish or request [alteration of *(I) pray thee*]

pri·va·cy \'prī-və-sē\ *n, pl* **-cies** 1 : the condition of being apart from company or observation : SECLUSION ⟨a yard with lots of *privacy*⟩ 2 : freedom from unauthorized intrusion ⟨a person's right to *privacy*⟩

¹pri·vate \'prī-vət\ *adj* 1 a : belonging to, concerning, or reserved for the use of a particular person or group : not public ⟨*private* property⟩ ⟨a *private* beach⟩ b : not under public control ⟨a *private* school⟩ 2 : not holding public office or employment ⟨a *private* citizen⟩ 3 a : offering privacy : SECLUDED ⟨a *private* office⟩ b : not publicly known : SECRET ⟨*private* agreements⟩ [Latin *privatus* "not holding public office, private", from *privare* "to deprive", from *privus* "private, set apart"] — **pri·vate·ly** *adv* — **pri·vate·ness** *n*

²private *n* 1 : a person of low or lowest rank in an organized group (as a police or fire department) 2 : the lowest enlisted rank in the Marine Corps and either of the two lowest enlisted ranks in the Army — **in private** : PRIVATELY, SECRETLY

private enterprise *n* : FREE ENTERPRISE

¹pri·va·teer \ˌprī-və-'tiər\ *n* 1 : an armed private ship commissioned to cruise against the commerce or warships of an enemy 2 : the commander or one of the crew of a privateer

²privateer *vi* : to cruise in or as a privateer

private first class *n* : an enlisted rank in the Army above private and below corporal and in the Marine Corps above private and below lance corporal

pri·va·tion \prī-'vā-shən\ *n* 1 : an act or instance of depriving : DEPRIVATION 2 : the state of being deprived especially of what is needed for existence : WANT [Middle French, from Latin *privatio*, from *privare* "to deprive"]

¹priv·a·tive \'priv-ət-iv\ *n* : a privative prefix or suffix

²privative *adj* : constituting or predicating privation or absence of a quality ⟨*a-, un-, non-* are *privative* prefixes⟩ — **priv·a·tive·ly** *adv*

priv·et \'priv-ət\ *n* : a shrub of the olive family with small white flowers that is widely used for hedges [origin unknown]

priv·i·lege \'priv-lij, -ə-lij\ *n* : something special one is allowed to have, be, or do [Old French, from Latin *privilegium* "law for or against a private person", from *privus* "private" + *leg-, lex* "law"]

priv·i·leged \-lijd\ *adj* 1 : having or enjoying one or more privileges ⟨*privileged* classes⟩ 2 : that need not be disclosed in a court of law ⟨a *privileged* communication⟩

priv·i·ly \'priv-ə-lē\ *adv* : PRIVATELY, SECRETLY

¹privy \'priv-ē\ *adj* 1 : belonging or relating to a person in his individual rather than his official capacity 2 : PRIVATE 3a ⟨a *privy* place⟩ 3 : sharing in a secret ⟨*privy* to the conspiracy⟩ [Old French *privé*, from Latin *privatus* "private"]

²privy *n, pl* **priv·ies** : a small building without plumbing that is used as a toilet; *also* : TOILET 2b

privy council *n* 1 *cap P&C* : an advisory council to the British crown usually functioning through its committees 2 : a usually appointive advisory council to an executive — **privy councillor** *n*

privy purse *n, often cap both Ps* : an allowance for the private expenses of the British sovereign

¹prize \'prīz\ *n* 1 : something won or to be won in competition or in contests of chance; *also* : a premium given as an inducement to buy 2 : something exceptionally desirable [Middle English *pris* "prize, price", from Old French, "price"]

²prize *adj* 1 a : awarded a prize ⟨a *prize* essay⟩ b : awarded as a prize ⟨*prize* money⟩ 2 : outstanding of its kind ⟨*prize* hogs⟩

³prize *vt* 1 : to estimate the value of : RATE 2 : to value highly : ESTEEM [Middle French *prisier*, from Late Latin *pretiare*, from Latin *pretium* "price, value"]

⁴prize *n* 1 : something taken by force, stratagem, or threat; *esp* : property lawfully captured in time of war 2 : an act of capturing or taking; *esp* : the wartime capture of a ship and its cargo at sea [Old French *prise* "act of taking", from *prendre* "to take", from Latin *prehendere*]

⁵prize *vb* : to press, force, or move with or as if with a lever : PRY [from earlier *prize* "lever", from ⁴*prize*]

prize·fight \'prīz-ˌfīt\ *n* : a professional boxing match — **prize·fight·er** \-ər\ *n* — **prize·fight·ing** \-ing\ *n*

prize ring *n* : a boxing ring

prize·win·ner \-ˌwin-ər\ *n* : a winner of a prize — **prize·win·ning** \-ˌwin-ing\ *adj*

¹pro \'prō\ *n, pl* **pros** \'prōz\ 1 : a favorable argument or piece of evidence ⟨*pros* and cons⟩ 2 : the affirmative position or one holding it [Latin, prep., "for"]

²pro *adv* : on the affirmative side

³pro *n or adj* : PROFESSIONAL

¹pro- *prefix* 1 a : prior to : prior ⟨*pro*gestational⟩ b : rudimentary : PROT- 2 2 : located in front of or at the front of ⟨*pro*thorax⟩ 3 : projecting ⟨*pro*gnathous⟩ [Latin, from Greek, from *pro* "before, forward, forth, for"]

²pro- *prefix* 1 : taking the place of : substituting for ⟨*pro*cathedral⟩ 2 : favoring : supporting : championing ⟨*pro*-American⟩ [Latin *pro* "in front of, before, for"]

prob·a·bil·i·ty \ˌpräb-ə-'bil-ət-ē\ *n, pl* **-ties** 1 : the quality, state, or degree of being probable ⟨some *probability* of war⟩ 2 : something probable 3 : a measure of the likelihood of an outcome or event expressed as the frequency with which it is theoretically expected to occur or as the ratio of the number of times it occurs in a test series to the total number of trials in the series

prob·a·ble \'präb-ə-bəl, 'präb-bəl\ *adj* 1 : supported by evidence strong enough to make it likely though not certain to be true ⟨a *probable* explanation⟩ 2 : likely to happen or to have happened ⟨the *probable* outcome of the game⟩ [Middle French, from Latin *probabilis*, from *probare* "to test, approve, prove", from *probus* "good, honest", from *pro* "for, in favor of"] — **prob·a·bly** \'präb-ə-blē, 'präb-lē\ *adv* □ SYN PROBABLE, POSSIBLE mean such as may be or may become true or actual. PROBABLE applies to what is supported by strong but not necessarily conclusive evidence ⟨the *probable* cause of the accident⟩ POSSIBLE refers to something which is within the limit of what may happen or of what a person or thing may do regardless of the chances for or against its actuality.

probable cause *n* : a reasonable ground for supposing that a criminal charge is well-founded

¹pro·bate \'prō-ˌbāt\ *n* 1 : proof before a probate court that the last will and testament of a deceased person is genuine 2 : judicial determination of the validity of a will [Latin *probatus*, past participle of *probare* "to test, prove, approve"]

²probate *vt* : to establish (a will) by probate as valid

probate court *n* : a court having jurisdiction chiefly over the probate of wills and the administration of estates of deceased persons

pro·ba·tion \prō-'bā-shən\ *n* 1 : critical examination and evaluation or subjection to such examination and evaluation 2 a : subjection of an individual to a period of testing and trial to ascertain fitness (as for a job or school) b : the suspending of a convicted offender's sentence during good behavior under the supervision of a probation officer c : the state or a period of being subject to probation — **pro·ba·tion·al** \-shnəl, -shən-l\ *adj* — **pro·ba·tion·al·ly** \-ē\ *adv* — **pro·ba·tion·ary** \-shə-ˌner-ē\ *adj*

pro·ba·tion·er \prō-'bā-shə-nər, -shnər\ *n* : a person (as a new student nurse or a convict on a suspended sentence) who is undergoing probation

privet

probation officer *n* : an officer appointed to investigate, report on, and supervise the conduct of convicted offenders on probation

pro·ba·tive \'prō-bət-iv\ *adj* **1** : serving to test or try **2** : serving to prove

pro·ba·to·ry \'prō-bə-ˌtōr-ē\ *adj* : PROBATIVE

¹probe \'prōb\ *n* **1** : a slender instrument for examining a cavity (as a wound) **2 a** : a pointed metal tip for making electrical contact with a circuit element being checked **b** : a device used to penetrate or send back information from outer space **3** : a searching examination; *esp* : an inquiry to discover evidence of wrongdoing ⟨a legislative *probe*⟩ [Medieval Latin *proba* "examination", from Latin *probare* "to test, prove"]

²probe *vb* **1** : to examine with or as if with a probe **2** : to investigate thoroughly **3** : to make an exploratory investigation — **prob·er** *n*

pro·bi·ty \'prō-bət-ē\ *n* : adherence to the highest principles and ideals : UPRIGHTNESS [Middle French *probité*, from Latin *probitas*, from *probus* "honest"]

¹prob·lem \'präb-ləm\ *n* **1 a** : a question raised for inquiry, consideration, or solution **b** : a proposition in mathematics or physics stating something to be done **2 a** : an intricate unsettled question **b** : a source of perplexity or vexation [Middle French *probleme*, from Latin *problema*, from Greek *problēma*, literally, "something thrown forward", from *proballein* "to throw forward", from *pro-* "forward" + *ballein* "to throw"]

²problem *adj* **1** : dealing with a problem of human conduct or social relationship ⟨a *problem* play⟩ **2** : difficult to deal with ⟨a *problem* child⟩

prob·lem·at·ic \ˌpräb-lə-'mat-ik\ *or* **prob·lem·at·i·cal** \-'mat-i-kəl\ *adj* : having the nature of a problem : difficult and uncertain : PUZZLING — **prob·lem·at·i·cal·ly** \-i-kə-lē, -klē\ *adv*

pro·bos·ci·de·an \prə-ˌbäs-ə-'dē-ən\ *or* **pro·bos·cid·i·an** \prə-ˌbäs-'id-ē-ən\ *n* : any of an order (Proboscidea) of large mammals comprising the elephants and extinct related forms [derived from Latin *proboscid-, proboscis* "proboscis"] — **pro·boscidean** *adj*

pro·bos·cis \prə-'bäs-əs, -kəs\ *n, pl* **-bos·cis·es** *also* **-bos·ci·des** \-'bäs-ə-ˌdēz\ **1** : the trunk of an elephant; *also* : a long, flexible, or prominent snout or nose **2** : an elongated sometimes extensible tubular process of the mouth region of an invertebrate (as a mosquito or butterfly) [Latin, from Greek *proboskis*, from *pro-* + *boskein* "to feed"]

pro·caine \'prō-ˌkān\ *n* : a drug resembling cocaine and used as a local anesthetic [²*pro-* + co*caine*]

pro·cam·bi·um \prō-'kam-bē-əm, 'prō-\ *n* : the part of a plant meristem that forms cambium and primary vascular tissues — **pro·cam·bi·al** \-bē-əl\ *adj*

procaryote *variant of* PROKARYOTE

pro·ca·the·dral \ˌprō-kə-'thē-drəl\ *n* : a parish church used as a cathedral

pro·ce·dure \prə-'sē-jər\ *n* **1 a** : a particular way of accomplishing something or of acting **b** : a step in a procedure **2 a** : a series of steps followed in a regular definite order ⟨legal *procedure*⟩ **b** : a series of instructions for a computer that has a name by which it can be called into action **3** : a traditional or established way of doing things — **pro·ce·dur·al** \prə-'sēj-rəl, -ə-rəl\ *adj* — **pro·ce·dur·al·ly** \-ē\ *adv*

pro·ceed \prō-'sēd, prə-\ *vi* **1** : to come forth from a source : ISSUE **2 a** : to continue after a pause or interruption **b** : to go on in an orderly regulated way **3 a** : to begin and carry on an action, process, or movement ⟨*proceed* to tell them off⟩ **b** : to be in the process of being accomplished ⟨the work's *proceeding* well⟩ **4** : to move along a course ⟨we *proceeded* south⟩ [Middle French *proceder*, from Latin *procedere*, from *pro-* "forward" + *cedere* "to go"]

pro·ceed·ing *n* **1** : PROCEDURE 2 **2** *pl* : things that take place ⟨talked over the day's *proceedings*⟩ **3 a** *pl* : legal action : LITIGATION ⟨divorce *proceedings*⟩ **b** : a suit or action at law **4** : a thing done **5** *pl* : an official record of things said or done

pro·ceeds \'prō-ˌsēdz\ *n pl* : the total amount or the profit arising (as from a business or tax) : RETURN

¹pro·cess \'präs-ˌes, 'prōs-, -əs\ *n, pl* **pro·cess·es** \-ˌes-əz, -ə-səz, -ə-ˌsēz\ **1 a** : PROGRESS, ADVANCE ⟨things will come right in the *process* of time⟩ **b** : something going on **2 a** : a natural phenomenon marked by gradual changes that lead toward a particular result ⟨the *process* of growth⟩ **b** : a series of actions, operations, or changes leading to an end ⟨education is a long *process*⟩ **3 a** : the proceedings or manner of proceeding in a legal action ⟨due *process* of law⟩ **b** : a legal summons or writ used by a court to compel the appearance of the defendant or obedience to its orders **4** : a prominent or projecting bodily part : OUTGROWTH ⟨a bony *process*⟩ [Middle French *proces*, from Latin *processus*, from *processus*, past participle of *procedere* "to proceed"]

²process *vt* **1** : to change or prepare by special treatment ⟨*process* foods⟩ **2 a** : to take care of according to a routine ⟨*process* insurance claims⟩ **b** : to take in and organize to be used in a variety of useful ways ⟨computers *process* data⟩

process cheese *n* : cheese made by blending different cheeses

pro·ces·sion \prə-'sesh-ən\ *n* **1** : continuous forward movement : PROGRESSION **2** : a group of individuals moving along in an orderly often ceremonial way ⟨a funeral *procession*⟩

¹pro·ces·sion·al \prə-'sesh-nəl, -ən-l\ *n* : a hymn sung during a procession (as of a choir entering the church at the beginning of a service); *also* : a ceremonial procession

²processional *adj* : of, relating to, or moving in a procession — **pro·ces·sion·al·ly** \-ē\ *adv*

pro·ces·sor \'präs-ˌes-ər, 'prōs-\ *n* **1** : one that processes **2** : the part of a computer that operates on data

pro·claim \prō-'klām\ *vt* : to announce publicly ⟨*proclaim* a holiday⟩ [Latin *proclamare*, from *pro-* "before" + *clamare* "to cry out"] SYN see DECLARE — **pro·claim·er** *n*

proc·la·ma·tion \ˌpräk-lə-'mā-shən\ *n* **1** : the action of proclaiming : an official publication ⟨*proclamation* of a new law⟩ **2** : something proclaimed [Middle French, from Latin *proclamatio*, from *proclamare* "to proclaim"]

pro·cliv·i·ty \prō-'kliv-ət-ē\ *n, pl* **-ties** : a tendency or inclination of the mind or temperament : DISPOSITION ⟨a child with a marked *proclivity* toward laziness⟩ [Latin *proclivitas*, from *proclivis* "sloping, prone", from *pro-* "forward" + *clivus* "hill"]

¹pro·con·sul \prō-'kän-səl, 'prō-\ *n* **1** : a governor or military commander of an ancient Roman province **2** : an administrator in a modern colony, dependency, or occupied area [Latin, from *pro consule* "for a consul"] — **pro·con·sul·ar** \-sə-lər, -slər\ *adj* — **pro·con·sul·ate** \-sə-lət, -slət\ *n* — **pro·con·sul·ship** \-səl-ˌship\ *n*

²proconsul *n* : an African Miocene fossil ape possibly ancestral to the anthropoid apes and man [¹*pro-* + *Consul*, a chimpanzee in the London Zoo]

pro·cras·ti·nate \prə-'kras-tə-ˌnāt\ *vb* **1** : to put off repeatedly **2** : to keep postponing something supposed to be done [Latin *procrastinare*, from *pro-* "forward" + *crastinus* "of tomorrow", from *cras* "tomorrow"] — **pro·cras·ti·na·tion** \-ˌkras-tə-'nā-shən\ *n* — **pro·cras·ti·na·tor** \-'kras-tə-ˌnāt-ər\ *n*

pro·cre·ate \'prō-krē-ˌāt\ *vb* : to beget or bring forth offspring : REPRODUCE [Latin *procreare*, from *pro-* "forth" + *creare* "to create"] — **pro·cre·a·tion** \ˌprō-krē-'ā-shən\ *n* — **pro·cre·a·tive** \'prō-krē-ˌāt-iv\ *adj* — **pro·cre·a·tor** \-ˌāt-ər\ *n*

pro·crus·te·an \prə-'krəs-tē-ən\ *adj, often cap* : marked by arbitrary often ruthless disregard of individual differences or special circumstances [*Procrustes*, legendary Greek robber who made his victims fit a certain bed by stretching or lopping off their legs]

pro·crustean bed *n, often cap P* : a scheme or pattern into which someone or something is arbitrarily forced

proc·tor \'präk-tər\ *n* : SUPERVISOR, MONITOR; *esp* : one appointed to supervise students (as at an examination) [Middle English *procutour* "procurator, proctor", alteration of *procuratour*] — **proctor** *vb* — **proc·to·ri·al** \präk-'tōr-ē-əl, -'tor-\ *adj* — **proc·tor·ship** \'präk-tər-,ship\ *n*

pro·cum·bent \prō-'kəm-bənt\ *adj* : lying face down [Latin *procumbens*, present participle of *procumbere* "tofall or lean forward"]

proc·u·ra·tor \'präk-yə-,rāt-ər\ *n* 1 : one that manages another's affairs : AGENT 2 : a Roman provincial administrator and financial manager 3 : a criminal prosecutor in various countries [Old French *procuratour*, from Latin *procurator*, from *procurare* "to take care of"] — **proc·u·ra·to·ri·al** \,präk-yə-rə-'tōr-ē-əl, -'tor-\ *adj*

pro·cure \prə-'kyùr\ *vb* 1 a : to get possession of : OBTAIN b : to make women available for promiscuous sexual intercourse 2 : to bring about : ACHIEVE [Late Latin *procurare*, from Latin, "to take care of", from *pro-* "for" + *cura* "care"] — **pro·cur·able** \-'kyùr-ə-bəl\ *adj* — **pro·cure·ment** \-'kyùr-mənt\ *n*

pro·cur·er \-'kyùr-ər\ *n* : one that procures; *esp* : PANDER 1b

Pro·cy·on \'prō-sē-,än, 'präs-ē-\ *n* : a bright star in Canis Minor [Latin, from Greek *Prokyōn*, literally, "fore-dog"; from its rising before the Dog Star]

¹prod \'präd\ *vt* **prod·ded; prod·ding** 1 a : to thrust a pointed instrument into b : to move to action : STIR 2 : to poke or stir as if with a prod [origin unknown] — **prod·der** *n*

²prod *n* 1 : a pointed instrument used to prod 2 : something that moves one to act

¹prod·i·gal \'präd-i-gəl\ *adj* 1 : recklessly extravagant ⟨a *prodigal* spender⟩ 2 : wastefully lavish ⟨*prodigal* entertainment⟩ [Latin *prodigus*, from *prodigere* "to drive away, squander", from *pro-, prod-* "forth" + *agere* "to drive"] — **prod·i·gal·i·ty** \,präd-ə-'gal-ət-ē\ *n* — **prod·i·gal·ly** \'präd-i-gə-lē, -glē\ *adv*

²prodigal *n* : a person who spends prodigally : SPENDTHRIFT

pro·di·gious \prə-'dij-əs\ *adj* 1 : exciting amazement or wonder 2 : extraordinary in bulk, quantity, or degree : ENORMOUS SYN see MONSTROUS — **pro·di·gious·ly** *adv* — **pro·di·gious·ness** *n*

prod·i·gy \'präd-ə-jē\ *n, pl* **-gies** 1 : something extraordinary or unexplainable 2 : an amazing instance, deed, or performance ⟨a *prodigy* of strength and skill⟩ 3 : a highly talented child [Latin *prodigium* "omen, monster"]

¹pro·duce \prə-'düs, -'dyüs\ *vb* 1 : to offer to view or notice : EXHIBIT ⟨*produce* evidence⟩ 2 : to give birth or rise to ⟨a tree *producing* good fruit⟩ 3 : to extend in length, area, or volume ⟨*produce* a side of a triangle⟩ 4 : to present to the public on the stage or screen or over radio or television ⟨*produce* a play⟩ 5 : to give being, form, or shape to : MAKE; *esp* : MANUFACTURE 6 : to bring or cause to bring in a profit ⟨income-*producing* investments⟩ 7 : to produce something [Latin *producere*, from *pro-* "forward" + *ducere* "to lead"]

²pro·duce \'präd-,üs, 'prōd- *also* -,yüs\ *n* 1 : something produced 2 : agricultural products; *esp* : fresh fruits and vegetables as distinguished from staple crops (as grain)

pro·duc·er \prə-'dü-sər, -'dyü-\ *n* 1 : one that produces; *esp* : one that grows agricultural products or manufactures articles 2 : a person who supervises or finances a stage or screen production or radio or television program 3 : an organism (as a green plant) which produces its own organic compounds from sim-

ple precursors (as carbon dioxide and inorganic nitrogen) and many of which are food sources for other organisms — compare CONSUMER b

producer gas *n* : a manufactured fuel gas consisting chiefly of carbon monoxide, hydrogen, and nitrogen

producer goods *n pl* : goods (as tools) that are used to produce other goods

pro·duc·ible \prə-'dü-sə-bəl, -'dyü-\ *adj* : capable of being produced

prod·uct \'präd-əkt, -,əkt\ *n* 1 : the number or expression resulting from the multiplication of two or more numbers or expressions 2 : something produced 3 : the amount, quantity, or total produced [Latin *productum* "something produced", from *productus*, past participle of *producere* "to produce"]

pro·duc·tion \prə-'dək-shən\ *n* 1 a : something produced : PRODUCT b (1) : a literary or artistic work (2) : a work presented on the stage or screen or over the air 2 a : the act or process of producing b : the making of goods available for human wants 3 : total output

pro·duc·tive \prə-'dək-tiv\ *adj* 1 : having the power to produce especially in abundance ⟨*productive* fishing waters⟩ 2 : effective in or bringing about a production ⟨an age *productive* of great men⟩ 3 : yielding or furnishing results, benefits, or profits ⟨a *productive* training program⟩ 4 a : effecting or helping to effect production b : yielding or devoted to the satisfaction of wants or the creation of utilities 5 : continuing to be used in the formation of new words or constructions ⟨*un-* is a *productive* English prefix⟩ — **pro·duc·tive·ly** *adv* — **pro·duc·tive·ness** *n*

pro·duc·tiv·i·ty \,prō-,dək-'tiv-ət-ē, ,präd-ək-, prə-,dək-\ *n* 1 : the quality or state of being productive 2 : rate of production especially of food by fixation of the sun's energy by producer organisms

pro·em \'prō-,em\ *n* 1 : PREFACE 2 2 : PRELUDE 1 [Middle French *proheme*, from Latin *prooemium*, from Greek *prooimion*, from *pro-* + *oimē* "song"]

prof \'präf\ *n, slang* : PROFESSOR 2

pro·fa·na·tion \,präf-ə-'nā-shən, ,prō-fə-\ *n* : the act of profaning

pro·fa·na·to·ry \prō-'fan-ə-,tōr-ē, -'fā-nə-, -,tor-\ *adj* : tending to profane

¹pro·fane \prō-'fān, prə-\ *vt* 1 : to violate or treat with irreverence, abuse, or contempt 2 : to put to a wrong, unworthy, or vulgar use — **pro·fan·er** *n*

²profane *adj* 1 : not concerned with religion or religious purposes 2 : not holy : not fit for religious uses 3 : serving to debase or defile what is holy : IRREVERENT [Middle French *prophane*, from Latin *profanus*, from *pro-* "before" + *fanum* "temple"] — **pro·fane·ly** *adv* — **pro·fane·ness** \-'fān-nəs\ *n*

pro·fan·i·ty \prō-'fan-ət-ē\ *n, pl* **-ties** 1 a : the quality or state of being profane b : the use of profane language 2 : profane language SYN see BLASPHEMY

pro·fess \prə-'fes\ *vt* 1 a : to receive formally into a religious community following a novitiate by acceptance of the required vows b : to take (vows) as a member of a religious community or order 2 a : to declare openly or freely ⟨*profess* confidence in a friend's honesty⟩ b : PRETEND, CLAIM ⟨*professed* to be a friend of mine⟩ 3 : to confess one's faith in or allegiance to ⟨*profess* Christianity⟩ 4 : to practice or claim to be versed in (a calling or profession) [derived from Latin *professus*, past participle of *profiteri* "to profess, confess", from *pro-* "before" + *fateri* "to acknowledge"]

pro·fessed \-'fest\ *adj* : openly declared whether truly or falsely

pro·fess·ed·ly \prə-'fes-əd-lē, -'fest-lē\ *adv* 1 : by one's own account 2 : supposedly but not really

pro·fes·sion \prə-'fesh-ən\ *n* 1 : the act of taking the vows of a religious community 2 : an act of openly declaring or publicly claiming a belief, faith, or opinion 3 : an avowed religious faith 4 a : a calling requiring specialized knowledge and academic preparation **b** : a principal employment **c** : the whole body of persons engaged in a calling

¹pro·fes·sion·al \prə-ˈfesh-nəl, -ən-l\ *adj* **1 a** : of, relating to, or characteristic of a profession **b** : engaged in one of the learned professions **2 a** : participating for gain or livelihood in an activity often engaged in by amateurs ⟨a *professional* golfer⟩ **b** : engaged in by persons receiving financial return ⟨*professional* football⟩ **3** : following a line of conduct as though it were a profession ⟨a *professional* patriot⟩ — **pro·fes·sion·al·ly** \-ē\ *adv*

²professional *n* : one that engages in an activity professionally

pro·fes·sion·al·ism \-ˌiz-əm\ *n* **1** : the conduct, aims, or qualities that mark a profession or a professional person **2** : the following of a profession (as athletics) for gain or livelihood

pro·fes·sion·al·ize \-ˌīz\ *vt* : to give a professional character to

pro·fes·sor \prə-ˈfes-ər\ *n* **1** : one that professes, avows, or declares **2 a** : a faculty member of the highest academic rank at an institution of higher education **b** : a teacher at a university, college, or sometimes secondary school — **pro·fes·so·ri·al** \ˌprō-fə-ˈsōr-ē-əl, ˌpräf-ə-, -ˈsȯr-\ *adj* — **pro·fes·so·ri·al·ly** \-ē-ə-lē\ *adv*

pro·fes·sor·ship \prə-ˈfes-ər-ˌship\ *n* : the office, duties, or position of an academic professor

¹prof·fer \ˈpräf-ər\ *vt* **prof·fered; prof·fer·ing** \ˈpräf-ring, -ə-ring\ : to present for acceptance : TENDER, OFFER [Anglo-French *profrer,* from Old French *poroffrir,* from *por-* "forth" (from Latin *pro-*) + *offrir* "to offer"]

²proffer *n* : something proffered : OFFER

pro·fi·cien·cy \prə-ˈfish-ən-sē\ *n, pl* **-cies 1** : advancement in knowledge or skill **2** : the quality or state of being proficient

pro·fi·cient \prə-ˈfish-ənt\ *adj* : well advanced in an art, occupation, or branch of knowledge [Latin *proficiens,* present participle of *proficere* "to go forward, accomplish", from *pro-* "forward" + *facere* "to make"] — **pro·fi·cient·ly** *adv* □ SYN PROFICIENT, ADEPT, SKILLFUL, EXPERT mean having great knowledge and experience in a trade or profession. PROFICIENT stresses competence derived from training and practice ⟨a *proficient* typist⟩ ADEPT adds to proficiency the implication of aptitude or cleverness ⟨an *adept* writer of dialogue⟩ SKILLFUL stresses dexterity in execution or performance ⟨*skillful* jugglers⟩ EXPERT implies extraordinary proficiency and often connotes knowledge and technical skill ⟨*expert* in accountancy⟩ ⟨*expert* mimicry⟩

¹pro·file \ˈprō-ˌfīl\ *n* **1** : a representation of something in outline; *esp* : a human head or face represented or seen in a side view **2** : an outline seen or represented in sharp relief **3** : a brief biographical sketch **4** : a vertical section of soil that shows the various zones **5** : degree or level of public exposure ⟨keep a low *profile*⟩ [Italian *profilo,* from *profilare* "to draw in outline", from *pro-* "forward" + *filare* "to spin"]

²profile *vt* **1** : to represent in profile : draw or write a profile of **2** : to shape the outline of by passing a cutter around

¹profile 1

¹prof·it \ˈpräf-ət\ *n* **1** : a valuable return : GAIN **2** : the gain after all expenses are subtracted from the total amount received **3** : the return coming to those who assume the risks of a business as distinguished from wages or rent [Middle French, from Latin *profectus* "advance, profit", from *proficere* "to go forward"] — **prof·it·less** \-ləs\ *adj*

²profit *vb* **1** : to be of service or advantage **2** : to derive benefit : GAIN ⟨*profit* by experience⟩ **3** : BENEFIT ⟨a business deal that *profited* no one⟩

prof·it·able \ˈpräf-ət-ə-bəl, ˈpräf-tə-bəl\ *adj* : yielding profits : PRODUCTIVE SYN see BENEFICIAL — **prof·it·abil·i·ty** \ˌpräf-ət-ə-ˈbil-ət-ē, ˌpräf-tə-ˈbil-\ *n* — **prof·it·able·ness** \ˈpräf-ət-ə-bəl-nəs, ˈpräf-tə-bəl-\ *n* — **prof·it·ably** \-blē\ *adv*

prof·i·teer \ˌpräf-ə-ˈtiər\ *n* : one who makes an unreasonable profit especially on the sale of essential goods during an emergency — **profiteer** *vi*

profit sharing *n* : the sharing with employees of a part of the profits of an enterprise

prof·li·ga·cy \ˈpräf-li-gə-sē\ *n* : the quality or state of being profligate

prof·li·gate \ˈpräf-li-gət\ *adj* **1** : loose in character or morals **2** : extremely wasteful [Latin *profligatus,* from *profligare* "to strike down, ruin"] — **profligate** *n* — **prof·li·gate·ly** *adv*

pro for·ma \prō-ˈfȯr-mə, ˈprō-\ *adj* : for the sake of or as a matter of form [Latin]

pro·found \prə-ˈfaund\ *adj* **1 a** : having intellectual depth and insight ⟨a *profound* scholar⟩ **b** : difficult to understand ⟨a *profound* work⟩ **2 a** : extending far below the surface **b** : coming from, reaching to, or situated at a depth ⟨a *profound* sigh⟩ **3 a** : deeply felt : INTENSE ⟨*profound* regret⟩ **b** : COMPLETE ⟨*profound* sleep⟩ [Middle French *profond* "deep", from Latin *profundus,* from *pro-* "before" + *fundus* "bottom"] — **pro·found·ly** *adv* — **pro·found·ness** \-ˈfaund-nəs, -ˈfaun-\ *n*

pro·fun·di·ty \prə-ˈfən-dət-ē\ *n, pl* **-ties 1 a** : intellectual depth **b** : something profound or hard to understand **2** : the quality or state of being very profound or deep [Middle French *profundité,* from Latin *profunditas* "depth", from *profundus* "deep"]

pro·fuse \prə-ˈfyüs\ *adj* **1** : very or too generous ⟨*profuse* in their thanks⟩ ⟨*profuse* spending⟩ **2** : exhibiting great abundance [Latin *profusus,* past participle of *profundere* "to pour forth", from *pro-* "forth" + *fundere* "to pour"] — **pro·fuse·ly** *adv* — **pro·fuse·ness** *n*

pro·fu·sion \prə-ˈfyü-zhən\ *n* **1** : profuse expenditure **2** : lavish display ⟨*profusion* of flowers⟩

pro·gen·i·tor \prō-ˈjen-ət-ər\ *n* **1 a** : a direct ancestor **b** : a biologically ancestral form **2** : one that originates or precedes [Middle French *progeniteur,* from Latin *progenitor,* from *progenitus,* past participle of *progignere* "to beget"]

prog·e·ny \ˈpräj-ə-nē\ *n, pl* **-nies** : offspring of animals or plants [Old French *progenie,* from Latin *progenies,* from *progignere* "to beget", from *pro-* "forth" + *gignere* "to beget"]

pro·ges·ta·tion·al \ˌprō-ˌjes-ˈtā-shnəl, -shən-l\ *adj* : preceding pregnancy or gestation; *esp* : of, relating to, inducing, or being the changes in a female mammal associated with ovulation and corpus luteum formation ⟨*progestational* hormones⟩

pro·ges·ter·one \prō-ˈjes-tə-ˌrōn\ *n* : a steroid progestational hormone $C_{21}H_{30}O_2$ that is produced by the corpus luteum and induces and maintains changes in the uterus to provide a suitable environment for a fertilized egg [*pro-* + *gestation* + *ster*ol + *-one,* alteration of *-ene*]

pro·glot·tid \prō-ˈglät-əd, ˈprō-\ *n* : a segment of a tapeworm containing both male and female reproductive organs [New Latin *proglottid-, proglottis,* from Greek *proglōttis,* "tip of the tongue", from *pro-* + *glōtta* "tongue"]

pro·glot·tis \-ˈglät-əs\ *n, pl* **-glot·ti·des** \-ˈglät-ə-ˌdēz\ : PROGLOTTID

prog·na·thous \ˈpräg-nə-thəs, präg-ˈnā-\ *adj* : having the jaws projecting beyond the upper part of the face [*pro-* + Greek *gnathos* "jaw"] — **prog·na·thism** \-ˌthiz-əm\ *n*

prog·no·sis \präg-ˈnō-səs\ *n, pl* **-no·ses** \-ˈnō-ˌsēz\ **1** : a forecast of the course of a disease; *also* : the outlook given by such a forecast **2** : FORECAST [Late Latin, from Greek *prognō-sis,* literally, "foreknowledge", from progignōskein "to know before", from *pro-* + *gig-nōskein* "to know"]

prog·nos·tic \präg-'näs-tik\ *n* **I** : something that foretells **2** : PROPHECY 2 [Middle French *pronostique,* from Latin *prognosticum,* from Greek *prognōstikon,* from *prognōstikos* "foretelling", from *progignōskein* "to know before"] — **prognostic** *adj*

prog·nos·ti·cate \präg-'näs-tə-ˌkāt\ *vt* **I** : to foretell from signs or symptoms : PREDICT **2** : to give an indication of in advance : FORESHOW — **prog·nos·ti·ca·tive** \-ˌkāt-iv\ *adj* — **prog·nos·ti·ca·tor** \-ˌkāt-ər\ *n*

prog·nos·ti·ca·tion \präg-ˌnäs-tə-'kā-shən\ *n* **I** : an indication in advance : FORETOKEN **2** : FORECAST

¹pro·gram \'prō-ˌgram, -grəm\ *n* **I** : a brief statement or written outline of something (as a concert) **2** : PERFORMANCE ⟨a television *program*⟩ **3** : a plan of action **4** : a sequence of coded instructions for a computer [French *programme* "agenda, public notice", from Greek *programma,* from *prographein* "to write before", from *pro* + *graphein* "to write"]

²program *vt* **pro·grammed** *or* **pro·gramed** \-ˌgramd, -grəmd\; **pro·gram·ming** *or* **pro·gram·ing** **I a** : to arrange or furnish a program of or for **b** : to enter in a program **2** : to provide (as a computer) with a program — **pro·gram·ma·ble** \'prō-ˌgram-ə-bəl\ *adj*

programme *chiefly British variant of* PROGRAM

programmed instruction *n* : instruction through information given in small steps with each step requiring a correct response before the learner can go on to the next

pro·gram·mer \'prō-ˌgram-ər\ *n* : a person who writes computer programs

¹prog·ress \'präg-rəs, -ˌres, *chiefly British* 'prō-ˌgres\ *n* **I a** : a royal journey or tour **b** : an official journey **c** : a journeying forword **2** : a forward movement : ADVANCE **3** : gradual improvement; *esp* : the progressive development of mankind [Latin *progressus* "advance", from *progressus,* past participle of *progredi* "to go forth", from *pro-* "forward" + *gradi* "to go"]

²pro·gress \prə-'gres\ *vi* **I** : to move forward : PROCEED **2** : to develop to a higher, better, or more advanced stage

pro·gres·sion \prə-'gresh-ən\ *n* **I** : a sequence of numbers in which each term is related to its predecessor by a uniform law: **a** : ARITHMETIC PROGRESSION **b** : GEOMETRIC PROGRESSION **2 a** : the action of progressing **b** : a connected series ⟨the rapid *progression* of incidents in a play⟩ **3 a** : series of musical chords **b** : the movement of voice parts in harmony — **pro·gres·sion·al** \-'gresh-nəl, -ən-l\ *adj*

¹pro·gres·sive \prə-'gres-iv\ *adj* **I a** : of, relating to, or characterized by progress or progression **b** : gradually increasing ⟨*progressive* income tax⟩ **2** : of, relating to, or constituting an educational theory marked by emphasis on the individual child, informal classroom procedure, and encouragement of self-expression **3** : moving forward or onward **4** : increasing in extent or severity ⟨a *progressive* disease⟩ **5** *often cap* : of or relating to political Progressives **6** : of, relating to, or constituting a verb form that expresses action or state in progress at the time of speaking or a time spoken of — **pro·gres·sive·ly** *adv* — **pro·gres·sive·ness** *n*

²progressive *n* **I a** : one that is progressive **b** : one believing in moderate political change and social improvement by governmental action **2** *cap* **a** : a member of a minor United States political party split off from the Republicans about 1912 : BULL MOOSE **b** : a follower of Robert M. La Follette in the presidential campaign of 1924 **c** : a follower of Henry A. Wallace in the presidential campaign of 1948

pro·gres·siv·ism \prə-'gres-iv-ˌiz-əm\ *n* **I** *often cap* : the principles or beliefs of progressives or of Progressives **2** : the theories of progressive education — **pro·gres·siv·ist** \-i-vəst\ *n or adj*

pro·hib·it \prō-'hib-ət\ *vt* **I** : to forbid by authority ⟨*prohibit* all-day parking⟩ **2 a** : to prevent from doing something **b** : to make impossible ⟨the high walls *prohibit* escape⟩ [Latin *prohibitus,* past participle of *prohibēre* "to hold away", from *pro-* "forward" + *habēre* "to hold"] SYN see FORBID

pro·hi·bi·tion \ˌprō-ə-'bish-ən\ *n* **I** : the act of prohibiting **2** : an order forbidding something **3** : the forbidding by law of the sale and sometimes the manufacture and transportation of alcoholic liquors as beverages

pro·hi·bi·tion·ist \-'bish-nəst, -ə-nəst\ *n* : a person who is in favor of prohibiting the manufacture and sale of alcoholic liquors as beverages

pro·hib·i·tive \prō-'hib-ət-iv\ *adj* : serving or tending to prohibit ⟨*prohibitive* prices⟩ — **pro·hib·i·tive·ly** *adv*

pro·hib·i·to·ry \prō-'hib-ə-ˌtōr-ē, -ˌtȯr-\ *adj* : PROHIBITIVE

¹proj·ect \'präj-ˌekt, -ikt\ *n* **I** : a particular plan or design : SCHEME **2** : a planned undertaking: as **a** : a definitely formulated piece of research **b** : a large usually government-supported undertaking **c** : a task or problem engaged in usually by a group of students to supplement and apply classroom studies **3** : a group of houses or apartment buildings constructed and arranged according to a single plan; *esp* : one built with government help to provide low-cost housing [Middle French *pourjet,* from *pourjeter* "to throw out, spy, plan", from *pour-* (from Latin *porro* "forward") + *jeter* "to throw"]

²pro·ject \prə-'jekt\ *vb* **I** : to devise in the mind : DESIGN ⟨*project* civic improvements⟩ **2** : to throw forward, upward, or outward **3** : to stick out ⟨a stone jetty *projecting* into the bay⟩ **4** : to cause (light or shadow) to fall into space or (an image) to fall on a surface ⟨*project* a beam of light⟩ ⟨*project* motion pictures on a screen⟩ **5** : to reproduce (as a point, line, or area) on a line, plane, or surface in a prescribed manner [partly from Middle French *pourjeter* "to throw out, plan"; partly from Latin *projectus,* past participle of *proicere* "to throw forward", from *pro-* + *jacere* "to throw"] — **pro·ject·able** \-'jek-tə-bəl\ *adj*

¹pro·jec·tile \prə-'jek-tl\ *n* **I** : a body projected by external force and continuing in motion by its own inertia; *esp* : a missile for a weapon (as a firearm or cannon) **2** : a self-propelling weapon (as a guided missile)

²projectile *adj* **I** : projecting or impelling forward ⟨a *projectile* force⟩ **2** : capable of being thrust forward

pro·jec·tion \prə-'jek-shən\ *n* **I a** : a method of projecting the curved surface of the earth or the celestial sphere on a flat surface map based on a systematic presentation of intersecting coordinate lines **b** (1) : the process of reproducing a spatial object upon a surface by projecting its points; *also* : the graphic reproduction so formed (2) : a set of points obtained by projecting another set of points onto a line, plane, or surface **2** : the act of throwing or shooting forward : EJECTION **3** : the forming of a plan **4 a** : a jutting out **b** : a part that juts out **5** : the making objective of what is primarily subjective **6** : the display of motion pictures by projecting an image from them upon a screen **7** : an estimate of future possibilities based on a current trend — **pro·jec·tion·al** \-shnəl, -shən-l\ *adj* □ SYN PROJECTION, PROTRUSION mean extension beyond a normal line or surface. PROJECTION implies a jutting out especially at a sharp angle; PROTRUSION suggests a thrusting or bulging out so as to seem a deformity.

pro·jec·tion·ist \-shə-nəst, -shnəst\ *n* : one that makes projections; *esp* : one that operates a motion-picture projector or television equipment

pro·jec·tive \prə-'jek-tiv\ *adj* **I** : of, relating to, or involving geometric projection or projective geometry **2** : jutting out

\ə\ abut		\ng\ sing	
\ər\ further		\ō\ bone	
\a\ mat		\ȯ\ saw	
\ā\ take		\ȯi\ coin	
\ä\ cot, cart		\th\ thin	
\au̇\ out		\t͟h\ this	
\ch\ chin		\ü\ food	
\e\ pet		\u̇\ foot	
\ē\ easy		\y\ yet	
\g\ go		\yü\ few	
\i\ tip		\yu̇\ cure	
\ī\ life		\zh\ vision	
\j\ job			

projective geometry *n* : a branch of mathematics concerned with the properties of geometric figures that remain unchanged by projection

pro·jec·tor \prə-'jek-tər\ *n* **1** : one that plans a project; *esp* : PROMOTER **2** : one that projects: as **a** : a device for projecting a beam of light **b** : an optical instrument or machine for projecting an image or pictures upon a surface

pro·kary·ote *also* **pro·cary·ote** \prō-'kar-ē-,ōt, 'prō-\ *n* : a cellular organism (as a bacterium or a blue-green alga) that does not have a distinct nucleus — compare EUKARYOTE [*pro-* + *kary-* "cell nucleus" (from Greek *karyon* "nut, kernel") + *-ote* (as in *zygote*)] — **pro·kary·ot·ic** \-,prō-,kar-ē-'ät-ik\ *adj*

pro·lac·tin \prō-'lak-tən\ *n* : a protein hormone of the pituitary gland that induces lactation — called also *luteotrophic hormone*

pro·lapse \prō-'laps\ *n* : the slipping of a body part from its usual position or relations [Late Latin *prolapsus* "fall", from Latin *prolabi* "to fall or slide forward", from *pro-* "forward" + *labi* "to slide"] — **prolapse** *vi*

pro·leg \'prō-,leg\ *n* : a fleshy leg on an abdominal segment of some insect larvae

pro·le·gom·e·non \,prō-li-'gäm-ə-,nän\ *n, pl* **-na** \-nə\ : introductory remarks; *esp* : a formal essay or critical discussion serving to introduce and interpret an extended work [Greek, neuter present passive participle of *prolegein* "to say beforehand", from *pro-* + *legein* "to say"] — **pro·le·gom·e·nous** \-nəs\ *adj*

¹pro·le·tar·i·an \,prō-lə-'ter-ē-ən\ *n* : a member of the proletariat [Latin *proletarius*, from *proles* "progeny"; from the fact that their chief contribution to the state was progeny rather than property]

²proletarian *adj* : of, relating to, or representative of the proletariat

pro·le·tar·i·at \,prō-lə-'ter-ē-ət, -'tar-, -ē-,at\ *n* **1** : the lowest social or economic class of a community **2** : industrial workers who sell their labor to live [French *prolétariat*, from Latin *proletarius* "proletarian"]

pro·lif·er·ate \prə-'lif-ə-,rāt\ *vi* : to grow or increase by rapid production of new units (as cells or offspring) [back-formation from *proliferation*, from French *prolifération*, from *proliférer* "to proliferate", from *prolifère* "proliferative", from Latin *proles* "progeny" + *-fer* "-ferous"] — **pro·lif·er·a·tion** \-,lif-ə-'rā-shən\ *n* — **pro·lif·er·a·tive** \-'lif-ə-,rāt-iv\ *adj*

pro·lif·ic \prə-'lif-ik\ *adj* **1** : producing young or fruit abundantly ⟨*prolific* orchard⟩ **2** : highly inventive : PRODUCTIVE ⟨a *prolific* mind⟩ **3** : causing or characterized by fruitfulness ⟨*prolific* growing season⟩ [French *prolifique*, from Latin *proles* "progeny"] SYN see FERTILE — **pro·lif·i·cal·ly** \-'lif-i-kə-lē, -klē\ *adv* — **pro·lif·ic·ness** *n*

pro·line \'prō-,lēn\ *n* : an amino acid $C_5H_9NO_2$ that can be synthesized by animals from glutamate [German *prolin*]

pro·lix \prō-'liks, 'prō-,liks\ *adj* : using or containing too many words : WORDY, LONG-WINDED [Latin *prolixus* "extended", from *pro-* "forward" + *liquēre* "to be fluid"] — **pro·lix·i·ty** \prō-'lik-sət-ē\ *n* — **pro·lix·ly** \prō-'liks-lē, 'prō-,\ *adv*

pro·logue \'prō-,lóg\ *n* **1** : the preface or introduction to a literary work **2 a** : a speech often in verse addressed to the audience by an actor at the beginning of a play **b** : the actor speaking such a prologue **3** : an introductory or preceding event or development [Old French, from Latin *prologus* "preface to a play", from Greek *prologos,* from *pro-* + *legein* "to speak"]

pro·long \prə-'lóng\ *vt* **1** : to make longer than usual : continue or lengthen in time ⟨a *prolonged* stay in the hospital⟩ **2** : to lengthen in extent or range ⟨*prolong* a boundary line⟩ [Middle French *prolonguer*, from Late Latin *prolongare*, from Latin *pro-* "forward" + *longus* "long"] SYN see EXTEND

pro·lon·ga·tion \prō-,lóng-'gā-shən\ *n* **1** : a lengthening in space or time **2** : something that prolongs or is prolonged

prom \'präm\ *n* : an often formal dance given by a high school or college class [short for *promenade*]

¹prom·e·nade \,präm-ə-'nād, -'näd\ *n* **1** : a leisurely walk or ride especially in a public place for pleasure or display **2** : a place for strolling **3** : a ceremonious opening of a formal ball consisting of a grand march of all the guests [French, from *promener* "to take for a walk", from Latin *prominare* "to drive forward", from *pro-* "forward" + *minare* "to drive"]

²promenade *vb* **1** : to take or go on a promenade **2** : to walk about in or on ⟨*promenading* the sun deck⟩ — **prom·e·nad·er** *n*

promenade deck *n* : an upper deck of a passenger ship where passengers stroll

Pro·me·the·an \prə-'mē-thē-ən\ *adj* : of, relating to, or resembling Prometheus; *esp* : daringly original or creative

pro·me·thi·um \-thē-əm\ *n* : a metallic chemical element obtained as a fission product of uranium or from neutron-irradiated neodymium — see ELEMENT table [New Latin, from *Prometheus,* a Titan]

prom·i·nence \'präm-ə-nəns\ *n* **1** : the quality, state, or fact of being prominent or conspicuous ⟨a person of *prominence*⟩ **2** : PROJECTION 4b **3** : a mass or stream of gas resembling a cloud that arises from the chromosphere of the sun

prom·i·nent \-nənt\ *adj* **1** : standing out or projecting beyond a surface or line : PROTUBERANT **2** : readily noticeable : CONSPICUOUS **3** : EMINENT, NOTABLE [Latin *prominens,* from *prominēre* "to jut forward"] — **prom·i·nent·ly** *adv*

prom·is·cu·i·ty \,präm-əs-'kyü-ət-ē, ,prō-məs-\ *n, pl* **-ties** **1** : a miscellaneous mingling of persons or things **2** : promiscuous sexual behavior

pro·mis·cu·ous \prə-'mis-kyə-wəs\ *adj* **1** : composed of all sorts of persons or things ⟨a *promiscuous* crowd of onlookers⟩ **2** : not restricted to one person or class ⟨give *promiscuous* praise⟩; *esp* : not restricted to one sexual partner **3** : HAPHAZARD, IRREGULAR ⟨*promiscuous* eating habits⟩ [Latin *promiscuus,* from *pro-* "forth" + *miscēre* "to mix"] — **pro·mis·cu·ous·ly** *adv* — **pro·mis·cu·ous·ness** *n*

¹prom·ise \'präm-əs\ *n* **1** : a statement assuring someone that the person making the statement will do or not do something : PLEDGE ⟨a *promise* to pay⟩ **2** : a cause or ground for hope or expectation especially of success or distinction ⟨the child shows *promise*⟩ **3** : something promised [Latin *promissum,* from *promissus,* past participle of *promittere* "to send forth, promise", from *pro-* "forth" + *mittere* "to send"]

²promise *vb* **1 a** : to pledge onself to do, bring about, or provide ⟨*promise* aid⟩ **b** : to tell as a promise ⟨*promised* them we'd wait⟩ **c** : to make a promise **2** : to suggest beforehand : FORETOKEN ⟨dark clouds *promising* rain⟩ — **prom·is·er** \'präm-ə-sər\ *or* **prom·i·sor** \,präm-ə-'sór\ *n*

promised land *n* **1** : the land of Canaan that God promised to Abraham and his descendants **2** : a better place that one hopes to reach or a better condition that one hopes to attain

prom·is·ing *adj* : full of promise : giving hope or assurance (as of success) ⟨a very *promising* pupil⟩ — **prom·is·ing·ly** \'präm-ə-sing-lē\ *adv*

prom·is·so·ry \'präm-ə-,sōr-ē, -,sór-\ *adj* : containing or conveying a promise or assurance ⟨a *promissory* note⟩

prom·on·to·ry \'präm-ən-,tōr-ē, -,tór-\ *n, pl* **-ries** : a high point of land or rock jutting out into a body of water : HEADLAND [Latin *promunturium*]

pro·mot·able \prə-'mōt-ə-bəl\ *adj* : likely or deserving to be promoted

pro·mote \prə-'mōt\ *vt* **1** : to advance in position, rank, or honor : ELEVATE ⟨*promote* pupils to a higher grade⟩ **2** : to contribute to the growth, success, or development of : FURTHER ⟨good food *promotes* health⟩ **3** : to take the first steps in organizing (as a business) [Latin *promotus*, past participle of *promovēre*, literally, "to move forward", from *pro-* "forward" + *movēre* "to move"]

pro·mot·er \prə-'mōt-ər\ *n* : one that promotes; *esp* : one taking on the financial responsibilities of a sporting event

pro·mo·tion \prə-'mō-shən\ *n* **1** : the act or fact of being raised in position or rank **2** : the act of furthering the growth or development of something — **pro·mo·tion·al** \-shnəl, -shən-l\ *adj*

¹prompt \'prämt, 'prämpt\ *vt* **1** : to move to action : CAUSE ⟨curiosity *prompted* me to ask the question⟩ **2** : to remind of something forgotten or poorly learned (as by suggesting the next few words in a speech) ⟨*prompt* an actor⟩ **3** : SUGGEST, INSPIRE ⟨pride *prompted* the act⟩ [Medieval Latin *promptare*, from Latin *promptus* "ready, prompt"]

²prompt *adj* **1 a** : being ready and quick as occasion demands ⟨*prompt* to answer⟩ **b** : PUNCTUAL ⟨*prompt* in arriving⟩ **2** : performed readily or immediately ⟨*prompt* assistance⟩ [Latin *promptus* "ready, prompt", from *promere* "to bring forth", from *pro-* "forth" + *emere* "to take"] — **prompt·ly** *adv* — **prompt·ness** *n*

prompt·book \'prämt-‚buk, 'prämp-\ *n* : a copy of a play with directions for performance used by a theater prompter

prompt·er \'präm-tər, 'prämp-\ *n* : a person who reminds another of the words to be spoken next (as in a play)

promp·ti·tude \'präm-tə-‚tüd, 'prämp-, -‚tyüd\ *n* : the quality or habit of being prompt : PROMPTNESS

prom·ul·gate \'präm-əl-‚gāt; prō-'məl-\ *vt* **1** : to make known by open declaration : PROCLAIM **2 a** : to make public the terms of (a proposed law) **b** : to issue or give out (a law) by way of putting into execution [Latin *promulgare*] — **prom·ul·ga·tion** \‚präm-əl-'gā-shən, ‚prō-məl-\ *n* — **prom·ul·ga·tor** \'präm-əl-‚gāt-ər, prō-'məl-\ *n*

pro·na·tion \prō-'nā-shən\ *n* : rotation of the hand or forearm so as to bring the palm facing downward or backward; *also* : rotation of a joint or part forward and toward the midline of the body [from *pronate*, from Late Latin *pronatus*, past participle of *pronare* "to bend forward", from Latin *pronus* "bent forward"] — **pro·nate** \'prō-‚nāt\ *vt*

pro·na·tor \'prō-‚nāt-ər\ *n* : a muscle that produces pronation

prone \'prōn\ *adj* **1** : having a tendency or inclination ⟨*prone* to laziness⟩ **2** : lying belly or face downward ⟨shoot from a *prone* position⟩ [Latin *pronus* "bent forward, tending"] — **prone·ness** \'prōn-nəs\ *n* □ SYN PRONE, PROSTRATE, SUPINE mean lying down. PRONE implies a position with the front of the body turned toward the supporting surface ⟨lying *prone* on the deck⟩ PROSTRATE implies lying at full length as in submission or physical collapse ⟨found the body *prostrate* on the floor⟩ SUPINE implies lying on one's back and may connote laziness or inertness.

¹prong \'prong, 'präng\ *n* **1** : a tine of a fork **2** : a slender pointed or projecting part (as of a tooth or an antler) [Middle English *pronge*] — **pronged** \'prongd, 'prängd\ *adj*

²prong *vt* : to stab, pierce, or break up with a pronged device

prong·horn \'prong-‚horn, 'präng-\ *n, pl* **pronghorn** *also* **pronghorns** : a cud-chewing mammal of treeless parts of western North America that resembles an antelope

pro·nom·i·nal \prō-'näm-ən-l\ *adj* **1** : of, relating to, or being a pronoun **2** : resembling a pronoun in identifying or specifying without describing ⟨the *pronominal* adjective *this* in "this dog"⟩ [Late Latin *pronominalis*, from Latin *pronomen* "pronoun"] — **pro·nom·i·nal·ly** \-l-ē\ *adv*

pro·noun \'prō-‚naun\ *n* : a word that is used as a substitute for a noun or a noun phrase, takes noun constructions, and refers to persons or things named or understood in the context [Latin *pronomen*, from *pro-* "for" + *nomen* "name"]

pro·nounce \prə-'nauns\ *vt* **1** : to declare officially or solemnly ⟨the minister *pronounced* them man and wife⟩ ⟨the judge *pronounced* sentence⟩ **2** : to assert as an opinion ⟨*pronounce* the book a success⟩ **3** : to utter the sounds of : speak aloud ⟨practice *pronouncing* foreign words⟩; *esp* : to say or speak correctly ⟨can't *pronounce* your name⟩ [Middle French *prononcier*, from Latin *pronuntiare*, from *pro-* "forth" + *nuntiare* "to report", from *nuntius* "messenger"] — **pro·nounce·able** \-'naun-sə-bəl\ *adj* — **pro·nounc·er** *n*

pro·nounced \-'naunst\ *adj* : strongly marked : DECIDED ⟨a *pronounced* change for the better⟩ — **pro·nounc·ed·ly** \-'naun-səd-lē\ *adv*

pro·nounce·ment \prə-'nauns-mənt\ *n* **1** : a formal declaration of opinion **2** : an authoritative announcement

pron·to \'prän-‚tō\ *adv* : right away : QUICKLY, PROMPTLY [Spanish, from Latin *promptus* "prompt"]

pro·nun·ci·a·men·to \prō-‚nən-sē-ə-'ment-ō\ *n, pl* **-tos** *or* **-toes** : PROCLAMATION 1, PRONOUNCEMENT [Spanish *pronunciamiento*, from *pronunciar* "to pronounce", from Latin *pronuntiare*]

pro·nun·ci·a·tion \prə-‚nən-sē-'ā-shən\ *n* : the act or manner of pronouncing something [Middle French *prononciation*, from Latin *pronuntiatio*, from *pronuntiare* "to pronounce"] — **pro·nun·ci·a·tion·al** \-shnəl, -shən-l\ *adj*

¹proof \'prüf\ *n* **1 a (1)** : evidence of truth or correctness ⟨gave *proof* of their statement⟩ **(2)** : the process of or an instance of establishing the validity of a statement (as a mathematical theorem) especially by derivation from other statements by accepted rules of reasoning **b** : a test to find out or show the essential facts or truth ⟨put the theory to the *proof*⟩ ⟨the *proof* of the pudding is in the eating⟩ **2 a** : a copy (as of composed text) made for correction or examination **b** : a test photographic print made from a negative **3** : alcoholic content (as of a beverage) indicated by a number that is twice the percent by volume of alcohol present ⟨whiskey of 90 *proof* is 45% alcohol⟩ [Old French *preuve*, from Late Latin *proba*, from Latin *probare* "to prove"]

²proof *adj* **1** : designed for or successful in repelling, resisting, or withstanding ⟨*proof* against tampering⟩ — usually used in combination ⟨bomb*proof*⟩ ⟨water*proof*⟩ **2** : used in proving or testing or as a standard of comparison ⟨use *proof* loads in testing a gun⟩

³proof *vt* : to test the activeness of (yeast)

proof·read \'prü-‚frēd\ *vb* : to read and make corrections (as in printer's proof) ⟨*proofread* a composition⟩

proof·read·er \-‚frēd-ər\ *n* : a person who reads and makes corrections in printer's proof

¹prop \'präp\ *n* : something that props or sustains : SUPPORT [Dutch *proppe* "stopper"]

²prop *vt* **propped; prop·ping** **1 a** : to hold up or keep from falling or slipping by placing something under or against ⟨*prop* the limb up⟩ **b** : to support by placing against something ⟨*prop* a rake against the tree⟩ **2** : SUSTAIN, STRENGTHEN ⟨*propped* up by faith in times of crisis⟩

³prop *n* : PROPERTY 5

⁴prop *n* : PROPELLER

pro·pa·gan·da \‚präp-ə-'gan-də, ‚prō-pə-\ *n* **1** *cap* : a congregation of the Roman Catholic curia having jurisdiction over missionary territories and related institutions **2** : the spreading of ideas, information, or rumor

pronghorn

\ə\ abut	\ng\ sing	
\ər\ further	\ō\ bone	
\a\ mat	\o\ saw	
\ā\ take	\oi\ coin	
\ä\ cot, cart	\th\ thin	
\au\ out	\th\ this	
\ch\ chin	\ü\ food	
\e\ pet	\u\ foot	
\ē\ easy	\y\ yet	
\g\ go	\yü\ few	
\i\ tip	\yu\ cure	
\ī\ life	\zh\ vision	
\j\ job		

for the purpose of helping or injuring a cause; *also* : the ideas, facts, or allegations so spread [New Latin, from *Congregatio de propaganda fide* "congregation for propagating the faith", organization established by Pope Gregory XV] — **pro·pa·gan·dist** \-dəst\ *n* — **pro·pa·gan·dis·tic** \-,gan·'dis-tik\ *adj* — **pro·pa·gan·dis·ti·cal·ly** \-ti-kə-lē, -klē\ *adv*

pro·pa·gan·dize \-'gan-,dīz\ *vb* **1** : to spread propaganda **2** : to influence or attempt to influence by propaganda

prop·a·gate \'präp-ə-,gāt\ *vb* **1** : to reproduce or increase by sexual or asexual means : MULTIPLY ⟨*propagate* an apple by grafting⟩ **2** : to pass along to offspring **3 a** : to cause to spread out and affect a greater number or greater area **b** : PUBLICIZE **c** : TRANSMIT 2 **4** : to increase in extent, number, or influence : EXTEND [Latin *propagare* "to set slips, propagate", from *propages* "slip, offspring", from *pro-* "before" + *pangere* "to fasten"] — **prop·a·ga·tive** \-,gāt-iv\ *adj* — **prop·a·ga·tor** \-,gāt-ər\ *n*

prop·a·ga·tion \,präp-ə-'gā-shən\ *n* : the act or process of propagating: as **a** : multiplication (as of a kind of organism) in number of individuals **b** : the spreading of something (as a belief) abroad or into new regions : DISSEMINATION ⟨*propagation* of a faith⟩ — **prop·a·ga·tion·al** \-shnəl, -shən-l\ *adj*

pro·pane \'prō-,pān\ *n* : a heavy flammable gaseous hydrocarbon C_3H_8 found in crude petroleum and natural gas and used especially as fuel and in chemical synthesis [*prop*ionic acid + *-ane*]

pro·pel \prə-'pel\ *vt* **pro·pelled; pro·pel·ling** **1** : to push or drive usually forward or onward ⟨a bicycle is *propelled* by pedals⟩ **2** : to give an impelling motive to : urge ahead ⟨people *propelled* by ambition⟩ [Latin *propellere*, from *pro-* "before" + *pellere* "to drive"] SYN see PUSH

¹pro·pel·lant *or* **pro·pel·lent** \-'pel-ənt\ *adj* : capable of propelling

²propellant *also* **propellent** *n* : something that propels: as **a** : an explosive for propelling projectiles **b** : fuel plus oxidizer used by a rocket engine **c** : a gas in a specially made container for expelling the contents when the pressure is released

pro·pel·ler *also* **pro·pel·lor** \prə-'pel-ər\ *n* : one that propels; *esp* : a device consisting of a hub with radiating blades that is used for propelling aircraft and boats

pro·pen·si·ty \prə-'pen-sət-ē\ *n, pl* **-ties** : a natural inclination or liking : BENT ⟨a *propensity* for drawing⟩ [derived from Latin *propensus,* past participle of *propendēre* "to incline", from *pro-* "before" + *pendēre* "to hang"]

¹prop·er \'präp-ər\ *adj* **1** : suitable by reason of essential nature or condition **2 a** : appointed for the liturgy of a particular day **b** : belonging to one : OWN **3** : belonging characteristically to a species or individual : PECULIAR **4** : strictly limited to a specified thing, place, or idea ⟨outside the city *proper*⟩ **5 a** : strictly accurate : CORRECT **b** : strictly decorous : GENTEEL [Old French *propre* "proper, own", from Latin *proprius* "own"] SYN see FIT

²proper *n, often cap* : the parts of the Mass or Divine Office that vary according to the day or feast

proper adjective *n* : an adjective formed from a proper noun

proper fraction *n* : a fraction in which the numerator is less in absolute value than the denominator

prop·er·ly \'präp-ər-lē\ *adv* **1** : in a suitable or fit manner ⟨behave *properly* in church⟩ **2** : strictly in accordance with fact : CORRECTLY ⟨goods not *properly* labeled⟩ ⟨*properly* speaking, whales are not fish⟩

proper noun *n* : a noun that designates a particular being or thing and in English is usually capitalized — called also *proper name*

proper subset *n* : a subset containing fewer elements than the set to which it belongs

prop·er·tied \'präp-ərt-ēd\ *adj* : owning property and especially much property

prop·er·ty \'präp-ərt-ē\ *n, pl* **-ties** **1** : a special quality or characteristic of a thing : a quality or attribute common to all things called by the same name ⟨sweetness is a *property* of sugar⟩ **2** : anything that is owned (as land, goods, or money) **3** : a piece of real estate with or without a structure on it ⟨a business *property*⟩ **4** : the legal right to property : OWNERSHIP **5** : an article to be used on the stage during a play or on the set of a motion picture except artificial scenery or actors' costumes [Middle French *propreté,* from Latin *proprietas,* from *proprius* "own"] SYN see QUALITY

prop·er·ty·less \-ləs\ *adj* : lacking property

property man *n* : one who is in charge of theater or motion-picture stage properties

pro·phage \'prō-,fāj, -,fäzh\ *n* : a form of a bacteriophage in which it is harmless to the host, is usually integrated into the hereditary material of the host, and reproduces when the host does

pro·phase \'prō-,fāz\ *n* **1** : the initial phase of mitosis in which chromosomes are condensed from the resting form and split into paired chromatids **2** : the initial stage of meiosis in which the chromosomes become visible, pairs of homologous chromosomes are associated and become shortened and thickened, individual chromosomes become visibly double as paired chromatids, cytological evidence of crossing-over appears, and the nuclear membrane disappears

proph·e·cy \'präf-ə-sē\ *n, pl* **-cies** **1** : the work or revelation of a prophet inspired by God **2** : the foretelling of the future ⟨the gift of *prophecy*⟩ **3** : something foretold of the future : PREDICTION [Old French *prophecie,* from Late Latin *prophetia,* from Greek *prophēteia,* from *prophētēs* "prophet"]

proph·e·sy \'präf-ə-,sī\ *vb* **-sied; -sy·ing** **1 a** : to speak or write as a prophet **b** : to utter by divine inspiration **2** : to predict on or as if on the basis of mystic knowledge ⟨*prophesy* bad weather⟩ [Middle French *prophesier,* from *prophecie* "prophecy"] SYN see FORETELL — **proph·e·si·er** \-,sī-ər, -,sīr\ *n*

proph·et \'präf-ət\ *n* **1** : a person who declares publicly a message that he or she believes has been divinely inspired; *esp, often cap* : the writer of one of the prophetic books of the Old Testament **2** : one gifted with more than ordinary spiritual and moral insight; *esp* : an inspired poet **3** : one who foretells future events **4** : an effective or leading spokesman for a cause, doctrine, or group ⟨a *prophet* of the revolution⟩ [Old French *prophete,* from Latin *propheta,* from Greek *prophētēs,* from *pro* "for" + *phanai* "to speak"]

proph·et·ess \-ət-əs\ *n* : a woman who is a prophet

pro·phet·ic \prə-'fet-ik\ *adj* **1** : of, relating to, or characteristic of a prophet or prophecy ⟨*prophetic* insight⟩ **2** : foretelling events : PREDICTIVE ⟨a *prophetic* statement⟩ — **pro·phet·i·cal** \-'fet-i-kəl\ *adj* — **pro·phet·i·cal·ly** \-i-kə-lē, -klē\ *adv*

Proph·ets \'präf-əts\ *n pl* : the second part of the Jewish scriptures — compare HAGIOGRAPHA, LAW 3b

pro·phy·lac·tic \,prō-fə-'lak-tik\ *adj* **1** : guarding from or preventing disease **2** : tending to prevent or ward off : PREVENTIVE [Greek *prophylaktikos,* from *prophylassein* "to keep guard before", from *pro-* "before" + *phylassein* "to guard", from *phylax* "guard"] — **prophylactic** *n* — **pro·phy·lac·ti·cal·ly** \-ti-kə-lē, -klē\ *adv*

pro·phy·lax·is \-'lak-səs\ *n, pl* **-lax·es** \-'lak-,sēz\ : measures designed to preserve health and prevent the spread of disease [New Latin, from Greek *prophylaktikos* "prophylactic"]

pro·pin·qui·ty \prō-'ping-kwət-ē\ *n* **1** : nearness of blood : KINSHIP **2** : nearness in place or time [Latin *propinquitas* "kinship, proximity", from *propinquus* "near, akin", from *prope* "near"]

pro·pi·on·ic acid \ˌprō-pē-ˌän-ik-\ *n* : a liquid sharp‑odored fatty acid $C_3H_6O_2$ found in milk and distillates of wood, coal, and petroleum [*pro-* + Greek *pīōn* "fat"]

pro·pi·ti·ate \prō-'pish-ē-ˌāt\ *vt* : to gain or regain the favor or goodwill of : APPEASE, CONCILIATE ⟨*propitiate* the angry gods with sacrifices⟩ [Latin *propitiare,* from *propitius* "propitious"] — **pro·pi·ti·a·tion** \-ˌpish-ē-'ā-shən\ *n* — **pro·pi·ti·a·tor** \-'pish-ē-ˌāt-ər\ *n* — **pro·pi·tia·to·ry** \-'pish-ē-ə-ˌtōr-ē, -'pish-ə-, -ˌtor-\ *adj*

pro·pi·tious \prə-'pish-əs\ *adj* **1** : favorably disposed ⟨the fates are *propitious*⟩ **2** : of good omen : PROMISING ⟨*propitious* signs⟩ **3** : likely to produce good results : OPPORTUNE ⟨the *propitious* moment for asking a favor⟩ [Latin *propitius,* from *pro-* "for" + *petere* "to seek"] — **pro·pi·tious·ly** *adv* — **pro·pi·tious·ness** *n*

prop·jet engine \ˌpräp-ˌjet-\ *n* : TURBO-PROPELLER ENGINE

prop·man \'präp-ˌman\ *n* : PROPERTY MAN

prop·o·lis \'präp-ə-ləs\ *n* : a brownish waxy resinous material collected by bees from the buds of trees and used as a cement [Latin, from Greek, from *pro-* "for" + *polis* "city"]

pro·po·nent \prə-'pō-nənt, 'prō-\ *n* : one who argues in favor of something : ADVOCATE [Latin *proponens,* present participle of *proponere* "to propound"]

¹pro·por·tion \prə-'pōr-shən, pə-, -'por-\ *n* **1** : the relation of one part to another or to the whole with respect to magnitude, quantity, or degree : RATIO **2** : balanced or pleasing arrangement **3** : a statement of the equality of two ratios (as $\frac{4}{5} = \frac{10}{5}$) **4 a** : fair or equal share **b** : QUOTA 1, PERCENTAGE **5** : relative dimensions : SIZE [Middle French, from Latin *proportio,* from *pro-* "for" + *portio* "portion"] — **pro·por·tioned** \-shənd\ *adj* — **in proportion** : PROPORTIONAL 1

²proportion *vt* **-tioned; -tion·ing** \-shə-ning, -shning\ **1** : to adjust (a part or thing) in size relative to other parts or things **2** : to make the parts of harmonious or symmetrical

¹pro·por·tion·al \prə-'pōr-shnəl, pə-, -'por-, -shən-l\ *adj* **1 a** : corresponding in size, degree, or intensity ⟨wages *proportional* to ability⟩ **b** : having the same or a constant ratio ⟨corresponding sides of similar triangles are *proportional*⟩ **2** : determined in size or degree with reference to proportions — **pro·por·tion·al·i·ty** \-ˌpōr-shə-'nal-ət-ē, -ˌpor-\ *n* — **pro·por·tion·al·ly** \-'pōr-shnə-lē, -'por-, -shən-l-ē\ *adv*

²proportional *n* : a number or quantity in a proportion

proportional parts *n pl* : fractional parts of the difference between successive entries in a table for use in linear interpolation

proportional representation *n* : an electoral system designed to represent in a legislative body each political group or party in proportion to its actual voting strength in the electorate

¹pro·por·tion·ate \prə-'pōr-shə-nət, pə-, -'por-, -shnət\ *adj* : PROPORTIONAL 1 — **pro·por·tion·ate·ly** *adv*

²pro·por·tion·ate \-shə-ˌnāt\ *vt* : to make proportionate

pro·pos·al \prə-'pō-zəl\ *n* **1** : an act of offering something for consideration **2 a** : something proposed : SUGGESTION **b** : OFFER 1b; *esp* : an offer of marriage

pro·pose \prə-'pōz\ *vb* **1** : to offer for consideration or discussion : SUGGEST ⟨*propose* terms of peace⟩ **2** : to make plans : INTEND ⟨*propose* to buy a new house⟩ **3** : to offer as a toast : suggest drinking to ⟨*propose* the health of a friend⟩ **4** : NAME, NOMINATE ⟨*propose* one for membership⟩ **5** : to make an offer of marriage [Middle French *proposer,* from Latin *proponere* "to propound"] — **pro·pos·er** *n*

prop·o·si·tion \ˌpräp-ə-'zish-ən\ *n* **1 a** : something offered for consideration or acceptance : PROPOSAL **b** : a theorem or problem to be demonstrated or performed **2** : an expression in language or signs of something that can be either true or false **3** : a project or situation

requiring action : UNDERTAKING — **prop·o·si·tion·al** \-'zish-nəl, -ən-l\ *adj*

pro·pound \prə-'paund\ *vt* : to offer for consideration : PROPOSE [alteration of earlier *propone,* from Latin *proponere* "to display, propound", from *pro-* "before" + *ponere* "to put, place"] — **pro·pound·er** *n*

¹pro·pri·etary \prə-'prī-ə-ˌter-ē\ *n, pl* **-tar·ies** **1** : PROPRIETOR 1 **2** : a drug whose name, composition, or process of manufacture is protected by secrecy, patent, or copyright against free competition : PATENT MEDICINE **3** : a business secretly owned and run as a cover for an intelligence organization

²proprietary *adj* **1** : of, relating to, or characteristic of a proprietor ⟨*proprietary* rights⟩ **2** : made and marketed by one having the exclusive right to manufacture and sell **3** : privately owned and managed ⟨a *proprietary* clinic⟩ [Late Latin *proprietarius,* from Latin *proprietas* "property"]

proprietary colony *n* : a colony granted to a proprietary with full prerogatives of government

pro·pri·etor \prə-'prī-ət-ər\ *n* **1** : one to whom ownership of a proprietary colony is granted **2** : one who holds something as property or a possession : OWNER — **pro·pri·etor·ship** \-ˌship\ *n*

pro·pri·etress \-'prī-ə-trəs\ *n* : a woman who is a proprietor

pro·pri·ety \prə-'prī-ət-ē\ *n, pl* **-ties** **1** : the quality or state of being proper **2** : correctness in manners or behavior : POLITENESS **3** *pl* : the rules and customs of polite society [Middle French *proprieté, propreté* "property"] SYN see DECORUM

pro·prio·cep·tor \ˌprō-prē-ō-'sep-tər\ *n* : a sensory receptor excited by stimuli arising within the organism [Latin *proprius* "own" + English *-ceptor* (as in *receptor*)] — **pro·prio·cep·tive** \-tiv\ *adj*

prop root *n* : a root that braces or supports a plant

pro·pul·sion \prə-'pəl-shən\ *n* **1** : the action or process of propelling **2** : something that propels [Latin *propulsus,* past participle of *propellere* "to propel"]

pro·pul·sive \-'pəl-siv\ *adj* : tending or having power to propel

pro·pyl·ene gly·col \ˌprō-pə-ˌlēn-'glī-ˌkol, -ˌkōl\ *n* : a sweet viscous liquid $C_3H_8O_2$ used as an antifreeze, solvent, and preservative [*propylene* from *prop*ionic acid + *-yl* + *-ene; glycol* from Greek *glykys* "sweet" + English *-ol*]

pro ra·ta \prō-'rāt-ə, 'prō-, -'rät-ə\ *adv* : according to share or liability : PROPORTIONATELY [Latin] — **pro rata** *adj*

pro·rate \prō-'rāt, 'prō-\ *vb* : to divide, distribute, or assess proportionately [*pro rata*] — **pro·ra·tion** \prō-'rā-shən\ *n*

pro·rogue \prə-'rōg, pə-'rōg\ *vb* **1** : DEFER, POSTPONE **2** : to suspend or end a legislative session [Middle French *proroguer* "to prolong, defer", from Latin *prorogare,* from *pro-* "before" + *rogare* "to ask"] — **pro·ro·ga·tion** \ˌprōr-ō-'gā-shən, ˌpror-\ *n*

pros *pl of* PRO

pro·sa·ic \prō-'zā-ik\ *adj* **1 a** : characteristic of prose as distinguished from poetry **b** : unimaginative in style or expression **2** : belonging to the everyday world : COMMONPLACE [Late Latin *prosaicus,* from Latin *prosa* "prose"] — **pro·sa·i·cal·ly** \-'zā-ə-kə-lē, -klē\ *adv*

pro·sce·ni·um \prō-'sē-nē-əm\ *n* **1** : the stage of an ancient theater **2** : the part of a modern stage in front of the curtain **3** : the wall that separates the stage from the auditorium and provides the arch that frames it [Latin, from Greek *proskēnion* "front of the building forming the background for a dramatic performance, stage", from *pro-* + *skēnē* "building forming the background for a dramatic performance"]

pro·scribe \prō-'skrīb\ *vt* **1** : to put outside the protection of the law : OUTLAW **2** : to condemn or forbid as harmful : PROHIBIT [Latin *proscribere* (past participle *proscriptus*) "to publish, proscribe", from *pro-* "be-

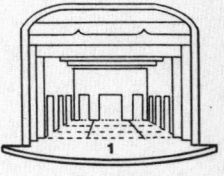

1 proscenium *2*

\ə\ **abut**	\ng\ **sing**
\ər\ **further**	\ō\ **bone**
\a\ **mat**	\o\ **saw**
\ā\ **take**	\oi\ **coin**
\ä\ **cot, cart**	\th\ **thin**
\au\ **out**	\th̲\ **this**
\ch\ **chin**	\ü\ **food**
\e\ **pet**	\u̇\ **foot**
\ē\ **easy**	\y\ **yet**
\g\ **go**	\yü\ **few**
\i\ **tip**	\yu̇\ **cure**
\ī\ **life**	\zh\ **vision**
\j\ **job**	

fore" + *scribere* "to write"] — **pro·scrib·er** *n* — **pro·scrip·tion** \-'skrip-shən\ *n* — **pro·scrip·tive** \-'skrip-tiv\ *adj* — **pro·scrip·tive·ly** *adv*

¹prose \'prōz\ *n* **1 a** : the ordinary language people use in speaking or writing **b** : a literary medium distinguished from poetry especially by its greater irregularity and variety of rhythm and its closer correspondence to the patterns of everyday speech **2** : a prosaic style, quality, character, or condition ⟨the *prose* of everyday life⟩ [Middle French, from Latin *prosa,* from *prorsus, prosus* "straightforward", from *proversus,* past participle of *provertere* "to turn forward", from *pro-* "forward" + *vertere* "to turn"] — **prose** *adj*

²prose *vi* **1** : to write prose **2** : to write or speak in a dull prosaic manner

pros·e·cute \'präs-i-ˌkyüt\ *vb* **1** : to press on with : carry on ⟨*prosecute* a war⟩ **2 a** : to carry on a legal action against (an accused person) in order to prove guilt **b** : to start legal proceedings with respect to ⟨*prosecute* a crime⟩ **c** : to start and carry on a legal suit or prosecution [Latin *prosecutus,* past participle of *prosequi* "to pursue"] — **pros·e·cut·able** \-ˌkyüt-ə-bəl\ *adj*

pros·e·cu·tion \ˌpräs-i-'kyü-shən\ *n* **1** : the act or process of prosecuting; *esp* : the starting and continuing of a criminal suit in court **2** : the party by whom criminal proceedings are begun or conducted

pros·e·cu·tor \'präs-i-ˌkyüt-ər\ *n* **1** : a person who institutes an official prosecution before a court **2** : an attorney who conducts proceedings in a court on behalf of the government : DISTRICT ATTORNEY

¹pros·e·lyte \'präs-ə-ˌlīt\ *n* : a new convert [Late Latin *proselytus* "proselyte, alien resident", from Greek *proselytos*]

²proselyte *vb* **1** : to convert from one religion, belief, or party to another **2** : to recruit members especially by the offer of special inducements — **pros·e·ly·tism** \-ˌlīt-ˌiz-əm, -lə-ˌtiz-\ *n*

pros·e·ly·tize \-lə-ˌtīz\ *vb* : PROSELYTE

pro·sim·i·an \prō-'sim-ē-ən, 'prō-\ *n* : a lower primate (as a lemur) — **prosimian** *adj*

pros·i·ness \'prō-zē-nəs\ *n* : the quality or state of being prosy

pro·sit \'prō-zət, -sət\ *or* **prost** \'prōst\ *interj* — used to wish good health especially before drinking [German, from Latin *prosit* "may it be beneficial", from *prodesse* "to be useful"]

pros·o·dist \'präs-əd-əst\ *n* : a specialist in prosody

pros·o·dy \'präs-əd-ē\ *n, pl* **-dies 1** : the study of versification; *esp* : METRICS **2** : a particular system, theory, or style of versification [Latin *prosodia* "accent of a syllable", from Greek *prosōidia* "song sung to instrumental music, accent", from *pros* "in addition to" + *ōidē* "song"] — **pro·sod·ic** \prə-'säd-ik\ *adj* — **pro·sod·i·cal·ly** \-i-kə-lē, -klē\ *adv*

¹pros·pect \'präs-ˌpekt\ *n* **1 a** : a wide view **b** : a viewing with the mind **2** : something extended to the view : SCENE **3 a** : act of looking forward : ANTICIPATION **b** : a mental picture of something to come : VISION **c** : something that is awaited or expected : POSSIBILITY **4 a** : a potential buyer or customer **b** : a candidate or a person likely to become a candidate ⟨presidential *prospects*⟩ [Latin *prospectus* "view, prospect", from *prospicere* "to look forward", from *pro-* "forward" + *specere* "to look"]

²prospect *vb* : to explore an area especially for mineral deposits — **pros·pec·tor** \-ˌpek-tər\ *n*

pro·spec·tive \prə-'spek-tiv *also* 'prä-ˌ, prō-, prä-'\ *adj* **1** : likely to come about : EXPECTED ⟨the *prospective* benefits of a law⟩ **2** : likely to be or become ⟨a *prospective* athlete⟩ — **pro·spec·tive·ly** *adv*

pro·spec·tus \prə-'spek-təs, prä-\ *n, pl* **-tus·es** : a printed statement describing an enterprise and distributed to prospective investors [Latin, "prospect"]

pros·per \'präs-pər\ *vb* **pros·pered; pros·per·ing** \-pə-ring, -pring\ **1** : SUCCEED; *esp* : to succeed financially **2** : FLOURISH 1, THRIVE **3** : to cause to succeed or thrive [Middle French *prosperer,* from Latin *prosperare* "to cause to succeed", from *prosperus* "favorable"]

pros·per·i·ty \prä-'sper-ət-ē\ *n* : the condition of being successful or thriving; *esp* : economic well-being

pros·per·ous \'präs-pə-rəs, -prəs\ *adj* **1** : AUSPICIOUS 1 **2** : marked by success or economic well-being — **pros·per·ous·ly** *adv* — **pros·per·ous·ness** *n*

pros·ta·glan·din \ˌpräs-tə-'glan-dən\ *n* : any of various fatty acids of animals that may perform a variety of physiological actions (as controlling blood pressure or smooth muscle contraction) [*prosta*te *gland* + *-in*; from its occurrence in the sexual glands of animals]

pros·tate \'präs-ˌtāt\ *n* : PROSTATE GLAND [Greek *prostatēs* "prostate gland", from *proïstanai* "to put in front", from *pro-* + *histanai* "to cause to stand"] — **pros·tat·ic** \präs-'tat-ik\ *adj*

prostate gland *n* : a firm partly muscular partly glandular body about the base of the mammalian male urethra

pros·the·sis \präs-'thē-səs, 'präs-thə-\ *n, pl* **-the·ses** \-ˌsēz\ : an artificial device to replace a missing part of the body [Greek, "addition", from *prostithenai* "to add to", from *pros-* "in addition to" + *tithenai* "to put"] — **pros·thet·ic** \präs-'thet-ik\ *adj* — **pros·thet·i·cal·ly** \-'thet-i-kə-lē, -klē\ *adv*

prosthetic group *n* : a nonprotein group of a conjugated protein

¹pros·ti·tute \'präs-tə-ˌtüt, -ˌtyüt\ *vt* : to devote to corrupt or unworthy purposes : DEBASE ⟨*prostitute* one's talents⟩ [Latin *prostitutus,* past participle of *prostituere* "to offer for prostitution", from *pro-* "before" + *statuere* "to set up, station", from *status* "position, state"]

²prostitute *n* : a person who engages in sexual activities for money

pros·ti·tu·tion \ˌpräs-tə-'tü-shən, -'tyü-\ *n* **1** : the acts or practices of a prostitute **2** : the state of being prostituted

pro·sto·mi·um \prō-'stō-mē-əm\ *n, pl* **-mia** \-mē-ə\ : the portion of the head of various worms and mollusks situated in front of the mouth and usually held not to be a true segment [New Latin, from Greek *pro-* + *stoma* "mouth"] — **pro·sto·mi·al** \-mē-al\ *adj*

¹pros·trate \'präs-ˌtrāt\ *adj* **1 a** : stretched out with face on the ground (as in adoration or submission) **b** : lying flat and stretched out **2** : lacking in vitality or will : OVERCOME **3** : trailing on the ground ⟨a *prostrate* shrub⟩ [Latin *prostratus,* past participle of *prosternere* "to prostrate", from *pro-* "before" + *sternere* "to spread out, throw down"] SYN see PRONE

²prostrate *vt* **1** : to throw or put into a prostrate position **2** : to make helpless or exhausted : OVERCOME

pros·tra·tion \prä-'strā-shən\ *n* **1** : the act of assuming or state of being in a prostrate position **2** : complete physical or mental exhaustion : COLLAPSE

prosy \'prō-zē\ *adj* **pros·i·er; -est 1** : PROSAIC 1 **2** : TEDIOUS

prot- *or* **proto-** *combining form* **1** : first in time ⟨*proto*history⟩ **2** : first formed : primary ⟨*proto*nema⟩ **3** *cap* : relating to or constituting the recorded or assumed language that is ancestral to a language or to a group of related languages or dialects [Greek *prōtos* "foremost, first"]

prot·ac·tin·i·um \ˌprōt-ˌak-'tin-ē-əm\ *n* : a shiny metallic radioactive chemical element of relatively short life — see ELEMENT table

pro·tag·o·nist \prō-'tag-ə-nəst\ *n* **1** : one who takes the leading part in a drama, novel, or story **2** : the leader of a cause : CHAMPION **3** : a muscle that by its contraction actually causes a particular movement [Greek *prōtagōnistēs,* from *prōtos* "first" + *agōnistēs* "competitor at games, actor", derived from *agōn* "contest"]

prot·amine \'prōt-ə-ˌmēn\ *n* : any of various simple strongly basic proteins that are not coagulable by heat but are soluble in water and dilute ammonia

pro·te·an \'prōt-ē-ən\ *adj* : readily assuming different shapes or roles ⟨the *protean* amoeba⟩ ⟨a *protean* actor⟩ [*Proteus,* Greek sea god]

pro·te·ase \'prōt-ē-ˌās\ *n* : PROTEINASE, PEPTIDASE

pro·tect \prə-'tekt\ *vt* **1** : to cover or shield from injury or destruction : GUARD **2** : to shield or foster (an industry) by trade controls [Latin *protectus,* past participle of *protegere* "to protect", from *pro-* "in front" + *tegere* "to cover"] SYN see DEFEND

pro·tec·tion \prə-'tek-shən\ *n* **1** : the act of protecting : the state of being protected **2 a** : one that protects **b** : the oversight or support of one that is smaller and weaker **3** : the freeing of the producers of a country from foreign competition especially by high duties on foreign goods **4** : money extorted by racketeers threatening violence **5** : COVERAGE 2b — **pro·tec·tive** \-'tek-tiv\ *adj* — **pro·tec·tive·ly** *adv*

pro·tec·tion·ist \-shə-nəst, -shnəst\ *n* : an advocate of government economic protection for domestic producers through restrictions on foreign competitors — **pro·tec·tion·ism** \-shə-ˌniz-əm\ *n* — **protectionist** *adj*

protective coloration *n* : coloration that makes an organism appear less visible or less attractive to predators

protective tariff *n* : a tariff intended primarily to protect domestic producers rather than to yield revenue

pro·tec·tor \prə-'tek-tər\ *n* **1 a** : one that protects : GUARDIAN **b** : a device used to prevent injury : GUARD **2** : one having the care of a kingdom (as during a king's minority) : REGENT — **pro·tec·tor·ship** \-ˌship\ *n*

pro·tec·tor·ate \prə-'tek-tə-rət, -ˌtrət\ *n* **1 a** : government by a protector; *esp* : the government of England (1653–59) under the Cromwells **b** : the rank, office, or period of rule of a protector **2 a** : the relationship of superior authority assumed by one state over a dependent one **b** : the dependent state in such a relationship

pro·té·gé \'prōt-ə-ˌzhā\ *n* : one under the care and protection of someone influential especially for the furthering of his or her career [French, from *protéger* "to protect", from Latin *protegere*]

pro·té·gée \-ˌzhā\ *n* : a girl or woman who is a protégé [French, feminine of *protégé*]

pro·tein \'prō-ˌtēn, 'prōt-ē-ən\ *n* **1** : any of numerous naturally occurring nitrogen-containing substances that consist of chains of amino acids and are essential constituents of all living cells **2** : the total nitrogenous material in plant or animal substances [French *protéine,* derived from Greek *prōtos* "first"] — **pro·tein·aceous** \ˌprō-tē-'nā-shəs, ˌprōt-ē-ə-'nā-\ *adj*

pro·tein·ase \'prō-ˌtē-ˌnās, 'prōt-ē-ə-\ *n* : an enzyme that hydrolyzes proteins especially to peptides

pro tem \prō-'tem\ *adv* : pro tempore

pro tem·po·re \prō-'tem-pə-rē\ *adv* : for the present : TEMPORARILY [Latin]

pro·teo·lyt·ic \ˌprōt-ē-ə-'lit-ik\ *adj* : of, relating to, or producing the hydrolysis of proteins or peptides to simpler and soluble products ⟨*proteolytic* enzymes⟩ — **pro·te·ol·y·sis** \ˌprōt-ē-'äl-ə-səs\ *n*

pro·te·ose \'prōt-ē-ˌōs, -ˌōz\ *n* : any of various water-soluble protein derivatives formed by partial hydrolysis

Prot·ero·zo·ic \ˌprät-ə-rə-'zō-ik, ˌprōt-\ *n* : the 2d of the three eons of geological history that perhaps exceeds in length all of subsequent geological time and is marked by rocks that contain a few fossils indicating the existence of annelid worms and algae; *also* : the corresponding system of rocks — see GEOLOGIC TIME table [Greek *proteros* "former, earlier", from *pro* "before"] — **Proterozoic** *adj*

¹pro·test \'prō-ˌtest\ *n* **1** : a formal declaration of opinion and usually of objection or complaint **2** : a declaration that payment of a note or bill has been refused and that all endorsers are liable for damages **3** : a complaint, objection, or display of unwillingness or disapproval

²pro·test \prə-'test, 'prō-ˌtest, prō-'\ *vb* **1 a** : to make solemn declaration of : ASSERT ⟨*protest* one's innocence⟩ **b** : to make a protestation **2 a** : to make a protest against ⟨*protested* the higher tax rate⟩ **b** : to object strongly ⟨*protest* against an arbitrary ruling⟩ [Middle French *protester,* from Latin *protestari,* from *pro-* "forth" + *testari* "to call to witness"] — **pro·test·er** *or* **pro·tes·tor** \-'tes-tər, -ˌtes-\ *n*

prot·es·tant \'prät-əs-tənt, *2 is also* prə-'tes-\ *n* **1** *cap* **a** : one of a group of German princes and cities presenting a defense of freedom of conscience against an edict of the Diet of Spires in 1529 intended to suppress the Lutheran movement **b** : a Christian denying the universal authority of the Pope and affirming the Reformation principles of justification by faith, the priesthood of all believers, and the primacy of the Bible **c** : a Christian not of a Catholic or Eastern church **2** : one who makes or enters a protest — **protestant** *adj, often cap* — **Prot·es·tant·ism** \'prät-əs-tənt-ˌiz-əm\ *n*

prot·es·ta·tion \ˌprät-əs-'tā-shən, ˌprō-ˌtes-\ *n* : the act of protesting : a solemn declaration or avowal

pro·thal·li·um \prō-'thal-ē-əm, 'prō-\ *or* **pro·thal·lus** \-'thal-əs\ *n, pl* **-lia** \-ē-ə\ *or* **-li** \-ˌī, -ˌē\ : a small flat green thallus attached to the soil by rhizoids that is the gametophyte of a pteridophyte (as a fern) [New Latin, from *pro-* + *thallus*] — **pro·thal·li·al** \-ē-əl\ *adj*

pro·tho·rax \prō-'thōr-ˌaks, 'prō-, -'thor-\ *n* : the first segment of the thorax of an insect — **pro·tho·rac·ic** \ˌprō-thə-'ras-ik\ *adj*

pro·throm·bin \prō-'thräm-bən, 'prō-\ *n* : a plasma protein produced in the liver in the presence of vitamin K and converted into thrombin in the clotting of blood

pro·tist \'prōt-əst\ *n* : any of a kingdom or group (Protista) of unicellular or noncellular organisms comprising bacteria, protozoans, various algae and fungi, and sometimes viruses [derived from Greek *prōtistos* "very first, primal", from *prōtos* "first"] — **pro·tis·tan** \prō-'tis-tən\ *adj or n*

pro·ti·um \'prōt-ē-əm, 'prō-shē-\ *n* : the ordinary light hydrogen isotope of atomic mass 1 [New Latin, from Greek *prōtos* "first"]

proto- — see PROT-

pro·to·coc·cus \ˌprōt-ə-'käk-əs\ *n* : any of a genus of globe-shaped and mostly terrestrial green algae [*prot-* + Greek *kokkos* "grain, seed"]

pro·to·col \'prōt-ə-ˌkȯl\ *n* **1** : an original draft, minute, or record of a document or transaction : MEMORANDUM **2** : a code of diplomatic or military etiquette and precedence [Middle French *prothocole,* from Medieval Latin *protocollum,* from Late Greek *prōtokollon* "first sheet of a papyrus roll bearing data of manufacture", from Greek *prōtos* "first" + *kollan* "to glue", from *kolla* "glue"]

pro·to·his·to·ry \ˌprōt-ō-'his-tə-rē, -trē\ *n* : the study of humanity of the period that just antedates recorded history — **pro·to·his·tor·ic** \-his-'tȯr-ik, -'tär-\ *adj*

pro·ton \'prō-ˌtän\ *n* : an elementary particle identical with the nucleus of the hydrogen atom that along with the neutron is a constituent of all other atomic nuclei and carries a positive charge numerically equal to the negative charge of an electron [Greek *prōton,* neuter of *prōtos* "first"] — **pro·ton·ic** \prō-'tän-ik\ *adj*

pro·to·ne·ma \ˌprōt-ə-'nē-mə\ *n, pl* **-ne·ma·ta** \-'nē-mət-ə, -'nem-ət-\ : the primary usually filamentous stage of the gametophyte in mosses and some liverworts that is comparable to the fern prothallium [*prot-* + Greek *nēmat-, nēma* "thread"] — **pro·to·ne·mal**

\ə\ abut	\ng\ sing
\ər\ further	\ō\ bone
\a\ mat	\ȯ\ saw
\ā\ take	\ȯi\ coin
\ä\ cot, cart	\th\ thin
\au̇\ out	\th\ this
\ch\ chin	\ü\ food
\e\ pet	\u̇\ foot
\ē\ easy	\y\ yet
\g\ go	\yü\ few
\i\ tip	\yu̇\ cure
\ī\ life	\zh\ vision
\j\ job	

\-'nē-məl\ *adj* — **pro·to·ne·ma·tal** \-'nē-mət-l, -'nem-ət-\ *adj*

pro·to·plan·et \'prōt-ō-,plan-ət\ *n* : a whirling mass of gas and dust that rotates around a star and that is held to be the source of a planet

pro·to·plasm \'prōt-ə-,plaz-əm\ *n* **1** : a colloidal complex of protein, various organic and inorganic substances, and water that constitutes the living nucleus, cytoplasm, plastids, and mitochondria of the cell and is held to be the physical basis of life **2** : CYTOPLASM [German *protoplasma,* from *prot-* "prot-" + *plasma* "plasma"] — **pro·to·plas·mic** \,prōt-ə-'plaz-mik\ *adj*

pro·to·plast \'prōt-ə-,plast\ *n* : the nucleus, cytoplasm, and plasma membrane of a cell constituting a living unit distinct from inert walls and inclusions [Middle French *protoplaste* "prototype, something formed first", from Late Latin *protoplastos* "first man", from Greek *prōtoplastos* "first formed", from *prōtos* "first" + *plastos* "formed", from *plassein* "to mold"]

pro·to·type \'prōt-ə-,tīp\ *n* **1** : an original model on which something is patterned **2** : an individual that exhibits the essential features of a later type — **pro·to·typ·al** \,prōt-ə-'tī-pəl\ *adj* — **pro·to·typ·i·cal** \-'tip-i-kəl\ *adj*

pro·to·zo·an \,prōt-ə-'zō-ən\ *n* : any of a phylum or group (Protozoa) of minute animals that are either single-celled or not obviously divided into cells, have varied structure and physiology and often complex life cycles, are represented in almost every kind of habitat, and include some which are serious parasites of man and domestic animals [*prot-* + Greek *zōion* "animal"] — **protozoan** *adj*

pro·to·zo·ol·o·gy \-zō-'äl-ə-jē, -zə-'wäl-\ *n* : a branch of zoology dealing with protozoans — **pro·to·zo·ol·o·gist** \-jəst\ *n*

pro·to·zo·on \-'zō-,än\ *n, pl* **-zoa** \-'zō-ə\ : PROTOZOAN

pro·tract \prō-'trakt\ *vt* : to prolong in time or space [Latin *protractus,* past participle of *protrahere* "to protract", literally, "to draw forward", from *pro-* "forward" + *trahere* "to draw"] SYN see EXTEND — **pro·trac·tion** \-'trak-shən\ *n*

pro·trac·tor \prō-'trak-tər, 'prō-,\ *n* **1 a** : one that protracts, prolongs, or delays **b** : a muscle that extends a part — compare RETRACTOR **2** : an instrument for laying down and measuring angles that is used in drawing and plotting

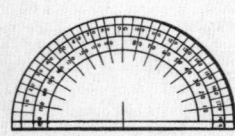

protractor 2

pro·trude \prō-'trüd\ *vb* **1** : to cause to stick out : PROJECT **2** : to jut out from the surroundings [Latin *protrudere* (past participle *protrusus*) "to thrust forward", from *pro-* "forward" + *trudere* "to thrust"] — **pro·tru·si·ble** \-'trü-sə-bəl, -zə-\ *adj*

pro·tru·sion \prō-'trü-zhən\ *n* **1** : the act of protruding : the state of being protruded **2** : something that protrudes SYN see PROJECTION

pro·tu·ber·ance \prō-'tü-bə-rəns, -'tyü-, -brəns\ *n* **1** : the quality or state of being protuberant **2** : something that is protuberant : BULGE

pro·tu·ber·ant \-bə-rənt, -brənt\ *adj* : bulging beyond the surrounding surface : PROMINENT [Late Latin *protuberans,* present participle of *protuberare* "to bulge out", from Latin *pro-* "forward" + *tuber* "hump, swelling"] — **pro·tu·ber·ant·ly** *adv*

proud \'praud\ *adj* **1** : feeling or showing pride: as **a** : having or displaying excessive self-esteem **b** : much pleased : EXULTANT ⟨*proud* parents of the valedictorian⟩ **c** : having proper self-respect ⟨too *proud* to beg⟩ **2** : MAGNIFICENT 1, STATELY **3** : VIGOROUS, SPIRITED ⟨a *proud* steed⟩ [Old English *prūd*] — **proud·ly** *adv*

prove \'prüv\ *vb* **proved; proved** *or* **prov·en** \'prü-vən\; **prov·ing** **1** : to test by an experiment or a standard — often used with *up* **2 a** : to establish the truth or validity of by evidence or demonstration **b** : to check the correctness of (as an arithmetic operation) **3 a** : to ascertain the genuineness of : VERIFY **b** : to obtain probate of (a will) **4** : to turn out especially after trial or

test ⟨the new drug *proved* effective⟩ [Old French *prover,* from Latin *probare* "to test, approve, demonstrate", from *probus* "good, honest"] — **prov·able** \'prü-və-bəl\ *adj*

prov·e·nance \'präv-nəns, -ə-nəns\ *n* : ORIGIN 2b, SOURCE [French, from *provenir* "to come forth, originate", from Latin *provenire,* from *pro-* "forth" + *venire* "to come"]

Pro·ven·çal \,prōv-ən-'säl, ,präv-, -,än-\ *n* **1** : a native or inhabitant of Provence **2** : a Romance language spoken in southeastern France [Middle French, from *provençal* "of Provence", from *Provence*] — **Provençal** *adj*

prov·en·der \'präv-ən-dər\ *n* **1** : dry food for domestic animals : FEED **2** : FOOD 2, VICTUALS [Middle French *provende, provendre,* from Medieval Latin *provenda,* alteration of *praebenda* "prebend"]

pro·ve·nience \prə-'vē-nyəns\ *n* : ORIGIN 2b, SOURCE [alteration of *provenance*]

pro·ven·tric·u·lus \,prō-ven-'trik-yə-ləs\ *n, pl* **-li** \-,lī, -,lē\ **1** : a pouch of the digestive tract (as of an insect or earthworm) **2** : the glandular stomach of a bird situated between the crop and gizzard [¹*pro-* + Latin *ventriculus* "stomach, ventricle"]

prov·erb \'präv-,ərb\ *n* : a brief popular saying or maxim : ADAGE [Middle French *proverbe,* from Latin *proverbium,* from *pro-* + *verbum* "word"]

pro·ver·bi·al \prə-'vər-bē-əl\ *adj* **1** : of, relating to, or resembling a proverb ⟨*proverbial* wisdom⟩ **2** : commonly spoken of ⟨the *proverbial* beginner's luck⟩ — **pro·ver·bi·al·ly** \-bē-ə-lē\ *adv*

Prov·erbs \'präv-,ərbz\ *n* — see BIBLE table

pro·vide \prə-'vīd\ *vb* **1** : to take precautionary measures ⟨*provide* against a possible shortage⟩ **2** : to include as a condition : STIPULATE ⟨the contract *provided* for 10 paid holidays⟩ **3** : to supply what is needed for sustenance or support ⟨*provides* for a large family⟩ **4 a** : OUTFIT, EQUIP ⟨*provide* the children with new shoes⟩ **b** : to supply for use : YIELD ⟨cows *provide* milk⟩ [Latin *providēre,* literally, "to see ahead", from *pro-* "forward" + *vidēre* "to see"] — **pro·vid·er** *n*

pro·vid·ed *conj* : on condition : IF — sometimes followed by *that*

prov·i·dence \'präv-əd-əns, -ə-,dens\ *n* **1 a** *often cap* : divine guidance or care **b** *cap* : God conceived as the power sustaining and guiding human destiny **2** : the quality or state of being provident : PRUDENCE [Middle French, from Latin *providentia,* from *providens* "provident"]

prov·i·dent \-əd-ənt, -ə-,dent\ *adj* **1** : making provision for the future : PRUDENT **2** : FRUGAL, THRIFTY [Latin *providens,* from *providēre* "to provide"] — **prov·i·dent·ly** *adv*

prov·i·den·tial \,präv-ə-'den-chəl\ *adj* **1** : of, relating to, or determined by Providence ⟨a *providential* plan⟩ **2** : occurring by or as if by an intervention of Providence : FORTUNATE ⟨a *providential* escape⟩ — **prov·i·den·tial·ly** \-'dench-lē, -ə-lē\ *adv*

pro·vid·ing \prə-'vīd-ing\ *conj* : PROVIDED

prov·ince \'präv-əns\ *n* **1 a** : a country or region brought under the control of the ancient Roman government **b** : an administrative district or division of a country **c** *pl* : all of a country except the metropolis **2** : a division of a country forming the jurisdiction of an archbishop or metropolitan **3** : proper or appropriate business or scope : SPHERE ⟨a legal question outside the physician's *province*⟩ [French, from Latin *provincia*]

¹**pro·vin·cial** \prə-'vin-chəl\ *n* **1** : the superior of a province of a religious order **2** : one living in or coming from a province **3 a** : a person of local or restricted outlook **b** : a person lacking urban polish or refinement

²**provincial** *adj* **1** : of, relating to, or coming from a province **2 a** : limited in outlook : NARROW **b** : lacking

the polish of urban society : UNSOPHISTICATED **3** : of or relating to a decorative style (as in furniture) marked by simplicity and relative plainness — **pro·vin·ci·al·i·ty** \-ˌvin-chē-'al-ət-ē\ *n* — **pro·vin·cial·ly** \-'vinch-lē, -ə-lē\ *adv*

pro·vin·cial·ism \prə-'vin-chə-ˌliz-əm\ *n* **1** : a dialectal or local word, phrase, or idiom **2** : the quality or state of being provincial

proving ground *n* **1** : a place for scientific experimentation or testing **2** : a place where something new is tried out

¹pro·vi·sion \prə-'vizh-ən\ *n* **1 a** : the act or process of providing ⟨*provision* of transportation for the trip⟩ **b** : a measure taken beforehand : PREPARATION ⟨make *provision* for emergencies⟩ **2** : a stock of needed materials or supplies; *esp* : a stock of food — usually used in pl. **3** : PROVISO 2, STIPULATION [Middle French, from Latin *provisio* "foresight", from *provisus,* past participle of *providēre* "to see ahead, provide"]

²provision *vt* **pro·vi·sioned; pro·vi·sion·ing** \-'vizh-ning, -ə-ning\ : to supply with provisions ⟨*provision* a military garrison⟩

pro·vi·sion·al \prə-'vizh-nəl, -ən-l\ *adj* : serving for the time being : TEMPORARY ⟨a *provisional* government⟩ — **pro·vi·sion·al·ly** \-ē\ *adv*

pro·vi·so \prə-'vī-zō\ *n, pl* **-sos** *or* **-soes** **1** : a part of a legal document that states a condition **2** : a requirement that is a condition ⟨given a bicycle with the *proviso* that it be kept in good repair⟩ [Medieval Latin *proviso quod* "provided that"]

pro·vi·ta·min \prō-'vīt-ə-mən, 'prō-\ *n* : a precursor of a vitamin convertible into the vitamin in an organism

prov·o·ca·tion \ˌpräv-ə-'kā-shən\ *n* **1** : the act of provoking : INCITEMENT **2** : something that provokes, arouses, or stimulates [Middle French, from Latin *provocatio,* from *provocare* "to provoke"]

pro·voc·a·tive \prə-'väk-ət-iv\ *adj* : serving as a provocation ⟨*provocative* comments⟩ — **pro·voc·a·tive·ly** *adv* — **pro·voc·a·tive·ness** *n*

pro·voke \prə-'vōk\ *vt* **1** : to arouse to action or feeling; *esp* : to excite to anger **2 a** : to call forth : EVOKE **b** : to stir up purposely **c** : to provide the needed stimulus for ⟨*provoke* a response from a nerve⟩ [Middle French *provoquer,* from Latin *provocare,* from *pro-* "forth" + *vocare* "to call"] □ SYN PROVOKE, EXCITE, STIMULATE mean to arouse as if by pricking. PROVOKE directs attention to the response called forth ⟨a joke that failed to *provoke* laughter⟩ ⟨such diplomatic moves as *provoke* nations to war⟩ EXCITE implies a stirring up or moving profoundly ⟨a performance that *excited* admiration⟩ STIMULATE suggests a rousing out of lethargy, inactivity, or indifference ⟨the need to *stimulate* the economy⟩

pro·vok·ing \-'vō-king\ *adj* : causing mild anger ⟨a *provoking* delay⟩ — **pro·vok·ing·ly** \-king-lē\ *adv*

pro·vost \'prō-ˌvōst, 'präv-əst\ *n* **1** : the chief dignitary of a collegiate or cathedral chapter **2** : a chief magistrate or a high-ranking administrative officer (as in a university) [Old English *profost* and Old French *provost,* both from Medieval Latin *propositus,* from Latin *praepositus* "one in charge", from *praeponere* "to place at the head"]

provost marshal \'prō-ˌvōst, 'präv-əst *also* ˌprō-vō-\ *n* : the head of the military police of a command

prow \'praù\ *n* **1** : the bow of a ship : STEM **2** : a pointed projecting front part [Middle French *proue,* probably from Italian dialect *prua,* from Latin *prora,* from Greek *prōira*]

prow·ess \'praù-əs\ *n* **1** : distinguished bravery; *esp* : military valor and skill **2** : extraordinary ability [Old French *proesse,* from *prou* "valiant", from Late Latin *prode* "advantageous", from Latin *prodesse* "to be advantageous"]

prowl \'praùl\ *vb* **1** : to move about or wander stealthily in the manner of a wild beast seeking prey **2** : to

roam over in a predatory manner ⟨*prowled* the streets⟩ [Middle English *prollen*] — **prowl** *n* — **prowl·er** *n*

prowl car *n* : SQUAD CAR

prox·i·mal \'präk-sə-məl\ *adj* **1** : being nearest : PROXIMATE **2** : near or next to the point of attachment or origin (as of a bone or a limb) — compare DISTAL **3** : of, relating to, or being the mesial and distal surfaces of a tooth [Latin *proximus*] — **prox·i·mal·ly** \-mə-lē\ *adv*

proximal convoluted tubule *n* : the convoluted portion of the vertebrate nephron that lies between Bowman's capsule and the loop of Henle and is held to be concerned especially with resorption of sugar, sodium and chloride ions, and water — called also *proximal tubule*

prox·i·mate \-mət\ *adj* **1 a** : very near : CLOSE **b** : soon forthcoming **2** : next preceding or following : DIRECT ⟨the *proximate* cause⟩ [Latin *proximatus,* past participle of *proximare* "to approach", from *proximus* "nearest, next", superlative of *prope* "near"] — **prox·i·mate·ly** *adv* — **prox·i·mate·ness** *n*

prox·im·i·ty \präk-'sim-ət-ē\ *n* : the quality or state of being proximate

prox·i·mo \'präk-sə-ˌmō\ *adj* : of or occurring in the next month after the present [Latin *proximo mense* "in the next month"]

proxy \'präk-sē\ *n, pl* **prox·ies** **1 a** : authority to act for another (as in voting) **b** : a document giving such authority **2** : a person authorized to act for another [Middle English *procucie,* from Anglo-French *procuracie,* from Medieval Latin *procuratia,* from Latin *procuratio* "management, act of taking charge", from *procurare* "to take care of"] — **proxy** *adj*

prude \'prüd\ *n* : a person overly or priggishly concerned with modesty and decorum [French, "good woman, prudish woman", short for *prudefemme* "good woman"] — **prud·ish** \'prüd-ish\ *adj* — **prud·ish·ly** *adv* — **prud·ish·ness** *n*

pru·dence \'prüd-ns\ *n* **1** : the ability to govern and discipline oneself by the use of reason **2** : discretion and shrewdness in the management of affairs **3** : skill and good judgment in the use of resources **4** : CAUTION 2, CIRCUMSPECTION

pru·dent \-nt\ *adj* **1** : marked by wisdom **2** : shrewdly practical **3** : CIRCUMSPECT, DISCREET **4** : FRUGAL, PROVIDENT [Middle French, from Latin *prudens,* from *providens* "provident"] — **pru·dent·ly** *adv*

pru·den·tial \prü-'den-chəl\ *adj* **1** : of, relating to, or resulting from prudence **2** : using prudence — **pru·den·tial·ly** \-chə-lē\ *adv*

prud·ery \'prüd-rē, -ə-rē\ *n, pl* **-er·ies** **1** : the quality or state of being prudish : exaggerated or priggish modesty **2** : a prudish remark or act

¹prune \'prün\ *n* : a plum dried or capable of drying without fermentation [Middle French, "plum", from Latin *prunum*]

²prune *vt* **1** : to cut off the dead or unwanted parts of (a woody plant) ⟨*prune* the hedge⟩ **2 a** : to reduce by eliminating superfluous matter ⟨*prune* an essay⟩ ⟨*prune* a budget⟩ **b** : to remove as superfluous [Middle French *proignier*] — **prun·er** *n*

pru·ri·ent \'prùr-ē-ənt\ *adj* **1** : having indecent desires or thoughts : LEWD **2** : inclined to or characterized by lasciviousness [Latin *pruriens,* present participle of *prurire* "to itch, crave, be wanton"] — **pru·ri·ence** \-ē-əns\ *n* — **pru·ri·ent·ly** *adv*

pru·ri·tus \prü-'rīt-əs, -'rēt-\ *n* : ITCH 1a [Latin, from *prurire* "to itch"] — **pru·rit·ic** \-'rit-ik\ *adj*

prus·sic acid \ˌprəs-ik-\ *n* : HYDROCYANIC ACID [French *acide prussique*]

¹pry \'prī\ *vi* **pried; pry·ing** : to look closely or inquisitively; *esp* : to invade another's privacy ⟨*pry* into other people's affairs⟩ [Middle English *prien*]

²pry *vt* **pried; pry·ing** **1** : to raise, move, or pull apart with a tool or lever **2** : to extract, detach, or open

\ə\ abut		\ng\ sing
\ər\ further		\ō\ bone
\a\ mat		\ȯ\ saw
\ā\ take		\ȯi\ coin
\ä\ cot, cart		\th\ thin
\aù\ out		\th\ this
\ch\ chin		\ü\ food
\e\ pet		\ u̇\ foot
\ē\ easy		\y\ yet
\g\ go		\yü\ few
\i\ tip		\yu̇\ cure
\ī\ life		\zh\ vision
\j\ job		

with difficulty ⟨*pry* a secret out of a person⟩ [alteration of ⁵*prize*]

pry·ing *adj* : impertinently or officiously inquisitive or interrogatory SYN see CURIOUS — **pry·ing·ly** \-ing-lē\ *adv*

psalm \'säm, 'sälm\ *n* : a sacred song or poem; *esp* : one of the hymns that make up the Old Testament Book of Psalms [Old English *psealm*, from Late Latin *psalmus*, from Greek *psalmos*, literally, "twanging of a harp", from *psallein* "to pluck"]

psalm·ist \-əst\ *n* : a writer or composer of psalms

psalm·o·dy \-əd-ē\ *n, pl* **-dies** **1** : the art or practice of singing psalms in worship **2** : a collection of psalms [Late Latin *psalmodia*, from Late Greek *psalmōidia*, literally, "singing to the harp", from Greek *psalmos* "psalm, twanging of a harp" + *aidein* "to sing"]

Psalms \'sämz, 'sälmz\ *n* — see BIBLE table

Psal·ter \'sol-tər\ *n* : the Book of Psalms; *also* : a collection of Psalms for liturgical or devotional use [Old English *psalter*, from Late Latin *psalterium*, from Late Greek *psaltērion*, from Greek, "psaltery"]

psal·tery *also* **psal·try** \'sol-tə-rē, -trē\ *n, pl* **-ter·ies** *also* **-tries** : an ancient stringed musical instrument resembling the zither [Middle French *psalterie*, from Latin *psalterium*, from Greek *psaltērion*, from *psallein* "to pluck, play on a stringed instrument"]

pseud- *or* **pseudo-** *combining form* : false : sham : spurious ⟨*pseudo*coel⟩ [Greek, from *pseudēs*]

pseu·do \'süd-ō\ *adj* : SHAM 1, FALSE [*pseudo-*]

pseu·do·coel \'süd-ə-ˌsēl\ *also* **pseu·do·coe·lom** \-ˌsē-ləm\ *n* : a body cavity of an invertebrate that is not structurally or in origin a true coelom — **pseu·do·coe·lo·mate** \ˌsüd-ə-'sē-lə-ˌmāt\ *adj or n*

pseu·do·nym \'süd-n-ˌim\ *n* : a fictitious name; *esp* : PEN NAME [French *pseudonyme*, from Greek *pseudōnymos* "bearing a false name", from *pseud-* + *onyma, onoma* "name"]

pseu·do·pod \'süd-ə-ˌpäd\ *n* : PSEUDOPODIUM — **pseu·dop·o·dal** \sü-'däp-əd-l\ *or* **pseu·do·po·di·al** \ˌsüd-ə-'pōd-ē-əl\ *adj*

pseu·do·po·di·um \ˌsüd-ə-'pōd-ē-əm\ *n, pl* **pseu·do·po·dia** \-ē-ə\ : a part of a cell that is temporarily protruded by moving cytoplasm (as in the amoeba) and that helps to move the cell and to take in its food [New Latin, from Greek *pseud-* + *podion* "little foot", from *pod-, pous* "foot"]

pshaw \'sho\ *interj* — used to express irritation, disapproval, contempt, or disbelief [imitative]

psi \'sī, 'psī\ *n* : the 23d letter of the Greek alphabet — Ψ or ψ

psi·lo·cy·bin \ˌsī-lə-'sī-bən\ *n* : a hallucinogenic organic compound $C_{12}H_{17}N_2O_4P$ obtained from a fungus [New Latin *Psilocybe*, genus name]

psi·lop·sid \sī-'läp-səd\ *n* : any of a major group (Psilopsida) of primitive rootless and often leafless vascular plants [derived from Greek *psilos* "bare" + *lykopsis*, a kind of plant] — **psilopsid** *adj*

psit·ta·cine \'sit-ə-ˌsīn\ *adj* : of or relating to the parrots [Latin *psittacinus*, from *psittacus* "parrot", from Greek *psittakos*] — **psittacine** *n*

psit·ta·co·sis \ˌsit-ə-'kō-səs\ *n* : PARROT FEVER

pso·ri·a·sis \sə-'rī-ə-səs\ *n* : a chronic skin disease characterized by circumscribed red patches covered with white scales [Greek *psōriasis*, from *psōrian* "to have the itch", from *psōra* "itch"] — **pso·ri·at·ic** \ˌsor-ē-'at-ik, ˌsor-\ *adj or n*

psych- *or* **psycho-** *combining form* **1** : mind : mental processes and activities ⟨*psycho*logy⟩ **2** : psychological methods ⟨*psycho*therapy⟩ **3** : brain ⟨*psycho*surgery⟩ **4** : mental and ⟨*psycho*somatic⟩ [Greek, from *psychē* "breath, principle of life, soul"]

psy·che \'sī-kē\ *n* : SOUL 1, SELF; *also* : MIND 2a [Greek *psychē*]

¹psy·che·del·ic \ˌsī-kə-'del-ik\ *adj* **1 a** : of, relating to, or being a drug (as LSD) that radically alters the mind

or mental processes usually only temporarily **b** : relating to the taking of psychedelic drugs ⟨a *psychedelic* experience⟩ **2 a** : imitating the effect of psychedelic drugs ⟨*psychedelic* art⟩ **b** : bright and glowing as a result of fluorescence ⟨*psychedelic* colors⟩ [Greek *psychē* "soul" + *dēloun* "to show"]

²psychedelic *n* : a psychedelic drug

psy·chi·a·try \sə-'kī-ə-trē, sī-\ *n* : a branch of medicine that deals with mental, emotional, or behavioral disorders — **psy·chi·at·ric** \ˌsī-kē-'a-trik\ *adj* — **psy·chi·at·ri·cal·ly** \-tri-kə-lē, -klē\ *adv* — **psy·chi·a·trist** \sə-'kī-ə-trəst, sī-\ *n*

¹psy·chic \'sī-kik\ *adj* **1** : of, relating to, affecting, or originating in the mind **2** : not physical; *esp* : not to be explained by knowledge of natural laws **3** : sensitive to influences or forces supposedly exerted from beyond the natural world — **psy·chi·cal** \-ki-kəl\ *adj* — **psy·chi·cal·ly** \-ki-kə-lē, -klē\ *adv*

²psychic *n* : a person (as a medium) apparently sensitive to nonphysical forces

psy·cho·ac·tive \ˌsī-kō-'ak-tiv\ *adj* : affecting the mind or behavior ⟨*psychoactive* drugs⟩

psy·cho·anal·y·sis \ˌsī-kō-ə-'nal-ə-səs\ *n, pl* **-y·ses** \-ˌsēz\ : a method of explaining and treating psychic and especially emotional disorders that emphasizes the importance of the patient's talking freely about himself or herself while under treatment and especially about dreams and early childhood memories and experiences — **psy·cho·an·a·lyst** \-'an-l-əst\ *n* — **psy·cho·an·a·lyt·ic** \-ˌan-l-'it-ik\ *or* **psy·cho·an·a·lyt·i·cal** \-'it-i-kəl\ *adj* — **psy·cho·an·a·lyt·i·cal·ly** \-'it-i-kə-lē, -klē\ *adv* — **psy·cho·an·a·lyze** \-'an-l-ˌīz\ *vb*

psy·cho·gen·ic \ˌsī-kə-'jen-ik\ *adj* : originating in the mind or in mental or emotional conflict

psy·cho·log·i·cal \ˌsī-kə-'läj-i-kəl\ *also* **psy·cho·log·ic** \-'läj-ik\ *adj* **1 a** : of or relating to psychology **b** : relating to, characteristic of, arising in, or acting through the mind : MENTAL **2** : intended to influence the will or mind ⟨*psychological* warfare⟩ — **psy·cho·log·i·cal·ly** \-i-kə-lē, -klē\ *adv*

psy·chol·o·gy \sī-'käl-ə-jē\ *n, pl* **-gies** **1** : the science or study of mind and behavior **2** : the mental or behavioral characteristics of an individual or group — **psy·chol·o·gist** \-jəst\ *n*

psy·cho·neu·ro·sis \ˌsī-kō-nù-'rō-səs, -nyù-\ *n* : NEUROSIS — **psy·cho·neu·rot·ic** \-'rät-ik\ *adj or n*

psy·cho·path \'sī-kə-ˌpath\ *n* : a person with a clear perception of reality but lacking a sense of social and moral obligation so that personal gain is sought by criminal acts, drug addiction, or sexual perversion without marked feelings of guilt; *also* : a mentally ill person — **psy·cho·path·ic** \ˌsī-kə-'path-ik\ *adj* — **psy·cho·path·i·cal·ly** \-i-kə-lē, -klē\ *adv*

psy·cho·pa·thol·o·gy \ˌsī-kō-pə-'thäl-ə-jē\ *n* : the study of mental disorders and of the associated psychologic and behavioral alterations and anomalies; *also* : such disordered state — **psy·cho·path·o·log·i·cal** \-ˌpath-ə-'läj-i-kəl\ *adj* — **psy·cho·path·o·log·i·cal·ly** \-i-kə-lē, -klē\ *adv* — **psy·cho·pa·thol·o·gist** \-pə-'thäl-ə-jəst\ *n*

psy·cho·sis \sī-'kō-səs\ *n, pl* **-cho·ses** \-'kō-ˌsēz\ : fundamental or severe personality disorder characterized by defective or lost contact with reality and often by delusions and hallucinations — **psy·chot·ic** \-'kät-ik\ *adj or n* — **psy·chot·i·cal·ly** \-'kät-i-kə-lē, -klē\ *adv*

psy·cho·so·mat·ic \ˌsī-kə-sə-'mat-ik\ *adj* : of, relating to, or being bodily symptoms or bodily and mental symptoms resulting from conflict and anxiety — **psy·cho·so·mat·i·cal·ly** \-i-kə-lē, -klē\ *adv*

psy·cho·sur·gery \ˌsī-kō-'sərj-rē, -ə-rē\ *n* : brain surgery employed in treating the symptoms of mental illness — **psy·cho·sur·geon** \-'sər-jən\ *n* — **psy·cho·sur·gi·cal** \-'sər-ji-kəl\ *adj*

psy·cho·ther·a·py \ˌsī-kō-'ther-ə-pē\ *n* : treatment of mental or emotional disorder or of related bodily ills

by psychological means — **psy·cho·ther·a·pist** \-pəst\
n

Psy·cho·zo·ic \ˌsī-kə-ˈzō-ik\ *adj* : QUATERNARY

psy·chrom·e·ter \sī-ˈkräm-ət-ər\ *n* : an instrument for
measuring the water vapor in the atmosphere by
means of the difference in the readings of two thermometers when one of them is kept wet so that it is
cooled by evaporation [Greek *psychros* "cold"] — **psy·chro·met·ric** \ˌsī-krō-ˈme-trik\ *adj*

psyl·la \ˈsil-ə\ *n* : any of a family of plant lice including
many economic pests [Greek, "flea"] — **psyl·lid** \-əd\
adj or n

ptar·mi·gan \ˈtär-mi-gən\ *n, pl* **ptarmigans** *or*
ptarmigan : any of various grouse of northern regions
with completely feathered feet [Scottish Gaelic
tàrmachan]

P T boat \ˈpē-ˈtē-\ *n* : a high-speed motorboat usually
equipped with torpedoes, machine guns, and depth
charges [*p*atrol *t*orpedo]

PTC \ˌpē-ˌtē-ˈsē\ *n* : PHENYLTHIOCARBAMIDE

pter·an·o·don \tə-ˈran-ə-ˌdän\ *n* : any of a genus of
Cretaceous flying reptiles with a wingspread of 8 meters [Greek *pteron* "wing, feather" + *anodōn* "toothless", from *an-* + *odōn* "tooth"]

pte·rid·o·phyte \tə-ˈrid-ə-ˌfīt\ *n* : any of a division
(Pteridophyta) of vascular plants that have roots,
stems, and leaves, lack flowers or seeds, and comprise
the ferns and related forms [derived from Greek *pter-
id-, pteris* "fern" + *phyton* "plant"] — **pte·rid·o·phyt·ic** \tə-ˌrid-ə-ˈfit-ik\ *adj*

ptero·dac·tyl \ˌter-ə-ˈdak-tl\ *n* : any of several extinct
flying reptiles with a featherless membrane extending
from the body along the arms and forming the supporting surface of the wings [Greek *pteron* "wing" + *daktylos* "finger"]

ptero·saur \ˈter-ə-ˌsȯr\ *n* : PTERODACTYL [derived from
Greek *pteron* "wing" + *sauros* "lizard"]

Ptol·e·ma·ic \ˌtäl-ə-ˈmā-ik\ *adj* : of, relating to, or characteristic of Ptolemy [Greek *Ptolemaikos,* from *Ptole-
maios* "Ptolemy"]

Ptolemaic system *n* : the system of planetary motions
according to which the earth is at the center with the
sun, moon, and planets revolving around it [*Ptolemy,*
2d century A. D. Alexandrian astronomer]

pto·maine \ˈtō-ˌmān, tō-ˈ\ *n* : any of various often poisonous organic compounds formed by bacteria-in-
duced rotting of nitrogenous matter (as proteins) [Ital-
ian *ptomaina,* from Greek *ptōma* "fall, fallen body,
corpse", from *piptein* "to fall"]

ptomaine poisoning *n* : food poisoning caused usually
by bacteria or bacterial products

pty·a·lin \ˈtī-ə-lən\ *n* : an amylase found in the saliva of
many animals [Greek *ptyalon* "saliva", from *ptyein*
"to spit"]

pub \ˈpəb\ *n, chiefly British* : PUBLIC HOUSE

pub crawler *n* : one that goes from bar to bar

pu·ber·ty \ˈpyü-bərt-ē\ *n* **1** : the condition of being or
the period of becoming first capable of reproducing
sexually **2** : the age at which puberty occurs often
construed legally as 14 in boys and 12 in girls [Latin
pubertas, from *puber* "pubescent"] — **pu·ber·tal**
\-bərt-l\ *adj*

pu·bes·cent \pyü-ˈbes-nt\ *adj* **1** : arriving at or having
reached puberty **2** : covered with fine soft short hairs
— **pu·bes·cence** \-ns\ *n*

pu·bic \ˈpyü-bik\ *adj* : of, relating to, or situated near
the pubis [Latin *pubes* "pubic hair, pubic region"]

pu·bis \ˈpyü-bəs\ *n, pl* **pu·bes** \-ˌbēz\ : the ventral and
anterior of the three principal bones composing each
hipbone — called also *pubic bone* [New Latin *os pubis,* literally, "bone of the pubic region"]

¹**pub·lic** \ˈpəb-lik\ *adj* **1 a** : of, relating to, or affecting
all the people ⟨*public* law⟩ **b** : of or relating to government **c** : relating to or engaged in the service of the
community or nation ⟨*public* life⟩ **2** : of or relating to

mankind in general : UNIVERSAL **3** : of or relating to
business or community interests as opposed to private
affairs **4** : devoted to the general welfare : HUMANITARI-
AN ⟨*public* spirit⟩ **5** : accessible to or shared by all
members of the community **6 a** : exposed to general
view : OPEN **b** : WELL-KNOWN, PROMINENT ⟨a *public* fig-
ure⟩ [Middle French *publique,* from Latin *publicus*] —
pub·lic·ly *adv* — **pub·lic·ness** *n*

²**public** *n* **1** : a place accessible or visible to the public
⟨seen together in *public*⟩ **2** : the people as a whole :
POPULACE ⟨a lecture open to the *public*⟩ **3** : a particular group of people ⟨a writer's *public*⟩

public address system *n* : an apparatus including one
or more loudspeakers for reproducing sound so that it
may be heard by a large audience in an auditorium or
outdoors

pub·li·can \ˈpəb-li-kən\ *n* **1** : a provincial tax collector
for the ancient Romans **2** *chiefly British* : a keeper of
a public house [Middle French, from Latin *publi-
canus,* from *publicum* "public revenue", from *publicus* "public"]

pub·li·ca·tion \ˌpəb-lə-ˈkā-shen\ *n* **1** : the act or process or an instance of publishing **2** : a published work
[Middle French, from Late Latin *publicatio,* from Latin
publicare "to publish"]

public domain *n* **1** : land owned directly by the government **2** : property rights that belong to the community
at large, are unprotected by copyright or patent, and
may be used by anyone

public house *n* **1** : INN 1, HOSTELRY **2** *chiefly British* : a
licensed saloon or bar

pub·li·cist \ˈpəb-lə-səst\ *n* **1 a** : an expert in international law **b** : an expert or commentator on public affairs **2** : one that publicizes; *esp* : PRESS AGENT

pub·lic·i·ty \pə-ˈblis-ət-ē, ˌpə-\ *n* **1** : the condition of
being public or publicly known **2** : something meant
to attract attention; *esp* : information with a news value designed to further the interests of a place, person,
or cause **3** : attention from the public and especially
the communications media

pub·li·cize \ˈpəb-lə-ˌsīz\ *vt* : to give publicity to : AD-
VERTISE, PROMOTE

public opinion *n* : the general attitude of the public on
some issue or the expression of this attitude ⟨*public
opinion* favored the government's policy⟩

public relations *n* : the business of inducing the public
to have understanding and goodwill for a person, firm,
or institution; *also* : the degree of understanding and
goodwill achieved

public school *n* **1** : any of various select endowed British schools that give a liberal education and prepare
students for the universities **2** : an elementary or secondary school maintained by a local government

public servant *n* : a governmental official or employee

public service *n* **1** : the business of supplying a commodity (as electricity or gas) or service (as transportation) to any or all members of a community **2** : governmental employment; *esp* : CIVIL SERVICE

public speaking *n* **1** : the act or process of making
speeches in public **2** : the art or science of effective
oral communication with an audience

pub·lic–spir·it·ed \ˌpəb-lik-ˈspir-ət-əd\ *adj* : motivated
by devotion to the general or national welfare — **pub·lic–spir·it·ed·ness** *n*

public utility *n* : a business organization (as a gas company) performing a public service and subject to special governmental regulation

public works *n pl* : works (as schools or highways) constructed for public use or enjoyment and financed and
owned by the government

pub·lish \ˈpəb-lish\ *vb* **1** : to make generally known :
make public announcement of ⟨*publish* a libel⟩ **2 a** :
to produce or release for publication; *esp* : PRINT **b** :
to issue the work of (an author) **3** : to have one's work
accepted for publication ⟨a *publishing* scholar⟩ [Mid-

ptarmigan

dle English *publishen,* from Middle French *publier,* from Latin *publicare,* from *publicus* "public"] **SYN** see DECLARE — **pub·lish·able** \-ə-bəl\ *adj*

pub·lish·er \-ər\ *n* : one that publishes; *esp* : one that issues and offers for sale printed matter (as books, periodicals, or newspapers)

puc·coon \pə-'kün\ *n* : any of several American plants (as the bloodroot) that yield a red or yellow pigment [of American Indian origin]

¹**puck** \'pək\ *n* **1** *archaic* : an evil spirit : DEMON **2** : a mischievous sprite : HOBGOBLIN 1 [Old English *pūca*]

²**puck** *n* : a hard rubber disk used in ice hockey [English dialect *puck* "to poke", alteration of English ²*poke*]

pucka *variant of* PUKKA

¹**puck·er** \'pək-ər\ *vb* **puck·ered; puck·er·ing** \'pək-ring, -ə-ring\ : to contract into folds or wrinkles ⟨the cloth *puckered* in shrinking⟩ [probably derived from ¹*poke*]

²**pucker** *n* : a fold or wrinkle in a normally even surface — **puck·ered** \'pək-ərd\ *adj* — **puck·ery** \'pək-rē, -ə-rē\ *adj*

puck·ish \'pək-ish\ *adj* : IMPISH, MISCHIEVOUS ⟨*puckish* humor⟩ [¹*puck*] — **puck·ish·ly** *adv* — **puck·ish·ness** *n*

pud·ding \'pùd-ing\ *n* **1** : a boiled or baked soft food usually with a cereal base ⟨corn *pudding*⟩ **2** : a dessert of a soft, spongy, or thick creamy consistency ⟨bread *pudding*⟩ **3** : a dish often containing suet or having a suet crust ⟨kidney *pudding*⟩ ⟨fig *pudding*⟩ [Middle English]

pudding stone *n* : conglomerate rock

¹**pud·dle** \'pəd-l\ *n* **1** : a very small pool of usually dirty or muddy water **2** : an earthy mixture (as of clay, sand, and gravel) worked while wet into a compact mass that becomes impervious to water when dry [Middle English *podel*]

²**puddle** *vt* **pud·dled; pud·dling** \'pəd-ling, -l-ing\ **1** : to make muddy or turbid **2 a** : to make a puddle of (as clay) **b** : to convert (melted pig iron) into wrought iron by stirring in the presence of an oxidizer **3** : to strew with puddles — **pud·dler** \-ler, -l-ər\ *n*

pu·den·cy \'pyüd-n-sē\ *n* : MODESTY [Latin *pudentia,* from *pudēre* "to be ashamed"]

pu·den·dum \pyù-'den-dəm\ *n, pl* **-den·da** \-'den-də\ : the external genital organs especially of a woman [New Latin, sing. of Latin *pudenda,* from *pudendus* "shameful", from *pudēre* "to be ashamed"] — **pu·den·dal** \-'den-dl\ *adj*

pudgy \'pəj-ē\ *adj* **pudg·i·er; -est** : short and plump : CHUBBY [origin unknown] — **pudg·i·ness** *n*

pu·eb·lo \pü-'eb-lō, 'pweb-, pyü-'eb-\ *n, pl* **-los 1** : an American Indian village of Arizona or New Mexico consisting of flat-roofed stone or adobe houses joined in groups sometimes several stories high **2** *cap* : a member of any of several American Indian peoples of the Southwest [Spanish, "village", literally, "people", from Latin *populus*]

pu·er·ile \'pyü-ər-əl, 'pyùr-, -ˌīl\ *adj* **1** : JUVENILE 3 **2** : CHILDISH, SILLY ⟨*puerile* remarks⟩ [Latin *puerilis,* from *puer* "boy, child"] — **pu·er·il·i·ty** \ˌpyü-ər-'il-ət-ē, ˌpyùr-\ *n*

pu·er·per·al \pyü-'ər-pə-rəl, -prəl\ *adj* : of or relating to parturition ⟨*puerperal* infection⟩ [Latin *puerpera* "woman in childbirth", from *puer* "child", + *parere* "to give birth to"]

puerperal fever *n* : an abnormal condition that results from infection of the placental site following delivery or abortion and is characterized in mild form by fever but in serious cases may spread through the wall of the uterus or into the bloodstream — called also *childbed fever*

¹**puff** \'pəf\ *vb* **1 a** (1) : to blow in short gusts (2) : to exhale forcibly **b** : to breathe hard : PANT ⟨*puffed* as we climbed the hill⟩ **c** : to emit, propel, blow, or expel by or as if by small whiffs or clouds (as of smoke) ⟨*puff* at a pipe⟩ ⟨a brisk breeze *puffed* the clouds away⟩

2 a : to speak or act in a scornful, conceited, or affected manner **b** : to make proud or conceited : ELATE **c** : to praise extravagantly (as in advertising) **3 a** : to distend or become distended with or as if with gas : SWELL ⟨the sprained ankle *puffed* up⟩ **b** : to open or appear in or as if in a puff [Old English *pyffan*]

²**puff** *n* **1 a** : an act or instance of puffing : WHIFF, GUST **b** : a slight explosive sound accompanying a puff **c** : a perceptible cloud (as of smoke or steam) emitted in a puff **2** : a light pastry that rises high in baking **3 a** : a slight swelling : PROTUBERANCE **b** : a fluffy mass: as (1) : a small fluffy pad for applying cosmetic powder (2) : a soft loose roll of hair (3) : a quilted bed covering **4** : a commendatory notice or review — **puff·i·ness** \'pəf-ē-nəs\ *n* — **puffy** \'pəf-ē\ *adj*

puff adder *n* : HOGNOSE SNAKE

puff·ball \'pəf-ˌbòl\ *n* : any of various mostly edible globe-shaped fungi that discharge ripe spores in a cloud resembling smoke when they are disturbed

puff·er \'pəf-ər\ *n* **1** : one that puffs **2** : any of various fishes that can inflate their bodies with air — called also *globefish*

puf·fin \'pəf-ən\ *n* : any of several short-necked northern seabirds that are related to the auks and have a deep grooved bill marked with different colors [Middle English *pophyn*]

puff paste *n* : dough used in making light flaky pastries

pug \'pəg\ *n* **1** : a small sturdy compact dog of Asian origin with a close coat, tightly curled tail, and broad wrinkled face **2 a** : PUG NOSE **b** : a close knot or coil of hair : BUN [obsolete *pug* "hobgoblin, monkey"]

pu·gi·list \'pyü-jə-ləst\ *n* : ¹BOXER [Latin *pugil* "boxer"] — **pu·gi·lism** \-ˌliz-əm\ *n* — **pu·gi·lis·tic** \ˌpyü-jə-'lis-tik\ *adj*

pug·na·cious \ˌpəg-'nā-shəs\ *adj* : having a quarrelsome or belligerent nature : TRUCULENT, COMBATIVE [Latin *pugnac-, pugnax,* from *pugnare* "to fight"] — **pug·na·cious·ly** *adv* — **pug·na·cious·ness** *n* — **pug·nac·i·ty** \-'nas-ət-ē\ *n*

pug nose *n* : a nose having a slightly concave bridge and flattened nostrils — **pug–nosed** \'pəg-'nōzd\ *adj*

puis·ne \'pyü-nē\ *adj, chiefly British* : inferior in rank ⟨a *puisne* judge⟩ [Middle French *puisné* "younger", literally, "born afterward"]

puis·sance \'pwis-ns, 'pyü-ə-səns\ *n* : ability to dominate or sway : MIGHT [Middle French, from *puissant* "powerful", from *poeir* "to be able, be powerful"] — **puis·sant** \-nt, -sənt\ *adj* — **puis·sant·ly** *adv*

puke \'pyük\ *vb* : VOMIT 1 [perhaps imitative]

puk·ka *or* **puc·ka** \'pək-ə\ *adj* : being genuine and authentic; *also* : FIRST-CLASS [Hindi *pakkā* "cooked, ripe, solid", from Sanskrit *pakva*]

pul·chri·tude \'pəl-krə-ˌtüd, -ˌtyüd\ *n* : physical comeliness : BEAUTY [Latin *pulchritudin-, pulchritudo,* from *pulcher* "beautiful"] — **pul·chri·tu·di·nous** \ˌpəl-krə-'tüd-n-əs, -'tyüd-\ *adj*

pule \'pyül\ *vi* : WHINE 1, WHIMPER ⟨a *puling* infant⟩ [probably imitative]

¹**pull** \'pùl\ *vb* **1** : to separate forcibly from a natural or firm attachment : PLUCK, EXTRACT ⟨*pull* a tooth⟩; *also* : to admit of being pulled ⟨the stump *pulled* hard⟩ **2 a** : to exert force upon so as to cause or tend to cause motion toward the force ⟨*pull* a wagon⟩ **b** : to stretch (cooling candy) repeatedly **c** : to strain by stretching abnormally ⟨*pull* a tendon⟩ **d** (1) : to use force in drawing, dragging, or tugging ⟨*pull* on that rope⟩ (2) : MOVE ⟨the car *pulled* away from the curb⟩ (3) : to take a drink (4) : to draw hard in smoking ⟨*pulled* at my pipe⟩ **e** : to work (an oar) by drawing back strongly **3** : to hit (a ball) to the left side of the field from a right-handed stance or to the right side from a left-handed stance **4** : to draw apart : REND, TEAR **5** : to print (as a proof) by impression **6** : REMOVE ⟨*pull* a crankshaft⟩ ⟨*pulled* the pitcher in the third inning⟩ **7** : to bring (a weapon) into the open ⟨*pulled* a knife⟩ **8** : to carry out

puffin

with skill or daring : COMMIT ⟨*pull* a robbery⟩ 9 : AT-
TRACT ⟨*pull* votes⟩ 10 : to feel or express strong sympathy : ROOT ⟨*pulling* for their team to win⟩ [Old English
pullian] — **pull·er** *n* — **pull oneself together** : to regain one's self-possession — **pull one's leg** : to deceive
someone playfully : HOAX — **pull stakes** *or* **pull up
stakes** : to move out : LEAVE — **pull strings** *or* **pull
wires** : to exert secret influence or control — **pull
together** : to work in harmony : COOPERATE

²**pull** *n* **1 a** : the act or an instance of pulling **b** (1) : a
draft of liquid (2) : an inhalation of smoke **c** : a route,
journey, or climb requiring effort ⟨a long *pull* uphill⟩
d : force required to overcome resistance to pulling **2
a** : ADVANTAGE ⟨the *pull* of a good family name⟩ **b** :
special influence ⟨got a job through *pull*⟩ **3** : PROOF 2a
4 : a device for pulling something or for operating by
pulling ⟨a bell *pull*⟩ **5** : a force that attracts, compels,
or influences : ATTRACTION ⟨the *pull* of gravity⟩

pull away *vi* : to draw oneself back or away : WITHDRAW
pull·back \'púl-ˌbak\ *n* : a pulling back; *esp* : an orderly
withdrawal of troops from a position
pull down *vt* **1** : to tear down : WRECK **2 a** : to bring to a
lower level : REDUCE **b** : to depress in health, strength,
or spirits **3** : to draw as wages or salary
pul·let \'púl-ət\ *n* : a young hen; *esp* : a hen of the common fowl less than a year old [Middle English *polet*
"young fowl", from Middle French *poulet*, from *poul*
"fowl", from Late Latin *pullus*, from Latin, "young of
an animal, chicken, sprout"]
pul·ley \'púl-ē\ *n, pl* **pulleys** **1** : a small wheel with a
grooved rim used singly with a rope or chain to
change the direction and point of application of a
pulling force and in combinations to increase the applied force especially for lifting weights; *also* : the
simple machine constituted by such a pulley with
ropes **2** : a wheel used to transmit power by means of
a band, belt, cord, rope, or chain [Middle French *pou-
lie*]
pull in *vb* **1** : CHECK, RESTRAIN ⟨*pull* a horse *in*⟩ **2** : AR-
REST ⟨*pull in* a suspect⟩ **3** : to arrive at a destination
⟨the train *pulled in* on time⟩
Pull·man \'púl-mən\ *n* : a railroad passenger car with
specially comfortable furnishings; *esp* : SLEEPING CAR
[George M. *Pullman*, died 1897, American inventor]
pull off *vt* : to accomplish successfully especially
against odds
pull·out \'púl-ˌaút\ *n* **1** : something that can be pulled
out **2** : the action in which an airplane goes from a
dive to horizontal flight **3** : PULLBACK
pull out \púl-'aút, 'púl-\ *vi* **1** : LEAVE, DEPART ⟨the ship
finally *pulled out*⟩ **2** : WITHDRAW ⟨*pulled out* at the
last minute and left us a player short⟩
¹**pull·over** \ˌpúl-ˌō-vər\ *adj* : put on by being pulled
over the head
²**pullover** \'púl-ˌō-vər\ *n* : a pullover garment
pull over \púl-'ō-vər, 'púl-\ *vi* : to steer one's vehicle to
the side of the road
pull through *vb* : to survive or help through a dangerous or difficult period or situation
pull up *vb* **1** : CHECK, REBUKE ⟨was *pulled up* for my bad
manners⟩ **2** : to bring or come to a stop : HALT ⟨*pulled*
the car *up* in front of the hotel⟩ **3** : to draw even with
others in a race
pul·mo·nary \'púl-mə-ˌner-ē, 'pəl-\ *adj* **1** : relating to
or associated with the lungs **2** : carried on by the
lungs [Latin *pulmonarius*, from *pulmon-, pulmo*
"lung"]
pulmonary artery *n* : an artery that conveys venous
blood from the heart to the lungs
pulmonary circulation *n* : the passage of blood from the
right side of the heart through arteries to the lungs
where it picks up oxygen and is returned to the left
side of the heart by veins
pulmonary vein *n* : a vein that returns oxygenated blood
from the lungs to the heart

pul·mo·nate \'púl-mə-ˌnāt, 'pəl-\ *adj* : having lungs or
organs resembling lungs; *also* : air-breathing ⟨*pulmo-
nate* snails⟩
pul·mo·tor \'púl-ˌmōt-ər, 'pəl-\ *n* : a respiratory apparatus for pumping oxygen or air into and out of the
lungs (as of an asphyxiated person) [from *Pulmotor*, a
former trademark]
¹**pulp** \'pəlp\ *n* **1 a** : the soft juicy or fleshy part of a
fruit or vegetable ⟨the *pulp* of an apple⟩ **b** : a mass of
vegetable matter from which the juice has been
pressed **2** : the soft sensitive tissue that fills the central cavity of a tooth **3** : a material prepared by chemical or mechanical means chiefly from wood and used
in making paper and cellulose products **4 a** : pulpy
condition **b** : something in a pulpy condition **5** : a
magazine or book using rough-surfaced paper made of
wood pulp and often dealing with sensational material
[Middle French *poulpe*, from Latin *pulpa* "flesh,
pulp"] — **pulp·i·ness** \'pəl-pē-nəs\ *n* — **pulpy** \'pəl-
pē\ *adj*
²**pulp** *vb* : to reduce to pulp : make or become pulpy —
pulp·er *n*
pul·pit \'púl-ˌpit, 'pəl-, -ˌpət\ *n* **1** : an elevated platform
or high reading desk used in preaching or conducting
a worship service **2 a** : the preaching profession **b** : a
position as a preacher [Late Latin *pulpitum*, from Latin, "staging, platform"]
pulp·wood \'pəlp-ˌwúd\ *n* : a wood (as aspen, hemlock, pine, or spruce) used in making pulp for paper
pul·que \'púl-ˌkā\ *n* : a fermented drink made in Mexico from the juice of various magueys [Mexican Span-
ish]
pul·sar \'pəl-ˌsär\ *n* : a celestial source of pulsating radio waves characterized by a short nearly constant interval (as .033 second) between pulses that is held to
be a rotating neutron star [*pulse* + *-ar* (as in *quasar*)]
pul·sate \'pəl-ˌsāt\ *vi* **1** : PULSE 1 ⟨a *pulsating* artery⟩
⟨*pulsating* drums⟩ **2** : to be vibrant with life, activity, or feeling ⟨a busy *pulsating* city⟩ [Latin *pulsare*,
from *pulsus*, past participle of *pellere* "to drive,
beat"]
pul·sa·tile \'pəl-sət-l, -sə-ˌtīl\ *adj* : that pulsates
pul·sa·tion \ˌpəl-'sā-shən\ *n* : pulsing movement or action (as of an artery); *also* : a single throb of such
movement
¹**pulse** \'pəls\ *n* : the edible seeds of several crops (as
peas, beans, or lentils) of the pea family; *also* : a plant
yielding pulse [Old French *pouls* "porridge", from
Latin *puls*]
²**pulse** *n* **1** : a regular throbbing caused in the arteries
by the contractions of the heart **2 a** : rhythmical beating, vibrating, or sounding **b** : BEAT 1c, THROB **3 a** : a
transient variation of a quantity (as electrical current
or voltage) whose value is normally constant **b** : an
electromagnetic wave or a sound wave of brief duration [Middle French *pouls*, from Latin *pulsus*, literally,
"beating", from *pulsus*, past participle of *pellere* "to
drive, beat"]
³**pulse** *vb* **1** : to exhibit a pulse or pulsation : THROB **2** :
to drive by or as if by a pulsation **3** : to cause to pulsate **4** : to produce or modulate (as electromagnetic
waves) in the form of pulses ⟨*pulsed* waves⟩
pul·ver·ize \'pəl-və-ˌrīz\ *vb* **1** : to reduce or become
reduced (as by beating or grinding) into a powder **2** :
to demolish as if by pulverizing : SMASH, ANNIHILATE
[Middle French *pulveriser*, from Late Latin *pulveri-
zare*, from Latin *pulver-, pulvis* "dust, powder"] —
pul·ver·iz·er *n*
pu·ma \'pü-mə, 'pyü-\ *n, pl* **pumas** *also* **puma** : COUGAR
[Spanish, from Quechua]
pum·ice \'pəm-əs\ *n* : a volcanic glass full of cavities
and very light in weight used especially in powder
form for smoothing and polishing — called also *pumice stone* [Middle French *pomis*, from Latin *pumic-,
pumex*]

pulley 1

\ə\ abut	\ng\ sing
\ər\ **further**	\ō\ **bone**
\a\ **mat**	\ȯ\ **saw**
\ā\ **take**	\ȯi\ **coin**
\ä\ **cot, cart**	\th\ **thin**
\au̇\ **out**	\th\ **this**
\ch\ **chin**	\ü\ **food**
\e\ **pet**	\u̇\ **foot**
\ē\ **easy**	\y\ **yet**
\g\ **go**	\yü\ **few**
\i\ **tip**	\yu̇\ **cure**
\ī\ **life**	\zh\ **vision**
\j\ **job**	

pum·mel \ˈpəm-əl\ *vb* **-meled** *or* **-melled; -mel·ing** *or* **-mel·ling** : POUND 2a, BEAT [alteration of *pommel*]

¹pump \ˈpəmp\ *n* : a device that raises, transfers, or compresses fluids especially by suction or pressure or both ⟨a water *pump*⟩ [Low German *pumpe* or Dutch *pompe*]

²pump *vb* **1** : to raise, transfer, or compress by means of a pump ⟨*pump* water⟩ **2** : to draw fluid from by the use of a pump ⟨*pump* a boat dry⟩ **3** : to draw, force, or drive onward in the manner of a pump ⟨the heart *pumps* blood into the arteries⟩ **4 a** : to question persistently **b** : to draw out by persistent questioning **5** : to move up and down like a pump handle ⟨*pump* the hand of a friend⟩ **6** : to fill by means of a pump ⟨*pump* up a tire⟩ **7** : to spurt out intermittently — **pump·er** *n*

³pump *n* : a low shoe without a fastening that grips the foot chiefly at the toe and heel [origin unknown]

pum·per·nick·el \ˈpəm-pər-ˌnik-əl\ *n* : a dark coarse sourdough rye bread [German]

pump·kin \ˈpəng-kən, ˈpəm-, ˈpəmp-\ *n* **1** : the usually round orange fruit of a vine of the gourd family widely used as food; *also* : a fruit (as a crookneck squash) of a closely related vine **2** : a usually hairy prickly vine that produces pumpkins [French *popon, pompon* "melon, pumpkin", from Latin *pepon-, pepo*, from Greek *pepōn*, from *pepōn* "ripened"]

pump·kin·seed \-ˌsēd\ *n* : a small brilliantly colored North American freshwater sunfish

¹pun \ˈpən\ *n* : the humorous use of a word in such a way as to suggest different meanings or applications or of words having the same or nearly the same sound but different meanings [perhaps from Italian *puntiglio* "fine point, quibble, scruple"]

²pun *vi* **punned; pun·ning** : to make puns

¹punch \ˈpənch\ *vb* **1 a** : PROD 2, POKE **b** : to act as herdsman of (range cattle) **2 a** : to strike with a forward thrust of the fist **b** : to drive or push forcibly by or as if by a punch **3** : to emboss, cut, perforate, or make with a punch **4** : to strike or press sharply the operating mechanism of [Middle French *poinçonner* "to prick, stamp", from *poinçon* "puncheon"] — **punch·er** *n*

²punch *n* **1** : the action of punching **2** : a quick blow with or as if with the fist **3** : energy or vigor that commands attention ⟨they lacked political *punch*⟩

³punch *n* **1** : a tool or machine for piercing, cutting (as a hole or notch), forming, driving the head of a nail below a surface or a bolt out of a hole, or impressing a design in a softer material **2** : a hole or notch resulting from a perforating operation [probably short for *puncheon*]

⁴punch *n* : a drink made of several ingredients (as fruit juices and spices) and often flavored with wine or distilled liquor [perhaps from Hindi *pãc* "five", from Sanskrit *pañca*; from the number of ingredients]

Punch–and–Judy show \ˌpən-chən-ˈjüd-ē-\ *n* : a traditional puppet show in which the hook-nosed humpback Punch fights comically with his wife Judy

punch bowl *n* : a large bowl from which a beverage (as punch) is served

punch card *n* : a card with holes punched in particular positions each with its own signification for use in data processing — called also *punched card*

punch–drunk \ˈpənch-ˌdrəngk\ *adj* **1** : suffering from brain injury received in prizefighting **2** : GROGGY ⟨*punch-drunk* with fatigue⟩ [²*punch*]

¹pun·cheon \ˈpən-chən\ *n* **1** : a pointed tool for piercing **2 a** : a short upright framing timber **b** : a split log or slab with the face smoothed **3** : a figured stamp die or punch used especially by goldsmiths and engravers [Middle French *poinçon*, derived from Latin *pungere* "to prick"]

²puncheon *n* **1** : a large cask of varying capacity **2** : any of various units of liquid capacity [Middle French *ponchon*]

punch in *vi* : to record the time of one's arrival or beginning work by punching a time clock

pun·chi·nel·lo \ˌpən-chə-ˈnel-ō\ *n* **1** *cap* : a fat short humpbacked clown or buffoon in Italian puppet shows **2** *pl* **-los** : a squat grotesque person [Italian dialect *polecenella*]

punching bag *n* : a usually suspended stuffed or inflated bag to be punched for exercise or for training in boxing

punch line *n* : the sentence, statement, or phrase (as in a joke) that makes the point

punch out *vi* : to record the time of one's stopping work or departure by punching a time clock

punch press *n* : a press for working on material (as metal) by the use of cutting, shaping, or combination dies

punchy \ˈpən-chē\ *adj* **punch·i·er; -est** : PUNCH-DRUNK

punc·tate \ˈpəng-ˌtāt, ˈpəngk-\ *adj* **1** : ending in or resembling a point **2** : marked with minute spots or depressions ⟨a *punctate* leaf⟩ [Latin *punctum* "point"] — **punc·ta·tion** \ˌpəng-ˈtā-shən, ˌpəngk-\ *n*

punc·til·io \ˌpəng-ˈtil-ē-ˌō, ˌpəngk-\ *n, pl* **-ios** **1** : a minute detail of conduct in a ceremony or in observance of a code **2** : careful observance of forms (as in social conduct) [Italian *puntiglio* "point of honor, scruple, quibble", from Spanish *puntillo*, from *punto* "point", from Latin *punctum*]

punc·til·i·ous \-ē-əs\ *adj* : marked by precise exact accordance with the details of codes or conventions SYN see CAREFUL — **punc·til·i·ous·ly** *adv* — **punc·til·i·ous·ness** *n*

punc·tu·al \ˈpəng-chə-wəl, ˈpəngk-\ *adj* **1** : PUNCTILIOUS **2 a** : being on time : PROMPT **b** : characterized by regular occurrence [Medieval Latin *punctualis*, from Latin *punctus* "pricking, point", from *pungere* "to prick"] — **punc·tu·al·i·ty** \ˌpəng-chə-ˈwal-ət-ē, ˌpəngk-\ *n* — **punc·tu·al·ly** \ˈpəng-chə-wə-lē, ˈpəngk-\ *adv* — **punc·tu·al·ness** \-wəl-nəs\ *n*

punc·tu·ate \ˈpəng-chə-ˌwāt, ˈpəngk-\ *vt* **1** : to mark or divide with punctuation marks **2** : to break into or interrupt at intervals ⟨a speech *punctuated* by coughs⟩ [Medieval Latin *punctuare*, from Latin *punctus* "point"] — **punc·tu·a·tor** \-ˌwāt-ər\ *n*

punctuated equilibrium *n* : evolution that is characterized by long periods of stability in the characteristics of an organism and short periods of rapid change during which new forms appear

punc·tu·a·tion \ˌpəng-chə-ˈwā-shən, ˌpəngk-\ *n* : the act, practice, or system of inserting standardized marks or signs in written matter to clarify the meaning and separate structural units

punctuation mark *n* : any of the standardized marks or signs used in punctuation

¹punc·ture \ˈpəng-chər, ˈpəngk-\ *n* **1** : the act of puncturing **2** : a hole or a narrow wound resulting from puncturing ⟨a *puncture* of the abdomen⟩ ⟨a tire with a *puncture*⟩ [Latin *punctura*, from *punctus*, past participle of *pungere* "to prick"]

²puncture *vb* **punc·tured; punc·tur·ing** \ˈpəng-chə-ring, ˈpəng-shring, ˈpəngk-\ **1** : to pierce with a pointed instrument or object **2** : to suffer a puncture of **3** : to become punctured **4** : to make useless or absurd as if by a puncture ⟨*puncture* an argument⟩

pun·dit \ˈpən-dət\ *n* : a wise or learned person : AUTHORITY [Hindi *paṇḍit*, from Sanskrit *paṇḍita*, from *paṇḍita* "learned"]

pun·gen·cy \ˈpən-jən-sē\ *n* : the quality or state of being pungent

pun·gent \ˈpən-jənt\ *adj* **1** : sharply stimulating to the mind ⟨*pungent* criticism⟩ ⟨*pungent* wit⟩ **2** : causing a sharp or irritating sensation; *esp* : ACRID [Latin *pungens*, present participle of *pungere* "to prick, sting"] — **pun·gent·ly** *adv*

Pu·nic \ˈpyü-nik\ *adj* : of or relating to Carthage or the Carthaginians [Latin *punicus*, from *Poenus* "inhabitant of Carthage", from Greek *Phoinix* "Phoenician"]

pun·ish \'pən-ish\ *vb* **1** : impose punishment on for a fault or offense ⟨*punish* the children for disobeying⟩ **2** : to inflict punishment for (as a crime) ⟨*punish* treason with death⟩ **3** : to deal with severely or roughly ⟨badly *punished* by my opponent⟩ **4** : to inflict punishment [Middle French *puniss-*, stem of *punir* "to punish", from Latin *punire,* from *poena* "penalty, pain"] — **pun·ish·abil·i·ty** \,pən-ish-ə-'bil-ət-ē\ *n* — **pun·ish·able** \'pən-ish-ə-bəl\ *adj* — **pun·ish·er** *n* □ SYN CHASTISE, DISCIPLINE: PUNISH implies subjection to penalty for wrongdoing; CHASTISE often implies corporal punishment but may suggest stern or painful verbal censure; DISCIPLINE may involve punishment but suggests action with the intent of bringing under control ⟨parents must *discipline* their children⟩

pun·ish·ing \'pən-ish-ing\ *adj* : very arduous, demanding, or painful ⟨a *punishing* race⟩ — **pun·ish·ing·ly** *adv*

pun·ish·ment \'pən-ish-mənt\ *n* **1** : the act of punishing **2 a** : suffering or pain that serves as retribution **b** : the penalty for a fault or crime ⟨the *punishment* for speeding⟩ **3** : severe, rough, or disastrous treatment ⟨trees showing the effects of *punishment* by a heavy storm⟩

pu·ni·tive \'pyü-nət-iv\ *adj* : inflicting, involving, or aiming at punishment [French *punitif,* from Medieval Latin *punitivus,* from Latin *punitus,* past participle of *punire* "to punish"] — **pu·ni·tive·ly** *adv* — **pu·ni·tive·ness** *n*

Pun·jabi \,pən-'jäb-ē, -'jab-\ *n* **1** : a native or inhabitant of the Punjab region of the Indian subcontinent **2** : PANJABI 1 — **Punjabi** *adj*

¹punk \'pəngk\ *n* **1** : a young inexperienced man **2** : a petty hoodlum [origin unknown]

²punk *adj* : very poor in quality : BAD, MISERABLE

³punk *n* **1** : wood so decayed as to be dry, crumbly, and useful for tinder **2** : a dry spongy substance prepared from fungi and used to ignite fuses especially of fireworks [perhaps alteration of *spunk* "tinder"]

pun·kah \'pəng-kə\ *n* : a large fan or a canvas-covered frame suspended from the ceiling and used especially in India for fanning a room [Hindi *pākhā*]

pun·kie *also* **pun·ky** \'pəng-kē\ *n, pl* **punkies** : a tiny biting fly : MIDGE [Dutch dialect *punki,* from Delaware *punk,* literally, "fine ashes, powder"]

pun·ster \'pən-stər\ *n* : one given to making puns

¹punt \'pənt\ *n* : a long narrow flat-bottomed square-ended boat usually propelled with a pole [Old English, from Latin *ponto,* from *pont-, pons* "bridge"]

²punt *vb* **1** : to propel (a boat) by pushing with a pole against the bottom of a body of water **2** : to go boating in a punt

³punt *vi* : to play at a gambling game against the banker [French *ponter,* from *ponte* "point in some games", from Spanish *punto* "point", from Latin *punctum*]

⁴punt *vb* **1** : to make a punt **2** : to kick (a ball) by means of a punt [origin unknown]

⁵punt *n* : a kick of a ball which is dropped from the hands and hit before it touches the ground

punt·er \'pənt-ər\ *n* : one that punts

punt formation *n* : an offensive football formation in which a back making a punt stands approximately 10 yards (about 9 meters) behind the line and the other backs are in blocking position close to the line of scrimmage

pu·ny \'pyü-nē\ *adj* **pu·ni·er; -est** : slight or inferior in power, size, or importance : WEAK [Middle French *puisné* "younger", from *puis* "afterward" + *né* "born"] — **pu·ni·ness** *n* □ ORIGIN *Puny* is a spelling adopted to reflect the pronunciation of *puisne,* from the Middle French *puisné,* "younger". The literal meaning of the French *puisné* is "born afterward", and in their earliest uses in English *puisne* and *puny* referred to someone younger than, or of inferior position to, someone else. In this sense it developed a spe-

cific legal meaning: a *puisne* (or *puny*) judge is a junior or subordinate judge in the superior courts. Very soon after being borrowed into English *puny* developed from its literal meaning the sense of "slight or inferior in power, vigor, size, or importance."

pup \'pəp\ *n* : a young dog; *also* : one of the young of various animals (as seals) [short for *puppy*]

pu·pa \'pyü-pə\ *n, pl* **pu·pae** \-,pē, -,pī\ *or* **pupas** : the stage of an insect (as a bee, moth, or beetle) having complete metamorphosis that occurs between the larva and the adult, is usually enclosed in a cocoon or case, and undergoes internal changes by which larval structures are replaced by those of the adult [Latin, "girl, doll"] — **pu·pal** \'pyü-pəl\ *adj*

pu·par·i·um \pyü-'par-ē-əm, -'per-\ *n, pl* **pu·par·ia** \-ē-ə\ : an outer shell that covers the pupae of some insects (as a fly) and is formed from the skin of the larva [New Latin, from *pupa*]

pu·pate \'pyü-,pāt\ *vi* : to become a pupa : pass through a pupal stage — **pu·pa·tion** \pyü-'pā-shən\ *n*

¹pu·pil \'pyü-pəl\ *n* **1** : a child or young person in school or in the charge of a tutor : STUDENT **2** : one who has been taught or influenced by a famous or distinguished person [Middle French *pupille* "minor ward", from Latin *pupillus* "male ward" (from *pupus* "boy") and *pupilla* "female ward", from *pupa* "girl, doll"] □ ORIGIN In Latin a *pupa* was either a girl or a doll. Its diminutive *pupilla* had two senses. A person can see himself or herself reflected in miniature, like a little doll, in the eye of another. For this reason the opening in the iris which seems to hold this image was called a *pupilla.* Our English *pupil* was borrowed from the Middle French descendent of the Latin word. In Latin a little girl who was an orphan and a ward was also called a *pupilla,* her masculine counterpart being a *pupillus.* Middle French *pupille* served for both sexes. English *pupil* was originally used for a ward, but in the 16th century the word developed a new meaning, and a *pupil* became a student in the charge of a tutor or in school.

²pupil *n* : the usually round opening in the iris of the eye that contracts and expands to control the amount of light falling on the retina [Middle French *pupille,* from Latin *pupilla,* from *pupa* "girl, doll"; from the tiny image of oneself seen reflected in another's eye]

pu·pil·age *or* **pu·pil·lage** \'pyü-pə-lij\ *n* : the state or period of being a pupil

pup·pet \'pəp-ət\ *n* **1 a** : a small-scale figure (as of a person) usually with a cloth body and hollow head that fits over and is moved by the hand **b** : MARIONETTE **2** : DOLL 1 **3** : one whose acts are controlled by an outside force or influence [Middle French *poupette,* derived from Latin *pupa* "doll"]

pup·pe·teer \,pəp-ə-'tiər\ *n* : one who manipulates puppets

pup·pet·ry \'pəp-ə-trē\ *n, pl* **-ries** : the production or creation of puppets or puppet shows

pup·py \'pəp-ē\ *n, pl* **puppies** : a young domestic dog; *esp* : one less than a year old [Middle French *poupée* "doll, toy", derived from Latin *pupa* "doll"] — **pup·py·ish** \-ē-ish\ *adj*

pup tent *n* : a small low tent for two persons usually consisting of two halves fastened together

pur·blind \'pər-,blīnd\ *adj* **1** : partly blind **2** : lacking in vision, insight, or understanding : OBTUSE [obsolete *purblind* "wholly blind", from Middle English *pur blind,* from *pur* "purely, wholly", from *pur* "pure"] — **pur·blind·ly** *adv* — **pur·blind·ness** \-,blīnd-nəs, -,blīn-nəs\ *n*

¹pur·chase \'pər-chəs\ *vt* **1 a** : to obtain by paying money or its equivalent : BUY ⟨*purchase* a house⟩ **b** : to obtain by labor, danger, or sacrifice : EARN **2** : to apply a device for obtaining a mechanical advantage to (as something to be moved); *also* : to move by a purchase [Old French *purchacier* "to seek to obtain", from *pur-*

\ə\ abut		\ng\ sing	
\ər\ further		\ō\ bone	
\a\ mat		\ȯ\ saw	
\ā\ take		\ȯi\ coin	
\ä\ cot, cart		\th\ thin	
\au̇\ out		\th\ this	
\ch\ chin		\ü\ food	
\e\ pet		\u̇\ foot	
\ē\ easy		\y\ yet	
\g\ go		\yü\ few	
\i\ tip		\yu̇\ cure	
\ī\ life		\zh\ vision	
\j\ job			

"forward" (from Latin *pro-*) + *chacier* "to chase"] — **pur·chas·able** \-chə-sə-bəl\ *adj* — **pur·chas·er** *n*

²**purchase** *n* **1** : an act or instance of purchasing **2** : something purchased **3 a** : a mechanical hold or advantage applied to the raising or moving of heavy bodies **b** : an apparatus or device by which advantage is gained **4** : a secure hold, grasp, or place to stand ⟨could not get a *purchase* on the ledge⟩

pur·dah \'pərd-ə\ *n* : seclusion of women from public observation among Muslims and some Hindus especially in India [Hindi *parda*, literally, "screen, veil"]

pure \'pyu̇r\ *adj* **1 a** : not mixed with anything else ⟨*pure* gold⟩ **b** : free from dust, dirt, or taint ⟨*pure* food⟩ **2 a** : nothing other than : SHEER ⟨*pure* nonsense⟩ **b** : ABSTRACT 3a, THEORETICAL ⟨*pure* science⟩ ⟨*pure* mathematics⟩ **3 a** : free from sin or moral guilt; *esp* : marked by chastity **b** : of unmixed ancestry **c** : breeding true for one or more characters [Old French *pur*, from Latin *purus*] SYN see CHASTE — **pure·ness** *n*

pure·blood \-ˌbləd\ *or* **pure-blood·ed** \-ˈbləd-əd\ *adj* : of unmixed ancestry : PUREBRED — **pureblood** *n*

pure·bred \-ˈbred\ *adj* : bred from members of a recognized breed, strain, or kind without admixture of other blood over many generations — **pure·bred** \-ˌbred\ *n*

¹**pu·ree** \pyu̇-ˈrā, -ˈrē\ *n* **1** : a paste or thick liquid suspension usually produced by rubbing cooked food through a sieve **2** : a thick soup having pureed vegetables as a base [French, from *purer* "to purify, strain", from Latin *purare* "to purify", from *purus* "pure"]

²**puree** *vt* **pu·reed; pu·ree·ing** : to reduce to a pulp by cooking and then rub through a sieve

pure line *n* : an essentially homozygous strain (as of Indian corn) usually formed by repeated selfing — **pure-line** *adj*

pure·ly \'pyu̇r-lē\ *adv* **1** : without admixture of anything injurious or foreign **2** : MERELY ⟨read *purely* for relaxation⟩ **3** : in a chaste manner **4** : WHOLLY 1

¹**pur·ga·tive** \'pər-gət-iv\ *adj* : purging or tending to purge; *esp* : causing a usually marked looseness of the bowels ⟨the *purgative* effect of green apples⟩

²**purgative** *n* : a strong laxative

pur·ga·to·ri·al \ˌpər-gə-ˈtōr-ē-əl, -ˈtȯr-\ *adj* **1** : cleansing of sin : EXPIATORY **2** : of or relating to purgatory

pur·ga·to·ry \'pər-gə-ˌtōr-ē, -ˌtȯr-\ *n, pl* **-ries 1** : an intermediate state after death in which according to Roman Catholic doctrine the souls of those who die in God's grace but without having made full satisfaction for their sins are purified by suffering **2** : a place or state of temporary punishment [Medieval Latin *purgatorium*, from Late Latin *purgatorius* "purging", from Latin *purgare* "to purge"]

¹**purge** \'pərj\ *vb* **1 a** : to clear of sin or guilt **b** : to cleanse or purify by separating and carrying off impurities **2** : to become free of impurities or excess matter through a cleansing process **3** : to remove by cleansing **4** : to have or cause vigorous and usually repeated evacuation of the bowels **5** : to get rid of (as undesirable persons) [Old French *purgier*, from Latin *purgare* "to purify, purge", from *purus* "pure"] — **pur·ga·tion** \ˌpər-ˈgā-shən\ *n* — **purg·er** *n*

²**purge** *n* **1 a** : an act or instance of purging **b** : a ridding of persons regarded as treacherous or disloyal **2** : something that purges; *esp* : PURGATIVE

pu·ri·fi·ca·tion \ˌpyu̇r-ə-fə-ˈkā-shən\ *n* : an act or instance of purifying or of being purified

pu·ri·fi·ca·tor \'pyu̇r-ə-fə-ˌkāt-ər\ *n* **1** : one that purifies **2** : a linen cloth used to wipe the chalice after celebration of the Eucharist

pu·rif·i·ca·to·ry \pyu̇r-ˈif-i-kə-ˌtōr-ē, 'pyu̇r-ə-fə-kə-, -ˌtȯr-\ *adj* : serving, tending, or intended to purify

pu·ri·fy \'pyu̇r-ə-ˌfī\ *vb* **-fied; -fy·ing 1** : to make pure : free from anything alien, extraneous, corrupting, polluting, or damaging **2** : to grow or become pure or clean — **pu·ri·fi·er** \-ˌfī-ər, -ˌfīr\ *n*

Pu·rim \'pu̇r-ˌim, pu̇r-ˈ\ *n* : a Jewish holiday celebrated in February or March in commemoration of the deliverance of the Jews from the massacre plotted by Haman [Hebrew *pūrīm*]

pu·rine \'pyu̇r-ˌēn\ *n* : any of a group of bases including several (as adenine and guanine) that are fundamental constituents of DNA and RNA [German *purin*, from Latin *purus* "pure" + New Latin *uricus* "uric" + German -*in* "ine"]

pur·ism \'pyu̇r-ˌiz-əm\ *n* : rigid adherence to or insistence of nicety especially in use of words — **pur·ist** \-əst\ *n* — **pu·ris·tic** \pyu̇r-ˈis-tik\ *adj*

pu·ri·tan \'pyu̇r-ət-n\ *n* **1** *cap* : a member of a 16th and 17th century Protestant group in England and New England opposing as unscriptural many traditional customs of the Church of England **2** : one who practices or preaches or follows a stricter moral code than that which prevails [probably from Late Latin *puritas* "purity"] — **puritan** *adj, often cap* — **pu·ri·tan·i·cal** \ˌpyu̇r-ə-ˈtan-i-kəl\ *adj* — **pu·ri·tan·i·cal·ly** \-kə-lē, -klē\ *adv* — **pu·ri·tan·ism** \'pyu̇r-ət-n-ˌiz-əm\ *n, often cap*

pu·ri·ty \'pyu̇r-ət-ē\ *n* : the quality or state of being pure [Old French *pureté*, from Late Latin *puritas*, from Latin *purus* "pure"]

¹**purl** \'pərl\ *n* : an intertwining of thread through the loop of a stitch along an edge (as in buttonholing) [obsolete *pirl* "to twist"]

²**purl** *vb* : to knit in purl stitch

³**purl** *n* **1** : a purling or swirling stream or rill **2** : a gentle murmur or movement (as of purling water) [perhaps of Scandinavian origin]

⁴**purl** *vi* **1** : EDDY, SWIRL **2** : to make a soft murmuring sound like that of a purling stream

pur·lieu \'pərl-ˌyü\ *n* **1 a** : a place of resort : HAUNT **b** *pl* : ²BOUND 3 **2 a** : an outlying or adjacent district **b** *pl* : ENVIRONMENT 1 [Middle English *purlewe* "land severed from a royal forest by perambulation", from Anglo-French *puralé* "perambulation", from Old French *puraler* "to go through", from *pur-* "for, through" + *aler* "to go"]

pur·lin \'pər-lən\ *n* : a horizontal member in a roof supporting the rafters [origin unknown]

pur·loin \pər-ˈlȯin, ˌpər-ˈ, 'pər-\ *vt* : STEAL 2a, FILCH [Anglo-French *purloigner* "to put away", from Old French *porloigner* "to put off, delay", from *por-* "forward" + *loing* "at a distance", from Latin *longe*, from *longus* "long"] — **pur·loin·er** *n*

purl stitch *n* : a knitting stitch usually made with the yarn at the front of the work by inserting the right needle into the front of a loop on the left needle from the right, catching the yarn with the right needle, and bringing it through to form a new loop — compare KNIT STITCH

¹**pur·ple** \'pər-pəl\ *adj* **1** : of the color purple **2** : highly rhetorical : ORNATE ⟨*purple* prose⟩ [Middle English *purpel*, alteration of *purper*, from Old English *purpuran* "of purple", from *purpure* "purple color", from Latin *purpura*, from Greek *porphyra*]

²**purple** *n* **1 a** : TYRIAN PURPLE **b** : a color about midway between red and blue **2 a** : cloth dyed purple **b** : a garment of purple cloth; *esp* : a robe worn as an emblem of rank or authority **3** : a mollusk yielding a purple dye and especially the Tyrian purple of ancient times **4** : a pigment or dye that colors purple **5** : imperial or regal rank or power : exalted station

³**purple** *vb* **pur·pled; pur·pling** \'pər-pə-ling, -pling\ : to turn purple

pur·plish \'pər-pə-lish, -plish\ *adj* : somewhat purple

¹**pur·port** \'pər-ˌpōrt, -ˌpȯrt\ *n* : meaning conveyed, professed, or implied : IMPORT; *also* : SUBSTANCE 1b, GIST [Anglo-French, "content, tenor", from *purporter* "to contain", from Old French *porporter* "to convey", from *por-* "forward" + *porter* "to carry"]

²pur·port \pər-'pōrt, ,pər-', -'pȯrt\ *vt* : to profess outwardly but often deceptively : CLAIM

pur·port·ed *adj* : REPUTED 2, RUMORED — **pur·port·ed·ly** *adv*

¹pur·pose \'pər-pəs\ *n* **1 a** : something set up as an end to be attained : INTENTION **b** : RESOLUTION 5b, DETERMINATION **2** : an object or result aimed at or achieved **3** : a subject under discussion [Old French *purpos*, from *purposer* "to purpose", from Latin *proponere* "to propose"] SYN see INTENTION — **pur·pose·ful** \-fəl\ *adj* — **pur·pose·ful·ly** \-fə-lē\ *adv* — **pur·pose·ful·ness** \-fəl-nəs\ *n* — **pur·pose·less** \-ləs\ *adj* — **on purpose** : by intent : INTENTIONALLY

²purpose *vt* : to have in mind as a purpose : INTEND, PROPOSE

pur·pose·ly \'pər-pəs-lē\ *adv* : with a deliberate or express purpose

pur·pos·ive \'pər-pə-siv\ *adj* **1** : serving or effecting a useful end though not clearly as a result of design **2** : having or tending to fulfill a conscious purpose or design : PURPOSEFUL — **pur·pos·ive·ly** *adv* — **pur·pos·ive·ness** *n*

purr \'pər\ *n* : the characteristic low vibrating murmur of an apparently contented or pleased cat [imitative] — **purr** *vb*

¹purse \'pərs\ *n* **1 a** : a small bag or pouch usually closed with a drawstring or snap and used to carry money **b** : a container (as a handbag) used to carry money and often small objects **2 a** : FUND 2b, RESOURCES **b** : a sum of money offered as a prize or present [Old English *purs*, from Medieval Latin *bursa*, from Late Latin, "hide of an ox", from Greek *byrsa*]

²purse *vt* **1** : to put into a purse **2** : PUCKER, KNIT ⟨*purse* one's lips⟩

purse–proud \-,praud\ *adj* : proud of one's wealth

purs·er \'pər-sər\ *n* : an official on a ship who keeps accounts and supervises the care of passengers

purs·lane \'pər-slən, -,slān\ *n* : a fleshy-leaved trailing plant with tiny bright yellow flowers that is a common troublesome weed but is sometimes used as a potherb or in salads [Middle French *porcelaine*, from Late Latin *porcillago*, from Latin *porcillaca*, alteration of *portulaca*]

pur·su·ance \pər-'sü-əns\ *n* : the act of pursuing or carrying out ⟨in *pursuance* of their plans⟩

pur·su·ant to \-ənt-\ *prep* : in carrying out : in conformance to : according to

pur·sue \pər-'sü\ *vt* **1** : to follow in order to overtake and capture or destroy **2** : to try to obtain or accomplish : SEEK ⟨*pursue* pleasure⟩ **3** : to proceed along : FOLLOW ⟨*pursue* a northerly course⟩ **4** : to engage in : PRACTICE ⟨*pursue* a hobby⟩ **5** : HARASS, HAUNT ⟨*pursued* by fears of bankruptcy⟩ **6** : COURT 2a, WOO [Anglo-French *pursuer*, from Old French *poursuir*, from Latin *prosequi*, from *pro-* "forward" + *sequi* "to follow"] SYN see CHASE — **pur·su·er** *n*

pur·suit \pər-'süt\ *n* **1** : the act of pursuing **2** : an activity that one engages in especially as a vocation [Old French *poursuite*, from *poursuir* "to pursue"]

pur·sui·vant \'pər-swi-vənt, -si-\ *n* : a person ranking below a herald but having similar duties [Middle French *poursuivant* "attendant of a herald", literally, "follower", from *poursuir*, *poursuivre* "to pursue"]

pur·sy \'pəs-ē, 'pər-sē\ *or* **pus·sy** \'pəs-ē\ *adj* **pur·si·er** *or* **pus·si·er; -est** **1** : short-winded especially because of corpulence **2** : too fat especially from self-indulgent or luxurious living [Anglo-French *pursif*, from Middle French *polsif*, from *poulser*, *polser* "to beat, push, pant"] — **pur·si·ness** *n*

pu·ru·lent \'pyur-yə-lənt, 'pyur-ə-\ *adj* : containing, consisting of, or accompanied by the formation of pus ⟨a *purulent* fever⟩ [Latin *purulentus*, from *pur-*, *pus* "pus"] — **pu·ru·lence** \-ləns\ *n*

pur·vey \pər-'vā, ,pər-', 'pər-,\ *vt* **1** : to supply (as provisions) usually as a business **2** : CIRCULATE 2b [Middle French *porveeir*, from Latin *providēre* "to provide"] — **pur·vey·ance** \-əns\ *n*

pur·vey·or \-ər\ *n* : one that purveys something (as provisions or news); *esp* : CATERER

pur·view \'pər-,vyü\ *n* **1** : the range or limit of authority, competence, responsibility, concern, or intention **2** : range of vision, understanding, or awareness [Middle English *purveu* "provision of a statute", from Anglo-French *purveu est* "it is provided" (opening phrase of a statute)]

pus \'pəs\ *n* : thick cloudy usually yellowish white fluid matter formed at a place of inflammation and infection (as an abscess) and containing white blood cells, tissue debris, and microorganisms [Latin]

¹push \'push\ *vb* **1 a** : to press against with force in order to drive or impel **b** : to exert or use pressure ⟨*push* on the door⟩ **2** : to thrust forward, downward, or outward ⟨plants *pushing* roots into the soil⟩ **3 a** : to press or urge forward **b** : to carry on with vigor or effectiveness ⟨*push* a campaign⟩ **4** : to bear hard upon so as to involve in difficulty ⟨was *pushed* for money⟩ **5** : to exert oneself continuously, vigorously, or obtrusively to gain an end (as social advancement) **6** : to engage in the sale of (illicit drugs) [Old French *poulser* "to beat, push", from Latin *pulsare*, from *pulsus*, past participle of *pellere* "to drive, strike"] — **push·er** *n* □ SYN PUSH, SHOVE, THRUST, PROPEL mean to cause to move ahead or aside by force. PUSH implies application of force by a body already in contact with the body to be moved; SHOVE implies a fast or rough pushing of something usually along a surface; THRUST suggests less steadiness and greater violence than PUSH ⟨*thrust* a knife into the crack⟩ PROPEL suggests rapidly driving forward or onward by force applied in any manner.

²push *n* **1** : a vigorous advance against obstacles **2** : a condition or occasion of stress : EMERGENCY **3** : an act of pushing: as **a** : a sudden thrust : SHOVE **b** : a steady application of physical force in a direction away from the body exerting it **c** : a stimulating effect or action ⟨the holiday business gave retail trade a *push*⟩

push–but·ton \-,push-,bət-n\ *adj* : using or dependent on complex and more or less automatic mechanisms ⟨*push-button* warfare⟩

push button *n* : a small button or knob that when pushed operates something especially by closing an electric circuit

push·cart \'push-,kärt\ *n* : a cart or barrow pushed by hand

push·ing *adj* **1** : ENTERPRISING **2** : tactlessly forward : PUSHY

push off *vi* : to set out : LEAVE

push·over \'push-,ō-vər\ *n* **1** : an opponent easy to defeat or a victim incapable of effective resistance **2** : someone unwilling or unable to resist the power of a particular attraction or appeal **3** : something accomplished without difficulty : SNAP ⟨the test was a *pushover*⟩

Push·tu \'pəsh-tü\ *variant of* PASHTO

push–up \'push-,əp\ *n* : a conditioning exercise performed in a prone position by bending and straightening the arms while keeping the body straight supported on the hands and toes

pushy \'push-ē\ *adj* **push·i·er; -est** : aggressive often to an objectionable degree : FORWARD — **push·i·ly** \'push-ə-lē\ *adv* — **push·i·ness** \'push-ē-nəs\ *n*

pu·sil·la·nim·i·ty \,pyü-sə-lə-'nim-ət-ē\ *n* : the quality or state of being pusillanimous

pu·sil·lan·i·mous \,pyü-sə-'lan-ə-məs\ *adj* : lacking courage and resolution : COWARDLY [Late Latin *pusillanimis*, from Latin *pusillus* "very small" (from *pusus* "small child") + *animus* "spirit"] — **pu·sil·lan·i·mous·ly** *adv*

¹puss \'pus\ *n* **1** : CAT 1a **2** : GIRL 1 [origin unknown]

²puss *n, slang* : FACE 1 [Irish Gaelic *pus* "mouth"]

\ə\ abut		\ng\ sing	
\ər\ further		\ō\ bone	
\a\ mat		\o\ saw	
\ā\ take		\oi\ coin	
\ä\ cot, cart		\th\ thin	
\au\ out		\th\ this	
\ch\ chin		\ü\ food	
\e\ pet		\u\ foot	
\ē\ easy		\y\ yet	
\g\ go		\yü\ few	
\i\ tip		\yu\ cure	
\ī\ life		\zh\ vision	
\j\ job			

puss·ley \'pəs-lē\ *n* : PURSLANE [by alteration]

¹pussy \'pùs-ē\ *n, pl* **puss·ies 1** : ¹PUSS 1 **2** : a catkin of the pussy willow

²pus·sy \'pəs-ē\ *adj* **pus·si·er; -est** : full of or resembling pus

³pus·sy *variant of* PURSY

pussy·foot \'pùs-ē-ˌfùt\ *vi* **1** : to tread or move warily or stealthily **2** : to avoid committing oneself : HEDGE

pussy willow \ˌpùs-ē-\ *n* : a willow having large cylindrical silky catkins

pus·tu·lar \'pəs-chə-lər\ *adj* **1** : of, relating to, marked by, or resembling pustules ⟨a *pustular* eruption⟩ **2** : covered with pustules ⟨a *pustular* leaf⟩

pus·tule \'pəs-chül\ *n* **1** : a small elevation of the skin having an inflamed base and containing pus **2** : a small elevation resembling a pimple or blister [Latin *pustula*]

¹put \'pùt\ *vb* **put; put·ting 1 a** : to place in a particular position or relationship ⟨*put* the book down⟩ **b** : to cause to move or go ⟨*put* a fist through the window⟩ ⟨*put* the ball into right field⟩ **c** : to throw with an overhand pushing motion ⟨*put* the shot⟩ **d** : to bring into a specified state or condition ⟨*put* it to use⟩ ⟨*put* the matter right⟩ **2 a** : to cause to suffer something ⟨*put* them to death⟩ **b** : IMPOSE, INFLICT ⟨*put* a special tax on luxuries⟩ **c** : to apply to some end ⟨*put* their skills to use⟩ **3** : to set before one for judgment or decision (as by a formal vote) **4** : to give expression to especially in intelligible language : TRANSLATE ⟨*put* your feelings into words⟩ ⟨*put* the poem into English⟩ **5 a** : to devote or urge to an activity or end ⟨*put* your mind to the problem⟩ ⟨*put* them to work⟩ **b** : INVEST ⟨*put* money in land⟩ **6 a** : to give as an estimate ⟨*put* the time at about eleven⟩ **b** : ATTACH, ATTRIBUTE ⟨*puts* a high value on friendship⟩ **c** : IMPUTE ⟨*put* the blame on your partner⟩ **7 a** : to commence a voyage ⟨the ship *put* to sea shorthanded⟩ **b** : to take a course ⟨*put* into a sheltered bay⟩ [Middle English *putten*] — **put forth 1** : to bring into action : EXERT **2** : to produce or send out by growth ⟨*put forth* leaves⟩ **3** : to start out — **put forward** : PROPOSE ⟨*put forward* a theory⟩ — **put in mind** : REMIND — **put to it** : to give difficulty to ⟨had been *put to it* to keep up⟩ — **put up with** : TOLERATE 1, ENDURE

²put *n* : a throw made usually with an overhand pushing motion

put about *vb* : to change or cause to change course or direction ⟨*put* the ship *about*⟩

put across *vt* : to achieve or convey successfully ⟨*put across* a plan⟩ ⟨*put* an idea *across*⟩

pu·ta·tive \'pyüt-ət-iv\ *adj* : commonly accepted or supposed to exist ⟨*putative* racial superiority⟩ ⟨a *putative* conspiracy⟩ [Late Latin *putativus*, from Latin *putare* "to think"] — **pu·ta·tive·ly** *adv*

put away *vt* **1** : DISCARD 2, RENOUNCE **2** : to consume by eating or drinking **3** : to confine especially in a mental institution

put by *vt* : to lay aside : SAVE ⟨had some money *put by*⟩

put down *vt* **1** : to bring to an end by force ⟨*put down* a riot⟩ **2 a** : DEPOSE 1, DEGRADE **b** : DISPARAGE, BELITTLE ⟨mentioned my poetry only to *put* it *down*⟩ **c** : DISAPPROVE, CRITICIZE ⟨were *put down* for the way they dressed⟩ **d** : HUMILIATE, SQUELCH ⟨was *put down* with a sharp retort⟩ **3** : to make ineffective : CHECK **4 a** : to write down (as in a list) **b** : to assign to a particular category or cause **5** : to preserve for future use ⟨*put down* a cask of pickles⟩

put in *vb* **1** : to make or make as a request, offer, or declaration ⟨*put in* a plea of not guilty⟩ ⟨*put in* for a job at the store⟩ **2** : to spend (time) at some activity or place ⟨*put in* six hours at the office⟩ **3** : PLANT ⟨*put in* a crop⟩ **4** : to call at or enter a place; *esp* : to enter a harbor or port

put off *vt* **1** : DISCONCERT, REPEL ⟨*put off* by their indifference⟩ **2 a** : to hold back to a later time : DEFER ⟨*put*

off a visit to the dentist⟩ **b** : to induce to wait ⟨*put* the bill collector *off*⟩ **b** : to rid oneself of

put on *vt* **1 a** : to dress oneself in **b** : to assume as if a garment : ADOPT ⟨*put on* airs⟩; *also* : FEIGN ⟨*put on* a show of anger⟩ **2** : EXAGGERATE 1 ⟨they are *putting* it *on* when they make such claims⟩ **3** : PERFORM, PRODUCE ⟨*put on* an entertaining act⟩ **4** : to mislead deliberately especially for amusement ⟨you're *putting* me *on*⟩ — **put-on** *adj*

put·out \'pùt-ˌaùt\ *n* : the act or an instance of causing a base runner or batter to be out in baseball

put out \pùt-'aùt, 'pùt-\ *vb* **1** : EXERT, USE ⟨*put out* all their strength to move the piano⟩ **2** : to cause to cease to burn or glow **3** : PRODUCE ⟨*puts out* a lot of work in eight hours⟩ **4 a** : IRRITATE, PROVOKE ⟨*put out* by our tardiness⟩ **b** : INCONVENIENCE ⟨don't *put* yourself *out* for us⟩ **5** : to cause to be out (as in baseball) **6** : to set out from shore

put over *vt* : to put across ⟨*put over* a scheme⟩ ⟨they're always trying to *put* something *over* on me⟩

pu·tre·fac·tion \ˌpyü-trə-'fak-shən\ *n* **1** : the rotting of organic matter; *esp* : bacterial or fungal decay of proteins with the formation of foul-smelling incompletely oxidized products **2** : the state of being putrefied : CORRUPTION [Late Latin *putrefactio*, from Latin *putrefacere* "to putrefy"] — **pu·tre·fac·tive** \-'fak-tiv\ *adj*

pu·tre·fy \'pyü-trə-ˌfī\ *vb* **-fied; -fy·ing** : to make or become putrid : DECOMPOSE, ROT [Latin *putrefacere*, from *putrēre* "to be rotten" + *facere* "to make"]

pu·tres·cent \pyü-'tres-nt\ *adj* : becoming putrid : ROTTING — **pu·tres·cence** \-ns\ *n*

pu·trid \'pyü-trəd\ *adj* **1 a** : being in a state of putrefaction : ROTTEN ⟨*putrid* meat⟩ **b** : characteristic of putrefaction : FOUL ⟨a *putrid* odor⟩ **2 a** : morally corrupt **b** : totally disagreeable or objectionable : VILE [Latin *putridus*, from *putrēre* "to be rotten", from *puter*, *putris* "rotten"] — **pu·trid·i·ty** \pyü-'trid-ət-ē\ *n* — **pu·trid·ly** \'pyü-trəd-lē\ *adv* — **pu·trid·ness** *n*

putsch \'pùch\ *n* : a secretly plotted and suddenly executed attempt to overthrow a government [German]

putt \'pət\ *n* : a golf stroke made on a putting green to cause the ball to roll toward the hole [alteration of ²*put*] — **putt** *vb*

put·tee \ˌpə-'tē, pù-; 'pət-ē\ *n* **1** : a cloth strip wrapped around the leg from ankle to knee **2** : a leather legging secured by a strap or catch or by laces [Hindi *paṭṭī* "strip of cloth", from Sanskrit *paṭṭikā*]

¹put·ter \'pùt-ər\ *n* : one that puts

²putt·er \'pət-ər\ *n* : a golf club used in putting

³put·ter \'pət-ər\ *vi* **1** : to move or act aimlessly or idly : DAWDLE **2** : to work at random : TINKER [alteration of *potter*] — **put·ter·er** \-ər-ər\ *n*

put through *vt* : to carry to a successful conclusion : EFFECT ⟨*put* a reform *through*⟩

putt·ing green \'pət-ing-\ *n* : a smooth usually grassy area around the hole into which the ball must be played in golf

put to *vi* : to put in to shore (as for shelter)

¹put·ty \'pət-ē\ *n, pl* **putties** : a cement usually made of whiting and boiled linseed oil beaten or kneaded to the consistency of dough and used in fastening glass in sashes and stopping crevices in woodwork; *also* : any of various substances resembling such cement in appearance, consistency, or use [French *potée*, literally, "potful", from *pot* "pot"]

²putty *vt* **put·tied; put·ty·ing** : to cement or seal with putty

put-up \ˌpùt-ˌəp\ *adj* : arranged secretly beforehand ⟨a *put-up* job⟩

put up \pùt-'əp, 'pùt-\ *vb* **1 a** : to prepare for later use ⟨*put up* a lunch⟩; *esp* : CAN ⟨*put up* peaches⟩ **b** : to put away out of use ⟨*put up* your sword⟩ **2** : to nominate for election **3** : to offer for public sale ⟨*put* the furniture *up* for auction⟩ **4** : to give or obtain food and shelter : LODGE ⟨*put* us *up* overnight⟩ **5** : BUILD 1, ERECT **6** :

CARRY ON 3 ⟨*put up* a struggle against odds⟩ **7** : to offer as a prize or stake — **put up to** : INCITE, INSTIGATE — **put up with** : TOLERATE 1, ENDURE

¹puz·zle \'pəz-əl\ *vb* **puz·zled; puz·zling** \'pəz-ling, -ə-ling\ **1** : to confuse the understanding of : PERPLEX, BEWILDER **2** : to solve with difficulty or ingenuity ⟨*puzzled* out the mystery⟩ **3** : to be uncertain as to action or choice **4** : to seek for or grope after something in a confused or uncertain manner ⟨*puzzle* over a problem⟩ [origin unknown] — **puz·zler** \'pəz-lər, -ə-lər\ *n* □ SYN PUZZLE, PERPLEX, MYSTIFY mean to baffle and disturb mentally. PUZZLE suggests some complication or contradiction difficult to understand or explain as a cause of mental confusion; PERPLEX usually adds an implication of causing worry and uncertainty in making a decision; MYSTIFY implies puzzling or perplexing thoroughly often by deliberate intent.

²puzzle *n* **1** : PUZZLEMENT 1 **2 a** : something that puzzles **b** : a question, problem, or contrivance designed for testing ingenuity

puz·zle·ment \'pəz-əl-mənt\ *n* **1** : the state of being puzzled : PERPLEXITY **2** : PUZZLE 2a

py- *or* **pyo-** *combining form* : pus ⟨*py*emia⟩ ⟨*pyo*rrhea⟩ [Greek *pyon*]

pyc·nom·e·ter \pik-'näm-ət-ər\ *n* : a standard vessel for measuring and comparing the densities of liquids or solids [Greek *pyknos* "dense"]

py·emia \pī-'ē-mē-ə\ *n* : infection of the blood with pus-forming bacteria accompanied by multiple abscesses — **py·emic** \-mik\ *adj*

py·gid·i·um \pī-'jid-ē-əm\ *n, pl* **-ia** \-ē-ə\ : a tail or terminal body region of an invertebrate [New Latin, from Greek *pygidion* "small rump", from *pygē* "rump"] — **py·gid·i·al** \-ē-əl\ *adj*

pyg·my *also* **pig·my** \'pig-mē\ *n, pl* **pygmies** **1** *often cap* : one of a race of dwarfs described by ancient Greek authors **2** *cap* : one of a small people of equatorial Africa ranging under five feet in height **3** : a person or thing very small for its kind : DWARF [Latin *pygmaeus* "of a pygmy, dwarfish", from Greek *pygmaios*, from *pygmē*, a measure of length, literally "fist"] — **pygmy** *adj*

py·ja·mas \pə-'jä-məz\ *chiefly British variant of* PAJAMAS

py·lon \'pī-,län, -lən\ *n* **1** : a usually massive gateway; *esp* : an ancient Egyptian one composed of two flat‐topped pyramids and a crosspiece **2** : a tower for supporting either end of a wire over a long span **3** : a projection (as a post or tower) marking a prescribed course of flight for an airplane [Greek *pylōn*, from *pylē* "gate"]

py·lo·ric \pī-'lōr-ik, pə-, -'lȯr-\ *adj* : of or relating to the pylorus; *also* : of, relating to, or situated in or near the posterior part of the stomach

py·lo·rus \-'lōr-əs, -'lȯr-\ *n, pl* **-lo·ri** \-'lōr-,ī, -'lȯr-, -,ē\ : the opening from the stomach to the intestine of a vertebrate [Late Latin, from Greek *pylōros*, literally, "one who guards a gate", from *pylē* "gate"]

pyo·gen·ic \,pī-ə-'jen-ik\ *adj* : producing pus : marked by pus production

py·or·rhea \,pī-ə-'rē-ə\ *n* : a pussy inflammation of the sockets of the teeth leading usually to loosening of the teeth — **py·or·rhe·al** \-'rē-əl\ *adj*

pyr- *or* **pyro-** *combining form* : fire : heat ⟨*pyro*mania⟩ [Greek *pyr* "fire"]

¹pyr·a·mid \'pir-ə-,mid\ *n* **1** : a massive structure built especially in ancient Egypt that usually has a square base and four triangular faces meeting at a point and contains tombs **2 a** : something felt to resemble a pyramid (as in shape or in broad-based organization) ⟨the social *pyramid*⟩ **b** : one of the conical masses that project from the medulla into the cavity of the kidney pelvis **3** : a polyhedron having for its base a plane figure with three or more angles and for its sides three or more triangles that meet to form the vertex [Latin *pyr*-

amid-, pyramis, from Greek] — **py·ram·i·dal** \pə-'ram-əd-l, ,pir-ə-'mid-l\ *adj* — **py·ram·i·dal·ly** \-ē\ *adv* — **pyr·a·mid·i·cal** \,pir-ə-'mid-i-kəl\ *adj*

²pyramid *vb* **1** : to increase rapidly and progressively step by step on a broad base **2** : to arrange or build up as if on the base of a pyramid

pyre \'pīr\ *n* : a combustible heap for burning a dead body as a funeral rite; *also* : a pile of material to be burned [Latin *pyra*, from Greek, from *pyr* "fire"]

py·re·noid \pī-'rē-,nȯid, 'pī-rə-\ *n* : one of the protein bodies in the chromatophores of various lower organisms (as some algae) that act as centers for starch deposition [Greek *pyrēn* "stone of a fruit"]

py·re·thrin \pī-'rē-thrən, -'reth-rən\ *n* : either of two oily liquid esters having insecticidal properties and occurring especially in pyrethrum flowers

py·re·thrum \-'rē-thrəm, -'reth-rəm\ *n* **1** : any of several chrysanthemums with finely divided often aromatic leaves including ornamentals as well as important sources of insecticides **2** : an insecticide made from the dried heads of some Old World pyrethrums [Latin, a plant resembling yarrow, from Greek *pyrethron*, from *pyr* "fire"]

Py·rex \'pī-,reks\ *trademark* — used for glass and glassware resistant to heat, chemicals, or electricity

pyr·i·dine \'pir-ə-,dēn\ *n* : a toxic water-soluble flammable liquid organic base C_5H_5N of pungent odor used as a solvent and in the manufacture of pharmaceuticals [derived from Greek *pyr* "fire"]

pyr·i·dox·ine *also* **pyr·i·dox·in** \,pir-ə-'däk-,sēn, -sən\ *n* : a crystalline alcohol of the vitamin B_6 group found especially in cereals and convertible in the organism into phosphate compounds that are essential coenzymes [*pyrid*ine + *ox-* + *-ine*]

pyr·i·form \'pir-ə-,fȯrm\ *adj* : having the form of a pear [Medieval Latin *pyrum* "pear", from Latin *pirum*]

py·rim·i·dine \pī-'rim-ə-,dēn, pə-\ *n* : any of a group of bases including several (as cytosine or thymine) that are fundamental constituents of DNA and RNA [alteration of *pyridine*]

py·rite \'pī-,rīt\ *n* : a common mineral FeS_2 that consists of iron disulfide, has a pale brass-yellow color and metallic luster, and is burned in making sulfur dioxide and sulfuric acid [Latin *pyrites* "flint"]

py·rites \pə-'rīt-ēz, pī-; 'pī-,rīts\ *n, pl* **pyrites** : any of various metallic-looking sulfides of which pyrite is the commonest [Latin, "flint", from Greek *pyritēs* "of fire", from *pyr* "fire"]

py·ro·lu·site \,pī-rō-'lü-,sīt\ *n* : a mineral MnO_2 consisting of manganese dioxide that is of an iron-black or dark steel-gray color and metallic luster, is usually soft, and is the most important ore of manganese [German *pyrolusit*, from Greek *pyr* "fire" + *lousis* "washing", from *louein* "to wash"]

py·rol·y·sis \pī-'räl-ə-səs\ *n* : chemical change brought about by the action of heat

py·ro·ma·nia \,pī-rō-'mā-nē-ə, -nyə\ *n* : a compulsive urge to start fires — **py·ro·ma·ni·ac** \-nē-,ak\ *n*

py·rom·e·ter \pī-'räm-ət-ər\ *n* : an instrument for measuring temperatures especially when above the range of mercurial thermometers — **py·ro·met·ric** \,pī-rə-'me-trik\ *adj* — **py·ro·met·ri·cal·ly** \-tri-kə-lē, -klē\ *adv* — **py·rom·e·try** \pī-'räm-ə-trē\ *n*

py·rope \'pī-,rōp\ *n* : a magnesium-aluminum garnet that is deep red in color and is frequently used as a gem [Middle French *pirope*, a red gem, from Latin *pyropus*, a red bronze, from Greek *pyrōpos*, literally, "fiery-eyed", from *pyr* "fire" + *ōps* "eye"]

py·ro·phor·ic \,pī-rə-'fȯr-ik, -'fär-\ *adj* **1** : igniting spontaneously **2** : emitting sparks when scratched or struck especially with steel [Greek *pyrophoros* "fire-bearing", from *pyr* "fire" + *-phoros* "carrying", from *pherein* "to carry"]

py·ro·tech·nic \,pī-rə-'tek-nik\ *n* **1** *pl* : the art of making or the manufacture and use of fireworks **2** *pl* **a** :

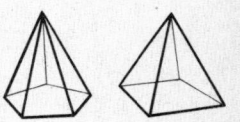

¹pyramid 3

materials (as fireworks) for flares or signals **b** : a display of fireworks **3** : a spectacular display (as of oratory) — usually used in pl. [derived from Greek *pyr* "fire" + *technē* "art"] — **pyrotechnic** *also* **py·ro·tech·ni·cal** \-ni·kəl\ *adj* — **py·ro·tech·ni·cal·ly** \-ni·kə-lē, -klē\ *adv* — **py·ro·tech·nist** \-'tek-nəst\ *n*

py·rox·ene \pī-'räk-ˌsēn\ *n* : any of various silicate minerals that usually contain magnesium or iron [French *pyroxène*, from Greek *pyr* "fire" + *xenos* "stranger"] — **py·rox·e·nic** \ˌpī-ˌrak-'sē-nik\ *adj*

py·rox·y·lin \pī-'räk-sə-lən\ *n* : a flammable substance resembling cotton that is produced chemically from cellulose and used in the manufacture of various products (as celluloid, lacquer, and some explosives) [*pyr-* + Greek *xylon* "wood"]

Pyr·rhic victory \ˌpir-ik-\ *n* : a victory won at excessive cost [*Pyrrhus*, died 272 B.C., king of Epirus who sustained heavy losses in defeating the Romans]

py·ru·vate \pī-'rü-ˌvāt\ *n* : a salt or ester of pyruvic acid

py·ru·vic acid \pī-'rü-vik-\ *n* : a 3-carbon liquid organic acid $C_3H_4O_3$ that is an important intermediate in carbohydrate metabolism and can be formed from either glucose or glycogen [*pyr-* + Latin *uva* "grape"; from its importance in fermentation]

Py·thag·o·re·an \pə-ˌthag-ə-'rē-ən, pī-\ *adj* : of, relating to, or associated with the Greek philosopher Pythagoras — **Pythagorean** *n*

Pythagorean numbers *n* : any set of three positive integers (as 3, 4, 5) that satisfy the equation $x^2 + y^2 = z^2$

Pythagorean theorem *n* : a theorem in geometry : the square of the length of the hypotenuse of a right triangle equals the sum of the squares of the lengths of the other two sides

Pyth·i·an \'pith-ē-ən\ *adj* : of or relating to the ancient Greek god Apollo especially as patron deity of Delphi [Latin *pythius* "of Delphi", from Greek *pythios*, from *Pythō* "Pytho", former name of Delphi]

Pythian Games *n pl* : an ancient Panhellenic festival similar to the Olympic Games celebrated at Delphi every four years in honor of Apollo

py·thon \'pī-ˌthän, -thən\ *n* : a large nonpoisonous constricting snake (as a boa); *esp* : any of an Old World genus of large snakes [Latin *Python*, a monstrous serpent killed by Apollo, from Greek *Pythōn*] — **py·tho·nine** \'pī-thə-ˌnīn\ *adj*

py·tho·ness \'pī-thə-nəs, 'pith-ə-\ *n* : a woman supposed to have a spirit of divination; *esp* : a priestess of Apollo held to have prophetic powers [Middle French *pithonisse*, from Late Latin *pythonissa*, from Greek *Pythōn*, spirit of divination, from *Pythō*, seat of the Delphic oracle] — **py·thon·ic** \pī-'thän-ik\ *adj*

pyx \'piks\ *n* : a small round case used to carry the Eucharist to the sick [Medieval Latin *pyxis*, from Latin, "box", from Greek]

python

Qq

q \'kyü\ *n, pl* **q's** *or* **qs** \'kyüz\ *often cap* : the seventeenth letter of the English alphabet

Q fever \'kyü-\ *n* : a disease marked by high fever, chills, and muscular pains, caused by a rickettsia, and transmitted by raw milk, by contact, or by ticks [*query*]

qt \'kyü-'tē\ *n, often cap Q&T* : QUIET — usually used in the phrase *on the qt* [abbreviation]

¹quack \'kwak\ *vi* : to utter the characteristic cry of a duck [imitative]

²quack *n* : a cry made by or as if by quacking

³quack *n* **1** : a person who pretends to have medical skill **2** : CHARLATAN [short for earlier *quacksalver*, from obsolete Dutch] — **quack·ery** \'kwak-rē, -ə-rē\ *n*

⁴quack *adj* : of, relating to, or characteristic of a quack; *esp* : pretending to cure diseases

quack grass *n* : a European grass that is naturalized throughout North America as a weed and spreads by creeping rhizomes — called also *couch grass, witchgrass* [derived from Old English *cwice*]

¹quad \'kwäd\ *n* : QUADRANGLE

²quad *n* : a type-metal space that is 1 en or more in width [derived from *quadrate*]

³quad *n* : QUADRUPLET

quad·ran·gle \'kwäd-ˌrang-gəl\ *n* **1** : a 4-sided enclosure especially when surrounded by buildings **2** : the buildings enclosing a quadrangle — **qua·dran·gu·lar** \kwä-'drang-gyə-lər\ *adj*

quad·rant \'kwäd-rənt\ *n* **1** : an instrument for measuring altitudes (as in astronomy or surveying) **2 a** : an arc of 90° : one quarter of a circle **b** : the area bounded by a quadrant and two radii **3** : any of the four quarters into which something is divided by two real or imaginary lines that intersect each other at right angles; *esp* : any of the four parts into which a plane is divided by rectangular coordinate axes lying in that plane [Latin *quadrans* "fourth part"] — **qua·dran·tal** \kwä-'drant-l\ *adj*

qua·draph·o·ny \kwä-'draf-ə-nē\ *n* : the transmission, recording, or reproduction of sound by techniques that utilize four transmission channels [derived from *quadri-* + *-phone*] — **quad·ra·phon·ic** \ˌkwäd-rə-'fän-ik\ *adj*

quad·rat \'kwäd-rət, -ˌrat\ *n* : a usually rectangular plot used for ecological or population studies [alteration of *quadrate*]

quad·rate \'kwäd-ˌrāt, -rət\ *n* : a bony or cartilaginous element on each side of the skull to which the lower jaw is attached in most lower vertebrates [earlier *quadrate* "square or cubical area or object", from Latin *quadratus*, past participle of *quadrare* "to make square"] — **quadrate** *adj*

qua·drat·ic \kwä-'drat-ik\ *adj* : involving terms of second degree at most ⟨a *quadratic* polynomial⟩ — **quadratic** *n*

quadratic equation *n* : an equation containing one term in which the unknown is squared and no term in which it is raised to a higher power

quad·ra·ture \'kwäd-rə-ˌchùr, -chər\ *n* **1** : the process of finding a square equal in area to a given area ⟨*quadrature* of the circle is impossible with ruler and compass⟩ **2** : a configuration in which two celestial bodies have a separation of 90 degrees ⟨Mars in *quadrature* with the sun⟩

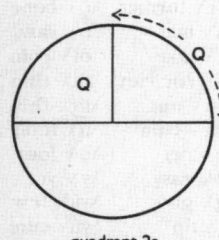

quadrant 2a

qua·dren·ni·al \kwä-'dren-ē-əl\ *adj* **1** : consisting of or lasting for four years **2** : occurring or being done every four years [Latin *quadriennium* "period of four years", from *quadri-* + *annus* "year"] — **qua·dren·ni·al·ly** \-ē-ə-lē\ *adv*

quadri- *or* **quadr-** *or* **quadru-** *combining form* **1** : four **2** : fourth [Latin]

quad·ri·ceps \'kwäd-rə-,seps\ *n* : the great extensor muscle of the front of the thigh [*quadri-* + *-ceps* (as in *biceps*)]

quadriceps fem·o·ris \-'fem-ə-rəs\ *n* : QUADRICEPS [New Latin]

¹quad·ri·lat·er·al \,kwäd-rə-'lat-ə-rəl, -'la-trəl\ *adj* : having four sides [Latin *quadrilaterus*, from *quadri-* + *later-, latus* "side"]

²quadrilateral *n* : a plane figure of four sides and four angles

qua·drille \kwä-'dril, kwə-, kə-\ *n* : a square dance for four couples or music for this dance [French, "group of knights in an exhibition tournament", from Spanish *cuadrilla* "troop"]

qua·dril·lion \kwä-'dril-yən\ *n* — see NUMBER table [French, from *quadri-* + *-illion* (as in *million*)]

quad·ri·par·tite \,kwäd-rə-'pär-,tīt\ *adj* **1** : consisting of four parts ⟨a *quadripartite* vault⟩ **2** : shared by four parties or persons ⟨a *quadripartite* agreement⟩

qua·droon \kwä-'drün\ *n* : a person of one-quarter Negro ancestry [Spanish *cuarterón*, from *cuarto* "fourth", from Latin *quartus*]

quad·ru·ped \'kwäd-rə-,ped\ *n* : an animal having four feet — **quadruped** *or* **qua·dru·pe·dal** \kwä-'drü-pəd-l, ,kwäd-rə-'ped-\ *adj*

¹qua·dru·ple \kwä-'drüp-əl, -'drəp-; 'kwäd-rəp-\ *vb* **qua·dru·pled; qua·dru·pling** \-ling, -ə-ling\ : to make or become four times as great or as many

²quadruple *adj* **1** : having four units or members **2** : being four times as great or as many **3** : marked by four beats per measure ⟨*quadruple* meter⟩ [Latin *quadruplus*, from *quadri-* + *-plus* "multiplied by"] — **quadruple** *n*

qua·drup·let \kwä-'drəp-lət, -'drüp-; 'kwäd-rəp-\ *n* **1** : one of four offspring born at one birth **2** : a combination of four of a kind

¹qua·dru·pli·cate \kwä-'drü-pli-kət\ *adj* : having or being four corresponding or identical parts or examples [Latin *quadruplicatus*, past participle of *quadruplicare* "to quadruple", from *quadruplic-, quadruplex* "fourfold"]

²qua·dru·pli·cate \-plə-,kāt\ *vt* **1** : QUADRUPLE **2** : to provide in quadruplicate — **qua·dru·pli·ca·tion** \kwä-,drü-plə-'kā-shən\ *n*

³qua·dru·pli·cate \kwä-'drü-pli-kət\ *n* **1** : one of four like things **2** : four copies all alike ⟨typed in *quadruplicate*⟩

quaes·tor \'kwes-tər\ *n* : one of numerous ancient Roman officials concerned chiefly with financial administration [Latin, from *quaestus*, past participle of *quaerere* "to seek, ask"]

quaff \'kwäf, 'kwaf\ *vb* : to drink deeply or repeatedly [origin unknown] — **quaff** *n*

quag \'kwag, 'kwäg\ *n* : MARSH, BOG [origin unknown]

quag·ga \'kwag-ə, 'kwäg-\ *n* : an extinct wild ass of southern Africa related to the zebras [obsolete Afrikaans]

quag·mire \'kwag-,mīr, 'kwäg-\ *n* **1** : soft miry land that gives under the feet **2** : a complex or uncertain position : PREDICAMENT

qua·hog \'kwò-,hòg, 'kwō-, 'kō-, -,häg\ *n* : a round thick-shelled American clam [of American Indian origin]

quai \'kā\ *n* : QUAY [French]

¹quail \'kwāl\ *n, pl* **quail** *or* **quails** : any of various game birds related to the common fowl: as **a** : a stocky short-winged Old World migratory bird occurring in many varieties **b** : any of various small American birds; *esp* : BOBWHITE [Middle French *quaille*, from Medieval Latin *quaccula*]

²quail *vi* : to shrink in dread or terror : COWER [Middle French *quailler* "to curdle", from Latin *coagulare*]

quaint \'kwānt\ *adj* **1** : unusual or different in character or appearance : ODD **2** : pleasingly old-fashioned or unfamiliar [Old French *cointe* "skilled", from Latin *cognitus*, past participle of *cognoscere* "to know"] — **quaint·ly** *adv* — **quaint·ness** *n*

¹quake \'kwāk\ *vi* **1** : to shake or vibrate usually from shock or instability **2** : to tremble or shudder usually from cold or fear [Old English *cwacian*]

²quake *n* : a shaking or trembling; *esp* : EARTHQUAKE

quak·er \'kwā-kər\ *n* **1** : one that quakes **2** *cap* : FRIEND 4

Quaker meeting *n* : a meeting of Friends for worship marked often by long periods of silence

qual·i·fi·ca·tion \,kwäl-ə-fə-'kā-shən\ *n* **1** : something that limits or restricts ⟨agreed without *qualification*⟩ **2 a** : a quality or skill that fits a person (as for an office) ⟨the applicant with the best *qualifications*⟩ **b** : a condition that must be met ⟨a *qualification* for membership⟩

qual·i·fied \'kwäl-ə-,fīd\ *adj* **1** : having the necessary skill, knowledge, or ability to do something ⟨a *qualified* accountant⟩ **2** : limited or modified in some way ⟨*qualified* agreement⟩ — **qual·i·fied·ly** \-,fī-əd-lē, -,fīd-lē\ *adv*

qual·i·fi·er \-,fī-ər, -,fīr\ *n* : one that qualifies: as **a** : one that satisfies specified requirements **b** : a word or word group that limits the meaning of another word or word group : MODIFIER

qual·i·fy \'kwäl-ə-,fī\ *vb* **-fied; -fy·ing** **1 a** : to make less general and more restricted : LIMIT **b** : to make less harsh or strict : MODERATE **c** : to alter the strength or flavor of ⟨*qualify* a liquor⟩ **d** : to limit the meaning of (as a noun) **2** : to characterize by naming a quality : DESCRIBE **3 a** : to fit by training, skill, or ability for a special purpose **b** : CERTIFY, LICENSE ⟨*qualified* to practice law⟩ **4** : to exhibit needed fitness, skill, or ability for some end [Middle French *qualifier*, from Medieval Latin *qualificare*, from Latin *qualis* "of what kind"]

qual·i·ta·tive \'kwäl-ə-,tāt-iv\ *adj* : of, relating to, or involving quality or kind — **qual·i·ta·tive·ly** *adv*

qualitative analysis *n* : chemical analysis designed to identify the components of a substance or mixture

qual·i·ty \'kwäl-ət-ē\ *n, pl* **-ties** **1 a** : peculiar and essential character : NATURE **b** : an inherent feature : PROPERTY ⟨hardness is a *quality* of steel⟩ **2** : degree of excellence : GRADE **3** : usually high social status : RANK **4** : a distinguishing attribute : CHARACTERISTIC **5 a** : vividness of hue **b** : TIMBRE [Old French *qualité*, from Latin *qualitas*, from *qualis* "of what kind"] □ SYN PROPERTY, ATTRIBUTE: QUALITY is a very general term applying to any trait, mark, or character of an individual or of a type; PROPERTY applies to a quality belonging to a thing's essential nature and helping to distinguish and identify its type or species; ATTRIBUTE is a quality ascribed to a thing or being often through lack of definite knowledge of it.

qualm \'kwäm, 'kwälm *also* 'kwòm\ *n* **1** : a sudden attack of illness, faintness, or nausea **2** : a sudden fear or misgiving **3** : a feeling of doubt or hesitation in matters of conscience ⟨had no *qualms* about lying⟩ [origin unknown] — **qualmy** \-ē\ *adj* □ SYN QUALM, SCRUPLE, COMPUNCTION mean a misgiving about what one is doing or going do do. QUALM implies an uneasy fear that one is not following one's conscience or better judgment; SCRUPLE implies doubt of the rightness of an act on grounds of principle; COMPUNCTION implies a spontaneous feeling that one is inflicting a wrong or injustice on someone.

qualm·ish \-ish\ *adj* **1 a** : feeling qualms : SQUEAMISH **b** : overly scrupulous **2** : of, relating to, or producing qualms — **qualm·ish·ly** *adv* — **qualm·ish·ness** *n*

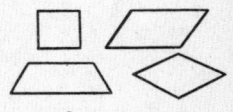

²quadrilateral

\ə\ abut	\ng\ sing
\ər\ further	\ō\ bone
\a\ mat	\ò\ saw
\ā\ take	\òi\ coin
\ä\ cot, cart	\th\ thin
\aù\ out	\th\ this
\ch\ chin	\ü\ food
\e\ pet	\ù\ foot
\ē\ easy	\y\ yet
\g\ go	\yü\ few
\i\ tip	\yù\ cure
\ī\ life	\zh\ vision
\j\ job	

quan·da·ry \'kwän-də-rē, -drē\ *n, pl* **-ries** : a state of puzzlement or doubt : DILEMMA [origin unknown] SYN see PREDICAMENT

quan·ti·fi·er \'kwänt-ə-,fī-ər, -,fīr\ *n* : a term (as *two, all, most,* or *no*) expressive of quantity; *esp* : one that binds the variables in a logical formula

quan·ti·ta·tive \'kwänt-ə-,tāt-iv, 'kwän-\ *adj* : of, relating to, expressible as, or involving the measurement of quantity — **quan·ti·ta·tive·ly** *adv* — **quan·ti·ta·tive-ness** *n*

quantitative analysis *n* : chemical analysis designed to determine the amounts or proportions of the components of a substance or mixture

quantitative inheritance *n* : inheritance of a character (as height or skin color in humans) controlled by a group of gene pairs at different chromosomal locations with each pair having a specific quantitative effect

quan·ti·ty \'kwänt-ət-ē, 'kwän-\ *n, pl* **-ties** **1 a** : an indefinite amount or number **b** : a large amount or number — often used in pl. **2 a** : the aspect in which a thing is measurable in terms of degree or magnitude **b** : a mathematical expression concerned with particular values **3** : duration of a speech sound as distinct from individual quality [Old French *quantité,* from Latin *quantitas,* from *quantus* "how much, how large"]

quan·tize \'kwän-,tīz\ *vt* **1** : to subdivide (as energy) into small units or amounts **2** : to calculate or express in terms of quantum mechanics — **quan·ti·za·tion** \,kwänt-ə-'zā-shən\ *n*

quan·tum \'kwänt-əm\ *n, pl* **quan·ta** \'kwänt-ə\ **1** : QUANTITY 1a, AMOUNT **2** : one of the very small parcels into which many forms of energy are subdivided [Latin, neuter of *quantus* "how much"]

quantum mechanics *n* : a general mathematical theory dealing with the interactions of matter and radiation in terms of observable quantities only — **quantum me-chanical** *adj*

quantum theory *n* : a branch of physical theory based on the concept of the subdivision of radiant energy into finite quanta and applied to numerous processes involving transference or transformation of energy on an atomic or molecular scale

¹quar·an·tine \'kwȯr-ən-,tēn, 'kwär-\ *n* **1** : a term during which a ship arriving in port and suspected of carrying contagious disease is forbidden contact with the shore **2** : a restraint upon the activities or movements of persons or the transport of goods designed to prevent the spread of disease or pests **3** : the period during which a person with a contagious disease is under quarantine **4** : a place (as a hospital) where individuals under quarantine are kept [Italian *quarantina* "period of 40 days", from Middle French *quarantaine,* from *quarante* "forty", from Latin *quadraginta*]

²quarantine *vt* : to detain in or exclude by or as if by quarantine : ISOLATE — **quar·an·tin·able** \-,tē-nə-bəl\ *adj*

¹quar·rel \'kwȯr-əl, 'kwär-əl, 'kwȯrl, 'kwärl\ *n* **1** : a cause of dispute or complaint **2** : a usually angry verbal dispute [Middle French *querele* "complaint", from Latin *querela,* from *queri* "to complain"]

²quarrel *vi* **-reled** *or* **-relled; -rel·ing** *or* **-rel·ling** **1** : to find fault ⟨*quarrel* with an idea⟩ **2** : to contend or dispute actively : SQUABBLE — **quar·rel·er** *or* **quar·rel·ler** *n*

quar·rel·some \'kwȯr-əl-səm, 'kwär-əl-, 'kwȯrl-, 'kwärl-\ *adj* : apt or inclined to quarrel : CONTENTIOUS — **quar·rel·some·ly** *adv* — **quar·rel·some·ness** *n*

¹quar·ry \'kwȯr-ē, 'kwär-\ *n, pl* **quarries** **1** : the object of a chase : GAME; *esp* : game hunted with hawks **2** : PREY 1 [Middle English *querre* "entrails of game given to the hounds", from Middle French *cuiree*] □ ORIGIN The *quarry* the hunter stalks is not related to the stonecutter's quarry. The first can be traced to a minor

ceremony that was once part of every successful hunt. The hounds were rewarded after the kill with a part of the slain animal's entrails. The French word for this hounds' portion was *cuiree. Cuiree* was borrowed into Middle English as *querre.* The word for the entrails of an animal was later transferred to the animal itself, when considered in the character of game pursued. Now anything pursued is its pursuer's *quarry.*

²quarry *n, pl* **quarries** : an open excavation usually for obtaining building stone, slate, or limestone [Middle French *quarriere,* derived from Latin *quadrum* "square"] □ ORIGIN The stone *quarry* is not so-called because it is sought after, as is game by a hunter, but rather takes its name from the building stones it provides. *Quarriere* was the Middle French word for a quarry, a source of squared stones. Its ultimate source was Latin *quadrum,* which means "square".

³quarry *vt* **quar·ried; quar·ry·ing** **1** : to dig or take from or as if from a quarry **2** : to make a quarry in — **quar·ri-er** *n*

quart \'kwȯrt\ *n* **1** : a unit of measure equal to ¼ gallon — see MEASURE table **2** : a vessel or measure having a capacity of one quart [Middle French *quarte* "fourth of a gallon", from *quart* "fourth", from Latin *quartus*]

¹quar·tan \'kwȯrt-n\ *adj* : characterized by an interval of approximately three days between occurrences : occurring on the fourth day [Old French *(fievre) quar-taine* "quartan fever", from Latin *(febris) quartana,* from *quartanus* "of the fourth", from *quartus* "fourth"]

²quartan *n* : an intermittent fever characterized by intervals of approximately 72 hours between attacks; *esp* : a quartan malaria

¹quar·ter \'kwȯrt-ər, 'kwȯt-\ *n* **1** : one of four equal parts **2** : a unit (as of weight or length) that equals one fourth of some larger unit **3 a** : any of four 3-month divisions of a year **b** : a school term of about 12 weeks **c** : QUARTER HOUR **d** : a coin worth a fourth of a dollar; *also* : the sum of 25 cents **e** : one limb of a 4-limbed animal or carcass with the parts near it ⟨a *quarter* of beef⟩ **f** : a fourth part of the moon's period ⟨a moon in its first *quarter*⟩ **g** : one of the four parts into which the horizon may be divided; *also* : a region or direction under such a part **h** : one of the four cardinal points corresponding to the four parts of the horizon; *also* : a compass point **4** : someone or something (as a place, direction, or group) not specified ⟨expecting trouble from another *quarter*⟩ **5 a** : a particular division or district of a city ⟨the foreign *quarter*⟩ **b** : an assigned place or duty station especially of a member of a naval crew ⟨a call to *quarters*⟩ **c** *pl* : living accommodations : LODGING **6** : MERCY; *esp* : a refraining from destroying a defeated enemy **7** : the stern area of a ship's side [Old French *quartier,* from Latin *quartar-ius,* from *quartus* "fourth"] — **at close quarters** : at close range or in immediate contact

²quarter *vb* **1 a** : to divide into four equal parts **b** : to separate into parts ⟨peel and *quarter* an orange⟩ **c** : DISMEMBER 1 **2** : to provide with or occupy a lodging **3** : to crisscross an area in many directions ⟨*quartered* the hills looking for the child⟩

³quarter *adj* : consisting of or equal to a quarter

¹quar·ter·back \-,bak\ *n* : an offensive football back who calls the signals and directs the offensive play of the team

²quarterback *vt* : to act as quarterback of (a football team)

quarter day *n, chiefly British* : the day which begins a quarter of the year and on which a quarterly payment falls due

quar·ter·deck \-,dek\ *n* **1** : the stern area of a ship's upper deck **2** : a part of a deck on a naval vessel set aside for ceremonial and official use

quarterdeck

quarterdeck I

quarter horse *n* : an alert stocky muscular horse capable of high speed for short distances and of great endurance under the saddle [from its high speed for distances up to a quarter of a mile]

quarter hour *n* **1** : 15 minutes **2** : any of the quarter points of an hour

quar·ter·ing *adj* : coming from a point well abaft the beam of a ship but not directly astern ⟨a *quartering* wind⟩

¹quar·ter·ly \'kwȯrt-ər-lē, 'kwȯt-\ *adv* : at 3-month intervals ⟨interest compounded *quarterly*⟩

²quarterly *adj* : coming during or at the end of each 3-month interval ⟨*quarterly* premium⟩ ⟨*quarterly* meeting⟩

³quarterly *n, pl* **-lies** : a periodical published four times a year

quar·ter·mas·ter \'kwȯrt-ər-‚mas-tər, 'kwȯt-\ *n* **1** : a petty officer who attends to a ship's steering and signals **2** : an army officer responsible for the clothing and subsistence of a body of troops

quar·tern \'kwȯrt-ərn, 'kwȯt-\ *n* : a fourth part : QUARTER [Old French *quarteron* "quarter of a pound, quarter of a hundred", from *quartier* "quarter"]

quarter note *n* : a musical note equal in value to one fourth of a whole note

quar·ter·saw \'kwȯrt-ər-‚sȯ, 'kwȯt-\ *vt* **-sawed; -sawed** *or* **-sawn** \-‚sȯn\; **-saw·ing** : to saw (a log) into quarters and then into planks in which the annual rings are nearly at right angles to the wide face

quarter section *n* : a tract of land that is half a mile square and contains 160 acres (about .647 square kilometer) in the United States government system of land surveying

quar·ter·staff \'kwȯrt-ər-‚staf\ *n, pl* **-staves** \-‚stavz, -‚stāvz\ : a long stout staff formerly used as a weapon

quar·tet *also* **quar·tette** \kwȯr-'tet\ *n* **1** : a musical composition for four instruments or voices **2** : a group or set of four [Italian *quartetto,* from *quarto* "fourth", from Latin *quartus*]

quar·tile \'kwȯr-‚tīl, 'kwȯrt-l\ *n* : one of three values that divide a frequency distribution into four equal intervals [derived from Latin *quartus* "fourth"]

quar·to \'kwȯrt-ō\ *n, pl* **quartos** : a book made of sheets of paper each folded twice to make four leaves or eight pages [Latin, ablative of *quartus* "fourth"]

quartz \'kwȯrts\ *n* : a common mineral SiO_2 consisting of silica often found in the form of colorless transparent crystals but sometimes (as in amethysts, agates, and jaspers) brightly colored [German *quarz*] — **quartz·ose** \'kwȯrt-‚sōs\ *adj*

quartz glass *n* : vitreous silica prepared from pure quartz and noted for its transparency to ultraviolet radiation

quartz·ite \'kwȯrt-‚sīt\ *n* : a compact granular rock composed of quartz and derived from sandstone

qua·sar \'kwā-‚zär *also* -‚sär\ *n* : any of various distant celestial objects that resemble stars but emit unusually bright blue and ultraviolet light and radio waves [*quas*i-stel*lar* radio source]

quash \'kwäsh, 'kwȯsh\ *vt* **1** : to make void by judicial action ⟨*quash* an indictment⟩ **2** : to suppress completely : QUELL ⟨*quash* a rebellion⟩ [Middle French *casser, quasser,* from Late Latin *cassare,* from Latin *cassus* "void"]

qua·si \'kwā-‚zī, -‚sī; 'kwäz-ē, 'kwäs-; 'kwā-zē\ *adj* : having or legally held to have a likeness to something else ⟨a *quasi* contract⟩

qua·si- \'kwā-‚zī, -‚sī; 'kwäz-ē, 'kwäs-; 'kwā-zē\ *combining form* : in some sense or degree : seemingly [Latin *quasi* "as if, as it were, approximately", from *quam* "as" + *si* "if"]

See *quasi-* and 2d element

quasi-academic	autobiographical	quasi-biography
quasi-apology	quasi-automatic	
quasi-	quasi-autonomous	

quasi-blockade	quasi-liberal	quasi-poetic
quasi-confidential	quasi-literary	quasi-poetical
quasi-criminal	quasi-living	quasi-poetry
quasi-diplomacy	quasi-medical	quasi-political
quasi-documentary	quasi-military	quasi-professional
quasi-dramatic	quasi-miraculous	quasi-public
quasi-experimental	quasi-mockery	quasi-realism
quasi-feudal	quasi-monopolistic	quasi-religious
quasi-fictional	quasi-monopoly	quasi-scholarly
quasi-governmental	quasi-mystic	quasi-scientific
quasi-historical	quasi-mystical	quasi-technical
quasi-history	quasi-national	quasi-tragic
quasi-independent	quasi-official	quasi-vigilante
quasi-intellectual	quasi-peace	quasi-voluntarily
quasi-judicial	quasi-permanence	quasi-voluntary
quasi-legal	quasi-permanent	quasi-war
quasi-legislative	quasi-philosophical	
quasi-legitimate	quasi-philosophy	

qua·si–stel·lar radio source \-'stel-ər-\ *n* : QUASAR

quas·sia \'kwäsh-ə\ *n* : a bitter tonic drug from the heartwood of several tropical trees sometimes used as a mild agent against parasitic worms or as an insecticide [*Quassi,* 18th century Surinam Negro slave who discovered the medicinal value of quassia]

Qua·ter·na·ry \'kwät-ər-‚ner-ē, kwə-'tər-nə-rē\ *n* : the period of the Cenozoic era from the end of the Tertiary to the present time; *also* : the corresponding system of rocks — see GEOLOGIC TIME table [Latin *quaternarius* "consisting of four each", from *quaterni* "four each"] — **Quaternary** *adj*

qua·train \'kwā-‚trān\ *n* : a unit or group of four lines of verse [French, from *quatre* "four", from Latin *quattuor*]

qua·tre·foil \'kat-ər-‚foil, 'ka-trə-\ *n* **1** : a conventionalized representation of a flower with four petals or of a leaf with four leaflets **2** : a 4-lobed foliation in architecture [Middle English *quaterfoil* "set of four leaves", from Middle French *quatre* "four" + Middle English *-foil* (as in *trefoil*)]

¹qua·ver \'kwā-vər\ *vb* **qua·vered; qua·ver·ing** \'kwāv-ring, -ə-ring\ **1** : TREMBLE, SHAKE ⟨*quavering* inwardly⟩ **2** : TRILL 2 **3** : to utter sound in tremulous uncertain tones ⟨a voice that *quavered*⟩ **4** : to utter quaveringly [Middle English *quaveren,* from *quaven* "to tremble"] — **qua·ver·ing·ly** \'kwāv-ring-lē, -ə-ring-\ *adv* — **qua·very** \'kwāv-rē, -ə-rē\ *adj*

²quaver *n* **1** : TRILL 1 **2** : a tremulous sound

quay \'kē, 'kā, 'kwā\ *n* : a paved bank or a solid artificial landing place beside water for convenience in loading and unloading ships [alteration of earlier *key,* from Middle French *cai,* of Celtic origin]

quean \'kwēn\ *n* : a disreputable woman [Old English *cwene*]

quea·sy *also* **quea·zy** \'kwē-zē\ *adj* **quea·si·er; -est** **1** : full of doubt : HAZARDOUS **2 a** : causing nausea ⟨*queasy* motion⟩ **b** : suffering from nausea **3 a** : causing uneasiness : DELICATE, SQUEAMISH ⟨a *queasy* conscience⟩ (2) : ill at ease ⟨*queasy* about our debts⟩ [Middle English *coysy, qwesye*] — **quea·si·ly** \-zə-lē\ *adv* — **quea·si·ness** \-zē-nəs\ *n*

que·bra·cho \kā-'bräch-ō, ki-\ *n, pl* **-chos** : a South American tree of the sumac family with dense wood rich in tannins; *also* : its wood or a tannin-rich extract of this used in tanning [American Spanish, alteration of *quiebracha,* from Spanish *quiebra* "it breaks" + *hacha* "ax"]

Que·chua \'kech-wə, -ə-wə\ *n* **1 a** : a member of an Amerindian people of central Peru **b** : a group of peoples constituting the dominant element of the Inca Empire **2** : the language of the Quechua people widely spoken by other Amerindian peoples of southern and western South America [Spanish, from Quechua *kkechúwa* "plunderer, robber"] — **Que·chu·an** \-wən\ *adj or n*

¹queen \'kwēn\ *n* **1** : the wife or widow of a king **2** : a woman who is a monarch **3 a** : a woman eminent in

quarter note

\ə\ abut	\ng\ sing
\ər\ further	\ō\ bone
\a\ mat	\ȯ\ saw
\ā\ take	\ȯi\ coin
\ä\ cot, cart	\th\ thin
\aù\ out	\t̲h̲\ this
\ch\ chin	\ü\ food
\e\ pet	\ù\ foot
\ē\ easy	\y\ yet
\g\ go	\yü\ few
\i\ tip	\yù\ cure
\ī\ life	\zh\ vision
\j\ job	

rank, power, or attractions ⟨a society *queen*⟩ **b** : a goddess or a thing personified as female and having supremacy in a specified realm ⟨*queen* of the ocean liners⟩ **c** : an attractive girl or woman; *esp* : a beauty contest winner **4** : the most privileged piece in chess having the power to move in any direction any number of unobstructed squares **5** : a playing card bearing the stylized figure of a queen **6 a** : the fertile fully developed female of social bees, ants, and termites whose function is to lay eggs **b** : a mature female cat [Old English *cwēn* "woman, wife, queen"] — **queen·like** \-ˌlīk\ *adj* — **queen·li·ness** \-lē-nəs\ *n* — **queen·ly** \-lē\ *adv or adj*

²**queen** *vb* **I** : to act like a queen; *esp* : to put on airs — usually used with *it* **2** : to become or promote to a queen in chess

Queen Anne \kwē-'nan\ *adj* **I** : of or relating to an early 18th century style of furniture characterized by extensive use of upholstery, marquetry, and Oriental fabrics **2** : of or relating to an early 18th century English style of building characterized by unpretentious design, modified classic ornament, and red brickwork in which relief ornament is carved [*Queen Anne* of England]

Queen Anne's lace *n* : WILD CARROT

queen consort *n, pl* **queens consort** : the wife of a reigning king

queen mother *n* : a dowager queen who is mother of the reigning sovereign

queen post *n* : one of two vertical tie posts in a truss (as of a roof)

queen post

¹**queer** \'kwiər\ *adj* **I a** : differing from what is usual or normal : ODD **b** (1) : ECCENTRIC 2, UNCONVENTIONAL (2) : mildly insane **2 a** *slang* : WORTHLESS 1a, COUNTERFEIT ⟨*queer* money⟩ **b** : QUESTIONABLE 2, SUSPICIOUS **3** : not quite well : QUEASY [origin unknown] SYN see STRANGE — **queer·ish** \-ish\ *adj* — **queer·ly** *adv* — **queer·ness** *n*

²**queer** *adv* : QUEERLY

³**queer** *vt* **I** : to spoil the effect or success of : DISRUPT ⟨*queer* one's plans⟩ **2** : to put or get into an embarrassing or unfavorable situation

quell \'kwel\ *vt* **I** : to put down : SUPPRESS ⟨*quell* a riot⟩ **2** : QUIET 1, PACIFY ⟨*quell* fears⟩ [Old English *cwellan* "to kill"] — **quell·er** *n*

quench \'kwench\ *vt* **I** : to put out ⟨*quench* a fire⟩ ⟨*quench* a lamp⟩ **2** : to bring to an end: as **a** : OVERCOME 1 ⟨*quench* anger⟩ **b** : REPRESS 3 ⟨*quench* rebellion⟩ **c** : SLAKE 2, SATISFY ⟨*quench* thirst⟩ **3** : to cool (as heated steel) suddenly by immersion (as in water or oil) [Old English *-cwencan*] — **quench·able** \'kwen-chə-bəl\ *adj* — **quench·er** *n* — **quench·less** \'kwench-ləs\ *adj*

quern \'kwərn\ *n* : a primitive hand mill for grinding grain [Old English *cweorn*]

quer·u·lous \'kwer-ə-ləs, -yə-ləs\ *adj* **I** : habitually complaining **2** : FRETFUL, PETULANT ⟨a *querulous* voice⟩ [Latin *querulus*, from *queri* "to complain"] — **quer·u·lous·ly** *adv* — **quer·u·lous·ness** *n*

¹**que·ry** \'kwiər-ē, 'kweər-\ *n, pl* **queries** **I** : QUESTION 1a(1), INQUIRY **2** : a question in the mind : DOUBT **3** : QUESTION MARK [Latin *quaere*, imperative of *quaerere* "to ask"]

²**query** *vt* **que·ried; que·ry·ing** **I** : to put as a question ⟨"When can I leave?" I *queried*⟩ **2** : to ask questions about especially in order to resolve a doubt ⟨*queried* a statement⟩ **3** : to ask questions of especially with a desire for authoritative information ⟨*queried* the professor about the lesson⟩ **4** : to mark with a query

¹**quest** \'kwest\ *n* **I** : an act or instance of seeking: **a** : PURSUIT, SEARCH ⟨in *quest* of game⟩ **b** : a chivalrous enterprise in medieval romance ⟨the *quest* of the Holy Grail⟩ **2** *obs* : ones who search or make inquiry [Middle French *queste* "search, pursuit", from Latin *quaestus*, past participle of *quaerere* "to seek, ask"]

²**quest** *vb* **I** : to go on a quest **2** : to search for : SEEK, PURSUE **3** : to ask for : DEMAND

¹**ques·tion** \'kwes-chən, 'kwesh-\ *n* **I a** (1) : an interrogative expression often used to test knowledge (2) : an interrogative sentence or clause **b** : a subject or aspect in dispute or open for discussion : ISSUE; *also* : MATTER 1b **c** (1) : a subject or point of debate or a proposition to be voted on in a meeting ⟨put the *question* to the members⟩ (2) : the bringing of this to a vote **d** : the specific point at issue **2 a** : an act or instance of asking : INQUIRY **b** (1) : OBJECTION, DISPUTE ⟨obey without *question*⟩ (2) : room for doubt or objection ⟨there's no *question* about their honesty⟩ (3) : CHANCE, POSSIBILITY ⟨no *question* of escape⟩ [Middle French, from Latin *quaestio*, from *quaestus*, past participle of *quaerere* "to seek, ask"]

²**question** *vb* **I a** : to ask questions of or about **b** : INQUIRE **2** ⟨a *questioning* mind⟩ **2** : CROSS-EXAMINE ⟨*question* a witness⟩ **3 a** : DOUBT, DISPUTE ⟨*question* a decision⟩ **b** : to subject to analysis : EXAMINE — **ques·tion·er** *n* — **ques·tion·ing·ly** \-chə-ning-lē\ *adv*

ques·tion·able \'kwes-chə-nə-bəl, 'kwesh-, *rapid* 'kwesh-nə-\ *adj* **I** : affording reason for being doubted, questioned, or challenged : PROBLEMATIC ⟨milk of *questionable* purity⟩ ⟨a *questionable* decision⟩ **2** : attended by well-grounded suspicions of being immoral, crude, false, or unsound : DUBIOUS ⟨*questionable* motives⟩ — **ques·tion·ably** \-blē\ *adv*

question mark *n* : a punctuation mark ? used chiefly at the end of a sentence to indicate a direct question

ques·tion·naire \ˌkwes-chə-'naər, -'neər\ *n* : a set of questions to be asked of a number of persons usually in order to gather statistics (as on opinions) [French, from *questionner* "to question"]

quet·zal \ket-'säl, -'sal\ *n, pl* **quet·zals** *or* **quet·za·les** \-'säl-ās\ **I** : a Central American bird with narrow crest and brilliant plumage and in the male tail feathers often more than one half meter in length **2** *pl usually* **quetzales** : the basic monetary unit of Guatemala; *also* : a coin or note representing this unit [American Spanish, from Nahuatl *quetzaltototl*, from *quetzalli* "brilliant tail feather" + *tototl* "bird"]

¹**queue** \'kyü\ *n* **I** : a braid of hair usually worn hanging at the back of the head **2** : a line especially of persons or vehicles **3** : a sequence of messages or jobs held in auxiliary storage in a computer awaiting transmission or processing [French, literally, "tail", from Latin *cauda*]

²**queue** *vb* **queued; queu·ing** *or* **queue·ing** **I** : to arrange or form in a queue **2** : to line up or wait in a queue ⟨the crowd *queued* up for tickets⟩ — **queu·er** *n*

¹**quib·ble** \'kwib-əl\ *n* **I** : an evasion of or shift from the point : EQUIVOCATION **2** : a trivial objection or criticism [probably from obsolete *quib* "quibble"]

²**quibble** *vi* **quib·bled; quib·bling** \'kwib-ling, -ə-ling\ **I** : to evade the issue : EQUIVOCATE **2 a** : CAVIL, CARP **b** : BICKER — **quib·bler** \'kwib-lər, -ə-lər\ *n*

¹**quick** \'kwik\ *adj* **I** *archaic* : not dead : LIVING, ALIVE **2** : RAPID, SPEEDY: as **a** : fast in understanding, thinking, or learning : mentally agile **b** : reacting with speed and sensitivity **c** : aroused immediately and intensely ⟨*quick* temper⟩ **d** : fast in development or occurrence ⟨a *quick* succession of events⟩ ⟨gave them a *quick* look⟩ **e** : marked by speed, readiness, or promptness of physical movement ⟨walked with *quick* steps⟩ **f** : capable of being speedily prepared ⟨a *quick* dinner⟩ **3** : having a sharp angle ⟨a *quick* turn in the road⟩ [Old English *cwic*] — **quick·ly** *adv* — **quick·ness** *n* □ SYN SPEEDY: QUICK stresses promptness and the shortness of time in which response, movement, or action takes place ⟨saved by *quick* thinking⟩ ⟨a *quick* answer⟩ SPEEDY implies quickness of successful accomplishment ⟨found a *speedy* solution of the problems⟩ or unusual velocity ⟨a *speedy* runner⟩

²**quick** *adv* : in a quick manner

³quick *n* **1** : a very sensitive area of flesh (as under a fingernail) **2** : the innermost sensibilities ⟨hurt to the *quick* by the remark⟩ **3** : the very center of something : HEART ⟨the *quick* of the matter⟩ [probably of Scandinavian origin]

quick bread *n* : a bread made with a leavening agent that permits immediate baking of the dough or batter mixture

quick·en \'kwik-ən\ *vb* **quick·ened; quick·en·ing** \'kwik-ning, -ə-ning\ **1 a** : to make or become alive : REVIVE **b** : to cause to be enlivened : STIMULATE ⟨curiosity *quickened* my interest⟩ **2** : to make or become more rapid : HASTEN, ACCELERATE ⟨*quickened* their steps⟩ ⟨my pulse *quickened* at the sight⟩ **3** : to show vitality or animation: as **a** : to commence active growth and development ⟨seeds *quickening* in the soil⟩ **b** : to reach the stage of fetal growth at which motion is felt by the mother **4** : to shine more brightly ⟨watched the dawn *quickening* in the east⟩ — **quick·en·er** \'kwik-nər, -ə-nər\ *n*

quick–freeze \'kwik-'frēz\ *vt* **-froze** \-'frōz\; **-fro·zen** \-'frōz-n\; **-freez·ing** : to freeze (food) for preservation so rapidly that ice crystals formed are too small to rupture the cells and the natural juices and flavor are preserved

quick·ie \'kwik-ē\ *n* : something done or made in a hurry

quick·lime \'kwik-,līm\ *n* : ¹LIME 2a

quick·sand \-,sand\ *n* : a deep mass of mixed loose sand and water into which heavy objects sink

quick·sil·ver \-,sil-vər\ *n* : MERCURY 1a [Old English *cwicseolfor,* from *cwic* "alive" + *seolfor* "silver"]
□ ORIGIN The metal mercury resembles silver in color, but, unlike silver, mercury is liquid at normal temperatures. It moves, then, like a living thing. The Old English word for mercury was *cwicseolfor,* a compound of *cwic* "alive" and *seolfor* "silver". The descriptive nature of the word *quicksilver,* however, is not native to English. The compound is a translation of the Latin *argentum vivum* found in Pliny and literally meaning "living silver".

quick·step \'kwik-,step\ *n* : a spirited march tune usually accompanying a march in quick time

quick–tem·pered \'kwik-'tem-pərd\ *adj* : easily angered

quick time *n* : a rate of marching in which 120 steps each 30 inches in length are taken in one minute

quick–wit·ted \-'wit-əd\ *adj* : quick in perception and understanding — **quick-wit·ted·ness** *n*

¹quid \'kwid\ *n, pl* **quid** *also* **quids** *British* : a pound sterling : SOVEREIGN [origin unknown]

²quid *n* : a wad of something chewable ⟨a *quid* of tobacco⟩ [Old English *cwidu* "cud"]

quid pro quo \,kwid-,prō-'kwō\ *n* : something given or received for something else [New Latin, "something for something"]

qui·es·cent \kwī-'es-nt, kwē-\ *adj* **1** : being at rest : IN-ACTIVE **2** : causing no trouble or symptoms [Latin *quiescens,* present participle of *quiescere* "to become quiet, rest", from *quies* "quiet"] SYN see LATENT — **qui·es·cence** \-ns\ *n* — **qui·es·cent·ly** *adv*

¹qui·et \'kwī-ət\ *n* : the quality or state of being quiet : TRANQUILLITY [Latin *quiet-, quies* "rest, quiet"] — **on the quiet** : in a secretive manner

²quiet *adj* **1 a** : marked by little or no motion or activity : CALM **b** : GENTLE, EASYGOING ⟨a *quiet* temperament⟩ **c** : not disturbed ⟨*quiet* reading⟩ **d** : enjoyed in peace and relaxation ⟨a *quiet* cup of tea⟩ **2 a** : free from noise or uproar : STILL **b** : UNOBTRUSIVE, CONSERVATIVE ⟨*quiet* clothes⟩ **3** : SECLUDED 1 ⟨a *quiet* nook⟩ [Middle French, from Latin *quietus,* from past participle of *quiescere* "to become quiet, rest", from *quies* "rest, quiet"] — **qui·et·ly** *adv* — **qui·et·ness** *n*

³quiet *adv* : in a quiet manner ⟨*quiet*-running engine⟩

⁴quiet *vb* **1** : to cause to be quiet : CALM **2** : to become quiet ⟨the audience *quieted* as the curtain rose⟩ — **qui·et·er** *n*

qui·etude \'kwī-ə-,tüd, -,tyüd\ *n* : a quiet state : REPOSE

qui·etus \kwī-'ēt-əs\ *n* **1** : a final freeing from something (as a debt, a duty, or life itself) **2** : something that quiets or represses **3** : a state of inactivity [Medieval Latin *quietus est* "he is quit", formula of discharge from obligation]

¹quill \'kwil\ *n* **1 a** : a bobbin, spool, or spindle on which filling yarn is wound **b** : a roll of dried bark (as of cinnamon) **c** : a hollow shaft often surrounding another shaft and used in various mechanical devices **2 a** : the hollow horny barrel of a feather; *also* : one of the large stiff feathers of a bird's wing or tail **b** : one of the hollow sharp spines of a porcupine or hedgehog **3** : an article made from or resembling the quill of a feather: as **a** : a pen for writing **b** : a float for a fishing line [Middle English *quil* "hollow reed, bobbin"]

²quill *vt* : to pierce with quills ⟨a dog *quilled* by a porcupine⟩

¹quilt \'kwilt\ *n* **1** : a bed coverlet having two layers of cloth filled with wool, cotton, or down held in place by patterned stitching **2** : something that is quilted or resembles a quilt [Middle English *quilte* "mattress, quilt", from Old French *cuilte,* from Latin *culcita* "mattress"]

²quilt *vb* **1 a** : to fill, pad, or line like a quilt **b** : to stitch, sew, or cover with lines or patterns like those used in quilts **c** : to fasten between two pieces of material **2** : to stitch or sew in layers with padding in between **3 a** : to make quilts **b** : to do quilted work — **quilt·er** *n*

quilt·ing *n* **1** : the act of one who quilts something **2** : material that is quilted or used for making quilts

quince \'kwins\ *n* : the fruit of an Asian tree of the rose family that resembles a hard-fleshed yellow apple and is used especially for marmalade, jelly, and preserves; *also* : this tree [Middle English *quynce* "quinces", pl. of *quyn* "quince", from Middle French *coin,* from Latin *cydonium,* from Greek *kydōnion*]

qui·nine \'kwī-,nīn *also* 'kwin-,īn\ *n* : a bitter crystalline alkaloid from cinchona bark used in medicine especially against malaria; *also* : a salt of this [Spanish *quina* "cinchona", short for *quinaquina,* from Quechua]

quinine water *n* : a carbonated beverage flavored with a small amount of quinine, lemon, and lime

Quin·qua·ge·si·ma \,kwing-kwə-'jes-ə-mə, -'jā-zə-\ *n* : the Sunday before Lent [Medieval Latin, from Latin *quinquagesimus* "fiftieth", from *quinquaginta* "fifty"]

quin·quen·ni·al \kwin-'kwen-ē-əl\ *adj* **1** : consisting of or lasting for five years **2** : occurring or being done every five years [Middle French, from Latin *quinquennium* "period of five years", from *quinque* "five" + *annus* "year"] — **quinquennial** *n* — **quin·quen·ni·al·ly** \-ē-ə-lē\ *adv*

quin·sy \'kwin-zē\ *n* : a severe inflammation of the throat or adjacent parts with swelling and fever [Middle French *quinancie,* from Late Latin *cynanche,* from Greek *kynanchē,* from *kyn-, kyōn* "dog" + *anchein* "to strangle"]

quint \'kwint\ *n* : QUINTUPLET

quin·tain \'kwint-n\ *n* : an object to be tilted at; *esp* : a post with a revolving crosspiece that has a target at one end and a sandbag at the other [Middle French *quintaine,* from Latin *quintana* "street in a Roman camp separating the 5th maniple from the 6th where military exercises were performed", from *quintanus* "5th in rank", from *quintus* "fifth"]

quin·tes·sence \kwin-'tes-ns\ *n* **1** : the purest form of something ⟨melody is the *quintessence* of music⟩ **2** : the most typical example or representative ⟨manners that were the *quintessence* of courtesy⟩ [derived from Medieval Latin *quinta essentia* "fifth essence, sup-

quince

\ə\ abut	\ng\ sing
\ər\ further	\ō\ bone
\a\ mat	\ȯ\ saw
\ā\ take	\ȯi\ coin
\ä\ cot, cart	\th\ thin
\au̇\ out	\th\ this
\ch\ chin	\ü\ food
\e\ pet	\u̇\ foot
\ē\ easy	\y\ yet
\g\ go	\yü\ few
\i\ tip	\yu̇\ cure
\ī\ life	\zh\ vision
\j\ job	

posed fifth element more subtle than earth, air, fire, or water''] — **quint·es·sen·tial** \ˌkwint-ə-'sen-chəl\ *adj*

quin·tet *also* **quin·tette** \kwin-'tet\ *n* **1** : a musical composition or movement for five instruments or voices **2** : a group or set of five (as musicians or basketball players) [Italian *quintetto*, from *quinto* "fifth", from Latin *quintus*]

quin·til·lion \kwin-'til-yən\ *n* — see NUMBER table [Latin *quintus* "fifth" + English *-illion* (as in *million*)] — **quin·til·lionth** \-yənth, -yəntth\ *adj or n*

¹quin·tu·ple \kwin-'tüp-əl, -'tyüp-, -'təp-; 'kwint-əp-\ *adj* **1** : having five units or members **2** : being five times as great or as many [Middle French, from Late Latin *quintuplex*, from Latin *quintus* "fifth" + *-plex* "-fold"] — **quintuple** *n*

²quintuple *vb* **quin·tu·pled; quin·tu·pling** \-ling, -ə-ling\ : to make or become five times as great or as many

quin·tup·let \kwin-'təp-lət, -'tüp-, -'tyüp-; 'kwint-əp-\ *n* **1** : a combination of five of a kind **2** : one of five offspring born at one birth

¹quin·tu·pli·cate \kwin-'tü-pli-kət, -'tyü-\ *adj* : having or being five corresponding or identical parts or examples [Latin *quintuplicatus*, past participle of *quintuplicare* "to quintuple", from *quintuplic-, quintuplex* "quintuple"]

²quin·tu·pli·cate \-pli-kət\ *n* **1** : one of five like things **2** : five copies all alike ⟨typed in *quintuplicate*⟩

³quin·tu·pli·cate \-plə-ˌkāt\ *vt* **1** : QUINTUPLE **2** : to provide in quintuplicate

¹quip \'kwip\ *n* **1 a** : a clever usually taunting remark : GIBE **b** : a witty or funny observation or response **2** : something strange or eccentric : ODDITY [earlier *quippy*, perhaps from Latin *quippe* "indeed", from *quid* "what"] SYN see JEST — **quip·ster** \-stər\ *n*

²quip *vb* **quipped; quip·ping** : to make quips; *also* : to make quips at

quire \'kwīr\ *n* : a collection of 24 or sometimes 25 sheets of paper of the same size and quality : ¹⁄₂₀ ream [Middle French *quaer* "four sheets of paper folded once, collection of sheets", derived from Latin *quaterni* "four each"]

quirk \'kwərk\ *n* **1** : an abrupt turn, twist, or curve ⟨some *quirk* of fate threw us together⟩ **2** : a peculiar trait : MANNERISM, IDIOSYNCRASY ⟨human beings with their *quirks* and foibles⟩ [origin unknown] — **quirk·i·ly** \'kwər-kə-lē\ *adv* — **quirk·i·ness** \-kē-nəs\ *n* — **quirky** \-kē\ *adj*

quirt \'kwərt\ *n* : a riding whip with a short handle and a rawhide lash [Mexican Spanish *cuarta*]

quis·ling \'kwiz-ling\ *n* : a traitor who collaborates with the invaders of his or her country especially by serving in a puppet government [Vidkun *Quisling*, died 1945, Norwegian politician]

¹quit \'kwit\ *adj* : released from obligation, charge, or penalty; *esp* : FREE ⟨*quit* of unnecessary fears⟩ [Old French *quite*, literally, "at rest", from Latin *quietus* "quiet, at rest"]

²quit *vb* **quit** *also* **quit·ted; quit·ting** **1** : to make full payment of ⟨*quit* a debt⟩ **2** : ACQUIT ⟨the youths *quit* themselves like adults⟩ **3 a** : to depart from or out of **b** : to bring (as a way of thought, acting, or living) to an end : STOP ⟨*quit* horsing around⟩ **c** : to give up (an action, activity, or employment) for good ⟨*quit* smoking⟩ ⟨*quit* a job⟩ **4** : to admit defeat : SURRENDER SYN see STOP

quit·claim \'kwit-ˌklām\ *vt* : to release or relinquish a legal claim to especially by a quitclaim deed — **quit·claim** *n*

quitclaim deed *n* : a legal instrument used to release a right, title, or interest in property to another without warranting the title

quite \'kwīt\ *adv* **1** : WHOLLY **1**, COMPLETELY ⟨not *quite* all⟩ **2** : to an extreme : POSITIVELY ⟨not *quite* sure⟩ **3** :

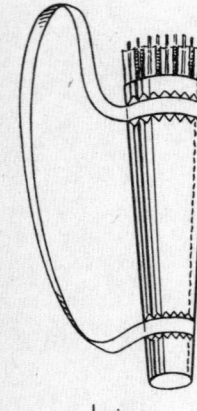

¹quiver

to a considerable extent : RATHER ⟨*quite* near⟩ [Middle English, from *quite* "free, quit"]

quit·rent \'kwit-ˌrent\ *n* : a fixed rent; *esp* : one payable to a feudal superior in the place of services

quits \'kwits\ *adj* : even or equal with another (as by repaying a debt or returning a favor)

quit·tance \'kwit-ns\ *n* **1 a** : discharge from a debt or an obligation **b** : a document evidencing quittance **2** : RECOMPENSE, REQUITAL

quit·ter \'kwit-ər\ *n* : one that quits; *esp* : one that gives up too easily

¹quiv·er \'kwiv-ər\ *n* : a case for holding arrows [Old French *quivre*, of Germanic origin]

²quiver *vi* **quiv·ered; quiv·er·ing** \'kwiv-ring, -ə-ring\ : to move with a slight trembling motion ⟨tall grass *quivering* in the breeze⟩ [Middle English *quiveren*]

³quiver *n* : the act or action of quivering

qui vive \kē-'vēv, 'kē-\ *n* **1** : CHALLENGE **2** **2** : ALERT, LOOKOUT ⟨on the *qui vive* for prowlers⟩ [French *qui vive?* "long live who?", challenge of a French sentry]

quix·ot·ic \kwik-'sät-ik\ *adj* : idealistic to an impractical degree; *esp* : marked by rash lofty romantic ideas or extravagantly chivalrous action [Don *Quixote*, hero of the novel *Don Quixote de la Mancha* by Cervantes] — **quix·ot·i·cal·ly** \-'sät-i-kə-lē, -klē\ *adv* — **quix·o·tism** \'kwik-sə-ˌtiz-əm\ *n*

¹quiz \'kwiz\ *n, pl* **quiz·zes** **1** : an eccentric or mocking person **2** : PRACTICAL JOKE **3** : the act or action of quizzing; *esp* : a short oral or written test [origin unknown]

²quiz *vt* **quizzed; quiz·zing** **1** : to make fun of : MOCK **2** : to look at inquisitively **3** : to question closely : EXAMINE — **quiz·zer** *n*

quiz·zi·cal \'kwiz-i-kəl\ *adj* **1** : slightly eccentric : ODD **2** : marked by bantering or teasing **3** : INQUISITIVE ⟨a *quizzical* look⟩ — **quiz·zi·cal·ly** \-kə-lē, -klē\ *adv*

quoin \'koin, 'kwoin\ *n* : a solid exterior angle (as of a building); *also* : one of the blocks forming it [alteration of earlier *coin* "corner, coin"]

quoit \'kwoit, 'kwāt, 'koit\ *n* **1** : a flattened ring of iron or circle of rope used in quoits **2** *pl* : a game in which quoits are tossed in an attempt to encircle a peg or come closer than one's opponent [Middle English *coite*]

quon·dam \'kwän-dəm, -ˌdam\ *adj* : FORMER **1**, SOMETIME ⟨a *quondam* friend⟩ [Latin, "at one time, formerly"]

Quon·set \'kwän-sət\ *trademark* — used for a prefabricated shelter set on a foundation of steel trusses and built of a semicircular arching roof of corrugated metal

quo·rum \'kwōr-əm, 'kwȯr-\ *n* : the number of officers or members of a body that when duly assembled is legally competent to transact business [Latin, "of whom"]

quo·ta \'kwōt-ə\ *n* **1** : a proportional part or share; *esp* : the share or proportion assigned to each member of a body **2** : the number or amount constituting a proportional share [Medieval Latin, from Latin *quota pars* "how great a part"]

quot·able \'kwōt-ə-bəl\ *adj* : fit for or worth quoting

quo·ta·tion \kwō-'tā-shən\ *n* **1** : something that is quoted; *esp* : a passage referred to or repeated **2 a** : the act or process of quoting **b** : the naming or publishing of current bids and offers or prices of securities or commodities; *also* : the bids, offers, or prices so named or published

quotation mark *n* : one of a pair of punctuation marks " " or ʺ ʺ or ' ' or ʹ ʹ used chiefly to indicate the beginning and the end of a quotation in which the exact phraseology of another or of a text is directly cited

¹quote \'kwōt\ *vb* **1 a** : to speak or write (a passage) from another usually with credit acknowledgment **b** : to repeat a passage from especially as authority or illustration ⟨*quote* Shakespeare⟩ **2** : to cite in illustration ⟨*quote* cases⟩ **3 a** : to name (the current price) of a commodity, stock, or bond **b** : to give exact information on **4** : to set off by quotation marks **5** : to give a quotation (the defendant said, and I *quote*, . . .) ⟨*quoted* from the Bible⟩ [Medieval Latin *quotare* "to mark the number of, number references", derived from Latin *quot* "how many"]

²quote *n* **1** : QUOTATION 1 **2** : QUOTATION MARK

quoth \kwōth, 'kwōth\ *vb past, archaic* : SAID — used chiefly in the first and third persons and placed before the subject [Old English *cwæth*, past of *cwethan* "to say"]

quo·tid·i·an \kwō-'tid-ē-ən\ *adj* **1** : belonging to each day ⟨*quotidian* routine⟩ **2** : COMMONPLACE, ORDINARY ⟨*quotidian* drabness⟩ [Middle French *cotidian*, from Latin *quotidianus, cotidianus,* from *quotidie* "every day", from *quot* "how many, (as) many as" + *dies* "day"]

quo·tient \'kwō-shənt\ *n* : the number resulting from the division of one number by another [Latin *quotiens* "how many times", from *quot* "how many"]

Rr

r \'är\ *n, pl* **r's** *or* **rs** \'ärz\ *often cap* : the 18th letter of the English alphabet

R *trademark* — used to certify that a motion picture is of such a nature that admission is restricted to persons over a specified age (as 17) unless accompanied by a parent or guardian; compare G, NC-17, PG, PG-13

rab·at \'rab-ē, 'rab-ət\ *n* : a black shirtfront often worn with a clerical collar [Middle French]

¹rab·bet \'rab-ət\ *n* : a groove or recess cut in the edge or face of a surface especially to receive the edge of another surface (as a panel) [Middle French *rabat* "act of beating down," from *rabattre* "to beat down"]

²rabbet *vt* **1** : to cut a rabbet in **2** : to join the edges of (as boards) by a rabbet

rab·bi \'rab-ī\ *n* **1** *often cap* : MASTER, TEACHER — used as a term of address for Jewish religious leaders **2** *often cap* : one of the scholars who developed the Talmudic basis of orthodox Judaism during the first centuries of the Christian era **3** : a Jew trained professionally and ordained as the official leader of a Jewish congregation [Late Latin, from Greek *rhabbi,* from Hebrew *rabbī* "my master", from *rabb* "master" + *-ī* "my"]

rab·bin·ate \'rab-ə-nət, -,nāt\ *n* **1** : the office or tenure of a rabbi **2** : the whole body of rabbis

rab·bin·ic \rə-'bin-ik, ra-\ *adj* **1** *often cap* : of or relating to rabbis or their writings **2** : of or preparing for the rabbinate — **rab·bin·i·cal** \-'bin-i-kəl\ *adj* — **rab·bin·i·cal·ly** \-i-kə-lē, -klē\ *adv*

rab·bin·ism \'rab-ə-,niz-əm\ *n* : rabbinic teachings and traditions

¹rab·bit \'rab-ət\ *n, pl* **rabbits** *also* **rabbit** : a small long-eared burrowing mammal differing from the related hares especially in producing naked young; *also* : its pelt [Middle English *rabet*]

²rab·bit *vi* : to hunt rabbits

rabbit fever *n* : TULAREMIA

rabbit punch *n* : a short chopping blow delivered to the back of the neck or the base of the skull [from the way a rabbit is stunned before being killed and butchered]

rab·ble \'rab-əl\ *n* **1** : a noisy and unruly crowd : MOB **2** : a body of people looked down upon as ignorant and disorderly [Middle English *rabel* "pack of animals"]

rab·ble-rous·er \-,raü-zər\ *n* : one that stirs up the masses of the people especially to hatred or violence

Ra·be·lai·sian \,rab-ə-'lā-zhən, -zē-ən\ *adj* **1** : of, relating to, or characteristic of Rabelais or his works **2** : marked by gross robust humor or extravagant caricature

rab·id \'rab-əd\ *adj* **1** : extremely violent : FURIOUS **2** : going to extreme lengths in expressing or pursuing a feeling, interest, or opinion ⟨a *rabid* sports fan⟩ **3** : affected with rabies ⟨a *rabid* dog⟩ [Latin *rabidus* "mad", from *rabere* "to rage, rave"] — **rab·id·ly** *adv* — **rab·id·ness** *n*

ra·bies \'rā-bēz\ *n* : an acute virus disease of the central nervous system of warm-blooded animals transmitted by the bite of an infected animal and always fatal when untreated — called also *hydrophobia* [Latin "madness", from *rabere* "to rage, rave"] — **ra·bic** \'rā-bik\ *adj*

rac·coon *also* **ra·coon** \ra-'kün\ *n, pl* **raccoon** *or* **raccoons** : a small flesh-eating mammal of North America that is chiefly gray, has a bushy ringed tail, and lives chiefly in trees; *also* : its pelt [of American Indian origin]

¹race \'rās\ *n* **1** : a strong or rapid current of water or its channel or passage; *esp* : a current of water used for industrial purposes (as turning a mill wheel) **2 a** : a set course or duration of time **b** : the course of life **3 a** : a running in competition **b** *pl* : a meeting for contests in the running especially of horses ⟨off to the *races*⟩ **c** : a contest involving progress toward a goal ⟨the *race* for the governorship⟩ **4** : a track or channel in which something rolls or slides; *esp* : a groove for the balls in a bearing [Old Norse *rās*]

²race *vb* **1** : to run in a race **2** : to go, move, or drive at top speed or out of control ⟨the flood *raced* through the valley⟩ **3 a** : to engage in a race with ⟨*race* the champion⟩ **b** : to enter in a race ⟨had a new horse to *race*⟩ **4** : to run (as an engine) at high speed without a load or with the transmission disengaged

³race **1 a** : a group of people of common ancestry or stock ⟨the English *race*⟩ ⟨scion of a noble *race*⟩ **b** : a class or kind of people unified by common interests, habits, or characteristics ⟨a new *race* of scientists⟩ **2 a** : a variety or breed of animals or plants **b** : a division of mankind possessing traits that are transmissible by descent and sufficient to characterize it as a distinct human type **3** : a major group of living things ⟨the human *race*⟩ ⟨the *race* of birds⟩

race·course \'rā-,skōrs, -,skȯrs\ *n* : a course for racing

race·horse \'rās-,hȯrs\ *n* : a horse bred or kept for racing

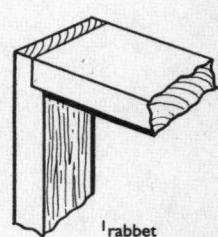

¹rabbet

raccoon

\ə\ abut		\ng\ sing	
\ər\ further		\ō\ bone	
\a\ mat		\ȯ\ saw	
\ā\ take		\ȯi\ coin	
\ä\ cot, cart		\th\ thin	
\aü\ out		\th\ this	
\ch\ chin		\ü\ food	
\e\ pet		\u̇\ foot	
\ē\ easy		\y\ yet	
\g\ go		\yü\ few	
\i\ tip		\yu̇\ cure	
\ī\ life		\zh\ vision	
\j\ job			

ra·ceme \rā-'sēm\ *n* : a simple inflorescence with a long axis bearing flowers on short stems in succession toward the apex [Latin *racemus* "bunch of grapes"] — **ra·ce·mose** \'ras-ə-ˌmōs, rā-'sē-\ *adj*

rac·er \'rā-sər\ *n* **1** : one that races **2** : any of various slender active American snakes; *esp* : common black-snake

race·track \'rās-ˌstrak\ *n* : a usually oval course for races

race·way \'rās-ˌwā\ *n* **1** : a channel for a current of water **2** : RACETRACK; *esp* : one for harness racing

ra·chis \'rā-kəs, 'rak-əs\ *n, pl* **ra·chis·es** *also* **ra·chi·des** \'rak-ə-ˌdēz, 'rā-kə-\ **1** : the axis of an inflorescence **2** : an extension of the petiole of a compound leaf that bears the leaflets **3** : the distal part of the shaft of a feather [Greek *rhachis* "spine, backbone"]

ra·cial \'rā-shəl\ *adj* **1** : of, relating to, or based on race **2** : existing or occurring between human races ⟨*racial* harmony⟩ — **ra·cial·ly** \-shə-lē\ *adv*

ra·cial·ism \'rā-shə-ˌliz-əm\ *n* : RACISM — **ra·cial·ist** \'rāsh-ləst, -ə-ləst\ *n or adj* — **ra·cial·is·tic** \ˌrā-shə-'lis-tik\ *adj*

rac·i·ly \'rā-sə-lē\ *adv* : in a racy manner

rac·i·ness \-sē-nəs\ *n* : the quality or state of being racy

rac·ism \'rā-ˌsiz-əm\ *n* **1** : belief that certain races of people are by birth and nature superior to others **2** : discrimination against the members of one or more races based upon racism — **rac·ist** \'rā-səst\ *n*

¹rack \'rak\ *n* **1** : a framework for holding fodder for livestock **2** : an instrument of torture on which a body is stretched **3** : a framework, stand, or grating on or in which articles are placed ⟨clothes *rack*⟩ ⟨bicycle *rack*⟩ **4** : a bar with teeth on one face for gearing with a pinion or worm gear [Middle English] — **on the rack** : under great mental or emotional stress

²rack *vt* **1** : to torture on the rack **2** : to cause to suffer torture, pain, or anguish ⟨*racked* by a cough⟩ **3** : to stretch or strain violently SYN see AFFLICT

³rack *vi* : to go at a rack [probably alteration of ¹*rock*]

⁴rack *n* : either of two gaits of a horse : **a** : PACE 2b **b** : a fast showy usually artifical 4-beat gait — called also *single-foot*

⁵rack *n* : DESTRUCTION ⟨went to *rack* and ruin⟩ [alteration of *wrack*]

¹rack·et *also* **rac·quet** \'rak-ət\ *n* : a usually long-handled implement used for hitting a ball or shuttlecock (as in tennis or badminton) that consists of an oval open frame strung with a netting (as of nylon) [Middle French *raquette*, from Arabic *rāḥah* "palm of the hand"]

¹racket: *top* tennis, *bottom* badminton

²racket *n* **1** : confused clattering noise : DIN **2 a** : a dishonest scheme; *esp* : one for obtaining money by cheating or through threats of violence **b** *slang* : OCCUPATION [probably imitative]

³racket *vi* **1** : to engage in active social life **2** : to move with or make a racket

¹rack·e·teer \ˌrak-ə-'tiər\ *n* : a person who engages in an illegal activity forgetting money especially by extortion

²racketeer *vi* : to operate an illegal racket

ra·con·teur \ˌrak-ˌän-'tər, rak-ən-\ *n* : one who excels in telling anecdotes [French, from *raconter* "to tell", from Old French, from *re-* "re-" + *aconter, acompter* "to tell, count"]

ra·coon *variant of* RACCOON

rac·quets \'rak-əts\ *n* : a game for two or four played with ball and racket on a 4-walled court

¹racy \'rā-sē\ *adj* **rac·i·er; -est** **1** : having the distinctive quality of something in its original or most characteristic form **2 a** : full of zest or vigor : LIVELY **b** : slightly indecent or improper : RISQUÉ, SUGGESTIVE ⟨*racy* stories⟩ [³*race*]

radial symmetry

²racy *adj* **rac·i·er; -est** : being long-bodied and lean ⟨a *racy* whippet⟩

ra·dar \'rā-ˌdär\ *n* : a device or system that sends out radio waves for detecting and locating an object by the reflection of the radio waves and that may use this reflection to find out the position and speed of the object [*ra*dio *d*etecting *a*nd *r*anging]

ra·dar·scope \-ˌskōp\ *n* : the part of a radar apparatus on which the spots of light appear that indicate the position and direction of motion of a distant object [*radar* + oscillo*scope*]

¹ra·di·al \'rād-ē-əl\ *adj* **1** : arranged or having parts arranged like rays coming from a common center **2** : relating to, placed like, or moving along a radius [Medieval Latin *radialis*, from Latin *radius* "spoke, radius, ray"] — **ra·di·al·ly** \-ē-ə-lē\ *adv*

²radial *n* **1** : a radial part **2** : a pneumatic tire in which the ply cords are laid at approximately 90° to the center line of the tread — called also *radial-ply tire, radial tire*

radial engine *n* : a usually internal-combustion engine with cylinders arranged radially like the spokes of a wheel

radial symmetry *n* : the condition of having similar parts regularly arranged around a central axis ⟨*radial* symmetry of the starfish⟩ — compare BILATERAL SYMMETRY — **radially symmetrical** *adj*

ra·di·an \'rād-ē-ən\ *n* : a unit of angular measure equal to approximately 57.25 degrees or to the central angle of a circle subtended by an arc equal in length to the radius [*radi*us + *-an*]

ra·di·ance \'rād-ē-əns\ *n* : the quality or state of being radiant : SPLENDOR

ra·di·ant \'rād-ē-ənt\ *adj* **1 a** : giving out or reflecting rays of light ⟨the *radiant* sun⟩ ⟨a *radiant* jewel⟩ **b** : vividly bright and shining ⟨*radiant* eyes⟩ **2** : marked by or expressive of love, confidence, or happiness **3 a** : emitted or transmitted by radiation ⟨*radiant* heat from the sun⟩ **b** : emitting or relating to radiant heat ⟨a *radiant* lamp⟩ — **ra·di·ant·ly** *adv*

radiant energy *n* : energy transmitted in the form of electromagnetic waves (as heat waves, light waves, radio waves, or X rays)

ra·di·ate \'rād-ē-ˌāt\ *vb* **1** : to send outrays of or as if of light **2 a** : to come or be sent out from a center in or as if in rays ⟨heat *radiates*⟩ ⟨a story that *radiated* widely⟩ **b** : to send out in rays or as if in rays ⟨stars *radiate* energy⟩ **3** : IRRADIATE 1a, ILLUMINATE **4** : to spread abroad or around : DISSEMINATE [Latin *radiare*, from *radius* "ray"]

ra·di·a·tion \ˌrād-ē-'ā-shən\ *n* **1** : the action or process of radiating; *esp* : the process of emitting radiant energy in the form of waves or particles **2** : something that is radiated: as **a** : energy radiated in the form of waves or particles **b** : biological evolution in a group of organisms that is characterized by spreading into different environments and by divergence of structure ⟨the Devonian *radiation* of fishes⟩ — **ra·di·a·tion·al** \-shnəl, -shən-l\ *adj* — **ra·di·a·tive** \'rād-ē-ˌāt-iv\ *adj*

radiation sickness *n* : sickness that results from exposure to radiation and is commonly marked by fatigue, nausea, vomiting, loss of teeth and hair, and in more severe cases by damage to blood-forming tissue with decrease in red and white blood cells and bleeding

ra·di·a·tor \'rād-ē-ˌāt-ər\ *n* : one that radiates; *esp* : any of various devices (as a set of pipes or tubes) for transferring heat from a fluid within to an area or object outside

¹rad·i·cal \'rad-i-kəl\ *adj* **1** : of, relating to, or proceeding from a root **2** : of or relating to the origin : FUNDAMENTAL ⟨*radical* differences⟩ **3 a** : marked by a sharp departure from the usual or traditional : EXTREME **b** : of, relating to, or disposed to the making of extreme changes in existing views, habits, conditions, or institutions ⟨*radical* ideas⟩; *esp* : of, relating to, or constituting a political group associated with views, practices, and policies of extreme change [Late Latin *radicalis*, from Latin *radic-, radix* "root"] SYN see LIBERAL — **rad·i·cal·ness** *n*

²radical *n* **1** : ROOT 5 **2** : one who is radical **3** : a group of atoms that is replaceable by a single atom and is capable of remaining unchanged during a series of reactions **4 a** : the indicated root of a mathematical expression **b** : RADICAL SIGN

radical expression *n* : a mathematical expression involving radical signs

rad·i·cal·ism \'rad-i-kə-ˌliz-əm\ *n* **1** : the quality or state of being radical **2** : the doctrines or principles of radicals

rad·i·cal·ize \-kə-ˌlīz\ *vt* : to make radical especially in politics — **rad·i·cal·iza·tion** \ˌrad-i-kə-lə-'zā-shən\ *n*

rad·i·cal·ly \'rad-i-kə-lē, -klē\ *adv* **1** : in origin or essence : NATURALLY **2** : in a radical or extreme manner

radical sign *n* : the sign √ placed before an expression in mathematics to indicate that the square root is to be extracted or that some other root is to be extracted when a corresponding index is placed over the sign

rad·i·cand \ˌrad-ə-'kand\ *n* : the expression under a radical sign [derived from Latin *radicari* "to take root", from *radic-, radix* "root"]

radices *pl of* RADIX

rad·i·cle \'rad-i-kəl\ *n* : the lower part of the axis of a plant embryo or seedling : the growing tip of the hypocotyl : HYPOCOTYL [Latin *radicula* "small root", from *radic-, radix* "root"] — **ra·dic·u·lar** \ra-'dik-yə-lər\ *adj*

radii *pl of* RADIUS

¹ra·dio \'rād-ē-ō\ *n, pl* **ra·di·os** **1** : the sending or receiving of messages or effects and especially sound by means of electromagnetic waves without a connecting wire **2** : a radio message **3** : a radio receiving set **4 a** : a radio transmitting station **b** : a radio broadcasting organization **c** : the radio broadcasting industry [short for *radiotelegraphy*]

²radio *adj* **1** : of, relating to, using, or operated by radiant energy ⟨*radio* communication⟩ **2** : of or relating to electric currents or phenomena of frequencies between about 15 kilohertz and 100,000 megahertz **3 a** : of, relating to, or used in radio or a radio set **b** : controlled or directed by radio

³radio *vb* **1** : to send or communicate by radio **2** : to send a radio message to

radio- *combining form* **1** : radial : radially ⟨*radio*symmetrical⟩ **2 a** : radiant energy : radiation ⟨*radio*active⟩ **b** : radioactive ⟨*radio*carbon⟩ **c** : radio ⟨*radio*telegraph⟩ [French, from Latin *radius* "spoke, radius, ray"]

ra·dio·ac·tive \ˌrād-ē-ō-'ak-tiv\ *adj* : of, caused by, or exhibiting radioactivity — **ra·dio·ac·tive·ly** *adv*

ra·dio·ac·tiv·i·ty \-ˌak-'tiv-ət-ē\ *n* : the property possessed by some elements (as uranium) of spontaneously emitting alpha, beta, and gamma rays by the disintegration of the nuclei of atoms

radio astronomy *n* : astronomy dealing with electromagnetic radiations of radio frequency received from outside the earth's atmosphere — **radio astronomer** *n*

ra·dio·au·to·graph \ˌrād-ē-ō-'ȯt-ə-ˌgraf\ *n* : AUTORADIOGRAPH — **ra·dio·au·tog·ra·phy** \-ȯ-'täg-rə-fē\ *n*

radio beacon *n* : a radio transmitting station that transmits radio signals for use (as on a landing field) in determining the direction or position of those receiving them

ra·dio·broad·cast \ˌrād-ē-ō-'brȯd-ˌkast\ *vt* : BROADCAST 3a — **ra·dio·broad·cast·er** *n*

radio car *n* : an automobile (as a police car) equipped with two-way radio communications

ra·dio·car·bon \-'kär-bən\ *n* : radioactive carbon; *esp* : CARBON 14

ra·dio·cast \'rād-ē-ō-ˌkast\ *vt* : BROADCAST 3a — **ra·dio·cast·er** *n*

ra·dio·el·e·ment \ˌrād-ē-ō-'el-ə-mənt\ *n* : a radioactive element

radio frequency *n* : any of the electromagnetic wave frequencies intermediate between audio frequencies and infrared frequencies used especially in radio and television transmission

ra·dio·gram \'rād-ē-ō-ˌgram\ *n* **1** : RADIOGRAPH **2** : a message sent by radiotelegraphy

¹ra·dio·graph \-ˌgraf\ *n* : a picture produced on a sensitive surface by a form of radiation other than light; *esp* : an X-ray photograph — **ra·dio·graph·ic** \ˌrād-ē-ō-'graf-ik\ *adj* — **ra·dio·graph·i·cal·ly** \-'graf-i-kə-lē, -klē\ *adv* — **ra·di·og·ra·phy** \ˌrād-ē-'äg-rə-fē\ *n*

²radiograph *vt* : to make a radiograph of

³radiograph *vt* : to send a radiogram to

ra·dio·iso·tope \ˌrād-ē-ō-'ī-sə-ˌtōp\ *n* : a radioactive isotope

ra·dio·lar·i·an \ˌrād-ē-ō-'lar-ē-ən, -'ler-\ *n* : any of a large order (Radiolaria) of marine protozoans with radiating threadlike pseudopodia and a siliceous skeleton [derived from Late Latin *radiolus* "small sunbeam", from Latin *radius* "ray"]

ra·di·ol·o·gy \ˌrād-ē-'äl-ə-jē\ *n* : the use of radiant energy in medicine — **ra·dio·log·ic** \ˌrād-ē-ō-'läj-ik\ *adj* — **ra·dio·log·i·cal** \-'läj-i-kəl\ *adj* — **ra·di·ol·o·gist** \ˌrād-ē-'äl-ə-jəst\ *n*

ra·di·om·e·ter \ˌrād-ē-'äm-ət-ər\ *n* : an instrument for measuring the intensity of radiant energy — **ra·dio·met·ric** \ˌrād-ē-ō-'me-trik\ *adj* — **ra·di·om·e·try** \-'äm-ə-trē\ *n*

ra·dio·nu·clide \ˌrād-ē-ō-'nü-ˌklīd, -'nyü-\ *n* : a radioactive nuclide

ra·dio·phone \'rād-ē-ə-ˌfōn\ *n* : RADIOTELEPHONE

ra·dio·pho·to \ˌrād-ē-ō-'fōt-ō\ *n* **1** : a picture transmitted by radio **2** : the process of transmitting a picture by radio

ra·dio·sonde \'rād-ē-ō-ˌsänd\ *n* : a miniature radio transmitter that is carried (as by a balloon) aloft with instruments for broadcasting data on humidity, temperature, and pressure [French *sonde* "sounding line"]

ra·dio·tel·e·graph \ˌrād-ē-ō-'tel-ə-ˌgraf\ *n* : telegraphy using radio waves — **ra·dio·te·leg·ra·phy** \-tə-'leg-rə-fē\ *n*

ra·dio·tel·e·phone \-'tel-ə-ˌfōn\ *n* : a telephone (as in a car) that utilizes radio waves wholly or partly instead of connecting wires — **ra·dio·te·le·pho·ny** \-tə-'lef-ə-nē, -'tel-ə-ˌfō-nē\ *n*

radio telescope *n* : a radio receiver-antenna combination used for observation in radio astronomy

ra·dio·ther·a·py \ˌrād-ē-ō-'ther-ə-pē\ *n* : the treatment of disease by means of X rays or radioactive substances — **ra·dio·ther·a·pist** \-pəst\ *n*

ra·dio–ul·na \ˌrād-ē-ō-'əl-nə\ *n* : a single bone in the forelimb of an amphibian (as a frog) equivalent to the separate radius and ulna of higher forms

radio wave *n* : an electromagnetic wave with radio frequency used in radio, television, or radar communication

rad·ish \'rad-ish, 'red-\ *n* : a pungent fleshy root usually eaten raw; *also* : a plant of the mustard family whose roots are radishes [Old English *rædic*, from Latin *radix* "root, radish"]

ra·di·um \'rād-ē-əm\ *n* : an intensely radioactive shining white metallic chemical element that occurs in combination in minute quantities in minerals (as pitchblende), emits alpha particles and gamma rays to form radon, and is used chiefly in luminous materials and in the treatment of cancer — see ELEMENT table [New Latin, from Latin *radius* "ray"]

ra·di·us \'rād-ē-əs\ *n, pl* **ra·dii** \-ē-ˌī\ *also* **-di·us·es** **1** : the bone on the thumb side of the human forearm; *also* : a corresponding part of vertebrates above fishes **2 a** : a line segment extending from the center of a circle or sphere to the circumference or surface; *also* : its length **b** : a circular area defined by a radius (deer may wander within a *radius* of several kilometers) **3** : a radial part or plane [Latin, "spoke, ray, radius"]

ra·dix \'rād-iks\ *n, pl* **ra·di·ces** \'rād-ə-ˌsēz, 'rad-\ *or* **ra·dix·es** : the base of a number system [Latin, "root"]

\ə\ abut		\ng\ sing	
\ər\ further		\ō\ bone	
\a\ mat		\ȯ\ saw	
\ā\ take		\ȯi\ coin	
\ä\ cot, cart		\th\ thin	
\au̇\ out		\th\ this	
\ch\ chin		\ü\ food	
\e\ pet		\u̇\ foot	
\ē\ easy		\y\ yet	
\g\ go		\yü\ few	
\i\ tip		\yu̇\ cure	
\ī\ life		\zh\ vision	
\j\ job			

ra·dome \'rā-ˌdōm\ *n* : a usually plastic housing sheltering the antenna assembly of a radar set [*ra*dar *dome*]

ra·don \'rā-ˌdän\ *n* : a heavy radioactive gaseous chemical element formed by disintegration of radium — see ELEMENT table [derived from *radium*]

rad·u·la \'raj-ə-lə\ *n, pl* **-lae** \-ˌlē, -ˌlī\ *also* **-las** : a toothed horny band in mollusks other than bivalves used to tear up and draw food into the mouth [Latin, "scraper", from *radere* "to scrape"] — **rad·u·lar** \-lər\ *adj*

raf·fia \'raf-ē-ə\ *n* : fiber from a pinnate-leaved palm of Madagascar used especially for baskets and hats [Malagasy *rafia*]

raff·ish \'raf-ish\ *adj* **1** : vulgarly crude or flashy **2** : marked by a carefree unconventionality [Middle English *raf* "rubbish"] — **raff·ish·ly** *adv* — **raff·ish·ness** *n*

¹raf·fle \'raf-əl\ *n* : a lottery in which the prize is won by one of the persons buying chances [Middle French *rafle*, a dice game]

²raffle *vt* **raf·fled; raf·fling** \'raf-ling, -ə-ling\ : to offer as a prize in a raffle ⟨*raffle* off a turkey⟩

¹raft \'raft\ *n* **1** : a collection of logs or timber fastened together for transportation by water **2** : a flat structure for support or transportation on water [Middle English *rafte* "rafter, raft", from Old Norse *raptr* "rafter"]

²raft *vb* **1** : to transport or move in or by means of a raft **2** : to make into a raft

³raft *n* : a large amount [alteration of earlier *raff* "jumble, rubbish", from Middle English *raf*]

raf·ter \'raf-tər\ *n* : any of the parallel beams that support a roof [Old English *ræfter*] — **raf·tered** \-tərd\ *adj*

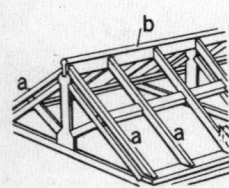

rafter: *a* rafters,
b ridgepole

¹rag \'rag\ *n* **1 a** : a waste or worn piece of cloth **b** *pl* : shabby or tattered clothing ⟨dressed in *rags*⟩ **2** : something felt to resemble a rag of cloth; *esp* : SCRAP 2, SHRED [Old Norse *rögg* "tuft, shagginess"]

²rag *vt* **ragged** \'ragd\; **rag·ging** **1** : to rail at : SCOLD **2** : TEASE 2a, HARASS [origin unknown]

rag·a·muf·fin \'rag-ə-ˌməf-ən\ *n* : a ragged often disreputable person; *esp* : a poorly clothed often dirty child [*Ragamoffyn*, a demon in *Piers Plowman* (1393), attributed to William Langland]

rag·bag \'rag-ˌbag\ *n* **1** : a bag for scraps **2** : a miscellaneous collection

rag doll *n* : a stuffed usually painted cloth doll

¹rage \'rāj\ *n* **1 a** : violent and uncontrolled anger : FURY **b** : a fit of violent anger **2** : violent action (as of wind or sea) **3** : CRAZE, VOGUE ⟨was all the *rage*⟩ [Middle French, derived from Latin *rabies* "madness, rage", from *rabere* "to rage, be mad"] SYN SEE ANGER

²rage *vi* **1** : to be in a rage **2** : to be in tumult ⟨the storm *raged*⟩ **3** : to persist or spread uncontrollably ⟨a *raging* epidemic⟩

rag·ged \'rag-əd\ *adj* **1** : roughly unkempt : STRAGGLY ⟨a *ragged* lawn⟩ **2** : having an irregular edge or outline : JAGGED ⟨*ragged* cliffs⟩ **3 a** : torn or worn to or as if to tatters ⟨a *ragged* dress⟩ **b** : wearing tattered clothes **4** : executed in an irregular or uneven manner ⟨played *ragged* defense⟩ — **rag·ged·ly** *adv* — **rag·ged·ness** *n*

rag·gedy \-əd-ē\ *adj* : somewhat ragged

rag·gle–tag·gle \'rag-əl-ˌtag-əl\ *adj* : MOTLEY [derived from *ragtag*]

rag·ing \'rā-jing\ *adj* **1** : causing great pain or distress **2** : VIOLENT 1, WILD

rag·lan sleeve \'rag-lən-\ *n* : a sleeve that extends to the neckline with slanted seams from the underarm to the neck [F. J. H. Somerset, Baron *Raglan*, died 1855, British field marshal]

rag·man \'rag-ˌman\ *n* : a collector of or dealer in rags

ra·gout \ra-'gü\ *n* : a highly seasoned meat stew with vegetables [French *ragoût*]

rag·pick·er \'rag-ˌpik-ər\ *n* : a person who collects rags and refuse for a living

rag·tag \'rag-ˌtag\ *adj* : RAGGED 1

rag·tag and bob·tail \ˌrag-ˌtag-ən-'bäb-ˌtāl\ *n* : RABBLE

rag·time \'rag-ˌtīm\ **1** : musical rhythm in which the melody has the accented notes falling on beats that are not usually accented **2** : music with ragtime rhythm [probably from *rag*ged + *time*]

rag·weed \'rag-ˌwēd\ *n* : any of various chiefly North American weedy herbs related to the daisies that produce pollen highly irritating to the eyes and nasal passages of some persons

rah \'rä, 'rȯ\ *interj* : HURRAH — used especially to cheer on a team ⟨*rah*, *rah*, team⟩

¹raid \'rād\ *n* **1 a** : an entering of something hostile or predatory **b** : a surprise attack by a small military force **2** : a sudden entry of officers of the law [Scottish dialect, from Old English *rād* "ride, raid"]

²raid *vt* : to make a raid on — **raid·er** *n*

¹rail \'rāl\ *n* **1 a** : a bar extending from one post or support to another and serving as a guard or barrier **b** : RAILING 1 **2 a** : a bar of rolled steel forming a track for wheeled vehicles **b** : TRACK 1c (2) **c** : RAILROAD [Middle French *reille* "ruler, bar", from Latin *regula* "ruler", from *regere* "to keep straight, rule"]

²rail *vt* : to provide with a railing

³rail *n, pl* **rails** *or* **rail** : any of a family of small wading birds related to the cranes [Middle French *raale*]

⁴rail *vi* : to criticize or scold in harsh or abusive language [Middle French *railler* "to mock, rally"] — **rail·er** *n*

rail·ing \'rā-ling\ *n* **1** : a barrier (as a fence or balustrade) consisting of rails and their supports **2** : material for making rails : RAILS

rail·lery \'rā-lə-rē\ *n, pl* **-ler·ies** : good-natured ridicule : BANTER [French *raillerie*, from *railler* "to mock, rally"]

¹rail·road \'rāl-ˌrōd\ *n* : a permanent road having a line of rails fixed to ties and laid on a roadbed and providing a track for cars and equipment drawn by locomotives or propelled by self-contained motors; *also* : such a road and its assets constituting a single property : a railroad company

²railroad *vb* **1 a** : to transport by railroad **b** : to work for a railroad company **2 a** : to push through hastily or without due consideration ⟨*railroad* a bill into law⟩ **b** : to convict with undue haste and by means of false charges or insufficient evidence — **rail·road·er** *n*

rail·road·ing *n* : construction or operation of a railroad

rail·way \'rāl-ˌwā\ *n* **1** : RAILROAD; *esp* : a railroad operating with light equipment or within a small area **2** : a line of track providing a runway for wheels

rai·ment \'rā-mənt\ *n* : CLOTHING, GARMENTS [Middle English *rayment*, short for *arrayment*, from *arrayen* "to array"]

¹rain \'rān\ *n* **1 a** : water falling in drops condensed from vapor in the atmosphere; *also* : the descent of such water **b** : RAINWATER **2 a** : a fall of rain : RAINSTORM **b** *pl* : the rainy season **3** : rainy weather **4** : a heavy fall of particles or bodies; *also* : a large outpouring ⟨a *rain* of abuse⟩ [Old English *regn*] — **rain·less** \-ləs\ *adj*

²rain *vb* **1** : to fall as water in drops from the clouds **2** : to send down rain **3** : to fall like rain **4** : to bestow abundantly — **rain cats and dogs** : to rain very hard : POUR

rain·bow \-ˌbō\ *n* **1** : an arc or circle that exhibits in concentric bands the colors of the spectrum and that is formed opposite the sun by the refraction and reflection of the sun's rays in raindrops, spray, or mist **2** : a multicolored array

rainbow runner *n* : a large brightly marked blue and yellow food and sport fish of warm seas

rainbow trout *n* : a large stout-bodied usually brightly marked trout native to western North America — called also *rainbow*; compare STEELHEAD

rain·coat \'rān-ˌkōt\ *n* : a coat of waterproof or water-resistant material

rain·drop \-ˌdräp\ *n* : a drop of rain

rain·fall \-ˌfol\ *n* **1** : RAIN 2a **2** : amount of precipitation ⟨an annual *rainfall* of 20 inches⟩

rain forest *n* : a usually tropical woodland with a high annual rainfall and lofty trees forming a continuous canopy

rain gauge *n* : an instrument for measuring rainfall

rain·mak·ing \'rān-ˌmā-king\ *n* : the act or process of producing or attempting to produce rain by artificial means — **rain·mak·er** \-kər\ *n*

rain·proof \'rān-ˈprüf\ *adj* : impervious to rain

rain·storm \-ˌstorm\ *n* : a storm of or with rain

rain·wa·ter \-ˌwot-ər, -ˌwät-\ *n* : water fallen as rain

rain·wear \-ˌwaər, -ˌweər\ *n* : waterproof or water-resistant clothing

rainy \'rā-nē\ *adj* **rain·i·er; -est** : having much rain : SHOWERY ⟨a *rainy* season⟩

rainy day *n* : a period of want or need ⟨lay something by for a *rainy day*⟩

¹raise \'rāz\ *vb* **1** : to cause or help to rise ⟨*raise* dust⟩ **2 a** : to rouse from sleep : AROUSE **b** : to stir up : INCITE ⟨*raise* a rebellion⟩ **c** : to establish radio communication with **3 a** : to set upright by lifting or building **b** : to lift to a higher position ⟨a fist *raised* in anger⟩ **c** : to place higher in rank or dignity : ELEVATE **d** : HEIGHTEN 1a, INVIGORATE **e** : to end or suspend the operation or validity of ⟨*raise* a siege⟩ **4** : COLLECT ⟨*raise* funds⟩ **5 a** : to foster the growth and development of : GROW ⟨*raise* corn⟩ ⟨*raise* pigs⟩ **b** : to bring up (a child) ⟨was *raised* in the city⟩ **6 a** : to give rise to : PROVOKE **b** : to give voice to ⟨*raise* a cheer⟩ **7** : to bring up for consideration or debate ⟨*raise* an issue⟩ **8 a** : to increase the strength, intensity, or pitch of **b** : to increase the degree or rate of ⟨*raise* the rent⟩ **c** : to multiply (a quantity) by itself a specified number of times **9** : to make light and porous ⟨*raise* dough⟩ **10** : to cause (an elevated injury) to form on the skin ⟨the blow *raised* a welt⟩ [Old Norse *reisa*] SYN see LIFT — **rais·er** *n* — **raise Cain** : to cause trouble

²raise *n* **1** : an act or method of raising or lifting **2** : an upward grade : RISE **3 a** : an increase in amount (as of a bet or bid) **b** : an increase in pay

rai·sin \'rāz-n\ *n* : a grape rich in sugar that is dried for food [Middle French, "grape", from Latin *racemus* "cluster of grapes or berries"]

rai·son d'être \ˌrā-ˌzōⁿ-ˈdetr\ *n* : reason or justification for existence [French]

ra·ja *or* **ra·jah** \'räj-ə, 'räzh-\ *n* : an Indian or Malay prince or chief [Hindi *rājā*, from Sanskrit *rājan* "king"]

Raj·put *or* **Raj·poot** \'räj-ˌpüt, 'räzh-\ *n* : a member of a former Indo-Aryan dominant military caste of northern India [Hindi *rājpūt*, from Sanskrit *rājaputra* "king's son", from *rājan* "king" + *putra* "son"]

¹rake \'rāk\ *n* : a long-handled garden tool having a bar with teeth or prongs; *also* : a machine for gathering hay [Old English *racu*]

²rake *vt* **1** : to gather, loosen, or smooth with or as if with a rake **2** : to gain (as money) quickly and in abundance **3 a** : BRUSH 3 **b** : SCRATCH 1 **4 a** : to search through : RANSACK **b** : to search out and gather together ⟨*rake* up old scandals⟩ **5** : to sweep the length of especially with gunfire **6** : to glance over rapidly — **rak·er** *n*

³rake *vi* : to incline from the perpendicular : SLANT [origin unknown]

⁴rake *n* : a slant or slope away from the perpendicular

⁵rake *n* : a dissolute person : LIBERTINE [short for earlier *rakehell*]

rake–off \'rā-ˌkof\ *n* : an improper or unlawful commission or profit received by one party in a business deal

¹rak·ish \'rā-kish\ *adj* : of, relating to, or characteristic of a rake — **rak·ish·ly** *adv* — **rak·ish·ness** *n*

²rakish *adj* **1** : having a smart stylish appearance suggestive of speed ⟨a *rakish* ship⟩ **2** : flashily unconventional or informal : JAUNTY ⟨*rakish* clothes⟩ [probably from ³*rake*; from the raking masts of pirate ships] — **rak·ish·ly** *adv* — **rak·ish·ness** *n*

rale \'ral, 'räl\ *n* : an abnormal sound accompanying breathing (as in pneumonia) [French *râle*]

ral·len·tan·do \ˌräl-ən-ˈtän-dō\ *adv or adj* : with a gradual decrease in tempo — used as a direction in music [Italian, literally, "slowing down"]

¹ral·ly \'ral-ē\ *vb* **ral·lied; ral·ly·ing** **1 a** : to bring together for a common purpose **b** : to bring back to order ⟨*rallying* the forces for a second assault⟩ **2** : to rouse for action or from depression or weakness ⟨the medicine *rallied* the patient⟩ **3** : to come together to renew an effort : join in a common cause **4** : RECOVER, REBOUND ⟨the market *rallied* after a slump⟩ **5** : to engage in a rally (as in tennis) [French *rallier*, from Old French *ralier*, from *re-* "re-" + *alier* "to unite, ally"]

²rally *n, pl* **rallies** **1** : the action of rallying **2** : a mass meeting intended to arouse group enthusiasm **3** : a series of strokes interchanged between players (as in tennis) before a point is won

³rally *vt* **ral·lied; ral·ly·ing** : to tease with good-natured or friendly ridicule [French *railler* "to mock, rally", from Provençal *ralhar* "to babble, joke", derived from Latin *ragere* "to neigh"]

¹ram \'ram\ *n* **1** : a male sheep **2** : BATTERING RAM **3** : a pointed beak on the prow of a ship for piercing an enemy ship **4** : a guided piece for exerting pressure or for driving or forcing something by impact [Old English *ramm*]

²ram *vb* **rammed; ram·ming** **1** : to strike or strike against with violence : CRASH **2** : to rush violently or forcibly ⟨*ram* through traffic⟩ **3** : to force in, down, or together by or as if by driving or pressing **4** : to force passage or acceptance of ⟨*ram* a bill through congress⟩ [Middle English *rammen*, probably from *ram*, n.] — **ram·mer** *n*

RAM \'ram\ *n* : RANDOM-ACCESS MEMORY

Ram·a·dan \'ram-ə-ˌdän, ˌräm-ə-'\ *n* : the 9th month of the Muhammadan year observed with daily fasting from dawn to sunset [Arabic *Ramadān*]

¹ram·ble \'ram-bəl\ *vb* **ram·bled; ram·bling** \-bə-ling, -bling\ **1 a** : to move aimlessly from place to place : WANDER, ROAM **b** : to explore idly **2** : to talk or write in a disjointed or disorganized fashion **3** : to grow or extend irregularly [perhaps from Middle English *romblen*, from *romen* "to roam"]

²ramble *n* : a leisurely excursion for pleasure; *esp* : a leisurely or aimless walk

ram·bler \'ram-blər\ *n* **1** : one that rambles **2** : a climbing rose with rather small often double flowers in large clusters

ram·bling \'ram-bling\ *adj* : lacking in logical organization : DISCURSIVE — **ram·bling·ly** \-bling-lē\ *adv*

ram·bouil·let \ˌram-bə-ˈlā\ *n, often cap* : a large sturdy sheep developed in France for mutton and wool [*Rambouillet*, France]

ram·bunc·tious \ram-ˈbəng-shəs, -ˈbəngk-\ *adj* : not restrained or orderly : UNRULY [probably derived from *robust*] — **ram·bunc·tious·ly** *adv* — **ram·bunc·tious·ness** *n*

ram·e·kin *or* **ram·e·quin** \'ram-i-kən\ *n* : an individual baking dish [French *ramequin*, a preparation of cheese baked with bread crumbs or eggs, from Low German *ramken*, from *ram* "cream"]

ra·mie \'rā-mē, 'ram-ē\ *n* : an Asian perennial plant of the nettle family; *also* : its strong lustrous bast fiber used as a textile fiber [Malay *rami*]

ram·i·fi·ca·tion \ˌram-ə-fə-ˈkā-shən\ *n* **1** : the act or process of branching **2** : BRANCH 2, OFFSHOOT **3** : OUTGROWTH, CONSEQUENCE ⟨the *ramifications* of a problem⟩

rambler 2

\ə\ abut	\ng\ sing
\ər\ further	\ō\ bone
\a\ mat	\o\ saw
\ā\ take	\oi\ coin
\ä\ cot, cart	\th\ thin
\au\ out	\th\ this
\ch\ chin	\ü\ food
\e\ pet	\u\ foot
\ē\ easy	\y\ yet
\g\ go	\yü\ few
\i\ tip	\yu\ cure
\ī\ life	\zh\ vision
\j\ job	

ram·i·fy \'ram-ə-ˌfī\ *vb* **-fied; -fy·ing** : to spread out or split up into branches or divisions [Middle French *ramifier,* from Medieval Latin *ramificare,* from Latin *ramus* "branch"]

ram·jet engine \ˌram-ˌjet-\ *n* : a jet engine having in its forward end a continuous inlet of air so that there is a compressing effect produced on the air taken in while the engine is in motion

¹ramp \'ramp\ *vi* **1** : to stand or advance menacingly with forelegs or with arms raised **2** : to move or act furiously : STORM [Old French *ramper* "to crawl, rear", of Germanic origin]

²ramp *n* : a sloping passage or roadway connecting different levels [French *rampe,* from *ramper* "to crawl, rear"]

¹ram·page \'ram-ˌpāj, ram-'\ *vi* : to rush wildly about : STORM [Scottish]

²ram·page \'ram-ˌpāj\ *n* : a course of violent, riotous, or reckless action or behavior — **ram·pa·geous** \ram-'pā-jəs\ *adj* — **ram·pa·geous·ly** *adv* — **ram·pa·geous·ness** *n*

ram·pant \'ram-pənt, -ˌpant\ *adj* **1** : rearing upon one or both hind legs with forelegs extended **2 a** : marked by a menacing wildness, extravagance, or absence of restraint **b** : unchecked in growth or spread [Middle French, present participle of *ramper* "to crawl, rear"] — **ram·pant·ly** *adv*

ram·part \'ram-ˌpärt, -pərt\ *n* : a broad wall or mound of earth raised as a fortification or protective barrier [Middle French]

¹ram·rod \'ram-ˌräd\ *n* **1** : a rod for ramming home the charge in a muzzle-loading firearm **2** : a cleaning rod for small arms

²ramrod *adj* : marked by rigidity, severity, or stiffness

ram·shack·le \'ram-ˌshak-əl\ *adj* : appearing ready to collapse: as **a** : DILAPIDATED **b** : carelessly or loosely constructed [alteration of earlier *ransackled,* derived from *ransack*]

ra·mus \'rā-məs\ *n, pl* **ra·mi** \-ˌmī\ : a projecting part or elongated process : BRANCH (the *rami* of the lower jaw) [Latin, "branch"]

ran *past of* RUN

¹ranch \'ranch\ *n* **1** : an establishment for raising horses, cattle, or sheep **2** : a farm devoted to a specialty (a fruit *ranch*) **3** : RANCH HOUSE 2 [Mexican Spanish *rancho* "small ranch", from Spanish, "camp, hut", from *ranchearse* "to settle", from Middle French *se ranger* "to arrange oneself"]

²ranch *vi* : to live or work or raise livestock on a ranch

ranch·er \'ran-chər\ *n* : one who owns or operates or works on a ranch

ran·che·ro \ran-'cheər-ō, rän-\ *n, pl* **-ros** : RANCHER [Mexican Spanish, from *rancho* "small ranch"]

ranch house *n* **1** : the main dwelling house on a ranch **2** : a one-story house typically with a low-pitched roof

ranch·man \'ranch-mən\ *n* : RANCHER

ran·cho \'ran-chō, 'rän-\ *n, pl* **ranchos** : RANCH 1 [Mexican Spanish, "small ranch"]

ran·cid \'ran-səd\ *adj* **1** : having the unpleasant smell or taste typical of decomposed oil or fat (*rancid* butter) **2** : distinctly unpleasant or distasteful; *also* : CORRUPT [Latin *rancidus,* from *rancēre* "to be rancid"] — **ran·cid·i·ty** \ran-'sid-ət-ē\ *n* — **ran·cid·ness** \'ran-səd-nəs\ *n*

ran·cor \'rang-kər\ *n* : intense hatred or spite [Middle French *ranc, ur,* from Late Latin *rancor* "rancidity, rancor", from Latin *rancēre* "to be rancid"] — **ran·cor·ous** \-kə-rəs, -krəs\ *adj* — **ran·cor·ous·ly** *adv*

¹ran·dom \'ran-dəm\ *n* : a haphazard course [Middle French *randon* "impetuosity", from *randir* "to run", of Germanic origin] — **at random** : without definite aim, direction, rule, or method

²random *adj* **1** : lacking a definite plan, purpose, or pattern **2** : having a definite and especially an equal probability of occurring (a *random* number); *also* :

consisting of or relating to such elements selected independently (*random* samples) — **ran·dom·ly** *adv* — **ran·dom·ness** *n* □ SYN RANDOM, HAPHAZARD, CASUAL mean determined by accident rather than design. RANDOM stresses lack of definite aim or fixed goal or avoidance of regular procedure (*random* collection of furniture) HAPHAZARD applies to what is done without regard for regularity or fitness or ultimate consequences (*haphazard* arrangement of furniture) CASUAL suggests working or acting without deliberation, intention, or purpose (a *casual* tour of the sights)

³random *adv* : in a random manner

ran·dom-ac·cess \ˌran-dəm-'ak-ˌses\ *adj* : permitting access to stored data in any order the user desires

random-access memory *n* : a computer memory that provides the main internal storage available to the user for programs and data — called also *RAM*; compare READ-ONLY MEMORY

ran·dom·ize \'ran-də-ˌmīz\ *vt* : to make random (carefully *randomized* sampling) — **ran·dom·iza·tion** \ˌran-də-mə-'zā-shən\ *n*

rang *past of* RING

¹range \'rānj\ *n* **1 a** : a series of things in a line : ROW (a *range* of mountains) **b** : an aggregate of individuals in one rank : CLASS, ORDER **2** : a cooking stove that has an oven and a flat top with plates or racks to hold utensils over flames or coils **3 a** : a place that may be ranged over **b** : open land over which livestock may roam and feed **c** : the region throughout which a kind of organism or ecological community naturally occurs **4** : the act of ranging about **5 a** (1) : the horizontal distance to which a projectile can be propelled (2) : the maximum distance a vehicle can travel without refueling **b** : a place where shooting is practiced; *also* : a special course (as over water) where missiles are tested **6 a** : the space or extent included, covered, or used : SCOPE **b** : the extent of pitch covered by a voice or a melody **7 a** : a variation between limits (a wide *range* of patterns) **b** : the difference between the least and greatest of a set of values **8** : the set of values a function may take on; *esp* : the set of values that the dependent variable may take on — compare DOMAIN 4 [Middle English, "row of persons", from Old French *renge,* from *rengier* "to range"]

²range *vb* **1 a** : to set in a row or in the proper order **b** : to place among others in a position or situation **c** : to assign to a category : CLASSIFY **2** : to rove over or through : roam at large or freely **3** : to raise (livestock) on a range **4** : to determine or give the elevation necessary for (a gun) to propel a projectile to a given distance **5 a** : to correspond in direction or line : ALIGN **b** : to extend in a particular direction **6** : to vary within limits **7** : to live or occur in or be native to a region [Middle French *ranger,* from Old French *rengier,* from *renc, reng* "line, place, row, rank"]

range finder *n* : a device used to determine the distance of an object (as a target)

range·land \'rānj-ˌland\ *n* : land used or suitable for range

rang·er \'rān-jər\ *n* **1 a** : the keeper of a British royal park or forest **b** : an officer charged with patrolling and protecting a forest **2** : an animal that ranges **3 a** : one of a body of organized armed men who range over a region **b** : a soldier in an army unit with special training (as parachute jumping and scuba diving) for carrying out surprise attacks and raids

rangy \'rān-jē\ *adj* **rang·i·er; -est 1** : having room for ranging **2** : able to range for considerable distances **3 a** : being long-limbed and long-bodied (*rangy* cattle) **b** : being tall and slender (*rangy* athletes) — **rang·i·ness** *n*

ra·ni *or* **ra·nee** \rä-'nē, 'rän-ē\ *n* : the wife of a raja : an Indian or Malay queen or princess [Hindi *rānī,* from Sanskrit *rājñī,* feminine of *rājan* "king"]

¹rank \'rangk\ *adj* **1** : strong and vigorous and usually coarse in growth ⟨*rank* weeds⟩ **2** : offensively gross or coarse ⟨*rank* language⟩ **3** : shockingly conspicuous ⟨*rank* cowardice⟩ **4** : EXTREME, UTTER ⟨a *rank* amateur⟩ **5** : unpleasantly strong-smelling : RANCID, FOUL [Old English *ranc* "overbearing, strong"] SYN SEE FLAGRANT — **rank·ness** *n*

²rank *n* **1** : ROW, SERIES ⟨*ranks* of houses⟩ **2** : a line of soldiers in close order side by side **3** *pl* : a group of individuals classed together ⟨in the *ranks* of the unemployed⟩ **4** : relative position or order : STANDING **5** : official grade or status (as in the army or navy) ⟨the *rank* of general⟩ **6** : position in regard to merit ⟨a musician of the highest *rank*⟩ **7** : a high social position **8** *pl* : the body of enlisted personnel (as in an army) [Middle French *renc, reng,* of Germanic origin]

³rank *vb* **1** : to arrange in lines or in a regular formation **2** : to determine the relative position of : RATE **3** : to take precedence of ⟨a captain *ranks* a lieutenant⟩ **4** : to take or have a position in relation to others : be in a class

rank and file *n* **1** : the enlisted personnel of an armed force **2** : the ordinary body of an organization or society as distinguished from the leaders

rank·er \'rang-kər\ *n* : one who serves or has served in the ranks; *esp* : a commissioned officer promoted from the ranks

rank·ing *adj* : having the highest rank or the foremost position

ran·kle \'rang-kəl\ *vb* **ran·kled; ran·kling** \-kə-ling, -kling\ **1** : to cause anger, irritation, or deep bitterness **2** : to cause resentment or bitterness in : irritate deeply [Middle French *rancler* "to fester", from Old French *draoncler, raoncler,* from *draoncle, raoncle* "festering sore", from Medieval Latin *dracunculus,* from Latin, "small serpent"] □ ORIGIN The modern senses of the verb *rankle* are figurative extensions of an earlier meaning, "to fester". The word was borrowed from Middle French *rancler.* The Old French noun *raoncle,* or *draoncle,* from which the verb is derived, means "a festering sore" and comes ultimately from Latin *dracunculus.* This word means literally "small serpent or dragon". In Medieval Latin *dracunculus* was used for a cancerous tumor or ulcer, probably because the form of a tumor was thought to be like that of a small serpent.

ran·sack \'ran-,sak, ran-', 'ran-'\ *vt* : to search thoroughly : RUMMAGE; *esp* : to search through and steal things of value [Old Norse *rannsaka*] — **ran·sack·er** *n*

¹ran·som \'ran-səm\ *n* **1** : something (as money) paid or demanded for the freedom of a captured person **2** : the act of ransoming [Old French *rançon,* from Latin *redemptio* "redemption"]

²ransom *vt* : to free from captivity or punishment by paying a price SYN SEE RESCUE — **ran·som·er** *n*

¹rant \'rant\ *vi* **1** : to talk noisily, excitedly, or wildly ⟨*rant* and rave in anger⟩ **2** : to scold violently [obsolete Dutch *ranten*] — **rant·er** *n*

²rant *n* : ranting speech : wild unrestrained language

¹rap \'rap\ *n* **1** : a sharp blow or knock **2** *slang* **a** : the blame for an action ⟨took the *rap*⟩ **b** : a criminal charge [Middle English *rappe*]

²rap *vb* **rapped; rap·ping** **1** : to give a quick sharp blow : KNOCK ⟨*rap* on the door⟩ **2** : to utter suddenly with force ⟨*rap* out an order⟩

³rap *n* : the least bit ⟨don't care a *rap*⟩ [perhaps from ¹*rap*]

⁴rap *n* **1** : CONVERSATION, TALK **2 a** : a rhythmic chanting often in unison of usually rhymed couplets to a musical accompaniment **b** : a piece so performed [perhaps from *repartee*]

⁵rap *vi* **rapped; rap·ping** **1** : to talk freely and frankly **2** : to perform rap music

ra·pa·cious \rə-'pā-shəs\ *adj* **1** : very grasping or greedy **2** : living on prey : PREDATORY [Latin *rapac-,*

rapax, from *rapere* "to seize"] — **ra·pa·cious·ly** *adv* — **ra·pa·cious·ness** *n* — **ra·pac·i·ty** \-'pas-ət-ē\ *n*

¹rape \'rāp\ *n* : a European herb of the mustard family grown as a forage crop and for its seeds which are used as a source of oil and as a bird food [Latin *rapa, rapum* "turnip, rape"]

²rape *vt* **1** *archaic* : to seize and take away by force **2** : to commit rape on : RAVISH [Latin *rapere*] — **rap·er** *n* — **rap·ist** \'rā-pəst\ *n*

³rape *n* **1** : a seizing by force **2** : sexual intercourse with a woman carried out without her consent and especially by force

ra·phe \'rā-fē, -,fē\ *n* : a seam or ridge (as at the union of the two lateral halves of an organ or on a seed) [Greek *rhaphē* "seam", from *rhaptein* "to sew"]

¹rap·id \'rap-əd\ *adj* : marked by a fast rate of motion, activity, succession, or occurrence : SWIFT [Latin *rapidus* "seizing, sweeping, rapid", from *rapere* "to seize, sweep away"] SYN SEE FAST — **rap·id·ly** *adv* — **rap·id·ness** *n*

²rapid *n* : a part of a river where the current is fast and the surface is usually broken by obstructions — usually used in pl.

rap·id-fire \,rap-əd-'fīr\ *adj* **1** : firing or adapted for firing shots in rapid succession **2** : marked by rapidity, liveliness, or sharpness ⟨*rapid-fire* questions⟩

ra·pid·i·ty \rə-'pid-ət-ē, ra-\ *n* : the quality or state of being rapid

rapid transit *n* : fast public passenger transportation (as by subway) in urban areas

ra·pi·er \'rā-pē-ər\ *n* : a straight 2-edged sword with a narrow pointed blade [Middle French *rapiere*]

rap·ine \'rap-ən, -,īn\ *n* : the seizing and carrying away of something by force : PILLAGE, PLUNDER [Latin *rapina,* from *rapere* "to seize"]

rap·port \ra-'pōr, -'pȯr\ *n* : harmonious accord or relation that makes communication possible or easy ⟨the teacher had good *rapport* with the pupils⟩ [French, from *rapporter* "to bring back, refer"]

rap·proche·ment \,rap-,rōsh-'mäⁿ\ *n* : the establishment or a state of cordial relations [French, from *rapprocher* "to bring together", from *re-* "re-" + *approcher* "to approach"]

rap·scal·lion \rap-'skal-yən\ *n* : RASCAL 1, SCAMP [alteration of earlier *rascallion,* from *rascal*]

rap sheet *n* : a police arrest record especially for an individual

rapt \'rapt\ *adj* **1** : carried away with emotion ⟨a *rapt* audience⟩ **2** : wholly absorbed ⟨listened with *rapt* attention⟩ [Latin *raptus,* past participle of *rapere* "to seize, sweep away"] — **rapt·ly** *adv* — **rapt·ness** \'rapt-nəs, 'rap-\ *n*

rap·tor \'rap-tər, -,tȯr\ *n* : a bird of prey [derived from Latin *raptor* "plunderer", from *rapere* "to seize"]

rap·to·ri·al \rap-'tōr-ē-əl, -'tȯr-\ *adj* **1** : adapted to seize prey **2** : of, relating to, or being a bird of prey

rap·ture \'rap-chər\ *n* : a deeply moving sense of joy, delight, or love — **rap·tur·ous** \'rap-chə-rəs, 'rap-shrəs\ *adj* — **rap·tur·ous·ly** *adv* — **rap·tur·ous·ness** *n*

ra·ra avis \,rar-ə-'ā-vəs, ,rer-; ,rär-ə-'äwəs\ *n, pl* **ra·ra avis·es** \-'ā-və-səz\ *or* **ra·rae aves** \,rär-,ī-'ā-,wās\ : a rare person or thing : RARITY [Latin, "rare bird"]

¹rare \'raər, 'reər\ *adj* : not cooked through — used of meat [Old English *brēre* "lightly boiled"]

²rare *adj* **1** : not thick or dense : THIN ⟨the *rare* atmosphere at high altitudes⟩ **2** : unusually fine : EXCELLENT, SPLENDID ⟨a person of *rare* charm⟩ **3** : seldom occurring or found : very uncommon **4** : valuable because of scarcity ⟨a collection of *rare* books⟩ [Latin *rarus*] — **rare·ness** *n*

rare·bit \'raər-bət, 'reər-\ *n* : WELSH RABBIT [by alteration]

rare earth element *n* : any of a series of naturally occurring metallic elements that includes the elements with

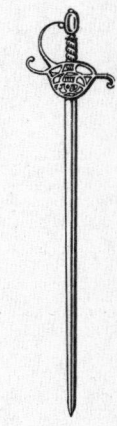

rapier

\ə\ abut	\ng\ sing
\ər\ further	\ō\ bone
\a\ mat	\ȯ\ saw
\ā\ take	\ȯi\ coin
\ä\ cot, cart	\th\ thin
\aů\ out	\th\ this
\ch\ chin	\ü\ food
\e\ pet	\ů\ foot
\ē\ easy	\y\ yet
\g\ go	\yü\ few
\i\ tip	\yů\ cure
\ī\ life	\zh\ vision
\j\ job	

ratchet wheel: *1* wheel,
2 reciprocating lever,
3 pawl for communicating
motion, *4* pawl for
preventing backward
motion

atomic numbers 58 through 71, usually lanthanum, and sometimes yttrium and scandium

rar·e·fac·tion \,rar-ə-'fak-shən, ,rer-\ *n* : the act or process of rarefying : the state of being rarefied [Medieval Latin *rarefactio,* from Latin *rarefacere* "to rarefy"] — **rar·e·fac·tion·al** \-shnəl, -shən-l\ *adj*

rar·e·fy *also* **rar·i·fy** \'rar-ə-,fī, 'rer-\ *vb* **-fied; -fy·ing 1** : to make or become thin, porous, or less dense **2** : to make or become more spiritual, refined, or abstruse [Middle French *rarefier,* from Latin *rarefacere,* from *rarus* "rare" + *facere* "to make"]

rare·ly \'raər-lē, 'reər-\ *adv* **1** : not often : SELDOM **2** : with rare skill : EXCELLENTLY **3** : UNUSUALLY ⟨a *rarely* beautiful view⟩

rare·ripe \-,rīp\ *adj* : early ripe [English dialect *rare* "early" + *ripe*] — **rareripe** *n*

rar·ing \-ing\ *adj* : full of enthusiasm or eagerness [from English dialect *rare* "to rear", alteration of English *rear*]

rar·i·ty \'rar-ət-ē, 'rer-\ *n, pl* **-ties 1** : the quality or state of being rarefied ⟨the *rarity* of the atmosphere⟩ **2** : the fact of being rare: as **a** : EXCELLENCE 1 **b** : SCARCITY **3** : one that is rare ⟨black pearls are *rarities*⟩

ras·cal \'ras-kəl\ *n* **1** : a mean, unprincipled, or dishonest person : ROGUE **2** : a mischievous person or animal [Middle English *rascaile* "rabble, one of the rabble"]

ras·cal·i·ty \ra-'skal-ət-ē\ *n, pl* **-ties** : the act, actions, or character of a rascal

ras·cal·ly \'ras-kə-lē\ *adj* : of or characteristic of a rascal ⟨a *rascally* trick⟩ — **rascally** *adv*

¹rash \'rash\ *adj* **1** : being too hasty in speech or action or in making decisions **2** : showing undue disregard for consequences : RECKLESS ⟨a *rash* act⟩ ⟨regret a *rash* promise⟩ [Middle English, *rasch* "quick"] **SYN** *see* **DARING** — **rash·ly** *adv* — **rash·ness** *n*

²rash *n* : a breaking out of the skin with red spots (as in measles) : ERUPTION [obsolete French *rache* "scurf", drived from Latin *rasus,* past participle of *radere* "to scrape, shave"]

rash·er \'rash-ər\ *n* : a thin slice of bacon or ham cut for broiling or frying; *also* : a portion consisting of several such slices [perhaps from obsolete *rash* "to cut", from Middle English *rashen*]

¹rasp \'rasp\ *vb* **1** : to rub with or as if with a rough file ⟨*rasp* off a rough edge⟩ **2** : to grate harshly upon : IRRITATE ⟨a voice that *rasps* the ear⟩ **3** : to speak or utter in a grating tone ⟨*rasp* out a complaint⟩ **4** : to produce a grating sound [Middle English *raspen*] — **rasp·er** *n*

²rasp *n* **1** : a coarse file with cutting points instead of lines **2 a** : an act of rasping **b** : a rasping sound, sensation, or effect

rasp·ber·ry \'raz-,ber-ē, -bə-rē, -brē\ *n* **1 a** : any of various black or red edible berries that consist of numerous small drupes on a fleshy receptacle and are rounder and smaller than the related blackberries **b** : a bramble that bears raspberries **2** : a sound of contempt made by protruding the tongue between the lips and expelling air so forcibly as to produce a vibration [English dialect *rasp* "raspberry" + English *berry*]

raspberry 1a

raspy \'ras-pē\ *adj* **rasp·i·er; -est 1** : HARSH, GRATING ⟨spoke with a *raspy* twang⟩ **2** : IRRITABLE

¹rat \'rat\ *n* **1** : a scaly-tailed gnawing rodent distinguished from the mouse chiefly by its larger size and by differences in the teeth **2** : a person who deserts a cause or betrays associates [Old English *ræt*]

²rat *vi* **rat·ted; rat·ting 1** : to desert or inform on one's associates **2** : to catch or hunt rats

rat·able *or* **rate·able** \'rāt-ə-bəl\ *adj* **1** : capable of being rated, estimated, or apportioned **2** *British* : TAXABLE — **rat·ably** \-blē\ *adv*

ratch \'rach\ *n* **1** : RATCHET 2 **2** : a notched bar with which a pawl or detent works to prevent reversal of motion [German *ratsche,* from *ratschen* "to rattle"]

rat cheese *n* : CHEDDAR

ratch·et \'rach-ət\ *n* **1** : a mechanism that consists of a bar or wheel having inclined teeth into which a pawl drops so as to allow motion in one direction only **2** : a pawl or detent for holding or propelling a ratchet wheel [alteration of earlier *rochet,* from French, from Middle French *rocquet* "lance head", of Germanic origin]

ratchet wheel *n* : a toothed wheel held in position or turned by an engaging pawl

¹rate \'rāt\ *vt* : to scold violently : BERATE [Middle English *raten*]

²rate *n* **1** : reckoned value : VALUATION **2 a** : a fixed ratio between two things — compare **RATE OF EXCHANGE b** (1) : a charge, payment, or price fixed according to a ratio, scale, or standard ⟨the tax *rate*⟩ (2) *British* : a local tax — usually used in pl. **3 a** : a quantity, amount, or degree of something measured per unit of something else **b** : an amount of payment or charge based on another amount ⟨interest at the *rate* of six percent⟩ **4** : relative condition or quality : CLASS [Middle French, from Medieval Latin *rata,* from Latin *pro rata parte* "according to a fixed proportion"] — **at any rate** : in any case : at least

³rate *vb* **1** : CONSIDER, REGARD ⟨was *rated* a good pianist⟩ **2** : to set an estimate or value on ⟨*rate* houses for tax purposes⟩ **3** : to determine the rank, class, or position of : GRADE ⟨*rate* a movie⟩ **4** : to have a rating or rank : be classed ⟨*rate* high⟩ **5** : to set a rate on **6** : to be qualified for ⟨*rate* a promotion⟩

rate of exchange : the amount of one currency that will buy a given amount of another

rate·pay·er \'rāt-,pā-ər\ *n, British* : TAXPAYER

rat·er \'rāt-ər\ *n* **1** : one that rates; *esp* : a person who estimates or determines a rating **2** : one having a specified rating or class — usually used in combination ⟨first-*rater*⟩

rath·er \'rath-ər, 'rəth-, 'räth\ *adv* **1** : more willingly : PREFERABLY ⟨I would *rather* not go⟩ **2** : on the contrary : INSTEAD ⟨things did not turn out well; *rather,* they turned out very badly⟩ **3** : more exactly : more properly : with better reason ⟨my friend, or, *rather,* my former friend⟩ ⟨to be pitied *rather* than blamed⟩ **4** : SOMEWHAT ⟨*rather* cold today⟩ [Old English *brathor,* comparative of *brathe* "quickly"]

raths·kel·ler \'räts-,kel-ər, 'rats-, 'raths-\ *n* : a restaurant patterned after the cellar of a German city hall where beer is sold [obsolete German (now *ratskeller*), "city-hall basement restaurant", from *rat* "council" + *keller* "cellar"]

rat·i·fy \'rat-ə-,fī\ *vt* **-fied; -fy·ing** : to approve and sanction formally : CONFIRM ⟨*ratify* a treaty⟩ ⟨*ratify* the decision of a subordinate⟩ [Middle French *ratifier,* from Medieval Latin *ratificare,* from Latin *ratus* "determined", from past participle of *reri* "to calculate"] — **rat·i·fi·ca·tion** \,rat-ə-fə-'kā-shən\ *n* — **rat·i·fi·er** \'rat-ə-,fī-ər, -,fīr\ *n*

rat·ing \'rāt-ing\ *n* **1 a** : a classification according to grade or rank **b** : a naval specialist classification **2** *chiefly British* : a naval enlisted man **3** : a relative estimate or evaluation : STANDING ⟨a good credit *rating*⟩

ra·tio \'rā-shō, -shē-,ō\ *n, pl* **ra·tios 1** : a fixed or approximate relation in number, quantity, or degree between things or to another thing ⟨the *ratio* of eggs to butter in a cake⟩ ⟨women outnumbered men in the *ratio* of three to one⟩ **2** : the quotient of one quantity divided by another ⟨the *ratio* of 6 to 3 may be expressed as 6:3, $^6/_3$, and 2⟩ [Latin, "computation, reason"]

ra·ti·o·ci·na·tion \,rat-ē-,ōs-n-'ā-shən, ,rash-ē-, -,äs-\ *n* **1** : the process of exact thinking : REASONING **2** : a reasoned train of thought [Latin *ratiocinatio,* from *ratiocinari* "to reckon", from *ratio* "computation, reason"] — **ra·ti·o·ci·na·tive** \-'ōs-n-,āt-iv, -'äs-\ *adj*

¹ra·tion \'rash-ən, 'rā-shən\ *n* **1 a** : a food allowance for one day **b** : FOOD, PROVISIONS — usually used in pl.

⟨had to pack supplies and *rations* on their backs⟩ **2** : a share especially as determined by supply or allotment by authority ⟨a wartime meat *ration*⟩ [French, from Latin *ratio* "computation, reason"]

²ration *vt* **ra·tioned; ra·tion·ing** \'rash-ning, 'rāsh-, -ə-ning\ **1** : to supply with rations ⟨*ration* cattle⟩ **2 a** : to distribute or allot as a ration ⟨the government *rationed* gas⟩ **b** : to use or allot sparingly ⟨the doctor *rations* a diabetic's sugar intake⟩

¹ra·tio·nal \'rash-nəl, -ən-l\ *adj* **1 a** : having reason or understanding ⟨*rational* beings⟩ **b** : relating to, based on, or agreeable to reason; *also* : SANE ⟨*rational* behavior⟩ **2** : relating to, consisting of, or being rational numbers ⟨a *rational* fraction⟩ [Latin *rationalis,* from *ratio* "computation, reason"] — **ra·tio·nal·i·ty** \,rash-ə-'nal-ət-ē\ *n* — **ra·tio·nal·ly** \'rash-nə-lē, -ən-l-ē\ *adv*

²rational *n* : something rational; *esp* : a rational number or fraction

ra·tio·nale \,rash-ə-'nal\ *n* : a basic reason or explanation [Latin, neuter of *rationalis* "rational"]

ra·tio·nal·ism \'rash-nə-,liz-əm, -ən-l-,iz-\ *n* : the theory or practice of guiding one's actions and opinions solely by what seems reasonable — **ra·tio·nal·ist** \-nə-ləst, -ən-l-əst\ *n* — **rationalist** *or* **ra·tio·nal·is·tic** \,rash-nə-'lis-tik, -ən-l-'is-\ *adj* — **ra·tio·nal·is·ti·cal·ly** \-ti-kə-lē, -klē\ *adv*

ra·tio·nal·ize \'rash-nə-,līz, -ən-l-,īz\ *vb* **1** : to free (a mathematical equation) from irrational expressions **2 a** : to provide a rational explanation of ⟨*rationalize* a myth⟩ **b** : to justify unreasonable actions or views by seemingly reasonable motives — **ra·tio·nal·iza·tion** \,rash-nə-lə-'zā-shən, -ən-l-ə-\ *n*

rational number *n* : a number expressible as an integer or the quotient of two integers

rational operation *n* : one of the arithmetic operations of addition, subtraction, multiplication, and division (except by 0)

rat·like \'rat-,līk\ *adj* : of, relating to, or resembling a rat

rat·line \'rat-lən\ *n* : one of the small cross ropes attached to the shrouds of a ship so as to form the steps of a rope ladder [origin unknown]

rat mite *n* : a widely distributed mite that usually feeds on rodents but may cause dermatitis in or transmit typhus to man

rat snake *n* : any of various large harmless rat-eating snakes

rat·tan \ra-'tan, rə-\ *n* **1 a** : a climbing palm with very long tough stems **b** : a part of one of these stems used especially for walking sticks and wickerwork **2** : a rattan cane or switch [Malay *rotan*]

rat·ter \'rat-ər\ *n* : one that catches rats; *esp* : a rat-catching dog or cat

¹rat·tle \'rat-l\ *vb* **rat·tled; rat·tling** \'rat-ling, -l-ing\ **1** : to make or cause to make a rattle **2** : to chatter incessantly and aimlessly **3** : to say or do in a brisk lively fashion ⟨*rattled* off the answers⟩ **4** : to disturb the composure of : UPSET ⟨*rattled* the speaker with questions⟩ [Middle English *ratelen*]

²rattle *n* **1** : a series of short sharp sounds : CLATTER ⟨the *rattle* of hail on a roof⟩ **2** : a device (as a toy) for making a rattling sound **3** : a rattling organ at the end of a rattlesnake's tail made up of horny joints **4** : a noise in the throat caused by air passing through mucus especially at the approach of death

rat·tler \'rat-lər, -l-ər\ *n* **1** : one that rattles **2** : RATTLESNAKE

rat·tle·snake \'rat-l-,snāk\ *n* : any of various venomous American snakes having at the end of the tail horny interlocking joints that rattle when shaken

rat·tle·trap \-,trap\ *n* : something rattly or rickety; *esp* : an old car — **rattletrap** *adj*

rat·tling \'rat-ling, -l-ing\ *adj* : LIVELY, BRISK ⟨moved at a *rattling* pace⟩ — **rat·tling·ly** \'rat-ling-lē\ *adv*

rat·tly \'rat-lē, -l-ē\ *adj* : likely to rattle : making a rattle ⟨a *rattly* old car⟩

rat·ty \'rat-ē\ *adj* **rat·ti·er; -est** **1** : infested with or suggestive of rats **2** : SHABBY, UNKEMPT ⟨a *ratty* old overcoat⟩

rau·cous \'ró-kəs\ *adj* **1** : disagreeably harsh or strident ⟨a *raucous* voice⟩ **2** : boisterously disorderly ⟨a *raucous* party⟩ [Latin *raucus* "hoarse"] — **rau·cous·ly** *adv* — **rau·cous·ness** *n*

rau·wol·fia \raủ-'wủl-fē-ə, ró-\ *n* : a medicinal extract from the root of an Indian tree of the dogbane family used in the treatment of hypertension and mental disorders; *also* : this tree [New Latin, a genus of trees, from Leonhard *Rauwolf,* died 1596, German botanist]

¹rav·age \'rav-ij\ *n* **1** : an act or practice of ravaging **2** : damage resulting from ravaging ⟨the *ravage* of time⟩ [French, from *ravir* "to ravish"]

²ravage *vb* **1** : to lay waste : PLUNDER **2** : DESTROY, RUIN ⟨a body *ravaged* by disease⟩ — **rav·ag·er** *n* □ SYN RAVAGE, DEVASTATE, WASTE mean to lay waste by plundering or destroying. RAVAGE suggests violent often repeated or continuing pillaging and destruction; DEVASTATE implies causing complete ruin and desolation over a wide area; WASTE may suggest destruction as a result of a slow process or may come close to *devastate* or *ravage.*

¹rave \'rāv\ *vb* **1** : to talk irrationally in or as if in delirium **2** : to declaim wildly **3** : to talk or utter with extreme enthusiasm [Middle English *raven*] — **rav·er** *n*

²rave *n* **1** : an act or instance of raving **2** : an extravagantly favorable criticism

¹rav·el \'rav-əl\ *vb* **rav·eled** *or* **rav·elled; rav·el·ing** *or* **rav·el·ling** \'rav-ling, -ə-ling\ **1** : to separate or undo the texture of : UNRAVEL **2** : to make plain : SIMPLIFY **3** : ENTANGLE, CONFUSE [Dutch *rafelen,* from *rafel* "loose thread"] — **rav·el·er** *or* **rav·el·ler** \'rav-lər, -ə-lər\ *n*

²ravel *n* : something that is raveled

rav·el·ing *or* **rav·el·ling** \'rav-ling, -ə-ling, -lən\ *n* : something raveled or frayed; *esp* : a thread raveled out of a fabric

¹ra·ven \'rā-vən\ *n* : a glossy black bird about one half meter long of northern regions that is related to the crow and has pointed throat feathers [Old English *hræfn*]

²raven *adj* : black or glossy like a raven

rav·en·ous \'rav-ə-nəs\ *adj* : very eager for food, satisfaction, or gratification ⟨a *ravenous* appetite⟩ [Middle French *ravineus* "rushing, rapacious", from *raviner* "to rush forward, ravish", from *ravine* "rapine", from Latin *rapina*] — **rav·en·ous·ly** *adv* — **rav·en·ous·ness** *n*

ra·vine \rə-'vēn\ *n* : a small narrow steep-sided valley larger than a gully, smaller than a canyon, and usually worn by running water [French, "mountain torrent", from Middle French, "rapine, rush", from Latin *rapina* "rapine"]

rav·i·o·li \,rav-ē-'ō-lē, ,räv-\ *n pl* : little cases of dough containing a filling (as of meat or cheese) that are usually boiled and served with a spicy tomato sauce [Italian, from Italian dialect *raviolo* "little turnip", from *rava* "turnip", from Latin *rapa*]

rav·ish \'rav-ish\ *vt* **1** : to seize and take away by violence **2** : to overcome with emotion **3** : RAPE 2 **4** : PLUNDER, ROB [Middle French *raviss-,* stem of *ravir* "to ravish", from Latin *rapere* "to seize"] — **rav·ish·er** *n* — **rav·ish·ment** \-mənt\ *n*

rav·ish·ing \'rav-i-shing\ *adj* : unusually attractive, pleasing, or striking — **rav·ish·ing·ly** \-shing-lē\ *adv*

¹raw \'ró\ *adj* **raw·er** \'ró-ər, 'rór\; **raw·est** \'ró-əst\ **1** : not cooked **2 a** (1) : being in or nearly in the natural state ⟨*raw* furs⟩ : not processed or manufactured ⟨*raw* milk⟩ ⟨*raw* data⟩ (2) : lacking a normal or usual finish **b** : not diluted or blended ⟨*raw* spirits⟩ **3** : having the surface abraded or chafed ⟨a *raw* wound⟩; *also* : irritat-

ratline

\ə\ abut		\ng\ sing	
\ər\ further		\ō\ bone	
\a\ mat		\ó\ saw	
\ā\ take		\ói\ coin	
\ä\ cot, cart		\th\ thin	
\aủ\ out		\th\ this	
\ch\ chin		\ü\ food	
\e\ pet		\ủ\ foot	
\ē\ easy		\y\ yet	
\g\ go		\yü\ few	
\i\ tip		\yủ\ cure	
\ī\ life		\zh\ vision	
\j\ job			

ed as if by chafing ⟨a *raw* sore throat⟩ **4 a** : lacking experience or understanding : GREEN ⟨a *raw* recruit⟩ **b** : lacking comforts or refinements ⟨a *raw* frontier village⟩ **c** : VULGAR, COARSE ⟨a *raw* story⟩ **5** : disagreeably damp or cold ⟨a *raw* blustery day⟩ [Old English *hrēaw*] — **raw·ly** \'rȯ-lē\ *adv* — **raw·ness** *n*

²raw *n* : a raw place or state — **in the raw 1** : in a natural or crude state ⟨life *in the raw*⟩ **2** : NAKED ⟨slept in the *raw*⟩

raw·boned \'rȯ-'bōnd\ *adj* : having little flesh : GAUNT SYN SEE LANK

raw deal *n* : an instance of unfair treatment

¹raw·hide \'rȯ-,hīd\ *n* **1** : untanned cattle skin **2** : a whip of untanned hide

²rawhide *vt* **-hid·ed; -hid·ing** : to whip or drive with or as if with a rawhide

raw material *n* : natural resources in an unprocessed state : material from which useful things can be produced

¹ray \'rā\ *n* : any of numerous flat broad fishes (as a skate) that live on the sea bottom and have their eyes on the upper surface of their bodies and the tail long and narrow [Middle French *raie*, from Latin *raia*]

²ray *n* **1 a** : one of the lines of light that appear to radiate from a bright object **b** : a thin beam of radiant energy (as light) **c** : a stream of particles traveling (as in radioactive phenomena) in the same line **2** : light cast by rays : RADIANCE **3** : a thin line suggesting a ray: as **a** : any of a group of lines diverging from a common center **b** : HALF LINE **4** : a plant or animal structure that resembles a ray: as **a** : a band of tissue extending radially in a woody plant stem and usually storing food or conducting raw material **b** : RAY FLOWER **5** : PARTICLE, TRACE ⟨a *ray* of hope⟩ [Middle French *rai*, from Latin *radius* "rod, spoke, ray"]

³ray *vb* **1** : to send out rays of or as if of light **2** : RADIATE 4 **3** : to subject to radiation

rayed \'rād\ *adj* : having rays or ray flowers

ray flower *n* : one of the flowers with a strap-shaped corolla in the head of a composite plant (as the aster) — called also *ray floret*

ray·less \'rā-ləs\ *adj* : lacking rays or ray flowers

ray·on \'rā-,än\ *n* **1** : any of a group of smooth textile fibers made from cellulosic material by extrusion through minute holes **2** : a rayon yarn, thread, or fabric [derived from ²*ray*]

raze \'rāz\ *vt* : to destroy utterly by tearing down : DEMOLISH ⟨*raze* a building⟩ [Middle English *rasen* "to erase", from Middle French *raser* "to scrape, erase", from Latin *rasus*, past participle of *radere* "to scrape, shave"]

ra·zor \'rā-zər\ *n* : a sharp cutting instrument used especially to shave off hair [Old French *raseor*, from *raser*, "to scrape, shave, erase"] — **razor** *adj*

ra·zor·back \-,bak\ *or* **razorback hog** *or* **razor–backed hog** \-,bakt-\ *n* : a thin-bodied long-legged half-wild mongrel hog chiefly of the southeastern United States

razor clam *n* : any of numerous marine bivalve mollusks having a long narrow curved thin shell

razz \'raz\ *vt* : to tease mockingly : KID [*raspberry*]

-rd *symbol* — used after the figure 3 to indicate the ordinal number third ⟨3*rd*⟩ ⟨53*rd*⟩

¹re \'rā\ *n* : the 2d note of the diatonic scale [Medieval Latin]

²re \'rā, 'rē\ *prep* : with regard to [Latin, ablative of *res* "thing"]

re- *prefix* **1** : again : anew ⟨*re*appear⟩ **2** : back : backward ⟨*re*call⟩ [Latin *re-, red-* "back, again, against"]

See *re-* and 2d element

reaccelerate	reacquisition
reaccept	readdress
reacclimatize	readjust
reaccredit	readjustment
reaccreditation	readmission
reacquaint	readmit
reacquire	readopt

reaffirm	recommencement
reaffirmation	recommission
reaffix	recompilation
realign	recompile
realignment	recomputation
reallocate	recompute
reallocation	reconceive
reanalysis	reconception
reanalyze	recondense
reannex	reconnect
reannexation	reconnection
reappear	reconquer
reappearance	reconquest
reapplication	reconsecrate
reapply	reconsecration
reappoint	reconsolidate
reappointment	recontact
reapportion	recontaminate
reapportionment	recontamination
reappraisal	recontour
reappraise	reconvene
reappropriate	reconvict
reapprove	reconviction
reargue	reconvince
reargument	recopy
rearousal	recross
rearouse	recultivate
rearrest	recut
reascend	redate
reascent	rededicate
reassemble	rededication
reassembly	redefine
reassert	redefinition
reassertion	redeliver
reassess	redelivery
reassessment	redeposit
reassign	redetermination
reassignment	redetermine
reassume	redevelop
reattach	rediscover
reattachment	rediscovery
reattain	redissolve
reattempt	redistill
reattribute	redistribute
reattribution	redistribution
reauthorize	redivide
reawaken	redivision
rebait	redraft
rebalance	redraw
rebaptism	reeligibility
rebaptize	reeligible
rebid	reemerge
rebind	reemergence
reboard	reemission
reboil	reemit
rebook	reemphasis
reburial	reemphasize
rebury	reenergize
rebuy	reengage
recalculate	reengagement
recalculation	reengrave
recalibrate	reenlist
recalibration	reenlistment
recast	reenroll
recentralization	reenter
recertification	reentrant
recertify	reequip
rechannel	reerect
recharge	reescalate
recheck	reescalation
rechristen	reestablish
recirculate	reestablishment
recirculation	reestimate
reclassification	reevaluate
reclassify	reevaluation
recodification	reexamination
recodify	reexamine
recolonization	reexperience
recolonize	reexplore
recolor	reexport
recombination	reexportation
recombine	reface
recommence	refeed

refight
refigure
refinance
refind
refire
refix
refloat
refocus
refold
reformulate
reformulation
refortification
refortify
reframe
refreeze
refry
regather
regild
reglaze
regrind
regroove
regrow
regrowth
rehear
reheat
rehire
rehospitalization
rehospitalize
rehouse
rehumanize
reidentify
reignite
reimmerse
reimplant
reimplantation
reimpose
reimposition
reincorporate
reindict
reindictment
reinfestation
reinflate
reinflation
reinitiate
reinject
reinjection
reinjure
reinoculate
reinoculation
reinsert
reinsertion
reinspect
reinspection
reinstall
reinstallation
reinstitute
reintegrate
reintegration
reinter
reintroduce
reintroduction
reinvade
reinvasion
reinvent
reinvention
reinvestigate
reinvestigation
reinvigorate
reinvigoration
rejudge
rekeyboard
rekindle
reknit
relabel
relandscape
relaunch
relearn
relend
relicense
relight
reline
reload
relock

relubricate
relubrication
remarry
remeet
remelt
remigration
remilitarization
remilitarize
remobilization
remobilize
remoisten
remold
remotivate
remotivation
rename
renationalization
renationalize
renegotiable
renegotiate
renegotiation
reobserve
reoccupation
reoccupy
reoccur
reoccurrence
reoffer
reoperate
reoperation
reorchestrate
reorchestration
reorient
reorientate
reorientation
repack
repaint
repattern
repave
rephotograph
replan
replaster
replay
replot
repolarization
repolarize
repolish
repoll
repopularize
repopulate
repopulation
repressurize
reprice
reprocess
reprogram
repurchase
rerecord
reregister
reregistration
reroof
reroute
resample
resaw
reschedule
reschool
rescore
rescreen
reseal
reseat
resee
resegregate
resegregation
resell
reseller
resentence
reset
resettle
resettlement
resew
reshoot
reshow
resilver
resoak
resocialization
resocialize

resod
resolder
resolidification
resolidify
resow
respray
restage
restamp
restimulate
restimulation
restock
restrengthen
restructure
restudy
restyle
resubmission
resubmit
resummon
resupply
resurface
resurge
resurvey
resynthesis
resynthesize
resystematize
retag
retarget
retaste
reteach
retell
retest

rethink
rethread
retie
retighten
retrain
retransfer
retransform
retransformation
retranslate
retransmission
retransmit
retry
retune
retype
reupholster
reutilization
reutilize
revaccinate
revaccination
revalidate
revalidation
revisit
rewarm
rewash
reweave
reweigh
rewet
rewind
rewire
rewrap

're \ər,r\ *vb* : ARE ⟨what *'re* you doing⟩ ⟨they *'re* very nice⟩

re·ab·sorb \ˌrē-əb-ˈsȯrb, -ˈzȯrb\ *vt* : to absorb again; *esp* : RESORB — **re·ab·sorp·tion** \-ˈsȯrp-shən, -ˈzȯrp-\ *n* — **re·ab·sorp·tive** \-ˈsȯrp-tiv, -ˈzȯrp-\ *adj*

¹reach \ˈrēch\ *vb* **1 a** : to stretch out : EXTEND ⟨*reach* out your hand⟩ **b** : to move the arm so as to make a grab ⟨*reached* for a knife⟩ **c** : to touch or grasp by extending a part of the body or an object ⟨couldn't *reach* the apple on the tree⟩ **2 a** : to go as far as ⟨the shadow *reached* the wall⟩ **b** : to extend continuously ⟨the field *reaches* to the highway⟩ **c** : to go or function effectively ⟨as far as the eye can *reach*⟩ **3 a** : to arrive at : come to ⟨*reached* home late⟩; *also* : ACHIEVE ⟨*reached* an understanding⟩ **b** : to get or be delivered to ⟨your message *reached* me⟩ **4** : to communicate with ⟨tried to *reach* you by phone⟩; *also* : to make an impression on : INFLUENCE ⟨couldn't *reach* my own child⟩ **5** : to hand over : PASS ⟨*reach* me the salt⟩ **6** : to sail on a reach [Old English *rǣcan*] — **reach·able** \ˈrē-chə-bəl\ *adj* — **reach·er** *n*

²reach *n* **1** : a continuous unbroken stretch or expanse; *esp* : a straight portion of a stream or river **2 a** : the action or an act of reaching **b** : the distance one can reach ⟨kept it in easy *reach*⟩ **c** : ability to stretch so as touch something ⟨you have a long *reach*⟩ **d** : the ability to reach something as if with the hands ⟨a new car is beyond our *reach*⟩ **3** : a course sailed approximately at right angles to the wind

re·act \rē-ˈakt\ *vb* **1** : to exert a reciprocal or counteracting force or influence — often used with *on* or *upon* **2** : to act or behave in response ⟨*reacted* violently to the suggestion⟩; *also* : to respond to a stimulus **3** : to act in opposition to a force or influence — usually used with *against* ⟨*reacted* against unfair treatment⟩ **4** : to move or tend in a reverse direction ⟨prices *reacted* strongly after a brief drop⟩ **5** : to undergo or make undergo chemical reaction [New Latin *reactus,* past participle of *reagere* "to react", from Latin *re-* + *agere* "to act"]

re·ac·tance \rē-ˈak-təns\ *n* : the part of the impedance of an alternating-current circuit due to capacitance and inductance and expressed in ohms

re·ac·tant \-tənt\ *n* : a chemically reacting substance

re·ac·tion \rē-ˈak-shən\ *n* **1 a** : the act or process or an instance of reacting **b** : tendency toward a former especially outmoded political or social order or policy

\ə\	abut	\ng\	sing
\ər\	further	\ō\	bone
\a\	mat	\ȯ\	saw
\ā\	take	\ȯi\	coin
\ä\	cot, cart	\th\	thin
\au̇\	out	\th\	this
\ch\	chin	\ü\	food
\e\	pet	\u̇\	foot
\ē\	easy	\y\	yet
\g\	go	\yü\	few
\i\	tip	\yu̇\	cure
\ī\	life	\zh\	vision
\j\	job		

2 : bodily response to or activity aroused by a stimulus : **a** : the response of tissues to a foreign substance (as an allergen or infective agent) **b** : mental or emotional response (as to exhausting effort or one's life situation) **3** : the force that a body subjected to the action of a force from another body exerts in the opposite direction **4 a** : chemical transformation or change : the action between atoms or molecules to form one or more new substances **b** : a process involving change in atomic nuclei — **re·ac·tion·al** \-shnəl, -shən-l\ *adj* — **re·ac·tion·al·ly** \-ē\ *adv*

¹re·ac·tion·ary \rē-'ak-shə-ˌner-ē\ *adj* : relating to, marked by, or favoring especially political reaction

²reactionary *n, pl* **-ar·ies** : a reactionary person

reaction time *n* : the time between the beginning of a stimulus and an individual's reaction to it

re·ac·ti·vate \rē-'ak-tə-ˌvāt, 'rē-\ *vb* : to make or become activated again — **re·ac·ti·va·tion** \ˌrē-ˌak-tə-'vā-shən\ *n*

re·ac·tive \rē-'ak-tiv\ *adj* **1** : of or relating to reaction or reactance **2** : reacting or tending to react — **re·ac·tive·ly** *adv* — **re·ac·tive·ness** *n* — **re·ac·tiv·i·ty** \ˌrē-ˌak-'tiv-ət-ē\ *n*

re·ac·tor \rē-'ak-tər\ *n* **1** : one that reacts; *esp* : one that reacts positively to a foreign substance (as in a test for hypersensitivity or a disease) **2 a** : a vat for an industrial chemical reaction **b** : an apparatus in which a chain reaction of fissionable material is initiated and controlled — called also *nuclear reactor*

¹read \'rēd\ *vb* **read** \'red\; **read·ing** \'rēd-ing\ **1 a** (1) : to go over systematically by sight or touch to take in and understand the meaning of (as letters or symbols) (2) : to study the movements of (a speaker's lips) and so understand what is being said (3) : to utter aloud the printed or written words of (4) : to understand the written form of ⟨*reads* French⟩ **b** : to learn from what one has seen in writing or printing ⟨*read* that they got married⟩ ⟨*read* about your promotion⟩ **c** : to deliver aloud by or as if by reading **d** : to make a study of ⟨*read* law⟩ **e** : PROOFREAD **f** : to hear and understand (a speaker or a transmission) in radio communications ⟨how do you *read* me — over⟩ **2 a** : to interpret the meaning or significance of ⟨*read* palms⟩ **b** : FORETELL, PREDICT **3** : to discover by interpreting outward expression or signs ⟨*read* guilt in their faces⟩ **4 a** : to attribute a meaning to : UNDERSTAND ⟨how do you *read* this passage⟩ **b** : to attribute as an assumption or conjecture ⟨*read* a nonexistent meaning into my words⟩ **5** : to use as a substitute for or in preference to another word or phrase in a particular passage, text, or version ⟨*read* "hurry" for "harry"⟩ **6** : INDICATE ⟨the thermometer *reads* zero⟩ **7 a** : to sense the meaning of (coded information) ⟨data must be *read* before it can be processed⟩ **b** : to sense the coded information on ⟨*read* a punch card⟩ **c** : to cause to be read and transferred to storage ⟨*read* data into memory⟩ **8** : to consist of specific words, phrases, or symbols ⟨the passage *reads* differently in older versions⟩ [Old English *rǣdan* "to advise, interpret, read"] — **read·abil·i·ty** \ˌrēd-ə-'bil-ət-ē\ *n* — **read·able** \'rēd-ə-bəl\ *adj* — **read·able·ness** *n* — **read·ably** \-blē\ *adv* — **read between the lines** : to understand more than is directly stated — **read the riot act 1** : to give an order or warning to cease something **2** : to give a severe reprimand

²read \'red\ *adj* : taught or informed by reading

read·er \'rēd-ər\ *n* **1** : one that reads **2 a** : a device that makes a readable image ⟨a microfiche *reader*⟩ **b** : a device that scans recorded data for input ⟨a card *reader*⟩ **3** : a book for instruction and practice especially in reading

read·er·ship \-ˌship\ *n* **1** : the office or position of a reader **2** : the mass or a particular group of readers

read·i·ly \'red-l-ē\ *adv* : in a ready manner: as **a** : WILLINGLY ⟨*readily* accepted advice⟩ **b** : EASILY ⟨reasons that were *readily* understood⟩

read·ing \'rēd-ing\ *n* **1 a** : material read or for reading **b** : extent of material read ⟨a person of vast *reading*⟩ **2** : something that is registered (as on a gauge) ⟨the thermometer *reading* was 70 degrees⟩ **3** : a particular interpretation or performance **4** : the introduction of a proposed bill to a legislative body by reading aloud all or a part of it

reading desk *n* : a desk to support a book in a convenient position for a standing reader

read–only memory *n* : a usually small computer memory that contains special-purpose information (as a program) which cannot be altered — called also *ROM*; compare RANDOM-ACCESS MEMORY

read·out \'rēd-ˌaut\ *n* : an electronic device that displays information (as data from a calculator); *also* : the information displayed

¹ready \'red-ē\ *adj* **read·i·er; -est 1** : prepared for use or action ⟨dinner is *ready*⟩ **2** : APT, LIKELY ⟨*ready* to cry⟩ **3** : WILLING ⟨*ready* to give aid⟩ **4** : notably dexterous, adroit, or skilled ⟨a *ready* wit⟩ **5** : PROMPT ⟨a *ready* answer⟩ **6** : AVAILABLE, HANDY ⟨*ready* money⟩ [Middle English *redy*] — **read·i·ness** \-nəs\ *n*

²ready *vt* **read·ied; ready·ing** : to make ready

³ready *n* : the state of being ready; *esp* : preparation of a gun for immediate aiming or firing

¹ready–made \ˌred-ē-'mād\ *adj* **1** : made beforehand for general sale ⟨*ready-made* clothes⟩ **2** : lacking individuality

²ready–made *n* : something (as a garment) that is ready-made

ready room *n* : a room in which pilots or astronauts are briefed and await takeoff orders

ready–to–wear \ˌred-ēt-ə-'waər, -'weər\ *adj* : READY-MADE 1

re·agent \rē-'ā-jənt\ *n* : one that reacts or induces a reaction; *esp* : a substance that takes part in or brings about a particular chemical reaction ⟨a fixing *reagent* for tissues⟩ ⟨a *reagent* for etching steel⟩ [New Latin *reagens*, present participle of *reagere* "to react"]

re·agin \rē-'ā-jən, -gən\ *n* : an antibody in the blood of some allergic individuals that can sensitize the skin of normal individuals [*reag*ent + *-in*] — **re·agin·ic** \ˌrē-ə-'jin-ik\ *adj* — **re·agin·i·cal·ly** \-'jin-i-kə-lē, -klē\ *adv*

¹re·al \'rī-əl, 'ril, 'rē-əl, 'rēl\ *adj* **1** : not artificial, deceptive, seeming, or false : GENUINE ⟨*real* gold⟩ **2 a** : not imaginary : ACTUAL ⟨in *real* life⟩ **b** (1) : belonging to the set of real numbers ⟨the *real* roots of an equation⟩ (2) : taking on only real numbers for values ⟨a *real* variable⟩ **3** : measured by purchasing power ⟨*real* income⟩ [Middle French, from Medieval Latin *realis* "relating to things" and Late Latin *realis* "real, actual", from Latin *res* "thing, fact"] — **re·al·ness** *n* □ SYN REAL, ACTUAL, TRUE mean corresponding to known facts. REAL implies an agreement between what a thing seems to be and what it is ⟨this is a *real* diamond⟩ ACTUAL stresses occurrence or existence as action or fact ⟨the *actual* temperature today is higher than predicted⟩ TRUE implies conforming to what is real or actual ⟨a *true* account of the incident⟩ or to a model or standard ⟨prove oneself a *true* friend⟩

²real *n* : a real thing; *esp* : REAL NUMBER

³real *adv* : VERY ⟨we had a *real* good time⟩

⁴re·al \rā-'äl\ *n, pl* **re·als** *or* **re·ales** \-'äl-ās\ : the chief former monetary unit of Spain [Spanish, from *real* "royal", from Latin *regalis*]

real estate *n* : property in houses and land

re·al·gar \rē-'al-ˌgär, -gər\ *n* : an orange-red mineral As_4S_4 or AsS consisting of a sulfide of arsenic and having a resinous luster [Medieval Latin, from Catalan, from Arabic *rahj al-ghār* "powder of the mine"]

real image *n* : an image of an object formed by rays of light coming to a focus (as after passing through a lens or after being reflected by a concave mirror)

re·al·ism \'rī-ə-ˌliz-əm, 'rē-ə-\ *n* **1** : the belief that objects we perceive through our senses are real and have an existence outside our own minds **2** : the tendency to see situations or difficulties in the light of facts and to deal with them practically **3** : the representation in literature and art of things as they are in life — **re·al·ist** \-ləst\ *n*

re·al·is·tic \ˌri-ə-'lis-tik, ˌrē-ə-\ *adj* **1** : true to life or nature ⟨a *realistic* painting⟩ **2** : having or showing an inclination to face facts and to deal with them sensibly ⟨a *realistic* approach⟩ — **re·al·is·it·cal·ly** \-ti-kə-lē, klē\ *adv*

re·al·i·ty \rē-'al-ət-ē\ *n, pl* **-ties** **1** : actual existence **2** : someone or something real or actual ⟨the *realities* of life⟩ **3** : the characteristic of being true to life or to fact

re·al·ize \'ri-ə-ˌlīz, 'rē-ə-\ *vt* **1** : to make actual : ACCOMPLISH ⟨*realize* a lifelong ambition⟩ **2** : to convert into money ⟨*realized* their assets⟩ **3** : to bring or get by sale, investment, or effort : GAIN ⟨*realize* a large profit⟩ **4** : to be aware of ⟨*realized* the danger⟩ — **re·al·iz·able** \'ri-ə-ˌlī-zə-bəl, 'rē-ə-\ *adj* — **re·al·iza·tion** \ˌri-ə-lə-'zā-shən, ˌrē-ə-\ *n* — **re·al·iz·er** *n*

real–life *adj* : happening in reality : based on actual events or situations ⟨*real-life* problems⟩ ⟨a *real-life* drama⟩

re·al·ly \'ril-ē, 'rēl-ē, 'ri-ə-lē, 'rē-ə-lē\ *adv* **1** : in reality : ACTUALLY ⟨didn't *really* mean what I said⟩ **2** : without question : TRULY ⟨a *really* beautiful day⟩ **3** : to be honest : FRANKLY ⟨*really*, you're being ridiculous⟩

realm \'relm\ *n* **1** : KINGDOM 1, 2 **2** : SPHERE, DOMAIN ⟨the *realm* of fancy⟩ [Old French *realme*, from Latin *regimen* "rule"]

real number *n* : any of the set of numbers (as −2, 3, ⅞, .25, √2 , π) that includes the rational numbers and the irrational numbers but not the imaginary numbers

real property *n* : property consisting of fixed, permanent, or immovable things (as lands, houses, or fixtures) — compare PERSONAL PROPERTY

Re·al·tor \'rē-əl-tər, 'rēl-, -ˌtȯr\ *collective mark* — used for a real estate agent who is a member of the National Association of Realtors

re·al·ty \'rē-əl-tē, 'rēl-\ *n, pl* **-ties** : REAL ESTATE [*real* + *-ty* (as in *property*)]

¹ream \'rēm\ *n* **1** : a quantity of paper being variously 480, 500, or 516 sheets **2** : a great amount — usually used in pl. [Middle French *raime*, from Arabic *rizmah*, literally, "bundle"]

²ream *vt* **1** : to widen the opening of (a hole) : COUNTERSINK **2** : to shape, enlarge, or dress (a hole) with a reamer **3** : to remove by reaming [perhaps from Old English dialect *rēman*]

ream·er \'rē-mər\ *n* **1** : a rotating tool with cutting edges for enlarging or shaping a hole **2** : a juice extractor with a ridged and pointed center rising from a shallow dish

re·an·i·mate \rē-'an-ə-ˌmāt, 'rē-\ *vb* : to give life to anew : REVIVE — **re·an·i·ma·tion** \-ˌan-ə-'mā-shən\ *n*

reap \'rēp\ *vb* **1 a** (1) : to cut with a sickle, scythe, or reaping machine ⟨*reap* rye⟩ (2) : to clear (as a field) of a crop by so cutting **b** : to gather (a crop) by so cutting : HARVEST **2** : to gain as a reward ⟨*reap* the benefit of hard work⟩ [Old English *reopan*]

reap·er \'rē-pər\ *n* : one that reaps; *esp* : a machine for reaping grain

¹rear \'riər\ *vb* **1** : to erect by building : CONSTRUCT **2 a** : to raise upright **b** : to rise high ⟨skyscrapers *rearing* above the city⟩ **c** : to rise up on the hind legs ⟨the horse *reared* in fright⟩ **3 a** : to undertake the breeding and raising of ⟨*rear* cattle⟩ **b** : to bring up (a person) [Old English *rēran*]

²rear *n* **1** : the back part of something: as **a** : the unit (as of an army) or area farthest from the enemy **b** : BUTTOCK 2 **2** : the space or position at the back ⟨the *rear* of a building⟩ [probably from *rear-* (in such terms as *rear guard*)]

³rear *adj* : being at the back

rear admiral *n* : an officer rank in the Navy and Coast Guard above captain and below vice admiral

rear guard *n* : a military detachment detailed to bring up and protect the rear of a main body or force [Middle French *reregarde*, from *rere* "backward, behind" (from Latin *retro*) + *garde* "guard"]

re·arm \rē-'ärm, 'rē-\ *vb* : to arm again especially with new or better weapons — **re·ar·ma·ment** \-'är-mə-mənt\ *n*

rear·most \'riər-ˌmōst\ *adj* : farthest in the rear

re·ar·range \ˌrē-ə-'rānj\ *vt* : to arrange again especially in a different way — **re·ar·range·able** \-'rān-jə-bəl\ *adj* — **re·ar·range·ment** \-'rānj-mənt\ *n*

rear·view mirror \ˌriər-ˌvyü-\ *n* : a mirror (as in a car) that gives a view to the rear

¹rear·ward \'riər-wərd\ *adj* **1** : located at, near, or toward the rear **2** : directed toward the rear — **rear·ward·ly** *adv*

²rearward *also* **rear·wards** \-wərdz\ *adv* : at, near, or toward the rear : BACKWARD

¹rea·son \'rēz-n\ *n* **1 a** : a statement offered in explanation or justification ⟨gave no *reason* for their absence⟩ **b** : a rational ground or motive ⟨*reasons* for thinking life may exist on Mars⟩ **c** : the thing that makes some fact intelligible : CAUSE **2 a** : the power of comprehending, inferring, or thinking especially in orderly logical ways : INTELLIGENCE **b** : SANITY ⟨almost lost my *reason*⟩ [Old French *raison*, from Latin *ratio* "computation, reason"] SYN *see* CAUSE — **in reason** : with reason — **within reason** : within reasonable limits — **with reason** : with good cause : JUSTIFIABLY

²reason *vb* **rea·soned; rea·son·ing** \'rēz-ning, -n-ing\ **1** : to talk persuasively or to present reasons in order to cause a change of mind ⟨*reason* with someone⟩ **2 a** : to use one's reason or to think in a logical way or manner **b** : to state, formulate, or conclude by use of reason ⟨*reasoned* that both statements couldn't be true⟩ SYN *see* THINK

rea·son·able \'rēz-nə-bəl, -n-ə-bəl\ *adj* **1 a** : agreeable to reason ⟨a *reasonable* theory⟩ **b** : not extreme or excessive : MODERATE ⟨a *reasonable* request⟩ **c** : INEXPENSIVE ⟨*reasonable* prices⟩ **2 a** : having the faculty of reason : RATIONAL **b** : possessing sound judgment — **rea·son·abil·i·ty** \ˌrēz-nə-'bil-ət-ē, -n-ə-\ *n* — **rea·son·able·ness** \'rēz-nə-bəl-nəs, -n-ə-\ *n* — **rea·son·ably** \-blē\ *adv*

rea·son·ing *n* **1** : the use of reason; *esp* : the drawing of inferences or conclusions through the use of reason **2** : the reasons used in and the proofs that result from thought

re·as·sur·ance \ˌrē-ə-'shur-əns\ *n* : the action of reassuring : the state of being reassured

re·as·sure \ˌrē-ə-'shur\ *vt* **1** : to assure anew **2** : to restore to confidence — **re·as·sur·ing·ly** \-'shur-ing-lē\ *adv*

re·ata \rē-'at-ə, -'ät-\ *n* : LARIAT [American Spanish]

Re·au·mur \ˌrā-ō-'myur\ *adj* : relating or conforming to a temperature scale on which the boiling point of water is at 80 degrees above the zero of the scale and the freezing point is at zero [René Antoine Ferchault de *Réaumur*, died 1757, French physicist]

reave \'rēv\ *vb* **reaved** *or* **reft** \'reft\; **reav·ing** *archaic* : PLUNDER, ROB [Old English *rēafian*] — **reav·er** *n*

reb \'reb\ *n* : JOHNNY REB [short for *rebel*]

¹re·bate \'rē-ˌbāt, ri-'\ *vt* : to make a rebate of : give as a rebate [Middle French *rabattre* "to beat down again", from Old French, from *re-* "re-" + *abattre* "to beat down"] — **re·bat·er** *n*

²re·bate \'rē-ˌbāt\ *n* : a return of a portion of a payment

¹reb·el \'reb-əl\ *adj* **1 a** : opposing or taking arms against the government or ruler **b** : of or relating to rebels **2** : REBELLIOUS 2, DISOBEDIENT [Old French *rebelle*, from Latin *rebellis*, from *re-* "re-, against" + *bellum* "war"]

²rebel *n* : one who rebels or participates in a rebellion

reamer 2

³**re·bel** \ri-'bel\ *vi* **re·belled; re·bel·ling 1 a :** to oppose or resist authority or control **b :** to renounce and resist by force the authority of one's government **2 :** to feel or exhibit anger or revulsion

re·bel·lion \ri-'bel-yən\ *n* **1 :** opposition to one in authority or dominance **2 a :** open defiance of or resistance to an established government **b :** an instance of such defiance or resistance : REVOLT, UPRISING □ **SYN** UPRISING, REVOLT, REVOLUTION: REBELLION implies open, organized, often armed resistance to authority; UPRISING implies no more than an effort at rebellion; REVOLT suggests an armed uprising that quickly succeeds or fails; REVOLUTION applies to a successful rebellion resulting in a change of government and often of social structure.

re·bel·lious \ri-'bel-yəs\ *adj* **1 :** engaged in rebellion **2 :** inclined to resist or disobey authority : INSUBORDINATE — **re·bel·lious·ly** *adv* — **re·bel·lious·ness** *n*

re·birth \rē-'bərth, 'rē-\ *n* **1 :** a new or second birth **2 :** RENAISSANCE 2, REVIVAL

re·born \-'bȯrn\ *adj* : experiencing a rebirth

¹**re·bound** \ri-'baȯnd\ *vt* **1 :** to spring back on striking something **2 :** to recover from setback or frustration [Middle French *rebondir,* from *re-* "re-" + *bondir* "to leap, bound"]

²**re·bound** \'rē-,baȯnd, ri-'\ *n* **1 a :** the action of rebounding : RECOIL **b :** an upward leap or movement ⟨a sharp *rebound* of the market⟩ **2 :** a basketball or hockey puck that rebounds **3 :** a reaction to setback, frustration, or crisis

re·bo·zo \ri-'bō-,zō, -,sō\ *n, pl* **-zos :** a long scarf worn chiefly by Mexican women [Spanish, shawl, from *rebozar* to muffle]

re·branch \rē-'branch, 'rē-\ *vi* : to form secondary branches

re·broad·cast \rē-'brȯd-,kast, 'rē-\ *vt* **-cast** *also* **-cast·ed; -cast·ing 1 :** to broadcast again ⟨a radio or television program being simultaneously received from another source⟩ **2 :** to repeat (a broadcast) at a later time — **rebroadcast** *n*

re·buff \ri-'bəf\ *vt* : to refuse or check sharply : SNUB [Middle French *rebuffer,* from obsolete Italian *ribuffare*] — **rebuff** *n*

re·build \rē-'bild\ *vb* **-built** \-'bilt\; **-build·ing 1 a :** to make extensive repairs to **b :** to restore to a previous state **2 :** to make extensive changes in : REMODEL **3 :** to build again ⟨planned to *rebuild* after the fire⟩

¹**re·buke** \ri-'byük\ *vt* : to scold or criticize sharply : REPRIMAND [Old North French *rebuker*] **SYN** see REPROVE — **re·buk·er** *n*

²**rebuke** *n* : REPRIMAND, REPROOF

re·bus \'rē-bəs\ *n* : a representation of words or syllables by pictures of objects whose names resemble the intended words or syllables in sound; *also* : a riddle made up of such pictures or symbols [Latin, "by things", from *res* "thing"]

rebus

re·but \ri-'bət\ *vt* **re·but·ted; re·but·ting 1 :** to contradict or oppose by formal argument, plea, or contrary proof **2 :** to expose the falsity of : REFUTE ⟨*rebut* a theory⟩ [Old French *reboter* "to drive back", from *re-* "re-" + *boter* "to butt"] — **re·but·ta·ble** \-'bət-ə-bəl\ *adj*

re·but·tal \ri-'bət-l\ *n* : the act of rebutting; *also* : argument or proof that rebuts

re·cal·ci·trance \ri-'kal-sə-trəns\ *or* **re·cal·ci·tran·cy** \-trən-sē\ *n* : the state of being recalcitrant

re·cal·ci·trant \-trənt\ *adj* **1 :** obstinately defiant of authority or restraint **2 :** not responsive to handling or treatment [Late Latin *recalcitrare* "to be stubbornly disobedient", from Latin, "to kick back", from *re-* + *calcitrare* "to kick", from *calc-, calx* "heel"] **SYN** see UNRULY — **recalcitrant** *n*

¹**re·call** \ri-'kȯl\ *vt* **1 a :** to call back ⟨*recalled* to duty⟩ ⟨*recall* a defective product⟩ **b :** to bring back to mind usually with some effort **2 :** CANCEL 2a, REVOKE **3 a :** to

bring back into existence **b :** to restore to consciousness or awareness **SYN** see REMEMBER — **re·call·able** \-'kȯ-lə-bəl\ *adj*

²**re·call** \ri-'kȯl, 'rē-,\ *n* **1 :** a summons to return **2 :** the right or procedure by which an official may be removed by vote of the people on petition **3 :** remembrance of what has been learned or experienced **4 :** the act of revoking **5 :** a public call by a manufacturer for the return of a product that may be defective or contaminated

re·cant \ri-'kant\ *vb* : to withdraw or repudiate a statement of opinion or belief formally and publicly : make an open confession of error [Latin *recantare,* from *re-* + *cantare* "to sing"] — **re·can·ta·tion** \,rē-,kan-'tā-shən\ *n* □ **SYN** RECANT, RETRACT mean to withdraw publicly something declared or professed. RECANT implies admission of error in something one has openly professed or taught ⟨the candidate *recanted* the challenged position⟩ RETRACT stresses the repudiation of something (as an accusation or an offer) previously put forward ⟨*retracted* their earlier offer⟩

¹**re·cap** \rē-'kap, 'rē-\ *vt* **re·capped; re·cap·ping :** ¹RETREAD

²**re·cap** \'rē-,kap\ *n* : a recapped tire : ²RETREAD 2

³**re·cap** \ri-'kap, 'rē-\ *vt* **re·capped; re·cap·ping :** RECAPITULATE ⟨now, to *recap* the news⟩

⁴**re·cap** \'rē-,kap, ri-\ *n* : RECAPITULATION

re·ca·pit·u·late \,rē-kə-'pich-ə-,lāt\ *vb* : to repeat briefly : SUMMARIZE [Late Latin *recapitulare,* from Latin *re-* + *capitulum* "division of a book", from *caput* "head"]

re·ca·pit·u·la·tion \-,pich-ə-'lā-shən\ *n* **1 :** a concise summary **2 :** the supposed repetition in the development of an individual of the evolutionary stages represented in its ancestral types **3 :** the third section of a sonata form — **re·ca·pit·u·la·to·ry** \-'pich-ə-lə-,tōr-ē, -,tȯr-\ *adj*

re·cap·ture \rē-'kap-chər, 'rē-\ *n* : the act of retaking : the fact of being retaken : RECOVERY — **recapture** *vt*

re·cede \ri-'sēd\ *vi* **1 a :** to move back or away : WITHDRAW ⟨the *receding* tide⟩ **b :** to slant backward ⟨a *receding* forehead⟩ **2 :** to grow less : CONTRACT [Latin *recedere* "to go back", from *re-* + *cedere* "to go"]

¹**re·ceipt** \ri-'sēt\ *n* **1 :** RECIPE **2 :** the act or process of receiving **3 :** something received — usually used in pl. **4 :** a writing acknowledging the receiving of goods or money [Old North French *receite,* from Medieval Latin *recepta,* derived from Latin *recipere* "to receive"]

²**receipt** *vt* **1 :** to give a receipt for or acknowledge the receipt of **2 :** to mark as paid

re·ceiv·able \ri-'sē-və-bəl\ *adj* **1 :** capable of being received **2 :** not yet paid : DUE ⟨accounts *receivable*⟩

re·ceiv·ables \-bəlz\ *n pl* : amounts of money receivable

re·ceive \ri-'sēv\ *vb* **1 :** to take possession or delivery of : come into possession of ⟨*receive* the money⟩ ⟨*receive* a letter⟩ **2 :** to permit to enter one's household or company : WELCOME, GREET ⟨*receive* friends⟩ **3 :** to hold a reception ⟨*receive* from four to six o'clock⟩ **4 :** to undergo or be subjected to ⟨an experience or treatment⟩ ⟨*receive* a shock⟩ **5 :** to change incoming radio waves into sounds or pictures [Old North French *receivre,* from Latin *recipere,* from *re-* + *capere* "to take"] □ **SYN** ACCEPT, TAKE: RECEIVE normally implies passiveness but usually suggests physical contact or presence; ACCEPT implies some element of consent or approval but a minimum of physical activity ⟨accepted the award and attended a dinner to *receive* it⟩ TAKE may imply seizing or picking up what is offered ⟨*take* a bribe⟩ ⟨*take* a hint⟩ or enduring what is inflicted ⟨*took* many heavy blows⟩

re·ceiv·er \ri-'sē-vər\ *n* : one that receives: as **a :** a person appointed to take control of property that is involved in a lawsuit or of a business that is bankrupt or is being reorganized **b** (1) : an apparatus for receiving radio or television broadcasts (2) : the portion of a telegraphic or telephonic apparatus that converts electric currents or waves into visible or audible signals **c** : an offensive football player who is eligible to catch a forward pass

re·ceiv·er·ship \-ˌship\ *n* **1** : the office or function of a receiver **2** : the state of being in the hands of a receiver

re·cen·cy \'rēs-n-sē\ *n* : the quality or state of being recent

re·cent \'rēs-nt\ *adj* **1 a** : of or relating to a time not long past **b** : having lately appeared or come into being **2** *cap* : HOLOCENE — **re·cent·ly** *adv* — **re·cent·ness** *n* □ SYN RECENT, MODERN, LATE mean having taken place, existed, or developed in times close to the present. RECENT is the least precise, suggesting only comparative nearness to the present ⟨*recent* discoveries in nuclear physics⟩ MODERN implies being characteristic of the present age ⟨*modern* methods of teaching⟩ LATE usually implies a series or succession of which the one described is the most recent ⟨the *late* war⟩

re·cep·ta·cle \ri-'sep-ti-kəl\ *n* **1** : something used to receive and contain smaller objects : CONTAINER **2** : the enlarged end of the flower stalk upon which the floral organs are borne **3** : an electrical fitting (as a socket) into which another fitting may be pushed or screwed for making an electrical connection [Latin *receptaculum,* from *receptare* "to receive", from *receptus,* past participle of *recipere* "to receive"]

re·cep·tion \ri-'sep-shən\ *n* **1** : the act or process of receiving, welcoming, or accepting ⟨our *reception* of the news⟩ ⟨got a cool *reception*⟩ **2** : the state or fact of being received (as into shelter or membership) **3** : a social gathering ⟨a wedding *reception*⟩ **4** : the receiving of a radio or television broadcast [Latin *receptio,* from *receptus,* past participle of *recipere* "to receive"]

re·cep·tion·ist \ri-'sep-shə-nəst, -shnəst\ *n* : an office employee who greets and assists callers

re·cep·tive \ri-'sep-tiv\ *adj* **1** : open and responsive to ideas **2** : able to receive and transmit stimuli : SENSORY — **re·cep·tive·ly** *adv* — **re·cep·tive·ness** *n* — **re·cep·tiv·i·ty** \ˌrē-ˌsep-'tiv-ət-ē, ri-\ *n*

re·cep·tor \ri-'sep-tər\ *n* : a cell or group of cells that receives stimuli : SENSE ORGAN

¹re·cess \'rē-ˌses, ri-'\ *n* **1** : a hidden, secret, or secluded place **2 a** : a space or little hollow set back (as from the main line of a coast) : INDENTATION **b** : ALCOVE 1 **3** : a suspension of business or procedure; *esp* : a brief period for relaxation between class or study periods of a school day [Latin *recessus,* from *recedere* "to recede"]

²recess *vb* **1** : to put into a recess ⟨*recessed* lighting⟩ **2** : to make a recess in **3** : to interrupt for or take a recess

re·ces·sion \ri-'sesh-ən\ *n* **1** : the act or fact of receding **2** : a departing procession (as of clergy and choir at the end of a church service) **3** : a downturn in business activity; *also* : the period of such a downturn

re·ces·sion·al \ri-'sesh-nəl, -ən-l\ *n* : a hymn or musical piece at the conclusion of a service or program; *also* : RECESSION 2

¹re·ces·sive \ri-'ses-iv\ *adj* **1** : tending to go back **2 a** : producing an effect on bodily characteristics only when homozygous ⟨*recessive* genes⟩ **b** : exhibited by the body only when the determining gene is homozygous ⟨*recessive* traits⟩ — **re·ces·sive·ly** *adv* — **re·ces·sive·ness** *n*

²recessive *n* : a recessive trait or gene; *also* : an organism expressing one or more recessive characters

re·cher·ché \rə-ˌsher-'shā\ *adj* **1** : being rare or exotic **2** : excessively refined : PRECIOUS [French, from *rechercher* "to seek out, research"]

rec·i·pe \'res-ə-pē, -ˌpē\ *n* **1** : PRESCRIPTION 3a **2** : a set of instructions for making something (as a food dish) from various ingredients **3** : method of procedure ⟨a *recipe* for happiness⟩ [Latin, "take", imperative of *recipere* "to take, receive"]

re·cip·i·ent \ri-'sip-ē-ənt\ *n* : one that receives ⟨the *recipient* of many honors⟩ [Latin *recipiens,* present participle of *recipere* "to receive"] — **recipient** *adj*

¹re·cip·ro·cal \ri-'sip-rə-kəl\ *adj* **1** : done or felt equally by both sides ⟨*reciprocal* affection⟩ **2** : related to each other in such a way that one completes the other or is the equivalent of the other : mutually corresponding **3** : of, constituting, or resulting from paired crosses in which the kind that supplies the male parent of the first cross supplies the female parent of the second cross and vice versa [Latin *reciprocus* "returning the same way, alternating", derived from *re-* "back" + *pro-* "forward"] — **re·cip·ro·cal·ly** \-kə-lē, -klē\ *adv* □ SYN RECIPROCAL, MUTUAL, COMMON mean shared or experienced by each of those involved. RECIPROCAL implies an equal return or counteraction by each of two sides ⟨*reciprocal* lowering of tariffs⟩ MUTUAL applies to feelings or effects shared by two jointly ⟨*mutual* affection⟩ COMMON implies only being shared by others ⟨united in a *common* purpose⟩

²reciprocal *n* **1** : something in a reciprocal relationship to another **2** : either of a pair of numbers (as ⅔ and ³⁄₂ or 9 and ⅑) whose product is one

re·cip·ro·cate \ri-'sip-rə-ˌkāt\ *vb* **1** : to give and take mutually : EXCHANGE **2** : to make a return for something **3** : to move forward and backward alternately ⟨a *reciprocating* mechanical part⟩ — **re·cip·ro·ca·tion** \-ˌsip-rə-'kā-shən\ *n* — **re·cip·ro·ca·tor** \-'sip-rə-ˌkāt-ər\ *n*

reciprocating engine *n* : an engine in which the to-and-fro motion of a piston is transformed into circular motion of the crankshaft

rec·i·proc·i·ty \ˌres-ə-'präs-ət-ē\ *n, pl* **-ties 1** : mutual dependence, cooperation, or exchange between persons, groups or states **2** : a mutual exchange of privileges; *esp* : a recognition by one of two countries or institutions of the validity of licenses or privileges granted by the other

re·cit·al \ri-'sīt-l\ *n* **1** : a reciting of something; *esp* : a story told in detail ⟨the *recital* of their troubles⟩ **2** : a program of one kind of music ⟨a piano *recital*⟩ **3** : a public performance by pupils (as music or dancing pupils) — **re·cit·al·ist** \-l-əst\ *n*

rec·i·ta·tion \ˌres-ə-'tā-shən\ *n* **1** : an enumeration or telling in detail **2** : the act or an instance of reading or repeating aloud especially publicly **3 a** : a student's oral reply to questions **b** : a class period

rec·i·ta·tive \ˌres-tə-'tēv, -ə-tə-\ *n* : a rhythmically free vocal style that imitates the natural inflections of speech and that is used for dialogue and narrative in operas and oratorios; *also* : a passage in this style [Italian *recitativo,* from *recitare* "to recite", from Latin] — **recitative** *adj*

re·cite \ri-'sīt\ *vb* **1** : to repeat from memory or read aloud publicly ⟨*recite* a poem⟩ **2 a** : to give a detailed narration of **b** : STATE 2 **3** : to answer (as to a teacher) questions about a lesson [Latin *recitare,* from *re-* + *citare* "to summon"] — **re·cit·er** *n*

reck \'rek\ *vi* **1** : CARE 1a, MIND **2** *archaic* : to be of interest : MATTER [Old English *reccan* "to take heed"]

reck·less \'rek-ləs\ *adj* **1** : marked by lack of caution : RASH **2** : NEGLIGENT 1, IRRESPONSIBLE ⟨*reckless* driving⟩ SYN see DARING — **reck·less·ly** *adv* — **reck·less·ness** *n*

reck·on \'rek-ən\ *vb* **reck·oned; reck·on·ing** \'rek-ning, -ə-ning\ **1 a** : COUNT 1a, COMPUTE ⟨*reckon* the days till Christmas⟩ **b** : to estimate by calculation ⟨*reckon* the height of a building⟩ **2** : CONSIDER 3, REGARD ⟨was *reckoned* among the leaders⟩ **3** *chiefly dialect* : THINK, SUPPOSE ⟨*reckoned* they might win⟩ **4** : to make up or settle an account **5** : to count on : DEPEND ⟨*reckon* on

\ə\ abut	\ng\ si**ng**
\ər\ fur**ther**	\ō\ b**o**ne
\a\ m**a**t	\o'\ s**aw**
\ā\ t**a**ke	\oi\ c**oi**n
\ä\ c**o**t, c**a**rt	\th\ **th**in
\au̇\ **ou**t	\ṯh\ **th**is
\ch\ **ch**in	\ü\ f**oo**d
\e\ p**e**t	\u̇\ f**oo**t
\ē\ **e**asy	\y\ **y**et
\g\ **g**o	\yü\ f**ew**
\i\ t**i**p	\yu̇\ c**u**re
\ī\ l**i**fe	\zh\ vi**s**ion
\j\ **j**ob	

support) [Old English *-recenian* (as in *gerecenian* "to narrate")] — **reck·on·er** \'rek-nər, -ə-nər\ *n* — **reckon with** : to take into account — **reckon without** : to fail to take into account

reck·on·ing *n* **1** : the act or an instance of reckoning: as **a** : ⁴BILL 4, ACCOUNT **b** : COMPUTATION **c** : calculation of a ship's position **2** : a settling of accounts ⟨a day of *reckoning*⟩ **3** : a summing up : APPRAISAL

re·claim \ri-'klām\ *vt* **1** : to recall from wrong or improper conduct : REFORM **2** : to alter from an undesirable or uncultivated state ⟨*reclaim* swampland for agriculture⟩ **3** : to obtain from a waste product or byproduct : RECOVER ⟨*reclaimed* wool⟩ [Old French *reclamer* "to call back", from Latin *reclamare* "to cry out against", from *re-* + *clamare* "to cry out"] — **re·claim·able** \-'klā-mə-bəl\ *adj* — **re·claim·er** *n*

rec·la·ma·tion \,rek-lə-'mā-shən\ *n* : the act or process of reclaiming : the state of being reclaimed

re·cline \ri-'klīn\ *vb* **1** : to lean or cause to lean backwards **2** : REPOSE, LIE ⟨*reclining* on the sofa⟩ [Latin *reclinare*, from *re-* + *clinare* "to bend"]

¹re·cluse \'rek-,lüs, ri-'klüs\ *adj* : marked by withdrawal from society : SOLITARY [Old French *reclus*, literally, "shut up", from Late Latin *reclusus*, past participle of *recludere* "to shut up", from Latin *re-* + *claudere* "to close"] — **re·clu·sive** \ri-'klü-siv, -ziv\ *adj*

²recluse *n* : a person (as a hermit) who lives away from others

rec·og·ni·tion \,rek-ig-'nish-ən, ,rek-əg-\ *n* **1** : the act of recognizing ⟨their *recognition* of me⟩ **2** : special attention or notice **3** : acknowledgment of something done or given (as by making an award) ⟨got a medal in *recognition* of bravery⟩ **4** : formal acknowledgment of the political existence of a government or nation [Latin *recognitio*, from *recognitus*, past participle of *recognoscere* '"to recognize"]

rec·og·niz·able \'rek-ig-,nī-zə-bəl, 'rek-əg-\ *adj* : capable of being recognized — **rec·og·niz·abil·i·ty** \,rek-ig-,nī-zə-'bil-ət-ē, ,rek-əg-\ *n* — **rec·og·niz·ably** \'rek-ig-,nī-zə-blē, -əg-\ *adv*

re·cog·ni·zance \ri-'käg-nə-zəns, -'kän-ə-\ *n* : a recorded legal promise to do something (as to appear in court)

rec·og·nize \'rek-ig-,nīz, 'rek-əg-\ *vt* **1** : to know and remember upon seeing ⟨*recognize* a person⟩ **2** : to consent to admit : ACKNOWLEDGE ⟨*recognize* one's faults⟩ **3** : to take approving notice of ⟨*recognize* an act of bravery⟩ **4** : to acknowledge acquaintance with ⟨*recognize* someone with a nod⟩ **5** : to acknowledge as entitled to be heard at a meeting ⟨the chair *recognizes* the delegate from Illinois⟩ **6** : to grant diplomatic recognition to ⟨*recognized* the new government⟩ [Middle French *reconoiss-*, stem of *reconoistre* "to recognize", from Latin *recognoscere*, from *re-* + *cognoscere* "to know", from *co-* + *gnoscere* "to come to know"]

¹re·coil \ri-'kȯil\ *vi* **1 a** : to fall back under pressure ⟨the soldiers *recoiled* before the enemy attack⟩ **b** : to shrink back ⟨*recoil* in horror⟩ **2** : to spring back to or as if to a starting point ⟨the spring *recoiled* upon release⟩ [Old French *reculer*, from *re-* "re-" + *cul* "backside", from Latin *culus*]

²re·coil \ri-'kȯil, 'rē-,\ *n* **1** : REBOUND 1 **2** : a springing back **3** : the distance through which something (as a spring) recoils

re·coil·less \ri-'kȯil-ləs, 'rē-,\ *adj* : having a minimum of recoil ⟨a *recoilless* gun⟩

rec·ol·lect \,rek-ə-'lekt\ *vb* **1** : to bring back to the level of conscious awareness **2** : to recall to (oneself) something forgotten or overlooked ⟨*recollected* myself and apologized⟩ [Medieval Latin *recollectus*, past participle of *recolligere* "to recollect", from Latin, "to gather again"] SYN see REMEMBER

re–col·lect \,rē-kə-'lekt\ *vt* : to collect again; *esp* : RE-COVER ⟨*re-collect* one's drooping spirits⟩

rec·ol·lec·tion \,rek-ə-'lek-shən\ *n* **1** : the action or power of recalling to mind : REMEMBRANCE **2** : something recalled to the mind SYN see MEMORY

re·com·bi·nant \rē-'käm-bə-nənt, 'rē-\ *n* : an individual exhibiting genetic recombination

recombinant DNA *n* : DNA prepared in the laboratory by breaking up and splicing together DNA from several different species of organisms

re·com·bi·na·tion \,rē-,käm-bə-'nā-shən\ *n* : the production of new combinations of genes especially through genetic crossing-over and the operation of the law of independent assortment

rec·om·mend \,rek-ə-'mend\ *vt* **1** : to make a statement in praise of; *esp* : to endorse as fit, worthy, or competent ⟨*recommend* a person for a position⟩ **2** : to put forward or suggest as one's advice, as one's choice, or as having one's support ⟨*recommend* that the matter be dropped⟩ **3** : to cause to receive favorable attention [Medieval Latin *recommendare* "to praise", from Latin *re-* + *commendare* "to commend"] — **rec·om·mend·able** \-'men-də-bəl\ *adj* — **rec·om·mend·er** *n*

rec·om·men·da·tion \,rek-ə-mən-'dā-shən, -,men-\ *n* **1** : the act of recommending **2** : something that recommends **3** : a thing or course of action recommended

re·com·mit \,rē-kə-'mit\ *vt* **1** : to refer (as a bill) again to a committee **2** : to commit again — **re·com·mit·ment** \-mənt\ *n* — **re·com·mit·al** \-'mit-l\ *n*

¹rec·om·pense \'rek-əm-,pens\ *vt* : to give compensation to or for [Middle French *recompenser*, from Late Latin *recompensare*, from Latin *re-* + *compensare* "to compensate"]

²recompense *n* : a return for something done, suffered, or given

rec·on·cil·abil·i·ty \,rek-ən-,sī-lə-'bil-ət-ē\ *n* : the quality or state of bring reconcilable

rec·on·cil·able \,rek-ən-'sī-lə-bəl\ *adj* : capable of being reconciled — **rec·on·cil·able·ness** *n*

rec·on·cile \'rek-ən-,sīl\ *vt* **1** : to make friendly again ⟨*reconcile* friends who have quarreled⟩ **2** : SETTLE, ADJUST ⟨*reconcile* differences of opinion⟩ **3** : to make agree ⟨a story that cannot be *reconciled* with the facts⟩ **4** : to cause to submit or accept ⟨*reconciled* to hardship⟩ [Latin *reconciliare*, from *re-* + *conciliare* "to conciliate"] — **rec·on·cile·ment** \-mənt\ *n* — **rec·on·cil·er** *n* — **rec·on·cil·ia·to·ry** \,rek-ən-'sil-yə-,tōr-ē, -,tȯr-\ *adj*

rec·on·cil·i·a·tion \,rek-ən-,sil-ē-'ā-shən\ *n* **1** : the action of reconciling : the state of being reconciled **2** : PENANCE 2

rec·on·dite \'rek-ən-,dīt, ri-'kän-\ *adj* **1** : hidden from sight : CONCEALED **2** : difficult to understand : DEEP ⟨a *recondite* subject⟩ **3** : of, relating to, or dealing with something little known [Latin *reconditus*, past participle of *recondere* "to conceal", from *re-* + *condere* "to store up"] — **rec·on·dite·ly** *adv* — **rec·on·dite·ness** *n*

re·con·di·tion \,rē-kən-'dish-ən\ *vt* : to restore to good condition (as by repairing or replacing parts) ⟨*recondition* a house⟩

re·con·firm \,rē-kən-'fərm\ *vt* : to confirm again; *also* : to establish more strongly — **re·con·fir·ma·tion** \,rē-,kän-fər-'mā-shən\ *n*

re·con·nais·sance \ri-'kän-ə-zəns\ *n* : a preliminary survey to gain information; *esp* : an exploratory military survey of enemy territory [French, literally, "recognition", from Middle French *reconoissance*, from *reconoistre* "to recognize"]

re·con·noi·ter \,rē-kə-'nȯit-ər, ,rek-ə-\ *vb* : to make a reconnaissance; *esp* : to survey in preparation for military action ⟨*reconnoiter* enemy territory⟩ [obsolete French *reconnoître*, literally, "to recognize", from Middle French *reconoistre*]

re·con·sid·er \,rē-kən-'sid-ər\ *vb* : to consider again especially with a view to change or reversal — **re·con·sid·er·a·tion** \-,sid-ə-'rā-shən\ *n*

re·con·sti·tute \rē-'kän-stə-ˌtüt, 'rē-, -ˌtyüt\ *vt* : to restore to a former condition by adding water

re·con·struct \ˌrē-kən-'strəkt\ *vt* : to construct again : REBUILD, REMODEL

re·con·struc·tion \ˌrē-kən-'strək-shən\ *n* **1 a** : the action of reconstructing : the state of being reconstructed **b** *often cap* : the reorganization and reestablishment of the seceded states in the Union after the American Civil War **2** : something reconstructed

re·con·ver·sion \ˌrē-kən-'vər-zhən\ *n* : conversion back to a previous state

re·con·vert \ˌrē-kən-'vərt\ *vb* : to convert back

¹re·cord \ri-'kord\ *vb* **1 a** (1) : to set down in writing (2) : to deposit an authentic official copy of ⟨*record* a deed⟩ **b** (1) : to register permanently (2) : INDICATE, READ ⟨the thermometer *recorded* 90°⟩ **2** : to cause (as sound or visual images) to be registered (as on a phonograph disc or magnetic tape) in reproducible form **3** : REPRODUCE 2 ⟨a voice that *records* well⟩ **4** : to give evidence of [Old French *recorder* "to recall to mind", from Latin *recordari*, from *re-* + *cord-, cor* "heart"]

²rec·ord \'rek-ərd, -ˌord\ *n* **1** : the state or fact of being recorded **2** : something that records: as **a** : something (as a monument) that recalls or reports past events **b** : an official writing that records the proceedings or acts of a group, organization, or official **c** : an authentic official copy of a document **3 a** : the known or recorded facts regarding something or someone ⟨my school *record*⟩ **b** : the best that has ever been done (as in a particular competition) ⟨broke the long jump *record*⟩ **4** : something on which sound or visual images have been recorded for later reproduction; *esp* : a disc with a spiral groove carrying recorded sound for phonograph reproduction — **off the record** : not for publication — **on record 1** : in the position of having publicly declared oneself **2** : in the status of being known, published, or documented

³rec·ord \'rek-ərd\ *adj* : setting a record : outstanding among other like things ⟨a *record* crop⟩

re·cord·er \ri-'kord-ər\ *n* **1** : one that records **2** : a municipal judge with criminal and sometimes limited civil jurisdiction **3** : a fipple flute with eight finger holes

re·cord·ing \ri-'kord-ing\ *n* : RECORD 4

re·cord·ist \ri-'kord-əst\ *n* : one who records sound especially on film

rec·ord player \'rek-ərd-\ *n* : an instrument for playing phonograph records through a loudspeaker

¹re·count \ri-'kaunt\ *vt* : to relate in detail ⟨*recount* an adventure⟩ [Middle French *reconter*, from *re-* "re-" + *conter* "to count, relate"]

²re·count \rē-'kaunt, 'rē-\ *vb* : to count again

³re·count \rē-'kaunt, 'rē-\ *n* : a second or fresh count

re·coup \ri-'küp\ *vt* **1** : to make up for : RECOVER ⟨*recoup* a loss⟩ **2** : REIMBURSE, COMPENSATE ⟨*recoup* a person for losses⟩ [French *recouper* "to cut back", from *re-* "re-" + *couper* "to cut"] — **re·coup·able** \-'kü-pə-bəl\ *adj* — **re·coup·ment** \-'küp-mənt\ *n*

re·course \'rē-ˌkōrs, -ˌkors, ri-'\ *n* **1** : a turning for assistance or protection ⟨have *recourse* to the law⟩ **2** : a source of help or strength [Middle French *recours*, from Late Latin *recursus*, from Latin, "act of running back", from *recurrere* "to run back", from *re-* + *currere* "to run"]

re·cov·er \ri-'kəv-ər\ *vb* **-cov·ered; -cov·er·ing** \-'kəv-ring, -ə-ring\ **1** : to get back : REGAIN ⟨*recover* a lost wallet⟩ **2** : to bring back to normal position or condition ⟨stumbled, then *recovered* myself⟩ **3 a** : to make up for ⟨*recover* lost time⟩ **b** : to gain by legal process ⟨*recover* damages⟩; *also* : to win damages at law **4** *archaic* : to come or return to : REACH **5** : RECLAIM ⟨*recover* gold from ore⟩ **6** : to regain health, consciousness, or self-control [Middle French *recoverer*, from Latin *recuperare*] — **re·cov·er·able** \-'kəv-rə-bəl, -ə-rə-\ *adj*

re–cov·er \ˌrē-'kəv-ər, 'rē-\ *vt* : to cover again or anew

re·cov·ery \ri-'kəv-rē, -ə-rē\ *n, pl* **-er·ies** : the act or process or an instance of recovering; *esp* : return to a former normal state

recovery room *n* : a hospital room equipped for meeting emergencies following surgery or childbirth

¹rec·re·ant \'rek-rē-ənt\ *adj* **1** : crying for mercy : COWARDLY **2** : unfaithful to duty or allegiance [Middle French, from *recroire* "to renounce one's cause in a trial by battle", from *re-* "re-" + *croire* "to believe", from Latin *credere*]

²recreant *n* **1** : COWARD **2** : one that is unfaithful : TRAITOR

¹rec·re·ate \'rek-rē-ˌāt\ *vt* : to give new life or freshness to [Latin *recreare* "to create anew, restore, refresh", from *re-* + *creare* "to create"] — **rec·re·ative** \-ˌāt-iv\ *adj*

²re·cre·ate \ˌrē-krē-'āt\ *vt* : to create anew especially in the imagination — **re·cre·ative** \-'āt-iv\ *adj*

rec·re·ation \ˌrek-rē-'ā-shən\ *n* : refreshment of strength and spirits after toil : DIVERSION; *also* : a means of refreshment or diversion (as a game or exercise) [Middle French, from Latin *recreatio* "restoration to health", from *recreare* "to restore, refresh"] — **rec·re·ation·al** \-shnəl, -shən-l\ *adj*

re·crim·i·nate \ri-'krim-ə-ˌnāt\ *vb* **1** : to make a return charge against an accuser **2** : to retort bitterly [Medieval Latin *recriminare*, from Latin *re-* + *criminari* "to accuse", from *crimen* "accusation, crime"] — **re·crim·i·na·tion** \-ˌkrim-ə-'nā-shən\ *n* — **re·crim·i·na·to·ry** \-'krim-ə-nə-ˌtōr-ē, -ˌtor-\ *adj*

re·cru·des·cence \ˌrē-krü-'des-ns\ *n* : a renewal or breaking out again especially of something unhealthful or dangerous [Latin *recrudescere* "to become raw again", from *re-* + *crudescere* "to become raw", from *crudus* "raw"] — **re·cru·desce** \-'des\ *vi* — **re·cru·des·cent** \-'des-nt\ *adj*

¹re·cruit \ri-'krüt\ *n* : a newcomer to a field or activity; *esp* : a newly enlisted or drafted member of the armed forces [French *recrute, recrue* "fresh growth, new levy of soldiers", from Middle French, from *recroistre* "to grow up again", from Latin *recrescere*, from *re-* + *crescere* "to grow"]

²recruit *vb* **1 a** : to fill up the number of (as an army) with new members **b** : to enlist new members **c** : to secure the services of : ENGAGE **2** : REPLENISH **3** : to restore or increase the health, vigor, or intensity of — **re·cruit·er** *n* — **re·cruit·ment** \-'krüt-mənt\ *n*

re·crys·tal·lize \rē-'kris-tə-ˌlīz, 'rē-\ *vb* : to form or cause to form crystals after being dissolved or melted — **re·crys·tal·li·za·tion** \rē-ˌkris-tə-lə-'zā-shən\ *n*

rect·an·gle \'rek-ˌtang-gəl\ *n* : a parallelogram all of whose angles are right angles [Medieval Latin *rectangulus* "having a right angle", from Latin *rectus* "right" + *angulus* "angle"]

rect·an·gu·lar \rek-'tang-gyə-lər\ *adj* **1** : having a flat surface shaped like a rectangle **2 a** : crossing, lying, or meeting at a right angle ⟨*rectangular* axes⟩ **b** : having edges and faces that meet at right angles and faces that are shaped like rectangles ⟨a *rectangular* solid⟩ — **rect·an·gu·lar·i·ty** \rek-ˌtang-gyə-'lar-ət-ē\ *n* — **rect·an·gu·lar·ly** \rek-'tang-gyə-lər-lē\ *adv*

rectangular coordinate *n* : a Cartesian coordinate of a Cartesian coordinate system whose straight-line axes are perpendicular

rec·ti·fi·er \'rek-tə-ˌfī-ər, -ˌfīr\ *n* : one that rectifies; *esp* : a device for converting alternating current into direct current

rec·ti·fy \'rek-tə-ˌfī\ *vt* **-fied; -fy·ing 1** : to set right : REMEDY **2** : to purify (as alcohol) especially by repeated or fractional distillation **3** : to correct by removing errors : ADJUST ⟨*rectify* the calendar⟩ **4** : to convert (an alternating current) into a direct current [Middle French *rectifier*, from Medieval Latin *rectificare*, from Latin *rectus* "right"] SYN see CORRECT — **rec·ti·fi·able**

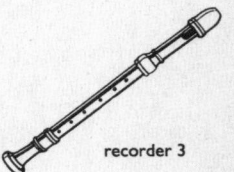

recorder 3

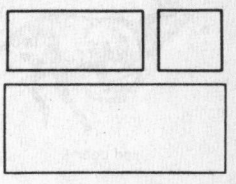

rectangle

\ə\ abut   \ng\ sing
\ər\ further \ō\ bone
\a\ mat   \o\ saw
\ā\ take   \oi\ coin
\ä\ cot, cart \th\ thin
\au\ out   \th\ this
\ch\ chin   \ü\ food
\e\ pet   \u\ foot
\ē\ easy   \y\ yet
\g\ go   \yü\ few
\i\ tip   \yu\ cure
\ī\ life   \zh\ vision
\j\ job

\'rek-tə-ˌfī-ə-bəl\ *adj* — **rec·ti·fi·ca·tion** \ˌrek-tə-fə-'kā-shən\ *n*

rec·ti·lin·e·ar \ˌrek-tə-'lin-ē-ər\ *adj* 1 : moving in, being in, or forming a straight line ⟨*rectilinear* motion⟩ 2 : characterized by straight lines [Late Latin *rectilineus,* from Latin *rectus* "straight, right" + *linea* "line"] — **rec·ti·lin·e·ar·ly** *adv*

rec·ti·tude \'rek-tə-ˌtüd, -ˌtyüd\ *n* 1 : the quality or state of being straight 2 : moral integrity [Middle French, from Late Latin *rectitudo,* from Latin *rectus* "straight, right"]

rec·to \'rek-tō\ *n, pl* **rectos** : a right-hand page — compare VERSO [New Latin *recto folio* "the page being straight"]

rec·tor \'rek-tər\ *n* 1 : a clergyman in charge of a church or parish 2 : the priest in charge of certain Roman Catholic religious houses for men 3 : the head of a university or school [Latin, "guide, director", from *rectus,* past participle of *regere* "to direct"]

rec·to·ry \'rek-tə-rē, -trē\ *n, pl* **-ries** : a rector's residence

rec·tum \'rek-təm\ *n, pl* **rectums** *or* **rec·ta** \-tə\ : the last part of the intestine linking the colon to the anus [New Latin, from *rectum intestinum,* literally, "straight intestine"] — **rec·tal** \-tl\ *adj*

rec·tus \'rek-təs\ *n, pl* **rec·ti** \-ˌtī, -ˌtē\ : any of several straight muscles (as of the abdomen) [New Latin, from *rectus musculus* "straight muscle"]

re·cum·bent \ri-'kəm-bənt\ *adj* 1 : being in a state of rest 2 : lying down [Latin *recumbens,* present participle of *recumbere* "to lie down"] — **re·cum·bent·ly** *adv*

re·cu·per·ate \ri-'kü-pə-ˌrāt, -'kyü-\ *vb* : to get back : RECOVER; *esp* : to regain health or strength [Latin *recuperare*] — **re·cu·per·a·tion** \-ˌkü-pə-'rā-shən, -ˌkyü-\ *n*

re·cu·per·a·tive \ri-'kü-pə-ˌrāt-iv, -'kyü-, -pə-rət-, -ˌprət-\ *adj* : of, relating to, or promoting recuperation

re·cur \ri-'kər\ *vi* **re·curred; re·cur·ring** 1 : to go or come back in thought or discussion ⟨*recur* to a subject in conversation⟩ 2 : to come again into the mind ⟨a memory that *recurred* over and over⟩ 3 : to occur again ⟨the fever *recurred*⟩ [Latin *recurrere* "to run back, return", from *re-* + *currere* "to run"] — **re·cur·rence** \-'kər-əns, -'kə-rəns\ *n*

re·cur·rent \ri-'kər-ənt, -'kə-rənt\ *adj* 1 : running or turning back in direction ⟨a *recurrent* vein⟩ 2 : happening time after time ⟨*recurrent* complaints⟩ [Latin *recurrens,* present participle of *recurrere* "to return"] — **re·cur·rent·ly** *adv*

re·curve \rē-'kərv, 'rē-\ *vb* : to curve backward or inward

re·cy·cle \rē-'sī-kəl, 'rē-\ *vt* : to process (as liquid body waste, glass, or cans) in order to regain for use — **re·cy·cla·ble** \-kə-lə-bəl, -klə-bəl\ *adj*

¹**red** \'red\ *adj* **red·der; red·dest** 1 a : of the color red b : having red as a distinguishing color 2 a (1) : flushed usually from emotion (2) : RUDDY 1 (3) : BLOODSHOT b : of a coppery hue c : being in the color range between a moderate orange and russet or bay d : REDDISH 3 a : stirring up or approving extreme social or political change especially by force b *cap* : COMMUNIST c : of or relating to a Communist country (as the Soviet Union) [Old English *rēad*] — **red·ly** *adv* — **red·ness** *n*

²**red** *n* 1 : a color whose hue resembles that of fresh blood or the ruby or is that of the long-wave extreme of the visible spectrum 2 : one that is of a red or reddish color 3 : a pigment or dye that colors red 4 a : a person who seeks the overthrow of an existing social or political order b *cap* : COMMUNIST 5 : the condition of showing a loss ⟨in the *red*⟩ [sense 5 from the bookkeeping practice of entering debit items in red ink]

re·dact \ri-'dakt\ *vt* 1 : to put in writing : FRAME 2 : to select or adapt for publication [back-formation from *redaction*] — **re·dac·tor** \-'dak-tər\ *n*

re·dac·tion \ri-'dak-shən\ *n* 1 : an act or instance of redacting 2 : EDITION 1 [French *rédaction,* derived from Latin *redigere* "to bring back, reduce", from *re-, red-* "re-" + *agere* "to lead"] — **re·dac·tion·al** \-shnəl, -shən-l\ *adj*

red alga *n* : an alga (division Rhodophyta) having predominantly red pigmentation

red·bird \'red-ˌbərd\ *n* : any of several birds (as a cardinal, several tanagers, or the bullfinch) with predominantly red plumage

red blood cell *n* : one of the hemoglobin-containing cells that carry oxygen to the tissues and are responsible for the red color of vertebrate blood — called also *red blood corpuscle*

red–blood·ed \'red-'bləd-əd\ *adj* : full of spirit and vigor

red·bone \'red-ˌbōn\ *n* : a speedy medium-sized dark red or red and tan American hound that is used especially for hunting raccoons

red·breast \-ˌbrest\ *n* : a bird (as a robin) with a reddish breast

red·bud \-ˌbəd\ *n* : an American tree of the pea family with usually pale rosy pink flowers and heart-shaped leaves

red·cap \-ˌkap\ *n* : a baggage porter

red–car·pet \'red-'kär-pət\ *adj* : marked by ceremonial courtesy ⟨*red-carpet* treatment⟩ [from the traditional laying down of a red carpet for important guests to walk on]

red cedar *n* : an American juniper with fragrant close-grained red wood; *also* : its wood

red cell *n* : RED BLOOD CELL

red cent *n* : a trivial amount

red clover *n* : a Eurasian clover with globe-shaped heads of reddish purple flowers widely grown as a hay, forage, and cover crop

red·coat \'red-ˌkōt\ *n* : a British soldier especially during the Revolutionary War

red corpuscle *n* : RED BLOOD CELL

red cross *n* : a red-colored cross on a white background used as a badge for hospitals and for members of an international organization that helps the suffering especially in war or disaster areas

¹**redd** \'red\ *vb* **redd·ed** *or* **redd; redd·ing** 1 *chiefly dialect* : to set in order 2 *chiefly dialect* : to make things tidy [Middle English *redden* "to clear"]

²**redd** *n* : the spawning place or nest of a fish [origin unknown]

red deer *n* : the common deer of temperate Europe and Asia related to but smaller than the American elk

red·den \'red-n\ *vb* **red·dened; red·den·ing** \'red-ning, -n-ing\ : to make or become red or reddish; *esp* : BLUSH 1

red·dish \'red-ish\ *adj* : somewhat red — **red·dish·ness** *n*

rede \'rēd\ *vt* 1 *dialect* : to give counsel to : ADVISE 2 *dialect* : INTERPRET 1, EXPLAIN [Old English *rǣdan* "to advise, interpret, read"]

red·ear \'red-ˌiər\ *n* : a common American sunfish with orange-red marks on the gill cover

re·dec·o·rate \rē-'dek-ə-ˌrāt, 'rē-\ *vb* 1 : to freshen or change in appearance : REFURBISH 2 : to freshen or change a decorative scheme — **re·dec·o·ra·tion** \ˌrē-ˌdek-ə-'rā-shən\ *n*

re·deem \ri-'dēm\ *vt* 1 a : to buy back : REPURCHASE b : to get or win back 2 a : to free from captivity usually by paying a ransom b : LIBERATE 1 c : to free from the bondage of sin 3 : to change for the better : REFORM 4 : REPAIR 1, RESTORE 5 a : to get back (a pledge) by payment of an amount secured thereby b : to remove the obligation of by payment c : to change into something of value 6 a : to atone for : EXPIATE b : to offset the bad effect of 7 : to make good : FULFILL ⟨*redeem* a promise⟩ [Middle French *redimer,* from Latin *redi-*

red deer

mere, from re-, red- "re-" + emere "to take, buy"] SYN see RESCUE — re·deem·able \-'dē-mə-bəl\ adj

re·deem·er \ri-'dē-mər\ n : one that redeems; esp, cap : JESUS

red eft n : an individual of the reddish terrestrial phase of a common American newt that has also a spotted aquatic phase

re·demp·tion \ri-'dem-shən, -'demp-\ n : the act or process or an instance of redeeming [Middle French, from Latin redemptio, from redemptus, past participle of redimere "to redeem"] — re·demp·tion·al \-shnəl, -shən-l\ adj — re·demp·tive \-'dem-tiv, -'demp-\ adj

Re·demp·tor·ist \ri-'dem-tə-rəst, -'demp-, -trəst\ n : a member of the Roman Catholic Congregation of the Most Holy Redeemer [French rédemptoriste, from Late Latin redemptor "redeemer", derived from Latin redimere "to redeem"]

re·de·sign \,rēd-i-'zīn\ vt : to revise in appearance, function, or content — redesign n

re·de·vel·op·ment \,rēd-i-'vel-əp-mənt\ n : the act or process of redeveloping; esp : renewal of a blighted area

red·fish \'red-,fish\ n : any of various reddish to bright red fishes

red fox n : a common fox with orange-red to dusky reddish brown fur

red giant n : a very large star with a relatively low surface temperature

red–green blindness n : a form of color blindness in which the spectrum is seen in tones of yellow and blue — called also red-green color blindness

red gum n : SWEET GUM

red–hand·ed \'red-'han-dəd\ adv or adj : in the act of committing a crime or misdeed

red·head \'red-,hed\ n 1 : a person having red hair 2 : an American duck related to the canvasback but having in the male a brighter reddish head and shorter bill

red heat n : the state of being red-hot; also : the temperature at which a substance is red-hot

red herring n 1 : a herring cured by salting and slow smoking to a dark brown color 2 : something intended to distract attention from the real issue [sense 2 from the practice of drawing a red herring across a trail to confuse hunting dogs]

red–hot \'red-'hät\ adj 1 : glowing red with heat 2 : exhibiting or marked by intense emotion, enthusiasm, or energy (a red-hot political campaign) 3 : FRESH, NEW (red-hot news)

re·dia \'rēd-ē-ə\ n, pl re·di·ae \-ē-,ē\ also re·di·as : a larva produced within the sporocyst of many trematodes that produces another generation of rediae or develops into a cercaria [Francesco Redi, died 1698?, Italian naturalist] — re·di·al \-ē-əl\ adj

Red Indian n : AMERICAN INDIAN

red·in·gote \'red-ing-,gōt\ n : a fitted outer garment: as a : a woman's lightweight coat open at the front b : a dress with a front gore of contrasting material [French, from English riding coat]

red·in·te·grate \ri-'dint-ə-,grāt, re-\ vt, archaic : to restore to a former or sound state [Latin redintegrare, from re-, red- "re-" + integrare "to integrate"] — red·in·te·gra·tion \-,dint-ə-'grā-shən, ,rē-, ,re-\ n, archaic

re·di·rect \,rēd-ə-'rekt, rē-dī-\ vt : to change the course or direction of — re·di·rec·tion \-'rek-shən\ n

¹re·dis·count \rē-'dis-,kaunt, 'rē-, ,rē-dis-\ vt : to discount again — re·dis·count·able \-ə-bəl\ adj

²re·dis·count \rē-'dis-,kaunt, 'rē-\ n : the act or process of rediscounting

re·dis·trict \rē-'dis-trikt, 'rē-\ vt : to divide anew into districts; esp : to revise the legislative districts of

red jasmine n : a widely cultivated frangipani with large terminal clusters of pink, red, or purple fragrant flowers

red lead n : a red lead oxide Pb_3O_4 used in storage-battery plates, in glass and ceramics, and as a paint pigment

red–let·ter \'red-'let-ər\ adj : memorable especially in a happy or joyful way (a red-letter day) [from the practice of marking holy days in red letters in church calendars]

red·line \'red-,līn\ vb : to withhold home-loan funds or insurance from neighborhoods held to be poor economic risks : discriminate against in lending or insuring — red·lin·ing \-ing\ n

Red Man n : AMERICAN INDIAN

red maple n : a common American maple with reddish twigs and rather soft wood

red marrow n : reddish bone marrow that is the seat of blood-cell production

red·neck \'red-,nek\ n : a member of the white Southern rural laboring class

re·do \rē-'dü, 'rē-\ vt -did \-'did\; -done \-'dən\; -do·ing : to do over or again; esp : REDECORATE (redid the bedroom in blue)

red oak n : any of numerous American oaks that have acorns with the inner surface of the shell lined with woolly hairs and leaf veins that usually run beyond the margin of the leaf to form bristles

red ocher n : a red earthy hematite used as a pigment

red·o·lence \'red-l-əns\ n 1 : SCENT 1b, AROMA 2 : the quality or state of being redolent

red·o·lent \-ənt\ adj 1 : exuding fragrance : AROMATIC 2 a : full of a specified fragrance (a room redolent of tobacco smoke) b : tending to suggest (a city redolent of ancient times) [Middle French, from Latin redolens, present participle of redolēre "to emit a scent", from re-, red- "re-" + olere "to smell"] — red·o·lent·ly adv

re·dou·ble \rē-'dəb-əl, 'rē-\ vb 1 : to make or become doubled (as in size, amount, or degree) (redouble one's efforts) 2 : to double back (the fox redoubled on its tracks) 3 : to double again

re·doubt \ri-'daut\ n : a small often temporary fortification (as for defending a hilltop) [French redoute, from Italian ridotto, from Medieval Latin reductus "secret place", from Latin, "withdrawn", from reducere "to lead back"]

re·doubt·able \ri-'daut-ə-bəl\ adj 1 : arousing fear or dread : FORMIDABLE (a redoubtable enemy) 2 : arousing admiring respect : EMINENT (a redoubtable scholar) [Middle French redoubtable, from redouter "to dread", from re- "re-" + douter "to doubt"] — re·doubt·ably \-blē\ adv

re·dound \ri-'daund\ vi 1 : to become reflected back especially so as to bring credit or discredit (actions that redound to one's credit) 2 : to become transferred or added : ACCRUE (additions that redound to the benefit of the library) [Middle French redonder "to overflow", from Latin redundare, from re-, red- "re-" + unda "wave"]

re·dox \'rē-,däks\ n : OXIDATION-REDUCTION [reduction + oxidation]

red–pen·cil \'red-'pen-səl\ vt 1 : CENSOR 2 : EDIT 1a, CORRECT, REVISE

red pepper n : CAYENNE PEPPER

red·poll \'red-,pōl\ n : any of several small finches which resemble siskins and in which the males usually have a red or rosy crown

¹re·dress \ri-'dres\ vt 1 : to set (as a wrong) right : make amends for : REMEDY, RELIEVE 2 : to correct or amend the faults of [Middle French redresser, from Old French redrecier, from re- "re-" + drecier "to make straight", from Latin directus "direct"]

²re·dress \ri-'dres, 'rē-,\ n 1 a : relief from distress b : means or possibility of seeking a remedy 2 : compensation for wrong or loss 3 a : an act or instance of redressing b : CORRECTION 1, RETRIBUTION

red salmon n : SOCKEYE

\ə\ abut	\ng\ sing
\ər\ further	\ō\ bone
\a\ mat	\ȯ\ saw
\ā\ take	\ȯi\ coin
\ä\ cot, cart	\th\ thin
\au̇\ out	\th\ this
\ch\ chin	\ü\ food
\e\ pet	\u̇\ foot
\ē\ easy	\y\ yet
\g\ go	\yü\ few
\i\ tip	\yu̇\ cure
\ī\ life	\zh\ vision
\j\ job	

red·shift \'red-'shift\ *n* : a displacement of the spectrum of a celestial body toward longer wavelengths that is a consequence of the Doppler effect or the gravitational field of the source — **red·shift·ed** *adj*

red siskin *n* : a South American finch that is scarlet with black head, wings, and tail and is often kept in captivity

red snapper *n* : any of several reddish sea fishes including some esteemed for food or sport

red snow *n* : snow reddened by various airborne dusts or especially by a growth of reddish algae

red spider *n* : any small web-spinning mite that attacks forage and crop plants

red spruce *n* : a cone-bearing tree of eastern North America that is an important source of lumber and pulpwood

red squirrel *n* : a common North American squirrel that has the upper parts chiefly red — called also *chickaree*

red star *n* : a star having a low surface temperature and a red color

red·start \'red-,stärt\ *n* **1** : a small red-tailed European thrush **2** : an American fly-catching warbler [*red* + obsolete *start* "tail", from Old English *steort*]

redstart 2

red tape *n* : official routine or procedure especially as marked by delay or inaction [from the red tape formerly used to bind legal documents in England]

red tide *n* : seawater discolored and made toxic by the presence of large numbers of dinoflagellates — compare GYMNODINIUM

red·top \'red-,täp\ *n* : any of several grasses with reddish panicles including an important forage and lawn grass of eastern North America

red-winged blackbird

re·duce \ri-'düs, -'dyüs\ *vb* **1 a** : to draw together or cause to converge : CONSOLIDATE **b** : to diminish in size, amount, extent, or number 〈*reduce* the number of accidents〉; *esp* : to lose weight by dieting **2** : to bring to a specified state or condition 〈*reduce* anarchy to order〉 **3** : to force to surrender **4 a** : to bring to a systematic form or character 〈*reduce* language to writing〉 〈*reduced* their observations to a theorem〉 **b** : to become converted or equated 〈their differences *reduced* to a question of semantics〉 **5** : to correct (as a fracture) by bringing displaced or broken parts back into normal position **6 a** : to lower in grade or rank : DEMOTE **b** : to lower in condition or status 〈*reduced* to panhandling〉 **c** : to diminish in strength or intensity **d** : to diminish in value **7 a** : to change the denominations or form of without changing the value **b** : to transpose from one form into another **c** : to change (a mathematical expression) to an equivalent but more fundamental expression 〈*reduce* a fraction〉 **8** : to break down (as by crushing or grinding) 〈*reduce* metal from its ore〉 **9 a** : to bring to the metallic state by removal of nonmetallic elements **b** : DEOXIDIZE **c** : to combine with or subject to the action of hydrogen **d** (1) : to change (an element or ion) from a higher to a lower oxidation state (2) : to add one or more electrons to (an atom or ion or molecule) [Latin *reducere* "to lead back", from *re-* + *ducere* "to lead"] — **re·duc·er** *n* — **re·duc·ibil·i·ty** \-,dü-sə-'bil-ət-ē, -,dyü-\ *n* — **re·duc·ible** \-'dü-sə-bəl, -'dyü-\ *adj* — **re·duc·ibly** \-blē\ *adv*

reducing agent *n* : a substance that reduces a chemical compound usually by donating electrons

re·duc·tase \ri-'dək-,tās, -,tāz\ *n* : an enzyme that catalyzes a chemical reduction

re·duc·tio ad ab·sur·dum \ri-'dək-tē-,ō,ad-əb-'sərd-əm, -'zərd-\ *n* : disproof of a proposition by showing that it contradicts accepted propositions when carried to its logical conclusion [Late Latin, literally, "reduction to the absurd"]

re·duc·tion \ri-'dək-shən\ *n* **1** : the act or process of reducing : the state of being reduced **2 a** : the amount by which something is reduced in price **b** : something

made by reducing **3** : a South American Indian settlement directed by Spanish missionaries **4** : MEIOSIS; *esp* : halving of the chromosome number usually in the first meiotic division [Middle French, from Latin *reductio* "restoration", from *reductus,* past participle of *reducere* "to lead back"] — **re·duc·tion·al** \-shnəl, -shən-l\ *adj* — **re·duc·tive** \-'dək-tiv\ *adj*

reduction division *n* : the division of meiosis in which chromosome reduction occurs and which is usually the first of the two meiotic division; *also* : MEIOSIS

re·dun·dan·cy \ri-'dən-dən-sē\ *n, pl* **-cies 1** : the quality or state of being redundant **2** : a lavish or excessive amount **3 a** : unnecessary repetition : PROLIXITY **b** : an act or instance of needless repetition

re·dun·dant \ri-'dən-dənt\ *adj* **1 a** : exceeding what is necessary or normal **b** : using more words than necessary : REPETITIOUS **2** : ABUNDANT, PROFUSE [Latin *redundare* "to overflow", from *re-, red-* "re-" + *unda* "wave"] — **re·dun·dant·ly** *adv*

re·du·pli·cate \ri-'dü-pli-,kāt, 'rē-, -'dyü-\ *vt* **1** : to make or perform again : COPY **2** : to form (a word) by reduplication — **re·du·pli·cate** \-kət\ *adj*

re·du·pli·ca·tion \ri-,dü-pli-'kā-shən, ,rē-, -,dyü-\ *n* **1** : an act or instance of doubling or reiterating : DUPLICATION **2** : repetition of a radical element or a part of it occurring usually at the beginning of a word and often accompanied by change of the radical vowel — **re·du·pli·ca·tive** \ri-'dü-pli-,kāt-iv, 'rē-, -'dyü-\ *adj* — **re·du·pli·ca·tive·ly** *adv*

red·wing \'red-,wing\ *n* **1** : a red-winged European thrush **2** : RED-WINGED BLACKBIRD

red–winged blackbird \,red-,wingd-, -,wing-\ *n* : a North American blackbird of which the adult male is black with a patch of bright scarlet on the wing

red·wood \'red-,wúd\ *n* : a tall cone-bearing timber tree of California that often reaches a height of 300 feet; *also* : its light durable brownish red wood

re·echo \rē-'ek-ō, 'rē-\ *vb* : to echo back : REVERBERATE 〈thunder *reechoed* through the valley〉

reed \'rēd\ *n* **1 a** : any of various tall grasses having slender often prominently jointed stems and growing especially in wet areas **b** : a stem of such a grass **c** : a mass or growth of reeds **2** : ARROW 1 **3** : a musical instrument made of the hollow joint of a plant **4** : an ancient Hebrew unit of length equal to 6 cubits (about 3 meters) **5 a** : a thin elastic tongue (as of cane, wood, metal, or plastic) fastened at one end to the mouthpiece of a musical instrument (as a clarinet) or to a fixture (as a reed block) over an air opening (as in an accordion) and set in vibration by an air current (as the breath) **b** : a reed instrument 〈the *reeds* of an orchestra〉 **6** : a device on a loom resembling a comb and used to space warp yarns evenly [Old English *hrēod*]

reed·buck \-,bək\ *n, pl* **reedbuck** *also* **reedbucks** : any of several fawn-colored African antelopes with hornless females

reed organ *n* : a keyboard wind instrument in which the wind acts on a set of metal reeds

re·ed·u·cate \rē-'ej-ə-,kāt, 'rē-\ *vt* : to train again; *esp* : to rehabilitate through education — **re·ed·u·ca·tion** \,rē-,ej-ə-'kā-shən\ *n* — **re·ed·u·ca·tive** \rē-'ej-ə-,kāt-iv, 'rē-\ *adj*

reedy \'rēd-ē\ *adj* **reed·i·er; -est 1** : abounding in or covered with reeds 〈a *reedy* marsh〉 **2** : made of or resembling reeds; *esp* : SLENDER, FRAIL 〈*reedy* arms〉 〈the *reedy* stem of a goblet〉 **3** : having the tone quality of a reed instrument 〈a *reedy* tenor voice〉 — **reed·i·ly** \'rēd-l-ē\ *adv* — **reed·i·ness** \'rēd-ē-nəs\ *n*

¹reef \'rēf\ *n* **1** : a part of a sail taken in or let out in regulating size **2** : the reduction in sail area made by reefing [Old Norse *rif*]

²reef *vt* : to reduce the area of (a sail) by rolling or folding and tying a portion

³reef *n* **1** : a chain of rocks or ridge of sand at or near the surface of water **2** : LODE [Dutch *rif*]

¹reef·er \'rē-fər\ *n* **1** : one that reefs **2** : a close-fitting usually double-breasted jacket of thick cloth

²reefer *n* : a marijuana cigarette [probably from Mexican Spanish *grifa*]

³ree·fer \'rē-fər\ *n* : REFRIGERATOR; *also* : a refrigerator car, truck, trailer, or ship [by alteration]

reef knot *n* : a square knot used in reefing a sail

¹reek \'rēk\ *n* **1** : VAPOR 1 **2** : a strong or disagreeable odor [Old English *rēc* "smoke"] — **reeky** \'rē-kē\ *adj*

²reek *vi* **1** : to emit smoke or vapor **2** : to have or give off a strong or unpleasant smell ⟨clothes *reeking* of tobacco smoke⟩ **3** : to give a strong impression ⟨she *reeks* of wealth⟩

¹reel \'rēl\ *n* **1** : a revolvable device on which something flexible is wound: as **a** : a small windlass at the butt of a fishing rod for the line **b** : a flanged spool for photographic film **2** : a quantity of something wound on a reel **3** : a frame for drying clothes usually having radial arms on a vertical pole [Old English *hrēol*]

²reel *vb* **1** : to wind on or as if on a reel **2** : to bring in (as a hooked fish) by reeling a fishing line : to wind or turn a reel — **reel·able** \'rē-lə-bəl\ *adj* — **reel·er** *n*

³reel *vi* **1 a** : to whirl around ⟨*reeling* in a dance⟩ **b** : to be in a whirl ⟨heads *reeling* with excitement⟩ **2** : to give way : fall back ⟨soldiers *reeling* in defeat⟩ **3** : STAGGER 1a [Middle English *relen*, probably from ¹*reel*]

⁴reel *n* : a reeling motion

⁵reel *n* : a lively dance originally of the Scottish Highlands; *also* : its music [probably from ⁴*reel*]

re·elect \,rē-ə-'lekt\ *vt* : to elect for another term in office — **re·elec·tion** \-'lek-shən\ *n*

reel off *vt* : to recite fluently ⟨*reeled off* the statistics⟩

re·en·act \,rē-ə-'nakt\ *vt* **1** : to enact again **2** : to perform again — **re·en·act·ment** \-'nakt-mənt, -'nak-\ *n*

re·en·trance \rē-'en-trəns, 'rē-\ *n* : REENTRY 2, 3

re·en·try \rē-'en-trē, 'rē-\ *n* **1** : a retaking possession especially from a tenant **2** : a second or new entry **3** : the action of reentering the earth's atmosphere after travel in space

¹reeve \'rēv\ *n* : a medieval English manor officer responsible chiefly for enforcing the discharge of feudal obligations [Old English *gerēfa*]

²reeve *vt* **rove** \'rōv\ *or* **reeved; reev·ing** **1** : to pass (as a rope) through a hole or opening **2** : to rig for operation by passing a rope through ⟨*reeve* up a set of blocks⟩ [origin unknown]

³reeve *n* : the female of the ruff [probably alteration of *ruff*]

ref \'ref\ *n* : REFEREE 2

re·fash·ion \rē-'fash-ən, 'rē-\ *vt* : to make over : ALTER

re·fec·tion \ri-'fek-shən\ *n* **1** : refreshment of mind, spirit, or body; *esp* : NOURISHMENT **2 a** : the taking of refreshment **b** : food and drink together : REPAST [Middle French, from Latin *refectio*, from *reficere* "to restore", from *re-* + *facere* "to make"]

re·fec·to·ry \ri-'fek-tə-rē, -trē\ *n, pl* **-ries** : a dining hall especially in a monastery or convent [Late Latin *refectorium*, from Latin *refectus*, past participle of *reficere* "to restore"]

refectory table *n* : a long narrow table with heavy legs

re·fer \ri-'fər\ *vb* **re·ferred; re·fer·ring** **1** : to place in a certain class so far as cause, relationship, or source is concerned ⟨*referred* the defeat to poor training⟩ **2** : to send or direct to a person or place for treatment, help, or information ⟨*refer* a child to a dictionary⟩ **3** : to go for information, advice, or aid ⟨*refer* to the dictionary for the meaning of a word⟩ **4** : to have relation or connection : RELATE ⟨the asterisk *refers* to a footnote⟩ **5** : to submit or hand over to someone else ⟨*refer* a patient to a specialist⟩ **6** : to direct attention : make reference [Latin *referre* "to bring back, report, refer", from *re-* + *ferre* "to carry"] — **re·fer·able** \'ref-rə-bəl, -ə-rə-; ri-

'fər-ə-\ *adj* — **re·fer·rer** \ri-'fər-ər\ *n* □ SYN REFER, ALLUDE mean to direct attention to something. REFER implies intentional introduction and distinct mention as by direct naming; ALLUDE suggests such indirect mention as is conveyed in a hint, a figure of speech, or other roundabout expression.

¹ref·er·ee \,ref-ə-'rē\ *n* **1** : a person to whom a legal matter is referred for investigation and report or for settlement **2** : a sports official usually having final authority in administering a game

²referee *vb* **-eed; -ee·ing** : to act or supervise as a referee

ref·er·ence \'ref-ərns, 'ref-rəns, -ə-rəns\ *n* **1** : the act of referring or consulting **2** : a bearing on a matter : RELATION ⟨with *reference* to what was said⟩ **3 a** : a remark referring to something : ALLUSION ⟨made *reference* to our agreement⟩ **b** : a sign or indication referring a reader to another passage or book **c** : consultation of information sources ⟨books for ready *reference*⟩ **4 a** : a person to whom inquiries as to the character or ability of another can be made **b** : a statement as to a person's character or ability given by someone familiar with them **c** : a book, passage, or document to which a reader is referred

reference book *n* : a book (as a dictionary, encyclopedia, or almanac) containing useful facts or information

reference mark *n* : a conventional mark (as *, †, or ‡) used in printing or writing to mark a reference

ref·er·en·dum \,ref-ə-'ren-dəm\ *n, pl* **-da** \-də\ *or* **-dums** : the principle or practice of submitting to popular vote a measure proposed or passed on by a legislative body or by popular initiative; *also* : a vote on such a measure [Latin, neuter of *referendus* "to be referred", from *referre* "to refer"]

re·fer·ent \'ref-rənt, -ə-rənt\ *n* : something that refers or is referred to; *esp* : the thing a word stands for [Latin *referens*, present participle of *referre* "to refer"] — **referent** *adj*

re·fer·ral \ri-'fər-əl\ *n* **1** : the act or an instance of referring **2** : one that is referred

¹re·fill \rē-'fil, 'rē-\ *vb* : to fill or become filled again — **re·fill·able** \-'fil-ə-bəl\ *adj*

²re·fill \'rē-,fil\ *n* **1** : material used to replace the exhausted supply of a device ⟨a lipstick *refill*⟩ **2** : something provided again; *esp* : a second filling of a medical prescription

re·fine \ri-'fīn\ *vb* **1 a** : to come or bring to a pure state ⟨*refine* sugar⟩ **b** : to distill (crude oil) and purify the resulting products **2** : to make or become improved or perfected by pruning or polishing **3** : to free from what is coarse, vulgar, or uncouth **4** : to make improvement by introducing subtleties or distinctions ⟨*refined* upon the older methods⟩ — **re·fin·er** *n*

re·fined \ri-'fīnd\ *adj* **1** : freed from impurities : PURE ⟨*refined* sugar⟩ **2** : WELL-BRED, CULTURED ⟨very *refined* manners⟩ **3** : carried to a fine point : EXACT ⟨*refined* measurements⟩

re·fine·ment \ri-'fīn-mənt\ *n* **1** : the act or process of refining **2** : the quality or state of being refined : CULTIVATION **3 a** : a refined feature or method **b** : SUBTLETY 2 **c** : a feature or device intended to improve or perfect

re·fin·ery \ri-'fīn-rē, -ə-rē\ *n, pl* **-er·ies** : a building and equipment for refining or purifying metals, oil, or sugar

re·fin·ish \rē-'fin-ish, 'rē-\ *vt* : to give (as furniture) a new surface — **re·fin·ish·er** *n*

re·fit \rē-'fit, 'rē-\ *vb* **re·fit·ted; re·fit·ting** : to get ready for use again : fit out or equip again ⟨*refit* a ship for service⟩ — **re·fit** \'rē-,fit, rē-', 'rē-\ *n*

re·flect \ri-'flekt\ *vb* **1** : to bend or throw back waves of light, sound, or heat ⟨a polished surface *reflects* light⟩ **2** : to give back an image or likeness of as if by a mirror **3** : to bring as a result ⟨your scholarship *reflects* credit on your school⟩ **4** : to cast reproach or blame ⟨our bad conduct *reflects* on our training⟩ **5** : to

\ə\ abut	\ng\ sing
\ər\ further	\ō\ bone
\a\ mat	\ȯ\ saw
\ā\ take	\ȯi\ coin
\ä\ cot, cart	\th\ thin
\au̇\ out	\th\ this
\ch\ chin	\ü\ food
\e\ pet	\u̇\ foot
\ē\ easy	\y\ yet
\g\ go	\yü\ few
\i\ tip	\yu̇\ cure
\ī\ life	\zh\ vision
\j\ job	

think seriously and carefully : MEDITATE [Latin *reflectere* "to bend back", from *re-* + *flectere* "to bend"] SYN see THINK

re·flec·tance \ri-'flek-təns\ *n* : the part of the light falling upon a surface that is reflected

reflecting telescope *n* : REFLECTOR 2

re·flec·tion \ri-'flek-shən\ *n* **1** : an instance of reflecting; *esp* : the return of light or sound waves from a surface **2** : the production of an image by or as if by a mirror **3 a** : the action of bending or folding back **b** : a reflected part : FOLD **4** : something produced by reflecting; *esp* : an image given back by a reflecting surface **5** : an often obscure or indirect criticism : REPROACH **6** : a thought, idea, or opinion formed or a remark made as a result of careful thinking **7** : consideration of some subject matter, idea, or purpose **8** : a geometric figure or a graph of an equation that is symmetric to another geometric figure or graph with respect to a line (as an axis of a coordinate system) — **re·flec·tion·al** \-shnəl, -shən-l\ *adj*

re·flec·tive \ri-'flek-tiv\ *adj* **1** : capable of reflecting light, images, or sound waves **2** : marked by reflection : THOUGHTFUL **3** : of, relating to, or caused by reflection — **re·flec·tive·ly** *adv* — **re·flec·tive·ness** *n* — **re·flec·tiv·i·ty** \,rē-,flek-'tiv-ət-ē, ri-\ *n*

re·flec·tor \ri-'flek-tər\ *n* **1** : one that reflects; *esp* : a polished surface for reflecting light or heat **2** : a telescope in which the principal focusing element is a mirror

¹re·flex \'rē-,fleks\ *n* **1 a** : reflected heat, light, or color **b** : a mirrored image **c** : a copy exact in essential or peculiar features **2 a** : an automatic and usually inborn response to a stimulus in which a nerve impulse passes inward from a receptor to a nerve center and thence outward to an effector (as a muscle or gland) without reaching the level of consciousness — compare HABIT **b** *pl* : the power of acting or responding with adequate speed [Latin *reflexus*, past participle of *reflectere* "to bend back"]

refraction: *1* light rays,
2 water

²reflex *adj* **1** : produced in reaction, resistance, or return **2** : of, relating to, or produced by a neural reflex ⟨*reflex* action⟩ — **re·flex·ly** *adv*

reflex arc *n* : the complete nervous path involved in a reflex

reflex camera *n* : a single- or double-lens camera in which the image formed by the focusing lens is reflected onto a usually ground-glass screen for viewing

re·flexed \'rē-,flekst, ri-'\ *adj* : bent or curved backward or downward ⟨*reflexed* petals⟩

re·flex·ion \ri-'flek-shən\ *chiefly British variant of* REFLECTION

¹re·flex·ive \ri-'flek-siv\ *adj* **1** : REFLEXED **2** : relating to, characterized by, or being a relation that exists between an entity and itself ⟨the relation "is equal to" is *reflexive* but the relation "is the parent of" is not⟩ **3** : of, relating to, or being an action directed back upon the doer or the grammatical subject ⟨*myself* in "I hurt myself" is a *reflexive* pronoun⟩ — **re·flex·ive·ly** *adv* — **re·flex·ive·ness** *n* — **re·flex·iv·i·ty** \,rē-,flek-'siv-ət-ē, ri-\ *n*

²reflexive *n* : a reflexive pronoun or verb

re·flux \'rē-,fləks\ *n* : a flowing back : EBB

re·for·est \rē-'fȯr-əst, 'rē-, -'fär-\ *vt* : to renew forest cover on by seeding or planting — **re·for·es·ta·tion** \rē-,fȯr-ə-'stā-shən, -,fär-\ *n*

¹re·form \ri-'fȯrm\ *vb* **1** : to make better by removal of faults ⟨*reform* the penal system⟩ **2** : to correct or improve one's own character or habits [Middle French *reformer*, from Latin *reformare*, from *re-* + *formare* "to form"] — **re·form·able** \-'fȯr-mə-bəl\ *adj*

²reform *n* **1** : improvement of what is bad or corrupt **2** : a removal or correction of an abuse, a wrong, or errors

re–form \rē-'fȯrm, 'rē-\ *vt* : to form or take form again

ref·or·ma·tion \,ref-ər-'mā-shən\ *n* **1** : the act of reforming : the state of being reformed **2** *cap* : a 16th century religious movement marked by rejection or modification of much of the Roman Catholic doctrine and practice and establishment of the Protestant churches — **ref·or·ma·tion·al** \-shnəl, -shən-l\ *adj*

re·for·ma·tive \ri-'fȯr-mət-iv\ *adj* : tending or inclined to reform

¹re·for·ma·to·ry \ri-'fȯr-mə-,tōr-ē, -,tȯr-\ *adj* : tending or intended to reform ⟨*reformatory* measures⟩

²reformatory *n, pl* **-ries** : a penal institution to which youthful or first offenders or women are committed for training and rehabilitation

re·formed *adj* **1** : changed for the better **2** *cap* : PROTESTANT; *esp* : of or relating to the Calvinist churches of continental Europe

reformed spelling *n* : any of several methods of spelling English words that use letters with more phonetic consistency than conventional spelling and usually discard some silent letters (as in *thoro* for thorough)

re·form·er \ri-'fȯr-mər\ *n* **1** : one that works for or urges reform **2** *cap* : a leader of the Reformation

re·form·ism \ri-'fȯr-,miz-əm\ *n* : a doctrine, policy, or movement of reform — **re·form·ist** \-məst\ *n*

Reform Judaism *n* : a 19th and 20th century development of Judaism marked by rationalization of belief, simplification of many observances, and affirmation of the religious rather than the national character of Judaism

reform school *n* : a reformatory for youthful offenders

re·fract \ri-'frakt\ *vt* : to subject to refraction [Latin *refractus*, past participle of *refringere* "to break open, break up, refract", from *re-* + *frangere* "to break"]

refracting telescope *n* : REFRACTOR

re·frac·tion \ri-'frak-shən\ *n* : the bending of a ray when it passes at an angle from one medium (as air) into another (as glass) in which its speed is different — **re·frac·tive** \-'frak-tiv\ *adj* — **re·frac·tiv·i·ty** \,rē-,frak-'tiv-ət-ē, ri-\ *n*

refractive index *n* : INDEX OF REFRACTION

re·frac·tor \ri-'frak-tər\ *n* : a telescope whose principal focusing element is usually an achromatic lens

¹re·frac·to·ry \ri-'frak-tə-rē, -trē\ *adj* **1** : resisting control or authority : STUBBORN ⟨a *refractory* child⟩ **2 a** : resistant to treatment **b** : unresponsive to stimulus **3** : difficult to fuse, corrode, or draw out; *esp* : capable of enduring high temperature [Latin *refractarius*, from *refragari* "to oppose"] SYN see UNRULY — **re·frac·to·ri·ly** \-tə-rə-lē, -trə-\ *adv* — **re·frac·to·ri·ness** \-tə-rē-nəs, -trē-\ *n*

²refractory *n, pl* **-ries** : something refractory; *esp* : a heat-resisting ceramic material

¹re·frain \ri-'frān\ *vt* : to hold oneself back from some often impulsive course of action ⟨*refrain* from laughing⟩ [Middle French *refraindre* "to restrain", from Latin *refringere* "to break up, check, refract"] — **re·frain·ment** \-mənt\ *n* □ SYN REFRAIN, ABSTAIN, FORBEAR mean to keep oneself from doing or indulging in something. REFRAIN suggests the checking of a momentary impulse or inclination ⟨*refrain* from smiling⟩ ABSTAIN implies deliberate renunciation or self-denial on principle ⟨*abstained* from alcohol in any form⟩ FORBEAR suggests self-restraint motivated by compassion, charity, or stoicism.

²refrain *n* : a regularly recurring phrase or verse especially at the end of each stanza of a poem or song : CHORUS; *also* : the melody of a refrain [Middle French, from *refraindre* "to resound", from Latin *refringere* "to break up, refract"]

re·fran·gi·ble \ri-'fran-jə-bəl\ *adj* : capable of being refracted [derived from Latin *refringere* "to refract"] — **re·fran·gi·bil·i·ty** \-,fran-jə-'bil-ət-ē\ *n* — **re·fran·gi·ble·ness** *n*

re·fresh \ri-'fresh\ *vb* **1** : to restore strength and animation to : REVIVE ⟨sleep *refreshes* the body⟩ **2 a** : to restore or maintain by renewing supply : REPLENISH **b** : STIMULATE ⟨let me *refresh* your memory⟩ **3** : to restore water to **4** : to take refreshment SYN see RENEW

re·fresh·en \-'fresh-ən\ *vt* : REFRESH 1, 2

re·fresh·er \ri-'fresh-ər\ *n* **1** : something that refreshes **2** : review or instruction designed especially to keep one up-to-date on professional developments

re·fresh·ing \-ing\ *adj* : serving to refresh; *esp* : agreeably stimulating because of freshness or newness — **re·fresh·ing·ly** \-ing-lē\ *adv*

re·fresh·ment \ri-'fresh-mənt\ *n* **1** : the act of refreshing : the state of being refreshed **2 a** : something that refreshes **b** *pl* : a light meal

re·frig·er·ant \ri-'frij-rənt, -ə-rənt\ *n* : a substance (as ice, ammonia, or carbon dioxide) used in refrigeration

re·frig·er·ate \ri-'frij-ə-,rāt\ *vt* : to make or keep cold or cool; *esp* : to freeze or chill (food) for preservation [Latin *refrigerare*, from *re-* + *frigerare* "to cool", from *frigor-, frigus* "cold"] — **re·frig·er·a·tion** \ri-,frij-ə-'rā-shən\ *n*

re·frig·er·a·tor \ri-'frij-ə-,rāt-ər\ *n* : a cabinet or room for keeping articles (as food) cool especially by means of a mechanical device

reft *past of* REAVE

re·fu·el \rē-'fyü-əl, 'rē-\ *vb* : to provide with or take on additional fuel

ref·uge \'ref-yüj, -,yüj\ *n* **1** : shelter or protection from danger or distress **2** : a place that provides shelter or protection ⟨a wildlife *refuge*⟩ [Middle French, from Latin *refugium*, from *refugere* "to escape", from *re-* + *fugere* "to flee"]

ref·u·gee \,ref-yu-'jē\ *n* : a person who flees for safety especially to a foreign country

re·ful·gence \ri-'ful-jəns, -'fəl-\ *n* : a radiant or resplendent quality or state : BRILLIANCE [Latin *refulgentia*, from *refulgēre* "to shine brightly", from *re-* + *fulgēre* "to shine"] — **re·ful·gent** \-jənt\ *adj*

¹re·fund \ri-'fənd, 'rē-,fənd\ *vt* : to return (money) in restitution or repayment [Latin *refundere*, literally, "to pour back", from *re-* + *fundere* "to pour"] — **re·fund·able** \-ə-bəl\ *adj*

²re·fund \'rē-,fənd\ *n* **1** : the act of refunding **2** : a sum refunded

³re·fund \rē-'fənd, 'rē-\ *vt* : to fund (a debt) again or anew

re·fur·bish \rē-'fər-bish, 'rē-\ *vt* : to brighten or freshen up : RENOVATE — **re·fur·bish·ment** \-mənt\ *n*

re·fus·al \ri-'fyü-zəl\ *n* **1** : the act of refusing **2** : the opportunity or right of refusing or taking before others

¹re·fuse \ri-'fyüz\ *vb* **1** : to decline to accept : REJECT ⟨*refused* the money⟩ **2 a** : to show or express positive unwillingness : fail deliberately ⟨*refused* to act⟩ **b** : DENY ⟨was *refused* entrance⟩ **3** : to withhold acceptance, compliance, or permission [Middle French *refuser*, from Latin *refusus*, past participle of *refundere* "to pour back"] — **re·fus·er** *n*

²ref·use \'ref-,yüs, -,yüz\ *n* **1** : worthless material **2** : RUBBISH, TRASH [Middle French *refus* "rejection", from *refuser* "to refuse"]

ref·u·ta·tion \,ref-yü-'tā-shən\ *n* : the act or process of refuting : DISPROOF

re·fute \ri-'fyüt\ *vt* : to prove wrong by argument or evidence : show to be false ⟨*refute* a witness's testimony⟩ [Latin *refutare*, literally, "to beat back"] — **re·fut·able** \-'fyüt-ə-bəl\ *adj* — **re·fut·ably** \-blē\ *adv* — **re·fut·er** *n*

re·gain \ri-'gān\ *vt* : to gain or reach again : RECOVER ⟨*regained* my health⟩

re·gal \'rē-gəl\ *adj* **1** : of, relating to, or suitable for a sovereign **2** : notably excellent or magnificent : SPLENDID [Latin *regalis*, from *reg-, rex* "king"] — **re·gal·i·ty** \ri-'gal-ət-ē\ *n* — **re·gal·ly** \'rē-gə-lē\ *adv*

re·gale \ri-'gāl\ *vb* **1** : to treat or entertain lavishly **2** : to give pleasure and amusement to ⟨*regaled* us with stories⟩ **3** : to feast oneself : FEED [French *régaler*, from

Middle French *regale* "party", from *re-* + *galer* "to have a good time"] — **re·gale·ment** \-mənt\ *n*

re·ga·lia \ri-'gāl-yə\ *n sing or pl* **1** : the emblems and symbols (as the crown and scepter) of royalty **2** : the insignia of an office or order **3** : special or official dress [Medieval Latin, from Latin *regalis* "regal"]

¹re·gard \ri-'gärd\ *n* **1 a** : CONSIDERATION 1, HEED **b** : LOOK 1, GAZE **2 a** : the worth or estimation in which something is held **b** (1) : a feeling of respect and affection : ESTEEM (2) *pl* : friendly greetings implying such feeling ⟨give them my *regards*⟩ **3** : REFERENCE, RESPECT ⟨this is in *regard* to your unpaid balance⟩ **4** : an aspect to be considered ⟨nothing to worry about in that *regard*⟩ [Middle French, from *regarder* "to look back at, regard", from *re-* + *garder* "to guard, look at"]

²regard *vt* **1** : to pay attention to **2 a** : to show respect or consideration for **b** : to hold in high esteem **3** : to look at steadily or attentively **4** : to take into consideration or account **5** : CONSIDER 3 ⟨*regarded* you as a friend⟩ □ SYN REGARD, RESPECT, ESTEEM, ADMIRE mean to recognize the worth of. REGARD is somewhat formal and requires some qualification ⟨one highly *regarded* in banking circles⟩ RESPECT implies having a good opinion of without suggesting real liking or warmth of feeling; ESTEEM implies high evaluation together with warmth of feeling; ADMIRE implies enthusiastic and often uncritical appreciation. — **as regards** : with respect to : REGARDING

re·gard·ful \ri-'gärd-fəl\ *adj* **1** : OBSERVANT 2, HEEDFUL **2** : full of or expressing regard : RESPECTFUL — **re·gard·ful·ly** \-fə-lē\ *adv* — **re·gard·ful·ness** *n*

re·gard·ing *prep* : with respect to : CONCERNING

¹re·gard·less \ri-'gärd-ləs\ *adj* : having or taking no regard : HEEDLESS — **re·gard·less·ly** *adv* — **re·gard·less·ness** *n*

²regardless *adv* : despite everything ⟨we are going there *regardless*⟩

re·gat·ta \ri-'gät-ə, -'gat-\ *n* : a boat race or a series of such races [Italian]

¹re·gen·cy \'rē-jən-sē\ *n, pl* **-cies** **1** : the office, jurisdiction, or government of a regent or body of regents **2** : the period of rule of a regent or body of regents

²regency *adj, often cap* : of, relating to, or resembling the furniture or the dress of the regency (1811–20) of George, Prince of Wales

re·gen·er·a·cy \ri-'jen-rə-sē, -ə-rə-\ *n* : the state of being regenerated

¹re·gen·er·ate \ri-'jen-rət, -ə-rət\ *adj* : having been regenerated; *esp* : spiritually reborn or converted — **re·gen·er·ate·ly** *adv* — **re·gen·er·ate·ness** *n*

²re·gen·er·ate \ri-'jen-ə-,rāt\ *vb* **1** : to cause to be reborn spiritually **2** : to reform radically for the better ⟨*regenerating* criminals⟩ **3** : to generate or produce anew; *esp* : to renew (a lost or damaged body part) by a new growth of tissue **4** : to restore to original strength or properties — **re·gen·er·a·tor** \-,rāt-ər\ *n*

re·gen·er·a·tion \ri-,jen-ə-'rā-shən, ,rē-\ *n* **1** : an act or the process of regenerating : the state of being regenerated **2** : spiritual renewal or revival

re·gen·er·a·tive \ri-'jen-ə-,rāt-iv\ *adj* **1** : of, relating to, or marked by regeneration **2** : tending to regenerate

re·gent \'rē-jənt\ *n* **1** : one who governs a kingdom during the minority, absence, or disability of the sovereign **2** : a member of a governing board (as of a state university) [Medieval Latin *regens*, from Latin *regere* "to direct, rule"] — **regent** *adj*

reg·gae \'reg-,ā, 'rā-,gā\ *n* : popular music of Jamaican origin that combines native styles with elements of U.S. black popular music and is performed at moderate tempos with the accent on the offbeat [origin unknown]

reg·i·cide \'rej-ə-,sīd\ *n* **1** : one who murders a king or assists in his death **2** : the murdering of a king [Latin *reg-, rex* "king"] — **reg·i·cid·al** \,rej-ə-'sīd-l\ *adj*

\ə\ abut   \ng\ sing
\ər\ further   \ō\ bone
\a\ mat   \ò\ saw
\ā\ take   \òi\ coin
\ä\ cot, cart   \th\ thin
\au̇\ out   \t͟h\ this
\ch\ chin   \ü\ food
\e\ pet   \u̇\ foot
\ē\ easy   \y\ yet
\g\ go   \yü\ few
\i\ tip   \yu̇\ cure
\ī\ life   \zh\ vision
\j\ job

re·gime also **ré·gime** \rā-'zhēm, ri-\ n **I a :** REGIMEN 1 **b :** a regular pattern of occurrence or action **2 a :** mode of rule or management **b :** a form of government ⟨a socialist *regime*⟩ **c :** a government in power **d :** a period of rule ⟨during the last *regime*⟩ [French *régime,* from Latin *regimen* "rule, guidance"]

reg·i·men \'rej-ə-mən, -,men\ n **I :** a systematic course of treatment ⟨a strict dietary *regimen*⟩ **2 :** REGIME 2b [Latin, "rule", from *regere* "to rule"]

¹reg·i·ment \'rej-mənt, -ə-mənt\ n **:** a military unit consisting of a number of battalions [Middle French, "rule, government", from Late Latin *regimentum,* from Latin *regere* "to rule"] — **reg·i·men·tal** \,rej-ə-'ment-l\ adj — **reg·i·men·tal·ly** \-l-ē\ adv

²reg·i·ment \'rej-ə-,ment\ vt **I :** to organize rigidly so as to regulate or control **2 :** to subject to order or uniformity — **reg·i·men·ta·tion** \,rej-ə-mən-'tā-shən, -,men-\ n

reg·i·men·tals \,rej-ə-'ment-lz\ n pl **I :** a regimental uniform **2 :** military dress

re·gion \'rē-jən\ n **I :** an administrative area, division, or district **2 a :** an often indefinite part, portion, or area ⟨cloudy *regions* of the sky⟩; also **:** VICINITY ⟨a pain in the *region* of the heart⟩ **b :** a broad continuous area (as of the earth) ⟨arctic *regions*⟩ **3 :** FIELD 2 **4 :** a set of points any two points of which can be connected by a line lying wholly within the set together with none, some, or all of the points on its boundary [Middle French, from Latin *regio,* from *regere* "to direct, rule"]

re·gion·al \'rēj-nəl, -ən-l\ adj **I :** of, relating to, or characteristic of a region ⟨a *regional* dialect⟩ **2 :** affecting a particular region **:** LOCAL ⟨*regional* pain⟩ — **re·gion·al·ly** \-ē\ adv

re·gion·al·ism \'rēj-nəl-,iz-əm, -ən-l-\ n **I :** consciousness of and loyalty to a distinct geographical region **2 :** emphasis on regional locale and characteristics in art or literature — **re·gion·al·ist** \-əst\ n or adj — **re·gion·al·is·tic** \,rēj-nəl-'is-tik, -ən-l-\ adj

¹reg·is·ter \'rej-ə-stər\ n **I a :** a written record containing regular entries of items or details **b :** a book for such a record ⟨a *register* of voters⟩ **2 a :** a set of organ pipes of like quality **:** STOP **b :** the range or a part of the range of a human voice or a musical instrument comprising tones similarly produced or of the same quality **3 :** a device (as in a floor or a wall) usually with a grille and shutters that regulate the flow of heated air from a furnace **4 :** REGISTRATION, REGISTRY ⟨a port of *register*⟩ **5 a :** an automatic device registering a number or a quantity **b :** a number or quantity so registered **6 :** a condition of correct alignment or proper relative position [Middle French *registre,* from Medieval Latin *registrum,* from Late Latin *regesta,* pl., "register", from Latin *regerere* "to bring back, record", from *re-* + *gerere* "to carry"]

²register vb **reg·is·tered; reg·is·ter·ing** \-stə-ring, -string\ **I a :** to make or secure official entry of in a register **:** RECORD ⟨*register* a deed⟩ **b :** to enroll formally especially as a voter or student **c :** to record automatically ⟨the thermometer *registered* zero⟩ **2 :** to make or adjust so as to correspond exactly **3 :** to obtain special protection for (a piece of mail) by prepayment of a fee **4 :** to convey an impression of ⟨your face *registered* fear⟩ **5 :** to be in correct alignment or register **6 :** to make an impression ⟨the name didn't *register*⟩

³register n **:** REGISTRAR

reg·is·tered adj **I :** having the owner's name entered in a register ⟨a *registered* security⟩ **2 :** recorded on the basis of pedigree or breed characteristics in the studbook of a breed association

registered nurse n **:** a graduate trained nurse licensed by a state authority

reg·is·tra·ble \'rej-ə-stə-rə-bəl, -strə-bəl\ adj **:** that can be registered

reg·is·trant \'rej-ə-strənt\ n **:** one that registers or is registered

reg·is·trar \'rej-ə-,strär\ n **:** an official recorder or keeper of records [Middle French *registreur,* from *registrer* "to register", from Medieval Latin *registrare,* from *registrum* "register"]

reg·is·tra·tion \,rej-ə-'strā-shən\ n **I :** the act of registering **2 :** an entry in a register **3 :** the number of individuals registered **:** ENROLLMENT **4 :** a document certifying an act of registering ⟨an automobile *registration*⟩

reg·is·try \'rej-ə-strē\ n, pl **-tries I :** REGISTRATION 3, ENROLLMENT **2 :** a ship's nationality as proved by its entry in a register **3 :** a place of registration **4 :** an official record book or an entry in one

reg·nal \'reg-nl\ adj **:** of or relating to a reign; esp **:** calculated from a monarch's accession to the throne ⟨during the second *regnal* year⟩ [Medieval Latin *regnalis,* from Latin *regnum* "reign"]

reg·nant \'reg-nənt\ adj **I :** exercising rule ⟨the queen *regnant*⟩ **2 :** having the chief power [Latin *regnare* "to reign", from *regnum* "reign"]

reg·o·lith \'reg-ə-,lith\ n **:** MANTLEROCK [Greek *rhēgos* "blanket" + English *-lith*]

¹re·gress \'rē-,gres\ n **I :** an act or the privilege of going or coming back **2 :** REENTRY 1 [Latin *regressus,* from *regredi* 'to go back", from *re-* + *gradi* "to go"]

²re·gress \ri-'gres\ vb **:** to go or cause to go back especially to a former level or condition — **re·gres·sor** \-'gres-ər\ n

re·gres·sion \ri-'gresh-ən\ n **:** an act or the fact of regressing: as **a :** progressive decline of something (as a manifestation of disease) **b :** gradual loss of differentiation and function by a body part **c :** reversion of thought or behavior to that characteristic of an earlier level of development

re·gres·sive \ri-'gres-iv\ adj **I :** of, relating to, or tending toward regression **2 :** decreasing in rate as the base increases ⟨a *regressive* tax⟩ — **re·gres·sive·ly** adv — **re·gres·sive·ness** n

¹re·gret \ri-'gret\ vb **re·gret·ted; re·gret·ting I a :** to mourn the loss or death of **b :** to miss very much **2 :** to be very sorry for **3 :** to experience regret [Middle French *regreter*] — **re·gret·ta·ble** \-'gret-ə-bəl\ adj — **re·gret·ta·bly** \-blē\ adv — **re·gret·ter** n

²regret n **I :** sorrow caused by circumstances beyond one's ability to remedy **2 a :** an expression of distressing emotion (as sorrow or disappointment) **b** pl **:** a note politely declining an invitation — **re·gret·ful** \-'gret-fəl\ adj — **re·gret·ful·ly** \-fə-lē\ adv — **re·gret·ful·ness** n

re·group \rē-'grüp, 'rē-\ vb **:** to form into a new grouping — **re·group·ment** \-mənt\ n

¹reg·u·lar \'reg-yə-lər\ adj **I :** belonging to a religious order ⟨*regular* clergy⟩ **2 a :** formed, built, arranged, or ordered according to an established rule, law, principle, or type **b** (1) **:** being both equilateral and equiangular ⟨a *regular* polygon⟩ (2) **:** having faces that are congruent regular polygons and all the polyhedral angles congruent ⟨a *regular* polyhedron⟩ **c :** perfectly symmetrical or even; esp **:** having radial symmetry ⟨*regular* flowers⟩ **d :** having or constituting an isometric system ⟨*regular* crystals⟩ **3 a :** ORDERLY, METHODICAL ⟨*regular* habits⟩ **b :** recurring or functioning at fixed or uniform intervals **4 a :** following established or prescribed usages, rules, or discipline **b :** NORMAL 2, CORRECT: as (1) **:** COMPLETE, ABSOLUTE ⟨a *regular* scoundrel⟩ (2) **:** thinking or behaving in an acceptable manner **c :** conforming to the normal or usual manner of inflection ⟨*regular* verbs⟩ **5 :** of, relating to, or constituting a regular army [Middle French *reguler,* from Late Latin *regularis,* from Latin *regula* "straightedge, rule"] — **reg·u·lar·i·ty** \,reg-yə-'lar-ət-ē\ n — **reg·u·lar·ly** \'reg-yə-lər-lē\ adv □ SYN NORMAL, TYPICAL: REGULAR stresses conformity to a rule, standard, or pattern; NORMAL implies lack of deviation from what has been established as the most usual or expected; TYPICAL implies showing all the important traits of a type, class, or group and may suggest lack of strong individuality.

²**regular** *n* : one who is regular: as **a** : one of the regular clergy **b** : a soldier in a regular army **c** : a player on an athletic team who usually starts every game

regular army *n* : a permanently organized body that is the standing army of a state

reg·u·lar·ize \'reg-yə-lə-ˌrīz\ *vt* : to make regular — **reg·u·lar·iz·er** *n*

reg·u·late \'reg-yə-ˌlāt\ *vt* **1 a** : to govern or direct according to rule **b** : to bring under the control of law or established authority **2** : to reduce to order, method, or uniformity 〈*regulated* their habits〉 **3** : to adjust for accurate functioning 〈*regulate* a clock〉 [Late Latin *regulare*, from Latin *regula* "rule"] — **reg·u·la·tive** \-ˌlāt-iv\ *adj* — **reg·u·la·tor** \-ˌlāt-ər\ *n* — **reg·u·la·to·ry** \-lə-ˌtōr-ē, -ˌtȯr-\ *adj*

¹**reg·u·la·tion** \ˌreg-yə-'lā-shən\ *n* **1** : the act of regulating : the state of being regulated **2 a** : an authoritative rule dealing with details **b** : a rule or order having the force of law issued by an executive authority SYN see LAW

²**regulation** *adj* : conforming to regulations : OFFICIAL

regulator gene *n* : a gene controlling the production of a genetic repressor

Reg·u·lus \'reg-yə-ləs\ *n* : a bright star in the constellation Leo [Latin, "petty king", from *reg-*, *rex* "king"]

re·gur·gi·tate \rē-'gər-jə-ˌtāt, 'rē-\ *vb* : to throw or be thrown back or out again 〈*regurgitate* undigested food〉 [Medieval Latin *regurgitare*, from Latin *re-* + Late Latin *gurgitare* "to engulf", from Latin *gurgit-*, *gurges* "whirlpool"] — **re·gur·gi·ta·tion** \rē-ˌgər-jə-'tā-shən\ *n*

re·ha·bil·i·tate \ˌrē-ə-'bil-ə-ˌtāt, ˌrē-hə-'bil-\ *vt* **1 a** : to restore to a former status : REINSTATE **b** : to restore to good repute : reestablish the good name of **2 a** : to restore to a state of efficiency, good management, or repair **b** : to restore to a condition of health or useful and constructive activity [Medieval Latin *rehabilitare*, derived from Latin *re-* + *habilitas* "aptness, ability", from *habilis* "handy, apt", from *habēre* "to have, hold"] — **re·ha·bil·i·ta·tion** \-ˌbil-ə-'tā-shən\ *n* — **re·ha·bil·i·ta·tive** \-'bil-ə-ˌtāt-iv\ *adj*

re·hash \rē-'hash, 'rē-\ *vt* : to present or use (as an argument) again in another form without substantial change or improvement — **re·hash** \'rē-ˌhash\ *n*

re·hears·al \ri-'hər-səl\ *n* : a rehearsing of something: as **a** : a private performance or practice session preparatory to a public appearance **b** : a practice exercise : TRIAL

re·hearse \ri-'hərs\ *vb* **1 a** : to say again : REPEAT **b** : to recount in order : ENUMERATE **2 a** : to practice (as a play) for public performance **b** : to train or make proficient (as actors) by rehearsal **3** : to engage in a rehearsal [Middle French *rehercier*, literally, "to harrow again", from *re-* "re-" + *hercier* "to harrow", from *herce* "harrow", from Latin *hirpex*] — **re·hears·er** *n*

re·hy·drate \rē-'hī-ˌdrāt, 'rē-\ *vt* : to restore fluid lost in dehydration to — **re·hy·dra·tion** \ˌrē-ˌhī-'drā-shən\ *n*

reichs·mark \'rīk-ˌsmärk\ *n, pl* **reichsmarks** *also* **reichsmark** : the German mark from 1925 to 1948 [German, from *reich* "empire" + *mark* "mark"]

¹**reign** \'rān\ *n* **1 a** : royal authority : SOVEREIGNTY **b** : the domination or influence of one resembling a monarch **2** : the time during which a monarch rules [Old French *regne*, from Latin *regnum*, from *reg-*, *rex* "king"]

²**reign** *vi* **1 a** : to have or exercise sovereign power : RULE **b** : to hold office as chief of state with only slight governing powers **2** : to exercise authority in the manner of a monarch **3** : to be predominant or prevalent

reign of terror : a period marked by violence that is often committed by those in power and produces widespread terror

re·im·burse \ˌrē-əm-'bərs\ *vt* : to pay back : REPAY [*re-* + obsolete *imburse* "to put in the pocket", from Middle French *embourser*, from Old French *em-* "en-" + *borser* "to get money", from *borse* "purse", from Medieval Latin *bursa*] — **re·im·burs·able** \-'bər-sə-bəl\ *adj* — **re·im·burse·ment** \-'bərs-mənt\ *n*

¹**rein** \'rān\ *n* **1** : a line or strap fastened to a bit on each side for controlling an animal — usually used in pl. **2 a** : a restraining influence : CHECK 〈kept the child under a tight *rein*〉 **b** : controlling or guiding power 〈seize the *reins* of government〉 **3** : complete freedom : SCOPE — usually used in the phrase *give rein to* [Middle French *rene*, derived from Latin *retinēre* "to hold back, restrain", from *re-* + *tenēre* "to hold"]

²**rein** *vb* : to check, control, or stop by or as if by reins

re·in·car·nate \ˌrē-ən-'kär-ˌnāt\ *vt* : to give a new or different body or form to

re·in·car·na·tion \ˌrē-ˌin-ˌkär-'nā-shən\ *n* **1** : the action of reincarnating : the state of being reincarnated **2** : rebirth in new bodies or forms of life; *esp* : a rebirth of a soul in a new human body

rein·deer \'rān-ˌdiər\ *n, pl* **reindeer** *also* **reindeers** : any of several large deer of northern regions having antlers in both sexes and including some used as meat and draft animals [Middle English *reindere*, from Old Norse *hreinn* "reindeer" + Middle English *dere* "deer"]

reindeer

reindeer moss *n* : a gray, erect, and much-branched lichen of northern and arctic regions important as reindeer food

re·in·fec·tion \ˌrē-ən-'fek-shən\ *n* : infection following another infection of the same type — **re·in·fect** \-'fekt\ *vt*

re·in·force \ˌrē-ən-'fōrs, -'fȯrs\ *vt* **1** : to strengthen with new force, assistance, material, or support 〈*reinforce* a wall〉 〈*reinforce* an argument〉 **2** : to strengthen with additional troops or ships **3** : to stimulate (as a student) so as to increase the frequency of a desired response; *also* : to increase the frequency of (a response) by such stimulation [*re-* + *inforce*, alteration of *enforce*]

reinforced concrete *n* : concrete in which metal rods, bars, or mesh are embedded for strengthening

re·in·force·ment \ˌrē-ən-'fōr-smənt, -'fȯr-\ *n* **1** : the action of reinforcing : the state of being reinforced **2** : something that reinforces

reins \'rānz\ *n pl* **1** : the kidneys or the region thereof **2** : the seat of the feelings or passions [Middle French, from Latin *renes*]

re·in·state \ˌrē-ən-'stāt\ *vt* : to restore to possession or to a former position, condition, or capacity 〈*reinstate* an official〉 — **re·in·state·ment** \-mənt\ *n*

re·in·ter·pret \ˌrē-ən-'tər-prət, *rapid* -pət\ *vt* : to interpret again; *esp* : to give a new or different interpretation to — **re·in·ter·pre·ta·tion** \-ˌtər-prə-'tā-shən, *rapid* -pə-'tā-\ *n*

re·in·vest \ˌrē-ən-'vest\ *vt* **1** : to invest again or anew **2 a** : to invest (as income from investments) in additional securities **b** : to invest (as earnings) in a business rather than distribute as dividends or profits — **re·in·vest·ment** \-'vest-mənt, -'ves-\ *n*

re·is·sue \rē-'ish-ü, 'rē-\ *vb* : to issue again 〈*reissued* the book in paperback form〉 — **reissue** *n*

re·it·er·ate \rē-'it-ə-ˌrāt\ *vt* : to say or do over again or repeatedly SYN see REPEAT — **re·it·er·a·tion** \rē-ˌit-ə-'rā-shən\ *n* — **re·it·er·a·tive** \rē-'it-ə-ˌrāt-iv, -rət-\ *adj* — **re·it·er·a·tive·ly** *adv* — **re·it·er·a·tive·ness** *ly*

¹**re·ject** \ri-'jekt\ *vt* **1** : to refuse to accept, submit to, or deal with **2** : DISCARD **2 3** : to refuse to grant or consider **4** : to subject to immunological rejection 〈*reject* a heart transplant〉 [Latin *rejectus*, past participle of *reicere* "to reject", from *re-* + *jacere* "to throw"]

\ə\ abut   \ng\ sing
\ər\ further   \ō\ bone
\a\ mat   \ȯ\ saw
\ā\ take   \ȯi\ coin
\ä\ cot, cart   \th\ thin
\au̇\ out   \th̄\ this
\ch\ chin   \ü\ food
\e\ pet   \u̇\ foot
\ē\ easy   \y\ yet
\g\ go   \yü\ few
\i\ tip   \yu̇\ cure
\ī\ life   \zh\ vision
\j\ job

□ SYN **REJECT, REPUDIATE, SPURN** mean to refuse to accept, receive, or consider something proposed or offered. **REJECT** stresses a casting back on the source and implies firmness and finality ⟨*rejected* all proposals for a truce⟩ **REPUDIATE** implies a usually scornful and public thrusting away as unworthy, untrue, or unjustified ⟨now *repudiate* former beliefs⟩ **SPURN** implies disdain or contempt more strongly than **REJECT** ⟨*spurned* all marriage proposals⟩

²**re·ject** \'rē-,jekt\ *n* : a rejected person or thing

re·jec·tion \ri-'jek-shən\ *n* **1 a** : the act of rejecting : the state of being rejected **b** : the immunological process of sloughing off foreign tissue or a transplanted organ **2** : something rejected

re·joice \ri-'jȯis\ *vb* **1** : to give joy to ⟨news that *rejoices* the heart⟩ **2** : to feel joy ⟨*rejoice* over a friend's good fortune⟩ [Middle French *rejoiss-*, stem of *rejoir* "to rejoice", from *re-* "re-" + *joir* "to rejoice", from Latin *gaudēre*] — **re·joic·er** *n* — **re·joic·ing·ly** \-'jȯi-sing-lē\ *adv*

re·joic·ing \-'jȯi-sing\ *n* **1** : the action of one that rejoices **2** : an instance, occasion, or expression of joy : **FESTIVITY**

re·join *vt* **1** \rē-'jȯin, 'rē-\ : to join again : return to ⟨*rejoined* my family after a trip⟩ **2** \ri-\ : **ANSWER 1, REPLY**

re·join·der \ri-'jȯin-dər\ *n* : **REPLY**; *esp* : an answer to a reply [Middle English *rejoiner*, from Middle French *rejoindre* "to rejoin", from *re-* "re-" + *joindre* "to join"]

re·ju·ve·nate \ri-'jü-və-,nāt\ *vt* : to make young or youthful again : give new vigor to [*re-* + Latin *juvenis* "young"] — **re·ju·ve·na·tion** \-,jü-və-'nā-shən\ *n* — **re·ju·ve·na·tor** \-'jü-və-,nāt-ər\ *n*

¹**re·lapse** \ri-'laps, 'rē-,\ *n* : the act or fact of relapsing; *esp* : a recurrence of illness after a period of improvement [Latin *relapsus,* past participle of *relabi* "to slide back", from *re-* + *labi* "to slide"]

²**relapse** *vi* **1** : to slip or fall back into a former worse state **2** : **SINK, SUBSIDE** ⟨*relapsed* into thought⟩ — **re·laps·er** *n*

relapsing fever *n* : an epidemic disease marked by recurring high fever lasting five to seven days and caused by a spirochete transmitted by the bites of lice or ticks

re·late \ri-'lāt\ *vb* **1** : to give an account of : **NARRATE** ⟨*relate* a story⟩ **2** : to show or establish a relationship between ⟨*relate* cause and effect⟩ **3** : to have relationship or connection : **REFER** **4** : to have meaningful social relationships [Latin *relatus,* past participle of *referre* "to carry back, refer"] — **re·lat·able** \-'lāt-ə-bəl\ *adj* — **re·lat·er** *or* **re·la·tor** \-'lāt-ər\ *n*

re·lat·ed *adj* : belonging to the same group on the basis of known or determinable qualities ⟨*related* phenomena⟩: as **a** (1) : having a common ancestry (2) : belonging to the same family by blood or marriage **b** : having close harmonic connection ⟨*related* chords⟩ — **re·lat·ed·ness** *n*

re·la·tion \ri-'lā-shən\ *n* **1** : the act of telling or recounting : **ACCOUNT** **2** : an aspect or quality (as resemblance) that connects two or more things or parts as being or belonging or working together or as being of the same kind **3 a** : **RELATIVE 3** **b** : relationship by blood or marriage : **KINSHIP** **4** : **REFERENCE 2, RESPECT** ⟨in *relation* to this⟩ **5** : the attitude which two or more individuals assume toward one another ⟨race *relations*⟩ **6 a** : the state of being mutually or reciprocally interested (as in social or commercial matters) **b** *pl* (1) : **AFFAIR 1a, DEALINGS** ⟨foreign *relations*⟩ (2) : **INTERCOURSE 1** — **re·la·tion·al** \-shnəl, -shən-l\ *adj*

re·la·tion·ship \-shən-,ship\ *n* **1** : the state or character of being related or interrelated **2** : **KINSHIP**; *also* : a specific instance or type of this **3** : a state of affairs existing between those having shared dealings

¹**rel·a·tive** \'rel-ət-iv\ *n* **1** : a word referring grammatically to an antecedent **2** : a thing having a relation to or connection with or necessary dependence upon another thing **3** : an individual connected with another by blood or marriage

²**relative** *adj* **1** : introducing a subordinate clause that qualifies an expressed or implied antecedent ⟨*relative* pronouns⟩; *also* : introduced by a connective having such an antecedent ⟨a *relative* clause⟩ **2** : **RELEVANT, PERTINENT** ⟨questions *relative* to the topic⟩ **3** : not absolute or independent : **COMPARATIVE** ⟨lived in *relative* isolation⟩ **4** : having the same key signature — used of major and minor keys and scales **5** : expressed as the ratio of the specified quantity (as an error in measuring) to the total magnitude (as the value of a measured quantity) or to the mean of all the quantities involved — **rel·a·tive·ly** *adj* — **rel·a·tive·ness** *n*

relative error *n* : the ratio of an error in a measured or calculated quantity to the magnitude of that quantity

relative humidity *n* : the ratio of the amount of water vapor actually present in the air to the greatest amount possible at the same temperature

relative to *prep* : with regard to : in connection with

rel·a·tiv·i·ty \,rel-ə-'tiv-ət-ē\ *n* **1** : the quality or state of being relative; *esp* : dependence on something else **2 a** : a theory in physics that equates mass and energy and that describes changes in mass, dimension, and time which are related to velocities approaching the speed of light **b** : an extension of the theory to include a discussion of gravitation and related acceleration phenomena — **rel·a·tiv·ist** \'rel-ət-iv-əst\ *n* — **rel·a·tiv·is·tic** \,rel-ət-iv-'is-tik\ *adj* — **rel·a·tiv·is·ti·cal·ly** \-ti-kə-lē, -klē\ *adv*

re·lax \ri-'laks\ *vb* **1** : to make or become less tense or rigid : **EASE** **2** : to make or become less severe or rigid ⟨*relax* immigration laws⟩ **3** : to cast off social restraint, nervous tension, anxiety, or suspicion ⟨couldn't *relax* in crowds⟩ **4** : to seek rest or recreation [Latin *relaxare,* from *re-* + *laxare* "to loosen", from *laxus* "loose"] — **re·lax·er** *n*

¹**re·lax·ant** \ri-'lak-sənt\ *adj* : producing relaxation

²**relaxant** *n* : a relaxing agent; *esp* : a drug causing muscular relaxation

re·lax·a·tion \,rē-,lak-'sā-shən, ri-\ *n* **1** : the act or fact of relaxing or being relaxed **2** : a relaxing state, activity, or pastime **3** : the lengthening that characterizes inactive muscles

re·laxed \ri-'lakst\ *adj* **1** : lacking in precision or strictness **2** : set at rest or at ease **3** : easy of manner : **INFORMAL** — **re·laxed·ly** \-'lak-səd-lē, -'laks-tlē\ *adv* — **re·laxed·ness** \-'lak-səd-nəs, -'lakst-nəs, -'laks-nəs\ *n*

re·lax·in \ri-'lak-sən\ *n* : a hormone of the corpus luteum that relaxes pelvic ligaments and facilitates childbirth

¹**re·lay** \'rē-,lā\ *n* **1** : a fresh supply (as of horses or men) arranged to relieve others at various stages especially of a journey or race **2 a** : a race between teams in which each team member successively covers a specified portion of the course or of the total distance **b** : one of the divisions of a relay **3 a** : an electromagnetic device in which the opening or closing of a circuit operates another device **b** : **SERVOMOTOR** **4** : the act of passing along by stages; *also* : one of such stages [Middle French *relais,* from *relaier* "to relay", from *re-* "re-" + *laier* "to leave", derived from Latin *laxare* "to loosen"]

²**re·lay** \'rē-,lā, ri-'lā\ *vt* **re·layed; re·lay·ing** **1** : to place in or provide with relays **2** : to pass along by relays **3** : to control or operate by a relay

³**re·lay** \rē-'lā, 'rē-\ *vt* **-laid** \-'lād\; **-lay·ing** : to lay again ⟨*relay* the patio flagstones⟩

¹**re·lease** \ri-'lēs\ *vt* **1** : to set free from restraint, confinement, or servitude **2** : to relieve from something that holds, burdens, or oppresses **3** : to give up in favor of another ⟨*release* a claim to property⟩ **4** : to give

permission for publication, performance, exhibition, or sale of at a specified date [Old French *relessier*, from Latin *relaxare* "to relax"] SYN see FREE — **re·leas·able** \-'lē-sə-bəl\ *adj*

²**release** *n* 1 : relief or deliverance from sorrow, suffering, or trouble 2 a : a discharge from an obligation (as a debt) b : a relinquishment of a right or claim; *esp* : a conveyance of a right in real property to another c : a document embodying a release 3 a : the act or an instance of liberating or freeing (as from physical restraint) b : the act or manner of ending a speech sound 4 : the state of being freed 5 : a device adapted to hold or release a mechanism as required 6 a : the act of permitting performance or publication b : the matter released; *esp* : a statement prepared for the press (a news *release*)

re·leas·er \ri-'lē-sər\ *n* : one that releases; *esp* : a stimulus that serves as the initiator of complex reflex behavior

rel·e·gate \'rel-ə-,gāt\ *vt* 1 : EXILE, BANISH 2 : to remove or dismiss to a less important or prominent place (*relegate* old books to the attic) 3 : to submit to someone or something for appropriate action [Latin *relegare*, from *re-* + *legare* "to send with a commission", from *leg-, lex* "law"] — **rel·e·ga·tion** \,rel-ə-'gā-shən\ *n*

re·lent \ri-'lent\ *vi* 1 : to become less severe, harsh, or strict 2 : to let up : SLACKEN [Middle English *relenten*]

re·lent·less \-ləs\ *adj* : mercilessly hard or harsh — **re·lent·less·ly** *adv* — **re·lent·less·ness** *n*

rel·e·vance \'rel-ə-vəns\ *also* **rel·e·van·cy** \-vən-sē\ *n, pl* **-vanc·es** *also* **-van·cies** : relation to the matter at hand : PERTINENCE

rel·e·vant \-vənt\ *adj* : having relevance (a *relevant* question) [Medieval Latin *relevans*, from Latin *relevare* "to raise up, relieve"] — **rel·e·vant·ly** *adv*

re·li·abil·i·ty \ri-,lī-ə-'bil-ət-ē\ *n* : the quality or state of being reliable

re·li·able \ri-'lī-ə-bəl\ *adj* : that can be relied on : DEPENDABLE — **re·li·able·ness** *n* — **re·li·ably** \-blē\ *adv*

re·li·ance \ri-'lī-əns\ *n* 1 : the act of relying 2 : the condition or attitude of one who relies : DEPENDENCE 3 : something or someone relied on

re·li·ant \-ənt\ *adj* : having reliance on something or someone : TRUSTING — **re·li·ant·ly** *adv*

rel·ic \'rel-ik\ *n* 1 : an object venerated because of association with a saint or martyr 2 : a surviving ruin or remnant (*relics* of ancient cities) 3 : a trace of some past or outmoded practice, custom, or belief : VESTIGE [Old French *relique*, derived from Late Latin *reliquiae* "remains of a martyr", from Latin, "remains", from *relinquere* "to leave behind"]

rel·ict \'rel-ikt\ *n* 1 : WIDOW 2 : a persistent remnant of an otherwise extinct flora or fauna [derived from Latin *relictus*, past participle of *relinquere* "to leave behind"]

re·lief \ri-'lēf\ *n* 1 a : removal or lightening of something oppressive, painful, or distressing b : aid in the form of money or necessities for the poor, aged, or handicapped c : military assistance to a post or force in extreme danger d : means of breaking monotony or boredom : DIVERSION 2 a : release from sentry or other duty b : one that takes the place of another on duty 3 : legal remedy or redress 4 a : projection from the background (as of figures in sculpture) b : a work of art with such raised figures c : vividness or sharpness of outline due to contrast (as of color or shading) 5 : the elevations or inequalities of a land surface [Middle French, from *relever* "to relieve"]

relief map *n* : a map representing topographic relief

relief pitcher *n* : a baseball pitcher who takes over for another during a game

re·lieve \ri-'lēv\ *vb* 1 : to free from pain, discomfort, or distress : give aid or help to (*relieve* the poor) (*relieved* by the news) 2 : to release from a post or duty espe-

cially by taking the place of (*relieve* a sentry) 3 : to remove or lessen the monotony of (a black dress *relieved* by a white collar) 4 : to put in or stand out in relief : give prominence to or set off by contrast (as in sculpture or painting) [Middle French *relever* "to raise up, relieve", from Latin *relevare*, from *re-* + *levare* "to raise"] — **re·liev·er** *n* □ SYN RELIEVE, ALLEVIATE, LIGHTEN mean to make something less grievous or more bearable. RELIEVE implies either removing entirely or lifting enough of a burden to make it tolerable; ALLEVIATE suggests temporary or partial lessening of pain or distress; LIGHTEN implies reducing a burdensome or depressing weight (the good news *lightened* their minds)

re·li·gion \ri-'lij-ən\ *n* 1 a : the service and worship of God or the supernatural b : belief in or devotion to religious faith or observance c : the state of a religious 2 : a set or system of religious attitudes, beliefs, and practices 3 : a cause, principle, or system of beliefs held to with zeal and faith [Latin *religio*]

re·li·gion·ist \ri-'lij-nəst, -ə-nəst\ *n* : a person adhering to a religion

¹**re·li·gious** \ri-'lij-əs\ *adj* 1 a : devoted to God or to the powers or principles believed to govern life (a very *religious* person) b : belonging to a religious order (a *religious* house) 2 : of or relating to religion (*religious* beliefs) 3 : DEPENDABLE, FAITHFUL SYN see DEVOUT — **re·li·gious·ly** *adv* — **re·li·gious·ness** *n*

²**religious** *n, pl* **religious** : a member of a religious order

re·lin·quish \ri-'ling-kwish\ *vt* 1 : to withdraw or retreat from : ABANDON 2 a : to desist from b : to release a claim to or possession or control of : RENOUNCE 3 : to release or let go (as a grip or hold) [Middle French *relinquiss-*, stem of *relinquir* "to relinquish", from Latin *relinquere* "to leave behind", from *re-* + *linquere* "to leave"] — **re·lin·quish·ment** \-mənt\ *n* □ SYN RELINQUISH, YIELD, RESIGN, SURRENDER mean to give up completely. RELINQUISH suggests that some regret, reluctance, or weakness is involved; YIELD implies concession or compliance or submission to force; RESIGN emphasizes voluntary and usually formal relinquishment; SURRENDER implies a giving up after a struggle to retain or resist.

rel·i·quary \'rel-ə-,kwer-ē\ *n, pl* **-quar·ies** : a small box or shrine in which sacred relics are kept

¹**rel·ish** \'rel-ish\ *n* 1 : a pleasing appetizing taste 2 : a small bit added for flavor : DASH 3 : personal liking (*relish* for hard work) 4 : keen enjoyment of something that satisfies one's tastes, inclination, or desires 5 : a highly seasoned sauce (as of pickles or mustard) eaten with other food to add flavor [Middle English *reles* "taste", from Old French, "something left behind", from *relessier* "to release"] SYN see TASTE

²**relish** *vt* 1 : to add relish to 2 : to be pleased or gratified by : ENJOY 3 : to eat or drink with pleasure — **rel·ish·able** \-ə-bəl\ *adj*

re·live \rē-'liv, 'rē-\ *vb* : to live again or over; *esp* : to experience again in imagination

re·lo·cate \rē-'lō-,kāt, 'rē-; ,rē-lō-'kāt\ *vb* 1 : to locate again 2 : to move to a new location (*relocate* a factory) — **re·lo·cat·able** \-ə-bəl\ *adj* — **re·lo·ca·tion** \,rē-lō-'kā-shən\ *n*

re·luc·tance \ri-'lək-təns\ *n* : the quality or state of being reluctant

re·luc·tan·cy \-tən-sē\ *n, pl* **-cies** : RELUCTANCE

re·luc·tant \ri-'lək-tənt\ *adj* : not willing (*reluctant* to go) [Latin *reluctari* "to struggle against", from *re-* + *luctari* "to struggle"] — **re·luc·tant·ly** *adv*

re·ly \ri-'lī\ *vi* **re·lied; re·ly·ing** 1 : to depend confidently (I know I can *rely* on you) 2 : to be dependent (*relied* on a spring for water) [Middle French *relier* "to connect, rally", from Latin *religare* "to tie back", from *re-* + *ligare* "to tie"]

¹**re·main** \ri-'mān\ *vi* 1 a : to be a part not destroyed, taken, or used up (little *remained* after the fire) b : to

relief 4b

\ə\ abut	\ng\ sing
\ər\ further	\ō\ bone
\a\ mat	\ȯ\ saw
\ā\ take	\ȯi\ coin
\ä\ cot, cart	\th\ thin
\au̇\ out	\t͟h\ this
\ch\ chin	\ü\ food
\e\ pet	\u̇\ foot
\ē\ easy	\y\ yet
\g\ go	\yü\ few
\i\ tip	\yu̇\ cure
\ī\ life	\zh\ vision
\j\ job	

be something yet to be shown, done, or treated ⟨that *remains* to be proved⟩ **2** : to stay in the same place or with the same person or group; *esp* : to stay behind **3** : to continue unchanged ⟨the weather *remained* cold⟩ [Middle French *remaindre*, from Latin *remanēre*, from *re-* + *manēre* "to stay, remain"] SYN see STAY

²remain *n* **1** : a remaining part or trace — usually used in pl. **2** *pl* : a dead body

¹re·main·der \ri-'mān-dər\ *n* **1 a** : a remaining group, part, or trace **b** (1) : the number left after a subtraction (2) : the final undivided part after division that is less than the divisor **2** : a book sold at a reduced price by the publisher after sales have slowed [Anglo-French, from Middle French *remaindre* "to remain"] SYN see BALANCE

²remainder *vt* **re·main·dered; re·main·der·ing** \-də-riŋ, -driŋ\ : to dispose of (books) as remainders

re·make \rē-'māk, 'rē-\ *vt* **-made** \-'mād\; **-mak·ing** : to make anew or in a different form — **re·make** \'rē-,māk\ *n*

¹re·mand \ri-'mand\ *vt* : to order back: as **a** : to send back (a case) to a lower court for further action **b** : to return to custody pending trial or for further detention [Middle French *remander*, from Late Latin *remandare* "to send back word", from Latin *re-* + *mandare* "to order"]

²remand *n* : the act of remanding : the state of being remanded

¹re·mark \ri-'märk\ *vb* **1** : to take notice of : OBSERVE **2** : to express as an observation or comment : SAY **3** : to make an observation or comment [French *remarquer*, from *re-* + *marquer* "to mark"]

²remark *n* **1** : the act of remarking : NOTICE **2** : mention of that which deserves attention or notice **3** : an expression of opinion or judgment

re·mark·able \ri-'mär-kə-bəl\ *adj* **1** : worthy of being or likely to be noticed **2** : UNCOMMON, EXTRAORDINARY ⟨a *remarkable* career⟩ — **re·mark·able·ness** *n* — **re·mark·ably** \-blē\ *adv*

re·mar·riage \rē-'mar-ij, 'rē-\ *n* : a second or later marriage

re·match \rē-'mach, 'rē-\ *n* : a second match between the same contestants or teams

re·me·di·able \ri-'mēd-ē-ə-bəl\ *adj* : capable of being remedied — **re·me·di·able·ness** *n* — **re·me·di·ably** \-blē\ *adv*

re·me·di·al \ri-'mēd-ē-əl\ *adj* : intended to remedy or improve ⟨*remedial* measures⟩ ⟨*remedial* reading courses⟩ — **re·me·di·al·ly** \-ē-ə-lē\ *adv*

¹rem·e·dy \'rem-əd-ē\ *n, pl* **-dies** **1** : a medicine or treatment that cures or relieves **2** : something that corrects an evil, rights a wrong, or makes up for a loss [Anglo-French *remedie*, from Latin *remedium*, from *re-* + *mederi* "to heal"]

²remedy *vt* **-died; -dy·ing** : to provide or serve as a remedy for : RELIEVE SYN see CURE

re·mem·ber \ri-'mem-bər\ *vb* **-bered; -ber·ing** \-bə-riŋ, -briŋ\ **1** : to bring to mind or think of again **2 a** : to keep in mind for attention or consideration **b** : to show remembrance of usually by kindness or giving ⟨*remembered* in the will⟩ **3** : to retain in the memory **4** : to convey greetings from [Middle French *remembrer*, from Late Latin *rememorari*, from *re-* + *memorari* "to be mindful of", from Latin *memor* "mindful"] — **re·mem·ber·able** \-bə-rə-bəl, -brə-bəl\ *adj* — **re·mem·ber·er** \-bər-ər\ *n* □ SYN RECOLLECT, RECALL, REMINISCE: REMEMBER implies a keeping in memory that may be effortless or unwilled; RECOLLECT implies bringing back to mind what is lost or scattered; RECALL suggests an effort to bring back to mind and often to recreate in speech; REMINISCE implies a casual often nostalgic recalling of experiences from long ago.

re·mem·brance \ri-'mem-brəns\ *n* **1** : the state of bearing in mind ⟨let us live in constant *remembrance* of our faults⟩ **2** : ability to remember : MEMORY **3** : an act

of calling to mind ⟨*remembrance* of past wrongs⟩ **4** : a memory of something ⟨had no *remembrance* of that day⟩ **5 a** : something that serves to keep in or bring to mind **b** : something (as a gift or greeting) expressive of friendly remembrance SYN see MEMORY

re·mind \ri-'mīnd\ *vt* : to cause to remember something ⟨*remind* a child that it is bedtime⟩ — **re·mind·er** *n*

rem·i·nisce \,rem-ə-'nis\ *vi* : to engage in reminiscence SYN see REMEMBER

rem·i·nis·cence \,rem-ə-'nis-ns\ *n* **1** : a recalling or telling of past experience ⟨spent an hour in *reminiscence*⟩ **2** : an account of a memorable experience SYN see MEMORY

rem·i·nis·cent \-nt\ *adj* **1** : of or relating to reminiscence : indulging in reminiscence **2** : tending to remind one (as of something seen or known before) [Latin *reminiscens*, present participle of *reminisci* "to remember"]

re·miss \ri-'mis\ *adj* **1** : negligent in the performance of work or duty : CARELESS **2** : showing neglect or disregard : LAX [Latin *remissus*, from *remittere* "to send back, relax"] SYN see NEGLIGENT — **re·miss·ly** *adv* — **re·miss·ness** *n*

re·mis·si·ble \ri-'mis-ə-bəl\ *adj* : capable of being forgiven ⟨*remissible* sins⟩ — **re·mis·si·bly** \-blē\ *adv*

re·mis·sion \ri-'mish-ən\ *n* : the act or process of remitting [Old French, from Latin *remissio*, from *remittere* "to send back, remit"]

re·mit \ri-'mit\ *vb* **re·mit·ted; re·mit·ting** **1 a** : to release from the guilt or penalty of : PARDON ⟨*remit* sins⟩ **b** : to refrain from exacting ⟨*remit* a penalty⟩ **c** : to give relief from (suffering) **2 a** : to lay aside ⟨do not *remit* your care of the garden⟩ **b** : to refrain from **c** : to let slacken : RELAX **3** : to submit or refer for consideration, judgment, decision, or action **4** : to restore or consign to a former status or condition **5** : POSTPONE, DEFER **6** : to send (money) especially in payment **7** : to lessen in intensity or severity often temporarily : MODERATE ⟨the fever *remitted*⟩ [Latin *remittere* "to send back, remit, relax", from *re-* + *mittere* "to send"] — **remit** *n* — **re·mit·ment** \-'mit-mənt\ *n* — **re·mit·ta·ble** \-'mit-ə-bəl\ *adj* — **re·mit·ter** *n*

re·mit·tal \ri-'mit-l\ *n* : REMISSION

re·mit·tance \ri-'mit-ns\ *n* **1** : a sum of money remitted **2** : a sending of money (as to a distant place)

re·mit·tent \ri-'mit-nt\ *adj* : marked by alternating periods of abatement and increase of symptoms ⟨a *remittent* fever⟩ [Latin *remittens*, present participle of *remittere* "to remit"] — **re·mit·tent·ly** *adv*

rem·nant \'rem-nənt\ *n* **1** : a surviving trace ⟨the *remnants* of a great civilization⟩ **2** : something left over ⟨a *remnant* of cloth⟩ [Middle French *remenant*, from *remenoir* "to remain", from Latin *remanēre*]

re·mod·el \rē-'mäd-l, 'rē-\ *vt* : to alter the structure of : partly rebuild

re·mon·strance \ri-'män-strəns\ *n* : an act or instance of remonstrating : PROTEST

re·mon·strant \-strənt\ *adj* : vigorously objecting or opposing — **remonstrant** *n* — **re·mon·strant·ly** *adv*

re·mon·strate \ri-'män-,strāt\ *vb* : to plead in opposition to something : speak in reproof : OBJECT, PROTEST ⟨*remonstrate* with a pupil for being disorderly⟩ [Medieval Latin *remonstrare* "to demonstrate", from Latin *re-* + *monstrare* "to show"]

rem·o·ra \'rem-ə-rə\ *n* : a fish having the front upper fin converted into a disk on the head by means of which it clings to other fishes and to ships [Latin, literally, "delay"]

re·morse \ri-'mórs\ *n* : a deep regret arising from a sense of guilt for past wrongs : SELF-REPROACH [Middle French *remors*, from Medieval Latin *remorsus*, from Latin *remordēre* "to bite again", from *re-* + *mordēre* "to bite"]

remora

re·morse·ful \-fəl\ *adj* : arising from or marked by remorse — **re·morse·ful·ly** \-fə-lē\ *adv* — **re·morse·ful·ness** *n*

re·morse·less \-ləs\ *adj* : being without remorse : MERCILESS — **re·morse·less·ly** *adv* — **re·morse·less·ness** *n*

re·mote \ri-'mōt\ *adj* 1 : far off in place or time : not near or recent ⟨the *remote* past⟩ 2 : OUT-OF-THE-WAY, SECLUDED ⟨a *remote* valley⟩ 3 : not closely connected or related 4 : not obvious or striking : SLIGHT ⟨*remote* likeness⟩ 5 : APART, ALOOF ⟨kept themselves *remote* from the dispute⟩ 6 : maintained or operating from a distance ⟨*remote* control⟩ [Latin *remotus*, from *removēre* "to remove"] SYN see DISTANT — **re·mote·ly** *adv* — **re·mote·ness** *n*

¹**re·mount** \rē-'maunt, 'rē-\ *vb* : to mount again

²**re·mount** \'rē-,maunt, rē-'\ *n* : a fresh horse to take the place of one disabled or exhausted

re·mov·abil·i·ty \ri-,mü-və-'bil-ət-ē\ *n* : the quality or state of being removable

re·mov·able \ri-'mü-və-bəl\ *adj* : that can be removed — **re·mov·able·ness** *n* — **re·mov·ably** \-blē\ *adv*

re·mov·al \ri-'mü-vəl\ *n* : the act of removing : the fact of being removed

¹**re·move** \ri-'müv\ *vb* 1 a : to change or cause to change to another location, position, station, or residence b : to go away 2 a : to move by lifting, pushing aside, or taking away or off b : to yield to being so moved ⟨this cap should *remove* easily⟩ 3 : to dismiss from office 4 : ELIMINATE ⟨*remove* a tumor surgically⟩ [Old French *removoir*, from Latin *removēre*, from *re-* + *movēre* "to move"] — **re·mov·er** *n*

²**remove** *n* 1 : REMOVAL; *esp* : a change of residence or location 2 a : a distance or interval separating one thing from another b : a degree or stage of separation ⟨at one *remove*⟩

re·moved \ri-'müvd\ *adj* 1 : far away : DISTANT ⟨a home far *removed* from cities⟩ 2 : distant in relationship ⟨the children of your first cousin are your first cousins once *removed*⟩ SYN see DISTANT

re·mu·da \ri-'müd-ə\ *n* : a herd of horses from which those to be used (as on a ranch) for the day are drawn [American Spanish, "relay of horses", from Spanish, "exchange", from *remudar* "to exchange", from *re-* "re-" + *mudar* "to change", from Latin *mutare*]

re·mu·ner·ate \ri-'myü-nə-,rāt\ *vt* : to pay an equivalent to for a service, loss, or expense : COMPENSATE [Latin *remunerare*, from *re-* + *munerare* "to give", from *muner-, munus* "gift"] SYN see PAY — **re·mu·ner·a·tor** \-,rāt-ər\ *n* — **re·mu·ner·a·to·ry** \ri-'myü-nə-rə-,tōr-ē, -,tȯr-\ *adj*

re·mu·ner·a·tion \ri-,myü-nə-'rā-shən\ *n* 1 : an act or fact of remunerating 2 : something that remunerates : COMPENSATION

re·mu·ner·a·tive \ri-'myü-nə-,rāt-iv\ *adj* 1 : serving to remunerate 2 : PROFITABLE ⟨made a *remunerative* investment⟩ — **re·mu·ner·a·tive·ly** *adv* — **re·mu·ner·a·tive·ness** *n*

Re·nais·sance \,ren-ə-'säns, -'zäns\ *n* 1 a : the movement or period in Europe between the 14th and 17th centuries marked by a revival of interest in classical arts and literature and by the beginnings of modern science b : the neoclassic style of architecture prevailing during the Renaissance 2 *often not cap* : a movement or period marked by a revival of vigorous artistic and intellectual activity [French, from Middle French, "rebirth", from *renaistre* "to be born again", from Latin *renasci*, from *re-* + *nasci* "to be born"]

re·nal \'rēn-l\ *adj* : of, relating to, or located in or near the kidneys [Late Latin *renalis*, from Latin *renes* "kidneys"]

renal artery *n* : either of the paired arteries that arise from the dorsal aorta and supply blood to the kidneys

renal vein *n* : either of the paired veins that drain blood from the kidneys into the vena cava

re·na·scence \ri-'nas-ns, -'nās-\ *n, often cap* : RENAISSANCE 2 — **re·na·scent** \-nt\ *adj*

rend \'rend\ *vt* **rent** \'rent\ *also* **rend·ed; rend·ing** 1 : to remove from place by violence : WREST 2 : to split or tear apart or in pieces by violence 3 : to tear (the hair or clothing) as a sign of anger, grief, or despair 4 a : to hurt mentally or emotionally b : to pierce with sound c : to divide (as a nation) into parties [Old English *rendan*]

ren·der \'ren-dər\ *vt* **ren·dered; ren·der·ing** \-də-ring, -dring\ 1 : DELIVER, GIVE ⟨*render* judgment⟩ 2 : to melt down : extract by heating ⟨*render* lard⟩ 3 : to give up : SURRENDER ⟨*render* one's life for a cause⟩ 4 : to give in return ⟨*render* thanks⟩ 5 : to present a statement of : bring to one's attention ⟨*render* a bill⟩ 6 : to cause to be or become : MAKE ⟨*render* a person helpless⟩ 7 : FURNISH, CONTRIBUTE ⟨*render* aid⟩ 8 : PRESENT, PERFORM ⟨*render* a song⟩ ⟨*render* a salute⟩ 9 : TRANSLATE ⟨*render* Latin into English⟩ [Middle French *rendre* "to give back, yield", derived from Latin *reddere*] — **ren·der·able** \-də-rə-bəl, -drə-bəl\ *adj* — **ren·der·er** \-dər-ər\ *n*

¹**ren·dez·vous** \'rän-di-,vü, -dā-\ *n, pl* **ren·dez·vous** \-,vüz\ 1 a : a place appointed for assembling or meeting b : a place where people get together : HAUNT 2 : an appointed meeting 3 : the process of bringing two spacecraft together [Middle French, from *rendez vous* "present yourselves"]

²**rendezvous** *vb* **ren·dez·voused** \-,vüd\; **ren·dez·vous·ing** \-,vü-ing\; **ren·dez·vous·es** \-,vüz\ : to come or bring together at a rendezvous

ren·di·tion \ren-'dish-ən\ *n* : the act or result of rendering: as a : TRANSLATION b : PERFORMANCE 3, INTERPRETATION [obsolete French, from Middle French *reddition*, from Late Latin *redditio*, from Latin *reddere* "to give back, yield"]

¹**ren·e·gade** \'ren-i-,gād\ *n* 1 : a deserter from one faith, cause, or allegiance to another 2 : one who rejects lawful or conventional behavior [Spanish *renegado*, from Medieval Latin *renegatus*, from *renegare* "to deny", from Latin *re-* + *negare* "to deny"]

²**renegade** *vi* : to become a renegade

³**renegade** *adj* : TRAITOROUS 1, APOSTATE

ren·e·ga·do \,ren-i-'gäd-ō, -'gad-\ *n, pl* **-does** : RENEGADE [Spanish]

re·nege \ri-'nig, -'neg, -'nēg, -'nāg\ *vi* 1 : to violate a rule in a card game by failing to follow suit when able 2 : to go back on a promise or commitment [Medieval Latin *renegare* "to deny"] — **re·neg·er** *n*

re·new \ri-'nü, -'nyü\ *vt* 1 : to make new again : restore to freshness or vigor ⟨strength *renewed* by a night's rest⟩ 2 : to restore to existence : REESTABLISH, RECREATE ⟨*renew* the splendor of a palace⟩ 3 : to do or make again : REPEAT ⟨*renew* a complaint⟩ 4 : to begin again : RESUME ⟨*renewed* efforts to make peace⟩ 5 : to put in a fresh supply of : REPLACE ⟨*renew* the water in a tank⟩ 6 : to grant or obtain an extension of ⟨*renew* a lease⟩

□ SYN RENEW, RESTORE, REFRESH, RENOVATE mean to make like new. RENEW can imply a replacing (as of worn parts or used-up supplies) or a recruiting (as of vigor or health); RESTORE suggests a returning to an original state of soundness or wholeness ⟨*restored* the old mansion⟩ REFRESH implies restoring qualities of liveliness or zest ⟨*refreshed* by a short nap⟩ RENOVATE applies chiefly to material things and suggests making like new but not necessarily like the original ⟨*renovate* the upstairs rooms⟩

re·new·able \ri-'nü-ə-bəl, -'nyü-\ *adj* : capable of being renewed; *esp* : capable of being replaced by natural ecological cycles or sound management procedures ⟨*renewable* resources like water, wildlife, forests, and grasslands⟩ — **re·new·abil·i·ty** \-,nü-ə-'bil-ət-ē, -,nyü-\ *n*

re·new·al \ri-'nü-əl, -'nyü-\ *n* 1 : the act of renewing : the state of being renewed 2 : something renewed

re·ni·form \'ren-ə-ˌfȯrm, 'rē-nə-\ *adj* : suggesting a kidney in outline ⟨a *reniform* leaf⟩ [Latin *renes* "kidneys"]

ren·net \'ren-ət\ *n* **1** : the contents of the stomach of an unweaned calf or other animal or the lining membrane of the stomach used for curdling milk **2** : rennin or a substitute used to curdle milk [Middle English, from Old English *gerennan* "to cause to coagulate"]

ren·nin \'ren-ən\ *n* : a stomach enzyme that coagulates casein and is used commercially to curdle milk in the making of cheese

re·nom·i·nate \rē-'näm-ə-ˌnāt, 'rē-\ *vt* : to nominate again especially for a succeeding term — **re·nom·i·na·tion** \-ˌnäm-ə-'nā-shən\ *n*

re·nounce \ri-'naůns\ *vt* **1** : to give up, abandon, or resign usually by formal declaration ⟨*renounced* the throne⟩ ⟨*renounce* one's errors⟩ **2** : to refuse further to follow, obey, or recognize : REPUDIATE ⟨*renounce* one's allegiance⟩ [Middle French *renoncer*, from Latin *renuntiare*, from *re-* + *nuntiare* "to report, announce", from *nuntius* "messenger"] — **re·nounce·ment** \-mənt\ *n* — **re·nounc·er** *n*

ren·o·vate \'ren-ə-ˌvāt\ *vt* : to make like new again : restore to a former state or to good condition [Latin *renovare*, from *re-* + *novare* "to make new", from *novus* "new"] SYN see RENEW — **ren·o·va·tion** \ˌren-ə-'vā-shən\ *n* — **ren·o·va·tor** \'ren-ə-ˌvāt-ər\ *n*

re·nown \ri-'naůn\ *n* : a state of being widely acclaimed and highly honored : FAME [Middle French *renon*, from *renomer* "to celebrate", from *re-* + *nomer* "to name", from Latin *nominare*, from *nomen* "name"]

re·nowned \-'naůnd\ *adj* : having renown : CELEBRATED SYN see FAMOUS

¹rent \'rent\ *n* **1** : property (as a house) rented or for rent **2** : money paid for the use of property : a periodic payment made by a tenant to the owner for the possession and use of real property **3** : the portion of the national income attributable to land as a factor of production [Old French *rente* "income from a property", derived from Latin *reddere* "to give back, yield"] — **for rent** : available for use or service at a price

²rent *vb* **1** : to take and hold property under an agreement to pay rent **2** : to grant the possession and enjoyment of for rent : LET **3** : to be for rent SYN see HIRE — **rent·able** \-ə-bəl\ *adj*

³rent *past of* REND

⁴rent *n* **1** : an opening made by or as if by rending **2** : an act or instance of rending

¹rent·al \'rent-l\ *n* **1** : an amount paid or collected as rent **2** : something rented **3** : an act of renting

²rental *adj* **1** : of, relating to, or available for rent **2** : dealing in rental property

rental library *n* : a commercially operated library (as in a store) that lends books at a fixed charge per book per day

rent·er \'rent-ər\ *n* : one that rents; *esp* : TENANT

rent·tier \rän-'tyā\ *n* : a person who receives a fixed income from investments [French, from *rente* "income from a property"]

re·num·ber \rē-'nəm-bər, 'rē-\ *vt* : to number again or differently

re·nun·ci·a·tion \ri-ˌnən-sē-'ā-shən\ *n* : the act or practice of renouncing [Latin *renuntiatio*, from *renuntiare* "to renounce"] — **re·nun·ci·a·tive** \-'nən-sē-ˌāt-iv\ *adj* — **re·nun·ci·a·to·ry** \-sē-ə-ˌtȯr-ē, -ˌtȯr\ *adj*

re·open \rē-'ō-pən, 'rē-, -'ōp-m\ *vb* **1** : to open again **2** : to take up again : RESUME

¹re·or·der \rē-'ȯrd-ər, 'rē-\ *vb* **1** : REORGANIZE **2** : to place a reorder or a reorder for

²reorder *n* : an order like a previous order from the same supplier

re·or·ga·ni·za·tion \rē-ˌȯrg-nə-'zā-shən, ˌrē-, -ə-nə-\ *n* : the act of reorganizing : the state of being reorganized; *esp* : the financial reconstruction of a business concern

re·or·ga·nize \rē-'ȯr-gə-ˌnīz, 'rē-\ *vb* : to organize again or anew; *esp* : to bring about a reorganization (as of a business concern) — **re·or·ga·niz·er** *n*

rep *or* **repp** \'rep\ *n* : a plain-woven fabric with prominent rounded crosswise ribs [French *reps*, from English *ribs*, pl. of *rib*]

re·pack·age \rē-'pak-ij, 'rē-\ *vt* : to package again and especially differently

¹re·pair \ri-'paǝr, -'peǝr\ *vi* : to make one's way : GO ⟨*repair* to an inner office⟩ [Middle French *repairier* "to go back to one's country", from Late Latin *repatriare*, from Latin *re-* + *patria* "native country"]

²repair *vb* **1 a** : to restore by replacing a part or putting together what is damaged : MEND **b** : to restore to a sound or healthy state : RENEW **2** : to make good : REMEDY **3** : to make up for : compensate for [Middle French *reparer*, from Latin *reparare*, from *re-* + *parare* "to prepare"] SYN see FIX — **re·pair·abil·i·ty** \-ˌpar-ə-'bil-ət-ē, -ˌper-\ *n* — **re·pair·able** \-'par-ə-bəl, -'per-\ *adj* — **re·pair·er** \-ər\ *n*

³repair *n* **1** : the action or process of repairing ⟨make *repairs*⟩ **2** : the result of repairing ⟨a tire with three *repairs*⟩ **3** : good or sound condition ⟨a house in *repair*⟩ **4** : condition with respect to soundness or need of repairing ⟨a house in bad *repair*⟩

re·pair·man \ri-'paǝr-ˌman, -'peǝr-, -mǝn\ *n* : one whose occupation is making repairs ⟨a TV *repairman*⟩

rep·a·ra·ble \'rep-rə-bəl, -ə-rə-\ *adj* : capable of being repaired

rep·a·ra·tion \ˌrep-ə-'rā-shən\ *n* **1** : the action or process of repairing or restoring : the state of being repaired or restored **2** : a making amends for a wrong or injury done : COMPENSATION **3** : the amends made for a wrong or injury; *esp* : money paid (as by one country to another) in compensation (as for damages in war) [Middle French, from Late Latin *reparatio*, from Latin *reparare* "to repair"]

re·par·a·tive \ri-'par-ət-iv\ *adj* **1** : of, relating to, or effecting repair **2** : serving to make amends

rep·ar·tee \ˌrep-ər-'tē, -ˌär-, -'tā\ *n* : a clever witty reply; *also* : the making of such replies [French *repartie*, from *repartir* "to retort", from *re-* "re-" + *partir* "to divide, part"]

re·pass \rē-'pas, 'rē-\ *vb* **1** : to pass again especially in the opposite direction : RETURN **2** : to cause to pass again **3** : to adopt again — **re·pas·sage** \-'pas-ij\ *n*

re·past \ri-'past\ *n* : something taken as food : MEAL [Middle French, from *repaistre* "to feed", from *re-* "re-" + *paistre* "to feed", from Latin *pascere*]

re·pa·tri·ate \rē-'pā-trē-ˌāt, 'rē-, -'pa-\ *vt* : to send or bring back to the country of which one is a citizen ⟨*repatriate* prisoners of war⟩ [Late Latin *repatriare* to go back to one's country", from Latin *re-* + *patria* "native country"] — **re·pa·tri·ate** \-trē-ət, -trē-ˌāt\ *n* — **re·pa·tri·a·tion** \ˌrē-ˌpā-trē-'ā-shən, -ˌpa-\ *n*

re·pay \rē-'pā, 'rē-\ *vb* **-paid; -pay·ing** **1** : to pay back ⟨I've already been *repaid*⟩ ⟨*repay* a loan⟩ **2** : to make return payment ⟨a lending bank requires proof of ability to *repay*⟩ — **re·pay·able** \-ə-bəl\ *adj* — **re·pay·ment** \-mənt\ *n*

re·peal \ri-'pēl\ *vt* : REVOKE, ANNUL; *esp* : to do away with by legislative enactment [Middle French *repeler*, from *re-* + *apeler* "to call, appeal"] — **repeal** *n* — **re·peal·able** \-'pē-lə-bəl\ *adj* — **re·peal·er** *n*

¹re·peat \ri-'pēt\ *vt* **1 a** : to say or state again : REITERATE **b** : to say over from memory : RECITE **c** : to say after another **d** : to tell to others ⟨*repeat* gossip⟩ **2** : to make, do, or perform again ⟨*repeat* a mistake⟩ **3** : to recur or cause to recur ⟨the cycle *repeats* itself indefinitely⟩ [Middle French *repeter*, from Latin *repetere*, from *re-* + *petere* "to go to, seek"] — **re·peat·able** \-ə-bəl\ *adj* □ SYN REPEAT, REITERATE mean to do or say again. REPEAT is the general term and may apply to one or many actions or utterances; **REITERATE** stresses exact repetition of something said and may be stronger in implying multiple repetition. — **repeat oneself** : to say or do the same thing more than once

²**re·peat** \ri-ˈpēt, ˈrē-,\ *n* **I** : the act of repeating **2 a** : something repeated **b** (1) : a musical passage to be repeated in performance (2) : a sign consisting of vertical dots placed before and after a passage to be repeated

re·peat·ed \ri-ˈpēt-əd\ *adj* : done or happening again and again : **FREQUENT** — **re·peat·ed·ly** *adv*

re·peat·er \ri-ˈpēt-ər\ *n* : one that repeats: as **a** : a watch that strikes the time when a spring is pressed **b** : a firearm that fires several times without reloading **c** : an habitual violator of the laws **d** : a student repeating a class or course

repeating decimal *n* : a decimal in which after a certain point a particular digit or sequence of digits repeats itself indefinitely — compare **TERMINATING DECIMAL**

re·pel \ri-ˈpel\ *vb* **re·pelled; re·pel·ling I a** : to drive back : **REPULSE b** : to fight against : **RESIST 2** : to turn away : **REJECT** ⟨*repelled* the insinuation⟩ **3 a** : to drive away : **DISCOURAGE b** : to be incapable of adhering to, mixing with, taking up, or holding **c** : to force away or apart or tend to do so by mutual action at a distance **4** : to cause aversion : **DISGUST** [Latin *repellere*, from *re-* + *pellere* "to drive"] — **re·pel·ler** *n*

re·pel·lant \ri-ˈpel-ənt\ *adj or n* : **REPELLENT**

¹**re·pel·lent** \-ənt\ *adj* **I** : serving or tending to drive away or ward off **2** : arousing aversion or disgust : **REPULSIVE** [Latin *repellens*, present participle of *repellere* "to repel"] **SYN see REPUGNANT** — **re·pel·len·cy** \-ən-sē\ *n* — **re·pel·lent·ly** *adv*

²**repellent** *n* : something that repels; *esp* : a substance employed to prevent insect attacks

re·pent \ri-ˈpent\ *vb* **I** : to feel sorrow for a wrong action and determine to do what is right **2** : to feel sorry for or dissatisfied with : **REGRET** ⟨*repent* a rash decision⟩ [Old French *repentir*, from *re-* "re-" + *pentir* "to be sorry", from Latin *paenitēre*] — **re·pent·er** *n*

re·pent·ance \ri-ˈpent-ns\ *n* : the action or process of repenting especially for misdeeds or moral shortcomings **SYN see PENITENCE**

re·pent·ant \ri-ˈpent-nt\ *adj* : feeling or showing repentance — **re·pent·ant·ly** *adv*

re·per·cus·sion \ˌrē-pər-ˈkəsh-ən, ˌrep-ər-\ *n* **I** : **REFLECTION 1, REVERBERATION 2 a** : a reciprocal action or effect **b** : a widespread, indirect, or unforeseen effect of an act, action, or event — **re·per·cus·sive** \-ˈkəs-iv\ *adj*

rep·er·toire \ˈrep-ə(r)-ˌtwär, -ər-\ *n* **I a** : a list or supply of dramas, operas, pieces, or parts that a company or person is prepared to perform **b** : a supply of skills, devices, or expedients possessed by a person **2 a** : the complete list or supply of dramas, operas, or musical works available for performance **b** : the complete list or supply of skills, devices, or ingredients used in a particular field, occupation, or practice [French *répertoire*, from Late Latin *repertorium* "list"]

rep·er·to·ry \ˈrep-ər-ˌtōr-ē, -ə-, -ˌtȯr-\ *n, pl* **-ries I a** : a stock or store of something : **COLLECTION** ⟨a *repertory* of unusual skills⟩ **2** : **REPERTOIRE** [Late Latin *repertorium* "list", from Latin *reperire* "to find", from *re-* + *parere* "to produce"]

rep·e·ti·tion \ˌrep-ə-ˈtish-ən\ *n* **I** : the act or an instance of repeating **2** : the fact of being repeated **3** : something repeated [Latin *repetitio*, from *repetere* "to repeat"]

rep·e·ti·tious \-ˈtish-əs\ *adj* : marked by repetition; *esp* : tediously repeating — **rep·e·ti·tious·ly** *adv* — **rep·e·ti·tious·ness** *n*

re·pet·i·tive \ri-ˈpet-ət-iv\ *adj* : **REPETITIOUS** — **re·pet·i·tive·ly** *adv* — **re·pet·i·tive·ness** *n*

re·phrase \rē-ˈfrāz, ˈrē-\ *vt* : to state in a different form ⟨let me *rephrase* the question⟩

re·pine \ri-ˈpīn\ *vi* **I** : to feel or express dejection or discontent : **COMPLAIN 2** : to wish discontentedly — **re·pin·er** *n*

re·place \ri-ˈplās\ *vt* **I** : to put back in a proper or former place ⟨*replace* a card in a file⟩ **2** : to take the place of : **SUPPLANT** ⟨paper money has *replaced* gold coins⟩ **3** : to fill the place of : supply an equivalent for ⟨*replace* a broken dish⟩ — **re·place·able** \-ˈplā-sə-bəl\ *adj* □ **SYN REPLACE, SUPPLANT, SUPERSEDE** mean to put out of place or into the place of another. **REPLACE** implies a supplying of a substitute or equivalent for something lost, destroyed, or no longer usable or adequate; **SUPPLANT** implies taking the place of one forced out by craft or fraud or the replacing of a thing with another newer or better ⟨coal *supplanted* wood for heating⟩ **SUPERSEDE** implies taking the place of one that has become outmoded, obsolete, or inferior.

re·place·ment \ri-ˈplā-smənt\ *n* **I** : the act of replacing : the state of being replaced : **SUBSTITUTION 2** : one that replaces another

replacement set *n* : a set of elements any one of which may be used to replace a given variable or placeholder in a mathematical expression (as an equation)

re·plant \rē-ˈplant, ˈrē-\ *vt* **I** : to set (a plant) to grow again or anew **2** : to provide with new plants ⟨*replanted* the park⟩

re·plen·ish \ri-ˈplen-ish\ *vt* : to fill again : bring back to a condition of being full or complete [Middle French *repleniss-*, stem of *replenir* "to fill", from *re-* "re-" + *plein* "full", from Latin *plenus*] — **re·plen·ish·er** *n* — **re·plen·ish·ment** \-ish-mənt\ *n*

re·plete \ri-ˈplēt\ *adj* **I** : filled to capacity : **FULL**; *esp* : full of food **2** : fully supplied or provided ⟨a book *replete* with illustrations⟩ **3** : **COMPLETE 1a** [Latin *repletus*, past participle of *replēre* "to fill up", from *re-* + *plēre* "to fill"] — **re·plete·ness** *n*

re·ple·tion \ri-ˈplē-shən\ *n* **I** : the act of eating to excess : the state of being fed to excess : **SURFEIT 2** : the condition of being filled up or overcrowded **3** : fulfillment of a need or desire : **SATISFACTION**

rep·li·ca \ˈrep-li-kə\ *n* **I** : a close reproduction or facsimile especially by the maker of the original **2** : **COPY 1, DUPLICATE** [Italian, "repetition", from *replicare* "to repeat", from Late Latin, from Latin, "to fold back"]

¹**rep·li·cate** \ˈrep-lə-ˌkāt\ *vb* **I** : **DUPLICATE 1, REPEAT 2** : to undergo replication ⟨*replicating* DNA⟩

²**rep·li·cate** \-li-kət\ *n* : one of several identical experiments, procedures, or samples

rep·li·ca·tion \ˌrep-lə-ˈkā-shən\ *n* **I** : **ANSWER 1a, REPLY 2** : precise copying or reproduction; *also* : an act or process of this

¹**re·ply** \ri-ˈplī\ *vb* **re·plied; re·ply·ing I a** : to respond in speech or writing **b** : to give as an answer **2** : to do something in response; *esp* : to return an attack [Middle French *replier* "to fold again", from Latin *replicare* "to fold back", from *re-* + *plicare* "to fold"] — **re·pli·er** \-ˈplī-ər, -ˈplīr\ *n*

²**reply** *n, pl* **replies** : something said, written, or done in response

¹**re·port** \ri-ˈpōrt, -ˈpȯrt\ *n* **I a** : common talk : an account spread by common talk : **RUMOR b** : **FAME, REPUTATION** ⟨a person of good *report*⟩ **2** : a usually detailed account or statement ⟨a news *report*⟩ **3** : an explosive noise ⟨the *report* of a gun⟩ [Middle French, from *reporter* "to report", from Latin *reportare*, from *re-* + *portare* "to carry"]

²**report** *vb* **I** : to give an account (as of an incident or of one's activities) **2** : to give an account of as a news item ⟨*report* a baseball game⟩ **3** : to make a charge of misconduct against ⟨*report* a schoolmate⟩ **4** : to present oneself ⟨*report* for duty⟩ ⟨*report* at the office⟩ **5** : to make known to the proper authorities ⟨*report* a fire⟩ **6** : to return or present (as a matter officially referred to a committee) with conclusions and recommendations — **re·port·able** \-ə-bəl\ *adj*

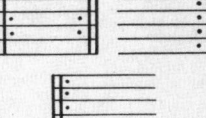

²repeat 2b (2)

\ə\ abut	\ng\ **sing**
\ər\ **further**	\ō\ **bone**
\a\ **mat**	\ȯ\ **saw**
\ā\ **take**	\ȯi\ **coin**
\ä\ **cot, cart**	\th\ **thin**
\aú\ **out**	\th\ **this**
\ch\ **chin**	\ü\ **food**
\e\ **pet**	\ú\ **foot**
\ē\ **easy**	\y\ **yet**
\g\ **go**	\yü\ **few**
\i\ **tip**	\yú\ **cure**
\ī\ **life**	\zh\ **vision**
\j\ **job**	

re·port·age \ri-'pōrt-ij, -'pȯrt-, *especially for 2* ‚rep-ər-'täzh\ *n* **1** : the act or process of reporting news **2** : writing intended to report observed or documented events [French, from *reporter* "to report"]

report card *n* : a report on a student's grades that is periodically submitted by a school to the student's parents or guardian

re·port·ed·ly \ri-'pōrt-əd-lē, -'pȯrt-\ *adv* : according to report

re·port·er \ri-'pōrt-ər, -'pȯrt-\ *n* : one that reports: as **a** : one that makes authorized statements of law decisions or legislative proceedings **b** : one employed by a newspaper or magazine to gather and write news **c** : one that broadcasts news — **rep·or·to·ri·al** \‚rep-ər-'tōr-ē-əl, ‚rēp-, -ə-'tōr-, -'tȯr-\ *adj* — **rep·or·to·ri·al·ly** \-ē-ə-lē\ *adv*

¹re·pose \ri-'pōz\ *vt* **1** : to place unquestioningly : SET ⟨*repose* trust in a friend⟩ **2** : to place for control, management, or use [derived from Latin *reponere* "to put back, put away, place", from *re-* + *ponere* "to put"]

²repose *vb* **1** : to lay at rest : put in a restful position ⟨*reposed* my head on a cushion⟩ **2** : to lie at rest : take rest ⟨*reposing* on the couch⟩ [Middle French, *reposer*, from Late Latin *repausare*, from *re-* + *pausare* "to stop", from Latin *pausa* "pause"]

³repose *n* **1** : a state of resting after exertion or strain; *esp* : rest in sleep **2** : CALM 2, PEACE **3** : cessation or absence of activity, movement, or animation ⟨a face in *repose*⟩

re·pose·ful \ri-'pōz-fəl\ *adj* : full of repose : QUIET — **re·pose·ful·ly** \-fə-lē\ *adv* — **re·pose·ful·ness** *n*

re·po·si·tion \‚rē-pə-'zish-ən\ *vt* : to change or restore the position of

re·pos·i·to·ry \ri-'päz-ə-‚tōr-ē, -‚tȯr-\ *n, pl* **-ries** **1** : a place or container where something is deposited or stored **2** : a side altar in a Roman Catholic church where the consecrated host is reserved from Holy Thursday until Good Friday **3** : one that contains or stores something nonmaterial ⟨libraries are *repositories* of knowledge⟩ **4** : a person to whom something is confided or entrusted [Latin *repositorium*, from *repositus*, past participle of *reponere* "to put away"]

re·pos·sess \‚rē-pə-'zes\ *vt* **1 a** : to regain possession of **b** : to retake possession of in default of the payment of installments due **2** : put in possession again — **re·pos·ses·sion** \-'zesh-ən\ *n*

re·pous·sé \rə-‚pü-'sā\ *adj* **1** : shaped or ornamented with patterns in relief made by hammering or pressing on the reverse side — used of metal **2** : formed in relief [French]

repp *variant of* REP

rep·re·hend \‚rep-ri-'hend\ *vt* : to voice disapproval of : CENSURE [Latin *reprehendere*, literally, "to hold back", from *re-* + *prehendere* "to grasp"]

rep·re·hen·si·ble \‚rep-ri-'hen-sə-bəl\ *adj* : worthy of or deserving censure or blame : CULPABLE — **rep·re·hen·si·ble·ness** *n* — **rep·re·hen·si·bly** \-blē\ *adv*

rep·re·hen·sion \-'hen-chən\ *n* : the act of reprehending : REPROOF [Latin *reprehensio*, from *reprehendere* "to reprehend"] — **rep·re·hen·sive** \-'hen-siv\ *adj*

rep·re·sent \‚rep-ri-'zent\ *vt* **1** : to present a picture, image, or likeness of : PORTRAY ⟨this picture *represents* a scene at King Arthur's court⟩ **2** : to serve as a sign or symbol of ⟨the flag *represents* our country⟩ **3 a** : to take the place of in some respect **b** : to act for or in the place of (as in a legislative body) **4** : to describe as having a specified character or quality **5** : to serve as a specimen, example, or instance of [Middle French *representer*, from Latin *repraesentare*, from *re-* + *praesentare* "to present"] — **rep·re·sent·able** \-ə-bəl\ *adj* — **rep·re·sent·er** *n*

rep·re·sen·ta·tion \‚rep-ri-‚zen-'tā-shən\ *n* **1** : one that represents: as **a** : an artistic likeness or image **b** : a sign or symbol of something **2** : a usually formal protest **3** : the act or action of representing or state of

being represented (as in a legislative body) — **rep·re·sen·ta·tion·al** \-shnəl, -shən-l\ *adj*

¹rep·re·sen·ta·tive \‚rep-ri-'zent-ət-iv\ *adj* **1** : being a representation ⟨a painting *representative* of a battle⟩ **2** : standing or acting for another especially through delegated authority **3** : of, based upon, or being a government in which the people are represented by persons chosen from among them usually by election **4** : serving as a typical or characteristic example ⟨a *representative* sample⟩ — **rep·re·sen·ta·tive·ly** *adv* — **rep·re·sen·ta·tive·ness** *n*

²representative *n* **1** : a typical example of a group, class, or quality : SPECIMEN **2 a** : one (as an agent or delegate) that represents another or others **b** : a member of the house of representatives of the United States Congress or a state legislature

re·press \ri-'pres\ *vt* **1** : to check by or as if by pressure : CURB **2** : to hold in by self-control ⟨*repress* a laugh⟩ **3** : to put down by force : SUBDUE ⟨*repress* a disturbance⟩ **4** : to prevent the natural or normal expression, activity, or development of ⟨*repress* one's anger⟩ **5** : to exclude from consciousness [Latin *repressus,* past participle of *reprimere* "to check, repress", from *re-* + *premere* "to press"] — **re·pres·sive** \-'pres-iv\ *adj* — **re·pres·sive·ly** *adv* — **re·pres·sive·ness** *n* — **re·pres·sor** \-'pres-ər\ *n*

re·pressed *adj* **1** : subjected to or marked by usually excessive repression **2** : characterized by restraint

re·pres·sion \ri-'presh-ən\ *n* **1** : the act of repressing : the state of being repressed **2** : a psychological process by which unacceptable wishes or impulses are kept from conscious awareness

re·pres·sor \ri-'pres-ər\ *n* : a gene product that interacts with a genetic operator to inhibit its function

¹re·prieve \ri-'prēv\ *vt* **1** : to delay the punishment of (as a condemned prisoner) **2** : to give relief or deliverance to for a time [perhaps from Middle French *repris,* past participle of *reprendre* "to take back"]

²reprieve *n* **1 a** : the act of reprieving : the state of being reprieved **b** : a formal temporary suspension of the execution of a sentence **2** : RESPITE 2

¹rep·ri·mand \'rep-rə-‚mand\ *n* : a severe or formal reproof [French *réprimande,* from Latin *reprimendus* "to be checked", from *reprimere* "to check, repress"]

²reprimand *vt* : to reprove severely and especially officially SYN see REPROVE

¹re·print \rē-'print, 'rē-\ *vt* : to print again — **re·print·er** *n*

²re·print \'rē-‚print\ *n* **1** : a new or additional printing without any change in the text of a book already published **2** : a separately printed text or excerpt

re·pri·sal \ri-'prī-zəl\ *n* **1** : the use of force short of war by one nation against another in retaliation for damage or loss suffered ⟨economic *reprisals*⟩ **2** : an act of retaliation especially in war [Middle French *reprisaille,* from obsolete Italian *ripresaglia,* from *ripreso,* past participle of *riprendere* "to take back", from *ri-* "re-" + *prendere* "to take", from Latin *prehendere*]

re·prise \ri-'prēz\ *n* : a recurrence, renewal, or resumption of an action or a musical passage [Middle French, from *reprendre* "to take back", from *re-* "re-" + *prendre* "to take", from Latin *prehendere*]

re·pro \'rē-prō\ *n, pl* **repros** : a clear sharp proof made especially from a letterpress printing surface to serve as photographic copy for a printing plate [short for *reproduction*]

¹re·proach \ri-'prōch\ *n* **1 a** : a cause or occasion of blame, discredit, or disgrace **b** : DISCREDIT 1, DISGRACE **2** : the act or action of reproaching : REBUKE [Middle French *reproche,* from *reprochier* "to reproach", derived from Latin *re-* + *prope* "near"] — **re·proach·ful** \-fəl\ *adj* — **re·proach·ful·ly** \-fə-lē\ *adv* — **re·proach·ful·ness** *n*

²reproach *vt* **1** : to find fault with : blame for a mistake or failure ⟨*reproached* me for my carelessness⟩ **2** : to

bring into discredit SYN SEE REPROVE — **re·proach·able** \-'prō-chə-bəl\ adj — **re·proach·er** n — **re·proach·ing·ly** \-'prō-ching-lē\ adv

¹**rep·ro·bate** \'rep-rə-ˌbāt\ vt : to condemn as unworthy or evil [Late Latin *reprobare,* from Latin *re-* + *probare* "to test, approve"] — **rep·ro·ba·tion** \ˌrep-rə-'bā-shən\ n — **rep·ro·ba·tive** \'rep-rə-ˌbāt-iv\ adj — **rep·ro·ba·to·ry** \-bə-ˌtōr-ē, -ˌtor-\ adj

²**reprobate** adj 1 : doomed to damnation 2 : thoroughly disreputable and morally abandoned

³**reprobate** n : a reprobate person

re·pro·duce \ˌrē-prə-'düs, -'dyüs\ vb 1 : to produce again: as a : to give rise to (new individuals of the same kind) b : to cause to exist again or anew ⟨*reproduce* water from steam⟩ c : to imitate closely ⟨*reproduce* the sound of thunder and footsteps by sound effects⟩ d : to present again e : to make an image or copy of f : to translate (a recording) into sound 2 : to undergo reproduction ⟨your voice *reproduces* well⟩ 3 : to produce offspring — **re·pro·duc·er** n — **re·pro·duc·ibil·i·ty** \-ˌdü-sə-'bil-ət-ē, -ˌdyü-\ n — **re·pro·duc·ible** \-'dü-sə-bəl, -'dyü-\ adj

re·pro·duc·tion \ˌrē-prə-'dək-shən\ n 1 : the act or process of reproducing; *esp* : the process by which plants and animals give rise to offspring 2 : something reproduced : COPY SYN SEE DUPLICATE

re·pro·duc·tive \ˌrē-prə-'dək-tiv\ adj : of, relating to, capable of, or concerned with reproduction — **re·pro·duc·tive·ly** adv — **re·pro·duc·tive·ness** n — **re·pro·duc·tiv·i·ty** \-ˌdək-'tiv-ət-ē\ n

re·proof \ri-'prüf\ n : censure for a fault : REBUKE [Middle French *reprove,* from *reprover* "to reprove"]

re·prove \ri-'prüv\ vt 1 : to scold usually gently or with kindly intent 2 : to express disapproval of : CENSURE [Middle French *reprover,* from Late Latin *reprobare* "to disapprove, reprobate"] — **re·prov·er** n □ SYN REPROVE, REBUKE, REPRIMAND, REPROACH mean to criticize for faulty behavior. REPROVE may imply a kindly intent and lack of harshness; REBUKE implies a stern or sharp reproving; REPRIMAND implies a severe, formal, often public or official rebuke; REPROACH often suggests displeasure or disappointment expressed in mild scolding.

¹**rep·tile** \'rep-tl, -ˌtīl\ n 1 : any of a class (Reptilia) of air-breathing vertebrates comprising the alligators and crocodiles, lizards, snakes, turtles, and extinct related forms and having a bony skeleton and a body usually covered with scales or bony plates 2 : a groveling or despicable person [Late Latin, from *reptilis* "creeping", from *repere* "to creep"]

²**reptile** adj : characteristic of a reptile : REPTILIAN

¹**rep·til·i·an** \rep-'til-ē-ən\ adj : of, relating to, or resembling reptiles

²**reptilian** n : REPTILE 1

re·pub·lic \ri-'pəb-lik\ n 1 a : a government having a chief of state who is not a monarch and who is usually a president b : a political unit having such a form of government 2 a : a government in which supreme power resides in a body of citizens entitled to vote and is exercised by elected officers and representatives responsible to them b : a political unit (as a nation) having such a form of government 3 : a constituent political and territorial unit of the Soviet Union or Yugoslavia [French *république,* from Latin *respublica,* from *res* "thing, wealth" + *publica,* feminine of *publicus* "public"]

¹**re·pub·li·can** \ri-'pəb-li-kən\ adj 1 a : of, relating to, or having the characteristics of a republic b : favoring, supporting, or advocating a republic 2 cap a : DEMOCRATIC-REPUBLICAN b : of, relating to, or constituting a political party in the United States evolving in the mid-19th century and historically associated with business, financial, and some agricultural interests and with favoring a restricted governmental role in social and economic life

²**republican** n 1 : one that favors or supports a republican form of government 2 cap a : a member of a political party advocating republicanism b : a member of the Republican party of the United States

re·pub·li·can·ism \-kə-ˌniz-əm\ n 1 : adherence to or sympathy for a republican form of government 2 : the principles or theory of republican government 3 cap : the principles, policy, or practices of the Republican party of the United States

re·pu·di·ate \ri-'pyüd-ē-ˌāt\ vt 1 : to divorce or separate formally from (a woman) 2 : to refuse to have anything to do with : DISOWN 3 a : to refuse to accept b : to reject as untrue or unjust ⟨*repudiate* a charge of favoritism⟩ 4 : to refuse to acknowledge or pay ⟨*repudiate* a debt⟩ [Latin *repudiare,* from *repudium* "divorce"] SYN SEE REJECT — **re·pu·di·a·tion** \-ˌpyüd-ē-'ā-shən\ n — **re·pu·di·a·tor** \-'pyüd-ē-ˌāt-ər\ n

re·pug·nance \ri-'pəg-nəns\ n : deep-rooted dislike : AVERSION, LOATHING

re·pug·nant \-nənt\ adj 1 : CONTRARY, INCOMPATIBLE ⟨punishments *repugnant* to the spirit of the law⟩ 2 : arousing distaste or aversion ⟨a *repugnant* idea⟩ [Middle French, "opposed, incompatible", from Latin *repugnare* "to fight against", from *re-* + *pugnare* "to fight"] — **re·pug·nant·ly** adv □ SYN REPELLENT, ABHORRENT: REPUGNANT implies arousing one's resistance or loathing by being alien to one's ideas, principles, or tastes; REPELLENT suggests a generally forbidding or unlovely quality that makes one back away; ABHORRENT adds to REPUGNANT an implication of stronger resistance or profound antagonism ⟨police methods *abhorrent* to a free people⟩

¹**re·pulse** \ri-'pəls\ vt 1 : to drive or beat back : REPEL ⟨*repulse* an attack⟩ 2 : to repel by discourtesy, coldness, or denial : REBUFF ⟨*repulsed* their advances⟩ 3 : to cause repulsion in : DISGUST ⟨*repulsed* at the sight⟩ [Latin *repulsus,* past participle of *repellere* "to repel"]

²**repulse** n 1 : a cold discourteous rebuff 2 a : the action of repelling an attacker b : the fact of being repelled

re·pul·sion \ri-'pəl-shən\ n 1 : the action of repulsing : the state of being repulsed 2 : the action of repelling : the force with which bodies, particles, or like forces repel one another 3 : a feeling of aversion : REPUGNANCE

re·pul·sive \ri-'pəl-siv\ adj 1 : tending or serving to repulse 2 : arousing aversion or disgust — **re·pul·sive·ly** adv — **re·pul·sive·ness** n

rep·u·ta·ble \'rep-yət-ə-bəl\ adj : having a good reputation : RESPECTED — **rep·u·ta·bil·i·ty** \ˌrep-yət-ə-'bil-ət-ē\ n — **rep·u·ta·bly** \'rep-yət-ə-blē\ adv

rep·u·ta·tion \ˌrep-yə-'tā-shən\ n 1 : overall quality or character as seen or judged by people in general ⟨has a bad *reputation*⟩ 2 : recognition by other people of some characteristic or ability ⟨has the *reputation* of being clever⟩ 3 : good name : a place in public esteem ⟨lose one's *reputation*⟩ 4 : FAME ⟨a worldwide *reputation*⟩

¹**re·pute** \ri-'pyüt\ vt : BELIEVE 4, CONSIDER ⟨is *reputed* to be a millionaire⟩ [Middle French *reputer,* from Latin *reputare* "to reckon up, think over", from *re-* + *putare* "to reckon"]

²**repute** n 1 : REPUTATION ⟨know a person by *repute*⟩ 2 : FAME, NOTE ⟨a scientist of *repute*⟩

re·put·ed \ri-'pyüt-əd\ adj 1 : having repute ⟨a highly *reputed* lawyer⟩ 2 : popularly supposed ⟨a *reputed* success⟩ — **re·put·ed·ly** adv

¹**re·quest** \ri-'kwest\ n 1 : an asking for something ⟨a *request* for help⟩ 2 : something asked for ⟨grant every *request*⟩ 3 : the condition of being requested ⟨tickets are available upon *request*⟩ 4 : DEMAND ⟨that book is in great *request*⟩ [Middle French *requeste,* derived from Latin *requirere* "to seek for, require"]

²**request** vt 1 : to make a request to or of 2 : to ask for ⟨*request* a loan⟩ SYN SEE ASK — **re·quest·er** n

\ə\	abut	\ng\	sing
\ər\	further	\ō\	bone
\a\	mat	\o\	saw
\ā\	take	\oi\	coin
\ä\	cot, cart	\th\	thin
\au̇\	out	\th\	this
\ch\	chin	\ü\	food
\e\	pet	\u̇\	foot
\ē\	easy	\y\	yet
\g\	go	\yü\	few
\i\	tip	\yu̇\	cure
\ī\	life	\zh\	vision
\j\	job		

re·qui·em \\'rek-wē-əm *also* 'rāk- *or* 'rēk-\\ *n* **1** : a mass for the dead; *also* : a musical setting for such a mass **2** : a musical service or hymn in honor of the dead [Latin, accusative of *requies* "rest"; first word of the introit of the requiem mass]

req·ui·es·cat \\,rek-wē-'es-,kät, ,rā-kwē-\\ *n* : a prayer for the repose of a dead person [Latin, "may he (or she) rest", from *requiescere* "to rest", from *re-* + *quiescere* "to be quiet", from *quies* "quiet"]

re·quire \\ri-'kwīr\\ *vt* **1** : ORDER, COMMAND ⟨the law *requires* drivers to observe traffic lights⟩ **2** : to demand as necessary or essential [Middle French *requerre,* derived from Latin *requirere,* from *re-* + *quaerere* "to seek, ask"] SYN see DEMAND

re·quire·ment \\-mənt\\ *n* : something required ⟨comply with all *requirements*⟩ ⟨sleep is a *requirement* for health⟩

req·ui·site \\'rek-wə-zət\\ *adj* : needed especially for the fulfillment of a special purpose [Latin *requisitus,* past participle of *requirere* "to require"] SYN see NECESSARY — **requisite** *n* — **req·ui·site·ness** *n*

¹req·ui·si·tion \\,rek-wə-'zish-ən\\ *n* **1** : the act of requiring or demanding **2** : an authoritative or formal demand or application ⟨a *requisition* for army supplies⟩ **3** : the condition of being demanded or put into use ⟨every car was in *requisition*⟩

²requisition *vt* **-si·tioned; -si·tion·ing** \\-'zish-ning, -ə-ning\\ : to take or get with a requisition ⟨*requisition* fresh supplies⟩

re·quit·al \\ri-'kwīt-l\\ *n* **1** : the act or action of requiting : the state of being requited **2** : something given in requital

re·quite \\ri-'kwīt\\ *vt* **1 a** : to make return for : REPAY **b** : to retaliate for : AVENGE **2** : to give something to in return for a benefit or service or for an injury [*re-* + obsolete *quite* "to quit, pay"] — **re·quit·er** *n*

¹re·run \\rē-'rən, 'rē-\\ *vt* : to run again or anew

²re·run \\'rē-,rən, rē-', 'rē-\\ *n* : the act or action or an instance of rerunning; *esp* : presentation of a motion-picture film or television program after its first run

re·sale \\'rē-,sāl, rē-', 'rē-\\ *n* : the act or an instance of selling again

re·scind \\ri-'sind\\ *vt* **1** : to make void : CANCEL ⟨*rescind* a contract⟩ **2** : REPEAL ⟨*rescind* a law⟩ [Latin *rescindere* "to cut apart, annul", from *re-* + *scindere* "to cut"] — **re·scind·er** *n*

re·scis·sion \\ri-'sizh-ən\\ *n* : an act of rescinding [Late Latin *rescissio,* from Latin *rescindere* "to annul"]

res·cue \\'res-kyü\\ *vt* : to free from confinement, danger, or evil : SAVE [Middle French *rescourre,* from *re-* + *escourre* "to shake out, wrest away", from Latin *excutere,* from *ex-* + *quatere* "to shake"] — **rescue** *n* — **res·cu·er** *n* □ SYN DELIVER, REDEEM, RANSOM: RESCUE implies freeing from imminent danger by prompt or viorgous action; DELIVER implies releasing from confinement, temptation, slavery, or suffering; REDEEM implies releasing from bondage or penalties by giving what is demanded or necessary; RANSOM applies specifically to buying out of captivity.

reservoir 1

re·search \\ri-'sərch, 'rē-,\\ *n* **1** : careful or diligent search **2** : studious inquiry or examination; *esp* : investigation or experimentation aimed at the discovery and interpretation of facts, revision of accepted theories or laws in the light of new facts, or practical application of such new or revised theories or laws [Middle French *recerche,* from *recerchier* "to investigate thoroughly", from *re-* + *cerchier* "to search"] — **research** *vb* — **re·search·er** *n*

re·sec·tion \\ri-'sek-shən\\ *n* : the surgical removal of part of an organ or structure [Latin *resectio* "act of cutting off", from *resecare* "to cut off", from *re-* + *secare* "to cut"] — **re·sect** \\-'sekt\\ *vt*

re·seed \\rē-'sēd, 'rē-\\ *vb* **1** : to sow seed on again or anew **2** : to maintain itself by self-sown seed

re·sem·blance \\ri-'zem-bləns\\ *n* **1 a** : the quality or state of resembling; *esp* : correspondence in appearance or superficial qualities **b** : a point of likeness **2** : REPRESENTATION 1a, IMAGE SYN see LIKENESS

re·sem·ble \\ri-'zem-bəl\\ *vt* **-bled; -bling** \\-bə-ling, -bling\\ : to be like or similar to [Middle French *resembler,* from *re-* "re-" + *sembler* "to be like, seem", from Latin *similare* "to copy", from *similis* "like"]

re·sent \\ri-'zent\\ *vt* : to feel or show annoyance or ill will over ⟨*resent* criticism⟩ [French *ressentir* "to feel, resent", from *re-* "re-" + *sentir* "to feel", from Latin *sentire*]

re·sent·ful \\-fəl\\ *adj* **1** : full of resentment : inclined to resent **2** : caused or marked by resentment — **re·sent·ful·ly** \\-fə-lē\\ *adv* — **re·sent·ful·ness** *n*

re·sent·ment \\ri-'zent-mənt\\ *n* : a feeling of angry displeasure at something regarded as a wrong, insult, or injury

re·ser·pine \\ri-'sər-,pēn, -pən\\ *n* : a drug obtained especially from and used similarly to rauwolfia [German *reserpin,* probably derived from New Latin *Rauwolfia serpentina,* a species of rauwolfia]

res·er·va·tion \\,rez-ər-'vā-shən\\ *n* **1** : the act of reserving **2** : an arrangement to have something (as a hotel room) held for one's use **3** : something reserved for a special use; *esp* : a tract of public lands so reserved ⟨an Indian *reservation*⟩ **4** : a limiting condition : EXCEPTION ⟨agree without *reservations*⟩

¹re·serve \\ri-'zərv\\ *vt* **1** : to keep in store for future or special use **2** : to retain or hold over to a future time or place : DEFER ⟨*reserve* one's comments on a plan⟩ **3** : to set or have set aside or apart ⟨*reserve* a hotel room⟩ [Middle French *reserver,* from Latin *reservare,* literally, "to keep back", from *servare* "to keep, save"]

²reserve *n* **1** : something stored or available for future use : STOCK ⟨oil *reserves*⟩ **2** : something reserved for a particular use: as **a** : military forces withheld or available for later use — usually used in pl. **b** : the military forces of a country not part of the regular services **c** : RESERVIST **d** : a tract set apart : RESERVATION **3** : an act of reserving : EXCEPTION **4** : restraint, closeness, or caution in one's words and bearing **5** : money or its equivalent kept on hand or set apart usually to meet obligations **6** : SUBSTITUTE ⟨the *reserves* on the football team⟩

re·served \\ri-'zərvd\\ *adj* **1** : restrained in words and actions ⟨very *reserved* in public⟩ **2** : set aside for future or special use SYN see SILENT — **re·serv·ed·ly** \\-'zər-vəd-lē\\ *adv* — **re·served·ness** \\-'zər-vəd-nəs, -'zərvd-nəs, -'zərv-nəs\\ *n*

re·serv·ist \\ri-'zər-vəst\\ *n* : a member of a military reserve

res·er·voir \\'rez-ərv-,wär, -əv-, -,wȯr, -,ȯr\\ *n* **1** : a place where something is kept in store; *esp* : an artificial lake where water is collected and kept in quantity for use **2** : an extra supply : RESERVE **3** : an organism in which a parasite that is harmful to some other species lives and multiplies [French *réservoir,* from *réserver* "to reserve"]

re·shape \\rē-'shāp, 'rē-\\ *vt* : to give a new form to

re·ship \\-'ship\\ *vb* : to ship again; *esp* : to put on board a second time — **re·ship·ment** \\-mənt\\ *n* — **re·ship·per** *n*

re·shuf·fle \\-'shəf-əl\\ *vt* **1** : to shuffle again **2** : to reorganize usually by redistribution of existing elements ⟨the President *reshuffled* the cabinet⟩ — **reshuffle** *n*

re·side \\ri-'zīd\\ *vi* **1** : to dwell permanently or continuously : have a fixed abode ⟨*reside* in St. Louis⟩ **2** : to be present as an element, quality, or right ⟨the power of veto *resides* in the president⟩ [Latin *residēre* "to sit back, abide", from *re-* + *sedēre* "to sit"] — **re·sid·er** *n*

res·i·dence \\'rez-əd-əns, -ə-,dens\\ *n* **1** : the act or fact of residing in a place as a dweller or in discharge of a duty ⟨physicians in *residence* in a hospital⟩ **2 a** : the place where one lives **b** : the status of a legal resident **3 a** : a building used as a home : DWELLING **b** : a unit of housing provided for students **4 a** : the period during which a person resides in a place **b** : a period of active study, research, or teaching at a collegeor university

res·i·den·cy \'rez-əd-ən-sē, -ə-,den-\ *n, pl* **-cies 1** : a usually official place of residence **2** : a territorial unit in which a political resident exercises authority **3** : a period of advanced training in a medical specialty

¹res·i·dent \'rez-əd-ənt, -ə-,dent\ *adj* **I a** : living in a place for some length of time **b** : serving in a regular or full-time capacity ⟨a *resident* engineer⟩ **c** : engaged in academic residence or professional residency ⟨a *resident* scholar⟩ ⟨*resident* physicians⟩ **2** : PRESENT 2b ⟨energy *resident* in matter⟩ **3** : not migratory ⟨*resident* birds⟩ [Latin *residens*, present participle of *residēre* "to sit back, abide"]

²resident *n* **I** : one who resides in a place **2** : a diplomatic agent exercising authority in a protected state **3** : one (as a physician) serving a residency

res·i·den·tial \,rez-ə-'den-chəl\ *adj* **I** : used as a residence or by residents ⟨a *residential* hotel⟩ **2** : adapted to or occupied by residences ⟨a *residential* neighborhood⟩ **3** : of or relating to residence or residences — **res·i·den·tial·ly** \-'dench-lē, -ə-lē\ *adv*

¹re·sid·u·al \ri-'zij-ə-wəl, -'zij-wəl\ *adj* : being or active as a residue : left over — **re·sid·u·al·ly** \-ē\ *adv*

²residual *n* **I** : a residual product, substance, or result : REMAINDER **2** : a payment (as to an actor or writer) for a rerun (as of a taped television program) after an initial showing

residual power *n* : power held to remain at the disposal of a government authority if neither forbidden (as by a constitution) or delegated to other authorities

re·sid·u·ary \ri-'zij-ə-,wer-ē\ *adj* : of, relating to, disposing of, or being a residue ⟨a *residuary* clause in a will⟩

res·i·due \'rez-ə-,dü, -,dyü\ *n* : whatever remains after a part is taken, set apart, or lost : REMNANT, REMAINDER; *esp* : the part of an estate remaining after the payment of all debts and specific devises and bequests [Middle French *residu*, from Latin *residuum*, from *residuus* "left over", from *residēre* "to sit back, remain"]

re·sid·u·um \ri-'zij-ə-wəm\ *n, pl* **re·sid·ua** \-ə-wə\ : something residual : RESIDUE, REMAINDER [Latin]

re·sign \ri-'zīn\ *vb* **I** : to give up by a formal or official act ⟨*resign* an office⟩ **2** : to give up an office or position **3** : to commit or give over or up : submit or yield deliberately ⟨*resign* oneself to disappointment⟩ [Middle French *resigner*, from Latin *resignare* "to unseal, cancel, resign", from *re-* + *signare* "to sign, seal"] SYN see RELINQUISH — **re·sign·er** *n*

res·ig·na·tion \,rez-ig-'nā-shən\ *n* **I a** : an act of resigning **b** : a written statement that gives notice of this act **2** : the quality or the feeling of a person who is resigned : quiet or patient submission or acceptance

re·signed \ri-'zīnd\ *adj* : submitting patiently (as to loss, sorrow, or misfortune) : SUBMISSIVE, UNCOMPLAINING — **re·sign·ed·ly** \-'zī-nəd-lē\ *adv* — **re·sign·ed·ness** \-'zī-nəd-nəs\ *n*

re·sil·ience \ri-'zil-yəns\ *or* **re·sil·ien·cy** \-yən-sē\ *n* **I** : the ability of a body to rebound, recoil, or resume its original size and shape after being compressed, bent, or stretched : ELASTICITY ⟨the *resilience* of rubber⟩ ⟨the *resiliency* of arteries⟩ **2** : the ability to recover from or adjust to misfortune or change

re·sil·ient \-yənt\ *adj* : having resilience: as **a** : capable of withstanding shock without permanent deformation or rupture **b** : SPRINGY ⟨*resilient* turf⟩ **c** : tending to recover readily from fatigue or depression [Latin *resiliens*, present participle of *resilire* "tojump back, recoil", from *re-* + *salire* "to leap"] SYN see ELASTIC — **re·sil·ient·ly** *adv*

res·in \'rez-n\ *n* **I a** : any of various solid or semisolid fusible natural organic substances that are usually transparent or translucent and yellowish to brown, are formed especially in plant secretions, are soluble in organic solvents but not in water, are electrical nonconductors, and are used chiefly in varnishes, printing inks, plastics, and sizes and in medicine **b** : ROSIN **2** : any of a large class of synthetic products that have some of the physical properties of natural resins but are different chemically and are used chiefly as plastics [Middle French *resine*, from Latin *resina*, from Greek *rhētinē* "pine resin"] — **res·in·ous** \-əs\ *adj*

res·in·oid \-,óid\ *n* : a somewhat resinous substance; *esp* : a thermosetting synthetic resin

¹re·sist \ri-'zist\ *vb* **I** : to withstand the force or effect of ⟨*resist* disease⟩ ⟨silver *resists* acids⟩ **2** : to exert oneself to check or defeat **3** : to exert force in opposition [Latin *resistere*, from *re-* + *sistere* "to take a stand"] SYN see OPPOSE — **re·sist·er** *n*

²resist *n* : something (as a coating) that resists or prevents a particular action

re·sis·tance \ri-'zis-təns\ *n* **I a** : an act or instance of resisting : OPPOSITION **b** : a means of resisting **2** : the ability to resist **3** : an opposing or retarding force **4 a** : the opposition offered by a body or substance to the passage through it of an electric current **b** : a source of electrical resistance **5** *often cap* : an underground organization of a conquered country engaging in sabotage and secret operations against occupation forces and collaborators

re·sis·tant \-tənt\ *adj* : giving or capable of resistance

re·sist·ibil·i·ty \ri-,zis-tə-'bil-ət-ē\ *n* **I** : the quality or state of being resistible **2** : the ability to resist

re·sist·ible \ri-'zis-tə-bəl\ *adj* : capable of being resisted

re·sis·tive \ri-'zis-tiv\ *adj* : marked by resistance

re·sis·tiv·i·ty \ri-,zis-'tiv-ət-ē\ *n, pl* **-ties 1** : capacity for resisting : RESISTANCE **2** : the longitudinal electrical resistance of a uniform rod of unit length and unit cross-sectional area : the reciprocal of conductivity

re·sist·less \ri-'zist-ləs\ *adj* **I** : IRRESISTIBLE **2** : offering no resistance — **re·sist·less·ly** *adv* — **re·sist·less·ness**

re·sis·tor \ri-'zis-tər\ *n* : a device offering electrical resistance

res·o·lute \'rez-ə-,lüt\ *adj* **I** : marked by firm determination **2** : BOLD 1, STEADY [Latin *resolutus*, past participle of *resolvere* "to break up, dissolve"] — **res·o·lute·ly** *adv* — **res·o·lute·ness** *n*

res·o·lu·tion \,rez-ə-'lü-shən\ *n* **I** : the act or process of reducing to simpler form: as **a** : the act of analyzing a complex idea into simpler ones **b** : the act of answering **c** : the act of determining **2** : the progression of a chord from dissonance to consonance **3** : the process or capability of making distinguishable individual parts, closely adjacent optical images, or sources of light **4** : the subsidence of inflammation especially in a lung **5 a** : something that is resolved **b** : firmness of resolve **6** : a formal expression of the opinion, will, or intent of an official body or assembled group **7** : the point in a literary work (as a play) at which the chief dramatic complication is worked out

¹re·solve \ri-'zälv, -'zólv\ *vb* **I a** : to break up or separate into component parts; *also* : to change by disintegration **b** : to reduce by analysis **c** : to distinguish between or make independently visible adjacent parts of **2 a** : to clear up : DISPEL ⟨*resolve* doubts⟩ **b** : to find an answer or solution to **3** : to reach a decision about : DETERMINE, DECIDE **4** : to declare or decide by a formal resolution and vote **5** : to work out the resolution of (as a play) **6** : to progress or cause to progress from dissonance to consonance [Latin *resolvere* "to unloose, break up, dissolve", from *re-* + *solvere* "to loosen"] — **re·solv·able** \-'zäl-və-bəl, -'zól-\ *adj* — **re·solv·er** *n*

²resolve *n* **I** : something resolved : DETERMINATION, RESOLUTION **2** : fixity of purpose

\ə\ abut	\ng\ sing
\ər\ further	\ō\ bone
\a\ mat	\ó\ saw
\ā\ take	\ói\ coin
\ä\ cot, cart	\th\ thin
\aú\ out	\th\ this
\ch\ chin	\ü\ food
\e\ pet	\ú\ foot
\ē\ easy	\y\ yet
\g\ go	\yü\ few
\i\ tip	\yú\ cure
\ī\ life	\zh\ vision
\j\ job	

re·solved \ri-'zälvd, -'zȯlvd\ *adj* : RESOLUTE 1, DETERMINED — **re·solv·ed·ly** \-'zäl-vəd-lē, -'zȯl-\ *adv*

res·o·nance \'rez-n-əns\ *n* **1 a** : the quality or state of being resonant **b** (1) : a vibration of large amplitude in a mechanical or electrical system caused by a relatively small periodic stimulus of the same or nearly the same period as the natural vibration period of the system (as when a radio receiving circuit is tuned to a broadcast frequency) (2) : the state of adjustment that produces resonance in a mechanical or electrical system (two circuits in *resonance* with each other) **2 a** : the intensification and enriching of a musical tone by supplementary vibration **b** : a quality imparted to voiced sounds by the configuration of the mouth and pharynx and in some cases also of the nasal cavity **3** : the condition of a molecule, ion, or radical in which two or more representative structures are needed to describe its characteristics

res·o·nant \-n-ənt\ *adj* **1** : continuing to sound : ECHOING **2** : of, relating to, or showing resonance **3** : intensified and enriched by resonance — **res·o·nant·ly** *adv*

res·o·nate \'rez-n-ˌāt\ *vi* **1** : to produce or exhibit resonance **2** : REECHO, RESOUND [Latin *resonare* "to resound"]

res·o·na·tor \-ˌāt-ər\ *n* : something (as a device for increasing the resonance of a musical instrument) that resounds or resonates

re·sorb \rē-'sȯrb, 'rē-, -'zȯrb\ *vt* : to break down and assimilate (something previously produced) (the tadpole's tail is gradually *resorbed*) [Latin *resorbēre* "to swallow again", from *re-* + *sorbēre* "to suck up"] — **re·sorp·tion** \-'sȯrp-shən, -'zȯrp-\ *n*

¹re·sort \ri-'zȯrt\ *n* **1 a** : one that is looked to for help : REFUGE, RESOURCE **b** : RECOURSE (have *resort* to force) **2 a** : frequent, habitual, or general visiting **b** (1) : a frequently visited place (2) : a place providing recreation and entertainment especially to vacationers [Middle French, "resource, recourse", from *resortir* "to rebound, resort", from *re-* + *sortir* "to escape"] SYN SEE RESOURCE

²resort *vi* **1** : to go especially frequently or habitually : REPAIR **2** : to have recourse (*resort* to violence)

re·sort·er \ri-'zȯrt-ər\ *n* : one that resorts; *esp* : a frequenter of resorts

re·sound \ri-'zaund\ *vb* **1** : to become filled with sound : REVERBERATE **2 a** : to sound loudly **b** : to sound or utter in full resonant tones **3** : to become renowned **4** : to extol loudly or widely : CELEBRATE [Middle French *resoner*, from Latin *resonare*, from *re-* + *sonare* "to sound"]

re·sound·ing *adj* **1** : producing or characterized by resonant sound : RESONATING **2 a** : impressively sonorous (a *resounding* name) **b** : DEFINITE, UNEQUIVOCAL (a *resounding* success) — **re·sound·ing·ly** \-'zaun-ding-lē\ *adv*

re·source \'rē-ˌsȯrs, -ˌzȯrs, -ˌsȯrs, -ˌzȯrs, ri-'\ *n* **1** : a new or a reserve source of supply or support **2** *pl* : a usable stock or supply (as of money, products, power, or energy) (America has great natural *resources*) **3** *archaic* : the possibility of relief or recovery **4** : the ability to meet and handle situations : RESOURCEFULNESS **5** : a means of handling a situation or of getting out of difficulty : EXPEDIENT [French *ressource*, from Old French *ressourse* "relief, resource", from *resourdre* "to relieve", literally, "to rise again", from Latin *resurgere*] □ SYN RESORT: RESOURCE applies to anything one falls back upon in the absence or failure of usual means (emergency power *resources*) RESORT implies usually one final resource called upon or used only under compulsion or in desperation (used the gun only as a last *resort*)

re·source·ful \-fəl\ *adj* : able to meet and deal with difficult situations — **re·source·ful·ly** \-fə-lē\ *adv* — **re·source·ful·ness** *n*

¹re·spect \ri-'spekt\ *n* **1** : a relation to or concern with something usually specified : REFERENCE (with *respect* to your last letter) **2** : an act of giving particular attention : CONSIDERATION **3 a** : deferential regard : ESTEEM (we've great *respect* for your opinion) **b** : the quality or state of being esteemed : HONOR **c** *pl* : expressions of respect or deference (pay one's *respects*) **4** : PARTICULAR, DETAIL (perfect in all *respects*) [Latin *respectus*, literally, "act of looking back", from *respicere* "to look back, regard", from *re-* + *specere* "to look"] SYN SEE DEFERENCE

²respect *vt* **1 a** : to consider worthy of high regard : ESTEEM **b** : to avoid interfering with (*respected* their privacy) **2** : to have reference to : CONCERN SYN SEE REGARD — **re·spect·er** *n*

re·spect·abil·i·ty \ri-ˌspek-tə-'bil-ət-ē\ *n* **1** : the quality or state of being respectable **2 a** : respectable persons **b** : a respectable custom : DECENCY

re·spect·able \ri-'spek-tə-bəl\ *adj* **1** : worthy of respect : ESTIMABLE **2** : decent or correct in character or behavior : PROPER (*respectable* people) **3 a** : fair in size or quantity (a *respectable* amount) **b** : moderately good : TOLERABLE **4** : fit to be seen : PRESENTABLE (*respectable* clothes) — **re·spect·able·ness** *n* — **re·spect·ably** \-blē\ *adv*

re·spect·ful \ri-'spekt-fəl\ *adj* : marked by or showing respect — **re·spect·ful·ly** \-fə-lē\ *adv* — **re·spect·ful·ness** *n*

re·spect·ing *prep* : CONCERNING

re·spec·tive \ri-'spek-tiv\ *adj* **1** *obsolete* : PARTIAL 1, DISCRIMINATIVE **2** : OWN, SEPARATE (their *respective* homes) — **re·spec·tive·ness** *n*

re·spec·tive·ly \ri-'spek-tiv-lē\ *adv* : as relating to each : each in the order given

re·spell \rē-'spel, 'rē-\ *vt* : to spell again or in another way; *esp* : to spell out according to a phonetic system (*respelled* pronunciations)

re·spi·ra·ble \'res-pə-rə-bəl, -prə-bəl; ri-'spī-rə-\ *adj* : fit for breathing

res·pi·ra·tion \ˌres-pə-'rā-shən\ *n* **1 a** : the placing (as by breathing) of air or dissolved gases in intimate contact with the circulating medium of a multicellular organism **b** : a single complete act of breathing **2** : the physical and chemical processes by which an organism supplies its cells and tissues with the oxygen needed for metabolism and relieves them of the carbon dioxide formed — **res·pi·ra·tion·al** \-shnəl, -shən-l\ *adj*

res·pi·ra·tor \'res-pə-ˌrāt-ər\ *n* **1** : a device covering the mouth or nose especially to prevent the inhalation of harmful vapors **2** : a device used in artificial respiration

res·pi·ra·to·ry \'res-pə-rə-ˌtōr-ē, -ˌprə-tōr-; ri-'spī-rə-; -ˌtȯr-\ *adj* : of or relating to respiration or the organs of respiration (*respiratory* diseases) (*respiratory* enzymes)

respiratory pigment *n* : any of various permanently or intermittently colored complex proteins (as hemoglobin and cytochrome) that function in the transfer of oxygen in cellular respiration

respiratory system *n* : a system of organs that functions in respiration and consists typically in air-breathing vertebrates of the lungs with their nerves and blood vessels, the organs by which the lungs connect with the outside air, and usually the muscles and parts of the skeleton concerned with support and with emptying and filling the lungs

re·spire \ri-'spīr\ *vb* : to engage in respiration; *esp* : BREATHE [Latin *respirare*, from *re-* + *spirare* "to blow, breathe"]

¹res·pite \'res-pət\ *n* **1** : a temporary delay : POSTPONEMENT; *esp* : REPRIEVE 1b **2** : an interval of rest or relief (a *respite* from toil) [Old French *respit*, from Medieval Latin *respectus*, from Latin, "act of looking back"]

²respite *vt* **1** : to grant a respite to **2** : to put off : DELAY

re·splen·dence \ri-'splen-dəns\ *n* : the quality or state of being resplendent : SPLENDOR — **re·splen·den·cy** \-dən-sē\ *n*

re·splen·dent \-dənt\ *adj* : marked by glowing splendor [Latin *resplendens,* present participle of *resplendēre* "to shine back", from *re-* + *splendēre* "to shine"] — **re·splen·dent·ly** *adv*

re·spond \ri-'spänd\ *vb* **1** : to say something in return : REPLY **2** : to react especially favorably in response ⟨*respond* to surgery⟩ [Middle French *respondre,* from Latin *respondēre* "to promise in return, answer", from *re-* + *spondēre* "to promise"]

¹re·spon·dent \ri-'spän-dənt\ *n* : one who responds: as **a** : one who maintains a thesis in reply **b** : one who answers in various legal proceedings (as in equity or to an appeal) [Latin *respondens,* present participle of *respondēre* "to answer"]

²respondent *adj* : RESPONSIVE 1; *esp* : being a respondent at law

re·sponse \ri-'späns\ *n* **1** : the act of replying : ANSWER **2** : words said or sung by the congregation or choir in a religious service **3** : a reaction of an organism to stimulation [Latin *responsum,* from *responsus,* past participle of *respondēre* "to answer"]

re·spon·si·bil·i·ty \ri-,spän-sə-'bil-ət-ē\ *n, pl* **-ties 1** : the quality or state of being responsible **2** : RELIABILITY, TRUSTWORTHINESS **3** : something for which one is responsible

re·spon·si·ble \ri-'spän-sə-bəl\ *adj* **1** : liable to be called upon to give satisfaction (as for losses or misdeeds) : ANSWERABLE ⟨*responsible* for the damage⟩ **2** : willing and able to fulfill one's obligations : RELIABLE ⟨*responsible* citizens⟩ **3** : requiring a person to take charge of or be trusted with important matters ⟨a *responsible* job⟩ **4** : able to choose for oneself between right and wrong — **re·spon·si·ble·ness** *n* — **re·spon·si·bly** \-blē\ *adv*

re·spon·sive \ri-'spän-siv\ *adj* **1** : giving response : ANSWERING ⟨*responsive* glances⟩ **2** : quick to respond or react sympathetically : SENSITIVE **3** : using responses ⟨*responsive* worship⟩ — **re·spon·sive·ly** *adv* — **re·spon·sive·ness** *n*

¹rest \'rest\ *n* **1** : REPOSE, SLEEP; *esp* : a bodily state characterized by minimal functional and metabolic activities **2 a** : freedom from activity **b** : a state of motionlessness or inactivity **c** : the repose of death **3** : a place for resting or lodging **4** : peace of mind or spirit **5 a** (1) : a silence in music equivalent in duration to a note of the same value (2) : a character representing such a silence **b** : a brief pause in reading **6** : something used for support ⟨leaned against the back *rest*⟩ [Old English]

²rest *vb* **1 a** (1) : to get rest by lying down; *esp* : SLEEP (2) : to give rest to ⟨*rest* yourself on the couch⟩ **b** : to lie dead **2** : to refrain from work or activity **3** : to place or be placed for or as if for support ⟨*rest* one's feet on a hassock⟩ **4 a** : to remain for action or accomplishment ⟨the decision *rests* with you alone⟩ **b** : DEPEND ⟨the success of the flight *rests* on the wing⟩ **c** : to fix or be fixed in trust or confidence ⟨*rested* our hopes on their promise⟩ **5** : to stop voluntarily the introduction of evidence in a law case ⟨the defense *rests*⟩

³rest *n* : something that is left over or behind : REMAINDER — used with *the* [Middle French *reste,* from *rester* "to remain", from Latin *restare,* literally, "to stand back", from *re-* + *stare* "to stand"] SYN see BALANCE

re·state \rē-'stāt, 'rē-\ *vt* : to state again or in another way — **re·state·ment** \-mənt\ *n*

res·tau·rant \'res-tə-rənt, -trənt, -tə-,ränt\ *n* : a public eating place [French, from *restaurer* "to restore", from Latin *restaurare*]

res·tau·ra·teur \,res-tə-rə-'tər\ *also* **res·tau·ran·teur** \-,rän-\ *n* : the operator or proprietor of a restaurant [French *restaurateur,* from Late Latin *restaurator* "restorer", from Latin *restaurare* "to restore"]

rest·ful \'rest-fəl\ *adj* **1** : giving rest ⟨a *restful* chair⟩ **2** : giving a feeling of rest : QUIET ⟨a *restful* scene⟩ — **rest·ful·ly** \-fə-lē\ *adv* — **rest·ful·ness** *n*

rest home *n* : an establishment that provides housing and care for the aged or for convalescents

rest house *n* : a building used for shelter by travelers

rest·ing *adj* **1** : DORMANT ⟨a *resting* spore⟩ **2** : VEGETATIVE 1a ⟨a *resting* nucleus⟩

res·ti·tu·tion \,res-tə-'tü-shən, -'tyü-\ *n* : the restoring of something to its rightful owner or the giving of an equivalent (as for loss or damage) ⟨make *restitution* for personal injuries⟩ [Old French, from Latin *restitutio,* from *restituere* "to restore", from *re-* + *statuere* "to set up", from *status* "position, condition, state"]

res·tive \'res-tiv\ *adj* **1** : stubbornly resisting control : BALKY **2** : fidgeting about : UNEASY [Middle French *restif,* from *rester* "to stop behind, remain", from Latin *restare*] — **res·tive·ly** *adv* — **res·tive·ness** *n* □ SYN RESTIVE, RESTLESS mean showing signs of unrest. RESTIVE implies unwillingness to submit to discipline or follow orders ⟨the colonies were becoming increasingly *restive*⟩ RESTLESS implies constant, aimless activity as from anxiety, boredom, discontent, or discomfort ⟨*restless* children in rainy weather⟩

rest·less \'rest-ləs\ *adj* **1** : lacking rest : giving no rest ⟨a *restless* night⟩ **2** : continuously moving : UNQUIET ⟨the *restless* sea⟩ **3** : marked by or showing unrest especially of mind ⟨*restless* pacing⟩ SYN see RESTIVE — **rest·less·ly** *adv* — **rest·less·ness** *n*

rest mass *n* : the mass of a body exclusive of additional mass acquired by the body when in motion according to the theory of relativity

re·stor·able \ri-'stōr-ə-bəl, -'stór-\ *adj* : fit to be restored or reclaimed

res·to·ra·tion \,res-tə-'rā-shən\ *n* **1** : an act of restoring or the condition of being restored: as **a** : a bringing back to a former position or condition **b** : RESTITUTION **c** : a restoring to an undamaged, fully functional, or improved condition **2** : something that is restored; *esp* : a representation or reconstruction of the original form (as of a fossil or a building) **3** *cap* : the reestablishment of the monarchy in England in 1660 under Charles II; *also* : the period in English history following this Restoration

¹re·stor·a·tive \ri-'stōr-ət-iv, -'stór-\ *adj* : of or relating to restoration; *esp* : having power to restore

²restorative *n* : something that serves to restore to consciousness or health

re·store \ri-'stōr, -'stór\ *vt* **1** : to give back : RETURN ⟨*restored* the package to its owner⟩ **2** : to put or bring back into existence or use ⟨*restore* harmony to the club⟩ **3** : to bring back to or put back into a former or original state : RENEW **4** : to put again in possession of something [Old French *restorer,* from Latin *restaurare* "to renew, rebuild", alteration of *instaurare*] SYN see RENEW — **re·stor·er** *n*

re·strain \ri-'strān\ *vt* **1 a** : to prevent from doing something **b** : CURB, REPRESS ⟨*restrain* one's anger⟩ **2** : to limit, restrict, or keep under control ⟨*restrain* trade⟩ **3** : to deprive of liberty; *esp* : to place under arrest or restraint [Middle French *restraindre,* from Latin *restringere,* from *re-* + *stringere* "to bind tight"] — **re·strain·able** \-'strā-nə-bəl\ *adj* — **re·strain·er** \-'strā-nər\ *n*

re·strained \ri-'strānd\ *adj* : marked by restraint : being without excess or extravagance — **re·strain·ed·ly** \-'strā-nəd-lē\ *adv*

re·straint \ri-'strānt\ *n* **1** : the act of restraining : the state of being restrained ⟨held in *restraint*⟩ **2** : a means of restraining : a restraining force or influence ⟨child *restraints* in a car⟩ ⟨place *restraints* on imports⟩ **3** : control over one's thoughts or feelings : RESERVE ⟨acted with admirable *restraint*⟩ [Middle French *restrainte,* from *restraindre* "to restrain"]

¹rest 5a (2)

\ə\ abut	\ng\ sing
\ər\ further	\ō\ bone
\a\ mat	\ò\ saw
\ā\ take	\òi\ coin
\ä\ cot, cart	\th\ thin
\aù\ out	\th\ this
\ch\ chin	\ü\ food
\e\ pet	\ù\ foot
\ē\ easy	\y\ yet
\g\ go	\yü\ few
\i\ tip	\yù\ cure
\ī\ life	\zh\ vision
\j\ job	

re·strict \ri-'strikt\ *vt* **1** : to confine within bounds : RESTRAIN **2** : to place under restrictions as to use [Latin *restrictus,* past participle of *restringere* "to restrain, restrict"] — **re·strict·ed** *adj* — **re·strict·ed·ly** *adv*

re·stric·tion \ri-'strik-shən\ *n* **1** : something (as a law or rule) that restricts **2** : an act of restricting : the condition of being restricted

re·stric·tive \ri-'strik-tiv\ *adj* **1** : serving or tending to restrict **2** : limiting the reference of a modified word or phrase ⟨*restrictive* clause⟩ — **re·stric·tive·ly** *adv* — **re·stric·tive·ness** *n*

rest room *n* : a room or suite of rooms providing personal facilities (as toilets)

¹**re·sult** \ri-'zəlt\ *vi* **1** : to come about as an effect of something ⟨disease *results* from infection⟩ **2** : to have something as an effect ⟨a disease that *results* in death⟩ [Medieval Latin *resultare,* from Latin, "to rebound", from *re-* + *saltare* "to leap", from *saltus,* past participle of *salire* "to leap"]

²**result** *n* **1** : something that results as a consequence, issue, or conclusion **2** : a beneficial or tangible effect ⟨this method gets *results*⟩ SYN see EFFECT — **re·sult·ful** \-fəl\ *adj* — **re·sult·less** \-ləs\ *adj*

¹**re·sult·ant** \ri-'zəlt-nt\ *adj* : derived from or resulting from something else — **re·sult·ant·ly** *adv*

²**resultant** *n* **1** : something that results : OUTCOME **2** : a vector equal to the sum of a given set of vectors

re·sume \ri-'züm\ *vb* **1** : to take or occupy again ⟨*resume* your seats⟩ **2** : to begin again or go back to (as after an interruption) ⟨*resume* speaking⟩ [Latin *resumere,* from *re-* + *sumere* "to take"]

ré·su·mé *or* **re·su·me** \'rez-ə-ˌmā\ *n* : SUMMARY; *esp* : a short account of one's career and qualifications prepared typically by someone applying for a job [French *résumé,* from *résumer* "to resume, summarize", from Latin *resumere* "to resume"]

re·sump·tion \ri-'zəm-shən, -'zəmp-\ *n* : the action of resuming ⟨*resumption* of work⟩ [Late Latin *resumptio,* from Latin *resumere* "to resume"]

re·sur·gence \ri-'sər-jəns\ *n* : a rising again into life, activity, or prominence [derived from Latin *resurgens,* present participle of *resurgere* "to rise again"] — **re·sur·gent** \-jənt\ *adj*

res·ur·rect \ˌrez-ə-'rekt\ *vt* **1** : to raise from the dead : bring back to life **2** : to bring to view or into use again ⟨*resurrect* an old song⟩ [back-formation from *resurrection*]

res·ur·rec·tion \ˌrez-ə-'rek-shən\ *n* **1 a** *cap* : the rising of Christ from the dead **b** *often cap* : the rising again to life of all the human dead before the final judgment **2** : RESURGENCE, REVIVAL [Late Latin *resurrectio,* from Latin *resurrectus,* past participle of *resurgere* "to rise again", from *re-* + *surgere* "to rise"] — **res·ur·rec·tion·al** \-shnəl, -shən-l\ *adj*

re·sus·ci·tate \ri-'səs-ə-ˌtāt\ *vb* : to revive from apparent death or from unconsciousness; *also* : REVITALIZE [Latin *resuscitare,* from *re-* + *suscitare* "to stir up", from *sub-, sus-* "up" + *citare* "to put in motion, stir"] — **re·sus·ci·ta·tion** \-ˌsəs-ə-'tā-shən\ *n* — **re·sus·ci·ta·tive** \-'səs-ə-ˌtāt-iv\ *adj*

re·sus·ci·ta·tor \ri-'səs-ə-ˌtāt-ər\ *n* : one that resuscitates; *esp* : an apparatus used to relieve asphyxiation

ret \'ret\ *vb* **ret·ted; ret·ting** : to soak so as to loosen the fiber from the woody tissue ⟨*ret* flax⟩ [Dutch *reten*]

¹**re·tail** \'rē-ˌtāl, *especially for 2 also* ri-'\ *vb* **1** : to sell in small quantities directly to the ultimate consumer **2** : TELL 2a, RETELL [Middle French *retaillier* "to cut back, divide into pieces", from *re-* "re-" + *taillier* "to cut", from Late Latin *taliare,* from Latin *talea* "twig, cutting"] — **re·tail·er** *n*

²**re·tail** \'rē-ˌtāl\ *n* : the sale of commodities or goods in small quantities directly to consumers — **at retail 1** : at a retailer's price **2** : ⁴RETAIL

³**re·tail** \'rē-ˌtāl\ *adj* : of, relating to, or engaged in the sale of commodities at retail ⟨*retail* trade⟩

⁴**re·tail** \'rē-ˌtāl\ *adv* **1** : in small quantities **2** : from a retailer

re·tain \ri-'tān\ *vt* **1 a** : to keep in possession or use ⟨*retain* knowledge⟩ **b** : to keep in one's employ or service; *esp* : to employ by paying a retainer **2** : to hold secure or intact ⟨lead *retains* heat⟩ [Middle French *retenir,* from Latin *retinēre* "to hold back, keep", from *re-* + *tenēre* "to hold"]

retained object *n* : an object in a passive construction ⟨*me* in *a book was given me* and *book* in *I was given a book* are *retained objects*⟩

¹**re·tain·er** \ri-'tā-nər\ *n* : a fee paid (as to a lawyer) for advice or services or for a claim upon services in case of need [Middle English *reteiner* "act of withholding", from *reteinen* "to retain" + Anglo-French *-er* (as in *weyver* "waiver")]

²**retainer** *n* **1** : one that retains **2** : a servant or follower in a wealthy household

¹**re·take** \rē-'tāk, 'rē-\ *vt* **-took** \-'tůk\; **-tak·en** \-'tā-kən\; **-tak·ing** : to take again; *esp* : to film again

²**re·take** \'rē-ˌtāk\ *n* : a second filming or photograph

re·tal·i·ate \ri-'tal-ē-ˌāt\ *vi* : to return like for like; *esp* : to get even [Late Latin *retaliare,* from Latin *re-* + *talio* "legal retaliation"] — **re·tal·i·a·tion** \-ˌtal-ē-'ā-shən\ *n* — **re·tal·i·a·tive** \-'tal-ē-ˌāt-iv\ *adj* — **re·tal·ia·to·ry** \-'tal-yə-ˌtōr-ē, -ˌtȯr-\ *adj*

re·tard \ri-'tärd\ *vt* : to slow up or hold back [Latin *retardare,* from *re-* + *tardus* "slow"] — **re·tard·er** *n*

re·tar·dant \ri-'tärd-nt\ *adj* : serving or tending to retard — **retardant** *n*

re·tar·date \ri-'tär-ˌdāt\ *n* : one who is retarded mentally

re·tar·da·tion \ˌrē-ˌtär-'dā-shən\ *n* **1** : an act or instance of retarding **2** : the extent to which something is retarded **3** : an abnormal slowness especially of mental or bodily development

re·tard·ed \ri-'tärd-əd\ *adj* : slow or limited in intellectual or emotional development or academic progress

retch \'rech, *especially British* 'rēch\ *vb* : VOMIT 1; *also* : to try to vomit [Old English *brǣcan* "to spit, clear the throat"]

re·te \'rēt-ē\ *n, pl* **re·tia** \-ē-ə\ : an anatomical network (as of nerves or blood vessels) [Latin, "net"]

re·ten·tion \ri-'ten-chən\ *n* **1** : the act of retaining : the state of being retained **2** : power of or capacity for retaining **3** : something retained [Latin *retentio,* from *retinēre* "to retain"]

re·ten·tive \ri-'tent-iv\ *adj* : having ability to retain; *esp* : having a good memory — **re·ten·tive·ly** *adv* — **re·ten·tive·ness** *n*

re·ten·tiv·i·ty \ˌrē-ˌten-'tiv-ət-ē\ *n* : the power of retaining; *esp* : the capacity for retaining magnetism after the action of the magnetizing force has ceased

ret·i·cence \'ret-ə-səns\ *n* : the quality or state of being reticent

ret·i·cent \-sənt\ *adj* **1** : inclined to be silent or secretive : UNCOMMUNICATIVE **2** : restrained in expression or presentation [Latin *reticens,* present participle of *reticēre* "to keep silent", from *re-* + *tacēre* "to be silent"] SYN see SILENT — **ret·i·cent·ly** *adv*

re·tic·u·lar \ri-'tik-yə-lər\ *adj* : RETICULATE; *also* : of, relating to, or being a reticulum

¹**re·tic·u·late** \-lət\ *adj* : resembling a net [Latin *reticulatus,* from *reticulum* "network", from *rete* "net"] — **re·tic·u·late·ly** *adv*

²**re·tic·u·late** \-ˌlāt\ *vb* **1** : to divide, mark, or construct so as to form a network **2** : to distribute by a network **3** : to become reticulated

re·tic·u·la·tion \ri-ˌtik-yə-'lā-shən\ *n* : a reticulate formation : NETWORK

ret·i·cule \'ret-i-ˌkyül\ *n* : a woman's drawstring bag used especially as a carryall [French *réticule,* from Latin *reticulum* "network, network bag", from *rete* "net"]

re·tic·u·lo·en·do·the·li·al system \ri-ˈtik-yə-lō-ˌen-də-ˈthē-lē-əl-\ *n* : a system of scattered cells derived from mesenchyme that includes all phagocytic cells in the body except circulating leukocytes [*reticulum* + *endothelium*]

re·tic·u·lum \ri-ˈtik-yə-ləm\ *n, pl* **-la** \-lə\ **1** : the second stomach of a ruminant mammal **2** : a netlike structure [Latin, "network", from *rete* "net"]

ret·i·na \ˈret-n-ə, ˈret-nə\ *n, pl* **retinas** or **ret·i·nae** \-n-ˌē, -n-ˌī\ : the sensory membrane that lines the eye, receives the image formed by the lens, is the immediate instrument of vision, and is connected with the brain by the optic nerve [Medieval Latin] — **ret·i·nal** \ˈret-n-əl, ˈret-nəl\ *adj*

ret·i·nal \ˈret-n-ˌal, -ˌȯl\ *n* : either a yellowish or an orange aldehyde derived from vitamin A that in combination with proteins forms the visual pigments of the retinal rods and cones [derived from *retina*]

ret·i·nene \ˈret-n-ˌēn\ *n* : RETINAL

ret·i·nue \ˈret-n-ˌü, -ˌyü\ *n* : the body of retainers who follow a distinguished person : SUITE [Middle French *retenue*, from *retenu*, past participle of *retenir* "to retain"]

re·tire \ri-ˈtīr\ *vb* **1** : to withdraw or cause to withdraw from action or danger : RETREAT **2** : to withdraw especially for privacy **3** : to give up or cause to give up one's position or occupation **4** : to go to bed **5 a** : to withdraw from circulation : RECALL **b** : to withdraw (as obsolete equipment) from usual use or service **6** : to put out (a batter or side) in baseball [Middle French *retirer*, from *re-* "re-" + *tirer* "to draw"]

re·tired \ri-ˈtīrd\ *adj* **1** : HIDDEN, SECLUDED ⟨a *retired* spot in the woods⟩ **2** : withdrawn from active duties or business **3** : received by or due to a person who has retired ⟨*retired* pay⟩ — **re·tired·ly** \-ˈtī-rəd-lē, -ˈtīrd-\ *adv* — **re·tired·ness** \-ˈtīrd-nəs\ *n*

re·tire·ment \ri-ˈtīr-mənt\ *n* : an act of retiring : the state of being retired; *esp* : a giving up of one's position or occupation

re·tir·ing \ri-ˈtīr-ing\ *adj* : RESERVED 1, SHY — **re·tir·ing·ly** \-ing-lē\ *adv* — **re·tir·ing·ness** *n*

re·tool \rē-ˈtül, ˈrē-\ *vt* : to equip anew with new or different tools ⟨*retool* a factory for making a new product⟩

¹re·tort \ri-ˈtȯrt\ *vb* **1** : to answer back : reply angrily or sharply **2** : to reply (as to an argument) with a counter argument [Latin *retortus*, past participle of *retorquēre* "to twist back, hurl back, retort", from *re-* + *torquēre* "to twist"]

²retort *n* : a quick, witty, or cutting reply; *esp* : one that turns the first speaker's words against him

³re·tort \ri-ˈtȯrt, ˈrē-ˌ\ *n* : a vessel in which substances are distilled or decomposed by heat [Middle French *retorte*, from Medieval Latin *retorta*, from Latin *retorquēre* "to twist back"; from its shape]

re·touch \rē-ˈtəch, ˈrē-\ *vt* : to touch up; *esp* : to alter (as a photographic negative) in order to produce a more desirable appearance — **re·touch** \ˈrē-ˌtəch, rē-ˈ, ˈrē-\ *n* — **re·touch·er** \rē-ˈtəch-ər, ˈrē-\ *n*

re·trace \rē-ˈtrās, ˈrē-\ *vt* : to trace again or back

re·tract \ri-ˈtrakt\ *vt* **1** : to draw or pull back or in ⟨a cat can *retract* its claws⟩ **2** : to take back (as an offer or accusation) : WITHDRAW [Latin *retractus*, past participle of *retrahere* "to retract", from *re-* + *trahere* "to draw"] SYN see RECANT — **re·tract·able** \-ˈtrak-tə-bəl\ *adj*

re·trac·tile \ri-ˈtrak-tl, -ˌtīl\ *adj* : capable of being drawn back or in ⟨the *retractile* claws of a cat⟩

re·trac·tion \ri-ˈtrak-shən\ *n* **1** : a statement retracting something previously said or published **2** : an act of retracting : the state of being retracted

re·trac·tor \ri-ˈtrak-tər\ *n* : one that retracts; *esp* : a muscle that draws an organ or part in or back — compare PROTRACTOR

¹re·tread \rē-ˈtred, ˈrē-\ *vt* **re·tread·ed; re·tread·ing** : to put a new tread on (a worn tire)

²re·tread \ˈrē-ˌtred\ *n* **1** : a new tread on a tire **2** : a retreaded tire

¹re·treat \ri-ˈtrēt\ *n* **1 a** : an act or process of withdrawing especially from what is difficult, dangerous, or disagreeable **b** : the usually forced withdrawal of troops from an enemy or from an advanced position **c** : a signal for retreating **d** : a signal given by bugle at the beginning of a military flag-lowering ceremony **e** : a military flag-lowering ceremony **2** : a place of privacy or safety : REFUGE **3** : a period of group withdrawal for prayer, meditation, and instruction under a director [Middle French *retrait*, from *retraire* "to withdraw", from Latin *retrahere* "to retract, withdraw"]

²retreat *vi* **1** : to make a retreat **2** : to slope backward

re·trench \ri-ˈtrench\ *vb* **1** : to cut down (as expenses) : REDUCE **2** : to reduce expenses : ECONOMIZE [obsolete French *retrencher*, from Middle French *retrenchier*, from *re-* + *trenchier* "to cut"] — **re·trench·ment** \-mənt\ *n*

re·tri·al \rē-ˈtrī-əl, ˈrē-, -ˈtrīl\ *n* : a second trial, experiment, or test

ret·ri·bu·tion \ˌre-trə-ˈbyü-shən\ *n* : something given in payment for an offense : PUNISHMENT [Middle French, from Late Latin *retributio*, from Latin *retribuere* "to pay back", from *re-* + *tribuere* "to pay"]

re·trib·u·tive \ri-ˈtrib-yət-iv\ *adj* : of, relating to, or marked by retribution — **re·trib·u·tive·ly** *adv*

re·trib·u·to·ry \-yə-ˌtōr-ē, -ˌtȯr-\ *adj* : RETRIBUTIVE

re·triev·al \ri-ˈtrē-vəl\ *n* **1** : an act or process of retrieving **2** : possibility of being retrieved or of recovering

¹re·trieve \ri-ˈtrēv\ *vb* **1** : to find and bring in killed or wounded game ⟨a dog that *retrieves* well⟩ **2** : to recover, restore, repair, or make good (as a loss or damage) ⟨*retrieve* a damaged reputation⟩ [Middle French *retrouver* "to find again", from *re-* "re-" + *trouver* "to find"] — **re·triev·able** \-ˈtrē-və-bəl\ *adj*

²retrieve *n* **1** : RETRIEVAL **2** : the successful return of a ball that is difficult to reach or control (as in tennis)

re·triev·er \ri-ˈtrē-vər\ *n* : one that retrieves; *esp* : a vigorous active medium-sized dog with heavy water-resistant coat developed by crossbreeding and used especially for retrieving game

ret·ro \ˈre-ˌtrō\ *adj* : relating to, reviving, or being the styles or especially the fashions of the past : fashionably nostalgic or old-fashioned ⟨a *retro* look⟩

retro- *prefix* : backward : back ⟨*retro*rocket⟩ [Latin, from *retro*]

ret·ro·ac·tive \ˌre-trō-ˈak-tiv\ *adj* : intended to apply or take effect at a date in the past ⟨a *retroactive* pay raise⟩ — **ret·ro·ac·tive·ly** *adv*

ret·ro·cede \ˌre-trō-ˈsēd\ *vb* **1** : to go back : RECEDE **2** : to cede back (as a territory or jurisdiction) [Latin *retrocedere*, from *retro-* + *cedere* "to go, cede"] — **ret·ro·ces·sion** \-ˈsesh-ən\ *n*

ret·ro·fit \ˈre-trə-ˌfit\ *vt* **1** : to furnish (as a computer, airplane, or building) with new or modified parts or equipment not available or considered necessary at the time of manufacture **2** : to install (new or modified parts or equipment) in something previously manufactured or constructed — **retrofit** *n*

ret·ro·flex \ˈre-trə-ˌfleks\ or **ret·ro·flexed** \-ˌflekst\ *adj* **1** : turned or bent abruptly backward **2** : pronounced with the tongue tip turned up or curled back just under the hard palate [Latin *retro-* + *flexus*, past participle of *flectere* "to bend"]

ret·ro·flex·ion or **ret·ro·flec·tion** \ˌre-trə-ˈflek-shən\ *n* : the act or process of bending back : the state of being bent back

¹ret·ro·grade \ˈre-trə-ˌgrād\ *adj* **1** : going or inclined to go from a better to a worse state **2** : having a backward direction, motion, or tendency [Latin *retrogradus* "moving backward", from *retro-* + *gradus* "step"]

³retort

\ə\ abut	\ng\ sing
\ər\ further	\ō\ bone
\a\ mat	\ȯ\ saw
\ā\ take	\ȯi\ coin
\ä\ cot, cart	\th\ thin
\aú\ out	\th\ this
\ch\ chin	\ü\ food
\e\ pet	\ú\ foot
\ē\ easy	\y\ yet
\g\ go	\yü\ few
\i\ tip	\yú\ cure
\ī\ life	\zh\ vision
\j\ job	

²**retrograde** *vi* **1** : to go back : RETREAT ⟨a glacier *retrogrades*⟩ **2** : to decline to a worse condition [Latin *retrogradi*, from *retro-* + *gradi* "to go"] — **ret·ro·gra·da·tion** \ˌre-trō-grā-'dā-shən\ *n*

ret·ro·gres·sion \ˌre-trə-'gresh-ən\ *n* : reversion to an earlier, lower, less specialized, or less developed state or condition [derived from Latin *retrogressus,* past participle of *retrogradi* "to move backward", from *retro-* + *gradi* "to step, go"] — **ret·ro·gress** \ˌre-trə-'gres\ *vi* — **ret·ro·gres·sive** \-'gres-iv\ *adj* — **ret·ro·gres·sive·ly** *adv*

ret·ro·rock·et \'re-trō-ˌräk-ət\ *n* : an auxiliary rocket on an airplane, missile, or spacecraft that produces thrust in a direction opposite to or at an oblique angle to the motion of the object for deceleration

ret·ro·spect \'re-trə-ˌspekt\ *n* : a looking back on things past : reflection on past events [*retro-* + *-spect* (as in *prospect*)]

ret·ro·spec·tion \ˌre-trə-'spek-shən\ *n* **1** : the act or power of recalling the past **2** : a review of past events

ret·ro·spec·tive \-'spek-tiv\ *adj* **1** : of, relating to, characteristic of, or given to retrospection **2** : affecting things past : RETROACTIVE — **ret·ro·spec·tive·ly** *adv*

ret·ro·vi·rus \'re-trō-ˌvī-rəs\ *n* : any of a group of RNA-containing viruses (as HIV) that include numerous tumor-producing viruses and that reproduce in infected host cells by going through an intermediate stage in which DNA is produced using reverse transcriptase as a catalyst and the viral RNA as a template — compare REVERSE TRANSCRIPTASE

¹**re·turn** \ri-'tərn\ *vb* **1** : to come or go back **2** : REPLY, ANSWER **3** : to make (as a report) officially by submitting a statement ⟨the jury *returned* a verdict⟩ **4** : to reelect to office ⟨a candidate *returned* by a large majority⟩ **5** : to bring, carry, send, or put back : RESTORE ⟨*return* a book to the library⟩ **6** : to bring in (as profit) : YIELD **7** : REPAY ⟨*return* borrowed money⟩ **8** : to send or say in response or reply ⟨*return* thanks⟩ [Middle French *retourner,* from *re-* "re-" + *tourner* "to turn"] — **re·turn·er** *n*

²**return** *n* **1 a** : the act of coming back to or from a place or condition **b** : a regular or frequent returning : RECURRENCE ⟨the *return* of spring⟩ **2 a** : a report of the results of balloting — usually used in pl. ⟨election *returns*⟩ **b** : a completed income tax form **3** : a means for conveying something (as water) back to its starting point **4 a** : the profit from labor, investment, or business : YIELD **b** : the rate of profit per unit of cost **5 a** : the act of returning something to a former place, condition, or ownership **b** : something returned **6** : an answering or retaliatory play: as **a** : the act of hitting a ball back to an opponent (as in tennis) **b** : the running with a football after receiving a kick or intercepting a pass of the other team

³**return** *adj* : played, delivered, or given in return ⟨a *return* call⟩ ⟨a *return* game⟩

re·turn·able \ri-'tər-nə-bəl\ *adj* **1** : that may be returned ⟨*returnable* bottles⟩ **2** : that must be returned ⟨a library book *returnable* in two weeks⟩

re·turn·ee \ri-ˌtər-'nē\ *n* : one who returns; *esp* : one returning to the United States after military service abroad

re·uni·fy \rē-'yü-nə-ˌfī, 'rē-\ *vt* : to restore unity to — **re·uni·fi·ca·tion** \rē-ˌyü-nə-fə-'kā-shən\ *n*

re·union \rē-'yü-nyən, 'rē-\ *n* **1** : the act of reuniting : the state of being reunited **2** : a reuniting of persons ⟨a class *reunion*⟩

re·unite \ˌrē-yü-'nīt\ *vb* : to come or bring together again after a separation

re·use \rē-'yüz, 'rē-\ *vt* : to use again — **re·us·able** \-'yü-zə-bəl\ *adj* — **re·use** \-'yüs\ *n*

¹**rev** \'rev\ *n* : a revolution of a motor

²**rev** *vb* **revved; rev·ving** : to operate or cause to operate at an increasing speed of revolution ⟨*rev* up a motor⟩

re·val·u·ate \rē-'val-yə-ˌwāt, 'rē-\ *vt* : REVALUE — **re·val·u·a·tion** \rē-ˌval-yə-'wā-shən\ *n*

re·val·ue \rē-'val-yü, 'rē-\ *vt* : to make a new valuation of

re·vamp \rē-'vamp, 'rē-\ *vt* **1** : RENOVATE, RECONSTRUCT **2** : to work over : REVISE

re·veal \ri-'vēl\ *vt* **1** : to make known ⟨*reveal* a secret⟩ **2** : to show plainly : DISPLAY [Middle French *reveler,* from Latin *revelare* "to uncover, reveal", from *re-* + *velare* "to cover", from *velum* "veil"] — **re·veal·able** \-'vē-lə-bəl\ *adj* — **re·veal·er** *n*

re·veal·ment \-'vēl-mənt\ *n* : an act of revealing : REVELATION

rev·eil·le \'rev-ə-lē\ *n* : a signal sounded at about sunrise on a bugle or drum to call soldiers or sailors to duty [French *réveillez,* imperative pl. of *réveiller* "to awaken", from *re-* "re-" + *éveiller* "to awaken", derived from Latin *ex-* + *vigilare* "to keep watch, stay awake"]

¹**rev·el** \'rev-əl\ *vi* **rev·eled** *or* **rev·elled; rev·el·ing** *or* **rev·el·ling** \'rev-ling, -ə-ling\ **1** : to take part in a revel **2** : to take intense satisfaction ⟨*reveling* in success⟩ [Middle French *reveler,* literally, "to rebel", from Latin *rebellare*] — **rev·el·er** *or* **rev·el·ler** \'rev-lər, -ə-lər\ *n*

²**revel** *n* : a noisy or merry celebration or party

rev·e·la·tion \ˌrev-ə-'lā-shən\ *n* **1** : an act of revealing or communicating divine truth **2 a** : an act of revealing to view **b** : something that is revealed; *esp* : an enlightening or astonishing disclosure [Middle French, from Late Latin *revelatio,* from Latin *revelare* "to reveal"]

Rev·e·la·tion \ˌrev-ə-'lā-shən\ *n* — see BIBLE table

rev·el·a·to·ry \'rev-ə-lə-ˌtōr-ē, -ˌtòr-, ri-'vel-ə-\ *adj* : of, relating to, or characteristic of revelation

rev·el·ry \'rev-əl-rē\ *n, pl* **-ries** : boisterous merrymaking

¹**re·venge** \ri-'venj\ *vt* **1** : to inflict injury in return for ⟨*revenge* an insult⟩ **2** : to avenge for a wrong done ⟨able to *revenge* themselves on their former persecutors⟩ [Middle French *revengier,* from *re-* + *vengier* "to avenge", from Latin *vindicare*] SYN see AVENGE — **re·veng·er** *n*

²**revenge** *n* **1** : an act or instance of revenging **2** : a desire to repay injury for injury **3** : an opportunity for getting satisfaction

re·venge·ful \-fəl\ *adj* : full of or given to revenge : VINDICTIVE — **re·venge·ful·ly** \-fə-lē\ *adv* — **re·venge·ful·ness** *n*

rev·e·nue \'rev-ə-ˌnü, -ˌnyü\ *n* **1** : the income from an investment **2** : the income that a government collects for public use **3** : the income produced by a given source [Middle French, from *revenir* "to return", from Latin *revenire,* from *re-* + *venire* "to come"]

rev·e·nu·er \-ˌnü-ər, -ˌnyü-\ *n* : a revenue officer or boat

revenue stamp *n* : a stamp (as on a cigar box) for use as evidence of payment of a tax

re·ver·ber·ant \ri-'vər-brənt, -bə-rənt\ *adj* : that reverberates — **re·ver·ber·ant·ly** *adv*

re·ver·ber·ate \ri-'vər-bə-ˌrāt\ *vi* : RESOUND, ECHO ⟨the shot *reverberated* among the hills⟩ [Latin *reverberare* "to cause to rebound", from *re-* + *verberare* "to lash", from *verber* "rod"] — **re·ver·ber·a·tion** \-ˌvər-bə-'rā-shən\ *n* — **re·ver·ber·a·tive** \-'vər-bə-ˌrāt-iv\ *adj*

¹**re·ver·ber·a·to·ry** \ri-'vər-bə-rə-ˌtōr-ē, -brə-, -ˌtòr-\ *adj* : acting by reverberation

²**reverberatory** *n, pl* **-tories** : a furnace or kiln in which heat is radiated from the roof onto the material treated

¹**re·vere** \ri-'viər\ *vt* : to show devotion and honor to [Latin *revereri,* from *re-* + *vereri* "to fear, respect"]

☐ SYN REVERE, REVERENCE, VENERATE, WORSHIP mean to hold in profound respect and honor. REVERE further implies deference and tenderness of feeling ⟨*revered* their grandparents⟩ REVERENCE suggests a self-denying acknowledging of what has a deep and inviolate claim to respect ⟨*reverence* truth⟩ VENERATE implies regarding as holy or sacrosanct especially because of age; WORSHIP implies paying homage to or as if to a divine being ⟨*worship* idols⟩

²**revere** *n* : REVERS [by alteration]

¹**rev·er·ence** \'rev-rəns, 'rev-ə-rəns, 'rev-ərns\ *n* **1 a** : honor or respect felt or shown : DEFERENCE **b** : a feeling of worshipful respect : VENERATION **2** : a gesture of respect (as a bow) **3** : the state of being revered or honored **4** : one held in reverence — used as a title for a member of the clergy SYN *see* DEFERENCE

²**reverence** *vt* : to regard or treat with reverence SYN *see* REVERE

¹**rev·er·end** \'rev-rənd, 'rev-ə-rənd, 'rev-ərnd\ *adj* **1** : worthy of reverence : REVERED **2** *often cap* : being a member of the clergy — used as a title usually preceded by *the* and followed by a title or a full name ⟨the *Reverend* Mr. Doe⟩ ⟨the *Reverend* John M. Doe⟩ [Middle French, from Latin *reverendus,* from *revereri* "to revere"]

²**reverend** *n* : a member of the clergy ⟨the *reverend* spoke at the meeting⟩

rev·er·ent \'rev-rənt, 'rev-ə-rənt, 'rev-ərnt\ *adj* : very respectful : showing reverence [Latin *reverens,* present participle of *revereri* "to revere"] — **rev·er·ent·ly** *adv*

rev·er·en·tial \,rev-ə-'ren-chəl\ *adj* **1** : proceeding from or expressing reverence ⟨*reverential* awe⟩ **2** : inspiring reverence — **rev·er·en·tial·ly** \-'rench-lē, -ə-lē\ *adv*

rev·er·ie *or* **rev·ery** \'rev-rē, -ə-rē\ *n, pl* **-er·ies 1** : DAYDREAM **2** : the condition of being lost in thought [French *rêverie,* from Middle French, "delirium", from *resver, rever* "to wander, be delirious"]

re·vers \ri-'viər, -'veər\ *n, pl* **revers** \-'viərz, -'veərz\ : a lapel especially on a woman's garment [French, from Middle French *revers* "turned back, reversed"]

re·vers·al \ri-'vər-səl\ *n* : an act or the process of reversing or being reversed

¹**re·verse** \ri-'vərs\ *adj* **1** : opposite or contrary to a previous or normal condition ⟨*reverse* order⟩ **2** : acting or operating in a manner contrary to the usual **3** : effecting reverse movement ⟨*reverse* gear⟩ [Middle French *revers,* from Latin *reversus,* past participle of *revertere* "to turn back"] — **re·verse·ly** *adv*

²**reverse** *vb* **1** : to turn completely about or upside down or inside out **2** : ANNUL: as **a** : to overthrow or set aside (a legal decision) by a contrary decision **b** : to cause to take an opposite point of view **c** : to change to the contrary ⟨*reverse* a policy⟩ **3 a** : to go or cause to go in the opposite direction **b** : to put (as a car) into reverse — **re·vers·er** *n* □ SYN REVERSE, TRANSPOSE, INVERT mean to change to the opposite position. REVERSE may imply change in order, direction of motion, or meaning; TRANSPOSE implies a change in order or relative position of units often through exchange of position; INVERT applies chiefly to turning upside down or inside out, less often end for end

³**reverse** *n* **1** : something directly contrary to something else : OPPOSITE **2** : an act or instance of reversing; *esp* : a change for the worse ⟨financial *reverses*⟩ **3** : the back part of something **4 a** : a gear that reverses something; *also* : the whole mechanism brought into play when such a gear is used **b** : movement in reverse

reverse tran·scrip·tase \-,tran-'skrip-,tās, -,tāz\ *n* : an enzyme that catalyzes the formation of DNA using RNA as a model and that is found especially in retroviruses (as HIV)

re·vers·ibil·i·ty \ri-,vər-sə-'bil-ət-ē\ *n* : the quality or state of being reversible

¹**re·vers·ible** \ri-'vər-sə-bəl\ *adj* : capable of being reversed or of reversing: as **a** : having two finished usable sides ⟨*reversible* fabric⟩ **b** : wearable with either side out ⟨a *reversible* coat⟩ — **re·vers·ibly** \-blē\ *adv*

²**reversible** *n* : a reversible fabric or garment

re·ver·sion \ri-'vər-zhən\ *n* **1** : a right of future possession (as of property or a title) **2 a** : an act or the process of returning (as to a former condition) **b** : reappearance of an ancestral character **3** : an act or instance of turning the opposite way : the state of being so turned **4** : a product of reversion (as an organism with atavistic characteristics) [Middle French, from Latin *reversio* "act of turning back", from *revertere* "to turn back"]

re·ver·sion·ary \-zhə-,ner-ē\ *adj* : of, relating to, constituting, or involving especially a legal reversion

re·vert \ri-'vərt\ *vi* **1** : to come or go back ⟨many *reverted* to savagery⟩ **2** : to undergo reversion [Middle French *revertir,* from *revertere* "to turn back", from *re-* + *vertere* "to turn"] — **re·vert·er** *n* — **re·vert·ible** \-'vərt-ə-bəl\ *adj*

re·vet \ri-'vet\ *vt* **re·vet·ted; re·vet·ting** : to face (as an embankment) with a revetment [French *revêtir,* literally, "to clothe again, dress up", from Latin *revestire,* from *re-* + *vestire* "to clothe"]

re·vet·ment \-mənt\ *n* **1** : a facing (as of stone) to sustain an embankment **2** : EMBANKMENT; *esp* : a protective barricade (as against bomb splinters)

re·vict·ual \rē-'vit-l, 'rē-\ *vb* : to resupply with provisions

¹**re·view** \ri-'vyü\ *n* **1 a** : a formal military inspection **b** : a military ceremony honoring a person or an event **2** : a general survey ⟨a *review* of the week's news⟩ **3** : an act of inspecting or examining ⟨the auditors' *review* was thorough⟩ **4** : judicial reexamination of the proceedings of a lower court **5 a** : a critical evaluation (as of a book or play) **b** : a magazine devoted chiefly to reviews and essays **6 a** : a retrospective view or survey **b** (1) : renewed study of material previously studied (2) : an exercise facilitating such study **7** : REVUE [Middle French *revue,* from *revoir* "to look over", from *re-* "re-" + *voir* "to see", from Latin *vidēre*]

²**review** *vb* **1** : to look at a thing again : study or examine again ⟨*review* a lesson⟩; *esp* : to reexamine judicially **2** : to make a formal inspection of (as troops) **3** : to give a criticism of (as a book or play) **4** : to look back on ⟨*review* accomplishments⟩ — **re·view·er** *n*

re·vile \ri-'vīl\ *vb* **1** : to subject to verbal abuse **2** : to use abusive language : RAIL [Middle French *reviler* "to despise", from *re-* "re-" + *vil* "vile"] — **re·vile·ment** \-mənt\ *n* — **re·vil·er** *n*

re·vis·able \ri-'vī-zə-bəl\ *adj* : capable of being revised

re·vis·al \-zəl\ *n* : an act of revising : REVISION

¹**re·vise** \ri-'vīz\ *vt* **1** : to look over again in order to correct or improve ⟨*revise* a manuscript⟩ **2** : to make a new, amended, improved, or up-to-date version or arrangement of ⟨*revise* a dictionary⟩ [French *reviser,* from Latin *revisere* "to look at again", from *revisus,* past participle of *revidēre* "to see again", from *re-* + *vidēre* "to see"] — **re·vis·er** *or* **re·vi·sor** \-'vī-zər\ *n*

²**re·vise** \'rē-,vīz, ri-'\ *n* : an act of revising : REVISION

re·vi·sion \ri-'vizh-ən\ *n* **1** : an act of revising (as a manuscript) **2** : a revised version — **re·vi·sion·ary** \-'vizh-ə-,ner-ē\ *adj*

re·vi·sion·ism \ri-'vizh-ə-,niz-əm\ *n* : a movement in revolutionary Marxian socialism favoring an evolutionary spirit — **re·vi·sion·ist** \-'vizh-nəst, -ə-nəst\ *adj or n*

re·vi·so·ry \ri-'vīz-rē, -ə-rē\ *adj* : having the power or purpose to revise ⟨*revisory* body⟩ ⟨a *revisory* function⟩

re·vi·tal·i·za·tion \rē-,vīt-l-ə-'zā-shən\ *n* **1** : an act or instance of revitalizing **2** : something revitalized

re·vi·tal·ize \rē-'vīt-l-,īz, 'rē-\ *vt* : to give new life or vigor to

re·viv·al \ri-'vī-vəl\ *n* : an act or instance of reviving : the state of being revived: as **a** : a reviving of interest (as in art, literature, or religion) **b** : a new publication or presentation (as of a book or play) **c** : a renewed flourishing ⟨a *revival* of business⟩ **d** : a meeting or se-

revers

ries of meetings conducted by a preacher to arouse religious emotions or to make converts

re·viv·al·ism \-'vī-və-₁liz-əm\ *n* : the often highly emotional spirit or methods characteristic of religious revivals

re·viv·al·ist \ri-'vī-və-ləst\ *n* : one who conducts revivals — **re·viv·al·is·tic** \-₁vī-və-'lis-tik\ *adj*

re·vive \ri-'vīv\ *vb* 1 : to bring back or come back to life, consciousness, or activity : make or become fresh or strong again 2 : to bring back into use ⟨trying to *revive* an old fashion⟩ [Middle French *revivre,* from Latin *revivere* "to live again", from *re-* + *vivere* "to live"] — **re·viv·er** *n*

re·viv·i·fy \rē-'viv-ə-₁fī\ *vt* **-fied; -fy·ing** : to give new life to : REVIVE — **re·viv·i·fi·ca·tion** \-₁viv-ə-fə-'kā-shən\ *n*

rev·o·ca·ble \'rev-ə-kə-bəl\ *adj* : capable of being revoked [Middle French, from Latin *revocabilis,* from *revocare* "to revoke"]

rev·o·ca·tion \₁rev-ə-'kā-shən\ *n* : an act or instance of revoking

re·voke \ri-'vōk\ *vb* : to put an end to (as a law, order, or privilege) by withdrawing, repealing, or canceling : ANNUL ⟨*revoke* a driver's license for speeding⟩ [Middle French *revoquer,* from Latin *revocare,* literally, "to call back", from *re-* + *vocare* "to call"] — **re·vok·er** *n*

¹re·volt \ri-'vōlt\ *vb* 1 : to renounce allegiance or subjection (as to a government) : REBEL 2 : to experience or cause to experience disgust or shock ⟨my tender nature *revolts* against such treatment⟩ [Middle French *revolter,* from Italian *rivoltare* "to overthrow", derived from Latin *revolvere* "to revolve, roll back"] — **re·volt·er** *n*

²revolt *n* 1 : an act or instance of revolting 2 : a renunciation of allegiance to a government or other legitimate authority; *esp* : INSURRECTION SYN SEE REBELLION

re·volt·ing *adj* : extremely offensive : NAUSEATING — **re·volt·ing·ly** \-'vōl-ting-lē\ *adv*

rev·o·lu·tion \₁rev-ə-'lü-shən\ *n* 1 : the action by a celestial body of going round in an orbit; *also* : the time taken to complete one such orbit 2 : completion of a course (as of years) ⟨a geologic *revolution*⟩ 3 a : the action or motion of revolving : a turning round a center or axis : ROTATION b : a single complete turn (as of a wheel or a phonograph record) 4 a : a sudden, radical, or complete change b : a fundamental change in political organization; *esp* : the overthrow of one government and the substitution of another by the governed [Middle French, from Late Latin *revolutio,* from Latin *revolvere* "to revolve, roll back"] SYN SEE REBELLION

¹rev·o·lu·tion·ary \-shə-₁ner-ē\ *adj* 1 a : of, relating to, or constituting a revolution ⟨*revolutionary* war⟩ b (1) : tending to or promoting revolution (2) : RADICAL 3, EXTREMIST 2 *cap* : of or relating to the American Revolution

²revolutionary *n, pl* **-ar·ies** : REVOLUTIONIST

rev·o·lu·tion·ist \₁rev-ə-'lü-shə-nəst, -shnəst\ *n* 1 : one engaged in a revolution 2 : one who holds or puts forward revolutionary doctrines — **revolutionist** *adj*

rev·o·lu·tion·ize \-shə-₁nīz\ *vt* 1 : to overthrow the established government of 2 : to imbue with revolutionary doctrines 3 : to change fundamentally or completely (as by a revolution) — **rev·o·lu·tion·iz·er** *n*

re·volve \ri-'välv, -'vȯlv\ *vb* 1 : to turn over at length in the mind ⟨*revolved* the story while I waited⟩ 2 a : to go round or cause to go round in an orbit b : to turn round on or as if on an axis : ROTATE 3 : to come around again : RECUR 4 : to move in response to or dependence on a specified agent ⟨the household *revolves* about the baby⟩ [Latin *revolvere* "to roll back, cause to return", from *re-* + *volvere* "to roll"] — **re·volv·able** \-'väl-və-bəl, -'vȯl-\ *adj*

rex

re·volv·er \ri-'väl-vər, -'vȯl-\ *n* : a handgun with a cylinder of several chambers brought successively into line with the barrel and discharged with the same hammer

rhea

re·volv·ing *adj* : tending to revolve or recur; *esp* : recurrently available ⟨*revolving* credit⟩

re·vue \ri-'vyü\ *n* : a theatrical production consisting typically of brief often satirical sketches and songs — compare MUSICAL [French, literally, "review"]

re·vul·sion \ri-'vəl-shən\ *n* 1 : a strong pulling or drawing away : WITHDRAWAL 2 a : a sudden or strong reaction or change b : a sense of utter repugnance : REPULSION [Latin *revulsio* "act of tearing away", from *revellere* "to pluck away", from *re-* + *vellere* "to pluck"] — **re·vul·sive** \-'vəl-siv\ *adj*

re·wake \rē-'wāk, 'rē-\ *or* **re·wak·en** \-'wā-kən\ *vb* : to waken again or anew

¹re·ward \ri-'wȯrd\ *vt* : to give a reward to or for ⟨*reward* them for their troubles⟩ ⟨*rewarded* our honesty⟩ [Old North French *rewarder* "to regard, reward", from *re-* "re-" + *warder* "to watch, guard", of Germanic origin] — **re·ward·able** \-ə-bəl\ *adj* — **re·ward·er** *n*

²reward *n* : something given or offered in return for a service; *esp* : money offered for the return of something lost or stolen or for the capture of a criminal

re·word \rē-'wərd, 'rē-\ *vt* : to state in different words ⟨*reword* a question⟩

re·work \rē-'wərk, 'rē-\ *vt* : to work again or anew: as a : REVISE b : to process (used or scrap material) for further use

¹re·write \rē-'rīt, 'rē-\ *vt* **-wrote** \-'rōt\; **-writ·ten** \-'rit-n\ *also* **-writ** \-'rit\; **-writ·ing** 1 : to write over again especially in a different form 2 : to put (material turned in by a reporter) into form for publication in a newspaper — **re·writ·er** *n*

²re·write \'rē-₁rīt\ *n* : something (as a newspaper article) rewritten

rex \'reks\ *n, pl* **rex·es** *or* **rex** : a mammal of a genetically variant strain characterized by a coat in which the normally longer and coarser guard hairs are shorter than the undercoat or lacking entirely [French *casto-rex,* a variety of rabbit, from Latin *castor* "beaver" + *rex* "king"]

rey·nard \'rān-ərd, 'ren-\ *n, often cap* : FOX 1a [Middle French *Renart, Renard,* the fox who is hero of the French beast epic *Roman de Renart*]

re·zone \rē-'zōn, 'rē-\ *vt* : to alter the zoning of

Rh \'är-'āch\ *adj* : of, relating to, or being an Rh factor ⟨an *Rh* antigen⟩

rhad·a·man·thine \₁rad-ə-'man-thən, -'mant-\ *adj, often cap* : rigorously strict or just [*Rhadamanthus,* mythical judge in the lower world]

Rhae·to–Ro·man·ic \₁rēt-ō-rō-'man-ik\ *n* : a Romance language of eastern Switzerland, northeastern Italy, and adjacent parts of Austria [Latin *rhaetus* "of Rhaetia (ancient Roman province)" + English *Romanic* "Romance"]

rhap·so·dize \'rap-sə-₁dīz\ *vi* : to speak or write rhapsodically ⟨*rhapsodize* about a book⟩ — **rhap·so·dist** \-səd-əst\ *n*

rhap·so·dy \'rap-səd-ē\ *n, pl* **-dies** 1 : a written or spoken expression of extravagant praise or ecstasy 2 : a musical composition of irregular form [Latin *rhapso-dia* "portion of an epic poem adapted for recitation", from Greek *rhapsōidia* "recitation of selections from epic poetry", from *rhaptein* "to sew, stitch together" + *aidein* "to sing"] — **rhap·sod·ic** \rap-'säd-ik\ *or* **rhap·sod·i·cal** \-i-kəl\ *adj* — **rhap·sod·i·cal·ly** \-i-kə-lē, -klē\ *adv*

rhea \'rē-ə\ *n* : any of several large tall flightless three-toed South American birds that resemble but are smaller than the ostrich [New Latin *Rhea,* genus name, probably from Latin, mother of Zeus, from Greek]

rhe·ni·um \'rē-nē-əm\ *n* : a rare heavy hard silvery white metallic chemical element that is used in catalysts and thermocouples — see ELEMENT table [New Latin, from Latin *Rhenus* "Rhine river"]

rhe·o·stat \'rē-ə-ˌstat\ *n* : a resistor for regulating an electric current by means of variable resistances [Greek *rhein* "to flow" + *-states* "one that stops or steadies", from *histanai* "to cause to stand"] — **rhe·o·stat·ic** \ˌrē-ə-'stat-ik\ *adj*

rhe·sus monkey \ˌrē-səs-\ *n* : a pale brown Indian monkey often kept in zoos and frequently used in medical research [New Latin *Rhesus,* genus of monkeys, from Latin, a mythical king of Thrace]

rhet·o·ric \'ret-ə-rik\ *n* **1** : the art of speaking or writing effectively; *also* : the study or application of the principles and rules of composition **2 a** : skill in the effective use of speech **b** : insincere or pretentious language [Middle French *rethorique,* from Latin *rhetorica,* from Greek *rhētorikē,* derived from *rhētōr* "orator, rhetorician", from *eirein* "to say, speak"]

rhe·tor·i·cal \ri-'tȯr-i-kəl, -'tär-\ *adj* **1 a** : of, relating to, or dealing with rhetoric ⟨*rhetorical* studies⟩ **b** : used solely for rhetorical effect ⟨a *rhetorical* question⟩ **2** : using rhetoric; *esp* : pretentious in language — **rhe·tor·i·cal·ly** \-kə-lē, -klē\ *adv* — **rhe·tor·i·cal·ness** \-kəl-nəs\ *n*

rhet·o·ri·cian \ˌret-ə-'rish-ən\ *n* **1 a** : a master or teacher of rhetoric **b** : ORATOR **2** : an eloquent or pretentious writer or speaker

rheum \'rüm\ *n* **1** : a watery discharge from the mucous membranes especially of the eyes or nose **2** : a condition (as a cold) marked by a rheum [Middle French *reume,* from Latin *rheuma,* from Greek, literally, "flow, flux", from *rhein* "to flow"] — **rheumy** \'rü-mē\ *adj*

¹rheu·mat·ic \rù-'mat-ik\ *adj* : of, relating to, characteristic of, or affected with rheumatism — **rheu·mat·i·cal·ly** \-'mat-i-kə-lē, -klē\ *adv*

²rheumatic *n* : one affected with rheumatism

rheumatic fever *n* : an acute disease especially of young people characterized by fever, by inflammation and pain in and around the joints, and by inflammation of the pericardium and heart valves

rheu·ma·tism \'rü-mə-ˌtiz-əm\ *n* : any of various conditions characterized by inflammation or pain in muscles, joints, or fibrous tissue ⟨muscular *rheumatism*⟩ — compare RHEUMATOID ARTHRITIS [Latin *rheumatismus* "flux, rheum", from Greek *rheumatismos,* derived from *rheuma* "flux, rheum", from *rhein* "to flow"]

rheu·ma·toid arthritis \ˌrü-mə-ˌtȯid-\ *n* : a usually chronic disease of unknown cause characterized especially by pain, stiffness, inflammation, and swelling of joints

Rh factor \är-'āch-\ *n* : a substance present in the red blood cells inherited according to Mendelian principles and capable of inducing intense antigenic reactions [*rh*esus monkey (in which it was first detected)]

rhine·stone \'rīn-ˌstōn\ *n* : a brilliant colorless imitation diamond made usually of glass or paste [*Rhine* river]

Rhine wine \'rīn-\ *n* : a typically light-bodied dry white wine produced in the Rhine valley; *also* : a similar wine made elsewhere

rhi·ni·tis \rī-'nīt-əs\ *n* : inflammation of the mucous membrane of the nose [Greek *rhin-, rhis* "nose"]

rhi·no \'rī-nō\ *n, pl* **rhino** *or* **rhinos** : RHINOCEROS

rhi·noc·er·os \rī-'näs-rəs, -ə-rəs\ *n, pl* **-er·os·es** *or* **-er·os** : a large thick-skinned three-toed plant-eating mammal of Africa and Asia that is related to the horse and has one or two heavy upright horns on the snout [Latin *rhinoceros,* from Greek *rhinokerōs,* from *rhin-, rhis* "nose" + *keras* "horn"]

rhiz- *or* **rhizo-** *combining form* : root ⟨*rhizo*sphere⟩ [Greek *rhiza*]

rhi·zo·bi·um \rī-'zō-bē-əm\ *n, pl* **-bia** \-bē-ə\ : any of a genus of small soil bacteria capable of forming symbiotic nodules on the roots of leguminous plants and of

there fixing atmospheric nitrogen [*rhiz-* + Greek *bios* "life"]

rhi·zoid \'rī-ˌzȯid\ *n* : a structure (as a fungal hypha) that functions like a root in absorption or support — **rhi·zoi·dal** \rī-'zȯid-l\ *adj*

rhi·zome \'rī-ˌzōm\ *n* : a somewhat elongate, often thickened, and usually horizontal underground plant stem that produces shoots above and roots below [Greek *rhizōma* "mass of roots", derived from *rhiza* "root"]

rhi·zo·pod \'rī-zə-ˌpäd\ *n* : any of a group (Rhizopoda) of usually creeping protozoans having pseudopodia and including the typical amoebas and related forms

rhi·zo·pus \'rī-zə-pəs\ *n* : any of a genus of mold fungi including economic pests (as the common black mold of bread) causing decay [*rhiz-* + Greek *pous* "foot"]

rhi·zo·sphere \'rī-zə-ˌsfiər\ *n* : the soil immediately about and influenced by plant roots : the rooting zone of a soil

Rh–negative \ˌär-ˌāch-'neg-ət-iv\ *adj* : lacking Rh factor in the red blood cells

rho \'rō\ *n* : the 17th letter of the Greek alphabet — Ρ or ρ

Rhode Is·land Red \rō-ˌdī-lənd-, -lən-\ *n* : any of an American breed of general-purpose domestic fowls with rich brownish red plumage [*Rhode Island,* United States]

Rho·de·sian man \rō-ˌdē-zhən-, -zhē-ən-\ *n* : an extinct African hominid with prominent brow ridges and large face but human palate and dentition [Northern *Rhodesia,* Africa]

rho·di·um \'rōd-ē-əm\ *n* : a white hard ductile metallic chemical element used in alloys with platinum — see ELEMENT table [New Latin, from Greek *rhodon* "rose"]

rho·do·den·dron \ˌrōd-ə-'den-drən\ *n* : any of a genus of the heath family of widely grown shrubs and trees with alternate leaves and showy flowers; *esp* : one with leathery evergreen leaves as distinguished from a deciduous azalea [Latin, "oleander", from Greek, from *rhodon* "rose" + *dendron* "tree"]

rho·dop·sin \rō-'däp-sən\ *n* : a red light-sensitive pigment in the retinal rods of marine fishes and most higher vertebrates that is important in vision in dim light — called also *visual purple;* compare IODOPSIN [Greek *rhodon* "rose" + *opsis* "sight, vision"]

rhomb·en·ceph·a·lon \ˌräm-ˌben-'sef-ə-ˌlän\ *n* : the parts of the vertebrate brain that develop from the embryonic hindbrain [Greek *rhombos* "rhombus" + English *encephalon*]

rhom·bic \'räm-bik\ *adj* **1** : having the form of a rhombus **2** : ORTHORHOMBIC

rhom·bo·he·dron \ˌräm-bō-'hē-drən\ *n, pl* **-drons** *or* **-dra** \-drə\ : a parallelepiped whose faces are rhombuses — **rhom·bo·he·dral** \-drəl\ *adj*

rhom·boid \'räm-ˌbȯid\ *n* : a parallelogram in which the angles are oblique and adjacent sides are unequal — **rhomboid** *adj* — **rhom·boi·dal** \räm-'bȯid-l\ *adj*

rhom·bus \'räm-bəs\ *n, pl* **rhom·bus·es** *or* **rhom·bi** \-ˌbī, -ˌbē\ : a parallelogram having the sides equal and the angles usually oblique [Latin, from Greek *rhombos*]

Rh–pos·i·tive \ˌär-ˌāch-'päz-ət-iv, -'päz-tiv\ *adj* : containing Rh factor in the red blood cells

rhu·barb \'rü-ˌbärb\ *n* **1** : a plant related to buckwheat that has broad green leaves borne on thick juicy pinkish stems often used for food **2** : a heated dispute or controversy ⟨the pitcher got into a *rhubarb* with the umpire⟩ [Middle French *reubarbe,* from Medieval Latin *reubarbarum,* alteration of *rha barbarum,* literally, "barbarian rhubarb"]

rhumba *variant of* RUMBA

rhumb line \'rəm-\ *n* : a line on the surface of the earth that makes equal oblique angles with all meridians [Spanish *rumbo*]

rhinoceros

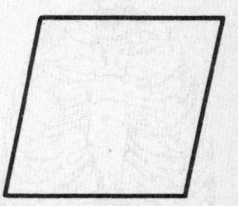

rhombus

\ə\ abut	\ng\ sing
\ər\ further	\ō\ bone
\a\ mat	\ȯ\ saw
\ā\ take	\ȯi\ coin
\ä\ cot, cart	\th\ thin
\au̇\ out	\t͟h\ this
\ch\ chin	\ü\ food
\e\ pet	\u̇\ foot
\ē\ easy	\y\ yet
\g\ go	\yü\ few
\i\ tip	\yu̇\ cure
\ī\ life	\zh\ vision
\j\ job	

¹rhyme *or* **rime** \'rīm\ *n* **1 a** : correspondence in terminal sounds of two or more words or lines of verse **b** : one of two or more words thus corresponding in sound **2 a** : rhyming verse **b** : a composition in verse that rhymes [Old French *rime*]

²rhyme *or* **rime** *vb* **1** : to make rhymes : put into rhyme; *also* : to compose rhyming verse **2** : to end in syllables that form rhymes ⟨words that *rhyme*⟩ **3** : to be in accord : HARMONIZE ⟨colors that *rhyme* well⟩ **4** : to cause to rhyme : use as rhyme ⟨*rhymed* "moon" with "June"⟩ — **rhym·er** *n*

rhyme scheme *n* : the arrangement of rhymes in a stanza or a poem

rhyme·ster *or* **rime·ster** \'rīm-stər\ *n* : an inferior poet : a maker of poor verse

rhyn·cho·ce·pha·lian \,ring-kō-sə-'fāl-yən\ *n* : the tuatara or a related extinct reptile [derived from Greek *rhynchos* "beak, snout" + *kephalē* "head"]

rhy·o·lite \'rī-ə-,līt\ *n* : a very acid volcanic rock that is the lava form of granite [German *rhyolith,* from Greek *rhyax* "stream, stream of lava" (from *rhein* "to flow") + German *-lith* "-lite"] — **rhy·o·lit·ic** \,rī-ə-'lit-ik\ *adj*

rhythm \'rith-əm\ *n* **1 a** : a flow of rising and falling sounds in language that is produced in verse by a regular recurrence of stressed and unstressed syllables : CADENCE **b** : a particular example or form of rhythm ⟨iambic *rhythm*⟩ **2 a** : a flow of sound in music marked by accented beats coming at regular intervals **b** : a characteristic rhythmic pattern ⟨waltz *rhythm*⟩ **c** : the group of instruments in a band providing the rhythm — called also *rhythm section* **3** : a movement or activity in which some action or element recurs regularly ⟨the *rhythm* of breathing⟩ [Latin *rhythmus,* from Greek *rhythmos,* from *rhein* "to flow"] — **rhyth·mic** \'rith-mik\ *or* **rhyth·mi·cal** \-mi-kəl\ *adj* — **rhyth·mi·cal·ly** \-mi-kə-lē, -klē\ *adv*

¹ri·al \rē-'ol, -'äl\ *n* **1** *also* **ri·yal** \-'ol, -'yol, -'äl, -'yäl\ : the basic monetary unit of Oman **2** : the basic monetary unit of Iran **3** : a coin or note representing one rial [Persian, from Arabic *riyāl* "riyal"]

²rial *variant of* RIYAL

ri·al·to \rē-'al-tō\ *n, pl* **-tos 1** : a center of business or financial activity **2** : a theater district [*Rialto,* island and district in Venice]

ri·ata \rē-'at-ə, -'ät-\ *n* : LARIAT [American Spanish *reata*]

¹rib \'rib\ *n* **1 a** : one of the paired curved bony or partly cartilaginous rods that are joined to the spinal column, stiffen the walls of the body of most vertebrates, and protect the viscera **b** : a cut of meat including a rib **2** : something (as a structural member of a ship or airplane) resembling a rib in shape or function **3** : an elongated ridge: as **a** : a major vein of an insect's wing or of a leaf **b** : one of the ridges in some knitted or woven fabrics [Old English]

²rib *vt* **ribbed; rib·bing 1** : to furnish or enclose with ribs **2** : to form ribs in (a fabric) especially in knitting — **rib·ber** *n*

³rib *vt* **ribbed; rib·bing** : to poke fun at : KID [probably from ¹*rib;* from the tickling of the ribs to cause laughter] — **rib·ber** *n*

rib·ald \'rib-əld\ *adj* : marked by or inclined to coarseness and indecency ⟨*ribald* language⟩ ⟨a *ribald* scoffer⟩ [Old French *ribauld* "rascal, wanton", from *riber* "to be wanton", of Germanic origin] SYN see COARSE — **rib·ald·ry** \-əl-drē\ *n*

rib·and \'rib-ənd\ *n* : a ribbon used especially as a decoration [Middle English, alteration of *riban*]

rib·bon \'rib-ən\ *n* **1 a** : a narrow closely woven strip of fabric used especially for trimming or for tying or ornamenting packages **b** : a piece of usually multicolored ribbon worn as a military decoration or as a symbol of a medal **c** : a strip of colored ribbon given for winning a place in competition **2** : a long narrow strip

¹rib 1a

resembling a ribbon: as **a** : a board framed into the studs to support the ceiling or floor joists **b** : a strip of inked fabric (as in a typewriter) **3** : SHRED, TATTER — usually used in pl. [Middle English *riban,* from Middle French *riban, ruban*] — **rib·bon·like** \-,līk\ *adj*

rib·bon·fish \-,fish\ *n* : any of various very long and greatly compressed sea fishes

ribbon worm *n* : NEMERTEAN

rib·by \'rib-ē\ *adj* : having prominent ribs; *also* : GAUNT

rib cage *n* : the bony enclosing wall of the chest consisting chiefly of the ribs and their connectives

ri·bo·fla·vin \,rī-bə-'flā-vən\ *n* : a yellow crystalline compound that is a growth-promoting member of the vitamin B complex occurring both free (as in milk) and combined (as in liver) [*ribo*se + Latin *flavus* "yellow"]

ri·bo·nu·cle·ase \,rī-bō-'nü-klē-,ās, -'nyü-, -,āz\ *n* : an enzyme that catalyzes the hydrolysis of RNA

ri·bo·nu·cle·ic acid \,rī-bō-nù-,klē-ik-, -nyù-, -,klā-\ *n* : RNA [*ribo*se + *nucleic acid*]

ri·bo·nu·cle·o·tide \-'nü-klē-ə-,tīd, -'nyü-\ *n* : a ribose-containing nucleotide that occurs especially in RNA

ri·bose \'rī-,bōs\ *n* : a pentose sugar $C_5H_{10}O_5$ found in the nucleotides of RNA [from *ribonic acid,* an acid obtained by oxidation of ribose, from German *ribonsäure*]

ribosomal RNA *n* : an RNA that is a fundamental structural part of the ribosomes

ri·bo·some \'rī-bə-,sōm\ *n* : a protoplasmic granule that contains RNA and is a site of protein synthesis [*ribo*nucleic acid + *-some*] — **ri·bo·som·al** \,rī-bə-'sō-məl\ *adj*

rice \'rīs\ *n* : an annual cereal grass grown in warm wet areas for its seed that is used especially for food; *also* : this seed [Old French *ris,* from Italian *riso,* from Greek *oryza*]

rice·bird \'rīs-,bərd\ *n* : any of several small birds common in rice fields; *esp* : BOBOLINK

ric·er \'rī-sər\ *n* : a kitchen utensil in which soft foods (as boiled potatoes) are pressed through a perforated container as slender strings

rich \'rich\ *adj* **1** : having or controlling great wealth **2 a** : having great value ⟨a *rich* harvest⟩ **b** : magnificently impressive : SUMPTUOUS **3** : well supplied with something pleasing or desirable ⟨a land *rich* in resources⟩: as **a** : vivid and deep in color ⟨a *rich* red⟩ **b** : full and mellow in tone and quality ⟨a *rich* voice⟩ **c** : of pleasingly strong odor ⟨*rich* perfumes⟩ **4** : highly productive : FRUITFUL ⟨a *rich* mine⟩ ⟨*rich* soil⟩ **5 a** : highly seasoned, fatty, oily, or sweet ⟨*rich* foods⟩ **b** : high in combustible content ⟨a *rich* fuel mixture⟩ **6** : giving amusement; *also* : LAUGHABLE [Old English *rīce*] — **rich·ness** *n*

rich·en \'rich-ən\ *vt* **rich·ened; rich·en·ing** \'rich-ning, -ə-ning\ : to make rich or richer

rich·es \'rich-əz\ *n pl* : things that make one rich : WEALTH [Old French *richesse* "richness", form *riche* "rich", of Germanic origin]

rich·ly \'rich-lē\ *adv* **1** : in a rich manner **2** : in full measure : AMPLY ⟨praise *richly* deserved⟩

Rich·ter scale \'rik-tər-\ *n* : a logarithmic scale for expressing the intensity of a seismic disturbance (as an earthquake) in terms of the energy dissipated in it [Charles R. *Richter,* born 1900, American seismologist]

¹rick \'rik\ *n* : a stack (as of hay) in the open air [Old English *hrēac*]

²rick *vt* : to pile (as hay) in ricks

rick·ets \'rik-əts\ *n* : a disease of the young marked especially by soft and deformed bones due to failure to assimilate and use calcium and phosphorus normally and caused by inadequate vitamin D [origin unknown]

rick·ett·sia \rik-'et-sē-ə\ *n, pl* **-si·as** *or* **-si·ae** \-sē-,ē, -sē-,ī\ : any of various microorganisms sometimes held to be intermediate between bacteria and true viruses that live in cells and include causers of serious diseases (as typhus) [Howard T. *Ricketts,* died 1910, American pathologist] — **rick·ett·si·al** \-sē-əl\ *adj*

rick·ety \'rik-ət-ē\ *adj* **1** : affected with rickets **2** : feeble in the joints ⟨a *rickety* old pensioner⟩ **3** : UNSOUND c, SHAKY ⟨a *rickety* wagon⟩

rick·ey \'rik-ē\ *n, pl* **rickeys** : a drink containing liquor, lime juice, sugar, and soda water; *also* : a similar drink without liquor [probably from the name *Rickey*]

rick·rack *or* **ric·rac** \'rik-,rak\ *n* : a flat braid woven to form zigzags and used especially as trimming on clothing [reduplication of ²*rack*]

rick·sha *or* **rick·shaw** \'rik-,shò\ *n* : a small 2-wheeled covered vehicle pulled by one man and used originally in Japan [alteration of *jinrikisha*]

¹ric·o·chet \'rik-ə-,shā, *British also* -,shet\ *n* : a glancing rebound (as of a bullet off a flat surface); *also* : an object that ricochets [French]

²ricochet *vi* **-cheted** \-,shād\ *or* **-chet·ted** \-,shet-əd\; **-chet·ing** \-,shā-ing\ *or* **-chet·ting** \-,shet-ing\ : to skip with or as if with glancing rebounds

ri·cot·ta \ri-'kòt-ə\ *n* : a white unripened whey cheese of Italy that resembles cottage cheese [Italian, from *ricuocere* "to cook again", from Latin *recoquere,* from *re-* + *coquere* "to cook"]

ric·tus \'rik-təs\ *n* : a gaping grin or grimace [Latin, "open mouth", from *rictus,* past participle of *ringi* "to gape"]

rid \'rid\ *vt* **rid** *also* **rid·ded; rid·ding** : to make free : RELIEVE — often used in the phrase *be rid of* or *get rid of* [Middle English *ridden* "to clear", from Old Norse *rythja*]

rid·able *or* **ride·able** \'rīd-ə-bəl\ *adj* : fit for riding

rid·dance \'rid-ns\ *n* : the act of ridding : the state of being rid of

rid·den \'rid-n\ *adj* : extremely concerned with or burdened by — usually used in combination ⟨guilt-*ridden*⟩ ⟨slum-*ridden*⟩

¹rid·dle \'rid-l\ *n* **1** : a mystifying, misleading, or puzzling question posed as a problem to be solved or guessed : CONUNDRUM **2** : something or someone difficult to understand [Old English *rædelse* "opinion, conjecture, riddle"] SYN SEE MYSTERY

²riddle *vb* **rid·dled; rid·dling** \'rid-ling, -l-ing\ **1** : to find the solution of **2** : to set a riddle for : PUZZLE **3** : to speak in riddles or set forth a riddle — **rid·dler** \-lər, -l-ər\ *n*

³riddle *n* : a coarse sieve (as for ashes) [Old English *hriddel*]

⁴riddle *vt* **1** : to sift or separate with or as if with a riddle **2 a** : to fill full of holes ⟨a boat *riddled* with shot⟩ **b** : to spread through : PERMEATE ⟨a story *riddled* with lies⟩

¹ride \'rīd\ *vb* **rode** \'rōd\; **rid·den** \'rid-n\; **rid·ing** \'rīd-ing\ **1 a** : to sit on and control so as to be carried along ⟨*ride* a horse⟩ ⟨*ride* a motorcycle⟩ **b** : to travel in or on as a conveyance ⟨*ride* a bus⟩ ⟨*ride* in an airplane⟩ **2 a** : to be supported by and move with ⟨a ship *riding* the waves⟩ ⟨the bearings *ride* on a cushion of grease⟩ **b** : to float at anchor **c** : to remain afloat through : SURVIVE ⟨*ride* out a storm⟩ **3 a** : to convey in or as if in a vehicle : give a ride to **b** : to travel over a surface ⟨the car *rides* well⟩ **4** : to torment by or as if by constant nagging or teasing **5 a** : to be contingent : DEPEND ⟨all our hopes *ride* on their success⟩ **b** : to be bet ⟨their money is *riding* on the favorite⟩ [Old English *rīdan*]

☐ SYN DRIVE: RIDE stresses being borne along on the back of an animal or in a conveyance ⟨*ride* in a train⟩ and implies control only when the rider is mounted astride ⟨*ride* a bicycle⟩ DRIVE implies the action of controlling the movements of an animal or a powered vehicle whether or not the agent is borne along ⟨*drive* a herd of sheep⟩ ⟨*drive* a bus⟩ — **ride for a fall** : to court

disaster — **ride roughshod over** : to treat with disdain or abuse

²ride *n* **1** : an act of riding; *esp* : a trip on horseback or by vehicle ⟨a *ride* in the country⟩ **2** : a way (as a road or path) for riding **3** : a mechanical device (as at an amusement park) for riding on **4** : a means of transportation ⟨needs a *ride* to work⟩

rid·er \'rīd-ər\ *n* **1** : one that rides **2 a** : an addition to a document often attached on a separate piece of paper **b** : a clause added to a legislative bill to secure a usually distinct object — **rid·er·less** \-ləs\ *adj*

¹ridge \'rij\ *n* **1** : a raised body part (as along the backbone) **2** : a range of hills or mountains **3** : a raised strip (as of plowed ground) **4** : the line made where two sloping surfaces come together ⟨the *ridge* of a roof⟩ [Old English *hrycg*]

²ridge *vb* : to form into or extend in ridges

ridge·ling *or* **ridg·ling** \'rij-ling\ *n* : a male domestic animal that is imperfectly developed sexually or imperfectly castrated [perhaps from ¹*ridge*]

ridge·pole \'rij-,pōl\ *n* **1** : the highest horizontal timber in a sloping roof to which the upper ends of the rafters are fastened **2** : a horizontal support for the top of a tent

ridgy \'rij-ē\ *adj* : having or rising in ridges

¹rid·i·cule \'rid-ə-,kyül\ *n* : the act of exposing to laughter : DERISION, MOCKERY [Latin *ridiculum* "jest", from *ridiculus* "laughable", from *ridēre* "to laugh"]

²ridicule *vt* : to make fun of — **rid·i·cul·er** *n* ☐ SYN RIDICULE, DERIDE, MOCK, TAUNT mean to make an object of laughter or scorn. RIDICULE implies an often malicious belittling; DERIDE suggests contemptuous and often bitter ridicule; MOCK implies scorn often expressed ironically as by mimicry or sham deference; TAUNT implies mockery and often jeering insults in an effort to challenge or reproach.

ri·dic·u·lous \rə-'dik-yə-ləs\ *adj* : arousing or deserving ridicule : ABSURD, PREPOSTEROUS SYN SEE LAUGHABLE — **ri·dic·u·lous·ly** *adv* — **ri·dic·u·lous·ness** *n*

¹rid·ing \'rīd-ing\ *n* : one of the three administrative jurisdictions into which Yorkshire, England, was formerly divided [Middle English, derived from Old Norse *thrithjungr* "third part", from *thrithi* "third"]

²rid·ing \'rīd-ing\ *n* : the action or state of one that rides

³rid·ing *adj* **1** : used for or when riding ⟨a *riding* horse⟩ **2** : operated by a rider ⟨a *riding* plow⟩

rid·ley \'rid-lē\ *n* : a large sea turtle of the western Atlantic [probably from the name *Ridley*]

rife \'rīf\ *adj* **1** : WIDESPREAD **2**, PREVALENT ⟨lands where famine is *rife*⟩ **2** : well supplied ⟨the air was *rife* with rumors⟩ [Old English *rȳfe*] — **rife** *adv* — **rife·ly** *adv*

¹riff \'rif\ *vb* : RIFFLE 3, SKIM ⟨*riff* pages⟩ [short for *riffle*]

²riff *n* : a repeated figure in jazz typically supporting a solo improvisation [probably from *refrain*]

³riff *vi* : to perform a jazz riff

Riff \'rif\ *n, pl* **Riffs** *or* **Riffi** \'rif-ē\ *or* **Riff** : a Berber of the Rif in northern Morocco

¹rif·fle \'rif-əl\ *n* **1 a** : a shallow extending across a stream bed and causing broken water **b** : a stretch of water flowing over a riffle **2** : a small wave or succession of small waves : RIPPLE [perhaps alteration of *ruffle*]

²riffle *vb* **rif·fled; rif·fling** \'rif-ling, -ə-ling\ **1** : to form, flow over, or move in riffles **2** : to ruffle slightly : RIPPLE **3 a** : to flip or leaf through hastily **b** : to manipulate or finger lightly or idly ⟨*riffle* a stack of coins⟩

riff·raff \'rif-,raf\ *n* **1 a** : disreputable persons **b** : RABBLE 2 **2** : RUBBISH, REFUSE [Middle English *ryffe raffe,* from *rif* and *raf* "every single one", from Middle French *rif et raf* "completely", from *rifler* "to scratch, plunder" + *raffe* "act of sweeping"] — **riffraff** *adj*

¹ri·fle \'rī-fəl\ *vb* **ri·fled; ri·fling** \'rī-fling, -fə-ling\ **1** : to ransack especially with the intent to steal ⟨*rifle* the

ricksha

mail) **2** : to steal and carry away **3** : to engage in ransacking and stealing [Middle French *rifler* "to scratch, file, plunder", of Germanic origin] — **ri·fler** \'rī-flər, -fə-lər\ □ ORIGIN The basic meaning of Middle French *rifler* was "to scratch or file". But it was in the extended sense "to plunder or ransack" that the Middle English borrowed the word from the French. Early in the 17th century the French word was borrowed again into English in something closer to its original sense, "to scratch". To *rifle* a gun was to cut spiral grooves into its bore. By functional shift *rifle* became a noun which named such a groove. And by the late 18th century a gun with a rifled bore was itself called a *rifle*.

²rifle *vt* **ri·fled; ri·fling** : to cut spiral grooves into the bore of ⟨*rifled* arms⟩ ⟨*rifled* pipe⟩ [French *rifler* "to scratch, file"]

³rifle *n* **1 a** : a weapon with a rifled bore intended to be fired from the shoulder **b** : a rifled artillery piece **2** *pl* : a body of soldiers armed with rifles

ri·fle·man \'rī-fəl-mən\ *n* **1** : a soldier armed with a rifle **2** : a person skilled in shooting with a rifle

ri·fle·ry \'rī-fəl-rē\ *n* : rifle shooting especially at targets

ri·fling \'rī-fling, -fə-ling\ *n* **1** : the act or process of making spiral grooves **2** : a system of spiral grooves in the bore of a gun causing a projectile when fired to rotate about its longer axis

¹rift \'rift\ *n* **1 a** : an opening (as a fissure or crevasse) made by splitting or separation **b** : FAULT 4 **2** : BREACH 3a, ESTRANGEMENT [of Scandinavian origin]

²rift *vb* : ²CLEAVE 1a, DIVIDE

¹rig \'rig\ *vt* **rigged; rig·ging** **1** : to fit out (as a ship) with rigging **2** : CLOTHE, DRESS ⟨was *rigged* out in my Sunday clothes⟩ **3** : to furnish with special gear : EQUIP **4** : to set up or fit up often as a makeshift ⟨*rig* a temporary shelter⟩ [Middle English *riggen*]

²rig *n* **1** : the distinctive shape, number, and arrangement of sails and masts of a ship ⟨a schooner *rig*⟩ **2** : EQUIPAGE; *esp* : a carriage with its horse **3** : CLOTHING, DRESS **4** : tackle, equipment, or machinery fitted for a specified purpose ⟨oil-drilling *rig*⟩

³rig *vt* **rigged; rig·ging** : to manipulate or control usually by deceptive or dishonest means ⟨*rig* an election⟩ ⟨*rig* a contest⟩ [from earlier *rig* "swindle", of unknown origin]

rig·a·doon \ˌrig-ə-'dün\ *or* **ri·gau·don** \rē-gō-'dōⁿ\ *n* : a lively dance of the 17th and 18th centuries; *also* : the music for a rigadoon [French *rigaudon*]

rigamarole *variant of* RIGMAROLE

Ri·gel \'rī-jəl, -gəl\ *n* : a bright star in the left foot of the constellation Orion [Arabic *Rijl*, literally, "foot"]

rig·ger \'rig-ər\ *n* **1** : one that rigs **2** : a ship of a specified rig ⟨square-*rigger*⟩

rig·ging \'rig-ing, -ən\ *n* **1 a** : the lines and chains used aboard a ship for supporting masts and spars and controlling sails **b** : a similar network (as in theater scenery) used for support and manipulation **2** : CLOTHING

¹right \'rīt\ *adj* **1** : RIGHTEOUS 1, UPRIGHT **2** : being in accordance with what is just, good, or proper ⟨*right* conduct⟩ **3 a** : conforming to a standard **b** : conforming to facts or truth : CORRECT ⟨the *right* answer⟩ **4** : SUITABLE, APPROPRIATE ⟨the *right* person for the job⟩ **5** : STRAIGHT ⟨a *right* line⟩ **6** : GENUINE 1, REAL **7 a** : of, relating to, situated on, or being the side of the body which is away from the heart and on which the hand is stronger and more skilled in most people ⟨*right* arm⟩ **b** : located in the same relative position as the right of the body when facing in the same direction as the observer : RIGHT-HAND ⟨the *right* side of the road⟩ **8** : having its axis perpendicular to the base ⟨a *right* cone⟩ **9** : of, relating to, or being the principal or more prominent side of an object ⟨turn the *right* side out⟩ **10** : acting or judging in accordance with truth or fact ⟨time proved them *right*⟩ **11 a** : physically or mentally

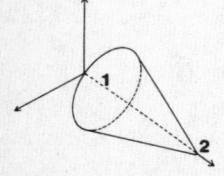

right circular cone: *1* axis, *2* vertex

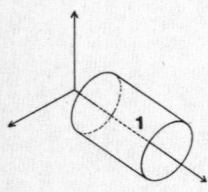

right circular cylinder: *1* axis

well ⟨did not feel *right*⟩ **b** : being in a correct or proper state ⟨put things *right*⟩ **12** : most favorable or desired : PREFERABLE ⟨live on the *right* side of town⟩ **13** *often cap* : of or adhering to the Right in politics [Old English *riht*] — **right·ness** *n*

²right *n* **1** : qualities (as adherence to duty and obedience to lawful authority) that together constitute the ideal of moral propriety **2** : something to which one has a just claim or which one may properly claim as due ⟨the *right* to respect⟩: as **a** : a power or privilege to which one is justly entitled ⟨one's *right* to vote⟩ **b** : an interest that one has in a property — often used in pl. ⟨mineral *rights*⟩ ⟨film *rights* of a novel⟩ **3** : the cause of truth or justice **4** : the location or direction of the right side ⟨the woods on my *right*⟩ **5 a** : the true account or correct interpretation **b** : the quality or state of being factually correct **6** *often cap* **a** : the part of a legislative chamber located to the right of the presiding officer **b** : the members of a continental European legislative body occupying the right and holding more conservative political views than other members **7 a** *cap* : individuals sometimes professing opposition to change in the established order and favoring traditional attitudes and practices and sometimes advocating the forced establishment of an authoritarian political order **b** *often cap* : a conservative position — **by rights** : with reason or justice : PROPERLY — **to rights** : into proper order

³right *adv* **1** : according to right ⟨live *right*⟩ **2** : EXACTLY, PRECISELY ⟨*right* at my fingertips⟩ **3** : in a suitable, proper, or desired manner ⟨hold your pen *right*⟩ **4** : in a direct line or course : DIRECTLY ⟨go *right* home⟩ **5** : according to fact or truth : TRULY ⟨guess *right*⟩ **6 a** : all the way ⟨windows *right* to the floor⟩ **b** : COMPLETELY ⟨felt *right* at home⟩ **7** : IMMEDIATELY ⟨*right* after lunch⟩ **8** : VERY ⟨a *right* pleasant day⟩ **9** : on or to the right ⟨looked *right* and left⟩

⁴right *vb* **1 a** : to relieve from wrong **b** : JUSTIFY 1a, VINDICATE **2 a** : to adjust or restore to the proper state or condition **b** : to bring or restore to an upright position ⟨*right* a capsized boat⟩ **3** : to become upright — **right·er** *n*

right angle *n* : the angle that is formed by two lines perpendicular to each other and measures 90 degrees — **right–an·gled** \'rīt-'ang-gəld\ *or* **right–an·gle** \-gəl\ *adj*

right circular cone *n* : a cone with a circular base and with the axis joining the vertex to the center of the base perpendicular to the plane of the base

right circular cylinder *n* : a cylinder with the bases circular and with the axis joining the two centers of the bases perpendicular to the planes of the two bases

right·eous \'rī-chəs\ *adj* **1** : acting rightly : UPRIGHT **2 a** : morally right or justifiable ⟨*righteous* actions⟩ **b** : arising from an outraged sense of justice or morality ⟨*righteous* indignation⟩ [alteration of earlier *rightuous*, from Middle English *rightwise*, *rightwos*, from Old English *rihtwīs*, from *riht* "right" + *wīs* "wise"] — **right·eous·ly** *adv* — **right·eous·ness** *n*

right field *n* **1** : the part of the baseball outfield to the right looking out from the home plate **2** : the position of the player defending right field — **right fielder** *n*

right·ful \'rīt-fəl\ *adj* **1** : morally right or good **2 a** : having a just or legally enforceable claim : LEGITIMATE ⟨the *rightful* owner⟩ **b** : held by right or just claim : LEGAL ⟨*rightful* authority⟩ **3** : PROPER 1, FITTING — **right·ful·ly** \-fə-lē\ *adv* — **right·ful·ness** *n*

right–hand \ˌrīt-ˌhand\ *adj* **1** : situated on the right **2** : RIGHT-HANDED 1 **3** : chiefly relied on : almost indispensable

right hand *n* **1 a** : the hand on a person's right side **b** : a reliable or indispensable person **2 a** : the right side **b** : a place of honor

right–hand·ed \'rīt-'han-dəd\ *adj* **1** : using the right hand more skillfully or freely than the left **2** : done or made with or for the right hand **3** : having or moving with a clockwise turn or twist — **right–hand·ed·ly** *or* **right–hand·ed** *adv* — **right–hand·ed·ness** *n*

right–hand·er \-'han-dər\ *n* **1** : a blow struck with the right hand **2** : a right-handed person

right·ist \'rīt-əst\ *n, often cap* : an advocate or adherent of the doctrines of the Right — **rightist** *adj, often cap*

right·ly \'rīt-lē\ *adv* **1** : FAIRLY 3, JUSTLY **2** : PROPERLY 1, FITLY **3** : according to truth or fact

right–of–way \,rīt-əv-'wā, -ə-\ *n, pl* **rights–of–way** *also* **right–of–ways 1** : a legal right of passage over another person's ground **2 a** : the area over which a right-of-way exists **b** : the strip of land over which a public road is built **c** : the land occupied by a railroad especially for its main line **d** : the land used by a public utility (as for a transmission line) **3** : the right of traffic to take precedence over other traffic

right prism *n* : a prism with the lateral edges perpendicular to the two bases and with all the lateral faces rectangles

Right Reverend — used as a title for some high religious officials (as Episcopal bishops)

right–to–work law \,rīt-tə-'wərk-\ *n* : a law banning the union shop and the closed shop

right triangle *n* : a triangle having a right angle

right·ward \-wərd\ *adv* : toward or on the right — **rightward** *adj*

right whale *n* : a large whalebone whale with no fin on the back, a very large head, and small eyes near the angles of the mouth

right wing *n* **1** : the rightist division of a group **2** : RIGHT 7 — **right–wing·er** \'rīt-'wing-ər\ *n*

rig·id \'rij-əd\ *adj* **1** : lacking flexibility : STIFF, HARD **2 a** : inflexibly set in opinion : UNYIELDING **b** : strictly observed : SCRUPULOUS **3** : HARSH, SEVERE ⟨*rigid* treatment⟩ **4** : precise and accurate in procedure [Latin *rigidus*, from *rigēre* "to be stiff"] — **ri·gid·i·ty** \rə-'jid-ət-ē\ *n* — **rig·id·ly** \'rij-əd-lē\ *adv* — **rig·id·ness** *n*
□ SYN RIGID, RIGOROUS, STRICT, STRINGENT mean very severe or stern. RIGID implies uncompromising inflexibility ⟨*rigid* and arbitrary rules⟩ RIGOROUS implies the imposing of hardship and difficulty ⟨*rigorous* training⟩ STRICT emphasizes close conformity to rules, standards, or requirements ⟨*strict* discipline⟩ STRINGENT suggests restrictions or limitations that curb or coerce ⟨*stringent* punishment⟩

rig·ma·role *or* **rig·a·ma·role** \'rig-ə-mə-,rōl, 'rig-mə-\ *n* **1** : confused or meaningless talk **2** : a complex and often unnecessary procedure [alteration of obsolete *ragman roll* "long list, catalog"]

rig·or \'rig-ər, 2 is also 'rī-,gȯr\ *n* **1 a** : harsh strictness : the quality of being unyielding : SEVERITY **b** : an act or instance of rigor **2** : a tremor caused by a chill **3** : a condition that makes life difficult or uncomfortable ⟨the *rigors* of frontier life⟩ **4** : strict precision ⟨logical *rigor*⟩ [Middle French *rigueur*, from Latin *rigor*, literally, "stiffness", from *rigēre* "to be stiff"]

rig·or mor·tis \,rig-ər-'mȯrt-əs\ *n* : transitory rigidity of muscles occurring after death [New Latin, "stiffness of death"]

rig·or·ous \'rig-rəs, -ə-rəs\ *adj* **1** : exercising or favoring rigor : very strict **2** : marked by extremes of temperature or climate : HARSH, SEVERE **3** : extremely accurate : PRECISE SYN see RIGID — **rig·or·ous·ly** *adv* — **rig·or·ous·ness** *n*

rile \'rīl\ *vt* **1** : ROIL 1 **2** : to make angry [alteration of *roil*]

¹rill \'ril\ *n* : a very small brook [Dutch *ril* or Low German *rille*]

²rill \'ril\ *or* **rille** \'ril, 'ril-ə\ *n* : any of several long narrow valleys on the moon's surface [German *rille*, literally, "channel made by a small stream", from Low German, "rill"]

¹rim \'rim\ *n* **1 a** : the outer often curved or circular edge or border of something **b** : BRINK 2 **2** : the outer part of a wheel joined to the hub usually by spokes [Old English *rima*] — **rim·less** \-ləs\ *adj* □ SYN BRIM: RIM applies to the edge of something circular or curving ⟨*rim* of a plate⟩ BRIM applies to the upper inside rim of something hollow ⟨fill the cup to the *brim*⟩

²rim *vb* **rimmed; rim·ming 1** : to furnish with a rim : serve as a rim for : BORDER **2** : to run around the rim of ⟨putts that *rim* the cup⟩ **3** : to form or show a rim

¹rime \'rīm\ *n* **1** : FROST 1c **2** : an accumulation of granular ice tufts on objects that resembles frost in appearance but is formed from supercooled fog or cloud **3** : CRUST 3a, INCRUSTATION [Old English *hrīm*]

²rime *vt* : to cover with or as if with rime

³rime, rimer, rimester *variant of* RHYME, RHYMER, RHYMESTER

rimy \'rī-mē\ *adj* **rim·i·er; -est** : covered with rime : FROSTY

rind \'rīnd\ *n* : the bark of a tree; *also* : a usually hard or tough outer layer (as the skin of a fruit) [Old English] — **rind·ed** \'rīn-dəd\ *adj*

rin·der·pest \'rin-dər-,pest\ *n* : an acute virus disease of cattle and sometimes sheep and goats [German, from *rinder* "cattle" + *pest* "pestilence"]

¹ring \'ring\ *n* **1** : a circular band for holding, connecting, hanging, or pulling ⟨a curtain *ring*⟩ ⟨a key *ring*⟩ or for packing or sealing **2** : a circlet often of precious metal worn on the finger **3 a** : a circular line, figure, or object **b** : an encircling arrangement ⟨a *ring* of suburbs⟩ **c** : a circular or spiral course **4 a** : an often circular space for exhibitions or competitions; *esp* : such a space at a circus **b** : a square enclosure in which boxing matches are held; *also* : the sport of boxing **5** : ANNUAL RING **6** : a combination of persons for a selfish and often corrupt purpose ⟨a drug *ring*⟩ **7** : an arrangement of atoms represented in formulas or models as a ring [Old English *hring*] — **ringed** \'ringd\ *adj* — **ring·like** \'ring-,līk\ *adj*

²ring *vb* **ringed; ring·ing** \'ring-ing\ **1** : to place or form a ring around : ENCIRCLE **2** : to provide with a ring **3** : GIRDLE 3 **4** : to throw a ring over (the mark) in a game where curved objects (as horseshoes) are tossed at a mark **5** : to form or take the shape of a ring

³ring *vb* **rang** \'rang\; **rung** \'rəng\; **ring·ing** \'ring-ing\ **1** : to sound clearly and reasonably when struck ⟨church bells *ringing*⟩ **2** : to cause to sound especially by striking ⟨*rang* the dinner bell⟩ **3** : to ring a bell as a signal ⟨*ring* for the attendant⟩ **4** : to announce by or as if by ringing ⟨*ring* in the new year⟩ **5 a** : to be filled with reverberating sound : RESOUND ⟨the hall *rang* with cheers⟩ **b** : to have the sensation of being filled with a humming sound ⟨my ears were *ringing*⟩ **6** : to be filled with talk or report ⟨the whole town *rang* with the story⟩ **7** : to repeat often or loudly or earnestly **8** : to have a sound or character expressive of some quality ⟨the story *rings* true⟩ **9 a** : to summon especially by bell **b** *chiefly British* : TELEPHONE 3 — usually used with up [Old English *hringan*] — **ring a bell** : to arouse a response ⟨that name *rings a bell*⟩ — **ring down the curtain** : to end a performance or an action — **ring the changes** : to run through a whole range of possibilities

⁴ring *n* **1** : a set of bells **2** : a clear resonant sound made by or as if by vibrating metal **3** : resonant tone : SONORITY **4** : a loud sound continued, repeated, or reverberated **5** : a sound or character expressive of a particular quality ⟨a story with the *ring* of truth⟩ **6 a** : the act or an instance of ringing **b** : a telephone call

ring–bolt \'ring-,bōlt\ *n* : a bolt with a ring through a loop at one end

¹ring·er \'ring-ər\ *n* **1** : one that sounds especially by ringing **2 a** : an often superior or ineligible competitor entered in competition under false representations ⟨charged that a *ringer* had won the feature race⟩ **b** :

ring-necked pheasant

one that strongly resembles another ⟨you're a dead *ringer* for my cousin⟩

²ring·er *n* : one (as a quoit or horseshoe) that encircles or puts a ring around a peg

Ring·er's solution \'ring-ərz-\ *n* : a balanced aqueous ionic solution that is used in physiological experiments to provide a medium essentially isotonic to many animal tissues [Sidney *Ringer*, died 1910, English physician]

ring finger *n* : the third finger of the hand

ring·lead·er \'ring-,lēd-ər\ *n* : a leader of a group engaged especially in improper or unlawful activities

ring·let \'ring-lət\ *n* **1** *archaic* : a small ring or circle **2** : CURL; *esp* : a long curl of hair

ring·mas·ter \'ring-,mas-tər\ *n* : one in charge of performances in a ring (as of a circus)

ring–necked \'ring-'nekt, -'nek, ,ring-, \ *or* **ring–neck** \,ring-,nek\ *adj* : having a ring of color about the neck

ring–necked pheasant *n* : an Old World pheasant with a white neck ring widely introduced in temperate regions as a game bird

ring·side \'ring-,sīd\ *n* **1** : the area just outside a ring especially in which a contest occurs **2** : a place from which one may have a close view — **ringside** *adj*

ring stand *n* : a metal stand consisting of an upright rod on a rectangular base used with rings and clamps for supporting laboratory apparatus

ring–tailed \'ring-'tāld\ *adj* : having a tail marked with rings of differing colors

ring·toss \-,tòs, -,täs\ *n* : a game the object of which is to toss a ring so that it will fall over an upright stick

ring·worm \-,wərm\ *n* : a contagious skin disease caused by fungi and characterized by ring-shaped discolored patches

rink \'ringk\ *n* **1 a** : a sheet of ice marked off for curling or ice hockey **b** : a usually artificial sheet of ice for ice-skating **c** : an enclosure for roller-skating **2** : a division of a bowling green large enough for a match **3** : a team in bowls or curling [Middle English *rinc* "area for a contest", from Middle French *renc* "row, rank, place"]

¹rinse \'rins\ *vt* **1** : to cleanse with liquid (as water) **2** : to treat (hair) with a rinse **3** : to remove (as dirt or impurities) by washing lightly or in water only [Middle French *rincer*, derived from Latin *recens* "fresh, recent"] — **rins·er** *n*

²rinse *n* **1** : the act or process of rinsing **2 a** : liquid used for rinsing **b** : a solution that temporarily tints hair

¹ri·ot \'rī-ət\ *n* **1** *archaic* **a** : DEBAUCHERY **b** : unrestrained revelry **2 a** : public violence, tumult, or disorder **b** : a tumultuous disturbance of the public peace by three or more persons assembled together **3** : a random or disorderly abundance especially of color **4** : one that is wildly amusing [Old French, "quarrel, dispute"]

²riot *vb* **1** : REVEL 1 **2** : to create or engage in a riot **3** : to waste or spend recklessly — **ri·ot·er** *n*

riot act *n* : a very strong reproof, reprimand, or warning — used in the phrase *read the riot act* [the *Riot Act*, English law of 1715 providing for the dispersal of riots upon command of legal authority]

riot gun *n* : a small arm used to disperse rioters rather than to inflict serious injury; *esp* : a short-barreled shotgun

ri·ot·ous \'rī-ət-əs\ *adj* **1** : PROFUSE 2, ABUNDANT **2 a** : of the nature of a riot : TURBULENT **b** : taking part in a riot — **ri·ot·ous·ly** *adv* — **ri·ot·ous·ness** *n*

¹rip \'rip\ *vb* **ripped**; **rip·ping 1** : to tear or split apart or open **2** : to saw or split (wood) with the grain **3** : to slash or slit with or as if with a sharp blade **4** : to rush headlong [probably from Flemish *rippen* "to strip off roughly"] — **rip·per** *n* — **rip into** : to tear into : ATTACK

²rip *n* : a rent made by ripping : TEAR

³rip *n* : a body of water made rough by the meeting of opposing currents or by passing over an irregular bottom [perhaps from ²*rip*]

⁴rip *n* **1** : a worn-out worthless horse **2** : a reckless or dissolute person [perhaps from *reprobate*]

ri·par·i·an \rə-'per-ē-ən, rī-\ *adj* : relating to or living or located on the bank of a natural watercourse (as a stream or river) or sometimes of a lake or a tidewater [Latin *riparius*, from *ripa* "bank, shore"]

rip cord *n* : a cord or wire pulled in making a descent to release the pilot parachute which lifts the main parachute out of its container

rip current *n* : a strong surface current flowing outward from a shore

ripe \'rīp\ *adj* **1** : fully grown and developed : MATURE **2** : having mature knowledge, understanding, or judgment **3** : of advanced years ⟨a *ripe* old age⟩ **4 a** : fully arrived : SUITABLE ⟨the time seemed *ripe*⟩ **b** : fully prepared : READY ⟨*ripe* for action⟩ **5** : brought by aging to full flavor or the best state : MELLOW ⟨*ripe* cheese⟩ **6** : ruddy, plump, or full like ripened fruit [Old English *rīpe*] — **ripe·ly** *adv* — **ripe·ness** *n*

rip·en \'rī-pən\ *vb* **rip·ened**; **rip·en·ing** \'rīp-ning, -ə-ning\ : to grow or make ripe — **rip·en·er** \'rīp-nər, -ə-nər\ *n*

rip–off \'rip-,óf\ *n* : an act or instance of stealing : THEFT; *also* : a financial exploitation

rip off \rip-'óf, 'rip-\ *vt* : ROB 1; *also* : STEAL

ri·poste \ri-'pōst\ *n* **1** : a fencer's quick return thrust following a parry **2** : a quick retort **3** : a retaliatory maneuver or measure [French, from Italian *risposta*, literally, "answer", from *rispondere* "to answer, respond", from Latin *respondēre*] — **riposte** *vi*

rip·ping \'rip-ing\ *adj* : MARVELOUS 3, TERRIFIC [probably from ¹*rip*]

¹rip·ple \'rip-əl\ *vb* **rip·pled**; **rip·pling** \'rip-ling, -ə-ling\ **1 a** : to become lightly ruffled or covered with small waves **b** : to flow in small waves **2** : to stir up small waves on ⟨wind *rippling* water⟩ **3** : to flow with a light rise and fall of sound or inflection ⟨laughter *rippling* over the audience⟩ **4** : to impart a wavy motion or appearance to [perhaps from ¹*rip*] — **rip·pler** \'rip-lər, -ə-lər\ *n*

²ripple *n* **1 a** : the ruffling of the surface of water **b** : a small wave **2** : a sound like that of rippling water

¹rip·rap \'rip-,rap\ *n* **1** : a foundation or sustaining wall of stones thrown together without order (as in deep water or on an embankment slope to prevent erosion) **2** : stone used for riprap [obsolete *riprap* "sound of rapping"]

²riprap *vt* **rip·rapped**; **rip·rap·ping 1** : to form a riprap in or on **2** : to strengthen or support with a riprap

rip–roar·ing \'rip-'rōr-ing, -'ròr-\ *adj* : noisily excited or exciting

rip·saw \'rip-,sò\ *n* : a coarse-toothed saw for cutting wood in the direction of the grain

rip·tide \'rip-,tīd\ *n* : RIP CURRENT

¹rise \'rīz\ *vi* **rose** \'rōz\; **ris·en** \'riz-n\; **ris·ing** \'rī-zing\ **1 a** : to get up especially from lying, kneeling, or sitting **b** : to get up from sleep or from one's bed **2** : to return from death **3** : to take up arms ⟨*rise* in rebellion⟩ **4** : to respond warmly : APPLAUD — usually used with *to* **5** : to end a session : ADJOURN ⟨the senate *rose* at noon⟩ **6** : to appear above the horizon ⟨the sun *rises* at six⟩ **7 a** : to move rose to starboard⟩ **7 a** : to move upward : ASCEND ⟨smoke *rises*⟩ **b** : to extend upward ⟨the hill *rises* to a great height⟩ **8** : to swell in size or volume ⟨the river is *rising*⟩ ⟨dough *rises*⟩ **9 a** : to become heartened or elated ⟨their spirits *rose*⟩ **b** : to increase in intensity ⟨felt my anger *rising*⟩ **10 a** : to go higher in rank : be promoted ⟨*rose* to colonel⟩ **b** : to increase in quantity or number ⟨production *rose* sharply⟩ **c** : to increase in price or be marked by increasing prices ⟨*rising* costs⟩ ⟨a *rising* stock market⟩ **11 a** : to come about : HAPPEN ⟨an ugly rumor had *risen*⟩ **b** : to have a source : ORIGINATE ⟨that river *rises* in the hills⟩ 12 : to exert oneself to meet a challenge ⟨*rise* to the occasion⟩ [Old English *rīsan*]

²**rise** \'rīz\ *n* 1 : an act of rising : a state of having risen 2 : ORIGIN 2a, BEGINNING 3 : the distance or elevation of one point above another 4 : an increase especially in amount, number, volume, or price 5 a : an upward slope b : a spot higher than surrounding ground 6 : an irritated or angry reaction ⟨got a *rise* out of you⟩

ris·er \'rī-zər\ *n* 1 : one that rises (as from sleep) 2 : the upright member between two stair treads

ris·i·bil·i·ty \,riz-ə-'bil-ət-ē\ *n, pl* **-ties** 1 : the ability or inclination to laugh — often used in pl. 2 : LAUGHTER, MERRIMENT

ris·i·ble \'riz-ə-bəl\ *adj* 1 : able or inclined to laugh 2 : provoking laughter : FUNNY [Late Latin *risibilis*, from Latin *risus*, past participle of *ridēre* "to laugh"] SYN see LAUGHABLE

¹**risk** \'risk\ *n* 1 : possibility of loss or injury : PERIL 2 a : the chance of loss or the perils to a person or thing that is insured b : a person or thing that is a hazard to an insurer ⟨a poor *risk*⟩ [French *risque*, from Italian *risco*] SYN see DANGER

²**risk** *vt* 1 : to expose to hazard or danger ⟨*risked* my life⟩ 2 : to take the risk or danger of ⟨*risked* breaking my neck⟩ — **risk·er** *n*

risky \'ris-kē\ *adj* **risk·i·er; -est** : involving risk or danger : HAZARDOUS — **risk·i·ness** *n*

ris·qué \ri-'skā\ *adj* : bordering on impropriety or indecency : OFF-COLOR [French, from *risquer* "to risk", from *risque* "risk"]

ri·tar·dan·do \ri-,tär-'dän-dō, ,rē-\ *adv or adj* : with a gradual slackening in tempo — used as a direction in music [Italian, literally, "retarding"] — **ritardando** *n*

rite \'rīt\ *n* 1 a : a prescribed form for a ceremony b : LITURGY 2 2 : a ceremonial act or action 3 : a division of the Christian church using a distinctive liturgy [Latin *ritus*]

¹**rit·u·al** \'rich-ə-wəl, 'rich-əl\ *adj* 1 : of or relating to rites or a ritual ⟨a *ritual* dance⟩ 2 : according to religious law or social custom ⟨*ritual* purity⟩ — **rit·u·al·ly** \-ē\ *adv*

²**ritual** *n* 1 : an established form for a ceremony 2 a : ritual observance; *esp* : a system of rites b : RITE 2 c : a formal and customarily repeated act or series of acts

rit·u·al·ism \-,iz-əm\ *n* 1 : the use of ritual 2 : excessive devotion to ritual — **rit·u·al·ist** \-əst\ *n* — **rit·u·al·is·tic** \,rich-ə-wəl-'is-tik, ,rich-əl-\ *adj* — **rit·u·al·is·ti·cal·ly** \-ti-kə-lē, -klē\ *adv*

ritzy \'rit-sē\ *adj* **ritz·i·er; -est** : showily elegant : POSH [*Ritz* hotels, noted for their opulence]

¹**ri·val** \'rī-vəl\ *n* 1 a : one of two or more trying to reach or obtain something that only one can possess b : one who tries to excel 2 : one that equals another in desired qualities : PEER [Latin *rivalis* "one using the same stream as another, rival in love", from *rivalis* "of a stream", from *rivus* "stream"] □ ORIGIN *Rival* is derived from Latin *rivalis*, which as an adjective means "of a brook or stream", from *rivus*, "brook or stream". As a noun *rivalis* (in its plural forms) refers literally to those who use the same stream as a source of water. Just as neighbors are likely to dispute each other's rights to a common source of water, so too contention is inevitable when two or more persons strive to obtain something that only one can possess. Latin *rivalis* developed a sense relating to rivalry in love, and in this sense it came into English.

²**rival** *adj* : having the same pretensions or claims

³**rival** *vt* **-valed** *or* **-valled; -val·ing** *or* **-val·ling** \'rīv-ling, -ə-ling\ 1 : to be in competition with 2 : to try to equal or excel 3 : EQUAL 2, MATCH

ri·val·ry \'rī-vəl-rē\ *n, pl* **-ries** : the act of rivaling : the state of being a rival : COMPETITION

rive \'rīv\ *vb* **rived** \'rīvd\; **riv·en** \'riv-ən\ *also* **rived; riv·ing** \'rī-ving\ 1 a : to tear apart : REND b : to split

with force or violence 2 a : to divide into pieces or factions ⟨the church was *riven* with discord⟩ b : FRACTURE ⟨a country *riven* by earthquakes⟩ [Old Norse *rifa*]

riv·er \'riv-ər\ *n* 1 : a natural stream of water larger than a brook or creek 2 : a large stream or flow ⟨a *river* of oil⟩ [Old French *rivere*, derived from Latin *riparius* "of a bank or shore", from *ripa* "bank, shore"]

riv·er·bank \'riv-ər-,bangk\ *n* : the bank of a river

riv·er·bed \-,bed\ *n* : the channel occupied or formerly occupied by a river

riv·er·boat \-,bōt\ *n* : a boat for use on a river

river horse *n* : HIPPOPOTAMUS

riv·er·ine \'riv-ə-,rīn, -,rēn\ *adj* 1 : relating to, formed by, or resembling a river 2 : living or situated on the banks of a river

riv·er·side \'riv-ər-,sīd\ *n* : the side or bank of a river

¹**riv·et** \'riv-ət\ *n* : a single-headed pin or bolt of metal used for uniting two or more pieces by passing the shank through a hole in each piece and then beating or pressing down the plain end so as to make a second head [Middle French, from *river* "to attach, clinch"]

²**rivet** *vt* 1 : to fasten with or as if with rivets 2 : to beat or press the end or point of (as a metallic pin, rod, or bolt) so as to form a head 3 : to attract and hold (as the attention) completely — **riv·et·er** *n*

ri·vi·era \,riv-ē-'er-ə, ri-'vyer-ə\ *n, often cap* : a coastal region frequented as a resort area and usually marked by a mild climate [*Riviera*, region in France and Italy]

riv·u·let \'riv-yə-lət, 'riv-ə-lət\ *n* : a small stream [Italian *rivoletto*, from *rivolo* "brook", from Latin *rivulus* "small stream", from *rivus* "brook, stream"]

¹**ri·yal** \rē-'ól, -'yól, -'äl, -'yäl\ *also* **ri·al** \-'ól, -'äl\ *n* 1 : the basic monetary unit of Saudi Arabia 2 : a coin or note representing one riyal [Arabic *riyāl*, from Spanish *real* "real"]

²**riyal** *variant of* RIAL

RNA \,är-,en-'ā\ *n* : any of various nucleic acids that contain ribose and uracil as structural components and are associated with the control of cellular chemical activities — compare DNA, MESSENGER RNA, RIBOSOMAL RNA, TRANSFER RNA [*ribon*ucleic *a*cid]

¹**roach** \'rōch\ *n, pl* **roach** *also* **roach·es** : a silver-white greenish-backed European freshwater fish related to the carp; *also* : any of several similar or related fishes [Middle French *roche*]

²**roach** *vt* : to brush (the hair) into an arched roll — often used with up [origin unknown]

³**roach** *n* : COCKROACH

road \'rōd\ *n* 1 : a place less enclosed than a harbor where ships may ride at anchor — often used in pl. 2 a : an open way for vehicles, persons, and animals; *esp* : one lying outside an urban district b : ROADBED 2 3 : ROUTE 2, PATH 4 : RAILWAY 5 : a series of visits to several places or the travel necessary to get there ⟨the team is on the *road*⟩ ⟨on tour with the musical's *road* company⟩ [Old English *rād* "ride, journey"]

road·abil·i·ty \,rōd-ə-'bil-ət-ē\ *n* : the qualities (as steadiness and balance) desirable in an automobile on the road

road·bed \'rōd-,bed\ *n* 1 : the foundation of a road or railroad 2 : the part of the surface of a road traveled by vehicles

road·block \-,bläk\ *n* 1 a : a barricade at a point on a road that can be covered by fire from a defending army b : a road barricade set up by law-enforcement officers 2 : an obstruction in a road 3 : something that hinders progress

road hog *n* : a motorist who obstructs others especially by occupying part of another's traffic lane

road·house \'rōd-,haus\ *n* : a nightclub usually outside a city

road metal *n* : broken stone or cinders used in making and repairing roads or ballasting railroads

road·run·ner \'rōd-,rən-ər\ *n* : a swift-running long-tailed cuckoo of the southwestern United States

riser 2

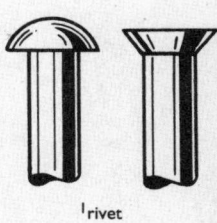

¹rivet

roadrunner

\ə\ abut		\ng\ sing	
\ər\ further		\ō\ bone	
\a\ mat		\ȯ\ saw	
\ā\ take		\ȯi\ coin	
\ä\ cot, cart		\th\ thin	
\au̇\ out		\th\ this	
\ch\ chin		\ü\ food	
\e\ pet		\u̇\ foot	
\ē\ easy		\y\ yet	
\g\ go		\yü\ few	
\i\ tip		\yu̇\ cure	
\ī\ life		\zh\ vision	
\j\ job			

¹road·side \'rōd-ˌsīd\ *n* : the strip of land along a road : the side of a road

²roadside *adj* : situated at the side of a road

road·stead \'rōd-ˌsted\ *n* : ROAD 1

road·ster \'rōd-stər\ *n* : an open automobile with one cross seat

road test *n* : a test (as of a vehicle or a person's ability to drive) made on the road

road·way \'rōd-ˌwā\ *n* **l a** : the strip of land over which a road passes **b** : ROAD; *esp* : ROADBED 2 **2** : a railroad right-of-way **3** : the part of a bridge used by vehicles

road·work \-ˌwərk\ *n* : conditioning for an athletic contest (as a boxing match) consisting mainly of long runs

roam \'rōm\ *vb* **l** : to go from place to place aimlessly : WANDER ⟨*roam* the hills⟩ **2** : to travel purposefully and unhindered through a wide area ⟨cattle *roaming* in search of water⟩ [Middle English *romen*] — **roam·er** *n*

¹roan \'rōn\ *adj* : of a base color (as black, red, or brown) dulled and lightened by white hairs [Middle French, from Old Spanish *roano*]

²roan *n* **l** : an animal (as a horse) with a roan coat **2** : the color of a roan horse

¹roar \'rōr, 'ror\ *vb* **l** : to utter the characteristic loud prolonged cry of a wild beast (as a lion) or a similar sound **2 a** : to make a loud reverberating sound **b** : to laugh loudly **3** : to be boisterous or disorderly **4** : to cause to roar ⟨*roar* a motor⟩ [Old English *rārian*] — **roar·er** \'rōr-ər, 'ror-\ *n*

²roar *n* **l a** : the deep loud cry of a wild beast **b** : a loud deep cry (as of pain or anger) **2** : a loud continuous confused sound ⟨the *roar* of the crowd⟩

roar·ing *adj* : very strong or active ⟨a *roaring* fire⟩ ⟨a *roaring* headache⟩

¹roast \'rōst\ *vb* **l a** : to cook by exposing to dry heat (as in an oven) **b** : to dry and parch by exposure to heat ⟨*roast* coffee⟩ **2** : to heat (inorganic material) with access of air and without fusing to effect change (as expulsion of volatile matter) ⟨*roast* a sulfide ore⟩ **3** : to criticize severely **4** : to undergo roasting [Old French *rostir*, of Germanic origin]

²roast *n* **l** : a piece of meat roasted or suitable for roasting **2** : an outing at which food is roasted **3** : an act of roasting; *esp* : severe banter or criticism

³roast *adj* : cooked by roasting ⟨*roast* beef⟩

roast·er \'rō-stər\ *n* **l** : one that roasts **2** : a pan or an appliance for roasting **3** : something (as a young chicken) suitable for roasting

rob \'räb\ *vb* **robbed; rob·bing l a** : to take something away from (a person or place) by force, threat, stealth, or trickery ⟨*rob* a store⟩ ⟨*rob* a pedestrian⟩ **b** : to commit robbery : STEAL **2 a** : to deprive of something due, expected, or desired **b** : to withhold unjustly or injuriously [Old French *rober*, of Germanic origin] — **rob·ber** *n*

robber fly *n* : any of various predaceous flies that usually resemble bumblebees

rob·bery \'räb-rē, -ə-rē\ *n, pl* **-ber·ies** : the act or practice of robbing; *esp* : larceny from the person or presence of another by violence or threat

¹robe \'rōb\ *n* **l** : a long loose or flowing garment: as **a** : one used for ceremonial occasions or as a symbol of office or profession **b** : a garment (as a dressing gown) replacing outer garments for informal wear **2** : a covering or wrap for the lower body ⟨wrapped the legs in a *robe* at the game⟩ [Old French, "plunder, robe", of Germanic origin]

²robe *vb* **l** : to clothe, invest, or cover with or as if with a robe **2** : to put on a robe **3** : DRESS 2a

rob·in \'räb-ən\ *n* **l** : a small European thrush with yellowish red throat and breast **2** : a large North American thrush with a gray back, streaked throat, and chief-

ly dull reddish breast and underparts [short for *Robin redbreast*, from *Robin*, nickname for *Robert*]

ro·bot \'rō-ˌbät, -bət\ *n* **l a** : a machine that looks like a human being and performs various complex acts (as walking or talking) of a human being **b** : an efficient, insensitive, often brutalized person **2** : a device that automatically performs tasks that are complicated and often continuously repeated **3** : something guided by automatic controls ⟨a *robot* airplane⟩ ⟨a *robot* factory⟩ [Czech, from *robota* "forced labor"] — **ro·bot·ic** \rō-'bät-ik\ *adj* □ ORIGIN In 1923 a play called *R.U.R.* opened in London and New York. The author, Karel Čapek, coined the term *robot* from the Czech *robota*, meaning "forced labor". In *R.U.R.* (which stands for "Rossum's Universal Robots") mechanical men originally designed to perform manual labor become so sophisticated that some advanced models develop the capacity to feel and hate, and eventually they destroy mankind.

ro·bust \rō-'bəst, 'rō-,\ *adj* **l** : strong and vigorously healthy : STURDY **2** : ROUGH, RUDE ⟨*robust* humor⟩ **3** : requiring strength or vigor ⟨*robust* work⟩ **4** : STRONG 7a [Latin *robustus* "oaken, strong", from *robur* "oak, strength"] — **ro·bust·ly** *adv* — **ro·bust·ness** *n*

roc \'räk\ *n* : a legendary bird of great size and strength believed to inhabit the Indian ocean area [Arabic *rukhkh*]

Ro·chelle salt \rō-ˌshel-\ *n* : a hydrated crystalline salt of potassium and sodium that is a mild purgative [La *Rochelle*, France]

roch·et \'räch-ət\ *n* : a white linen vestment resembling a surplice worn by bishops and privileged prelates [Middle French]

¹rock \'räk\ *vb* **l** : to move back and forth in or as if in a cradle **2 a** : to sway or cause to sway back and forth **b** (1) : DAZE 1, STUN (2) : DISTURB 2a, b, UPSET [Old English *roccian*] SYN see SHAKE

²rock *n* **l** : a rocking movement **2** : music usually played on amplified instruments and marked by a heavy beat, repetition of simple phrases, and often country, folk, or blues elements

³rock *n* **l** : a large mass of stone forming a cliff, promontory, or peak **2** : consolidated or unconsolidated solid mineral matter; *also* : a particular mass of it **3** : something (as a support or refuge) like a rock in firmness **4** *slang* **a** : GEM 1 **b** : DIAMOND 1a [Old North French *roque*] — **on the rocks l** : in or into a state of destruction or wreckage **2** : on ice cubes ⟨bourbon *on the rocks*⟩

rock bottom *n* : the lowest or most basic part or level — **rock–bottom** *adj*

rock·bound \'räk-ˌbau̇nd\ *adj* : fringed, surrounded, or covered with rocks : ROCKY

rock candy *n* : sugar crystallized in large masses

rock crystal *n* : transparent quartz

rock·er \'räk-ər\ *n* **l a** : a curving piece of wood or metal on which an object (as a cradle) rocks **b** : a structure or device (as a chair) that rocks upon rockers **2** : a mechanism that works with a rocking motion **3** : a rock singer, musician, or song

¹rock·et \'räk-ət\ *n* **l** : a firework consisting of a case containing a combustible composition fastened to a guiding stick and projected through the air by the reaction resulting from the rearward discharge of the gases liberated by combustion **2** : a jet engine that operates on the same principle as the firework rocket, carries the fuel and oxygen needed for combustion and thus makes the engine independent of the oxygen of the air, and is used especially for the propulsion of a missile or a vehicle (as an airplane) — called also *rocket engine* **3** : a rocket-propelled bomb, missile, or projectile [Italian *rocchetta*, literally, "small distaff", from *rocca* "distaff", of Germanic origin]

²rocket *vb* **l** : to convey by means of a rocket ⟨*rocket* a satellite into orbit⟩ **2** : to rise up swiftly, spectacularly,

robin 2

and with force **3** : to travel rapidly in or as if in a rocket

rock·e·teer \‚räk-ə-'tiər\ *n* **I** : one who fires, pilots, or
rides in a rocket **2** : a scientist who specializes in rock-
etry

rocket plane *n* : an airplane propelled by rockets or
armed with rocket launchers

rock·et·ry \'räk-ə-trē\ *n* : the study of, experimentation with, or use of rockets

rocket ship *n* : a rocket-propelled spaceship

rock·fish \'räk-‚fish\ *n* : any of various valuable market
and sport fishes (as a greenling or striped bass) that
live among rocks or on rocky bottoms

rock garden *n* : a garden laid out among rocks or decorated with rocks and adapted for the growth of particular kinds of plants (as alpines)

rocking chair *n* : a chair mounted on rockers

rocking horse *n* : a toy horse mounted on rockers —
called also *hobbyhorse*

rock lobster *n* : SPINY LOBSTER

rock 'n' roll \‚räk-ən-'rōl\ *n* : ²ROCK 2

rock pigeon *n* : a wild bluish gray Old World pigeon

rock–ribbed \'räk-'ribd\ *adj* **I** : ¹ROCKY 1 **2** : INFLEX-
IBLE 2, 3

rock salt *n* : common salt in large crystals or masses

rock·weed \'räk-‚wēd\ *n* : any of various brown algae
commonly growing attached to rocks along shores —
called also *fucus*

rock wool *n* : mineral wool made by blowing a jet of
steam through molten rock or through slag and used
chiefly for heat and sound insulation

¹rocky \'räk-ē\ *adj* **rock·i·er; -est** **I** : abounding in or
consisting of rocks **2** : difficult to impress or affect :
INSENSITIVE **3** : firmly held : STEADFAST — **rock·i·ness**
n

²rocky *adj* **rock·i·er; -est** **I** : not stable : WOBBLY **2** :
physically upset : UNWELL — **rock·i·ness** *n*

Rocky Mountain goat *n* : MOUNTAIN GOAT [*Rocky
mountains*, North America]

Rocky Mountain sheep *n* : BIGHORN

Rocky Mountain spotted fever *n* : an acute rickettsial
disease marked by chills, fever, prostration, pains in
muscles and joints, and a red to purple eruption and
transmitted by the bite of a tick

ro·co·co \rə-'kō-kō, ‚rō-kə-'kō\ *adj* **I** : of or relating to
an 18th century artistic style marked especially by fanciful curved forms **2** : excessively ornate [French,
from *rocaille* "rock-work", from *roc* "rock", from
Middle French *roche*] — **rococo** *n*

rod \'räd\ *n* **I** : a straight slender stick or bar (a curtain
rod): as **a** : a stick used to punish; *also* : PUNISHMENT
b : a pole with a line and usually a reel attached for
fishing **c** : a bar for measuring **2 a** : a unit of length —
see MEASURE table **b** : a square rod **3** : any of the rod-
shaped sensory bodies in the retina responsive to faint
light **4** : a bacterium shaped like a rod **5** *slang* : PISTOL
[Old English *rodd*] — **rod·less** \-ləs\ *adj* — **rod·like**
\-‚līk\ *adj*

rode *past of* RIDE

ro·dent \'rōd-nt\ *n* : any of an order (Rodentia) of relatively small gnawing mammals (as mice, squirrels, or
beavers) having a single pair of upper incisors with a
chisel-shaped edge — compare LAGOMORPH [derived
from Latin *rodens*, present participle of *rodere* "to
gnaw"] — **rodent** *adj*

ro·den·ti·cide \rō-'dent-ə-‚sīd\ *n* : an agent that kills or
repels rodents — **ro·den·ti·cid·al** \-‚dent-ə-'sīd-l\ *adj*

ro·deo \'rōd-ē-‚ō, rə-'dā-ō\ *n, pl* **-de·os** **I** : ROUNDUP 1
2 : a contest or exhibition of cowboy skills (as riding
and roping) [Spanish, from *rodear* "to surround",
from *rueda* "wheel", from Latin *rota* "wheel"]

¹roe \'rō\ *n, pl* **roe** *or* **roes** : DOE [Old English *rā*]

²roe *n* : the eggs of a fish especially while still bound
together in a membrane [Middle English *roof, roughe,
row*]

roe·buck \'rō-‚bək\ *n, pl* **roebuck** *or* **roebucks** : ROE
DEER; *esp* : the male roe deer

roe deer *n* : a small active deer of Europe and Asia that
has erect antlers forked at the tip and is reddish brown
in summer and grayish in winter

¹roent·gen *also* **rönt·gen** \'rent-gən, 'rənt-, -jən\ *adj* :
of or relating to X rays (*roentgen* examinations) [Wil-
helm *Röntgen*, died 1923, German physicist]

²roentgen *also* **röntgen** *n* : a unit of x-radiation or gamma radiation equal to the amount of radiation that produces in one cubic centimeter of dry air ionization
equal to one electrostatic unit of charge

roentgen ray *n, often cap 1st R* : X RAY

Ro·ga·tion Day \rō-'gā-shən-\ *n* : one of the days of
prayer especially for the harvest observed on the three
days before Ascension Day and by Roman Catholics also on April 25 [Latin *rogatio* "questioning", from *rogare* "to ask"]

rogations *n pl* : the ceremonies of the Rogation Days

rog·er \'räj-ər\ *interj* — used especially in radio and
signaling to indicate that a message has been received
and understood [*Roger*, former communications code
word for *r*, initial letter of *received*]

¹rogue \'rōg\ *n* **I a** : TRAMP 1, VAGRANT **b** : a dishonest
or worthless person : SCOUNDREL **c** : a pleasantly mischievous person : SCAMP **2** : a vicious or lazy animal
3 : an individual plant or animal with a chance and
usually inferior biological variation [origin unknown]
— **rogu·ish** \'rō-gish\ *adj* — **rogu·ish·ly** *adv* — **rogu-
ish·ness** *n*

²rogue *vi* **rogued; rogu·ing** *or* **rogue·ing** : to weed out
inferior individuals from a crop

³rogue *adj* : being vicious and destructive (*rogue* elephants)

rogu·ery \'rō-gə-rē, -grē\ *n, pl* **-er·ies** **I** : the practices
or an act characteristic of a rogue **2** : mischievous play

rogues' gallery *n* : a collection of pictures of persons
arrested as criminals

roil \'rȯil, *2 is also* 'rīl\ *vt* **I** : to make cloudy or muddy
by stirring up sediment **2** : RILE 2 [origin unknown]

roily \'rȯi-lē\ *adj* **roil·i·er; -est** **I** : full of sediment or
dregs : MUDDY **2** : TURBULENT 2

rois·ter \'rȯi-stər\ *vi* **rois·tered; rois·ter·ing** \-stə-riŋ,
-striŋ\ : REVEL 1 [from earlier *roister* "roisterer",
probably from Middle French *rustre* "boor, lout", derived from Latin *rusticus* "rustic, rural"] — **rois·ter·er**
\-stər-ər\ *n*

role *also* **rôle** \'rōl\ *n* **I a** : a character assigned or as-
sumed **b** : a part played by an actor or singer **2** : FUNC-
TION 2, 4 [French *rôle*, literally, "roll", from Old
French *rolle*]

role model *n* : a person whose behavior in a particular
role is imitated by others

role–play *vt* : to act out (*role-play* an interview)

¹roll \'rōl\ *n* **I a** : a written document that may be
rolled up : SCROLL **b** : an official list especially of
members of a body (as a legislature) **2** : something
that is rolled or rounded: as **a** : a quantity (as of fabric
or paper) rolled up to form a single package **b** (1) : a
food preparation rolled up for cooking or serving (2) :
a small piece of baked yeast dough **c** : paper money
folded or rolled **3** : something that rolls : ROLLER [Old
French *rolle*, from Latin *rotula*, "small wheel", from
rota "wheel"]

²roll *vb* **I a** : to move along a surface by rotation without sliding **b** : to turn over and over **c** : to move about
or as if about an axis or point **2 a** : to put a wrapping
around **b** : to form into a ball or roll **3** : to make
smooth, even, or compact with or as if with a roller **4
a** : to move on rollers or wheels **b** : to begin operating
or moving (the new shop got *rolling*) **5 a** : to make or
cause to make a full reverberating or continuous beating sound (*roll* a drum) (thunder *rolled*) **b** : to utter
with a trill (you *roll* your *r*'s) **6** : to rob (as an unconscious person) usually by going through the pockets

roe deer

\ə\ abut	\ng\ sing
\ər\ further	\ō\ bone
\a\ mat	\o\ saw
\ā\ take	\ȯi\ coin
\ä\ cot, cart	\th\ thin
\au̇\ out	\th\ this
\ch\ chin	\ü\ food
\e\ pet	\u̇\ foot
\ē\ easy	\y\ yet
\g\ go	\yü\ few
\i\ tip	\yu̇\ cure
\ī\ life	\zh\ vision
\j\ job	

7 : to luxuriate in an abundant supply ⟨*rolling* in money⟩ **8** : ELAPSE, PASS ⟨time *rolls* by⟩ **9** : to flow in a continuous stream ⟨money was *rolling* in⟩ **10** : to have a wavy surface ⟨*rolling* prairies⟩ **11** : to sway from side to side : ROCK ⟨the ship heaved and *rolled*⟩ **12** : to respond to rolling in a specified way ⟨a good paint *rolls* on smoothly⟩ **13** : to move forward : develop and maintain impetus

³**roll** *n* **1 a** : a sound produced by rapid strokes on a drum **b** : a sonorous and often rhythmical flow of speech **c** : a heavy reverberating sound ⟨the *roll* of cannon⟩ **2** : a rolling movement or an action or process involving such movement; *esp* : a swaying or side=to-side movement

roll bar *n* : an overhead metal bar on an automobile that is designed to protect the occupant in case of a turnover

roll call *n* : the act of calling off a list of names (as for checking attendance); *also* : a time for a roll call

¹**roll·er** \'rō-lər\ *n* **1 a** : a revolving cylinder over or on which something is moved or which is used to press, shape, spread, or smooth something **b** : a rod on which something (as a map) is rolled up **c** : a small wheel (as of a roller skate) **2** : a long heavy wave on the sea **3** : one that rolls or rolls over

²**roll·er** \'rō-lər\ *n* : a canary with a soft trilling song [German, from *rollen* "to roll, reverberate", from Middle French *roller*, derived from Latin *rotula* "small wheel"]

roller bearing *n* : a bearing in which a revolving part turns on rollers held in a circular frame or cage

roll·er coaster \'rō-lər-ˌkō-stər, 'rō-lē-ˌkō-\ *n* : an amusement park ride consisting of an elevated railway with sharp curves and steep inclines on which cars roll

roller rink *n* : RINK 1c

roll·er skate *n* : a skate that has wheels instead of a runner — **roller–skate** *vi*

rol·lick \'räl-ik\ *vi* : FROLIC [origin unknown] — **rollick** *n* — **rol·lick·ing** *adj*

rolling mill *n* : an establishment where metal is rolled into plates and bars

rolling pin *n* : a cylinder (as of wood) for rolling out dough

rolling stock *n* : wheeled vehicles owned or used by a railroad or motor carrier

roll·top desk \ˌrōl-ˌtäp-\ *n* : a writing desk with a cover that rolls back into the frame

roll up *vb* **1** : ACCUMULATE ⟨*rolled up* a majority⟩ **2** : to arrive in a vehicle

ro·ly–po·ly \ˌrō-lē-'pō-lē\ *n, pl* **-lies** **1** : a short stout person or thing **2** : a pudding made of rolled-out dough spread with a filling, rolled up into a cylinder shape, and baked or steamed [reduplication of *roly*, from ²*roll*] — **roly–poly** *adj*

ROM \'räm\ *n* : READ-ONLY MEMORY

ro·maine \rō-'mān\ *n* : a lettuce with long spoon-shaped leaves and columnar heads [French, from *romain* "Roman", from Latin *Romanus*]

¹**Ro·man** \'rō-mən\ *n* **1 a** : a native or resident of Rome **b** : a citizen of the Roman Empire **2** : ROMAN CATHOLIC — often taken to be offensive **3** *not cap* : roman letters or type

²**Roman** *adj* **1** : of or relating to ancient or modern Rome, the people of Rome, or the empire of which Rome was the original capital; *esp* : characteristic of the ancient Romans ⟨*Roman* fortitude⟩ **2** : LATIN 2 **3** *not cap* : of or relating to a type style with upright characters (as in "these words are roman") **4** : of or relating to the see of Rome or the Roman Catholic Church **5** : having a prominent slightly aquiline bridge ⟨a *Roman* nose⟩

ro·man à clef \rō-ˌmänⁿ-ä-'klä\ *n, pl* **ro·mans à clef** *same or* -ˌmänⁿz-ä-\ : a novel in which real persons or

roller skate

actual events figure but with their names disguised [French, literally, "novel with a key"]

Roman candle *n* : a cylindrical firework that discharges at intervals balls or stars of fire

Roman Catholic *adj* : of or relating to the body of Christians having a hierarchy under the pope, a liturgy centered in the Mass, and a body of dogma formulated by the church as the infallible interpreter of revealed truth — **Roman Catholic** *n* — **Roman Catholicism** *n*

¹**ro·mance** \rō-'mans, 'rō-ˌ\ *n* **1 a** : a medieval tale based on legend, chivalric love and adventure, and the supernatural **b** : a prose narrative dealing with imaginary characters involved in heroic, adventurous, or mysterious events remote in time or place **c** : a love story **2** : something that lacks basis in fact **3** : the adventurous or glamorous attractiveness of something ⟨the *romance* of the old West⟩ **4** : a love affair **5** *cap* : the Romance languages [Old French *romans* "French, something written in French, romance", from Latin *romanice* "in the Roman manner", derived from *Romanus* "Roman"] □ ORIGIN In the last centuries of the Roman Empire the wide variety and distribution of the peoples recognized as Roman citizens led to the gradual change of the Latin language. The developing languages, which in their early stages were local dialects of Latin, were called *romans* (to use the Old French term) to distinguish them from the formal and official language. Most serious literature was still written in Latin, but in France entertaining verse tales were often written in the more popular spoken language, *romans*. The word *romans* came to be used for such a tale and was borrowed, in this sense, into English. Because many of these tales dealt with love, *romance* came to mean simply "a love story", and eventually it developed the sense of "a love affair".

²**romance** *vb* **1** : to exaggerate or invent details or incidents ⟨would *romance* about meeting great people⟩ **2 a** : to entertain romantic thoughts or ideas **b** : to carry on a love affair with ⟨a fine place in which to *romance* their girls⟩

Ro·mance \rō-'mans, 'rō-ˌ\ *adj* : of, relating to, or being the languages (as French, Italian, or Spanish) developed from Latin

Roman collar *n* : CLERICAL COLLAR

Ro·man·esque \ˌrō-mə-'nesk\ *adj* : of or relating to an architectural style developed in Italy and western Europe and characterized in its development after 1000 A. D. by the use of the round arch and vault, decorative use of arcades, and profuse ornament — **Romanesque** *n*

Ro·ma·ni·an *variant of* RUMANIAN

Ro·man·ic \rō-'man-ik\ *adj* : ROMANCE — **Romanic** *n*

Roman numeral *n* : a numeral in a system of notation based on the ancient Roman system — see NUMBER table

Ro·ma·no \rə-'män-ō, rō-\ *n* : a sharp hard Italian cheese [Italian, "Roman", from Latin *Romanus*]

Ro·mans \'rō-mənz\ *n* — see BIBLE table

Ro·mansh *or* **Ro·mansch** \rō-'mänch\ *n* : the Rhaeto=Romanic dialects spoken in the Grisons, Switzerland, and adjacent parts of Italy [Romansh *romonsch*]

¹**ro·man·tic** \rō-'mant-ik\ *adj* **1 a** : consisting of or resembling a romance ⟨*romantic* writing⟩ **b** : not factual : IMAGINARY ⟨a too *romantic* report of your adventure⟩ **2 a** : UNREALISTIC, IMPRACTICAL **b** *often cap* : of, relating to, or exhibiting romanticism **3** : having a strong emotional or imaginative appeal or association ⟨a *romantic* spot⟩ **4** : marked by or being passionate love [French *romantique*, from obsolete *romant* "romance", from Old French *romans*] — **ro·man·ti·cal·ly** \-i-kə-lē, -klē\ *adv*

²**romantic** *n* **1** : a romantic person, trait, or component **2** *cap* : a romantic writer, artist, or composer

ro·man·ti·cism \rō-'mant-ə-ˌsiz-əm\ *n* **1** : the quality or state of being romantic **2** *often cap* : a literary, artistic, and philosophical movement marked by emphasis on the imagination and emotions and especially by an exaltation of primitive and the common people, appreciation of nature, and interest in the remote or melancholy — **ro·man·ti·cist** \-səst\ *n, often cap*

ro·man·ti·cize \rō-'mant-ə-ˌsīz\ *vb* **1** : to make romantic : present romantically **2** : to have romantic ideas — **ro·man·ti·ci·za·tion** \-ˌmant-ə-sə-'zā-shən\ *n*

Ro·ma·ny \'räm-ə-nē, 'rō-mə-\ *n* **1** : GYPSY 1 **2** : the Indic language of the Gypsies [Romany *romani*, adj., "gypsy", from *rom* "gypsy man", from Sanskrit *ḍomba* "man of a low caste of musicians"] — **Romany** *adj*

¹romp \'rämp\ *n* **1** : ROMPER 1 **2** : boisterous play : FROLIC [derived from ¹*ramp*]

²romp *vi* : to play in a boisterous way : FROLIC

romp·er \'räm-pər\ *n* **1** : one that romps **2** : a child's one-piece garment including pants and a top — usually used in pl.

ron·do \'rän-dō\ *n, pl* **rondos** : a musical composition or movement in which the principal theme recurs several times with contrasting themes in between [Italian *rondò*, from Middle French *rondeau* "song with frequent repetitions of its two themes, rondeau"]

röntgen *variant of* ROENTGEN

rood \'rüd\ *n* **1** : CROSS 1b, CRUCIFIX **2** : any of various units of land area; *esp* : a British unit equal to ¼ acre (about 1011.7 square meters) [Old English *rōd* "rod, rood"]

¹roof \'rüf, 'ruf\ *n, pl* **roofs** \'rüfs, 'rufs *also* 'rüvz, 'ruvz\ **1** : the upper covering part of a building; *also* : ROOFING **2** : something (as the vaulted upper boundary of the mouth) resembling a roof in form, position, or function [Old English *hrōf*] — **roofed** \'rüft, 'ruft\ *adj* — **roof·less** \-ləs\ *adj* — **roof·like** \-ˌlīk\ *adj*

²roof *vt* : to cover with or as if with a roof — **roof·er** *n*

roof·ing *n* : material for a roof

roof·top \'rüf-ˌtäp, 'ruf-\ *n* : ROOF 1; *esp* : the outer surface of a usually flat roof (sunning themselves on the *rooftop*)

roof·tree \-ˌtrē\ *n* : RIDGEPOLE 1

¹rook \'ruk\ *n* : a common Old World gregarious bird about the size and color of the related American crow [Old English *hrōc*]

²rook *vt* : to defraud by cheating or swindling

³rook *n* : a chess piece that can move parallel to the edges of the board across any number of unoccupied squares — called also *castle* [Middle French *roc*, from Arabic *rukhkh*, from Persian]

rook·ery \'ruk-ə-rē\ *n, pl* **-er·ies** **1** : the breeding place of a colony of gregarious birds (as rooks) or mammals; *also* : the colony itself **2** : a crowded dilapidated tenement or group of dwellings

rook·ie \'ruk-ē\ *n* **1** : RECRUIT 1 **2** : a person who is in the first year of participation in a professional sport [perhaps alteration of *recruit*]

¹room \'rüm, 'rum\ *n* **1** : unoccupied area : SPACE (*room* to turn the car) **2 a** : a partitioned part of the inside of a building **b** : the people in a room **c** *pl* : LODGING 2, APARTMENT **3** : opportunity or occasion for something : CHANCE (*room* for improvement) [Old English *rūm*] — **roomed** \'rümd, 'rumd\ *adj*

²room *vb* : to provide with or occupy lodgings

room·er \'rü-mər, 'rum-ər\ *n* : LODGER

room·ette \rü-'met, rum-'et\ *n* : a small private single room on a railroad sleeping car

room·ful \'rüm-ˌful, 'rum-\ *n, pl* **roomfuls** \-ˌfulz\ *or* **rooms·ful** \'rümz-ˌful, 'rumz-\ : as much or as many as a room will hold; *also* : the persons or objects in a room

rooming house *n* : a house where rooms are rented to lodgers

room·mate \'rüm-ˌmāt, 'rum-\ *n* : one of two or more persons occupying the same room

roomy \'rü-mē, 'rum-ē\ *adj* **room·i·er; -est** : having plenty of room : SPACIOUS — **room·i·ness** *n*

¹roost \'rüst\ *n* **1** : PERCH 2a **2** : a place where birds customarily roost [Old English *hrōst*]

²roost *vb* : to settle on or as if on a roost : PERCH

roost·er \'rü-stər\ *n* : an adult male domestic fowl; *also* : an adult male bird

¹root \'rüt, 'rut\ *n* **1 a** : the usually underground part of a seed plant body that functions as an organ of absorption, aeration, and food storage or as a means of anchorage and support and that differs from a stem especially in lacking nodes, buds, and leaves **b** : a subterranean plant part especially when fleshy and edible **2 a** : the part of a tooth within the socket **b** : the enlarged basal part of a hair within the skin **c** : the basal or central part of a bodily structure or the part by which it is attached (nerve *roots*) (the *root* of the tongue) **3 a** : the cause or origin of something : SOURCE **b** : an underlying support : BASIS **c** : the essential core : HEART **4 a** : a number that when taken as a factor an indicated number of times gives a specified number (2 is a 4th *root* of 16) **b** : a solution of a polynomial equation in one unknown **5** : a word or part of a word from which other words are derived by adding a prefix or suffix **6** : the lowest tone of a chord in normal position — compare INVERSION [Old English *rōt*, from Old Norse] SYN see ORIGIN — **root·ed** \-əd\ *adj* — **root·less** \-ləs\ *adj* — **root·like** \-ˌlīk\ *adj*

²root *vb* **1 a** : to form or enable to form roots **b** : to fix or become fixed by or as if by roots : take root **2** : to remove altogether often by force (*root* out dissenters)

³root *vb* **1** : to turn up or dig in the earth with the snout **2** : to poke or dig about [Old English *wrōtan*]

⁴root \'rüt *also* 'rut\ *vi* **1** : to applaud noisily : CHEER (a group of students *rooting* for the football team) **2** : to encourage or lend support to someone or something (*rooted* for the reform candidate) [perhaps from earlier *rout* "to bellow", from Old Norse *rauta*] — **root·er** *n*

root beer *n* : a sweetened carbonated beverage flavored with extracts of roots and herbs

root cap *n* : a protective cap of parenchyma cells that covers the terminal meristem in most root tips

root cellar *n* : an underground storage area for vegetables (as root crops)

root crop *n* : a crop (as turnips or sweet potatoes) grown for its enlarged roots

root hair *n* : one of the filamentous outgrowths near the tip of a rootlet that function in absorption of water and minerals

root·let \'rüt-lət, 'rut-\ *n* : a small root

root pressure *n* : the chiefly osmotic pressure that contributes to the rise of water into the stems of plants from the roots

root·stock \'rüt-ˌstäk, 'rut-\ *n* **1** : RHIZOME **2** : a stock for grafting consisting of a root or a piece of root

rooty \'rüt-ē, 'rut-\ *adj* **root·i·er; -est** : full or consisting of roots (*rooty* soil)

¹rope \'rōp\ *n* **1 a** : a large stout cord of strands (as of fiber or wire) twisted or braided together **b** : a length of material (as rope or rawhide) suitable for a use; *esp* : LARIAT **c** : a hangman's noose **2** : a row or string consisting of things united by or as if by braiding, twining, or threading (a *rope* of daisies) **3** *pl* : special techniques or procedures (show them the *ropes*) [Old English *rāp*]

²rope *vb* **1 a** : to bind, fasten, or tie with a rope or cord **b** : to set off or divide by a rope (*rope* off the street) **c** : LASSO **2** : to draw as if with a rope : LURE **3** : to take the form of or twist in the manner of rope — **rop·er** *n*

rope·danc·er \'rōp-ˌdan-sər\ *n* : one that dances, walks, or performs acrobatic feats on a rope high in the air — **rope·danc·ing** \-sing\ *n*

rope·walk \-ˌwok\ *n* : a place where rope is made

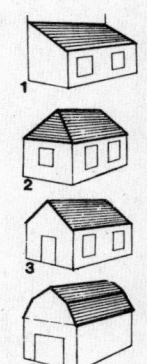

¹roof 1. *1* lean-to, 2 hip, 3 saddle, 4 gambrel

\ə\ abut	\ng\ sing
\ər\ further	\ō\ bone
\a\ mat	\o\ saw
\ā\ take	\oi\ coin
\ä\ cot, cart	\th\ thin
\au\ out	\th\ this
\ch\ chin	\ü\ food
\e\ pet	\u\ foot
\ē\ easy	\y\ yet
\g\ go	\yü\ few
\i\ tip	\yu\ cure
\ī\ life	\zh\ vision
\j\ job	

rosette 1

rope·walk·er \-,wȯ-kər\ *n* : an acrobat who walks on a rope high in the air

ropy \'rō-pē\ *adj* **rop·i·er; -est** **1** : capable of being drawn into a sticky thread **2** : suggesting rope : **STRINGY, SINEWY** ⟨*ropy* muscles⟩ — **rop·i·ness** *n*

Roque·fort \'rōk-fərt\ *trademark* — used for a cheese made of ewes' milk and ripened in caves

ror·qual \'rȯr-kwəl, -,kwȯl\ *n* : any of several large whalebone whales having the skin of the throat marked with deep longitudinal furrows [French, from Norwegian *rørhval*, from Old Norse *reytharhvalr*, from *reythr* "rorqual" + *hvalr* "whale"]

Ror·schach test \,rȯr-,shäk-, ,rōr-\ *n* : a personality and intelligence test in which the way a subject interprets blots of ink of varying designs and colors is used to interpret emotional and intelligence factors [Herman *Rorschach*, died 1922, Swiss psychiatrist]

ro·sar·i·an \rō-'zar-ē-ən, -'zer-\ *n* : a grower or fancier of roses

ro·sa·ry \'rōz-rē, -ə-rē\ *n, pl* **-ries** **1** : a string of beads used in counting prayers especially of the Roman Catholic rosary **2** *often cap* : a Roman Catholic devotion consisting of meditation on usually five sacred mysteries during recitation of five decades of Hail Marys of which each is preceded by the Lord's Prayer and followed by the Gloria Patri [Medieval Latin *rosarium*, from Latin, "rose garden", derived from *rosa* "rose"] □ **ORIGIN** *Rosary* comes from Medieval Latin *rosarium*, which in earlier Latin meant literally "a rose garden". It was used metaphorically to refer to a series of prayers, thought of perhaps as a garden of prayers and perhaps influenced by the association in Christian symbolism of the rose with the Virgin Mary and the rose garden with paradise. *Rosarium* was applied by extension to the string of beads as well as to the prayers themselves.

¹rose *past of* **RISE**

²rose \'rōz\ *n* **1 a** : any of a genus of usually prickly dicotyledonous shrubs with pinnate leaves and showy flowers having five petals in the wild state but being often double in cultivation **b** : the flower of a rose **2** : **COMPASS CARD** **3** : a moderate purplish red [Old English, from Latin *rosa*] — **rose·like** \-,līk\ *adj*

³rose *adj* **1** : of, relating to, resembling, or used for the rose **2** : of the color rose

ro·se·ate \'rō-zē-ət, -zē-,āt\ *adj* **1** : resembling a rose especially in color **2** : overly optimistic — **ro·se·ate·ly** *adv*

rose·bay \'rōz-,bā\ *n* : **RHODODENDRON**; *esp* : one of eastern North America with rosy bell-shaped flowers

rose–breast·ed grosbeak \,rōz-,bres-təd-\ *n* : a grosbeak of eastern North America that in the male is chiefly black and white with the breast and lining of the wings rose red and in the female is a streaky grayish brown with the lining of the wings orange

rose·bud \'rōz-,bəd\ *n* : the bud of a rose

rose·bush \-,bu̇sh\ *n* : a shrub that produces roses

rose–col·ored \'rōz-,kəl-ərd\ *adj* **1** : having a rose color **2** : seeing or seen in a promising light : **OPTIMISTIC**

rose fever *n* : hay fever occurring in the spring or early summer

rose·fish \'rōz-,fish\ *n* : a marine food fish of northern Atlantic coasts that is usually rosy red when adult

rose mallow *n* : a usually rosy-flowered hibiscus or hollyhock

rose·mary \'rōz-,mer-ē\ *n* : a fragrant shrubby mint of southern Europe and Asia Minor used in cookery and in perfumery [Latin *rosmarinus*, from *ros* "dew" + *marinus* "of the sea"]

rose of Shar·on \-'shar-ən, -'sher-\ : a commonly cultivated Asian small shrubby hibiscus having showy rose, purple, or white flowers [Plain of *Sharon*, Palestine]

ro·se·o·la \,rō-zē-'ō-lə, rō-'zē-ə-lə\ *n* : a spotty rose-colored eruption or a condition marked by this; *esp* : **GER-**

MAN MEASLES [New Latin, from Latin *roseus* "rosy", from *rosa* "rose"] — **ro·se·o·lar** \-lər\ *adj*

Ro·set·ta stone \rō-'zet-ə-\ *n* : a stone found in 1799 that bears an inscription in hieroglyphics, demotic characters, and Greek and is known for giving the first clue in deciphering Egyptian hieroglyphics [*Rosetta*, Egypt]

ro·sette \rō-'zet\ *n* **1** : an ornament (as of cloth or paper) resembling a rose **2** : a cluster of leaves developed on a plant in crowded whorls either basally (as in a dandelion) or at the apex (as in palms)

rose water *n* : a watery solution of the fragrant constituents of the rose used as a perfume

rose·wood \'rōz-,wu̇d\ *n* **1** : any of various tropical trees yielding valuable cabinet woods of a dark red or purplish color streaked and variegated with black **2** : the wood of a rosewood

Rosh Ha·sha·nah \,rōsh-hə-'shō-nə, ,rōsh-ə-, ,räsh-, -'shän-ə\ *n* : the Jewish New Year observed as a religious holiday in September or October [Hebrew *rōsh hashshānāh*, literally, "beginning of the year"]

¹ros·in \'räz-n, 'rȯz-\ *n* : a translucent amber-colored to almost black brittle resin that is obtained by chemical means from pine trees or from tall oil and is used in making varnish, paper size, soap, and soldering flux and on violin bows [Middle French *resine* "resin"] — **ros·in·ous** \'räz-n-əs, 'räz-nəs, 'rȯz-\ *adj*

²rosin *vt* : to rub (as the bow of a violin) with rosin

ros·ter \'räs-tər\ *n* : a list usually of personnel; *esp* : one assigning duties [Dutch *rooster*, literally, "gridiron", from *roosten* "to roast"; from the parallel lines]

ros·trum \'räs-trəm\ *n, pl* **rostrums** *or* **ros·tra** \-trə\ **1** : a stage or platform for public speaking **2** : a bodily part or process (as a snout or median projection) suggesting a bird's bill [Latin, "beak, ship's beak", from *rodere* "to gnaw"; sense 1 from Latin *Rostra*, speakers' platform in the Roman Forum, from pl. of *rostrum* "beak"] — **ros·tral** \-trəl\ *adj* — **ros·trate** \-,trāt\ *adj* □ **ORIGIN** The Latin word *rostrum*, whose primary meaning is "beak", was derived from the verb *rodere*, "to gnaw". Eventually *rostrum* came to be used to refer to the prow or beak of a ship. In 338 B. C. the beaks of ships captured from the people of Antium (now called Anzio) were used to decorate the orators' platform in the Roman Forum. From this time on, this platform was called *Rostra*, the plural form of *rostrum*. Later *rostra* was used to refer to any platform from which a speaker addressed an assembly. In English the singular form *rostrum* is still so used.

rosy \'rō-zē\ *adj* **ros·i·er; -est** **1 a** : of the color rose **b** : having a healthy pink complexion **c** : marked by blushes **2** : characterized by or tending to promote optimism ⟨*rosy* prospects⟩ — **ros·i·ly** \-zə-lē\ *adv* — **ros·i·ness** \-zē-nəs\ *n*

¹rot \'rät\ *vb* **rot·ted; rot·ting** **1 a** : to undergo decomposition from the action of bacteria or fungi **b** : to become unsound or weak (as from use or chemical action) **2 a** : to go to ruin : **DETERIORATE** **b** : to become morally corrupt : **DEGENERATE** **3** : to cause to decompose or deteriorate with rot [Old English *rotian*] **SYN** *see* **DECAY**

²rot *n* **1 a** : the process of rotting : the state of being rotten **b** : something rotten or rotting **2** : a disease of plants or animals marked by the breaking down of tissue; *also* : an area of broken-down tissue **3** : **NONSENSE 1** — often used interjectionally

Ro·ta \'rōt-ə\ *n* : a tribunal of the papal curia exercising jurisdiction especially in matrimonial cases appealed from diocesan courts [Medieval Latin, from Latin, "wheel"]

Ro·tar·i·an \rō-'ter-ē-ən\ *n* : a member of one of the major service clubs [*Rotary (club)*]

¹ro·ta·ry \'rōt-ə-rē\ *adj* **1 a** : turning on an axis like a wheel ⟨a *rotary* blade⟩ **b** : taking place about an axis ⟨*rotary* motion⟩ **2** : having an important part that turns on an axis (a *rotary* cutter) **3** : characterized by rotation [Medieval Latin *rotarius,* from Latin *rota* "wheel"]

²rotary *n, pl* **-ries 1** : a rotary machine **2** : a road junction formed around a central circle about which traffic moves in one direction only

rotary engine *n* **1** : any of various engines (as a turbine) in which power is applied to vanes or similar parts that move in a circular path **2** : a radial engine in which the cylinders revolve about a stationary crankshaft

rotary–wing aircraft *n* : an aircraft supported in flight partially or wholly by rotating airfoils

ro·tate \'rō-ˌtāt\ *vb* **1** : to turn or cause to turn about an axis or a center : REVOLVE (the earth *rotates*) **2 a** : to do or cause to do something in turn : ALTERNATE (*rotate* on the night shift) **b** : to pass in a series (the seasons *rotate*) **3** : to grow in rotation (*rotate* alfalfa and corn) [Latin *rotare,* from *rota* "wheel"] — **ro·tat·able** \'rō-ˌtāt-ə-bəl *also* rō-'\ *adj* — **ro·tat·or** \'rō-ˌtāt-ər *also* rō-'\ *n*

ro·ta·tion \rō-'tā-shən\ *n* **1 a** : the act of rotating especially on or as if on an axis **b** : one complete turn **2 a** : return or succession in a recurring series (*rotation* of the seasons) **b** : CROP ROTATION — **ro·ta·tion·al** \-shnəl, -shən-l\ *adj* — **in rotation** : one after another in an orderly sequence

ro·ta·to·ry \'rōt-ə-ˌtōr-ē, -ˌtȯr-\ *adj* **1** : of, relating to, or producing rotation **2** : occurring in rotation

¹rote \'rōt\ *n* **1** : the use of memory usually with little intelligence (learn by *rote*) **2** : routine or repetition carried out mechanically or without understanding [Middle English]

²rote *adj* : learned or memorized by rote

ro·te·none \'rōt-n-ˌōn\ *n* : a crystalline insecticide obtained from plants (as derris) that is of low toxicity for warm-blooded animals and is used especially in home gardens [Japanese *roten* "derris plant"]

ro·ti·fer \'rōt-ə-fər\ *n* : any of a class (Rotifera) of minute aquatic animals having at one end a disk with circles of cilia which in motion look like revolving wheels [derived from Latin *rota* "wheel" + *ferre* "to bear, carry"] — **ro·tif·er·an** \rō-'tif-ə-rən\ *adj or n*

ro·tis·ser·ie \rō-'tis-rē, -ə-rē\ *n* : an appliance fitted with a spit on which food is rotated before or over a source of heat [French *rôtisserie* "restaurant", from Middle French *rostisserie,* from *rostir* "to roast"]

ro·to \'rōt-ō\ *n, pl* **rotos** : ROTOGRAVURE

ro·to·gra·vure \ˌrōt-ə-grə-'vyu̇r\ *n* **1** : PHOTOGRAVURE **2** : a section of a newspaper devoted to rotogravure pictures [Latin *rota* "wheel" + English *-o-* + *gravure*]

ro·tor \'rōt-ər\ *n* **1** : a part that revolves in a stationary part (as in an electrical machine) **2** : a complete system of horizontal rotating blades that supplies the force supporting an aircraft in flight (the *rotor* of a helicopter) [contraction of *rotator*]

rot·ten \'rät-n\ *adj* **1** : having rotted : PUTRID (*rotten* fruit) **2** : morally corrupt **3** : extremely unpleasant or inferior (*rotten* weather) [Old Norse *rotinn*] — **rot·ten·ly** *adv* — **rot·ten·ness** \-n-nəs\ *n*

rot·ten·stone \'rät-n-ˌstōn\ *n* : a decomposed siliceous limestone used for polishing

rot·ter \'rät-ər\ *n* : a thoroughly objectionable person

ro·tund \rō-'tənd, 'rō-,\ *adj* **1** : marked by roundness **2** : FULL, SONOROUS (*rotund* voices) **3** : PLUMP, CHUBBY [Latin *rotundus*] — **ro·tun·di·ty** \rō-'tən-dət-ē\ *n* — **ro·tund·ly** \rō-'tən-dlē, 'rō-,\ *adv* — **ro·tund·ness** \rō-'tənd-nəs, -'tən-, 'rō-,\ *n*

ro·tun·da \rō-'tən-də\ *or* **ro·ton·da** \-'tän-\ *n* **1** : a round building; *esp* : one covered by a dome **2 a** : a large round room **b** : a large central area (as in a hotel) [Italian *rotonda,* from Latin *rotundus* "round"]

roué \ru̇-'ā\ *n* : a usually male libertine [French, literally, "broken on the wheel", from *rouer* "to break on the wheel", from Medieval Latin *rotare,* from Latin,

"to rotate"; from the feeling that such a person deserves this punishment]

¹rouge \'rüzh, *especially Southern* 'rüj\ *n* **1** : any of various cosmetics to color the cheeks or lips red **2** : a red powder consisting essentially of ferric oxide used in polishing (as gems) and as a pigment [French, from *rouge* "red", from Latin *rubeus* "reddish"]

²rouge *vb* **1** : to apply rouge to **2** : to use rouge

¹rough \'rəf\ *adj* **1 a** : having an uneven surface : not smooth **b** : covered with or made up of coarse and often shaggy hair or bristles (a *rough*-coated terrier) **c** : difficult to travel over or penetrate : WILD (*rough* country) **2 a** : characterized by harshness, violence, or force **b** : DIFFICULT, TRYING (a *rough* day at the office) **3** : coarse or rugged in character or appearance: as **a** : harsh to the ear **b** : crude in style or expression **c** : marked by a lack of refinement or grace : UNCOUTH **4** : marked by incompleteness or inexactness (a *rough* draft) (*rough* estimates) [Old English *rūh*] — **rough·ly** *adv* — **rough·ness** *n* □ SYN ROUGH, HARSH, RUGGED mean not smooth or even. ROUGH implies having points, bristles, ridges, or projections on the surface (*rough* wood) HARSH implies having a surface or texture that is unpleasant to the touch (*harsh* sand) RUGGED implies irregularity or unevenness of land surface and connotes difficulty of travel (*rugged* mountain roads)

²rough *n* **1** : uneven ground covered with high grass, brush, and stones; *esp* : such ground bordering a golf fairway **2** : the disagreeable side or aspect (take the *rough* with the smooth) **3** : something in a crude, unfinished, or preliminary state; *also* : such a state (diamonds in the *rough*) **c** : a hasty preliminary drawing or layout **4** : ROWDY, TOUGH (a gang of *roughs*)

³rough *adv* : in a rough manner

⁴rough *vt* **1** : ROUGHEN **2 a** : MANHANDLE, BEAT (*roughed* up by hoodlums) **b** : to subject to unnecessary and intentional violence in a sport **3** : to shape, make, or dress in a rough or preliminary way (*rough* out a plan) — **rough·er** *n* — **rough it** : to live under primitive conditions

rough·age \'rəf-ij\ *n* : coarse bulky food (as bran) that is relatively high in fiber and low in digestible nutrients and assists in movement of materials through the digestive tract

rough–and–ready \ˌrəf-ən-'red-ē\ *adj* : crude in nature, method, or manner but effective in action or use

rough–and–tum·ble \-ən-'təm-bəl\ *n* : a rough disorderly unrestrained struggle — **rough–and–tumble** *adj*

¹rough·cast \'rəf-ˌkast\ *n* **1** : a rough model **2** : a plaster of lime mixed with shells or pebbles used for covering buildings

²roughcast *vt* **-cast; -cast·ing 1** : to plaster (as a wall) with roughcast **2** : to shape or form roughly

rough–dry \-'drī\ *vt* : to dry (laundry) without smoothing or ironing — **roughdry** *adj*

rough·en \'rəf-ən\ *vb* **rough·ened; rough·en·ing** \'rəf-ning, -ə-ning\ : to make or become rough

rough fish *n* : a fish that is neither a sport fish nor an important food for sport fishes

rough–hew \'rəf-'hyü\ *vt* **-hewed; -hewed** *or* **-hewn** \-'hyün\; **-hew·ing** \-'hyü-\ **1** : to hew (as timber) coarsely without smoothing or finishing **2** : to form crudely

rough–hewn \'rəf-'hyün\ *adj* : lacking polish or social graces

rough·house \'rəf-ˌhau̇s\ *n* : violence or rough rowdy play — **rough·house** \-ˌhau̇s, -ˌhau̇z\ *vb* — **rough·house** \-ˌhau̇s\ *adj*

rough·ish \'rəf-ish\ *adj* : somewhat rough

rough·neck \'rəf-ˌnek\ *n* **1** : a rough person; *esp* : ROWDY, TOUGH **2** : a worker on an oil-drilling crew

Rough Rid·er *n* : a member of the 1st United States Volunteer Cavalry regiment in the Spanish-American War commanded by Theodore Roosevelt

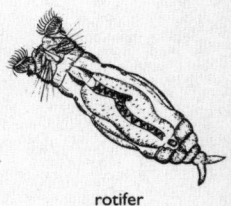

rotifer

\ə\ abut		\ng\ sing	
\ər\ further		\ō\ bone	
\a\ mat		\ȯ\ saw	
\ā\ take		\ȯi\ coin	
\ä\ cot, cart		\th\ thin	
\au̇\ out		\th\ this	
\ch\ chin		\ü\ food	
\e\ pet		\u̇\ foot	
\ē\ easy		\y\ yet	
\g\ go		\yü\ few	
\i\ tip		\yu̇\ cure	
\ī\ life		\zh\ vision	
\j\ job			

¹rough·shod \-'shäd\ *adj* **1** : shod with calked shoes **2** : marked by force without justice or consideration

²roughshod *adv* : in a roughshod manner

rou·lade \rü-'läd\ *n* : a slice of meat rolled with or without a stuffing [French, from *rouler* "to roll"]

¹rou·lette \rü-'let\ *n* **1** : a gambling game in which players bet on which compartment of a revolving wheel a small ball will come to rest in **2 a** : a toothed wheel or disk (as for producing rows of dots on engraved plates or for making short consecutive incisions in paper to facilitate subsequent division) **b** : tiny slits in a sheet of stamps made by a roulette [French, literally, "small wheel", from Old French *roelete,* from *roele* "wheel", from Late Latin *rotella* "small wheel", from Latin *rota* "wheel"]

²roulette *vt* : to make roulettes in

Rou·ma·ni·an \rü-'mā-nē-ən\ *variant of* RUMANIAN

¹round \'raund\ *adj* **1 a** : shaped like a disk or a ball : having every part of the surface or circumference equidistant from the center **b** : CYLINDRICAL **c** : having a curved outline **2** : well fleshed : PLUMP **3 a** : COMPLETE, FULL ⟨a *round* dozen⟩ **b** : approximately correct; *esp* : exact only to a specific decimal **c** : LARGE ⟨a good *round* sum⟩ **4 a** : BLUNT, OUTSPOKEN **b** : not restrained or toned down ⟨a *round* oath⟩ **5** : moving in or forming a circle **6 a** : brought to completion or perfection : FINISHED **b** : presented with lifelike fullness or vividness **7 a** : having full or unimpeded resonance or tone **b** : pronounced with rounded lips **8** : of or relating to handwriting predominantly curved rather than angular [Old French *roont,* from Latin *rotundus*] — **round·ly** *adv* — **round·ness** \'raund-nəs, 'raun-\ *n*

²round *adv* : ¹AROUND

³round \'raund\ *n* **1 a** : something (as a circle, globe, or ring) that is round **b** : a knot or circle of people or things **2** : ROUND DANCE 1 **3** : a song in which three or four voices follow each other around and sing the same melody and words **4 a** : a rung of a ladder or a chair **b** : a rounded molding **5 a** : a circling path or course **b** : motion in a circle or a curving path **6** : a route or circuit habitually covered : a series of customary calls or stops **7** : a drink apiece served at one time to each person in a group **8** : a series of recurring routine or repetitive actions or events ⟨a *round* of parties⟩ **9** : a period of time that recurs in a fixed pattern **10 a** : one shot fired by a weapon or by each man in a military unit **b** : a unit of ammunition consisting of the parts necessary to fire one shot **11** : a unit of action in a contest or game that occupies a stated period, covers a prescribed distance, includes a specified number of plays, or gives each player one turn **12** : a demonstrative outpouring or burst ⟨a *round* of applause⟩ **13** : a cut of beef especially between the rump and the lower leg **14** : a rounded or curved part — **in the round 1** : in full sculptured form unattached to a background : FREESTANDING **2** : with a comprehensive view or representation **3** : with a center stage surrounded by an audience on all sides ⟨theater *in the round*⟩ — **out of round** : not perfectly or adequately round or circular

⁴round \'raund\ *vb* **1 a** : to make round **b** : to become round or plump **c** : to pronounce (a sound) with rounding of the lips **2 a** : to go around **b** : to pass part way around **3** : to form a circle around **4 a** : to bring to completion ⟨*round* out a career⟩ **b** : to become complete **c** : to bring to perfection of style : POLISH **3 5** : to express as a round number ⟨*round* off to three decimal places⟩ **6** : to follow a winding course ⟨horses *rounding* into the homestretch⟩ — **round on** : to turn against

⁵round \raund, 'raund\ *prep* : ²AROUND

¹round·about \'raun-də-ˌbaut\ *n* **1** : an indirect route : DETOUR **2** *British* **a** : MERRY-GO-ROUND **b** : ROTARY 2

²round·about \ˌraun-də-'baut\ *adj* : not direct

round clam *n* : QUAHOG

round dance *n* **1** : a folk dance in which dancers form a ring and move in a prescribed direction **2** : a ballroom dance in which couples progress around the room **3** : a series of movements performed by a bee to indicate that a source of food is nearby

round·ed \'raun-dəd\ *adj* **1** : curving or round in shape **2** : fully developed — **round·ed·ness** *n*

roun·del \'raun-dl\ *n* : a round figure or object; *esp* : a circular panel, window, or niche [Old French *rondel,* from *roont* "round"]

roun·de·lay \'raun-də-ˌlā\ *n* **1** : a simple song with a refrain **2** : a poem with a refrain recurring frequently or at fixed intervals [Middle French *rondelet,* literally, "small circle", from *rondel* "small circle, roundel"]

round·er \'raun-dər\ *n* **1** : a person of loose morals or conduct **2** *pl* : an English game played with ball and bat somewhat resembling baseball **3 a** : one that rounds by hand or by machine **b** : a tool for making an edge or a surface round

Round·head \'raund-ˌhed\ *n* : a Puritan or member of the parliamentary party in England at the time of Charles I and Oliver Cromwell [from the Puritans' cutting their hair short in contrast to the Cavaliers]

round·head·ed \-'hed-əd\ *adj* : having a round head; *esp* : BRACHYCEPHALIC — **round·head·ed·ness** *n*

round·house \'raund-ˌhaus\ *n* **1** : a circular building for housing and repairing locomotives **2** : a cabin or apartment on the after part of a quarterdeck **3** : a blow in boxing delivered with a wide swing **4** : a slow wide curve in baseball

round·ish \'raun-dish\ *adj* : somewhat round

round robin *n* **1 a** : a written petition or protest with signatures in a circle so as not to indicate who signed first **b** : a letter sent in turn to the members of a group each of whom signs and forwards it sometimes after adding comment **2** : a tournament in which every contestant meets every other contestant in turn **3** : SERIES 1, ROUND [from the name *Robin*]

round–shoul·dered \'raund-'shōl-dərd, 'raun-\ *adj* : having the shoulders stooping or rounded

round table *n* **1** *cap R&T* **a** : a large circular table for King Arthur and his knights **b** : the knights of King Arthur **2** : a meeting of a group of persons for discussion; *also* : the persons meeting

round–the–clock *adj* : being in effect, continuing, or lasting 24 hours a day

round trip *n* : a trip to a place and back usually over the same route

round·up \'raun-ˌdəp\ *n* **1** : the gathering together of cattle on the range by riding around them and driving them in **2** : a gathering together of scattered persons or things **3** : SUMMARY, RÉSUMÉ ⟨the 6 o'clock news *roundup*⟩

round up \raun-'dəp, 'raun-\ *vt* **1** : to collect (cattle) by means of a roundup **2** : to gather in or bring together

round·worm \'raun-ˌdwərm\ *n* : a nematode worm (as a hookworm or a trichina); *also* : a related round-bodied unsegmented worm as distinguished from a flatworm

¹rouse \'rauz\ *vb* **1** : to arouse or become aroused from or as if from sleep : AWAKEN **2** : to become stirred **3** : to stir up : EXCITE [Middle English *rousen*]

²rouse *n* : an act or instance of rousing; *esp* : an excited stir

³rouse *n, archaic* : CAROUSE

rous·ing \'rau-zing\ *adj* **1 a** : EXCITING ⟨played a *rousing* march⟩ **b** : BRISK, LIVELY ⟨a *rousing* cheer⟩ **2** : EXCEPTIONAL 2

roust·about \'rau-stə-ˌbaut\ *n* : one who does heavy or unskilled labor (as a deckhand or longshoreman, a laborer in an oil field, or a circus worker who erects and dismantles tents) [from *roust* "to rouse", alteration of *rouse*]

¹rout \ˈrau̇t\ *n* **1** : a crowd of people; *esp* : RABBLE **2** : DISTURBANCE 3 **3** : a fashionable gathering : RECEPTION [Middle French *route* "troop, defeat", derived from Latin *ruptus,* past participle of *rumpere* "to break"]

²rout *vb* **1** : to search haphazardly : RUMMAGE **2** : to find or bring to light especially with difficulty : DISCOVER **3** : to gouge out or make a furrow in (as wood or metal) **4 a** : to expel by force : EJECT ⟨*routed* out of their homes⟩ **b** : to cause to emerge especially from bed : ROUSE [alteration of ³*root*]

³rout *n* **1** : a state of wild confusion and disorderly retreat **2 a** : a disastrous defeat **b** : an act or instance of routing [Middle French *route* "troop, defeat"]

⁴rout *vt* **1** : to disorganize or defeat completely **2** : to drive out : DISPEL

¹route \ˈrüt, ˈrau̇t\ *n* **1 a** : a traveled way : HIGHWAY **b** : a means of access : CHANNEL **2** : an established, selected, or assigned course of travel ⟨a newspaper *route*⟩ [Old French, derived from Latin *ruptus,* past participle of *rumpere* "to break"]

²route *vt* **1** : to send, forward, or transport by a certain route ⟨*route* traffic around the city⟩ **2** : to arrange and direct the order and carrying out of (as a series of operations in a factory)

route·man \-mən, -ˌman\ *n* : one who sells or makes deliveries on an assigned route

¹rout·er \ˈrau̇t-ər\ *n* : a machine with a revolving vertical spindle for milling out the surface of wood or metal

²rout·er \ˈrüt-ər, ˈrau̇t-\ *n* : one that routes

¹rou·tine \rü-ˈtēn\ *n* **1** : a regular or customary course of procedure **2** : an often repeated speech **3** : a fixed piece of entertainment often repeated : ACT; *esp* : a theatrical number [French, from *route* "route"]

²routine *adj* **1** : being commonplace or uninspired **2** : done or happening regularly ⟨*routine* inspection⟩ — **rou·tine·ly** *adv*

¹rove \ˈrōv\ *vb* **1** : to move aimlessly : ROAM ⟨*rove* about the country⟩ **2** : to wander through or over ⟨*rove* the seas⟩ [Middle English *roven* "to shoot arrows at marks chosen at random"]

²rove *past of* REEVE

rove beetle *n* : any of numerous often predatory active beetles with a long body and very short wing cases [perhaps from ¹*rove*]

¹ro·ver \ˈrō-vər\ *n* : PIRATE [Dutch, from *roven* "to rob"]

²rov·er \ˈrō-vər\ *n* : one that roves : WANDERER, ROAMER

rov·ing \ˈrō-ving\ *n* : a twisted roll or strand of fibers

¹row \ˈrō\ *vb* **1** : to propel a boat by means of oars **2** : to move by or as if by the propulsion of oars **3** : to be equipped with (a specified number of oars) **4** : to engage in rowing **5** : to transport in or as if in a boat propelled by oars [Old English *rōwan*] — **row·er** \ˈrō-ər, ˈrȯr\ *n*

²row *n* : an act or instance of rowing

³row *n* **1** : a group forming a more or less straight line ⟨a *row* of bottles⟩ ⟨corn planted in *rows*⟩ **2** : an urban street or district

⁴row \ˈrau̇\ *n* : a noisy disturbance or quarrel : BRAWL [origin unknown]

⁵row \ˈrau̇\ *vi* : to engage in a row : FIGHT, QUARREL

row·an \ˈrau̇-ən, ˈrō-ən\ *n* **1** : a Eurasian tree of the rose family with flat clusters of white flowers followed by small red pomes; *also* : the closely related American mountain ash **2** *or* **row·an·ber·ry** \-ˌber-ē\ : the fruit of a rowan [of Scandinavian origin]

row·boat \ˈrō-ˌbōt\ *n* : a boat designed to be rowed

¹row·dy \ˈrau̇d-ē\ *adj* **row·di·er; -est** : coarse or boisterous in behavior : ROUGH [perhaps from ⁴*row*] — **row·di·ness** *n* — **row·dy·ish** \-ē-ish\ *adj* — **row·dy·ism** \-ē-ˌiz-əm\ *n*

²rowdy *n, pl* **rowdies** : a rowdy person : TOUGH

¹row·el \ˈrau̇-əl, ˈrau̇l\ *n* : a revolving disk at the end of a spur with sharp points for goading a horse [Middle French *rouelle* "small wheel", from Late Latin *rotella,* from Latin *rota* "wheel"]

²rowel *vt* **-eled** *or* **-elled; -el·ing** *or* **-el·ling** : to goad with or as if with a rowel : SPUR

row·en \ˈrau̇-ən\ *n* **1** : a stubble field left unplowed for late grazing **2** : AFTERMATH 1 — often used in pl. [Middle English *rowein*]

row house \ˈrō-\ *n* : one of a series of houses connected by common sidewalls

row·ing \ˈrō-ing\ *n* : the sport of racing long narrow boats propelled by oars

rowing boat *n, chiefly British* : ROWBOAT

row·lock \ˈräl-ək, ˈrəl-; ˈrō-ˌläk\ *n, chiefly British* : OARLOCK

¹roy·al \ˈrȯi-əl, ˈrȯil\ *adj* **1 a** : of kingly ancestry **b** : of, relating to, or subject to the crown **c** : being in the crown's service ⟨*Royal* Navy⟩ **2 a** : suitable for royalty : MAGNIFICENT ⟨a *royal* welcome⟩ **b** : requiring no exertion : EASY ⟨no *royal* road to victory⟩ **3 a** : of great size or high quality **b** : established or chartered by the crown ⟨a *royal* colony⟩ [Middle French *roial,* from Latin *regalis,* from *reg-, rex* "king"] — **roy·al·ly** \ˈrȯi-ə-lē\ *adv*

²royal *n* : a small sail on the mast immediately above the topgallant sail

royal blue *n* : a vivid purplish blue

roy·al·ist \ˈrȯi-ə-ləst\ *n* **1** : a supporter (as during a time of civil war) of a king **2** : a believer in monarchy as a form of government — **royalist** *adj*

royal jelly *n* : a highly nutritious secretion of the pharyngeal glands of the honeybee that is fed to all very young larvae and continuously to queen larvae

royal palm *n* : a tall graceful American palm widely planted as an ornamental tree in tropical regions

royal poinciana *n* : a showy tropical tree widely planted for its immense racemes of scarlet and orange flowers

roy·al·ty \ˈrȯi-əl-tē, ˈrȯil-tē\ *n, pl* **-ties 1 a** : royal standing or power **b** : a right or privilege of a sovereign (as a percentage of gold or silver taken from mines) **2** : regal character or bearing : NOBILITY **3 a** : persons of royal lineage **b** : a person of royal rank **c** : a privileged class **4 a** : a share of the product or profit reserved by the grantor especially of an oil or mining lease **b** : a payment made to the owner of a patent or copyright for the use of it

-rrhea *also* **-rrhoea** *n combining form* : flow : discharge ⟨sebor*rhea*⟩ [Greek *-rrhoia,* from *rhoia,* from *rhein* "to flow"]

¹rub \ˈrəb\ *vb* **rubbed; rub·bing 1 a** : to move or make move along the surface of a body with pressure **b** (1) : to fret or chafe with friction ⟨the new shoes *rubbed*⟩ (2) : to cause or cause to feel discontent, irritation, or anger ⟨*rubbed* me the wrong way⟩ **2 a** : to apply or spread by rubbing ⟨*rub* ointment on your chest⟩ **b** : to treat in some way by rubbing ⟨*rub* the surface clean⟩ [Middle English *rubben*]

²rub *n* **1 a** : DIFFICULTY ⟨that's the *rub*⟩ **b** : something (as sharp criticism) that grates the feelings **c** : something that mars or upsets serenity **2** : the application of friction with pressure ⟨an alcohol *rub*⟩

ru·ba·to \rü-ˈbät-ō\ *n, pl* **-tos** : fluctuation of speed within a musical phrase typically against a rhythmically steady accompaniment [Italian, literally, "robbed"]

¹rub·ber \ˈrəb-ər\ *n* **1 a** : one that rubs **b** : an instrument or object (as a rubber eraser) used in rubbing, polishing, scraping, or cleaning **c** : something that prevents rubbing or chafing **2 a** : an elastic substance obtained by coagulating the milky juice of various tropical plants **b** : any of various synthetic rubberlike substances **c** : natural or synthetic rubber modified by chemical treatment to increase its useful properties (as toughness and resistance to wear) and used in tires, electrical insulation, and waterproof materials **3** : something made of or resembling rubber; *esp* : a

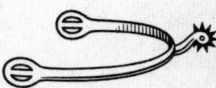

¹rowel

\ə\ abut	\ng\ sing
\ər\ further	\ō\ bone
\a\ mat	\ȯ\ saw
\ā\ take	\ȯi\ coin
\ä\ cot, cart	\th\ thin
\au̇\ out	\th\ this
\ch\ chin	\ü\ food
\e\ pet	\u̇\ foot
\ē\ easy	\y\ yet
\g\ go	\yü\ few
\i\ tip	\yu̇\ cure
\ī\ life	\zh\ vision
\j\ job	

rubber overshoe [sense 2 from its use in erasers] — **rub·ber·like** \-,līk\ *adj* — **rub·bery** \'rəb-rē, -ə-rē\ *adj*

²rubber *n* : a contest that consists of an odd number of games and is won by the side that takes a majority (as two out of three) [origin unknown]

rubber band *n* : a continuous band of rubber used in various ways (as to hold a bunch of things together)

rub·ber·ized \'rəb-ə-,rīzd\ *adj* : coated or saturated with rubber or a rubber preparation (*rubberized* raincoats)

rub·ber·neck \'rəb-ər-,nek\ *n* **1** : an inquisitive person **2** : TOURIST; *esp* : one on a guided tour — **rubberneck** *vi*

rubber plant *n* : a tall tropical Asian fig tree that is often dwarfed in pots as a houseplant

rub·ber-stamp \,rəb-ər-'stamp\ *vt* : to approve, endorse, or dispose of as a matter of routine usually without exercise of judgment or at the command of another

rubber stamp *n* **1** : a stamp of rubber for making imprints **2 a** : a person who echoes or imitates others **b** : a person or body given to rubber-stamping

rubber tree *n* : a South American tree that is a source of rubber and is cultivated in plantations; *also* : any tree that yields rubber

rub·bing \'rəb-ing\ *n* : an image of a raised, indented, or textured surface obtained by placing paper over it and rubbing the paper with colored material

rubbing alcohol *n* : a watery solution of an alcohol used externally especially to soothe or refresh

rub·bish \'rəb-ish\ *n* : useless waste or rejected matter : TRASH [Middle English *robys*] — **rub·bishy** \'rəb-i-shē\ *adj*

rub·ble \'rəb-əl\ *n* **1** : rough stone as it comes from the quarry **2** : waterworn or rough broken stones or bricks used in coarse masonry or in filling courses of walls; *also* : RUBBLEWORK **3** : a mass of rough irregular pieces ⟨a town bombed to *rubble*⟩ [Middle English *robyl*]

rub·down \'rəb-,daůn\ *n* : a brisk rubbing of the body (as after a bath)

rube \'rüb\ *n* : an awkward unsophisticated rustic [*Rube*, nickname for *Reuben*]

¹ru·be·fa·cient \,rü-bə-'fā-shənt\ *adj* : causing redness (as of the skin) [Latin *rubefaciens*, present participle of *rubefacere* "to make red", from *rubeus* "reddish" + *facere* "to make"]

²rubefacient *n* : a substance for external application that produces redness of the skin — **ru·be·fac·tion** \-'fak-shən\ *n*

ru·bel·la \rü-'bel-ə\ *n* : GERMAN MEASLES [New Latin, from Latin *rubellus* "reddish", from *ruber* "red"]

ru·be·o·la \rü-'bē-ə-lə, ,rü-bē-'ō-\ *n* : MEASLES [New Latin, from Latin *rubeus* "reddish"] — **ru·be·o·lar** \-lər\ *adj*

Ru·bi·con \'rü-bi-,kän\ *n* : a deliberate irrevocable step or act [Latin *Rubicon-, Rubico*, river of northern Italy forming part of the boundary between Cisalpine Gaul and Italy whose crossing by Julius Caesar in 49 B. C. was regarded by the Senate as an act of war]

ru·bi·cund \'rü-bi-,kənd, -kənd\ *adj* : somewhat red : RUDDY [Latin *rubicundus*, from *rubēre* "to be red"] — **ru·bi·cun·di·ty** \,rü-bi-'kən-dət-ē\ *n*

ru·bid·i·um \rü-'bid-ē-əm\ *n* : a soft silvery metallic chemical element that decomposes water with violence and bursts into flame spontaneously in air — see ELEMENT table [New Latin, from Latin *rubidus* "red", from *rubēre* "to be red"]

ru·big·i·nous \rü-'bij-ə-nəs\ *adj* : of a rusty red color [Latin *robiginosus, rubiginosus* "rusty", from *robigo* "rust"]

ru·ble \'rü-bəl\ *n* **1** : the basic monetary unit of the Soviet Union **2** : a coin representing one ruble [Russian *rubl'*]

rub out *vt* **1** : to obliterate by rubbing **2** : KILL 1

rubber tree

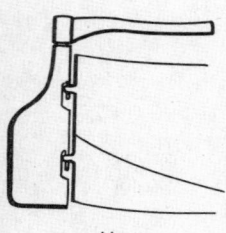

rudder

ru·bric \'rü-brik\ *n* **1** : a heading of a part of a book or manuscript done or underlined in a color (as red) different from the rest **2 a** (1) : NAME, TITLE; *esp* : the title of a law (2) : something under which a thing is classed : CATEGORY **b** : an authoritative rule; *esp* : a rule for conduct of a liturgical service **c** : an explanatory or introductory comment or gloss; *esp* : an editorial interpolation **3** : an established rule or custom [Middle French *rubrique*, literally, "red ocher", from Latin *rubrica*, from *ruber* "red"] — **rubric** *or* **ru·bri·cal** \-bri-kəl\ *adj* □ ORIGIN Derived ultimately from Latin *ruber*, "red", *rubric* was originally used in Middle English to name red ocher, a red pigment. Yet in present-day English *rubric* is used to mean "an authoritative rule" or "an explanatory commentary". This semantic transformation is derived from the practice originated centuries ago of putting instructions or explanations in a manuscript or printed book in red ink to contrast with the black ink of the text.

¹ru·by \'rü-bē\ *n, pl* **rubies 1** : a precious stone that is a deep red corundum **2 a** : the dark red color of the ruby **b** : something resembling a ruby in color [Middle French *rubi*, from Latin *rubeus* "reddish"]

²ruby *adj* : of the color ruby

ruby glass *n* : glass of a deep red color containing selenium, an oxide of copper, or chloride of gold

ruck \'rək\ *n* : the usual run of persons or things [Middle English *ruke* "pile of combustible material", of Scandinavian origin]

ruck·sack \'rək-,sak, 'růk-\ *n* : KNAPSACK [German]

ruck·us \'rək-əs, 'rük-, 'růk-\ *n* : ⁴ROW, DISTURBANCE [probably blend of *ruction* and *rumpus*]

ruc·tion \'rək-shən\ *n* **1** : a noisy fight **2** : UPROAR [perhaps from *insurrection*]

rud·der \'rəd-ər\ *n* : a flat piece of wood or metal attached to the stern of a boat or the after end of the keel for steering a boat; *also* : a similar piece attached to the rear of an aircraft [Old English *rōther* "paddle"]

rud·dle \'rəd-l\ *n* : RED OCHER [from earlier *rud* "red ocher", from Old English *rudu* "redness"]

rud·dle·man \-mən\ *n* : a dealer in red ocher

rud·dy \'rəd-ē\ *adj* **rud·di·er; -est 1** : having a healthy reddish color **2** : REDDISH [Old English *rudig*, from *rudu* "redness"] — **rud·di·ly** \'rəd-l-ē\ *adv* — **rud·di·ness** \'rəd-ē-nəs\ *n*

rude \'rüd\ *adj* **1** : being in a rough or unfinished state : CRUDE **2** : lacking refinement, delicacy, or culture **3** : offensive in manner or action : DISCOURTEOUS **4** : FORCEFUL, ABRUPT ⟨a *rude* awakening⟩ [Middle French, from Latin *rudis*] — **rude·ly** *adv* — **rude·ness** *n*

ru·di·ment \'rüd-ə-mənt\ *n* **1** : an elementary principle or skill — usually used in pl. ⟨the *rudiments* of chess⟩ **2** : something unformed or undeveloped : BEGINNING — usually used in pl. [Latin *rudimentum* "beginning", from *rudis* "raw, rude"]

ru·di·men·ta·ry \,rüd-ə-'ment-ə-rē, -'men-trē\ *adj* **1** : ELEMENTARY 1a, FUNDAMENTAL **2** : very imperfectly developed or represented only by a small part compared to the fully developed form

¹rue \'rü\ *vt* **rued; ru·ing** : to feel penitence, remorse, or regret for [Old English *hrēowan*]

²rue *n* : REGRET 1, SORROW

³rue *n* : a woody perennial herb with yellow flowers, a strong smell, and bitter-tasting leaves [Middle French, from Latin *ruta*, from Greek *rhytē*]

rue anemone *n* : a delicate spring herb of the buttercup family with white flowers

rue·ful \'rü-fəl\ *adj* **1** : exciting pity or sympathy : PITIABLE ⟨a *rueful* tale⟩ **2** : MOURNFUL, REGRETFUL ⟨took defeat with a *rueful* smile⟩ — **rue·ful·ly** \-fə-lē\ *adv* — **rue·ful·ness** *n*

ru·fes·cent \rü-'fes-nt\ *adj* : REDDISH [Latin *rufescens*, present participle of *rufescere* "to become red", from *rufus* "red"]

¹ruff \'rəf\ *n* **1** : a large round collar of pleated muslin worn by men and women of the late 16th and early 17th centuries **2 a** : a fringe of long hairs or feathers growing around or on the neck **b** : a common Eurasian sandpiper whose male during the breeding season has a large ruff [probably from *ruffle*] — **ruffed** \'rəft\ *adj*

²ruff *n* : the act of trumping [Middle French *roffle*] — **ruff** *vb*

ruffed grouse *n* : a North American grouse with tufts of shiny black feathers on the sides of the neck

ruf·fi·an \'rəf-ē-ən\ *n* : a coarse brutal person [Middle French *rufian*] — **ruffian** *adj* — **ruf·fi·an·ism** \-ē-ə-,niz-əm\ *n* — **ruf·fi·an·ly** \-ē-ən-lē\ *adj*

¹ruf·fle \'rəf-əl\ *vb* **ruf·fled; ruf·fling** \'rəf-ling, -ə-ling\ **1 a** : to disturb the smoothness of : ROUGHEN ⟨*ruffle* the waters of a pond⟩ **b** : TROUBLE 1a, VEX **2** : to erect (as feathers) in or like a ruff **3** : RIFFLE 3, SHUFFLE **4** : to make into a ruffle [Middle English *ruffelen*]

²ruffle *n* **1** : a state or cause of irritation **2** : an unevenness or disturbance of surface : RIPPLE **3 a** : a strip of lace or cloth gathered or pleated on one edge **b** : ¹RUFF 2a — **ruf·fly** \'rəf-lē, -ə-lē\ *adj*

³ruffle *n* : a low vibrating drumbeat that is less loud than a roll [from earlier *ruff* "drumbeat", of imitative origin]

ru·fous \'rü-fəs\ *adj* : REDDISH [Latin *rufus* "red"]

rug \'rəg\ *n* **1** : a piece of thick heavy fabric usually with a nap or pile used as a floor covering **2** : a floor mat of an animal pelt ⟨bearskin *rug*⟩ **3** : a lap robe [of Scandinavian origin]

rug·by \'rəg-bē\ *n, often cap* : a football game played by teams of 15 players and marked by continuous play featuring kicking, running with the ball, lateral passing, and tackling but without blocking or forward passing [*Rugby* School, Rugby, England]

rug·ged \'rəg-əd\ *adj* **1** : having a rough uneven surface : JAGGED ⟨*rugged* mountains⟩ **2** : STORMY 2 **3** : showing signs of strength : STURDY ⟨*rugged* pioneers⟩ **4 a** : STERN ⟨*rugged* times⟩ **b** : COARSE 3, RUDE **5** : presenting a severe test of ability, endurance, or resolution ⟨*rugged* course of training⟩ [Middle English, "shaggy"] SYN see ROUGH — **rug·ged·ly** *adv* — **rug·ged·ness** *n*

ru·gose \'rü-,gōs\ *adj* : full of folds or wrinkles ⟨*rugose* leaves⟩ [Latin *rugosus,* from *ruga* "wrinkle"] — **ru·gose·ly** *adv* — **ru·gos·i·ty** \rü-'gäs-ət-ē\ *n*

¹ru·in \'rü-ən, -,in\ *n* **1** : physical, moral, economic, or social collapse **2 a** : the state of being ruined **b** : the remains of something destroyed — usually used in pl. ⟨the *ruins* of a city⟩ **3** : a cause of destruction ⟨greed was my *ruin*⟩ **4** : the action of destroying, laying waste, or wrecking **5** : a ruined building, person, or object [Middle French *ruine* "collapse", from Latin *ruina*]

²ruin *vt* **1** : to reduce to ruins : DEVASTATE ⟨a *ruined* city⟩ **2 a** : to damage irreparably ⟨*ruined* our chances⟩ **b** : BANKRUPT, IMPOVERISH ⟨*ruined* by the depression⟩ — **ru·in·er** *n*

ru·in·ation \,rü-ə-'nā-shən\ *n* : RUIN 3

ru·in·ous \'rü-ə-nəs\ *adj* **1** : DILAPIDATED **2** : causing or tending to cause ruin : DESTRUCTIVE ⟨*ruinous* tax laws⟩ — **ru·in·ous·ly** *adv*

¹rule \'rül\ *n* **1 a** : a prescribed guide for conduct or action **b** : the laws laid down by the founder of a religious order **c** : an accepted procedure, custom, or habit **d** : a legal precept or doctrine **e** : REGULATION, BYLAW ⟨the *rules* of the club⟩ **2 a** : a usually valid generalization **b** : a generally prevailing quality, state, or mode **c** : a regulating principle ⟨the *rules* of harmony⟩ **3 a** : the exercise of authority or control : DOMINION **b** : a period of such rule : REIGN ⟨during the *rule* of King George III⟩ **4 a** : a strip of material marked off in units used for measuring or ruling off lengths **b** (1) : a metal strip that prints a linear design (2) : a linear design produced by or as if by such a strip [Old French *reule,*

from Latin *regula* "straightedge, norm, rule", from *regere* "to lead straight, rule"]

²rule *vb* **1 a** : CONTROL 2a, DIRECT **b** : MANAGE 2 **2 a** : to exercise authority or power over : GOVERN **b** : to be preeminent in : DOMINATE **3** : to declare authoritatively; *esp* : to lay down a legal rule **4** : to mark with lines drawn along or as if along the straight edge of a ruler **5 a** : to exercise supreme authority **b** : PREDOMINATE 2, PREVAIL SYN see GOVERN

rule·less \'rül-ləs\ *adj* : not restrained or regulated by law

rule of thumb 1 : a method based on experience and common sense **2** : a general principle regarded as roughly correct but not scientifically accurate

rule out *vt* **1** : to eliminate as a possibility **2** : to make impossible : PREVENT

rul·er \'rü-lər\ *n* **1** : one that rules; *esp* : SOVEREIGN **2** : a smooth-edged strip (as of wood or metal) used as a guide in drawing lines or for measuring

¹rul·ing \'rü-ling\ *n* : an official or authoritative decision or interpretation (as by a judge on a point of law)

²ruling *adj* **1** : exerting power or authority **2** : CHIEF ⟨a *ruling* ambition⟩

rum \'rəm\ *n* **1** : an alcoholic liquor distilled from a fermented cane product (as molasses) **2** : alcoholic liquor [probably from obsolete *rumbullion* "rum"]

Ru·ma·nian *or* **Ro·ma·nian** *also* **Rou·ma·nian** \rù-'mā-nē-ən, -nyən\ *n* **1** : a native or inhabitant of Rumania **2** : the Romance language of the Rumanians — **Ruma·nian** *adj*

rum·ba *also* **rhum·ba** \'rəm-bə, 'rùm-\ *n* **1** : a Cuban dance marked by violent movements **2** : a ballroom dance imitative of the Cuban rumba [American Spanish]

¹rum·ble \'rəm-bəl\ *vb* **rum·bled; rum·bling** \-bə-ling, -bling\ **1** : to make a low heavy rolling sound **2** : to travel with a low reverberating sound **3** : to speak or utter in a low rolling tone [Middle English *rumblen*]

²rumble *n* : a low heavy continuous reverberating often muffled sound

rumble seat *n* : a folding seat in the back of an automobile (as a coupe or roadster) not covered by the top

ru·men \'rü-mən\ *n, pl* **ru·mi·na** \-mə-nə\ *or* **rumens** : the large first compartment of the stomach of a ruminant in which cellulose is broken down by the action of symbionts [Latin *rumin-, rumen* "gullet"] — **ru·mi·nal** \-mən-l\ *adj*

¹ru·mi·nant \'rü-mə-nənt\ *n* : a ruminant mammal

²ruminant *adj* **1 a** : chewing the cud **b** : of or relating to a group (Ruminantia) of even-toed hoofed mammals (as sheep, giraffes, deer, and camels) that chew the cud and have a complex 3- or 4-chambered stomach **2** : given to or engaged in contemplation : MEDITATIVE — **ru·mi·nant·ly** *adv*

ru·mi·nate \'rü-mə-,nāt\ *vb* **1** : to engage in contemplation : MUSE, MEDITATE **2** : to chew the cud : bring up and chew again what has been chewed slightly and swallowed [Latin *ruminari* "to chew the cud, muse upon", from *rumen* "gullet"] — **ru·mi·na·tion** \,rü-mə-'nā-shən\ *n* — **ru·mi·na·tive** \'rü-mə-,nāt-iv\ *adj* — **ru·mi·na·tive·ly** *adv* — **ru·mi·na·tor** \-,nāt-ər\ *n*

¹rum·mage \'rəm-ij\ *n* : a thorough search especially among a confusion of objects or into every section [Middle French *arrimage* "act of packing cargo"]

²rummage *vb* **1** : to make a thorough search especially by moving about, turning over, or looking through the contents of a place or receptacle ⟨*rummage* through an attic⟩ **2** : to discover by searching ⟨*rummaged* up what they needed for costumes⟩

rummage sale *n* : a sale of miscellaneous and often donated articles

rum·my \'rəm-ē\ *n* : a card game in which each player tries to be the first to play all cards held in the hand by laying them down in groups of three or more of the

ruffed grouse

\ə\	abut	\ng\	sing
\ər\	further	\ō\	bone
\a\	mat	\ò\	saw
\ā\	take	\òi\	coin
\ä\	cot, cart	\th\	thin
\aù\	out	\th̲\	this
\ch\	chin	\ü\	food
\e\	pet	\ù\	foot
\ē\	easy	\y\	yet
\g\	go	\yü\	few
\i\	tip	\yù\	cure
\ī\	life	\zh\	vision
\j\	job		

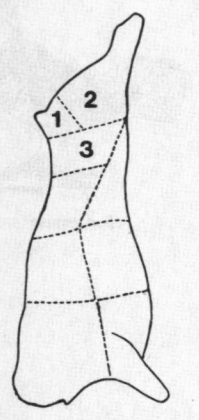

rump 1: *1* rump, 2 round,
3 loin

same kind or in sequence [perhaps derived from earlier *rum* "queer, odd"]

¹ru·mor \'rü-mər\ *n* **1** : talk or opinion widely current but having no known source : HEARSAY **2** : a statement or report going around without known authority for its truth [Middle French *rumour,* from Latin *rumor*]

²rumor *vt* **ru·mored; ru·mor·ing** \'rüm-riŋ, -ə-riŋ\ : to tell or spread by rumor

ru·mor·mon·ger \'rü-mər-,məŋ-gər, -,mäŋ-\ *n* : one who spreads rumors

rump \'rəmp\ *n* **1** : the back part of an animal's body where the hips and thighs join generally including the buttocks **2** : a cut of beef between the loin and round **3** : a small fragment remaining after the separation of the larger part of a group or an area; *esp* : a group (as a parliament) carrying on in the name of the original body after the departure or expulsion of a large number of its members [of Scandinavian origin] — **rumped** \'rəmt, 'rəmpt\ *adj*

rum·ple \'rəm-pəl\ *vb* **rum·pled; rum·pling** \-pə-liŋ, -pliŋ\ **1** : WRINKLE, CRUMPLE ⟨*rumple* the bedclothes⟩ **2** : to make unkempt : TOUSLE ⟨*rumpled* my hair⟩ [Dutch *rompelen*]

rum·pus \'rəm-pəs\ *n* : a noisy commotion [origin unknown]

rumpus room *n* : a room (as in the basement of a home) set apart for games, parties, and recreation

¹run \'rən\ *vb* **ran** \'ran\; **run; run·ning** **1 a** : to go faster than a walk; *esp* : to go steadily by springing steps so that both feet leave the ground for an instant in each step **b** : to move at a fast gallop ⟨*running* horses⟩ **c** : FLEE 1, RETREAT, ESCAPE ⟨dropped the gun and *ran*⟩ **2 a** : to move freely about at will ⟨let the dog *run* loose⟩ **b** : to keep company ⟨*running* with a bad crowd⟩ **c** : to sail in the same direction the wind is blowing **d** : to go about ⟨*running* around without a coat⟩ **3 a** : to go or cause to go rapidly or hurriedly : HASTEN **b** : to do or accomplish by or as if by running ⟨*run* errands⟩ **4 a** : to compete in a race **b** : to enter or put forward as a contestant in an election contest **5 a** : to move on or as if on wheels : GLIDE ⟨file drawers *running* on ball bearings⟩ **b** : to roll forward rapidly or freely **c** : to ravel lengthwise **6** : to sing or play a musical passage quickly ⟨*run* up the scale⟩ **7 a** : to go back and forth : PLY **b** : to migrate or move in schools; *esp* : to ascend a river to spawn ⟨shad are *running* in the river⟩ **8** : FUNCTION, OPERATE ⟨keep the car *running*⟩ **9** : to continue in force or operation ⟨the contract has two years to *run*⟩ **10** : to pass into a specified condition ⟨*run* into debt⟩ **11 a** : to move as a fluid : FLOW **b** : MELT ⟨solder *runs* at low heat⟩ **c** : to spread out : DISSOLVE ⟨colors guaranteed not to *run*⟩ **d** : to discharge a fluid ⟨a *running* sore⟩ **12** : to tend to develop a specified quality or feature ⟨they *run* to big noses in that family⟩ **13 a** : to extend through space or time ⟨the boundary line *runs* east⟩ ⟨a family line that *runs* back to a notorious horse thief⟩ **b** : to be in a certain form or expression ⟨the letter *runs* as follows⟩ or order of succession ⟨house numbers *run* in odd numbers from 3 to 57⟩ **14 a** : to occur persistently : RECUR ⟨musical talent *runs* in the family⟩ **b** : to exist or occur in a continuous range of variation ⟨the quality *runs* from good to terrible⟩ **c** : to play on stage ⟨the play *ran* for six months⟩ **15 a** : to spread or pass quickly from point to point ⟨chills *ran* up my spine⟩ **b** : to be current : CIRCULATE ⟨speculation *ran* rife on who it would be⟩ **16 a** : to bring to a specified condition by or as if by running ⟨*ran* themselves to death⟩ **b** : TRACE ⟨*ran* the rumor to its source⟩ **c** : to keep or maintain (livestock) on or as if on pasturage **17 a** : to pass over or traverse ⟨*ran* the whole range of emotions⟩ **b** : to slip through or past ⟨*run* a blockade⟩ **18 a** : to cause to penetrate or enter : THRUST ⟨*ran* a splinter into my toe⟩ **b** : STITCH ⟨*run* a basting⟩ **c** : to cause to pass : LEAD ⟨*run* a wire in from the antenna⟩ **d** : to cause to collide ⟨*ran* my head into a post⟩ **e** :

SMUGGLE ⟨*run* guns⟩ **19** : to cause to pass lightly or quickly over, along, or into something ⟨*ran* my eye down the list⟩ **20 a** : to cause or allow to go in a specified manner or direction ⟨*ran* the car off the road⟩ **b** : to carry on : MANAGE ⟨*run* a factory⟩ **21 a** : to flow with ⟨streets *ran* blood⟩ **b** : ASSAY ⟨the ore *runs* high in silver⟩ **22** : to make oneself liable to : INCUR ⟨*ran* the risk of discovery⟩ **23** : to mark out : DRAW ⟨*run* a contour line on a map⟩ **24** : to permit charges to accumulate before settling ⟨*run* an account⟩ ⟨*ran* up a big bill⟩ **25** : PRINT ⟨*run* the advertisement for three days⟩ [Middle English *rinnen,* v.i. (from Old English *rinnan* and Old Norse *rinna*) and *rennen,* v.t., from Old Norse *renna*] — **run across** : to meet with or discover by chance — **run a fever** *or* **run a temperature** : to have a fever — **run foul of** **1** : to collide with ⟨*ran foul of* a hidden reef⟩ **2** : to run into conflict with or hostility to ⟨*run foul of* the law⟩ — **run into** **1** : to mount up to ⟨a boat like that one *runs into* money⟩ **2 a** : to collide with **b** : ENCOUNTER, MEET ⟨*ran into* an old friend⟩ — **run riot** **1** : to act wildly or without restraint **2** : to occur in profusion — **run short** : to become insufficient — **run to seed** : to exhaust vitality in or as if in producing seed

²run *n* **1 a** : an act or the action of running : continued rapid movement ⟨broke into a *run*⟩ **b** : a fast gallop **c** : a migrating of fish; *also* : fish migrating especially to spawn **d** : a running race ⟨a mile *run*⟩ **e** : a score made in baseball by a base runner reaching home plate **2 a** *chiefly Midland* : CREEK **2 b** : something that flows in the course of an operation or during a particular time ⟨the first *run* of maple sap⟩ **3 a** : the horizontal distance from one point to another **b** : general tendency or direction **4** : a continuous series or unbroken period especially of things of identical or similar sort: as **a** : a rapid scale passage in vocal or instrumental music **b** : an unbroken course of theatrical performances **c** : an unbroken stretch ⟨a *run* of bad luck⟩ **d** : sudden heavy demands from depositors, creditors, or customers ⟨a *run* on a bank⟩ **5** : the quantity of work turned out in a continuous operation **6** : the usual or normal kind ⟨average *run* of college graduates⟩ **7 a** : the distance covered in a period of continuous traveling or sailing ⟨logged the day's *run*⟩ **b** : regular course : TRIP ⟨the bus makes four *runs* daily⟩ **c** : freedom of movement in or access to a place or area ⟨has the *run* of the house⟩ **8 a** : a way, track, or path frequented by animals ⟨a deer *run*⟩ **b** : an enclosure for livestock where they may feed or exercise **9 a** : an inclined course (as for skiing) **b** : a track or guide on which something runs **10** : a ravel in a knitted fabric (as in hosiery) caused by the breaking of stitches — **run·less** \-ləs\ *adj*

run·about \'rən-ə-,baut\ *n* **1** : one who wanders about : STRAY **2** : a light open wagon, roadster, or motorboat

run·a·gate \'rən-ə-,gāt\ *n* **1** : FUGITIVE 1, RUNAWAY **2** : VAGABOND [from obsolete *renegate* "renegade", from Medieval Latin *renegatus*]

run·around \'rən-ə-,raund\ *n* : deceptive or delaying action especially in response to a request

¹run·away \'rən-ə-,wā\ *n* **1** : FUGITIVE 1 **2** : the act of running away out of control; *also* : a horse that is running out of control **3** : a one-sided victory

²runaway *adj* **1** : running away : FUGITIVE **2** : accomplished by elopement or during flight ⟨a *runaway* marriage⟩ **3** : won by or having a long lead **4** : subject to uncontrolled changes ⟨*runaway* inflation⟩

run away \,rən-ə-'wā\ *vi* **1** : FLEE 1, DESERT ⟨*ran away* from the fight⟩ **2** : to leave home; *esp* : ELOPE ⟨*ran away* to get married⟩ **3** : to run out of control : STAMPEDE, BOLT

run·down \'rən-,daun\ *n* : an item-by-item report : SUMMARY

run-down \'rən-'daun\ *adj* **1** : being in poor repair : DILAPIDATED **2** : being in poor health **3** : completely unwound ⟨a *run-down* clock⟩

run down \'rən-'daun, ,rən-\ *vb* **1 a :** to collide with and knock down **b :** to run against and cause to sink **2 a :** to chase until exhausted or captured **b :** to find by search : trace the source of **3 :** DISPARAGE 2 **4 :** to cease to operate because of the exhaustion of motive power **5 :** to deteriorate in physical condition

rune \'rün\ *n* **1 :** one of the characters of an alphabet used by the Germanic peoples from about the 3d to the 13th centuries **2 :** mystic utterance or inscription **3 :** a Finnish or Old Norse poem [Old Norse and Old English *rūn* "mystery, runic character, writing"; sense 3 from Finnish *runo,* of Germanic origin] — **ru·nic** \'rü-nik\ *adj*

¹rung *past participle of* RING

²rung \'rəng\ *n* **1 a :** a rounded part placed as a crosspiece between the legs of a chair **b :** one of the crosspieces of a ladder **2 :** STEP 5a, LEVEL (down a few *rungs* in the social scale) [Old English *hrung* "crossbar, spoke"]

run–in \'rən-,in\ *n* **:** ALTERCATION, QUARREL

run·let \'rən-lət\ *n* **:** RUNNEL

run·nel \'rən-l\ *n* **:** RIVULET, STREAMLET [Old English *rynel*]

run·ner \'rən-ər\ *n* **1 a :** one that runs : RACER **b :** BALL-CARRIER **c :** BASE RUNNER **2 :** MESSENGER (was a *runner* on Wall Street) **3 :** any of various large active sea fishes **4 a :** either of the longitudinal pieces on which a sled or sleigh slides **b :** the blade of a skate **c :** the support of a drawer or a sliding door **5 a :** a slender creeping branch of a plant; *esp* **:** STOLON 1 **b :** a plant that forms or spreads by runners **6 a :** a long narrow carpet **b :** a narrow decorative cloth cover for a table or dresser top

run·ner–up \'rən-ər-,əp\ *n* **:** the competitor in a contest that finishes next to the winner

¹run·ning *n* **:** the action of running — **in the running :** having a chance to win a contest — **out of the running :** having no chance to win a contest

²running *adj* **1 :** FLUID, RUNNY (a *running* sore) **2 :** INCESSANT, CONTINUOUS (a *running* battle) **3 :** measured in a straight line (buy cloth by the *running* meter) **4 :** initiated or performed while running or with a running start (a *running* leap)

³running *adv* **:** in succession (four days *running*)

running board *n* **:** a footboard especially at the side of an automobile

running knot *n* **:** a knot that slips along the line round which it is tied

running light *n* **:** one of the lights carried by a vehicle (as a ship) under way at night that indicate position, size, and direction

running mate *n* **:** a candidate running for a subordinate office (as of vice-president) who is paired with the candidate for the top office on the same ticket

running stitch *n* **:** a small even stitch run in and out in cloth

run·ny \'rən-ē\ *adj* **run·ni·er; -est :** having a tendency to run (a *runny* nose)

run·off \'rən-,óf\ *n* **1 :** water that is removed from soil by natural drainage **2 :** a final contest to decide a previous indecisive contest or series of contests

run off \'rən-'óf, ,rən-\ *vb* **1 :** to produce by or as if by printing (*ran off* a few more copies) **2 :** to cause to be run or played to a finish **3 :** to steal (as cattle) by driving away **4 :** to run away — **run off with :** to carry off : STEAL

run-of-the-mill \,rən-əv-thə-'mil, ,rən-ə-thə-\ *adj* **:** not outstanding in quality or rarity : AVERAGE

¹run–on \'rən-'ón, -'än\ *adj* **:** continuing without rhetorical pause from one line of verse into another

²run–on \'rən-,ón, -,än\ *n* **:** something (as a dictionary entry) that is run on

run on \'rən-'ón, ,rən-, -'än\ *vb* **1 :** PERSIST 2 **2 :** to talk or narrate at length **3 :** to continue (matter in type) without a break or a new paragraph **4 :** to place or add (as an entry in a dictionary) at the end of a paragraphed item

run–on sentence *n* **:** a sentence containing a comma fault

run out *vi* **1 :** to come to an end : EXPIRE **2 :** to become exhausted or used up : FAIL — **run out of :** to use up the available supply of

run over *vb* **1 :** OVERFLOW 2, 3 **2 :** to exceed a limit **3 :** to go over, examine, repeat, or rehearse quickly **4 :** to collide with, knock down, and often drive over

runt \'rənt\ *n* **:** an unusually small person or animal [origin unknown] — **runty** \-ē\ *adj*

run through *vt* **1 :** PIERCE 1 **2 :** to spend or consume wastefully and rapidly **3 :** to read or rehearse without pausing

run·way \'rən-,wā\ *n* **1 :** RUN 8 **2 :** a paved strip of ground on a landing field for the landing and takeoff of airplanes **3 :** a support (as a track, pipe, or trough) on which something runs

ru·pee \rü-'pē, 'rü-,pē\ *n* **1 :** the basic monetary unit of India, Mauritius, Nepal, Pakistan, Seychelles, and Sri Lanka **2 :** a coin or note representing one rupee [Hindi *rūpaiyā,* from Sanskrit *rūpya* "coined silver", from *rūpa* "form, beauty"]

ru·pi·ah \rü-'pē-ə\ *n* **1 :** the basic monetary unit of Indonesia **2 :** a coin or note representing one rupiah [Hindi *rūpaiyā* "rupee"]

¹rup·ture \'rəp-chər\ *n* **1 :** breach of peace or concord; *esp* **:** open hostility or war between nations **2 :** a breaking or tearing apart (as of body tissue) or the resulting state **3 :** HERNIA [Latin *ruptura* "fracture", from *ruptus,* past participle of *rumpere* "to break"] SYN SEE FRACTURE

²rupture *vb* **rup·tured; rup·tur·ing** \-chə-ring, -shring\ **1 :** to part by violence : BREAK **2 :** to produce a rupture in **3 :** to have a rupture

ru·ral \'rúr-əl\ *adj* **:** of or relating to the country, country people or life, or agriculture [Middle French, from Latin *ruralis,* from *rur-, rus* "open land, country"]

rural free delivery *n* **:** the free delivery of mail on routes in country districts — called also *rural delivery*

rural route *n* **:** a mail-delivery route in a rural free delivery area

rur·ban \'rər-bən, 'rúr-\ *adj* **:** of, relating to, or constituting an area which is chiefly residential but where some farming is carried on [blend of *rural* and *urban*]

ruse \'rüs, 'rüz\ *n* **:** a deceptive stratagem : ARTIFICE, SUBTERFUGE SYN SEE TRICK [French, from Middle French *ruser* "to dodge, deceive"]

¹rush \'rəsh\ *n* **:** any of various monocotyledonous often tufted marsh plants with cylindrical often hollow stems used in chair seats and mats [Old English *risc, rysc*] — **rushy** \-ē\ *adj*

²rush *vb* **1 :** to move forward, progress, or act with haste or eagerness or without preparation (*rush* out the door) **2 :** to push or impel on or forward with speed or violence (*rush* them to the hospital) **3 :** to perform in a short time or at a high speed (*rush* a job through) **4 :** CHARGE 4 (*rushed* the hijackers) **5 :** to carry the football in a running play **6 :** to lavish attention on : COURT [Middle French *ruser* "to put to flight, dodge, deceive", from Latin *recusare* "to refuse"] — **rush·er** *n*

³rush *n* **1 a :** a violent forward motion (a *rush* of wind) **b :** CHARGE 7, ONSET (led the *rush* on the enemy position) **2 :** a burst of activity, productivity, or speed **3 :** a thronging of people usually to a new place and in search of wealth (gold *rush*) **4 :** a running play in football **5 :** a round of attention usually involving extensive social activity **6 :** the first rapid excitation produced by a narcotic drug

⁴rush *adj* **:** requiring or marked by special speed or urgency (*rush* orders) (the *rush* season)

rusk \'rəsk\ *n* **:** a sweet or plain bread baked, sliced, and baked again until dry and crisp [Spanish and Portuguese *rosca* "coil, twisted roll"]

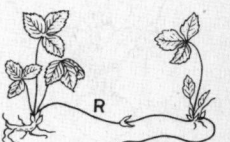

rune 1

R runner 5a

\ə\ abut	\ng\ sing
\ər\ further	\ō\ bone
\a\ mat	\ȯ\ saw
\ā\ take	\ȯi\ coin
\ä\ cot, cart	\th\ thin
\au̇\ out	\th\ this
\ch\ chin	\ü\ food
\e\ pet	\u̇\ foot
\ē\ easy	\y\ yet
\g\ go	\yü\ few
\i\ tip	\yu̇\ cure
\ī\ life	\zh\ vision
\j\ job	

Russ \'rəs\ *n, pl* **Russ** *or* **Russ·es** : RUSSIAN 1a [Russian *Rus'*] — **Russ** *adj*

rus·set \'rəs-ət\ *n* **1** : coarse homespun usually reddish brown cloth **2** : a strong brown **3** : any of various winter apples with rough russet skins [Old French *rousset,* from *rousset* "reddish brown", from *rous* "reddish brown", from Latin *russus* "red"] — **russet** *adj*

Rus·sian \'rəsh-ən\ *n* **1 a** : any of the people of the Soviet Union; *esp* : a member of the dominant Slavic-speaking Great Russian ethnic group of Russia **b** : a person of Russian descent **2** : a Slavic language of the Russian people that is the official language of Russia and formerly of the Soviet Union — **Russian** *adj*

Russian olive *n* : a small Eurasian tree or shrub with usually silvery leaves widely grown in dry windy regions as a hedge and shelter plant

Russian thistle *n* : a prickly European herb that is a serious weed in North America

Russian wolfhound *n* : BORZOI

Russo- *combining form* **1** : Russia : Russians **2** : Russian and

¹rust \'rəst\ *n* **1 a** : the reddish brittle coating chiefly of ferric oxide formed on iron especially when chemically attacked by moist air **b** : a comparable coating produced on other metals by corrosion **2** : corrosive or injurious influence or effect **3 a** : any of numerous destructive diseases of plants caused by fungi and marked by reddish brown pustular lesions **b** : any of an order (Uredinales) of parasitic fungi that cause plant rusts — compare WHITE RUST **4** : a strong reddish brown [Old English *rūst*]

²rust *vb* **1** : to form or cause to form rust : become oxidized ⟨iron *rusts*⟩ **2** : to weaken or degenerate or cause to degenerate especially from inaction, lack of use, or passage of time : CORRODE ⟨diplomatic skill that had not *rusted*⟩ **3** : to turn the color of rust

¹rus·tic \'rəs-tik\ *adj* **1** : of, relating to, or suitable for the country : RURAL ⟨*rustic* sports⟩ **2** : made of the rough limbs of trees ⟨*rustic* furniture⟩ **3** : AWKWARD, BOORISH ⟨*rustic* manners⟩ [Middle French *rustique,* from Latin *rusticus,* from *rus* "open land, country"] — **rus·ti·cal·ly** \-ti-kə-lē, -klē\ *adv* — **rus·tic·i·ty** \ˌrəs-'tis-ət-ē\ *n*

²rustic *n* : an inhabitant of a rural area; *esp* : an unsophisticated one

rus·ti·cate \'rəs-ti-ˌkāt\ *vb* **1** : to go into or reside in the country **2** : to suspend from school or college — **rus·ti·ca·tion** \ˌrəs-ti-'kā-shən\ *n* — **rus·ti·ca·tor** \'rəs-ti-ˌkāt-ər\ *n*

¹rus·tle \'rəs-əl\ *vb* **rus·tled; rus·tling** \'rəs-ling, -ə-ling\ **1** : to make or cause to make a rustle **2** : to act or move with energy or speed **3** : to get by or as if by foraging ⟨*rustle* up some food⟩ **4** : to steal (as cattle) from the range [Middle English *rustelen*]

²rustle *n* : a quick succession or confusion of small sounds ⟨the *rustle* of leaves⟩ ⟨the *rustle* among a theater audience⟩

rus·tler \'rəs-lər, -ə-lər\ *n* : one that rustles cattle

rust·proof \'rəst-ˌprüf\ *adj* : incapable of rusting

rusty \'rəs-tē\ *adj* **rust·i·er; -est** **1** : affected by or as if by rust; *esp* : stiff with or as if with rust **2** : inept and slow through lack of practice or old age **3 a** : of the color rust **b** : dulled in color or appearance by age and use — **rust·i·ly** \'rəs-tə-lē\ *adv* — **rust·i·ness** \-tē-nəs\ *n*

¹rut \'rət\ *n* : a state of sexual excitement especially in the male deer; *also* : a period in which this occurs [Middle French *rut, ruit* "roar", from Late Latin *rugitus,* from Latin *rugire* "to roar"]

²rut *n* **1** : a track worn by a wheel or by habitual passage **2** : a usual or fixed practice : a regular course; *esp* : a monotonous routine ⟨my life's in a *rut*⟩ [perhaps from Middle French *route* "way, route"] — **rut·ty** \'rət-ē\ *adj*

³rut *vt* **rut·ted; rut·ting** : to make a rut in : FURROW

ru·ta·ba·ga \ˌrüt-ə-'bā-gə, ˌrüt-, -'beg-ə\ *n* : a turnip with a very large yellowish root [Swedish dialect *rotabagge,* from Swedish *rot* "root" + *bagge* "bag"]

ruth \'rüth\ *n* **1** : compassion for the misery of another : PITY **2** : sorrow for one's own faults : REMORSE [Middle English *ruthe,* from *ruen* "to rue"]

Ruth \'rüth\ *n* — see BIBLE table

ru·the·ni·um \rü-'thē-nē-əm\ *n* : a hard brittle grayish rare metallic chemical element used in hardening platinum alloys — see ELEMENT table [New Latin, from Medieval Latin *Ruthenia* "Russia"]

ruth·less \'rüth-ləs\ *adj* : having no ruth : MERCILESS, CRUEL — **ruth·less·ly** *adv* — **ruth·less·ness** *n*

ru·tile \'rü-ˌtēl\ *n* : a mineral TiO_2 that consists of titanium dioxide usually with a little iron, is mostly of a reddish brown color, and is a major source of titanium [German *rutil,* from Latin *rutilus* "reddish"]

-ry \rē\ *n suffix, pl* **-ries** : -ERY ⟨citizen*ry*⟩ ⟨wizard*ry*⟩ [Old French *-erie, -rie* "-ery"]

rye \'rī\ *n* **1** : a hardy annual cereal grass widely grown for grain and as a cover crop; *also* : its seeds **2** : whiskey distilled from rye or from rye and malt [Old English *ryge*]

rye bread *n* : bread made wholly or partly from rye flour

rye·grass \'rī-ˌgras\ *n* : either of two grasses that are used especially for pasture and as cover crops

rutabaga

s \'es\ *n, pl* **s's** *or* **ss** \'es-əz\ *often cap* **1** : the 19th letter of the English alphabet **2** : a grade rating a student's work as satisfactory **3** : something shaped like the letter S

¹**-s** \s\ *after a voiceless consonant sound,* z *after a voiced consonant sound or a vowel sound* \ *n pl suffix* **1** — used to form the plural of most nouns that do not end in *s, z, sh, ch,* or *y* following a consonant ⟨heads⟩ ⟨books⟩ ⟨boys⟩ ⟨beliefs⟩, to form the plural of proper nouns that end in *y* following a consonant ⟨Marys⟩, and with or without a preceding apostrophe to form the plural of abbreviations, numbers, letters, and symbols used as nouns ⟨MCs⟩ ⟨4s⟩ ⟨#s⟩ ⟨B's⟩; compare ¹-ES 1 **2** — used to form adverbs denoting usual or repeated action or state ⟨always at home Sundays⟩ ⟨mornings we stop by the newsstand⟩ ⟨goes to school nights⟩ [Old English -*as,* nominative and accusative pl. ending of some masculine nouns; sense 2 from Old English -*es,* genitive sing. ending of nouns (functioning adverbially)]

²**-s** *like* ¹-s\ *vb suffix* — used to form the third person singular present of most verbs that do not end in *s, z, sh, ch,* or in *y* following a consonant ⟨falls⟩ ⟨takes⟩ ⟨plays⟩; compare ²-ES

¹**'s** *like* -'s\ *vb* **1** : IS ⟨someone's here⟩ **2** : HAS ⟨who's seen them?⟩ **3** : DOES ⟨what's it need?⟩

²**'s** \s\ *pron* : US — used with let ⟨let's⟩

-'s \s\ *after voiceless consonant sounds other than* s, sh, ch; z *after vowel sounds or voiced consonant sounds other than* z, zh, j; əz *after* s, sh, ch, z, zh, j\ *n suffix or pron suffix* — used to form the possessive of singular nouns ⟨child's⟩, of plural nouns not ending in s ⟨children's⟩, of some pronouns ⟨anyone's⟩, and of word groups functioning as nouns ⟨the book on the shelf's cover⟩ or pronouns ⟨someone else's⟩ [Old English -*es,* genitive singular ending]

sab·a·dil·la \,sab-ə-'dil-ə, -'dē-ə, -'dē-yə\ *n* : a Mexican plant of the lily family; *also* : its seeds used as a source of a poisonous irritant alkaloid and in insecticides [Spanish *cebadilla*]

Sab·ba·tar·i·an \,sab-ə-'ter-ē-ən\ *n* **1** : one who keeps the 7th day of the week as holy **2** : one who favors strict observance of the Sabbath [Latin *sabbatarius,* from *sabbatum* "Sabbath"] — **Sabbatarian** *adj* — **Sab·ba·tar·i·an·ism** \-,iz-əm\ *n*

Sab·bath \'sab-əth\ *n* **1** : the 7th day of the week observed from Friday evening to Saturday evening as a day of rest and worship by Jews and some Christians **2** : the day of the week (as among Christians) set aside in a religion for rest and worship [Old French and Old English *sabat,* from Latin *sabbatum,* from Greek *sabbaton,* from Hebrew *shabbāth,* literally, "rest"] SYN see SUNDAY

sab·bat·i·cal \sə-'bat-i-kəl\ *or* **sab·bat·ic** \-'bat-ik\ *adj* **1** : of or relating to the Sabbath **2** : of or relating to a sabbatical year

sabbatical year *n* : a leave granted (as to a professor) usually every 7th year for rest, travel, or research — called also *sabbatical leave*

¹**sa·ber** *or* **sa·bre** \'sā-bər\ *n* **1** : a cavalry sword with a curved blade, thick back, and guard **2 a** : a fencing sword with an arched guard that covers the back of the hand and an imaginary full-length cutting edge **b** : the sport of fencing with a saber [French *sabre,* from German dialect *sabel,* of Slavic origin]

²**saber** *or* **sabre** *vt* **sa·bered** *or* **sa·bred; sa·ber·ing** *or* **sa·bring** \-bə-ring, -bring\ : to strike, cut, or kill with a saber

saber rattling *n* : aggressive display of military power

sa·ber–toothed tiger \,sā-bər-,tüth-'tī-gər, -,tütht-\ *n* : any of various large prehistoric cats with very long curved upper canine teeth — called also *saber·toothed cat*

Sa·bine \'sā-,bīn\ *n* : a member of an ancient people of the Apennines northeast of Latium conquered by Rome in 290 B.C. [Latin *Sabinus*] — **Sabine** *adj*

¹**sa·ble** \'sā-bəl\ *n, pl* **sable** *or* **sables** **1 a** : the color black **b** : black clothing worn in mourning — usually used in pl. **2 a** : a flesh-eating mammal of northern Europe and Asia related to the martens and valued for its soft rich brown fur; *also* : a related animal **b** : the fur or pelt of a sable [Middle French, "sable or its fur, the heraldic color black", from Low German *sabel,* of Slavic origin]

¹sable 2a

²**sable** *adj* **1** : BLACK 1a **2** : DARK ⟨the *sable* sky⟩

sa·ble·fish \'sā-bəl-,fish\ *n* : a large dark spiny-finned fish of the Pacific coast that is a leading market fish with a liver rich in vitamins

sa·bot \sa-'bō, 'sab-ō\ *n* : a wooden shoe worn especially in various European countries [French]

¹**sab·o·tage** \'sab-ə-,täzh\ *n* **1** : destruction of an employer's property (as tools or materials) or the hindering of manufacturing by discontented workers **2** : destructive or obstructive action carried on by enemy agents or sympathizers to hinder a nation's war or defense effort [French, from *saboter* "to clatter with sabots, botch, sabotage", from *sabot* "sabot"]

²**sabotage** *vt* : to practice sabotage on

sab·o·teur \,sab-ə-'tər, -'tùr\ *n* : a person who commits sabotage [French, from *saboter* "to sabotage"]

sa·bra \'sä-brə\ *n, often cap* : a native Israeli [Modern Hebrew *ṣabbār,* literally, "prickly pear"]

sac \'sak\ *n* : a pouch within an animal or plant often containing a fluid ⟨a synovial *sac*⟩ [French, literally, "bag", from Latin *saccus*] — **sac·cate** \'sak-,āt\ *adj* — **sac·like** \'sak-,līk\ *adj*

sac·cha·ride \'sak-ə-,rīd\ *n* : a simple sugar, combination of sugars, or polymerized sugar

sac·cha·rim·e·ter \,sak-ə-'rim-ət-ər\ *n* : a device for measuring the amount of sugar in a solution

sac·cha·rin \'sak-rən, -ə-rən\ *n* : a very sweet white coal tar derivative that is a calorie-free sweetener

sac·cha·rine \'sak-rən, -ə-rən, -ə-,rēn, -ə-,rīn\ *adj* **1 a** : of, relating to, or resembling that of sugar ⟨*saccharine* taste⟩ ⟨*saccharine* fermentation⟩ **b** : yielding or containing sugar ⟨*saccharine* fluids⟩ **2** : overly or ingratiatingly sweet ⟨a *saccharine* smile⟩ [Latin *saccharum* "sugar", from Greek *sakcharon,* derived from San-

\ə\ abut	\ng\ sing
\ər\ further	\ō\ bone
\a\ mat	\ó\ saw
\ā\ take	\oi\ coin
\ä\ cot, cart	\th\ thin
\aú\ out	\th\ this
\ch\ chin	\ü\ food
\e\ pet	\ú\ foot
\ē\ easy	\y\ yet
\g\ go	\yü\ few
\i\ tip	\yú\ cure
\ī\ life	\zh\ vision
\j\ job	

skrit *śarkarā* "gravel, sugar"] — **sac·cha·rin·i·ty** \,sak-ə-'rin-ət-ē\ *n*

sac·cule \'sak-yül\ *n* : a little sac; *esp* : the smaller chamber of the membranous labyrinth of the ear — compare UTRICLE [Latin *sacculus* "little bag", from *saccus* "bag"]

sac·cu·lus \'sak-yə-ləs\ *n, pl* **-li** \-,lī, -,lē\ : SACCULE

sac·er·do·tal \,sas-ər-'dōt-l, ,sak-\ *adj* : PRIESTLY [Middle French, from Latin *sacerdotalis,* from *sacerdos* "priest", from *sacer* "sacred"] — **sac·er·do·tal·ly** \-l-ē\ *adv*

sac·er·do·tal·ism \-l-,iz-əm\ *n* : religious belief emphasizing the powers of priests as essential mediators between God and man — **sac·er·do·tal·ist** \-l-əst\ *n*

sac fungus *n* : ASCOMYCETE

sa·chem \'sā-chəm\ *n* : a North American Indian chief; *esp* : an Algonquian chief [of American Indian origin] — **sa·chem·ic** \sā-'chem-ik\ *adj*

sa·chet \sa-'shā\ *n* : a small bag that contains a perfumed powder and is used to scent clothes and linens [French, literally, "small bag", from *sac* "bag"]

¹**sack** \'sak\ *n* **1 a** : a large bag made of coarse strong material **b** : a small container made of light material (as paper) **2** : the amount contained in a sack **3 a** : a woman's loose-fitting dress **b** : a short usually loose-fitting coat for women and children **4** : DISMISSAL — usually used with *get* or *give* **5** : BUNK 2, BED [Old English *sacc* "bag", from Latin *saccus,* from Greek *sakkos,* of Semitic origin]

²**sack** *vt* **1** : to put in a sack **2** : to dismiss especially in a summary manner

³**sack** *n* : a usually dry and strong white wine imported to England from the south of Europe especially during the 16th and 17th centuries [Middle French *sec* "dry", from Latin *siccus*]

⁴**sack** *n* : the plundering of a captured town [Middle French *sac,* from Italian *sacco* literally, "bag", from Latin *saccus*]

⁵**sack** *vt* **1** : to plunder after capture **2** : to strip of valuables : LOOT

sack·but \'sak-,bət, -bət\ *n* : a medieval trombone [Middle French *saqueboute,* literally, "hooked lance", from *saquer* "to pull" + *bouter* "to push"]

sack·cloth \'sak-,klòth\ *n* **1** : a coarse cloth suitable for sacks : SACKING **2** : a garment of sackcloth worn as a sign of mourning or penitence

sack coat *n* : a man's jacket with a straight unfitted back

sack·ful \'sak-,fùl\ *n, pl* **sackfuls** \-,fùlz\ *or* **sacks·ful** \'saks-,fùl\ : the quantity that fills a sack

sack·ing \'sak-ing\ *n* : strong coarse cloth (as burlap) from which sacks are made

sack race *n* : a jumping race in which the legs of each competitor are enclosed in a sack

sacque \'sak\ *n* : a loose lightweight jacket; *esp* : an infant's short jacket fastened at the neck [alteration of ¹*sack*]

sa·cral \'sak-rəl, 'sā-krəl\ *adj* : of, relating to, or lying near the sacrum

sac·ra·ment \'sak-rə-mənt\ *n* **1** : a formal religious act that is sacred as a sign or symbol of a spiritual reality; *esp* : one instituted by Jesus Christ as a means of grace **2** *cap* : BLESSED SACRAMENT 2 [Late Latin *sacramentum,* from Latin, "oath of allegiance, obligation", from *sacrare* "to consecrate", from *sacer* "holy, sacred"] — **sac·ra·men·tal** \,sak-rə-'ment-l\ *adj* — **sac·ra·men·tal·ly** \-l-ē\ *adv*

sac·ra·men·tal \,sak-rə-'ment-l\ *n* : an action (as a rite) or object (as a rosary) originating in the church but serving as an indirect means of grace by producing devotion

sac·ra·men·tal·ism \-l-,iz-əm\ *n* : belief in or use of sacramental rites, acts, or objects; *esp* : belief that the sacraments are in themselves effective and necessary for salvation — **sac·ra·men·tal·ist** \-l-əst\ *n*

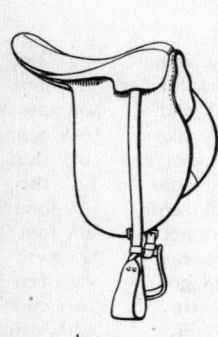

¹saddle 1a

sa·cred \'sā-krəd\ *adj* **1** : set apart in honor of someone ⟨a monument *sacred* to the memory of our heroes⟩ **2** : HOLY ⟨the *sacred* name of Jesus⟩ **3** : RELIGIOUS ⟨*sacred* songs⟩ **4** : requiring or deserving to be held in highest esteem and protected from violation or encroachment ⟨a *sacred* right⟩ ⟨one's *sacred* word⟩ [Middle English, from past participle of *sacren* "to consecrate", from Old French *sacrer,* from Latin *sacrare,* from *sacer* "sacred, holy, cursed"] — **sa·cred·ly** *adv* — **sa·cred·ness** *n*

sacred cow *n* : a person or thing immune from criticism [from the veneration of the cow by Hindus]

¹**sac·ri·fice** \'sak-rə-,fīs, -fəs\ *n* **1** : an act of offering to deity something precious; *esp* : the killing of a victim on an altar **2** : something offered in sacrifice **3** : a giving up of something for the sake of something else; *also* : something so given up ⟨the *sacrifices* made by parents⟩ **4** : loss of something and especially of a profit ⟨sell goods at a *sacrifice*⟩ [Old French, from Latin *sacrificium,* from *sacer* "sacred" + *facere* "to make"]

²**sac·ri·fice** \-,fīs, -,fīz\ *vb* **1** : to offer as a sacrifice or perform sacrificial rites **2** : to give up for the sake of something else ⟨*sacrifice* one's free time to help a friend⟩ ⟨*sacrificed* everything to win the election⟩ **3** : to sell at a loss **4** : to make a sacrifice hit — **sac·ri·fic·er** *n*

sacrifice fly *n* : an outfield fly in baseball that is caught but that is long enough to permit a base runner to score

sacrifice hit *n* : a bunt in baseball that allows a base runner to advance one base while the batter is put out

sac·ri·fi·cial \,sak-rə-'fish-əl\ *adj* : of or relating to sacrifice — **sac·ri·fi·cial·ly** \-'fish-ə-lē\ *adv*

sac·ri·lege \'sak-rə-lij\ *n* **1** : theft or violation of something consecrated to God **2** : gross misuse or disrespect of something sacred or precious ⟨it would be a *sacrilege* to cut such splendid trees⟩ [Old French, from Latin *sacrilegium,* derived from *sacer* "sacred" + *legere* "to gather, steal"] — **sac·ri·le·gious** \,sak-rə-'lij-əs, -'lē-jəs\ *adj* — **sac·ri·le·gious·ly** *adv* — **sac·ri·le·gious·ness** *n*

sac·ris·tan \'sak-rə-stən\ *n* : an officer of a church in charge of the sacristy and ceremonial equipment; *also* : SEXTON

sac·ris·ty \'sak-rə-stē\ *n, pl* **-ties** : a room in a church where sacred utensils and vestments are kept [Medieval Latin *sacristia,* from *sacrista* "sacristan", from Latin *sacer* "sacred"]

sac·ro·il·i·ac \,sak-rō-'il-ē-,ak, ,sā-krō-\ *n* : the region in which the sacrum and ilium join — **sacroiliac** *adj*

sac·ro·sanct \'sak-rō-,sangt, -,sangkt\ *adj* : SACRED 4, INVIOLABLE [Latin *sacrosanctus,* probably from *sacro sanctus* "hallowed by a sacred rite"] — **sac·ro·sanc·ti·ty** \,sak-rō-'sang-tət-ē, -'sangk-\ *n*

sa·crum \'sak-rəm, 'sā-krəm\ *n, pl* **sa·cra** \'sak-rə, 'sā-krə\ : the part of the vertebral column that is directly connected with or forms a part of the pelvis and in man consists of five united vertebrae [Late Latin *os sacrum* "last bone of the spine", literally, "sacred bone"]

sad \'sad\ *adj* **sad·der; sad·dest 1** : affected with or expressive of grief or unhappiness ⟨*sad* at the loss⟩ ⟨*sad* songs⟩ **2 a** : causing or associated with grief or unhappiness : DEPRESSING ⟨*sad* news⟩ **b** : DEPLORABLE, WRETCHED ⟨a *sad* loss of confidence⟩ [Old English *sæd* "sated"] — **sad·ly** *adv*

sad·den \'sad-n\ *vb* **sad·dened; sad·den·ing** \'sad-ning, -n-ing\ : to make or become sad

¹**sad·dle** \'sad-l\ *n* **1 a** : a girthed usually padded and leather-covered seat for a rider on horseback; *also* : a comparable part of a driving harness **b** : a seat to be straddled on a vehicle (as a bicycle) **2** : a ridge connecting two higher land elevations **3** : a cut of meat consisting of both sides of the back including the loins **4** : something like a saddle in shape, position, or use;

esp : a support for an object **5** : a piece of leather across the instep of a shoe [Old English *sadol*] — **in the saddle** : in control or command

²**saddle** *vb* **sad·dled; sad·dling** \'sad-ling, -l-ing\ **1** : to put a saddle on or on a horse ⟨quickly *saddled* and rode off⟩ **2** : ENCUMBER 1, BURDEN

sad·dle·bag \'sad-l-,bag\ *n* : a large pouch carried hanging from a saddle or over the rear wheel of a bicycle or motorcycle

saddle blanket *n* : a blanket or pad placed under a saddle

sad·dle·bow \'sad-l-,bō\ *n* : the arch in the front of a saddle

sad·dle·cloth \-,klóth\ *n* : a cloth placed under or over a saddle

saddle horse *n* : a horse suited for or trained for riding

saddle leather *n* : vegetable-tanned leather from cattle hide that is used for saddlery; *also* : smooth polished leather simulating this

sad·dler \'sad-lər\ *n* : one that makes, repairs, or sells equipment for horses (as saddles)

sad·dlery \'sad-lə-rē, 'sad-l-rē\ *n, pl* **-dler·ies** : the work, articles of trade, or shop of a saddler

saddle shoe *n* : an oxford-style shoe having a saddle of contrasting color or leather

saddle soap *n* : a mild oily soap used for cleansing and conditioning leather

saddle sore 1 : a sore on the back of a horse from an ill-fitting saddle **2** : an irritation or sore on parts of a rider's body chafed by the saddle

sad·dle·tree \'sad-l-,trē\ *n* : the frame of a saddle

Sad·du·cee \'saj-ə-,sē, 'sad-yə-\ *n* : a member of a Jewish party of the time of Christ that consisted largely of a priestly aristocracy and that rejected doctrines not in the Law [Old English *sadduce*, from Late Latin *sadducaeus*, from Greek *saddoukaios*, from Hebrew *ṣāddūqī*] — **Sad·du·ce·an** \,saj-ə-'sē-ən, ,sad-yə-\ *adj* — **Sad·du·cee·ism** \'saj-ə-,sē-,iz-əm, 'sad-yə-\ *n*

sad·iron \'sad-,ī-ərn, -,īrn\ *n* : a flatiron pointed at both ends and having a removable handle [*sad* "compact, heavy" (from Old English *sæd* "sated") + *iron*]

sa·dism \'sād-,iz-əm, 'sad-\ *n* **1** : a perversion in which pleasure is obtained by inflicting physical or mental pain especially upon a loved one **2 a** : pleasure taken in cruelty **b** : excessive cruelty [Marquis de *Sade*, died 1814, French soldier and pervert] — **sa·dist** \-əst\ *n* — **sa·dis·tic** \sə-'dis-tik, sā-\ *adj* — **sa·dis·ti·cal·ly** \-ti-kə-lē, -klē\ *adv*

sad·ness \'sad-nəs\ *n* : the quality, state, or fact of being sad **SYN** see MELANCHOLY

sad sack *n* : a very inept person

sa·fa·ri \sə-'fär-ē, -'far-\ *n, pl* **-ris 1** : the caravan and equipment of a hunting expedition especially in eastern Africa **2** : a hunting expedition in eastern Africa **3** : EXPEDITION 1a [Arabic *safariy* "of a trip"]

¹**safe** \'sāf\ *adj* **1** : freed from harm or risk : UNHURT **2 a** : secure from threat of danger, harm, or loss **b** : successful in reaching base in baseball **3** : affording safety **4** : not threatening danger : HARMLESS ⟨*safe* medicine⟩ **5 a** : CAUTIOUS ⟨a *safe* policy⟩ **b** : TRUSTWORTHY, RELIABLE ⟨a *safe* guide⟩ [Old French *sauf*, from Latin *salvus* "safe, healthy"] — **safe·ly** *adv* — **safe·ness** *n* □ **SYN** SAFE, SECURE mean free from danger. SAFE often implies danger successfully avoided or risk run without harm ⟨arrived *safe* on the other bank of the river⟩ and always suggests present or immediate freedom from threatening harm ⟨stayed *safe* at home⟩ SECURE implies freedom from anxiety or apprehension of loss or danger ⟨locks and alarms designed to make people feel *secure*⟩

²**safe** *n* : a place or container to keep articles (as valuables) safe

safe–con·duct \'sāf-'kän-,dəkt, -,dəkt\ *n* **1** : protection given a person passing through a military zone or occupied area **2** : a document authorizing safe-conduct

safe·crack·er \'sāf-,krak-ər\ *n* : one that breaks open safes to steal their contents

safe–de·pos·it box \,sāf-di-'päz-ət-\ *n* : a box (as in the vault of a bank) for the safe storage of valuables

¹**safe·guard** \'sāf-,gärd\ *n* : something that protects and gives safety : DEFENSE

²**safeguard** *vt* : to make safe or secure : PROTECT

safe·keep·ing \'sāf-'kē-ping\ *n* : a keeping or being kept in safety

safe·light \'sā-,flīt\ *n* : a darkroom lamp with a filter to screen out rays that are harmful to sensitive film or paper

safe sex *n* : sexual activity and especially sexual intercourse in which various measures (as the use of latex condoms or the practice of monogamy) are taken to avoid disease (as AIDS) transmitted by sexual contact

safe·ty \'sāf-tē\ *n, pl* **safeties 1** : the state of being safe : SECURITY **2** : a protective device (as on a firearm) to prevent accidental operation **3 a** : a situation in football in which a member of the offensive team is tackled behind his own goal line and which counts two points for the defensive team — compare TOUCHBACK **b** : a defensive football back who plays the deepest position in the secondary

safety belt *n* : a belt fastening a person to an object to prevent falling or injury

safety glass *n* : glass that resists shattering and is formed of two sheets of glass with a sheet of transparent plastic between them

safety lamp *n* : a miner's lamp constructed to avoid explosion in an atmosphere containing flammable gas usually by enclosing the flame in fine wire gauze

safety match *n* : a match that can be ignited only by striking on a specially prepared surface

safety pin *n* : a pin in the form of a clasp with a guard covering its point

safety razor *n* : a razor with a guard for the blade to prevent deep cuts

safety valve *n* **1** : a valve that opens automatically to prevent accident (as when steam pressure becomes too great) **2** : OUTLET 2

saf·flow·er \'saf-,laù-ər, -,laùr\ *n* : a widely grown Old World herb of the daisy family with large orange or red flower heads yielding a dyestuff and seeds rich in edible oil [Middle French *saffleur*, from Italian *saffiore*, from Arabic *aṣfar*, a yellow plant]

saf·fron \'saf-rən\ *n* **1 a** : a purple-flowered crocus whose deep orange aromatic pungent dried stigmas are used especially to color and flavor foods **b** : these dried usually powdered stigmas **2** : a moderate orange to orange yellow [Old French *safran*, from Medieval Latin *safranum*, from Arabic *za'farān*]

saf·ra·nine *or* **saf·ra·nin** \'saf-rə-,nēn, -nən\ *n* : any of various usually red synthetic dyes [from French or German *safran* "saffron"]

¹**sag** \'sag\ *vi* **sagged; sag·ging 1** : to droop, sink, or settle from or as if from pressure or loss of tautness **2** : to lose firmness, resiliency, or vigor ⟨*sagging* spirits⟩ **3** : to decline from a thriving position ⟨a *sagging* economy⟩

²**sag** *n* : a sagging part or area ⟨the *sag* in a rope⟩; *also* : an instance or amount of sagging

sa·ga \'säg-ə\ *n* **1** : a tale of historic or legendary figures and events of Norway and Iceland **2** : a story of heroic deeds **3** : a long detailed account [Old Norse]

sa·ga·cious \sə-'gā-shəs\ *adj* : keen and farsighted in understanding and judgment : DISCERNING ⟨a *sagacious* judge of character⟩ [Latin *sagac-, sagax*] **SYN** see SHREWD — **sa·ga·cious·ly** *adv* — **sa·ga·cious·ness** *n* — **sa·gac·i·ty** \-'gas-ət-ē\ *n*

sag·a·more \'sag-ə-,mōr, -,mór\ *n* **1** : an Algonquian Indian chief subordinate to a sachem **2** : SACHEM [of American Indian origin]

¹**sage** \'sāj\ *adj* : WISE, PRUDENT ⟨*sage* advice⟩ [Old French, derived from Latin *sapere* "to taste, be wise"] — **sage·ly** *adv* — **sage·ness** *n*

\ə\ abut	\ng\ si**ng**
\ər\ fur**ther**	\ō\ b**one**
\a\ m**at**	\ó\ s**aw**
\ā\ t**ake**	\ói\ c**oin**
\ä\ c**ot, cart**	\th\ **thin**
\aù\ **out**	\t̲h̲\ **this**
\ch\ **chin**	\ü\ f**ood**
\e\ p**et**	\u̇\ f**oot**
\ē\ **easy**	\y\ **yet**
\g\ **go**	\yü\ f**ew**
\i\ t**ip**	\yu̇\ c**ure**
\ī\ l**ife**	\zh\ vi**sion**
\j\ **job**	

saguaro

sailboat

Saint Bernard

²**sage** *n* : a very wise person

³**sage** *n* **1** : a mint with grayish green aromatic leaves used especially in flavoring meats; *also* : SALVIA **2** : SAGEBRUSH [Middle French *sauge,* from Latin *salvia,* from *salvus* "healthy, safe"]

sage·brush \'sāj-ˌbrəsh\ *n* : any of several low shrubby North American plants of the daisy family; *esp* : a common plant with a bitter juice and an odor like a sage that is widespread on alkaline plains of the western United States

sag·it·tal \'saj-ət-l, sə-'jit-\ *adj* : of, relating to, or being the median longitudinal plane of the body [Latin *sagitta* "arrow"] — **sag·it·tal·ly** \-l-ē\ *adv*

Sag·it·tar·i·us \ˌsaj-ə-'ter-ē-əs\ *n* **1** : a zodiacal southern constellation pictured as a centaur shooting an arrow **2** : the 9th sign of the zodiac; *also* : one born under this sign [Latin, literally, "archer", from *sagitta* "arrow"]

sa·go \'sā-gō\ *n, pl* **sagos** : a dry granulated or powdered starch prepared from the pith of a sago palm [Malay *sagu* "sago palm"]

sago palm *n* : a palm or cycad that yields sago; *esp* : any of a genus of tall pinnate-leaved East Indian palms

sa·gua·ro \sə-'wär-ə, -'wär-ō, -'gwär-ō\ *n, pl* **-ros** : a cactus of desert regions of the southwestern United States and Mexico that has a columnar spiny sparsely branched trunk of up to 20 meters and bears white flowers and edible fruit [Mexican Spanish]

sa·hib \'sā-ˌhib, -ˌib, -ˌhēb, -ˌēb, sä-'\ *n* **1** : SIR, MASTER — used especially among Hindus and Muslims in colonial India when addressing or speaking of a European of some social or official status **2** : a European man of some social status living in India — compare MEMSAHIB

said \'sed\ *adj* : AFOREMENTIONED (the *said* parties will abide by the terms of the contract) [from past participle of *say*]

¹**sail** \'sāl, *as last element in compounds often* səl\ *n* **1 a** : a usually rectangular or triangular piece of fabric by means of which wind is used to propel a wind-powered vessel or craft **b** : the sails of a ship **2** *pl usually* **sail** : a ship equipped with sails **3** : a passage by a sailing boat or ship (go for a *sail*) [Old English *segl*]

²**sail** *vb* **1 a** : to travel on water in a sailing vessel; *also* : to travel or begin a journey by water (*sailed* for England on the first steamer) **b** : to move or pass over by ship (*sail* the seas) **c** : to function in sailing (a boat that *sails* well); *also* : to handle or manage the sailing of (experienced in *sailing* small craft) **2** : to move effortlessly or gracefully — **sail into** : to attack vigorously or sharply (*sailed into* their *dinner*) (*sailed into* me for being late)

sail·boat \'sāl-ˌbōt\ *n* : a boat equipped with sails

sail·cloth \-ˌklóth\ *n* : a heavy canvas formerly much used for sails and tents

sail·er \'sā-lər\ *n* : a ship or boat especially having specified sailing qualities

sail·fish \'sāl-ˌfish\ *n* : any of a genus of large sea fishes related to the swordfish but having teeth, scales, and a very large fin on the back

sail·ing \'sā-ling\ *n* **1** : the technical skill of managing a ship : NAVIGATION **2** : the sport of navigating or riding in a sailboat

sail·or \'sā-lər\ *n* **1** : one that sails: as **a** : a member of a ship's crew **b** : a person of the rank of seaman in the Navy **c** : a traveler by water **2** : a stiff straw hat with a low flat crown and straight circular brim

sail·plane \'sāl-ˌplān\ *n* : a glider designed to rise in an upward current of air

¹**saint** \'sānt; *when a name follows* ˌsānt *or* sānt *or* sənt\ *n* **1** : a holy and godly person; *esp* : one who is canonized **2** : a very pious or virtuous person **3** *cap* : LATTER-DAY SAINT [Middle French, from Late Latin *sanctus,* from Latin, "sacred", from *sancire* "to make sacred"]

²**saint** \'sānt\ *vt* : CANONIZE

Saint Ag·nes's Eve \-ˌag-nə-səz-'ēv, -ˌag-nəs-'ēv\ *n* : the night of January 20 when a woman is traditionally held to have a revelation of her future husband [*Saint Agnes*]

Saint An·drew's cross \-ˌan-ˌdrüz-\ *n* : a cross having two intersecting oblique bars [*Saint Andrew,* died about 60 A. D., one of the 12 apostles]

Saint An·tho·ny's fire \-ˌan-thə-nēz-, -ˌant-\ *n* : an inflammatory or gangrenous skin condition (as erysipelas); *esp* : one usually caused by eating rye (as in bread) infected with a particular fungus [*Saint Anthony,* died about 350, Egyptian monk]

Saint Ber·nard \ˌsānt-bər-'närd, -bə-\ *n* : any of a Swiss alpine breed of tall powerful dogs used especially formerly in aiding lost travelers [the hospice of Grand *Saint Bernard,* where such dogs were first bred]

saint·dom \'sānt-dəm\ *n* : SAINTHOOD 1

saint·ed \'sānt-əd\ *adj* **1** : SAINTLY, PIOUS **2** : DECEASED

Saint El·mo's fire \-ˌel-mōz-\ *n* : a luminous discharge of electricity sometimes seen in stormy weather at prominent points on an airplane or ship [*Saint Elmo (Erasmus),* died 303, Italian bishop and patron saint of sailors]

saint·hood \'sānt-ˌhud\ *n* **1** : the quality or state of being a saint **2** : saints as a group

Saint–John's–wort \-'jänz-ˌwərt, -ˌwórt\ *n* : any of a large genus of mostly weedy herbs and shrubs with showy yellow flowers [*Saint John* the Baptist]

saint·ly \'sānt-lē\ *adj* **saint·li·er; -est** : relating to, resembling, or befitting a saint : HOLY — **saint·li·ness** *n*

Saint Mar·tin's summer \-ˌmärt-nz-'səm-ər, -ˌmärt-n-\ *n* : Indian summer when occurring in November [*Saint Martin's Day,* November 11]

Saint Pat·rick's Day \-'pa-triks-\ *n* : March 17 observed by the Roman Catholic Church in honor of St. Patrick and celebrated as a legal holiday in Ireland in commemoration of his death

saint·ship \'sānt-ˌship\ *n* : SAINTHOOD 1

Saint Val·en·tine's Day \-'val-ən-ˌtīnz-\ *n* : February 14 observed as a time for sending valentines [*Saint Valentine,* died about 270, Italian priest]

Saint Vi·tus' dance *or* **Saint Vi·tus's dance** \-ˌvīt-əs-, -əs-əz-\ *n* : CHOREA [*Saint Vitus,* 3d century Christian child martyr]

saith \seth, 'seth, 'sā-əth\ *archaic present 3d sing of* SAY

¹**sake** \'sāk\ *n* **1** : END, PURPOSE (for the *sake* of argument) **2** : GOOD, ADVANTAGE (the *sake* of my country) [Middle English, "dispute, guilt, purpose", from Old English *sacu* "guilt, action at law"]

²**sa·ke** *or* **sa·ki** \'säk-ē\ *n* : a Japanese alcoholic beverage of fermented rice usually served hot [Japanese *sake*]

sal \'sal\ *n* : SALT (*sal* soda) [Latin]

sa·laam \sə-'läm\ *n* **1** : a salutation or ceremonial greeting in the East **2** : deference shown by bowing very low and placing the right palm on the forehead [Arabic *salām,* literally, "peace"] — **salaam** *vb*

sal·able *or* **sale·able** \'sā-lə-bəl\ *adj* : capable of being or fit to be sold : MARKETABLE — **sal·abil·i·ty** \ˌsā-lə-'bil-ət-ē\ *n*

sa·la·cious \sə-'lā-shəs\ *adj* **1** : arousing sexual desire or imagination : LASCIVIOUS **2** : LUSTFUL, LECHEROUS [Latin *salac-, salax* "fond of leaping, lustful", from *salire* "to leap"] — **sa·la·cious·ly** *adv* — **sa·la·cious·ness** *n*

sal·ad \'sal-əd\ *n* **1** : a cooked or uncooked food prepared with a savory dressing and usually served cold: as **a** : raw vegetables (as lettuce and tomatoes) served with dressing **b** : a cold dish (as of meat or fish) served singly or in combinations usually on lettuce and with a dressing **2** : a green vegetable or herb grown for salad [Middle French *salade,* from Pro-

vençal *salada,* from *salar* "to salt", from *sal* "salt",
from Latin]

salad days *n pl* : time of youthful inexperience or indiscretion

salad dressing *n* : a sauce for a salad

salad oil *n* : a vegetable oil suitable for use in salad
dressings

sal·a·man·der \'sal-ə-ˌman-dər\ *n* **1** : a mythical being
having the power to endure fire without harm **2** : any
of an order (Caudata) of amphibians superficially resembling lizards but scaleless and covered with a soft
moist skin **3** : something (as a utensil for browning
pastry or a portable stove or incinerator) used in connection with fire [Middle French *salamandre,* from
Latin *salamandra,* from Greek] — **sal·a·man·drine**
\ˌsal-ə-'man-drən\ *adj*

sa·la·mi \sə-'läm-ē\ *n* : highly seasoned sausage of
pork and beef often dried for storage [Italian, pl. of
salame "salami", from *salare* "to salt", from *sale*
"salt", from Latin *sal*]

sal am·mo·ni·ac \ˌsal-ə-'mō-nē-ˌak\ *n* : AMMONIUM
CHLORIDE [Latin *sal ammoniacus,* literally, "salt of
Ammon"]

sal·a·ried \'sal-rēd, -ə-rēd\ *adj* : receiving or yielding a
salary

sal·a·ry \'sal-rē, -ə-rē\ *n, pl* **-ries** : money paid regularly
(as by the year or month) for work or services [Latin
salarium "salt money, pension, salary", derived from
sal "salt"] SYN see WAGE □ ORIGIN In the Roman army
soldiers were allowed a sum of money to buy salt
with, since salt was not always easily come by and was
important for more than increasing the savor of food
in the days before refrigeration. Later *salarium,* the
name for this money, came to be used for the stipend
or pension paid to soldiers and still later for payments
made to officials of the empire. Latin *salarium,* the
source of English *salary,* is derived from *sal,* "salt".

sale \'sāl\ *n* **1** : the act of selling; *esp* : the transfer of
ownership of property from one person to another for
a price **2** : public disposal to the highest bidder : AUCTION **3** : a selling of goods at bargain prices **4** *pl* **a** :
the business of selling **b** : gross receipts ⟨*sales* are up⟩
— **for sale** : available for purchase — **on sale 1** : for
sale **2** : available for purchase at a reduced price [Old
English *sala,* from Old Norse]

sales \'sālz\ *adj* : of, relating to, or used in selling

sales check *n* : a piece of paper used by retail stores as a
memorandum, record, or receipt of a sale

sales·clerk \-ˌklərk\ *n* : a person employed to sell merchandise in a store

Sa·le·sian \sə-'lē-zhən, sā-\ *n* : a member of the Society
of St. Francis de Sales founded by St. John Bosco in
Turin, Italy in the 19th century and devoted chiefly to
education

sales·man \'sālz-mən\ *n* : one who is employed to sell
merchandise either in a territory or in a store — **salesman·ship** \-ˌship\ *n*

sales·peo·ple \-ˌpē-pəl\ *n pl* : people employed to sell
goods or services

sales·per·son \-ˌpər-sən\ *n* : a person employed to sell
goods or services

sales register *n* : CASH REGISTER

sales·room \'sālz-ˌrüm, -ˌrùm\ *n* : a place where goods
are displayed for sale

sales tax *n* : a tax on the sale of goods and services that
is usually calculated as a percentage of the purchase
price and collected by the seller

sales·wom·an \'sālz-ˌwùm-ən\ *n* : a woman employed
to sell merchandise

Sa·lic \'sā-lik, 'sal-ik\ *adj* : of, relating to, or being a
Frankish people that settled on the IJssel river early in
the 4th century [Medieval Latin *Salicus,* from Late Latin *Salii* "Salic Franks"]

sal·i·cin \'sal-ə-sən\ *n* : a bitter white crystalline compound found in the bark and leaves of several willows

and poplars and used in medicine like salicylic acid
[French *salicine,* from Latin *salic-, salix* "willow"]

sa·lic·y·late \sə-'lis-ə-ˌlāt\ *n* : a salt or ester of salicylic
acid; *also* : SALICYLIC ACID

sal·i·cyl·ic acid \ˌsal-ə-ˌsil-ik-\ *n* : a crystalline organic
acid $C_7H_6O_3$ used especially in the form of salts to relieve pain or fever and in the treatment of rheumatism
[derived from Latin *salic-, salix* "willow"]

sa·lience \'sāl-yəns, 'sā-lē-əns\ *n* **1** : the quality or state
of being salient **2** : a striking point or feature : HIGHLIGHT

¹sa·lient \'sāl-yənt, 'sā-lē-ənt\ *adj* **1** : jetting upward ⟨a
salient fountain⟩ **2 a** : projecting beyond a line,
surface, or level ⟨a *salient* angle⟩ **b** : standing out conspicuously : PROMINENT ⟨*salient* traits⟩ [Latin *saliens,*
present participle of *salire* "to leap"] — **sa·lient·ly**
adv

²salient *n* : something that projects outward; *esp* : an
outwardly projecting part of a fortification or line of
defense

¹sa·line \'sā-ˌlēn, -ˌlīn\ *adj* **1** : consisting of or containing salt ⟨a *saline* solution⟩ **2** : of, relating to, or resembling salt : SALTY ⟨a *saline* taste⟩ ⟨*saline* compounds⟩
[Latin *salinus,* from *sal* "salt"] — **sa·lin·i·ty** \sā-'lin-ət-ē, sə-\ *n*

²saline *n* **1** : a metallic salt; *esp* : a salt of potassium,
sodium, or magnesium with a cathartic action **2** : a
saline solution

sal·i·nom·e·ter \ˌsal-ə-'näm-ət-ər\ *n* : an instrument for
measuring the amount of salt in a solution

Salis·bury steak \ˌsolz-ˌber-ē-, ˌsalz-, -bə-rē, -brē-\ *n* :
ground beef mixed with egg, milk, bread crumbs, and
seasoning and formed into large patties for cooking [J.
H. *Salisbury,* 19th century English physician]

sa·li·va \sə-'lī-və\ *n* : a slightly alkaline secretion of
water, mucin, protein, salts, and often a starch-splitting enzyme secreted into the mouth by salivary glands
[Latin]

sal·i·vary \'sal-ə-ˌver-ē\ *adj* : of or relating to saliva or
the glands that secrete it; *esp* : producing or carrying
saliva ⟨*salivary* glands⟩

sal·i·vate \'sal-ə-ˌvāt\ *vi* : to secrete saliva especially in
large amounts — **sal·i·va·tion** \ˌsal-ə-'vā-shən\ *n*

Salk vaccine \'sok-, 'solk-\ *n* : a polio vaccine that contains virus inactivated with formaldehyde and is administered by injection [Jonas *Salk,* born 1914, American physician]

¹sal·low \'sal-ō\ *n* : any of various Old World broadleaved willows used especially as sources of charcoal
and tanbark [Old English *sealh*]

²sallow *adj* : of a grayish greenish yellow color [Old English *salu*] — **sal·low·ish** \'sal-ə-wish\ *adj* — **sal·low·ness** \'sal-ō-nəs\ *n*

³sallow *vt* : to make sallow

¹sal·ly \'sal-ē\ *n, pl* **sallies 1** : an action of rushing or
bursting forth; *esp* : a sortie of troops from a defensive
position to attack the enemy **2 a** : a brief outbreak :
OUTBURST **b** : a witty remark : QUIP **3** : an excursion
usually off the beaten track : JAUNT [Middle French
saillie, from *saillir* "to rush forward", from Latin *salire* "to leap"]

²sally *vi* **sal·lied; sal·ly·ing 1** : to leap out or burst forth
suddenly **2** : to set out : DEPART — usually used with
forth

Sal·ly Lunn \ˌsal-ē-'lən\ *n* : a slightly sweetened yeast-leavened bread [*Sally Lunn,* 18th century English baker]

sal·ma·gun·di \ˌsal-mə-'gən-dē\ *n* **1** : a salad of
chopped meats, anchovies, eggs, and vegetables arranged in rows for contrast and served with dressing
2 : a varied mixture : POTPOURRI [French *salmigondis*]

salm·on \'sam-ən\ *n, pl* **salmon** *also* **salmons 1 a** : a
large soft-finned game fish of the northern Atlantic related to the trouts and chars and noted as a table fish
b : any of various related fishes; *esp* : any of a genus of

salamander 2

salmon 1a

\ə\ abut	\ng\ sing
\ər\ **further**	\ō\ bone
\a\ mat	\ò\ saw
\ā\ take	\òi\ coin
\ä\ cot, cart	\th\ thin
\aù\ out	\th\ this
\ch\ chin	\ü\ food
\e\ pet	\ù\ foot
\ē\ easy	\y\ yet
\g\ go	\yü\ few
\i\ tip	\yù\ cure
\ī\ life	\zh\ vision
\j\ job	

saltbox

saluki

fishes that breed in rivers tributary to the northern Pacific **2** : a strong yellowish pink color resembling that of the flesh of some salmons [Middle French, from Latin *salmo*] — **salm·on·oid** \'sam-ə-ˌnȯid\ *adj or n*

salm·on·ber·ry \-ˌber-ē\ *n* : a showy red-flowered raspberry of the Pacific coast; *also* : its edible salmon-colored fruit

sal·mo·nel·la \ˌsal-mə-'nel-ə\ *n*, *pl* **-nellas** *or* **-nella** *also* **-nel·lae** \-'nel-ˌē, -ˌī\ : any of a genus of rod-shaped bacteria that cause food poisoning, gastrointestinal inflammation, or diseases of the genital tract of warm-blooded animals [New Latin, from Daniel E. *Salmon*, died 1914, American veterinarian]

sal·mo·nel·lo·sis \ˌsal-mə-ˌnel-'ō-səs\ *n*, *pl* **-lo·ses** \-ˌsēz\ : infection with or disease caused by salmonellas

salmon pink *n* : a strong yellowish pink

sa·lon \sə-'län, 'sal-ˌän, sa-'lōⁿ\ *n* **1** : an elegant apartment or living room **2** : a fashionable gathering of notables customarily held at the home of a prominent person **3 a** : a place for the exhibition of art **b** *cap* : an annual art exhibition **4** : a stylish business establishment [French]

sa·loon \sə-'lün\ *n* **1** : an elaborately decorated public apartment or hall (as a large cabin for the social use of a ship's passengers) **2** : a place in which alcoholic beverages are sold and consumed [French *salon*, from Italian *salone*, from *sala* "hall", of Germanic origin]

sal·pi·glos·sis \ˌsal-pə-'gläs-əs\ *n* : any of a genus of Chilean herbs of the potato family that are sometimes grown for their large multicolored funnel-shaped flowers [New Latin, from Greek *salpinx* "trumpet" + *glōssa* "tongue"]

sal·sa \'sȯl-sə, 'säl-\ *n* **1** : a spicy sauce of tomatoes, onions, and hot peppers **2** : popular music of Latin American origin that has absorbed characteristics of rhythm and blues, jazz, and rock [Spanish, literally, "sauce", from Latin, feminine of *salsus* "salted"]

sal·si·fy \'sal-sə-fē, -ˌfī\ *n*, *pl* **-fies** : a purple-flowered herb of the daisy family that is grown for its long fleshy edible root — called also *oyster plant* [French *salsifis*, from Italian *sassefrica*, from Late Latin *saxifrica*, any of various herbs, from Latin *saxum* "rock" + *fricare* "to rub"]

sal soda \'sal-'sōd-ə\ *n* : a transparent crystalline hydrated sodium carbonate $Na_2CO_3 \cdot 10H_2O$ used in washing and bleaching textiles

¹salt \'sȯlt\ *n* **1 a** : a compound in the form of crystals that consists of sodium chloride, is abundant in nature, and is used especially for seasoning or preserving food — called also *common salt* **b** *pl* (1) : a mineral or saline mixture (as Epsom salts) used as a laxative or cathartic (2) : SMELLING SALTS **c** : a compound formed by replacement of part or all of the acid hydrogen of an acid by a metal or a group acting like a metal **2 a** : an ingredient that gives savor, piquancy, or zest : FLAVOR **b** : sharpness of wit : PUNGENCY **c** : COMMON SENSE **d** : DOUBT **3** — often used in the phrase with a *grain of salt* **e** : the sprinkling of people thought to set a model of excellence for or to give tone to the rest — usually used in the phrase *salt of the earth* **3** : SAILOR ⟨a tale told by an old *salt*⟩ [Old English *sealt*]

²salt *vt* **1 a** : to treat, flavor, or supply with salt ⟨*salt* a dish to taste⟩ **b** : to preserve (food) with salt **2** : to add flavor or zest to (as a story) **3** : to make (as a mine) appear richer by secretly adding valuable mineral

³salt *adj* **1 a** : SALINE, SALTY ⟨*salt* water⟩ **b** : being or inducing the one of the four basic taste sensations produced by table salt **2** : cured or seasoned with salt ⟨*salt* pork⟩ **3** : flooded by the sea ⟨a *salt* pond⟩ **4** : SALTY 3a — **salt·ness** *n*

sal·ta·tion \sal-'tā-shən, sȯl-\ *n* : the action of leaping or jumping [Latin *saltatio*, from *saltare* "to leap, dance", from *saltus*, past participle of *salire* "to leap"]

salt away *vt* : to lay away (as money) safely : SAVE

salt·box \'sȯlt-ˌbäks\ *n* : a frame dwelling with two stories in front and one behind and a roof with a long rear slope

salt·cel·lar \-ˌsel-ər\ *n* : a small container for holding salt at the table [Middle English *salt saler*, from *salt* + *saler* "saltcellar", from Middle French, from Latin *salarius* "of salt", from *sal* "salt"]

salt·er \'sȯl-tər\ *n* **1** : one that manufactures or deals in salt **2** : one that salts something (as meat, fish, or hides)

sal·tern \'sȯl-tərn\ *n* : a place where salt is made by boiling or evaporation [Old English *sealtern*, from *sealt* "salt" + *ærn* "house"]

salt flat *n* : an area of salt-encrusted land left by evaporation of water (as from a former lake)

salt gland *n* : a gland (as of a seabird) capable of excreting a concentrated salt solution

sal·tine \sȯl-'tēn\ *n* : a thin crisp cracker sprinkled with salt

salt lick *n* : LICK 3

salt marsh *n* : flat land subject to overflow by salt water

salt out *vt* : to precipitate, coagulate, or separate (a dissolved substance or sol) from a solution by adding salt

salt·pe·ter \'sȯlt-ˌpēt-ər\ *n* **1** : POTASSIUM NITRATE **2** : SODIUM NITRATE [Middle French *salpetre*, from Medieval Latin *sal petrae*, literally, "salt of the rock"]

salt·shak·er \-ˌshā-kər\ *n* : a container with a perforated top for sprinkling salt

salt·wa·ter \ˌsȯlt-ˌwȯt-ər, -ˌwät-\ *adj* : relating to, living in, or consisting of salt water

salt·works \'sȯlt-ˌwərks\ *n sing or pl* : a plant where salt is prepared commercially

salty \'sȯl-tē\ *adj* **salt·i·er; -est** **1** : seasoned with or containing salt often to excess **2** : suggesting the sea or nautical life **3 a** : CAUSTIC ⟨*salty* wit⟩ **b** : SPICY **4**, RACY — **salt·i·ness** *n*

sa·lu·bri·ous \sə-'lü-brē-əs\ *adj* : favorable to or promoting health [Latin *salubris*] SYN see HEALTHFUL — **sa·lu·bri·ous·ly** *adv* — **sa·lu·bri·ous·ness** *n* — **sa·lu·bri·ty** \-brət-ē\ *n*

sa·lu·ki \sə-'lü-kē\ *n* : any of an old northern African and Asian breed of tall slender swift-footed keen-eyed hunting dogs having long narrow skulls and a smooth silky coat ranging from white or cream to black or black and tan [Arabic *salūqīy* "of Saluq", from *Salūq* "Saluq (ancient city in Arabia)"]

sal·u·tary \'sal-yə-ˌter-ē\ *adj* **1** : promoting health : CURATIVE **2** : producing a beneficial effect ⟨*salutary* advice⟩ [Middle French *salutaire*, from Latin *salutaris*, from *salut-, salus* "health"] SYN see HEALTHFUL — **sal·u·tar·i·ly** \ˌsal-yə-'ter-ə-lē\ *adv* — **sal·u·tar·i·ness** \'sal-yə-ˌter-ē-nəs\ *n*

sal·u·ta·tion \ˌsal-yə-'tā-shən\ *n* **1 a** : an expression of greeting, goodwill, or courtesy **b** *pl* : REGARD 2b (2) **2** : the word or phrase of greeting that conventionally begins a letter — **sal·u·ta·tion·al** \-shnəl, -shən-l\ *adj*

sal·u·ta·to·ri·an \sə-ˌlüt-ə-'tōr-ē-ən, -'tȯr-\ *n* : the graduating student usually second highest in rank who gives the salutatory address

¹sa·lu·ta·to·ry \sə-'lüt-ə-ˌtōr-ē, -ˌtȯr-\ *adj* : expressing salutations or welcome

²salutatory *n*, *pl* **-ries** : a salutatory address given at a commencement exercise

¹sa·lute \sə-'lüt\ *vb* **1** : to greet with courteous words or with a sign of respect or goodwill **2 a** : to honor by a conventional military ceremony **b** : to show respect and recognition by assuming a prescribed position or making a prescribed gesture ⟨*salute* an officer⟩ **c** : PRAISE 1 [Latin *salutare*, from *salut-, salus* "health, safety, greeting"] — **sa·lut·er** *n*

²salute *n* **1** : SALUTATION 1, GREETING **2 a** : a sign, token, or ceremony (as a kiss or a bow) expressing goodwill, compliment, or respect **b** : the position or gesture of a person saluting a superior

salv·able \\'sal-və-bəl\\ *adj* : capable of being saved or salvaged [Late Latin *salvare* "to save"]

¹sal·vage \\'sal-vij\\ *n* **1** : money paid for saving a wrecked or endangered ship, its cargo, or its passengers **2 a** : the act of saving a ship **b** : the act of saving property in danger **3** : property saved or recovered (as from a wreck or fire) [French, from Middle French *salver* "to save"]

²salvage *vt* : to rescue or save especially from wreckage or ruin — **sal·vage·able** \\-ə-bəl\\ *adj* — **sal·vag·er** *n*

Sal·var·san \\'sal-vər-,san\\ *trademark* — used for arsphenamine

sal·va·tion \\sal-'vā-shən\\ *n* **1** : deliverance from sin **2** : preservation from destruction or failure **3** : something that saves ⟨the medicine was the patient's *salvation*⟩ [Old French, from Late Latin *salvatio,* from *salvare* "to save"] — **sal·va·tion·al** \\-shnəl, -shən-l\\ *adj*

¹salve \\'sav, 'sáv\\ *n* **1** : a healing ointment **2** : an influence or agent that remedies or soothes [Old English *sealf*]

²salve *vt* : to ease or soothe with or as if with a salve

sal·ver \\'sal-vər\\ *n* : a serving tray [French *salve,* from Spanish *salva* "sampling of food to detect poison, tray", from *salvar* "to save, sample food to detect poison", from Late Latin *salvare* "to save"]

sal·via \\'sal-vē-ə\\ *n* : any of a large and widely distributed genus of herbs or shrubs of the mint family; *esp* : a scarlet-flowered sage widely grown for ornament [Latin]

sal·vo \\'sal-vō\\ *n, pl* **salvos** *or* **salvoes 1 a** : a firing at one time of two or more guns in military action or as a salute **b** : the release all at once of a rack of bombs or rockets **c** : a discharge of one gun after another in a battery **d** : the bombs or projectiles released in a salvo **2** : SALUTE 2a, TRIBUTE **3** : a sudden burst (as of cheers) [Italian *salva,* from French *salve,* from Latin, "hail!", imperative of *salvēre* "to be healthy", from *salvus* "healthy, safe"]

sa·ma·ra \\'sam-ə-rə; sə-'mar-ə, -'mär-\\ *n* : a dry usually one-seeded winged fruit (as of an ash or elm tree) that does not split open when ripe — called also *key* [Latin, "elm seed"]

Sa·mar·i·tan \\sə-'mar-ət-n, -'mer-\\ *n* **1** : a native or inhabitant of Samaria **2** *often not cap* : one ready and generous in helping those in distress [Late Latin *samaritanus,* from Greek *samaritēs,* from *Samaria* "Samaria"; sense 2 from the parable of the good Samaritan, Luke 10:30-37] — **samaritan** *adj, often cap*

sa·mar·i·um \\sə-'mer-ē-əm, -'mar-\\ *n* : a pale gray lustrous metallic chemical element — see ELEMENT table [New Latin, from French *samarskite,* a mineral, from Colonel von *Samarski,* 19th century Russian mine official]

sam·ba \\'sam-bə, 'säm-\\ *n* : a Brazilian dance characterized by a dip and spring upward at each beat of the music [Portuguese] — **samba** *vi*

Sam Browne belt \\,sam-,braun-\\ *n* : a leather belt for a dress uniform supported by a light strap passing over the right shoulder [Sir *Sam*uel James *Browne,* died 1901, British army officer]

¹same \\'sām\\ *adj* **1 a** : resembling in every relevant respect **b** : conforming in every respect ⟨gave the *same* answer as before⟩ **2 a** : being one without addition, change, or discontinuance : IDENTICAL **b** : being the one under discussion or already referred to ⟨quoted from this *same* book⟩ **3** : corresponding so closely as to be indistinguishable ⟨on the *same* day last year⟩ [Old Norse *samr*]

²same *pron* **1** : something identical with or similar to another **2** : something previously defined or described

³same *adv* : in the same manner

same·ness \\'sām-nəs\\ *n* **1** : the quality or state of being the same : IDENTITY **2** : lack of variety : MONOTONY

sam·i·sen \\'sam-ə-,sen\\ *n* : a 3-stringed Japanese musical instrument resembling a banjo [Japanese]

sa·mite \\'sam-,īt, 'sā-,mīt\\ *n* : a rich medieval silk fabric interwoven with gold or silver [Middle French *samit,* from Medieval Latin *examitum,* from Middle Greek *hexamiton,* from Greek *hexanitos* "of 6 threads", from *hex* "six" + *mitos* "warp thread"]

Samoa time *n* : the time of the 11th time zone west of Greenwich that includes American Samoa

sam·o·var \\'sam-ə-,vär\\ *n* **1** : an urn with a spigot at its base used especially in Russia to boil water for tea **2** : an urn similar to a Russian samovar with a device for heating the contents [Russian, from *samo-* "self" + *varit'* "to boil"]

samp \\'samp\\ *n* : coarse hominy or a boiled cereal made from it [of American Indian origin]

sam·pan \\'sam-,pan\\ *n* : a flat-bottomed Chinese skiff usually propelled by two short oars [Chinese (Pekingese dialect) *san¹pan³,* from *san¹* "three" + *pan³* "plank"]

¹sam·ple \\'sam-pəl\\ *n* **1** : a representative part or a single item from a larger whole or group : SPECIMEN **2** : a part of a statistical population whose properties are studied to gain information about the whole [Middle French *essample* "example, sample", from Latin *exemplum*]

²sample *vt* **sam·pled; sam·pling** \\-pə-ling, -pling\\ : to take a sample of; *esp* : to judge the quality of by a sample

¹sam·pler \\'sam-plər\\ *n* : a piece of needlework typically having letters or verses embroidered on it in various stitches as an example of skill

²sampler *n* **1** : one that collects, prepares, or examines samples **2** : a collection of samples

sample room *n* : a room where samples of merchandise are displayed for the inspection of buyers for retail stores

sample space *n* : a set in which all the possible outcomes of a statistical experiment (as tossing a pair of dice) are represented as points

sam·pling *n* **1** \\'sam-pling\\ : SAMPLE 1 **2** \\-pə-ling, -pling\\ : the act, process, or technique of selecting a suitable sample

Sam·u·el \\'sam-yə-wəl, 'sam-yəl\\ *n* — see BIBLE table

sam·u·rai \\'sam-ə-,rī, -yə-,rī\\ *n, pl* **samurai 1** : a feudal military retainer of a Japanese daimyo **2** : the warrior aristocracy of Japan [Japanese]

san·a·tar·i·um \\,san-ə-'ter-ē-əm\\ *n, pl* **-i·ums** *or* **-ia** \\-ē-ə\\ : SANATORIUM

san·a·to·ri·um \\,san-ə-'tōr-ē-əm, -'tor-\\ *n, pl* **-ri·ums** *or* **-ria** \\-ē-ə\\ : an establishment for the care and treatment especially of convalescents or the chronically ill [New Latin, derived from Latin *sanare* "to heal, cure", from *sanus* "healthy"]

sanc·ti·fy \\'sang-tə-,fī, 'sangk-\\ *vt* **-fied; -fy·ing 1** : to set apart as sacred : CONSECRATE **2** : to make free from sin : PURIFY **3** : to give moral or social sanction to [Middle French *sanctifier,* from Late Latin *sanctificare,* from Latin *sanctus* "sacred", from *sancire* "to make sacred"] — **sanc·ti·fi·ca·tion** \\,sang-tə-fə-'kā-shən, ,sangk-\\ *n* — **sanc·ti·fi·er** \\'sang-tə-,fī-ər, 'sangk-,-,fīr\\ *n*

sanc·ti·mo·ni·ous \\,sang-tə-'mō-nē-əs, ,sangk-\\ *adj* : hypocritically devout — **sanc·ti·mo·ni·ous·ly** *adv* — **sanc·ti·mo·ni·ous·ness** *n*

sanc·ti·mo·ny \\'sang-tə-,mō-nē, 'sangk-\\ *n* : hypocritical piety [Middle French *sanctimonie* "holiness", from Latin *sanctimonia,* from *sanctus* "holy, sacred"]

¹sanc·tion \\'sang-shən, 'sangk-\\ *n* **1** : a binding or compelling force; *esp* : one that determines action in accordance with morality **2** : explicit or official permission or approval **3** : an economic or military measure adopted usually by several nations against another nation violating international law [Latin *sanctio,* from

samisen

sampan

\\ə\\ abut	\\ng\\ sing
\\ər\\ further	\\ō\\ bone
\\a\\ mat	\\o\\ saw
\\ā\\ take	\\oi\\ coin
\\ä\\ cot, cart	\\th\\ thin
\\au\\ out	\\th\\ this
\\ch\\ chin	\\ü\\ food
\\e\\ pet	\\u\\ foot
\\ē\\ easy	\\y\\ yet
\\g\\ go	\\yü\\ few
\\i\\ tip	\\yu\\ cure
\\ī\\ life	\\zh\\ vision
\\j\\ job	

sanctus, past participle of *sancire* "to make sacred, sanction"]

²sanction *vt* **sanc·tioned; sanc·tion·ing** \-shə-ning, -shning\ **1** : to make valid or binding usually by a formal procedure **2** : to give effective or authoritative approval or consent to **SYN** see **APPROVE**

sanc·ti·ty \'sang-tət-ē, 'sangk-\ *n, pl* **-ties 1** : holiness of life and character **2 a** : inviolable quality (the *sanctity* of a promise) **b** *pl* : sacred objects, obligations, or rights

sanc·tu·ary \'sang-chə-,wer-ē, 'sangk-\ *n, pl* **-ar·ies 1** : a holy or sacred place **2** : a building or room for religious worship **3** : the most sacred part (as near the altar) of a place of worship **4** : a refuge for wildlife where predators are controlled and hunting is illegal **5 a** : a place of refuge **b** : safety or protection afforded by a sanctuary [Middle French *sainctuarie,* from Late Latin *sanctuarium,* from Latin *sanctus* "sacred"]

sanc·tum \'sang-təm, 'sangk-\ *n, pl* **sanctums** *also* **sancta** \-tə\ **1** : **SANCTUARY** 1 **2** : a place where one is free from intrusion [Late Latin, from Latin *sanctus* "sacred"]

Sanc·tus \'sang-təs, 'sangk-, 'säng-, 'sängk-\ *n* : an ancient Christian hymn closing the preface of most Christian liturgies and commencing with the words *Sanctus, sanctus, sanctus* or *Holy, holy, holy*

¹sand \'sand\ *n* **1 a** : a loose granular material resulting from the disintegration of rocks **b** : soil containing 85 percent or more of sand and a maximum of 10 percent of clay **2** : a tract of sand : **BEACH 3** : the sand in an hourglass; *also* : the moments of a lifetime — usually used in pl. **4** : firm resolution : **COURAGE** (hasn't the *sand* to object) [Old English]

²sand *vt* **1** : to sprinkle with or as if with sand **2** : to cover or fill with sand **3** : to smooth with an abrasive and especially with sandpaper — **sand·er** \'san-dər\ *n*

san·dal \'san-dl\ *n* **1** : a shoe consisting of a sole strapped to the foot **2** : a low-cut shoe that fastens by an ankle strap **3** : a rubber overshoe cut very low [Latin *sandalium,* from Greek *sandalion,* from *sandalon* "sandal"] — **san·daled** *or* **san·dalled** \'san-dld\ *adj*

san·dal·wood \'san-dl-,wůd\ *n* : the close-grained fragrant yellowish heartwood of an Indo-Malayan tree much used in ornamental carving and cabinetwork; *also* : the tree that yields this wood [Middle French *sandal,* from Medieval Latin *sandalum,* from Late Greek *santalon,* derived from Sanskrit *candana*]

¹sand·bag \'sand-,bag, 'san-\ *n* : a bag filled with sand (as for use as ballast or as a weapon or in a wall or fortification)

²sandbag *vt* **1** : to bank, stop up, or weight with sandbags **2 a** : to hit or stun with a sandbag **b** : to force by crude means — **sand·bag·ger** *n*

sand·bank \-,bangk\ *n* : a large deposit of sand

sand·bar \-,bär\ *n* : a ridge of sand formed in water by tides or currents

¹sand·blast \-,blast\ *n* : a stream of sand projected by compressed air (as for engraving, cutting, or cleaning glass or stone)

²sandblast *vt* : to engrave, cut, or clean with a high-velocity stream of sand — **sand·blast·er** *n*

sand·box \-,bäks\ *n* : a box for holding sand especially for children to play in

sand·bur \-,bər\ *n* : any of several weeds of waste places with burry fruit

sand dollar *n* : a flat circular sea urchin that lives chiefly in shallow water and on sandy bottoms

sand·er·ling \'san-dər-ling\ *n* : a small largely gray and white sandpiper [perhaps derived from *sand* + *-ling*]

sand flea *n* **1** : a flea found in sandy places **2** : **BEACH FLEA**

sand fly *n* : any of various small biting two-winged flies

sand·glass \'sand-,glas, 'san-\ *n* : an instrument like an hourglass for measuring time by the running of sand

sand dollar

sand·hog \'sand-,hóg, -,häg\ *n* : a laborer who works in a caisson in driving underwater tunnels

sand·lot \'san-,dlät, -,lät\ *n* : a vacant lot especially when used by youngsters for unorganized sports — **sandlot** *adj* — **sand·lot·ter** *n*

sand·man \'sand-,man, 'san-\ *n* : a character in folklore who makes children sleepy supposedly by sprinkling sand in their eyes

¹sand·pa·per \-,pā-pər\ *n* : paper covered on one side with abrasive material (as sand) glued fast and used for smoothing and polishing

²sandpaper *vt* : to rub with sandpaper

sand·pile \-,pīl\ *n* : a pile of sand especially for children to play in

sand·pip·er \-,pī-pər\ *n* : any of numerous small shorebirds distinguished from the related plovers chiefly by the longer and soft-tipped bill

sand·stone \'sand-,stōn, 'san-\ *n* : a sedimentary rock consisting of usually quartz sand and a natural cement

sand·storm \-,stórm\ *n* : a storm of wind (as in a desert) that drives clouds of sand

sand trap *n* : an artificial hazard on a golf course consisting of a depression containing sand

¹sand·wich \'san-,dwich, -,wich\ *n* **1** : slices of bread with a filling (as of meat, cheese, or a spread) between them **2** : something resembling a sandwich [John Montagu, 4th Earl of *Sandwich,* died 1792, English diplomat]

²sandwich *vt* **1** : to insert between two or more things (plastic *sandwiched* between layers of glass to make safety glass) **2** : to make a place for : **CROWD** (*sandwich* another activity into a busy schedule)

sandwich board *n* : two usually hinged boards designed for hanging from the shoulders with one board before and one behind and used especially for advertising

sandwich man *n* : a person who advertises or pickets a place of business by wearing a sandwich board

sand·worm \'san-,dwərm, -,wərm\ *n* : any of various sand-dwelling polychaete worms; *esp* : any of several large burrowing worms often used as bait

sand·wort \'san-,dwərt, -,wərt, -,dwórt, -,wórt\ *n* : any of various low tufted chickweeds growing in sandy or gritty soil

sandy \'san-dē\ *adj* **sand·i·er; -est 1** : consisting of, containing, or sprinkled with sand **2** : of a yellowish gray color

sane \'sān\ *adj* **1** : mentally sound and healthy **2** : **SENSIBLE** 4, **RATIONAL** [Latin *sanus* "healthy, sane"] — **sane·ly** *adv* — **sane·ness** \'sān-nəs\ *n*

sang *past of* **SING**

sang-froid \'sän-'frwä\ *n* : self-possession or imperturbability especially under strain [French *sang-froid,* literally, "cold blood"]

san·gui·nary \'sang-gwə-,ner-ē\ *adj* **1** : **BLOODTHIRSTY, MURDEROUS 2** : **BLOODY** (a *sanguinary* battle) [Latin *sanguinarius,* from *sanguin-, sanguis* "blood"] — **san·gui·nar·i·ly** \,sang-gwə-'ner-ə-lē\ *adv*

san·guine \'sang-gwən\ *adj* **1 a** : having the color of blood **b** : **RUDDY** (a *sanguine* complexion) **2** : **SANGUINARY** 1 **3** : having a bodily conformation and temperament marked by sturdiness, high color, and cheerfulness **4** : **CONFIDENT, OPTIMISTIC** (*sanguine* about the future) [Middle French *sanguin,* from Latin *sanguineus,* from *sanguin-, sanguis* "blood"] — **san·guine·ly** *adv* — **san·guine·ness** \-gwən-nəs\ *n* — **san·guin·i·ty** \sang-'gwin-ət-ē, san-\ *n*

san·i·cle \'san-i-kəl\ *n* : any of several plants held to have healing powers [Middle French, from Medieval Latin *sanicula,* probably from *sanus* "healthy"]

san·i·tar·i·an \,san-ə-'ter-ē-ən\ *n* : a specialist in sanitary science and public health (milk *sanitarian*)

san·i·tar·i·um \,san-ə-'ter-ē-əm\ *n, pl* **-i·ums** *or* **-ia** \-ē-ə\ : **SANATORIUM** [New Latin, from Latin *sanitas* "health, sanity"]

san·i·tary \'san-ə-ˌter-ē\ adj 1 : of or relating to health : HYGIENIC ⟨*sanitary* laws⟩ 2 : free from filth, infection, or dangers to health [French *sanitaire,* from Latin *sanitas* "health"] — **san·i·tar·i·ly** \ˌsan-ə-'ter-ə-lē\ adv

sanitary landfill n : LANDFILL

sanitary napkin n : a disposable absorbent pad in a gauzecovering used to absorb uterine flow (as during menstruation)

san·i·ta·tion \ˌsan-ə-'tā-shən\ n 1 : the act or process of making sanitary 2 : the promotion of community hygiene and disease prevention especially by supervision and maintenance of sewage disposal systems, collection and disposal of trash and garbage, and cleaning of streets

san·i·tize \'san-ə-ˌtīz\ vt : to make sanitary (as by cleaning or sterilizing) — **san·i·ti·za·tion** \ˌsan-ət-ə-'zā-shən\ n

san·i·ty \'san-ət-ē\ n : the quality or state of being sane [Latin *sanitas* "health, sanity", from *sanus* "healthy, sane"]

San Jo·se scale \ˌsan-ə-ˌzā-\ n : a scale insect that is naturalized in the United States probably from Asia and is a most damaging pest to fruit trees [*San Jose,* California]

sank past of SINK

sans \sanz, ˌsanz\ prep : WITHOUT [Middle French, from Latin *sine*]

San·skrit \'san-ˌskrit\ n : an ancient Indic language that is the classical language of India and of Hinduism [Sanskrit *saṃskṛta,* literally, "perfected"] — **Sanskrit** adj

sans ser·if or **san·ser·if** \san-'ser-əf\ n : a letter or typeface with no serifs

san·se·vie·ria \ˌsan-sə-'vir-ē-ə\ n : any of a genus of tropical Old World herbs with mottled or striped sword-shaped leaves [Raimondo di Sangro, prince of *San Severo,* died 1774, Italian scholar]

San·ta Claus \'sant-ē-ˌkloz, 'sant-ē-\ n : the spirit of Christmas personified as a fat, jolly old man in a red suit who distributes toys to children [Dutch *Sinterklaas,* alteration of *Sint Nikolaas* "Saint Nicholas"]

San·ta Ger·tru·dis \ˌsant-ə-ˌgər-'trüd-əs\ n : any of an American breed of cherry-red beef cattle developed from a Brahman-Shorthorn cross and noted for their ability to withstand heat and their resistance to insects [*Santa Gertrudis,* section of the King Ranch, Kingsville, Texas]

san·ton·i·ca \san-'tän-i-kə\ n : the dried unopened flower heads of a wormwood sometimes used as a worm remedy [Latin *herba santonica,* a kind of herb, from *santonicus* "of the Santoni", from *Santoni,* a people of Aquitania]

¹sap \'sap\ n 1 : the fluid part of a plant; *esp* : a watery solution that circulates through a vascular plant 2 : VITALITY 2b 3 : a foolish gullible person [Old English *sæp*]

²sap vt **sapped; sap·ping** 1 : UNDERMINE ⟨heavy tides *sapped* the seawall⟩ 2 : to weaken gradually ⟨the heat *sapped* my strength⟩ [earlier *sap* "extension of a trench to a point beneath an enemy's fortifications", from Middle French *sappe* "hoe", from Italian *zappa*]

sap·head \'sap-ˌhed\ n : a weak-minded or foolish person : SAP — **sap·head·ed** \-'hed-əd\ adj

sa·pi·ence \'sā-pē-əns, 'sap-ē-\ n : WISDOM 1a

sa·pi·ent \'sā-pē-ənt, 'sap-ē-\ adj : WISE 1, DISCERNING [Middle French, from Latin *sapiens,* from *sapere* "to taste, be wise"] — **sa·pi·ent·ly** adv

sap·less \'sap-ləs\ adj 1 : destitute of sap : DRY 2 : lacking vitality or vigor : FEEBLE — **sap·less·ness** n

sap·ling \'sap-ling\ n : a young tree usually not over four inches in diameter at breast height

sap·o·dil·la \ˌsap-ə-'dil-ə\ n : a tropical American evergreen tree with hard reddish wood, an edible brownish berry, and a latex that yields chicle [Spanish *zapotillo,* from *zapote* "sapodilla", from Nahuatl *tzapotl*]

sap·o·na·ceous \ˌsap-ə-'nā-shəs\ adj : resembling or having the qualities of soap : SOAPY [Latin *sapon-, sapo* "soap", of Germanic origin] — **sap·o·na·ceous·ness** n

sa·pon·i·fy \sə-'pän-ə-ˌfī\ vb **-fied; -fy·ing** 1 : to convert (as fat) into soap; *specif* : to hydrolyze (a fat) with alkali to form a soap and glycerol 2 : to undergo saponifying — **sa·pon·i·fi·able** \-ˌfī-ə-bəl\ adj — **sa·pon·i·fi·ca·tion** \-ˌpän-ə-fə-kā-shən\ n — **sa·pon·i·fi·er** \-'pän-ə-ˌfī-ər, -ˌfīr\ n

sap·per \'sap-ər\ n 1 : a military engineer who constructs field fortifications 2 : an engineer who lays, detects, and disarms mines

sap·phire \'saf-ˌīr\ n 1 : a gem variety of corundum occurring in transparent or translucent colorless or colored forms except red; *esp* : a transparent rich blue gemstone 2 : a deep purplish blue [Old French *safir,* from Latin *sapphirus,* from Greek *sappheiros,* from Hebrew *sappīr,* from Sanskrit *śanipriya,* literally, "dear to the planet Saturn", from *Sani* "Saturn" + *priya* "dear"] — **sapphire** adj

sap·py \'sap-ē\ adj **sap·pi·er; -est** 1 : abounding with sap 2 : containing much sapwood 3 a : foolishly sentimental b : lacking in good sense : SILLY — **sap·pi·ness** n

sapr- or **sapro-** combining form 1 : rotten : putrid 2 : dead or decaying organic matter ⟨*sapro* phyte⟩ [Greek *sapros*]

sap·ro·phyte \'sap-rə-ˌfīt\ n : a plant living on dead or decaying organic matter; *also* : any saprophytic organism

sap·ro·phyt·ic \ˌsap-rə-'fit-ik\ adj : obtaining food by absorbing dissolved organic material and especially the products of organic breakdown and decay — **sap·ro·phyt·i·cal·ly** \-'fit-i-kə-lē, -klē\ adv

sap·suck·er \'sap-ˌsək-ər\ n : any of various small American woodpeckers reputed to feed on sap

sap·wood \-ˌwu̇d\ n : the younger softer sap-containing and usually lighter-colored wood in the outer portion of a woody stem — compare HEARTWOOD

Sar·a·cen \'sar-ə-sən\ n 1 : a member of a nomadic people of the deserts of Syria and northern Arabia 2 : ARAB 1 [Late Latin *Saracenus,* from Late Greek *Sarakēnos*] — **Saracen** adj — **Sar·a·cen·ic** \ˌsar-ə-'sen-ik\ adj

sa·ran \sə-'ran\ n : a tough flexible thermoplastic resin that can be formed into waterproof and chemically resistant products (as filaments, tubing, and coating) [from *Saran Wrap,* a trademark]

sa·ra·pe variant of SERAPE

sarc- or **sarco-** combining form : flesh [Greek *sark-, sarx*]

sar·casm \'sär-ˌkaz-əm\ n 1 : a cutting and often ironic remark 2 : the use of sarcasms in speech or writing ⟨this is no time to indulge in *sarcasm*⟩ [French *sarcasme,* from Late Latin *sarcasmos,* from Greek *sarkasmos,* from *sarkazein* "to tear flesh, bite the lips, sneer", from *sark-, sarx* "flesh"]

sar·cas·tic \sär-'kas-tik\ adj 1 : given to sarcasm 2 : containing sarcasm ⟨a *sarcastic* remark⟩ — **sar·cas·ti·cal·ly** \-ti-kə-lē, -klē\ adv

sar·co·lem·ma \ˌsär-kə-'lem-ə\ n : the thin sheath of a muscle fiber [*sarc-* + Greek *lemma* "husk", from *lepein* "to peel"]

sar·co·ma \sär-'kō-mə\ n : a malignant tumor arising in tissue of mesodermal origin (as connective tissue or striated muscle) — **sar·co·ma·tous** \sär-'käm-ət-əs, -'kōm-\ adj

sar·coph·a·gus \sär-'käf-ə-gəs\ n, pl **-gi** \-ˌgī, -ˌjī, -ˌgē\ or **-gus·es** : a stone coffin; *esp* : one exposed to view in the open air or in a tomb [Latin *sarcophagus (lapis)* "limestone used for coffins", from Greek (lithos) *sarkophagos,* literally, "flesh-eating stone", from *sark-, sarx* "flesh" + *phagein* "to eat"]

Santa Gertrudis

sapsucker

\ə\ abut	\ng\ sing
\ər\ **further**	\ō\ bone
\a\ mat	\ȯ\ saw
\ā\ take	\ȯi\ coin
\ä\ cot, cart	\th\ thin
\au̇\ out	\th\ this
\ch\ chin	\ü\ food
\e\ pet	\u̇\ foot
\ē\ easy	\y\ yet
\g\ go	\yü\ few
\i\ tip	\yu̇\ cure
\ī\ life	\zh\ vision
\j\ job	

sari

sar·dine \sär-'dēn\ *n, pl* **sardines** *also* **sardine** **1** : any of several small or immature fishes of the herring family; *esp* : the young of the European pilchard when of a size suitable for preserving for food **2** : any of various small fishes (as an anchovy) resembling the true sardines or similarly preserved for food [Middle French, from Latin *sardina*]

sar·don·ic \sär-'dän-ik\ *adj* : bitterly scornful : CYNICAL [French *sardonique*, from Greek *sardonios*] — **sar·don·i·cal·ly** \-'dän-i-kə-lē, -klē\ *adv*

sard·on·yx \sär-'dän-iks, 'särd-n-\ *n* : onyx having layers of carnelian [Latin, from Greek]

sar·gas·so \sär-'gas-ō\ *n, pl* **-sos** **1** : GULFWEED, SARGASSUM **2** : a mass of floating vegetation and especially sargassums [Portuguese *sargaço*]

sar·gas·sum \sär-'gas-əm\ *n* : any of a genus of branching brown algae with lateral outgrowths forming leafy segments, air bladders, or spore-bearing structures [New Latin, from *sargasso*]

sa·ri *or* **sa·ree** \'sär-ē\ *n* : a garment of Hindu women that consists of a long cloth draped so that one end forms a skirt and the other a head or shoulder covering [Hindi *sāṛī*, from Sanskrit *śāṭī*]

sa·rong \sə-'róng, -'räng\ *n* : a loose skirt made of a long strip of cloth wrapped loosely around the body and worn by men and women of the Malay archipelago and the Pacific islands [Malay *kain sarong* "cloth sheath"]

sar·sa·pa·ril·la \ˌsas-pə-'ril-ə, ˌsärs-, -ə-pə-\ *n* **1 a** : any of various tropical American smilaxes **b** : the dried roots of a sarsaparilla plant used especially as a flavoring **2** : a sweetened carbonated beverage flavored chiefly with birch oil and sassafras [Spanish *zarzaparilla*]

sar·to·ri·al \sär-'tōr-ē-əl, -'tòr-\ *adj* : of or relating to a tailor or tailored clothes ⟨the *sartorial* appearance of a politician⟩ ⟨*sartorial* splendor⟩ [Latin *sartor* "tailor", from *sartus*, past participle of *sarcire* "to mend"] — **sar·to·ri·al·ly** \-ē-ə-lē\ *adv*

sar·to·ri·us \-ē-əs\ *n* : a muscle that crosses the front of the thigh obliquely and assists in rotating the leg outward to the position assumed in sitting cross-legged [New Latin, from Latin *sartor* "tailor"]

¹sash \'sash\ *n* : a broad band (as of silk) worn around the waist or over the shoulder [Arabic *shāsh* "muslin"]

²sash *n, pl* **sash** *or* **sash·es** : the framework in which panes of glass are set in a window or door; *also* : the movable part of a window ⟨raised the *sash* to let in air⟩ [probably from French *châssis* "chassis"]

sa·shay \sa-'shā\ *vi* **1** : to strut or move about in an ostentatious manner **2** : to proceed in a diagonal or sideways manner [French *chassé*, a dance step, from *chasser* "to chase"]

¹sass \'sas\ *n* : impudent speech [back-formation from *sassy*]

²sass *vt* : to talk impudently or disrespectfully to

sas·sa·fras \'sas-ˌfras, -ə-ˌfras\ *n* : a tall eastern North American tree of the laurel family having fragrant yellow flowers and blue-black berries; *also* : its dried root bark used especially in medicine or as a flavoring agent [Spanish *sasafrás*]

sassafras

sassy \'sas-ē\ *adj* **sass·i·er; -est** : given to back talk : FRESH [alteration of *saucy*]

sat *past of* SIT

Sa·tan \'sāt-n\ *n* : DEVIL 1 [Old English, from Late Latin, from Greek, from Hebrew *śāṭān*] — **sa·tan·ic** \sə-'tan-ik, sā-\ *adj* — **sa·tan·i·cal·ly** \-'tan-i-kə-lē, -klē\ *adv*

satch·el \'sach-əl\ *n* : a small bag for carrying clothes or books [Middle French *sachel*, from Latin *sacellus* "small bag", from *saccus* "bag"]

sate \'sāt\ *vt* **1** : SURFEIT, GLUT **2** : SATIATE 1 [probably from *satiate*]

sa·teen \sa-'tēn\ *n* : a glossy cotton fabric resembling satin [alteration of *satin*]

sat·el·lite \'sat-l-ˌīt\ *n* **1** : a servile follower **2 a** : a celestial body orbiting another of larger size **b** : a man-made object or vehicle intended to orbit the earth, the moon, or another celestial body **3** : one that is subordinate to or dependent on another; *esp* : a country dominated or controlled by another more powerful country [Middle French, from Latin *satellit-, satelles* "attendant"] — **satellite** *adj*

sa·tia·ble \'sā-shə-bəl\ *adj* : possible to appease or satisfy

¹sa·tiate \'sā-shē-ət, -shət\ *adj* : marked by or feeling satiety

²sa·ti·ate \'sā-shē-ˌāt\ *vt* **1** : to satisfy (as a person or an appetite) fully **2** : SURFEIT [Latin *satiare*, from *satis* "enough"] — **sa·ti·a·tion** \ˌsā-shē-'ā-shən, ˌsā-sē-\ *n*

sa·ti·e·ty \sə-'tī-ət-ē\ *n* **1** : SURFEIT 1, REPLETION **2** : revulsion or disgust that follows overindulgence [Middle French *satieté*, from Latin *satietas*, from *satis* "enough"]

sat·in \'sat-n\ *n* : a fabric (as of silk) with smooth lustrous face and dull back [Middle French] — **satin** *adj*

sat·in·et *or* **sat·in·ette** \ˌsat-n-'et\ *n* : a usually thin silk satin

satin weave *n* : a weave in which warp threads interlace with filling threads to produce a smooth-faced fabric

sat·in·wood \'sat-n-ˌwùd\ *n* **1** : a hard yellowish brown wood with a satiny luster **2** : a tree yielding satinwood; *esp* : an East Indian tree of the mahogany family

sat·iny \'sat-n-ē\ *adj* : having the soft lustrous smoothness of satin : resembling satin ⟨*satiny* skin⟩

sat·ire \'sa-ˌtīr\ *n* **1** : a literary work holding up human vices and follies to ridicule or scorn **2** : biting wit, irony, or sarcasm used to expose and discredit vice or folly [Middle French, from Latin *satura, satira*, from *(lanx) satura* "full plate, medley", from *satur* "sated"] — **sa·tir·ic** \sə-'tir-ik\ *or* **sa·tir·i·cal** \-'tir-i-kəl\ *adj* — **sa·tir·i·cal·ly** \-i-kə-lē, -klē\ *adv* □ ORIGIN English *satire* is derived from Latin *satira* and its earlier form *satura*, which in classical times meant "a satirical poem". Before the development of this style of satiric poetry, the *satura* was a poem dealing with a number of different subjects. It is this sense of "a poetic medley" that gives us a clue to the early development of the word. This sense of *satura* evolved from the phrase *lanx satura*, literally "a full plate". *Satura* is a form of *satur*, which means "sated" or "full of food". *Lanx satura* once meant a plate filled with various fruits or a dish made from a mixture of many ingredients.

sat·i·rist \'sat-ə-rəst\ *n* : one that satirizes; *esp* : a satirical writer

sat·i·rize \-ˌrīz\ *vb* **1** : to utter or write satires **2** : to criticize or ridicule by means of satire

sat·is·fac·tion \ˌsat-əs-'fak-shən\ *n* **1 a** : fulfillment of a need or want **b** : the quality or state of being satisfied : CONTENTMENT **c** : a cause or means of enjoyment : GRATIFICATION **2** : compensation for a loss or injury : RESTITUTION **3** : convinced assurance or certainty ⟨proved to the *satisfaction* of the court⟩ [Middle French, from Latin *satisfactio* "reparation, amends", from *satisfacere* "to satisfy"]

sat·is·fac·to·ry \ˌsat-əs-'fak-tə-rē, -trē\ *adj* : sufficient or adequate to satisfy : meeting what is asked or demanded — **sat·is·fac·to·ri·ly** \-tə-rə-lē, -trə-\ *adv* — **sat·is·fac·to·ri·ness** \-tə-rē-nəs, -trē-\ *n*

sat·is·fy \'sat-əs-ˌfī\ *vb* **-fied; -fy·ing** **1 a** : to carry out the terms of ⟨*satisfy* a contract⟩ **b** : to meet a financial obligation to : PAY **2 a** : to make happy : PLEASE **b** : to gratify to the full : APPEASE ⟨*satisfied* my hunger⟩ **3 a** : CONVINCE ⟨*satisfied* that the defendant is innocent⟩ **b** : to put an end to : DISPEL ⟨*satisfied* all their objections⟩ **4 a** : to conform or be adequate to : MEET ⟨*satisfy* a need⟩ **b** : to make true by fulfilling a condition ⟨values that *satisfy* an equation⟩ ⟨*satisfy* a hypothesis⟩ [Middle French *satisfier*, from Latin *satisfacere*, from *satis*

sat·is·fi·able \ˌsat-əs-ˈfī-ə-bəl\ *adj* — **sat·is·fy·ing·ly** \ˈsat-əs-ˌfī-ing-lē\ *adv*

sa·trap \ˈsā-ˌtrap, ˈsa-\ *n* **1** : the governor of a province in ancient Persia **2** : a subordinate ruler; *esp* : a petty tyrant [Latin *satrapes,* from Greek *satrapēs,* from Persian *xshathrapāvan,* literally, "protector of the dominion"]

sa·tra·py \ˈsā-trə-pē, ˈsa-, -ˌtrap-ē\ *n, pl* **-pies** : the territory or jurisdiction of a satrap

sat·u·rant \ˈsach-ə-rənt\ *n* : something that saturates

sat·u·rate \ˈsach-ə-ˌrāt\ *vt* **1** : to treat, furnish, or charge with something to the point where no more can be absorbed, dissolved, or retained ⟨air *saturated* with water vapor⟩ **2** : to fill completely with something that permeates or pervades [Latin *saturare,* from *satur* "sated"] — **sat·u·ra·ble** \ˈsach-rə-bəl, -ə-rə-\ *adv* — **sat·u·ra·tor** \ˈsach-ə-ˌrāt-ər\ *n*

sat·u·rat·ed \ˈsach-ə-ˌrāt-əd\ *adj* **1** : steeped in moisture : SOAKED **2 a** : being a solution is unable to absorb or dissolve any more of a substance at a given temperature and pressure **b** : being a carbon compound having no double or triple bonds between carbon atoms **3** : not diluted with white ⟨a *saturated* color⟩

sat·u·ra·tion \ˌsach-ə-ˈrā-shən\ *n* **1** : the act of saturating : the state of being saturated **2** : chromatic purity : freedom from dilution with white **3** : an overwhelming concentration of military forces or firepower

Sat·ur·day \ˈsat-ərd-ē\ *n* : the 7th day of the week [Old English *sæterndæg,* literally, "Saturn's day", derived from Latin *Saturnus* "Saturn"]

Sat·urn \ˈsat-ərn\ *n* : the planet 6th in order from the sun — see PLANET table [*Saturn,* Roman god] — **Sa·tur·ni·an** \sa-ˈtər-nē-ən\ *adj*

sat·ur·na·lia \ˌsat-ər-ˈnāl-yə\ *n sing or pl* **1** *cap* : the festival of Saturn in ancient Rome beginning on December 17 **2** : an unrestrained often licentious celebration : ORGY [Latin, derived from *Saturnus* "Saturn"] — **sat·ur·na·lian** \-yən\ *adj*

sat·ur·nine \ˈsat-ər-ˌnīn\ *adj* : having a sullen or sardonic aspect : GLOOMY, GRAVE [from the supposed character of those born under the planet Saturn] — **sat·ur·nine·ly** *adv*

sa·tyr \ˈsāt-ər, ˈsat-\ *n* **1** : a forest god in Greek mythology often represented as having the ears and tail of a horse or goat and given to boisterous pleasures **2** : a man of lustful or lecherous habits **3** : any of a family of usually brown and gray butterflies often with eyespots on the wings [Latin *satyrus,* from Greek *satyros*] — **sa·tyr·ic** \sā-ˈtir-ik, sə-, sa-\ *adj*

¹sauce \ˈsȯs, 4 usually ˈsas\ *n* **1** : a condiment or relish for food; *esp* : one in the form of a liquid or semisolid : DRESSING **2** : something that adds zest or piquancy **3** : cooked fruit eaten with other food or as a dessert ⟨apple *sauce*⟩ **4** : pert or impudent language or actions [Middle French, from Latin *salsus* "salted", from *sallere* "to salt", from *sal* "salt"]

²sauce \ˈsȯs, 2 usually ˈsas\ *vt* **1** : to add relish or seasoning to **2** : to be rude or impudent to

sauce·pan \ˈsȯs-ˌpan\ *n* : a small deep cooking pan with a handle

sau·cer \ˈsȯ-sər\ *n* **1** : a small round shallow dish in which a cup is set at table **2** : something like a saucer especially in shape [Middle French *saussier* "dish for sauce", from *sausse, sauce* "sauce"]

saucy \ˈsas-ē also ˈsȯs-ē\ *adj* **sauc·i·er; -est 1** : IMPUDENT, BOLD **2** : IRREPRESSIBLE, PERT **3** : SMART, TRIM ⟨a *saucy* little hat⟩ — **sauc·i·ly** \-ə-lē\ *adv* — **sauc·i·ness** \-ē-nəs\ *n*

sau·er·bra·ten \ˈsaú-ər-ˌbrät-n, ˈsaúr-\ *n* : pot-roasted beef marinated in vinegar with seasonings before cooking [German, from *sauer* "sour" + *braten* "roast meat"]

sau·er·kraut \ˈsaú-ər-ˌkraút, ˈsaúr-\ *n* : finely cut cabbage fermented in brine [German, from *sauer* "sour" + *kraut* "cabbage"]

sau·ger \ˈsȯ-gər\ *n* : a pike perch similar to the walleye but smaller; *also* : WALLEYE [origin unknown]

sau·na \ˈsȯ-nə, ˈsaú-nə\ *n* : a Finnish steam bath; *also* : a bathhouse with steam provided usually by water thrown on hot stones [Finnish]

saun·ter \ˈsȯnt-ər, ˈsänt-\ *vi* : to walk along in an idle or leisurely manner : STROLL [probably from Middle English *santren* "to muse"] — **saunter** *n* — **saun·ter·er** \-ər-ər\ *n*

sau·ri·an \ˈsȯr-ē-ən\ *n* : any of a group (Sauria) of reptiles including the lizards and in older classifications the crocodiles and various extinct forms (as the dinosaurs) suggesting lizards [derived from Greek *sauros* "lizard"] — **saurian** *adj*

saur·is·chi·an \sȯ-ˈris-kē-ən\ *n* : any of an order (Saurischia) of four-footed dinosaurs with a typically reptilian pelvic girdle [derived from Greek *sauros* "lizard" + *ischion* "hip joint"] — **saurischian** *adj*

sau·ro·pod \ˈsȯr-ə-ˌpäd\ *n* : any of a group (Sauropoda) of large long-necked plant-eating saurischian dinosaurs — **sauropod** *adj*

sau·sage \ˈsȯ-sij\ *n* : highly seasoned minced meat (as pork) usually stuffed in casings [Old North French *saussiche,* from Late Latin *salsicia,* from Latin *salsus* "salted", from *sallere* "to salt", from *sal* "salt"]

¹sau·té \sȯ-ˈtā, sō-\ *n* : a sautéed dish [French, "sautéed", from *sauter* "to jump", from Latin *saltare*] — **sauté** *adj*

²sauté *vt* **sau·téed** *or* **sau·téd; sau·té·ing** : to fry quickly in shallow fat

sau·terne \sō-ˈtərn, sȯ-, -ˈteərn\ *n* : a semisweet golden-colored table wine [French *sauternes,* from *Sauternes,* commune in France]

¹sav·age \ˈsav-ij\ *adj* **1** : not domesticated or under human control ⟨a *savage* bear⟩ **2** : CRUEL 2, FEROCIOUS **3 a** : RUDE **3 b** : lacking complex or advanced culture : UNCIVILIZED [Middle French *sauvage,* derived from Latin *silvaticus* "of the woods, wild", from *silva* "wood, forest"] SYN see BARBARIAN — **sav·age·ly** *adv* — **sav·age·ness** *n*

²savage *n* **1** : a person belonging to a primitive society **2** : a brutal person **3** : a rude or unmannerly person

³savage *vt* : to attack or treat violently or brutally

sav·age·ry \ˈsav-ij-rē, -ə-rē\ *n, pl* **-ries 1** : the quality of being savage **2** : an act of cruelty or violence **3** : an uncivilized state

sa·van·na *or* **sa·van·nah** \sə-ˈvan-ə\ *n* : a tropical or subtropical grassland containing scattered trees [Spanish *zavana,* of American Indian origin]

sa·vant \sa-ˈvänt, -ˈväⁿ; sə-ˈvant, ˈsav-ənt\ *n* : a learned person : SCHOLAR [French, from *savoir* "to know", from Latin *sapere* "to taste, be wise"]

¹save \ˈsāv\ *vb* **1 a** : to deliver from sin **b** : to rescue from danger or harm **c** : to preserve or guard from injury, destruction, or loss **2** : to put aside as a store or reserve; *also* : to put aside money **3 a** : to make unnecessary : AVOID **b** : to prevent an opponent from making, scoring, or winning ⟨a diving catch that *saved* a goal⟩ **4** : MAINTAIN, PRESERVE ⟨*save* appearances⟩ **5** : to avoid unnecessary waste or expense : ECONOMIZE [Old French *salver,* from Late Latin *salvare,* from Latin *salvus* "safe"] — **sav·able** *or* **save·able** \ˈsā-və-bəl\ *adj* — **sav·er** *n*

²save *n* : a play that prevents an opponent from scoring or winning; *also* : a game that has been saved

³save \sāv, ˌsāv\ *prep* : EXCEPT ⟨no hope *save* one⟩ [Old French *sauf,* from *sauf,* adj., "safe"]

⁴save \sāv, ˌsāv\ *conj* : were it not : ONLY — used with *that*

sav·in \ˈsav-ən\ *n* : any of several mostly low-growing junipers [Middle French *savine,* from Latin *sabina*]

¹sav·ing \ˈsā-ving\ *n* **1** : the act of rescuing ⟨the *saving* of lives⟩ **2 a** : something saved ⟨made a *saving* of 50 percent⟩ **b** *pl* : money saved over a period of time

\ə\ abut	\ng\ sing
\ər\ further	\ō\ bone
\a\ mat	\ȯ\ saw
\ā\ take	\ȯi\ coin
\ä\ cot, cart	\th\ thin
\aú\ out	\th\ this
\ch\ chin	\ü\ food
\e\ pet	\ú\ foot
\ē\ easy	\y\ yet
\g\ go	\yü\ few
\i\ tip	\yú\ cure
\ī\ life	\zh\ vision
\j\ job	

²**saving** *adj* **1** : ECONOMICAL 1, THRIFTY **2** : making up for something : COMPENSATORY ⟨a *saving* sense of humor⟩

³**saving** *prep* **1** : EXCEPT, SAVE **2** : without disrespect to

⁴**saving** *conj* : EXCEPT

savings account *n* : an interest-bearing account with a bank

savings bank *n* : a bank that receives and invests savings accounts and pays interest to depositors

savings bond *n* : a registered United States bond issued in denominations of $25 to $1000

sav·ior *or* **sav·iour** \'sāv-yər\ *n* **1** : one that saves from harm **2** *cap* : a bringer of salvation; *esp* : JESUS [Middle French *saveour,* from Late Latin *salvator,* from *salvare* "to save"]

sa·voir faire \,sav-,wär-'faər, -'feər\ *n* : ability to do or say the right or graceful thing : TACT [French *savoir-faire,* literally, "knowing how to do"]

¹**sa·vor** \'sā-vər\ *n* **1** : the taste and odor of something ⟨the *savor* of roast meat⟩ **2** : a distinctive quality [Old French, from Latin *sapor*] — **sa·vor·less** \-ləs\ *adj*

²**savor** *vb* **sa·vored; sa·vor·ing** \'sāv-ring, -ə-ring\ **1** : to have a specified smell or quality **2** : to give flavor to : SEASON **3 a** : to have experience of **b** : to taste or smell with pleasure : RELISH **c** : to delight in : ENJOY — **sa·vor·er** \'sā-vər-ər\ *n*

¹**sa·vory** \'sāv-rē, -ə-rē\ *adj* **sa·vor·i·er; -est** : pleasing to the taste or smell : APPETIZING — **sa·vor·i·ness** *n*

²**sa·vo·ry** \'sāv-rē, -ə-rē\ *n, pl* **-ries** : any of a genus of aromatic mints used to season food [Middle English *saverey*]

¹**sav·vy** \'sav-ē\ *vb* **sav·vied; sav·vy·ing** : GET 7c, UNDERSTAND ⟨you *savvy* what I mean?⟩ [Spanish *sabe* "he, she, or it knows", from *saber* "to know", from Latin *sapere* "to taste, be wise"]

²**savvy** *n* : practical understanding ⟨political *savvy*⟩

¹**saw** *past of* SEE

²**saw** \'sȯ\ *n* **1** : a hand or power tool used to cut hard material (as wood, metal, or bone) with a toothed blade or disk **2** : a machine mounting a saw (as a band saw or circular saw) [Old English *sagu*] — **saw·like** \-,līk\ *adj*

³**saw** *vb* **sawed** \'sȯd\; **sawed** *or* **sawn** \'sȯn\; **saw·ing** \'sȯ-ing, 'sȯing\ **1** : to cut or form by cutting with a saw **2** : to slice as though with a saw **3** : to make motions as though using a saw ⟨*sawed* at the reins⟩ — **saw·er** \'sȯ-ər, 'sȯr\ *n*

⁴**saw** *n* : a common saying : PROVERB [Old English *sagu* "talk"]

saw·buck \'sȯ-,bək\ *n* **1** : SAWHORSE **2** *slang* : a 10-dollar bill [sense 2 probably from the resemblance of the Roman numeral X to the ends of a sawhorse]

saw·dust \'sȯ-,dəst\ *n* : dust or fine particles of wood made by a saw in cutting

saw–edged \'sȯ-'ejd\ *adj* : having a toothed or nicked edge

sawed–off \'sȯ-,dȯf\ *adj* **1** : having an end sawed off ⟨a *sawed-off* shotgun⟩ **2** : being of less than average height

saw·fish \'sȯ-,fish\ *n* : any of several mostly tropical rays with a long flattened snout bearing a row of stout toothlike structures along each edge

saw·fly \-,flī\ *n* : any of numerous insects that are related to the wasps and bees and usually have in the female a pair of organs for making slits in leaves or stems into which eggs are laid

saw grass *n* : a sedge with sharply toothed leaves

saw·horse \'sȯ-,hȯrs\ *n* : a frame or rack on which wood is rested while being sawed by hand

saw·log \-,lȯg, -,läg\ *n* : a log fit for sawing into lumber

saw·mill \-,mil\ *n* : a mill or machine for sawing logs

saw·tim·ber \'sȯ-,tim-bər\ *n* : timber suitable for sawing into lumber

saw·tooth \-,tüth\ *adj* : SAW-TOOTHED

sawhorse

saxophone

saw–toothed \-'tütht\ *adj* : having an edge or outline like the teeth of a saw

saw–whet \-,hwet, -,wet\ *n* : a very small harsh-voiced North American owl largely dark brown above and white beneath [from the resemblance of its cry to the sound of filing a saw]

saw·yer \'sȯ-yər, 'sȯi-ər\ *n* **1** : one that saws timber **2** : any of several large beetles whose larvae bore large holes in timber

sax \'saks\ *n* : SAXOPHONE

sax·horn \'saks-,hȯrn\ *n* : one of a family of valved brass instruments having a conical tube, oval shape, and cup-shaped mouthpiece [Antoine J. *Sax,* died 1894, Belgian maker of musical instruments]

sax·i·frage \'sak-sə-frij, -,frāj\ *n* : any of a genus of plants with showy 5-parted flowers and usually with leaves growing in tufts close to the ground [Middle French, from Late Latin *saxifraga,* derived from Latin *saxum* "rock" + *frangere* "to break"]

Sax·on \'sak-sən\ *n* **1** : a member of a Germanic people invading and conquering England with the Angles and Jutes in the 5th century A. D. and merging with them to form the Anglo-Saxon people **2** : a native or inhabitant of Saxony [Late Latin *Saxones* "Saxons", of Germanic origin] — **Saxon** *adj*

sax·o·phone \'sak-sə-,fōn\ *n* : a wind instrument with reed mouthpiece, curved conical metal tube, and finger keys [French, from Antoine J. *Sax,* died 1894, Belgian maker of musical instruments] — **sax·o·phon·ic** \,sak-sə-'fän-ik\ *adj* — **sax·o·phon·ist** \'sak-sə-,fō-nəst\ *n*

sax·tu·ba \'saks-'tü-bə, -'tyü-\ *n* : a bass saxhorn

¹**say** \'sā\ *vt* **said** \'sed\; **say·ing** \'sā-ing\; **says** \'sez\ **1 a** : to express in words : STATE **b** : to state as opinion or belief : DECLARE **2 a** : UTTER 1b, PRONOUNCE **b** : RECITE, REPEAT ⟨*said* their prayers⟩ **3** : INDICATE, SHOW ⟨the clock *says* five minutes after twelve⟩ [Old English *secgan*] — **say·er** \'sā-ər\ *n*

²**say** *n* **1** : an expression of opinion ⟨had my *say*⟩ **2** : the power to decide or help decide

³**say** *adv* **1** : ABOUT, APPROXIMATELY ⟨the property is worth, *say,* four million dollars⟩ **2** : for example : AS ⟨if we compress any gas, *say* oxygen⟩

say·ing \'sā-ing\ *n* : something frequently said : PROVERB

say–so \'sā-,sō\ *n* **1 a** : one's unsupported word or assurance **b** : an authoritative pronouncement ⟨acted on the doctor's *say-so*⟩ **2** : a right of final decision : AUTHORITY

¹**scab** \'skab\ *n* **1** : scabies of domestic animals **2** : a crust of hardened blood and serum over a wound **3 a** : a contemptible person **b** : a worker who takes the place of a striking worker **4** : any of various plant diseases characterized by crusted spots [of Scandinavian origin]

²**scab** *vi* **scabbed; scab·bing** **1** : to become covered with a scab **2** : to act as a scab

scab·bard \'skab-ərd\ *n* : a sheath for a sword, dagger, or bayonet [Anglo-French *escauberz* "scabbards", of Germanic origin] — **scabbard** *vt*

scab·by \'skab-ē\ *adj* **scab·bi·er; -est** **1 a** : covered with or full of scabs ⟨*scabby* skin⟩ **b** : diseased with scab ⟨a *scabby* animal⟩ ⟨*scabby* potatoes⟩ **2** : MEAN, CONTEMPTIBLE ⟨a *scabby* trick⟩

sca·bies \'skā-bēz\ *n, pl* **scabies** : an itch or mange caused by mites living as parasites under the skin [Latin]

sca·brous \'skab-rəs *also* 'skāb-\ *adj* **1** : DIFFICULT, KNOTTY ⟨a *scabrous* problem⟩ **2** : rough to the touch ⟨a *scabrous* leaf⟩ **3** : unpleasant, repulsive, or reprehensible in some way [Latin *scaber* "rough, scurfy"] — **sca·brous·ly** *adv* — **sca·brous·ness** *n*

¹**scad** \'skad\ *n, pl* **scad** *also* **scads** : any of several mostly small sea fishes related to the pompanos [origin unknown]

²scad *n* **1** : a large number or quantity **2** *pl* : a great abundance ⟨*scads* of money⟩ [probably from English dialect *scald* "a multitude", from ²*scald*]

scaf·fold \'skaf-əld *also* -ˌōld\ *n* **1 a** : a temporary or movable platform for workmen **b** : a platform on which a criminal is executed (as by hanging) **2** : a supporting framework [Old North French *escafaut*]

scaf·fold·ing \-ing\ *n* : a system of scaffolds; *also* : materials for scaffolds

¹sca·lar \'skā-lər, -ˌlär\ *adj* **1** : arranged like a ladder : GRADUATED ⟨a *scalar* chain of authority⟩ **2** : capable of being represented by a point on a scale **3** : of, relating to, or being a scalar or a scalar product [Latin *scalaris*, from *scalae* "stairs, ladders"]

²scalar *n* **1** : a real number rather than a vector **2** : a quantity (as mass or time) that has a magnitude describable by a real number but no direction

sca·la·re \skə-'laər-ē, -'leər-, -'lär-\ *n* : a black and silver laterally compressed South American fish popular in aquariums [derived from Latin *scalaris* "scalar"; from the barred pattern on its body]

scalar product *n* : a real number that is the product of the lengths of two vectors and the cosine of the angle between them

scal·a·wag *or* **scal·ly·wag** \'skal-i-ˌwag\ *n* **1** : RASCAL 1, SCAMP **2** : a white Southerner acting as a Republican in the time of reconstruction after the Civil War [origin unknown]

¹scald \'skȯld\ *vt* **1** : to burn with or as if with hot liquid or steam **2 a** : to subject to the action of boiling water or steam ⟨*scald* dishes⟩ **b** : to bring to a temperature just below the boiling point ⟨*scald* milk⟩ **3** : SCORCH 1a [Old North French *escalder,* from Late Latin *excaldare* "to wash in warm water", from Latin *ex-* + *calida, calda* "warm water", from *calidus* "warm"]

²scald *n* **1** : an injury to the body caused by scalding **2** : an act or process of scalding **3** : a plant disease marked especially by discoloration suggesting injury by heat

scald·ing \'skȯl-ding\ *adj* **1** : causing the sensation of scalding or burning **2** : BOILING ⟨*scalding* water⟩ **3** : very hot : SCORCHING ⟨the *scalding* sun⟩ **4** : SCATHING, CUTTING ⟨a *scalding* editorial⟩

¹scale \'skāl\ *n* **1 a** : either pan of a balance **b** : BALANCE — usually used in pl. **2** : a device for weighing ⟨a bathroom *scale*⟩ [Old Norse *skāl* "bowl, scale of a balance"]

²scale *vb* **1** : to weigh in scales **2** : to have a specified weight

³scale *n* **1** : one of the small rigid flattened plates forming an outer covering on the body especially of a fish or reptile **2** : a small thin part or structure suggesting a fish scale: as **a** : a modified leaf covering a bud of a seed plant **b** : a small dry flake of skin ⟨dandruff *scales*⟩ **3** : SCALE INSECT **4** : a thin layer, coating, or incrustation forming especially on metal (as iron) ⟨boiler *scale*⟩ [Middle French *escale,* of Germanic origin] — **scaled** \'skāld\ *adj* — **scale·less** \'skāl-ləs\ *adj* — **scale·like** \'skāl-ˌlīk\ *adj*

⁴scale *vb* **1** : to remove scale or the scales from ⟨*scale* a boiler⟩ ⟨*scale* fish⟩ **2** : to take off in scales or thin layers **3** : to form scale on **4** : to come off in scales or shed scales : FLAKE **5** : to become encrusted with scale **6** : to throw (a flat object) and cause to sail in the air or skip on the water ⟨*scaling* cards into a hat⟩

⁵scale *n* **1** : something graduated especially when used as a measure or rule: as **a** : a series of spaces marked by lines and used to measure distances or to register something (as the height of the mercury in a thermometer) **b** : a divided line on a map or chart indicating the length (as an inch) used to represent a larger unit of measure (as a mile) **c** : an instrument consisting of a strip (as of wood, plastic, or metal) with one or more sets of spaces graduated and numbered on its surface for measuring or laying off distances or dimensions **2** : a basis for a system of numbering ⟨the deci-

mal *scale*⟩ **3** : a graduated series ⟨the *scale* of prices⟩ **4** : the size of a picture, plan, or model of a thing in proportion to the size of the thing itself **5** : relative size or degree ⟨do things on a large *scale*⟩ **6** : a standard by which something can be measured or judged **7** : a graduated series of tones going up or down in pitch [Late Latin *scala* "ladder, staircase", from Latin *scalae,* pl., "stairs, ladder"]

⁶scale *vb* **1** : to climb by or as if by means of a ladder or rope **2 a** : to arrange in a graduated series ⟨*scale* a test⟩ **b** : to measure by or as if by a scale **c** : to make, regulate, or estimate according to a rate or standard ⟨*scale* down a budget⟩ SYN see ASCEND

scale insect *n* : any of numerous small insects that are related to the plant lice, include many destructive plant pests, and have winged males, scale-covered females usually structurally degenerate and permanently attached to the host plant, and young that suck the juices of plants

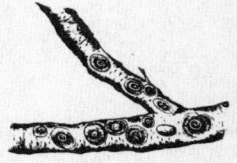

scale insect

scale leaf *n* : a modified usually small and scaly leaf (as of a cypress)

sca·lene \'skā-ˌlēn, skā-'\ *adj* : having the sides unequal ⟨a *scalene* triangle⟩ [Late Latin *scalenus,* from Greek *skalēnos,* literally, "uneven"]

scale·pan \'skāl-ˌpan\ *n* : a pan of a scale for weighing

scal·er \'skā-lər\ *n* : one that scales

scal·lion \'skal-yən\ *n* : a young onion pulled before the bulb has enlarged [Anglo-French *scalun,* derived from Latin *ascalonia caepa* "onion of Ascalon (a seaport in Palestine)"]

¹scal·lop \'skäl-əp, 'skal-\ *n* **1 a** : any of a family of marine bivalve mollusks with the shell radially ribbed **b** : the adductor muscle of a scallop as an article of food **2** : a scallop-shell valve or a similarly shaped dish used for baking **3** : one of a continuous series of circle segments or angular projections forming a border [Middle French *escalope* "shell", of Germanic origin]

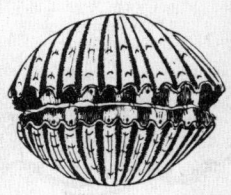

¹scallop 1a

²scallop *or* **es·cal·lop** \is-'käl-əp, -'kal-\ *vt* **1** : to bake in a sauce usually covered with seasoned bread or cracker crumbs ⟨*scalloped* potatoes⟩ **2** : to shape, cut, or finish in scallops — **scal·lop·er** *n*

scal·ly·wag *variant of* SCALAWAG

¹scalp \'skalp\ *n* **1** : the part of the skin and flesh of the head usually covered with hair **2** : a part of the human scalp cut or torn from an enemy as a token of victory [of Scandinavian origin]

²scalp *vt* **1 a** : to deprive of the scalp **b** : to remove an upper or better part from **2 a** : to buy and sell so as to make small quick profits **b** : to buy and resell at greatly increased prices ⟨*scalp* theater tickets⟩ — **scalp·er** *n*

scal·pel \'skal-pəl *also* skal-'pel\ *n* : a small straight thin-bladed knife used especially in surgery [Latin *scalpellum* "small knife", from *scalprum* "chisel, knife", from *scalpere* "to carve"]

scalp lock *n* : a long tuft of hair on the crown of the otherwise shaved head of a warrior of some American Indian tribes

scaly \'skā-lē\ *adj* **scal·i·er; -est** **1 a** : covered with, composed of, or rich in scale or scales **b** : FLAKY 2 **2** : infested with scale insects ⟨*scaly* fruit⟩ — **scal·i·ness** *n*

¹scamp \'skamp\ *n* **1** : RASCAL 1, ROGUE **2** : an impish or playful young person [obsolete *scamp* "to roam about idly"]

²scamp *vt* : to perform in a hasty, neglectful, or imperfect manner : SKIMP ⟨*scamp* one's work⟩ [perhaps of Scandinavian origin]

scam·per \'skam-pər\ *vi* **scam·pered; scam·per·ing** \-pə-ring, -pring\ : to run nimbly and playfully [perhaps from obsolete Dutch *schampen* "to flee", from Middle French *escamper,* derived from Latin *ex-* + *campus* "field"] — **scamper** *n*

scan \'skan\ *vb* **scanned; scan·ning** **1 a** : to read or mark so as to show metrical structure **b** : to conform to a metrical pattern **2 a** : to examine intensively **b** : to make a wide sweeping search of ⟨a fire lookout *scan-*

\ə\ abut	\ng\ sing
\ər\ further	\ō\ bone
\a\ mat	\ȯ\ saw
\ā\ take	\ȯi\ coin
\ä\ cot, cart	\th\ thin
\aú\ out	\th\ this
\ch\ chin	\ü\ food
\e\ pet	\ú\ foot
\ē\ easy	\y\ yet
\g\ go	\yü\ few
\i\ tip	\yú\ cure
\ī\ life	\zh\ vision
\j\ job	

ning the hills⟩ **c** : to look through or over hastily ⟨*scan* the newspaper⟩ **3** : to move across in successive lines to form an image on a cathode-ray tube ⟨the electron beam *scans* the face of the picture tube⟩ [Late Latin *scandere*, from Latin, "to climb"] **SYN** see **SCRUTINIZE** — **scan** *n*

scan·dal \'skan-dl\ *n* **1** : an offense against faith or morals that causes another to sin **2** : loss of or damage to reputation caused by actual or apparent violation of morality or propriety : **DISGRACE** ⟨to the *scandal* of the school⟩ **3 a** : something that offends propriety or accepted moral standards or disgraces those associated with it ⟨the slum is a *scandal*⟩ **b** : a person whose conduct offends propriety or morality **4** : malicious or defamatory gossip ⟨untouched by *scandal*⟩ [Late Latin *scandalum* "stumbling block, offense", from Greek *skandalon*]

scan·dal·ize \'skan-də-ˌlīz\ *vt* **1** : to speak falsely or maliciously of : **MALIGN** **2** : to offend the moral sense of : **SHOCK** ⟨their actions *scandalized* the neighbors⟩ — **scan·dal·iza·tion** *n* — **scan·dal·iz·er** *n*

scan·dal·mon·ger \'skan-dl-ˌməng-gər, -ˌmäng-\ *n* : a person who spreads scandal

scan·dal·ous \'skan-də-ləs, -dləs\ *adj* **1** : **DEFAMATORY** ⟨a *scandalous* story⟩ **2** : offensive to propriety or morality : **SHOCKING** ⟨*scandalous* behavior⟩ — **scan·dal·ous·ly** *adv* — **scan·dal·ous·ness** *n*

scandal sheet *n* : a newspaper or periodical dealing to a large extent in scandal and gossip

Scan·di·na·vian \ˌskan-də-'nā-vē-ən, -vyən\ *n* **1 a** : a native or inhabitant of Scandinavia **b** : a person of Scandinavian descent **2** : the Germanic languages of the Scandinavian peoples including Icelandic, Norwegian, Swedish, and Danish — **Scandinavian** *adj*

scan·di·um \'skan-dē-əm\ *n* : a silvery white metallic chemical element — see **ELEMENT** table [New Latin, from Latin *Scandia*, southern part of the Scandinavian peninsula]

scan·ner \'skan-ər\ *n* : one that scans: as **a** : a device that senses recorded information **b** : a device used for scanning (as in television) or for making a series of images of parts of the human body

scan·sion \'skan-chən\ *n* : the analysis of verse to show its meter [Late Latin *scansio*, from *scandere* "to scan"]

¹scant \'skant\ *adj* **1** *dialect* : excessively frugal : **PARSIMONIOUS** **2 a** : barely or scarcely sufficient ⟨paid *scant* attention to me⟩; *esp* : not quite coming up to a stated measure ⟨a *scant* cup of milk⟩ **b** : lacking in amplitude or quantity : **MEAGER, SCANTY** ⟨a *scant* amount⟩ **3** : having a small or insufficient supply ⟨*scant* of breath⟩ [Old Norse *skamt*, neuter of *skammr* "short"] — **scant·ly** *adv* — **scant·ness** *n*

²scant *adv, dialect* : **SCARCELY, HARDLY**

³scant *vt* **1** : to provide with a meager or inadequate portion or share : **STINT** **2** : to make small, narrow, or meager : **SKIMP** **3** : to provide an incomplete supply of ⟨*scant* one's efforts⟩ **4** : to give scant attention to : **SLIGHT** ⟨a subject *scanted* in textbooks⟩

scant·ling \'skant-ling, -lən\ *n* : a small piece of lumber; *esp* : one of the upright pieces in the frame of a house [Middle English *scantilon*, literally, "mason's or carpenter's gauge", from Old North French *escantillon*]

scanty \'skant-ē\ *adj* **scant·i·er; -est** **1** : barely enough **2** : less than normal or needed : **INSUFFICIENT SYN** see **MEAGER** — **scant·i·ly** \'skant-l-ē\ *adv* — **scant·i·ness** \'skant-ē-nəs\ *n*

¹scape \'skāp\ *vb* : **ESCAPE**

²scape *n* **1** : a leafless flower stalk (as in the tulip) that begins at or beneath the surface of the ground **2** : the shaft of an animal part (as an antenna or a feather) [Latin *scapus* "shaft, stalk"]

-scape \ˌskāp\ *n combining form* : a (specified) type of scene; *also* : a pictorial representation of (such a scene) ⟨moon*scape*⟩ [*landscape*]

scarab 1

scape·goat \'skāp-ˌgōt\ *n* **1** : a goat upon whose head are symbolically placed the sins of the people after which he is sent into the wilderness in the biblical ceremony for Yom Kippur **2** : a person or thing bearing the blame for others [¹*scape*]

scape·grace \-ˌgrās\ *n* : an incorrigible rascal

scap·u·la \'skap-yə-lə\ *n, pl* **-lae** \-ˌlē, -ˌlī\ *or* **-las** : **SHOULDER BLADE** [Latin, "shoulder, shoulder blade"]

¹scap·u·lar \'skap-yə-lər\ *n* **1 a** : a long wide band of cloth with an opening for the head worn front and back over the shoulders as part of a monastic habit **b** : a pair of small cloth squares joined by shoulder tapes and worn under the clothing on the breast and back as a sacramental and often also as a badge of a third order or confraternity **2** : one of the feathers covering the base of a bird's wing [Late Latin *scapulare*, from Latin *scapula* "shoulder"]

²scapular *adj* : of or relating to the shoulder or the shoulder blade

scapular medal *n* : a medal worn in place of a sacramental scapular

¹scar \'skär\ *n* **1** : an isolated or protruding rock **2** : a steep rocky eminence : a bare place on the side of a mountain [Old Norse *sker* "skerry"]

²scar *n* **1 a** : a mark remaining after injured tissue has healed **b** : a mark resembling a scar and usually marking the former point of attachment of some other structure; *esp* : one on a stem where a leaf or fruit has separated **2** : a lasting moral or emotional injury [Middle French *escare* "scab", from Late Latin *eschara*, from Greek, "hearth, scab"] — **scar·less** \-ləs\ *adj*

³scar *vb* **scarred; scar·ring** *vb* **1** : to mark with or form a scar **2** : to do lasting injury to **3** : to become scarred

scar·ab \'skar-əb\ *n* **1** : a large black or nearly black dung beetle regarded by the ancient Egyptians as symbolic of resurrection and immortality; *also* : any of various related beetles **2** : an ornament or a gem made to represent a scarab [Middle French *scarabee*, from Latin *scarabaeus*]

scar·a·mouch *or* **scar·a·mouche** \'skar-ə-ˌmüsh, -ˌmüch, -ˌmaùch\ *n* **1** : a cowardly buffoon **2** : **RASCAL, SCAMP** [French *Scaramouche*, a stock character in Italian comedy, from Italian *Scaramuccia*]

¹scarce \'skeərs, 'skaərs\ *adj* : deficient in quantity or number : not plentiful or abundant [Old North French *escars*, derived from Latin *excerpere* "to pluck out, excerpt"] — **scarce·ness** *n*

²scarce *adv* : **SCARCELY, HARDLY**

scarce·ly \'sker-slē, 'skar-\ *adv* **1 a** : only just ⟨had *scarcely* got there when they started⟩ **b** : almost not ⟨*scarcely* ever goes out⟩ **2 a** : certainly not ⟨could *scarcely* tell them they were wrong⟩ **b** : probably not ⟨could *scarcely* have found a neater solution⟩

scar·ci·ty \'sker-sət-ē, 'skar-\ *n, pl* **-ties** : the quality or condition of being scarce

¹scare \'skeər, 'skaər\ *vb* **1** : to frighten suddenly : **ALARM** **2** : to become frightened ⟨they *scare* easily⟩ [Old Norse *skirra*, from *skjarr* "shy, timid"] — **scar·er** *n*

²scare *n* **1** : a sudden fright **2** : a widespread state of alarm : **PANIC**

scare·crow \'skeər-ˌkrō, 'skaər-\ *n* **1 a** : an object usually suggesting a human figure that is set up to scare birds away from crops **b** : something frightening but harmless **2** : a skinny or ragged person

scare·head \-ˌhed\ *n* : a big, sensational, or alarming newspaper headline

scare·mon·ger \-ˌməng-gər, -ˌmäng-\ *n* : **ALARMIST**

scare up *vt* : to bring to light or get together with considerable labor or difficulty ⟨managed to *scare up* the money⟩

¹scarf \'skärf\ *n, pl* **scarves** \'skärvz\ *or* **scarfs** \'skärfs\ **1** : a broad band (as of cloth) worn about the shoulders, around the neck, over the head, or about the waist **2** : TIPPET 3 **3** : RUNNER 6 [Old North French *es-carpe* "sash, sling"]

²scarf *n* **1** : either of the ends that fit together to form a scarf joint **2** : a joint made by beveling, halving, or notching two pieces to correspond and lapping and bolting them [Middle English *skarf*]

³scarf *or* **scarph** \'skärf\ *vt* : to unite by a scarf joint

scarf·pin \'skärf-,pin\ *n* : TIEPIN

scarf·skin \'skärf-,skin\ *n* : EPIDERMIS 1, CUTICLE; *esp* : that about the base of a nail [¹*scarf*]

scar·i·fy \'skar-ə-,fī, 'sker-\ *vt* **-fied; -fy·ing 1** : to make scratches or small cuts in ⟨*scarify* skin for vaccination⟩ ⟨*scarify* seeds to help them germinate⟩ **2** : to lacerate the feelings of : FLAY [Middle French *scarifier*, from Late Latin *scarificare*, from Latin *scarifare*, from Greek *skariphasthai* "to scratch an outline, sketch"] — **scar·i·fi·ca·tion** \,skar-ə-fə-'kā-shən, ,sker-\ *n* — **scar·i·fi·er** \'skar-ə-,fī-ər, 'sker-, -,fīr\ *n*

scar·la·ti·na \,skär-lə-'tē-nə\ *n* : a usually mild scarlet fever [New Latin, from Medieval Latin *scarlata* "scarlet"] — **scar·la·ti·nal** \-'tēn-l\ *adj*

¹scar·let \'skär-lət\ *n* **1** : scarlet cloth or clothes **2** : a bright red [Medieval Latin *scarlata*, from Persian *saqalāt*, a kind of rich cloth]

²scarlet *adj* : bright red

scarlet fever *n* : an acute contagious disease caused by a blood-attacking streptococcus and marked by fever, inflammation of the nose, throat, and mouth, and a red rash

scarlet pimpernel *n* : a common pimpernel having scarlet, white, or purplish flowers that close in cloudy weather

scarlet runner *n* : a tropical American high-climbing bean with large bright red flowers and red-and-black seeds grown widely as an ornamental and in Great Britain as a preferred table bean

scarlet sage *n* : any of several red-flowered salvias

scarlet tanager *n* : a common American tanager of which the male is scarlet with black wings and the female and young are chiefly olive

scarp \'skärp\ *n* **1** : a line of cliffs produced by faulting or erosion **2** : a low steep slope along a beach caused by wave erosion [Italian *scarpa*] — **scarped** \'skärpt\ *adj*

scar tissue *n* : connective tissue forming a bodily scar

scary *also* **scar·ey** \'skeər-ē, 'skaər-\ *adj* **scar·i·er; -est 1** : causing fright : ALARMING ⟨a *scary* movie⟩ **2** : easily scared : TIMID **3** : marked by fear ⟨a *scary* feeling⟩

¹scat \'skat\ *vi* **scat·ted; scat·ting 1** : to go away quickly — often used interjectionally to drive away an animal (as a cat) **2** : to move fast : SCOOT [*scat*, interj. used to drive away a cat]

²scat *n* : jazz singing with nonsense syllables [perhaps imitative]

³scat *vi* **scat·ted; scat·ting** : to improvise nonsense syllables to an instrumental accompaniment : sing scat

¹scathe \'skāth\ *n* : HARM, INJURY [Old Norse *skathi*] — **scathe·less** \-ləs\ *adj*

²scathe *vt* **1** : to do harm to; *esp* : to injure by fire **2** : to assail with withering denunciation

scath·ing \'skā-thing\ *adj* : bitterly severe ⟨a *scathing* rebuke⟩ — **scath·ing·ly** \-thing-lē\ *adv*

sca·tol·o·gy \skə-'täl-ə-jē, ska-\ *n* : interest in or treatment of obscene matters especially in literature [Greek *skat-*, *skōr* "dung"] — **scat·o·log·i·cal** \,skat-l-'äj-i-kəl\ *adj*

scat·ter \'skat-ər\ *vb* **1** : to cause to separate widely **2** : to distribute irregularly **3** : to sow broadcast : STREW **4** : to diffuse, disperse, or reflect (a beam of radiation) in a random manner **5** : to separate from each other and go in various directions ⟨we all *scattered* after graduation⟩ **6** : to occur or fall irregularly or at random [Middle English *scateren*] — **scat·ter·er** \-ər-ər\ *n* □ SYN SCATTER, DISPERSE, DISPEL, DISSIPATE mean to cause to separate or break up. SCATTER implies forcefully driving parts or units irregularly in many directions; DISPERSE implies a wider separation and complete breaking up of mass or group; DISPEL stresses a driving away or getting rid of as if by scattering; DISSIPATE stresses complete disintegration or dissolution and final disappearance.

scat·ter·brain \-,brān\ *n* : a giddy heedless person incapable of concentration — **scat·ter·brained** \-,brānd\ *adj*

scat·tered \'skat-ərd\ *adj* **1** : not closely associated or organized ⟨*scattered* thoughts⟩ **2** : separated by or occurring at wide irregular intervals ⟨*scattered* showers⟩ **3** : spread over a wide area ⟨a *scattered* settlement⟩ SYN see INFREQUENT

¹scat·ter·ing \'skat-ə-ring\ *n* **1** : an act or process in which something scatters or is scattered **2** : something scattered; *esp* : a small number or quantity interspersed here and there ⟨a *scattering* of visitors⟩

²scattering *adj* **1** : going in various directions **2** : found or placed far apart and in no order — **scat·ter·ing·ly** *adv*

scatter pin *n* : a small pin used as jewelry and worn usually in groups of two or more on a woman's dress

scatter rug *n* : a rug of such a size that several can be used (as to fill vacant places) in a room

scaup \'skȯp\ *n, pl* **scaup** *or* **scaups** : any of several diving ducks [perhaps from *scalp* "bed of shellfish"; from its fondness for shellfish]

scav·enge \'skav-inj\ *vb* **1** : to remove dirt or refuse from an area **2** : to salvage (usable material) from what has been discarded [back-formation from *scavenger*]

scav·en·ger \'skav-ən-jer\ *n* **1** *chiefly British* : a person employed to remove dirt and refuse from streets **2** : one that scavenges **3** : an organism (as a vulture) that feeds habitually on refuse or carrion [Middle English *skawager* "collector of a toll on goods sold by nonresident merchants", from *skawage* "toll on goods sold by nonresident merchants", from Old North French *escauwage* "inspection"] □ ORIGIN In the 14th, 15th, and 16th centuries many English towns and cities levied a tax on goods shown for sale by nonresident merchants in order to put outsiders at a disadvantage in their trade in comparison with local merchants. Middle English *skawage*, the name for this tax, was borrowed from Old North French *escauwage*, "inspection", a word of Germanic origin, related to English *show*. The *skawagers* (or later *scavengers*) of London were officers who collected the *skawage*. The responsibility for keeping the streets clean later fell on their shoulders as well. Now anyone who collects junk is a *scavenger*.

scavenger hunt *n* : a party contest in which players are sent out usually in pairs to obtain without buying unusual objects within a time limit

sce·nar·io \sə-'nar-ē-,ō, -'ner-\ *n, pl* **-i·os 1 a** : an outline or synopsis of a play **b** : the libretto of an opera **2** : SCREENPLAY **3** : an account or synopsis of a projected course of action or events [Italian, from Latin *scaenarium*, from *scaena*, *scena* "stage, scene"]

sce·nar·ist \-'nar-əst, -'ner-\ *n* : a writer of scenarios

send \'send\ *n* **1** : the lift of a wave **2** : the upward movement of a pitching ship [perhaps short for *ascend*]

scene \'sēn\ *n* **1** : one of the subdivisions of a play: as **a** : a division of an act presenting continuous action in one place **b** : a single situation or unit of dialogue in a play **c** : a motion picture or television episode or sequence **2 a** : a stage setting ⟨change *scenes*⟩ **b** : a view or sight having pictorial quality ⟨a winter *scene*⟩ **3** : the place of an occurrence or action : LOCALE ⟨*scene* of a riot⟩ **4** : an exhibition of anger or indecorous behavior ⟨create a *scene*⟩ [Middle French, "stage", from Latin *scena* "stage, scene", from Greek *skēnē* "temporary shelter, tent, building forming the background for

\ə\ abut		\ng\ sing
\ər\ **further**		\ō\ bone
\a\ mat		\o\ saw
\ā\ take		\oi\ coin
\ä\ cot, cart		\th\ thin
\au̇\ out		\th\ this
\ch\ chin		\ü\ food
\e\ pet		\u̇\ foot
\ē\ easy		\y\ yet
\g\ go		\yü\ few
\i\ tip		\yu̇\ cure
\ī\ life		\zh\ vision
\j\ job		

a dramatic performance, stage''] — **behind the scenes**
1 : out of public view : in secret 2 : in a position to see
or control the hidden workings ⟨the person *behind the
scenes*⟩

scen·ery \'sēn-rē, -ə-rē\ *n* 1 : the painted scenes or
hangings and accessories used on a theater stage 2 : a
picturesque view or landscape ⟨mountain *scenery*⟩

scene·shift·er \'sēn-,shif-tər\ *n* : a worker who moves
the scenes in a theater

scene-steal·er \-,stē-lər\ *n* : an actor who is not the intended center of attraction but who draws attention to
himself

sce·nic \'sē-nik\ *adj* 1 : of or relating to the stage, a
stage setting, or stage representation ⟨*scenic* effects⟩
2 : of, relating to, or marked by natural scenery ⟨a *scenic* route⟩ 3 : representing graphically an action,
event, or episode ⟨a *scenic* frieze⟩ — **sce·ni·cal** \-ni-
kəl\ *adj* — **sce·ni·cal·ly** \-ni-kə-lē, -klē\ *adv*

scenic railway *n* : a miniature railway (as in an amusement park) with artificial scenery along the way

¹**scent** \'sent\ *n* 1 **a** : an odor left by an animal on a
surface passed over; *also* : a course of pursuit or discovery ⟨throw one off the *scent*⟩ **b** : a characteristic or
particular and usually agreeable odor 2 **a** : sense of
smell ⟨a keen *scent*⟩ **b** : power of detection ⟨a *scent*
for heresy⟩ 3 : INKLING, INTIMATION ⟨a *scent* of trouble⟩
4 : PERFUME 2 5 : bits of paper dropped in the game of
hare and hounds 6 : an odorous lure for an animal SYN
SEE SMELL

²**scent** *vt* 1 **a** : SMELL ⟨the dog *scented* a rabbit⟩ **b** : to get
or have an inkling of ⟨*scent* trouble⟩ 2 : to imbue or
fill with odor ⟨*scent* a handkerchief⟩ [Middle French
sentir "to feel, smell", from Latin *sentire* "to perceive, feel"]

scent·ed *adj* : having scent; *esp* : PERFUMED

scent·less \'sent-ləs\ *adj* : lacking scent; *esp* : ODORLESS
— **scent·less·ness** *n*

scep·ter \'sep-tər\ *n* 1 : a staff or baton borne by a sovereign as an emblem of authority 2 : royal or imperial
authority : SOVEREIGNTY [Old French *ceptre*, from Latin
sceptrum, from Greek *skēptron*] — **scep·tered**
\-tərd\ *adj*

scep·tic \'skep-tik\ *variant of* SKEPTIC

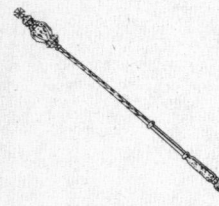

scepter 1

¹**sched·ule** \'skej-ül, -əl, *Canadian also* 'shej-, *British
usually* 'shed-yül\ *n* 1 **a** : a written or printed list,
catalog, or inventory **b** : TIMETABLE 2 : PROGRAM 3,
AGENDA [Middle French *cedule* "slip of paper, note",
from Late Latin *schedula* "slip of paper", from Latin
scheda "sheet of papyrus"]

²**schedule** *vt* 1 : to place in or as if in a schedule ⟨*schedule* a meeting⟩ 2 : to make a schedule of

schee·lite \'shā-,līt\ *n* : a mineral CaWO₄ that is a souce
of tungsten and its compounds [German *scheelit*, from
Karl W. *Scheele*, died 1786, Swedish chemist]

sche·mat·ic \ski-'mat-ik\ *adj* : of, relating to, or forming a scheme, plan, or diagram : DIAGRAMMATIC —
scematic *n* — **sche·mat·i·cal·ly** \-'mat-i-kə-lē, -klē\
adv

sche·ma·tize \'skē-mə-,tīz\ *vt* 1 : to form or form into a
scheme or systematic arrangement 2 : to express or
depict schematically — **sche·ma·ti·za·tion** \,skē-mət-
ə-'zā-shən\ *n*

¹**scheme** \'skēm\ *n* 1 : a graphic sketch or outline 2 : a
concise statement or table 3 : a plan or program of
action; *esp* : a crafty or secret one 4 : a systematic or
organized design ⟨the color *scheme* of a room⟩ ⟨their
whole *scheme* of life⟩ [Latin *schemat-*, *schema* "arrangement, figure", from Greek *schēmat-*, *schēma*,
from *echein* "to have, hold, be in (such) a position"]
SYN SEE PLAN

²**scheme** *vb* 1 : to form a scheme for 2 : to form plans;
also : to engage in intrigue : PLOT — **schem·er** *n*

schem·ing *adj* : given to forming schemes; *esp* :
shrewdly devious and intriguing

scher·zan·do \skert-'sän-dō\ *adv or adj* : in a sportive
manner : PLAYFULLY — used as a direction in music
indicating style and tempo ⟨allegretto *scherzando*⟩
[Italian, from *scherzare* "to joke", of Germanic origin]

scher·zo \'skert-sō\ *n, pl* **scherzos** *or* **scher·zi** \-sē\ : a
sprightly humorous instrumental musical composition
or movement commonly in quick triple time [Italian,
literally, "joke", from *scherzare* "to joke"]

Schick test \'shik-\ *n* : a serological test to determine
whether an individual is susceptible to diphtheria
[Béla *Schick*, died 1967, American pediatrician]

schil·ler \'shil-ər\ *n* : a bronzy iridescent luster (as of a
mineral) [German]

schil·ling \'shil-ing\ *n* 1 : the basic monetary unit of
Austria 2 : a coin representing one schilling [German]

schism \'siz-əm, 'skiz-\ *n* 1 : DIVISION 5, SEPARATION;
also : lack of harmony : DISCORD 2 **a** : formal division
in or separation from a church or religious body **b** :
the religious offense of promoting schism [Middle
French *cisme*, from Late Latin *schismat-*, *schisma*,
from Greek, "cleft, division", from *schizein* "to
split"]

¹**schis·mat·ic** \siz-'mat-ik, skiz-\ *n* : one who creates or
takes part in schism

²**schismatic** *adj* : of, relating to, or guilty of schism —
schis·mat·i·cal \-'mat-i-kəl\ *adj* — **schis·mat·i·cal·ly**
\-i-kə-lē, -klē\ *adv*

schis·ma·tist \'siz-mət-əst, 'skiz-\ *n* : SCHISMATIC

schis·ma·tize \-mə-,tīz\ *vb* : to take part in or induce
into schism

schist \'shist\ *n* : a metamorphic crystalline rock that
can be split along approximately parallel planes
[French *schiste*, derived from Greek *schizein* "to
split"] — **schis·tose** \'shis-,tōs\ *adj*

schis·to·some \'shis-tə-,sōm\ *n* : any of various elongated trematode worms with the sexes separate that
mostly parasitize the blood vessels of birds and mammals and in man cause serious diseases [Greek *schistos*
"that may be split" (from *schizein* "to split") + *sōma*
"body"] — **schistosome** *adj*

schis·to·so·mi·a·sis \,shis-tə-sə-'mī-ə-səs\ *n, pl* **-a·ses**
\-ə-,sēz\ : infestation with or disease caused by
schistosomes

schiz- *or* **schizo-** *combining form* 1 : split : cleft ⟨*schizo*carp⟩ 2 : characterized by or involving cleavage
⟨*schizo*gony⟩ [Greek *schizein* "to split"]

schiz·o·carp \'skiz-ə-,kärp, 'skit-sə-\ *n* : a dry compound fruit that splits at maturity into closed one=
seeded carpels — **schiz·o·car·pous** \,skiz-ə-'kär-pəs,
,skit-sə-\ *adj*

schiz·oid \'skit-,sȯid\ *adj* : characterized by a personality exhibiting shyness, oversensitivity, daydreaming,
avoidance of competition or close relationships with
people, and often eccentric behavior — **schizoid** *n*

schiz·o·phre·nia \,skit-sə-'frē-nē-ə\ *n* : a psychosis
characterized by abnormalities of thought, emotion,
and behavior including distorted perception of reality,
withdrawal from social interaction, emotions inappropriate to the thoughts or behavior associated with
them, delusions, and hallucinations [New Latin, from
schiz- + Greek *phrēn* "mind"] — **schiz·o·phren·ic**
\-'fren-ik\ *adj or n*

schle·miel \shlə-'mēl\ *n* : an unlucky bungler : CHUMP
[Yiddish *shlumiel*]

schlock \'shläk\ *adj* : of low quality or value ⟨*schlock*
merchandise⟩ [Yiddish *shlak*, from *shlak* "curse,
cheap merchandise", literally, "blow", from Middle
High German *slag, slac*] — **schlock** *n*

schm- *or* **shm-** \shm\ *combining form* — used to form
a rhyming term of derision by replacing the initial
consonant or consonant cluster of a word or by preceding the initial vowel ⟨art, *schm*art, that's just
kitsch⟩ ⟨fancy, *schm*ancy, I prefer plain⟩ [Yiddish
shm-]

schmaltz *or* **schmalz** \'shmȯlts\ *n* : sentimental or florid music or art [Yiddish *shmalts*, literally, "rendered fat", from Middle High German *smalz*] — **schmaltzy** \'shmȯlt-sē\ *adj*

schmear \'shmiər\ *n* : a mass or body of similar things — usually used in the phrase *the whole schmear* [Yiddish *shmir* "smear", from *shmiren* "to smear", from Middle High German *smiren*]

schmuck *or* **shmuck** \'shmək\ *n* : a stupid, naive, or foolish person [Yiddish *shmok* "penis, fool", from German *schmuck* "adornment"]

schnapps \'shnaps\ *n, pl* **schnapps** : any of various distilled liquors; *esp* : strong Holland gin [German *schnaps*]

schnau·zer \'shnaut-sər, 'shnau̇-zər, 'snau̇-\ *n* : any of an old German breed of terriers with a long head, small ears, and wiry coat [German, from *schnauze* "snout"]

schnit·zel \'shnit-səl, 'snit-\ *n* : a seasoned and garnished veal cutlet [German, "cutlet, shaving, chip"]

schnoz·zle \'shnäz-əl, 'snäz-\ *n, slang* : NOSE [probably from Yiddish *shnoitsl*, from *shnoits* "snout", from German *schnauze*]

scho·la can·to·rum \,skō-lə-,kan-'tōr-əm, -'tȯr-\ *n, pl* **scho·lae cantorum** \-,lē-, -,lā-, -,lī-\ : a liturgical choir or choir school [Medieval Latin, "school of singers"]

schol·ar \'skäl-ər\ *n* **1** : one who attends a school or studies under a teacher : PUPIL **2 a** : one who has done advanced study in a special field **b** : a learned person **3** : a holder of a scholarship [Old English *scolere* and Old French *escoler*, from Medieval Latin *scholaris*, derived from Latin *schola* "school"]

schol·ar·ly \-ər-lē\ *adj* : characteristic of or suitable to learned persons : LEARNED, ACADEMIC

schol·ar·ship \-ər-,ship\ *n* **1** : financial aid given to a student (as by a college or foundation) to assist in the cost of education **2** : the character, qualities, or attainments of a scholar : LEARNING

¹scho·las·tic \skə-'las-tik\ *adj* **1 a** *often cap* : of or relating to Scholasticism ⟨*scholastic* theology⟩ **b** : excessively dogmatic or formal in instruction : PEDANTIC **2** : of or relating to schools or scholars [Latin *scholasticus* "of a school", from Greek *scholastikos*, derived from *scholē* "school"] — **scho·las·ti·cal·ly** \-ti-kə-lē, -klē\ *adv*

²scholastic *n* **1** *cap* : a Scholastic philosopher **2** : a person who prefers or uses scholastic or traditional methods (as in art)

scho·las·ti·cism \skə-'las-tə-,siz-əm\ *n* **1** *cap* : a dominant movement in medieval thought typically using methods of reasoning adapted from Aristotle to interpret systematically the dogmas of Christian faith **2** : close adherence to traditional teachings or methods (as of a school or sect)

scho·li·ast \'skō-lē-,ast, -lē-əst\ *n* : a maker of scholia : COMMENTATOR, ANNOTATOR [Middle Greek *scholiastēs*, derived from Greek *scholion* "scholium"]

scho·li·um \'skō-lē-əm\ *n, pl* **-lia** \-lē-ə\ *or* **-li·ums** **1** : a marginal annotation or comment (as on the text of a classic by an early grammarian) **2** : explanatory or elaborative matter appended to but not essential to a demonstration or a train of reasoning [New Latin, from Greek *scholion* "comment, scholium", from *scholē* "lecture, school"]

¹school \'skül\ *n* **1 a** : a place or establishment for teaching and learning ⟨a *school* of design⟩ ⟨public *schools*⟩ **b** : a faculty or division of an institution of higher learning devoted to teaching, study, and research in a particular field of knowledge ⟨graduate *school*⟩ ⟨the *school* of law⟩ **2** : the physical plant of a school : SCHOOLHOUSE **3 a** : the process of learning or being instructed at a school ⟨found *school* very difficult⟩ **b** : attendance at a school ⟨my last year of *school*⟩ **c** : a session of school ⟨missed *school* yesterday⟩ **d** : the students or the students and faculty of a school ⟨is pop-

ular with the whole *school*⟩ **4** : persons holding the same opinions and beliefs or accepting the same intellectual methods or leadership ⟨certain *schools* of thought⟩ [Old English *scōl*, from Latin *schola*, from Greek *scholē* "leisure, discussion, lecture, school"]

□ **ORIGIN** The original meaning of the Greek word *scholē*, from which our *school* is derived, was "leisure". To the Greeks it seemed only natural to occupy one's leisure with learning and thinking, and *scholē* came to mean "a place for learning" as well as "leisure". The Romans borrowed the Greek word as *schola* and employed Greek slaves as teachers. Christian missionaries later established schools throughout Europe, and Latin *schola* became Old English *scōl*.

²school *vt* : TEACH, TRAIN; *esp* : to drill in or habituate to something ⟨*school* oneself in patience⟩

³school *n* : a large number of aquatic animals of one kind (as bass) swimming together [Dutch *schole*]

⁴school *vi* : to swim or feed in a school ⟨bluefish are *schooling*⟩

school age *n* : the period of life during which a child is considered mentally and physically fit to attend school and is commonly required to do so by law

school·bag \'skül-,bag\ *n* : a bag for carrying schoolbooks and school supplies

school board *n* : a board in charge of local public schools

school·book \'skül-,bu̇k\ *n* : a school textbook

school·boy \-,bȯi\ *n* : a boy attending elementary or secondary school

school bus *n* : a vehicle used for transporting children to or from school or on activities connected with school

school·child \'skül-,chīld\ *n* : a child attending school

school·fel·low \-,fel-ō\ *n* : SCHOOLMATE

school·girl \-,gərl\ *n* : a girl attending elementary or secondary school

school·house \-,hȧu̇s\ *n* : a building used as a school

school·ing *n* **1** : instruction in school : EDUCATION **2** : the cost of instruction and maintenance at school **3** : the training of an animal and especially a horse to service

school·man \'skül-mən, -,man\ *n* : SCHOLASTIC 1

school·marm \-,märm, -,mäm\ *or* **school·ma'am** \-,mäm, -,mam\ *n* **1** : a woman schoolteacher especially in an old-type rural or small-town school **2** : a person who exhibits characteristics (as pedantry and priggishness) popularly attributed to schoolteachers [*school* + *marm*, alteration of *ma'am*]

school·mas·ter \-,mas-tər\ *n* : a male schoolteacher

school·mate \-,māt\ *n* : a school companion

school·mis·tress \-,mis-trəs\ *n* : a woman schoolteacher

school·room \-,rüm, -,ru̇m\ *n* : CLASSROOM

school·teach·er \-,tē-chər\ *n* : a person who teaches in a school

school·time \-,tīm\ *n* **1** : the time for beginning a session of school or during which school is held **2** : the period of life spent in school or in study — usually used in pl.

school·work \-,wərk\ *n* : lessons done in classes at school or assigned to be done at home

school·yard \-,yärd\ *n* : the playground of a school

schoo·ner \'skü-nər\ *n* **1** : a fore-and-aft rigged sailing vessel with two masts; *also* : any large fore-and-aft rigged ship **2** : a large tall glass (as for beer) **3** : PRAIRIE SCHOONER [origin unknown]

schot·tische \'shät-ish, shä-'tēsh\ *n* **1** : a round dance similar to but slower than the polka **2** : music for the schottische [German, from *schottisch* "Scottish"]

schuss \'shu̇s, 'shüs\ *n* **1** : a straight high-speed run on skis **2** : a straightaway downhill skiing course [German, literally, "shot"] — **schuss** *vb*

schwa \'shwä\ *n* **1** : an unstressed vowel that is the usual sound of the first and last vowels of the English

schnauzer

schooner 1

\ə\ abut	\ng\ sing
\ər\ further	\ō\ bone
\a\ mat	\ȯ\ saw
\ā\ take	\ȯi\ coin
\ä\ cot, cart	\th\ thin
\au̇\ out	\t͟h\ this
\ch\ chin	\ü\ food
\e\ pet	\u̇\ foot
\ē\ easy	\y\ yet
\g\ go	\yü\ few
\i\ tip	\yu̇\ cure
\ī\ life	\zh\ vision
\j\ job	

word *America* **2** : the symbol ə commonly used for a schwa and sometimes also for a similarly articulated stressed vowel (as in *cut*) [German, from Hebrew *shĕwā*]

sci·at·ic \sī-'at-ik\ *adj* **1** : of, relating to, or situated near the hip **2** : of, relating to, or caused by sciatica [Middle French *sciatique*, from Late Latin *sciaticus*, from Latin *ischiadicus* "of sciatica", from Greek *ischiadikos*, from *ischiad-*, *ischias* "sciatica", from *ischion* "ischium"]

sci·at·i·ca \sī-'at-i-kə\ *n* : pain along the course of a sciatic nerve especially in the back of a thigh; *also* : pain in or near the hips [Medieval Latin, from Late Latin *sciaticus* "sciatic"]

sciatic nerve *n* : either of the pair of largest nerves in the body each of which supplies a leg and the pelvic region and passes out of the pelvis and down the back of the thigh

sci·ence \'sī-əns\ *n* **1 a** : a department of systematized knowledge that is an object of study ⟨the *science* of theology⟩; *esp* : one of the natural sciences ⟨chemistry is a *science*⟩ **b** : something (as a sport or technique) that may be studied or learned like systematized knowledge **2** : knowledge covering general truths or the operation of general laws especially as obtained and tested through the scientific method [Middle French, from Latin *scientia*, from *sciens* "having knowledge", from *scire* "to know"]

science fiction *n* : fiction dealing with the impact of actual or imagined scientific developments upon society or individuals; *also* : futuristic fiction using an aspect of science as an essential component of the plot

sci·en·tial \sī-'en-chəl\ *adj* **1** : relating to or producing knowledge or science **2** : having efficient knowledge : CAPABLE

sci·en·tif·ic \,sī-ən-'tif-ik\ *adj* : of, relating to, or exhibiting the methods or principles of science — **sci·en·tif·i·cal·ly** \-'tif-i-kə-lē, -klē\ *adv*

scientific method *n* : principles and procedures for the systematic pursuit of knowledge involving the recognition and formulation of a problem, the collection of data through observation and experiment, and the formulation and testing of hypotheses

scientific notation *n* : the representation of numbers as the product of a decimal between 1 and 10 and a power of 10

sci·en·tism \'sī-ən-,tiz-əm\ *n* **1** : methods and attitudes typical of or attributed to the natural scientist **2** : an exaggerated trust in scientific and especially materialistic methods (as for seeking knowledge or solving problems)

sci·en·tist \'sī-ən-təst\ *n* **1** : one learned in science and especially natural science : a scientific investigator **2** *cap* : CHRISTIAN SCIENTIST

sci·en·tis·tic \,sī-ən-'tis-tik\ *adj* **1** : professedly scientific **2** : relating to or characterized by scientism

scil·la \'sil-ə, 'skil-ə\ *n* : any of a genus of Old World bulbous herbs of the lily family often grown for their clusters of pink, blue, or white flowers [Latin, "squill"]

scim·i·tar \'sim-ət-ər, -ə-,tär\ *n* : a curved sword used especially by Arabs and Turks [Italian *scimitarra*]

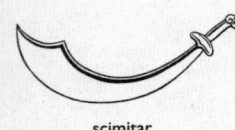

scimitar

scin·til·la \sin-'til-ə\ *n* : a very small amount : IOTA, TRACE [Latin]

scin·til·late \'sint-l-,āt\ *vi* **1** : to emit quick flashes of light; *also* : SPARKLE 1, TWINKLE **2** : to perform brilliantly [Latin *scintillare* "to sparkle", from *scintilla* "spark"] SYN see GLISTEN — **scin·til·lant** \-l-ənt\ *adj* — **scin·til·lant·ly** *adv* — **scin·til·la·tion** \,sint-l-'ā-shən\ *n* — **scin·til·la·tor** \'sint-l-,āt-ər\ *n*

scintillation counter *n* : a device for detecting and registering individual scintillations (as in radioactive emission)

sci·o·lism \'sī-ə-,liz-əm\ *n* : a superficial show of learning [Late Latin *sciolus* "one whose knowledge is su-

sconce

perficial", from Latin *scius* "knowing", from *scire* "to know"] — **sci·o·list** \-ləst\ *n* — **sci·o·lis·tic** \,sī-ə-'lis-tik\ *adj*

sci·on *also* **ci·on** \'sī-ən\ *n* **1** : a detached living portion of a plant joined to a stock in grafting and usually supplying only aerial parts to a graft **2** : DESCENDANT, CHILD ⟨a *scion* of a royal stock⟩ [Middle French, *cion*, of Germanic origin]

scis·sion \'sizh-ən\ *n* : a dividing of or split in a group or union [French, "division, split", from Late Latin *scissio*, from Latin *scindere* "to split"]

¹scis·sor \'siz-ər\ *n* : SCISSORS [Middle French *cisoire*, from Late Latin *cisorium* "cutting instrument", derived from Latin *caedere* "to cut"]

²scissor *vt* : to cut, cut up, or cut off with scissors

scis·sors \'siz-ərz\ *n sing or pl* **1** : a cutting instrument having two blades so fastened together that the sharp edges slide past each other **2** : a gymnastic or wrestling feat in which the leg movements suggest the action of scissors

scissors kick *n* : a swimming kick used especially in the sidestroke in which the legs come together like scissors

scler- *or* **sclero-** *combining form* : hard ⟨*scler*ite⟩ [Greek *sklēros*]

scle·ra \'skler-ə\ *n* : the dense fibrous white or bluish white tissue that covers that portion of the eyeball not covered by the cornea [New Latin, from Greek *sklēros* "hard"]

scler·e·id \'skler-ē-əd\ *n* : a supporting cell of a plant that is lignified and often mineralized — called also *stone cell* [derived from *sclerenchyma*]

scle·ren·chy·ma \sklə-'reng-kə-mə\ *n* : a protective or supporting tissue in higher plants composed of cells with walls thickened and lignified and often mineralized — compare COLLENCHYMA [*scler-* + *-enchyma* (as in *parenchyma*)] — **scler·en·chy·ma·tous** \,skler-ən-'kim-ət-əs, -'kī-mət-\ *adj*

scler·ite \'skliər-,īt, 'skleər-\ *n* : a hard chitinous or calcareous plate or piece (as of the arthropod skeleton)

scle·ro·sis \sklə-'rō-səs\ *n* : a usually pathological hardening of tissue especially from increase of connective tissue

scle·rot·ic \sklə-'rät-ik\ *adj* **1** : being or relating to the sclera **2** : of, relating to, or affected with or as if with sclerosis

¹scoff \'skäf, 'skóf\ *n* : an expression of scorn, derision, or contempt [Middle English *scof*]

²scoff *vb* : to show or treat with contempt by derisive acts or words : MOCK — **scoff·er** *n* □ SYN SCOFF, SNEER, JEER mean to show contempt in derision or mockery. SCOFF implies insolent or irreverent mockery or derision ⟨*scoffed* at the coach's training rules⟩ SNEER implies an ill-natured contempt often half concealed and conveyed only in the tone of voice or facial expression; JEER suggests loud laughter and coarse or vulgar derision.

scoff·law \-,ló\ *n* : a contemptuous law violator

¹scold \'skōld\ *n* **1** : one addicted to abusive language **2** : one that scolds habitually or persistently [Middle English *scald*, *scold*]

²scold *vb* **1** : to find fault noisily **2** : to rebuke severely or angrily — **scold·er** *n*

sco·lex \'skō-,leks\ *n*, *pl* **sco·li·ces** *also* **sco·le·ces** \-lə-,sēz\ *or* **sco·lex·es** \-,lek-səz\ : the head of a tapeworm [Greek *skōlēx* "worm"]

sco·li·o·sis \,skō-lē-'ō-səs, ,skäl-ē-\ *n*, *pl* **-o·ses** \-,sēz\ : a lateral curvature of the spine — compare KYPHOSIS, LORDOSIS [Greek *skoliōsis* "crookedness of a bodily part", from *skolios* "crooked"] — **sco·li·ot·ic** \-'ät-ik\ *adj*

sconce \'skäns\ *n* : a candlestick or group of candlesticks mounted on a plaque and fastened to a wall [Middle French *esconse* "screened lantern", from *escondre* "to hide", from Latin *abscondere*]

scone \'skōn, 'skän\ *n* : a quick bread usually made with oatmeal or barley flour and baked on a griddle [perhaps from Dutch *schoonbrood* "fine white bread", from *schoon* "pure, clean" + *brood* "bread"]

¹scoop \'sküp\ *n* **1 a** : a large shovel (as for shoveling coal) **b** : a tool or utensil shaped like a shovel or a deep spoon for taking up a portion of a loose or soft material ⟨an ice cream *scoop*⟩ **c** : a cutting or gouging tool with a rounded blade **2** : an act or the action of scooping : a motion made with or as if with a scoop **3 a** : the amount held by a scoop ⟨a *scoop* of sugar⟩ **b** : a hole made by scooping **4** : information of immediate interest; *also* : an exclusive news report [Dutch *schope*] — **scoop·ful** \-,fùl\ *n*

²scoop *vt* **1** : to take out or up or empty with or as if with a scoop **2** : to make hollow : dig out **3** : BEAT 5a (2) — **scoop·er** *n*

scoot \'süt\ *vi* : to go suddenly and swiftly : DART [probably of Scandinavian origin] — **scoot** *n*

scoot·er \'sküt-ər\ *n* **1** : a child's vehicle that consists of a narrow board mounted between two wheels one behind the other with an upright steering handle attached to the front wheel **2** : MOTOR SCOOTER

scop \'shōp, 'skōp, 'skäp\ *n* : an Old English bard or poet [Old English]

¹scope \'skōp\ *n* **1** : space or opportunity for unhampered action or thought ⟨given full *scope* to develop new solutions⟩ **2** : something sought : OBJECT **3** : extent covered, reached, or viewed : RANGE ⟨a subject broad in *scope*⟩ [Italian *scopo* "purpose, goal", from Greek *skopos*]

²scope *n* : any of various instruments for viewing: as **a** : MICROSCOPE **b** : TELESCOPE **c** : OSCILLOSCOPE **d** : RADAR-SCOPE [-*scope*]

-scope \,skōp\ *n combining form* : means (as an instrument) for viewing or observing ⟨micro*scope*⟩ [Greek -*skopion*]

sco·pol·amine \skō-'päl-ə-,mēn, -mən\ *n* : a poisonous alkaloid found in some plants of the potato family and used as a truth serum or especially with morphine as a sedative [German *scopolamin*, from New Latin *Scopolia*, genus of plants + German *amin* "amine"]

-s·co·py \s-kə-pē\ *n combining form, pl* **-pies** : viewing : observation ⟨stereo*scopy*⟩ [Greek -*skopia*, from *skeptesthai* "to watch, look at"]

scor·bu·tic \skȯr-'byüt-ik\ *adj* : of, relating to, or resembling scurvy; *also* : diseased with scurvy [New Latin *scorbutus* "scurvy"] — **scor·bu·ti·cal·ly** \-'byüt-i-kə-lē, -klē\ *adv*

¹scorch \'skȯrch\ *vb* **1 a** : to burn superficially usually to the point of changing color, texture, or flavor ⟨*scorch* a roast⟩ ⟨linen *scorches* easily⟩ **b** : to parch and discolor with or as if with intense heat ⟨lawns *scorched* by summer suns⟩ **2** : to distress or embarrass with usually sarcastic censure [Middle English *scorchen*]

²scorch *n* **1** : a result of scorching **2** : a browning of plant tissues usually from disease or heat

scorched earth *n* : land stripped of anything that could be of use to an invading enemy force

scorch·er \'skȯr-chər\ *n* : one that scorches; *esp* : a very hot day

¹score \'skōr, 'skȯr\ *n, pl* **scores 1** *or pl* **score a** : TWENTY **b** : a group of 20 things — often used in combination with a cardinal number ⟨five*score*⟩ **c** *pl* : an indefinite large number ⟨*scores* of cars in the parking lot⟩ **2 a** : a line made with or as if with a sharp instrument **b** : a mark used as a starting point or goal or for keeping account **3 a** : a reckoning kept by making marks on a tally **b** : ACCOUNT 1 **c** : amount due : INDEBTEDNESS **4** : an obligation or grudge kept in mind for requital ⟨looking for an opportunity to settle the *score*⟩ **5 a** : REASON, GROUND ⟨you have nothing to fear on that *score*⟩ **b** : SUBJECT 3c, TOPIC **6** : a musical composition in written or printed notation **7** : a number expressing accomplishment (as in a game or test) or quality (as of a product) ⟨a *score* of 80 out of a possible 100⟩ **8** : the true facts or prospects of a situation ⟨know the *score* on the unemployment situation⟩ [Old Norse *skor* "notch, tally, twenty"]

²score *vb* **1 a** : to record by or as if by notches on a tally **b** : to keep score in a game or contest **2** : to mark with lines, grooves, scratches, or notches **3** : BERATE, SCOLD **4 a** : to make a score in or as if in a game : TALLY ⟨*score* a run⟩ **b** : to enable (a base runner) to make a score ⟨*scored* the runner from second base with a single⟩ **c** : to have as a value in a game or contest : COUNT ⟨a touchdown *scores* six points⟩ **d** : ACHIEVE 2, WIN **5** : to determine the merit of : GRADE **6** : to write or arrange music for **7 a** : to gain or have the advantage **b** : to be successful — **scor·er** *n*

score·board \'skōr-,bōrd, 'skȯr-,bȯrd\ *n* : a large board for displaying the score of a game or match

score·card \-,kärd\ *n* : a card for recording the score (as of a game)

score·keep·er \-,kē-pər\ *n* : an official who records the score during the progress of a game or contest

score·less \-ləs\ *adj* : having no score; *esp* : involving no points or runs

sco·ria \'skōr-ē-ə, 'skȯr-\ *n, pl* **-ri·ae** \-ē-,ē, -ē-,ī\ **1** : the refuse from melting of metals or reduction of ores : SLAG **2** : rough vesicular cindery lava [Latin, from Greek *skōria*, from *skōr* "excrement"] — **sco·re·a·ceous** \,skōr-ē-'ā-shəs, ,skȯr-\ *adj*

¹scorn \'skȯrn\ *n* **1** : a feeling of contempt and loathing toward something considered inferior or unworthy **2** : an object of extreme disdain, contempt, or derision [Old French *escarn*, of Germanic origin]

²scorn *vt* **1** : to hold in or reject with bitter or angry contempt ⟨*scorned* all weaklings⟩ ⟨*scorn* a bribe⟩ **2** : to refuse because of scorn : DISDAIN ⟨*scorned* to reply to the charge⟩ SYN see DESPISE — **scorn·er** *n*

scorn·ful \'skȯrn-fəl\ *adj* : full of scorn : CONTEMPTUOUS — **scorn·ful·ly** \-fə-lē\ *adv* — **scorn·ful·ness** *n*

Scor·pio \'skȯr-pē-,ō\ *n* **1** : a zodiacal southern constellation that is located partly in the Milky Way and adjoins Libra **2** : the 8th sign of the zodiac; *also* : one born under this sign [Latin, from Greek *Skorpios*, literally, "scorpion"]

scor·pi·on \'skȯr-pē-ən\ *n* : any of an order (Scorpionida) of arachnids having an elongated body and a narrow segmented tail with a venomous sting at the tip [Old French, from Latin *scorpio*, from Greek *skorpios*]

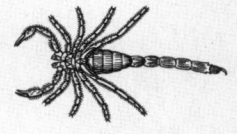
scorpion

scorpion fish *n* : any of a family of large-headed spiny-finned sea fishes including some with poisonous spines

Scor·pi·us \'skȯr-pē-əs\ : SCORPIO 1 [Latin, from Greek *Skorpios*, literally, "scorpion"]

Scot \'skät\ *n* **1** : any of a Gaelic people of northern Ireland settling in Scotland about A. D. 500 **2 a** : a native or inhabitant of Scotland **b** : a person of Scotch descent [Old English *Scottas* "Irishmen, Scotsmen", from Late Latin *Scotus* "Irishman"]

scotch \'skäch\ *vt* **1** *archaic* : to injure so as to make temporarily harmless **2** : to stamp out : CRUSH ⟨*scotch* a rebellion⟩; *esp* : to end decisively by showing the falsity of ⟨*scotch* a rumor⟩ [Middle English *scocchen* "to gash"]

¹Scotch \'skäch\ *adj* **1** : of, relating to, or characteristic of Scotland, the Scotch, or Scots **2** : ECONOMICAL 1, FRUGAL [contraction of *Scottish*]

²Scotch *n* **1** : SCOTS **2** **Scotch** *pl* : the people of Scotland **3** : whiskey distilled in Scotland especially from barley

Scotch broth *n* : a soup made from beef or mutton and vegetables and thickened with barley

Scotch–Irish *adj* : of, relating to, or characteristic of the population of northern Ireland that is descended from Scotch settlers or their descendants who emigrated to the United States before 1846 — **Scotch–Irish** *n*

SCOW

Scotch·man \'skäch-mən\ *n* : a man who is a Scot or is of Scotch descent

Scotch terrier *n* : SCOTTISH TERRIER

Scotch·wom·an \'skäch-,wùm-ən\ *n* : a woman who is a Scot or is of Scotch descent

sco·ter \'skōt-ər\ *n, pl* **scoters** *or* **scoter** : any of several sea ducks of northern coasts of Europe and North America [origin unknown]

scot–free \'skät-'frē\ *adj* : totally free from obligation, harm, or penalty [from *scot* "money assessed or paid", from Old Norse *skot* "shot, contribution"]

¹Scots \'skäts\ *adj* : SCOTCH 1 [Middle English *Scottis*, alteration of *Scottish*]

²Scots *n* : the English language of Scotland

Scots·man \'skät-smən\ *n* : SCOTCHMAN

Scots·wom·an \-,swùm-ən\ *n* : SCOTCHWOMAN

Scot·tie \'skät-ē\ *n* : SCOTTISH TERRIER

¹Scot·tish \'skät-ish\ *adj* : SCOTCH 1

²Scottish *n* : SCOTS

Scottish Gaelic *n* : the Gaelic language of Scotland

Scottish terrier *n* : any of an old Scottish breed of terrier with short legs, large head, small erect ears, broad deep chest, and a hard coat of wiry hair

scoun·drel \'skaùn-drəl\ *n* : a mean worthless person : VILLAIN [origin unknown] — **scoundrel** *adj* — **scoundrel·ly** \-drə-lē\ *adj*

¹scour \'skaùr\ *vb* 1 : to move about or through quickly especially in search 2 : to examine minutely and rapidly [Middle English *scuren*] — **scour·er** *n*

²scour *vb* 1 **a** : to rub hard in order to clean **b** : to remove by rubbing hard and washing ⟨*scour* spots from the stove⟩ 2 : to free from foreign matter or impurities by or as if by washing ⟨*scour* wool⟩ 3 **a** : to clear, dig, or remove by a powerful current of water **b** : to wear away (as by water) : ERODE ⟨a stream *scouring* its banks⟩ 4 : to suffer from diarrhea or dysentery 5 : to become clean and bright by rubbing [Middle English *scouren*] — **scour·er** *n*

³scour *n* 1 : an action or result of scouring 2 *pl* : DIARRHEA, DYSENTERY

¹scourge \'skərj\ *n* 1 : WHIP 1, LASH 2 **a** : an instrument of punishment or criticism **b** : a cause of widespread or great affliction [Anglo-French *escorge*, derived from Old French *es-* "ex-" + Latin *corrigia* "whip"]

²scourge *vt* 1 : to whip severely : FLOG 2 : to subject to affliction : DEVASTATE ⟨a region *scourged* by malaria⟩ — **scourg·er** *n*

scouring rush *n* : EQUISETUM; *esp* : one with harsh abrasive stems formerly used for scouring

¹scout \'skaùt\ *vb* 1 : to go about and observe in search of information ⟨*scout* an area for minerals⟩ ⟨*scouted* around the enemy position⟩ 2 **a** : to make a search ⟨*scout* about for firewood⟩ **b** : to find by searching [Middle French *escouter* "to listen", from Latin *auscultare*]

²scout *n* 1 : the act or an instance of scouting : RECONNAISSANCE 2 **a** : one sent to obtain information and especially to reconnoiter in war **b** : LOOKOUT 1 **c** : a person who searches for talented newcomers 3 *often cap* **a** : BOY SCOUT **b** : GIRL SCOUT 4 : FELLOW 4a, GUY

³scout *vb* 1 : to make fun of : MOCK 2 : to reject scornfully as absurd : SCOFF ⟨*scout* a theory⟩ [of Scandinavian origin]

scout car *n* : a fast armored military reconnaissance vehicle with four-wheel drive and open top

scout·craft \-,kraft\ *n* : the craft, skill, or practice of a scout

scout·er \-ər\ *n* 1 : one that scouts 2 *often cap* : an adult leader of the Boy Scouts of America

scout·ing \'skaùt-ing\ *n* 1 : the action of one that scouts 2 *often cap* : the activities of the various organizations for youth intended to develop character, citizenship, and individual skills

scout·mas·ter \'skaùt-,mas-tər\ *n* : the leader of a band of scouts and especially of a troop of Boy Scouts

scow \'skaù\ *n* : a large flat-bottomed boat with broad square ends used chiefly for transporting sand, gravel, or refuse [Dutch *schouw*]

¹scowl \'skaùl\ *vb* 1 : FROWN 1, GLOWER ⟨*scowled* at my impudence⟩ 2 : to exhibit or express with a scowl ⟨*scowl* one's displeasure⟩ [Middle English *skoulen*] — **scowl·er** *n*

²scowl *n* : a facial expression of displeasure : FROWN

¹scrab·ble \'skrab-əl\ *vb* **scrab·bled; scrab·bling** \'skrab-ling, -ə-ling\ 1 : SCRAWL, SCRIBBLE 2 : to scratch or claw about clumsily or frantically 3 **a** : to struggle for a foothold : SCRAMBLE **b** : to struggle by or as if by scraping or scratching ⟨*scrabble* for a living⟩ [Dutch *schrabbelen* "to scratch"] — **scrab·bler** \'skrab-lər, -ə-lər\ *n*

²scrabble *n* : an act or instance of scrabbling

scrab·bly \'skrab-lē, -ə-lē\ *adj* **scrab·bli·er; -est** 1 : RASPY 1, SCRATCHY 2 : SPARSE, SCRUBBY ⟨a *scrabbly* garden⟩

¹scrag \'skrag\ *n* 1 : a rawboned or scrawny person or animal 2 : the lean end of a neck of mutton or veal [perhaps from *crag* "neck, throat", from Dutch *craghe*]

²scrag *vt* **scragged; scrag·ging** : KILL, MURDER

scrag·gly \'skrag-lē, -ə-lē\ *adj* **scrag·gli·er; -est** : of rough or irregular outline; *also* : RAGGED, UNKEMPT

scrag·gy \'skrag-ē\ *adj* **scrag·gi·er; -est** 1 : ROUGH 1c, JAGGED 2 : being lean and long : SCRAWNY

scram \'skram\ *vi* **scrammed; scram·ming** : to go away at once ⟨*scram,* you're not wanted⟩ [short for *scramble*]

scram·ble \'skram-bəl\ *vb* **scram·bled; scram·bling** \-bə-ling, -bling\ 1 : to move or climb hastily on all fours 2 : to move or act urgently or unceremoniously in trying to win or escape something ⟨*scramble* for front seats⟩ 3 : SPRAWL 3, STRAGGLE 4 **a** : to toss or mix together : JUMBLE **b** : to prepare (eggs) by stirring during cooking [perhaps alteration of *¹scrabble*] — **scramble** *n* — **scram·bler** \-bə-lər, -blər\ *n*

¹scrap \'skrap\ *n* 1 *pl* : fragments of discarded or left-over food 2 : a small bit : FRAGMENT ⟨*scraps* of cloth⟩ ⟨not a *scrap* of truth in the story⟩ 3 : discarded or waste material (as metal) for reprocessing [Old Norse *skrap* "scraps"]

²scrap *vt* **scrapped; scrap·ping** 1 : to break up into scrap ⟨*scrap* a battleship⟩ 2 : to discard as worthless

³scrap *n* : ¹QUARREL, FIGHT [origin unknown]

⁴scrap *vi* **scrapped; scrap·ping** : QUARREL 2, FIGHT — **scrap·per** *n*

scrap·book \'skrap-,bùk\ *n* : a blank book for mementos (as clippings and pictures)

¹scrape \'skrāp\ *vb* 1 **a** : to remove by repeated strokes of an edged tool ⟨*scrape* off rust⟩ **b** : to clean or smooth by rubbing with an edged tool or abrasive 2 : to move along or over something with a grating noise : GRATE; *also* : to damage by such an action ⟨*scrape* a fender⟩ 3 **a** : to gather with difficulty and little by little ⟨*scrape* together a few dollars⟩ **b** : to barely make one's way ⟨*scraped* through with low grades⟩ [Old Norse *skrapa*] — **scrap·er** *n*

²scrape *n* 1 **a** : the act or process of scraping **b** : a sound, mark, or injury made by scraping 2 : a bow made by drawing back the foot 3 : a disagreeable predicament

scrap·ple \'skrap-əl\ *n* : a seasoned ground mush of cornmeal and bits of meat set in a mold and served sliced and fried [derived from *¹scrap*]

¹scrap·py \'skrap-ē\ *adj* **scrap·pi·er; -est** : consisting of scraps

²scrappy *adj* **scrap·pi·er; -est** 1 : likely or tending to quarrel : QUARRELSOME 2 : aggressive and determined in spirit — **scrap·pi·ness** *n*

¹scratch \'skrach\ *vb* 1 : to scrape or dig with or as if with the claws or nails 2 : to rub and tear or mark the surface of with something sharp 3 **a** : SCRAPE 3 **b** : to work hard and save ⟨have to *scratch* for a living⟩ **4** : to write or draw on a surface especially hastily or carelessly : SCRAWL **5 a** : ERASE, CANCEL **b** : to withdraw (an entry) from competition **6 a** : to use the claws or nails in digging, tearing, or wounding **b** : to scrape or rub oneself (as to relieve itching) **7** : to make a thin grating sound [blend of English dialect *scrat* "to scratch" and obsolete English *cratch* "to scratch"] — **scratch·er** *n*

²**scratch** *n* **1 a** : an act or sound of scratching **b** : a mark (as a line) or injury made by scratching **2 a** : the starting line in a race **b** : NOTHING ⟨start from *scratch*⟩ **3** : satisfactory condition or performance ⟨not up to *scratch*⟩ **4** : poultry feed scattered especially to induce birds to exercise

³**scratch** *adj* **1** : made tentatively or casually ⟨a *scratch* shot⟩ **2** : put together with little selection ⟨a *scratch* team⟩

scratch hit *n* : a batted ball not solidly hit or cleanly played yet credited to the batter as a base hit

scratch paper *n* : paper suitable for casual writing

scratch test *n* : a test for allergic susceptibility made by rubbing an extract of an allergy-producing substance into small breaks or scratches in the skin

scratchy \'skrach-ē\ *adj* **scratch·i·er; -est 1** : likely to scratch or irritate : PRICKLY ⟨*scratchy* woolens⟩ **2** : making a scratching noise **3** : marked or made with scratches ⟨a *scratchy* surface⟩ **4** : uneven in quality — **scratch·i·ly** \'skrach-ə-lē\ *adv* — **scratch·i·ness** \'skrach-ē-nəs\ *n*

scrawl \'skrȯl\ *vb* : to write or draw awkwardly, hastily, or carelessly : SCRIBBLE [origin unknown] — **scrawl** *n* — **scrawl·er** *n* — **scrawl·i·ness** \'skrȯ-lē-nəs\ *n* — **scrawly** \'skrȯ-lē\ *adj*

scraw·ny \'skrȯ-nē\ *adj* **scraw·ni·er; -est** : ill-nourished : SKINNY ⟨*scrawny* cattle⟩ [origin unknown] — **scraw·ni·ness** *n*

¹**scream** \'skrēm\ *vb* **1** : to utter a loud shrill prolonged cry or sound; *also* : to utter with such a sound ⟨*screamed* my name⟩ **2** : to produce or give a vivid, startling, or alarming effect ⟨a *screaming* red⟩ ⟨*screaming* headlines⟩ [Middle English *scremen*]

²**scream** *n* **1** : a loud shrill prolonged cry or sound **2** : one that provokes great laughter ⟨you're a *scream*⟩ □ SYN SHRIEK, SCREECH: SCREAM is the general term for utterance that is sharpened and prolonged by intensity of feeling. SHRIEK may imply an intensified scream or suggest a degree of wildness or lack of control ⟨*shrieks* of dismay⟩ ⟨hysterical *shrieks* of laughter⟩ SCREECH implies a harsh shrillness painful to the hearer and suggesting an unearthly or, often, a comic effect ⟨the *screech* of an angry parrot⟩

scream·er \'skrē-mər\ *n* **1** : one that screams **2** : any of several large South American birds with spurs on the wings **3** : a sensationally startling headline

scream·ing·ly \'skrē-ming-lē\ *adv* : to an extreme degree ⟨*screamingly* funny⟩

¹**screech** \'skrēch\ *n* **1** : a shrill harsh cry usually of terror or pain **2** : a sound like a screech ⟨*screech* of brakes⟩ SYN see SCREAM

²**screech** *vb* **1** : to utter a high shrill piercing cry usually in terror or pain; *also* : to utter with a screech ⟨*screeched* a warning⟩ **2** : to make a sound like a screech [Middle English *scrichen*] — **screech·er** *n*

screech owl *n* : any of numerous small reddish brown or gray New World owls with a pair of tufts of lengthened feathers on the head that resemble ears

screed \'skrēd\ *n* : a lengthy discourse [Old English *scrēade* "fragment, shred"]

¹**screen** \'skrēn\ *n* **1 a** : a device or partition used to hide, restrain, protect, or decorate ⟨a window *screen*⟩; *also* : something that serves to shelter, protect, or conceal ⟨a *screen* of fighter planes⟩ ⟨used the store as a *screen* for illegal activities⟩ **b** : a maneuver in various sports whereby a defender is legally cut off from the

play **2** : a sieve or perforated material set in a frame and used for separating finer parts from coarser parts (as of sand) **3 a** : a flat surface upon which a picture or series of pictures is projected **b** : the surface (as of a cathode-ray tube) upon which the image appears in an electronic device (as in a television set or computer terminal) **4** : the motion-picture industry [Middle French *escren*, from Dutch *scherm*]

²**screen** *vb* **1** : to guard from injury or danger **2 a** : to shelter, protect, or separate with or as if with a screen **b** : to pass (as coal, gravel, or ashes) through a screen to separate the fine part from the coarse; *also* : to remove by or as if by a screen **c** : to examine systematically in order to separate into groups; *also* : to select or eliminate by this means ⟨*screened* the applicants⟩ **3** : to provide with a screen especially to keep out insects ⟨*screen* a porch⟩ **4 a** : to project (as a motion-picture film) on a screen **b** : to present in a motion picture **c** : to appear on a motion-picture screen **5** : to cut off an opponent from a play — **screen·able** \'skrē-nə-bəl\ *adj* — **screen·er** *n*

screen·ing \'skrē-ning\ *n* **1** *pl* : material (as fine coal) separated out by passage through or retention on a screen **2** : a mesh (as of metal or plastic) used especially for screens

screen pass *n* : a forward pass in football in which the receiver is protected by a screen of blockers

screen·play \'skrēn-ˌplā\ *n* : the written form of a story prepared for motion-picture or television production

screen test *n* : a short film sequence testing the ability of a prospective movie actor or actress — **screen–test** *vt*

screen·writ·er \'skrēn-ˌrīt-ər\ *n* : a writer of screenplays

¹**screw** \'skrü\ *n* **1 a** : a simple machine consisting of a spirally grooved solid cylinder and a correspondingly grooved cylindrical hollow part into which it fits **b** : a nail-shaped or rod-shaped metal piece with a spiral groove and a slotted or recessed head used for fastening pieces of solid material together **2 a** : a screw-shaped form : SPIRAL **b** : a turn of a screw; *also* : a twist like the turn of a screw **c** : a screw-shaped device (as a corkscrew) **3** : PROPELLER **4** : THUMBSCREW 2 [Middle French *escroe* "screw nut", from Medieval Latin *scrofa*, from Latin, "sow"] — **screw·like** \-ˌlīk\ *adj*

²**screw** *vb* **1 a** (1) : to attach, fasten, or close by means of a screw ⟨*screw* a hinge to a door⟩ (2) : to operate, tighten, or adjust by means of a screw ⟨*screw* up a sagging beam with a jack⟩ **b** : to move or cause to move spirally as a screw does; *also* : to close or set in position by such an action ⟨*screw* on a lid⟩ ⟨*screw* a jar shut⟩ **2 a** : to twist out of shape : CONTORT ⟨a face *screwed* up in pain⟩ SQUINT **2 3** : to increase in amount or capability ⟨*screwed* up my nerve⟩ — **screw·er** *n*

¹**screw·ball** \'skrü-ˌbȯl\ *n* **1** : a baseball pitch that spins and breaks in the opposite direction to a curve **2** : NUT 4a

²**screwball** *adj* : NUTTY 2

screw·driv·er \'skrü-ˌdrī-vər\ *n* : a tool for turning screws

screw eye *n* : a screw having a head in the form of a loop

screw pine *n* : any of a genus of tropical plants with slender palmlike stems, often huge prop roots, and terminal crowns of swordlike leaves — called also *pandanus*

screw propeller *n* : PROPELLER

screw thread *n* : the projecting spiral rib of a screw between the grooves

screw·worm \'skrü-ˌwərm\ *n* : the grub of a two=winged fly of warm parts of America that develops especially in sores or wounds of mammals

screech owl

screwy \'skrü-ē\ *adj* **screw·i·er; -est** 1 : crazily absurd, eccentric, or unusual 2 : CRAZY 2a, INSANE

scrib·al \'skrī-bəl\ *adj* : of, relating to, or due to a scribe ⟨a *scribal* error⟩

scrib·ble \'skrib-əl\ *vb* **scrib·bled; scrib·bling** \'skrib-ling, -ə-ling\ : to write or draw hastily or carelessly [Medieval Latin *scribillare*, from Latin *scribere* "to write"] — **scribble** *n*

scrib·bler \'skrib-lər\ *n* 1 : one that scribbles 2 : a minor or inferior author

¹scribe \'skrīb\ *n* 1 : a scholar of the Jewish law in New Testament times 2 a : an official or public secretary or clerk b : a copier of manuscripts 3 : AUTHOR 1; *esp* : JOURNALIST [Latin *scriba* "official writer", from *scribere* "to write"]

²scribe *vt* : to mark or make by cutting or scratching with a pointed instrument ⟨*scribe* a line on metal⟩ [probably short for *describe*]

scrib·er \'skrī-bər\ *n* : a sharp-pointed tool for marking off material (as wood or metal) to be cut

scrim \'skrim\ *n* : a durable plain-woven usually cotton fabric [origin unknown]

¹scrim·mage \'skrim-ij\ *n* 1 : a confused fight : SCUFFLE 2 : the interplay between two football teams that begins with the snap of the ball and continues until the ball is dead 3 : practice play between a team's squads or a practice game between two teams [alteration of ¹*skirmish*]

²scrimmage *vi* : to take part in a scrimmage — **scrim·mag·er** *n*

scrimp \'skrimp\ *vb* 1 : STINT 1, SKIMP 2 : ECONOMIZE 1 [perhaps of Scandinavian origin] — **scrimpy** \'skrim-pē\ *adj*

scrim·shaw \'skrim-,shȯ\ *n* : carved or engraved articles made especially by American whalers and from whale ivory [origin unknown] — **scrimshaw** *vb*

scrip \'skrip\ *n* 1 : a document showing that the holder or bearer is entitled to something (as stock or land) 2 : paper currency or a token issued temporarily (as in an emergency) [short for *script*]

script \'skript\ *n* 1 a : something written : TEXT b : an original or principal legal document c (1) : MANUSCRIPT 1 (2) : the written text of a stage play, a movie, or a broadcast 2 a : printed lettering resembling handwritten lettering b : written characters : HANDWRITING c : ALPHABET 1 [Latin *scriptum* "thing written", from *scribere* "to write"]

scrip·to·ri·um \skrip-'tōr-ē-əm, -'tȯr-\ *n, pl* **-ria** \-ē-ə\ : a copying room in a medieval monastery set apart for the scribes [Medieval Latin, from Latin *scribere* "to write"]

scrip·tur·al \'skrip-chə-rəl, 'skrip-shrəl\ *adj* : of, relating to, or being in accordance with a sacred writing; *esp* : BIBLICAL — **scrip·tur·al·ly** \-ē\ *adv*

scrip·ture \'skrip-chər\ *n* 1 a *cap* : the books of the Old and New Testaments or of either of them : BIBLE — often used in pl. b *often cap* : a passage from the Bible 2 : the sacred writings of any religion 3 : a body of writings considered authoritative [Latin *scriptura* "writing", from *scribere* "to write"]

script·writ·er \'skrip-,trīt-ər\ *n* : one that writes scripts for motion pictures or for radio or television programs

scriv·e·ner \'skriv-nər, -ə-nər\ *n* : a professional copyist or writer : SCRIBE [Middle French *escrivein*, derived from Latin *scriba* "scribe"]

scrod \'skräd\ *n* : a young fish (as a cod or haddock); *esp* : one split and boned for cooking [perhaps from obsolete Dutch *schrood* "shred"]

scrof·u·la \'skrȯf-yə-lə, 'skräf-\ *n* : tuberculosis of the lymph glands especially in the neck [Medieval Latin, from Late Latin *scrofulae* "swellings of the lymph glands of the neck", from Latin *scrofa* "sow"] — **scrof·u·lous** \-ləs\ *adj*

scroll 1

scroll \'skrōl\ *n* 1 : a roll (as of paper or parchment) providing a writing surface; *esp* : one on which something is written or engraved 2 : an ornament suggesting a loosely or partly rolled scroll [Middle English *scrowle*, alteration of *scrowe*, from Middle French *escroue* "scrap, scroll", of Germanic origin]

scroll saw *n* : a saw with a thin blade for cutting curves or irregular designs

scroll·work \'skrōl-,wərk\ *n* : ornamental work (as in metal or wood) having a scroll or scrolls as its chief feature

scrooge \'skrüj\ *n, often cap* : a miserly person [Ebenezer *Scrooge*, character in *A Christmas Carol*, story by Charles Dickens]

scro·tum \'skrōt-əm\ *n, pl* **scro·ta** \'skrōt-ə\ *or* **scro·tums** : the external pouch that in most mammals contains the testes [Latin] — **scro·tal** \'skrōt-l\ *adj*

scrounge \'skraunj\ *vb* 1 : to hunt or collect by or as if by foraging ⟨*scrounge* around for firewood⟩ 2 : CADGE, WHEEDLE ⟨*scrounge* a dollar from a friend⟩ [from English dialect *scrunge* "to wander about idly"] — **scroung·er** *n*

¹scrub \'skrəb\ *n* 1 a : a stunted tree or shrub b : vegetation consisting chiefly of or a tract covered with scrubs 2 : a usually inferior domestic animal of mixed or unknown parentage 3 a : a person of insignificant size or standing b : a player not on the first team [Old English *scrybb* "brushwood"] — **scrub** *adj*

²scrub *vb* **scrubbed; scrub·bing** 1 : to clean with hard rubbing : SCOUR b : to remove by or as if by scrubbing 2 : to subject to friction : RUB [of Low German or Scandinavian origin] — **scrub·ber** *n*

³scrub *n* 1 : an act or instance of scrubbing 2 : one that scrubs

scrub brush *n* : a brush with hard bristles for heavy cleaning

scrub·by \'skrəb-ē\ *adj* **scrub·bi·er; -est** 1 : inferior in size or quality : STUNTED ⟨*scrubby* cattle⟩ 2 : covered with or consisting of vegetational scrub 3 : lacking distinction : SHABBY [¹*scrub*]

scrub typhus *n* : an acute rickettsial disease of the western Pacific area that resembles typhus and is transmitted by larval mites — called also *tsutsugamushi disease*

scrub·wom·an \'skrəb-,wum-ən\ *n* : a woman who hires herself out for cleaning : CHARWOMAN

scruff \'skrəf\ *n* : the loose skin of the back of the neck : NAPE [alteration of earlier *scuff*, of unknown origin]

scruffy \-ē\ *adj* **scruff·i·er; -est** : poor and shabby ⟨a *scruffy* hippie⟩ ⟨put on my *scruffiest* jeans⟩ [English dialect *scruff* "something worthless", alteration of *scurf*]

scrump·tious \'skrəm-shəs, 'skrəmp-\ *adj* : DELIGHTFUL, EXCELLENT [probably alteration of *sumptuous*] — **scrump·tious·ly** *adv*

¹scrunch \'skrənch\ *vb* 1 a : to crush together : CRUMPLE b : to make or move with a crunching sound 2 : CROUCH 1 [alteration of ¹*crunch*]

²scrunch *n* : a crunching sound

¹scru·ple \'skrü-pəl\ *n* 1 — see MEASURE table 2 : a tiny part or quantity [Latin *scrupulus*, a unit of weight, from *scrupulus* "small sharp stone"]

²scruple *n* 1 : an ethical consideration or principle that makes one uneasy or inhibits action 2 : SCRUPULOSITY 1 [Middle French *scrupule*, from Latin *scrupulus* "small sharp stone, scruple", from *scrupus* "sharp stone"] SYN see QUALM

³scruple *vi* **scru·pled; scru·pling** \-pə-ling, -pling\ : to have scruples

scru·pu·los·i·ty \,skrü-pyə-'läs-ət-ē\ *n, pl* **-ties** 1 : the quality or state of being scrupulous 2 : ²SCRUPLE 1

scru·pu·lous \'skrü-pyə-ləs\ *adj* 1 : having or full of scruples 2 : PUNCTILIOUS SYN see CAREFUL — **scru·pu·lous·ly** *adv* — **scru·pu·lous·ness** *n*

scru·ta·ble \'skrüt-ə-bəl\ *adj* : capable of being deciphered : COMPREHENSIBLE [Late Latin *scrutabilis* "searchable", from Latin *scrutari* "to search, examine"]

scru·ti·nize \'skrüt-n-ˌīz\ *vt* : to examine very closely or critically : INSPECT — **scru·ti·niz·er** *n* □ SYN SCRUTINIZE, SCAN, EXAMINE mean to look at searchingly and critically. SCRUTINIZE stresses close attention to minute detail ⟨*scrutinized* every line of the contract⟩ SCAN suggests a rapid but thorough covering of an entire surface or body of printed matter ⟨*scanned* several newspapers each morning⟩ EXAMINE suggests scrutinizing in order to determine the nature, condition, or quality of a thing ⟨*examined* the gem for flaws⟩

scru·ti·ny \'skrüt-n-ē, 'skrüt-nē\ *n, pl* **-nies** 1 : a thorough study, inquiry, or inspection : EXAMINATION 2 : a searching look [Latin *scrutinium,* from *scrutari* "to search, examine", from *scruta* "trash"]

scu·ba \'skü-bə, 'skyü-\ *n* : an apparatus that provides air for breathing while swimming underwater [*s*elf-*c*ontained *u*nderwater *b*reathing *a*pparatus]

scuba diver *n* : a person who dives with scuba gear

¹scud \'skəd\ *vi* **scud·ded; scud·ding** : to move or run swiftly especially as if driven forward [probably of Scandinavian origin]

²scud *n* 1 : the act of scudding 2 : wind-driven clouds or water

¹scuff \'skəf\ *vb* 1 : to scrape the feet in walking : SHUFFLE ⟨*scuff* one's feet on the ground⟩ ⟨*scuffed* along the path⟩ 2 : to become rough or scratched through wear ⟨some leathers *scuff* easily⟩ [probably of Scandinavian origin]

²scuff *n* 1 : a noise or act of scuffing 2 : a flat-soled house slipper

scuf·fle \'skəf-əl\ *vb* **scuf·fled; scuf·fling** \'skəf-ling, -ə-ling\ 1 : to struggle in a confused way at close quarters 2 : to move with a quick shuffling gait; *also* : SCUFF [probably of Scandinavian origin] — **scuffle** *n* — **scuf·fler** \'skəf-lər, -ə-lər\ *n*

¹scull \'skəl\ *n* 1 **a** : an oar used at the stern of a boat to propel it forward with a side-to-side motion **b** : one of a pair of short oars for use by one person 2 : a long narrow boat usually for racing propelled by one or more persons using sculls [Middle English *sculle*]

²scull *vb* 1 : to propel by a scull or sculls 2 : to scull a boat — **scull·er** *n*

scul·lery \'skəl-rē, -ə-rē\ *n, pl* **-ler·ies** : a room for cleaning and storing dishes and culinary utensils, washing vegetables, and similar domestic work [Middle French *escuelerie* "department of household in charge of dishes", from *escuelle* "bowl", from Latin *scutella* "drinking bowl, tray", from *scutra* "platter"]

scul·lion \'skəl-yən\ *n* : a kitchen helper [Middle French *escouillon* "dishcloth", from *escouve* "broom", from Latin *scopa*, literally, "twig"]

scul·pin \'skəl-pən\ *n, pl* **sculpins** *also* **sculpin** 1 : any of numerous spiny large-headed broad-mouthed usually scaleless fishes 2 : a scorpion fish of the southern California coast sought for food and sport [origin unknown]

sculpt \'skəlpt\ *vb* : SCULPTURE 1, CARVE [French *sculpter,* derived from Latin *sculpere*]

sculp·tor \'skəlp-tər\ *n* : one that sculptures [Latin, from *sculpere* "to carve"]

sculp·tress \-trəs\ *n* : a woman who sculptures

sculp·tur·al \'skəlp-chə-rəl, 'skəlp-shrəl\ *adj* : of, relating to, or resembling sculpture — **sculp·tur·al·ly** \-ē\ *adv*

¹sculp·ture \'skəlp-chər\ *n* 1 : the act, process, or art of carving or cutting hard materials or modeling plastic materials into works of art 2 : work produced by sculpture; *also* : a piece of such work [Latin *sculptura,* from *sculpere* "to carve" alteration of *scalpere*]

²sculpture *vb* 1 **a** : to represent or produce by or subject to sculpture ⟨*sculpture* a model's head⟩ ⟨*sculpture* a statue⟩ ⟨*sculpture* marble⟩ **b** : to adorn with sculpture ⟨*sculpture* a tomb⟩ 2 : to work as a sculptor

¹scum \'skəm\ *n* 1 **a** : extraneous matter or impurities risen to or formed on the surface of a liquid **b** : a slimy coating especially on stagnant water 2 **a** : foul or worthless things **b** : the lowest class : RABBLE [Dutch *schum*] — **scum·my** \'skəm-ē\ *adj*

²scum *vi* **scummed; scum·ming** : to form or become covered with or as if with scum

scun·ner \'skən-ər\ *n* : an unreasonable or extreme dislike or prejudice [Middle English *skunniren* "to be disgusted"]

scup \'skəp\ *n, pl* **scup** *also* **scups** : either of two porgies of the Atlantic coast of the United States [of American Indian origin]

scup·per \'skəp-ər\ *n* : an opening in the bulwarks of a boat through which water drains overboard [Middle English *skopper*]

scup·per·nong \-ˌnȯng, -ˌnäng\ *n* 1 : MUSCADINE; *esp* : a cultivated muscadine with yellowish green plum-flavored fruits 2 : a wine made from scuppernongs [*Scuppernong,* river and lake in North Carolina]

scurf \'skərf\ *n* 1 : thin dry scales given off by the skin especially in an abnormal skin condition 2 : a substance that sticks to a surface in flakes; *also* : a scaly deposit or covering (as on a plant surface) [of Scandinavian origin] — **scurfy** \'skər-fē\ *adj*

scur·ri·lous \'skər-ə-ləs, 'skə-rə-\ *adj* 1 **a** : using or given to coarse language **b** : being vulgar and evil 2 : containing obscenities or crude abuse ⟨*scurrilous* verse⟩ [Latin *scurrilis,* from *scurra* "buffoon"] — **scur·ril·i·ty** \skə-'ril-ət-ē\ *n* — **scur·ri·lous·ly** \'skər-ə-ləs-lē, 'skə-rə-\ *adv* — **scur·ri·lous·ness** *n*

scur·ry \'skər-ē, 'skə-rē\ *vi* **scur·ried; scur·ry·ing** : to move briskly : SCAMPER [short for *hurry-scurry,* reduplication of *hurry*] — **scurry** *n*

¹scur·vy \'skər-vē\ *n* : a deficiency disease caused by lack of ascorbic acid and marked by spongy gums, loosened teeth, and bleeding into the skin and mucous membranes

²scurvy *adj* **scur·vi·er; -est** : disgustingly mean or contemptible ⟨*scurvy* tricks⟩ [*scurf*] SYN see CONTEMPTIBLE — **scur·vi·ly** \-və-lē\ *adv* — **scur·vi·ness** \-vē-nəs\ *n*

scut \'skət\ *n* : a short erect tail (as of a rabbit) [origin unknown]

¹scutch \'skəch\ *vt* : to separate the woody fiber from (flax or hemp) by beating [obsolete French *escoucher,* derived from Latin *excutere* "to beat out", from *ex-* + *quatere* "to shake, strike"]

²scutch *n* : SCUTCHER

scutch·eon \'skəch-ən\ *n* : ESCUTCHEON

scutch·er \'skəch-ər\ *n* : an implement or machine for scutching

scute \'sküt, 'skyüt\ *n* : an external bony or horny plate or large scale [Latin *scutum* "shield"]

scu·tel·lum \skü-'tel-əm, skyü-\ *n, pl* **-tel·la** \-'tel-ə\ : any of several small shield-shaped plant structures [New Latin, from Latin *scutum* "shield"] — **scu·tel·late** \-'tel-ət\ *adj*

scut·ter \'skət-ər\ *vi* : SCURRY, SCUTTLE [alteration of *⁴scuttle*]

¹scut·tle \'skət-l\ *n* 1 : a shallow open basket (as for grain or garden produce) 2 : a metal pail for carrying coal [Latin *scutella* "drinking bowl, tray", from *scutra* "platter"]

²scuttle *n* : a small opening (as in the side or deck of a ship or the roof of a house) furnished with a lid; *also* : its lid [Middle English *skottell*]

³scuttle *vt* **scut·tled; scut·tling** \'skət-ling, -l-ing\ 1 : to sink (a boat) intentionally by making holes in the sides or bottom 2 : to injure or end by a deliberate act ⟨*scuttle* a conference⟩

⁴scuttle *vi* **scut·tled; scut·tling** \'skət-ling, -l-ing\ : SCURRY [probably blend of *scud* and *shuttle*]

⁵scuttle *n* 1 : a quick shuffling pace 2 : a short swift run

scuba diver

sculpin 1

\ə\ abut	\ng\ sing
\ər\ further	\ō\ bone
\a\ mat	\ȯ\ saw
\ā\ take	\ȯi\ coin
\ä\ cot, cart	\th\ thin
\au̇\ out	\th\ this
\ch\ chin	\ü\ food
\e\ pet	\u̇\ foot
\ē\ easy	\y\ yet
\g\ go	\yü\ few
\i\ tip	\yu̇\ cure
\ī\ life	\zh\ vision
\j\ job	

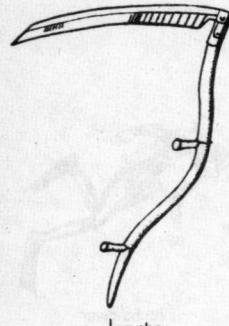

¹scythe

sea horse 2

scut·tle·butt \'skət-l-,bət\ *n* : RUMOR 1, GOSSIP [earlier *scuttlebutt* "cask fitted with a spigot to provide drinking water on shipboard, drinking fountain on a ship", from ²*scuttle*]

scy·pha \'sī-fə\ *n* : any of various small mostly cup-shaped calcareous sponges [New Latin, from Latin *scyphus* "cup"]

scy·phis·to·ma \sī-'fis-tə-mə\ *n, pl* -**mae** \-,mē\ *also* -**mas** : a sexually produced scyphozoan larva that repeatedly constricts transversely to form free-swimming medusae [Latin *scyphus* "cup" + Greek *stoma* "mouth"]

scy·pho·zo·an \,sī-fə-'zō-ən\ *n* : any of a class (Scyphozoa) of coelenterates comprising mostly large jellyfishes that lack a true polyp stage [Latin *scyphus* "cup" + Greek *zōion* "animal"] — **scyphozoan** *adj*

¹scythe \'sīth, 'sī\ *n* : an implement used for mowing (as grass) and composed of a long curving blade fastened at an angle to a long handle [Old English *sīthe*]

²scythe *vt* : to cut with or as if with a scythe : MOW

sea \'sē\ *n* **1 a** : the great body of salty water that covers much of the earth; *also* : the waters of the earth as distinguished from the land and air **b** : a body of salt water less extensive than an ocean (the Mediterranean *sea*) **c** : OCEAN 2 **d** : an inland body of water either salt or fresh (the *Sea* of Galilee) **2 a** : surface motion on a large body of water or its direction (a following *sea*) **b** : rough water : a heavy swell or wave (a high *sea* swept the deck) **3** : something suggesting the sea (as in vastness) (a golden *sea* of wheat) **4** : the seafaring life [Old English *sǣ*] — **sea** *adj* — **at sea 1** : on the sea; *esp* : on a sea voyage **2** : LOST 2c, BEWILDERED — **to sea** : to or on the open waters of the sea

sea anchor *n* : a drag typically of canvas thrown overboard to retard the drifting of a ship or seaplane and to keep its head to the wind

sea anemone *n* : any of numerous usually solitary polyps (order Actiniaria) that have bright and varied colors and a cluster of tentacles and that superficially resemble a flower in form

sea·bag \'sē-,bag\ *n* : a cylindrical canvas bag used especially by a sailor for gear (asclothes)

sea bass *n* **1** : any of numerous marine fishes related to but usually smaller and more active than the groupers; *esp* : a food and sport fish of the Atlantic coast of the United States **2** : any of numerous croakers or drums including noted sport and food fishes

sea·bed \'sē-,bed\ *n* : the floor of a sea or ocean

Sea·bee \'sē-,bē\ *n* : a member of a construction battalion of the United States Navy [alteration of *cee* + *bee*; from the initials of *construction battalion*]

sea·bird \'sē-,bərd\ *n* : a bird (as a gull or albatross) frequenting the open ocean

sea biscuit *n* : HARDTACK

sea·board \'sē-,bōrd, -,bȯrd\ *n* : SEACOAST; *also* : the country bordering a seacoast — **seaboard** *adj*

sea·boot \'sē-,büt\ *n* : a very high waterproof boot used especially by sailors and fishermen

sea·borne \-,bōrn, -,bȯrn\ *adj* **1** : borne over or upon the sea (a *seaborne* invasion) **2** : engaged in or carried on by overseas shipping (*seaborne* trade)

sea bream *n* : any of numerous sea fishes related to the perches

sea breeze *n* : a breeze blowing inland from the sea

sea change *n* **1** : a change brought about by the sea **2** : TRANSFORMATION 1

sea chest *n* : a sailor's storage chest for personal property

sea·coast \'sē-,kōst\ *n* : the shore or border of the land adjacent to the sea

sea cow *n* : MANATEE, DUGONG

sea·craft \'sē-,kraft\ *n* **1** : seagoing ships **2** : skill in navigation

sea cucumber *n* : any of a class (Holothurioidea) of echinoderms having a long flexible tough muscular body often resembling a cucumber — called also *holothurian*

sea dog *n* : a veteran sailor

sea duty *n* : duty in the United States Navy performed outside the continental United States or specified dependencies thereof

sea eagle *n* : any of various eagles that feed largely on fish

Sea Explorer *n* : an Explorer in a scouting program that teaches seamanship

sea fan *n* : a coelenterate with a fan-shaped skeleton that is related to the corals and sea anemones

sea·far·er \'sē-,far-ər, -,fer-\ *n* : MARINER

sea·far·ing \-,far-ing, -,fer-\ *n* **1** : traveling over the sea **2** : the occupation of a sailor — **seafaring** *adj*

sea·food \'sē-,füd\ *n* : edible marine fish and shellfish

sea·front \-,frənt\ *n* : the waterfront of a seaside place

sea·girt \-,gərt\ *adj* : surrounded by the sea

sea·go·ing \-,gō-ing\ *adj* : adapted or used for sea travel (*seagoing* ships); *also* : SEAFARING (a *seagoing* nation)

sea green *n* **1** : a moderate green or bluish green **2** : a moderate yellow green

sea gull *n* : GULL; *esp* : one frequenting the sea

sea hare *n* : any of various large naked sea mollusks with arched backs and front tentacles that project like ears

sea horse *n* **1** : a fabulous animal half horse and half fish **2** : a small long-snouted fish that is covered with bony plates and has a head that looks like a horse's head

sea is·land cotton \,sē-,ī-lənd-, -,ī-lən-\ *n, often cap S&I* : a cotton with especially long silky fiber [*Sea Islands*, chain of islands in the Atlantic]

sea king *n* : a Viking chief

¹seal \'sēl\ *n, pl* **seals** *also* **seal 1** : any of numerous marine flesh-eating mammals chiefly of cold regions with limbs modified into webbed flippers adapted primarily to swimming **2 a** : the pelt of a seal **b** : leather made from the skin of a seal [Old English *seolh*]

²seal *vi* : to hunt seals — **seal·er** *n*

³seal *n* **1** : a device with an identifying design or words cut into or raised on its surface that can be pressed or stamped (as into paper or wax) to form a mark (as for certifying a signature or authenticating a document); *also* : a piece of wax or a wafer bearing such an impressed mark or the mark itself **2** : a usually ornamental adhesive stamp that may be used to close a letter or package; *esp* : one sold in a fund-raising campaign **3 a** : something (as a pledge) that makes safe or secure (under *seal* of secrecy) **b** : a closure that can be opened only by breaking or tearing (a *seal* on the door of a boxcar) **c** : a tight and perfect closure (test the *seal* of the jars); *also* : a device or an arrangement of material designed to produce such a closure (covered the joint with a thick *seal* of rosin) (the water *seal* of a toilet) [Old French *seel*, from Latin *sigillum*, from *signum* "sign, seal"] — **under seal** : with an authenticating seal affixed

⁴seal *vt* **1** : to mark with or certify or authenticate by or as if by a seal (*seal* a deed) **2** : to close or make fast with or as if with a seal often to prevent or disclose tampering (the sheriff *sealed* the premises) (*seal* a letter with glue) (ice *sealed* the ships into the harbor) **3** : to determine finally and irrevocably (this answer *sealed* our fate) — **seal·er** *n*

sea lamprey *n* : a large lamprey sometimes used as food that is a pest destructive of native fish in the Great Lakes

sea–lane \'sē-,lān\ *n* : an established sea route

seal·ant \'sē-lənt\ *n* : a sealing agent (radiator *sealant*)

sea lavender *n* : any of several salt-marsh plants with basal leaves and branching sprays of tiny usually lavender flowers

sea legs *n* : bodily adjustment to the motion of a ship at sea indicated especially by ability to walk steadily and by freedom from seasickness

sea lettuce *n* : ULVA

sea level *n* : the height of the surface of the sea midway between the average high and low tides

sea lily *n* : CRINOID; *esp* : a stalked crinoid

sealing wax *n* : a resinous composition that is plastic when warm and is used for sealing (as letters or dry cells)

sea lion *n* : any of several large Pacific eared seals

seal·skin \'sēl-ˌskin\ *n* **1** : the fur or pelt of a fur seal **2** : a garment (as a coat) of sealskin — **sealskin** *adj*

¹**seam** \'sēm\ *n* **1** : the joining or the mark made by the joining of two pieces or edges of material by sewing **2** : the space between adjacent planks of a ship **3 a** : a line left by a cut or wound; *also* : WRINKLE **b** : a layer or stratum (as of mineral) between distinctive layers ⟨coal *seams*⟩ [Old English *sēam*] — **seam·less** \-ləs\ *adj* — **seam·like** \-ˌlīk\ *adj*

²**seam** *vt* **1** : to join by or as if by sewing **2** : to mark with lines suggesting seams : FURROW ⟨creeks *seam* the valley⟩ — **seam·er** *n*

sea·man \'sē-mən\ *n* **1** : SAILOR 1a, MARINER **2** : an enlisted rank in the Navy and Coast Guard above seaman apprentice and below petty officer third class

seaman apprentice *n* : an enlisted rank in the Navy and Coast Guard above seaman recruit and below seaman

seaman recruit *n* : the lowest enlisted rank in the Navy and Coast Guard

sea·man·ship \'sē-mən-ˌship\ *n* : the art or skill of handling, working, and navigating a ship

sea·mark \-ˌmärk\ *n* **1** : a line on a coast marking the tidal limit **2** : an elevated object serving as a beacon to mariners

sea mile *n* : NAUTICAL MILE

sea·mount \'sē-ˌmaunt\ *n* : a submarine mountain

seam·stress \'sēm-strəs, 'sēmp-\ *also* **semp·stress** \'sem-strəs, 'semp-\ *n* : a woman who sews especially for a living [*seamster, sempster* "tailor" (from Old English *sēamestre,* from *sēam* "seam") + *-ess*]

seamy \'sē-mē\ *adj* **seam·i·er; -est** **1** : having or showing seams ⟨*seamy* ledges⟩ **2** : UNPLEASANT, SORDID ⟨the *seamy* side of life⟩ — **seam·i·ness** *n*

sé·ance \'sā-ˌäns, -ˌäⁿs\ *n* **1** : SESSION 1 **2** : a meeting of persons seeking to communicate with spirits [French, literally, "sitting", from *seoir* "to sit", from Latin *sedēre*]

sea nettle *n* : a stinging jellyfish

sea otter *n* : a large marine otter of northern Pacific coasts that attains a maximum length of nearly six feet and feeds largely on shellfish

sea pen *n* : any of numerous coelenterates that are related to the corals and form colonies of a feathery form

sea·plane \'sē-ˌplān\ *n* : an airplane designed to take off from and land on the water

sea·port \-ˌpōrt, -ˌpȯrt\ *n* : a port, harbor, or town accessible to seagoing ships

sea power *n* **1** : a nation having formidable naval strength **2** : naval strength

¹**sear** \'siər\ *vb* **1** : to cause withering or drying : PARCH ⟨harsh winds that *sear* and burn⟩ **2** : to burn, scorch, brown, or injure with or as if with sudden application of intense heat [Old English *sēarian* "to become sere", from *sēar* "sere"]

²**sear** *n* : a mark or scar left by searing

¹**search** \'sərch\ *vb* **1 a** : to go through or look carefully and thoroughly in an effort to find or discover ⟨*search* a room⟩ ⟨*search* for a lost child⟩ **b** : to examine for articles concealed on the person **c** : to examine or explore with painstaking care often with a particular objective in view : PROBE ⟨*searching* for an escape from a problem⟩ **2** : to find or come to know by or as if by careful investigation or scrutiny ⟨*searching* out every weakness in an adversary's argument⟩ [Middle French *cerchier,* from Late Latin *circare* "to go about", from Latin *circum* "round about", from circus "circle"] — **search·able** \'sər-chə-bəl\ *adj* — **search·er** \-chər\ *n* — **search·ing·ly** \-ching-lē\ *adv*

²**search** *n* **1 a** : an act of searching **b** : an act of boarding and inspecting a ship on the high seas (as by a belligerent seeking contraband goods) **2** : a person or party that searches

search·light \'sərch-ˌlīt\ *n* : an apparatus for projecting a powerful beam of light; *also* : a beam of light projected by such an apparatus

search warrant *n* : a warrant authorizing a search of a specified place for stolen goods or unlawful possessions

sea robin *n* : any of several gurnards

sea-run \ˌsē-ˌrən\ *adj* : ANADROMOUS ⟨a *sea-run* salmon⟩

sea·scape \'sē-ˌskāp\ *n* **1** : a view of the sea **2** : a picture representing a scene at sea

sea scorpion *n* : SCULPIN

Sea Scout *n* : SEA EXPLORER

sea serpent *n* : a large marine animal resembling a snake often reported to have been seen but never proved to exist

sea·shell \'sē-ˌshel\ *n* : the shell of a marine animal and especially a mollusk

sea·shore \-ˌshōr, -ˌshȯr\ *n* **1** : land adjacent to the sea : SEACOAST **2** : the ground between the ordinary high-water and low-water marks

sea·sick \-ˌsik\ *adj* : affected with or suggestive of seasickness

sea·sick·ness \-nəs\ *n* : motion sickness experienced on the water

sea·side \'sē-ˌsīd\ *n* : country adjacent to the sea : SEASHORE

sea slug *n* **1** : SEA CUCUMBER **2** : a naked marine gastropod mollusk

sea snake *n* **1** : SEA SERPENT **2** : any of numerous venomous aquatic snakes of warm seas

¹**sea·son** \'sēz-n\ *n* **1 a** : a suitable or natural time or occasion ⟨a *season* for all things⟩ **b** : a usually brief period of time ⟨willing to wait a *season*⟩ **c** : a particular point in a period or in the course of events ⟨visitors at all *seasons*⟩ **2 a** : a period of the year associated with some recurrent phenomenon or activity ⟨the growing *season*⟩ **b** : a period characterized by a particular kind of weather ⟨a long dry *season*⟩ **c** : one of the four quarters into which the year is commonly divided — compare AUTUMN, SPRING, SUMMER, WINTER **d** : a period of the year associated with a particular event (as a holiday) or phase of human activity (as agriculture, sport, or business) ⟨the Christmas *season*⟩ ⟨the baseball *season*⟩ [Old French *saison,* from Latin *satio* "act of sowing", from *satus,* past participle of *serere* "to sow"] — **in season** **1** : at the right or fitting time **2** : at the stage of greatest fitness (as for eating) ⟨peaches are *in season*⟩ **3** : legal to take by hunting or fishing — **out of season** : not in season ⟨fined for hunting *out of season*⟩

²**season** *vb* **sea·soned; sea·son·ing** \'sēz-ning, -n-ing\ **1** : to give food better flavor or more zest by adding seasoning ⟨a perfectly *seasoned* stew⟩; *also* : to add seasoning ⟨*season* to taste⟩ **2 a** : to treat so as to be fit for use; *esp* : to prepare (lumber) for use by controlled drying **b** : to make fit by experience ⟨*seasoned* veterans⟩ **3** : to become seasoned [Middle French *assaisoner* "to ripen, season", from *saison* "season"] — **sea·son·er** \'sēz-nər, -n-ər\ *n*

sea·son·able \'sēz-nə-bəl, -n-ə-bəl\ *adj* **1** : suitable to the season or circumstances : TIMELY ⟨a *seasonable* frost⟩ ⟨*seasonable* temperatures⟩ **2** : occurring in good or proper time : OPPORTUNE ⟨*seasonable* advice⟩ ⟨a *seasonable* time to open discussions⟩ — **sea·son·able·ness** *n* — **sea·son·ably** \-blē\ *adv*

sea lion

sea otter

\ə\ abut		\ng\ sing	
\ər\ further		\ō\ bone	
\a\ mat		\ȯ\ saw	
\ā\ take		\oi\ coin	
\ä\ cot, cart		\th\ thin	
\au\ out		\th\ this	
\ch\ chin		\ü\ food	
\e\ pet		\u\ foot	
\ē\ easy		\y\ yet	
\g\ go		\yü\ few	
\i\ tip		\yu\ cure	
\ī\ life		\zh\ vision	
\j\ job			

sea·son·al \'sēz-nəl, -n̥-əl\ *adj* **1** : of, relating to, or varying in occurrence with the seasons ⟨*seasonal* storms⟩ **2** : affected or caused by seasonal need or availability ⟨*seasonal* industries⟩ ⟨*seasonal* unemployment⟩ — **sea·son·al·ly** \-ē\ *adv*

sea·son·ing \'sēz-ning, -n̥-ing\ *n* : an ingredient (as a condiment, spice, or herb) added to food primarily for savor

season ticket *n* : a ticket (as to all of a club's home games) valid during a specified time

sea spider *n* : any of a class (Pycnogonida) of small long-legged marine arthropods superficially resembling spiders

sea squirt *n* : any of various simple pouched tunicates

sea star *n* : STARFISH

sea stores *n pl* : supplies (as of foodstuffs) laid in before starting on a sea voyage

¹seat \'sēt\ *n* **1 a** : something (as a chair) intended to be sat in or on **b** : the particular part of something on which one rests in sitting ⟨*seat* of the trousers⟩ ⟨a chair *seat*⟩ **c** : the part of the body that bears the weight in sitting : BUTTOCKS **2 a** : a seating accommodation ⟨had three *seats* for the game⟩ **b** : a right of sitting usually as a member ⟨a *seat* in the senate⟩ **c** : MEMBERSHIP ⟨a *seat* on the stock exchange⟩ **3** : a place or area where something is situated or centered ⟨*seats* of higher learning⟩; *esp* : a place (as a capital city) from which authority is exercised ⟨the new *seat* of the government⟩ **4** : posture in or way of sitting especially on horseback **5** : a part or surface on which another part or surface rests ⟨a valve *seat*⟩ [Old Norse *sæti*] — **seat·ed** \-əd\ *adj*

²seat *vb* **1 a** : to cause to sit or assist in finding a seat ⟨*seat* a guest⟩ **b** : to provide seats for ⟨a theater *seating* 1000 persons⟩ **c** : to put in a sitting position ⟨*seat* oneself at table⟩ **2** : to repair the seat of or provide a new seat for **3** : to fit to, on, or with a seat ⟨*seat* a valve⟩ — **seat·er** *n*

seat belt *n* : straps (as in an automobile or airplane) designed to hold a person steady in a seat

sea train *n* **1** : a seagoing ship equipped for carrying a train of railroad cars **2** : several army or navy transports forming a convoy at sea

sea trout *n* **1** : a trout or char that as an adult inhabits the sea but ascends rivers to spawn **2** : any of various sea fishes (as a weakfish or greenling) resembling trouts

sea urchin *n* : any of a class (Echinoidea) of echinoderms enclosed in shells that are usually flattened and globe-shaped and covered with movable spines

sea urchin

sea·wall \'sē-,wȯl\ *n* : a wall or embankment to protect the shore from erosion or to act as a breakwater

¹sea·ward \'sē-wərd\ *n* : the direction or side away from land and toward the open sea

²seaward *also* **sea·wards** \-wərdz\ *adv or adj* : toward the sea

sea·wa·ter \'sē-,wȯt-ər, -,wät-\ *n* : water in or from the sea

sea·way \-,wā\ *n* **1** : a route for travel on the sea; *also* : an ocean traffic lane **2** : a moderate or rough sea **3** : a deep inland waterway that admits ocean shipping

sea·weed \-,wēd\ *n* : a plant growing in the sea; *esp* : a marine alga (as a kelp)

sea·worn \-,wȯrn, -,wȯrn\ *adj* **1** : impaired or eaten away by the sea ⟨*seaworn* shores⟩ **2** : worn out by sea voyaging

sea·wor·thy \-,wər-t͟hē\ *adj* : fit or safe for a sea voyage ⟨a *seaworthy* ship⟩ — **sea·wor·thi·ness** *n*

sea wrack *n* : SEAWEED; *esp* : seaweed growing or washed ashore in large masses

se·ba·ceous gland \si-,bā-shəs-\ *n* : one of the skin glands that secrete an oily lubricating substance into the hair follicles [Latin *sebaceus* "made of tallow", from *sebum* "tallow"]

seb·or·rhea \,seb-ə-'rē-ə\ *n* : excessive secretion and discharge of sebum — **seb·or·rhe·ic** \-'rē-ik\ *adj*

se·bum \'sē-bəm\ *n* : the secretion of the sebaceous glands [Latin, "tallow, grease"]

se·cant \'sē-,kant, -kənt\ *n* **1** : a straight line cutting a curve at two or more points **2** : a trigonometric function that for an acute angle is the ratio of the hypotenuse of a right triangle of which the angle is considered part and the side adjacent to the angle — abbreviation *sec* [Latin *secans*, present participle of *secare* "to cut"]

se·cede \si-'sēd\ *vi* : to withdraw from an organization (as a nation, church, or political party) [Latin *secedere*, from *se-* "apart" + *cedere* "to go"] — **se·ced·er** *n*

se·ces·sion \si-'sesh-ən\ *n* **1** : the act of seceding : a formal withdrawal **2** *often cap* : the withdrawal of the 11 southern states from the Union at the start of the Civil War [Latin *secessio*, from *secedere* "to secede"] — **se·ces·sion·ism** \-'sesh-ə-,niz-əm\ *n* — **se·ces·sion·ist** \-'sesh-nəst, -ə-nəst\ *n*

se·clude \si-'klüd\ *vt* : to keep or shut away from others : make inaccessible ⟨*secluded* themselves with a few old friends⟩ [Latin *secludere*, from *se-* "apart" + *claudere* "to close"]

se·clud·ed *adj* **1** : screened or hidden from view **2** : living in seclusion — **se·clud·ed·ly** *adv* — **se·clud·ed·ness** *n*

se·clu·sion \si-'klü-zhən\ *n* **1** : the act of secluding : the condition of being secluded **2** : a secluded or isolated place [Medieval Latin *seclusio*, from Latin *secludere* "to seclude"] — **se·clu·sive** \-'klü-siv, -ziv\ *adj* — **se·clu·sive·ly** *adv* — **se·clu·sive·ness** *n*

seco·bar·bi·tal \,sek-ō-'bär-bə-,tȯl\ *n* : a barbiturate $C_{12}H_{18}N_2O_3$ that is used chiefly in the form of its bitter powdery sodium salt as a hypnotic and sedative [*Seco*nal, a trademark + *barbital*]

Sec·o·nal \'sek-ə-,nȯl\ *trademark* — used for secobarbital

¹sec·ond \'sek-ənd *also* -ənt\ *adj* **1** : being number two in a countable series **2** : being next after the first (as in order, time, or importance) **3** : ALTERNATE, OTHER ⟨elects a mayor every *second* year⟩ **4** : resembling or suggesting a prototype : ANOTHER ⟨a *second* Solomon⟩ **5** : having a musical part lower in pitch than or subordinate to another of its kind ⟨*second* violin⟩ [Old French, from Latin *secundus* "following, second", from *sequi* "to follow"] — **second** *adv* — **sec·ond·ly** *adv*

²second *n* **1 a** : number two in a countable series ⟨the *second* of the month⟩ — see NUMBER table **b** : one next after the first (as in the time, order, or importance) **2** : one who assists or supports another (as in a duel or a boxing match) **3 a** : a musical interval embracing two diatonic degrees **b** : the tone at this interval **4** : an inferior or flawed article (as of merchandise) **5** : the act of seconding a motion **6** : the second gear or speed in an automotive vehicle **7** *pl* : a second helping of food

³second *n* **1 a** : the 60th part of a minute of angular measure **b** : the 60th part of a minute of time; *esp* : the international unit of time related to the period of the radiation corresponding to a change between the two levels of the ground state of a particular isotope of the cesium atom **2** : an instant of time : MOMENT ⟨I'll be back in a *second*⟩ [Medieval Latin *secunda*, from Latin *secundus* "second"; from its being the second sexagesimal division of a unit, as a minute is the first]

⁴second *vt* **1** : to give support or encouragement to : ASSIST **2** : to endorse (a motion or a nomination) so that debate or voting may begin [Latin *secundare*, from *secundus* "second, favorable"] — **sec·ond·er** *n*

¹sec·ond·ary \'sek-ən-,der-ē\ *adj* **1 a** : of second rank, importance, or value ⟨*secondary* streams⟩ **b** : of, relating to, or constituting the second strongest of the three or four degrees of stress ⟨the fourth syllable of basketball team carries *secondary* stress) **2 a :** derived from something original, primary, or basic **b :** of, relating to, or being the current created by a change in the primary current or the circuit of the created current in an induction coil or transformer **c :** produced by activity of formative tissue and especially cambium other than that at the growing point **3 a :** of, relating to, or being a second order or stage in a sequence or series **b :** of, relating to, or being the second segment of the wing of a bird or the quills of this segment **c :** intermediate between elementary and collegiate ⟨*secondary* school⟩ — **sec·ond·ar·i·ly** \ˌsek-ən-'der-ə-lē\ *adv* — **sec·ond·ar·i·ness** \'sek-ən-ˌder-ē-nəs\ *n*

²**secondary** *n, pl* **-ar·ies :** one that is secondary: as **a :** a defensive football backfield **b :** a secondary feather of a bird **c :** the coil through which the secondary current passes in an induction coil or transformer — called also *secondary coil*

secondary cell *n* : STORAGE CELL

secondary emission *n* : the emission of electrons from a surface that is bombarded by charged particles

secondary road *n* **1 :** a road not of primary importance **2 :** a road that feeds traffic to a more important road (as a turnpike)

secondary sex characteristic *n* : a physical or mental characteristic that appears in members of one sex at puberty or in seasonal breeders at the breeding season and is not directly concerned with reproduction

second base *n* **1 :** the base that must be touched second by a base runner in baseball **2 :** the position of the player defending the area to the right of second base

second base·man \-'bā-smən\ *n* : a player defending the area to the right of second base

sec·ond–best \ˌsek-ən-'best\ *adj* : next to the best

second childhood *n* : a state of feebleness or childishness of mind caused by or accompanying old age

sec·ond–class \ˌsek-ng-'klas, -ən-, -ənd-\ *adj* **1 :** of or relating to a second class **2 a :** INFERIOR 3, MEDIOCRE **b :** socially or economically deprived ⟨*second-class* citizens⟩

second class *n* **1 :** the second and usually next to highest group in a classification **2 :** a class of United States or Canadian mail comprising newspapers and periodicals sent to subscribers

Second Coming *n* : the coming of Christ on Judgment Day

second–degree burn *n* : a burn marked by pain, blistering, and superficial destruction of the skin with fluid infiltration and reddening of the tissues beneath the burn

second growth *n* : forest trees that come up naturally after removal of the first growth by cutting or by fire

sec·ond–guess \ˌsek-ng-'ges, -ən-\ *vt* **1 :** to think out alternative strategies or explanations for after the event **2 a :** OUTWIT **b :** PREDICT — **sec·ond–guess·er** *n*

sec·ond·hand \ˌsek-ən-'hand\ *adj* **1 :** taken from someone else ⟨*secondhand* information⟩ **2 :** having had a previous owner ⟨a *secondhand* car⟩ **3 :** selling used goods ⟨a *secondhand* store⟩ — **secondhand** *adv*

second hand \'sek-ən-ˌhand\ *n* : the hand marking seconds on a timepiece

second lieutenant *n* : the lowest officer rank in the Army, Marine Corps, and Air Force

second person *n* : a set of words or forms (as verb forms or pronouns) referring to the person or thing addressed in the utterance in which they occur; *also* : a word or form belonging to such a set

sec·ond–rate \ˌsek-ən-'drāt, -'rāt\ *adj* : of second or inferior quality or value : MEDIOCRE — **sec·ond–rate·ness** *n* — **sec·ond–rat·er** \-'drāt-ər, -'rāt-\ *n*

second sight *n* : CLAIRVOYANCE 1

second–story man *n* : a burglar who enters a house by an upstairs window

sec·ond–string \ˌsek-ən-'string, -ng-\ *adj* : being a substitute player as distinguished from a regular [from the reserve bowstring carried by an archer in case the first breaks]

se·cre·cy \'sē-krə-sē\ *n, pl* **-cies 1 :** the habit or practice of keeping secrets **2 :** the quality or state of being hidden or concealed [Middle English *secretee,* from *secre* "secret", from Middle French *secré,* from Latin *secretus*]

¹**se·cret** \'sē-krət\ *adj* **1 a :** hidden or kept from knowledge or view **b :** working with hidden aims or methods : UNDERCOVER ⟨a *secret* agent⟩ **2 :** SECLUDED 1 ⟨a *secret* valley⟩ [Middle French, from Latin *secretus,* from *secernere* "to separate, distinguish", from *se-* "apart" + *cernere* "to sift"] — **se·cret·ly** *adv* ☐ SYN SECRET, COVERT, CLANDESTINE, SURREPTITIOUS mean done without attracting observation. SECRET may imply concealment on any grounds or for any motive ⟨*secret* diplomatic negotiations⟩ COVERT stresses the mere fact of not being open or declared ⟨*covert* envy of a friend⟩ CLANDESTINE implies secrecy usually of a forbidden act ⟨*clandestine* drug trade⟩ SURREPTITIOUS stresses the careful and skillful avoidance of detection as in violating a law or custom or right ⟨*surreptitious* copying from notes⟩

²**secret** *n* **1 a :** something kept hidden or unexplained : MYSTERY **b :** something kept from the knowledge of others or shared only confidentially with a few **2 :** a secret condition or place : SECRECY ⟨conspired in *secret*⟩ **3 :** something taken to be a key to a desired end ⟨the *secret* of longevity⟩

sec·re·tar·i·at \ˌsek-rə-'ter-ē-ət\ *n* **1 :** the clerical staff of an organization **2 :** the administrative department of a governmental organization ⟨the United Nations *secretariat*⟩ [French *secrétariat* "office of a secretary, secretariat", from Medieval Latin *secretariatus* "office of a secretary", from *secretarius* "secretary"]

sec·re·tary \'sek-rə-ˌter-ē\ *n, pl* **-tar·ies 1 :** a person employed to handle correspondence and routine or detail work for a superior **2 :** an officer of a business corporation or society who has charge of the correspondence and records **3 :** a government official in charge of the affairs of a department ⟨*Secretary* of State⟩ **4 :** a writing desk with a top section for books [Medieval Latin *secretarius* "confidential employee, secretary", derived from Latin *secretus* "secret"] — **sec·re·tari·al** \ˌsek-rə-'ter-ē-əl\ *adj* — **sec·re·tary·ship** \'sek-rə-ˌter-ē-ˌship\ *n*

secretary–general *n, pl* **secretaries–general :** a principal administrative officer

secret ballot *n* : AUSTRALIAN BALLOT

¹**se·crete** \si-'krēt\ *vb* : to produce and give off a secretion ⟨glands that *secrete* intermittently⟩ [back-formation from *secretion*]

²**se·crete** \si-'krēt, 'sē-krət\ *vt* : to deposit or conceal in a hiding place ⟨*secrete* money in one's shoe⟩ [¹*secret*]

se·cre·tin \si-'krēt-n\ *n* : an intestinal hormone capable of stimulating the pancreas and liver to secrete [*secret*ion + *-in*]

se·cre·tion \si-'krē-shən\ *n* **1 :** a concealing or hiding of something **2 a :** the act or process of secreting **b :** a product of glandular activity; *esp* : one (as a hormone or enzyme) that performs a specific useful function in the organism [French *sécrétion,* from Latin *secretio* "separation", from *secernere* "to separate", from *se-* "apart" + *cernere* "to sift"] — **se·cre·tion·ary** \-shə-ˌner-ē\ *adj*

se·cre·tive \'sē-krət-iv, si-'krēt-\ *adj* : disposed to secrecy or concealment : not frank or open — **se·cre·tive·ly** *adv* — **se·cre·tive·ness** *n*

se·cre·to·ry \si-'krēt-ə-rē\ *adj* : of, relating to, or active in secretion

secret police *n* : a police organization operating largely in secrecy and especially to further the political purposes of its government often with terroristic methods

secretary 4

\ə\ abut	\ng\ sing
\ər\ further	\ō\ bone
\a\ mat	\ȯ\ saw
\ā\ take	\ȯi\ coin
\ä\ cot, cart	\th\ thin
\au̇\ out	\t͟h\ this
\ch\ chin	\ü\ food
\e\ pet	\u̇\ foot
\ē\ easy	\y\ yet
\g\ go	\yü\ few
\i\ tip	\yu̇\ cure
\ī\ life	\zh\ vision
\j\ job	

Secret Service *n* : a division of the United States Treasury Department charged chiefly with the suppression of counterfeiting and the protection of the president

sect \'sekt\ *n* **1 a** : a dissenting or schismatic religious body; *esp* : one regarded as extreme or heretical **b** : a religious denomination **2 a** : a group adhering to a distinctive doctrine or to a leader **b** : PARTY 1 **c** : FACTION 1 [Latin *secta* "way of life, class of persons", from *sequi* "to follow"]

¹sec·tar·i·an \sek-'ter-ē-ən\ *adj* **1** : of, relating to, or characteristic of a sect or sectarian **2** : limited in character or scope : PAROCHIAL — **sec·tar·i·an·ism** \-ē-ə-,niz-əm\ *n*

²sectarian *n* **1** : a member of a sect **2** : a narrow or bigoted person

sec·tar·i·an·ize \sek-'ter-ē-ə-,nīz\ *vb* **1** : to act as sectarians **2** : to make sectarian

sec·ta·ry \'sek-tə-rē\ *n, pl* **-ries** : a member of a sect

¹sec·tion \'sek-shən\ *n* **1 a** : the action or an instance of cutting or separating by cutting **b** : a part set off by or as if by cutting : PORTION, SLICE **2** : a distinct part or portion of a writing: as **a** : a subdivision of a chapter **b** : a distinct component part of a newspaper ⟨sports *section*⟩ **3** : CROSS SECTION 1b **4** : a character § used chiefly as a reference mark or to show the beginning of a section **5** : a piece of land one square mile (about 2.6 square kilometers) in area forming one of the 36 subdivisions of a township **6** : a distinct part of an area, community, or group of people **7 a** : a division of a railroad sleeping car with an upper and a lower berth **b** : a part of a permanent railroad way under the care of a particular set of men **c** : one of two or more vehicles that run on the same schedule **8** : one of several component parts (as of a bookcase) that may be assembled or reassembled **9** : a division of an orchestra composed of one class of instruments ⟨brass *section*⟩ [Latin *sectio,* from *secare* "to cut"]

²section *vb* **sec·tioned; sec·tion·ing** \-shə-ning, -shning\ **1** : to cut or separate into or become cut or separated into parts or sections **2** : to represent in sections (as by a drawing)

sec·tion·al \'sek-shnəl, -shən-l\ *adj* **1 a** : of or relating to a section **b** : local or regional rather than general in character ⟨*sectional* interests⟩ **2** : made up of or divided into sections ⟨a *sectional* sofa⟩ — **sec·tion·al·ly** \-ē\ *adv*

sec·tion·al·ism \'sek-shnə-,liz-əm, -shən-l-,iz-\ *n* : an exaggerated devotion to the interests of a region

section gang *n* : a gang or crew of track workers employed to maintain a railroad section

section hand *n* : a laborer belonging to a section gang

sec·tor \'sek-tər, -,tor\ *n* **1** : the part of a circle between two radii and their intercepted arc on the circumference **2** : an area assigned to a military commander to defend **3** : a distinctive part (as of an economy) ⟨the industrial *sector*⟩ [Latin, "cutter", from *secare* "to cut"] — **sec·to·ri·al** \sek-'tōr-ē-əl, -'tor-\ *adj*

¹sec·u·lar \'sek-yə-lər\ *adj* **1 a** : of or relating to the worldly or temporal ⟨*secular* concerns⟩ **b** : not openly or specifically religious ⟨*secular* music⟩ **c** : not ecclesiastical or clerical ⟨*secular* courts⟩ **2** : of or relating to clergy not belonging to a religious order ⟨a *secular* priest⟩ **3 a** : occurring once in an age or a century **b** : existing or continuing through ages or centuries ⟨*secular* enmities⟩ [Old French *seculer,* from Late Latin *saecularis,* from Latin, "coming once in an age", from *saeculum* "breed, generation, age"] — **sec·u·lar·ly** *adv*

²secular *n* **1** : a secular ecclesiastic (as a parish priest) **2** : LAYMAN

sec·u·lar·ism \-lə-,riz-əm\ *n* : indifference to or rejection or exclusion of religion and religious considerations — **sec·u·lar·ist** \-rəst\ *n* — **secularist** *or* **sec·u·lar·is·tic** \,sek-yə-lə-'ris-tik\ *adj*

sec·u·lar·ize \'sek-yə-lə-,rīz\ *vt* **1** : to make secular **2** : to transfer from ecclesiastical to civil or lay use, possession, or control — **sec·u·lar·iza·tion** \,sek-yə-lə-rə-'zā-shən\ *n* — **sec·u·lar·iz·er** \'sek-yə-lə-,rī-zər\ *n*

se·cur·ance \si-'kyur-əns\ *n* : the act of making secure

¹se·cure \si-'kyur\ *adj* **1 a** : easy in mind : CONFIDENT **b** : assured in opinion or expectation : having no doubt **2 a** : free from danger **b** : free from risk of loss **c** : affording safety : INVIOLABLE ⟨a *secure* hideaway⟩ **d** : TRUSTWORTHY, DEPENDABLE ⟨a *secure* foundation⟩ **3** : SURE 5a, CERTAIN ⟨our victory is *secure*⟩ [Latin *securus* "safe, secure", from *se* "without" + *cura* "care"] SYN see SAFE — **se·cure·ly** *adv* — **se·cure·ness** *n*

²secure *vb* **1 a** : to relieve from exposure to danger : GUARD, SHIELD ⟨*secure* a supply line from enemy raids⟩ **b** : to put beyond hazard of losing or of not receiving : GUARANTEE **c** : to give pledge of payment to (a creditor) or of (an obligation) ⟨*secure* a note with collateral⟩ **2 a** : to take (a person) into custody ⟨*secure* the prisoner⟩ **b** : to make fast : SEAL ⟨*secure* a door⟩ **c** : to tie up : BERTH ⟨*secure* a boat for the night⟩ **3 a** : to get secure possession of : PROCURE ⟨*secure* employment⟩ **b** : to bring about : EFFECT **4** : to release (naval personnel) from work or duty; *also* : to stop work — **se·cur·er** *n*

se·cure·ment \si-'kyur-mənt\ *n* : the act or process of making secure

se·cu·ri·ty \si-'kyur-ət-ē\ *n, pl* **-ties** **1** : the quality or state of being secure: as **a** : freedom from danger : SAFETY **b** : freedom from fear or anxiety **2 a** : something given, deposited, or pledged to make certain the fulfillment of an obligation ⟨*security* for a loan⟩ **b** : SURETY 3 **3** : an evidence of debt or of property ⟨bonds and stock certificates are *securities*⟩ **4 a** : something that secures : PROTECTION **b** : measures taken especially to guard against espionage or sabotage ⟨concern over internal *security*⟩

Security Council *n* : a permanent council of the United Nations having primary responsibility for the maintenance of peace and security

se·dan \si-'dan\ *n* **1** : a portable often covered chair that is designed to carry one person and is borne on poles by two men **2 a** : an enclosed automobile that seats four to seven persons including the driver in a single compartment and has a permanent top **b** : CRUISER 3 [origin unknown]

se·date \si-'dāt\ *adj* : SERIOUS 1, STAID ⟨*sedate* manners⟩ [Latin *sedatus,* from *sedare* "to calm"] — **se·date·ly** *adv* — **se·date·ness** *n*

se·da·tion \si-'dā-shən\ *n* **1** : the inducing of a relaxed easy state especially by the use of sedatives **2** : a state resulting from or like that resulting from sedation

¹sed·a·tive \'sed-ət-iv\ *adj* : tending to calm, moderate, or relieve tension or irritability

²sedative *n* : a sedative agent or drug

sed·en·tary \'sed-n-,ter-ē\ *adj* **1** : not migratory : SETTLED ⟨*sedentary* birds⟩ **2** : doing or requiring much sitting ⟨a *sedentary* job⟩ **3** : permanently attached ⟨*sedentary* barnacles⟩ [Middle French *sedentaire,* from Latin *sedentarius,* from *sedens,* present participle of *sedēre* "to sit"]

se·der \'sād-ər\ *n, pl* **se·da·rim** \si-'där-əm\ *or* **seders** *often cap* : a Jewish home or community service and ceremonial dinner held on the first and by Orthodox Jews outside Israel on the second evening of the Passover in commemoration of the exodus from Egypt [Hebrew *sēdher* "order"]

sedge \'sej\ *n* : any of a family of usually tufted marsh plants differing from the related grasses in having achenes and solid stems [Old English *secg*] — **sedgy** \'sej-ē\ *adj*

sed·i·ment \'sed-ə-mənt\ *n* **1** : material that settles to the bottom of a liquid **2** : material (as stones and sand) deposited by water, wind, or glaciers [Middle

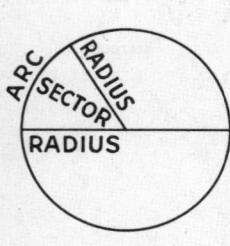

sector 1

French, from Latin *sedimentum* "settling", from *sedēre* "to sit, sink down"] — **sed·i·ment** \-,ment\ *vb*

sed·i·men·ta·ry \,sed-ə-'ment-ə-rē, -'men-trē\ *adj* **1** : of, relating to, or containing sediment ⟨*sedimentary* deposits⟩ **2** : formed by or from deposits of sediment ⟨limestone and sandstone are *sedimentary* rocks⟩

sed·i·men·ta·tion \,sed-ə-mən-'tā-shən, -,men-\ *n* : the action or process of depositing sediment

se·di·tion \si-'dish-ən\ *n* : incitement of resistance to or of insurrection against lawful authority [Middle French, from Latin *seditio,* literally, "separation", from *sed-, se-* "apart" + *itio* "act of going", from *ire* "to go"] □ **SYN SEDITION, TREASON** mean a serious breach of allegiance. **SEDITION** implies acts leading to or exciting commotion or resistance to authority but not including overt acts of violence or betrayal; **TREASON** implies an overt act aiming at overthrow of government or betrayal to the enemy.

se·di·tious \si-'dish-əs\ *adj* **1** : disposed to arouse, take part in, or be guilty of sedition ⟨a *seditious* agitator⟩ **2** : being or tending to cause sedition ⟨*seditious* statements⟩ — **se·di·tious·ly** *adv* — **se·di·tious·ness** *n*

se·duce \si-'düs, -'dyüs\ *vt* **1** : to persuade to disobedience or disloyalty **2** : to lead astray ⟨*seduced* into crime⟩ **3** : to entice to sexual intercourse **4** : **ATTRACT** [Latin *seducere* "to lead away", from *se-* "apart" + *ducere* "to lead"] — **se·duce·ment** \-'dü-smənt, -'dyü-\ *n* — **se·duc·er** *n*

se·duc·tion \si-'dək-shən\ *n* **1** : the act of seducing **2** : something that seduces [Latin *seductio* "act of leading aside", from *seducere* "to lead away"]

se·duc·tive \si-'dək-tiv\ *adj* : tending or having the qualities to seduce — **se·duc·tive·ly** *adv* — **se·duc·tive·ness** *n*

se·duc·tress \-trəs\ *n* : a woman who seduces [obsolete *seductor* "male seducer" + *-ess*]

sed·u·lous \'sej-ə-ləs\ *adj* : diligent in application or pursuit : **ASSIDUOUS** [Latin *sedulus,* from *sedulo* "sincerely, diligently", from *se* "without" + *dolus* "guile"] — **sed·u·lous·ly** *adv* — **sed·u·lous·ness** *n*

se·dum \'sēd-əm\ *n* : any of a genus of fleshy-leaved herbs including the orpine : **STONECROP** [Latin, a plant related to sedum]

¹see \'sē\ *vb* **saw** \'so\; **seen** \'sēn\; **see·ing** \'sē-ing\ **1 a** : to perceive by the eye or have the power of sight ⟨*see* a bird⟩ ⟨a person who cannot *see*⟩ **b** : to give or pay attention ⟨*see,* the bus is coming⟩ **c** : to look about **2 a** : to have experience of : **UNDERGO** ⟨*see* army service⟩ **b** : to come to know : **DISCOVER 3 a** : to form a mental picture of : **VISUALIZE b** : to perceive the meaning or importance of : **UNDERSTAND c** : to be aware of : **RECOGNIZE d** : to imagine as a possibility : **SUPPOSE** ⟨can't *see* how we can lose⟩ **4 a** : to make investigation or inquiry : **EXAMINE, WATCH** ⟨want to *see* how they handle the problem⟩ **b** : **READ** ⟨*saw* the story in the paper⟩ **c** : to attend as a spectator ⟨*see* a play⟩ **5 a** : to take care of : provide for ⟨enough to *see* us through⟩ **b** : **FINISH** ⟨*see* the job through⟩ **c** : **HELP, SUPPORT** ⟨*saw* me through a bad time⟩ **6** : to make sure ⟨*see* that order is kept⟩ **7 a** : to regard as : **JUDGE b** : to prefer to have ⟨I'll *see* you dead before I accept your terms⟩ **c** : to find acceptable or attractive ⟨still can't *see* the design⟩ **8 a** : to call on : **VISIT** ⟨*see* a sick friend⟩ **b** (1) : to keep company with especially in courtship or dating ⟨had been *seeing* each other for a year⟩ (2) : to grant an interview to : **RECEIVE** ⟨the president will *see* you now⟩ **9** : **ACCOMPANY, ESCORT** ⟨*see* the babysitter home⟩ **10** : to meet (a bet) in poker or to equal the bet of (a player) : **CALL** [Old English *sēon*]

²see *n* **1** : the city in which a bishop's church is located **2** : the jurisdiction of a bishop : **DIOCESE** [Old French *se,* from Latin *sedes* "seat"]

see·able \'sē-ə-bəl\ *adj* : capable of being seen

¹seed \'sēd\ *n, pl* **seed** *or* **seeds 1 a** : the grains or ripened ovules of plants used for sowing **b** : the fertilized ripened ovule of a flowering plant containing an embryo and capable normally of germination to produce a new plant; *also* : a plant structure (as a spore or small dry fruit) capable of producing a new plant **2 a** : **MILT, SEMEN b** : a developmental form of a lower animal suitable for transplanting; *esp* : **SPAT 3** : **PROGENY** ⟨the *seed* of David⟩ **4** : a source of development or growth : **GERM** ⟨sowed the *seeds* of discord⟩ **5** : something (as a small bubble in glass) that resembles a seed in shape or size [Old English *sǣd*] — **seed** *adj* — **seed·ed** \-əd\ *adj* — **seed·like** \'sēd-,līk\ *adj*

²seed *vb* **1 a** : **SOW** 1a, c, **PLANT** ⟨*seed* land to grass⟩ **b** : to bear or shed seeds ⟨weeds that *seed* freely⟩ **c** : to remove seeds from ⟨*seed* raisins⟩ **2** : to supply with nuclei (as of crystallization or condensation); *esp* : to treat (a cloud) with solid particles to convert water droplets into ice crystals in an attempt to produce rain **3** : to schedule (tournament players or teams) so that superior ones will not meet in early rounds

seed·bed \'sēd-,bed\ *n* : soil or a bed of soil prepared for planting seed

seed·case \-,kās\ *n* : a dry hollow fruit (as a pod) enclosing seeds

seed coat *n* : the hardened integuments of a ripened plant ovule forming an outer protective cover on a seed

seed·eat·er \'sēd-,ēt-ər\ *n* : a bird (as a finch) whose diet consists basically of seeds

seed·er \'sēd-ər\ *n* **1** : a machine for planting or sowing seeds **2** : a device for seeding fruit

seed fern *n* : any of an order (Cycadofilicales) of extinct plants with fronds like ferns and naked seeds

seed leaf *n* : **COTYLEDON** 2

seed·less \'sēd-ləs\ *adj* : having no seeds ⟨*seedless* grapes⟩

seed·ling \-ling\ *n* **1** : a young plant grown from seed **2** : a young tree before it becomes a sapling — **seed·ling** *adj*

seed oyster *n* : a young oyster especially of a size for transplantation

seed pearl *n* : a very small and often irregular pearl

seed plant *n* : a plant that bears seeds : **SPERMATOPHYTE**

seed·pod \'sēd-,päd\ *n* : **POD** 1

seeds·man \'sēdz-mən\ *n* **1** : one that sows seed **2** : a dealer in seeds

seed·time \'sēd-,tīm\ *n* : the season of sowing

seedy \'sēd-ē\ *adj* **seed·i·er; -est 1 a** : containing or full of seeds ⟨a *seedy* fruit⟩ **b** : containing many small similar inclusions ⟨glass *seedy* with air bubbles⟩ **2** : inferior in condition or quality: as **a** : **SHABBY, RUN-DOWN** ⟨*seedy* clothes⟩ **b** : somewhat disreputable : **SQUALID** ⟨a *seedy* district⟩ ⟨*seedy* entertainment⟩ **c** : slightly unwell ⟨felt *seedy* and went home early⟩ — **seed·i·ly** \'sēd-l-ē\ *adv* — **seed·i·ness** \'sēd-ē-nəs\ *n*

see·ing \'sē-ing\ *conj* : in view of the fact : inasmuch as — often used with *that* or *as*

Seeing Eye *trademark* — used for a guide dog trained to lead the blind

seek \'sēk\ *vb* **sought** \'sot\; **seek·ing 1** : to resort to : go to ⟨*seek* the shade on a hot day⟩ **2 a** : to go in search of : look for ⟨*seek* a friend⟩ **b** : to make a search or inquiry **c** : to try to discover ⟨*seek* the truth⟩ **3** : to ask for ⟨*seek* advice⟩ **4** : to try to acquire or gain ⟨*seek* one's fortune⟩ **5** : to make an attempt : **TRY** ⟨*seek* to find a way⟩ [Old English *sēcan*] — **seek·er** *n*

seel \'sēl\ *vt* : to close the eyes of (as a hawk) by drawing threads through the eyelids [Middle French *siller,* from Medieval Latin *ciliare,* from Latin *cilium* "eyelid"]

seem \'sēm\ *vi* **1 a** (1) : to give the impression of being : **APPEAR** ⟨*seem* reasonable⟩ (2) : to pretend to be **b** : to appear to the observation or understanding ⟨*seemed* to know⟩ **c** : to appear to one's own mind or opinion ⟨*seem* to feel no pain⟩ **2** : to give evidence of existing or being present ⟨there *seems* no reason for worry⟩ [of Scandinavian origin]

¹seem·ing \'sē-ming\ *n* : external appearance as distinguished from true character : LOOK

²seeming *adj* : apparent on superficial view : OSTENSIBLE ⟨*seeming* enthusiasm⟩ — **seem·ing·ly** \'sē-ming-lē\ *adv*

seem·ly \'sēm-lē\ *adj* **seem·li·er; -est** **1** : good-looking : HANDSOME, ATTRACTIVE **2** : conventionally proper : DECOROUS ⟨*seemly* behavior⟩ **3** : suited to the occasion, purpose, or person : FIT ⟨a *seemly* reply⟩ [Old Norse *sœmiligr*, from *sœmr* "becoming"] — **seem·li·ness** *n* — **seemly** *adv*

seen *past participle of* SEE

seep \'sēp\ *vi* : to flow or pass slowly through fine pores or small openings : OOZE ⟨water *seeped* through the wall⟩ [Old English *sipian*]

seep·age \'sē-pij\ *n* **1** : the process of seeping **2** : fluid that has seeped through porous material

seer \'siər, *esp for 1 also* 'sē-ər\ *n* **1** : one that sees **2 a** : one that predicts events or developments : PROPHET **b** : a person credited with extraordinary moral and spiritual insight

seer·ess \'siər-əs\ *n* : a woman who is a seer

seer·suck·er \'siər-ˌsək-ər\ *n* : a light fabric of linen, cotton, or rayon usually striped and slightly puckered [Hindi *śīrśaker,* from Persian *shīr-o-shakar,* literally, "milk and sugar"]

¹see·saw \'sē-ˌsȯ\ *n* **1** : an alternating up-and-down or backward-and-forward motion or movement; *also* : a contest or struggle in which now one side now the other has the lead **2 a** : a pastime in which two children or groups of children ride on opposite ends of a plank balanced in the middle so that one end goes up as the other goes down **b** : the plank or apparatus so used [probably from reduplication of ³*saw*] — **seesaw** *adj*

²seesaw *vb* **see·sawed; see·saw·ing** **1 a** : to move backward and forward or up and down **b** : to play on a seesaw **2** : ALTERNATE

seethe \'sēth\ *vb* **1** *archaic* : BOIL, STEW **2** : to soak or saturate in a liquid **3 a** : to be in a state of rapid agitated movement **b** : to churn or foam as if boiling ⟨the river rapids *seethed*⟩ **4** : to suffer violent internal excitement ⟨*seethed* with rage⟩ [Old English *sēothan*]

¹seg·ment \'seg-mənt\ *n* **1** : any of the parts into which a thing is divided or naturally separates : SECTION, DIVISION **2 a** : a part cut off from a geometrical figure (as a circle or sphere) by a line or plane; *esp* : the part of a circle bounded by a chord and an arc of that circle **b** : a part of a straight line included between two points — called also *line segment* [Latin *segmentum,* from *secare* "to cut"] SYN see PART — **seg·men·tary** \'seg-mən-ˌter-ē\ *adj* — **seg·ment·ed** \'seg-ˌment-əd, seg-'ment-\ *adj*

²seg·ment \'seg-ˌment\ *vb* : to separate into segments : give off as segments

seg·men·tal \seg-'ment-l\ *adj* **1** : of, relating to, or having the form of a segment or sector of a circle ⟨*segmental* fanlight⟩ ⟨*segmental* pediment⟩ **2** : METAMERIC **3** : of, relating to, or resulting from segmentation : SUBSIDIARY ⟨*segmental* data⟩ — **seg·men·tal·ly** \-l-ē\ *adv*

seg·men·ta·tion \ˌseg-mən-'tā-shən, -ˌmen-\ *n* : the process of dividing into segments; *esp* : the formation of many cells from a single cell (as in a developing egg)

se·go lily \ˌsē-gō-\ *n* : a western North American perennial herb of the lily family with an edible bulb and bell-shaped flowers that are white with purple, yellow, and lilac markings [Paiute *sego* "bulb of the sego lily"]

¹seg·re·gate \'seg-ri-ˌgāt\ *vb* **1** : to separate or set apart from others or from the general mass : ISOLATE **2** : to cause or force the segregation of **3** : to separate during

meiosis [Latin *segregare,* from *se-* "apart" + *greg-, grex* "herd"] — **seg·re·ga·tive** \-ˌgāt-iv\ *adj*

²seg·re·gate \-gət, -ˌgāt\ *n* : a segregated individual or class of individuals

seg·re·ga·tion \ˌseg-ri-'gā-shən\ *n* **1** : the act or process of segregating : the state of being segregated **2** : the separation or isolation of a race, class, or ethnic group by discriminatory means (as restriction to an area, barriers to social intercourse, or separate educational facilities)

seg·re·ga·tion·ist \-shə-nəst, -shnəst\ *n* : an advocate of segregation especially of races

se·gue \'sāg-ˌwā, 'seg-\ *imperative verb* : proceed to what follows without pause — used as a direction in music [Italian, "there follows", from *seguire* "to follow", from Latin *sequi*]

sei·del \'sīd-l\ *n* : a large glass for beer [German, from Latin *situla* "bucket"]

sei·gneur \sān-'yər\ *n, often cap* : LORD 1a, b, SEIGNIOR [Middle French, from Medieval Latin *senior,* from Latin, adj., "senior"] — **sei·gneur·ial** \-ē-əl\ *adj*

sei·gnior \sān-'yȯr, 'sān-,\ *n* : a man of rank or authority; *esp* : the feudal lord of a manor [Middle French *seigneur*]

sei·gniory *or* **sei·gnory** \'sān-yə-rē\ *n, pl* **-gnior·ies** *or* **-gnor·ies** : the territory of a lord : DOMAIN

sei·gno·ri·al \sān-'yȯr-ē-əl, -'yȯr-\ *adj* : of, relating to, or befitting a seignior : MANORIAL

¹seine \'sān\ *n* : a large fishing net kept vertical in the water by weights and floats [Old English *segne,* from Latin *sagena,* from Greek *sagēnē*]

²seine *vb* : to fish with or catch with a seine — **sein·er** *n*

seism- *or* **seismo-** *combining form* : earthquake : vibration ⟨*seismo*graph⟩ [Greek *seismos* "shock, earthquake", from *seiein* "to shake"]

seis·mic \'sīz-mik, 'sīs-\ *adj* : of, subject to, or caused by an earthquake or an artificially produced earth vibration — **seis·mi·cal·ly** \-mi-kə-lē, -klē\ *adv*

seis·mo·gram \'sīz-mə-ˌgram, 'sīs-\ *n* : the record of an earth tremor made by a seismograph

seis·mo·graph \-ˌgraf\ *n* : an apparatus for recording the intensity, direction, and duration of earthquakes or similar vibrations of the ground — **seis·mo·graph·ic** \ˌsīz-mə-'graf-ik, ˌsīs-\ *adj* — **seis·mog·ra·phy** \sīz-'mäg-rə-fē, sīs-\ *n*

seis·mol·o·gy \sīz-'mäl-ə-jē, sīs-\ *n* : a science that deals with earthquakes and with artificially produced vibrations of the earth — **seis·mo·log·i·cal** \ˌsīz-mə-'läj-i-kəl, ˌsīs-\ *adj* — **seis·mo·log·i·cal·ly** \-kə-lē, -klē\ *adv* — **seis·mol·o·gist** \sīz-'mäl-ə-jəst, sīs-\ *n*

seis·mom·e·ter \sīz-'mäm-ət-ər\ *n* : a seismograph that measures actual movements of the ground (as on the earth or the moon)

seize \'sēz\ *vb* **1** : to take possession of : CONFISCATE **2** : to take possession of by force ⟨*seize* a fortress⟩ **3** : to take hold of suddenly or with force : CLUTCH **4** : UNDERSTAND, COMPREHEND ⟨*seize* an idea quickly⟩ **5** : to take prisoner : ARREST **6** : to bind together by lashing (as with small cord) ⟨*seize* two ropes⟩ **7** : to attack or overwhelm suddenly ⟨was *seized* with a fever⟩ **8 a** : to stick fast to or jam with a part in relative motion ⟨the piston *seized*⟩ **b** : to fail to operate due to the seizing of a part ⟨the engine *seized*⟩ [Old French *saisir* "to put in possession of", from Medieval Latin *sacire,* of Germanic origin] SYN see TAKE — **seiz·er** *n*

seiz·ing \'sē-zing\ *n* **1 a** : the cord used in seizing **b** : the fastening so made **2** : the operation of fastening together or lashing with small rope or cord

sei·zure \'sē-zhər\ *n* **1** : the act or process of seizing : the state of being seized **2** : a sudden attack (as of disease) : FIT

se·lag·i·nel·la \sə-ˌlaj-ə-'nel-ə\ *n* : any of a genus of mossy lower vascular plants [New Latin, from Latin *selagin-, selago,* a kind of plant]

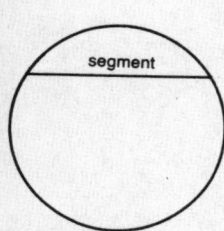

¹segment 2a

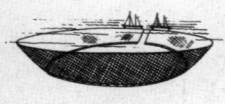

¹seine

se·lah \'sē-lə, -ˌlä\ *interj* — a term of uncertain meaning found in the Hebrew text of the Psalms and Habakkuk carried over untranslated into some English versions [Hebrew *selāh*]

sel·dom \'sel-dəm\ *adv* : in few instances : RARELY [Old English *seldan*]

¹se·lect \sə-'lekt\ *adj* **1** : chosen from a number or group by fitness or preference **2 a** : of special value or excellence : SUPERIOR, CHOICE ⟨a *select* hotel⟩ **b** : carefully or fastidiously chosen often with regard to social, economic, or cultural characteristics ⟨a *select* membership⟩ **3** : judicious or restrictive in choice : DISCRIMINATING [Latin *selectus,* past participle of *seligere* "to select", from *se-* "apart" + *legere* "to gather, pick"] — **se·lect·ness** *n*

²select *vb* : to take by preference from a number or group : pick out : CHOOSE

se·lect·ee \sə-ˌlek-'tē\ *n* : one inducted into military service under selective service

se·lec·tion \sə-'lek-shən\ *n* **1** : the act or process of selecting : the state of being selected **2** : one that is selected : CHOICE; *also* : a collection of selected things **3** : a natural or artificial process that results or tends to result in the survival and reproduction of some individuals or organisms but not of others with the result that the inherited traits of the survivors are perpetuated

se·lec·tive \sə-'lek-tiv\ *adj* : of, relating to, or characterized by selection : selecting or tending to select — **se·lec·tive·ly** *adv* — **se·lec·tive·ness** *n* — **se·lec·tiv·i·ty** \si-ˌlek-'tiv-ət-ē, ˌsē-\ *n*

selective service *n* : a system under which individuals are called up for military service : DRAFT

se·lect·man \sə-'lekt-ˌman, -'lek-, -mən; -ˌlekt-'man, -ˌlek-\ *n* : one of a board of elected town officials in all New England states except Rhode Island

se·lec·tor \sə-'lek-tər\ *n* : one that selects

sel·e·nite \'sel-ə-ˌnīt\ *n* : a variety of gypsum occurring in transparent colorless crystals or crystalline masses [Latin *selenites,* from Greek *selēnitēs lithos,* literally, "stone of the moon", from *selēnē* "moon"; from the belief that it waxed and waned with the moon]

se·le·ni·um \sə-'lē-nē-əm\ *n* : a nonmetallic chemical element resembling sulfur in chemical properties that is used chiefly in electronic devices — see ELEMENT table [New Latin, from Greek *selēnē* "moon"]

¹self \'self, *South also* 'sef\ *pron* : MYSELF, HIMSELF, HERSELF ⟨check payable to *self*⟩ [Old English, intensive pron.]

²self *adj* **1** : having a single character or quality throughout; *esp* : having one color only ⟨a *self* flower⟩ **2** : of the same kind (as in color, material, or pattern) as something with which it is used ⟨a *self* belt⟩ ⟨*self* trimming⟩

³self \'self\ *n, pl* **selves** \'selvz, *South also* 'sevz\ **1** : a person regarded as an individual apart from everyone else **2** : a typical or particular aspect of one's behavior or character ⟨one's true *self*⟩ ⟨your better *self*⟩ **3** : personal interest or advantage ⟨without thought of *self*⟩

⁴self *vb* **1** : INBREED **2** : SELF-POLLINATE

self- *combining form* **1 a** : oneself or itself ⟨*self*-devouring⟩ **b** : of oneself or itself ⟨*self*-abasement⟩ **c** : by oneself or itself ⟨*self*-made⟩ **2 a** : to, with, for, or toward oneself or itself ⟨*self*-addressed⟩ ⟨*self*-satisfaction⟩ **b** : of or in oneself or itself inherently ⟨*self*-evident⟩ **c** : from or by means of oneself or itself ⟨*self*-fertile⟩

self-aban·doned \ˌsel-fə-'ban-dənd\ *adj* : abandoned by oneself; *esp* : given up to one's impulses

self-abase·ment \ˌsel-fə-'bās-mənt\ *n* : humiliation of oneself based on feelings of inferiority, guilt, or shame

self-ab·ne·gat·ing \'sel-'fab-ni-ˌgāt-ing\ *adj* : SELF-DENYING

self-ab·ne·ga·tion \ˌsel-ˌfab-ni-'gā-shən\ *n* : SELF-DENIAL

self-ab·sorbed \ˌsel-fəb-'sorbd, -'zorbd\ *adj* : absorbed in one's own thoughts, activities, or interests

self-ab·sorp·tion \-'sorp-shən, -'zorp-\ *n* : preoccupation with oneself

self-abuse \ˌsel-fə-'byüs\ *n* **1** : reproach of oneself **2** : MASTURBATION

self-ac·cu·sa·tion \ˌsel-ˌfak-yə-'zā-shən\ *n* : the act or an instance of accusing oneself

self-ac·quired \ˌsel-fə-'kwīrd\ *adj* : acquired by oneself

self-act·ing \'sel-'fak-ting\ *adj* : acting or capable of acting of or by itself

self-ad·dressed \ˌsel-fə-'drest, 'sel-'fad-ˌrest\ *adj* : addressed for return to the sender ⟨*self*-addressed envelopes⟩

self-ad·just·ing \ˌsel-fə-'jəs-ting\ *adj* : adjusting by itself ⟨a *self*-adjusting wrench⟩

self-ad·min·is·tered \ˌsel-fəd-'min-ə-stərd\ *adj* : administered, managed, or dispensed by oneself

self-ad·mi·ra·tion \ˌsel-ˌfad-mə-'rā-shən\ *n* : SELF-CONCEIT

self-ad·vance·ment \ˌsel-fəd-'van-smənt\ *n* : the act of advancing oneself

self-af·fect·ed \ˌsel-fə-'fek-təd\ *adj* : VAIN 3, CONCEITED

self-ag·gran·dize·ment \ˌsel-fə-'gran-dəz-mənt, -ˌdīz-; ˌsel-ˌfag-rən-'dīz-\ *n* : the act or process of making oneself greater (as in power or influence)

self-ag·gran·diz·ing \ˌsel-fə-'gran-ˌdī-zing, 'sel-'fag-rən-\ *adj* : acting or seeking to make oneself greater

self-anal·y·sis \ˌsel-fə-'nal-ə-səs\ *n* : a systematic attempt by an individual to understand his or her own personality without the aid of another person — **self-an·a·lyt·i·cal** \ˌsel-ˌfan-l-'it-i-kəl\ *adj*

self-ap·plause \ˌsel-fə-'ploz\ *n* : an expression or feeling of approval of oneself

self-ap·point·ed \ˌsel-fə-'point-əd\ *adj* : appointed by oneself usually without justification or qualifications ⟨a *self*-appointed censor⟩

self-ap·pro·ba·tion \ˌsel-ˌfap-rə-'bā-shən\ *n* : satisfaction with one's actions and achievements

self-as·sert·ing \ˌsel-fə-'sərt-ing\ *adj* **1** : asserting oneself or one's own rights, opinions, or claims **2** : putting oneself forward in a confident or arrogant manner

self-as·ser·tion \ˌsel-fə-'sər-shən\ *n* **1** : the act of asserting oneself or one's own rights, opinions, or claims **2** : the act of asserting one's superiority over others

self-as·ser·tive \-'sərt-iv\ *adj* : given to or marked by self-assertion — **self-as·ser·tive·ly** *adv* — **self-as·ser·tive·ness** *n*

self-as·sur·ance \ˌsel-fə-'shur-əns\ *n* : SELF-CONFIDENCE

self-as·sured \-'shurd\ *adj* : SELF-CONFIDENT — **self-as·sured·ness** \-'shur-əd-nəs, -'shurd-\ *n*

self-aware·ness \ˌsel-fə-'waər-nəs, -'weər-\ *n* : an awareness of one's own personality or individuality

self-born \'self-'born\ *adj* **1** : arising within the self ⟨*self*-born sorrows⟩ **2** : springing from a prior self ⟨a phoenix rising *self*-born from the fire⟩

self-cen·tered \'self-'sent-ərd\ *adj* : interested chiefly in one's own self : SELFISH — **self-cen·tered·ly** *adv* — **self-cen·tered·ness** *n*

self-charg·ing \-'chär-jing\ *adj* : that charges itself

self-clos·ing \-'klō-zing\ *adj* : closing or shutting automatically after being opened

self-com·mand \ˌself-kə-'mand\ *n* : control of one's own behavior and emotions : SELF-CONTROL

self-com·pat·i·ble \ˌself-kəm-'pat-ə-bəl\ *adj* : capable of effective self-pollination — compare SELF-INCOMPATIBLE

self-com·pla·cent \ˌself-kəm-'plās-nt\ *adj* : SELF-SATISFIED, COMPLACENT — **self-com·pla·cen·cy** \-'plās-n-sē\ *n* — **self-com·pla·cent·ly** *adv*

self-com·posed \ˌself-kəm-'pōzd\ *adj* : having one's emotions under control — **self-com·pos·ed·ly** \-'pō-zəd-lē\ *adv*

self-con·ceit \,self-kən-'sēt\ *n* : too high an opinion of one's qualities or abilities — **self-con·ceit·ed** \-əd\ *adj*

self-con·cern \,self-kən-'sərn\ *n* : selfish or morbid concern for oneself — **self-con·cerned** \-'sərnd\ *adj*

self-con·dem·na·tion \,self-,kän-,dem-'nā-shən, -dəm-\ *n* : condemnation of one's own character or actions

self-con·fessed \,self-kən-'fest\ *adj* : openly acknowledged

self-con·fi·dence \'self-'kän-fəd-əns, -fə-,dens\ *n* : confidence in oneself and in one's powers and abilities — **self-con·fi·dent** \-fəd-ənt, -fə-,dent\ *adj* — **self-con·fi·dent·ly** *adv*

self-con·scious \'self-'kän-chəs\ *adj* **1** : aware of oneself as an individual **2** : uncomfortably conscious of oneself as an object of the observation of others : ill at ease — **self-con·scious·ly** *adv* — **self-con·scious·ness** *n*

self-con·sis·tent \,self-kən-'sis-tənt\ *adj* : having each part logically consistent with the rest — **self-con·sis·ten·cy** \-tən-sē\ *n*

self-con·sti·tut·ed \'self-'kän-stə-,tüt-əd, -,tyüt-\ *adj* : constituted by oneself

self-con·tained \,self-kən-'tānd\ *adj* **1** : complete in itself **2 a** : showing self-control **b** : formal and reserved in manner — **self-con·tained·ly** \-'tā-nəd-lē, -'tān-dlē\ *adv* — **self-con·tained·ness** \-'tā-nəd-nəs, -'tānd-nəs, -'tān-nəs\ *n* — **self-con·tain·ment** \-'tān-mənt\ *n*

self-con·tempt \,self-kən-'temt, -'tempt\ *n* : contempt for oneself

self-con·tent·ed \,self-kən-'tent-əd\ *adj* : SELF-SATIS-FIED, COMPLACENT — **self-con·tent** \-'tent\ *n* — **self-con·tent·ed·ly** *adv* — **self-con·tent·ed·ness** *n* — **self-con·tent·ment** \-'tent-mənt\ *n*

self-con·tra·dic·to·ry \,self-,kän-trə-'dik-tə-rē, -trē\ *adj* : consisting of two contradictory members or parts ⟨a *self-contradictory* statement⟩

self-con·trol \,self-kən-'trōl\ *n* : control over one's own impulses, emotions, or acts — **self-con·trolled** \-'trōld\ *adj*

self-cor·rect·ing \,self-kə-'rek-ting\ *adj* : correcting or compensating for one's own errors or weaknesses

self-cor·rec·tive \-'rek-tiv\ *adj* : SELF-CORRECTING

self-cre·at·ed \,self-krē-'āt-əd\ *adj* : created or appointed by oneself

self-crit·i·cism \'self-'krit-ə-,siz-əm\ *n* : the act of or capacity for criticizing one's own faults or shortcomings

self-de·ceiv·ing \,self-di-'sē-ving\ *adj* **1** : given to self-deception ⟨a *self-deceiving* hypocrite⟩ **2** : serving to deceive oneself ⟨*self-deceiving* excuses⟩

self-de·cep·tion \,self-di-'sep-shən\ *n* : the act of deceiving oneself : the state of being deceived by oneself — **self-de·cep·tive** \-'sep-tiv\ *adj*

self-ded·i·ca·tion \,self-,ded·i-'kā-shən\ *n* : dedication of oneself to a cause or ideal

self-de·feat·ing \,self-di-'fēt-ing\ *adj* : acting to defeat its own purpose

self-de·fense \,self-di-'fens\ *n* : the act of defending oneself, one's property, or a close relative

self-de·ni·al \,self-di-'nī-əl, -'nīl\ *n* : the act of refraining from gratifying one's own desires — **self-de·ny·ing** \-'nī-ing\ *adj*

self-de·pen·dence \,self-di-'pen-dəns\ *n* : SELF-RELI-ANCE — **self-de·pen·dent** \-dənt\ *adj*

self-de·pre·ci·a·tion \,self-di-,prē-shē-'ā-shən\ *n* : belittlement or undervaluation of oneself

self-de·spair \,self-di-'spaər, -'speər\ *n* : despair of oneself : HOPELESSNESS

self-de·struct \,self-di-'strəkt\ *vi* : to destroy itself

self-de·struc·tion \,self-di-'strək-shən\ *n* : destruction of oneself; *esp* : SUICIDE — **self-de·struc·tive** \-'strək-tiv\ *adj*

self-de·ter·mi·na·tion \,self-di-,tər-mə-'nā-shən\ *n* **1** : the act or power of deciding things for oneself **2** : the right of a people to determine the form of government they will have — **self-de·ter·min·ing** \-'tər-mə-ning\ *adj*

self-de·ter·mined \-'tər-mənd\ *adj* : determined by oneself

self-de·vel·op·ment \,self-di-'vel-əp-mənt\ *n* : development of one's own capabilities or possibilities

self-de·vo·tion \,self-di-'vō-shən\ *n* : devotion of oneself especially in service or sacrifice

self-de·vour·ing \,self-di-'vaủr-ing\ *adj* : devouring itself

self-di·rect·ed \,self-də-'rek-təd, -dī-\ *adj* : directed by oneself; *esp* : not guided or impelled by an outside force or agency ⟨a *self-directed* personality⟩

self-dis·ci·pline \'self-'dis-ə-plən\ *n* : correction or regulation of oneself for the sake of improvement — **self-dis·ci·plined** \-plənd\ *adj*

self-dis·cov·ery \,self-dis-'kəv-rē, -ə-rē\ *n* : the act or process of achieving self-knowledge

self-dis·trust \,self-dis-'trəst\ *n* : a lack of confidence in oneself : DIFFIDENCE — **self-dis·trust·ful** \-fəl\ *adj*

self-doubt \'self-'daủt\ *n* : a lack of faith in oneself — **self-doubt·ing** \-ing\ *adj*

self-ed·u·cat·ed \'sel-'fej-ə-,kāt-əd\ *adj* : educated by one's own efforts without formal instruction — **self-ed·u·ca·tion** \,sel-,fej-ə-'kā-shən\ *n*

self-ef·fac·ing \,sel-fə-'fā-sing\ *adj* : tending to keep oneself in the background : UNASSERTIVE — **self-ef·face·ment** \-'fā-smənt\ *n* — **self-ef·fac·ing·ly** \-'fā-sing-lē\ *adv*

self-em·ployed \,sel-fim-'plóid\ *adj* : earning income directly from one's own business, trade, or profession rather than as salary or wages from an employer — **self-em·ploy·ment** \-'plói-mənt\ *n*

self-es·teem \,sel-fə-'stēm\ *n* **1** : a proper satisfaction with one's own worth **2** : an inflated opinion of one's own worth

self-ev·i·dent \'sel-'fev-əd-ənt, -ə-,dent\ *adj* : evident without proof or argument — **self-ev·i·dent·ly** *adv*

self-ex·am·i·na·tion \,sel-fig-,zam-ə-'nā-shən\ *n* : an act of examining oneself; *esp* : INTROSPECTION

self-ex·e·cut·ing \'sel-'fek-sə-,kyüt-ing\ *adj* : taking effect immediately without implementing legislation ⟨a *self-executing* treaty⟩

self-ex·plain·ing \,sel-fik-'splā-ning\ *adj* : SELF-EXPLAN-ATORY

self-ex·plan·a·to·ry \-'splan-ə-,tōr-ē, -,tór-\ *adj* : understandable without explanation

self-ex·pres·sion \,sel-fik-'spresh-ən\ *n* : the expression of one's own personality : assertion of one's individual traits — **self-ex·pres·sive** \-'spres-iv\ *adj*

self-feed·er \'self-'fēd-ər\ *n* : a device for feeding livestock equipped with a feed hopper that automatically supplies a trough

self-fer·tile \'self-'fərt-l\ *adj* : fertile by means of its own pollen or sperm — **self-fer·til·i·ty** \,self-fər-'til-ət-ē\ *n*

self-fer·til·iza·tion \,self-,fərt-l-ə-'zā-shən\ *n* : fertilization by pollen or sperm from the same individual — **self-fer·til·ize** \'self-'fərt-l-,īz\ *vb*

self-flat·tery \'self-'flat-ə-rē\ *n* : the glossing over of one's own weaknesses or mistakes and the exaggeration of one's own good qualities and achievements

self-for·get·ful \,self-fər-'get-fəl\ *adj* : having or showing no thought of self or selfish interests — **self-for·get·ful·ly** \-fə-lē\ *adv* — **self-for·get·ful·ness** *n*

self-formed \'self-'fórmd\ *adj* : formed or developed by one's own efforts

self-fruit·ful \'self-'früt-fəl\ *adj* : capable of setting a crop of self-pollinated fruit — **self-fruit·ful·ness** *n*

self-ful·fill·ing \,self-fủl-'fil-ing\ *adj* : marked by or achieving self-fulfillment

self-ful·fill·ment \-'fil-mənt\ *n* : fulfillment of oneself

self-giv·ing \'self-'giv-ing\ *adj* : inclined to self-sacrifice : UNSELFISH

self·glo·ri·fi·ca·tion \self-ˌglȯr-ə-fə-ˈkā-shən, -ˌglȯr-\ *n* : a feeling or expression of one's own superiority

self·glo·ry \ˈself-ˈglȯr-ē, -ˈglȯr-\ *n* : personal vanity : PRIDE

self·gov·ern·ment \ˈself-ˈgəv-ər-mənt; -ˈgəb-m-ənt, -ˈgəv-; -ˈgəv-ərn-mənt\ *n* **1** : SELF-CONTROL **2** : government of a political unit by action of its own people; *esp* : democratic government — **self·gov·erned** \-ˈgəv-ərnd\ *adj* — **self·gov·ern·ing** \-ər-niŋ\ *adj*

self·grat·i·fi·ca·tion \self-ˌgrat-ə-fə-ˈkā-shən\ *n* : the act of pleasing oneself or of satisfying one's desires

self·heal \ˈself-ˌhēl\ *n* : a low-growing blue-flowered mint supposed to have healing powers

self·help \ˈself-ˈhelp\ *n* : the act or an instance of providing for or helping oneself without depending on others

self·hyp·no·sis \ˌself-hip-ˈnō-səs\ *n* : hypnosis of oneself

self·ig·nite \ˌsel-fig-ˈnīt\ *vi* : to become ignited without flame or spark (as under high compression) — **self·ig·ni·tion** \-ˈnish-ən\ *n*

self·im·age \ˈsel-ˈfim-ij\ *n* : one's conception of oneself or of one's role

self·im·mo·la·tion \ˌsel-ˌfim-ə-ˈlā-shən\ *n* : a deliberate and willing sacrifice of oneself

self·im·por·tance \ˌsel-fim-ˈpȯrt-ns, -əns\ *n* **1** : an exaggerated estimate of one's own importance : SELF-CONCEIT **2** : arrogant or pompous behavior — **self·im·por·tant** \-nt, -ənt\ *adj* — **self·im·por·tant·ly** *adv*

self·im·posed \ˌsel-fim-ˈpōzd\ *adj* : imposed on one by oneself : voluntarily assumed (a *self-imposed* exile)

self·im·prove·ment \ˌsel-fim-ˈprüv-mənt\ *n* : improvement of oneself by one's own action

self·in·clu·sive \ˌsel-fin-ˈklü-siv, -ziv\ *adj* : SELF-CONTAINED 1

self·in·com·pat·i·ble \ˌsel-ˌfin-kəm-ˈpat-ə-bəl\ *adj* : incapable of effective self-pollination — compare SELF-COMPATIBLE

self·in·crim·i·na·tion \ˌsel-fin-ˌkrim-ə-ˈnā-shən\ *n* : incrimination of oneself; *esp* : the giving of evidence or answering of questions which could make one subject to criminal prosecution — **self·in·crim·i·nat·ing** \-ˈkrim-ə-ˌnāt-iŋ\ *adj*

self·in·duced \ˌsel-fin-ˈdüst, -ˈdyüst\ *adj* **1** : induced by oneself **2** : produced by self-induction (a *self-induced* voltage)

self·in·duc·tance \-ˈdək-təns\ *n* : inductance in which an electromotive force is produced by self-induction

self·in·duc·tion \-ˈdək-shən\ *n* : induction of an electromotive force in a circuit by a varying current in the same circuit

self·in·dul·gence \ˌsel-fin-ˈdəl-jəns\ *n* : overindulgence of one's own appetites, desires, or whims — **self·in·dul·gent** \-jənt\ *adj* — **self·in·dul·gent·ly** *adv*

self·in·flict·ed \ˌsel-fin-ˈflik-təd\ *adj* : inflicted by oneself (a *self-inflicted* wound)

self·in·struct·ed \ˌsel-fin-ˈstrək-təd\ *adj* : SELF-TAUGHT

self·in·ter·est \ˈsel-ˈfin-trəst, -ˈfint-ə-rəst\ *n* **1** : one's own interest or advantage **2** : a concern for one's own advantage and well-being — **self·in·ter·est·ed** \-əd\ *adj* — **self·in·ter·est·ed·ness** *n*

self·in·volved \ˌsel-fin-ˈvälvd, -ˈvȯlvd\ *adj* : SELF-ABSORBED

self·ish \ˈsel-fish\ *adj* **1** : concerned excessively or exclusively with oneself : seeking or concentrating on one's own advantage, pleasure, or well-being without regard for others **2** : arising from concern with one's own welfare or advantage in disregard of others (a *selfish* act) — **self·ish·ly** *adv* — **self·ish·ness** *n*

self·jus·ti·fi·ca·tion \ˌself-ˌjəs-tə-fə-ˈkā-shən\ *n* : the act or an instance of making excuses for oneself

self·knowl·edge \ˈself-ˈnäl-ij\ *n* : knowledge of one's own capabilities, character, feelings, or motivations

self·less \ˈself-fləs\ *adj* : having or showing no concern for self : UNSELFISH — **self·less·ly** *adv* — **self·less·ness** *n*

self·lim·it·ing \ˈsel-ˈflim-ət-iŋ\ *adj* : limiting oneself or itself

self·lock·ing \ˈsel-ˈfläk-iŋ\ *adj* : locking by its own action

self·love \ˈsel-ˈfləv\ *n* : love of self : **a** : CONCEIT 1, SELF-CONCEIT **b** : regard for one's own happiness or advantage — **self·lov·ing** \-iŋ\ *adj*

self·lu·bri·cat·ing \ˈsel-ˈflü-brə-ˌkāt-iŋ\ *adj* : lubricating itself

self·lu·mi·nous \ˈsel-ˈflü-mə-nəs\ *adj* : having in itself the property of emitting light

self·made \ˈself-ˈmād\ *adj* **1** : made by oneself or itself **2** : raised from poverty or obscurity by one's own efforts

self·mas·tery \ˈself-ˈmas-tə-rē, -trē\ *n* : SELF-COMMAND, SELF-CONTROL

self·ob·ser·va·tion \ˌsel-ˌfäb-sər-ˈvā-shən, -zər-\ *n* **1** : observation of one's own appearance **2** : INTROSPECTION

self·op·er·at·ing \ˈsel-ˈfäp-ə-ˌrāt-iŋ\ *or* **self·op·er·a·tive** \-ˈfäp-rət-iv, -ə-rət-; -ˈfäp-ə-ˌrāt-\ *adj* : SELF-ACTING

self·opin·ion·at·ed \ˌsel-fə-ˈpin-yə-ˌnāt-əd\ *adj* **1** : CONCEITED **2** : stubbornly holding to one's own opinion

self·orig·i·nat·ed \ˌsel-fə-ˈrij-ə-ˌnāt-əd\ *adj* : originated by oneself or itself

self·per·pet·u·at·ing \ˌself-pər-ˈpech-ə-ˌwāt-iŋ\ *adj* : capable of continuing or renewing itself indefinitely (*self-perpetuating* board of trustees)

self·pity \ˈself-ˈpit-ē\ *n* : pity for oneself — **self·pity·ing** \-ē-iŋ\ *adj* — **self·pity·ing·ly** \-iŋ-lē\ *adv*

self·poised \ˈself-ˈpȯizd\ *adj* **1** : balanced without support **2** : having poise through self-command

self·pol·li·nate \ˈself-ˈpäl-ə-ˌnāt\ *vb* : to undergo or cause to undergo self-pollination

self·pol·li·na·tion \ˌself-ˌpäl-ə-ˈnā-shən\ *n* : the transfer of pollen from the anther of a flower to the stigma of the same flower or sometimes to that of a genetically identical flower (as of the same plant or clone)

self·por·trait \ˈself-ˈpōr-trət, -ˈpȯr-, -ˌtrāt\ *n* : a portrait of oneself done by oneself

self·pos·sessed \ˌself-pə-ˈzest\ *adj* : composed in mind or manner : CALM — **self·pos·sessed·ly** \-ˈzes-əd-lē, -ˈzest-lē\ *adv*

self·pos·ses·sion \ˌself-pə-ˈzesh-ən\ *n* : control of one's emotions or reactions : COMPOSURE

self·praise \ˈself-ˈprāz\ *n* : praise of oneself

self·pres·er·va·tion \ˌself-ˌprez-ər-ˈvā-shən\ *n* : the keeping of oneself from destruction, injury, or loss

self·pride \ˌself-ˈprīd\ *n* : pride in oneself or in that which relates to oneself

self·pro·claimed \ˌself-prō-ˈklāmd\ *adj* : SELF-STYLED (a *self-proclaimed* genius)

self·pro·duced \ˌself-prə-ˈdüst, -ˈdyüst\ *adj* : produced by oneself or itself

self·pro·pelled \ˌself-prə-ˈpeld\ *adj* : containing within itself the means for its own propulsion

self·pro·pel·ling \-ˈpel-iŋ\ *adj* : SELF-PROPELLED

self·pro·tec·tion \ˌself-prə-ˈtek-shən\ *n* : protection of oneself : SELF-DEFENSE

self·pun·ish·ment \ˈself-ˈpən-ish-mənt\ *n* : punishment of oneself

self·pu·ri·fi·ca·tion \ˌself-ˌpyur-ə-fə-ˈkā-shən\ *n* : purification of oneself (moral *self-purification*)

self·ques·tion·ing \ˈself-ˈkwes-chə-niŋ\ *n* : INTROSPECTION

self·re·al·iza·tion \ˌsel-ˌfrē-ə-lə-ˈzā-shən\ *n* : fulfillment by oneself of the possibilities of one's character or personality

self·re·cord·ing \ˌsel-fri-ˈkȯrd-iŋ\ *adj* : making a record automatically (*self-recording* instruments)

self·re·gard \ˌsel-fri-ˈgärd\ *n* **1** : regard for or consideration of oneself or one's own interests **2** : SELF-RESPECT 1 — **self·re·gard·ing** \-iŋ\ *adj*

\ə\ abut	\ŋ\ sing	
\ər\ further	\ō\ bone	
\a\ mat	\ȯ\ saw	
\ā\ take	\ȯi\ coin	
\ä\ cot, cart	\th\ thin	
\au̇\ out	\t̲h̲\ this	
\ch\ chin	\ü\ food	
\e\ pet	\u̇\ foot	
\ē\ easy	\y\ yet	
\g\ go	\yü\ few	
\i\ tip	\yu̇\ cure	
\ī\ life	\zh\ vision	
\j\ job		

self–reg·u·lat·ing \'sel-'freg-yə-,lāt-ing\ *adj* : regulating oneself or itself; *esp* : AUTOMATIC ⟨a *self-regulating* mechanism⟩ — **self–reg·u·la·tion** \,sel-,freg-yə-'lā-shən\ *n*

self–re·li·ance \,sel-fri-'lī-ənts\ *n* : reliance on one's own efforts and abilities — **self–re·li·ant** \-ənt\ *adj*

self–re·nun·ci·a·tion \,sel-fri-,nən-sē-'ā-shən\ *n* : renunciation of one's own desires or ambitions

self–rep·li·cat·ing \'sel-'frep-lə-,kāt-ing\ *adj* : duplicating itself ⟨DNA is a *self-replicating* molecule⟩

self–re·proach \,sel-fri-'prōch\ *n* : the act of blaming or accusing oneself — **self–re·proach·ful** \-fəl\ *adj* — **self–re·proach·ing** \-'prō-ching\ *adj*

self–re·pro·duc·ing \'sel-,frē-prə-'dü-sing, -'dyü-\ *adj* : SELF-REPLICATING

self–re·spect \,sel-fri-'spekt\ *n* **1** : a proper respect for oneself as a human being **2** : regard for one's own standing or position — **self–re·spect·ing** \-'spek-ting\ *adj*

self–re·straint \,sel-fri-'strānt\ *n* : restraint imposed on oneself : SELF-CONTROL

self–re·veal·ing \,sel-fri-'vē-ling\ *adj* : marked by self-revelation

self–rev·e·la·tion \,sel-,frev-ə-'lā-shən\ *n* : revelation of one's own thoughts, feelings, and attitudes especially without deliberate intent

self–re·ward·ing \,sel-fri-'wȯrd-ing\ *adj* : containing or producing its own reward ⟨a *self-rewarding* virtue⟩

self–righ·teous \'sel-'frī-chəs\ *adj* : convinced of one's own righteousness especially in contrast with the actions and beliefs of others — **self–righ·teous·ly** *adv* — **self–righ·teous·ness** *n*

self–ris·ing \'sel-'frī-zing\ *adj* : rising without the use of leaven ⟨*self-rising* flour⟩

self–sac·ri·fice \'self-'sak-rə-,fīs, -fəs\ *n* : sacrifice of oneself or one's interest for others or for a cause or ideal — **self–sac·ri·fic·ing** \-,fī-sing\ *adj* — **self–sac·ri·fic·ing·ly** \-sing-lē\ *adv*

self·same \'self-,sām\ *adj* : precisely the same : IDENTICAL — **self·same·ness** *n*

self–sat·is·fac·tion \,self-,sat-əs-'fak-shən\ *n* : a usually smug satisfaction with oneself, one's position, or one's achievements

self–sat·is·fied \'self-'sat-əs-,fīd\ *adj* : feeling or showing self-satisfaction

self–sat·is·fy·ing \-,fī-ing\ *adj* : giving satisfaction to oneself

self–seal·ing \'self-'sē-ling\ *adj* : capable of sealing itself (as after puncture) ⟨a *self-sealing* tire⟩

self–search·ing \'self-'sər-ching\ *adj* : SELF-QUESTIONING

self–seek·er \'self-'sē-kər\ *n* : a person who is interested only in his or her own advantage or pleasure — **self–seek·ing** \-king\ *n or adj*

self–serve \'self-'sərv\ *adj* : permitting self-service

self–ser·vice \'self-'sər-vəs\ *n* : the serving of oneself (as in a cafeteria or market) with things to be paid for usually upon leaving — **self–service** *adj*

self–slaugh·ter \'self-'slȯt-ər\ *n* : SUICIDE 1a

self–sow \'self-'sō\ *vi* : to sow itself by dropping seeds or by natural action (as of wind or water)

self–start·er \'self-'stärt-ər\ *n* **1** : more or less automatic attachment for starting an internal-combustion engine **2** : a person who has initiative

self–start·ing \-'stärt-ing\ *adj* : capable of starting by itself

self–ster·ile \'self-'ster-əl\ *adj* : sterile to its own pollen or sperm — **self–ste·ril·i·ty** \,self-stə-'ril-ət-ē\ *n*

self–styled \'self-'stīld\ *adj* : called by oneself ⟨*self-styled* experts⟩

self–suf·fi·cient \,self-sə-'fish-ənt\ *adj* **1** : able to take care of oneself without outside help **2** : having great confidence in one's own ability or worth : SECURE — **self–suf·fi·cien·cy** \-ən-sē\ *n*

self–suf·fic·ing \,self-sə-'fī-sing\ *adj* : SELF-SUFFICIENT 1 — **self–suf·fic·ing·ly** \-'fī-sing-lē\ *adv* — **self–suf·fic·ing·ness** *n*

self–sup·port \,self-sə-'pōrt, -'pȯrt\ *n* : independent support of oneself or itself — **self–sup·port·ed** \-əd\ *adj*

self–sup·port·ing \-ing\ *adj* : characterized by self-support: as **a** : meeting one's needs by one's own efforts or output **b** : supporting itself or its own weight ⟨a *self-supporting* wall⟩

self–sus·tained \,self-sə-'stānd\ *adj* : sustained by oneself

self–sus·tain·ing \-'stā-ning\ *adj* **1** : maintaining or able to maintain oneself by independent effort : SELF-SUPPORTING **2** : maintaining or able to maintain itself once started ⟨a *self-sustaining* nuclear reaction⟩

self–taught \'self-'tȯt\ *adj* **1** : having knowledge or skills acquired by one's own efforts without formal instruction **2** : learned by oneself ⟨*self-taught* knowledge⟩

self–treat·ment \'self-'trēt-mənt\ *n* : medication of oneself or treatment of one's ailment without outside medical supervision

self–trust \'self-'trəst\ *n* : SELF-CONFIDENCE

self–un·der·stand·ing \,sel-,fən-dər-'stan-ding\ *n* : SELF-KNOWLEDGE

self–will \'self-'wil\ *n* : stubborn or willful adherence to one's own desires or ideas : OBSTINACY — **self–willed** \-'wild\ *adj*

self–wind·ing \'self-'wīn-ding\ *adj* : not needing to be wound by hand : winding by itself ⟨a *self-winding* watch⟩

Sel·juk \'sel-,jük, sel-'\ *or* **Sel·ju·ki·an** \sel-'jü-kē-ən\ *adj* **1** : of or relating to any of several Turkish dynasties ruling in western Asia in the 11th, 12th, and 13th centuries **2** : of, relating to, or characteristic of a Turkish people ruled over by a Seljuk dynasty [Turkish *Selçuk,* ancestor of the dynasties] — **Seljuk** *or* **Seljukian** *n*

¹sell \'sel\ *vb* **sold** \'sōld\; **sell·ing** **1** : to deliver up in violation of duty, trust, or loyalty : BETRAY ⟨the traitors *sold* their king to the enemy⟩ **2 a** : to give in exchange especially for money ⟨they *sold* us some fish⟩; *also* : to give in exchange foolishly or dishonorably ⟨*sell* one's birthright for a mess of pottage⟩ **b** : to work at or deal in the sale of : have or offer for sale ⟨*sells* insurance⟩ ⟨that store *sells* imported foods⟩; *also* : to achieve the sale of ⟨tried *selling* encyclopedias for a while⟩ **3 a** : to find buyers : be bought ⟨that model didn't *sell* very well⟩ **b** : to be for sale ⟨they *sell* for $15 apiece⟩ **4 a** : to make acceptable, believable, or desirable by persuasion ⟨the President couldn't *sell* the program to Congress⟩ **b** : to bring around to a favorable way of thinking ⟨tried to *sell* me on the idea⟩ **c** : to gain acceptance or approval ⟨your idea won't *sell* with them⟩ [Old English *sellan*] — **sell·able** \'sel-ə-bəl\ *adj* — **sell short 1** : to make a short sale of ⟨*sell* a stock short⟩ **2** : to underestimate the ability, strength, or importance of

²sell *n* **1** : a deliberate deception : HOAX **2** : the act or a type of selling : SALESMANSHIP

sell·er \'sel-ər\ *n* **1** : one that offers for sale or makes a sale **2** : a product selling well or to a specified extent ⟨a good *seller*⟩

seller's market *n* : a market with few goods at relatively high prices — compare BUYER'S MARKET

sell·out \'sel-,aut\ *n* **1** : the act or an instance of selling out **2** : a performance or exhibition for which all seats are sold

sell out \sel-'aut, 'sel-\ *vb* **1 a** : to dispose of one's goods by sale **b** : to sell the goods of usually to meet an obligation **2** : to betray one's cause or associates

selt·zer \'selt-sər\ *n* : an artificially prepared water containing carbon dioxide [German *Selterser wasser* "water of Selters", from *Nieder Selters,* Germany]

sel·va \'sel-və\ *n* : a tropical rain forest [Spanish and Portuguese, "forest", from Latin *silva* "wood, grove"]

sel·vage *or* **sel·vedge** \'sel-vij\ *n* : the edge of cloth so woven that it will not ravel [Middle English *selvage*, probably from Flemish *selvegge*, *selvage*, from *selv* "self" + *egge* "edge"]

selves *pl of* SELF

se·man·tic \si-'mant-ik\ *adj* **1** : of or relating to meaning in language **2** : of or relating to semantics [Greek *sēmantikos* "significant", from *sēmanein* "to signify, mean", from *sēma* "sign, token"] — **se·man·ti·cal·ly** \-'mant-i-kə-lē, -klē\ *adv*

se·man·ti·cist \si-'mant-ə-səst\ *n* : a specialist in semantics

se·man·tics \si-'mant-iks\ *n* **1** : the study of meanings **2 a** : the meaning or relationship of meaning of a word or set of words ⟨it's just a question of *semantics*⟩ **b** : the careful use of words (as in advertising or political propaganda) to achieve a desired effect on an audience

¹sem·a·phore \'sem-ə-,fōr, -,fȯr\ *n* **1** : an apparatus for visual signaling (as by the position of one or more movable arms) **2** : a system of visual signaling by two flags held one in each hand [Greek *sēma* "sign, signal"]

²semaphore *vb* : to signal by or as if by semaphore

sem·blance \'sem-bləns\ *n* **1** : outward appearance or show **2 a** : one that resembles another **b** : SIMILARITY 1 [Middle French, from *sembler* "to be like, seem", from Latin *similare* "to copy", from *similis* "like, similar"]

se·men \'sē-mən\ *n, pl* **sem·i·na** \'sem-ə-nə\ *or* **semens** : a viscid whitish fluid of the male reproductive tract consisting of spermatozoa suspended in secretions of accessory glands [Latin, "seed"]

se·mes·ter \sə-'mes-tər\ *n* : one of two usually 18-week terms into which an academic year is often divided [German, from Latin *semestris* "half-yearly", from *sex* "six" + *mensis* "month"] — **se·mes·tral** \-trəl\ *or* **se·mes·tri·al** \-trē-əl\ *adj*

semi- \,sem-i, 'sem-, -,ē, -,ī\ *prefix* **1 a** : precisely half of **b** : half in quantity or value : half of or occurring halfway through a specified period of time ⟨*semi*annual⟩ ⟨*semi*centennial⟩ — compare BI- **2** : to some extent : partly : incompletely ⟨*semi*dry⟩ ⟨*semi*independent⟩ — compare DEMI-, HEMI- **3 a** : partial : incomplete ⟨*semi*darkness⟩ **b** : having some of the characteristics of ⟨*semi*desert⟩ **c** : in some sense or degree ⟨*semi*governmental⟩ [Latin]

semi·ab·strac·tion \,sem-ē-ab-'strak-shən, ,sem-,ī-\ *n* : a composition or creation (as in painting or sculpture) in which the subject matter is easily recognizable though the form is stylized — **semi·ab·stract** \-ab-'strakt, -'ab-,\ *adj*

semi·an·nu·al \,sem-ē-'an-yə-wəl, ,sem-,ī-, -'an-yəl\ *adj* : occurring twice a year — **semi·an·nu·al·ly** \-ē\ *adv*

semi·aquat·ic \-ə-'kwät-ik, -'kwat-\ *adj* : growing in or adjacent to water; *also* : frequenting but not living wholly in water

semi·ar·bo·re·al \-,är-'bōr-ē-əl, -'bȯr-\ *adj* : often inhabiting and frequenting trees

semi·ar·id \-'ar-əd\ *adj* : characterized by light rainfall; *esp* : having from about 10 to 20 inches (25 to 50 centimeters) of annual precipitation

semi·au·to·mat·ic \-,ȯt-ə-'mat-ik\ *adj* : not fully automatic — **semiautomatic** *n* — **semi·au·to·mat·i·cal·ly** \-'mat-i-kə-lē, -klē\ *adv*

semi·au·ton·o·mous \-ȯ-'tän-ə-məs\ *adj* : chiefly self-governing within a larger political or organizational entity

semi·cen·ten·a·ry \,sem-i-,sen-'ten-ə-rē, ,sem-,ī-, -'sent-n-,er-ē\ *n or adj* : SEMICENTENNIAL

semi·cen·ten·ni·al \-,sen-'ten-ē-əl\ *n* : a 50th anniversary or its celebration — **semicentennial** *adj*

semi·cir·cle \'sem-i-,sər-kəl\ *n* : a half of a circle bounded by a diameter and half the circumference — **semi·cir·cu·lar** \,sem-i-'sər-kyə-lər\ *adj*

semicircular canal *n* : any of the loop-shaped tubular parts in the inner ear of vertebrates that together constitute a sensory organ concerned with the maintenance of sense of balance

semi·civ·i·lized \,sem-i-'siv-ə-,līzd, ,sem-,ī-\ *adj* : partly civilized

semi·clas·si·cal \-'klas-i-kəl\ *adj* **1** : having some of the characteristics of the classical: as **a** : of, relating to, or being a musical composition that acts as a bridge between classical and popular music **b** : of, relating to, or being a classical composition that has developed popular appeal **2** : of less importance or of lower quality than the classical ⟨a *semiclassical* theory in physics⟩

semi·co·lon \'sem-i-,kō-lən\ *n* : a punctuation mark ; used chiefly to separate independent clauses not joined by a conjunction, to separate independent clauses the second of which begins with a conjunctive adverb, or to separate phrases and clauses containing commas

semi·con·duc·tor \,sem-i-kən-'dək-tər, ,sem-,ī-\ *n* : any of a class of solids (as germanium or silicon) whose electrical conductivity is between that of a conductor and that of an insulator — **semi·con·duct·ing** \-'ting\ *adj* — **semi·con·duc·tive** \-tiv\ *adj*

semi·con·scious \-'kän-chəs\ *adj* : incompletely conscious — **semi·con·scious·ly** *adv* — **semi·con·scious·ness** *n*

semi·crys·tal·line \-'kris-tə-lən\ *adj* : partly crystalline

semi·dark·ness \-'därk-nəs\ *n* : partial darkness

semi·des·ert \-'dez-ərt\ *n* : an area having some of the characteristics of a desert and often lying between a desert and grassland

semi·de·tached \-di-'tacht\ *adj* : forming one of a pair of residences joined into one building by a common sidewall

semi·di·vine \-də-'vīn\ *adj* : more than mortal but not fully divine

semi·do·mes·ti·cat·ed \-də-'mes-ti-,kāt-əd\ *adj* : of, relating to, or living in semidomestication

semi·do·mes·ti·ca·tion \-də-,mes-ti-'kā-shən\ *n* : a captive state of a wild animal in which its living conditions and often its breeding are controlled by man

semi·dry \,sem-i-'drī\ *adj* : fairly dry

semi·dry·ing \,sem-i-'drī-ing\ *adj* : that dries imperfectly or slowly ⟨cottonseed oil is a *semidrying* oil⟩

¹semi·fi·nal \,sem-i-'fīn-l\ *adj* **1** : being next to the last in an elimination tournament ⟨*semifinal* pairings⟩ **2** : of or participating in a semifinal

²semi·fi·nal \'sem-i-,fīn-l\ *n* : a semifinal match or round — **semi·fi·nal·ist** \,sem-i-'fīn-l-əst\ *n*

semi·fit·ted \,sem-i-'fit-əd, ,sem-,ī-\ *adj* : partly fitted

semi·flex·i·ble \-'flek-sə-bəl\ *adj* : somewhat flexible

semi·flu·id \,sem-i-'flü-əd, ,sem-,ī-\ *adj* : having the qualities of both a fluid and a solid : VISCOUS ⟨fluid and *semifluid* greases⟩ — **semifluid** *n*

semi·for·mal \-'fȯr-məl\ *adj* : being or suitable for an occasion of moderate formality ⟨a *semiformal* dinner⟩

semi·gloss \'sem-i-,gläs, 'sem-,ī-, -,glȯs\ *adj* : having a low luster ⟨*semigloss* paint⟩

semi·gov·ern·men·tal \,sem-i-,gəv-ər-'ment-l, ,sem-,ī-, -,gəv-ərn-'ment-l\ *adj* : having some governmental functions and powers

semi·hard \-'härd\ *adj* : moderately hard

semi·hol·i·day \,sem-i-'häl-ə-,dā, ,sem-,ī-\ *n* : a weekday during a religious festival (as Passover) on which ceremonial observances continue but activities forbidden on full festival days are permitted though discouraged

semi·in·de·pen·dent \,sem-ē-,in-də-'pen-dənt, ,sem-,ī-\ *adj* : partially independent; *esp* : SEMIAUTONOMOUS

semi·leg·end·ary \,sem-i-'lej-ən-,der-ē, ,sem-,ī-\ *adj* : elaborated in legend but having a possible historical existence

¹semaphore 2

\ə\	abut	\ng\	sing
\ər\	further	\ō\	bone
\a\	mat	\ȯ\	saw
\ā\	take	\ȯi\	coin
\ä\	cot, cart	\th\	thin
\au̇\	out	\th̲\	this
\ch\	chin	\ü\	food
\e\	pet	\u̇\	foot
\ē\	easy	\y\	yet
\g\	go	\yü\	few
\i\	tip	\yu̇\	cure
\ī\	life	\zh\	vision
\j\	job		

semi·liq·uid \,sem-i-'lik-wəd, ,sem-,ī-\ *adj* : having the qualities of both a liquid and a solid : SEMIFLUID ⟨*semiliquid* ice cream⟩ — **semiliquid** *n*

semi·lit·er·ate \-'lit-ə-rət, -'li-trət\ *adj* **1** : able to read and write on an elementary level **2** : able to read but unable to write

semi·log·a·rith·mic \-,lóg-ə-'rith-mik, -,läg-\ *also* **semi·log** \'sem-i-,lóg, 'sem-,ī-, -,läg\ *adj* : having one scale logarithmic and the other arithmetic ⟨*semilogarithmic* graph paper⟩

semi·lu·nar \,sem-i-'lü-nər, ,sem-,ī-\ *adj* : shaped like a crescent

semilunar valve *n* : any of the crescent-shaped valvular cusps that occur as a set of three between the heart and the aorta and another of three between the heart and the pulmonary artery

semi·lus·trous \,sem-i-'ləs-trəs, ,sem-,ī-\ *adj* : slightly lustrous

semi·mat *or* **semi·matt** *or* **semi·matte** \,sem-i-'mat, ,sem-,ī-\ *adj* : having little luster

semi·moist \-'móist\ *adj* : slightly moist

semi·mo·nas·tic \-mə-'nas-tik\ *adj* : having some features characteristic of a monastic order

¹semi·month·ly \-'mənth-lē, -'məntth-\ *adj* : done, appearing, or occurring twice a month

²semimonthly *n* : a semimonthly publication

³semimonthly *adv* : twice a month

semi·mys·ti·cal \-'mis-ti-kəl\ *adj* : having some of the qualities of mysticism

sem·i·nal \'sem-ən-l\ *adj* **1** : of, relating to, or consisting of seed or semen **2** : having the character of a creative power, principle, or source : containing or contributing the seeds of later development [Middle French, from Latin *seminalis,* from *semin-, semen* "seed"] — **semi·nal·ly** \-l-ē\ *adv*

seminal vesicle *n* : a pouch on either side of the male reproductive tract that serves for the temporary storage of semen

sem·i·nar \'sem-ə-,när\ *n* **1** : a course of study pursued by a group of advanced students doing original research under a professor and exchanging results and discussions **2** : a meeting of a seminar or a room for such meetings [German, from Latin *seminarium* "seedbed"]

sem·i·nar·i·an \,sem-ə-'ner-ē-ən\ *n* : a student in a seminary especially of the Roman Catholic Church

sem·i·nary \'sem-ə-,ner-ē\ *n, pl* **-nar·ies 1** : an institution of secondary education; *esp* : an academy for girls **2** : an institution for training clergymen [Latin *seminarium* "seedbed", from *semin-, semen* "seed"]

sem·i·nif·er·ous \,sem-ə-'nif-rəs, -ə-rəs\ *adj* : producing or bearing seed or semen [Latin *semin-, semen* "seed" + English *-iferous*]

seminiferous tubule *n* : any of the coiled threadlike tubules that make up the bulk of the testis and are lined with a germinal epithelium from which the spermatozoa are produced

Sem·i·nole \'sem-ə-,nōl\ *n* : a member of an Amerindian people of what is now Florida [Creek *simalóni, simanóli,* literally, "wild", from American Spanish *cimarrón*]

semi·no·mad \,sem-i-'nō-,mad, ,sem-,ī-\ *n* : a member of a people living usually in portable or temporary dwellings and practicing seasonal migration but having a base camp at which some crops are cultivated — **semi·no·mad·ic** \-nō-'mad-ik\ *adj*

semi·of·fi·cial \,sem-ē-ə-'fish-əl, ,sem-,ī-\ *adj* : having some official authority or standing ⟨a *semiofficial* statement⟩ — **semi·of·fi·cial·ly** \-'fish-lē, -ə-lē\ *adv*

semi·opaque \-ō-'pāk\ *adj* : nearly opaque

semi·pal·mat·ed \,sem-i-'pal,māt-əd, ,sem-,ī-, -'päm,āt-, -'päl,māt-\ *adj* : having the anterior toes joined only part way down with a web

semi·per·ma·nent \-'pər-mə-nənt\ *adj* **1** : permanent in some respects **2** : lasting for an indefinite time

semi·per·me·able \-'pər-mē-ə-bəl\ *adj* : partially but not freely or wholly permeable; *esp* : permeable to some usually small molecules but not to other usually larger particles ⟨a *semipermeable* membrane⟩ — **semi·per·me·abil·i·ty** \-,pər-mē-ə-'bil-ət-ē\ *n*

semi·po·lit·i·cal \-pə-'lit-i-kəl\ *adj* : of, relating to, or involving some political features or activity

semi·post·al \-'pōs-tl\ *n* : a postage stamp sold (as for various humanitarian purposes) at a premium over its postal value

semi·pre·cious \-'presh-əs\ *adj* : of somewhat less commercial value than precious ⟨*semiprecious* gemstones⟩

semi·pri·vate \-'prī-vət\ *adj* : shared with one other or a few others ⟨a *semiprivate* room in a hospital⟩

semi·pro \'sem-i-,prō, 'sem-,ī-\ *adj or n* : SEMIPROFESSIONAL

semi·pro·fes·sion·al \,sem-i-prə-'fesh-nəl, -ən-l, ,sem-,ī-\ *adj* **1** : engaging in an activity for pay or gain but not as a full-time occupation **2** : engaged in by semiprofessional players ⟨*semiprofessional* baseball⟩ — **semiprofessional** *n* — **semi·pro·fes·sion·al·ly** \-ē\ *adv*

semi·pub·lic \-'pəb-lik\ *adj* **1** : having some features of a public institution; *esp* : maintained as a public service by a private nonprofit organization **2** : open to some persons outside the regular membership

semi·re·li·gious \-ri-'lij-əs\ *adj* : somewhat religious in character

semi·rig·id \-'rij-əd\ *adj* **1** : rigid to some degree or in some parts **2** : having a flexible cylindrical gas container with an attached stiffening keel that carries the load ⟨*semirigid* airships⟩

semi·sa·cred \-'sā-krəd\ *adj* : SEMIRELIGIOUS

semi·skilled \,sem-i-'skild, ,sem-,ī-\ *adj* : having or requiring less training than skilled labor and more than unskilled labor

semi·soft \-'sóft\ *adj* : fairly soft; *esp* : firm but easily cut ⟨*semisoft* cheese⟩

semi·sol·id \-'säl-əd\ *adj* : having the qualities of both a solid and a liquid ⟨jelly is *semisolid*⟩ — **semisolid** *n*

semi·sweet \-'swēt\ *adj* : slightly sweetened ⟨*semisweet* chocolate⟩

Sem·ite \'sem-,īt\ *n* **1** : a member of any of the peoples descended from Shem **2** : a member of any of a group of peoples of southwestern Asia chiefly represented by the Jews and Arabs [French *sémite,* from *Sem* "Shem (eldest son of Noah)", from Late Latin, from Greek *Sēm,* from Hebrew *Shēm*]

semi·ter·res·tri·al \,sem-i-tə-'res-trē-əl, ,sem-,ī-, -'res-chəl, -'resh-chəl\ *adj* **1** : growing on boggy ground **2** : frequenting but not living wholly on land

¹Se·mit·ic \sə-'mit-ik\ *adj* **1** : of, relating to, or characteristic of the Semites; *esp* : JEWISH **2** : of, relating to, or constituting a branch of the Afro-Asiatic language family that includes Hebrew, Aramaic, Arabic, and Ethiopic

²Semitic *n* : any or all of the Semitic languages

Sem·i·tism \'sem-ə-,tiz-əm\ *n* **1 a** : Semitic character or qualities **b** : a Semitic idiom or expression **2** : policy favorable to Jews : predisposition in favor of Jews

semi·ton·al \,sem-i-'tōn-l, ,sem-,ī-\ *adj* : CHROMATIC 2, SEMITONIC — **semi·ton·al·ly** \-l-ē\ *adv*

semi·tone \'sem-i-,tōn, 'sem-,ī-\ *n* : the tone at a half step; *also* : HALF STEP — **semi·ton·ic** \,sem-i-'tän-ik, ,sem-,ī-\ *adj* — **semi·ton·i·cal·ly** \-'tän-i-kə-lē, -klē\ *adv*

semi·trail·er \'sem-i-,trā-lər, 'sem-,ī-\ *n* : a freight trailer that in use is supported at its forward end by the truck tractor; *also* : a semitrailer with attached tractor

semi·trans·lu·cent \,sem-i-,trans-'lüs-nt, ,sem-,ī-, -,tranz-\ *adj* : partly translucent

semi·trans·par·ent \-'par-ənt, -'per-\ *adj* : imperfectly transparent — **semi·trans·par·en·cy** \-ən-sē\ *n*

semi·trop·i·cal \-'träp-i-kəl\ *adj* : SUBTROPICAL

semi·trop·ics \-'träp-iks\ *n pl* : SUBTROPICS

¹semi·week·ly \-'wē-klē\ *adj* : done, appearing, or occurring twice a week — **semiweekly** *adv*

²semiweekly *n* : a semiweekly publication

semi·works \'sem-i-ˌwərks, 'sem-ˌī-\ *n pl* : a manufacturing plant operating on a limited commercial scale to provide final tests of a new product or process

semi·year·ly \ˌsem-i-'yiər-lē, ˌsem-ˌī-\ *adj* : done, appearing, or occurring twice a year

sem·o·li·na \ˌsem-ə-'lē-nə\ *n* : the purified middlings of hard wheat (as durum) used for pasta (as macaroni or spaghetti) [Italian *semolino,* from *semola* "bran", from Latin *simila* "finest wheat flour"]

sem·per·vi·vum \ˌsem-pər-'vī-vəm\ *n* : any of a large genus of Old World fleshy herbs of the orpine family often grown as ornamentals [New Latin, from Latin *sempervivus* "ever-living", from *semper* "ever" + *vivus* "living"]

sem·pi·ter·nal \ˌsem-pi-'tərn-l\ *adj* : of never-ending duration : ETERNAL [Late Latin *sempiternalis,* from Latin *sempiternus,* from *semper* "ever, always"] — **sem·pi·ter·nal·ly** \-l-ē\ *adv* — **sem·pi·ter·ni·ty** \-'tər-nət-ē\ *n*

sem·pre \'sem-prā\ *adv* : ALWAYS — used in music directions [Italian, from Latin *semper*]

semp·stress *variant of* SEAMSTRESS

¹sen \'sen\ *n, pl* **sen** 1 : a Japanese monetary unit equal to ¹/₁₀₀ yen 2 : a coin representing one sen [Japanese]

²sen *n, pl* **sen** 1 : an Indonesian monetary unit equal to ¹/₁₀₀ rupiah 2 : a coin representing one sen [Indonesian *sén,* probably from English *cent*]

sen·ate \'sen-ət\ *n* 1 a : the supreme council of the ancient Roman republic and empire b : the higher chamber in some bicameral legislatures 2 : the hall or chamber in which a senate meets 3 : a governing body of some universities charged with maintaining academic standards and regulations [Old French *senat,* from Latin *senatus,* from *senex* "old, old man"]

sen·a·tor \'sen-ət-ər\ *n* : a member of a senate — **sen·a·tor·ship** \-ˌship\ *n*

sen·a·to·ri·al \ˌsen-ə-'tōr-ē-əl, -'tȯr-\ *adj* : of, relating to, or befitting a senator or a senate ⟨*senatorial* office⟩ ⟨*senatorial* rank⟩

senatorial courtesy *n* : a custom of the United States Senate of refusing to confirm a presidential appointment of an official in or from a state when the appointment is opposed by the senators or senior senator of the president's party from that state

send \'send\ *vb* **sent** \'sent\; **send·ing** 1 : to cause to go : DISPATCH ⟨*sent* the student home⟩ ⟨*send* a message⟩; *esp* : to drive or propel physically ⟨*sent* the ball into right field⟩ 2 : to cause to happen ⟨whatever fate may *send*⟩ 3 : to have an agent, order, or request go or be transmitted ⟨*send* out for coffee⟩ ⟨*sent* for their price list⟩; *esp* : to transmit an order or request to come or return ⟨the principal *sent* for me⟩ 4 : to put or bring into a certain condition ⟨the request *sent* them into a tizzy⟩ [Old English *sendan*] — **send·er** *n* — **send packing** : to send off roughly or in disgrace

send–off \'sen-ˌdȯf\ *n* : a demonstration of goodwill and enthusiasm for the beginning of a new venture (as a trip)

Sen·e·ca \'sen-i-kə\ *n, pl* **Seneca** *or* **Senecas** : a member of an Iroquoian people of what is now western New York [Dutch *Sennecaas* "the Seneca, Oneida, Onondaga, and Cayuga people", from Mohican *A'sinnika* "Oneida", translation of Iroquois *Onĕyóde',* literally, "standing rock"]

sen·e·schal \'sen-ə-shəl\ *n* : an agent or bailiff who managed a lord's estate in feudal times [Middle French, of Germanic origin]

se·nes·cence \si-'nes-ns\ *n* 1 : the process of growing old 2 : the state of being old [Latin *senescens,* present participle of *senescere* "to grow old", from *senex* "old"] — **se·nesce** \si-'nes\ *vi* — **se·nes·cent** \-nt\ *adj*

se·nhor \si-'nyōr, -'nyȯr\ *n, pl* **senhors** *or* **se·nho·res** \-'nyōr-ēs, -'nyȯr-, -ˌēsh, -ˌēz, -ˌēzh\ — used by or to Portuguese-speaking people as a courtesy title equivalent to *Mr.* [Portuguese, from Medieval Latin *senior* "lord, superior", from Latin, adj., "senior"]

se·nho·ra \si-'nyōr-ə, -'nyȯr-\ *n* — used by or to Portuguese-speaking people as a courtesy title equivalent to *Mrs.* [Portuguese, feminine of *senhor*]

se·nho·ri·ta \ˌsē-nyə-'rēt-ə\ *n* — used by or to Portuguese-speaking people as a courtesy title equivalent to *Miss* [Portuguese, from *senhora*]

se·nile \'sēn-ˌīl *also* 'sen-\ *adj* : of or relating to old age : resulting from old age ⟨*senile* weaknesses⟩; *also* : having infirmities associated with old age ⟨a *senile* oldster⟩ [Latin *senilis,* from *senex* "old, old man"] — **se·nile·ly** \-ˌīl-lē\ *adv*

se·nil·i·ty \si-'nil-ət-ē\ *n* : the quality or state of being senile; *esp* : the physical and mental infirmity of old age

¹se·nior \'sē-nyər\ *n* 1 : a person older or of higher rank than another 2 : a student in the last year before graduating from a school of secondary or higher level [Latin, from *senior,* adj.]

²senior *adj* 1 a : OLDER — used chiefly to distinguish a father with the same given name as his son and usually placed in its abbreviated form after a surname ⟨John M. Doe, *Sr.*⟩ b : having reached the age of retirement ⟨*senior* citizens⟩ 2 : higher in standing or rank ⟨*senior* partner⟩ 3 : of or relating to seniors ⟨the *senior* class⟩ [Latin, "older, elder, senior", comparative of *senex* "old"]

senior airman *n* : a rank in the Air Force comparable to sergeant that is usually held temporarily by an airman before being appointed sergeant

senior chief petty officer *n* : an enlisted rank in the Navy and Coast Guard above chief petty officer and below master chief petty officer

senior high school *n* : a school usually including grades 10-12

se·nior·i·ty \sēn-'yȯr-ət-ē, -'yär-\ *n* 1 : the quality or state of being senior 2 : a privileged status attained by length of service

senior master sergeant *n* : an enlisted rank in the Air Force above master sergeant and below chief master sergeant

sen·na \'sen-ə\ *n* 1 : CASSIA 2; *esp* : one used medicinally 2 : the dried leaflets of various cassias used as a purgative [Arabic *sanā*]

sen·net \'sen-ət\ *n* : a signal call on a trumpet or cornet for entrance or exit on the stage [probably from obsolete *signet* "signal"]

sen·night *also* **se'n·night** \'sen-ˌīt\ *n, archaic* : one week [Old English *seofon nihta* "seven nights"]

sen·nit \'sen-ət\ *n* 1 : a braided cord or fabric of plaited rope yarns or other small stuff 2 : a straw or grass braid for hats [perhaps from French *coussinet* "small cushion, pad", from *coussin* "cushion"]

se·nor *or* **se·ñor** \sān-'yȯr\ *n, pl* **senors** *or* **se·ño·res** \-'yȯr-ās, -'yȯr-\ — used by or to Spanish-speaking people as a courtesy title equivalent to *Mr.* [Spanish *señor,* from Medieval Latin *senior* "superior, lord", from Latin, adj., "senior"]

se·no·ra *or* **se·ño·ra** \sān-'yȯr-ə, -'yȯr-\ *n* — used by or to Spanish-speaking people as a courtesy title equivalent to *Mrs.* [Spanish *señora,* feminine of *señor*]

se·no·ri·ta *or* **se·ño·ri·ta** \ˌsān-yə-'rēt-ə\ *n* — used by or to Spanish-speaking people as a courtesy title equivalent to *Miss* [Spanish *señorita,* from *señora*]

sen·sa·tion \sen-'sā-shən, sən-\ *n* 1 a : awareness (as of noise or heat) or a mental process (as seeing, hearing, or smelling) due to stimulation of a sense organ b : an indefinite bodily feeling ⟨a *sensation* of buoyancy⟩ 2 : something that causes or is the object of sensation 3 a : a state of excited interest or feeling b : a cause of such excitement ⟨the play was a *sensation*⟩

sen·sa·tion·al \-shnəl, -shən-l\ *adj* **1** : of or relating to sensation or the senses **2** : arousing or tending to arouse (as by lurid details) an intense and usually superficial interest or emotional reaction ⟨*sensational* news⟩ **3** : exceedingly or unexpectedly excellent or great ⟨a *sensational* diving catch⟩ — **sen·sa·tion·al·ly** \-ē\ *adv*

sen·sa·tion·al·ism \-,iz-əm\ *n* : the use or effect of sensational subject matter or treatment — **sen·sa·tion·al·ist** \-əst\ *n* — **sen·sa·tion·al·is·tic** \-,sā-shnəl-'is-tik, -shən-l-\ *adj*

¹sense \'sens\ *n* **1** : a meaning conveyed or intended; *esp* : one of the meanings a word may bear **2 a** : a specialized animal function or mechanism (as sight, hearing, smell, taste, or touch) basically involving interaction of a stimulus and a sense organ ⟨the pain *sense*⟩ **b** : the sensory mechanisms constituting a unit distinct from other functions (as movement or thought) **3** : conscious awareness or rationality ⟨when they came to their *senses* they saw what they had done⟩ **4 a** : a particular sensation or kind or quality of sensation ⟨a good *sense* of balance⟩ **b** : a definite but often vague awareness ⟨a *sense* of danger⟩ **c** : intellectual appreciation ⟨a *sense* of humor⟩ **5** : INTELLIGENCE 1a, JUDGMENT; *esp* : good judgment **6** : one of two opposite directions describable by the motion of a point, line, or surface [Latin *sensus* "sensation, feeling, meaning", from *sentire* "to perceive, feel"] SYN see MEANING

²sense *vt* **1 a** : to perceive by the senses **b** : to be or become conscious of ⟨*sense* danger⟩ **2** : UNDERSTAND 1 **3** : to detect (as radiation) automatically

sense·ful \'sens-fəl\ *adj* : full of sense : REASONABLE

sense·less \'sen-sləs\ *adj* : destitute of, deficient in, or contrary to sense: as **a** : UNCONSCIOUS ⟨knocked *senseless*⟩ **b** : FOOLISH, STUPID **c** : MEANINGLESS, PURPOSELESS ⟨a *senseless* act⟩ — **sense·less·ly** *adv* — **sense·less·ness** *n*

sense organ *n* : a bodily structure affected by a stimulus (as heat or sound waves) in such a manner as to activate associated sensory nerve fibers which convey impulses to the central nervous system where they are interpreted as corresponding sensations

sen·si·bil·i·ty \,sen-sə-'bil-ət-ē\ *n, pl* **-ties 1** : ability to receive sensations : SENSITIVITY ⟨tactile *sensibility*⟩ **2** : peculiar susceptibility to a pleasurable or painful impression (as praise or a slight) — often used in pl. **3** : awareness of and responsiveness toward something (as emotion in another) **4** : refined sensitiveness in emotion and taste

sen·si·ble \'sen-sə-bəl\ *adj* **1 a** : capable of being perceived by the senses or by reason or understanding **b** : perceptibly large : CONSIDERABLE ⟨a *sensible* error⟩ **2** : capable of receiving sense impressions ⟨*sensible* to pain⟩ **3** : COGNIZANT, AWARE **4** : having or containing good sense or reason : REASONABLE ⟨a *sensible* arrangement⟩ — **sen·si·ble·ness** *n* — **sen·si·bly** \-blē\ *adv*

sen·si·tive \'sen-sət-iv, 'sen-stiv\ *adj* **1** : subject to excitation by or responsive to stimuli **2** : easily or strongly affected or hurt ⟨a *sensitive* child⟩; *esp* : HYPERSENSITIVE ⟨*sensitive* to egg protein⟩ **3 a** : capable of indicating minute differences : DELICATE ⟨*sensitive* scales⟩ **b** : readily affected or changed by various agents or causes (as light or mechanical shock) **c** : high in radio sensitivity **4** : concerned with or involving highly classified government information ⟨appointed to a *sensitive* government post⟩ [Middle French *sensitif*, from Medieval Latin *sensitivus*, from Latin *sentire* "to feel"] — **sen·si·tive·ly** *adv* — **sen·si·tive·ness** *n*

sensitive fern *n* : a common American fern with fronds very susceptible to frost injury

sensitive plant *n* : any of several mimosas having leaves that fold or droop when touched

sen·si·tiv·i·ty \,sen-sə-'tiv-ət-ē\ *n, pl* **-ties** : the quality or state of being sensitive: as **a** : the capacity of an organism or sense organ to respond to stimulation : IR-

RITABILITY **b** : HYPERSENSITIVITY **c** : the degree to which a radio receiving set responds to incoming waves

sen·si·tize \'sen-sə-,tīz\ *vb* : to make or become sensitive or hypersensitive — **sen·si·ti·za·tion** \,sen-sət-ə-'zā-shən\ *n* — **sen·si·tiz·er** \'sen-sə-,tī-zər\ *n*

sen·si·tom·e·ter \,sen-sə-'täm-ət-ər\ *n* : an instrument for measuring sensitivity of photographic material — **sen·si·to·met·ric** \,sen-sət-ə-'me-trik\ *adj* — **sen·si·tom·e·try** \,sen-sə-'täm-ə-trē\ *n*

sen·sor \'sen-,sȯr, 'sen-sər\ *n* : a device that responds to a physical stimulus (as heat or light) and transmits a resulting impulse (as for operating a control)

sen·so·ri·mo·tor \,sens-rē-'mōt-ər, -ə-rē-\ *adj* : of, relating to, or functioning in both sensory and motor aspects of bodily activity

sen·so·ry \'sens-rē, -ə-rē\ *adj* **1** : of or relating to sensation or to the senses **2** : conveying nerve impulses from the sense organs : AFFERENT ⟨*sensory* neurons⟩

sen·su·al \'sench-wəl, -ə-wəl; 'sen-shəl\ *adj* **1** : SENSORY 1 **2** : relating to or consisting in the gratification of the senses or the indulgence of appetite **3 a** : devoted to or preoccupied with the senses or appetites **b** : VOLUPTUOUS 1 **c** : deficient in moral, spiritual, or intellectual interests : WORLDLY; *esp* : IRRELIGIOUS [Late Latin *sensualis*, from Latin *sensus* "sense"] — **sen·su·al·i·ty** \,sen-chə-'wal-ət-ē\ *n* — **sen·su·al·ly** \'sench-wə-lē, -ə-wə-; 'sen-shə-lē\ *adv*

sen·su·al·ism \'sench-wə-,liz-əm, -ə-wə-, 'sen-shə-,liz-\ *n* : persistent pursuit of sensual pleasures — **sen·su·al·ist** \-ləst\ *n* — **sen·su·al·is·tic** \,sench-wə-'lis-tik, -ə-wə-; ,sen-shə-'lis-\ *adj*

sen·su·al·ize \'sench-wə-,līz, -ə-wə-; 'sen-shə-,līz\ *vt* : to make sensual — **sen·su·al·iza·tion** \,sench-wə-lə-'zā-shən, -ə-wə-; ,sen-shə-lə-\ *n*

sen·su·ous \'sench-wəs, -ə-wəs\ *adj* **1 a** : of or relating to the senses **b** : having strong sensory appeal ⟨*sensuous* pleasure⟩ **2** : characterized by sense impressions or imagery aimed at the senses ⟨*sensuous* description⟩ **3** : highly susceptible to influence through the senses — **sen·su·ous·ly** *adv* — **sen·su·ous·ness** *n*

sent *past of* SEND

¹sen·tence \'sent-ns, -nz\ *n* **1 a** : JUDGMENT 2a; *esp* : one formally pronounced by a court in a criminal proceeding and specifying the punishment to be inflicted **b** : the punishment so imposed ⟨serve a *sentence* for robbery⟩ **2** *archaic* : AXIOM 1 **3 a** : a grammatically self-contained speech unit that expresses an assertion, a question, a command, a wish, or an exclamation, that in writing usually begins with a capital letter and concludes with appropriate end punctuation, and that in speaking is phonetically distinguished by various patterns of stress, pitch, and pauses **b** : a statement in words or symbols (as $3 + 5 = 8$) expressing a relationship between mathematical entities [Old French, from Latin *sententia*, literally, "feeling, opinion", from *sentire* "to feel"] — **sen·ten·tial** \sen-'ten-chəl\ *adj* — **sen·ten·tial·ly** \-chə-lē\ *adv*

²sentence *vt* **1** : to pronounce sentence on **2** : to condemn to a specified punishment

sentence fragment *n* : a word, phrase, or clause that lacks the grammatically self-contained structure of a sentence but has in speech the intonation of a sentence and is written and punctuated as if it were a complete sentence

sentence stress *n* : the manner in which stresses are distributed on the syllables of words assembled into sentences — called also *sentence accent*

sen·ten·tious \sen-'ten-chəs\ *adj* **1** : being concise and forceful : PITHY **2** : containing, using, or inclined to use high-sounding empty phrases or pompous sayings [Latin *sententiosus*, from *sententia* "sentence, maxim, feeling"] — **sen·ten·tious·ly** *adv* — **sen·ten·tious·ness** *n*

sen·tient \'sen-chē-ənt, -chənt\ *adj* : capable of feeling : conscious of sense impressions ⟨the lowest of *sentient* creatures⟩ [Latin *sentiens*, present participle of *sentire* "to feel"] — **sentience** \-chē-ənts, -chəns\ *n* — **sen·tient·ly** *adv*

sen·ti·ment \'sent-ə-mənt\ *n* **1 a** : an attitude, thought, or judgment prompted by feeling **b** : a specific view or notion : OPINION **2 a** : EMOTION **b** : refined feeling : delicate sensibility **c** : emotional idealism **d** : a romantic or nostalgic feeling [Medieval Latin *sentimentum*, from Latin *sentire* "to feel"] SYN see FEELING

sen·ti·men·tal \,sent-ə-'ment-l\ *adj* **1 a** : marked or governed by feeling, sensibility, or emotional idealism **b** : resulting from feeling rather than reason or thought **2** : having an excess or affectation of sentiment or sensibility — **sen·ti·men·tal·ly** \-l-ē\ *adv*

sen·ti·men·tal·ism \-l-,iz-əm\ *n* **1** : the disposition to favor or indulge in sentiment **2** : SENTIMENTALITY 2 — **sen·ti·men·tal·ist** \-l-əst\ *n*

sen·ti·men·tal·i·ty \,sent-ə-,men-'tal-ət-ē, -mən-\ *n, pl* **-ties 1** : the quality or state of being sentimental especially to excess or in affectation **2** : a sentimental idea or its expression

sen·ti·men·tal·ize \-'ment-l-,īz\ *vb* **1** : to indulge in sentiment **2** : to look upon or imbue with sentiment — **sen·ti·men·tal·iza·tion** \-,ment-l-ə-'zā-shən\ *n*

¹sen·ti·nel \'sent-nəl, -n-əl\ *n* : one that watches or guards [Middle French *sentinelle*, from Italian *sentinella*, from *sentina* "vigilance", from *sentire* "to perceive", from Latin]

²sentinel *vt* **-neled;** *or* **-nelled; -nel·ing** *or* **-nel·ling 1** : to watch over as a sentinel **2** : to furnish with a sentinel **3** : to post as sentinel

sen·try \'sen-trē\ *n, pl* **sentries** : GUARD, WATCH; *esp* : a soldier standing guard at a point of passage [perhaps from obsolete *sentry* "sanctuary, watch tower"]

sentry box *n* : a shelter for a sentry on duty

se·pal \'sēp-əl, 'sep-\ *n* : one of the modified leaves comprising a flower calyx [New Latin *sepalum*, derived from Greek *skepē* "covering"]

sep·a·ra·ble \'sep-rə-bəl, -ə-rə-\ *adj* : capable of being separated or distinguished — **sep·a·ra·bil·i·ty** \,sep-rə-'bil-ət-ē, -ə-rə-\ *n* — **sep·a·ra·ble·ness** \'sep-rə-bəl-nəs, -ə-rə-\ *n*

¹sep·a·rate \'sep-ə-,rāt, 'sep-,rāt\ *vb* **1 a** : to set or keep apart : DISCONNECT **b** : to keep distinct in the mind : DISTINGUISH ⟨*separate* religion from magic⟩ **c** : SORT ⟨*separate* mail⟩ **d** : to disperse in space or time : SCATTER ⟨widely *separated* homesteads⟩ **2** : to release officially : DISCHARGE ⟨was *separated* from the army⟩ **3** : to block off : SEGREGATE **4** : to isolate or become isolated from a mixture ⟨*separate* cream from milk⟩ **5** : to become divided or detached : come apart **6 a** : to break off an association : WITHDRAW **b** : to cease to be or live together especially as husband and wife **7** : to go in different directions [Latin *separare*, from *se-* "apart" + *parare* "to prepare, procure"] □ SYN SEPARATE, DIVIDE, SEVER mean to break or keep apart. SEPARATE may imply any one of several ways or causes such as dispersion, removal of one from others, or presence of an intervening thing; DIVIDE implies separating by cutting or breaking into pieces or sections; SEVER implies violence especially in the removal of a part or member.

²sep·a·rate \'sep-rət, -ə-rət\ *adj* **1** : set or kept apart : DETACHED **2** : not shared with another : INDIVIDUAL ⟨*separate* rooms⟩ **3 a** : existing by itself **b** : dissimilar in nature or identity ⟨the *separate* pieces of a puzzle⟩ — **sep·a·rate·ly** \-rət-lē, 'sep-ərt-lē\ *adv* — **sep·a·rate·ness** \-rət-nəs\ *n*

³sep·a·rate \'sep-rət, -ə-rət\ *n* : an article of dress designed to be worn interchangeably with others to form various costume combinations

sep·a·ra·tion \,sep-ə-'rā-shən\ *n* **1** : the act or process of separating : the state of being separated **2 a** : a point, line, or means of division **b** : an intervening

space : GAP **3 a** : a formal separating of husband and wife by agreement but without divorce **b** : termination of a contractual relationship (as employment or military service)

sep·a·rat·ist \'sep-rət-əst, -ə-rət-\ *n, often cap* : one that favors separation: as **a** *cap* : one of a group of 16th and 17th century English Protestants preferring to separate from rather than to reform the Church of England **b** : an advocate of independence or autonomy for a part of a nation — **sep·a·rat·ism** \-rə-,tiz-əm\ *n* — **sep·a·ra·tis·tic** \,sep-rə-'tis-tik, -ə-rə-\ *adj*

sep·a·ra·tive \'sep-ə-,rāt-iv, 'sep-rət-, 'sep-ə-rət-\ *adj* : tending toward, causing, or expressing separation

sep·a·ra·tor \'sep-ə-,rāt-ər\ *n* : one that separates; *esp* : a device for separating liquids (as cream from milk) of different specific gravities or liquids from solids — compare CENTRIFUGE

Se·phar·di \sə-'färd-ē\ *n, pl* **Se·phar·dim** \-'färd-əm\ : a member of one of the two great divisions of Jews comprising the occidental branch of European Jews settling in Spain and Portugal — compare ASHKENAZI [Hebrew *sĕphāradhī*, from *Sĕphāradh* "Spain", from *sĕphāradh*, a region where Jews were once exiled (Obadiah 1:20)] — **Se·phar·dic** \-'färd-ik\ *adj*

¹se·pia \'sē-pē-ə\ *n* **1** : a brown melanin-containing pigment from the ink of cuttlefishes **2** : a brownish gray to dark olive brown [Latin, "cuttlefish", from Greek *sēpia*]

²sepia *adj* **1** : of the color sepia **2** : made of or done in sepia ⟨*sepia* print⟩

se·poy \'sē-,pȯi\ *n* : a native of India employed as a soldier by a European power [Portuguese *sipai*, from Hindi *sipāhī*, from Persian, "cavalryman"]

sep·sis \'sep-səs\ *n, pl* **sep·ses** \'sep-,sēz\ : a poisoned condition resulting from the spread of bacteria or their poisonous products from a center of infection [Greek *sēpsis* "decay", from *sēpein* "to make putrid"]

sep·tate \'sep-,tāt\ *adj* : divided by or having a septum

Sep·tem·ber \sep-'tem-bər, səp-\ *n* : the 9th month of the year [Old French *Septembre*, from Latin *September*, from *septem* "seven"; from its having been originally the 7th month of the Roman calendar]

sep·ten·ni·al \sep-'ten-ē-əl\ *adj* **1** : consisting of or lasting for seven years **2** : occurring or being done every seven years [Late Latin *septennium* "period of 7 years", from Latin *septem* "seven" + *-ennium* (as in *biennium* "biennium")] — **sep·ten·ni·al·ly** \-ē-ə-lē\ *adv*

sep·tet *also* **sep·tette** \sep-'tet\ *n* **1** : a musical composition for seven instruments or voices **2** : a group or set of seven [German *septett*, from Latin *septem* "seven"]

sep·tic \'sep-tik\ *adj* **1** : of, relating to, or causing putrefaction **2** : produced by putrefaction or by disease germs ⟨*septic* poisoning⟩ [Latin *septicus*, from Greek *sēptikos*, from *sēpein* "to make putrid"]

sep·ti·ce·mia \,sep-tə-'sē-mē-ə\ *n* : BLOOD POISONING — **sep·ti·ce·mic** \-'sē-mik\ *adj*

septic sore throat *n* : a severe sore throat caused by streptococci and accompanied by fever, prostration, and toxemia

septic tank *n* : a tank in which the solid matter of continuously flowing sewage is broken down by bacteria

sep·til·lion \sep-'til-yən\ *n* — see NUMBER table [French, from Latin *septem* "seven" + French *-illion* (as in *million*)]

sep·tu·a·ge·nar·i·an \,sep-,tü-ə-jə-'ner-ē-ən, -,tyü-; ,sep-tə-wə-jə-\ *n* : a person who is 70 or more but less than 80 years old [Late Latin *septuagenarius* "70 years old", derived from Latin *septuaginta* "seventy"] — **septuagenarian** *adj*

Sep·tu·a·ges·i·ma \,sep-tə-wə-'jes-ə-mə\ *n* : the 3d Sunday before Lent [Late Latin, from Latin *septuagesimus* "70th", from *septuaginta* "seventy"]

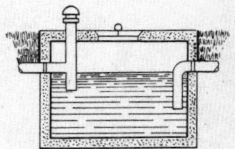

septic tank

serape

Sep·tu·a·gint \sep-'tü-ə-jənt, -'tyü-; 'sep-tə-wə-,jint\ *n* : a pre-Christian Greek version of the Old Testament used by Greek-speaking Christians [Latin *septuaginta* "seventy"; from the approximate number of its translators]

sep·tum \'sep-təm\ *n, pl* **sep·ta** \-tə\ : a dividing wall or membrane especially between bodily spaces or masses of soft tissue [Latin *saeptum* "enclosure, wall", from *saepire* "to fence in", from *saepes* "fence"] — **sep·tal** \'sep-tl\ *adj*

¹sep·ul·cher *or* **sep·ul·chre** \'sep-əl-kər\ *n* **1** : a place of burial : TOMB **2** : a receptacle for religious relics especially in an altar [Old French *sepulcre,* from Latin *sepulcrum, sepulchrum,* from *sepelire* "to bury"]

²sepulcher *or* **sepulchre** *vt* **-chered** *or* **-chred; -cher·ing** *or* **-chring** \-kə-ring, -kring\ *archaic* : to place in or as if in a sepulcher : BURY

se·pul·chral \sə-'pəl-krəl\ *adj* **1** : of or relating to burial, the grave, or monuments to the dead ⟨a *sepulchral* stone⟩ **2** : DISMAL 1, GLOOMY — **se·pul·chral·ly** \-krə-lē\ *adv*

sep·ul·ture \'sep-əl-,chủr\ *n* **1** : BURIAL **2** : SEPULCHER [Old French, from Latin *sepultura,* from *sepelire* "to bury"]

se·qua·cious \si-'kwā-shəs\ *adj* **1** *archaic* : inclined to follow : TRACTABLE **2** : intellectually servile [Latin *sequac-, sequax* "inclined to follow", from *sequi* "to follow"] — **se·qua·cious·ly** *adv* — **se·quac·i·ty** \-'kwas-ət-ē\ *n*

se·quel \'sē-kwəl\ *n* **1** : an event that follows or comes afterward : RESULT **2** : a work (as a novel or movie) that continues a story begun in another [Middle French *sequelle,* from Latin *sequela,* from *sequi* "to follow"]

se·que·la \si-'kwel-ə, -'kwē-lə\ *n, pl* **-que·lae** \-'kwel-,ē, -,ī; -'kwē-,lē\ **1** : an aftereffect of disease or injury **2** : a secondary result : CONSEQUENCE [Latin, "sequel"]

¹se·quence \'sē-kwəns, -,kwens\ *n* **1** : a continuous or connected series: as **a** : an extended series of poems united by a single theme ⟨a sonnet *sequence*⟩ **b** : three or more playing cards usually of the same suit in consecutive order of rank **c** : a succession of repetitions of a melodic phrase each in a new position **d** : a set of numbers having a definite order fixed by a rule **e** : a succession of scenes developing a single subject or phase of a film story **2** : order of succession **3 a** : CONSEQUENCE 1, RESULT **b** : a subsequent development **4** : continuity of progression [derived from Late Latin *sequentia* "sequel", from Latin *sequi* "to follow"] SYN see SUCCESSION

²sequence *vt* : to arrange in a sequence

se·quenc·er \'sē-kwən-sər, -,kwen-sər\ *n* : a device that determines a sequence

se·quen·cy \-kwən-sē\ *n, pl* **-cies** : SEQUENCE 2, 4

se·quent \'sē-kwənt\ *adj* : following in time or as an effect [Latin *sequens,* present participle of *sequi* "to follow"] — **sequent** *n*

se·quen·tial \si-'kwen-chəl\ *adj* **1** : of, relating to, or arranged in a sequence : SERIAL 1 ⟨*sequential* file systems⟩ **2** : following in sequence — **se·quen·tial·ly** \-chə-lē\ *adv*

se·ques·ter \si-'kwes-tər\ *vt* **-tered; -ter·ing** \-tə-ring, -tring\ **1** : to set apart : SEGREGATE, WITHDRAW **2** : to take custody of (as personal property) until a demand is satisfied [Middle French *sequestrer,* from Late Latin *sequestrare* "to surrender for safekeeping, set apart", from Latin *sequester* "agent, depositary"]

se·ques·tra·tion \,sē-kwəs-'trā-shən, si-,kwes-\ *n* : the act of sequestering : the state of being sequestered

se·quin \'sē-kwən\ *n* **1** : an old gold coin of Italy and Turkey **2** : a spangle used as an ornament on clothes [French, from Italian *zecchino,* from *zecca* "mint", from Arabic *sikkah* "die, coin"]

se·quined *or* **se·quinned** \-kwənd\ *adj* : ornamented with or as if with sequins

se·quoia \si-'kwoi-ə\ *n* : either of two huge cone-bearing California trees of the pine family that reach a height of over 90 meters : **a** : BIG TREE **b** : REDWOOD [*Sequoya* (George Guess), died 1843, American Indian scholar]

sera *pl of* SERUM

se·rac \sə-'rak\ *n* : a pinnacle, sharp ridge, or block of ice among the crevasses of a glacier [French *sérac,* literally, a kind of white cheese, from Medieval Latin *seracium* "whey", from Latin *serum*]

se·ra·glio \sə-'ral-yō\ *n, pl* **-glios** *also* **-gli** \-yē\ : HAREM 1a [Italian *serraglio* "enclosure, seraglio", partly from Medieval Latin *serraculum* "bar of a door, bolt", from Late Latin *serare* "to bolt"; partly from Turkish *saray* "palace"]

se·ra·pe *or* **sa·ra·pe** \sə-'räp-ē, -'rap-\ *n* : a colorful woolen shawl worn over the shoulder especially by Mexican men [Mexican Spanish *sarape*]

ser·aph \'ser-əf\ *n, pl* **ser·a·phim** \-ə-,fim\ *or* **seraphs** : an angel of the highest order [Late Latin *seraphim* "seraphs", from Hebrew *śĕrāphīm*]

Serb \'sərb\ *n* **1** : a native or inhabitant of the former kingdom of Serbia or of the federal republic of Serbia in Yugoslavia **2** : SERBIAN [Serbian *Srb*] — **Serb** *adj*

Ser·bi·an \'sər-bē-ən\ *n* **1** : SERB 1 **2 a** : the Serbo-Croatian language as spoken in Serbia **b** : a literary form of Serbo-Croatian using the Cyrillic alphabet — **Serbian** *adj*

Ser·bo–Cro·atian \,sər-bō-krō-'ā-shən\ *n* **1** : the Slavic language of the Serbs and Croats which is called Serbian when written in the Cyrillic alphabet and Croatian when written in the Roman alphabet **2** : one whose native language is Serbo-Croatian — **Serbo–Croatian** *adj*

sere \'siər\ *adj* : dried up [Old English *sēar* "dry"]

¹ser·e·nade \,ser-ə-'nād\ *n* **1 a** : a complimentary vocal or instrumental performance; *esp* : one given outdoors at night for a woman **b** : a work so performed **2** : a work for chamber orchestra resembling a suite [French *sérénade,* from Italian *serenata,* from *sereno* "clear, calm (of weather)", from Latin *serenus*]

²serenade *vb* : to entertain with or perform a serenade — **ser·e·nad·er** *n*

ser·en·dip·i·tous \,ser-ən-'dip-ət-əs\ *adj* : obtained or characterized by serendipity ⟨*serendipitous* discoveries⟩

ser·en·dip·i·ty \,ser-ən-'dip-ət-ē\ *n* : the gift of accidentally finding valuable or agreeable things [from its possession by the heroes of the Persian fairy tale *The Three Princes of Serendip*]

¹se·rene \sə-'rēn\ *adj* **1 a** : being clear and free of storms ⟨*serene* skies⟩ **b** : shining bright and steady **2** : marked by utter calm : TRANQUIL **3** : AUGUST — used as part of a title ⟨Your *Serene* Highness⟩ [Latin *serenus*] SYN see CALM — **se·rene·ly** *adv* — **se·rene·ness** \-'rēn-nəs\ *n*

²serene *n* **1** : a serene condition or expanse (as of sky, sea, or light) **2** : SERENITY, TRANQUILLITY

se·ren·i·ty \sə-'ren-ət-ē\ *n* : the quality or state of being serene

serf \'sərf\ *n* : a member of a servile feudal class bound to the soil [French, from Latin *servus* "slave, servant, serf"] — **serf·age** \'sər-fij\ *n* — **serf·dom** \'sərf-dəm\ *n* — **serf·hood** \-,hủd\ *n* — **serf·ish** \'sər-fish\ *adj* — **serf·ism** \-,fiz-əm\ *n*

serge \'sərj\ *n* : a durable twilled fabric having a smooth clear face and a diagonal rib on the front and the back [Middle French *sarge,* derived from Latin *sericus* "of silk", from Greek *sērikos,* from *Sēres,* an ancient Asian people producing silk]

ser·gean·cy \'sär-jən-sē\ *n* : the function, office, or rank of a sergeant

ser·geant *also* **ser·jeant** \'sär-jənt\ *n* **1** : an enlisted rank in the Army and Marine Corps above corporal and below staff sergeant and in the Air Force above airman first class and below staff sergeant **2** : a police officer ranking in the United States just below captain or sometimes lieutenant [Middle English, literally, "servant", from Old French *sergent,* from Latin *serviens,* present participle of *servire* "to serve"]

sergeant at arms *n* : an officer of an organization (as a court of law) appointed to keep order

sergeant first class *n* : an enlisted rank in the Army above staff sergeant and below master sergeant

sergeant major *n, pl* **sergeants major** *or* **sergeant majors** **1** : a noncommissioned officer (as in the Army) serving as chief enlisted assistant in a headquarters **2 a** : an enlisted rank in the Marine Corps above master sergeant **b** : COMMAND SERGEANT MAJOR, STAFF SERGEANT MAJOR

¹se·ri·al \'sir-ē-əl\ *adj* **1** : of, consisting of, or arranged in a series, rank, or row ⟨*serial* order⟩ **2** : appearing in parts or numbers that follow regularly ⟨a *serial* story⟩ **3** : relating to or being a connection in a computer system in which the bits of a byte are transmitted in sequence over a single line — **se·ri·al·ly** \-ē-ə-lē\ *adv*

²serial *n* **1** : a work appearing (as in a magazine or on television) in parts at intervals **2** : one part of a serial work : INSTALLMENT — **se·ri·al·ist** \-ē-ə-ləst\ *n*

se·ri·al·ize \'sir-ē-ə-ˌlīz\ *vt* : to arrange or present in serial form — **se·ri·al·iza·tion** \ˌsir-ē-ə-lə-'zā-shən\ *n*

se·ri·a·tim \ˌsir-ē-'āt-əm, -'at-\ *adv* : in a series : SERIALLY [Medieval Latin, from Latin *series* "series"]

seri·cul·ture \'ser-ə-ˌkəl-chər\ *n* : the raising of silkworms for silk production [Latin *sericum* "silk" + English *culture*] — **seri·cul·tur·al** \ˌser-ə-'kəlch-rəl, -ə-rəl\ *adj*

se·ries \'siər-ēz, -ˌēz\ *n, pl* **series** **1 a** : a number of things or events of the same class coming one after another **b** : a group with an order of arrangement exhibiting progression **2** : the indicated sum of a usually infinite sequence of numbers **3** : a succession of volumes or issues published with related subjects or authors, similar format and price, or continuous numbering **4** : a division of rock formations smaller than a system comprising rocks deposited during an epoch **5** : an arrangement of the parts of or elements in an electric circuit whereby all the current passes through each part or element without branching **6** : a group of chemical compounds related in composition and structure **7** : a group of successive coordinate sentence elements joined together [Latin, from *serere* "to join, link together"] SYN see SUCCESSION — **in series** : in a serial arrangement

ser·if \'ser-əf\ *n* : any of the short lines that cross the ends of the strokes of a printed letter [probably from Dutch *schreef* "stroke, line", from *schriven* "to write", from Latin *scribere*]

seri·graph \'ser-ə-ˌgraf\ *n* : an original silk-screen color print made by an artist [Latin *sericum* "silk" + Greek *graphein* "to write, draw"] — **se·rig·ra·pher** \sə-'rig-rə-fər\ *n* — **se·rig·ra·phy** \-fē\ *n*

ser·ine \'seər-ˌēn\ *n* : a crystalline amino acid $C_3H_7NO_3$ that occurs as a structural part of many proteins [derived from Latin *sericum* "silk"]

se·rio·com·ic \ˌsir-ē-ō-'käm-ik\ *adj* : having a mixture of the serious and the comic — **se·rio·com·i·cal·ly** \-'käm-i-kə-lē, -klē\ *adv*

se·ri·ous \'sir-ē-əs\ *adj* **1** : thoughtful or subdued in appearance or manner : SOBER **2 a** : requiring much thought or work ⟨*serious* study⟩ **b** : of or relating to a matter of importance ⟨a *serious* play⟩ **3** : not joking or trifling : EARNEST **4 a** : not easily answered or solved ⟨*serious* objections⟩ **b** : having important or dangerous possible consequences ⟨a *serious* injury⟩ [Late Latin *seriosus,* alteration of Latin *serius*] — **se·ri·ous·ly** *adv* — **se·ri·ous·ness** *n* □ SYN EARNEST, GRAVE, SOLEMN: SERIOUS implies showing or having a concern for what really matters; EARNEST adds an implication of sincerity or intensity of purpose; GRAVE implies both serious-

ness and dignity in expression or attitude; SOLEMN suggests an impressive gravity free from levity.

se·ri·ous–mind·ed \ˌsir-ē-ə-'smīn-dəd\ *adj* : having a serious disposition or trend of thought — **se·ri·ous–mind·ed·ly** *adv* — **se·ri·ous–mind·ed·ness** *n*

ser·jeant *variant of* SERGEANT

serjeant–at–law \ˌsär-jənt-ət-'lò\ *n, pl* **serjeants–at–law** : a barrister of the highest rank

ser·mon \'sər-mən\ *n* **1** : a public speech usually by a member of the clergy giving religious instruction or exhortation **2** : a lecture on conduct or duty [Old French, from Medieval Latin *sermo,* from Latin, "speech, conversation", from *serere* "to join, link together"] — **ser·mon·ic** \ˌsər-'män-ik\ *adj*

ser·mon·ize \'sər-mə-ˌnīz\ *vb* **1** : to compose or deliver a sermon : PREACH **2** : to speak or write as if delivering a sermon : LECTURE — **ser·mon·iz·er** *n*

Sermon on the Mount : a talk by Jesus recorded in Matthew 5–7 and Luke 6:20–49

se·rol·o·gy \sə-'räl-ə-jē\ *n* : a science dealing with serums and especially their reactions and properties — **se·ro·log·ic** \ˌsir-ə-'läj-ik\ *or* **se·ro·log·i·cal** \-'läj-i-kəl\ *adj* — **se·ro·log·i·cal·ly** \-i-kə-lē, -klē\ *adv* — **se·rol·o·gist** \sə-'räl-ə-jəst\ *n*

se·ro·sa \sə-'rō-zə\ *n* : a usually enclosing serous membrane [New Latin, from *serosus* "serous", from Latin *serum* "serum"] — **se·ro·sal** \-'rō-zəl\ *adj*

se·ro·to·nin \ˌsir-ə-'tō-nən, ˌser-\ *n* : an amine that causes narrowing of blood vessels and is found especially in the blood serum and gastric mucous membrane of mammals [*serum* + *ton*ic + -*in*]

se·rous \'sir-əs\ *adj* : of, relating to, resembling, or producing serum; *esp* : thin and watery ⟨a *serous* fluid⟩

serous membrane *n* : a thin membrane (as the peritoneum) with cells that secrete a serous fluid; *esp* : SEROSA

ser·pent \'sər-pənt\ *n* **1** : SNAKE 1; *esp* : a large snake **2** : DEVIL 1 **3** : a treacherous person [Middle French, from Latin *serpens,* from *serpere* "to creep"]

¹ser·pen·tine \'sər-pən-ˌtēn, -ˌtīn\ *adj* **1** : of or resembling a serpent **2** : subtly wily or tempting **3** : winding or turning one way and another ⟨a *serpentine* path⟩ — **ser·pen·tine·ly** *adv*

²serpentine *n* : something that winds sinuously

³ser·pen·tine \-ˌtēn\ *n* : a mineral consisting essentially of a hydrous silicate of magnesium usually having a dull green color and often a mottled appearance

serpent star *n* : BRITTLE STAR

¹ser·rate \sə-'rāt, 'seər-ˌāt\ *vt* : to mark with serrations : NOTCH [Late Latin *serrare* "to saw", from Latin *serra* "saw"]

²ser·rate \'seər-ˌāt, sə-'rāt\ *or* **ser·rat·ed** \'ser-ˌāt-əd, sə-'rāt-\ *adj* : having a saw-toothed edge ⟨a *serrate* leaf⟩ [Latin *serratus,* from *serra* "saw"]

ser·ra·tion \sə-'rā-shən, se-\ *n* **1** : a serrate condition or formation **2** : one of the teeth in a serrate margin

ser·ried \'ser-ēd\ *adj* : crowded together ⟨*serried* ranks of soldiers⟩ — **ser·ried·ly** *adv* — **ser·ried·ness** *n* [from earlier *serry* "to crowd together", from Middle French *serrer* "to press, crowd", from Late Latin *serare* "to bolt"]

se·rum \'sir-əm\ *n, pl* **serums** *or* **se·ra** \-ə\ : the watery portion of a bodily fluid remaining after coagulation: as **a** : BLOOD SERUM **b** : immune blood serum that contains specific immune bodies (as antitoxins or agglutinins) [Latin, "whey, serum"]

serum albumin *n* : an albumin or mixture of albumins normally constituting more than half of the blood serum protein and serving to maintain the blood osmotic pressure

serum globulin *n* : a globulin or mixture of globulins occurring in blood serum and containing most of the antibodies of the blood

serum sickness *n* : an allergic reaction to the injection of foreign serum

\ə\ abut		\ng\ sing	
\ər\ further		\ō\ bone	
\a\ mat		\ò\ saw	
\ā\ take		\òi\ coin	
\ä\ cot, cart		\th\ thin	
\aù\ out		\th\ this	
\ch\ chin		\ü\ food	
\e\ pet		\ù\ foot	
\ē\ easy		\y\ yet	
\g\ go		\yü\ few	
\i\ tip		\yù\ cure	
\ī\ life		\zh\ vision	
\j\ job			

serval

ser·val \'sər-vəl, ,sər-'val\ *n* : a tawny black-spotted African wildcat with large ears and long legs [French, from Portuguese *lobo serval* "lynx", from Medieval Latin *lupus cervalis,* literally, "cervine wolf"]

ser·vant \'sər-vənt\ *n* : one that serves others; *esp* : one that performs household or personal services [Old French, from *servir* "to serve"]

¹**serve** \'sərv\ *vb* **1 a** : to be a servant **b** : to give the service and respect due to (a superior); *also* : WORSHIP ⟨*serve* God⟩ **c** : to comply with the commands or demands of : GRATIFY **d** (1) : to work through or perform a term of service especially in an army or navy (2) : to put in : SPEND ⟨*serve* 30 days in jail⟩ **2 a** : to officiate as a priest or member of the clergy **b** : to assist as server at mass **3 a** : to be of use : answer a purpose ⟨the tree *serves* as shelter⟩ **b** : to be favorable, opportune, or convenient ⟨when the time *serves*⟩ **c** : to be enough or satisfactory for ⟨a pie that will *serve* eight people⟩ **d** : to hold an office : discharge a duty or function ⟨*serve* on a jury⟩ **4 a** : to wait on (as at a table or counter) **b** : to set out or bring portions of (food or drink) **5 a** : to supply with something (as heat or light) needed or desired **b** : to furnish professional services to **6** : to make a serve (as in tennis) **7** : to treat or act toward in a specified way ⟨they *served* me ill⟩ **8 a** : to bring to notice, deliver, or execute as required by law **b** : to make legal service on (a person named in a writ) [Old French *servir,* from Latin *servire* "to be a slave, serve", from *servus* "slave, servant"]

²**serve** *n* : the act or privilege of putting the ball or shuttlecock in play (as in tennis or badminton); *also* : a stroke that begins a rally

serv·er \'sər-vər\ *n* **1** : one that serves food or drink **2** : the player who puts a ball or shuttlecock in play **3** : the celebrant's assistant at low mass **4** : something (as a tray) used in serving food or drink

¹**ser·vice** \'sər-vəs\ *n* **1** : the occupation or function of serving ⟨in active *service*⟩; *esp* : employment as a servant **2 a** : the work or action performed by one that serves ⟨gives good and quick *service*⟩ **b** : HELP, USE, BENEFIT ⟨be of *service* to them⟩ **c** : contribution to the welfare of others **d** : disposal for use ⟨at your *service*⟩ **3 a** : a form followed in worship or in a religious ceremony ⟨the burial *service*⟩ **b** : a meeting for worship ⟨held an evening *service*⟩ **4** : the act of serving: as **a** : a helpful act : good turn ⟨did us a *service*⟩ **b** : useful labor that does not produce a tangible commodity — usually used in pl. ⟨charge for professional *services*⟩ **c** : the act or privilege of serving (as in tennis) **5** : a set of articles for a particular use ⟨a coffee *service*⟩ **6 a** : an administrative division (as of a government) ⟨the consular *service*⟩ **b** : a nation's military forces or one of these forces ⟨called into the *service*⟩ **7** : a facility supplying some public demand ⟨bus *service*⟩; *esp* : one providing maintenance and repair [Old French, from Latin *servitium* "condition of a slave", from *servus* "slave"]

¹service 5

²**service** *adj* **1 a** : of or relating to the armed services **b** : of, relating to, or constituting a branch of an army that provides service and supplies **2** : used in serving or supplying **3** : intended for everyday use : DURABLE **4** : providing services (as repairs or maintenance)

³**service** *vt* : to perform services for : repair or provide maintenance for

⁴**service** *n* : an Old World tree resembling the related mountain ashes but having larger flowers and larger edible fruit; *also* : a related Old World tree with small speckled brown fruits [Old English *syrfe,* from Latin *sorbus*]

ser·vice·able \'sər-və-sə-bəl\ *adj* **1** : HELPFUL, USEFUL **2** : wearing well in use — **ser·vice·abil·i·ty** \,sər-və-sə-'bil-ət-ē\ *n* — **ser·vice·ably** \-blē\ *adv*

ser·vice·ber·ry \'sər-vəs-,ber-ē, 2 *is also* 'sär-\ *n* **1** : the fruit of a service tree **2** : any of various North American trees and shrubs of the rose family that bear showy white flowers and edible purple or red fruits — called also *Juneberry, shadblow, shadbush*

service book *n* : a book setting forth forms of worship used in religious services

service box *n* : the area of the court in which a player stands while serving in various wall and net games

service charge *n* : a fee charged for a particular service often in addition to a standard or basic fee

service club *n* **1** : a club of business or professional people organized for their common benefit and active in community service **2** : a recreation center for enlisted men provided by one of the armed services

service court *n* : a part of the court into which the ball or shuttlecock must be served (as in tennis or badminton)

ser·vice·man \'sər-vəs-,man, -mən\ *n* **1** : a man who is in the armed forces **2** : a man who repairs or maintains equipment

service mark *n* : a mark or device used to identify a service (as transportation or insurance) offered to customers

service medal *n* : a medal awarded to a person who does military service in a specified war or campaign

service module *n* : a space vehicle module that contains propellant tanks, fuel cells, and the main rocket engine

service station *n* : a retail station for servicing motor vehicles especially with gasoline and oil

service stripe *n* : a stripe worn on the left sleeve of a military uniform to indicate three years of service in the Army or Air Force or four years in the Navy

ser·vice tree \'sər-vəs-\ *n* : ⁴SERVICE

ser·vice·wom·an \'ser-və-,swùm-ən\ *n* : a female member of the armed forces

ser·vi·ette \,sər-vē-'et\ *n, chiefly British* : a table napkin [French, from *servir* "to serve"]

ser·vile \'sər-vəl, -,vīl\ *adj* **1** : of or befitting a slave or an enslaved or menial class ⟨*servile* work⟩ ⟨*servile* flattery⟩ **2** : lacking spirit or independence : SUBMISSIVE ⟨*servile* to authority⟩ [Latin *servilis,* from *servus* "slave"] — **ser·vile·ly** \-vəl-lē, -,vīl-lē\ *adv* — **ser·vile·ness** \-vəl-nəs, -,vīl-\ *n* — **ser·vil·i·ty** \,sər-'vil-ət-ē\ *n* [Latin *servilis,* from *servus* "slave"]

serv·ing \'sər-ving\ *n* : a helping of food or drink

Ser·vite \'sər-,vīt\ *n* : a member of the mendicant Order of Servants of Mary founded at Florence in 1233 [Medieval Latin *Servitae* "Servites", from Latin *servus* "slave, servant"]

ser·vi·tor \'sər-vət-ər, -və-,tȯr\ *n* : a male servant [Middle French *servitour,* from Late Latin *servitor,* from Latin *servire* "to serve"]

ser·vi·tude \'sər-və-,tüd, -,tyüd\ *n* : a state of subjection to another that constitutes or resembles slavery or serfdom [Middle French, from Latin *servitudo* "slavery", from *servus* "slave"]

ser·vo \'sər-vō\ *n, pl* **servos** **1** : SERVOMOTOR **2** : SERVOMECHANISM

ser·vo·mech·a·nism \'sər-vō-,mek-ə-,niz-əm\ *n* : a device for automatically correcting the performance of a mechanism [*servo-* (as in *servomotor*) + *mechanism*]

ser·vo·mo·tor \'sər-vō-,mōt-ər\ *n* : a motor in a servomechanism that supplements a primary control by correcting position or motion [French *servo-moteur,* from Latin *servus* "slave, servant" + French *moteur* "motor", from Latin *motor* "one that moves"]

ses·a·me \'ses-ə-mē\ *n* **1** : an annual erect hairy herb of warm regions; *also* : its small somewhat flat seeds used as a source of oil and a flavoring agent **2** : OPEN SESAME [Latin *sesama,* from Greek *sēsamē,* of Semitic origin]

sesqui- *combining form* : one and a half times ⟨*sesqui*centennial⟩ [Latin, "one and a half", literally, "and a half", from *semis* "half" + *-que* "and"]

ses·qui·cen·ten·ni·al \,ses-kwi-sen-'ten-ē-əl\ *n* : a 150th anniversary or its celebration — **sesquicentennial** *adj*

ses·qui·pe·da·lian \,ses-kwə-pə-'dāl-yən\ *adj* **1** : having many syllables : LONG **2** : given to or characterized by the use of long words [Latin *sesquipedalis,* literally, "a foot and a half long", from *sesqui-* + *ped-, pes* "foot"]

ses·sile \'ses-,īl, -əl\ *adj* **1** : attached directly by the base and not raised upon a stalk or peduncle ⟨a *sessile* leaf⟩ **2** : permanently attached and not free to move about : SEDENTARY ⟨*sessile* polyps⟩ [Latin *sessilis* "of or fit for sitting, low", from *sessus,* past participle of *sedēre* "to sit"]

ses·sion \'sesh-ən\ *n* **1** : a meeting or series of meetings of a body (as a court or legislature) to transact business **2** : the period between the first and last of a series of meetings of a legislative or judicial body **3** : the ruling body of a Presbyterian congregation **4** : the period during the year or day in which a school conducts classes **5** : a meeting or period devoted to an activity ⟨a recording *session*⟩ [Middle French, from Latin *sessio,* literally, "act of sitting", from *sessus,* past participle of *sedēre* "to sit"] — **ses·sion·al** \'sesh-nəl, -ən-l\ *adj*

ses·terce \'ses-,tərs\ *n* : an ancient Roman coin equal to ¼ denarius [Latin *sestertius*]

ses·tet \se-'stet\ *n* : a stanza or poem of six lines; *esp* : the last six lines of an Italian sonnet — compare OCTAVE 2 [Italian *sestetto,* from *sesto* "sixth", from Latin *sextus,* from *sex* "six"]

¹set \'set\ *vb* **set; set·ting 1** : to cause to sit : place in or on a seat **2** : to give (a fowl) eggs to hatch or provide (eggs) with suitable conditions for hatching **3 a** : to put or fix in a place, condition, or position ⟨*set* a dish on the table⟩ ⟨*set* a trap⟩ **b** : to put (dough) aside to rise **4** : to direct with fixed attention ⟨*set* your mind to it⟩ **5** : to cause to assume a specified condition, relation, or occupation ⟨slaves were *set* free⟩ **6** : to appoint or assign an office or duty ⟨*set* pickets around the camp⟩ **7** : APPLY ⟨*set* a match to kindling⟩ **8** : FIX, PRESCRIBE ⟨*set* a date⟩ **9 a** : to establish as the highest level or best performance ⟨*set* a speed record⟩ **b** : to furnish as a pattern or model ⟨*set* a good example⟩ **c** : to allot as a task ⟨I was *set* the job of dusting⟩ **10** : to arrange or put into a desired and especially a normal position ⟨*set* a broken bone⟩ ⟨*set* the sails⟩ **11 a** : to put in order for use ⟨*set* the table⟩ **b** : to make scenically ready for a performance ⟨*set* the stage⟩ **c** (1) : to arrange (type) for printing (2) : to put into type or its equivalent **12** : to dress (hair) especially by curling or waving **13 a** : to adorn with something attached or separate ⟨a sky *set* with stars⟩ **b** : to fix (as a jewel) in a setting **14 a** : to place in a relative rank or category ⟨*set* duty before pleasure⟩ **b** : VALUE, ESTIMATE ⟨*set* the loss at $2000⟩ **15 a** : to direct to action **b** : to incite to attack or antagonism ⟨war *sets* country against country⟩ **16** : to put and fix in a direction ⟨*set* our faces toward home⟩ **17 a** : to fix firmly : make immobile ⟨*set* my jaw in determination⟩ **b** : to make unyielding or obstinate ⟨*set* your mind against all appeals⟩ **18** : to become or cause to become firm or solid ⟨the jelly is *setting*⟩ **19** : to form and bring (fruit or seed) to maturity **20** *chiefly dialect* : SIT 1a **21** : to be becoming : be suitable : FIT ⟨your behavior doesn't *set* well with your years⟩ **22** : to cover and warm eggs to hatch them ⟨*setting* hens⟩ **23** : to become lodged or fixed ⟨the pudding *sets* heavily on the stomach⟩ **24** : to pass below the horizon : go down ⟨the sun *sets*⟩ **25** : to apply oneself ⟨*set* to work⟩ **26** : to have a specified direction in motion : FLOW ⟨a current that *sets* to the north⟩ **27** : to dance face-to-face with another in a square dance ⟨*set* to your partner and turn⟩ **28** : to become permanent ⟨a dye that will not *set*⟩ **29** : to become whole by knitting ⟨the bone has not *set*⟩ [Old English *settan*] — **set about** : to begin to do ⟨*set about* proving it could be done⟩ — **set aside 1** : to put to one side : DISCARD **2** : to save for future use **3** : to reject from consideration **4** : ANNUL, OVERRULE ⟨the verdict was *set aside* by the court⟩ — **set at** : ATTACK 1, ASSAIL — **set forth 1** : to make known : PUBLISH **2** : to start out on a journey : set out — **set forward 1** : PROMOTE 2, FURTHER **2** : to set out on a journey — **set one's heart on** : RESOLVE 3 — **set store** : to consider valuable or worthwhile — used with *by* or *on* — **set to music** : to provide music for (lyrics) — **set upon** : to attack with violence ⟨*set upon* by a band of robbers⟩

²set *adj* **1** : INTENT, DETERMINED ⟨were *set* on going⟩ **2** : fixed by authority ⟨a *set* wage⟩ **3** : INTENTIONAL, PREMEDITATED ⟨did it of *set* purpose⟩ **4** : reluctant to change : OBSTINATE ⟨very *set* in your ways⟩ **5 a** : IMMOVABLE, RIGID ⟨a *set* frown⟩ **b** : BUILT-IN **6** : remaining unchanged : PERSISTENT ⟨*set* defiance⟩ **7 a** : READY 1, PREPARED ⟨all *set* for an early start⟩ **b** : poised to start running or to dive in at the instant a signal is given ⟨ready, get *set,* go⟩

³set *n* **1** : the act or action of setting : the condition of being set **2** : mental inclination, tendency, or habit : BENT **3** : a number of persons or things of the same kind that belong or are used together **4** : direction of flow ⟨the *set* of the wind⟩ **5** : form or carriage of the body or of its parts ⟨the *set* of your shoulders⟩ **6** : the manner of fitting or of being placed or suspended ⟨the *set* of a coat⟩ **7** : amount of deflection from a straight line **8** : permanent change of form (as of metal) due to repeated or excessive stress **9** : a young plant or a plant part (as a corm or a piece of tuber) suitable for planting or transplanting **10** : an artificial setting for a scene of a play or movie **11** : a division of a tennis match won usually by the player or side that first wins six games **12** : SETTING 6 **13** : the basic formation in a country-dance or square dance **14** : a collection of mathematical elements (as numbers or points) **15** : an electronic apparatus ⟨a radio *set*⟩ ⟨a television *set*⟩

se·ta \'sēt-ə\ *n, pl* **se·tae** \'sē-,tē\ : a slender usually rigid or bristly and springy organ or part of an animal or plant [Latin *saeta, seta* "bristle"] — **se·tal** \'sēt-l\ *adj*

set·back \'set-,bak\ *n* **1** : a checking of progress **2** : an unexpected reverse or defeat

set down *vt* **1** : to cause to sit down : SEAT **2** : to cause or allow to get off a vehicle : DELIVER **3** : to land (an aircraft) on the ground or water **4** : to put in writing **5 a** : REGARD, CONSIDER ⟨*set* them *down* as crooks⟩ **b** : ATTRIBUTE ⟨*set down* their success to perseverance⟩

¹set-in \,set-in\ *adj* **1** : placed, located, or built as a part of another construction ⟨*set-in* bookcases⟩ **2** : cut separately and stitched in ⟨*set-in* sleeves⟩

²set-in \'set-,in\ *n* : something that is set in : INSERT

set in *vb* **1** : INSERT; *esp* : to stitch (a small part) within a larger article **2** : to enter upon a particular state ⟨winter *set in* early⟩ **3** : to begin to work

set·off \'set-,óf\ *n* **1** : something that is set off against another thing : **a** : DECORATION 2, ORNAMENT **b** : COUNTERBALANCE 2 **2** : the discharge of a debt by setting against it a distinct claim in favor of the debtor; *also* : the claim itself

set off \set-'óf, 'set-\ *vb* **1 a** : to show up by contrast ⟨a pale face *set off* by dark eyes⟩ **b** : ADORN, EMBELLISH ⟨that pin *sets off* the dress⟩ **c** : to set apart : make distinct or outstanding ⟨commas *set off* words in a series⟩ **2 a** : OFFSET 1b, COMPENSATE **b** : to make a setoff of **3 a** : to set in motion : cause to begin ⟨that story *set* me *off* laughing⟩ **b** : to cause to explode **4** : to measure off on a surface : lay off **5** : to start out on a course or a journey ⟨*set off* for home⟩

set on *vb* **1** : ATTACK 1 **2 a** : to urge (as a dog) to attack or pursue **b** : to incite to action : INSTIGATE ⟨*set* students *on* to riot⟩ **c** : to set to work **3** : to go on : ADVANCE

set out *vb* **1** : to state, describe, or recite at length **2 a** : to arrange and present graphically or systematically **b** : to mark out (as a design) : lay out the plan of **3** : to

\ə\ abut	\ng\ si**ng**
\ər\ fur**ther**	\ō\ b**one**
\a\ m**at**	\ȯ\ s**aw**
\ā\ t**ake**	\ȯi\ c**oin**
\ä\ c**ot, cart**	\th\ **thin**
\au̇\ **out**	\t̲h̲\ **this**
\ch\ **chin**	\ü\ f**ood**
\e\ p**et**	\u̇\ f**oot**
\ē\ **easy**	\y\ **yet**
\g\ **go**	\yü\ f**ew**
\i\ t**ip**	\yu̇\ c**ure**
\ī\ l**ife**	\zh\ vi**sion**
\j\ **job**	

begin with a definite purpose : INTEND ⟨*set out* to win⟩ **4** : to start out on a course, a journey, or a career

set piece *n* **1** : a realistic piece of stage scenery standing by itself **2** : a composition (as in literature) executed in a fixed or ideal form often with great artistry and brilliant effect

set point *n* : a point that decides a tennis set if won by the side having an advantage in the score

set·screw \'set-ˌskrü\ *n* **1** : a screw screwed through one part and tightly upon or into another part to prevent relative movement **2** : a screw for regulating a valve opening or a spring tension

set·tee \se-'tē\ *n* **1** : a long seat with a back **2** : a medium-sized sofa with arms and a back [alteration of ¹*settle*]

set·ter \'set-ər\ *n* **1** : one that sets **2** : a large long-coated bird dog of a type formerly trained to crouch on finding game but now to point

set theory *n* : a branch of mathematics that deals with the nature and relations of sets — **set–theoretic** *adj*

set·ting \'set-ing\ *n* **1** : the way, position, or direction in which something is set **2** : the frame or bed in which a gem is set **3 a** : BACKGROUND 3a, b(1), ENVIRONMENT **b** : the time and place of the action of a play or movie **c** : the scenery used in a play or a movie **4** : the music composed for a text (as a poem) **5** : the tableware required for arranging a place at a table **6** : a batch of eggs for incubation

¹**set·tle** \'set-l\ *n* : a wooden bench with arms, a high solid back, and an enclosed base [Old English *setl* "seat, chair"]

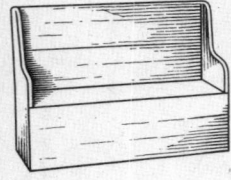

¹settle

²**settle** *vb* **set·tled; set·tling** \'set-ling, -l-ing\ **1** : to place so as to stay **2 a** : to establish residence in : COLONIZE ⟨*settled* the West⟩ **b** : to make one's home ⟨*settle* in the country⟩ **3 a** : to cause to pack down or to become compact by sinking : sink gradually or to the bottom **b** : to clarify by causing dregs or impurities to sink **c** : to become clear by depositing sediment **4 a** : to make or become quiet or orderly ⟨reading *settles* my nerves⟩ **b** : to take up an ordered or stable life ⟨marry and *settle* down⟩ **5 a** : to fix or resolve conclusively ⟨*settle* the question⟩ **b** : to establish or secure permanently **6** : to arrange in a desired position **7 a** : to make or arrange for final disposition of ⟨*settle* an estate⟩ **b** : to bestow or give possession of legally ⟨*settled* property on the child⟩ **c** : to pay in full ⟨*settle* a bill⟩ **8** : to adjust differences or accounts [Old English *setlan* "to seat, place, settle", from *setl* "seat"]

set·tle·ment \'set-l-mənt\ *n* **1** : the act or process of settling **2** : final payment (as of a bill) **3 a** : a place or region newly settled **b** : a small village **4** : an institution providing various community services especially to residents of large cities — called also *settlement house* **5** : an agreement composing differences

set·tler \'set-lər, -l-ər\ *n* : one that settles (as in a new region)

set·tling \'set-ling, -l-ing\ *n* : something that settles at the bottom of a liquid : SEDIMENT — usually used in pl.

set·tlor \'set-ˌlȯr, -l-ˌȯr\ *n* : one that makes a settlement or creates a trust of property

set-to \'set-ˌtü\ *n, pl* **set-tos** \-ˌtüz\ : a usually brief and vigorous fight or argument

set to \set-'tü, 'set-\ *vi* **1** : to begin actively and earnestly ⟨*set to* and ate with a will⟩ **2** : to begin fighting

set-up \'set-ˌəp\ *n* **1** : glass, ice, and mixer served to patrons who supply their own liquor **2** : a task or contest intentionally made easy **3** : the way in which something is set up : ARRANGEMENT

set up \set-'əp, 'set-\ *vb* **1 a** : to assemble the parts of and erect ⟨*set up* a printing press⟩ **b** : to put (a machine) in readiness or adjustment for a tooling operation **2** : CAUSE, CREATE ⟨*set up* a clamor⟩ **3 a** : ELATE, GRATIFY ⟨*set up* by the victory⟩ **b** : to make proud or vain **4 a** : to put forward or extol as a model **b** : to

claim (oneself) to be ⟨*set* yourself *up* as an authority⟩ **5** : FOUND 3, INAUGURATE **6** : to provide with a means of making a living ⟨*set* them *up* in a new shop⟩ **7** : to make careful plans for ⟨*set up* a robbery⟩ **8 a** : to treat to (drinks) **b** : to treat (someone) to something **9** : to make pretensions ⟨*setting up* to be a wise man⟩ — **set up housekeeping** : to establish one's living quarters — **set up shop** : to establish one's business

sev·en \'sev-ən\ *n* **1** : one more than six; *also* : a symbol representing this — see NUMBER table **2** : the seventh in a set or series **3** : something having seven units or members [Old English *seofon*] — **seven** *adj or pron*

sev·en·teen \ˌsev-ən-'tēn, 'sev-ən-\ *n* : one more than 16; *also* : a symbol representing this — see NUMBER table [Old English *seofontēne*] — **seventeen** *adj or pron* — **sev·en·teenth** \-'tēnth, -'tēntth\ *adj or n*

seventeen–year locust *n* : a cicada of the United States with a life of 17 years in the North and 13 years in the South of which the greatest part is spent as a wingless underground nymph that feeds on roots and emerges from the soil to become a short-lived winged adult

sev·enth \'sev-ənth, -əntth\ *n, pl* **sev·enths** \'sev-əns, -ənths, -əntths\ **1** : number seven in a countable series — see NUMBER table **2 a** : a musical interval embracing seven degrees **b** : LEADING TONE **c** : the harmonic combination of two tones a seventh apart — **seventh** *adj or adv*

Seventh Day Adventist *n* : a member of an evangelical Protestant denomination organized in the United States in 1863 and marked by emphasis on preparation for Christ's Second Coming

seventh heaven *n* : a state of extreme joy [from the 7th being the highest of the 7 heavens of Muslim and cabalist doctrine]

sev·en·ty \'sev-ən-tē\ *n, pl* **-ties** : ten more than 60; *also* : a symbol representing this — see NUMBER table [Old English *seofontig*] — **sev·en·ti·eth** \-tē-əth\ *adj or n* — **seventy** *adj or pron*

sev·en·ty–eight \ˌsev-ən-tē-'āt\ *n* : a phonograph record for play at 78 revolutions per minute

sev·er \'sev-ər\ *vb* **sev·ered; sev·er·ing** \'sev-ring, -ə-ring\ **1** : to put or keep apart : DIVIDE; *esp* : to remove (as a part) by or as if by cutting **2** : to come or break apart [Middle French *severer,* from Latin *separare*] SYN see SEPARATE — **sev·er·abil·i·ty** \ˌsev-rə-'bil-ət-ē, -ə-rə-\ *n* — **sev·er·able** \'sev-rə-bəl, -ə-rə-\ *adj*

¹**sev·er·al** \'sev-rəl, -ə-rəl\ *adj* **1 a** : separate or distinct from one another : DIFFERENT ⟨federal union of the *several* states⟩ **b** : PARTICULAR, RESPECTIVE ⟨specialists in their *several* fields⟩ **2** : more than two but fewer than many ⟨moved *several* inches⟩ [Anglo-French, from Medieval Latin *separalis,* derived from the Latin *separare* "to separate"] — **sev·er·al·ly** \-ē\ *adv*

²**several** *pron, pl in construction* : an indefinite number more than two and fewer than many ⟨*several* of the guests⟩

sev·er·al·fold \ˌsev-rəl-'fōld, -ə-rəl-\ *adj* **1** : having several parts or aspects **2** : being several times as large, as great, or as many as some understood size, degree, or amount ⟨a *severalfold* increase⟩ — **severalfold** *adv*

sev·er·al·ty \'sev-rəl-tē, -ə-rəl-\ *n* : the quality or state of being several : DISTINCTNESS, SEPARATENESS

sev·er·ance \'sev-rəns, -ə-rəns\ *n* : the act or process of severing : the state of being severed

severance pay *n* : an allowance usually based on length of service that is payable to an employee on termination of employment

se·vere \sə-'viər\ *adj* **1 a** : strict in judgment, discipline, or government **b** : strict or stern in bearing or manner : AUSTERE **2** : rigorous in restraint, punishment, or requirement : STRINGENT **3** : strongly critical **4** : sober or restrained in decoration or manner : PLAIN **5 a** : inflicting physical discomfort or hardship : HARSH ⟨*severe* winters⟩ **b** : inflicting pain or distress : GRIEVous ⟨a *severe* wound⟩ **6** : requiring great effort : **ARDU-OUS** ⟨a *severe* test⟩ **7** : of a great degree : **MARKED** ⟨a *severe* economic depression⟩ [Latin *severus*] — **se·vere·ly** *adv* — **se·vere·ness** *n* □ SYN SEVERE, STERN, AUSTERE mean showing or requiring strict discipline or firm restraint. SEVERE implies enforcing standards without indulgence or laxity and may suggest harshness; STERN stresses inflexibility and inexorability of temper or character; AUSTERE suggests absence of warmth, color, or feeling and may apply to rigorous simplicity or self-denial.

se·ver·i·ty \sə-'ver-ət-ē\ *n, pl* **-ties** : the quality or state of being severe

Sè·vres \'sev-rə, 'sev, 'sevr\ *n* : an often elaborately decorated French porcelain [*Sèvres,* France]

sew \'sō\ *vb* **sewed; sewn** \'sōn\ *or* **sewed; sew·ing** **1** : to join or fasten by stitches made with a flexible thread or filament ⟨*sew* on a button⟩ **2** : to close or enclose by sewing ⟨*sew* the money in a bag⟩ **3** : to practice or engage in sewing [Old English *sīwian*]

sew·age \'sü-ij\ *n* : refuse liquids or waste matter carried off by sewers [³*sewer*]

¹sew·er \'sō-ər, 'sōr\ *n* : one that sews

²sew·er \'sü-ər, 'sù-ər, 'sùr\ *n* : a covered usually underground passage to carry off water and sewage [Middle French *essewer, seweur,* from *essewer* "to drain", derived from Latin *ex-* + *aqua* "water"]

sew·er·age \'sü-ə-rij, 'sù-ər-ij, 'sùr-ij\ *n* **1** : SEWAGE **2** : the removal and disposal of sewage and surface water by sewers **3** : a system of sewers

sew·ing \'sō-ing\ *n* **1** : the act, method, or occupation of one that sews **2** : material that has been or is to be sewed

sew up *vt* **1** : to get exclusive use or control of **2** : to make certain of : ASSURE ⟨*sew up* a deal⟩

sex \'seks\ *n* **1** : either of two divisions of organisms distinguished respectively as male and female **2** : the sum of the structural, functional, and behavioral characteristics of living beings that are ultimately related to reproduction by two interacting parents and that serve to distinguish males and females **3** : sexual activity or intercourse [Latin *sexus*]

sex- *or* **sexi-** *combining form* : six [Latin *sex*]

sex·a·ge·nar·i·an \,sek-sə-jə-'ner-ē-ən, sek-,saj-ə-\ *n* : a person who is 60 or more but less than 70 years old [Latin *sexagenarius* "60 years old, of 60", derived from *sexaginta* "sixty"] — **sexagenarian** *adj*

Sex·a·ges·i·ma \,sek-sə-'jes-ə-mə, -'jā-zə-mə\ *n* : the second Sunday before Lent [Late Latin, from Latin *sexagesimus* "sixtieth"]

sex·a·ges·i·mal \-'jes-ə-məl\ *adj* : of, relating to, or based on the number 60 ⟨*sexagesimal* measurement of angles⟩ [Latin *sexagesimus* "sixtieth", from *sexaginta* "sixty"]

sex appeal *n* : personal appeal or physical attractiveness for members of the opposite sex

sex cell *n* : GAMETE

sex chromosome *n* : a chromosome inherited differently in the two sexes that is or is held to be concerned directly with the inheritance of sex

sexed \'sekst\ *adj* : having sex or sexual instincts

sex gland *n* : GONAD

sex hormone *n* : a hormone that affects the growth or function of the reproductive organs or the development of secondary sex characteristics

sex·ism \'sek-,siz-əm\ *n* : prejudice or discrimination based on sex — **sex·ist** \'sek-səst\ *adj or n*

sex·less \'sek-sləs\ *adj* : lacking sex : NEUTER — **sex·less·ness** *n*

sex–linked \'sek-,slingt, -,slingkt\ *adj* **1** : located on one sex chromosome but not on the other so that one sex has one allele and the other has two ⟨a *sex-linked* gene⟩ **2** : characterized by or controlled by sex-linked genes ⟨a *sex-linked* character⟩ — **sex–link·age** \-,sling-kij\ *n*

sext \'sekst\ *n, often cap* : the fourth of the canonical hours [Latin *sexta* "6th hour of the day", from *sextus* "sixth", from *sex* "six"]

sex·tant \'sek-stənt\ *n* : a navigational instrument for measuring the angle between the horizon and the sun or a star in order to determine the latitude (as of a ship) [New Latin *sextans* "6th part of a circle", from Latin, "6th part", from *sextus* "sixth"]

sex·tet \sek-'stet\ *n* **1** : a musical composition for six instruments or voices **2** : a group or set of six [alteration of *sestet*]

sex·til·lion \sek-'stil-yən\ *n* — see NUMBER table [French, from Latin *sex* "six" + French *-illion* (as in *million*)]

sex·ton \'sek-stən\ *n* : a church officer or employee who takes care of the church property and sometimes rings the bell for services and digs graves [Middle French *secrestain,* from Medieval Latin *sacristanus* "sacristan"]

¹sex·tu·ple \sek-'stüp-əl, -'styüp-, -'stəp-; 'sek-stəp-\ *adj* **1** : having six units or members **2** : being six times as great or as many [probably from Medieval Latin *sextuplus,* from Latin *sextus* "sixth"] — **sextuple** *n*

²sextuple *vb* **sex·tu·pled; sex·tu·pling** \-ling, -ə-ling\ : to make or become six times as much or as many

sex·tup·let \sek-'stəp-lət, -'stüp-, -'styüp-; 'sek-stəp-\ *n* **1** : a combination of six of a kind **2** : one of six offspring born at one birth

sex·u·al \'seksh-wəl, -ə-wəl; 'sek-shəl\ *adj* **1** : of, relating to, or associated with sex or the sexes ⟨*sexual* differentiation⟩ ⟨*sexual* conflict⟩ **2** : having or involving sex ⟨*sexual* reproduction⟩ ⟨*sexual* spores⟩ — **sex·u·al·i·ty** \,sek-shə-'wal-ət-ē\ *n* — **sex·u·al·ly** \'seksh-wə-lē, -ə-wə-; 'seksh-lē, -ə-lē\ *adv*

sexual intercourse *n* : sexual union especially involving penetration of the vagina by the penis

sexual relations *n pl* : SEXUAL INTERCOURSE

sexually transmitted disease *n* : STD

sexy \'sek-sē\ *adj* **sex·i·er; -est** : sexually suggestive or stimulating : EROTIC — **sex·i·ness** *n*

sfer·ics \'sfiər-iks, 'sfer-\ *n pl* : ATMOSPHERICS [by shortening]

¹sfor·zan·do \sfòrt-'sän-dō, -'san-\ *adj or adv* : played with prominent stress or accent — used of a single note or chord as a direction in music [Italian, literally, "forcing", from *sforzare* "to force"]

²sforzando *n, pl* **-dos** *or* **-di** \-dē\ : an accented tone or chord

sh \sh often prolonged\ *interj* — used often in prolonged or reduplicated form to urge or command silence or less noise [imitative]

shab·by \'shab-ē\ *adj* **shab·bi·er; -est** **1 a** : threadbare and faded from wear **b** : ill kept : DILAPIDATED **2** : dressed in worn clothes **3 a** : MEAN, UNFAIR ⟨*shabby* treatment⟩ **b** : inferior in quality [obsolete *shab* "scab, low fellow", from Old English *sceabb* "scab"] — **shab·bi·ly** \'shab-ə-lē\ *adv* — **shab·bi·ness** \'shab-ē-nəs\ *n*

Sha·bu·oth \shə-'vü-,ōt, -,ōth, -,ōs, -əs\ *n* : a Jewish holiday celebrated in May or June to commemorate the revelation of the Ten Commandments at Mount Sinai and in biblical times as a harvest festival [Hebrew *shābhu'ōth,* literally, "weeks"]

shack \'shak\ *n* **1** : HUT, SHANTY **2** : a room or similar enclosed structure for a particular person or use ⟨a radio *shack*⟩ ⟨an ammunition *shack*⟩ [probably from English dialect *shackly* "rickety"]

¹shack·le \'shak-əl\ *n* **1** : something (as a manacle or fetter) that confines the legs or arms **2** : something that checks or prevents free action as if by fetters — usually used in pl. **3** : a device (as a clevis) for making something fast [Old English *sceacul*]

²shackle *vt* **shack·led; shack·ling** \'shak-ling, -ə-ling\ **1 a** : to bind with shackles **b** : to make fast with a shackle **2** : to deprive of freedom of action : HINDER ⟨*shack-*

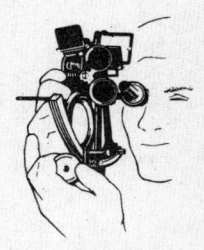

sextant

\ə\ abut	\ng\ sing
\ər\ further	\ō\ bone
\a\ mat	\ò\ saw
\ā\ take	\òi\ coin
\ä\ cot, cart	\th\ thin
\au̇\ out	\th\ this
\ch\ chin	\ü\ food
\e\ pet	\u̇\ foot
\ē\ easy	\y\ yet
\g\ go	\yü\ few
\i\ tip	\yu̇\ cure
\ī\ life	\zh\ vision
\j\ job	

led by poverty) SYN see HAMPER — **shack·ler** \'shak-lər, -ə-lər\ *n*

shad \'shad\ *n, pl* **shad** : any of several deep-bodied food fishes that are closely related to the herrings but ascend rivers in the spring to spawn [Old English *sceadd*]

shad·blow \'shad-,blō\ *n* : SERVICEBERRY 2

shad·bush \-,bush\ *n* : SERVICEBERRY 2

shad·dock \'shad-ək\ *n* : a large thick-rinded usually pear-shaped citrus fruit closely related to the grapefruit but often having coarse dry pulp; *also* : the tree that bears it [Captain *Shaddock*, 17th century English ship commander]

¹shade \'shād\ *n* **1 a** : partial darkness caused by interception of the rays of light **b** : relative obscurity or retirement **2** : space sheltered from sunlight **3** : a vaporous or unreal appearance **4** *pl* **a** : the shadows that gather as darkness comes on **b** : UNDERWORLD 2, HADES **5** : a disembodied spirit : GHOST **6** : something that intercepts or shelters from light, sun, or heat: as **a** : a device partially covering a lamp so as to reduce glare **b** : a screen usually on a roller for regulating the light or the view through a window **7 a** : the representation of the effect of shade in painting or drawing **b** : a subdued or somber feature **8 a** : a color produced by a pigment or dye mixture having some black in it **b** : a color slightly different from the one under consideration **9** : a minute difference or variation ⟨*shades* of meaning⟩ **10** : a facial expression of sadness or displeasure [Old English *sceadu*] SYN see COLOR — **shade·less** \-ləs\ *adj*

²shade *vb* **1 a** : to shelter or screen by intercepting radiated light or heat **b** : to cover with a shade **2** : to hide partly by or as if by a shadow **3** : to darken with or as if with a shadow **4** : to cast into the shade : OBSCURE **5 a** : to represent the effect of shade or shadow on **b** : to add shading to **c** : to color so that the shades pass gradually from one to another **6** : to change by gradual transition or qualification **7** : to reduce (as a price) slightly — **shad·er** *n*

shad·ing \'shād-ing\ *n* : a filling up within outlines to suggest different degrees of light and dark in a picture or drawing

sha·doof \shə-'düf, sha-\ *n* : a counterbalanced sweep used since ancient times especially in Egypt for raising water (as for irrigation) [Arabic *shādūf*]

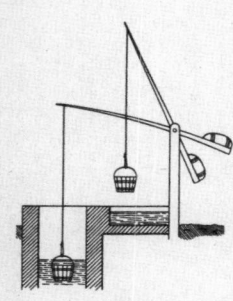
shadoof

¹shad·ow \'shad-ō\ *n* **1** : shade within defined bounds **2** : a reflected image **3** : shelter from danger or observation **4 a** : an imperfect and faint representation **b** : IMITATION 2, COPY **5** : the dark figure cast upon a surface by a body blocking rays from a light source **6** : PHANTOM 1a **7** : a shaded part of a picture **8** : a form without substance : REMNANT, VESTIGE ⟨are only a *shadow* of your former self⟩ **9 a** : an inseparable companion or follower **b** : one that shadows as a spy or detective **10** : a small degree or portion : TRACE ⟨not a *shadow* of a doubt⟩ **11** : a gloomy influence [Old English *sceadu* "shade, shadow"] — **shad·ow·less** \-ləs\ *adj* — **shad·ow·like** \-,līk\ *adj*

²shadow *vb* **1 a** : to cast a shadow on **b** : to cast a gloom over : CLOUD **2** : to represent or indicate obscurely or faintly **3** : to follow especially secretly : TRAIL **4** : to pass gradually or by degrees **5** : to become overcast with or as if with shadows — **shad·ow·er** \'shad-ə-wər\ *n*

³shadow *adj* **1 a** : set up in order to function if the opportunity arises ⟨a *shadow* government⟩ **b** : belonging to a shadow cabinet or shadow government ⟨*shadow* minister of foreign affairs⟩ **2** : having an indistinct pattern ⟨a *shadow* plaid⟩

shad·ow·box \'shad-ō-,bäks, -ə-\ *vi* : to go through the motions of boxing as if with an imaginary opponent especially during training — **shad·ow·box·ing** *n*

shadow box *n* : a shallow enclosing case usually with a glass front in which something is displayed

shadow play *n* : a play in which the shadows of the actors are projected on a screen

shad·owy \,shad-ə-wē\ *adj* **1 a** : being or resembling a shadow : UNREAL **b** : faintly visible : INDISTINCT **2** : being in or obscured by shadow **3** : SHADY 1

shady \'shād-ē\ *adj* **shad·i·er; -est** **1** : producing or affording shade **2** : sheltered from the sun **3 a** : of questionable merit **b** : DISREPUTABLE — **shad·i·ly** \'shād-l-ē\ *adv* — **shad·i·ness** \'shād-ē-nəs\ *n*

¹shaft \'shaft\ *n, pl* **shafts** \'shafs, 'shafts, *in sense 3 also* 'shavz\ **1 a** : the long handle of a weapon (as a spear) **b** : ¹SPEAR 1, LANCE **2 a** : the slender stem of an arrow **b** : ARROW 1 **3** : POLE; *esp* : one of two poles between which a horse is hitched to pull a vehicle **4** : a narrow beam of light **5** : something resembling the shaft of an arrow or spear: as **a** : the handle of a tool **b** : a tall monument (as a column) **c** : a vertical opening or passage through the floors of a building ⟨an air *shaft*⟩ **d** : a commonly cylindrical bar used to support rotating pieces or to transmit power or motion by rotation **e** : a vertical or inclined opening of uniform and limited cross section made for finding or mining ore, raising water, or ventilating underground workings **f** : the midrib of a feather **6 a** : a projectile thrown like a spear or shot like an arrow **b** : a scornful or satirical remark : BARB **c** : harsh or unfair treatment [Old English *sceaft*]

²shaft *vt* : to fit with a shaft

¹shag \'shag\ *n* **1 a** : a shaggy tangled mass or covering **b** : long coarse or matted fiber or nap **2** : CORMORANT 1 [Old English *sceacga*]

²shag *vb* **shagged; shag·ging** **1** : to fall or hang in shaggy masses **2** : to make rough or shaggy

³shag *vt* **shagged; shag·ging** **1** : to chase after; *esp* : to run after and return (as a ball) **2** : to chase away [origin unknown]

shag·bark \'shag-,bärk\ *n* : a hickory with a gray shaggy outer bark that peels off in long strips

shag·gy \'shag-ē\ *adj* **shag·gi·er; -est** **1 a** : covered with or made up of long, coarse, or matted hair or thick, tangled, or unkempt vegetation **b** : having a rough or hairy surface **2** : UNKEMPT, SHABBY — **shag·gi·ly** \'shag-ə-lē\ *adv* — **shag·gi·ness** \'shag-ē-nəs\ *n*

sha·green \sha-'grēn, shə-\ *n* **1** : an untanned leather covered with small round granulations and usually dyed green **2** : the rough skin of various sharks and rays [French *chagrin*, from Turkish *çağrı, sağrı*] — **shagreen** *adj*

shah \'shä, 'shò\ *n* : the sovereign of Iran [Persian *shāh* "king"] — **shah·dom** \'shäd-əm, 'shòd-\ *n*

¹shake \'shāk\ *vb* **shook** \'shuk\; **shak·en** \'shā-kən\; **shak·ing** **1** : to move irregularly to and fro : QUIVER, TREMBLE ⟨*shaking* with cold⟩ **2** : to become unsteady : TOTTER **3** : to brandish, wave, or flourish often in a threatening way **4** : to cause to move in a quick jerky way **5** : to free oneself from ⟨*shake* off a cold⟩ **6** : to cause to waver : WEAKEN ⟨*shake* one's faith⟩ **7** : to dislodge or eject by quick jerky movements ⟨*shake* the dust from a cloth⟩ **8** : to clasp (hands) in greeting or as a sign of goodwill or agreement **9** : to stir the feelings of : UPSET ⟨*shook* me up⟩ [Old English *sceacan*] — **shak·able** *or* **shake·able** \'shā-kə-bəl\ *adj* □ SYN SHAKE, AGITATE, ROCK mean to move up and down or back and forth with some violence. SHAKE applies to short, rapid movements often for a particular purpose; AGITATE suggests more violent and prolonged tossing or stirring ⟨the washer cleans by *agitating*⟩ ROCK implies a swinging or swaying motion resulting from violent impact or upheaval ⟨a city *rocked* by an earthquake⟩ — **shake a leg 1** : DANCE 1 **2** : to hurry up

²shake *n* **1** : an act of shaking: as **a** : an act of shaking hands **b** : an act of shaking oneself **2 a** : a blow or shock that upsets the equilibrium or disturbs the balance of something **b** : EARTHQUAKE **3** *pl* : a condition of trembling (as from chill) **4** : something produced by shaking: as **a** : a fissure in strata **b** : MILK SHAKE **5** : a wavering, quivering, or alternating motion caused by a blow or shock **6** : TRILL 1a **7** : a very brief period of time : INSTANT ⟨ready in two *shakes*⟩ **8** *pl* : one of importance or ability — usually used in the phrase *no great shakes* **9** : a shingle split from a piece of log usually three to four feet long ⟨cedar *shakes*⟩ **10** : ³DEAL 2 ⟨a fair *shake*⟩

shake·down \'shāk-,daùn\ *n* **1** : an improvised bed (as one made up on the floor) **2** : a boisterous dance **3** : an act or instance of shaking someone down; *esp* : EXTORTION **4** : a process or period of adjustment **5** : a test under operating conditions of something new (as a ship) for defects or to familiarize the operators with it

shake down \shāk-'daùn, 'shāk-\ *vb* **1 a** : to take up temporary quarters **b** : to occupy a makeshift bed **2 a** : to become accustomed especially to new surroundings or duties **b** : to settle down **c** : to give a shakedown test to **3** : to obtain money from in a dishonest or illegal manner and especially by extortion **4** : to bring about a reduction of

shake·out \'shā-,kaùt\ *n* : a minor economic recession

shak·er \'shā-kər\ *n* **1** : one that shakes; *esp* : any of various utensils or machines used in shaking **2** *cap* : a member of a millenarian sect originating in England in 1747 and practicing celibacy and communal living — **Shaker** *adj*

Shake·spear·ean *or* **Shake·spear·ian** \shāk-'spir-ē-ən\ *adj* : of, relating to, or characteristic of William Shakespeare or his writings

Shakespearean sonnet *n* : ENGLISH SONNET

shake-up \'shā-,kəp\ *n* : an act or instance of shaking up; *esp* : an extensive and often drastic reorganization ⟨lost my job in an office *shake-up*⟩

shake up \shā-'kəp, 'shā-\ *vt* **1** : to jar by or as if by a physical shock ⟨the collision *shook* both drivers *up*⟩ **2** : to make an extensive often drastic reorganization of

sha·ko \'shā-kō, 'shak-ō\ *n, pl* **sha·kos** *or* **sha·koes** : a stiff military cap with a high crown and plume [French, from Hungarian *csákó*]

shaky \'shā-kē\ *adj* **shak·i·er; -est 1 a** : lacking stability **b** : lacking in firmness (as of beliefs) **c** : lacking in authority or reliability : QUESTIONABLE **2 a** : somewhat unsound in health **b** : characterized by shaking **3** : likely to give way or break down — **shak·i·ly** \-kə-lē\ *adv* — **shak·i·ness** \-kē-nəs\ *n*

shale \'shāl\ *n* : a rock that is formed by the consolidation of clay, mud, or silt, has a finely layered structure, and splits easily [Old English *scealu* "shell, scale"] — **shaley** \'shā-lē\ *adj*

shall \shəl, shal, 'shal\ *auxiliary verb, past* **should** \shəd, shud, 'shùd\; *present sing & pl* **shall 1 a** — used to express a command or exhortation ⟨you *shall* go⟩ **b** — used in laws, regulations, or directives to express what is mandatory ⟨it *shall* be unlawful to carry firearms⟩ **2 a** — used to express what is inevitable or what is likely to happen in the future ⟨we *shall* have to be ready⟩ ⟨we *shall* see⟩ **b** — used to express simple futurity ⟨when *shall* we expect you⟩ **3** — used to express determination ⟨they *shall* not pass⟩ [Old English *sceal* "owe, owes, ought to, must"]

shal·lop \'shal-əp\ *n* : a small open boat propelled by oars or sails [Middle French *chaloupe*]

shal·lot \shə-'lät\ *n* : a bulbous perennial herb that resembles the related onion and produces small clustered bulbs used in cooking [French *échalote*]

¹shal·low \'shal-ō\ *adj* **1** : having little depth ⟨*shallow* water⟩ ⟨a *shallow* pan⟩ **2** : lacking in depth of knowledge, thought, or feeling [Middle English *schalowe*] SYN see SUPERFICIAL — **shal·low·ly** *adv* — **shal·low·ness** *n*

²shallow *vb* : to make or become shallow

³shallow *n* : a shallow place or area in a body of water — usually used in pl.

sha·lom \shä-'lōm, shə-\ *interj* — used as a Jewish greeting and farewell [Hebrew *shālōm* "peace"]

sha·lom alei·chem \,shò-lə-mə-'lā-kəm, ,shō-, -kəm\ *interj* — used as a traditional Jewish greeting [Hebrew *shālōm ʼalēkhem* "peace unto you"]

shalt \shəlt, shalt, 'shalt\ *archaic present 2d sing of* SHALL

¹sham \'sham\ *n* **1** : HOAX 1 **2** : cheap falseness : HYPOCRISY **3** : a decorative piece of cloth simulating an article of personal or household linen and used in place of or over it **4** : an imitation or counterfeit intended to appear genuine **5** : a person who shams [perhaps from English dialect *sham* "shame"]

²sham *vb* **shammed; sham·ming** : to act intentionally so as to give a false impression : FEIGN

³sham *adj* **1** : not genuine : FALSE **2** : having such poor quality as to seem false

sha·man \'shäm-ən, 'shā-mən\ *n, pl* **shamans** : a priest held to cure the sick, to discover the hidden, and to control events by magic [Russian, of Altaic origin]

sha·man·ism \-,iz-əm\ *n* : a religion of the Ural-Altaic peoples of northern Asia and Europe marked by belief in gods, demons, and ancestral spirits responsive only to the shamans; *also* : any similar religion — **sha·man·ist** \-əst\ *n or adj* — **sha·man·is·tic** \,shäm-ən-'is-tik, ,shā-mən-\ *adj*

sham·ble \'sham-bəl\ *vi* **sham·bled; sham·bling** \-bə-ling, -bling\ : to walk awkwardly with dragging feet : SHUFFLE [*shamble legs* "malformed legs", from *shamble* "table for exhibition of meat for sale", from Old English *sceamul* "stool, table"] — **shamble** *n*

sham·bles \'sham-bəlz\ *n sing or pl* **1** : a place of mass slaughter **2** : a scene or state of great confusion, disorder, or destruction [*shamble* "table for exhibition of meat for sale, meat market"]

sham·bling *adj* : marked by slow awkward movement

¹shame \'shām\ *n* **1 a** : a painful emotion caused by consciousness of guilt, shortcoming, or impropriety **b** : the susceptibility to such emotion **2** : a condition of humiliating disgrace or disrepute **3 a** : something that brings strong regret, censure, or reproach **b** : a cause of feeling shame [Old English *scamu*]

²shame *vt* **1** : to bring shame to : DISGRACE **2** : to put to shame by outdoing **3** : to cause to feel shame **4** : to force by causing to feel guilty ⟨*shamed* into confessing⟩

shame·faced \'shām-'fāst\ *adj* **1** : showing modesty : BASHFUL **2** : ASHAMED 1 [alteration of earlier *shamefast*, from Old English *scamfæst*, from *scamu* "shame" + *fæst* "fixed, fast"] — **shame·faced·ly** \-'fā-səd-lē, -'fāst-lē\ *adv* — **shame·faced·ness** \-'fā-səd-nəs, -'fāst-nəs, -'fās-nəs\ *n* □ ORIGIN Some English words have been altered so as to give them an apparent relationship to other better-known or better-understood words. Such a process of alteration is called folk etymology. A common word formed by folk etymology is *shamefaced*. Old English *scamfæst* meant "bashful" or "modest" or, more literally, "held fast by shame". The second element of *shamefaced*, then, was originally the same as that of *steadfast*. The similarity of consonant sounds between *-fast* and *-faced* contributed to the alteration of *shamefast* to *shamefaced*, and the belief that modesty or bashfulness is reflected in a person's face probably had some influence too.

shame·ful \'shām-fəl\ *adj* **1** : bringing shame : DISGRACEFUL **2** : arousing the feeling of shame : INDECENT — **shame·ful·ly** \-fə-lē\ *adv* — **shame·ful·ness** *n*

shame·less \'shām-ləs\ *adj* **1** : having no shame : BRAZEN **2** : showing lack of shame : DISGRACEFUL — **shame·less·ly** *adv* — **shame·less·ness** *n*

sham·mer \'sham-ər\ *n* : one that shams

sham·my \'sham-ē\ *variant of* CHAMOIS

¹sham·poo \sham-'pü\ *vt* **1** *archaic* : MASSAGE **2 a** : to wash (as the hair) with soap and water or with a spe-

shako

cial preparation **b** : to wash the hair of [Hindi *căpo,* imperative of *căpnă* "to press, shampoo"] — **shampoo·er** *n*

²shampoo *n, pl* **shampoos 1** : an act or instance of shampooing **2** : a preparation used in shampooing

sham·rock \'sham-ˌräk\ *n* : any of several plants (as a wood sorrel or some clovers) having leaves with three leaflets and used as a floral emblem by the Irish [Irish Gaelic *seamróg*]

sha·mus \'shäm-əs, 'shā-məs\ *n* **1** *slang* : POLICEMAN **2** *slang* : a private detective [probably from Yiddish *shames* "sexton of a synagogue"]

shang·hai \shang-'hī, 'shang-\ *vt* **shang·haied; shang·haiing 1 a** : to put aboard a ship by force often with the help of liquor or drugs **b** : to put by force or threat of force into a place of detention **2** : to put by trickery into an undesirable position [*Shanghai,* China; from the former use of this method to secure sailors for voyages to the Orient] — **shang·hai·er** \-'hī-ər, -'hīr\ *n*

Shan·gri–la \ˌshang-gri-'lä\ *n* **1** : a beautiful imaginary place where life approaches perfection : UTOPIA **2** : a remote usually idyllic hideaway [*Shangri-La,* imaginary community depicted in the novel *Lost Horizon* by James Hilton]

shank \'shangk\ *n* **1 a** : the part of the leg between the knee and the ankle in humans or the corresponding part in various other vertebrates **b** : a cut of meat from usually the upper part of a leg **2** : a straight narrow usually essential part of an object: as **a** : a straight shaft (as of an anchor or fishhook) **b** : the stem of a tobacco pipe or the part between the stem and the bowl **c** : the narrow part of the sole of a shoe beneath the instep **3** : a part of a tool that connects the acting part with a part (as a handle) by which it is held or moved (the *shank* of a drill bit) (the *shank* of a key) **4 a** : the latter part of a period of time **b** : the early or main part of a period of time [Old English *scanca*]

shan't \shant, 'shant, shȧnt, 'shȧnt\ : shall not

shan·tung \shan-'təng, 'shan-\ *n* : a fabric in plain weave having a slightly irregular surface [*Shantung,* China]

shan·ty \'shant-ē\ *n, pl* **shanties** : a small roughly built shelter or dwelling : HUT [Canadian French *chantier,* from French, "frame for supporting barrels", from Latin *cantherius* "trellis"]

shan·ty·town \-ˌtaun\ *n* : a town or section of a town consisting mostly of shanties

shap·able *or* **shape·able** \'shā-pə-bəl\ *adj* **1** : capable of being shaped **2** : SHAPELY

¹shape \'shāp\ *vb* **1** : FORM 1, CREATE; *esp* : to give a particular form or shape to **2** : to adapt in shape so as to fit neatly and closely **3** : DEVISE 2, PLAN **4** : to embody in definite form (*shaping* a tradition into an epic) **5** : to make fit : ADAPT (learn to *shape* your aims to your abilities) **6** : to determine or direct the course of (as life) **7** : to take on or approach a definite form : DEVELOP — often used with *up* [Old English *scieppan*]

²shape *n* **1 a** : the visible characteristic of a particular thing **b** : spatial form **c** : a standard or universally recognized spatial form **2** : bodily contour especially of the trunk : FIGURE **3 a** : PHANTOM 1a, APPARITION **b** : assumed appearance : GUISE **4** : form of embodiment (as in words) : a form (as of thought) that is definite and organized (a plan took *shape*) (got the speech into *shape*) **5** : something having a particular form (the *shape* of society now) **6** : the condition in which one exists at a particular time (in good *shape* for your age) SYN see FORM — **shaped** *adj*

shape·less \'shā-pləs\ *adj* **1** : having no definite shape **2 a** : deprived of usual or normal shape : MISSHAPEN **b** : not shapely — **shape·less·ly** *adv* — **shape·less·ness** *n*

shape·ly \'shā-plē\ *adj* **shape·li·er; -est** : having a regular or pleasing shape — **shape·li·ness** *n*

shap·en \'shā-pən\ *adj* : fashioned in or provided with a definite shape — usually used in combination (an ill-*shapen* body)

shard \'shärd\ *also* **sherd** \'shərd\ *n* **1** : a fragment of something brittle (as pottery) **2** : a small piece : SCRAP [Old English *sceard*]

¹share \'sheər, 'shaər\ *n* **1 a** : a portion belonging to, due to, or contributed by an individual **b** : a fair portion **2 a** : the part allotted or belonging to one of a number owning something together **b** : any of the equal portions or interests into which the property of a corporation is divided [Old English *scearu* "cutting, tonsure"]

²share *vb* **1** : to divide and distribute in shares : APPORTION — usually used with *out* **2** : to partake of, use, experience, or enjoy with others **3 a** : to give or be given a share in **b** : to have a share — used with *in* — **shar·er** *n*

³share *n* : PLOWSHARE [Old English *scear*]

share-crop \'sheər-ˌkräp, 'shaər-\ *vb* : to farm or produce as a sharecropper

share-crop·per \-ˌkräp-ər\ *n* : a farmer who works land for a landlord in return for a share of the crop

share-hold·er \-ˌhōl-dər\ *n* : one that owns a share in a property; *esp* : STOCKHOLDER

¹shark \'shärk\ *n* : any of numerous usually rather large and typically gray marine elasmobranch fishes most of which are active predators and are of economic importance especially for their large livers which are a source of oil and for their hides from which leather is made [origin unknown]

²shark *n* **1** : a greedy crafty person who takes advantage of the needs of others (a loan *shark*) **2** : a person who excels especially in a particular field (a *shark* at math) [probably from German *schurke* "scoundrel"]

shark·skin \-ˌskin\ *n* **1** : the hide of a shark or leather made from it **2 a** : a smooth durable woolen or worsted suiting in twill or basket weave with small woven designs **b** : a smooth crisp fabric with a dull finish made usually of rayon in basket weave

shark sucker *n* : REMORA

¹sharp \'shärp\ *adj* **1** : adapted to cutting or piercing: as **a** : having a thin keen edge or fine point **b** : briskly cold : CHILLY **2 a** : keen in intellect : QUICK-WITTED **b** : keen in perception : ACUTE, VIGILANT **c** : keen in attention to one's own interest sometimes to the point of being unethical **3** : keen in spirit or action: as **a** : full of activity : BRISK **b** : capable of acting or reacting strongly; *esp* : CAUSTIC 1 **4** : SEVERE, HARSH: as **a** : inclined to or marked by irritability or anger **b** : causing intense mental or physical distress **c** : cutting in language or import (a *sharp* retort) **5 a** : having a strong odor or flavor (*sharp* cheese) **b** : ACRID 1 **c** : having a strong piercing sound **6 a** : terminating in a point or edge (*sharp* features) **b** : involving an abrupt change in direction (a *sharp* turn) **c** : clear in outline or detail : DISTINCT **d** : set forth with clarity and distinctness (*sharp* contrast) **7 a** : higher by a half step (tone of G *sharp*) **b** : higher than the proper pitch **c** : having a sharp in the signature (key of F *sharp*) **8** : STYLISH, DRESSY [Old English *scearp*] — **sharp·ly** *adv* — **sharp·ness** *n* □ SYN SHARP, KEEN, ACUTE mean having or showing alert competence and clear understanding. SHARP implies quick perception, clever resourcefulness, or sometimes questionable trickiness (*sharp* traders) KEEN suggests quickness, enthusiasm, and a penetrating mind (a *keen* student of history) ACUTE implies a power to penetrate and may suggest subtlety and sharpness of discrimination (*acute* mathematical reasoning)

²sharp *adv* **1** : in a sharp manner : SHARPLY **2** : EXACTLY 1, PRECISELY (4 o'clock *sharp*)

³sharp *n* **1** : a musical note or tone one half step higher than a specified note or tone; *also* : a character # on a line or space of the staff indicating such a note or tone **2** : a real or self-styled expert; *also* : SHARPER

⁴sharp *vb* **1** : to raise in pitch especially by a half step **2** : to sing or play above the proper pitch

sharp·en \\'shär-pən\\ *vb* **sharp·ened; sharp·en·ing** \\'shärp-ning, -ə-ning\\ : to make or become sharp or sharper — **sharp·en·er** \\'shärp-nər, -ə-nər\\ *n*

sharp·er \\'shär-pər\\ *n* : CHEAT 2, SWINDLER

sharp–eyed \\'shär-'pīd\\ *adj* : having keen sight; *also* : keen in observing or penetrating

sharp·ie *or* **sharpy** \\'shär-pē\\ *n, pl* **sharp·ies** 1 : a long narrow shallow-draft boat with flat or slightly V=shaped bottom and one or two masts that bear a triangular sail 2 a : SHARPER b : an exceptionally keen or alert person

sharp–nosed \\'shärp-'nōzd\\ *adj* : keen in smelling

sharp practice *n* : unscrupulous seeking or taking of advantage (as in business)

sharp–set \\'shärp-'set\\ *adj* 1 : set at a sharp angle or so as to present a sharp edge 2 : eager in appetite or desire — **sharp–set·ness** *n*

sharp·shoot·er \\'shärp-ˌshüt-ər\\ *n* : a good marksman especially with a rifle — **sharp·shoot·ing** \\-ˌshüt-ing\\ *n*

sharp–sight·ed \\-'sīt-əd\\ *adj* 1 : having acute sight 2 : mentally keen or alert

sharp–tongued \\-'təngd\\ *adj* : harsh or bitter in speech

sharp–wit·ted \\-'wit-əd\\ *adj* : having or showing a keen mind

Shas·ta daisy \\'shast-ə-\\ *n* : a large-flowered garden daisy that resembles the oxeye daisy [Mount *Shasta*, northern California]

¹**shat·ter** \\'shat-ər\\ *vb* 1 : to cause to drop or be dispersed 2 : to break at once into pieces 3 : to damage badly : RUIN (my health had been *shattered*) 4 : to drop or scatter parts (as leaves, petals, or fruit) [Middle English *schateren*]

²**shatter** *n* : FRAGMENT 1, SHRED (the vase lay in *shatters*)

shat·ter·proof \\ˌshat-ər-'prüf\\ *adj* : made so as not to shatter (*shatterproof* glass)

¹**shave** \\'shāv\\ *vb* **shaved; shaved** *or* **shav·en** \\'shā-vən\\; **shav·ing** 1 a : to cut off thin slices from (as a board with a plane) b : to cut off closely (a lawn *shaven* close) 2 : to make bare or smooth by cutting the hair from (had my head *shaved*) 3 : to cut or pare off by means of an edged instrument (as a razor); *esp* : to remove hair close to the skin with a razor 4 : to come close to or touch lightly in passing [Old English *scafan*]

²**shave** *n* 1 : any of various tools for shaving or cutting thin slices 2 : a thin slice : SHAVING 3 : an act or process of shaving 4 : an act of coming very near to

shave·ling \\'shāv-ling\\ *n* 1 : a tonsured clergyman : PRIEST — usually used disparagingly 2 : STRIPLING

shav·er \\'shā-vər\\ *n* 1 : one that shaves; *esp* : an electric razor 2 : BOY 1, YOUNGSTER

shave·tail \\'shāv-ˌtāl\\ *n* 1 : a pack mule especially when newly broken in 2 : SECOND LIEUTENANT — usually used disparagingly [from the practice of shaving the tails of newly broken mules]

Sha·vi·an \\'shā-vē-ən\\ *n* : an admirer or devotee of G. B. Shaw, his writings, or his social and political theories [New Latin *Shavius*, latinized form of George Bernard *Shaw*] — **Shavian** *adj*

shav·ing \\'shā-ving\\ *n* 1 : the act of one that shaves 2 : something shaved off (wood *shavings*)

shaw \\'shȯ\\ *n, dialect* : COPPICE, THICKET [Old English *sceaga*]

¹**shawl** \\'shȯl\\ *n* : a square or oblong piece of fabric used especially as a covering for the head or shoulders [Persian *shāl*]

²**shawl** *vt* : to wrap in or as if in a shawl

shawm \\'shȯm\\ *n* : a medieval double-reed woodwind instrument [Middle French *chalemie*, derived from Latin *calamus* "reed", from Greek *kalamos*]

Shaw·nee \\shȯ-'nē, shä-\\ *n, pl* **Shawnee** *or* **Shawnees** : a member of an Algonquian people originally of the central Ohio valley [Shawnee *Shaawanwaaki*]

shay \\'shā\\ *n, chiefly dialect* : CHAISE 1 [back-formation from *chaise*, taken as pl.]

¹**she** \\shē, 'shē\\ *pron* 1 : that female one who is neither speaker nor hearer (*she* is a doctor) — compare HE, HER, HERS, IT, THEY 2 — used to refer to one regarded as feminine (as by personification) (*she* was a fine ship) [Middle English]

²**she** \\'shē\\ *n* : a female person or animal — often used in combination (*she*-cat) (*she*-cousin)

sheaf \\'shēf\\ *n, pl* **sheaves** \\'shēvz\\ 1 : a bundle of stalks and ears of grain 2 : something resembling or suggesting a sheaf of grain (a *sheaf* of papers) [Old English *scēaf*] — **sheaf·like** \\'shē-ˌflīk\\ *adj*

¹**shear** \\'shiər\\ *vb* **sheared; sheared** *or* **shorn** \\'shȯrn, 'shȯrn\\; **shear·ing** 1 : to cut the hair or wool from (*shearing* sheep) 2 : to deprive of by or as if by cutting (*shorn* of their power) 3 : to cut or cut through with or as if with shears (*shear* a metal sheet in two) 4 : to become divided or broken under the action of a shear (bolts may *shear* off) [Old English *scieran*] — **shear·er** *n*

²**shear** *n* 1 a : a cutting implement similar or identical to a pair of scissors but typically larger — usually used in pl.; *also* : one blade of a pair of shears b : any of various cutting machines operating by the action of opposed cutting edges of metal — usually used in pl. 2 : an action or force that causes or tends to cause two parts of a body to slide on each other in a direction parallel to their plane of contact

sheared \\'shiərd\\ *adj* : formed or finished by shearing; *esp* : having the pile cut to uniform length (*sheared* beaver)

shear·wa·ter \\'shiər-ˌwȯt-ər, -ˌwät-\\ *n* : any of numerous oceanic birds related to the petrels and albatrosses that in flight usually skim close to the waves

sheath \\'shēth\\ *n, pl* **sheaths** \\'shēthz, 'shēths\\ 1 : a case for a blade (as of a knife) 2 : a covering especially of an anatomical structure suggesting a sheath in form or use 3 : a woman's close-fitting dress [Old English *scēath*]

sheathe \\'shēth\\ *vt* 1 : to put into or as if into a sheath 2 : to encase or cover with something (as sheets of metal) that protects [Middle English *shethen*, from *shethe* "sheath"] — **sheath·er** *n*

sheath·ing \\'shē-thing, -thing\\ *n* : material used to sheathe something; *esp* : the first covering of boards or of waterproof material on the outside wall of a frame house or on a timber roof

sheath knife *n* : a knife having a fixed blade and designed to be carried in a sheath

¹**sheave** \\'shiv, 'shēv\\ *n* : a grooved wheel : PULLEY [Middle English *sheve*]

²**sheave** \\'shēv\\ *vt* : to gather and bind into a sheaf [*sheaf*]

she·bang \\shi-'bang\\ *n* : everything involved in what is under consideration — usually used in the phrase *the whole shebang* [origin unknown]

¹**shed** \\'shed\\ *vb* **shed; shed·ding** 1 a : to pour forth in drops (*shed* tears) b : to cause (blood) to flow by cutting or wounding c : to give off or out (the sun *sheds* light) 2 : to throw off : REPEL (the duck's plumage *sheds* water) 3 a : to rid of : DISCARD (*shed* excess weight) (*shed* spores) b : to cast aside or let fall (some natural covering) (a snake *sheds* its skin) (the cat is *shedding*) [Old English *scēadan* "to divide, separate"] — **shed·der** *n*

²**shed** *n* 1 : a slight structure built for shelter or storage (tool *shed*) 2 : a single-storied building with one or more sides unenclosed (customs *shed*) [probably from Middle English *shade*]

³**shed** *vt* **shed·ded; shed·ding** : to put or house in a shed

she'd \\shēd, ˌshēd\\ : she had : she would

sheen \\'shēn\\ *n* 1 : a bright or shining condition 2 : subdued shininess of surface (the *sheen* of satin) [Old English *scīene*] — **sheeny** \\'shē-nē\\ *adj*

sheep 1: *top* karakul,
bottom merino

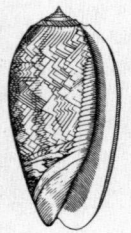

¹shell 2

sheep \'shēp\ *n, pl* **sheep** **1** : any of a genus of cud‑chewing mammals related to the goats but stockier and lacking a beard in the male; *esp* : one long domesticated for its flesh, wool, and other products **2** : one that is like a sheep (as in being timid, defenseless, or easily led) **3** : SHEEPSKIN 1 [Old English *scēap*] — **sheep** *adj*

sheep·cote \-,kōt, -,kät\ *n, chiefly British* : SHEEPFOLD

sheep–dip \-,dip\ *n* : a liquid preparation of toxic chemicals into which sheep are plunged especially to destroy parasitic arthropods

sheep dog *n* : a dog used or trained to tend, drive, or guard sheep

sheep·fold \'shēp-,fōld\ *n* : a pen or shelter for sheep

sheep·herd·er \'shēp-,hərd-ər\ *n* : a worker in charge of sheep especially on open range — **sheep·herd·ing** \-,hərd-ing\ *n*

sheep·ish \'shē-pish\ *adj* **1** : resembling a sheep in meekness, stupidity, or timidity **2** : embarassed by consciousness of a fault ⟨a *sheepish* look⟩ — **sheep·ish·ly** *adv* — **sheep·ish·ness** *n*

sheep's eye *n* : a shy, longing, and usually amorous glance

sheeps·head \'shēps-,hed\ *n* : any of several fishes; *esp* : a food fish of the Atlantic and Gulf coasts of the United States with broad incisor teeth

sheep·shear·er \'shēp-,shir-ər\ *n* : one that shears sheep

sheep·shear·ing \-,shiər-ing\ *n* **1** : the act of shearing sheep **2** : the time or season for shearing sheep

sheep·skin \'shēp-,skin\ *n* **1** : the skin of a sheep or leather prepared from it; *also* : PARCHMENT 1 **2** : DIPLOMA

¹**sheer** \'shiər\ *adj* **1** : very thin or transparent ⟨*sheer* stockings⟩ **2 a** : UTTER ⟨*sheer* nonsense⟩ **b** : taken or acting apart from everything else ⟨by *sheer* force⟩ **3** : marked by great and unbroken steepness [Middle English *schere* "free from guilt"] SYN see STEEP — **sheer·ly** *adv* — **sheer·ness** *n*

²**sheer** *adv* **1** : WHOLLY 1, ALTOGETHER **2** : straight up or down

³**sheer** *vi* : to turn from a course : SWERVE [perhaps alteration of ¹*shear*]

⁴**sheer** *n* : a turning from or change in the course of a ship

⁵**sheer** *n* : the fore-and-aft curvature from bow to stern of a ship's deck as shown in side elevation [perhaps alteration of ²*shear*]

¹**sheet** \'shēt\ *n* **1** : a broad piece of cloth; *esp* : an oblong of cloth used as an article of bedding next to the person **2 a** : a usually rectangular piece of paper **b** *pl* : the unbound pages of a book **c** : a newspaper, periodical, or occasional publication **d** : the unseparated postage stamps printed by one impression of a plate on a single piece of paper **3** : a broad expanse or surface ⟨a *sheet* of ice⟩ **4** : a portion of something that is thin in comparison to its length and breadth ⟨a *sheet* of plastic⟩ [Old English *scȳte*]

²**sheet** *vt* **1** : to cover with a sheet : SHROUD **2** : to furnish with sheets

³**sheet** *n* **1** : a rope or chain that regulates the angle at which a sail is set in relation to the wind **2** *pl* : the spaces at either end of an open boat not taken up by seats [Old English *scēata* "lower corner of a sail"]

sheet anchor *n* **1** : an unusually large anchor especially for use in an emergency **2** : something that constitutes a main support or dependence in danger

sheet·ing \'shēt-ing\ *n* : material in the form of sheets or suitable for forming into sheets

sheet lightning *n* : lightning in diffused or sheet form

sheet metal *n* : metal in the form of sheets

sheet music *n* : music printed on unbound sheets of paper

sheikh *or* **sheik** \'shēk, *for 1 also* 'shāk\ *n* **1** : an Arab chief **2** *usually* **sheik** : a man held to be irresistibly attractive to romantic young women [Arabic *shaykh*] — **sheik·dom** \-dəm\ *n*

shek·el \'shek-əl\ *n* **1** : an ancient unit of weight or value; *esp* : a Hebrew unit equal to about 252 grains troy (about 16.3 grams) **2** : a coin weighing one shekel [Hebrew *sheqel*]

shel·drake \'shel-,drāk\ *n* **1** : any of several Old World ducks; *esp* : a common mostly black-and-white European duck slightly larger than the mallard **2** : MERGANSER [Middle English]

shelf \'shelf\ *n, pl* **shelves** \'shelvz\ **1 a** : a thin flat usually long and narrow piece of firm material fastened horizontally (as on a wall) at a distance from the floor to hold objects **b** : the contents of a shelf **2** : something resembling a shelf: as **a** : a sandbank or ledge of rocks usually partially submerged **b** : a flat projecting layer of rock [Middle English] — **shelf·like** \'shel-,flīk\ *adj* — **on the shelf** : in a state of inactivity or uselessness

shelf fungus *n* : a fungus that forms shelflike fruiting bodies

shelf life *n* : the period of time during which a material may be stored and remain suitable for use

¹**shell** \'shel\ *n* **1 a** : a hard rigid outer covering of an animal (as a turtle, oyster, or beetle) **b** : the outer covering of an egg and especially of a bird's egg **c** : the outer covering of a nut, fruit, or seed especially when hard or toughly fibrous **2** : shell material or shells especially of mollusks; *also* : a shell-bearing mollusk **3** : something that resembles a shell: as **a** : a framework or exterior structure **b** : a casing without substance ⟨the *shell* of my former self⟩ **c** : an edible case for holding a filling ⟨a pastry shell⟩ **d** : a reinforced concrete arched or domed roof used primarily over large unpartitioned areas **4** : an impersonal manner that conceals the presence or absence of feeling **5** : a narrow light racing boat propelled by two, four, or eight persons pulling oars; *also* : SCULL **6** : any of the spheres defined by the orbits of a group of electrons of approximately equal energy surrounding the nucleus of an atom **7 a** : a hollow projectile for artillery containing an explosive bursting charge **b** : a metal or metal and plastic or paper case which holds the charge of powder and shot or a bullet used with breech-loading small arms **8** : a plain usually sleeveless blouse or sweater [Old English *sciell*] — **shell** *adj* — **shelled** \'sheld\ *adj* — **shell·work** \'shel-,wərk\ *n* — **shelly** \'shel-ē\ *adj*

²**shell** *vb* **1 a** : to remove or fall from a natural enclosing cover (as a shell or husk) ⟨*shell* peas⟩ **b** : to remove the grains from (as an ear of Indian corn) **2** : to shoot shells at, upon, or into : BOMBARD

she'll \shēl, shil, ,shēl\ : she shall : she will

¹**shel·lac** \shə-'lak\ *n* **1** : purified lac **2** : a preparation of lac dissolved in alcohol that is used in finishing wood [*shell* + *lac*]

²**shellac** *vt* **shel·lacked; shel·lack·ing** **1** : to coat with shellac **2** : to defeat decisively

shel·lack·ing \shə-'lak-ing\ *n* : a decisive defeat or sound drubbing ⟨took a *shellacking* in last year's election⟩

shell·back \'shel-,bak\ *n* : an old or veteran sailor

shell bean *n* : a bean grown primarily for its edible seeds; *also* : these seeds — compare SNAP BEAN

shell·fire \'shel-,fīr\ *n* : a firing or exploding of shells

shell·fish \-,fish\ *n* : an aquatic invertebrate animal with a shell; *esp* : an edible mollusk or crustacean

shell out *vb* : PAY 1

shell pink *n* : a light yellowish pink

shell·proof \'shel-'prüf\ *adj* : capable of resisting shells or bombs

shell shock *n* : a neurotic condition appearing in soldiers exposed to modern warfare — **shell–shock** \'shel-,shäk\ *vt*

¹shel·ter \'shel-tər\ *n* **1** : something that covers or affords protection : a means or place of protection ⟨fallout *shelter*⟩ **2** : the state of being covered and protected [origin unknown] — **shel·ter·less** \-ləs\ *adj*

²shelter *vb* **shel·tered; shel·ter·ing** \-tə-ring, -tring\ **1** : to constitute or provide a shelter for : PROTECT **2** : to place under shelter or protection **3** : to take shelter — **shel·ter·er** \-tər-ər\ *n*

shel·ter·belt \-tər-,belt\ *n* : a barrier of trees and shrubs that protects (as soil and crops) from wind and storm and lessens erosion

shelter half *n* : one of the halves of a shelter tent

shelter tent *n* : a small tent for two persons usually consisting of two interchangeable pieces of waterproof cotton duck that fasten together at an overlap

shel·ty *or* **shel·tie** \'shel-tē\ *n, pl* **shelties** **1** : SHETLAND PONY **2** : SHETLAND SHEEPDOG [probably of Scandinavian origin]

shelve \'shelv\ *vb* **1** : to furnish with shelves ⟨*shelve* a closet⟩ **2** : to place on a shelf ⟨*shelve* books⟩ **3 a** : to remove from active service **b** : to put off or aside ⟨*shelve* a bill⟩ **4** : to slope in a formation like a shelf : INCLINE — **shelv·er** *n*

shelves *pl of* SHELF

shelv·ing \'shel-ving\ *n* **1** : material for shelves **2** : a number of shelves

She·ma \shə-'mä\ *n* : the central creed of Judaism comprising Deuteronomy 6:4–9 and 11:13–21 and Numbers 15:37–41 [Hebrew *shĕma'* ''hear'', first word of Deuteronomy 6:4]

she·nan·i·gan \shə-'nan-i-gən\ *n* **1** : an underhand trick **2 a** : tricky or questionable conduct **b** : high-spirited or mischievous activity — usually used in pl. [origin unknown]

She·ol \shē-'ōl, 'shē-,\ *n* **1** : the dwelling place of the dead in ancient Hebrew belief **2** : HELL 1 [Hebrew *Shĕ'ōl*]

¹shep·herd \'shep-ərd\ *n* **1** : a man or boy who tends and guards sheep : PASTOR [Old English *scēaphyrde*, from *scēap* ''sheep'' + *hierde* ''herdsman'']

²shepherd *vt* **1** : to tend as a shepherd **2** : to guide or guard in the manner of a shepherd ⟨*shepherd* tourists through a museum⟩

shepherd dog *n* : SHEEP DOG

shep·herd·ess \-'shep-ərd-əs\ *n* : a woman or girl who tends and guards sheep

shepherd's check *n* : a pattern of small even black and white checks; *also* : a fabric woven in this pattern — called also *shepherd's plaid*

shepherd's pie *n* : a meat pie topped with mashed potatoes

Sher·a·ton \'sher-ət-n\ *adj* : of or relating to an early 19th century English furniture style characterized by delicate construction, graceful proportions, and the use of straight lines [Thomas *Sheraton,* died 1806, English cabinetmaker]

sher·bet \'shər-bət\ *also* **sher·bert** \-bərt\ *n* **1** : a cold drink of sweetened and diluted fruit juice **2** : an ice with milk, egg white, or gelatin added [Turkish *serbet*, from Persian *sharbat*, from Arabic *sharbah* ''drink'']

sherd *variant of* SHARD

sher·iff \'sher-əf\ *n* : a county official charged with keeping the peace and with judicial duties (as executing the processes and orders of courts) [Old English *scīrgerēfa*, from *scīr* ''shire'' + *gerēfa* ''reeve'']

sher·lock \'shər-,läk\ *n, often cap* : DETECTIVE [*Sherlock* Holmes, detective in stories by Sir Arthur Conan Doyle]

Sher·pa \'sheər-pə, 'shər-\ *n* : a member of a Tibetan people living on the high southern slopes of the Himalayas and skilled in mountain climbing

sher·ry \'sher-ē\ *n, pl* **sherries** : a fortified wine with a distinctive nutty flavor [*Xeres* (now *Jerez*), Spain] ☐ ORIGIN Many wines are named after the places where they are made. The region around the town of

Xeres (the modern name is *Jerez*) in Spain produced a type of white wine that was introduced to England in the 16th century. At that time the name of the town *Xeres* was often spelled *Sherries* in English—the *sh* represented the best English approximation to the contemporary pronunciation of the Spanish *x*. And the wine from *Xeres* was called *sherris*. But some, judging from the form of the word *sherris* that it was a plural, began to use what they believed was its singular form, *sherry*. This type of derivation by subtraction of a real or supposed affix is called back-formation.

she's \shēz, ,shēz\ : she is : she has

Shet·land \'shet-lənd\ *n* **1 a** : SHETLAND PONY **b** : SHETLAND SHEEPDOG **2** *often not cap* **a** : a lightweight loosely twisted yarn of Shetland wool used for knitting and weaving **b** : a fabric of Shetland wool

Shetland pony *n* : any of a breed of small stocky shaggy hardy ponies originating in the Shetland islands

Shetland sheepdog *n* : any of a breed of dogs resembling miniature collies with a profuse long coat developed in the Shetland islands

Shetland wool *n* : fine wool from sheep raised in the Shetland islands; *also* : yarn spun from this wool

shew \'shō\ *British variant of* SHOW

shib·bo·leth \'shib-ə-ləth also -,leth\ *n* **1 a** : SLOGAN **2 b** : an idea or saying that is commonly believed **2** : a custom or usage that is a criterion for distinguishing members of one group [Hebrew *shibbōleth* ''stream''] ☐ ORIGIN In the 12th chapter of the book of Judges there is an account of a battle between the Gileadites and the Ephraimites. The Ephraimite army was routed, and the retreating Ephraimites tried to cross the Jordan river at a ford held by the Gileadites. Anyone wishing to pass was asked if he were an Ephraimite. If the reply was ''no'' he was asked to say the word *shibbōleth*. In Hebrew *shibbōleth* means ''stream'', but on this occasion its meaning was of no importance. Unlike the Gileadites, the Ephraimites could not pronounce an *sh* sound. If a man replied ''*sibbōleth*'' the Gileadites knew he was an Ephraimite and slew him.

¹shield \'shēld\ *n* **1** : a broad piece of defensive armor carried on the arm **2** : one that protects or defends : DEFENSE **3** : ESCUTCHEON **4 a** : a device or part that serves as a protective cover or barrier **b** : a protective structure (as a carapace) of some animals **5** : the ancient mass of hard rock that forms the core of a continent **6** : something shaped like or resembling a shield: as **a** : a policeman's badge **b** : a decorative or identifying emblem [Old English *scield*]

²shield *vt* **1** : to protect with or as if with a shield **2** : to cut off from observation : HIDE SYN see DEFEND

¹shift \'shift\ *vb* **1** : to exchange for or replace by another : CHANGE **2 a** : to change the place, position, or direction of : MOVE **b** : to make a change in place, position, or direction **c** : to change the gear rotating the transmission shaft of an automobile **3** : to change phonetically **4** : to get along : MANAGE ⟨left the others to *shift* for themselves⟩ [Old English *sciftan* ''to divide, arrange''] — **shift·er** *n*

²shift *n* **1 a** : a means or device for effecting an end **b** : a deceitful scheme : DODGE **c** : an expedient tried in difficult circumstances : EXTREMITY **2** : SLIP 5a, CHEMISE **3** : a change in direction ⟨a *shift* in the wind⟩ **4 a** : change in place or position **5** : a group who work together in alternation with other groups; *also* : the period during which one such group works **6** : a removal from one person or thing to another : TRANSFER ⟨a *shift* of responsibility⟩ **7** : GEARSHIFT

shift key *n* : a key on a keyboard (as of a typewriter) that when pressed enables an alternate character set to be printed

shift·less \'shift-ləs, 'shif-\ *adj* **1** : lacking in resourcefulness : INEFFICIENT **2** : lacking in ambition or incentive : LAZY — **shift·less·ly** *adv* — **shift·less·ness** *n*

Shetland pony

\ə\ abut	\ng\ sing
\ər\ further	\ō\ bone
\a\ mat	\ȯ\ saw
\ā\ take	\ȯi\ coin
\ä\ cot, cart	\th\ thin
\au̇\ out	\th\ this
\ch\ chin	\ü\ food
\e\ pet	\u̇\ foot
\ē\ easy	\y\ yet
\g\ go	\yü\ few
\i\ tip	\yu̇\ cure
\ī\ life	\zh\ vision
\j\ job	

shifty \'shif-tē\ *adj* **shift·i·er; -est** **1 a :** given to deception, evasion, or fraud **: TRICKY b :** capable of evasive movement **: ELUSIVE 2 :** indicative of a tricky nature ⟨*shifty* eyes⟩ — **shift·i·ly** \-tə-lē\ *adv* — **shift·i·ness** \-tē-nəs\ *n*

shil·le·lagh *also* **shil·la·lah** \shə-'lā-lē\ *n* **: CUDGEL, CLUB** [*Shillelagh,* town in Ireland famed for its oak trees]

shil·ling \'shil-ing\ *n* **1 a :** a former British monetary unit equal to 12 pence or ¹⁄₂₀ pound **b :** a coin representing this unit **2 :** a monetary unit equal to ¹⁄₂₀ pound and a corresponding coin in any of several countries in or formerly in the British Commonwealth **3 :** any of several early American coins **4 a :** the basic monetary unit of Kenya, Somalia, Tanzania, and Uganda **b :** a coin representing this unit [Old English *scilling*]

¹shil·ly–shal·ly \'shil-ē-,shal-ē\ *adj* **: IRRESOLUTE** [reduplication of *shall I*]

²shilly–shally *n* **: INDECISION, IRRESOLUTION**

³shilly–shally *vi* **shil·ly–shal·lied; shil·ly–shal·ly·ing 1 :** to show hesitation or lack of decisiveness **: VACILLATE 2 :** to waste time **: DAWDLE**

¹shim \'shim\ *n* **:** a thin often tapered piece of wood, metal, or stone used to fill in space (as for support or leveling) [origin unknown]

²shim *vt* **shimmed; shim·ming :** to fill out or level up by the use of a shim

¹shim·mer \'shim-ər\ *vi* **shim·mered; shim·mer·ing** \'shim-ring, -ə-ring\ **1 :** to shine with a wavering light **: GLIMMER** ⟨leaves *shimmering* in the sunshine⟩ **2 :** to appear in a constantly changing wavy form [Old English *scimerian*]

²shimmer *n* **1 :** a wavering light **:** subdued sparkle or sheen **2 :** a wavering image or effect especially when produced by heat waves — **shim·mery** \'shim-rē, -ə-rē\ *adj*

¹shim·my \'shim-ē\ *n, pl* **shimmies 1 :** a jazz dance characterized by a shaking of the body from the shoulders down **2 :** an abnormal vibration especially in the front wheels of an automobile [short for *shimmy-shake,* from *shimmy,* alteration of *chemise*]

²shimmy *vi* **shim·mied; shim·my·ing 1 :** to shake or quiver in or as if in dancing a shimmy **2 :** to vibrate abnormally

¹shin \'shin\ *n* **:** the front part of the vertebrate leg below the knee [Old English *scinu*]

²shin *vb* **shinned; shin·ning 1 :** to climb by moving oneself along alternately with the arms or hands and legs ⟨*shin* a tree⟩ **2 :** to move forward rapidly on foot

shin·bone \'shin-'bōn, -,bōn\ *n* **: TIBIA** 1a

shin·dig \'shin-,dig\ *n* **:** a festive occasion: as **a :** a social gathering with dancing **b :** a usually large or lavish party [probably alteration of *shindy*]

shin·dy \'shin-dē\ *n, pl* **shindys** *or* **shindies 1 : SHINDIG** a **2 : FRACAS, UPROAR** [probably alteration of ¹*shinny*]

¹shine \'shīn\ *vb* **shone** \'shōn\ *or* **shined; shin·ing 1 :** to send out rays of light **2 :** to be bright by reflection of light **: GLEAM 3 :** to show brilliance **:** be eminent or distinguished ⟨*shine* in conversation⟩ **4 :** to have a bright glowing appearance **5 :** to be conspicuously evident or clear ⟨human sympathy *shone* through all their actions⟩ **6 :** to throw or flash the light of **7** *past & past participle* **shined :** to make bright by polishing ⟨*shine* your shoes⟩ [Old English *scīnan*]

²shine *n* **1 :** brightness caused by the emission or reflection of light **2 :** a brilliance of quality or appearance **3 :** fair weather **: SUNSHINE** ⟨will go, rain or *shine*⟩ **4 :** a stupid trick or silly caper — usually used in pl. **5 : LIKING, FANCY** ⟨took a *shine* to them⟩ **6 :** a polish given to shoes

shin·er \'shī-nər\ *n* **1 :** one that shines **2 :** a silvery fish; *esp* **:** any of numerous freshwater American fishes related to the carp **3 : BLACK EYE**

¹shin·gle \'shing-gəl\ *n* **1 :** a small thin piece of building material (as of wood or a composition of asphalt)

for laying in overlapping rows as a covering for the roof or sides of a building **2 :** a small signboard [Middle English *schingel*]

²shingle *vt* **shin·gled; shin·gling** \-gə-ling, -gling\ **1 :** to cover with or as if with shingles **2 :** to cut (a woman's hair) with a short tapered line at the back

³shingle *n* **1 :** coarse pebbly gravel on the seashore **2 :** a place (as a beach) strewn with shingle [probably of Scandinavian origin]

shin·gler \'shing-gə-lər, -glər\ *n* **:** one that shingles

shin·gles \'shing-gəlz\ *n* **:** a virus disease marked by inflammation of one or more ganglia and by pain and skin eruption usually along the course of a single nerve [Medieval Latin *cingulus,* from Latin *cingulum* "girdle", from *cingere* "to gird"]

shin·gly \'shing-gə-lē, -glē\ *adj* **:** composed of or abounding in shingle ⟨a *shingly* beach⟩

shin·ing *adj* **1 :** giving forth or reflecting light **2 :** splendidly bright ⟨*shining* newness⟩ **3 :** having a distinguished quality ⟨*shining* prose⟩; *esp* **: ILLUSTRIOUS** ⟨a *shining* example of integrity⟩ — **shin·ing·ly** \'shī-ning-lē\ *adv*

¹shin·ny \'shin-ē\ *n* **:** the game of hockey played with a curved stick and a ball or block of wood by youngsters [perhaps from ¹*shin*]

²shinny *vi* **shin·nied; shin·ny·ing : SHIN** 1 [²*shin*]

shin·plas·ter \'shin-,plas-tər\ *n* **:** a piece of paper currency especially in denominations of less than one dollar

Shin·to \'shin-,tō\ *n* **:** a religious cult of Japan consisting chiefly in the reverence of the spirits of natural forces, emperors, and heroes [Japanese *shintō*] — **Shin·to·ism** \-,iz-əm\ *n* — **Shin·to·ist** \-əst\ *n or adj*

shiny \'shī-nē\ *adj* **shin·i·er; -est :** bright in appearance **: SHINING** ⟨*shiny* kitchenware⟩ — **shin·i·ness** *n*

¹ship \'ship\ *n* **1 a :** a large seagoing vessel **b :** a square-rigged sailing vessel with three or more masts — compare ⁵**BARK, BRIG 2 :** the crew of a ship **3 a : AIRSHIP b : AIRPLANE c : SPACESHIP** [Old English *scip*]

²ship *vb* **shipped; ship·ping 1 a :** to place or receive on board a ship for transportation by water **b :** to cause to be transported ⟨*ship* grain by rail⟩ **2 :** to put in place for use ⟨*ship* the tiller⟩ **3 :** to take into a ship or boat ⟨*ship* oars⟩ **4 :** to take (as water) over the side **5 :** to engage to serve on shipboard

-ship \,ship\ *n suffix* **1 :** state **:** condition **:** quality ⟨friend*ship*⟩ **2 :** office **:** dignity **:** profession ⟨author*ship*⟩ ⟨clerk*ship*⟩ ⟨lord*ship*⟩ **3 :** art **:** skill ⟨seaman*ship*⟩ **4 :** something showing, exhibiting, or embodying a quality or state ⟨town*ship*⟩ **5 :** one entitled to a (specified) rank, title, or appellation ⟨your Lady*ship*⟩ [Old English *-scipe*]

ship biscuit *n* **: HARDTACK**

ship·board \'ship-,bōrd, -,bòrd\ *n* **1 :** the side of a ship **2 :** the deck or interior of a ship ⟨met on *shipboard*⟩

ship bread *n* **: HARDTACK**

ship·build·er \'ship-,bil-dər\ *n* **:** one who designs or builds ships — **ship·build·ing** \-ding\ *n*

ship·lap \'ship-,lap\ *n* **:** wooden sheathing in which the boards are rabbeted so that the edges of each board lap over the edges of adjacent boards to make a flush joint

ship·load \-'lōd, -,lōd\ *n* **:** enough to fill a ship

ship·man \'ship-mən\ *n* **1 : SAILOR** 1a **2 : SHIPMASTER**

ship·mas·ter \-,mas-tər\ *n* **:** the master or commander of a ship other than a warship

ship·mate \-,māt\ *n* **:** a fellow sailor

ship·ment \'ship-mənt\ *n* **1 :** the act or process of shipping **2 :** the goods shipped

ship of the line : a warship large enough to be used for direct engagement of the enemy

ship·own·er \'ship-,ō-nər\ *n* **:** the owner of a ship

ship·pa·ble \'ship-ə-bəl\ *adj* **:** suitable for shipping

ship·per \'ship-ər\ *n* **:** one that sends goods by any form of conveyance

ship·ping \'ship-ing\ *n* **1** : the body of ships in one place or belonging to one port or country **2** : the act or business of one that ships

shipping clerk *n* : one who is employed in a shipping room to assemble, pack, and send out or receive goods

ship·shape \'ship-,shāp\ *adj* : TRIM, TIDY

ship·side \-,sīd\ *n* : the area adjacent to shipping that is used for storage and loading of freight and passengers

ship's papers *n pl* : documents required on board a ship including certificates of ownership and registry, logbook, customs clearance, and crew, passenger, and cargo lists

ship·way \'ship-,wā\ *n* : the ways on which a ship is built

ship·worm \'ship-,wərm\ *n* : any of various long-bodied marine clams that resemble worms, burrow in submerged wood, and damage wharf piles and wooden ships

¹ship·wreck \-,rek\ *n* **1** : a wrecked ship or its parts : WRECKAGE **2** : the destruction or loss of a ship **3** : total loss or failure : RUIN [Old English *scipwræc,* from *scip* "ship" + *wræc* "something driven by the sea"]

²shipwreck *vt* **1 a** : to cause to experience shipwreck **b** : RUIN **2** : to destroy (a ship) by grounding or foundering

ship·wright \-,rīt\ *n* : a carpenter skilled in ship construction and repair

ship·yard \-,yärd\ *n* : a place where ships are built or repaired

shire \'shīr, *in place-name compounds* ,shiər, shər\ *n* : a territorial division of England usually identical with a county [Old English *scīr* "office, shire"]

shirk \'shərk\ *vb* **1** : to evade the performance of an obligation **2** : AVOID [origin unknown] — **shirk·er** *n*

shirr \'shər\ *vt* **1** : to draw (as cloth) together in a shirring **2** : to bake (eggs removed from the shell) until set [origin unknown]

shirr·ing \'shər-ing\ *n* : a decorative gathering (as of cloth) made by drawing up the material along two or more parallel lines of stitching

shirt \'shərt\ *n* : a garment for the upper part of the body: as **a** : a loose cloth garment usually having a collar, sleeves, a front opening, and a tail long enough to be tucked inside trousers or a skirt **b** : UNDERSHIRT [Old English *scyrte*]

shirt·front \-,frənt\ *n* : the front of a shirt

shirt·ing \'shərt-ing\ *n* : fabric suitable for shirts

shirt·mak·er \'shərt-,mā-kər\ *n* : one that makes shirts

shirt·sleeve \-,slēv\ *n* : the sleeve of a shirt — **in shirt-sleeves** : wearing a shirt but no coat

shirt·tail \'shərt-,tāl\ *n* : the part of a shirt that reaches below the waist especially in the back

shirt·waist \'shərt-,wāst\ *n* : a woman's tailored garment (as a dress or blouse) with details copied from men's shirts

shish ke·bab \'shish-kə-,bäb\ *n* : kabob cooked on skewers [Armenian *shish kabab*]

shiv·a·ree \,shiv-ə-'rē, 'shiv-ə-,rē\ *n* : a noisy mock serenade to a newly married couple [French *charivari*] — **shivaree** *vt*

¹shiv·er \'shiv-ər\ *n* : one of the small pieces into which a brittle thing is broken by sudden violence [Middle English]

²shiver *vb* **shiv·ered; shiv·er·ing** \'shiv-ring, -ə-ring\ : to break into many small pieces : SHATTER

³shiver *vi* **shiv·ered; shiv·er·ing** \'shiv-ring, -ə-ring\ : to undergo trembling (as from cold or fear) : QUIVER [Middle English *chiveren*]

⁴shiver *n* **1** : an instance of shivering **2** : a thrill of emotion and especially fear — usually used in pl.

shiv·ery \'shiv-rē, -ə-rē\ *adj* **1** : characterized by shivers **2** : causing shivers ⟨*shivery* ghost stories⟩

shm- — see SCHM-

shmuck *variant of* SCHMUCK

¹shoal \'shōl\ *adj* : SHALLOW ⟨*shoal* water⟩ [Old English *sceald*]

²shoal *n* **1** : a shallow place in a body of water (as the sea or a river) **2** : a sandbank or sandbar that makes the water shallow

³shoal *vi* : to become shallow

⁴shoal *n* : a large group (as of fish) : SCHOOL, CROWD [Old English *scolu* "multitude"]

⁵shoal *vi* : ⁴SCHOOL, THRONG

shoat \'shōt\ *n* : a young hog usually less than one year old [Middle English *shote*]

¹shock \'shäk\ *n* : a pile of sheaves of grain or stalks of Indian corn with the butt ends down [Middle English]

²shock *vt* : to collect into shocks

³shock *n* **1** : the impact or encounter of individuals or groups in combat **2** : a violent shake or jar : CONCUSSION ⟨an earthquake *shock*⟩ **3 a** : a disturbance in the equilibrium or permanence of something **b** : a sudden or violent disturbance in the mental or emotional faculties **4** : a state of profound bodily depression associated with reduced blood volume and pressure and caused usually by severe especially crushing injuries, hemorrhage, or burns **5** : sudden stimulation of the nerves and convulsive contraction of the muscles caused by the discharge of electricity through the animal body **6 a** : STROKE 5 **b** : CORONARY THROMBOSIS [Middle French *choc,* from *choquer* "to strike against"]

⁴shock *vt* **1 a** : to strike with surprise, terror, horror, or disgust ⟨*shocked* by the city's slums⟩ **b** : to subject to the action of an electrical discharge **2** : to drive by or as if by a shock

⁵shock *n* : a thick bushy mass (as of hair) [perhaps from ¹*shock*]

shock absorber *n* : a device for absorbing the energy of sudden impulses or shocks in machinery or structures

shock·er \'shäk-ər\ *n* : one that shocks; *esp* : a sensational work of fiction or drama

shock·ing *adj* : extremely startling and offensive ⟨a *shocking* crime⟩ — **shock·ing·ly** \-ing-lē\ *adv*

shock therapy *n* : the treatment of mental disorder by causing coma or convulsions especially through use of electricity — called also *shock treatment*

shock troops *n pl* : troops chosen for offensive work because of their high morale, training, and discipline

shock wave *n* : a wave formed by the sudden compression (as by an earthquake or supersonic aircraft) of the substance through which the wave travels

shod \'shäd\ *adj* **1** : wearing shoes **2** : furnished or equipped with a shoe

¹shod·dy \'shäd-ē\ *n* **1** : a fabric manufactured wholly or partly from reclaimed wool **2** : inferior, imitation, or pretentious articles or matter [origin unknown]

²shoddy *adj* **shod·di·er; -est** **1** : made of shoddy **2 a** : cheaply imitative : vulgarly pretentious **b** : hastily or poorly done : INFERIOR **c** : SHABBY 1a — **shod·di·ly** \'shäd-l-ē\ *adv* — **shod·di·ness** \'shäd-ē-nəs\ *n*

¹shoe \'shü\ *n* **1** : an outer covering for the human foot typically made of leather with a thick or stiff sole and an attached heel **2** : something that resembles a shoe in appearance or use: as **a** : HORSESHOE 1 **b** : the runner of a sled **c** : the part of a brake that presses on the wheel of a vehicle **3** : the outside casing of an automobile tire [Old English *scōh*]

²shoe *vt* **shod** \'shäd\ *also* **shoed** \'shüd\; **shoe·ing** **1** : to furnish with a shoe or shoes **2** : to cover for protection, strength, or ornament

shoe·black \'shü-,blak\ *n* : BOOTBLACK

shoe·box \-,bäks\ *n* : a box designed to hold a pair of shoes for retail sale

shoe·horn \-,horn\ *n* : a curved piece (as of metal or plastic) to aid in slipping on a shoe

shoe·lace \-,lās\ *n* : a lace or string for fastening a shoe

shoe·mak·er \-,mā-kər\ *n* : one whose business is making or repairing shoes

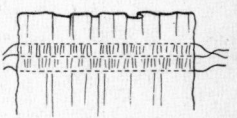
shirring

shoehorn

\ə\	abut	\ng\	sing
\ər\	**further**	\ō\	bone
\a\	mat	\ȯ\	saw
\ā\	take	\oi\	coin
\ä\	cot, cart	\th\	thin
\aů\	out	\th\	this
\ch\	chin	\ü\	food
\e\	pet	\u̇\	foot
\ē\	easy	\y\	yet
\g\	go	\yü\	few
\i\	tip	\yů\	cure
\ī\	life	\zh\	vision
\j\	job		

shoe·string \-ˌstriŋ\ *n* **1** : SHOELACE **2** : a small or barely adequate amount of money or capital ⟨start a business on a *shoestring*⟩ [sense 2 from shoestrings' being a typical item sold by itinerant vendors]

shoe tree *n* : a foot-shaped device for inserting in a shoe to preserve its shape

sho·far \'shō-ˌfär, -fər\ *n, pl* **sho·froth** \shō-'frōt, -'frōth, -'frōs\ : a ram's-horn trumpet used in some synagogue observances [Hebrew *shōphār*]

sho·gun \'shō-gən\ *n* : one of a line of military governors ruling Japan until the revolution of 1867–68 [Japanese *shōgun* "general"] — **sho·gun·ate** \'shō-gə-nət, -ˌnāt\

shone *past of* SHINE

shoo \'shü\ *vt* : to scare, drive, or send away by or as if by crying shoo [Middle English *schowe,* interj. used in frightening away an animal]

¹shook *past or chiefly dialect past participle of* SHAKE

²shook \'shūk\ *n* **1** : a set of pieces of lumber for assembling one hogshead, cask, or barrel **2** : a bundle of parts (as of boxes) ready to be put together [origin unknown]

¹shoot \'shüt\ *vb* **shot** \'shät\; **shoot·ing 1 a** : to let fly or cause to be driven forward with force ⟨*shoot* an arrow⟩ **b** : to cause a missile to be driven forth from : DISCHARGE ⟨*shoot* off a gun⟩ **c** : to cause a weapon to discharge a missile ⟨*shoot* at a target⟩ **d** : to carry when discharged ⟨guns that *shoot* many miles⟩ **e** : to send forth with suddenness or intensity ⟨*shot* us a meaningful look⟩ **f** : to propel (as a ball or puck) toward a goal; *also* : to score by so doing ⟨*shoot* a basket⟩ **g** : PLAY ⟨*shoot* a round of golf⟩ ⟨*shoot* craps⟩ **2 a** : to strike with a missile especially from a bow or gun; *esp* : to wound or kill with a missile discharged from a firearm ⟨*shoot* deer⟩ ⟨*shot* a burglar⟩ **b** : to remove or destroy by use of firearms ⟨*shoot* off a lock⟩ **3** : to push or slide into or out of a fastening ⟨*shot* the door bolt⟩ **4** : to set off : DETONATE ⟨*shoot* off fireworks⟩ **5 a** : to push or thrust forward usually abruptly or swiftly ⟨lizards *shooting* out their tongues⟩ **b** : to sprout or grow rapidly ⟨children *shooting* up into adulthood⟩ **6** : to utter or emit rapidly, suddenly, or with force ⟨*shot* out the answer⟩ **7 a** : to go or pass rapidly and precipitately ⟨*shot* out of the office⟩ ⟨the pain *shot* down my arm⟩ **b** : to pass swiftly along ⟨*shoot* the rapids in a canoe⟩ **c** : to stream out suddenly : SPURT **8 a** : to take the altitude of ⟨*shoot* the sun with a sextant⟩ **b** : to take a picture of : PHOTOGRAPH **c** : to film a scene ⟨the director is ready to *shoot*⟩ [Old English *scēotan*] — **shoot·er** *n* — **shoot at** *or* **shoot for** : to aim at : strive for — **shoot the works** : to put forth all one's efforts or available capital

²shoot *n* **1 a** : the aerial part of a plant : a stem with its leaves and appendages; *also* : a branch or part of a plant developed from a single bud **b** : OFFSHOOT **2 a** : an act or the action of shooting **b** : a hunting trip or party **c** : a shooting match ⟨skeet *shoot*⟩

shooting gallery *n* : a range usually covered and equipped with targets for practice with firearms

shooting iron *n* : FIREARM

shooting star *n* **1** : a meteor appearing as a temporary streak of light in the night sky **2** : a North American perennial herb of the primrose family with entire oblong leaves and showy flowers

¹shop \'shäp\ *n* **1** : a building or room stocked with merchandise for sale : STORE **2** : FACTORY 2, MILL **3 a** : a school laboratory equipped for instruction in manual arts **b** : the art or science of working with tools and machinery **4 a** : a business establishment; *esp* : OFFICE **b** : SHOPTALK [Old English *sceoppa* "booth"]

²shop *vb* **shopped; shop·ping 1** : to examine goods or services with intent to buy or in search of the best buy **2** : to make a search : HUNT ⟨*shopped* around for the best-qualified person⟩ **3** : to examine the stock or offerings of ⟨*shop* the stores for gift ideas⟩

shop·keep·er \'shäp-ˌkē-pər\ *n* : STOREKEEPER

shop·lift·er \'shäp-ˌlif-tər\ *n* : a thief who steals merchandise on display in stores — **shop·lift·ing** \-tiŋ\ *n*

shop·per \'shäp-ər\ *n* **1** : one that shops **2** : one whose occupation is shopping as an agent for customers or for an employer

shopping center *n* : a group of retail and service stores located in a suburban area and provided with extensive parking space

shop steward *n* : a union member elected as the union representative of a shop or department in dealings with the management

shop·talk \'shäp-ˌtok\ *n* : the jargon or subject matter peculiar to an occupation or a special area of interest

shop·worn \-ˌworn, -ˌworn\ *adj* **1** : faded, soiled, or impaired by remaining too long in a store ⟨*shopworn* merchandise⟩ **2** : stale from excessive use or familiarity ⟨a story on a *shopworn* theme⟩ ⟨full of clichés and *shopworn* anecdotes⟩

¹shore \'shōr, 'shor\ *n* : the land bordering a usually large body of water; *esp* : COAST [Middle English]

²shore *vt* : to give support to : BRACE [Middle English *shoren*]

³shore *n* : a prop or brace placed beneath or against something to support it

shore·bird \-ˌbərd\ *n* : any of a group (Charadrii) of birds that frequent the seashore

shore leave *n* : a leave of absence to go on shore granted to a sailor or naval officer

shore·line \-ˌlīn\ *n* : the line where a body of water touches the shore; *also* : the strip of land along this line

shore patrol *n* : a branch of a navy that exercises guard and police functions

shor·ing \'shōr-iŋ, 'shor-\ *n* : a group of shores ⟨the *shoring* for a wall⟩

shorn *past participle of* SHEAR

¹short \'short\ *adj* **1 a** : having little length **b** : not tall : LOW **2 a** : not extended in time : BRIEF ⟨a *short* life⟩ **b** : not retentive ⟨a *short* memory⟩ **c** : QUICK, SPEEDY ⟨made *short* work of the job⟩ **d** : seeming to pass quickly ⟨a few *short* years later⟩ **3 a** : being a syllable or speech sound of relatively little duration **b** : being the member of a pair of similarly spelled vowel or vowel-containing sounds that is descended from a vowel short in duration ⟨*short a* in *fat*⟩ ⟨*short i* in *sin*⟩ **4** : limited in distance ⟨a *short* walk⟩ **5 a** : not sufficient in quantity : INADEQUATE ⟨in *short* supply⟩ **b** : not reaching far enough **c** : inherently or basically weak ⟨*short* on brains⟩ **6 a** : ABRUPT 2b, CURT **b** : quickly provoked ⟨a *short* temper⟩ **7** : containing or cooked with shortening ⟨*short* pastry⟩ **8 a** : not lengthy or drawn out **b** : ABBREVIATED ⟨doc is *short* for doctor⟩ [Old English *scort*] — **short·ish** \-ish\ *adj*

²short *adv* **1** : in a curt manner **2** : BRIEFLY ⟨*short*-lasting⟩ **3** : at a disadvantage : UNAWARES ⟨caught *short*⟩ **4** : so as to interrupt ⟨took us up *short*⟩ **5** : ABRUPTLY, SUDDENLY ⟨stopped *short*⟩ **6** : at some point before a goal or limit aimed at ⟨the arrow fell *short*⟩

³short *n* **1** : the sum and substance : UPSHOT ⟨the *short* of it⟩ **2 a** : a short syllable **b** : a short sound or signal **3** *pl* **a** : a by-product of wheat milling that includes the germ, fine bran, and some flour **b** : refuse, clippings, or trimmings discarded in various manufacturing processes **4** : something that is shorter than the usual or regular length **5** *pl* **a** : knee-length or less than knee-length trousers **b** : short underpants **6** : SHORT CIRCUIT — **in short** : by way of summary : BRIEFLY

⁴short *vt* : SHORT-CIRCUIT

short·age \'short-ij\ *n* : a lack in the amount needed : DEFICIT ⟨a *shortage* in the accounts⟩

short·bread \'short-ˌbred\ *n* : a thick cookie made of flour, sugar, and much shortening

short·cake \-ˌkāk\ *n* **1** : a crisp and often unsweetened biscuit or cookie **2** : a dessert made of usually very short baking-powder-biscuit dough baked and spread with sweetened fruit

short·change \-'chānj\ *vt* **1** : to give less than the correct amount of change to **2** : to deprive of something due : CHEAT — **short·chang·er** *n*

short–cir·cuit \'shȯrt-'sər-kət\ *vb* **1** : to make a short circuit in or have a short circuit **2** : BYPASS

short circuit *n* : a connection of comparatively low resistance accidentally or intentionally made between points in an electric circuit between which the resistance is normally much greater

short·com·ing \'shȯrt-,kəm-ing, shȯrt-'kəm-, 'shȯrt-'kəm-\ *n* : the state, fact, or an instance of falling below a standard

short·cut \'shȯrt-,kət, -'kət\ *n* **1** : a route more direct than that usually taken **2** : a quicker way of doing something

short–day \'shȯrt-,dā\ *adj* : flowering or developing to maturity only in response to alternating short light and long dark periods — compare DAY-NEUTRAL, LONG-DAY

short division *n* : mathematical division in which the successive steps are performed without writing out the remainders

short·en \'shȯrt-n\ *vb* **short·ened; short·en·ing** \'shȯrt-ning, -n-ing\ : to make or become short or shorter — **short·en·er** \'shȯrt-nər, -n-ər\ *n* □ SYN CURTAIL, ABBREVIATE: SHORTEN may imply reduction either in extent or duration; CURTAIL adds an implication of a cutting off that deprives of completeness or adequacy ⟨rain *curtailed* the ceremony⟩ ABBREVIATE applies chiefly to the shortening of the written form of a word or phrase by omission of parts ⟨Doctor can be *abbreviated* to Dr.⟩

short·en·ing \'shȯrt-ning, -n-ing\ *n* **1** : a making or becoming short or shorter **2** : an edible fat (as butter or lard) used in baking

short·hand \'shȯrt-,hand\ *n* : a method of writing rapidly by substituting characters, abbreviations, or symbols for letters, words, or phrases : STENOGRAPHY — **shorthand** *adj*

short·hand·ed \-'han-dəd\ *adj* : having or working with fewer than the usual number of people

short–haul \-,hȯl\ *adj* : traveling or involving a short distance ⟨*short-haul* flights⟩

short·horn \'shȯrt-,hȯrn\ *n, often cap* : any of a breed of red, roan, or white beef cattle originating in the north of England and including good milk-producing strains from which a distinct breed has been evolved — called also *Durham*

short–horned \-'hȯrnd\ *adj* : having short horns or antennae

short–horned grasshopper *n* : any of a family of grasshoppers with short antennae

short hundredweight *n* : HUNDREDWEIGHT 1

short–lived \'shȯrt-'līvd, -'livd\ *adj* : not living or lasting long

short·ly \'shȯrt-lē\ *adv* **1 a** : in a few words : BRIEFLY **b** : in an abrupt manner : CURTLY **2 a** : in a short time : SOON ⟨will arrive *shortly*⟩ **b** : at a short interval ⟨*shortly* after⟩

short·ness \'shȯrt-nəs\ *n* : the quality or state of being short

short–or·der \-,ȯrd-ər\ *adj* : preparing or serving food that can be cooked quickly when a customer orders it

short ribs *n pl* : a cut of beef consisting of rib ends between the rib roast and the plate

short shrift *n* **1** : a brief respite from death **2** : little consideration

short·sight·ed \'shȯrt-'sīt-əd\ *adj* **1** : NEARSIGHTED, MYOPIC **2** : characterized by lack of foresight — **short·sight·ed·ly** *adv* — **short·sight·ed·ness** *n*

short·stop \'shȯrt-,stäp\ *n* **1** : the position of the baseball player defending the area on the third-base side of second base **2** : the player stationed in the shortstop position

short story *n* : an invented prose narrative usually dealing with a few characters and aiming at developing a single episode or creating a single mood

short–tem·pered \'shȯrt-'tem-pərd\ *adj* : having a quick temper : easily angered

short–term \-'tərm\ *adj* **1** : occurring over or involving a relatively short period of time **2** : of or relating to a financial transaction based on a term usually of less than a year

short ton *n* : a unit of weight — see MEASURE table

short·wave \-'wāv\ *n* : a radio wave having a wavelength between 10 and 100 meters

short–wind·ed \-'win-dəd\ *adj* : affected with or characterized by shortness of breath

Sho·shone \shə-'shō-nē, -'shōn; 'shō-,shōn\ *or* **Sho·sho·ni** \shə-'shō-nē\ *n, pl* **Shoshones** *or* **Shoshoni** *also* **Shoshone** *or* **Shoshonis** : a member of a group of Indian peoples of the Great Basin having an Aztec-related language

¹shot \'shät\ *n* **1 a** : an action of shooting **b** : a directed propelling of a missile (as an arrow, stone, or rocket); *esp* : a directed discharge of a gun or cannon **c** : a stroke or throw in a game; *esp* : an attempt at scoring **d** : a setting off of an explosive ⟨a nuclear *shot*⟩ **e** : an injection of something (as a medicine or antibody) into the body **2 a** *pl* **shot** : something propelled by shooting; *esp* : small lead or steel pellets fired from a shotgun **b** : a metal sphere of iron or brass that is put for distance **3 a** : the distance that a missile is or can be thrown **b** : RANGE, REACH ⟨not within rifle *shot*⟩ **4** : one that shoots : MARKSMAN **5 a** : ATTEMPT, TRY ⟨take another *shot* at the puzzle⟩ **b** : CHANCE ⟨the horse was a 10 to 1 *shot*⟩ **6** : a remark so directed as to have telling effect **7 a** : PHOTOGRAPH **b** : a single sequence of a motion picture or a television program shot by one camera without interruption **8 a** : a single drink of liquor **b** : a portion (as of medicine) taken at one time [Old English *scot*]

²shot *past and past participle of* SHOOT

³shot *adj* **1 a** : having contrasting and changeable color effects : IRIDESCENT ⟨blue silk *shot* with silver⟩ **b** : suffused or streaked with a color ⟨hair *shot* with gray⟩ **c** : pervaded by a contrasting element ⟨satire *shot* with sympathy⟩ **2** : reduced to ruin or collapse ⟨the business was *shot*⟩

shot·gun \'shät-,gən\ *n* : a gun with a smooth bore used to fire shot at short range

shot hole *n* **1** : a drilled hole in which a charge of dynamite is exploded **2** : a hole made usually by a boring insect

shot put *n* : a field event in which the shot is put for distance — **shot–put·ter** \-,pu̇t-ər\ *n* — **shot–put·ting** \-,pu̇t-ing\ *n*

should \shəd, shu̇d, 'shu̇d\ *past of* SHALL — used as an auxiliary verb to express (1) condition or possibility ⟨if you *should* see them, tell them this⟩, (2) obligation or propriety ⟨you *should* brush your teeth regularly⟩, (3) futurity from the point of view in the past ⟨thought I *should* soon be free⟩, (4) what is probable or expected ⟨they *should* be here soon⟩, and (5) politeness in softening a request or assertion ⟨I *should* like some coffee⟩ [Old English *sceolde* "owed, was obliged to"]

¹shoul·der \'shōl-dər\ *n* **1 a** : the laterally projecting part of the human body formed of the bones and joints by which the arm is connected with the trunk together with the muscles covering these **b** : the corresponding but usually less projecting part of a lower vertebrate **2** : a cut of meat including the upper joint of the foreleg and adjacent parts **3** : the part of a garment at the wearer's shoulder **4** : a part or projection resembling a human shoulder ⟨*shoulder* of a hill⟩ **5** : either edge of a road; *esp* : the part of a road outside of the traveled way [Old English *sculdor*]

²shoulder *vb* **shoul·dered; shoul·der·ing** \-də-ring, -dring\ **1** : to push or thrust with the shoulder : JOSTLE

shorthorn

⟨*shouldered* my way through the crowd⟩ **2 a :** to place or bear on the shoulder ⟨*shouldered* the knapsack⟩ **b :** to assume the burden or responsibility of ⟨*shoulder* the blame⟩

shoulder blade *n* : a large triangular bone of the back part of the shoulder that is the principal bone of the corresponding half of the shoulder girdle and articulates with the corresponding clavicle or coracoid to form a socket for the humerus of the arm — called also *scapula*

shoulder girdle *n* : PECTORAL GIRDLE

shoulder strap : a strap that passes over the shoulder and holds up an article or garment

should·est \'shūd-əst\ *archaic past 2d sing of* SHALL

shouldn't \'shūd-nt\ : should not

shouldst \shədst, shūdst, 'shūdst\ *archaic past 2d sing of* SHALL

¹shout \'shaut\ *vb* **1 :** to utter a sudden loud cry ⟨*shouted* with delight⟩ **2 :** to utter in a loud voice ⟨*shouted* insults⟩ [Middle English *shouten*] — **shout·er** *n*

²shout *n* : a loud cry or call

shouting distance *n* : easy reach ⟨lived within *shouting distance* of their cousins⟩

¹shove \'shəv\ *vb* **1 :** to push with steady force **2 :** to push carelessly or rudely ⟨*shove* a person out of the way⟩ [Old English *scūfan* "to thrust away"] SYN *see* PUSH — **shov·er** *n*

²shove *n* : an act or instance of shoving : a forcible push

¹shov·el \'shəv-əl\ *n* **1 :** an implement consisting of a broad often curved blade attached to a long handle used for lifting and throwing loose material **2 :** SHOV-ELFUL [Old English *scofl*]

²shovel *vb* **shov·eled** *or* **shov·elled; shov·el·ing** *or* **shov·el·ling** \'shəv-ling, -ə-ling\ **1 :** to take up and throw with a shovel **2 :** to dig or clean out with a shovel **3 :** to throw or convey roughly or in the mass as if with a shovel ⟨*shovel* food into one's mouth⟩

shov·el·er *or* **shov·el·ler** \'shəv-lər, -ə-lər\ *n* **1 :** one that shovels **2 :** any of several river ducks having a large and very broad bill

shov·el·ful \'shəv-əl-ˌful\ *n, pl* **shovelfuls** \-ˌfulz\ *or* **shov·els·ful** \-əlz-ˌful\ : the amount held by a shovel

shov·el·man \-ˌman, -mən\ *n* : one who works with a hand or power shovel

shov·el–nosed \ˌshəv-əl-'nōzd\ *adj* : having a broad flat head, nose, or beak

¹show \'shō\ *vb* **showed; shown** \'shōn\ *or* **showed; showing** **1 :** to place in sight : DISPLAY **2 :** to reveal by one's condition, nature, or behavior **3 :** GRANT, BE-STOW ⟨the king *showed* no mercy⟩ **4 :** TEACH ⟨*showed* me how to knit⟩ **5 :** PROVE ⟨the result *showed* that we were right⟩ **6 :** DIRECT, GUIDE ⟨*show* a visitor to the door⟩ **7 :** APPEAR ⟨anger *showed* in their faces⟩ **8 :** to be noticeable ⟨the patch hardly *shows*⟩ **9 :** to finish third or at least third in a horse race [Old English *scēawian* "to look, look at, see"] □ SYN SHOW, EXHIB-IT, DISPLAY mean to present so as to invite notice or attention. SHOW implies enabling another to see or examine ⟨*showed* me a picture of the lake⟩ EXHIBIT implies putting forward openly or publicly ⟨*exhibit* paintings at a gallery⟩ DISPLAY stresses putting in position where others may see to advantage ⟨*display* sale items⟩

²show *n* **1 :** a demonstrative display ⟨a *show* of strength⟩ **2 a :** a false semblance : PRETENSE ⟨made a *show* of friendship⟩ **b :** a more or less true appearance of something : SIGN ⟨a *show* of reason⟩ **c :** an impressive display **3 :** something exhibited especially for wonder or ridicule : SPECTACLE **4 :** a public presentation: as **a :** a competitive exhibition (as of animals) to demonstrate quality **b :** a theatrical presentation **c :** a radio or television program **d :** ENTERTAINMENT 3 **5 :** ENTERPRISE, AFFAIR ⟨ran the whole *show*⟩ **6 :** third place at the finish of a horse race

shrew 1

show·biz \'shō-ˌbiz\ *n* : SHOW BUSINESS

show·boat \'shō-ˌbōt\ *n* : a river steamboat containing a theater and carrying a troupe of actors to give plays at river communities

show business *n* : the arts, occupations, and businesses (as theater, motion pictures, and television) that comprise the entertainment industry

show·case \-ˌkās\ *n* : a glass case or box to display and protect wares in a store or articles in a museum

show·down \-ˌdaun\ *n* : the final settlement of a contested issue; *also* : the test of strength by which a contested issue is resolved

¹show·er \'shau-ər, 'shaur\ *n* **1 a :** a fall of rain of short duration **b :** a like fall of sleet, hail, or snow **2 :** something resembling a rain shower ⟨a *shower* of sparks⟩ ⟨a *shower* of tears⟩ **3 :** a party given by friends who bring gifts often of a particular kind ⟨a linen *shower* for a bride⟩ **4 :** SHOWER BATH [Old English *scūr*] — **show·ery** \-ē\ *adj*

²shower *vb* **1 :** to fall in or as if in a shower **2 :** to bathe in a shower bath **3 :** to wet copiously in a spray, fine stream, or drops **4 :** to give in abundance ⟨*showered* them with gifts⟩

³show·er \'shō-ər, 'shōr\ *n* : one that shows : EXHIBITOR

shower bath *n* : a bath in which water is sprayed on the person; *also* : the apparatus that provides such a bath

show·ing \'shō-ing\ *n* **1 :** an act of putting something on view : EXHIBITION ⟨a *showing* of fall fashions⟩ ⟨a *showing* of a new feature film⟩ **2 :** PERFORMANCE, RE-CORD ⟨made a good *showing* in the tournament⟩

show·man \'shō-mən\ *n* **1 :** the producer of a theatrical show **2 :** a person having a sense or knack for dramatization or visual effectiveness — **show·man·ship** \-ˌship\ *n*

show–off \'shō-ˌof\ *n* **1 :** conspicuous behavior **2 :** one that shows off

show off \shō-'of, 'shō-\ *vb* **1 :** to display proudly **2 :** to seek to attract attention by conspicuous behavior

show·piece \-ˌpēs\ *n* : a prime or outstanding example used for exhibition

show·place \-ˌplās\ *n* : a place exhibited or regarded as an example of beauty or excellence

show·room \-ˌrüm, -ˌrum\ *n* : a room used for the display of merchandise or of samples

show up *vb* **1 :** to reveal the true nature of : EXPOSE ⟨*showed up* their ignorance⟩ **2 :** ARRIVE ⟨*showed up* late⟩ **3 :** to be visible or evident ⟨*shows up* well in this light⟩

showy \'shō-ē\ *adj* **show·i·er; -est** **1 :** making an attractive show ⟨*showy* blossoms⟩ **2 :** GAUDY — **show·i·ly** \'shō-ə-lē\ *adv* — **show·i·ness** \'shō-ē-nəs\ *n*

shrap·nel \'shrap-nəl\ *n, pl* **shrapnel** **1 :** a projectile that consists of a case provided with a powder charge and a large number of usually lead balls and is exploded in flight **2 :** bomb, mine, or shell fragments [Henry *Shrapnel,* died 1842, English artillery officer]

¹shred \'shred\ *n* : a long narrow strip from a larger body of the same material ⟨*shreds* of cloth⟩; *also* : PAR-TICLE, SCRAP ⟨hadn't a *shred* of evidence⟩ [Old English *scrēade*]

²shred *vb* **shred·ded; shred·ding** **1 :** to cut or tear into shreds **2 :** to break up into shreds — **shred·der** *n*

shrew \'shrü\ *n* **1 :** any of numerous small chiefly nocturnal mammals related to the moles, somewhat resembling mice, but having a long pointed snout, very small eyes, and velvety fur **2 :** a woman who scolds or quarrels constantly [Old English *scrēawa*]

shrewd \'shrüd\ *adj* **1 a :** SEVERE, HARD ⟨a *shrewd* blow⟩ **b :** CUTTING 2 ⟨a *shrewd* wind⟩ **2 :** marked by cleverness, discernment, or sagacity ⟨*shrewd* observer⟩ [Middle English *shrewed* "shrewish, evil, severe", from *shrewe* "shrew" + *-ed*] — **shrewd·ly** *adv* — **shrewd·ness** *n* □ SYN SHREWD, ASTUTE, SAGACIOUS mean acute in perception and sound in judgment. SHREWD implies native cleverness, hardheadedness, and an ability to see beneath the surface; **ASTUTE** stresses shrewdness in practical affairs and especially connotes an ability to act successfully in one's own interests; **SAGACIOUS** suggests native shrewdness matured by experience into practical wisdom and far-sightedness.

shrew·ish \'shrü-ish\ *adj* : **QUARRELSOME, ILL-TEMPERED** — **shrew·ish·ly** *adv* — **shrew·ish·ness** *n*

¹shriek \'shrēk\ *vb* **1** : to utter a loud shrill cry or sound **2** : to utter with a shriek or sharply and shrilly [probably from Middle English *shriken*]

²shriek *n* **1** : a shrill usually wild or involuntary cry **2** : a sound like a shriek ⟨a *shriek* of escaping steam⟩ **SYN** see **SCREAM**

shrie·val \'shrē-vəl\ *adj* : of or relating to a sheriff [obsolete *shrieve* "sheriff", from Old English *scīrgerēfa*] — **shrie·val·ty** \-tē\ *n*

shrift \'shrift\ *n, archaic* : the confession of sins to a priest or the hearing of a confession by a priest [Old English *scrift*, from *scrīfan* "to shrive"]

shrike \'shrīk\ *n* : any of numerous usually largely gray or brownish singing birds that have a strong notched bill hooked at the tip, feed chiefly on insects, and often impale their prey on thorns [perhaps from Old English *scrīc* "thrush"]

¹shrill \'shril\ *vb* : to utter or emit a sharp piercing sound : **SCREAM** [Middle English *shrillen*]

²shrill *adj* **1** : having, emitting, or being a sharp high-pitched tone or sound ⟨a *shrill* whistle⟩ **2** : accompanied by sharp high-pitched sounds or cries ⟨*shrill* gaiety⟩ **3** : having an intense or vivid effect on the senses — **shrill** *adv* — **shrill·ness** *n* — **shril·ly** \'shril-lē\ *adv*

³shrill *n* : a shrill sound

¹shrimp \'shrimp\ *n, pl* **shrimp** *or* **shrimps** **1** : any of numerous small mostly marine crustaceans related to the lobsters and having a long slender body, compressed abdomen, and long legs; *also* : any small crustacean resembling a true shrimp **2** : a very small or puny person or thing [Middle English *shrimpe*]

²shrimp *vi* : to fish for or catch shrimp

¹shrine \'shrīn\ *n* **1** : a case or box for sacred relics (as the bones of a saint) **2 a** : the tomb of a saint **b** : a place in which devotion is paid to a saint or deity **c** : a niche containing a religious image **3** : a place or object hallowed because of its associations ⟨Westminster Abbey is a *shrine* for tourists⟩ [Old English *scrīn*, from Latin *scrinium* "case, chest"]

²shrine *vt* : **ENSHRINE**

shrin·er \'shrī-nər\ *n* : a member of a secret fraternal society called the Ancient Arabic Order of Nobles of the Mystic Shrine

¹shrink \'shringk\ *vb* **shrank** \'shrangk\ *also* **shrunk** \'shrəngk\; **shrunk**; **shrink·ing** **1** : to contract or curl up the body or part of it : **HUDDLE, COWER** ⟨*shrink* in horror⟩ **2 a** : to become or cause to become smaller or more compacted ⟨the sweater *shrank* when it was washed⟩ **b** : to lose substance or weight ⟨meat *shrinks* in cooking⟩ **c** : to lessen in amount or value ⟨their fortune *shrank* during the depression⟩ **3** : to draw back ⟨*shrink* from a quarrel⟩ [Old English *scrincan*] — **shrink·able** \'shring-kə-bəl\ *adj* — **shrink·er** *n*

²shrink *n* **1** : the act of shrinking **2** *slang* : **PSYCHIATRIST**

shrink·age \'shring-kij\ *n* **1** : the act or process of shrinking **2** : the amount lost by shrinkage

shrinking violet *n* : a bashful or retiring person; *esp* : one who shrinks from public recognition

shrive \'shrīv\ *vb* **shrived** *or* **shrove** \'shrōv\; **shriv·en** \'shriv-ən\ *or* **shrived**; **shriv·ing** \'shrī-ving\ **1** : to hear the confession of and administer the sacrament of penance to : **PARDON** **2** : to confess one's sins especially to a priest [Old English *scrīfan* "to shrive, prescribe", from Latin *scribere* "to write"]

shriv·el \'shriv-əl\ *vb* **shriv·eled** *or* **shriv·elled**; **shriv·el·ing** *or* **shriv·el·ling** \'shriv-ling, -ə-ling\ **1** : to draw into wrinkles especially with a loss of moisture **2** : to

reduce or become reduced to weakness, helplessness, or inefficiency [origin unknown] **SYN** see **WITHER**

Shrop·shire \'shräp-,shiər, -shər, *especially in the United States* -,shir\ *n* : any of an English breed of dark-faced hornless mutton-type sheep that yield a heavy fleece [*Shropshire,* England]

¹shroud \'shraud\ *n* **1** : burial garment : **WINDING-SHEET** **2** : something that covers, screens, or guards ⟨a *shroud* of secrecy⟩ **3 a** : one of the lines leading usually in pairs from the top of a mast to provide lateral support to the mast **b** : one of the cords that suspend the harness of a parachute from the canopy [Old English *scrūd* "garment"]

²shroud *vt* **1 a** : to cut off from view : **SCREEN** ⟨trees *shrouded* in heavy mist⟩ **b** : to veil under another appearance ⟨*shrouded* in mystery⟩ **2** : to dress for burial

Shrove·tide \'shrōv-,tīd\ *n* : the period of three days immediately preceding Ash Wednesday [Middle English *schroftide*]

Shrove Tuesday \'shrōv-\ *n* : the Tuesday before Ash Wednesday

¹shrub \'shrəb\ *n* : a low usually several-stemmed woody plant — compare **HERB, TREE** [Old English *scrybb* "brushwood"]

²shrub *n* **1** : a beverage that consists of an alcoholic liquor, fruit juice, fruit rind, and sugar **2** : a beverage made by adding acidulated fruit juice to iced water [Arabic *sharāb* "beverage"]

shrub·bery \'shrəb-rē, -ə-rē\ *n, pl* **-ber·ies** : a planting or growth of shrubs

shrub·by \'shrəb-ē\ *adj* **shrub·bi·er; -est** **1** : consisting of or covered with shrubs **2** : resembling a shrub

¹shrug \'shrəg\ *vb* **shrugged; shrug·ging** : to raise or draw in the shoulders especially to express lack of interest or dislike [Middle English *schruggen*]

²shrug *n* **1** : an act of shrugging **2** : a woman's small waist-length or shorter jacket

shrug off *vt* **1** : to brush aside : **MINIMIZE** **2** : to shake off **3** : to remove (a garment) by wriggling out

shrunk·en \'shrəng-kən\ *adj* **1** : diminished or contracted especially in size or value ⟨the *shrunken* dollar⟩ **2** : having been subjected to a shrinking process

¹shuck \'shək\ *n* **1** : **SHELL, HUSK**: as **a** : the outer covering of a nut or Indian corn **b** : the shell of an oyster or clam **2** : something of little value ⟨not worth *shucks*⟩ [origin unknown]

²shuck *vt* **1** : to strip of shucks **2** : **REMOVE** ⟨*shucked* their clothes off⟩

¹shud·der \'shəd-ər\ *vi* **shud·dered; shud·der·ing** \'shəd-ring, -ə-ring\ **1** : to tremble convulsively : **SHIVER** ⟨*shuddered* to think of the accident⟩ **2** : **QUIVER** ⟨the train *shuddered* to a halt⟩ [Middle English *shodderen*]

²shudder *n* : an act of shuddering — **shud·dery** \-ə-rē\ *adj*

¹shuf·fle \'shəf-əl\ *vb* **shuf·fled; shuf·fling** \'shəf-ling, -ə-ling\ **1** : to mix in a mass confusedly : **JUMBLE** **2** : to put or thrust aside or under cover **3 a** : to mix (as a pack of cards) so that cards will later appear in random order **b** : to move about, back and forth, or from one place to another **4 a** : to move (as the feet) by sliding along or dragging back and forth without lifting **b** : to perform (as a dance) with a dragging sliding step **5** : to get into or out of (a situation) especially by trickery : **WORM** ⟨*shuffle* out of a difficulty⟩ **6** : to act or speak in an evasive manner [perhaps from ¹*shove*] — **shuf·fler** \-lər, -ə-lər\ *n*

²shuffle *n* **1** : evasion of an issue : **EQUIVOCATION** **2 a** : an act of shuffling **b** : a right or turn to shuffle cards **c** : **JUMBLE** **3 a** : a dragging sliding movement; *esp* : a sliding or scraping step in dancing **b** : a dance characterized by such a step

shuf·fle·board \'shəf-əl-,bōrd, -,bord\ *n* **1** : a game in which players try to push disks into scoring areas of a diagram marked on a smooth surface **2** : the diagram

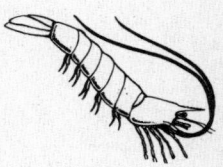

¹shrimp 1

or court on which shuffleboard is played [alteration of obsolete *shove-board*]

shul \'shul\ *n* : SYNAGOGUE [Yiddish, school, synagogue]

shun \'shən\ *vt* **shunned; shun·ning** : to avoid deliberately and especially habitually [Old English *scunian*] — **shun·ner** *n*

shun·pike \'shən-,pīk\ *n* : a side road used to avoid tolls on a turnpike

¹shunt \'shənt\ *vb* 1 : to turn off to one side : SHIFT; *esp* : to switch (as a train) from one track to another 2 : to provide with or divert by means of an electrical shunt 3 : to travel back and forth [Middle English *shunten* "to flinch"] — **shunt·er** *n*

²shunt *n* : a means or mechanism for turning or thrusting aside: as **a** *chiefly British* : a railroad switch **b** : a conductor joining two points in an electrical circuit so as to form a parallel or alternative path through which a portion of the current may pass

shush \'shəsh, 'shùsh\ *n* : a sibilant sound uttered to demand silence [imitative] — **shush** *vt*

shut \'shət\ *vb* **shut; shut·ting** 1 : to close or become closed by bringing openings or covering parts together ⟨*shut* one's eyes⟩ 2 : to prevent entrance to or passage to or from 3 : to hold within limits by or as if by enclosure : IMPRISON ⟨*shut* up in a stalled elevator⟩ 4 : to cease or cause to cease operation ⟨the epidemic *shut* down the school⟩ [Old English *scyttan*]

shut·down \'shət-,daùn\ *n* : a temporary or permanent ending of an activity (as work in a factory)

shut–eye \'shət-,ī\ *n* : SLEEP 1

shut–in \,shət-,in\ *adj* : confined by illness or incapacity — **shut–in** \'shət-,in\ *n*

shut·off \'shət-,óf\ *n* 1 : something that shuts off 2 : INTERRUPTION, STOPPAGE

shut·out \'shət-,aùt\ *n* : a game or contest in which one side is prevented from scoring

shut out \'shət-'aùt, ,shət-\ *vt* 1 : to keep out : EXCLUDE 2 : to prevent (an opponent) from scoring in a game or contest

¹shut·ter \'shət-ər\ *n* 1 : one that shuts 2 : a usually movable cover or screen for a window or door 3 : the part of a camera that opens and closes to expose the film

²shutter *vt* : to close with or by shutters

shut·ter·bug \-,bəg\ *n* : a photography enthusiast

¹shut·tle \'shət-l\ *n* 1 **a** : an instrument used in weaving to carry the thread back and forth from side to side through the threads that run lengthwise **b** : a spindle-shaped device holding the thread in tatting or netting **c** : any of various thread holders for the lower thread of a sewing machine that carry the lower thread through a loop of the upper thread to make a stitch 2 **a** : a going back and forth regularly over a specified and often short route by a vehicle **b** : a vehicle used in a shuttle ⟨a *shuttle* bus⟩ [Middle English *shittle, schutylle*]

²shuttle *vb* **shut·tled; shut·tling** \'shət-ling, -l-ing\ 1 : to move or travel back and forth frequently 2 : to move by or as if by a shuttle

¹shut·tle·cock \'shət-l-,käk\ *n* : a lightweight conical object with a rounded often rubber-covered nose used in badminton and usually made of molded plastic or a rounded cork with feathers stuck in one side

²shuttlecock *vb* : to send, toss, or go to and fro

shut up *vb* 1 : to cause (a person) to stop talking 2 : to stop writing or speaking

¹shy \'shī\ *adj* **shi·er** *or* **shy·er** \'shī-ər, 'shīr\; **shi·est** *or* **shy·est** \'shī-əst\ 1 : easily frightened : TIMID 2 : disposed to avoid a person or thing : DISTRUSTFUL 3 : hesitant in committing oneself : CHARY 4 : marked by sensitive diffidence : BASHFUL 5 : having less than the proper amount or number : SHORT [Old English *scēoh*] — **shy·ly** *adv* — **shy·ness** *n* □ SYN BASHFUL, MODEST, COY: SHY implies a timid shrinking from contact or fa-

miliarity with others; BASHFUL implies a hesitant shyness characteristic of childhood; MODEST suggests an absence of undue confidence or conceit; COY implies deliberately assumed or affected shyness.

²shy *vi* **shied; shy·ing** 1 : to draw back in sudden dislike or distaste : RECOIL ⟨*shied* from publicity⟩ ⟨*shied* at the idea of encouraging revolutionaries⟩ 2 : to start suddenly aside through fright or alarm ⟨the horse *shied* at a blowing paper⟩

³shy *n, pl* **shies** : a sudden start aside (as of a horse)

⁴shy *vt* **shied; shy·ing** : to throw with a jerk : FLING [perhaps from **¹shy**]

⁵shy *n, pl* **shies** : the act of shying : TOSS

shy·ster \'shī-stər\ *n* : an unscrupulous lawyer or politician [probably from *Scheuster,* 19th century American attorney frequently rebuked in a New York court for pettifoggery]

si \'sē\ *n* : the 7th note of the diatonic scale : TI [Italian]

¹Si·a·mese \,sī-ə-'mēz, -'mēs\ *adj* 1 : of, relating to, or characteristic of Thailand, the Thais, or their language 2 : exhibiting great resemblance : very like [*Siam* (Thailand); sense 2 from *Siamese twin*]

²Siamese *n, pl* **Siamese** 1 : THAI 1 2 : THAI 2

Siamese cat *n* : a slender blue-eyed short-haired domestic cat of a breed of oriental origin with pale body and darker ears, paws, tail, and face

Siamese twin *n* : either of a pair of human or animal twins born joined together [Chang, died 1874, and Eng, died 1874, congenitally united twins born in Siam]

sib \'sib\ *n* 1 : KINDRED; *also* : a group of persons descended from the same real or supposed ancestor 2 : one closely related to another : a blood relation 3 : SIBLING [Old English *sibb* "related by blood", from *sibb* "kinship"] — **sib** *adj*

Si·be·ri·an husky \sī-,bir-ē-ən-\ *n* : any of a breed of medium-sized compact dogs developed as sled dogs in northeastern Siberia that resemble the Alaskan malamutes

¹sib·i·lant \'sib-ə-lənt\ *adj* : having, containing, or producing the sound of or a sound resembling that of the *s* or the *sh* in *sash* [Latin *sibilare* "to hiss, whistle"]

²sibilant *n* : a sibilant speech sound (as English \s\, \z\, \sh\, \zh\, \ch (=tsh)\, or \j (=dzh)\)

sib·ling \'sib-ling\ *n* : a brother or sister without regard to sex; *also* : one of two or more individuals having one common parent

sib·yl \'sib-əl\ *n, often cap* 1 : any of several ancient prophetesses 2 **a** : a female prophet **b** : FORTUNE-TELLER [Latin *sibylla,* from Greek] — **si·byl·ic** *or* **si·byl·lic** \sə-'bil-ik\ *adj* — **sib·yl·line** \'sib-ə-,līn\ *adj*

¹sic *or* **sick** \'sik\ *vt* **sicced** *or* **sicked** \'sikt\; **sic·cing** *or* **sick·ing** \'sik-ing\ : to attack or cause to attack or chase — usually used as a command to a dog ⟨*sic* 'em⟩ [alteration of *seek*]

²sic \'sik, 'sēk\ *adv* : intentionally so written — used after a printed word or passage to indicate that it reproduces an original ⟨said they seed [*sic*] it all⟩ [Latin, "so, thus"]

sic·ca·tive \'sik-ət-iv\ *n* : DRIER 2 [Late Latin *siccativus* "making dry", from Latin *siccare* "to dry", from *siccus* "dry"]

sick \'sik\ *adj* 1 **a** (1) : affected with disease or ill health (2) : of, relating to, or intended for use in sickness ⟨*sick* pay⟩ ⟨a *sick* ward⟩ **b** : NAUSEATED, QUEASY ⟨*sick* to one's stomach⟩ **c** : undergoing menstruation 2 : spiritually or morally unsound or corrupt 3 **a** : sickened by strong emotion ⟨*sick* with shame⟩ **b** : disgusted by some excess ⟨*sick* of flattery⟩ **c** : depressed and longing for something ⟨*sick* at heart⟩ 4 : mentally or emotionally unsound or disordered ⟨*sick* thoughts⟩ 5 : lacking or declining in vigor ⟨a *sick* market⟩ [Old English *sēoc*] □ SYN SICK, ILL mean not being in good health. SICK is the common general term in American

Siamese cat

use but not in British use where ILL is preferred and SICK usually restricted to mean violently nauseated.

sick bay *n* : a compartment in a ship used as a dispensary and hospital

sick·bed \'sik-,bed\ *n* : the bed of a sick person

sick call *n* : a scheduled time when persons (as soldiers) may report as sick to the medical officer

sick·en \'sik-ən\ *vb* **sick·ened; sick·en·ing** \'sik-ning, -ə-ning\ : to make or become sick — **sick·en·er** \'sik-nər, -ə-nər\ *n*

sick·en·ing *adj* : causing sickness : NAUSEATING — **sick·en·ing·ly** \'sik-ning-lē, -ə-ning-\ *adv*

sick headache *n* : MIGRAINE

sick·ish \'sik-ish\ *adj* **1** : somewhat nauseated : QUEASY **2** : somewhat sickening ⟨a *sickish* odor⟩ — **sick·ish·ly** *adv* — **sick·ish·ess** *n*

¹sick·le \'sik-əl\ *n* **1 a** : a cutting tool consisting of a curved metal blade with a short handle **b** : a cutting mechanism (as of a combine) consisting of a bar with a series of cutting elements **2** *cap* : a group of six stars in the constellation Leo [Old English *sicol*, from Latin *secula*] — **sickle** *adj*

²sickle *vb* **sick·led; sick·ling** \'sik-ling, -ə-ling\ : to form into a crescent ⟨the ability of red blood cells to *sickle*⟩

sick leave *n* **1** : an absence from duty or work permitted because of illness **2** : the number of days per year allowed an employee for sickness

sickle cell *n* : an abnormal red blood cell of crescent shape

sickle–cell anemia *n* : a chronic inherited anemia that occurs especially in Negroes and is characterized by sickle cells in the circulating blood

sickle–cell trait *n* : an inherited blood condition in which some red blood cells tend to sickle but not usually enough to produce anemia and which occurs especially in Negroes

sick·ly \'sik-lē\ *adj* **sick·li·er; -est 1** : somewhat unwell; *also* : habitually ailing **2** : produced by or associated with sickness ⟨a *sickly* complexion⟩ ⟨a *sickly* appetite⟩ **3** : producing or tending to sickness ⟨a *sickly* climate⟩ **4** : appearing as if sick: **a** : LANGUID, PALE ⟨a *sickly* flame⟩ **b** : WRETCHED, UNEASY ⟨a *sickly* smile⟩ **c** : lacking in vigor : WEAK ⟨a *sickly* plant⟩ **5** : SICKENING — **sick·li·ness** \'sik-lē-nəs\ *n* — **sickly** *adv*

sick·ness \'sik-nəs\ *n* **1** : ill health : ILLNESS **2** : a specific disease : MALADY **3** : NAUSEA 1

sick·room \'sik-,rüm, -,rùm\ *n* : a room in which a person is confined by sickness

sid·dur \'sid-ər, -,ùr\ *n, pl* **sid·du·rim** \sə-'dùr-əm\ : a Jewish prayer book containing Hebrew and Aramaic prayers used in the daily liturgy [Late Hebrew *siddūr*, literally, "order, arrangement"]

¹side \'sīd\ *n* **1** : the right or left part of the trunk or wall of the body; *also* : the entire right or left half of an animal body ⟨a *side* of beef⟩ **2** : a place, space, or direction with respect to a center line (as of an aisle, river, or street) **3** : a surface forming a border or face of an object **4** : an outer portion of a thing considered as facing in a particular direction ⟨the upper *side*⟩ **5** : a slope or declivity of a hill or ridge **6 a** : a bounding line of a geometrical figure ⟨*side* of a square⟩ **b** : one of the surfaces that delimit a solid; *esp* : one of the longer surfaces **c** : either surface of a thin object ⟨one *side* of a record⟩ **7** : the space beside one **8** : the attitude or activity of one person or group with respect to another : PART **9** : a body of partisans or contestants ⟨victory for neither *side*⟩ **10** : a line of descent traced through either parent **11** : an aspect or part of something held to be contrasted with some other aspect or part ⟨the better *side* of one's nature⟩ **12** : MEMBER 3b [Old English *side*] — **on the side 1** : in addition to the main portion **2** : in addition to a principal occupation ⟨selling insurance *on the side*⟩

²side *adj* **1** : of, relating to, or situated on the side ⟨a *side* window⟩ **2 a** : directed toward or from the side

⟨*side* thrust⟩ **b** : in addition to or secondary to something primary ⟨*side* issue⟩ **c** : additional to the main portion ⟨a *side* order of salad⟩

³side *vb* **1** : to take sides : join or form sides ⟨*sided* with the rebels⟩ **2** : to furnish with sides or siding ⟨*side* a house⟩

⁴side *n* : swaggering or arrogant manner [obsolete *side* "proud, boastful", from Middle English, "wide"]

side·arm \'sīd-,ärm\ *adj* : thrown with a sideways sweep of the arm between shoulder and hip — **side·arm** *adv*

side arm *n* : a weapon (as a sword or pistol) worn at the side or in the belt

side·board \'sīd-,bōrd, -,bòrd\ *n* : a piece of dining-room furniture with drawers and compartments for dishes, silverware, and table linen

side·burns \'sīd-,bərnz\ *n pl* **1** : short side-whiskers worn with a smooth chin **2** : continuations of the hairline in front of the ears [anagram of *burnsides*] □ ORIGIN During the American Civil War, the Union general Ambrose Everett Burnside wore long bushy side-whiskers. His appearance struck the fancy of Washingtonians as he conducted parades and maneuvers with his regiment of Rhode Island volunteers in the early days of the war. This early popularity fostered the fashion for such whiskers, which came to be called *burnsides*. A later anagram of this word gives us *sideburns*.

side·car \'sīd-,kär\ *n* : a one-wheeled car attached to the side of a motorcycle

sid·ed \'sīd-əd\ *adj* : having sides often of a specified number or kind ⟨one-*sided*⟩ ⟨glass-*sided*⟩

side dish *n* : food served in addition to the main course

side effect *n* : a secondary and usually unfavorable effect (as of a drug) — called also *side reaction*

side·glance \'sīd-,glans\ *n* **1** : a glance directed to the side **2** : an indirect or slight reference

side issue *n* : an issue apart from the main point

side·kick \'sīd-,kik\ *n* : a person closely associated with another as subordinate or partner

side·light \-,līt\ *n* **1 a** : light from the side **b** : incidental or additional information **2** : the red light on the port side or the green light on the starboard side carried by ships or boats under way at night

¹side·line \-,līn\ *n* **1** : a line at right angles to a goal line or end line and marking a side of a court or field of play **2 a** : a line of goods sold in addition to one's principal line **b** : a business or activity pursued in addition to one's regular occupation **3 a** : the space immediately outside the lines along either side of a playing area **b** : the standpoint of persons not immediately participating or concerned — usually used in pl.

²sideline *vt* : to make unable to play in a game or sport ⟨*sidelined* by an injury⟩

side·lin·er \'sīd-,lī-nər\ *n* : one that remains on the sidelines during an activity : one that does not participate

¹side·ling *or* **sid·ling** \'sīd-ling\ *adv* : in a sidelong direction : SIDEWAYS

²sideling *or* **sidling** *adj* **1** : directed toward one side **2** : SLOPING ⟨*sideling* ground⟩

¹side·long \'sīd-,lòng\ *adv* **1** : SIDEWAYS ⟨glanced *sidelong* at them⟩ **2** : on the side [alteration of ¹*sideling*]

²sidelong *adj* **1** : lying or inclining to one side : SLANTING **2 a** : directed to one side ⟨*sidelong* looks⟩ **b** : indirect rather than straightforward

side·man \'sīd-,man\ *n* : a member of a band or orchestra and especially a jazz or swing band or orchestra

side·piece \-,pēs\ *n* : a piece contained in or forming the side of something

si·de·re·al \sī-'dir-ē-əl\ *adj* **1** : of or relating to the stars or constellations **2** : measured by the apparent motion of fixed stars ⟨*sidereal* time⟩ [Latin *sidereus*, from *sider-, sidus* "star, constellation"]

sid·er·ite \'sid-ə-,rīt\ *n* : a natural carbonate of iron $FeCO_3$ that is a valuable iron ore [German *siderit*, from Greek *sidēros* "iron"]

¹sickle 1a

side·sad·dle \'sīd-,sad-l\ *n* : a saddle in which the rider sits with both legs on the same side of the horse — **sidesaddle** *adv*

side·show \-,shō\ *n* **1** : a minor show offered in addition to a main exhibition (as of a circus) **2** : an incidental diversion

side·slip \-,slip\ *vi* **1** : to skid sideways — used especially of an automobile **2** : to slide sideways through the air in a downward direction — **sideslip** *n*

side·spin \-,spin\ *n* : a rotary motion that causes a ball to spin around a vertical axis

side·split·ting \-,split-ing\ *adj* : extremely funny

side·step \'sīd-,step\ *vb* **1** : to take a side step **2** : to avoid by a step to the side **3** : to avoid meeting issues

side step *n* **1** : a step to the side (as in boxing to avoid a blow) **2** : a step taken sideways (as in climbing on skis)

side·stroke \-,strōk\ *n* : a swimming stroke performed on the side in which the arms are alternately pulled back and down while the legs do a scissors kick

¹side·swipe \-,swīp\ *vt* : to strike with a glancing blow along the side ⟨*sideswiped* a parked car⟩

²sideswipe *n* **1 a** : the action of sideswiping **b** : an instance of sideswiping : a glancing blow **2** : an incidental disapproving remark, allusion, or reference

¹side·track \-,trak\ *n* **1** : SIDING 1 **2** : a position or state of secondary importance

²sidetrack *vt* **1** : to transfer from a main railroad line to a siding ⟨*sidetrack* a train⟩ **2** : to turn aside from a main purpose or use

side·walk \'sīd-,wȯk\ *n* : a usually paved walk for pedestrians at the side of a street

sidewalk superintendent *n* : a passerby who stops to watch construction or demolition work

side·wall \'sīd-,wȯl\ *n* **1** : a wall forming the side of something **2** : the side of an automotive tire between the tread shoulder and the bead

side·ward \-wərd\ *or* **side·wards** \-wərdz\ *adv or adj* : toward the side

side·way \-,wā\ *adv or adj* : SIDEWAYS

side·ways \-,wāz\ *adv or adj* **1** : from one side **2** : with one side forward **3** : toward one side; *also* : ASKANCE

side·wheel·er \'sīd-,hwē-lər, 'sīd-,wē-\ *n* : a steamboat having a paddle wheel on each side

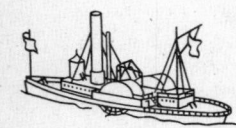

side-wheeler

side·whis·kers \'sīd-,hwis-kərz, 'sīd-,wis-\ *n pl* : whiskers on the side of the face usually worn long with the chin shaven

side·wind·er \'sīd-,wīn-dər\ *n* **1** : a heavy swinging blow from the side **2** : a small rattlesnake of the southwestern United States that moves over sand by thrusting its body diagonally forward in a series of flat S= shaped loops

side·wise \-,wīz\ *adv or adj* : SIDEWAYS

sid·ing \'sīd-ing\ *n* **1** : a short railroad track connected with the main track by switches at one or more places **2** : material (as boards or metal pieces) used to cover the outside walls of frame buildings

si·dle \'sīd-l\ *vb* **si·dled; si·dling** \'sīd-ling, -l-ing\ **1** : to advance obliquely usually in a furtive or unobtrusive way **2** : to cause to move or turn sideways [probably back-formation from ²*sideling*] — **sidle** *n*

siege \'sēj\ *n* **1** : a military blockade of a fortified place **2** : a continued attempt to gain possession of something **3** : a persistent attack (as of illness) [Old French *sege* "seat, blockade", derived from Latin *sedēre* "to sit"]

si·en·na \sē-'en-ə\ *n* : an earthy substance containing oxides of iron and usually of manganese that is brownish yellow when raw and orange red or reddish brown when burnt and is used as a pigment [Italian *terra di Siena,* literally, "Siena earth", from *Siena,* Italy]

si·er·ra \sē-'er-ə\ *n* **1** : a range of mountains especially with jagged peaks **2** : the country about a sierra [Spanish, literally, "saw", from Latin *serra*]

si·es·ta \sē-'es-tə\ *n* : an afternoon nap or rest [Spanish, from Latin *sexta hora* "noon", literally, "sixth hour"]

sie·va bean \'sē-və-, 'siv-ē-\ *n* : any of several small= seeded beans closely related to and sometimes classed as lima beans [origin unknown]

¹sieve \'siv\ *n* : a device with meshes or perforations through which finer particles of a mixture (as of ashes, flour, or sand) of various sizes are passed to separate them from coarser ones, through which the liquid is drained from liquid-containing material, or through which soft materials are forced for reduction to fine particles [Old English *sife*]

²sieve *vb* : to put through a sieve : SIFT

sieve plate *n* **1** : a perforated structure through which water passes into the body of a starfish or other echinoderm **2** : an area in the end wall of a sieve tube pierced by fine pores

sieve tube *n* : a tube that consists of an end-to-end series of thin-walled living cells, is the characteristic element of the phloem, and is held to function chiefly in translocation of organic solutes

sift \'sift\ *vb* **1 a** : to put through a sieve ⟨*sift* flour⟩ **b** : to separate by putting through a sieve **2 a** : to screen out the valuable or good : SELECT **b** : to study or investigate thoroughly **3** : to scatter by or as if by sifting **4** : to pass through or as if through a sieve [Old English *siftan*] — **sift·er** *n*

sift·ing *n* **1** : the act or process of sifting **2** *pl* : sifted material ⟨bran mixed with *siftings*⟩

sigh \'sī\ *vb* **1** : to take or exhale a deep audible breath (as in weariness or grief) **2** : to make a sound like sighing ⟨wind *sighing* in the branches⟩ **3** : GRIEVE ⟨*sighing* for the days of my youth⟩ **4** : to express by sighs [Old English *sīcan*] — **sigh** *n* — **sigh·er** \'sī-ər, 'sīr\ *n*

¹sight \'sīt\ *n* **1** : something that is seen : SPECTACLE **2 a** : a thing that is worth seeing **b** : something ridiculous or disorderly in appearance **3 a** : the process, power, or function of seeing; *esp* : the animal sense of which the eye is the receptor organ and by which the position, shape, and color of objects are perceived **b** : mental or spiritual perception **c** : mental view; *esp* : JUDGMENT **4 a** : the act of looking at or beholding **b** : INSPECTION ⟨this letter is for your *sight* only⟩ **c** : VIEW, GLIMPSE ⟨I caught *sight* of a friend⟩ **d** : an observation to determine direction or position (as by a navigator) **5 a** : perception of an object by the eye **b** : the range of vision **6 a** : a device (as a small metal bead on a gun barrel) that aids the eye in aiming or in determining the direction of an object **b** : an aim or observation taken by means of such a device [Old English *gesiht* "faculty or act of sight, thing seen"]

²sight *adj* **1** : based on recognition or comprehension without previous study ⟨*sight* translation⟩ **2** : payable on presentation ⟨a *sight* draft⟩

³sight *vb* **1** : to get sight of **2** : to look at through or as if through a sight **3** : to aim by means of sights **4** : to look carefully in a particular direction

sight·ed \'sīt-əd\ *adj* : having sight ⟨clear-*sighted*⟩

sight·less \'sīt-ləs\ *adj* : lacking sight : BLIND — **sight·less·ness** *n*

sight·ly \'sīt-lē\ *adj* **1** : pleasing to the sight : HANDSOME **2** : affording a good view — **sight·li·ness** *n*

sight–read \'sīt-,rēd\ *vb* **sight–read** \-,red\; **sight–read·ing** \-,rēd-ing\ : to read a foreign language or perform music at first sight — **sight reader** \-,rēd-ər\ *n*

¹sight–see·ing \'sīt-,sē-ing\ *adj* : engaged in, devoted to, or used for seeing things and places of interest

²sight–seeing *n* : the act or pastime of seeing places of interest — **sight–se·er** \'sīt-,sē-ər, -,si-ər, -,sir\ *n*

sight unseen *adv* : without inspection or appraisal

sig·il \'sij-əl, 'sig-,il\ *n* **1** : SEAL 1, SIGNET **2** : a sign, word, or device of supposed occult power in astrology or magic [Latin *sigillum,* from *signum* "sign, seal"]

sig·ma \'sig-mə\ *n* : the 18th letter of the Greek alphabet — Σ or σ or ς

sig·moid \'sig-ˌmȯid\ *adj* **1 a** : curved like the letter C **b** : curved in two directions like the letter S **2** : of, relating to, or being the contracted and crooked part of the colon immediately above the rectum [Greek *sigmoeidēs,* from *sigma* "sigma"; from a common form of sigma shaped like the Roman letter C] — **sig·moi·dal·ly** \sig-ˈmȯid-l-ē\ *adv*

¹sign \'sīn\ *n* **1 a** : a motion or gesture by which a thought is expressed or a command made known **b** : SIGNAL 1a **2** : a mark having a conventional meaning and used in place of words or to represent a complex notion **3** : one of the 12 divisions of the zodiac **4 a** : a character (as a flat or sharp) used in musical notation **b** : a character (as ÷ or √) indicating a mathematical operation; *also* : one of two characters + and − characterizing a number as positive or negative **5 a** : a lettered board or other display used to identify or advertise a place of business **b** : a posted command, warning, or direction **c** : SIGNBOARD **6 a** : something that serves to indicate the presence or existence of something : TOKEN **b** : PRESAGE 1, PORTENT **c** : an objective evidence of plant or animal disease — compare SYMPTOM [Old French *signe,* from Latin *signum* "mark, sign, image, seal"]

²sign *vb* **1 a** : to place a sign upon **b** : to represent or indicate by a sign **2** : to affix one's signature to **3** : to communicate by making a sign **4** : to hire by securing the signature of [Middle French *signer,* from Latin *signare,* from *signum* "sign"] — **sign·er** *n*

¹sig·nal \'sig-nᵊl\ *n* **1 a** : an act, event, or watchword that serves to start some action **b** : something that stirs to action **2** : a sound or gesture made to give warning or command **3** : an object placed to give notice or warning **4 a** : the message, sound, or effect transmitted in electronic communication (as radio or television) **b** : a radio wave or electric current that transmits a message or effect (as in radio, television, or telephony) [Middle French, from Medieval Latin *signale,* derived from Latin *signum* "sign"]

²signal *vb* **-naled** *or* **-nalled; -nal·ing** *or* **-nal·ling** **1** : to notify by a signal **2** : to communicate by signals **3** : to make or send a signal — **sig·nal·er** *n*

³signal *adj* **1** : distinguished from the ordinary : OUTSTANDING ⟨a *signal* achievement⟩ **2** : used in signaling ⟨a *signal* beacon⟩ — **sig·nal·ly** \'sig-nᵊl-ē\ *adv*

sig·nal·ize \'sig-nᵊl-ˌīz\ *vt* **1** : to make conspicuous : DISTINGUISH **2** : to point out carefully or distinctly **3** : to make signals to : SIGNAL; *also* : INDICATE 1 — **sig·nal·iza·tion** \ˌsig-nᵊl-ə-ˈzā-shən\ *n*

sig·nal·man \'sig-nᵊl-mən, -ˌman\ *n* : one who signals or works with signals

sig·nal·ment \-mənt\ *n* : description by peculiar, appropriate, or characteristic marks

sig·na·to·ry \'sig-nə-ˌtōr-ē, -ˌtȯr-\ *n, pl* **-ries** : a signer with another or others; *esp* : a government bound with others by a signed convention — **signatory** *adj*

sig·na·ture \'sig-nə-ˌchür, -chər\ *n* **1** : the name of a person written with his or her own hand **2** : a letter at the bottom of the first page of a sheet of printed pages (as of a book) to ensure placement in the right order in binding; *also* : the sheet itself which when folded becomes one unit of the book **3 a** : KEY SIGNATURE **b** : TIME SIGNATURE **4** : a tune, musical number, or sound effect or in television a characteristic title or picture used to identify a program, entertainer, or orchestra [Medieval Latin *signatura,* from Latin *signare* "to sign, seal"]

sign·board \'sīn-ˌbōrd, -ˌbȯrd\ *n* : a board bearing a notice or sign

¹sig·net \'sig-nət\ *n* **1** : a seal used in place of a signature on a document **2** : the impression made by or as if by a signet **3** : a small intaglio seal [Middle French, from *signe* "sign, seal"]

²signet *vt* : to stamp or authenticate with a signet

signet ring *n* : a finger ring engraved with a signet

sig·ni·fi·able \'sig-nə-ˌfī-ə-bəl\ *adj* : capable of being represented by a sign or symbol

sig·nif·i·cance \sig-ˈnif-i-kəns\ *n* **1 a** : something that is conveyed as a meaning often obscurely or indirectly **b** : the quality of communicating or implying **2 a** : IMPORTANCE **b** : the quality of being statistically significant SYN see MEANING

sig·nif·i·can·cy \-kən-sē\ *n* : SIGNIFICANCE

sig·nif·i·cant \-kənt\ *adj* **1** : having meaning : SUGGESTIVE, EXPRESSIVE **2** : suggesting or containing a disguised or special meaning **3 a** : IMPORTANT 1, WEIGHTY **b** : probably caused by something other than chance ⟨statistically *significant* correlations⟩ **c** : DISTINCTIVE ⟨the difference between the initial sounds of *keel* and *cool* is not *significant* in English⟩ [Latin *significare* "to signify"] — **sig·nif·i·cant·ly** *adv*

significant figures *n pl* : the figures of a number beginning with the first figure to the left that is not zero and ending with the last figure to the right that is not zero or is a zero that is considered to be exact — called also *significant digits*

sig·ni·fi·ca·tion \ˌsig-nə-fə-ˈkā-shən\ *n* **1** : a signifying by signs **2** : IMPORT; *esp* : the meaning that a term, symbol, or character regularly conveys or is intended to convey SYN see MEANING

sig·nif·i·ca·tive \'sig-ˈnif-ə-ˌkāt-iv\ *adj* **1** : INDICATIVE 2 **2** : SIGNIFICANT 1, SUGGESTIVE — **sig·nif·i·ca·tive·ly** *adv* — **sig·nif·i·ca·tive·ness** *n*

sig·ni·fi·er \'sig-nə-ˌfī-ər, -ˌfīr\ *n* : one that signifies : SIGN

sig·ni·fy \'sig-nə-ˌfī\ *vb* **-fied; -fy·ing** **1** : MEAN 2, DENOTE **2** : to show by a word, signal, or gesture **3** : to have significance or importance [Old French *signifier,* from Latin *significare* "to indicate, signify", from *signum* "sign"]

sign in *vi* : to make a record of one's arrival or presence

sign language *n* : a system of hand gestures used for communication by the deaf or by people speaking different languages

sign off *vi* : to announce the end (as of a program or broadcast)

sign of the cross : a gesture of the hand forming a cross especially on forehead, shoulders, and breast to profess Christian faith or ask divine care and blessing

sign on *vi* **1** : to hire oneself by or as if by a signature **2** : to announce the beginning of broadcasting

si·gnor \sēn-ˈyȯr, -ˈyōr\ *n, pl* **signors** *or* **si·gno·ri** \sēn-ˈyȯr-ē, -ˈyȯr-\ — used by or to Italian-speaking people as a courtesy title equivalent to *Mr.* [Italian *signore, signor,* from Medieval Latin *senior* "superior, lord", from Latin, adj., "senior"]

si·gno·ra \sēn-ˈyȯr-ə, -ˈyȯr-\ *n, pl* **-gnoras** *or* **-gno·re** \-ˈyȯr-ā, -ˈyȯr-ā\ — used by or to Italian-speaking people as a courtesy title equivalent to *Mrs.* [Italian, feminine of *signore, signor*]

si·gno·ri·na \ˌsēn-yə-ˈrē-nə\ *n, pl* **-nas** *or* **-ne** \-nā\ — used by or to Italian-speaking people as a courtesy title equivalent to *Miss* [Italian, from *signora*]

sign·post \'sīn-ˌpōst\ *n* : a post with a sign on it to direct travelers

Sikh \'sēk\ *n* : a believer in a monotheistic religion of India founded about 1500 by a Hindu under Islamic influence and marked by rejection of idolatry and caste [Hindi, literally, "disciple"] — **Sikh** *adj* — **Sikh·ism** \-ˌiz-əm\ *n*

si·lage \'sī-lij\ *n* : fodder converted into succulent feed for livestock through processes of anaerobic acid fermentation (as in a silo) [short for *ensilage*]

sild \'sil, 'sild\ *n* : a young herring other than a brisling canned as a sardine in Norway [Norwegian]

¹si·lence \'sī-ləns\ *n* **1** : forbearance from speech or noise — often used interjectionally **2** : absence of

\ə\	abut	\ng\	sing
\ər\	further	\ō\	bone
\a\	mat	\ȯ\	saw
\ā\	take	\ȯi\	coin
\ä\	cot, cart	\th\	thin
\aü\	out	\t̶h\	this
\ch\	chin	\ü\	food
\e\	pet	\u̇\	foot
\ē\	easy	\y\	yet
\g\	go	\yü\	few
\i\	tip	\yu̇\	cure
\ī\	life	\zh\	vision
\j\	job		

sound or noise : STILLNESS **3** : absence of mention: **a** : OBLIVION **2**, OBSCURITY **b** : SECRECY **2**

²**silence** *vt* **1** : to stop the noise or speech of : reduce to silence **2** : to restrain from expression **3** : to cause to cease hostile firing by return fire or by destroying

si·lenc·er \'sī-lən-sər\ *n* : one that silences; *esp* : a silencing device for small arms

si·lent \'sī-lənt\ *adj* **1 a** : not speaking : MUTE, SPEECHLESS **b** : unwilling to speak **2** : free from sound or noise : STILL **3** : UNSPOKEN ⟨*silent* disapproval⟩ **4 a** : making no mention ⟨history is *silent* about this person⟩ **b** : INACTIVE; *esp* : taking no active part in the conduct of a business ⟨a *silent* partner⟩ **5** : not pronounced ⟨*silent b* in doubt⟩ [Latin *silens*, from *silēre* "to be silent"] — **si·lent·ly** *adv* □ SYN TACITURN, RETICENT, RESERVED: SILENT implies a habit of saying no more than is necessary and often less than expected; TACITURN suggests a temperamental disinclination to talk and a sullen avoidance of sociability; RETICENT implies a reluctance to speak out plainly especially about one's personal affairs; RESERVED suggests the restraining influence of caution or formality in checking easy conversation.

silent butler *n* : a container with hinged lid for collecting table crumbs and the contents of ashtrays

si·lex \'sī-,leks\ *n* : SILICA [Latin, "flint, quartz"]

¹**sil·hou·ette** \,sil-ə-'wet\ *n* **1** : a drawing or cutout of the outline of an object filled in with black; *esp* : a profile portrait of this kind **2** : characteristic shape of an object (as an airplane) seen or as if seen against the light [French, from Étienne de *Silhouette*, died 1767, French controller general of finances] □ ORIGIN Étienne de Silhouette was French controller general of finances in the mid-18th century. He was extremely close with the state's money as well as his own, so close, in fact, that *à la Silhouette* came to mean "cheaply" for a time. His niggardliness was greeted with ridicule. It was even suggested that one of his economies was the decoration of his house with his outlines, which he made himself, rather than more expensive paintings. Outline drawings, as stingy of detail as Silhouette was of money, were given his name.

²**silhouette** *vt* : to represent by a silhouette; *also* : to project upon a background like a silhouette ⟨a flock of geese *silhouetted* against the evening sky⟩

sil·i·ca \'sil-i-kə\ *n* : the dioxide of silicon SiO₂ occurring in crystalline, amorphous, and impure forms (as in quartz, opal, and sand) [New Latin, from Latin *silic-*, *silex* "flint, quartz"]

silica gel *n* : colloidal silica resembling coarse white sand in appearance but possessing many fine pores and therefore extremely adsorbent

sil·i·cate \'sil-i-kət, 'sil-ə-,kāt\ *n* : a compound formed from silica and any of various oxides of metals

si·li·ceous *or* **si·li·cious** \sə-'lish-əs\ *adj* : of, relating to, or containing silica or a silicate ⟨*siliceous* limestone⟩

si·lic·ic \sə-'lis-ik\ *adj* : of, relating to, or derived from silica or silicon

silicic acid *n* : any of various weakly acid substances obtained as gelatinous masses by treating silicates with acids

silicified wood *n* : chalcedony in the form of petrified wood

si·lic·i·fy \sə-'lis-ə-,fī\ *vt* **-fied; -fy·ing** : to convert into or impregnate with silica — **si·lic·i·fi·ca·tion** \-,lis-ə-fə-'kā-shən\ *n*

sil·i·con \'sil-i-kən, 'sil-ə-,kän\ *n* : a tetravalent nonmetallic chemical element that occurs combined as the most abundant element next to oxygen in the earth's crust and is used especially in alloys — see ELEMENT table [*silica* + *-on* (as in *carbon*)]

silicon carbide *n* : a hard brittle crystalline compound SiC of silicon and carbon used as an abrasive

silicon dioxide *n* : SILICA

sil·i·cone \'sil-ə-,kōn\ *n* : any of various polymeric organic silicon compounds obtained as oils, greases, or plastics and used especially for water-resistant and heat-resistant lubricants, varnishes, binders, and electric insulators [derived from *silicon*]

sil·i·co·sis \,sil-ə-'kō-səs\ *n* : a disease of the lungs marked by formation of scar tissue and shortness of breath and caused by prolonged inhaling of silica dusts — **sil·i·cot·ic** \-'kät-ik\ *adj or n*

si·lique \sə-'lēk\ *n* : a long narrow 2-valved usually many-seeded capsule characteristic of the mustard family [French, from Latin *siliqua* "pod, husk"]

¹**silk** \'silk\ *n* **1** : a fine continuous protein fiber produced by various insect larvae usually for cocoons; *esp* : a lustrous tough elastic fiber produced by silkworms and used for textiles **2 a** : thread, yarn, or fabric made from silk **b** : a garment of silk **3** : a silky material or filament (as that produced by a spider) ⟨milkweed *silk*⟩; *esp* : the styles of an ear of Indian corn [Old English *seolc*] — **silk** *adj*

²**silk** *vi* : to develop the silk ⟨the corn is *silking*⟩

silk cotton *n* : the silky or cottony covering of seeds of a silk-cotton tree; *esp* : KAPOK

silk–cotton tree *n* : any of various tropical trees with palmate leaves and large fruits with the seeds enveloped by silk cotton

silk·en \'sil-kən\ *adj* **1** : made or consisting of silk **2** : resembling silk especially in soft lustrous smoothness

silk hat *n* : a hat with a tall cylindrical crown and a silk-plush finish worn by men as a dress hat

silk moth *n* : the silkworm moth

silk screen *n* : a stencil process in which coloring matter is forced onto the material to be printed through the meshes of a silk or organdy screen — called also *silk-screen process*

silk–stocking *adj* **1** : fashionably dressed ⟨a *silk-stocking* audience⟩ **2** : ARISTOCRATIC, WEALTHY ⟨the *silkstocking* districts of a city⟩

silk·worm \'sil-,kwərm\ *n* : a moth larva that spins a large amount of strong silk in constructing its cocoon; *esp* : the rough wrinkled hairless yellowish caterpillar of an Asian moth long grown as a source of silk

silky \'sil-kē\ *adj* **silk·i·er; -est** **1** : SILKEN 2 **2** : having or covered with fine soft hairs, plumes, or scales — **silk·i·ly** \-kə-lē\ *adv* — **silk·i·ness** \-kē-nəs\ *n*

sill \'sil\ *n* **1** : a horizontal piece (as a timber) that forms the lowest member of a framework or supporting structure (as of a house or bridge): as **a** : the horizontal member at the base of a window **b** : the timber or stone at the foot of a door : THRESHOLD **2** : a flat mass of igneous rock injected while molten between other rocks [Old English *syll*]

sillabub *variant of* SYLLABUB

sil·li·man·ite \'sil-ə-mə-,nīt\ *n* : a brown, grayish, or pale green crystalline mineral that consists of an aluminum silicate [Benjamin *Silliman*, died 1864, American geologist]

sil·ly \'sil-ē\ *adj* **sil·li·er; -est** **1** : mentally feeble : FOOLISH **2** : contrary to reason : ABSURD **3** : lacking in seriousness : TRIFLING [Middle English *sely* "happy, innocent, pitiable, feeble", from Old English *sǣl* "happiness"] — **sil·li·ly** \'sil-ə-lē\ *adv* — **sil·li·ness** \'sil-ē-nəs\ *n* — **silly** *n or adv*

si·lo \'sī-lō\ *n, pl* **silos** **1** : a trench, pit, or especially a tall cylinder (as of wood or concrete) used for making and storing silage **2** : a deep bin for housing a missile underground [Spanish]

¹**silt** \'silt\ *n* **1** : loose sedimentary material with rock particles usually ¹⁄₂₀ millimeter or less in diameter; *also* : soil containing 80 percent or more of such silt and less than 12 percent of clay **2** : a deposit of sediment (as by a river) [Middle English *cylte*] — **silty** \'sil-tē\ *adj*

²**silt** *vb* : to become or make choked, obstructed, or covered with silt — **silt·a·tion** \sil-'tā-shən\ *n*

silkworm

silo 1

Si·lu·ri·an \sī-'lùr-ē-ən, sə-\ *n* : the period of the Paleozoic era between the Ordovician and Devonian marked by the appearance of very large crustaceans and of the first land plants; *also* : the corresponding system of rocks — see GEOLOGIC TIME table [Latin *Silures*, a people of ancient Britain] — **Silurian** *adj*

silvan *variant of* SYLVAN

¹sil·ver \'sil-vər\ *n* **1** : a white ductile and malleable metallic chemical element that takes a high polish, is usually univalent in compounds, and has high thermal and electric conductivity — see ELEMENT table **2 a** : coin made of silver **b** : articles (as tableware) made of or plated with silver **3** : a medium gray [Old English *seolfor*]

²silver *adj* **1** : relating to, made of, or yielding silver ⟨*silver* jewelry⟩ ⟨*silver* ore⟩ **2** : SILVERY

³silver *vt* **sil·vered; sil·ver·ing** \'silv-riŋ, -ə-riŋ\ **1 a** : to cover with silver (as by electroplating) **b** : to coat with a substance (as a metal) resembling silver ⟨*silver* glass with an amalgam⟩ **2** : to give a silvery appearance to — **sil·ver·er** \'sil-vər-ər\ *n*

silver bromide *n* : a compound AgBr extremely sensitive to light and much used for photographic emulsions

silver bullet *n* : something that acts as a magical weapon; *esp* : one that instantly solves a long-standing problem

silver chloride *n* : a compound AgCl sensitive to light and used especially for photographic emulsions

sil·ver·fish \'sil-vər-,fish\ *n* **1** : any of various silvery fishes (as a tarpon) **2** : any of various small wingless insects (order Thysanura); *esp* : one found in houses and sometimes injurious to sized papers or starched clothes

silver fox *n* : a genetically determined color phase of the common red fox in which the pelt is black tipped with white

silver iodide *n* : a compound AgI that is sensitive to light and is used in photography, rainmaking, and medicine

silver lining *n* : a consoling or hopeful prospect

silver maple *n* : a common North American maple with deeply cut leaves that are light green above and silvery white below; *also* : its hard close-grained but brittle light brown wood

sil·vern \'sil-vərn\ *adj* **1** : made of silver **2** : resembling or characteristic of silver : SILVERY

silver nitrate *n* : an irritant compound AgNO₃ that is used as a chemical reagent, in photography, and in medicine especially as an antiseptic

silver paper *n* : a metallic paper with a coating or lamination resembling silver

silver perch *n* : any of various somewhat silvery fishes that resemble perch

silver plate *n* **1** : a plating of silver **2** : domestic flatware and hollowware of silver or of a base metal plated with silver

silver protein *n* : a colloidal light-sensitive preparation of silver and protein used as an antiseptic

silver screen *n* **1** : a motion-picture screen **2** : SCREEN 3b

sil·ver·sides \'sil-vər-,sīdz\ *n sing or pl* : any of a family of small fishes with a silvery stripe along each side of the body

sil·ver·smith \-,smith\ *n* : a person who makes articles of silver

silver spoon *n* : WEALTH; *esp* : inherited wealth [from the phrase *born with a silver spoon in one's mouth* "born wealthy"]

silver standard *n* : a monetary standard under which the currency unit is defined by a stated quantity of silver

sil·ver–tongued \,sil-vər-'təŋd\ *adj* : ELOQUENT ⟨a *silver-tongued* orator⟩

sil·ver·ware \'sil-vər-,waər, -,weər\ *n* : SILVER PLATE 2; *also* : FLATWARE

sil·very \'silv-rē, -ə-rē\ *adj* **1** : having a soft clear ring ⟨a *silvery* voice⟩ **2** : having the white lustrous sheen of silver — **sil·ver·i·ness** *n*

sil·vi·cul·ture *or* **syl·vi·cul·ture** \'sil-və-,kəl-chər\ *n* : FORESTRY; *esp* : the science of the culture of forest trees [French, from Latin *silva* "forest" + *cultura* "culture"] — **sil·vi·cul·tur·al** \,sil-və-'kəlch-rəl, -ə-rəl\ *adj* — **sil·vi·cul·tur·al·ly** \-ē\ *adv* — **sil·vi·cul·tur·ist** \-'kəlch-rəst, -ə-rəst\ *n*

Sim·chas To·rah \,sim-käs-'tòr-ə, -'tór-\ *n* : a Jewish holiday observed in October or November in celebration of the completion of the annual reading of the Torah [Hebrew *śimḥath tōrāh* "rejoicing of the Torah"]

¹sim·i·an \'sim-ē-ən\ *adj* : of, relating to, or resembling monkeys [Latin *simia* "ape", from *simus* "snub-nosed", from Greek *simos*]

²simian *n* : MONKEY 1

sim·i·lar \'sim-ə-lər\ *adj* **1** : having characteristics in common : COMPARABLE **2** : not differing in shape but only in size or position ⟨*similar* triangles⟩ [French *similaire*, from Latin *similis* "like, similar"] — **sim·i·lar·ly** *adv* □ SYN SIMILAR, ANALOGOUS, PARALLEL mean closely resembling each other. SIMILAR implies the possibility of being mistaken for each other; ANALOGOUS applies to things belonging in essentially different categories but nevertheless having many similarities ⟨*analogous* political systems⟩ PARALLEL suggests a marked likeness in the development of two things ⟨the *parallel* careers of two movie stars⟩

sim·i·lar·i·ty \,sim-ə-'lar-ət-ē\ *n, pl* **-ties 1** : the quality or state of being similar : RESEMBLANCE **2** : a point in which things are similar : CORRESPONDENCE SYN see LIKENESS

sim·i·le \'sim-ə-lē, -,lē\ *n* : a figure of speech in which things different in kind or quality are compared by the use of the word *like* or *as* (as in *cheeks like roses*) — compare METAPHOR [Latin, "comparison", from *similis* "like, similar"]

si·mil·i·tude \sə-'mil-ə-,tüd, -,tyüd\ *n* **1** : a visible likeness : IMAGE **2** : an imaginative comparison **3** : SIMILARITY

sim·mer \'sim-ər\ *vb* **sim·mered; sim·mer·ing** \'sim-riŋ, -ə-riŋ\ **1** : to stew gently below or just at the boiling point **2 a** : to be in a state of early development ⟨an idea *simmering* in the back of my mind⟩ **b** : to be in inward turmoil : SEETHE ⟨*simmered* with fury at the insult⟩ [Middle English *simperen*] — **simmer** *n*

si·mo·ni·ac \sī-'mō-nē-,ak, sə-\ *n* : one who practices simony — **simoniac** *or* **si·mo·ni·a·cal** \,sī-mə-'nī-ə-kəl, ,sim-ə-\ *adj* — **si·mo·ni·a·cal·ly** \-'nī-ə-kə-lē, -klē\ *adv*

si·mo·nize \'sī-mə-,nīz\ *vt* : to polish with or as if with wax [from *Simoniz*, a trademark]

si·mon–pure \,sī-mən-'pyùr\ *adj* : of untainted purity or integrity; *also* : pretentiously or hypocritically pure [from *the real Simon Pure,* alluding to a character impersonated by another in the play *A Bold Stroke for a Wife* (1718) by Susanna Centlivre]

si·mo·ny \'sī-mə-nē, 'sim-ə-\ *n* : the buying or selling of a church office [Late Latin *simonia*, from *Simon Magus* (Acts 8:9–24)]

si·moom \sə-'müm, sī-\ *or* **si·moon** \-'mün\ *n* : a hot dry violent wind laden with dust from Asian and African deserts [Arabic *samūm*]

sim·pa·ti·co \sim-'pät-i-,kō, -'pat-\ *adj* **1** : LIKABLE **2** : CONGENIAL 2 [Italian, from *simpatia* "sympathy, congeniality", from Latin *sympathia* "sympathy"]

¹sim·per \'sim-pər\ *vi* **sim·pered; sim·per·ing** \-pə-riŋ, -priŋ\ : to smile in a foolish affected manner [perhaps of Scandinavian origin] — **sim·per·er** \-pər-ər\ *n*

²simper *n* : a silly smile : SMIRK

sim·ple \'sim-pəl\ *adj* **sim·pler** \-pə-lər, -plər\; **sim·plest** \-pə-ləst, -pləst\ **1** : free from deceit or vanity **2 a** : of humble origin **b** : lacking in education, experience, or intelligence **3 a** (1) : free from complexity or complications ⟨a *simple* melody⟩ (2) : expressed in a form in which the indicated operations have been carried out and radicals have been eliminated as far as possible ⟨3x is *simpler* than 6x−3x⟩ **b** : consisting of only one main clause and no subordinate clauses ⟨*simple* sentence⟩ **c** : not compound ⟨the *simple* noun "boat"⟩ **d** (1) : not subdivided into branches or leaflets (2) : developing from a single ovary ⟨*simple* fruits⟩ **4 a** : UTTER, ABSOLUTE ⟨the *simple* truth⟩ **b** : easily understood or performed ⟨a *simple* task⟩ [Old French, "plain, uncomplicated, artless", from Latin *simplus, simplex,* literally, "single"] — **sim·ple·ness** \-pəl-nəs\ *n* □ SYN SIMPLE, EASY mean not demanding great effort or involving difficulty. SIMPLE stresses lack of complexity or subtlety ⟨a *simple* case of theft⟩ EASY implies offering little resistance to being understood or accomplished or dealt with ⟨an *easy* problem⟩ ⟨an *easy* victory⟩

simple eye *n* : an eye having a single lens — compare COMPOUND EYE

simple fraction *n* : a fraction having whole numbers for the numerator and denominator — compare COMPLEX FRACTION

simple fracture *n* : a breaking of a bone in such a way that the skin is not broken and bone fragments do not protrude

simple interest *n* : interest paid or computed on the original principal only of a loan or on the amount of an account

simple machine *n* : any of various elementary mechanisms formerly considered as the elements of which all machines are composed and including the lever, the wheel and axle, the pulley, the inclined plane, the wedge, and the screw

sim·ple·mind·ed \,sim-pəl-'mīn-dəd\ *adj* : not subtle : UNSOPHISTICATED; *also* : FOOLISH — **sim·ple·mind·ed·ly** *adv* — **sim·ple·mind·ed·ness** *n*

simple sugar *n* : MONOSACCHARIDE

sim·ple·ton \'sim-pəl-tən\ *n* : a person lacking in common sense [*simple* + *-ton* (as in surnames such as *Washington*)]

sim·plex \'sim-,pleks\ *n, pl* **sim·pli·cia** \sim-'plish-ə, -ē-ə\ *or* **sim·pli·ces** \'sim-plə-,sēz\ : a word that is not a compound [Latin *simplic-, simplex* "simple, single"] — **sim·pli·cial** \sim-'plish-əl\ *adj*

sim·plic·i·ty \sim-'plis-ət-ē\ *n, pl* **-ties 1** : the quality or state of being simple **2** : freedom from pretense or guile : HONESTY **3 a** : directness or clarity of expression **b** : restraint in ornamentation **4** : FOLLY 2, SILLINESS [Middle French *simplicité,* from Latin *simplicitas,* from *simplic-, simplex* "simple"]

sim·pli·fy \'sim-plə-,fī\ *vt* **-fied; -fy·ing** : to make simple or simpler — **sim·pli·fi·ca·tion** \,sim-plə-fə-'kā-shən\ *n* — **sim·pli·fi·er** \'sim-plə-,fī-ər, -,fīr\ *n*

sim·ply \'sim-plē\ *adv* **1 a** : CLEARLY ⟨stated the directions *simply*⟩ **b** : PLAINLY ⟨*simply* dressed⟩ **c** : DIRECTLY, CANDIDLY ⟨told the story as *simply* as a child would⟩ **2 a** : MERELY, SOLELY ⟨eats *simply* to keep alive⟩ **b** : REALLY 1 ⟨*simply* marvelous⟩

sim·u·late \'sim-yə-,lāt\ *vt* : to give the appearance or effect of : IMITATE [Latin *simulare* "to copy, represent, feign", from *similis* "like, similar"] — **sim·u·la·tive** \-,lāt-iv\ *adj* — **sim·u·la·tor** \-,lāt-ər\ *n*

sim·u·la·tion \,sim-yə-'lā-shən\ *n* **1** : the act or process of simulating **2** : a sham object : COUNTERFEIT **3** : the imitation of the workings of one system or process using another ⟨a computer *simulation* of space flight⟩

si·mul·cast \'sī-məl-,kast\ *vb* : to broadcast simultaneously by AM and FM radio or by radio and television [*simul*taneous broad*cast*] — **simulcast** *n*

si·mul·ta·neous \,sī-məl-'tā-nē-əs, -nyəs\ *adj* **1** : existing or occurring at the same time : COINCIDENT **2** : satisfied by the same values of the variables ⟨*simultaneous* equations⟩ [derived from Latin *simul* "at the same time"] SYN see CONTEMPORARY — **si·mul·ta·ne·i·ty** \-tə-'nē-ət-ē, -'nā-\ *n* — **si·mul·ta·neous·ly** \-'tā-nē-ə-slē, -nyə-slē\ *adv* — **si·mul·ta·neous·ness** *n*

¹sin \'sin\ *n* **1** : an offense against God **2** : MISDEED, FAULT [Old English *synn*]

²sin *vi* **sinned; sin·ning** : to commit a sin

Sin·an·thro·pus \sī-'nan-thrə-pəs, -'nant-; ,sī-,nan-'thrō-\ *n* : PEKING MAN [Late Latin *Sinae,* pl., "Chinese" + Greek *anthrōpos* "man"]

¹since \sins, 'sins\ *adv* **1** : from a definite past time until now ⟨has stayed there ever *since*⟩ **2** : before the present time : AGO ⟨long *since* dead⟩ **3** : after a time in the past : SUBSEQUENTLY ⟨has *since* become rich⟩ [Middle English *sithens, sins,* from *sithen,* from Old English *siththan,* from *sith tham* "since that"]

²since *prep* : from or after a specified time in the past ⟨improvements made *since* 1928⟩ ⟨happy *since* then⟩

³since *conj* **1** : at a time or times in the past after or later than ⟨have held two jobs *since* I graduated⟩ **2** : from the time in the past when ⟨ever *since* we were children⟩ **3** : in view of the fact that : BECAUSE ⟨*since* it was raining I wore a hat⟩

sin·cere \sin-'siər\ *adj* **1 a** : free from deceit : HONEST ⟨a *sincere* friend⟩ **b** : free from adulteration : PURE ⟨a *sincere* doctrine⟩ **2** : GENUINE 1, REAL ⟨a *sincere* work of art⟩ [Middle French, from Latin *sincerus*] — **sin·cere·ly** *adv* — **sin·cere·ness** *n* — **sin·cer·i·ty** \-'ser-ət-ē, -'sir-\ *n*

sine \'sīn\ *n* : a trigonometric function that for an acute angle in a right triangle is the ratio between the side opposite the angle and the hypotenuse — abbreviation sin [Medieval Latin *sinus,* from Latin, "curve"]

si·ne·cure \'sī-ni-kyùr, 'sin-i-\ *n* : an office or position that requires little or no work [Medieval Latin *sine cura* "without cure of souls"]

si·ne die \,sī-nē-'dī-,ē, -'dī; sin-ē-'dē-,ā\ *adv* : for an unspecified period of time : INDEFINITELY ⟨the meeting adjourned *sine die*⟩ [Latin, "without day"]

si·ne qua non \,sin-i-,kwä-'nän, -'nōn; *also* ,sī-nē-,kwä-'nän\ *n* : something absolutely essential or indispensable [Late Latin, "without which not"]

sin·ew \'sin-yü, 'sin-ü\ *n* **1** : TENDON; *esp* : one dressed for use as a cord or thread **2** : solid resilient strength : POWER [Old English *seono*]

sine wave *n* : a wave form that represents periodic oscillations in which the amplitude of displacement at each point is proportional to the sine of the angle of the displacement

sin·ewy \'sin-yə-wē, 'sin-ə-wē\ *adj* **1** : full of sinews : TOUGH, STRINGY ⟨*sinewy* meat⟩ **2** : STRONG ⟨*sinewy* arms⟩

sin·fo·nia \,sin-fə-'nē-ə\ *n, pl* **-nie** \-'nē-,ā\ **1** : an orchestral musical composition found in 18th century opera **2** : SYMPHONY 2 [Italian, from Latin *symphonia* "symphony"]

sin·ful \'sin-fəl\ *adj* : marked by or full of sin : WICKED — **sin·ful·ly** \-fə-lē\ *adv* — **sin·ful·ness** *n*

¹sing \'sing\ *vb* **sang** \'sang\ *or* **sung** \'səng\; **sung; sing·ing** \'sing-ing\ **1 a** : to produce musical sounds by means of the voice ⟨*sing* for joy⟩ **b** : to utter with musical sounds ⟨*sing* a song⟩ **c** : CHANT, INTONE ⟨*sing* mass⟩ **2** : to make pleasing musical sounds ⟨birds *singing* at dawn⟩ **3** : to make a slight shrill sound ⟨a kettle *singing* on the stove⟩ **4 a** : to tell a story in poetry : relate in verse **b** : to express vividly and enthusiastically ⟨*sing* their praises⟩ **5** : BUZZ, RING ⟨ears *singing* from the sudden descent⟩ **6** : to act on or affect by singing ⟨*sing* a baby to sleep⟩ **7 a** : to call aloud : cry out ⟨*sing* out when you find them⟩ **b** : to divulge information or give evidence [Old English *singan*] — **sing·able** \'sing-ə-bəl\ *adj*

²**sing** *n* : a singing especially in company

¹**singe** \'sinj\ *vb* **singed** \'sinjd\; **singe·ing** \'sin-jing\ : to burn superficially or lightly : SCORCH; *esp* : to remove hair, down, or fuzz from usually by passing briefly over a flame [Old English *sengan*]

²**singe** *n* : a slight burn : SCORCH

¹**sing·er** \'sing-ər\ *n* : one that sings

²**sing·er** \'sin-jər\ *n* : one that singes

singing bird *n* **1** : SONGBIRD 1 **2** : a passerine bird

¹**sin·gle** \'sing-gəl\ *adj* **1** : not married **2** : unaccompanied by others **3 a** (1) : consisting of or having only one part or feature (2) : of or relating to one of two or more aspects or parts **b** : having but one whorl of petals or ray flowers ⟨a *single* rose⟩ **4 a** : consisting of a separate unique whole : INDIVIDUAL ⟨every *single* citizen⟩ **b** : of, relating to, or involving only one person **5** : FRANK, HONEST ⟨a *single* devotion⟩ **6** : being a whole ⟨a *single* world⟩ **7** : engaged in one to one ⟨fight in *single* combat⟩ **8** : having no equal or like : SINGULAR **9** : designed for the use of one person or family ⟨a *single* house⟩ [Middle French, from Latin *singulus* "one only"] — **sin·gle·ness** *n* □ **SYN** SOLITARY, SOLE, UNIQUE: SINGLE implies being unaccompanied or unassisted by any other ⟨operated by a *single* worker⟩ ⟨a *single* line of trees⟩ SOLITARY implies being both single and isolated ⟨a *solitary* oak in a field⟩ SOLE implies being the only one existing or acting ⟨the *sole* reason for refusing⟩ ⟨the *sole* survivor of the wreck⟩ UNIQUE implies being the only one of its kind or character in existence ⟨a *unique* mineral specimen⟩

²**single** *n* **1** : a separate individual person or thing **2** : a base hit that permits the batter to reach first base **3** *pl* : a game (as of tennis or handball) between two players

³**single** *vb* **sin·gled; sin·gling** \'sing-gə-ling, -gling\ **1** : to select or distinguish (a person or thing) from a number or group — usually used with *out* **2** : to make a single in baseball

single bond *n* : a chemical bond in which one pair of electrons is shared by two atoms in a molecule especially when the atoms can share more than one pair of electrons — compare DOUBLE BOND, TRIPLE BOND

sin·gle-breast·ed \,sing-gəl-'bres-təd\ *adj* : having a center closing with one row of buttons and no lap

single entry *n* : a method of bookkeeping that shows only one side of a business transaction and usually consists only of a record of accounts with debtors and creditors

single file *n* : a line of persons or things arranged one behind another — **single file** *adv*

¹**sin·gle-foot** \'sing-gəl-,fut\ *n, pl* **single-foots** : ⁴RACK b

²**single-foot** *vi* : to go at a rack — **sin·gle-foot·er** *n*

sin·gle-hand·ed \,sing-gəl-'han-dəd\ *adj* **1** : managed or done by one person **2** : working alone : lacking help — **single-handed** *adv* — **sin·gle-hand·ed·ly** *adv*

sin·gle-heart·ed \-'härt-əd\ *adj* : characterized by sincerity and unity of purpose — **sin·gle-heart·ed·ly** *adv* — **sin·gle-heart·ed·ness** *n*

sin·gle-mind·ed \-'mīn-dəd\ *adj* **1** : SINCERE, SINGLE-HEARTED **2** : having one overriding purpose — **sin·gle-mind·ed·ly** *adv* — **sin·gle-mind·ed·ness** *n*

sin·gle-space \-'spās\ *vt* : to type or print with no blank lines between lines of copy

sin·gle-stick \'sing-gəl-,stik\ *n* : fighting or fencing with a wooden stick or sword held in one hand; *also* : the weapon used

sin·glet \'sing-glət\ *n, chiefly British* : an athletic jersey : UNDERSHIRT [from its having only one thickness of cloth]

single tax *n* : a tax levied on a single item (as real estate) as the sole source of public revenue

sin·gle·ton \'sing-gəl-tən\ *n* **1** : a playing card that is the only one of its suit originally held in a hand **2** : an individual distinct from others grouped with it [French, from English *single*]

sin·gle·tree \-,trē\ *n* : WHIFFLETREE

sin·gly \'sing-gə-lē, -glē\ *adv* : by or with oneself

¹**sing·song** \'sing-,sòng\ *n* : voice delivery marked by a narrow range or a monotonous rise and fall of pitch

²**singsong** *adj* : having a monotonous cadence or rhythm

¹**sin·gu·lar** \'sing-gyə-lər\ *adj* **1 a** : of or relating to a separate person or thing : INDIVIDUAL **b** : of, relating to, or being a word form denoting one person, thing, or instance **c** : of or relating to a single instance or to something considered by itself **2 a** : EXCEPTIONAL **2 b** : UNIQUE 2 **3** : being at variance with others : PECULIAR [Middle French *singuler*, from Latin *singularis*, from *singulus* "only one"] — **sin·gu·lar·ly** *adv*

²**singular** *n* : something that is singular; *esp* : the singular number, the inflectional form denoting it, or a word in that form

sin·gu·lar·i·ty \,sing-gyə-'lar-ət-ē\ *n, pl* **-ties 1** : the quality or state of being singular **2** : something that is peculiar

sin·gu·lar·ize \'sing-gyə-lə-,rīz\ *vt* : to make singular

Sin·ha·lese *or* **Sin·gha·lese** \,sing-gə-'lēz, -sin-ə-, -sin-hə-,-,lēs\ *n* **1** : a member of a people forming a major part of the population of Sri Lanka **2** : the Indic language of the Sinhalese people [Sanskrit *Siṁhala* "Ceylon"] — **Sinhalese** *adj*

sin·is·ter \'sin-ə-stər\ *adj* **1** : singularly evil or productive of evil : BAD **2** : of, relating to, or situated to the left or on the left side of something **3** : seriously threatening trouble or disaster : OMINOUS [Latin, "on the left side, unlucky"] — **sin·is·ter·ly** *adv* — **sin·is·ter·ness** *n*

sin·is·tral \'sin-ə-strəl\ *adj* : of, relating to, or inclined to the left; *esp* : LEFT-HANDED — **sin·is·tral·ly** \-strə-lē\ *adv*

¹**sink** \'singk\ *vb* **sank** \'sangk\ *or* **sunk** \'səngk\; **sunk; sink·ing 1** : to move or cause to move downward usually so as to be submerged or buried ⟨feet *sinking* into deep mud⟩ ⟨*sink* a ship⟩ **2 a** : to fall to a lower level ⟨the lake *sank* during the drought⟩ **b** : to make or become lower in pitch or volume ⟨my voice *sank* to a whisper⟩ **c** : to fall to or into an inferior status : DECLINE ⟨*sink* into decay⟩ **d** : SET 24 **3 a** : to penetrate or cause to penetrate ⟨*sank* the ax into the tree⟩ **b** : to become absorbed ⟨water *sinking* into dry sand⟩; *also* : to be apprehended and retained ⟨the lesson *sank* in⟩ **4** : to fail in strength, spirits, or health ⟨my heart *sank* as I saw the wreck⟩ ⟨the patient is *sinking* fast⟩ **5** : to form by digging or boring usually in the earth ⟨*sink* a well⟩ **6** : RESTRAIN, SUPPRESS ⟨*sinking* my pride, I apologized⟩ **7** : to invest especially unwisely [Old English *sincan*] — **sink·able** \'sing-kə-bəl\ *adj*

²**sink** *n* **1 a** : CESSPOOL **b** : SEWER **c** : a stationary basin for washing (as in a kitchen) connected with a drain and usually a water supply **2** : a place marked by vice, corruption, and filth **3** : a depression in the land surface; *esp* : one having a saline lake with no outlet

sink·age \'sing-kij\ *n* : the act, process, or extent of sinking

sink·er \'sing-kər\ *n* **1** : one that sinks; *esp* : a weight for sinking a line or net **2** : DOUGHNUT

sink·hole \'singk-,hōl\ *n* : a hollow place in which drainage collects

sinking fund *n* : a fund set up and accumulated by usually regular deposits for paying off the principal of a debt

sin·less \'sin-ləs\ *adj* : free from sin — **sin·less·ly** *adv* — **sin·less·ness** *n*

sin·ner \'sin-ər\ *n* : one that sins

Sino- *combining form* **1** : Chinese **2** : Chinese and [Late Latin *Sinae*, pl., "Chinese", from Greek *Sinai*, from Arabic *Sīn* "China"]

si·no·atri·al node \,sī-nō-,ā-trē-əl-\ *n* : a small mass of tissue that is embedded in the musculature of the right

\ə\	abut	\ng\	sing
\ər\	further	\ō\	bone
\a\	mat	\ò\	saw
\ā\	take	\òi\	coin
\ä\	cot, cart	\th\	thin
\aù\	out	\th\	this
\ch\	chin	\ü\	food
\e\	pet	\ù\	foot
\ē\	easy	\y\	yet
\g\	go	\yü\	few
\i\	tip	\yù\	cure
\ī\	life	\zh\	vision
\j\	job		

atrium of higher vertebrates and that originates the impulses stimulating the heartbeat [*sinus* + *atrium*]

sin·ter \'sint-ər\ *vt* : to cause to become a coherent mass by heating without melting [German *sinter* "deposit formed by the evaporation of lake water", from Old High German *sintar* "slag"] — **sinter** *n*

sin·u·os·i·ty \,sin-yə-'wäs-ət-ē\ *n, pl* **-ties** 1 : the quality or state of being sinuous 2 : something that is sinuous

sin·u·ous \'sin-yə-wəs\ *adj* 1 a : of a serpentine or wavy form : WINDING b : marked by strong lithe movements 2 : INTRICATE, COMPLEX [Latin *sinuosus*, from *sinus* "curve"] — **sin·u·ous·ly** *adv* — **sin·u·ous·ness** *n*

si·nus \'sī-nəs\ *n* : CAVITY, HOLLOW: as a : a narrow passage by which pus is discharged b : any of several cavities in the skull mostly communicating with the nostrils c : a dilatation in a bodily canal or vessel; *also* : a space forming a channel (as for the passage of blood) d : a cleft or indentation between adjoining lobes (as of a leaf) [Latin, "curve, fold, hollow"]

si·nus·itis \,sī-nə-'sīt-əs\ *n* : inflammation of a sinus especially of the skull

si·nus ve·no·sus \,sī-nəs-vi-'nō-səs\ *n* : an enlarged pouch which adjoins the heart and through which venous blood enters the heart in lower vertebrates and embryos [New Latin, "venous sinus"]

Si·on \'sī-ən\ *variant of* ZION

Siou·an \'sü-ən\ *n* 1 : a stock of Indian languages spoken in central and eastern North America 2 : a member of the Indian peoples speaking Siouan languages

Sioux \'sü\ *n, pl* **Sioux** \'sü, 'süz\ : a member of an Amerindian people of the Missouri and northern Mississippi valleys : SIOUAN [French, from *Nadowessioux*, from Ojibwa *Nadoweisiw*]

¹sip \'sip\ *vb* **sipped; sip·ping** 1 : to drink in small quantities or little by little 2 : to take sips from : TASTE [Middle English *sippen*] — **sip·per** *n*

²sip *n* 1 : the act of sipping 2 : a small amount taken by sipping

¹si·phon *also* **sy·phon** \'sī-fən\ *n* 1 a : a tube bent to form two legs of unequal length by which a liquid can be transferred to a lower level over an intermediate elevation by the pressure of the atmosphere in forcing the liquid up the shorter branch of the tube immersed in it while the excess of weight of the liquid in the longer branch when once filled causes a continuous flow b *usually* **syphon** : a bottle for holding carbonated water that is driven out through a bent tube in its neck by the pressure of the gas when a valve in the tube is opened 2 : any of various tubular organs in animals and especially mollusks or arthropods used for drawing in or ejecting fluids [French, from Latin *sipho* "tube, pipe, siphon", from Greek *siphōn*]

²siphon *also* **syphon** *vb* **si·phoned; si·phon·ing** \'sīf-ning, -ə-ning\ : to draw off or pass off by or as if by a siphon

si·pho·no·phore \sī-'fän-ə-,fōr, 'sī-fə-nə-, -,fȯr\ *n* : any of an order (Siphonophora) of mostly delicate, transparent, and colored compound hydrozoans

sir \sər, 'sər\ *n* 1 *often cap* : a male member of an order of knighthood or a man holding the rank of baronet — used as a title before a full name or a given name ⟨*Sir* Winston Churchill⟩ ⟨*Sir* Winston⟩ 2 a — used as a usually respectful form of direct address ⟨yes, *sir*⟩ b *cap* — used sometimes as a salutation in a letter addressed to high-ranking officials (as a governor) ⟨*Sir:*⟩ [Middle English, from *sire*]

Si·rach \'sī-rak *also* sə-'räk\ *n* — see BIBLE table

sir·dar \'sər-,där\ *n* : a person of high rank or one holding a position of responsibility especially in India [Hindi *sardār*, from Persian]

¹sire \'sīr\ *n* 1 a : FATHER 1a b *archaic* : a male ancestor : FOREFATHER c : AUTHOR 2, ORIGINATOR 2 a *archaic* : a man of high station or great authority — used formerly as a form of address (as to a king) or as a title b — a form of respectful address formerly used for a

reigning sovereign 3 : the male parent of an animal and especially of a domestic animal [Old French, from Latin *senior*, adj., "senior"]

²sire *vt* 1 : BEGET 1, PROCREATE — used especially of domestic animals 2 : to bring into being : ORIGINATE

¹si·ren \'sī-rən, *for 3 also* sī-'rēn\ *n* 1 *often cap* : one of a group of creatures in Greek mythology depicted as birds with the heads and sometimes the breasts and arms of women that lured mariners to destruction by their singing 2 : a woman held to be insidiously seductive : TEMPTRESS 3 a : an apparatus producing musical tones by the rapid interruption of a current (as of air or steam) by a perforated rotating disk b : a device often electrically operated for producing a penetrating warning sound ⟨an ambulance *siren*⟩ ⟨an air-raid *siren*⟩ 4 a : any of a genus of eel-shaped amphibians with small forelimbs but neither hind legs nor pelvis and with permanent external gills as well as lungs b : SIRENIAN [Latin, from Greek *seirēn*]

²si·ren \'sī-rən\ *adj* : of, relating to, or resembling a siren

si·re·ni·an \sī-'rē-nē-ən\ *n* : any of an order (Sirenia) of aquatic plant-eating mammals including the manatee and dugong

siren song *n* : an alluring utterance or appeal; *esp* : one that is seductive or deceptive

Sir·i·us \'sir-ē-əs\ *n* : a star of the constellation Canis Major constituting the brightest star in the heavens — called also *Dog Star* [Latin, from Greek *Seirios*, literally, "glowing"]

sir·loin \'sər-,lȯin\ *n* : a cut of meat and especially of beef from the part of the hindquarter just in front of the round [Middle French *surlonge*, from *sur* "over" (from Latin *super*) + *loigne, longe* "loin"]

si·roc·co \sə-'räk-ō\ *n, pl* **-cos** 1 a : a hot dust-laden wind from the Libyan desert that blows on the northern Mediterranean coast chiefly in Italy, Malta, and Sicily b : a warm moist oppressive southeast wind in the same regions 2 : a hot or warm wind of cyclonic origin from an arid or heated region [Italian *scirocco, sirocco*, from Arabic *sharq* "east"]

sir·rah *also* **sir·ra** \'sir-ə\ *n, obsolete* — used as a form of address implying inferiority in the person addressed [alteration of *sir*]

sir·ree *also* **sir·ee** \sər-'ē, ,sər-'ē\ *n* : SIR 2a — used as an emphatic form usually after *yes* or *no*

sirup, sirupy *variant of* SYRUP, SYRUPY

si·sal \'sī-səl, -zəl\ *n* 1 : a strong durable white fiber used for cordage 2 : a widely grown West Indian agave whose leaves yield sisal [Mexican Spanish, from *Sisal*, Yucatán, Mexico]

sis·kin \'sis-kən\ *n* : a small chiefly greenish and yellowish Old World finch related to the goldfinch [German dialect *sisschen*, of Slavic origin]

sis·si·fied \'sis-i-,fīd\ *adj* : SISSY

sis·sy \'sis-ē\ *n, pl* **sissies** : an effeminate man or boy; *also* : a timid or cowardly person [*sis*, short for *sister*] — **sissy** *adj*

sis·ter \'sis-tər\ *n* 1 : a female who has one or both parents in common with another 2 *often cap* : a woman who is a member of a religious order — often used as a title ⟨*Sister* Mary Angelica⟩ 3 a : a woman related to another person by a common tie or interest b : one having characteristics similar to another ⟨*sister* ships⟩ 4 *chiefly British* : NURSE 2 [Old English *sweoster*]

sis·ter·hood \-,hu̇d\ *n* 1 a : the state of being a sister b : sisterly relationship 2 : a community or society of sisters; *esp* : a religious society of women

sis·ter-in-law \'sis-tə-rən-,lȯ, -trən-,lȯ, -tərn-,lȯ\ *n, pl* **sis·ters-in-law** \-tər-zən-\ 1 : the sister of one's spouse 2 a : the wife of one's brother b : the wife of one's spouse's brother

sis·ter·ly \'sis-tər-lē\ *adj* : of, relating to, or typical of a sister — **sisterly** *adv*

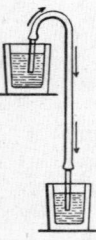

¹siphon 1a

sis·trum \'sis-trəm\ *n, pl* **sistrums** *or* **sis·tra** \-trə\ : an ancient Egyptian percussion instrument having a thin metal frame with many metal rods that jingle when shaken [Latin, from Greek *seistron,* from *seiein* "to shake"]

¹sit \'sit\ *vb* **sat** \'sat\; **sit·ting 1 a** : to rest or cause to rest on the buttocks or haunches ⟨*sit* in a chair⟩ ⟨*sat* the baby down to eat⟩ **b** : PERCH 2, ROOST **c** : to keep one's seat upon ⟨*sit* a horse⟩ **d** : SEAT 1b **2** : to occupy a place as a member of an official body ⟨*sit* in Congress⟩ **3** : to hold a session **4** : to cover eggs for hatching : BROOD **5 a** : to pose for a portrait or photograph **b** : to serve as a model **6** : to lie or hang relative to a wearer ⟨the collar *sits* awkwardly⟩ **7** : to lie or rest in any condition or location ⟨the vase *sits* on the table⟩ ⟨the house *sits* well back from the road⟩ **8** : to remain inactive ⟨the car *sits* in the garage⟩ **9** : BABY-SIT [Old English *sittan*] — **sit on 1** : to hold deliberations about **2** : REPRESS 4, SQUELCH **3** : to delay action or decision concerning — **sit on one's hands 1** : to withhold applause **2** : to fail to take action — **sit pretty** : to be in a very favorable position — **sit tight** : to maintain one's position without change

²sit *n* **1** : an act or period of sitting **2** : the way in which a garment fits

si·tar \si-'tär\ *n* : an Indian lute with a long neck and a varying number of strings [Hindi *sitār*]

sit–down \'sit-,daůn\ *n* : a work stoppage in which protesting employees cease working but refuse to leave their place of employment — called also *sit-down strike*

¹site \'sīt\ *n* **1** : the actual or planned location (as of a building or town) **2** : the place or scene of something ⟨famous battle *sites*⟩ ⟨a camp *site*⟩ [Latin *situs* "place, position", from *sinere* "to leave, place, lay"]

²site *vt* : to place on a site or in position : LOCATE

sith \'sith, 'sith\ *archaic variant of* SINCE

sit–in \'sit-,in\ *n* **1** : SIT-DOWN **2** : an act of occupying seats especially in a racially segregated establishment in organized protest

sit out *vt* : to refrain from participating in ⟨will *sit* the next dance *out*⟩ ⟨*sat* the war *out*⟩

sit·ter \'sit-ər\ *n* : one that sits; *esp* : BABY-SITTER

¹sit·ting \'sit-ing\ *n* **1** : an act of one that sits; *esp* : a single occasion of continuous sitting **2 a** : a brooding over eggs for hatching **b** : SETTING 6 **3** : SESSION 1

²sitting *adj* **1** : that is setting ⟨a *sitting* hen⟩ **2** : easily hit ⟨a *sitting* target⟩ **3 a** : used in or for sitting ⟨a *sitting* position⟩ **b** : performed while sitting ⟨a *sitting* shot⟩

sitting duck *n* : an easy or defenseless target for attack, criticism, or unscrupulous dealings

sitting room *n* : LIVING ROOM

¹sit·u·ate \'sich-ə-wət, -,wāt\ *adj* : SITUATED 1 [Medieval Latin *situatus,* past participle of *situare* "to place", from Latin *situs* "place, site"]

²sit·u·ate \'sich-ə-,wāt\ *vt* : to place in a site or situation

sit·u·at·ed \-,wāt-əd\ *adj* **1** : having a site : LOCATED **2** : CIRCUMSTANCED ⟨not rich but comfortably *situated*⟩

sit·u·a·tion \,sich-ə-'wā-shən\ *n* **1 a** : the way in which something is placed in relation to its surroundings **b** : SITE 1 **2 a** : position or place of employment : POST, JOB **b** : position in life : STATUS **3** : position with respect to conditions and circumstances ⟨the military *situation*⟩ **4 a** : relative position or combination of circumstances at a certain moment ⟨the *situation* at the beginning of the trial⟩ **b** : a particular or striking complex of affairs at a stage in the action of a narrative or drama — **sit·u·a·tion·al** \-shnəl, -shən-l\ *adj* — **sit·u·a·tion·al·ly** \-ē\ *adv*

sit–up \'sit-,əp\ *n* : a conditioning exercise performed in a supine position by raising the trunk to a sitting position usually while keeping the legs straight and returning to the original position

sit up \sit-'əp\ *vi* **1** : to rise from a lying to a sitting position **2** : to show interest, alertness, or surprise **3** : to stay up beyond the usual bedtime

si·tus \'sīt-əs\ *n* : the place where something exists or originates [Latin, "place, site"]

sitz bath \'sits-\ *n* : a tub in which one bathes in a sitting position; *also* : a bath so taken especially therapeutically [German *sitzbad,* from *sitz* "act of sitting" + *bad* "bath"]

sitz·mark \'sit-,smärk, 'zit-\ *n* : a depression left in the snow by a skier falling backward [German *sitzmarke,* from *sitz* "act of sitting" + *marke* "mark"]

six \'siks\ *n* **1** : one more than five; *also* : a symbol representing this — see NUMBER table **2** : the sixth in a set or series **3** : something having six units or members; *esp* : a 6-cylinder engine or automobile [Old English *siex*] — **six** *adj or pron* — **at sixes and sevens** : in disorder

six–gun \'siks-,gən\ *n* : a 6-chambered revolver

six–o–six *or* **606** \,sik-,sō-'siks\ *n* : ARSPHENAMINE [from its having been the 606th compound tested and introduced by Paul Ehrlich, died 1915, German bacteriologist]

six–pack \'sik-,spak\ *n* **1** : a package of six items (as bottles or cans) **2** : the contents of a six-pack

six·pence \'sik-spəns, *in the United States also* -,spens\ *n* : the sum of six pence; *also* : a British coin no longer issued worth six pence or half a shilling

six·pen·ny \-spə-nē, *in the United States also* -,spen-ē\ *adj* : costing or worth sixpence

six–shoot·er \'sik-'shüt-ər, ,siks-\ *n* : SIX-GUN

six·teen \sik-'stēn, 'sik-\ *n* : one more than 15; *also* : a symbol representing this — see NUMBER table [Old English *sixtȳne*] — **sixteen** *adj or pron* — **six·teenth** \-'stēnth, -stēntth\ *adj or n*

sixteenth note *n* : a musical note with the time value of $\frac{1}{16}$ of a whole note

sixth \'siksth, 'sikstth, 'sikst\ *n* : number six in a countable series — see NUMBER table — **sixth** *adj or adv* — **sixth·ly** \-lē\ *adv*

sixth sense *n* : a keen intuitive power

six·ty \'sik-stē\ *n, pl* **sixties** : ten more than 50; *also* : a symbol representing this — see NUMBER table [Old English *siextig*] — **six·ti·eth** \-stē-əth\ *adj or n* — **sixty** *adj or pron*

six·ty–fourth note \,sik-stē-'fōrth-, -'fȯrth-\ *n* : a musical note with the time value of $\frac{1}{64}$ of a whole note

siz·able *or* **size·able** \'sī-zə-bəl\ *adj* : fairly large — **siz·able·ness** *n* — **siz·ably** \-blē\ *adv*

¹size \'sīz\ *n* **1 a** : physical magnitude, extent, or bulk : relative or proportionate dimensions **b** : considerable proportions : BIGNESS **2** : one of a series of graduated measures especially of manufactured articles (as of clothing) conventionally identified by numbers or letters ⟨a *size* 7 hat⟩ **3** : character or status of a person or thing especially with reference to importance, merit, or correspondence to needs **4** : actual state of affairs : true condition ⟨that's about the *size* of it⟩ [Middle French *sise* "assize", short for *assise*]

²size *vt* **1** : to make a particular size : bring to proper or suitable size **2** : to arrange, grade, or classify as to size or bulk **3** : to form a judgment of — usually used with *up* ⟨*size* a job up⟩ ⟨*sizing* up the candidates⟩

³size *n* : a gluey material (as a preparation of glue, flour, varnish, or resins) used for filling the pores in a surface (as of plaster), as a stiffener (as of fabric), or as an adhesive for applying color or leaf to book edges or covers [Middle English *sise*]

⁴size *vt* : to apply size to

⁵size *adj* : SIZED 1 ⟨bite-*size*⟩

sized \'sīzd\ *adj* **1** : having a specified size or bulk ⟨a small-*sized* house⟩ **2** : arranged or adjusted by size

siz·ing \'sī-zing\ *n* : ³SIZE

siz·zle \'siz-əl\ *vb* **siz·zled**; **siz·zling** \'siz-ling, -ə-ling\ **1** : to burn up or sear with or as if with a hissing sound

sitar

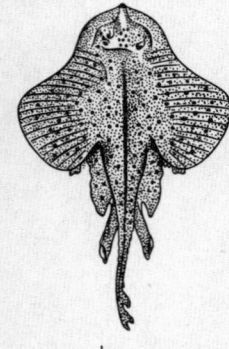
¹skate

2 : to make a hissing sound in or as if in burning or frying **3** : SEETHE **4** [perhaps from earlier *siss* "to hiss"] — **siz·zle** *n* — **siz·zler** \'siz-lər, -ə-lər\ *n*

ska \'skä\ *n* : popular music of Jamaican origin that combines elements of traditional Caribbean rhythms and jazz [origin unknown]

skald \'skold, 'skäld\ *n* : an ancient Scandinavian poet or writer of history [Old Norse *skäld*] — **skald·ic** \-ik\ *adj*

¹**skate** \'skāt\ *n* : any of numerous rays with broadly winglike lateral fins [Old Norse *skata*]

²**skate** *n* : a metal runner or a set of two pairs of wheels in tandem on a frame that may be attached to the bottom of a boot for use in gliding over ice or rolling over a hard flat surface; *also* : a boot with an attached runner or wheels [Dutch *schaats* "stilt, skate"]

³**skate** *vi* **1** : to glide on skates propelled by the alternate pushing action of the legs **2** : to slip or glide as if on skates — **skat·er** *n*

⁴**skate** *n* **1** : a thin awkward-looking or decrepit horse : NAG **2** : FELLOW 4a [probably from English dialect *skite* "offensive person"]

skate·board \'skāt-,bord, -,bord\ *n* : a short narrow board with two pairs of wheels mounted on the bottom in such a way that they will turn in the direction that the board is tilted — **skate·board·er** \-,bord-ər, -,bord-\ *n* — **skate·board·ing** \-ing\ *n*

skat·ing \'skāt-ing\ *n* : the sport or pastime of gliding on skates; *esp* : competition that involves racing or the performance of fancy maneuvers or dance patterns on skates

ske·dad·dle \ski-'dad-l\ *vi* **-dad·dled; -dad·dling** \-'dad-ling, -l-ing\ : to run away; *esp* : to flee in a panic [origin unknown]

skeet \'skēt\ *n* : clay pigeon shooting on a semicircular range with targets thrown from either of two traps so as to provide a variety of shooting angles [Old Norse *skjōta* "to shoot"]

¹**skein** \'skān\ *n* : a looped length of yarn or thread put up in a loose twist after it is taken from the reel [Middle French *escaigne*]

²**skein** *vt* : to wind into skeins ⟨*skein* yarn⟩

skel·e·tal \'skel-ət-l\ *adj* : of, relating or attached to, forming, or resembling a skeleton ⟨*skeletal* muscles⟩ ⟨the *skeletal* system⟩ — **skel·e·tal·ly** \-l-ē\ *adv*

¹**skel·e·ton** \'skel-ət-n\ *n* **1** : a usually rigid supporting or protecting structure or framework of an organism; *esp* : the framework of bone or sometimes cartilage that supports the soft tissues and protects the internal organs of a vertebrate (as a fish or human) **2** : something reduced to its minimum form or essential parts **3** : an emaciated person or animal **4** : something forming a structural framework **5** : something shameful and kept secret (as in a family) [Greek, neuter of *skeletos* "dried up"]

skep

²**skeleton** *adj* : of, consisting of, or resembling a skeleton ⟨a *skeleton* crew⟩

skel·e·ton·ize \'skel-ət-n-,īz\ *vt* : to produce in or reduce to skeleton form

skel·e·ton·iz·er \-,ī-zər\ *n* : a moth or butterfly larva that feeds on leaves reducing them to a skeleton of veins

skeleton key *n* : a key made to open many locks

skel·ter \'skel-tər\ *vi* : SCURRY [from *helter-skelter*]

skep \'skep\ *n* : a domed beehive made of twisted straw [Old English *sceppe* "basketful", from Old Norse *skeppa* "bushel"]

skep·tic *or* **scep·tic** \'skep-tik\ *n* **1** : an adherent or advocate of skepticism **2** : a person slow to believe or ready to question : DOUBTER [Greek *skeptikos*, from *skeptikos* "thoughtful", from *skeptesthai* "to look, consider"]

skep·ti·cal \-ti-kəl\ *adj* : relating to, characteristic of, or marked by skepticism — **skep·ti·cal·ly** \-kə-lē, -klē\ *adv*

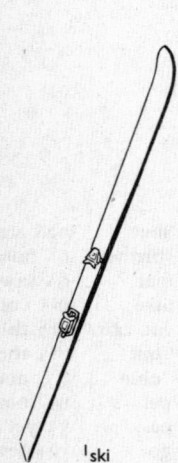
¹ski

skep·ti·cism \'skep-tə-,siz-əm\ *n* **1** : the philosophical doctrine that true and absolute knowledge is unattainable **2** : an attitude of doubt, suspicion, or uncertainty especially about religious matters

sker·ry \'sker-ē\ *n, pl* **skerries** : a rocky isle : REEF [of Scandinavian origin]

¹**sketch** \'skech\ *n* **1 a** : a rough drawing representing the chief features of an object or scene and often made as a preliminary study **b** : a tentative draft (as for a literary work) **2** : a brief description or outline **3 a** : a short literary composition somewhat resembling the short story and the essay but intentionally casual in treatment and familiar in tone **b** : a short instrumental composition **c** : a theatrical piece having a single scene; *esp* : a brief comic skit [Dutch *schets*, from Italian *schizzo* "sketch, splash", from *schizzare* "to splash"]

²**sketch** *vb* **1** : to make a sketch, rough draft, or outline of **2** : to draw or paint sketches — **sketch·er** *n*

sketch·book \'skech-,buk\ *n* : a book of or for sketches

sketchy \'skech-ē\ *adj* **sketch·i·er; -est 1** : of the nature of a sketch : roughly outlined **2** : lacking in completeness, clearness, or polish — **sketch·i·ly** \'skech-ə-lē\ *adv* — **sketch·i·ness** \'skech-ē-nəs\ *n*

¹**skew** \'skyü\ *vb* **1** : to take an oblique course : move or turn aside : TWIST, SWERVE **2** : to make, set, or cut on the skew **3** : to distort from a true value or symmetrical form [Old North French *escuer* "to shun", of Germanic origin]

²**skew** *adj* **1** : set, placed, or running obliquely to something else **2** : neither parallel nor intersecting ⟨*skew* lines⟩ — **skew·ness** \'skyü-nəs\ *n*

³**skew** *n* : a deviation from a straight line : SLANT

skew·bald \'skyü-,bold\ *adj* : marked with spots and patches of white and some other color ⟨a *skewbald* horse⟩ [earlier *skewed* "skewbald" + *bald*]

¹**skew·er** \'skyü-ər, 'skyu-ər, 'skyur\ *n* **1** : a pin for keeping meat in form while roasting or for holding small pieces of meat and vegetables for broiling **2** : something shaped or used like a meat skewer [probably from earlier *skiver* "cutter", from *skive* "to cut, pare", of Scandinavian origin]

²**skewer** *vt* : to fasten or pierce with or as if with a skewer

skew quadrilateral *n* : a quadrilateral in which not all four vertices lie in the same plane

¹**ski** \'skē\ *n, pl* **skis** : one of a pair of narrow strips of wood, metal, or plastic curving upward in front that are worn by people for gliding over snow or water [Norwegian, from Old Norse *skith* "stick, ski"]

²**ski** *vi* **skied; ski·ing** : to glide on skis — **ski·er** *n*

ski boot *n* : a boot or shoe used for skiing; *esp* : a heavy rigid boot that extends above the ankle

¹**skid** \'skid\ *n* **1** : a log or plank for supporting something (as above the ground) ⟨put a boat on *skids*⟩ **2** : one of the logs, planks, or rails along or on which something heavy is rolled or slid **3** : a device placed under a carriage wheel to prevent its turning : DRAG **4** : a runner used as part of the landing gear of an airplane or helicopter **5** : the act of skidding : SLIDE [perhaps of Scandinavian origin] — **on the skids** : declining sharply (as in value, status, or prominence)

²**skid** *vb* **skid·ded; skid·ding 1** : to slow or halt by use of a skid **2** : to haul along, slide, hoist, or store on skids **3 a** : to fail to grip the roadway; *esp* : to slip sideways on the road ⟨the car *skidded* on an icy road⟩ **b** : to slide sideways away from the center of curvature when turning ⟨a *skidding* airplane⟩ **c** : SLIDE, SLIP ⟨*skid* across ice⟩ **4** : to fall rapidly, steeply, or far ⟨the temperature *skidded* to zero⟩

skid·doo *or* **ski·doo** \skid-'ü\ *vi* : to go away : DEPART [probably alteration of *skedaddle*]

skid row \'skid-'rō\ *n* : a district of cheap saloons and rooming houses frequented by vagrants and derelicts

[from *skid road* "road along which logs are dragged, section of town frequented by loggers"]

skiff \'skif\ *n* **1** : a small rowboat or sailboat **2** : a small fast motorboat [Italian *schifo*, of Germanic origin]

ski·ing *n* : the art or sport of sliding and jumping on skis

ski jump *n* : a jump made by a person wearing skis; *also* : a course or track especially prepared for such jumping — **ski jump** *vi*

ski lift *n* : a power-driven conveyor for transporting skiers or sightseers up a long slope or mountainside

skill \'skil\ *n* **1** : ability or dexterity that comes from training or practice **2** : a developed or acquired ability : ACCOMPLISHMENT ⟨reading *skills*⟩ [Old Norse *skil* "distinction, knowledge"] SYN see ART

skilled \'skild\ *adj* **1** : having acquired mastery of a skill : EXPERT ⟨a *skilled* mason⟩ **2** : requiring skill and training ⟨a *skilled* trade⟩ ⬜ SYN SKILLFUL: SKILLED applies to one who has mastered the details and technique of a trade, art, or profession ⟨*skilled* craftsmen⟩ SKILLFUL stresses adeptness and dexterity as individual qualities rather than standards ⟨*skillful* performance of a concerto⟩

skil·let \'skil-ət\ *n* : a frying pan [Middle English *skelet*]

skill·ful *or* **skil·ful** \'skil-fəl\ *adj* **1** : having or displaying skill : EXPERT, DEXTEROUS ⟨a *skillful* debater⟩ **2** : accomplished with skill ⟨*skillful* defense⟩ SYN see PROFICIENT, SKILLED — **skill·ful·ly** \-fə-lē\ *adv* — **skill·ful·ness** *n*

skill·less *or* **skil·less** \'skil-ləs\ *adj* : having no skill — **skill·less·ness** *n*

¹skim \'skim\ *vb* **skimmed; skim·ming** **1 a** : to clear (a liquid) of scum or floating substance : remove (as film or scum) from the surface of a liquid **b** : to remove cream from by skimming **2** : to read, study, or examine superficially and rapidly; *esp* : to glance through (as a book) for the chief ideas or the plot **3** : to throw so as to ricochet along the surface of water **4** : to cover or become covered with or as if with a film or scum **5** : to pass swiftly or lightly over : glide above or near a surface [Middle English *skimmen*]

²skim *n* **1** : a thin layer, coating, or film **2** : the act of skimming **3** : something (as milk) that is skimmed

³skim *adj* **1** : that has been skimmed **2** : made of skim milk ⟨*skim* cheese⟩

skim·mer \'skim-ər\ *n* **1** : one that skims; *esp* : a flat perforated scoop or spoon used for skimming **2** : any of several long-winged seabirds related to the terns that fly low over the water **3** : a usually straw flat-crowned hat with a wide straight brim

skim milk *also* **skimmed milk** *n* : milk from which the cream has been taken

skim·ming \'skim-ing\ *n* **1** : material skimmed from a liquid **2** : the practice of concealing gambling profits so as to avoid taxes

ski·mo·bile \'skē-mō-ˌbēl\ *n* : SNOWMOBILE

skimp \'skimp\ *vb* **1** : to give insufficient or barely sufficient attention or effort to or funds for **2** : to save by or as if by skimping [perhaps alteration of *scrimp*]

skimpy \'skim-pē\ *adj* **skimp·i·er; -est** : deficient (as in supply) especially through skimping : SCANTY — **skimp·i·ly** \-pə-lē\ *adv* — **skimp·i·ness** \-pē-nəs\ *n*

¹skin \'skin\ *n* **1 a** : the integument of an animal and especially of a small animal or furbearer when separated from the body — compare HIDE **b** : a sheet of parchment or vellum made from a hide **c** : BOTTLE 1b **2 a** : the external limiting layer of an animal body especially when forming a tough but flexible cover; *also* : the 2-layered tissue of which this is formed in a vertebrate — compare DERMIS, EPIDERMIS **b** : an outer or surface layer (as a rind) ⟨a sausage *skin*⟩ ⟨apple *skins*⟩ **3** : the life or physical well-being of a person ⟨save one's *skin*⟩ **4** : a sheathing or casing forming the outside surface of a structure (as a ship or airplane) [Old Norse *skinn*] — **skin·less** \-ləs\ *adj* — **skinned** \'skind\ *adj* — **by the skin of one's teeth** : by a very

narrow margin — **under one's skin** : beneath one's surface powers of resistance to the point of distressing or irritating

²skin *vb* **skinned; skin·ning** **1** : to cover or become covered with or as if with skin **2 a** : to strip, scrape, or rub off the skin of ⟨*skin* a fruit⟩ ⟨*skin* one's knee⟩ **b** : to strip or peel off **3 a** : CHEAT 1, FLEECE **b** : OUTDO **c** : CENSURE, REPRIMAND **4 a** : to climb up or down ⟨*skin* up and down a rope⟩ **b** : to pass or get by with scant room to spare

skin–deep \'skin-'dēp\ *adj* **1** : as deep as the skin **2** : SUPERFICIAL; *esp* : not thorough or lasting in impression

skin–dive \'skin-ˌdīv\ *vi* : to engage in skin diving — **skin diver** *n*

skin diving *n* : the sport of swimming underwater with a mask, swim fins, and usually a snorkel especially without scuba equipment

skin·flint \'skin-ˌflint\ *n* : a person who is very hard and grasping in money matters

skin·ful \-ˌfu̇l\ *n* **1** : the contents of a skin bottle **2** : a large or satisfying quantity especially of liquor

skin game *n* : a swindling game or trick

skin graft *n* : a piece of skin transferred from a donor area to grow new skin at a place denuded (as by burning)

skink \'skingk\ *n* : any of a family of mostly small lizards with small scales [Latin *scincus*, from Greek *skinkos*]

skin·ner \'skin-ər\ *n* **1** : one that removes and processes or deals in skins, pelts, or hides **2** : a driver of draft animals and especially mules

skin·ny \'skin-ē\ *adj* **skin·ni·er; -est** **1** : resembling skin : MEMBRANOUS ⟨a *skinny* layer⟩ **2** : very thin : LEAN, EMACIATED — **skin·ni·ness** *n*

skin·ny–dip·ping \'skin-ē-ˌdip-ing\ *n* : swimming in the nude — **skin·ny–dip·per** \-ˌdip-ər\ *n*

skin test *n* : a test (as a scratch test) performed on the skin and used in detecting allergic hypersensitivity

skin·tight \'skin-'tīt\ *adj* : closely fitted to the figure

¹skip \'skip\ *vb* **skipped; skip·ping** **1 a** : to move or proceed with leaps and bounds **b** : to bound or cause to bound off one point after another **c** : to leap over lightly and nimbly **2** : to depart hurriedly or secretly ⟨*skip* town⟩ **3 a** : to pass over or omit (as an interval, item, or step) **b** : to omit or cause to omit a grade in school in advancing to the next **c** : to pass over without notice or mention **d** : to fail to attend ⟨*skipped* the meeting⟩ **e** : MISFIRE 1 [Middle English *skippen*]

²skip *n* **1 a** : a light bounding step **b** : a gait composed of alternating hops and steps **2** : an act of omission or the thing omitted

³skip *n* : the captain of a side in some games (as curling or lawn bowling) [short for ²*skipper*]

⁴skip *vt* **skipped; skip·ping** : to act as skipper of

skip·jack \'skip-ˌjak\ *n, pl* **skipjacks** *or* **skipjack** : any of various fishes (as a bonito or bluefish) that jump above or play at the surface of the water

ski pole *n* : a pointed pole or stick used as an aid in skiing that is fitted with a strap for the hand at the top and an encircling disk set a little above the point

¹skip·per \'skip-ər\ *n* **1** : one that skips **2 a** : any of numerous small stout-bodied insects of swift erratic flight that differ from the typical butterflies in wing venation and the form of the antennae **b** : any of several small leaping insects ⟨cheese *skippers*⟩

²skipper *n* : the master of a ship; *esp* : the master of a fishing, small trading, or pleasure boat [Dutch *schipper*, from *schip* "ship"]

¹skirl \'skərl, 'skirl\ *vb* : to sound the high shrill tone of the bagpipe [of Scandinavian origin]

²skirl *n* : the high shrill sound of a bagpipe

¹skir·mish \'skər-mish\ *n* **1** : a minor fight in war **2** : a brisk preliminary conflict [Middle French *escar-*

¹skunk ¹

mouche, from Italian *scaramuccia,* of Germanic origin]

²**skirmish** *vi* **1** : to engage in a skirmish **2** : to search about (as for supplies) — **skir·mish·er** *n*

¹**skirr** \'skər\ *vb* **1** : to leave hurriedly : FLEE; *also* : to move rapidly **2** : to pass rapidly over especially in search of something [perhaps from ¹*scour*]

²**skirr** *n* : WHIR, ROAR [probably imitative]

¹**skirt** \'skərt\ *n* **1 a** : a free hanging part of a garment extending from the waist down **b** : a separate free hanging garment for women and girls covering the body from the waist down **c** : either of two flaps on a saddle covering the bars on which the stirrups are hung **2** *pl* : the outlying parts of a town or city : OUTSKIRTS **3** : a part or attachment serving as a rim, border, or edging **4** *slang* : GIRL 1b, WOMAN [Old Norse *skyrta* "shirt, kirtle"]

²**skirt** *vb* **1** : to form or run along the edge of : BORDER **2** : to provide a skirt or border for **3 a** : to go or pass around or about; *esp* : to go around or keep away from in order to avoid danger or discovery **b** : to evade or miss by a narrow margin **4** : to be, lie, or move along an edge, border, or margin — **skirt·er** *n*

skirt·ing \'skərt-ing\ *n* **1** : something that skirts: as **a** : BORDER 1, MARGIN **b** *British* : BASEBOARD **2** : fabric suitable for skirts

ski run *n* : a slope or trail suitable for skiing

ski suit *n* : a warm outfit for winter sports made in onepiece or two-piece style with a jacket top and pants

skit \'skit\ *n* **1** : a satirical or humorous story or sketch; *esp* : a sketch included in a dramatic performance (as a revue) **2** : a short serious dramatic piece; *esp* : one done by amateurs [origin unknown]

ski tow *n* **1** : a power-driven conveyor for pulling skiers to the top of a slope that consists usually of an endless motor-driven moving rope which the skier grasps **2** : SKILIFT

skit·ter \'skit-ər\ *vb* : to glide or skip lightly or quickly : skim along a surface [probably from English dialect *skite* "to move quickly"]

skit·tish \'skit-ish\ *adj* **1** : lively or frivolous in nature or action **2** : easily frightened : RESTIVE ⟨a *skittish* horse⟩ **3** : hard to deal with or manage : TRICKY **4 a** : tensely nervous or cautious : WARY **b** : inclined to be shy : COY [Middle English] — **skit·tish·ly** *adv* — **skittish·ness** *n*

skit·tle \'skit-l\ *n* **1** *pl* : an English version of ninepins played either with wooden disks or a ball **2** : one of the pins used in skittles [perhaps of Scandinavian origin]

skoal \'skōl\ *n* : TOAST 3, HEALTH — often used interjectionally [Danish *skaal,* literally, "cup"]

skua \'skyü-ə\ *n* : JAEGER; *esp* : a large North Atlantic jaeger [New Latin, of Scandinavian origin]

skul·dug·gery *or* **skull·dug·gery** \,skəl-'dəg-rē, -ə-rē\ *n, pl* **-ger·ies** : underhanded or unscrupulous behavior [origin unknown]

¹**skulk** \'skəlk\ *vi* **1** : to move in a stealthy or furtive manner : SNEAK **2** : to hide or conceal oneself from cowardice or fear or with treacherous intent [of Scandinavian origin] — **skulk·er** *n* □ SYN SKULK, SLINK, SNEAK mean to go or act so as to escape attention. SKULK may imply shyness or cowardice but often suggests an intent to spy or waylay; SLINK stresses a moving so as to avoid notice rather than keeping actually out of sight; SNEAK may add an implication of furtively entering or leaving a place or of accomplishing a purpose by indirect and underhanded methods.

²**skulk** *n* : one that skulks

skull \'skəl\ *n* **1** : the vertebrate head skeleton that forms a bony or cartilaginous case enclosing the brain and chief sense organs and supporting the jaws **2** : the seat of understanding or intelligence : MIND [of Scandinavian origin]

¹skylark

skull and crossbones *n, pl* **skulls and crossbones** : a representation of a human skull over crossbones usually used as a warning of danger to life

skull·cap \'skəl-,kap\ *n* : a close-fitting cap; *esp* : a light cap without brim for indoor wear

skull practice *n* : a strategy class for an athletic team

¹**skunk** \'skəngk\ *n, pl* **skunks** *also* **skunk** **1** : any of various common black-and-white New World mammals related to the weasels and having glands near the anus from which a secretion of pungent and offensive odor is ejected when the animal is startled **2** : an obnoxious person [of American Indian origin]

²**skunk** *vt* : to defeat decisively; *esp* : to shut out in a game

skunk cabbage *n* : an American perennial marsh herb of the arum family that sends up in early spring a cowl= shaped ill-smelling brownish purple spathe

sky \'skī\ *n, pl* **skies** **1** : the expanse of space that appears to constitute a vault over the earth **2** : HEAVEN 2 **3** : WEATHER, CLIMATE ⟨the weatherman predicts sunny *skies*⟩ [Old Norse *skȳ* "cloud"]

sky blue *n* : a pale to light blue

sky·borne \'skī-,bōrn, -,bȯrn\ *adj* : AIRBORNE ⟨*skyborne* troops⟩

sky·box \'skī-,bäks\ *n* : a roofed enclosure of private seats situated high in a sports stadium and typically featuring luxurious amenities

sky·cap \-,kap\ *n* : a person employed to carry hand luggage at an airport [*sky* + -*cap* (as in *redcap*)]

sky·div·ing \-,dī-ving\ *n* : the sport of jumping from an airplane with a parachute at a moderate altitude (as 2000 meters) and performing various maneuvers before opening the parachute and attempting to land on a small target on the ground — **sky diver** *n*

sky·ey \'skī-ē\ *adj* : of or resembling the sky : ETHEREAL

sky-high \'skī-'hī\ *adv or adj* **1 a** : high into the air **b** : to a very high level ⟨our spirits rose *sky-high*⟩ ⟨profits were *sky-high*⟩ **2** : in an enthusiastic manner **3** : to bits : APART ⟨blown *sky-high*⟩

sky·jack·er \-,jak-ər\ *n* : one who commandeers a flying airplane (as by coercing the pilot at gunpoint) [*sky* + -*jacker* (as in *hijacker*)] — **sky·jack·ing** \-,jaking\ *n*

¹**sky·lark** \'skī-,lärk\ *n* : a common Old World lark that sings as it rises in almost perpendicular flight

²**skylark** *vi* : to play wild boisterous pranks : FROLIC — **sky·lark·er** *n*

sky·light \'skī-,līt\ *n* : a window or group of windows in a roof or ceiling

sky·line \-,līn\ *n* **1** : the line where earth and sky seem to meet : HORIZON **2** : an outline against the sky ⟨a *skyline* of tall buildings⟩

sky pilot *n* : CLERGYMAN; *esp* : CHAPLAIN

¹**sky·rock·et** \'skī-,räk-ət\ *n* : ROCKET 1

²**skyrocket** *vb* : to rise or cause to rise abruptly and rapidly ⟨prices are *skyrocketing*⟩

sky·scrap·er \'skī-,skrā-pər\ *n* : a very tall building

sky·ward \'skī-wərd\ *adv or adj* **1** : toward the sky ⟨gaze *skyward*⟩ **2** : to a higher level

sky·way \'skī-,wā\ *n* **1** : a route used by airplanes : AIR LANE **2** : an elevated highway

sky·writ·ing \'skī-,rīt-ing\ *n* : writing formed in the sky by means of a visible substance (as smoke) emitted from an airplane — **sky·writ·er** \-,rīt-ər\ *n*

slab \'slab\ *n* **1** : a thick slice or plate (as of stone, wood, or bread) **2** : the outside piece cut from a log in squaring it [Middle English *slabbe*]

slab·ber \'slab-ər\ *vb* **slab·bered; slab·ber·ing** \'slabring, -ə-ring\ : SLOBBER 1, DROOL [probably from Dutch *slabberen,* from *slabben* "to slaver"] — **slabber** *n*

slab-sid·ed \'slab-'sīd-əd\ *adj* : having flat sides; *also* : being tall or long and lank

¹**slack** \'slak\ *adj* **1** : not properly diligent, careful, or prompt : NEGLIGENT **2** : marked by slowness or lack of energy ⟨a *slack* pace⟩ **3 a** : not tight or tightly drawn ⟨a

slack rope) **b** : lacking in firmness : WEAK ⟨*slack* control⟩ **4** : wanting in activity : DULL ⟨the *slack* season⟩ [Old English *sleac*] — **slack·ly** *adv* — **slack·ness** *n*

²**slack** *vb* **1 a** : to be or become slack or negligent in performing or doing ⟨*slack* one's vigilance⟩ **b** : MODERATE 1 ⟨the wind *slacked* off⟩ **2** : to shirk or evade work or duty **3** : LOOSEN 2 **4 a** : to cause to abate **b** : SLAKE 4

³**slack** *n* **1** : cessation in movement or flow **2** : a part of something that hangs loose without strain ⟨the *slack* of a rope⟩ **3** *pl* : pants especially for casual wear **4** : a dull season or period : LULL

⁴**slack** *n* : fine screenings of coal containing wastes that make it unusable as fuel unless cleaned [Middle English *sleck*]

slack·en \'slak-ən\ *vb* **slack·ened; slack·en·ing** \'slak-ning, -ə-ning\ **1** : to make or become less active : slow up ⟨*slacken* speed⟩ **2** : to make less taut : LOOSEN ⟨*slacken* sail⟩ : SLACK 1a

slack·er \'slak-ər\ *n* : one who shirks work or evades an obligation especially for military service in time of war

slack water *n* : the period at the turn of the tide when there is little or no horizontal motion of tidal water

slag \'slag\ *n* : waste left after the smelting of ore [Low German *slagge*] — **slag·gy** \'slag-ē\ *adj*

slain *past participle of* SLAY

slake \'slāk, 3 & 4 are also 'slak\ *vb* **1** *archaic* : to make or become less violent, intense, or severe : ABATE, MODERATE **2** : to relieve or satisfy with water or liquid : QUENCH ⟨*slake* one's thirst⟩ **3** : to become slaked ⟨lime may *slake* spontaneously in moist air⟩ **4 a** : to cause (lime) to heat and crumble by treatment with water : HYDRATE **b** : to alter (lime) by exposure to air with conversion at least in part to a carbonate [Old English *slacian*, from *sleac* "slack"]

sla·lom \'släl-əm\ *n* **1** : skiing in a zigzag or wavy course between upright obstacles (as flags) **2** : a race against time over a zigzag course [Norwegian, literally, "sloping track"]

¹**slam** \'slam\ *n* : the winning of all or all but one of the tricks of a deal in bridge [origin unknown]

²**slam** *n* **1** : a heavy impact **2 a** : a noisy violent closing **b** : a banging noise especially from the slamming of a door **3** : a cutting or violent criticism [probably of Scandinavian origin]

³**slam** *vb* **slammed; slam·ming 1** : to strike or beat hard **2** : to shut forcibly and noisily : BANG ⟨*slam* the door⟩ **3 a** : to set or slap down violently or noisily ⟨*slammed* my fist on the table⟩ **b** : to put or set hard : JAM 2 ⟨*slammed* on the brakes⟩ **4** : to make a banging noise **5** : to criticize harshly

slam–bang \'slam-'bang\ *adv or adj* **1** : with noisy violence **2** : HEADLONG, RECKLESSLY

slam dunk *n* : DUNK SHOT — **slam–dunk** \'slam-'dəngk\ *vb*

¹**slan·der** \'slan-dər\ *n* **1** : the utterance of false charges or misrepresentations which defame and damage another's reputation **2** : a false and defamatory oral statement about a person — compare LIBEL [Old French *esclandre*, from Late Latin *scandalum* "stumbling block, offense", from Greek *skandalon*] — **slan·der·ous** \-də-rəs, -drəs\ *adj* — **slan·der·ous·ly** *adv* — **slan·der·ous·ness** *n*

²**slander** *vt* **slan·dered; slan·der·ing** \-də-ring, -dring\ : to utter slander against — **slan·der·er** \-dər-ər\ *n* □ SYN SLANDER, DEFAME, MALIGN mean to injure by speaking ill of. SLANDER stresses the suffering of the victim regardless of the intent of the slanderer ⟨*slandered* by thoughtless tongues⟩ DEFAME stresses the actual loss of or injury to one's good name and repute ⟨turning traitor forever *defamed* the family name⟩ MALIGN usually suggests the operation of hatred, prejudice, or bigotry often by subtle misrepresentation rather than direct accusation ⟨*maligned* and persecuted by evil forces⟩

¹**slang** \'slang\ *n* **1** : language peculiar to a particular group, trade, or pursuit ⟨baseball *slang*⟩ **2** : an informal nonstandard vocabulary composed typically of often short-lived coinages, arbitrarily changed words, and extravagant, forced, or facetious figures of speech [origin unknown] SYN see DIALECT — **slang** *adj*

²**slang** *vb* **1** *chiefly British* : to abuse with harsh or coarse language **2** : to use slang or vulgar abuse

slangy \'slang-ē\ *adj* **slang·i·er; -est 1** : of, relating to, or being slang : containing slang **2** : addicted to the use of slang — **slang·i·ly** \'slang-ə-lē\ *adv* — **slang·i·ness** \'slang-ē-nəs\ *n*

¹**slant** \'slant\ *vb* **1** : to turn or incline from a straight line or a level : SLOPE **2** : to interpret or present in accordance with a special viewpoint ⟨stories *slanted* toward young adults⟩ [of Scandinavian origin]

²**slant** *n* **1** : a slanting direction, line, or plane : SLOPE **2 a** : something that slants **b** : DIAGONAL 3 **3** : a way of looking at something ⟨considered the problem from a new *slant*⟩ **4** : GLANCE 3, LOOK — **slant** *adj*

slant height *n* **1** : the length of a line segment lying in the lateral surface of a right circular cone **2** : the altitude of a lateral face of a regular pyramid

slant·ways \'slant-,wāz\ *adv* : SLANTWISE

slant·wise \-,wīz\ *adv or adj* : so as to slant : at a slant : in a slanting direction or position

¹**slap** \'slap\ *n* **1** : a quick sharp blow especially with the open hand; *also* : a noise suggesting that of a slap **2** : INSULT 1, SNUB [Low German *slapp*]

²**slap** *vb* **slapped; slap·ping 1 a** : to strike with or as if with the open hand **b** : to make a sound like that of a slap **2** : to put, place, or throw with careless haste or force ⟨*slapped* down the paper⟩ **3** : to assail verbally : INSULT

³**slap** *adv* : DIRECTLY 1, SMACK

slap·dash \'slap-,dash, -'dash\ *adv or adj* : in a slipshod manner : HAPHAZARD; *also* : HASTILY

slap down *vt* **1** : to prohibit or restrain usually abruptly and with censure from acting in a specified way : SQUELCH **2** : to put an abrupt stop to : SUPPRESS

slap·jack \'slap-,jak\ *n* **1** : PANCAKE **2** : a card game for children in which each player tries to be first to slap a hand on any jack that is turned face up [²*slap* + *-jack* (as in *flapjack*)]

slap shot *n* : a shot in ice hockey made with a full swing that usually causes the puck to fly through the air

slap·stick \'slap-,stik\ *n* **1** : a device made of two flat sticks so fastened as to make a loud noise when used (as by a clown) to strike a person **2** : comedy stressing farce and horseplay — **slapstick** *adj*

¹**slash** \'slash\ *vb* **1** : to cut with rough sweeping blows : GASH **2** : to whip or strike with or as if with a cane **3** : to criticize without mercy **4** : to cut slits in (as a skirt) to reveal a color beneath **5** : to reduce sharply : CUT ⟨*slash* prices⟩ [Middle English *slaschen*] — **slash·er** *n*

²**slash** *n* **1** : an act or result of slashing: as **a** : a long cut or stroke made by slashing **b** : an ornamental slit in a garment **c** : a sharp reduction ⟨budget *slash*⟩ **2** : an open debris-strewn tract in a forest; *also* : the debris in such a tract **3** : DIAGONAL 3

³**slash** *n* : a low swampy area often overgrown with brush [probably from Old English *plæsc* "marshy pool"]

slash pine *n* : a southern pine important as a source of turpentine and lumber

slash pocket *n* : a pocket suspended on the wrong side of a garment from a finished slit on the right side that serves as its opening

slat \'slat\ *n* : a thin narrow flat strip of wood, plastic, or metal ⟨the *slats* of a blind⟩ [Middle French *esclat* "splinter", from *esclater* "to burst, splinter"] — **slat·ted** \'slat-əd\ *adj*

slack–
slat

965

\ə\ abut	\ng\ sing
\ər\ further	\ō\ bone
\a\ mat	\ȯ\ saw
\ā\ take	\ȯi\ coin
\ä\ cot, cart	\th\ thin
\aù\ out	\th\ this
\ch\ chin	\ü\ food
\e\ pet	\ù\ foot
\ē\ easy	\y\ yet
\g\ go	\yü\ few
\i\ tip	\yù\ cure
\ī\ life	\zh\ vision
\j\ job	

¹slate \'slāt\ *n* **1** : a fine-grained and usually bluish gray rock that is formed by compression of shales or other rocks and that splits readily into thin layers or plates; *also* : a piece of this (as a shingle) dressed for use **2** : a tablet of material (as slate) used for writing on **3** : something (as a list of candidates) recorded or made public as if written on a slate **4 a** : a dark purplish gray **b** : a gray similar in color to common roofing slate [Middle French *esclat* "splinter"] — **slate** *adj* — **slate·like** \-,līk\ *adj*

²slate *vt* **1** : to cover with slate or a slatelike substance ⟨*slate* a roof⟩ **2** : to register or schedule on or as if on a slate ⟨*slate* a meeting⟩ — **slat·er** \'slāt-ər\ *n*

slath·er \'slath-ər\ *vt* **slath·ered; slath·er·ing** \'slath·ring, -ə-ring\ **1** : to spread thickly or lavishly ⟨*slather* jam on bread⟩ **2** : to cover thickly or lavishly ⟨*slather* bread with jam⟩ [from earlier *slather* "great quantity", of unknown origin]

slat·tern \'slat-ərn\ *n* : an untidy slovenly woman [probably from German *schlottern* "to hang loosely, slouch"] — **slat·tern·li·ness** \-lē-nəs\ *n* — **slat·tern·ly** \-lē\ *adj or adv*

slaty \'slāt-ē\ *adj* : of, containing, or characteristic of slate; *also* : gray like slate

¹slaugh·ter \'slȯt-ər\ *n* **1** : the act of killing; *esp* : the butchering of livestock for market **2** : destruction of human lives especially in battle : CARNAGE [of Scandinavian origin]

²slaughter *vt* **1** : to kill (an animal) for food : BUTCHER **2** : to kill ruthlessly or in large numbers : MASSACRE — **slaugh·ter·er** \'slȯt-ər-ər\ *n*

slaugh·ter·house \'slȯt-ər-,haus\ *n* : an establishment where animals are butchered

slaugh·ter·ous \'slȯt-ə-rəs\ *adj* : of or relating to slaughter : MURDEROUS — **slaugh·ter·ous·ly** *adv*

Slav \'släv, 'slav\ *n* : a native speaker of a Slavic language [Medieval Latin *Sclavus*, from Late Greek *Sklabos*, from *Sklabēnoi* "Slavs", of Slavic origin]

¹slave \'slāv\ *n* **1** : a person held in servitude as the property of another **2** : a person who has lost self-control and is dominated by something or someone ⟨a *slave* to drink⟩ **3** : DRUDGE, TOILER [Medieval Latin *sclavus*, from *Sclavus* "Slav"] — **slave** *adj* □ ORIGIN In the Middle Ages the warring Germanic peoples subjugated a great part of the Slavic population of east-central Europe. Conquered Slavs were bought and sold as slaves throughout the West. The Slavs' own name for themselves became *Sclavus* in the Latin that served medieval Europe as a universal language. By the 9th or 10th century *sclavus* was used for any human chattel of no matter what origin. This *sclavus* is the ancestor of our English *slave*.

²slave *vi* : to work like a slave : DRUDGE

slave driver *n* **1** : a supervisor of slaves at work **2** : a harsh taskmaster

slave·hold·er \'slāv-,hōl-dər\ *n* : an owner of slaves — **slave·hold·ing** \-ding\ *adj or n*

¹sla·ver \'slav-ər, 'slāv-\ *vi* **sla·vered; sla·ver·ing** \'slav-ring, 'slāv-, -ə-ring\ : DROOL 1b, SLOBBER [of Scandinavian origin]

²slaver *n* : saliva dribbling from the mouth

³slav·er \'slā-vər\ *n* : a person or ship engaged in the slave trade

slav·ery \'slāv-rē, -ə-rē\ *n* **1** : DRUDGERY, TOIL **2 a** : the state of being a slave : SERVITUDE **b** : the practice of owning slaves

slave state *n* : a state of the United States in which slavery was legal until the Civil War

slave trade *n* : traffic in slaves; *esp* : the buying and selling of Negroes for profit prior to the American Civil War

slav·ey \'slā-vē\ *n, pl* **slaveys** : DRUDGE; *esp* : a servant who does general housework

¹Slav·ic \'slav-ik, 'släv-\ *adj* : of, relating to, or characteristic of the Slavs or their languages

²Slavic *n* : a branch of the Indo-European language family including Bulgarian, Czech, Polish, Serbo-Croatian, Slovene, Russian, and Ukrainian

slav·ish \'slā-vish\ *adj* **1** : of or characteristic of a slave : SERVILE **2** : lacking in independence or originality especially of thought ⟨*slavish* dependence on customary ways⟩ ⟨*slavish* imitators⟩ — **slav·ish·ly** *adv* — **slav·ish·ness** *n*

¹Sla·von·ic \slə-'vän-ik\ *adj* : SLAVIC [Medieval Latin *Sclavonia, Slavonia* "land of the Slavs"]

²Slavonic *n* **1** : SLAVIC **2** : OLD CHURCH SLAVONIC

slaw \'slȯ\ *n* : COLESLAW

slay \'slā\ *vb* **slew** \'slü\; **slain** \'slān\; **slay·ing** : to put to death violently : KILL [Old English *slēan* "to strike, slay"] SYN see KILL — **slay·er** *n*

sleave \'slēv\ *n* : SKEIN [derived from Old English -*slǣfan* "to cut"]

slea·zy \'slē-zē, 'slā-\ *adj* **slea·zi·er; -est** **1** : not firmly or closely woven : FLIMSY **2** : made carelessly of inferior material : SHODDY **3** : cheap in character or quality [origin unknown] — **slea·zi·ly** \-zə-lē\ *adv* — **slea·zi·ness** \-zē-nəs\ *n*

¹sled \'sled\ *n* **1** : a vehicle on runners for conveying loads especially over snow or ice **2** : a sled used for coasting on snow-covered slopes [Dutch *sledde*]

²sled *vb* **sled·ded; sled·ding** : to ride or carry on a sled or sleigh — **sled·der** *n*

sled·ding *n* **1** : the use of a sled; *also* : the conditions under which a sled is used **2** : GOING 2 ⟨tough *sledding*⟩

sled dog *n* : a dog trained to draw a sledge especially in the Arctic regions — called also *sledge dog*

¹sledge \'slej\ *n* : SLEDGEHAMMER [Old English *slecg*]

²sledge *n* : a strong heavy sled [Dutch dialect *sleedse*]

³sledge *vb* : to travel with or transport on a sledge

sledge·ham·mer \'slej-,ham-ər\ *n* : a large heavy hammer usually wielded with both hands [¹*sledge*] — **sledgehammer** *adj or vb*

¹sleek \'slēk\ *vb* **1** : to make or become sleek **2** : to cover up : gloss over [Middle English *sliken*]

²sleek *adj* **1 a** : smooth and glossy as if polished ⟨*sleek* dark hair⟩ **b** : having a smooth healthy well-groomed look ⟨*sleek* cattle⟩ **2** : having a prosperous air — **sleek·ly** *adv* — **sleek·ness** *n*

¹sleep \'slēp\ *n* **1** : the natural periodic suspension of consciousness during which the powers of the body are restored **2** : a state resembling sleep: as **a** : a state of torpid inactivity **b** : DEATH 4; *also* : TRANCE, COMA [Old English *slǣp*] — **sleep·like** \-,līk\ *adj*

²sleep *vb* **slept** \'slept\; **sleep·ing** **1** : to rest or be in a state of sleep **2** : to have sexual relations **3** : to get rid of or spend in or by sleep ⟨*slept* away my cares⟩ **4** : to provide sleeping space for ⟨the boat *sleeps* six⟩

sleep·er \'slē-pər\ *n* **1** : one that sleeps **2** : a horizontal beam to support something at or near ground level **3** : SLEEPING CAR **4** : something unpromising or unnoticed that suddenly attains prominence or value

sleeping bag *n* : a bag that is warmly lined or padded for use in sleeping outdoors

sleeping car *n* : a railroad passenger car having berths for sleeping

sleeping pill *n* : a drug and especially a barbiturate that is taken as a tablet or capsule to induce sleep

sleeping sickness *n* **1** : a serious disease found in much of tropical Africa that is marked by fever, protracted lethargy, tremors, and loss of weight and is caused by either of two trypanosomes, and is transmitted by tsetse flies **2** : any of various virus diseases of which lethargy or drowsiness is a prominent feature

sleep·less \'slē-pləs\ *adj* **1** : not able to sleep : INSOMNIAC **2** : affording no sleep **3** : unceasingly alert or active — **sleep·less·ly** *adv* — **sleep·less·ness** *n*

sleep out *vi* **1** : to sleep outdoors **2** : to sleep away from home

sleep·walk·er \'slēp-ˌwȯ-kər\ *n* : one that walks in one's sleep : SOMNAMBULIST — **sleep·walk·ing** \-king\ *n*

sleepy \'slē-pē\ *adj* **sleep·i·er; -est** **1** : ready to fall asleep : DROWSY **2** : quietly inactive ⟨a *sleepy* village⟩ — **sleep·i·ly** \-pə-lē\ *adv* — **sleep·i·ness** \-pē-nəs\ *n*

sleepy·head \'slē-pē-ˌhed\ *n* : a sleepy person

¹sleet \'slēt\ *n* : frozen or partly frozen rain [Middle English *slete*] — **sleety** \'slēt-ē\ *adj*

²sleet *vi* : to shower sleet

sleeve \'slēv\ *n* **1** : the part of a garment covering the arm **2** : something like a sleeve in shape or use; *esp* : a tubular part fitting over another part [Old English *slīefe*] — **sleeved** \'slēvd\ *adj* — **sleeve·less** \'slēv-ləs\ *adj*

sleeve·let \'slēv-lət\ *n* : a covering for the forearm to protect clothing from wear or dirt

sleeve target *n* : a tubular cloth target towed by an airplane for use in air and ground antiaircraft gunnery practice

¹sleigh \'slā\ *n* : an open usually horse-drawn vehicle with runners for use on snow or ice [Dutch *slede, slee*]

²sleigh *vi* : to drive or travel in a sleigh

sleigh bell *n* : any of various bells commonly attached to a sleigh or to the harness of a horse drawing a sleigh

sleight \'slīt\ *n* : deceitful craftiness : CUNNING; *also* : STRATAGEM [Old Norse *slægth*, from *slægr* "sly"]

sleight of hand **1** : skill and dexterity especially in magic tricks **2** : a magic trick requiring sleight of hand

slen·der \'slen-dər\ *adj* **1 a** : spare in frame or flesh; *esp* : gracefully slight **b** : small in circumference in proportion to length or height **2** : limited or inadequate in amount : MEAGER [Middle English *sclendre, slendre*] SYN see THIN — **slen·der·ly** *adv* — **slen·der·ness** *n*

slen·der·ize \-də-ˌrīz\ *vt* : to make slender

¹sleuth \'slüth\ *n* : DETECTIVE [short for *sleuthhound*]

☐ **ORIGIN** A modern English *sleuth* is a detective, but in Middle English the word *sleuth* meant "the track of an animal or person". The word was a borrowing from Old Norse *slōth*. After the 15th century, *sleuth* was seldom used except in compounds like *sleuth-dog* and *sleuthhound*. These were terms for a dog trained to follow a track. The sleuthhound became a symbol of the eager and thorough pursuit of an object. In the 19th century United States the metaphoric *sleuth-hound* acquired a more specific meaning and became an epithet for a detective. This new term was soon shortened to *sleuth*.

²sleuth *vi* : to act as a detective

sleuth·hound \-ˌhau̇nd\ *n* : a dog that tracks by scent; *esp* : BLOODHOUND [Middle English, from *sleuth* "track of an animal or person", from Old Norse *slōth*]

¹slew \'slü\ *past of* SLAY

²slew *variant of* SLOUGH

³slew *variant of* SLUE

⁴slew *also* **slue** *n* : a large number : LOT ⟨a whole *slew* of letters to write⟩ ⟨*slews* of work⟩ [Irish Gaelic *sluagh*]

¹slice \'slīs\ *n* **1** : a thin flat piece cut from something ⟨a *slice* of bread⟩ **2** : a spatula or knife with wedge-shaped blade ⟨fish *slice*⟩ **3** : a path of a ball that deviates from a straight course to the same side as the dominant hand of the player propelling it [Middle French *esclice* "splinter", from *esclicier* "to splinter", of Germanic origin]

²slice *vb* **1 a** : to cut with or as if with a knife **b** : to cut into slices **2** : to hit (a ball) so that a slice results — **slic·er** *n*

¹slick \'slik\ *vt* : to make sleek or smooth [Middle English *sliken*]

²slick *adj* **1 a** : having a smooth surface : SLIPPERY **b** : GLIB, TRITE **2 a** : characterized by subtlety or nimble wit; *esp* : WILY **b** : DEFT, SKILLFUL — **slick·ly** *adv* — **slick·ness** *n*

³slick *n* **1** : something that is smooth or slippery; *esp* : a smooth patch of water covered with a film of oil **2** : a popular magazine printed on coated stock

slick·er \'slik-ər\ *n* **1** : a long loose raincoat often of oilskin or plastic **2 a** : a clever crook **b** : a usually sophisticated or stylish person : DUDE

¹slide \'slīd\ *vb* **slid** \'slid\; **slid·ing** \'slīd-ing\ **1 a** : to move or cause to move smoothly over a surface : GLIDE, SLIP ⟨*slide* a dish across the table⟩ ⟨the pen *slides* smoothly over the paper⟩ **b** : to coast on snow or ice **2** : to slip and fall by a loss of footing, balance, or support ⟨the package *slid* from the heap⟩ **3 a** : to move or pass smoothly and easily ⟨the dog *slid* through the brush⟩ **b** : to move, pass, or put unobtrusively, stealthily, or imperceptibly ⟨*slid* quietly into the seat⟩ ⟨time *slid* by⟩ ⟨*slide* the note into my hand⟩ [Old English *slīdan*]

²slide *n* **1** : the act or motion of sliding **2** : the descent of a mass (as of earth, rock, or snow) down a slope **3 a** : a surface down which a person or thing slides **b** : something (as a cover for an opening) that operates or adjusts by sliding **4 a** : a glass plate on which is placed an object to be examined under a microscope **b** : a photographic transparency arranged for projection

slide fastener *n* : ZIPPER

slid·er \'slīd-ər\ *n* **1** : one that slides or operates a slide **2** : a pitch in baseball that is thrown like a fastball but breaks slightly in the same direction as a curve

slide rule *n* : an instrument used for rapid calculation that consists in its simple form of a ruler with a lengthwise central sliding piece each of which is graduated with similar logarithmic scales labeled with the corresponding antilogarithms

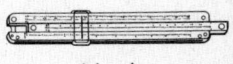

slide rule

slide·way \'slīd-ˌwā\ *n* : a way along which something slides

sliding board *n* : a playground slide

¹slight \'slīt\ *adj* **1 a** : having a slim or delicate build : not stout or massive in body **b** : lacking in strength or substance : FLIMSY, FRAIL **c** : deficient in weight, solidity, or importance : TRIVIAL **2** : small of its kind or in amount : SCANTY, MEAGER [Middle English, "smooth, slight"] SYN see THIN — **slight·ly** *adv* — **slight·ness** *n*

²slight *vt* : to treat as slight or unimportant: as **a** : to treat with disdain or discourteous indifference **b** : to perform or attend to carelessly and inadequately

³slight *n* **1** : an act or an instance of slighting **2** : a humiliating discourtesy

slight·ing *adj* : characterized by disregard or disrespect ⟨a *slighting* remark⟩ — **slight·ing·ly** \-ing-lē\ *adv*

sli·ly *variant of* SLYLY

¹slim \'slim\ *adj* **slim·mer; slim·mest** **1** : of small diameter or thickness in proportion to the height or length : SLENDER **2 a** : inferior in quality or amount : SLIGHT **b** : SCANTY, SMALL [Dutch, "bad, inferior"] SYN see THIN — **slim·ly** *adv* — **slim·ness** *n*

²slim *vb* **slimmed; slim·ming** : to make or become slender

slime \'slīm\ *n* **1** : soft moist earth or clay; *esp* : sticky slippery mud **2** : a soft slippery substance; *esp* : a skin secretion (as of a slug or catfish) [Old English *slīm*]

slime mold *n* : any of a group (Myxomycetes or Mycetozoa) of organisms that are usually held to be lower fungi but sometimes are considered protozoans and that live vegetatively as mobile plasmodia and reproduce by spores

slim–jim \'slim-'jim\ *n* : one that is notably slender [*slim* + *Jim*, nickname for *James*]

slimy \'slī-mē\ *adj* **slim·i·er; -est** **1** : of, relating to, or resembling slime : VISCOUS; *also* : covered with or yielding slime **2** : VILE, OFFENSIVE ⟨a *slimy* traitor⟩ — **slim·i·ly** \-mə-lē\ *adv* — **slim·i·ness** \-mē-nəs\ *n*

¹sling \'sling\ *vt* **slung** \'sləng\; **sling·ing** \'sling-ing\ **1** : to toss casually or forcibly : FLING **2** : to throw with a sling [Middle English *slingen*] — **sling·er** \'sling-ər\ *n*

\ə\ abut   \ng\ **sing**
\ər\ **further**   \ō\ **bone**
\a\ **mat**   \ȯ\ **saw**
\ā\ **take**   \ȯi\ **coin**
\ä\ **cot, cart**   \th\ **thin**
\au̇\ **out**   \th\ **this**
\ch\ **chin**   \ü\ **food**
\e\ **pet**   \u̇\ **foot**
\ē\ **easy**   \y\ **yet**
\g\ **go**   \yü\ **few**
\i\ **tip**   \yu̇\ **cure**
\ī\ **life**   \zh\ **vision**
\j\ **job**

²sling *n* : a slinging or hurling of or as if of a missile

³sling *n* **1 a** : a device for throwing something (as stones) that usually consists of a short strap with strings fastened to its ends and is whirled round to discharge its missile **b** : SLINGSHOT **2 a** : a usually looped line (as of rope) used to hoist, lower, support, or carry something; *esp* : a hanging bandage suspended from the neck to support an arm or hand **b** : a device (as a rope net) for enclosing material to be hoisted by a tackle or crane

⁴sling *vt* **slung** \'sləng\; **sling·ing** \'sling-ing\ **1** : to put in or move or support with a sling ⟨*sling* cargo from a ship's hold⟩ **2** : to cause to become suspended ⟨*sling* a hammock⟩

sling·shot \'sling-,shät\ *n* : a forked stick with an elastic band attached for shooting small stones

slink \'slingk\ *vb* **slunk** \'sləngk\; **slink·ing** : to move or go stealthily (as in fear or shame) [Old English *slincan* "to creep"] SYN see SKULK

slinky \'sling-kē\ *adj* **slink·i·er; -est 1** : stealthily quiet ⟨*slinky* movements⟩ **2** : sleek and sinuous in outline ⟨a *slinky* evening gown⟩

¹slip \'slip\ *vb* **slipped; slip·ping 1 a** : to move easily and smoothly : SLIDE ⟨the bolt *slipped* back⟩ ⟨*slip* the knife into its sheath⟩ **b** : to move or place quietly or stealthily **c** : to pass without being noted or used ⟨time *slipped* by⟩ ⟨let the opportunity *slip*⟩ **2 a** : to get away from : ELUDE ⟨*slipped* their pursuers⟩ **b** : to get free from ⟨the dog *slipped* its collar⟩ **c** : to escape the attention of ⟨*slipped* my mind⟩ **d** : to utter or become uttered inadvertently or casually ⟨the secret *slipped* out⟩ **e** : to let loose or let go of ⟨*slip* a dog from a leash⟩ **f** : to cause to slide open : RELEASE ⟨*slip* a bolt⟩ **g** : to let (a knitting stitch) pass from one needle to another without working a new stitch **3 a** : to slide out of place, away from a support, or from one's grasp ⟨the dish *slipped* to the floor⟩ **b** : to slide so as to fall or lose balance ⟨*slip* on a grease spot⟩ **c** : to slide or cause to slide especially in putting, passing, or inserting easily or quickly ⟨*slip* into a coat⟩ ⟨*slip* a dress on⟩ **d** : DISLOCATE ⟨*slipped* my shoulder⟩ **e** : to fail to progress or hold normally from or as if from sliding ⟨the loose belt continued to *slip*⟩ **4** : to fall from some level or standard (as of conduct or activity) usually gradually or by degrees ⟨the market *slipped* from an earlier high⟩ [Middle English *slippen*, from Dutch or Low German] — **slip something over** : to foist something on another : get the better of another by trickery

²slip *n* **1 a** : a sloping ramp that extends out into the water and serves for landing or repairing ships **b** : a ship's berth between two piers **2** : the act or an instance of departing secretly or hurriedly **3 a** : a mistake in judgment, policy, or procedure **b** : an unintentional and trivial mistake or fault **4** : the act or an instance of slipping down or out of place ⟨a *slip* on the ice⟩ ⟨a *slip* in stock prices⟩ **5 a** : an undergarment made in dress length with shoulder straps **b** : PILLOWCASE SYN see ERROR

³slip *n* **1** : a small shoot or twig cut for planting or grafting : CUTTING **2 a** : a long narrow strip of material **b** : a piece of paper used for a memorandum or record ⟨sales *slip*⟩ **3** : a young and slender person [Middle English *slippe*]

⁴slip *vt* **slipped; slip·ping** : to take cuttings from (a plant)

⁵slip *n* : thin wet clay used in pottery for casting, for decoration, or as a cement [Old English *slypa* "slime, paste"]

slip·case \'slip-,kās\ *n* : a protective container for books with one open end

slip·cov·er \'slip-,kəv-ər\ *n* : a removable protective covering for an article of furniture

slip·knot \'slip-,nät\ *n* : a knot that slips along a line around which it is made; *esp* : one made by tying an overhand knot around a rope to form an adjustable loop

slip noose *n* : a noose with a slipknot

slip–on \'slip-,ȯn, -,än\ *n* : an article of clothing (as a glove, shoe, or girdle) that is easily slipped on or off

slip·page \'slip-ij\ *n* **1** : an act, instance, or process of slipping **2 a** : power lost in transmission **b** : the difference between theoretical and actual output (as of power)

slipped disk *n* : a protrusion of one of the cartilage disks between vertebrae with pressure on spinal nerves resulting in low back pain

slip·per \'slip-ər\ *n* : a light low shoe without laces that is easily slipped on or off — **slip·pered** \-ərd\ *adj*

slip·pery \'slip-rē, -ə-rē\ *adj* **slip·per·i·er; -est 1** : having a surface smooth enough to cause one to slide or lose one's hold ⟨a *slippery* floor⟩ **2** : not worthy of trust : TRICKY, UNRELIABLE [Old English *slipor*] — **slip·per·i·ness** *n*

slippery elm *n* : a North American elm with hard wood and fragrant inner bark; *also* : its wood or bark

slip·shod \'slip-'shäd\ *adj* : very careless : SLOVENLY [earlier *slipshod* "wearing loose shoes, shabby", from ¹*slip* + *shod*]

slip·stick \'slip-,stik\ *n* : SLIDE RULE

slip stitch *n* : a concealed stitch for sewing folded edges (as hems) made by alternately running the needle inside the fold and picking up a thread or two from the body of the article

slip·stream \'slip-,strēm\ *n* : the stream of air driven aft by the propeller of an aircraft

slip·up \'slip-,əp\ *n* **1** : MISTAKE **2** : MISCHANCE

slip up \slip-'əp, 'slip-\ *vi* : to make a mistake : BLUNDER

¹slit \'slit\ *vt* **slit; slit·ting 1 a** : to make a slit in : SLASH **b** : to cut off or away : SEVER **2** : to cut into long narrow strips [Middle English *slitten*] — **slit·ter** *n*

²slit *n* : a long narrow cut or opening — **slit** *adj* — **slit·like** \-,līk\ *adj*

slith·er \'slith-ər\ *vb* **slith·ered; slith·er·ing** \'slith-ring, -ə-ring\ **1** : to slide or cause to slide on or as if on a loose gravelly surface **2** : to slip or slide like a snake [Old English *slidrian*, from *slīdan* "to slide"]

slith·ery \'slith-rē, -ə-rē\ *adj* : having a slippery surface, texture, or quality

¹sliv·er \'sliv-ər, 2 is usually 'slīv-\ *n* **1** : a long slender piece cut or torn off : SPLINTER **2** : an untwisted strand of textile fiber as it comes from a carding or combining machine [Middle English *slivere*, from *sliven* "to slice off", from Old English -*slīfan*]

²sliv·er \'sliv-ər\ *vb* **sliv·ered; sliv·er·ing** \'sliv-ring, -ə-ring\ : to cut or form into slivers : SPLINTER

slob \'släb\ *n* : a slovenly or boorish person [Irish Gaelic *slab* "mud"]

¹slob·ber \'släb-ər\ *vb* **slob·bered; slob·ber·ing** \'släb-ring, -ə-ring\ **1** : to let saliva or liquid dribble from the mouth : DROOL **2** : to show feeling to excess : GUSH [Middle English *sloberen*] — **slob·ber·er** \'släb-ər-ər\ *n*

²slobber *n* **1** : dripping saliva **2** : silly excessive show of feeling — **slob·bery** \'släb-rē, -ə-rē\ *adj*

sloe \'slō\ *n* : the tart bluish black globe-shaped fruit of the blackthorn; *also* : BLACKTHORN 1 [Old English *slāh*]

sloe–eyed \'slō-'īd\ *adj* **1** : having soft dark bluish or purplish black eyes **2** : having slanted eyes

sloe gin *n* : a sweet reddish liqueur flavored chiefly with sloes

slog \'släg\ *vb* **slogged; slog·ging 1** : to hit hard : BEAT **2** : to plod or work doggedly on [origin unknown] — **slog·ger** *n*

slo·gan \'slō-gən\ *n* **1** : a word or phrase that calls to battle **2** : a word or phrase used by a party, a group, or a business to attract attention [Scottish Gaelic *sluagh-ghairm* "army cry"]

slo·gan·eer \,slō-gə-'niər\ *n* : a coiner or user of slogans — **sloganeer** *vi*

sloop \\'slüp\\ *n* : a fore-and-aft rigged sailing boat with one mast and a single jib [Dutch *sloep*]

¹slop \\'släp\\ *n* **1** : soft mud : SLUSH **2** : thin tasteless drink or liquid food — usually used in pl. **3** : liquid spilled or splashed **4 a** : food waste (as garbage) or a thin gruel fed to animals **b** : excreted body waste — usually used in pl. [Middle English *sloppe*]

²slop *vb* **slopped; slop·ping 1** : to spill on or over ⟨*slop* milk from a glass⟩ ⟨*slopped* my shirt with gravy⟩ **2** : to feed slop to ⟨*slop* the hogs⟩ **3** : to slouch or lounge about in a sloppy manner ⟨*slop* about the house⟩

¹slope \\'slōp\\ *adj* : being slanted or at an angle [Middle English *slope*, adv., "obliquely"]

²slope *vb* : to take a slanting direction : give a slant to : INCLINE — **slop·er** *n*

³slope *n* **1** : ground that forms a natural or artificial incline **2** : upward or downward slant or inclination or degree of slant **3** : the part of a continent draining to a particular ocean **4 a** : the tangent of the angle made by a straight line with the x-axis **b** : the slope of the line tangent to a plane curve at a point

slop·py \\'släp-ē\\ *adj* **slop·pi·er; -est 1 a** : wet so as to spatter easily : SLUSHY ⟨a *sloppy* racetrack⟩ **b** : wet with or as if with something slopped over **2** : SLOVENLY, CARELESS ⟨a *sloppy* dresser⟩ **3** : excessively sentimental — **slop·pi·ly** \\'släp-ə-lē\\ *adv* — **slop·pi·ness** \\'släp-ē-nəs\\ *n*

¹slosh \\'släsh\\ *n* **1** : SLUSH 1, 2 **2** : the slap or splash of liquid [probably blend of *slop* and *slush*]

²slosh *vb* **1** : to flounder through or splash about in or with water, mud, or slush **2** : to move with a splash

¹slot \\'slät\\ *n* : a long narrow opening, groove, or passage : SLIT, NOTCH [Middle English, "hollow running down the middle of the breast", from Middle French *esclot*]

²slot *vt* **slot·ted; slot·ting** : to cut a slot in

³slot *n, pl* **slot** : the track of an animal (as a deer) [Middle French *esclot* "track"]

sloth \\'slóth, 'slōth\\ *n* **1** : INDOLENCE, LAZINESS **2** : any of several slow-moving mammals of Central and South America that are related to the armadillos and live in trees where they hang back downward and feed on leaves, shoots, and fruits [Middle English *slouthe*, from *slow*]

sloth·ful \\-fəl\\ *adj* : LAZY 1, INDOLENT — **sloth·ful·ly** \\-fə-lē\\ *adv* — **sloth·ful·ness** *n*

slot machine *n* : a machine whose operation is begun when a coin is dropped into a slot

¹slouch \\'slaùch\\ *n* **1** : an awkward, lazy, or incompetent person **2** : a gait or posture characterized by ungainly stooping of head and shoulders [origin unknown]

²slouch *vi* : to walk with or assume a slouch — **sloucher** *n*

slouch hat *n* : a soft usually felt hat with a flexible brim

slouchy \\'slaù-chē\\ *adj* **slouch·i·er; -est** : slouching or slovenly in appearance — **slouch·i·ly** \\-chə-lē\\ *adv* — **slouch·i·ness** \\-chē-nəs\\ *n*

¹slough \\'slü, 'slaù; *in the United States (except New England)* 'slü *is usual for sense 1;* 'slaù *is more frequent for sense 2*\\ *n* **1** *also* **slew** *or* **slue** \\'slü\\ : a wet and marshy or muddy place (as a swamp or backwater) **2** : a discouraged, degraded, or dejected state [Old English *slōh*]

²slough \\'sləf\\ *also* **sluff** *n* **1** : the cast-off skin of a snake **2** : a mass of dead tissue separating from an ulcer **3** : something that may be shed or cast off [Middle English *slughe*]

³slough \\'sləf\\ *also* **sluff** *vb* : to cast off or become cast off: as **a** : to cast off one's skin or dead tissue from living tissue **b** : to get rid of or discard as irksome, objectionable, or disadvantageous

slough of de·spond \\,slaù-əv-di-'spänd, ,slü-\\ : a state of extreme depression [from the *Slough of Despond*,

deep bog into which Christian falls in the allegory *Pilgrim's Progress* (1678) by John Bunyan]

slough over \\,sləf-\\ *vt* : to treat as slight or unimportant ⟨trying to *slough over* their own mistakes⟩

Slo·vak \\'slō-,väk, -,vak\\ *n* **1** : a member of a Slavic people of eastern Czechoslovakia **2** : the Slavic language of the Slovak people [Slovak *Slovák*] — **Slovak** *adj* — **Slo·vak·i·an** \\slō-'väk-ē-ən, -'vak-\\ *adj or n*

slov·en \\'sləv-ən\\ *n* : one habitually negligent of neatness or cleanliness [Middle English *sloveyn* "rascal"]

Slo·vene \\'slō-,vēn\\ *n* **1 a** : a member of a southern Slavic group of people usually classed with the Serbs and Croats and living in Yugoslavia **b** : a native or inhabitant of Slovenia **2** : the language of the Slovenes [German, from Slovene *Sloven*] — **Slovene** *adj* — **Slo·ve·ni·an** \\slō-'vē-nē-ən\\ *adj or n*

slov·en·ly \\'sləv-ən-lē\\ *adj* **1 a** : untidy especially in dress or person **b** : lazily slipshod **2** : characteristic of a sloven — **slov·en·li·ness** *n* — **slovenly** *adv*

¹slow \\'slō\\ *adj* **1 a** : mentally dull : STUPID **b** : naturally inert or sluggish **2 a** : lacking in readiness, promptness, or willingness **b** : not hasty **3 a** : moving, flowing, or proceeding without speed or at less than usual speed ⟨*slow* traffic⟩ **b** : not vigorous or active ⟨a *slow* fire⟩ **c** : taking place at a low rate or over a considerable period of time ⟨*slow* growth⟩ **4** : having qualities that hinder or stop rapid progress or action ⟨a *slow* racetrack⟩ **5 a** : registering behind or below what is correct ⟨the clock is *slow*⟩ **b** : that is behind the time at a specified time or place **6** : lacking in activity or liveliness ⟨a *slow* market⟩ ⟨a *slow* party⟩ [Old English *slāw*] — **slow·ly** *adv* — **slow·ness** *n*

²slow *adv* : SLOWLY ⟨drive *slow*⟩

³slow *vb* : to make or go slow or slower

slow·down \\'slō-,daùn\\ *n* : a slowing down

slow–foot·ed \\'slō-'fùt-əd\\ *adj* : moving at a very slow pace — **slow–foot·ed·ness** *n*

slow·ish \\'slō-ish\\ *adj* : somewhat slow ⟨a *slowish* reader⟩

slow match *n* : a match or fuse made so as to burn slowly and evenly and used for firing (as of blasting charges)

slow motion *n* : action in a projected motion picture or television program that proceeds at a rate slower than the action photographed or taped

slow·poke \\'slō-,pōk\\ *n* : a very slow person

slow–wit·ted \\-'wit-əd\\ *adj* : SLOW 1a

sludge \\'sləj\\ *n* **1** : MUD, MIRE **2** : a muddy or slushy mass, deposit, or sediment; *esp* : precipitated solid matter produced by water and sewage treatment processes [probably alteration of *slush*] — **sludgy** \\'sləj-ē\\ *adj*

¹slue \\'slü\\ *variant of* SLOUGH

²slue *vb* : to turn, twist, or swing about especially out of a course : VEER [origin unknown]

³slue *n* : an act or instance of sluing

⁴slue *variant of* SLEW

¹slug \\'sləg\\ *n* **1** : SLUGGARD **2** : any of numerous chiefly terrestrial mollusks that are closely related to the land snails but are long and wormlike and have only a rudimentary shell or none **3** : a smooth soft larva of a sawfly or moth that creeps like a snail [of Scandinavian origin]

²slug *n* **1** : a small piece of shaped metal: as **a** : a musket ball or bullet **b** : a metal disk for insertion in a slot machine in place of a coin **2** : a line of type cast as one piece **3** : a single drink of liquor : SHOT **4** : the gravitational unit of mass in the fps system to which a pound force can impart an acceleration of one foot per second per second that is equal to about 14.59 kilograms [probably from ¹*slug*]

³slug *n* : a heavy blow especially with the fist [perhaps from ²*slug*]

⁴slug *vb* **slugged; slug·ging** : to strike heavily with or as if with the fist or a bat

sloth 2

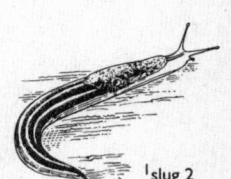

¹slug 2

\\ə\\ abut	\\ng\\ sing
\\ər\\ further	\\ō\\ bone
\\a\\ mat	\\ò\\ saw
\\ā\\ take	\\òi\\ coin
\\ä\\ cot, cart	\\th\\ thin
\\aù\\ out	\\th\\ this
\\ch\\ chin	\\ü\\ food
\\e\\ pet	\\ù\\ foot
\\ē\\ easy	\\y\\ yet
\\g\\ go	\\yü\\ few
\\i\\ tip	\\yù\\ cure
\\ī\\ life	\\zh\\ vision
\\j\\ job	

slug·abed \'sləg-ə-,bed\ *n* : one who stays in bed too long; *also* : SLUGGARD

slug·fest \'sləg-,fest\ *n* : a fight or boxing match marked by exchange of heavy blows

slug·gard \'sləg-ərd\ *n* : an habitually lazy person [Middle English *sluggart*] — **sluggard** *adj* — **slug·gard·ly** *adj*

slug·ger \'sləg-ər\ *n* : one (as a batter or boxer) that strikes hard or with heavy blows

slug·gish \'sləg-ish\ *adj* : slow and inactive in movement or reaction by habit or condition — **slug·gish·ly** *adv* — **slug·gish·ness** *n*

¹**sluice** \'slüs\ *n* **1** : an artificial passage for water with a gate for controlling its flow or changing its direction **2** : a body of water held back by a gate or a stream flowing through a gate **3** : a device (as a water gate) for controlling the flow of water **4** : a channel that carries off surplus water **5** : a long inclined trough (as for washing gold-bearing earth or for floating logs to a sawmill) [Middle French *escluse,* from Late Latin *exclusa,* from Latin *excludere* "to shut off, exclude"]

²**sluice** *vt* **1** : to draw off by or through a sluice **2 a** : to wash with or in water running through or from a sluice **b** : to drench with a sudden flow

sluice·way \'slü-,swā\ *n* : an artificial channel into which water is let by a sluice

¹**slum** \'sləm\ *n* : a thickly populated usually urban area marked by crowding, run-down housing, and generally wretched living conditions [origin unknown]

²**slum** *vi* **slummed; slum·ming** : to visit slums especially out of curiosity or for pleasure — **slum·mer** *n*

slum·ber \'sləm-bər\ *vi* **slum·bered; slum·ber·ing** \-bə-ring, -bring\ **1** : to sleep or lie asleep : DOZE **2** : to lie dormant ⟨a *slumbering* volcano⟩ [Middle English *slumberen,* from *slumen* "to doze"] — **slumber** *n* — **slum·ber·er** \-bər-ər\ *n*

slum·ber·ous *or* **slum·brous** \'sləm-bə-rəs, -brəs\ *adj* **1 a** : SLEEPY 1 **b** : QUIET 1a **2** : inviting slumber ⟨a *slumberous* sound⟩

slumber party *n* : an overnight gathering of teenage girls usually at one of their homes at which they dress in nightclothes but pass the night more in talking than sleeping

slum·gul·lion \'sləm-,gəl-yən\ *n* : a meat stew [perhaps from earlier *slum* "slime" + English dialect *gullion* "mud, cesspool"]

slum·lord \'sləm-,lord\ *n* : a landlord who receives unusually large profits from substandard properties [*slum* + land*lord*]

¹**slump** \'sləmp\ *vi* **1** : to drop or slide down suddenly : COLLAPSE **2** : to assume a drooping posture or carriage : SLOUCH **3** : to fall sharply ⟨sales *slumped*⟩ [probably of Scandinavian origin]

²**slump** *n* : a large or prolonged decline especially in economic activity or prices

slung *past of* SLING

slunk *past of* SLINK

¹**slur** \'slər\ *vb* **slurred; slur·ring** **1 a** : to slide or slip over without due mention, consideration, or emphasis **b** : to perform hurriedly : SKIMP **c** : to perform (successive musical notes of different pitch) in a smooth or connected manner **3** : to speak indistinctly [probably from Low German *slurren* "to shuffle"]

²**slur** *n* **1 a** : a curved line ⌢ or ⌣ connecting notes to be sung or performed without a break **b** : the combination of two or more slurred tones **2** : a slurring manner of speech

³**slur** *vb* **slurred; slur·ring** **1** : to cast aspersions upon : DISPARAGE **2** : to make indistinct : OBSCURE [Middle English *sloor* "thin mud"]

⁴**slur** *n* **1** : an insulting or disparaging remark **2** : a shaming or degrading effect

slurp \'slərp\ *vb* : to eat or drink noisily or with a sucking sound [Dutch *slurpen*] — **slurp** *n*

slur·ry \'slər-ē, 'slə-rē\ *n, pl* **slurries** : a watery mixture of insoluble matter (as mud, lime, or pulverized ore) [Middle English *slory*]

slush \'sləsh\ *n* **1** : partly melted or watery snow **2** : soft mud : MIRE **3** : RUBBISH, DRIVEL [perhaps of Scandinavian origin]

slush fund *n* : a fund for carrying on corrupt activities (as bribing public officials)

slushy \'sləsh-ē\ *adj* **slush·i·er; -est** : full of or resembling slush ⟨a *slushy* road⟩ ⟨soft *slushy* ice⟩ — **slush·i·ness** *n*

slut \'slət\ *n* **1** : a slovenly woman **2** : a lewd woman; *esp* : PROSTITUTE [Middle English *slutte*] — **slut·tish** \'slət-ish\ *adj* — **slut·tish·ly** *adv* — **slut·tish·ness** *n*

sly \'slī\ *adj* **sli·er** *also* **sly·er** \'slī-ər, 'slīr\; **sli·est** *also* **sly·est** \'slī-əst\ **1 a** : clever in concealing one's aims or ends ⟨too *sly* to be trusted⟩ **b** : lacking in straightforwardness and candor ⟨a *sly* explanation⟩ **2** : lightly mischievous : ROGUISH [Old Norse *slœgr*] — **sly·ly** *adv* — **sly·ness** *n* □ SYN SLY, CRAFTY, ARTFUL, WILY mean apt to attain an end by devious means. SLY stresses furtiveness, lack of candor, and skill in concealing one's aims and methods ⟨a *sly* scheme⟩ CRAFTY suggests skill in deception acquired by experience ⟨a *crafty* trial lawyer⟩ ARTFUL suggests insinuating or ingratiating craftiness ⟨an *artful* matchmaker⟩ WILY stresses cleverness in setting or avoiding traps ⟨the *wily* fox⟩ — **on the sly** : in a stealthy or furtive manner

¹**smack** \'smak\ *n* **1** : characteristic or perceptible taste or flavor **2** : a small quantity [Old English *smæc*]

²**smack** *vi* : to have a flavor, trace, or suggestion ⟨the roast *smacks* of thyme⟩ ⟨such actions *smack* of treachery⟩

³**smack** *vb* **1** : to close and open (lips) noisily especially in eating **2** : to kiss usually loudly or boisterously **3 a** : to make a smack **b** : to hit so as to make a smack [related to Dutch *smacken* "to strike"]

⁴**smack** *n* **1** : a quick sharp noise made by rapidly compressing and opening the lips **2** : a loud kiss **3** : a sharp slap or blow

⁵**smack** *adv* : in a square and sharp manner : DIRECTLY ⟨it hit me *smack* in the face⟩

⁶**smack** *n* : a sailing ship (as a sloop or cutter) used chiefly in coasting and fishing [Dutch *smak* or Low German *smack*]

smack–dab \'smak-'dab\ *adv, dialect* : SQUARELY, EXACTLY

smack·er \'smak-ər\ *n* **1** : one that smacks **2** *slang* : DOLLAR 3

¹**small** \'smol\ *adj* **1** : little in size **2** : few in numbers or members ⟨a *small* crowd⟩ **3** : little in amount ⟨a *small* supply⟩ **4** : not very much or big ⟨*small* success⟩ **5** : UNIMPORTANT ⟨a *small* matter⟩ **6** : operating on a limited scale ⟨*small* dealers⟩ **7** : GENTLE, SOFT ⟨a *small* voice⟩ **8** : not generous : MEAN ⟨a *small* nature⟩ **9** : made up of small units **10** : HUMBLE, MODEST ⟨a *small* beginning⟩ **11** : HUMILIATED, HUMBLED ⟨felt very *small* to be caught cheating⟩ **12** : LOWERCASE [Old English *smæl*] — **small·ness** *n* □ SYN LITTLE: SMALL and LITTLE are often interchangeable but SMALL, contrasting with large or great, applies more to relative size determined by capacity, value, number ⟨a *small* mouth⟩ ⟨a *small* quantity of salt⟩ LITTLE, contrasting with big or much, is more absolute in implication and may suggest pettiness, petiteness, insignificance, immaturity ⟨a *little* child⟩ ⟨had *little* hope of success⟩

²**small** *adv* **1** : in or into small pieces ⟨cut the meat *small*⟩ **2** : without force or loudness ⟨speak *small*⟩ **3** : in a small manner ⟨most businesses begin *small*⟩

³**small** *n* **1** : a part smaller and especially narrower than the remainder ⟨the *small* of the back⟩ **2 a** *pl* : small-sized products **b** *pl, British* : SMALLCLOTHES 2

small arm *n* : a firearm fired while held in the hands

small beer *n* **1** : a weak or inferior beer **2** : something of small importance : TRIVIA

small calorie *n* : CALORIE 1a

small change *n* **1** : money consisting of small coins **2** : something trifling or petty

small circle *n* : a circle on the surface of a sphere whose plane does not pass through the center of the sphere; *esp* : such a circle on the surface of the earth — compare GREAT CIRCLE

small·clothes \'smȯl-ˌklōz, -ˌklōthz\ *n pl* **1** : close-fitting knee breeches worn especially in the 18th century **2** : small articles of clothing

small–fry \-ˌfrī\ *adj* **1** : MINOR ⟨a *small-fry* politician⟩ **2** : of or relating to children

small game *n* : birds and small mammals (as rabbits) hunted for sport

small hours *n pl* : the early morning hours

small intestine *n* : the part of the intestine that lies between the stomach and colon, consists of duodenum, jejunum, and ileum, secretes digestive enzymes, and is the chief seat of the absorption of digested nutrients

small·ish \'smȯ-lish\ *adj* : somewhat small

small–mind·ed \'smȯl-'mīn-dəd\ *adj* : lacking breadth of mind; *also* : typical of a small-minded person — **small–mind·ed·ly** *adv* — **small–mind·ed·ness** *n*

small potatoes *n* : someone or something of trivial importance or worth

small·pox \'smȯl-ˌpäks\ *n* : an acute contagious virus disease marked by fever and skin eruption with pustules, sloughing, and scar formation

small–scale \-'skāl\ *adj* **1** : small in scope; *esp* : small in output or operation **2** : having a scale (as one inch to 25 miles) that permits plotting of comparatively little detail ⟨a *small-scale* map⟩

small stores *n pl* : articles of clothing sold by a naval supply officer to naval personnel

small talk *n* : light or casual conversation

small–time \'smȯl-ˌtīm\ *adj* : of insignificant standing : SMALL-SCALE, MINOR — **small–tim·er** \-'tī-mər\ *n*

smarmy \'smär-mē\ *adj* : exhibiting or marked by smug, ingratiating, or false earnestness : UNCTUOUS [earlier *smarm* "to gush, slobber", of unknown origin]

¹smart \'smärt\ *vi* **1** : to cause or feel a sharp stinging pain **2** : to feel or endure distress, remorse, or embarrassment ⟨*smarts* under criticism⟩ [Old English *smeortan*]

²smart *adj* **1** : causing smarting **2** : marked by forceful activity or vigorous strength **3** : BRISK 1, SPIRITED **4 a** : mentally alert : BRIGHT **b** : sharp in scheming : SHREWD **5 a** : WITTY, CLEVER **b** : PERT, SAUCY ⟨don't get *smart* with me⟩ **6 a** : stylish or elegant in dress or appearance **b** : SOPHISTICATED 3 **c** : FASHIONABLE 1 SYN see CLEVER — **smart·ly** *adv* — **smart·ness** *n*

³smart *adv* : SMARTLY

⁴smart *n* **1** : a smarting pain **2** : deep grief or remorse

smart al·eck \'smärt-ˌal-ik, -ˌel-\ *n* : an offensively conceited and bumptious person [*Aleck*, nickname for *Alexander*] — **smart–al·ecky** \-ˌal-ə-kē, -ˌel-\ *or* **smart–aleck** *adj*

smart·en \'smärt-ⁿ\ *vb* **smart·ened; smart·en·ing** \'smärt-ning, -ⁿ-ing\ **1** : to make smart or smarter : SPRUCE, FRESHEN ⟨*smarten* up an old dress with a new collar⟩ **2** : to make or become more alert or informed ⟨*smarten* up if you don't want to get into trouble⟩

smart set *n* : extremely fashionable society

smart·weed \'smärt-ˌwēd\ *n* : any of various weedy plants with strong acrid juice that are related to the buckwheats

smarty *or* **smart·ie** \'smärt-ē\ *n, pl* **smart·ies** : SMART ALECK

¹smash \'smash\ *vb* **1** : to break in pieces by force : SHATTER ⟨*smash* down a door⟩ ⟨the dish *smashed* on the floor⟩ **2** : to drive, throw, or move with a destructive effect ⟨the ball *smashed* through the window⟩ **3** : WRECK 1b **4** : to go to pieces suddenly : COLLAPSE [perhaps blend of *smack* and *mash*] — **smash·er** *n*

²smash *n* **1 a** : a smashing blow or attack **b** : a hard overhand stroke (as in tennis) **2** : the condition of being smashed **3 a** : the action or sound of smashing; *esp* : SMASHUP 2 **b** : utter collapse : RUIN; *esp* : BANKRUPTCY **4** : a striking success : HIT ⟨the new play is a *smash*⟩

smash·ing \'smash-ing\ *adj* **1** : that smashes ⟨a *smashing* defeat⟩ **2** : extremely moving, effective, or attractive ⟨a *smashing* performance⟩

smash·up \'smash-ˌəp\ *n* **1** : a complete collapse **2** : a destructive collision of motor vehicles

smat·ter \'smat-ər\ *n* : SMATTERING 2 [Middle English *smatteren* "to chatter, talk ignorantly"]

smat·ter·ing \'smat-ə-ring\ *n* **1** : superficial piecemeal knowledge **2** : a small scattered number

smaze \'smāz\ *n* : a combination of haze and smoke similar to smog in appearance but less damp in consistency [*sm*oke + h*aze*]

¹smear \'smiər\ *n* **1** : a spot made by or as if by an oily or sticky substance : SMUDGE **2** : material smeared on a surface; *esp* : material prepared for microscopic examination by smearing on a slide **3** : a usually unproven charge or accusation [Old English *smeoru*]

²smear *vt* **1 a** : to spread or daub with something oily or sticky **b** : to spread over a surface **2** : to stain, smudge, or dirty by or as if by smearing; *also* : to blacken the reputation of **3** : to blot out or blur by or as if by smearing — **smear·er** *n*

smear·case *or* **smier·case** \'smiər-ˌkās\ *n, chiefly Midland* : COTTAGE CHEESE [German *schmierkäse*, from *schmieren* "to smear" + *käse* "cheese"]

smear word *n* : an epithet intended to smear a person or group

smeary \'smiər-ē\ *adj* **smear·i·er; -est** **1** : marked by smears **2** : tending to smear

¹smell \'smel\ *vb* **smelled** \'smeld\ *or* **smelt** \'smelt\; **smell·ing** **1** : to get the odor of through stimuli affecting the olfactory sense organs of the nose **2** : to detect or become aware of as if by the sense of smell **3** : to exercise the sense of smell **4 a** : to give off an odor **b** : to give off a suggestion of something and especially of something unwholesome or evil ⟨the plan *smells* of trickery⟩ [Middle English *smellen*] — **smell·er** *n* — **smell a rat** : to have a suspicion of something wrong

²smell *n* **1 a** : the process or power of smelling **b** : the special sense used to perceive odor **2** : the property of a thing that affects the olfactory organs : ODOR **3** : a pervading quality : AURA **4** : an act of smelling □ SYN ODOR, SCENT, AROMA: SMELL and ODOR may imply either a pleasant or unpleasant sensation though SMELL may cover a wider range of quality, intensity, or source; SCENT implies less strength and suggests a substance, an animal, or a plant giving off a characteristic smell ⟨the *scent* of pine⟩ AROMA suggests a pungent, pervasive, usually pleasant smell ⟨the *aroma* of fresh coffee⟩

smelling salts *n pl* : a usually scented aromatic preparation of an ammonium salt and ammonia water used to relieve faintness

smelly \'smel-ē\ *adj* **smell·i·er; -est** : having a smell and especially a bad smell

¹smelt \'smelt\ *n, pl* **smelts** *or* **smelt** : any of several very small food fishes of coastal or fresh waters that resemble and are related to the trout [Old English]

²smelt *vt* : to melt or fuse (as ore) usually in order to separate the metal [Dutch or Low German *smelten*]

smelt·er \'smel-tər\ *n* : one that smelts : **a** : a worker in or an owner of a smeltery **b** *or* **smelt·ery** \-tə-rē, -trē\ : an establishment for smelting

smid·gen *or* **smid·geon** *or* **smid·gin** \'smij-ən\ *n* : a small amount : BIT [perhaps from English dialect *smitch* "soiling mark"]

smi·lax \'smī-ˌlaks\ *n* **1** : GREENBRIER **2** : a delicate greenhouse twining plant related to the garden asparagus and having ovate bright green terminal branches in place of leaves [Latin, "bindweed, yew", from Greek]

\ə\ abut		\ng\ sing
\ər\ further		\ō\ bone
\a\ mat		\ȯ\ saw
\ā\ take		\ȯi\ coin
\ä\ cot, cart		\th\ thin
\au̇\ out		\th\ this
\ch\ chin		\ü\ food
\e\ pet		\u̇\ foot
\ē\ easy		\y\ yet
\g\ go		\yü\ few
\i\ tip		\yu̇\ cure
\ī\ life		\zh\ vision
\j\ job		

¹**smile** \'smīl\ *vb* **I** : to have, produce, or exhibit a smile **2 a** : to look with amusement or ridicule **b** : to be propitious or agreeable ⟨weather *smiled* on our plans⟩ **3** : to express by a smile [Middle English *smilen*] — **smil·er** *n* — **smil·ing·ly** \'smī-ling-lē\ *adv*

²**smile** *n* : a change of facial expression in which the eyes brighten and the lips curve slightly upward especially in expression of amusement, pleasure, approval, or scorn — **smile·less** \'smīl-ləs\ *adj* — **smile·less·ly** *adv*

smirch \'smərch\ *vt* **I** : to make dirty, stained, or discolored especially by smearing with something that soils **2** : to bring discredit or disgrace on [Middle English *smorchen*] — **smirch** *n*

smirk \'smərk\ *vi* : to smile in an affected manner : SIMPER [Old English *smearcian* "to smile"] — **smirk** *n*

smirky \'smər-kē\ *adj* : marked by or given to smirking

smite \'smīt\ *vb* **smote** \'smōt\; **smit·ten** \'smit-n\ *or* **smote**; **smit·ing** \'smīt-ing\ **I** : to strike sharply or heavily with the hand or a hand weapon **2 a** : to kill or injure by smiting **b** : to attack or afflict suddenly and injuriously ⟨*smitten* by disease⟩ **3** : to affect like a sudden hard blow ⟨*smitten* with terror⟩ [Old English *smītan*] — **smit·er** \'smīt-ər\ *n*

smith \'smith\ *n* **I** : a worker in metals **2** : MAKER — often used in combination ⟨gun*smith*⟩ ⟨tune*smith*⟩ [Old English]

smith·er·eens \,smith-ə-'rēnz\ *n pl* : small pieces [Irish Gaelic *smidirīn* "small fragment"]

smith·ery \'smith-ə-rē\ *n* **I** : the work, art, or trade of a smith **2** : SMITHY

smith·son·ite \'smith-sə-,nīt\ *n* : a usually white or nearly white native zinc carbonate ZnCO₃ [James *Smithson,* died 1829, British chemist]

smithy \'smith-ē, 'smith-\ *n, pl* **smith·ies** **I** : the workshop of a smith **2** : BLACKSMITH

¹**smock** \'smäk\ *n* **I** *archaic* : a woman's undergarment; *esp* : CHEMISE **2** : a light loose garment worn usually over regular clothing for protection from dirt [Old English *smoc*]

²**smock** *vt* : to embroider or shirr with smocking

smock·ing \'smäk-ing\ *n* : a decorative embroidery or shirring made by gathering cloth in regularly spaced round tucks

smog \'smäg *also* 'smóg\ *n* : a thick haze caused by the action of sunlight on air polluted by smoke and automobile exhaust fumes [blend of *smoke* and *fog*] — **smog·gy** \-ē-\ *adj*

smok·able *or* **smoke·able** \'smō-kə-bəl\ *adj* : fit for smoking

¹**smoke** \'smōk\ *n* **I a** : the gas of burning organic materials (as coal, wood, or tobacco) made visible by small particles of carbon **b** : a suspension of solid or liquid particles in a gas **2** : a mass or column of smoke **3** : fume or vapor often resulting from the action of heat on moisture **4** : something of little substance, permanence, or value **5** : something that obscures **6** : something to smoke (as a cigarette); *also* : the smoking of this [Old English *smoca*] — **smoke·like** \'smō-,klīk\ *adj*

²**smoke** *vb* **I a** : to emit or exhale smoke **b** : to emit excessive smoke **2** : to inhale and exhale the fumes of burning plant material (as tobacco); *also* : to use in smoking ⟨*smoke* a cigar⟩ **3** : to act on with smoke: **a** : to drive away by smoke **b** : to blacken or discolor with smoke **c** : to cure by exposure to smoke ⟨*smoked* meat⟩ **d** : to stun (as bees) by smoke

smoke and mirrors *n pl* : something intended to disguise or draw attention away especially from an embarrassing or unpleasant issue

smoke·chas·er \-,chā-sər\ *n* : one that fights forest fires

smoke–filled room \,smōk-,fild-\ *n* : a room (as in a hotel) in which a small group of politicians carry on negotiations

smoke·house \'smōk-,haús\ *n* : a building where meat or fish is cured by means of dense smoke

smoke jumper *n* : a forest-fire fighter who parachutes to locations otherwise difficult to reach

smoke·less \'smō-kləs\ *adj* : producing or containing little or no smoke ⟨*smokeless* powder⟩ ⟨a *smokeless* sky⟩

smokeless tobacco *n* : pulverized or shredded tobacco chewed or placed between cheek and gum

smoke out *vt* **I** : to drive out by or as if by smoke **2** : to bring to public knowledge

smok·er \'smō-kər\ *n* **I** : one that smokes **2** : a railroad car or compartment in which smoking is allowed **3** : an informal social gathering for men

smoke screen *n* : a screen of or as if of smoke to hinder observation or detection

smoke·stack \'smōk-,stak\ *n* : a chimney or funnel through which smoke and gases are discharged (as from a ship or factory)

smoke tree *n* : a small shrubby tree of the sumac family often grown for its large panicles of tiny flowers suggesting a cloud of smoke

smoking jacket *n* : a man's easy jacket for home wear

smoking lamp *n* : a lamp on a ship kept lighted during the hours when smoking is allowed

smoking room *n* : a room (as in a hotel or club) set apart for smokers

smoky \'smō-kē\ *adj* **smok·i·er; -est** **I** : giving off smoke especially in large quantities ⟨*smoky* stoves⟩ **2** : resembling or suggestive of smoke ⟨a *smoky* flavor⟩ **3** : filled with or darkened by smoke ⟨a *smoky* room⟩ ⟨*smoky* ceilings⟩ — **smok·i·ly** \-kə-lē\ *adv* — **smok·i·ness** \-kē-nəs\ *n*

smoky quartz *n* : a yellow or smoky-brown often transparent crystalline quartz

¹**smol·der** *or* **smoul·der** \'smōl-dər\ *n* : a slow smoky fire [Middle English *smolder*]

²**smolder** *or* **smoulder** *vi* **smol·dered** *or* **smoul·dered**; **smol·der·ing** *or* **smoul·der·ing** \'smōl-də-ring, -dring\ **I** : to burn sluggishly with smoke and usually without flame ⟨fire was *smoldering* in the grate⟩ **2** : to exist in a state of suppressed activity ⟨a *smoldering* rebellion⟩; *also* : to indicate a suppressed emotion ⟨eyes *smoldering* with anger⟩

smolt \'smōlt\ *n* : a salmon or sea trout when it is about two years old and silvery and first descends to the sea [Middle English]

smooch \'smüch\ *vi* : KISS, PET [alteration of earlier *smouch* "to kiss loudly", of imitative origin] — **smooch** *n*

¹**smooth** \'smüth\ *adj* **I a** : having a continuous even curve or surface : not rough ⟨a *smooth* skin⟩ **b** : being without hairs or projections : GLABROUS **c** : causing no resistance to sliding **2** : free from obstacles or difficulties ⟨a *smooth* path⟩ **3** : even and uninterrupted in flow or flight **4** : excessively and often artfully suave : INGRATIATING **5 a** : calm or unruffled in manner or behavior **b** : generally agreeable : COURTEOUS **6** : not sharp or acid : BLAND ⟨a *smooth* sherry⟩ [Old English *smōth*] SYN see SUAVE — **smooth·ly** *adv* — **smooth·ness** *n*

²**smooth** *vt* **I** : to make smooth **2 a** : to free from what is harsh or disagreeable : POLISH ⟨*smoothed* out my style⟩ **b** : to make calm : SOOTHE **3** : to minimize (as a fault) in order to allay ill will ⟨*smoothed* things over with apologies⟩ **4** : to free from obstruction or difficulty **5** : to cause to lie evenly and in order ⟨*smooth* out the tablecloth⟩ — **smooth·er** *n*

smooth·bore \'smüth-'bōr, -'bor\ *adj* : having a smooth-surfaced bore — **smooth·bore** \'smüth-,\ *n*

smooth·en \'smü-thən\ *vb* : to make or become smooth

smooth muscle *n* : muscle made up of spindle-shaped cells with single nuclei and no cross striations that is typical of visceral organs, occurs especially in sheets and rings, and is not under voluntary control — called also *involuntary muscle*; compare STRIATED MUSCLE

smooth–tongued \'smüth–·təngd\ *adj* : ingratiating in speech

smoothy *or* **smooth·ie** \'smü–thē\ *n, pl* **smooth·ies** 1 : a smooth-tongued person 2 a : a person with polished manners b : a man with an ingratiating manner toward women

smor·gas·bord \'smör·gəs–·bord, –·bord\ *n* : a buffet offering a large variety of foods and dishes [Swedish *smörgåsbord*, from *smörgås* "open sandwich" + *bord* "table"]

smote *past of* SMITE

¹smoth·er \'sməth–ər\ *n* 1 : a dense cloud (as of fog, foam, or dust) 2 : a confused multitude of things [Middle English *smorther* "dense smoke", from *smoren* "to smother", from Old English *smorian* "to suffocate"]

²smother *vb* **smoth·ered; smoth·er·ing** \'sməth–·ring, –ə–ring\ 1 a : to overcome by depriving of air or exposing to smoke or fumes : SUFFOCATE b : to prevent the development or activity of ⟨*smother* a child with too much care⟩ 2 : to become suffocated 3 a : to cover up : SUPPRESS ⟨*smother* a yawn⟩ b : to overlay thickly : BLANKET ⟨broiled steak *smothered* with mushrooms⟩ c : OVERWHELM 1 d : CONQUER 3

¹smudge \'sməj\ *vb* 1 a : to make a smudge on b : to soil as if by smudging 2 : to smoke or protect by a smudge fire 3 : to make a smudge 4 : to become smudged [Middle English *smogen*]

²smudge *n* 1 a : a blurry spot or streak : SMEAR b : STAIN 2 2 : a fire made to smoke (as for driving away mosquitoes or protecting fruit from frost) — **smudg·i·ly** \'sməj–ə–lē\ *adv* — **smudg·i·ness** \'sməj–ē–nəs\ *n* — **smudgy** \'sməj–ē\ *adj*

smudge pot *n* : a container in which fuel (as oil) is burned to produce a smudge

smug \'sməg\ *adj* **smug·ger; smug·gest** : highly self-satisfied : COMPLACENT [probably from Low German *smuck* "neat"] — **snug·ly** *adv* — **snug·ness** *n*

smug·gle \'sməg–əl\ *vb* **smug·gled; smug·gling** \'sməg–ling, –ə–ling\ 1 : to export or import secretly and unlawfully (as to avoid paying duty) ⟨*smuggle* jewels⟩ 2 : to take, bring, or introduce secretly or stealthily [Low German *smuggeln* and Dutch *smokkelen*] — **smug·gler** \'sməg–lər\ *n*

¹smut \'smət\ *vb* **smut·ted; smut·ting** 1 : to stain, taint, or affect with smut 2 : to become affected by smut [probably from Middle English *smotten* "to stain"]

²smut *n* 1 : matter that soils or blackens; *esp* : a particle of soot 2 : any of various destructive diseases of plants and especially of cereal grasses caused by parasitic fungi that transform plant structures (as seeds) into dark masses of spores; *also* : a fungus causing a smut 3 : obscene or indecent language or matter

smutch \'sməch\ *n* : a dark stain : SMUDGE [probably from ¹*smudge*] — **smutch** *vt* — **smutchy** \–ē\ *adj*

smut·ty \'smət–ē\ *adj* **smut·ti·er; –est** 1 : soiled with smut ⟨a *smutty* face⟩ 2 : affected with smut fungus 3 : INDECENT ⟨*smutty* jokes⟩ — **smut·ti·ly** \'smət–l–ē\ *adv* — **smut·ti·ness** \'smət–ē–nəs\ *n*

snack \'snak\ *n* : a light meal : LUNCH [Middle English *snake* "bite", from *snaken* "to bite"]

snack bar *n* : a public eating place where snacks are served usually at a counter

snaf·fle \'snaf–əl\ *n* : a simple jointed bit for a bridle [origin unknown] — **snaffle** *vt*

sna·fu \sna–'fü\ *adj* : being in a state of confusion : AWRY [*s*ituation *n*ormal *a*ll *f*ouled *u*p] — **snafu** *n* — **snafu** *vt*

¹snag \'snag\ *n* 1 : a stump or stub of a tree branch especially when embedded under water and not visible from the surface 2 : an uneven or broken projection from a smooth or finished surface 3 : a concealed

or unexpected difficulty or hindrance [of Scandinavian origin] — **snag·gy** \'snag–ē\ *adj*

²snag *vt* **snagged; snag·ging** 1 a : to catch and usually damage on or as if on a snag ⟨*snagged* my sleeve on a nail⟩ b : to halt or impede as if on a snag ⟨the bill was *snagged* in committee⟩ 2 : to catch or obtain by quick action ⟨*snagged* two tickets for the big game⟩

snag·gle·tooth \'snag–əl–·tüth\ *n* : an irregular, broken, or projecting tooth [English dialect *snaggle* "irregular tooth", from ¹*snag*] — **snag·gle·toothed** \·snag–əl–·tütht\ *adj*

snail \'snāl\ *n* 1 : a gastropod mollusk especially when having an external enclosing spiral shell 2 : a slow-moving person or thing [Old English *snægl*]

¹snake \'snāk\ *n* 1 : any of numerous limbless reptiles (suborder Serpentes or Ophidia) with a long tapering body and salivary glands often modified to produce venom which is injected through grooved or tubular fangs 2 : a despicable or treacherous person [Old English *snaca*] — **snake·like** \'snā–·klīk\ *adj*

²snake *vb* 1 : to crawl or move sinuously, silently, or secretly 2 : to move (as logs) by dragging

snake·bird \'snāk–·bərd\ *n* : any of several fish-eating birds related to the cormorants but distinguished by a longer neck and sharp-pointed bill

snake·bite \–·bīt\ *n* : the bite of a snake and especially a venomous snake

snake charmer *n* : an entertainer who exhibits a professed power to charm or fascinate venomous snakes

snake dance *n* : a group of people moving single file in a wavy path (as in celebration of an athletic victory)

snake doctor *n* : DRAGONFLY

snake fence *n* : WORM FENCE

snake in the grass : a treacherous person pretending to be a friend

snake oil *n* : any of various substances or mixtures sold (as by a traveling medicine show) as medicine usually without regard to their medical worth or properties

snake·root \'snā–·krüt, –·krút\ *n* : any of various plants mostly with roots reputed to cure snakebites; *also* : the root of such a plant

snake·skin \'snāk–·skin\ *n* : the skin of a snake or leather made from it

snaky \'snā–kē\ *adj* **snak·i·er; –est** 1 : of or resembling a snake 2 : abounding in snakes — **snak·i·ly** \–kə–lē\ *adv*

¹snap \'snap\ *vb* **snapped; snap·ping** 1 a : to close the jaws suddenly : seize something sharply with the mouth ⟨fish *snapping* at bait⟩ b : to grasp at something eagerly ⟨*snapped* at the chance to travel⟩ c : to take possession of promptly and decisively ⟨*snap* up a bargain⟩ 2 : to speak or utter sharply or irritably ⟨*snap* at a friend⟩ ⟨*snapped* out an answer⟩ 3 a : to break or break apart suddenly and especially with a sharp sound ⟨the twig *snapped*⟩ b : to give way or cause to give way suddenly under stress ⟨my nerves *snapped*⟩ c : to bring to a sudden end ⟨*snapped* the opposing team's winning streak⟩ 4 : to make or cause to make a sharp or crackling sound ⟨*snap* a whip⟩ 5 a : to close or fit in place with an abrupt movement ⟨the lid *snapped* shut⟩ b : to put into or remove from a position by a sudden movement or with a snapping sound ⟨*snap* off a switch⟩ c : to close by means of snaps or fasteners ⟨*snapped* up the back of the dress⟩ 6 : FLASH ⟨eyes *snapping* in anger⟩ 7 a : to move briskly or sharply ⟨*snapped* to attention⟩ b : to put (a football) in play especially by passing or handing backward between the legs c : to take a snapshot of [Dutch or Low German *snappen*]

²snap *n* 1 : an abrupt closing (as of the mouth in biting or of scissors in cutting); *esp* : a biting or snatching with the teeth or jaws 2 : CINCH 3a 3 : a small amount : BIT ⟨don't care a *snap*⟩ 4 a : a sudden snatching at something b : a quick short movement c : a sudden sharp breaking 5 : a sound made by snapping some-

snail 1

thing ⟨shut the book with a *snap*⟩ **6** : a sudden interval of harsh weather ⟨a cold *snap*⟩ **7** : a catch or fastening that closes or locks with a click ⟨the *snap* of a bracelet⟩ **8** : a thin brittle cookie **9** : SNAPSHOT **10 a** : ENERGY 2 **b** : a pleasing vigorous quality **11** : an act or instance of snapping a football

³**snap** *adj* **1** : made suddenly or without deliberation ⟨a *snap* judgment⟩ **2** : shutting or fastening with a click or by means of a device that snaps ⟨a *snap* lock⟩ **3** : unusually easy ⟨a *snap* course⟩

snap·back \'snap-,bak\ *n* : a sudden rebound or recovery

snap back \snap-'bak, 'snap-\ *vi* : to make a quick or vigorous recovery ⟨*snap back* after an illness⟩

snap bean *n* : a bean grown primarily for its young pods usually used broken in pieces as a cooked vegetable — compare SHELL BEAN

snap·drag·on \'snap-,drag-ən\ *n* : any of several garden plants having showy white, crimson, or yellow 2-lipped flowers [from the fancied resemblance of the flowers to the face of a dragon]

snap·per \'snap-ər\ *n, pl* **snappers 1 a** : one that snaps **b** : SNAPPING TURTLE **2** *pl also* **snapper a** : any of a large family of active flesh-eating fishes of warm seas important as food and sport fishes **b** : any of several immature fishes (as the young of the bluefish) that resemble a snapper

snapping turtle *n* : any of several large edible American aquatic turtles with powerful jaws and a strong musky odor

snap·pish \'snap-ish\ *adj* **1** : marked by or given to curt irritable speech : IRASCIBLE **2** : inclined to bite ⟨a *snappish* dog⟩ — **snap·pish·ly** *adv* — **snap·pish·ness** *n*

snap·py \'snap-ē\ *adj* **snap·pi·er; -est 1** : SNAPPISH 1 **2 a** : LIVELY 4 **b** : briskly cold **c** : SMART 6a, STYLISH — **snap·pi·ly** \'snap-ə-lē\ *adv* — **snap·pi·ness** \'snap-ē-nəs\ *n*

snap·shot \'snap-,shät\ *n* : a casual photograph made by rapid exposure usually with a small hand-held camera

¹**snare** \'snaər, 'sneər\ *n* **1** : a trap often consisting of a noose for catching small animals or birds **2** : something by which one is entangled, trapped, or deceived **3** : one of the catgut strings or metal spirals of a snare drum [Old English *sneare,* from Old Norse *snara*]

²**snare** *vt* **1** : to capture or entangle by or as if by use of a snare **2** : to win or attain by skillful or deceptive maneuvers SYN see CATCH — **snar·er** *n*

snare drum *n* : a small double-headed drum with one or more snares stretched across its lower head

¹**snarl** \'snärl\ *n* **1** : a tangle especially of hairs or thread : KNOT **2** : a tangled situation ⟨a traffic *snarl*⟩ [Middle English *snarle*]

²**snarl** *vb* : to become or cause to become tangled

³**snarl** *vb* **1** : to growl with a snapping or gnashing of teeth **2** : to express anger in a surly harsh way **3** : to utter with a snarl [obsolete *snar* "to growl"] — **snarl·er** *n*

⁴**snarl** *n* : a surly angry growl

¹**snatch** \'snach\ *vb* **1** : to seize or try to seize something quickly or suddenly ⟨*snatched* at the rope⟩ **2** : to grasp or take suddenly without permission, ceremony, or right [Middle English *snacchen* "to snap, seize"] SYN see TAKE — **snatch·er** *n*

²**snatch** *n* **1 a** : a short period ⟨slept in *snatches*⟩ **b** : something brief, fragmentary, or hurried ⟨*snatches* of old tunes⟩ **2 a** : a snatching at or of something **b** *slang* : an act or instance of kidnapping

snatchy \'snach-ē\ *adj* : marked by breaks in continuity

snaz·zy \'snaz-ē\ *adj* **snaz·zi·er; -est** : conspicuously or flashily attractive [origin unknown]

¹**sneak** \'snēk\ *vb* **sneaked** \'snēkt\ *or* **snuck** \'snək\; **sneak·ing 1** : to go stealthily or furtively : SLINK **2** : to

put, bring, or take in a furtive or sly manner [related to Old English *snīcan* "to sneak along"] SYN see SKULK

²**sneak** *n* **1** : a person who acts in a stealthy, furtive, or sly manner **2** : the act or an instance of sneaking

³**sneak** *adj* **1** : carried on secretly : CLANDESTINE **2** : occurring without warning ⟨a *sneak* attack⟩

sneak·er \'snē-kər\ *n* **1** : one that sneaks **2** : a usually canvas sports shoe with a pliable rubber sole

sneak·ing \'snē-king\ *adj* **1** : UNDERHAND 1, FURTIVE **2 a** : not openly expressed or acknowledged ⟨a *sneaking* sympathy⟩ **b** : that is a persistent conjecture ⟨a *sneaking* suspicion⟩ — **sneak·ing·ly** \'snē-king-lē\ *adv*

sneak preview *n* : a special advance showing of a movie before its release for public viewing

sneak thief *n* : a thief who steals without using violence or forcibly breaking into buildings

sneaky \'snē-kē\ *adj* **sneak·i·er; -est** : UNDERHAND 1 — **sneak·i·ly** \-kə-lē\ *adv* — **sneak·i·ness** \-kē-nəs\ *n*

¹**sneer** \'sniər\ *vb* **1** : to smile with facial contortions expressing scorn or contempt **2 a** : to speak or write in a scornfully jeering manner **b** : to express with a sneer [probably related to Middle High German *snerren* "to chatter, gossip"] SYN see SCOFF — **sneer·er** *n*

²**sneer** *n* : a sneering expression or remark

¹**sneeze** \'snēz\ *vi* : to expel the breath in a sudden violent audible spasm [Middle English *snesen,* alteration of *fnesen,* from Old English *fnēosan*] — **sneez·er** *n* — **sneeze at** : to treat as unimportant ⟨a cool million is nothing to *sneeze at*⟩

²**sneeze** *n* : an act or fact of sneezing

sneeze·weed \'snēz-,wēd\ *n* : a North American yellow-flowered perennial herb whose odor is said to cause sneezing

sneezy \'snē-zē\ *adj* : given to or causing sneezing

snell \'snel\ *n* : a short line by which a fishhook is attached to a longer line [origin unknown]

¹**snick** \'snik\ *vt* : to cut slightly : NICK [probably from obsolete *snick or snee* "to cut and thrust", from Dutch *steken of snijden* "to thrust or cut"]

²**snick** *n* : a slight often metallic sound : CLICK [imitative]

¹**snick·er** \'snik-ər\ *vi* **snick·ered; snick·er·ing** \'snik-ring, -ə-ring\ : to laugh in a covert or partly suppressed way especially at the embarrassment of someone else [imitative]

²**snicker** *n* : an act or sound of snickering

snide \'snīd\ *adj* **1** : MEAN, LOW ⟨a *snide* trick⟩ **2** : slyly disparaging : INSINUATING ⟨*snide* remarks⟩ [origin unknown]

sniff \'snif\ *vb* **1** : to draw air audibly up the nose **2** : to show or express disdain or scorn ⟨*sniffed* at menial jobs⟩ **3** : to smell or take by inhalation through the nose : INHALE ⟨*sniff* perfume⟩ **4** : to detect by or as if by smelling ⟨*sniff* out trouble⟩ [Middle English *sniffen*] — **sniff** *n* — **sniff·er** *n*

sniff·ish \'snif-ish\ *adj* : SNIFFY, HAUGHTY — **sniff·ish·ly** *adv* — **sniff·ish·ness** *n*

¹**snif·fle** \'snif-əl\ *vi* **snif·fled; snif·fling** \'snif-ling, -ə-ling\ **1** : to sniff repeatedly : SNUFFLE **2** : to speak with or as if with sniffling [derived from *sniff*] — **snif·fler** \'snif-lər, -ə-lər\ *n*

²**sniffle** *n* **1** *pl* : a head cold marked by nasal discharge **2** : an act or sound of sniffling

sniffy \'snif-ē\ *adj* : inclined to sniff haughtily : SUPERCILIOUS — **sniff·i·ly** \'snif-ə-lē\ *adv* — **sniff·i·ness** \'snif-ē-nəs\ *n*

snif·ter \'snif-tər\ *n* : a short-stemmed goblet with a bowl narrowing toward the top [Middle English *snifteren* "to sniff, snort"]

snig·ger \'snig-ər\ *vi* **snig·gered; snig·ger·ing** \'snig-ring, -ə-ring\ : SNICKER [by alteration] — **snigger** *n*

¹**snip** \'snip\ *n* **1** : a small piece that is snipped off; *also* : FRAGMENT **2** : an act or sound of snipping **3** : a presumptuous or impertinent person [Dutch or Low German]

¹snipe

²snip *vb* **snipped; snip·ping** : to cut or cut off with or as if with shears or scissors; *esp* : to clip suddenly or by bits

¹snipe \'snīp\ *n, pl* **snipes** *or* **snipe** : any of several game birds especially of marshy areas that resemble the related woodcocks [of Scandinavian origin]

²snipe *vi* **1** : to shoot at a person or persons from a usually concealed vantage point **2** : to aim a snide attack [earlier *snipe* "to shoot snipe"] — **snip·er** \'snī-pər\ *n*

snip·pet \'snip-ət\ *n* : a small part, piece, or thing

snip·py \'snip-ē\ *adj* **snip·pi·er; -est 1** : SHORT-TEM-PERED, IRASCIBLE **2** : unduly brief or curt **3** : putting on airs — **snip·pi·ness** *n*

snips \'snips\ *n pl* : hand shears used especially for cutting sheet metal ⟨tin *snips*⟩

snit \'snit\ *n* : a state of irritated agitation [origin unknown]

¹snitch \'snich\ *vb* **1** : INFORM, TATTLE ⟨always *snitching* on someone⟩ **2** : to take by stealth; *esp* : PILFER ⟨*snitched* a dime from me⟩ [origin unknown] — **snitch·er** *n*

²snitch *n* : one that snitches; *esp* : INFORMANT

sniv·el \'sniv-əl\ *vi* **sniv·eled** *or* **sniv·elled; sniv·el·ing** *or* **sniv·el·ling** \'sniv-ling, -ə-ling\ **1** : to run at the nose **2** : to snuff mucus up the nose audibly : SNUFFLE **3** : to cry or whine with snuffling **4** : to speak or act in a whining or weakly emotional way [Middle English *snivelen*] — **sniv·el·er** \'sniv-lər, -ə-lər\ *n*

snob \'snäb\ *n* **1** : one who obviously imitates, fawningly admires, or vulgarly seeks association with those in a superior position **2 a** : one who looks down on those in an inferior position **b** : one whose attitude is offensively superior (as in matters of taste) [obsolete *snob* "member of the lower classes", from English dialect, "shoemaker"]

snob appeal *n* : qualities in a product (as high price or foreign origin) that appeal to the snobbery in a purchaser

snob·bery \'snäb-rē, -ə-rē\ *n, pl* **-ber·ies** : snobbish conduct or outlook

snob·bish \'snäb-ish\ *adj* : characteristic of or befitting a snob — **snob·bish·ly** *adv* — **snob·bish·ness** *n* — **snob·bism** \'snäb-,iz-əm\ *n*

snob·by \'snäb-ē\ *adj* : SNOBBISH

snood \'snüd\ *n* : a net or fabric bag pinned or tied on at the back of a woman's head for holding the hair [Old English *snōd* "hair band"]

snook \'snuk, 'snük\ *n, pl* **snook** *or* **snooks** : a large vigorous sport and food fish of warm seas related to the perches but resembling a pike [Dutch *snoek*]

snook·er \'snuk-ər\ *n* : a variation of pool played with 15 red object balls and 6 object balls of different colors [origin unknown]

¹snoop \'snüp\ *vi* : to look or pry especially in a sneaky or meddlesome way [Dutch *snoepen* "to buy or eat on the sly"] — **snoop·er** \'snü-pər\ *n*

²snoop *n* : one that snoops

snoop·er·scope \'snü-pər-,skōp\ *n* : a device utilizing infrared radiation for enabling a person to see an object obscured (as by darkness)

snoopy \'snü-pē\ *adj* : given to snooping : PRYING

snoot \'snüt\ *n* **1** : SNOUT 1 **2** : NOSE 1, 3 [Middle English *snute*]

snooty \'snüt-ē\ *adj* **snoot·i·er; -est** : haughtily contemptuous : SNOBBISH — **snoot·i·ly** \'snüt-l-ē\ *adv* — **snoot·i·ness** \'snüt-ē-nəs\ *n*

¹snooze \'snüz\ *vi* : NAP 1, DOZE [origin unknown] — **snooz·er** *n*

²snooze *n* : a short sleep : NAP

snore \'snōr, 'snór\ *vi* : to breathe during sleep with a rough hoarse noise [Middle English *snoren*] — **snore** *n* — **snor·er** *n*

¹snor·kel \'snór-kəl\ *n* **1** : a tube or tubes that can be extended above the surface of the water to supply air to and remove exhaust from a submerged submarine

2 : a tube used by swimmers for breathing with the face under water [German *schnorchel*]

²snorkel *vi* **snor·keled; snor·kel·ing** \-kə-ling, -kling\ : to swim on the surface with the face in the water using a snorkel; *also* : to engage in skin diving

¹snort \'snórt\ *vb* **1 a** : to force air violently through the nose with a rough harsh sound **b** : to express scorn, anger, indignation, or surprise by a snort **2** : to express with a snort ⟨*snort* one's disgust⟩ **3** : to take in (a drug) by inhaling through the nose [Middle English *snorten*] — **snort·er** *n*

²snort *n* **1** : an act or sound of snorting **2** : a drink of usually straight liquor taken in one draft

snout \'snaut\ *n* **1 a** : a long projecting nose or muzzle (as of a swine); *also* : the projecting front of the head of various animals (as a weevil) **b** : the human nose especially when large or grotesque **2** : something resembling an animal's snout [Middle English *snute*] — **snout·ed** \-əd\ *adj*

snout beetle *n* : WEEVIL

¹snow \'snō\ *n* **1 a** : small white crystals of frozen water formed directly from the water vapor of the air **b** : a fall of snow crystals : a mass of snow crystals fallen to earth **2** : something resembling snow: as **a** : a congealed or crystallized substance resembling snow in appearance ⟨carbon dioxide *snow*⟩ **b** *slang* : COCAINE **c** : small transient light or dark spots on a television or radar screen [Old English *snāw*]

²snow *vb* **1** : to fall or cause to fall in or as snow ⟨*snowed* messages on the senators⟩ **2 a** : to cover, shut in, or imprison with or as if with snow **b** : to charm, persuade, or deceive glibly

¹snow·ball \'snō-,ból\ *n* : a round mass of snow pressed or rolled together

²snowball *vb* **1** : to throw snowballs at **2** : to increase or expand at a rapidly accelerating rate

snow·bank \'snō-,bangk\ *n* : a mound or slope of snow

snow·ber·ry \-,ber-ē\ *n* : a low-growing North American shrub of the honeysuckle family with clusters of pink flowers and white berries

snow·bird \-,bərd\ *n* : any of several small birds (as a junco) seen chiefly in winter

snow–blind \-,blīnd\ *or* **snow–blind·ed** \-'blīn-dəd\ *adj* : affected with snow blindness

snow blindness *n* : inflammation and inability to tolerate light caused by exposure of the eyes to ultraviolet rays reflected from snow or ice

snow·bound \'snō-'baund\ *adj* : shut in or blockaded by snow

snow·cap \-,kap\ *n* : a covering cap of snow (as on a mountain peak) — **snow·capped** \-,kapt\ *adj*

snow·drift \-,drift\ *n* : a bank of drifted snow

snow·drop \-,dräp\ *n* : an early-blooming plant of the amaryllis family that bears nodding white flowers

snow·fall \-,fól\ *n* **1** : a fall of snow **2** : the amount of snow that falls in a single storm or in a given period

snow fence *n* : a fence placed across the usual path of the wind to protect something (as a road) from snow drifts

snow·field \-,fēld\ *n* : a broad level expanse of snow; *esp* : a mass of perennial snow (as at the head of a glacier)

snow·flake \-,flāk\ *n* : a flake or crystal of snow

snow leopard *n* : a large cat of central Asia with a long heavy pelt blotched with brownish black in summer and white in winter

snow line *n* : the lower edge of an area of permanent snow (as on a mountain peak)

snow·man \'snō-,man\ *n* : snow shaped to resemble a human figure

snow·mo·bile \'snō-mō-,bēl\ *n* : any of various automotive vehicles for travel on snow [*snow* + auto*mobile*] — **snow·mo·bil·er** \-,bē-lər\ *n* — **snow·mo·bil·ing** \-,bē-ling\ *n*

\ə\ abut	\ng\ sing
\ər\ further	\ō\ bone
\a\ mat	\ó\ saw
\ā\ take	\ói\ coin
\ä\ cot, cart	\th\ thin
\au\ out	\th\ this
\ch\ chin	\ü\ food
\e\ pet	\u\ foot
\ē\ easy	\y\ yet
\g\ go	\yü\ few
\i\ tip	\yu\ cure
\ī\ life	\zh\ vision
\j\ job	

snow–on–the–mountain–snow–on–the–mountain *n* : a showy white-bracted spurge native to the western United States

snow·plow \'snō-ˌplau̇\ *n* **1** : any of various devices used for clearing away snow **2** : a method of stopping in skiing in which the tails of the skis are pushed out to either side

¹snow·shoe \-ˌshü\ *n* : a light oval wooden frame strung with thongs that is attached to the foot to enable a person to walk on soft snow without sinking

²snowshoe *vi* **snow·shoed; snow·shoe·ing** : to travel on snowshoes

snowshoe rabbit *n* : a rather large rabbit of northern North America with heavy fur on the hind feet and a coat that is brown in the summer but usually white in winter — called also *snowshoe hare*

snowshoe rabbit

snow·slide \'snō-ˌslīd\ *n* : an avalanche of snow

snow·storm \-ˌstȯrm\ *n* : a storm of falling snow

snow·suit \-ˌsüt\ *n* : a one-piece or two-piece and usually lined garment for winter wear by children

snow tire *n* : an automobile tire with a tread designed to give added traction on snow

snow under *vt* **1** : to overwhelm especially beyond capacity to absorb or deal with something **2** : to defeat by a large margin

snow–white \'snō-'hwīt -'wīt\ *adj* : white as snow

snowy \'snō-ē\ *adj* **snow·i·er; -est 1 a** : marked by snow ⟨a *snowy* day⟩ **b** : covered with snow ⟨*snowy* mountaintops⟩ **2** : whitened by or as if by snow ⟨an orchard *snowy* with apple blossoms⟩ **3** : SNOW-WHITE — **snow·i·ly** \'snō-ə-lē\ *adv* — **snow·i·ness** \'snō-ē-nəs\ *n*

snowy owl *n* : a large chiefly arctic owl that is white or white spotted with brown

snowy owl

¹snub \'snəb\ *vt* **snubbed; snub·bing 1** : to check or stop with a cutting reply : REBUKE **2** : to check (as a line or cable that is running out) suddenly especially by turning around a fixed object (as a post) **3** : to treat with contempt or neglect **4** : to extinguish by stubbing ⟨*snub* out a cigarette⟩ [of Scandinavian origin]

²snub *n* : an act or an instance of snubbing : REBUFF

³snub *or* **snubbed** \'snəbd\ *adj* : BLUNT, STUBBY ⟨a *snub* nose⟩ — **snub·ness** *n*

snub·ber \'snəb-ər\ *n* **1** : one that snubs **2** : SHOCK ABSORBER

snub–nosed \'snəb-'nōzd\ *adj* : having a stubby and usually slightly turned-up nose

snuck *past of* SNEAK

¹snuff \'snəf\ *n* : the charred part of the wick of a candle [Middle English *snoffe*]

²snuff *vt* **1** : to cut or pinch off the snuff of (a candle) so as to brighten the light **2** : EXTINGUISH ⟨*snuff* out a life⟩

³snuff *vb* **1** : to draw forcibly through or into the nostrils **2** : to sniff inquiringly [related to Dutch *snuffen* "to sniff, snuff"]

⁴snuff *n* : the act of snuffing : SNIFF

⁵snuff *n* : a preparation of pulverized tobacco to be chewed, placed against the gums, or inhaled through the nostrils [Dutch *snuf*, short for *snuftabak*, from *snuffen* "to sniff, snuff" + *tabak* "tobacco"] — **up to snuff** : meeting an acceptable standard

snuff·box \'snəf-ˌbäks\ *n* : a small box for holding snuff

¹snuff·er \'snəf-ər\ *n* **1** : a device somewhat like a pair of scissors for cutting and holding the snuff of a candle — usually used in pl. **2** : a device for extinguishing candles

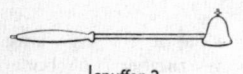

¹snuffer 2

²snuffer *n* : one that snuffs or sniffs

¹snuf·fle \'snəf-əl\ *vb* **snuf·fled; snuf·fling** \'snəf-ling, -ə-ling\ **1** : to snuff or sniff usually noisily and repeatedly **2** : to breathe through an obstructed nose with a sniffing sound **3** : to speak in a nasal tone; *also* : WHIMPER, WHINE [related to Dutch *snuffelen* "to snuffle"] — **snuf·fler** \'snəf-lər, -ə-lər\ *n*

²snuffle *n* : the sound made in snuffling

¹snug \'snəg\ *adj* **snug·ger; snug·gest 1 a** : SEAWORTHY **b** : fitting closely and comfortably ⟨a *snug* coat⟩ **2** : enjoying or affording warm secure shelter and comfort : COZY ⟨a *snug* cottage⟩ **3** : offering safe concealment ⟨a *snug* hideout⟩ [perhaps of Scandinavian origin] — **snug** *adv* — **snug·ly** *adv* — **snug·ness** *n*

²snug *vb* **snugged; snug·ging 1** : to settle or lie down : NESTLE **2** : to make snug

snug·gery \'snəg-rē, -ə-rē\ *n, pl* **-ger·ies** *chiefly British* : a snug place; *esp* : DEN 4

snug·gle \'snəg-əl\ *vb* **snug·gled; snug·gling** \'snəg-ling, -ə-ling\ **1** : to curl up comfortably or cozily **2** : to draw close especially for comfort or in affection [derived from ²*snug*]

¹so \sō, 'sō, *especially before an adj or adv followed by "that"* sə\ *adv* **1 a** : in a manner or way that is indicated or suggested ⟨do you really think *so*⟩ ⟨it *so* happened that all were wrong⟩ **b** : in the same manner or way : ALSO ⟨you worked hard and *so* did we⟩ **c** : SUBSEQUENTLY, THEN ⟨and *so* home and to bed⟩ **2 a** : to an indicated or suggested extent or degree ⟨had never been *so* happy⟩ **b** : to a great extent or degree : VERY, EXTREMELY ⟨came home because we loved it *so*⟩ **c** : to a definite but unspecified extent or degree ⟨can only do *so* much in a day⟩ **d** : most certainly : INDEED ⟨you did *so* do it⟩ **3** : THEREFORE, CONSEQUENTLY [Old English *swā*]

²so \sō, 'sō\ *conj* **1 a** : with the result that ⟨your diction is good, *so* every word is clear⟩ **b** : in order that ⟨be quiet *so* I can sleep⟩ **2** *archaic* : provided that **3 a** : for that reason : THEREFORE ⟨I want to go, *so* I will⟩ **b** — used as an introductory particle ⟨*so* here we are⟩ often to belittle a point being discussed ⟨*so* what?⟩

³so \'sō\ *adj* **1** : conforming with actual facts : TRUE ⟨said things that were not *so*⟩ **2** : marked by a definite order ⟨your books are always just *so*⟩

⁴so \ˌsō, 'sō\ *pron* **1** : such as has been specified : the same ⟨became insane and remained *so*⟩ **2** : approximately that ⟨20 years or *so*⟩

⁵so \'sō\ *variant of* SOL

¹soak \'sōk\ *vb* **1 a** : to remain steeping in liquid (as water) **b** : to place in a medium to wet or permeate thoroughly **2 a** : to enter or pass through something by or as if by pores : SATURATE **b** : to capture one's full attention ⟨let the remark *soak* in⟩ **3** : to extract by or as if by steeping ⟨*soak* the dirt out⟩ **4** : to draw in by or as if by suction or absorption ⟨*soaked* up the sunshine⟩ **5** : to levy an exorbitant charge against ⟨*soaked* the taxpayers⟩ [Old English *socian*] — **soak·er** *n*

²soak *n* **1** : the act or process of soaking : the state of being soaked **2** : DRUNKARD

soak·age \'sō-kij\ *n* **1** : liquid gained by absorption or lost by seepage **2** : the act or process of soaking : the state of being soaked

so–and–so \'sō-ən-ˌsō\ *n, pl* **so–and–sos** *or* **so–and–so's** \-ən-ˌsōz\ : an unnamed or unspecified person or thing

¹soap \'sōp\ *n* **1** : a substance that is usually made by the action of alkali on fat, dissolves in water, and is used for washing **2** : a salt of a fatty acid [Old English *sāpe*]

²soap *vt* : to rub soap over or into

soap·ber·ry \'sōp-ˌber-ē\ *n* : any of a genus of chiefly tropical woody plants; *also* : the fruit of a soapberry and especially one used as a soap substitute

soap·box \-ˌbäks\ *n* : an improvised platform used by a self-appointed, spontaneous, or informal speaker — **soapbox** *adj*

Soap Box Derby *service mark* — used for a downhill race for youngsters' homemade racing cars without motors or pedals

soap bubble *n* : a hollow iridescent globe formed by blowing a film of soapsuds (as from a pipe)

soap opera *n* : a radio or television serial drama performed usually on a daytime commerical program [from its frequently being sponsored by soap manufacturers]

soap plant *n* : a plant with a part (as leaves or root) that can be used as a soap substitute

soap·stone \'sōp-,stōn\ *n* : a soft stone having a soapy feel and composed essentially of talc, chlorite, and often some magnetite

soap·suds \-,sədz\ *n pl* : SUDS 1

soap·wort \-,wərt, -,wȯrt\ *n* : BOUNCING BET

soapy \'sō-pē\ *adj* **soap·i·er; -est** 1 : smeared with or full of soap ⟨a *soapy* face⟩ 2 : containing or combined with soap ⟨*soapy* ammonia⟩ 3 : resembling or having the qualities of soap — **soap·i·ly** \-pə-lē\ *adv* — **soap·i·ness** \-pē-nəs\ *n*

¹soar \'sōr, 'sȯr\ *vi* **a** : to fly aloft or about **b** : to sail or hover in the air often at a great height : GLIDE 2 : to rise or increase dramatically (as in position or price) 3 : to ascend to a higher or more exalted level 4 : to rise majestically [Middle French *essorer* "to air, soar" derived from Latin *ex-* + *aura* "air"] — **soar·er** *n*

²soar *n* : the act of soaring : upward flight

¹sob \'säb\ *vb* **sobbed; sob·bing** 1 : to cry with convulsive catching of the breath 2 : to make a sound like that of sobbing ⟨the wind *sobbed* through the trees⟩ 3 : to bring to a specified state by sobbing ⟨*sobbed* myself to sleep⟩ 4 : to utter with sobs ⟨*sobbed* out the story⟩ [Middle English *sobben*]

²sob *n* 1 : an act of sobbing 2 : a sound of or like that of sobbing

¹so·ber \'sō-bər\ *adj* **so·ber·er** \-bər-ər\; **so·ber·est** \-bə-rəst, -brəst\ 1 **a** : sparing or temperate in the use of food and drink **b** : not drunk 2 : SERIOUS 1 3 : subdued in tone, color, or intensity 4 : having or showing self-control : avoiding extremes of behavior [Middle French *sobre*, from Latin *sobrius*] — **so·ber·ly** \-bər-lē\ *adv* — **so·ber·ness** *n*

²sober *vb* **so·bered; so·ber·ing** \-bə-ring, -bring\ : to make or become sober — often used with *up*

so·ber·sid·ed \,sō-bər-'sīd-əd\ *adj* : SERIOUS 1

so·ber·sides \'sō-bər-'sīdz\ *n sing or pl* : one who is sobersided

so·bri·e·ty \sə-'brī-ət-ē\ *n* : the quality or state of being sober [Middle French *sobrieté*, from Latin *sobrietas*, from *sobrius* "sober"]

so·bri·quet \'sō-bri-,kā, -,ket, ,sō-bri-'\ *or* **sou·bri·quet** \'sü-, ,sü-, 'sü-, ,sü-\ *n* : a fanciful name or epithet [French]

sob story *n* : a sentimental story designed chiefly to evoke sympathy or sadness

so-called \'sō-'kȯld\ *adj* 1 : commonly or popularly named ⟨the *so-called* pocket veto⟩ 2 : falsely or inaccurately named ⟨your *so-called* friend⟩

soc·cer \'säk-ər\ *n* : a football game with 11 players on a side in which a round ball is advanced by kicking or by propelling it with any part of the body except the hands and arms [by shortening and alteration from *association football*]

so·cia·bil·i·ty \,sō-shə-'bil-ət-ē\ *n, pl* **-ties** : the quality or state of being sociable : AFFABILITY; *also* : the act or an instance of being sociable

¹so·cia·ble \'sō-shə-bəl\ *adj* 1 : inclined to seek or enjoy companionship : AFFABLE, FRIENDLY ⟨*sociable* people⟩ 2 : leading to friendliness or pleasant social relations [Latin *sociabilis*, from *sociare* "to join, associate", from *socius* "companion"] — **so·cia·ble·ness** *n* — **so·cia·bly** \-blē\ *adv*

²sociable *n* : SOCIAL

¹so·cial \'sō-shəl\ *adj* 1 **a** : marked by, devoted to, or engaged in for sociability ⟨*social* events⟩ ⟨my *social* life⟩ **b** : SOCIABLE 1 2 : of or relating to human society, the interaction of the group and its members, and the welfare of these members ⟨*social* institutions⟩ ⟨*social* legislation⟩ 3 **a** : tending to form cooperative and interdependent relationships with one's fellows ⟨humans are *social* beings⟩ **b** : naturally living or growing in groups or communities ⟨bees are *social* insects⟩ 4 : of, relating to, or based on status in a particular society

⟨different *social* circles⟩; *also* : of or relating to fashionable society ⟨a *social* leader⟩ [Latin *socialis*, from *socius* "companion, associate"]

²social *n* : an informal social gathering frequently involving a special activity or interest

social climber *n* : one who attempts to gain a higher social position or acceptance in fashionable society

social democracy *n* : a political movement advocating a gradual and peaceful transition from capitalism to socialism by democratic means — **social democrat** *n* — **social democratic** *adj*

social disease *n* 1 : VENEREAL DISEASE 2 : a disease (as tuberculosis) whose frequency is directly related to social and economic factors

so·cial·ism \'sō-shə-,liz-əm\ *n* 1 : any of various economic and political theories or social systems based on collective or governmental ownership and administration of the means of production and distribution of goods 2 : a stage of society in Marxist theory transitional between capitalism and communism and distinguished by unequal distribution of goods and pay according to work done — **so·cial·ist** \'sōsh-ləst, -ə-ləst\ *n* — **socialist** *or* **so·cial·is·tic** \,sō-shə-'lis-tik\ *adj* — **so·cial·is·ti·cal·ly** \-ti-kə-lē, -klē\ *adv*

so·cial·ite \'sō-shə-,līt\ *n* : a socially prominent person

so·ci·al·i·ty \,sō-shē-'al-ət-ē\ *n, pl* **-ties** 1 : SOCIABILITY 2 : the tendency to associate in or to form social groups

so·cial·ize \'sō-shə-,līz\ *vb* 1 : to make social; *esp* : to train so as to develop the qualities essential to group living 2 **a** : to regulate according to the theory or practice of socialism ⟨*socialize* industry⟩ **b** : to adapt to social needs and uses 3 : to take part in the social life around one — **so·cial·iza·tion** \,sō-shə-lə-'zā-shən\ *n* — **so·cial·iz·er** \'sō-shə-,lī-zər\ *n*

socialized medicine *n* : medical and hospital services for the members of a class or population administered by an organized group (as a state agency) and paid for from funds obtained usually by assessments, philanthropy, or taxation

so·cial·ly \'sōsh-lē, -ə-lē\ *adv* 1 : in a social manner ⟨*socially* popular⟩ 2 : with respect to society ⟨*socially* prominent⟩ 3 : by or through society ⟨*socially* prescribed values⟩

so·cial–mind·ed \,sō-shəl-'mīn-dəd\ *adj* : having an interest in society; *esp* : actively interested in social welfare or the well-being of society as a whole

social science *n* 1 : a science (as psychology or sociology) that deals with the institutions and functioning of human society and with the interrelationships of individuals as members of society 2 : a science (as economics) dealing with a particular phase or aspect of human society — **social scientist** *n*

social secretary *n* : a personal secretary employed to handle social correspondence and appointments

social security *n* 1 : the principle or practice of public provision for the economic security and social welfare of the individual and the family 2 *often cap* : a United States government program established in 1935 to include old-age and survivors insurance, contributions to state unemployment insurance, and old-age and disability assistance

social service *n* : an activity designed to promote social welfare

social studies *n pl* : studies (as history, civics, economics, and geography) that deal with human relationships and the functions of society

social welfare *n* : organized public or private social services for the assistance of disadvantaged groups

social work *n* : the art, practice, or profession of extending the benefits of organized society especially through assistance to the economically underprivileged and the socially maladjusted — **social worker** *n*

¹so·ci·ety \sə-'sī-ət-ē\ *n, pl* **-et·ies** 1 : companionship with one's associates : COMPANY 2 : the social order or

\ə\ abut   \ng\ sing
\ər\ further \ō\ bone
\a\ mat   \ȯ\ saw
\ā\ take   \ȯi\ coin
\ä\ cot, cart \th\ thin
\aú\ out   \th\ this
\ch\ chin   \ü\ food
\e\ pet   \ú\ foot
\ē\ easy   \y\ yet
\g\ go   \yü\ few
\i\ tip   \yú\ cure
\ī\ life   \zh\ vision
\j\ job

community life considered as a system within which the individual lives ⟨rural *society*⟩ **3** : people in general ⟨the benefit of *society*⟩ **4** : an association of persons for some purpose ⟨a mutual aid *society*⟩ **5** : a part of a community regarded as a unit distinguished by common interests or standards; *esp* : the group or set of fashionable persons **6** : a system of interdependent organisms or biological units; *also* : an assemblage of plants usually of a single species or habit within a larger ecological community [Middle French *societé,* from Latin *societas,* from *socius* "companion"] — **so·ci·etal** \-ət-l\ *adj*

²**society** *adj* : of, relating to, or characteristic of fashionable society

so·cio·eco·nom·ic \,sō-sē-ō-,ek-ə-'näm-ik, ,sō-shē-, -,ē-kə-\ *adj* : of, relating to, or involving a combination of social and economic factors

so·ci·ol·o·gy \,sō-sē-'äl-ə-jē, -shē-\ *n* : the science of society, social institutions, and social relationships [French *sociologie,* from Latin *socius* "companion"] — **so·cio·log·i·cal** \,sō-sē-ə-'läj-i-kəl, -shē-\ *also* **so·cio·log·ic** \-ə-'läj-ik\ *adj* — **so·cio·log·i·cal·ly** \-i-kə-lē, -klē\ *adv* — **so·ci·ol·o·gist** \-'äl-ə-jəst\ *n*

so·cio·po·lit·i·cal \,sō-sē-ō-pə-'lit-i-kəl, ,sō-shē-\ *adj* : of, relating to, or involving both social and political factors

¹**sock** \'säk\ *n, pl* **socks** *or* **sox** \'säks\ : a knitted or woven covering for the foot usually extending above the ankle and sometimes to the knee [Old English *socc* "low shoe", from Latin *soccus*]

²**sock** *vb* : to hit, strike, or apply forcefully : deliver a blow [probably of Scandinavian origin]

³**sock** *n* : a vigorous or violent blow : PUNCH

sock·et \'säk-ət\ *n* : an opening or hollow that receives and holds something ⟨the eye *socket*⟩ [Anglo-French *soket* "small plowshare", from Old French *soc* "plowshare"]

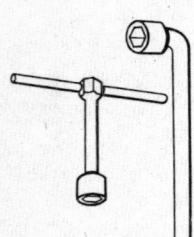

socket wrench

socket wrench *n* : a wrench usually in the form of a bar and removable socket made to fit a bolt or nut

sock·eye \'säk-,ī\ *n* : a small but commercially important Pacific salmon that spawns in late summer or fall — called also *red salmon* [of American Indian origin]

So·crat·ic \sə-'krat-ik\ *adj* : of or relating to Socrates, his followers, or his philosophical method of systematic doubt and questioning of another

¹**sod** \'säd\ *n* **1 a** : TURF 1 **b** : the grass- and forb-covered surface of the ground **2** : one's native land [Dutch or Low German *sode*]

²**sod** *vt* **sod·ded; sod·ding** : to cover with sod or turfs

so·da \'sōd-ə\ *n* **1 a** : SODIUM CARBONATE **b** : SODIUM BICARBONATE **c** : SODIUM HYDROXIDE **d** : sodium oxide Na_2O **e** : SODIUM — used in combination ⟨*soda* alum⟩ **2 a** : SODA WATER **b** : SODA POP **c** : a sweet drink consisting of soda water, flavoring, and often ice cream [Italian]

soda ash *n* : commercial sodium carbonate

soda cracker *n* : a cracker leavened with bicarbonate of soda and cream of tartar

soda fountain *n* **1** : an apparatus for drawing soda water **2** : the equipment and counter for the preparation and serving of sodas, sundaes, and ice cream

soda jerk *n* : one who dispenses carbonated drinks and ice cream at a soda fountain

soda lime *n* : a mixture of sodium hydroxide and slaked lime used especially to absorb moisture and gases

so·da·list \'sōd-l-əst, sō-'dal-\ *n* : a sodality member

so·dal·i·ty \sō-'dal-ət-ē\ *n, pl* **-ties** : an organized society or fellowship; *esp* : a devotional or charitable association of Roman Catholic laity [Latin *sodalitas* "comradeship, club", from *sodalis* "comrade"]

soda pop *n* : a bottled soft drink consisting of soda water with added flavoring and a sweet syrup

soda water *n* : a beverage consisting of water highly charged with carbonic acid gas

¹**sod·den** \'säd-n\ *adj* **1 a** : dull or lacking in expression ⟨*sodden* features⟩ **b** : SLUGGISH, UNIMAGINATIVE ⟨*sodden* minds⟩ **2** : heavy with moisture : SATURATED ⟨*sodden* ground⟩ [Middle English *soden,* from past participle of *sethen* "to seethe"] — **sod·den·ly** *adv* — **sod·den·ness** \-n-nəs, -n-əs\ *n*

²**sodden** *vb* : to make or become sodden

so·di·um \'sōd-ē-əm\ *n* : a soft waxy silver-white metallic element chemically very active and found abundantly in nature always in combined form — see ELEMENT table [New Latin, from English *soda*]

sodium ben·zo·ate \-'ben-zə-,wāt\ *n* : a crystalline or granular sodium salt $NaC_7H_5O_2$ used chiefly as a food preservative

sodium bicarbonate *n* : a white crystalline weakly alkaline salt $NaHCO_3$ used especially in baking powders, fire extinguishers, and medicine

sodium carbonate *n* : a sodium salt of carbonic acid: as **a** : a strongly alkaline compound Na_2CO_3 used in making glass, soaps, and chemicals **b** : SAL SODA

sodium chloride *n* : an ionic chemical compound NaCl that consists of crystals having equal numbers of sodium and chlorine atoms : SALT 1a

sodium cyanide *n* : a white poisonous salt NaCN used especially in electroplating, fumigating and treating steel

sodium fluoride *n* : a poisonous crystalline salt NaF that is used in the fluoridation of water and as a pesticide

sodium hydroxide *n* : a white brittle solid NaOH that is a strong caustic base used in making soap, rayon, and paper

sodium hypochlorite *n* : an unstable salt NaOCl used asa bleaching agent and disinfectant

sodium nitrate *n* : a deliquescent crystalline salt $NaNO_3$ found in crude form in Chile and used as a fertilizer and an oxidizing agent and in curing meat

sodium silicate *n* : WATER GLASS 3

sodium sulfate *n* : a bitter salt Na_2SO_4 used especially in detergents, in the manufacture of wood pulp and rayon, and in dyeing and finishing textiles

sodium thiosulfate *n* : a hygroscopic crystalline salt $Na_2S_2O_3$ used especially as a photographic fixing agent and a reducing or bleaching agent

sodium–vapor lamp *n* : an electric lamp that contains sodium vapor and electrodes between which a luminous discharge takes place

Sod·om \'säd-əm\ *n* : a place notorious for vice or corruption [*Sodom,* city of ancient Palestine destroyed by God for its wickedness (Genesis 18:20, 21; 19:24–28)]

so·fa \'sō-fə\ *n* : a long upholstered seat usually with arms and a back and often convertible into a bed [Arabic *ṣuffah* "long bench"]

so far as *conj* : insofar as

sof·fit \'säf-ət\ *n* : the underside of a part or member of a building and especially of an arch [French *soffite,* from Italian *soffitto,* derived from Latin *suffigere* "to fasten underneath"]

1 soffit

soft \'sȯft\ *adj* **1 a** : having a pleasing, comfortable, or soothing quality or effect : GENTLE, MILD ⟨*soft* breezes⟩ **b** : quiet in pitch or volume ⟨*soft* voices⟩ **c** : not bright or glaring ⟨*soft* lighting⟩ **d** : demanding little effort : EASY ⟨a *soft* job⟩ **e** : smooth or delicate in appearance or texture ⟨*soft* cashmere⟩ **f** : pleasingly mild in taste or odor **2 a** : having a mild gentle nature : DOCILE **b** : lacking in strength or vigor : unfit for prolonged exertion or severe stress : FEEBLE ⟨*soft* from good living⟩ **c** : weak or deficient mentally **d** : advocating or being a moderate or conciliatory policy ⟨took a *soft* stand toward the rebels⟩ **3 a** : yielding to physical pressure ⟨a *soft* mattress⟩ ⟨*soft* metals such as lead⟩ **b** : relatively lacking in hardness ⟨*soft* iron⟩ ⟨*soft* wood⟩ **4** : gently or gradually curved or rounded : not harsh or jagged ⟨a range of *soft* hills⟩ **5** : sounding as in *ace* and *gem* respectively — used of *c* and *g* **6 a** : deficient in or free from substances (as calcium and magnesium salts) that prevent lathering of soap ⟨*soft* water⟩ **b** : containing no alcohol ⟨*soft* drinks⟩ **7** : having relatively low penetrating power ⟨*soft* X rays⟩ **8** : occurring at such a speed as to avoid destructive impact ⟨*soft* landing of a spacecraft on the moon⟩ [Old English *sēfte, sōfte*] — **soft·ly** \'soft-lē\ *or* **soft** *adv* — **soft·ness** \'soft-nəs, 'sof-\ *n*

soft·ball \'soft-,bol, 'sof-\ *n* : a variation of baseball played on a smaller diamond with a larger ball that is pitched underhanded; *also* : the ball used in this game

soft–boiled \-'boild\ *adj* : lightly boiled so that the contents are only partly coagulated ⟨*soft-boiled* eggs⟩

soft coal *n* : BITUMINOUS COAL

soft·en \'so-fən\ *vb* **soft·ened; soft·en·ing** \'sof-ning, -ə-ning\ **1** : to make or become soft or softer **2** : to lessen the strength or resistance of — **soft·en·er** \'sof-nər, -ə-nər\ *n*

soft–finned \'soft-'find, 'sof-\ *adj* : having fins in which the membrane is supported entirely or mostly by soft or jointed rays — compare SPINY-FINNED

soft–head·ed \'soft-'hed-əd\ *adj* : having a weak, unrealistic, or uncritical mind : IMPRACTICAL — **soft–head·ed·ly** *adv* — **soft–head·ed·ness** *n*

soft–heart·ed \-'härt-əd\ *adj* : emotionally responsive : SYMPATHETIC — **soft–heart·ed·ly** *adv* — **soft–heart·ed·ness** *n*

soft–land \-'land\ *vb* : to make or cause to make a soft landing on a celestial body (as the moon) — **soft–land·er** *n*

soft palate *n* : a fold at the back of the hard palate that partially separates the mouth and pharynx

soft–ped·al \'soft-'ped-l, 'sof-\ *vt* **1** : to use the soft pedal in playing **2** : to play down ⟨*soft-pedal* the issue⟩

soft pedal *n* : a foot pedal on a piano that reduces the volume of sound

soft rot *n* : a mushy, watery, or slimy decay of a plant or plant part usually caused by bacteria or fungi

soft sell *n* : the use of suggestion or persuasion in selling rather than aggressive pressure

soft–shell \'soft-,shel, 'sof-\ *or* **soft–shelled** \-'sheld\ *adj* : having a soft or fragile shell especially as a result of recent shedding

soft–shoe \'soft-'shü, 'sof-\ *adj* : of or relating to tap dancing done in soft-soled shoes without metal taps

soft–soap \-'sōp\ *vb* : to soothe or coax with flattery — **soft–soap·er** *n*

soft soap *n* **1** : a semifluid soap **2** : FLATTERY 2

soft–spo·ken \'soft-'spō-kən, 'sof-\ *adj* : having a mild or gentle voice

soft·ware \'sof-,twaər, -,tweər\ *n* : the programs and related documentation associated with a computer system

soft wheat *n* : a wheat with soft starchy kernels high in starch but usually low in gluten

¹soft·wood \'soft-,twüd\ *n* **1** : the wood of a cone-bearing tree including both soft and hard woods **2** : a tree that yields softwood

²softwood *adj* : having or made of softwood

soft–wood·ed \'sof-'twüd-əd\ *adj* **1** : having soft wood that is easy to work or finish **2** : SOFTWOOD 1

soft·y *or* **sof·tie** \'sof-tē\ *n, pl* **soft·ies** **1** : WEAKLING **2** : a silly or sentimental person

sog·gy \'säg-ē\ *adj* **sog·gi·er; -est** : saturated or heavy with water or moisture [English dialect *sog* "to soak"] — **sog·gi·ly** \'säg-ə-lē\ *adv* — **sog·gi·ness** \'säg-ē-nəs\ *n*

¹soil \'soil\ *vb* : to make or become dirty or corrupt [Old French *soiller* "to wallow, soil", from *soil* "pigsty", probably from Latin *suile,* from *sus* "pig"]

²soil *n* **1 a** : SOILAGE, STAIN **b** : moral defilement : CORRUPTION **2** : something that soils or pollutes

³soil *n* **1** : firm land : EARTH **2** : the loose surface material of the earth in which plants grow **3** : COUNTRY 2a, LAND ⟨our native *soil*⟩ **4** : the agricultural life or call-

ing **5** : a medium in which something may take root and grow ⟨slums are fertile *soil* for crime⟩ [Anglo-French, from Latin *solium* "seat"]

soil·age \'soi-lij\ *n* : the act of soiling : the condition of being soiled

soil bank *n* : acreage retired from crop cultivation and planted with soil-building crops under a federally sponsored plan that provides subsidies to farmers for the retired land

soil conservation *n* : soil management designed to obtain good yields while improving and protecting the soil

soil·less \'soil-ləs\ *adj* : carried on without soil

soil profile *n* : PROFILE 4

soil science *n* : the science of soils — **soil scientist** *n*

soi·ree *or* **soi·rée** \swä-'rā\ *n* : an evening party or reception [French *soirée* "evening period, evening party", from *soir* "evening", from Latin *sero* "at a late hour", from *serus* "late"]

¹so·journ \'sō-,jərn, sō-'\ *n* : a temporary stay [Old French *sojorn,* from *sojorner* "to sojourn", derived from Latin *sub* "under, during" + Late Latin *diurnum* "day"]

²sojourn *vi* : to stay as a temporary resident — **so·journ·er** *n*

¹sol \'sōl\ *also* **so** \'sō\ *n* : the 5th note of the diatonic scale [Medieval Latin]

²sol \'säl, 'sol\ *n, pl* **so·les** \'sō-,lās\ **1** : the basic monetary unit of Peru **2** : a coin or note representing one sol [American Spanish, from Spanish, "sun", from Latin]

³sol \'säl, 'sol\ *n* : a fluid colloidal system [*solution*]

Sol \'säl\ *n* : SUN 1a [Latin]

¹sol·ace \'säl-əs\ *n* : a relieving of grief or anxiety or a source of this [Old French *solas,* from Latin *solacium,* from *solari* "to console"]

²solace *vt* **1** : to give solace to **2** : to make cheerful **3** : ALLAY, SOOTHE ⟨*solace* grief⟩ SYN see COMFORT — **sol·ac·er** *n*

so·la·num \sə-'lā-nəm, -'län-, -'lan-\ *n* : any of a large genus of herbs, shrubs, and trees that includes several economically important plants (as the potato) [Latin, "nightshade"]

so·lar \'sō-lər, -,lär\ *adj* **1** : of, derived from, or relating to the sun **2** : measured by the earth's course in relation to the sun ⟨*solar* time⟩ ⟨*solar* year⟩ **3 a** : produced or operated by the action of the sun's light or heat **b** : using the sun's rays especially to produce heat or electricity [Latin *solaris,* from *sol* "sun"]

solar cell *n* : a photoelectric cell that converts sunlight into electrical energy and is used as a power source

solar collector *n* : any of various devices for the absorption of solar radiation for the heating of water or buildings or the production of electricity

solar flare *n* : a sudden temporary outburst of gases from a small area of the sun's surface

so·lar·i·um \sō-'lar-ē-əm, sə-, -'ler-\ *n, pl* **-ia** \-ē-ə\ *also* **-i·ums** : a room exposed to the sun [Latin, from *sol* "sun"]

solar panel *n* : a group of solar cells forming a flat surface (as on a spacecraft)

so·lar plexus \'sō-lər-\ *n* **1** : a nerve plexus in the abdomen behind the stomach and in front of the aorta that contains ganglia distributing nerve fibers to the viscera **2** : the pit of the stomach [from the radiating nerve fibers]

solar system *n* : a star with the group of heavenly bodies that revolve around it; *esp* : the sun with the planets, moons, asteroids, and comets that orbit it

solar wind *n* : plasma continuously ejected from the sun's surface into interplanetary space

sold *past of* SELL

¹sol·der \'säd-ər, 'sod-\ *n* : a metal or metallic alloy used when melted to join metallic surfaces; *esp* : an alloy of lead and tin so used [Middle French *soudure,*

\ə\ abut		\ng\ sing	
\ər\ further		\ō\ bone	
\a\ mat		\o\ saw	
\ā\ take		\oi\ coin	
\ä\ cot, cart		\th\ thin	
\au\ out		\th\ this	
\ch\ chin		\ü\ food	
\e\ pet		\ù\ foot	
\ē\ easy		\y\ yet	
\g\ go		\yü\ few	
\i\ tip		\yù\ cure	
\ī\ life		\zh\ vision	
\j\ job			

from *souder* "to solder", from Latin *solidare* "to make solid", from *solidus* "solid"]

²**solder** *vb* **sol·dered; sol·der·ing** \'säd-ring, 'sód-, -ə-ring\ **1** : to unite or repair with solder **2** : to become joined or renewed by or as if by the use of solder — **sol·der·er** \-ər-ər\ *n*

soldering iron *n* : a metal device for applying heat in soldering

¹**sol·dier** \'sōl-jər\ *n* **1 a** : one engaged in military service and especially in the army **b** : an enlisted man or woman **2** : a worker in a cause **3** : a member of a caste of wingless individuals with large heads and jaws among termites and some ants [Old French *soudier*, from *soulde* "pay", from Late Latin *solidus*, a kind of coin, from Latin, "solid"] — **sol·dier·ly** \-lē\ *adj*

²**soldier** *vi* **sol·diered; sol·dier·ing** \'sōlj-ring, -ə-ring\ **1** : to serve as or act like a soldier **2** : to make a show of activity while really loafing

soldier of fortune : one who follows a military career wherever there is promise of profit, adventure, or pleasure

sol·diery \'sōlj-rē, -ə-rē\ *n, pl* **-dier·ies** : a body of soldiers

¹**sole** \'sōl\ *n* **1** : the undersurface of a foot **2** : the part of footwear on which the sole of the foot rests **3** : the bottom or lower part of something : the base on which something rests [Middle French, from Latin *solea* "sandal"] — **soled** \'sōld\ *adj*

²**sole** *vt* : to furnish with a sole ⟨*sole* shoes⟩

³**sole** *n* : any of a family of small-mouthed flatfishes having reduced fins and small closely set eyes and including valued food fishes; *also* : any of several other market flatfishes [Middle French, from Latin *solea* "sandal, a kind of flatfish"]

⁴**sole** *adj* **1** *archaic* : having no companion : ALONE **2 a** : having no sharer ⟨*sole* owner⟩ **b** : being the only one **3** : functioning independently and without assistance or interference ⟨the *sole* judge⟩ **4** : belonging exclusively to the one person, unit, or group named ⟨given *sole* authority⟩ [Middle French *seul*, from Latin *solus*] SYN see SINGLE — **sole·ness** *n*

so·le·cism \'säl-ə-ˌsiz-əm, 'sō-lə-\ *n* **1** : an ungrammatical combination of words in a sentence **2** : a breach of etiquette or decorum [Latin *soloecismus*, from Greek *soloikismos*, from *soloikos* "speaking incorrectly", literally, "inhabitant of Soloi", from *Soloi*, city in ancient Cilicia where a substandard form of Greek was spoken] — **so·le·cis·tic** \ˌsäl-ə-'sis-tik, ˌsō-lə-\ *adj*

sole·ly \'sōl-lē, 'sō-lē\ *adv* **1** : without another : SINGLY, ALONE **2** : EXCLUSIVELY, ENTIRELY ⟨done *solely* for money⟩

sol·emn \'säl-əm\ *adj* **1** : celebrated with religious rites or ceremony : SACRED **2** : FORMAL, STATELY ⟨a *solemn* procession⟩ **3** : done or made seriously and thoughtfully ⟨*solemn* promise⟩ **4** : gravely sober and serious ⟨at this *solemn* moment⟩ **5** : SOMBER ⟨robe of *solemn* black⟩ [Middle French *solemne*, from Latin *sollemnis* "regularly appointed, solemn"] SYN see SERIOUS — **so·lem·ni·ty** \sə-'lem-nət-ē\ *n* — **sol·emn·ly** \'säl-əm-lē\ *adv* — **sol·emn·ness** \-əm-nəs\ *n*

sol·em·nize \'säl-əm-ˌnīz\ *vt* **1** : to observe or honor with solemnity **2** : to perform with pomp or ceremony; *esp* : to celebrate ⟨a marriage⟩ with religious rites **3** : to make solemn : DIGNIFY — **sol·em·ni·za·tion** \ˌsäl-əm-nə-'zā-shən\ *n*

so·le·noid \'sō-lə-ˌnóid, 'säl-ə-\ *n* : a coil of wire commonly in the form of a cylinder that when carrying a current resembles a bar magnet so that a movable core is drawn into the coil when a current flows [French *solénoïde*, derived from Greek *sōlēn* "pipe"] — **so·le·noi·dal** \ˌsō-lə-'nóid-l, ˌsäl-ə-\ *adj*

sole·plate \'sōl-ˌplāt\ *n* : the undersurface of a flatiron

sole·print \-ˌprint\ *n* : a print of the sole of the foot; *esp* : one made in the manner of a fingerprint and used for the identification of an infant

¹**sol–fa** \sōl-'fä, 'sōl-\ *vb* **1** : to sing the sol-fa syllables **2** : to sing (as a melody) to sol-fa syllables

²**sol–fa** *n* **1** : SOL-FA SYLLABLES **2** : SOLMIZATION; *also* : an exercise thus sung

sol–fa syllables *n pl* : the syllables *do, re, mi, fa, sol, la, ti* used in singing the tones of the scale

soli *pl of* SOLO

so·lic·it \sə-'lis-ət\ *vb* **1** : BEG, ENTREAT; *esp* : to approach with a request or plea ⟨*soliciting* employers for jobs⟩ **2** : to appeal for ⟨*solicit* funds⟩ **3** : to accost a person for immoral purposes [Middle French *solliciter* "to disturb, take charge of", from Latin *sollicitare* "to disturb", from *sollicitus* "solicitous"] — **so·lic·i·ta·tion** \-ˌlis-ə-'tā-shən\ *n*

so·lic·i·tant \sə-'lis-ət-ənt\ *n* : one who solicits

so·lic·i·tor \sə-'lis-ət-ər\ *n* **1** : one that solicits; *esp* : an agent that solicits (as contributions to charity) **2** : a British lawyer who advises clients, represents them in the lower courts, and prepares cases for barristers to plead in the higher courts **3** : the chief law officer of a municipality, county, or government department — **so·lic·i·tor·ship** *n*

so·lic·i·tous \sə-'lis-ət-əs\ *adj* **1** : full of concern or fears : APPREHENSIVE **2** : extremely careful **3** : anxiously willing : EAGER [Latin *sollicitus*, from *sollus* "whole" + *citus*, past participle of *ciēre* "to move"] SYN see THOUGHTFUL — **so·lic·i·tous·ly** *adv* — **so·lic·i·tous·ness** *n*

so·lic·i·tude \sə-'lis-ə-ˌtüd, -ˌtyüd\ *n* **1** : the state of being solicitous : ANXIETY **2** : excessive care or attention

¹**sol·id** \'säl-əd\ *adj* **1 a** : having an interior filled with matter : not hollow **b** : written as one word without a hyphen ⟨a *solid* compound⟩ **2** : having, involving, or dealing with three dimensions or with solids ⟨*solid* geometry⟩ **3 a** : not loose or spongy : COMPACT ⟨a *solid* mass of rock⟩ **b** : neither gaseous nor liquid : HARD, RIGID ⟨*solid* ice⟩ **4** : of good substantial quality or kind ⟨*solid* comfort⟩ ⟨*solid* reasons⟩ **5 a** : not interrupted ⟨for three *solid* hours⟩ **b** : UNANIMOUS, UNITED ⟨we are *solid* for pay increases⟩ **6 a** : thoroughly dependable : RELIABLE ⟨a *solid* citizen⟩ **b** : serious in purpose or character ⟨*solid* reading⟩ **7** : of one substance or character: as **a** : entirely of one metal or containing the minimum of alloy necessary to impart hardness ⟨*solid* gold⟩ **b** : of a single color or tone [Middle French *solide*, from Latin *solidus*] — **solid** *adv* — **sol·id·ly** *adv* — **sol·id·ness** *n*

²**solid** *n* **1** : a geometrical figure or element (as a cube or sphere) having three dimensions **2** : a solid substance : a substance that does not flow perceptibly under moderate stress

sol·i·dar·i·ty \ˌsäl-ə-'dar-ət-ē\ *n, pl* **-ties** : unity based on community of interests, objectives, or standards [French *solidarité*, derived from Latin *solidus* "solid"] SYN see UNITY

solid geometry *n* : a branch of geometry that deals with figures of three-dimensional space — compare PLANE GEOMETRY

so·lid·i·fy \sə-'lid-ə-ˌfī\ *vb* **-fied; -fy·ing** : to make or become solid, compact, or hard — **so·lid·i·fi·ca·tion** \sə-ˌlid-ə-fə-'kā-shən\ *n*

so·lid·i·ty \sə-'lid-ət-ē\ *n, pl* **-ties** **1** : the quality or state of being solid **2** : moral, mental, or financial soundness

solid–state *adj* **1** : relating to the properties, structure, or reactivity of solid material **2** : utilizing the electric, magnetic, or photic properties of solid materials : not utilizing electron tubes

so·lil·o·quist \sə-'lil-ə-kwəst\ *n* : one who soliloquizes

so·lil·o·quize \sə-'lil-ə-ˌkwīz\ *vi* : to utter a soliloquy : talk to oneself — **so·lil·o·quiz·er** *n*

so·lil·o·quy \sə-'lil-ə-kwē\ *n, pl* **-quies** **1** : the act of talking to oneself **2** : a dramatic monologue that gives the illusion of being a series of unspoken thoughts [Late Latin *soliloquium*, from Latin *solus* "alone" + *loqui* "to speak"]

sol·i·taire \\'säl-ə-ˌtaər, -ˌteər\\ *n* **1** : a single gem (as a diamond) set alone **2** : a card game played by one person alone [French, from *solitaire*, adj., "solitary", from Latin *solitarius*]

¹sol·i·tary \\'säl-ə-ˌter-ē\\ *adj* **1** : being or going alone ⟨a *solitary* traveler⟩ **2** : seldom visited : UNFREQUENTED **3** : being the only one : SOLE ⟨the *solitary* example⟩ **4** : growing or living alone : not forming part of a group or cluster ⟨flowers terminal and *solitary*⟩ ⟨the *solitary* bees⟩ [Latin *solitarius*, from *solitas* "solitude", from *solus* "alone"] — **sol·i·tar·i·ly** \\ˌsäl-ə-'ter-ə-lē\\ *adv* — **sol·i·tar·i·ness** \\'säl-ə-ˌter-ē-nəs\\ *n* □ SYN SOLITARY, FORLORN, DESOLATE mean isolated from others. SOLITARY implies the absence of any others of the same kind; FORLORN and DESOLATE imply absence or loss of friends and family; applied to places they suggest dreariness and desertion by former inhabitants; DESOLATE may also imply a sense of final and irreparable loss and loneliness. SYN see in addition SINGLE

²solitary *n, pl* **-tar·ies** **1** : RECLUSE, HERMIT **2** : solitary confinement in prison

sol·i·tude \\'säl-ə-ˌtüd, -ˌtyüd\\ *n* **1** : the quality or state of being alone or remote from society **2** : a lonely place

sol·mi·za·tion \\ˌsäl-mə-'zā-shən\\ *n* : the act, practice, or system of using a set of syllables to denote the tones of a musical scale [French *solmisation*, from *solmiser* "to sing the syllables do, re, mi, fa, sol, la, ti", from *sol* "sol" + *mi* "mi" + *-iser* "-ize"]

¹so·lo \\'sō-lō\\ *n, pl* **solos 1** *or pl* **so·li** \\'sō-lē\\ **a** : a musical composition for a single voice or instrument with or without accompaniment **b** : the featured part of a concerto or similar work **2** : an action in which there is only one performer [Italian, from *solo* "alone", from Latin *solus*]

²solo *adv or adj* : without a companion : ALONE

³solo *vi* **so·loed; so·lo·ing** : to perform by oneself; *esp* : to fly an airplane without one's instructor

so·lo·ist \\'sō-lə-wəst, -ˌlō-əst\\ *n* : one who performs a solo

Solomon's seal *n* **1** : any of a genus of perennial herbs of the lily family with gnarled rhizomes **2** : an emblem consisting of two triangles forming a 6-pointed star and formerly used as an amulet especially against fever

so·lon \\'sō-lən, -ˌlän\\ *n* **1** : a wise and skillful lawgiver **2** : a member of a legislative body [*Solon,* died about 559 B.C., Athenian lawgiver]

so long \\sō-'lȯng\\ *interj* — used to express farewell [probably by folk etymology from Irish Gaelic *slán,* literally, "health, security"]

so long as *conj* **1** : during and up to the end of the time that : WHILE **2** : provided that

sol·stice \\'säl-stəs, 'sōl-, 'sȯl-\\ *n* **1** : the point in the path of the sun at which the sun is farthest from the equator either north or south **2** : the time of the sun's passing a solstice which occurs on June 22d to begin summer in the northern hemisphere and on December 22d to begin winter in the northern hemisphere [Old French, from Latin *solstitium,* from *sol* "sun" + *sistere* "to come to a stop, cause to stand"] — **sol·sti·tial** \\säl-'stish-əl, sōl-, sȯl-\\ *adj*

sol·u·bil·i·ty \\ˌsäl-yə-'bil-ət-ē\\ *n, pl* **-ties 1** : the quality or state of being soluble **2** : the amount of a substance that will dissolve in a given amount of another substance

sol·u·ble \\'säl-yə-bəl\\ *adj* **1** : capable of being dissolved in a liquid ⟨sugar is *soluble* in water⟩ **2** : capable of being solved or explained [Middle French, from Late Latin *solubilis,* from Latin *solvere* "to loosen, solve, dissolve"] — **sol·u·ble·ness** *n* — **sol·u·bly** \\-blē\\ *adv*

sol·ute \\'säl-ˌyüt\\ *n* : a dissolved substance [Latin *solutus,* past participle of *solvere* "to dissolve"]

so·lu·tion \\sə-'lü-shən\\ *n* **1 a** : an action or process of solving **b** (1) : an answer to a problem : EXPLANATION (2) : SOLUTION SET; *also* : a member of a solution set **2 a** : an act or the process by which a solid, liquid, or gaseous substance is uniformly mixed with a liquid or sometimes a gas or solid **b** : a typically liquid uniform mixture formed by the process of solution **c** : the condition of being dissolved **d** : a liquid containing a dissolved substance **3** : a bringing or coming to an end or into a state of discontinuity [Middle French, from Latin *solutio,* from *solvere* "to loosen, solve, dissolve"]

solution set *n* : a set of values that satisfy an equation or inequality; *also* : TRUTH SET

solv·able \\'säl-və-bəl, 'sȯl-\\ *adj* : capable of being solved — **solv·abil·i·ty** \\ˌsäl-və-'bil-ət-ē, ˌsȯl-\\ *n*

¹sol·vate \\'säl-ˌvāt, 'sȯl-\\ *n* : a combination of a solute with a solvent or of a dispersed phase with a dispersion medium [*solvent* + *-ate*]

²solvate *vt* : to convert into a solvate — **sol·va·tion** \\säl-'vā-shən, sȯl-\\ *n*

solve \\'sälv, 'sȯlv\\ *vt* : to find a solution for [Latin *solvere* "to loosen, solve, dissolve", from *sed-, se-* "apart" + *luere* "to release"]

sol·ven·cy \\'säl-vən-sē, 'sȯl-\\ *n, pl* **-cies** : the quality or state of being solvent

¹sol·vent \\-vənt\\ *adj* : able to pay all legal debts [Latin *solvens,* present participle of *solvere* "to dissolve, pay"] — **sol·vent·ly** *adv*

²solvent *n* **1** : a usually liquid substance capable of dissolving or dispersing one or more other substances **2** : something that provides a solution

So·ma·li \\sō-'mäl-ē, sə-\\ *n* : a member of a people of Somaliland apparently of mixed Mediterranean and Negroid stock — **Somali** *adj*

so·mat·ic \\sō-'mat-ik, sə-\\ *adj* **1** : of, relating to, or affecting the body especially as distinguished from the germ plasm or the psyche ⟨*somatic* cells⟩ **2** : of or relating to the wall of the body : PARIETAL [Greek *sōmatikos,* from *sōmat-, sōma* "body"] — **so·mat·i·cal·ly** \\-'mat-i-kə-lē, -klē\\ *adv*

somatic mutation *n* : a mutation occurring in a somatic cell and inducing a chimera

so·mato·tro·phic hormone \\sō-ˌmat-ə-, -ˌtrō-fik-\\ *or* **so·mato·tro·pic hormone** \\-ˌtrō-pik-\\ *n* : GROWTH HORMONE 1

som·ber *or* **som·bre** \\'säm-bər\\ *adj* **1** : so shaded as to be dark and gloomy **2** : GRAVE, MELANCHOLY ⟨a *somber* mood⟩ **3** : dull or dark colored [French *sombre*] — **som·ber·ly** *or* **som·bre·ly** *adv* — **som·ber·ness** *or* **som·bre·ness** *n*

som·bre·ro \\səm-'breər-ō, säm-\\ *n, pl* **-ros** : a high-crowned hat of felt or straw with a very wide brim worn especially in the Southwest and Mexico [Spanish, from *sombra* "shade"]

¹some \\'səm, *sense 2* 'səm *or* səm\\ *adj* **1** : being unknown, undetermined, or unspecified ⟨*some* stranger was looking for you⟩ **2 a** : being one, a part, or an unspecified number of something (as a class or group) named or implied ⟨*some* gems are hard⟩ **b** : being of an unspecified amount or number ⟨give me *some* water⟩ ⟨have *some* apples⟩ **3** : worthy of notice or consideration ⟨that was *some* party⟩ [Old English *sum*]

²some \\'səm\\ *pron, sing or pl in construction* **1** : one indeterminate quantity, portion, or number as distinguished from the rest ⟨*some* of the milk⟩ ⟨*some* of the apples⟩ **2** : an indefinite additional amount ⟨ran a mile and then *some*⟩

³some \\'səm, səm\\ *adv* **1** : ABOUT ⟨*some* eighty houses⟩ **2 a** : SOMEWHAT ⟨felt *some* better⟩ **b** : to some degree : a little ⟨the cut bled *some*⟩

¹-some \\səm\\ *adj suffix* : characterized by a (specified) thing, quality, state, or action ⟨awe*some*⟩ ⟨burden*some*⟩ [Old English *-su*]

²-some \\səm\\ *n suffix* : group of (so many) members and especially persons ⟨four*some*⟩ [Middle English *sum,* pron., "one, some"]

Solomon's seal 2

sombrero

\ə\ abut		\ng\ sing
\ər\ further		\ō\ bone
\a\ mat		\ȯ\ saw
\ā\ take		\ȯi\ coin
\ä\ cot, cart		\th\ thin
\au̇\ out		\th\ this
\ch\ chin		\ü\ food
\e\ pet		\u̇\ foot
\ē\ easy		\y\ yet
\g\ go		\yü\ few
\i\ tip		\yu̇\ cure
\ī\ life		\zh\ vision
\j\ job		

³-some \,sōm\ *n combining form* : body ⟨chromo*some*⟩ [Greek *sōma*]

¹some·body \'səm-,bäd-ē, -bəd-\ *pron* : one or some person of unspecified or indefinite identity ⟨*some-body* will come in⟩

²somebody *n* : a person of position or importance

some·day \'səm-,dā\ *adv* : at some future time

some·how \'səm-,haủ\ *adv* : in one way or another not known or designated : by some means

some·one \-,wən, -,wən\ *pron* : some person : SOME-BODY

some·place \-,plās\ *adv* : SOMEWHERE 1

som·er·sault \'səm-ər-,sólt\ *n* : a leap or roll in which a person turns forward or backward in a complete revolution with the feet moving up over the head [Middle French *sombresaut* "leap", derived from Latin *super* "over" + *saltus* "leap", from *salire* "to jump"] — **somersault** *vi*

som·er·set \-,set\ *n or vi* : SOMERSAULT [by alteration]

¹some·thing \'səm-thing, 'səmp-, *especially in rapid speech or for 2* 'səmp-m\ *pron* 1 : some undetermined or unspecified thing 2 : a person or thing of consequence

²something *adv* 1 : in some degree : SOMEWHAT 2 : EXTREMELY ⟨swears *something* awful⟩

¹some·time \'səm-,tīm\ *adv* 1 : at some time in the future ⟨I'll do it *sometime*⟩ 2 : at some not specified or definitely known point of time ⟨*sometime* last night⟩

²sometime *adj* : having been formerly : FORMER ⟨*sometime* mayor of the city⟩

some·times \'səm-,tīmz; ,səm-', səm-'\ *adv* : at times : now and then : OCCASIONALLY

some·way \'səm-,wā\ *also* **some·ways** \-,wāz\ *adv* : in some way : SOMEHOW

¹some·what \-,hwät, -,hwət, -,wät, -,wət; ,səm-', səm-'\ *pron* : SOMETHING 2

²somewhat *adv* : in some degree or measure : SLIGHTLY ⟨*somewhat* relieved⟩

¹some·where \'səm-,hwear, -,hwaər, -,hwər, -,wear, -,waər, -wər\ *adv* 1 : in, at, or to a place unknown or unspecified 2 : to or into a stage or period of positive accomplishment ⟨now we're getting *somewhere*⟩ 3 : APPROXIMATELY ⟨*somewhere* about nine o'clock⟩

²somewhere *n* : an undetermined or unnamed place

some·wheres \-,hwearz, -,hwaərz, -,hwərz, -,wearz, -,waərz, -wərz\ *adv* : SOMEWHERE 1

so·mite \'sō-,mīt\ *n* : one segment of the longitudinal series of segments into which the body of vertebrates and many other animals is divided : METAMERE [Greek *sōma* "body"] — **so·mit·ic** \sō-'mit-ik\ *adj*

som·me·lier \,səm-əl-'yā\ *n, pl* **sommeliers** \-'yā, -'yāz\ : an employee of a restaurant who has charge of wines and their serving [French, from Middle French, "court official charged with transportation of supplies", from Provençal *saumalier* "pack animal driver", from *sauma* "pack animal", from Late Latin *sagma* "packsaddle", from Greek]

som·nam·bu·lant \säm-'nam-byə-lənt\ *adj* : walking or addicted to walking while asleep

som·nam·bu·lism \säm-'nam-byə-,liz-əm\ *n* : a sleeping state in which motor acts (as walking) are performed; *also* : actions characteristic of this state [derived from Latin *somnus* "sleep" + *ambulare* "to walk"] — **som·nam·bu·list** \-ləst\ *n* — **som·nam·bu·lis·tic** \säm-,nam-byə-'lis-tik\ *adj*

som·nif·er·ous \säm-'nif-rəs, -ə-rəs\ *adj* : SOPORIFIC 1a [Latin *somnifer*, from *somnus* "sleep" + *-fer* "-ferous"] — **som·nif·er·ous·ly** *adv*

som·no·lence \'säm-nə-ləns\ *n* : the quality or state of being drowsy

som·no·lent \-lənt\ *adj* : inclined to or heavy with sleep : DROWSY ⟨a *somnolent* village⟩ [Middle French *sompnolent*, from Latin *somnolentus*, from *somnus* "sleep"] — **som·no·lent·ly** *adv*

son \'sən\ *n* 1 **a** : a male offspring especially of human beings **b** : a male adopted child **c** : a male descendant 2 *cap* : the second person of the Trinity 3 : a person closely associated with or deriving from a formative agent (as a nation, school, or race) ⟨*sons* of modern technology⟩ [Old English *sunu*]

so·nant \'sō-nənt\ *adj* 1 : VOICED 2 2 : SYLLABIC 2 [Latin *sonare* "to sound"] — **sonant** *n*

so·nar \'sō-,när\ *n* : an apparatus that detects the presence and location of submerged objects (as submarines) by reflected sound waves [*so*und *na*vigation *r*anging]

so·na·ta \sə-'nät-ə\ *n* : an instrumental musical composition typically of three or four movements in contrasting forms and keys [Italian, from *sonare* "to sound", from Latin]

sonata form *n* : a musical form consisting basically of an exposition, a development, and a recapitulation used especially for the first movement of a sonata

son·a·ti·na \,sän-ə-'tē-nə\ *n* : a short usually simplified sonata [Italian, from *sonata*]

song \'sóng\ *n* 1 : the act or art of singing 2 : poetical composition : POETRY 3 **a** : a short musical composition of words and music **b** : a collection of such compositions 4 **a** : a melody for a lyric poem or ballad **b** : a poem easily set to music 5 : a small amount ⟨can be bought for a *song*⟩ [Old English *sang*]

song·bird \-,bərd\ *n* 1 : a bird that utters a succession of musical tones 2 : SINGING BIRD 2

song·fest \-,fest\ *n* : an informal session of group singing of popular or folk songs

song·ful \-fəl\ *adj* : given to singing : MELODIOUS — **song·ful·ly** \-fə-lē\ *adv* — **song·ful·ness** *n*

song·less \'sóng-ləs\ *adj* : lacking in, incapable of, or not given to song — **song·less·ly** *adv*

Song of Sol·o·mon \-'säl-ə-mən\ — see BIBLE table

song·smith \'sóng-,smith\ *n* : a composer of songs

song sparrow *n* : a common sparrow of eastern North America noted for its sweet cheerful song

song·ster \'sóng-stər\ *n* : one skilled in song : SINGER

song·stress \-strəs\ *n* : a female singer

song thrush *n* : a largely olive-brown Old World thrush noted for its song — called also *mavis, throstle*

song·writ·er \'sóng-,rīt-ər\ *n* : a person who composes words or music or both especially for popular songs

son·ic \'sän-ik\ *adj* 1 : using, produced by, or relating to sound waves ⟨*sonic* altimeter⟩ 2 : having a frequency within the audibility range of the human ear — used of waves and vibrations [Latin *sonus* "sound"] — **son·i·cal·ly** \'sän-i-kə-lē, -klē\ *adv*

sonic boom *n* : a sound resembling an explosion produced when a pressure wave formed at the nose of an aircraft traveling at supersonic speed reaches the ground

son–in–law \'sən-ən-,lò\ *n, pl* **sons–in–law** \'sən-zən-\ : the husband of one's daughter

son·net \'sän-ət\ *n* : a poem of 14 lines usually in iambic pentameter rhyming according to a prescribed scheme — compare ENGLISH SONNET, ITALIAN SONNET [Italian *sonetto*, from Provençal *sonet* "little song", from *son* "sound, song", from Latin *sonus* "sound"]

son·ne·teer \,sän-ə-'tiər\ *n* : a writer of sonnets

sonnet sequence *n* : a series of sonnets often having a unifying theme

son·ny \'sən-ē\ *n* : a young boy — usually used in address

so·nor·i·ty \sə-'nór-ət-ē, -'när-\ *n, pl* **-ties** 1 : the quality or state of being sonorous : RESONANCE 2 : a sonorous tone or speech

so·no·rous \sə-'nōr-əs, -'nór-; 'sän-ə-rəs\ *adj* 1 : producing sound (as when struck) 2 : full or loud in sound : RESONANT 3 : imposing or impressive in effect or style [Latin *sonorus*] — **so·no·rous·ly** *adv* — **so·no·rous·ness** *n*

son·ship \'sən-,ship\ *n* : the relationship of son to father

soon \'sün, *especially New England* 'sun\ *adv* **1** : before long : without undue time lapse ⟨*soon* after sunrise⟩ **2** : PROMPTLY, SPEEDILY ⟨as *soon* as possible⟩ **3** *archaic* : before the usual time **4** : by choice : WILLINGLY ⟨I'd *sooner* stay than go⟩ [Old English *sōna* "soon, immediately"]

soot \'sut, 'sət, 'süt\ *n* : a black substance that is formed by combustion, rises in fine particles, and adheres to the sides of the chimney or pipe conveying the smoke; *esp* : the fine powder consisting chiefly of carbon that colors smoke [Old English *sōt*]

¹sooth \'süth\ *adj, archaic* : agreeing with or telling the truth [Old English *sōth*]

²sooth *n, archaic* : the quality or state of being true

soothe \'süth\ *vb* **1 a** : to please by or as if by attention or concern : PLACATE **b** : RELIEVE 1, ALLEVIATE **2** : to bring comfort, solace, or reassurance [Old English *sōthian* "to prove the truth", from *sōth* "true"]

sooth·ing \'sü-thing\ *adj* : tending to calm or allay — **sooth·ing·ly** \-thing-lē\ *adv* — **sooth·ing·ness** *n*

sooth·ly \'süth-lē\ *adv, archaic* : in truth : TRULY

sooth·say·er \'süth-,sā-ər\ *n* : a person who claims to foretell events — **sooth·say·ing** \-,sā-ing\ *n*

sooty \'sut-ē, 'sət-, 'süt-\ *adj* **soot·i·er; -est** **1 a** : of, relating to, or producing soot **b** : soiled with soot **2** : of the color of soot — **soot·i·ly** \-l-ē\ *adv* — **soot·i·ness** \-ē-nəs\ *n*

sooty mold *n* : a dark layer of fungus mycelium growing in insect honeydew on the leaves of plants; *also* : a fungus producing this

¹sop \'säp\ *n* **1** *chiefly dialect* : a piece of food dipped or steeped in a liquid (as bread dipped in milk or gravy) **2** : a bribe, gift, or gesture meant to pacify or win favor [Old English *sopp*]

²sop *vt* **sopped; sop·ping** **1 a** : to steep or dip in or as if in liquid **b** : to wet thoroughly : SOAK **2** : to mop up (as water) **3** : to give a bribe or conciliatory gift to

soph·ism \'säf-,iz-əm\ *n* : an unsound misleading argument that on the surface seems reasonable

soph·ist \'säf-əst\ *n* **1** *cap* : one of a class of ancient Greek teachers of rhetoric, philosophy, and the art of successful living noted for their subtle often specious reasoning **2** : one who argues by the use of sophisms [Latin *sophista*, from Greek *sophistēs*, literally, "expert, wise man", from *sophizesthai* "to become wise, deceive", from *sophos* "wise"]

so·phis·tic \sə-'fis-tik\ *or* **so·phis·ti·cal** \-ti-kəl\ *adj* : being clever and subtle but misleading — **so·phis·ti·cal·ly** \-ti-kə-lē, -klē\ *adv*

¹so·phis·ti·cate \sə-'fis-tə-,kāt\ *vt* **1** : to alter deceptively; *esp* : ADULTERATE **2** : to deprive of genuineness, naturalness, or simplicity; *esp* : to deprive of naiveté and make worldly-wise — **so·phis·ti·ca·tion** \-,fis-tə-'kā-shən\ *n*

²so·phis·ti·cate \-'fis-ti-kət, -tə-,kāt\ *n* : a sophisticated person

so·phis·ti·cat·ed \-tə-,kāt-əd\ *adj* **1** : not in a natural, pure, or original state ⟨a *sophisticated* oil⟩ **2** : deprived of native or original simplicity: as **a** : highly complicated : COMPLEX ⟨*sophisticated* instruments⟩ **b** : WORLDLY-WISE, KNOWING ⟨a *sophisticated* person⟩ **3** : devoid of grossness : SUBTLE: as **a** : finely experienced and aware ⟨a *sophisticated* columnist⟩ **b** : intellectually appealing ⟨*sophisticated* novels⟩ — **so·phis·ti·cat·ed·ly** *adv*

soph·ist·ry \'säf-ə-strē\ *n, pl* **-ries** : subtle but deceptive reasoning or argumentation

soph·o·more \'säf-m-,ōr, -,ór; 'säf-,mōr, -,mór\ *n* : a student in the second year at college or a 4-year secondary school [probably from Greek *sophos* "wise" + *mōros* "foolish"]

soph·o·mor·ic \,säf-ə-'mōr-ik, -'mòr-, -'mär-\ *adj* **1** : of, relating to, or characteristic of a sophomore **2** : conceited and overconfident of knowledge but poorly informed and immature

So·pho·ni·as \,säf-ə-'nī-əs, ,sō-fə-\ *n* — see BIBLE table

¹so·po·rif·ic \,säp-ə-'rif-ik, ,sō-pə-\ *adj* **1 a** : causing or tending to cause sleep **b** : tending to dull awareness or alertness **2** : of, relating to, or characterized by sleepiness or lethargy [derived from Latin *sopor* "deep sleep"]

²soporific *n* : a soporific agent or drug

sop·ping \'säp-ing\ *adj* : very wet : drenched through

sop·py \'säp-ē\ *adj* **sop·pi·er; -est** **1** : SOPPING **2** : very wet or slushy

¹so·pra·no \sə-'pran-ō, -'prän-\ *n, pl* **-pran·os** **1** : the highest singing voice of women or boys; *also* : a singer having such a voice **2** : the highest voice part in a 4-part chorus — compare ALTO, BASS, TENOR [Italian, from *sopra* "above", from Latin *supra*]

²soprano *adj* **1** : relating to the soprano voice or part **2** : having a high range ⟨*soprano* sax⟩

so·ra \'sōr-ə, 'sòr-\ *n* : a small short-billed North American rail common in marshes [origin unknown]

sorb \'sòrb\ *vt* : to take up and hold by either adsorption or absorption [back-formation from *absorb* and *adsorb*]

sor·cer·er \'sòrs-rər, -ə-rər\ *n* : a person who practices sorcery : WIZARD

sor·cer·ess \'sòrs-rəs, -ə-rəs\ *n* : a female sorcerer

sor·cer·ous \'sòrs-rəs, -ə-rəs\ *adj* : of or relating to sorcery

sor·cery \'sòrs-rē, -ə-rē\ *n* : the use of power gained from the assistance or control of evil spirits especially for divining : WITCHCRAFT [Old French *sorcerie*, from *sorcier* "sorcerer", derived from Latin *sors* "chance, lot"]

sor·did \'sòrd-əd\ *adj* **1** : DIRTY, FILTHY ⟨*sordid* surroundings⟩ **2** : marked by baseness or grossness : VILE ⟨*sordid* motives⟩ **3** : meanly greedy : COVETOUS **4** : of a dull or muddy color [Latin *sordidus*, from *sordes* "dirt"] — **sor·did·ly** *adv* — **sor·did·ness** *n*

sor·di·no \sòr-'dē-nō\ *n, pl* **-di·ni** \-nē\ : MUTE 2 [Italian, from *sordo* "silent", from Latin *surdus*]

¹sore \'sōr, 'sòr\ *adj* **1 a** : causing or tending to cause mental distress ⟨a *sore* subject⟩ **b** : painfully sensitive : TENDER ⟨*sore* muscles⟩ **c** : hurt or inflamed so as to be or seem painful ⟨*sore* runny eyes⟩ **2** : attended by difficulties, hardship, or exertion ⟨in *sore* straits⟩ **3** : made angry ⟨*sore* over a remark⟩ [Old English *sār*] — **sore·ness** *n*

²sore *n* **1** : a localized sore spot on the body; *esp* : one (as an ulcer) with the tissues broken and usually infected **2** : a source of pain or vexation : AFFLICTION

³sore *adv* : SORELY

sore·head \-,hed\ *n* : a person easily angered or disgruntled — **sorehead** *or* **sore·head·ed** \-'hed-əd\ *adj*

sore·ly \-lē\ *adv* : in a sore manner : VERY, EXTREMELY

sore throat *n* : painful throat due to inflammation of the fauces and pharynx

sor·ghum \'sòr-gəm\ *n* **1** : any of an economically important genus of Old World tropical grasses similar to Indian corn in habit but with the spikelets in pairs on a hairy axis; *esp* : one cultivated for grain, forage, or syrup — compare SORGO **2** : syrup from sorgo [New Latin, from Italian *sorgo*]

sor·go \'sòr-gō\ *n, pl* **sorgos** : a sorghum grown primarily for its sweet juice from which syrup is made but also used for fodder and silage [Italian]

so·ro·ral \sə-'rōr-əl, -'ror-\ *adj* : of, relating to, or characteristic of a sister : SISTERLY [Latin *soror* "sister"]

so·ror·i·ty \sə-'ròr-ət-ē, -'rär-\ *n, pl* **-ties** : a club of girls or women especially at a college [Medieval Latin *sororitas* "sisterhood", from Latin *soror* "sister"]

sorp·tion \'sòrp-shən\ *n* : the process of sorbing : the state of being sorbed [back-formation from *absorption* and *adsorption*]

\ə\ abut	\ng\ sing
\ər\ further	\ō\ bone
\a\ mat	\ò\ saw
\ā\ take	\òi\ coin
\ä\ cot, cart	\th\ thin
\aú\ out	\th\ this
\ch\ chin	\ü\ food
\e\ pet	\ú\ foot
\ē\ easy	\y\ yet
\g\ go	\yü\ few
\i\ tip	\yú\ cure
\ī\ life	\zh\ vision
\j\ job	

¹sor·rel \'sȯr-əl, 'sär-\ *n* **1** : an animal (as a horse) of a sorrel color **2** : a brownish orange to light brown [Middle French *sorel,* from *sor* "reddish brown"]

²sorrel *n* : any of various plants with sour juice: as **a** : ¹DOCK **b** : WOOD SORREL [Middle French *surele,* from *sur* "sour", of Germanic origin]

¹sor·row \'sär-ō, 'sȯr-\ *n* **1 a** : sadness or anguish due to loss (as of something loved) **b** : a cause of grief or sadness **2** : CONTRITION, REPENTANCE [Old English *sorg*] □ SYN SORROW, GRIEF, ANGUISH mean distress of mind. SORROW implies a sense of loss often with feelings of guilt and remorse; GRIEF implies a sharp feeling of distress for a definite and immediate cause; ANGUISH implies a torturing grief or dread.

²sorrow *vi* : to feel or express sorrow : GRIEVE

sor·row·ful \-fəl\ *adj* **1** : full of or marked by sorrow **2** : expressive of or inducing sorrow — **sor·row·ful·ly** \-fə-lē\ *adv* — **sor·row·ful·ness** *n*

sor·ry \'sär-ē, 'sȯr-\ *adj* **sor·ri·er; -est 1** : feeling sorrow, regret, or penitence **2** : MOURNFUL 2, SAD **3** : inspiring sorrow, pity, scorn, or ridicule : WRETCHED [Old English *sārig,* from *sār* "sore"] — **sor·ri·ly** \'sär-ə-lē, 'sȯr-\ *adv* — **sor·ri·ness** \'sär-ē-nəs, 'sȯr-\ *n*

¹sort \'sȯrt\ *n* **1** : a group set up on the basis of any characteristic in common : CLASS, KIND **2** : method or manner of acting : WAY **3** : general character or disposition; *also* : PERSON, INDIVIDUAL (you're not a bad *sort* at heart) [Middle French *sorte,* probably from Latin *sors* "chance, lot"] SYN see KIND — **after a sort** : in a rough or haphazard way — **of sorts** *or* **of a sort** : of an inconsequential or mediocre quality (a poet *of sorts*) — **out of sorts 1** : out of temper : IRRITABLE **2** : not well

²sort *vb* **1** : to put in a certain place or rank according to kind, class, or nature : CLASSIFY (*sort* mail) (*sort* out colors) **2** : AGREE 6, SUIT — **sort·able** \'sȯrt-ə-bəl\ *adj* — **sort·er** *n*

sor·tie \'sȯrt-ē, sȯr-'tē\ *n* **1** : a sudden issuing of troops from a defensive position against the enemy : SALLY **2** : one mission or attack by a single plane [French, from *sortir* "to go out"] — **sortie** *vi*

sort of \,sȯrt-əv, -ə, -ər\ *adv* : to a moderate degree : RATHER

so·rus \'sōr-əs, 'sȯr-\ *n, pl* **so·ri** \'sōr-ī, 'sȯr-, -ē\ : a cluster of plant reproductive bodies; *esp* : one of the dots on the underside of a fertile fern frond consisting of a cluster of spores [New Latin, from Greek *sōros* "heap"]

SOS \,es-ō-'es, ,es-ə-'wes\ *n* **1** : an internationally recognized signal of distress in radio code ···−−−··· used especially by ships calling for help **2** : a call or request for help or rescue

¹so-so \'sō-'sō\ *adv* : neither very badly nor very well

²so-so *adj* : neither very good nor very bad

so·ste·nu·to \,sō-stə-'nüt-ō, ,sȯ-\ *adv or adj* : sustained to or beyond the note's full value — used as a direction in music [Italian, from *sostenere* "to sustain", from Latin *sustinēre*]

sot \'sät\ *n* : an habitual drunkard [Old English *sott* "fool"]

sot·ted \'sät-əd\ *adj* : become stupid or drunken : SOTTISH

sot·tish \'sät-ish\ *adj* : resembling a sot (as in folly or intemperance) — **sot·tish·ly** *adv* — **sot·tish·ness** *n*

sot·to vo·ce \,sät-ō-'vō-chē\ *adv or adj* **1** : under the breath : in an undertone; *also* : PRIVATELY **2** : very softly [Italian *sottovoce,* from *sotto* "under" + *voce* "voice"]

sou \'sü\ *n* : a French bronze coin of the period before 1914 worth 5 centimes or one twentieth of a franc [French, from Old French *sol,* from Late Latin *solidus,* a kind of coin, from Latin, "solid"]

sou·brette \sü-'bret\ *n* **1 a** : a coquettish maid or frivolous young woman in comedies **b** : an actress who

plays such a part **2** : a soprano who sings supporting roles in comic opera [French]

sou·bri·quet *variant of* SOBRIQUET

¹souf·flé \sü-'flā, 'sü-,\ *n* : a delicate spongy hot dish lightened in baking by stiffly beaten egg whites [French, from *souffler* "to puff up", from Latin *sufflare,* from *sub-* + *flare* "to blow"]

²soufflé *or* **souf·fléed** \-'flād, -,flād\ *adj* : puffed by or in cooking (*soufflé* omelets)

sough \'sau̇, 'səf\ *vi* : to make a moaning or sighing sound [Old English *swōgan*] — **sough** *n*

sought *past of* SEEK

¹soul \'sōl\ *n* **1** : the spiritual part of a person believed to give life to the body and in many religions regarded as immortal **2 a** : a person's moral and emotional nature (my *soul* rebels against cruelty) **b** : spiritual force : FERVOR **3** : the essential part of something **4** : the moving spirit : LEADER (the *soul* of an enterprise) **5** : EMBODIMENT (a friend who is the *soul* of honor) **6** : a human being : PERSON (a kind *soul*) **7** : a disembodied spirit **8** : a strong positive feeling (as of intense sensitivity and emotional fervor) conveyed especially by black American performers [Old English *sāwol*] □ SYN SOUL, SPIRIT mean an immaterial entity distinguishable from and superior to the body. SOUL is preferred when the entity is considered as having functions, responsibilities, or a certain destiny (to save one's *soul*) (sell one's *soul* to the devil) SPIRIT is preferred when the quality, movement, or activity is stressed (their *spirits* were refreshed) or opposition to the material part is intended (the *spirit* is willing but the flesh is weak)

²soul *adj* **1** : of, relating to, or characteristic of black Americans or their culture **2** : designed for or controlled by blacks

soul·ful \-fəl\ *adj* : full of or expressing feeling or emotion — **soul·ful·ly** \-fə-lē\ *adv* — **soul·ful·ness** *n*

soul·less \'sōl-ləs\ *adj* : having no soul or no greatness or nobleness of mind or feeling — **soul·less·ly** *adv*

soul–search·ing \'sōl-,sər-ching\ *n* : examination of one's conscience especially with regard to motives and values

¹sound \'sau̇nd\ *adj* **1** : free from flaw, defect, or decay **2** : free from injury or disease : HEALTHY (a *sound* mind in a *sound* body) **3** : SOLID, FIRM (a building of *sound* construction) **4** : free from error or fallacy : VALID (a *sound* argument) **5** : showing good sense : WISE (*sound* advice) **6** : HONORABLE, HONEST (*sound* principles) **7** : THOROUGH (a *sound* beating) **8** : not disturbed : DEEP (a *sound* sleep) [Old English *gesund*] SYN see HEALTHY, VALID — **sound·ly** *adv* — **sound·ness** \'sau̇nd-nəs, 'sau̇n-\ *n*

²sound *adv* : SOUNDLY (*sound* asleep)

³sound *n* **1 a** : the sensation experienced through the sense of hearing **b** : a particular auditory impression : NOISE, TONE **c** : mechanical energy that is transmitted by longitudinal pressure waves in a material medium (as air) and is the objective cause of hearing **2 a** : one of the noises that together make up human speech (the *sound* of *th* in *this*) **b** : a sequence of spoken noises (*-cher* of *teacher* and *-ture* of *creature* have the same *sound*) **3 a** : meaningless noise **b** : impression conveyed (the excuse has a suspicious *sound*) **4** : hearing distance : EARSHOT [Old French *son,* from Latin *sonus*]

⁴sound *vb* **1 a** : to make or cause to make a sound **b** : RESOUND 1, 2 **c** : to give a summons by sound **2 a** : PRONOUNCE 3 **b** : to put into words : VOICE **3 a** : to make known : PROCLAIM **b** : to order, signal, or indicate by a sound **4** : to make or convey the impression of being : SEEM (*sounds* incredible) **5** : to examine by causing to emit sounds (*sound* the lungs) — **sound·able** \'sau̇n-də-bəl\ *adj*

⁵sound *n* **1** : a long passage of water that is wider than a strait and often connects two larger bodies of water or forms a channel between the mainland and an island

2 : the air bladder of a fish [Old English *sund* "sea" and Old Norse *sund* "strait"]

⁶sound *vb* **I a** : to measure the depth of (as with a sounding line) : FATHOM **b** : to look into or investigate the possibility **2** : to try to find out the views or intentions of : PROBE **3** : to dive down suddenly ⟨a *sounding* whale⟩ [Middle French *sonder*, from *sonde* "sounding line"]

sound barrier *n* : the sudden large increase in resistance that the air offers to an airplane nearing the speed of sound

sound·board \'saund-,bōrd, 'saun-, -,bȯrd\ *n* **I** : a thin resonant board so placed in a musical instrument as to reinforce its tones by sympathetic vibration **2** : SOUNDING BOARD 1a

sound box *n* : a hollow chamber in a musical instrument for increasing its sonority

sound effects *n pl* : variously produced effects that are imitative of sounds called for in a script (as of a play or movie)

sound·er \'saun-dər\ *n* : one that sounds; *esp* : a device for making soundings

¹sound·ing \'saun-ding\ *adj* **1** : SONOROUS **2**, RESONANT **2** : POMPOUS **1**, HIGH-SOUNDING — **sound·ing·ly** \-ding-lē\ *adv*

²sounding *n* **I a** : measurement by sounding **b** : the depth so ascertained **2** : a probe, test, or sampling of opinion or intention

sounding board *n* **I a** : a structure behind or over a pulpit, rostrum, or platform to give distinctness and sonority to sound **b** : a device or agency that helps spread opinions or utterances **2** : SOUNDBOARD 1

sounding line *n* : a line, wire, or cord weighted at one end and often marked at intervals for sounding

¹sound·less \'saun-dləs\ *adj* : incapable of being sounded : UNFATHOMABLE

²soundless *adj* : making no sound — **sound·less·ly** *adv*

sound off *vi* **1** : to count cadence while marching **2 a** : to speak up in a loud voice **b** : to voice one's opinions freely and vigorously

sound pollution *n* : NOISE POLLUTION

¹sound·proof \'saund-'prüf, 'saun-\ *adj* : impervious to sound

²soundproof *vt* : to insulate so as to obstruct the passage of sound

sound track *n* **1** : the area on a motion-picture film that carries the sound record **2** : a recording of the musical score of a motion picture

sound truck *n* : a truck equipped with a loudspeaker

sound waves *n pl* : longitudinal pressure waves in a material medium regardless of whether they constitute audible sound

soup \'süp\ *n* **1** : a liquid food with a meat, fish, or vegetable stock as a base and often containing pieces of solid food **2** : something (as a heavy fog) having or suggesting the consistency of soup **3** : an unfortunate predicament ⟨in the *soup*⟩ [French *soupe* "sop, soup", of Germanic origin]

soup·çon \süp-'sōⁿ, 'süp-,sän\ *n* : a little bit : TRACE [French, literally, "suspicion"]

souped–up \'süpt-'əp\ *adj* : increased in power or efficiency ⟨a *souped-up* hot rod⟩ [English slang *soup* "dope injected into a racehorse to improve its performance", from *soup*] — **soup up** \süp-'əp, 'süp-\ *vt*

soup kitchen *n* : an establishment dispensing free food (as soup and bread) to the needy

soupy \'sü-pē\ *adj* **soup·i·er**; **-est** **1** : having the consistency of soup **2** : densely foggy or cloudy

¹sour \'saur\ *adj* **1** : being or inducing the one of the four basic taste sensations characterized by an acid or tart taste ⟨*sour* as vinegar⟩ **2 a** : having undergone a usually acid fermentation ⟨*sour* milk⟩ **b** : indicative of decay : PUTRID ⟨a *sour* odor⟩ **3** : UNPLEASANT, DISAGREEABLE ⟨a *sour* look⟩ ⟨hit a *sour* note⟩ **4** : acid in reaction ⟨*sour* soil⟩ [Old English *sūr*] — **sour·ish** \-ish\ *adj*

sour·ly *adv* — **sour·ness** *n* □ SYN ACID, TART: SOUR usually implies having lost sweetness or freshness through fermentation or spoiling ⟨*sour* cream⟩ ACID applies to things having naturally or normally a biting or stinging taste ⟨*acid* fruits like lemons⟩ TART suggests a sharp but agreeable acidity ⟨*tart* applesauce⟩

²sour *n* **1** : something sour **2** : the primary taste sensation produced by sour stimuli

³sour *vb* : to become or make sour

sour ball *n* : a spherical piece of hard candy having a tart flavor

source \'sōrs, 'sȯrs\ *n* **I a** : a generative force : CAUSE **b** (1) : a point of origin (2) : one that initiates : AUTHOR; *also* : PROTOTYPE **2**, MODEL (3) : one that supplies information **2** : the point of origin of a stream of water : FOUNTAINHEAD **3** : a firsthand document or primary reference work [Middle French *sourse*, from *sourdre* "to rise, spring forth", from Latin *surgere*] SYN see ORIGIN

source book *n* : a fundamental document or record on which subsequent writings, beliefs, or practices are based

sour cherry *n* : a small Old World cherry tree widely grown for its soft tart bright red to nearly black fruits; *also* : its fruit

sour·dough \'saur-,dō\ *n* **1** : a leaven of dough in which fermentation is active **2** : an old-time prospector in Alaska or northwestern Canada [sense 2 from the use of sourdough for making bread in prospectors' camps]

sour grapes *n pl* : the belittling of something that has proven unattainable [from the fable ascribed to Aesop of the fox who being unable to reach some grapes he had desired disparaged them as sour]

sour gum *n* : a timber tree of the eastern United States with blue-black fruits and close-grained grayish wood

sour·sop \'saur-,säp\ *n* : a small tropical American tree related to the custard apple; *also* : its large edible fruit

sou·sa·phone \'sü-zə-,fōn\ *n* : a large circular tuba with a flaring adjustable bell [John P. *Sousa*]

¹souse \'saus\ *vb* **1** : PICKLE **2 a** : to plunge in liquid : IMMERSE **b** : DRENCH **2**, SATURATE **3** : to make or become drunk : INEBRIATE [Middle French *souce* "pickling solution", of Germanic origin]

²souse *n* **1** : something pickled; *esp* : seasoned and chopped pork trimmings, fish, or shellfish **2** : an act or instance of drenching **3** : an habitual drunkard

sou·tane \sü-'tän, -'tan\ *n* : CASSOCK [French, from Italian *sottana*, literally, "undergarment", derived from Latin *subtus* "underneath"]

¹south \'saúth; *in compounds, as* "southwest", *also* saú *or* 'saú *especially by seamen* \ *adv* : to, toward, or in the south [Old English *sūth*]

²south *adj* **1** : situated toward or at the south **2** : coming from the south

³south *n* **I a** : the direction to the right of one facing east **b** : the compass point directly opposite to north **2** *cap* : regions or countries south of a specified or implied point

South African *n* : a native or inhabitant of the Republic of South Africa; *esp* : AFRIKANER — **South African** *adj*

south·bound \'saúth-,baúnd\ *adj* : headed south

¹south·east \saú-'thēst, *nautical* saú-'ēst\ *adv* : to, toward, or in the southeast

²southeast *n* **I a** : the general direction between south and east **b** : the compass point midway between south and east : S 45° E **2** *cap* : regions or countries southeast of a specified or implied point

³southeast *adj* **1** : coming from the southeast **2** : situated toward or at the southeast

south·east·er \saú-'thē-stər, saú-'ē-stər\ *n* **1** : a strong southeast wind **2** : a storm with southeast winds

south·east·er·ly \saú-'thē-stər-lē\ *adv or adj* **1** : from the southeast **2** : toward the southeast

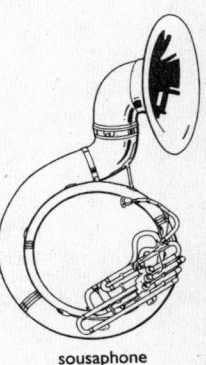

sousaphone

\ə\ abut	\ng\ sing
\ər\ further	\ō\ bone
\a\ mat	\ȯ\ saw
\ā\ take	\ȯi\ coin
\ä\ cot, cart	\th\ thin
\aú\ out	\th\ this
\ch\ chin	\ü\ food
\e\ pet	\ú\ foot
\ē\ easy	\y\ yet
\g\ go	\yü\ few
\i\ tip	\yú\ cure
\ī\ life	\zh\ vision
\j\ job	

south·east·ern \saủ-'thē-stərn\ *adj* **I** *often cap* : of, relating to, or characteristic of a region conventionally designated Southeast **2** : lying toward or coming from the southeast — **south·east·ern·most** \-stərn-,mōst\ *adj*

South·east·ern·er \-stər-nər, -stə-nər\ *n* : a native or inhabitant of a southeastern region (as of the United States)

¹south·east·ward \saủ-'thēs-twərd\ *adv or adj* : toward the southeast — **south·east·wards** \-twərdz\ *adv*

²southeastward *n* : SOUTHEAST

south·er \'saủ-thər\ *n* : a southerly wind

south·er·ly \'səth-ər-lē\ *adv or adj* **I** : from the south **2** : toward the south

south·ern \'səth-ərn\ *adj* **I** *often cap* : of, relating to, or characteristic of a region conventionally designated South **2** : lying toward or coming from the south [Old English *sūtherne*] — **south·ern·most** \-,mōst\ *adj*

Southern *n* : the dialect of English spoken in most of the Chesapeake Bay area, the Coastal plain and the greater part of the upland plateau in Virginia, No. Carolina, So. Carolina, and Georgia, and the Gulf states at least as far west as the valley of the Brazos river in central Texas

Southern Cross *n* : four bright stars in the southern hemisphere situated as if at the extremities of a Latin cross; *also* : the constellation of which these four stars are the brightest

South·ern·er \'səth-ər-nər, 'səth-ə-nər\ *n* : a native or inhabitant of the South (as of the United States)

southern hemisphere *n* : the half of the earth that lies south of the equator

southern lights *n pl* : AURORA AUSTRALIS

south·ing \'saủ-thing, -thing\ *n* **I** : difference in latitude to the south from the last preceding point of reckoning **2** : southerly progress

south·land \'saủth-,land, -lənd\ *n, often cap* : land in the south : the south of a country or region

south·paw \'saủth-,pȯ\ *n* : LEFT-HANDER; *esp* : a left-handed baseball pitcher — **southpaw** *adj*

south pole *n* **I** *often cap S&P* : the southernmost point of the earth : the southern end of the earth's axis **2** : the pole of a magnet that points toward the south

South·ron \'səth-rən\ *n* : SOUTHERNER: as **a** *chiefly Scottish* : ENGLISHMAN **b** *chiefly Southern* : a native or inhabitant of the southern states of the United States [Middle English *southren* "southern", from Old English *sūtherne*]

south–seeking pole *n* : SOUTH POLE 2

south–southeast *n* : two points east of south : S 22° 30' E

south–southwest *n* : two points west of south : S 22° 30' W

¹south·ward \'saủth-wərd\ *adv or adj* : toward the south — **south·wards** \-wərdz\ *adv*

²southward *n* : southward direction or part

¹south·west \saủth-'west, *nautical* saủ-'west\ *adv* : to, toward, or in the southwest

²southwest *n* **I a** : the general direction between south and west **b** : the compass point midway between south and west : S 45° W **2** *cap* : regions or countries southwest of a specified or implied point

³southwest *adj* **I** : coming from the southwest **2** : situated toward or at the southwest

south·west·er \saủth-'wes-tər, saủ-'wes-\ *n* **I** : a strong southwest wind **2** : a storm with southwest winds

south·west·er·ly \-'wes-tər-lē\ *adv or adj* **I** : from the southwest **2** : toward the southwest

south·west·ern \saủth-'wes-tərn\ *adj* **I** *often cap* : of, relating to, or characteristic of a region conventionally designated Southwest **2** : lying toward or coming from the southwest — **south·west·ern·most** \-stərn-,mōst\ *adj*

South·west·ern·er \-tər-nər, -tə-nər\ *n* : a native or inhabitant of a southwestern region (as of the United States)

¹south·west·ward \saủth-'wes-twərd\ *adv or adj* : toward the southwest — **south·west·wards** \-twərdz\ *adv*

²southwestward *n* : SOUTHWEST

sou·ve·nir \'sü-və-,niər, ,sü-və-'\ *n* : something that serves as a reminder : MEMENTO [French, literally, "act of remembering", from (*se*) *souvenir* "to remember", from Latin *subvenire* "to come up, come to mind", from *sub-* "up" + *venire* "to come"]

sou'·west·er \saủ-'wes-tər\ *n* **I** : SOUTHWESTER **2 a** : a long oilskin coat worn especially at sea during stormy weather **b** : a waterproof hat with wide slanting brim longer in back than in front

¹sov·er·eign *also* **sov·ran** \'säv-rən, -ərn, -ə-rən, 'səv-\ *n* **I a** : one possessing or held to possess sovereignty; *esp* : a monarch exercising supreme authority **b** : one that exercises supreme authority within a limited sphere : CHIEF **c** : an acknowledged leader : ARBITER **2** : a British gold coin no longer used worth one pound sterling

²sovereign *also* **sovran** *adj* **I a** : supreme in power or authority ⟨a *sovereign* ruler⟩ **b** : politically independent : AUTONOMOUS ⟨a *sovereign* state⟩ **2 a** : SUPREME 2, SUPERLATIVE **b** : EFFECTUAL, POTENT ⟨a *sovereign* remedy for colds⟩ [Middle French *soverain,* derived from Latin *super* "over, above"] SYN see FREE — **sov·er·eign·ly** *adv*

sov·er·eign·ty \-tē\ *n, pl* **-ties I a** : supreme power especially over a political unit **b** : freedom from external control **2** : one that is sovereign; *esp* : an autonomous state

so·vi·et \'sōv-ē-,et, 'säv-, -ē-ət\ *n* **I** : an elected governmental council in a Communist country **2** *pl, cap* **a** : BOLSHEVIK 1 **b** : the people and especially the political and military leaders of the Soviet Union [Russian *sovet*] — **soviet** *adj, often cap* — **so·vi·et·ism** \-,iz-əm\ *n, often cap*

so·vi·et·ize \-,īz\ *vt, often cap* **I** : to bring under Soviet control **2** : to force into conformity with Soviet cultural patterns or governmental policies — **so·vi·et·iza·tion** \,sōv-ē-,et-ə-'zā-shən, ,säv-ē-, -ē-ət-\ *n, often cap*

sov·khoz \säf-'kȯz\ *n, pl* **sov·kho·zy** \-'kȯ-zē\ *or* **sov·khoz·es** : a state-owned farm of the Soviet Union paying wages to the workers — compare KOLKHOZ [Russian, from *sovetskoe khoz*yaĭstvo "soviet farm"]

¹sow \'saủ\ *n* : an adult female swine [Old English *sugu*]

²sow \'sō\ *vb* **sowed; sown** \'sōn\ *or* **sowed; sow·ing I a** : to plant seed for growth especially by scattering **b** : PLANT 1a **c** : to strew with or as if with seed **d** : to introduce into a selected environment : IMPLANT **2** : to set in motion : FOMENT ⟨*sow* suspicion⟩ **3** : to spread abroad : DISSEMINATE [Old English *sāwan*] — **sow·er** \'sō-ər, 'sȯr\ *n*

sow·bel·ly \'saủ-,bel-ē\ *n* : fat salt pork or bacon

sow bug \'saủ-\ *n* : WOOD LOUSE

sow thistle \'saủ-\ *n* : any of a genus of spiny weedy European herbs of the sunflower family widely naturalized (as in North America)

sox *pl of* SOCK

soy \'sȯi\ *n* **I** : an oriental brown sauce made from soybeans fermented in brine **2** : SOYBEAN [Japanese *shōyu*]

soya \'sȯi-ə, 'sȯi-yə\ *n* : SOYBEAN [Dutch *soja,* from Japanese *shōyu* "soy"]

soy·bean \'sȯi-,bēn, -,bēn\ *n* : a hairy annual Asian plant of the pea family widely grown for its oil-rich and protein-rich edible seeds and for forage and soil improvement; *also* : its seed

spa \'spä, 'spȯ\ *n* **I a** : a mineral spring **b** : a resort with mineral springs **2** : a fashionable resort or hotel [*Spa,* watering place in Belgium]

sou'wester 2b

soybean

¹space \'spās\ *n* **1 :** a period of time; *also* **:** its duration **2 a :** a limited extent in one, two, or three dimensions **b :** an extent set apart or available ⟨parking *space*⟩ ⟨floor *space*⟩ **3 :** one of the degrees between or above or below the lines of a musical staff **4 :** a boundless three-dimensional extent in which objects and events occur and have relative position and direction **5 :** the region beyond the earth's atmosphere **6 a :** a blank area separating words or lines **b :** something (as a piece of type) used to produce such a blank area **7 :** a set of mathematical points each defined by one or more coordinates **8 :** an interval in operation during which a telegraph key is not in contact **9 a :** LINAGE 1 **b :** broadcast time available especially to advertisers [Old French *espace*, from Latin *spatium* "area, room, interval of space or time"]

²space *vt* **:** to place at intervals or arrange with space between — **spac·er** *n*

space–age \'spā-ˌsāj\ *adj* **:** of or relating to the age of space exploration; *esp* **:** MODERN

space charge *n* **:** an electric charge (as the electrons in the region near the filament of a vacuum tube) distributed throughout a three-dimensional region

space·craft \'spā-ˌskraft\ *n, pl* **spacecraft :** a vehicle designed to operate outside the earth's atmosphere

spaced–out \'spā-ˈstaut\ *adj* **:** dazed or stupefied by or as if by a drug

space·flight \'spās-ˌflīt\ *n* **:** flight beyond the earth's atmosphere

space heater *n* **:** a device for heating an enclosed space; *esp* **:** an often portable device that heats the space in which it is located and has no external heating ducts

space·less \'spā-sləs\ *adj* **1 :** having no limits : BOUNDLESS **2 :** occupying no space

space medicine *n* **:** a branch of medicine that deals with the effect on the human body of spaceflight

space·port \'spā-ˌspōrt, -ˌspȯrt\ *n* **:** an installation for testing and launching rockets, missiles, and satellites

space·ship \'spās-ˌship, 'spāsh-\ *n* **:** SPACECRAFT

space shuttle *n* **:** a spacecraft designed to transport people and cargo between earth and space that can be used repeatedly

space station *n* **:** an artificial satellite designed to stay in orbit permanently and be occupied by humans for long periods

space suit *n* **:** a suit equipped to make life in space possible for its wearer

space walk *n* **:** a period of activity outside a spacecraft by an astronaut in space

spa·cial *variant of* SPATIAL

spac·ing \'spā-sing\ *n* **1 :** an arrangement in space **2 :** the distance between any two objects in a usually regular series

spa·cious \'spā-shəs\ *adj* **1 :** vast or ample in extent : ROOMY ⟨a *spacious* hall⟩ **2 :** large or magnificent in scale : EXPANSIVE — **spa·cious·ly** *adv* — **spa·cious·ness** *n*

¹spade \'spād\ *n* **1 :** a digging implement adapted for being pushed into the ground with the foot **2 :** a spade-shaped instrument [Old English *spadu*] — **spade·ful** *n* — **call a spade a spade 1 :** to call a thing by its right name however coarse **2 :** to speak frankly

²spade *vb* **:** to dig with or use a spade — **spad·er** *n*

³spade *n* **:** a black figure resembling an inverted heart with a short stem at the bottom used to distinguish a suit of playing cards; *also* **:** a card of the suit bearing spades [Italian *spada* or Spanish *espada* "broad sword"; both from Latin *spatha*, from Greek *spathē* "blade"]

spade·foot \'spād-ˌfut\ *n, pl* **spadefoots :** any of several burrowing toads with the feet modified for digging — called also *spadefoot toad*

spade·work \'spād-ˌwərk\ *n* **1 :** work done with a spade **2 :** the preliminary hard work in an undertaking

spa·dix \'spād-iks\ *n, pl* **spa·di·ces** \'spād-ə-ˌsēz\ **:** a floral spike (as in the arums) with a fleshy or succulent axis usually enclosed in a spathe [Latin, "frond torn from a palm tree", from Greek, from *span* "to draw, pull"]

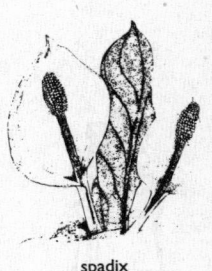

spadix

spa·ghet·ti \spə-'get-ē\ *n* **:** pasta made in thin solid strings [Italian, from pl. of *spaghetto* "little string", from *spago* "string"]

spake \'spāk\ *archaic past of* SPEAK

¹span \'span\ *archaic past of* SPIN

²span *n* **1 :** the distance from the end of the thumb to the end of the little finger of a spread hand; *also* **:** an English unit of length equal to 9 inches (about 22.9 centimeters) **2 :** an extent, stretch, reach, or spread between two limits: as **a :** a limited space of time ⟨*span* of life⟩ **b :** the spread of an arch, beam, truss, or girder from one support to another; *also* **:** the portion thus extended [Old English *spann*]

³span *vt* **spanned; span·ning 1 a :** to measure by or as if by the hand with fingers and thumb extended **b :** MEASURE 3 **2 a :** to reach or extend across **b :** to place or construct a span over

⁴span *n* **:** a pair of animals (as mules) driven together [Dutch, from *spannen* "to hitch up"]

span·dex \'span-ˌdeks\ *n* **:** any of various synthetic elastic textile fibers

span·drel *or* **span·dril** \'span-drəl\ *n* **:** the sometimes ornamented space between the right or left exterior curve of an arch and an enclosing right angle [derived from Old French *espandre* "to spread out, expand", from Latin *expandere*]

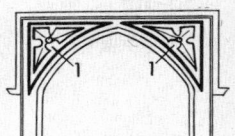

1 spandrel

¹span·gle \'spang-gəl\ *n* **1 :** a small piece of shining metal or plastic used for ornamentation especially on clothes **2 :** a small glittering object [Middle English *spangel*]

²spangle *vb* **span·gled; span·gling** \'spang-gə-ling, -gling\ **1 :** to set or sprinkle with or as if with spangles **2 :** to glitter as if covered with spangles : SPARKLE

Span·glish \'spang-glish, -lish\ *n* **:** Spanish marked by many borrowings from English; *also* **:** any of various combinations of Spanish and English

Span·iard \'span-yərd\ *n* **:** a native or inhabitant of Spain [Middle French *Espaignart*, from *Espaigne* "Spain", from Latin *Hispania*]

span·iel \'span-yəl\ *n* **1 :** any of numerous small or medium-sized mostly short-legged dogs usually having long wavy hair, feathered legs and tail, and large drooping ears **2 :** TOADY [Middle French *espaignol*, literally, "Spaniard", derived from Latin *Hispania* "Spain"]

Span·ish \'span-ish\ *n* **1 :** the Romance language of the largest part of Spain and of the countries colonized by Spaniards **2** *pl in construction* **:** the people of Spain [Middle English *Spainish*, from *Spain*] — **Spanish** *adj*

Spanish American *n* **1 :** a native or inhabitant of one of the countries of America in which Spanish is the national language **2 :** a resident of the United States whose native language is Spanish and whose culture is of Spanish origin — **Spanish–American** *adj*

Spanish fly *n* **:** a green blister beetle of southern Europe; *also* **:** a dried preparation of these formerly used as an aphrodisiac

Spanish mackerel *n* **:** any of various usually large fishes chiefly of warm seas that resemble or are related to the common mackerel

Spanish moss *n* **:** an epiphytic plant related to the pineapple that forms pendent tufts of grayish green filaments on trees in the southern United States, Mexico, and the West Indies

Spanish moss

Spanish omelet *n* **:** an omelet served with a sauce of chopped green pepper, onion, and tomato

Spanish rice *n* **:** rice cooked with onions, green pepper, and tomatoes

spank \'spangk\ *vt* **:** to strike especially on the buttocks with the open hand [imitative] — **spank** *n*

\ə\ abut	\ng\ sing
\ər\ further	\ō\ bone
\a\ mat	\ȯ\ saw
\ā\ take	\ȯi\ coin
\ä\ cot, cart	\th\ thin
\au̇\ out	\th\ this
\ch\ chin	\ü\ food
\e\ pet	\u̇\ foot
\ē\ easy	\y\ yet
\g\ go	\yü\ few
\i\ tip	\yu̇\ cure
\ī\ life	\zh\ vision
\j\ job	

spark plug 1

spank·er \'spang-kər\ *n* : the fore-and-aft sail on the mast nearest the stern of a square-rigged ship [origin unknown]

spank·ing \'spang-king\ *adj* 1 : remarkable of its kind 2 a : moving or able to move briskly b : being fresh and strong ⟨a *spanking* wind⟩ [origin unknown]

span·ner \'span-ər\ *n* 1 *chiefly British* : WRENCH 2 2 : a wrench having a jaw or socket to fit a nut or head of a bolt, a pipe, or hose coupling; *esp* : one having a tooth or pin in its jaw to fit a hole or slot in an object [German, "instrument for winding springs", from *spannen* "to stretch"]

span–new \'span-'nü, -'nyü\ *adj* : BRAND-NEW [Old Norse *spānnȳr*, from *spānn* "chip of wood" + *nȳr* "new"]

span·worm \'span-,wərm\ *n* : LOOPER 1

¹spar \'spär\ *n* 1 : a stout pole 2 : a stout rounded wood or metal piece (as a mast, boom, or yard) used to support sail rigging 3 : one of the main longitudinal members of the wing of an airplane that carry the ribs [Middle English *sparre*]

²spar *vi* **sparred; spar·ring** 1 a : BOX; *esp* : to gesture without landing a blow to draw one's opponent or create an opening b : to engage in a practice or exhibition bout of boxing 2 : SKIRMISH 1, WRANGLE [probably alteration of ²*spur*]

³spar *n* : a sparring match or session

¹spare \'spaər, 'speər\ *vb* 1 : to refrain from destroying, punishing, or harming : be lenient ⟨*spare* a prisoner⟩ 2 : to refrain from attacking or reprimanding ⟨the sermon *spared* no one⟩ 3 : to free from a liability or requirement : EXEMPT ⟨*spare* yourself the trouble⟩ 4 : to refrain from : AVOID ⟨*spare* no cost⟩ 5 : to be frugal or use frugally : STINT ⟨don't *spare* the syrup⟩ 6 a : to give up as not strictly needed ⟨can you *spare* a dollar⟩ b : to have left over or as margin ⟨time to *spare*⟩ [Old English *sparian*]

²spare *adj* 1 : not being used; *esp* : held for emergency use ⟨a *spare* tire⟩ 2 : being over and above what is needed : SUPERFLUOUS ⟨*spare* time⟩ 3 : not liberal or profuse : MEAGER ⟨a *spare* diet⟩ 4 : healthily lean ⟨a *spare* build⟩ 5 : not abundant or plentiful : SCANTY [Old English *spær*] — **spare·ly** *adv* — **spare·ness** *n*

³spare *n* 1 : a spare or duplicate piece or part (as an automobile tire) 2 a : the knocking down of all 10 pins with 2 bowls in a frame in bowling b : the score made by this action

spare·able \'spar-ə-bəl, 'sper-\ *adj* : that can be spared

spare·ribs \'spaər-,ribz, 'speər-, -,ibz\ *n pl* : a cut of pork ribs separated from the bacon strip [by folk etymology from Low German *ribbesper* "pickled pork ribs roasted on a spit", from *ribbe* "rib" + *sper* "spear, spit"]

spar·ing \'spaər-ing, 'speər-\ *adj* 1 : tending to save; *esp* : FRUGAL 2 : SCANTY 2 — **spar·ing·ly** \-ing-lē\ *adv*

¹spark \'spärk\ *n* 1 a : a small particle of a burning substance b : a hot glowing particle struck from a larger mass; *esp* : one heated by friction 2 : a luminous electrical discharge of very short duration between two conductors 3 : SPARKLE 1, FLASH 4 : something that sets off a sudden force ⟨the *spark* that set off the riot⟩ 5 : SEED 4, GERM [Old English *spearca*]

²spark *vb* 1 a : to throw out or produce sparks b : to flash or fall like sparks 2 : to respond with enthusiasm 3 : to set off in a burst of activity : ACTIVATE 4 : to stir to activity : INCITE ⟨the captain *sparked* the team to victory⟩ — **spark·er** *n*

³spark *n* 1 : a foppish young man : GALLANT 2 : SUITOR 3, SWAIN [perhaps of Scandinavian origin]

⁴spark *vb* : WOO 1a, COURT — **spark·er** *n*

spark coil *n* : an induction coil for producing a spark for an internal-combustion engine

sparking plug *n, British* : SPARK PLUG 1

¹spar·kle \'spär-kəl\ *vi* **spar·kled; spar·kling** \-kə-ling, -kling\ 1 a : SPARK 1a b : to give off or reflect bright

moving points of light 2 : to perform brilliantly 3 : EFFERVESCE ⟨wine that *sparkles*⟩ 4 : to become lively or animated [derived from *spark*] SYN see FLASH

²sparkle *n* 1 : a little spark : SCINTILLATION ⟨the *sparkle* of a diamond⟩ 2 : the quality of sparkling 3 a : ANIMATION, LIVELINESS ⟨the *sparkle* of your wit⟩ b : EFFERVESCENCE

spar·kler \'spär-klər\ *n* : one that sparkles: as a : DIAMOND 1a b : a firework that throws off brilliant sparks on burning

sparkling wine *n* : an effervescent red or white wine

spark plug *n* 1 : a part that fits into the cylinder head of an internal-combustion engine and produces the spark for combustion 2 : one that activates or gives impetus to an undertaking — **spark·plug** \'spärk-,pləg\ *vt*

sparky \'spär-kē\ *adj* **spark·i·er; -est** : being lively and active

sparring partner *n* : one with whom a boxer spars for practice during training

spar·row \'spar-ō\ *n* 1 : any of several small usually brownish or grayish songbirds related to the finches; *esp* : ENGLISH SPARROW 2 : any of various finches resembling the true sparrows [Old English *spearwa*]

sparrow hawk *n* : any of various small hawks or falcons

sparse \'spärs\ *adj* : of few and scattered elements; *esp* : not thickly grown or settled [Latin *sparsus* "spread out", from *spargere* "to scatter"] SYN see MEAGER — **sparse·ly** *adv* — **sparse·ness** *n* — **spar·si·ty** \'spär-sət-ē\ *n*

¹Spar·tan \'spärt-n\ *n* 1 : a native or inhabitant of ancient Sparta 2 : a person of great courage and fortitude

²Spartan *adj* 1 : of or relating to ancient Sparta 2 a : marked by strict self-discipline and self-denial ⟨a *Spartan* athlete⟩ b : marked by simplicity and frugality ⟨*Spartan* living conditions⟩ c : undaunted by pain or danger ⟨*Spartan* courage⟩

spar varnish *n* : an exterior waterproof varnish [¹*spar*]

spasm \'spaz-əm\ *n* 1 : an involuntary and abnormal muscular contraction 2 : a sudden violent and temporary effort or emotion [Middle French *spasme*, from Latin *spasmus*, from Greek *spasmos*, from *span* "to draw, pull"]

spas·mod·ic \spaz-'mäd-ik\ *adj* 1 : relating to or affected or characterized by spasm ⟨*spasmodic* movements⟩ 2 : acting or proceeding fitfully : INTERMITTENT ⟨*spasmodic* interest⟩ 3 : subject to outbursts of emotional excitement : EXCITABLE [Greek *spasmōdēs*, from *spasmos* "spasm"] — **spas·mod·i·cal·ly** \-'mäd-i-kə-lē, -klē\ *adv*

spas·tic \'spas-tik\ *adj* 1 : of, relating to, or characterized by spasm ⟨*spastic* colon⟩ 2 : suffering from spastic paralysis ⟨a *spastic* child⟩ [Latin *spasticus*, from Greek *spastikos* "drawing in", from *span* "to draw, pull"] — **spastic** *n* — **spas·ti·cal·ly** \-ti-kə-lē, -klē\ *adv* — **spas·tic·i·ty** \spa-'stis-ət-ē\ *n*

spastic paralysis *n* : paralysis from rigidly contracted muscles and increased tendon reflexes — compare CEREBRAL PALSY

¹spat \'spat\ *past of* SPIT

²spat *n, pl* **spat** *or* **spats** : a young bivalve mollusk (as an oyster) — usually used collectively [origin unknown]

³spat *n* : a cloth or leather gaiter covering the instep and ankle [short for *spatterdash*, a kind of legging worn as protection from water and mud]

⁴spat *n* 1 : a brief petty quarrel : TIFF 2 *chiefly dialect* : SLAP 1 3 : a sound like that of rain falling in large drops ⟨the *spat* of bullets⟩ [probably imitative]

⁵spat *vb* **spat·ted; spat·ting** 1 *chiefly dialect* : SLAP 1a 2 : to quarrel pettily or briefly : TIFF 3 : to strike with a sound like that of rain falling in large drops

spate \'spāt\ *n* 1 : FLOOD 1a, FRESHET 2 a : a large number or amount b : a sudden or strong outburst : RUSH [Middle English]

spathe \'spāth\ *n* : a sheathing bract or pair of bracts enclosing an inflorescence and especially a spadix [Latin *spatha* "broad sword", from Greek *spathē* "blade"] — **spathed** \'spāthd\ *adj*

spa·tial *or* **spa·cial** \'spā-shəl\ *adj* : relating to, occupying, or having the character of space [Latin *spatium* "space"] — **spa·ti·al·i·ty** \ˌspā-shē-'al-ət-ē\ *n* — **spa·tial·ly** \'spāsh-lē, -ə-lē\ *adv*

¹**spat·ter** \'spat-ər\ *vb* 1 : to splash with or as if with a liquid; *also* : to soil or spot in this way 2 : to scatter by splashing ⟨*spatter* mud⟩ 3 : to injure by aspersion : DEFAME ⟨*spatter* a good reputation⟩ 4 **a** : to spurt out in scattered drops **b** : to drop with a sound like rain [related to Flemish *spetteren* "to spatter"]

²**spatter** *n* 1 : the act or sound of spattering : the state of being spattered 2 **a** : a drop or splash spattered on something **b** : a small amount or number : SPRINKLE ⟨a *spatter* of applause⟩

spat·ter·dock \'spat-ər-ˌdäk\ *n* : a common yellow North American water lily

spat·u·la \'spach-ə-lə\ *n* : a flat thin usually metal implement used especially for spreading or mixing soft substances, scooping, or lifting [Late Latin, "spoon, spatula", from Latin *spatha* "sword, spoon", from Greek *spathē* "blade"]

spat·u·late \'spach-ə-lət\ *adj* : shaped like a spatula

spav·in \'spav-ən\ *n* : a bony enlargement of the hock of a horse associated with strain [Middle French *espavain*] — **spav·ined** \-ənd\ *adj*

¹**spawn** \'spȯn, 'spän\ *vb* 1 **a** : to produce or deposit eggs or spawn — used of an aquatic animal **b** : to induce (fish) to spawn 2 : to bring forth : GENERATE ⟨*spawn* ideas⟩ 3 : to produce young especially in large numbers [Anglo-French *espaundre,* from Old French *espandre* "to spread out, expand", from Latin *expandere*] — **spawn·er** *n*

²**spawn** *n* 1 : the eggs of aquatic animals (as fishes or oysters) that lay many small eggs 2 **a** : PRODUCT 2 **b** : offspring produced in large quantities 3 : the seed, germ, or source of something 4 : mycelium especially prepared (as in bricks) for propagating mushrooms

spay \'spā\ *vt* : to remove the ovaries of (a female animal) [Middle French *espeer* "to cut with a sword", from *espee* "sword", from Latin *spatha,* from Greek *spathē* "blade"]

speak \'spēk\ *vb* **spoke** \'spōk\; **spo·ken** \'spō-kən\; **speak·ing** 1 : to utter words with the voice : TALK 2 : to utter by means of words ⟨*speak* the truth⟩ 3 : to address a gathering 4 : to mention in speech or writing 5 : to carry a meaning as if by speech ⟨wore clothes that *spoke* of poverty⟩ 6 : to make a natural or characteristic sound ⟨the big gun *spoke*⟩ 7 : to use in talking ⟨*speak* French⟩ [Old English *sprecan, specan*] — **speak·able** \'spē-kə-bəl\ *adj* □ **SYN TALK**: SPEAK may apply to any articulated sounds ranging from the least to the most coherent; TALK is less technical and less formal and implies a listener and connected discourse or exchange of thoughts. — **speak for** 1 : to speak in behalf of : represent the opinions of 2 : to apply for : CLAIM — **speak out** 1 : to speak loudly and distinctly 2 : to speak freely — **speak to** : REPROVE 2, REBUKE — **speak up** : to speak out — **speak well for** : to be evidence in favor of — **speak with** : to talk to

speak·easy \'spē-ˌkē-zē\ *n* : a place where alcoholic drinks are illegally sold

speak·er \'spē-kər\ *n* 1 **a** : one that speaks **b** : a person who makes a public speech or acts as a spokesman 2 : the presiding officer of a deliberative assembly ⟨*Speaker* of the House of Representatives⟩ 3 : LOUDSPEAKER

speak·er·ship \-ˌship\ *n* : the position of speaker especially of a legislative body

speak·ing \'spē-king\ *adj* 1 : highly significant or expressive : ELOQUENT ⟨*speaking* eyes⟩ 2 : closely resembling an original

speaking tube *n* : a pipe through which conversation may be conducted (as between different parts of a building)

¹**spear** \'spiər\ *n* 1 : a thrusting or throwing a weapon with a long shaft and sharp head or blade 2 : a sharp-pointed instrument with barbs used in spearing fish 3 : SPEARMAN [Old English *spere*]

²**spear** *adj* : PATERNAL 1, MALE ⟨the *spear* side of the family⟩ [¹*spear* — see DISTAFF origin]

³**spear** *vb* 1 : to pierce or strike with or as if with a spear 2 : to thrust with or as if with a spear — **spear·er** *n*

⁴**spear** *n* : a usually young blade, shoot, or sprout (as of grass) [alteration of ¹*spire*]

¹**spear·fish** \'spiər-ˌfish\ *n* : any of several large sea fishes related to the marlins and sailfishes

²**spearfish** *vi* : to fish with a spear

spear·gun \'spiər-ˌgən\ *n* : a gun that shoots a spear and is used for spearfishing

¹**spear·head** \'spiər-ˌhed\ *n* 1 : the sharp-pointed head of a spear 2 : a leading element, force, or influence

²**spearhead** *vt* : to serve as leader or leading element of

spear·man \'spiər-mən\ *n* : one (as a soldier) armed with a spear

spear·mint \-ˌmint, -mənt\ *n* : a common mint grown for flavoring and especially for its aromatic oil

¹**spe·cial** \'spesh-əl\ *adj* 1 **a** : distinguished by some unusual quality ⟨a *special* occasion⟩ **b** : regarded with particular favor ⟨a *special* friend⟩ 2 **a** : distinctive in character : PECULIAR ⟨a *special* case⟩ **b** : of, relating to, or constituting a species : SPECIFIC ⟨a *special* concept⟩ 3 : additional to what is usual ⟨a *special* edition⟩ 4 : designed for a particular purpose or occasion ⟨a *special* diet⟩ [Latin *specialis* "individual, particular", from *species* "species"] — **spe·cial·ly** \'spesh-lē, -ə-lē\ *adv*

²**special** *n* 1 : one that is used for a special service ⟨caught a commuter *special*⟩ 2 : something (as a television program) that is not part of a regular series

special delivery *n* : a messenger delivery of a piece of mail ahead of the regular carrier delivery for an extra fee

spe·cial·ist \'spesh-ləst, -ə-ləst\ *n* 1 : one who devotes himself or herself to a special occupation or branch of learning ⟨eye *specialist*⟩ 2 : any of four enlisted ranks in the Army comparable to corporal through sergeant first class — **specialist** *or* **spe·cial·is·tic** \ˌspesh-ə-'lis-tik\ *adj*

spe·ci·al·i·ty \ˌspesh-ē-'al-ət-ē\ *n, pl* **-ties** 1 : a special mark or quality 2 : a special object or class of objects 3 **a** : a special aptitude or skill **b** : a particular occupation or branch of learning

spe·cial·iza·tion \ˌspesh-lə-'zā-shən, -ə-lə-\ *n* 1 : a making or becoming specialized 2 **a** : structural adaptation of a body part to a particular function or of an organism for life in a particular environment **b** : a body part or an organism adapted by specialization

spe·cial·ize \'spesh-ə-ˌlīz\ *vb* 1 : to make particular mention of : PARTICULARIZE 2 : to apply or direct to a specific end or use ⟨*specialized* study⟩ 3 : to concentrate one's efforts in a special activity or field ⟨*specialize* in French⟩ 4 : to undergo specialization; *esp* : to change adaptively

spe·cial·ty \'spesh-əl-tē\ *n, pl* **-ties** 1 : a distinctive mark or quality 2 **a** : a special object or class of objects; *esp* : a product of a special kind or of special excellence ⟨pancakes were the cook's *specialty*⟩ **b** : the state of being special, distinctive, or peculiar 3 : something in which one specializes or has special knowledge

spe·ci·a·tion \ˌspē-shē-'ā-shən, ˌspē-sē-\ *n* : differentiation into new biological species — **spe·ci·ate** \'spē-shē-ˌāt, -sē-\ *vi*

spe·cie \'spē-shē, -sē\ *n* : money in coin especially of gold or silver [from in *specie* "in kind, in coin", from Latin, "in kind"] — **in specie** : in the same or like form

spearmint

\ə\ abut	\ng\ sing
\ər\ further	\ō\ bone
\a\ mat	\ȯ\ saw
\ā\ take	\ȯi\ coin
\ä\ cot, cart	\th\ thin
\au̇\ out	\th\ this
\ch\ chin	\ü\ food
\e\ pet	\u̇\ foot
\ē\ easy	\y\ yet
\g\ go	\yü\ few
\i\ tip	\yu̇\ cure
\ī\ life	\zh\ vision
\j\ job	

¹spe·cies \'spē-,shēz, -shēz, -,sēz, -sēz\ *n, pl* **species** **1**
a : a class of individuals with common qualities and a
common name : KIND, SORT **b** (1) : a category of biological classification ranking below the genus, comprising related organisms or populations potentially
capable of interbreeding, and being designated by a
binomial that consists of the name of its genus followed by a Latin or latinized uncapitalized noun or
adjective agreeing grammatically with the genus name
(2) : an individual or kind belonging to such a species
2 : the consecrated eucharistic elements [Latin, "appearance, kind, species"]

²species *adj* : belonging to a biological species as distinguished from a horticultural variety ⟨a *species* rose⟩

spec·i·fi·able \'spes-ə-,fī-ə-bəl\ *adj* : capable of being
specified

¹spe·cif·ic \spi-'sif-ik\ *adj* **1** : of, relating to, or constituting a species **2** : precisely and accurately formulated ⟨a *specific* statement of faith⟩ **3** : having a unique
relation to something ⟨*specific* antibodies⟩; *esp* : exerting a distinctive and usually a causative or curative
influence ⟨quinine is *specific* for malaria⟩ [Late Latin
specificus, from Latin *species* "species"] SYN see EX-
PLICIT — **spe·cif·i·cal·ly** \-'sif-i-kə-lē, -klē\ *adv* —
spec·i·fic·i·ty \,spes-ə-'fis-ət-ē\ *n*

²specific *n* **1 a** : something peculiarly adapted to a purpose or use **b** : a drug or remedy specific for a particular disease **2 a** : a characteristic quality or trait **b** : precise details or distinctions : PARTICULARS **c** *pl* : SPECIFI-
CATION 2a

spec·i·fi·ca·tion \,spes-fə-'kā-shən, -ə-fə-\ *n* **1** : the act
or process of specifying **2 a** (1) : a detailed precise
presentation of something or of a plan or proposal for
something — often used in pl. ⟨the architect's *specifi-
cations* for a new building⟩ (2) : a written description
of an invention for which a patent is sought **b** : a single item in such a detailed presentation

specific gravity *n* : the ratio of the density of a substance to the density of some other substance (as water) taken as a standard when both densities are obtained by weighing in air

specific heat *n* **1** : the ratio of the quantity of heat required to raise the temperature of a body one degree
to that required to raise the temperature of an equal
mass of water one degree **2** : the heat in calories required to raise the temperature of one kilogram of a
substance one degree Celsius

spec·i·fy \'spes-ə-,fī\ *vt* **-fied; -fy·ing** **1** : to name or state
explicitly or in detail ⟨*specify* the reason for absence⟩
2 : to include as an item in a specification ⟨*specify* oak
flooring⟩ [Old French *specifier,* from Late Latin *specifi-
care,* from *specificus* "specific"] — **spec·i·fi·er** \-,fī-
ər, -,fir\ *n*

spec·i·men \'spes-ə-mən\ *n* **1** : an item or part typical
of a group or whole : SAMPLE **2** : PERSON, SORT ⟨a tough
specimen⟩ [Latin, from *specere* "to look at"]

spe·ci·os·i·ty \,spē-shē-'äs-ət-ē\ *n* : the quality or state
of being specious

spe·cious \'spē-shəs\ *adj* : having a false look of truth,
fairness, or genuineness ⟨a *specious* argument⟩ [Latin
speciosus "beautiful, plausible", from *species* "appearance, species"] SYN see PLAUSIBLE — **spe·cious·ly**
adv — **spe·cious·ness** *n*

¹speck \'spek\ *n* **1** : a small discoloration or spot especially from dirt or decay **2** : PARTICLE 2a, BIT **3** : something marked or marred with specks [Old English *spec-
ca*]

²speck *vt* : to produce specks on or in

¹speck·le \'spek-əl\ *n* : a little speck [Middle English]

²speckle *vt* **speck·led; speck·ling** \'spek-ling, -ə-ling\ **1** :
to mark with speckles **2** : to be distributed in or on
like speckles ⟨small lakes *speckled* the land⟩

specs \'speks\ *n pl* : GLASS 2c [contraction of
spectacles]

spec·ta·cle \'spek-ti-kəl\ *n* **1 a** : something exhibited
to view as unusual, notable, or entertaining; *esp* : an
eye-catching or dramatic public display **b** : an object
of curiosity or contempt ⟨made a *spectacle* of herself at
the party⟩ **2** *pl* : GLASS 2c [Middle French, from Latin
spectaculum, from *spectare* "to watch", from *specere*
"to look at"]

spec·ta·cled \-kəld\ *adj* : having or wearing spectacles

¹spec·tac·u·lar \spek-'tak-yə-lər, spək-\ *adj* : of, relating to, or constituting a spectacle — **spec·tac·u·lar·ly**
adv

²spectacular *n* : something (as an elaborate television
show) that is spectacular

spec·ta·tor \'spek-,tāt-ər, spek-'\ *n* : one who watches
without being involved or taking part [Latin, from
spectare "to watch"] — **spectator** *adj*

spec·ter *or* **spec·tre** \'spek-tər\ *n* **1** : GHOST 2 **2** : something that haunts or perturbs the mind [French *spectre,*
from Latin *spectrum* "appearance, specter", from *specere* "to look, look at"]

spec·tral \'spek-trəl\ *adj* **1** : of, relating to, or suggesting a specter : GHOSTLY **2** : of, relating to, or made by a
spectrum ⟨*spectral* color⟩ — **spec·tral·ly** \-trə-lē\ *adv*
— **spec·tral·ness** *n*

spec·tro·gram \'spek-trə-,gram\ *n* : a photograph or diagram of a spectrum

spec·tro·graph \'spek-trə-,graf\ *n* : an instrument for
spreading radiation into a spectrum and photographing or mapping the spectrum — **spec·tro·graph·ic**
\,spek-trə-'graf-ik\ *adj* — **spec·tro·graph·i·cal·ly**
\-'graf-i-kə-lē, -klē\ *adv*

spec·trom·e·ter \spek-'träm-ət-ər\ *n* **1** : an instrument
used in determining the index of refraction **2** : a spectroscope fitted for measurements of the spectra observed with it — **spec·tro·met·ric** \,spek-trə-'me-trik\
adj — **spec·trom·e·try** \spek-'träm-ə-trē\ *n*

spec·tro·pho·tom·e·ter \,spek-trō-fə-'täm-ət-ər\ *n* : an
instrument for measuring the relative intensities of the
light in different parts of a spectrum

spec·tro·scope \'spek-trə-,skōp\ *n* : an instrument that
produces spectra from or by means of electromagnetic
radiation — **spec·tro·scop·ic** \,spek-trə-'skäp-ik\ *adj*
— **spec·tro·scop·i·cal·ly** \-'skäp-i-kə-lē, -klē\ *adv* —
spec·tros·co·pist \spek-'träs-kə-pəst\ *n* — **spec·tros·
co·py** \-pē\ *n*

spec·trum \'spek-trəm\ *n, pl* **spec·tra** \-trə\ *or* **spec·
trums** **1 a** : a series of colors formed when a beam of
white light is dispersed (as by passing through a
prism) so that the component waves are arranged in
the order of their wavelengths from red continuing
through orange, yellow, green, blue, indigo, and violet **b** : a series of radiations arranged in regular order
according to some varying characteristic especially
wavelength — compare ELECTROMAGNETIC SPECTRUM
2 : a continuous sequence or range ⟨a wide *spectrum*
of political opinions⟩ [Latin, "appearance, specter"]

spec·u·lar \'spek-yə-lər\ *adj* : of, relating to, or having
the qualities of a mirror [Latin *specularis,* from *specu-
lum* "mirror"] — **spec·u·lar·ly** *adv*

spec·u·late \'spek-yə-,lāt\ *vi* **1 a** : to meditate on or
ponder a subject : REFLECT **b** : to think or theorize
about something in which evidence is too slight for
certainty to be reached **2** : to assume a business risk in
hope of gain; *esp* : to buy or sell in expectation of
profiting from market fluctuations [Latin *speculari* "to
spy out, examine", from *specula* "watchtower", from
specere "to look"] SYN see THINK — **spec·u·la·tion**
\,spek-yə-'lā-shən\ *n* — **spec·u·la·tive** \'spek-yə-lət-
iv, -,lāt-\ *adj* — **spec·u·la·tive·ly** *adv* — **spec·u·la·tor**
\-,lāt-ər\ *n*

spec·u·lum \'spek-yə-ləm\ *n, pl* **-la** \-lə\ *also* **-lums** **1** :
a tubular instrument inserted into a body passage for
inspection or medication **2** : a reflector in an optical
instrument [Latin, "mirror", from *specere* "to look"]

speech \'spēch\ *n* **1 a** : the communication or expression of thoughts in spoken words **b** : CONVERSATION **2 a** : something that is spoken **b** : a public discourse **3 a** : LANGUAGE 1a, DIALECT **b** : an individual manner or style of speaking **4** : the power of expressing or communicating thoughts by speaking [Old English *sprǣc, spǣc*]

speech community *n* : a group of people sharing characteristic patterns of vocabulary, grammar, and pronunciation

speech·ify \'spē-chə-,fī\ *vi* **-ified; -ify·ing** : to make a speech : HARANGUE

speech·less \'spēch-ləs\ *adj* **1** : lacking or deprived of the power of speaking **2** : not speaking for a time : SILENT ⟨*speechless* with surprise⟩ SYN *see* DUMB — **speech·less·ly** *adv* — **speech·less·ness** *n*

¹speed \'spēd\ *n* **1** *archaic* : prosperity in an undertaking : SUCCESS **2 a** : the act or state of moving swiftly : SWIFTNESS **b** : rate of motion : VELOCITY 1, 3 **3** : swiftness or rate of performance or action : QUICKNESS **4 a** : the sensitivity of a photographic film, plate, or paper **b** : the light-gathering power of a lens expressed as relative aperture **5** : a transmission gear in automotive vehicles ⟨shift to low *speed*⟩ **6** : METHAMPHETAMINE; *also* : a related drug [Old English *spēd*] SYN *see* HASTE

²speed *vb* **sped** \'sped\ *or* **speed·ed; speed·ing 1 a** : to prosper in an undertaking : to help to succeed : AID **2 a** : to make haste **b** : to go or drive at excessive or illegal speed **3** : to move, work, or take place faster : ACCELERATE **4 a** : to cause to move quickly : HASTEN **b** : to wish Godspeed to **c** : to increase the speed of : ACCELERATE — **speed·er** *n*

³speed *adj* : of, relating to, or regulating speed

speed·ball \'spēd-,bol\ *n* : a game between 2 teams of 11 players on a football field which is similar to soccer but in which the ball may be kicked or played with the hands

speed·boat \'spēd-,bōt\ *n* : a fast launch or motorboat

speed bump *n* : a low raised ridge across a roadway (as in a parking lot) to limit vehicle speed

speed limit *n* : the highest speed a vehicle may legally travel at

speed·om·e·ter \spi-'däm-ət-ər\ *n* **1** : an instrument that measures speed **2** : an instrument that both measures speed and records distance traveled

speed–read·ing \'spēd-,rēd-ing\ *n* : a method of reading rapidly by skimming

speed·ster \'spēd-stər\ *n* : one that speeds or is capable of great speed

speed trap *n* : a stretch of road policed by concealed officers or devices (as radar) to catch speeders

speed·up \'spēd-,əp\ *n* **1** : ACCELERATION 2 **2** : an employer's demand for accelerated output without increased pay

speed·way \'spēd-,wā\ *n* : a racecourse for motor vehicles

speed·well \'spēd-,wel\ *n* : any of a genus of herbs of the snapdragon family; *esp* : a creeping perennial European herb with small bluish flowers

speedy \'spēd-ē\ *adj* **speed·i·er; -est** : rapid in motion or action SYN *see* QUICK — **speed·i·ly** \'spēd-l-ē\ *adv* — **speed·i·ness** *n*

spe·le·ol·o·gy \,spē-lē-'äl-ə-jē, spel-ē-\ *n* : the scientific study or exploration of caves [Latin *speleum* "cave" (from Greek *spēlaion*) + English *-logy*] — **spe·le·o·log·i·cal** \,spē-lē-ə-'läj-i-kəl, ,spel-ē-\ *adj* — **spe·le·ol·o·gist** \-'äl-ə-jəst\ *n*

¹spell \'spel\ *n* **1 a** : a spoken word or form of words believed to have magic power : INCANTATION **b** : a state of enchantment **2** : a strong compelling influence or attraction [Old English, "talk, tale"]

²spell *vt* : to put under a spell : BEWITCH

³spell *vb* **spelled** \'speld, 'spelt\; **spell·ing 1** : to read or discern slowly and with difficulty — often used with *out* **2 a** : to name, write, or print the letters of in order ⟨*spell* a word⟩ **b** : to constitute the letters of ⟨*c-a-t* spells "cat"⟩ **3** : MEAN, SIGNIFY ⟨another drought may *spell* famine⟩ **4** : to form words with letters [Old French *espeller*, of Germanic origin]

⁴spell *vb* **spelled** \'speld\; **spell·ing 1** : to take the place of for a time : RELIEVE ⟨if we *spell* each other we won't get tired⟩ **2** : to allow an interval of rest to : REST [Old English *spelian*]

⁵spell *n* **1** : one's turn at work **2** : a period spent in a job or occupation **3 a** : a short period of time **b** : a stretch of a specified type of weather **4** : a period of bodily or mental distress or disorder : ATTACK, FIT ⟨a *spell* of coughing⟩ ⟨a fainting *spell*⟩

spell·bind \'spel-,bīnd\ *vt* **-bound** \-,baund\; **-bind·ing** : to hold by or as if by a spell : FASCINATE [back-formation from *spellbound*]

spell·bind·er \-,bīn-dər\ *n* : a speaker of compelling eloquence

spell·bound \-'baund\ *adj* : held by or as if by a spell

spell·down \'spel-,daun\ *n* : SPELLING BEE

spell·er \'spel-ər\ *n* **1** : one that spells words **2** : a book with exercises for teaching spelling

spell·ing \'spel-ing\ *n* : the forming of words from letters according to accepted usage; *also* : the letters of a word

spelling bee *n* : a spelling contest in which each contestant is eliminated as soon as he or she misspells a word

spell out *vt* : to make very explicit or emphatic

¹spelt \'spelt\ *n* : a wheat with loose spikes and spikelets that each contain two light-red kernels [Old English, from Late Latin *spelta*, of Germanic origin]

²spelt *chiefly British past of* SPELL

spel·ter \'spel-tər\ *n* : ZINC; *esp* : zinc cast in slabs for commercial use [probably from Dutch *speauter*]

spe·lunk·er \spi-'ləng-kər, 'spē-,\ *n* : a person who makes a hobby of exploring and studying caves [Latin *spelunca* "cave", from Greek *spēlynx*] — **spe·lunk·ing** \-king\ *n*

spend \'spend\ *vt* **spent** \'spent\; **spend·ing 1** : to use up or pay out : EXPEND **2 a** : to wear out : EXHAUST **b** : to consume wastefully : SQUANDER **3** : to cause or permit to elapse : PASS ⟨*spent* the evening reading⟩ [partly from Old English *spendan*, from Latin *expendere* "to expend"; partly from Old French *despendre*, from Latin *dispendere* "to weigh out", from *dis-* + *pendere* "to weigh"] — **spend·er** *n*

spend·able \'spen-də-bəl\ *adj* : available for spending

spending money *n* : money for small personal expenses

spend·thrift \'spend-,thrift, 'spen-\ *n* : one who spends lavishly or wastefully — **spendthrift** *adj*

Spen·se·ri·an \spen-'sir-ē-ən\ *adj* : of, relating to, or characteristic of Edmund Spenser or his writings

Spenserian stanza *n* : a stanza consisting of eight lines of iambic pentameter and an alexandrine with a rhyme scheme *ababbcbcc*

spent \'spent\ *adj* **1** : used up **2** : drained of energy or effectiveness [past participle of *spend*]

sperm \'spərm\ *n, pl* **sperm** *or* **sperms 1 a** : SEMEN **b** : a male gamete **2** : a product (as oil) of the sperm whale [Middle French *esperme*, from Late Latin *sperma*, from Greek, literally, "seed"]

sperm- *or* **spermo-** *or* **sperma-** *or* **spermi-** *combining form* : seed : germ : sperm ⟨*sperma*theca⟩ [Greek *sperma*]

sper·ma·ce·ti \,spər-mə-'sēt-ē, -'set-\ *n* : a waxy solid obtained from the oil of cetaceans and especially the sperm whale and used in ointments, cosmetics, and candles [Medieval Latin *sperma ceti* "whale sperm"]

sper·ma·ry \'spərm-rē, -ə-rē\ *n, pl* **-ries** : an organ in which male gametes are developed

spermat- *or* **spermato-** *combining form* : seed : spermatozoon ⟨*spermato*cyte⟩ [Greek *spermat-, sperma* "seed, sperm"]

sper·ma·the·ca \,spər-mə-'thē-kə\ *n* : a sac for sperm storage in the female reproductive tract of many lower animals — **sper·ma·the·cal** \-kəl\ *adj*

sperm whale

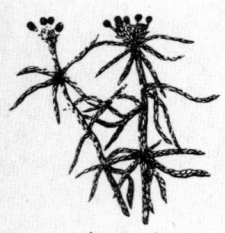

sphagnum 1

sphere 1b

sphinx 2

sper·mat·ic \,spər-'mat-ik\ *adj* : of or relating to sperm or the male gonad

sper·ma·tid \'spər-mət-əd\ *n* : one of the cells produced in meiosis that differentiate into spermatozoa [derived from Greek *sperma* "seed, sperm"]

sper·ma·ti·um \,spər-'mā-shē-əm\ *n, pl* **-tia** \-shē-ə\ : a nonmotile cell functioning or held to function as a male gamete in some lower plants [New Latin, derived from Greek *sperma* "seed, sperm"] — **sper·ma·tial** \-shē-əl, -shəl\ *adj*

sper·mato·cyte \,spər-'mat-ə-,sīt, 'spər-mət-\ *n* : a cell giving rise to sperm cells

sper·mato·gen·e·sis \,spər-mət-ə-'jen-ə-səs, spər-,mat-\ *n, pl* **-e·ses** \-ə-,sēz\ : the process of male gamete formation including meiosis and transformation of the four resulting spermatids into spermatozoa — **sper·mato·ge·net·ic** \spər-,mat-ə-jə-'net-ik, ,spər-mət-ō-\ *adj*

sper·mato·go·ni·um \,spər-mət-ə-'gō-nē-əm, spər-,mat-\ *n, pl* **-nia** \-nē-ə\ : a primitive male germ cell [*spermat-* + *gonium* "primitive germ cell", from Greek *gonos* "offspring, seed"] — **sper·mato·go·ni·al** \-nē-əl\ *adj*

sper·mato·phyte \,spər-'mat-ə-,fīt\ *n* : any of a group (Spermatophyta) of higher plants comprising those that produce seeds and including the gymnosperms and angiosperms — **sper·mato·phyt·ic** \spər-,mat-ə-'fit-ik, ,spər-mət-\ *adj*

sper·mato·zo·on \,spər-,mat-ə-'zō-,än, ,spər-mət-, -'zō-ən\ *n, pl* **-zoa** \-'zō-ə\ : SPERM CELL [*spermat-* + Greek *zōion* "animal"] — **sper·mato·zo·al** \-'zō-əl\ *adj*

sperm cell *n* : a motile male gamete of an animal usually with rounded or elongate head and a long posterior flagellum — called also *spermatozoon*

sper·mi·cide \'spər-mə-,sīd\ *n* : a preparation or substance (as in a contraceptive) used to kill sperm

sperm nucleus *n* : either of two nuclei derived from the generative nucleus of a pollen grain that function in the double fertilization of a seed plant

sperm oil *n* : a pale yellow oil from the sperm whale used especially as a lubricant

sperm whale \'spərm-\ *n* : a large toothed whale with a closed cavity in the head containing a fluid mixture of spermaceti and oil [short for *spermaceti whale*]

¹spew \'spyü\ *vb* : to pour forth : VOMIT [Old English *spīwan*] — **spew·er** *n*

²spew *n* : matter that is spewed

sphag·num \'sfag-nəm\ *n* **1** : any of a large genus of atypical mosses that grow only in wet acid areas where their remains become compacted with other plant debris to form peat **2** : a mass of sphagnum plants [New Latin, from Latin *sphagnos,* a kind of moss, from Greek] — **sphag·nous** \-nəs\ *adj*

sphal·er·ite \'sfal-ə-,rīt\ *n* : a widely distributed ore of zinc composed essentially of zinc sulfide [German *sphalerit,* from Greek *sphaleros* "deceitful"; from its often being mistaken for galena]

sphe·no·don \'sfē-nə-,dän, 'sfen-ə-\ *n* : TUATARA [derived from Greek *sphēn* "wedge" + *odōn* "tooth"]

¹sphe·noid \'sfē-,nóid\ or **sphe·noi·dal** \sfi-'nóid-l\ *adj* : of, relating to, or being a winged bone of the base of the cranium [Greek *sphēnoeidēs* "wedge-shaped", from *sphēn* "wedge"]

²sphenoid *n* : a sphenoid bone

sphe·nop·sid \sfi-'näp-səd\ *n* : any of a major group (Sphenopsida) of primitive, jointed, and mostly extinct vascular plants including the equisetums [derived from Greek *sphēn* "wedge" + *opsis* "appearance, vision"]

sphere \'sfiər\ *n* **1 a** (1) : the apparent surface of the heavens of which half forms the dome of the visible sky (2) : one of the concentric and eccentric revolving spherical transparent shells in which according to ancient astronomy stars, sun, planets, and moon are set **b** : a globe representing the earth **2 a** : a globular

body : BALL **b** : a surface all points of which are equally distant from a center; *also* : the space enclosed by such a surface **3** : natural, normal, or proper place; *esp* : social order or rank **4** : a field or range of influence or significance : PROVINCE [Middle French *espere* "globe, celestial sphere", from Latin *sphaera,* from Greek *sphaira,* literally, "ball"] — **spher·ic** \'sfiər-ik, 'sfer-\ *adj* — **sphe·ric·i·ty** \sfir-'is-ət-ē\ *n*

sphere of influence : an area within which the interests of one nation are paramount

spher·i·cal \'sfir-i-kəl, 'sfer-\ *adj* **1** : having the form of a sphere or of one of its segments **2** : relating to or dealing with a sphere or its properties — **spher·i·cal·ly** \-kə-lē, -klē\ *adv*

spherical aberration *n* : aberration caused by the spherical form of a lens or mirror that gives different foci for central and marginal rays

spherical angle *n* : the angle between two intersecting arcs of great circles of a sphere

spherical triangle *n* : a figure analogous to a plane triangle formed by three intersecting arcs of great circles of a sphere

sphe·roid \'sfiər-,óid, 'sfeər-\ *n* : a figure resembling a flattened sphere — **sphe·roi·dal** \sfir-'óid-l\ *adj* — **sphe·roi·dal·ly** \-'óid-l-ē\ *adv*

spher·ule \'sfiər-ül, 'sfeər-, -yül\ *n* : a little sphere or spherical body

sphery \'sfiər-ē\ *adj* : suggestive of the heavenly spheres ⟨*sphery* eyes⟩ ⟨*sphery* music⟩

sphinc·ter \'sfing-tər, 'sfingk-\ *n* : a muscular ring surrounding and able to contract or close a bodily opening [Late Latin, from Greek *sphinktēr,* literally, "band", from *sphingein* "to bind tight"]

sphinx \'sfings, 'sfingks\ *n* **1 a** : a monster in Greek mythology having typically a lion's body, wings, and the head and bust of a woman **b** : a person whose character, motives, or feelings are enigmatic **2** : an ancient Egyptian image in the form of a recumbent lion having a man's head, a ram's head, or a hawk's head **3** : HAWKMOTH — called also *sphinx moth* [Latin, from Greek]

sphyg·mo·ma·nom·e·ter \,sfig-mō-mə-'näm-ət-ər\ *n* : an instrument for measuring blood pressure and especially arterial blood pressure [Greek *sphygmos* "pulse" + English *manometer*] — **sphyg·mo·ma·nom·e·try** \-mə-'näm-ə-trē\ *n*

Spi·ca \'spī-kə\ *n* : a bright star in the constellation Virgo [Latin, literally, "spike of grain"]

spi·cate \'spī-,kāt\ *adj* : arranged in the form of a spike ⟨a *spicate* inflorescence⟩ [Latin *spicatus,* past participle of *spicare* "to arrange in a spike", from *spica* "spike of grain"]

¹spice \'spīs\ *n* **1** : any of various aromatic plant products (as pepper or nutmeg) used to season or flavor foods **2** : something that gives zest or relish **3** : a pungent or fragrant odor : PERFUME [Old French *espice,* from Late Latin *species* "spices", from Latin, "species"]

²spice *vt* : to season with or as if with spices

spice·bush \-,bùsh\ *n* : an aromatic shrub of the laurel family with small early yellow flowers

spick-and-span \,spik-ən-'span\ *adj* **1** : BRAND-NEW, FRESH **2** : spotlessly clean and neat [derived from obsolete *spick* "spike" + *span-new*]

spic·ule \'spik-yül\ *n* : a minute slender pointed usually hard body; *esp* : one of the minute calcium or silica-containing bodies that support the tissues of various invertebrates [Latin *spiculum* "point", from *spica* "spike of grain"]

spicy \'spī-sē\ *adj* **spic·i·er; -est** **1** : having the quality, flavor, or fragrance of spice **2** : producing or abounding in spices **3** : LIVELY, SPIRITED ⟨a *spicy* temper⟩ **4** : somewhat scandalous or lewd ⟨*spicy* gossip⟩ — **spic·i·ly** \-sə-lē\ *adv* — **spic·i·ness** \-sē-nəs\ *n*

spi·der \'spīd-ər\ *n* **1** : any of an order (Araneida) of arachnids having a body with two main divisions, four pairs of walking legs, and two or more pairs of abdominal organs for spinning threads of silk used in making cocoons for their eggs, nests for themselves, or webs for entangling their prey **2** : a cast-iron frying pan originally made with short feet to stand among coals on the hearth [Middle English *spithre*]

spider crab *n* : any of numerous crabs with extremely long legs and nearly triangular bodies

spider mite *n* : RED SPIDER

spider monkey *n* : any of a genus of New World monkeys with long slender limbs, the thumb absent or rudimentary, and a very long prehensile tail

spi·der·web \'spīd-ər-,web\ *n* **1** : the silken web spun by most spiders and used as a resting place and a trap for small prey **2** : something like a spiderweb in appearance or function

spi·der·wort \-,wərt, -,wȯrt\ *n* : any of a genus of monocotyledonous plants with short-lived usually blue or violet flowers

spi·dery \'spīd-ə-rē\ *adj* **1** : resembling a spider; *also* : long and thin like the legs of a spider **2** : resembling a spiderweb **3** : full of spiders

spie·gel·ei·sen \'spē-gə-,līz-n\ *also* **spie·gel** \'spē-gəl\ *n* : a pig iron containing 15 to 30 percent manganese and 4.5 to 6.5 percent carbon [German *spiegeleisen*, from *spiegel* "mirror" + *eisen* "iron"]

¹spiel \'spēl\ *vb* : to talk volubly or extravagantly [German *spielen* "to play"] — **spiel·er** *n*

²spiel *n* : voluble mechanical often extravagant talk; *esp* : a sales pitch

spiffy \'spif-ē\ *adj* **spiff·i·er; -est 1** : fine looking : SMART **2** : EXCELLENT, DELIGHTFUL ⟨a *spiffy* party⟩ [English dialect *spiff* "dandified"]

spig·ot \'spig-ət, 'spik-ət\ *n* **1** : a pin or peg used to stop the vent in a cast **2** : FAUCET [Middle English]

¹spike \'spīk\ *n* **1** : a very large nail **2 a** : one of a row of pointed irons placed (as on the top of a wall) to prevent passage **b** : one of several metal projections set in the sole and heel of a shoe to improve traction in sports **3** : an unbranched antler of a young deer **4** : a pointed element (as in a graph) [Middle English]

²spike *vt* **1** : to fasten or furnish with spikes **2 a** : to disable (a muzzle-loading cannon) temporarily by driving a spike into the vent **b** : to suppress or block completely : QUASH **3** : to pierce or impale with or on a spike **4** : to add alcohol or liquor to (a drink) **5** : to drive (a volleyball) down into the opponent's court with a hard blow

³spike *n* **1** : an ear of grain **2** : a long usually rather narrow flower cluster in which the blossoms grow close to the central stem [Latin *spica*]

spiked \'spīkt\ *adj* **1 a** : bearing ears **b** : having a spiky inflorescence ⟨*spiked* flowers⟩ **2** : SPIKY

spike heel *n* : a very high tapering heel used on women's shoes

spike lavender *n* : a European mint related to and used like the true lavender

spike·let \'spī-klət\ *n* : a small or secondary spike; *esp* : one of the small few-flowered bracted spikes that make up the compound inflorescence of a grass or sedge

spike·like \'spī-,klīk\ *adj* : resembling a spike

spike·nard \'spīk-,närd\ *n* **1 a** : a fragrant ointment of the ancients **b** : an East Indian aromatic plant of the valerian family from which the ointment may have been derived **2** : an American herb of the ginseng family with an aromatic root and round flower clusters branching off the main stem [Medieval Latin *spica nardi*, literally, "spike of nard"]

spiky \'spī-kē\ *adj* **spik·i·er; -est 1** : having a sharp projecting point **2** : having spikes

spile \'spīl\ *n* **1** : ¹PILE **2** : a small plug used to stop the vent of a cask : BUNG **3** : a spout inserted in a tree to draw off sap [probably from Dutch *spijl* "stake"] — **spile** *vt*

spil·ing \'spī-ling\ *n* : a set of piles : PILING

¹spill \'spil\ *vb* **spilled** \'spild, 'spilt\ *also* **spilt** \'spilt\; **spill·ing 1** : to cause (blood) to flow **2 a** : to cause or allow unintentionally to fall, flow, or run out **b** : to fall or run out so as to be lost or wasted **3** : to relieve or lessen the pressure of (the wind) on sails by movement of the boat or adjustment of the sail **4** : to fall or cause to fall from one's place ⟨the horse *spilled* its rider⟩ **5** : to let out : DIVULGE **6** : to spread beyond bounds ⟨crowds *spilled* into the street⟩ [Old English *spillan* "to kill, spill"] — **spill·able** \'spil-ə-bəl\ *adj*

²spill *n* **1** : an act or instance of spilling; *esp* : a fall from a horse or vehicle **2** : something spilled

³spill *n* : a roll or cone of paper serving as a container [Middle English *spille* "wooden splinter"]

spill·age \'spil-ij\ *n* **1** : the act or process of spilling **2** : the quantity that spills

spil·li·kin \'spil-i-kən\ *n* : JACKSTRAW [probably from Dutch *spelleken* "small peg"]

spill·way \'spil-,wā\ *n* : a passage for surplus water to run over or around a dam or similar obstruction

spilth \'spilth\ *n* **1** : an act or instance of spilling **2 a** : something spilled **b** : TRASH 1a, RUBBISH

¹spin \'spin\ *vb* **spun** \'spən\; **spin·ning 1** : to draw out and twist into yarn or thread ⟨*spin* flax⟩ **2 a** : to produce by drawing out and twisting fibers ⟨*spin* thread⟩ **b** : to form threads or a web or cocoon by extruding a viscous rapidly hardening fluid **3 a** : to revolve rapidly : GYRATE **b** : to be dizzy : feel as if turning rapidly **4** : to cause to whirl : TWIRL ⟨*spin* a top⟩ **5 a** : to extend to great length : PROLONG **b** : to make up with the imagination ⟨*spun* a story⟩ **6** : to move swiftly on wheels or in a vehicle **7** : to shape into threadlike form in manufacture; *also* : to manufacture by a whirling process [Old English *spinnan*]

²spin *n* **1 a** : the act of spinning or twirling something **b** : whirling motion imparted by spinning : rapid rotation **c** : an excursion in a vehicle especially on wheels **2 a** : an aerial maneuver or flight condition in which an airplane moves downward in a somewhat corkscrew path **b** : a plunging descent or downward spiral **c** : a state of mental confusion **3** : a special point of view, emphasis, or interpretation

spin·ach \'spin-ich\ *n* : a potherb of the goosefoot family widely grown for its edible leaves [Middle French *espinache*, from Spanish *espinaca*, from Arabic *isfānākh*, from Persian]

¹spi·nal \'spīn-l\ *adj* **1** : of, relating to, or situated near the backbone **2** : of, relating to, or affecting the spinal cord ⟨*spinal* nerve cells⟩ — **spi·nal·ly** \-l-ē\ *adv*

²spinal *n* : an anesthetic administered by way of the spinal cord

spinal column *n* : the axial skeleton of the trunk and tail of a vertebrate that consists of a jointed series of vertebrae enclosing and protecting the spinal cord — called also *backbone*

spinal cord *n* : the cord of nervous tissue that extends from the brain along the back in the cavity of the spinal column, branches to form the spinal nerves, carries nerve impulses to and from the brain, and serves as a center for initiating and coordinating many reflex acts

spinal nerve *n* : any of the paired nerves which arise from the spinal cord and pass to various parts of the trunk and limbs and of which there are normally 31 pairs in man

¹spin·dle \'spin-dl\ *n* **1 a** : a round stick with tapered ends used to form and twist the yarn in hand spinning **b** : a rod holding a bobbin in a textile machine **2** : something shaped like a spindle (as a figure along which the chromosomes are distributed during mitosis) **3 a** : the bar that actuates the bolt of a lock **b** (1) : a turned often decorative piece of furniture or woodwork ⟨*spindles* of a chair⟩ (2) : NEWEL 2 **c** : a revolving piece usually smaller than a shaft **d** : the part of an

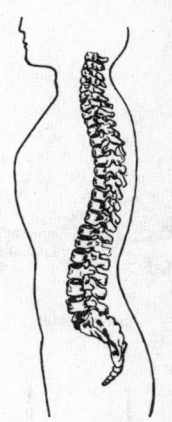

spinal column

\ə\ abut	\ng\ sing
\ər\ further	\ō\ bone
\a\ mat	\ȯ\ saw
\ā\ take	\ȯi\ coin
\ä\ cot, cart	\th\ thin
\au̇\ out	\th\ this
\ch\ chin	\ü\ food
\e\ pet	\u̇\ foot
\ē\ easy	\y\ yet
\g\ go	\yü\ few
\i\ tip	\yu̇\ cure
\ī\ life	\zh\ vision
\j\ job	

axle on which a vehicle wheel turns [Old English *spi-nel*]

²**spindle** *vi* **spin·dled; spin·dling** \'spin-dling, -ling, -dl-ing\ : to form a long slender stalk usually without flower or fruit

spin·dle–legged \,spin-dl-'leg-əd, -'legd\ *adj* : having long thin legs

spin·dle–shanked \,spin-dl-'shangt, -'shangkt\ *adj* : SPINDLE - LEGGED

spin·dling \'spin-dling, -ling, -dl-ing\ *adj* : SPINDLY ⟨*spindling* stems⟩

spin·dly \'spin-dlē, -lē, -dl-ē\ *adj* **spin·dli·er; -est** : excessively or abnormally long or tall and thin ⟨*spindly* legs⟩

spin·drift \'spin-,drift\ *n* : spray blown from waves [Scottish *speendrift,* from *speen* "to drive before a wind" + English *drift*]

spine \'spīn\ *n* **1 a** : SPINAL COLUMN **b** : something resembling a spinal column or constituting a central axis or chief support **c** : the back of a book usually lettered with the title and the author's and publisher's names **2** : a stiff pointed process; *esp* : one on a plant that is a modified leaf or leaf part [Latin *spina* "thorn, spinal column"] — **spined** \'spīnd\ *adj*

spi·nel \spə-'nel\ *n* **1** : a hard crystalline mineral consisting of an oxide of magnesium and aluminum that varies from colorless to ruby-red to black and is used as a gem **2** : any of a group of minerals that are essentially oxides of magnesium, ferrous iron, zinc, or manganese [Italian *spinella,* from *spina* "thorn", from Latin]

spine·less \'spīn-ləs\ *adj* **1** : free from spines, thorns, or prickles **2** : having no spinal column : INVERTEBRATE **3** : lacking courage or strength of character — **spine·less·ly** *adv* — **spine·less·ness** *n*

spin·et \'spin-ət\ *n* **1** : a small early harpsichord usually without legs **2 a** : a small upright piano **b** : a small electronic organ [Italian *spinetta*]

spin·na·ker \'spin-i-kər\ *n* : a large triangular sail set on a long light pole in front of the mast and used when reaching or when running before the wind [origin unknown]

¹spinnaker

spiny lobster

¹spire 3a

spin·ner \'spin-ər\ *n* **1** : one that spins **2** : a fishing lure that revolves when drawn through the water

spin·ner·et \,spin-ə-'ret\ *n* **1** : an organ especially of a spider or caterpillar for producing threads of silk from the secretion of silk glands **2** *or* **spin·ner·ette** : a small metal plate, thimble, or cap with fine holes through which a cellulose or chemical solution is forced in the spinning of man-made filaments (as rayon or nylon)

spin·ning \'spin-ing\ *n* : a method of fishing in which bait or a lure is cast by means of a light flexible rod, a spinning reel, and a light line

spinning frame *n* : a machine that draws, twists, and winds yarn

spinning jen·ny \'spin-ing-,jen-ē\ *n* : an early multiple-spindle machine for spinning wool or cotton [*Jenny,* nickname for *Jane*]

spinning reel *n* : a fishing reel with an open-faced nonrevolving spool on which line is wound by a moving arm which is locked out of the way during casting to permit the line to spiral off the reel freely

spinning wheel *n* : a small domestic hand-driven or foot-driven machine for spinning yarn or thread in which a wheel drives a single spindle

spin–off \'spin-,óf\ *n* : a secondary or derived product or effect : BY-PRODUCT ⟨household products that are *spin-offs* of missile research⟩

spi·nous \'spī-nəs\ *adj* : SPINY 1, 3

spin·ster \'spin-stər\ *n* **1** : a woman whose occupation is to spin **2** : an unmarried woman; *esp* : one who seems unlikely to marry — **spin·ster·hood** \-,hùd\ *n* — **spin·ster·ish** \-stə-rish, -strish\ *adj*

spin·thari·scope \spin-'thar-ə-,skōp\ *n* : an instrument consisting of a fluorescent screen and a magnifying

lens system for visual detection of alpha rays [Greek *spintharis* "spark"]

spin the bottle *n* : a kissing game in which a bottle is spun to point to the one to be kissed

spi·nule \'spī-nyül\ *n* : a tiny spine — **spi·nu·lose** \-nyə-,lōs\ *adj*

spiny \'spī-nē\ *adj* **spin·i·er; -est 1** : having spines, prickles, or thorns **2** : full of difficulties, obstacles, or annoyances : THORNY **3** : resembling a spine especially in slender pointed form — **spin·i·ness** *n*

spiny anteater *n* : ECHIDNA

spiny–finned \,spī-nē-'find\ *adj* : having fins with one or more stiff unbranched rays without transverse segmentation — compare SOFT-FINNED

spiny–head·ed worm \,spī-nē-,hed-əd-\ *n* : any of a small phylum (Acanthocephala) of unsegmented parasitic worms with a hooked proboscis used for attachment to the intestinal wall of the host

spiny lobster *n* : an edible crustacean distinguished from the related true lobster by the simple unenlarged first pair of legs and by the spiny carapace

spir·a·cle \'spir-i-kəl, 'spī-ri-\ *n* : a breathing orifice (as a blowhole of a whale or a tracheal opening of an insect) [Latin *spiraculum,* from *spirare* "to breathe"] — **spi·rac·u·lar** \spə-'rak-yə-lər, spī-\ *adj*

¹spi·ral \'spī-rəl\ *adj* **1** : winding around a center or pole and gradually receding from or approaching it **2** : HELICAL ⟨the *spiral* form of the thread of a screw⟩ **3** : of, relating to, or resembling a spiral ⟨a *spiral* staircase⟩ [Medieval Latin *spiralis,* from Latin *spira* "coil"] — **spi·ral·ly** \-rə-lē\ *adv*

²spiral *n* **1 a** : the path of a point in a plane moving around a central point while continuously moving away from or approaching it **b** : a three-dimensional curve (as a helix) turning about an axis **2** : a single turn or coil in a spiral object **3** : something having a spiral form **4** : a continuously spreading and accelerating increase or decrease ⟨a wage *spiral*⟩

³spiral *vb* **-raled** *or* **-ralled; -ral·ing** *or* **-ral·ling 1** : to move in a spiral course **2** : to form into a spiral

spiral galaxy *n* : a galaxy with a central nucleus from which extend concentrations of matter forming curved arms

spi·rant \'spī-rənt\ *n* : a consonant (as \f\, \s\, \sh\) uttered with friction of the breath against some part of the oral passage [Latin *spirans,* present participle of *spirare* "to breathe"] — **spirant** *adj*

¹spire \'spīr\ *n* **1** : a slender tapering blade or stalk (as of grass) **2** : a sharp pointed tip (as of a tree or antler) **3 a** : a pointed roof especially of a tower **b** : STEEPLE [Old English *spīr*]

²spire *vi* : to shoot up like a spire

³spire *n* : the upper part of a spiral mollusk shell [Latin *spira* "coil", from Greek *speira*]

⁴spire *vi* : to rise in or as if in a spiral

spi·rea *or* **spi·raea** \spī-'rē-ə\ *n* : any of a genus of shrubs of the rose family with small perfect white or pink flowers in dense clusters [Latin, a kind of plant, from Greek *speiraia*]

spired \'spīrd\ *adj* : having a spire ⟨a *spired* church⟩

spi·ril·lum \spī-'ril-əm\ *n, pl* **-ril·la** \-'ril-ə\ : any of a genus of long curved flagellate bacteria; *also* : any spiral filamentous bacterium (as a spirochete) [New Latin, from Latin *spira* "coil"]

¹spir·it \'spir-ət\ *n* **1** : a life-giving force; *esp* : a force within a person held to endow the body with life, energy, and power : SOUL **2 a** *cap* : HOLY SPIRIT **b** : a supernatural being : GHOST, DEVIL **c** : a supernatural being that enters into and controls a person **d** : a bodiless being inhabiting a place or thing **3** : MOOD, DISPOSITION ⟨in good *spirits*⟩ **4** : mental vigor or animation : VIVACITY **5** : real meaning or intention ⟨the *spirit* of the law⟩ **6** : an emotion, frame of mind, or inclination governing one's actions ⟨said in a *spirit* of fun⟩ ⟨school *spirit*⟩ **7** : PERSON ⟨a bold *spirit*⟩ **8 a** : a distilled alcoholic liquor — usually used in pl. **b** : an alcoholic solution of a volatile substance 〈*spirit* of camphor〉 — often used in pl. [Latin *spiritus,* literally, "breath"] SYN see SOUL

²**spirit** *vt* **1** : ANIMATE 2, ENCOURAGE **2** : to carry off or convey secretly or mysteriously

spir·it·ed \'spir-ət-əd\ *adj* : full of spirit, courage, or energy — **spir·it·ed·ly** *adv* — **spir·it·ed·ness** *n*

spirit gum *n* : a solution (as of gum arabic in ether) used especially for attaching false hair to the skin

spir·it·ism \'spir-ət-,iz-əm\ *n* : SPIRITUALISM 2a — **spir·it·ist** \-ət-əst\ *n* — **spir·it·is·tic** \,spir-ət-'is-tik\ *adj*

spir·it·less \'spir-ət-ləs\ *adj* : lacking animation, cheer, or courage — **spir·it·less·ly** *adv* — **spir·it·less·ness** *n*

spirit level *n* : a level using the position of a bubble in a small tube of liquid (as alcohol) as an indicator

spirits of turpentine *or* **spirit of turpentine** : TURPENTINE 2a

¹**spir·i·tu·al** \'spir-ich-wel, -ə-wəl, -ich-əl\ *adj* **1** : of, relating to, or consisting of spirit : not bodily or material **2 a** : RELIGIOUS, SACRED 〈*spiritual* songs〉 **b** : ecclesiastical rather than lay or temporal **3** : related or joined in spirit : having a spiritual rather than physical relationship **4 a** : of or relating to supernatural beings **b** : of, relating to, or involving spiritualism : SPIRITUALISTIC — **spir·i·tu·al·ly** \-ē\ *adv* — **spir·i·tu·al·ness** *n*

²**spiritual** *n* : a religious song originated by blacks especially of the southern United States

spir·i·tu·al·ism \'spir-ich-wə-,liz-əm, -liz-əm, -ə-wə-, -ich-ə-,liz-\ *n* **1** : the belief that spirit is the principal aspect of reality **2 a** : a belief that the spirits of the dead communicate with the living **b** *cap* : a movement comprising religious organizations emphasizing spiritualism — **spir·i·tu·al·ist** \-ləst\ *n, often cap* — **spir·i·tu·al·is·tic** \,spir-ich-wə-'lis-tik, -ə-wə-, -ich-ə-'lis-\ *adj*

spir·i·tu·al·i·ty \,spir-ich-ə-'wal-ət-ē\ *n* **1** : concern with religious rather than material values **2** : the quality or state of being spiritual

spir·i·tu·al·ize \'spir-ich-wə-,līz, -ə-wə-, -ich-ə-,līz\ *vt* **1** : to make spiritual especially by freeing from worldly influences **2** : to give a spiritual meaning to or understand in a spiritual sense — **spir·i·tu·al·iza·tion** \,spir-ich-wə-lə-'zā-shən, -ə-wə-, -ich-ə-lə-\ *n*

spir·i·tu·ous \'spir-ich-wəs, -ə-wəs, -ich-əs, 'spir-ət-əs\ *adj* : containing or being distilled alcohol 〈*spirituous* liquors〉 — **spir·i·tu·os·i·ty** \,spir-ich-ə-'wäs-ət-ē\ *n*

spi·ro·chete *or* **spi·ro·chaete** \'spī-rə-,kēt\ *n* : any of an order (Spirochaetales) of slender spirally undulating bacteria including those causing syphilis and relapsing fever [Latin *spira* "coil" (from Greek *speira*) + Greek *chaitē* "long hair"] — **spi·ro·che·tal** \,spī-rə-'kēt-l\ *adj*

spi·ro·gy·ra \,spī-rə-'jī-rə\ *n* : any of a genus of freshwater green algae with spiral chlorophyll bands [Greek *speira* "coil" + *gyros* "ring, circle"]

spi·rom·e·ter \spī-'räm-ət-ər\ *n* : an instrument for measuring the air entering and leaving the lungs [Latin *spirare* "to breathe"] — **spi·ro·met·ric** \,spī-rə-'me-trik\ *adj* — **spi·rom·e·try** \spī-'räm-ə-trē\ *n*

spiry \'spīr-ē\ *adj* : resembling a spire especially in slender tapering form; *also* : having spires

¹**spit** \'spit\ *n* **1** : a slender pointed rod for holding meat over a fire **2** : a small point of land especially of sand or gravel running into a body or water [Old English *spitu*]

²**spit** *vt* **spit·ted; spit·ting** : to put on or as if on a spit

³**spit** *vb* **spit** *or* **spat** \'spat\; **spit·ting** **1 a** : to eject saliva from the mouth : EXPECTORATE **b** : to express by or as if by spitting or make a spitting sound 〈the cat *spat* angrily〉 〈*spitting* a contemptuous reply〉 **2 a** : to give off usually briskly or vigorously : EMIT 〈the fire *spat* sparks〉 **b** : to rain or snow in flurries [Old English *spittan*] — **spit·ter** *n*

⁴**spit** *n* **1 a** : SALIVA **b** : the act of spitting **2** : a frothy secretion produced by spittlebugs **3** : perfect likeness

spit and polish *n* : extreme attention to smartness of appearance especially at the expense of operational efficiency [from the practice of polishing objects such as shoes by moistening them and then rubbing them with a cloth]

spit·ball \'spit-,bȯl\ *n* **1** : paper chewed and rolled into a ball to be used as a missile **2** : a baseball pitch delivered after the ball has been moistened (as with saliva or sweat) so that it moves erratically

spit curl *n* : a small spiral curl that is usually pressed flat against the forehead, temple, or cheek

¹**spite** \'spīt\ *n* : petty ill will or malice with a desire to irritate, annoy, or thwart [Middle English, short for *despite*] — **in spite of** : in defiance or contempt of : NOTWITHSTANDING

²**spite** *vt* **1** : to treat maliciously (as by shaming or thwarting) **2** : ANNOY, OFFEND 〈did it to *spite* me〉

spite·ful \'spīt-fəl\ *adj* : filled with or showing spite : MALICIOUS — **spite·ful·ly** \-fə-lē\ *adv* — **spite·ful·ness** *n*

spit·fire \'spit-,fīr\ *n* : a quick-tempered person

spit·ting image \,spit-n-, ,spit-ing-\ *n* : perfect likeness

spit·tle \'spit-l\ *n* **1** : SALIVA **2** : ⁴SPIT 2 [Old English *spǣtl*]

spit·tle·bug \-,bəg\ *n* : any of numerous leaping insects that are related to the cicadas and aphids and have larvae which secrete froth

spittle insect *n* : SPITTLEBUG

spit·toon \spi-'tün\ *n* : a receptacle for spit — called also *cuspidor* [⁴*spit* + *-oon* (as in *balloon*)]

spitz \'spits\ *n* : any of several stocky heavy-coated dogs of northern origin with erect ears and a heavily furred tail tightly curled over the back [German, from *spitz* "pointed"]

splanch·nic \'splangk-nik\ *adj* : of or relating to the viscera : VISCERAL [Greek *splanchnikos,* from *splanchna* "viscera"]

¹**splash** \'splash\ *vb* **1 a** : to strike or move through a liquid or semifluid substance and cause it to spatter 〈*splash* water〉 〈*splash* through mud〉 **b** : to wet or soil by dashing a liquid on : SPATTER 〈*splashed* by a passing car〉; *also* : to cause to soil something by splashing 〈*splashed* ink on the paper〉 **2** : to make a splashing sound (as in falling or moving) 〈a brook *splashing* over rocks〉 **3 a** : to spread or scatter like a splashed liquid 〈a painting *splashed* with color〉 〈sunbeams *splashed* through the curtain〉 **b** : to display prominently 〈a scandal *splashed* all over the newspaper〉 [alteration of *plash*] — **splash·er** *n*

²**splash** *n* **1** : splashed material; *also* : a spot or daub from or as if from splashed liquid **2** : the sound or action of splashing **3** : a vivid impression created especially by showy activity or appearance; *also* : a showy display — **splash·i·ly** \'splash-ə-lē\ *adv* — **splash·i·ness** \'splash-ē-nəs\ *n* — **splashy** \'splash-ē\ *adj*

splash·down \'splash-,daún\ *n* : the controlled landing of a spacecraft in the ocean — **splash down** \splash-'daún, 'splash-\ *vi*

splash guard *n* : a flap suspended behind a rear wheel to prevent tire splash from muddying windshields of following vehicles

¹**splat** \'splat\ *n* : a single flat thin usually vertical member of a back of a chair [obsolete *splat* "to spread flat", from Middle English *splatten*]

²**splat** *n* : a splattering or splashing sound [imitative]

splat·ter \'splat-ər\ *vb* : SPATTER 1, 2, 4 [probably blend of *splash* and *spatter*] — **splatter** *n*

¹**splay** \'splā\ *vb* **1** : to spread out **2** : to make or become slanting [Middle English *splayen,* short for *displayen* "to display"]

²**splay** *n* **1** : a slope or bevel especially of the sides of a door or window **2** : degree of outward slope

³**splay** *adj* **1** : turned outward **2** : AWKWARD 2a, UNGAINLY

\ə\	abut	\ng\	sing
\ər\	further	\ō\	bone
\a\	mat	\ȯ\	saw
\ā\	take	\ȯi\	coin
\ä\	cot, cart	\th\	thin
\aú\	out	\th\	this
\ch\	chin	\ü\	food
\e\	pet	\ú\	foot
\ē\	easy	\y\	yet
\g\	go	\yü\	few
\i\	tip	\yú\	cure
\ī\	life	\zh\	vision
\j\	job		

splay·foot \'splā-,fût, -'fût\ *n* : a foot abnormally flattened and spread out : FLATFOOT — **splayfoot** *or* **splay·foot·ed** \-'fût-əd\ *adj*

spleen \'splēn\ *n* **1** : a very vascular ductless organ near the stomach or intestine of most vertebrates concerned with final destruction of blood cells, storage of blood, and production of lymphocytes **2** : ANGER, MALICE [Latin *splen,* from Greek *splēn*]

spleen·ful \-fəl\ *adj* : SPLENETIC

spleen·wort \-,wərt, -,wórt\ *n* : any of a genus of ferns having linear or oblong clusters of spores borne obliquely on the upper side of the frond [from the belief in its power to cure disorders of the spleen]

spleeny \'splē-nē\ *adj* : full of or displaying spleen

splen·dent \'splen-dənt\ *adj* **1** : SHINING 1, LUSTROUS **2** : ILLUSTRIOUS, BRILLIANT [Late Latin *splendens,* from Latin *splendēre* "to shine"]

splen·did \'splen-dəd\ *adj* **1** : possessing or displaying splendor: as **a** : brilliantly shining : RADIANT **b** : SHOWY 1, MAGNIFICENT **2** : ILLUSTRIOUS, GRAND **3** : PRAISEWORTHY, EXCELLENT [Latin *splendidus,* from *splendēre* "to shine"] — **splen·did·ly** *adv* — **splen·did·ness** *n* □ SYN SPLENDID, GLORIOUS, GORGEOUS mean extraordinarily impressive. SPLENDID implies outshining the usual in brilliance or excellence; GLORIOUS suggests beauty and distinction heightened by radiance; GORGEOUS implies a rich splendor especially in display of color.

splen·dif·er·ous \splen-'dif-rəs, -ə-rəs\ *adj* **1** : SPLENDID 1, MAGNIFICENT **2** : deceptively splendid [*splendor* + *-i- + -ferous*] — **splen·dif·er·ous·ly** *adv* — **splen·dif·er·ous·ness** *n*

splen·dor \'splen-dər\ *n* **1 a** : great brightness or luster : BRILLIANCY ⟨the *splendor* of the sun⟩ **b** : sumptuous display : MAGNIFICENCE, POMP ⟨an affair of great *splendor*⟩ **2** : something splendid or contributing to splendor ⟨surrounded by *splendors* and luxuries⟩ [Anglo-French *splendur,* from Latin *splendor,* from *splendēre* "to shine"] — **splen·dor·ous** *also* **splen·drous** \-də-rəs, -drəs\ *adj*

sple·net·ic \spli-'net-ik\ *adj* : marked by bad temper, hatred, or spite [Late Latin *spleneticus,* from Latin *splen* "spleen"] — **sple·net·i·cal·ly** \spli-'net-i-kə-lē, -klē\ *adv*

splen·ic \'splen-ik\ *adj* : of, relating to, or located in the spleen

¹splice \'splīs\ *vt* **1** : to unite (as two ropes) by weaving the strands together **2** : to unite (as rails or timbers) by lapping the ends together and making them fast [obsolete Dutch *splissen*] — **splic·er** *n*

²splice *n* : a joining or joint made by splicing

²splice

spline \'splīn\ *n* **1** : a thin wood or metal strip used in building construction **2** : a key that is fixed to one of two connected mechanical parts and fits into a keyway in the other; *also* : a keyway for such a key [origin unknown]

¹splint \'splint\ *n* **1 a** : a thin strip of wood interwoven with others incaning **b** : SPLINTER 1 **c** : material or a device used to protect and immobilize a body part (as a broken arm) **2** : a bony enlargement on the cannon bone of a horse [Low German *splinte, splente*]

²splint *vt* : to support and immobilize with or as if with a splint or splints

splint bone *n* : one of the slender rudimentary bones on each side of the cannon bone in the limb of a horse

¹splin·ter \'splint-ər\ *n* **1 a** : a thin piece split or torn off lengthwise : SLIVER **b** : a small jagged particle **2** : a group or faction broken away from a parent body [Dutch] — **splinter** *adj* — **splin·tery** \'splint-ə-rē\ *adj*

²splinter *vb* : to divide or break into splinters

¹split \'split\ *vb* **split; split·ting 1 a** : to divide lengthwise usually along a grain or seam or by layers : CLEAVE ⟨wood that *splits* easily⟩ ⟨*split* slate into shingles⟩ **b** : to separate the parts of by interposing something ⟨*split* an infinitive⟩ ⟨the river *splits* the town⟩ **2 a** : to tear or break apart : BURST ⟨the pants *split* at the seams⟩ **b** : to subject (an atom or atomic nucleus) to artificial disintegration especially by fission **c** : to affect as if by breaking up or tearing apart : SHATTER **3** : to divide into parts or portions: as **a** : to divide between individuals : SHARE ⟨the winning team *split* the prize⟩ **b** : to divide into factions, parties, or groups **c** : to mark (a ballot) or cast (a vote) for candidates of different parties **d** : to break down (a chemical compound) into constituents ⟨*split* a fat into glycerol and fatty acids⟩; *also* : to remove by such separation ⟨*split* off carbon dioxide⟩ **e** : to divide (stock) by issuing a larger number of shares to existing shareholders usually without increase in total face value **4** : LEAVE ⟨they *split* town⟩ **5** *British* : INFORM 2, TELL — usually used with *on* [Dutch *splitten*] — **split·ter** *n* — **split hairs** : to make trivial distinctions

²split *n* **1** : a product or result of splitting: as **a** : a narrow break made by or as if by splitting : CRACK **b** : a part split off or made thin by splitting **c** : a group or faction formed by splitting **d** : a situation in bowling in which two or more pins are left standing after a delivery with one or more pins missing between them **2** : the act or process of splitting : DIVISION ⟨a stock *split*⟩; *esp* : a dividing into divergent or antagonistic elements **3** : the feat of lowering oneself to the floor or leaping into the air with the legs extended in a straight line and in opposite directions

³split *adj* : divided by or as if by splitting ⟨a *split* lip⟩ ⟨*split* families⟩; *also* : prepared for use by splitting ⟨*split* hides⟩

split decision *n* : a decision in a boxing match reflecting a division of opinion among the referee and judges

split end *n* : an offensive end in football who lines up several yards wide of the formation

split infinitive *n* : an infinitive with *to* having a modifier between the *to* and the verbal (as in "to really start")

split–lev·el \'split-'lev-əl\ *adj* : divided vertically so that the floor level of rooms in one part is about midway between the levels of two successive stories in an adjoining part ⟨*split-level* houses⟩ — **split–lev·el** \-,lev-əl\ *n*

split personality *n* : a personality structure composed of two or more groups of behavior tendencies and attitudes each expressed independently

split rail *n* : a fence rail split from a log

split second *n* : a very brief period : FLASH, INSTANT ⟨happened in a *split second*⟩

split shift *n* : a shift of working hours divided into two or more working periods (as morning and evening)

split ticket *n* : a ballot cast by a voter who votes for candidates of more than one party

split·ting \'split-ing\ *adj* : very severe ⟨a *splitting* headache⟩

splotch \'spläch\ *n* : BLOTCH 2, SPOT [perhaps blend of *spot* and *blotch*] — **splotch** *vt* — **splotchy** \'spläch-ē\ *adj*

¹splurge \'splərj\ *n* **1** : a showy display **2** : liberal indulgence [perhaps blend of *splash* and *surge*]

splurge *vb* **1** : to make a showy display **2** : to indulge oneself or spend lavishly

¹splut·ter \'splət-ər\ *n* **1** : a confused noise (as of hasty speaking) **2** : a splashing or sputtering sound [probably alteration of *sputter*] — **splut·tery** \'splət-ə-rē\ *adj*

²splutter *vb* **1** : to make a noise as if spitting **2** : to speak or utter hastily and confusedly — **splut·ter·er** \'splət-ər-ər\ *n*

¹spoil \'spóil\ *n* **1 a** : plunder taken from an enemy in war or a victim in robbery : LOOT **b** : something won usually by effort or skill : PREY — usually used in pl. ⟨the *spoils* of the chase⟩ **2** : earth and rock excavated or dredged **3** : an object damaged or flawed in the making [Middle French *espoille,* from Latin *spolia,* pl. of *spolium*]

²spoil *vb* **spoiled** \'spȯild, 'spȯilt\ *or* **spoilt** \'spȯilt\; **spoil·ing** **1** : PLUNDER, ROB **2 a** : to damage seriously : RUIN ⟨a crop *spoiled* by floods⟩ **b** : to impair the quality or effect of ⟨a quarrel *spoiled* the celebration⟩ **c** : to decay or lose freshness, value, or usefulness usually through being kept too long **3** : to damage the character or disposition of by pampering **4** : to have an eager desire ⟨*spoiling* for a fight⟩ SYN see DECAY — **spoil·able** \'spȯi-lə-bəl\ *adj* — **spoil·er** *n*

spoil·age \'spȯi-lij\ *n* **1** : the act or process of spoiling **2** : something spoiled or wasted **3** : loss by spoilage

spoils·man \'spȯilz-mən\ *n* : one who serves a political party in expectation of receiving a public office

spoil·sport \'spȯil-,spōrt, -,spȯrt\ *n* : one who spoils the sport or pleasure of others

spoils system *n* : the practice of distributing public offices and their privileges as plunder to members of the victorious political party

¹spoke \'spōk\ *past & archaic past participle of* SPEAK

²spoke *n* : one of the bars radiating from the hub of a wheel to support the rim [Old English *spāca*]

spo·ken \'spō-kən\ *adj* **1 a** : expressed in speech rather than writing : ORAL ⟨a *spoken* message⟩ **b** : used in speaking ⟨*spoken* English⟩ **2** : speaking in (such) a manner — used in combination ⟨soft-*spoken*⟩ ⟨plain*spoken*⟩ [past participle of *speak*]

spoke·shave \'spōk-,shāv\ *n* : a two-handled tool that is used for planing curved pieces of wood [²*spoke*]

spokes·man \'spōk-smən\ *n* : a man who is a spokesperson [probably from ¹*spoke*]

spokes·per·son \'spōk-,spərs-n\ *n, pl* **spokespersons** *or* **spokes·peo·ple** \-,spē-pəl\ : a person who speaks as a representative of another person or of a group

spokes·wom·an \'spōk-,swu̇m-ən\ *n* : a woman who is a spokesperson

spo·li·a·tion \,spō-lē-'ā-shən\ *n* : the act of plundering : the state of being plundered especially in war [Latin *spoliatio*, from *spoliare* "to plunder", from *spolium* "spoil"]

spon·dee \'spän-,dē\ *n* : a metrical foot consisting of two accented syllables (as in *tom-tom*) [Middle French, from Latin *spondeum* "foot of 2 long syllables", from Greek *spondeios*, from *spondē* "libation"; from its use in music accompanying libations] — **spon·da·ic** \spän-'dā-ik\ *adj*

¹sponge \'spənj\ *n* **1 a** : an elastic porous mass of fibers that forms the internal skeleton of various marine animals (phylum Porifera) and is able when wetted to absorb water; *also* : a piece of this material or of a porous rubber or cellulose product of similar properties used especially for cleaning **b** : any of a phylum (Porifera) of lowly aquatic animals that are essentially double-walled cell colonies and permanently attached as adults **2** : a pad (as of folded gauze) used in surgery and medicine (as to remove discharges or apply medication) **3** : one who lives upon others **4 a** : raised dough **b** : a whipped dessert usually containing whites of eggs or gelatin **c** : a metal (as platinum) obtained in porous form usually by reduction without fusion [Old English, from Latin *spongia*, from Greek]

²sponge *vb* **1 a** : to cleanse, wipe, or moisten with or as if with a sponge **b** : to erase or destroy with or as if with a sponge **2** : to absorb with or as if with or like a sponge **3** : to get something from or live on another by imposing on hospitality or good nature **4** : to dive or dredge for sponges — **spong·er** *n*

sponge cake *n* : a cake made without shortening

sponge rubber *n* : cellular rubber resembling a natural sponge in structure used especially for cushions and in weather-stripping

spon·gin \'spən-jən\ *n* : a fibrous protein that is the chief constituent of the flexible fibers in sponge skeletons [German, from Latin *spongia* "sponge"]

spongy \'spən-jē\ *adj* **spong·i·er; -est 1** : resembling a sponge in appearance or absorbency **2** : soft and full of holes or moisture : not firm or solid — **spong·i·ness** *n*

spongy parenchyma *n* : a spongy layer of irregular chlorophyll-bearing cells interspersed with air spaces that fills the part of a leaf between the palisade layer and the lower epidermis — called also *spongy layer, spongy tissue*

spon·son \'spän-sən\ *n* **1** : a projection (as a gun platform) from the side of a ship or a tank **2** : an air chamber along a canoe or seaplane to increase stability and buoyancy on water [probably from *expansion*]

¹spon·sor \'spän-sər\ *n* **1** : a person who takes the responsibility for some other person or thing ⟨agreed to be their *sponsor* at the club⟩ **2** : GODPARENT **3** : a person or an organization that pays for or plans and carries out a project or activity; *esp* : one that pays the cost of a radio or television program usually in return for limited advertising time [Latin, "guarantor, surety", from *spondēre* "to promise"] — **spon·sor·ship** \'spän-sər-,ship\ *n*

²sponsor *vt* **spon·sored; spon·sor·ing** \'späns-ring, -ə-ring\ : to be or act as sponsor for

spon·ta·ne·ity \,spänt-ən-'ē-ət-ē, ,spänt-n-, -'ā-ət-\ *n* **1** : the quality or state of being spontaneous **2** : spontaneous action or movement

spon·ta·ne·ous \spän-'tā-nē-əs\ *adj* **1** : done, said, or produced freely and naturally ⟨*spontaneous* laughter⟩ **2** : acting or taking place without apparent external cause or influence ⟨*spontaneous* rebellion⟩ ⟨*spontaneous* recovery from illness⟩ [Late Latin *spontaneus*, from Latin *sponte* "of one's free will"] — **spon·ta·ne·ous·ly** *adv* — **spon·ta·ne·ous·ness** *n* □ SYN SPONTANEOUS, IMPULSIVE, INSTINCTIVE, AUTOMATIC mean acting or activated without deliberation. SPONTANEOUS implies lack of prompting and connotes genuineness ⟨*spontaneous* applause⟩ IMPULSIVE implies acting under immediate stress of emotion or spirit of the moment ⟨an *impulsive* act of generosity⟩ INSTINCTIVE stresses spontaneous action involving neither judgment nor conscious intention ⟨*instinctive* shrinking from snakes⟩ AUTOMATIC implies action engaging neither the mind nor the emotions and connotes a predictable response ⟨a soldier's *automatic* obedience to commands⟩

spontaneous combustion *n* : a bursting into flame of combustible material through heat produced within itself by chemical action (as oxidation)

spontaneous generation *n* : spontaneous origin of organisms directly from lifeless matter — called also *abiogenesis*

¹spoof \'spüf\ *vt* **1** : to deceive by a hoax **2** : to make good-natured fun of ⟨a skit *spoofing* big business⟩ [*Spoof*, a hoaxing game invented by Arthur Roberts, died 1933, English comedian]

²spoof *n* **1** : HOAX, DECEPTION **2** : a light good-natured parody

¹spook \'spük\ *n* : GHOST 2 [Dutch] — **spook·ish** \'spü-kish\ *adj*

²spook *vb* : to make or become frightened or frantic

spooky \'spü-kē\ *adj* **spook·i·er; -est 1** : relating to, resembling, or suggesting spooks ⟨a *spooky* movie⟩ **2** : NERVOUS, SKITTISH ⟨a *spooky* horse⟩ — **spook·i·ness** *n*

spool \'spül\ *n* **1** : a cylinder which has a rim at each end and usually a hollow center and on which material (as thread or tape) is wound **2** : material wound on a spool [Middle French *espole*, from Dutch *spoele*] — **spool** *vb*

¹spoon \'spün\ *n* **1** : an implement that consists of a small shallow bowl with a handle and is used especially in eating and cooking **2** : something that resembles a spoon in shape [Old English *spōn* "splinter, chip"]

²spoon *vb* **1** : to take up and usually transfer in or as if in a spoon **2** : to make love with kissing and caressing [sense 2 probably from the Welsh custom of an engaged man's presenting his fiancée with an elaborately carved wooden spoon]

'sponge 1b

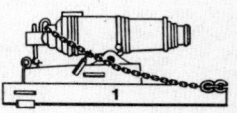

' sponson '

\ə\ abut		\ng\ sing	
\ər\ further		\ō\ bone	
\a\ mat		\o̧\ saw	
\ā\ take		\o̧i\ coin	
\ä\ cot, cart		\th\ thin	
\au̇\ out		\th\ this	
\ch\ chin		\ü\ food	
\e\ pet		\u̇\ foot	
\ē\ easy		\y\ yet	
\g\ go		\yü\ few	
\i\ tip		\yu̇\ cure	
\ī\ life		\zh\ vision	
\j\ job			

spoonbill 1

spoon·bill \'spün-ˌbil\ *n* **1** : any of several wading birds related to the ibises that have the bill broad and flat at the tip **2** : any of several broad-billed ducks

spoon bread *n* : soft bread made of cornmeal mixed with milk, eggs, shortening, and leavening and served with a spoon

spoo·ner·ism \'spü-nə-ˌriz-əm\ *n* : a transposition of usually initial sounds of two or more words (as in tons of soil for sons of toil) [William A. *Spooner,* died 1930, English clergyman and educator]

spoon–feed \'spün-ˌfēd\ *vt* **-fed** \-ˌfed\; **-feed·ing** **1** : to feed by means of a spoon **2** : to present information to in so complete a manner as to prevent independent thought

spoon·ful \'spün-ˌfül\ *n, pl* **spoonfuls** \-ˌfülz\ *also* **spoons·ful** \'spünz-ˌfül\ : as much as a spoon can hold; *esp* : TEASPOONFUL

¹spoor \'spür, 'spōr, 'spȯr\ *n* : a track or trail especially of a wild animal [Afrikaans]

²spoor *vb* : to track something by a spoor

spor- *or* **sporo-** *combining form* : seed : spore ⟨*sporo*cyst⟩ [New Latin *spora*]

spo·rad·ic \spə-'rad-ik\ *adj* : occurring occasionally, singly, or in scattered instances ⟨*sporadic* outbreaks of disease⟩ [Medieval Latin *sporadicus,* from Greek *sporadikos,* from *sporadēn* "here and there", from *sporas* "scattered"] SYN see INFREQUENT — **spo·rad·i·cal·ly** \-'rad-i-kə-lē, -klē\ *adv*

spo·ran·gi·o·phore \spə-'ran-jē-ə-ˌfōr, -ˌfȯr\ *n* : a stalk (as a fungal hypha) that bears sporangia

spo·ran·gi·um \spə-'ran-jē-əm\ *n, pl* **-gia** \-jē-ə\ : a sac or case within which usually asexual spores are produced [New Latin, from *spor-* + Greek *angeion* "vessel"] — **spo·ran·gial** \-jē-əl, -jəl\ *adj*

¹spore \'spōr, 'spȯr\ *n* : a primitive usually one-celled body produced by plants and some lower animals and capable of developing either directly or after fusion with another spore into a new individual in some cases unlike the parent [New Latin *spora* "seed, spore", from Greek, "act of sowing, seed", from *speirein* "to sow"] — **spored** \'spōrd, 'spȯrd\ *adj*

²spore *vi* : to produce spores or reproduce by spores

spore case *n* : SPORANGIUM

spore mother cell *n* : a cell whose final divisions produce spores usually in groups of four

spo·ro·cyst \'spōr-ə-ˌsist, 'spȯr-\ *n* **1** : a resting cell (as in a slime mold) that may give rise to asexual spores **2** : a sac that is the first asexual reproductive form of some trematode worms and buds off cells from its inner surface — **spo·ro·cys·tic** \ˌspōr-ə-'sis-tik, ˌspȯr-\ *adj*

spo·ro·cyte \'spōr-ə-ˌsīt, 'spȯr-\ *n* : SPORE MOTHER CELL

spo·rog·e·nous \spə-'räj-ə-nəs\ *adj* **1** : producing or adapted to the production of spores ⟨*sporogenous* hyphae⟩ **2** : reproducing by spores

spo·ro·phore \'spōr-ə-ˌfōr, 'spȯr-ə-ˌfȯr\ *n* : the part or organ of a sporophyte that actually produces spores

spo·ro·phyll \'spōr-ə-ˌfil, 'spȯr-\ *n* : a spore-bearing and usually greatly modified leaf (as a stamen or carpel)

spo·ro·phyte \-ˌfīt\ *n* : the individual or generation of a plant having alternating sexual and asexual generations that bears asexual spores — compare GAMETOPHYTE — **spo·ro·phyt·ic** \ˌspōr-ə-'fit-ik, ˌspȯr-\ *adj*

spo·ro·zo·an \ˌspōr-ə-'zō-ən, ˌspȯr-\ *n* : any of a large class (Sporozoa) of strictly parasitic protozoans that have a complicated life cycle usually involving both asexual and sexual generations often in different hosts and that include important pathogens (as the malaria parasites) [derived from *spor-* + Greek *zōion* "animal"] — **sporozoan** *adj*

spo·ro·zo·ite \-'zō-ˌīt\ *n* : a usually motile infective form of some sporozoans that is formed by division of a zygote and initiates an asexual cycle in the new host

spor·ran \'spȯr-ən, 'spär-\ *n* : a pouch of skin with the hair or fur on that is worn in front of the kilt by Highlanders in full dress [Scottish Gaelic *sporan*]

1 sporran

¹sport \'spōrt, 'spȯrt\ *vb* **1 a** : to amuse oneself : FROLIC **b** : to engage in a sport **2** : to speak or act in jest or mockingly : TRIFLE **3** : to display or wear proudly : show off ⟨*sport* a new hat⟩ **4** : to deviate or vary abruptly from type : MUTATE [Middle English *sporten,* short for *disporten* "to disport"]

²sport *n* **1 a** : a source of diversion : RECREATION **b** : physical activity engaged in for pleasure; *esp* : a particular activity (as hunting or an athletic game) so engaged in **2 a** : PLEASANTRY 2, JEST **b** : MOCKERY 1, DERISION **3 a** : something tossed or driven about in or as if in play ⟨the battered boat became the *sport* of wind and waves⟩ **b** : LAUGHINGSTOCK, BUTT **4 a** : a person who engages in sport **b** : one who lives up to the ideals of sportsmanship **5** : a usually conspicuous mutant individual

³sport *or* **sports** \'spōrts, 'spȯrts\ *adj* : relating to, suitable for, or sought for sport ⟨*sport* fish⟩

sport·ing \'spōrt-ing, 'spȯrt-\ *adj* **1 a** : used or suitable for sport; *esp* : bred or trained for use in hunting ⟨a *sporting* dog⟩ **b** : marked by or calling for sportsmanship **c** : involving such risk as a sports contender may expect to take or encounter ⟨a *sporting* chance⟩ **2** : of or relating to dissipation (as gambling)

sport·ive \'spōrt-iv, 'spȯrt-\ *adj* : engaging in sport : FROLICSOME — **sport·ive·ly** *adv* — **sport·ive·ness** *n*

sports car *also* **sport car** *n* : a low usually two-seat open automobile that is especially fast and maneuverable

sports·cast \'spōrt-ˌskast, 'spȯrt-\ *n* : a broadcast dealing with sports events [*sport* + broad*cast*] — **sports·cast·er** *n*

sport shirt *n* : a shirt for casual wear with open neck

sports·man \'spōrt-smən, 'spȯrt-\ *n* **1** : a person who engages in or is interested in sports and especially outdoor sports **2** : a person who is fair and generous and a good loser and a graceful winner — **sports·man·like** \-ˌlīk\ *adj* — **sports·man·ly** \-lē\ *adj*

sports·man·ship \-smən-ˌship\ *n* **1** : skill in or devotion to sports **2** : conduct befitting a good sportsman

sports·wear \-ˌswaər, -ˌsweər\ *n* : clothes suitable for casual wear especially while engaging in or watching sports

sports·wom·an \'spōrt-ˌswüm-ən, 'spȯrt-\ *n* : a woman who engages in sports and especially in outdoor sports

sports·writ·er \'spōrts-ˌrīt-ər, 'spȯrts-\ *n* : one who writes about sports especially for a newspaper

sporty \'spōrt-ē, 'spȯrt-\ *adj* **sport·i·er; -est** **1** : characteristic of a sportsman **2 a** : notably gay or dissipated : FAST ⟨a *sporty* crowd⟩ **b** : FLASHY, SHOWY ⟨*sporty* new clothes⟩ **3** : SPORT ⟨a *sporty* boat⟩ — **sport·i·ly** \'spōrt-l-ē, 'spȯrt-\ *adv* — **sport·i·ness** \'spōrt-ē-nəs, 'spȯrt-\ *n*

spor·u·la·tion \ˌspōr-yə-'lā-shən, ˌspȯr-\ *n* : formation of or division into spores [New Latin *sporula* "small spore", from *spora* "spore"] — **spor·u·late** \'spōr-yə-ˌlāt, 'spȯr-\ *vi* — **spor·u·la·tive** \-ˌlāt-iv\ *adj*

¹spot \'spät\ *n* **1** : a blemish or stain on character or reputation : FAULT **2 a** : a small area visibly different (as in color, finish, or material) from the surrounding area **b** : an area marred or marked (as by dirt); *also* : a circumscribed surface lesion of disease (as measles) **3 a** : a small quantity or amount **b** : a small or particular place or extent of space ⟨a good *spot* for a picnic⟩ **4 a** : a particular position (as in an organization or on a program) ⟨have a *spot* open in sales⟩ **b** : a position usually of difficulty or embarrassment : FIX [Middle English] — **on the spot** **1** : at once : IMMEDIATELY **2** : at the place of action ⟨make an investigation *on the spot*⟩ **3** : in difficulty or danger

²spot *vb* **spot·ted; spot·ting** **1** : to mark or become marked with or as if with spots : STAIN, BLEMISH ⟨a *spotted* reputation⟩ ⟨white *spots* so easily⟩ **2** : to single out : IDENTIFY, DETECT ⟨*spot* a friend⟩ ⟨*spot* an opportunity⟩; *also* : to locate precisely ⟨*spot* an enemy's position) **3 a** : to lie or occur at intervals in or on ⟨slopes *spotted* with plowed fields⟩ **b** : to place at intervals or in a desired spot ⟨*spot* a picture on the wall⟩ **4** : to remove spots from **5** : to allow a handicap or advantage ⟨was *spotted* 5 points⟩ — **spot·ta·ble** \'spät-ə-bəl\ *adj*

³**spot** *adj* **1** : being, originating, or done on the spot or in or for a particular spot ⟨*spot* coverage of the news⟩ **2 a** : paid out upon delivery ⟨*spot* cash⟩ **b** : broadcast between scheduled programs ⟨*spot* announcements⟩ **3** : made at random or restricted to a few places or instances ⟨a *spot* check⟩

spot–check \'spät-,chek\ *vb* : to sample or investigate quickly or at random : make a spot check

spot·less \'spät-ləs\ *adj* : free from spot or blemish : perfectly clean or pure — **spot·less·ly** *adv* — **spot·less·ness** *n*

¹**spot·light** \'spät-,līt\ *n* **1 a** : a projected spot of light used to illuminate something (as a person on a stage) brilliantly **b** : conspicuous public notice **2** : a light designed to direct a narrow intense beam of light on a small area

²**spotlight** *vt* : to illuminate with or as if with a spotlight

spot·ted \'spät-əd\ *adj* **1 a** : marked with spots **b** : being sullied : TARNISHED **2** : accompanied by an eruption ⟨a *spotted* fever⟩ **3** : SPOTTY

spotted owl *n* : a rare large dark brown dark-eyed owl that has barred and spotted underparts and is found from British Columbia to Southern California and central Mexico

spotted turtle *n* : a small American freshwater turtle that has a blackish shell covered with round yellow spots

spot·ter \'spät-ər\ *n* **1** : one that makes, applies, or removes spots **2** : one that keeps watch : OBSERVER; *esp* : a civilian who watches for approaching enemy airplanes

spot·ty \'spät-ē\ *adj* **spot·ti·er; -est 1** : SPOTTED 1a **2** : lacking uniformity ⟨did a *spotty* job of cleaning up⟩ — **spot·ti·ly** \'spät-l-ē\ *adv* — **spot·ti·ness** \'spät-ē-nəs\ *n*

spou·sal \'spaů-zəl, -səl\ *n* : MARRIAGE 2, WEDDING — usually used in pl. — **spousal** *adj*

spouse \'spaůs *also* 'spaůz\ *n* : a married person [Old French *espous,* from Latin *sponsus* "betrothed, newly married", from *spondēre* "to promise, betroth"]

¹**spout** \'spaůt\ *vb* **1** : to eject (as liquid) in a stream or jet ⟨wells *spouting* oil⟩ **2** : to speak or utter readily, volubly, and at length **3** : to issue with force or in a jet : SPURT ⟨blood *spouted* from the wound⟩ [Middle English *spouten*] — **spout·er** *n*

²**spout** *n* **1** : a tube, pipe, or hole through which something (as rainwater) spouts **2** : a jet of liquid; *esp* : WATERSPOUT

¹**sprain** \'sprān\ *n* **1** : a sudden or violent twist or wrench of a joint with stretching or tearing of ligaments **2** : a sprained condition [origin unknown] SYN see STRAIN

²**sprain** *vt* : to injure by a sudden or severe twist

sprat \'sprat\ *n* : a small European herring closely related to the common herring; *also* : a small or young herring or similar fish (as an anchovy) [Old English *sprott*]

sprawl \'spról\ *vb* **1** : to creep or clamber awkwardly **2** : to lie or sit with arms and legs spread out **3** : to spread or cause to spread out irregularly or awkwardly ⟨a factory *sprawling* over a vast area⟩ [Old English *sprēawlian* "to thrash about"] — **sprawl** *n*

¹**spray** \'sprā\ *n* **1** : a usually flowering branch or shoot **2** : a decorative flat arrangement of flowers and foliage **3** : something (as an ornament) resembling a spray [Middle English]

²**spray** *n* **1** : water flying in small drops or particles (as when blown from waves or thrown up by a waterfall)

2 a : a jet of vapor or finely divided liquid (as from an atomizer) **b** : a device (as an atomizer or sprayer) by which a spray is dispersed or applied [obsolete *spray* "to sprinkle", from Dutch *sprayen*]

³**spray** *vb* **1** : to disperse or apply in a spray **2** : to project spray on or into — **spray·er** *n*

spray gun *n* : a device for spraying paints or insecticides

¹**spread** \'spred\ *vb* **spread; spread·ing 1 a** : to open or expand over a larger area ⟨*spread* out a map⟩ **b** : to stretch out or apart : EXTEND ⟨*spread* your arms wide⟩ **2 a** : SCATTER, STREW ⟨*spread* fertilizer⟩ **b** : to distribute over a period or among a group ⟨*spread* the work to be done⟩ **c** : to apply on a surface ⟨*spread* butter on bread⟩ **d** : COVER, OVERLAY ⟨*spread* a floor with carpet⟩ **e** (1) : to prepare or furnish for dining : SET ⟨*spread* a table⟩ (2) : SERVE ⟨*spread* a banquet⟩ **3 a** : to become or cause to become widely known ⟨the news *spread* rapidly⟩ **b** : to extend the range or incidence of ⟨*spread* a disease⟩ [Old English *sprǣdan*] — **spread·er** *n*

²**spread** *n* **1 a** : the act or process of spreading **b** : extent of spreading ⟨the *spread* of a bird's wings⟩ **2** : something spread out: as **a** : EXPANSE **b** *West* : RANCH 1 **c** : a prominent display in a periodical **3** : something spread on or over a surface: as **a** : a food to be spread (as on bread or crackers) **b** : FEAST 1a **c** : a cover for a table or bed **4** : distance between two points

spread–ea·gle \'spred-,ē-gəl\ *vb* **spread–ea·gled; spread–ea·gling** \-gə-ling, -gling\ **1** : to stand or move with arms and legs stretched out **2** : to spread over : stretch across

spread eagle *n* **1** : a representation of an eagle with wings raised and legs extended **2** : something resembling or suggesting a spread eagle

spread·sheet \'spred-,shēt\ *n* : an accounting program for a computer; *also* : the ledger layout simulated by such a program

spree \'sprē\ *n* : an unrestrained indulgence in or outburst of an activity ⟨a buying *spree*⟩; *esp* : BINGE [perhaps from Scottish *spreath* "cattle raid, foray", from Scottish Gaelic *sprēidh* "cattle", from Latin *praeda* "booty, prey"]

¹**sprig** \'sprig\ *n* **1** : a small shoot : TWIG **2** : an ornament resembling a sprig, stemmed flower, or leaf **3** : a small headless nail : BRAD [Middle English *sprigge*]

²**sprig** *vt* **sprigged; sprig·ging** : to drive sprigs into

spright·ful \'sprīt-fəl\ *adj* : SPRIGHTLY — **spright·ful·ly** \-fə-lē\ *adv* — **spright·ful·ness** *n*

spright·ly \'sprīt-lē\ *adj* **spright·li·er; -est** : marked by a gay lightness and liveliness [obsolete *spright* "sprite", alteration of *sprite*] — **spright·li·ness** *n* — **sprightly** *adv*

¹**spring** \'spring\ *vb* **sprang** \'sprang\ *or* **sprung** \'sprəng\; **sprung; spring·ing** \'spring-ing\ **1 a** (1) : DART 2, SHOOT (2) : to be resilient or elastic; *also* : to move by elastic force ⟨the lid *sprang* shut⟩ **b** : to become warped **2** : to issue with speed and force or as a stream **3 a** : to grow as a plant **b** : to issue by birth or descent **c** : to come into being : ARISE **4 a** : to make a leap or series of leaps **b** : to jump up suddenly **5** : to stretch out in height : RISE **6 a** : SPLIT, CRACK ⟨wind *sprang* the mast⟩ **b** : to have (a leak) develop **7** : to cause to operate suddenly ⟨*spring* a trap⟩ **8** : to produce or disclose suddenly or unexpectedly ⟨*sprung* a surprise on us⟩ **9** : to release or cause to be released from custody or confinement [Old English *springan*] — **spring·er** \'spring-ər\ *n*

²**spring** *n* **1 a** : a source of supply; *esp* : a source of water issuing from the ground **b** : an ultimate source especially of action or motion **2 a** : the season between winter and summer comprising in the northern hemisphere usually the months of March, April, and May or as reckoned astronomically extending from the March equinox to the June solstice **b** : a time or season

\ə\ abut		\ng\ sing	
\ər\ further		\ō\ bone	
\a\ mat		\ó\ saw	
\ā\ take		\ói\ coin	
\ä\ cot, cart		\th\ thin	
\aů\ out		\th\ this	
\ch\ chin		\ü\ food	
\e\ pet		\ů\ foot	
\ē\ easy		\y\ yet	
\g\ go		\yü\ few	
\i\ tip		\yů\ cure	
\ī\ life		\zh\ vision	
\j\ job			

of growth or development **3** : an elastic body or device that recovers its original shape when released after being distorted **4 a** : the act or an instance of leaping up or forward : BOUND **b** : capacity for springing : RESILIENCE, BOUNCE

spring beauty *n* : a spring herb that sends up a 2-leaved stem bearing delicate pink flowers

spring·board \\'spring-ˌbōrd, -ˌbȯrd\\ *n* **1** : a flexible board usually secured at one end and used to gain height for gymnastic stunts or diving **2** : a point of departure

spring·bok \\'spring-ˌbäk\\ *n, pl* **springbok** or **springboks** : a swift and graceful southern African gazelle [Afrikaans, from *spring* "to jump" + *bok* "male goat"]

spring–clean·ing \\-'klē-ning\\ *n* : the act or process of cleaning a place thoroughly

spring·er spaniel \\ˌspring-ər-\\ *n* : a medium-sized largely white sporting dog of English or Welsh origin used chiefly for finding and flushing small game

spring fever *n* : a lazy or restless feeling often associated with the onset of spring

spring·house \\'spring-ˌhaùs\\ *n* : a small building over a spring used for cool storage (as of dairy products or meat)

spring peeper *n* : a small brown tree toad of the eastern United States and Canada with a shrill piping call

spring·tail \\'spring-ˌtāl\\ *n* : any of an order (Collembola) of small primitive wingless arthropods that are related to or classed among the insects

spring·tide \\'spring-ˌtīd\\ *n* : SPRINGTIME

spring tide *n* : a greater than usual tide occurring at each new moon and full moon

spring·time \\'spring-ˌtīm\\ *n* : the season of spring

spring wagon *n* : a light wagon equipped with springs

spring·wood \\'spring-ˌwüd\\ *n* : the softer more porous portion of an annual ring of wood that develops early in the growing season — compare SUMMERWOOD

springy \\'spring-ē\\ *adj* **spring·i·er; -est** : having an elastic quality : RESILIENT — **spring·i·ly** \\'spring-ə-lē\\ *adv* — **spring·i·ness** \\'spring-ē-nəs\\ *n*

¹sprin·kle \\'spring-kəl\\ *vb* **sprin·kled; sprin·kling** \\-kə-ling, -kling\\ **1** : to scatter in drops or particles **2 a** : to scatter over **b** : to scatter at intervals in or among : DOT **c** : to wet lightly **3** : to rain lightly in scattered drops [Middle English *sprinclen*] — **sprin·kler** \\-kə-lər, -klər\\ *n*

²sprinkle *n* **1** : the act or an instance of sprinkling; *esp* : a light rain **2** : SPRINKLING

sprinkler system *n* : a system for protection against fire in which pipes are distributed for conveying an extinguishing fluid (as water) to outlets

sprin·kling \\'spring-kling\\ *n* : a limited quantity or amount; *esp* : SCATTERING

¹sprint \\'sprint\\ *vi* : to run at top speed especially for a short distance [of Scandinavian origin] — **sprint·er** *n*

²sprint *n* **1** : the act or an instance of sprinting **2** : a race run at or near top speed the whole way : DASH

sprit \\'sprit\\ *n* : a spar attached to the mast that runs diagonally across a rectangular fore-and-aft sail to support it [Old English *sprēot* "pole, spear"]

sprite \\'sprīt\\ *n* **1** : GHOST 2 **2 a** : an often mischievous supernatural being **b** : an elfish person [Old French *esprit* "spirit", from Latin *spiritus*]

sprit·sail \\'sprit-ˌsāl, -səl\\ *n* : a sail extended by a sprit

sprock·et \\'spräk-ət\\ *n* **1** : a projection on the rim of a wheel shaped so as to interlock with the links of a chain **2** : a wheel having sprockets [origin unknown]

¹sprout \\'spraùt\\ *vb* **1** : to send out new growth **2** : to grow rapidly **3** : to cause to sprout ⟨*sprout* oats⟩ [Old English -*sprūtan*]

²sprout *n* **1** : SHOOT 1a; *esp* : a young shoot (as from a seed or root) **2** *pl* : edible shoots especially of a plant of the mustard family; *also* : a plant (as brussels sprouts) producing them

¹spruce \\'sprüs\\ *n* : any of a genus of evergreen trees of the pine family with a conical head of dense foliage and with soft light wood; *also* : its wood [Middle English *Spruce* "Prussia", alteration of *Pruce,* from Old French] □ ORIGIN Prussia was formerly called *Pruce* or *Spruce* in English. A number of goods imported from Prussia—*spruce* canvas, *spruce* iron, *spruce* leather—were all very well-thought-of. Perhaps the most important of these Prussian or *Spruce* products was the spruce tree, a tall, straight conifer that was especially desirable for use as the mast of a ship. About the middle of the 17th century, *Spruce* as the name for the country was largely supplanted by Prussia. But by this time *spruce* had become well established as the name of the tree.

²spruce *adj* : neat or smart in appearance : TRIM [perhaps from obsolete *spruce leather* "leather imported from Prussia"] — **spruce·ly** *adv* — **spruce·ness** *n*

³spruce *vb* : to make or make oneself spruce ⟨*spruce* up a room⟩ ⟨*spruce* up before dinner⟩

sprue \\'sprü\\ *n* : a chronic disease marked especially by fatty diarrhea and dietary deficiency symptoms [Dutch *spruw*]

sprung *past of* SPRING

spry \\'sprī\\ *adj* **spri·er** or **spry·er** \\'sprī-ər, 'sprīr\\; **spri·est** or **spry·est** \\'sprī-əst\\ : light and easy in motion : NIMBLE, SPRIGHTLY [perhaps of Scandinavian origin] — **spry·ly** *adv* — **spry·ness** *n*

¹spud \\'spəd\\ *n* **1** : a tool or device (as for digging, lifting, or cutting) combining the characteristics of spade and chisel **2** : POTATO 2b [Middle English *spudde* "dagger"]

²spud *vb* **spud·ded; spud·ding** : to dig with a spud

¹spume \\'spyüm\\ *n* : frothy matter on liquids : FOAM [Middle French, from Latin *spuma*] — **spu·mous** \\'spyü-məs\\ *adj* — **spumy** \\'spyü-mē\\ *adj*

²spume *vi* : FROTH 3, FOAM

spu·mo·ni or **spu·mo·ne** \\spù-'mō-nē\\ *n* : ice cream in layers of different colors, flavors, and textures often with candied fruits and nuts [Italian *spumone,* from *spuma* "foam", from Latin]

spun *past of* SPIN

spun glass *n* : FIBERGLASS

spunk \\'spəngk\\ *n* : SAND 4, PLUCK [earlier *spunk* "tinder", from Scottish Gaelic *spong* "sponge, tinder", from Latin *spongia* "sponge"]

spunky \\'spəng-kē\\ *adj* **spunk·i·er; -est** : full of spunk : SPIRITED — **spunk·i·ly** \\-kə-lē\\ *adv* — **spunk·i·ness** \\-kē-nəs\\ *n*

spun sugar *n* : a confection or garnish made from boiled sugar syrup drawn out into fine threads and variously shaped or heaped up

¹spur \\'spər\\ *n* **1 a** : a pointed device secured to a rider's heel and used to urge on the horse **b** *pl* : recognition for achievement **2** : a goad to action : STIMULUS **3** : something projecting like or suggesting a spur: as **a** : a stiff sharp projecting part (as a broken branch of a tree or a horny process on a cock's leg) **b** : a hollow projecting appendage of a corolla or calyx (as in larkspur or columbine) **4** : a ridge that extends laterally from a mountain **5** : a railroad track diverging from a main line [Old English *spura*] — **on the spur of the moment** : on impulse

²spur *vb* **spurred; spur·ring** **1** : to urge a horse on with spurs **2** : INCITE, STIMULATE ⟨*spur* the team to victory⟩

spurge \\'spərj\\ *n* : any of a family of mostly shrubby plants with a bitter milky juice and often showy bracts surrounding insignificant flowers — compare POINSETTIA [Middle French, "purge, spurge", from *espurgier* "to purge", from Latin *expurgare*]

spur gear *n* : a gear wheel with radial teeth parallel to its axis

spu·ri·ous \\'spyùr-ē-əs\\ *adj* : not genuine or authentic : FALSE, COUNTERFEIT [Late Latin *spurius,* from Latin, "bastard"] — **spu·ri·ous·ly** *adv* — **spu·ri·ous·ness** *n*

sprocket 1, 2

¹spur 1a

¹spurn \'spərn\ *vt* **1** : to kick aside **2** : to reject with disdain [Old English *spurnan*] SYN see REJECT — **spurn·er** *n*

²spurn *n* **1** : KICK 1a (1) **2** : disdainful rejection

spur-of-the-moment *adj* : occurring or developing without prior planning ⟨a *spur-of-the-moment* decision⟩

spurred \'spərd\ *adj* **1** : wearing spurs **2** : having one or more spurs ⟨a *spurred* violet⟩

¹spurt \'spərt\ *n* : a sudden brief burst of increased effort or activity [origin unknown]

²spurt *vi* : to make a spurt

³spurt *vb* **1** : SPOUT 3 **2** : SQUIRT [perhaps related to *sprout*]

⁴spurt *n* : a sudden gush : JET

spur track *n* : a track that diverges from a main line

sput·nik \'sput-nik, 'spət-\ *n* : SATELLITE 2b [Russian, literally, "traveling companion", from *s* "with" + *put'* "path"]

¹sput·ter \'spət-ər\ *vb* **1** : to spit or squirt particles of food or saliva noisily from the mouth **2** : to speak or utter hastily or explosively in confusion or excitement ⟨*sputtered* out their protests⟩ **3** : to make explosive popping sounds ⟨the motor *sputtered* and died⟩ [related to Dutch *sputteren* "to sputter"] — **sput·ter·er** \'-ər-ər\ *n*

²sputter *n* : the act or sound of sputtering

spu·tum \'spyüt-əm, 'spüt-\ *n, pl* **spu·ta** \'-ə\ : material spit or coughed up and made up of saliva and mucous discharges from the respiratory passages [Latin, from *spuere* "to spit"]

¹spy \'spī\ *vb* **spied; spy·ing** **1** : to watch, inspect, or examine secretly : act as a spy **2** : to catch sight of : SEE ⟨*spied* a friend in the crowd⟩ **3** : to search or search out usually by close study or examination [Old French *espier*, of Germanic origin]

²spy *n, pl* **spies** **1** : one that secretly watches another so as to obtain information **2** : a person who tries secretly to obtain information for one country in the territory of another usually hostile country

spy·glass \'spī-ˌglas\ *n* : a small telescope

squab \'skwäb\ *n, pl* **squabs** *or* **squab** : a fledgling bird; *esp* : a fledgling pigeon about four weeks old [probably of Scandinavian origin]

¹squab·ble \'skwäb-əl\ *n* : a noisy quarrel usually over trifles [probably of Scandinavian origin]

²squabble *vi* **squab·bled; squab·bling** \'skwäb-ling, -ə-ling\ : to quarrel noisily and to no purpose : WRANGLE — **squab·bler** \'-ler, -ə-lər\ *n*

squad \'skwäd\ *n* **1** : a small organized group of military personnel; *esp* : a tactical unit that can be easily directed in the field **2** : a small group engaged in a common effort or occupation ⟨a football *squad*⟩ [Middle French *esquade*, from Spanish *escuadra* and Italian *squadra*, both derived from Latin *quadrare* "to square"]

squad car *n* : a police automobile connected by a two-way radio with headquarters — called also *cruiser*, *prowl car*

squad·ron \'skwäd-rən\ *n* : any of several units of military organization [Italian *squadrone*, from *squadra* "squad"]

squad room *n* **1** : a room in a barracks used to billet soldiers **2** : a room in a police station where members of the force assemble

squal·id \'skwäl-əd\ *adj* **1** : marked by filthiness and degradation from neglect or poverty **2** : morally debased : SORDID [Latin *squalidus*] — **squal·id·ly** *adv* — **squal·id·ness** *n*

¹squall \'skwȯl\ *vb* : to utter a raucous cry [of Scandinavian origin] — **squall·er** *n*

²squall *n* : a raucous cry

³squall *n* **1** : a sudden violent wind often with rain or snow **2** : a short-lived commotion [probably of Scandinavian origin]

⁴squall *vi* : to blow a squall

squal·ly \'skwȯl-lē\ *adj* **squall·i·er; -est** : marked by squalls : GUSTY, STORMY

squal·or \'skwäl-ər\ *n* : the quality or state of being squalid [Latin]

squa·mo·sal \skwə-'mō-səl, -zəl\ *adj* : of, relating to, or being a bone of the skull of many vertebrates corresponding to the squamous portion of the temporal bone of humans

squa·mous \'skwä-məs, 'skwä-\ *adj* **1** : covered with or consisting of scales : SCALY **2** : of, relating to, or being the anterior upper portion of the temporal bone of human beings and some other mammals [Latin *squamosus*, from *squama* "scale"]

squan·der \'skwän-dər\ *vb* **squan·dered; squan·der·ing** \'-də-ring, -dring\ : to spend extravagantly or wastefully [origin unknown] — **squan·der·er** \'-dər-ər\ *n*

¹square \'skwaər, 'skweər\ *n* **1** : an instrument having at least one right angle and two straight edges used to mark or test right angles **2** : a rectangle with all four sides equal **3** : any of the quadrilateral spaces marked out on a board for playing games **4** : the product of a number multiplied by itself **5 a** : an open place or area formed at the meeting of two or more streets **b** : BLOCK 5b, 5c **6** : a person who is overly conventional or conservative [Middle French *esquarre*, derived from Latin *ex-* + *quadrare* "to square"] — **on the square** **1** : at right angles **2** : in a fair open manner : HONESTLY — **out of square** : not at an exact right angle

²square *adj* **1 a** : having four equal sides and four right angles **b** : forming a right angle ⟨a *square* corner⟩ **2** : raised to the second power **3 a** : of a shape suggesting strength and solidity ⟨a *square* jaw⟩ ⟨*square* shoulders⟩ **b** : rectangular and equilateral in section ⟨a *square* tower⟩ **c** : having a rectangular rather than curving outline **4 a** : converted from a linear unit into a square unit of area having the same length of side ⟨a *square* meter is the area of a square each side of which is a meter⟩ **b** : being of a specified length in each of two equal dimensions ⟨10 meters *square*⟩ **5 a** : exactly adjusted or aligned **b** : FAIR 5a, JUST **c** : leaving no balance : SETTLED **d** : TIED ⟨the golfers were all *square* at the end of the 6th hole⟩ **e** : SUBSTANTIAL 2 ⟨a *square* meal⟩ **6** : being unsophisticated, conservative, or conventional — **square·ly** *adv* — **square·ness** *n*

³square *vb* **1** : to make square or rectangular ⟨*square* a building stone⟩ **2** : to bring approximately to a right angle ⟨*squared* my shoulders⟩ **3 a** : to multiply (a number) by itself **b** : to find a square equal in area to ⟨*square* a circle⟩ **4** : to agree or make agree : HARMONIZE ⟨your story does not *square* with the facts⟩ **5** : BALANCE, SETTLE ⟨*square* an account⟩ **6** : to mark off into squares **7** : to influence or settle by or as if by a bribe

square away *vb* : to put in order or readiness

square bracket *n* : BRACKET 3a

square dance *n* : a dance for four couples who form the sides of a square — **square dancer** *n* — **square dancing** *n*

square deal *n* : an honest and fair transaction or trade

square knot *n* : a knot made of two reverse half-knots and typically used to join the ends of two cords

square measure *n* : a unit or system of units for measuring area — see MEASURE table, METRIC SYSTEM table

square-rigged \'skwaər-'rigd, 'skweər-\ *adj* : having the principal sails extended on yards fastened to the masts horizontally and at their center

square-rig·ger \'-'rig-ər\ *n* : a square-rigged vessel

square root *n* : a factor of a number that when squared gives the number ⟨the *square root* of 9 is ±3⟩

square sail \'-ˌsāl, -səl\ *n* : a 4-sided sail used on a square-rigged vessel

square shooter *n* : a just or honest person

square-shoul·dered \'-'shōl-dərd\ *adj* : having the shoulders high and well braced back

spyglass

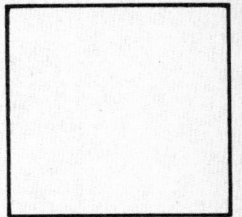

¹square 2

\ə\ abut	\ng\ sing
\ər\ further	\ō\ bone
\a\ mat	\ȯ\ saw
\ā\ take	\ȯi\ coin
\ä\ cot, cart	\th\ thin
\aú\ out	\th\ this
\ch\ chin	\ü\ food
\e\ pet	\ú\ foot
\ē\ easy	\y\ yet
\g\ go	\yü\ few
\i\ tip	\yú\ cure
\ī\ life	\zh\ vision
\j\ job	

squar·ish \'skwaər-ish, 'skweər-\ *adj* : somewhat square in form or appearance — **squar·ish·ly** *adv*

¹squash \'skwäsh, 'skwȯsh\ *vb* **1** : to press or beat into a pulp or flat mass **2** : to put down : SUPPRESS **3** : SQUEEZE, PRESS ⟨*squashed* into the seat⟩ [Middle French *esquasser,* from Latin *ex-* + *quassare* "to shake"] — **squash·er** *n*

²squash *n* **1** : the sudden fall of a heavy soft body or the sound of such a fall **2** : a squelching sound made by walking on oozy ground or in water-soaked boots **3** : a crushed mass **4** : SQUASH RACQUETS

³squash *n, pl* **squash·es** *or* **squash** : a fruit of any of various widely grown plants of the gourd family that is used especially as a vegetable and for livestock feed; *also* : a plant that bears squashes [of American Indian origin]

squash bug *n* : a large black American bug injurious to squash vines

squash racquets *n* : a singles or doubles game in a 4-wall court with rackets and a rubber ball

squash tennis *n* : a game resembling squash racquets played with an inflated ball the size of a tennis ball

squashy \'skwäsh-ē, 'skwȯsh-\ *adj* **squash·i·er; -est** : easily squashed : SOFT ⟨a *squashy* pillow⟩ — **squash·i·ly** \'skwäsh-ə-lē, 'skwȯsh-\ *adv* — **squash·i·ness** \'skwäsh-ē-nəs, 'skwȯsh-\ *n*

¹squat \'skwät\ *vb* **squat·ted; squat·ting** **1** : to sit or cause (oneself) to sit on one's haunches **2** : to occupy land as a squatter **3** : CROUCH, COWER ⟨a *squatting* hare⟩ [Middle French *esquatir,* from *es-* "ex-" + *quatir* "to press", derived from Latin *cogere* "to drive together"]

²squat *n* **1** : the act of squatting **2** : a squatting posture

³squat *adj* **squat·ter; squat·test** **1** : sitting with the haunches close above the heels **2 a** : low to the ground **b** : being short and thick — **squat·ly** *adv* — **squat·ness** *n*

squat·ter \'skwät-ər\ *n* **1** : one that squats **2 a** : one that settles on land without right or title or payment of rent **b** : one that settles on public land under government regulation with the purpose of acquiring title

squat·ty \'skwät-ē\ *adj* **squat·ti·er; -est** : SQUAT 2

squaw \'skwȯ\ *n* : an American Indian woman [of American Indian origin]

squaw·fish \-ˌfish\ *n* : any of several mostly freshwater fishes of western North America

¹squawk \'skwȯk\ *vi* **1** : to utter a harsh abrupt scream **2** : to complain or protest loudly or vehemently [probably blend of *squall* and *squeak*] — **squawk·er** *n*

²squawk *n* **1** : a harsh abrupt scream **2** : a noisy complaint

squawk box *n* : an intercom speaker

squaw·root \'skwȯ-ˌrüt, -ˌrút\ *n* : a North American herb that is parasitic on oak and hemlock roots and has a thick stem with yellow fleshy scales

¹squeak \'skwēk\ *vb* **1** : to utter a sharp shrill cry or noise **2** : to pass, succeed, or win by a narrow margin ⟨barely *squeaked* by⟩ **3** : to utter in a shrill piping tone [Middle English *squeken*]

²squeak *n* **1** : a sharp shrill cry or sound **2** : ESCAPE 1 ⟨a close *squeak*⟩ — **squeaky** \'skwē-kē\ *adj*

¹squeal \'skwēl\ *vb* **1** : to utter a shrill cry or sound **2 a** : to turn informer **b** : COMPLAIN 1, PROTEST **3** : to utter with or as if with a squeal [Middle English *squelen*] — **squeal·er** *n*

²squeal *n* : a shrill cry or sound

squea·mish \'skwē-mish\ *adj* **1 a** : easily nauseated : QUEASY **b** : affected with nausea **2** : easily shocked or disgusted [Anglo-French *escoymous*] — **squea·mish·ly** *adv* — **squea·mish·ness** *n*

squee·gee \'skwē-ˌjē\ *n* : a blade of leather or rubber set on a handle and used for spreading or wiping liquid material on, across, or off a surface (as a window) [probably imitative] — **squeegee** *vt*

¹squeeze \'skwēz\ *vb* **1 a** : to exert pressure especially on opposite sides of : COMPRESS **b** : to extract or emit under pressure ⟨*squeeze* juice from a lemon⟩ **c** : to force or thrust by compression : CROWD ⟨two more *squeezed* into the car⟩ **2 a** : to extort money, goods, or services from ⟨*squeezed* their tenants mercilessly⟩ **b** : to cause hardship to : OPPRESS **c** : to reduce the amount of ⟨rising costs *squeezed* profits⟩ **3** : to gain or win by a narrow margin [Old English *cwȳsan*] — **squeez·er** *n*

²squeeze *n* **1 a** : an act or instance of squeezing : COMPRESSION **b** : HANDSHAKE; *also* : EMBRACE **2** : financial pressure caused by narrowing margins (as between costs and selling price) or by shortages

squeeze bottle *n* : a bottle of flexible plastic that dispenses its contents by being pressed

squeeze play *n* : a baseball play in which a batter attempts to score a runner from third base by bunting

¹squelch \'skwelch\ *n* **1** : a sound of or as if of semiliquid matter under suction ⟨the *squelch* of mud⟩ **2** : a retort that silences an opponent [imitative]

²squelch *vb* **1 a** : to fall or stamp on so as to crush **b** : to completely suppress : QUELL, SILENCE **2** : to emit or cause to emit a sucking sound **3** : to splash through water, slush, or mire — **squelch·er** *n*

sque·teague \skwi-'tēg\ *n, pl* **squeteague** : any of various weakfishes [of American Indian origin]

squib \'skwib\ *n* **1 a** : a small firecracker **b** : a broken firecracker that burns out with a fizz **2** : a short humorous or satiric writing or speech [origin unknown]

squid \'skwid\ *n, pl* **squid** *or* **squids** : any of numerous 10-armed cephalopod mollusks with a long tapered body, a fin on each side, and usually a slender internal chitinous support [origin unknown]

squig·gle \'skwig-əl\ *n* : a short wavy twist or line : CURLICUE [from earlier *squiggle* "to wriggle", blend of *squirm* and *wriggle*]

squill \'skwil\ *n* **1** : a Mediterranean bulbous herb of the lily family with narrow leaves and white flowers; *also* : its bulb used in medicine and in rat poisons **2** : SCILLA [Latin *squilla, scilla,* from Greek *skilla*]

¹squint \'skwint\ *adj* : affected with cross-eye [Middle English *asquint*]

²squint *vi* **1 a** : to look in a squint-eyed manner **b** : to be cross-eyed **2** : to look or peer with eyes closed — **squint·er** *n*

³squint *n* : STRABISMUS; *also* : an action or instance of squinting — **squinty** \'skwint-ē\ *adj*

squint–eyed \'skwint-ˌīd\ *adj* : having eyes that squint

¹squire \'skwīr\ *n* **1** : one who bears the shield or armor of a knight **2 a** : a male attendant on a great personage **b** : LADIES' MAN, ESCORT **3 a** : a member of the British gentry ranking below a knight and above a gentleman **b** : an owner of a country estate **c** : JUSTICE OF THE PEACE [Old French *esquier,* from Late Latin *scutarius* "guard armed with a shield", from Latin *scutum* "shield"]

²squire *vt* : to attend as a squire or escort

squire·archy *or* **squir·archy** \'skwīr-ˌär-kē\ *n* **1** : the gentry or landed-proprietor class **2** : government by a landed gentry

squirm \'skwərm\ *vi* **1** : to twist about like an eel or a worm **2** : to feel acutely embarrassed ⟨undeserved praise made us *squirm*⟩ [perhaps imitative] — **squirmy** \'skwər-mē\ *adj*

squir·rel \'skwər-əl, 'skwə-rəl, 'skwərl\ *n, pl* **squirrels** *also* **squirrel** **1** : any of various small or medium-sized rodents (family Sciuridae); *esp* : one with a long bushy tail and strong hind legs adapted to leaping from branch to branch **2** : the fur of a squirrel [Middle French *esquireul,* derived from Latin *sciurus,* from Greek *skiouros,* from *skia* "shadow" + *oura* "tail"]

squirrel monkey *n* : a small soft-haired South American monkey having a long tail not used for grasping and

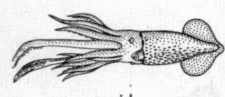

squid

squirrel 1

being colored chiefly yellowish gray with a white face and black nose

¹squirt \'skwərt\ *vb* : to come forth, drive, or eject in a sudden rapid stream : SPURT [Middle English *squirten*]

²squirt *n* **1 a** : an instrument (as a syringe) for squirting a liquid **b** : a small quick stream : JET **c** : the action of squirting **2** : an impudent youngster

squirt gun *n* : WATER PISTOL

squirting cucumber *n* : a Mediterranean plant of the gourd family having a fruit that bursts when ripe forcibly ejecting the seeds

squishy \'skwish-ē\ *adj* : being soft, yielding, and damp [from earlier *squish* "to squash"]

SRO \,es-,är-'ō\ *n* : a house, apartment building, or residential hotel in which low-income or welfare tenants live in single rooms [*single-r*oom *o*ccupancy]

SS \es-'es, 'es-\ *n* : a unit of Nazis created to serve as bodyguard to Hitler and later expanded to take charge of central security and extermination of undesirables [German, abbreviation for *Schutzstaffel*, literally, "protection echelon"]

¹-st — see -EST

²-st *symbol* — used after the figure 1 to indicate the ordinal number *first* ⟨1*st*⟩ ⟨71*st*⟩

¹stab \'stab\ *n* **1** : a wound produced by a pointed weapon **2** : a thrust of a pointed weapon **3** : EFFORT 2, TRY [Middle English *stabbe*]

²stab *vt* **stabbed; stab·bing** **1** : to wound or pierce by the thrust of a pointed weapon **2** : STICK 2 ⟨*stab* a needle into thick cloth⟩ — **stab·ber** *n*

sta·bil·i·ty \stə-'bil-ət-ē\ *n, pl* **-ties** : the quality, state, or degree of being stable: as **a** : the property of a body that causes it to return to its original condition when disturbed (as in balance) **b** : resistance to chemical change or to physical disintegration

sta·bi·lize \'stā-bə-,līz\ *vb* : to make or become stable, steadfast, or firm; *also* : to hold steady (as by means of a stabilizer) — **sta·bi·li·za·tion** \,stā-bə-lə-'zā-shən\ *n*

sta·bi·liz·er \'stā-bə-,lī-zər\ *n* : one (as a chemical or a device) that stabilizes something; *esp* : a fixed surface for stabilizing the motion of an airplane

¹sta·ble \'stā-bəl\ *n* **1** : a building in which domestic animals are sheltered and fed; *esp* : such a building having stalls or compartments ⟨horse *stable*⟩ **2 a** : the racehorses of one owner **b** : a group of athletes (as boxers) under one management [Old French *estable*, from Latin *stabulum*, from *stare* "to stand"] — **sta·ble-man** \-mən, -,man\ *n*

²stable *vb* **sta·bled; sta·bling** \-bə-ling, -bling\ : to put, keep, or live in or as if in a stable

³stable *adj* **sta·bler** \-bə-lər, -blər\; **sta·blest** \-bə-ləst, -bləst\ **1 a** : firmly established : FIXED ⟨a *stable* community⟩ **b** : not changing or fluctuating ⟨a *stable* income⟩ **c** : LASTING, PERMANENT ⟨*stable* institutions⟩ **2** : steady in purpose : CONSTANT ⟨*stable* personalities⟩ **3 a** : designed so as to develop forces that restore the original condition when disturbed from a condition of equilibrium or steady motion ⟨a *stable* airplane⟩ **b** : able to resist alteration in chemical, physical, or biological properties ⟨a *stable* compound⟩ ⟨*stable* emulsions⟩ [Old French *estable*, from Latin *stabilis*, from *stare* "to stand"] — **sta·ble·ness** \-bəl-nəs\ *n* — **sta·bly** \-bə-lē, -blē\ *adv*

sta·bler \-bə-lər, -blər\ *n* : one that keeps a stable

sta·bling *n* : accommodation for animals in a building ⟨*stabling* for six horses⟩

stac·ca·to \stə-'kät-ō\ *adj* **1 a** : cut short or apart in performing : DISCONNECTED ⟨*staccato* notes⟩ **b** : marked by short clear-cut playing or singing of tones or chords ⟨a *staccato* style⟩ **2** : ABRUPT, DISJOINTED ⟨the *staccato* noises of a skipping motor⟩ [Italian, from *staccare* "to detach", derived from Old French *desta-chier*] — **staccato** *adv* — **staccato** *n*

¹stack \'stak\ *n* **1** : a large usually conical pile (as of hay, straw, or grain) **2** : an orderly pile of objects usually one on top of the other ⟨a *stack* of dishes⟩ **3** : a vertical pipe (as for carrying off smoke or vapor) **4 a** : a rack with shelves for storing books **b** *pl* : the part of a library in which books are stored in racks **5** : three or more rifles arranged together to stand in the form of a pyramid [Old Norse *stakkr*]

²stack *vb* : to arrange in or form a stack : PILE ⟨*stacked* the dishes on the table⟩ — **stack·er** *n*

stack up *vi* : to measure : COMPARE

sta·dia \'stād-ē-ə\ *n* : a surveying method for determination of distances and differences of elevation that uses a telescopic instrument having two horizontal lines through which the marks on a graduated rod are observed; *also* : the instrument or the rod used in this method [Italian, probably from Latin, pl. of *stadium*]

sta·di·um \'stād-ē-əm\ *n, pl* **-dia** \-ē-ə\ *or* **-di·ums** **1** : an ancient Greek or Roman unit of length ranging from about 185 to 225 meters **2 a** : a course for footraces in ancient Greece with tiers of seats for spectators **b** *pl usu* **stadiums** : a large usually unroofed building with tiers of seats for spectators at modern sports events [Latin, from Greek *stadion*]

¹staff \'staf\ *n, pl* **staffs** \'stafs, 'stavz\ *or* **staves** \'stāvz, 'stavz\ **1 a** : a pole, stick, rod, or bar used as a support or as a sign of authority ⟨a flag hanging limp on its *staff*⟩ **b** : the long handle of a weapon (as a lance or pike) **c** : CLUB 1a, CUDGEL **2** : something that props or sustains ⟨bread is the *staff* of life⟩ **3** : the five horizontal lines with their spaces on which music is written **4** *pl* **staffs a** : a group of persons serving as assistants to or employees under a chief ⟨a hospital *staff*⟩ **b** : a group of officers or aides appointed to assist a civil executive or commanding officer **c** : military officers not eligible for operational command but having administrative duties [Old English *stæf*] — **staff** *adj*

²staff *vt* : to supply with a staff (as of workers)

staff·er \'staf-ər\ *n* : a member of a staff

staff sergeant *n* : an enlisted rank in the Army above sergeant and below sergeant first class, in the Marine Corps above sergeant and below gunnery sergeant, and in the Air Force above sergeant and below technical sergeant

staff sergeant major *n* : an enlisted rank in the Army above master sergeant

¹stag \'stag\ *n, pl* **stag** *or* **stags** **1** : an adult male red deer; *also* : the male of various other large deer **2** : a male animal castrated after maturity **3 a** : a social gathering of men only **b** : a man who attends a dance or party unaccompanied by a woman [Old English *stagga*]

²stag *adj* **1** : intended or suitable for men only ⟨a *stag* party⟩ **2** : unaccompanied by someone of the opposite sex — **stag** *adv*

stag beetle *n* : any of numerous mostly large beetles whose males have long and often branched mandibles

¹stage \'stāj\ *n* **1** : one of the horizontal levels into which a structure is divisible: as **a** : a floor of a building **b** : a shelf or layer especially as one of a series **c** : any of the levels attained by a river above an arbitrary zero point ⟨flood *stage*⟩ **2** : a raised platform (as a scaffold or landing stage): as **a** : a part of a theater including the acting area **b** : the small platform on which an object is placed for microscopic examination **3 a** : a center of attention : scene of action **b** : the theatrical profession or art **4** : a division or a dividing point: as **a** : a stopping place especially for a stagecoach providing fresh horses and refreshments **b** : the distance between stopping places in a journey **c** : a degree of advance attained (as in a process or undertaking) ⟨an early *stage* of a disease⟩ **d** : one of the distinguishable periods of the growth and development of a plant or animal ⟨the larval *stage* of a beetle⟩; *also* : an individual in such a stage **e** : one complete process or step in a sequential or recurrent activity **5** : STAGECOACH **6** : one of two or more sections of a rocket each

¹staff 3 with clef

\ə\ abut	\ng\ sing
\ər\ further	\ō\ bone
\a\ mat	\ȯ\ saw
\ā\ take	\ȯi\ coin
\ä\ cot, cart	\th\ thin
\au̇\ out	\th\ this
\ch\ chin	\ü\ food
\e\ pet	\u̇\ foot
\ē\ easy	\y\ yet
\g\ go	\yü\ few
\i\ tip	\yu̇\ cure
\ī\ life	\zh\ vision
\j\ job	

having its own fuel and engine [Old French *estage,* derived from Latin *stare* "to stand"] — **on the stage** : in or into the acting profession

²stage *vt* : to produce or show publicly on or as if on the stage

stage·coach \'stāj-ˌkōch\ *n* : a horse-drawn passenger and mail coach running on a regular schedule

stage·craft \-ˌkraft\ *n* : the effective management of theatrical devices or techniques

stage direction *n* : a description or direction written or printed in a play

stage fright *n* : nervousness felt at appearing before an audience

stage·hand \'stāj-ˌhand\ *n* : a stage worker who handles scenery, properties, or lights

stage manager *n* : a person who is in charge of the stage and physical aspects of a theatrical production

stag·er \'stā-jər\ *n* : an experienced person (an old *stager*)

stage·struck \'stāj-ˌstrək\ *adj* : fascinated by the stage; *esp* : having a strong desire to become an actor

stage whisper *n* : a loud whisper by an actor audible to the spectators but supposed not be to heard by persons on the stage

¹stag·ger \'stag-ər\ *vb* **stag·gered; stag·ger·ing** \'stag-ring, -ə-ring\ **1 a** : to move unsteadily from side to side as if about to fall : REEL **b** : to cause to reel or totter **2 a** : to begin to doubt and waver : become less confident **b** : to cause to doubt, waver, or hesitate **3** : to place or arrange in a zigzag or alternate but regular way [Old Norse *stakra,* from *staka* "to push"] — **stag·ger·er** \'stag-ər-ər\ *n*

²stagger *n* **1** *pl* : an abnormal condition of domestic mammals and birds associated with damage to the central nervous system and marked by incoordination and a reeling unsteady gait **2** : a reeling or unsteady gait or stance

stag·ger·ing *adj* : serving to stagger : ASTONISHING, OVERWHELMING — **stag·ger·ing·ly** \'stag-ring-lē, -ə-ring-\ *adv*

stag·ing \'stā-jing\ *n* **1** : SCAFFOLDING **2** : the putting of a play on the stage **3** : the assembling of troops or supplies in a particular place

stag·nant \'stag-nənt\ *adj* **1 a** : not flowing in a current or stream **b** : STALE (*stagnant* air) **2** : DULL, INACTIVE (*stagnant* business) — **stag·nan·cy** \-nən-sē\ *n* — **stag·nant·ly** *adv*

stag·nate \'stag-ˌnāt\ *vi* : to be or become stagnant [Latin *stagnare,* from *stagnum* "body of standing water"] — **stag·na·tion** \stag-'nā-shən\ *n*

stagy \'stā-jē\ *adj* **stag·i·er; -est** : of or resembling the stage; *esp* : theatrical or artificial in manner — **stag·i·ly** \-jə-lē\ *adv* — **stag·i·ness** \-jē-nəs\ *n*

¹staid \'stād\ *adj* : marked by sedateness and often prim self-restraint : SOBER, GRAVE [from past participle of ³*stay*] — **staid·ly** *adv* — **staid·ness** *n*

²staid *past of* STAY

¹stain \'stān\ *vb* **1** : to soil or discolor especially in spots **2** : to give color to (as by dyeing) **3** : to taint with guilt, vice, or corruption [partly from Middle French *desteindre* "to discolor", from *des-* "dis-" + *teindre* "to dye", from Latin *tingere;* partly of Scandinavian origin] — **stain·abil·i·ty** \ˌstā-nə-'bil-ət-ē\ *n* — **stain·able** \'stā-nə-bəl\ *adj* — **stain·er** *n*

²stain *n* **1** : a soiled or discolored spot **2** : a taint of guilt : STIGMA **3** : a preparation (as of dye or pigment) used in staining; *esp* : one capable of penetrating the pores of wood — **stain·less** \'stān-ləs\ *adj* — **stain·less·ly** *adv*

stained glass *n* : glass colored or stained (as for windows)

stainless steel *n* : steel alloyed with chromium and highly resistant to stain, rust, and corrosion

stair \'staər, 'steər\ *n* **1** : a series of steps or flights of steps for passing from one level to another — often

used in pl. (ran down the *stairs*) **2** : one step of a stairway [Old English *stǣger*]

stair·case \-ˌkās\ *n* : a flight of stairs with the supporting framework, casing, and balusters

stair·way \-ˌwā\ *n* : one or more flights of stairs usually with landings to pass from one level to another

stair·well \-ˌwel\ *n* : a vertical shaft in which stairs are located

¹stake \'stāk\ *n* **1** : a pointed piece (as of wood) driven or to be driven into the ground especially as a marker or support; *also* : a similar upright support (as for the load of a vehicle) **2 a** : a post to which a person is bound for execution by burning **b** : execution by burning at a stake **3 a** : something that is staked for gain or loss **b** : the prize in a contest **c** : an interest or share in a commercial venture **4** : a Mormon territorial unit comprising a number of wards **5** : GRUBSTAKE [Old English *staca*] — **at stake** : at issue : in jeopardy

²stake *vt* **1 a** : to mark the limits of by stakes (*stake* out a mining claim) **b** : to tether to a stake **c** : to fasten up or support (as plants) with stakes **2 a** : BET 1, HAZARD **b** : to back financially; *esp* : GRUBSTAKE

sta·lac·tite \stə-'lak-ˌtīt\ *n* : a deposit of calcium carbonate resembling an icicle hanging from the roof or sides of a cavern [Greek *stalaktos* "dripping" from *stalassein* "to let drip"] — **stal·ac·tit·ic** \ˌstal-ˌak-'tit-ik\ *adj*

sta·lag·mite \stə-'lag-ˌmīt\ *n* : a deposit like an inverted stalactite found on the floor of a cave [Greek *stalagma* "drop" or *stalagmos* "dripping"] — **stal·ag·mit·ic** \ˌstal-ˌag-'mit-ik\ *adj*

¹stale \'stāl\ *adj* **1** : tasteless, unpleasant, or unwholesome from age (*stale* food) **2** : tedious from familiarity (*stale* news) **3** : WEAK, INEFFECTIVE (felt *stale* and listless after a long illness) [Middle English, "aged" (of ale)] — **stale·ly** \'stāl-lē\ *adv* — **stale·ness** *n*

²stale *vb* : to make or become stale

¹stale·mate \'stāl-ˌmāt\ *n* **1** : a drawing position in chess in which only the king can move and although not in check can move only into check **2** : a drawn contest : DEADLOCK [obsolete *stale* "stalemate" (derived from Old French *estal* "position, stall") + *mate*]

²stalemate *vt* : to bring into a stalemate

Sta·lin·ism \'stäl-ə-ˌniz-əm, 'stal-\ *n* : the theory and practice of communism developed by Stalin from Marxism-Leninism and characterized especially by rigid authoritarianism, widespread use of terror, and often by Russian nationalism — **Sta·lin·ist** \-nəst\ *n or adj*

¹stalk \'stók\ *vb* **1** : to hunt stealthily (a *stalking* cat) (*stalk* a deer); *also* : to go through (an area) in stalking prey **2** : to walk with haughty or pompous bearing **3** : to move through or follow usually in a persistent or furtive way (famine *stalked* the land) (*stalk* a criminal) [Old English *bestealcian*] — **stalk·er** *n*

²stalk *n* **1** : the act of stalking **2** : a stalking gait

³stalk *n* **1** : a plant stem; *esp* : the main stem of an herbaceous plant **2** : a slender supporting or connecting structure : PEDUNCLE (the *stalk* of a crinoid) [Middle English *stalke*] — **stalked** \'stókt\ *adj* — **stalk·less** \'stók-ləs\ *adj* — **stalky** \'stó-kē\ *adj*

stalk·ing-horse \'stó-king-ˌhórs\ *n* **1** : a horse or a figure like a horse behind which a hunter stalks game **2** : something used to mask a purpose

¹stall \'stól\ *n* **1 a** : a compartment for a domestic animal in a stable or barn **b** : a space set off (as for parking a motor vehicle) **2 a** : a seat in the chancel of a church with back and sides wholly or partly enclosed **b** *British* : a front orchestra seat in a theater **3** : a booth, stand, or counter at which articles are displayed for sale **4** : a protective sheath for a finger or toe [Old English *steall*]

²stall *vb* **1** : to put into or keep in a stall **2** : to bring or come to a standstill: as **a** : MIRE **b** (1) : to stop running

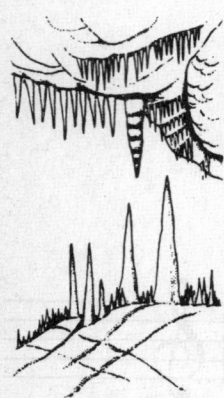
stalactite and stalagmite

⟨the car *stalled*⟩ (2) : to cause (an engine) to stop usually unintentionally **c** : to go or cause (as an airplane) to go into a stall

³stall *n* : the condition of an aircraft or a wing of an aircraft in which lift is lost and the aircraft or wing tends to drop

⁴stall *n* : a ruse to deceive or delay [English dialect *stale* "lure, decoy", from Anglo-French *estale*]

⁵stall *vb* : to hold off, divert, or delay by evasion or deception

stal·lion \'stal-yən\ *n* : a male horse; *esp* : one kept primarily as a stud [Middle French *estalon,* of Germanic origin]

¹stal·wart \'stȯl-wərt\ *adj* **1** : STURDY 1a, STOUT **2** : VALIANT 1, RESOLUTE [Old English *stælwierthe* "serviceable"] — **stal·wart·ly** *adv* — **stal·wart·ness** *n*

²stalwart *n* **1** : a stalwart person **2** : an unwavering partisan (as in politics)

sta·men \'stā-mən\ *n, pl* **stamens** *also* **sta·mi·na** \'stā-mə-nə, 'stam-ə-\ : an organ of a flower that produces male gametes, consists of an anther and a filament, and is morphologically a sporophyll [Latin, "warp, thread"]

stam·i·na \'stam-ə-nə\ *n* : the capacity or ability to endure or perform a lot or for a long time [Latin, pl. of *stamen* "warp, thread, thread of life"]

sta·mi·nate \'stā-mə-nət, 'stam-ə-, -,nāt\ *adj* : having stamens; *esp* : having stamens but no pistils

¹stam·mer \'stam-ər\ *vb* **stam·mered; stam·mer·ing** \'stam-ring, -ə-ring\ : to utter with or make involuntary stops and repetitions in speaking [Old English *stamerian*] — **stam·mer·er** \'stam-ər-ər\ *n* □ SYN STAMMER, STUTTER mean to speak haltingly or stumblingly. STAMMER often suggests a temporary inhibition through fear, embarrassment, or shock ⟨breathlessly *stammered* out thanks⟩ STUTTER suggests an habitual defect of speech although it may imply merely the effect of haste or excitement.

²stammer *n* : an act or instance of stammering

¹stamp \'stamp; *1b & 2 are also* 'stamp *or* 'stȯmp\ *vb* **1 a** : to pound or crush with a heavy instrument **b** : to strike or beat forcibly with the bottom of the foot **c** : to bring down forcibly or noisily ⟨*stamp* one's feet⟩ **d** : to extinguish or destroy by or as if by stamping with the foot ⟨*stamp* out racism⟩ **2** : to walk heavily or noisily **3 a** : IMPRESS, IMPRINT ⟨*stamp* the bill "paid"⟩ **b** : to attach a stamp to ⟨*stamp* a letter⟩ **4** : to form with a stamp or die **5** : CHARACTERIZE 1 [Middle English *stampen*] — **stamp·er** *n*

²stamp \'stamp\ *n* **1** : a device or instrument for stamping **2** : the impression or mark made by stamping **3** : a distinctive character, indication, or mark **4** : the act of stamping **5** : a stamped or printed paper affixed in evidence that a tax has been paid; *also* : POSTAGE STAMP

¹stam·pede \stam-'pēd\ *n* **1** : a wild headlong rush or flight of frightened animals **2** : a mass movement of people at a common impulse [American Spanish *estampida,* from Spanish, "crash", from *estampar* "to stamp", of Germanic origin]

²stampede *vb* **1** : to run away or cause (as cattle) to run away in panic **2** : to act together or cause to act together suddenly and without thought (as in panic)

stamp·ing ground \'stamp-, 'stamp-, 'stȯmp-\ *n* : a favorite or habitual resort

stance \'stans\ *n* **1** : way of standing or being placed : POSTURE **2** : intellectual or emotional attitude ⟨an antiwar *stance*⟩ [Middle French *estance* "position, posture, stay", derived from Latin *stare* "to stand"]

¹stanch *also* **staunch** \'stȯnch, 'stänch\ *vt* : to stop the flowing of; *also* : to stop the flow of blood from (a wound) [Middle French *estancher,* derived from Latin *stare* "to stand"] — **stanch·er** *n*

²stanch *variant of* STAUNCH

¹stan·chion \'stan-chən\ *n* **1** : an upright bar, post, or support **2** : a device that fits loosely around an ani-

mal's neck and limits forward and backward motion (as in a stall) [Middle French *estanchon,* from *estance* "stance, stay, prop"]

²stanchion *vt* : to provide with stanchions : support or secure with or as if with a stanchion

¹stand \'stand\ *vb* **stood** \'stud\; **stand·ing** **1 a** : to support oneself on the feet in an erect position **b** : to be a specified height when fully erect ⟨*stands* two meters tall⟩ **c** : to rise to one's feet **2 a** : to take up or maintain a specified position or posture ⟨*stand* aside⟩ ⟨*stands* first in the class⟩ ⟨where do we *stand* on this question⟩ **b** : to maintain one's position ⟨*stand* fast⟩ **3** : to be in a particular state or situation ⟨*stands* accused⟩ **4** : to hold a course at sea ⟨*standing* away from the shore⟩ **5** *chiefly British* : to be a candidate : RUN **6 a** : to rest, remain, or set upright on a base or lower end ⟨the clock *stood* on the mantle⟩ **b** : to occupy a place or location ⟨a house *standing* on a knoll⟩ **7 a** : to remain stationary or inactive ⟨the car *stood* in the garage⟩ ⟨rainwater *standing* in pools⟩ **b** : to remain in effect ⟨the order *stands*⟩ **8** : to exist in a definite form ⟨you must take or leave the offer as it *stands*⟩ **9 a** : to endure or undergo successfully : BEAR, WITHSTAND ⟨*stand* pain⟩ ⟨able to *stand* an operation⟩ **b** : to submit to ⟨*stand* trial⟩ **10** : to perform the duty of ⟨*stand* guard⟩ **11** : to pay for ⟨*stand* drinks⟩ [Old English *standan*] — **stand·er** *n* — **stand by** : to be or remain loyal to ⟨*stood by* us in our hour of need⟩ — **stand for** **1** : to be a symbol for : REPRESENT **2** : to put up with : PERMIT — **stand on** **1** : to depend upon **2** : to insist on — **stand one's ground** : to maintain one's position — **stand pat** : to oppose or resist change

²stand *n* **1** : an act or instance of stopping or staying in one place: as **a** : a halt for defense or resistance ⟨a goal-line *stand*⟩ **b** : a stop made to give a theatrical performance **2 a** : a place or post where one stands **b** : a position with respect to an issue **3 a** : the place occupied by a witness testifying in court **b** : a tier of seats for spectators of an outdoor sport or spectacle **c** : a raised platform (as for a speaker) **4** : a small often open-air structure for a small retail business **5** : a support (as a rack or table) on or in which something may be placed ⟨umbrella *stands*⟩ **6** : a group of plants growing in a continuous area ⟨a good *stand* of wheat⟩

¹stan·dard \'stan-dərd\ *n* **1 a** : a figure adopted as an emblem by an organized body of people ⟨the eagle was the Roman legion's *standard*⟩ **b** : the personal flag of the ruler of a state **2 a** : something set up by authority or by general consent as a rule for measuring or as a model ⟨a *standard* of weight⟩ ⟨*standards* of good manners⟩ **b** : the basis of value in a monetary system **3** : a structure that serves as a support ⟨a lamp *standard*⟩ **4** : an enlarged upper petal of a flower; *esp* : one of the three inner usually erect and incurved petals of an iris [Middle French *estandard* "rallying point, standard", of Germanic origin] □ SYN STANDARD, GAUGE, CRITERION denote a means of determining what a thing should be. STANDARD applies to any definite rule, principle, or measure established by authority or custom ⟨*standards* of education⟩ GAUGE applies to a means of testing a particular dimension (as thickness, depth, or diameter) or a particular quality or aspect ⟨viewed awards as a *gauge* of quality in books⟩ CRITERION may apply to anything used as a test of quality whether or not it is formulated as a rule or principle ⟨the sole *criterion* for passing⟩

²standard *adj* **1 a** : constituting or conforming to a standard established by law or custom ⟨*standard* weight⟩ **b** : being sound and usable but not of special or the highest quality ⟨*standard* beef⟩ **2** : regularly and widely used ⟨*standard* practice in the trade⟩ **3** : having recognized and permanent value ⟨a *standard* reference work⟩ **4** : substantially uniform and well established by usage in the speech and writing of the educated and widely recognized as acceptable

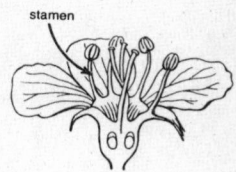

stamen

stamen

¹stanchion 2

\ə\ abut   \ng\ sing
\ər\ further \ō\ bone
\a\ mat   \ȯ\ saw
\ā\ take   \ȯi\ coin
\ä\ cot, cart \th\ thin
\aů\ out   \th\ this
\ch\ chin   \ü\ food
\e\ pet   \ů\ foot
\ē\ easy   \y\ yet
\g\ go   \yü\ few
\i\ tip   \yů\ cure
\ī\ life   \zh\ vision
\j\ job

STANDARD TIME IN 50 PLACES THROUGHOUT THE WORLD WHEN IT IS 12:00 NOON IN NEW YORK

CITY	TIME	CITY	TIME
[1]Amsterdam, Netherlands	6:00 P.M.	[2]Montevideo, Uruguay	2:00 P.M.
Anchorage, Alaska	8:00 A.M.	Montreal, Quebec	12:00 NOON
Bangkok, Thailand	12:00 MIDNIGHT	[1]Moscow, Russia	8:00 P.M.
Beijing, China	1:00 A.M. next day	Ottawa, Ontario	12:00 NOON
Berlin, Germany	6:00 P.M.	[1]Paris, France	6:00 P.M.
Bombay, India	10:30 P.M.	Perth, Australia	1:00 A.M. next day
[1]Brussels, Belgium	6:00 P.M.	Rio de Janeiro, Brazil	2:00 P.M.
[2]Buenos Aires, Argentina	2:00 P.M.	Rome, Italy	6:00 P.M.
Calcutta, India	10:30 P.M.	Saint John's, Newfoundland	1:30 P.M.
Cape Town, South Africa	7:00 P.M.	Salt Lake City, Utah	10:00 A.M.
Chicago, Illinois	11:00 A.M.	San Francisco, California	9:00 A.M.
Delhi, India	10:30 P.M.	San Juan, Puerto Rico	1:00 P.M.
Denver, Colorado	10:00 A.M.	Santiago, Chile	1:00 P.M.
Djakarta, Indonesia	12:00 MIDNIGHT	Shanghai, China	1:00 A.M. next day
Halifax, Nova Scotia	1:00 P.M.	Singapore	1:00 A.M. next day
Hong Kong	1:00 A.M. next day	Stockholm, Sweden	6:00 P.M.
Honolulu, Hawaii	7:00 A.M.	Sydney, Australia	3:00 A.M. next day
Istanbul, Turkey	7:00 P.M.	Tehran, Iran	8:30 P.M.
Juneau, Alaska	9:00 A.M.	Tokyo, Japan	2:00 A.M. next day
Karachi, Pakistan	10:00 P.M.	Toronto, Ontario	12:00 NOON
London, England	5:00 P.M.	Vancouver, British Columbia	9:00 A.M.
Los Angeles, California	9:00 A.M.	[1]Vladivostok, Russia	3:00 A.M. next day
[1]Madrid, Spain	6:00 P.M.	Washington, D.C.	12:00 NOON
Manilla, Philippines	1:00 A.M. next day	Wellington, New Zealand	5:00 A.M.
Mexico City, Mexico	11:00 A.M.	Winnipeg, Manitoba	11:00 A.M.

[1]Time in France, Spain, Netherlands, Belgium, and Russia is one hour in advance of the standard meridians.
[2]Time in Argentina and Uruguay is one hour in advance of the standard meridian.

stan·dard–bear·er \-ˌbar-ər, -ˌber-\ *n* **1** : one that bears a standard or banner **2** : the leader of an organization or movement

stan·dard·bred \-ˌbred\ *n* : any of an American breed of light trotting and pacing horses bred for speed and noted for endurance

Standard English *n* : the English that with respect to spelling, grammar, pronunciation, and vocabulary is substantially uniform though not devoid of regional differences, that is well established by usage in the formal and informal speech and writing of the educated, and that is widely recognized as acceptable wherever English is spoken and understood

stan·dard·ize \'stan-dər-ˌdīz\ *vt* : to compare with or bring into conformity with a standard — **stan·dard·iza·tion** \ˌstan-dərd-ə-'zā-shən\ *n*

standard of living : the necessities, comforts, and luxuries that a person or group is accustomed to

standard time *n* : the time established by law or by general usage over a region or country — compare ALASKA TIME, ATLANTIC TIME, CENTRAL TIME, EASTERN TIME, HAWAII-ALEUTIAN TIME, MOUNTAIN TIME, PACIFIC TIME, YUKON TIME
SEE TIME CHART ABOVE

stand·by \'stand-ˌbī, 'stan-\ *n, pl* **stand·bys** : one available or to be relied upon especially in emergencies

stand by \stand-'bī, 'stand-, stan-, 'stan-\ *vi* **1** : to be present; *also* : to remain aloof **2** : to be waiting in a state of readiness ⟨please *stand by*⟩

stand down *vi* : to leave the witness stand

stand·ee \stan-'dē\ *n* : one who occupies standing room

stand–in \'stan-ˌdin\ *n* **1** : someone employed to occupy a performer's place while lights and camera are readied **2** : SUBSTITUTE

stand in \stan-'din, 'stan-\ *vi* : to act as a stand-in — **stand in with** : to be in a specially favored position with

¹stand·ing \'stan-ding\ *adj* **1** : upright on the feet or base : ERECT ⟨*standing* timber⟩ **2 a** : not flowing : STAGNANT **b** : remaining the same for an indeterminate period ⟨a *standing* offer⟩ **c** : continuing in existence or use indefinitely : PERMANENT ⟨a *standing* army⟩ ⟨*standing* committees⟩ **3** : done from a standing position ⟨*standing* jump⟩

²standing *n* **1** : the action or position of one that stands **2** : DURATION ⟨a quarrel of long *standing*⟩; *esp* : length of service or experience especially as determining status ⟨postgraduate *standing*⟩ **3** : position or comparative rank (as in society, a profession, or a competitive activity) ⟨had the highest *standing* on the test⟩; *also* : good reputation ⟨people of *standing* in the community⟩

standing room *n* : space for standing; *esp* : accommodation available for spectators or passengers after all seats are filled

standing wave *n* : a vibration of a body or physical system in which the amplitude varies from place to place, is constantly zero at fixed points, and has maxima at other points

stand-off \'stan-ˌdȯf\ *n* **1** : a standing off; *esp* : ALOOFNESS **2 a** : a counterbalancing effect **b** : TIE 4b, DRAW

stand off \stan-'dȯf, 'stan-\ *vb* : to keep or hold at a distance (as in social intercourse)

stand·off·ish \stan-'dȯ-fish\ *adj* : lacking cordiality

stand·out \'stan-ˌdau̇t\ *n* : one that is prominent or conspicuous especially because of excellence

stand out \stan-'dau̇t, 'stan-\ *vi* **1 a** : to appear as if in relief : PROJECT **b** : to be prominent or conspicuous **2** : to be stubborn in resolution or resistance

stand-pat \'stand-ˌpat, 'stan-\ *adj* : stubbornly conservative — **stand·pat·ter** \-ˌpat-ər\ *n*

stand-pipe \'stand-ˌpīp, 'stan-\ *n* : a high vertical pipe or reservoir used to deliver water at uniform pressure

stand-point \-ˌpȯint\ *n* : a position from which objects or principles are viewed and according to which they are compared and judged

stand-still \-ˌstil\ *n* : a complete stop

stand up *vb* **1** : to remain sound and intact **2** : to fail to keep an appointment with — **stand up for** : DEFEND ⟨*stand up for* one's beliefs⟩ — **stand up to 1** : to meet fairly and fully **2** : to face boldly

stank *past of* STINK

stan·nic \'stan-ik\ *adj* : of, relating to, or containing tin especially with a valence of four [derived from Late Latin *stannum* "tin"]

stan·nous \'stan-əs\ *adj* : of, relating to, or containing tin especially when bivalent

stan·za \'stan-zə\ *n* : a division of a poem consisting of a series of lines arranged together in a usually recurring pattern of meter and rhyme [Italian, "stay, abode, room, stanza", derived from Latin *stare* "to stand"] — **stan·za·ic** \stan-'zā-ik\ *adj*

sta·pes \'stā-,pēz\ *n, pl* **stapes** *or* **sta·pe·des** \'stā-pə-,dēz\ : the innermost ossicle of the ear of a mammal — compare INCUS, MALLEUS [Medieval Latin, "stirrup"] — **sta·pe·di·al** \stā-'pēd-ē-əl, stə-\ *adj*

staph \'staf\ *n* : STAPHYLOCOCCUS

staph·y·lo·coc·cus \,staf-ə-lō-'käk-əs\ *n, pl* **-coc·ci** \-'käk-,sī, -,ī, -,sē, -,ē\ : any of various nonmotile spherical bacteria that occur especially in irregular clusters and include parasites of skin and mucous membranes [derived from Greek *staphylē* "bunch of grapes" + *kokkos* "grain, seed"] — **staph·y·lo·coc·cal** \-'käk-əl\ *adj* — **staph·y·lo·coc·cic** \-'käk-sik, -ik\ *adj*

¹sta·ple \'stā-pəl\ *n* **1** : a U-shaped piece of metal usually with sharp points to be driven into a surface to hold something (as fence wire) in place **2** : a U-shaped piece of thin wire to be driven through layers of thin material (as paper) and bent over at the ends to fasten them together [Old English *stapol* "post"]

²staple *vt* **sta·pled; sta·pling** \-pə-ling, -pling\ : to fasten with staples

³staple *n* **1** : a town established formerly as a center for the sale or exportation of commodities in bulk **2** : a place of supply : SOURCE **3** : a chief commodity or product of a place **4 a** : something in widespread and constant use or demand **b** : the sustaining or principal element : SUBSTANCE **5** : RAW MATERIAL **6** : textile fiber (as wool or rayon) of relatively short length that when spun and twisted forms a yarn rather than a filament [Dutch *stapel* "emporium"]

⁴staple *adj* **1** : used, needed, or enjoyed constantly usually by many individuals **2** : produced regularly or in large quantities **3** : PRINCIPAL, CHIEF ⟨our *staple* crop⟩

sta·pler \'stā-plər\ *n* : a device that staples

¹star \'stär\ *n* **1** : a natural luminous body visible in the sky especially at night **2** : a self-luminous gaseous celestial body (as the sun) of great mass whose shape is usually spheroidal and whose size may be as small as the earth's or larger than the earth's orbit **3 a** : a planet or a configuration of the planets that is held in astrology to influence one's destiny or fortune — usually used in pl. **b** : FORTUNE 2, FAME **c** *obsolete* : DESTINY **2 4 a** : a conventional figure with five or more points that represents or resembles a star; *esp* : ASTERISK **b** : an often star-shaped ornament or medal worn as a badge of honor, authority, or rank or as the insignia of an order **5 a** : the principal member of a theatrical or operatic company **b** : an outstandingly talented performer **c** : one who stands out among one's peers ⟨one of the brightest *stars* in the legal profession⟩ [Old English *steorra*] — **star·less** \-ləs\ *adj* — **star·like** \-,līk\ *adj*

²star *vb* **starred; star·ring** **1** : to sprinkle or adorn with stars **2 a** : to mark with a star as being superior **b** : to mark with an asterisk **3** : to present in the role of a star **4** : to play the most prominent or important role ⟨will *star* in a new play⟩ **5** : to perform outstandingly ⟨*starred* at shortstop⟩

³star *adj* **1** : of, relating to, or being a star **2** : being of outstanding excellence ⟨a *star* athlete⟩

¹star·board \'stär-bərd\ *n* : the right side of a ship or aircraft looking forward — compare ³PORT [Old English *stēorbord,* from *stēor-* "steering oar" + *bord* "ship's side"]

²starboard *adj* : of, relating to, or situated to starboard

¹starch \'stärch\ *vt* : to stiffen with or as if with starch [Middle English *sterchen*]

²starch *n* **1** : a white odorless tasteless granular or powdery complex carbohydrate $(C_6H_{10}O_5)_x$ that is the chief storage form of carbohydrate in plants, is an important foodstuff, and is used also in adhesives and sizes, in laundering, and in pharmacy and medicine **2** : a stiff formal manner : FORMALITY **3** : resolute vigor : ENERGY

Star Chamber *n* : a court existing in England from the 15th century until 1641 with wide civil and criminal jurisdiction and marked by secret often arbitrary and oppressive procedures

starchy \'stär-chē\ *adj* **starch·i·er; -est** **1** : containing, consisting of, or resembling starch **2** : consisting of or marked by formality or stiffness — **starch·i·ness** *n*

star–crossed \'stär-,kröst\ *adj* : not favored by the stars : ILL-FATED

star·dom \'stärd-əm\ *n* : the status or position of a star ⟨rose to *stardom* in Hollywood⟩

star·dust \'stär-,dəst\ *n* : a feeling or impression of romance, magic, or ethereality

¹stare \'staər, 'steər\ *vb* **1** : to look fixedly often with wide-open eyes ⟨*stare* at a stranger⟩ **2** : to show up conspicuously **3** : to have an effect upon by looking fixedly [Old English *starian*] — **star·er** *n*

²stare *n* : the act or an instance of staring

stare down *vt* : to cause to waver or submit by or as if by staring ⟨*stare down* a dog⟩

star·fish \'stär-,fish\ *n* : any of a class (Asteroidea) of echinoderms having a body of usually five arms radially arranged about a central disk and feeding largely on mollusks (as oysters)

star·flow·er \-,flaù-ər, -,flaùr\ *n* : any of several plants (as a star-of-Bethlehem) having star-shaped 5-petaled flowers

star·gaze \-,gāz\ *vi* **1** : to gaze at stars **2** : to stare absentmindedly : DAYDREAM [back-formation from *stargazer*]

star·gaz·er \-,gā-zər\ *n* : one that gazes at the stars: as **a** : ASTROLOGER **b** : ASTRONOMER

¹stark \'stärk\ *adj* **1** : STRONG 1, ROBUST **2 a** : rigid in or as if in death **b** : INFLEXIBLE **3**, STRICT ⟨*stark* discipline⟩ **3** : SHEER, UTTER ⟨*stark* nonsense⟩ **4 a** : BARREN, DESOLATE ⟨a *stark* landscape⟩ **b** (1) : having few or no ornaments : BARE (2) : HARSH, UNADORNED ⟨*stark* realism⟩ **5** : sharply delineated [Old English *stearc* "stiff, strong"] — **stark·ly** *adv* — **stark·ness** *n*

²stark *adv* **1** : in a stark manner **2** : WHOLLY 1 ⟨*stark* mad⟩

star·let \'stär-lət\ *n* : a young movie actress being coached and publicized for starring roles

star·light \-,līt\ *n* : the light given by the stars

star·ling \'stär-ling\ *n* : any of a family of usually dark passerine birds that tend to flock together; *esp* : a dark brown or in summer glossy greenish black European bird naturalized and often a pest in the United States [Old English *stærlinc,* from *stær* "starling" + *-ling, -linc* "-ling"]

star·lit \'stär-,lit\ *adj* : lighted by the stars

star–of–Bethlehem *n* : any of a genus of plants of the lily family with 5-petaled usually greenish white flowers

star of Beth·le·hem \-'beth-li-,hem, -lē-həm, -lē-əm\ : a star held to have guided the three wise men to the infant Jesus in Bethlehem

Star of Da·vid \-'dā-vəd\ : a hexagram used as a symbol of Judaism

star·ry \'stär-ē\ *adj* **star·ri·er; -est** **1** : adorned with stars ⟨*starry* heavens⟩ **2** : of, relating to, or consisting of the stars : STELLAR ⟨*starry* light⟩ **3** : shining like stars : SPARKLING ⟨*starry* eyes⟩

star·ry–eyed \,stär-ē-'īd\ *adj* : regarding an object or a prospect in an overly favorable light

Stars and Bars *n sing or pl* : the first flag of the Confederate States of America having three bars of red, white, and red respectively and a blue union with white stars in a circle representing the seceded states

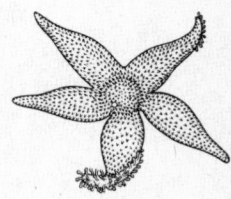

starfish

\ə\ abut   \ng\ sing
\ər\ further   \ō\ bone
\a\ mat   \ó\ saw
\ā\ take   \oi\ coin
\ä\ cot, cart   \th\ thin
\aú\ out   \t͟h\ this
\ch\ chin   \ü\ food
\e\ pet   \ú\ foot
\ē\ easy   \y\ yet
\g\ go   \yü\ few
\i\ tip   \yù\ cure
\ī\ life   \zh\ vision
\j\ job

Stars and Stripes *n sing or pl* : the flag of the United States having 13 alternately red and white horizontal stripes and a blue union with one white star for each state

star–span·gled \'stär-ˌspang-gəld\ *adj* : studded with stars

Star–Spangled Banner *n* : STARS AND STRIPES

¹**start** \'stärt\ *vb* 1 : to move suddenly and sharply : react with a quick involuntary movement 2 a : to issue with sudden force ⟨blood *starting* from the wound⟩ b : to come into being, activity, or operation : BEGIN 3 : BULGE ⟨eyes *starting* from their sockets⟩ 4 : to become or cause to become loosened or forced out of place 5 a : to begin a course or journey b : to range from a specified initial point ⟨the rates *start* at ten dollars⟩ 6 : to be or cause to be a participant in a game or contest; *esp* : to be or cause to be in the lineup at the beginning of a game 7 : to cause to leave a place of concealment : FLUSH 8 *archaic* : STARTLE 2, ALARM 9 : to bring up for consideration or discussion 10 : to bring into being ⟨*start* a rumor⟩ 11 : to begin the use or employment of ⟨*start* a fresh loaf of bread⟩ 12 a : to cause to move, act, or operate ⟨*start* the motor⟩ b : to care for during early stages ⟨*start* seedlings indoors⟩ 13 : to perform the first stages or action of ⟨*started* studying music⟩ [Middle English *sterten*]

²**start** *n* 1 a : a quick involuntary bodily reaction b : a brief and sudden action or movement c : a sudden impulse or outburst 2 : a beginning of movement, activity, or development 3 : a lead or advantage at the beginning of a race or competition : HEAD START 4 : a place of beginning 5 : the act or an instance of being a competitor in a race or a member of a lineup at the beginning of a game

start·er \'stärt-ər\ *n* 1 : one that initiates or sets going: as a : an official who gives the signal to begin a race b : one who dispatches vehicles 2 a : one that enters a competition or that regularly appears in a lineup at the beginning of games b : one that begins to engage in an activity or process 3 : one that causes something to begin operating: as a : SELF-STARTER b : material containing microorganisms used to induce a desired fermentation 4 : something that is the beginning of a process, activity, or series

¹**star·tle** \'stärt-l\ *vb* **star·tled; star·tling** \'stärt-ling, -l-ing\ 1 : to move or jump suddenly as in surprise or alarm 2 : to frighten suddenly and usually not seriously 3 : to cause to start [Middle English *stertlen*, from *sterten* "to start"]

²**startle** *n* : a sudden mild shock (as of surprise or alarm)

star·tling *adj* : causing a momentary fright, surprise, or astonishment — **star·tling·ly** \'stärt-ling-lē, -l-ing-\ *adv*

star·va·tion \stär-'vā-shən\ *n* : the act or an instance of starving : the state of being starved

starve \'stärv\ *vb* 1 : to die or suffer greatly from lack of food 2 *archaic* : to die of or suffer greatly from cold b : to kill with cold 3 : to suffer or perish or cause to suffer or perish from deprivation ⟨a child *starving* for affection⟩ 4 a : to kill or subdue with hunger b : to deprive of nourishment c : to cause to submit as if by depriving of nourishment [Old English *steorfan* "to die"]

starve·ling \-ling\ *n* : one thin and weakened by or as if by lack of food

¹**stash** \'stash\ *vt* : to store in a usually secret place for future use [origin unknown]

²**stash** *n* 1 : hiding place : CACHE 2 : something stored or hidden away

sta·sis \'stā-səs, 'stas-əs\ *n, pl* **sta·ses** \'stā-ˌsēz, 'stas-ˌēz\ 1 : a slowing or stoppage of a normal bodily flow (as of blood) or rhythmic movement (as of the intestine) 2 : a state of static balance among opposing tendencies or forces : STAGNATION [Greek, "act or condi-

tion of standing, stopping", from *histasthai* "to stand"]

stat·able *or* **state·able** \'stāt-ə-bəl\ *adj* : capable of being stated

¹**state** \'stāt\ *n* 1 a : mode or condition of being ⟨water in the gaseous *state*⟩ ⟨a *state* of readiness⟩ b (1) : condition of mind or temperament ⟨in a highly nervous *state*⟩ (2) : a condition of abnormal tension or excitement 2 a : social positon; *esp* : high rank b (1) : elaborate or luxurious style of living (2) : formal dignity ⟨travel in *state*⟩ 3 a : ESTATE 3 b *obsolete* : a person of high rank : NOBLE 4 a : a politically organized body of people usually occupying a definite territory; *esp* : one that is sovereign b : the political organization of such a body of people 5 : the operations or concerns of the government of a country 6 : one of the units which make up a nation having a federal government ⟨the United *States* of America⟩ 7 : the territory of a state [Latin *status*, from *stare* "to stand"] — **state·less** \-ləs\ *adj* — **state·less·ness** *n*

²**state** *adj* 1 : suitable or used for ceremonial or formal occasions ⟨*state* robes⟩ 2 : of or relating to a national state or to one of the units which make up a federal government ⟨a *state* church⟩ ⟨a *state* legislature⟩ 3 : GOVERNMENTAL ⟨*state* secrets⟩

³**state** *vt* 1 : to set by regulation or authority 2 : to express the particulars of especially in words; *also* : to express in words ⟨*state* an opinion⟩

state bank *n* : a bank chartered by and operating under the laws of a state especially of the United States

state capitalism *n* : an economic system in which capital is largely under government ownership and control while other economic relations are little changed from capitalism

state college *n* : a college that is financially supported by a state government and often specializes in a branch of technical or professional education

state·craft \'stāt-ˌkraft\ *n* : the art of conducting government affairs

stat·ed \'stāt-əd\ *adj* 1 : FIXED, REGULAR ⟨at *stated* times⟩ 2 : set down definitely — **stat·ed·ly** *adv*

stated clerk *n* : an executive officer of a Presbyterian governing body (as a synod) ranking below the moderator

State flower *n* : a flowering plant selected as the floral emblem of a state of the United States

state·hood \'stāt-ˌhùd\ *n* : the condition of being a state; *esp* : the condition or status of one of the states of the United States

state·house \-ˌhaùs\ *n* : the building in which a state legislature sits

state·ly \'stāt-lē\ *adj* **state·li·er; -est** 1 a : HAUGHTY, UNAPPROACHABLE b : marked by lofty or imposing dignity 2 : impressive in size or proportions — **state·li·ness** *n* — **stately** *adv*

state·ment \'stāt-mənt\ *n* 1 : the act or process of stating or presenting orally or on paper 2 : something stated: as a : a report of facts or opinions b : a single declaration or remark : ASSERTION 3 : PROPOSITION 2 4 : a brief summarized record of a financial account ⟨a monthly bank *statement*⟩ 5 : an instruction in a computer program

state·room \'stāt-ˌrüm, -ˌrùm\ *n* : a private room on a boat or ship or on a railroad car

state's evidence *n, often cap S* 1 : one who gives evidence for the prosecution in United States state or federal criminal proceedings 2 : evidence for the prosecution in a criminal proceeding

States General *n pl* : the assembly of the three orders of clergy, nobility, and third estate in France before the Revolution

¹**state·side** \'stāt-ˌsīd\ *adj* : of or relating to the United States as regarded from outside its conterminous limits [(*United*) *States* + *side*]

²state·side *adv* : in or to the conterminous states of the United States

states·man \'stāt-smən\ *n* : a person engaged in fixing the policies and conducting the affairs of a government; *esp* : one having unusual wisdom in such matters — **states·man·like** \-ˌlīk\ *adj* — **states·man·ly** \-lē\ *adj* — **states·man·ship** \-ˌship\ *n*

state socialism *n* : an economic system with limited socialist characteristics introduced by usually gradual political action

states' rights *n pl* : all rights not vested by the Constitution of the United States in the federal government nor forbidden by it to the separate states

state·wide \'stāt-'wīd\ *adj* : including all parts of a state

¹stat·ic \'stat-ik\ *adj* **1** : exerting force by reason of weight alone without motion ⟨*static* load⟩ **2** : of or relating to bodies at rest or forces in equilibrium **3** : showing little change **4 a** : marked by a lack of movement, animation, or progress **b** : producing an effect of rest or interruption **5** : standing or fixed in one place : STATIONARY **6** : of, relating to, producing, or being stationary charges of electricity (as those produced by friction or induction) **7** : of, relating to, or caused by radio static [Greek *statikos* "causing to stand", from *histanai* "to cause to stand, weigh"] — **stat·i·cal·ly** \'stat-i-kə-lē, -klē\ *adv*

²static *n* : noise produced in a radio or television receiver by atmospheric or electrical disturbances; *also* : the electrical disturbances producing this noise [*static electricity*]

static line *n* : a cord attached to a parachute pack and to an airplane to open the parachute after a jumper clears the plane

stat·ics \'stat-iks\ *n* : a branch of mechanics dealing with the relations of forces that produce equilibrium among material bodies

¹sta·tion \'stā-shən\ *n* **1** : the place or position in which something or someone stands or is assigned to stand or remain **2** : the act or manner of standing : POSTURE **3** : a stopping place: as **a** : a regular stopping place in a transportation route **b** : a building at such a stopping place : DEPOT **4 a** : a post or sphere of duty or occupation **b** : a stock farm of Australia or New Zealand **5** : social standing : RANK **6** : a place for specialized observation and study of scientific phenomena ⟨a weather *station*⟩ **7 a** : a place established to provide a public service ⟨police *station*⟩ ⟨power *station*⟩ **b** : a branch post office **8 a** : a complete assemblage of radio or television equipment for transmitting or receiving **b** : the place in which such a station is located [Middle French, from Latin *statio*, from *stare* "to stand"]

²station *vt* **sta·tioned; sta·tion·ing** \'stā-shə-ning, -shning\ : to assign or set in a station or position : POST

sta·tion·ary \'stā-shə-ˌner-ē\ *adj* **1** : fixed in a station, course, or mode : IMMOBILE **2** : unchanging in condition : STABLE

station break *n* : a pause in a radio or television broadcast for announcement of the identity of the network or station

sta·tio·ner \'stā-shə-nər, -shnər\ *n* **1** *archaic* **a** : BOOKSELLER **b** : PUBLISHER **2** : one that sells stationery [Medieval Latin *stationarius*, from *statio* "shop", from Latin, "station"]

sta·tio·nery \'stā-shə-ˌner-ē\ *n* **1** : materials (as paper, pens, and ink) for writing or typing **2** : letter paper usually with matching envelopes [*stationer*]

station house *n* : a police station

sta·tion·mas·ter \'stā-shən-ˌmas-tər\ *n* : an official in charge of the operation of a railroad station

stations of the cross *often cap S&C* **1** : a series of usually 14 images or pictures especially in a church that represent the stages of Christ's passion **2** : a devotion involving commemorative meditation before the stations of the cross

station wagon *n* : an automobile that has an interior longer than a sedan's, has one or more rear seats readily lifted out or folded to facilitate light trucking, has no separate luggage compartment, and often has a door at the rear end

stat·ism \'stāt-ˌiz-əm\ *n* : a concentration of economic controls and planning in the hands of a highly centralized government

sta·tis·tic \stə-'tis-tik\ *n* : a single term or datum in a collection of statistics [back-formation from *statistics*]

stat·is·ti·cian \ˌstat-ə-'stish-ən\ *n* : one versed in or engaged in compiling statistics

sta·tis·tics \stə-'tis-tiks\ *n sing or pl* : a branch of mathematics dealing with the collection, analysis, interpretation, and presentation of masses of numerical data; *also* : a collection of such numerical data [German *statistik* "study of political data", derived from Latin *status* "state"] — **sta·tis·ti·cal** \-'tis-ti-kəl\ *adj* — **sta·tis·ti·cal·ly** \-ti-kə-lē, -klē\ *adv*

stato- *combining form* **1** : resting **2** : equilibrium ⟨*stato*cyst⟩ [Greek *statos* "stationary", from *histasthai* "to stand"]

stat·o·cyst \'stat-ə-ˌsist\ *n* : an organ of equilibrium occurring especially in invertebrate animals and consisting usually of a fluid-filled vesicle in which are suspended calcium-containing particles

stat·o·lith \'stat-l-ˌith\ *n* : a calcium-containing body in a statocyst

sta·tor \'stāt-ər\ *n* : a stationary part in a machine in or about which a rotor revolves [Latin, "one that stands", from *stare* "to stand"]

stat·u·ary \'stach-ə-ˌwer-ē\ *n, pl* **-ar·ies** **1 a** : the art of making statues **b** : a collection of statues **2** : SCULPTOR — **statuary** *adj*

stat·ue \'stach-ü\ *n* : a likeness (as of a person or animal) sculptured, modeled, or cast in a solid substance [Middle French, from Latin *statua*, from *statuere* "to set up", from *status* "position, state"]

stat·u·esque \ˌstach-ə-'wesk\ *adj* : resembling a statue especially in well-proportioned or massive dignity — **stat·u·esque·ly** *adv* — **stat·u·esque·ness** *n*

stat·u·ette \ˌstach-ə-'wet\ *n* : a small statue

stat·ure \'stach-ər\ *n* **1** : natural height (as of a person) in an upright position **2** : quality or status gained by growth, development, or achievement ⟨reached adult *stature*⟩ [Old French, from Latin *statura*, from *stare* "to stand"]

sta·tus \'stāt-əs, 'stat-\ *n* **1** : position or rank in relation to others : STANDING **2** : CONDITION, SITUATION ⟨the economic *status* of a country⟩ [Latin, "position, state, status"]

sta·tus quo \ˌstāt-əs-'kwō, ˌstat-\ *n* : the existing state of affairs [Latin, "state in which"]

stat·ute \'stach-üt, -ət\ *n* : a law enacted by the legislative branch of a government [Old French *statut*, from Late Latin *statutum* "law, regulation", from Latin *statuere* "to set up", from *status* "position, state"] **syn** see LAW

statute mile *n* : MILE 1

statute of limitations : a statute assigning a certain time after which rights cannot be enforced by legal action

stat·u·to·ry \'stach-ə-ˌtōr-ē, -ˌtor-\ *adj* **1** : of, relating to, or of the nature of a statute **2** : enacted, created or regulated by statute

¹staunch *variant of* STANCH

²staunch *or* **stanch** \'stȯnch, 'stänch\ *adj* **1 a** : WATERTIGHT, SOUND ⟨a *staunch* ship⟩ **b** : strongly built : SUBSTANTIAL ⟨*staunch* foundations⟩ **2** : steadfast in loyalty or principle ⟨a *staunch* friend⟩ [Middle French *estanc*, from *estancher* "to stanch"] — **staunch·ly** *adv* — **staunch·ness** *n*

¹stave \'stāv\ *n* **1** : a wooden stick **2** : one of the narrow strips of wood or narrow iron plates placed edge

\ə\ abut		\ng\ sing	
\ər\ further		\ō\ bone	
\a\ mat		\o\ saw	
\ā\ take		\oi\ coin	
\ä\ cot, cart		\th\ thin	
\au̇\ out		\th\ this	
\ch\ chin		\ü\ food	
\e\ pet		\u̇\ foot	
\ē\ easy		\y\ yet	
\g\ go		\yü\ few	
\i\ tip		\yu̇\ cure	
\ī\ life		\zh\ vision	
\j\ job			

stave

¹stave 2

to edge to form the sides, covering, or lining of a vessel (as a barrel) or structure **3** : STANZA **4** : STAFF 3 [back-formation from *staves*]

²**stave** *vb* **staved** *or* **stove** \'stōv\; **stav·ing** **I** : to break in the stave of (a cask) **2** : to smash a hole in ⟨*stave* in a boat⟩; *also* : to crush or break inward ⟨*staved* in several ribs⟩ **3** : to drive or thrust away **4** : to become stove in — used of a boat or ship

stave off *vt* : to ward or fend off ⟨*stave off* trouble⟩

staves *pl of* STAFF

¹**stay** \'stā\ *n* : a strong rope or wire used to steady or brace something (as a mast) [Old English *stæg*]

²**stay** *vb* **I** : to fasten (as a smokestack) with stays **2** : to go about : TACK

³**stay** *vb* **stayed** \'stād\ *or* **staid** \'stād\; **stay·ing I** : to stop going forward : PAUSE **2** : to continue in a place or condition : REMAIN **3** : to stand firm **4** : to take up residence : LODGE **5** : WAIT 1 **6** : to last out (as a race) **7** : CHECK, HALT ⟨*stay* an execution⟩ **8** : ALLAY ⟨*stayed* the unrest⟩ [Middle French *ester* "to stand, stay", from Latin *stare*] □ SYN STAY, REMAIN, ABIDE, LINGER mean to continue in a place. STAY often implies the status of a guest or visitor; REMAIN suggests a continuing after others have gone; ABIDE may imply either continuing indefinitely in a residence or waiting patiently for an outcome; LINGER implies failing to depart when it is time to do so.

⁴**stay** *n* **I** : the action of halting : the state of being stopped **2** : a residence or visit in a place

⁵**stay** *n* **I a** : something that serves as a prop : SUPPORT **b** : a thin firm strip (as of whalebone, steel, or plastic) used for stiffening a garment (as a corset) or part (as a shirt collar) **2** : a corset stiffened with stays — usually used in pl. [Middle French *estaie*, of Germanic origin]

⁶**stay** *vt* **I** : to provide physical or moral support for : SUSTAIN **2** : to fix on something as a foundation : REST

stay-at-home \'stā-ət-ˌhōm\ *n* : one that seldom travels or wanders from home : HOMEBODY

staying power *n* : capacity for endurance

stay·sail \'stā-ˌsāl, -səl\ *n* : a fore-and-aft sail hoisted on a stay

STD \ˌes-ˌtē-'dē\ *n* : any of various diseases transmitted by direct sexual contact that include the classic venereal diseases (as syphilis and gonorrhea) and other diseases (as hepatitis and AIDS) that are often or sometimes contracted by other than sexual means [*s*exually *t*ransmitted *d*isease]

stead \'sted\ *n* **I** : ADVANTAGE, SERVICE ⟨my knowledge of French stood me in good *stead*⟩ **2** : the office, place, or function ordinarily occupied or carried out by someone or something else ⟨acted in the mayor's *stead*⟩ [Old English *stede* "place, position"]

stead·fast \'sted-ˌfast\ *adj* **I a** : firmly fixed in place **b** : not subject to change ⟨a *steadfast* purpose⟩ **2** : firm in belief, determination, or adherence : LOYAL ⟨*steadfast* friends⟩ [Old English *stedefæst*, from *stede* "place" + *fæst* "fixed, fast"] SYN see FAITHFUL — **stead·fast·ly** *adv* — **stead·fast·ness** \-ˌfast-nəs, -ˌfas-\ *n*

stead·ing \'sted-ing\ *n* : a small farm or homestead [Middle English *steding*, from *stede* "place, farm"]

¹**steady** \'sted-ē\ *adj* **stead·i·er; -est I a** : firm in position : FIXED **b** : direct or sure in movement : UNFALTERING **2 a** : REGULAR, UNIFORM ⟨a *steady* pace⟩ **b** : not changing constantly or varying widely **3 a** : not easily moved or upset **b** : constant in feeling, principle, purpose, or attachment : DEPENDABLE **c** : not given to dissipation or disorderly behavior [obsolete *stead* "place, position", from Old English *stede*] — **stead·i·ly** \'sted-l-ē\ *adv* — **stead·iness** \'sted-ē-nəs\ *n* □ SYN STEADY, EVEN, UNIFORM mean not varying throughout a course or extent. STEADY implies lack of fluctuation or interruption of movement; EVEN suggests an absence of variation in quality or character; UNIFORM stresses

the sameness or alikeness of all the elements of an aggregate, a series, or a set.

²**steady** *vb* **stead·ied; steady·ing** : to make, keep, or become steady

³**steady** *adv* **I** : in a steady manner : STEADILY **2** : on the course set — used as a direction to the helmsman of a ship

⁴**steady** *n, pl* **stead·ies** : one that is steady; *esp* : a boyfriend or girl friend with whom one goes steady

steady state *n* : a dynamically balanced conditon of a system or process that when once established tends to persist

steady state theory *n* : a theory in astronomy : the universe has always existed and has always been expanding with hydrogen being created continuously — compare BIG BANG THEORY

steak \'stāk\ *n* **I a** : a slice of meat cut from a fleshy part of a beef carcass **b** : a similar slice of a specified meat other than beef **2** : a cross-sectional slice of a large fish (as salmon) [Old Norse *steik*]

steak knife *n* : a table knife having a blade with a sharp often serrated edge

¹**steal** \'stēl\ *vb* **stole** \'stōl\; **sto·len** \'stō-lən\; **steal·ing I** : to come or go secretly, quietly, gradually, or unexpectedly ⟨*stole* out of the room⟩ **2 a** : to take and carry away without right and with intent to keep the property of another **b** : to take entirely to oneself or beyond one's proper share ⟨*steal* the show⟩ **3 a** : to move, transfer, or introduce secretly : SMUGGLE **b** : to accomplish or get in a concealed or unobserved manner ⟨*steal* a nap⟩ **4 a** : to seize, gain, or win by trickery, skill, or daring **b** : to reach a base in baseball by running without the aid of a hit or an error [Old English *stelan*] — **steal·er** *n*

²**steal** *n* **I** : the act or an instance of stealing **2** : something offered or purchased at a low price : BARGAIN

stealth \'stelth\ *n* **I** : furtive or secret action ⟨entered the building by *stealth*⟩ **2** : an aircraft-design style intended to make an airplane difficult to detect by radar [Middle English *stelthe*]

stealthy \'stel-thē\ *adj* **stealth·i·er; -est I** : slow and secret in action or character **2** : intended to escape observation ⟨*stealthy* glances⟩ — **stealth·i·ly** \-thə-lē\ *adv* — **stealth·i·ness** \-thē-nəs\ *n*

¹**steam** \'stēm\ *n* **I a** : the invisible vapor into which water is converted when heated to the boiling point **b** : the mist formed by the condensation on cooling of water vapor **2 a** : water vapor kept under pressure so as to supply energy for heating, cooking, or mechanical work; *also* : the power so generated **b** : driving force : POWER ⟨arrived under their own *steam*⟩ **c** : emotional tension ⟨needed to let off a little *steam* after exams⟩ **3 a** : STEAMER 2a **b** : travel by or a trip in a steamer [Old English *stēam*]

²**steam** *vb* **I** : to rise or pass off as vapor **2** : to give off steam or vapor **3** : to move or travel by or as if by the agency of steam **4** : to be angry : BOIL **5** : to expose to the action of steam (as for softening or cooking)

steam·boat \-ˌbōt\ *n* : a boat propelled by steam power

steam engine *n* : an engine driven by steam; *esp* : a reciprocating engine having a piston driven in a closed cylinder by steam

steam·er \'stē-mər\ *n* **I** : a vessel in which something is steamed **2 a** : a ship propelled by steam **b** : an engine, machine, or vehicle operated by steam

steamer rug *n* : a warm covering for the lap and feet especially of a person sitting on a ship's deck

steamer trunk *n* : a trunk suitable for use in a stateroom of a steamer

steam fitter *n* : one that installs or repairs equipment (as steam pipes) for heating, ventilating, or refrigerating systems — **steam fitting** *n*

steam iron *n* : a pressing iron with a compartment holding water that is converted to steam by the iron's heat and emitted through the bottom onto the fabric being pressed

¹steam·roll·er \\'stēm-'rō-lər\\ *n* **1** : a machine formerly driven by steam that is equipped with heavy wide rollers for compacting roads and pavements **2** : a power or force that crushes opposition

²steamroller *also* **steam·roll** \\-'rōl\\ *vb* **1** : to crush with a steamroller **2 a** : to overcome by greatly superior force **b** : to exert crushing force or pressure with respect to **3** : to move or proceed with irresistible force

steam·ship \\'stēm-,ship\\ *n* : STEAMER 2a

steam shovel *n* : a power shovel formerly operated by steam

steam table *n* : a table having openings to hold containers of cooked food over steam or hot water circulating beneath them

steam turbine *n* : a turbine that is driven by the pressure of steam discharged at high velocity against the turbine vanes

steamy \\'stē-mē\\ *adj* **steam·i·er; -est** : consisting of, characterized by, or full of steam — **steam·i·ly** \\-mə-lē\\ *adv* — **steam·i·ness** \\-mē-nəs\\ *n*

ste·ap·sin \\stē-'ap-sən\\ *n* : a fat-digesting enzyme in pancreatic juice [Greek *stear* "fat" + English *-psin* (as in *pepsin*)]

stea·rate \\'stē-ə-,rāt, 'sti-ər-,āt, 'stir-,āt\\ *n* : a salt or ester of stearic acid

stea·ric acid \\stē-,ar-ik-, ,stiər-ik-\\ *n* : a white crystalline fatty acid obtained by saponifying tallow or other hard fats containing stearin [derived from Greek *stear* "fat, suet"]

stea·rin \\'stē-ə-rən, 'sti-ər-ən, 'stir-ən\\ *n* **1** : an ester of glycerol and stearic acid **2** *also* **stea·rine** \\same or -,rēn, -,ēn\\ : the solid portion of a fat

ste·atite \\'stē-ə-,tīt\\ *n* : a massive talc having a grayish green or brown color : SOAPSTONE [Latin *steatitis*, a precious stone, from Greek, from *steat-, stear* "fat"]

steed \\'stēd\\ *n* : HORSE; *esp* : a spirited horse [Old English *stēda* "stallion"]

¹steel \\'stēl\\ *n* **1** : commercial iron that contains carbon in any amount up to about 1.7 percent as an essential alloying constituent and is distinguished from cast iron by its malleability and lower carbon content **2** : an instrument or implement of or characteristically of steel: as **a** : a thrusting or cutting weapon **b** : an instrument (as a fluted round rod with a handle) for sharpening knives **c** : a piece of steel for striking sparks from flint **3** : a hard cold quality suggestive of steel [Old English *stȳle, stēle*]

²steel *vt* **1** : to overlay, point, or edge with steel **2** : to make hard or unbending ⟨*steel* one's heart⟩

³steel *adj* **1** : made of or resembling steel **2** : of or relating to the production of steel

steel guitar *n* : HAWAIIAN GUITAR

steel·head \\'stēl-,hed\\ *n* : a large silvery western North American seagoing trout that ascends rivers to breed and is usually held to be a race of the rainbow trout

steel·ie *also* **steely** \\'stē-lē\\ *n, pl* **steelies** : a small steel ball used in playing marbles

steel wool *n* : an abrasive material composed of long fine steel shavings and used especially for scouring and burnishing

steel·work \\'stēl-,wərk\\ *n* **1** : work in steel **2** *pl* : an establishment where steel is made — **steel·work·er** \\-,wər-kər\\ *n*

steely \\'stē-lē\\ *adj* **steel·i·er; -est** **1** : made of steel **2** : resembling steel ⟨*steely* determination⟩ — **steel·i·ness** *n*

steel·yard \\'stēl-,yärd\\ *n* : a balance on which something to be weighed is hung from the shorter arm of a lever and is balanced by a weight that slides along the longer arm which is marked with a scale

¹steep \\'stēp\\ *adj* **1** : making a large angle with the plane of the horizon : almost straight up and down **2** : being or characterized by a very rapid decline or in-

crease ⟨a *steep* rise in costs⟩ **3** : difficult to accept, meet, or perform : STIFF ⟨*steep* prices⟩ [Old English *stēap* "high, deep"] — **steep·ly** *adv* — **steepness** *n*

□ SYN PRECIPITOUS, SHEER: STEEP implies such sharpness of pitch that ascent or descent is very difficult ⟨*steep* hills⟩ ⟨a *steep* roof⟩ PRECIPITOUS suggests an incline closely approaching the vertical ⟨*precipitous* canyon walls⟩ SHEER implies an unbroken perpendicular expanse ⟨a *sheer* cliff⟩

²steep *n* : a place with steep sides or slope

³steep *vb* **1 a** : to soak in a liquid (as for softening, bleaching, or extracting a flavor) at a temperature under the boiling point ⟨*steep* tea⟩ **b** : to undergo the process of soaking in a liquid **2** : BATHE, WET **3** : to saturate with or subject thoroughly to (some strong or pervading influence) ⟨*steeped* in learning⟩ [Middle English *stepen*] — **steep·er** *n*

steep·en \\'stē-pən\\ *vb* **steep·ened; steep·en·ing** \\'stēp-ning, -ə-ning\\ : to make or become steeper ⟨the trail *steepened*⟩

stee·ple \\'stē-pəl\\ *n* : a tall structure that tops a church tower and usually bears a small spire at the top; *also* : a church tower [Old English *stēpel* "tower"] — **stee·pled** \\-pəld\\ *adj*

stee·ple·chase \\'stē-pəl-,chās\\ *n* **1 a** : a cross-country race on horseback **b** : a race on a closed course over obstacles (as hedges, walls, and a water jump) **2** : a footrace of usually 3000 meters run over hurdles and a water jump [from the use of church steeples as landmarks to guide the riders] — **stee·ple·chas·er** \\-,chā-sər\\ *n*

stee·ple·jack \\-,jak\\ *n* : one whose work is building smokestacks, towers, or steeples or climbing up the outside of such structures to paint and make repairs

¹steer \\'stiər\\ *n* : a domestic bull castrated before sexual maturity; *esp* : an ox being raised for beef [Old English *stēor* "young ox"]

²steer *vb* **1 a** : to direct the course or the course of ⟨*steer* by the stars⟩ ⟨*steer* a conversation⟩ **b** : to take or maintain a course ⟨*steer* for home⟩ **c** : to set and hold to (a course) ⟨*steer* a course for home⟩ **2** : to pursue a course of action **3** : to respond to steering ⟨a car that *steers* well⟩ [Old English *stīeran*] — **steer·able** \\'stir-ə-bəl\\ *adj* — **steer·er** \\'stir-ər\\ *n* — **steer clear** : to keep entirely away ⟨*steer clear* of arguments⟩

³steer *n* : a hint as to procedure : TIP ⟨gave us a bum *steer*⟩

steer·age \\'stir-ij\\ *n* **1** : the act or practice of steering; *also* : DIRECTION 1 **2** : a section in a passenger ship for passengers paying the lowest fares [sense 2 from its originally being located near the rudder]

steer·age·way \\-,wā\\ *n* : sufficient forward motion of a boat or ship for it to be able to respond to steering

steering column *n* : the column that encloses the connections to the steering gear of a vehicle (as an automobile)

steering committee *n* : a managing or directing committee

steering gear *n* : a mechanism by which something is steered

steering wheel *n* : a hand-operated wheel by means of which one steers something

steers·man \\'stiərz-mən\\ *n* : one who steers : HELMSMAN

stego·saur \\'steg-ə-,sȯr\\ *n* : any of a suborder of dinosaurs with strongly developed dorsal bony armor [derived from New Latin *stegosaurus*]

stego·sau·rus \\,steg-ə-'sȯr-əs\\ *n* : any of a genus of large armored dinosaurs of the Upper Jurassic rocks of Colorado and Wyoming [New Latin, from Greek *stegos* "roof" + *sauros* "lizard"]

stein \\'stīn\\ *n* : an earthenware mug especially for beer often having a hinged top; *also* : the quantitiy of beer that a stein holds [probably from German *steingut* "stoneware", from *stein* "stone" + *gut* "goods"]

¹steamroller 1

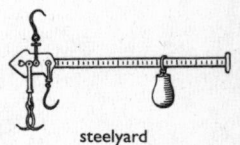

steelyard

stegosaur

\\ə\\ abut   \\ng\\ sing
\\ər\\ further   \\ō\\ bone
\\a\\ mat   \\ȯ\\ saw
\\ā\\ take   \\ȯi\\ coin
\\ä\\ cot, cart   \\th\\ thin
\\au̇\\ out   \\th\\ this
\\ch\\ chin   \\ü\\ food
\\e\\ pet   \\u̇\\ foot
\\ē\\ easy   \\y\\ yet
\\g\\ go   \\yü\\ few
\\i\\ tip   \\yu̇\\ cure
\\ī\\ life   \\zh\\ vision
\\j\\ job

stele \'stēl, 'stē-lē\ *n* : the usually cylindrical central vascular portion of the axis of a vascular plant [Greek *stēlē* "pillar"] — **ste·lar** \'stē-lər\ *adj*

stel·lar \'stel-ər\ *adj* **1 a** : of or relating to the stars : ASTRAL ⟨*stellar* light⟩ **b** : composed of stars **2** : of or relating to a theatrical or film star **3** : OUTSTANDING 3 ⟨a *stellar* production⟩ ⟨a *stellar* performance⟩ [Late Latin *stellaris,* from Latin *stella* "star"]

¹stem \'stem\ *n* **1 a** : the main axis of a plant that develops buds and shoots instead of roots **b** : a plant part (as a petiole or stipe) that supports another **2** : the bow of a ship **3** : a line of ancestry : STOCK; *esp* : a fundamental line from which others have arisen **4** : the part of an inflected word that remains unchanged throughout an inflection **5** : something felt to resemble a plant stem: as **a** : a main or heavy stroke of a letter **b** : the short perpendicular line extending from the head of a musical note **c** : the part of a tobacco pipe from the bowl outward **d** : the slender support of a piece of stemware (as a goblet) **e** : a shaft of a watch [Old English *stefn, stemn*] — **stem·less** \-ləs\ *adj* — **stemmed** \'stemd\ *adj* — **from stem to stern** : THROUGHOUT, THOROUGHLY

²stem *vt* **stemmed; stem·ming 1** : to make headway against (as an adverse tide, current, or wind) **2** : to go counter to (something adverse) ⟨*stem* an angry crowd⟩

³stem *vb* **stemmed; stem·ming 1** : to have or trace an origin or development : DERIVE ⟨illness that *stems* from an accident⟩ **2** : to remove the stem from — **stem·mer** *n*

⁴stem *vb* **stemmed; stem·ming 1** : to stop, check, or restrain by or as if by damming; *also* : to become checked **2 a** : to push (a ski) out to the side in preparation for turning or to slow down **b** : to retard oneself by forcing the heels of both skis outward from the line of progress [Old Norse *stemma* "to dam up"]

⁵stem *n* : an act or instance of stemming on skis

stem·my \'stem-ē\ *adj* **stem·mi·er; -est** : abounding in stems ⟨*stemmy* hay⟩

stem·ware \'stem-,waər, -,weər\ *n* : stemmed glass hollowware

stem–wind·ing \-'wīn-ding\ *adj* : wound by an inside mechanism turned by the knurled knob at the outside end of the stem ⟨a *stem-winding* watch⟩ — **stem–wind·er** \-dər\ *n*

stench \'stench\ *n* : an extremely disagreeable smell : STINK [Old English *stenc*]

¹sten·cil \'sten-səl\ *n* **1** : impervious material (as paper or metal) perforated with lettering or a design through which a substance (as ink) is forced onto a surface to be printed **2** : a pattern, design, or print produced by means of a stencil **3** : a printing process that uses a stencil [Middle French *estanceler* "to ornament with sparkling colors", from *estancele* "spark", derived from Latin *scintilla*]

²stencil *vt* **-ciled** *or* **-cilled; -cil·ing** *or* **-cil·ling** \-sə-ling, -sling\ **1** : to mark or paint with a stencil **2** : to produce by stencil

stencil paper *n* : strong tissue paper impregnated or coated (as with paraffin) for stencils

steno \'sten-ō\ *n, pl* **sten·os** : STENOGRAPHER

ste·nog·ra·pher \stə-'näg-rə-fər\ *n* **1** : a writer of shorthand **2** : one employed chiefly to take and transcribe dictation

ste·nog·ra·phy \-fē\ *n* **1** : the art or process of writing in shorthand **2** : shorthand especially written from dictation or oral discourse **3** : the making of shorthand notes and subsequent transcription of them [Greek *stenos* "narrow"] — **sten·o·graph·ic** \,sten-ə-'graf-ik\ *adj* — **sten·o·graph·i·cal·ly** \-'graf-i-kə-lē, -klē\ *adv*

ste·no·sis \stə-'nō-səs\ *n, pl* **-no·ses** \-'nō-,sēz\ : a narrowing or constriction of a bodily passage or orifice [Greek *stenōsis* "act of narrowing", from *stenoun* "to narrow", from *stenos* "narrow"] — **ste·nosed** \-'nōzd, -'nōst\ *adj* — **ste·not·ic** \-'nät-ik\ *adj*

sten·tor \'sten-,tȯr, 'stent-ər\ *n* **1** : a person having a loud voice **2** : any of a genus of trumpet-shaped ciliate protozoans [Latin, from Greek *Stentōr,* a Greek herald in the Trojan War noted for his loud voice]

sten·to·ri·an \sten-'tōr-ē-ən, -'tȯr-\ *adj* : extremely loud ⟨a *stentorian* voice⟩

¹step \'step\ *n* **1** : a rest for the foot in ascending or descending: as **a** : STAIR 2 **b** : a ladder rung **2 a** (1) : an advance or movement made by raising the foot and bringing it down elsewhere (2) : a combination of foot or foot and body movements constituting a unit or a repeated pattern (as in a dance) (3) : manner of walking : STRIDE ⟨know you by your *step*⟩ **b** : FOOTPRINT **c** : the sound of a footstep **3 a** : the space passed over in one step **b** : a short distance ⟨only a *step* away⟩ **c** : the height of one stair **4** *pl* : COURSE, WAY ⟨directed their *steps* for home⟩ **5 a** : a degree, grade, or rank in a scale ⟨one *step* nearer graduation⟩ **b** : a stage in a process **6** : a block supporting the heel of a mast **7** : an action, proceeding, or measure often occurring as one in a series **8** : a steplike offset or part usually occurring in a series **9** : a musical scale degree [Old English *stæpe*] — **step·like** \-,līk\ *adj* — **stepped** \'stept\ *adj*

²step *vb* **stepped; step·ping 1 a** : to move or take by raising the foot and bringing it down elsewhere or by moving each foot in succession ⟨*stepped* off the curb⟩ ⟨*step* a pace forward⟩ **b** : DANCE 1 **2 a** : to go on foot : WALK ⟨*step* outside⟩ **b** : to move briskly ⟨kept us *stepping*⟩ **3** : to press down with the foot ⟨*step* on a nail⟩ **4** : to come as if at a single step ⟨*step* into a good job⟩ **5** : to erect (a mast) by fixing the lower end in a step **6** : to measure by steps ⟨*step* off 50 meters⟩ **7** : to make steps in **8** : to construct or arrange in or as if in steps — **step on it** : to hurry up

step- *combining form* : related by virtue of a remarriage (as of a parent) and not by blood ⟨*step*parent⟩ ⟨*step*sister⟩ [Old English *stēop-*]

step·broth·er \'step-,brəth-ər\ *n* : a son of one's stepparent by a former marriage

step–by–step \,step-bə-'step\ *adj* : marked by successive degrees usually of limited extent : GRADUAL

step·child \'step-,chīld\ *n* : a child of one's spouse by a former marriage

step·daugh·ter \-,dȯt-ər\ *n* : a daughter of one's spouse by a former marriage

step down \step-'daun, 'step-\ *vb* **1** : to give up a position **2** : to lower the voltage of (a current) by means of a transformer — **step–down** \'step-,daun\ *adj*

step·fa·ther \'step-,fäth-ər\ *n* : the husband of one's mother by a subsequent marriage

step–in \'step-,in\ *n* **1** : an article of clothing that is put on by being stepped into **2** *pl* : a woman's brief panties

step·lad·der \'step-,lad-ər\ *n* : a ladder that has broad flat steps and two pairs of legs connected by a hinge at the top and that opens at the bottom to become freestanding

step·moth·er \-,məth-ər\ *n* : the wife of one's father by a subsequent marriage

step out *vi* **1** : to go away from a place usually for a short distance and for a short time **2** : to go or march at a vigorous or increased pace **3** : to engage in social activity away from home

step·par·ent \'step-,par-ənt, -,per-\ *n* : the spouse of one's parent by a subsequent marriage

steppe \'step\ *n* : dry usually level largely grass-covered land in regions of wide temperature range (as in southeastern Europe and parts of Asia) [Russian *step'*]

stepped–up \'step-'təp\ *adj* : made more vigorous and intensive ⟨a *stepped-up* advertising program⟩

step·per \'step-ər\ *n* : one that steps lively (as a fast horse or a dancer)

step·ping–off place \,step-ing-'ȯf-\ *n* **1** : the outbound end of a transportation line **2** : a place from which one leaves

step·ping–stone \\'step-ing-,stōn\ *n* **1** : a stone to step on (as in crossing a stream) **2** : a means of progress or advancement ⟨a *stepping-stone* to success⟩

step·sis·ter \\'step-,sis-tər\ *n* : a daughter of one's stepparent by a former marriage

step·son \-,sən\ *n* : a son of one's spouse by a former marriage

step stool *n* : a stool with one or two steps that often fold away beneath the seat

step–up \\'step-,əp\ *n* : an increase in size or amount

step up \step-'əp, 'step-\ *vb* **1** : to increase the voltage of (a current) by means of a transformer **2** : to increase, augment, or advance ⟨*step up* production⟩ **3** : to come forward — **step–up** \\'step-,əp\ *adj*

step·wise \\'step-,wīz\ *adj* : marked by steps : GRADUAL

-ster \stər\ *n combining form* **1** : one that does or handles or operates ⟨spin*ster*⟩ ⟨tap*ster*⟩ ⟨team*ster*⟩ **2** : one that makes or uses ⟨pun*ster*⟩ ⟨song*ster*⟩ **3** : one that is associated with or participates in ⟨game*ster*⟩ ⟨gang*ster*⟩ **4** : one that is ⟨old*ster*⟩ ⟨young*ster*⟩ [Old English *-estre* "female agent"]

stere- *or* **stereo-** *combining form* **1** : solid ⟨*stereo*scope⟩ **2** : stereoscopic ⟨*stereo*microscope⟩ [Greek *stereos*]

ste·reo \\'ster-ē-,ō, 'stir-\ *n* **1** : STEREOTYPE 1 **2 a** : a stereoscopic method, system, or effect **b** : a stereoscopic photograph **3 a** : stereophonic reproduction **b** : a stereophonic sound system — **stereo** *adj*

ste·re·og·ra·phy \,ster-ē-'äg-rə-fē, ,stir-\ *n* : stereoscopic photography — **ste·reo·graph·ic** \-ē-ə-'graf-ik\ *adj*

ste·reo·isom·er·ism \,ster-ē-ō-ī-'säm-ə-,riz-əm, ,stir-\ *n* : isomerism in which atoms are linked in the same order but differ in their spatial arrangement — **ste·reo·iso·mer** \-'ī-sə-mər\ *n* — **ste·reo·iso·mer·ic** \-,ī-sə-'mer-ik\ *adj*

ste·reo·mi·cro·scope \-'mī-krə-,skōp\ *n* : a microscope having a set of lenses for each eye to make an object appear in three dimensions

ste·reo·phon·ic \,ster-ē-ə-'fän-ik, ,stir-\ *adj* : giving, relating to, or constituting a three-dimensional effect of reproduced sound — compare MONOPHONIC

ste·re·op·ti·con \,ster-ē-'äp-ti-kən, ,stir-\ *n* : a projector for transparent slides [*stere-* + Greek *optikon*, neuter of *optikos* "optic"]

ste·reo·scope \\'ster-ē-ə-,skōp, 'stir-\ *n* : an optical instrument with two eyeglasses for helping the observer to combine the images of two pictures taken from points of view a little way apart and thus to get the effect of solidity or depth

ste·reo·scop·ic \,ster-ē-ə-'skäp-ik, ,stir-\ *adj* **1** : of or relating to the stereoscope **2** : characterized by stereoscopy ⟨*stereoscopic* vision⟩ — **ste·reo·scop·i·cal·ly** \-i-kə-lē, -klē\ *adv*

ste·re·os·co·py \,ster-ē-'äs-kə-pē, ,stir-\ *n* : the seeing of objects in three dimensions

ste·reo·tax·ic \,ster-ē-ə-'tak-sik, ,stir-\ *adj* : of, relating to, or being a technique or apparatus used in neurological research or surgery for directing the tip of a delicate instrument (as a needle or an electrode) in three planes in an attempt to reach a predetermined place in the nervous system and especially the brain [derived from *stere-* + *taxis*] — **ste·reo·tax·i·cal·ly** \-si-kə-lē, -klē\ *adv*

¹ste·reo·type \\'ster-ē-ə-,tīp, 'stir-\ *n* **1** : a plate made by molding a matrix of a printing surface and making from this a cast in type metal **2** : something conforming to a general pattern and lacking individual distinguishing marks or qualities; *esp* : a standardized mental picture that is held in common by members of a group and that represents an oversimplified opinion, emotional attitude, or uncritical judgment

²stereotype *vt* **1** : to make a stereotype from **2 a** : to repeat without variation **b** : to develop a mental stereotype about — **ste·reo·typ·er** *n*

ste·reo·typed \-,tīpt\ *adj* : lacking originality or individuality SYN see TRITE

ste·reo·ty·py \-,tī-pē\ *n* : the art or process of making or of printing from stereotype plates

ste·rig·ma \stə-'rig-mə\ *n, pl* **-ma·ta** \-mət-ə\ : a filament that supports a spore or chain of spores [Greek *stērigma* "support", from *stērizein* "to prop"]

ster·ile \\'ster-əl\ *adj* **1** : not able to bear fruit, crops, or offspring : not fertile : BARREN ⟨*sterile* soil⟩ **2** : free from living organisms and especially microorganisms ⟨*sterile* dressing for a wound⟩ **3** : lacking in ideas or originality [Latin *sterilis*] — **ste·ril·i·ty** \stə-'ril-ət-ē\ *n*

ster·il·ize \\'ster-ə-,līz\ *vt* : to make sterile: as **a** : to deprive of the power of reproducing or germinating **b** : to make powerless or useless **c** : to free from living organisms (as bacteria) — **ster·il·iza·tion** \,ster-ə-lə-'zā-shən\ *n* — **ster·il·iz·er** \\'ster-ə-,lī-zər\ *n*

¹ster·ling \\'stər-ling\ *n* **1** : British money **2** : sterling silver or articles of it [Middle English, "silver penny"]

²sterling *adj* **1** : of, relating to, or calculated in terms of British sterling **2 a** : a fixed standard of purity usually defined legally as represented by an alloy of 925 parts of silver with 75 parts of copper ⟨*sterling* silver⟩ **b** : made of sterling silver **3** : conforming to the highest standard ⟨a person of *sterling* quality⟩ — **ster·ling·ly** \-ling-lē\ *adv* — **ster·ling·ness** *n*

¹stern \\'stərn\ *adj* **1 a** : hard and severe in nature or manner ⟨a *stern* judge⟩ **b** : showing severity : HARSH **2** : not inviting or attractive : FORBIDDING **3** : FIRM, RESOLUTE ⟨a *stern* resolve to win⟩ [Old English *styrne*] SYN see SEVERE — **stern·ly** *adv* — **stern·ness** \\'stərn-nəs\ *n*

²stern *n* **1** : the rear end of a boat or ship **2** : a rear part [Middle English "rudder"]

stern·most \\'stərn-,mōst\ *adj* : farthest astern

stern·post \-,pōst\ *n* : the principal member at the stern of a ship extending from keel to deck

stern·num \\'stər-nəm\ *n, pl* **sternums** *or* **ster·na** \-nə\ : a compound ventral bone or cartilage connecting the ribs or the pectoral girdle or both — called also *breastbone* [New Latin, from Greek *sternon* "chest, breastbone"] — **ster·nal** \\'stərn-l\ *adj*

stern–wheel·er \-'hwē-lər, -'wē-lər\ *n* : a steamboat having a single paddle wheel at the stern instead of on the sides

ste·roid \\'stiər-,óid *also* 'steər-\ *n* : any of numerous compounds containing the carbon ring system of the sterols and including the sterols and various hormones and glycosides

ste·rol \\'stiər-,ól, 'steər-, -,ōl\ *n* : any of various solid alcohols (as cholesterol) widely distributed in animal and plant lipids [*cholesterol*]

ster·to·rous \\'stərt-ə-rəs\ *adj* : characterized by a harsh snoring or gasping sound ⟨*stertorous* breathing⟩ [derived from Latin *stertere* "to snore"] — **ster·to·rous·ly** *adv* — **ster·to·rous·ness** *n*

stet \\'stet\ *vt* **stet·ted; stet·ting** : to annotate (a word or passage) with or as if with the word *stet* in order to nullify a previous order to delete or omit from a manuscript or printer's proof [Latin, "let it stand", from *stare* "to stand"]

stetho·scope \\'steth-ə-,skōp *also* 'steth-\ *n* : an instrument used for listening to sounds produced in the body and especially in the chest [French *stéthoscope*, from Greek *stēthos* "chest"] — **stetho·scop·ic** \,steth-ə-'skäp-ik *also* ,steth-\ *adj*

ste·ve·dore \\'stē-və-,dōr, -,dór\ *n* : a person whose work is to load and unload ships or boats in port [Spanish *estibador*, from *estibar* "to pack", from Latin *stipare* "to press together"] — **stevedore** *vb*

¹stew \\'stü, 'styü\ *n* **1** : food (as meat with vegatables) prepared by slow boiling **2** : a state of excitement, worry, or confusion

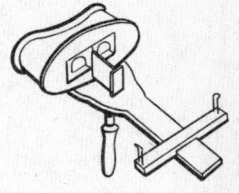

stereoscope

\ə\ abut		\ng\ sing
\ər\ further		\ō\ bone
\a\ mat		\ó\ saw
\ā\ take		\ói\ coin
\ä\ cot, cart		\th\ thin
\aú\ out		\th\ this
\ch\ chin		\ü\ food
\e\ pet		\ú\ foot
\ē\ easy		\y\ yet
\g\ go		\yü\ few
\i\ tip		\yú\ cure
\ī\ life		\zh\ vision
\j\ job		

stickleback

²**stew** *vb* **1** : to cook in liquid over a low heat **2** : to become agitated or worried : FRET [Middle French *estuver*]

stew·ard \'stü-ərd, 'stú-, 'styü-, 'styú-, 'stùrd, 'styúrd\ *n* **1** : a manager of a large household, estate, or organization **2 a** : a person employed to supervise the provision and distribution of food (as on a ship) **b** : a worker who serves and attends the needs of passengers (as on a train or ship) [Old English *stīweard,* from *stī, stig* "hall, sty" + *weard* "ward"]

stew·ard·ess \-əs\ *n* : a woman who performs the duties of a steward; *esp* : one who attends passengers on an airplane

stew·ard·ship \-,ship\ *n* : the office, duties, and obligations of a steward; *also* : the individual's responsibility to manage his life and property with proper regard to the rights of others

stib·nite \'stib-,nīt\ *n* : a mineral Sb_2S_3 consisting of a sulfide of antimony occurring in lead-gray crystals of metallic luster [French *stibine,* from Latin *stibium* "antimony", from Greek *stibi,* from Egyptian *sṭm*]

¹**stick** \'stik\ *n* **1** : a cut or broken branch or twig especially when dry and dead **2** : a long slender piece of wood: as **a** : a club or staff used as a weapon **b** : WALKING STICK 1 **c** : an implement used for striking or propelling an object in a game **3** : something like a stick in shape, origin, or use ⟨a *stick* of dynamite⟩; *esp* : an airplane lever operating the elevators and ailerons **4** : a person who is dull, stiff, and lifeless **5** *pl* : remote or rural districts ⟨way out in the *sticks*⟩ [Old English *sticca*]

²**stick** *vb* **stuck** \'stək\; **stick·ing** **1 a** : PIERCE 1, STAB **b** : to kill by piercing **2** : to cause (as a pointed instrument) to penetrate — used with *in, into,* or *through* ⟨*stuck* a needle in my finger⟩ **3 a** : to fasten by thrusting in **b** : IMPALE **c** : to push out, up, or under ⟨*stuck* out my hand⟩ **4** : to put or set in a specified place or position **5** : to attach by or as if by causing to adhere to a surface **6** : to halt the movement or action of ⟨cars got *stuck* in the mud⟩ **7** : BAFFLE 1, STUMP **8 a** : CHEAT 1, DEFRAUD **b** : to saddle with something disadvantageous or disagreeable ⟨*stuck* with the job of cleaning up⟩ **9** : to hold to something firmly by or as if by adhesion ⟨the glue *stuck* to my fingers⟩ **10 a** : to remain in a place, situation, or environment **b** : to hold fast or adhere resolutely : CLING **11 a** : to become blocked, wedged, or jammed **b** : to be unable to proceed through fear or scruple **12** : PROJECT 3, PROTRUDE [Old English *stician*] □ SYN STICK, ADHERE, COHERE, CLING mean to become or remain closely attached. STICK implies being embedded, glued, or cemented in or on something; ADHERE implies a growing together or a process like it; COHERE suggests a sticking together of parts so as to form a unified mass or whole; CLING implies attachment by hanging on with arms or tendrils. — **stick one's neck out** : to make oneself vulnerable unnecessarily — **stuck on** : infatuated with

³**stick** *n* **1** : a thrust with a pointed instrument : STAB **2** : adhesive quality or substance

stick around *vi* : to stay or wait about : LINGER

stick·ball \'stik-,ból\ *n* : baseball adapted for play in small areas using a broomstick and a lightweight ball

stick·er \'stik-ər\ *n* **1** : one (as a brier or knife) that pierces with a point **2 a** : something that adheres (as a bur) or causes adhesion (as glue) **b** : a slip of paper with gummed back that when moistened adheres to a surface

stick·han·dler \'stik-,han-dlər, -lər, -dl-ər\ *n* : a hockey or lacrosse player adept at maneuvering the ball or puck

stick insect *n* : any of various usually wingless insects that are distantly related to the mantises and have a long round body resembling a stick

stick-in-the-mud \'stik-ən-<u>th</u>ə-,məd\ *n* : one who is slow, old-fashioned, or unprogressive; *esp* : an old fogy

stick·le \'stik-əl\ *vi* **stick·led; stick·ling** \'stik-ling, -ə-ling\ **1** : to contend especially stubbornly and usually on insufficient grounds **2** : to feel often excessive scruples [Middle English *stightlen,* from *stighten* "to arrange", from Old English *stihtan*]

stick·le·back \'stik-əl-,bak\ *n* : any of numerous small scaleless fishes having two or more free spines in front of the dorsal fin [Old English *sticel* "goad"]

stick·ler \'stik-lər, -ə-lər\ *n* **1** : one that insists on exactitude or rigid propriety (as of conduct or dress) **2** : POSER, PUZZLE

stick·man \'stik-,man, -mən\ *n* : one who handles a stick: as **a** : one who supervises the play at a dice table, calls the decisions, and retrieves the dice **b** : a player in any of various games (as lacrosse) played with a stick

stick out *vb* **1 a** : to jut out : PROJECT **b** : to be conspicuous **2** : to be persistent ⟨*stuck out* for higher wages⟩ **3** : to put up with : ENDURE

stick·pin \'stik-,pin\ *n* : an ornamental pin worn in a necktie

stick shift *n* : a manually operated gearshift mounted on the steering column or floor of an automobile vehicle

stick·tight \'stik-,tīt\ *n* : BUR MARIGOLD

stick-to-it·ive·ness \stik-tü-ət-iv-nəs\ *n* : dogged perseverance : TENACITY

stick up \stik-'əp, 'stik-\ *vt* : to rob at the point of a gun — **stick·up** \'stik-,əp\ *n*

stick·work \'stik-,wərk\ *n* : the use (as in lacrosse) of one's stick in offensive and defensive techniques

sticky \'stik-ē\ *adj* **stick·i·er; -est** **1 a** : ADHESIVE, GLUEY ⟨*sticky* syrup⟩ **b** : coated with a sticky substance **2** : HUMID, MUGGY ⟨a hot, *sticky* day⟩ **3** : tending to stick ⟨a *sticky* valve⟩ **4 a** : DISAGREEABLE 1, PAINFUL **b** : DIFFICULT, TROUBLESOME ⟨a *sticky* situation⟩ — **stick·i·ly** \'stik-ə-lē\ *adv* — **stick·i·ness** \'stik-ē-nəs\ *n*

¹**stiff** \'stif\ *adj* **1 a** : not easily bent : RIGID **b** : lacking in normal or usual suppleness or mobility ⟨*stiff* muscles⟩ **2 a** : marked by moral courage **b** : STUBBORN 2, UNYIELDING **c** : formally reserved in manner; *also* : lacking in ease or grace **3** : hard fought ⟨drives a *stiff* bargain⟩ **4 a** : exerting great force : STRONG ⟨a *stiff* wind⟩ **b** : POTENT ⟨a *stiff* dose⟩ **5 a** : HARSH, SEVERE ⟨a *stiff* penalty⟩ **b** : difficult to do or cope with ⟨a *stiff* task⟩; *also* : RUGGED ⟨*stiff* terrain⟩ **6** : EXPENSIVE 2, STEEP [Old English *stīf*] — **stiff·ly** *adv* — **stiff·ness** *n*

²**stiff** *adv* **1** : in a stiff manner ⟨frozen *stiff*⟩ **2** : to an extreme degree ⟨bored *stiff*⟩

³**stiff** *n* **1** : CORPSE **2** : PERSON, FELLOW ⟨you lucky *stiff*⟩

stiff-arm \'stif-,ärm\ *vb* : STRAIGHT-ARM — **stiff-arm** *n*

stiff·en \'stif-ən\ *vb* **stiff·ened; stiff·en·ing** \'stif-ning, -ə-ning\ : to make or become stiff or stiffer — **stiff·en·er** \-nər, -ə-nər\ *n*

stiff-necked \'stif-'nekt\ *adj* : arrogantly stubborn

¹**sti·fle** \'stī-fəl\ *n* : the joint next above the hock in the hind leg of a four-footed animal (as a horse) corresponding to the knee in humans [Middle English]

²**stifle** *vb* **sti·fled; sti·fling** \-fə-ling, -fling\ **1 a** : to kill by depriving of or die from lack of oxygen or air **b** : to smother by or as if by depriving of air ⟨*stifle* a fire⟩ **2** : to check or keep in check by deliberate effort : REPRESS ⟨*stifled* my anger⟩ [Middle English *stuflen*] — **sti·fling·ly** \-fə-ling-lē, -fling-\ *adv*

stig·ma \'stig-mə\ *n, pl* **stig·ma·ta** \stig-'mät-ə, 'stig-mət-ə\ *or* **stigmas** **1 a** : a mark of shame or discredit : STAIN **b** : an identifying mark or characteristic; *esp* : a specific diagnostic sign of a disease **2** *pl* : bodily marks or pains resembling the wounds of the crucified Christ **3 a** : a small spot, scar, or opening on a plant or animal **b** : the part of the pistil of a flower which receives the pollen grains and on which they germinate [Latin *stigmat-, stigma* "mark, brand", from Greek, from *stizein* "to tattoo"] — **stig·mal** \'stig-məl\ *adj* — **stig·mat·ic** \stig-'mat-ik\ *adj* — **stig·mat·i·cal·ly** \-'mat-i-klē, -kə-lē\ *adv*

stig·ma·tize \'stig-mə-ˌtīz\ *vt* : to mark with a stigma; *esp* : to characterize or identify as disgraceful or shameful — **stig·ma·ti·za·tion** \ˌstig-mət-ə-'zā-shən\ *n*

¹**stile** \'stīl\ *n* : a step or set of steps for passing over a fence or wall; *also* : TURNSTILE [Old English *stigel*]

²**stile** *n* : one of the vertical members in a frame or panel (as of a window or door) into which the secondary members are fitted [probably from Dutch *stijl* "post"]

sti·let·to \stə-'let-ō\ *n, pl* **-tos** *or* **-toes** **1** : a slender dagger with a blade thick in proportion to its width **2** : a pointed instrument for piercing holes for eyelets or embroidery [Italian, from *stilo* "stylus, dagger", from Latin *stilus* "stylus"]

¹**still** \'stil\ *adj* **1 a** : not moving ⟨lying quiet and *still*⟩ **b** : not carbonated ⟨*still* wine⟩ **c** : of, relating to, or being an ordinary photograph as distinguished from a motion picture **2** : uttering no sound ⟨be *still* and listen⟩ **3 a** : CALM, TRANQUIL ⟨a *still* lake⟩ **b** : free from noise or turbulence : PEACEFUL [Old English *stille*] — **still·ness** *n*

²**still** *vb* **1 a** : ALLAY 2, CALM ⟨*still* their fears⟩ **b** : to put an end to **2** : to make or become motionless or silent

³**still** *adv* **1** : without motion ⟨sit *still*⟩ **2** *archaic* : ALWAYS, CONTINUALLY **3** — used as a function word to indicate the continuance of an action or condition ⟨*still* lived there⟩ ⟨it's *still* hot⟩ **4** : in spite of that : NEVERTHELESS ⟨those who take the greatest care *still* make mistakes⟩ **5 a** : EVEN ⟨a *still* more difficult problem⟩ **b** : in addition : YET ⟨won *still* another game⟩

⁴**still** *n* **1** : QUIET, SILENCE **2** : a still photograph; *esp* : one of actors or scenes of a motion picture for publicity or documentary purposes

⁵**still** *n* **1** : DISTILLERY **2** : apparatus used in distillation [Middle English *stillen* "to distill", short for *distillen*]

still alarm *n* : a fire alarm transmitted (as by telephone call) without sounding the signal apparatus

still·birth \'stil-ˌbərth\ *n* : the birth of a dead fetus

still·born \-'bȯrn\ *adj* **1** : dead at birth **2** : failing from the start : ABORTIVE — **still·born** \-ˌbȯrn\ *n*

still hunt *n* : a quiet pursuing or ambushing (as of game) — **still-hunt** \'stil-ˌhənt\ *vb*

still life *n, pl* **still lifes** \-ˌlīfs, -ˌlīvz\ : a picture consisting predominantly of inanimate objects

still·man \'stil-mən\ *n* **1** : one who runs or operates a still **2** : one who tends distillation equipment (as in an oil refinery)

¹**stilt** \'stilt\ *n* **1 a** : one of two poles each with a rest or strap for the foot used to elevate the wearer above the ground in walking **b** : a pile or post serving as one of the supports of a structure above ground or water level **2** *pl also* **stilt** : any of various long-legged three-toed birds related to the avocets that frequent inland ponds and marshes and nest in small colonies [Middle English *stilte*]

²**stilt** *vt* : to raise on or as if on stilts

stilt·ed \'stil-təd\ *adj* **1** : stiffly formal : not easy and natural ⟨*stilted* speech⟩ **2** : raised on or as if on stilts ⟨a *stilted* arch⟩ — **stilt·ed·ly** *adv* — **stilt·ed·ness** *n*

stim·u·lant \'stim-yə-lənt\ *n* **1** : an agent (as a drug) that temporarily increases the functional activity or efficiency of a tissue or organ **2** : STIMULUS ⟨a *stimulant* to trade⟩ **3** : an alcoholic beverage — **stimulant** *adj*

stim·u·late \-ˌlāt\ *vt* **1** : to make active or more active : ANIMATE, AROUSE ⟨*stimulate* industry⟩ **2** : to act on as a physiological stimulus or stimulant [Latin *stimulare*, from *stimulus* "goad, stimulus"] SYN see PROVOKE — **stim·u·la·tion** \ˌstim-yə-'lā-shən\ *n* — **stim·u·la·tive** \'stim-yə-ˌlāt-iv\ *adj* — **stim·u·la·tor** \-ˌlāt-ər\ *n* — **stim·u·la·to·ry** \-lə-ˌtōr-ē, -ˌtȯr-\ *adj*

stim·u·lus \'stim-yə-ləs\ *n, pl* **-li** \-ˌlī, -ˌlē\ **1** : something that rouses or incites to activity : INCENTIVE ⟨new *stimuli* to business⟩ **2** : an agent (as an environmental change) that directly influences the activity of living protoplasm (as by exciting a sensory organ) [Latin]

¹**sting** \'sting\ *vb* **stung** \'stəng\; **sting·ing** \'sting-ing\ **1 a** : to prick painfully especially with a sharp or poisonous process **b** : to affect with or feel sharp, quick, and usually burning pain or smart ⟨hail *stung* their faces⟩ ⟨faces *stinging* from the cold⟩ **2** : to cause to suffer severely ⟨*stung* with remorse⟩ **3** : OVER-CHARGE, CHEAT ⟨some people always get *stung*⟩ **4** : to use a stinger [Old English *stingan*]

²**sting** *n* **1 a** : the act of stinging **b** : a wound or pain caused by or as if by stinging **2** : STINGER 2 **3** : a stinging element, force, or quality — **sting·less** \'sting-ləs\ *adj*

sting·a·ree \'sting-ə-ˌrē\ *n* : STINGRAY [by alteration]

sting·er \'sting-ər\ *n* **1** : one that stings; *esp* : a sharp blow or remark **2** : a sharp organ of offense and defense (as of a bee or scorpion) usually adapted to wound by piercing and injecting a poisonous secretion

stinging cell *n* : NEMATOCYST

sting·ray \'sting-ˌrā\ *n* : any of numerous rays with one or more large sharp barbed spines near the base of the whiplike tail capable of inflicting severe wounds

stin·gy \'stin-jē\ *adj* **stingier; -est** **1** : not generous or liberal : sparing or scant in giving or spending **2** : SCANTY, MEAGER ⟨*stingy* portions⟩ [probably related to *sting*] — **stin·gily** \-jə-lē\ *adv* — **stin·gi·ness** \-jē-nəs\ *n* □ SYN CLOSE, PENURIOUS, MISERLY: STINGY implies an unwillingness to spend, give, or share freely and a marked lack of generosity; CLOSE suggests keeping a tight grip on one's money and possessions; PENURIOUS implies a frugality that gives an appearance of actual poverty; MISERLY suggests a sordid avariciousness and a morbid pleasure in hoarding.

¹**stink** \'stingk\ *vb* **stank** \'stangk\ *or* **stunk** \'stəngk\; **stunk; stink·ing** **1** : to give forth or cause to have a strong and offensive smell ⟨*stink* up a room⟩ **2** : to be offensive or have something to an offensive degree **3** : to be of extremely poor quality [Old English *stincan*]

²**stink** *n* **1** : a strong offensive odor : STENCH **2** : a public outcry against something offensive ⟨raised a *stink* about gambling⟩ — **stinky** \'sting-kē\ *adj*

stink·bug \'stingk-ˌbəg\ *n* : any of various true bugs that emit a disagreeable odor

stink·er \'sting-kər\ *n* **1** : one that stinks **2** : an offensive or contemptible person

¹**stint** \'stint\ *vb* **1** : to limit in share or portion : cut short in amount ⟨*stint* the children's milk⟩ **2** : to be sparing or frugal [Old English *styntan* "to blunt, dull"] — **stint·er** *n*

²**stint** *n* **1** : RESTRICTION 1, LIMITATION **2** : a definite quantity of work assigned

stipe \'stīp\ *n* : a short plant stalk; *esp* : one supporting a fern frond or the cap of a mushroom [Latin *stipes* "tree trunk"] — **stiped** \'stīpt\ *adj*

sti·pend \'stī-ˌpend, -pənd\ *n* : a fixed sum of money paid periodically for services or to defray expenses [Latin *stipendium*, from *stips* "gift" + *pendere* "to weigh, pay"] SYN see WAGE

stip·ple \'stip-əl\ *vt* **stip·pled; stip·pling** \'stip-ling, -ə-ling\ **1** : to engrave by means of dots and flicks **2 a** : to make (as in paint or ink) by small short touches that together produce an even or softly graded shadow **b** : to apply (as paint) by repeated small touches **3** : SPECKLE 1, FLECK [Dutch *stippelen* "to spot, dot"] — **stipple** *n* — **stip·pler** \-lər, -ə-lər\ *n*

stip·u·late \'stip-yə-ˌlāt\ *vb* : to make an agreement or arrange as part of an agreement; *esp* : to demand or insist on as a condition in an agreement [Latin *stipulari*] — **stip·u·la·tor** \-ˌlāt-ər\ *n* — **stip·u·la·to·ry** \-lə-ˌtōr-ē, -ˌtȯr-\ *adj*

stip·u·la·tion \ˌstip-yə-'lā-shən\ *n* **1** : an act of stipulating **2** : something stipulated; *esp* : a condition required as part of an agreement

stip·ule \'stip-ˌyül\ *n* : either of a pair of small appendages at the base of the leaf in many plants [Latin *stipu-*

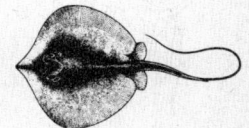
stingray

la "stalk"] — **stip·u·lar** \-yə-lər\ *adj* — **stip·u·late** \-yə-lət\ *adj*

¹stir \'stər\ *vb* **stirred; stir·ring** **1 a :** to make or cause to make a usually slight movement or change of position **b :** to disturb the quiet of : AGITATE **2 a :** to alter the relative position of the particles or parts of especially by a continued circular movement **b :** to mix by or as if by stirring **3 :** BESTIR **4 :** to bring into notice or debate : RAISE 〈the answer *stirred* our hopes〉 **5 a :** to rouse to activity : INCITE, QUICKEN 〈their emotions *stirred*〉 **b :** to call forth (as a memory) : EVOKE 〈*stirred* thoughts of home〉 **6 :** to be active or busy [Old English *styrian*] — **stir·rer** *n*

²stir *n* **1 a :** a state of disturbance or activity **b :** widespread notice and discussion : IMPRESSION **2 :** a slight movement **3 :** a stirring movement

stir·ring \'stər-ing\ *adj* **1 :** ACTIVE 4 **2 :** giving rise to excitement

stir·rup \'stər-əp *also* 'stir-əp *or* 'stə-rəp\ *n* **1 :** either of a pair of small light frames often of metal hung by straps from a saddle and used as a support for the foot of a horseback rider **2 a :** something (as a support or clamp) resembling or functioning like a stirrup **b :** STAPES [Old English *stigrāp*, literally, "mounting rope"]

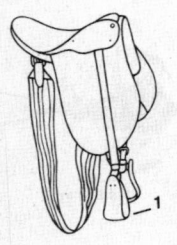

| stirrup |

stirrup cup *n* **1 :** a cup of drink (as wine) taken by a rider about to depart **2 :** a farewell cup

¹stitch \'stich\ *n* **1 :** a local sharp and sudden pain especially in the side **2 a :** one in-and-out movement of a threaded needle in sewing, embroidery, or suturing **b :** a portion of thread left in the material after one stitch **3 :** a single piece of clothing 〈didn't have a *stitch* on〉 **4 :** a single loop of thread or yarn around an implement (as a knitting needle or crochet hook) **5 :** a stitch or series of stitches formed in a particular way 〈basting *stitch*〉 [Old English *stice*] — **in stitches :** in a state of uncontrollable laughter

²stitch *vb* **1 a :** to join with or as if with stitches **b :** to make, mend, or decorate with or as if with stitches **2 :** to unite by means of staples **3 :** to do needlework : SEW — **stitch·er** *n*

stithy \'stith-ē, 'stith-\ *n, pl* **stith·ies** **1 :** ANVIL 1 **2 :** SMITHY 1 [Old Norse *stethi*]

sti·ver \'stī-vər\ *n* **1 a :** a former monetary unit of the Netherlands equal to ¹⁄₂₀ gulden **b :** a coin representing one stiver **2 :** something of little value [Dutch *stuiver*]

stoat \'stōt\ *n* **:** the European ermine especially in its brown summer coat [Middle English *stote*]

stob \'stäb\ *n, chiefly dialect* **:** STAKE 1, POST [Middle English, "stump"]

¹stock \'stäk\ *n* **1 a :** STUMP 1b **b** *archaic* **:** a log or block of wood **c (1) :** something without life or consciousness **(2) :** a dull, stupid, or lifeless person **2 a :** a supporting framework or part: as **a** *pl* **:** a timber frame with holes to contain the feet or feet and hands of an offender undergoing public punishment **b :** the wooden part by which a rifle or shotgun is held during firing **c :** the butt of an implement **3 a :** the main stem of a plant : TRUNK **b :** a plant or plant part united with a scion in grafting and supplying mostly underground parts to a graft **4 :** the crosspiece of an anchor **5 a :** the original (as a person, race, or language) from which others derive : SOURCE **b :** the descendants of one individual : FAMILY, LINEAGE **6 a (1) :** the equipment of an establishment **(2) :** farm animals : LIVESTOCK **b :** a store or supply accumulated; *esp* **:** the inventory of goods of a merchant or manufacturer **7 :** the proprietorship element in a corporation divided into shares giving to the owners an interest in its assets and earnings and usually voting power **8 :** any of a genus of herbaceous or shrubby plants of the mustard family with clusters of usually sweet-scented flowers **9 :** a wide band or scarf worn about the neck especially by some members of the clergy **10 a :** liquid in which meat, fish, or vegeta-

bles have been simmered that is used as a basis for soup, gravy, or sauce **b :** RAW MATERIAL **11 a :** the estimation in which one is held **b :** confidence placed in one **12 :** the production and presentation of plays by a stock company [Old English *stocc*]

²stock *vb* **1 :** to fit to or with a stock **2 :** to provide with or acquire stock or a stock 〈*stock* a family with linens〉 〈*stock* up on sundries〉 **3 :** to procure or keep a stock of 〈a store that *stocks* only the finest goods〉 **4 :** to graze (livestock) on land

³stock *adj* **1 a :** kept regularly in stock 〈comes in *stock* sizes〉 〈a *stock* model〉 **b :** commonly used or brought forward : STANDARD 〈the *stock* answer〉 **2 a :** kept for breeding purposes 〈a *stock* mare〉 **b :** devoted to or used or intended for livestock 〈*stock* train〉 〈*stock* farm〉 **3 :** employed in taking care of the stock of merchandise on hand 〈a *stock* clerk〉

¹stock·ade \stä-'kād\ *n* **1 :** a line of stout posts set firmly to form a defense **2 a :** an enclosure or pen made with posts and stakes **b :** an enclosure in which prisoners are kept [Spanish *estacada*, from *estaca* "stake", of Germanic origin]

²stockade *vt* **:** to fortify or surround with a stockade

stock·bro·ker \'stäk-,brō-kər\ *n* **:** one that carries out orders to buy and sell securities — **stock·brok·ing** \-,brō-king\ *or* **stock·bro·ker·age** \-kə-rij, -krij\ *n*

stock car *n* **:** a racing car having the basic chassis and body lines of a commercially produced assembly-line model

stock company *n* **1 :** a corporation or joint-stock company whose capital is represented by stock **2 :** a theatrical company attached to a repertory theater; *esp* **:** one without outstanding stars

stock exchange *n* **1 :** a place where organized trading in securities is conducted **2 :** an association of people organized to provide a market among themselves for the purchase and sale of securities

stock·fish \'stäk-,fish\ *n* **:** fish (as cod, haddock, or hake) dried hard in the open air without salt [Dutch *stocvisch*, from *stoc* "stick" + *visch* "fish"]

stock·hold·er \-,hōl-dər\ *n* **:** an owner of stocks : SHAREHOLDER

stock·i·nette *or* **stock·i·net** \,stäk-ə-'net\ *n* **:** a soft elastic usually cotton fabric used especially for bandages and infants' wear [alteration of earlier *stocking net*]

stock·ing \'stäk-ing\ *n* **1 a :** a usually knit close-fitting covering for the foot and leg **b :** SOCK **2 :** something resembling a stocking; *esp* **:** a ring of distinctive color on the lower part of the leg of an animal [obsolete *stock* "to cover with a stocking", from English dialect *stock* "stocking"] — **stock·inged** \-ingd\ *adj*

stocking cap *n* **:** a long knitted cone-shaped cap usually with a tassel or pom-pom worn especially for winter sports or play

stock–in–trade \,stäk-ən-'trād, 'stäk-ən-,\ *n* **1 :** the equipment necessary to or used in a trade or business **2 :** something held to resemble the standard equipment of a business or person with a trade

stock·man \'stäk-mən, -,man\ *n* **:** one occupied as an owner or worker in the raising of livestock

stock market *n* **1 :** STOCK EXCHANGE 1 **2 :** a market for stocks or for a particular stock

stock·pile \'stäk-,pīl\ *n* **:** a reserve supply especially of something essential accumulated within a country for use during a shortage — **stockpile** *vt*

stock·pot \-,pät\ *n* **:** a pot in which soup stock is prepared

stock·room \-,rüm, -,rum\ *n* **:** a storage place for supplies or goods used in a business

stock–still \-'stil\ *adj* **:** very still : MOTIONLESS

stocky \'stäk-ē\ *adj* **stock·i·er; -est :** compact, sturdy, and relatively thick in build : THICKSET — **stock·i·ly** \'stäk-ə-lē\ *adv* — **stock·i·ness** \'stäk-ē-nəs\ *n*

stock·yard \-,yärd\ *n* **:** a yard for stock; *esp* **:** one in which livestock are kept temporarily for slaughter, market, or shipping

stodgy \'stäj-ē\ *adj* **stodg·i·er; -est** **1** : having a thick gluey consistency : HEAVY ⟨*stodgy* bread⟩ **2** : moving in a slow plodding way especially as a result of physical bulkiness **3** : having no excitement : DULL **4** : extremely old-fashioned in attitude or outlook **5 a** : DRAB **2 b** : DOWDY [earlier *stodge* "to stuff with food"] — **stodg·i·ly** \'stäj-ə-lē\ *adv* — **stodg·i·ness** \'stäj-ē-nəs\ *n*

sto·gie *or* **sto·gy** \'stō-gē\ *n, pl* **stogies** : a slender cylindrical cigar; *also* : CIGAR [*Conestoga*, Pennsylvania]

¹**sto·ic** \'stō-ik\ *n* **1** *cap* : a member of an ancient Greek school of philosophy holding that the wise person should be free from passion, unmoved by joy or grief, and submissive to natural law **2** : one who appears or claims to be indifferent to pleasure or pain [Latin *stoicus,* from Greek *stōïkos,* from *Stoa Poikilē* "the Painted Portico (portico at Athens where Zeno taught)"]

²**stoic** *adj* **1** *cap* : of or relating to the Stoics or their doctrines **2** : indifferent to pleasure or pain — **sto·i·cal** \'stō-i-kəl\ *adj* — **sto·i·cal·ly** \-i-kə-lē, -klē\ *adv*

sto·icism \'stō-ə-,siz-əm\ *n* **1** *cap* : the philosophy of the Stoics **2** : indifference to pleasure or pain : IMPASSIVENESS

stoke \'stōk\ *vb* **1** : to stir up or tend (as a fire) : supply (as a furnace) with fuel **2** : to stir up a fire : tend the fires of furnaces **3** : to feed (as oneself) abundantly [Dutch *stoken*]

stoke·hold \-,hōld\ *n* **1** : a room containing a ship's boilers **2** : the space in front of the boilers of a ship from which the furnaces are fed

stok·er \'stō-kər\ *n* **1** : one that tends a furnace; *esp* : one that tends a ship's steam boiler **2** : a machine for feeding a fire

¹**stole** *past of* STEAL

²**stole** \'stōl\ *n* **1** : a long loose garment : ROBE **2** : a long narrow band worn around the neck by bishops and priests and over the left shoulder by deacons in ceremonies **3** : a long wide scarf or similar covering worn usually across the shoulders [Old English, from Latin *stola,* from Greek *stolē*]

stolen *past participle of* STEAL

stol·id \'stäl-əd\ *adj* : having or expressing little or no sensibility : not easily aroused or excited : UNEMOTIONAL ⟨*stolid* peasants⟩ ⟨waited in *stolid* silence⟩ [Latin *stolidus* "dull, stupid"] SYN see IMPASSIVE — **sto·lid·i·ty** \stä-'lid-ət-ē, stə-\ *n* — **stol·id·ly** \'stäl-əd-lē\ *adv*

sto·lon \'stō-lən, -,län\ *n* **1** : a horizontal branch from the base of a plant that produces new plants from buds at its tip or nodes (as in the strawberry) — called also *runner* **2** : a branch of fungus mycelium spreading over the surface of the medium on which it is growing [Latin *stolon-, stolo* "branch, sucker"] — **sto·lon·if·er·ous** \,stō-lə-'nif-rəs, -ə-rəs\ *adj*

sto·ma \'stō-mə\ *n* **1** *pl* **stomas** : any of various small simple bodily openings especially in a lower animal **2** *pl* **sto·ma·ta** \-mət-ə\ : any of the minute openings in the epidermis of a leaf through which moisture and gases pass [Greek *stomat-, stoma* "mouth"] — **sto·ma·tal** \'stō-mət-l\ *adj*

¹**stom·ach** \'stəm-ək, -ik\ *n* **1 a** : a pouch of the vertebrate alimentary canal into which food goes for further mixing and digestion after passing from the mouth down the throat **b** : a cavity with a similar function in an invertebrate animal **c** : the part of the body that contains the stomach : BELLY, ABDOMEN **2 a** : desire for food caused by hunger : APPETITE **b** : INCLINATION, DESIRE ⟨had no *stomach* for bloodshed⟩ **3** *obsolete* **a** : VALOR, SPIRIT **b** : PRIDE 1a **c** : RESENTMENT [Middle French *estomac,* from Latin *stomachus* "gullet, esophagus, stomach", from Greek *stomachos,* from *stoma* "mouth"] — **stomach** *adj*

²**stomach** *vt* **1** *archaic* : to take offense at **2** : to bear without open reaction or resentment : BROOK

stom·ach·ache \-,āk\ *n* : pain in or in the region of the stomach

stom·ach·er \'stəm-i-kər, -i-chər\ *n* : the center front section of a bodice appearing between the laces of an outer garment (as in 16th century costume); *also* : a jeweled ornament for the front of a bodice

¹**sto·mach·ic** \stə-'mak-ik\ *adj* : of or relating to the stomach ⟨*stomachic* vessels⟩

²**stomachic** *n* : a stimulant or tonic for the stomach

stomach pump *n* : a suction pump with a flexible tube for removing liquids from the stomach

sto·mate \'stō-,māt\ *n* : STOMA 2 [derived from *stoma*]

¹**stomp** \'stämp, 'stómp\ *vb* : STAMP 2 — **stomp·er** *n*

²**stomp** *n* **1** : STAMP 4 **2** : a jazz dance characterized by heavy stamping

¹**stone** \'stōn\ *n* **1** : earth or mineral matter hardened in a mass **2** : a piece of rock not as fine as gravel ⟨throw *stones*⟩ **3** : rock used as a material especially for building **4** : a piece of rock used for some special purpose (as for a monument at a grave) **5** : JEWEL, GEM ⟨precious *stones*⟩ **6** : CALCULUS 1 **7** : a hard stony seed or one (as of a plum) enclosed in a stony cover **8** *pl usually* **stone** : any of various units of weight; *esp* : an official British unit equal to 14 pounds (about 6.35 kilograms) [Old English *stān*]

²**stone** *adj* : of, relating to, or made of stone

³**stone** *vt* **1** : to hurl stones at; *esp* : to kill by hitting with stones **2** : to remove the stones of (a fruit) **3 a** : to rub, scour, or polish (as leather or machined metal) with a stone **b** : to sharpen with a whetstone — **ston·er** *n*

⁴**stone** *adv* : in a complete manner : ENTIRELY, UTTERLY — used as an intensive ⟨the soup is *stone* cold⟩; often used in combination ⟨*stone*-broke⟩

Stone Age *n* : the first known period of prehistoric human culture characterized by the use of stone tools

stone-blind \'stōn-'blīnd\ *adj* : totally blind — **stone-blind·ness** \-'blīnd-nəs, -'blīn-\ *n*

stone cell *n* : SCLEREID

stone·crop \'stōn-,kräp\ *n* : SEDUM; *esp* : a mossy evergreen creeping sedum with pungent leaves

stone·cut·ter \-,kət-ər\ *n* **1** : one that cuts, carves, or dresses stone **2** : a machine for dressing stone — **stone·cut·ting** \-,kət-ing\ *n*

stoned \'stōnd\ *adj* **1** : DRUNK 1 **2** : being under the influence of a drug

stone-deaf \'stōn-'def\ *adj* : totally deaf — **stone-deaf·ness** *n*

stone fly *n* : any of an order (Plecoptera) of 4-winged insects with aquatic gilled nymphs used by anglers for bait

stone fruit *n* : DRUPE

stone-ground \'stōn-'graúnd\ *adj* : ground by millstones rather than by some other process

stone·ma·son \'stōn-,mās-n\ *n* : a mason who builds with stone — **stone·ma·son·ry** \-rē\ *n*

stone wall *n* **1** *chiefly Northern* : a fence made of stones; *esp* : one built of rough stones without mortar to enclose a field **2** : an immovable block or obstruction (as in public affairs)

stone·ware \'stōn-,waər, -,weər\ *n* : a strong opaque ceramic ware that is high-fired, well vitrified, and nonporous

stone·work \-,wərk\ *n* **1** : a structure or part built of stone : MASONRY **2** : the shaping, preparation, or setting of stone — **stone·work·er** \-,wər-kər\ *n*

stone·wort \-,wərt, -,wórt\ *n* : any of a family of freshwater green algae that resemble the equisetums and are often encrusted with calcium-containing deposits

stony *also* **ston·ey** \'stō-nē\ *adj* **ston·i·er; -est** **1** : abounding in or having the nature of stone : ROCKY **2 a** : insensitive as stone : PITILESS, HARDHEARTED **b** : showing no movement or reaction : EXPRESSIONLESS **3** : STONE-BROKE — **ston·i·ly** \'stōn-l-ē\ *adv* — **ston·i·ness** \'stō-nē-nəs\ *n*

stood *past of* STAND

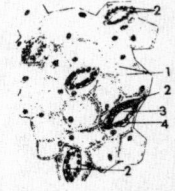

stoma: *1* epithelial cells, *2* guard cells, *3* stoma, *4* chloroplasts

\ə\ abut		\ng\ sing	
\ər\ further		\ō\ bone	
\a\ mat		\ó\ saw	
\ā\ take		\oi\ coin	
\ä\ cot, cart		\th\ thin	
\aú\ out		\th\ this	
\ch\ chin		\ü\ food	
\e\ pet		\ú\ foot	
\ē\ easy		\y\ yet	
\g\ go		\yü\ few	
\i\ tip		\yú\ cure	
\ī\ life		\zh\ vision	
\j\ job			

stooge \'stüj\ *n* **1** : one who slavishly follows or serves another **2** : STRAIGHT MAN [origin unknown] — **stooge** *vi*

stool \'stül\ *n* **1 a** : a seat usually without back or arms supported by three or four legs or by a central pedestal **b** : FOOTSTOOL **2 a** : a seat used while defecating or urinating **b** : a discharge of fecal matter [Old English *stōl*]

stool pigeon *n* **1** : a pigeon used as a decoy to draw others within a net **2** : a person acting as a spy or informer especially for the police [probably from the early practice of fastening the decoy bird to a stool]

¹stoop \'stüp\ *vb* **1** : to bend forward and downward **2** : to carry the head and shoulders or the upper part of the body bent forward **3** : to descend to doing something that is beneath one : degrade or debase oneself ⟨*stoop* to lying⟩ **4** : to descend swiftly on prey : SWOOP ⟨a hawk *stooping* after a mouse⟩ [Old English *stūpian*] □ SYN STOOP, CONDESCEND, DEIGN mean to descend from one's real or pretended level of dignity. STOOP may imply a descent from a relatively high plane to a much lower one morally or socially; CONDESCEND implies an unbending by one of high position to meet a social inferior on the same level; DEIGN suggests a haughty or reluctant condescension; CONDESCEND and DEIGN are used chiefly in irony or mild derision.

²stoop *n* **1 a** : an act of bending the body forward **b** : a temporary or habitual forward bend of the back and shoulders **2** : the descent of a bird especially on its prey **3** : a lowering of oneself either in condescension or in submission

³stoop *n* : a porch, platform, or entrance stairway at a house door [Dutch *stoep*]

¹stop \'stäp\ *vb* **stopped; stop·ping** **1** : to close an opening by filling or blocking it : PLUG ⟨nose *stopped* up by a cold⟩ ⟨*stopped* their ears with cotton⟩ **2** : CHECK, RESTRAIN ⟨*stop* a person from going⟩ **3** : to halt the movement or progress of ⟨*stop* the car⟩ **4** : to instruct one's bank not to honor or pay ⟨*stop* payment on a check⟩ **5** : to change the pitch of (as a violin string) by pressing with the finger **6 a** : to cease activity or operation **b** : to come to an end **7** : to break one's journey [Old English -*stoppian*, from Latin *stuppa* "oakum, tow"] □ SYN CEASE, DESIST, QUIT : STOP applies to action or progress or to what is operating or progressing and may imply suddenness or definiteness ⟨*stopped* at the red signal⟩ CEASE applies to states, conditions, or existence and may add a suggestion of gradualness and a degree of finality ⟨*ceased* raining during the night⟩ DESIST implies forbearance or restraint as a motive for stopping or ceasing ⟨*desisted* from further efforts to persuade them⟩ QUIT may stress either finality or abruptness in stopping or ceasing ⟨the engine faltered, sputtered, then *quit*⟩

²stop *n* **1 a** : CESSATION, END **b** : a pause or breaking off in speech **2** : a graduated set of organ pipes of like kind and tone quality **3 a** : something that impedes, obstructs, or brings to a halt : IMPEDIMENT, OBSTACLE **b** : the aperture of a camera lens **c** : a drain plug : STOPPER **4** : a device for arresting or limiting motion **5** : the act of stopping : the state of being stopped : CHECK **6 a** : a halt in a journey : STAY **b** : a stopping place **7 a** *chiefly British* : any of several punctuation marks **b** — used in telegrams and cables to indicate a period **8** : a consonant in the articulation of which there is a stage (as in the *p* of *apt* or the *g* of *tiger*) when the breath passage is completely closed

³stop *adj* : serving to stop : designed to stop ⟨*stop* line⟩ ⟨*stop* signal⟩ ⟨*stop* valve⟩

stop bath *n* : an acid bath used to stop the development of a photographic negative or print

stop·cock \'stäp-ˌkäk\ *n* : a cock for stopping or regulating flow (as through a pipe)

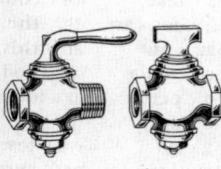
stopcock

stop down *vt* : to reduce the aperture of (a lens) by means of a diaphragm

¹stope \'stōp\ *n* : a usually steplike excavation underground for the removal of ore [probably from Low German *stope*, literally, "step"]

²stope *vb* : to mine by means of a stope

stop·gap \'stäp-ˌgap\ *n* : something that serves as a temporary substitute : MAKESHIFT

stop knob *n* : one of the handles by which an organist draws or shuts off a particular stop

stop·light \'stäp-ˌlīt\ *n* : TRAFFIC SIGNAL

stop·over \'stäp-ˌō-vər\ *n* **1** : a stop at an intermediate point in one's journey **2** : a stopping place on a journey

stop·page \'stäp-ij\ *n* : the act of stopping : the state of being stopped : HALT, OBSTRUCTION

¹stop·per \'stäp-ər\ *n* **1** : one that brings to a halt : CHECK **2** : one that closes, shuts, or fills up; *esp* : something (as a bung or cork) used to plug an opening

²stopper *vt* : to close or secure with or as if with a stopper

stop·ple \'stäp-əl\ *n* : something that closes an aperture : STOPPER, PLUG [Middle English *stoppell*, from *stoppen* "to stop"] — **stopple** *vt*

stop street *n* : a street on which a vehicle must stop just before entering a through street

stop·watch \'stäp-ˌwäch\ *n* : a watch having a hand that can be started and stopped at will for exact timing (as of a race)

stor·able \'stōr-ə-bəl, 'stȯr-\ *adj* : that may be stored ⟨*storable* commodities⟩ — **storable** *n*

stor·age \'stōr-ij, 'stȯr-\ *n* **1 a** : space or a place for storing **b** : an amount stored **c** : MEMORY 4 **2 a** : the act of storing : the state of being stored **b** : the price charged for storing something

storage battery *n* : a cell or connected group of cells that converts chemical energy into electrical energy by reversible chemical reactions and that may be recharged by passing a current through it in the direction opposite to that of its discharge — called also *storage cell*

sto·rax \'stōr-ˌaks, 'stȯr-\ *n* **1** : a resin related to benzoin and formerly used in incense **2** : a fragrant balsam from trees of the witchhazel family [Late Latin, from Latin *styrax*, from Greek]

¹store \'stōr, 'stȯr\ *vt* **1** : FURNISH, SUPPLY ⟨*store* a ship with provisions⟩ **2** : to lay away : ACCUMULATE ⟨*store* vegetables for winter use⟩ **3 a** : to deposit in a place (as a warehouse) for safekeeping or disposal ⟨*stored* my furniture until I found a new apartment⟩ **b** : to place (as data) in a computer for later use **4** : to provide storage room for : HOLD [Old French *estorer* "to construct, restore, store", from Latin *instaurare* "to renew, restore"]

²store *n* **1** *pl* : accumulated supplies (as of food) ⟨a ship's *stores*⟩ **2** : something stored : STOCK ⟨a *store* of good jokes⟩ **3** : a place where goods are sold : SHOP — **in store** : in a state of imminence : WAITING ⟨there's trouble *in store* for you⟩

³store *adj* : purchased from a store : READY-MADE ⟨*store* clothes⟩ ⟨*store* bread⟩

store cheese *n* : CHEDDAR

store·front \'stōr-ˌfrənt, 'stȯr-\ *n* **1** : the front side of a store or store building facing a street **2** : a building, room, or group of rooms having a storefront — **storefront** *adj*

storefront church *n* : a city church that uses storefront facilities as a meeting place

store·house \'stōr-ˌhaus, 'stȯr-\ *n* **1** : a building for storing goods : WAREHOUSE **2** : an abundant supply or source ⟨a *storehouse* of knowledge⟩

store·keep·er \-ˌkē-pər\ *n* **1** : one that is in charge of supplies **2** : the operator of a retail store

store·room \-ˌrüm, -ˌrum\ *n* : a room in which goods are stored

store·wide \-'wīd\ *adj* : including all or most merchandise in a store 〈a *storewide* sale〉

¹sto·ried \'stōr-ēd, 'stór-\ *adj* **1** : decorated with designs representing scenes from story or history 〈a *storied* tapestry〉 **2** : having an interesting history : celebrated in story or history 〈a *storied* castle〉

²storied *or* **sto·reyed** *adj* : having stories 〈a two-*storied* house〉

stork \'stórk\ *n* : any of various large mostly Old World wading birds having a long stout bill and being related to the herons [Old English *storc*]

storks·bill \'stórks-,bil\ *n* : any of several plants of the geranium family with long beaked fruits

¹storm \'stórm\ *n* **1 a** : a disturbance of the atmosphere accompanied by wind and usually by rain, snow, hail, sleet, or thunder and lightning **b** : a heavy fall of rain, snow, or hail **c** : wind having a speed of 103 to 116 kilometers per hour **2** : a disturbed or agitated state : a sudden or violent commotion **3** : a sudden heavy influx or onset **4** : a heavy discharge of objects (as missiles) **5** : a tumultuous outburst 〈a *storm* of protests〉 **6** : a violent assault on a defended position [Old English]

²storm *vb* **1 a** : to blow with violence **b** : to rain, hail, snow, or sleet heavily **2** : to attack by storm 〈*stormed* ashore at zero hour〉 〈*storm* the fort〉 **3** : to show violent emotion : RAGE 〈*storming* at the delay〉 **4** : to rush about violently 〈the mob *stormed* through the streets〉 SYN see ATTACK

storm·bound \-,baùnd\ *adj* : cut off from outside communication by a storm or its effects : stopped or delayed by storms

storm door *n* : an additional door placed outside an ordinary outside door for protection against severe weather

storm petrel *n* : any of various small petrels; *esp* : a small sooty black white-marked petrel frequenting the north Atlantic and Mediterranean — called also *Mother Carey's chicken, stormy petrel*

storm trooper *n* : a member of a private Nazi army noted for aggressiveness, violence, and brutality

storm window *n* : a framed glass window placed outside an ordinary window as a protection against severe weather — called also *storm sash*

stormy \'stór-mē\ *adj* **storm·i·er; -est 1** : relating to, characterized by, or indicative of a storm 〈a *stormy* day〉 〈*stormy* skies〉 **2** : marked by turmoil or fury : PASSIONATE, TURBULENT 〈a *stormy* life〉 — **storm·i·ly** \-mə-lē\ *adv* — **storm·i·ness** \-mē-nəs\ *n*

¹sto·ry \'stōr-ē, 'stór-\ *n, pl* **stories 1 a** : an account of incidents or events **b** : ANECDOTE **2 a** : a fictional narrative shorter than a novel; *esp* : SHORT STORY **b** : the plot of a narrative or dramatic work **3** : a widely circulated rumor **4** : FALSEHOOD 1 **5** : LEGEND 1a, ROMANCE **6** : a news article or broadcast [Old French *estorie* "story, history", from Latin *historia*]

²story *vt* **sto·ried; sto·ry·ing 1** *archaic* : to narrate or describe in story **2** : to adorn with a story or a scene from history

³story *or* **sto·rey** *n, pl* **stories** *or* **storeys 1** : a set of rooms on one floor level of a building **2** : a horizontal division of a building's exterior not necessarily corresponding exactly with the stories within [Medieval Latin *historia* "picture, story of a building", from Latin, "history"; probably from pictures adorning the windows of medieval buildings]

sto·ry·book \'stōr-ē-,búk, 'stór-\ *n* : a book of stories (as for children)

sto·ry·tell·er \-,tel-ər\ *n* : a teller of stories: as **a** : a relator of anecdotes **b** : a reciter of tales (as in a children's library) **c** : one that tells lies : FIBBER **d** : a writer of stories — **sto·ry·tell·ing** \-,tel-ing\ *adj or n*

stoup \'stüp\ *n* **1** : a container (as a large glass or a tankard) for beverages **2** : a basin for holy water at the entrance of a church [Middle English *stowp*]

¹stout \'staút\ *adj* **1** : strong of character: as **a** : BOLD 1a, BRAVE **b** : firmly resolute : STAUNCH **2 a** : physically strong : POWERFUL **b** : STURDY 2a, VIGOROUS **c** : sturdily constructed : SOLID 〈*stout* boots〉 **3** : full of energy : FORCEFUL **4** : bulky in body : FAT [Old French *estout*, of Germanic origin] — **stout·ish** \'staút-ish\ *adj* — **stout·ly** *adv* — **stout·ness** *n*

²stout *n* **1** : a heavy-bodied dark brew made with roasted malt and a relatively high percentage of hops **2 a** : a fat person **b** : a clothing size for the large figure

stout·en \'staút-n\ *vb* **stout·ened; stout·en·ing** \'staút-ning, -n-ing\ : to make or become stout

stout·heart·ed \'staút-'härt-əd\ *adj* : BOLD 1a, BRAVE — **stout·heart·ed·ly** *adv* — **stout·heart·ed·ness** *n*

¹stove \'stōv\ *n* **1** : an apparatus that burns fuel or uses electricity to provide heat (as for cooking or heating) **2** : KILN [Dutch or Low German, "heated room"]

²stove *past of* STAVE

stove·pipe \'stōv-,pīp\ *n* **1** : a metal pipe for carrying off smoke from a stove **2** : a tall silk hat

sto·ver \'stō-vər\ *n* : dried stalks of grain with the ears removed that are used as feed for livestock [Anglo-French *estovers* "necessary supplies", from Old French *estoveir* "to be necessary", from Latin *est opus* "there is need"]

stow \'stō\ *vt* **1** : HOUSE 1a, LODGE **2** : to put away : STORE **3 a** : to dispose in an orderly fashion : ARRANGE, PACK **b** : to fill with cargo : LOAD **4** *slang* : to put aside : STOP — usually used in the phrase *stow it* **5** : to cram in (food) — usually used with *away* [Middle English *stowen* "to place", from *stowe* "place", from Old English *stōw*]

stow·age \'stō-ij\ *n* **1 a** : an act or process of stowing **b** : goods stowed or to be stowed **2 a** : storage capacity **b** : a place for storage **3** : STORAGE 2a

stow·away \'stō-ə-,wā\ *n* : one that stows away

stow away \,stō-ə-'wā, 'stō-ə-,\ *vi* : to conceal oneself aboard a vehicle as a way to obtain transportation

STP \,es-,tē-'pē\ *n* : a powerful hallucinogenic drug that is chemically related to amphetamine [from *STP*, a trademark for a motor fuel additive]

stra·bis·mus \strə-'biz-məs\ *n* : an eye disorder in which the two eyes cannot be directed to the same point because of a fault of the muscles of the eyeball [Greek *strabismos* "condition of squinting", from *strabizein* "to squint", from *strabos* "squint-eyed"] — **stra·bis·mic** \-mik\ *adj*

¹strad·dle \'strad-l\ *vb* **strad·dled; strad·dling** \'strad-ling, -l-ing\ **1** : to part the legs wide : stand, sit, or walk with the legs wide apart **2** : to stand, sit, or be astride of 〈*straddle* a horse〉 **3** : SPRAWL 3 **4** : to be noncommittal : favor or seem to favor two apparently opposite sides 〈*straddle* an issue〉 [derived from *stride*] — **strad·dler** \'strad-lər, -l-ər\ *n*

²straddle *n* **1** : the act or position of one that straddles **2** : a noncommittal or uncertain position

strafe \'sträf\ *vt* : to fire on (as troops) at close range and especially with machine guns from low-flying airplanes [German *Gott strafe England* "God punish England", slogan of the Germans in World War I] — **straf·er** *n*

strag·gle \'strag-əl\ *vi* **strag·gled; strag·gling** \'strag-ling, -ə-ling\ **1** : to wander from a direct course or way : ROVE, STRAY **2** : to trail off from others of its kind : spread out irregularly [Middle English *straglen*] — **strag·gler** \-lər, -ə-lər\ *n*

strag·gly \'strag-lē, -ə-lē\ *adj* **strag·gli·er; -est** : spread out or scattered irregularly 〈a *straggly* beard〉

¹straight \'strāt\ *adj* **1 a** : free from curves, bends, angles, or irregularities 〈*straight* hair〉 〈*straight* timber〉 **b** : generated by a point moving continuously in the same direction 〈a *straight* line〉 **2** : DIRECT, UNINTERRUPTED: as **a** : lying along or holding to a direct or proper course or method 〈a *straight* thinker〉 **b** : CANDID, FRANK 〈a *straight* answer〉 **c** : coming directly

storm petrel

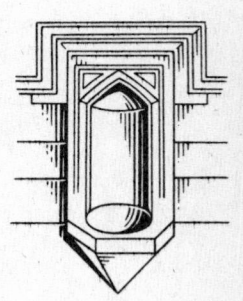

stoup 2

\ə\ abut		\ng\ sing	
\ər\ further		\ō\ bone	
\a\ mat		\ó\ saw	
\ā\ take		\ói\ coin	
\ä\ cot, cart		\th\ thin	
\aú\ out		\th\ this	
\ch\ chin		\ü\ food	
\e\ pet		\ú\ foot	
\ē\ easy		\y\ yet	
\g\ go		\yü\ few	
\i\ tip		\yú\ cure	
\ī\ life		\zh\ vision	
\j\ job			

from a trustworthy source 〈a *straight* tip on the horses〉 **d** : made up of elements arranged in a logical order; *also* : CONSECUTIVE 〈five *straight* hours〉 **e** : VERTICAL 2, UPRIGHT **3 a** : JUST, FAIR 〈*straight* dealings〉 **b** : properly ordered or arranged 〈set the kitchen *straight*〉; *also* : CORRECT 〈get the facts *straight*〉 **c** : free from extraneous matter 〈*straight* whiskey〉 **d** : making no exceptions in one's support of a party 〈vote a *straight* ticket〉 **e** : not deviating from the general norm or prescribed pattern 〈a *straight* dramatic part〉 **f** : CONVENTIONAL 1; *esp* : SQUARE 6 **4** : being the only form of financial compensation 〈salespeople on *straight* commission〉 [Middle English, from past participle of *strecchen* "to stretch"] — **straight·ness** *n*

²straight *adv* : in a straight manner, course, or line

³straight *n* **1** : something that is straight: as **a** : a straight line or arrangement **b** : STRAIGHTAWAY; *esp* : HOMESTRETCH **c** : a true or honest report or course **2 a** : a sequence (as of shots, strokes, or moves) resulting in a perfect score in a game or contest **b** : first place at the finish of a horse race : WIN **3** : a combination of five cards in sequence in a poker hand **4** : a conventional person

straight A \ˌstrāt-ˈā\ *adj* : having or being a first-class record of achievement

straight angle *n* : an angle whose sides lie in the same straight line and that equals two right angles

straight–arm \ˈstrāt-ˌärm\ *vb* : to ward off an opponent with the arm held straight — **straight–arm** *n*

¹straight·away \ˈstrāt-ə-ˌwā\ *adj* **1** : proceeding in a straight line : continuous in direction : STRAIGHTFORWARD **2** : IMMEDIATE 〈made a *straightaway* reply〉

²straightaway *n* : a straight course: as **a** : the straight part of a closed racecourse : STRETCH **b** : a straight and unimpeded stretch of road or way

³straight·away \ˌstrāt-ə-ˈwā\ *adv* : without hesitation or delay : IMMEDIATELY

straight·edge \ˈstrāt-ˌej\ *n* : a bar of wood, metal, or plastic with a straight edge for testing straight lines and surfaces or drawing straight lines

straight·en \ˈstrāt-n\ *vb* **straight·ened**; **straight·en·ing** \ˈstrāt-ning, -n-ing\ **1** : to make or become straight — usually used with *up* or *out* **2** : to put in order 〈*straighten* up a room〉 〈*straightened* out my accounts〉 — **straight·en·er** \ˈstrāt-nər, -n-ər\ *n*

straight face *n* : a face showing no emotion and especially no merriment — **straight–faced** \ˈstrāt-ˈfāst\ *adj*

straight flush *n* : a combination of five cards of the same suit in sequence in a poker hand

¹straight·for·ward \strāt-ˈfȯr-wərd, ˈstrāt-\ *adj* **1 a** : OUTSPOKEN, CANDID 〈a *straightforward* reply〉 **b** : CLEAR 3c, UNMISTAKABLE **2** : proceeding in a straight course or manner : DIRECT, UNDEVIATING — **straight·for·ward·ly** *adv* — **straight·for·ward·ness** *n*

²straight·for·ward *also* **straight·for·wards** \-wərdz\ *adv* : in a straightforward way

straight man *n* : an entertainer who feeds lines to a comedian

straight off *adv* : at once : IMMEDIATELY

straight razor *n* : a razor with a rigid cutting blade hinged to a case that forms a handle when the razor is open for use

straight·way \ˈstrāt-ˌwā, -ˈwā\ *adv* **1** : in a direct course : DIRECTLY **2** : right away : IMMEDIATELY

¹strain \ˈstrān\ *n* **1 a** : LINEAGE, ANCESTRY **b** : a group of presumed common ancestry that is physiologically but usually not morphologically distinct 〈a high-yielding *strain* of winter wheat〉 **c** : SORT 1, KIND **2 a** : inherited or inherent character, quality, or disposition 〈a *strain* of madness in the family〉 **b** : TRACE, STREAK 〈a *strain* of sadness in the story〉 **3 a** : TUNE 1b, AIR **b** : a passage of verbal or musical expression **4 a** : the general tone of an utterance or of a course of action or conduct **b** : TEMPER 4c, MOOD [Middle English *streen* "progeny, lineage", from Old English *strēon* "gain, acquisition"]

²strain *vb* **1 a** : to draw tight : cause to clasp firmly **b** : to stretch to maximum extension and tautness **2 a** : to exert oneself to the utmost : STRIVE **b** : to injure or undergo injury by overuse, misuse, or excessive pressure 〈*strain* the heart by overwork〉 **c** : to cause a change of form or size in (a body) by application of external force **3** : to squeeze or clasp tightly: as **a** : HUG 1 **b** : to compress painfully : CONSTRICT **4 a** : to pass or cause to pass through or as if through a strainer : FILTER **b** : to remove by straining 〈*strain* lumps out of the gravy〉 **5** : to stretch beyond a proper limit 〈*strain* the truth〉 **6** : to make great difficulty or resistance : BALK 〈a horse *straining* at the lead〉 [Middle French *estraindre*, from Latin *stringere*]

³strain *n* : an act of straining or the condition of being strained: as **a** : excessive physical or mental tension **b** : bodily injury from excessive tension, effort, or use 〈heart *strain*〉; *esp* : one resulting from a wrench or twist and involving undue stretching of muscles or ligaments 〈back *strain*〉 **c** : deformation of a material body under the action of applied forces □ SYN STRAIN, SPRAIN mean damage to muscles or tendons through overstretching or overexertion. STRAIN may apply to any part of the body; SPRAIN applies chiefly to the tearing of ligaments at a joint by sharp wrenching or twisting.

strained \ˈstrānd\ *adj* **1** : FORCED 〈a *strained* smile〉 **2** : pushed by antagonism near to open conflict 〈*strained* relations between countries〉

strain·er \ˈstrā-nər\ *n* : one that strains; *esp* : a device (as a screen, sieve, or filter) to retain solid pieces while a liquid passes through

¹strait \ˈstrāt\ *adj* **1** *archaic* **a** : NARROW 1 **b** : limited in space or time **c** : closely fitting : TIGHT **2** *archaic* : RIGOROUS, EXACTING **3 a** : causing distress : DIFFICULT **b** : limited as to means or resources [Old French *estreit*, from Latin *strictus* "strait, strict"] — **strait·ly** *adv* — **strait·ness** *n*

²strait *n* **1 a** *archaic* : a narrow space or passage **b** : a comparatively narrow passageway connecting two large bodies of water — often used in pl. **c** : ISTHMUS **2** : a situation of perplexity or distress — often used in pl. 〈dire *straits*〉

strait·en \ˈstrāt-n\ *vt* **strait·ened**; **strait·en·ing** \ˈstrāt-ning, -n-ing\ **1 a** : to make strait or narrow **b** : to hem in : CONFINE **2** *archaic* : to restrict in freedom or scope : HAMPER **3** : to subject to distress, privation, or deficiency 〈in *straitened* circumstances〉

strait·jack·et *also* **straight·jack·et** \ˈstrāt-ˌjak-ət\ *n* : a cover or overgarment of strong material (as canvas) used to bind the body and especially the arms closely in restraining a violent prisoner or patient

strait·laced *or* **straight·laced** \ˈstrāt-ˈlāst\ *adj* : excessively strict in manners, morals, or opinion — **strait·laced·ly** \-ˈlā-səd-lē, -lās-tlē\ *adv* — **strait·laced·ness** \-ˈlāst-nəs, -ˈlās-; -ˈlā-səd-nəs\ *n*

strake \ˈstrāk\ *n* : a continuous band of hull planking or plates on a ship; *also* : the width of such a band [Middle English]

stra·mo·ni·um \strə-ˈmō-nē-əm\ *n* : the dried leaves of the jimsonweed used in medicine similarly to belladonna especially in asthma [New Latin, "jimsonweed"]

¹strand \ˈstrand\ *n* : the land bordering a body of water : SHORE, BEACH [Old English]

²strand *vb* **1** : to run, drive, or cause to drift onto a strand : run aground : BEACH **2** : to leave in a strange or an unfavorable place especially without funds or means to depart 〈*stranded* in a strange city〉

³strand *n* **1** : one of the threads, strings, or wires twisted to make a cord, rope, or cable; *also* : the rope, cord, or cable into which these strands are twisted **2** : an elongated or twisted and plaited body resembling a rope 〈a *strand* of pearls〉 **3** : one of the elements of a complex whole 〈the *strands* of a legal argument〉 [Middle English *strond*]

⁴strand *vt* **1** : to form (as a rope) from strands **2** : to play out, twist, or arrange in a strand

strange \'strānj\ *adj* **1 a** *archaic* : FOREIGN **2 b** : not native to or naturally belonging in a place : of external origin, kind, or character **2 a** : not known, heard, or seen before ⟨*strange* surroundings⟩ **b** : causing surprise or wonder : UNUSUAL, BIZARRE ⟨*strange* clothes⟩ **3** : ill at ease ⟨feel *strange* on your first day in school⟩ [Old French *estrange*, from Latin *extraneus*, literally, "external", from *extra* "outside"] — **strange·ly** *adv* — **strange·ness** *n* □ SYN QUEER, PECULIAR, OUTLANDISH: STRANGE emphasizes unfamiliarity and may apply to what is foreign or unnatural or unaccountable ⟨*strange* behavior⟩ QUEER suggests a dubious, unexpected, often sinister strangeness ⟨a *queer* taste⟩ PECULIAR implies a marked difference from the usual ⟨a *peculiar* hobbling gait⟩ OUTLANDISH implies an uncouth or barbaric strangeness ⟨*outlandish* clothes⟩ ⟨*outlandish* customs⟩

strang·er \'strān-jər\ *n* **1** : one who is strange: as **a** : FOREIGNER **b** : one in the house of another as a guest, visitor, or intruder **c** : a person or thing that is unknown or with whom one is unacquainted **d** : one who does not belong to or is kept from the activities of a group **2** : one ignorant of or unacquainted with someone or something ⟨a *stranger* to good manners⟩

stran·gle \'strang-gəl\ *vb* **stran·gled; stran·gling** \-gə-ling, -gling\ **1** : to choke to death by squeezing the throat **2** : to suppress or hinder the rise, expression, or growth of **3** : to become strangled [Middle French *estrangler*, from Latin *strangulare*, from Greek *strangalan*, from *strangalē* "halter"] — **stran·gler** \-gə-lər, -glər\ *n*

stran·gle·hold \'strang-gəl-,hōld\ *n* **1** : a wrestling hold by which one's opponent is choked **2** : a force or influence that chokes or suppresses freedom of movement or expression

stran·gu·late \'strang-gyə-,lāt\ *vb* **1** : STRANGLE 1, CONSTRICT **2** : to become constricted so as to stop circulation ⟨a hernia may *strangulate*⟩ [Latin *strangulare*]

stran·gu·la·tion \,strang-gyə-'lā-shən\ *n* **1** : an act or process of strangling or strangulating **2** : the state of being strangled or strangulated

¹strap \'strap\ *n* **1** : a band, plate, or loop of metal for binding objects together or for clamping an object in position **2 a** : a narrow usually flat strip or thong of a flexible material and especially leather used variously (as for securing, holding together, or wrapping) **b** : something made of a strap forming a loop ⟨a boot *strap*⟩ **c** : a strip of leather used for flogging **d** : STROP [alteration of *strop*]

²strap *vt* **strapped; strap·ping 1 a** : to secure with or attach by means of a strap **b** : BIND, CONSTRICT; *also* : to support (as a sprained joint) with strips of adhesive plaster **2** : to beat or punish with a strap **3** : STROP **4** : to cause to suffer from an extreme scarcity ⟨I'm *strapped* for cash⟩

strap·hang·er \'strap-,hang-ər\ *n* : a standing passenger in a subway, streetcar, bus, or train who clings for support to one of the devices (as short straps) placed along the aisle

strap·less \-ləs\ *adj* : having no strap; *esp* : made or worn without shoulder straps ⟨a *strapless* gown⟩

strap·per \'strap-ər\ *n* : one that is unusually large or robust

strap·ping \'strap-ing\ *adj* : having a vigorously sturdy constitution : ROBUST

strat·a·gem \'strat-ə-jəm\ *n* **1 a** : a trick in war for deceiving and outwitting the enemy **b** : a cleverly contrived trick or scheme for gaining an end **2** : skill in ruses or trickery [Italian *stratagemma*, from Latin *stratagema*, from Greek *stratēgēma*, from *stratēgein* "to be a general, maneuver", from *stratēgos* "general"] SYN see TRICK

stra·te·gic \strə-'tē-jik\ *adj* **1** : of, relating to, or marked by strategy ⟨a *strategic* retreat⟩ **2 a** : important in strategy : required for the conduct of war ⟨*strategic* materials⟩ **b** : of great importance within an integrated whole or to a planned effect ⟨emphasized the *strategic* points of the argument⟩ **3** : designed or trained to strike at the sources of an enemy's power ⟨*strategic* bombers⟩ — **stra·te·gi·cal** \-ji-kəl\ *adj* — **stra·te·gi·cal·ly** \-ji-kə-lē, -klē\ *adv*

strat·e·gist \'strat-ə-jəst\ *n* : one skilled in strategy

strat·e·gy \'strat-ə-jē\ *n, pl* **-gies 1 a** (1) : the science and art of using the political, economic, psychological, and military forces of a country so as to support adopted policies in peace or war (2) : the science and art of military command exercised to meet the enemy in combat under advantageous conditions **b** : a variety of or instance of the use of strategy **2 a** : a careful plan or method : STRATAGEM **b** : the art of devising or employing plans or stratagems to achieve a goal [Greek *stratēgia* "generalship", from *stratēgos* "general", from *stratos* "army" + *agein* "to lead"] □ SYN TACTICS: STRATEGY applies to the devising of a general plan of attack, defense, or action so as to achieve an end with the forces or means available ⟨attempting to trade blows at close range with a stronger hitter is a mistake in *strategy*⟩ TACTICS applies to the technique of utilizing forces properly or skillfully in action or combat ⟨failing to protect the jaw is poor boxing *tactics*⟩

strath \'strath\ *n* : a flat wide river valley or the low-lying grassland along it [Scottish Gaelic *srath*]

stra·tic·u·late \strə-'tik-yə-lət, stra-\ *adj* : characterized by thin parallel strata [derived from *stratum*]

strat·i·fy \'strat-ə-,fī\ *vb* **-fied; -fy·ing 1** : to form, deposit, or arrange in strata ⟨*stratified* epithelium⟩ ⟨a society *stratified* by custom⟩ **2** : to become arranged in strata — **strat·i·fi·ca·tion** \,strat-ə-fə-'kā-shən\ *n*

stra·tig·ra·phy \strə-'tig-rə-fē\ *n* **1** : geology that deals with the origin, composition, distribution, and succession of strata **2** : the arrangement of strata — **strat·i·graph·ic** \,strat-ə-'graf-ik\ *adj*

stra·to·cu·mu·lus \,strāt-ō-'kyü-myə-ləs, ,strat-\ *n* : stratified cumulus consisting of large balls or rolls of dark cloud which often cover the whole sky especially in winter

strato·sphere \'strat-ə-,sfiər\ *n* : an upper portion of the atmosphere above approximately 11 kilometers depending on latitude, season, and weather in which temperature changes but little with altitude and clouds of water are rare [French *stratosphère*, from New Latin *stratum* "stratum" + French *sphère* "sphere"] — **strato·spher·ic** \,strat-ə-'sfiər-ik, -'sfer-\ *adj*

stra·tum \'strāt-əm, 'strat-\ *n, pl* **stra·ta** \-ə\ **1** : a layer of a substance; *esp* : one having parallel layers of other kinds lying above or below or both above and below it ⟨a rock *stratum*⟩ ⟨a cold *stratum* in a lake⟩ ⟨deep *stratum* of the skin⟩ **2 a** : a stage of historical or cultural development **b** : a level of society made up of persons with the same or similar social, economic, or cultural status [Latin, "spread, bed", from *sternere* "to spread out"]

stra·tus \'strāt-əs, 'strat-\ *n, pl* **stra·ti** \'strāt-,ī, 'strat-\ : a cloud form extending horizontally over a relatively large area at an altitude of from 600 to 2100 meters [Latin, past participle of *sternere* "to spread out"]

¹straw \'strȯ\ *n* **1 a** : stalks of grain after threshing; *also* : any dry stalky plant residue ⟨pea *straw*⟩ ⟨pine *straw*⟩ **b** : a natural or artificial heavy fiber used for weaving, plaiting, or braiding **2** : a dry coarse stem especially of a cereal grass **3 a** (1) : something of little value or significance ⟨not worth a *straw*⟩ (2) : something too insubstantial to give support or help in a desperate situation ⟨clutch at *straws*⟩ **b** : CHAFF 2 **4** : a tube for sucking up a beverage [Old English *strēaw*] — **strawy** \'strȯ-i, 'strȯi\ *adj*

strawberry

²straw *adj* **1 a** : made of straw ⟨a *straw* rug⟩ **b** : of, relating to, or used for straw ⟨a *straw* barn⟩ **2** : of the color of straw **3** : of little or no value : WORTHLESS

straw·ber·ry \'stró-ber-ē, -bə-rē, -brē\ *n* : an edible juicy red pulpy fruit of a low herb of the rose family with white flowers and long slender runners; *also* : this plant [from the appearance of the achenes on the surface] — **strawberry** *adj*

strawberry mark *n* : a usually red and elevated birthmark that is a small tumor of a blood vessel

strawberry roan *n* : a roan horse with a decidedly red ground color

straw boss *n* : a foreman of a small gang of workers

straw·flow·er \'stró-flaù-ər, -flaùr\ *n* : any of several everlasting flowers

straw·hat theater \,stró-,hat-\ *n* : a summer theater [from the former fashion of men's wearing straw hats in summer]

straw man *n* **1** : a weak or imaginary argument or adversary set up only to be easily confuted **2** : a person set up to serve as a cover for a questionable transaction

straw vote *n* : an unofficial vote (as one taken at a chance gathering) to test the relative strength of opposing candidates or issues

¹stray \'strā\ *n* **1** : a domestic animal wandering at large or lost **2** : a person or thing that strays : a detached individual : STRAGGLER, WAIF

²stray *vi* **1** : to wander from company, restraint, or proper limits : ROAM **2 a** : to wander from a direct course or at random **b** : ERR **2** [Middle French *estraier,* derived from Latin *extra-* "outside" + *vagari* "to wander"] — **stray·er** *n*

³stray *adj* **1** : having strayed ⟨a *stray* cow⟩ **2** : occurring at random or as detached individuals ⟨a few *stray* hairs⟩ ⟨*stray* remarks⟩

¹streak \'strēk\ *n* **1** : a line or mark that is not the same color or texture as its background : STRIPE **2 a** : the color of the fine powder of a mineral obtained by scratching or rubbing against a hard white surface **b** : microorganisms implanted in a line on a solid culture medium **3 a** : a narrow band of light **b** : a lightning bolt **4 a** : TRACE, STRAIN ⟨a *streak* of stubbornness⟩ **b** : a brief run (as of luck) **c** : a consecutive series ⟨a winning *streak*⟩ **5** : a narrow layer ⟨a *streak* of lean in bacon⟩ ⟨a *streak* of ore⟩ [Old English *strica*]

²streak *vb* **1** : to make streaks on or in **2** : to move swiftly : RUSH

streaked \'strēkt, 'strē-kəd\ *adj* : marked with stripes or linear discolorations

streaky \'strē-kē\ *adj* **streak·i·er; -est 1** : marked with streaks **2** : VARIABLE 1a, CHANGEABLE ⟨a *streaky* hitter in baseball⟩ — **streak·i·ness** *n*

¹stream \'strēm\ *n* **1** : a body of running water (as a river or brook) flowing on the earth; *also* : a body of flowing fluid (as water or gas) **2 a** : a steady succession **b** : a constantly renewed supply **c** : a continuous moving procession **3** : an unbroken flow (as of gas or particles of matter) **4** : a ray or beam of light **5** : a dominant attitude, group, or line of development [Old English *strēam*] — **on stream** : into production

²stream *vb* **1 a** : to flow or cause to flow in or as if in a stream **b** : to leave a bright trail **2 a** : to exude a bodily fluid profusely **b** : to become soaked **3** : to trail out at full length **4** : to pour in large numbers **5** : to display fully extended

stream·er \'strē-mər\ *n* **1 a** : a flag that streams in the wind; *esp* : PENNANT **b** : a long narrow wavy strip like or suggesting a banner floating in the wind **c** : BANNER **2** **2** *pl* : AURORA BOREALIS

stream·let \'strēm-lət\ *n* : a small stream

stream·line \-'līn, -,līn\ *vt* **1** : to design or construct with a contour for decreasing resistance to motion through water or air or as if for this purpose **2** : to bring up to date : MODERNIZE **3** : to make simpler or more efficient

stream·lined \-'līnd, -,līnd\ *also* **stream·line** *adj* **1 a** : contoured to reduce resistance to motion through water or air or as if for this purpose **b** : stripped of nonessentials **2** : brought up to date

¹street \'strēt\ *n* **1 a** : a thoroughfare especially in a city, town, or village usually including sidewalks and being wider than an alley or lane **b** : the part of a street reserved for vehicles **c** : a thoroughfare and the property along it (lived on Maple *Street*) **2** : the people occupying property on a street ⟨the whole *street* was excited⟩ [Old English *strēt,* from Late Latin *strata* "paved road", from Latin *stratus,* past participle of *sternere* "to spread out"]

²street *adj* **1** : of or relating to the street or streets ⟨a *street* door⟩ ⟨a *street* map⟩ ⟨*street* clothes⟩ **2** : of or relating to the environment of the streets ⟨*street* people⟩

street ar·ab \-'ar-əb, -'ā-,rab\ *n, often cap A* : a homeless vagabond and especially an outcast boy or girl in the streets of a city

street·car \'strēt-,kär\ *n* : a vehicle on rails used primarily for transporting passengers and typically operating on city streets

street·light \-,līt\ *n* : a light usually mounted on a pole that forms one in a series spaced at intervals along a public road

street railway *n* : a company operating streetcars or buses

street–smart \'strēt-,smärt\ *adj* : STREETWISE

street smarts *n pl* : the quality of being streetwise

street·wise \'strēt-,wīz\ *adj* : possessing the skills and attitudes necessary to survive in an often violent urban environment

strength \'strength, 'strengkth\ *n* **1** : the quality or state of being strong : inherent power **2** : power to resist force : SOLIDITY, TOUGHNESS **3** : power of resisting attack : INVULNERABILITY **4** : legal, logical, or moral force **5 a** : degree of potency of effect or of concentration **b** : intensity of light, color, sound, or odor **6** : force as measured in numbers ⟨an army at full *strength*⟩ **7** : SUPPORT ⟨has enough *strength* in the senate to pass the bill⟩ [Old English *strengthu*] SYN see POWER — **strength·less** \-ləs\ *adj* — **strength·less·ness** *n*

strength·en \'streng-thən, 'strengk-\ *vb* **strength·ened; strength·en·ing** \'strength-ning, 'strengkth-, -ə-ning\ : to make or become stronger — **strength·en·er** \'strength-nər, 'strengkth-, -ə-nər\ *n*

stren·u·os·i·ty \,stren-yə-'wäs-ət-ē\ *n* : the quality or state of being strenuous

stren·u·ous \'stren-yə-wəs\ *adj* **1 a** : vigorously active : ENERGETIC ⟨leads a *strenuous* life⟩ **b** : FERVENT, ZEALOUS ⟨*strenuous* protest⟩ **2** : marked by or calling for energy or stamina : ARDUOUS ⟨*strenuous* work⟩ [Latin *strenuus*] SYN see VIGOROUS — **stren·u·ous·ly** *adv* — **stren·u·ous·ness** *n*

strep \'strep\ *n* : STREPTOCOCCUS

strep throat *n* : SEPTIC SORE THROAT

strep·to·ba·cil·lus \,strep-tō-ba-'sil-əs\ *n* : any of various bacilli in which the individual cells are joined in a chain [Greek *streptos* "twisted, pliant" (from *strephein* "to twist, turn") + New Latin *bacillus*]

strep·to·coc·cus \,strep-tə-'käk-əs\ *n, pl* **strep·to·coc·ci** \-'käk-,sī, -,ī, -,sē, -,ē\ : any of various nonmotile mostly parasitic spherical bacteria that occur in pairs or chains and include important pathogens of humans and domestic animals [derived from Greek *streptos* "twisted" + *kokkos* "grain, seed"] — **strep·to·coc·cal** \-'käk-əl\ *adj*

strep·to·my·ces \,strep-tə-'mī-,sēz\ *n, pl* **streptomyces** *or* **strep·to·my·cetes** \-'mī-,sēts, -mī-'; -mī-'sēt-ēz\ : any of a genus of mostly soil actinomycetes including some that form antibiotics as by-products of their metabolism [derived from Greek *streptos* "twisted" + *mykēs* "fungus"]

strep·to·my·cin \,strep-tə-'mīs-n\ *n* : an antibiotic base produced by a soil streptomyces and used especially in the treatment of tuberculosis

¹stress \'stres\ *n* **1** : constraining force or influence: as **a** : mutual force or action between surfaces in contact caused by external force (as tension or shear) **b** : a force that tends to distort a body **c** : a factor that induces bodily or mental tension and may be a factor in the causing of disease; *also* : a state of tension resulting from a stress **2** : EMPHASIS, WEIGHT (lay *stress* on a point) **3** : intensity of utterance given to a speech sound, syllable, or word **4** : relative force or prominence of sound in verse; *also* : a syllable having this stress **5** : ACCENT 6a [Middle English *stresse* "stress, distress", from *destresse,* from Old French] — **stress·less** \-ləs\ *adj* — **stress·less·ness** *n*

²stress *vt* **1** : to subject to physical or psychological stress **2** : ACCENT (*stress* the first syllable) **3** : to lay stress on : EMPHASIZE

stressed–out \'strest-'aut\ *adj* : suffering from high levels of physical or especially psychological stress

stress fracture *n* : a usually hairline fracture of a bone that has been subjected to repeated stress

stress·ful \-fəl\ *adj* : full of or tending to induce stress — **stress·ful·ly** \-fə-lē\ *adv*

stress mark *n* : a mark used with (as before, after, or over) a written syllable in the respelling of a word to show that this syllable is to be stressed when spoken : ACCENT MARK

¹stretch \'strech\ *vb* **1** : to extend (as one's limbs or body) in a reclining position (*stretch* oneself out on the bed) **2** : to reach out (*stretch* forth an arm) **3 a** : to extend in length or breadth or both : SPREAD **b** : to extend over a continuous period **4** : to cause the limbs of (a person) to be pulled especially in torture **5** : to draw up (one's body) from a cramped, stooping, or relaxed position (awoke and *stretched* myself) **6** : to pull taut **7 a** : to enlarge or distend especially by force **b** : STRAIN 2b **8** : to cause to reach or continue (*stretch* a wire between two posts) **9** : to extend often unduly the scope or meaning of (*stretch* the truth) **10** : to become extended without breaking [Middle English *strecchen,* from Old English *streccan*] — **stretch·abil·i·ty** \,strech-ə-'bil-ət-ē\ *n* — **stretch·able** \'strech-ə-bəl\ *adj* — **stretch one's legs** : to take a walk for exercise

²stretch *n* **1 a** : an exercise of something (as the imagination or understanding) beyond ordinary or normal limits **b** : an extension of the scope or application of something **2** : the extent to which something may be stretched **3** : the act of stretching : the state of being stretched **4 a** : an extent in length or area **b** : a continuous period of time (silent for a *stretch*) **5** : a walk to relieve fatigue **6** : a term of imprisonment **7 a** : either of the straight sides of a racecourse; *esp* : HOMESTRETCH **b** : a final stage **8** : the capacity for being stretched : ELASTICITY

³stretch *adj* : easily stretched : ELASTIC (*stretch* hosiery)

stretch·er \'strech-ər\ *n* **1** : one that stretches; *esp* : a device or machine for stretching or expanding something (as curtains) **2** : a litter (as of canvas) for carrying a disabled or dead person **3** : a rod or bar extending between two legs of a chair or table

stretch·er–bear·er \-,bar-ər, -,ber-\ *n* : one who carries one end of a stretcher

strew \'strü\ *vt* **strewed; strewed** *or* **strewn** \'strün\; **strew·ing** **1** : to spread (as seeds or flowers) by scattering **2** : to cover by or as if by scattering something over or on **3** : to become dispersed over **4** : to spread abroad : DISSEMINATE [Old English *strewian*]

stria \'strī-ə\ *n, pl* **stri·ae** \'strī-,ē\ **1** : a tiny groove or channel **2** : a narrow line, band, or groove especially when one of a series [Latin, "furrow, channel"]

stri·at·ed \'strī-,āt-əd\ *adj* : marked with lines, bands, or grooves — **stri·a·tion** \strī-'ā-shən\ *n*

striated muscle *n* : muscle that is made up of usually elongated cells with many nuclei and with alternate light and dark cross striations, is typical of the muscles which move the vertebrate skeleton, and is mostly under voluntary control — compare CARDIAC MUSCLE, SMOOTH MUSCLE

strick·en \'strik-ən\ *adj* **1** : hit or wounded by or as if by a missile **2** : afflicted with disease, misfortune, or sorrow [from past participle of *strike*]

strict \'strikt\ *adj* **1 a** : stringent in requirement or control (under *strict* orders) **b** : severe in discipline **2 a** : inflexibly maintained or adhered to : COMPLETE, ABSOLUTE (*strict* secrecy) **b** : rigorously conforming to principle or to a norm (a *strict* Catholic) **3** : EXACT, PRECISE (in the *strict* meaning of the word) [Latin *strictus,* from *stringere* "to bind tight"] SYN see RIGID — **strict·ly** *adv* — **strict·ness** \'strikt-nəs, 'strik-\ *n*

stric·ture \'strik-chər\ *n* **1** : an abnormal narrowing of a bodily passage; *also* : the narrowed part **2** : something that closely restrains or limits : RESTRICTION **3** : an adverse criticism : CENSURE [Late Latin *strictura,* from Latin *stringere* "to bind tight"]

¹stride \'strīd\ *vb* **strode** \'strōd\; **strid·den** \'strid-n\; **strid·ing** \'strīd-ing\ **1** : BESTRIDE, STRADDLE **2** : to step over **3** : to move over, through, or along with or as if with long measured steps **4** : to take a very long step [Old English *strīdan*] — **strid·er** \'strīd-ər\ *n*

²stride *n* **1 a** : a cycle of locomotor movements (as of a horse) completed when the feet regain their initial relative positions; *also* : the distance covered by this **b** : the most effective natural pace — often used in the phrase *hit one's stride* **2** : a long step **3** : an act of striding **4** : a stage of progress : ADVANCE (the *strides* made in the control of tuberculosis) **5** : a manner of striding (a purposeful *stride*)

stri·dent \'strīd-nt\ *adj* **1** : sounding harsh, grating, or shrill **2** : unpleasantly discordant (*strident* colors) [Latin *stridens,* past participle of *stridere, stridēre* "to make a harsh noise"] — **stri·den·cy** \-n-sē\ *n* — **stri·dent·ly** *adv*

stri·dor \'strīd-ər, 'strī-,dòr\ *n* : a strident noise [Latin, from *stridere, stridēre* "to make a harsh noise"]

strid·u·late \'strij-ə-,lāt\ *vi* : to make a shrill creaking noise by rubbing together special bodily structures — used especially of male insects (as crickets or grasshoppers) [derived from Latin *stridulus* "shrill", from *stridere, stridēre* "to make a harsh noise"] — **strid·u·la·tion** \,strij-ə-'lā-shən\ *n*

strid·u·lous \'strij-ə-ləs\ *adj* : making a shrill creaking sound [Latin *stridulus*] — **strid·u·lous·ly** *adv*

strife \'strīf\ *n* **1** : bitter sometimes violent conflict or dissension (political *strife*) **2** : an act of contention : FIGHT, STRUGGLE [Old French *estrif*]

strife·less \-ləs\ *adj* : free from strife

¹strike \'strīk\ *vb* **struck** \'strək\; **struck** *also* **strick·en** \'strik-ən\; **strik·ing** \'strī-king\ **1** : to take a course : GO (*strike* across the field) **2 a** : to deliver a stroke, blow, or thrust : HIT **b** : to drive or remove by or as if by a blow (*struck* the knife from my hand) **c** : to attack or seize especially with fangs or claws (*struck* by a snake) **3** : to come into contact or collision with **4** : to remove or cancel with or as if with a stroke of the pen (*struck* out a word in the text) **5** : to lower, take down, or take apart (*strike* a flag) (*strike* the tents) **6 a** : to indicate or become indicated by a bell or chime (as of a clock) **b** : to indicate by sounding **7** : to pierce or penetrate or to cause to pierce or penetrate **8** : to make a military attack : FIGHT (*strike* for freedom) **9** : to seize the bait (a fish *struck*) **10** : to begin or cause to grow : take root or cause to take root (some plant cuttings *strike* quickly) **11** : to stop work in order to force an employer to comply with demands **12** : to make a beginning : LAUNCH (the orchestra *struck* into another waltz) **13** : to afflict suddenly : lay low (*struck* down at the height of one's career) **14 a** : to bring into

\ə\ abut		\ng\ sing	
\ər\ further		\ō\ bone	
\a\ mat		\ò\ saw	
\ā\ take		\òi\ coin	
\ä\ cot, cart		\th\ thin	
\aù\ out		\th\ this	
\ch\ chin		\ü\ food	
\e\ pet		\ù\ foot	
\ē\ easy		\y\ yet	
\g\ go		\yü\ few	
\i\ tip		\yù\ cure	
\ī\ life		\zh\ vision	
\j\ job			

forceful contact ⟨*struck* my knee against the dash⟩ **b** : to thrust oneself forward **c** : to fall on ⟨sunlight *struck* the glass⟩ **d** : to become audible to ⟨a loud sound *strikes* the ear⟩ **15 a** : to affect with a mental or emotional state or a strong emotion ⟨*struck* with horror⟩ **b** : to bring about : INDUCE, CAUSE ⟨the words *struck* fear in them⟩ **c** : to cause to become by or as if by a sudden blow ⟨*struck* them dead⟩ **d** : to produce by stamping with a die or punch ⟨*strike* a medal⟩ **e** : to produce (as fire) by or as if by striking or rubbing **f** : to cause to ignite by friction ⟨*strike* a match⟩ **16** : to agree on the terms of ⟨*strike* a bargain⟩ **17 a** : to play by strokes on the keys or strings **b** : to produce by or as if by playing a musical instrument ⟨*strike* a chord on the piano⟩ **18 a** : to occur to **b** : to appear to **c** : to make a strong impression on : IMPRESS ⟨I was *struck* by its beauty⟩ **19** : to arrive at by computation ⟨*strike* an average⟩ **20 a** : to come to ⟨*strike* the main road⟩ **b** : to run across ⟨the best story I ever *struck*⟩ **21** : to take on : ASSUME ⟨*strike* a pose⟩ [Old English *strīcan* "to stroke, go"]

²strike *n* **1** : an act or instance of striking **2 a** : a work stoppage by a body of workers to force an employer to comply with demands **b** : a temporary stoppage of activities in protest against an act or condition **3** : the direction of the line of intersection of a horizontal plane with an uptilted geological stratum **4** : a pull on a line by a fish in striking **5** : a stroke of good luck; *esp* : a discovery of a valuable mineral deposit **6** : a pitched baseball that passes through the strike zone or that is swung at and is charged against the batter **7** : DISADVANTAGE 2, HANDICAP **8** : an act or instance of knocking down all the bowling pins with the first bowl **9 a** : a military attack; *esp* : an air attack on a single objective **b** : a group of airplanes taking part in such an attack

strike·bound \'strīk-ˌbau̇nd\ *adj* : subjected to or shut down by a strike ⟨a *strikebound* factory⟩

strike·break·er \'strīk-ˌbrā-kər\ *n* : a person hired to help break up a strike by workers

strike·break·ing \-ˌking\ *n* : action designed to break up a strike

strike off *vt* **1** : to produce with ease ⟨*strike off* a poem for the occasion⟩ **2** : to depict clearly and exactly

strike·out \'strī-ˌkau̇t\ *n* : an out in baseball resulting from a batter's being charged with three strikes

strike out \strī-'kau̇t, 'strī-\ *vb* **1** : to enter upon a course of action ⟨*strike out* on one's own⟩ **2** : to set out vigorously ⟨*struck out* for home immediately⟩ **3** : to retire or be retired by a strikeout

strike·over \'strī-ˌkō-vər\ *n* : an act or instance of striking a typewriter character on a spot already occupied by another character

strik·er \'strī-kər\ *n* : one that strikes: as **a** : a player in any of several games who strikes **b** : the hammer of the striking mechanism of a clock or watch **c** : a worker on strike

strike up *vb* **1** : to begin to play or be played ⟨the band *struck up*⟩ ⟨a waltz *struck up*⟩ **2** : to cause to begin ⟨*strike up* a conversation⟩

strike zone *n* : the area (as between the knees and armpits of a batter) over home plate through which a pitched baseball must pass to be called a strike

strik·ing \'strī-king\ *adj* : REMARKABLE, IMPRESSIVE ⟨a *striking* costume⟩ ⟨a *striking* resemblance⟩ — **strik·ing·ly** \-king-lē\ *adv*

¹string \'string\ *n* **1** : a small cord used to bind, fasten, or tie **2** : a thin tough plant structure; *esp* : the fiber connecting the halves of a bean pod **3 a** : the gut, wire, or plastic cord of a musical instrument **b** *pl* (1) : the stringed instruments of an orchestra (2) : the players of such instruments **4 a** : a group of objects threaded on a string **b** : a series arranged in or as if in a line ⟨a *string* of victories⟩ **c** : the animals and especially horses belonging to or used by one individual **5** : LINE

14 6 *pl* **a** : contingent conditions or obligations ⟨an agreement with no *strings* attached⟩ **b** : CONTROL 1, DOMINATION [Old English *streng*] — **string·less** \'string-ləs\ *adj* — **on the string** : subject to one's pleasure or influence

²string *vb* **strung** \'strəng\; **string·ing** \'string-ing\ **1** : to equip with strings **2** : to make tense **3 a** : to thread on or as if on a string ⟨*string* beads⟩ **b** : to thread with objects **c** : to tie, hang, or fasten with string **4** : to hang by the neck ⟨*strung* up from a high tree⟩ **5** : to remove the strings of ⟨*string* beans⟩ **6 a** : to extend or stretch like a string ⟨*string* wires from tree to tree⟩ **b** : to set out in a line or series **c** : to move, progress, or lie in a string **d** : to form into strings **7** : FOOL 3, HOAX

string along *vb* **1** : to go along : AGREE ⟨*string along* with the majority⟩ **2** : to keep dangling or waiting ⟨*stringing* customers *along* with false promises⟩

string bass *n* : DOUBLE BASS

string bean *n* : a bean of one of the older varieties of kidney bean that have stringy fibers on the lines of separation of the pods; *also* : SNAP BEAN

string·course \'string-ˌkōrs, -ˌkȯrs\ *n* : a horizontal band (as of bricks) in a building forming a part of the design

stringed instrument \'stringd-\ *n* : a musical instrument (as a violin, harp, or piano) sounded by plucking or striking or by drawing a bow across tense strings

strin·gent \'strin-jənt\ *adj* **1** : binding, drawing, or pressing tight **2** : marked by rigor, strictness, or severity especially with regard to rule or standard [Latin *stringens,* present participle of *stringere* "to bind tight"] SYN see RIGID — **strin·gen·cy** \-jən-sē\ *n* — **strin·gent·ly** *adv*

string·er \'string-ər\ *n* **1** : one that strings **2 a** : a long horizontal member in a framed structure or a bridge **b** : one of the inclined sides of a stair supporting the treads and risers **3** : a longitudinal member (as in an airplane fuselage or wing) to reinforce the skin **4** : one estimated to be of specified excellence or quality or efficiency — usually used in combination ⟨first-*stringer*⟩ ⟨second-*stringer*⟩

string·halt \'string-ˌhȯlt\ *n* : lameness of the hind legs of a horse due to muscular spasm — **string·halt·ed** \-ˌhȯl-təd\ *adj*

string·ing \'string-ing\ *n* : the gut, silk, or nylon with which a racket is strung

string tie *n* : a narrow necktie

stringy \'string-ē\ *adj* **string·i·er; -est 1 a** : containing, consisting of, or resembling fibrous matter or a string ⟨*stringy* root⟩ ⟨*stringy* hair⟩ **b** : lean and sinewy in build : WIRY **2** : capable of being drawn out to form a string : ROPY ⟨a *stringy* precipitate⟩ — **string·i·ness** *n*

¹strip \'strip\ *vb* **stripped** *also* **stript** \'stript\; **strip·ping 1 a** : to remove clothing, covering, or surface matter from ⟨*stripped* the baby for a bath⟩ **b** : to remove (as clothing) from a person ⟨*stripped* the gloves from my hands⟩ **c** : UNDRESS ⟨*stripped* and showered⟩ **d** : SKIN, PEEL ⟨*strip* bark from a tree⟩ **2** : to divest of honors, privileges, or functions **3 a** : to remove unnecessary or superficial matter from ⟨a prose style *stripped* to the bones⟩ **b** : to remove furniture, equipment, or accessories from **4** : PLUNDER, SPOIL ⟨troops *stripped* the captured town⟩ **5** : to make bare or clear (as by cutting or grazing) **6** : DISMANTLE 2, DISASSEMBLE ⟨*strip* a rifle⟩ **7** : to tear or damage the screw thread of (as a bolt or nut) [Old English *-strīpan*] — **strip·per** *n*

²strip *n* **1** : a long narrow piece or area ⟨*strips* of bacon⟩ ⟨a *strip* of land⟩ **2** : AIRSTRIP [perhaps from Low German *strippe* "strap"]

strip–crop·ping \'strip-ˌkräp-ing\ *n* : the growing of a cultivated crop (as corn) in strips alternating with strips of a sod-forming crop (as hay) arranged to follow land contours and minimize erosion — **strip–crop** \-ˌkräp\ *vb*

¹**stripe** \'strīp\ *n* : a stroke or blow with a rod or lash [Middle English]

²**stripe** *vt* : to make stripes on

³**stripe** *n* **1** : a line or long narrow section differing in color or texture from parts adjoining **2** : a piece of braid (as on the sleeve) to indicate military rank or length of service **3** : a distinct variety or sort : TYPE ⟨persons of the same political *stripe*⟩ [probably from Dutch] — **stripe·less** \'strī-pləs\ *adj*

striped \'strīpt, 'strī-pəd\ *adj* : having stripes or streaks

striped bass *n* : a large sea bass of the Atlantic coast of the United States that has been introduced along the Pacific coast

strip·ling \'strip-ling\ *n* : a youth just passing from boyhood to manhood [Middle English]

strip mine *n* : a mine that is worked from the earth's surface by the stripping away of overlying material — **strip-mine** *vt* — **strip miner** *n*

strive \'strīv\ *vi* **strove** \'strōv\ *also* **strived** \'strīvd\; **striv·en** \'striv-ən\ *or* **strived**; **striv·ing** \'strī-ving\ **1** : to struggle in opposition : CONTEND **2** : to devote serious effort or energy : ENDEAVOR ⟨*strive* to win⟩ [Old French *estriver*, of Germanic origin] SYN see TRY — **striv·er** \'strī-vər\ *n*

strobe \'strōb\ *n* **1** : STROBOSCOPE **2** : a device that uses a flashtube for high-speed illumination (as in photography) — called also *strobe light*

stro·bi·lus \strō-'bī-ləs, 'strō-bə-\ *n, pl* **-li** \-,lī\ **1** : an aggregation of sporophylls resembling a cone (as in a club moss or equisetum) **2** : the cone of a gymnosperm [Late Latin, "pinecone", from Greek *strobilos* "top, pinecone", from *strobos* "whirl"]

stro·bo·scope \'strō-bə-,skōp\ *n* : an instrument for determining speeds of rotation or frequencies of vibration especially by means of a rapidly flashing light that illuminates an object intermittently [Greek *strobos* "whirl"] — **stro·bo·scop·ic** \,strō-bə-'skäp-ik\ *adj* — **stro·bo·scop·i·cal·ly** \-'skäp-i-kə-lē, -klē\ *adv*

strode *past of* STRIDE

¹**stroke** \'strōk\ *vt* **1** : to pass the hand over gently in one direction **2** : to caress by stroking [Old English *strācian*] — **strok·er** *n*

²**stroke** *n* **1** : the act of striking; *esp* : a blow with a weapon or implement **2** : a single unbroken movement; *esp* : one of a series of repeated or to-and-fro movements **3** : a striking of the ball in a game; *esp* : a striking or attempt to strike the ball that constitutes the scoring unit in golf **4** : a sudden action or process producing an impact ⟨a *stroke* of lightning⟩ or unexpected result ⟨a *stroke* of luck⟩ **5** : sudden weakening or loss of consciousness, sensation, and voluntary motion caused by rupture or obstruction of an artery of the brain (as by a clot) — called also *apoplexy* **6** : one of a series of propelling movements against a resisting medium ⟨*strokes* of an oar⟩ **7 a** : a vigorous or energetic effort **b** : a delicate or clever touch in a narrative, description, or construction **8** : HEARTBEAT **9** : the movement or the distance of the movement in either direction of a mechanical part (as a piston rod) having a reciprocating motion **10** : the sound of a bell being struck **11 a** : a mark made by a single movement of a tool **b** : one of the lines of a letter of the alphabet [Middle English]

³**stroke** *vt* **1** : to mark or cancel with a line ⟨*stroked* out my name⟩ **2** : HIT 1a

stroll \'strōl\ *vb* : to walk in a leisurely or idle manner : RAMBLE [probably from German dialect *strollen*] — **stroll** *n*

stroll·er \'strō-lər\ *n* **1** : one that strolls **2** : a wheeled seat in which a baby may be pushed

stro·ma \'strō-mə\ *n, pl* **stro·ma·ta** \-mət-ə\ : a supporting framework in or of an organism: as **a** : the network of connective tissue that supports an animal organ **b** : an irregular mass of fungal hyphae supporting and enclosing spore-bearing structures [Latin, "bed covering", from Greek *strōma*, from *stornynai* "to spread out"]

strong \'strȯng\ *adj* **strong·er** \'strȯng-gər\; **strong·est** \'strȯng-gəst\ **1** : having or marked by great physical power : ROBUST **2** : having moral or intellectual power **3** : having great resources (as of wealth) **4** : of a specified number ⟨an army ten thousand *strong*⟩ **5** : being great or striking : CLOSE ⟨bears a *strong* resemblance to me⟩ **6** : FORCEFUL, COGENT ⟨*strong* arguments⟩ **7** : not mild or weak : INTENSE: as **a** : rich in some active agent (as a flavor or extract) ⟨*strong* coffee⟩ **b** : high in saturation and medium in lightness ⟨a *strong* red⟩ **c** : ionizing freely in solution ⟨*strong* acids and bases⟩ **d** : magnifying by refracting greatly ⟨a *strong* lens⟩ **8** : moving with rapidity or force ⟨*strong* wind⟩ **9** : ARDENT, ZEALOUS ⟨*strong* advocates of peace⟩ **10 a** : able to withstand stress : not easily injured : SOLID **b** : not easily subdued or taken ⟨a *strong* fort⟩ **11** : well established : FIRM ⟨*strong* beliefs⟩ **12** : having or being an offensive or intense odor or flavor : RANK **13** : of, relating to, or constituting a verb or verb conjugation that forms the past tense by a change in the root vowel and the past participle usually by the addition of *-en* with or without change of the root vowel (as *strive, strove, striven* or *drink, drank, drunk*) [Old English *strang*] — **strong** *adv* — **strong·ly** \'strȯng-lē\ *adv*

¹**strong–arm** \'strȯng-,ärm\ *adj* : having, using, or involving undue force : VIOLENT ⟨*strong-arm* methods⟩

²**strong–arm** *vt* **1** : to use force on : ASSAULT **2** : to rob by force

strong·box \'strȯng-,bäks\ *n* : a strongly made container for money or valuables

strong force *n* : the force between the particles of an atomic nucleus that acts to hold the nucleus together and is the strongest known force

strong·hold \-,hōld\ *n* : a fortified place : FORTRESS

strong–mind·ed \-'mīn-dəd\ *adj* : markedly independent in thought and judgment — **strong–mind·ed·ly** *adv* — **strong–mind·ed·ness** *n*

strong suit *n* **1** : a long suit containing high cards **2** : something in which one excels : FORTE

stron·tium \'strän-chē-əm, -chəm; 'stränt-ē-əm\ *n* : a soft malleable ductile metallic element occurring only in combined form — see ELEMENT table [New Latin, from *strontia* "strontium monoxide", from *Strontian*, village in Scotland]

strontium 90 *n* : a heavy radioactive isotope of strontium having the mass number 90 that is present in the fallout from nuclear explosions

¹**strop** \'sträp\ *n* : STRAP; *esp* : a usually leather band for sharpening a razor [Old English, "thong for securing an oar", from Latin *struppus* "band, strap", from Greek *strophos*]

²**strop** *vt* **stropped; strop·ping** : to sharpen (a razor) on a strop

stro·phe \'strō-fē\ *n* : a division of a poem : STANZA [Greek *strophē*, literally, "turn", from *strephein* "to turn, twist"] — **stro·phic** \'strō-fik, 'sträf-ik\ *adj*

strove *past & chiefly dialect past participle of* STRIVE

struck \'strək\ *adj* : closed or affected by a labor strike [past participle of *strike*]

struc·tur·al \'strək-chə-rəl, 'strək-shrəl\ *adj* **1** : of, relating to, or affecting structure ⟨*structural* defects⟩ ⟨*structural* principles⟩ **2** : used or formed for use in construction ⟨*structural* steel⟩ — **struc·tur·al·ly** \-ē\ *adv*

structural formula *n* : an expanded molecular formula showing the arrangement within the molecule of atoms and of bonds

¹**struc·ture** \'strək-chər\ *n* **1** : the action of building : CONSTRUCTION **2 a** : something constructed **b** : something made up of interdependent parts in a definite pattern of organization **3** : manner of construction : MAKEUP **4** : the arrangement or relationship of elements (as particles, parts, or organs) in a substance,

\ə\ abut	\ng\ sing
\ər\ further	\ō\ bone
\a\ mat	\ȯ\ saw
\ā\ take	\ȯi\ coin
\ä\ cot, cart	\th\ thin
\au̇\ out	\th\ this
\ch\ chin	\ü\ food
\e\ pet	\u̇\ foot
\ē\ easy	\y\ yet
\g\ go	\yü\ few
\i\ tip	\yu̇\ cure
\ī\ life	\zh\ vision
\j\ job	

body, or system ⟨soil *structure*⟩ ⟨the *structure* of a language⟩ [Latin *structura,* from *struere* "to heap up, build"] — **struc·ture·less** \-ləs\ *adj*

²structure *vt* **struc·tured; struc·tur·ing** \'strək-chə-ring, 'strək-shring\ : to form into a structure : ORGANIZE

stru·del \'strüd-l, 'shtrüd-l\ *n* : a pastry made from a sheet of thin dough rolled up with filling and baked [German, literally, "whirlpool"]

¹strug·gle \'strəg-əl\ *vi* **strug·gled; strug·gling** \'strəg-ling, -ə-ling\ **1** : to make violent strenuous efforts against opposition : STRIVE **2** : to proceed with difficulty or with great effort ⟨*struggle* through deep snow⟩ [Middle English *struglen*] — **strug·gler** \-lər, -ə-lər\ *n*

²struggle *n* **1** : a violent effort or exertion **2** : CONTEST 1, STRIFE

struggle for existence : the competition (as for food, space, or light) between members of a natural population that tends to eliminate less efficient individuals and thereby to increase the chance that the more efficient will pass on their traits

strum \'strəm\ *vb* **strummed; strum·ming** : to play on a stringed instrument by brushing the strings with the fingers [imitative] — **strum·mer** *n*

strum·pet \'strəm-pət\ *n* : PROSTITUTE, HARLOT [Middle English]

strung *past of* STRING

¹strut \'strət\ *vb* **strut·ted; strut·ting** **1** : to walk with a stiff proud gait **2** : to parade (as clothes) with a show of pride [Old English *strūtian* "to exert oneself"] — **strut·ter** *n* □ SYN STRUT, SWAGGER mean to assume an air of importance. STRUT emphasizes pompous dignity and vanity as expressed by one's gait or bearing; SWAGGER suggests ostentatiousness and insolence or boastfulness especially in one's manners and movements.

²strut *n* **1** : a bar or brace that resists pressure in the direction of its length **2** : a pompous step or walk

strych·nine \'strik-,nīn, -nən, -,nēn\ *n* : a bitter poisonous alkaloid that is obtained from nux vomica and related plants, acts as a stimulant to the central nervous system, and is used especially as a rat poison [French, from Latin *strychnos* "nightshade", from Greek]

¹stub \'stəb\ *n* **1** : STUMP 1b **2** : something having or worn to a short or blunt shape: as **a** : a pen with a short blunt nib **b** : a short part left after a larger part has been broken off or used up ⟨pencil *stub*⟩ **3 a** : a small part of a check kept as a record of the contents of the check **b** : the part of a ticket returned to the user [Old English *stybb*]

²stub *vt* **stubbed; stub·bing** **1** : to extinguish (as a cigarette) by crushing **2** : to strike (as one's toe) against an object

stub·ble \'stəb-əl\ *n* **1** : the stem ends of herbaceous plants and especially cereal grasses remaining attached to the soil after harvest **2** : a rough surface or growth resembling stubble; *esp* : a short growth of beard [Old French *estuble,* from Latin *stipula, stupula,* "stalk, straw"] — **stub·bly** \'stəb-lē, -ə-lē\ *adj*

stub·born \'stəb-ərn\ *adj* **1 a** : hard to convince, persuade, or move to action : OBSTINATE ⟨*stubborn* as a mule⟩ **b** : having a firm idea or purpose : DETERMINED **2** : done or continued in an obstinate or persistent manner ⟨*stubborn* refusal⟩ **3** : difficult to handle, manage, or treat ⟨*stubborn* hair⟩ [Middle English *stuborn*] SYN see OBSTINATE — **stub·born·ly** *adv* — **stub·born·ness** \-ərn-nəs\ *n*

stub·by \'stəb-ē\ *adj* **stub·bi·er; -est** **1** : resembling a stub especially in shortness and broadness ⟨*stubby* fingers⟩ **2** : abounding with stubs : BRISTLY — **stub·bi·ness** *n*

stuc·co \'stək-ō\ *n, pl* **stuccos** *or* **stuccoes** : a plaster (as of portland cement, sand, and lime) used to cover exterior walls or ornament interior walls [Italian, of Germanic origin] — **stucco** *vt*

stuc·co·work \'stək-ō-,wərk\ *n* : work done in stucco

stuck *past of* STICK

stuck–up \'stək-'əp\ *adj* : CONCEITED, SELF-IMPORTANT

¹stud \'stəd\ *n* **1** : a group of animals and especially horses kept primarily for breeding; *also* : the place where they are kept **2** : a male animal (as a stallion) kept for breeding [Old English *stōd*] — **at stud** : for breeding as a stud

²stud *n* **1** : one of the smaller uprights in the framing of the walls of a building to which sheathing, paneling, or laths are fastened : SCANTLING **2 a** : a boss, rivet, or nail with a large head used for ornament or protection **b** : a solid button with a shank or eye on the back inserted through an eyelet in a garment as a fastener or ornament **3** : a piece (as a rod or pin) projecting from a machine and serving chiefly as a support or axis [Old English *studu* "post"]

³stud *vt* **stud·ded; stud·ding** **1** : to furnish (as a building or wall) with studs **2** : to adorn, cover, or protect with studs **3** : to mark, decorate, or dot at random ⟨a sky *studded* with stars⟩

stud·book \'stəd-,bůk\ *n* : an official record of the pedigree of purebred animals (as horses or dogs)

stud·ding \'stəd-ing\ *n* : the studs of a building or wall

stud·ding sail \'stəd-ing-,sāl, 'stən-səl\ *n* : a light sail set at the side of a principal square sail of a ship [origin unknown]

stu·dent \'stüd-nt, 'styüd-, *especially South* -ənt\ *n* **1** : LEARNER, SCHOLAR; *esp* : one who attends a school or college **2** : one who studies : an attentive and systematic observer ⟨a *student* of life⟩ [Latin *studens,* from *studēre* "to study"]

student government *n* : the organization and management of student life, activities, or discipline by various student organizations in a school or college

student teacher *n* : a student engaged in practice teaching

stud·horse \'stəd-,hȯrs\ *n* : a stallion kept especially for breeding

stud·ied \'stəd-ēd\ *adj* **1** : KNOWLEDGEABLE, LEARNED ⟨well *studied* in math⟩ **2** : carefully considered or prepared : THOUGHTFUL **3** : produced or marked by conscious design ⟨*studied* indifference⟩ — **stud·ied·ly** *adv* — **stud·ied·ness** *n*

stu·dio \'stüd-ē-,ō, 'styüd-\ *n, pl* **-di·os** **1 a** : the working place of an artist **b** : a place for the study of an art ⟨a dance *studio*⟩ **2** : a place where motion pictures are made **3** : a place maintained and equipped for the transmission of radio or television programs [Italian, literally, "study", from Latin *studium*]

studio couch *n* : an upholstered usually backless couch that can be made to serve as a double bed by sliding from underneath it the frame of a single cot

stu·di·ous \'stüd-ē-əs, 'styüd-\ *adj* **1** : given to, concerned with, or tending to promote study ⟨*studious* habits⟩ **2** : marked by purposeful effort : EARNEST — **stu·di·ous·ly** *adv* — **stu·di·ous·ness** *n*

¹study \'stəd-ē\ *n, pl* **stud·ies** **1** : a state of contemplation : REVERIE **2 a** : application of the mind to the acquisition of knowledge often about a particular field or topic **b** : a careful examination or analysis of something; *also* : a report or publication on such a study **3** : a building or room devoted to study or literary pursuits **4 a** : a branch or department of learning : SUBJECT **b** : the activity or work of a student **5** : a usually preliminary or elementary artistic production concerned especially with problems of technique ⟨a series of *studies* of classic heads⟩ [Old French *estudie,* from Latin *studium*]

²study *vb* **stud·ied; study·ing** **1** : to engage in study or the study of **2** : ENDEAVOR, TRY ⟨*studied* to please the boss⟩ **3** : to consider attentively or in detail especially with the intent of fixing in the mind or of appraising ⟨*studied* the question carefully⟩

study hall *n* **1** : a room in a school set aside for study **2** : a period in a student's day set aside for study and homework

¹stuff \'stəf\ *n* **1** : materials, supplies, or equipment used in some activity: as **a** : a person's or a family's movable possessions (as household goods or baggage) **b** : material to be manufactured, wrought, or used in construction **c** : a finished textile suitable for clothing; *esp* : wool or worsted material **2 a** : writing, discourse, or ideas often of little or temporary worth **b** : actions or talk of a particular and often objectionable kind ⟨how do they get away with such *stuff*⟩ **3 a** : an aggregate of matter ⟨volcanic rock is curious *stuff*⟩ **b** : matter of a particular kind often unspecified ⟨sold tons of the *stuff*⟩ **4 a** : fundamental material : SUBSTANCE ⟨*stuff* of greatness⟩ **b** : subject matter **5** : special knowledge or capability ⟨has the *stuff* to do well here⟩ [Middle French *estoffe,* from *estoffer* "to equip, stock"]

²stuff *vb* **1 a** : to fill by or as if by packing things in : CRAM **b** : to eat gluttonously **c** : to fill with a stuffing **d** : to stop up : PLUG **2** : to put or push into something especially carelessly or casually ⟨*stuffed* the clothes into the drawer⟩ — **stuff·er** *n*

stuffed shirt *n* : a smug, conceited, and usually pompous person

stuff·ing \'stəf-ing\ *n* : material used to stuff something; *esp* : a seasoned mixture used to stuff meat, vegetables, eggs, or poultry

stuff shot *n* : DUNK SHOT

stuffy \'stəf-ē\ *adj* **stuff·i·er; -est 1** : SULLEN 1, ILL-HUMORED **2 a** : oppressive to the breathing : CLOSE ⟨a *stuffy* room⟩ **b** : stuffed or choked up ⟨a *stuffy* feeling in my head⟩ **3** : lacking in vitality or interest : DULL **4** : narrowly inflexible in standards of conduct : SELF-RIGHTEOUS — **stuff·i·ly** \'stəf-ə-lē\ *adv* — **stuff·i·ness** \'stəf-ē-nəs\ *n*

stul·ti·fy \'stəl-tə-ˌfī\ *vt* **-fied; -fy·ing 1** : to cause to appear or be stupid, foolish, or absurdly illogical **2** : to make futile or useless especially through weakening or repressive influences ⟨*stultify* initiative⟩ [Late Latin *stultificare* "to make foolish", from Latin *stultus* "foolish"] — **stul·ti·fi·ca·tion** \ˌstəl-tə-fə-ˈkā-shən\ *n*

stum·ble \'stəm-bəl\ *vi* **stum·bled; stum·bling** \-bə-ling, -bling\ **1** : to trip in walking or running; *also* : to walk unsteadily **2 a** : to blunder morally **b** : to speak or act in a blundering or clumsy manner **3** : to come or happen unexpectedly or by chance ⟨*stumbled* on a discovery⟩ [Middle English *stumblen*] — **stumble** *n* — **stum·bler** \-bə-lər, -blər\ *n* — **stum·bling·ly** \-bə-ling-lē, -bling-\ *adv*

stum·bling block \'stəm-bling-\ *n* **1** : an impediment to belief or understanding **2** : an obstacle to progress

¹stump \'stəmp\ *n* **1 a** : the base of a bodily part (as an arm or leg) remaining after the rest is removed **b** : the part of a plant and especially a tree remaining attached to the root after the top is cut off **2** : a part (as of a tooth or pencil) remaining after the rest is worn away or lost : STUB **3** : a place or occasion for political public speaking [Middle English *stumpe*]

²stump *vb* **1 a** : STUB 2 **b** : to walk or walk over heavily or clumsily **2 a** : CHALLENGE 4, DARE **b** : BEWILDER 2, CONFOUND **3** : to clear (land) of stumps **4** : to go about making political speeches or supporting a cause ⟨*stump* the state for the reform candidate⟩ — **stump·er** *n*

stump·age \'stəm-pij\ *n* : the value of standing timber; *also* : uncut timber or the right to cut it

stumpy \'stəm-pē\ *adj* **stump·i·er; -est 1** : full of stumps **2** : being short and thick : SQUAT

stun \'stən\ *vt* **stunned; stun·ning 1** : to make senseless or dizzy by or as if by a blow **2** : to overcome with astonishment or disbelief : SHOCK ⟨*stunned* by the news⟩ [Old French *estoner* "to astonish", from Latin *ex-* + *tonare* "to thunder"]

stung *past of* STING

stunk *past of* STINK

stun·ner \'stən-ər\ *n* : one that stuns; *esp* : an unusually attractive person

stun·ning \'stən-ing\ *adj* **1** : causing astonishment or disbelief **2** : strikingly impressive especially in beauty or excellence — **stun·ning·ly** \-ing-lē\ *adv*

¹stunt \'stənt\ *vt* : to hinder the normal growth of : DWARF [English dialect *stunt* "stunted, abrupt"]

²stunt *n* : a plant disease in which dwarfing occurs

³stunt *n* : an unusual or difficult feat performed or undertaken usually to gain attention or publicity [probably alteration of *stump* "challenge"]

⁴stunt *vi* : to perform stunts

stupe \'stüp, 'styüp\ *n* : a hot wet often medicated cloth applied externally (as to stimulate circulation) [Latin *stuppa* "coarse part of flax, tow", from Greek *styppē*]

stu·pe·fy \'stü-pə-ˌfī, 'styü-\ *vt* **-fied; -fy·ing 1** : to make stupid, groggy, or insensible **2** : ASTONISH, BEWILDER [Middle French *stupefier,* from Latin *stupefacere,* from *stupēre* "to be astonished" + *facere* "to make, do"] — **stu·pe·fac·tion** \ˌstü-pə-ˈfak-shən, ˌstyü-\ *n* — **stu·pe·fi·er** \'stü-pə-ˌfī-ər, 'styü-, -ˌfīr\ *n*

stu·pen·dous \stu̇-ˈpen-dəs, styu̇-\ *adj* : stupefying or amazing especially because of size, complexity, or greatness [Latin *stupendus* "to be wondered at", from *stupēre* "to be astonished"] SYN see MONSTROUS — **stu·pen·dous·ly** *adv* — **stu·pen·dous·ness** *n*

stu·pid \'stü-pəd, 'styü-\ *adj* **1 a** : slow of mind : OBTUSE **b** : given to unwise decisions or actions **2** : dulled in feeling or sensation **3** : marked by or resulting from dullness : SENSELESS ⟨a *stupid* mistake⟩ **4** : DREARY, BORING ⟨a *stupid* plot⟩ [Middle French *stupide,* from Latin *stupidus,* from *stupēre* "to be benumbed, be astonished"] — **stu·pid·ly** *adv* — **stu·pid·ness** *n* □ SYN STUPID, DULL, DENSE mean lacking in power to take in ideas or impressions. STUPID implies a slow-witted or dazed state of mind that may be either congenital or temporary; DULL suggests a slow or sluggish mind such as results from disease, depression, or shock; DENSE implies a relative imperviousness to new or complex ideas.

stu·pid·i·ty \stu̇-ˈpid-ət-ē, styu̇-\ *n, pl* **-ties 1** : the quality or state of being stupid **2** : something (as an idea or act) that is stupid

stu·por \'stü-pər, 'styü-\ *n* **1** : a condition characterized by great dulling or suspension of sense or feeling ⟨a drunken *stupor*⟩ **2** : a state of extreme apathy or torpor resulting often from stress or shock [Latin, from *stupēre* "to be benumbed, be astonished"] SYN see LETHARGY — **stu·por·ous** \-pə-rəs, -prəs\ *adj*

stur·dy \'stərd-ē\ *adj* **stur·di·er; -est 1 a** : firmly built or made **b** : HARDY 3 **2 a** : marked by or reflecting physical strength or vigor : ROBUST **b** : FIRM 3, RESOLUTE [Middle English, "brave, stubborn", from Old French *estourdi* "stunned, rash", from *estourdir* "to stun", derived from Latin *ex-* + *turdus* "thrush"] — **stur·di·ly** \'stərd-l-ē\ *adv* — **stur·di·ness** \'stərd-ē-nəs\ *n* □ ORIGIN In early medieval Europe the thrush had a reputation for drunkenness and dullwittedness. This bird was believed to gorge itself on grapes until it became quite dizzy. Indeed, the French still have a proverbial phrase *soûl comme une grive,* "drunk as a thrush". A person who is stunned acts dizzy or drunk, and the Old French verb *estourdir,* "to stun", was derived from the Latin name, *turdus,* of the drunk and dizzy thrush. Middle English *sturdy,* borrowed from Old French *estourdi,* "stunned, rash", originally meant "rashly or recklessly brave". *Sturdy* later developed the senses "stubborn, hardy, robust, firm".

stur·geon \'stər-jən\ *n* : any of various usually large long-bodied fishes that have a thick skin with rows of bony plates and are valued for their flesh and especially for their roe which is made into caviar [Old French *estourjon,* of Germanic origin]

sturgeon

\ə\ abut	\ng\ sing
\ər\ further	\ō\ bone
\a\ mat	\ȯ\ saw
\ā\ take	\ȯi\ coin
\ä\ cot, cart	\th\ thin
\au̇\ out	\th\ this
\ch\ chin	\ü\ food
\e\ pet	\u̇\ foot
\ē\ easy	\y\ yet
\g\ go	\yü\ few
\i\ tip	\yu̇\ cure
\ī\ life	\zh\ vision
\j\ job	

¹**stut·ter** \'stət-ər\ *vb* : to speak or utter with involuntary repetition, disruption, or blocking of vocal sounds [Middle English *stutten*] **syn** see **STAMMER** — **stut·ter·er** \'stət-ər-ər\ *n*

²**stutter** *n* **1** : an act or instance of stuttering **2** : a speech disorder involving stuttering accompanied by emotional turmoil

¹**sty** \'stī\ *n, pl* **sties** *also* **styes** \'stīz\ **1** : a pen or enclosed housing for swine **2** : a filthy, low, or vicious place [Old English *stig*]

²**sty** *or* **stye** \'stī\ *n, pl* **sties** *or* **styes** \'stīz\ : an inflamed swelling of a skin gland on the edge of an eyelid [from obsolete *styan,* from Old English *stigend,* from *stigan* "ro rise"]

sty·gian \'stij-ən, 'stij-ē-ən\ *adj, often cap* : **INFERNAL, GLOOMY** ⟨*stygian* darkness⟩ [Latin *stygius,* from Greek *stygios,* from *Styg-, Styx* "Styx"]

¹**style** \'stīl\ *n* **1 a** : an instrument used by the ancients in writing on waxed tablets **b** : the shadow-producing indicator of a sundial **c** : **GRAVER 2 d** : **NEEDLE 3d e** : a slender prolongation of a plant ovary bearing a stigma at its apex **f** : a slender bodily process of an animal **2** : mode of expressing thought in language; *esp* : one characteristic of an individual, period, school, or nation ⟨ornate *style*⟩ **3** : the custom or plan followed in spelling, capitalization, punctuation, and typographic arrangement and display **4** : mode of address : **TITLE 5 a** (1) : manner or method of acting or performing especially in accordance with some standard (2) : a distinctive or characteristic manner **b** : a fashionable manner or mode ⟨dining in *style*⟩ ⟨that dress is out of *style*⟩ **c** : overall excellence, skill, or grace in performance, manner, or appearance [Latin *stilus* "stake, stylus, style of writing"] **syn** see **DICTION, FASHION** — **style·less** \'stīl-ləs\ *adj*

²**style** *vt* **1** : **NAME, CALL** ⟨*style* themselves scientists⟩ **2 a** : to cause to conform to a customary style **b** : to design and make in accord with the current fashion — **styl·er** *n*

style·book \'stīl-,bùk\ *n* : a book explaining, describing, or illustrating the prevailing, accepted, or authorized style ⟨a *stylebook* for printers⟩

sty·let \'stī-lət\ *n* **1** : a slender surgical probe **2** : a style on an animal [French, from Middle French *stilet* "stiletto", from Italian *stiletto*]

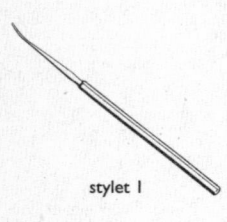

stylet 1

styl·ish \'stī-lish\ *adj* : having style; *esp* : conforming to current fashion — **styl·ish·ly** *adv* — **styl·ish·ness** *n*

styl·ist \'stī-ləst\ *n* **1** : a master or model of style; *esp* : a writer or speaker eminent in matters of style **2** : one who develops, designs, or advises on styles — **sty·lis·tic** \stī-'lis-tik\ *also* **sty·lis·ti·cal** \-ti-kəl\ *adj* — **sty·lis·ti·cal·ly** \-ti-kə-lē, -klē\ *adv*

styl·ize \'stīl-,īz\ *vt* : to conform to a style; *esp* : to represent or design according to a style or stylistic pattern rather than according to nature — **styl·iza·tion** \,stī-lə-'zā-shən\ *n* — **styl·iz·er** \'stīl-,ī-zər\ *n*

sty·lo·bate \'stī-lə-,bāt\ *n* : a continuous flat coping or pavement on which a row of architectural columns is supported [Latin *stylobates,* from Greek *stylobatēs,* from *stylos* "pillar" + *bainein* "to walk, go"]

sty·loid \'stīl-,ȯid\ *adj* : resembling a style ⟨the slender pointed *styloid* process of the ulna⟩

sty·lus \'stī-ləs\ *n, pl* **sty·li** \'stīl-,ī\ *also* **sty·lus·es** \'stī-lə-səz\ **1** : an instrument for writing or marking **2** : **NEEDLE 3d** [Latin *stilus* "stake, stylus"]

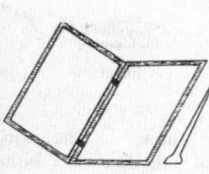

stylus 1 with Roman wax tablet

¹**sty·mie** \'stī-mē\ *n* : a very distressing and thwarting situation [perhaps from Scottish *stymie* "person with poor eyesight"]

²**stymie** *vt* **sty·mied; sty·mie·ing** : to present an obstacle to : stand in the way of

styp·tic \'stip-tik\ *adj* : tending to contract or bind : **ASTRINGENT**; *esp* : tending to check bleeding ⟨*styptic* effect of cold⟩ [Latin *stypticus,* from Greek *styptikos,* from *styphein* "to contract"] — **styptic** *n*

styptic pencil *n* : a cylindrical stick of medicated styptic substance used especially in shaving to stop the bleeding from small cuts

sty·rene \'stī-,rēn\ *n* : a fragrant liquid hydrocarbon used chiefly in making synthetic rubber, resins, and plastics [derived from Latin *styrax* "storax"]

Sty·ro·foam \'stī-rə-,fōm\ *trademark* — used for an expanded rigid polystyrene plastic

sua·sion \'swā-zhən\ *n* : the act of influencing or persuading [Latin *suasio,* from *suadēre* "to urge, persuade"] — **sua·sive** \'swā-siv, -ziv\ *adj* — **sua·sive·ly** *adv* — **sua·sive·ness** *n*

suave \'swäv\ *adj* : smoothly but often superficially polite and agreeable [Middle French, "pleasant, sweet", from Latin *suavis*] — **suave·ly** *adv* — **suave·ness** *n* — **sua·vi·ty** \'swäv-ət-ē\ *n* □ **syn** SUAVE, URBANE, BLAND, SMOOTH mean pleasingly tactful and well-mannered. SUAVE implies a specific ability to deal with others easily and without friction ⟨a *suave* headwaiter⟩ URBANE suggests courtesy and poise developed by wide social experience ⟨an *urbane* outlook on life⟩ BLAND emphasizes mildness of manner and absence of irritating qualities ⟨a *bland,* kindly old soul⟩ SMOOTH usually suggests a deliberately assumed suavity ⟨a *smooth* liar⟩

¹**sub** \'səb\ *n* : **SUBSTITUTE**

²**sub** *vi* **subbed; sub·bing** : to act as a substitute

³**sub** *n* : **SUBMARINE**

sub- *prefix* **1** : under : beneath : below ⟨*sub*aqueous⟩ ⟨*sub*soil⟩ **2 a** : subordinate : secondary ⟨*sub*station⟩ **b** : subdivision of ⟨*sub*committee⟩ ⟨*sub*species⟩ **c** : with repetition (as of a process) so as to form, stress, or deal with subordinate parts or relations ⟨*sub*let⟩ **3** : less than completely, perfectly, or normally : somewhat ⟨*sub*dominant⟩ **4** : falling nearly in the category of and often adjoining : bordering upon ⟨*sub*arctic⟩ [Latin, "under, below, secretly, from below, up, near", from *sub* "under, close to"]

See *sub-* and 2d element

subadolescent	subdialect	subparagraph
subagency	subdirector	subpart
subagent	subdiscipline	subproblem
suballocation	subdistrict	subprocess
subaverage	subfield	subproduct
subbase	subfile	subprogram
subbasement	subframe	subproject
subbranch	subgenre	subregion
subcabinet	subglacial	subroutine
subcaste	subgoal	subsea
subcategorization	subgroup	subsite
subcategorize	subhumid	subsociety
subcategory	subindustry	subspecialty
subclassification	sublethal	subsystem
subclassify	sublevel	subtask
subcluster	sublot	subtest
subcollege	submarket	subtheme
subcollegiate	subminimal	subtotal
subcolony	subnetwork	subtreasury
subcommission	subniche	subtribe
subcommunity	suboceanic	subtype
subcomponent	suboptimal	subunit
subcult	suborganization	subvisible
subdepartment	subpar	subzone
subdevelopment		

sub·aer·i·al \,səb-'ar-ē-əl, 'səb-, -'er-; ,səb-ā-'ir-ē-əl\ *adj* : situated or occurring on or close to the surface of the earth ⟨*subaerial* habitat⟩ ⟨*subaerial* roots⟩ — **sub·aer·i·al·ly** \-ē-ə-lē\ *adv*

sub·al·pine \,səb-'al-,pīn, 'səb-\ *adj* **1** : of or relating to the region about the foot and lower slopes of the Alps **2** *cap* : of, relating to, or growing on upland slopes near timberline

¹**sub·al·tern** \sə-'bȯl-tərn, *especially British* 'səb-əl-tərn\ *adj* : of low or lower rank : **SUBORDINATE** [Late Latin *subalternus,* from Latin *sub-* + *alternus* "alternate"]

²subaltern *n* : SUBORDINATE; *esp* : a commissioned officer in the British army below the rank of captain

sub·aque·ous \ˌsəb-'ā-kwē-əs, 'səb-, -'ak-wē-\ *adj* : formed, occurring, or existing in or under water

sub·arc·tic \-'ärk-tik, -'ärt-ik\ *adj* : of, relating to, or being regions immediately outside of the arctic circle or regions similar to these in climate or conditions of life

sub·as·sem·bly \ˌsəb-ə-'sem-blē\ *n* : an assembled unit designed to be incorporated with other units in a finished product

sub·atom·ic \ˌsəb-ə-'täm-ik\ *adj* : of or relating to the inside of the atom or particles smaller than atoms

sub·cel·lu·lar \ˌsəb-'sel-yə-lər, 'səb-\ *adj* : of less than cellular scope or level of organization

sub·class \'səb-ˌklas\ *n* : a primary division of a class (as in taxonomy)

¹sub·cla·vi·an \ˌsəb-'klā-vē-ən\ *adj* **1** : located under the clavicle **2** : of, relating to, or being a subclavian part

²subclavian *n* : a subclavian part (as an artery or vein)

sub·clin·i·cal \ˌsəb-'klin-i-kəl, 'səb-\ *adj* : not severe enough to be detectable by the usual clinical tests ⟨a *subclinical* infection⟩ — **sub·clin·i·cal·ly** \-kə-lē, -klē\ *adv*

sub·com·mit·tee \'səb-kə-ˌmit-ē, ˌsəb-kə-'\ *n* : a subdivision of a committee usually organized for a specific purpose

sub·com·pact \'səb-ˈkäm-ˌpakt\ *n* : an automobile smaller than a compact

¹sub·con·scious \ˌsəb-'kän-chəs, 'səb-\ *adj* **1** : existing in the mind but not immediately available to consciousness **2** : imperfectly conscious ⟨a *subconscious* state⟩ — **sub·con·scious·ly** *adv* — **sub·con·scious·ness** *n*

²subconscious *n* : the mental activities just below the threshold of consciousness

sub·con·ti·nent \'səb-'känt-n-ənt, -'känt-nənt\ *n* : a large landmass smaller than a continent; *esp* : a major subdivision of a continent ⟨the Indian *subcontinent*⟩ — **sub·con·ti·nen·tal** \ˌsəb-ˌkänt-n-'ent-l\ *adj*

¹sub·con·tract \ˌsəb-'kän-ˌtrakt, 'səb-; ˌsəb-kən-'\ *vb* **1** : to engage a third party to perform (work included in an original contract) under a subcontract **2** : to let out or undertake work under a subcontract — **sub·con·trac·tor** \-ˌtrak-tər\ *n*

²sub·con·tract \'səb-'kän-ˌtrakt, -ˌkän-\ *n* : a contract between a party to an original contract and a third party who usually agrees to supply work or materials required in the original

sub·crit·i·cal \ˌsəb-'krit-i-kəl, 'səb-\ *adj* **1** : less or lower than critical **2** : of insufficient size to sustain a chain reaction ⟨*subcritical* mass of fissionable material⟩

sub·cul·ture \'səb-ˌkəl-chər\ *n* **1** : a culture (as of bacteria) derived from another culture; *also* : an act or instance of producing a subculture **2** : a distinguishable subdivision of a culture ⟨a criminal *subculture*⟩

sub·cu·ta·ne·ous \ˌsəb-kyù-'tā-nē-əs\ *adj* : being, living, used, or made under the skin ⟨*subcutaneous* fat⟩ ⟨a *subcutaneous* needle⟩ — **sub·cu·ta·ne·ous·ly** *adv*

sub·dea·con \ˌsəb-'dē-kən, 'səb-\ *n* : a cleric ranking below a deacon; *esp* : a cleric in the lowest of the former major orders of the Roman Catholic church

sub·deb \'səb-ˌdeb\ *n* : SUBDEBUTANTE

sub·deb·u·tante \'səb-'deb-yu-ˌtänt, 'səb-\ *n* : a young girl who is about to become a debutante; *also* : a girl in her middle teens

sub·di·ac·o·nate \ˌsəb-dī-'ak-ə-nət\ *n* : the office or rank of a subdeacon

sub·di·vide \ˌsəb-də-'vīd\ *vb* **1** : to divide the parts of into more parts **2** : to divide into several parts; *esp* : to divide (a tract of land) into building lots — **sub·di·vid·able** \-də-'vīd-ə-bəl\ *adj*

sub·di·vi·sion \ˌsəb-də-'vizh-ən, 'səb-də-ˌ\ *n* **1** : the act or process of subdividing **2** : one of the parts into which something is subdivided

sub·dom·i·nant \ˌsəb-'däm-ə-nənt, 'səb-\ *n* **1** : the 4th tone of the major or minor scale (as F in the scale of C) **2** : an ecologically important life form subordinate in influence to the dominants of a community — **subdominant** *adj*

sub·due \səb-'dü, -'dyü\ *vt* **1** : to conquer and bring into subjection : VANQUISH **2** : to bring under control especially by willpower ⟨*subdued* fear⟩ **3** : to reduce the intensity or degree of ⟨*subdued* light⟩ [Middle French *soduire* "to seduce" from Latin *subducere* "to withdraw", from *sub-* + *ducere* "to lead, draw"] SYN see CONQUER — **sub·du·er** *n*

sub·en·try \'səb-ˌen-trē\ *n* : an entry made under a more general entry

su·ber·in \'sü-bə-rən\ *n* : a complex fatty substance that is the basis of cork [French *subérine,* from Latin *suber* "cork"]

sub·fam·i·ly \'səb-ˌfam-lē, -ə-lē\ *n* : a taxonomic category next below a family

sub·freez·ing \'səb-'frē-zing\ *adj* : lower than is required to produce freezing

sub·ge·nus \'səb-ˌjē-nəs\ *n* : a category in biological taxonomy below a genus and above a species

sub·grade \'səb-ˌgrād\ *n* : a surface of earth or rock leveled off to receive a foundation (as of a road)

sub·head \'səb-ˌhed\ *or* **sub·head·ing** \-ing\ *n* **1** : a heading of a subdivision (as in an outline) **2** : a subordinate caption, title, or headline

sub·hu·man \ˌsəb-'hyü-mən, 'səb-, -'yü-\ *adj* : less than human: as **a** : failing to reach the level (as of intelligence) associated with normal human beings **b** : unsuitable to or unfit for human beings

sub·ja·cent \ˌsəb-'jās-nt\ *adj* : lying under or below; *also* : lower than but not directly below ⟨hills and *subjacent* valleys⟩ [Latin *subjacens,* present participle of *subjacēre* "to lie under", from *sub-* + *jacēre* "to lie"] — **sub·ja·cen·cy** \-n-sē\ *n* — **sub·ja·cent·ly** *adv*

¹sub·ject \'səb-jikt\ *n* **1** : one that is placed under authority or control: as **a** : one subject to a monarch and governed by the monarch's law **b** : one who lives in the territory of, enjoys the protection of, and owes allegiance to a sovereign power or state **2** : the thing or person of which a quality, attribute, or relation is affirmed **3 a** : a department of knowledge or learning **b** : an individual (as a person or plant) that is studied or experimented on; *esp* : a dead body for anatomical dissection **c** (1) : something about which something is said or done (2) : something (as a scene or figure) that is represented or dealt with in a work of art **4** : a noun or noun equivalent about which something is stated by the predicate **5** : the principal melodic phrase on which a musical composition or movement is based [Middle French, from Latin *subjectus* "one under authority" and *subjectum* "subject of a proposition", both from *subicere* "to throw under, subject", from *sub-* + *jacere* "to throw"] SYN see CITIZEN

²subject *adj* **1** : owing obedience or allegiance to another (as a parent or ruler) **2 a** : LIABLE 2b, INCLINED ⟨*subject* to temptation⟩ **b** : SUSCEPTIBLE, PRONE ⟨*subject* to colds⟩ **3** : CONDITIONAL, CONTINGENT ⟨*subject* to approval⟩

³sub·ject \səb-'jekt\ *vt* **1 a** : to bring under control or dominion : SUBJUGATE **b** : to make amenable to the discipline and control of a superior **2 a** : to make liable : PREDISPOSE **b** : to make accountable : SUBMIT **3** : to cause to undergo : EXPOSE ⟨*subject* one to ridicule⟩ — **sub·jec·tion** \səb-'jek-shən\ *n*

sub·jec·tive \səb-'jek-tiv\ *adj* **1** : of, relating to, or being a subject **2** : of, relating to, or arising within one's self or mind in contrast to what is outside : PERSONAL ⟨*subjective* experience⟩ ⟨*subjective* symptoms of dis-

\ə\ abut		\ng\ sing	
\ər\ further		\ō\ bone	
\a\ mat		\ò\ saw	
\ā\ take		\òi\ coin	
\ä\ cot, cart		\th\ thin	
\aù\ out		\th\ this	
\ch\ chin		\ü\ food	
\e\ pet		\ù\ foot	
\ē\ easy		\y\ yet	
\g\ go		\yü\ few	
\i\ tip		\yù\ cure	
\ī\ life		\zh\ vision	
\j\ job			

ease) — **sub·jec·tive·ly** *adv* — **sub·jec·tiv·i·ty** \səb-,jek-'tiv-ət-ē, ,səb-\ *n*

subjective complement *n* : a grammatical complement relating to the subject of an intransitive verb ⟨in "I had fallen sick" *sick* is a *subjective complement*⟩

subject matter *n* : matter presented for consideration in discussion, thought, or study

sub·join \səb-'jȯin, ,səb-\ *vt* : APPEND, ANNEX

sub·ju·gate \'səb-jə-,gāt\ *vt* **1** : to force to submit to control : MASTER **2** : to bring into servitude : ENSLAVE [Latin *subjugare,* literally, "to bring under the yoke", from *sub-* + *jugum* "yoke"] SYN see CONQUER — **sub·ju·ga·tion** \,səb-jə-'gā-shən\ *n* — **sub·ju·ga·tor** \'səb-jə-,gāt-ər\ *n*

¹sub·junc·tive \səb-'jəng-tiv, -'jəngk-\ *adj* : of, relating to, or being the grammatical mood that represents a denoted act or state not as fact but as conditional or possible or viewed emotionally (as with doubt or desire) ⟨in "if I were you, I wouldn't go" *were* is in the *subjunctive* mood⟩ [Late Latin *subjunctivus,* from Latin *subjungere* "to subordinate", from *sub-* + *jungere* "to join"]

²subjunctive *n* : the subjunctive mood of a language; *also* : a verb in this mood

sub·king·dom \'səb-,king-dəm\ *n* : a primary division of a taxonomic kingdom

sub·lease \'səb-'lēs, -,lēs\ *n* : a lease by a tenant of part or all of leased premises to another person — **sublease** *vb*

sub·let \'səb-'let\ *vb* **sub·let; sub·let·ting 1** : to lease or rent all or part of a leased or rented property **2** : SUBCONTRACT 1

sub·li·mate \'səb-lə-,māt\ *vt* : to direct the expression of (instinctive desires and impulses) from a primitive form to a more socially or culturally acceptable form — **sub·li·ma·tion** \,səb-lə-'mā-shən\ *n*

¹sub·lime \sə-'blīm\ *vb* **1** : to pass or cause to pass from a solid to a gaseous state on heating and back to solid form on cooling without apparently passing through a liquid state; *also* : to release or purify by such action ⟨*sublime* sulfur from a mixture⟩ **2** : to make finer or more worthy : convert (something inferior) into something of higher worth [Middle French *sublimer,* from Medieval Latin *sublimare* "to refine, sublime", from Latin, "to elevate", from *sublimis* "sublime, raised on high"] — **sub·lim·er** *n*

²sublime *adj* **1 a** : lofty, grand, or exalted in thought, expression, or manner ⟨a *sublime* prose style⟩ **b** : of outstanding spiritual, intellectual, or moral worth ⟨*sublime* devotion to duty⟩ **2** : inspiring awe : SOLEMN ⟨*sublime* beauty⟩ [Latin *sublimis,* literally, "raised on high", from *sub* "under, up to" + *limen* "threshold, lintel"] — **sub·lime·ly** *adv* — **sub·lime·ness** *n*

sub·lim·i·nal \səb-'lim-ən-l, 'səb-\ *adj* **1** : inadequate to produce a sensation or a perception ⟨*subliminal* stimuli⟩ **2** : existing or functioning outside the area of conscious awareness ⟨the *subliminal* mind⟩ ⟨*subliminal* techniques in advertising⟩ [*sub-* + Latin *limin-, limen* "threshold"] — **sub·lim·i·nal·ly** \-l-ē\ *adv*

sub·lim·i·ty \sə-'blim-ət-ē\ *n, pl* **-ties 1** : something sublime **2** : the quality or state of being sublime

sub·lin·gual \,səb-'ling-yə-wəl, 'səb-, -'ling-wəl\ *adj* : situated or occurring under the tongue ⟨*sublingual* salivary glands⟩

sub·lux·a·tion \,səb-,lək-'sā-shən\ *n* : a partial dislocation of a bone or joint [*sub-* + Late Latin *luxatio* "dislocation", from Latin *luxare* "to dislocate", from *luxus* "dislocated"]

sub·ma·chine gun \,səb-mə-'shēn-,gən\ *n* : a lightweight automatic or semiautomatic portable firearm fired from the shoulder or hip

sub·mar·gin·al \,səb-'märj-nəl, 'səb-, -ən-l\ *adj* : less than marginal; *esp* : inadequate for some end or use ⟨farming *submarginal* land⟩ — **sub·mar·gin·al·ly** \-ē\ *adv*

¹sub·ma·rine \'səb-mə-,rēn, ,səb-mə-'\ *adj* : UNDERWATER; *esp* : UNDERSEA

²submarine *n* **1** : something that functions or operates underwater: as **a** : an underwater explosive mine **b** : a naval combat vessel designed for on-the-surface or underwater operations **2** : a large sandwich made from a long roll filled usually with cold cuts, cheese, onion, lettuce, and tomato

sub·ma·rin·er \'səb-mə-,rē-nər, ,səb-mə-'; ,səb-'mar-ə-\ *n* : a member of a submarine crew

¹sub·max·il·lary \,səb-'mak-sə-,ler-ē, 'səb-\ *adj* : of, relating to, or situated below the lower jaw

²submaxillary *n, pl* **-lar·ies** : a submaxillary part (as an artery or gland)

sub·me·di·ant \,səb-'mēd-ē-ənt, 'səb-\ *n* : the 6th tone above the tonic in a diatonic scale

sub·merge \səb-'mərj\ *vb* **1** : to put or go under water ⟨the whale *submerged*⟩ **2** : to cover or become covered with or as if with water ⟨floodwaters *submerged* the town⟩ ⟨memories *submerged* by time⟩ [Latin *submergere,* from *sub-* + *mergere* "to plunge"] — **sub·mer·gence** \-'mər-jəns\ *n* — **sub·merg·ible** \-'mər-jə-bəl\ *adj*

sub·mersed \səb-'mərst\ *adj* **1** : covered with water **2** : growing or adapted to grow underwater [Latin *submersus,* past participle of *submergere* "to submerge"]

¹sub·mers·ible \'səb-mər-sə-bəl\ *adj* : capable of being submerged

²submersible *n* : a boat that is capable of submerging : SUBMARINE

sub·mer·sion \səb-'mər-zhən, -shən\ *n* : the action of submerging : the state of being submerged

sub·mi·cro·scop·ic \,səb-,mī-krə-'skäp-ik\ *adj* : too small to be seen in an ordinary light microscope

sub·min·i·a·ture \,səb-'min-ē-ə-,chùr, 'səb-, -'min-i-,chùr, -chər\ *adj* : very small ⟨*subminiature* electronic equipment⟩

sub·mis·sion \səb-'mish-ən\ *n* **1** : an act of submitting something (as for consideration, inspection, or comment) **2** : the condition of being submissive, humble, or compliant **3** : an act of submitting to the authority or control of another [Middle French, from Latin *submissio* "act of lowering", from *submittere* "to lower, submit"]

sub·mis·sive \-'mis-iv\ *adj* : inclined or willing to submit to others : YIELDING, MEEK — **sub·mis·sive·ly** *adv* — **sub·mis·sive·ness** *n*

sub·mit \səb-'mit\ *vb* **sub·mit·ted; sub·mit·ting 1 a** : to give over or leave to the judgment or approval of someone else : REFER ⟨*submit* an issue for arbitration⟩ **b** : to make available : OFFER ⟨*submit* a report⟩ **2** : to subject to a process or practice **3** : to put forward as an opinion : AFFIRM **4** : to yield to the power or will of another [Latin *submittere* "to lower, submit", from *sub-* + *mittere* "to send"] SYN see YIELD

sub·mu·co·sa \,səb-myū-'kō-zə\ *n* : a supporting layer of loose connective tissue just under a mucous membrane — **sub·mu·co·sal** \-zəl\ *adj* — **sub·mu·cous** \,səb-'myū-kəs, 'səb-\ *adj*

¹sub·nor·mal \,səb-'nȯr-məl, 'səb-\ *adj* : being below what is normal — **sub·nor·mal·i·ty** \,səb-nȯr-'mal-ət-ē\ *n* — **sub·nor·mal·ly** \,səb-'nȯr-mə-lē, 'səb-\ *adv*

²subnormal *n* : one that is below normal; *esp* : a person of subnormal intelligence

sub·or·bit·al \,səb-'ȯr-bət-l, 'səb-\ **1** : situated beneath the eye or its orbit **2** : being or involving less than one orbit ⟨a spacecraft's *suborbital* flight⟩

sub·or·der \'səb-,ȯrd-ər\ *n* : a subdivision of an order

¹sub·or·di·nate \sə-'bȯrd-n-ət, -'bȯrd-nət\ *adj* **1** : placed in or occupying a lower class or rank : INFERIOR **2** : submissive to or controlled by authority **3 a** : of, relating to, or being a clause that functions as a noun, adjective, or adverb **b** : grammatically subordinating [Medieval Latin *subordinatus,* past participle of *subordinare* "to subordinate", from Latin *sub-* + *ordi-*

nare "to order"] — **sub·or·di·nate·ly** *adv* — **sub·or·di·nate·ness** *n*

²**subordinate** *n* : one that is subordinate

³**sub·or·di·nate** \sə-'bȯrd-n-ˌāt\ *vt* : to make subordinate — **sub·or·di·na·tion** \-ˌbȯrd-n-'ā-shən\ *n* — **sub·or·di·na·tive** \-'bȯrd-n-ˌāt-iv\ *adj*

sub·orn \sə-'bȯrn\ *vt* : to induce secretly to do an unlawful thing and especially to commit perjury ⟨*suborn* a witness⟩ [Middle French *suborner*, from Latin *subornare*, from *sub-* "secretly" + *ornare* "to furnish, equip"] — **sub·or·na·tion** \ˌsəb-ˌȯr-'nā-shən\ *n* — **sub·orn·er** \sə-'bȯr-nər\ *n*

sub·phy·lum \'səb-ˌfī-ləm\ *n* : a primary division of a phylum

sub·plot \-ˌplät\ *n* : a subordinate plot in fiction or drama

¹**sub·poe·na** \sə-'pē-nə\ *n* : a writ commanding a person designated in it to appear in court under a penalty for failure to appear [Latin *sub poena* "under penalty"]

²**subpoena** *vt* **-naed; -na·ing** : to serve or summon with a writ of subpoena

sub·po·lar \ˌsəb-'pō-lər, 'səb-\ *adj* : SUBANTARCTIC, SUBARCTIC

sub·pop·u·la·tion \ˌsəb-ˌpäp-yə-'lā-shən\ *n* : an identifiable part of a population

sub ro·sa \ˌsəb-'rō-zə\ *adv* : in confidence : SECRETLY [New Latin, literally, "under the rose"; from the old custom of hanging a rose over the council table to indicate that all present were sworn to secrecy]

sub·rou·tine \ˌsəb-rü-'tēn, -'rü-\ *n* : a sequence of computer instructions for performing a specified task that can be used repeatedly

sub–Sa·ha·ran \ˌsəb-sə-'har-ən, ˌsəb-, -'her-, -'här-\ *adj* : of, relating to, or being the part of Africa south of the Sahara

sub·scribe \səb-'skrīb\ *vb* **1 a** : to write (one's name) underneath : SIGN **b** : to give consent or approval by or as if by signing one's name ⟨unwilling to *subscribe* to the agreement⟩ **2 a** : to pledge (a gift or contribution) by writing one's name with the amount ⟨*subscribed* $100 to the fund⟩ **b** : to agree to contribute something; *also* : to make an agreed contribution **3 a** : to enter one's name for a publication or service; *also* : to receive a periodical or service regularly on order ⟨*subscribe* to a newspaper⟩ **b** : to agree to buy and pay for securities especially of a new offering ⟨*subscribed* for 1000 shares⟩ [Latin *subscribere*, literally, "to write beneath", from *sub-* + *scribere* "to write"] — **sub·scrib·er** *n*

sub·script \'səb-ˌskript\ *n* : a distinguishing symbol or letter written immediately below or below and to the right or left of another character [Latin *subscriptus*, past participle of *subscribere* "to write beneath"] — **subscript** *adj*

sub·scrip·tion \səb-'skrip-shən\ *n* **1** : an act or instance of subscribing **2** : an amount or thing that is subscribed **3** : a purchase of future issues of a periodical [Latin *subscriptio* "signature", from *subscribere* "to write beneath, subscribe"]

sub·sense \'səb-ˌsen(t)s\ *n* : a subordinate division of a sense (as in a dictionary)

sub·se·quent \'səb-si-kwənt, -sə-ˌkwent\ *adj* : following in time, order, or place : SUCCEEDING [Latin *subsequens*, present participle of *subsequi* "to follow close", from *sub-* "near" + *sequi* "to follow"] — **sub·se·quence** \-sə-ˌkwens, -si-kwəns\ *n* — **subsequent** *n* — **sub·se·quent·ly** \-ˌkwent-lē, -kwənt-\ *adv* — **sub·se·quent·ness** \-ˌkwent-, -kwənt-\ *n*

sub·serve \səb-'sərv\ *vt* **1** : to serve as a means in carrying on or out or in aiding **2** : to promote the welfare or purposes of [Latin *subservire*, from *sub-* + *servire* "to serve"]

sub·ser·vi·ence \səb-'sər-vē-əns\ *also* **sub·ser·vi·en·cy** \-ən-sē\ *n, pl* **-enc·es** *also* **-en·cies** **1** : a subservient or subordinate place or function **2** : slavish obedience

sub·ser·vi·ent \-ənt\ *adj* **1** : useful in an inferior capacity : SUBORDINATE **2** : slavishly obedient : OBSEQUIOUS [Latin *subserviens*, present participle of *subservire* "to subserve"] — **sub·ser·vi·ent·ly** *adv*

sub·set \'səb-ˌset\ *n* : a mathematical set each of whose elements is included in another set

sub·side \səb-'sīd\ *vi* **1** : to sink or fall to the bottom : SETTLE **2** : to tend downward : DESCEND ⟨the flood *subsided* slowly⟩ **3** : to let oneself settle down ⟨*subside* into a chair⟩ **4** : to become quiet or less : ABATE ⟨as the fever *subsides*⟩ ⟨my anger *subsided*⟩ [Latin *subsidere*, from *sub-* + *sidere* "to sit down, sink"] — **sub·sid·ence** \səb-'sīd-ns, 'səb-səd-əns\ *n*

¹**sub·sid·i·ary** \səb-'sid-ē-ˌer-ē, -'sid-ə-rē\ *adj* **1 a** : furnishing aid or support : AUXILIARY ⟨*subsidiary* details⟩ **b** : of secondary importance : TRIBUTARY ⟨*subsidiary* streams⟩ **2** : of, relating to, affected by, or being a subsidy ⟨*subsidiary* payments⟩ [Latin *subsidiarius*, from *subsidium* "reserve troops"] — **sub·sid·i·ar·i·ly** \-ˌsid-ē-'er-ə-lē\ *adv*

²**subsidiary** *n, pl* **-ar·ies** : one that is subsidiary; *esp* : a company wholly controlled by another

sub·si·dize \'səb-sə-ˌdīz, -zə-\ *vt* : to aid or furnish with a subsidy — **sub·si·di·za·tion** \ˌsəb-səd-ə-'zā-shən, ˌsəb-zəd-\ *n*

sub·si·dy \'səb-səd-ē, -zəd-\ *n, pl* **-dies** : a grant or gift of money; *esp* : a grant by a government to a private individual, a company, or another government to aid an enterprise beneficial to the public [Latin *subsidium* "reserve troops, support, assistance", from *sub-* "near" + *sedēre* "to sit"]

sub·sist \səb-'sist\ *vi* **1** : to have or continue to have existence **2** : to receive maintenance (as food and clothing) : LIVE [Late Latin *subsistere*, from Latin, "to halt, remain", from *sub-* + *sistere* "to come to a stand"]

sub·sis·tence \səb-'sis-təns\ *n* **1 a** : real being : EXISTENCE **b** : the condition of remaining in existence **2 a** : means of subsisting **b** : the minimum (as of food and shelter) necessary to support life [Late Latin *subsistentia*, from *subsistere* "to subsist"] — **sub·sist·ent** \-tənt\ *adj*

¹**sub·soil** \'səb-ˌsȯil\ *n* : a layer of weathered material that lies just under the surface soil

²**subsoil** *vt* : to turn, break, or stir the subsoil of

sub·son·ic \ˌsəb-'sän-ik, 'səb-\ *adj* **1** : of, relating to, or being a speed less than that of sound in air **2** : moving, capable of moving, or utilizing air currents moving at a subsonic speed **3** : INFRASONIC 1

sub·spe·cies \'səb-ˌspē-shēz, -sēz\ *n* : a subdivision of a species: as **a** : a taxonomic category that ranks immediately below a species and designates a physically distinguishable and geographically isolated group whose members interbreed with those of other subspecies of the same species where their ranges overlap **b** : a named subdivision (as a race or variety) of a taxonomic species — **sub·spe·cif·ic** \ˌsəb-spi-'sif-ik\ *adj*

sub·stage \'səb-ˌstāj\ *n* : an attachment to a microscope by means of which accessories (as a mirror or lamp) are held in place beneath the stage of the instrument

sub·stance \'səb-stəns\ *n* **1 a** : essential nature : ESSENCE ⟨divine *substance*⟩ **b** : a fundamental or characteristic part or quality ⟨the *substance* of the speech⟩ **2 a** : physical material from which something is made or which has discrete existence **b** : matter of particular or definite chemical constitution **c** : something (as drugs or alcoholic beverages) deemed harmful and usually subject to legal restriction ⟨has a *substance* problem⟩ **3** : material possessions : PROPERTY ⟨a person of *substance*⟩ [Old French, from Latin *substantia*, from *substare* "to stand under", from *sub-* + *stare* "to stand"]

substance abuse *n* : excessive use of a drug (as alcohol or narcotics) : use of a drug without medical justification — **substance abuser** *n*

\ə\ abut \ˌ\ \ng\ sing
\ər\ **further** \ō\ bone
\a\ mat \ȯ\ saw
\ā\ take \ȯi\ coin
\ä\ cot, cart \th\ thin
\aú\ out \th\ this
\ch\ chin \ü\ food
\e\ pet \ú\ foot
\ē\ easy \y\ yet
\g\ go \yü\ few
\i\ tip \yú\ cure
\ī\ life \zh\ vision
\j\ job

sub·stan·dard \ˌsəb-'stan-dərd, 'səb-\ *adj* **1** : deviating from or falling short of a standard or norm **2** : conforming to a pattern of linguistic usage existing within a speech community but not that of the prestige group in that community

sub·stan·tial \səb-'stan-chəl\ *adj* **1 a** : existing as or in substance : MATERIAL **b** : not imaginary or illusory : REAL ⟨the *substantial* world⟩ **c** : IMPORTANT 1, ESSENTIAL ⟨a *substantial* difference in the stories⟩ **2** : ample to satisfy and nourish ⟨a *substantial* diet⟩ **3 a** : having means : WELL-TO-DO ⟨a *substantial* farmer⟩ **b** : considerable in quantity : significantly large ⟨a *substantial* increase⟩ ⟨a *substantial* wage⟩ **4** : well and sturdily built ⟨*substantial* buildings⟩ **5** : being largely but not wholly what is specified ⟨a *substantial* lie⟩ — **sub·stan·ti·al·i·ty** \-ˌstan-chē-'al-ət-ē\ *n* — **sub·stan·tial·ly** \-'stanch-lē-, -ə-lē\ *adv*

sub·stan·ti·ate \səb-'stan-chē-ˌāt\ *vt* **1** : to provide evidence for : PROVE ⟨*substantiate* claims in court⟩ **2** : to give substance or body to : EMBODY — **sub·stan·ti·a·tion** \-ˌstan-chē-'ā-shən\ *n*

¹sub·stan·tive \'səb-stən-tiv\ *n* : a word or word group functioning syntactically as a noun [Middle French *substantif*, derived from Late Latin *substantivus* "having or expressing substance"] — **sub·stan·ti·val** \ˌsəb-stən-'tī-vəl\ *adj* — **sub·stan·ti·val·ly** \-və-lē\ *adv*

²substantive *adj* **1** : of, relating to, or being something totally independent **2 a** : real rather than apparent **b** : belonging to the substance of a thing : ESSENTIAL ⟨*substantive* rights⟩ **c** : expressing existence ⟨the *substantive* verb is the verb *to be*⟩ **3** : functioning as a grammatical substantive ⟨a *substantive* clause⟩ **4** : considerable in amount or numbers : SUBSTANTIAL **5** : creating and defining rights and duties ⟨*substantive* law⟩ [Late Latin *substantivus* "having substance", from Latin *substantia* "substance"] — **sub·stan·tive·ly** *adv* — **sub·stan·tive·ness** *n*

sub·sta·tion \'səb-ˌstā-shən\ *n* : a station subordinate to another station

¹sub·sti·tute \'səb-stə-ˌtüt, -ˌtyüt\ *n* : a person or thing that takes the place of another [Latin *substitutus*, past participle of *substituere* "to put in place of", from *sub-* + *statuere* "to set up, place"] — **substitute** *adj*

²substitute *vb* **1** : to put in the place of another : EXCHANGE **2** : to serve as a substitute : REPLACE — **sub·sti·tu·tion** \ˌsəb-stə-'tü-shən, -'tyü-\ *n* — **sub·sti·tu·tion·al** \-shnəl, shən-l\ *adj* — **sub·sti·tu·tion·al·ly** \-ē\ *adv* — **sub·sti·tu·tion·ary** \-shə-ˌner-ē\ *adj*

sub·strate \'səb-ˌstrāt\ *n* **1** : SUBSTRATUM a **2** : the base on which an organism lives or over which it moves ⟨the soil is the *substrate* of most seed plants⟩ **3** : a substance acted upon (as by an enzyme)

sub·stra·tum \'səb-ˌstrāt-əm, -ˌstrat-\ *n* : an underlying support : FOUNDATION: as **a** : the material of which something is made and from which it derives its special qualities **b** : a layer beneath the surface soil : SUBSOIL [Medieval Latin, from Latin *substernere* "to spread under", from *sub-* + *sternere* "to spread"]

sub·struc·ture \'səb-ˌstrək-chər\ *n* : FOUNDATION 2, GROUNDWORK

sub·sume \səb-'süm\ *vt* : to classify within a larger category or under a general principle [Latin *sub-* + *sumere* "to take up"] — **sub·sump·tion** \səb-'səm-shən, -'səmp-\ *n*

sub·sur·face \'səb-ˌsər-fəs\ *adj* : of, relating to, or involving an area or material beneath a surface (as of the earth) ⟨*subsurface* water⟩

sub·teen \'səb-'tēn\ *n* : a child approaching adolescence

sub·ten·ant \ˌsəb-'ten-ənt, 'səb-\ *n* : one who rents from a tenant — **sub·ten·an·cy** \-'ten-ən-sē\ *n*

sub·tend \səb-'tend\ *vt* **1 a** : to be opposite to and extend from one side to the other of ⟨a hypotenuse *subtends* a right angle⟩ **b** : to fix the angular extent of

with respect to a fixed point or object taken as the vertex ⟨a central angle *subtended* by an arc⟩ **c** : to determine the measure of by marking off the endpoints of ⟨a chord *subtends* an arc⟩ **2** : to underlie so as to include [Latin *subtendere* "to stretch beneath", from *sub-* + *tendere* "to stretch"]

sub·ter·fuge \'səb-tər-ˌfyüj\ *n* : a device (as a scheme or trick) used to avoid an unpleasant circumstance (as blame) : a deceptive evasion [Late Latin *subterfugium*, from Latin *subterfugere* "to evade", from *subter-* "beneath, secretly" + *fugere* "to flee"]

sub·ter·ra·nean \ˌsəb-tə-'rā-nē-ən, -nyən\ *or* **sub·ter·ra·neous** \-nē-əs, -nyəs\ *adj* **1** : being, living, or operating under the surface of the earth **2** : existing or working in secret : HIDDEN [Latin *subterraneus*, from *sub* "under" + *terra* "earth"] — **sub·ter·ra·ne·an·ly** *adv*

sub·tile \'sət-l, 'səb-tl\ *adj* **sub·til·er** \'sət-lər, -l-ər, 'səb-tə-lər\; **sub·til·est** \'sət-ləst, -l-əst, 'səb-tə-ləst\ **1** : SUBTLE 1a, ELUSIVE **2** : ARTFUL 3b, CRAFTY [Latin *subtilis*] — **sub·tile·ly** \'sət-lē, -l-lē, -l-ē; 'səb-tə-lē\ *adv* — **sub·tile·ness** \'sət-l-nəs, 'səb-tl-\ *n*

sub·til·ty \'sət-l-tē, 'səb-tl-\ *n, pl* **-ties** : SUBTLETY

sub·ti·tle \'səb-ˌtīt-l\ *n* **1** : a secondary or explanatory title **2** : a printed statement or fragment of dialogue appearing on the screen between the scenes of a silent motion picture or appearing as a translation at the bottom of the screen during the scenes especially of a foreign-language movie — **subtitle** *vt*

sub·tle \'sət-l\ *adj* **sub·tler** \'sət-lər, -l-ər\; **sub·tlest** \'sət-ləst, -l-əst\ **1 a** : DELICATE 1a, ELUSIVE ⟨a *subtle* aroma⟩ **b** : difficult to understand or distinguish : OBSCURE ⟨*subtle* differences in vowel sounds⟩ **2 a** : marked by insight and sensitivity : PERCEPTIVE ⟨a *subtle* mind⟩ **b** : SKILLFUL, EXPERT ⟨*subtle* workmanship⟩; *also* : cleverly made or contrived ⟨a *subtle* mechanism⟩ **3 a** : ARTFUL 3b, WILY **b** : INSIDIOUS ⟨a *subtle* poison⟩ [Old French *soutil*, from Latin *subtilis*, literally, "finely woven", from *sub-* + *tela* "web"] — **sub·tle·ness** \'sət-l-nəs\ *n* — **sub·tly** \'sət-lē, -l-lē, -l-ē\ *adv*

sub·tle·ty \'sət-l-tē\ *n, pl* **-ties** **1** : the quality or state of being subtle **2** : something subtle; *esp* : a fine distinction

sub·ton·ic \ˌsəb-'tän-ik, 'səb-\ *n* : LEADING TONE [from its being a half tone below the upper tonic]

sub·top·ic \'səb-ˌtäp-ik\ *n* : a secondary topic : one of the subdivisions into which a topic may be divided

sub·tract \səb-'trakt\ *vb* : to take away by deducting : perform a subtraction ⟨*subtract* 5 from 9⟩ [Latin *subtractus*, past participle of *subtrahere* "to draw from beneath, withdraw", from *sub-* + *trahere* "to draw"] — **sub·tract·er** *n*

sub·trac·tion \səb-'trak-shən\ *n* **1** : an act or instance of subtracting **2** : the operation of deducting one number from another

sub·trac·tive \-'trak-tiv\ *adj* **1** : tending to subtract **2** : constituting or involving subtraction ⟨a *subtractive* correction⟩

sub·tra·hend \'səb-trə-ˌhend\ *n* : a number that is to be subtracted from a minuend [Latin *subtrahendus* "to be withdrawn", from *subtrahere* "to withdraw"]

sub·trop·i·cal \ˌsəb-'träp-i-kəl, 'səb-\ *also* **sub·trop·ic** \-'träp-ik\ *adj* : of, relating to, or being the regions bordering on the tropical zone

sub·trop·ics \-'träp-iks\ *n pl* : subtropical regions

sub·urb \'səb-ˌərb\ *n* **1 a** : an outlying part of a city or town **b** : a smaller community adjacent to a city **2** *pl* : the residential area adjacent to a city or large town; *also* : ENVIRONS 1 [Latin *suburbium*, from *sub-* "near" + *urbs* "city"] — **sub·ur·ban** \sə-'bər-bən\ *adj or n*

sub·ur·ban·ite \sə-'bər-bə-ˌnīt\ *n* : one who lives in the suburbs

sub·ur·bia \sə-'bər-bē-ə\ *n* **1** : the suburbs of a city **2** : suburbanites as a distinctive social group **3** : the manners, styles, and customs typical of suburban life

sub·ven·tion \səb-'ven-chən\ *n* : financial support especially in the form of an endowment or a subsidy [Late Latin *subventio* "assistance", from Latin *subvenire* "to come up, come to the rescue", from *sub-* "up" + *venire* "to come"]

sub·ver·sion \səb-'vər-zhən\ *n* : the act of subverting : the state of being subverted; *esp* : a systematic attempt to overthrow or undermine a government or political system by persons working secretly within the country involved [Middle French, from Late Latin *subversio,* from Latin *subvertere* "to subvert"] — **sub·ver·sive** \-'vər-siv, -ziv\ *adj or n* — **sub·ver·sive·ly** *adv*

sub·vert \səb-'vərt\ *vt* : to overturn or overthrow from the foundation : RUIN 2 : to corrupt by undermining the morals, allegiance, or faith of [Middle French *subvertir,* from Latin *subvertere,* literally, "to turn from beneath", from *sub-* + *vertere* "to turn"] — **sub·vert·er** *n*

sub·way \'səb-,wā\ *n* : an underground way; *esp* : a usually electric underground railway

suc·ceed \sək-'sēd\ *vb* 1 a : to come next after another in possession of an office or estate; *esp* : to inherit sovereignty b : to follow after another in order 2 : to turn out well : be successful [Latin *succedere,* from *sub-* "near" + *cedere* "to go"] SYN see FOLLOW — **suc·ceed·er** *n*

suc·cess \sək-'ses\ *n* 1 a : degree or measure of succeeding b : a favorable completion of something c : the gaining of wealth, favor, or prestige 2 : one that succeeds [Latin *successus,* from *succedere* "to succeed"]

suc·cess·ful \-fəl\ *adj* 1 : resulting or terminating in success 2 : gaining or having gained success — **suc·cess·ful·ly** \-fə-lē\ *adv* — **suc·cess·ful·ness** *n*

suc·ces·sion \sək-'sesh-ən\ *n* 1 : the order, action, or right of succeeding to a throne, title, or property 2 a : a repeated following of one person or thing after another b : a process of one-way ecological change in which organisms of one kind are replaced by those of another kind 3 : a number of persons or things that follow one after another [Latin *successio,* from *succedere* "to succeed"] — **suc·ces·sion·al** \-'sesh-nəl, -ən-l\ *adj* — **suc·ces·sion·al·ly** \-ē\ *adv* □ SYN SEQUENCE, SERIES: SUCCESSION may apply to things of any sort that follow in order of time or place and usually without interruption; SEQUENCE suggests a uniform, logical, or regular succession; SERIES implies that the objects are of a similar nature or stand in similar relation to each other ⟨a *series* of monthly payments⟩

suc·ces·sive \sək-'ses-iv\ *adj* : following in succession or serial order : following each other without interruption ⟨failed in three *successive* tries⟩ SYN see CONSECUTIVE — **suc·ces·sive·ly** *adv* — **suc·ces·sive·ness** *n*

suc·ces·sor \sək-'ses-ər\ *n* : one that follows: as a : one who succeeds to a throne, title, estate, or office b : a positive integer obtained from another positive integer by adding 1

suc·cinct \sək-'singt, sek-, ,sə-, -'singkt\ *adj* 1 *archaic* a : being girded b : close-fitting 2 : marked by briefness and compactness of expression : CONCISE [Latin *succinctus,* from *succingere* "to gird from below, tuck up", from *sub-* + *cingere* "to gird"] — **suc·cinct·ly** *adv* — **suc·cinct·ness** *n*

¹suc·cor \'sək-ər\ *n* : RELIEF 1a; *also* : AID, HELP [Old French *sucors,* from Medieval Latin *succursus,* from Latin *succurrere* "to run up, run to help", from *sub-* "up" + *currere* "to run"]

²succor *vt* : to go to the aid of (one in need or distress) : RELIEVE — **suc·cor·er** *n*

suc·co·ry \'sək-rē, -ə-rē\ *n, pl* **-ries** : CHICORY [Middle English *cicoree*]

suc·co·tash \'sək-ə-,tash\ *n* : lima or shell beans and corn cooked together [of American Indian origin]

suc·cu·bus \'sək-yə-bəs\ *n, pl* **suc·cu·bi** \-,bī, -,bē\ : a female demon that lies on people in their sleep [Medieval Latin, from Late Latin *succuba* "prostitute", from Latin *succubare* "to lie under", from *sub-* + *cubare* "to lie, recline"]

¹suc·cu·lent \'sək-yə-lənt\ *adj* 1 a : full of juice : JUICY b : having fleshy tissues designed to conserve moisture ⟨*succulent* plants⟩ 2 : full of vitality, freshness, or richness [Latin *suculentus,* from *sucus* "juice"] — **suc·cu·lence** \-ləns\ *n* — **suc·cu·lent·ly** *adv*

²succulent *n* : a succulent plant (as a cactus)

suc·cumb \sə-'kəm\ *vi* 1 : to yield to superior strength or force or overpowering appeal or desire 2 : to cease to exist : DIE [Latin *succumbere,* from *sub-* + *-cumbere* "to lie down"] SYN see YIELD

¹such \'səch, 'səch, sich, ,sich\ *adj* 1 a : of a kind or character to be stated or suggested ⟨a bag *such* as a doctor carries⟩ b : having a quality to a degree to be indicated ⟨our excitement was *such* that we shouted⟩ 2 : having a quality already specified ⟨deeply moved by *such* acts of kindness⟩ 3 : of so extreme a degree or quality ⟨you're *such* a snob⟩ 4 : of the same class, type, or sort ⟨other *such* clinics throughout the state⟩ [Old English *swilc*]

²such *pron* 1 : such a person or thing ⟨had a plan if it may be called *such*⟩ 2 : someone or something stated, implied, or exemplified ⟨*such* were the Romans⟩ ⟨*such* was the result⟩ 3 : someone or something similar ⟨ships and planes and *such*⟩ — **as such** : in itself ⟨as *such* the gift was worth little⟩

³such *adv* 1 : to such a degree : so ⟨*such* tall buildings⟩ ⟨*such* a fine person⟩ 2 : VERY, ESPECIALLY ⟨hasn't been in *such* good spirits lately⟩ 3 : in such a way

¹such and such *pron* : something not specified ⟨it's easy to say we want the system to produce *such and such*⟩

²such and such *adj* : not named or specified ⟨what we mean when we say that *such and such* a people is civilized⟩

¹such·like \'səch-,līk\ *adj* : of like kind : SIMILAR

²suchlike *pron* : someone or something of the same sort : a similar person or thing

¹suck \'sək\ *vb* 1 a : to draw in (liquid) or draw liquid from through suction created by movements of the mouth ⟨*suck* venom from a snakebite⟩ b : to draw milk from a breast or udder with the mouth ⟨young pigs *sucking* well⟩ c (1) : to consume by applying the lips or tongue to ⟨*suck* a lollipop⟩ (2) : to apply the mouth to and create a sucking action on ⟨*suck* a bruised finger⟩ 2 : to take something in or up or remove something from by or as if by suction ⟨plants *sucking* moisture from the soil⟩ ⟨a well *sucked* dry by constant pumping⟩ 3 : to make or cause to make a sound or motion like that of sucking ⟨*suck* in your stomach⟩ 4 : to act in an obsequious way ⟨*sucking* up to the boss⟩ [Old English *sūcan*]

²suck *n* 1 : the act of sucking 2 : a sucking movement or force

¹suck·er \'sək-ər\ *n* 1 : one that sucks 2 : a part of an animal's body used for sucking or for clinging by suction 3 : a secondary shoot from the roots or lower part of a plant 4 : any of numerous freshwater fishes related to the carps but having usually thick soft lips for sucking in food 5 : LOLLIPOP 6 a : a person easily cheated or deceived b : a person irresistibly attracted to something ⟨a *sucker* for new cars⟩

²sucker *vb* **suck·ered; suck·er·ing** \'sək-ring, -ə-ring\ 1 : to remove suckers from 2 : to have or send out suckers

sucker punch *vt* : to punch (a person) suddenly without warning and often without apparent provocation — **sucker punch** *n*

sucking louse *n* : any of an order (Anoplura) of wingless insects comprising the true lice with mouthparts adapted to sucking body fluids

suck·le \'sək-əl\ *vt* **suck·led; suck·ling** \'sək-ling, -ə-ling\ 1 a : to give milk to from the breast or udder ⟨a mother *suckling* her child⟩ b : to bring up : NOURISH 2 : to draw milk from the breast or udder of ⟨lambs

¹sucker 4

\ə\ abut	\ng\ sing
\ər\ further	\ō\ bone
\a\ mat	\ȯ\ saw
\ā\ take	\ȯi\ coin
\ä\ cot, cart	\th\ thin
\au̇\ out	\th\ this
\ch\ chin	\ü\ food
\e\ pet	\u̇\ foot
\ē\ easy	\y\ yet
\g\ go	\yü\ few
\i\ tip	\yu̇\ cure
\ī\ life	\zh\ vision
\j\ job	

suckling the ewes) [probably back-formation from *suckling*]

suck·ling \'sək-ling\ *n* : a young unweaned mammal

su·crase \'sü-ˌkrās\ *n* : INVERTASE [French *sucre* "sugar"]

su·cre \'sü-krā\ *n* **1** : the basic monetary unit of Ecuador **2** : a coin representing one sucre [Spanish, from Antonio José de *Sucre,* died 1830, South American liberator]

su·crose \'sü-ˌkrōs\ *n* : a sweet crystalline disaccharide sugar $C_{12}H_{22}O_{11}$ that occurs naturally in most land plants and is the sugar obtained from sugarcane or sugar beets [French *sucre* "sugar"]

suc·tion \'sək-shən\ *n* **1** : the act or process of sucking **2 a** : the action of exerting a force upon something by means of reduced air pressure over part of its surface so that the normal air pressure on another part of its surface pushes or tends to push it toward the region of reduced pressure **b** : force so exerted [Late Latin *suctio,* from Latin *sugere* "to suck"] — **suc·tion·al** \-shən-l, -shnəl\ *adj*

suction cup *n* : a cup-shaped device in which a partial vacuum can be produced when applied to a surface

Su·dan grass \sü-ˈdan-, -ˈdän-\ *n* : a vigorous tall-growing annual sorghum widely grown for hay and fodder

Su·dan·ic \sü-ˈdan-ik\ *n* : the languages neither Bantu nor Hamitic spoken in a belt extending from Senegal to southern Sudan — **Sudanic** *adj*

¹sud·den \'səd-n\ *adj* **1 a** : happening quickly and unexpectedly ⟨a *sudden* shower⟩ **b** : come upon unexpectedly ⟨a *sudden* turn in the road⟩ **c** : rising or dropping sharply : STEEP ⟨a *sudden* descent to the sea⟩ **2** : marked by or showing hastiness : RASH ⟨a *sudden* decision⟩ **3** : made or brought about in a short time : PROMPT ⟨a *sudden* cure⟩ [Middle French *sodain,* from Latin *subitaneus,* from *subitus* "sudden", from *subire* "to come up", from *sub-* "up" + *ire* "to go"] — **sud·den·ly** *adv* — **sud·den·ness** \'səd-n-nəs, 'səd-n-əs\ *n*

²sudden *n, obsolete* : an unexpected occurrence : EMERGENCY — **all of a sudden** *or* **on a sudden** : sooner than was expected : SUDDENLY

sudden death *n* : a period of play to break a tie that terminates a game the moment one side scores or gains a lead

sudden infant death syndrome *n* : death of an apparently healthy infant usually before one year of age that is of unknown cause and occurs usually during sleep — abbreviation *SIDS*

su·do·rif·ic \-ˈrif-ik\ *adj* : causing or inducing sweat ⟨*sudorific* herbs⟩ [Latin *sudor* "sweat"] — **sudorific** *n*

¹suds \'sədz\ *n pl* **1** : water mixed with soap or detergent especially when frothy; *also* : the froth on such water **2** : BEER 1 [probably from Dutch *sudse* "marsh"]

²suds *vb* **1** : to wash in suds **2** : to form suds

sudsy \'səd-zē\ *adj* **suds·i·er; -est** : full of suds : FROTHY

sue \'sü\ *vb* **1** : to pay court to : WOO **2** : to seek justice from a person by bringing a legal action **3** : to make a request or application : PLEAD — usually used with *for* or *to* ⟨the nation *sued* for peace⟩ [Old French *suivre,* derived from Latin *sequi* "to follow"] — **su·er** *n*

suede *or* **suède** \'swād\ *n* **1** : leather with a napped surface **2** : a cloth fabric finished with a short nap to resemble suede [French *gants de Suède* "Swedish gloves"]

su·et \'sü-ət\ *n* : the hard fat about the kidneys and loins in beef and mutton that yields tallow [Anglo-French *sue,* from Latin *sebum* "tallow, suet"]

suf·fer \'səf-ər\ *vb* **suf·fered; suf·fer·ing** \'səf-ring, -ə-ring\ **1** : to feel or endure pain **2** : EXPERIENCE, UNDERGO ⟨*suffer* a defeat⟩ **3** : to bear loss or damage ⟨the business *suffered* during your illness⟩ **4** : to allow especially because of indifference [Old French *souffrir,* from Latin *suffere,* from *sub-* "up" + *ferre* "to bear"]

— **suf·fer·able** \'səf-rə-bəl, -ə-rə-\ *adj* — **suf·fer·able·ness** *n* — **suf·fer·ably** \-blē\ *adv* — **suf·fer·er** \'səf-ər-ər\ *n*

suf·fer·ance \'səf-rəns, -ə-rəns\ *n* **1** : consent or approval implied by a lack of interference or failure to enforce a prohibition **2** : power or ability to withstand ⟨pain beyond *sufferance*⟩

suf·fer·ing *n* **1** : the state or experience of one that suffers **2** : mental or physical pain SYN see DISTRESS

suf·fice \sə-ˈfīs\ *vb* **1** : to meet or satisfy a need : be sufficient **2** : to be competent or capable **3** : to be enough for [Middle French *suffis-,* stem of *suffire* "to suffice", from Latin *sufficere,* literally, "to put under", from *sub-* + *facere* "to make, do"]

suf·fi·cien·cy \sə-ˈfish-ən-sē\ *n, pl* **-cies 1** : sufficient means to meet one's needs : COMPETENCY **2** : the quality or state of being sufficient : ADEQUACY

suf·fi·cient \sə-ˈfish-ənt\ *adj* **1** : enough to meet the needs of a situation or a proposed end **2** : being a proposition whose truth is adequate to insure the truth of another proposition ⟨*p* is necessary and *sufficient* for *q*⟩ [Latin *sufficiens,* from *sufficere* "to suffice"] — **suf·fi·cient·ly** *adv* □ SYN ENOUGH, ADEQUATE: SUFFICIENT suggests a fairly exact meeting of a need; ENOUGH is less exact or less formal than SUFFICIENT; ADEQUATE may imply barely meeting a requirement or a moderate standard.

¹suf·fix \'səf-ˌiks\ *n* : an affix occurring at the end of a word [Latin *suffixus,* past participle of *suffigere* "to fasten underneath", from *sub-* + *figere* "to fasten"] — **suf·fix·al** \-ik-səl\ *adj* — **suf·fix·less** \-ˌiks-ləs\ *adj*

²suf·fix \'səf-ˌiks, sə-ˈfiks\ *vt* : to attach as a suffix — **suf·fix·a·tion** \ˌsəf-ˌik-ˈsā-shən\ *n*

suf·fo·cate \'səf-ə-ˌkāt\ *vb* **1 a** : to stop the breath of (as by strangling or asphyxiation) **b** : to deprive of oxygen; *also* : distress by want of cool fresh air **2** : to hinder or stop the development of **3** : to be or become suffocated; *esp* : to die or suffer from lack of breathable air [Latin *suffocare,* from *sub-* + *fauces* "throat"] — **suf·fo·cat·ing·ly** \-ˌkāt-ing-lē\ *adv* — **suf·fo·ca·tion** \ˌsəf-ə-ˈkā-shən\ *n* — **suf·fo·ca·tive** \'səf-ə-ˌkāt-iv\ *adj*

¹suf·fra·gan \'səf-ri-gən\ *n* **1** : a diocesan bishop (as in the Roman Catholic Church and the Church of England) of lower rank than a metropolitan **2** : an Anglican bishop assisting a diocesan bishop and not having the right of succession [Middle French, from Medieval Latin *suffraganeus,* from Latin *suffragium* "support"]

²suffragan *adj* **1** : of or being a suffragan **2** : of lower rank than a metropolitan or archiepiscopal see

suf·frage \'səf-rij\ *n* **1** : an intercessory prayer **2** : a vote given in deciding a disputed question or in electing a person to office **3** : the right of voting : FRANCHISE; *also* : the exercise of such right [Latin *suffragium* "vote, support"]

suf·frag·ette \ˌsəf-ri-ˈjet\ *n* : a woman who supports suffrage for her sex

suf·frag·ist \'səf-ri-jəst\ *n* : one who supports extension of suffrage especially to women

suf·fuse \sə-ˈfyüz\ *vt* : to spread over or through in the manner of fluid or light : FLUSH, FILL [Latin *suffusus,* past participle of *suffundere* "to pour beneath, suffuse", from *sub-* + *fundere* "to pour"] — **suf·fu·sion** \-ˈfyü-zhən\ *n* — **suf·fu·sive** \-ˈfyü-siv, -ziv\ *adj*

Su·fi \'sü-fē\ *n* : a Muslim mystic [Arabic *ṣūfīy*] — **Sufi** *adj* — **Su·fic** \-fik\ *adj* — **Su·fism** \-ˌfiz-əm\ *n*

¹sug·ar \'shug-ər\ *n* **1** : a sweet crystallizable material that consists wholly or essentially of sucrose, is colorless or white when pure, is obtained commercially from sugarcane or sugar beet and less extensively from sorghum, maples, and palms, and is nutritionally important as a source of dietary carbohydrate and as a sweetener and preservative of other foods **2** : any of various water-soluble compounds that vary widely in sweetness and comprise the simpler carbohydrates [Middle French *sucre*, from Medieval Latin *zuccarum*, from Italian *zucchero*, from Arabic *sukkar*, from Persian *shakar*, from Sanskrit *śarkarā*]

²sug·ar *vb* **sug·ared; sug·ar·ing** \'shüg-ring, -ə-ring\ **1** : to mix, cover, or sprinkle with sugar **2** : to make something less hard to take or bear **3** : to change to crystals of sugar

sugar beet *n* : a white-rooted beet grown for the sugar in its roots

sugar bush *n* : woods in which sugar maples predominate

sug·ar·cane \'shüg-ər-ˌkān\ *n* : a stout tall perennial grass that has broad leaves and is widely grown in warm regions as a source of sugar

sug·ar·coat \-ˌshüg-ər-ˈkōt\ *vt* **1** : to coat with sugar **2** : to make attractive or agreeable on the surface

sug·ar·house \'shüg-ər-ˌhaús\ *n* : a building where sugar is made or refined; *esp* : one where maple sap is boiled in the making of maple syrup and maple sugar

sug·ar·less \'shüg-ər-ləs\ *adj* : containing no sugar

sug·ar·loaf \-ˌlōf\ *n* **1** : refined sugar molded into a cone **2** : a hill or mountain shaped like a sugarloaf — **sugarloaf** *adj*

sugar maple *n* : a maple of eastern North America with 3-lobed to 5-lobed leaves, hard close-grained wood much used for cabinetwork, and sap that is the chief source of maple syrup and maple sugar

sugar of lead : LEAD ACETATE

sugar pine *n* : a lofty pine of California and Oregon that has large cones often 18 inches long and a soft reddish brown wood

sug·ar·plum \'shüg-ər-ˌpləm\ *n* : a round piece of candy

sug·ary \'shüg-rē, -ə-rē\ *adj* **1** : containing, resembling, or tasting of sugar **2** : affectedly or over sweet

sug·gest \səg-ˈjest, sə-ˈjest\ *vt* **1 a** : to put (as a thought, plan, or desire) into a person's mind **b** : to propose as an idea or possibility ⟨*suggest* going for a walk⟩ **2** : to call to mind through close connection or association [Latin *suggestus*, past participle of *suggerere* "to put under, furnish, suggest", from *sub-* + *gerere* "to carry"] — **sug·gest·er** *n* □ SYN SUGGEST, HINT, INTIMATE mean to convey an idea indirectly. SUGGEST stresses putting into the mind by association of ideas; HINT implies the use of slight or remote suggestion with a minimum of overt statement; INTIMATE stresses delicacy of suggestion without connoting any lack of candor.

sug·gest·ible \səg-ˈjes-tə-bəl, sə-ˈjes-\ *adj* : easily influenced by suggestion — **sug·gest·ibil·i·ty** \-ˌjes-tə-ˈbil-ət-ē\ *n*

sug·ges·tion \səg-ˈjes-chən, sə-ˈjes-, -ˈjesh-\ *n* **1 a** : the act or process of suggesting **b** : something suggested **2 a** : the process by which one thought leads to another especially through association of ideas **b** : a means or process of influencing attitudes and behavior hypnotically **3** : a slight indication : TRACE

sug·ges·tive \səg-ˈjes-tiv, sə-ˈjes-\ *adj* **1 a** : giving a suggestion : INDICATIVE **b** : full of suggestions : PROVOCATIVE **c** : stirring mental associations **2** : suggesting or tending to suggest something indelicate : RISQUÉ — **sug·ges·tive·ly** *adv* — **sug·ges·tive·ness** *n*

sui·cid·al \ˌsü-ə-ˈsīd-l\ *adj* **1** : relating to or of the nature of suicide **2** : marked by an impulse to kill oneself **3 a** : very dangerous to life ⟨*suicidal* risks⟩ **b** : destructive of one's own interests — **sui·cid·al·ly** \-l-ē\ *adv*

sui·cide \'sü-ə-ˌsīd\ *n* **1 a** : the act of taking one's own life voluntarily **b** : ruin of one's own interests **2** : one that commits or attempts suicide [Latin *sui* "of oneself" + English *-cide*]

sui gen·er·is \ˌsü-ˌī-ˈjen-ə-rəs, ˌsü-ē-ˈjen-, -ˈgen-\ *adj* : forming a class alone : PECULIAR [Latin, "of its own kind"]

¹suit \'süt\ *n* **1** : an action or process in a court for enforcing a right or claim **2** : an act or instance of suing or seeking by entreaty; *esp* : COURTSHIP **3** : a number of things used together : SET **4** : a set of garments: as **a** : an outer costume of two or more pieces **b** : a costume to be worn for a special purpose or under particular conditions ⟨gym *suit*⟩ **5 a** : all the playing cards of one kind (as spades or hearts) in a pack; *also* : all the cards of the same suit held by a player ⟨a 5-card *suit*⟩ **b** : all the dominoes bearing the same number on one half of the face [Old French *siute* "act of following, suite", derived from Latin *sequi* "to follow"]

²suit *vb* **1** : to be in harmony : AGREE **2** : to be appropriate or acceptable **3** : to outfit with clothes : DRESS **4** : ADAPT ⟨*suit* the action to the word⟩ **5 a** : to be proper for : BEFIT **b** : to be becoming to **6** : to meet the needs or desires of

suit·able \'süt-ə-bəl\ *adj* **1** : adapted to a use or purpose **2** : satisfying propriety : PROPER ⟨clothes *suitable* to the occasion⟩ **3** : QUALIFIED 1 ⟨*suitable* candidates⟩ SYN see FIT — **suit·abil·i·ty** \ˌsüt-ə-ˈbil-ət-ē\ *n* — **suit·able·ness** \'süt-ə-bəl-nəs\ *n* — **suit·ably** \-blē\ *adv*

suit·case \'süt-ˌkās\ *n* : TRAVELING BAG; *esp* : a rigid flat rectangular one

suite \'swēt, *2c is also* 'süt\ *n* **1** : RETINUE; *esp* : the personal staff accompanying a ruler, diplomat, or dignitary on official business **2** : a group of things forming a unit or making up a collection : SET: as **a** : a group of rooms occupied as a unit : APARTMENT **b** (1) : a 17th and 18th century instrumental musical form consisting of a series of dances in the same or related keys (2) : a modern instrumental composition in a number of usually descriptive movements (3) : an orchestral concert arrangement in suite form of material drawn from a longer work (as a ballet) **c** : a set of matched furniture for a room [French, from Old French *siute*]

suit·ing \'süt-ing\ *n* : fabric for suits of clothes

suit·or \'süt-ər\ *n* **1** : one that petitions or pleads **2** : a party to a suit at law **3** : a man who courts a woman or seeks to marry her

su·ki·ya·ki \ˌskē-ˈäk-ē, ˌsúk-ē-ˈäk-ē -ˈyäk-\ *n* : a dish prepared from meat, soybean curd, and vegetables (as onions, celery, bamboo sprouts, and mushrooms) cooked in soy sauce, sake, and sugar [Japanese, from *suki* "spade" + *yaki* "roast"]

Suk·koth \'súk-ˌōt, -ˌōth, -ˌōs\ *n* : a Jewish holiday celebrated in September or October as a harvest festival of thanksgiving and to commemorate the temporary shelters used by the Jews during their wanderings in the wilderness [Hebrew *ḥag has-sukkōth* "feast of the tabernacles"]

sul·cus \'səl-kəs\ *n, pl* **sul·ci** \-ˌkī, -ˌkē\ : an anatomical furrow or groove; *esp* : a shallow furrow on the surface of the brain separating adjacent convolutions [Latin] — **sul·cate** \-ˌkāt\ *adj*

sulf- *combining form* : sulfur : containing sulfur ⟨*sulf*ide⟩

sul·fa \'səl-fə\ *adj* **1** : related chemically to sulfanilamide **2** : of, relating to, or employing sulfa drugs [short for *sulfanilamide*]

sul·fa·di·a·zine \ˌsəl-fə-ˈdī-ə-ˌzēn\ *n* : a sulfa drug used especially in the treatment of meningitis, pneumonia, and intestinal infections [*sulfa* + *di-* + *az-* "containing nitrogen" (from French *azote* "nitrogen") + *-ine*]

sulfa drug *n* : any of various synthetic organic bacteria-inhibiting drugs that are sulfonamides closely related chemically to sulfanilamide

sul·fa·mer·a·zine \ˌsəl-fə-ˈmer-ə-ˌzēn\ *n* : a sulfa drug with uses similar to those of sulfadiazine [*sulfa* + *-mer* (from Greek *meros* "part") + *-azine* (as in *sulfadiazine*)]

sul·fa·nil·a·mide \ˌsəl-fə-ˈnil-ə-ˌmīd, -məd\ *n* : a crystalline compound that is the amide of sulfanilic acid

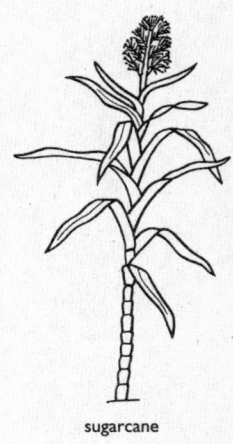

sugarcane

\ə\ abut	\ng\ sing
\ər\ further	\ō\ bone
\a\ mat	\ȯ\ saw
\ā\ take	\ȯi\ coin
\ä\ cot, cart	\th\ thin
\aú\ out	\th\ this
\ch\ chin	\ü\ food
\e\ pet	\ú\ foot
\ē\ easy	\y\ yet
\g\ go	\yü\ few
\i\ tip	\yú\ cure
\ī\ life	\zh\ vision
\j\ job	

and the parent compound of most of the sulfa drugs [*sulfanil*ic + *amide*]

sul·fa·nil·ic acid \,səl-fə-,nil-ik-\ *n* : a crystalline acid obtained from aniline and used especially in making dyes [*sulf-* + *anil*ine + *-ic*]

sul·fate \'səl-,fāt\ *n* : a salt or ester of sulfuric acid

sul·fide \'səl-,fīd\ *n* : a compound of sulfur with one or more other elements : a salt of hydrogen sulfide

sul·fite \'səl-,fīt\ *n* : a salt or ester of sulfurous acid — **sul·fit·ic** \,səl-'fit-ik\ *adj*

sul·fon·amide \,səl-'fän-ə-,mīd, -'fō-nə-, -məd\ *n* : the amide (as sulfanilamide) of a sulfonic acid; *also* : SULFA DRUG

sul·fon·ic acid \,səl-,fän-ik-, -'fōn-\ *n* : any of numerous acids that may be derived from sulfuric acid by replacement of a hydroxyl group by either an inorganic anion or a univalent organic radical [derived from *sulf-*]

sul·fur *or* **sul·phur** \'səl-fər\ *n* : a nonmetallic element that occurs either free or in combined form, is a constituent of proteins, exists in several forms including yellow crystals, and is used especially in the chemical and paper industries, in rubber vulcanization, and in medicine for treating skin diseases — see ELEMENT table [Latin]

sulfur dioxide *n* : a heavy strong-smelling gas SO_2 that is used especially in making sulfuric acid, in bleaching, as a preservative, and as a refrigerant and is a major air pollutant especially in industrial areas

sul·fu·ric *or* **sul·phu·ric** \,səl-'fyûr-ik\ *adj* : of, relating to, or containing sulfur especially in a higher valence

sulfuric acid *n* : a heavy corrosive oily strong acid H_2SO_4 that is colorless when pure and is a vigorous oxidizing and dehydrating agent

sul·fu·rous *or* **sul·phu·rous** \'səl-fyə-rəs, -fə-, *also esp for 1* ,səl-'fyûr-əs\ *adj* 1 : of, relating to, or containing sulfur especially in a lower valence 2 a : of, relating to, or dealing with the fire of hell : INFERNAL b : FIERY, INFLAMED ⟨*sulfurous* sermons⟩ c : PROFANE, BLASPHEMOUS ⟨*sulfurous* language⟩ — **sul·fu·rous·ly** *adv* — **sul·fu·rous·ness** *n*

sulfurous acid *n* : a weak unstable acid H_2SO_3 known in solution and through its salts and used as a reducing and bleaching agent

sulfur trioxide *n* : a compound SO_3 that is a heavy corrosive liquid when first produced but that changes into a solid form and is a powerful oxidizing agent

¹sulk \'səlk\ *vt* : to be moodily silent or ill-humored : nurse a grievance [back-formation from *sulky*]

²sulk *n* 1 : the state of one sulking — often used in pl. ⟨had a case of the *sulks*⟩ 2 : a sulky mood or spell ⟨was in a *sulk*⟩

¹sulky \'səl-kē\ *adj* **sulk·i·er; -est** 1 : inclined to sulk : given to fits of sulking 2 : MALCONTENT, GLOOMY [probably from obsolete *sulke* "sluggish"] SYN see SULLEN — **sulk·i·ly** \-kə-lē\ *adv* — **sulk·i·ness** \-kē-nəs\ *n*

²sulky *n, pl* **sulk·ies** : a light 2-wheeled vehicle having a seat for the driver only and usually no body [probably from ¹*sulky*]

²sulky

sul·len \'səl-ən\ *adj* 1 a : gloomily or resentfully silent or repressed b : suggesting a sullen state ⟨a *sullen* refusal⟩ 2 : dull or somber in sound or color 3 : DISMAL 1, GLOOMY [Middle English *solain* "sullen, solitary"] — **sul·len·ly** *adv* — **sul·len·ness** \'səl-ən-nəs, -ən-əs\ *n* □ SYN SULLEN, SURLY, SULKY mean showing a forbidding or disagreeable mood. SULLEN implies a gloomy silent bad humor and a refusal to be sociable; SURLY implies rudeness and gruffness especially in response to requests or questions; SULKY suggests childish resentment expressed in fits of peevish sullenness.

sul·ly \'səl-ē\ *vb* **sul·lied; sul·ly·ing** : to make soiled or tarnished [probably from Middle French *soiller* "to soil"]

sul·phur butterfly \,səl-fər-\ *n* : any of numerous rather small butterflies having usually yellow or orange wings with a black border

sulphur yellow *n* : a brilliant greenish yellow

sul·tan \'səlt-n\ *n* : a sovereign especially of a Muslim state [Middle French, from Arabic *sulṭān*]

sul·tana \,səl-'tan-ə\ *n* 1 : a female member of a sultan's family; *esp* : a sultan's wife 2 a : a pale yellow seedless grape grown for raisins and wine b : the raisin of this grape [Italian, from *sultano* "sultan", from Arabic *sulṭān*]

sul·tan·ate \'səlt-n-,āt\ *n* 1 : the office, dignity, or power of a sultan 2 : a state or country governed by a sultan

sul·try \'səl-trē\ *adj* **sul·tri·er; -est** 1 : very hot and humid 2 : burning hot ⟨the *sultry* sun⟩ 3 : SENSUAL, VOLUPTUOUS ⟨*sultry* glances⟩ [derived from *swelter*] — **sul·tri·ly** \-trə-lē\ *adv* — **sul·tri·ness** \-trē-nəs\ *n*

¹sum \'səm\ *n* 1 : an indefinite or specified amount of money 2 : the whole amount 3 a : SUMMARY b : GIST 4 a : the result obtained by the mathematical operation of addition ⟨the *sum* of 5 and 7 is 12⟩ b : the limit of the sum of the first *n* terms of an infinite series as *n* increases indefinitely c : a problem in arithmetic [Old French *summe,* from Latin *summa,* from *summus* "highest"] □ SYN AMOUNT, AGGREGATE, TOTAL: SUM indicates the result of simple addition of numbers or particulars; AMOUNT implies the result of accumulating or successive additions; AGGREGATE stresses the notion of the grouping or massing together of distinct individuals; TOTAL stresses the completeness or inclusiveness of the addition.

²sum *vb* **summed; sum·ming** 1 : to calculate the sum of : COUNT 2 : to reach a sum : AMOUNT — usually used with *to* 3 : SUMMARIZE — usually used with *up* ⟨*sum* up the evidence⟩

su·mac *or* **su·mach** \'sü-,mak, 'shü-\ *n* 1 : any of a genus of trees, shrubs, and woody vines with feathery compound leaves turning to brilliant red in autumn and spikes or loose clusters of red or whitish berries — compare POISON IVY, POISON OAK 2 : a material used in tanning and dyeing made of the leaves and other parts of sumac [Middle French *sumac,* from Arabic *summāq*]

Su·mer·i·an \sû-'mer-ē-ən, -'mir-\ *n* 1 : a native of Sumer 2 : the language of the Sumerians surviving as a literary language after the rise of Akkadian — **Sumerian** *adj*

sum·ma cum lau·de \,sûm-ə-,kûm-'laùd-ə, -'laùd-ē; ,səm-ə-,kəm-'lȯd-ē\ *adv or adj* : with highest academic distinction ⟨graduated *summa cum laude*⟩ [Latin, "with highest praise"]

sum·mand \'səm-,and, ,sə-'mand\ *n* : a term in a summation : ADDEND [Medieval Latin *summandus,* from *summare* "to sum", from Latin *summa* "sum"]

sum·ma·rize \'səm-ə-,rīz\ *vb* 1 : to tell in or reduce to a summary 2 : to make a summary — **sum·ma·ri·zation** \,səm-rə-'zā-shən, -ə-rə-\ *n* — **sum·ma·riz·er** \'səm-ə-,rī-zər\ *n*

¹sum·ma·ry \'səm-ə-rē\ *adj* 1 : expressing or covering the main points briefly 2 : done without delay or formality : quickly carried out [Medieval Latin *summarius,* from Latin *summa* "sum"] — **sum·mar·i·ly** \,sə-'mer-ə-lē, 'səm-ə-rə-lē\ *adv*

²summary *n, pl* **-ries** : a concise statement of the main ideas (as of a book)

sum·ma·tion \,sə-'mā-shən\ *n* 1 : the act or process of forming a sum : ADDITION 2 : SUM 2, 3a, 4a 3 : a final part of an argument reviewing points made and expressing conclusions — **sum·ma·tion·al** \-shnəl, -shən-l\ *adj*

¹sum·mer \'səm-ər\ *n* 1 a : the season between spring and autumn comprising usually the months of June, July, and August or as determined astronomically extending from the June solstice to the September equinox b : the warmer half of the year 2 : YEAR ⟨a youth of 16 *summers*⟩ 3 : a time or season of fulfillment [Old English *sumor*]

²summer *vb* **sum·mered; sum·mer·ing** \'səm-ring, -ə-ring\ **1** : to pass the summer **2** : to keep or carry through the summer; *esp* : to provide with pasture during the summer

³summer *n* : a large horizontal beam or stone used especially in building (as for the lintel of a door or window) [Middle French *somier* "packhorse, beam", derived from Late Latin *sagma* "packsaddle", from Greek]

sum·mer·house \'səm-ər-,haus\ *n* : a rustic covered structure in a garden or park to provide a cool shady retreat in summer

summer kitchen *n* : a small building or shed built adjacent to a house and used as a kitchen in warm weather

sum·mer·sault *archaic variant of* SOMERSAULT

summer school *n* : a school or school session conducted in summer enabling students to accelerate progress toward a degree, to make up credits lost through absence or failure, or to round out professional education

summer squash *n* : any of various garden squashes closely related to the typical pumpkins and used as a vegetable while immature and before hardening of the seeds and rind

sum·mer·time \'səm-ər-,tīm\ *n* : the summer season or a period like summer

summer time *n, chiefly British* : DAYLIGHT SAVING TIME

sum·mer·wood \'səm-ər-,wùd\ *n* : the harder less porous portion of an annual ring of wood that develops late in the growing season — compare SPRINGWOOD

sum·mery \'səm-rē, -ə-rē\ *adj* : of, resembling, or fit for summer

sum·mit \'səm-ət\ *n* **1** : TOP, APEX; *esp* : the highest point (as of a mountain) **2** : the highest level attainable : PINNACLE **3** : the highest level (as of officials) [Middle French *somete*, from *sum* "top", from Latin *summus* "highest"] □ SYN SUMMIT, PEAK, PINNACLE, APEX mean the highest point attained or attainable. SUMMIT implies the topmost level attainable ⟨a view from the *summit*⟩ PEAK suggests the highest among other high points ⟨*peak* of excitement⟩ PINNACLE suggests a dizzying often insecure height ⟨reach a *pinnacle* of success on the stage⟩ APEX implies the point at which all ascending lines converge and contrasts with *base* ⟨*apex* of cultural achievement⟩

sum·mon \'səm-ən\ *vt* **1** : to issue a call to convene **2** : to command by service of a summons to appear in court **3** : to send for : CALL ⟨*summon* a physician⟩ **4** : to call forth or arouse ⟨*summon* up enough courage to act⟩ [Old French *somondre*, from Latin *summonēre* "to remind secretly", from *sub-* "secretly" + *monēre* "to warn"] — **sum·mon·er** *n*

¹sum·mons \'səm-ənz\ *n, pl* **sum·mons·es** **1** : the act of summoning; *esp* : a call by authority to appear at a place named or to attend to some duty **2** : a warning or notice to appear in court **3** : a call, signal, or knock that summons

²summons *vt* : SUMMON 2

sum·mum bo·num \,sùm-əm-'bō-nəm, ,səm-\ *n* : the supreme or greatest good [Latin]

su·mo \'sü-mō\ *n* : a Japanese form of wrestling in which each competitor seeks to force the opponent out of the ring or make the opponent touch the ground with any part of the body other than the soles of the feet [Japanese *sumō*]

sump \'səmp\ *n* : a pit or reservoir serving as a receptacle or as a drain for fluids [Middle English *sompe* "swamp"]

sump·ter \'səm-tər, 'səmp-\ *n* : a pack animal [Middle French *sometier* "driver of a packhorse", derived from Late Latin *sagma* "packsaddle", from Greek]

sump·tu·ary \'səm-chə-,wer-ē, 'səmp-\ *adj* **1** : designed to regulate personal expenses and especially to prevent luxury **2** : designed to regulate habits on moral or religious grounds [Latin *sumptuarius*, from *sumptus* "expense"]

sump·tu·ous \'səm-chə-wəs, 'səmp-, -chəs\ *adj* : involving large expense : LUXURIOUS ⟨a *sumptuous* feast⟩ [Middle French *sumptueux*, from Latin *sumptuosus*, from *sumptus* "expense", from *sumere* "to take, spend"] — **sump·tu·ous·ly** *adv* — **sump·tu·ous·ness** *n*

sum total *n* **1** : a total arrived at through the counting of sums **2** : total result : TOTALITY ⟨the *sum total* of weeks of discussion was a deadlock⟩

¹sun \'sən\ *n* **1 a** : the luminous celestial body around which the planets revolve, from which they receive heat and light, and which has a mean distance from the earth of 93,000,000 miles (150,000,000 kilometers) and a diameter of 864,000 miles (1,390,000 kilometers) **b** : a celestial body like the sun **2** : the heat or light radiated from the sun : SUNSHINE **3** : one resembling the sun usually in brilliance **4** : the rising or setting of the sun ⟨from *sun* to *sun*⟩ [Old English *sunne*]

²sun *vb* **sunned; sun·ning** **1** : to expose to or as if to the rays of the sun **2** : to sun oneself

sun·baked \'sən-,bākt\ *adj* **1** : baked by exposure to sunlight ⟨*sunbaked* bricks⟩ **2** : heated, parched, or compacted especially by excessive sunlight

sun·bath \'sən-,bath, -,bàth\ *n* : exposure to sunlight or a sunlamp

sun·bathe \-,bāth\ *vi* : to take a sunbath — **sun·bath·er** \-,bā-thər\ *n*

sun·beam \-,bēm\ *n* : a ray of sunlight

sun·bird \-,bərd\ *n* : any of a family of brightly colored Old World birds suggesting hummingbirds

sun·block \-,bläk\ *n* : a preparation designed to block out more of the sun's rays than a sunscreen

sun·bon·net \-,bän-ət\ *n* : a woman's bonnet with a wide brim framing the face and usually a ruffle at the back to protect the neck from the sun

¹sun·burn \-,bərn\ *vb* **1** : to burn or discolor by the sun **2** : to cause or undergo sunburn

²sunburn *n* : a skin inflammation caused by excessive exposure to sunlight

sun·burst \'sən-,bərst\ *n* **1** : a burst of sunlight especially through a break in the clouds **2** : a stylized representation of a sun surrounded by rays

sun·dae \'sən-dē\ *n* : a portion of ice cream served with topping (as crushed fruit or nuts) [probably alteration of *Sunday*]

¹Sun·day \'sən-dē\ *n* : the 1st day of the week : the Christian Sabbath [Old English *sunnandæg*, literally, "day of the sun"] □ SYN SABBATH: SUNDAY is the name of the first day of the week; SABBATH is the institution of observing one day of the week as a period of rest and worship, the day being Sunday for most Christians, Saturday for Jews and some Christians

²Sunday *adj* **1** : of, relating to, or associated with Sunday **2** : AMATEUR, DILETTANTE ⟨*Sunday* painters⟩

³Sunday *vi* : to spend Sunday ⟨was *Sundaying* in the country⟩

Sunday best *n* : one's best clothes

Sunday punch *n* : a blow in boxing capable of knocking out an opponent; *also* : a devastating blow

Sunday School *n* : a school held on Sunday for religious education

sun deck *n* : a deck of a ship or a roof or terrace used for sunbathing

sun·der \'sən-dər\ *vb* **sun·dered; sun·der·ing** \-də-ring, -dring\ : to break, force, or come apart or in two : sever especially with violence [Old English *gesundrian, syndrian*]

sun·dew \'sən-,dü, -,dyü\ *n* : any of a genus of bog herbs that trap and digest insects with their hairy glandular leaves

sun·di·al \-,dī-əl, -,dīl\ *n* : a device to show the time of day by the position of the shadow cast on a plate or disk typically by an upright indicator

sundew

\ə\ abut	\ng\ sing
\ər\ further	\ō\ bone
\a\ mat	\ò\ saw
\ā\ take	\òi\ coin
\ä\ cot, cart	\th\ thin
\aú\ out	\th\ this
\ch\ chin	\ü\ food
\e\ pet	\ù\ foot
\ē\ easy	\y\ yet
\g\ go	\yü\ few
\i\ tip	\yù\ cure
\ī\ life	\zh\ vision
\j\ job	

sunfish 1

sun dog *n* : PARHELION

sun·down \'sən-,daùn\ *n* : SUNSET 2

sun·dries \'sən-drēz\ *n pl* : miscellaneous small articles or items (as pins, needles, or thread)

sun·drops \'sən-,dräps\ *n sing or pl* : a day-flowering herb similar to the related evening primrose

¹**sun·dry** \'sən-drē\ *adj* : VARIOUS 3 ⟨for *sundry* reasons⟩ [Old English *syndrig* "separate, distinct"]

²**sundry** *pron, pl in construction* : various ones — usually used in the phrase *all and sundry*

sun·fish \'sən-,fish\ *n* **1** : a large sea fish with a very deep, short, and flat body, high fins, and a small mouth **2** : any of a family of American freshwater fishes that are related to the perches and usually have a deep compressed body and a metallic luster

sun·flow·er \-,flaü-ər, -,flaür\ *n* : any of a genus of tall herbs related to the daisies that are often grown for their showy yellow-rayed flower heads and for their oil-rich seeds

sung *past of* SING

Sung \'sùng\ *n* : a Chinese dynasty dated A.D. 960–1279 and marked by cultural refinement and achievements in philosophy, literature, and art [Chinese (Pekingese dialect) *Sung*⁴]

sun·glass·es \'sən-,glas-əz\ *n pl* : tinted glasses that protect the eyes from sunlight

sun–god \'sən-,gäd\ *n* : a god that represents or personifies the sun in various religions

sunk *past of* SINK

sunk·en \'səng-kən\ *adj* **1** : submerged especially in the depths of a body of water ⟨*sunken* ships⟩ **2** : fallen in : HOLLOW ⟨*sunken* cheeks⟩ **3 a** : lying in a depression ⟨a *sunken* garden⟩ **b** : constructed below the general floor level ⟨a *sunken* living room⟩

sun·lamp \'sən-,lamp\ *n* : an electric lamp designed to emit radiation of wavelengths from ultraviolet to infrared

sun·less \'sən-ləs\ *adj* : lacking sunlight : GLOOMY

sun·light \-,līt\ *n* : the light of the sun : SUNSHINE

sun·lit \-,lit\ *adj* : lighted by or as if by the sun

sun·ny \'sən-ē\ *adj* **sun·ni·er; -est** **1** : bright with or warmed by sunshine ⟨a *sunny* day⟩ ⟨*sunny* rooms⟩ **2** : MERRY 1, CHEERFUL ⟨*sunny* dispositions⟩ — **sun·ni·ly** \'sən-l-ē\ *adv* — **sun·ni·ness** \'sən-ē-nəs\ *n*

sun parlor *n* : a glass-enclosed porch or living room with a sunny exposure — called also *sun porch, sunroom*

sun·rise \'sən-,rīz\ *n* **1** : the apparent rising of the sun above the horizon; *also* : the accompanying atmospheric effects **2** : the time at which the sun rises

sun·screen \-,skrēn\ *n* : a substance (as para-aminobenzoic acid) used in suntan preparations to protect the skin from excessive ultraviolet radiation

sun·set \-,set\ *n* **1** : the apparent descent of the sun below the horizon; *also* : the accompanying atmospheric effects **2** : the time at which the sun sets **3** : a period of decline; *esp* : old age

sun·shade \-,shād\ *n* : something used as a protection from the sun's rays: as **a** : PARASOL **b** : AWNING

sun·shine \-,shīn\ *n* **1 a** : the sun's light or direct rays **b** : the warmth and light given by the sun's rays **c** : a spot or surface on which the sun's light shines **2** : something that radiates warmth, cheer, or happiness — **sun·shiny** \-,shī-nē\ *adj*

sun·spot \-,spät\ *n* : one of the dark spots that appear from time to time on the sun's surface and are usually visible only with the telescope

sun·stroke \-,strōk\ *n* : heatstroke caused by direct exposure to the sun

sun·struck \-,strək\ *adj* : affected or touched by the sun

sun·suit \-,süt\ *n* : an outfit (as of halter and shorts) worn usually for sunbathing and play

sun·tan \-,tan\ *n* **1** : a browning of the skin from exposure to the rays of the sun **2** *pl* : a tan-colored summer uniform — **sun·tanned** \-,tand\ *adj*

sun·up \'sən-,əp\ *n* : SUNRISE

¹**sun·ward** \-wərd\ *or* **sun·wards** \-wərdz\ *adv* : toward the sun

²**sunward** *adj* : facing the sun

sun·wise \'sən-,wīz\ *adv* : CLOCKWISE

¹**sup** \'səp\ *vb* **supped; sup·ping** **1** : to take or drink in swallows or gulps **2** *chiefly dialect* : to take food and especially liquid food into the mouth a little at a time (as from a spoon) [Old English *sūpan, suppan*]

²**sup** *n* : a mouthful especially of liquor or broth : SIP; *also* : a small quantity of liquid ⟨a *sup* of tea⟩

³**sup** *vi* **supped; sup·ping** **1** : to eat the evening meal **2** : to make one's supper — used with *on* or *off* ⟨*supped* on roast beef⟩ [Old French *souper*, from *soupe* "sop, soup"]

¹**su·per** \'sü-pər\ *n* **1 a** : SUPERNUMERARY **2 b** : SUPERINTENDENT, SUPERVISOR **2** : a removable upper story of a beehive **3** : a superfine grade or extra large size

²**super** *adj* **1** : very good or valuable **2** : very large, powerful, or great ⟨a *super* bomb⟩ ⟨*super* secrecy⟩ [short for *superfine*] — **super** *adv*

super- *prefix* **1 a** : over and above : higher in quantity, quality, or degree than : more than ⟨*super*human⟩ **b** : in addition : extra ⟨*super*tax⟩ **c** : exceeding or so as to exceed a norm ⟨*super*heat⟩ **2 a** : situated or placed above, on, or at the top of ⟨*super*structure⟩ **b** : next above or higher ⟨*super*tonic⟩ **3** : constituting a more inclusive category than that specified ⟨*super*family⟩ **4** : superior in status, title, or position ⟨*super*power⟩ [Latin, "over, above, in addition to", from *super* "over, above, on top of"]

See *super-* and 2d element

superadministrator	superintelligence	supersmooth
superambitious	superintelligent	supersoft
superathlete	superintensity	supersophisticated
superbomb	superluxury	superspecial
superbomber	supermasculine	superspecialist
superbright	supermassive	superspecialization
superbureaucrat	supermodern	superspecialized
supercautious	supernation	superspectacle
superchic	supernational	superspectacular
superclean	superpatriot	superspy
supercolossal	superpatriotic	superstate
supercomfortable	superpatriotism	superstore
supercompetitive	superpersonal	superstrength
superconfident	superplane	superstrong
superconservative	superplayer	supersubtle
superconvenient	superpolite	supersubtlety
supercop	superport	supersurgeon
supercorporation	superpowerful	supersweet
superdiplomat	superrich	supersystem
supereffective	superromantic	supertanker
superefficiency	supersafe	superthick
superefficient	supersalesman	superthin
superfast	superscout	superthriller
supergood	supersecrecy	supertight
supergovernment	supersecret	supervirtuoso
supergroup	supersize	superwave
superheroine	supersized	superweapon
superhit	supersleuth	superwide
superintellectual	superslick	

su·per·a·ble \'sü-pə-rə-bəl, -prə-bəl\ *adj* : capable of being overcome or conquered ⟨*superable* odds⟩ [Latin *superabilis*, from *superare* "to surmount", from *super* "over"] — **su·per·a·ble·ness** *n* — **su·per·a·bly** \-blē\ *adv*

su·per·abound \,sü-pə-rə-'baund\ *vi* : to abound or prevail greatly or to excess

su·per·abun·dant \-'bən-dənt\ *adj* : more than ample : EXCESSIVE — **su·per·abun·dance** \-dəns\ *n* — **su·per·abun·dant·ly** *adv*

su·per·add \,sü-pə-'rad\ *vt* : to add over and above something or in extra or superfluous amount — **su·per·ad·di·tion** \'pə-rə-'dish-ən\ *n*

su·per·an·nu·ate \,sü-pə-'ran-yə-,wāt\ *vb* **1 a** : to make or declare obsolete or out-of-date **b** : to retire and pension because of age or infirmity **2** : to become retired or antiquated [back-formation from *superannuated*] — **su·per·an·nu·a·tion** \-₊ran-yə-'wā-shən\ *n*

su·per·an·nu·at·ed *adj* **1** : too old or outmoded for work or use **2** : retired on a pension [Medieval Latin *superannuatus*, past participle of *superannuari* "to be too old", from Latin *super-* + *annus* "year"]

su·perb \su̇-'pərb\ *adj* : extremely fine, brilliant, or splendid ⟨a *superb* craftsman⟩ ⟨*superb* palaces⟩ [Latin *superbus* "excellent, proud", from *super* "above"] — **su·perb·ly** *adv* — **su·perb·ness** *n*

su·per·car·go \₊sü-pər-'kär-gō\ *n* : an officer on a merchant ship in charge of the commercial concerns of the voyage [Spanish *sobrecargo*, from *sobre-* "over" (from Latin *super-*) + *cargo* "load, charge"]

su·per·charge \'sü-pər-₊chärj\ *vt* **1** : to supply a charge to the intake of (as an engine) at a pressure higher than that of the surrounding atmosphere **2** : PRESSURIZE 1

su·per·char·ger \-₊chär-jər\ *n* : a device (as a blower or compressor) for increasing the volume air charge of an internal-combustion engine or for pressurizing the cabin of an airplane

su·per·cil·i·ous \₊sü-pər-'sil-ē-əs\ *adj* : haughtily scornful [Latin *superciliosus*, from *supercilium* "eyebrow, haughtiness"] — **su·per·cil·i·ous·ly** *adv* — **su·per·cil·i·ous·ness** *n*

su·per·com·put·er \'sü-pər-kəm-₊pyüt-ər\ : a large very fast mainframe used especially for scientific computations

su·per·con·duc·tiv·i·ty \₊sü-pər-₊kän-₊dək-'tiv-ət-ē\ *n* : a complete disappearance of electrical resistance in various metals at temperatures near absolute zero — **su·per·con·duc·tive** \-kən-'dək-tiv\ *adj* — **su·per·con·duc·tor** \-kən-'dək-tər\ *n*

su·per·cool \₊sü-pər-'kül\ *vt* : to cool below the freezing point without solidification or crystallization

su·per·ego \₊sü-pə-'rē-gō\ *n* : the one of the three divisions of the psyche in psychoanalytic theory that is only partly conscious, represents the incorporation of parental conscience and the rules of society, and functions to reward and punish through a system of moral attitudes, conscience, and a sense of guilt — compare EGO 3, ID

su·per·em·i·nent \-'rem-ə-nənt\ *adj* : extremely high, distinguished, or conspicuous — **su·per·em·i·nence** \-nəns\ *n* — **su·per·em·i·nent·ly** *adv*

su·per·er·o·ga·tion \₊sü-pə-₊rer-ə-'gā-shən\ *n* : the act of performing more than is required by duty, obligation, or need [Medieval Latin *supererogatio*, from *supererogare* "to perform beyond the call of duty", derived from Latin *super-* + *e-* + *rogare* "to ask"]

su·per·erog·a·to·ry \₊sü-pə-ri-'räg-ə-₊tōr-ē, -₊tȯr-\ *adj* **1** : observed or performed to an extent not demanded or needed **2** : SUPERFLUOUS, NONESSENTIAL

su·per·fam·i·ly \'sü-pər-₊fam-lē, -ə-lē\ *n* : a category of taxonomic classification ranking next above a family

su·per·fi·cial \₊sü-pər-'fish-əl\ *adj* **1 a** : of or relating to a surface **b** : situated on or near or affecting only the surface **2** : concerned only with the obvious or apparent : not profound or thorough : SHALLOW [Late Latin *superficialis*, from Latin *superficies* "surface", from *super-* + *facies* "face"] — **su·per·fi·ci·al·i·ty** \-₊fish-ē-'al-ət-ē\ *n* — **su·per·fi·cial·ly** \-fish-lē, -ə-lē\ *adv* — **su·per·fi·cial·ness** \-fish-əl-nəs\ *n* □ SYN SUPERFICIAL, CURSORY, SHALLOW mean lacking in depth, solidity, or completeness. SUPERFICIAL implies a concern only with what appears at the surface or at first glance; CURSORY suggests a neglect of details through haste or indifference; SHALLOW is usually derogatory and implies lack of depth in knowledge, reasoning, emotions, or character.

su·per·fi·cies \-'fish-ēz, -ē-₊ēz\ *n, pl* **superficies** **1** : the surface of a body or the boundary of a region of space

2 : the external aspects or appearance of a thing [Latin, "surface"]

su·per·fine \₊sü-pər-'fīn\ *adj* **1** : very refined : FINICKY **2** : very finely divided **3** : of high quality or grade

su·per·flu·i·ty \₊sü-pər-'flü-ət-ē\ *n, pl* **-ties** **1** : EXCESS 1a, OVERSUPPLY **2** : something unnecessary or more than enough

su·per·flu·ous \su̇-'pər-flə-wəs\ *adj* : exceeding what is sufficient or necessary : EXTRA [Latin *superfluus*, from *superfluere* "to overflow", from *super-* + *fluere* "to flow"] — **su·per·flu·ous·ly** *adv* — **su·per·flu·ous·ness** *n*

su·per·gi·ant \'sü-pər-₊jī-ənt\ *n* : a star of very great luminosity and enormous size

su·per·glue \-₊glü\ *n* : a very strong glue; *esp* : a glue whose chief ingredient is a substance that becomes adhesive by polymerization rather than evaporation of a solvent

su·per·heat \₊sü-pər-'hēt\ *vt* **1 a** : to heat (steam) to a higher temperature than the normal boiling point of water **b** : to heat (a liquid) above the boiling point without converting to vapor **2** : to heat very much or excessively — **su·per·heat·er** *n*

su·per·hero \'sü-per-₊hē-rō, -₊hiər-ō\ *n* : a fictional hero having extraordinary or superhuman powers; *also* : a very successful person

su·per·het·er·o·dyne \₊sü-pər-'het-ə-rə-₊dīn\ *adj* : of or relating to a form of radio reception in which beats are produced of a frequency above audibility but below that of the received signals and the current of the beat frequency is then rectified, amplified, and finally rectified again so as to reproduce the sound [*super*sonic + *heterodyne*] — **superheterodyne** *n*

su·per·high frequency \'sü-pər-₊hī-\ *n* : a radio frequency in the range between 3000 and 30,000 megacycles — abbreviation SHF

su·per·high·way \₊sü-pər-'hī-₊wā\ *n* : a broad highway designed for high-speed traffic

su·per·hu·man \-'hyü-mən, -'yü-\ *adj* **1** : being above the human : DIVINE **2** : exceeding normal human power, size, or capability : HERCULEAN ⟨*superhuman* effort⟩ — **su·per·hu·man·ly** *adv*

su·per·im·pose \₊sü-pə-rim-'pōz\ *vt* : to place or lay over or above something — **su·per·im·pos·able** \-'pō-zə-bəl\ *adj* — **su·per·im·po·si·tion** \-₊rim-pə-'zish-ən\ *n*

su·per·in·cum·bent \-rin-'kəm-bənt\ *adj* : lying or resting and usually exerting pressure on something else [Latin *superincumbens*, present participle of *superincumbere* "to lie on top of", from *super-* + *incumbere* "to lie down on"] — **su·per·in·cum·bent·ly** *adv*

su·per·in·duce \-rin-'düs, -'dyüs\ *vt* : to introduce as an addition over or above something already existing [Latin *superinducere*, from *super-* + *inducere* "to lead in"] — **su·per·in·duc·tion** \-'dək-shən\ *n*

su·per·in·tend \₊sü-pə-rin-'tend, ₊sü-prin-, ₊sü-pərn-\ *vt* : to have or exercise the charge and oversight of : DIRECT [Late Latin *superintendere*, from Latin *super-* + *intendere* "to attend, direct attention to"]

su·per·in·tend·ence \-'ten-dəns\ *or* **su·per·in·tend·en·cy** \-dən-sē\ *n, pl* **-enc·es** *or* **-en·cies** : the act, duty, or office of superintending or overseeing

su·per·in·tend·ent \-'ten-dənt\ *n* : a person who oversees, manages, or maintains something ⟨a building *superintendent*⟩ ⟨*superintendent* of schools⟩ [Medieval Latin *superintendens*, from Late Latin *superintendere* "to superintend"]

¹su·pe·ri·or \su̇-'pir-ē-ər\ *adj* **1** : situated higher up : UPPER: as **a** : situated above or anterior or dorsal to another and especially a corresponding part ⟨a *superior* artery⟩ **b** : attached to and arising from a plant ovary ⟨a *superior* calyx⟩ **c** : free from the calyx or other floral envelope ⟨a *superior* plant ovary⟩ **2 a** : of higher rank, quality, or importance **b** : greater in quantity or numbers **3** : courageously or serenely indifferent (as to something painful or disheartening) **4 a :** excellent of its kind **b :** affecting or assuming an air of superiority **: SUPERCILIOUS 5 :** more comprehensive ⟨a genus is *superior* to a species⟩ [Middle French *superieur,* from Latin *superior,* comparative of *superus* "upper", from *super* "over, above"] — **su·pe·ri·or·i·ty** \-,pir-ē-'ȯr-ət-ē, -'är-\ *n* — **su·pe·ri·or·ly** \-'pir-ē-ər-lē\ *adv*

²superior *n* **I :** one who is above another in rank, station, or office; *esp :* the head of a religious house or order **2 :** one that surpasses another in quality or merit

superior court *n* **I :** a court intermediate between inferior courts and higher appellate courts **2 :** a court with juries having original jurisdiction

superiority complex *n :* an exaggerated opinion of oneself

superior vena cava *n :* a large vein that returns blood from the head and forelimbs to the heart

su·per·jet \'sü-pər-,jet\ *n :* a supersonic jet airplane

¹su·per·la·tive \su̇-'pər-lət-iv\ *adj* **I :** of, relating to, or constituting the degree of grammatical comparison that denotes an extreme or unsurpassed level or extent **2 :** surpassing all others **: SUPREME 3 : EXCESSIVE, EXAGGERATED** [Middle French *superlatif,* from Late Latin *superlativus,* from Latin *superlatus,* past participle of *superferre* "to carry over, raise high", from *super-* + *ferre* "to carry"] — **su·per·la·tive·ly** *adv* — **su·per·la·tive·ness** *n*

²superlative *n* **I :** the superlative degree or a superlative form in a language **2 :** the superlative or utmost degree of something **: ACME;** *also :* something that is superlative

su·per·man \'sü-pər-,man\ *n :* a man with exceptional powers [translation of German *übermensch*]

su·per·mar·ket \-,mär-kət\ *n :* a self-service retail market selling foods and household merchandise

su·per·mi·cro \-,mī-,krō\ *n :* a very fast and powerful microcomputer

su·per·mini \-,min-ē\ *n :* **SUPERMINICOMPUTER**

su·per·mini·com·put·er \-'min-ē-kəm-,pyüt-ər\ *n :* a very fast and powerful minicomputer

su·per·nal \su̇-'pərn-l\ *adj* **I a :** being or coming from on high **b :** being or seeming more than earthly ⟨*supernal* beauty⟩ ⟨*supernal* joy⟩ **2 :** located or originating in the sky [Middle French, from Latin *supernus,* from *super* "over, above"] — **su·per·nal·ly** \-l-ē\ *adv*

su·per·na·tant \,sü-pər-'nāt-nt\ *adj :* floating on the surface [Latin *supernatare* "to float", from *super-* + *natare* "to swim"] — **supernatant** *n*

su·per·nat·u·ral \,sü-pər-'nach-rəl, -ə-rəl\ *adj* **I :** of or relating to an order of existence beyond the visible observable universe; *esp :* of or relating to God or a god, demigod, spirit, or demon **2 a :** departing from what is usual or normal especially so as to appear to transcend the laws of nature **b :** attributed to an invisible agent (as a ghost or spirit) — **supernatural** *n* — **su·per·nat·u·ral·ly** \-'nach-rə-lē, -ə-rə-; -'nach-ər-lē\ *adv* — **su·per·nat·u·ral·ness** \-'nach-rəl-nəs, -ə-rəl-\ *n*

su·per·nat·u·ral·ism \-'nach-rə-,liz-əm, -ə-rə-\ *n* **I :** the quality or state of being supernatural **2 :** belief in a supernatural power and order of existence — **su·per·nat·u·ral·ist** \-ləst\ *n or adj* — **su·per·nat·u·ral·is·tic** \-,nach-rə-'lis-tik, -ə-rə-\ *adj*

su·per·nor·mal \-'nȯr-məl\ *adj* **I :** exceeding the normal or average **2 :** being beyond natural human powers — **su·per·nor·mal·ly** \-mə-lē\ *adv*

su·per·no·va \-'nō-və\ *n :* the explosion of a very large star in which the star temporarily radiates up to one billion times more energy than the sun

¹su·per·nu·mer·ary \,sü-pər-'nü-mə-,rer-ē, -'nyü-\ *adj* **I :** exceeding the stated or prescribed number **2 : SUPERFLUOUS** [Late Latin *supernumerarius,* from Latin *super-* + *numerus* "number"]

²supernumerary *n, pl* **-ar·ies I :** a supernumerary person or thing **2 :** an actor employed to play a small usually nonspeaking part (as in a mob scene or spectacle)

su·per·phos·phate \,sü-pər-'fäs-,fāt\ *n :* a soluble mixture of phosphates used as fertilizer

su·per·po·si·tion \,sü-pər-pə-'zish-ən\ *n :* the act or process of laying one thing over or above another especially so that they coincide [French, from Late Latin *superpositio,* from Latin *superponere* "to superpose", from *super-* + *ponere* "to place"] — **su·per·pose** \,sü-pər-'pōz\ *vt*

su·per·pow·er \'sü-pər-,pau̇-ər, -,pau̇r\ *n :* an extremely powerful nation

su·per·sat·u·rate \,sü-pər-'sach-ə-,rāt\ *vt :* to add something to beyond saturation

su·per·sat·u·rat·ed \-'sach-ə-,rāt-əd\ *adj :* containing an amount of something greater than the amount required for saturation by having been cooled from a higher temperature to a temperature below that at which saturation occurs ⟨a *supersaturated* solution⟩ ⟨air *supersaturated* with water vapor⟩

su·per·sat·u·ra·tion \-,sach-ə-'rā-shən\ *n :* the state of being supersaturated

su·per·scribe \'sü-pər-,skrīb\ *vt :* to write or engrave on the top or outside; *esp :* to write (as a name or address) on the outside or cover of [Latin *superscribere,* from *super-* + *scribere* "to write"]

su·per·script \'sü-pər-,skript\ *n :* a distinguishing symbol or letter written immediately above or above and to the right or left of another character [Latin *superscriptus,* past participle of *superscribere* "to superscribe"] — **superscript** *adj*

su·per·scrip·tion \,sü-pər-'skrip-shən\ *n* **I :** the act of superscribing **2 :** something superscribed on something else **: INSCRIPTION;** *esp :* **ADDRESS**

su·per·sede \,sü-pər-'sēd\ *vt* **I :** to force out of use as inferior **2 :** to take the place, room, or position of **3 :** to displace in favor of another **: SUPPLANT** [Middle French *superseder* "to refrain from", from Latin *supersedēre* "to be superior to, refrain from", from *super-* + *sedēre* "to sit"] **SYN see REPLACE** — **su·per·sed·er** *n* — **su·per·se·dure** \-'sē-jər\ *n*

su·per·sen·si·tive \-'sen-sət-iv, -'sen-stiv\ *adj :* **HYPERSENSITIVE** — **su·per·sen·si·tive·ly** *adv* — **su·per·sen·si·tive·ness** *n* — **su·per·sen·si·tiv·i·ty** \-,sen-sə-'tiv-ət-ē\ *n*

su·per·ses·sion \,sü-pər-'sesh-ən\ *n :* the act of superseding **:** the state of being superseded [Medieval Latin *supersessio,* from Latin *supersedēre* "to refrain from"] — **su·per·ses·sive** \-'ses-iv\ *adj*

su·per·son·ic \-'sän-ik\ *adj* **I : ULTRASONIC 2 :** of, being, or relating to speeds from one to five times the speed of sound in air **3 :** moving, capable of moving, or utilizing air currents moving at supersonic speed ⟨a *supersonic* airplane⟩ — **su·per·son·i·cal·ly** \-'sän-i-kə-lē, -klē\ *adv*

su·per·son·ics \-'sän-iks\ *n :* the science of supersonic phenomena

su·per·star \'sü-pər-,stär\ *n :* a star who is considered extremely talented, has great public appeal, and who can usually command a high salary — **su·per·star·dom** \-dəm\ *n*

su·per·sti·tion \,sü-pər-'stish-ən\ *n* **I :** beliefs or practices resulting from ignorance, fear of the unknown, or belief in fate, omens, magic, or chance as governing principles **2 :** an attitude of resignation toward or fear of nature, the unknown, or God resulting from superstition [Middle French *supersticion,* from Latin *superstitio,* from *superstes* "standing over (as witness or survivor)", from *super-* + *stare* "to stand"] — **su·per·sti·tious** \-'stish-əs\ *adj* — **su·per·sti·tious·ly** *adv* — **su·per·sti·tious·ness** *n*

su·per·store \'sü-pər-,stōr, -,stȯr\ *n :* a very large store offering a wide variety of merchandise for sale

su·per·struc·ture \'sü-pər-,strək-chər\ *n :* something (as the part of a building above the basement or of a ship above the main deck) built upon an underlying or more fundamental base ⟨the social *superstructure*⟩

— **su·per·struc·tur·al** \-,strək-chə-rəl, -,strək-shrəl\ *adj*

su·per·tax \'sü-pər-,taks\ *n* : SURTAX

su·per·ton·ic \,sü-pər-'tän-ik\ *n* : the second tone of the musical scale

su·per·vene \,sü-pər-'vēn\ *vi* : to take place as an additional or unexpected development [Latin *supervenire,* from *super-* + *venire* "to come"]

su·per·vise \'sü-pər-,vīz\ *vt* : to be in charge of : SUPERINTEND [Medieval Latin *supervisus,* past participle of *supervidēre* "to supervise", from Latin *super-* + *vidēre* "to see"] — **su·per·vi·sion** \,sü-pər-'vizh-ən\ *n*

su·per·vi·sor \'sü-pər-,vī-zər\ *n* : one that supervises; *esp* : an administrative officer in charge of a business, government, or school unit or operation — **su·per·vi·so·ry** \,sü-pər-'vīz-rē, -ə-rē\ *adj*

su·per·wom·an \'sü-pər-,wùm-ən\ *n* : an exceptional woman; *esp* : a woman who succeeds in having a career and raising a family

su·pi·na·tion \,sü-pə-'nā-shən\ *n* : rotation of the hand or forearm so as to bring the palm facing upward or forward [Latin *supinare* "to lay on the back", from *supinus* "supine"] — **su·pi·nate** \'sü-pə-,nāt\ *vb*

su·pi·na·tor \'sü-pə-,nāt-ər\ *n* : a muscle that produces the motion of supination

¹**su·pine** \sù-'pīn\ *adj* **1** : lying on the back or with the face upward **2** : showing mental or moral slackness : APATHETIC [Latin *supinus*] SYN see PRONE — **su·pine·ly** *adv* — **su·pine·ness** \-'pīn-nəs\ *n*

²**su·pine** \'sü-,pīn\ *n* : a Latin verbal noun having an accusative of purpose in *-um* and an ablative of specification in *-u*

sup·per \'səp-ər\ *n* **1** : the evening meal when dinner is taken at midday **2** : refreshments or a meal served late in the evening [Old French *souper,* from *souper* "to sup"]

sup·plant \sə-'plant\ *vt* **1** : to take the place of (another) especially by force or treachery **2 a** : to remove and supply a substitute for ⟨efforts to *supplant* the vernacular⟩ **b** : to gain the place of especially by reason of superiority [Middle French *supplanter,* from Latin *supplantare* "to overthrow by tripping up", from *sub-* + *planta* "sole of the foot"] SYN see REPLACE — **sup·plan·ta·tion** \sə-,plan-'tā-shən\ *n* — **sup·plant·er** \sə-'plant-ər\ *n*

¹**sup·ple** \'səp-əl\ *adj* **sup·pler** \'səp-lər, -ə-lər\; **sup·plest** \'səp-ləst, -ə-ləst\ **1 a** : yielding easily and often submissively to the wishes of others **b** : readily adaptable to new situations **2 a** : capable of being bent or folded without creases or breaks : PLIANT ⟨*supple* leather⟩ **b** : able to bend or twist with ease and grace : LIMBER ⟨*supple* legs of a dancer⟩ [Old French *souple,* from Latin *supplex* "submissive, suppliant", literally, "bending under"] — **sup·ple·ness** \-əl-nəs\ *n*

²**supple** *vt* **sup·pled; sup·pling** \'səp-ling, -ə-ling\ : to make supple

¹**sup·ple·ment** \'səp-lə-mənt\ *n* **1** : something that completes or makes an addition ⟨diet *supplements*⟩ ⟨the *supplement* at the back of the book⟩ **2** : an angle or arc that when added to a given angle or arc equals 180 degrees [Latin *supplementum,* from *supplēre* "to fill up, complete, supply"] — **sup·ple·men·tal** \,səp-lə-'ment-l\ *adj* — **sup·ple·men·ta·tion** \,səp-lə-,men-'tā-shən\ *n*

²**sup·ple·ment** \'səp-lə-,mənt\ *vt* : to add to : fill a deficiency of

sup·ple·men·ta·ry \,səp-lə-'ment-ə-rē, -'men-trē\ *adj* **1** : added as a supplement : ADDITIONAL **2** : being or related to a supplement or a supplementary angle

supplementary angle *n* : either of two angles or arcs whose sum is 180 degrees — usually used in pl.

¹**sup·pli·ant** \'səp-lē-ənt\ *n* : one who supplicates [Middle French, from *supplier* "to supplicate", from Latin *supplicare*]

²**suppliant** *adj* : earnestly and humbly imploring — **sup·pli·ant·ly** *adv*

sup·pli·cant \'səp-li-kənt\ *n* : one who supplicates — **supplicant** *adj* — **sup·pli·cant·ly** *adv*

sup·pli·cate \'səp-lə-,kāt\ *vb* **1** : to make a humble appeal; *esp* : to pray to God **2** : to ask for or of earnestly and humbly : BESEECH [Latin *supplicare,* from *supplex* "submissive, suppliant"] — **sup·pli·ca·tion** \,sep-lə-'kā-shən\ *n* — **sup·pli·ca·to·ry** \'səp-li-kə-,tōr-ē-,tòr-\ *adj*

¹**sup·ply** \sə-'plī\ *vt* **sup·plied; sup·ply·ing** **1** : to add as a supplement **2** : to provide for : SATISFY ⟨to *supply* their wants⟩ **3** : to provide or furnish with ⟨*supply* provisions⟩ **4** : to satisfy the needs or wishes of ⟨*supply* them with fuel⟩ [Middle French *soupleier,* from Latin *supplēre* "to fill up, supply", from *sub-* "up" + *plēre* "to fill"] — **sup·pli·er** \-'plī-ər, -'plīr\ *n*

²**supply** *n, pl* **supplies** **1 a** : the quantity or amount (as of a commodity) needed or available **b** : PROVISION 2, STORE — usually used in pl. **2** : the act or process of filling a want or need : PROVISION **3** : the quantities of goods or services offered for sale at a particular time or at one price

¹**sup·port** \sə-'pōrt, -'pòrt\ *vt* **1** : to endure bravely or quietly : BEAR **2 a** (1) : to promote the interests or cause of (2) : to uphold or defend as valid or right : ADVOCATE (3) : to argue or vote for **b** : ASSIST, HELP **c** : to act in a lesser role with (a star actor) **d** : SUBSTANTIATE 1, VERIFY **3** : to pay the costs of : MAINTAIN **4 a** : to hold up or in position or serve as a foundation or prop for **b** : to maintain (the price of a commodity) at a high level by purchases or loans **5** : to keep (something) going : SUSTAIN [Middle French *supporter,* from Latin *supportare* "to carry", from *sub-* + *portare* "to carry"] — **sup·port·able** \-ə-bəl\ *adj*

²**support** *n* **1** : the act or process of supporting : the condition of being supported **2** : one that supports

sup·port·er \sə-'pōrt-ər, -'pòrt-\ *n* : one that supports; *esp* : ADVOCATE 2

sup·port·ive \sə-'pōrt-iv, -'pòrt-\ *adj* : furnishing or intended to furnish support

sup·pose \sə-'pōz\ *vb* **1** : to take as true or as a fact for the sake of argument : lay down as a hypothesis ⟨*suppose* a fire should break out⟩ **2** : to hold as an opinion : BELIEVE ⟨they *supposed* they were on the right bus⟩ **3** : THINK, GUESS ⟨who do you *suppose* will win⟩ ⟨I *suppose* so⟩ [Middle French *supposer,* derived from Latin *supponere* "to put under, substitute", from *sub-* + *ponere* "to put, place"]

sup·posed \sə-'pōzd, *in the phrase* "supposed to" *often* -'pōz, -'pōs, -'pōst\ *adj* **1** : usually mistakenly believed **2 a** : required by authority ⟨she was *supposed* to practice two hours daily⟩ **b** : given permission ⟨you're not *supposed* to do that⟩ — **sup·pos·ed·ly** \-'pō-zəd-lē\ *adv*

sup·po·si·tion \,səp-ə-'zish-ən\ *n* **1** : something that is supposed : HYPOTHESIS **2** : the act of supposing [Late Latin *suppositio,* derived from Latin *supponere* "to put under"] — **sup·po·si·tion·al** \-'zish-nəl, -ən-l\ *adj* — **sup·po·si·tion·al·ly** \-ē\ *adv*

sup·po·si·tious \-'zish-əs\ *adj* : SUPPOSITITIOUS

sup·pos·i·ti·tious \sə-,päz-ə-'tish-əs\ *adj* **1** : fraudulently substituted : SPURIOUS **2** : of the nature of a supposition : HYPOTHETICAL [Latin *supposoticius,* from *supponere* "to put under, substitute"] — **sup·pos·i·ti·tious·ly** *adv* — **sup·pos·i·ti·tious·ness** *n*

sup·pos·i·to·ry \sə-'päz-ə-,tōr-ē, -,tòr-\ *n, pl* **-ries** : a solid but readily meltable cone or cylinder of usually medicated material for insertion into a bodily passage or cavity (as the rectum) [Medieval Latin *suppositorium,* derived from Latin *supponere* "to put under"]

sup·press \sə-'pres\ *vt* **1** : to put down by authority or force : SUBDUE **2 a** : to keep from being made known **b** : to stop the publication or circulation of **3 a** : to exclude from consciousness **b** : to hold back : RE-

\ə\ abut   \ng\ sing
\ər\ further   \ō\ bone
\a\ mat   \ò\ saw
\ā\ take   \òi\ coin
\ä\ cot, cart   \th\ thin
\aù\ out   \th\ this
\ch\ chin   \ü\ food
\e\ pet   \ù\ foot
\ē\ easy   \y\ yet
\g\ go   \yü\ few
\i\ tip   \yù\ cure
\ī\ life   \zh\ vision
\j\ job

STRAIN ⟨*suppress* a cough⟩ **4** : to inhibit the growth or development of : STUNT [Latin *suppressus*, past participle of *supprimere* "to suppress", from *sub-* + *premere* "to press"] — **sup·press·ible** \-ə-bəl\ *adj* — **sup·pres·sion** \-'presh-ən\ *n* — **sup·pres·sive** \-'pres-iv\ *adj* — **sup·pres·sor** \-'pres-ər\ *n*

sup·pres·sor T cell \sə-,pres-ər-'tē-\ *n* : a T cell that suppresses the immune response of B cells and other T cells to an antigen — called also *suppressor cell*

sup·pu·rate \'səp-yə-,rāt\ *vi* : to form or give off pus [Latin *suppurare*, from *sub-* + *pur-, pus* "pus"] — **sup·pu·ra·tion** \,səp-yə-'rā-shən\ *n* — **sup·pu·ra·tive** \'səp-yə-,rāt-iv\ *adj*

supra- *prefix* **1** : SUPER- 2a ⟨*supra*orbital⟩ **2** : transcending ⟨*supra*national⟩ [Latin, from *supra* "above, beyond"]

su·pra·na·tion·al \,sü-prə-'nash-nəl, -'nash-ən-l\ *adj* : transcending national boundaries or authority

su·pra·or·bit·al \-'ȯr-bət-l\ *adj* : situated or occurring above the orbit of the eye

¹su·pra·re·nal \-'rēn-l\ *adj* : situated above or in front of the kidneys; *esp* : ADRENAL

²suprarenal *n* : a suprarenal part; *esp* : ADRENAL GLAND

su·prem·a·cist \sù-'prem-ə-səst\ *n* : an advocate of supremacy of a particular group (as a race)

su·prem·a·cy \sù-'prem-ə-sē\ *n, pl* **-cies** : the quality or state of being supreme; *also* : supreme authority or power [*supreme* + *-acy* (as in *primacy*)] □ SYN SUPREMACY, ASCENDANCY mean a being first in rank, power, or influence. SUPREMACY implies definite superiority over all others ⟨*supremacy* in steel production⟩ ASCENDANCY implies domination of one by another which may or may not involve supremacy ⟨seeking to keep one's *ascendancy* over an old rival⟩

su·preme \sù-'prēm\ *adj* **1** : highest in rank or authority **2** : highest in degree or quality **3** : ULTIMATE, FINAL ⟨the *supreme* sacrifice⟩ [Latin *supremus*, superlative of *superus* "upper", from *super* "over, above"] — **su·preme·ly** *adv* — **su·preme·ness** *n*

Supreme Being *n* : GOD 1

supreme court *n* : the highest court of the United States consisting of a chief justice and eight associate justices; *also* : a similar body in many states

sur- *prefix* : over : above ⟨*sur*tax⟩ [Old French, from Latin *super-*]

sur·cease \'sər-,sēs, ,sər-'\ *n* : CESSATION; *esp* : a temporary respite or end [Middle French *sursis*, past participle of *surseoir* "to desist, take a respite", from Latin *supersedēre* "to be superior to, refrain from", from *super-* + *sedēre* "to sit"]

¹sur·charge \'sər-,chärj\ *vt* **1 a** : OVERCHARGE 1 **b** : to charge an extra fee usually for a special service **2** : to burden with an excess physical or emotional load **3** : to mark (as a stamp) with a surcharge

²surcharge *n* **1** : an additional tax or charge **2** : an excessive load **3 a** : an overprint on a stamp; *esp* : one that alters the denomination **b** : a stamp bearing such an overprint

sur·cin·gle \'sər-,sing-gəl\ *n* : a band or girth passing around the body of a horse to bind a saddle or pack fast to the horse's back [Middle French *surcengle*, from *sur-* + *cengle* "girdle", from Latin *cingulum*]

sur·coat \'sər-,kōt\ *n* : an outer coat or cloak; *esp* : a tunic worn over armor

¹surd \'sərd\ *adj* : VOICELESS — used of speech sounds [Latin *surdus* "deaf, silent, stupid"]

²surd *n* **1** : an irrational root (as $\sqrt{3}$) **2** : a surd speech sound

¹sure \'shur, *especially South* 'shōr\ *adj* **1** : firmly established : STEADFAST ⟨a *sure* foundation⟩ **2** : RELIABLE, TRUSTWORTHY **3** : marked by or given to feelings of intuitive certainty **4** : admitting of no doubt : CERTAIN **5 a** : bound to happen : INEVITABLE ⟨*sure* disaster⟩ **b** : destined as if by fate ⟨*sure* to win⟩ [Middle French *sur*, from Latin *securus* "secure"] — **sure·ness** *n* □ SYN

SURE, CERTAIN, POSITIVE mean having no doubt of one's opinion or conclusion. SURE usually stresses the subjective or intuitive feeling of assurance ⟨I am *sure* I have seen that face before⟩ CERTAIN implies basing a conclusion on definite grounds or indubitable evidence; POSITIVE intensifies sureness and may imply opinionated conviction or forceful expression of it. — **for sure** : without doubt : with certainty — **to be sure 1** : SURELY 1b, CERTAINLY **2** : it must be acknowledged

²sure *adv* : SURELY

sure·fire \-'fīr\ *adj* : certain to get results : DEPENDABLE

sure·foot·ed \-'fût-əd\ *adj* : not liable to stumble or fall — **sure·foot·ed·ness** *n*

sure·ly \'shur-lē\ *adv* **1 a** : with assurance : CONFIDENTLY **b** : without doubt : CERTAINLY ⟨will *surely* be there⟩ **2** : INDEED 1, REALLY — often used as an intensive ⟨I *surely* am tired this afternoon⟩

sure·ty \'shur-ət-ē, 'shurt-ē\ *n, pl* **sureties 1** : sure knowledge : CERTAINTY **2** : a pledge for the fulfillment of an undertaking : GUARANTEE **3** : one who assumes legal liability for another's debt, default, or failure to do a duty — **sure·ty·ship** \-ē-,ship\ *n*

¹surf \'sərf\ *n* **1** : the swell of the sea that breaks upon the shore **2** : the foam, splash, and sound of breaking waves [origin unknown]

²surf *vi* : to ride the surf : engage in surfing — **surf·er** *n*

¹sur·face \'sər-fəs\ *n* **1** : the outside of an object or body **2** : a plane or curved two-dimensional locus of points ⟨the *surface* of a sphere⟩ **3** : the external or superficial aspect of something ⟨on the *surface*, the statement appears to be true⟩ **4** : a complete airfoil [French, from *sur-* + *face*] — **surface** *adj* — **sur·faced** \-fəst\ *adj*

²surface *vb* **1** : to give a surface to: as **a** : to plane (as lumber) smooth **b** : to apply a surface layer to **2** : to come to the surface ⟨the submarine *surfaced*⟩ — **sur·fac·er** *n*

surface tension *n* : the attractive force felt by surface molecules of a liquid from the molecules beneath that tends to draw the surface molecules into the mass of the liquid and makes the liquid assume the shape having the least surface area

sur·fac·ing \'sər-fə-sing\ *n* : material forming or used to form a surface (as on a road)

surf·board \'sərf-,bōrd, -,bȯrd\ *n* : a buoyant board used in the sport of surfing — **surfboard** *vi* — **surf·board·er** *n*

surf·boat \-,bōt\ *n* : a boat for use in heavy surf

surf casting *n* : the technique or act of casting artificial or natural bait into the open ocean or in a bay where waves break on a beach — **surf caster** *n*

¹sur·feit \'sər-fət\ *n* **1** : an overabundant supply : EXCESS **2** : an intemperate indulgence in something (as food or drink) **3** : disgust caused by excess : SATIETY [Middle French *surfait*, from *surfaire* "to overdo", from *sur-* + *faire* "to do", from Latin *facere*]

²surfeit *vb* : to feed, supply, or indulge to the point of surfeit : CLOY

surfing \'sər-fing\ *n* : the sport of riding the surf especially on a surfboard

¹surge \'sərj\ *vi* **1** : to rise and fall actively **2** : to rise and move or roll forward in or as if in waves or billows ⟨the sea *surged*⟩ ⟨a crowd of people *surged* toward the door⟩ **3** : to rise suddenly to an abnormal value — used especially of current or voltage [Middle French *sourge-*, stem of *sourdre* "to rise, surge", from Latin *surgere* "to go straight up, rise", from *sub-* "up" + *regere* "to lead straight"]

²surge *n* **1** : a swelling, rolling, or sweeping forward like that of a wave **2** : a large wave or billow : SWELL **3** : a transient sudden rise of current or voltage in an electrical circuit

sur·geon \'sər-jən\ *n* : a physician who specializes in surgery [Anglo-French *surgien*, from Old French *cirurgien*, from *cirurgie* "surgery"]

1 surcingle

surfboard

sur·gery \'sərj-rē, -ə-rē\ *n, pl* **-ger·ies** **1** : a branch of medicine concerned with the correction of physical defects, the repair and healing of injuries, and the treatment of diseased conditions especially by operations **2** : work done by a surgeon : OPERATION **3 a** *British* : a physician's or dentist's office **b** : a room or area where surgery is performed [Old French *cirurgie, surgerie,* from Latin *chirurgia,* from Greek *cheirourgia,* derived from *cheir* "hand" + *ergon* "work"]

sur·gi·cal \'sər-ji-kəl\ *adj* : of, relating to, or associated with surgeons or surgery ⟨*surgical* skills⟩ ⟨*surgical* implements⟩ ⟨*surgical* fevers⟩ — **sur·gi·cal·ly** \-kə-lē, -klē\ *adv*

sur·ly \'sər-lē\ *adj* **sur·li·er; -est** : irritably sullen and churlish in mood or manner [Middle English *sirly* "lordly, imperious", from *sir*] SYN see SULLEN — **sur·li·ness** *n*

¹sur·mise \sər-'mīz\ *vb* : to imagine or infer on slight grounds : GUESS [Middle French *surmis,* past participle of *surmetre* "to accuse", from Latin *supermittere* "to throw on", from *super-* + *mittere* "to send"] SYN see CONJECTURE

²sur·mise \sər-'mīz, 'sər-\ *n* : a thought or idea based on scanty evidence : CONJECTURE

sur·mount \sər-'maúnt\ *vt* **1** : to rise above or prevail over : OVERCOME ⟨*surmount* an obstacle⟩ **2** : to get to the top of : CLIMB **3** : to stand or lie at the top of : CROWN ⟨a cross *surmounts* the church steeple⟩ — **sur·mount·able** \-ə-bəl\ *adj*

¹sur·name \'sər-ˌnām\ *n* : the name borne in common by members of a family [earlier *surname* "added name, nickname"]

²surname *vt* : to give a surname to

sur·pass \sər-'pas\ *vt* **1** : to be greater, better, or stronger than : EXCEED **2** : to go beyond the reach, powers, or capacity of SYN see EXCEED — **sur·pass·able** \-ə-bəl\ *adj*

sur·plice \'sər-pləs\ *n* : a loose white tunic worn at service by a member of the clergy or choir [Old French *surpliz,* from Medieval Latin *superpellicium,* from *super-* + *pellicium* "coat of skins", derived from Latin *pellis* "skin"]

sur·plus \'sər-ˌpləs, -pləs\ *n* : the amount that remains when use or need is satisfied : EXCESS [Middle French, from Medieval Latin *superplus,* from Latin *super-* + *plus* "more"] — **surplus** *adj*

sur·plus·age \-ij\ *n* **1** : SURPLUS **2** : excessive or nonessential matter

surplus value *n* : the difference in Marxist theory between the value of work done by labor and the wages paid by the employer

¹sur·prise \sər-'prīz, sə-'prīz\ *n* **1 a** : an attack made without warning **b** : a taking unawares ⟨we were taken by *surprise*⟩ **2** : something that surprises **3** : the state of being surprised : ASTONISHMENT [Middle French, from *surprendre* "to take over, surprise", from *sur-* + *prendre* "to take"]

²surprise *vt* **1** : to attack unexpectedly; *also* : to capture by an unexpected attack **2** : to take unawares : come upon unexpectedly **3** : to strike with wonder or amazement because unexpected □ SYN SURPRISE, ASTONISH, ASTOUND mean to impress strongly through unexpectedness. SURPRISE stresses causing an effect through being unexpected at a particular time or place rather than by being essentially unusual or novel; ASTONISH implies surprising so greatly as to seem incredible; ASTOUND stresses the shock of astonishment.

sur·pris·ing *adj* : of a kind to cause surprise — **sur·pris·ing·ly** \-'prī-zing-lē\ *adv*

sur·re·al·ism \sə-'rē-ə-ˌliz-əm\ *n* : a modern movement in art and literature with the aim of expressing subconscious mental activities through fantastic or incongruous imagery or unnatural juxtapositions and combinations — **sur·re·al·ist** \-ləst\ *n or adj* — **sur·re·al·**

is·tic \-ˌrē-ə-'lis-tik\ *adj* — **sur·re·al·is·ti·cal·ly** \-ti-kə-lē, -klē\ *adv*

¹sur·ren·der \sə-'ren-dər\ *vb* **sur·ren·dered; sur·ren·der·ing** \-də-ring, -dring\ **1** : to give over to the power, control, or possession of another especially under compulsion ⟨*surrendered* the fort⟩ **2** : to give oneself up into the power of another especially as a prisoner **3** : to give oneself over to something (as an influence or course of action) [Middle French *surrendre,* from *sur-* + *rendre* "to yield"] SYN see RELINQUISH

²surrender *n* : the giving of oneself or something into the power of another person or thing

sur·rep·ti·tious \ˌsər-əp-'tish-əs, ˌsə-rəp-\ *adj* : done, made, or acquired by stealth : CLANDESTINE, STEALTHY [Latin *surrepticius,* from *surripere* "to snatch secretly", from *sub-* + *rapere* "to seize"] SYN see SECRET — **sur·rep·ti·tious·ly** *adv* — **sur·rep·ti·tious·ness** *n*

sur·rey \'sər-ē, 'sə-rē\ *n, pl* **surreys** : a four-wheel two-seated horse-drawn pleasure carriage [*Surrey,* England]

sur·ro·gate \'sər-ə-ˌgāt, 'sə-rə-, -gət\ *n* **1** : DEPUTY 1, SUBSTITUTE **2** : a local judicial officer in some states having jurisdiction over the settling of estates [Latin *surrogatus,* past participle of *surrogare* "to substitute", from *sub-* + *rogare* "to ask"] — **surrogate** *adj*

¹sur·round \sə-'raúnd\ *vt* : to enclose on all sides : ENCIRCLE, ENCOMPASS [Middle French *suronder* "to overflow", from Late Latin *superundare,* from Latin *super-* + *unda* "wave"]

²surround *n* : something (as a border or edging) that surrounds

sur·round·ings \-'raún-dingz\ *n pl* : ENVIRONMENT 1

sur·sum cor·da \ˌsúr-səm-'kórd-ə\ *n* **1** *often cap S&C* : a versicle exhorting thanksgiving to God **2** : something inspiriting [Late Latin, "(lift) up (your) hearts"]

sur·tax \'sər-ˌtaks\ *n* : an additional tax over and above a general tax

sur·tout \sər-'tü, ˌsər-\ *n* : a long close-fitting overcoat [French, from *sur* "over" + *tout* "all"]

sur·veil·lance \sər-'vā-ləns *also* -'vāl-yəns *or* -'vā-əns\ *n* : close watch [French, from *surveiller* "to watch over", from *sur-* + *veiller* "to watch", from Latin *vigilare,* from *vigil* "watchful"]

sur·veil·lant \-'vā-lənt *also* -'vāl-yənt *or* -'vā-ənt\ *n* : one that keeps another under surveillance

¹sur·vey \sər-'vā, 'sər-\ *vt* **sur·veyed; sur·vey·ing** **1** : to look over and examine closely **2** : to determine the form, boundaries, and position of (as a piece of land) **3** : to view or study as a whole : make a survey of [Middle French *surveeir,* from *sur-* + *veeir* "to see", from Latin *vidēre*] — **sur·vey·or** \sər-'vā-ər\ *n*

²sur·vey \'sər-ˌvā, sər-'\ *n, pl* **surveys** : the act or an instance of surveying: as **a** : a broad treatment of a subject **b** : POLL 4a **2** : something that is surveyed

sur·vey·ing \sər-'vā-ing\ *n* **1** : the occupation of making land surveys **2** : a branch of applied mathematics concerned with the accurate measurement and representation of the earth's surface

sur·viv·al \sər-'vī-vəl\ *n* **1** : a living or continuing longer than another or beyond something ⟨*survival* of the soul after death⟩ **2** : the continuation of life despite difficult conditions ⟨techniques for *survival* in the desert⟩ **3** : one that survives

survival of the fittest : NATURAL SELECTION

sur·vive \sər-'vīv\ *vb* **1** : to remain alive or in existence : live on **2** : to remain alive after the death of ⟨the parents *survived* their child⟩ **3** : to continue to exist or live after ⟨*survived* the flood⟩ [Middle French *survivre* "to outlive", from Latin *supervivere,* from *super-* + *vivere* "to live"] — **sur·vi·vor** \-'vī-vər\ *n*

sus·cep·ti·bil·i·ty \sə-ˌsep-tə-'bil-ət-ē\ *n, pl* **-ties** **1** : the quality or state of being susceptible; *esp* : lack of ability to resist some outside agent (as a pathogen or drug) : SENSITIVITY **2 a** : a susceptible temperament or constitution **b** *pl* : FEELING 2b, SENSIBILITIES

surplice

surrey

sus·cep·ti·ble \sə-'sep-tə-bəl\ *adj* **1** : capable of submitting to an action, process, or operation ⟨a theory *susceptible* to proof⟩ **2** : open, subject, or unresistant to some stimulus, influence, or agency ⟨persons *susceptible* to colds⟩ **3** : easily influenced or affected [Late Latin *susceptibilis,* from Latin *suscipere* "to take up", from *sub-, sus-* "up" + *capere* "to take"] — **sus·cep·ti·ble·ness** *n* — **sus·cep·ti·bly** \-blē\ *adv*

¹sus·pect \'səs-ˌpekt, sə-'spekt\ *adj* : regarded with or deserving suspicion [Middle French, from Latin *suspectus,* from *suspicere* "to suspect"]

²sus·pect \'səs-ˌpekt\ *n* : one who is suspected

³sus·pect \sə-'spekt\ *vb* **1** : to have doubts of : DISTRUST **2** : to believe to be guilty on slight evidence or without proof ⟨*suspected* me of theft⟩ **3** : to imagine to be or be true, likely, or probable : SURMISE **4** : to be suspicious [Latin *suspectare,* from *suspicere* "to look up at, regard with awe, suspect", from *sub-* "up" + *specere* "to look at"]

sus·pend \sə-'spend\ *vb* **1** : to bar temporarily from any privilege or office ⟨*suspend* a student from school⟩ **2 a** : to stop or do away with (as an activity) for a time ⟨*suspend* publication⟩ **b** : to defer on specified conditions ⟨*suspend* sentence on an offender⟩ ⟨*suspend* judgment⟩ **3** : to cease for a time from operation or activity **4 a** : HANG; *esp* : to hang so as to be free on all sides except at the point of support ⟨*suspend* a ball by a thread⟩ **b** : to keep from falling or sinking by some invisible support (as buoyancy) ⟨dust *suspended* in the air⟩ [Old French *suspendre,* from Latin *suspendere,* from *sub-, sus-* "up" + *pendere* "to cause to hang, weigh"]

suspended animation *n* : temporary suspension of the vital functions (as in persons nearly drowned)

sus·pend·er \sə-'spen-dər\ *n* **1** : one that suspends **2** : a device by which something may be suspended; *esp* : either of two supporting bands worn across the shoulders to support pants, skirt, or belt — usually used in pl. ⟨a pair of *suspenders*⟩

sus·pense \sə-'spens\ *n* **1** : temporary cessation : SUSPENSION **2** : mental uncertainty : **a** : ANXIETY 1a **b** : pleasant excitement as to a decision or outcome ⟨a novel of *suspense*⟩ **3** : the state of being undecided : lack of certainty ⟨our next move was still in *suspense*⟩ [Middle French, from *suspendre* "to suspend"] — **sus·pense·ful** \-fəl\ *adj*

sus·pen·sion \sə-'spen-chən\ *n* **1** : the act of suspending or the state or period of being suspended: as **a** : temporary removal from office or privileges **b** : temporary withholding (as of belief or decision) **c** : temporary setting aside of a law or rule **2** : the act of hanging : the state of being hung **3 a** : the state of a substance when its particles are mixed with but undissolved in a fluid or solid; *also* : a substance in this state **b** : a system consisting of a solid dispersed in a solid, liquid, or gas usually in particles of larger than colloidal size **4** : something suspended **5 a** : a device by which something is suspended **b** : the system of devices (as springs) supporting the upper part of a vehicle on the axles [Late Latin *suspensio,* from Latin *suspendere* "to suspend"]

suspension bridge *n* : a bridge that has its roadway suspended from two or more cables usually passing over towers and securely anchored at the ends

suspension points *n pl* : usually three spaced periods used to show the omission of a word or word group

sus·pen·sive \sə-'spen-siv\ *adj* **1** : stopping temporarily **2** : characterized by suspense, suspended judgment, or indecisiveness — **sus·pen·sive·ly** *adv*

sus·pen·sor \sə-'spen-sər\ *n* : a suspending part or structure; *esp* : a group of cells supporting a plant embryo or zygospore

sus·pen·so·ry \sə-'spens-rē, -ə-rē\ *adj* **1** : fitted or serving to suspend something **2** : temporarily leaving something undetermined

suspensory ligament *n* : a fibrous membrane holding the iris of the eye in place

¹sus·pi·cion \sə-'spish-ən\ *n* **1** : the act or an instance of suspecting or being suspected **2** : a state of mental uneasiness and uncertainty : DOUBT **3** : a slight touch or trace : SUGGESTION ⟨just a *suspicion* of garlic⟩ [Latin *suspicio,* from *suspicere* "to suspect"] SYN see DOUBT

²suspicion *vt* **sus·pi·cioned; sus·pi·cion·ing** \-'spish-ning, -ə-ning\ *chiefly substandard* : SUSPECT

sus·pi·cious \sə-'spish-əs\ *adj* **1** : arousing or tending to arouse suspicion **2** : disposed to suspect : DISTRUSTFUL **3** : indicative of suspicion ⟨a *suspicious* glance⟩ — **sus·pi·cious·ly** *adv* — **sus·pi·cious·ness** *n*

sus·pire \sə-'spīr\ *vi* : to draw a long deep breath : SIGH [Latin *suspirare,* from *sub-* + *spirare* "to breathe"] — **sus·pi·ra·tion** \ˌsəs-pə-'rā-shən\ *n*

sus·tain \sə-'stān\ *vt* **1** : to give support or relief to **2** : to supply with sustenance : NOURISH **3** : to keep up : PROLONG ⟨*sustain* the growth in the economy⟩ **4** : to support the weight of : CARRY **5** : to keep up the spirits or courage of **6 a** : to bear up under : ENDURE **b** : UNDERGO 1 ⟨*sustained* a serious wound⟩ **7** : to support as true, legal, valid, or just ⟨the court *sustained* the earlier verdict⟩ **8** : PROVE 2a, CONFIRM [Old French *sustenir,* from Latin *sustinēre* "to hold up, sustain", from *sub-, sus-* "up" + *tenēre* "to hold"] — **sus·tain·able** \-'stā-nə-bəl\ *adj* — **sus·tain·er** *n*

sustaining program *n* : a radio or television program that is paid for by a station or network and has no commercial sponsor

sus·te·nance \'səs-tə-nəns\ *n* **1 a** : means of support, maintenance, or subsistence **b** : FOOD; *also* : NOURISHMENT **2** : the act of sustaining : the state of being sustained; *esp* : a supplying with the necessaries of life [Old French, from *sustenir* "to sustain"]

su·sur·ra·tion \ˌsü-sə-'rā-shən\ *n* : a rustling or whispering sound [Late Latin *susurratio,* from Latin *susurrare* "to whisper"]

sut·ler \'sət-lər\ *n* : one formerly let to follow an army or establish a store on a post and sell food and provisions [Dutch *soeteler,* from Low German *suteler* "sloppy worker, camp cook"]

sut·tee \sə-'tē, ˌsə-'tē\ *n* : the act or custom of a Hindu widow allowing herself to be cremated on the funeral pile of her husband; *also* : a woman so cremated [Sanskrit *satī* "wife who performs suttee", literally, "good woman", from *sat* "true, good"]

¹su·ture \'sü-chər\ *n* **1 a** : a strand or fiber used to sew parts of the living body; *also* : a stitch made with this **b** : the act or process of sewing with sutures **2 a** : the line of union in an immovable joint (as between the bones of the skull); *also* : such a joint **b** : a furrow at the junction of adjacent bodily parts; *esp* : a line along which a fruit dehisces [Latin *sutura* "seam, suture", from *suere* "to sew"] — **su·tur·al** \'süch-rəl, -ə-rəl\ *adj* — **su·tur·al·ly** \-ē\ *adv*

²suture *vt* **su·tured; su·tur·ing** \'süch-ring, -ə-ring\ : to unite, close, or secure with sutures ⟨*suture* a wound⟩

su·zer·ain \'süz-rən, -ə-rən, 'süz-ə-ˌrān\ *n* **1** : a feudal lord : OVERLORD **2** : a state controlling the foreign relations of another but allowing it internal sovereignty [French, from Middle French *sus* "up" + *-erain* (as in *soverain* "sovereign")] — **su·zer·ain·ty** \-tē\ *n*

svelte \'sfelt\ *adj* **1** : slender and graceful in form **2** : URBANE, SUAVE [French, from Italian *svelto,* from *svellere* "to pluck out", from Latin *evellere,* from *e-* + *vellere* "to pluck"]

Sven·ga·li \sfen-'gäl-ē\ *n* : one who attempts to exert a dominant and sometimes evil influence over another [*Svengali,* evil hypnotist in the novel *Trilby* by George du Maurier, died 1896, British artist and novelist]

¹swab \'swäb\ *n* **1 a** : MOP; *esp* : a yarn mop **b** : a wad of absorbent material usually wound around one end of a small stick and used for applying medication or for removing material (as from a wound or lesion);

also : a specimen taken with a swab **2** : SAILOR 1a [probably from Dutch *swabbe*]

²**swab** *vt* **swabbed; swab·bing** : to use a swab on

swad·dle \'swäd-l\ *vt* **swad·dled; swad·dling** \'swäd-ling, -l-ing\ **1** : to wrap (an infant) with swaddling clothes **2** : to wrap closely : SWATHE [Middle English *swadelen*]

swaddling clothes *n pl* **1** : narrow strips of cloth wrapped around an infant to restrict movement **2** : limitations or restrictions imposed upon the immature or inexperienced

swag \'swag\ *n* **1 a** : something hanging in a curve between two points : FESTOON **b** : a suspended cluster **2** : goods acquired by unlawful means : LOOT [earlier *swag* "to sway", probably of Scandinavian origin]

¹**swag·ger** \'swag-ər\ *vi* **swag·gered; swag·ger·ing** \'swag-ring, -ə-ring\ **1** : to conduct oneself in an arrogant or overbearing manner; *esp* : to walk with an air of superiority **2** : BOAST 1, 2, BRAG [probably from *swag* "to sway"] SYN see STRUT — **swag·ger·er** \'swag-ər-ər\ *n* — **swag·ger·ing·ly** \-ring-lē, -ə-ring-\ *adv*

²**swagger** *n* : an act or instance of swaggering

swagger stick *n* : a short light stick usually covered with leather or tipped with metal

Swa·hi·li \swä-'hē-lē\ *n* **1** : a member of a Bantu-speaking people of Zanzibar and the adjacent coast of Africa **2** : a Bantu language that is a trade and governmental language over much of East Africa and in the Congo region [Arabic *sawāḥil*, pl. of *sāḥil* "coast"]

swain \'swān\ *n* **1** : RUSTIC, PEASANT; *esp* : SHEPHERD **2** : a male admirer or suitor : BEAU [Old Norse *sveinn* "boy, servant"]

swale \'swāl\ *n* : a small, low-lying and usually wet stretch of land [Middle English, "shade"]

¹**swal·low** \'swäl-ō\ *n* **1** : any of a family of small long-winged migratory passerine birds that are noted for their graceful flight and have usually a deeply forked tail **2** : any of several swifts that superficially resemble swallows [Old English *swealwe*]

²**swallow** *vb* **1 a** : to take into the stomach through the mouth and throat **b** : to perform the actions used in swallowing something **2** : to envelop or take in as if by swallowing ⟨was *swallowed* up by the crowd⟩ **3** : to accept without question, protest, or resentment ⟨a hard story to *swallow*⟩ **4** : to take back : RETRACT ⟨had to *swallow* those words⟩ **5** : to keep from expressing or showing : REPRESS ⟨*swallow* one's anger⟩ **6** : to utter (as words) indistinctly [Old English *swelgan*] — **swal·low·er** \'swäl-ə-wər\ *n*

³**swallow** *n* **1** : an act of swallowing **2** : an amount that can be swallowed at one time

swal·low·tail \'swäl-ō-,tāl\ *n* **1** : a deeply forked and tapering tail (as of a swallow) **2** : any of various large butterflies with the border of the hind wing drawn out into a process resembling a tail — **swal·low·tailed** \,swäl-ō-'tāld\ *adj*

swam *past of* SWIM

swa·mi \'swäm-ē\ *n* : a Hindu mystic or religious teacher — used as a title [Hindi *svāmī*, from Sanskrit *svāmin* "owner, lord", from *sva* "one's own"]

¹**swamp** \'swämp, 'swómp\ *n* : wet spongy land or a tract of this often partially or intermittently covered with water and usually overgrown with shrubs and trees — compare MARSH [Middle English *sompe*, from Dutch *somp* "morass"] — **swamp·i·ness** \-pē-nəs\ *n* — **swampy** \'swäm-pē, 'swóm-\ *adj*

²**swamp** *vb* **1 a** : to cause to capsize in water or fill with water and sink **b** : to fill with or as if with water : SUBMERGE **2** : to overwhelm by an excess of something (as enemies or work)

swamp buggy *n* : a vehicle designed to travel over swampy terrain; *esp* : a four-wheeled motor vehicle with oversize tires

swamp·land \'swäm-,pland, 'swóm-\ *n* : SWAMP

swampy \'swäm-pē, 'swóm-\ *adj* **swamp·i·er; -est** : consisting of or resembling swamp : MARSHY ⟨frogs in a *swampy* place among the trees⟩ — **swamp·i·ness** *n*

swan \'swän\ *n, pl* **swans** *also* **swan** : any of various heavy-bodied long-necked mostly pure white aquatic birds related to but larger than the geese [Old English]

swan dive *n* : a headfirst forward dive made with the back arched, the head back, the arms out to either side, and the legs together

¹**swank** \'swangk\ *vi* : to show off : SWAGGER [perhaps from Middle High German *swanken* "to sway"]

²**swank** *n* : a sometimes flashy show of elegance or pretense

³**swank** *or* **swanky** \'swang-kē\ *adj* **swank·er** *or* **swank·i·er; -est** **1** : characterized by showy display : OSTENTATIOUS **2** : fashionably elegant : SMART — **swank·i·ly** \'swang-kə-lē\ *adv* — **swank·i·ness** \-kē-nəs\ *n*

swans·down \'swänz-,daún\ *n* **1** : the very soft white down of the swan **2** : a heavy cotton flannel with a thick nap on the face

swan song *n* **1** : a song of unusual beauty formerly thought to be sung by a dying swan **2** : a farewell appearance or final act or pronouncement

¹**swap** *also* **swop** \'swäp\ *vb* **swapped; swap·ping** : to give in exchange : make an exchange : BARTER [Middle English *swappen* "to strike"; from the practice of striking hands in closing a business deal]

²**swap** *n* : EXCHANGE 1, TRADE

sward \'sword\ *n* : the grassy surface of land : TURF [Old English *sweard* "skin, rind"]

¹**swarm** \'sworm\ *n* **1** : a great number of honeybees emigrating together from a hive in company with a queen to start a new colony elsewhere; *also* : a colony of honeybees settled in a hive **2** : an extremely large number massed together and usually in motion [Old English *swearm*]

²**swarm** *vb* **1** : to form and depart from a hive in a swarm **2** : to migrate, move, or gather in a crowd : THRONG **3** : to contain or fill with a swarm : TEEM — **swarm·er** *n*

³**swarm** *vb* : to climb with the hands and feet; *esp* : SHIN ⟨*swarm* up a pole⟩ [origin unknown]

swarm spore *n* : a tiny motile spore

swart \'sword\ *adj* : SWARTHY [Old English *sweart*] — **swart·ness** *n*

swar·thy \'swor-thē, -thē\ *adj* **swar·thi·er; -est** : of a dark color, complexion, or cast : DUSKY [derived from *swart*] — **swar·thi·ness** *n*

¹**swash** \'swäsh\ *vb* **1** : BLUSTER 2, SWAGGER **2** : to make violent noisy movements **3** : to move or cause to move with a splashing sound

²**swash** *n* **1** : SWAGGER **2** : a dashing of water against or upon something [probably imitative]

swash·buck·ler \-,bək-lər\ *n* : a boasting soldier or blustering ruffian : BRAVO [¹*swash* + *buckler*] — **swash·buck·le** \-,bək-əl\ *vt* — **swash·buck·ling** \-,bək-ling\ *adj or n*

swas·ti·ka \'swäs-ti-kə *also* swä-'stē-kə\ *n* : a symbol or ornament in the form of a Greek cross with the ends of the arms extended at right angles all in the same rotary direction [Sanskrit *svastika*, from *svasti* "welfare", from *su-* "well" + *asti* "he is"; from its being regarded as a good luck symbol]

swat \'swät\ *vb* **swat·ted; swat·ting** : to hit with a quick hard blow [English dialect *swat* "to squat", alteration of *squat*] — **swat** *n* — **swat·ter** *n*

swatch \'swäch\ *n* **1 a** : a sample piece (as of fabric) or a collection of samples **b** : a typical sample **2** : PATCH ⟨a *swatch* of color⟩ [origin unknown]

swath \'swäth, 'swóth\ *or* **swathe** \'swäth, 'swóth, 'swäth\ *n* **1 a** : the sweep of a scythe or machine in mowing or the path cut in one course **b** : a row of cut grain or grass **2** : a long broad strip or belt ⟨a long *swath* of land⟩ **3** : a space devastated as if by a scythe [Old English *swæth* "footstep, trace"]

swan

\ə\ abut	\ng\ sing
\ər\ further	\ō\ bone
\a\ mat	\ó\ saw
\ā\ take	\ói\ coin
\ä\ cot, cart	\th\ thin
\aú\ out	\th\ this
\ch\ chin	\ü\ food
\e\ pet	\ú\ foot
\ē\ easy	\y\ yet
\g\ go	\yü\ few
\i\ tip	\yú\ cure
\ī\ life	\zh\ vision
\j\ job	

¹**swathe** \'swā<u>th</u>, 'swȯ<u>th</u>, 'swä<u>th</u>\ *vt* **1** : to bind, wrap, or swaddle with or as if with a bandage **2** : ENVELOP [Old English *swathian*]

²**swathe** \'swä<u>th</u>, 'swȯ<u>th</u>, 'swä<u>th</u>\ *or* **swath** \'swä<u>th</u>, 'swä<u>th</u>, 'swȯ<u>th</u>, 'swȯ<u>th</u>\ *n* **1** : a band used in swathing **2** : an enveloping medium

¹**sway** \'swā\ *vb* **1 a** : to swing or cause to swing slowly back and forth from a base or pivot **b** : to move gently from an upright to a leaning position **2** : to hold sway : act as ruler or governor **3** : to fluctuate or veer between one point, position, or opinion and another **4** : to cause to turn aside (as from a thought or course of action) **5** : to exert a guiding or controlling influence upon [Middle English *sweyen* "to fall, swoon"] SYN see INFLUENCE — **sway·er** *n* □ SYN SWAY, OSCILLATE, VIBRATE, WAVER mean to move back and forth. SWAY implies a slow swinging or teetering movement as of something large and heavy; OSCILLATE suggests a relatively rapid and rhythmic alternation of direction; VIBRATE applies especially to the very rapid oscillation of an elastic body under stress or impact; WAVER stresses irregular movement suggestive of reeling or tottering. SYN see in addition INFLUENCE

²**sway** *n* **1** : the action or an instance of swaying or of being swayed : an oscillating, fluctuating, or sweeping motion **2** : an inclination or deflection caused by or as if by swaying **3 a** : a controlling force or influence **b** : sovereign power : DOMINION

sway·backed \'swā-,bakt\ *also* **sway·back** \'swā-'bak\ *adj* : having an unusually hollow or sagging back (a *swaybacked* mare) — **sway·back** *n*

swear \'swaər, 'sweər\ *vb* **swore** \'swōr, 'swȯər\; **sworn** \'swōrn, 'swȯrn\; **swear·ing** **1** : to utter or take solemnly (an oath) **2 a** : to assert as true or promise under oath **b** : to assert or promise emphatically or earnestly **3 a** : to administer an oath to (*swear* the witness) **b** : to bind by an oath (*swore* them to secrecy) **4** : to bring into a specified state by swearing (*swear* your life away) **5** : to take an oath **6** : to use profane or obscene language : CURSE [Old English *swerian*] — **swear·er** *n* — **swear by** : to place great confidence in — **swear off** : to vow to abstain from (*swear off* smoking)

swear in *vt* : to induct into office by administration of an oath

swear out *vt* : to procure (a warrant for arrest) by making a sworn accusation

swear·word \'swaər-,wərd, 'sweər-\ *n* : a profane or dirty word

¹**sweat** \'swet\ *vb* **sweat** *or* **sweat·ed**; **sweat·ing** **1** : to give off perceptible salty moisture through the openings of the sweat glands : PERSPIRE **2** : to give off or cause to give off moisture **3** : to collect drops of moisture (stones *sweat* at night) **4 a** : to work so hard that one perspires : TOIL (*sweat* over a lesson) **b** : to undergo anxiety or mental distress **5** : to soak with sweat (*sweat* a collar) **6** : to get rid of or lose by perspiring (*sweat* off weight) (*sweat* out a fever) **7** : to drive hard : OVERWORK; *esp* : to force to work hard at low wages and under bad conditions (a factory that *sweats* its employees) **8** : to heat (as solder) so as to melt and cause to run especially between surfaces to unite them; *also* : to unite by such means (*sweat* a pipe joint) [Old English *swǣtan*, from *swāt* "sweat"] — **sweat blood** : to work or worry intensely

²**sweat** *n* **1** : hard work : DRUDGERY **2** : fluid excreted from the sweat glands of the skin : PERSPIRATION **3** : moisture issuing from or gathering in drops on a surface **4** : the condition of one sweating or sweated **5** : a state of anxiety or impatience

sweat·band \'swet-,band\ *n* **1** : a band lining the inner edge of a hat or cap to prevent sweat damage **2** : a band of material worn around the head or wrist to absorb sweat

sweat·er \'swet-ər\ *n* **1** : one that sweats or causes sweating **2** : a knitted or crocheted jacket or pullover

sweat gland *n* : a gland of the skin that secretes perspiration and opens by a minute pore in the skin

sweat lodge *n* : a hut, lodge, or cavern heated by steam from water poured on hot stones and used especially by American Indians for ritual or therapeutic sweating

sweat out *vt* **1** : to endure or wait through the course of **2** : to work one's way painfully through or to

sweat pants *n pl* : pants having a drawstring waist and elastic cuffs at the ankle that are worn especially by athletes in warming up

sweat shirt *n* : a loose collarless usually long-sleeved pullover of heavy cotton jersey

sweat·shop \'swet-,shäp\ *n* : a shop or factory in which workers are employed for long hours at low wages and under unhealthy conditions

sweaty \'swet-ē\ *adj* **sweat·i·er; -est** **1** : wet or stained with or smelling of sweat **2** : causing sweat (*sweaty* work) — **sweat·i·ly** \'swet-l-ē\ *adv* — **sweat·i·ness** \'swet-ē-nəs\ *n*

swede \'swēd\ *n* **1** *cap* **a** : a native or inhabitant of Sweden **b** : a person of Swedish descent **2** : RUTABAGA

Swed·ish \'swēd-ish\ *n* **1** : the Germanic language spoken in Sweden **2** *pl in construction* : the people of Sweden — **Swedish** *adj*

¹**sweep** \'swēp\ *vb* **swept** \'swept\; **sweep·ing** **1 a** : to remove from a surface with or as if with a broom or brush **b** : to remove or take with a single continuous forceful action **c** : to drive or carry along with irresistible force **2 a** : to clean with or as if with a broom or brush **b** : to move across or along swiftly, violently, or overwhelmingly **c** : to win an overwhelming victory in or on (*sweep* the elections) **3** : to touch in passing with a swift continuous movement **4** : to go with stately or sweeping movements **5** : to trace the outline of (as a curve or angle) **6** : to cover the entire range of **7** : to move or extend in a wide curve or range [Middle English *swepen*] — **sweep·er** *n*

²**sweep** *n* **1** : something that sweeps or works with a sweeping motion: as **a** : a long pole pivoted on a post and used to raise and lower a bucket (as in a well) **b** : a long oar **c** : a windmill sail **2 a** : an act or instance of sweeping; *esp* : a clearing out or away with or as if with a broom **b** : an overwhelming victory (as the winning of all the contests or prizes in a competition) **3 a** : a movement of great range and force **b** : a curving or circular course or line **c** : the compass of a sweeping movement : SCOPE **d** : a broad extent **4** : CHIMNEY SWEEP

²sweep 1a

sweep·back \'swēp-,bak\ *n* : the backward slant of an airplane wing in which the outer portion of the wing is downstream from the inner portion

sweep hand *n* : SWEEP-SECOND HAND

¹**sweep·ing** *n* **1** : the act or action of one that sweeps (gave the room a good *sweeping*) **2** *pl* : things collected by sweeping : REFUSE

²**sweeping** *adj* **1 a** : moving or extending in a wide curve or over a wide area **b** : having a curving line or form **2 a** : EXTENSIVE (*sweeping* reforms) **b** : broadly and indiscriminately inclusive (*sweeping* generalizations) — **sweep·ing·ly** \'swē-ping-lē\

sweep net *n* : a bag-shaped net with a handle used by entomologists for catching insects by sweeping it over vegetation

sweep–sec·ond hand \'swēp-,sek-ənd-, -ənt-\ *n* : a hand marking seconds on a timepiece mounted concentrically with the other hands and read on the same dial

sweep·stakes \-,stāks\ *n sing or pl, also* **sweep·stake** \-,stāk\ **1 a** : a race or contest in which the entire prize may be awarded to the winner **b** : a horse race in which the stake awarded to the winner or distributed among the top finishers is made up at least in part of the entry fees or money contributed by the owners of the horses **2** : CONTEST 1, COMPETITION **3** : any of various lotteries [Middle English *swepestake* "one who wins all the stakes in a game", from *swepen* "to sweep" + *stake*]

¹sweet \'swēt\ *adj* **1 a** : pleasing to the taste **b** : being or inducing the one of the four basic taste sensations that is typically induced by table sugar **c** : having a relatively large sugar content **2 a** : pleasing to the mind or feelings : AGREEABLE **b** : marked by gentle good humor or kindliness **c** : FRAGRANT **d** : delicately pleasing to the ear or eye **e** : SACCHARINE 2, CLOYING **3** : much loved : DEAR **4 a** : not sour or rancid : not decaying or stale : WHOLESOME **b** : not salt or salted : FRESH ⟨*sweet* water⟩ **c** : free from excessive acidity ⟨*sweet* soil⟩ **d** : free from noxious gases and odors [Old English *swēte*] — **sweet·ly** *adv* — **sweet·ness** *n* — **sweet on** : in love with

²sweet *adv* : in a sweet way

³sweet *n* **1** : something that is sweet to the taste: as **a** : a food (as a candy or preserve) having a high sugar content **b** *British* : DESSERT **c** *British* : CANDY 2 **2** : a sweet taste sensation **3** : a pleasant or gratifying experience, possession, or state **4** : DARLING

sweet alyssum *n* : a perennial European herb of the mustard family often grown for its clusters of small fragrant usually white flowers

sweet basil *n* : a common basil that has white flowers tinged with purple and is used especially in seasoning

sweet·bread \'swēt-ˌbred\ *n* : the thymus or pancreas especially of a young animal used as food

sweet·bri·er *also* **sweet·bri·ar** \-ˌbrī-ər, -ˌbrīr\ *n* : an Old World rose with stout recurved prickles and white to deep rosy pink single flowers — called also *eglantine*

sweet cherry *n* : a white-flowered Eurasian cherry widely grown for its large sweet-flavored fruits; *also* : its fruit

sweet cic·e·ly \-'sis-lē, -ə-lē\ *n, pl* **-lies** : any of several herbs of the carrot family with white flowers and an aromatic root [*cicely* from Latin *seselis,* from Greek]

sweet clover *n* : any of a genus of tall erect plants of the pea family widely grown for soil improvement or hay

sweet corn *n* : an Indian corn with kernels containing much sugar and adapted for table use when immature

sweet·en \'swēt-n\ *vb* **sweetened; sweet·en·ing** \'swēt-ning, -n-ing\ : to make or become sweet — **sweeten·er** \'swēt-nər, -n-ər\ *n*

sweet·en·ing *n* **1** : the act or process of making sweet **2** : something that sweetens

sweet fern *n* : a small North American shrub of the wax-myrtle family with sweet-scented or aromatic leaves

sweet flag *n* : a perennial marsh herb of the arum family with long leaves and a pungent rhizome

sweet gum *n* : an American timber tree with palmately lobed leaves, hard reddish wood, and a long-stemmed woody fruit resembling a bur; *also* : its wood

sweet·heart \'swēt-ˌhärt\ *n* **1** : DARLING **2** : the person one is in love with : LOVER

sweet·ing \'swēt-ing\ *n* **1** *archaic* : SWEETHEART **2** : a sweet apple

sweet·ish \'swēt-ish\ *adj* : somewhat and often unpleasantly sweet — **sweet·ish·ly** *adv*

sweet marjoram *n* : an aromatic European herb with dense spikelike flower clusters

sweet·meat \'swēt-ˌmēt\ *n* : a food rich in sugar: as **a** : a candied or crystallized fruit **b** : CANDY 2

sweet pea *n* : a garden plant with slender climbing stems and large fragrant flowers; *also* : its flower

sweet pepper *n* : a large mild-flavored thick-walled capsicum fruit; *also* : a plant bearing this

sweet potato *n* **1** : a tropical vine related to the morning glory with variously shaped leaves and purplish flowers; *also* : its large sweet starchy tuberous root that is cooked and eaten as a vegetable **2** : OCARINA

sweet·shop \'swēt-ˌshäp\ *n, chiefly British* : a candy store

sweet sorghum *n* : SORGO

sweet tooth *n* : a craving or fondness for sweet food

sweet wil·liam \swēt-'wil-yəm\ *n, often cap W* : a widely grown Eurasian pink with small white to deep red or purple flowers often showily spotted, banded, or mottled and borne in flat clusters on erect stalks [from the name *William*]

¹swell \'swel\ *vb* **swelled; swelled** *or* **swol·len** \'swō-lən\; **swell·ing 1 a** : to expand (as in size, volume, or numbers) gradually beyond a normal or original limit ⟨the population *swelled*⟩ **b** : to be distended or puffed up ⟨the ankle is badly *swollen*⟩ **c** : to form a bulge or rounded elevation **2** : to fill or become filled with pride and arrogance **3** : to fill or become filled with emotion [Old English *swellan*]

²swell *n* **1 a** : a rounded elevation **b** : the condition of being protuberant **2** : a long often massive crestless wave or succession of waves **3 a** : a gradual increase and decrease of the loudness of a musical sound; *also* : a sign ⟨⟩ indicating a swell ⟨⟩ : a device used in an organ for governing loudness **4 a** : a person dressed in the height of fashion **b** : a person of high social position or outstanding competence

³swell *adj* **1** : STYLISH, FASHIONABLE **2** : EXCELLENT, FIRST-RATE

swelled head *n* : an exaggerated opinion of oneself : SELF-CONCEIT — **swelled–head·ed** \'sweld-'hed-əd\ *adj* — **swelled–head·ed·ness** *n*

swell·ing \'swel-ing\ *n* **1** : something that is swollen; *esp* : an abnormal bodily protuberance or localized enlargement **2** : the condition of being swollen

¹swel·ter \'swel-tər\ *vb* **swel·tered; swel·ter·ing** \'swel-tring, -tə-ring\ **1** : to suffer, sweat, or be faint from heat **2** : to oppress with heat [Middle English *sweltren,* from *swelten* "to die, be overcome by heat", from Old English *sweltan* "to die"]

²swelter *n* **1** : a state of oppressive heat **2** : an excited or overwrought state of mind ⟨in a *swelter*⟩

swel·ter·ing *adj* : oppressively hot — **swel·ter·ing·ly** \-tə-ring-lē, -tring-\ *adv*

swept *past of* SWEEP

swept–back \'swept-'bak, 'swep-\ *adj* : possessing sweepback

¹swerve \'swərv\ *vb* : to turn aside suddenly from a straight line or course ⟨*swerved* to avoid an oncoming car⟩ [Old English *sweorfan* "to wipe, grind away"] □ SYN SWERVE, VEER mean to turn aside from a straight course. SWERVE may suggest a physical, mental, or moral turning that may be small in degree but is usually sudden or sharp; VEER implies a sharp change in course or direction.

²swerve *n* : an act or instance of swerving

¹swift \'swift\ *adj* **1** : moving or capable of moving with great speed **2** : occurring suddenly or within a very short time ⟨*swift* changes⟩ **3** : quick to act or respond ⟨*swift* in thought and deed⟩ [Old English] SYN see FAST — **swift·ly** *adv* — **swift·ness** \'swift-nəs, 'swif-\ *n*

²swift *adv* : SWIFTLY ⟨*swift*-flowing⟩

³swift *n* **1** : any of several lizards that run swiftly **2** : any of numerous small and usually sooty black birds that are related to the hummingbirds but superficially resemble swallows

¹swig \'swig\ *n* : a quantity drunk at one time : DRAFT [origin unknown]

²swig *vb* **swigged; swig·ging** : to drink in gulps ⟨*swig* cider⟩ — **swig·ger** *n*

¹swill \'swil\ *vb* **1** : WASH 2, DRENCH **2** : to drink great drafts of : consume freely, greedily, or to excess **3** : to feed (as a pig) with swill [Old English *swillan*] — **swill·er** *n*

²swill *n* **1** : food for animals (as swine) composed of edible refuse mixed with liquid **2** : GARBAGE, REFUSE **3** : a draft of liquor

sweet gum

sweet pea

\ə\ abut		\ng\ sing
\ər\ further		\ō\ bone
\a\ mat		\ȯ\ saw
\ā\ take		\ȯi\ coin
\ä\ cot, cart		\th\ thin
\au̇\ out		\th\ this
\ch\ chin		\ü\ food
\e\ pet		\u̇\ foot
\ē\ easy		\y\ yet
\g\ go		\yü\ few
\i\ tip		\yu̇\ cure
\ī\ life		\zh\ vision
\j\ job		

¹swim \'swim\ *vb* **swam** \'swam\; **swum** \'swəm\; **swim·ming** **1 a** : to move through water by natural means (as the action of limbs, fins, or tail) **b** : to move quietly and smoothly : GLIDE **2 a** : to float on or in or be covered with or as if with a liquid ⟨toy boats *swimming* in the tub⟩ ⟨meat that *swam* in fat⟩ **b** : to experience or suffer from or as if from vertigo ⟨my head *swam* in the stuffy room⟩ **3** : to surmount difficulties **4** : to cross by propelling oneself through water ⟨*swim* a stream⟩ [Old English *swimman*] — **swim·ma·ble** \'swim-ə-bəl\ *adj* — **swim·mer** *n*

²swim *n* **1** : an act or period of swimming **2** : a temporary dizziness or unconsciousness **3** : the main current of activity ⟨be in the *swim*⟩

swim bladder *n* : the air bladder of a fish

swim fin *n* : a rubber shoe with the front expanded into a paddle for use in skin diving or scuba diving

swim·mer·et \,swim-ə-'ret\ *n* : one of a series of small appendages under the abdomen of many crustaceans that are used especially for swimming or for carrying eggs

swimmer's itch *n* : an itchy skin inflammation caused by superficial invasion of the skin by larval trematode worms that are not normally parasites of human beings

swim·ming *adj* : marked by, adapted to, or used in or for swimming

swim·ming·ly \-ing-lē\ *adv* : very well : SPLENDIDLY

swimming pool *n* : a tank (as of concrete or plastic) made for swimming

swim·my \'swim-ē\ *adj* : verging on, causing, or affected by dizziness — **swim·mi·ly** \'swim-ə-lē\ *adv* — **swim·mi·ness** \'swim-ē-nəs\ *n*

swim·suit \'swim-,süt\ *n* : a suit for wear for swimming

¹swin·dle \'swin-dl\ *vb* **swin·dled; swin·dling** \-dling, -dl-ing\ : to deprive of something by deception or fraud [back-formation from *swindler*, from German *schwindler* "giddy person", from *schwindeln* "to be dizzy"] SYN see CHEAT — **swin·dler** \-dlər, -dl-ər\ *n*

²swindle *n* : an act or instance of swindling : FRAUD

swine \'swīn\ *n, pl* **swine** **1** : any of a family of stout-bodied short-legged hoofed mammals with a thick bristly skin and a long flexible snout; *esp* : a domesticated animal derived from the European wild boar and widely raised for meat **2** : a contemptible person [Old English *swīn*]

swine·herd \-,hərd\ *n* : one who tends swine

¹swing \'swing\ *vb* **swung** \'swəng\; **swing·ing** \'swing-ing\ **1 a** : to wield with a sweep or flourish ⟨*swing* an axe⟩ **b** : to cause to sway to and fro or turn on an axis; *also* : to face or move in another direction **2 a** : to hang or be hung so as to permit swaying or turning ⟨*swing* a hammock⟩ **b** : to die by hanging **c** : to move freely to and fro from or rotate about a point of suspension ⟨the door *swung* open⟩ **d** : to hang freely from a support **e** : to shift or fluctuate between extremes ⟨the market *swung* sharply downward⟩ **3** : to handle successfully : MANAGE ⟨learning to *swing* a new job⟩ **4** : to play or sing (as a melody) in the style of swing music : perform swing music **5 a** : to move along rhythmically **b** : to start up in a smooth vigorous manner ⟨*swing* into action⟩ **c** : to hit at something with a sweeping movement [Old English *swingan* "to beat, fling oneself, rush"] — **swing·able** \'swing-ə-bəl\ *adj* — **swing·ably** \-blē\ *adv* — **swing·er** \'swing-ər\ *n*

²swing *n* **1** : an act of swinging **2** : a swinging movement, blow, or rhythm: as **a** : a regular to-and-fro movement of or as if of a suspended body **b** : a steady pulsing rhythm (as in poetry or music); *also* : dancing to swing music **c** : a repeated shifting from one condition, form, or position to another **3** : the distance through which something swings ⟨a pendulum with a 25-centimeter *swing*⟩ **4** : a swinging seat usually hung by overhead ropes **5** : a curving course or outline or one beginning and ending at the same point ⟨took a *swing* through the hills⟩ **6** : a style of jazz in which the

melody is freely interpreted and improvised on by the individual players within a steadily maintained rhythm — **swing** *adj*

swin·gle·tree \'swing-gəl-,trē\ *n* : WHIFFLETREE [Middle English *swingel* "instrument for beating flax, cudgel"]

swing shift *n* : the work shift between the day and night shifts (as from 4 p.m. to midnight)

swin·ish \'swī-nish\ *adj* : of, suggesting, or befitting swine : BEASTLY — **swin·ish·ly** *adv* — **swin·ish·ness** *n*

¹swipe \'swīp\ *n* : a strong sweeping blow [probably alteration of *sweep*]

²swipe *vb* **1** : to strike or wipe with a sweeping motion **2** : STEAL 2a, PILFER

¹swirl \'swərl\ *n* **1** : a whirling mass or motion : EDDY **2** : whirling confusion **3** : a twisting shape or mark [Middle English]

²swirl *vb* **1** : to move with or pass in a swirl **2** : to be marked with or arranged in swirls **3** : to cause to swirl — **swirl·ing·ly** \'swər-ling-lē\ *adv*

¹swish \'swish\ *vb* : to make, move, or strike with a rustling or hissing sound [imitative] — **swish·ing·ly** \-ing-lē\ *adv*

²swish *n* **1** : a prolonged hissing sound (as of a whip cutting the air) or a light rustling sound (as of silk in friction) **2** : a swishing movement — **swishy** \-ē\ *adj*

Swiss \'swis\ *n* **1** *pl* **Swiss** **a** : a native or inhabitant of Switzerland **b** : a person of Swiss decent **2** *often not cap* : a fine sheer cotton fabric often with raised dots originally made in Switzerland **3** : a mild elastic hard cheese with large holes [Middle French *Suisse*, from Middle High German *Swīzer*, from *Swīz* "Switzerland"] — **Swiss** *adj*

Swiss chard *n* : CHARD

¹switch \'swich\ *n* **1** : a slender flexible whip, rod, or twig **2** : an act of switching: as **a** : a blow with a switch **b** : a shift from one to another ⟨a *switch* of political parties⟩ **3** : a tuft of long hairs at the end of the tail of an animal (as a cow) **4 a** : a device made usually of two movable rails and necessary connections and designed to turn a locomotive or train from one track to another **b** : a railroad siding **5** : a device for making, breaking, or changing the connections in an electrical circuit **6** : a strand of added or artificial hair used in some coiffures [perhaps from Dutch *swijch* "twig"]

²switch *vb* **1** : to strike or whip with or as if with a switch **2** : to lash from side to side : WHISK ⟨a cat *switching* its tail⟩ **3** : to turn, shift, or change by operating a switch ⟨*switch* a train onto a siding⟩ ⟨*switch* off the light⟩ **4** : to change one for another : EXCHANGE ⟨*switched* methods to improve production⟩ ⟨*switched* to a different brand⟩ — **switch·er** *n*

switch·back \'swich-,bak\ *n* : a zigzag road, trail, or section of railroad tracks for climbing a steep hill

switch·blade knife \,swich-,blād-\ *n* : a pocketknife having the blade spring-operated so that pressure on a release catch causes it to fly open

switch·board \'swich-,bōrd, -,bȯrd\ *n* : a device (as in a telephone exchange) consisting of a panel on which are mounted electric switches so arranged that a number of circuits may be connected, combined, and controlled

switch–hit·ter \'swich-'hit-ər\ *n* : a baseball player who can bat either left-handed or right-handed

switch·man \'swich-mən\ *n* : one who attends a railroad switch

switch·yard \-,yärd\ *n* : a place where railroad cars are switched from one track to another and trains are made up

Swit·zer \'swit-sər\ *n* : SWISS 1 [Middle High German *Swīzer*]

¹swiv·el \'swiv-əl\ *n* : a device joining two parts so that one or both can pivot freely (as on a bolt or pin) [Middle English]

²swivel *vb* **swiv·eled** *or* **swiv·elled; swiv·el·ing** *or* **swiv·el·ling** \'swivling, -ə-ling\ : to turn on or as if on a swivel

swivel chair *n* : a chair that swivels on its base

swiv·et \'swiv-ət\ *n* : a state of extreme agitation ⟨in a *swivet*⟩ [origin unknown]

swiz·zle stick \'swiz-əl-\ *n* : a stick used to stir mixed drinks [*swizzle*, a kind of cocktail]

swob *archaic variant of* SWAB

swollen *past participle of* SWELL

¹swoon \'swün\ *vi* **1** : FAINT **2 2** : to drift or fade imperceptibly [Middle English *swounen*] — **swoon·er** *n* — **swoon·ing·ly** \'swü-ning-lē\ *adv*

²swoon *n* **1** : a partial or total loss of consciousness; *also* : a dazed enraptured state **2** : a dreamy flow (as of music)

¹swoop \'swüp\ *vb* **1** : to descend or pounce suddenly ⟨the eagle *swooped* down on its prey⟩ **2** : to carry off abruptly [Old English *swāpan* "to sweep"]

²swoop *n* : an act or instance of swooping

swoosh \'swüsh, 'swùsh,\ *vb* : to make, move, or discharge with a rushing sound [imitative] — **swoosh** *n*

swop *variant of* SWAP

sword \'sōrd, 'sórd\ *n* **1** : a weapon having a long usually sharp-pointed and sharp-edged blade **2** : something that kills or punishes as effectively as a sword **3** : military power or the use of it : WAR [Old English *sweord*] — **sword·like** \-,līk\ *adj* — **at swords' points** : mutually antagonistic

sword cane *n* : a cane that conceals a sword or dagger blade

sword dance *n* : any of several folk dances in which performers hold, swing, or dance around swords — **sword dancer** *n*

sword·fish \'sōrd-,fish, 'sórd-\ *n* : a very large oceanic food fish having a long swordlike beak formed by the bones of the upper jaw

sword grass *n* : a grass or sedge having leaves with a sharp or toothed edge

sword knot *n* : an ornamental cord or tassel tied to the hilt of a sword

sword·play \-,plā\ *n* : the art or skill of using a sword especially in fencing

swords·man \'sōrdz-mən, 'sórdz-\ *n* **1** : one who fights with a sword **2** : one skilled in the use of the sword : FENCER

swords·man·ship \-,ship\ *n* : SWORDPLAY

sword·tail \'sōrd-,tāl, 'sórd-\ *n* : a small brightly marked Central American topminnow with many color varieties that is often kept in tropical aquariums

swore *past of* SWEAR

sworn *past participle of* SWEAR

swum *past participle of* SWIM

swung *past of* SWING

syc·a·more \'sik-ə-,mōr, -,mór\ *n* **1** : a common fig tree of Egypt and Asia Minor **2** : a Eurasian maple with yellow flowers in long clusters **3** : a large spreading American plane tree with light-brown flaky bark and round fruits like buttons [Middle French *sicamor*, from Latin *sycomorus*, from Greek *sykomoros*]

syc·o·phant \'sik-ə-fənt\ *n* : a servile self-seeking flatterer : PARASITE [Latin *sycophanta* "informer, swindler, sycophant", from Greek *sykophantēs* "informer"] — **syc·o·phan·cy** \-fən-sē\ *n* — **syc·o·phan·tic** \,sik-ə-'fant-ik\ *adj* — **syc·o·phan·ti·cal·ly** \-'fant-i-kə-lē, -klē\ *adv*

sy·enite \'sī-ə-,nīt\ *n* : an igneous rock composed chiefly of feldspar [Latin *Syenites lapis* "stone of Syene", from *Syene*, ancient city in Egypt] — **sy·enit·ic** \,sī-ə-'nit-ik\ *adj*

syl·la·bary \'sil-ə-,ber-ē\ *n, pl* **-bar·ies** : a series or set of written characters each one of which is used to represent a syllable

syl·lab·ic \sə-'lab-ik\ *adj* **1** : of, relating to, or denoting syllables ⟨*syllabic* accent⟩ **2** *of a consonant* : not accompanied in the same syllable by a vowel ⟨\n\ is syl-

labic in \'bät-n-ē\ botany but is nonsyllabic in \'bät-nē\⟩ **3** : characterized by distinct enunciation or separation of syllables — **syl·lab·i·cal·ly** \-'lab-i-kə-lē, -klē\ *adv*

syl·lab·i·ca·tion \sə-,lab-ə-'kā-shən\ *n* : the forming of syllables : the division of words into syllables — **syl·lab·i·cate** \-'lab-ə-,kāt\ *vb*

syl·lab·i·fi·ca·tion \sə-,lab-ə-fə-'kā-shən\ *n* : SYLLABICATION

syl·lab·i·fy \sə-'lab-ə-,fī\ *vt* **-fied; -fy·ing** : to form or divide into syllables

¹syl·la·ble \'sil-ə-bəl\ *n* **1** : a unit of spoken language that consists of one or more vowel sounds alone or of a syllabic consonant alone or of either with one or more consonant sounds preceding or following **2** : one or more letters (as *syl, la,* and *ble*) in a word (as *syl-la-ble*) usually set off from the rest of the word by a centered dot or a hyphen and treated as guides to dividing a word at the end of a line **3** : the smallest conceivable expression or unit of something ⟨not the least *syllable* of wit⟩ [Middle French *sillabe*, from Latin *syllaba*, from Greek *syllabē*, from *syllambanein* "to combine", from *syn-* + *lambanein* "to take"]

²syllable *vt* **syl·la·bled; syl·la·bling** \-bə-ling, -bling\ : to express or utter in syllables

syl·la·bub *or* **sil·la·bub** \'sil-ə-,bəb\ *n* **1** : a drink or dessert made by curdling milk or cream usually with wine **2** : a dessert of sweetened milk or cream beaten to a froth and flavored with wine or liquor [origin unknown]

syl·la·bus \-bəs\ *n, pl* **-bi** \-,bī, -,bē\ *or* **-bus·es** : a summary outline (as of a course of study) [Latin *sillybus* "label for a book", from Greek *sillybos*]

syl·lo·gism \'sil-ə-,jiz-əm\ *n* **1** : a brief form for stating an argument from the general to the particular that consists of two statements and a conclusion that must be true if these two statements are true ⟨"all lawbreakers deserve punishment; this person is a lawbreaker; therefore this person deserves punishment" is a *syllogism*⟩ **2** : deductive reasoning [Middle French *silogisme*, from Latin *syllogismus*, from Greek *syllogismos*, from *syllogizesthai* "to reason deductively", derived from *syn-* + *logos* "reckoning, word"] — **syl·lo·gis·tic** \,sil-ə-'jis-tik\ *adj* — **syl·lo·gis·ti·cal·ly** \-ti-kə-lē, -klē\ *adv*

sylph \'silf\ *n* **1** : an imaginary aerial spirit **2** : a slender graceful woman [New Latin *sylphus*] — **sylph·like** \'sil-,flīk\ *adj*

syl·van *also* **sil·van** \'sil-vən\ *adj* **1 a** : living or located in the woods or forest **b** : of, relating to, or characteristic of the woods or forest **2** : abounding in woods or trees : WOODED [Medieval Latin *silvanus, sylvanus*, from Latin *silva, sylva* "woods"]

syl·vat·ic \sil-'vat-ik\ *adj* : occurring in or affecting wild animals ⟨*sylvatic* plague⟩ [Latin *silvaticus* "of the woods, wild", from *silva* "woods"]

sylviculture *variant of* SILVICULTURE

sym- — see SYN-

sym·bi·ont \'sim-,bī-änt, -bē-\ *n* : an organism living in symbiosis; *esp* : the smaller member of a symbiotic pair [derived from Greek *symbioun* "to live together"] — **sym·bi·on·tic** \,sim-bī-'änt-ik, -bē-\ *adj*

sym·bi·o·sis \,sim-bī-'ō-səs, -bē-\ *n, pl* **-o·ses** \-'ō-,sēz\ : the living together in intimate association or close union of two unlike organisms especially when mutually beneficial [German *symbiose*, from Greek *symbiōsis* "state of living together", from *symbioun* "to live together", derived from *syn-* + *bios* "life"] — **sym·bi·ot·ic** \-'ät-ik\ *adj* — **sym·bi·ot·i·cal·ly** \-i-kə-lē, -klē\ *adv*

sym·bol \'sim-bəl\ *n* **1** : something that stands for something else; *esp* : something concrete that represents or suggests another thing that cannot in itself be represented or visualized : EMBLEM ⟨the cross is the *symbol* of Christianity⟩ **2** : a letter, character, or sign

swordfish

sycamore 3

\ə\ abut	\ng\ sing
\ər\ further	\ō\ bone
\a\ mat	\ó\ saw
\ā\ take	\oi\ coin
\ä\ cot, cart	\th\ thin
\au̇\ out	\t͟h\ this
\ch\ chin	\ü\ food
\e\ pet	\u̇\ foot
\ē\ easy	\y\ yet
\g\ go	\yü\ few
\i\ tip	\yu̇\ cure
\ī\ life	\zh\ vision
\j\ job	

used (as to represent a quantity, position, relation-ship, direction, or something to be done) instead of a word or group of words (the sign + is the *symbol* for addition) [derived from Greek *symbolon* "token of identity to be verified by matching it with its other half, symbol", from *symballein* "to throw together, compare", from *syn-* + *ballein* "to throw"]

sym·bol·ic \sim-'bäl-ik\ *or* **sym·bol·i·cal** \-'bäl-i-kəl\ *adj* **1** : of, relating to, or using symbols or symbolism (a *symbolic* meaning) **2** : having the function or signif-icance of a symbol — **sym·bol·i·cal·ly** \-i-kə-lē, -klē\ *adv*

sym·bol·ism \'sim-bə-,liz-əm\ *n* **1** : the art or practice of using symbols or indicating symbolically (as in art or literature) **2** : a system of symbols or representa-tions (the language and *symbolism* of set theory)

sym·bol·ist \-ləst\ *n* **1** : a user of symbols or symbol-ism (as in artistic expression) **2** : an expert in the in-terpretation or explanation of symbols — **symbolist** *or* **sym·bol·is·tic** \,sim-bə-'lis-tik\ *adj*

sym·bol·ize \'sim-bə-,līz\ *vb* **1** : to serve as a symbol of (a lion *symbolizes* courage) **2** : to use symbols : repre-sent by a symbol or set of symbols — **sym·bol·iza·tion** \,sim-bə-lə-'zā-shən\ *n* — **sym·bol·iz·er** \'sim-bə-,līz-ər\ *n*

sym·met·ri·cal \sə-'me-tri-kəl\ *or* **sym·met·ric** \-trik\ *adj* **1** : having, involving, or exhibiting symmetry: as **a** : having corresponding points whose connecting lines are bisected by a given point or perpendicularly bisected by a given line or plane (*symmetrical* curves) **b** : capable of division by a longitudinal plane into similar halves (a *symmetrical* leaf) **c** : having the same number of members in each whorl of floral leaves (*symmetrical* flowers) **2** *symmetric* : being a relation or expression for which the terms may be inter-changed without altering the value, character, or truth (*R* is a *symmetric* relation if *aRb* implies *bRa*) — **sym·met·ri·cal·ly** \-tri-kə-lē, -klē\ *adv* — **sym·met·ri·cal·ness** \-kəl-nəs\ *n*

sym·me·try \'sim-ə-trē\ *n, pl* **-tries** **1** : balanced pro-portions; *also* : beauty of form arising from balanced proportions **2** : correspondence in size, shape, and relative position of parts on opposite sides of a divid-ing line or median plane or about a center of axis — compare BILATERAL SYMMETRY, RADIAL SYMMETRY [Latin *symmetria*, from Greek, derived from *syn-* + *metron* "measure"]

sym·pa·thet·ic \,sim-pə-'thet-ik\ *adj* **1 a** : appropriate to one's mood or disposition : CONGENIAL (a *sympa-thetic* environment) **b** : favorably impressed or in-clined (*sympathetic* with their aims) **c** : marked by kindly or pleased appreciation **2** : given to or arising from sympathy, compassion, friendliness, and sensitiv-ity to others (a *sympathetic* person) (*sympathetic* strikes) (a *sympathetic* remark) **3 a** : of or relating to the sympathetic nervous system **b** : mediated by or acting on the sympathetic nerves — **sym·pa·thet·i·cal·ly** \-'thet-i-kə-lē, -klē\ *adv*

sympathetic nervous system *n* : the part of the auto-nomic nervous system that prepares the body to react to stressful situations, has primary control over the di-lation of blood vessels, pupils, and breathing passages, and is composed of nerve fibers that trigger the release of epinephrine and norepinephrine — compare PARASYMPATHETIC NERVOUS SYSTEM

sympathetic vibration *n* : a vibration produced in one body by vibrations of exactly the same period in a neighboring body

sym·pa·thize \'sim-pə-,thīz\ *vi* **1** : to react or respond in sympathy **2** : to be in accord or harmony **3 a** : to share in some distress, suffering, or grief **b** : to express sympathy **4** : to be in sympathy intellectually (*sympa-thize* with a proposal) — **sym·pa·thiz·er** *n*

sym·pa·tho·mi·met·ic \,sim-pə-thō-mə-'met-ik, -mī-\ *adj* : resembling the action of the sympathetic nervous

system in physiological effect (*sympathomimetic* drugs)

sym·pa·thy \'sim-pə-thē\ *n, pl* **-thies** **1** : a relationship between persons or things wherein whatever affects one similarly affects the other **2 a** : inclination to think or feel alike : emotional or intellectual accord forming a bond of goodwill **b** : tendency to favor or support **3** : the act of or capacity for entering into or sharing the feelings or interests of another [Latin *sym-pathia,* from Greek *sympatheia,* derived from *syn-* + *pathos* "feelings, experience"]

sym·pat·ric \sim-'pa-trik\ *adj* : occurring in the same area or region (*sympatric* species of birds) [*syn-* + Greek *patra* "fatherland", from *patēr* "father"]

sym·phon·ic \sim-'fän-ik\ *adj* **1** : HARMONIOUS 1 **2** : of, relating to, or suggesting a symphony or symphony or-chestra — **sym·phon·i·cal·ly** \-'fän-i-kə-lē, -klē\ *adv*

sym·pho·ny \'sim-fə-nē, 'simp-\ *n, pl* **-nies** **1** : harmoni-ous arrangement (as of sound or color) **2 a** : a usually long and complex sonata for symphony orchestra **b** : something resembling a symphony in complexity or variety **3 a** : SYMPHONY ORCHESTRA **b** : a symphony or-chestra concert [Old French *symphonie* "harmony of sounds", from Latin *symphonia,* from Greek *sym-phōnia,* derived from *syn-* + *phōnē* "voice, sound"]

symphony orchestra *n* : a large orchestra of wind, string, and percussion instruments that plays sym-phonic works

sym·phy·sis \'sim-fə-səs, 'simp-\ *n, pl* **-phy·ses** \-fə-,sēz\ : a largely or completely immovable joint be-tween bones especially with the surfaces connected by pads of cartilage without a joint membrane [Greek, "state of growing together", from *symphyesthai* "to grow together", from *syn-* + *phyein* "to make grow, bring forth"] — **sym·phy·se·al** \,sim-fə-'sē-əl, ,simp-\ *adj*

sym·po·si·um \sim-'pō-zē-əm *also* -zhē-əm, -zhəm\ *n, pl* **-sia** \-zē-ə, -zhē-ə, -zhə\ *or* **-si·ums** **1** : a formal meeting at which several speakers deliver short ad-dresses on a topic or on related topics **2 a** : a collec-tion of opinions on a subject **b** : DISCUSSION **2** [Latin, "drinking party after a banquet", from Greek *sympo-sion,* from *sympinein* "to drink together", from *syn-* + *pinein* "to drink"]

symp·tom \'sim-təm, 'simp-\ *n* **1** : a change in an or-ganism indicative of disease or physical abnormality; *esp* : one (as headache) that is directly perceptible on-ly to the individual affected — compare SIGN 6c **2** : INDICATION 2; *also* : ¹TRACE 5a [Late Latin *symptomat-, symptoma,* from Greek *symptōma* "occurrence, attri-bute, symptom", from *sympiptein* "to occur", from *syn-* + *piptein* "to fall"] — **symp·tom·less** \-ləs\ *adj*

symp·tom·at·ic \,sim-tə-'mat-ik, ,simp-\ *adj* **1 a** : be-ing a symptom (as of disease) (*symptomatic* of small-pox) **b** : concerned with or affecting symptoms (*symp-tomatic* medicine) **2** : CHARACTERISTIC, INDICATIVE (re-action to a scandal as *symptomatic* of the public's concern) — **symp·tom·at·i·cal·ly** \-'mat-i-kə-lē, -klē\ *adv*

syn- *or* **sym-** *prefix* : with : along with : together (*sym*patric) (*syn*gamy) [Greek, from *syn* "with, to-gether with"]

syn·a·gogue *or* **syn·a·gog** \'sin-ə-,gäg\ *n* **1** : a Jewish congregation **2** : the house of worship and communal center of a Jewish congregation [Old French *synagoge,* from Late Latin *synagoga,* from Greek *synagōgē* "as-sembly, synagogue", from *synagein* "to bring togeth-er", from *syn-* + *agein* "to lead"] — **syn·a·gog·al** \,sin-ə-'gäg-əl\ *adj*

¹syn·apse \'sin-,aps, sə-'naps\ *n* : the point at which a nervous impulse passes from one neuron to another [Green *synapsis* "juncture", from *synaptein* "to fas-ten together", from *syn-* + *haptein* "to fasten"]

²synapse *vi* : to form a synapse or come together in syn-apsis

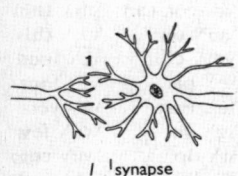

1 : ¹synapse

syn·ap·sis \sə-'nap-səs\ *n, pl* **-ap·ses** \-ˌsēz\ *n* : the association of homologous chromosomes that occurs in the first meiotic prophase and is the mechanism for crossing over [Greek, "juncture"] — **syn·ap·tic** \-'nap-tik\ *adj*

¹sync \'singk\ *n* : SYNCHRONIZATION, SYNCHRONISM — **sync** *adj*

²sync *vb* **synced** \'singt, 'singkt\; **sync·ing** \'sing-king\ : SYNCHRONIZE

synchro- *combining form* : synchronized : synchronous ⟨*synchro* flash⟩ ⟨*synchro* mesh⟩

syn·chro·cy·clo·tron \ˌsing-krō-'sī-klə-ˌträn, ˌsin-\ *n* : a modified cyclotron that achieves greater energies for the charged particles

syn·chro·flash \'sing-krō-ˌflash, 'sin-\ *adj* : employing or produced with a mechanism that fires a flash bulb the instant the camera shutter opens

syn·chro·mesh \-ˌmesh\ *adj* : designed for effecting synchronized shifting of gears — **synchromesh** *n*

syn·chro·nism \'sing-krə-ˌniz-əm, 'sin-\ *n* 1 : the quality or state of being synchronous 2 : chronological arrangement of historical events and personages so as to indicate coincidence or coexistence — **syn·chro·nis·tic** \ˌsing-krə-'nis-tik, ˌsin-\ *adj*

syn·chro·nize \'sing-krə-ˌnīz, 'sin-\ *vb* 1 : to happen at the same time 2 a : to agree in time b : to cause to agree in time ⟨*synchronize* your watches⟩ b : to represent, arrange, or tabulate according to dates or time ⟨*synchronize* the events of European history⟩ 3 : to make (as two gears) synchronous in operation — **syn·chro·ni·za·tion** \ˌsing-krə-nə-'zā-shən, ˌsin-\ *n* — **syn·chro·niz·er** \'sing-krə-ˌnī-zər, 'sin-\ *n*

synchronized swimming *n* : exhibition or competitive swimming in which usually two or more swimmers move in such a way as to form constantly changing patterns in the water with their movements synchronized with each other and with a musical accompaniment

syn·chro·nous \'sing-krə-nəs, 'sin-\ *adj* 1 : happening or existing at the same time : SIMULTANEOUS ⟨*synchronous* meetings⟩ 2 : working, moving, or occurring together at the same rate and at the proper time with respect to each other ⟨*synchronous* beat of a bird's wings⟩; *esp* : having the same period and phase ⟨*synchronous* vibration⟩ [Late Latin *synchronos,* from Greek, from *syn-* + *chronos* "time"] — **syn·chro·nous·ly** *adv* — **syn·chro·nous·ness** *n*

synchronous motor *n* : an electric motor having a speed strictly proportional to the frequency of the operating current

syn·chro·tron \'sing-krə-ˌträn, 'sin-\ *n* : an apparatus for imparting very high speeds to charged particles

syn·cline \'sin-ˌklīn\ *n* : a place in the earth's crust where the rock layers form a trough — compare ANTI-CLINE [back-formation from *synclinal,* from Greek *syn-* + *klinein* "to lean"] — **syn·cli·nal** \sin-'klīn-l\ *adj*

syn·co·pate \'sing-kə-ˌpāt, 'sin-\ *vt* 1 a : to shorten or produce by syncope b : to cut short 2 : to modify or affect (musical rhythm) by syncopation — **syn·co·pa·tor** \-ˌpāt-ər\ *n*

syn·co·pa·tion \ˌsing-kə-ˌpā-shən, ˌsin-\ *n* 1 : a shifting of the regular metrical accent in music caused typically by stressing the weak beat 2 : a syncopated rhythm, passage, or dance step — **syn·co·pa·tive** \'sing-kə-ˌpāt-iv, 'sin-\ *adj*

syn·co·pe \'sing-kə-pē, 'sin-\ *n* 1 : FAINT, SWOON 2 : the loss of one or more sounds or letters in the interior of a word (as fo'c'sle from forecastle) [Late Latin, from Greek *synkopē,* literally, "cutting short", from *syn-koptein* "to cut short", from *syn-* + *koptein* "to cut"]

syn·cy·tium \sin-'sish-əm, -'sish-ē-əm\ *n, pl* **-tia** \-ə\ : a multinucleate mass of protoplasm usually resulting from fusion of cells [New Latin, from *syn-* + *cyt-*] — **syn·cy·tial** \-'sish-əl\ *adj*

syn·di·cal·ism \'sin-di-kə-ˌliz-əm\ *n* 1 : a revolutionary doctrine advocating seizure of control of the economy and the government by workers through use of direct means (as the general strike) 2 : a system of economic organization in which industries are owned and managed by the workers [French *syndicalisme,* from *chambre syndicale* "trade union"] — **syn·di·cal** \'sin-di-kəl\ *adj* — **syn·di·cal·ist** \-ləst\ *adj or n*

¹syn·di·cate \'sin-di-kət\ *n* 1 : an association of persons officially authorized to undertake some duty or negotiate some business 2 a : a group of persons or concerns who combine to carry out a particular transaction b : a loose association of racketeers in control of organized crime c : a European labor union 3 : a business concern that sells materials for publication in a number of newspapers or periodicals simultaneously 4 : a group of newspapers under one management [French *syndicat,* from *syndic* "municipal magistrate", from Latin *syndicus* "representative", from Greek *syndikos* "advocate, representative", from *syn-* + *dikē* "judgment, case at law"] SYN see MONOPOLY

²syn·di·cate \'sin-də-ˌkāt\ *vb* 1 : to subject to or manage as a syndicate 2 : to sell (as a cartoon) to a publication syndicate 3 : to unite to form a syndicate — **syn·di·ca·tion** \ˌsin-də-'kā-shən\ *n* — **syn·di·ca·tor** \'sin-də-ˌkāt-ər\ *n*

syn·drome \'sin-ˌdrōm\ *n* : a group of signs and symptoms that occur together and characterize a particular abnormality [Greek *syndromē,* from *syn-* + *dramein* "to run"]

syn·er·gid \sə-'nər-jəd, 'sin-ər-\ *n* : either of two small cells of the embryo sac of a seed plant lying near the micropyle of the ovule [derived from Greek *synergos* "working together"]

syn·er·gism \'sin-ər-ˌjiz-əm\ *n* : cooperative action of discrete agencies such that the total effect is greater than the sum of the effects taken independently [derived from Greek *synergos* "working together", from *syn-* + *ergon* "work"] — **syn·er·gist** \-jəst\ *n*

syn·er·gis·tic \ˌsin-ər-'jis-tik\ *adj* : of, relating to, or able to function in synergism ⟨a *synergistic* reaction⟩ ⟨*synergistic* drugs⟩ — **syn·er·gis·ti·cal·ly** \-ti-kə-lē, -klē\ *adv*

syn·ga·my \'sing-gə-mē\ *n* : FERTILIZATION b

syn·od \'sin-əd\ *n* 1 : an ecclesiastical assembly or council: as a : the governing assembly of an Episcopal province b : a Presbyterian governing body ranking above the presbytery c : a regional or national organization of Lutheran congregations 2 : a group assembled (as for consultation) : MEETING, CONVENTION ⟨a *synod* of cooks⟩ [Late Latin *synodus,* from Greek *synodos* "meeting, assembly", from *syn-* + *hodos* "way, journey"] — **syn·od·al** \-əd-l\ *adj*

syn·od·i·cal \sə-'näd-i-kəl\ *or* **syn·od·ic** \-'näd-ik\ *adj* 1 : of or relating to a synod : SYNODAL 2 : relating to conjunction; *esp* : relating to the period between two successive conjunctions of the same celestial bodies

syn·o·nym \'sin-ə-ˌnim\ *n* 1 : one of two or more words of the same language that have the same or nearly the same meaning in some or all senses 2 : a symbolic or figurative name 3 : a taxonomic name rejected as being incorrectly applied or incorrect in form [Latin *synonymum,* from Greek *synōnymon,* derived from *syn-* + *onyma* "name"] — **syn·o·nym·i·ty** \ˌsin-ə-'nim-ət-ē\ *n*

syn·on·y·mize \sə-'nän-ə-ˌmīz\ *vt* : to give or analyze the synonyms of (a word)

syn·on·y·mous \sə-'nän-ə-məs\ *adj* : having the character of a synonym; *also* : alike in meaning or significance — **syn·on·y·mous·ly** *adv*

syn·on·y·my \sə-'nän-ə-mē\ *n, pl* **-mies** 1 a : the study or discrimination of synonyms b : a list or collection of synonyms often defined and discriminated from each other 2 : the quality or state of being synonymous

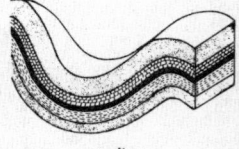

syncline

\ə\ abut	\ng\ sing
\ər\ further	\ō\ bone
\a\ mat	\o\ saw
\ā\ take	\oi\ coin
\ä\ cot, cart	\th\ thin
\au\ out	\th\ this
\ch\ chin	\ü\ food
\e\ pet	\u̇\ foot
\ē\ easy	\y\ yet
\g\ go	\yü\ few
\i\ tip	\yu̇\ cure
\ī\ life	\zh\ vision
\j\ job	

syn·op·sis \sə-'näp-səs\ *n, pl* **-op·ses** \-'äp-,sēz\ : a condensed statement or outline (as of a narrative or treatise) : SUMMARY, ABSTRACT [Late Latin, from Greek, literally, "comprehensive view", from *synopsesthai* "to be going to see together", from *syn-* + *opsesthai* "to be going to see"]

syn·op·tic \sə-'näp-tik\ *adj* 1 : affording a general view of a whole ⟨a daily *synoptic* weather chart of Canada⟩ 2 : showing or characterized by comprehensiveness or breadth of view ⟨a *synoptic* genius⟩ 3 a : presenting or sharing the same or a common view b *often cap* : of or relating to the first three Gospels of the New Testament [Greek *synoptikos*, from *synopsesthai* "to be going to see together"] — **syn·op·ti·cal** \-ti-kəl\ *adj* — **syn·op·ti·cal·ly** \-ti-kə-lē, -klē\ *adv*

syn·o·vi·al \sə-'nō-vē-əl\ *adj* : of or relating to the connective tissue membrane that lines joint capsules and secretes a transparent viscid lubricating fluid [New Latin *synovia* "fluid secreted by synovial membranes"]

syn·tac·tic \sin-'tak-tik\ *adj* : of, relating to, or according to the rules of syntax [Greek *syntaktikos* "arranging together", from *syntassein* "to arrange together"] — **syn·tac·ti·cal** \-ti-kəl\ *adj* — **syn·tac·ti·cal·ly** \-ti-kə-lē, -klē\ *adv*

syn·tax \'sin-,taks\ *n* 1 : connected or orderly system or arrangement 2 a : the way in which words are put together to form phrases, clauses, or sentences b : the part of grammar dealing with this [Late Latin *syntaxis*, from Greek, from *syntassein* "to arrange together", from *syn-* + *tassein* "to arrange"]

syn·the·sis \'sin-thə-səs, 'sint-\ *n, pl* **-the·ses** \-thə-,sēz\ 1 : the composition or combination of parts or elements so as to form a whole; *esp* : the production of a substance by union of chemically simpler substances 2 a : the combining of often diverse conceptions into a coherent whole; *also* : the complex so formed b : deductive reasoning from general principles or causes to particular effects c : the final stage of a dialectic process combining thesis and antithesis into a new whole [Greek, from *syntithenai* "to put together", from *syn-* + *tithenai* "to put, place"] — **syn·the·sist** \-səst\ *n*

syn·the·size \-,sīz\ *vt* : to combine or produce by synthesis

syn·the·siz·er \-,sī-zər\ *n* 1 : one that synthesizes 2 : a computer-controlled device that creates and modifies sound (as for producing music)

¹syn·thet·ic \sin-'thet-ik\ *adj* 1 : relating to or involving synthesis 2 : of, relating to, or produced by chemical synthesis; *esp* : produced artificially : MAN-MADE ⟨*synthetic* drugs⟩ ⟨*synthetic* fibers⟩ [Greek *synthetikos* "of composition", from *syntithenai* "to put together"] SYN see ARTIFICIAL — **syn·thet·i·cal·ly** \-'thet-i-kə-lē, -klē\ *adv*

²synthetic *n* : a product of chemical synthesis

synthetic division *n* : a simplified method for dividing a polynomial by another polynomial of the first degree by writing down only the coefficients of the several powers of the variable and changing the sign of the constant term in the divisor in order to replace the usual subtractions by additions

syph·i·lis \'sif-ləs, -ə-ləs\ *n* : a chronic contagious usually venereal disease caused by a spirochete and marked by three stages extending over many years [New Latin, from *Syphilus*, hero of the poem *Syphilis sive Morbus Gallicus* (*Syphilis or the French disease*) (1530) by Girolamo Fracastoro] — **syph·i·lit·ic** \,sif-ə-'lit-ik\ *adj or n*

sy·phon *variant of* SIPHON

Syr·a·cuse watch glass \'sir-ə-,kyüs-, -,kyüz-\ *n* : a small circular flat-bottomed dish of thick glass that has a shallow depression and is used in biology (as for culturing or staining) — called also *Syracuse dish* [*Syracuse*, New York]

¹syringe

Syr·i·ac \'sir-ē-,ak\ *n* 1 : a literary language based on an eastern Aramaic dialect and used as the literary and liturgical language by several Eastern Christian churches 2 : Aramaic spoken by Christian communities [Latin *syriacus* "Syrian", from Greek *syriakos*, from *Syria*, ancient country in Asia] — **Syriac** *adj*

sy·rin·ga \sə-'ring-gə\ *n* : PHILADELPHUS [New Latin, "lilac", from Greek *syring-, syrinx* "panpipe"]

¹sy·ringe \sə-'rinj *also* 'sir-inj\ *n* : a device used to inject fluids into or withdraw them from the body or its cavities [Medieval Latin *syringa*, from Greek *syring-, syrinx* "panpipe, tube"]

²syringe *vt* : to irrigate or cleanse with or as if with a syringe

syr·inx \'sir-ings, -ingks\ *n, pl* **sy·rin·ges** \sə-'ring-gēz, -'rin-jēz\ *or* **syr·inx·es** \'sir-ing-səz, -ingk-\ 1 : PANPIPE 2 : the vocal organ of birds that is a special modification of the lower part of the trachea or of the bronchi or of both [Greek] — **sy·rin·ge·al** \sə-'ring-gē-əl, -'rin-jē-\ *adj*

syr·up *or* **sir·up** \'sər-əp, 'sir-əp, 'sə-rəp\ *n* 1 : a thick sticky solution of sugar and water often flavored or medicated 2 : the concentrated juice of a fruit or plant [Middle French *sirop*, from Medieval Latin *syrupus*, from Arabic *sharāb*] — **syr·upy** *or* **sir·upy** \-ē\ *adj*

sys·op \'sis-,äp\ *n* : the administrator of a computer bulletin board [*sys*tem *op*erator]

sys·tem \'sis-təm\ *n* 1 a (1) : a group of objects or units so combined as to form a whole and work, function, or move interdependently and harmoniously ⟨a railroad *system*⟩ ⟨steam heating *systems*⟩ ⟨a park *system*⟩ (2) : a set of simultaneous equations or inequalities b (1) : a body that functions as a whole ⟨a *system* weakened by disease⟩ (2) : a group of bodily organs that together carry on one or more vital functions ⟨the nervous *system*⟩ c : a particular form of societal organization ⟨the capitalist *system*⟩ d : a major division of rocks usually greater than a series 2 a : an organized set of doctrines or principles usually designed to explain the ordering or functioning of some whole b : a method of classifying, symbolizing, or schematizing ⟨a decimal *system* of numbers⟩ ⟨taxonomic *systems*⟩ 3 : harmonious arrangement or pattern [Late Latin *systemat-, systema*, from Greek *systēmat-, systēma*, from *synistanai* "to combine", from *syn* + *histanai* "to cause to stand"] — **sys·tem·less** \-ləs\ *adj*

sys·tem·at·ic \,sis-tə-'mat-ik\ *adj* 1 : relating to or forming a system ⟨*systematic* thought⟩ 2 : presented or formulated as a system 3 a : methodical in procedure or plan ⟨*systematic* investigation⟩ b : carried on or acting with thoroughness or persistency 4 : of, relating to, or concerned with classification : TAXONOMIC — **sys·tem·at·i·cal** \-'mat-i-kəl\ *adj* — **sys·tem·at·i·cal·ly** \-i-kə-lē, -klē\ *adv* — **sys·tem·at·ic·ness** *n*

systematic error *n* : an error in data that is due to the method of measurement or observation and not due to chance

sys·tem·at·ics \-'mat-iks\ *n sing or pl* 1 a : the science or technique of classification b : the classification and study of organisms with regard to their natural relationships : TAXONOMY 2 : a system of classification

sys·tem·a·tist \'sis-tə-mət-əst, sis-'tem-ət-\ *n* 1 : a maker or follower of a system 2 : TAXONOMIST

sys·tem·a·tize \'sis-tə-mə-,tīz\ *vt* : to make into or arrange according to a system — **sys·tem·a·ti·za·tion** \,sis-tə-mət-ə-'zā-shən\ *n* — **sys·tem·a·tiz·er** \'sis-tə-mə-,tī-zər\ *n*

sys·tem·ic \sis-'tem-ik\ *adj* : of, relating to, or common to a system: as a : affecting the body generally ⟨a *systemic* disease⟩ b : relating to or being part of the systemic circulation ⟨*systemic* arteries⟩ c : acting by being taken into bodily systems and making the organism toxic to a pest (as a mite or insect) — **sys·tem·i·cal·ly** \-'tem-i-kə-lē, -klē\ *adv*

systemic circulation *n* : the part of the blood circulation concerned with distribution of blood to the tissues as distinguished from the part concerned with gaseous exchange in the lungs

sys·tem·ize \'sis-tə-ˌmīz\ *vt* : SYSTEMATIZE — **sys·tem·iza·tion** \ˌsis-tə-mə-'zā-shən\ *n*

systems analyst *n* : a person who studies an activity (as a procedure or business) to find out its goals and to discover the most efficient ways to accomplish them

sys·to·le \'sis-tə-lē\ *n* : the contraction of the heart by which the blood is forced onward and the circulation kept up [Greek *systolē* "contraction", from *systellein* "to contract", from *syn-* + *stellein* "to send"] — **sys·tol·ic** \sis-'täl-ik\ *adj*

Tt

t \'tē\ *n, pl* **t's** *or* **ts** \'tēz\ *often cap* : the 20th letter of the English alphabet — **to a T** : to perfection [short for *to a tittle*]

't \t\ *pron* : IT ⟨*'t*will do⟩

¹**tab** \'tab\ *n* **1 a** : a short projection used as an aid for filing, pulling, or hanging **b** : a small insert, addition, or remnant ⟨license plate *tab*⟩ **c** : an appendage or extension of something; *esp* : one of a series of small pendants forming a decorative border or edge of a garment **d** : a small auxiliary airfoil hinged to a control surface (as a trailing edge) to help stabilize an airplane in flight **2 a** : SURVEILLANCE, WATCH ⟨keep *tab* on the situation⟩ **b** : a creditor's statement : BILL, CHECK **3** : TABULATOR 6 [origin unknown]

²**tab** *vt* **tabbed; tab·bing 1** : to furnish or ornament with tabs **2** : to single out ⟨*tabbed* as a bright prospect⟩

tab·ard \'tab-ərd\ *n* **1** : a tunic worn by a knight over his armor and emblazoned with his arms **2** : a herald's official cape or coat displaying his lord's arms [Old French *tabart*]

¹**tab·by** \'tab-ē\ *n, pl* **tabbies** : a domestic cat with a gray or tawny coat striped and mottled with black; *also* : a female cat [French *tabis* "silk taffeta with moiré finish", from Medieval Latin *attabi*, from Arabic *'attābī*]

²**tabby** *adj* : striped and mottled with darker color ⟨*tabby* fur⟩

tab·er·na·cle \'tab-ər-ˌnak-əl\ *n* **1 a** *often cap* : a tent sanctuary used by the Israelites during the Exodus **b** : a dwelling place **2** : an ornamental locked box fixed to the middle of the altar and used for reserving bread consecrated at Mass **3** : a house of worship; *esp* : a building or shelter used for evangelistic services [Old French, from Latin *tabernaculum* "tent", from *taberna* "hut, tavern"]

¹**ta·ble** \'tā-bəl\ *n* **1** : TABLET 1a **2 a** : a piece of furniture consisting of a smooth flat slab fixed on legs **b** : FOOD, FARE ⟨sets a good *table*⟩ **c** : an act of assembling to eat : MEAL **d** : a group of people assembled at or as if at a table **3 a** : a systematic arrangement of data in rows or columns for ready reference ⟨a *table* of weights⟩ **b** : LIST ⟨the *table* of contents⟩ **4 a** : TABLELAND **b** : a horizontal stratum [Old English *tabule* and Old French *table*, both from Latin *tabula* "board, tablet, list"]

²**table** *vt* **ta·bled; ta·bling** \-bə-ling, -bling\ **1** : TABULATE **2** : to remove (a parliamentary motion) from consideration indefinitely **3** : to put on a table

tab·leau \'tab-ˌlō, ta-'blō\ *n, pl* **tableaus** *or* **tab·leaux** \-ˌlōz, -'blōz\ : a lifelike representation of a scene or event by an appropriate grouping of persons who remain silent and motionless [French, derived from Old French *table* "table"]

ta·ble·cloth \'tā-bəl-ˌklȯth\ *n* : a covering spread over a dining table before the places are set

ta·ble d'hôte \ˌtäb-əl-'dōt, ˌtab-\ *n* **1** : a meal served to all guests of a hotel at a stated hour and fixed price **2** : a complete meal of several courses offered in a restaurant or hotel at a fixed price — compare A LA CARTE [French, literally, "host's table"]

ta·ble·land \'tā-bəl-ˌland, -ˌand\ *n* : a broad level elevated area : PLATEAU

table linen *n* : linen (as tablecloths and napkins) for the table

table salt *n* : salt for use at the table and in cooking

ta·ble·spoon \'tā-bəl-ˌspün\ *n* **1** : a large spoon used for serving rather than eating **2** : TABLESPOONFUL

ta·ble·spoon·ful \ˌtā-bəl-'spün-ˌfül, 'tā-bəl-ˌ\ *n, pl* **-spoonfuls** \-ˌfülz\ *or* **-spoons·ful** \-'spünz-ˌfül, -ˌspünz-\ **1** : as much as a tablespoon can hold **2** : a unit of measure used especially in cookery equal to one half fluid ounce (about 14.8 milliliters) or three teaspoonfuls

table sugar *n* : SUGAR 1; *esp* : granulated sugar

tab·let \'tab-lət\ *n* **1 a** : a flat slab or plaque suited for or bearing an inscription **b** : a collection of sheets of writing paper glued together at one edge **2 a** : a compressed or molded block of a solid material : CAKE **b** : a small mass of medicated material usually in the shape of a disk [Middle French *tablete*, from *table* "tablet, table"]

table talk *n* : informal conversation at or as if at a dining table

table tennis *n* : a game resembling tennis that is played on a 9-by-5-foot table with wooden paddles and a small hollow plastic ball

ta·ble·top \'tā-bəl-ˌtäp\ *n* : the top of a table — **tabletop** *adj*

ta·ble·ware \'tā-bəl-ˌwaər, -ˌweər\ *n* : utensils (as of china, glass, or silver) for table use

table wine *n* : a still wine of not more than 14 percent alcohol by volume usually served with food

¹**tab·loid** \'tab-ˌlȯid\ *adj* : compressed or condensed into small scope ⟨*tabloid* information⟩ [from *Tabloid*, a trademark applied to a concentrated form of drugs and chemicals]

²**tabloid** *n* : a newspaper about half the page size of an ordinary newspaper that contains news in condensed form and much photographic matter

¹**ta·boo** *also* **ta·bu** \tə-'bü, ta-\ *adj* : prohibited by a taboo [Tongan (a Polynesian language of the Tonga islands) *tabu*]

\ə\ abut		\ng\ sing	
\ər\ **further**		\ō\ bone	
\a\ mat		\ȯ\ saw	
\ā\ take		\ȯi\ coin	
\ä\ cot, cart		\th\ thin	
\aú\ out		\th\ this	
\ch\ chin		\ü\ food	
\e\ pet		\ú\ foot	
\ē\ easy		\y\ yet	
\g\ go		\yü\ few	
\i\ tip		\yú\ cure	
\ī\ life		\zh\ vision	
\j\ job			

tabor

²**taboo** *also* **tabu** *n, pl* **taboos** *also* **tabus** **1** : a prohibition against touching, saying, or doing something for fear of immediate harm from a mysterious superhuman force **2** : a prohibition imposed by social custom

³**taboo** *also* **tabu** *vt* : to place under a taboo

ta·bor \'tā-bər\ *n* : a small drum with one head used to accompany a pipe played by the same person [Old French] — **ta·bor·er** \-bər-ər\ *n*

tab·o·ret *or* **tab·ou·ret** \,tab-ə-'ret, -'rā\ *n* **1** : a low stool without arms or back **2** : a small ornamental stand (as for a plant) [French *tabouret*, literally, "small drum", from Middle French *tabor*, *tabour* "drum"]

tab·u·lar \'tab-yə-lər\ *adj* **1** : having a flat surface **2 a** : arranged or entered in a table **b** : computed by means of a table [Latin *tabularis* "of boards", from *tabula* "board, tablet"] — **tab·u·lar·ly** *adv*

ta·bu·la ra·sa \,tab-yə-lə-'räz-ə, -'räs-\ *n, pl* **ta·bu·lae ra·sae** \-,lī-'räz-,ī, -'räs-\ : the mind in its hypothetical primary blank or empty state before receiving outside impressions [Latin, "smoothed (wax) tablet"]

tab·u·late \'tab-yə-,lāt\ *vt* : to put into tabular form — **tab·u·la·tion** \,tab-yə-'lā-shən\ *n*

tab·u·la·tor \'tab-yə-,lāt-ər\ *n* : one that tabulates: as **a** : a business machine that sorts and selects information from marked or perforated cards **b** : a device on a typewriter or billing machine for arranging data in columns

tac·a·ma·hac \'tak-ə-mə-,hak\ *n* **1** : any of several aromatic oleoresins used in ointments and plasters and for incense **2** : BALSAM POPLAR [Spanish *tacamahaca*, from Nahuatl *tecamaca*]

tach \'tak\ *n* : TACHOMETER

ta·chis·to·scope \tə-'kis-tə-,skōp\ *n* : an apparatus for the brief exposure of visual stimuli [Greek *tachistos*, superlative of *tachys* "swift"]

ta·chom·e·ter \ta-'käm-ət-ər, tə-\ *n* : a device for indicating speed of rotation (as of the crankshaft of an automobile engine) [Greek *tachos* "speed"]

tachy·car·dia \,tak-i-'kärd-ē-ə\ *n* : rapid heart action [Greek *tachys* "swift" + *kardia* "heart"]

ta·chym·e·ter \ta-'kim-ət-ər, tə-\ *n* : a surveying instrument (as a transit) for determining quickly the distances, bearings, and elevations of distant objects [Greek *tachys* "swift"]

tac·it \'tas-ət\ *adj* **1** : expressed or carried on without words or speech **2** : implied or indicated but not actually expressed ⟨*tacit* consent⟩ [Latin *tacitus* "silent", from *tacēre* "to be silent"] — **tac·it·ly** *adv* — **tac·it·ness** *n*

tac·i·turn \'tas-ə-,tərn\ *adj* : habitually or temperamentally disinclined to talk [Latin *taciturnus*, from *tacitus* "silent"] SYN see SILENT — **tac·i·tur·ni·ty** \,tas-ə-'tər-nət-ē\ *n* — **tac·i·turn·ly** \'tas-ə-,tərn-lē\ *adv*

¹**tack** \'tak\ *vb* **1** : ATTACH; *esp* : to fasten or affix with tacks **2** : to join in a slight or hasty manner **3** : to add as a supplement **4** : to change the direction of a sailing vessel when sailing close-hauled by putting the helm alee and shifting the sails **5 a** : to sail in a different direction by a tack **b** : to follow a zigzag course **c** : to modify one's policy or an attitude abruptly — **tack·er** *n*

²**tack** *n* **1** : a small short sharp-pointed nail usually with a broad flat head for fastening some light object or material to a solid surface ⟨a carpet *tack*⟩ **2 a** : a rope used to hold in place the forward lower corner of the lowest sail on any square-rigged mast of a ship **b** : the lower forward corner of a fore-and-aft sail **3 a** : the direction a vessel is sailing as shown by the way the sails are trimmed; *also* : the movement of a vessel with respect to the direction of the wind ⟨on the port *tack*⟩ **b** : a change of course from one tack to another **4** : a zigzag movement on land **5** : a course or method of action ⟨on the wrong *tack*⟩ **6** : a slight or temporary sewing or fastening [Middle English *tak* "fastener"]

tadpole

³**tack** *n* : STUFF 3b; *esp* : FOODSTUFF [origin unknown]

⁴**tack** *n* : equipment for riding horses : stable gear [perhaps short for *tackle*]

tack·i·ness \'tak-ē-nəs\ *n* : the quality or state of being tacky

¹**tack·le** \'tak-əl, *nautical often* 'tāk-\ *n* **1** : a set of the equipment used in a particular activity : GEAR ⟨fishing *tackle*⟩ **2 a** : a ship's rigging **b** : an assemblage of ropes and pulleys arranged to gain mechanical advantage for hoisting and pulling **3 a** : the act or an instance of tackling **b** : either of two football linemen who line up inside the ends [Middle English *takel*]

²**tackle** *vt* **tack·led; tack·ling** \'tak-ling, -ə-ling\ **1** : HARNESS ⟨*tackle* up the horses⟩ **2 a** : to seize, take hold of, or grapple with especially in order to stop or subdue **b** : to seize and stop or throw down (a player) in football **3** : to set about dealing with ⟨*tackle* the job of cleaning up⟩ — **tack·ler** \-lər, -ə-lər\ *n*

¹**tacky** \'tak-ē\ *adj* **tack·i·er; -est** : barely sticky to the touch : ADHESIVE ⟨*tacky* varnish⟩

²**tacky** *adj* **tack·i·er; -est** **1 a** : characterized by lack of good breeding **b** : SHABBY 1b, SEEDY **2 a** : marked by lack of style or good taste : DOWDY **b** : marked by cheap showiness : GAUDY [from earlier *tacky* "low-class person"]

ta·co \'täk-ō\ *n, pl* **tacos** \-ōz\ : a usually fried tortilla that is folded or rolled and stuffed with a mixture (as of seasoned meat, cheese and lettuce) [Mexican Spanish]

tac·o·nite \'tak-ə-,nīt\ *n* : a flinty rock high enough in iron content to be used as a low-grade iron ore [*Taconic* mountain range, United States]

tact \'takt\ *n* : a keen understanding of how to act in getting along with others; *esp* : the ability to deal with others without offending them [French, "sense of touch", from Latin *tactus*, from *tangere* "to touch"]

tact·ful \'takt-fəl\ *adj* : having or showing tact — **tact·ful·ly** \-fə-lē\ *adv* — **tact·ful·ness** *n*

¹**tac·tic** \'tak-tik\ *adj* : of, relating to, or showing biological taxis [Greek *taktikos* "of order", from *tassein* "to arrange"]

²**tactic** *n* **1** : a method of employing forces in combat **2** : a planned action or maneuver for accomplishing an end

tac·ti·cal \'tak-ti-kəl\ *adj* **1 a** : of or relating to combat tactics **b** : of, relating to, or designed for air attack in close support of friendly ground forces ⟨*tactical* air force⟩ **2 a** : of or relating to small-scale actions serving a larger purpose **b** : skillful in planning or maneuvering — **tac·ti·cal·ly** \-kə-lē, -klē\ *adv*

tac·ti·cian \tak-'tish-ən\ *n* : one skilled in tactics

tac·tics \'tak-tiks\ *n sing or pl* **1 a** : the science and art of disposing and maneuvering forces in combat **b** : the art or skill of employing available means to accomplish an end **2** : a system or mode of procedure [Greek *taktika*, from *taktikos* "of order, of tactics", from *tassein* "to arrange, place in battle formation"] SYN see STRATEGY

tac·tile \'tak-tl, -,tīl\ *adj* **1** : perceptible by touch **2** : of, relating to, or used in the sense of touch [Latin *tactilis*, from *tangere* "to touch"] — **tac·til·i·ty** \tak-'til-ət-ē\ *n*

tact·less \'tak-tləs\ *adj* : having or showing no tact — **tact·less·ly** *adv* — **tact·less·ness** *n*

tac·tu·al \'tak-chə-wəl, -chəl\ *adj* : TACTILE [Latin *tactus* "sense of touch", from *tangere* "to touch"] — **tac·tu·al·ly** \-ē\ *adv*

tad \'tad\ *n* : BOY 1 [probably from Old English *tāde* "toad"]

tad·pole \'tad-,pōl\ *n* : an aquatic frog or toad larva typically having a long tail, rounded body, and gills [Middle English *taddepol*, from *tode* "toad" + *polle* "head, poll"]

taw kwon do \'tī-'kwän-'dō\ *n, often cap T & K & D* : a Korean martial art resembling karate [Korean *t'aekwŏndo*]

tael \'tāl\ *n* **1** : any of various units of weight of eastern Asia **2** : any of various Chinese units of value based on the value of a tael weight of silver [Portuguese, from Malay *tahil*]

tae·nia \'tē-nē-ə\ *n, pl* **-ni·ae** \-nē-ˌē\ *or* **-ni·as 1** : an ancient Greek fillet **2** : a band on a Doric order separating the frieze from the architrave **3** : TAPEWORM [Latin, from Greek *tainia*]

taf·fe·ta \'taf-ət-ə\ *n* : a crisp plain-woven lustrous fabric of various fibers used especially for women's clothing [Middle French *taffetas*, from Italian *taffetà*, from Turkish *tafta*, from Persian *tāftah* "woven"]

taff·rail \'taf-ˌrāl, -rəl\ *n* : the rail around the stern of a ship [Dutch *tafereel*]

taf·fy \'taf-ē\ *n, pl* **taffies** : a candy usually of molasses or brown sugar boiled and pulled until porous and light-colored [origin unknown]

¹tag \'tag\ *n* **1** : a loose hanging piece of cloth : TATTER **2** : a metal or plastic binding on an end of a shoelace **3** : a piece of hanging or attached material **4 a** : a brief quotation used for emphasis or effect **b** : TAG LINE **5** : a marker used for identification or classification ⟨price *tag*⟩ [Middle English *tagge*]

²tag *vb* **tagged; tag·ging 1** : to provide or mark with or as if with a tag **2** : to attach as an addition **3** : APPEND **3** : to follow closely and persistently **4** : LABEL 2

³tag *n* **1** : a children's game in which one player is it and chases the others and tries to tag one of them to make that player it **2** : an act or instance of touching a base runner with the ball in baseball [origin unknown]

⁴tag *vt* **tagged; tag·ging 1 a** : to touch in or as if in a game of tag **b** : to put out (a runner in baseball) by touching with the ball **2** : to hit solidly : catch with a blow

Ta·ga·log \tə-'gäl-əg, -ˌóg\ *n* **1** : a member of a people of central Luzon **2** : an Austronesian language of the Tagalog people [Tagalog]

tag·along \'tag-ə-ˌlóng\ *n* : one that persistently and often annoyingly follows the lead of another

tag end *n* **1** : the last part **2** : a miscellaneous or random bit

tag line *n* **1** : a final line (as in a play or joke); *esp* : one that serves to clarify a point or create a dramatic effect **2** : a phrase identified with an individual, group, or product : SLOGAN

tag up *vi* : to touch a base in baseball before running after a fly ball is caught

Ta·hi·tian \tə-'hē-shən\ *n* **1** : a native or inhabitant of Tahiti **2** : the Polynesian language of the Tahitians — **Tahitian** *adj*

Tai \'tī\ *n, pl* **Tai** : a member of a group of peoples of southeast Asia

tai·ga \'tī-gə\ *n* : swampy northern forest of cone-bearing trees (as pines, spruces, and firs) beginning where the tundra ends [Russian *taiga*]

¹tail \'tāl\ *n* **1** : the rear end or a lengthened growth from the rear end of the body of an animal **2** : something resembling an animal's tail ⟨*tail* of a kite⟩ **3** *pl* : full evening dress for men **4** : the back, last, lower, or inferior part of something **5** : the reverse of a coin — usually used in pl. ⟨*tails*, I win⟩ **6** : a spy (as a detective) who follows someone **7** : the rear part of an airplane consisting of horizontal and vertical stabilizing surfaces with attached control surfaces **8** : the trail of a fugitive in flight [Old English *tægel*] — **tailed** \'tāld\ *adj* — **tail·less** \'tāl-ləs\ *adj* — **tail·like** \'tāl-ˌlīk\ *adj*

²tail *adj* **1** : being at the rear ⟨*tail* gunner⟩ **2** : coming from the rear ⟨*tail* wind⟩

³tail *vb* **1 a** : to make or furnish with a tail **b** : to follow or be drawn behind like a tail **2** : to place the end of (as a rafter) in a wall or other support **3** : to follow closely for purposes of observation : SHADOW **4** : to grow progressively smaller, fainter, or more scattered — usually used with *off*

tail·back \'tāl-ˌbak\ *n* : the offensive football back who lines up farthest from the line of scrimmage

tail·board \-ˌbórd, -ˌbord\ *n* : TAILGATE

tail·bone \-'bōn, -ˌbōn\ *n* : a hind or lower vertebra; *also* : COCCYX

tail end *n* **1** : the hindmost end ⟨the *tail end* of the line⟩ **2** : the concluding period ⟨the *tail end* of the season⟩

tail fin *n* : CAUDAL FIN

¹tail·gate \'tāl-ˌgāt\ *n* : a gate at the back end of a vehicle (as a station wagon) that can be let down for loading and unloading

²tailgate *vb* : to drive dangerously close behind

tail·ing \'tā-ling\ *n* **1** *pl* : refuse material separated as residue in the preparation of various products (as grain or ores) **2** : the part of a projecting stone or brick inserted in a wall

tail lamp *n* : TAILLIGHT

tail·light \'tāl-ˌlīt\ *n* : a red warning light mounted at the rear of a vehicle

¹tai·lor \'tā-lər\ *n* : one whose occupation is making or altering outer garments [Old French *tailleur*, from *taillier* "to cut", from Late Latin *taliare*, from Latin *talea* "twig, cutting"]

²tailor *vt* **1 a** : to make or fashion as the work of a tailor **b** : to make or adapt to suit a special need or purpose **2** : to fit with clothes **3** : to style with trim straight lines and details completed by hand

tai·lored \-lərd\ *adj* **1** : made by a tailor **2** : fashioned or fitted to resemble a tailor's work **3** : CUSTOM-MADE

tai·lor·ing *n* **1 a** : the business or occupation of a tailor **b** : the work or workmanship of a tailor **2** : the making or adapting of something to suit a particular purpose

tai·lor–made \ˌtā-lər-'mād\ *adj* **1** : made by or as if by a tailor; *esp* : characterized by precise fit and simplicity of style **2** : made or as if made to suit a particular need

tail·piece \'tāl-ˌpēs\ *n* **1** : a piece added at the end **2** : a device from which the strings of a stringed instrument are stretched to the pegs **3** : an ornament placed below the text matter of a page (as at the end of a chapter) **4** : a beam tailed in a wall and supported by a header

tail pipe *n* : an outlet by which the exhaust gases are removed from an engine (as of an automobile or jet aircraft)

tail plane *n* : the horizontal tail surfaces of an airplane

tail·race \'tāl-ˌrās\ *n* : the part of a millrace below the waterwheel or turbine

tail·spin \-ˌspin\ *n* **1** : SPIN 2a **2** : a collapse into depression or confusion

tail wind *n* : a wind having the same general direction as the course of a moving object (as an aircraft)

¹taint \'tānt\ *vt* **1** : to touch or affect slightly with something bad **2** : SPOIL 2c **3** : to contaminate morally : CORRUPT [Middle English *taynten* "to affect by attainder", from Middle French *ataint*, past participle of *ataindre* "to affect by attainder, attain"]

²taint *n* **1** : a trace of decay : STAIN, BLEMISH **2** : a contaminating influence — **taint·less** \-ləs\ *adj*

¹take \'tāk\ *vb* **took** \'tük\; **tak·en** \'tā-kən\; **tak·ing 1** : to get into one's hands : GRASP ⟨*take* my hand⟩ **2** : CAPTURE ⟨*take* a fort⟩ **3** : WIN ⟨*take* first prize⟩ **4** : to get possession of (as by buying or capturing) ⟨decided to *take* the house⟩ ⟨*took* several trout with hook and line⟩ **5** : to seize and affect suddenly ⟨*taken* with a fever⟩ **6** : CHARM, DELIGHT ⟨were much *taken* with our new acquaintance⟩ **7** : EXTRACT ⟨*take* material from an encyclopedia⟩ **8** : REMOVE, SUBTRACT ⟨*take* 78 from 112⟩; *also* : to put an end to (as life) **9** : to find out by testing or examining ⟨*take* a patient's temperature⟩ **10** : SELECT ⟨*take* your choice⟩ **11** : ASSUME ⟨*take* office⟩ **12** : ABSORB ⟨this cloth *takes* dye well⟩ **13 a** : to be affected by : CONTRACT ⟨*took* a fit⟩ ⟨*took* cold⟩ **b** : BECOME ⟨*took* sick⟩ **14** : ACCEPT, FOLLOW ⟨*take* my advice⟩ **15** : to introduce into the body ⟨*take* medicine⟩ **16 a** : to submit to ⟨*took* the punishment without complaint⟩

| tailing

\ə\ abut \ng\ sing
\ər\ further \ō\ bone
\a\ mat \ó\ saw
\ā\ take \ói\ coin
\ä\ cot, cart \th\ thin
\aú\ out \th\ this
\ch\ chin \ü\ food
\e\ pet \ú\ foot
\ē\ easy \y\ yet
\g\ go \yü\ few
\i\ tip \yú\ cure
\ī\ life \zh\ vision
\j\ job

b : WITHSTAND ⟨*takes* a punch well⟩ **17** : to subscribe to ⟨*takes* two newspapers⟩ **18** : UNDERSTAND ⟨*take* a nod to mean yes⟩ **19** : FEEL ⟨*take* pride in one's work⟩ ⟨*take* offense⟩ **20** : to be formed or used with ⟨a noun that *takes* an *s* in the plural⟩ ⟨this verb *takes* an object⟩ **21** : to convey, lead, carry, or cause to come along with one **22 a** : to avail oneself of ⟨*take* shelter⟩ **b** : to proceed to occupy ⟨*take* a chair⟩ **23** : NEED, REQUIRE ⟨this job *takes* a lot of time⟩ **24** : to obtain an image or copy of ⟨*take* a photograph⟩ ⟨*take* fingerprints⟩ **25** : to set out to make, do, or perform ⟨*take* a walk⟩ — often used with *on* ⟨*took* on a new assignment⟩ **26** : to have effect (as by adherence or absorption) ⟨a dye that *takes* well⟩; *also* : to establish a take ⟨the vaccination *took*⟩ **27** : to go or get away ⟨*take* to the hills⟩ [Old English *tacan*, from Old Norse *taka*] □ SYN SEIZE, GRASP, SNATCH: TAKE applies to any manner of getting something into one's possession or control; SEIZE suggests sudden forcible taking of something tangible ⟨*seized* the thief in the act of *taking* the money⟩ GRASP stresses a laying hold so as to have firmly in possession ⟨*grasped* the handrail⟩ SNATCH suggests more suddenness but less force than SEIZE ⟨*snatched* a doughnut and ran out⟩ SYN see in addition BRING, RECEIVE — **take advantage of 1** : to use to advantage : profit by **2** : to impose upon : EXPLOIT — **take after 1** : to take as an example : FOLLOW **2** : to look like : RESEMBLE — **take care** : to be careful : exercise caution or prudence — **take care of** : to attend to or provide for the needs, operation, or treatment of — **take effect 1** : to become operative **2** : to produce a result as expected or intended : be effective — **take for** : to suppose to be; *esp* : to suppose mistakenly to be — **take for granted 1** : to assume as true, real, or expected **2** : to value too lightly — **take hold** : to become attached or established : take effect — **take into account** : to make allowance for — **take in vain** : to use (a name) profanely or without proper respect — **take issue** : to take up the opposite side — **take part** : PARTICIPATE — **take place** : to come about or occur : HAPPEN — **take stock** : INVENTORY, ASSESS — **take the cake** : to be remarkable or unbelievable — **take the count 1** : to be knocked out in a boxing match **2** : to go down in defeat — **take the floor** : to rise (as in a meeting) to make an address — **take to 1** : to take in hand : take care of **2** : to apply or devote oneself to (as a practice, habit, or occupation) ⟨*take to* begging⟩ **3** : to adapt oneself to : respond to **4** : to conceive a liking for — **take to task** : to call to account for a shortcoming : REPROVE

²take *n* **1** : an act or the action of taking (as by seizing, accepting, or coming into possession) **2** : something that is taken : **a** : money taken in **b** : SHARE, CUT ⟨wanted a bigger *take*⟩ **c** : the quantity (as of game) taken at one time : CATCH **d** (1) : a scene recorded (as on film or videotape) at one time without stopping the camera (2) : a sound recording made during a single recording period (3) : a trial recording **3 a** : a bodily reaction that indicates a successful immunization especially against smallpox **b** : a successful union of a graft **4** : mental response or reaction ⟨delayed *take*⟩

take back *vt* : RETRACT, WITHDRAW ⟨*take back* what you said⟩

¹take·down \'tāk-,daùn\ *adj* : constructed so as to be readily taken apart ⟨a *takedown* rifle⟩

²takedown *n* : the action or an act of taking down: as **a** : the action of humiliating **b** : the action of taking apart **c** : the act of bringing one's wrestling opponent to the mat from a standing position

take down \tāk-'daùn, 'tāk-\ *vb* **1 a** : to pull to pieces **b** : DISASSEMBLE **2** : to lower the spirit or vanity of **3 a** : to write down **b** : to record by mechanical means **4** : to become seized or attacked especially by illness ⟨*took down* with the mumps⟩

take-home pay \'tāk-,hōm-\ *n* : the money left in one's pay after all deductions (as taxes) have been made : the money one actually gets on payday

take in *vt* **1** : to draw into a smaller compass ⟨*take in* a slack line⟩ : **a** : FURL ⟨*take in* the sail⟩ **b** : to make (a garment) smaller by enlarging seams or tucks **2 a** : to receive as a guest or inmate **b** : to give shelter to **3 a** : to receive in payment or as a return **b** : to receive (work) into one's house to be done for pay ⟨*take in* washing⟩ **4** : to encompass within fixed limits : COMPRISE, INCLUDE **5** : ATTEND ⟨*take in* a movie⟩ **6** : to receive into the mind : PERCEIVE ⟨paused to *take* the situation *in*⟩ **7** : CHEAT, DECEIVE ⟨*taken in* by a hard luck story⟩

taken *past participle of* TAKE

take·off \'tā-,kòf\ *n* **1** : an imitation especially in the form of caricature **2 a** : a rise or leap from a surface in making a jump or flight or an ascent in an airplane **b** : an action of starting out or setting out **3** : a spot at which one takes off **4** : a mechanism for transmission of the power of an engine or vehicle to operate some other mechanism

take off \tā-'kòf, 'tā-\ *vb* **1 1** : REMOVE ⟨*take* your hat *off*⟩ **2** : RELEASE ⟨*take* the brake *off*⟩ **3** : to spend (time) away from work or duty ⟨*took* two weeks *off* in August⟩ **4 a** : to copy from an original : REPRODUCE **b** : MIMIC 1, 2 **5** : to take away : DETRACT **6 a** : to start off or away : set out ⟨*took off* without delay⟩ **b** : to branch off (as from a main stream or stem) **c** : to begin a leap or spring **d** : to leave the surface : begin flight

take on *vb* **1** : to contend with or face as an opponent **2** : ENGAGE, HIRE ⟨*took* me *on* for the summer⟩ **3** : to assume or acquire (as an appearance or quality) as or as if one's own **4** : to show one's feelings especially of grief or anger in a demonstrative way

take·out \'tā-,kaùt\ *n* : the action or an act of taking out

take out \tā-'kaùt, 'tā-\ *vb* **1** : to remove by cleansing **2** : to find release for : EXPEND ⟨*took* their frustration *out* on us⟩ **3** : to escort and usually pay the way especially on a social occasion **4** : to take as an equivalent in another form ⟨*took* the debt *out* in goods⟩ **5** : to obtain from the proper authority ⟨*take out* a charter⟩ **6** : to start on a course : set out — **take it out on** : to expend anger, vexation, or frustration in harassment of

take·over \'tā-,kō-vər\ *n* : the action or an act of taking over

take over \tā-'kō-vər, 'tā-\ *vb* : to assume control or possession of or responsibility for something ⟨*took over* the government⟩

take-up \'tā-,kəp\ *n* **1** : the action of taking something up (as by gathering, contraction, absorption, or adjustment) **2** : a device for tightening or drawing in

take up \tā-'kəp, 'tā-\ *vb* **1** : to remove by lifting or pulling up **2** : to accept or adopt for the purpose of assisting **3** : to take or accept (as a belief, idea, or practice) as one's own **4** : to respond favorably to (as a bet, challenge, or proposal) **5** : to make a beginning where another has left off — **take up for** : to take the part or side of — **take up with** : to begin to associate with

¹tak·ing \'tā-king\ *n* **1** : a state of violent agitation and distress **2** *pl* : receipts especially of money : PROFIT

²taking *adj* **1** : very attractive **2** : CONTAGIOUS

talc \'talk\ *n* : a soft mineral consisting of a basic silicate of magnesium that is usually whitish, greenish, or grayish with a soapy feel and occurs in flaky, granular, or fibrous masses [Middle French, "mica", from Medieval Latin *talk*, from Arabic *talq*]

tal·cum powder \'tal-kəm-\ *n* : a cosmetic powder composed of perfumed talc or talc and a mild antiseptic [Medieval Latin *talcum* "mica", from earlier *talk*]

tale \'tāl\ *n* **1** : an oral relation or recital ⟨a *tale* of woe⟩ **2** : a story about an imaginary event ⟨a fairy *tale*⟩ **3** : a false story : LIE **4** : a piece of harmful gossip ⟨all sorts of *tales* were going around about them) **5 a** : COUNT 1, TALLY **b** : a number of things taken together : TOTAL [Old English *talu*]

tale·bear·er \-,bar-ər, -,ber-\ *n* : one that spreads gossip, scandal, or idle rumors : GOSSIP — **tale·bear·ing** \-ing\ *adj or n*

tal·ent \'tal-ənt\ *n* **1** : any of several ancient units of weight and money value (as a unit of Palestine and Syria equal to 3000 shekels (about 49 kilograms) or a Greek unit equal to 6000 drachmas (about 26 kilograms) **2** : the abilities, power, and gifts a person is born with **3 a** : a special often creative or artistic aptitude **b** : general intelligence or mental power : ABILITY **4** : persons of talent in a field or activity [Old English *talente*, from Latin *talentum*, from Greek *talanton*; senses 2-4 from the parable of the talents in Matthew 25:14-30] — **tal·ent·ed** \-ən-təd\ *adj* □ SYN GENIUS: TALENT suggests a marked special ability without implying a mind of extraordinary power ⟨a *talent* for singing⟩ GENIUS may also imply marked talent but more often suggests an inborn creative intelligence far above ordinary ⟨true *genius* usually appears very early in life⟩

talent scout *n* : a person engaged in discovering and recruiting people of talent (as in music or a sport)

talent show *n* : a show consisting of a series of individual performances (as singing) by amateurs who may be selected for special recognition as performing talent

ta·ler *also* **tha·ler** \'täl-ər\ *n* : any of numerous silver coins issued by various German states from the 15th to the 19th centuries [German *thaler*, *taler*, short for *joachimsthaler*, from Sankt *Joachimsthal*, Bohemia, where the first talers were made]

tales·man \'tālz-mən, 'tā-lēz-\ *n* : a person added to a jury usually from among bystanders to make up a deficiency in the available number of jurors [Middle English *tales* "talesmen", from Medieval Latin *tales de circumstantibus* "such (persons) of the bystanders"; from the wording of the writ summoning them]

tale–tell·er \'tāl-,tel-ər\ *n* **1** : one who tells tales or stories **2** : TALEBEARER — **tale–tell·ing** \-ing\ *adj or n*

tal·is·man \'tal-ə-smən, -əz-mən\ *n, pl* **talismans** : a ring or stone carved with symbols and believed to have magical powers : CHARM [French, from Italian *talismano*, from Arabic *ṭilsam*, from Middle Greek *telesma*, literally, "consecration"] — **tal·is·man·ic** \,tal-ə-'sman-ik, -əz'man-\ *adj* — **tal·is·man·i·cal·ly** \-i-kə-lē, -klē\ *adv*

¹talk \'tȯk\ *vb* **1** : to deliver or express in speech : UTTER ⟨*talk* sense⟩ **2** : to make the subject of conversation or discourse : DISCUSS ⟨*talk* business⟩ **3** : to persuade, affect, or cause by talking ⟨*talked* them into agreeing⟩ **4** : to use (a language) for conversing or communicating : SPEAK ⟨can *talk* Italian⟩ **5 a** : to express or exchange ideas by means of spoken words : CONVERSE **b** : to convey information or communicate in any way (as with signs or sounds) **c** : to use speech : SPEAK ⟨babies can't *talk*⟩ **6 a** : to speak idly : PRATE **b** : GOSSIP **c** : to reveal secret or confidential information **7** : to give a talk : LECTURE [Middle English *talken*] SYN see SPEAK — **talk·er** *n* — **talk back** : to answer impertinently — **talk turkey** : to speak frankly or bluntly

²talk *n* **1** : the act or an instance of talking : SPEECH **2** : a way of speaking : LANGUAGE **3** : pointless or fruitless discussion : VERBIAGE **4** : a formal discussion, negotiation, or exchange of views **5** : RUMOR, GOSSIP **6** : the topic of interested comment, conversation, or gossip ⟨it's the *talk* of the village⟩ **7** : an analysis or discussion presented in an informal manner

talk·ative \'tȯ-kət-iv\ *adj* : fond of talking — **talk·ative·ness** *n* □ SYN TALKATIVE, GARRULOUS, VOLUBLE mean fond of talking. TALKATIVE implies a readiness to talk and engage in conversation; GARRULOUS suggests wordy, rambling, or tedious talkativeness ⟨a *garrulous*

old politician⟩ VOLUBLE suggests keeping up an uninterrupted seemingly endless flow of talk ⟨a *voluble* salesclerk who wouldn't quit⟩

talk down *vb* **1** : to overcome or silence by argument or by loud talking **2** : to speak in a condescending or superior way

talk·ie \'tȯ-kē\ *n* : a motion picture with a synchronized sound track [*talk* + mov*ie*]

talking book *n* : a phonograph or tape recording of a reading of a book or magazine designed chiefly for the use of the blind

talking machine *n* : PHONOGRAPH

talk·ing-to \'tȯ-king-,tü\ *n* : REPRIMAND, LECTURE ⟨father gave them a severe *talking-to*⟩

talk out *vt* : to clarify or settle by oral discussion ⟨*talk out* their differences⟩

talk over *vt* : to have a talk about : DISCUSS

talk up *vt* **1** : to discuss favorably : ADVOCATE **2** : to speak clearly or directly

talky \'tȯ-kē\ *adj* **talk·i·er; -est** **1** : fond of talking : TALKATIVE **2** : containing too much talk

tall \'tȯl\ *adj* **1 a** : great in stature or height **b** : of a specified height ⟨five feet *tall*⟩ **2 a** : large or formidable in amount, extent, or degree ⟨a *tall* order to fill⟩ **b** : FLOWERY, GRANDILOQUENT ⟨*tall* talk⟩ **c** : INCREDIBLE, IMPROBABLE ⟨a *tall* story⟩ [Middle English "brave, handsome"] — **tall** *adv* — **tall·ish** \'tȯ-lish\ *adj* — **tall·ness** *n*

tall·boy \'tȯl-,bȯi\ *n* **1** : HIGHBOY **2** : a double chest of drawers

tal·lith \'täl-əs, -ət, -əth\ *n, pl* **tal·li·thim** \,täl-ə-'sēm, -'tēm, -'thēm\ : a shawl with fringed corners traditionally worn over the head or shoulders by Jewish men during morning prayers [Hebrew *ṭallīth* "cover, cloak"]

tall oil \'täl-, 'tȯl-\ *n* : a resinous by-product from the manufacture of chemical wood pulp used especially in making soaps, coatings, and oils [German *tallöl*, from Swedish *tallolja*, from *tall* "pine" + *olja* "oil"]

tal·low \'tal-ō\ *n* : the white nearly tasteless solid rendered fat of cattle and sheep used chiefly in soap, margarine, candles, and lubricants [Middle English *talgh*, *talow*] — **tal·lowy** \'tal-ə-wē\ *adj*

¹tal·ly \'tal-ē\ *n, pl* **tallies** **1** : a device for recording business transactions; *esp* : a rod notched with marks representing numbers and serving as a record of a transaction and of the amount due or paid **2 a** : a reckoning or recorded account; *also* : a total recorded **b** : a score or point made (as in a game) **3 a** : a part that corresponds to an opposite or companion member : COMPLEMENT **b** : CORRESPONDENCE 1a [Medieval Latin *talea*, from Latin, "twig, cutting"]

²tally *vb* **tal·lied; tal·ly·ing** **1** : to keep a reckoning of : COUNT **2** : to make a tally : SCORE **3** : MATCH **4**, AGREE

tal·ly·ho \,tal-ē-'hō\ *n, pl* **tallyhos** : a call of a huntsman at the sight of the fox [probably from French *taïaut*, a cry used to excite hounds in deer hunting]

tal·ly·man \'tal-ē-mən\ *n* **1** *British* : one who sells goods on the installment plan **2** : one who tallies, checks, or keeps an account or record (as of a receipt of goods)

Tal·mud \'täl-,mud, 'tal-məd\ *n* : the authoritative body of Jewish tradition [Hebrew *talmūdh*, literally, "instruction"] — **Tal·mu·dic** \tal-'müd-ik, -'myüd-, -'məd-, täl-'mud-\ *also* **Tal·mu·di·cal** \-i-kəl\ *adj, often cap* — **Tal·mud·ism** \'täl-,mud-,iz-əm, 'tal-məd-\ *n, often cap* — **Tal·mud·ist** \-əst\ *n, often cap*

tal·on \'tal-ən\ *n* **1** : the claw of an animal and especially of a bird of prey **2** : a part or object shaped like or suggestive of a claw [Middle French, "heel, spur", derived from Latin *talus* "ankle, anklebone"] — **tal·oned** \-ənd\ *adj*

¹ta·lus \'tā-ləs\ *n* : rock debris at the base of a cliff [French, "sloping ground", from Latin *talutium* "slope indicating presence of gold under the soil"]

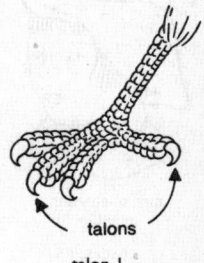

talons

talon 1

\ə\ abut	\ng\ sing
\ər\ further	\ō\ bone
\a\ mat	\ȯ\ saw
\ā\ take	\ȯi\ coin
\ä\ cot, cart	\th\ thin
\aú\ out	\th\ this
\ch\ chin	\ü\ food
\e\ pet	\ú\ foot
\ē\ easy	\y\ yet
\g\ go	\yü\ few
\i\ tip	\yú\ cure
\ī\ life	\zh\ vision
\j\ job	

²**talus** *n, pl* **ta·li** \'tā-,lī\ **I** : the bone that in man bears the weight of the body and with the tibia and fibula forms the ankle joint — called also *anklebone* **2** : the entire ankle [Latin]

tam \'tam\ *n* : TAM-O'-SHANTER

tam·able *or* **tame·able** \'tā-mə-bəl\ *adj* : capable of being tamed

ta·ma·le \tə-'mäl-ē\ *n* : ground meat seasoned with chili, rolled in cornmeal dough, wrapped in corn husks, and steamed [Mexican Spanish *tamales*, pl. of *tamal* "tamale", from Nahuatl *tamalli*]

tam·a·rack \'tam-ə-,rak\ *n* : any of several American larches; *also* : their wood [origin unknown]

tam·a·rind \'tam-ə-rənd, -,rind\ *n* : a tropical tree of the pea family with hard yellowish wood, feathery leaves, and red-striped yellow flowers; *also* : its pod which has an acid pulp used for preserves or in drinks [Spanish *tamarindo*, from Arabic *tamr hindī*, literally, "Indian date"]

tam·a·risk \'tam-ə-,risk\ *n* : any of a genus of chiefly desert shrubs having tiny narrow leaves and masses of minute flowers [Late Latin *tamariscus*, from Latin *tamarix*]

¹**tam·bour** \'tam-,bùr, tam-'\ *n* **I** : ¹DRUM 1 **2 a** : an embroidery frame; *esp* : a set of two interlocking hoops between which cloth is stretched before stitching **b** : embroidery made on a tambour frame **3** : a rolling top or front (as of a desk) of narrow strips of wood glued on canvas [French, from Arabic *ṭanbūr*, from Persian *tabīr*]

²**tambour** *vb* **I** : to embroider (cloth) with tambour **2** : to work at a tambour frame — **tam·bour·er** *n*

tam·bou·rine \,tam-bə-'rēn\ *n* : a small drum; *esp* : a shallow one-headed drum with loose metallic disks at the sides that is played by shaking, striking with the hand, or rubbing with the thumb

tambourine

¹**tame** \'tām\ *adj* **I** : reduced from a state of native wildness especially so as to be tractable and useful to humans : DOMESTICATED **2** : made docile and submissive : SUBDUED **3** : lacking spirit, zest, or interest : INSIPID [Old English *tam*] — **tame·ly** *adv* — **tame·ness** *n*

²**tame** *vb* **I a** : to make or become tame **b** : to subject to cultivation **2** : to deprive of spirit : HUMBLE, SUBDUE **3** : to tone down : SOFTEN — **tam·er** *n*

tame·less \'tām-ləs\ *adj* : not tamed or tamable

Ta·mil \'tam-əl, 'täm-\ *n* **I** : a Dravidian language of Tamil Nadu state and of northern and eastern Sri Lanka **2** : a Tamil-speaking person

tam-o'-shan·ter \'tam-ə-,shant-ər\ *n* : a cap of Scottish origin with a tight headband, wide flat circular crown, and often a pompon in the center [*Tam o' Shanter*, hero of the poem *Tam o' Shanter* by Robert Burns]

tam-o'-shanter

tamp \'tamp\ *vt* **I** : to drive in or down by a succession of light or medium blows : COMPACT ⟨*tamp* wet concrete⟩ **2** : to put a check on : LESSEN [probably from Middle English *tampion* "plug", from Middle French *tapon*, *tampon*, of Germanic origin] — **tamp·er** *n*

tam·per \'tam-pər\ *vi* **tam·pered; tam·per·ing** \-pə-ring, -pring\ **I** : to use underhand or improper methods (as bribery) **2 a** : to interfere so as to cause a weakening or change for the worse **b** : to try foolish or dangerous experiments : MEDDLE [probably from Middle French *temprer* "to temper, mix, meddle"] — **tam·per·er** \-pər-ər\ *n*

tam·pi·on \'tam-pē-ən, 'täm-\ *n* : a wooden plug or a metal or canvas cover for the muzzle of a gun [Middle English, "plug"]

¹**tam·pon** \'tam-,pän\ *n* : a plug (as of cotton) introduced into a cavity usually to check bleeding or absorb secretions [French, literally, "plug"]

²**tampon** *vt* : to plug with a tampon

tam–tam \'tam-,tam, 'täm-,täm\ *n* **I** : TOM-TOM **2** : GONG 1 [Hindi *ṭamṭam*]

tandem bicycle

¹**tan** \'tan\ *vb* **tanned; tan·ning** **I** : to convert (hide) into leather by treatment with a solution (as of tannin-rich bark) **2** : to make or become tan or brown by exposure to the sun **3** : THRASH 2, WHIP [Middle French *tanner*, from Medieval Latin *tannare*, from *tannum* "tanbark"]

²**tan** *n* **I** : TANBARK 1 **2** : a tanning material or its active agent (as tannin) **3** : a brown color imparted to the skin by exposure to the sun or weather **4** : a light yellowish brown [French, from Medieval Latin *tannum*]

³**tan** *adj* **tan·ner; tan·nest** : of the color tan

tan·a·ger \'tan-i-jər\ *n* : any of a family of small brightly colored mostly tropical American birds that are related to the finches but have larger thicker bills [Portuguese *tangará*, from Tupi]

tan·bark \'tan-,bärk\ *n* **I** : bark rich in tannin that is used in tanning **2** : a surface (as a circus ring) covered with spent tanbark

¹**tan·dem** \'tan-dəm\ *n* **I a** : a 2-seated carriage drawn by horses harnessed one before the other; *also* : a team so harnessed **b** : TANDEM BICYCLE **2** : a group of two or more arranged one behind the other or used or acting in conjunction [Latin, "at last, at length" (taken to mean "lengthwise")] □ ORIGIN When a pair of horses pulls a carriage, the two are usually harnessed side by side. But there is a type of carriage that is drawn by two horses harnessed one before the other. This carriage owes its name, *tandem*, to a rather contorted Latin-English pun. The Latin word *tandem* means "at length, at last, finally". We do not know who the punster was who first suggested that a carriage pulled by horses arranged lengthwise, "at length", should be called a *tandem*, but he or she need not have been a scholar. The Latin word is not a rare one and would be known to any student, however shallow, of the language. In English *tandem* came eventually to be used for any arrangement of things or of people one behind another.

²**tandem** *adv or adj* : one after or behind another

tandem bicycle *n* : a bicycle for two or more persons sitting tandem

¹**tang** \'tang\ *n* **I** : a projecting part (as on a knife, file, or sword) to connect with the handle **2 a** : a sharp distinctive often lingering flavor **b** : a pungent odor **3 a** : a faint suggestion : TRACE **b** : a distinguishing characteristic that sets apart or gives a special individuality [of Scandinavian origin] — **tanged** \'tangd\ *adj*

²**tang** *n* : any of various large coarse seaweeds (as a rockweed) [of Scandinavian origin]

³**tang** *vb* : CLANG, RING [imitative]

⁴**tang** *n* : a sharp twanging sound

Tang \'täng\ *n* : a Chinese dynasty dated A. D. 618–907 and marked by wide contacts with other cultures and by the development of printing and the flourishing of poetry and art [Chinese (Pekingese dialect) *t'ang*²]

tan·ge·lo \'tan-jə-,lō\ *n, pl* **-los** : a hybrid between a tangerine and a grapefruit; *also* : its fruit [blend of *tangerine* and *pomelo* "grapefruit" (from Dutch *pompelmoes*)]

tan·gen·cy \'tan-jən-sē\ *n, pl* **-cies** : the quality or state of being tangent

¹**tan·gent** \-jənt\ *adj* **I a** : touching a curve or surface at only one point in the given location ⟨straight line *tangent* to a curve⟩ **b** (1) : having a common tangent line at a point ⟨*tangent* curves⟩ (2) : having a common tangent plane at a point ⟨*tangent* surfaces⟩ **2** : diverging from an original purpose or course : IRRELEVANT ⟨*tangent* remarks⟩ [Latin *tangens*, present participle of *tangere* "to touch"]

²**tangent** *n* **I** : the trigonometric function that for an acute angle is the ratio between the side opposite to the angle when it is considered part of a right triangle and the side adjacent — abbreviation tan **2 a** : a line tangent to a curve **b** : the part of a tangent to a plane curve between the point of tangency and the horizon-

tal axis **3** : an abrupt change of course : DIGRESSION ⟨went off on a *tangent* and never got to the point⟩

tan·gen·tial \tan-'jen-chəl\ *adj* **1** : TANGENT **2** : acting along or lying in a tangent ⟨*tangential* forces⟩ **3** : DIVERGENT, DIGRESSIVE ⟨*tangential* comment⟩ — **tan·gen·tial·ly** \-'jench-lē, -ə-lē\ *adv*

tan·ger·ine \'tan-jə-,rēn, ,tan-jə-'-\ *n* **1** : MANDARIN 3; *esp* : one grown for its deep orange loose-skinned fruit especially in the United States and southern Africa **2** : the fruit of the tangerine [French *Tanger* "Tangier, Morocco"]

¹tan·gi·ble \'tan-jə-bəl\ *adj* **1 a** : capable of being perceived especially by the sense of touch : PALPABLE **b** : having substance or reality ⟨a *tangible* advantage⟩ : MATERIAL **2** : capable of being appraised at an actual or approximate value ⟨*tangible* assets⟩ [Late Latin *tangibilis*, from Latin *tangere* "to touch"] — **tan·gi·bil·i·ty** \,tan-jə-'bil-ət-ē\ *n* — **tan·gi·ble·ness** \'tan-jə-bəl-nəs\ *n* — **tan·gi·bly** \-blē\ *adv*

²tangible *n* : something tangible; *esp* : a tangible asset

¹tan·gle \'tang-gəl\ *vb* **tan·gled; tan·gling** \-gə-ling, -gling\ **1** : to make or become involved so as to hamper or embarrass : be or become entangled ⟨hopelessly *tangled* in argument⟩ **2** : to twist or become twisted together into a mass hard to straighten out again [Middle English *tanglen*]

²tangle *n* **1** : a tangled twisted mass (as of vines) confusedly interwoven **2** : a complicated or confused state or condition **3** : DISPUTE, ARGUMENT ⟨had a *tangle* with their neighbor⟩

tan·gle·ment \'tang-gəl-mənt\ *n* : ENTANGLEMENT

tan·gly \'tang-gə-lē, -glē\ *adj* **tan·gli·er; -est** : full of tangles

¹tan·go \'tang-gō\ *n, pl* **tangos** : a ballroom dance of Spanish-American origin with a variety of steps and postures; *also* : music for this dance [American Spanish]

²tango *vi* : to dance the tango

tan·gram \'tang-grəm, 'tan-\ *n* : a Chinese puzzle made by cutting a square of thin material into a number of pieces which can be recombined into many different figures [perhaps from Chinese (Pekingese dialect) *t'ang*² "Chinese" + English *-gram*]

tangy \'tang-ē\ *adj, sometimes* **tangos tang·i·er; -est** : having or suggestive of a tang ⟨a *tangy* smell⟩ — **tang·i·ness** *n*

¹tank \'tangk\ *n* **1** : a usually large receptacle for holding, transporting, or storing liquids **2** : an enclosed heavily armed and armored combat vehicle that moves on tracks [Portuguese *tanque*, alteration of *estanque*, from *estancar* "to stanch"]

²tank *vt* : to place, store, or treat in a tank

tank·age \'tang-kij\ *n* **1** : the capacity or contents of a tank **2** : dried animal residues usually freed from the fat and gelatin and used as fertilizer and in feeds **3** : fees charged for storage in tanks

tan·kard \'tang-kərd\ *n* : a tall one-handled drinking vessel; *esp* : a silver or pewter mug with a lid [Middle English]

tank·er \'tang-kər\ *n* : a vehicle (as a ship, truck, or aircraft) designed for the transportation of liquids

tank farm *n* : an area with tanks for storage of oil

tank town *n* : a small town [from the fact that formerly trains stopped at such towns only to take on water]

tan·nage \'tan-ij\ *n* : the act, process, or result of tanning

tan·ner \'tan-ər\ *n* : one that tans hides

tan·nery \'tan-rē, -ə-rē\ *n, pl* **tan·ner·ies** : a place where tanning is carried on

tan·nic acid \,tan-ik-\ *n* : TANNIN

tan·nin \'tan-ən\ *n* : any of various substances of plant origin used in tanning and dyeing, in inks, and as an astringent [French, from *tanner* "to tan"]

tan·ning *n* **1** : the art or process by which a skin is tanned **2** : a browning of the skin by sunlight **3** : WHIPPING

tan·nish \'tan-ish\ *adj* : somewhat tan

tan·sy \'tan-zē\ *n, pl* **tansies** : any of a genus of mostly weedy herbs related to the daisies; *esp* : one with finely cut leaves, aromatic odor, and very bitter taste [Old French *tanesie*, from Medieval Latin *athanasia*, from Greek, "immortality"]

tan·ta·lite \'tant-l-,īt\ *n* : a mineral consisting of a dark shiny oxide of iron, manganese, tantalum, and niobium

tan·ta·lize \'tant-l-,īz\ *vt* : to tease or torment by or as if by presenting something desirable to the view but continually keeping it out of reach [*Tantalus*] — **tan·ta·liz·er** *n*

tan·ta·liz·ing *adj* : possessing a quality that arouses or stimulates desire or interest; *also* : mockingly out of reach — **tan·ta·liz·ing·ly** \-,ī-zing-lē\ *adv*

tan·ta·lum \'tant-l-əm\ *n* : a hard ductile gray-white acid-resisting metallic chemical element found combined in rare minerals — see ELEMENT table [New Latin, from Latin *Tantalus* "Tantalus"; from its inability to absorb acid]

tan·ta·mount \'tant-ə-,maunt\ *adj* : equal in value, meaning, or effect [obsolete *tantamount*, n., "equivalent", from Anglo-French *tant amunter* "to amount to as much"]

tan·tara \tan-'tar-ə, -'tär-\ *n* : the blare of a trumpet or horn [Latin *taratantara*]

¹tan·tivy \tan-'tiv-ē\ *adv or adj* : at a gallop [origin unknown]

²tantivy *n* : a rapid gallop or ride : a headlong rush

tan·trum \'tan-trəm\ *n* : a fit of bad temper [origin unknown]

tan·yard \'tan-,yärd\ *n* : the section or part of a tannery housing tanning vats

Tao \'daù, 'taù\ *n* : the ultimate principle of the universe in Taoism [Chinese (Pekingese dialect) *tao*⁴, literally, "way"]

Tao·ism \-,iz-əm\ *n* **1** : a Chinese mystical philosophy traditionally founded by Lao-tzu in the 6th century B.C. that teaches conformity to the Tao by unassertive action and simplicity **2** : a religion developed from Taoist philosophy and Buddhist and folk religion and concerned with obtaining long life and good fortune often by magical means — **Tao·ist** \-əst\ *adj or n* — **Tao·is·tic** \daù-'is-tik, taù-\ *adj*

¹tap \'tap\ *n* **1 a** : FAUCET, SPIGOT **b** : liquor drawn through a tap **2** : the procedure of removing fluid from a container or cavity by tapping **3** : a tool for forming an internal screw thread **4** : an intermediate point in an electric circuit where a connection may be made [Old English *tæppa* "tap of a cask"] — **on tap 1** : ready to be drawn ⟨ale *on tap*⟩ **2** : on hand : AVAILABLE

²tap *vt* **tapped; tap·ping** **1** : to release or cause to flow by piercing or by drawing a plug from the containing vessel or cavity ⟨*tap* wine from a cask⟩ **2 a** : to pierce so as to let out or draw off a fluid ⟨*tap* maple trees⟩ **b** : to draw from or upon ⟨*tap* the nation's resources⟩ **c** : to connect into (a telephone or telegraph wire) to get information; *also* : to connect into (an electrical circuit) **3** : to form a female screw in by means of a tap — **tap·per** *n*

³tap *vb* **tapped; tap·ping** **1** : to strike or rap lightly especially with a slight sound ⟨*tap* the desk with a pencil⟩ ⟨*tap* on the window⟩ **2** : to make or produce by repeated light blows ⟨a woodpecker *tapped* a hole in the tree⟩ **3** : to repair (a shoe) by putting a half sole on **4** : SELECT; *esp* : to elect to membership (as in a fraternity or sorority) [Middle French *taper* "to strike with the flat of the hand", of Germanic origin] — **tap·per** *n*

⁴tap *n* **1** : a light usually audible blow; *also* : its sound **2** : HALF SOLE **3** : a small metal plate for the sole or heel of a shoe (as for tap dancing)

ta·pa \'täp-ə, 'tap-\ *n* : the bark of a tree pounded to make a coarse cloth usually decorated with geometric patterns; *also* : this cloth [Tahitian]

tankard

tap dance *n* : a dance tapped out audibly with the feet — **tap–dance** \'tap-,dans\ *vi* — **tap dancer** *n* — **tap dancing** *n*

¹tape \'tāp\ *n* **1** : a narrow band of woven fabric **2** : a string stretched breast-high above the finishing line of a footrace **3** : a narrow flexible strip or band; *esp* : MAGNETIC TAPE **4** : a recording on magnetic tape [Old English *tæppe*]

²tape *vt* **1** : to fasten, tie, bind, cover, or support with tape **2** : to measure with a tape measure **3** : to record on magnetic tape

tape deck *n* : a device used to play back and often to record on magnetic tapes that usually has to be connected to a separate audio system

tape·line \'tā-,plīn\ *n* : TAPE MEASURE

tape measure *n* : a tape marked off in units (as inches or centimeters) and used for measuring

¹ta·per \'tā-pər\ *n* **1 a** : a long waxed wick used especially for lighting lamps, pipes, or fires; *also* : a slender candle **b** : a feeble light **2 a** : a tapering form or figure **b** : gradual lessening of thickness, diameter, or width in an elongated object **c** : a gradual decrease [Old English]

²taper *vb* **ta·pered; ta·per·ing** \-pə-ring, -pring\ **1** : to make or become gradually smaller toward one end **2** : to diminish gradually

tape–re·cord \,tā-pri-'kȯrd\ *vt* : to make a recording of on magnetic tape — **tape recording** *n*

tape recorder *n* : a device for recording on and playing back magnetic tapes

taper off *vb* : to stop or decrease gradually

tap·es·try \'tap-ə-strē\ *n, pl* **-tries** : a heavy textile used especially as a wall hanging or furniture covering [Middle French *tapisserie*, from *tapisser* "to carpet", from *tapis* "carpet", from Greek *tapēs*] — **tap·es·tried** \-strēd\ *adj*

tapestry carpet *n* : a carpet in which the designs are printed in colors on the threads before the fabric is woven

tape·worm \'tāp-,wərm\ *n* : a flatworm with a segmented body that is parasitic when adult in the intestine of vertebrates : CESTODE

tap·hole \'tap-,hōl\ *n* : a hole for a tap; *esp* : a hole at or near the bottom of a furnace or ladle through which molten metal or slag can be tapped

tap·i·o·ca \,tap-ē-'ō-kə\ *n* : a usually granular preparation of cassava starch used especially in puddings and as a thickening in liquid foods [Spanish and Portuguese, from Tupi *typyóca*]

ta·pir \'tā-pər\ *n, pl* **tapir** *or* **tapirs** : any of several large chiefly nocturnal hoofed mammals of tropical America, Malaya, and Sumatra that have long flexible snouts and are related to the horses and rhinoceroses [Tupi *tapiíra*]

tapir

tap·pet \'tap-ət\ *n* : a lever or projection moved by some other piece (as a cam) or intended to tap or touch something else to cause a particular motion [³*tap*]

tap·room \'tap-,rüm, -,rùm\ *n* : BARROOM

tap·root \-,rüt, -,rùt\ *n* : a large strong root that grows vertically downward and gives off smaller lateral roots — compare FIBROUS ROOT [¹*tap*]

taps \'taps\ *n sing or pl* : the last bugle call at night blown as a signal that lights are to be put out; *also* : a similar call blown at military funerals and memorial services [probably from earlier *taptoo* "tattoo"]

tap·ster \'tap-stər\ *n* : BARTENDER

¹tar \'tär\ *n* **1** : a dark usually odorous viscous liquid obtained by destructive distillation of organic material (as wood, coal, or peat) **2** : a residue present in tobacco smoke that contains combustion by-products (as resins, acids, and phenols) [Old English *teoru*]

²tar *vt* **tarred; tar·ring** : to treat or smear with or as if with tar

tar·an·tel·la \,tar-ən-'tel-ə\ *n* : a vivacious folk dance of southern Italy in ⁶/₈ time [Italian, from *Taranto*, Italy]

ta·ran·tu·la \tə-'ranch-lə, -ə-lə; -'rant-l-ə\ *n* **1** : a large European spider whose bite was once thought to cause an uncontrollable desire to dance **2** : any of a family of large hairy American spiders that are mostly rather sluggish and essentially harmless to humans [Medieval Latin, from Italian *tarantola*, from *Taranto*, Italy]

tar·boosh *also* **tar·bush** \tär-'büsh, 'tär-,\ *n* : a usually red hat similar to the fez worn alone or aspart of a turban especially by Muslim men [Arabic *ṭarbūsh*]

tar·dy \'tärd-ē\ *adj* **tar·di·er; -est** **1** : moving or progressing slowly **2** : being late or delayed [Middle French *tardif*, derived from Latin *tardus*] — **tar·di·ly** \'tärd-l-ē\ *adv* — **tar·di·ness** \'tärd-ē-nəs\ *n*

¹tare \'taər, 'teər\ *n* **1 a** : VETCH; *also* : its seed **b** : a weed of grainfields mentioned in the Bible **2** *pl* : an undesirable element [Middle English]

²tare *n* : a deduction of weight made to allow for the weight of a container or vehicle [Middle French, from Italian *tara*, from Arabic *ṭarḥa*] — **tare** *vt*

targe \'tärj\ *n, archaic* : a light shield [Old French]

tar·get \'tär-gət\ *n* **1 a** : a mark to shoot at **b** : an object of ridicule or criticism **c** : a goal to be achieved : OBJECTIVE **2** : the surface usually of platinum or tungsten upon which the cathode rays within an X-ray tube are focused and from which the X rays are emitted [Middle French *targette* "small shield", from *targe* "light shield", of Germanic origin]

target date *n* : the date set for an event or for the completion of a project, goal, or quota

tar·iff \'tar-əf\ *n* **1 a** : a schedule of duties imposed by a government on imported or in some countries exported goods **b** : a duty or rate of duty imposed in such a schedule **2** : a schedule of rates or charges of a business or public utility [Italian *tariffa*, from Arabic *ta'rīf* "notification"]

tar·la·tan \'tär-lət-n\ *n* : a thin stiff transparent muslin [French *tarlatane*]

tar·mac \'tär-,mak\ *n* : a tarmacadam road, apron, or runway [from *Tarmac*, a trademark]

Tar·mac \'tär-,mak\ *trademark* — used for a bituminous binder for surfacing roads

tar·mac·ad·am \,tär-mə-'kad-əm\ *n* **1** : a pavement made by putting tar over courses of crushed stone and then rolling **2** : a material of tar and aggregates mixed in a plant and shaped on the roadway [*tar* + *macadam*]

tarn \'tärn\ *n* : a small mountain lake or pool usually of glacial origin [of Scandinavian origin]

¹tar·nish \'tär-nish\ *vb* **1** : to make or become dull, dim, or discolored ⟨silver *tarnishes*⟩ **2** : to lessen the prestige or quality of ⟨a *tarnished* reputation⟩ [Middle French *terniss-*, stem of *ternir* "to tarnish"] — **tar·nish·able** \-ə-bəl\ *adj*

²tarnish *n* : something that tarnishes; *esp* : a film of chemically altered material on the surface of a metal (as silver)

ta·ro \'tär-ō, 'tar-, 'ter-\ *n, pl* **taros** : a plant of the arum family grown throughout the tropics for its edible starchy tuberous rootstocks; *also* : this rootstock [Tahitian and Maori]

tarp \'tärp\ *n* : TARPAULIN

tar paper *n* : a heavy paper coated or saturated with tar for use especially in building

tar·pau·lin \tär-'pȯ-lən, 'tär-pə-\ *n* : a piece of material (as waterproof canvas) used for protecting exposed objects [probably derived from *tar* + *pall*]

tar·pon \'tär-pən\ *n, pl* **tarpon** *or* **tarpons** : a large silvery sport fish found in tropical waters [origin unknown]

tar·ra·gon \'tar-ə-,gän, -gən\ *n* : a small European wormwood grown for its pungent aromatic foliage used especially in vinegar and cookery [Middle French targon, from Medieval Latin *tarchon*, from Arabic *ṭarkhūn*]

¹**tar·ry** \'tar-ē\ *vi* **tar·ried; tar·ry·ing 1** : to be tardy : DELAY, LINGER **2** : to stay in or at a place [Middle English *tarien*]

²**tar·ry** \'tär-ē\ *adj* : of, resembling, or covered with tar

¹**tar·sal** \'tär-səl\ *adj* : of or relating to the tarsus

²**tarsal** *n* : a tarsal part (as a bone or cartilage)

tar sand *n* : a natural saturation of sand or sandstone with heavy sticky portions of petroleum

tar·si·er \'tär-sē-ər, -sē-,ā\ *n* : any of several small nocturnal arboreal East Indian mammals related to the lemurs [French, from *tarse* "tarsus"] — **tar·si·oid** \-sē-,ȯid\ *adj or n*

tar·so·meta·tar·sus \'tär-sō-'met-ə-,tär-səs\ *n* : the large compound bone of the tarsus of a bird; *also* : the segment of the limb it supports

tar·sus \'tär-səs\ *n, pl* **tar·si** \-,sī, -,sē\ **1** : the part of the vertebrate foot between the metatarsus and the leg; *also* : the small bones that support this part of the foot **2** : the shank of a bird's leg **3** : the distal part of the limb of an arthropod [New Latin, from Greek *tarsos* "wickerwork mat, flat of the foot, ankle"]

¹**tart** \'tärt\ *adj* **1** : agreeably sharp to the taste : pleasantly acid **2** : SARCASTIC 1, CAUSTIC [Old English *teart* "sharp, severe"] SYN see SOUR — **tart·ly** *adv* — **tart·ness** *n*

²**tart** *n* **1** : a small pie or pastry shell containing jelly, custard, or fruit **2** : PROSTITUTE [Middle French *tarte*]

tar·tan \'tärt-n\ *n* **1** : a plaid textile design of Scottish origin usually distinctively patterned to designate a clan **2** : a fabric or garment with tartan design [probably from Middle French *tiretaine* "linsey-woolsey"]

¹**tar·tar** \'tärt-ər\ *n* **1** : a substance consisting essentially of cream of tartar found in the juice of grapes and deposited in wine casks as a reddish crust or sediment **2** : a hard crust of saliva, food residue, and various calcium salts that forms on the teeth [Medieval Latin *tartarum*]

²**tartar** *n* **1** *cap* : a native or inhabitant of Tatary **2** : a bad-tempered or unexpectedly formidable person [Middle French *Tartare*, probably from Medieval Latin *Tartarus*, from Persian *Tātār*] — **Tartar** *adj* — **Tar·tar·i·an** \tär-'tar-ē-ən, -'ter-\ *adj*

tartar emetic *n* : a poisonous salt of sweetish metallic taste that is used in dyeing and in medicine especially in the treatment of amebic dysentery

tar·tar·ic acid \tär-,tar-ik-\ *n* : a strong organic acid $C_4H_6O_6$ that occurs in four forms, is usually obtained from grape tartar, and is used especially in food and medicines and in photography

tar·tar sauce *or* **tar·tare sauce** \,tärt-ər-\ *n* : mayonnaise with chopped pickles, olives, capers, and parsley [French *sauce tartare*]

tart·ish \'tärt-ish\ *adj* : somewhat tart — **tart·ish·ly** *adv*

tart·let \'tärt-lət\ *n* : a small tart

tar·trate \'tär-,trāt\ *n* : a salt or ester of tartaric acid

Tar·zan \'tärz-n, 'tär-,zan\ *n* : a strong agile person of heroic proportions and bearing [*Tarzan*, hero of adventure stories by Edgar Rice Burroughs]

task \'task\ *n* : a piece of work especially as assigned by another : DUTY, FUNCTION [Old North French *tasque*, from Medieval Latin *tasca* "tax or service imposed by a feudal superior", from *taxare* "to tax"] □ SYN TASK, DUTY, ASSIGNMENT, JOB mean a piece of work to be done. TASK implies work imposed by one in authority or by circumstance ⟨every child had a daily *task* to perform⟩ DUTY implies an obligation to perform or responsibility for performance ⟨the limits of their *duties* as guardians⟩ ASSIGNMENT implies a definite limited task assigned by one in authority; JOB applies to a piece of work one is asked to do or agrees to do voluntarily ⟨a helper to do *jobs* around the house⟩

and often stresses quality or difficulty of performance ⟨did a good *job* on the research project⟩

task force *n* : a temporary grouping especially of military units to accomplish a particular objective

task·mas·ter \'task-,mas-tər\ *n* : one who imposes a task or burdens another with labor

task·mis·tress \-,mis-trəs\ *n* : a woman who is a taskmaster

task·work \-,wərk\ *n* **1** : PIECEWORK **2** : hard work

Tas·ma·ni·an devil \taz-,mā-nē-ən-\ *n* : a powerful stocky burrowing flesh-eating marsupial of Tasmania

Tasmanian wolf *n* : a somewhat doglike flesh-eating marsupial formerly common in Australia but now considered extinct

¹**tas·sel** \'tas-əl, *oftenest of corn* 'täs-, 'tȯs-\ *n* **1** : a hanging ornament made of a bunch of cords of even length fastened at one end **2** : something resembling a tassel; *esp* : the terminal male inflorescence of some plants and especially Indian corn [Old French, "clasp, tassel", from Latin *taxillus* "small die"]

²**tassel** *vb* **-seled** *or* **-selled; -sel·ing** *or* **-sel·ling** \-ə-ling, -ling\ : to adorn with or put forth tassels

¹**taste** \'tāst\ *vb* **1** : EXPERIENCE ⟨*taste* the joy of flying⟩ **2** : to try or determine the flavor of by taking a little into the mouth **3** : to eat or drink especially in small quantities **4** : to distinguish or recognize as if by the sense of taste **5** : to have a specific flavor [Old French *taster* "to touch, taste", derived from Latin *taxare* "to touch"]

²**taste** *n* **1 a** : a small amount tasted **b** : a small sample of experience ⟨first *taste* of battle⟩ **2** : the one of the special senses that perceives and distinguishes the sweet, sour, bitter, or salty quality of a dissolved substance and is mediated by receptors in the taste buds of the tongue **3 a** : the objective quality of a dissolved substance perceptible to the sense of taste **b** : a complex sensation resulting from usually combined stimulation of the senses of taste, smell, and touch : FLAVOR **4** : the distinctive quality of an experience **5** : individual preference : INCLINATION **6 a** : critical judgment, discernment, or appreciation **b** : manner or aesthetic quality indicative of discernment or appreciation □ SYN TASTE, RELISH, GUSTO, ZEST mean a liking for something that gives pleasure. TASTE may imply a natural or acquired specific liking or interest; RELISH suggests a capability for keen gratification of appetite or other senses; GUSTO implies a heartiness in relishing that goes with vitality or high spirits; ZEST implies an eagerness for and keen perception of a thing's peculiar pleasure.

taste bud *n* : any of the sensory organs by which taste is perceived and which lie chiefly in the tongue

taste·ful \'tāst-fəl\ *adj* : having, showing, or conforming to good taste — **taste·ful·ly** \-fə-lē\ *adv* — **taste·ful·ness** *n*

taste·less \'tāst-ləs\ *adj* **1** : lacking flavor : FLAT, INSIPID **2** : not having or showing good taste ⟨*tasteless* decorations⟩ — **taste·less·ly** *adv* — **taste·less·ness** *n*

tast·er \'tā-stər\ *n* : one that tastes: as **a** : a person who samples food or drink prepared for another usually to test for poison **b** : a person able to taste the chemical phenylthiocarbamide

tasty \'tā-stē\ *adj* **tast·i·er; -est 1** : pleasing to the taste : SAVORY **2** : TASTEFUL — **tast·i·ly** \-stə-lē\ *adv* — **tast·i·ness** \-stē-nəs\ *n*

tat \'tat\ *vb* **tat·ted; tat·ting** : to work at or make by tatting [back-formation from *tatting*]

Ta·tar \'tät-ər\ *n* : a member of any of a group of Turkic peoples found mainly in the Tatar Republic of Russia and parts of Siberia and central Asia [Persian *Tātār*, of Turkic origin]

tat·ter \'tat-ər\ *n* **1** : a part torn and left hanging : SHRED **2** *pl* : tattered clothing [of Scandinavian origin] — **tatter** *vb*

tartan 1

Tasmanian wolf

\ə\ abut		\ng\ sing	
\ər\ further		\ō\ bone	
\a\ mat		\ȯ\ saw	
\ā\ take		\ȯi\ coin	
\ä\ cot, cart		\th\ thin	
\au̇\ out		\th\ this	
\ch\ chin		\ü\ food	
\e\ pet		\u̇\ foot	
\ē\ easy		\y\ yet	
\g\ go		\yü\ few	
\i\ tip		\yu̇\ cure	
\ī\ life		\zh\ vision	
\j\ job			

tat·ter·de·ma·lion \,tat-ərd-i-'māl-yən, -'mal-, -ē-ən\ *n* : a person dressed in ragged clothing : RAGAMUFFIN [origin unknown]

tat·tered \'tat-ərd\ *adj* **1** : wearing ragged clothes ⟨a *tattered* barefoot child⟩ **2** : torn in shreds : RAGGED ⟨a *tattered* flag⟩

tat·ter·sall \'tat-ər-,sòl\ *n* **1** : a pattern of colored lines enclosing squares of solid background **2** : a fabric woven or printed in a tattersall pattern [*Tattersall's* horse market, London, England]

tat·ting \'tat-ing\ *n* **1** : a handmade lace formed usually by looping and knotting with a single thread and a small shuttle **2** : the act or process of making tatting [origin unknown]

¹tat·tle \'tat-l\ *vb* **tat·tled; tat·tling** \'tat-ling, -l-ing\ **1** : CHATTER 2, PRATTLE **2** : to tell secrets [Dutch *tatelen*]

²tattle *n* **1** : idle talk : CHATTER **2** : GOSSIP 2, TALEBEARING

tat·tler \'tat-lər, -l-ər\ *n* **1** : TATTLETALE **2** : any of various slender long-legged shorebirds (as the willet and yellowlegs) with a loud and frequent call

tat·tle·tale \'tat-l-,tāl\ *n* : one that tattles : INFORMER

¹tat·too \ta-'tü\ *n, pl* **tattoos 1 a** : a call sounded shortly before taps as notice to go to quarters **b** : an outdoor military exercise given by troops as evening entertainment **2** : a rapid rhythmic rapping ⟨hoofs beating a *tattoo* on the road⟩ [Dutch *taptoe*, from the phrase *tap toe!* "taps shut!"]

²tattoo *n* : an indelible mark or figure fixed on the body by insertion of pigment under the skin or by production of scars [Tahitian *tatau*]

³tattoo *vt* **1** : to mark or color (the skin) with a tattoo **2** : to mark the skin with (a tattoo) — **tat·too·er** *n*

tau \'tau, 'tò\ *n* : the 19th letter of the Greek alphabet — T or τ

taught *past of* TEACH

taunt \'tònt, 'tänt\ *vt* : to reproach or challenge in a mocking or insulting way : jeer at [perhaps from Middle French *tenter* "to try, tempt"] SYN see RIDICULE — **taunt** *n* — **taunt·er** *n* — **taunt·ing·ly** \-ing-lē\ *adv*

taupe \'tōp\ *n* : a brownish gray [French, literally, "mole", from Latin talpa]

tau·rine \'tòr-,īn\ *adj* **1** : of or relating to a bull **2** : of or relating to the common domestic cattle as distinguished from Indian humped cattle [Latin *taurinus*, from *taurus* "bull"]

Tau·rus \'tòr-əs\ *n* **1** : a zodiacal constellation that contains the Pleiades and Hyades **2** : the 2d sign of the zodiac; *also* : one born under this sign [Latin, literally, "bull"]

taut \'tòt\ *adj* **1 a** : tightly drawn : not slack ⟨a *taut* rope⟩ **b** : HIGH-STRUNG, TENSE ⟨*taut* nerves⟩ **2 a** : kept in proper order or condition ⟨a *taut* ship⟩ **b** : not loose or flabby : FIRM [Middle English *tought*] SYN see TIGHT — **taut·ly** *adv* — **taut·ness** *n*

taut·en \'tòt-n\ *vb* **taut·ened; taut·en·ing** \'tòt-ning, -n-ing\ : to make or become taut

tau·tog \'tò-,tòg\ *n* : an edible fish related to the wrasses and found along the Atlantic coast of the United States — called also *blackfish* [of American Indian origin]

tau·tol·o·gy \tò-'täl-ə-jē\ *n, pl* **-gies** : needless repetition of an idea, statement, or word; *also* : an instance of such repetition ⟨"a beginner who has just started" is a *tautology*⟩ [Late Latin *tautologia*, from Greek, from *tautologos* "tautologous", from *tauto* "the same" (contraction of *to auto*) + *legein* "to say"] — **tau·to·log·i·cal** \,tòt-l-'äj-i-kəl\ *adj* — **tau·to·log·i·cal·ly** \-kə-lē, -klē\ *adv* — **tau·tol·o·gous** \tò-'täl-ə-gəs\ *adj* — **tau·tol·o·gous·ly** *adv*

tav·ern \'tav-ərn\ *n* **1** : an establishment where alcoholic beverages are sold to be drunk on the premises **2** : INN 1 [Old French *taverne*, from Latin *taberna*, literally, "shed, hut, shop", from *trabs* "beam"]

tav·ern·er \'tav-ər-nər,'tav-ə-nər\ *n* : one that keeps a tavern

taw \'tò\ *n* **1** : a playing marble used as a shooter **2** : the line from which players shoot at marbles [origin unknown]

taw·dry \'tòd-rē, 'täd-\ *adj* **taw·dri·er; -est** : cheap and gaudy in appearance and quality [*tawdry lace* "tie of lace for the neck", from *Saint Audrey* (Etheldreda), died 679, queen of Northumbria] SYN see GAUDY — **taw·dri·ly** \-rə-lē\ *adv* — **taw·dri·ness** \-rē-nəs\ *n*
□ ORIGIN When Etheldreda, queen of Northumbria, renounced her husband and her royal position and became a nun, she was soon appointed abbess of a monastery in the Isle of Ely. She was renowned for her saintliness and is said to have died of a swelling in her throat, which she took as a judgment upon her fondness for wearing necklaces in her youth. An annual fair was held in Saint Etheldreda's honor on 17 October, and her name became simplified to *Saint Audrey*. At these fairs cheap knickknacks were sold, among them a type of necklace called "Saint Audrey's lace", which was eventually altered to "tawdry lace". *Tawdry* came to be used for other cheap finery and is now an adjective meaning "cheap and gaudy".

¹taw·ny \'tò-nē, 'tän-ē\ *adj* **taw·ni·er; -est** : of the color tawny [Middle French *tanné*, past participle of *tanner* "to tan"] — **taw·ni·ness** *n*

²tawny *n, pl* **tawnies** : a brownish orange to light brown color

¹tax \'taks\ *vt* **1** : to levy a tax on **2** : to call to account : CENSURE ⟨*taxed* them with neglect of their duties⟩ **3** : to make heavy and rigorous demands on : subject to excessive stress ⟨the job *taxed* my strength⟩ [Middle French *taxer*, from Medieval Latin *taxare*, from Latin, "to feel, estimate, censure", from *tangere* "to touch"] — **tax·abil·i·ty** \,tak-sə-'bil-ət-ē\ *n* — **tax·able** \'tak-sə-bəl\ *adj* — **tax·er** *n*

²tax *n* **1 a** : a charge usually of money imposed by authority upon persons or property for public purposes **b** : a sum levied on members of an organization to defray expenses **2** : a heavy demand ⟨the trip would be too great a *tax* on your health⟩

tax·a·tion \tak-'sā-shən\ *n* **1** : the action of taxing; *esp* : the imposition of taxes **2** : income obtained from taxes

tax evasion *n* : deliberate failure to pay taxes usually by false reports of taxable income or property

tax–ex·empt \,tak-sig-'zemt, -'zempt\ *adj* **1** : exempted from a tax **2** : bearing interest free from federal or state income tax ⟨*tax-exempt* securities⟩

¹taxi \'tak-sē\ *n, pl* **tax·is** \-sēz\ *also* **tax·ies** : TAXICAB; *also* : a similarly operated boat or airplane

²taxi *vb* **tax·ied; taxi·ing** *or* **taxy·ing; tax·is** *or* **tax·ies 1** : to operate or move at low speed along the surface of the ground ⟨the plane *taxied* to the hangar⟩ **2 a** : to ride in a taxicab **b** : to transport by taxi

taxi·cab \'tak-sē-,kab\ *n* : an automobile that carries passengers for a fare usually determined by the distance traveled and often shown by a meter [earlier *taxi*meter *cab*]

taxi dancer *n* : a girl employed by a dance hall, café, or cabaret to dance with patrons who pay a certain amount for each dance

taxi·der·my \'tak-sə-,dər-mē\ *n* : the art of preparing, stuffing, and mounting skins of animals [derived from Greek *taxis* "arrangement" + *derma* "skin"] — **taxi·der·mic** \,tak-sə-'dər-mik\ *adj* — **taxi·der·mist** \'tak-sə-,dər-məst\ *n*

taxi·me·ter \'tak-sē-,mēt-ər\ *n* : an instrument for use in a hired vehicle (as a taxicab) for automatically showing the fare due [French *taximètre*, from German *taxameter*, from Medieval Latin *taxa* "tax, charge" (from *taxare* "to tax") + German *-meter* "-meter"]

tax·is \'tak-səs\ *n, pl* **tax·es** \'tak-,sēz\ : reflex movement by a freely motile organism in relation to a source of stimulation (as a light or a temperature or chemical gradient); *also* : a reflex reaction involving such movement — compare TROPISM [Greek, "arrangement", from *tassein* "to arrange"]

taxi stand *n* : a place where taxis may park awaiting hire

tax·on \'tak-ˌsän\ *n, pl* **taxa** \-sə\ *also* **tax·ons** : a taxonomic group or entity; *also* : its name in a formal system of nomenclature [back-formation from *taxonomy*]

tax·on·o·my \tak-'sän-ə-mē\ *n* 1 : the study of scientific classification : SYSTEMATICS 2 a : CLASSIFICATION 2a(1) b : orderly classification of plants and animals according to their presumed natural relationships [French *taxonomie,* from Greek *taxis* "arrangement" + *nemein* "to control, distribute"] — **tax·o·nom·ic** \ˌtak-sə-'näm-ik\ *adj* — **tax·o·nom·i·cal·ly** \-'näm-i-kə-lē, -klē\ *adv* — **tax·on·o·mist** \tak-'sän-ə-məst\ *n*

tax·pay·er \'tak-ˌspā-ər\ *n* : one that pays or is subject to a tax

tax·us \'tak-səs\ *n, pl* **tax·us** \-səs\ : YEW 1a [Latin]

Tay–Sachs disease \'tā-ˌsaks-\ *n* : a fatal hereditary disease that is caused by an enzyme deficiency, is marked by a build-up of lipids especially in nerve tissues, and occurs especially in individuals of eastern European Jewish ancestry — called also *Tay-Sachs*

TB \ˌtē-'bē, 'tē-\ *n* : TUBERCULOSIS [*TB* (abbreviation for *tubercle bacillus*)]

T–bone \'tē-ˌbōn\ *n* : a small beefsteak from behind the ribs containing a T-shaped bone and a small piece of tenderloin

T cell \'te-ˌsel\ *n* : any of several lymphocytes (as a helper T cell) that differentiate in the thymus and include some that exert control over immune functions and others that destroy antigen-bearing cells — called also *T lymphocyte*; compare B CELL [*t*hymus-derived *cell*]

tea \'tē\ *n* 1 a : a shrub related to the camellia that has lance-shaped leaves and fragrant white flowers and is grown mainly in China, Japan, India, and Sri Lanka b : the leaves and leaf buds of this plant prepared for use in beverages usually by immediate curing by heat or by such curing following a period of fermentation 2 : an aromatic beverage prepared from tea leaves by steeping them in boiling water 3 : any of various plants used like tea; *also* : an infusion from their leaves used medicinally or as a beverage 4 a : a late afternoon serving of tea and a light meal b : a party or reception at which tea is served 5 *slang* : MARIJUANA 2 [Chinese (Amoy dialect) *t'e*]

tea bag *n* : a cloth or filter-paper bag holding enough tea for an individual serving

tea ball *n* : a perforated metal ball that holds tea leaves and is used in brewing tea in a pot or cup

tea·ber·ry \'tē-ˌber-ē\ *n* : CHECKERBERRY [from the use of its leaves as a substitute for tea]

tea biscuit *n, British* : CRACKER 2, COOKIE

teach \'tēch\ *vb* **taught** \'tȯt\; **teach·ing** 1 a : to cause to know or understand ⟨*taught* us German⟩ b : to assist in learning how to do something : show how ⟨*teach* a child to read⟩ 2 : to guide the studies of : INSTRUCT ⟨*teach* a class⟩ 3 : to give lessons in : instruct pupils in ⟨*teach* music⟩ 4 : to be or work as a teacher ⟨was *teaching* in Chicago⟩ 5 : to cause to learn : cause to know the consequences of an action ⟨*taught* by experience⟩ [Old English *tǣcan*] □ SYN INSTRUCT, EDUCATE, TRAIN: TEACH applies to any manner of imparting information or skill so that others may learn; INSTRUCT suggests methodical or formal teaching ⟨*instructed* them in swimming⟩ EDUCATE suggests providing formal schooling for fostering mental, moral, and physical growth and maturity and usually stresses book learning; TRAIN stresses the end in view and usually implies practice and drill as the means to that end ⟨*train* an

apprentice in a trade⟩ ⟨toilet-*train* a young child⟩ SYN see in addition LEARN

teach·able \'tē-chə-bəl\ *adj* 1 : capable of being taught; *esp* : apt and willing to learn 2 : well adapted for use in teaching ⟨a *teachable* textbook⟩ — **teach·abil·i·ty** \ˌtē-chə-'bil-ət-ē\ *n*

teach·er \'tē-chər\ *n* : one that teaches; *esp* : one whose occupation is to instruct

teachers college *n* : a college for the training of teachers usually offering a full 4-year course and granting a bachelor's degree

teach–in \'tē-ˌchin\ *n* : a get-together especially of college students and faculty for discussion especially of a controversial public issue

teach·ing *n* 1 : the act, practice, or profession of a teacher 2 : something taught; *esp* : DOCTRINE — **teaching** *adj*

teaching aid *n* : a device (as a record player, map, or picture) used by a teacher to supplement classroom instruction

tea·cup \'tē-ˌkəp\ *n* : a cup usually holding less than 250 milliliters that is used with a saucer for hot beverages — **tea·cup·ful** \'tē-kəp-ˌfúl\ *n*

tea dance *n* : a dance held in the late afternoon

tea·house \'tē-ˌhaús\ *n* : a public house or restaurant where tea and light refreshments are sold

teak \'tēk\ *n* 1 : a tall East Indian timber tree of the vervain family 2 : the hard durable yellowish brown wood of teak [Portuguese *teca,* of Dravidian origin]

tea·ket·tle \'tē-ˌket-l\ *n* : a covered kettle that is used for boiling water and that has a handle and spout

teak·wood \'tē-ˌkwúd\ *n* : TEAK

teal \'tēl\ *n, pl* **teal** *or* **teals** : any of several small short-necked ducks of Europe and America [Middle English *tele*]

¹**team** \'tēm\ *n* 1 : a group of animals: as a : two or more draft animals harnessed to the same vehicle or implement; *also* : one or more animals with harness and attached vehicle b : a brood especially of young pigs or ducks c : a matched group of animals for exhibition 2 : a number of persons associated together in work or activity: as a : a group on one side (as in football or a debate) b : CREW 2, GANG [Old English *tēam* "group of draft animals"]

²**team** *vb* 1 : to yoke or join in a team 2 : to haul with or drive a team 3 : to form a team ⟨*team* up together⟩

team handball *n* : a game developed from soccer which is played between two teams of seven players and in which the ball is thrown, caught, and dribbled with the hands

team·mate \'tēm-ˌmāt\ *n* : a fellow member of a team

team·ster \'tēm-stər, 'tēmp-\ *n* : one who drives a team or truck especially as an occupation

team·work \'tēm-ˌwərk\ *n* : the work or activity of a number of persons acting in close association as members of a unit ⟨*teamwork* won the game⟩

tea·pot \'tē-ˌpät\ *n* : a vessel that is used for brewing and serving tea and that has a spout

¹**tear** \'tiər\ *n* 1 : a drop of the salty liquid that keeps the eye and the inner eyelids moist 2 : a transparent drop of fluid or hardened fluid matter (as resin) 3 *pl* : an act of crying or grieving ⟨burst into *tears*⟩ [Old English *tæhher, tēar*] — **teary** \'tiər-ē\ *adj*

²**tear** *vi* : to shed tears

³**tear** \'taər, 'teər\ *vb* **tore** \'tōr, 'tȯr\; **torn** \'tōrn, 'tȯrn\; **tear·ing** 1 a : to separate or pull apart by force : REND b : LACERATE ⟨*tear* the skin⟩ 2 : to divide or disrupt by the pull of contrary forces ⟨a mind *torn* by doubts⟩ 3 : to remove by force ⟨children *torn* from their families⟩ 4 : to cause or make by force or violent means ⟨*tore* a hole in the wall⟩ 5 : to move or act with violence, haste, or force ⟨*tore* down the street⟩ [Old English *teran*] — **tear·er** *n*

⁴**tear** \'taər, 'teər\ *n* 1 a : the act of tearing b : damage from being torn; *esp* : a torn place 2 a : a hurried pace : HURRY b : SPREE ⟨go on a *tear*⟩

tea 1a

\ə\ abut		\ng\ sing	
\ər\ further		\ō\ bone	
\a\ mat		\ȯ\ saw	
\ā\ take		\ȯi\ coin	
\ä\ cot, cart		\th\ thin	
\aú\ out		\th\ this	
\ch\ chin		\ü\ food	
\e\ pet		\ú\ foot	
\ē\ easy		\y\ yet	
\g\ go		\yü\ few	
\i\ tip		\yú\ cure	
\ī\ life		\zh\ vision	
\j\ job			

tear down *vt* **1 a** : to cause to decompose or disintegrate : DESTROY **b** : VILIFY 2, DENIGRATE **2** : to take apart

tear·drop \'tiər-,dräp\ *n* **1** : ¹TEAR 1 **2** : something (as a pendent gem) shaped like a dropping tear

tear·ful \'tiər-fəl\ *adj* : flowing with, accompanied by, or causing tears — **tear·ful·ly** \-fə-lē\ *adv* — **tear·ful·ness** *n*

tear gas *n* : a solid, liquid, or gaseous substance that on dispersion in the atmosphere blinds the eyes with tears — **tear-gas** \'tiər-,gas\ *vt*

tear·jerk·er \'tiər-,jər-kər\ *n* : an extravagantly pathetic story, play, film, or broadcast — **tear·jerk·ing** \-king\ *adj*

tea·room \'tē-,rüm, -,rùm\ *n* : a small restaurant serving light meals

tea rose *n* : any of numerous hybrid garden bush roses descended chiefly from a Chinese rose and valued especially for their abundant large usually tea-scented blossoms

tear·stain \'tiər-,stān\ *n* : a spot or streak left by tears — **tear·stained** \-,stānd\ *adj*

¹tease \'tēz\ *vt* **1 a** : to disentangle and lay parallel by combing or carding ⟨*tease* wool⟩ **b** : TEASEL **2 a** : to annoy persistently : PESTER **b** : TANTALIZE [Old English *tǣsan*] — **teas·er** *n*

²tease *n* **1** : the act of teasing : the state of being teased **2** : one that teases

¹tea·sel *or* **tea·zel** *or* **tea·zle** \'tē-zəl\ *n* **1 a** : an Old World prickly herb with flower heads that are covered with stiff hooked bracts — called also *fuller's teasel* **b** : a plant related to the teasel **2 a** : a dried flower head of the fuller's teasel used to raise a nap on woolen cloth **b** : a wire substitute for the fuller's teasel [Old English *tǣsel*]

²teasel *vt* **tea·seled** *or* **tea·selled; tea·sel·ing** *or* **tea·sel·ling** \'tēz-ling, -ə-ling\ : to raise a nap on (cloth) with teasels

¹teasel 1a

tea·spoon \'tē-,spün, -,spün\ *n* **1** : a small spoon used especially for eating soft foods and stirring beverages **2** : TEASPOONFUL

tea·spoon·ful \-,fùl\ *n, pl* **-spoonfuls** \-,fùlz\ *or* **-spoons·ful** \-,spünz-,fùl, -,spünz-\ **1** : as much as a teaspoon can hold **2** : a unit of measure used especially in cookery equal to 1⅓ fluidrams (about 4.9 milliliters) or one third of a tablespoonful

teat \'tit, 'tēt\ *n* **1** : the protuberance through which milk is drawn from an udder or breast : NIPPLE **2** : a small projection (as on a mechanical part) [Old French *tete,* of Germanic origin] — **teat·ed** \-əd\ *adj*

tea time \'tē-,tīm\ *n* : the customary time for tea : late afternoon or early evening

tea wagon *n* : a small table on wheels used in serving tea and light refreshments

tech·ne·tium \tek-'nē-shē-əm, -shəm\ *n* : a metallic chemical element obtained by bombarding molybdenum and in the fission of uranium — see ELEMENT table [New Latin, from Greek *technētos,* derived from *technē* "art"]

tech·nic \'tek-nik, *for 1 also* tek-'nēk\ *n* **1** : TECHNIQUE 1 **2** *pl* : TECHNOLOGY 1a

tech·ni·cal \'tek-ni-kəl\ *adj* **1 a** : having special usually practical knowledge especially of a mechanical or scientific subject ⟨*technical* experts⟩ **b** : marked by or characteristic of specialization ⟨a *technical* language⟩ **2** : of or relating to a particular subject; *esp* : of or relating to a practical subject organized on scientific principles ⟨*technical* training⟩ **3** : existing by application of laws or rules **4** : of or relating to technique **5** : of, relating to, or produced by commercial processes ⟨*technical* sulfuric acid⟩ [Greek *technikos* "of art, skillful", from *technē* "art, skill"] — **tech·ni·cal·ly** \-kə-lē, -klē\ *adv*

technical foul *n* : a foul that is less serious than a personal foul or that involves unsportsmanlike conduct

tech·ni·cal·i·ty \,tek-nə-'kal-ət-ē\ *n, pl* **-ties** **1** : the quality or state of being technical **2** : something technical; *esp* : a detail meaningful only to a specialist

technical knockout *n* : the termination of a boxing match when one boxer is unable or is declared by the referee to be unable to continue

technical sergeant *n* : an enlisted rank in the Air Force above staff sergeant and below master sergeant

tech·ni·cian \tek-'nish-ən\ *n* : a specialist in the technical details or in the technique of a subject, art, or occupation

tech·nique \tek-'nēk\ *n* **1** : the way in which technical details are treated (as by a writer) or basic physical movements are used (as by a dancer); *also* : ability in such treatment or use ⟨faultless piano *technique*⟩ **2 a** : technical methods (as in scientific research) ⟨laboratory *technique*⟩ **b** : a method of accomplishing a desired aim [French, from *technique* "technical", from Greek *technikos*]

tech·noc·ra·cy \tek-'näk-rə-sē\ *n* : management of society by technical experts — **tech·no·crat** \'tek-nə-,krat\ *n*

tech·no·log·i·cal \,tek-nə-'läj-i-kəl\ *or* **tech·no·log·ic** \-'läj-ik\ *adj* : of, relating to, or characterized or caused by technology — **tech·no·log·i·cal·ly** \-'läj-i-kə-lē, -klē\ *adv*

tech·nol·o·gy \tek-'näl-ə-jē\ *n, pl* **-gies** **1 a** : applied science **b** : a technical method of achieving a practical purpose **2** : the means employed to provide objects for human sustenance and comfort [Greek *technologia* "systematic treatment of an art", from *technē* "art" + *-logia* "-logy"] — **tech·nol·o·gist** \-jəst\ *n*

tech·no-pop \'tek-nō-,päp\ *n* : pop music featuring extensive use of synthesizers

tec·ton·ic \tek-'tän-ik\ *adj* : of or relating to changes in the shape of the crust of a moon or planet (as the earth), the forces involved in or producing such changes, and the resulting forms [Greek *tektonikos* "of a builder", from *tektōn* "builder"]

tec·ton·ics \-iks\ *n sing or pl* **1** : a branch of geology concerned with the structure of the earth's crust and especially with the formation of folds and faults in it **2** : the process of change in the earth's crust that produces continents, ocean basins, plateaus, mountains, folds, and faults

ted·dy bear \'ted-ē-\ *n* : a stuffed toy bear [*Teddy,* nickname of President Theodore Roosevelt; from a cartoon showing him sparing the life of a bear cub while hunting]

Te Deum \tā-'dā-əm, tē-'dē-\ *n, pl* **Te Deums** : a hymn of praise to God [Late Latin *Te Deum laudamus* "Thee, God, we praise"]

te·dious \'tēd-ē-əs, 'tē-jəs\ *adj* : tiresome because of length or dullness : BORING — **te·dious·ly** *adv* — **te·dious·ness** *n*

te·di·um \'tēd-ē-əm\ *n* : the quality or state of being tedious : TEDIOUSNESS, BOREDOM [Latin *taedium* "disgust, irksomeness", from *taedēre* "to disgust, weary"]

tee \'tē\ *n* : the area from which a golf ball is struck in starting play on a hole; *also* : a tiny mound or a small peg with concave top on which the ball is set to be struck [origin unknown]

teem \'tēm\ *vi* **1** : to become filled to overflowing : ABOUND ⟨lakes *teeming* with fish⟩ **2** : to be present in large quantity [Old English *tīeman, tǣman* "to bring forth, give birth to"]

teen \'tēn\ *adj* : TEENAGE

teen·age \'tēn-,nāj\ *or* **teen·aged** \'tē-,nājd\ *adj* : of, being, or relating to people in their teens

teen·ag·er \-,nā-jər\ *n* : a teenage person

teens \'tēnz\ *n pl* **1** : the numbers 13 through 19; *esp* : the years 13 through 19 in a lifetime or century **2** : teenage people [*-teen* (as in *thirteen*)]

tee·ny \'tē-nē\ *adj* **tee·ni·er; -est** : TINY [by alteration]

tee off *vi* **1** : to drive a golf ball from a tee at the beginning of play on a hole **2** : BEGIN 1, START

tee·pee *variant of* TEPEE

tee shirt *variant of* T-SHIRT

tee·ter \'tēt-ər\ *vi* **1 a** : to move unsteadily **b** : WAVER 1, VACILLATE **2** : SEESAW 1b [Middle English *titeren*] — **teeter** *n*

tee·ter-board \-,bōrd, -,bȯrd\ *n* **1** : SEESAW 2b **2** : a board placed on a raised support in such a way that a person standing on one end of the board is thrown into the air if another person jumps on the opposite end

tee·ter–tot·ter \'tēt-ər-,tät-ər\ *n* : SEESAW 2b

teeth *pl of* TOOTH

teethe \'tēth\ *vi* **teethed**; **teeth·ing** : to cut one's teeth : grow teeth

teeth·ridge \'tē-,thrij\ *n* : the inner surface of the gums of the upper front teeth

tee·to·tal·er *or* **tee·to·tal·ler** \'tē-'tōt-l-ər\ *n* : a person who practices or advocates teetotalism [*t*otal + *total* (abstinence)]

tee·to·tal·ism \-l-,iz-əm\ *n* : the principle or practice of complete abstinence from drinking alcoholic beverages

Tef·lon \'tef-,län\ *trademark* — used for synthetic fluorine-containing resins used especially for nonstick coatings

tek·tite \'tek-,tīt\ *n* : a glassy body of probably meteoric origin and of rounded but indefinite shape [Greek *tēktos* "molten", from *tēkein* "to melt"]

tele- *or* **tel-** *combining form* **1** : at a distance ⟨*tele*communication⟩ ⟨*tele*pathy⟩ **2 a** : telegraph ⟨*tele*typewriter⟩ **b** : television ⟨*tele*course⟩ [Greek *tēle* "far off"]

tele·cast \'tel-i-,kast\ *vb* **telecast** *also* **tele·cast·ed**; **tele·cast·ing** [*tele-* + broad*cast*] : to broadcast by television — **telecast** *n* — **tele·cast·er** *n*

tele·com·mu·ni·ca·tion \,tel-i-kə-,myü-nə-'kā-shən\ *n* **1** : communication at a distance (as by cable, radio, telegraph, telephone, or television) **2** : a science that deals with telecommunication

tele·course \'tel-i-,kōrs, -,kȯrs\ *n* : a course of study conducted over television

tele·ge·nic \,tel-ə-'jen-ik, -'jēn-\ *adj* : suitable for television broadcast — **tele·ge·ni·cal·ly** \-i-kə-lē, -klē\ *adv*

tele·gram \'tel-ə-,gram, *Southern also* -grəm\ *n* : a message sent by telegraph

¹tele·graph \-,graf\ *n* : an apparatus for communication at a distance by coded signals; *esp* : an apparatus, system, or process for communication at a distance by electric transmission of such signals over wire — **tele·graph·ic** \,tel-ə-'graf-ik\ *adj* — **tele·graph·i·cal·ly** \-'graf-i-kə-lē, -klē\ *adv*

²telegraph *vt* **1 a** : to send by or as if by telegraph **b** : to send a telegram to **c** : to send (as flowers or money) by means of a telegraphic order **2** : to make known by signs especially unknowingly and in advance ⟨*tele*graph a punch⟩ — **te·leg·ra·pher** \tə-'leg-rə-fər\ *n* — **te·leg·ra·phist** \-fəst\ *n*

te·leg·ra·phy \tə-'leg-rə-fē\ *n* : the use or operation of a telegraph apparatus or system

tele·ki·ne·sis \,tel-i-kə-'nē-səs, -kī-\ *n* : the apparent production of motion in objects (as by a spiritualistic medium) without physical contact or other explainable means [*tele-* + Greek *kinēsis* "motion", from *kinein* "to move"]

tele·mar·ket·ing \,tel-ə-'mär-kət-ing\ *n* : the marketing of goods or services by telephone — **tele·mar·ket·er** \-kət-ər\ *n*

tele·me·ter \'tel-ə-,mēt-ər\ *n* : an electrical apparatus for measuring something (as pressure, speed, or temperature), transmitting the result especially by radio to a distant station, and there indicating the measurement — **telemeter** *vb* — **tele·met·ric** \,tel-ə-'me-trik\ *adj* — **tele·met·ri·cal·ly** \-tri-kə-lē, -klē\ *adv* — **te·lem·e·try** \tə-'lem-ə-trē\ *n*

---

te·le·ol·o·gist \,tel-ē-'äl-ə-jəst, ,tē-lē-\ *n* : a specialist or believer in teleology

te·le·ol·o·gy \,tel-ē-'äl-ə-jē, ,tē-lē-\ *n* : a doctrine that attributes a purpose to nature or that explains natural phenomena as directed toward a goal [Greek *telos* "end, purpose"] — **te·le·o·log·i·cal** \,tel-ē-ə-'läj-i-kəl, ,tē-lē-\ *adj*

te·le·ost \'tel-ē-,äst, ,tē-lē-\ *n* : any of a group (Teleostei or Teleostomi) of fishes comprising those with a bony rather than a cartilaginous skeleton [derived from Greek *teleios* "complete, perfect" (from *telos* "end") + *osteon* "bone"] — **teleost** *adj* — **te·le·os·te·an** \,tel-ē-'äs-tē-ən, ,tē-lē-\ *adj or n*

te·lep·a·thy \tə-'lep-ə-thē\ *n* : apparent communication from one mind to another by means other than the known physical senses — **tele·path** \'tel-ə-,path\ *n* — **tele·path·ic** \,tel-ə-'path-ik\ *adj* — **tele·path·i·cal·ly** \-'path-i-kə-lē, -klē\ *adv*

¹tele·phone \'tel-ə-,fōn\ *n* : an instrument for transmitting and receiving sounds over long distances by electricity

²telephone *vb* **1** : to communicate by telephone **2** : to send by telephone **3** : to speak to by telephone — **tele·phon·er** *n*

telephone booth *n* : an enclosure within which one may stand or sit while making a telephone call

tele·phon·ic \,tel-ə-'fän-ik\ *adj* **1** : conveying sound to a distance **2** : of, relating to, or conveyed by telephone

¹tele·pho·to \,tel-ə-'fōt-ō\ *adj* : being a camera lens system designed to give a large image of a distant object; *also* : relating to or being photography done with a telephoto lens

²telephoto *n* : a telephoto lens

Telephoto *trademark* — used for an apparatus for transmitting photographs electrically or for a photograph so transmitted

tele·play \'tel-ə-,plā\ *n* : a play written for television

tele·print·er \'tel-ə-,print-ər\ *n* : a device capable of producing hard copy from signals received over a communications circuit; *esp* : TELETYPEWRITER

Tele·Promp·Ter \'tel-ə-,präm-tər, -,prämp-\ *trademark* — used for a device for presenting a script in front of an actor or speaker on television

¹tele·scope \'tel-ə-,skōp\ *n* **1** : a usually tubular optical instrument for viewing distant objects by means of the refraction of light rays through a lens or the reflection of light rays by a concave mirror — compare REFLECTOR, REFRACTOR **2** : any of various tubular magnifying optical instruments **3** : RADIO TELESCOPE

²telescope *vb* **1** : to slide or pass or cause to slide or pass one within another like the cylindrical sections of a hand telescope **2** : CONDENSE 1, COMPRESS

tele·scop·ic \,tel-ə-'skäp-ik\ *adj* **1 a** : of, with, or relating to a telescope **b** : suitable for seeing or magnifying distant objects **2** : seen or discoverable only by a telescope ⟨*telescopic* stars⟩ **3** : able to discern objects at a distance **4** : having parts that telescope — **tele·scop·i·cal·ly** \-'skäp-i-kə-lē, -klē\ *adv*

tele·thon \'tel-ə-,thän\ *n* : a long television program usually to solicit funds (as for a charity) [*tele-* + *-thon* (as in *marathon*)]

Tele·type \'tel-ə-,tīp\ *trademark* — used for a teletypewriter

tele·type·writ·er \,tel-ə-'tīp-,rīt-ər\ *n* : a printing device resembling a typewriter that is used to send and receive telephonic signals

tel·evan·ge·list \,tel-i-'van-jə-ləst\ *n* : an evangelist who conducts regularly televised religious programs — **tel·evan·ge·lism** \-,liz-əm\ *n*

tele·view \'tel-ə-,vyü\ *vi* : to observe or watch by means of a television receiver — **tele·view·er** *n*

tele·vise \'tel-ə-,vīz\ *vt* : to pick up and usually broadcast (as a sports event) by television [back-formation from *television*]

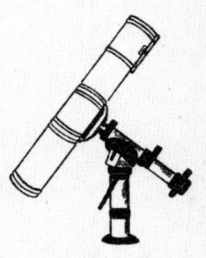

¹**telescope** ¹

tele·vi·sion \'tel-ə-,vizh-ən\ *n* **1** : an electronic system of transmitting images of fixed or moving objects together with sound over a wire or through space by apparatus that converts light and sound into electrical waves and reconverts them into visible light rays and audible sound **2** : a television receiving set **3 a** : the television broadcasting industry **b** : television as a medium of communication

tel·ex \'tel-,eks\ *n* : a communication service involving teletypewriters connected by wire through automatic exchanges [*tele*printer + *ex*change]

te·lio·spore \'tē-lē-ə-,spōr, -,spȯr\ *n* : a thick-walled spore forming the final stage in the life cycle of a rust fungus and giving rise to a basidium [Greek *teleios* "complete" (from *telos* "end") + English *spore*]

tell \'tel\ *vb* **told** \'tōld\; **tell·ing 1** : COUNT, ENUMERATE 〈all *told*, there were 30 students〉 **2 a** : to relate in detail : NARRATE 〈*tell* a story〉 **b** : to make a narration 〈*told* about our trip〉 **c** : SAY, UTTER 〈*tell* a lie〉 **3 a** : to make known : REVEAL 〈*tell* a secret〉 **b** : to express in words 〈can't *tell* you how pleased we are〉 **4** : to report to : INFORM **5** : ORDER, DIRECT 〈*told* me to wait〉 **6** : to ascertain by observing : find out 〈can *tell* you're honest〉 **7** : to act as a talebearer 〈*tell* on a cheater〉 **8** : to have a marked effect 〈the pressure *told* on them〉 **9** : to serve as evidence 〈smiles *telling* of success〉 [Old English *tellan*]

tell·er \'tel-ər\ *n* **1** : one that relates or communicates 〈a *teller* of tales〉 **2** : a person appointed to count votes **3** : a bank employee who receives and pays out money

tell·ing \'tel-ing\ *adj* : producing a marked effect 〈a *telling* argument〉 〈a *telling* blow〉 — **tell·ing·ly** \-ing-lē\ *adv*

tell off *vt* **1 a** : to number and set apart **b** : to assign to a special duty **2** : SCOLD 2, TONGUE-LASH

tell·tale \'tel-,tāl\ *n* **1 a** : GOSSIP 1, TALEBEARER **b** : an outward sign : INDICATION **2 a** : a device for indicating or recording something **b** : a railroad warning device (as a row of long strips hanging over tracks near the approach to a low overhead bridge) — **telltale** *adj*

tel·lu·ride \'tel-yə-,rīd\ *n* : a binary compound of tellurium with another element or a radical

tel·lu·ri·um \tə-'luṙ-ē-əm, te-\ *n* : a chemical element that resembles selenium and sulfur in properties and that occurs in crystalline form, in a dark amorphous form, or combined with metals — see ELEMENT table [New Latin, from Latin *tellur-, tellus* "earth"]

tel·ly \'tel-ē\ *n, pl* **tellys** *also* **tellies** *chiefly British* : TELEVISION

telo·phase \'tē-lə-,fāz, 'tel-ə-\ *n* : the final stage of mitosis in which the spindle disappears and two new nuclei appear each with a set of chromosomes; *also* : a corresponding stage in meiosis [Greek *telos* "end"]

tel·son \'tel-sən\ *n* : the terminal segment of the body of an arthropod or segmented worm; *esp* : that of a crustacean forming the middle lobe of the tail [Greek, "end of a plowed field"]

tem·blor \'tem-blər, -,blȯr, -,blōr\ *n* : EARTHQUAKE [Spanish, literally, "trembling", from *temblar* "to tremble", from Medieval Latin *tremulare*]

tem·er·ar·i·ous \,tem-ə-'rer-ē-əs, -'rar-\ *adj* : marked by temerity : rashly or presumptuously daring [Latin *temerarius*, from *temere* "at random, rashly"] — **tem·er·ar·i·ous·ly** *adv*

te·mer·i·ty \tə-'mer-ət-ē\ *n, pl* **-ties** : unreasonable or foolhardy contempt of danger or opposition : RECKLESSNESS [Latin *temeritas*, from *temere* "at random, rashly"] □ SYN AUDACITY: TEMERITY suggests boldness arising from reckless or heedless contempt of danger 〈had the *temerity* to challenge the dictatorial order〉 AUDACITY implies a disregard of restraints imposed by prudence or convention 〈had the *audacity* to come to the party uninvited〉

¹tem·per \'tem-pər\ *vb* **tem·pered; tem·per·ing** \'tem-pə-ring, -pring\ **1** : MODERATE, SOFTEN 〈*temper* justice with mercy〉 **2** : to control by reducing : SUBDUE 〈*temper* one's anger〉 **3** : to bring to the desired consistency or texture 〈*temper* modeling clay〉 **4** : to bring (as steel) to the desired hardness by heating and cooling **5** : to be or become tempered [Old English *temprian* and Old French *temprer*, both from Latin *temperare* "to moderate, mix, temper"] — **tem·per·able** \-pə-rə-bəl, -prə-bəl\ *adj*

²temper *n* **1** : characteristic tone : TREND, TENDENCY 〈the *temper* of the times〉 **2** : high quality of mind or spirit : COURAGE, METTLE **3** : the state of a substance with respect to certain desired qualities (as hardness, elasticity, or workability) 〈the *temper* of a knife blade〉 **4 a** : a characteristic cast of mind or state of feeling : DISPOSITION **b** : calmness of mind : COMPOSURE 〈lost my *temper*〉 **c** : state of feeling or frame of mind at a particular time usually dominated by a single strong emotion **d** : a state of anger **e** : a tendency to anger 〈has a hot *temper*〉 SYN see MOOD

tem·pera \'tem-pə-rə\ *n* : a process of painting in which an albuminous or colloidal medium (as egg yolk) is employed as a vehicle instead of oil [Italian *tempera*, literally, "temper"]

tem·per·a·ment \'tem-pə-rə-mənt, -prə-mənt\ *n* **1** : characteristic mode of emotional response 〈is of a nervous *temperament*〉 **2** : excessive sensitiveness or irritability [Latin *temperamentum* "mixture, makeup, constitution", from *temperare* "to mix, temper"]

tem·per·a·men·tal \,tem-pə-rə-'ment-l, -prə-'ment-\ *adj* **1** : of, relating to, or arising from temperament 〈*temperamental* peculiarities〉 **2 a** : marked by extreme sensitivity and impulsive changes of mood 〈a *temperamental* singer〉 **b** : unpredictable in behavior or performance 〈a *temperamental* car〉 — **tem·per·a·men·tal·ly** \-l-ē\ *adv*

tem·per·ance \'tem-pə-rəns, -prəns, -pərns\ *n* **1** : moderation in action, thought, or feeling : RESTRAINT **2** : habitual moderation in the indulgence of the appetites or passions; *esp* : moderation in or abstinence from the use of intoxicating drink

tem·per·ate \'tem-pə-rət, -prət\ *adj* **1** : marked by moderation: as **a** : not excessive or extreme **b** : moderate in satisfying one's needs or desires **c** : moderate in the use of liquor **d** : marked by self-control : RESTRAINED 〈*temperate* speech〉 **2** : having, found in, or associated with a moderate climate 〈*temperate* heat〉 **3** : existing as a prophage in infected cells and rarely causing lysis 〈*temperate* bacteriophages〉 SYN see MODERATE — **tem·per·ate·ly** *adv* — **tem·per·ate·ness** *n*

temperate zone *n, often cap T&Z* : the area or region between the tropic of Cancer and the arctic circle or between the tropic of Capricorn and the antarctic circle

tem·per·a·ture \'tem-pər-,chuṙ, -pə-,chuṙ, -pə-rə-,chuṙ, -prə-,chuṙ, -chər\ *n* **1** : the degree of hotness or coldness of something (as air, water, or the body) as shown by a thermometer **2** : FEVER 1 〈has a *temperature*〉

temperature inversion *n* : INVERSION 3

tem·pered \'tem-pərd\ *adj* **1** : made moderate 〈stylishness *tempered* with good taste〉 **2** : brought to the desired state (as of hardness, toughness, or flexibility) 〈*tempered* steel〉 〈*tempered* glass〉 **3** : having a particular kind of temper — used in combination 〈short-*tempered*〉

tem·pest \'tem-pəst\ *n* **1** : an extensive violent wind; *esp* : one accompanied by rain, hail, or snow **2** : TUMULT 1, UPROAR [Old French *tempeste*, from Latin *tempestas* "season, weather, storm", from *tempus* "time"]

tem·pes·tu·ous \tem-'pes-chə-wəs, -'pesh-\ *adj* : STORMY 2 — **tem·pes·tu·ous·ly** *adv* — **tem·pes·tu·ous·ness** *n*

Tem·plar \'tem-plər\ *n* **1** : a knight of a religious military order established early in the 12th century in Jerusalem to protect pilgrims and Christ's burial place

2 : KNIGHT TEMPLAR 2 [Old French *templier,* from Medieval Latin *templarius,* from Latin *templum* "temple"]

tem·plate *or* **tem·plet** \'tem-plət\ *n* 1 : a gauge, pattern, or mold (as a thin plate or board) used as a guide to the form of a piece being made 2 : a molecule (as of RNA) in a biological system that carries the genetic code for another molecule [probably derived from French *temple,* a part of a loom]

¹**tem·ple** \'tem-pəl\ *n* 1 : a building for worship: as **a** *often cap* : one of three successive national sanctuaries in ancient Jerusalem **b** : a building for Mormon sacred ordinances **c** : a synagogue of Reform or Conservative Judaism 2 : a local lodge of a fraternal order [Old English *tempel* and Old French *temple,* both from Latin *templum*] — **tem·pled** \-pəld\ *adj*

²**temple** *n* : the flattened space on each side of the forehead of man and some other mammals [Middle French, derived from Latin *tempora,* pl., "temples"]

tem·po \'tem-pō\ *n, pl* **tem·pi** \-pē\ *or* **tempos** 1 : the rate of speed of a musical piece or passage indicated by one of a series of directions (as largo, presto, or allegro) and often by an exact metronome marking 2 : rate of motion or activity : PACE [Italian, literally, "time", from Latin *tempus*]

¹**tem·po·ral** \'tem-pə-rəl, -prəl\ *adj* 1 : of or relating to time as opposed to eternity 2 **a** : of or relating to earthly life **b** : of or relating to nonreligious matters [Latin *temporalis,* from *tempor-, tempus* "time"] — **tem·po·ral·ly** \-ē\ *adv*

²**temporal** *adj* : of or relating to the temples or to the sides of the skull behind the orbits [Middle French, derived from Latin *tempora* "temples"] — **tem·po·ral·ly** \-ē\ *adv*

temporal bone *n* : a compound bone of the side of the human skull

tem·po·ral·i·ty \,tem-pə-'ral-ət-ē\ *n, pl* **-ties** 1 **a** : civil or political as distinguished from spiritual or church power or authority **b** : church property or income — often used in pl. 2 : the quality or state of being temporal

tem·po·rary \'tem-pə-,rer-ē\ *adj* : lasting for a limited time [Latin *temporarius,* from *tempor-, tempus* "time"] — **tem·po·rar·i·ly** \,tem-pə-'rer-ə-lē\ *adv* — **tem·po·rar·i·ness** \'tem-pə-,rer-ē-nəs\ *n*

temporary duty *n* : temporary military service away from one's regular unit

tem·po·rize \'tem-pə-,rīz\ *vi* 1 : to act to suit the time or occasion : yield to current or dominant opinion 2 : to draw out negotiations so as to gain time [Middle French *temporiser,* from Medieval Latin *temporizare* "to pass the time", from Latin *tempor-, tempus* "time"] — **tem·po·ri·za·tion** \,tem-pə-rə-'zā-shən\ *n* — **tem·po·riz·er** \'tem-pə-,rī-zər\ *n*

tempt \'temt, 'tempt\ *vt* 1 : to entice to do wrong by promising pleasure or gain 2 **a** *obsolete* : to make trial of : TEST **b** : to try presumptuously : PROVOKE (*tempted* fate by speeding) **c** : to risk the dangers of 3 **a** : to induce to do something : INCITE (*tempt* one to folly) **b** : to cause to be strongly inclined : almost move or persuade (was *tempted* to call it quits) [Old French *tempter, tenter,* from Latin *temptare, tentare* "to feel, try, tempt"] — **tempt·able** \'tem-tə-bəl, 'temp-\ *adj*

temp·ta·tion \tem-'tā-shən, temp-\ *n* 1 : the act of tempting : the state of being tempted especially to evil : ENTICEMENT 2 : something tempting

tempt·er \'tem-tər, 'temp-\ *n* : one that tempts

tempt·ing *adj* : that attracts strongly (a *tempting* offer) — **tempt·ing·ly** \'tem-ting-lē, 'temp-\ *adv*

tempt·ress \'tem-trəs, 'temp-\ *n* : a woman who tempts

ten \'ten\ *n* 1 : one more than nine; *also* : a symbol representing this — see NUMBER table 2 : the tenth in a set or series 3 : something having ten units or members 4 : a 10-dollar bill [Old English *tīene*] — **ten** *adj or pron*

ten·a·ble \'ten-ə-bəl\ *adj* : capable of being held, maintained, or defended (a *tenable* argument) (retreated since the position was not *tenable*) [French, from *tenir* "to hold", from Latin *tenēre*] — **ten·a·bil·i·ty** \,ten-ə-'bil-ət-ē\ *n* — **ten·a·ble·ness** \'ten-ə-bəl-nəs\ *n* — **ten·a·bly** \-blē\ *adv*

te·na·cious \tə-'nā-shəs\ *adj* 1 **a** : not easily pulled apart : COHESIVE, TOUGH (a *tenacious* metal) **b** : tending to adhere to another substance : STICKY (*tenacious* burs) 2 **a** : holding fast or tending to hold fast : PERSISTENT, STUBBORN (*tenacious* of their rights) **b** : RETENTIVE (a *tenacious* memory) [Latin *tenac-, tenax* "tending to hold fast", from *tenēre* "to hold"] — **te·na·cious·ly** *adv* — **te·na·cious·ness** *n*

te·nac·i·ty \tə-'nas-ət-ē\ *n* : the quality or state of being tenacious

ten·an·cy \'ten-ən-sē\ *n, pl* **-cies** 1 : the temporary possession or occupancy of another's property; *also* : the period of such occupancy or possession 2 : the ownership of property

¹**ten·ant** \'ten-ənt\ *n* 1 **a** : the owner or possessor of real estate or sometimes personal property **b** : one who occupies or temporarily possesses property of another; *esp* : one who rents or leases (as a house) from a landlord 2 : OCCUPANT, DWELLER [Middle French, from *tenir* "to hold"]

²**tenant** *vt* : to hold or occupy as a tenant : INHABIT — **ten·ant·able** \-ən-tə-bəl\ *adj*

tenant farmer *n* : a farmer who works land owned by another and pays rent either in cash or in shares of produce

ten·ant·less \'ten-ənt-ləs\ *adj* : having no tenants

ten·ant·ry \'ten-ən-trē\ *n, pl* **-ries** 1 : the condition of being a tenant 2 : a group of tenants

ten–cent store \'ten-'sent-\ *n* : FIVE-AND-TEN

tench \'tench\ *n, pl* **tench** *or* **tench·es** : a Eurasian freshwater fish related to the dace and noted for its ability to survive outside water [Middle French *tenche,* from Late Latin *tinca*]

Ten Commandments *n pl* : the commandments of God given to Moses on Mount Sinai

¹**tend** \'tend\ *vb* 1 : to pay attention (*tend* to business) 2 : to take care of (*tend* a garden) 3 : to have charge of as caretaker or overseer 4 : to manage the operation of (*tend* a machine) [Middle English *tenden,* short for *attenden* "to attend"]

²**tend** *vi* 1 : to move or turn in a certain direction : LEAD (the road *tends* to the right) 2 : to have a tendency : to be likely (people who *tend* to slouch) [Middle French *tendre* "to stretch, tend", from Latin *tendere*]

ten·dance \'ten-dəns\ *n* : watchful care : ATTENDANCE

ten·den·cy \'ten-dən-sē\ *n, pl* **-cies** 1 **a** : direction or approach toward a place, object, effect, or limit **b** : a proneness to a particular kind of thought or action : PROPENSITY 2 : the purposeful trend of something written or said : AIM [Medieval Latin *tendentia,* from Latin *tendere* "to stretch, tend"] □ SYN TENDENCY, TREND, DRIFT, TENOR mean movement in a particular direction. TENDENCY implies an ever-present inclination or force sending one in a particular direction (had a *tendency* to exaggerate) (counteracts the *tendency* of engines to knock) TREND implies a general direction maintained in spite of irregularities and more often subject to change than TENDENCY (*trends* in current fiction) DRIFT suggests a tendency determined by external influences (the present *drift* toward centralization) or it may apply to an underlying trend of a discourse (lost the *drift* of the conversation) TENOR stresses a clearly perceptible direction and a continuous, undeviating course.

ten·den·tious *also* **ten·den·cious** \ten-'den-chəs\ *adj* : marked by a tendency in favor of a particular point of view : BIASED — **ten·den·tious·ly** *adv* — **ten·den·tious·ness** *n*

\ə\ abut		\ng\ sing	
\ər\ further		\ō\ bone	
\a\ mat		\ȯ\ saw	
\ā\ take		\ȯi\ coin	
\ä\ cot, cart		\th\ thin	
\au̇\ out		\th\ this	
\ch\ chin		\ü\ food	
\e\ pet		\u̇\ foot	
\ē\ easy		\y\ yet	
\g\ go		\yü\ few	
\i\ tip		\yu̇\ cure	
\ī\ life		\zh\ vision	
\j\ job			

¹**ten·der** \'ten-dər\ *adj* **1 a** : having a soft or yielding texture : easily broken, cut, or damaged : FRAGILE **b** : easily chewed : SUCCULENT **2 a** : physically weak : DELICATE **b** : IMMATURE, YOUNG ⟨children of *tender* years⟩ **c** : incapable of resisting cold ⟨*tender* shrubs⟩ **3** : FOND, LOVING ⟨a *tender* look⟩ **4 a** : showing care : CONSIDERATE ⟨*tender* regard⟩ **b** : highly susceptible to impressions or emotions : IMPRESSIONABLE ⟨a *tender* conscience⟩ **5 a** : appropriate or conducive to a delicate or sensitive constitution or character : GENTLE, MILD ⟨*tender* breeding⟩ ⟨*tender* irony⟩ **b** : delicate or soft in quality or tone **6 a** : sensitive to touch : easily hurt ⟨a *tender* scar⟩ **b** : sensitive to injury or insult : TOUCHY ⟨*tender* pride⟩ **c** : demanding careful and sensitive handling : TICKLISH ⟨a *tender* situation⟩ [Old French *tendre*, Latin *tener*] — **ten·der·ly** *adv* — **ten·der·ness** *n*

²**tender** *vt* **ten·dered; ten·der·ing** \-də-riŋ, -driŋ\ **1** : to make a tender of ⟨*tender* the amount of rent⟩ **2** : to present for acceptance : PROFFER ⟨*tendered* my resignation⟩

³**tender** *n* **1** : an offer of money in payment of a debt **2** : an offer or proposal made for acceptance; *esp* : an offer of a bid for a contract **3** : something that may by law be offered in payment; *esp* : MONEY [Middle French *tendre* "to stretch, stretch out, offer, tend"]

⁴**tend·er** \'ten-dər\ *n* : one that tends or takes care: as **a** : a ship employed to serve other ships (as by supplying provisions) **b** : a boat that carries passengers or freight between shore and a larger ship **c** : a vehicle attached to a locomotive for carrying a supply of fuel and water

ten·der·foot \'ten-dər-ˌfut\ *n, pl* **-feet** \-ˌfēt\ *also* **-foots** **1** : a person who is not hardened to a rough outdoor life; *esp* : a newcomer in a recent settlement (as on a frontier) **2** : an inexperienced beginner : NOVICE

ten·der·heart·ed \ˌten-dər-'härt-əd\ *adj* : easily moved to love, pity, or sorrow : COMPASSIONATE — **ten·der·heart·ed·ly** *adv* — **ten·der·heart·ed·ness** *n*

ten·der·ize \'ten-də-ˌrīz\ *vt* : to make (meat) tender — **ten·der·iza·tion** \ˌten-də-rə-'zā-shən\ *n* — **ten·der·iz·er** \'ten-də-ˌrī-zər\ *n*

ten·der·loin \'ten-dər-ˌloin\ *n* **1** : a strip of tender meat on each side of the backbone : a fillet of beef or pork **2** : a district of a city largely devoted to vice [sense 2 from such a district's making possible a luxurious diet for a corrupt police officer]

ten·di·nous \'ten-də-nəs\ *adj* **1** : of, relating to, or resembling a tendon **2** : consisting of tendons : SINEWY [New Latin *tendinosus*, from *tendin-, tendo* "tendon", from Medieval Latin *tendon-, tendo*]

ten·don \'ten-dən\ *n* : a tough cord or band of fibrous tissue connecting a muscle to some other part (as a bone) and transmitting the force exerted by the muscle [Medieval Latin *tendon-, tendo*, from Latin *tendere* "to stretch"]

tendon of Achilles \-ə-'kil-ēz\ : ACHILLES TENDON

ten·dril \'ten-drəl\ *n* **1** : a leaf, stipule, or stem modified into a slender spirally coiling sensitive organ serving to attach a plant to its support **2** : something (as a ringlet of hair) that curls like a tendril [perhaps from Middle French *tendron*, alteration of *tendon*, literally, "tendon"] — **ten·driled** *or* **ten·drilled** \-drəld\ *adj* — **ten·dril·ous** \-drə-ləs\ *adj*

Ten·e·brae \'ten-ə-ˌbrā, -ˌbrī, -ˌbrē\ *n sing or pl* : the office of matins and lauds for the three days before Easter commemorating the sufferings and death of Christ with a progressive extinguishing of candles [Medieval Latin, from Latin, "darkness"]

1080 *also* **ten–eighty** \te-'nāt-ē\ *n* : a poisonous substance used to kill rodents [from its laboratory serial number]

ten·e·ment \'ten-ə-mənt\ *n* **1 a** : a house used as a dwelling **b** : APARTMENT 1, FLAT **c** : TENEMENT HOUSE **2** : a dwelling place ⟨the soul's *tenement*, the body⟩ [Middle French, from Medieval Latin *tenementum*, from Latin *tenēre* "to hold"]

tenement house *n* : APARTMENT BUILDING; *esp* : one barely meeting minimum standards of sanitation, safety, and comfort and housing poorer families

ten·et \'ten-ət\ *n* : a principle, belief, or doctrine generally held to be true; *esp* : one held in common by members of an organization, group, or profession [Latin, "he holds", from *tenēre* "to hold"] SYN see DOCTRINE

ten·fold \'ten-ˌfōld, -'fōld\ *adj* **1** : having 10 units or members **2** : of or equal to 1000 percent — **tenfold** *adv*

ten·nis \'ten-əs\ *n* : a game that is played with rackets and a light elastic ball by two players or pairs of players on a level court divided by a low net [Middle English *tenetz, tenys*]

tennis shoe *n* : a lightweight canvas or leather shoe with a pliable sole for wear when playing tennis

¹**ten·on** \'ten-ən\ *n* : a projecting part in a piece of material (as wood) for insertion into a mortise to make a joint [Old French, from *tenir* "to hold", from Latin *tenēre*]

²**tenon** *vt* **1** : to unite by a tenon **2** : to cut or fit for insertion in a mortise

¹**ten·or** \'ten-ər\ *n* **1** : the general drift of something spoken or written **2 a** : the voice part next to the lowest in a 4-part chorus — compare ALTO, BASS, SOPRANO **b** : the highest natural adult male voice **c** : a singer having such a voice **d** : an instrument playing a part between that of an alto and a bass **3** : a continuance in a course, movement or activity : TREND [Old French, from Latin *tenor* "uninterrupted course", from *tenēre* "to hold"] SYN see TENDENCY

²**tenor** *adj* : of, relating to, or being the tenor in music

ten·pen·ny \ˌten-ˌpen-ē\ *adj* : equal to, worth, or costing ten pennies

tenpenny nail *n* : a nail 3 inches (7.62 centimeters) long [from its original price per hundred]

ten·pin \'ten-ˌpin\ *n* **1** : a bottle-shaped bowling pin 15 inches (38.1 centimeters) high **2** *pl* : a bowling game using 10 tenpins and a large ball with each player allowed to bowl 2 balls in each of 10 frames

ten·pound·er \'ten-'paun-dər\ *n* : LADYFISH

tens digit *n* : the numeral (as 5 in 456) occupying the tens place in a number expressed in the Arabic system of writing numbers

¹**tense** \'tens\ *n* **1** : a distinction of form in a verb to express distinction of time **2** : a particular inflectional form or set of inflectional forms of a verb expressing a specific time distinction [Middle French *tens* "time, tense", from Latin *tempus*]

²**tense** *adj* **1** : stretched tight : made taut : RIGID **2 a** : feeling or showing nervous tension : HIGH-STRUNG **b** : marked by strain or suspense **3** : produced with the speech muscles in a relatively tense state ⟨the *tense* vowels \ē\ and \ü\⟩ — compare LAX [Latin *tensus*, from *tendere* "to stretch"] SYN see TIGHT — **tense·ly** *adv* — **tense·ness** *n*

³**tense** *vb* : to make or become tense

ten·sile \'ten-səl *also* 'ten-ˌsīl\ *adj* **1** : capable of stretching or being stretched : DUCTILE **2** : of or relating to tension

tensile strength *n* : the greatest longitudinal stress a substance can bear without tearing apart

¹**ten·sion** \'ten-chən\ *n* **1 a** : the act or action of stretching or the condition or degree of being stretched to stiffness : TAUTNESS ⟨*tension* of a muscle⟩ **b** : STRESS 1c **2 a** : either of two balancing forces causing or tending to cause extension of a body **b** : the condition in an elastic body resulting from elongation **c** : PRESSURE ⟨oxygen *tension* in lake water⟩ **3 a** : a state of mental unrest often with signs of physiological stress **b** : a state of latent hostility or opposition between individuals or groups **4** : a device to produce a

desired tension [Latin *tensio*, from *tendere* "to stretch"] — **ten·sion·al** \'tench-nəl, -ən-l\ *adj* — **tension·less** \'ten-chən-ləs\ *adj*

²tension *vt* : to subject to tension

ten·si·ty \'ten-sət-ē\ *n, pl* **-ties** : the quality or state of being tense

ten·sor \'ten-sər, 'ten-,sȯr\ *n* : a muscle that stretches a part

ten–speed \'ten-,spēd\ *n* : a bicycle with a derailleur that has ten possible combinations of gears

tens place *n* : the place two to the left of the decimal point in a number expressed in the Arabic system of writing numbers

ten–strike \'ten-,strīk\ *n* : a strike in bowling

¹tent \'tent\ *n* **1** : a collapsible shelter (as of canvas or nylon) stretched and held in place by poles and used especially as temporary housing (as by campers) **2** : something that resembles a tent or that serves as a shelter; *esp* : a canopy or enclosure placed over the head and shoulders to retain vapors or oxygen administered medically **3** : the web of a tent caterpillar [Old French *tente*, derived from Latin *tendere* "to stretch"]

²tent *vb* **1** : to live or lodge in a tent **2** : to cover with or as if with a tent

ten·ta·cle \'tent-i-kəl\ *n* **1** : one of the long flexible processes usually about the head or mouth of an animal (as a worm or fish) used especially for feeling, grasping, or handling **2** : something suggesting a tentacle; *esp* : a sensitive hair on a plant [New Latin *tentaculum*, from Latin *tentare* "to feel, touch"] — **ten·ta·cled** \-kəld\ *adj* — **ten·tac·u·lar** \ten-'tak-yə-lər\ *adj*

ten·ta·tive \'tent-ət-iv\ *adj* **1** : not fully worked out or developed : not final ⟨*tentative* plans⟩ **2** : HESITANT, UNCERTAIN ⟨a *tentative* smile⟩ [Medieval Latin *tentativus*, from Latin *tentare* "to feel, try"] — **ten·ta·tive·ly** *adv* — **ten·ta·tive·ness** *n*

tent caterpillar *n* : any of several destructive gregarious caterpillars that construct large silken webs on trees

ten·ter \'tent-ər\ *n* : a frame or endless track with hooks or clips along two sides that is used for drying and stretching cloth [Middle English *teyntur*]

ten·ter·hook \'tent-ər-,hu̇k\ *n* : a sharp hooked nail used especially for fastening cloth on a tenter — **on tenterhooks** : in a state of uneasiness, strain, or suspense

tenth \'tenth, 'tentth\ *n* **1** : number 10 in a countable series — see NUMBER table **2** : one of 10 equal parts — **tenth** *adj or adv*

tent stitch *n* : a short stitch slanting to the right that is used (as in embroidery) to form even lines of solid background

ten·u·ous \'ten-yə-wəs\ *adj* : having little substance or strength : FLIMSY, WEAK ⟨a *tenuous* hold on reality⟩ [Latin *tenuis* "thin, tenuous"] — **te·nu·i·ty** \te-'nü-ət-ē, tə-, -'nyü-\ *n* — **ten·u·ous·ly** \'ten-yə-wəs-lē\ *adv* — **ten·u·ous·ness** *n*

ten·ure \'ten-yər\ *n* **1** : the act, right, manner, or term of holding something (as real property, a position, or an office) **2** : GRASP 3, HOLD [Old French, derived from Latin *tenēre* "to hold"] — **ten·u·ri·al** \te-'nyu̇r-ē-əl\ *adj* — **ten·u·ri·al·ly** \-ē-ə-lē\ *adv*

ten·ured \'ten-yərd\ *adj* : having tenure ⟨*tenured* teachers⟩

te·o·sin·te \,tā-ō-'sint-ē\ *n* : a large annual fodder grass of Mexico and Central America closely related to and possibly ancestral to maize [Mexican Spanish, from Nahuatl *teocentli*, from *teotl* "god" + *centli* "ear of corn"]

te·pee *or* **ti·pi** *also* **tee·pee** \'tē-,pē\ *n* : a conical tent usually of skins used by some American Indians [of American Indian origin]

tep·id \'tep-əd\ *adj* **1** : moderately warm : LUKEWARM ⟨a *tepid* bath⟩ **2** : lacking enthusiasm or conviction : HALFHEARTED ⟨a *tepid* interest⟩ [Latin *tepidus*, from *tepēre* "to be moderately warm"] — **te·pid·i·ty** \tə-

'pid-ət-ē, te-\ *n* — **tep·id·ly** \'tep-əd-lē\ *adv* — **tep·id·ness** *n*

te·qui·la \tə-'kē-lə\ *n* : a Mexican liquor made by redistilling mescal [Spanish, from *Tequila*, district of Mexico]

tera- \'ter-ə\ *combining form* : trillion [Greek *teras* "monster"]

ter·bi·um \'tər-bē-əm\ *n* : a usually trivalent metallic highly reactive chemical element — see ELEMENT table [New Latin, from *Ytterby*, Sweden]

terce \'tərs\ *or* **tierce** \'tiərs\ *n, often cap* : the third of the canonical hours [Middle French *terce*, *tierce*, from *terz* "third", from Latin *tertius*]

ter·cen·ten·a·ry \,tər-,sen-'ten-ə-rē; tər-'sent-n-,er-ē, 'tər-\ *n, pl* **-ries** : a 300th anniversary or its celebration [Latin *ter* "three times"] — **tercentenary** *adj*

ter·cen·ten·ni·al \,tər-,sen-'ten-ē-əl\ *adj or n* : TERCENTENARY

ter·cet \'tər-sət\ *n* : a unit or group of three lines of verse [Italian *terzetto*, from *terzo* "third", from Latin *tertius*]

ter·e·binth \'ter-ə-,binth, -,bintth\ *n* : a small European tree related to the sumac that yields an oleoresin [Middle French *terebinthe*, from Latin *terebinthus*, from Greek *terebinthos*]

te·re·do \tə-'rēd-ō, -'rād-\ *n, pl* **-re·dos** *or* **-red·i·nes** \-'red-n-,ēz\ : SHIPWORM [Latin, from Greek *terēdōn*]

ter·gi·ver·sate \'tər-ji-vər-,sāt\ *vi* : to desert one's party or position; *esp* : EQUIVOCATE 1 [Latin *tergiversari* "to turn the back, shuffle", from *tergum* "back" + *versare* "to turn," from *versus*, past participle of *vertere* "to turn"] — **ter·gi·ver·sa·tion** \,tər-ji-vər-'sā-shən\ *n* — **ter·gi·ver·sa·tor** \'tər-ji-vər-,sāt-ər\ *n*

ter·gum \'tər-gəm\ *n, pl* **ter·ga** \-gə\ : the back of an animal; *also* : a plate on the back of an arthropod [Latin, "back"]

¹term \'tərm\ *n* **1** : END, TERMINATION; *also* : a point in time assigned to something (as payment of rent or interest) **2** : a fixed extent of time especially as set by law, custom, or some recurrent phenomenon ⟨the governor served two *terms*⟩ ⟨ready for the new school *term*⟩ **3** *pl* : provisions determining the nature and scope of something and especially of an agreement **4 a** : a word or expression that has a precise meaning in some uses or is peculiar to a particular field ⟨legal *terms*⟩ **b** *pl* : diction of a specified kind ⟨spoke in glowing *terms* of their prospects⟩ **5 a** : a mathematical expression connected with another by a plus or minus sign **b** : an element of a fraction or proportion or of a series or sequence **6** *pl* **a** : mutual relationship : FOOTING ⟨on good *terms*⟩ **b** : AGREEMENT, CONCORD ⟨came to *terms* with their employer⟩ [Old French *terme* "boundary, end", from Latin *terminus*] — **in terms of** : with respect to ⟨considered *in terms of* today's wages⟩

²term *vt* : to apply a term to : CALL, NAME

¹ter·ma·gant \'tər-mə-gənt\ *n* : an overbearing quarrelsome woman : SHREW [Middle English *Termagant*, an imaginary Muslim deity represented in medieval plays as a boisterous character]

²termagant *adj* : noisily quarrelsome

¹ter·mi·nal \'tər-mən-l\ *adj* **1 a** : of or relating to an end, extremity, boundary, or terminus ⟨*terminal* pillar⟩ **b** : growing at the end of a branch or stem ⟨*terminal* bud⟩ **2 a** : of, relating to, or occurring in a term or each term **b** : occurring at or contributing to the end of life ⟨*terminal* illness⟩ **3** : occurring at or constituting the end of a period or series — **ter·mi·nal·ly** \-l-ē\ *adv*

²terminal *n* **1** : a part that forms the end **2** : a device attached to the end (as of a wire) for convenience in making electrical connections **3 a** : either end of a carrier line (as a railroad or shipping line) with its handling and storage facilities, offices, and stations; *also* : a usually major freight or passenger station **b** : a town

tepee

\ə\ abut	\ng\ sing
\ər\ further	\ō\ bone
\a\ mat	\ȯ\ saw
\ā\ take	\ȯi\ coin
\ä\ cot, cart	\th\ thin
\au̇\ out	\th\ this
\ch\ chin	\ü\ food
\e\ pet	\u̇\ foot
\ē\ easy	\y\ yet
\g\ go	\yü\ few
\i\ tip	\yu̇\ cure
\ī\ life	\zh\ vision
\j\ job	

at the end of a carrier line : TERMINUS **4** : a device (as a teletypewriter) through which a user can communicate with a computer

terminal side *n* : a straight line that rotates about a point on another line in generating an angle

ter·mi·nate \'tər-mə-ˌnāt\ *vb* **1 a** : to bring to or come to an end : CLOSE **b** : to form the conclusion of : form an ending **2** : to serve as a limit to : BOUND **3** : to extend only to a limit (as a point or line); *esp* : to reach a terminus [Latin *terminare,* from *terminus* "end"] SYN see CLOSE — **ter·mi·na·ble** \-mə-nə-bəl\ *adj* — **ter·mi·na·tive** \-ˌnāt-iv\ *adj*

terminating decimal *n* : a decimal that can be expressed in a finite number of figures — compare RE-PEATING DECIMAL

ter·mi·na·tion \ˌtər-mə-'nā-shən\ *n* **1** : end in time or existence : CONCLUSION ⟨*termination* of life⟩ **2** : a limit in space or extent : BOUND **3** : the last part of a word : SUFFIX; *esp* : an inflectional ending **4** : the act of terminating SYN see END — **ter·mi·na·tion·al** \-shnəl, -shən-l\ *adj*

ter·mi·na·tor \'tər-mə-ˌnāt-ər\ *n* **1** : one that terminates **2** : the dividing line between the illuminated and the unilluminated part of the moon's or a planet's disk

ter·mi·nol·o·gy \ˌtər-mə-'näl-ə-jē\ *n, pl* **-gies** : the technical or special terms used in a business, art, science, or special subject ⟨the *terminology* of law⟩ [Medieval Latin *terminus* "term, expression", from Latin, "boundary, end"] — **ter·mi·no·log·i·cal** \ˌtərm-nə-'läj-i-kəl, ˌtərm-ən-l-'äj-\ *adj*

term insurance *n* : insurance for a specified period that pays only for losses suffered during this period

ter·mi·nus \'tər-mə-nəs\ *n, pl* **-ni** \-ˌnī, -ˌnē\ *or* **-nus·es** **1** : final goal : finishing point **2** : a post or stone marking a boundary **3 a** : either end of a transportation line or travel route **b** : the station or the town or city at such a place **4** : EXTREMITY, TIP ⟨the *terminus* of a glacier⟩ [Latin, "boundary, end"]

ter·mite \'tər-ˌmīt\ *n* : any of an order (Isoptera) of pale-colored soft-bodied social insects that have winged sexual forms, wingless sterile workers, and often soldiers, feed on wood, and include some very destructive to wooden structures and trees — called also *white ant* [Late Latin *termit-, termes,* a worm that eats wood]

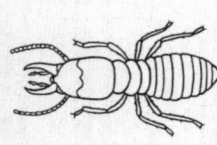

termite

term paper *n* : a major written assignment in a school or college course representative of a student's individual research and study in a subject area — called also *term report*

tern \'tərn\ *n* : any of numerous seabirds that usually have a forked tail, black cap, and white body and that in comparison to the related gulls have a smaller and more slender body and bill and narrower wings [of Scandinavian origin]

ter·na·ry \'tər-nə-rē\ *adj* **1** : of, relating to, or proceeding by threes **2** : having three elements or parts [Latin *ternarius,* from *terni* "three each"]

ter·pene \'tər-ˌpēn\ *n* : any of various hydrocarbons $(C_5H_8)_n$ found especially in essential oils, resins, and balsams and used mostly as solvents and in organic synthesis [German *terpentin* "turpentine"]

terp·si·cho·re·an \ˌtərp-sik-ə-'rē-ən\ *adj* : of or relating to dancing [*Terpsichore,* Greek muse of dancing]

¹ter·race \'ter-əs\ *n* **1 a** : a flat roof or open platform : BALCONY, DECK **b** : a relatively level paved or planted area adjoining a building **2** : a raised embankment with the top leveled; *also* : one of a series of banks or ridges formed in a slope to conserve moisture and soil for agriculture **3 a** (1) : a row of houses on raised ground or a sloping site (2) : a group of such houses **b** : a strip of park in the middle of a street **c** : STREET [Middle French, "pile of earth, terrace", from Provençal *terrassa,* from *terra* "earth", from Latin]

²terrace *vt* : to make into a terrace or supply with terraces ⟨the front yard had been *terraced* down to the road⟩

ter·ra–cot·ta \ˌter-ə-'kät-ə\ *n, pl* **terra–cottas** **1** : glazed or unglazed fired earthenware **2** : a brownish orange [Italian *terra cotta,* literally, "baked earth"]

ter·ra fir·ma \-'fər-mə\ *n* : dry land : solid ground [New Latin; literally, "solid land"]

ter·rain \tə-'rān, te-\ *n* : the surface features of a tract of land ⟨a rough *terrain*⟩ [French, "land, ground", from Latin *terrenum,* derived from *terra* "earth, land"]

ter·ra·pin \'ter-ə-pən, 'tar-\ *n* : any of various edible North American turtles living in fresh or brackish water [of American Indian origin]

ter·rar·i·um \tə-'rar-ē-əm, -'rer-\ *n, pl* **-ia** \-ē-ə\ *or* **-iums** : a vivarium without standing water [Latin *terra* "earth land" + *-arium* (as in *aquarium*)]

ter·raz·zo \tə-'raz-ō, -'rät-sō\ *n* : a mosaic flooring made by embedding small pieces of marble or granite in mortar [Italian, literally, "terrace"]

ter·res·tri·al \tə-'res-trē-əl, -'res-chəl, -'resh-chəl\ *adj* **1 a** : of or relating to the earth or its inhabitants ⟨*terrestrial* magnetism⟩ **b** : PROSAIC 2, COMMONPLACE **2** : of or relating to land as distinct from air or water ⟨*terrestrial* transportation⟩ **3 a** : living on or in or growing from land ⟨*terrestrial* plants⟩ ⟨*terrestrial* birds⟩ **b** : of or relating to terrestrial organisms ⟨*terrestrial* habits⟩ [Latin *terrestris,* from *terra* "earth"] — **terrestrial** *n* — **ter·res·tri·al·ly** \-ē\ *adv*

ter·ri·ble \'ter-ə-bəl\ *adj* **1** : causing terror or awe : FEARFUL, DREADFUL ⟨a *terrible* disaster⟩ **2 a** : hard to bear usually because of excess of some quality ⟨*terrible* cold⟩ **b** : very bad or extremely unpleasant ⟨had a *terrible* time⟩ **c** : of notably inferior quality ⟨a *terrible* movie⟩ [Middle French, from Latin *terribilis,* from *terrēre* "to frighten"] — **ter·ri·bly** \-blē\ *adv*

ter·ri·er \'ter-ē-ər\ *n* : any of various usually small dogs originally used by hunters to dig for small game and attack the quarry underground or drive it out [French *chien terrier,* literally, "earth dog"]

ter·rif·ic \tə-'rif-ik\ *adj* **1** : TERRIBLE 1, FRIGHTFUL ⟨*terrific* destruction⟩ **2** : EXTRAORDINARY, ASTOUNDING ⟨*terrific* speed⟩; *esp* : TREMENDOUS ⟨a *terrific* explosion⟩ **3** : unusually fine : MAGNIFICENT ⟨the party was *terrific*⟩ — **ter·rif·i·cal·ly** \-'rif-i-kə-lē, -klē\ *adv*

ter·ri·fy \'ter-ə-ˌfī\ *vt* **-fied; -fy·ing** : to fill with or move to some action by terror

ter·ri·fy·ing \-ˌfī-ing\ *adj* : causing terror or great apprehension — **ter·ri·fy·ing·ly** *adv*

¹ter·ri·to·ri·al \ˌter-ə-'tōr-ē-əl, -'tor-\ *adj* **1 a** : of or relating to territory or a territory ⟨a *territorial* government⟩ **b** : of or relating to or organized chiefly for home defense ⟨a *territorial* army⟩ **2** : of, relating to, or exhibiting territoriality ⟨*territorial* birds⟩ — **ter·ri·to·ri·al·ly** \-ē-ə-lē\ *adv*

²territorial *n* : a member of a territorial military unit

ter·ri·to·ri·al·ism \ˌter-ə-'tōr-ē-ə-ˌliz-əm, -'tor-\ *n* : TERRITORIALITY

ter·ri·to·ri·al·i·ty \ˌter-ə-ˌtōr-ē-'al-ət-ē, -ˌtor-\ *n* : the pattern of behavior associated with the defense of a male animal's territory

ter·ri·to·ri·al·ize \-'tōr-ē-ə-ˌlīz, -'tor-\ *vt* : to organize on a territorial basis — **ter·ri·to·ri·al·iza·tion** \-ˌtōr-ē-ə-lə-'zā-shən, -ˌtor-\ *n*

territorial waters *n pl* : the waters under the sovereign jurisdiction of a nation or state including both marginal sea and inland waters

ter·ri·to·ry \'ter-ə-ˌtōr-ē, -ˌtor-\ *n, pl* **-ries** **1** : a geographical area belonging to or under the jurisdiction of a government **a** : an administrative subdivision of a country (as the Soviet Union) **c** : a part of the United States not included within any state but organized with a separate legislature **d** : a geographical area dependent upon an external government but having some degree of autonomy **2 a** : an indeterminate geographical area **b** : a field of knowledge or interest **3 a** : an assigned area 〈a salesman's *territory*〉 **b** : an area that is occupied and defended by a male bird or mammal [Latin *territorium,* from *terra* "land"]

ter·ror \'ter-ər\ *n* **1** : a state of intense fear **2 a** : a cause of fear or anxiety **b** : a dreadful person or thing; *esp* : an obnoxious child **3 a** : REIGN OF TERROR **b** : the deliberate use of violence and brutality especially as a political weapon [Middle French *terreur,* from Latin *terror,* from *terrēre* "to frighten"]

ter·ror·ism \'ter-ər-ˌiz-əm\ *n* : systematic use of terror especially as a means of gaining some political end — **ter·ror·ist** \-ər-əst\ *adj or n* — **ter·ror·is·tic** \ˌter-ər-'is-tik\ *adj*

ter·ror·ize \'ter-ər-ˌīz\ *vt* **1** : to fill with terror or anxiety **2** : to coerce by threat or violence — **ter·ror·iza·tion** \ˌter-ər-ə-'zā-shən\ *n*

ter·ry \'ter-ē\ *n, pl* **terries** : an absorbent fabric with a loose pile of uncut loops — called also *terry cloth* [perhaps from French *tiré,* past participle of *tirer* "to draw"]

terse \'tərs\ *adj* : using as few words as possible without loss of force or clearness : being brief and effective : SUCCINCT [Latin *tersus* "clean, neat", from *tergēre* "to wipe off"] — **terse·ly** *adv* — **terse·ness** *n*

¹ter·tian \'tər-shən\ *adj* : recurring at approximately 48-hour intervals 〈a *tertian* fever〉 [Latin *tertianus,* from *tertius* "third"]

²tertian *n* : an intermittent fever that recurs at approximately 48-hour intervals; *esp* : a tertian malaria

¹ter·ti·ary \'tər-shē-ˌer-ē\ *n, pl* **-ar·ies** **1** : a member of a monastic third order especially of lay people **2** *cap* : the Tertiary period or system of rocks

²tertiary *adj* **1 a** : of 3d rank, importance, or value **b** : of, relating to, or constituting the 3d strongest of three or four degrees of stress 〈the 3d syllable of *basketball team* carries *tertiary* stress〉 **2** *cap* : of, relating to, or being the first period of the Cenozoic era or the corresponding system of rocks marked by the formation of high mountains (as the Alps and Himalayas) and the dominance of mammals on land — see GEOLOGIC TIME table **3** : formed by the substitution of three atoms or groups 〈a *tertiary* salt〉 **4** : occurring in or being a 3d stage [Latin *tertiarius,* from *tertius* "third"]

ter·za rima \ˌtert-sə-'rē-mə\ *n* : a verse form consisting of tercets usually in iambic pentameter with an interlaced rhyme scheme (as *aba, bcb, cdc*) [Italian, literally, "third rhyme"]

tes·la \'tes-lə\ *n* : a unit of magnetic flux density in the mks system [Nikola *Tesla,* died 1943, American electrician and inventor]

tes·sel·late \'tes-ə-ˌlāt\ *vt* : to form into or adorn with mosaic [Late Latin *tessellare* "to pave with tesserae", from Latin *tessella* "small tessera", from *tessera*] — **tes·sel·la·tion** \ˌtes-ə-'lā-shən\ *n*

tes·sel·lat·ed \'tes-ə-ˌlāt-əd\ *adj* : made of or resembling mosaic; *esp* : having a checkered appearance

tes·sera \'tes-ə-rə\ *n, pl* **-ser·ae** \-ˌrē, -ˌrī\ **1** : a small tablet (as of wood, bone, or ivory) used by the ancient Romans as a ticket, tally, voucher, or means of identification **2** : a small piece (as of marble, glass, or tile) used in mosaic work [Latin]

¹test \'test\ *n* **1 a** : a critical examination, observation, or evaluation : TRIAL 〈put their courage to the *test*〉 **b** : something that tries quality or resistance 〈ideas that can only be judged by the *test* of time〉 **2** : a means of testing: as **a** : a procedure, reaction, or reagent used to identify or differentiate something 〈a *test* for starch〉 〈a series of allergy *tests*〉 **b** : an examination (as in school) intended to measure the skill, knowledge, intelligence, capacities, or aptitudes **3** : a result of or rating based on a test 〈a boiler of 300 kilograms *test*〉 [Middle French, "vessel in which metals were assayed,

cupel", from Latin *testum* "earthen vessel"] □ ORIGIN Latin *testum* was a general word for an earthen vessel. In the Middle Ages its French descendant, *test,* was the word for a specific type of vessel used in the assaying of precious metals, a cupel. A cupel is a shallow porous cup. When impure silver or gold is heated in it, the impurities are absorbed in the porous material, leaving a relatively pure button of silver or gold. As the name for a cupel, *test* was borrowed into English in the 14th century. It was later used figuratively. To "put something to the test" was to make trial of it, to determine its quality or genuineness, as a precious metal might be tried in a cupel.

²test *vb* **1** : to put to test or proof : TRY **2 a** : to undergo a test **b** : to achieve a rating on the basis of tests **3** : to use tests as a means of analysis or diagnosis 〈*test* for copper〉 〈*test* for allergens〉 — **test·able** \'tes-tə-bəl\ *adj*

³test *n* : a firm or rigid outer covering (as a shell) of many invertebrates [Latin *testa* "shell"]

tes·ta \'tes-tə\ *n, pl* **tes·tae** \-ˌtē, -ˌtī\ : the hard outer coat of a seed [Latin, "shell"]

tes·ta·ceous \tes-'tā-shəs\ *adj* **1** : consisting of or resembling shell 〈stone of *testaceous* composition〉 **2** : of reddish to yellowish brown

tes·ta·cy \'tes-tə-sē\ *n, pl* **-cies** : the state of being testate

tes·ta·ment \'tes-tə-mənt\ *n* **1 a** *archaic* : a covenant between God and the human race **b** *cap* : either of two chief divisions of the Bible **2 a** : a tangible proof or tribute **b** : an expression of conviction : CREDO **3** : a legal instrument by which a person determines the disposition of his or her property after death [Late Latin *testamentum* "covenant, holy scripture", from Latin, "last will", from *testari* "to call to witness, make a will", from *testis* "witness"] — **tes·ta·men·ta·ry** \ˌtes-tə-'ment-ə-rē, -'men-trē\ *adj*

tes·tate \'tes-ˌtāt, -tət\ *adj* : having left a valid will 〈he died *testate*〉 [Latin *testatus,* past participle of *testari* "to make a will"]

tes·ta·tor \'tes-ˌtāt-ər, tes-'\ *n* : a person who leaves a will in force at death

tes·ta·trix \tes-'tā-triks\ *n* : a female testator

test ban *n* : a self-imposed ban on the atmospheric testing of nuclear weapons by countries having such weapons

test case *n* **1** : a representative case whose outcome is likely to serve as a precedent **2** : a proceeding brought by agreement or on an understanding of the parties to obtain a decision as to the constitutionality of a statute

test·cross \'test-ˌkrȯs, 'tes-\ *n* : a cross between an individual expressing a recessive trait and one expressing a dominant trait to determine whether or not the latter is heterozygous

test·ed \'tes-təd\ *adj* : subjected to or qualified through testing 〈time-*tested* principles〉 〈tuberculin-*tested* cattle〉

¹tes·ter \'tēs-tər, 'tes-\ *n* : a canopy over a bed, pulpit, or altar [Middle French *testiere* "head covering", from *teste* "head", from Late Latin *testa* "skull", from Latin, "shell"]

²test·er \'tes-tər\ *n* : one that tests

tes·ti·cle \'tes-ti-kəl\ *n* : TESTIS [Latin *testiculus,* from *testis*] — **tes·tic·u·lar** \tes-'tik-yə-lər\ *adj*

tes·ti·fy \'tes-tə-ˌfī\ *vb* **-fied; -fy·ing** **1 a** : to make a statement based on personal knowledge or belief : give evidence 〈*testify* in court〉 **b** : to declare solemnly (as under oath) 〈*testified* that the signature was genuine〉 **2** : to serve as a sign 〈smiles *testifying* to contentment〉 [Latin *testificari,* from *testis* "witness"] — **tes·ti·fi·er** \-ˌfī-ər, -ˌfīr\ *n*

¹tes·ti·mo·ni·al \ˌtes-tə-'mō-nē-əl\ *adj* **1** : of, relating to, or being testimony **2** : expressive of appreciation or esteem 〈a *testimonial* dinner〉

\ə\	abut	\ng\	sing
\ər\	further	\ō\	bone
\a\	mat	\ȯ\	saw
\ā\	take	\ȯi\	coin
\ä\	cot, cart	\th\	thin
\aú\	out	\th\	this
\ch\	chin	\ü\	food
\e\	pet	\ú\	foot
\ē\	easy	\y\	yet
\g\	go	\yü\	few
\i\	tip	\yú\	cure
\ī\	life	\zh\	vision
\j\	job		

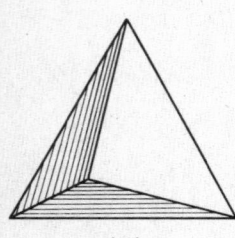

tetrahedron

²testimonial *n* **1** : an indication of worth or quality: as **a** : an endorsement of a product or service ⟨writing *testimonials* for patent medicines⟩ **b** : a character reference : letter of recommendation **2** : an expression of appreciation : TRIBUTE

tes·ti·mo·ny \'tes-tə-ˌmō-nē\ *n, pl* **-nies 1 a** : the tablets inscribed with the Mosaic law or the ark containing them **b** : a divine decree attested in the Scriptures **2 a** : evidence based on observation or knowledge : authoritative evidence **b** : a solemn declaration usually made orally by a witness under oath in response to interrogation by a lawyer or authorized public official **3** : an open acknowledgement or profession (as of religious experience) [Latin *testimonium* "evidence, witness", from *testis* "witness"]

tes·tis \'tes-təs\ *n, pl* **tes·tes** \'tes-ˌtēz\ : a typically paired male reproductive gland that produces sperm and secretes various male hormones and in most mammals is contained within the scrotum [Latin, "witness, testis"]

tes·tos·ter·one \te-'stäs-tə-ˌrōn\ *n* : a potent male sex hormone that is produced by special cells of the testis or made synthetically [derived from *testis* + *sterol*]

test paper *n* : paper saturated with a reagent that changes color in testing for various substances

test pilot *n* : a pilot employed to put new airplanes through severe tests

test tube *n* : a usually plain tube of thin glass closed at one end and used especially in chemistry and biology

tes·tu·do \tes-'tüd-ō, -'tyüd-\ *n, pl* **-dos** : a cover of overlapping shields or a shed wheeled up to a wall used by the ancient Romans to protect an attacking force [Latin, literally, "tortoise, tortoise shell"]

tes·ty \'tes-tē\ *adj* **tes·ti·er; -est 1** : easily annoyed : IRRITABLE **2** : marked by impatience or ill humor ⟨*testy* remarks⟩ [Anglo-French *testif* "headstrong", from Old French *teste* "head"] SYN see IRASCIBLE — **tes·ti·ly** \-tə-lē\ *adv* — **tes·ti·ness** \-tē-nəs\ *n*

te·tan·ic \te-'tan-ik\ *adj* : of, relating to, or being tetanus or tetany — **te·tan·i·cal·ly** \-'tan-i-kə-lē, -klē\ *adv*

tet·a·nus \'tet-n-əs, 'tet-nəs\ *n* **1** : an acute infectious disease characterized by tonic spasm of voluntary muscles especially of the jaw and caused by the toxin of a clostridium bacillus which usually enters a wound and multiplies in damaged tissue **2** : prolonged contraction of a muscle resulting from rapidly repeated motor impulses [Latin, from Greek *tetanos*, from *tetanos* "stretched, rigid"]

tet·a·ny \'tet-n-ē, 'tet-nē\ *n* : a condition marked by tonic spasm of muscles and associated usually with deficient parathyroid secretion and faulty mineral balance

tetchy \'tech-ē\ *adj* **tetchi·er; -est** : irritably or peevishly sensitive : TOUCHY [perhaps from obsolete *tetch* "habit"]

¹tête-à-tête \ˌtāt-ə-'tāt\ *adv* : in private [French, literally, "head to head"]

²tête-à-tête \'tāt-ə-ˌtāt, *2 is also* 'tēt-ə-ˌtēt\ *n* **1** : a private conversation between two persons **2** : a seat for two persons facing each other

³tête-à-tête \ˌtāt-ə-ˌtāt\ *adj* : being face to face : PRIVATE

¹teth·er \'teth-ər\ *n* **1** : a line (as of rope or chain) by which an animal is fastened so as to restrict its range **2** : the limit of one's strength or resources : SCOPE ⟨at the end of my *tether*⟩ [Middle English *tethir*]

²tether *vt* **teth·ered; teth·er·ing** \'teth-ring, -ə-ring\ : to fasten or restrain by or as if by a tether

tet·ra \'te-trə\ *n* : any of various small brightly colored South American fishes often bred in tropical aquariums [New Latin *Tetragonopterus*, former genus name, from Late Latin *tetragonum* "quadrangle" + Greek *pteron* "wing"]

tetra- *or* **tetr-** *combining form* : four : having four : having four parts ⟨*tetra*valent⟩ [Greek]

tet·ra·chlo·ride \ˌte-trə-'klōr-ˌīd, -'klȯr-\ *n* : a chloride containing four atoms of chlorine

tet·ra·chord \'te-trə-ˌkȯrd\ *n* : a diatonic series of four tones : half an octave

tet·ra·cy·cline \ˌte-trə-'sī-ˌklēn\ *n* : a yellow crystalline broad-spectrum antibiotic produced by a soil actinomycete or synthetically

tet·rad \'te-ˌtrad\ *n* : a group or arrangement of four: as **a** : a group of four cells produced by the successive divisions of a mother cell **b** : an arrangement of chromosomes by fours in the first meiotic prophase due to early splitting of paired chromosomes [Greek *tetrad-, tetras*, from *tetra-*] — **te·trad·ic** \te-'trad-ik\ *adj*

tet·ra·eth·yl·lead \ˌte-trə-ˌeth-əl-'led\ *n* : a heavy oily poisonous liquid PbC_4H_{20} used as an antiknockagent

tet·ra·he·dron \ˌte-trə-'hē-drən\ *n, pl* **-drons** *or* **-dra** \-drə\ : a polyhedron of four faces — **tet·ra·he·dral** \-drəl\ *adj*

te·tra·hy·dro·can·nab·i·nol \-ˌhī-drə-kə-'nab-ə-ˌnȯl, -ˌnōl\ *n* : THC [*tetra-* + *hydr-* "hydrogen" + *cannab*is + *-in* + *-ol*]

tet·ral·o·gy \te-'träl-ə-jē, -'tral-\ *n, pl* **-gies** : a series of four connected works (as operas or novels)

te·tram·e·ter \te-'tram-ət-ər\ *n* : a line of verse consisting of four metrical feet [Greek *tetrametron*, derived from *tetra-* + *metron* "measure"]

tet·ra·ploid \'te-trə-ˌplȯid\ *adj* : having or being a chromosome number four times the monoploid number ⟨a *tetraploid* cell⟩ — **tetraploid** *n* — **tet·ra·ploi·dy** \-ˌplȯid-ē\ *n*

tet·ra·pod \'te-trə-ˌpäd\ *n* : a vertebrate (as a frog, bird, or cat) with two pairs of limbs

tet·rarch \'te-ˌträrk, 'tē-\ *n* : a governor of the 4th part of a province (as of ancient Rome) [Latin *tetrarcha*, from Greek *tetrarchēs*, from *tetra-* + *archein* "to rule"] — **te·trar·chic** \te-'trär-kik, tē-\ *adj*

te·trar·chy \'te-ˌträr-kē, 'tē-\ *n, pl* **-chies** : government by four persons ruling jointly

tet·ra·va·lent \ˌte-trə-'vā-lənt\ *adj* : having a valence of four

tet·rode \'te-ˌtrōd\ *n* : a vacuum tube with four electrodes

te·trox·ide \te-'träk-ˌsīd\ *n* : a compound of an element or radical with four atoms of oxygen

Teu·ton \'tüt-n, 'tyüt-n\ *n* **1** : a member of an ancient probably Germanic or Celtic people **2** : a member of a people speaking a language of the Germanic branch of the Indo-European language family; *esp* : GERMAN [Latin *Teutoni* "Teutons"]

¹Teu·ton·ic \tü-'tän-ik, tyü-\ *adj* : of, relating to, or characteristic of the Teutons — **Teu·ton·i·cal·ly** \-'tän-i-kə-lē, -klē\ *adv*

²Teutonic *n* : GERMANIC

tex·as \'tek-səs, -siz\ *n* : a structure on an upper deck of a steamer containing the officers' cabins and having the pilothouse in front or on top [*Texas*, state of the United States; from the fact that cabins on Mississippi steamboats were once named after states and the officers' cabins were the largest]

Texas fever *n* : an infectious disease of cattle transmitted by a tick and caused by a protozoan that multiplies in the blood and destroys the red blood cells

texas leaguer *n* : a fly that falls between the infielders and the outfielders [*Texas League*, a baseball minor league]

Texas Ranger *n* : a member of a mounted police force in Texas

text \'tekst\ *n* **1 a** : the original written or printed words and form of a literary work **b** : an edited or emended copy of an original work ⟨several *texts* of the play are in print⟩ **2 a** : the main body of printed or written matter on a page **b** : the principal part of a book exclusive of front and back matter **3 a** : a passage of Scripture chosen for the subject of a sermon; *also* : a passage providing a basis (as for a speech) **b** : a source of information or authority **4** : a subject on which one writes or speaks : TOPIC **5** : matter handled with a computer that is chiefly in the form of words **6** : TEXTBOOK [Middle French *texte,* from Latin *textus* "texture, context", from *texere* "to weave"]

text·book \'tekst-ˌbu̇k, 'teks-\ *n* : a book used in the study of a subject; *esp* : one that presents the principles of a subject

tex·tile \'tek-ˌstīl 'teks-tl\ *n* **1** : CLOTH 1; *esp* : a woven or knit cloth **2** : a fiber, filament, or yarn used in making cloth [Latin, from *textilis* "woven", from *texere* "to weave"] — **textile** *adj*

tex·tu·al \'teks-chə-wəl, -chəl\ *adj* : of, relating to, or based on a text — **tex·tu·al·y** \-ē\ *adv*

textual criticism *n* **1** : the study of a literary work that aims to establish the original text **2** : a critical study of literature emphasizing a close reading and analysis of the text — **textual critic** *n*

¹**tex·ture** \'teks-chər\ *n* **1** : something (as cloth) formed by or as if by weaving **2 a** : the structure, feel, and appearance of a textile that result from the kind and arrangement of its threads ⟨the harsh *texture* of burlap⟩ **b** : similar qualities dependent on the nature and arrangement of the constituent particles of a substance ⟨a gritty *texture*⟩ ⟨a fine *texture*⟩ **3** : an essential or identifying part or quality ⟨the truly American *texture* of the experience⟩ [Latin *textura,* from *texere* "to weave"] — **tex·tur·al** \-chə-rəl\ *adj* — **tex·tured** \-chərd\ *adj*

²**texture** *vt* : to give a particular and especially a rough texture to ⟨*texture* a ceiling⟩

T formation *n* : an offensive football formation in which the fullback lines up behind the quarterback and one halfback lines up on either side of the fullback

¹**-th** — see -ETH

²**-th** *or* **-eth** *adj suffix* — used in forming ordinal numbers ⟨hundred*th*⟩ ⟨fortie*th*⟩ [Old English -*tha*]

³**-th** *n suffix* **1** : act or process ⟨spil*th*⟩ **2** : state or condition ⟨dear*th*⟩ [Old English]

Thai \'tī\ *n* **1** : a native or inhabitant of Thailand **2** : the official language of Thailand — **Thai** *adj*

thal·a·mus \'thal-ə-məs\ *n, pl* **-mi** \-ˌmī, -ˌmē\ : the largest subdivision of the diencephalon forming a coordinating center through which incoming nerve impulses are directed to appropriate parts of the brain cortex [New Latin, from Greek *thalamos* "chamber"] — **tha·lam·ic** \thə-'lam-ik\ *adj*

tha·las·sic \thə-'las-ik\ *adj* **1** : of or relating to the sea or ocean **2** : of or relating to seas or gulfs as distinguished from oceans [French *thalassique,* from Greek *thalassa* "sea"]

tha·ler *variant of* TALER

tha·lid·o·mide \thə-'lid-ə-ˌmīd, -məd\ *n* : a sedative and hypnotic drug $C_{13}H_{10}N_2O_4$ found to cause malformation of infants born to mothers using it during pregnancy [derived from *naphthalene* + *amide*]

thal·lic \'thal-ik\ *adj* : of, relating to, or containing thallium especially with a valence of three

thal·li·um \'thal-ē-əm\ *n* : a poisonous metallic chemical element resembling lead in physical properties — see ELEMENT table [New Latin, from Greek *thallos* "young shoot"; from the green line in its spectrum]

thal·lo·phyte \'thal-ə-ˌfīt\ *n* : any of a primary division (Thallophyta) of the plant kingdom comprising plants with single-celled sex organs or with sex organs of which all cells give rise to gametes and including the algae, fungi, and lichens [derived from Greek *thallos* "young shoot" + *phytos* "plant"] — **thal·lo·phyt·ic** \ˌthal-ə-'fit-ik\ *adj*

thal·lous \'thal-əs\ *adj* : of, relating to, or containing thallium with a valence of one

thal·lus \'thal-əs\ *n, pl* **thal·li** \'thal-ˌī, -ˌē\ *or* **thal·lus·es** : the thallophytic plant body characterized by lack of differentiation into distinct members (as stem,

leaves, or roots) and by growth that is not confined to an apical point [New Latin, from Greek *thallos* "young shoot", from *thallein* "to sprout"] — **thal·loid** \'thal-ˌȯid\ *adj*

than \thən, than, 'than\ *conj* **1** — used as a function word after a comparative adjective or adverb to introduce the second part of a comparison expressing inequality ⟨older *than* I am⟩ ⟨easier said *than* done⟩ **2** — used as a function word to indicate difference of kind, manner, or identity; used especially with some adjectives and adverbs that express diversity ⟨anywhere else *than* at home⟩ [Old English *thonne, thænne* "then, than"]

thane \'thān\ *n* **1** : a free retainer of an Anglo-Saxon lord; *esp* : one holding lands of the king and performing military service **2** : a Scottish feudal lord [Old English *thegn*]

thank \'thangk\ *vt* **1** : to express gratitude to ⟨*thanked* them for the present⟩ **2** : to hold responsible ⟨had only themselves to *thank* for their loss⟩ [Old English *thancian*]

thank·ful \'thangk-fəl\ *adj* **1** : conscious of benefit received **2** : expressive of thanks **3** : well pleased : GLAD SYN see GRATEFUL — **thank·ful·ly** \-fə-lē\ *adv* — **thank·ful·ness** *n*

thank·less \'thang-kləs\ *adj* **1** : not expressing or feeling gratitude : UNGRATEFUL **2** : not likely to obtain thanks ⟨a *thankless* task⟩ — **thank·less·ly** *adv* — **thank·less·ness** *n*

thanks \'thangks\ *n pl* **1** : kindly or grateful thoughts : GRATITUDE ⟨express my *thanks* for their kindness⟩ **2** : an expression of gratitude ⟨return *thanks* before the meal⟩ — often used in an utterance containing no verb and serving as a courteous and somewhat informal expression of gratitude ⟨many *thanks*⟩ [Old English *thanc* "thought, gratitude"]

thanks·giv·ing \thangs-'giv-ing, thangks-\ *n* **1** : the act of giving thanks **2** : a prayer expressing gratitude **3** *cap* : THANKSGIVING DAY

Thanksgiving Day *n* : the 4th Thursday in November observed as a legal holiday in the United States for public thanksgiving to God

thank·wor·thy \'thang-ˌkwər-thē\ *adj* : worthy of thanks or gratitude : MERITORIOUS

thank–you–ma'am \'thangk-yu̇-ˌmam, -yē, -ē-\ *n* : a bump or depression in a road [probably from its causing a nodding of the head]

¹**that** \that, 'that\ *pron, pl* **those** \thōz, 'thōz\ **1 a** : the person, thing, or idea indicated, mentioned, or understood from the situation ⟨*that* is my father⟩ **b** : the time, action, or event specified ⟨after *that* we went to bed⟩ **c** : the kind or thing specified as follows ⟨the purest water is *that* produced by distillation⟩ **2 a** : the one farther away or less immediately under observation or discussion ⟨*those* are elms and these are maples⟩ **b** : the former one **3 a** : the one : the thing : the kind : SOMETHING, ANYTHING ⟨what's *that* you say⟩ **b** *pl* : some persons ⟨*those* who think the time has come⟩ [Old English *thæt,* neuter demonstrative pron. and definite article]

²**that** \thət, that, ˌthat\ *conj* **1 a** (1) — used to introduce a noun clause that is usually the subject or object of a verb or a predicate nominative ⟨said *that* they were afraid⟩ (2) — used to introduce a subordinate clause that is joined as complement to a noun or adjective ⟨certain *that* this is true⟩ ⟨the certainty *that* this is true⟩ ⟨the fact *that* you are here⟩ **b** — used to introduce an exclamatory clause expressing surprise, sorrow, or indignation ⟨*that* it should come to this⟩ **2 a** — used to introduce a subordinate clause expressing purpose or desired result ⟨saved money so *that* they could buy bicycles⟩ **b** — used to introduce an exclamatory clause expressing a wish ⟨oh, *that* they were here⟩ **3** — used to introduce a subordinate clause expressing a reason or cause ⟨delighted *that* you could

come) **4** — used to introduce a subordinate clause expressing result, consequence, or effect ⟨worked so hard *that* they became exhausted⟩

³that *adj, pl* **those 1** : being the person, thing, or idea specified, mentioned, or understood ⟨*that* child did it⟩ **2** : the farther away or less immediately under observation or discussion ⟨this chair or *that* one⟩

⁴that \thət,that, ˌthat\ *pron* **1** — used as a function word to introduce a relative clause and to serve as a substitute within that clause for the substantive modified by that clause ⟨the house *that* Jack built⟩ **2 a** : at which : in which : on which : by which : with which : to which ⟨each year *that* the lectures are given⟩ **b** : according to what : to the extent of what — used after a negative ⟨has never been there *that* I know of⟩ SYN see WHO

⁵that \ˈthat\ *adv* **1** : to such an extent ⟨a nail about *that* long⟩ **2** : VERY, EXTREMELY ⟨it's not *that* important⟩

¹thatch \ˈthach\ *vt* : to cover with or as if with thatch [Old English *theccan* "to cover"] — **thatch·er** *n*

²thatch *n* **1** : a plant material (as straw) for use as roofing **2** : a cover (as a roof) of thatch or as if of thatch ⟨a *thatch* of unruly hair⟩

¹thaw \ˈthȯ\ *vb* **1** : to melt or cause to melt : reverse the effect of freezing ⟨ice on the pond is *thawing*⟩ **2 a** : to become so warm or mild as to melt ice or snow **b** : to recover from chilling ⟨the skiers *thawed* out in front of the fire⟩ **3** : to grow less cold or reserved in manner : become more friendly [Old English *thawian*]

²thaw *n* **1** : the action, fact, or process of thawing **2** : a warmth of weather sufficient to thaw ice

THC \ˌtē-ˌäch-ˈsē\ *n* : a physiologically active liquid from hemp plant resin that is the chief intoxicant in marijuana — called also *tetrahydrocannabinol* [*tetrahydrocannabinol*]

¹the \ *before consonant and especially South sometimes vowel sounds* thə; *before vowel sounds* thē; *1g is often* ˈthē\ *definite article* **1 a** : that (one) or those (ones) previously mentioned or clearly understood from the context or situation ⟨put *the* cat out⟩ **b** : that unique (one) : that (one) existing as only one at a time ⟨*the* Lord⟩ ⟨*the* Pope⟩ **c** : that (one) or those (ones) near in space, time, or thought ⟨news of *the* day⟩ **d** : that (one) or those (ones) best known to the speaker or writer or to the hearer or reader ⟨*the* President⟩ ⟨*the* courts will decide⟩ **e** : MY, YOUR, HIS, HER, ITS, OUR, THEIR ⟨grabbed me by *the* collar⟩ ⟨how's *the* family⟩ ⟨*the* ankle is better today⟩ **f** : EACH, EVERY ⟨eighty crackers to *the* box⟩ **g** : that (one) or those (ones) considered best, most typical, or most worth singling out ⟨*the* poet of the decade⟩ ⟨my friend Adams is not one of *the* Adamses⟩ **2 a** : any (one) typical of or standing for an entire class so named ⟨courtesy distinguishes *the* gentleman⟩ ⟨good for *the* soul⟩ **b** : that which is ⟨an essay on *the* sublime⟩ **3** : all those that are ⟨*the* Greeks⟩ ⟨*the* aristocracy⟩ [Old English *thē*, masculine demonstrative pron. and definite article, alteration of *sē*]

²the *adv* **1** : than before : than otherwise — used before a comparative ⟨none *the* wiser for attending⟩ **2 a** : to what extent ⟨*the* sooner the better⟩ **b** : to that extent ⟨the sooner *the* better⟩ **3** : beyond all others ⟨likes this *the* best⟩ [Old English *thӯ* "by that", from *thæt* "that"]

the- *or* **theo-** *combining form* : god : God ⟨*the*ism⟩ [Greek *theos*]

the·ater *or* **the·atre** \ˈthē-ət-ər, *sometimes* ˈthē-ˌat-ər\ *n* **1** : a building or area for dramatic performances or for showing movies **2** : a place resembling a theater in form or use; *esp* : a room often with rising tiers of seats for assemblies (as for a lecture) **3** : a place of enactment of significant events or action ⟨a *theater* of war⟩ **4** : dramatic literature or performance [Middle French *theatre*, from Latin *theatrum*, from Greek *theatron*, from *theasthai* "to view", from *thea* "act of seeing"]

the·a·ter·go·er \-ˌgō-ər, -ˌgȯr\ *n* : a person who frequently goes to the theater — **the·a·ter·go·ing** \-ˌgō-ing\ *n*

theater–in–the–round *n* : ARENA THEATER

the·at·ri·cal \thē-ˈa-tri-kəl\ *adj* **1** : of or relating to the theater or the presentation of plays ⟨a *theatrical* costume⟩ **2** : marked by pretense or artificiality of emotion : not natural and simple ⟨a *theatrical* acceptance speech⟩ SYN see DRAMATIC — **the·at·ri·cal·ism** \-kə-ˌliz-əm\ *n* — **the·at·ri·cal·i·ty** \-ˌa-trə-ˈkal-ət-ē\ *n* — **the·at·ri·cal·ly** \-ˈa-tri-kə-lē, -klē\ *adv*

the·at·ri·cals \thē-ˈa-tri-kəlz\ *n pl* **1** : the performance of plays ⟨amateur *theatricals*⟩ **2** : the arts of acting and stagecraft

the·at·rics \-ˈtriks\ *n pl* **1** : THEATRICALS 1 **2** : staged or contrived effects

the·ca \ˈthē-kə\ *n, pl* **the·cae** \ˈthē-ˌsē, -ˌkē\ : an envelope or sheath enclosing an organism or one of its parts : CAPSULE, TEST [New Latin, from Greek *thēkē* "case"] — **the·cal** \ˈthē-kəl\ *adj* — **the·cate** \-ˌkāt\ *adj*

the·co·dont \ˈthē-kə-ˌdänt\ *n* : any of an order (Thecodontia) of Triassic reptiles held to be ancestral to the dinosaurs, crocodiles, and birds [derived from Greek *thēkē* "case" + *odont-, odous* "tooth"] — **thecodont** *adj*

thee \thē, ˈthē\ *pron, objective case of* THOU

theft \ˈtheft\ *n* : the act of stealing: as **a** : LARCENY **b** : unlawful taking (as by embezzlement or burglary) of property [Old English *thīefth*]

thegn \ˈthān\ *n* : THANE 1 [Old English]

their \thər, theər, thaər, ˌtheər, ˌthaər\ *adj* **1** : of or relating to them or themselves especially as possessors, agents, or objects of an action ⟨*their* clothes⟩ ⟨*their* deeds⟩ ⟨*their* being seen⟩ **2** : his or her : HIS, HER, ITS — used with an indefinite 3d person singular antecedent ⟨anyone in *their* right mind⟩ [Old Norse *theirra*, pron.]

theirs \ˈtheərz, ˈthaərz\ *pron, sing or pl in construction* **1** : that which belongs to them : those which belong to them — used without a following noun as an equivalent in meaning to the adjective *their* **2** : his or hers : HIS, HERS — used with an indefinite 3d person singular antecedent ⟨I will do my part if everybody else will do *theirs*⟩

the·ism \ˈthē-ˌiz-əm\ *n* : belief in the existence of a god or gods; *esp* : belief in the existence of God as creator and ruler of the universe — **the·ist** \ˈthē-əst\ *n* — **the·is·tic** \thē-ˈis-tik\ *adj* — **the·is·ti·cal** \-ˈis-ti-kəl\ *adj* — **the·is·ti·cal·ly** \-ti-kə-lē, -klē\ *adv*

-theism *n combining form* : belief in (such) a god or (such or so many) gods ⟨mono*theism*⟩

-theist *n combining form* : believer in (such) a god or (such or so many) gods ⟨mono*theist*⟩

them \thəm, əm, them, ˈthem, *after* p, b, v, f *also* ᵊm\ *pron, objective case of* THEY

theme \ˈthēm\ *n* **1** : a subject of discourse, artistic representation, or musical composition **2** : a written exercise : COMPOSITION [Latin *themat-, thema*, from Greek, literally, "something laid down", from *tithenai* "to put"] — **the·mat·ic** \thi-ˈmat-ik\ *adj* — **the·mat·i·cal·ly** \-ˈmat-i-kə-lē, -klē\ *adv*

theme song *n* **1** : a melody recurring so often in a musical play that it characterizes the production or one of its characters **2** : SIGNATURE 4

them·selves \thəm-ˈselvz, them-\ *pron pl* **1 a** : those identical ones that are they — used reflexively or for emphasis ⟨nations that govern *themselves*⟩ ⟨they *themselves* were present⟩; compare THEY **b** : himself or herself : HIMSELF, HERSELF — used with an indefinite 3d person singular antecedent ⟨nobody can call *themselves* worthy⟩ **2** : their normal, healthy, or sane condition or selves ⟨were *themselves* again after a night's rest⟩

¹then \then, 'then\ *adv* **1** : at that time **2 a** : soon after that ⟨walked to the door, *then* turned⟩ **b** : following next after in order **c** : in addition : BESIDES **3 a** : in that case **b** : according to that ⟨your mind is made up, *then*⟩ **c** : as it appears ⟨the cause, *then*, is established⟩ **d** : as a necessary consequence ⟨if you were there, *then* you saw them⟩ [Old English *thonne*, *thænne*]

²then \'then\ *n* : that time ⟨wait until *then*⟩

³then \'then\ *adj* : existing or acting at or belonging to the time mentioned ⟨the *then* king⟩

thence \'thens, 'thens\ *adv* **1** : from that place **2** *archaic* : from that time : THENCEFORTH **3** : from that fact or circumstance : THEREFROM [Middle English *thanne*, *thannes*, from Old English *thanon*]

thence·forth \-,fōrth, -,fȯrth\ *adv* : from that time forward : THEREAFTER

thence·for·ward \thens-'fȯr-wərd, thens-\ *also* **thence·for·wards** \-wərdz\ *adv* : onward from that place or time : THENCEFORTH

theo- — see THE-

the·oc·ra·cy \thē-'äk-rə-sē\ *n*, *pl* **-cies** **1** : government of a country by officials regarded as divinely guided **2** : a country governed by a theocracy — **theo·crat** \'thē-ə-,krat\ *n* — **theo·crat·ic** \,thē-ə-'krat-ik\ *adj* — **theo·crat·i·cal·ly** \-'krat-i-kə-lē, -klē\ *adv*

the·od·o·lite \thē-'äd-l-,īt\ *n* : a surveyor's instrument for measuring horizontal and usually also vertical angles [New Latin *theodelitus*]

theo·lo·gian \,thē-ə-'lō-jən\ *n* : a specialist in theology

theo·log·i·cal \,thē-ə-'läj-i-kəl\ *adj* : of or relating to theology — **theo·log·i·cal·ly** \-kə-lē, -klē\ *adv*

theological virtue *n* : a spiritual grace (as faith, hope, or charity) held to perfect the natural virtues

the·ol·o·gy \thē-'äl-ə-jē\ *n*, *pl* **-gies** **1** : the study and interpretation of religious faith, practice, and experience; *esp* : thought about God and his relation to the world **2** : a course of professional religious training

the·o·rem \'thē-ə-rəm, 'thi-ər-əm, 'thir-əm\ *n* **1** : a formula, proposition, or statement (as in logic) that has been or is to be proved from other formulas or propositions **2** : an idea accepted or proposed as a demonstrable truth [Late Latin *theorema*, from Greek *theōrēma*, from *theōrein* "to look at", derived from *thea* "act of seeing"]

the·o·ret·i·cal \,thē-ə-'ret-i-kəl\ *also* **the·o·ret·ic** \-'ret-ik\ *adj* **1 a** : relating to or having the character of theory : ABSTRACT **b** : confined to theory or speculation : SPECULATIVE ⟨*theoretical* mechanics⟩ **2** : given to or skilled in theorizing **3** : existing only in theory : HYPOTHETICAL [Late Latin *theoreticus*, from Greek *theōrētikos*, from *theōrein* "to look at"] — **the·o·ret·i·cal·ly** \-i-kə-lē, -klē\ *adv*

the·o·re·ti·cian \,thē-ə-rə-'tish-ən\ *n* : THEORIST

the·o·rist \'thē-ə-rəst, 'thi-ər-əst, 'thir-əst\ *n* : a person who theorizes

the·o·rize \'thē-ə-,rīz\ *vb* **-rized; -riz·ing** : to form a theory : SPECULATE — **the·o·ri·za·tion** \,thē-ə-rə-'zā-shən\ *n* — **the·o·riz·er** \'thē-ə-,rī-zər\ *n*

the·o·ry \'thē-ə-rē, 'thi-ər-ē, 'thir-ē\ *n*, *pl* **-ries** **1** : the general or abstract principles of a body of fact, a science, or an art ⟨music *theory*⟩ — compare PRACTICE **2** : a plausible or scientifically acceptable general principle or body of principles offered to explain phenomena ⟨the wave *theory* of light⟩ **3 a** : a hypothesis assumed for the sake of argument or investigation **b** : SUPPOSITION 1, CONJECTURE **4** : abstract thought : SPECULATION [Late Latin *theoria*, from Greek *theōria*, from *theōrein* "to look at"] SYN see HYPOTHESIS

the·os·o·phy \thē-'äs-ə-fē\ *n* **1** : belief about God and the world held to be based on mystical insight **2** *often cap* : the beliefs of a modern movement originating in the United States in 1875, following chiefly Buddhist and Hindu philosophies, and seeking to promote universal brotherhood and spiritual growth [Medieval Latin *theosophia*, from Late Greek, from Greek *theos*

"god" + *sophia* "wisdom"] — **the·o·soph·i·cal** \,thē-ə-'säf-i-kəl\ *adj* — **the·o·soph·i·cal·ly** \-'säf-i-kə-lē, -klē\ *adv* — **the·os·o·phist** \thē-'äs-ə-fəst\ *n*

ther·a·peu·tic \,ther-ə-'pyüt-ik\ *adj* : of, relating to, or dealing with healing and especially with remedies for diseases : MEDICINAL ⟨a *therapeutic* dose of arsenic⟩ ⟨*therapeutic* studies⟩ [Greek *therapeutikos*, from *therapeuein* "to attend, treat", from *theraps* "attendant"] — **ther·a·peu·ti·cal·ly** \-'pyüt-i-kə-lē, -klē\ *adv*

ther·a·peu·tics \-'pyüt-iks\ *n* : a branch of medical science dealing with the use of remedies

ther·a·pist \'ther-ə-pəst\ *n* : one specializing in therapy; *esp* : a person trained in methods of treatment and rehabilitation other than the use of drugs or surgery ⟨a speech *therapist*⟩

the·rap·sid \thə-'rap-səd\ *n* : any of an order (Therapsida) of Permian and Triassic reptiles held to be ancestral to the mammals [perhaps from Greek *theraps* "attendant"]

ther·a·py \'ther-ə-pē\ *n*, *pl* **-pies** : therapeutic treatment of bodily, mental, or social disorders or maladjustment [Greek *therapeia*, from *therapeuein* "to treat"]

¹there \'thaer, 'thear\ *adv* **1** : in or at that place ⟨stand over *there*⟩ **2** : to or into that place **3** : at that point or stage ⟨*there* the plot thickens⟩ **4** : in that matter, respect, or relation ⟨*there* you have a choice⟩ **5** — used interjectionally to express satisfaction, approval, soothing, or defiance ⟨*there*, I'm through⟩ [Old English *thær*]

²there \thaer, thear, ,thaer, ,thear, *1 is also* thər\ *pron* **1** — used as the grammatical subject in a sentence in which the logical subject appears in the predicate (1) usually after a form of *be* as an auxiliary verb ⟨*there* are some people waiting to see you⟩ or as a full verb ⟨*there* might be something wrong⟩ or (2) rarely after a full verb other than *be* ⟨*there* arose a great howl⟩ **2** — used as an indefinite substitute for a name ⟨hi *there*⟩

³there \like¹\ *n* **1** : that place or position **2** : that point ⟨you take it from *there*⟩

⁴there \like¹\ *adj* — used for emphasis especially after a demonstrative pronoun or a noun modified by a demonstrative adjective ⟨those people *there* can tell you⟩

there·abouts *or* **there·about** \,thar-ə-'baùts, ,ther-, -ə-'baùt\ *adv* **1** : near that place or time **2** : about that amount or number ⟨fifty people or *thereabouts*⟩

there·af·ter \tha-'raf-tər, the-\ *adv* : after that

there·at \-'rat\ *adv* **1** : at that place **2** : at that occurrence : on that account

there·by \thaer-'bī, thear-\ *adv* **1** : by that : by that means ⟨made a friend *thereby*⟩ **2** : connected with or with reference to that ⟨*thereby* hangs a tale⟩

there·for \-'fȯr\ *adv* : for or in return for that ⟨issued bonds *therefor*⟩

there·fore \'thaer-,fōr, 'thear-, -,fȯr\ *adv* **1 a** : for that reason : CONSEQUENTLY **b** : because of that **c** : on that ground **2** : to that end

there·from \thaer-'frəm, thear-, -'främ\ *adv* : from that or it ⟨learned much *therefrom*⟩

there·in \tha-'rin, the-\ *adv* **1** : in or into that place, time, or thing ⟨the world and all *therein*⟩ **2** : in that particular or respect ⟨*therein* they disagreed⟩

there·in·af·ter \,thar-in-'af-tər, ,ther-\ *adv* : in the following part of that matter (as writing, document, or speech)

there·of \tha-'rəv, the-, -'räv\ *adv* **1** : of that or it **2** : from that cause or particular : THEREFROM

there·on \-'ȯn, -'rän\ *adv* : on that

there·to \thaer-'tü, thear-\ *adv* : to that

there·to·fore \'thart-ə-,fōr, 'thert-, -,fȯr\ *adv* : up to that time

there·up·on \'thar-ə-,pȯn, 'ther-, -,pän\ *adv* **1** : on that matter : THEREON ⟨they disagreed *thereupon*⟩ **2** : THEREFORE **3** : immediately after that : at once

theodolite

there·with \tha͟ar-'wi͟th, thea͟r-, -'with\ *adv* : with that ⟨led a simple life and was happy *therewith*⟩

there·with·al \'tha͟ar-with-,ȯl, 'thea͟r-, -with-\ *adv* **1** *archaic* : BESIDES **2** : THEREWITH

therm- *or* **thermo-** *combining form* : heat ⟨*therm*ion⟩ ⟨*thermo*stat⟩ [Greek *thermē*]

¹ther·mal \'thər-məl\ *adj* : of, relating to, or caused by heat : WARM, HOT — **ther·mal·ly** \-mə-lē\ *adv*

²thermal *n* : a rising body of warm air

thermal pollution *n* : the discharge of heated liquid (as water) into a natural body of water at a temperature harmful to the environment

thermal printer *n* : a dot matrix printer (as for a computer) in which heat is applied to the pins of the matrix to form dots on usually heat-sensitive paper

thermal spring *n* : a spring whose water is warmer than the locality in which it is situated

therm·ion \'thər-,mī-ən, -,mī-,än\ *n* : an electrically charged particle emitted by an incandescent substance — **therm·ion·ic** \,thər-mī-'än-ik\ *adj*

therm·is·tor \'thər-,mis-tər\ *n* : an electrical resistor made of a material whose resistance varies sharply in a known manner with the temperature [*therm*al re*sistor*]

ther·mo·cline \'thər-mə-,klīn\ *n* : a layer of water in a body of water (as a lake) separating an upper warmer lighter oxygen-rich zone from a lower colder heavier oxygen-poor zone

ther·mo·cou·ple \'thər-mə-,kəp-əl\ *n* : a device for measuring temperature in which a pair of wires of dissimilar metals (as copper and iron) are joined and the free ends of the wires are connected to an instrument (as a voltmeter) that measures the difference in potential created at the junction of the two metals

ther·mo·dy·nam·ics \,thər-mō-dī-'nam-iks, -də-\ *n* : physics that deals with the mechanical action or relations of heat — **ther·mo·dy·nam·ic** \-ik\ *adj* — **ther·mo·dy·nam·i·cal·ly** \-'nam-i-kə-lē, -klē\ *adv*

ther·mo·elec·tric \,thər-mō-i-'lek-trik\ *adj* : of or relating to phenomena involving relations between the temperature and the electrical condition in a metal or in contacting metals

ther·mo·elec·tric·i·ty \,thər-mō-i-,lek-'tris-ət-ē, -'tris-tē\ *n* : electricity produced by the direct action of heat (as by the unequal heating of a circuit composed of two dissimilar metals)

ther·mo·gram \'thər-mə-,gram\ *n* : a photograph that shows differences in temperature between different parts of an object (as the body or a building)

ther·mo·graph \'-,graf\ *n* : a self-recording thermometer

ther·mo·la·bile \,thər-mō-'lā-,bīl, -bəl\ *adj* : unstable when heated ⟨many enzymes and vitamins are *thermolabile*⟩ — compare THERMOSTABLE — **ther·mo·la·bil·i·ty** \-lā-'bil-ət-ē\ *n*

ther·mom·e·ter \thər-'mäm-ət-ər, thə-'mäm-\ *n* : an instrument for measuring temperature commonly by means of the expansion or contraction of mercury or alcohol as indicated by its rise or fall in a thin glass tube alongside a scale — **ther·mo·met·ric** \,thər-mə-'me-trik\ *adj* — **ther·mo·met·ri·cal·ly** \-tri-kə-lē, -klē\ *adv*

ther·mom·e·try \thər-'mäm-ə-trē, thə-'mäm-\ *n* : the measurement of temperature

ther·mo·nu·cle·ar \,thər-mō-'nü-klē-ər, -'nyü-\ *adj* **1** : of or relating to the transformations in the nucleus of atoms of low atomic weight (as hydrogen) that require a very high temperature (as in the hydrogen bomb or in the sun) ⟨a *thermonuclear* reaction⟩ ⟨a *thermonuclear* weapon⟩ **2** : of, utilizing, or relating to a thermonuclear bomb ⟨*thermonuclear* war⟩

ther·mo·phile \'thər-mə-,fīl\ *n* : an organism growing at a high temperature — **ther·mo·phil·ic** \,thər-mə-'fil-ik\ *adj*

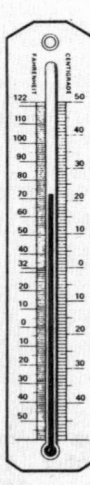

thermometer

ther·mo·pile \'thər-mə-,pīl\ *n* : an apparatus consisting of a number of thermoelectric couples combined so as to multiply the effect and used for generating electric currents or for determining intensities of radiation

ther·mo·plas·tic \,thər-mə-'plas-tik\ *adj* : having the property of softening or fusing when heated and of hardening again when cooled ⟨*thermoplastic* synthetic resins⟩ — **thermoplastic** *n*

ther·mo·reg·u·la·tor \,thər-mō-'reg-yə-,lāt-ər\ *n* : a device (as a thermostat) for the regulation of temperature

ther·mos \'thər-məs\ *n* : VACUUM BOTTLE [from *Thermos*, a former trademark]

ther·mo·set·ting \'thər-mō-,set-ing\ *adj* : having the property of becoming permanently rigid when heated or cured ⟨a *thermosetting* synthetic resin⟩

ther·mo·sphere \'thər-mə-,sfiər\ *n* : the part of the earth's atmosphere that begins at about 80 kilometers above the earth's surface and is characterized by a steady increase in temperature with height

ther·mo·sta·ble \,thər-mō-'stā-bəl\ *adj* : stable when heated ⟨*thermostable* enzymes⟩ — compare THERMOLABILE

ther·mo·stat \'thər-mə-,stat\ *n* : an automatic device for regulating temperature (as of a heating system); *also* : a device for actuating fire alarms or for controlling automatic sprinklers [*therm-* + Greek *-statēs* "one that stops or steadies", from *histanai* "to cause to stand"] — **ther·mo·stat·ic** \,thər-mə-'stat-ik\ *adj* — **ther·mo·stat·i·cal·ly** \-'stat-i-kə-lē, -klē\ *adv*

ther·mo·tax·is \,thər-mə-'tak-səs\ *n* : a taxis in which a temperature gradient constitutes the directive factor — **ther·mo·tac·tic** \-'tak-tik\ *adj*

ther·mot·ro·pism \,thər-'mä-trə-,piz-əm\ *n* : a tropism in which a temperature gradient determines the orientation — **ther·mo·trop·ic** \,thər-mə-'träp-ik\ *adj*

the·sau·rus \thi-'sȯr-əs\ *n, pl* **-sau·ri** \-'sȯr-,ī, -,ē\ *or* **-sau·rus·es** \-'sȯr-ə-səz\ **1** : a book of words or of information about a particular field; *esp* : a dictionary of synonyms **2** : TREASURY **3**, STOREHOUSE [Latin, "treasure, collection", from Greek *thēsauros*]

these *pl of* THIS

the·sis \'thē-səs\ *n, pl* **the·ses** \'thē-,sēz\ **1** : a proposition to be proved or advanced without proof : HYPOTHESIS **2** : an essay bringing together the results of original research; *esp* : one written by a candidate for an academic degree [Latin, from Greek, literally, "act of laying down", from *tithenai* "to put"]

¹thes·pi·an \'thes-pē-ən\ *adj, often cap* : relating to the drama : DRAMATIC [from the tradition that Thespis was the originator of the actor's role]

²thespian *n* : ACTOR 1b

Thes·sa·lo·nians \,thes-ə-'lō-nyənz, -nē-ənz\ *n* — see BIBLE table

the·ta \'thāt-ə\ *n* : the 8th letter of the Greek alphabet — Θ or θ

they \thā, 'thā\ *pron, pl in construction* **1 a** : those ones — used as 3d person pronoun serving as the plural of *he, she,* or *it* or referring to a group of two or more individuals not all of the same sex ⟨*they* dance well⟩ **b** : ¹HE 2 — often used with an indefinite 3d person singular antecedent ⟨anyone can leave if *they* like⟩ **2** : PEOPLE 1 — used in a generic sense ⟨as lazy as *they* come⟩ ⟨*they* say it will rain⟩ [Old Norse *their*]

they'd \thād, thād\ : they had : they would

they'll \thāl, thāl, thel\ : they shall : they will

they're \thər, theər, theər, thā-ər\ : they are

they've \thāv, thāv\ : they have

thi- *or* **thio-** *combining form* : containing sulfur ⟨*thio*urea⟩ [Greek *theion* "sulfur"]

thi·a·mine \'thī-ə-mən, -,mēn\ *also* **thi·a·min** \-mən\ *n* : a vitamin of the vitamin B complex essential to normal metabolism and nerve function and widely distributed in plants and animals — called also *vitamin*

B, vitamin B₁ [*thiamine* alteration of *thiamin*, from *thi-* + -*amin* (as in *vitamin*)]

¹**thick** \'thik\ *adj* **I a** : having or being of relatively great depth or extent from one surface to its opposite ⟨a *thick* plank⟩ **b** : heavily built : THICKSET **2 a** : close-packed : DENSE ⟨*thick* forest⟩ **b** : occurring in large numbers : NUMEROUS **c** : viscous in consistency ⟨*thick* syrup⟩ **d** : STUFFY ⟨air *thick* with smoke⟩ **e** : marked by haze, fog, or mist ⟨*thick* weather⟩ **f** : impenetrable to the eye ⟨*thick* fog⟩ **g** : extremely intense ⟨*thick* silence⟩ **3** : measuring in thickness ⟨two meters *thick*⟩ **4 a** : imperfectly articulated : INDISTINCT ⟨*thick* speech⟩ **b** : PRONOUNCED ⟨a *thick* French accent⟩ **c** : producing inarticulate speech ⟨a *thick* tongue⟩ **5** : OBTUSE 1, STUPID **6** : associated on close terms [Old English *thicce*] — **thick·ish** \-ish\ *adj* — **thick·ly** *adv*

²**thick** *n* **I** : the most crowded or active part ⟨in the *thick* of battle⟩ **2** : the part of greatest thickness

³**thick** *adv* : THICKLY

thick and thin *n* : every difficulty and obstacle ⟨stood by their friend through *thick and thin*⟩

thick·en \'thik-ən\ *vb* **thick·ened; thick·en·ing** \'thik-ning, -ə-ning\ **I** : to make or become thick, dense, or viscous **2** : to add to the depth or diameter of **3 a** : to make inarticulate ⟨alcohol *thickened* their speech⟩ **b** : to grow blurred or obscure **4** : to grow broader or bulkier **5** : to grow complicated or keen ⟨the plot *thickens*⟩ — **thick·en·er** \'thik-nər, -ə-nər\ *n*

thick·en·ing *n* **I** : the act of making or becoming thick **2** : something used to thicken (as flour in a gravy) **3** : a thickened part or place

thick·et \'thik-ət\ *n* **I** : a thick usually circumscribed growth of shrubbery, small trees, or underbrush **2** : something resembling a thicket in density or impenetrability [Old English *thiccet*, from *thicce* "thick"] — **thick·et·ed** \-ət-əd\ *adj*

thick·head·ed \'thik-'hed-əd\ *adj* **I** : having a thick head **2** : mentally dull

thick·ness \'thik-nəs\ *n* **I** : the quality or state of being thick **2** : the smallest of the three dimensions of something (length, width, and *thickness* of a board) **3** : viscous consistency ⟨the *thickness* of honey⟩ **4** : the thick part of something **5** : CONCENTRATION 3, DENSITY **6** : dullness of mind **7** : LAYER, PLY, SHEET ⟨a single *thickness* of canvas⟩

thick·set \'thik-'set\ *adj* : of short stout build : STOCKY

thick·skinned \-'skind\ *adj* **I** : having a thick skin **2** : CALLOUS 2, INSENSITIVE

thick–wit·ted \-'wit-əd\ *adj* : dull or slow of mind : STUPID

thief \'thēf\ *n, pl* **thieves** \'thēvz\ : one that steals [Old English *thēof*] — **thiev·ish** \'thē-vish\ *adj* — **thiev·ish·ly** *adv* — **thiev·ish·ness** *n*

thieve \'thēv\ *vb* **I** : to commit a theft **2** *chiefly British* : to take by stealth : STEAL

thiev·ery \'thēv-rē, -ə-rē\ *n, pl* **-er·ies** : the action of stealing

thigh \'thī\ *n* **I a** : the segment of the vertebrate hind limb extending from the hip to the knee and supported by a single large bone; *also* : the next outer segment in a bird or in a four-footed animal in which the true thigh is obscured **b** : the femur of an insect **2** : something resembling or covering a thigh [Old English *thēoh*]

thigh·bone \-'bōn, -,bōn\ *n* : FEMUR 1

thig·mo·tax·is \,thig-mə-'tak-səs\ *n* : a taxis in which contact (as with a rigid surface) is the directive factor [Greek *thigma* "contact", from *thinganein* "to touch"]

thig·mot·ro·pism \thig-'mä-trə-,piz-əm\ *n* : a tropism in which contact (as with a rigid surface) is the orienting factor

thim·ble \'thim-bəl\ *n* **I** : a cap or cover used in sewing to protect the finger that pushes the needle **2** : a grooved ring of thin metal used to fit in a loop in a wire or rope **3** : a fixed or movable ring, tube, or lining in a hole [Middle English *thymbyl*, probably from Old English *thȳmel* "covering for the thumb", from *thūma* "thumb"]

thim·ble·ber·ry \-,ber-ē\ *n* : any of several American raspberries or blackberries with thimble-shaped fruit

thim·ble·ful \-,fůl\ *n* **I** : as much as a thimble will hold **2** : a very small quantity

¹**thim·ble·rig** \'thim-bəl-,rig\ *n* : a swindling trick in which a small ball or pea is quickly shifted from under one to another of three small cups to fool a spectator guessing its location

²**thimblerig** *vt* **I** : to swindle by thimblerig **2** : to cheat by trickery — **thim·ble·rig·ger** *n*

¹**thin** \'thin\ *adj* **thin·ner; thin·nest** **I a** : having little extent from one surface to its opposite ⟨*thin* paper⟩ **b** : measuring little in cross section or diameter ⟨*thin* rope⟩ **2** : not dense in arrangement or distribution ⟨*thin* hair⟩ **3** : not plump or fat : LEAN **4 a** : more fluid or rarefied than normal ⟨*thin* air⟩ **b** : not well filled or supplied : SCANTY ⟨a *thin* market⟩ **5** : lacking substance or strength ⟨*thin* broth⟩ ⟨a *thin* excuse⟩ **6** : somewhat feeble, shrill, and lacking in resonance ⟨a *thin* voice⟩ [Old English *thynne*] — **thin·ly** *adv* — **thin·ness** \'thin-nəs\ *n* — **thin·nish** \'thin-ish\ *adj*

□ SYN THIN, SLENDER, SLIM, SLIGHT mean not thick, broad, abundant, or dense. THIN implies comparatively little extension between surfaces or in diameter ⟨a *thin* layer of ice⟩ ⟨*thin* wire⟩ or it may imply lack of substance, richness, or abundance ⟨*thin* soup⟩ ⟨a *thin* hedge⟩ SLENDER implies leanness often with graceful proportions ⟨*slender* columns⟩ SLIM suggests scantiness or fragile slenderness ⟨a *slim* paycheck⟩ SLIGHT implies thinness and smallness ⟨a person of *slight* build⟩

²**thin** *adv* **thin·ner; thin·nest** : THINLY ⟨*thin*-clad⟩

³**thin** *vb* **thinned; thin·ning** : to make or become thin or thinner: **a** : to reduce in thickness or depth **b** : to make less dense or viscous **c** : DILUTE 2, WEAKEN **d** : to cause to lose flesh **e** : to reduce in number or bulk

¹**thine** \thīn, 'thīn\ *adj, archaic* : THY — used especially before a word beginning with a vowel [Old English *thīn*]

²**thine** \'thīn\ *pron, sing or pl in construction* : that which belongs to thee : those which belong to thee — used without a following noun as an equivalent in meaning to the adjective *thy*; used especially in ecclesiastical or literary language

thing \'thing\ *n* **I a** : a matter of concern : AFFAIR ⟨many *things* to do⟩ **b** *pl* : state of affairs in general or within a specified or implied sphere ⟨*things* are improving⟩ **c** : a particular state of affairs : SITUATION ⟨look at this *thing* another way⟩ **d** : EVENT, CIRCUMSTANCE ⟨that shooting was a terrible *thing*⟩ **2 a** : DEED, ACT, ACCOMPLISHMENT ⟨do great *things*⟩ **b** : a product of work or activity ⟨likes to build *things*⟩ **c** : the aim of effort or activity ⟨the *thing* is to get well⟩ **3 a** : a separate and distinct item or object : ENTITY; *esp* : a physical object **b** : an inanimate object as distinguished from a living being **4 a** *pl* : PERSONAL PROPERTY ⟨pack your *things*⟩ **b** : an article of clothing ⟨not a *thing* to wear⟩ **c** *pl* : equipment or utensils especially for a particular purpose ⟨bring the tea *things*⟩ **5** : an object or entity not precisely designated or capable of being designated ⟨how do you use this *thing*⟩ **6 a** : DETAIL, POINT ⟨checks every little *thing*⟩ **b** : a material or substance of a specified kind ⟨avoid starchy *things*⟩ **7 a** : a spoken or written observation or point **b** : IDEA, NOTION ⟨say the first *thing* you think of⟩ **c** : a piece of news or information ⟨couldn't get a *thing* out of the prisoner⟩ **8** : INDIVIDUAL; *esp* : PERSON ⟨you poor *thing*⟩ **9** : the proper or fashionable way of behaving, talking, or dressing ⟨it is the *thing* to do⟩ **10 a** : an irrational fear or obsession ⟨have a *thing* about snakes⟩ **b** : something with strong personal appeal ⟨allowed to do their own *thing*⟩ [Old English, "thing, assembly"]

\ə\ abut		\ng\ sing	
\ər\ further		\ō\ bone	
\a\ mat		\ò\ saw	
\ā\ take		\th\ thin	
\ä\ cot, cart		\th\ this	
\aů\ out		\ü\ food	
\ch\ chin		\ů\ foot	
\e\ pet		\y\ yet	
\ē\ easy		\yü\ few	
\g\ go		\yů\ cure	
\i\ tip		\zh\ vision	
\ī\ life			
\j\ job			

thing·am·a·bob \'thing-ə-mə-,bäb\ *n* : THINGAMAJIG
thing·am·a·jig *or* **thing·um·a·jig** \'thing-ə-mə-,jig\ *n* : something that is hard to classify or whose name is unknown or forgotten [derived from *thing*]
thing·um·my \'thing-ə-mē\ *n, pl* **-mies** : THINGAMAJIG [derived from *thing*]
¹**think** \'thingk\ *vb* **thought** \'thȯt\; **think·ing** **1** : to form or have in the mind **2** : INTEND, PLAN ⟨*thought* to return early⟩ **3 a** : to have as an opinion : BELIEVE ⟨*think* it's so⟩ **b** : to regard as : CONSIDER ⟨*think* the rule unfair⟩ **4** : to reflect on : PONDER ⟨*think* the matter over⟩ **5** : to call to mind : REMEMBER ⟨couldn't *think* of the name⟩ **6** : to create or devise by thinking ⟨*think* up a caption for the picture⟩ **7** : to subject to the processes of logical thought ⟨*think* things out⟩ **8** : to exercise the powers of judgment, conception, or inference : REASON **9 a** : to have the mind engaged in reflection : MEDITATE ⟨*thinking* sadly of the past⟩ **b** : to consider the suitability ⟨*thought* of you for captain⟩ **10** : to have a view or opinion ⟨*think* of myself as a skier⟩ **11** : to have concern ⟨*think* of just yourself⟩ **12** : EXPECT 4a ⟨*thought* to find them at home⟩ [Old English *thencan*] — **think·able** \'thing-kə-bəl\ *adj* — **think·er** *n* □ SYN THINK, REFLECT, REASON, SPECULATE mean to use one's powers of conception, judgment, or inference. THINK may apply to any mental activity but often suggests attainment of clear ideas or conclusions; REFLECT suggests unhurried consideration of something recalled to mind; REASON stresses orderly logical thinking especially in reaching a conclusion; SPECULATE implies reasoning but stresses the uncertain, theoretical, or problematic character of the conclusions ⟨*speculated* on the probable consequences of a nuclear war⟩ — **think better of** : to reconsider and make a wiser decision — **think much of** : to view with satisfaction — usually used in negative constructions ⟨didn't *think much of* the idea⟩
²**think** *n* : an act of thinking ⟨has another *think* coming⟩
¹**think·ing** *n* **1** : the action of using one's mind to produce thoughts **2 a** : OPINION, JUDGMENT ⟨it is, to my *thinking*, utter nonsense⟩ **b** : THOUGHT 3b
²**thinking** *adj* : marked by use of the intellect : RATIONAL — **think·ing·ly** \'thing-king-lē\ *adv* — **think·ing·ness** *n*
thinking cap *n* : a state or mood in which one thinks ⟨put on your *thinking cap*⟩
think piece *n* : a news article consisting chiefly of background material and personal opinion and analysis
thin·ner \'thin-ər\ *n* : one that thins; *esp* : a volatile liquid (as turpentine) used to thin paint
thin–skinned \'thin-'skind\ *adj* **1** : having a thin skin **2** : unduly sensitive to criticism or insult : TOUCHY
thio- — see THI-
thio·urea \,thī-ō-yu̇-'rē-ə\ *n* : a colorless crystalline bitter compound $CS(NH_2)_2$ analogous to and resembling urea that is used especially as a photographic and organic chemical reagent
thi·ram \'thī-,ram\ *n* : a sulfur-containing fungicide and seed disinfectant [derived from Greek *theion* "sulfur"]
¹**third** \'thərd\ *adj* **1** : being number three in a countable series **2** : being next after the second (as in order, time, or importance) **3** : being one of three equal parts [Old English *thridda, thirdda*] — **third** *adv* — **third·ly** *adv*
²**third** *n* **1** : number three in a countable series — see NUMBER table **2** : one of three equal parts **3 a** : a musical interval of three degrees or a tone at this interval **b** : the harmonic combination of two tones a third apart **4** : the third gear or speed of an automotive vehicle **5** : one next after a second (as in time, order, or importance)
third base *n* **1** : the base that must be touched third by a base runner in baseball **2** : the position of the player defending the area around third base

third base·man \-'bā-smən\ *n* : the player defending the area around third base
third class *n* : the class next below second class in a classification ⟨travel by *third class* to Europe⟩; *esp* : a class of United States mail including various printed matter and merchandise that weighs less than 16 ounces and is open to inspection — **third–class** *adj or adv*
third degree *n* : severe or brutal treatment of a prisoner (as by police) in order to get information or a confession
third–degree burn *n* : a burn in which there is destruction of the whole thickness of the skin and sometimes of deeper tissues with loss of fluid and often shock
third dimension *n* : thickness, depth, or apparent thickness or depth that confers solidity on an object — **third–di·men·sion·al** *adj*
third estate *n* : the third of the traditional political orders : COMMON 3a; *also* : MIDDLE CLASS
third force *n* : a grouping (as of political parties or international powers) intermediate between two opposing political forces
third order *n, often cap T&O* **1** : an organization composed of lay people living in secular society under a religious rule and directed by a religious order **2** : a congregation especially of teaching or nursing sisters affiliated with a religious order
third party *n* **1** : a person other than the principals ⟨a *third party* to a divorce proceeding⟩ **2** : a political party operating usually for a limited time in addition to the two major parties in a 2-party system
third person *n* : a set of words or forms (as verb forms or pronouns) referring to someone or something that is neither the speaker or writer of the utterance in which they occur nor the one to whom that utterance is addressed; *also* : a word or form belonging to such a set
third rail *n* : a metal rail which is parallel to the tracks and through which electric current is led to the motors of an electric locomotive
third–rate \'thər-'drāt\ *adj* : of third quality or value; *esp* : worse than second-rate — **third–rat·er** \-'drāt-ər\ *n*
third world *n, often cap T&W* **1** : a group of nations mostly of Africa and Asia claiming to be aligned with neither the Communist nor non-Communist blocs **2** : the underdeveloped nations of the world
¹**thirst** \'thərst\ *n* **1** : a feeling of dryness in the mouth and throat associated with a desire for liquids; *also* : the bodily condition (as of dehydration) that induces this **2** : an ardent desire : LONGING ⟨a *thirst* for knowledge⟩ [Old English *thurst*]
²**thirst** *vi* **1** : to suffer thirst **2** : to have a strong desire : LONG
thirsty \'thər-stē\ *adj* **thirst·i·er; -est** **1 a** : feeling thirst **b** : lacking moisture : ARID ⟨*thirsty* land⟩ **c** : highly absorbent ⟨*thirsty* towels⟩ **2** : having a strong desire : AVID ⟨*thirsty* for knowledge⟩ — **thirst·i·ly** \-stə-lē\ *adv* — **thirst·i·ness** \-stē-nəs\ *n*
thir·teen \,thər-'tēn, ,thərt-, 'thər-, 'thərt-\ *n* : one more than 12; *also* : a symbol representing this — see NUMBER table [Old English *thrēotīne*] — **thirteen** *adj or pron* — **thir·teenth** \-'tēnth, -'tēntth\ *adj or n*
thir·ty \'thərt-ē\ *n, pl* **thirties** **1** : ten more than 20; *also* : a symbol representing this — see NUMBER table **2** *pl* : the numbers 30 to 39; *esp* : the years 30 to 39 in a lifetime or century **3** : a mark or sign of completion **4** : the 2d point scored by a side in a game of tennis **5** : a 30 caliber machine gun — usually written .30 [Old English *thrītig*] — **thir·ti·eth** \-ē-əth\ *n or adj* — **thirty** *adj or pron*
thir·ty–eight \,thərt-ē-'āt\ *n* : a 38 caliber pistol — usually written .38
thirty–second note *n* : a musical note having the time value of one thirty-second of a whole note

thir·ty–thir·ty \,thərt-ē-'thərt-ē\ *n* : a rifle that fires a 30 caliber cartridge having a 30 grain powder charge — usually written .30-30

thir·ty–three \-'thrē\ *n* : a phonograph record for play at 33⅓ revolutions per minute — usually written 33

thir·ty–two \-'tü\ *n* : a 32 caliber pistol — usually written .32

¹**this** \this, 'this, thəs\ *pron, pl* **these** \thēz 'thēz\ **1 a** (1) : the person, thing, or idea that is present or near in place, time, or thought or that has just been mentioned 〈*these* are my hands〉 (2) : what is stated in the following phrase, clause, or discourse 〈I can only say *this:* they aren't here〉 **b** : this time or place 〈hoped to return before *this*〉 **2 a** : the one nearer or more immediately under observation 〈*this* is iron and that is tin〉 **b** : the latter one [Old English *thes* (masculine), *this* (neuter)]

²**this** *adj, pl* **these 1 a** : being the one that is present or near in place, time, or thought or that has just been mentioned 〈*this* book is mine〉 〈early *this* morning〉 〈all *these* years〉 **b** : being one not previously mentioned — used especially in narrative to give a sense of immediacy or vividness 〈I had on *this* bright red shirt〉 **2** : being the nearer at hand or more immediately under observation or discussion 〈*this* car or that one〉

³**this** \'this\ *adv* : to the degree or extent indicated by something immediately present 〈didn't expect to wait *this* long〉

this·tle \'this-əl\ *n* : any of various prickly plants of the daisy family with often showy heads of mostly tubular flowers [Old English *thistel*] — **this·tly** \'this-lē, -ə-lē\ *adj*

this·tle·down \-əl-,daun\ *n* : the down from the ripe flower head of a thistle

thistle tube *n* : a funnel tube usually of glass with a bulging top and flaring mouth

¹**thith·er** \'thith-ər also 'thith-\ *adv* : to that place : THERE [Old English *thider*]

²**thither** *adj* : being on the other and farther side : more remote

thith·er·to \-,tü\ *adv* : until that time

tho \'thō, thō, ,thō\ *adv or conj* : THOUGH

thole \'thōl\ *also* **thole·pin** \-,pin\ *n* : a pin set in the gunwale of a boat as a pivot for an oar [Old English *thol*]

Tho·mism \'tō-,miz-əm\ *n* : the scholastic philosophical and theological system of Saint Thomas Aquinas — **Tho·mist** \-məst\ *n or adj* — **Tho·mis·tic** \tō-'mis-tik\ *adj*

Thomp·son submachine gun \'täm-sən-, 'tämp-\ *n* : a submachine gun with a pistol grip and stock for firing from the shoulder — called also *tommy gun* [John T. *Thompson,* died 1940, American army officer]

thong \'thȯng\ *n* : a strip of leather used especially for fastening something [Old English *thwong*]

thoracic duct *n* : the chief lymphatic vessel carrying lymph back to the bloodstream especially from the abdomen and lower limbs, lying along the front of the spinal column, and opening into the left subclavian vein

tho·rax \'thōr-,aks, 'thȯr-\ *n, pl* **tho·rax·es** *or* **tho·ra·ces** \'thōr-ə-,sēz, 'thȯr-\ **1** : the part of the body of a mammal between the neck and the abdomen; *also* : its cavity in which the heart and lungs lie **2** : the middle of the three chief divisions of the body of an insect [Latin *thorac-, thorax* "breastplate, thorax", from Greek *thōrak-, thōrax*] — **tho·rac·ic** \thə-'ras-ik\ *adj*

Tho·ra·zine \'thōr-ə-,zēn, 'thȯr-\ *trademark* — used for chlorpromazine

tho·ria \'thōr-ē-ə, 'thȯr-\ *n* : a powdery white oxide of thorium used especially in crucibles and optical glass [New Latin, from *thorium*]

tho·ri·um \'thōr-ē-əm, 'thȯr-\ *n* : a radioactive metallic chemical element that occurs combined in minerals — see ELEMENT table [New Latin, from Old Norse *Thōrr* "Thor"]

thorn \'thȯrn\ *n* **1** : a woody plant bearing sharp processes (as briers, prickles, or spines); *esp* : HAWTHORN **2 a** : a sharp rigid process on a plant; *esp* : one that is a short, rigid, sharp-pointed, and leafless branch **b** : a sharp rigid process on an animal **3** : something that causes distress or irritation [Old English] — **thorned** \'thȯrnd\ *adj* — **thorn·less** \'thȯrn-ləs\ *adj* — **thorn·like** \-,līk\ *adj*

thorn apple *n* **1** : the fruit of a hawthorn; *also* : HAWTHORN **2** : JIMSONWEED

thorn-bush \'thȯrn-,bush\ *n* **1** : any of various spiny or thorny shrubs or small trees **2** : a low growth of thorny shrubs especially of dry tropical regions

thorny \'thȯr-nē\ *adj* **thorn·i·er; -est 1** : full of or covered with thorns : SPINY **2** : DIFFICULT, TRYING 〈a *thorny* problem〉 — **thorn·i·ness** *n*

thoro \'thər-ō, 'thə-rō\ *nonstandard variant of* THOROUGH

thor·ough \'thər-ō, 'thə-rō\ *adj* **1** : being such to the fullest degree : EXHAUSTIVE, COMPLETE 〈a *thorough* search〉 〈*thorough* success〉 **2** : careful about detail 〈a very *thorough* worker〉 [Middle English *thorow,* from *thorow* "through", from Old English *thurh*] — **thor·ough·ly** *adv* — **thor·ough·ness** *n*

¹**thor·ough·bred** \'thər-ə-,bred, 'thə-rə-\ *adj* **1 a** *cap* : of, relating to, or being a member of the Thoroughbred breed of horses **b** : PUREBRED 〈*thoroughbred* dogs〉 **2** : marked by grace and elegance

²**thoroughbred** *n* **1** *cap* : any of an English breed of light speedy horses kept chiefly for racing and originating from crosses between English mares of uncertain ancestry and Arab stallions **2** : a purebred or pedigreed animal **3** : a person of sterling qualities

thor·ough·fare \-,faər, -,feər\ *n* **1** : a public way connecting two streets : a street or road open at both ends **2** : a main road : a busy street

thor·ough·go·ing \,thər-ə-'gō-ing, ,thə-rə-\ *adj* : marked by thoroughness or zeal 〈*thoroughgoing* cooperation〉

thorp \'thȯrp\ *n, archaic* : VILLAGE 1, HAMLET [Old English]

those *pl of* THAT

¹**thou** \thau, 'thau\ *pron* : the one spoken to — used especially in ecclesiastical or literary language; compare THEE, THINE, THY, YE, YOU [Old English *thū*]

²**thou** \'thau\ *n, pl* **thou** *or* **thous** : a thousand of something (as dollars)

¹**though** \'thō\ *adv* : HOWEVER 2, NEVERTHELESS 〈not for long, *though*〉 [of Scandinavian origin]

²**though** \thō, ,thō\ *conj* **1** : in spite of the fact that 〈*though* it was raining, we went for a walk〉 **2** : even if : even supposing 〈determined to fight for truth *though* they should die for it〉

¹**thought** *past of* THINK

²**thought** \'thȯt\ *n* **1 a** : the act or process of thinking **b** : serious consideration : careful attention 〈give *thought* to the future〉 **2 a** : power of thinking and especially of reasoning and judging **b** : power of imagining or comprehending 〈beauty beyond *thought*〉 **3 a** : a product of thinking (as an idea, fancy, or invention) 〈idle *thoughts*〉 〈a pleasing *thought*〉 **b** : the intellectual product or the organized views and principles of a period, place, group, or individual 〈modern scientific *thought*〉 **4** : a slight amount : BIT 〈add just a *thought* more salt to the stew〉 [Old English *thōht*]

thought·ful \'thȯt-fəl\ *adj* **1 a** : absorbed in thought : MEDITATIVE **b** : characterized by careful reasoned thinking **2 a** : having thought : HEEDFUL **b** : given to heedful anticipation of the needs of others — **thought·ful·ly** \-fə-lē\ *adv* — **thought·ful·ness** *n* □ SYN THOUGHTFUL, CONSIDERATE, SOLICITOUS mean mindful of others. THOUGHTFUL implies unselfish concern and ability to anticipate another's needs; CONSIDERATE im-

\ə\ abut		\ng\ sing	
\ər\ further		\ō\ bone	
\a\ mat		\ȯ\ saw	
\ā\ take		\ȯi\ coin	
\ä\ cot, cart		\th\ thin	
\au\ out		\th\ this	
\ch\ chin		\ü\ food	
\e\ pet		\u̇\ foot	
\ē\ easy		\y\ yet	
\g\ go		\yü\ few	
\i\ tip		\yu̇\ cure	
\ī\ life		\zh\ vision	
\j\ job			

plies kind concern for the feelings of others; SOLICI-
TOUS implies deep concern and suggests anxiety for
the welfare of another ⟨solicitous about our family⟩

thought·less \'thȯt-ləs\ adj **1 a** : insufficiently alert :
CARELESS **b** : RECKLESS 1, RASH **2** : devoid of thought :
INSENSATE **3** : lacking concern for others : INCONSIDER-
ATE — **thought·less·ly** adv — **thought·less·ness** n

thought–out \-'aȯt\ adj : produced or arrived at
through careful and thorough consideration

thou·sand \'thaȯ-znd, 'thaȯz-n̄\ n, pl **thousands** or
thousand 1 : ten times 100; also : a symbol representing this — see NUMBER table **2** : a very large or indefinitely great number [Old English thūsend] —
thousand adj

thou·sand–leg·ger \,thaȯz-n-'leg-ər, -'dleg-ər\ n : MIL-
LIPEDE

thousands digit n : the numeral (as 1 in 1456) occupying the thousands place in a number expressed in the
Arabic system of writing numbers

thousands place n : the place four to the left of the
decimal point in a number expressed in the Arabic
system of writing numbers

thou·sandth \'thaȯz-nth, -ntth\ n **1** : one of 1000
equal parts **2** : number 1000 in a countable series —
see NUMBER table — **thousandth** adj

thrall \'thrȯl\ n **1** : SLAVE 1; also : SERF **2** : the condition of a thrall : SLAVERY [Old English thrǣl, from Old
Norse thrǣll] — **thrall·dom** or **thral·dom** \-dəm\ n

¹**thrash** \'thrash\ vb **1** : THRESH 1 **2** : to beat soundly or
strike about with or as if with a stick or whip : FLOG;
also : DEFEAT **3** : to swing, beat, or stir about in the
manner of a rapidly moving flail ⟨thrash one's arms⟩
4 : to go over again and again ⟨thrash the matter over
in your mind⟩ [alteration of thresh]

²**thrash** n : an act of thrashing

¹**thrash·er** \'thrash-ər\ n : one that thrashes or threshes

²**thrasher** n : any of numerous long-tailed American
singing birds that resemble thrushes and include notable singers and mimics [probably alteration of thrush]

¹**thread** \'thred\ n **1** : a thin continuous filament ⟨the
spider's sticky thread⟩; esp : a textile cord made by
twisting together strands of spun fiber (as cotton, flax,
or silk) **2 a** : something (as a streak or slender stream)
suggesting a filament ⟨a thread of light⟩ **b** : SCREW
THREAD **3** : a line of reasoning or train of thought that
connects the parts in a sequence of ideas or events
⟨lost the thread of the story⟩ [Old English thrǣd] —
thread·like \-,līk\ adj

²**thread** vb **1** : to put a thread in working position in (as
a needle) **2 a** : to pass something through in the manner of a thread ⟨thread a pipe with wire⟩ **b** : to make
one's way through or between : wind a way ⟨threading
narrow alleys⟩ **3** : to put together on or as if on a
thread : STRING ⟨thread beads⟩ **4** : to interweave with
or as if with threads : INTERSPERSE ⟨dark hair threaded
with silver⟩ **5** : to form a screw thread on or in **6** : to
draw out into a thread when dripped from a spoon —
thread·er n

thread·bare \'thred-,baȧr, -,beȧr\ adj **1** : having the
nap worn off so that the thread shows **2** : having lost
freshness and interest from overuse SYN see TRITE —
thread·bare·ness n

thread·worm \-,wərm\ n : a slender nematode worm
(as a pinworm)

thready \'thred-ē\ adj **thread·i·er; -est 1** : consisting of
or bearing fibers or filaments ⟨a thready bark⟩ **2** : having the form or appearance of a thread **3** : lacking in
fullness, body, or vigor ⟨a thready voice⟩ ⟨a thready
pulse⟩ — **thread·i·ness** n

threat \'thret\ n **1** : an expression of an intent to do
harm or something wrong or foolish **2** : something
that threatens [Old English threat "coercion"]

threat·en \'thret-n\ vb **threat·ened; threat·en·ing**
\'thret-ning, -n-ing\ **1** : to utter threats : make threats
against ⟨threaten trespassers⟩ **2** : to give signs or warn-

ing of : PORTEND ⟨clouds threatening rain⟩ **3** : to be an
imminent danger to : MENACE — **threat·en·er** \'thret-
nər, -n-ər\ n — **threat·en·ing·ly** \'thret-ning-lē, -n-
ing-lē\ adv □ SYN THREATEN, MENACE mean to announce or forecast impending danger or evil. THREAT-
EN applies to a probable occurrence of evil or affliction; it may imply an impersonal warning of trouble,
punishment, or retribution ⟨the drought threatened
starvation⟩ MENACE implies alarming by a hostile or
fearful aspect or character ⟨nuclear arms that menace
humanity⟩

three \'thrē\ n **1** : one more than two; also : a symbol
representing this — see NUMBER table **2** : the third in a
set or series **3** : something having three units or members [Old English thrīe (masculine), thrēo (feminine
and neuter)] — **three** adj or pron

three–base hit n : TRIPLE 2

3–D \'thrē-'dē\ n : the three-dimensional form or a picture produced in it

three–deck·er \'thrē-'dek-ər\ n **1** : a ship having three
decks; also : a warship carrying guns on three decks
2 : something having three floors, tiers, or layers; esp :
a sandwich with three slices of bread and two layers of
filling

three–dimensional adj **1** : of, relating to, or having
three dimensions **2** : giving the illusion of depth or
varying distances — used of a pictorial representation
or a sound system

three·fold \'thrē-,fōld, -'fōld\ adj **1** : having three units
or members **2** : of or amounting to 300 percent —
threefold adv

three–gait·ed \-'gāt-əd\ adj : trained to use the walk,
trot, and canter ⟨three-gaited saddle horses⟩

three–hand·ed \-'han-dəd\ adj : played or to be played
by three players ⟨three-handed bridge⟩

Three Hours n : a service of devotion between noon and
three o'clock on Good Friday

three–legged \'thrē-'leg-əd, -'legd\ adj : having three
legs

three–legged race n : a race between pairs of competitors with each pair having their adjacent legs bound
together

three–mile limit n : an area of the sea extending three
miles out from shore included in the territorial jurisdiction of a state

three·pence \'threp-əns, 'thrip-, 'thrəp-, United States
also 'thrē-,pens\ n, pl **threepence** or **three·penc·es** :
the sum of three pence; also : a former British coin
worth threepence

three·pen·ny \'threp-nē, 'thrip-, 'thrəp-, -ə-nē, United
States also 'thrē-,pen-ē\ adj **1** : costing or worth
threepence **2** : of little value : POOR

three–point landing n : an airplane landing in which
the two main wheels of the landing gear and the tail
wheel or skid or the nose wheel touch the ground simultaneously

three–ring circus n **1** : a circus with simultaneous performances in three rings **2** : something confusing, engrossing, or entertaining

three R's n pl : the fundamentals taught in elementary
school; esp : reading, writing, and arithmetic [from
the phrase reading, 'riting, and 'rithmetic]

three·score \'thrē-'skōr, -'skȯr\ adj : SIXTY

three·some \'thrē-səm\ n : a group of three persons or
things

three–spined stickleback \,thrē-,spīnd-, -,spīn-\ n : a
stickleback of fresh and brackish waters that typically
has three dorsal spines

three–toed sloth : any of several sloths of the genus
Bradypus that have three claws on each foot and nine
vertebrae in the neck — compare TWO-TOED SLOTH

thren·o·dy \'thren-əd-ē\ n, pl **-dies** : a song of lamentation or sorrow : DIRGE [Greek thrēnōidia, from
thrēnos "dirge" + aeidein "to sing"]

thre·o·nine \'thrē-ə-,nēn\ *n* : an amino acid that is essential to normal nutrition [probably derived from *threose*, a sugar, probably derived from Greek *erythros* "red"]

thresh \'thrash, 'thresh\ *vb* **1 a** : to separate seed from (a harvested plant) mechanically **b** : to separate (grain) from straw **2** : THRASH ⟨*thresh* over a problem⟩ ⟨*threshed* about in bed⟩ [Old English *threscan*]

thresh·er \-ər\ *n* **1** : one that threshes; *esp* : THRESHING MACHINE **2** : a large common shark having a long curved upper lobe on its tail with which it is said to thresh the water to round up the fish on which it feeds — called also *thresher shark*

threshing machine *n* : a machine for separating grain or seeds from straw

thresh·old \'thresh-,hōld, -,ōld\ *n* **1** : the sill of a door **2 a** : GATE 1, DOOR, ENTRANCE **b** : a place of beginning : OUTSET ⟨at the *threshold* of an adventure⟩ **3** : the point or level at which a physiological or psychological effect begins to be produced ⟨*threshold* of pain⟩ [Old English *threscwald*] — **threshold** *adj*

threw *past of* THROW

thrice \'thrīs\ *adv* **1** : three times **2** : to a high degree [Middle English *thrie*, *thries*, from Old English *thriga*]

thrift \'thrift\ *n* **1** : careful management especially of money **2** : a tufted stemless herb having heads of pink or white flowers growing on mountains and seacoasts [Old Norse, "prosperity", from *thrīfask* "to thrive"]

thrift·less \'thrift-ləs\ *adj* : wasteful of money or resources — **thrift·less·ness** *n*

thrifty \'thrif-tē\ *adj* **thrift·i·er; -est** **1** : inclined to save : SAVING **2** : thriving through industry and frugality : PROSPEROUS **3** : thriving in health and growth ⟨*thrifty* cattle⟩ — **thrift·i·ly** \-tə-lē\ *adv* — **thrift·i·ness** \-tē-nəs\ *n*

thrill \'thril\ *vb* **1 a** : to experience or cause to experience a sudden intense feeling of excitement **b** : to have or cause to have a shivering or tingling sensation **2** : VIBRATE **3**, TREMBLE ⟨a voice *thrilling* with emotion⟩ [Old English *thyrlian* "to pierce", from *thyrel* "hole", from *thurh* "through"] — **thrill** *n*

thrill·er \-ər\ *n* : one that produces thrills; *esp* : a work of fiction or drama designed to hold the interest by the use of a high degree of action, intrigue, adventure, or suspense

thrips \'thrips\ *n, pl* **thrips** : any of an order (Thysanoptera) of small to tiny sucking insects most of which feed often destructively on plant juices [Latin, "worm that bores in wood", from Greek]

thrive \'thrīv\ *vi* **thrived** *or* **throve** \'thrōv\; **thriv·en** \'thriv-ən\ *or* **thrived; thriv·ing** \'thrī-ving\ **1** : to grow vigorously : do well **2** : to gain in wealth or possessions : PROSPER, FLOURISH [Old Norse *thrīfask*] — **thriv·er** \'thrī-vər\ *n* — **thriv·ing·ly** \-ving-lē\ *adv*

throat \'thrōt\ *n* **1** : the part of the neck in front of the spinal column; *also* : the passages through it to the stomach and lungs **2** : something resembling the throat especially in being an entrance, a passageway, a constriction, or a narrowed part [Old English *throte*] — **throat·ed** \-əd\ *adj*

throat·latch \-,lach\ *n* : a strap of a bridle or halter passing under a horse's throat

throaty \'thrōt-ē\ *adj* **throat·i·er; -est** : uttered or produced from or as if from low in the throat ⟨a *throaty* voice⟩ — **throat·i·ly** \'thrōt-l-ē\ *adv* — **throat·i·ness** \'thrōt-ē-nəs\ *n*

¹throb \'thräb\ *vi* **throbbed; throb·bing** **1** : to pulsate or pound with abnormal force or rapidity : PALPITATE **2** : to beat or vibrate rhythmically [Middle English *throbben*]

²throb *n* : a single beat of a pulsating movement or sensation

throe \'thrō\ *n* : a condition of struggle and anguish : PANG, SPASM — usually used in pl. ⟨death *throes*⟩

⟨*throes* of childbirth⟩ [Old English *thrawu*, *thrēa* "threat, pain"]

thromb- *or* **thrombo-** *combining form* : blood clot : clotting of blood ⟨*thromb*in⟩ ⟨*thrombo*plastic⟩ [Greek *thrombos* "clot"]

throm·bin \'thräm-bən\ *n* : a proteolytic enzyme that is formed from prothrombin and assists the clotting of blood by promoting conversion of fibrinogen to fibrin

throm·bo·cyte \-bə-,sīt\ *n* : BLOOD PLATELET; *also* : an invertebrate cell with similar function — **throm·bo·cyt·ic** \,thräm-bə-'sit-ik\ *adj*

throm·bo·em·bo·lism \,thräm-bō-'em-bə-,liz-əm\ *n* : a blocking of a blood vessel by an embolus that has broken away from a thrombus and become lodged elsewhere

throm·bo·plas·tin \-'plas-tən\ *n* : a complex protein substance found especially in blood platelets that functions in the clotting of blood — **throm·bo·plas·tic** \-'plas-tik\ *adj*

throm·bo·sis \thräm-'bō-səs\ *n, pl* **-bo·ses** \-'bō-,sēz\ : the formation or presence of a blood clot within a blood vessel during life — **throm·bot·ic** \-'bät-ik\ *adj*

throm·bus \'thräm-bəs\ *n, pl* **throm·bi** \-,bī, -,bē\ : a clot of blood formed within a blood vessel and remaining attached to its place of origin — compare EMBOLUS [New Latin, from Greek *thrombos* "clot"]

¹throne \'thrōn\ *n* **1 a** : the chair occupied by a high dignitary (as a king, queen, or bishop) during formal or ceremonial occasions **b** : the seat of a deity or devil **2** : royal power and dignity : SOVEREIGNTY [Old French *trone*, from Latin *thronus*, from Greek *thronos*]

²throne *vt* : to seat on a throne : ENTHRONE

throne room *n* : a formal audience room containing the throne of a sovereign

¹throng \'throng\ *n* **1 a** : a multitude of assembled persons **b** : a large number : CROWD **2** : a crowding together of many individuals [Old English *thrang*] SYN see MULTITUDE

²throng *vb* **thronged; throng·ing** \'throng-ing\ **1** : to crowd upon or into ⟨shoppers *thronged* the store⟩ **2** : to crowd together in great numbers

thros·tle \'thräs-əl\ *n* : ¹THRUSH; *esp* : SONG THRUSH [Old English]

¹throt·tle \'thrät-l\ *vb* **throt·tled; throt·tling** \'thrät-ling, -l-ing\ **1 a** : to impede or check the breathing of : CHOKE, STRANGLE **b** : to prevent or check expression or activity of : SUPPRESS **2 a** : to obstruct the flow of (as fuel to an engine) by closing a valve **b** : to reduce the speed of (an engine) by such means [Middle English *throtlen*, from *throte* "throat"] — **throt·tler** \'thrät-lər, -l-ər\ *n*

²throttle *n* : a valve controlling the volume of steam or of fuel (as gasoline) delivered to the cylinders of an engine; *also* : a lever controlling this valve [perhaps from English dialect *thropple* "throat"]

throt·tle·hold \'thrät-l-,hōld\ *n* : a vicious, strangling, or repressive control

¹through *also* **thru** \'thrü, 'thrü\ *prep* **1 a** : in at one side and out at the opposite side of ⟨drove *through* the town⟩ **b** : by way of ⟨left *through* the window⟩ **c** : in the midst of : AMONG ⟨highway *through* the trees⟩ **2 a** : by means of ⟨succeeded *through* perseverance⟩ **b** : because of ⟨failed *through* ignorance⟩ **3** : over the whole surface or extent of ⟨all *through* the country⟩ **4 a** : from the beginning to the end of : DURING ⟨*through* the summer⟩ **b** : to and including ⟨Monday *through* Friday⟩ [Old English *thurh, thuruh*] SYN see BY

²through *also* **thru** \'thrü\ *adv* **1 a** : from one end or side to the other ⟨the shield was pierced *through*⟩ **b** : over the whole distance ⟨shipped *through* to Boston⟩ **2 a** : from beginning to end ⟨read the book *through* at one sitting⟩ **b** : to completion, conclusion, or accomplishment ⟨see it *through*⟩ **3** : to the core : COMPLETELY ⟨was wet *through*⟩ **4** : into the open : OUT ⟨break *through*⟩

thresher 2

\ə\ abut \ng\ sing
\ər\ further \ō\ bone
\a\ mat \o\ saw
\ā\ take \oi\ coin
\ä\ cot, cart \th\ thin
\au\ out \th\ this
\ch\ chin \ü\ food
\e\ pet \u\ foot
\ē\ easy \y\ yet
\g\ go \yü\ few
\i\ tip \yu\ cure
\ī\ life \zh\ vision
\j\ job

³through *also* **thru** \'thrü\ *adj* **1 a** : extending from one surface to another ⟨a *through* mortise⟩ **b** (1) : admitting free or continuous passage : DIRECT ⟨a *through* street⟩ (2) : affording right of way **2 a** (1) : going from point of origin to destination without change or reshipment ⟨a *through* train⟩ (2) : of or relating to such movement ⟨a *through* ticket⟩ **b** : initiated at and destined for points outside a local zone ⟨*through* traffic⟩ **3 a** : arrived at completion or accomplishment ⟨*through* with the job⟩ **b** : having no further strength or resources; *also* : no longer needed or wanted ⟨you're *through*—that was your last chance⟩

¹through·out \thrü-'aút\ *adv* **1** : in or to every part ⟨of one color *throughout*⟩ **2** : during the whole time or action : from beginning to end ⟨remained loyal *throughout*⟩

²throughout *prep* **1** : in or to every part of ⟨*throughout* the house⟩ **2** : during the whole time of ⟨*throughout* the evening⟩

through·way *variant of* THRUWAY

throve *past of* THRIVE

¹throw \'thrō\ *vb* **threw** \'thrü\; **thrown** \'thrōn\; **throw·ing** **1** : to propel through the air by a forward motion of the hand and arm **2** : to propel through the air in any way **3** : to cause to fall ⟨the wrestler *threw* the opponent⟩ ⟨a horse shied and *threw* the rider⟩ **4 a** : to put suddenly in a certain condition or position ⟨*thrown* out of work by automation⟩ **b** : to form or shape on a potter's wheel **5** : to put on or take off hastily ⟨*throw* on a coat⟩ **6** : to twist two or more fibers of (as silk) to form one thread **7** : to make a cast of or at dice **8** : SHED ⟨a snake *throws* its skin⟩ **9** : to move quickly ⟨*throw* in reinforcements⟩ **10** : to lose (a game or contest) intentionally ⟨was paid to *throw* the fight⟩ **11** : to move (as a switch or a lever) to an open or closed position **12** : to act as host for : put on ⟨*throw* a party⟩ [Old English *thrāwan* "to cause to twist or turn"] — **throw·er** \'thrō-ər, 'thrōr\ *n* □ SYN FLING, HURL, TOSS: THROW is interchangeable with the other terms but basically implies a movement of the arm propelling an object through the air; FLING stresses less control and more force in throwing and may suggest an emotional basis for the action ⟨madly rushed to the window and *flung* it open⟩ HURL implies power as in throwing a massive weight ⟨ocean waves *hurling* their weight upon the shore⟩ TOSS suggests a light or aimless upward throwing ⟨leaves *tossed* by the wind⟩

²throw *n* **1 a** : an act of throwing, hurling, or flinging **b** (1) : one's turn to throw something (as dice) (2) : the number thrown with a cast of dice **c** : a method of throwing an opponent in wrestling or judo **2** : the distance a missile is or may be thrown **3 a** : a light coverlet **b** : a woman's scarf or light wrap

throw·away \'thrō-ə-ˌwā\ *n* : a handbill or circular distributed free

throw away \ˌthrō-ə-'wā\ *vt* **1** : to get rid of : DISCARD **2** : SQUANDER, WASTE

throw·back \'thrō-ˌbak\ *n* : reversion to an earlier type or phase; *also* : an instance or product of such reversion

throw back \thrō-'bak, 'thrō-\ *vt* **1** : to cause to rely : make dependent **2** : REFLECT 1

throw in *vt* : to add as a supplement or bonus

throw off *vt* **1 a** : to free oneself from **b** : to cast off often in a hurried or vigorous manner **c** : DIVERT 1 ⟨was *thrown off* the scent⟩ **2** : to give up : EMIT **3** : to produce in an offhand manner **4** : to cause to make a mistake : MISLEAD ⟨was *thrown off* in my calculations⟩

throw out *vt* **1 a** : to remove from a place, office, or employment usually in a sudden or unexpected manner **b** : to reject or get rid of as worthless or unnecessary **2** : to give expression to : UTTER ⟨*threw out* some thoughts for consideration⟩ **3** : to give forth from within : EMIT ⟨the flowers *threw out* a nice fragrance⟩ **4** : to

cause to project : EXTEND **5** : to make a throw that enables a teammate in baseball to put out (a base runner) **6** : DISENGAGE ⟨*throw out* the clutch⟩

throw over *vt* : to forsake despite bonds of attachment or duty

throw rug *n* : SCATTER RUG

throw up *vb* **1** : to raise quickly ⟨*throw up* the window⟩ **2** : to give up : QUIT ⟨just want to *throw* the whole thing *up*⟩ **3** : to build hurriedly **4** : VOMIT 1 **5** : to mention repeatedly by way of reproach ⟨*throw up* a past mistake⟩

thru *variant of* THROUGH

¹thrum \'thrəm\ *vb* **thrummed; thrum·ming** **1** : to play or pluck a stringed instrument idly : STRUM **2** : to sound with a monotonous hum : recite tiresomely or monotonously [imitative]

²thrum *n* : the monotonous sound of thrumming

¹thrush \'thrəsh\ *n* : any of a large family of small or medium-sized birds that are mostly of a plain color often with spotted underparts and include many excellent singers [Old English *thrysce*]

²thrush *n* : a fungal disease especially of infants marked by white patches in the mouth [probably of Scandinavian origin]

¹thrust \'thrəst\ *vb* **thrust; thrust·ing** **1** : to push or drive with force : SHOVE **2** : to cause to enter or pierce something by or as if by pushing **3** : to push forth : EXTEND ⟨*thrust* out roots⟩ **4** : INTERJECT, INTERPOLATE **5** : to press or force the acceptance of upon someone **6** : to make a thrust, stab, or lunge with or as if with a pointed weapon [Old Norse *thrȳsta*] SYN see PUSH

²thrust *n* **1 a** : a push or lunge with a pointed weapon **b** : a verbal attack **c** : a military assault **2 a** : a strong continued pressure **b** : the sideways pressure of one part of a structure against another part (as of an arch against an abutment) **c** : the force produced by a propeller or jet or rocket engine that drives an aircraft or rocket forward **3 a** : a forward or upward push **b** : a movement in a specified direction

thrust·er \'thrəs-tər\ *n* : one that thrusts; *esp* : an engine that produces thrust by discharging a jet of fluid or a stream of particles

thru·way *or* **through·way** \'thrü-ˌwā\ *n* : EXPRESSWAY

¹thud \'thəd\ *vi* **thud·ded; thud·ding** : to move or strike so as to make a thud [probably from Old English *thyddan* "to thrust"]

²thud *n* **1** : ⁵BLOW 1 **2** : a dull sound : THUMP

thug \'thəg\ *n* : a brutal ruffian or assassin : GANGSTER, KILLER [Hindi *thag*] — **thug·gery** \'thəg-ə-rē\ *n* □ ORIGIN *Thug* was used in English in the early 19th century as a transliteration of Hindi *thag*, which literally means "thief", but which was applied specifically to the members of a group of professional robbers and murderers active in India from the 16th to the 19th century who strangled their victims. The word caught on in English, especially in the United States, and is now used to label any brutal ruffian, gangster, or killer.

Thu·le \'thü-lē, 'thyü-\ *n* : the northernmost part of the habitable ancient world [Latin, from Greek *Thoulē*]

thu·li·um \'thü-lē-əm, 'thyü-\ *n* : a rare metallic chemical element — see ELEMENT table [New Latin, from Latin *Thule* "Thule"]

¹thumb \'thəm\ *n* **1** : the short thick first digit of the human hand opposable to the other fingers; *also* : the corresponding digit in lower animals **2** : the part of a glove or mitten that covers the thumb [Old English *thūma*]

²thumb *vt* **1 a** : to leaf through with the thumb : TURN ⟨*thumb* the pages of a book⟩ **b** : to soil or wear by or as if by repeated thumbing ⟨a well-*thumbed* book⟩ **2** : to request or obtain (a ride) in a passing automobile by signaling with the thumb

¹thumb·nail \'thəm-ˌnāl, -'nāl\ *n* : the nail of the thumb

²thumb·nail \,thəm-,nāl\ *adj* : CONCISE, BRIEF ⟨a *thumbnail* sketch⟩

thumb·print \'thəm-,print\ *n* : a print or impression made by the thumb

thumb·screw \'thəm-,skrü\ *n* **1** : a screw having a flat=sided or knurled head so that it may be turned by the thumb and forefinger **2** : an instrument of torture for squeezing the thumb by a screw

thumb·tack \-,tak\ *n* : a tack with a broad flat head for pressing into a board or wall with the thumb

¹thump \'thəmp\ *vb* **1** : to strike or beat with or as if with something thick or heavy so as to cause a dull sound **2** : to beat heavily : POUND ⟨my heart *thumped* at the sight⟩ **3** : to inflict or emit a thump [imitative]

²thump *n* : a blow or knock with or as if with something blunt or heavy; *also* : the sound made by such a blow

thump·ing *adj* : impressively large, great, or excellent ⟨a *thumping* majority⟩

¹thun·der \'thən-dər\ *n* **1 a** : the loud sound that follows a flash of lightning and is caused by sudden expansion of the air in the path of the electrical discharge **b** *archaic* : a discharge of lightning **2** : a loud utterance or threat **3** : BANG, RUMBLE ⟨the *thunder* of guns⟩ [Old English *thunor*]

²thunder *vb* **thun·dered; thun·der·ing** \-də-ring, -dring\ **1** : to produce thunder ⟨it *thundered*⟩ **2** : to produce a sound like thunder ⟨horses *thundered* down the road⟩ **3** : ROAR ⟨the crowd *thundered* its approval⟩ — **thun·der·er** \-dər-ər\ *n*

thun·der·bolt \'thən-dər-,bōlt\ *n* **1** : a single discharge of lightning with the accompanying thunder **2 a** : a person or thing likened to lightning in suddenness, effectiveness, or destructive power **b** : a verbal lambasting

thun·der·clap \-,klap\ *n* **1** : a crash of thunder **2** : something sharp, loud, or sudden like a clap of thunder

thun·der·cloud \-,klaud\ *n* : a dark storm cloud that produces lightning and thunder

thun·der·head \-,hed\ *n* : a rounded mass of cumulus cloud often appearing before a thunderstorm

thun·der·ing *adj* : awesomely great, intense, or unusual ⟨a *thundering* success⟩ — **thun·der·ing·ly** \-də-ring-lē, -dring-\ *adv*

thunder lizard *n* : BRONTOSAURUS

thun·der·ous \'thən-də-rəs, -drəs\ *adj* **1** : full of or marked by thunder ⟨*thunderous* clouds⟩ **2** : as loud as thunder : very loud ⟨*thunderous* applause⟩ — **thun·der·ous·ly** *adv*

thun·der·show·er \'thən-dər-,shau-ər, -,shaur\ *n* : a shower accompanied by lightning and thunder

thun·der·storm \-,stórm\ *n* : a storm accompanied by lightning and thunder

thun·der·struck \-,strək\ *adj* : stunned or astonished as if struck by a thunderbolt ⟨*thunderstruck* at the news⟩

thu·ri·ble \'thùr-ə-bəl, 'thyùr-, 'thər-\ *n* : CENSER [Middle French, from Latin *thuribulum*, from *thur-, thus* "incense", from Greek *thyos*, from *thyein* "to sacrifice"]

thu·ri·fer \-ə-fər\ *n* : one who carries a censer [Latin, "incense-bearing", from *thur-, thus* "incense" + *ferre* "to carry"]

Thurs·day \'thərz-dē\ *n* : the 5th day of the week [Old English *thursdæg*, from Old Norse *thōrsdagr*, literally, "day of Thor"]

thus \'thəs\ *adv* **1** : in this or that manner or way **2** : to this degree or extent : so ⟨a mild winter *thus* far⟩ **3** : because of this or that : HENCE **4** : as an example [Old English]

thwack \'thwak\ *vt* : to strike with or as if with something flat or heavy : WHACK [imitative] — **thwack** *n*

¹thwart \'thwórt, *nautical often* 'thórt\ *adv* : ATHWART [Old Norse *thvert*, from *thverr* "transverse, oblique"]

²thwart *adj* : situated or placed across something else : TRANSVERSE, OBLIQUE

³thwart *vt* **1** : OPPOSE **2**, BAFFLE **2** : to defeat the hopes or aspirations of SYN see FRUSTRATE — **thwart·er** *n*

⁴thwart *n* : a rower's seat extending across a boat

thwart·wise \-,wīz\ *adv or adj* : CROSSWISE 2

thy \thī, ,thī\ *adj, archaic* : of or relating to thee or thyself especially as possessor, agent, or object of an action — used especially in ecclesiastical or literary language [Old English *thīn*]

thyme \'tīm *also* 'thīm\ *n* : any of a genus of mints with small pungent aromatic leaves; *esp* : one grown for use in seasoning and formerly in medicine [Middle French *thym*, from Latin *thymum*, from Greek *thymon*, from *thyein* "to make a burnt offering, sacrifice"]

thy·mine \'thī-,mēn\ *n* : a pyrimidine base $C_5H_6N_2O_2$ that is one of the four bases coding genetic information in the polynucleotide chain of DNA — compare ADENINE, CYTOSINE, GUANINE [German *thymin*, from New Latin *thymus* "thymus"]

thy·mol \'thī-,mòl, -,mōl\ *n* : a crystalline compound $C_{10}H_{14}O$ of aromatic odor and antiseptic properties used as a fungicide and preservative [*thyme*]

thy·mus \'thī-məs\ *n, pl* **thy·mus·es** *or* **thy·mi** \-,mī\ : a largely lymphoid glandular structure that is present in most young vertebrates typically at the base of the neck, that before and for a time after birth has very important effects on the production, development, and activity of the white blood cells which attack and destroy or make inactive cells and substances foreign to the body, and that becomes less active and gradually shrinks or disappears with age [New Latin, from Greek *thymos*] — **thy·mic** \-mik\ *adj*

thymy *or* **thym·ey** \'tī-mē *also* 'thī-\ *adj* : abounding in or fragrant with thyme

thy·ro·cal·ci·to·nin \,thī-rō-,kal-sə-'tō-nən\ *n* : a protein hormone from the thyroid gland that tends to lower the level of calcium in the blood plasma — called also *calcitonin*

¹thy·roid \'thī-,róid\ *adj* **1** : of, relating to, or being a large endocrine gland of most vertebrates that lies at the base of the neck and produces an iodine-containing hormone which affects especially growth, development, and metabolic rate **2** : of, relating to, or being the chief cartilage of the larynx [Greek *thyreoeidēs* "shield-shaped, thyroid", from *thyreos* "oblong shield", from *thyra* "door"]

²thyroid *n* **1** : a thyroid gland or cartilage; *also* : a part (as an artery or nerve) associated with either of these **2** : a preparation of mammalian thyroid gland used medicinally

thyroid–stimulating hormone *n* : a hormone secreted by the pituitary gland that regulates the formation and secretion of thyroid hormone

thy·ro·tro·pic hormone \,thī-rə-,trō-pik-, -,träp-ik-\ *n* : THYROID-STIMULATING HORMONE

thy·rox·ine *or* **thy·rox·in** \thī-'räk-,sēn, -sən\ *n* : the hormone of the thyroid gland or a preparation or derivative of this used to treat thyroid disorders

thy·self \thī-'self\ *pron, archaic* : YOURSELF — used especially in ecclesiastical or literary language

ti \'tē\ *n* : the 7th note of the diatonic scale [alteration of *si*]

ti·ara \tē-'ar-ə, -'er-, -'är-\ *n* **1** : a 3-tiered crown worn by the pope **2** : a decorative band or semicircular ornament for the head for formal wear by women [Latin, "royal Persian headdress", from Greek]

Ti·bet·an \tə-'bet-n\ *n* **1** : a member of the Mongoloid native race of Tibet modified in the west and south by intermixture with Indian peoples and in the east with Chinese **2** : the language of the Tibetan people — **Tibetan** *adj*

tib·ia \'tib-ē-ə\ *n, pl* **-i·ae** \-ē-,ē, -ē-,ī\ *also* **-i·as 1 a** : the inner and usually larger of the two bones of the vertebrate hind limb between the knee and ankle — called also *shinbone* **b** : the fourth joint of the leg of

tiara 2

\ə\ abut	\ng\ sing
\ər\ further	\ō\ bone
\a\ mat	\ò\ saw
\ā\ take	\òi\ coin
\ä\ cot, cart	\th\ thin
\au\ out	\th\ this
\ch\ chin	\ü\ food
\e\ pet	\ù\ foot
\ē\ easy	\y\ yet
\g\ go	\yü\ few
\i\ tip	\yù\ cure
\ī\ life	\zh\ vision
\j\ job	

an insect between the femur and tarsus **2** : an ancient flute originally fashioned from an animal's leg bone [Latin] — **tib·i·al** \-ē-əl\ *adj*

tib·io·fib·u·la \ˌtib-ē-ō-ˈfib-yə-lə\ *n* : a single bone that replaces the tibia and fibula in a frog or toad

tic \ˈtik\ *n* : local and habitual twitching of particular muscles especially of the face [French]

¹tick \ˈtik\ *n* : any of numerous bloodsucking arachnids that are larger than the related mites, attach themselves to warm-blooded vertebrates to feed, and include important vectors of infectious diseases [Middle English *tyke*]

²tick *n* **1** : a light rhythmic audible tap or beat (as of a clock); *also* : a series of such ticks **2** : a small spot or mark; *esp* : one used to direct attention to something, to check an item on a list, or to represent a point on a scale [Middle English *tek*]

³tick *vb* **1 a** : to make the sound of a tick or a series of ticks **b** : to mark, count, or announce by or as if by ticking beats ⟨a meter *ticking* off the cab fare⟩ **2** : to operate as or in the manner of a functioning mechanism : RUN ⟨tried to understand what made them *tick*⟩ **3** : to mark with a written tick : CHECK ⟨*ticking* off names on a list⟩

⁴tick *n* **1** : the fabric case of a mattress, pillow, or bolster; *also* : a mattress consisting of a tick and its filling **2** : TICKING [Middle English *tike*, probably derived from Latin *theca* "cover", from Greek *thēkē* "case"]

⁵tick *n* : CREDIT, TRUST; *also* : a credit account ⟨bought on *tick*⟩ [short for *ticket*]

ticked \ˈtikt\ *adj* **1** : marked with small spots **2** : banded with two or more colors ⟨*ticked* hairs in the coat of a rabbit⟩

tick·er \ˈtik-ər\ *n* : something that ticks or produces a ticking sound: as **a** : WATCH 6 **b** : a telegraphic receiving instrument that automatically prints off stock quotations or news on a paper ribbon **c** *slang* : HEART 1a

ticker tape *n* : the paper ribbon on which a telegraphic ticker prints off its information

¹tick·et \ˈtik-ət\ *n* **1 a** : a document that serves as a certificate, license, or permit; *esp* : a mariner's or airman's certificate **b** : TAG, LABEL ⟨price *ticket*⟩ **2** : a summons or warning issued to a traffic offender **3** : a document or token showing that a fare or admission fee has been paid **4** : a list of candidates for nomination or election **5** : a slip or card recording a transaction or undertaking or giving instructions ⟨sales *ticket*⟩ ⟨a driver's trip *ticket*⟩ ⟨repair *ticket*⟩ [obsolete French *etiquet* (now *étiquette*) "label", from Middle French *estiquet*, from *estiquier* "to attach", from Dutch *steken* "to stick"]

²ticket *vt* **1** : to attach a ticket to : LABEL; *also* : DESIGNATE **2** : to serve with a traffic ticket

ticket agent *n* **1** : one who acts as an agent of a transportation company to sell tickets for travel **2** : one who sells theater and entertainment tickets — **ticket agency** *n*

ticket–of–leave *n, pl* **tickets–of–leave** : a license or permit formerly given in the United Kingdom and the British Commonwealth to a convict to go free subject to certain conditions

tick·ing \ˈtik-ing\ *n* : a strong fabric used in upholstering and as a covering for mattresses and pillows

¹tick·le \ˈtik-əl\ *vb* **tick·led; tick·ling** \ˈtik-ling, -ə-ling\ **1** : to have a tingling or prickling sensation ⟨my back *tickles*⟩ **2 a** : to excite or stir up agreeably : PLEASE ⟨food that *tickles* the palate⟩ **b** : to provoke to laughter or merriment : AMUSE **3** : to touch a body part lightly so as to excite the surface nerves and cause uneasiness, laughter, or spasmodic movements [Middle English *tikelen*]

²tickle *n* **1** : something that tickles **2** : a tickling sensation **3** : the act of tickling

tick·ler \ˈtik-lər, -ə-lər\ *n* **1** : one that tickles **2** : a file arranged to bring matters to timely attention

tick·lish \ˈtik-lish, -ə-lish\ *adj* **1** : sensitive to tickling **2 a** : TOUCHY, OVERSENSITIVE ⟨*ticklish* about being bald⟩ **b** : easily overturned : UNSTABLE ⟨a canoe is *ticklish* to handle⟩ **3** : requiring delicate handling : CRITICAL ⟨a *ticklish* subject⟩ ⟨a *ticklish* situation⟩ — **tick·lish·ly** *adv* — **tick·lish·ness** *n*

tick·tack·toe *also* **tic–tac–toe** \ˌtik-ˌtak-ˈtō\ *or* **tit–tat–toe** \ˌti-ˌtat-ˈtō, ˌti-ˌta-ˈtō\ *n* : a game in which two players alternately put Xs and Os in compartments of a figure formed by two vertical lines crossing two horizontal lines with each player trying to get a row of three Xs or three Os before the opponent does [*tic-tac-toe*, a former game in which players with eyes shut brought down a pencil on a slate marked with numbers and scored the number hit]

tick·tock \ˈtik-ˌtäk, -ˌtäk\ *n* : the ticking sound of a large clock [imitative]

tick trefoil *n* : any of various plants of the pea family having leaves with three leaflets and rough sticky fruits [¹*tick*]

tid·al \ˈtīd-l\ *adj* **1** : of or relating to tides : periodically rising and falling or flowing and ebbing ⟨*tidal* waters⟩ **2** : dependent (as to the time of arrival or departure) on the state of the tide ⟨a *tidal* steamer⟩ — **tid·al·ly** \-l-ē\ *adv*

tidal wave *n* **1 a** : an unusually high sea wave that sometimes follows an earthquake **b** : an unusual rise of water alongshore due to strong winds **2** : something overwhelming (as a sweeping majority vote or an irresistible impulse)

tid·bit \ˈtid-ˌbit\ *or* **tit·bit** \ˈtit-ˌbit\ *n* **1** : a choice morsel of food **2** : a choice or pleasing bit (as of news) [perhaps from *tit-* (as in *titmouse*) + *bit*]

tid·dle·dy·winks *or* **tid·dly·winks** \ˈtid-l-ē-ˌwings, ˈtid-l-dē-, ˈtid-lē-, -ˌwingks\ *n* : a game in which players try to snap small disks from a flat surface into a small container [probably from English dialect *tiddly* "little"]

¹tide \ˈtīd\ *n* **1 a** *obsolete* : a space of time : PERIOD **b** : a fit or opportune time : OPPORTUNITY **c** : an ecclesiastical anniversary or festival; *also* : its season **2 a** (1) : the alternate rising and falling of the surface of the ocean that occurs twice a day and is caused by the gravitational attraction of the sun and moon occurring unequally on different parts of the earth (2) : a less marked rising and falling of an inland body of water **b** : FLOOD TIDE 1 **3** : something that fluctuates like the tides of the sea : VICISSITUDE ⟨the *tides* of fortune⟩ **4** : a flowing stream : CURRENT [Old English *tīd* "time"]

²tide *vb* **1** : to drift or cause to drift with the tide **2** : to enable to surmount or endure a difficulty ⟨the money *tided* us over⟩

tide·land \-ˌland, -lənd\ *n* **1** : land overflowed during flood tide **2** : land underlying the ocean beyond the low-water limit of the tide but within a nation's territorial waters — often used in pl.

tide·mark \ˈtīd-ˌmärk\ *n* **1 a** : a high-water or sometimes low-water mark left by tidal water or a flood **b** : a mark placed to indicate this point **2** : the point to which something has risen or below which it has fallen

tide pool *n* : a pool left (as in a rock basin) by an ebbing tide

tide·wa·ter \ˈtīd-ˌwȯt-ər, -ˌwät-\ *n* **1** : water overflowing land at flood tide **2** : low-lying coastal land

tid·ing \ˈtīd-ing\ *n* : a piece of news — usually used in pl. ⟨good *tidings*⟩ [Old English *tīdung*, from *tīdan* "to happen"]

¹ti·dy \ˈtīd-ē\ *adj* **ti·di·er; -est** **1** : properly filled out : PLUMP **2** : ADEQUATE, SATISFACTORY ⟨a *tidy* arrangement⟩ **3 a** : neat and orderly in appearance or habits : well ordered and cared for **b** : METHODICAL, PRECISE ⟨a *tidy* mind⟩ **4** : LARGE, SUBSTANTIAL ⟨a *tidy* sum⟩ [Middle English, "timely, in good condition", from *tide* "time"] — **ti·di·ly** \ˈtīd-l-ē\ *adv* — **ti·di·ness** \ˈtīd-ē-nəs\ *n*

²tidy *vb* **ti·died; ti·dy·ing** 1 : to put in order ⟨*tidy* a room⟩ 2 : to make things tidy ⟨*tidying* up after supper⟩

³tidy *n, pl* **tidies** : a piece of fancywork used to protect the back, arms, or headrest of a chair or sofa from wear or soiling

¹tie \'tī\ *n* 1 **a** : a line, ribbon, or cord used for fastening, uniting, or drawing something closed; *esp* : SHOELACE **b** (1) : a structural element (as a beam) holding two pieces together : a tension member in a construction (2) : one of the transverse supports to which railroad rails are fastened 2 : something that serves as a connecting link : as **a** : a moral or legal obligation to someone or something **b** : a bond of kinship or affection 3 : a curved line that joins two musical notes indicating the same pitch used to denote a single tone sustained through the time value of the two 4 **a** : an equality in number (as of votes or scores) **b** : equality in a contest; *also* : a contest that ends in a draw 5 : a method or style of tying or knotting 6 : something that is knotted or is to be knotted when worn: as **a** : NECKTIE **b** : a low laced shoe : OXFORD [Old English *tēag*]

²tie *vb* **tied; ty·ing** \'tī-ing\ *or* **tie·ing** 1 **a** : to fasten, attach, or close by means of a tie **b** : to form a knot or bow in ⟨*tie* your scarf⟩ **c** : to make by tying separate parts together ⟨*tied* a wreath⟩ ⟨*tie* a fishing fly⟩ 2 **a** : to unite in marriage **b** : to unite (musical notes) by a tie 3 : to restrain or constrain the acts of 4 **a** (1) : to make or have an equal score with in a contest (2) : to cause to be a tie ⟨*tied* the score⟩ **b** : to come up with something equal to : EQUAL 5 : to make a tie: as **a** : to make a bond or connection **b** : to make the same score **c** : to be connected : fit in

tie–in \'tī-,in\ *n* : something that ties in, relates, or connects

tie in \tī-'in, 'tī-\ *vb* : to connect mechanically or logically in a system ⟨the pipeline *ties in* here⟩

tie·pin \-,pin\ *n* : an ornamental pin used to hold the ends of a necktie in place

¹tier \'tiər\ *n* : a row, rank, or layer of articles; *esp* : one of two or more rows arranged one above another [Middle French *tire* "rank", of Germanic origin]

²tier *vb* 1 : to place or arrange in tiers 2 : to rise in tiers

³ti·er \'tī-ər, 'tīr\ *n* : one that ties

tierce \'tiərs\ *often cap, variant of* TERCE

tier·cel \'tiər-səl\ *n* : a male hawk — compare FALCON [Middle French *tercel*, derived from Latin *tertius* "third"]

tiered \'tiərd\ *adj* : having or arranged in tiers, rows, or layers

tie–up \'tī-,əp\ *n* 1 : a suspension of traffic or business (as by a strike or lockout or a mechanical breakdown) 2 : CONNECTION 4b, ASSOCIATION ⟨looking for a helpful financial *tie-up*⟩

tie up \tī-'əp, 'tī-\ *vt* 1 : to attach, fasten, or bind securely; *also* : to wrap up and fasten 2 **a** : to use in such a manner as to make unavailable for other purposes **b** : to restrain from operation or progress ⟨traffic was *tied up* for miles⟩ 3 : DOCK ⟨the ferry *ties up* at the south slip⟩ 4 : to place in or assume a relationship with something else ⟨this *ties up* with what was said before⟩

¹tiff \'tif\ *n* : a petty quarrel [origin unknown]

²tiff *vi* : to have a minor quarrel

tif·fin \'tif-ən\ *n* : a midday meal : LUNCHEON [probably derived from obsolete English *tiff* "to eat between meals"]

ti·ger \'tī-gər\ *n, pl* **tigers** *also* **tiger** 1 **a** : a large Asian flesh-eating mammal of the cat family having a tawny coat transversely striped with black **b** : any of several large wildcats (as the jaguar or cougar) **c** : TIGER CAT 2 2 : a fierce and bloodthirsty person or quality [Old English *tiger* and Old French *tigre*, both from Latin *tigris*, from Greek, of Iranian origin] — **ti·ger·like** \-gər-,līk\ *adj*

tiger beetle *n* : any of numerous active flesh-eating beetles having larvae that tunnel in the soil

tiger cat *n* 1 : any of various wildcats (as the serval, ocelot, or margay) of moderate size and variegated coloration 2 : a striped or sometimes blotched tabby cat

ti·ger·ish \'tī-gə-rish, -grish\ *adj* : suggesting a tiger (as in grace, fierceness, or vigor) — **ti·ger·ish·ly** *adv* — **ti·ger·ish·ness** *n*

tiger lily *n* : a common Asian lily widely grown for its nodding orange-colored flowers densely spotted with black

tiger moth *n* : any of a family of stout-bodied moths usually with broad striped or spotted wings

tiger salamander *n* : a common black or brown yellow-blotched North American salamander

tiger shark *n* : a large brown or gray shark of warm seas that is often a man-eater

¹tight \'tīt\ *adj* 1 : so close in structure as not to permit passage of a fluid or light ⟨a *tight* roof⟩ 2 **a** : fixed very firmly in place ⟨loosen a *tight* jar cover⟩ **b** : not slack or loose : TAUT ⟨a *tight* knot⟩ **c** : fitting too closely for comfort or free movement 3 : neat and orderly in arrangement or design : SNUG 4 : difficult to get through or out of : TRYING ⟨in a *tight* situation⟩ 5 **a** : firm in control ⟨kept a *tight* hand on the business⟩ **b** : STINGY 1, MISERLY 6 : packed or compressed to the limit : entirely full 7 : DRUNK 1 8 : low in supply : SCARCE ⟨*tight* loan money⟩ 9 : sound and free from cracks or breaks ⟨*tight* lumber⟩ [of Scandinavian origin] — **tight·ly** *adv* — **tight·ness** *n* □ SYN TIGHT, TAUT, TENSE mean drawn or stretched to the limit. TIGHT may imply a binding, constricting, or jamming encirclement, or the removal of the smallest opening or looseness; TAUT suggests the pulling of a rope or fabric until there is no give or slack; TENSE often adds to TAUT the suggestion of strain impairing normal functioning ⟨*tense* muscles⟩

²tight *adv* 1 : in a tight manner ⟨the door was shut *tight*⟩ 2 : SOUND ⟨sleep *tight*⟩

tight·en \'tīt-n\ *vb* **tight·ened; tight·en·ing** \'tīt-ning, -n-ing\ : to make or become tight or tighter — **tight·en·er** \'tīt-nər, -n-ər\ *n*

tight end *n* : an offensive football end who lines up within two yards of the tackle

tight–fist·ed \'tīt-'fis-təd\ *adj* : MISERLY, STINGY

tight–lipped \-'lipt\ *adj* 1 : having the lips closed tight (as in determination) 2 : reluctant to speak

tight·rope \'tīt-,rōp\ *n* : a rope or wire stretched taut for acrobats to perform on

tights \'tīts\ *n pl* : a skintight garment covering the body from the neck down or from the waist down

tight·wad \'tīt-,wäd\ *n* : a stingy person

tight·wire \-,wīr\ *n* : a tightrope made of wire

ti·gress \'tī-grəs\ *n* : a female tiger

tike *variant of* TYKE

til·de \'til-də\ *n* : a mark ˜ placed especially over the letter (as in Spanish *señor* "sir") to denote the sound \nʸ\ or over vowels (as in Portuguese *profissão* "profession") to indicate nasality [Spanish, from Medieval Latin *titulus* "tittle"]

¹tile \'tīl\ *n* 1 *pl* **tiles** *or* **tile a** : a flat or curved piece of fired clay, stone, or concrete used especially for roofs, floors, or walls **b** : a hollow or concave piece of fired clay or concrete used for a drain 2 : TILING 2b 3 : a thin piece of resilient material (as linoleum or rubber) for covering floors or walls [Old English *tigele*, from Latin *tegula*]

²tile *vt* 1 : to cover with tiles 2 : to install drainage tile in — **til·er** *n*

til·ing \'tī-ling\ *n* 1 : the act of one who tiles 2 **a** : TILES **b** : a surface of tiles

¹till \tl, təl, til, ,til\ *prep or conj* : UNTIL [Old English *til*]

²till \'til\ *vt* : to work (land) by plowing, sowing, and raising crops [Old English *tilian*] — **till·able** \-ə-bəl\ *adj*

tiger 1a

\ə\ abut   \ng\ sing
\ər\ further   \ō\ bone
\a\ mat   \o´\ saw
\ā\ take   \oi\ coin
\ä\ cot, cart   \th\ thin
\au̇\ out   \th\ this
\ch\ chin   \ū\ food
\e\ pet   \u´\ foot
\ē\ easy   \y\ yet
\g\ go   \yü\ few
\i\ tip   \yu´\ cure
\ī\ life   \zh\ vision
\j\ job

³till \'til\ *n* : a receptacle (as a drawer) for money [Anglo-French *tylle*]

⁴till \'til\ *n* : unstratified glacial drift consisting of clay, sand, gravel, and boulders intermingled [origin unknown]

till·age \'til-ij\ *n* **1** : the operation of tilling land **2** : cultivated land

¹till·er \'til-ər\ *n* : one that tills : CULTIVATOR

²til·ler \'til-ər\ *n* **1** : a lever used to turn the rudder of a boat from side to side **2** : a steering wheel for the rear wheels or trailer section of a vehicle (as a fire truck) — called also *tiller wheel* [Middle French *telier* "stock of a crossbow", literally, "beam of a loom", from Medieval Latin *telarium*, from Latin *tela* "web"]

³til·ler *n* : SPROUT 1, STALK; *esp* : one from the base of a cereal grass [Old English *telgor*, *telgra* "twig, shoot"]

⁴til·ler *vi* : to put forth tillers ⟨the oats are *tillering*⟩

til·ler·man \'til-ər-mən\ *n* : STEERSMAN

¹tilt \'tilt\ *vb* **1** : to cause to slope : INCLINE **2** : to move or shift so as to lean or incline : SLANT **3** : to engage in a combat with lances : JOUST [Middle English *tilten*] — **tilt·er** *n*

²tilt *n* **1** : a contest on horseback in which two combatants charging with lances try to unhorse each other : JOUST **2 a** : a verbal encounter involving sharp exchanges : ALTERCATION **b** : SPEED 2a — used in the phrase *at full tilt* **3 a** : the act of tilting : the state or position of being tilted **b** : a sloping surface

tilth \'tilth\ *n* **1** : cultivation of the soil **2** : cultivated land : TILLAGE **3** : the state of being tilled [Old English, from *tilian* "to till"]

tilt·me·ter \'tilt-ˌmēt-ər\ *n* : an instrument to measure the tilting of the earth's surface

tim·bal \'tim-bəl\ *n* : KETTLEDRUM [French *timbale*, from Spanish *atabal*, from Arabic *aṭ-ṭabl* "the drum"]

¹tim·ber \'tim-bər\ *n* **1** : wood for use in making something **2** : a squared or dressed and usually large piece of wood **3** : wooded land or growing trees constituting a source of timber **4** : a curving frame branching outward from the keel of a ship that is usually composed of several pieces united : RIB [Old English, "building, wood"] — **timber** *adj*

²timber *vt* **tim·bered; tim·ber·ing** \-bə-ring, -bring\ : to frame, cover, or support with timbers

tim·bered \'tim-bərd\ *adj* **1** : furnished with, made of, or covered with timber **2** : having walls framed by exposed timbers

timber hitch *n* : a knot used to secure a line to a log or spar

tim·ber·ing \'tim-bə-ring, -bring\ *n* : a set of timbers : timber construction

tim·ber·land \'tim-bər-ˌland\ *n* : wooded land especially with marketable timber

tim·ber·line \-ˌlīn\ *n* : the upper limit of tree growth in mountains or high latitudes

timber wolf *n* : a large usually gray North American wolf extinct over much of the eastern and southern parts of its range

tim·ber·work \'tim-bər-ˌwərk\ *n* : a timber construction

tim·bre \'tam-bər, 'tim-\ *n* : the quality given to a sound by its overtones: as **a** : the resonance by which the ear recognizes and identifies a voiced speech sound **b** : the tone distinctive of a singing voice or a musical instrument [French, from Middle French, "bell struck by a hammer", from Old French, "drum", derived from Greek *tympanon*]

tim·brel \'tim-brəl\ *n* : a small hand drum or tambourine [Middle English *timbre* "tambourine", from Old French, "drum"] — **tim·brelled** \-brəld\ *adj*

¹time \'tīm\ *n* **1 a** : the measured or measurable period during which an action, process, or condition exists or continues : DURATION **b** : LEISURE ⟨*time* for reading⟩ **2** : the point or period when something occurs : OCCASION **3** : an appointed, fixed, or customary moment or hour

timber wolf

for something to happen, begin, or end ⟨arrived ahead of *time*⟩ **4 a** : an historical period : AGE **b** : a division of geologic chronology **c** : conditions at present or at some specified period — usually used in pl. ⟨*times* are hard⟩ ⟨move with the *times*⟩ **d** : the present time ⟨issues of the *time*⟩ **5 a** : LIFETIME **b** : a period or term especially of military service **c** : a prison sentence **6** : SEASON 2 **7 a** : rate of speed : TEMPO **b** : the grouping of the beats of music : RHYTHM **8 a** : a moment, hour, day, or year as indicated by a clock or calendar ⟨what *time* is it⟩ **b** : any of various systems (as sidereal or solar) of reckoning time **9 a** : one of a series of recurring instances or repeated actions ⟨told you many *times*⟩ **b** *pl* (1) : added or accumulated quantities or instances ⟨five *times* greater⟩ (2) : equal fractional parts of which an indicated number equals a comparatively greater quantity ⟨seven *times* smaller⟩ **c** : TURN ⟨three *times* at bat⟩ **10** : finite as contrasted with infinite duration **11** : a person's experience during a specified period or on a particular occasion ⟨a good *time*⟩ **12 a** : the period of one's work ⟨make up *time*⟩ **b** : an hourly pay rate **13 a** : the playing time of a game **b** : TIME-OUT ⟨called *time* to make a substitution⟩ [Old English *tīma*] — **at the same time** : HOWEVER 2, NEVERTHELESS — **at times** : now and then — **from time to time** : once in a while : OCCASIONALLY — **in no time** : in the shortest possible time — **in time 1** : early enough **2** : in the course of time : EVENTUALLY **3** : in correct rhythm or tempo — **on time 1** : at the time set : PUNCTUALLY **2** : on an installment payment plan : on credit

²time *vt* **1 a** : to arrange or set the time of : SCHEDULE **b** : to regulate (a watch) to keep correct time **2** : to set the tempo, speed, or duration of **3** : to cause to keep time with something **4** : to determine or record the time, duration, or rate of **5** : to adjust (as a mechanical part) so that an action occurs at a desired instant

³time *adj* **1 a** : of or relating to time **b** : recording time **2** : timed to ignite or explode at a specific moment ⟨a *time* bomb⟩

time and a half *n* : payment of a worker (as for overtime) at one and a half times the regular wage rate

time capsule *n* : a container holding historical records or objects representative of current culture that is deposited (as in a cornerstone) for preservation until discovery by some future age

time card *n* : a card used with a time clock to record an employee's starting and quitting times each day or on each job

time clock *n* : a clock that stamps an employee's starting and quitting times on a time card

timed \'tīmd\ *adj* **1** : made to occur at or in a set time ⟨a *timed* explosion⟩ **2** : done or taking place at a time of a specified sort ⟨an ill-*timed* arrival⟩

time deposit *n* : a bank deposit payable a specified number of days after deposit or upon advance notice to the bank

time exposure *n* : exposure of a photographic film for a definite time usually of more than one half second; *also* : a photograph taken by such exposure

time–hon·ored \'tī-ˌmän-ərd\ *adj* : honored or respected because of age or long-established usage

time·keep·er \'tīm-ˌkē-pər\ *n* **1** : TIMEPIECE **2** : a clerk who keeps records of the time worked by employees **3** : an official who keeps track of the time in an athletic game or contest — **time·keep·ing** \-ping\ *n*

time·less \'tīm-ləs\ *adj* **1 a** : having no beginning or end : UNENDING **b** : not restricted to a particular time or date **2** : not affected by time — **time·less·ly** *adv* — **time·less·ness** *n*

time lock *n* : a lock controlled by clockwork to prevent its being opened before a set time

time·ly \'tīm-lē\ *adj* **time·li·er; -est 1** : coming early or at the right time : OPPORTUNE **2** : appropriate or adapted to the times or the occasion ⟨a *timely* book⟩ — **time·li·ness** *n*

time–out \'tī-'maut\ *n* : a suspension of play in an athletic game

time·piece \'tīm-,pēs\ *n* : a device (as a clock or watch) to measure the passage of time

tim·er \'tī-mər\ *n* : one that times: as **a** : TIMEPIECE; *esp* : a stopwatch for timing races **b** : TIMEKEEPER **c** : a device (as a clock) that indicates by an audible signal the end of an interval of time or that automatically starts or stops a device

times \,tīmz\ *prep* : multiplied by ⟨two *times* two is four⟩

time–sav·er \'tīm-,sā-vər\ *n* : something that saves time

time–sav·ing \'tīm-,sā-ving\ *adj* : intended or serving to lessen the amount of time needed to do something ⟨a *timesaving* device⟩

time·serv·er \-,sər-vər\ *n* : a person who only does what everyone else does or what pleases a supervisor — **time·serv·ing** \-,ving\ *adj or n*

time–sharing \'tīm-,sheər-ing, -,shaər-\ *n* : use of a computer system by many individuals at the same time in such a way that each user has the impression of being the only user of the system

time signature *n* : a sign used to indicate musical meter and usually written with one number above another with the bottom number indicating the kind of note used as a unit of measurement and the top number indicating the number of these units in each bar

time·ta·ble \'tīm-,tā-bəl\ *n* **1** : a table of departure and arrival times (as of trains, buses, or airplanes) **2** : a schedule showing a planned order or sequence

time·worn \-,wōrn, -,wórn\ *adj* **1** : worn or impaired by time **2 a** : AGE-OLD, ANCIENT ⟨*timeworn* procedures⟩ **b** : HACKNEYED, STALE ⟨a *timeworn* joke⟩

time zone *n* : a geographical region within which the same standard time is used

tim·id \'tim-əd\ *adj* : lacking in courage or self-confidence : FEARFUL, SHY [Latin *timidus*, from *timēre* "to fear"] — **ti·mid·i·ty** \tə-'mid-ət-ē\ *n* — **tim·id·ly** \'tim-əd-lē\ *adv*

tim·ing *n* **1** : selection for maximum effect of the precise moment for beginning or doing something **2** : observation and recording (as by a stopwatch) of the elapsed time of an act, action, or process

tim·o·rous \'tim-rəs, -ə-rəs\ *adj* **1** : of a timid disposition : AFRAID **2** : expressing or suggesting timidity [Middle French *timoureus*, from Medieval Latin *timorosus*, from Latin *timor* "fear", from *timēre* "to fear"] — **tim·o·rous·ly** *adv* — **tim·o·rous·ness** *n*

tim·o·thy \'tim-ə-thē\ *n* : a European grass with long cylindrical spikes widely grown for hay [probably after *Timothy* Hanson, 18th century American farmer said to have introduced it from New England to the southern states]

Tim·o·thy \'tim-ə-thē\ *n* — see BIBLE table

tim·pa·ni *or* **tym·pa·ni** \'tim-pə-nē\ *n pl* : a set of two or three kettledrums played by one performer [Italian *timpani*, pl. of *timpano* "kettledrum", from Latin *tympanum* "drum"] — **tim·pa·nist** \-nəst\ *n*

¹tin \'tin\ *n* **1** : a soft bluish white lustrous crystalline metallic chemical element that is malleable and ductile at ordinary temperatures and that is used as a protective coating in tinfoil and in soft solders and alloys — see ELEMENT table **2 a** : a box, can, pan, vessel, or a sheet made of tinplate **b** : a sealed can holding food [Old English] — **tin** *adj*

²tin *vt* **tinned; tin·ning** **1** : to cover or plate with tin or an alloy of tin **2** : to put up or pack in tins : CAN

tinct \'tingt, 'tingkt\ *n* : TINCTURE 1 — **tinct** *adj*

¹tinc·ture \'ting-chər, 'tingk-\ *n* **1** : a substance that colors, dyes, or stains **2** : a slight admixture : TRACE **3** : an alcoholic solution of a medicinal substance [Latin *tinctura* "act of dyeing", from *tingere* "to tinge"]

²tincture *vt* **1** : to tint or stain with a color : TINGE **2** : to infuse or instill with a property or quality : IMPREGNATE

tin·der \'tin-dər\ *n* : a very flammable substance that can be used as kindling [Old English *tynder*] — **tin·dery** \-də-rē\ *adj*

tin·der·box \-,bäks\ *n* **1 a** : a metal box for holding tinder and usually a flint and steel for striking a spark **b** : a highly flammable object or place **2** : a person, place, or situation likely to erupt into strife or conflict

tine \'tīn\ *n* : a slender pointed projecting part : PRONG ⟨the *tines* of a fork⟩ [Old English *tind*]

tin·ea \'tin-ē-ə\ *n* : any of several fungous diseases of the skin; *esp* : RINGWORM [Latin, "worm, moth"] — **tin·e·al** \-ē-əl\ *adj*

tin fish *n, slang* : TORPEDO 2b

tin·foil \'tin-,fóil\ *n* **1** : a thin metal sheeting usually of aluminum or tin-lead alloy **2** : SILVER PAPER

ting \'ting\ *n* : a high-pitched sound (as from a light stroke on a glass) [Middle English *tingen* "to ting"] — **ting** *vb*

tinge \'tinj\ *vt* **tinged; tinge·ing** *or* **ting·ing** \'tin-jing\ **1 a** : to color slightly : TINT **b** : to affect or modify with a slight odor or taste **2** : to modify in character ⟨respect *tinged* with envy⟩ [Latin *tingere* "to dip, tinge"] — **tinge** *n*

tin·gle \'ting-gəl\ *vi* **tin·gled; tin·gling** \-gə-ling, -gling\ : to feel a ringing, stinging, prickling, or thrilling sensation; *also* : to cause such a sensation ⟨the story *tingles* with suspense⟩ [Middle English *tinglen*, alteration of *tinklen* "to tinkle, tingle"] — **tingle** *n* — **tin·gly** \-gə-lē, -glē\ *adj*

tin hat *n* : a metal helmet

tin·horn \'tin-,hórn\ *n* : a pretentious or boastful person (as a gambler) with little money, power, or ability

¹tin·ker \'ting-kər\ *n* **1** : a mender of household utensils (as pots and pans) who usually travels from place to place **2** : an unskilled mender : BUNGLER [Middle English *tinkere*]

²tinker *vi* **tin·kered; tin·ker·ing** \-kə-ring, -kring\ : to work in the manner of a tinker; *esp* : to repair or adjust something in an unskilled or experimental manner — **tin·ker·er** \-kər-ər\ *n*

tinker's damn *or* **tinker's dam** *n* : something absolutely worthless [probably from the tinkers' reputation for blasphemy]

¹tin·kle \'ting-kəl\ *vb* **tin·kled; tin·kling** \-kə-ling, -kling\ **1** : to make or emit a tinkle **2 a** : to cause to make a tinkle **b** : to produce by tinkling ⟨*tinkle* a tune on the piano⟩ [Middle English *tinklen*, from *tinken* "to tinkle"]

²tinkle *n* : a series of short high ringing or clinking sounds — **tin·kly** \-kə-lē, -klē\ *adj*

tin·man \'tin-mən\ *n* : TINSMITH

tin·ni·tus \'tin-ə-təs\ *n* : a usually subjective sensation of noise (as a ringing or roaring) [Latin, "ringing, tinnitus", from *tinnire* "to ring"]

tin·ny \'tin-ē\ *adj* **tin·ni·er; -est** **1** : of, abounding in, or yielding tin **2** : resembling or suggestive of tin: as **a** : LIGHT, CHEAP ⟨a *tinny* watch⟩ **b** : thin in tone ⟨a *tinny* voice⟩ — **tin·ni·ly** \'tin-l-ē\ *adv* — **tin·ni·ness** \'tin-ē-nəs\ *n*

Tin Pan Alley *n* : a district occupied chiefly by composers or publishers of popular music; *also* : the body of such composers or publishers

tin·plate \'tin-'plāt\ *n* : thin sheet iron or steel coated with tin — **tin–plate** *vt*

¹tin·sel \'tin-səl\ *n* **1** : a thread, strip, or sheet of metal, paper, or plastic used to produce a glittering and sparkling appearance (as in fabrics, yarns, or decorations) **2** : something superficially attractive or glamorous but of little real worth [Middle French *estincelle*, *etincelle* "spark, spangle", from Latin *scintilla* "spark"]

²tinsel *adj* **1** : made of or covered with tinsel **2** : cheaply gaudy : TAWDRY

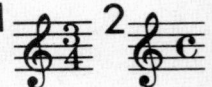

time signature: *1* 3/4 time, *2* common time

³tinsel *vt* **-seled** *or* **-selled; -sel·ing** *or* **-sel·ling** \-sə-ling, -sling\ **1** : to adorn with or as if with tinsel **2** : to give a superficial brightness to

tin·sel·ly \'tin-sə-lē, -slē\ *adj* : TINSEL

tin·smith \'tin-ˌsmith\ *n* : a worker who makes or repairs things of metal (as tin)

¹tint \'tint\ *n* **1** : a slight or pale coloring : TINGE ⟨white without a *tint* of yellow⟩ **2** : a color produced by a pigment or dye mixture having some white in it **3** : a usually slight modifying quality or characteristic **4** : a dye for the hair [Latin *tinctus* "act of dyeing", from *tingere* "to tinge"] SYN see COLOR — **tint·er** *n*

²tint *vt* : to impart or apply a tint to : COLOR

tin·tin·nab·u·la·tion \ˌtin-tə-ˌnab-yə-'lā-shən\ *n* **1** : the ringing or sounding of bells **2** : a jingling or tinkling sound as if of bells [Latin *tintinnabulum* "bell", from *tintinnare* "to ring, jingle"]

tin·type \'tin-ˌtīp\ *n* : an early photograph consisting of a positive image taken directly on a thin iron plate having a darkened surface

tin·ware \-ˌwaər, -ˌweər\ *n* : articles made of tinplate

tin·work \-ˌwərk\ *n* **1** : work in tin **2** *pl* : an establishment where tin is smelted, rolled, or otherwise worked

ti·ny \'tī-nē\ *adj* **ti·ni·er; -est** : very small or diminutive : MINUTE [Middle English *tine*] — **ti·ni·ness** *n*

¹tip \'tip\ *n* **1** : the pointed or rounded end of something : END **2** : a small piece or part serving as an end, cap, or point [Middle English] — **tipped** \'tipt\ *adj*

²tip *vt* **tipped; tip·ping** **1 a** : to furnish with a tip **b** : to cover or decorate the tip of **2** : to affix (an insert) in a book — often used with *in* **3** : to remove the ends of (as plant shoots)

³tip *vb* **tipped; tip·ping** **1** : OVERTURN, UPSET ⟨*tipped* over a glass⟩ **2** : TILT 2 ⟨the bench *tipped* on the uneven floor⟩ **3** : to raise and tilt forward in salute ⟨*tipped* my hat⟩ [Middle English *tipen*] — **tip the scales** **1** : to register weight **2** : to shift the balance of power or influence

⁴tip *n* : the act or an instance of tipping : TILT

⁵tip *n* : a light touch or blow : TAP [Middle English *tippe*]

⁶tip *vt* **tipped; tip·ping** : to strike lightly : TAP

⁷tip *vb* **tipped; tip·ping** **1** : to give a gratuity to ⟨*tip* a waitress⟩ **2** : to give gratuities ⟨was miserly about *tipping*⟩ [perhaps from ⁶*tip*]

⁸tip *n* : a gift or small sum of money tendered for a service : GRATUITY

⁹tip *n* : an item of authoritative or confidential information ⟨a *tip* on a sure winner in a horse race⟩ [perhaps from ⁷*tip*]

¹⁰tip *vt* **tipped; tip·ping** : to give information or advice often in a secret or confidential manner ⟨was *tipped* off as to what would happen⟩

tip·cart \'tip-ˌkärt\ *n* : a cart whose body can be tipped on the frame to empty its contents

tip·cat \-ˌkat\ *n* : a game in which one player using a bat lightly strikes a tapered wooden peg and as it flies up strikes it again to drive it as far as possible while fielders try to recover it; *also* : the peg used in this game

ti·pi *variant of* TEPEE

tip-off \'tip-ˌȯf\ *n* : ⁹TIP, WARNING

tip·per \'tip-ər\ *n* : one that tips

tip·pet \'tip-ət\ *n* **1** : a long hanging part of a garment (as on a sleeve or cape) **2** : a shoulder cape usually with hanging ends **3** : a long black scarf worn over the robe by members of the Anglican clergy [Middle English *tipet*]

¹tip·ple \'tip-əl\ *vi* **tip·pled; tip·pling** \'tip-ling, -ə-ling\ : to drink liquor especially continuously in small amounts [back-formation from obsolete *tippler* "barkeeper", from Middle English *tipeler*] — **tip·pler** \'tip-lər, -ə-lər\ *n*

²tipple *n* : an intoxicating beverage : DRINK

³tipple *n* **1** : an apparatus by which loaded cars are emptied by tipping **2** : the place where tipping is done; *esp* : a coal-screening plant [derived from *tip*]

tip·staff \'tip-ˌstaf\ *n, pl* **tip·staves** \-ˌstavz, -ˌstävz\ : an officer (as a constable or bailiff) who bears a staff [obsolete *tipstaff* "staff tipped with metal"]

tip·ster \'tip-stər\ *n* : one who gives or sells tips especially for gambling or speculation

tip·sy \'tip-sē\ *adj* **tip·si·er; -est** **1** : unsteady, staggering, or foolish from the effects of alcohol : somewhat drunk **2** : ASKEW ⟨a *tipsy* angle⟩ [³*tip* + -*sy* (as in *tricksy*)] — **tip·si·ly** \-sə-lē\ *adv* — **tip·si·ness** \-sē-nəs\ *n*

¹tip·toe \'tip-ˌtō, -'tō\ *n* : the tip of a toe; *also* : the ends of the toes — **on tiptoe** **1** : on the tips of one's toes **2** : ALERT 1, EXPECTANT

²tiptoe *adv* : on or as if on tiptoe ⟨walk *tiptoe*⟩

³tiptoe *adj* **1** : marked by standing or walking on tiptoe **2** : CAUTIOUS ⟨a *tiptoe* approach⟩

⁴tiptoe *vi* : to stand, raise oneself, or walk on or as if on tiptoe

¹tip-top \'tip-'täp, -ˌtäp\ *n* : the highest point : SUMMIT

²tip-top *adj* : EXCELLENT, FIRST-RATE — **tip-top** *adv*

ti·rade \'tī-ˌrād, 'tī-ˌ\ *n* : a long furious usually abusive speech [French, "shot, tirade", from Italian *tirata*, from *tirare* "to draw, shoot"]

¹tire \'tīr\ *vb* **1** : to become weary **2** : to exhaust or greatly decrease the physical strength of : FATIGUE **3** : to wear out the patience or attention of : bore completely [Old English *tēorian, tȳrian*]

²tire *n* **1** : a metal hoop forming the tread of a wheel **2 a** : a rubber cushion that encircles a wheel and usually consists of a rubber-and-fabric covering containing a cavity or a separate inner tube that is filled with compressed air **b** : the external rubber-and-fabric covering of a pneumatic tire that uses an inner tube [probably from earlier *tire* "headband", from Middle English *attire* "attire"]

tired \'tīrd\ *adj* **1** : WEARY 1 **2 a** : FED UP ⟨I'm *tired* of all this nonsense⟩ **b** : HACKNEYED ⟨*tired* old jokes⟩ — **tired·ly** *adv* — **tired·ness** *n*

tire·less \'tīr-ləs\ *adj* : not easily tired ⟨a *tireless* worker⟩ — **tire·less·ly** *adv* — **tire·less·ness** *n*

tire·some \'tīr-səm\ *adj* : WEARISOME, TEDIOUS — **tire·some·ly** *adv* — **tire·some·ness** *n*

tire·wom·an \'tīr-ˌwùm-ən\ *n* : a lady's maid [derived from *attire*]

tir·ing-room \'tī-ring-ˌrüm, -ˌrùm\ *n* : a dressing room especially in a theater [derived from *attire*]

'tis \tiz, 'tiz\ : it is

tis·sue \'tish-ü\ *n* **1 a** : a fine lightweight often sheer fabric **b** : MESH, NETWORK, WEB ⟨a *tissue* of lies⟩ **2** : a piece of soft absorbent paper used especially as a handkerchief or for removing cosmetics **3** : a mass or layer of cells usually of one kind that together with their intercellular substance form one of the structural materials of a plant or an animal — compare ORGAN; CONNECTIVE TISSUE, EPITHELIUM, PARENCHYMA [Old French *tissu*, a rich fabric, from *tistre* "to weave", from Latin *texere*]

tissue paper *n* : a thin gauzy paper often used to wrap delicate articles

¹tit \'tit\ *n* : TEAT [Old English]

²tit *n* : TITMOUSE; *also* : any of various small plump often long-tailed birds

ti·tan \'tīt-n\ *n* **1** *cap* : one of a family of giants ruling the universe until overthrown by the Olympian gods **2** : one of gigantic size, power, or achievement [Greek]

ti·ta·nate \'tīt-n-ˌāt\ *n* **1** : any of various oxides of titanium and another metal **2** : a titanium ester

ti·tan·ess \'tīt-n-əs\ *n, often cap* : a female titan

ti·tan·ic \tī-'tan-ik\ *adj* **1** *cap* : of, relating to, or resembling the Titans **2** : vast in size, force, or power : COLOSSAL

ti·ta·ni·um \tī-'tā-nē-əm, tə-\ *n* : a silvery gray light strong metallic chemical element found combined in various minerals and used in alloys (as steel) — see ELEMENT table [New Latin, from Greek *Titan* "Titan"]

titanium dioxide *n* : an oxide TiO_2 of titanium used especially as a white pigment

titanium white *n* : titanium dioxide used as a pigment

ti·tan·o·there \tī-'tan-ə-ˌthiər\ *n* : any of various large often horned extinct mammals distantly related to the horses [derived from Greek *Titan* "Titan" + *thērion* "wild animal"]

tit·bit *variant of* TIDBIT

tit for tat \ˌtit-fər-'tat\ : an equivalent given in return (as for an injury) : RETALIATION [alteration of earlier *tip for tap*]

¹tithe \'tīth\ *vb* **1** : to pay or give a tithe **2** : to levy a tithe on [Old English *teogothian*, from *teogotha* "tenth"] — **tith·er** *n*

²tithe *n* **1** : a tenth part paid in kind or money as a voluntary contribution or as a tax especially for the support of a religious establishment **2 a** : TENTH 2 **b** : a small part

ti·tian \'tish-ən\ *adj, often cap* : of a brownish orange color [*Titian,* Italian painter]

tit·il·late \'tit-ə-ˌlāt\ *vt* **1** : TICKLE 2 **2** : to excite pleasurably [Latin *titillare*] — **tit·il·la·tion** \ˌtit-l-'ā-shən\ *n* — **tit·il·la·tive** \'tit-l-ˌāt-iv\ *adj*

tit·i·vate *or* **tit·ti·vate** \'tit-ə-ˌvāt\ *vb* : to dress up : spruce up : SMARTEN [perhaps from *tidy* + *-vate* (as in *renovate*)] — **tit·i·va·tion** \ˌtit-ə-'vā-shən\ *n*

¹ti·tle \'tīt-l\ *n* **1 a** : RIGHT, PRIVILEGE; *esp* : the elements constituting legal ownership **b** : a legal document (as a deed) that is evidence of a right **2** : something that justifies or substantiates a claim **3 a** : a descriptive or general heading (as of a chapter in a book) **b** : the heading of an act or statute or of a legal action or proceeding **4** : the distinguishing name of a written, printed, or filmed production or of a musical composition or a work of art **5** : a division of a legal document or a book or bill; *esp* : one larger than a section or article **6** : an appellation of dignity or honor attached to a person or family (as by hereditary right) (a *title* of nobility) **7** : CHAMPIONSHIP 2a (won the batting *title*) [Old French, from Latin *titulus* "inscription, title"]

²title *vt* **ti·tled; ti·tling** \'tīt-ling, -l-ing\ : to call by a title : TERM

ti·tled \'tīt-ld\ *adj* : having a title especially of nobility

title deed *n* : the deed constituting the evidence of a person's legal ownership

ti·tle·hold·er \'tīt-l-ˌhōl-dər\ *n* : one that holds a title; *esp* : CHAMPION

title page *n* : a page of a book bearing the title and usually the names of the author and publisher and the place of publication

title role *n* : a part or character that gives a play or movie its name

ti·tlist \'tīt-l-əst, 'tīt-ləst\ *n* : TITLEHOLDER

tit·mouse \'tit-ˌmaús\ *n, pl* **tit·mice** \-ˌmīs\ : any of numerous small tree-dwelling and insect-eating birds related to the nuthatches but longer tailed [Middle English *titmose*]

Ti·to·ism \'tēt-ō-ˌiz-əm\ *n* : nationalistic policies and practices followed by a communist state independently of the Soviet Union especially as practiced in Yugoslavia by Marshal Tito

ti·trate \'tī-ˌtrāt\ *vt* : to subject to titration [French *titre* "title, proportion of gold or silver in a coin", from Old French *title* "label, title"]

ti·tra·tion \tī-'trā-shən\ *n* : the process of determining the strength of a solution or the concentration of a substance in solution by finding the smallest amount of a reagent required to cause a given effect (as color change) in reaction with a known volume of the test solution

ti·tri·met·ric \ˌtī-trə-'me-trik\ *adj* : determined by titration — **ti·tri·met·ri·cal·ly** \-tri-kə-lē, -klē\ *adv*

tit-tat-toe *variant of* TICKTACKTOE

tit·ter \'tit-ər\ *vi* : to laugh in a nervous or partly suppressed manner [imitative] — **titter** *n*

tit·tle \'tit-l\ *n* **1** : a point or small sign used as a diacritical mark in writing or printing **2** : a very small part or amount [Medieval Latin *titulus,* from Latin, "inscription, title"]

tit·tle-tat·tle \'tit-l-ˌtat-l\ *n* **1** : GOSSIP 2 [reduplication of *tattle*] — **tittle-tattle** *vi*

tit·u·lar \'tich-lər, -ə-lər\ *adj* **1 a** : existing in title only **b** : having the title belonging to an office or dignity without its duties or responsibilities **2** : bearing a title **3** : of, relating to, or being a title [Latin *titulus* "title"] — **tit·u·lar·ly** *adv*

titular bishop *n* : a Roman Catholic bishop with the title of but without jurisdiction in a defunct see

tiz·zy \'tiz-ē\ *n, pl* **tizzies** : a highly excited and distracted state of mind [origin unknown]

T lymphocyte *n* : T CELL

tme·sis \'mē-səs, tə-'mē-səs\ *n* : separation of parts of a compound word by the intervention of one or more words (as *what place soever* for *whatsoever place*) [Late Latin, from Greek *tmēsis* "act of cutting", from *temnein* "to cut"]

TNT \ˌtē-ˌen-'tē\ *n* : TRINITROTOLUENE [*tri*nitro*t*oluene]

¹to \tə, tù, tü; *before vowels usually* tə; *after* -t *(as in "want") often* ə\ *prep* **1 a** : in the direction of and reaching (walked *to* school) **b** : in the direction of : so as to approach (on the way *to* town) **c** : close against : ON (applied polish *to* the table) **d** : as far as (stripped *to* the waist) **2 a** : for the purpose of : FOR (came *to* our aid) **b** : in honor of (a toast *to* the winner) **c** : so as to become or bring about (broken *to* pieces) **3 a** : BEFORE (ten minutes *to* five) **b** : UNTIL (from eight *to* five) **4 a** : being a part or accessory of (a key *to* the door) **b** : with the accompaniment of (sang *to* the music) **5 a** : in an indicated relation with (similar *to* that one) **b** (1) : in accordance with (add salt *to* taste) (2) : within the range of (*to* my knowledge) **c** : contained, occurring, or included in (400 *to* the box) **6 a** : as regards (agreeable *to* everyone) **b** : affecting as the receiver or beneficiary of an action (gave it *to* me) **c** : for no one except (had a room *to* myself) **7** — used to indicate that the following verb is an infinitive (wants *to* go) and often used by itself at the end of a clause to stand for an infinitive (don't want *to*) [Old English *tō*]

²to \'tü\ *adv* **1** — used as a function word to indicate direction toward (run *to* and fro) **2** : into contact, position, or attachment especially with a frame (as of a door) (wind blew the door *to*) **3** : to the matter or business at hand (the boxers set *to* with a flurry of blows) **4** : to a state of consciousness or awareness (brought me *to* with smelling salts) **5** : at hand : BY (saw the moose close *to*)

toad \'tōd\ *n* : any of numerous tailless leaping amphibians that as compared with the related frogs are generally more terrestrial in habit and squatter and shorter in build and have weaker hind limbs and rough, dry, and warty rather than smooth and moist skin [Old English *tāde*]

toad·eat·er \-ˌēt-ər\ *n* : TOADY

toad·fish \-ˌfish\ *n* : any of various marine fishes with a large thick head, a wide mouth, and scaleless slimy skin

toad·flax \-ˌflaks\ *n* : BUTTER-AND-EGGS

toad·stone \'tōd-ˌstōn\ *n* : a stone or similar object held to have formed in the head or body of a toad and formerly often worn as a charm or an antidote to poison

toad·stool \'tōd-ˌstül\ *n* : a fungus having an umbrella-shaped cap : MUSHROOM; *esp* : one that is poisonous or inedible

\ə\ abut		\ng\ sing	
\ər\ **further**		\ō\ bone	
\a\ **mat**		\ó\ saw	
\ā\ take		\ói\ coin	
\ä\ cot, cart		\th\ thin	
\aú\ out		\th\ this	
\ch\ chin		\ū\ food	
\e\ pet		\ú\ foot	
\ē\ easy		\y\ yet	
\g\ go		\yü\ few	
\i\ tip		\yú\ cure	
\ī\ life		\zh\ vision	
\j\ job			

¹toady \'tōd-ē\ n, pl **toad·ies** : a person who flatters or fawns upon another in the hope of receiving favors

²toady vi **toad·ied; toady·ing** : to behave as a toady — **toady·ism** \-ē-,iz-əm\ n

to–and–fro \,tü-ən-'frō\ adj : forward and backward

¹toast \'tōst\ vb **1** : to make (as bread) crisp, hot, and brown by heat **2** : to warm thoroughly; also : to become toasted [Middle French toster, from Late Latin tostare "to roast", from Latin torrēre "to dry, parch"]

²toast n **1** : sliced toasted bread browned on both sides by heat **2 a** : a person whose health is drunk or something in honor of which persons drink **b** : a highly admired person **3** : an act of proposing or of drinking in honor of a toast [sense 2 from the use of pieces of spiced toast to flavor drinks]

³toast vt : to propose or drink to as a toast

toast·er \'tō-stər\ n : one that toasts; esp : an electrical appliance for toasting

toaster oven n : an electric kitchen appliance that bakes, broils, and toasts and that fits on a counter top

toast·mas·ter \'tōst-,mas-tər, 'tōs-\ n : a person who presides at a banquet and introduces the after-dinner speakers

toast·mis·tress \-,mis-trəs\ n : a girl or woman who presides as toastmaster

to·bac·co \tə-'bak-ō\ n, pl **-cos 1** : any of a genus of chiefly American plants of the potato family with sticky foliage and tubular flowers; esp : a tall erect annual South American herb grown for its leaves **2** : the leaves of cultivated tobacco prepared for use in smoking or chewing or as snuff **3** : manufactured products of tobacco (as cigars or cigarettes); also : smoking as a practice [Spanish tabaco, of American Indian origin]

tobacco mosaic n : any of a complex of virus diseases of tobacco and related plants

to·bac·co·nist \tə-'bak-ə-nəst\ n : a dealer in tobacco especially at retail

to–be \tə-'bē\ adj : that is to be : FUTURE — usually used in combination ⟨a bride-to-be⟩

To·bit \'tō-bət\ n — see BIBLE table

¹to·bog·gan \tə-'bäg-ən\ n **1** : a long flat-bottomed light sled made without runners and curved up at the front **2** : a downward course or a sharp decline [Canadian French tobogan, of American Indian origin]

²toboggan vi **1** : to coast on a toboggan **2** : to decline suddenly and sharply (as in value) — **to·bog·gan·er** n — **to·bog·gan·ist** \tə-'bäg-ə-nəst\ n

| toboggan |

to·by \'tō-bē\ n, pl **tobies** often cap : a small jug, pitcher, or mug modeled in the form of a stout man with a cocked hat for the brim [Toby, nickname from the name Tobias]

toc·ca·ta \tə-'kät-ə\ n : a musical composition usually for organ or harpsichord in a free style [Italian, from toccare "to touch"]

to·coph·er·ol \tō-'käf-ə-,rōl, -,rōl\ n : any of various fat-soluble phenolic compounds with varying degrees of antioxidant and vitamin E activity [derived from Greek tokos "childbirth, offspring" + pherein "to carry, bear"]

toc·sin \'täk-sən\ n **1** : an alarm bell or the ringing of it **2** : a warning signal [Middle French toquassen, from Provençal tocasenh, from tocar "to touch, ring" + senh "sign, bell", from Latin signum "sign"]

¹to·day \tə-'dā\ adv **1** : on or for this day **2** : at the present time : NOWADAYS

²today n : the present day, time, or age

tod·dle \'täd-l\ vi **tod·dled; tod·dling** \'täd-ling, -l-ing\ : to walk with short tottering steps in the manner of a young child [origin unknown] — **toddle** n — **tod·dler** \'täd-lər, -l-ər\ n

tod·dy \'täd-ē\ n, pl **toddies 1** : the sap of various mostly East Indian palms often fermented to form an alcoholic liquor **2** : a hot drink consisting of an alcoholic liquor, water, sugar, and spices [Hindi tāṛī, from tāṛ, a kind of palm, from Sanskrit tāla]

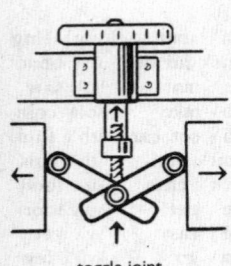

| toga |

| toggle joint |

to–do \tə-'dü\ n, pl **to–dos** \-'düz\ : BUSTLE, STIR

¹toe \'tō\ n **1 a** : one of the jointed members that make up the front end of a vertebrate foot **b** : the front end or part of a foot or hoof **c** : the forepart of something (as a shoe) worn on the foot **2** : something that resembles the toe of a foot especially in form or position ⟨the toe of a golf club⟩ [Old English tā] — **toe·less** \-ləs\ adj

²toe vb **toed; toe·ing 1** : to furnish with a toe ⟨toe off a sock in knitting⟩ **2** : to touch, reach, or drive with the toe ⟨toe a football⟩ **3** : to drive (as a nail) slantwise; also : to fasten by nails so driven **4** : to stand or walk so that the toes assume an indicated position or direction ⟨toe in⟩ — **toe the line** : to conform rigorously to a rule or standard

toed \'tōd\ adj **1** : having a toe or such or so many toes — used especially in combination ⟨5-toed⟩ **2** : driven obliquely ⟨a toed nail⟩; also : secured by toed nails

toe dance n : a dance executed on the tips of the toes — **toe–dance** \'tō-,dans\ vi — **toe dancer** n

toe·hold \'tō-,hōld\ n **1** : a small foothold : a means of progressing **2** : a hold in which the offensive wrestler bends or twists the opponent's foot

¹toe·nail \'tō-,nāl, -'nāl\ n : a nail of a toe

²toenail vt : to fasten by toed nails : TOE

tof·fee or **tof·fy** \'tò-fē, 'täf-ē\ n, pl **toffees** or **toffies** : brittle but tender candy made by boiling sugar and butter together [alteration of taffy]

tog \'täg, 'tòg\ vt **togged; tog·ging** : to put togs on : DRESS

to·ga \'tō-gə\ n : the loose outer garment worn in public by citizens of ancient Rome; also : a similar loose wrap or a professional, official, or academic gown [Latin] — **to·gaed** \-gəd\ adj

to·geth·er \tə-'geth-ər\ adv **1** : in or into one group, body, or place ⟨gathered together⟩ **2** : in or into association, union, or contact with each other ⟨in business together⟩ ⟨the doors banged together⟩ **3 a** : at one time ⟨they all cheered together⟩ **b** : in succession : without intermission ⟨work for hours together⟩ **4 a** : in or by combined effort : JOINTLY ⟨worked together to clear the road⟩ **b** : in or into agreement ⟨get together on a plan⟩ **c** : so as to form an integrated or coherent whole ⟨put words together in sentences⟩ **5** : considered as a whole ⟨more than all the others together⟩ [Old English togædere, from tō "to" + gædere "together"] — **to·geth·er·ness** n

tog·gery \'täg-rē, 'tòg-, -ə-rē\ n, pl **-ger·ies** : CLOTHING

¹tog·gle \'täg-əl\ n : a crosspiece attached to the end of or to a loop in a rope, chain, or belt to prevent slipping or to serve as a fastening or as a grip for tightening [origin unknown]

²toggle vt **tog·gled; tog·gling** \'täg-ling, -ə-ling\ **1** : to fasten with or as if with a toggle **2** : to furnish with a toggle

toggle bolt n : a bolt that has a nut with wings that close for passage through a small hole and spring open after passing through the hole to keep the bolt from slipping back through

toggle joint n : a device consisting of two bars jointed together end to end but not in line so that when a force is applied to the joint tending to straighten it pressure will be exerted on the parts fixed at the ends of the bars

toggle switch n : an electric switch depending on a toggle joint with a spring to open or close the circuit when a projecting lever is pushed through a small arc

togs \'tägz, 'tògz\ n pl : CLOTHING; esp : a set of clothes and accessories for a specified use ⟨riding togs⟩ [English slang tog "coat", probably derived from Latin toga "toga"]

¹toil \'tòil\ n : long hard tiring labor : DRUDGERY [Anglo-French toyl "struggle, battle", from Old French toeil "battle, confusion", from toeillier "to disturb, dispute", from Latin tudiculare "to crush, grind", derived from *tudes* "hammer"] — **toil·ful** \-fəl\ *adj* — **toil·ful·ly** \-fə-lē\ *adv*

²**toil** *vi* **1** : to work hard and long : LABOR **2** : PLOD 1, TRUDGE ⟨*toiling* up a steep hill⟩ — **toil·er** *n*

³**toil** *n* : something that involves or holds one fast : SNARE, TRAP — usually used in pl. [Middle French *toile* "cloth, net", from Latin *tela* "web", from *texere* "to weave"]

¹**toi·let** \'tȯi-lət\ *n* **1** : the act or process of dressing and grooming oneself **2 a** : BATHROOM **b** : a fixture for defecation and urination; *esp* : WATER CLOSET [Middle French *toilette* "cloth put over the shoulders while dressing the hair or shaving", from *toile* "cloth", from Latin *tela* "web"]

²**toilet** *vb* **1** : to dress and groom oneself **2** : to help (a child) use the toilet

toilet paper *n* : a thin sanitary absorbent paper for bathroom use chiefly after defecation or urination

toi·let·ry \'tȯi-lə-trē\ *n, pl* **-ries** : an article or preparation used in grooming oneself — usually used in pl.

toilet soap *n* : a mild often perfumed and colored soap

toi·lette \twä-'let\ *n* **1** : TOILET 1 **2 a** : formal or fashionable attire or style of dressing **b** : a particular costume or outfit [French]

toilet water *n* : a perfumed liquid containing a high percentage of alcohol for use in or after a bath or as a skin freshener

toil·some \'tȯil-səm\ *adj* : marked by or full of toil or fatigue : LABORIOUS — **toil·some·ly** *adv* — **toil·some·ness** *n*

toil·worn \-,wōrn, -,wȯrn\ *adj* : showing the effects of or worn out by long hard work

To·kay \tō-'kā\ *n* : a sweet usually dark gold dessert wine made near Tokaj, Hungary; *also* : a similar wine made elsewhere

toke \'tōk\ *n, slang* : a puff on a marijuana cigarette [American Spanish *toque*, from Spanish, "touch, test"]

¹**to·ken** \'tō-kən\ *n* **1** : an outward sign or expression ⟨*tokens* of grief⟩ **2** : SYMBOL, EMBLEM ⟨the white flag is a *token* of surrender⟩ **3 a** : SOUVENIR, KEEPSAKE **b** : a small part representing the whole : INDICATION ⟨a mere *token* of future benefits⟩ **4 a** : something given or shown as a guarantee (as of identity, right, or authority) **b** : a piece resembling a coin issued for use (as for fare on a bus) [Old English *tācen*] — **by the same token** : for the same reason

²**token** *adj* **1** : done or given in partial fulfillment of an obligation or undertaking ⟨a *token* payment⟩ **2** : MINIMAL, PERFUNCTORY ⟨*token* resistance⟩

to·ken·ism \'tō-kə-,niz-əm\ *n* : the policy or practice of making only a token effort (as in integrating races)

token money *n* **1** : money of regular government issue having a greater face value than intrinsic value **2** : privately issued tokens for use as money

tol·booth \'tōl-,büth, 'tō-, 'täl-, 'tōl-\ *n* **1** *Scottish* : a town or market hall **2** *Scottish* : JAIL, PRISON [Middle English *tolbothe* "tollbooth, town hall, jail"]

tol·bu·ta·mide \täl-'byüt-ə-,mīd\ *n* : a sulfonamide that lowers blood sugar level and is used in the treatment of diabetes [*tolu*ene + *but*yric + *amide*]

told *past of* TELL

tole \'tōl\ *n* : usually japanned or painted sheet metal (as tinplate) used mostly for decorative objects (as trays or boxes) and finished in various colors often with stenciled designs [French *tôle* "sheet metal", from French dialect, "table, slab", from Latin *tabula* "board, tablet"]

To·le·do \tə-'lēd-ō\ *n, pl* **-dos** : a finely tempered sword of a kind made in Toledo, Spain

tol·er·a·ble \'täl-rə-bəl, -ə-rə-; 'täl-ər-bəl\ *adj* **1** : capable of being borne or endured **2** : moderately good or agreeable : PASSABLE — **tol·er·a·bil·i·ty** \,täl-rə-'bil-ət-ē, -ə-rə-\ *n* — **tol·er·a·bly** \'täl-rə-blē, -ə-rə-; 'täl-ər-blē\ *adv*

tol·er·ance \'täl-rəns, -ə-rəns\ *n* **1** : relative capacity to endure or adapt physiologically to an unfavorable environmental factor **2 a** : sympathy or indulgence for beliefs or practices differing from one's own **b** : the act of allowing something : TOLERATION **3** : allowable deviation from a standard — **tol·er·ant** \-rənt\ *adj* — **tol·er·ant·ly** *adv*

tol·er·ate \'täl-ə-,rāt\ *vt* **1** : to allow to be done or to exist : put up with : ENDURE **2** : to show tolerance toward ⟨plants that *tolerate* drought⟩ ⟨*tolerate* a drug⟩ [Latin *tolerare*] — **tol·er·a·tion** \,täl-ə-'rā-shən\ *n* — **tol·er·a·tor** \'täl-ə-,rāt-ər\ *n*

¹**toll** \'tōl\ *n* **1** : a tax paid for a privilege (as the use of a highway or bridge) **2** : a charge paid for a service (as placing a long-distance telephone call) **3** : a ruinous price; *esp* : cost in life or misery [Old English]

²**toll** *vt* : to take as toll; *also* : to take a toll from

³**toll** *vb* **1** : to sound (a bell) by pulling the rope **2** : to signal or announce by the sounding of a bell ⟨the clock *tolled* the hour⟩ ⟨bells *tolling* the alarm⟩ **3** : to sound with slow measured strokes [Middle English *tollen*]

⁴**toll** *n* : the sound of a tolling bell

toll·booth \'tōl-,büth\ *n* : a booth where tolls are paid

toll call *n* : a long-distance telephone call at charges above a local rate

toll·gate \'tōl-,gāt\ *n* : a point where vehicles stop to pay a toll

toll·house \-,haůs\ *n* : a house or booth where tolls are collected

Tol·tec \'tōl-,tek, 'täl-\ *n* : a member of a Nahuatlan people of central and southern Mexico [Spanish *tolteca*, of American Indian origin] — **Tol·tec·an** \-ən\ *adj*

tol·u·ene \'täl-yə-,wēn\ *n* : a hydrocarbon similar to benzene but less volatile, less flammable, and less toxic that is used especially as a solvent and in organic synthesis [Spanish *tolú*, a balsam from which toluene was distilled, from Santiago de *Tolú*, Colombia]

tom \'täm\ *n* : the male of various animals ⟨a *tom* swan⟩: as **a** : TOMCAT **b** : GOBBLER [*Tom*, nickname for *Thomas*]

¹**tom·a·hawk** \'täm-i-,hȯk\ *n* : a light ax used as a weapon by North American Indians [of American Indian origin]

²**tomahawk** *vt* : to cut, strike, or kill with a tomahawk

to·ma·to \tə-'māt-ō, -'mät-\ *n, pl* **-toes** **1** : any of a genus of South American herbs of the potato family; *esp* : one widely grown for its edible fruits **2** : the usually large, rounded, and red or yellow pulpy fruit of a tomato [Spanish *tomate*, from Nahuatl *tomatl*]

tomb \'tüm\ *n* **1 a** : GRAVE **b** : a place of burial **2** : a house, chamber, or vault for the dead **3** : a building or structure resembling a tomb [Anglo-French *tumbe*, from Late Latin *tumba* "sepulchral mound", from Greek *tymbos*]

tom·boy \'täm-,bȯi\ *n* : a girl of boyish behavior — **tom·boy·ish** \-ish\ *adj* — **tom·boy·ish·ness** *n*

tomb·stone \'tüm-,stōn\ *n* : GRAVESTONE

tom·cat \'täm-,kat\ *n* : a male cat

tom·cod \-,käd\ *n* : any of several small fishes resembling the related common codfish

Tom, Dick, and Harry \,täm-,dik-ən-'har-ē\ *n* : the ordinary person : ANYONE — often used with every ⟨helps every *Tom, Dick, and Harry* in need⟩

tome \'tōm\ *n* : BOOK 1a; *esp* : a large or scholarly book [Latin *tomus*, from Greek *tomos* "section, tome", from *temnein* "to cut"]

to·men·tose \tō-'men-,tōs, 'tō-mən-\ *adj* : covered with densely matted hairs ⟨a *tomentose* leaf⟩ [Latin *tomentum* "cushion stuffing"]

tom·fool \'täm-'fül\ *n* : a great fool : BLOCKHEAD — **tomfool** *adj* — **tom·fool·ery** \täm-'fül-rē, -ə-rē\ *n*

Tom·my \'täm-ē\ *n, pl* **Tommies** : a British soldier [*Thomas* Atkins, name used as model in official army forms]

\ə\ **abut**		\ng\ **sing**	
\ər\ **further**		\ō\ **bone**	
\a\ **mat**		\ȯ\ **saw**	
\ā\ **take**		\ȯi\ **coin**	
\ä\ **cot, cart**		\th\ **thin**	
\aů\ **out**		\th\ **this**	
\ch\ **chin**		\ü\ **food**	
\e\ **pet**		\ů\ **foot**	
\ē\ **easy**		\y\ **yet**	
\g\ **go**		\yü\ **few**	
\i\ **tip**		\yů\ **cure**	
\ī\ **life**		\zh\ **vision**	
\j\ **job**			

tom·my gun \'täm-ē-,gən\ *n* : SUBMACHINE GUN [*Thompson* submachine gun]

tom·my·rot \'täm-ē-,rät\ *n* : NONSENSE 1 [English dialect *tommy* "fool" + *rot*]

to·mo·gram \'tō-mə-,gram\ *n* : an X-ray photograph of a section of the body in which shadows of structures in front of and behind the section being studied do not show [Greek *tomos* "section"]

¹to·mor·row \tə-'mär-ō, -'mȯr-\ *adv* : on or for the day after today [Old English *tō morgen,* from *tō* "to" + *morgen* "morrow, morning"]

²tomorrow *n* **1** : the day after today **2** : FUTURE 1a

Tom Thumb \'täm-'thəm\ *n* : a very small individual [*Tom Thumb,* legendary English dwarf]

tom–tom \'täm-,täm, 'təm-,təm\ *n* : a usually long narrow small-headed drum commonly beaten with the hands [Hindi *ṭamṭam*]

-t·o·my \t-ə-mē\ *n combining form, pl* **-tomies** : cutting : incision ⟨tracheo*tomy*⟩ [Greek *-tomos* "that cuts", from *temnein* "to cut"]

ton \'tən\ *n, pl* **tons** *also* **ton 1** : any of various units of weight : **a** — see MEASURE table **b** : METRIC TON **2 a** : a unit of internal capacity for ships equal to 100 cubic feet (about 2.83 cubic meters) **b** : a unit approximately equal to the volume of a long ton weight of seawater used in reckoning the displacement of ships and equal to 35 cubic feet (about .99 cubic meters) **c** : a unit of volume for cargo freight usually reckoned at 40 cubic feet (about 1.13 cubic meters) **3** : a great quantity : LOT — often used in pl. ⟨*tons* of money⟩ [Middle English *tunne,* a unit of weight or capacity, from Old English *tunne* "tun"]

ton·al \'tōn-l\ *adj* **1** : of, relating to, or having tonality **2** : of or relating to tone or tonicity — **ton·al·ly** \-l-ē\ *adv*

to·nal·i·ty \tō-'nal-ət-ē\ *n, pl* **-ties** : tonal quality: as **a** : the character of a musical composition dependent on its key or on the relation of its tones and chords to a keynote **b** : the arrangement or interrelation of color tones of a picture

¹tone \'tōn\ *n* **1 a** : quality of vocal or musical sound **b** : a sound of definite pitch or vibration **c** : pitch, inflection, or modulation of voice especially as an individual characteristic, a mode of emotional expression, or a linguistic device ⟨a shrill *tone*⟩ ⟨in angry *tones*⟩ **2** : a style or way of speaking or writing ⟨a scholarly *tone*⟩ **3** : general character, quality, or trend ⟨the depressing *tone* of your thoughts⟩ **4 a** : color quality or value : a tint or shade of color ⟨decorated in soft *tones*⟩ **b** : a color that modifies another ⟨gray with a blue *tone*⟩ **5 a** : a healthy state of the body or any of its parts; *also* : a state of normal tension and responsiveness to stimulation **b** : healthy elasticity : RESILIENCY [Latin *tonus* "tension, tone", from Greek *tonos,* literally "act of stretching"] — **toned** \'tōnd\ *adj*

²tone *vb* **1** : to give a particular intonation or inflection to **2** : to impart tone to : STRENGTHEN **3** : to soften, blend, or harmonize in color, appearance, or sound — **ton·er** *n*

tone arm *n* : the movable part of a phonograph that carries the pickup and permits the needle to follow the record groove

tone–deaf \'tōn-,def\ *adj* : relatively insensitive to differences in musical pitch

tone language *n* : a language (as Chinese) in which variations in tone distinguish words of different meaning that otherwise would sound alike

tong \'täng, 'tȯng\ *vb* **1** : to take, hold, or handle with tongs **2** : to use tongs especially in taking or handling something — **tong·er** \'täng-ər, 'tȯng-\ *n*

tongs \'tängz, 'tȯngz\ *n pl* : any of numerous grasping devices commonly having two pieces joined at one end by a pivot or hinged like scissors [Old English *tang*]

¹tongue \'təng\ *n* **1 a** : a fleshy movable process of the floor of the mouth in most vertebrates that bears sensory organs and small glands and functions especially in taking and swallowing food and in human beings as a speech organ **b** : an analogous part of various invertebrate animals **2** : the flesh of a tongue (as of the ox or sheep) used as food **3** : the power of communication through speech **4 a** : LANGUAGE; *esp* : a spoken language **b** : manner or quality of utterance with respect to tone or sound, meaning, or the intention of the speaker ⟨a clever *tongue*⟩ **c** : ecstatic usually unintelligible utterance accompanying religious excitation — usu. used in pl. **5** : something resembling an animal's tongue in being elongated and fastened at one end only: as **a** : a movable pin in a buckle **b** : a metal piece suspended inside a bell so as to strike against the sides as the bell is swung **c** : the flap under the lacing of a shoe **6** : a projecting ridge or rib (as on one edge of a board) [Old English *tunge*] — **tongue·less** \-ləs\ *adj* — **tongue·like** \-,līk\ *adj* — **on the tip of one's tongue 1** : about to be spoken **2** : just escaping mental recall

²tongue *vb* **tongued; tongu·ing** \'təng-ing\ **1** : to touch or lick with or as if with the tongue **2** : to cut a tongue on **3** : to articulate notes on a wind instrument by means of the tongue

tongue and groove *n* : a joint made by a tongue on one edge of a board fitting into a corresponding groove on the edge of another board

tongue in cheek *adv* : with insincerity, irony, or whimsical exaggeration — **tongue-in-cheek** *adj*

tongue–lash \'təng-,lash\ *vb* : SCOLD 2, BERATE — **tongue–lash·ing** *n*

tongue–tied \-,tīd\ *adj* : unable to speak clearly or freely (as from shyness)

tongue twister *n* : a word, phrase, or sentence difficult to articulate because of a succession of similar consonant sounds

¹ton·ic \'tän-ik\ *adj* **1 a** : of, relating to, or marked by tension and especially muscular tension : exhibiting tonus **b** : producing or tending to produce healthy muscular condition and reaction **c** : being or marked by excessive and prolonged muscular contraction ⟨*tonic* convulsions⟩ **2 a** : improving physical or mental tone : INVIGORATING **b** : yielding a tonic substance **3** : relating to or based on the first tone of a scale ⟨*tonic* harmony⟩ **4** : bearing a principal stress or accent ⟨a *tonic* syllable⟩ [Greek *tonikos,* from *tonos* "tension, tone"] — **ton·i·cal·ly** \'tän-i-kə-lē, -klē\ *adv*

²tonic *n* **1** : a tonic agent (as a drug) **2** : the first degree of a major or minor musical scale **3** : a voiced sound

to·nic·i·ty \tō-'nis-ət-ē\ *n* : the quality of having tone and especially healthy vigor of body or mind

¹to·night \tə-'nīt\ *adv* : on this present night or the night following this present day

²tonight *n* : the night that ends the present day

ton·nage \'tən-ij\ *n* **1 a** : a duty on ships based on cargo capacity **b** : a duty on goods per ton transported **2** : ships in terms of the total number of tons registered or carried or of their carrying capacity **3 a** : the cubical content of a merchant ship in units of 100 cubic feet (about 2.83 cubic meters) **b** : the displacement of a warship **4** : total weight in tons shipped, carried, or mined [Middle English, "duty levied on every tun of imported wine", from Old French *tonne* "tun", from Medieval Latin *tunna,* of Celtic origin]

ton·neau \tə-'nō\ *n* : the rear seating compartment of an automobile; *also* : the entire seating compartment [French, literally, "tun", derived from Old French *tonne*]

ton·sil \'tän-səl\ *n* : either of a pair of masses of lymphoid tissue that lie one on each side of the throat at the back of the mouth [Latin *tonsillae* "tonsils"] — **ton·sil·lar** \-sə-lər\ *adj*

ton·sil·lec·to·my \ˌtän-sə-'lek-tə-mē\ *n, pl* **-mies** : the surgical removal of the tonsils

ton·sil·li·tis \-'līt-əs\ *n* : inflammation of the tonsils

ton·so·ri·al \tän-'sōr-ē-əl, -'sòr-\ *adj* : of or relating to a barber or a barber's work [Latin *tonsorius,* from *tondēre* "to shear"]

ton·sure \'tän-chər\ *n* **1** : the Roman Catholic or Eastern rite of admission to the clergy by the clipping or shaving of the head **2** : the shaven crown or patch worn by monks and many clerics [Latin *tonsura* "act of shearing", from *tondēre* "to shear"] — **ton·sured** \-chərd\ *adj*

to·nus \'tō-nəs\ *n* : TONE 5a; *esp* : the state of partial contraction characteristic of normal muscle [Latin, "tension, tone"]

too \tü, 'tü\ *adv* **1** : ALSO, BESIDES ⟨sell the house and furniture *too*⟩ **2 a** : OVER 3, EXCESSIVELY ⟨it's *too* late⟩ **b** : to such a degree as to be regrettable ⟨this has gone *too* far⟩ **c** : VERY ⟨only *too* glad to help⟩ **3** : so 2d, INDEED ⟨I didn't! You did *too*!⟩ [Old English *tō* "to, too"]

took *past of* TAKE

¹tool \'tül\ *n* **1** : an instrument (as a hammer, saw, or wrench) used or worked by hand or by a machine; *also* : a machine that operates tools for shaping work **2 a** : an instrument or apparatus used in performing an operation or necessary in the practice of a vocation or profession ⟨a scholar's books are *tools*⟩ **b** : a means to an end **3** : a person used or manipulated by another : DUPE [Old English *tōl*] SYN see IMPLEMENT

²tool *vb* **1** : DRIVE ⟨*tooled* along the road⟩ **2** : to shape, form, or finish with a tool; *esp* : to letter or ornament (as a book cover) by means of hand tools **3** : to equip a plant or industry with machines and tools for production — often used with *up*

tool·box \'tül-ˌbäks\ *n* : a chest for tools

tool·head \'tül-ˌhed\ *n* : a part of a machine in which a tool or toolholder is clamped and which is provided with adjustments to bring the tool into the desired position

tool·hold·er \-ˌhōl-dər\ *n* : a short steel bar having a shank at one end to fit into the toolhead of a machine and a clamp at the other end to hold small interchangeable cutting bits

tool·house \-ˌhaus\ *n* : a building (as in a garden) for storing tools

tool·mak·er \'tül-ˌmā-kər\ *n* : a machinist who specializes in the construction, repair, maintenance, and calibration of the tools, jigs, fixtures, and instruments of a machine shop

tool·mak·ing \-ˌmā-king\ *n* : the act, process, or art of making tools

tool·room \-ˌrüm, -ˌrùm\ *n* : a room where tools are kept; *esp* : a room in a machine shop in which tools are made, stored, or loaned out to the workers

tool·shed \-ˌshed\ *n* : TOOLHOUSE

¹toot \'tüt\ *vb* **1** : to sound a short blast ⟨a horn *tooted*⟩ **2** : to blow or sound (an instrument) especially so as to produce short blasts ⟨*toot* a whistle⟩ [probably imitative] — **toot·er** *n*

²toot *n* : a short blast (as on a horn); *also* : a sound resembling such a blast

³toot *n* : a drinking bout : SPREE ⟨went on a *toot*⟩ [Scottish *toot* "to drink heavily"]

tooth \'tüth\ *n, pl* **teeth** \'tēth\ **1 a** : one of the hard bony structures borne especially on the jaws of vertebrates and used for seizing and chewing food and as weapons **b** : any of various usually hard and sharp processes especially about the mouth of an invertebrate **2** : TASTE, LIKING ⟨a *tooth* for sweets⟩ **3** : a projection resembling or suggesting the tooth of an animal in shape, arrangement, or action ⟨the *tooth* of a saw⟩ **4** : one of the projections on the rim of a cogwheel : COG **5 a** : something that injures, tortures, devours, or destroys ⟨sailed into the *teeth* of the hurricane⟩ **b** *pl* : effective means of enforcement **6** : a roughness of

surface produced by mechanical or artificial means [Old English *tōth*] — **toothed** \'tütht\ *adj* — **tooth·less** \'tüth-ləs\ *adj* — **tooth·like** \-ˌlīk\ *adj* — **to the teeth** : FULLY, COMPLETELY ⟨armed *to the teeth*⟩

tooth·ache \'tü-ˌthāk\ *n* : pain in or about a tooth

tooth and nail *adv* : with every available means : all out ⟨fight *tooth and nail*⟩

tooth·brush \'tüth-ˌbrəsh\ *n* : a brush for cleaning the teeth

toothed whale *n* : any of a group (Odontoceti) of whales with numerous simple conical teeth

tooth·paste \'tüth-ˌpāst\ *n* : a paste dentifrice

tooth·pick \-ˌpik\ *n* : a pointed instrument (as a small tapering piece of wood) used for removing food particles lodged between the teeth

tooth powder *n* : a dentifrice in powder form

tooth shell *n* : any of a class (Scaphopoda) of marine mollusks with a tapering tubular shell; *also* : this shell

tooth·some \'tüth-səm\ *adj* **1** : pleasing to the taste : DELICIOUS ⟨a *toothsome* dessert⟩ **2** : physically attractive : LOVELY — **tooth·some·ly** *adv* — **tooth·some·ness** *n*

toothy \'tü-thē\ *adj* **tooth·i·er; -est** : having or showing prominent teeth ⟨a *toothy* grin⟩ — **tooth·i·ly** \-thə-lē\ *adv*

¹top \'täp\ *n* **1 a** : the highest point, level, or part ⟨the *top* of the hill⟩ **b** : the upper end, edge, or surface ⟨the *top* of the page⟩ ⟨filled the glass to the *top*⟩ **2** : the stalk and leaves of a plant and especially of one with edible roots ⟨beet *tops*⟩ **3** : an integral part serving as an upper piece, lid, or covering ⟨a pajama *top*⟩ ⟨put the *top* on the jar⟩ **4** : the highest position or rank : ACME ⟨reached the *top* of the profession⟩; *also* : one in such a position ⟨secrets known only to the *top*⟩ [Old English] — **topped** \'täpt\ *adj* — **off the top of one's head** : in an impromptu way — **on top of 1** : in control of ⟨was *on top of* the job⟩ **2** : in sudden unexpected nearness to ⟨the motorboat was *on top of* us⟩ **3** : in addition to — **on top of the world** : in a position of great success, happiness, or fame

²top *vt* **topped; top·ping** **1** : to remove or cut the top of ⟨*top* a tree⟩ **2 a** : to cover with a top : provide, form, or serve as a top for **b** : to supply with a decorative or protective finish or a final touch ⟨*topped* the sundae with nuts⟩ ⟨a meal *topped* off with coffee⟩ **3 a** : to be or become higher than ⟨the flood *topped* the dike⟩ **b** : to be superior to ⟨*topped* the record⟩ **c** : to gain ascendancy over : DOMINATE **4 a** : to rise to, reach, or be at the top of **b** : to go over the top of **5** : to strike (a ball) above the center creating topspin or sometimes making a weak stroke

³top *adj* **1** : of, relating to, or being at the top **2** : LEADING 1, CHIEF **3** : of the highest quality, amount, or degree ⟨*top* value⟩

⁴top *n* : a commonly cylindrical or cone-shaped toy that has a point on which it is made to spin [Old English]

to·paz \'tō-ˌpaz\ *n* **1** : a hard mineral consisting of a silicate of aluminum and occurring in crystals of various colors with the yellow variety being the one usually cut and prized as a gem **2** : a gem (as a yellow sapphire) resembling the true topaz [Old French *topace,* from Latin *topazus,* from Greek *topazos*]

top billing *n* **1** : the position at the top of a theatrical bill usually featuring the star's name **2** : prominent emphasis, featuring, or advertising

top boot *n* : a high boot often with light-colored leather bands around the upper part

top·coat \'täp-ˌkōt\ *n* : a lightweight overcoat

top·cross \-ˌkros\ *n* : a cross between a superior or purebred male and inferior female stock to improve the average quality of the progeny; *also* : an offspring from such a cross

top dog *n* : one that is in a position of authority especially by winning in a hard-fought competition

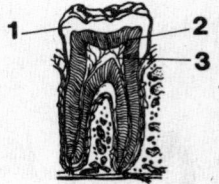

tooth 1a: *1* enamel, *2* dentine, *3* pulp

top dollar *n* : the highest amount being paid for a commodity or service ⟨paid *top dollar* for the tickets⟩

top drawer *n* : the highest level of society, authority, or excellence

tope \ˈtōp\ *n* : a widely distributed small shark with a liver rich in vitamin A [origin unknown]

to·pee *or* **to·pi** \tō-ˈpē, ˈtō-pē\ *n* : a lightweight helmet-shaped hat made of pith or cork [Hindi *ṭopī*]

top·er \ˈtō-pər\ *n* : a heavy drinker; *esp* : DRUNKARD [obsolete *tope,* interjection used to wish good health before drinking]

top flight *n* : TOP DRAWER — **top·flight** \ˈtäp-ˈflīt\ *adj*

Top 40 *n pl* : the 40 best-selling phonograph records for a given period

top·gal·lant \täp-ˈgal-ənt, ˈtäp-, tə-ˈgal-\ *n* : the sail just above a topsail and below the royal on a square-rigged ship

top hat *n* : a tall-crowned hat usually of beaver or silk

top–heavy \ˈtäp-ˌhev-ē\ *adj* : having the top part too heavy for the lower part

To·phet \ˈtō-fət\ *n* : HELL 2 [Hebrew *tōpheth,* shrine south of ancient Jerusalem where human sacrifices were performed to Moloch (Jeremiah 7:31)]

¹**to·pi·ary** \ˈtō-pē-ˌer-ē\ *adj* : of, relating to, or being the training and trimming of woody plants into odd or ornamental shapes; *also* : characterized by such work [Latin *topiarius,* from *topia* "ornamental gardening", from Greek *topos* "place"]

²**topiary** *n, pl* **-ar·ies** : topiary art or gardening; *also* : a topiary garden

top·ic \ˈtäp-ik\ *n* **1** : a heading in an outlined argument or exposition **2** : the subject of a discourse or a section of it : THEME [Latin *Topica,* a work by Aristotle on forms of argument, from Greek *Topika,* derived from *topos* "place, commonplace"]

top·i·cal \ˈtäp-i-kəl\ *adj* **1 a** : of or relating to a place **b** : local or designed for local application ⟨a *topical* remedy⟩ ⟨a *topical* anesthetic⟩ **2 a** : of, relating to, or arranged by topics ⟨a *topical* outline⟩ **b** : referring to the topics of the day or place : of local or temporary interest [Greek *topikos,* from *topos* "place"] — **top·i·cal·i·ty** \ˌtäp-ə-ˈkal-ət-ē\ *n* — **top·i·cal·ly** \ˈtäp-i-kə-lē, -klē\ *adv*

topic sentence *n* : a sentence that states the main thought of a paragraph or of a larger unit of discourse

top·knot \ˈtäp-ˌnät\ *n* **1** : an ornament (as a bow) forming a headdress or worn as part of a hairstyle **2** : a crest of feathers or hair on the top of the head

/ topknot 2

top·less \ˈtäp-ləs\ *adj* **1** : being without a top **2 a** : wearing no clothing on the upper body **b** : featuring topless waitresses or entertainers

top·lofty \ˈtäp-ˌlof-tē\ *also* **top·loft·i·cal** \täp-ˈlof-ti-kəl\ *adj* : very superior in air or attitude : HAUGHTY — **top·loft·i·ness** \ˈtäp-ˌlof-tē-nəs\ *n*

top·mast \-ˌmast, -məst\ *n* : the mast that is next above the lower mast and topmost in a fore-and-aft rig

top milk *n* : the cream-rich upper layer of unhomogenized milk that has stood in a container

top·min·now \ˈtäp-ˌmin-ō\ *n* : any of a large family of small viviparous surface-feeding fishes

top·most \-ˌmōst\ *adj* : highest of all : UPPERMOST

top·notch \-ˈnäch\ *adj* : of the highest quality : FIRST-RATE — **top·notch·er** \-ˈnäch-ər\ *n*

to·pog·ra·pher \tə-ˈpäg-rə-fər\ *n* : one skilled in topography

to·po·graph·ic \ˌtäp-ə-ˈgraf-ik, ˌtō-pə-\ *adj* : of, relating to, or concerned with topography ⟨a *topographic* map⟩

to·po·graph·i·cal \-ˈgraf-i-kəl\ *adj* **1** : TOPOGRAPHIC **2** : of, relating to, or concerned with the artistic representation of a particular locality ⟨*topographical* paintings⟩ — **to·po·graph·i·cal·ly** \-kə-lē, -klē\ *adv*

to·pog·ra·phy \tə-ˈpäg-rə-fē\ *n* **1** : the art or practice of detailing on maps or charts natural and man-made features of a place or region especially so as to show elevations **2** : the configuration of a surface including

toque

its relief and the position of its natural and man-made features ⟨a map showing *topography*⟩ [Late Latin *topographia,* from Greek, from *topographein* "to describe a place", from *topos* "place" + *graphein* "to write"]

to·pol·o·gy \tə-ˈpäl-ə-jē, tä-\ *n* **1** : topographical study of a particular place; *esp* : the history of a region as indicated by its topography **2** : the anatomy of a particular region of the body **3** : a branch of mathematics concerned with those properties of geometric figures that do not change when the shape of the figure is subjected to continuous change — **to·po·log·i·cal** \ˌtäp-ə-ˈläj-i-kəl, ˌtō-pə-\ *adj* — **to·pol·o·gist** \tə-ˈpäl-ə-jəst, tō-\ *n*

top·per \ˈtäp-ər\ *n* **1** : one that is at or on the top **2 a** : SILK HAT **b** : OPERA HAT **3** : something (as a joke) that caps everything preceding **4** : a woman's usually short and loose-fitting lightweight outer coat

¹**top·ping** \ˈtäp-ing\ *n* **1** : something that forms a top; *esp* : a garnish (as a sauce, bread crumbs, or whipped cream) placed on top of a food **2** : the action of one that tops

²**topping** *adj* **1** : highest in rank or eminence **2** *chiefly British* : SUPERIOR 4a, EXCELLENT

top·ple \ˈtäp-əl\ *vb* **top·pled; top·pling** \ˈtäp-ling, -ə-ling\ **1** : to fall or cause to fall from or as if from being top-heavy **2** : to be or seem unsteady : TOTTER **3** : OVERTHROW ⟨*topple* a government⟩ [derived from ²*top*]

tops \ˈtäps\ *adj* : topmost in quality, ability, popularity, or eminence ⟨*tops* in your profession⟩

top·sail \ˈtäp-ˌsāl, -səl\ *also* **top·s'l** \-səl\ *n* **1** : the sail next above the lowermost sail on a mast in a square-rigged ship **2** : the sail set above and sometimes on the gaff in a fore-and-aft rigged ship

top secret *adj* : demanding inviolate secrecy among top officials or a select few

top sergeant *n* : FIRST SERGEANT 1

top·side \ˈtäp-ˈsīd\ *adv or adj* **1** : on deck **2** : to or on the top or surface

top·soil \-ˌsoil\ *n* : surface soil; *esp* : the organic layer in which plants have most of their roots and which the farmer turns over in plowing

top·spin \ˈtäp-ˌspin\ *n* : rotary motion imparted to a ball causing it to rotate forward in the direction of movement [¹*top*]

top·sy–tur·vi·ness \ˌtäp-sē-ˈtər-vē-nəs\ *n* : the quality or state of being topsy-turvy

¹**top·sy–tur·vy** \ˌtäp-sē-ˈtər-vē\ *adv* **1** : upside down **2** : in utter confusion or disorder [probably derived from ¹*top* + obsolete *terve* "to turn upside down"]

²**topsy–turvy** *adj* : turned topsy-turvy : totally disordered — **top·sy–tur·vi·ly** \-ˈtər-və-lē\ *adv* — **top·sy–tur·vy·dom** \-ˈtər-vēd-əm\ *n*

³**topsy–turvy** *n* : TOPSY-TURVINESS

toque \ˈtōk\ *n* : a woman's small hat without a brim made in any of various soft close-fitting shapes [Middle French, "soft hat with a narrow brim", from Spanish *toca* "headdress"]

tor \ˈtor\ *n* : a high craggy hill [Old English *torr*]

To·rah \ˈtōr-ə, ˈtor-; ˈtoi-rə\ *n* **1** : LAW 3b **2** : the body of wisdom and law found in the Jewish Scripture and oral tradition **3** : a leather or parchment scroll of the Pentateuch used in a synagogue for liturgical purposes [Hebrew *tōrāh*]

¹**torch** \ˈtorch\ *n* **1** : a flaming light made of something (as resinous wood) that burns brightly and usually carried in the hand **2** : something (as wisdom or knowledge) likened to a torch as giving light or guidance **3** : any of various portable devices for producing a hot flame — compare BLOWTORCH **4** *chiefly British* : FLASHLIGHT 3 [Old French *torche* "bundle of twisted straw or tow"]

²**torch** *vt* : to set on fire with or as if with a torch

torch·bear·er \ˈtorch-ˌbar-ər, -ˌber-\ *n* **1** : one that carries a torch **2** : one that is in the forefront of a movement, campaign, or crusade

torch·light \'torch-,līt\ *n* : light given by torches

torch singer *n* : a singer of torch songs

torch song *n* : a popular sentimental song of unrequited love

tore *past of* TEAR

to·re·ador \'tor-ē-ə-,dor, 'tōr-, 'tär-\ *n* : BULLFIGHTER [Spanish, from *torear* "to fight bulls", from *toro* "bull", from Latin *taurus*]

to·re·ro \tə-'rear-ō\ *n, pl* **-ros** : BULLFIGHTER [Spanish, from Late Latin *taurarius*, from Latin *taurus* 'bull']

tori *pl of* TORUS

to·rii \'tōr-ē-,ē, 'tor-\ *n, pl* **torii** : a Japanese gateway of light construction built at the approach to a Shinto temple [Japanese]

¹tor·ment \'tor-,ment\ *n* **1** : the infliction of torture (as by rack or wheel) **2** : extreme physical or mental pain or anguish : AGONY **3** : a source of irritation or pain [Old French, from Latin *tormentum* "torture", from *torquēre* "to twist"]

²tor·ment \tor-'ment, 'tor-,\ *vt* **1 a** : to cause severe suffering of body or mind to **b** : to cause worry or vexation to : TROUBLE ⟨a mystery that has *tormented* us for years⟩ **2** : DISTORT 1, TWIST SYN see AFFLICT — **tor·men·tor** \-ər\ *n*

torn *past participle of* TEAR

tor·na·dic \tor-'nād-ik, -'nad-\ *adj* : relating to, characteristic of, or being a tornado

tor·na·do \tor-'nād-ō\ *n, pl* **-does** *or* **-dos** : a violent destructive whirling wind accompanied by a funnel-shaped cloud that progresses in a narrow path over the land [Spanish *tronada* "thunderstorm", from *tronar* "to thunder", from Latin *tonare*]

¹tor·pe·do \tor-'pēd-ō\ *n, pl* **-does** **1** : ELECTRIC RAY **2 a** : a submarine mine **b** : a self-propelled cigar-shaped submarine missile filled with an explosive charge **3 a** : a charge of explosive enclosed in a container or case **b** : a small firework that explodes when thrown against a hard object [Latin, literally, "numbness", from *torpēre* "to be numb"]

²torpedo *vt* **1** : to hit or sink (a ship) with a naval torpedo **2** : to destroy or nullify altogether : WRECK ⟨*torpedo* a plan⟩

torpedo boat *n* : a small fast boat for firing torpedoes

torpedo–boat destroyer *n* : a large, fast, and powerful armed torpedo boat originally intended principally for the destruction of torpedo boats but later used also as a formidable torpedo boat

tor·pid \'tor-pəd\ *adj* **1 a** : having lost motion or the power of exertion or feeling : DORMANT ⟨a bear *torpid* in its winter sleep⟩ **b** : sluggish in functioning or acting ⟨a *torpid* mind⟩ **2** : lacking in energy or vigor : APATHETIC, DULL [Latin *torpidus*, from *torpēre* "to be numb"] — **tor·pid·i·ty** \tor-'pid-ət-ē\ *n* — **tor·pid·ly** \'tor-pəd-lē\ *adv*

tor·por \'tor-pər\ *n* **1** : temporary loss or suspension of motion or feeling : extreme sluggishness ⟨the *torpor* of bears in winter⟩ **2** : APATHY 2, DULLNESS [Latin, from *torpēre* "to be numb"] SYN see LETHARGY

torque \'tork\ *n* : a force which produces or tends to produce rotation or twisting [Latin *torquēre* "to twist"]

tor·rent \'tor-ənt, 'tär-\ *n* **1** : a violent or rushing stream of a liquid (as water or lava) **2** : a large, rapid, or violent flow (as of orders, activity, or abuse) : SURGE [French, from Latin *torrens*, from *torrens* "burning, seething, rushing", from *torrēre* "to parch, burn"]

tor·ren·tial \to-'ren-chəl, tə-\ *adj* **1 a** : relating to or having the character of a torrent ⟨*torrential* rains⟩ **b** : caused by or resulting from action of rapid streams ⟨*torrential* gravel⟩ **2** : resembling a torrent in violence or rapidity of flow — **tor·ren·tial·ly** \-'rench-lē, -ə-lē\ *adv*

tor·rid \'tor-əd, 'tär-\ *adj* **1 a** : parched with heat especially of the sun ⟨*torrid* sands⟩ **b** : giving off intense heat **2** : ARDENT, PASSIONATE ⟨*torrid* love letters⟩ [Latin

torridus, from *torrēre* "to parch"] — **tor·rid·i·ty** \to-'rid-ət-ē\ *n* — **tor·rid·ly** \'tor-əd-lē, 'tär-\ *adv* — **tor·rid·ness** *n*

torrid zone *n* : the belt of the earth between the tropics over which the sun is vertical at some period of the year

tor·sion \'tor-shən\ *n* **1** : the act or process of turning or twisting **2** : the state of being twisted [Late Latin *torsus*, past participle of Latin *torquēre* "to twist"] — **tor·sion·al** \-shnəl, -shən-l\ *adj*

torsion bar *n* : a long metal piece in an automobile suspension that has one end firmly attached to the frame and the other end twisted and connected to the axle and that acts like a spring

tor·so \'tor-sō\ *n, pl* **torsos** *or* **tor·si** \-,sē\ **1** : the trunk of a sculptured representation of a human body; *esp* : the trunk of a statue whose head and limbs are mutilated **2** : something (as a piece of writing) that is mutilated or left unfinished **3** : the human trunk [Italian, literally, "stalk", from Latin *thyrsus*, from Greek *thyrsos*]

tort \'tort\ *n* : a wrongful act which does not involve a breach of contract and for which the injured party can recover damages in a civil action [Middle French, from Medieval Latin *tortum*, from Latin *tortus* "twisted", from *torquēre* "to twist"]

torte \'tort-ə, 'tort\ *n, pl* **tor·ten** \'tort-n\ *or* **tortes** : a cake made of many eggs and often grated nuts or dry bread crumbs and usually covered with a rich frosting [German]

tor·ti·lla \tor-'tē-ə, -'tē-yə\ *n* : a round thin cake made from cornmeal or flour [American Spanish, from Spanish *torta* "cake", from Late Latin, "round loaf of bread"]

tor·toise \'tort-əs\ *n* : any of an order (Testudinata) of reptiles : TURTLE; *esp* : a land turtle [Middle French *tortue*]

¹tor·toise·shell \'tort-əs-,shel, -əsh-,shel\ *n* : a mottled horny substance that covers the bony shell of some sea turtles and is used in inlaying and in making various ornamental articles

²tortoiseshell *adj* : made of or resembling tortoiseshell especially in spotted brown and yellow coloring

tor·to·ni \tor-'tō-nē\ *n* : ice cream made of heavy cream often with minced almonds and chopped maraschino cherries and often flavored with rum [probably from *Tortoni*, 19th century Italian restaurateur in Paris]

tor·tu·ous \'torch-wəs, -ə-wəs\ *adj* **1** : marked by repeated twists, bends, or turns : WINDING ⟨a *tortuous* stream⟩ **2 a** : marked by devious or indirect tactics : CROOKED, TRICKY **b** : confusingly roundabout ⟨the *tortuous* workings of the law⟩ [Middle French *tortueux*, from Latin *tortuosus*, from *tortus* "twist", from *torquēre* "to twist"] — **tor·tu·ous·ly** *adv* — **tor·tu·ous·ness** *n*

¹tor·ture \'tor-chər\ *n* **1** : the infliction of intense pain especially to punish or obtain a confession **2 a** : physical or mental anguish : AGONY **b** : something that causes agony [French, from Late Latin *tortura*, from Latin *torquēre* "to twist"]

²torture *vt* **tor·tured; tor·tur·ing** \'torch-ring, -ə-ring\ **1** : to punish or coerce by inflicting excruciating pain **2** : to cause intense suffering to : TORMENT **3** : to twist or wrench out of shape : DISTORT SYN see AFFLICT — **tor·tur·er** \'tor-chər-ər\ *n*

tor·tur·ous \'torch-rəs, -ə-rəs\ *adj* : causing torture : cruelly painful — **tor·tur·ous·ly** *adv*

to·rus \'tōr-əs, 'tor-\ *n, pl* **to·ri** \'tōr-,ī, 'tor-, -,ē\ **1** : a large molding of convex profile commonly occurring as the lowest molding in the base of a column **2** : a doughnut-shaped surface generated by a circle rotated about an axis in its plane that does not intersect the circle [Latin, "protuberance, bulge, torus molding"]

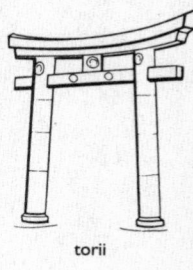

torii

\ə\ abut	\ng\ sing
\ər\ **further**	\ō\ bone
\a\ mat	\o\ saw
\ā\ take	\oi\ coin
\ä\ cot, cart	\th\ thin
\aù\ out	\th\ this
\ch\ chin	\ü\ food
\e\ pet	\ù\ foot
\ē\ easy	\y\ yet
\g\ go	\yü\ few
\i\ tip	\yù\ cure
\ī\ life	\zh\ vision
\j\ job	

To·ry \'tōr-ē, 'tór-\ *n, pl* **Tories** **1 a** : a member of a British political group of the 18th and early 19th centuries favoring royal authority and the established church and seeking to preserve the traditional political structure — compare WHIG **b** : CONSERVATIVE 1b **2** : an American supporting the cause of the British Crown during the American Revolution : LOYALIST **3** *often not cap* : an extreme conservative especially in politics and economics [Irish Gaelic *tōraidhe* "pursued man, robber"; from Irish royalists outlawed in the 17th century] — **Tory** *adj*

¹toss \'tós, 'täs\ *vb* **1** : to keep throwing here and there or backward and forward : cause to pitch or roll ⟨waves *tossed* the ship about⟩ **2** : to throw with a quick light motion ⟨*toss* a ball into the air⟩ **3** : to lift with a sudden motion ⟨*toss* the head⟩ **4** : to pitch or bob about rapidly ⟨a canoe *tossing* on the waves⟩ **5** : to accomplish, provide, or dispose of easily ⟨*tossed* off a few verses⟩ **6** : to be restless : fling oneself about ⟨*toss* in one's sleep⟩ **7** : to stir or mix lightly ⟨*toss* a salad⟩ **8** : to decide an issue by flipping a coin [probably of Scandinavian origin] SYN see THROW

²toss *n* **1** : the state or fact of being tossed **2 a** : an act or instance of tossing **b** : a deciding by chance and especially by flipping a coin

toss-up \-,əp\ *n* **1** : TOSS 2b **2** : an even chance

¹tot \'tät\ *n* **1** : a small child : TODDLER **2** : SHOT 8a [origin unknown]

²tot *vb* **tot·ted; tot·ting** : to add together : TOTAL — usually used with *up* [*tot.*, abbreviation of *total*]

¹to·tal \'tōt-l\ *adj* **1** : making up or being the whole : ENTIRE ⟨the *total* amount⟩ **2** : ABSOLUTE 4, UTTER ⟨*total* ruin⟩ **3** : making use of every available means to accomplish a single objective ⟨*total* war⟩ [Middle French, from Medieval Latin *totalis*, from Latin *totus* "whole, entire"]

²total *n* **1** : a product of addition : SUM **2** : an entire quantity : AMOUNT SYN see SUM

³total *vt* **to·taled** *or* **to·talled; to·tal·ing** *or* **to·tal·ling** **1** : to add up : COMPUTE **2** : to amount to : NUMBER

total eclipse *n* : an eclipse in which one celestial body is completely obscured by the shadow or body of another

to·tal·i·tar·i·an \tō-,tal-ə-'ter-ē-ən\ *adj* **1** : of, relating to, or being a political regime based on subordination of the individual to the state and strict control of all aspects of life especially by use of force **2** : advocating or characteristic of such a regime [*total* + *-itarian* (as in *authoritarian*)] — **totalitarian** *n* — **to·tal·i·tar·i·an·ism** \-ē-ə-,niz-əm\ *n*

to·tal·i·ty \tō-'tal-ət-ē\ *n, pl* **-ties** **1** : an aggregate amount : SUM, WHOLE **2** : the quality or state of being total : ENTIRETY

to·tal·ize \'tōt-l-,īz\ *vt* **1** : to add up : TOTAL **2** : to express as a whole

to·tal·ly \'tōt-l-ē\ *adv* **1** : in a total manner : WHOLLY **2** : as a whole : in toto

¹tote \'tōt\ *vt* **1** : to carry by hand : LUG **2** : HAUL 1c, CONVEY [origin unknown] — **tot·er** *n*

²tote *n* : a large handbag — called also **tote bag**

to·tem \'tōt-əm\ *n* : an object (as an animal or plant) or a representation of an object serving as the emblem of a family or clan and often as a reminder of its ancestry [Ojibwa *ototeman* "his totem"] — **to·tem·ic** \tō-'tem-ik\ *adj*

totem pole

totem pole *n* : a pole carved and painted with totemic symbols that is erected before the houses of some northwest coast Indians

¹tot·ter \'tät-ər\ *vi* **1 a** : to tremble or rock as if about to fall : SWAY **b** : to become unstable : threaten to collapse **2** : to move unsteadily : STAGGER, WOBBLE [Middle English *toteren*] — **tot·ter·ing·ly** \'tät-ə-ring-lē\ *adv* — **tot·tery** \'tät-ə-rē\ *adj*

²totter *n* : an unsteady gait : WOBBLE

toucan

tou·can \'tü-,kan, tü-'\ *n* : any of a family of fruit-eating birds of tropical America with brilliant coloring and a very large but light and thin-walled bill [French, from Portuguese *tucano*, from Tupi]

¹touch \'təch\ *vb* **1** : to feel or handle (as with fingers or hands) ⟨loved to *touch* soft velvet⟩ **2** : to come close : VERGE ⟨actions *touching* on treason⟩ **3 a** : to take into the hands or mouth ⟨never *touches* meat⟩ **b** : to put hands on in any way or degree ⟨don't *touch* the exhibits⟩ ⟨wouldn't *touch* your money⟩; *esp* : HARM ⟨swore they hadn't *touched* the child⟩ **4** : to persuade to give or lend ⟨*touched* me for $10⟩ **5** : to cause to be briefly in contact with something ⟨*touched* spurs to the horse⟩ ⟨*touch* a match to kindling⟩ **6 a** : to meet without overlapping or penetrating : ADJOIN **b** : to rival in quality or value ⟨this car doesn't *touch* my old one⟩ **7** : to speak or tell of especially in passing ⟨barely *touched* on domestic politics⟩ **8** : to affect the interest of : CONCERN ⟨a problem *touching* everyone⟩ **9 a** : to affect physically; *esp* : to harm slightly by or as if by contact ⟨fruit *touched* by frost⟩ **b** : to give a delicate tint, line, or expression to ⟨lips *touched* with a smile⟩ **10** : to move emotionally ⟨*touched* by your loyalty⟩ **11** : to make a brief incidental stop in part ⟨*touched* at several ports⟩ [Old French *tuchier*] — **touch·able** \-ə-bəl\ *adj* — **touch·er** *n*

²touch *n* **1** : a light stroke, tap, or blow **2** : the act or fact of touching or being touched **3 a** : the special sense by which light pressure is perceived ⟨fabric soft to the *touch*⟩ **b** : a particular sensation conveyed by this sense : FEEL ⟨the soft *touch* of silk⟩ **4** : quality or kind especially as attested by authority; *also* : an attesting mark (as on silver) **5** : a small amount : TRACE ⟨a *touch* of garlic⟩; *esp* : a light attack ⟨a *touch* of fever⟩ **6** : a manner of touching or striking the keys of a keyboard ⟨a firm *touch* on the piano⟩; *also* : the character of response of the keys to being struck ⟨a typewriter with a stiff *touch*⟩ **7** : an effective and subtle detail in creating or improving an artistic work ⟨applied finishing *touches* to the portrait⟩ **8** : distinctive manner or method ⟨the *touch* of a genius⟩ **9** : a characteristic or distinguishing trait or quality ⟨a classic *touch* to your writing⟩ **10** *slang* : an act of seeking or getting a gift or loan **11** : a state of contact or communication ⟨let's keep in *touch*⟩

touch and go *n* : a highly uncertain or precarious situation — **touch–and–go** *adj*

touch·back \'təch-,bak\ *n* : a situation in football in which the defending team downs the ball behind its own goal line after receiving a kick or intercepting a pass

touch·down \-,daún\ *n* **1 a** : the act of touching a football to the ground behind an opponent's goal **b** : a score of six points in American football made by carrying the ball over the opponent's goal line **2** : the act or moment of touching down (as with an airplane or spacecraft)

touch down \təch-'daún, 'təch-\ *vi* : to reach the ground : LAND

tou·ché \tü-'shā\ *interj* — used to acknowledge a hit in fencing or the success of an argument [French, from *toucher* "to touch", from Old French *tuchier*]

touched \'təcht\ *adj* : slightly unbalanced mentally

touch football *n* : football chiefly characterized by the substitution of touching for tackling

touch·hole \'təch-,hōl\ *n* : the vent in old-time cannons or firearms through which the charge was ignited

¹touch·ing *prep* : in reference to : CONCERNING

²touching *adj* : arousing tenderness or compassion — **touch·ing·ly** \-ing-lē\ *adv*

touch-me-not \'təch-mē-,nät\ *n* : IMPATIENS [from the bursting of the ripe pods when touched]

touch off *vt* **1** : to describe or characterize with precision **2 a** : to cause to explode by or as if by touching with fire **b** : to release or start with sudden violence ⟨*touched off* a riot⟩

touch pad *n* : a keypad for an electronic device (as a microwave oven) that consists of a flat surface divided into several differently marked areas which are touched to choose options

touch screen *n* : a display screen (as for a computer) on which the user selects options by touching the screen

touch·stone \'təch-ˌstōn\ *n* **1** : a black stone formerly used to test the purity of gold and silver by the streak left on the stone when rubbed by the metal **2** : a test or standard for judging something

touch system *n* : a method of typewriting that assigns a particular finger to each key and makes it possible to type without looking at the keyboard

Touch–Tone \'təch-ˌtōn, -ˌtōn\ *trademark* — used for a telephone having push buttons that produce tones corresponding to numbers

touch–type \'təch-ˌtīp\ *vi* : to type by the touch system

touch up *vt* **1** : to improve or perfect by small additional strokes or alterations **2** : to stimulate by or as if by a flick of a whip

touch·wood \'təch-ˌwud\ *n* : ³PUNK

touchy \'təch-ē\ *adj* **touch·i·er; -est 1** : marked by readiness to take offense on slight provocation **2** : acutely sensitive or irritable ⟨a *touchy* swelling⟩ **3** : calling for tact, care, or caution in treatment ⟨a *touchy* subject⟩ SYN see IRASCIBLE — **touch·i·ly** \'təch-ə-lē\ *adv* — **touch·i·ness** \'təch-ē-nəs\ *n*

touchy-feely \ˌtəch-ē-'fē-lē\ *adj* : characterized by or encouraging interpersonal touching in the free expression of emotions ⟨*touchy-feely* therapy⟩; *also* : openly or excessively emotional and personal ⟨*touchy-feely* management⟩

¹tough \'təf\ *adj* **1** : able to undergo great strain : flexible and not brittle ⟨*tough* fibers⟩ **2** : not easily chewed ⟨*tough* meat⟩ **3** : able to stand hard work and hardship : ROBUST ⟨a *tough* body⟩ **4 a** : hard to influence : STUBBORN ⟨a *tough* bargainer⟩ **b** : very difficult ⟨a *tough* problem⟩ **5** : ROWDY, LAWLESS ⟨a *tough* neighborhood⟩ **6** : free from softness or sentimentality ⟨a *tough* approach to delinquency⟩; *esp* : marked by firm uncompromising determination ⟨a *tough* foreign policy⟩ [Old English *tōh*] — **tough·ly** *adv* — **tough·ness** *n*

²tough *n* : a vicious and unruly person; *also* : ROWDY

tough·en \'təf-ən\ *vb* **tough·ened; tough·en·ing** \'təf-ning, -ə-ning\ : to make or become tough

tough–mind·ed \'təf-'mīn-dəd\ *adj* : realistic or unsentimental in temper or habitual point of view

tou·pee \tü-'pā\ *n* : a usually small wig or hairpiece for a man [French *toupet* "forelock", of Germanic origin]

¹tour \'tur, *1 is also* 'taur\ *n* **1** : a period of work or duty ⟨a long *tour* abroad⟩ **2** : a trip or excursion usually ending at the point of beginning ⟨a *tour* of the city⟩ [Middle French, from Old French *tourn, tour* "lathe, circuit, turn", from Latin *tornus* "lathe"]

²tour *vb* : to make a tour of : travel as a tourist

tour de force \ˌturd-ə-'fōrs, -'fors\ *n, pl* **tours de force** *same*\ : a feat of strength, skill, or ingenuity [French]

touring car *n* : an old-fashioned open automobile with two cross seats, usually four doors, and a folding top

tour·ist \'tur-əst\ *n* : one who travels for pleasure — **tourist** *adj*

tourist class *n* : economy accommodation on a ship, airplane, or train

tourist court *n* : MOTEL

tourist home *n* : a house in which rooms are available for rent to transients

tour·ma·line \'tur-mə-lən, -lēn\ *n* : a mineral of variable color that is a complex silicate and when transparent is cut for use as a gemstone [Sinhalese *toramalli* "carnelian"]

tour·na·ment \'tur-nə-mənt *also* 'tər- *or* 'tor-\ *n* **1 a** : a contest of skill and courage between armored knights fighting with blunted lances or swords **b** : a series of knightly contests occurring at one time and place **2** : a series of athletic contests, sports events, or games for a championship ⟨a tennis *tournament*⟩ [Old French *torneiement* "to engage in a tournament", from torn, tourn "lathe, circuit, turn"]

tour·ney \'tur-nē *also* 'tər- *or* 'tor-\ *n, pl* **tourneys** : TOURNAMENT [Middle French *tornei*, from *torneier* "to engage in a tournament"]

tour·ni·quet \'tur-ni-kət, 'tər-\ *n* : a device (as a bandage twisted tight with a stick) to check bleeding [French, from *tourner* "to turn"]

¹tou·sle \'tau-zəl, -səl\ *vt* **tou·sled; tou·sling** \'tauz-ling, 'taus-, -ə-ling\ : DISHEVEL, RUMPLE ⟨*tousled* hair⟩ [Middle English *touselen*]

²tousle *n* : a tangled mass or condition

¹tout \'taut\ *vb* **1** : to solicit or canvass for patronage, trade, votes, or support **2 a** *chiefly British* : to spy about at racing stables and tracks to get information to be used in betting **b** : to provide tips on racehorses [Middle English *tuten* "to peer"]

²tout *n* : one who touts: as **a** : one who solicits patronage **b** : one who gives tips or solicits bets on a horse race

³tout *vt* : to praise or publicize insistently or excessively [alteration of ¹*toot*]

tout·er \'taut-ər\ *n* : TOUT

¹tow \'tō\ *vt* : to draw or pull along behind : HAUL [Old English *togian*]

²tow *n* **1** : an act or instance of towing or the fact or condition of being towed **2** : a line or rope for towing **3** : something (as a tugboat or barge) that tows or is towed — **in tow 1** : in the state or course of being towed **2** : under guidance or protection : in the position of a follower

³tow *n* **1** : short broken fiber from flax, hemp, or jute used for yarn, twine, or stuffing **2** : yarn or cloth made of tow [Old English *tow-* "spinning"]

tow·age \'tō-ij\ *n* **1** : the act of towing **2** : the price paid for towing

¹to·ward \'tō-ərd, 'to-ərd, 'tōrd, 'tord\ *adj* **1** *also* **to·wards** \'tō-ərdz, 'to-ərdz, 'tōrdz, 'tordz\ **a** : coming soon : IMMINENT ⟨could move fast enough if a meal was *toward*⟩ **b** : happening at the moment : AFOOT **2 a** *obsolete* : quick to learn : APT **b** : PROPITIOUS **3** ⟨a *toward* breeze⟩ [Old English *tōweard* "facing, imminent", from *tō* "to" + *-weard* "-ward"]

²to·ward \tō-ərd, 'tō-, twō-, 'twō-; tōrd, 'tōrd, twōrd, 'twōrd; tə-'word\ *or* **to·wards** *same followed by* z\ *prep* **1** : in the direction of ⟨driving *toward* town⟩ **2 a** : along a course leading to ⟨efforts *toward* reconciliation⟩ **b** : in relation to ⟨attitude *toward* life⟩ **3** : so as to face ⟨the back was *toward* me⟩ **4** : not long before ⟨*toward* noon⟩ **5** : in order to provide part of the payment for ⟨save *toward* a college education⟩

tow·boat \'tō-ˌbōt\ *n* **1** : TUGBOAT **2** : a compact shallow-draft boat for pushing barges on inland waterways

¹tow·el \'tau-əl, 'taul\ *n* : a cloth or piece of absorbent paper for wiping or drying [Old French *toaille*, of Germanic origin]

²towel *vb* **-eled** *or* **-elled; -el·ing** *or* **-el·ling 1** : to rub or dry with a towel **2** : to use a towel

tow·el·ing *or* **tow·el·ling** \'tau-ling, -ə-ling\ *n* : material for towels

¹tow·er \'tau-ər, 'taur\ *n* **1** : a building or structure typically higher than it is wide and high relative to its surroundings that may stand apart (as a campanile) or be attached (as a church belfry) to a larger structure and that may be of skeleton framework (as an observation or transmission tower) **2** : a towering citadel : FORTRESS [Old English *torr* and Old French *tur*, both from Latin *turris*, from Greek *tyrsis*] — **tow·ered** \'tau-ərd, 'taurd\ *adj*

²tower *vi* : to reach or rise to a great height

tow·er·ing *adj* **1** : impressively high or great : IMPOSING **2** : reaching a high point of intensity ⟨a *towering* rage⟩

¹tower 1

3 : going beyond proper bounds : EXCESSIVE ⟨*towering* ambition⟩

tower wagon *n* : a wagon or motortruck with a high adjustable platform on which workers can stand

tow·head \'tō-ˌhed\ *n* : a person having flaxen hair — **tow·head·ed** \-ˈhed-əd\ *adj*

to·whee \'tō-ˌhē, 'tō-ē, tō-'hē\ *n* **1** : a finch of eastern North America having the male black, white, and rufous — called also *chewink* **2** : any of numerous American finches related to the towhee [imitative]

to wit \tə-'wit\ *adv* : that is to say : NAMELY [Middle English *to witen,* literally, "to know"]

tow·line \'tō-ˌlīn\ *n* : a line used in towing

town \'taùn\ *n* **1 a** : a heavily populated area as distinguished from surrounding rural territory; *esp* : one larger than a village but smaller than a city **b** : CITY 1a **c** : an English village having a periodic fair or market **2 a** : the city or urban life as contrasted with the country **b** : TOWNSPEOPLE 1 **3** : a New England territorial and political unit usually containing both rural and urban areas under a single town government — called also *township* [Old English *tūn* "enclosure, village, town"] — **town** *adj*

town clerk *n* : an official who keeps the town records

town crier *n* : an old-time town officer making public proclamations

town hall *n* : a public building used for town-government offices and meetings

town house *n* **1** : the city residence of one having a countryseat or a chief residence elsewhere **2** : a house connected to another by a common sidewall

town meeting *n* : a meeting of inhabitants or taxpayers of a town to transact public business

towns·folk \'taùnz-ˌfōk\ *n pl* : TOWNSPEOPLE

town·ship \'taùn-ˌship\ *n* **1 a** : TOWN 3 **b** : a unit of local government in some northeastern and north central states **c** : a subdivision of the county especially in the southern United States **2** : a division of territory in surveys of United States public land containing 36 sections or 36 square miles (about 93.2 square kilometers)

towns·man \'taùnz-mən\ *n* **1** : a native or resident of a town or city **2** : a fellow citizen of a town

towns·peo·ple \-ˌpē-pəl\ *n pl* **1** : the inhabitants of a town or city **2** : town-dwelling or town-bred persons

towns·wom·an \-ˌwùm-ən\ *n* **1** : a woman native or resident of a town or city **2** : a woman who is a fellow citizen of a town

tow·path \'tō-ˌpath, -ˌpath\ *or* **towing path** *n* : a path (as along a canal) traveled by men or animals towing boats

tow·rope \'tō-ˌrōp\ *n* : a line used in towing

tow truck *n* : WRECKER 4

tox- *or* **toxi-** *or* **toxo-** *combining form* : poisonous : poison ⟨*tox*emia⟩ [Latin *toxicum* "poison"]

tox·a·phene \'täk-sə-ˌfēn\ *n* : a chlorine-containing insecticide [from *Toxaphene,* a former trademark]

tox·emia \täk-'sē-mē-ə\ *n* : an abnormal condition associated with the presence of toxic substances in the blood — **tox·emic** \-mik\ *adj*

tox·ic \'täk-sik\ *adj* **1** : of, relating to, or caused by a poison or toxin **2** : POISONOUS [Late Latin *toxicus,* from Latin *toxicum* "poison", from Greek *toxikon* "arrow poison", derived from *toxon* "bow, arrow"] — **tox·ic·i·ty** \täk-'sis-ət-ē\ *n*

tox·i·col·o·gy \ˌtäk-si-'käl-ə-jē\ *n* : a science that deals with poisonous materials and their effect and with the problems involved in their use and control — **tox·i·co·log·i·cal** \-kə-'läj-i-kəl\ *adj* — **tox·i·co·log·i·cal·ly** \-i-kə-lē, -klē\ *adv* — **tox·i·col·o·gist** \-'käl-ə-jəst\ *n*

tox·in \'täk-sən\ *n* : a complex usually unstable substance that is a metabolic product of a living organism (as a bacterium), that is very poisonous when introduced directly into the tissues but is usually destroyed by the digestive process when taken by mouth, and that typically induces antibody formation ⟨tetanus *toxin*⟩ — compare ANTITOXIN, TOXOID

tox·in-an·ti·tox·in \'täk-sə-'nant-i-ˌtäk-sən\ *n* : a mixture of a toxin and its antitoxin used especially formerly in immunizing against a disease (as diphtheria)

tox·oid \'täk-ˌsóid\ *n* : a toxin (as of tetanus) treated so as to destroy its poisonous effects while leaving it still capable of causing the formation of antibodies when injected into the body

¹toy \'tói\ *n* **1** : something (as a trinket) of small or no real value or importance : TRIFLE **2** : something for a child to play with **3** : something tiny; *esp* : an animal of a breed or variety characterized by exceptionally small size [Middle English *toye* "dalliance"] — **toy** *adj* — **toy·like** \-ˌlīk\ *adj*

²toy *vi* : to amuse oneself as if with a toy : PLAY, TRIFLE ⟨*toy* with an idea⟩ — **toy·er** *n*

toy·on \'tói-ˌän\ *n* : an ornamental evergreen shrub of the rose family that is native to the North American Pacific coast and has white flowers succeeded by persistent bright red berries [American Spanish *tollon*]

tra·bec·u·la \trə-'bek-yə-lə\ *n, pl* **-lae** \-ˌlē, -ˌlī\ *also* **-las** : a small anatomical bar, rod, or septum often bridging a gap or forming part of a framework ⟨spleen *trabeculae*⟩ [Latin, "little beam", from *trabs, trabes* "beam"] — **tra·bec·u·lar** \-lər\ *adj*

¹trace \'trās\ *n* **1** : a mark or line left by something that has passed : TRAIL, TRACK; *also* : FOOTPRINT **2** : a sign or evidence of some past thing : VESTIGE ⟨*traces* of an earlier civilization⟩ **3** : something traced or drawn (as a line); *esp* : the marking made by a recording instrument (as a seismograph or kymograph) **4** : the intersection of a line or plane with a plane **5 a** : a minute amount or indication ⟨a *trace* of red⟩ **b** : an amount of a chemical constituent not quantitatively determined because of minuteness [Middle French, from *tracier* "to trace"] □ SYN TRACE, VESTIGE, TRACK mean a sign left by something that has passed. TRACE may suggest any line or mark or discernible effect ⟨*traces* of a deer in the snow⟩ ⟨*traces* of their native dialect in their speech⟩ VESTIGE applies to tangible remains, as a fragment, remnant, or relic ⟨*vestiges* of a primitive society⟩ TRACK suggests a continuous line that can be followed ⟨hounds on the *track* of a fox⟩

²trace *vb* **1 a** : DELINEATE 1, SKETCH **b** : to form (as letters or figures) carefully or painstakingly **c** : to copy (as a drawing) by following lines or letters seen through a transparent superimposed sheet **d** : to make a graphic instrumental record of ⟨*trace* the heart action⟩ **e** : to adorn with linear ornamentation (as tracery) **2 a** : to follow the footprints, track, or trail of **b** : to study out or follow the development and progress of in detail or step by step **3** : to be traceable historically ⟨a family that *traces* to the Norman conquest⟩ [Middle French *tracier,* derived from Latin *trahere* "to pull, draw"]

³trace *n* **1** : either of two straps, chains, or lines of a harness for attaching a horse to something (as a vehicle) to be drawn **2** : one or more vascular bundles supplying a leaf or twig [Middle French *trais,* pl. of *trait* "pull, draft, tract", from Latin *tractus* "act of drawing", from *trahere* "to pull, draw"]

trace·able \'trā-sə-bəl\ *adj* **1** : capable of being traced **2** : that can be attributed ⟨a failure *traceable* to laziness⟩ — **trace·ably** \-blē\ *adv*

trace element *n* : a chemical element used by organisms in minute quantities and held essential to their physiology

trace·less \'trās-ləs\ *adj* : having or leaving no trace — **trace·less·ly** *adv*

trac·er \'trā-sər\ *n* **1 a** : a person who traces missing persons or property **b** : an inquiry sent out in tracing something lost in transit **2** : a draftsman who traces designs, patterns, or markings **3** : a device (as a stylus) used in tracing **4 a** : ammunition containing a chemical composition to mark the flight of projectiles by a trail of smoke or fire **b** : a substance and especially a labeled element or atom used to trace the course of a chemical or biological process

trac·ery \ˈtrās-rē, -ə-rē\ *n, pl* **-er·ies** **1** : architectural ornamental work with branching lines; *esp* : decorative openwork in the upper part of a Gothic window **2** : a decorative interlacing of lines suggestive of Gothic tracery — **trac·er·ied** \-rēd\ *adj*

tra·chea \ˈtrā-kē-ə\ *n, pl* **-che·ae** \-kē-ē, -kē-ˌī\ *also* **-che·as** **1** : the main trunk of the system of tubes by which air passes to and from the lungs in vertebrates **2** : one of the air-conveying tubules forming the respiratory system of most insects and many other arthropods [Medieval Latin, from Late Latin *trachia,* from Greek *tracheia artēria* "rough artery", from *trachys* "rough"] — **tra·che·al** \-kē-əl\ *adj* — **tra·che·ate** \-kē-ˌāt, -ət\ *adj*

tracheal gill *n* : one of the external gills that connect with the tracheae of some aquatic insect larvae or nymphs

tra·cheid \ˈtrā-kē-əd, -ˌkēd\ *n* : a long tubular xylem cell that functions in conduction and support and has tapering closed ends and thickened lignified walls [derived from *trachea*]

tra·cheo·phyte \ˈtrā-kē-ə-ˌfīt\ *n* : any of a division (Tracheophyta) comprising green plants with a vascular system that contains tracheids or tracheal elements and including ferns and related plants and the seed plants

tra·che·ot·o·my \ˌtrā-kē-ˈät-ə-mē\ *n, pl* **-mies** : the surgical operation of cutting into the trachea especially through the skin

tra·cho·ma \trə-ˈkō-mə\ *n* : a chronic contagious eye disease marked by inflammation of the conjunctiva, caused by a rickettsia, and sometimes causing blindness [Greek *trachōma,* from *trachys* "rough"] — **tra·chom·a·tous** \-ˈkäm-ət-əs, -ˈkōm-\ *adj*

trac·ing \ˈtrā-sing\ *n* **1** : the act of one that traces **2** : something that is traced

¹track \ˈtrak\ *n* **1 a** : detectable evidence (as the wake of a ship, a line of footprints, or a wheel rut) that something has passed **b** : a path made by repeated footfalls : TRAIL **c** (1) : a course laid out especially for racing (2) : the parallel rails of a railroad **d** : any of a series of parallel paths on a magnetic tape **2** : the course along which something moves **3 a** : a sequence of events or a train of ideas : SUCCESSION **b** : awareness of a fact or progression ⟨lose *track* of the time⟩ **4 a** : the width of a wheeled vehicle from wheel to wheel **b** : either of two endless metal belts on which a track-laying vehicle (as a tank) travels **5** : track-and-field sports; *esp* : those performed on a racing track [Middle French *trac*] SYN see TRACE — **in one's tracks** : where one is at the moment : on the spot : INSTANTLY ⟨dropped the deer *in its tracks*⟩

²track *vb* **1** : to follow the tracks or traces of : TRAIL **2** : to observe or plot the moving path of (as a spacecraft or missile) with instruments **3** : to pass over : TRAVERSE **4** : to make tracks upon or with ⟨*track* up the floor with muddy feet⟩ ⟨*track* mud all over the floor⟩ — **track·er** *n*

track·age \ˈtrak-ij\ *n* **1** : lines of railway track **2 a** : a right to use the tracks of another railroad **b** : the charge for such right

track–and–field \ˌtrak-ən-ˈfēld\ *adj* : of, relating to, or being any of various competitive athletic events (as running, jumping, and weight throwing) performed on a running track or on the adjacent field

track·ball \ˈtrak-ˌból\ *n* : a ball that is mounted usually in a computer console so as to be only partially exposed and is rotated to control the movement of a cursor on a display

track·lay·ing \ˈtrak-ˌlā-ing\ *adj* : of, relating to, or being a vehicle that travels on two endless metal belts

track·less \ˈtrak-ləs\ *adj* : having no track : PATHLESS — **track·less·ly** *adv* — **track·less·ness** *n*

¹tract \ˈtrakt\ *n, often cap* : verses of Scripture (as from the Psalms) used between the gradual and the Gospel at some masses [Medieval Latin *tractus,* from Latin, "action of drawing, extension"; from its being sung without a break by one voice]

²tract *n* : a pamphlet or leaflet intended to draw attention or gain support for something (as a political or religious movement) [Latin *tractatus* "treatise", from *tractare* "to draw out, handle, treat"]

³tract *n* **1 a** : an indefinite stretch especially of land ⟨broad *tracts* of prairie⟩ **b** : a defined area especially of land ⟨a garden *tract*⟩ **2** : a system of body parts or organs that collectively serve some special purpose ⟨the digestive *tract*⟩ [Latin *tractus* "action of drawing, extension", from *trahere* "to pull, draw"]

trac·ta·ble \ˈtrak-tə-bəl\ *adj* **1** : easily led, taught, or controlled : DOCILE ⟨a *tractable* horse⟩ **2** : easily handled, managed, or wrought : MALLEABLE [Latin *tractabilis,* from *tractare* "to handle, treat"] — **trac·ta·bil·i·ty** \ˌtrak-tə-ˈbil-ət-ē\ *n* — **trac·ta·ble·ness** \ˈtrak-tə-bəl-nəs\ *n* — **trac·ta·bly** \-blē\ *adv*

trac·tion \ˈtrak-shən\ *n* **1** : the act of drawing : the state of being drawn; *also* : the force exerted in drawing **2** : the drawing of a vehicle by motive power; *also* : the motive power employed **3** : the adhesive friction of a body on a surface on which it moves ⟨the *traction* of a wheel on a rail⟩ **4** : a pulling force exerted on a skeletal structure (as in a fracture) by means of a special device; *also* : a state of tension caused by such a pulling force ⟨a leg in *traction*⟩ [Medieval Latin *tractio,* from Latin *trahere* "to draw"] — **trac·tion·al** \-shnəl, -shən-l\ *adj*

trac·tive \ˈtrak-tiv\ *adj* : serving to pull : used in pulling

trac·tor \ˈtrak-tər\ *n* **1** : a 4-wheeled or tracklaying rider-controlled automotive vehicle used especially for drawing implements (as agricultural) or for bearing and propelling such implements **2** : a smaller 2-wheeled apparatus controlled usually through handlebars by a walking operator **3** : a truck with short chassis and no body used in combination with a trailer for the highway hauling of freight [Latin *tractus,* past participle of *trahere* "to pull, draw"]

¹trade \ˈtrād\ *n* **1** : a customary course of action : PRACTICE **2 a** : the business or work in which one engages regularly : OCCUPATION **b** : an occupation requiring manual or mechanical skill : CRAFT **c** : the persons engaged in an occupation, business, or industry **3 a** : the business of buying and selling or bartering commodities : COMMERCE **b** : BUSINESS 1b ⟨was in the novelty *trade*⟩ **4 a** : an act or instance of trading : TRANSACTION; *esp* : an exchange of property without use of money **b** : a firm's customers : CLIENTELE **c** : the concerns engaged in a business or industry [Middle English, "path, track, course of action", from Low German, "path"] SYN see BUSINESS

²trade *vb* **1 a** : to give in exchange for another commodity : BARTER; *also* : to make an exchange of **b** : to buy and sell (as stock) regularly **2 a** : to engage in the exchange, purchase, or sale of goods **b** : to make one's purchases : SHOP

³trade *adj* **1** : of, relating to, or used in trade **2** : intended for persons in a business or industry ⟨a *trade* journal⟩ **3** : of, composed of, or representing the trades or trade unions **4** : of or associated with a trade wind ⟨the *trade* belts⟩

trade acceptance *n* : a time draft for the amount of a purchase drawn by the seller on the buyer and bearing the buyer's acceptance

trade dollar *n* : a United States silver dollar issued from 1873 to 1885 for use in oriental trade

trade–in \ˈtrād-ˌin\ *n* : something given in trade usually as part payment of the price of another

tracery 1

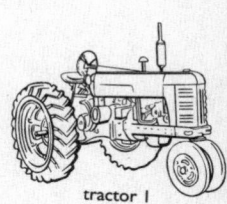

tractor 1

\ə\ abut		\ng\ sing	
\ər\ further		\ō\ bone	
\a\ mat		\ó\ saw	
\ā\ take		\ói\ coin	
\ä\ cot, cart		\th\ thin	
\aú\ out		\th\ this	
\ch\ chin		\ü\ food	
\e\ pet		\ú\ foot	
\ē\ easy		\y\ yet	
\g\ go		\yü\ few	
\i\ tip		\yú\ cure	
\ī\ life		\zh\ vision	
\j\ job			

trade in \'trād-'in, 'trād-\ *vt* : to turn in as usually part payment for a purchase ⟨*trade* an old car *in* on a new one⟩

¹**trade·mark** \-,märk\ *n* : a device (as a word) pointing distinctly to the origin or ownership of merchandise to which it is applied and legally reserved to the exclusive use of the owner as maker or seller

²**trademark** *vt* : to secure trademark rights for : register the trademark of

trade name *n* 1 : the name by which an article is called in its own trade 2 : a name that is given by a manufacturer or merchant to a product to distinguish it as made or sold by him and that may be used and protected as a trademark 3 : the name under which a firm does business

trad·er \'trād-ər\ *n* 1 : a person who trades 2 : a ship engaged in trade

trade school *n* : a secondary school teaching the skilled trades

trades·man \'trādz-mən\ *n* 1 : one who runs a retail store : SHOPKEEPER 2 : a worker in a skilled trade : CRAFTSMAN

trades·peo·ple \-,pē-pəl\ *n pl* : people (as shopkeepers) engaged in trade

trade union *n* : LABOR UNION; *esp* : CRAFT UNION — compare INDUSTRIAL UNION — **trade unionism** *n* — **trade unionist** *n*

trade wind *n* : a wind blowing almost continually in the same course, from northeast to southwest in a belt north of the equator and from southeast to northwest in one south of the equator [¹*trade* ("habitual course")]

trading post *n* : a station or store of a trader or trading company established in a sparsely settled region

trading stamp *n* : a printed stamp given as a premium to a retail customer to be accumulated and redeemed in merchandise

tra·di·tion \trə-'dish-ən\ *n* : the handing down of information, beliefs, or customs from one generation to another; *also* : something thus handed down [Latin *traditio* "action of handing over, tradition", from *tradere* "to hand over, hand down", from *trans-* + *dare* "to give"] — **tra·di·tion·al** \-'dish-nəl, -ən-l\ *adj* — **tra·di·tion·al·ly** \-ē\ *adv*

tra·di·tion·al·ism \-'dish-nə-,liz-əm, -ən-l-,iz-\ *n* : the doctrines or practices of those who follow or accept tradition — **tra·di·tion·al·ist** \-nə-ləst, -ən-l-əst\ *n or adj* — **tra·di·tion·al·is·tic** \-,dish-nə-'lis-tik, -ən-l-'is-\ *adj*

tra·duce \trə-'düs, -'dyüs\ *vt* : to injure the reputation of by falsehood or misrepresentation : DEFAME [Latin *traducere* "to lead across, transfer, degrade", from *trans-* + *ducere* 'to lead"] — **tra·duce·ment** \-mənt\ *n* — **tra·duc·er** *n*

¹**traf·fic** \'traf-ik\ *n* 1 a : import and export trade b : the business of buying and selling 2 : communication or dealings between individuals or groups 3 a : the movement (as of vehicles or pedestrians) through an area or along a route b : the vehicles or pedestrians moving along a route 4 : the passengers or cargo carried by a transportation system [Middle French *trafique*, from Italian *traffico*, from *trafficare* "to traffic"]

²**traffic** *vb* **traf·ficked; traf·fick·ing** : to carry on traffic : TRADE, DEAL — **traf·fick·er** *n*

traffic circle *n* : ROTARY 2

traffic island *n* : a paved or planted island in a roadway designed to guide the flow of traffic

traffic signal *n* : an electrically operated signal (as a system of colored lights) for controlling traffic — called also *traffic light*

trag·a·canth \'traj-ə-,kanth, 'trag-, -,kantth\ *n* : a gum from various Old World plants related to the American locoweeds that swells in water and is used in the arts and in pharmacy — called also *gum tragacanth* [Mid-

dle French *tragacanthe*, from Latin *tragacantha*, from Greek *tragakantha*, from *tragos* "goat" + *akantha* "thorn"]

tra·ge·di·an \trə-'jēd-ē-ən\ *n* 1 : a writer of tragedies 2 : an actor of tragic roles

tra·ge·di·enne \trə-,jēd-ē-'en\ *n* : an actress who plays tragic roles [French *tragédienne*, from *tragédie* "tragedy"]

trag·e·dy \'traj-əd-ē\ *n, pl* **-dies** 1 : a serious drama having a sorrowful or disastrous conclusion 2 a : a disastrous event : CALAMITY b : MISFORTUNE 2 3 : tragic quality or element [Middle French *tragedie*, from Latin *tragoedia*, from Greek *tragōidia*, from *tragos* "goat" + *aeidein* "to sing"] □ ORIGIN Our word *tragedy* is derived from Greek *tragōidia*, a compound of *tragos*, "goat", and *aeidein*, "to sing". The Greeks' reasons for calling this dramatic form "goat song" are obscure. Tragedy developed in the 6th and 5th centuries B. C. out of the performance of originally lyric recitations. Prizes were sometimes given for dramatic performances, and it may be that competition for the prize of a goat accounts for the word *tragōidia*. Another possibility is that a goat was sacrificed in earlier religious rituals out of which tragedy may have developed. A third theory is that tragedy developed out of the performance of lyric hymns to the god Dionysus in which the chorus was dressed as satyrs, mythical beings with some of the attributes of goats.

trag·ic \'traj-ik\ *adj* 1 : of, marked by, or expressive of tragedy 2 a : dealing with or treated in tragedy ⟨the *tragic* hero⟩ b : appropriate to or typical of tragedy 3 a : regrettably serious or unpleasant b : marked by a sense of tragedy — **trag·i·cal** \-i-kəl\ *adj* — **trag·i·cal·ly** \-i-kə-lē, -klē\ *adv* — **trag·i·cal·ness** \-i-kəl-nəs\ *n*

tragi·com·e·dy \,traj-i-'käm-əd-ē\ *n* : a drama or a situation blending tragic and comic elements — **tragi·com·ic** \-'käm-ik\ *or* **tragi·com·i·cal** \-'käm-i-kəl\ *adj*

¹**trail** \'trāl\ *vb* 1 a : to drag or draw along behind ⟨the horse *trailed* its reins⟩ b : to hang down or rest on or creep over the ground ⟨*trailing* vines⟩ 2 : to lag behind : do poorly in relation to others 3 : to carry or bring along as a burden or bother 4 : to follow in the tracks of : PURSUE ⟨dogs *trailing* a fox⟩ 5 : to hang or let hang so as to touch the ground ⟨a *trailing* skirt⟩ 6 : to form a trail : STRAGGLE ⟨smoke *trailed* from the chimney⟩ 7 : DWINDLE ⟨the sound *trailed* off⟩ [Middle French *trailler* "to tow", derived from Latin *tragula* "sledge, dragnet"] SYN see CHASE

²**trail** *n* 1 : something that trails or is trailed: as a : the train of a gown b : the part of a gun carriage that rests on the ground when the piece is ready for action 2 a : something that follows or moves along as if being drawn along : TRAIN b (1) : the streak produced by a meteor (2) : a line produced photographically by the moving image of a celestial body ⟨star *trails*⟩ 3 a : a trace or mark left by something that has passed or been drawn along ⟨a *trail* of blood⟩ b : a track made by passage through a wilderness : a beaten path c : a marked path through a forest or mountainous region

trail·blaz·er \-,blā-zər\ *n* 1 : one that marks or points out a trail to guide others : PATHFINDER 2 : PIONEER 1 — **trail·blaz·ing** \-zing\ *adj*

trail·er \'trā-lər\ *n* 1 : a trailing plant 2 a : a vehicle designed to be hauled (as by a tractor) b : a vehicle designed to serve wherever parked as a dwelling or as a place of business

trailer park *n* : an area equipped to provide space for house trailers — called also *trailer camp, trailer court*

trailing arbutus *n* : ARBUTUS 2

trailing edge *n* : the rearmost edge of an airfoil

¹**train** \'trān\ *n* 1 : a part of a gown that trails behind the wearer 2 : RETINUE 3 : a moving file of persons, vehicles, or animals 4 a : order designed to lead to some result b : an orderly succession or sequence ⟨a

train of thought) **c** : accompanying circumstances **d** : SEQUEL 1, AFTERMATH **5** : a line of combustible material (as gunpowder) laid to lead fire to a charge **6** : a series of moving machine parts (as gears) for transmitting and modifying motion **7 a** : a connected line of railroad cars with or without a locomotive **b** : an automotive tractor with one or more trailer units [Middle French, from *trainer* "to draw, drag"]

²**train** *vb* **1** : to direct the growth of (a plant) usually by bending, pruning, and tying **2 a** : to teach something (as a skill, profession, or trade) to ⟨was *trained* in the law⟩ **b** : to teach (an animal) to obey **3** : to make ready (as by exercise) for a test of skill **4** : to aim (as a gun) at a target **5** : to undergo instruction, discipline, or drill [Middle French *trainer* "to draw, drag"] SYN see TEACH — **train·able** \ˈtrā-nə-bəl\ *adj* — **train·ee** \trā-ˈnē\ *n*

train·er \ˈtrā-nər\ *n* **1** : one that trains **2** : a member of the staff for an athletic team responsible for treating ailments and minor injuries

train·ing \ˈtrā-niŋ\ *n* **1** : the course followed by one who trains or is being trained ⟨take nursing *training*⟩ **2** : the condition of one who has trained for a test or contest SYN see EDUCATION

train·load \ˈtrān-ˈlōd\ *n* : the full freight or passenger capacity of a railroad train

train·man \ˈtrān-mən, -ˌman\ *n* : a member of a railroad train crew supervised by a conductor

traipse \ˈtrāps\ *vi* : to walk or tramp about [origin unknown] — **traipse** *n*

trait \ˈtrāt\ *n* : a distinguishing quality (as of personality or physical makeup) : PECULIARITY, CHARACTERISTIC [Middle French, literally, "act of drawing", from Latin *tractus*, from *trahere* "to draw, drag"]

trai·tor \ˈtrāt-ər\ *n* **1** : one who betrays another's trust or is false to an obligation or duty **2** : one who commits treason [Old French *traitre*, from Latin *traditor*, from *tradere* "to hand over, betray", from *trans-* + *dare* "to give"]

trai·tor·ous \ˈtrāt-ə-rəs, ˈtrā-trəs\ *adj* **1** : guilty or capable of treason **2** : constituting treason — **trai·tor·ous·ly** *adv*

trai·tress \ˈtrā-trəs\ *or* **trai·tor·ess** \ˈtrāt-ə-rəs, ˈtrā-trəs\ *n* : a girl or woman who is a traitor

tra·jec·to·ry \trə-ˈjek-tə-rē, -trē\ *n, pl* -**ries** : the curve that a moving body (as a planet in its orbit, a projectile, or a rocket) describes in space [Latin *trajectus*, past participle of *traicere* "to cause to cross, cross", from *trans-* + *jacere* "to throw"]

tram \ˈtram\ *n* **1** : a cart or wagon running on rails (as in a mine) **2** *chiefly British* : STREETCAR **3** : the carriage of an overhead conveyor [English dialect, "shaft of a wheelbarrow"]

tram·car \ˈtram-ˌkär\ *n* **1** *chiefly British* : STREETCAR **2** : TRAM 1

tram·line \ˈtram-ˌlīn\ *n, British* : a streetcar line

¹**tram·mel** \ˈtram-əl\ *n* **1** : a net for catching birds or fish **2** : something hindering activity, progress, or freedom : RESTRAINT — usually used in pl. **3** : an adjustable pothook for a fireplace crane **4** : a compass for drawing large circles that consists of a beam with two sliding parts — usually used in pl. [Middle French *tremail*, from Late Latin *tremaculum*, from Latin *tres* "three" + *macula* "mesh, spot"]

²**trammel** *vt* **tram·meled** *or* **tram·melled; tram·mel·ing** *or* **tram·mel·ling** \ˈtram-liŋ, -ə-liŋ\ **1** : to catch or hold in or as if in a net : ENMESH **2** : to prevent or hinder the free play of : CONFINE

¹**tramp** \ˈtramp, *1 & 2 are also* ˈträmp, ˈtromp\ *vb* **1** : to walk heavily **2** : to tread on forcibly and repeatedly : TRAMPLE **3 a** : to wander through or travel on foot **b** : to travel as a tramp [Middle English *trampen*] — **tramp·er** *n*

²**tramp** \ˈtramp, *3 is also* ˈträmp, ˈtromp\ *n* **1** : a begging or thieving vagrant **2** : a walking trip : HIKE **3** :

the succession of sounds made by the beating of marching feet **4** : a ship not making regular trips but taking cargo to any port whenever it is offered — called also *tramp steamer*

tram·ple \ˈtram-pəl\ *vb* **tram·pled; tram·pling** \-pə-liŋ, -pliŋ\ **1** : to tramp or tread heavily so as to bruise, crush, or injure ⟨the cattle *trampled* on the young wheat⟩ **2** : to tread underfoot : stamp on **3** : to inflict pain, injury, or loss by ruthless or heartless treatment ⟨*trample* on the rights of a friend⟩ [Middle English *tramplen*, from *trampen* "to tramp"] — **trample** *n* — **tram·pler** \-pə-lər, -plər\ *n*

tram·po·line \ˌtram-pə-ˈlēn, ˈtram-pə-ˌ\ *n* : a resilient canvas sheet or web supported by springs in a metal frame used as a springboard and landing area for performing jumps and flips [Spanish *trampolín*, from Italian *trampolino*, of Germanic origin] — **tram·po·lin·er** \-ˈlē-nər, -ˌlē-\ *n* — **tram·po·lin·ist** \-nəst\ *n*

tram·po·lin·ing \-ˈlē-niŋ, -ˌlē-\ *n* : the sport of jumping and performing acrobatic feats on a trampoline

tram·way \ˈtram-ˌwā\ *n* **1** : a road or way for trams **2** *British* : a streetcar line

trance \ˈtrans\ *n* **1** : a state of partly suspended animation or inability to function : STUPOR **2** : a sleeplike state (as of deep hypnosis) **3** : a state of profound abstraction or absorption : ECSTASY [Middle French *transe*, from *transir* "to pass away, swoon", from Latin *transire* "to cross over, pass away", from *trans-* + *ire* "to go"]

tran·quil \ˈtraŋ-kwəl, ˈtran-\ *adj* **1** : free from agitation, disturbance, or turmoil : SERENE **2** : STABLE 1b [Latin *tranquillus*] SYN see CALM — **tran·quil·ly** \-kwə-lē\ *adv* — **tran·quil·ness** *n*

tran·quil·ize *or* **tran·quil·lize** \-kwə-ˌlīz\ *vb* : to make or become tranquil or relaxed; *esp* : to relieve of mental tension and anxiety usually by means of drugs

tran·quil·iz·er \-ˌlī-zər\ *n* : one that tranquilizes; *esp* : a drug used to reduce mental disturbance (as anxiety and tension)

tran·quil·li·ty *or* **tran·quil·i·ty** \tran-ˈkwil-ət-ē, traŋ-\ *n* : the quality or state of being tranquil

trans- *prefix* **1** : on or to the other side of : across : beyond ⟨*trans*atlantic⟩ **2** : through **3** : so or such as to change or transfer ⟨*trans*location⟩ ⟨*trans*ship⟩ [Latin *trans-*, *tra-*, from *trans* "across, beyond"]

See *trans-* and 2d element

transbay	transculturally	transinsular
transborder	transdesert	transisthmian
transchannel	transequatorial	transpeninsular
transcultural	transgenerational	transworld

trans·act \trans-ˈakt, tranz-\ *vt* **1** : to carry through : bring about : NEGOTIATE ⟨*transact* a sale⟩ **2** : to carry on : CONDUCT ⟨*transact* business⟩ [Latin *transactus*, past participle of *transigere* "to drive through, transact", from *trans-* + *agere* "to drive"] — **trans·ac·tor** \-ˈak-tər\ *n*

trans·ac·tion \-ˈak-shən\ *n* **1** : an act, process, or instance of transacting **2 a** : something transacted; *esp* : a business deal **b** *pl* : the record of the meeting of a society — **trans·ac·tion·al** \-shnəl, -shən-əl\ *adj*

trans·at·lan·tic \ˌtrans-ət-ˈlant-ik, ˌtranz-\ *adj* : extending across or situated beyond the Atlantic ocean

trans·ceiv·er \trans-ˈē-vər, tranz-\ *n* : a radio transmitter-receiver that uses many of the same components for transmission and reception [*trans*mitter + *re*ceiver]

tran·scend \tran-ˈsend\ *vt* **1** : to rise above or go beyond the limits of : EXCEED **2** : SURPASS ⟨a poem *transcending* all others⟩ [Latin *transcendere* "to climb across, transcend", from *trans-* + *scandere* "to climb"] SYN see EXCEED

tran·scend·ence \-ˈsen-dəns\ *also* **tran·scend·en·cy** \-dən-sē\ *n* : the quality or state of being transcendent

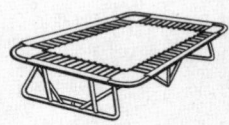

trampoline

\ə\ abut \ŋ\ sing
\ər\ **further** \ō\ **bone**
\a\ **mat** \ȯ\ **saw**
\ā\ **take** \ȯi\ **coin**
\ä\ **cot, cart** \th\ **thin**
\au̇\ **out** \th̶\ **this**
\ch\ **chin** \ū̶\ **food**
\e\ **pet** \u̇\ **foot**
\ē\ **easy** \y\ **yet**
\g\ **go** \yū̶\ **few**
\i\ **tip** \yu̇\ **cure**
\ī\ **life** \zh\ **vision**
\j\ **job**

tran·scend·ent \-dənt\ *adj* **1** : exceeding usual limits **2** : extending or lying beyond the limits of ordinary experience [Latin *transcendens,* present participle of *transcendere* "to transcend"] — **tran·scend·ent·ly** *adv*

tran·scen·den·tal \,tran-,sen-'dent-l, ,tran-sən-\ *adj* **1** : TRANSCENDENT 1 **2** : incapable of being the root of an algebraic equation with rational coefficients ⟨π is a *transcendental* number⟩ **3** : of or relating to transcendentalism — **tran·scen·den·tal·ly** \-l-ē\ *adv*

tran·scen·den·tal·ism \-l-,iz-əm\ *n* : a philosophy holding that ultimate reality is unknowable and asserting the primacy of the spiritual over the material and empirical — **tran·scen·den·tal·ist** \-l-əst\ *adj or n*

trans·con·ti·nen·tal \,trans-,känt-n-'ent-l\ *adj* : extending or going across a continent ⟨*transcontinental* flight⟩

tran·scribe \tran-'skrīb\ *vt* **1 a** : to make a written copy of **b** : to make a copy of (dictated or recorded matter) in longhand or on a typewriter **2 a** : to represent (speech sounds) by means of phonetic symbols **b** : to transfer (data) from one recording form to another **c** : to record (as on magnetic tape) for later broadcast **3** : to make a musical transcription of **4** : to broadcast by electrical transcription **5** : to cause (as DNA) to undergo genetic transcription [Latin *transcribere,* from *trans-* + *scribere* "to write"] — **tran·scrib·er** *n*

tran·script \'tran-,skript\ *n* **1** : a written, printed, or typed copy **2** : an official copy (as of a student's educational record) [Medieval Latin *transcriptum,* from Latin *transcribere* "to transcribe"]

tran·scrip·tion \tran-'skrip-shən\ *n* **1** : an act, process, or instance of transcribing **2** : COPY 1, TRANSCRIPT: as **a** : an arrangement of a musical composition for some instrument or voice other than the original **b** : ELECTRICAL TRANSCRIPTION **3** : the process of constructing a messenger RNA molecule using a DNA molecule as a template with resulting transfer of genetic information to the messenger RNA — compare TRANSLATION 4 — **tran·scrip·tion·al** \-shnəl, -shən-l\ *adj* — **tran·scrip·tion·al·ly** \-ē\ *adv*

trans·duc·er \trans-'dü-sər, tranz-, -'dyü-\ *n* : a device that is actuated by power from one system and supplies power in any other form to a second system [Latin *transducere* "to lead across", from *trans-* + *ducere* "to lead"]

¹tran·sect \tran-'sekt\ *vt* : to cut transversely [*trans-* + Latin *sectus,* past participle of *secare* "to cut"] — **tran·sec·tion** \-'sek-shən\ *n*

²tran·sect \'tran-,sekt\ *n* : a sample area (as of vegetation) usually in the form of a long continuous strip

tran·sept \'tran-,sept\ *n* : the part forming the arms of a cross-shaped church [Latin *trans-* + *saeptum* "enclosure, wall", from *saepire* "to fence in", from *saepes* "fence"]

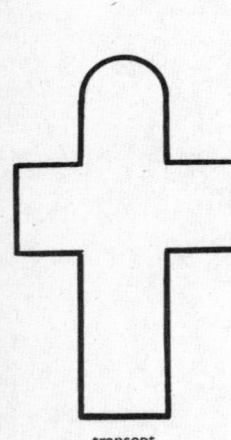

transept

¹trans·fer \trans-'fər, 'trans-,\ *vb* **trans·ferred; trans·fer·ring** **1 a** : to convey from one person, place, or situation to another : TRANSPORT **b** : to cause to pass from one to another : TRANSMIT **2** : to make over the possession or ownership of : CONVEY **3** : to print or otherwise copy from one surface to another by contact **4** : to move to a different place, region, or situation; *esp* : to withdraw from one educational institution to enroll at another **5** : to change from one vehicle or transportation line to another [Latin *transferre,* from *trans-* + *ferre* "to carry"] — **trans·fer·abil·i·ty** \,trans-,fər-ə-'bil-ət-ē\ *n* — **trans·fer·able** \trans-'fər-ə-bəl\ *adj* — **trans·fer·al** \-'fər-əl\ *n* — **trans·fer·rer** \-'fər-əl\ *n*

²trans·fer \'trans-,fər\ *n* **1** : conveyance of right, title, or interest in real or personal property from one person to another **2** : an act, process, or instance of transferring : TRANSFERENCE **3** : one that transfers or is transferred; *esp* : a graphic image transferred by contact from one surface to another **4** : a place where a transfer is made (as of trains to ferries) **5** : a ticket entitling

a passenger on a public conveyance to continue the journey on another route

trans·fer·ee \,trans-fər-'ē\ *n* **1** : a person to whom a conveyance is made **2** : one transferred

trans·fer·ence \trans-'fər-əns\ *n* : an act, process, or instance of transferring : TRANSFER

trans·fer·or \,trans-fər-'òr\ *n* : one that transfers a title, right, or property

trans·fer RNA \'trans-,fər-\ *n* : a relatively small RNA that transfers a particular amino acid to a growing protein at the site of protein synthesis during genetic translation

trans·fig·u·ra·tion \,trans-,fig-yə-'rā-shən, -,fig-ə-'rā-\ *n* **1** : a change of form or appearance; *esp* : a glorifying or exalting change **2** *cap* **a** : the supernatural change in the appearance of Jesus on the mountain **b** : a church festival on August 6 commemorating this

trans·fig·ure \trans-'fig-yər, *especially British* -'fig-ər\ *vt* : to give a new and typically exalted or spiritual appearance to SYN see TRANSFORM

trans·fix \trans-'fiks\ *vt* **1** : to pierce through with or as if with a pointed weapon : IMPALE **2** : to hold motionless by or as if by piercing — **trans·fix·ion** \-'fik-shən\ *n*

trans·form \trans-'fòrm\ *vb* **1 a** : to change in composition, structure, or character : CONVERT **b** : to change in outward appearance **2** : to change in mathematical form without altering value or meaning — **trans·form·able** \-'fòr-mə-bəl\ *adj* — **trans·for·ma·tive** \-'fòr-mət-iv\ *adj* □ SYN TRANSFORM, METAMORPHOSE, TRANSMUTE, TRANSFIGURE mean to change something into a different thing. TRANSFORM implies a change in form, nature, or function ⟨*transform* a desert into a fertile plain⟩ METAMORPHOSE suggests an abrupt or striking alteration induced as if supernaturally or by natural (as chemical) agencies ⟨the ugly duckling *metamorphosed* into a swan⟩ TRANSMUTE implies a change from a lower to a higher element or thing ⟨the artist *transmutes* ordinary scenes into extraordinary ones⟩ TRANSFIGURE implies a change that exalts and glorifies.

trans·for·ma·tion \,trans-fər-'mā-shən\ *n* **1** : an act, process, or instance of transforming or being transformed **2** : the operation of changing (as by rotation or mapping) one mathematical configuration or expression into another in accordance with a mathematical rule **3** : genetic modification of a cell and especially of a bacterium by introduction of DNA from a genetically different source

trans·form·er \trans-'fòr-mər\ *n* : one that transforms; *esp* : a device without moving parts for changing an electric current into one of different voltage by electromagnetic induction

trans·fuse \trans-'fyüz\ *vt* **1 a** : to cause to pass from one to another : TRANSMIT **b** : to spread into or through : PERMEATE **2 a** : to transfer (as blood or saline) into a vein of a human or animal **b** : to subject (a patient) to transfusion [Latin *transfusus,* past participle of *transfundere* "to transfuse", from *trans-* + *fundere* "to pour"] — **trans·fus·able** \-'fyü-zə-bəl\ *adj* — **trans·fu·sion** \-'fyü-zhən\ *n*

trans·gress \trans-'gres, tranz-\ *vb* **1** : to go beyond limits set by : VIOLATE ⟨*transgress* the divine law⟩ **2** : to pass beyond or go over a limit or boundary **3** : to violate a command or law : SIN [French *transgresser,* from Latin *transgressus,* past participle of *transgredi* "to step beyond or across", from *trans-* + *gradi* "to step"] — **trans·gres·sor** \-'gres-ər\ *n*

trans·gres·sion \-'gresh-ən\ *n* : an act, process, or instance of transgressing; *esp* : violation of a law, command, or duty

tran·sience \'tran-chəns\ *n* : the quality or state of being transient

¹tran·sient \-chənt\ *adj* **1** : not lasting or staying long ⟨a *transient* population⟩ **2** : changing in form or appearance ⟨a *transient* scene⟩ [Latin *transiens,* present participle of *transire* "to cross, pass", from *trans-* + *ire* "to go"] — **tran·sient·ly** *adv* □ **SYN TRANSITORY:** **TRANSIENT** applies to what is short in duration and passes quickly ⟨*transient* guests⟩ ⟨*transient* as music⟩ **TRANSITORY** stresses the inevitability of changing, ending, or dying out ⟨*transitory* fads and fashions⟩

²**transient** *n* : one that is transient: as **a** : a transient guest **b** : a person traveling about usually in search of work

tran·sis·tor \tran-'zis-tər, -'sis-\ *n* **1** : an electronic device similar to the electron tube in use (as amplification and rectification) consisting of a small block of a semiconductor (as germanium) that has at least three electrodes **2** : a radio having transistors — called also *transistor radio* [¹*tran*sfer + re*sistor;* from its transferring an electrical signal across a resistor]

tran·sis·tor·ize \-tə-,rīz\ *vt* : to equip (a device) with transistors

¹**tran·sit** \'trans-ət, 'tranz-\ *n* **1 a** : an act, process, or instance of passing through or over : **PASSAGE** **b** : transporting of persons or things from one place to another ⟨goods lost in *transit*⟩ **c** : local transportation of people by public conveyance or a system of such transportation **2 a** : passage of a celestial body over the meridian of a place or through the field of a telescope **b** : passage of a smaller body (as Venus) across the disk of a larger (as the sun) **3** : a theodolite with the telescope mounted so that it can be transited [Latin *transitus,* from *transire* "to cross, pass", from *trans-* + *ire* "to go"]

²**transit** *vb* **1** : to make a transit **2 a** : to pass or cause to pass over or through **b** : to pass across **3** : to turn (a telescope) about the horizontal transverse axis in surveying

transit instrument *n* **1** : a telescope mounted at right angles to a horizontal east-west axis and used with a clock andchronograph for observing the time of transit of a celestial body over the meridian of a place **2** : **TRANSIT 3**

tran·si·tion \trans-'ish-ən, tranz-\ *n* **1** : a passing from one state, stage, place, or subject to another **2** : a musical passage leading from one section of a piece to another — **tran·si·tion·al** \-'ish-nəl, -ən-l\ *adj* — **tran·si·tion·al·ly** \-ē\ *adv*

transition element *n* : any of various metallic elements (as chromium, iron, and nickel) that can form bonds using electrons from two energy levels instead of only one

tran·si·tive \'trans-ət-iv, 'tranz-\ *adj* **1** : characterized by having or containing a direct object ⟨a *transitive* verb⟩ **2** : relating to or being a relation such that if *A* is so related to *B* and *B* is so related to *C,* then *A* is so related to *C* ⟨equality is a *transitive* relation⟩ **3** : of, relating to, or involving transition — **tran·si·tive·ly** *adv* — **tran·si·tive·ness** *n* — **tran·si·tiv·i·ty** \,trans-ə-'tiv-ət-ē, ,tranz-\ *n*

tran·si·to·ry \'trans-ə-,tōr-ē, 'tranz-, -,tòr-\ *adj* : lasting only a short time : **SHORT-LIVED, TEMPORARY** ⟨the *transitory* pleasures of the world⟩ **SYN** see **TRANSIENT** — **tran·si·to·ri·ly** \,trans-ə-'tōr-ə-lē, ,tranz-, -'tòr-\ *adv* — **tran·si·to·ri·ness** \'trans-ə-,tōr-ē-nəs, 'tranz-, -,tòr-\ *n*

trans·late \trans-'lāt, tranz-\ *vb* **1** : to bear or change from one place, state, form, or appearance to another : **TRANSFER, TRANSFORM** ⟨*translate* plans into action⟩ **2 a** : to turn from one language into another **b** : to transfer or turn from one set of symbols into another : **TRANSCRIBE** **c** : to express in different words : **PARAPHRASE** **3** : to subject (as genetic information) to translation in protein synthesis [Latin *translatus,* past participle of *transferre* "to transfer, translate"] — **trans·lat·abil·i·ty** \-,lāt-ə-'bil-ət-ē\ *n* — **trans·lat·able** \-'lāt-ə-bəl\ *adj* — **trans·la·tor** \-'lāt-ər\ *n*

trans·la·tion \trans-'lā-shən, tranz-\ *n* **1** : an act, process, or instance of translating **2** : the product of translating ⟨a German *translation* of the novel⟩ **3** : a rigid motion of a mathematical figure equivalent to a transformation of coordinates in which the new axes are parallel to the old ones **4** : the process of forming a protein molecule at the site of protein synthesis from information contained in messenger RNA — compare **TRANSCRIPTION 3** — **trans·la·tion·al** \-shnəl, -shən-l\ *adj*

trans·lit·er·ate \trans-'lit-ə-,rāt, tranz-\ *vt* : to represent or spell in the characters of another alphabet [*trans-* + Latin *littera* "letter"] — **trans·lit·er·a·tion** \-,lit-ə-'rā-shən\ *n*

trans·lo·cate \'trans-lō-,kāt, 'tranz-, trans-', tranz-'\ *vt* : to transfer by translocation

trans·lo·ca·tion \,trans-lō-'kā-shən, ,tranz-\ *n* : a changing of location : **DISPLACEMENT:** as **a** : the conducting of soluble material from one part of a plant to another **b** : exchange of parts between nonhomologous chromosomes

trans·lu·cence \trans-'lüs-ns, tranz-\ *or* **trans·lu·cen·cy** \-n-sē\ *n* : the quality or state of being translucent

trans·lu·cent \-nt\ *adj* **1** : shining or glowing through **2** : admitting and diffusing light so that objects beyond cannot be clearly distinguished [Latin *translucens,* present participle of *translucēre* "to shine through", from *trans-* + *lucēre* "to shine"] **SYN** see **CLEAR** — **trans·lu·cent·ly** *adv*

trans·ma·rine \,trans-mə-'rēn, ,tranz-\ *adj* : being or coming from beyond or across the sea

trans·mi·gra·tion \,trans-,mī-'grā-shən, ,tranz-\ *n* **1** : the changing of one's home from one country to another : **MIGRATION** **2** : the passing of a soul into another body after death — **trans·mi·grate** \trans-'mī-,grāt, tranz-\ *vi* — **trans·mi·gra·to·ry** \-'mī-grə-,tōr-ē, -,tòr-\ *adj*

trans·mis·si·ble \trans-'mis-ə-bəl, tranz-\ *adj* : capable of being transmitted ⟨*transmissible* diseases⟩ — **trans·mis·si·bil·i·ty** \-,mis-ə-'bil-ət-ē\ *n*

trans·mis·sion \-'mish-ən\ *n* **1** : an act, process, or instance of transmitting something **2** : the passage of radio waves in the space between transmitting and receiving stations; *also* : the act or process of transmitting by radio or television **3** : an assembly of parts including the speed-changing gears and the propeller shaft by which power is transmitted from an automobile engine to the live axle **4** : something transmitted [Latin *transmissio,* from *transmittere* "to transmit"] — **trans·mis·sive** \-'mis-iv\ *adj* — **trans·mis·siv·i·ty** \,trans-mis-'iv-ət-ē, ,tranz-\ *n*

trans·mit \trans-'mit, tranz-\ *vb* **trans·mit·ted; trans·mit·ting** **1 a** : to send or transfer from one person or place to another : **FORWARD** **b** : to transfer by or as if by inheritance **c** : to convey (infection) abroad or to another **2 a** (1) : to cause (as light or force) to pass or be passed through space or a medium (2) : to admit the passage of ⟨glass *transmits* light⟩ **b** : to send out a signal either by radio waves or over a wire [Latin *transmittere,* from *trans-* + *mittere* "to send"] — **trans·mit·ta·ble** \-'mit-ə-bəl\ *adj* — **trans·mit·tal** \-'mit-l\ *n*

trans·mit·ter \-'mit-ər\ *n* **1** : one that transmits **2** : the part of a telephone that includes the mouthpiece and a mechanism that picks up sound waves and sends them over the wire **3** : the device in a telegraph system that sends out messages **4** : the apparatus that sends out radio or television signals

trans·mog·ri·fy \trans-'mäg-rə-,fī, tranz-\ *vt* **-fied; -fy·ing** : to change or alter often with grotesque or humorous effect [origin unknown] — **trans·mog·ri·fi·ca·tion** \-,mäg-rə-fə-'kā-shən\ *n*

trans·mu·ta·tion \,trans-myù-'tā-shən, ,tranz-\ *n* : an act or instance of transmuting or being transmuted: as **a** : the hypothetical changing of base metals into gold or silver **b** : the changing of one element or nuclide into another either naturally or artificially — **trans·mut·a·tive** \trans-'myüt-ət-iv, tranz-\ *adj*

\ə\	abut	\ng\	sing
\ər\	further	\ō\	bone
\a\	mat	\ò\	saw
\ā\	take	\òi\	coin
\ä\	cot, cart	\th\	thin
\aù\	out	\th\	this
\ch\	chin	\ü\	food
\e\	pet	\ù\	foot
\ē\	easy	\y\	yet
\g\	go	\yü\	few
\i\	tip	\yù\	cure
\ī\	life	\zh\	vision
\j\	job		

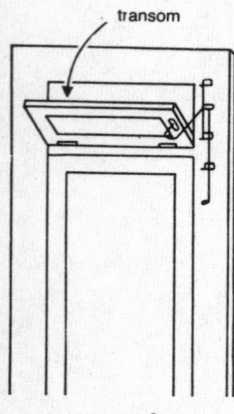

transom 2

trans·mute \trans-'myüt, tranz-\ *vb* 1 : to change in form, appearance, or nature especially to a higher form 2 : to subject to transmutation 3 : to undergo transmutation [Latin *transmutare,* from *trans-* + *mutare* "to change"] SYN see TRANSFORM — **trans·mut·able** \-'myüt-ə-bəl\ *adj*

trans·na·tion·al \trans-'nash-nəl, 'trans-, tranz-, 'tranz-, -ən-l\ *adj* : extending beyond national boundaries

trans·oce·an·ic \,trans-ō-shē-'an-ik, ,tranz-\ *adj* 1 : being or living beyond the ocean 2 : crossing or extending across the ocean ⟨*transoceanic* cables⟩

tran·som \'tran-səm\ *n* 1 : a transverse piece in a structure : CROSSPIECE: as **a** : LINTEL **b** : a horizontal crossbar in a window, over a door, or between a door and a window or fanlight above it 2 : a window above a door or above another window built on and commonly hinged to a transom [probably from Latin *transtrum,* from *trans* "across"]

tran·son·ic *also* **trans–son·ic** \trans-'sän-ik, tran-'sän-\ *adj* 1 : being or relating to a speed approximating the speed of sound in air — often used of aeronautical speeds between 600 and 900 miles per hour (about 950 to 1450 kilometers per hour) 2 : moving, capable of moving, or utilizing air currents moving at a transonic speed ⟨*transonic* bomber⟩ [*trans-* + *-sonic* (as in *supersonic*)]

trans·pa·cif·ic \,trans-pə-'sif-ik\ *adj* : crossing, extending across, or situated beyond the Pacific ocean

trans·par·ence \trans-'par-əns, -'per-\ *n* : TRANSPARENCY 1

trans·par·en·cy \-ən-sē\ *n, pl* **-cies** 1 : the quality or state of being transparent 2 : a picture or design on glass, thin cloth, paper, or film viewed by light shining through it or by projection

trans·par·ent \-ənt\ *adj* 1 **a** (1) : having the property of transmitting light so that bodies lying beyond are entirely visible (2) : allowing the passage of a specified form of radiation (as X rays or ultraviolet light) **b** : fine or sheer enough to be seen through 2 **a** : FRANK 1, GUILELESS **b** : easily detected or seen through : OBVIOUS [Medieval Latin *transparens,* present participle of *transparēre* "to show through", from Latin *trans-* + *parēre* "to show oneself, appear"] SYN see CLEAR — **trans·par·ent·ly** *adv* — **trans·par·ent·ness** *n*

tran·spi·ra·tion \,trans-pə-'rā-shən\ *n* : the act or process or an instance of transpiring; *esp* : the passage of watery vapor from a living body through a membrane or pores — compare PERSPIRATION

tran·spire \trans-'pīr\ *vb* 1 **a** : to pass off or give passage to (a fluid) through small openings; *esp* : to excrete (watery vapor) through a membrane or pores ⟨a large tree may *transpire* tons of water in a season⟩ **b** : to escape in the form of a vapor especially from a living body 2 : to give off vaporous material (as watery vapor from the surfaces of leaves) 3 : to pass in the form of a vapor from a living body 4 : to become known or apparent 5 : to come to pass [Middle French *transpirer,* from Latin *trans-* + *spirare* "to breathe"] SYN see HAPPEN

¹trans·plant \trans-'plant\ *vb* 1 : to lift and reset (a plant) in another soil or situation 2 : to remove from one place and settle elsewhere 3 : to transfer (an organ or tissue) from one part or individual to another 4 : to tolerate being transplanted — **trans·plant·able** \-ə-bəl\ *adj* — **trans·plan·ta·tion** \,trans-,plan-'tā-shən\ *n* — **trans·plant·er** \trans-'plant-ər\ *n*

²trans·plant \'trans-,plant\ *n* 1 : the act or process of transplanting 2 : something or someone transplanted

trans·po·lar \trans-'pō-lər, 'trans-\ *adj* : going or extending across either of the polar regions

¹trans·port \trans-'pōrt, -'pȯrt\ *vt* 1 : to convey from one place to another : CARRY 2 : ENRAPTURE ⟨*transported* with delight⟩ 3 : to send to a penal colony overseas [Latin *transportare,* from *trans-* + *portare*

"to carry"] — **trans·port·abil·i·ty** \-,pōrt-ə-'bil-ət-ē -,pȯrt-\ *n* — **trans·port·able** \-'pōrt-ə-bəl, -'pȯrt-\ *adj* — **trans·port·er** *n*

²trans·port \'trans-,pōrt, -,pȯrt\ *n* 1 : the act of transporting : TRANSPORTATION 2 : strong or intensely pleasurable emotion : ECSTASY, RAPTURE ⟨*transports* of joy⟩ 3 **a** : a ship for carrying soldiers or military equipment **b** : a vehicle used to transport persons or goods **c** : a system of public transportation

trans·por·ta·tion \,trans-pər-'tā-shən\ *n* 1 : an act, process, or instance of transporting or being transported 2 : banishment to a penal colony 3 **a** : means of conveyance or travel from one place to another **b** : public conveyance of passengers or goods especially as a commercial enterprise

trans·pose \trans-'pōz\ *vt* 1 : TRANSFORM 1a 2 : TRANSLATE 2 3 : to transfer from one place or period to another : SHIFT 4 : to change the relative place or normal order of 5 : to write or perform (a musical composition) in a different key 6 : to bring (a term) from one side of an algebraic equation to the other with change of sign [Middle French *transposer,* from Latin *transponere* "to change the position of", from *trans-* + *ponere* "to put, place"] SYN see REVERSE — **trans·pos·able** \-'pō-zə-bəl\ *adj* — **trans·po·si·tion** \,trans-pə-'zish-ən\ *n*

trans·sex·u·al \trans-'seksh-wəl, 'trans-, -ə-wəl, -'sek-shəl\ *n* : a person genetically of one sex who has a strong urge to belong to the opposite sex which may be carried to the point of undergoing surgery to modify the sex organs to mimic those of the opposite sex — **transsexual** *adj* — **trans·sex·u·al·ism** \-wə-,liz-əm, -shə-,liz-\ *n*

trans·ship \tran-'ship, trans-\ *vb* : to transfer for further transportation from one means of transport to another — **trans·ship·ment** \-mənt\ *n*

tran·sub·stan·ti·ate \,tran-səb-'stan-chē-,āt\ *vb* : to change into another substance [Medieval Latin *transubstantiare,* from Latin *trans-* + *substantia* "substance"]

tran·sub·stan·ti·a·tion \-,stan-chē-'ā-shən\ *n* 1 : an act or instance of transubstantiating or being transubstantiated 2 : the change in the consecrated bread and wine at Mass in substance but not in appearance to the body and blood of Christ

trans·ura·ni·um \,tran-shə-'rā-nē-əm, ,tran-zhə-\ *or* **trans·ura·nic** \-'ran-ik, -'rā-nik\ *adj* : having an atomic number greater than that of uranium

trans·ver·sal \trans-'vər-səl, tranz-\ *n* : a line that intersects a system of lines

¹trans·verse \trans-'vərs, tranz-', 'trans-,, 'tranz-\ *adj* : lying or being across : set crosswise [Latin *transversus,* from *transvertere* "to turn across", from *trans-* + *vertere* "to turn"] — **trans·verse·ly** *adv*

²trans·verse \'trans-,vərs, 'tranz-\ *n* : something transverse

transverse wave *n* : a wave in which the vibrating element moves in a direction perpendicular to the direction of advance of the wave

trans·ves·tism \trans-'ves-,tiz-əm, tranz-\ *n* : adoption of the dress and often the behavior of the opposite sex [German *transvestismus,* from Latin *trans-* + *vestire* "to clothe"] — **trans·ves·tite** \-'ves-,tīt\ *adj or n*

¹trap \'trap\ *n* 1 : a device (as a snare or pitfall) for catching animals; *esp* : one that holds by springing shut suddenly 2 : something by which one is caught or stopped unawares 3 **a** : a device for hurling clay pigeons into the air **b** : SAND TRAP 4 : a light usually one-horse carriage with springs 5 : any of various devices for preventing passage of something often while allowing other matter to proceed 6 : a device for drains or sewers consisting of a bend or partitioned chamber in which the liquid forms a seal to prevent the passage of sewer gas [Old English *treppe* and Old French *trape*]

²trap *vb* **trapped; trap·ping 1 a** : to catch in or as if in a trap **b** : to place in a restricted position : CONFINE **2** : to provide with a trap **3** : to separate out (as water from steam) **4** : to engage in trapping animals SYN see CATCH — **trap·per** *n*

³trap *vt* **trapped; trap·ping** : to decorate with or as if with trappings [Middle English *trappen*, from *trappe* "cloth", from Middle French *drap*]

⁴trap *or* **trap–rock** \'trap-,räk\ *n* : any of various fine-grained igneous rocks used especially in road making [Swedish *trapp*, from *trappa* "stair", from Low German *trappe*]

trap·door \'trap-'dōr, -'dȯr\ *n* : a lifting or sliding door covering an opening in a roof, ceiling, or floor

trap–door spider *n* : any of various spiders that build silk-lined underground nests topped with a hinged lid

tra·peze \tra-'pēz\ *n* : an acrobatic apparatus consisting of a short horizontal bar suspended at a height by two parallel ropes [French *trapèze*, from New Latin *trapezium* "trapezium"]

tra·pez·ist \-'pē-zəst\ *n* : a performer on the trapeze

tra·pe·zi·um \tra-'pē-zē-əm\ *n, pl* **-zi·ums** *or* **-zia** \-ze-ə\ **1** : a quadrilateral having no two sides parallel **2** *British* : TRAPEZOID 2 [New Latin, from Greek *trapezion*, literally, "small table", from *trapeza* "table", from *tra-* "four" + *peza* "foot"]

tra·pe·zi·us \-zē-əs\ *n* : a large flat triangular superficial muscle of each side of the back [New Latin, from *trapezium*; from the figure formed by the two muscles]

trap·e·zoid \'trap-ə-,zȯid\ *n* **1** *British* : TRAPEZIUM 1 **2** : a quadrilateral having only two sides parallel — **trap·e·zoi·dal** \,trap-ə-'zȯid-l\ *adj*

trap·ping \'trap-ing\ *n* **1** : CAPARISON 1 — usually used in pl. **2** *pl* : outward decoration or signs ⟨the *trappings* of success⟩

Trap·pist \'trap-əst\ *n* : a monk of an austere branch of the Cistercian Order [French *trappiste*, from La *Trappe*, France, where the branch was established] — **Trappist** *adj*

traps \'traps\ *n pl* : personal belongings : LUGGAGE [Middle English *trappe* "cloth"]

trap·shoot·ing \'trap-,shüt-ing\ *n* : shooting at clay pigeons thrown from a trap into the air away from the shooters — **trap·shoot·er** \-,shüt-ər\ *n*

trash \'trash\ *n* **1** : something worth little or nothing: as **a** : ¹JUNK 2a, RUBBISH **b** : empty talk : NONSENSE **c** : low-grade or worthless artistic matter **2** : something in a crumbled or broken condition or mass; *esp* : debris from pruning or processing plant material **3** : a worthless or shameful person; *also* : RIFFRAFF [of Scandinavian origin]

trashy \'trash-ē\ *adj* **trash·i·er; -est** : resembling trash : WORTHLESS — **trash·i·ness** *n*

trat·to·ria \,trät-ə-'rē-ə\ *n* : an eating house : RESTAURANT [Italian]

trau·ma \'traü-mə, 'trȯ-\ *n, pl* **trau·ma·ta** \-mət-ə\ *or* **traumas 1 a** : a bodily injury caused by a physical force applied from without ⟨surgical *trauma*⟩ **b** : a disordered psychic or behavioral state resulting from stress or injury **2** : a cause of trauma [Greek *traumat-, trauma* "wound"] — **trau·mat·ic** \tra-'mat-ik, trȯ-, traü-\ *adj* — **trau·mat·i·cal·ly** \-'mat-i-kə-lē, -klē\ *adv*

¹tra·vail \tra-'vāl, 'trav-,āl\ *n* **1 a** : work especially of a painful or laborious nature : TOIL **b** : a piece of work : TASK **c** : AGONY 1a, TORMENT **2** : LABOR 1c, CHILDBIRTH [Old French from *travaillier* "to torture, travail", derived from Latin *tripalis* "having 3 stakes", from *tri-* + *palus* "stake"] □ ORIGIN Late Latin *trepalium* was the name of an instrument of torture. We do not know exactly what the *trepalium* looked like, but we can get some idea from the word's etymology. *Trepalium* is a derivative of Latin *tripalis*, which means "having 3 stakes". Although only *trepalium* is found in docu-

ments that still exist, we can assume that there was also another form, *tripalium*. *Travaillier*, "to torture", an Old French descendant of this *tripalium*, early developed the extended and milder senses "to trouble", "to labor or toil", and "to weary". The noun *travail*, "labor, toil", derived from the verb *travaillier*, was borrowed from Old French into English.

²travail *vi* : to work hard : TOIL

¹trav·el \'trav-əl\ *vb* **trav·eled** *or* **trav·elled; trav·el·ing** *or* **trav·el·ling** \'trav-ling, -ə-ling\ **1** : to journey from place to place or to a distant place **2** : to journey from place to place selling or taking orders **3 a** : to move or advance from one place to another **b** : to undergo transportation **c** : to walk or run with a basketball in violation of the rules **4** : to journey through or over : TRAVERSE ⟨this trail can be *traveled* only on horseback⟩ [Old French *travaillier* "to travail"] □ ORIGIN In the Middle Ages the most striking thing about *travel* was its difficulty. A journey cost a great deal of wearisome effort, so that a pilgrimage to a distant religious shrine, for example, was an act of real devotion. The verb *travail* developed in English the specific sense "to go on a journey". *Travel*, originally a variant spelling of *travail*, has attached itself to this particular sense and so become a separate word.

²travel *n* **1 a** : the act of traveling : PASSAGE **b** : JOURNEY, TRIP — often used in pl. **2** *pl* : an account of one's travels **3** : the number traveling : TRAFFIC **4 a** : MOVEMENT ⟨the *travel* of satellites around the earth⟩ **b** : the motion of a piece of machinery; *esp* : reciprocating motion

travel agency *n* : an agency engaged in selling, arranging, or furnishing information about personal transportation or travel — called also *travel bureau* — **travel agent** *n*

trav·eled *or* **trav·elled** \'trav-əld\ *adj* **1** : experienced in travel **2** : used by travelers ⟨a *traveled* road⟩

trav·el·er *or* **trav·el·ler** \'trav-lər, -ə-lər\ *n* : one that travels

traveler's check *n* : a draft purchased from a bank or express company and signed by the purchaser at the time of purchase and again at the time of cashing

traveling bag *n* : a bag carried by hand and designed to hold a traveler's clothing and personal articles

traveling salesman *n* : a traveling representative of a business concern who solicits orders

trav·el·ogue *also* **trav·el·og** \'trav-ə-,lȯg, -,läg\ *n* : a usually illustrated lecture on travel [*travel* + *-logue*]

tra·vers·al \tra-'vər-səl\ *n* : the act or an instance of traversing

¹trav·erse \'trav-ərs, *especially for 5 also* tra-'vərs\ *n* **1** : something that crosses or lies across **2** : OBSTACLE, ADVERSITY **3** : a gallery extending from side to side in a large building **4** : a route or way across or over (as a zigzag course) **5** : the act or an instance of traversing : CROSSING **6** : a protective projecting wall or bank of earth in a trench **7** : a line surveyed across a plot of ground [Middle French, from *traverser* "to cross", from Late Latin *transversare*, from Latin *transvertere* "to turn across"]

²tra·verse \tra-'vərs\ *vb* **1** : to go against or act in opposition to : OPPOSE **2** : to pass through, across, or over **3** : to make a study of : EXAMINE **4** : to ascend, descend, or cross (a slope or gap) at an angle **5** : to move back and forth or from side to side **6** : to move or turn laterally : SWIVEL **7** : to climb or ski at an angle or in a zigzag course — **tra·vers·able** \-'vər-sə-bəl\ *adj* — **tra·vers·er** *n*

³trav·erse \'trav-ərs, -,ərs; tra-'vərs\ *adj* : lying across : TRANSVERSE

traverse jury \'trav-ərs-\ *n* : PETIT JURY

trav·er·tine \'trav-ər-,tēn, -tən\ *n* : a massive usually layered calcium carbonate formed by deposition from spring waters or especially from hot springs [French

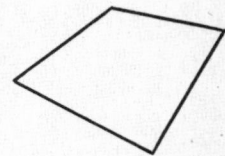

trapezium 1

travertin, from Italian *tivertino, travertino,* from Latin *tiburtinus* "of Tivoli", from *Tibur* "Tivoli"]

¹trav·es·ty \'trav-ə-stē\ *n, pl* **-ties** **1** : a burlesque and usually grotesque translation or imitation **2** : an inferior imitation or likeness ⟨a *travesty* of justice⟩ [obsolete *travesty* "disguised, parodied", from French *travestir* "to disguise", from Italian *travestire,* from *tra-* "trans-" + *vestire* "to dress", from Latin, from *vestis* "garment"] **SYN** see **CARICATURE**

²travesty *vt* **-tied; -ty·ing** : to make a travesty of : **PARODY**

tra·vois \trə-'vȯi, 'trav-,ȯi\ *n, pl* **tra·vois** \-'vȯiz, -,ȯiz\ *also* **tra·vois·es** \-'vȯi-zəz, -,ȯi-zəz\ : a vehicle used by the Amerindians of the Great Plains consisting of two trailing poles serving as shafts and bearing a platform or net for the load [Canadian French *travois*]

¹trawl \'trȯl\ *vb* : to fish or catch with a trawl [probably from Dutch *tragelen*]

²trawl *n* : a large conical net dragged along the sea bottom in fishing

trawl·er \'trȯ-lər\ *n* : a person or vessel that fishes by trawling

tray \'trā\ *n* : an open receptacle with flat bottom and low rim for holding, carrying, or exhibiting articles ⟨a serving *tray*⟩ ⟨the *trays* of a trunk⟩ [Old English *trīg, trēg*]

treach·er·ous \'trech-rəs, -ə-rəs\ *adj* **1** : guilty of or inclined to treachery **2 a** : not reliable ⟨a *treacherous* memory⟩ **b** : giving a false appearance of safety ⟨*treacherous* quicksand⟩ — **treach·er·ous·ly** *adv* — **treach·er·ous·ness** *n*

treach·ery \'trech-rē, -ə-rē\ *n, pl* **-er·ies** **1** : violation of allegiance or of faith and confidence : **TREASON** **2** : an act of treason [Old French *trecherie,* from *trechier* "to deceive"]

trea·cle \'trē-kəl\ *n* **1** *chiefly British* : **MOLASSES** **2** : something (as a tone of voice) heavily sweet and cloying [Middle French *triacle,* an antidote against poison, from Latin *theriaca,* from Greek *thēriakē* "antidote against a poisonous bite", derived from *thēr* "wild animal"] — **trea·cly** \-kə-lē, -klē\ *adj*

¹tread \'tred\ *vb* **trod** \'träd\; **trod·den** \'träd-n\ *or* **trod; tread·ing** **1 a** : to step or walk on or over **b** : to walk along : **FOLLOW** **2 a** : to beat or press with the feet : **TRAMPLE** **b** : to bring under control or put down by force **3 a** : to form by treading ⟨*tread* a path⟩ **b** : to execute by stepping or dancing ⟨*tread* a measure⟩ **4 a** : to set foot **b** : to put one's foot : **STEP** [Old English *tredan*] — **tread·er** *n* — **tread water** : to keep the body nearly upright in the water and the head above water by a treading motion of the feet usually aided by the hands

²tread *n* **1** : a mark made by or as if by treading **2** : the action, manner, or sound of treading **3 a** : the part of a sole that touches the ground **b** : the part of a wheel that bears on a road or rail; *esp* : the thickened face of an automobile tire **4** : the distance between the points of contact with the ground of the two front wheels or the two rear wheels of a vehicle **5** : the horizontal part of a step

¹trea·dle \'tred-l\ *n* : a lever or other device pressed by the foot to drive a machine [Old English *tredel* "step of a stair", from *tredan* "to tread"]

²treadle *vb* **trea·dled; trea·dling** \'tred-ling, -l-ing\ : to operate a treadle or operate the treadle of

tread·mill \'tred-,mil\ *n* **1** : a device moved by persons treading on steps set around the rim of a wide wheel or by animals walking on an endless belt **2** : a wearisome or monotonous routine

trea·son \'trēz-n\ *n* **1** : the betrayal of a trust : **TREACHERY** **2** : the offense of attempting by overt acts to overthrow the government of the state to which one owes allegiance or to bring about its defeat in war [Old French *traison,* from Medieval Latin *traditio,* from Latin, "act of handing over, teaching, tradition"] **SYN**

see **SEDITION** ☐ **ORIGIN** *Treason* and *tradition* are derived from the same Latin source. Latin *traditio* means "teaching" or "tradition", but these senses are developed from its literal sense, "the act of handing over something". Tradition is maintained by passing information from one generation to another, whereas treason is committed when someone who has been entrusted with information passes it on to someone else. The difference in form between the two words can be accounted for by the fact that *treason* came to us through Old French, where *traditio* underwent sound change, while *tradition* was later borrowed directly from Latin.

trea·son·able \'trēz-nə-bəl, -n-ə-bəl\ *adj* : relating to, consisting of, or involving treason — **trea·son·ably** \-blē\ *adv*

trea·son·ous \'trēz-nəs, -n-əs\ *adj* : **TREASONABLE**

¹trea·sure \'trezh-ər, 'trāzh-\ *n* **1 a** (1) : wealth (as money, jewels, or precious metals) stored up or hoarded ⟨buried *treasure*⟩ (2) : **RICHES** **b** : a store of money in reserve **2** : something of great worth or value; *also* : a person esteemed as rare or precious [Old French *tresor,* from Latin *thesaurus,* from Greek *thēsauros*]

²treasure *vt* **trea·sured; trea·sur·ing** \'trezh-ring, 'trāzh-, -ə-ring\ **1** : to collect and store up (something of value) for future use **2** : to hold or keep as precious : **CHERISH** — **trea·sur·able** \'trezh-rə-bəl, 'trāzh-, -ə-rə-\ *adj*

treasure hunt *n* : any of various games in which each player or team tries to be first to find whatever has been hidden (as by finding and following a series of hidden clues)

trea·sur·er \'trezh-rər, 'trezh-ər-ər, 'trāzh-\ *n* : a person trusted with charge of a treasure or a treasury; *esp* : an officer of a club, business, or government who has charge of money taken in and paid out — **trea·sur·er·ship** \-,ship\ *n*

treasure trove \'trezh-ər-,trōv, 'trāzh-\ *n* **1** : treasure found buried in the ground or hidden away and of unknown ownership **2** : a discovery or something discovered that is full of things to be treasured [Anglo-French *tresor trové,* literally, "found treasure"]

trea·sury \'trezh-rē, 'trāzh-, -ə-rē\ *n, pl* **trea·sur·ies** **1 a** : a place in which stores of wealth are kept **b** : the place of deposit and disbursement of collected funds; *esp* : one where public revenues are deposited, kept, and disbursed **c** : funds kept in a place of deposit **2** *cap* : a governmental department in charge of finances **3** : a repository for treasures ⟨a *treasury* of poems⟩

treasury note *n* : a currency note issued by the United States Treasury in payment for silver bullion purchased under the Sherman Silver Purchase Act of 1890

¹treat \'trēt\ *vb* **1** : to discuss terms of accommodation or settlement : **NEGOTIATE** **2 a** : to deal with a matter especially in writing : **DISCOURSE** ⟨books *treating* of crime⟩ **b** : to present or represent artistically **c** : to deal with : **HANDLE** **3 a** : to pay for another's entertainment **b** : to provide with free food, entertainment, or enjoyment **4 a** : to behave or act toward : **USE** ⟨*treat* a horse cruelly⟩ **b** : to regard and deal with in a specified manner ⟨*treat* as confidential⟩ **5** : to care for or deal with medically or surgically **6** : to subject to some action ⟨*treat* soil with lime⟩ [Old French *traitier,* from Latin *tractare* "to handle, deal with, treat", from *trahere* "to draw"] — **treat·er** *n*

²treat *n* **1** : an entertainment given without expense to those invited **2** : an especially unexpected source of pleasure or amusement ⟨the *treat* of seeing you again⟩

treat·able \'trēt-ə-bəl\ *adj* : that can be treated; *esp* : responsive to medical or surgical treatment — **treat·abil·i·ty** \,trēt-ə-'bil-ət-ē\ *n*

trea·tise \'trēt-əs\ *n* : a book or an article treating a subject systematically ⟨a *treatise* on war⟩ [Anglo-French *tretiz,* from Old French *traitier* "to treat"]

treat·ment \'trēt-mənt\ *n* **1** : the act or manner or an instance of treating someone or something **2** : a substance or technique used in treating

trea·ty \'trēt-ē\ *n, pl* **treaties** : an agreement or arrangement made by negotiation; *esp* : a contract between two or more states or sovereigns [Middle French *traité,* from Medieval Latin *tractatus,* from Latin, "treatment", from *tractare* "to treat"]

treaty port *n* : a port or inland city of China, Japan, and Korea formerly open by treaty to foreign commerce

¹tre·ble \'treb-əl\ *n* **1 a** : the highest of the four voice parts in vocal music : SOPRANO **b** : a singer or instrument taking this part **c** : a high-pitched voice, tone, or sound **d** : the upper half of the musical pitch range **2** : something triple in construction, uses, amount, number, or value [Middle English]

²treble *adj* **1 a** : having three parts **b** : triple in number or amount **2 a** : relating to or having the range of a musical treble ⟨*treble* voices⟩ **b** : high-pitched : SHRILL [Middle French, from Latin *triplus* "triple"] — **tre·bly** \'treb-lē, -ə-lē\ *adv*

³treble *vb* **tre·bled; tre·bling** \'treb-ling, -ə-ling\ **1** : to make or become three times the size, amount, or number ⟨*treble* its weight⟩ **2** : to sing treble

treble clef *n* **1** : a clef that places G above middle C on the second line of the staff **2** : TREBLE STAFF [from its use for the notation of treble parts]

treble staff *n* : the musical staff carrying the treble clef

¹tree \'trē\ *n* **1 a** : a woody perennial plant having a single usually tall main stem with few or no branches on its lower part **b** : a shrub or herb that looks like a tree ⟨rose *trees*⟩ ⟨a banana *tree*⟩ **2** : a piece of wood (as a post or pole) usually adapted to a particular use or forming part of a structure or implement **3** : something in the form of or felt to resemble a tree: as **a** : a diagram that depicts a branching from an original stem ⟨genealogical *tree*⟩ **b** : a much-branched system of channels especially in an animal body ⟨the vascular *tree*⟩ [Old English *trēow*] — **tree·less** \-ləs\ *adj* — **tree·like** \-,līk\ *adj*

²tree *vt* **treed; tree·ing** **1 a** : to drive to or up a tree ⟨*treed* by a bull⟩ **b** : to bring to bay **2** : to furnish or fit with a tree

tree farm *n* : an area of forest land managed to ensure continuous commercial production — **tree farmer** *n*

tree fern *n* : a tropical fern with a woody stalk and a crown of large often feathery fronds

tree frog *n* : any of numerous tailless amphibians that frequent trees — called also *tree toad;* compare SPRING PEEPER

tree house *n* : a structure (as a playhouse) built among the branches of a tree

tree line *n* : TIMBERLINE

tree of heaven : AILANTHUS

tree ring *n* : ANNUAL RING

tree shrew *n* : any of a family of tree-dwelling insect-eating mammals sometimes classified as true insectivores and sometimes as primitive primates

tree toad *n* : TREE FROG

tree·top \'trē-,täp\ *n* : the topmost part of a tree

tre·foil \'trē-,fȯil, 'tref-,ȯil\ *n* **1 a** : CLOVER **b** : any of several herbs of the pea family having leaves with three leaflets **2** : an ornament or symbol in the form of a 3-parted leaf [Middle French *trefeuil,* from Latin *trifolium,* from *tri-* + *folium* "leaf"]

trek \'trek\ *vi* **trekked; trek·king** **1** *chiefly southern Africa* : to migrate by ox wagon or in a train of such wagons **2** : to make one's way arduously [Afrikaans, from Dutch *trecken* "to pull, haul, migrate"] — **trek** *n* — **trek·ker** *n*

¹trel·lis \'trel-əs\ *n* : a frame of latticework used especially as a screen or a support for climbing plants [Middle French *treliz* "fabric of coarse weave, trellis", derived from Latin *tri-* + *liceum* "thread"]

²trellis *vt* **1** : to provide with or train on a trellis ⟨*trellis* a vine⟩ **2** : to cross or interlace on or through : INTERWEAVE

trel·lis·work \'trel-ə-,swərk\ *n* : LATTICEWORK

trem·a·tode \'trem-ə-,tōd\ *n* : any of a class (Trematoda) of parasitic flatworms including the flukes [derived from Greek *trēmatōdēs* "pierced with holes", from *trēma* "hole", from *tetrainein* "to bore"] — **trematode** *adj*

¹trem·ble \'trem-bəl\ *vi* **trem·bled; trem·bling** \-bə-ling, -bling\ **1** : to shake involuntarily (as with fear or cold) : SHIVER **2** : to move, sound, or occur as if shaken or tremulous **3** : to be affected with fear or doubt ⟨*tremble* for the safety of a friend⟩ [Middle French *trembler,* from Medieval Latin *tremulare,* from Latin *tremulus* "tremulous"] — **trem·bler** \-bə-lər, -blər\ *n*

²tremble *n* **1** : a fit or spell of involuntary shaking or quivering **2** : a tremor or series of tremors

trem·bly \'trem-bə-lē, -blē\ *adj* : marked by trembling

tre·men·dous \tri-'men-dəs\ *adj* **1** : such as may excite trembling or arouse dread, awe, or terror **2** : astonishing by reason of extreme size, power, greatness, or excellence [Latin *tremendus,* from *tremere* "to tremble"] SYN see MONSTROUS — **tre·men·dous·ly** *adv* — **tre·men·dous·ness** *n*

trem·o·lo \'trem-ə-,lō\ *n, pl* **-los** **1 a** : the rapid reiteration of a musical tone or of alternating tones to produce a tremulous effect **b** : a perceptible rapid variation of pitch in singing similar to the vibrato of a stringed instrument **2** : a mechanical device in an organ for causing a tremulous effect [Italian, from *tremolo* "tremulous", from Latin *tremulus*]

trem·or \'trem-ər\ *n* **1** : a trembling or shaking usually from weakness or disease **2** : a quivering or vibratory motion (as of the earth or a leaf) **3** : a feeling of uncertainty or insecurity [Middle French *tremour,* from Latin *tremor,* from *tremere* "to tremble"]

trem·u·lous \'trem-yə-ləs\ *adj* **1** : characterized by or affected with trembling or tremors ⟨*tremulous* hands⟩ **2** : affected with timidity : TIMOROUS ⟨a shy *tremulous* child⟩ **3** : such as is caused by a tremulous state ⟨a *tremulous* smile⟩ **4** : exceedingly sensitive [Latin *tremulus,* from *tremere* "to tremble"] — **trem·u·lous·ly** *adv* — **trem·u·lous·ness** *n*

¹trench \'trench\ *n* **1 a** : a long narrow cut in land : DITCH **b** : a long ditch protected by a bank of earth thrown before it that is used to shelter soldiers **2** : a long narrow steep-sided depression in the ocean floor [Middle French *trenche* "act of cutting", from *trenchier* "to cut"]

²trench *vb* **1** : to protect with or as if with a trench **2** : to cut a trench in : DITCH **3** : to come close : VERGE ⟨the answer *trenched* on impudence⟩

tren·chan·cy \'tren-chən-sē\ *n* : the quality of being trenchant

tren·chant \'tren-chənt\ *adj* **1** : having a sharp edge or point : CUTTING ⟨a *trenchant* blade⟩ ⟨*trenchant* sarcasm⟩ **2** : sharply clear : PENETRATING ⟨a *trenchant* analysis of a situation⟩ **3** : mentally energetic [Middle French, present participle of *trenchier* "to cut"] SYN see INCISIVE — **tren·chant·ly** *adv*

trench coat *n* **1** : a waterproof overcoat with a removable lining designed for wear in trenches **2** : a loose double-breasted raincoat with deep pockets, a belt, and straps on the shoulders

¹tren·cher \'tren-chər\ *n* : a wooden platter for serving food [Middle French *trencheoir* "platter for carving", from *trenchier* "to cut"]

²trench·er \'tren-chər\ *n* : one that digs trenches

tren·cher·man \-mən\ *n* **1** : a hearty eater **2** *archaic* : HANGER-ON, SPONGER

trench fever *n* : a rickettsial disease marked by fever and pain (as in joints) and transmitted by the body louse

trefoil 2

trench foot *n* : a painful foot disorder resembling frostbite and resulting from exposure to cold and wet

trench knife *n* : a knife with a strong double-edged 8-inch blade suited for hand-to-hand fighting

trench mouth *n* **1** : VINCENT'S ANGINA **2** : VINCENT'S INFECTION

¹**trend** \'trend\ *vi* **1 a** : to extend in a general direction **b** : to veer in a new direction : BEND **2 a** : to show a tendency : INCLINE **b** : SHIFT ⟨opinions *trending* toward conservatism⟩ [Old English *trendan* "to turn, revolve"]

²**trend** *n* **1** : general direction taken ⟨easterly *trend* of the shoreline⟩ **2 a** : a prevailing tendency or inclination ⟨economic *trends*⟩ **b** : a general movement : SWING **c** : a current style or preference **d** : a line of development SYN see TENDENCY

tre·pan \tri-'pan\ *vt* **tre·panned; tre·pan·ning** : to remove a disk from (the skull) [Medieval Latin *trepanum* "trephine", from Greek *trypanon* "auger", from *trypan* "to bore", from *trypa* "hole"] — **trep·a·na·tion** \,trep-ə-'nā-shən\ *n*

tre·pang \tri-'pang\ *n* : any of several large Pacific sea cucumbers that are used dried especially by the Chinese for making soup — called also *bêche-de-mer* [Malay *tĕripang*]

tre·phine \'trē-,fīn\ *n* : a surgical instrument for cutting out circular sections (as of bone or corneal tissue) [French *tréphine*, from obsolete English *trafine*, from Latin *tres fines* "three ends"]

trep·i·da·tion \,trep-ə-'dā-shən\ *n* **1** *archaic* : a tremulous motion **2** : a state of alarm : FEAR [Latin *trepidatio*, from *trepidare* "to tremble", from *trepidus* "agitated"]

trepo·ne·ma \,trep-ə-'nē-mə\ *n, pl* **-ma·ta** \-mət-ə\ *or* **-mas** : any of a genus of spirochetes that parasitize warm-blooded animals and include organisms causing syphilis and yaws [New Latin, derived from Greek *trepein* "to turn" + *nēma* "thread"] — **trepo·ne·mal** \-məl\ *adj*

¹**tres·pass** \'tres-pəs, -,pas\ *n* **1 a** : a violation of morals : TRANSGRESSION; *esp* : SIN **b** : an unwarranted infringement **2 a** (1) : an unlawful act committed on the person, property, or rights of another (2) : a court action for injuries done by such an act **b** : the tort of wrongful entry on real property [Old French *trespas*, from *trespasser* "to go across, trespass", from *tres* "across" (from Latin *trans*) + *passer* "to pass"]

²**trespass** *vi* **1** : ERR 1, SIN **2** : to commit a trespass; *esp* : to enter unlawfully upon the land of another — **tres·pass·er** *n*

tress \'tres\ *n* **1** *archaic* : a plait of hair : BRAID **2 a** : a long lock of hair **b** *pl* : long unbound hair [Old French *trece*]

tres·tle \'tres-əl\ *n* **1** : a braced frame that consists usually of a horizontal piece with spreading legs at each end and that supports something (as a tabletop or drawing board) **2** : a braced framework of timbers or steel for carrying a road or railroad over a depression [Middle French *trestel*, derived from Latin *transtillum* "small beam", from *transtrum* "traverse beam, transom"]

tres·tle·work \-,wərk\ *n* : a system of connected trestles supporting a structure (as a bridge)

trews \'trüz\ *n pl* : close-cut tartan shorts worn under the kilt in Highland dress [Scottish Gaelic *triubhas*]

trey \'trā\ *n, pl* **treys** : a card or die with three spots [Middle French *treis, treie*, from Latin *tres* "three"]

tri- *combining form* **1** : three : having three elements or parts ⟨*tri*axial⟩ ⟨*tri*graph⟩ **2** : into three ⟨*tri*sect⟩ **3 a** : thrice ⟨*tri*weekly⟩ **b** : every third ⟨*tri*monthly⟩ [Latin (from *tri-, tres*) and Greek, from *tri-, treis*]

tri·able \'trī-ə-bəl\ *adj* : liable or subject to judicial or quasi-judicial examination or trial ⟨a case *triable* without a jury⟩ — **tri·able·ness** *n*

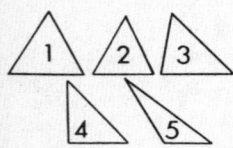

triangle 1: *1* equilateral, 2 isosceles, 3 scalene, 4 right, 5 obtuse

tri·ac·e·tate \trī-'as-ə-,tāt, 'trī-\ *n* : a textile fiber or fabric made by the chemical addition of acetate groups to cellulose

tri·ad \'trī-,ad *also* -əd\ *n* **1** : a union or group of three usually closely related persons or things **2** : a chord of three tones consisting of a root with its third and fifth and constituting the harmonic basis of tonal music [Latin *triad-, trias*, from Greek, from *treis* "three"] — **tri·ad·ic** \trī-'ad-ik\ *adj* — **tri·ad·i·cal·ly** \-'ad-i-kə-lē, -klē\ *adv*

¹**tri·al** \'trī-əl, 'trīl\ *n* **1** : the action or process of testing something (as by use or examination) **2** : formal examination before a court of justice of the matter in issue in a civil or criminal case **3** : a test of faith, patience, or stamina **4** : a tryout or experiment to test quality, value, or usefulness **5** : ATTEMPT, EFFORT [Anglo-French, from *trier* "to try"]

²**trial** *adj* **1** : of, relating to, or used in a trial **2** : made or done as a test or experiment **3** : used or tried out in a test or experiment

trial and error *n* : the trying of this and that until something succeeds

trial balance *n* : a list of the debit and credit balances of accounts in a ledger made primarily to verify their equality

trial balloon *n* **1** : a balloon sent up to test air currents and wind velocity **2** : a project or scheme tentatively announced in order to test public opinion

trial run *n* : a testing exercise

tri·an·gle \'trī-,ang-gəl\ *n* **1** : a polygon having three sides **2 a** : a musical percussion instrument made of a rod of steel bent into the form of a triangle open at one angle **b** : a drafting instrument consisting of a thin flat right-angled triangle with acute angles of 45 degrees or of 30 degrees and 60 degrees

tri·an·gu·lar \trī-'ang-gyə-lər\ *adj* **1 a** : of, relating to, or having the form of a triangle **b** : having a triangular base or principal surface ⟨a *triangular* pyramid⟩ **2** : of, relating to, or involving three parts or persons ⟨a *triangular* love affair⟩ — **tri·an·gu·lar·i·ty** \trī-,ang-gyə-'lar-ət-ē\ *n* — **tri·an·gu·lar·ly** \trī-'ang-gyə-lər-lē\ *adv*

¹**tri·an·gu·late** \trī-'ang-gyə-lət\ *adj* : consisting of or marked with triangles

²**tri·an·gu·late** \-,lāt\ *vt* **1** : to divide into triangles **2** : to survey, map, or determine by triangulation

tri·an·gu·la·tion \trī-,ang-gyə-'lā-shən\ *n* : the measurement of the elements necessary to determine the network of triangles into which any part of the earth's surface is divided in surveying

Tri·as·sic \trī-'as-ik\ *n* : the earliest period of the Mesozoic era; *also* : the corresponding system of rocks — see GEOLOGIC TIME table [Latin *trias* "triad"; from the 3 subdivisions of the European Triassic] — **Triassic** *adj*

tri·ath·lete \,trī-'ath-,lēt\ *n* : an athlete who competes in a triathlon

tri·ath·lon \-'ath-,län\ *n* : an athletic contest that is a long-distance race consisting of three phases (as swimming, bicycling, and running) [*tri-* + *-athlon* (as in *decathlon*)]

tri·atom·ic \,trī-ə-'täm-ik\ *adj* : having three atoms in the molecule

tri·ax·i·al \trī-'ak-sē-əl, 'trī-\ *adj* : having or involving three axes

trib·al \'trī-bəl\ *adj* : of, relating to, or characteristic of a tribe ⟨*tribal* customs⟩ — **trib·al·ly** \-bə-lē\ *adv*

trib·al·ism \-bə-,liz-əm\ *n* **1** : tribal consciousness and loyalty; *esp* : exaltation of the tribe above other groups **2** : strong loyalty within a social group

tribe \'trīb\ *n* **1** : a social group comprising numerous families, clans, or generations **2** : a group of persons having a common character, occupation, or interest **3** : a taxonomic category of variable rank; *also* : a natural group irrespective of taxonomic rank ⟨the cat *tribe*⟩ [Latin *tribus* "a division of the Roman people, tribe"]

tribes·man \'trībz-mən\ *n* : a member of a tribe

trib·u·la·tion \,trib-yə-'lā-shən\ *n* : distress or suffering resulting from oppression, persecution, or affliction; *also* : a trying experience [Old French *tribulacion,* from Latin *tribulatio,* from *tribulare* "to press, oppress", from *tribulum* "nail-studded board used in threshing", from *terere* "to rub"]

tri·bu·nal \trī-'byün-l, trib-'yün-\ *n* **1** : the seat of a judge : TRIBUNE **2** : a court of justice **3** : something that decides or determines ⟨the *tribunal* of public opinion⟩ [Latin, "platform for magistrates", from *tribunus* "tribune"]

trib·u·nate \'trib-yə-,nāt, trib-'yü-nət\ *n* : the office, function, or term of office of a tribune

¹trib·une \'trib-,yün, trib-'yün\ *n* **1 a** : one of six officers of a Roman legion who functioned in turn as its commander **b** : a Roman official under the monarchy and the republic with the function of protecting the plebeian citizen from arbitrary action by patrician magistrates **2** : a defender of the people especially against arbitrary abuse of authority [Latin *tribunus,* from *tribus* "tribe"] — **trib·une·ship** \-,ship\ *n*

²tribune *n* : a platform from which an assembly is addressed [French, from Italian *tribuna,* from Latin *tribunal*]

¹trib·u·tary \'trib-yə-,ter-ē\ *adj* **1** : paying tribute to another : SUBJECT **2** : paid or owed as tribute **3** : CONTRIBUTORY **4** : flowing into a larger stream or lake

²tributary *n, pl* **-tar·ies 1** : a ruler or state that pays tribute **2** : a stream feeding a larger stream or a lake

trib·ute \'trib-,yüt, -yət\ *n* **1 a** : a payment made by one ruler or nation to another to show submission or to secure peace or protection **b** : a tax to raise money for this payment **c** : the obligation to pay tribute ⟨nations under *tribute*⟩ **2** : something given or contributed voluntarily as due or deserved : a gift or service showing respect, gratitude, or affection ⟨a floral *tribute*⟩; *esp* : PRAISE, CREDIT [Latin *tributum,* from *tribuere* "to allot, pay", from *tribus* "tribe"]

trice \'trīs\ *n* : a brief space of time : INSTANT — used chiefly in the phrase *in a trice* [Middle English *trise,* literally, "pull", from *trisen* "to pull", from Dutch, "to hoist"]

tri·ceps \'trī-,seps\ *n, pl* **tri·ceps·es** *also* **triceps** : a muscle that arises from three heads; *esp* : the great extensor muscle along the back of the upper arm [Latin, "3-headed", from *tri-* + *caput* "head"]

tri·cer·a·tops \trī-'ser-ə-,täps\ *n* : a large plant-eating Cretaceous dinosaur with three horns, a bony hood or crest on the neck, and hoofed toes [Greek *tri-* + *kerat-, keras* "horn" + *ōps* "face"]

-trices *pl of* -TRIX

tri·chi·na \trə-'kī-nə\ *n, pl* **-nae 1** : a small slender nematode worm that in the larval state is parasitic in the voluntary muscles of flesh-eating mammals (as human and hog) **2** : TRICHINOSIS [New Latin, from Greek *trichinos* "made of hair", from *trich-, thrix* "hair"] — **tri·chi·nal** \trə-'kīn-l\ *adj* — **tri·chi·nous** \'trik-ə-nəs, trə-'kī-nəs\ *adj*

trich·i·no·sis \,trik-ə-'nō-səs\ *n, pl* **-no·ses** \-'nō-,sēz\ : a disease caused by trichinae and marked especially by muscular pain, difficulty in breathing, fever, and edema

tricho·cyst \'trik-ə-,sist\ *n* : any of the minute lassoing or stinging organs of a protozoan [Greek *trich-, thrix* "hair"]

tri·chome \'trik-,ōm, 'trī-,kōm\ *n* : a threadlike outgrowth; *esp* : an epidermal filament on a plant [German *trichom,* from Greek *trichōma* "growth of hair", from *trich-, thrix* "hair"]

tricho·mo·nad \,trik-ə-'mō-,nad, -'mō-nəd\ *n* : any of a genus of flagellated protozoans parasitic in various animals including humans [Greek *trich-, thrix* "hair" + Late Latin *monad-, monas* "monad"]

tricho·mo·ni·a·sis \,trik-ə-mə-'nī-ə-səs\ *n, pl* **-a·ses** \-ə-,sēz\ : infection with or disease caused by trichomonads; *esp* : a human vaginal inflammation with a persistent discharge

tri·chot·o·mous \trī-'kät-ə-məs\ *adj* : divided or dividing into three parts or into threes : THREEFOLD ⟨*trichotomous* branching⟩ [Late Greek *trichotomein* "to trisect", from Greek *tricha* "in three" (from *treis* "three") + *temnein* "to cut"] — **tri·chot·o·mous·ly** *adv* — **tri·chot·o·my** \-mē\ *n*

¹trick \'trik\ *n* **1 a** : a crafty procedure or practice meant to deceive or defraud **b** : a mischievous act : PRANK **c** : an indiscreet or childish action **d** : a dexterous or ingenious feat designed to puzzle or amuse ⟨a juggler's *tricks*⟩ **2 a** : an habitual peculiarity of behavior or manner **b** : a characteristic and identifying feature ⟨a *trick* of speech⟩ **c** : an optical illusion ⟨a mere *trick* of the light⟩ **3 a** : a quick or artful way of getting a result : KNACK **b** : a technical device (as of an art or craft) ⟨the *tricks* of stage technique⟩ **4** : the cards played in one round of a card game often used as a scoring unit **5** : a working shift [Old North French *trique,* from *trikier* "to deceive, cheat"] □ SYN TRICK, RUSE, STRATAGEM, WILE mean an indirect means to gain an end. TRICK may imply deception, roguishness, or illusion and either an evil or harmless end; RUSE stresses an attempt to mislead by a false impression; STRATAGEM implies a ruse to entrap or outwit and suggests a more or less carefully laid-out plan; WILE suggests an attempt to entrap or deceive with false allurements.

²trick *adj* **1** : of, relating to, or involving tricks or trickery ⟨*trick* dice⟩ **2** : somewhat defective and unreliable ⟨a *trick* knee⟩

³trick *vt* **1** : to deceive by cunning or artifice : CHEAT **2** : to dress or adorn especially fancifully or ornately ⟨*tricked* out in a gaudy uniform⟩

trick·ery \'trik-rē, -ə-rē\ *n, pl* **-er·ies** : the use of tricks to deceive or defraud SYN see DECEPTION

¹trick·le \'trik-əl\ *vi* **trick·led; trick·ling** \'trik-ling, -ə-ling\ **1** : to flow or fall in drops **2** : to flow in a thin gentle stream [Middle English *triklen*]

²trickle *n* : a trickling stream

trick or treat *n* : a children's Halloween practice of asking for treats from door to door under threat of playing tricks on householders who refuse

trick·ster \'trik-stər\ *n* : one who tricks or cheats

tricky \'trik-ē\ *adj* **trick·i·er; -est 1** : of or characteristic of a trickster : SLY **2** : requiring skill, aptitude, or caution : DELICATE **3** : TRICK 2 — **trick·i·ly** \'trik-ə-lē\ *adv* — **trick·i·ness** \'trik-ē-nəs\ *n*

tri·clin·ic \trī-'klin-ik, 'trī-\ *adj* : having three unequal axes intersecting at oblique angles — used especially of a crystal

¹tri·col·or \'trī-,kəl-ər\ *n* : a flag of stripes of three colors ⟨the French *tricolor*⟩

²tricolor *or* **tri·col·ored** \'trī-,kəl-ərd\ *adj* : having or using three colors

tri·corn \'trī-,korn\ *adj* : having three horns or corners [Latin *tricornis,* from *tri-* + *cornu* "horn"]

tri·corne *or* **tri·corn** \'trī-,korn\ *n* : COCKED HAT

tri·cor·nered \'trī-'kor-nərd\ *adj* : having three corners

tri·cot \'trē-kō, 'trī-kət\ *n* **1** : a plain run-resistant knitted fabric (as for underwear) **2** : a twilled clothing fabric of wool or wool and cotton [French, from *tricoter* "to knit"]

¹tri·cus·pid \trī-'kəs-pəd, 'trī-\ *adj* : having three cusps

²tricuspid *n* : a tooth having three cusps

tri·cus·pid valve \trī-,kəs-pəd-\ *n* : a valve of three flaps that prevents return of blood from the right ventricle to the right atrium [Latin *tricuspid-, tricuspis* "having 3 points", from *tri-* + *cuspis* "point"]

tri·cy·cle \'trī-,sik-əl\ *n* : a 3-wheeled vehicle propelled by pedals, hand levers, or a motor [French from Greek *tri-* + *kykles* "wheel"]

triceratops

\ə\ abut		\ng\ sing	
\ər\ further		\ō\ bone	
\a\ mat		\o'\ saw	
\ā\ take		\oi\ coin	
\ä\ cot, cart		\th\ thin	
\au̇\ out		\th\ this	
\ch\ chin		\ü\ food	
\e\ pet		\u̇\ foot	
\ē\ easy		\y\ yet	
\g\ go		\yü\ few	
\i\ tip		\yu̇\ cure	
\ī\ life		\zh\ vision	
\j\ job			

tri·dent \'trīd-nt\ *n* : a 3-pronged spear [Latin *trident-, tridens,* from *tri-* + *dent-, dens* "tooth"]

tri·di·men·sion·al \,trīd-ə-'mench-nəl, -ən-l\ *adj* : of or relating to three dimensions

trid·u·um \'trij-ə-wəm, 'trid-yə-\ *n* : a period of three days of prayer usually preceding a Roman Catholic feast [Latin, "period of 3 days"]

tried \'trīd\ *adj* : found good, faithful, or trustworthy through experience or testing [from past participle of *try*]

tri·en·ni·al \trī-'en-ē-əl, 'trī-\ *adj* **1** : consisting of or lasting for three years **2** : occurring or being done every three years — **triennial** *n* — **tri·en·ni·al·ly** \-ē-ə-lē\ *adv*

tri·en·ni·um \trī-'en-ē-əm\ *n, pl* **-ni·ums** *or* **-nia** \-ē-ə\ : a period of three years [Latin, from *tri-* + *annus* "year"]

tri·er \'trī-ər, 'trīr\ *n* : one that tries

¹tri·fle \'trī-fəl\ *n* **1** : something of little value or importance; *esp* : an insignificant amount **2** : a dessert of sponge cake spread with jam or jelly covered with custard and whipped cream [Old French *trufe, trufle* "mockery"]

²trifle *vb* **tri·fled; tri·fling** \-fə-ling, -fling\ **1 a** : to talk in a jesting or mocking manner with intent to mislead **b** : to act in a heedless or frivolous way : PLAY **2** : to waste time **3** : to spend or waste in trifling or on trifles ⟨*trifle* away money⟩ **4** : to handle something idly : TOY — **tri·fler** \-fə-lər, -flər\ *n*

tri·fling \'trī-fling\ *adj* : lacking in significance or solid worth: as **a** : FRIVOLOUS ⟨*trifling* talk⟩ **b** : TRIVIAL ⟨a *trifling* gift⟩

tri·fo·li·ate \trī-'fō-lē-ət, 'trī-\ *adj* : having three leaves ⟨a *trifoliate* plant⟩ **2** : TRIFOLIOLATE

tri·fo·li·o·late \trī-'fō-lē-ə-,lāt, 'trī-\ *adj* : having three leaflets ⟨a *trifoliolate* leaf⟩

tri·fur·cate \trī-'fər-kət, 'trī-, -,kāt; 'trī-fər-,kāt\ *adj* : TRICHOTOMOUS [Latin *trifurcus,* from *tri-* + *furca* "fork"] — **tri·fur·cate** \'trī-fər-,kāt, trī-'fər-\ *vi* — **tri·fur·ca·tion** \,trī-fər-'kā-shən\ *n*

¹trig \'trig\ *adj* : stylishly trim : SMART, NEAT [Middle English, "trusty, nimble", of Scandinavian origin]

²trig *n* : TRIGONOMETRY

tri·gem·i·nal nerve \trī-,jem-ən-l-\ *n* : either of the 5th pair of cranial nerves that supply motor and sensory fibers mostly to the face — called also *trigeminal* [Latin *trigeminus* "threefold", from *tri-* + *geminus* "twin"]

¹trig·ger \'trig-ər\ *n* : a movable lever attached to a catch that when released by pressure allows a mechanism to go into action; *esp* : the part of the lock of a firearm that releases the hammer and so fires the gun [Dutch *trekker,* from *trekken* "to pull, draw"] — **trigger** *adj* — **trig·gered** \-ərd\ *adj*

²trigger *vb* **trig·gered; trig·ger·ing** \'trig-ring, -ə-ring\ **1** : to fire by pulling a mechanical trigger ⟨*trigger* a rifle⟩; *also* : to cause the explosion of (as a missile) **2** : to initiate or set in motion as if by pulling a trigger ⟨*triggered* a fight⟩

trig·ger–hap·py \'trig-ər-,hap-ē\ *adj* : irresponsible in the use of firearms; *esp* : inclined to shoot before clearly identifying the target

tri·glyph \'trī-,glif\ *n* : a slightly projecting rectangular tablet in a Doric frieze with two vertical channels and two corresponding half channels on the vertical sides [Latin *triglyphus,* from Greek *triglyphos,* from *tri-* + *glyphein* "to carve"]

trig·o·no·met·ric \,trig-ə-nə-'me-trik\ *also* **trig·o·no·met·ri·cal** \-tri-kəl\ *adj* : of, relating to, or in accordance with trigonometry — **trig·o·no·met·ri·cal·ly** \-tri-kə-lē, -klē\ *adv*

trigonometric function *n* : a function (as the sine, cosine, tangent, cotangent, secant, or cosecant) of an arc or angle most simply expressed in terms of the ratios of pairs of sides of a right-angled triangle — called also *circular function*

trig·o·nom·e·try \,trig-ə-'näm-ə-trē\ *n* : the study of the properties of triangles and trigonometric functions and of their applications [Greek *trigōnon* "triangle", derived from *tri-* + *gōnia* "angle"]

tri·graph \'trī-,graf\ *n* : three letters spelling a single consonant, vowel, or diphthong — **tri·graph·ic** \trī-'graf-ik\ *adj*

tri·he·dral \trī-'hē-drəl, 'trī-\ *adj* **1** : having three faces ⟨*trihedral* angle⟩ **2** : of or relating to a trihedral angle — **trihedral** *n*

tri·lat·er·al \trī-'lat-ə-rəl, 'trī-, -'la-trəl\ *adj* : having three sides — **tri·lat·er·al·i·ty** \,trī-,lat-ə-'ral-ət-ē\ *n* — **tri·lat·er·al·ly** \trī-'lat-ə-rə-lē, 'trī-, -'la-trə-\ *adv*

tri·lin·gual \trī-'ling-gwəl, -gyə-wəl\ *adj* **1** : of, containing, or expressed in three languages **2** : using or able to use three languages especially with the fluency characteristic of a native speaker — **tri·lin·gual·ly** \-gwə-lē\ *adv*

¹trill \'tril\ *n* **1 a** : the alternation of two musical tones a scale degree apart — called also *shake* **b** : VIBRATO 1 **2** : a sound resembling a musical trill : WARBLE **3** : the rapid vibration of one speech organ against another (as of the tip of the tongue against the teethridge); *also* : a speech sound so made [Italian *trillo,* from *trillare* "to thrill"]

²trill *vb* **1** : to utter as or with a trill **2** : to play or sing with a trill : QUAVER — **trill·er** *n*

tril·lion \'tril-yən\ *n* **1** — see NUMBER table **2** : a very large number [French, from *tri-* "tri-" + *-illion* (as in *million*)] — **trillion** *adj* — **tril·lionth** \-yənth, -yəntth\ *adj or n*

tril·li·um \'tril-ē-əm\ *n* : any of a genus of herbs of the lily family with short rhizomes and an erect stem bearing a whorl of three leaves and a large solitary 3-petaled flower [New Latin, from Swedish *trilling* "triplet"; from its 3 leaves]

tri·lo·bite \'trī-lə-,bīt\ *n* : any of a group (Trilobita) of extinct Paleozoic marine arthropods having a segmented body divided by longitudinal furrows on the back into three lobes [derived from Greek *trilobos* "three-lobed", from *tri-* + *lobos* "lobe"]

tril·o·gy \'tril-ə-jē\ *n, pl* **-gies** : a series of three literary or musical compositions that are closely related and develop a single theme

¹trim \'trim\ *vb* **trimmed; trim·ming** **1 a** : to decorate with something (as ribbons or ornaments) : ADORN **b** : to arrange a display of goods in (a shop window) **2 a** : to administer a beating or defeat to **b** : CHEAT 1, SWINDLE **3 a** : to make trim and neat especially by cutting or clipping **b** : to free of excess or unnecessary matter by or as if by cutting ⟨*trim* a budget⟩ **4 a** : to cause (a ship or boat) to assume a desirable position in the water by arrangement of ballast, cargo, or passengers; *also* : to adjust (as an airplane, blimp, or submarine) for horizontal movement or for motion upward or downward **b** : to adjust (as a sail) to a desired position **5** : to maintain neutrality between opposing parties [Old English *trymian* "to strengthen, arrange", from *trum* "strong, firm"]

²trim *adj* **trim·mer; trim·mest** : neat, orderly, and compact in line or structure — **trim·ly** *adv* — **trim·ness** *n*

³trim *adv* : TRIMLY

⁴trim *n* **1 a** : the readiness of a ship for sailing **b** : the readiness of a person or thing for action or use : FITNESS **2 a** : material used for ornament or trimming **b** : the woodwork in the finish of a building especially around openings **c** : the interior furnishings of an automobile **3 a** : the position of a ship or boat especially with reference to the horizontal **b** : the relation between the plane of a sail and the direction of the ship **c** : the position of an airplane at which it will continue in level flight with no adjustments to the controls **4** : something trimmed off

tri·ma·ran \'trī-mə-ˌran, ˌtrī-mə-'\ *n* : a sailboat consisting of three hulls side by side [*tri-* + *-maran* (as in *catamaran*)]

tri·mes·ter \trī-'mes-tər, 'trī-ˌ\ *n* **1** : a period of three or about three months **2** : one of three terms into which an academic year is sometimes divided [French *trimestre*, from Latin *trimestris* "of 3 months", from *tri-* + *mensis* "month"] — **tri·mes·tral** \trī-'mes-trəl\ *adj* — **tri·mes·tri·al** \trī-'mes-trē-əl\ *adj*

trim·e·ter \'trim-ət-ər\ *n* : a line consisting of three metrical feet [Latin *trimetrus*, from Greek *trimetros* "having 3 measures", from *tri-* + *metron* "measure"]

trim·mer \'trim-ər\ *n* **1 a** : one that trims articles **b** : something with which trimming is done **2** : a beam that holds the end of a header in floor framing **3** : WEATHERCOCK 2

trim·ming \'trim-ing\ *n* **1** : the action of one that trims **2** : a severe defeat **3** : something that trims, ornaments, or completes ⟨the *trimming* on a hat⟩ ⟨roast turkey and all the *trimmings*⟩ **4** *pl* : parts removed by trimming

tri·month·ly \trī-'mənth-lē, 'trī-ˌ, -'mənth-\ *adj* : occurring every three months

tri·mo·tor \'trī-ˌmōt-ər\ *n* : an airplane with three engines

trine \'trīn\ *adj* : THREEFOLD, TRIPLE [Middle French *trin*, from Latin *trinus*, from *trini* "three each"]

trin·i·tar·i·an \ˌtrin-ə-'ter-ē-ən\ *adj* **1** *cap* : of or relating to the Trinity, the doctrine of the Trinity, or adherents to that doctrine **2** : having three parts or aspects

Trinitarian *n* : one who subscribes to the doctrine of the Trinity — **Trin·i·tar·i·an·ism** \-ē-ə-ˌniz-əm\ *n*

tri·ni·tro·tol·u·ene \ˌtrī-nī-trō-'täl-yə-ˌwēn\ *n* : a flammable toxic compound $C_7H_5N_3O_6$ obtained by nitrating toluene and used as a high explosive and in chemical synthesis

Trin·i·ty \'trin-ət-ē\ *n, pl* **-ties** **1** : the unity of Father, Son, and Holy Spirit as three persons in one Godhead **2** *not cap* : TRIAD 1 **3** : TRINITY SUNDAY [Old French *trinité*, from Late Latin *trinitas* "state of being threefold", from Latin *trinus* "threefold"]

Trinity Sunday *n* : the 8th Sunday after Easter

Trin·i·ty·tide \'trin-ət-ē-ˌtīd\ *n* : the season of the church year between Trinity Sunday and Advent

trin·ket \'tring-kət\ *n* **1** : a small ornament (as a jewel or ring) **2** : a thing of little value : TRIFLE [perhaps from Middle English *trenket* "small knife", from Old North French *trenquet*]

trin·ket·ry \'tring-kə-trē\ *n* : small items of personal ornament

¹tri·no·mi·al \trī-'nō-mē-əl\ *n* **1** : a polynomial of three terms **2** : a biological taxonomic name consisting of three terms of which the first denotes the genus, the second the species, and the third the particular variety or subspecies named in full by the combination [*tri-* + *-nomial* (as in *binomial*)]

²trinomial *adj* **1** : consisting of three terms **2** : of or relating to trinomials

trio \'trē-ō\ *n, pl* **tri·os** **1 a** : a musical composition for three voice parts or three instruments **b** : a dance by three people **c** : the performers of a musical or dance trio **2** : a group or set of three [French, from Italian, from Latin *tri-, tres* "three"]

tri·ode \'trī-ˌōd\ *n* : a vacuum tube with three electrodes

tri·o·let \'trī-ə-lət, 'trē-\ *n* : a poem or stanza of eight lines in which the first line is repeated as the fourth and seventh and the second line as the eighth and which has a rhyme scheme of ABaAabAB [French]

tri·ose \'trī-ˌōs\ *n* : either of two monosaccharides containing three carbon atoms

tri·ox·ide \trī-'äk-ˌsīd, 'trī-\ *n* : an oxide containing three atoms of oxygen

¹trip \'trip\ *vb* **tripped; trip·ping** **1 a** : to move (as in dancing or walking) with light quick steps **b** : to perform (as a dance) lightly or nimbly **2** : to catch one's foot while walking or running : cause to stumble **3 a** : to make or cause to make a mistake : SLIP, BLUNDER **b** : to catch in a misstep, fault, or blunder; *also* : EXPOSE **4** : to put (as a mechanism) into operation usually by release of a catch or detent; *also* : to become operative [Middle French *triper*, of Germanic origin]

²trip *n* **1** : an act of causing another to lose footing **2 a** : VOYAGE, JOURNEY ⟨a *trip* to Europe⟩ **b** : a single visit or round having a specific aim or recurring regularly ⟨a *trip* to the dentist's⟩ ⟨the milkman's daily *trip*⟩ **3** : ERROR 4, MISSTEP **4** : a quick light step **5** : a faltering step : STUMBLE **6 a** : the action of tripping mechanically **b** : a device (as a catch) for tripping a mechanism **7** : an intense sensory and especially visionary experience undergone by a person who has taken a psychedelic drug

tri·par·tite \trī-'pär-ˌtīt, 'trī-\ *adj* **1** : having three parts **2** : having three corresponding parts or copies **3** : made between or involving three parties — **tri·par·tite·ly** *adv*

tripe \'trīp\ *n* **1** : stomach tissue of a ruminant and especially of the ox for use as food **2** : TRASH 1 [Old French]

trip–ham·mer \'trip-ˌham-ər\ *n* : a massive hammer raised by machinery and then tripped to fall on the work below

triph·thong \'trif-ˌthong, 'trip-\ *n* **1** : a 3-element speech sound **2** : TRIGRAPH [*tri-* + *-phthong* (as in *diphthong*)]

¹tri·ple \'trip-əl\ *vb* **tri·pled; tri·pling** \'trip-ling, -ə-ling\ **1** : to make or become three times as great or as many : multiply by three **2** : to make a triple in baseball

²triple *n* **1 a** : a triple sum, quantity, or number **b** : a combination, group, or series of three **2** : a base hit that enables the batter to reach third base

³triple *adj* **1** : having three units or members **2** : being three times as great or as many **3** : three times repeated [Latin *triplus*, from *tri-* + *-plus* "-fold"]

triple bond *n* : a chemical bond in which three pairs of electrons are shared by two atoms in a molecule — compare DOUBLE BOND, SINGLE BOND

triple jump *n* : a track-and-field event in which competitors jump for distance from a running start combining in succession a hop, a stride, and a jump

triple play *n* : a play in baseball by which three players are put out

triple point *n* : the condition of temperature and pressure under which the gaseous, liquid, and solid phases of a substance can exist in equilibrium

tri·ple–space \ˌtrip-əl-'spās\ *vb* **1** : to type (copy) leaving two blank lines between lines of copy **2** : to type on every third line

tri·plet \'trip-lət\ *n* **1** : a unit of three lines of verse **2** : a combination, set, or group of three **3** : one of three offspring born at one birth **4** : a group of three notes played in the time of two of the same value **5** : CODON

¹tri·plex \'trip-ˌleks, 'trī-ˌpleks\ *adj* : TRIPLE 1 [Latin, from *tri-* + *plex* "-fold"]

²triplex *n* : something that is triplex

¹trip·li·cate \'trip-li-kət\ *adj* : having or being three corresponding or identical parts or examples [Latin *triplicatus*, past participle of *triplicare* "to triple", from *triplic-, triplex* "triplex"]

²triplicate *n* **1** : one of three like things **2** : three copies all alike

³trip·li·cate \-lə-ˌkāt\ *vt* **1** : to make triple **2** : to provide in triplicate — **trip·li·ca·tion** \ˌtrip-lə-'kā-shən\ *n*

trip·lo·blas·tic \ˌtrip-lō-'blas-tik\ *adj* : having three primary germ layers

trip·loid \'trip-ˌlóid\ *adj* : having or being a chromosome number three times the monoploid number — **triploid** *n* — **trip·loi·dy** \-ˌlóid-ē\ *n*

\ə\ abut		\ng\ sing	
\ər\ further		\ō\ bone	
\a\ mat		\ó\ saw	
\ā\ take		\ói\ coin	
\ä\ cot, cart		\th\ thin	
\aú\ out		\th\ this	
\ch\ chin		\ü\ food	
\e\ pet		\ú\ foot	
\ē\ easy		\y\ yet	
\g\ go		\yü\ few	
\i\ tip		\yú\ cure	
\ī\ life		\zh\ vision	
\j\ job			

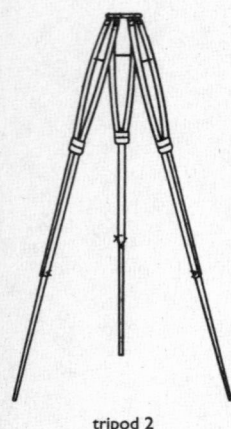

tripod 2

tri·ply \'trip-lē, -ə-lē\ *adv* : in a triple degree, amount, or manner

tri·pod \'trī-,päd\ *n* **1** : something (as a container or stool) resting on three legs **2** : a three-legged stand (as for a camera) [Latin *tripod-, tripus,* from Greek *tripod-, tripous,* derived from *tri- + pod-, pous* "foot"] — **tripod** *or* **trip·o·dal** \'trip-əd-l, 'trī-,päd-\ *adj*

trip·per \'trip-ər\ *n* **1** *chiefly British* : EXCURSIONIST **2** : a tripping device or mechanism

trip·ping·ly \'trip-ing-lē\ *adv* **1** : in a nimble manner **2** : in a fluent manner

trip·tych \'trip-tik, -,tik\ *n* **1** : an ancient Roman writing tablet with three waxed leaves hinged together **2** : a picture or carving in three panels side by side [Greek *triptychos* "having 3 folds", from *tri- + ptychē* "fold"]

tri·reme \'trī-,rēm\ *n* : an ancient galley having three banks of oars [Latin *triremis,* from *tri- + remus* "oar"]

tri·sac·cha·ride \trī-'sak-ə-,rīd, 'trī-\ *n* : any sugar that yields on complete hydrolysis three monosaccharide molecules

tri·sect \'trī-,sekt, trī-'\ *vt* : to divide into three usually equal parts [*tri- +* Latin *sectus,* past participle of *secare* "to cut"] — **tri·sec·tion** \'trī-,sek-shən, trī-'\ *n* — **tri·sec·tor** \'trī-,sek-tər, trī-'\ *n*

tri·so·di·um \,trī-'sōd-ē-əm\ *adj* : containing three atoms of sodium in the molecule

tri·so·mic \trī-'sō-mik, 'trī-\ *adj* : having one or a few chromosomes triploid in an otherwise diploid set — **trisomic** *n* — **tri·so·my** \'trī-,sō-mē\ *n*

triste \'trēst\ *adj* : SAD, MOURNFUL; *also* : WISTFUL [French, from Latin *tristis*]

tri·syl·lab·ic \,trī-sə-'lab-ik\ *adj* : having three syllables — **tri·syl·lab·i·cal·ly** \-'lab-i-kə-lē, -klē\ *adv* — **tri·syl·la·ble** \'trī-,sil-ə-bəl, trī-', 'trī-'\ *n*

trite \'trīt\ *adj* : so common that the novelty has worn off : STALE, HACKNEYED ⟨a *trite* remark⟩ [Latin *tritus,* from *terere* "to rub, wear away"] — **trite·ly** *adv* — **trite·ness** *n* □ SYN TRITE, HACKNEYED, STEREOTYPED, THREADBARE mean lacking freshness and power to interest or compel attention. TRITE applies to a once effective phrase or idea spoiled by long familiarity; HACKNEYED stresses being worn out by overuse so as to become dull and meaningless; STEREOTYPED implies falling invariably into the same pattern or form; THREADBARE applies to something that has been used so often it no longer can be interesting.

tri·ti·um \'trit-ē-əm, 'trish-ē-\ *n* : a radioactive isotope of hydrogen with atoms of about three times the mass of ordinary light hydrogen atoms [New Latin, from Greek *tritos* "third"]

trit·o·ma \'trit-ə-mə\ *n* : any of a genus of African herbs of the lily family often grown for their spikes of showy red or yellow flowers [New Latin, from Greek *tritomos* "cut thrice", from *tri- + temnein* "to cut"]

tri·ton \'trīt-n\ *n* : any of various large sea snails with a heavy conical shell; *also* : this shell [*Triton,* son of Poseidon]

trit·u·rate \'trich-ə-,rāt\ *vt* **1** : CRUSH 3, GRIND **2** : to reduce to a fine powder by rubbing or grinding [Late Latin *triturare* "to thresh", from Latin *tritura* "act of rubbing, threshing", from *tritus,* past participle of *terere* "to rub"] — **trit·u·ra·ble** \-rə-bəl\ *adj* — **trit·u·rate** \-rət\ *n* — **trit·u·ra·tion** \,trich-ə-'rā-shən\ *n* — **trit·u·ra·tor** \'trich-ə-,rāt-ər\ *n*

¹tri·umph \'trī-əmf, -əmpf\ *n* **1** : an ancient Roman ceremonial honoring a victorious general **2** : joy or exultation over victory or success **3 a** : a military victory or conquest **b** : a notable success [Middle French *triumphe,* from Latin *triumphus*] SYN SEE VICTORY

²triumph *vi* **1** : to celebrate victory or success often boastfully or rejoicingly **2** : to obtain victory : PREVAIL, WIN

tri·um·phal \trī-'əm-fəl, -'əmp-\ *adj* : of, relating to, or used in a triumph ⟨a *triumphal* march⟩

tri·um·phant \trī-'əm-fənt, -'əmp-\ *adj* **1** : VICTORIOUS, CONQUERING **2** : rejoicing for or celebrating victory : EXULTANT — **tri·um·phant·ly** *adv*

tri·um·vir \trī-'əm-vər\ *n* : one of a commission or ruling body of three especially in ancient Rome [Latin, back-formation from *triumviri,* pl., "commission of 3 men", from *trium virum* "of 3 men"]

tri·um·vi·rate \-və-rət\ *n* **1** : the office or term of office of a triumvir **2** : government by three persons who share authority and responsibility **3** : a group of three persons who share power or office

tri·une \'trī-,ün, -,yün\ *adj* : three in one; *esp* : of or relating to the Trinity ⟨the *triune* God⟩ [Latin *tri- + unus* "one"]

tri·va·lent \trī-'vā-lənt, 'trī-\ *adj* : having a valence of three — **tri·va·lence** \-ləns\ *or* **tri·va·len·cy** \-lən-sē\ *n*

triv·et \'triv-ət\ *n* **1** : a three-legged stand or support; *esp* : one for holding a kettle near the fire **2** : an ornamental metal plate on very short legs used under a hot dish to protect the table [Old English *trefet*]

triv·ia \'triv-ē-ə\ *n sing or pl* : unimportant matters or facts [Latin, "crossroads", pl. of *trivium*]

triv·i·al \'triv-ē-əl\ *adj* **1** : ORDINARY 2a, COMMONPLACE **2** : of little worth or importance : INSIGNIFICANT [Latin *trivialis* "found everywhere, commonplace, trivial", from *trivium* "crossroads", from *tri- + via* "way"] — **triv·i·al·ly** \-ē-ə-lē\ *adv*

triv·i·al·i·ty \,triv-ē-'al-ət-ē\ *n, pl* **-ties 1** : the quality or state of being trivial **2** : something trivial : TRIFLE

trivial name *n* **1** : the second term of a taxonomic binomial **2** : a common or vernacular name of an organism or chemical

¹tri·week·ly \trī-'wē-klē, 'trī-\ *adj* **1** : occurring, appearing, or done three times a week **2** : occurring, appearing, or done every three weeks — **triweekly** *adv*

²triweekly *n* : a triweekly publication

-trix \triks, ,triks\ *n suffix, pl* **-tri·ces** \trə-,sēz, 'trī-sēz\ *or* **-trix·es** \trik-sez, ,trik-\ **1** : female that does or is associated with a (specified) thing ⟨avia*trix*⟩ **2** : geometric line, point, or surface ⟨genera*trix*⟩ [Latin, feminine of *-tor,* suffix denoting an agent]

tRNA \,tē-,är-,en-'ā, 'tē-,är-,en-,ā\ *n* : TRANSFER RNA

tro·chan·ter \trō-'kant-ər\ *n* : a small segment immediately external to the coxa of the leg of an insect [Greek *trochantēr* "rough process at the upper part of the femur"]

tro·che \'trō-kē, *British also* 'trōsh\ *n* : a usually circular medicinal tablet or lozenge used especially as a demulcent [earlier *trochisk,* from Late Latin *trochiscus,* from Greek *trochiskos,* from *trochos* "wheel", from *trechein* "to run"]

tro·chee \'trō-,kē\ *n* : a metrical foot consisting of one accented syllable followed by one unaccented syllable (as in *hungry*) [French *trochée,* from Latin *trochaeus,* from Greek *trochaios,* derived from *trochē* "run, course", from *trechein* "to run"] — **tro·cha·ic** \trō-'kā-ik\ *adj*

troch·le·ar nerve \,träk-lē-ər-\ *n* : either of the 4th pair of cranial nerves which control movements of some of the eye muscles — called also *trochlear* [*trochlea* "anatomical structure resembling a pulley", from Latin, "block of pulleys", from Greek *trochileia*]

trocho·phore \'träk-ə-,fōr, -,for\ *n* : a free-swimming ciliated larva typical of marine annelid worms but occurring also in several other invertebrate groups [derived from Greek *trochos* "wheel" + *pherein* "to carry"]

trod *past of* TREAD

trodden *past participle of* TREAD

trog·lo·dyte \'träg-lə-,dīt\ *n* : CAVEMAN 1; *also* : a person felt to resemble a troglodyte especially in unsocial habits [Latin *troglodytae,* pl., from Greek *trōglodytai,* from *trōglē* "hole, cave" + *dyein* "to enter"] — **trog·lo·dyt·ic** \,träg-lə-'dit-ik\ *adj*

troi·ka \'tròi-kə\ *n* **1** : a Russian vehicle drawn by three horses abreast; *also* : a team for such a vehicle **2** : a group of three [Russian *troĭka*, from *troe* "three"]

Tro·jan \'trō-jən\ *n* **1** : a native or inhabitant of ancient Troy **2** : one who shows pluck, endurance, or determined energy [Latin *trojanus* "of Troy", from *Troia*, *Troja* "Troy", from Greek *Trōia*] — **Trojan** *adj*

Trojan horse *n* : one intended to undermine or subvert from within [from the large hollow wooden horse filled with Greek soldiers and introduced within the walls of Troy by a stratagem during the Trojan War]

¹troll \'trōl\ *vb* **1 a** : to sing the parts of (as a round or catch) in succession **b** : to sing loudly or in a jovial way **2** : to speak or recite in a rolling voice **3** : to fish or fish for with a hook and line drawn through the water (as behind a slowly moving boat) [Middle English *trollen* "to roll"] — **troll·er** *n*

²troll *n* **1** : a lure or a line with its lure and hook used in trolling **2** : a song sung in parts successively : ROUND

³troll *n* : a dwarf or giant of Teutonic folklore inhabiting caves or hills [Norwegian *troll* and Danish *trold*, from Old Norse *troll* "giant, demon"]

trol·ley *or* **trol·ly** \'träl-ē\ *n*, *pl* **trolleys** *or* **trollies 1 a** : a device for carrying current from a wire to an electrically driven vehicle **b** : TROLLEY CAR **2** : a wheeled carriage running on an overhead rail or track [probably from earlier *troll* "to roll", from Middle English *trollen*]

trolley bus *n* : a bus powered by electric power from two overhead wires

trolley car *n* : a streetcar that runs on tracks and gets its electric power through a trolley

trol·lop \'träl-əp\ *n* **1** : a slovenly woman : SLATTERN **2** : a loose woman : WANTON [probably from German dialect *trolle*]

trom·bone \träm-'bōn, trəm-, ,tram-\ *n* : a brass wind instrument that has a cupped mouthpiece, that consists of a long cylindrical metal tube bent twice upon itself and ending in a bell, and that has a movable slide with which to vary the pitch [Italian, from *tromba* "trumpet", of Germanic origin] — **trom·bon·ist** \-'bō-nəst\ *n*

-tron \,trän\ *n suffix* **1** : vacuum tube **2** : device for the manipulation of subatomic particles ⟨cyclo*tron*⟩ [Greek, suffix denoting an instrument]

¹troop \'trüp\ *n* **1 a** : a group of soldiers **b** : a cavalry unit corresponding to an infantry company **c** *pl* : armed forces **2** : a collection of beings or things : COMPANY **3** : a unit of boy or girl scouts under a leader [Middle French *troupe* "company, herd", of Germanic origin]

²troop *vi* **1** : to move or gather in crowds **2** : ASSOCIATE 1 (a dove *trooping* with crows)

troop·er \'trü-pər\ *n* **1** : an enlisted member of a cavalry unit **2 a** : a mounted police officer **b** : a state police officer

troop·ship \'trüp-,ship\ *n* : a ship for carrying troops

trop- *or* **tropo-** *combining form* : turn : turning : change ⟨*trop*ism⟩ ⟨*tropo*sphere⟩ [Greek *tropos*, from *trepein* "to turn"]

trope \'trōp\ *n* : the use of a word or expression in a figurative sense : FIGURE OF SPEECH [Latin *tropus*, from Greek *tropos* "turn, way, trope"]

tro·phic \'trō-fik\ *adj* **1** : of or relating to nutrition : NUTRITIONAL ⟨*trophic* disorders⟩ **2** : ³TROPIC [French *trophique*, from Greek *trophikos*, from *trophē* "nourishment", from *trephein* "to nourish"] — **tro·phi·cal·ly** \-fi-kə-lē, -klē\ *adv*

tro·phy \'trō-fē\ *n*, *pl* **trophies 1 a** : a memorial of an ancient Greek or Roman victory raised on the field of battle **b** : a representation of such a memorial (as on a medal) **2** : something won or given in victory or con-

quest especially when preserved or mounted as a memorial **3** : MEMENTO [Middle French *trophee*, from Latin *tropaeum*, *trophaeum*, from Greek *trepaion*, derived from *tropē* "turn, rout", from *trepein* "to turn"] — **tro·phied** \-fēd\ *adj*

-tro·phy \trə-fē\ *n combining form*, *pl* **-trophies** : nutrition : nurture : growth ⟨hyper*trophy*⟩ [Greek *-trophia*, from *trephein* "to nourish"]

¹trop·ic \'träp-ik\ *n* **1** : either of the two parallels of the earth's latitude that are approximately 23½ degrees north of the equator and approximately 23½ degrees south of the equator **2** *pl, often cap* : the region lying between the two tropics [Latin *tropicus* "of the solstice", from Greek *tropikos*, from *tropē* "turn"; from the fact that their projections on the celestial sphere mark the sun's declination at the solstices]

²tropic *adj* : of, relating to, or occurring in the tropics : TROPICAL

³tro·pic \'trō-pik\ *adj* **1** : of, relating to, or characteristic of tropism or of a tropism **2** *of a hormone* : influencing the activity of a specified gland

trop·i·cal *for 1* 'träp-i-kəl, *for 2* 'trōp- *also* 'träp-\ *adj* **1** : of, located in, or used in the tropics **2** : FIGURATIVE 2 — **trop·i·cal·ly** \-kə-lē, -klē\ *adv*

tropical aquarium *n* : an aquarium kept at a uniform warmth and used especially for tropical fish

tropical cyclone *n* : a cyclone in the tropics usually characterized by winds rotating at the rate of 75 miles (about 120 kilometers) an hour or more

tropical fish *n* : any of various small usually showy fishes of exotic origin often kept in the tropical aquarium

tropical storm *n* : a tropical cyclone with strong winds of less than hurricane intensity

tropic bird *n* : any of several web-footed oceanic birds related to the gannets that are mostly white with a little black and a very long central pair of tail feathers

tropic of Cancer : the parallel of latitude that is approximately 23½ degrees north of the equator and is the northernmost latitude reached by the overhead sun [from the sign of the zodiac which its celestial projection intersects]

tropic of Capricorn : the parallel of latitude that is approximately 23½ degrees south of the equator and is the southernmost latitude reached by the overhead sun [from the sign of the zodiac which its celestial projection intersects]

tro·pism \'trō-,piz-əm\ *n* : involuntary orientation by an organism or one of its parts that involves turning or curving and is a positive or negative response to a source of stimulation; *also* : a reflex reaction involving such movement [Greek *tropos* "turn", from *trepein* "to turn"] — **tro·pis·tic** \trō-'pis-tic\ *adj*

tro·po·pause \'trōp-ə-,pòz, 'träp-\ *n* : the region at the top of the troposphere

tro·po·sphere \'trōp-ə-,sfiər, 'träp-\ *n* : the portion of the atmosphere which is below the stratosphere, which extends outward about 11 to 16 kilometers from the earth's surface, and in which generally temperature decreases rapidly with altitude and clouds form [Greek *tropos* "turn"] — **tro·po·spher·ic** \,trōp-ə-'sfiər-ik, ,träp-, -'sfer-\ *adj*

¹trot \'trät\ *n* **1 a** (1) : a moderately fast gait of a four-footed animal (as a horse) in which the legs move in diagonal pairs (2) : a jogging gait of humans that falls between a walk and a run **b** : a ride on horseback **2** : PONY 3 [Middle French, from *troter* "to trot", of Germanic origin]

²trot *vb* **trot·ted; trot·ting 1 a** : to ride, drive, or go at a trot **b** : to cause to go at a trot **2** : to proceed briskly : HURRY

¹troth \'träth, 'trȯth, 'trōth *or with* th\ *n* **1** : loyal or pledged faithfulness : FIDELITY **2** : one's pledged word; *also* : BETROTHAL [Old English *trēowth*]

²troth *vt* : BETROTH, PLEDGE

¹trombone

\ə\ abut	\ng\ sing
\ər\ further	\ō\ bone
\a\ mat	\ȯ\ saw
\ā\ take	\òi\ coin
\ä\ cot, cart	\th\ thin
\aù\ out	\th\ this
\ch\ chin	\ü\ food
\e\ pet	\ù\ foot
\ē\ easy	\y\ yet
\g\ go	\yü\ few
\i\ tip	\yù\ cure
\ī\ life	\zh\ vision
\j\ job	

trot out *vt* : to bring forward for display

Trots·ky·ism \'trät-skē-,iz-əm, 'tról-\ *n* : the Communist principles developed by or associated with Leon Trotsky and usually including adherence to the concept of worldwide revolution — **Trots·ky·ist** \-skē-əst\ *n or adj* — **Trots·ky·ite** \-skē-,īt\ *n or adj*

trot·ter \'trät-ər\ *n* : one that trots; *esp* : a standardbred horse trained for harness racing

trou·ba·dour \'trü-bə-,dōr, -,dór, -,dùr\ *n* : a poet-musician of medieval France and Italy [French, from Provençal *trobador,* from *trobar* "to compose"]

¹**trou·ble** \'trəb-əl\ *vb* **trou·bled; trou·bling** \'trəb-ling, -ə-ling\ **1 a** : to agitate or become agitated mentally or spiritually : WORRY, DISTURB **b** : to produce physical disorder in : AFFLICT ⟨*troubled* with deafness⟩ **c** : to put to exertion or inconvenience ⟨may I *trouble* you for the salt⟩ **2** : to put into confused motion ⟨wind *troubled* the sea⟩ **3** : to make an effort : take pains ⟨do not *trouble* to come⟩ [Old French *tourbler, troubler,* derived from Latin *turbidare,* from *turbidus* "turbid, troubled"]

²**trouble** *n* **1 a** : the quality or state of being troubled : MISFORTUNE ⟨help people in *trouble*⟩ **b** : an instance of distress or annoyance **2 a** : civil disorder or agitation ⟨labor *trouble*⟩ **b** : an effort made : PAIN 4 ⟨took the *trouble* to call⟩ **c** (1) : a condition of physical distress (2) : DISEASE, AILMENT (3) : MALFUNCTION ⟨engine *trouble*⟩ ⟨*trouble* with the plumbing⟩ **d** : a personal characteristic that is a handicap or a source of distress ⟨laziness is your *trouble*⟩ **e** : a troubling thing ⟨the *trouble* is that you're wrong⟩ SYN see EFFORT

trou·ble·mak·er \'trəb-əl-,mā-kər\ *n* : a person who causes dissension

trou·ble·shoot·er \-,shüt-ər\ *n* **1** : a skilled worker employed to locate trouble and make repairs in machinery and technical equipment **2** : one that is expert in resolving disputes or problems — **trou·ble·shoot** \-,shüt\ *vb*

trou·ble·some \'trəb-əl-səm\ *adj* **1** : giving trouble or anxiety : VEXATIOUS ⟨a *troublesome* infection⟩ **2** : DIFFICULT 2a, BURDENSOME — **trou·ble·some·ly** *adv* — **trou·ble·some·ness** *n*

trou·blous \'trəb-ləs, -ə-ləs\ *adj* **1 a** : full of trouble ⟨*troublous* times⟩ **b** : STORMY ⟨*troublous* seas⟩ **2** : that disturbs or troubles ⟨*troublous* dreams⟩ — **trou·blous·ly** *adv* — **trou·blous·ness** *n*

trough \'tróf, 'tróth\ *n, pl* **troughs** \'trófs, 'tróvz, 'tróths, 'tróthz, 'tróz\ **1 a** : a long shallow often V-shaped receptacle for the drinking water or feed of domestic animals **b** : any of various domestic or industrial containers **2 a** : a conduit, drain, or channel for water; *esp* : a gutter along the eaves **b** : a long and narrow or shallow depression (as between waves or hills) **3** : the low point in a cycle; *esp* : an elongated area of low barometric pressure [Old English *trog*]

trounce \'traúns\ *vt* : to thrash or punish severely: as **a** : FLOG, CUDGEL **b** : to defeat decisively [origin unknown]

¹**troupe** \'trüp\ *n* : COMPANY, TROOP; *esp* : a group of stage performers [Middle French, of Germanic origin]

²**troupe** *vi* : to travel in a troupe; *also* : to perform as a member of a stage troupe — **troup·er** *n*

trou·sers \'traú-zərz\ *n pl* : PANTS 1 [earlier *trouse,* from Scottish Gaelic *triubhas*]

trous·seau \'trü-,sō\ *n, pl* **trous·seaux** \-,sōz\ *or* **trous·seaus** : the personal possessions of a bride [French, from *trousse* "bundle", from *trousser* "to truss"]

trout \'traút\ *n, pl* **trout** *also* **trouts 1** : any of various food and sport fishes mostly smaller than the related salmons and restricted to cool clear fresh waters **2** : any of various fishes felt to resemble the true trouts — compare SEA TROUT [Old English *trùht,* from Late Latin *trocta, tructa,* a kind of fish with sharp teeth, from Greek *tróktēs,* literally, "gnawer", from *trógein* "to gnaw"]

trout lily *n* : DOGTOOTH VIOLET [probably from its speckled leaves]

trove \'trōv\ *n* **1** : DISCOVERY 2, FIND **2** : a valuable collection : TREASURE; *also* : HAUL 1a [short for *treasure trove*]

trow \'trō\ *vb* **1** *obsolete* : BELIEVE 2, 3, TRUST **2** *archaic* : THINK 3, SUPPOSE [Old English *trēowan*]

¹**trow·el** \'traú-əl, 'traúl\ *n* **1** : a small hand tool consisting of a flat blade with a handle used for spreading and smoothing mortar or plaster **2** : a small hand tool with a curved blade used by gardeners [Middle French *truelle,* from Late Latin *truella,* derived from Latin *trua* "ladle"]

²**trowel** *vt* **-eled** *or* **-elled; -el·ing** *or* **-el·ling** : to smooth, mix, or apply with a trowel

troy \'trói\ *adj* : expressed in troy weight [*Troyes,* France]

troy weight *n* : a series of units of weight based on a pound of 12 ounces and the ounce of 20 pennyweights or 480 grains — see MEASURE table

tru·ant \'trü-ənt\ *n* : one who shirks duty; *esp* : one who stays out of school without permission [Old French, "vagrant", of Celtic origin] — **tru·an·cy** \-ən-sē\ *n* — **truant** *adj*

truant officer *n* : one employed by a public-school system to investigate cases of truancy

truce \'trüs\ *n* **1** : a temporary interruption of fighting by mutual agreement of the combatants : ARMISTICE **2** : a temporary rest especially from a disagreeable state or activity [Middle English *trewes,* pl. of *trewe* "agreement", from Old English *trēow* "fidelity"]

¹**truck** \'trək\ *vb* : to exchange goods : BARTER [Old French *troquer*]

²**truck** *n* **1** : BARTER **2** : goods for barter or for small trade **3** : close association : TRAFFIC **4** : payment of wages in goods instead of cash **5** : vegetables grown for market **6** : small articles of little value; *also* : RUBBISH

³**truck** *n* **1** : a small wooden cap at the top of a flagpole or mast **2** : a vehicle (as a small flat-topped car on wheels, a two-wheeled barrow with long handles, or a strong heavy wagon or automobile) for carrying heavy articles **3 a** : a swiveling carriage with springs and one or more pairs of wheels used to carry an end of a railroad car or a locomotive **b** : a short heavy-duty automotive vehicle equipped with a swiveling device for hauling a trailer; *also* : a truck with attached trailer [probably from Latin *trochus* "iron hoop", from Greek *trochos* "wheel"]

⁴**truck** *vb* **1** : to transport on or by truck **2** : to be employed as a truck driver

truck·age \'trək-ij\ *n* **1** : money paid for hauling on a truck **2** : carriage by truck

truck·er \'trək-ər\ *n* **1** : one whose business is transporting goods by truck **2** : a truck driver

truck farm *n* : a farm growing vegetables for market — **truck farmer** *n*

truck·ing \'trək-ing\ *n* : the process or business of transporting goods on trucks

truck·le \'trək-əl\ *vt* **truck·led; truck·ling** \'trək-ling, -ə-ling\ : to act in a servile way : yield to the will of another : SUBMIT ⟨*truckle* to a conqueror⟩ [from the lower position of the truckle bed] — **truck·ler** \-lər, -ə-lər\ *n*

truckle bed *n* : TRUNDLE BED [Middle English *trocle* "small wheel, pulley", from Latin *trochlea* "block of pulleys"]

truck·line \'trək-,līn\ *n* : a carrier using trucks and related freight vehicles

truck·man \'trək-mən\ *n* **1** : TRUCKER **2** : a member of a fire department unit that operates a ladder truck

truck system *n* : the system of paying wages in goods instead of cash

truc·u·lent \'trək-yə-lənt *also* 'trük-\ *adj* **1** : feeling or displaying ferocity : CRUEL, SAVAGE **2** : DESTRUCTIVE,

DEADLY **3 :** very bitter and harsh **4 :** AGGRESSIVE, BEL-LIGERENT [Latin *truculentus,* from *truc-, trux* "fierce"] — **truc·u·lence** \-ləns\ *also* **truc·u·len·cy** \-lən-sē\ *n* — **truc·u·lent·ly** *adv*

¹trudge \'trəj\ *vb* **1 :** to walk or march steadily and usually laboriously **2 :** to walk or march along or over [origin unknown] — **trudg·er** *n*

²trudge *n* **:** a long tiring walk **:** TRAMP

trud·gen stroke \'trəj-ən-\ *n* **:** a swimming stroke in which a double overarm motion is combined with a scissors kick [John *Trudgen,* 19th century English swimmer]

¹true \'trü\ *adj* **1 :** STEADFAST **2,** LOYAL **2** *archaic* **:** TRUTHFUL **3 :** that can be relied on **:** CERTAIN **4 a :** corresponding to fact or actuality **:** ACCURATE, CORRECT **b :** logically necessary **5 :** SINCERE ⟨*true* friendship⟩ **6 :** properly so called **:** GENUINE ⟨lichens have no *true* stems⟩ ⟨whales are *true* but not typical mammals⟩; *also* **:** TYPICAL ⟨the *true* cats⟩ **7 :** that is fitted or formed or that functions accurately **8 :** RIGHTFUL, LE-GITIMATE ⟨the *true* owner⟩ ⟨our *true* ruler⟩ **9 :** determined with reference to the earth's axis rather than the magnetic poles ⟨*true* north⟩ [Old English *trēowe*] SYN SEE REAL — **true·ness** *n*

²true *n* **1 :** TRUTH 2a(1), REALITY — usually used with *the* **2 :** the quality or state of being accurate (as in alignment or adjustment) — used in the phrases *in true* and *out of true*

³true *vt* **trued; true·ing** *also* **tru·ing :** to make level, square, balanced, or concentric **:** bring to desired mechanical accuracy or form

⁴true *adv* **1 :** in a truthful manner **2 a :** TRULY **3** ⟨the bullet flew straight and *true*⟩ **b :** without variation from type ⟨breed *true*⟩

true bill *n* **:** a bill of indictment endorsed by a grand jury as justifying prosecution of the accused

true–blue \'trü-'blü\ *adj* **:** marked by unswerving loyalty (as to a party)

true·born \-,bórn\ *adj* **:** genuinely such by birth ⟨a *trueborn* American⟩

true bug *n* **:** BUG 1b

true–false test *n* **:** a test consisting of a series of statements to be marked as true or false

true-heart·ed \'trü-'härt-əd\ *adj* **:** STEADFAST 2, LOYAL

true–life \-,trü-,līf\ *adj* **:** true to life ⟨a *true-life* story⟩

true·love \'trü-,ləv\ *n* **:** one truly beloved or loving **:** SWEETHEART

true lover's knot *n* **:** a complicated ornamental knot not easily untied and symbolic of mutual love — called also *truelove knot*

true rib *n* **:** one of the ribs connected directly with the sternum by cartilages and in human beings constituting the first seven pairs

truf·fle \'trəf-əl, 'trüf-\ *n* **:** the usually dark wrinkled edible subterranean fruiting body of a European fungus; *also* **:** this fungus [Middle French *truffe,* from Provençal *trufa,* derived from Latin *tuber* "tuber, truffle"]

tru·ism \'trü-,iz-əm\ *n* **:** an obvious truth — **tru·is·tic** \trü-'is-tik\ *adj*

trull \'trəl\ *n* **:** TROLLOP 2, STRUMPET [obsolete German *trulle*]

tru·ly \'trü-lē\ *adv* **1 :** SINCERELY — often used in a letter as a complimentary close after *yours* **2 :** ⁴TRUE 1 **3 :** with exactness of construction or operation **:** ACCU-RATELY **4 a :** INDEED — often used as an intensive ⟨*truly,* you are nice⟩ or interjectionally to express astonishment or doubt **b :** without pretense **:** GENUINELY **5 :** as it ought to be

¹trump \'trəmp\ *n* **1 :** TRUMPET 1 **2 :** a sound of trumpeting [Old French *trompe*]

²trump *n* **1 a :** a card of a suit whose cards will win over any card of any other suit **b :** the suit whose cards are trumps for a particular hand — often used in pl.

2 : a dependable and exemplary person [alteration of ¹*triumph*]

³trump *vb* **1 :** to take with a trump ⟨*trump* a trick⟩ **2 :** to play a trump **3 :** to get the better of **:** OUTDO

trumped–up \'trəm-,təp, 'trəmp-\ *adj* **:** MADE-UP 2, SPU-RIOUS ⟨*trumped-up* charges⟩

trum·pery \'trəm-pə-rē, -prē\ *n, pl* **-per·ies 1 a :** trivial or useless articles **:** JUNK **b :** worthless nonsense **2** *archaic* **:** tawdry finery [Middle French *tromperie* "deceit", from *tromper* "to deceive"] — **trumpery** *adj*

¹trum·pet \'trəm-pət\ *n* **1 :** a wind instrument consisting of a long cylindrical metal tube commonly once or twice curved and ending in a bell **2 :** a trumpet player **3 :** something that resembles a trumpet or its tonal quality: as **a :** a funnel-shaped instrument (as a megaphone) for collecting, directing, or intensifying sound ⟨an ear *trumpet*⟩ **b** (1) **:** a very loud voice (2) **:** a penetrating cry (as of an elephant) [Middle French *trompette,* from Old French *trompe*] — **trum·pet·like** \-,līk\ *adj*

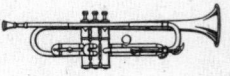
¹trumpet 1

²trumpet *vb* **1 :** to blow a trumpet **2 :** to sound or proclaim on or as if on a trumpet ⟨*trumpeted* the news⟩ **3 :** to make a sound similar to that of a trumpet

trumpet creeper *n* **:** a North American woody vine with pinnate leaves and large red trumpet-shaped flowers — called also *trumpet vine*

trum·pet·er \'trəm-pət-ər\ *n* **1 :** a trumpet player; *esp* **:** one that gives signals with a trumpet **2 a :** a rare pure white North American wild swan noted for its sonorous voice **b :** any of an Asian breed of pigeons with a rounded crest and heavily feathered feet

trump up *vt* **1 :** to concoct especially with intent to deceive **:** FABRICATE, INVENT ⟨*trump up* false charges⟩ **2** *archaic* **:** to cite as support for an action or claim **:** AL-LEGE

trun·cate \'trəng-,kāt, 'trən-\ *vt* **:** to shorten by or as if by cutting off [Latin *truncare,* from *truncus* "trunk"] — **trun·ca·tion** \,trəng-'kā-shən, ,trən-\ *n*

trun·cat·ed \-,kāt-əd\ *adj* **1 :** having the apex replaced by a plane section and especially by one parallel to the base ⟨a *truncated* cone⟩ **2 a :** cut short **b :** lacking an expected or normal element (as a syllable) at beginning or end

¹trun·cheon \'trən-chən\ *n* **1 :** a shattered spear or lance **2 a** *obsolete* **:** CLUB 1a **b :** BATON 1 **c :** a police officer's club [Middle French *tronchon,* derived from Latin *truncus* "trunk"]

²truncheon *vt, archaic* **:** to beat with a truncheon

¹trun·dle \'trən-dl\ *n* **1 :** a small wheel or roller **2 :** a low-wheeled cart or truck [Old English *trendel* "circle, ring, wheel"]

²trundle *vb* **trun·dled; trun·dling** \'trən-dling, -dl-ing\ **1 a :** to propel by causing to rotate **:** ROLL ⟨*trundled* a wheelbarrow⟩ **b :** to progress by revolving **2 :** to transport in a wheeled vehicle — **trun·dler** \-dlər, -dl-ər\ *n*

trundle bed *n* **:** a low bed usually on casters that can be slid under a higher bed — called also *truckle bed*

trunk \'trəngk\ *n* **1 a :** the main stem of a tree apart from branches or roots **b :** the body of a person or lower animal apart from the head and limbs **c :** the main or basal part of something ⟨the *trunk* of an artery⟩ **2 a :** a box or chest for holding clothes or other goods especially for traveling **b :** the enclosed space usually in the rear of an automobile for carrying articles (as luggage) **3 :** the long flexible muscular nose of an elephant; *also* **:** PROBOSCIS **4 :** TRUNK LINE [Middle French *tronc,* from Latin *truncus* "tree trunk, torso"]

trunk hose *n pl* **:** short full breeches reaching about halfway down the thigh worn chiefly in the late 16th and early 17th centuries

trunk line *n* **1 :** a system handling long-distance through traffic **2 a :** a main supply channel **b :** a direct link

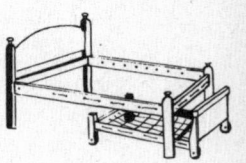
trundle bed

\ə\ **abut**	\ng\ **sing**
\ər\ **further**	\ō\ **bone**
\a\ **mat**	\ó\ **saw**
\ā\ **take**	\ói\ **coin**
\ä\ **cot, cart**	\th\ **thin**
\aú\ **out**	\t͟h\ **this**
\ch\ **chin**	\ü\ **food**
\e\ **pet**	\ú\ **foot**
\ē\ **easy**	\y\ **yet**
\g\ **go**	\yü\ **few**
\i\ **tip**	\yú\ **cure**
\ī\ **life**	\zh\ **vision**
\j\ **job**	

trun·nion \\'trən-yən\\ *n* : PIVOT 1, PIN; *esp* : either of two opposite projections on which a cannon is supported and elevated [French *trognon* "core, stump"]

¹**truss** \\'trəs\\ *vt* **1 a** : to secure tightly : BIND ⟨they *trussed* up their victim⟩ **b** : to arrange for cooking by binding close the wings or legs of ⟨*truss* a turkey⟩ **2** : to support, strengthen, or stiffen by a truss [Old French *trousser*] — **truss·er** *n*

²**truss** *n* **1** : a rigid framework of beams, bars, or rods ⟨a *truss* for a roof⟩ **2** : a device worn to hold a hernia in place

truss bridge *n* : a bridge supported mainly by trusses

¹**trust** \\'trəst\\ *n* **1 a** : assured reliance on the character, ability, strength, or truth of someone or something **b** : one in which confidence is placed **2 a** : dependence on something future or contingent : HOPE **b** : reliance on future payment for goods delivered : CREDIT **3 a** : a legal right or interest in property that one does not actually own ⟨income received under a *trust* established by their parents⟩ **b** : property held or managed by one person or concern (as a bank or trust company) for the benefit of another **c** : a combination of firms or corporations formed by a legal agreement; *esp* : one that reduces or threatens to reduce competition **4 a** : something (as a public office) committed to one to be used or cared for in the interest of another **b** : responsible charge or office **c** : CUSTODY, CARE [Middle English] SYN see MONOPOLY — **in trust** : in the care or possession of a trustee

²**trust** *vb* **1 a** : to place confidence : DEPEND ⟨*trust* in God⟩ ⟨*trust* to luck⟩ **b** : to be confident : HOPE **2** : to commit or place in one's care or keeping : ENTRUST **3 a** : to rely on the truthfulness or accuracy of : BELIEVE **b** : to place confidence in : rely on **c** : to hope or expect confidently ⟨*trusted* to find oil on the land⟩ **4 a** : to sell or deliver on credit **b** : to extend credit to — **trust·er** *n*

trust·bust·er \\'trəst-,bəs-tər\\ *n* : one that seeks to break up business trusts; *esp* : a federal official who prosecutes trusts under the antitrust laws — **trust–bust·ing** \\-,ting\\ *n*

trust company *n* : a corporation and especially a bank organized to perform fiduciary functions

trust·ee \\,trəs-'tē\\ *n* **1** : a person to whom property is legally committed in trust **2** : a country charged with the supervision of a trust territory

trust·ee·ship \\-,ship\\ *n* **1** : the office or function of a trustee **2** : supervisory control by one or more countries over a trust territory

trust·ful \\'trəst-fəl\\ *adj* : full of trust : CONFIDING — **trust·ful·ly** \\-fə-lē\\ *adv* — **trust·ful·ness** *n*

trust fund *n* : property (as money or securities) settled or held in trust

trust·ing \\'trəs-ting\\ *adj* : having trust, faith, or confidence : TRUSTFUL — **trust·ing·ly** \\-ting-lē\\ *adv*

trust territory *n* : a non-self-governing territory placed under an administrative authority by the Trusteeship Council of the United Nations

trust·wor·thy \\'trəst-,wər-the̲\\ *adj* : worthy of confidence : DEPENDABLE — **trust·wor·thi·ly** \\-the̲-lē\\ *adv* — **trust·wor·thi·ness** \\-the̲-nəs\\ *n*

¹**trusty** \\'trəs-tē\\ *adj* **trust·i·er**; **-est** : TRUSTWORTHY

²**trusty** \\'trəs-tē, ,trəs-'tē\\ *n, pl* **trust·ies** : a trusty or trusted person; *esp* : a convict considered trustworthy and allowed special privileges

truth \\'trüth\\ *n, pl* **truths** \\'trü_t̲hz, 'trüths\\ **1 a** *archaic* : FIDELITY 1a, CONSTANCY **b** : sincerity in action, character, and utterance **2** : something that is real or true: as **a** (1) : the real state of things : FACT (2) : the body of real things, events, and facts : ACTUALITY **b** (1) : a judgment, proposition, idea, or statement that is true or accepted as true ⟨the *truths* of science⟩ (2) : the body of such truths **3** : the property of being in accord with what is, has been, or must be [Old English *trēowth* "fidelity"] — **in truth** : in fact : ACTUALLY

truth·ful \\'trüth-fəl\\ *adj* : telling or inclined to tell the truth — **truth·ful·ly** \\-fə-lē\\ *adv* — **truth·ful·ness** *n*

truth serum *n* : a hypnotic or anesthetic held to induce a subject under questioning to talk freely

truth set *n* : a set of the elements that can be substituted to make a set of open sentences true

¹**try** \\'trī\\ *vb* **tried**; **try·ing** **1 a** : to examine or investigate judicially **b** : to conduct the trial of **2 a** : to put to test or trial **b** : to test to the limit or breaking point : STRAIN ⟨*try* one's patience⟩ **3** : to melt down and obtain in a pure state : RENDER ⟨*try* lard from fat pork⟩ **4** : to make an attempt : ENDEAVOR [Anglo-French *trier*, from Old French, "to pick out, sift"] □ SYN ATTEMPT, STRIVE: TRY suggests effort or experiment made in the hope of determining facts or of testing or proving something ⟨*tried* various occupations⟩ ATTEMPT suggests a beginning of or venturing upon something and often implies failure ⟨*attempted* to break through the enemy lines⟩ STRIVE implies great exertion against great difficulty and suggests persistent effort ⟨*strive* to achieve lasting peace⟩ — **try one's hand** : to attempt something for the first time

²**try** *n, pl* **tries** : an experimental trial : ATTEMPT

try for point : an attempt made after scoring a touchdown in football to kick a goal so as to score an additional point or to again carry the ball across the opponents' goal line or complete a forward pass in the opponents' end zone so as to score one or two additional points

try·ing \\'trī-ing\\ *adj* : causing distress or annoyance

try on \\trī-'ȯn, 'trī-, -'än\\ *vt* : to put on (a garment) in order to test the fit — **try–on** \\'trī-,ȯn, -,än\\ *n*

try–out \\'trī-,aut\\ *n* : an experimental performance or demonstration: as **a** : a testing of one's ability to perform especially as an athlete or actor **b** : a test performance of a play before its formal opening

try out \\trī-'aut, 'trī-\\ *vi* : to compete for a position especially on an athletic team or for a part in a play

try·pano·so·ma \\trip-,an-ə-'sō-mə\\ *n* : TRYPANOSOME

try·pano·some \\trip-'an-ə-,sōm\\ *n* : any of a genus of parasitic flagellate protozoans that invade the blood of various vertebrates including man, are usually transmitted by the bite of an insect, and include causers of serious disease (as sleeping sickness) [New Latin *Trypanosoma*, genus name, from Greek *trypanon* "auger" + *sōma* "body"]

try·pano·so·mi·a·sis \\trip-,an-ə-sə-'mī-ə-səs\\ *n, pl* **-a·ses** \\-ə-,sēz\\ : infection with or disease caused by trypanosomes

tryp·sin \\'trip-sən\\ *n* : an enzyme from pancreatic juice that breaks down protein in an alkaline medium [Greek *tryein* "to wear down" + English *-psin* (as in *pepsin*)] — **tryp·tic** \\'trip-tik\\ *adj*

tryp·sin·o·gen \\trip-'sin-ə-jən\\ *n* : the inactive form of trypsin present in the pancreas

tryp·to·phan \\'trip-tə-,fan\\ *or* **tryp·to·phane** \\-,fān\\ *n* : a crystalline amino acid that is widely distributed in protein and that is essential to animal life [derived from *trypsin* + Greek *phanēs* "appearing", from *phainein* "to show"]

try square *n* : an instrument used for laying off right angles and testing whether work is square

tryst \\'trist, *especially British* 'trīst\\ *n* **1** : an agreement (as between lovers) to meet **2** : an appointed meeting or meeting place [Old French *triste* "watch post"]

tsar \\'zär, 'tsär, 'sär\\ *variant of* CZAR

tset·se \\'set-sē, 'tset-, 'sēt-, 'tsēt-, 'tēt-\\ *n, pl* **tsetse** *or* **tseses** : any of a genus of two-winged flies mostly of Africa south of the Sahara desert that include vectors of human and animal trypanosomes — called also *tsetse fly* [of Bantu origin]

T–shirt \\'tē-,shərt\\ *n* : a collarless short-sleeved cotton undershirt for men; *also* : a jersey outer shirt of similar design [from its being shaped like a T]

T square *n* : a ruler with a crosspiece or head at one end used in making parallel lines

tsu·na·mi \sù-'näm-ē, tsù-\ *n* : TIDAL WAVE 1a [Japanese] — **tsu·na·mic** \-'näm-ik\ *adj*

tsu·tsu·ga·mu·shi disease \,süt-sə-gə-'mü-shē-, ,tsüt-, ,tüt-, -'gäm-ù-shē-\ *n* : SCRUB TYPHUS [Japanese *tsutsugamushi* "scrub typhus mite", from *tsutsuga* "sickness" + *mushi* "insect"]

Tua·reg \'twä-,reg\ *n* : a member of the dominant nomadic people of the central and western Sahara and the Middle Niger [Arabic *Tawārig*]

tu·a·ta·ra \,tü-ə-'tär-ə\ *n* : a large spiny four-footed reptile of islands off the coast of New Zealand that has a vestigial third eye and is the only survivor of a once widely distributed order [Maori *tuatàra*]

¹tub \'təb\ *n* **1** : a wide low vessel originally formed with wooden staves, round bottom, and hoops **2** : an old or slow boat **3** : BATHTUB; *also* : BATH 2a **4** : the amount that a tub will hold [Dutch *tubbe*]

²tub *vb* **tubbed; tub·bing** : to wash or bathe in a tub — **tub·ba·ble** \'təb-ə-bəl\ *adj*

tu·ba \'tü-bə, 'tyü-\ *n* : a large usually oval low-pitched brass wind instrument; *esp* : one with a conical tube and a cup-shaped mouthpiece [Italian, from Latin, "trumpet"]

tub·al \'tü-bəl, 'tyü-\ *adj* : of, relating to, or involving a tube

tub·by \'təb-ē\ *adj* **tub·bi·er; -est** : PUDGY, CHUBBY

tube \'tüb, 'tyüb\ *n* **1 a** : a hollow elongated cylinder; *esp* : one to convey fluids **b** : a slender channel within a plant or animal body : DUCT **2** : any of various usually cylindrical structures or devices: as **a** : a round container from which a paste is dispensed by squeezing **b** (1) : TUNNEL (2) *British* : SUBWAY **c** : the basically cylindrical part connecting the mouthpiece and bell of a wind instrument **d** : INNER TUBE **e** : ELECTRON TUBE **f** : TELEVISION ⟨watching the *tube*⟩ [French, from Latin *tubus*] — **tubed** \'tübd, 'tyübd\ *adj* — **tube·like** \'tü-,blīk, 'tyü-\ *adj*

tube foot *n* : one of the small flexible tubular processes of most echinoderms that are extensions of the water-vascular system used especially in locomotion and grasping

tube·less \'tü-bləs, 'tyü-\ *adj* : lacking a tube; *esp* : being a pneumatic tire that does not depend on an inner tube for airtightness

tube nucleus *n* : a nucleus of a pollen grain that is held to control growth of the pollen tube — compare GENERATIVE NUCLEUS

tu·ber \'tü-bər, 'tyü-\ *n* : a plant underground resting stage consisting of a short fleshy stem bearing minute scale leaves each with a bud in its axil potentially able to produce a new plant — compare BULB, CORM **2** : a fleshy root or rhizome resembling a tuber [Latin, "lump, tuber, truffle"]

tu·ber·cle \'tü-bər-kəl, 'tyü-\ *n* **1** : a small knobby prominence or outgrowth especially on a plant or animal **2** : a small abnormal lump in the substance of an organ or in the skin; *esp* : one caused by tuberculosis [Latin *tuberculum*, from *tuber* "lump, tuber"] — **tu·ber·cled** \-kəld\ *adj*

tubercle bacillus *n* : the bacterium that causes tuberculosis

tu·ber·cu·lar \tù-'bər-kyə-lər, tyù-\ *adj* **1** : relating to, resembling, or constituting a tubercle **2** : characterized by tubercular lesions ⟨*tubercular* leprosy⟩ **3** : of, relating to, or affected with tuberculosis : TUBERCULOUS ⟨*tubercular* meningitis⟩ — **tu·ber·cu·lar·ly** *adv*

tu·ber·cu·lin \tù-'bər-kyə-lən, tyù-\ *n* : a sterile liquid containing substances from the tubercle bacillus that is used in the diagnosis of tuberculosis

tuberculin test *n* : a test for hypersensitivity to tuberculin as an indication of past or present tubercular infection

tu·ber·cu·lo·sis \tù-,bər-kyə-'lō-səs, tyü-\ *n* : a communicable disease of some vertebrates caused by the tubercle bacillus and typically marked by wasting, fever, and formation of cheesy tubercles that in human beings occur mostly in the lungs

tu·ber·cu·lous \tù-'bər-kyə-ləs, tyü-\ *adj* **2** : TUBERCULAR 1 **2** : being or affected or associated with tuberculosis ⟨a *tuberculous* process⟩ — **tu·ber·cu·lous·ly** *adv*

tube·rose \'tü-,brōz, 'tyü- (by folk etymology); *also* 'tü-bə-,rōz, 'tyü-, -bə-,rōs\ *n* : a Mexican bulbous herb of the amaryllis family grown for its spike of fragrant white flowers [Latin *tuberosus* "tuberous", from *tuber* "tuber"]

tu·ber·os·i·ty \,tü-bə-'räs-ət-ē, ,tyü-\ *n, pl* **-ties** : a rounded prominence; *esp* : one on a bone usually serving for the attachment of muscles or ligaments

tu·ber·ous \'tü-bə-rəs, 'tyü-, -brəs\ *adj* **1 a** : consisting of or resembling a tuber **b** : bearing tubers **2** : of, relating to, or being a plant tuber or tuberous root — **tu·ber·ous·ly** *adv*

tu·bi·fex \'tü-bə-,feks, 'tyü-\ *n, pl* **-fex** *or* **-fex·es** : any of a genus of slender reddish oligochaete worms that live in tubes in fresh or brackish water and are widely used as food for aquarium fish [New Latin *Tubifex*, genus name, from Latin *tubus* "tube" + *facere* "to make"]

tub·ing \'tü-bing, 'tyü-\ *n* **1** : material in the form of a tube; *also* : a length or piece of tube **2** : a series or system of tubes

tu·bu·lar \'tü-byə-lər, 'tyü-\ *adj* **1** : having the form of or consisting of a tube **2** : made or provided with tubes — **tu·bu·lar·i·ty** \,tü-byə-'lar-ət-ē, ,tyü-\ *n*

tu·bule \'tü-byül, 'tyü-\ *n* : a small tube; *esp* : a long slender anatomical channel

¹tuck \'tək\ *vb* **1 a** : to pull up or draw together into folds **b** : to make a tuck in **2** : to put or fit into a snug position or place ⟨a cottage *tucked* away in the hill⟩ **3 a** : to push in the loose end of so as to hold tightly ⟨*tuck* in your shirt⟩ **b** : to cover by tucking in bedclothes ⟨a child *tucked* in for the night⟩ [Old English *tūcian* "to ill-treat"]

²tuck *n* **1** : a fold stitched into cloth to shorten, decorate, or control fullness **2** : an act or instance of tucking

³tuck *n* : VIGOR 1, ENERGY [probably from ²*tuck*]

¹tuck·er \'tək-ər\ *n* **1** : one that tucks **2** : a piece of lace or cloth in the neckline of a dress

²tucker *vt* **tuck·ered; tuck·er·ing** \'tək-ring, -ə-ring\ : EXHAUST — often used with *out* [derived from Old English *tūcian* "to ill-treat"]

-tude \,tüd, ,tyüd\ *n suffix* : -NESS ⟨exact*itude*⟩ [Latin *-tudin-, -tudo*]

Tu·dor \'tüd-ər, 'tyüd-\ *adj* **1** : of or relating to the English royal family ruling from 1485 to 1603 **2** : of, relating to, or characteristic of the Tudor period [Henry *Tudor* (Henry VII of England)] — **Tudor** *n*

Tues·day \'tüz-dē, 'tyüz-\ *n* : the 3d day of the week [Old English *tīwesdæg*, literally, "day of Tiu (god of war)"]

tu·fa \'tü-fə, 'tyü-\ *n* **1** : TUFF **2** : a porous rock formed as a deposit from springs or streams [Italian *tufo*, from Latin *tophus*] — **tu·fa·ceous** \tü-'fā-shəs, tyü-\ *adj*

tuff \'təf\ *n* : a rock composed of the finer kinds of volcanic detritus [Middle French *tuf*, from Italian *tufo*] — **tuff·a·ceous** \,tə-'fā-shəs\ *adj*

tuf·fet \'təf-ət\ *n* **1** : TUFT 1a **2** : a low seat [alteration of *tuft*]

¹tuft \'təft\ *n* **1 a** : a small cluster of long flexible outgrowths (as hairs or feathers) **b** : a bunch of soft fluffy threads cut off short and used as ornament **2** : CLUMP 1, CLUSTER **3** : one of the projections of yarns drawn through a fabric or otherwise making up a fabric so as to produce a surface of raised loops or cut pile [Middle French *tufe*] — **tuft·ed** \'təf-təd\ *adj* — **tufty** \'təf-tē\ *adj*

tuatara

tuba

\ə\ abut	\ng\ sing
\ər\ further	\ō\ bone
\a\ mat	\ò\ saw
\ā\ take	\òi\ coin
\ä\ cot, cart	\th\ thin
\aù\ out	\t̶h̶\ this
\ch\ chin	\ü\ food
\e\ pet	\ù\ foot
\ē\ easy	\y\ yet
\g\ go	\yü\ few
\i\ tip	\yù\ cure
\ī\ life	\zh\ vision
\j\ job	

²tuft *vt* **1** : to provide or adorn with a tuft **2** : to make (as a mattress) firm by stitching at intervals and sewing on tufts **3** : to make (a fabric) of or with tufts

¹tug \'təg\ *vb* **tugged; tug·ging 1 a** : to pull hard **b** : to move by pulling hard : DRAG, HAUL **2** : to struggle in opposition **3** : to tow with a tugboat [Middle English *tuggen*] — **tug·ger** *n*

²tug *n* **1 a** : a harness trace **b** : a rope or chain used for pulling **2 a** : an act or instance of tugging : PULL **b** : a strong pulling force **3 a** : a straining effort **b** : a struggle between opposing individuals or opposite forces **4** : TUGBOAT

tug·boat \'təg-,bōt\ *n* : a strongly built powerful boat used for towing and pushing (as ships in harbors)

tug–of–war \,təg-əv-'wȯr, ,təg-ə-\ *n, pl* **tugs–of–war 1** : a struggle for supremacy **2** : an athletic contest in which two teams pull against each other at opposite ends of a rope

tu·i·tion \tu̇-'ish-ən, tyu̇-\ *n* **1** : the act or profession of teaching : INSTRUCTION **2** : the price of or payment for instruction [Old French *tuicion* "guardianship", from Latin *tuitio*, from *tueri* "to look at, look after"] — **tu·i·tion·al** \-'ish-nəl, -ən-l\ *adj*

tu·la·re·mia \,tü-lə-'rē-mē-ə, ,tyü-\ *n* : an infectious bacterial disease of rodents, man, and some domestic animals transmitted especially by the bites of insects and in man marked by symptoms (as fever) of toxemia [New Latin, from *Tulare* county, California] — **tu·la·re·mic** \-mik\ *adj*

tu·le \'tü-lē\ *n* : either of two large coarse sedges growing on wet land of the southwestern United States [Spanish, from Nahuatl *tullin*]

tulip

tu·lip \'tü-ləp, 'tyü-\ *n* : any of a genus of Eurasian bulbous herbs of the lily family that have linear or broadly lance-shaped leaves and are widely grown for their showy flowers; *also* : the flower or bulb of a tulip [New Latin *tulipa*, from Turkish *tülbend* "turban"]

tulip tree *n* : a tall North American timber tree of the magnolia family with large greenish yellow tulip-shaped flowers and soft white wood used especially for cabinetwork and woodenware

tulle \'tül\ *n* : a sheer often stiffened silk, rayon, or nylon net used chiefly for veils, evening dresses, or ballet costumes [French, from *Tulle*, France]

tul·li·bee \'təl-ə-bē\ *n* : any of several American whitefishes; *esp* : a common cisco that is a commercially important food fish [Canadian French *toulibi*]

¹tum·ble \'təm-bəl\ *vb* **tum·bled; tum·bling** \-bə-ling, -bling\ **1 a** : to perform gymnastic feats of rolling and turning **b** : to turn end over end in falling or flight **2 a** : to fall suddenly and helplessly **b** : to suffer a sudden decline, downfall, or defeat : COLLAPSE **3** : to move or go hurriedly and confusedly **4** : to come to understand **5** : to cause to tumble (as by pushing) **6 a** : to toss together into a confused mass **b** : RUMPLE [Middle English *tumblen*, from *tumben* "to dance", from Old English *tumbian*]

²tumble *n* **1** : something tumbled **2** : an act or instance of tumbling

tum·ble·bug \'təm-bəl-,bəg\ *n* : a large stout-bodied beetle that rolls dung into small balls, buries them in the ground, and lays eggs in them

tum·ble·down \,təm-bəl-'daun\ *adj* : DILAPIDATED

tumble dry *vt* : to dry (as clothes) in a dryer

tum·bler \'təm-blər\ *n* **1** : one that tumbles: as **a** : GYMNAST, ACROBAT **b** : a pigeon that habitually somersaults backward in flight **2** : a drinking glass without foot or stem and originally with pointed or convex base **3** : a movable part in a lock that must be adjusted (as by a key) before the bolt can be thrown **4** : a device or mechanism for tumbling

tumbleweed

tum·ble·weed \'təm-bəl-,wēd\ *n* : a plant that breaks away from its roots in autumn and is blown about by the wind

²tuna

tum·bling \'təm-bə-ling, -bling\ *n* : the skill, practice, or sport of executing acrobatic feats (as somersaults, rolls, and handsprings) on a mat usually without apparatus

tum·brel *or* **tum·bril** \'təm-brəl\ *n* : a farmer's cart used during the French Revolution to carry condemned persons to the guillotine [Old French *tumberel* "tipcart", from *tomber* "to tumble", of Germanic origin]

tu·mes·cence \tü-'mes-ns, tyü-\ *n* : a swelling or becoming swollen or the resulting state [Latin *tumescens*, present participle of *tumescere* "to swell up", from *tumēre* "to swell"] — **tu·mes·cent** \-nt\ *adj*

tu·mid \'tü-məd, 'tyü-\ *adj* **1** : marked by swelling ⟨*tumid* flesh⟩ **2** : TURGID 2, BOMBASTIC [Latin *tumidus*, from *tumēre* "to swell"] — **tu·mid·i·ty** \tü-'mid-ət-ē, tyü-\ *n*

tum·my \'təm-ē\ *n, pl* **tummies** : STOMACH 1c [baby-talk for *stomach*]

tu·mor \'tü-mər, 'tyü-\ *n* : a swollen or distended part; *esp* : an abnormal mass of tissue that is not inflammatory, arises without obvious cause from cells of preexistent tissue, and possesses no physiologic function [Latin, from *tumēre* "to swell"] — **tu·mor·like** \-,līk\ *adj* — **tu·mor·ous** \'tüm-rəs, 'tyüm-, -ə-rəs\ *adj*

tump·line \'təm-,plin\ *n* : a sling formed by a strap slung over the forehead or chest used for carrying a pack on the back or in hauling loads [*tump* of American Indian origin]

tu·mult \'tü-,məlt, 'tyü-\ *n* **1** : violent and disorderly commotion or disturbance (as of a crowd) with uproar and confusion **2** : violent agitation of mind or feelings [Middle French *tumulte*, from Latin *tumultus*]

tu·mul·tu·ous \tü-'məl-chə-wəs, tyü-, -chəs\ *adj* : marked by tumult and especially by violent turbulence or upheaval — **tu·mul·tu·ous·ly** *adv* — **tu·mul·tu·ous·ness** *n*

tu·mu·lus \'tü-myə-ləs, 'tyü-\ *n, pl* **-li** \-,lī, -,lē\ : an artificial hillock or mound usually over an ancient grave [Latin]

tun \'tən\ *n* **1** : a large cask for liquids and especially wine **2** : the capacity of a tun as a varying liquid measure; *esp* : a measure of 252 gallons (about 954 liters) [Old English *tunne*]

¹tu·na \'tü-nə\ *n* : any of several flat-jointed prickly pears; *also* : the edible fruit of a tuna [Spanish, of American Indian origin]

²tu·na \'tü-nə, 'tyü-\ *n, pl* **tuna** *or* **tunas** : any of several mostly large active sea fishes (as an albacore or bonito) related to the mackerels and valued for food and sport [American Spanish, from Spanish *atún*, from Arabic *tūn*, from Latin *thunnus*, from Greek *thynnos*]

tun·able \'tü-nə-bəl, 'tyü-\ *adj* : capable of being tuned — **tun·able·ness** *n* — **tun·ably** \-blē\ *adv*

tun·dra \'tən-drə *also* 'tun-\ *n* : a treeless plain of arctic and subarctic regions [Russian, of Finno-Ugric origin]

¹tune \'tün, 'tyün\ *n* **1 a** : a musical composition or air **b** : a dominant theme **2** : correct musical pitch or consonance ⟨the piano was not in *tune*⟩ **3 a** : AGREEMENT, HARMONY ⟨in *tune* with the times⟩ **b** : general attitude ⟨you'll change your *tune* after you read this⟩ **4** : AMOUNT, EXTENT ⟨a subsidy to the *tune* of $5,000,000⟩ [Middle English, alteration of *tone*]

²tune *vb* **1** : to come or bring into harmony : ATTUNE **2** : to adjust a radio or television receiver to either receive or reject a broadcast **3** : to adjust in musical pitch **4** : to adjust for precise functioning ⟨*tune* a motor⟩

tune·ful \'tün-fəl, 'tyün-\ *adj* : MELODIOUS 1, MUSICAL — **tune·ful·ly** \-fə-lē\ *adv* — **tune·ful·ness** *n*

tun·er \'tü-nər, 'tyü-\ *n* **1** : one that tunes ⟨piano *tuner*⟩ **2** : something used for tuning; *esp* : the part of a receiving set that selects radio signals for conversion into audio or visual signals

tune–up \'tü-ˌnəp, 'tyü-\ *n* **1** : a general adjustment to ensure efficient functioning ⟨a motor *tune-up*⟩ **2** : a preliminary trial : WARM-UP

tung \'təng\ *n* : TUNG TREE

tung·sten \'təng-stən, 'təngk-\ *n* : a gray-white heavy ductile hard metallic chemical element that is used especially for electrical purposes and in hardening alloys (as steel) — called also *wolfram*; see ELEMENT table [Swedish, from *tung* "heavy" + *sten* "stone"]

tung tree *n* : any of several trees whose seeds yield a drying oil; *esp* : a Chinese tree widely grown in warm regions [Chinese (Pekingese dialect) *t'ung*²]

Tun·gu·sic \tùng-'gü-zik, tən-\ *n* : a subfamily of Altaic languages spoken in Manchuria and northward [*Tungus*, a Mongoloid people of eastern Siberia, from Russian] — **Tungusic** *adj*

tu·nic \'tü-nik, 'tyü-\ *n* **1** : a simple belted knee-length or longer slip-on garment worn by ancient Greeks and Romans **2** : a long usually plain and close-fitting jacket with high collar worn especially as part of a uniform **3** : a blouse or jacket reaching to or just below the hips [Latin *tunica*, of Semitic origin]

tu·ni·ca \'tü-ni-kə, 'tyü-\ *n, pl* **-cae** \-nə-ˌkē, -ˌkī\ : an enveloping integument, membrane, or layer of animal or plant tissue [Latin, "tunic, membrane"]

tu·ni·cate \'tü-ni-kət, 'tyü-, -nə-ˌkāt\ *n* : any of a major group (Tunicata) of lowly marine chordates with a reduced nervous system and an outer cuticular covering : SEA SQUIRT — **tunicate** *adj*

tuning fork *n* : a 2-pronged metal instrument that gives a fixed tone when struck and is useful for tuning musical instruments and ascertaining standard pitch

¹tun·nel \'tən-l\ *n* : an enclosed passage (as a tube or conduit); *esp* : one underground (as under an obstruction or in a mine [Middle French *tonel* "tun", from Old French *tonne*, from Medieval Latin *tunna*, of Celtic origin] — **tun·nel·like** \-l-ˌlīk, -l-ˌīk\ *adj*

²tunnel *vb* **-neled** *or* **-nelled**; **-nel·ing** *or* **-nel·ling** \'tən-ling, -l-ing\ : to make or use a tunnel or form a tunnel in — **tun·nel·er** \'tən-lər, -l-ər\ *n*

tun·ny \'tən-ē\ *n, pl* **tunnies** *also* **tunny** : ²TUNA [derived from Latin *thunnus*]

tu·pe·lo \'tü-pə-ˌlō, 'tyü-\ *n, pl* **-los** **1** : any of a genus of mostly North American trees of the dogwood family; *esp* : BLACK GUM **2** : the pale soft easily worked wood of a tupelo [Creek *ito opilwa* "swamp tree"]

Tu·pi \tü-'pē, 'tü-,\ *n* **1** : a member of a group of peoples of the Amazon valley **2** : the language of the Tupi people

tup·pence *variant of* TWOPENCE

tuque \'tük, 'tyük\ *n* : a warm knitted usually pointed stocking cap [Canadian French, from French *toque*]

tur·ban \'tər-bən\ *n* **1** : a headdress worn chiefly in countries of the eastern Mediterranean and southern Asia especially by Muslims and made of a cap around which is wound a long cloth **2** : a headdress resembling a turban; *esp* : a woman's close-fitting hat without a brim [Middle French *turbant*, from Italian *turbante*, from Turkish *tülbend*, from Persian *dulband*] — **tur·baned** *or* **tur·banned** \-bənd\ *adj*

tur·bel·lar·i·an \ˌtər-bə-'ler-ē-ən, -'lar-\ *n* : any of a class (Turbellaria) of mostly aquatic and free-living flatworms; *esp* : PLANARIAN [derived from Latin *turbellae* "bustle, stir", from *turba* "confusion, crowd"] — **turbellarian** *adj*

tur·bid \'tər-bəd\ *adj* **1 a** : thick or opaque with matter in suspension ⟨a *turbid* stream⟩ **b** : heavy with smoke or mist : DENSE **2** : confused in thought or feeling [Latin *turbidus* "confused, turbid", from *turba* "confusion, crowd"] — **tur·bid·i·ty** \ˌtər-'bid-ət-ē\ *n* — **tur·bid·ly** \'tər-bəd-lē\ *adv* — **tur·bid·ness** *n*

¹tur·bi·nate \'tər-bə-nət\ *adj* : of, relating to, or being the thin bony or cartilaginous plates on the walls of the nasal passages [Latin *turbinatus* "shaped like a top", from *turbo* "top"]

²turbinate *n* : a turbinate bone or cartilage

tur·bine \'tər-bən, -ˌbīn\ *n* : an engine whose central driving shaft is fitted with vanes whirled around by the pressure of water or hot gases (as steam or exhaust gases) [French, from Latin *turbo* "top, whirlwind"]

tur·bo \'tər-bō\ *n, pl* **turbos** **1** : TURBINE **2** : TURBOSUPERCHARGER

tur·bo- *combining form* **1** : coupled directly to a driving turbine **2** : consisting of or incorporating a turbine ⟨*turbo*jet engine⟩

tur·bo·charg·er \'tər-bō-ˌchär-jər\ *n* : a blower driven by exhaust gas turbines and used to supercharge an engine

tur·bo·jet \'tər-bō-ˌjet\ *n* : an airplane powered by turbojet engines

turbojet engine *n* : a jet engine in which a turbine drives a compressor that supplies air to a burner and hot gases from the burner drive the turbine before being discharged rearward

tur·bo·prop \'tər-bō-ˌpräp\ *n* **1** : TURBOPROPENGINE **2** : an airplane powered by turboprop engines

turboprop engine *n* : a jet engine designed to produce thrust principally by means of a propeller driven by a turbine with additional thrust usually obtained by the rearward discharge of hot exhaust gases

tur·bo·su·per·charg·er \-'sü-pər-ˌchär-jər\ *n* : a turbine compressor driven by hot exhaust gases of an airplane engine for feeding rarefied air at high altitudes into the carburetor of the engine at sea-level pressure so as to increase engine power

tur·bot \'tər-bət\ *n, pl* **turbot** *also* **turbots** : a large brownish European flatfish that is a popular food fish; *also* : any of various flatfishes resembling this [Old French *tourbot*]

tur·bu·lence \'tər-byə-ləns\ *n* : the quality or state of being turbulent: as **a** : wild commotion **b** : irregular atmospheric motion especially when characterized by up and down currents **c** : departure in a fluid from a smooth flow

tur·bu·len·cy \-lən-sē\ *n, pl* **-cies** *archaic* : TURBULENCE

tur·bu·lent \-lənt\ *adj* **1** : causing unrest, violence, or disturbance **2** : characterized by agitation or tumult : TEMPESTUOUS [Latin *turbulentus*, from *turba* "confusion, crowd"] — **tur·bu·lent·ly** *adv*

turbulent flow *n* : a fluid flow in which the velocity at a given point varies erratically in magnitude and direction

Tur·co- *or* **Tur·ko-** *combining form* : Turkish : Turkish and

tu·reen \tə-'rēn, tyü-\ *n* : a deep bowl from which food (as soup) is served [French *terrine*, from *terrin* "earthen", derived from Latin *terra* "earth"]

turf \'tərf\ *n, pl* **turfs** \'tərfs\ *or* **turves** \'tərvz\ **1** : the upper layer of soil bound by grass and plant roots into a thick mat; *also* : a piece of this — called also *sod* **2 a** : PEAT **2 b** : a piece of peat dried for fuel **3 a** : a track or course for horse racing **b** : the sport or business of horse racing [Old English] — **turfy** \'tər-fē\ *adj*

turf·man \'tərf-mən\ *n* : a devotee of horse racing; *esp* : one who owns and races horses

tur·ges·cent \ˌtər-'jes-nt\ *adj* : becoming turgid, distended, or inflated [Latin *turgescens*, present participle of *turgescere* "to swell", from *turgēre* "to be swollen"] — **tur·ges·cence** \-ns\ *n*

tur·gid \'tər-jəd\ *adj* **1 a** : affected with swelling ⟨*turgid* limbs⟩ **b** : exhibiting turgor **2** : excessively embellished in style or language : BOMBASTIC, POMPOUS [Latin *turgidus*, from *turgēre* "to be swollen"] — **tur·gid·i·ty** \ˌtər-'jid-ət-ē\ *n* — **tur·gid·ly** \'tər-jəd-lē\ *adv* — **tur·gid·ness** *n*

tur·gor \'tər-gər, -ˌgòr\ *n* : the normal state of firmness and tension typical of living cells [Late Latin, "turgidity", from Latin *turgēre* "to be swollen"]

Turk \'tərk\ *n* **1** : a member of any of numerous Asian peoples speaking Turkic languages who live in a re-

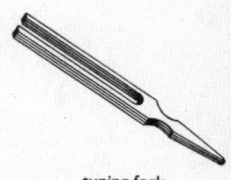

tuning fork

\ə\ abut	\ng\ sing
\ər\ further	\ō\ bone
\a\ mat	\ò\ saw
\ā\ take	\òi\ coin
\ä\ cot, cart	\th\ thin
\aú\ out	\th\ this
\ch\ chin	\ü\ food
\e\ pet	\ú\ foot
\ē\ easy	\y\ yet
\g\ go	\yü\ few
\i\ tip	\yú\ cure
\ī\ life	\zh\ vision
\j\ job	

turkey 1

gion ranging from the Balkans to eastern Siberia and western China **2** : a native or inhabitant of Turkey [Middle French *Turc*, from Medieval Latin *Turcus*, from Turkish *Türk*]

tur·key \'tər-kē\ *n, pl* **turkeys 1** : a large American bird which is related to the common fowl, is of wide range in North America, and is domesticated in most parts of the world **2** : FLOP 2, FAILURE **3** *slang* **a** : SUCKER 6a **b** : FOOL 1, DOPE [*Turkey*; from confusion with the guinea fowl, supposed to be imported from Turkish territory]

turkey buzzard *n* : an American vulture common in South and Central America and in the southern United States — called also **turkey vulture**

tur·key-cock \'tər-kē-ˌkäk\ *n* **1** : GOBBLER **2** : a strutting pompous person

turkey shoot *n* : a contest of marksmanship with a gun at a moving target with a turkey offered as a prize

Tur·ki \'tər-ˌkē, 'túr-\ *n* : any central Asian Turkic language [Persian *turkī*, from *Turk* "Turk", from Turkish *Türk*]

Turk·ic \'tər-kik\ *n* : a subfamily of Altaic languages including Turkish — **Turkic** *adj*

¹Turk·ish \'tər-kish\ *adj* **1** : of, relating to, or characteristic of Turkey, the Turks, or Turkish **2** : TURKIC

²Turkish *n* : the Turkic language of Turkey

Turkish bath *n* : a bath in which the bather passes through a series of steam rooms of increasing temperature and then receives a rubdown, massage, and cold shower

Turkish coffee *n* : a drink made by boiling powdered coffee in a thin sugar syrup

Turkish delight *n* : a jellylike or gummy confection usually cut in cubes and dusted with sugar — called also *Turkish paste*

Turkish towel *n* : a towel made of cotton terry cloth

Tur·ko·man *or* **Tur·co·man** \'tər-kə-mən\ *n, pl* **Turkomans** *or* **Turcomans** : a member of a group of peoples living chiefly in Turkmenistan, Afghanistan, and Iran [Medieval Latin *Turcomannus*, from Persian *Turkmān*, from *turkmān* "resembling a Turk", from *Turk* "Turk", from Turkish *Türk*]

tur·mer·ic \'tər-mə-rik *also* 'tü-mə-, 'tyü-\ *n* **1** : an East Indian herb of the ginger family; *also* : its aromatic rootstock powdered for use as a condiment, yellow dye, or stimulant **2** : any of several plants resembling turmeric [Middle French *terre merite* "saffron", from Medieval Latin *terra merita*, literally, "deserving or deserved earth"]

tur·moil \'tər-ˌmóil\ *n* : an utterly confused or extremely agitated state or condition [origin unknown]

¹turn \'tərn\ *vb* **1 a** : to move or cause to move around an axis or center : ROTATE, REVOLVE ⟨wheels *turning* slowly⟩ ⟨*turn* a crank⟩; *also* : to operate or cause to operate by so turning ⟨*turn* a key in a lock⟩ **b** : to whirl giddily : become dizzy ⟨your head will *turn* at the height⟩ **c** : to have as a center (as of interest) or a decisive factor ⟨their decision must *turn* on circumstances⟩ ⟨the story *turns* about the fate of a family⟩ **d** : to think over : PONDER **e** : to execute by revolving ⟨*turn* handsprings⟩ **2 a** : to alter or reverse in position usually by moving through an arc ⟨*turn* toward your partner⟩: as **(1)** : to dig or plow so as to invert ⟨*turn* the soil⟩ **(2)** : to make over by reversing the material and resewing ⟨*turn* a collar⟩ **b** : to disturb or upset the order or state or balance of ⟨everything was *turned* topsy-turvy⟩ **c** : to injure by a sudden twist : WRENCH ⟨*turned* my ankle⟩ **3** : to change or cause to change ⟨water *turned* to ice⟩: as **a (1)** : TRANSFORM ⟨*turn* wild land into fruitful farms⟩ **(2)** : BECOME ⟨*turn* traitor⟩ **b** : TRANSLATE 2a, PARAPHRASE **c** : to exchange for something else ⟨*turn* property into cash⟩ **d** : to cause to spoil : SOUR ⟨*turned* milk⟩ **e** : to change in color ⟨leaves *turning* in the fall⟩ **f** : to cause to be : MAKE ⟨hair *turned* white by sorrow⟩ **g** : to be inconstant : VARY **4 a** : to take or cause to take

or move in another, an opposite, or a particular direction ⟨*turned* the overflow into an old stream bed⟩ ⟨the road *turns* to the left⟩ ⟨*turned* the car around⟩ ⟨when the tide *turns*⟩; *also* : to go around ⟨*turn* a corner⟩ **b** : to alter from a previous or anticipated course ⟨these few votes *turned* the election⟩ **c (1)** : to change one's behavior or attitude to opposition or hostility ⟨felt the world had *turned* against them⟩; *also* : DEFECT **(2)** : to attack suddenly and usually unexpectedly and violently ⟨the dog *turned* on a neighbor⟩ **d** : to bring to bear : TRAIN ⟨*turn* a weapon on an enemy⟩; *also* : to direct or point usually toward or away from something ⟨*turned* their thoughts homeward⟩ **e** : to influence toward a change (as in one's way of life) **f** : DEVOTE 1, APPLY ⟨*turned* their skills to the service of the poor⟩ **g** : to cause to recoil ⟨*turns* their own argument against them⟩ **h** : to drive or send from or to a specified place or condition ⟨*turn* cattle into a field⟩ ⟨*turn* mutineers adrift⟩ **i** : to seek out as a source ⟨*turn* to a friend for help⟩ **5 a** : to give a rounded form to by means of a lathe and cutting tool **b** : to give a well-rounded or graceful shape or form to ⟨*turn* the heel of a sock⟩ ⟨*turned* a phrase⟩ **c** : to become or cause to become bent or curved ⟨the edge of the knife had *turned*⟩ **6** : to gain in the course of business ⟨*turning* a quick profit⟩ [Old English *tyrnan*, *turnian* and Old French *torner*, *tourner*, both from Latin *tornare* "to turn on a lathe", from *tornus* "lathe", from Greek *tornos*] — **turn a deaf ear** : to refuse to listen — **turn a hair** : to be or become upset or frightened — **turn one's back on 1** : REJECT 1 **2** : ABANDON **3** — **turn one's hand** *or* **turn a hand** : to set to work : apply oneself usefully — **turn one's head** : to cause to have great notions of pride or conceit — **turn tail** : to run away : FLEE — **turn the scale** : to prove decisive — **turn the trick** : to bring about the desired result or effect — **turn turtle** : CAPSIZE, OVERTURN

²turn *n* **1** : the action or an act of turning about a center or axis ⟨each *turn* of the wheel⟩ **2 a** : a change or changing of direction, course, or position **b** : a place where something turns : BEND, CURVE ⟨at the *turn* of the road⟩ **c (1)** : a change or changing of condition or trend ⟨took a *turn* for the better⟩ ⟨a *turn* in the weather⟩ **(2)** : a usually sudden and brief attack or spell of nerves or faintness ⟨gave me a *turn*⟩ **d** : a musical ornament consisting of a group of notes including the one next above and next below the principal note **3** : an act affecting another ⟨did me a very bad *turn*⟩ **4 a** : a period of action or activity : SPELL ⟨each took a *turn* at the job⟩ **b** : place or appointed time in a succession or scheduled order ⟨wait one's *turn* at the dentist's⟩ **5** : special purpose or need ⟨it served my *turn*⟩ **6** : a short walk or ride ⟨took a *turn* through the park⟩ **7 a** : distinctive quality or character ⟨a neat *turn* of phrase⟩ **b** : the form in accord with which something is fashioned : CAST ⟨a peculiar *turn* of mind⟩ **c** : the state or manner of being coiled or twisted; *also* : a single round (as of a rope) ⟨took a *turn* around a post to hold the horse⟩ **d** : a special twist or interpretation ⟨gave the old tale a new *turn*⟩ **8** : particular or special aptitude or skill : BENT ⟨a *turn* for languages⟩ — **at every turn** : CONSTANTLY, CONTINUOUSLY — **to a turn** : to perfection

turn·about \'tər-nə-ˌbaút\ *n* : a change or reversal of direction, trend, policy, or role

turn·around \-ˌraúnd\ *n* : a space permitting the turning around of a vehicle

turn away *vb* **1** : DEFLECT, AVERT **2 a** : to send away : REJECT, DISMISS **b** : to refuse admittance or acceptance to **3** : to start to go away : DEPART

turn back *vb* **1** : to refer to an earlier time or place **2** : to drive back or away **3** : to stop the advance of : CHECK

turn·buck·le \'tərn-ˌbək-əl\ *n* : a link with a screw thread at one or both ends used for tightening a rod or stay by pulling together the ends that it connects

turn·coat \'tərn-ˌkōt\ *n* : one who forsakes his or her party or principles; *esp* : TRAITOR

turn down \ˌtərn-'daùn, 'tərn-\ *vt* 1 : to turn upside down : INVERT 2 : to reduce in intensity by turning a control ⟨*turn down* the volume⟩ 3 : REJECT ⟨*turned down* the offer⟩ — **turn·down** \ˌtərn-ˌdaùn\ *adj or n*

turn·er \'tər-nər\ *n* 1 : one that turns or is used for turning ⟨cake *turner*⟩; *esp* : one that forms articles with a lathe

Tur·ner's syndrome \'tər-nərz-\ *n* : a genetically determined condition associated with the presence of one X chromosome and no Y chromosome and characterized by an outwardly female bodily type with incomplete and infertile sex organs [Henry Hubert *Turner*, died 1970, American physician]

turn·ery \'tər-nə-rē\ *n, pl* **-er·ies** : the work, products, or shop of a turner

turn in *vb* 1 : to give up or hand over ⟨*turn in* extra supplies⟩ 2 : to inform on : BETRAY 3 : PRODUCE, DO ⟨*turn in* good work⟩ 4 : to turn from a road or path so as to enter ⟨*turn in* at the gate⟩ 5 : to go to bed

turning point *n* : a point at which a significant change occurs

tur·nip \'tər-nəp\ *n* : either of two biennial herbs of the mustard family with thick roots eaten as a vegetable or fed to stock : **a** : one with hairy leaves and usually white and flattened roots **b** : RUTABAGA [probably from [superscript]1*turn* + English dialect *neep* "turnip", from the rounded root]

turn·key \'tərn-ˌkē\ *n, pl* **turnkeys** : one who has charge of a prison's keys : JAILER

turn·off \'tər-ˌnóf\ *n* 1 : a turning off 2 : a place where one turns off

turn off \ˌtər-'nóf, 'tər-\ *vt* 1 : DISMISS, DISCHARGE ⟨*turn off* employees⟩ 2 : to turn aside or aside from something ⟨*turn off* a puzzling question⟩ ⟨*turned off* into a side road⟩ 3 : to stop the functioning or flow of by or as if by turning a control ⟨*turn* the light *off*⟩ 4 : to cause to lose interest or responsiveness

turn on *vt* 1 : to cause to function or flow by or as if by turning a control ⟨*turn* the water *on* full⟩ ⟨*turn on* the lights⟩ ⟨*turned on* all my charm⟩ 2 **a** : to undergo or cause to undergo an intense often visionary experience by taking a drug; *also* : to cause to get high **b** : to excite or become excited pleasurably ⟨rock music *turns* me *on*⟩

turn·out \'tər-ˌnaùt\ *n* 1 : an act of turning out 2 : a gathering of people for a special purpose 3 : a widened space (as in a highway) for vehicles to pass or park 4 : a clearing out and cleaning 5 **a** : a carriage with its team and equipment **b** : an outfit of clothes : COSTUME 6 : YIELD, OUTPUT

turn out \ˌtər-'naùt, 'tər-\ *vb* 1 : to put out of some shelter : EVICT 2 : to empty of contents; *also* : CLEAN 3 : to make with rapidity or regularity 4 : to equip, dress, or finish in a careful or elaborate way 5 : to turn off (as a light) 6 : to call (as a guard) from rest or shelter 7 **a** : to come out in answer to a summons ⟨*turn out* for practice⟩ **b** : to get out of bed 8 **a** : to prove in the end ⟨*turned out* to be a spy⟩ **b** : END 2 ⟨how did the game *turn out*⟩

[superscript]1**turn·over** \'tər-ˌnō-vər\ *n* 1 : an act or result of turning over : UPSET 2 : a shifting usually in position or opinion 3 : a reorganization especially of personnel 4 : a filled pastry with one half of the crust turned over the other 5 : the amount of business done or work accomplished; *also* : the rate at which material is processed 6 : the buying, selling, and replacing of goods considered as one complete process ⟨the annual *turnover* in shoes⟩ 7 : the number of employees hired in a given time to replace those leaving or discharged

[superscript]2**turn·over** \ˌtər-ˌnō-vər\ *adj* : capable of being turned over

turn over \ˌtər-'no-vər, 'tər-\ *vb* 1 **a** : to turn from an upright position : OVERTURN **b** : OPERATE, RUN ⟨engines

turning over slowly⟩ 2 : to examine or search by shifting item by item ⟨*turning over* old letters⟩ 3 : to think over : meditate on ⟨*turn over* a problem in search of a solution⟩ 4 : to hand over : TRANSFER 5 **a** : to receive and dispose of (as a stock of merchandise) usually in the course of business **b** : to do business to the amount of ⟨expected to *turn over* $1000 a week⟩ 6 : to heave with nausea ⟨your stomach will *turn over* with shock⟩

turn·pike \'tərn-ˌpīk\ *n* 1 : a toll bar : TOLLGATE 2 **a** : a toll road; *esp* : a toll expressway **b** : a main road [Middle English *turnepike* "revolving frame bearing spikes and serving as a barrier", from *turnen* "to turn" + *pike*]

turn·spit \-ˌspit\ *n* 1 : one that turns a spit 2 : a rotatable spit

turn·stile \-ˌstīl\ *n* : a post with arms pivoted on the top set in a passageway so that persons can pass through only on foot one by one

turn·stone \-ˌstōn\ *n* : any of various widely distributed migratory shorebirds resembling the related plovers and sandpipers

turn·ta·ble \-ˌtā-bəl\ *n* : a revolvable platform: as **a** : a platform with a track for turning wheeled vehicles **b** : LAZY SUSAN **c** : a rotating platform that carries a phonograph record

turn to \'tərn-ˌtü\ *vi* : to apply oneself to work : act vigorously

turn-up \ˌtər-ˌnəp\ *adj* 1 : turned up ⟨a *turnup* nose⟩ 2 : made or fitted to be turned up ⟨a *turnup* collar⟩

turn up \ˌtər-'nəp, 'tər-\ *vb* 1 : to bring or come to light unexpectedly or after being lost ⟨the papers will *turn up*⟩ 2 : to raise or increase by or as if by adjusting a control ⟨*turn up* the heat⟩ 3 **a** : to turn out to be ⟨*turned up* missing⟩ **b** : to become evident : APPEAR ⟨that name is always *turning up*⟩ **c** : to put in an appearance ⟨*turned up* half an hour late⟩ 4 : to happen unexpectedly — **turn up one's nose** : to show scorn or disdain

tur·pen·tine \'tər-pən-ˌtīn\ *n* 1 : an oleoresin obtained from various conifers (as some pines and firs) 2 **a** : an essential oil obtained from turpentines by distillation and used especially as a solvent and thinner — called also *gum turpentine* **b** : a similar oil obtained by distillation or carbonization of pinewood — called also *wood turpentine* [Medieval Latin *terbentina* "oleoresin obtained from the terebinth", derived from Latin *terebinthus* "terebinth"]

tur·pi·tude \'tər-pə-ˌtüd, -ˌtyüd\ *n* : inherent baseness : DEPRAVITY ⟨moral *turpitude*⟩ [Middle French, from Latin *turpitudo*, from *turpis* "vile, base"]

turps \'tərps\ *n* : TURPENTINE

tur·quoise \'tər-ˌkwóiz, -ˌkòiz\ *n* 1 : a mineral that is a blue, bluish green, or greenish gray hydrous basic copper aluminum phosphate, takes a high polish, and sometimes is valued as a gem 2 : a light greenish blue [Middle French *turquoyse*, from *turquoys* "Turkish", from *Turc* "Turk"]

tur·ret \'tər-ət, 'tə-rət, 'tùr-ət\ *n* 1 : a little tower often at a corner of a building 2 **a** : a pivoted and revolvable holder in a machine tool **b** : a device (as on a microscope or television camera) for holding several lenses 3 : a gunner's fixed or movable enclosure in an airplane **4** : a revolving structure on a warship or on a tank in which guns are mounted [Middle French *torete*, from *tor, tur* "tower"] — **tur·ret·ed** \-əd\ *adj*

[superscript]1**tur·tle** \'tərt-l\ *n, archaic* : TURTLEDOVE [Old English *turtla*, from Latin *turtur*]

[superscript]2**turtle** *n, pl* **turtles** *also* **turtle** : any of an order (Testudinata) of land, freshwater, and marine reptiles with a toothless horny beak and a bony shell which encloses the trunk and into which the head, limbs, and tail usually may be withdrawn — compare TERRAPIN, TORTOISE [probably from French *tortue*]

turnstone

\ə\ abut	\ng\ sing
\ər\ **further**	\ō\ bone
\a\ mat	\ó\ saw
\ā\ take	\oi\ coin
\ä\ cot, cart	\th\ thin
\aù\ out	\th\ this
\ch\ chin	\ü\ food
\e\ pet	\ù\ foot
\ē\ easy	\y\ yet
\g\ go	\yü\ few
\i\ tip	\yù\ cure
\ī\ life	\zh\ vision
\j\ job	

tutu

tur·tle·back \'tərt-l-,bak\ *n* : a raised convex surface — **turtleback** *or* **tur·tle–backed** \,tərt-l-'bakt\ *adj*

tur·tle·dove \'tərt-l-,dəv\ *n* : any of several small wild pigeons especially of an Old World genus noted for cooing [¹*turtle*]

tur·tle·neck \-,nek\ *n* : a high close-fitting turnover collar used especially for sweaters; *also* : a sweater with a turtleneck

tur·tling \'tərt-ling, -l-ing\ *n* : the action or process of catching turtles

turves *pl of* TURF

¹**Tus·can** \'təs-kən\ *n* **1** : a native or inhabitant of Tuscany **2 a** : the Italian language spoken in Tuscany **b** : the standard literary dialect of Italian [Latin *tuscanus*, adj., "Etruscan", from *Tusci* "Etruscans"]

²**Tuscan** *adj* : of, relating to, or characteristic of Tuscany, the Tuscans, or Tuscan

Tus·ca·ro·ra \,təs-kə-'rōr-ə, -'ror-\ *n* : a member of an Iroquoian people originally of what is now North Carolina and later of New York and Ontario [Tuscarora *Ska-ru-rēⁿ*, literally, "Indian hemp gatherers"]

¹**tush** \'təsh\ *n* : a long pointed tooth [Old English *tūsc*] — **tushed** \'təsht\ *adj*

²**tush** *interj* — used to express disdain or reproach [Middle English *tussch*]

¹**tusk** \'təsk\ **1** : a long greatly enlarged tooth (as of an elephant, walrus, or boar) that projects when the mouth is closed and serves for gathering food or as a weapon **2** : a tooth-shaped part [Old English *tūx*] — **tusked** \'təskt\ *adj*

²**tusk** *vt* : to dig up or gash with a tusk

tusk·er \'təs-kər\ *n* : an animal with tusks; *esp* : a male elephant with two normally developed tusks

¹**tus·sle** \'təs-əl\ *vi* **tus·sled; tus·sling** \'təs-ling, -ə-ling\ : to struggle roughly : SCUFFLE [Middle English *tussillen*]

²**tussle** *n* **1** : a physical contest or struggle : SCUFFLE **2** : a rough argument, controversy, or struggle against difficult odds

tus·sock \'təs-ək\ *n* : a compact tuft especially of grass or sedge; *also* : a hummock in marsh bound together by plant roots [origin unknown] — **tus·socky** \'təs-ə-kē\ *adj*

tussock moth *n* : any of numerous dull-colored moths that usually have wingless females and larvae with long tufts of hair

tut *a t-sound made by suction rather than explosion; often read as* 'tət\ *or* **tut–tut** *interj* — used to express disapproval or disbelief [origin unknown]

tu·tee \tü-'tē, tyü-\ *n* : one who is being tutored

tu·te·lage \'tüt-l-ij, 'tyüt-\ *n* **1** : an act of guarding or protecting : GUARDIANSHIP **2** : the state of being under a guardian or tutor; *also* : the right, power, or influence of a tutor over a pupil **3** : INSTRUCTION [Latin *tutela* "protection, guardian", from *tueri* "to look at, guard"]

tu·te·lar \'tüt-l-ər, 'tyüt-\ *adj* : TUTELARY

tu·te·lary \'tüt-l-,er-ē, 'tyüt-\ *adj* **1** : having the guardianship of a person or a thing ⟨*tutelary* deities⟩ **2** : of or relating to a guardian ⟨*tutelary* authority⟩

¹**tu·tor** \'tüt-ər, 'tyüt-\ *n* : a person charged with the instruction and guidance of another: as **a** : a private teacher **b** : a college teacher especially in a British university who guides the individual studies of undergraduates in a particular field **c** : a college or university teacher ranking below an instructor **d** : a college or university officer having administrative or counseling functions [Latin, "guardian, tutor", from *tueri* "to look at, guard"] — **tu·tor·ship** \-,ship\ *n*

²**tutor** *vb* : to teach usually individually

¹**tu·to·ri·al** \tü-'tōr-ē-əl, tyü-, -'tor-\ *adj* : of, relating to, or involving a tutor

²**tutorial** *n* : a class conducted by a tutor for one student or a small number of students

tut·ti–fruit·ti \,tüt-ē-'früt-ē\ *n* : a confection or ice cream containing chopped usually candied fruits [Italian *tutti frutti*, literally, "all fruits"]

tu·tu \'tü-tü\ *n* : a very short projecting skirt worn by a ballerina [French, from baby talk *cucu*, *tutu* "backside", alteration of *cul*]

tu–whit tu–whoo \tə-,hwit-tə-'hwü, -,wit-tə-'wü\ *n* : the cry of an owl [imitative]

tux \'təks\ *n* : TUXEDO

tux·e·do \,tək-'sēd-ō\ *n, pl* **-dos** *or* **-does** : a semiformal dress suit for men [*Tuxedo* Park, New York] □ ORIGIN *Tuxedo* can be traced back to a Delaware Indian word meaning "wolf". The Delawares of eastern North America belonged to three groups named from the turkey, the turtle, and the wolf. *P'tuksit*, the Delaware word for "wolf", was used as a name for the third group. In the 18th century European Americans gave the name of the P'tuksit, anglicized as *Tuxedo*, to a village in southeastern New York. In the 1880's a large tract of land called Tuxedo Park, near the village and on the shore of Tuxedo Lake, became a fashionable resort community. It was here, near the turn of the century, that some young men began to wear dress jackets without tails. The new style which they made popular was soon called *tuxedo*.

tu·yere \twē-'eər\ *n* : a nozzle through which an air blast is delivered to a forge or blast furnace [French *tuyère*, from *tuyau* "pipe"]

TV \'tē-'vē\ *n* : TELEVISION [*tele*v*ision*]

twa \'twä\ *or* **twae** \'twä, 'twē\ *Scottish variant of* TWO

twad·dle \'twäd-l\ *n* : silly idle talk : DRIVEL [probably alteration of English dialect *twattle*]

twain \'twān\ *n* **1** : TWO **2** : COUPLE, PAIR [Old English *twēgen*, adj. and pron., "two"]

¹**twang** \'twang\ *n* **1** : a harsh quick ringing sound like that of a plucked bowstring **2 a** : nasal speech or resonance **b** : the characteristic speech of a region, locality, or group of people [imitative]

²**twang** *vb* **twanged; twang·ing** \'twang-ing\ **1** : to sound or cause to sound with a twang **2** : to speak with a nasal intonation

¹**tweak** \'twēk\ *vt* : to pinch and pull with a sudden jerk and twist [Old English *twiccian* "to pluck"]

²**tweak** *n* : an act of tweaking : PINCH

tweed \'twēd\ *n* **1** : a rough woolen fabric made usually in twill weaves **2** *pl* : tweed clothing; *esp* : a tweed suit [Scottish *tweel* "twill", from Middle English *twyll*]

tweedy \'twēd-ē\ *adj* **tweed·i·er; -est** **1** : of or resembling tweed **2 a** : given to wearing tweeds **b** : informal or suggestive of the outdoors in taste or habits

tweet \'twēt\ *n* : CHIRP [imitative] — **tweet** *vb*

tweet·er \'twēt-ər\ *n* : a small loudspeaker responsive only to the higher acoustic frequencies and reproducing sounds of high pitch — compare WOOFER

tweeze \'twēz\ *vt* : to pluck or remove with tweezers [back-formation from *tweezers*]

tweez·ers \'twē-zərz\ *n pl* : a small metal instrument that is used for plucking, holding, or manipulating, and consists of two legs joined at one end [obsolete *tweeze* "case for small implements", from French *étui*]

Twelfth Day *n* : EPIPHANY 1

Twelfth Night *n* **1** : the eve preceding Epiphany **2** : the evening of Epiphany

twelve \'twelv\ *n* **1** : one more than 11; *also* : a symbol representing this — see NUMBER table **2** *cap* : the twelve original disciples of Jesus **3** : the 12th in a set or series **4** : something having 12 units or members [Old English *twelf*] — **twelve** *adj or pron* — **twelfth** \'twelfth, 'twelftth\ *n* — **twelfth** *adj or adv*

twelve·month \-,mənth, -,məntth\ *n* : YEAR

twen·ty \'twent-ē\ *n, pl* **twenties** : one more than 19; *also* : a symbol representing this — see NUMBER table

[Old English *twēntig*] — **twenty** *adj or pron* — **twen-ti-eth** \-ē-əth\ *adj or n*

twen-ty-one \,twent-ē-'wən\ *n* : BLACKJACK 3

twen-ty-twen-ty *or* **20/20** \,twent-ē-'twent-ē\ *adj* : of normal acuity ⟨*twenty-twenty* vision⟩ [from the custom of testing vision chiefly at a distance of 20 feet]

twen-ty-two \,twent-ē-'tü\ *n* : a 22-caliber rifle or pistol — usually written .22

twerp *also* **twirp** \'twərp\ *n* : a silly, insignificant, or contemptible person [origin unknown]

twice \'twīs\ *adv* : two times ⟨*twice* absent⟩ ⟨*twice* two is four⟩ [Middle English *twiges*, *twies*, from Old English *twiga*]

twice-born \-'bȯrn\ *adj* : having undergone a spiritual rebirth or regeneration through religious conversion or renewal or by an initiation ceremony

twice-laid \-'lād\ *adj* : made from the ends of rope and strands of used rope ⟨*twice-laid* rope⟩

twice-told \,twīs-'tōld\ *adj* 1 : narrated twice 2 : HACKNEYED, TRITE — used chiefly in the phrase *a twice-told tale*

¹**twid-dle** \'twid-l\ *vb* **twid-dled; twid-dling** \'twid-ling, -l-ing\ 1 : to be busy with trifles : FIDDLE 2 : to rotate lightly or idly ⟨*twiddle* one's thumbs⟩ [origin unknown]

²**twiddle** *n* : an act of twiddling : TURN, TWIST

¹**twig** \'twig\ *n* : a small shoot or branch [Old English *twigge*] — **twigged** \'twigd\ *adj* — **twig-gy** \'twig-ē\ *adj*

²**twig** *vb* **twigged; twig-ging** : to catch on : NOTICE, UNDERSTAND [perhaps from Scottish Gaelic *tuig* "I understand"]

twi-light \'twī-,līt\ *n* 1 a : the light from the sky between full night and sunrise or between sunset and full night b : the time of twilight 2 a : a state of indistinctness b : a period of decline [Middle English, from *twi-* "two" + *light*] — **twilight** *adj*

twilight sleep *n* : a state produced by injection of morphine and scopolamine in which awareness and memory of pain is dulled or effaced

¹**twill** \'twil\ *n* 1 : a fabric with a twill weave 2 : a textile weave that produces a pattern of diagonal lines or ribs [Middle English *twyll*, from Old English *twilic* "having a double thread", from Latin *bilic-, bilix*, from *bi-* + *licium* "thread"]

²**twill** *vt* : to make (cloth) with a twill weave

¹**twin** \'twin\ *adj* 1 : born with one other or as a pair at one birth ⟨my *twin* brother⟩ ⟨*twin* girls⟩ 2 a : made up of two similar, related, or connected members or parts b : paired in a close or necessary relationship c : having or consisting of two identical units d : being one of a pair ⟨*twin* city⟩ [Old English *twinn* "twofold"]

²**twin** *n* 1 : either of two offspring born together 2 : one of two persons or things closely related to or resembling each other

³**twin** *vb* **twinned; twin-ning** 1 : to bring together in close association : COUPLE 2 : MATCH 4 3 : to bring forth twins

twin bill *n* : DOUBLEHEADER

¹**twine** \'twīn\ *n* 1 : a strong string of two or more strands twisted together 2 a : an act of interlacing b : TANGLE [Old English *twīn*]

²**twine** *vb* 1 a : to twist together b : to form by twining 2 a : to coil or cause to coil about a support b : WRAP ⟨*twined* their arms about each other⟩ 3 : MEANDER 1, WIND

¹**twinge** \'twinj\ *vb* **twinged; twing-ing** *or* **twinge-ing** : to affect with or feel a sudden sharp local pain [Old English *twengan* "to pinch"]

²**twinge** *n* 1 : a sudden sharp stab of pain 2 : a moral or emotional pang

¹**twin-kle** \'twing-kəl\ *vb* **twin-kled; twin-kling** \'twing-kə-ling, -kling\ 1 : to shine or cause to shine with a flickering or sparkling light : SCINTILLATE 2 : to appear bright with merriment 3 : to move or flutter rapidly :

FLIT [Old English *twinclian*] — **twin-kler** \-kə-lər, -klər\ *n*

²**twinkle** *n* 1 : a wink of the eyelids 2 : a very brief period : TWINKLING 3 : SPARKLE, FLICKER ⟨that *twinkle* in your eye⟩ — **twin-kly** \-kə-lē, -klē\ *adj*

twin-kling \'twing-kə-ling, -kling, *for 1b* -kling\ *n* 1 a : a winking of the eye b : INSTANT ⟨in a *twinkling*⟩ 2 : SCINTILLATION

twin-screw \'twin-'skrü\ *adj* : having a right-handed and a left-handed propeller parallel to each other on each side of the plane of the keel

¹**twirl** \'twərl\ *vb* 1 : to revolve or cause to revolve rapidly : SPIN, WHIRL ⟨*twirl* a baton⟩ 2 : to pitch in a baseball game 3 : CURL, TWIST ⟨*twirl* one's hair⟩ [perhaps of Scandinavian origin] — **twirl-er** *n*

²**twirl** *n* 1 : an act of twirling 2 : COIL, WHORL

twirp *variant of* TWERP

¹**twist** \'twist\ *vb* 1 : to unite by winding one thread, strand, or wire around another 2 : TWINE 2a, COIL 3 a : to turn so as to sprain or hurt ⟨*twisted* my ankle⟩ b : to alter the meaning of : PERVERT ⟨*twisted* the facts⟩ c : CONTORT ⟨*twist* one's face into a grin⟩ d : to pull off, rotate, or break by a turning force 4 : to follow a winding course 5 a : to turn or change shape under a turning force b : SQUIRM, WRITHE ⟨*twisting* in their seats⟩ 6 : to turn around [Middle English *twisten*, from Old English *-twist* "rope"]

²**twist** *n* 1 : something formed by twisting or winding: as a : a thread, yarn, or cord formed by twisting two or more strands together b : a baked piece of twisted dough c : tobacco leaves twisted into a thick roll 2 a : an act of twisting : the state of being twisted b : a spiral turn or curve 3 a : a turning aside : DEFLECTION b : ECCENTRICITY ⟨a *twist* of speech⟩ c : a distortion of meaning ⟨gave the facts a *twist*⟩ 4 a : an unexpected turn or development b : GIMMICK ⟨a new *twist* in advertising⟩

twist-er \'twis-tər\ *n* 1 : one that twists 2 : a tornado, waterspout, or dust devil in which the rotatory ascending movement of a column of air is visible

twit \'twit\ *vt* **twit-ted; twit-ting** : to poke fun at gently [Old English *ætwītan* "to reproach", from *æt* "at" + *wītan* "to blame"]

¹**twitch** \'twich\ *vb* 1 : to move or pull with a sudden motion 2 : PLUCK ⟨*twitched* at my sleeve⟩ 3 : to move jerkily [Middle English *twicchen*]

²**twitch** *n* 1 : an act of twitching 2 a : a short sharp contraction of muscle fibers b : a slight jerk of a body part

¹**twit-ter** \'twit-ər\ *vb* 1 : to utter successive chirping sounds 2 a : to talk in a chattering fashion b : GIGGLE, TITTER 3 : to shake with agitation : FLUTTER [Middle English *twiteren*]

²**twitter** *n* 1 : a trembling agitation 2 : a succession of chirping sounds 3 : a light chattering — **twit-tery** \-ə-rē\ *adj*

twixt \twikst, 'twikst\ *prep* : BETWEEN [Middle English *twix*, short for *betwix, betwixt*]

two \'tü\ *n* 1 : one more than one; *also* : a symbol representing this — see NUMBER table 2 : the second in a set or series 3 : something having two units or members [Old English *twā*, adj. and pron. (feminine and neuter)] — **two** *adj or pron*

two-base hit *n* : DOUBLE 1b

two-bit \,tü-'bit\ *adj* 1 : of the value of two bits 2 : being cheap, petty, or small-time

two bits *n sing or pl* 1 : QUARTER 3d 2 : something of small worth or importance

¹**two-by-four** \,tü-bə-'fȯr, -'fȯr\ *n* : a piece of lumber approximately 2 by 4 inches (5.1 by 10.2 centimeters) as sawed and usually 1⅝ by 3⅝ inches (4.1 by 9.2 centimeters) if dressed

²**two-by-four** *adj* 1 : measuring two units (as inches) by four 2 : very small or petty

two–dimensional *adj* **1** : having two dimensions **2** : lacking depth of characterization ⟨*two-dimensional* fiction⟩

two–faced \'tü-'fāst\ *adj* **1** : having two faces **2** : deceptively false — **two-faced·ly** \-'fā-səd-lē, -'fāst-lē\ *adv*

two–fist·ed \'tü-'fis-təd\ *adj* : VIRILE, VIGOROUS

two–fold \'tü-,fōld, -'fōld\ *adj* **1** : having two units or members **2** : of or equaling 200 percent — **twofold** *adv*

2, 4–D \,tü-,fōr-'dē, -,for-\ *n* : a white crystalline organic compound used as a weed killer

two–hand·ed \'tü-'han-dəd\ *adj* **1** : used with both hands ⟨a *two-handed* sword⟩ **2** : requiring two persons ⟨a *two-handed* saw⟩ **3** : having or efficient with two hands

two·pence \'təp-əns, *United States also* 'tü-,pens\ *also* **tup·pence** \'təp-əns\ *n* : the sum of two pence

two·pen·ny \'təp-nē, -ə-nē, *United States also* 'tü-,pen-ē\ *adj* : of the value of or costing twopence

two–ply \'tü-'plī\ *adj* : consisting of two strands or thicknesses

two·some \'tü-səm\ *n* : a group of two persons or things

two–step \'tü-,step\ *n* **1** : a ballroom dance in march or polka time **2** : a piece of music for the two-step — **two–step** *vi*

two–time \'tü-,tīm\ *vt* : to be unfaithful or treacherous to; *esp* : to be sexually unfaithful to (a spouse or lover)

two–toed sloth : any of several sloths of the genus Choloepus having two claws on each front foot and six or seven vertebrae in the neck — compare THREE-TOED SLOTH

two–way *adj* : involving two elements or allowing movement or use in two directions or manners

two–winged fly \,tü-,wingd-\ *n* : any of a large order (Diptera) of winged or rarely wingless insects (as a housefly, mosquito, or gnat) that have the anterior wings functional and the posterior wings reduced to balancers and that have segmented often headless, eyeless, and legless larvae

-ty *n suffix* : -ITY [Old French *-té*, from Latin *-tat-*, *-tas*]

ty·coon \tī-'kün\ *n* **1** : SHOGUN **2** : a business executive of exceptional wealth and power [Japanese *taikun*, from Chinese (Pekingese dialect) *ta*[4] "great" + *chün*[1] "ruler"] □ ORIGIN The shoguns were commanders-in-chief of the Japanese army, and so great was their influence that for centuries they were the real rulers of Japan, though they acted in the name of the emperor. When Commodore Matthew Perry went to Japan in 1853, he seems to have thought that he was negotiating with the emperor when in fact his antagonist was the shogun. The honorific *taikun* was used to describe the shogun to visiting Westerners. This title, borrowed from Chinese *ta*[4] *chün*[1], "great ruler", was more impressive than *shogun*, "general". Japanese *taikun*, usually spelled *tycoon* in English, caught on in the United States after Perry's expedition fired the public imagination. It was occasionally extended to describe any powerful person. Later specialization of meaning set in and *tycoon* became a term for an industrial magnate.

tying *present participle of* TIE

tyke *also* **tike** \'tīk\ *n* **1** : DOG 1a, CUR **2** : a small child [Old Norse *tīk* "bitch"]

tympani *variant of* TIMPANI

tym·pan·ic \tim-'pan-ik\ *adj* **1** : of, relating to, or being a tympanum **2** : resembling a drum

tympanic membrane *n* : EARDRUM

tym·pa·num \'tim-pə-nəm\ *n, pl* **-na** \-nə\ *also* **-nums** **1 a** (1) : EARDRUM (2) : MIDDLE EAR **b** : a thin tense membrane covering an organ of hearing or of sound-production of an insect **2 a** : the recessed usually triangular face of a pediment within the frame made by

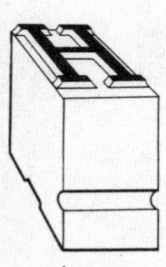

[1]type 2a

the upper and lower cornices **b** : the space within an arch and above a lintel or a subordinate arch [Latin, "drum, architectural panel", from Greek *tympanon* "drum"]

[1]**type** \'tīp\ *n* **1 a** : a person or thing believed to foreshadow or symbolize another **b** (1) : one having qualities of a higher category : MODEL (2) : a specimen or series of specimens on which a taxonomic species or subspecies is actually based **2 a** : a rectangular block typically of metal or wood bearing a relief character from which an inked print is made **b** : a collection of such blocks or the letters printed from them **c** : characters (as numbers, letters, or punctuation marks) for printing ⟨the *type* for this book has been photocomposed⟩ **3 a** : general form or character common to a number of individuals that distinguishes them as an identifiable class ⟨horses of draft *type*⟩ **b** : a particular kind, class, or group : SORT ⟨a seedless *type* of orange⟩ [Latin *typus* "image", from Greek *typos* "blow, impression, model", from *typtein* "to strike, beat"] SYN see KIND

[2]**type** *vb* **1** : TYPIFY **2** : TYPEWRITE **3** : to identify as belonging to a type: as **a** : to determine the natural type of (as a blood sample) **b** : TYPECAST — **typ·able** *or* **type·able** \'tī-pə-bəl\ *adj*

type·cast \'tīp-,kast\ *vt* **1** : to cast (an actor or actress) in a part calling for the same characteristics as those he or she possesses **2** : to cast (an actor or actress) repeatedly in the same type of role

type·face \'tīp-,fās\ *n* : all type of a single design

type·found·er \-,faún-dər\ *n* : one engaged in the design and production of metal printing type for hand composition — **type·found·ing** \-ding\ *n* — **type·found·ry** \-drē\ *n*

type metal *n* : an alloy that consists essentially of lead, antimony, and tin and is used in making printing type

type·script \-,skript\ *n* : something that is typewritten [*type* + manu*script*]

type·set \'tīp-,set\ *vt* **-set; -set·ting** : to set in type : COMPOSE

type·set·ter \-,set-ər\ *n* : one that sets type for printing — **type·set·ting** \-,set-ing\ *n*

type·write \'tī-,prīt\ *vb* : to write with a typewriter

type·writ·er \'tī-,prīt-ər\ *n* **1** : a machine for writing in characters similar to those produced by printer's type by means of keyboard-operated types striking through an inked ribbon **2** : TYPIST

type·writ·ing \-,prīt-ing\ *n* **1** : the act or study of or skill in using a typewriter **2** : the printing done with a typewriter

typh·lo·sole \'tif-lə-,sōl\ *n* : a fold of the wall that projects into the cavity of the intestine of some invertebrates (as the earthworm) [Greek *typhlos* "blind" + *sōlēn* "pipe"]

ty·phoid \'tī-,foid, tī-'-, 'tī-'\ *adj* : of, relating to, or being typhoid fever

typhoid fever *n* : a communicable bacterial disease marked especially by fever, diarrhea, prostration, headache, and intestinal inflammation — called also *typhoid* [derived from New Latin *typhus*]

ty·phoon \tī-'fün\ *n* : a tropical cyclone occurring in the region of the Philippines or the China sea [earlier *touffon*, from Arabic *tūfān* "hurricane", from Greek *typhōn* "whirlwind"]

ty·phus \'tī-fəs\ *n* : a severe rickettsial disease marked by high fever, stupor alternating with delirium, intense headache, and a dark red rash and transmitted especially by body lice [New Latin, from Greek *typhos* "fever"]

typ·i·cal \'tip-i-kəl\ *adj* **1** : being or having the nature of a type ⟨*typical* species⟩ **2** : combining or exhibiting the essential characteristics of a group ⟨a *typical* suburban house⟩ SYN see REGULAR — **typ·i·cal·i·ty** \,tip-ə-'kal-ət-ē\ *n* — **typ·i·cal·ly** \'tip-i-kə-lē, -klē\ *adv* — **typ·i·cal·ness** \-kəl-nəs\ *n*

typ·i·fy \'tip-ə-,fī\ *vt* **-fied; -fy·ing 1 :** PREFIGURE 1, REP-
RESENT **2 :** to have or embody the essential or main
characteristics of
typ·ist \'tī-pəst\ *n* : one who typewrites
ty·po \'tī-pō\ *n, pl* **typos** : a typographical error
ty·pog·ra·pher \tī-'päg-rə-fər\ *n* **1 :** COMPOSITOR **2 :**
PRINTER a **3 :** a specialist in the choice and arrangement of type matter
ty·pog·ra·phy \-fē\ *n* : the style, arrangement, or appearance of typeset matter — **ty·po·graph·ic** \,tī-pə-
'graf-ik\ *adj* — **ty·po·graph·i·cal** \-'graf-i-kəl\ *adj* —
ty·po·graph·i·cal·ly \-i-kə-lē, -klē\ *adv*
typy *or* **typ·ey** \'tī-pē\ *adj* **typ·i·er; -est** : of superior
bodily conformation ⟨a *typy* steer⟩
ty·ran·ni·cal \tə-'ran-i-kəl, tī-\ *also* **ty·ran·nic** \-'ran-ik\
adj : of, relating to, or characteristic of a tyrant or tyranny : DESPOTIC — **ty·ran·ni·cal·ly** \-'ran-i-kə-lē, -klē\
adv
tyr·an·nize \'tir-ə-,nīz\ *vb* **1 :** to act like a tyrant **2 :** to
treat tyrannically — **tyr·an·niz·er** *n*
ty·ran·no·saur \tə-'ran-ə-,sòr, tī-\ *n* : a very large American flesh-eating dinosaur of the Cretaceous having
small forelegs and walking on its hind legs [derived
from Greek *tyrannos* "tyrant" + *sauros* "lizard"]
ty·ran·no·sau·rus \tə-,ran-ə-'sòr-əs, tī-\ *n* : TYRANNO-
SAUR
tyr·an·nous \'tir-ə-nəs\ *adj* : marked by tyranny; *esp* :
unjustly severe — **tyr·an·nous·ly** *adv*

tyr·an·ny \'tir-ə-nē\ *n, pl* **-nies 1 a :** a government in
which absolute power is held by a single ruler **b :** the
office, authority, and administration of such a ruler **2 :**
arbitrary and despotic government; *esp* : rigorous, cruel, and oppressive government **3 :** SEVERITY, RIGOR ⟨the
tyranny of the alarm clock⟩ **4 :** a tyrannical act [Mid-
dle French *tyrannie*, from Medieval Latin *tyrannia*,
from Latin *tyrannus* "tyrant"]
ty·rant \'tī-rənt\ *n* **1 :** an absolute ruler unrestrained
by law or constitution **2 a :** a ruler who exercises absolute power in an oppressive or brutal manner **b :**
one resembling such a tyrant in the harsh use of authority or power [Old French *tyran*, *tyrant*, from Latin *tyrannus*, from Greek *tyrannos*]
tyrant flycatcher *n* : any of a family of large American
flycatchers with a flattened bill usually hooked at the
tip
tyre *chiefly British variant of* TIRE
Tyr·i·an purple \,tir-ē-ən-\ *n* : a synthetic crimson or
purple dye formerly obtained by the ancient Greeks
and Romans from gastropod mollusks [*Tyre*, city of ancient Phoenicia]
ty·ro \'tī-rō\ *n, pl* **tyros** : a beginner in learning [Latin
tiro "young soldier, tyro"]
ty·ro·sine \'tī-rə-,sēn\ *n* : an amino acid obtained by
hydrolysis of proteins [derived from Greek *tyros*
"cheese"]
tzar \'zär, 'tsär, 'sär\ *variant of* CZAR

tyrannosaur

Uu

u \'yü\ *n, pl* **u's** *or* **us** \'yüz\ *often cap* : the 21st letter
of the English alphabet
ubiq·ui·tous \yü-'bik-wət-əs\ *adj* : existing or being everywhere at the same time : widely or generally present [from *ubiquity*, from Latin *ubique* "everywhere"]
— **ubiq·ui·tous·ly** *adv* — **ubiq·ui·tous·ness** *n* — **ubiq-
ui·ty** \-wət-ē\ *n*
U-boat \'yü-'bōt\ *n* : a German submarine [German *u-
boot*, short for *unterseeboot*, literally, "undersea
boat"]
ud·der \'əd-ər\ *n* **1 :** a large bag-shaped organ consisting of two or more mammary glands enclosed in a
common envelope and each provided with a nipple
2 : a mammary gland [Old English *ūder*]
UFO \,yü-ef-'ō\ *n, pl* **UFO's** *or* **UFOs** \-'ōz\ : an unidentified flying object; *esp* : FLYING SAUCER [*u*nidentified
*f*lying *o*bject]
ugh *often read as* 'əg *or* 'ək *or* 'ə\ *interj* — used to
indicate the sound of a cough or grunt or to express
disgust or horror [probably imitative]
ug·li·fy \'əg-li-,fī\ *vt* **-fied; -fy·ing** : to make ugly
ug·ly \'əg-lē\ *adj* **ug·li·er; -est 1 :** FRIGHTFUL ⟨an *ugly*
wound⟩ **2 a :** offensive to the sight : UNSIGHTLY **b :** offensive or unpleasing to any sense ⟨an *ugly* smell⟩ **3 :**
morally offensive or objectionable **4 a :** likely to cause
inconvenience or discomfort : TROUBLESOME ⟨an *ugly*
situation⟩ **b :** SURLY ⟨an *ugly* disposition⟩ — **ug·li·ness**
n [Old Norse *uggligr*, from *uggr* "fear"]
ugly duckling *n* : an unpromising child or thing actually
capable of developing into a person or thing worthy of
attention or respect [*The Ugly Duckling*, story by Hans

Christian Andersen in which a supposed ugly duckling
develops into a swan]
Ugri·an \'ü-grē-ən, 'yü-\ *n* : a member of the eastern
division of the Finno-Ugric peoples [Old Russian *Ugre*
"Hungarians"] — **Ugrian** *adj*
uh–huh *two m's separated by the voiceless sound* h,
ən-'hən, 'ən-,hən\ *interj* — used to indicate affirmation,
agreement, or gratification [probably imitative]
uh·lan \'ü-,län, 'ü-lən, 'yü-lən\ *n* : one of a body of Prussian light cavalry originally modeled on Tatar lancers
[German, from Polish *ulan*, from Turkish *oğlan* "boy,
servant"]
uin·ta·there \yu-'int-ə-,thiər\ *n* : any of a genus of extinct plant-eating ungulate mammals that somewhat
resembled elephants [*Uinta* county, Wyoming +
Greek *thērion* "beast"]
ukase \yü-'kās, -'kāz, 'yü-,; 'ü-,kāz\ *n* : an edict especially of a Russian emperor or government [French, from
Russian *ukaz*]
Ukrai·ni·an \yü-'krā-nē-ən\ *n* **1 :** a native or inhabitant
of the Ukraine **2 :** the Slavic language of the Ukrainian
people — **Ukrainian** *adj*
uku·le·le \,yü-kə-'lā-lē, ,ü-kə-\ *n* : a small guitar popularized in Hawaii that is strung usually with four
strings and is played with the fingers or a pick
[Hawaiian *'ukulele*, from *'uku* "flea" + *lele* "jumping"]
-u·lar \yə-lər, ə-lər\ *adj suffix* : of, relating to, or resembling ⟨valv*ular*⟩ [Latin *-ularis*, from *-ulus, -ula,
-ulum* "-ule" + *-aris* "-ar"]

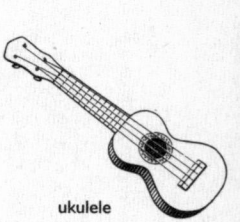

ukulele

\ə\ abut		\ng\ sing
\ər\ further		\ō\ bone
\a\ mat		\ò\ saw
\ā\ take		\òi\ coin
\ä\ cot, cart		\th\ thin
\aú\ out		\th\ this
\ch\ chin		\ü\ food
\e\ pet		\ú\ foot
\ē\ easy		\y\ yet
\g\ go		\yü\ few
\i\ tip		\yú\ cure
\ī\ life		\zh\ vision
\j\ job		

ul·cer \'əl-sər\ *n* **1** : a slow-healing open sore that often discharges pus **2** : something that festers and corrupts like an open sore [Latin *ulcer-, ulcus*]

ul·cer·ate \'əl-sə-ˌrāt\ *vb* : to become affected with or cause an ulcer : cause an ulcer in ⟨an *ulcerated* wound⟩ — **ul·cer·ation** \ˌəl-sə-'rā-shən\ *n*

ul·cer·ous \'əls-rəs, -ə-rəs\ *adj* **1** : of or marked by ulceration ⟨*ulcerous* lesions⟩ **2** : affected with an ulcer

-ule \ˌül, ˌyül\ *n suffix* : little one ⟨lob*ule*⟩ [Latin *-ulus, -ula, -ulum*]

ul·lage \'əl-ij\ *n* : the amount that a container (as a cask) lacks of being full [Middle French *eullage* "act of filling a cask", from *eullier* "to fill a cask", from Old French *ouil* "eye, bunghole", from Latin *oculus* "eye"]

ul·na \'əl-nə\ *n, pl* **ulnas** *or* **ul·nae** \-ˌnē, -ˌnī\ : the bone on the little-finger side of the human forearm; *also* : a corresponding part of vertebrates above fishes [Latin, "elbow"] — **ul·nar** \-nər\ *adj*

ul·ster \'əl-stər\ *n* : a long loose overcoat of heavy material [*Ulster,* Ireland]

ul·te·ri·or \ˌəl-'tir-ē-ər\ *adj* **1 a** : lying farther away : more remote **b** : situated beyond or on the farther side **2** : going beyond what is openly said or shown ⟨*ulterior* motives⟩ [Latin, "farther, further", derived from *uls* "beyond"] — **ul·te·ri·or·ly** *adv*

ul·ti·ma \'əl-tə-mə\ *n* : the last syllable of a word [Latin, feminine of *ultimus* "last"]

¹ul·ti·mate \'əl-tə-mət\ *adj* **1 a** : most remote in space or time : FARTHEST **b** : last in a progression : FINAL **c** : EVENTUAL **d** : EXTREME **3 2** : arrived at as the last result ⟨the *ultimate* question⟩ **3 a** : BASIC ⟨*ultimate* reality⟩ **b** : not capable of further division or separation : ELEMENTAL **4** : being the greatest [Medieval Latin *ultimatus* "last", from Late Latin *ultimare* "to come to an end", from Latin *ultimus* "last, farthest", derived from *uls* "beyond"] SYN see LAST — **ul·ti·mate·ly** *adv* — **ul·ti·mate·ness** *n*

²ultimate *n* : something ultimate

Ul·ti·ma Thu·le \ˌəl-tə-mə-'thü-lē, -'thyü-\ *n* : THULE [Latin, "farthest Thule"]

ul·ti·ma·tum \ˌəl-tə-'māt-əm, -'mät-\ *n, pl* **-tums** *or* **-ta** \-ə\ : a final proposition, condition, or demand; *esp* : one whose rejection will bring about an end of negotiations and a resort to direct action (as by force) [New Latin, from Medieval Latin *ultimatus* "last"]

ul·ti·mo \'əl-tə-ˌmō\ *adj* : of or occurring the month preceding the present [Latin *ultimo mense* "in the last month"]

¹ul·tra \'əl-trə\ *adj* : going beyond others or beyond due limit : EXTREME [*ultra-*]

²ultra *n* : EXTREMIST

ultra- *prefix* **1** : beyond in space : on the other side of ⟨*ultra*violet⟩ **2** : beyond the range or limits of : transcending ⟨*ultra*microscopic⟩ ⟨*ultra*sonic⟩ **3** : beyond what is ordinary, proper, or moderate : excessively ⟨*ultra*modern⟩ [Latin, from *ultra* "beyond", derived from *uls* "beyond"]

See *ultra-* and 2d element

ultracareful	ultraleftist	ultrarare
ultracasual	ultraliberal	ultrarational
ultracautious	ultraliberalism	ultrarealism
ultrachic	ultralow	ultrarealist
ultracivilized	ultramasculine	ultrarealistic
ultraclean	ultramilitant	ultrarefined
ultracommercial	ultranationalism	ultrarespectable
ultraconservative	ultranationalist	ultrarevolutionary
ultraconvenient	ultranationalistic	ultrarich
ultrafast	ultraorthodox	ultrarightist
ultrafastidious	ultrapatriotic	ultraromantic
ultrafeminine	ultrapowerful	ultrasafe
ultraglamorous	ultrapractical	ultrasecret
ultrahazardous	ultraprecision	ultrasensitive
ultrahigh	ultrapure	ultraserious
ultraleft	ultraradical	ultrasharp
ultraleftism	ultrarapid	ultrasmall

ul·tra·cen·tri·fuge \ˌəl-trə-'sen-trə-ˌfyüj\ *n* : a high-speed centrifuge able to separate small (as colloidal) particles — **ul·tra·cen·trif·u·gal** \-ˌsen-'trif-yə-gəl, -'trif-i-gəl\ *adj*

ul·tra·high frequency \ˌəl-trə-ˌhī-\ *n* : any radio frequency in the range between 300 and 3000 megahertz — abbreviation UHF

ul·tra·light \ˌəl-trə-'līt\ *adj* : extremely light in mass or weight ⟨an *ultralight* alloy⟩

¹ul·tra·ma·rine \ˌəl-trə-mə-'rēn\ *n* **1** : a deep blue pigment **2** : a vivid blue

²ultramarine *adj* : situated beyond the sea

ul·tra·mi·cro \ˌəl-trə-'mī-krō\ *adj* : being or dealing with something smaller than micro

ul·tra·mi·cro·scope \ˌəl-trə-'mī-krə-ˌskōp\ *n* : an apparatus that uses scattered light to view particles too small to be seen with an ordinary microscope

ul·tra·mi·cro·scop·ic \-ˌmī-krə-'skäp-ik\ *adj* **1** : too small to be seen with an ordinary microscope **2** : of or relating to an ultramicroscope — **ul·tra·mi·cro·scop·i·cal·ly** \-'skäp-i-kə-lē, -klē\ *adv*

ul·tra·mod·ern \ˌəl-trə-'mäd-ərn\ *adj* : extremely or excessively modern in idea, style, or tendency — **ul·tra·mod·ern·ist** \-ər-nəst\ *n*

ul·tra·short \-'shȯrt\ *adj* : very short

¹ul·tra·son·ic \-'sän-ik\ *adj* **1** : having a frequency above the human ear's ability to hear **2** : using, produced by, or relating to ultrasonic waves or vibrations — **ul·tra·son·i·cal·ly** \-'sän-i-kə-lē, -klē\ *adv*

²ultrasonic *n* : an ultrasonic wave or frequency

ul·tra·son·ics \-'sän-iks\ *n* : the science or technology of ultrasonic phenomena

ul·tra·sound \ˌəl-trə-'saund\ *n* **1** : vibrations of the same physical nature as sound but with frequencies above the range of human hearing **2** : the medical use of ultrasound and especially the diagnostic or therapeutic use of ultrasound and especially a technique involving the formation of a two-dimensional image used for the examination and measurement of internal body structures and the detection of bodily abnormalities **3** : a diagnostic examination using ultrasound

ul·tra·vi·o·let \-'vī-ə-lət\ *adj* **1** : situated beyond the visible spectrum at its violet end and having a wavelength shorter than those of visible light but longer than those of X rays **2** : relating to, producing, or using ultraviolet radiation — **ultraviolet** *n*

ultraviolet light *n* : ultraviolet radiation

ul·u·late \'əl-yə-ˌlāt\ *vi* : to utter a howl or wail [Latin *ululare*] — **ul·u·lant** \-lənt\ *adj* — **ul·u·la·tion** \ˌəl-yə-'lā-shən\ *n*

ul·va \'əl-və\ *n* : any of a genus of green marine algae with a thin flat edible thallus — called also *sea lettuce* [Latin, "sedge"]

um·bel \'əm-bəl\ *n* : an inflorescence typical of the carrot family in which the flower stalks appear to spring from the same point to form a flat or rounded flower cluster [Latin *umbella* "umbrella"] — **um·beled** *or* **um·belled** \-bəld\ *adj* — **um·bel·late** \'əm-bə-ˌlāt, ˌəm-'bel-ət\ *adj*

um·ber \'əm-bər\ *n* **1** : a brown earth valued as a pigment **2 a** : a moderate to dark yellowish brown **b** : a moderate brown [probably from obsolete *umber* "shade, color", from Middle French *umbre* "shade, shadow", from Latin *umbra*] — **umber** *adj*

um·bil·i·cal \ˌəm-'bil-i-kəl\ *adj* : of, relating to, or adjacent to the navel

umbilical cord *n* : a cord arising from the navel that connects the fetus with the placenta

um·bil·i·cate \ˌəm-'bil-i-kət\ *or* **um·bil·i·cat·ed** \-'bil-ə-ˌkāt-əd\ *adj* : having or suggesting an umbilicus — **um·bil·i·ca·tion** \ˌəm-ˌbil-ə-'kā-shən\ *n*

um·bil·i·cus \ˌəm-'bil-i-kəs\ *n, pl* **-bil·i·ci** \-'bil-ə-ˌkī, -ˌkē, -ˌsī\ *or* **-bil·i·cus·es** **1 a** : a depression in the abdominal wall at the point of attachment of the umbilical cord to the fetus **b** : any of several morphological depressions (as the hilum of a seed) **2** : a central point [Latin]

um·bles \\'əm-bəlz\\ *n pl* : the entrails of an animal and especially of a deer used as food [Middle English *nombles, umbles,* from Middle French *nomble* "fillet of beef, pork loin", from Latin *lumbulus* "little loin", from *lumbus* "loin"]

um·bo \\'əm-bō\\ *n, pl* **um·bo·nes** \\,əm-'bō-nēz\\ *or* **um·bos** **1** : the boss of a shield **2** : a rounded anatomical elevation; *esp* : one of the lateral prominences just above the hinge of a bivalve shell [Latin] — **um·bo·nate** \\'əm-bə-,nāt\\ *adj*

um·bra \\'əm-brə\\ *n, pl* **umbras** *or* **um·brae** \\-brē, -,brī\\ **1** : a shaded area **2** : the conical part of the shadow of a celestial body excluding all light from the primary source [Latin, "shade, shadow"]

um·brage \\'əm-brij\\ *n* **1 a** : SHADE 1a **b** : a growth (as of tangled branches) that gives shade **2** : RESENTMENT, OFFENSE (take *umbrage* at a remark) [Middle French, derived from Latin *umbra*] — **um·bra·geous** \\,əm-'brā-jəs\\ *adj* □ ORIGIN English *umbrage* originally meant "shade, shadow". This is also the meaning of its ultimate Latin source, *umbra. Umbrage* was often used figuratively, and in the 17th century the word took on the pejorative sense "a shadow of suspicion cast on someone". From this usage it was but a short semantic leap to "resentment, offense", which is the sense used in the common phrases "give umbrage" and "take umbrage".

um·brel·la \\,əm-'brel-ə\\ *n* **1** : a collapsible shade for protection against weather consisting of fabric stretched over hinged ribs radiating from a center pole; *esp* : a small one for carrying in the hand **2** : the bell-shaped or saucer-shaped largely jellylike body proper of most jellyfishes [Italian *ombrella,* from Latin *umbella,* from *umbra* "shade"]

umbrella plant *n* : an African sedge that has large terminal whorls of slender leaves and is often grown as a houseplant

umbrella tree *n* **1** : an American magnolia having large leaves clustered at the ends of the branches **2** : any of various trees or shrubs resembling an umbrella especially in the arrangement of leaves or the shape of the crown

Um·bri·an \\'əm-brē-ən\\ *n* **1 a** : a member of a people of ancient Italy occupying Umbria **b** : a native or inhabitant of the Italian province of Umbria **2** : the Italic language of ancient Umbria — **Umbrian** *adj*

umi·ak *also* **oo·mi·ak** \\'ü-mē-,ak\\ *n* : an open Eskimo boat made of a wooden frame covered with hide [Eskimo]

¹um·laut \\'um-,laut, 'üm-\\ *n* **1 a** : the change of a vowel caused by partial assimilation to a succeeding sound **b** : a vowel resulting from such partial assimilation **2** : a diacritical mark ¨ placed especially over a German vowel to indicate umlaut [German, from *um-* "around" + *laut* "sound"]

²umlaut *vt* **1** : to produce by umlaut **2** : to write or print an umlaut over

¹um·pire \\'əm-,pīr\\ *n* **1** : one having authority to decide finally a controversy or question between parties **2** : an official in a sport who conducts the game and rules on plays [Middle English *oumpere,* from *noumpere* (the phrase *a noumpere* being understood as *an oumpere*), from Middle French *nomper* "not equal, not paired", from *non-* + *per* "equal", from Latin *par*]

²umpire *vb* : to supervise or act as umpire (*umpire* a baseball game)

ump·teen \\'əmp-'tēn, 'əmp-, ,əm-, ,əmp-\\ *adj* : very many : indefinitely numerous [blend of earlier *umpty* "such and such" and *-teen* (as in *thirteen*)] — **umpteenth** \\-'tēnth, -'tēnth\\ *adj*

¹un- \\,ən, 'ən\\ *prefix* **1** : not : IN-, NON- — in adjectives formed from adjectives (*un*certain) (*un*skilled) or par-

ticiples (*un*dressed) and in nouns formed from nouns (*un*concern) **2** : opposite of : contrary to — in adjectives formed from adjectives (*un*constitutional) or participles (*un*believing) and in nouns formed from nouns (*un*reason) [Old English]

²un- *prefix* **1** : do the opposite of : reverse (a specified action) : DE- 1a, DIS- 1a — in verbs formed from verbs (*un*bend) (*un*dress) (*un*fold) **2 a** : deprive of : remove (a specified thing) from : remove — in verbs formed from nouns (*un*frock) (*un*sex) **b** : release from : free from — in verbs formed from nouns (*un*hand) **c** : remove from : extract from — in verbs formed from nouns (*un*bosom) **d** : cause to cease to be — in verbs formed from nouns (*un*man) **3** : completely (*un*loose) [Old English *on-, un-,* alteration of *and-* "against"]

See *un-* and 2d element

unabsorbed	unappreciated	unburied
unabsorbent	unappreciative	unburnable
unacademic	unapproachability	unburned
unacademically	unapproachable	unburnt
unaccented	unapproachably	unbusinesslike
unacceptability	unappropriated	uncalcified
unacceptable	unapproved	uncalled
unacceptably	unarguable	uncanceled
unaccepted	unarguably	uncanonical
unacclimated	unarmored	uncapitalized
unacclimatized	unarrogant	uncared-for
unaccommodating	unarticulated	uncaring
unaccredited	unartistic	uncarpeted
unachieved	unashamed	uncastrated
unacknowledged	unashamedly	uncataloged
unacquainted	unaspirated	uncatchable
unactable	unassailed	uncaught
unacted	unassigned	uncelebrated
unadaptable	unassimilable	uncensored
unadapted	unassimilated	uncensured
unaddressed	unassisted	uncertified
unadjusted	unassociated	unchallenged
unadmitted	unassuaged	unchallenging
unadoptable	unathletic	unchanged
unadventurous	unattainable	unchanging
unadvertised	unattended	unchaperoned
unaesthetic	unattested	uncharacteristic
unaffectionate	unattractive	uncharacteristically
unaffectionately	unattractively	uncharismatic
unaffiliated	unattractiveness	uncharming
unaffluent	unattributable	unchecked
unaffordable	unaudited	unchic
unafraid	unauthentic	unchivalrous
unaged	unauthorized	unchivalrously
unaggressive	unavailability	unchristened
unaging	unavailable	unchronicled
unaided	unavowed	unciliated
unair-conditioned	unawakened	unclad
unalienated	unawarded	unclaimed
unalike	unbaptized	unclarity
unalleviated	unbeautiful	unclassifiable
unallocated	unbeautifully	unclear
unaltered	unbelligerent	uncleared
unambiguous	unbeloved	unclimbable
unambiguously	unbemused	unclimbed
unambitious	unbitter	unclog
unamenable	unbleached	unclouded
unamended	unblemished	uncluttered
unamiable	unblended	uncoated
unamplified	unbookish	uncoerced
unamusing	unborrowed	uncollected
unanalyzable	unbought	uncollectible
unanalyzed	unbowdlerized	uncolored
unannotated	unbracketed	uncombed
unannounced	unbranded	uncombined
unanswered	unbreakable	uncomely
unanticipated	unbridgeable	uncomic
unapologetic	unbridged	uncommercial
unapologetically	unbrilliant	uncommon
unapparent	unbruised	uncompensated
unappeased	unbrushed	uncompetitive
unappetizing	unbudgeted	uncompetitiveness
unappetizingly	unbudging	uncomplaining

umbrella 1

umiak

\\ə\\ abut	\\ng\\ sing
\\ər\\ **further**	\\ō\\ bone
\\a\\ mat	\\ȯ\\ saw
\\ā\\ take	\\ȯi\\ coin
\\ä\\ cot, cart	\\th\\ **thin**
\\aú\\ **out**	\\th\\ **this**
\\ch\\ **chin**	\\ü\\ food
\\e\\ pet	\\ú\\ foot
\\ē\\ **easy**	\\y\\ **yet**
\\g\\ **go**	\\yü\\ few
\\i\\ tip	\\yú\\ cure
\\ī\\ life	\\zh\\ vision
\\j\\ **job**	

uncomplainingly
uncompleted
uncomplicated
uncompounded
uncomprehended
uncomprehending
unconcealed
unconfessed
unconfined
unconfirmed
unconfuse
uncongenial
unconnected
unconquered
unconsecrated
unconsolidated
unconstrained
unconsumed
uncontainable
uncontaminated
uncontemporary
uncontested
uncontradicted
uncontrived
uncontrolled
uncontroversial
uncontroversially
unconverted
unconvinced
unconvincing
unconvincingly
uncooked
uncooperative
uncoordinated
uncordial
uncorrected
uncorroborated
uncorrupt
uncountable
uncourageous
uncreative
uncredited
uncrippled
uncropped
uncrossable
uncrowded
uncultivable
uncultivated
uncultured
uncured
uncurious
uncurtained
uncustomarily
uncustomary
uncynical
uncynically
undamaged
undamped
undated
undecidable
undecipherable
undecked
undeclared
undecorated
undefeated
undefended
undefiled
undefinable
undefined
undeformed
undeliverable
undelivered
undemanding
undemocratic
undemocratically
undenominational
undependable
undescribable
undeserved
undeserving
undesired
undetectable

undetected
undeterminable
undetermined
undeterred
undeveloped
undiagnosable
undiagnosed
undialectical
undifferentiated
undigested
undigestible
undignified
undiluted
undiminished
undiminishing
undimmed
undiplomatic
undiplomatically
undischarged
undisciplined
undisclosed
undiscouraged
undiscoverable
undiscovered
undiscriminating
undiscussed
undismayed
undisputable
undisputed
undissolved
undistinguished
undistorted
undistracted
undistributed
undisturbed
undivided
undoctored
undoctrinaire
undocumented
undogmatic
undomesticated
undoubtable
undoubting
undrained
undramatic
undrinkable
undutiful
undutifully
undutifulness
undynamic
uneager
uneatable
uneaten
unedifying
unedited
uneducable
uneducated
unelected
unembarrassed
unembellished
unemotional
unemotionally
unemphatic
unemphatically
unenclosed
unencouraging
unencumbered
unendurable
unendurably
unenforceable
unenforced
unengaged
unenlarged
unenlightened
unenlightening
unenterprising
unenthusiastic
unenthusiastically
unenviable
unenvious
unescapable
unessential

unethical
unevaluated
unexamined
unexcelled
unexcitable
unexcited
unexciting
unexotic
unexpended
unexpired
unexplainable
unexplained
unexploded
unexploited
unexplored
unexposed
unexpressed
unexpurgated
unfading
unfaltering
unfalteringly
unfashionable
unfashionably
unfastidious
unfathomable
unfazed
unfeasible
unfeminine
unfenced
unfermented
unfertile
unfertilized
unfilled
unfiltered
unfired
unflamboyant
unflattering
unflyable
unfocused
unfond
unforced
unforeseeable
unforeseen
unforgivable
unforgiving
unformulated
unfortified
unfossiliferous
unframed
unfree
unfrozen
unfulfilled
unfunny
unfurnished
unfused
unfussy
ungallant
ungallantly
ungarnished
ungenial
ungenteel
ungentle
ungentlemanly
ungerminated
ungifted
unglamorized
unglamorous
ungraded
ungrammatical
ungrammatically
ungraspable
unguessable
unguided
unhackneyed
unhampered
unharmed
unharvested
unhatched
unhealed
unheated
unheeded
unheeding

unhelpful
unheralded
unheroic
unhesitating
unhesitatingly
unhindered
unhip
unhistorical
unhonored
unhoused
unhumorous
unhurt
unhygienic
unhysterical
unidentifiable
unidentified
unideological
unidiomatic
unilluminated
unimaginable
unimaginably
unimaginative
unimpaired
unimpassioned
unimpeded
unimportant
unimposing
unimpressed
unimpressive
unincorporated
unincubated
unindexed
unindicted
unindustrialized
uninfected
uninflected
uninfluenced
uninformed
uninhabitable
uninhabited
uninitiated
uninjured
uninoculated
uninspected
uninspired
uninspiring
uninstructed
uninstructive
uninsulated
uninsurable
uninsured
unintegrated
unintellectual
unintelligible
unintelligibly
unintended
unintentional
unintentionally
uninteresting
unintimidated
uninventive
uninvited
uninviting
uninvolved
unirradiated
unirrigated
unissued
unjointed
unjustifiable
unjustifiably
unjustified
unkept
unknowable
unknowing
unknowingly
unknowledgeable
unkosher
unlabeled
unladylike
unlamented
unleavened
unliberated

unlicensed
unlighted
unlikable
unlined
unlit
unliterary
unlobed
unlovable
unloved
unloving
unmalicious
unmanageable
unmanly
unmapped
unmarked
unmarketable
unmarred
unmarried
unmasculine
unmatchable
unmatched
unmated
unmeasurable
unmeasured
unmechanized
unmediated
unmelodious
unmemorable
unmentioned
unmerited
unmet
unmetabolized
unmilitary
unmilled
unmindful
unmixed
unmodernized
unmodified
unmolested
unmonitored
unmotivated
unmounted
unmovable
unmusical
unnameable
unnamed
unnecessary
unneeded
unnewsworthy
unnoticeable
unnoticed
unnourishing
unobjectionable
unobservable
unobserved
unobstructed
unobtainable
unofficial
unofficially
unopenable
unopened
unopposed
unordered
unoriginal
unorthodox
unorthodoxly
unostentatious
unostentatiously
unowned
unoxygenated
unpaid
unpainted
unpalatable
unparasitized
unpardonable
unpartitioned
unpassable
unpasteurized
unpatentable
unpatriotic
unpaved
unpedantic

unperceived
unperceptive
unperformable
unperformed
unpersuaded
unpersuasive
unperturbed
unpicturesque
unplanned
unplausible
unplayable
unpleased
unpleasing
unplowed
unpoetic
unpoliced
unpolished
unpolluted
unposed
unpractical
unpredictability
unpredictable
unpredictably
unpremeditated
unprepared
unpreparedness
unprepossessing
unpressed
unpressured
unpressurized
unpretty
unprocessed
unproductive
unprogrammed
unprogressive
unprompted
unpronounceable
unpronounced
unpropitious
unprosperous
unprotected
unprovable
unproved
unproven
unprovided
unprovoked
unpruned
unpublicized
unpublishable
unpublished
unpunctual
unpunctuality
unpunished
unquenchable
unquestioned
unraised
unranked
unrationed
unravished
unreachable
unrealizable
unrealized
unreasoned
unreceptive
unreclaimable
unrecognizable
unrecognizably
unrecognized
unreconcilable
unreconciled
unrecorded
unrecoverable
unredeemed
unredressed
unrefined
unreflective
unreformed
unregarded
unregistered
unregulated
unrehearsed
unreinforced

Note: column 4 items partial list: unhelpful ... uninvolved continues with:
unirradiated
unirrigated
unissued
unjointed

(the following entries also appear in column 4:)
uninvolved
unirradiated

unrelated	unserious	unsystematized
unrelaxed	unserved	untactful
unreliability	unserviceable	untagged
unreliable	unshaded	untainted
unrelieved	unshakable	untalented
unreluctant	unshaken	untamable
unremarkable	unshapely	untamed
unremembered	unshared	untapped
unreminiscent	unsharp	untarnished
unremovable	unshaven	untaxed
unrepentant	unshorn	unteachable
unrepentantly	unsifted	untechnical
unreported	unsigned	untempered
unrepresentative	unsinkable	untenanted
unrepresented	unslaked	untended
unrepressed	unsmiling	untestable
unrequited	unsoiled	untested
unresistant	unsold	unthreatening
unresolvable	unsoldierly	unthrifty
unresolved	unsolicited	untillable
unrespectable	unsolvable	untilled
unrestful	unsolved	untiring
unrestricted	unsorted	untouched
unretouched	unsown	untraceable
unreturnable	unspecialized	untraditional
unrevealed	unspecifiable	untrained
unreviewed	unspecific	untrammeled
unrevised	unspecified	untranslatable
unrevolutionary	unspectacular	untranslated
unrewarded	unspent	untraveled
unrewarding	unspiritual	untreated
unrhymed	unsplit	untrimmed
unrhythmic	unspoiled	untrod
unridable	unspoken	untrodden
unripened	unsportsmanlike	untroubled
unromantic	unsprayed	untrustworthy
unromantically	unsquared	untufted
unromanticized	unstained	untypical
unroofed	unstandardized	untypically
unrushed	unsterile	ununderstandable
unsafe	unsterilized	unusable
unsaid	unstinted	unutilized
unsalable	unstinting	unvaried
unsalaried	unstratified	unvarying
unsalted	unstructured	unventilated
unsalvageable	unstylish	unverifiable
unsanctioned	unsubdued	unversed
unsanitary	unsubsidized	unviable
unsatisfactorily	unsubstantiated	unvisited
unsatisfactoriness	unsubtle	unwanted
unsatisfactory	unsuited	unwarlike
unsatisfied	unsullied	unwarranted
unscalable	unsupervised	unwavering
unscarred	unsupported	unwaveringly
unscented	unsure	unwaxed
unscheduled	unsurpassable	unweaned
unscholarly	unsurpassed	unwearable
unscreened	unsurprised	unweathered
unscriptural	unsurprising	unwed
unseasoned	unsurprisingly	unwelcome
unseaworthy	unsusceptible	unwilling
unsecured	unsuspected	unwillingly
unsegmented	unsuspecting	unwillingness
unselfconscious	unsuspicious	unwinnable
unselfconsciously	unsustainable	unwomanly
unselfconsciousness	unswayed	unwon
unsensational	unsweetened	unworkable
unsensitized	unsympathetic	unworked
unsent	unsynchronized	unworried
unsentimental	unsystematic	unwounded
unseparated	unsystematically	unwoven

un·abashed \,ən-ə-'basht\ *adj* : not abashed — **un·abash·ed·ly** \-'bash-əd-lē\ *adv*

un·abat·ed \,ən-ə-'bāt-əd\ *adj* : not abated : at full strength or force — **un·abat·ed·ly** *adv*

un·able \,ən-'ā-bəl, 'ən-\ *adj* : not able : INCAPABLE

un·abridged \,ən-ə-'brijd\ *adj* **1** : not abridged : COMPLETE ⟨an *unabridged* reprint of a novel⟩ **2** : complete of its class : not based on one larger ⟨an *unabridged* dictionary⟩

un·ac·com·mo·dat·ed \,ən-ə-'käm-ə-,dāt-əd\ *adj* : not accommodated : UNPROVIDED

un·ac·com·pa·nied \,ən-ə-'kəmp-nēd, -ə-nēd\ *adj* : not accompanied; *esp* : being without instrumental accompaniment

un·ac·count·able \,ən-ə-'kaunt-ə-bəl\ *adj* **1** : not to be accounted for : INEXPLICABLE **2** : not to be called to account : not responsible — **un·ac·count·abil·i·ty** \-,kaunt-ə-'bil-ət-ē\ *n* — **un·ac·count·ably** \,ən-ə-'kaunt-ə-blē\ *adv*

un·ac·count·ed \-'kaunt-əd\ *adj* : not accounted or made clear — often used with for

un·ac·cus·tomed \,ən-ə-'kəs-təmd\ *adj* **1** : UNUSUAL, UNFAMILIAR ⟨*unaccustomed* scenes⟩ **2** : not used : not habituated ⟨*unaccustomed* to travel⟩

una cor·da \,ü-nə-'kord-ə\ *adv or adj* : with soft pedal depressed — used as a direction in piano music [Italian, literally, "one string"]

una corda pedal *n* : SOFT PEDAL 1

un·adorned \,ən-ə-'dornd\ *adj* : not adorned : lacking embellishment or decoration

un·adul·ter·at·ed \,ən-ə-'dəl-tə-,rāt-əd\ *adj* : free from adulterants : PURE — **un·adul·ter·at·ed·ly** *adv*

un·ad·vised \,ən-əd-'vīzd\ *adj* **1** : done without due consideration : RASH **2** : not prudent — **un·ad·vis·ed·ly** \-'vī-zəd-lē\ *adv*

un·af·fect·ed \,ən-ə-'fek-təd\ *adj* **1** : not influenced or changed mentally, physically, or chemically **2** : free from affectation : GENUINE — **un·af·fect·ed·ly** *adv* — **un·af·fect·ed·ness** *n*

un·alien·able \,ən-'āl-yə-nə-bəl, 'ən-, -'ā-lē-ə-nə-\ *adj* : INALIENABLE

un·aligned \,ən-l-'īnd\ *adj* : not associated with any one of competing international blocs ⟨*unaligned* nations⟩

un·al·loyed \,ən-l-'oid\ *adj* : free from all admixture : PURE ⟨*unalloyed* metal⟩ ⟨*unalloyed* bliss⟩

un·al·ter·able \,ən-'ol-trə-bəl, -tə-rə-, 'ən-\ *adj* : not capable of being changed ⟨*unalterable* hatred⟩ — **un·al·ter·ably** \-blē\ *adv*

un–Amer·i·can \,ən-ə-'mer-ə-kən\ *adj* : not American : not characteristic of or consistent with American customs or principles — **un–Amer·i·can·ism** \-kə-,niz-əm\ *n*

un·aneled \,ən-ə-'nēld\ *adj, archaic* : not having received extreme unction [earlier *anele* "to anoint", from Old English *an* "on" + *ele* "oil", from Latin *oleum*]

una·nim·i·ty \,yü-nə-'nim-ət-ē\ *n* : the quality or state of being unanimous

unan·i·mous \yu-'nan-ə-məs\ *adj* **1** : being of one mind : agreeing completely **2** : assented to by all ⟨a *unanimous* vote⟩ [Latin *unanimus,* from *unus* "one" + *animus* "mind"] — **unan·i·mous·ly** *adv*

un·an·swer·able \,ən-'ans-rə-bəl, -ə-rə-, 'ən-\ *adj* : not answerable; *esp* : IRREFUTABLE ⟨the arguments were *unanswerable*⟩

un·ap·peal·able \,ən-ə-'pē-lə-bəl\ *adj* : not appealable : not subject to appeal

un·ap·peal·ing \,ən-ə-'pē-ling\ *adj* : lacking appeal

un·ap·peas·able \,ən-ə-'pē-zə-bəl\ *adj* : not to be appeased : IMPLACABLE — **un·ap·peas·ably** \-blē\ *adv*

un·apt \,ən-'apt, 'ən-\ *adj* **1** : UNSUITABLE, INAPPROPRIATE **2** : not accustomed and not likely **3** : DULL, BACKWARD ⟨*unapt* students⟩ — **un·apt·ly** \-'ap-tlē, -lē\ *adv* — **un·apt·ness** \-'ap-nəs, -'apt-\ *n*

un·arm \,ən-'ärm, 'ən-\ *vt* : DISARM 1

un·armed \-'ärmd\ *adj* : not armed or armored

un·asked \,ən-'askt, -'ast, -'askt, -'ast, 'ən-\ *adj* : not asked or asked for

un·as·sail·able \,ən-ə-'sā-lə-bəl\ *adj* : not assailable : not liable to doubt, attack, or question — **un·as·sail·ably** \-blē\ *adv*

un·as·ser·tive \,ən-ə-'sərt-iv\ *adj* : not assertive : MODEST, SHY

\ə\ abut	\ng\ sing
\ər\ further	\ō\ bone
\a\ mat	\o\ saw
\ā\ take	\oi\ coin
\ä\ cot, cart	\th\ thin
\au\ out	\th\ this
\ch\ chin	\ü\ food
\e\ pet	\u\ foot
\ē\ easy	\y\ yet
\g\ go	\yü\ few
\i\ tip	\yu\ cure
\ī\ life	\zh\ vision
\j\ job	

un·as·sum·ing \‚ən-ə-'sü-ming\ *adj* : not bold or forward : MODEST — **un·as·sum·ing·ly** \-ming-lē\ *adv* — **un·as·sum·ing·ness** *n*

un·at·tached \‚ən-ə-'tacht\ *adj* **1** : not attached **2** : not married or engaged

un·avail·ing \‚ən-ə-'vā-ling\ *adj* : of no avail : not successful : VAIN — **un·avail·ing·ly** \-ling-lē\ *adv*

un·avoid·able \‚ən-ə-'vȯid-ə-bəl\ *adj* : not avoidable — **un·avoid·ably** \-blē\ *adv*

¹**un·aware** \‚ən-ə-'waər, -'weər\ *adv* : UNAWARES

²**unaware** *adj* : not aware : IGNORANT — **un·aware·ness** *n*

un·awares \-'waərz, -'weərz\ *adv* **1** : without knowing **2** : without warning : by surprise ⟨taken *unawares*⟩

un·backed \‚ən-'bakt, 'ən-\ *adj* : not supported or encouraged

un·bal·ance \‚ən-'bal-əns, 'ən-\ *vt* : to put out of balance

un·bal·anced \-ənst\ *adj* **1** : not in equilibrium **2** : mentally deranged **3** : not adjusted so as to make credits equal to debits ⟨an *unbalanced* account⟩

un·bal·last·ed \‚ən-'bal-ə-stəd, 'ən-\ *adj* : not furnished with or steadied by ballast : UNSTEADY

un·bar \‚ən-'bär, 'ən-\ *vt* : to remove a bar from : UNBOLT, OPEN

un·barred \-'bärd\ *adj* **1** : not secured by a bar : UNLOCKED **2** : not marked with bars

un·bear·able \‚ən-'bar-ə-bəl, 'ən-, -'ber-\ *adj* : greater than can be borne ⟨*unbearable* pain⟩ — **un·bear·ably** \-blē\ *adv*

un·beat·able \-'bēt-ə-bəl\ *adj* : not capable of being defeated

un·beat·en \-'bēt-n̩\ *adj* **1** : not pounded or beaten **2** : not traveled **3** : not defeated

un·be·com·ing \‚ən-bi-'kəm-ing\ *adj* : not becoming : UNSUITABLE SYN see INDECOROUS — **un·be·com·ing·ly** \-ing-lē\ *adv* — **un·be·com·ing·ness** *n*

un·be·known \‚ən-bi-'nōn\ *or* **un·be·knownst** \-'nōnst\ *adj* : happening without one's knowledge : UNKNOWN — usually used with to

un·be·lief \‚ən-bə-'lēf\ *n* : the withholding or absence of belief : DOUBT □ SYN DISBELIEF, INCREDULITY: UNBELIEF suggests withholding of belief especially in religious matters ⟨warned against skepticism and *unbelief*⟩ DISBELIEF stresses rejection of what is asserted or stated ⟨a firm *disbelief* in ghosts⟩ INCREDULITY implies a skeptical attitude ⟨received the news with *incredulity*⟩ and suggests rejection on general grounds rather than immediate evidence

un·be·liev·able \-'lē-və-bəl\ *adj* : too improbable for belief — **un·be·liev·ably** \-blē\ *adv*

un·be·liev·er \-'lē-vər\ *n* **1** : one who does not believe : DOUBTER **2** : one who does not believe in a particular religious faith

un·be·liev·ing \-'lē-ving\ *adj* : marked by unbelief — **un·be·liev·ing·ly** \-ving-lē\ *adv*

un·bend \‚ən-'bend, 'ən-\ *vb* **-bent** \-'bent\; **-bend·ing** **1** : to free from being bent : make or become straight **2** : to make or become less stiff or more affable : RELAX

un·bend·ing \‚ən-'ben-ding, 'ən-\ *adj* : formal and distant in manner

un·be·seem·ing \‚ən-bi-'sē-ming\ *adj* : not befitting : UNBECOMING

un·bi·ased \‚ən-'bī-əst, 'ən-\ *adj* : free from bias ⟨an *unbiased* opinion⟩; *esp* : UNPREJUDICED SYN see FAIR

un·bid·den \-'bid-n̩\ *also* **un·bid** \-'bid\ *adj* : not bidden : UNASKED

un·bind \-'bīnd\ *vt* **-bound** \-'baund\; **-bind·ing** **1** : to remove a band from : free from fastenings **2** : to set free : RELEASE

un·bit·ted \-'bit-əd\ *adj* : UNRESTRAINED 1, UNBRIDLED

un·blenched \-'blencht\ *adj* : not disconcerted : UNDAUNTED

un·blessed *also* **un·blest** \-'blest\ *adj* **1** : not blessed **2** : EVIL 1a

un·blush·ing \-'bləsh-ing\ *adj* **1** : not blushing **2** : SHAMELESS, UNABASHED — **un·blush·ing·ly** \-ing-lē\ *adv*

un·bod·ied \-'bäd-ēd\ *adj* **1** : having no body; *also* : freed from the body **2** : FORMLESS

un·bolt \‚ən-'bōlt, 'ən-\ *vt* : to open or unfasten by withdrawing a bolt

un·bolt·ed \-'bōl-təd\ *adj* : not sifted ⟨*unbolted* flour⟩

un·born \-'bȯrn\ *adj* **1** : not born : not brought into life **2** : still to appear : FUTURE ⟨*unborn* generations⟩

un·bos·om \-'bùz-əm\ *vb* **1** : to give expression to : DISCLOSE, REVEAL **2** : to disclose one's thoughts or feelings

un·bound \-'baund\ *adj* : not bound: as **a** (1) : not fastened or tied up (2) : not confined ⟨an *unbound* spirit⟩ **b** : not having the leaves fastened together ⟨an *unbound* book⟩

un·bound·ed \-'baun-dəd\ *adj* : having no limits ⟨*unbounded* space⟩ ⟨*unbounded* enthusiasm⟩

un·bowed \‚ən-'baud, 'ən-\ *adj* : not bowed down; *esp* : not subdued

un·brace \-'brās\ *vt* **1** : to free or detach by or as if by untying or removing a brace or bond **2** : to make feeble : WEAKEN

un·braid \-'brād\ *vt* : to separate the strands of

un·branched \‚ən-'brancht, 'ən-\ *adj* : free from or not divided into branches ⟨a straight *unbranched* trunk⟩ ⟨a leaf with *unbranched* veins⟩

un·bred \-'bred\ *adj* : not bred : never having been bred ⟨an *unbred* heifer⟩

un·bri·dled \-'brīd-l̩d\ *adj* **1** : UNRESTRAINED ⟨greeted the star's appearance with *unbridled* enthusiasm⟩ **2** : not confined by a bridle

un·bro·ken \-'brō-kən\ *adj* **1** : not damaged : WHOLE **2** : not subdued or tamed ⟨an *unbroken* colt⟩ **3** : not interrupted : CONTINUOUS ⟨an *unbroken* row of trees⟩

un·buck·le \‚ən-'bək-əl, 'ən-\ *vt* : to unfasten the buckle of

un·build \-'bild\ *vt* : to pull down : DEMOLISH, RAZE

un·built \-'bilt\ *adj* **1** : not built : not yet constructed **2** : not built on ⟨an *unbuilt* plot⟩

un·bur·den \-'bərd-n̩\ *vt* **1** : to free from a burden **2** : to relieve oneself of ⟨as cares, fears, or worries⟩ : cast off

un·but·ton \-'bət-n̩\ *vt* : to unfasten the buttons of ⟨as a garment⟩

un·but·toned \-nd\ *adj* **1 a** : not buttoned **b** : not provided with buttons **2** : not under constraint

un·cage \‚ən-'kāj, 'ən-\ *vt* : to release from or as if from a cage

un·called–for \-'kȯld-‚fȯr\ *adj* : not called for : not needed or wanted : not proper ⟨an *uncalled-for* remark⟩

un·can·ny \-'kan-ē\ *adj* **1** : seeming to have a supernatural character or origin : MYSTERIOUS **2** : being beyond what is normal or expected : suggesting superhuman or supernatural powers ⟨an *uncanny* sense of direction⟩ SYN see WEIRD — **un·can·ni·ly** \-'kan-l-ē\ *adv*

un·cap \-'kap\ *vt* : to remove a cap or covering from

un·ceas·ing \-'sē-sing\ *adj* : never ceasing : CONTINUOUS, INCESSANT — **un·ceas·ing·ly** \-'sē-sing-lē\ *adv*

un·cer·e·mo·ni·ous \‚ən-‚ser-ə-'mō-nē-əs\ *adj* : acting without or lacking ordinary courtesy — **un·cer·e·mo·ni·ous·ly** *adv* — **un·cer·e·mo·ni·ous·ness** *n*

un·cer·tain \‚ən-'sərt-n̩, 'ən-\ *adj* **1** : not determined or fixed ⟨an *uncertain* quantity⟩ **2** : subject to chance or change : not dependable ⟨an *uncertain* temper⟩ **3** : not sure ⟨*uncertain* of the truth⟩ **4** : not definitely known — **un·cer·tain·ly** *adv* — **un·cer·tain·ness** \-n-nəs, -n-əs\ *n*

un·cer·tain·ty \-n-tē\ *n* **1** : lack of certainty **2** : something that is uncertain SYN see DOUBT

un·chain \‚ən-'chān, 'ən-\ *vt* : to free by or as if by removing a chain : set loose

un·chancy \-'chan-sē\ *adj* **1** *chiefly Scottish* : ILL-FATED **2** *chiefly Scottish* : DANGEROUS

un·change·able \-'chān-jə-bəl\ *adj* : not changing or to be changed : IMMUTABLE — **un·change·able·ness** *n* — **un·change·ably** \-blē\ *adv*

un·charged \-'chärjd\ *adj* : having no electric charge

un·char·i·ta·ble \-'char-ət-ə-bəl\ *adj* : lacking in charity; *esp* : severe in judging others — **un·char·i·ta·ble·ness** *n* — **un·char·i·ta·bly** \-blē\ *adv*

un·chart·ed \-'chärt-əd\ *adj* : not recorded or plotted on a map, chart, or plan : UNKNOWN

un·chaste \-'chāst\ *adj* : not chaste : lacking in chastity — **un·chaste·ly** *adv* — **un·chaste·ness** \-'chāst-nəs, -'chās-\ *n* — **un·chas·ti·ty** \-'chas-tət-ē\ *n*

un·chris·tian \-'kris-chən\ *adj* **1** : not of the Christian faith **2 a** : contrary to the Christian spirit or character **b** : BARBAROUS **2** UNCIVILIZED

un·cir·cum·cised \,ən-'sər-kəm-,sīzd, 'ən-\ *adj* **1** : not circumcised **2** : spiritually impure : HEATHEN — **un·cir·cum·ci·sion** \,ən-,sər-kəm-'sizh-ən\ *n*

un·civ·il \,ən-'siv-əl, 'ən-\ *adj* **1** : not civilized : BARBAROUS **2** : lacking in courtesy : ILL-MANNERED

un·civ·i·lized \-'siv-ə-,līzd\ *adj* **1** : not civilized : BARBAROUS **2** : remote from civilization : WILD

un·clasp \-'klasp\ *vb* **1** : to open the clasp of **2** : to loosen a hold or grip or the hold or grip of

un·clas·si·fied \-'klas-ə-,fīd\ *adj* : not classified; *esp* : not subject to a security classification

un·cle \'əng-kəl\ *n* **1** : the brother of one's father or mother **2** : the husband of one's aunt **3** — used as a cry of surrender ⟨was forced to cry *uncle*⟩ [Old French, from Latin *avunculus* "mother's brother"]

un·clean \,ən-'klēn, 'ən-\ *adj* **1** : morally or spiritually impure **2** : prohibited by ritual law for use or contact **3** : DIRTY **1**, FILTHY — **un·clean·ness** \-'klēn-nəs\ *n*

¹un·clean·ly \-'klen-lē\ *adj* : morally or physically unclean — **un·clean·li·ness** *n*

²un·clean·ly \-'klēn-lē\ *adv* : in an unclean manner

un·clench \-'klench\ *vb* : to open from a clenched position : RELAX

Un·cle Sam \,əng-kəl-'sam\ *n* **1** : the United States government personified **2** : the American nation or people [expansion of *U.S.*, abbreviation of *United States*]

Uncle Tom \-'täm\ *n* : a black eager to win the approval of whites and willing to cooperate with them [*Uncle Tom*, pious and faithful slave in the novel *Uncle Tom's Cabin* by Harriet Beecher Stowe]

un·cloak \,ən-'klōk, 'ən-\ *vb* **1** : to remove a cloak or cover from **2** : REVEAL **1**, UNMASK **3** : to take off a cloak

un·close \-'klōz\ *vb* : OPEN

un·closed \-'klōzd\ *adj* : not closed or settled : not concluded

un·clothe \-'klōth̲\ *vt* : to strip of clothes or a covering

un·clothed \-'klōth̲d\ *adj* : not clothed

un·coil \,ən-'kȯil, 'ən-\ *vb* : to release or become released from a coiled state : UNWIND

un·coined \-'kȯind\ *adj* **1** : not minted ⟨*uncoined* metal⟩ **2** : not fabricated : NATURAL

un·com·fort·able \-'kəm-fərt-ə-bəl, -'kəmp-; -'kəmf-tə-bəl, -'kəmp-, -'kəmpf-, -'kəm-, -tər-\ *adj* **1** : causing discomfort ⟨an *uncomfortable* chair⟩ **2** : feeling discomfort : UNEASY — **un·com·fort·ably** \-blē\ *adv*

un·com·mit·ted \,ən-kə-'mit-əd\ *adj* : not committed; *esp* : not pledged to a particular belief, allegiance, or program

un·com·mon \,ən-'käm-ən, 'ən-\ *adj* **1** : not ordinarily encountered : UNUSUAL ⟨when airplanes were *uncommon*⟩ **2** : EXTRAORDINARY **1**, EXCEPTIONAL ⟨a run of *uncommon* luck⟩ — **un·com·mon·ly** *adv* — **un·com·mon·ness** \-ən-nəs\ *n*

un·com·mu·ni·ca·tive \,ən-kə-'myü-nə-,kāt-iv, -ni-kət-\ *adj* : not inclined to talk or give out information : RESERVED

un·com·pli·men·ta·ry \,ən-,käm-plə-'ment-ə-rē, -'men-trē\ *adj* : not complimentary : DEROGATORY

un·com·pro·mis·ing \,ən-'käm-prə-,mī-zing, 'ən-\ *adj* : not making or accepting a compromise : making no concessions — **un·com·pro·mis·ing·ly** \-zing-lē\ *adv*

un·con·cern \,ən-kən-'sərn\ *n* **1** : lack of care or interest : INDIFFERENCE **2** : freedom from excessive concern or anxiety SYN see INDIFFERENCE

un·con·cerned \-'sərnd\ *adj* **1** : not involved : having no part or interest **2** : not anxious or upset : free of worry — **un·con·cern·ed·ly** \-'sər-nəd-lē\ *adv* — **un·con·cern·ed·ness** \-nəd-nəs\ *n*

un·con·di·tion·al \,ən-kən-'dish-nəl, -'dish-ən-l\ *adj* : not limited : ABSOLUTE, UNQUALIFIED ⟨*unconditional* surrender⟩ — **un·con·di·tion·al·ly** \-ē\ *adv*

un·con·di·tioned \-'dish-ənd\ *adj* **1** : not subject to conditions **2** : not dependent on conditioning or learning : INHERENT

un·con·form·able \,ən-kən-'fȯr-mə-bəl\ *adj* **1** : not conforming **2** : exhibiting geological unconformity — **un·con·form·ably** \-blē\ *adv*

un·con·for·mi·ty \,ən-kən-'fȯr-mət-ē\ *n* **1** : lack of continuity in deposition between rock strata in contact due especially to weathering **2** : the surface of contact between strata exhibiting unconformity

un·con·quer·able \,ən-'käng-krə-bəl, -kə-rə-, 'ən-\ *adj* : incapable of being conquered or overcome — **un·con·quer·ably** \-blē\ *adv*

un·con·scio·na·ble \-'känch-nə-bəl, -ə-nə-\ *adj* **1** : not guided or controlled by conscience **2** : EXCESSIVE, UNREASONABLE ⟨paid an *unconscionable* price⟩ **3** : shockingly unfair or unjust ⟨*unconscionable* sales practices⟩ [earlier *conscionable* "conscientious", derived from *conscience*] — **un·con·scio·na·bly** \-blē\ *adv*

¹un·con·scious \-'kän-chəs\ *adj* **1** : not aware ⟨*unconscious* of the risk⟩ **2 a** : of or relating to the unconscious **b** : having lost consciousness ⟨knocked *unconscious* by a fall⟩ **3** : not realized by oneself : not consciously done ⟨an *unconscious* mistake⟩ — **un·con·scious·ly** *adv* — **un·con·scious·ness** *n*

²unconscious *n* : the part of one's mental life that is not ordinarily available to consciousness and is manifested in spontaneous overt behavior (as slips of the tongue) or in dreams

un·con·sid·ered \,ən-kən-'sid-ərd\ *adj* **1** : not considered or worth consideration **2** : not resulting from consideration or study

un·con·sti·tu·tion·al \,ən-,kän-stə-'tüsh-nəl, -'tyüsh-, -ən-l\ *adj* : not according to or consistent with the constitution of a state or society — **un·con·sti·tu·tion·al·i·ty** \-,tü-shə-'nal-ət-ē, -,tyü-\ *n* — **un·con·sti·tu·tion·al·ly** \-'tüsh-nə-lē, -'tyüsh-, -ən-l-ē\ *adv*

un·con·trol·la·ble \,ən-kən-'trō-lə-bəl\ *adj* : incapable of being controlled : UNGOVERNABLE — **un·con·trol·la·bly** \-blē\ *adv*

un·con·ven·tion·al \,ən-kən-'vench-nəl, -ən-l\ *adj* : not conventional: as **a** : not bound by or in accordance with convention **b** : being out of the ordinary — **un·con·ven·tion·al·i·ty** \-,vench-ə-'nal-ət-ē\ *n* — **un·con·ven·tion·al·ly** \-'vench-nə-lē, -ən-l-ē\ *adv*

un·cork \,ən-'kȯrk, 'ən-\ *vt* **1** : to draw a cork from **2 a** : to release from a sealed or pent-up state ⟨*uncork* a surprise⟩ **b** : to let go : RELEASE ⟨*uncork* a wild pitch⟩

un·count·ed \-'kaunt-əd\ *adj* **1** : not counted **2** : INNUMERABLE

un·cou·ple \-'kəp-əl\ *vt* **-cou·pled; -cou·pling** \-'kəp-ling, -ə-ling\ **1** : to loose (hunting dogs) to seek game **2** : DISCONNECT ⟨*uncouple* railroad cars⟩

un·couth \-'küth\ *adj* **1** : strange, awkward, and clumsy in shape or appearance **2** : vulgar in conduct or speech : CRUDE [Old English *uncūth* "strange, unfamiliar", from ¹*un-* + *cūth* "known"]

un·cov·er \-'kəv-ər\ *vb* **1** : to make known : bring to light : DISCLOSE, REVEAL **2** : to expose to view by removing some covering **3 a** : to take the cover from **b** :

\ə\ abut		\ng\ sing	
\ər\ further		\ō\ bone	
\a\ mat		\ȯ\ saw	
\ā\ take		\ȯi\ coin	
\ä\ cot, cart		\th\ thin	
\au̇\ out		\th̲\ this	
\ch\ chin		\ü\ food	
\e\ pet		\u̇\ foot	
\ē\ easy		\y\ yet	
\g\ go		\yü\ few	
\i\ tip		\yu̇\ cure	
\ī\ life		\zh\ vision	
\j\ job			

to remove the hat from; *also* : to take off the hat as a token of respect

un·cov·ered \-'kəv-ərd\ *adj* : not covered or supplied with a covering

un·cre·at·ed \‚ən-krē-'āt-əd\ *adj* **1** : not existing by creation : ETERNAL **2** : not yet created

un·crit·i·cal \‚ən-'krit-i-kəl, 'ən-\ *adj* **1** : not critical : lacking in discrimination **2** : showing lack or improper use of critical standards or procedures — **un·crit·i·cal·ly** \-kə-lē, -klē\ *adv*

un·cross \-'krós\ *vb* : to change from a crossed position

un·crown \-'kraùn\ *vt* : to take the crown from : DEPOSE

un·crys·tal·lized \-'kris-tə-‚līzd\ *adj* : not crystallized; *esp* : not in final form ⟨an *uncrystallized* plan⟩

unc·tion \'əng-shən, 'əngk-\ *n* **1** : the act of anointing as a rite of consecration or healing **2** : exaggerated, assumed, or superficial earnestness of language or manner [Latin *unctio,* from *unguere* "to anoint"]

unc·tu·ous \'əng-chə-wəs, -chəs, 'əngk-; 'əngsh-wəs, 'əngksh-\ *adj* **1** : being like an ointment especially in smooth greasy texture or appearance **2** : full of unction in speech and manner; *esp* : insincerely smooth [Medieval Latin *unctuosus,* from Latin *unctum* "ointment", from *unguere* "to anoint"] — **unc·tu·ous·ly** *adv* — **unc·tu·ous·ness** *n*

un·curl \‚ən-'kərl, 'ən-\ *vb* : to make or become straightened out from a curled or coiled position

un·cut \‚ən-'kət, 'ən-\ *adj* **1** : not cut down or cut into **2** : not shaped by cutting ⟨an *uncut* diamond⟩ **3** *of a book* : not having the folds of the leaves slit **4** : not abridged or curtailed

un·daunt·ed \‚ən-'dónt-əd, -'dänt-\ *adj* : not daunted : not discouraged or dismayed : FEARLESS — **un·daunt·ed·ly** *adv*

un·dead \‚ən-'ded\ *n, pl* **undead 1** : VAMPIRE **1 2** : ZOMBIE

un·de·ceive \‚ən-di-'sēv\ *vt* : to free from deception, illusion, or error

un·de·cid·ed \‚ən-di-'sīd-əd\ *adj* **1** : not yet decided : not settled ⟨the question is still *undecided*⟩ **2** : not having decided : uncertain what to do ⟨still *undecided* about it⟩ — **un·de·cid·ed·ly** *adv*

un·de·mon·stra·tive \‚ən-di-'män-strət-iv\ *adj* : restrained or reserved in expression of feeling — **un·de·mon·stra·tive·ly** *adv* — **un·de·mon·stra·tive·ness** *n*

un·de·ni·able \‚ən-di-'nī-ə-bəl\ *adj* **1** : plainly true : INCONTESTABLE **2** : unquestionably excellent or genuine ⟨an applicant with *undeniable* references⟩ — **un·de·ni·able·ness** *n* — **un·de·ni·ably** \-blē\ *adv*

¹un·der \'ən-dər\ *adv* **1** : in or into a position below or beneath something ⟨the duck surfaced, then went *under* again⟩ **2** : below some quantity, level, or norm ⟨10 dollars or *under*⟩ — often used in combination ⟨*under* played the part⟩ **3** : in or into a condition of subjection, subordination, or unconsciousness ⟨the ether put me *under*⟩ **4** : so as to be covered or hidden ⟨turned *under* by the plow⟩ [Old English]

²un·der \‚ən-dər, 'ən-\ *prep* **1** : below or beneath so as to be overhung, surmounted, covered, protected, or concealed by ⟨*under* a tree⟩ ⟨*under* sunny skies⟩ ⟨*under* cover of darkness⟩ **2 a** : subject to the authority or guidance of ⟨served *under* the general⟩ **b** : subject to the action, operation, or effect of ⟨*under* pressure⟩ ⟨*under* an anesthetic⟩ **3** : within the group or designation of ⟨*under* this heading⟩ **4 a** : less or lower than (as in size, amount, or rank) ⟨all weights *under* 12 ounces⟩ ⟨nobody *under* a colonel⟩ **b** : below the standard or required degree of ⟨*under* legal age⟩ SYN see BELOW

³under \'ən-dər\ *adj* **1 a** : lying or placed below, beneath, or on the ventral side **b** : facing or protruding downward — often used in combination ⟨*under*surface of a leaf⟩ **2** : lower in rank or authority : SUBORDINATE **3** : lower than usual, proper, or desired in amount, quality, or degree

/ undercarriage 2

un·der·achiev·er \‚ən-də-rə-'chē-vər\ *n* : a student who fails to reach his or her scholastic potential

un·der·act \‚ən-də-'rakt\ *vb* : to perform feebly or with restraint: as **a** : to perform (a dramatic part) with less than the necessary skill or vigor **b** : to perform with restraint for greater dramatic impact or personal force

un·der·ac·tive \‚ən-də-'rak-tiv\ *adj* : having an abnormally low degree of activity ⟨an *underactive* thyroid gland⟩ — **un·der·ac·tiv·i·ty** \-rak-'tiv-ət-ē\ *n*

un·der·age \‚ən-də-'rāj\ *adj* : of less than mature or legal age

¹un·der·arm \‚ən-də-'rärm\ *adj* **1** : UNDERHAND **2** ⟨an *underarm* toss⟩ **2** : placed under or on the underside of the arm ⟨*underarm* seams⟩

²un·der·arm \‚ən-də-'rärm\ *adv* : with an underarm motion

³un·der·arm \'ən-də-‚rärm\ *n* **1** : ARMPIT **2** : the part of a garment that covers the underside of the arm

un·der·bel·ly \'ən-dər-‚bel-ē\ *n* : the under surface of a body or mass; *also* : a vulnerable area

un·der·bid \‚ən-dər-'bid\ *vb* **-bid; -bid·ding 1** : to bid less than (a competing bidder) **2** : to bid too low (as in cards) — **un·der·bid·der** *n*

un·der·body \'ən-dər-‚bäd-ē\ *n* : the lower or ventral part of an animal's body

un·der·bred \‚ən-dər-'bred\ *adj* : marked by lack of good breeding : ILL-BRED

un·der·brush \'ən-dər-‚brəsh\ *n* : shrubs and small trees growing among large trees : UNDERGROWTH

un·der·car·riage \-‚kar-ij\ *n* **1** : a supporting framework (as of an automobile) **2** : the landing gear of an airplane

un·der·charge \‚ən-dər-'chärj\ *vt* : to charge (as a person) too little — **un·der·charge** \'ən-dər-‚\ *n*

un·der·class·man \‚ən-dər-'klas-mən\ *n* : a member of the freshman or sophomore class

un·der·clothes \'ən-dər-‚klōz, -‚klōthz\ *n pl* : UNDERWEAR

un·der·cloth·ing \-‚klō-thing\ *n* : UNDERWEAR

un·der·coat \-‚kōt\ *n* **1** : a coat or jacket worn under another **2** : a growth of short hair or fur partly concealed by a longer growth ⟨a dog's *undercoat*⟩ **3** : a coat (as of paint) applied as a base for another coat **4** : UNDERCOATING — **undercoat** *vt*

un·der·coat·ing \-‚kōt-ing\ *n* : a special waterproof coating applied to the undersurfaces of a vehicle

un·der·cool \‚ən-dər-'kül\ *vt* : SUPERCOOL

un·der·cov·er \-'kəv-ər\ *adj* : acting or done in secret; *esp* : employed or engaged in spying or secret investigation

un·der·croft \'ən-dər-‚króft\ *n* : a subterranean room; *esp* : a vaulted chamber under a church [Middle English, from *under* + *crofte* "crypt", from Dutch, from Latin *crypta*]

un·der·cur·rent \'ən-dər-‚kər-ənt, -‚kə-rənt\ *n* **1** : a current below the upper currents or surface **2** : a hidden tendency of opinion or feeling often contrary to the one publicly shown

¹un·der·cut \‚ən-dər-'kət\ *vb* **-cut; -cut·ting 1 a** : to cut away the under part of ⟨*undercut* a vein of ore⟩ **b** : to cut away a base or material below a surface **2** : to cut away material from the underside of (an object) so as to leave an overhanging portion in relief **3** : to offer to sell at lower prices than or to work for lower wages than (a competitor) **4** : to strike (the ball) in golf or tennis obliquely downward so as to give a backspin or height to the shot

²un·der·cut \'ən-dər-‚kət\ *n* : the action or result of cutting away from the underside of something

un·der·de·vel·oped \‚ən-dər-di-'vel-əpt\ *adj* **1** : not normally or adequately developed ⟨*underdeveloped* muscles⟩ **2** : failing to reach a potential level of economic development (as from lack of capital) ⟨the *underdeveloped* nations⟩

un·der·do \,ən-dər-'dü\ *vt* **-did** \-'did\; **-done** \-'dən\; **-do·ing** \-'dü-ing\ **1** : to do less thoroughly than one can; *esp* : to cook (as meat) rare

un·der·dog \'ən-dər-,dȯg\ *n* **1** : the loser or predicted loser in a struggle **2** : a victim of injustice or persecution

un·der·done \,ən-dər-'dən\ *adj* : not thoroughly cooked : RARE ⟨*underdone* steak⟩

un·der·draw·ers \'ən-dər-,drȯ-ərz, -,drȯrz\ *n pl* : UNDERPANTS

un·der·es·ti·mate \,ən-də-'res-tə-,māt\ *vt* **1** : to estimate as being less than the actual size, quantity, or number **2** : to place too low a value on : UNDERRATE — **un·der·es·ti·mate** \-mət\ *n* — **un·der·es·ti·ma·tion** \-,res-tə-'mā-shən\ *n*

un·der·ex·pose \,ən-də-rik-'spōz\ *vt* : to expose (a photographic plate or film) for less time than is needed — **un·der·ex·po·sure** \-'spō-zhər\ *n*

un·der·feed \,ən-dər-'fēd\ *vt* **-fed** \-'fed\; **-feed·ing** **1** : to feed too little **2** : to feed with fuel from the underside

un·der·foot \,ən-dər-'fut\ *adv* **1** : under the feet **2** : in the way ⟨a puppy always *underfoot*⟩

un·der·fur \'ən-dər-,fər\ *n* : the thick soft fur lying beneath the longer and coarser hair of a mammal

un·der·gar·ment \-,gär-mənt\ *n* : a garment to be worn under another

un·der·gird \,ən-dər-'gərd\ *vt* **1** : to make secure underneath **2** : to brace up : STRENGTHEN

un·der·go \,ən-dər-'gō\ *vt* **-went** \-'went\; **-gone** \-'gȯn, -'gän\; **-go·ing** \-'gō-ing\ **1** : to submit or be subjected to : ENDURE ⟨*undergo* an operation⟩ **2** : to pass through : EXPERIENCE ⟨*undergo* a change⟩

un·der·grad·u·ate \-'graj-wət, -ə-wət, -ə-,wāt\ *n* : a student at a college or university who has not received a first degree

¹**un·der·ground** \,ən-dər-'graund\ *adv* **1** : beneath the surface of the earth **2** : in or into hiding or secret operation ⟨the party went *underground*⟩

²**un·der·ground** \'ən-dər-,graund\ *n* **1** : a space under the surface of the ground; *esp* : an underground railway **2** : a secret political movement or group; *esp* : an organized body working in secret to overthrow a government or an occupying power **3** : a group or movement that functions outside the establishment

³**un·der·ground** \'ən-dər-,graund\ *adj* **1** : being, growing, operating, or situated below the surface of the ground ⟨an *underground* stream⟩ **2** : conducted by secret means ⟨*underground* resistance movement⟩ **3** : produced or published outside the establishment ⟨*underground* newspapers⟩; *also* : of or relating to the avant-garde underground ⟨an *underground* theater⟩

Underground Railroad *n* : a system of cooperation among active antislavery people in the United States before 1863 by which fugitive slaves were secretly helped to reach the North or Canada

un·der·growth \'ən-dər-,grōth\ *n* : low growth on the floor of a forest including seedlings and saplings, shrubs, and herbs

¹**un·der·hand** \'ən-dər-,hand\ *adv* **1** : in an underhand or secret way **2** : with an underhand motion ⟨bowl *underhand*⟩ ⟨pitch *underhand*⟩

²**underhand** *adj* **1** : marked by secrecy, chicanery, and deception : SLY **2** : performed with the hand brought forward and up from below the level of the shoulder ⟨an *underhand* pitch⟩

un·der·hand·ed \,ən-dər-'han-dəd\ *adj or adv* : UNDERHAND — **un·der·hand·ed·ly** *adv* — **un·der·hand·ed·ness** *n*

¹**un·der·lay** \,ən-dər-'lā\ *vt* **-laid** \-'lād\; **-lay·ing** **1** : to provide a layer of something beneath often as a support or backing ⟨*underlay* shingles with tar paper⟩ **2** : to raise or support by something laid under

²**un·der·lay** \'ən-dər-,lā\ *n* : something that is laid under

un·der·lie \,ən-dər-'lī\ *vt* **-lay** \-'lā\; **-lain** \-'lān\; **-ly·ing** \-'lī-ing\ **1** : to be situated under **2** : to form the foundation of : SUPPORT ⟨ideas *underlying* the revolution⟩

un·der·line \'ən-dər-,līn, ,ən-dər-'\ *vt* **1** : to draw a line under : STRESS **3** — **un·der·line** \'ən-dər-,līn\ *n*

un·der·ling \'ən-dər-ling\ *n* : one who is under the orders of another : SUBORDINATE, INFERIOR

un·der·lip \,ən-dər-'lip\ *n* : the lower lip

un·der·ly·ing \,ən-dər-,lī-ing\ *adj* **1** : lying under or below ⟨the *underlying* rock is shale⟩ **2** : FUNDAMENTAL, BASIC ⟨*underlying* principles⟩

un·der·mine \,ən-dər-'mīn\ *vt* **1** : to dig out or wear away the supporting earth beneath ⟨*undermine* a wall⟩ **2** : to weaken or wear away secretly or gradually ⟨*undermine* a government⟩

un·der·most \'ən-dər-,mōst\ *adj* : lowest in relative position — **undermost** *adv*

¹**un·der·neath** \,ən-dər-'nēth\ *prep* **1** : directly under **2** : under subjection to [Old English *underneothan,* from *under* + *neothan* "below"]

²**underneath** *adv* **1** : under or below an object or a surface : BENEATH **2** : on the lower side

un·der·nour·ished \,ən-dər-'nər-isht, -'nə-risht\ *adj* : supplied with insufficient nourishment and especially foods for sound health and growth — **un·der·nour·ish·ment** \-'nər-ish-mənt, -'nə-rish-\ *n*

un·der·pants \'ən-dər-,pans\ *n pl* : short or long pants worn under an outer garment

un·der·part \-,pärt\ *n* **1** : a part lying on the lower side especially of a bird or mammal **2** : a subordinate or auxiliary part or role

un·der·pass \-,pas\ *n* : a passage underneath something (as for a road passing under a railroad or another road)

un·der·pay \,ən-dər-'pā\ *vt* **-paid** \-'pād\; **-pay·ing** : to pay too little

un·der·pin \-'pin\ *vt* **1** : to form part of, strengthen, or replace the foundation of ⟨*underpin* a structure⟩ **2** : SUPPORT, SUBSTANTIATE ⟨*underpin* an argument with evidence⟩

un·der·pin·ning \'ən-dər-,pin-ing\ *n* **1** : the material and construction (as a foundation) used for support of a structure **2** : PROP, SUPPORT **3** : a person's legs — usually used in pl.

un·der·play \,ən-dər-'plā\ *vb* : to handle without exaggeration; *esp* : to play down ⟨*underplay* a dramatic role⟩

un·der·plot \'ən-dər-,plät\ *n* : a dramatic plot that is subordinate to the main action

un·der·priv·i·leged \,ən-dər-'priv-lijd, -ə-lijd\ *adj* **1** : deprived of some of the basic economic and social rights that others enjoy **2** : of or relating to underprivileged people

un·der·pro·duc·tion \,ən-dər-prə-'dək-shən\ *n* : production of less than enough to satisfy demand or of less than the usual amount

un·der·rate \,ən-dər-'rāt, -də-'rāt\ *vt* : to rate too low : UNDERVALUE

un·der·run \-'rən\ *n* : the amount by which something produced falls below an estimate

un·der·score \'ən-dər-,skōr, -,skȯr\ *vt* **1** : to draw a line under : UNDERLINE **2** : STRESS **3** — **underscore** *n*

¹**un·der·sea** \,ən-dər-,sē\ *adj* **1** : being or carried on under the sea or under the surface of the sea ⟨*undersea* oil deposits⟩ **2** : designed for use under the surface of the sea ⟨an *undersea* fleet⟩

²**un·der·sea** \,ən-dər-,sē\ *or* **un·der·seas** \-,sēz\ *adv* : under the sea : beneath the surface of the sea

under secretary *n* : a secretary immediately subordinate to a principal secretary ⟨*under secretary* of state⟩

un·der·sell \,ən-dər-'sel\ *vt* **-sold** \-'sōld\; **-sell·ing** : to sell articles cheaper than ⟨*undersell* a competitor⟩

un·der·sexed \-'sekst\ *adj* : having little sexual desire

un·der·shirt \'ən-dər-,shərt\ *n* : a collarless undergarment with or without sleeves

underpass

\ə\	abut	\ng\	sing
\ər\	further	\ō\	bone
\a\	mat	\ȯ\	saw
\ā\	take	\ȯi\	coin
\ä\	cot, cart	\th\	thin
\au̇\	out	\th\	this
\ch\	chin	\ü\	food
\e\	pet	\u̇\	foot
\ē\	easy	\y\	yet
\g\	go	\yü\	few
\i\	tip	\yu̇\	cure
\ī\	life	\zh\	vision
\j\	job		

un·der·shoot \,ən-dər-'shüt\ *vt* **-shot** \-'shät\; **-shoot-ing** : to shoot or fall short of or below (a target) ⟨an airplane *undershooting* the runway⟩

un·der·shot \,ən-dər-,shät\ *adj* **1** : having the lower incisor teeth or lower jaw projecting beyond the upper when the mouth is closed **2** : moved by water passing beneath ⟨*undershot* wheel⟩

un·der·side \'ən-dər-,sīd, ,ən-dər-'\ *n* : the side or surface lying underneath

un·der·signed \'ən-dər-,sīnd\ *n, pl* **undersigned** : one who signs his or her name at the end of a document

un·der·sized \,ən-dər-'sīzd\ *adj* : smaller than is usual or standard ⟨*undersized* trout⟩

un·der·skirt \'ən-dər-,skərt\ *n* : a skirt worn under an outer skirt; *esp* : PETTICOAT

un·der·slung \,ən-dər-'sləng\ *adj* **1** : suspended so as to extend below the axles ⟨an *underslung* automobile frame⟩ **2** : having a low center of gravity

un·der·spin \'ən-dər-,spin\ *n* : BACKSPIN

un·der·stand \,ən-dər-'stand\ *vb* **-stood** \-'stüd\; **-stand-ing 1** : to grasp the meaning of : COMPREHEND **2** : to have thorough knowledge of ⟨*understand* the arts⟩ **3** : GATHER, INFER ⟨we *understand* that you're leaving today⟩ **4** : INTERPRET, EXPLAIN ⟨I *understand* the letter to be a refusal⟩ **5** : to have a sympathetic attitude ⟨you just don't *understand* about these things⟩ **6** : to accept as settled ⟨it is *understood* that I will pay⟩ **7** : to supply in thought as if expressed ⟨"to be married" is commonly *understood* after the word *engaged*⟩ [Old English *understandan,* from *under* + *standan* "to stand"] — **un·der·stand·abil·i·ty** \-,stan-də-'bil-ət-ē\ *n* — **un·der·stand·able** \-'stan-də-bəl\ *adj* — **un·der·stand·ably** \-blē\ *adv*

¹un·der·stand·ing \,ən-dər-'stan-ding\ *n* **1** : mental grasp : COMPREHENSION **2** : the ability to understand and judge ⟨a person of *understanding*⟩ **3 a** : agreement of opinion and feeling **b** : a mutual agreement informally or tacitly entered into ⟨an economic *understanding* between two nations⟩

²understanding *adj* **1** : endowed with understanding **2** : PATIENT 2, TOLERANT, SYMPATHETIC — **un·der·stand·ing·ly** \-'stan-ding-lē\ *adv*

un·der·state \,ən-dər-'stāt\ *vt* **1** : to represent as less than is the case **2** : to state with restraint especially for greater effect — **un·der·state·ment** \-mənt\ *n*

un·der·stood \,ən-dər-'stüd\ *adj* **1** : fully apprehended **2** : agreed on **3** : IMPLICIT 1

un·der·sto·ry \'ən-dər-,stōr-ē, -,stór-\ *n* : the plants of a forest undergrowth; *also* : an underlying layer of low vegetation

¹un·der·study \'ən-dər-,stəd-ē, ,ən-dər-'\ *vb* **1** : to study an actor's part in order to substitute in an emergency **2** : to prepare as understudy to (as an actor)

²un·der·study \'ən-dər-,stəd-ē\ *n* : one who is prepared to act another's part or take over another's duties

un·der·sur·face \-,sər-fəs\ *n* : UNDERSIDE

un·der·take \,ən-dər-'tāk\ *vt* **-took** \-'tük\; **-tak·en** \-'tā-kən\; **-tak·ing 1** : to take in hand : set about ⟨*undertake* a task⟩ **2** : to put oneself under obligation to perform : AGREE ⟨*undertake* to deliver a package⟩ **3** : GUARANTEE 2, PROMISE

un·der·tak·er \'ən-dər-,tā-kər\ *n* : one whose business is to prepare the dead for burial and to take charge of funerals

un·der·tak·ing \'ən-dər-,tā-king, ,ən-dər-'; *2 is* 'ən-dər-,only\ *n* **1** : the act of one that undertakes something (as a project) **2** : the business of an undertaker **3** : something undertaken : ENTERPRISE **4** : PROMISE 1, GUARANTEE

un·der·ten·ant \'ən-dər-,ten-ənt\ *n* : SUBTENANT

un·der-the-count·er *adj* : covert and usually unlawful ⟨*under-the-counter* liquor sales⟩ [from the hiding of illicit wares under the counters of stores where they are sold]

un·der·tone \'ən-dər-,tōn\ *n* **1** : a low or subdued tone ⟨spoke in an *undertone*⟩ **2** : a subdued color

un·der·tow \-,tō\ *n* : a current beneath the surface of the water that moves away from or along the shore while the surface water above it moves toward the shore

un·der·val·ue \,ən-dər-'val-yü\ *vt* **1** : to value below the real worth **2** : to set little value on — **un·der·val·u·a·tion** \-,val-yə-'wā-shən\ *n*

un·der·wa·ter \,ən-dər-,wót-ər, -,wät-\ *adj* : lying, growing, worn, or operating below the surface of the water — **un·der·wa·ter** \-'wót-, -'wät-\ *adv*

un·der·way \,ən-dər-'wā\ *adj* : occurring, performed, or used while traveling or in motion ⟨*underway* refueling⟩

under way \-'wā\ *adv* **1** : in motion; *esp* : not at anchor or aground **2** : into motion from a standstill **3** : in progress : AFOOT ⟨preparations were *under way*⟩ [probably from Dutch *onderweg,* from earlier *onderwegen,* literally, "under or among the ways"]

un·der·wear \'ən-dər-,waər, -,weər\ *n* : clothing worn next to the skin and under other clothing

¹un·der·weight \,ən-dər-'wāt\ *n* : weight below what is normal, average, or necessary

²underweight *adj* : weighing less than the normal or requisite amount

¹un·der·wing \'ən-dər-,wing\ *n* : either of the posterior pair of wings of an insect

²underwing *adj* : located or growing beneath or on the under surface of a wing ⟨*underwing* coverts⟩

un·der·wood \'ən-dər-,wùd\ *n* : UNDERBRUSH, UNDERGROWTH

un·der·wool \-,wùl\ *n* : short woolly underfur

un·der·world \-,wərld\ *n* **1** *archaic* : EARTH **2** : the place of departed souls : HADES **3** : a social level regarded as below the level of ordinary life; *esp* : the world of organized crime

un·der·write \'ən-dər-,rīt, -də-; ,ən-dər-', -də-\ *vt* **-wrote** \-,rōt, -'rōt\; **-writ·ten** \-,rit-n, -'rit-n\; **-writ·ing** \-,rīt-ing, -'rīt-\ **1** : to write under or at the end of something else **2 a** : to put one's name to (an insurance policy) and thereby become answerable for a designated loss or damage **b** : to insure life or property **3** : to subscribe to : agree to ⟨refused to *underwrite* the government's foreign policy⟩ **4 a** : to agree to purchase (a security issue) usually on a fixed date at a fixed price with a view to public resale **b** : to guarantee financial support of ⟨*underwrite* an expedition⟩ — **un·der·writ·er** \'ən-dər-,rīt-ər, 'ən-də-\ *n*

¹un·de·sir·able \-'zī-rə-bəl\ *adj* : not desirable : OBJECTIONABLE — **un·de·sir·abil·i·ty** \,zī-rə-'bil-ət-ē\ *n* — **un·de·sir·able·ness** \-'zī-rə-bəl-nəs\ *n* — **un·de·sir·ably** \-blē\ *adv*

²undesirable *n* : one that is undesirable

un·de·vi·at·ing \,ən-'dē-vē-,āt-ing, 'ən-\ *adj* : keeping a true course : UNSWERVING — **un·de·vi·at·ing·ly** \-ing-lē\ *adv*

un·dies \'ən-dēz\ *n pl* : UNDERWEAR; *esp* : women's underwear

un·dine \,ən-'dēn, 'ən-,\ *n* : WATER NYMPH [New Latin *undina,* from Latin *unda* "wave"]

un·di·rect·ed \,ən-də-'rek-təd, -dī-\ *adj* : not directed, planned, or guided ⟨*undirected* efforts⟩

un·dis·guised \,ən-dis-'gīzd\ *adj* : OPEN 2c

un·do \,ən-'dü, 'ən-\ *vb* **-did** \-'did\; **-done** \-'dən\; **-do·ing** \-'dü-ing\ **1** : to make or become unfastened or loosened **2** : to make of no effect or as if not done : NULLIFY **3 a** : to ruin the worldly means, reputation, or hopes of ⟨*undone* by greed⟩ **b** : UPSET 3a — **un·do·er** *n*

un·do·able \-'dü-ə-bəl\ *adj* : that cannot be done

un·do·ing \,ən-'dü-ing\ *n* **1** : the act of loosening or unfastening **2** : RUIN; *also* : a cause of ruin **3** : ANNULMENT, REVERSAL

un·done \,ən-'dən, 'ən-\ *adj* : not done or finished

un·doubt·ed \-'dauṫ-əd\ *adj* : not doubted or doubtful : CERTAIN ⟨*undoubted* proof of guilt⟩ — **un·doubt·ed·ly** *adv*

un·drape \-'drāp\ *vt* : to strip of drapery : UNVEIL

un·draw \-'drȯ\ *vt* **-drew** \-'drü\; **-drawn** \-'drȯn\; **-draw·ing** : to draw (as a curtain) aside : OPEN

un·dreamed \ən-'dremt, -'drempt, -'drēmd, 'ən-\ *also* **undreamt** \-'dremt, -'drempt\ *adj* : not dreamed or thought of — usually used with of

¹un·dress \ən-'dres, 'ən-\ *vb* **1** : to remove the clothes of **2** : to take off one's clothes

²undress *n* **1** : informal dress: as **a** : a loose robe or dressing gown **b** : ordinary dress **2** : a state of nudity

un·dressed \-'drest\ *adj* : not dressed: as **a** : partially, improperly, or informally clothed **b** : not fully processed or finished ⟨*undressed* hides⟩ **c** : not cared for or tended ⟨an *undressed* wound⟩ ⟨*undressed* fields⟩

un·due \-'dü, -'dyü\ *adj* **1** : not due : not yet payable **2** : going beyond what is proper or fit

un·du·lant \'ən-jə-lənt, 'ən-dyə-, -də-\ *adj* : rising and falling in waves

undulant fever *n* : a persistent human bacterial disease marked by fluctuating fever, pain and swelling in the joints, and great weakness

un·du·late \'ən-jə-ˌlāt, 'ən-dyə-, -də-\ *vb* **1** : to form or move in waves : FLUCTUATE **2** : to rise and fall in volume, pitch, or cadence **3** : to present a wavy appearance [Late Latin *undula* "small wave", from Latin *unda* "wave"]

un·du·la·tion \ˌən-jə-'lā-shən, ˌən-dyə-, -də-\ *n* **1 a** : the action of undulating **b** : a wavelike motion to and fro in a fluid or elastic medium : VIBRATION **2** : a wavy appearance or form

un·du·la·to·ry \'ən-jə-lə-ˌtōr-ē, 'ən-dyə-, -də-, -ˌtȯr-\ *adj* : of or relating to undulation; *also* : UNDULANT

un·du·ly \ˌən-'dü-lē, -'dyü-, 'ən-\ *adv* : in an undue manner : EXCESSIVELY

un·dy·ing \-'dī-ing\ *adj* : not dying : IMMORTAL

un·earned \-'ərnd\ *adj* : not gained by labor, service, or skill ⟨*unearned* income⟩

un·earth \ˌən-'ərth, 'ən-\ *vt* **1** : to dig up out of or as if out of the earth ⟨*unearth* a forgotten photo⟩ **2** : to make known : bring to light ⟨*unearth* a plot⟩

un·earth·ly \-lē\ *adj* **1** : not earthly: as **a** : SUPERNATURAL 2 ⟨*unearthly* beings⟩ **b** : STRANGE 2b, EERIE ⟨an *unearthly* light⟩ **2** : not usual or reasonable ⟨an *unearthly* hour to get up⟩ — **un·earth·li·ness** *n*

un·easy \ˌən-'ē-zē, 'ən-\ *adj* **1** : not easy in manner : AWKWARD **2** : disturbed by pain or worry : RESTLESS **3** : UNSTABLE ⟨an *uneasy* truce⟩ — **un·eas·i·ly** \-'ē-zə-lē\ *adv* — **un·eas·i·ness** \-'ē-zē-nəs\ *n*

un·em·ploy·able \ˌən-im-'plȯi-ə-bəl\ *adj* : not acceptable for employment — **unemployable** *n*

un·em·ployed \-'plȯid\ *adj* : not employed: **a** : not being used **b** : not engaged in a gainful occupation — **unemployed** *n*

un·em·ploy·ment \ˌən-im-'plȯi-mənt\ *n* : the state of being out of work : involuntary idleness of workers

unemployment benefit *n* : money paid at regular intervals to an unemployed worker (as by an employer or a government agency)

un·end·ing \ˌən-'en-ding, 'ən-\ *adj* : being without ending : ENDLESS — **un·end·ing·ly** \-ding-lē\ *adv*

¹un·equal \-'ē-kwəl\ *adj* **1 a** : not of the same measurement, quantity, or number as another **b** : not like or not the same as another in degree, worth, or status **2** : not uniform : VARIABLE, UNEVEN **3** : badly balanced or matched ⟨an *unequal* fight⟩ **4** : INADEQUATE, INSUFFICIENT ⟨timber *unequal* to the strain⟩ — **un·equal·ly** \-kwə-lē\ *adv*

²unequal *n* : one that is not equal to another

un·equaled \-'ē-kwəld\ *adj* : not equaled : MATCHLESS

un·equiv·o·cal \ˌən-i-'kwiv-ə-kəl\ *adj* : leaving no doubt : CLEAR — **un·equiv·o·cal·ly** \-kə-lē, -klē\ *adv*

un·err·ing \ˌən-'eər-ing, -'ər-ing, 'ən-\ *adj* : making no errors : UNFAILING — **un·err·ing·ly** \-ing-lē\ *adv*

un·even \ˌən-'ē-vən, 'ən-\ *adj* **1** : ODD 2a **2 a** : not even : not level or smooth : RUGGED ⟨large *uneven* teeth⟩ ⟨*uneven* handwriting⟩ **b** : varying from the straight or parallel **c** : not uniform : IRREGULAR ⟨*uneven* combustion⟩ **d** : varying in quality ⟨an *uneven* performance⟩ **3** : UNEQUAL 3 — **un·even·ly** *adv* — **un·even·ness** \-vən-nəs\ *n*

un·event·ful \ˌən-i-'vent-fəl\ *adj* : not eventful : lacking interesting or noteworthy happenings ⟨an *uneventful* trip⟩ — **un·event·ful·ly** \-fə-lē\ *adv*

un·ex·am·pled \ˌən-ig-'zam-pəld\ *adj* : having no example or parallel : UNPRECEDENTED

un·ex·cep·tion·able \ˌən-ik-'sep-shnə-bəl, -shə-nə-\ *adj* : not open to objection or criticism : beyond reproach : UNIMPEACHABLE [¹*un-* + obsolete *exception* "to take exception, object" + *-able*] — **un·ex·cep·tion·able·ness** *n* — **un·ex·cep·tion·ably** \-blē\ *adv*

un·ex·cep·tion·al \-'sep-shnəl, -shən-l\ *adj* : ORDINARY 1

un·ex·pect·ed \ˌən-ik-'spek-təd\ *adj* : not expected or foreseen — **un·ex·pect·ed·ly** *adv* — **un·ex·pect·ed·ness** *n*

un·ex·pres·sive \ˌən-ik-'spres-iv\ *adj* : INEXPRESSIVE

un·fail·ing \-'fā-ling\ *adj* **1** : CONSTANT 1 **2** : EVERLASTING, INEXHAUSTIBLE ⟨an *unfailing* topic of interest⟩ **3** : INFALLIBLE 2, SURE — **un·fail·ing·ly** *adv* — **un·fail·ing·ness** *n*

un·fair \-'faər, -'feər\ *adj* **1** : marked by injustice, partiality, or deception : UNJUST, DISHONEST **2** : not equitable in business dealings — **un·fair·ly** *adv* — **un·fair·ness** *n*

un·faith \ˌən-'fāth, 'ən-', 'ən-,\ *n* : absence of faith : DISBELIEF

un·faith·ful \ˌən-'fāth-fəl, 'ən-\ *adj* : not faithful : **a** : not adhering to vows, allegiance, or duty : DISLOYAL **b** : not faithful to marriage vows **c** : INACCURATE ⟨an *unfaithful* translation⟩ — **un·faith·ful·ly** \-fə-lē\ *adv* — **un·faith·ful·ness** *n*

un·fa·mil·iar \ˌən-fə-'mil-yər\ *adj* **1** : not well known : STRANGE ⟨an *unfamiliar* place⟩ **2** : not well acquainted ⟨*unfamiliar* with the subject⟩ — **un·fa·mil·iar·i·ty** \-ˌmil-'yar-ət-ē, -ˌmil-ē-'ar-\ *n* — **un·fa·mil·iar·ly** \-'mil-yər-lē\ *adv*

un·fas·ten \ˌən-'fas-n, 'ən-\ *vb* : to make or become loose : UNDO

un·fa·vor·able \-'fāv-rə-bəl, -ə-rə-; -'fā-vər-bəl\ *adj* **1 a** : not disposed to favor **b** : expressing disapproval : NEGATIVE **2** : not propitious : DISADVANTAGEOUS — **un·fa·vor·able·ness** *n* — **un·fa·vor·ably** \-blē\ *adv*

un·feel·ing \-'fē-ling\ *adj* **1** : lacking feeling : INSENSATE **2** : lacking kindness or sympathy : HARDHEARTED — **un·feel·ing·ly** \-ling-lē\ *adv* — **un·feel·ing·ness** *n*

un·feigned \ˌən-'fānd, 'ən-\ *adj* : not feigned or hypocritical : GENUINE — **un·feign·ed·ly** \-'fā-nəd-lē, -'fān-dlē\ *adv*

un·fet·ter \ˌən-'fet-ər, 'ən-\ *vt* : LIBERATE 1, EMANCIPATE

un·fil·ial \-'fil-ē-əl, -'fil-yəl\ *adj* : not observing the obligations of a child to a parent : UNDUTIFUL

un·fin·ished \-'fin-isht\ *adj* : not finished; *esp* : not brought to the final desired state

¹un·fit \-'fit\ *adj* : not fit : **a** : not adapted to a purpose : UNSUITABLE **b** : not qualified : INCOMPETENT **c** : physically or mentally unsound — **un·fit·ly** *adv* — **un·fit·ness** *n*

²unfit *vt* : to make unfit : DISABLE, DISQUALIFY

un·fix \ˌən-'fiks, 'ən-\ *vt* **1** : to loosen from a fastening : DETACH, DISENGAGE **2** : to make unstable : UNSETTLE

un·flag·ging \-'flag-ing\ *adj* : CONSTANT 1 — **un·flag·ging·ly** *adv*

un·flap·pa·ble \-'flap-ə-bəl\ *adj* : not easily upset or panicked : COOL [¹*un-* + *flap* "state of excitement" (from ¹*flap*) + *-able*]

un·fledged \-'flejd\ *adj* **1** : not feathered or ready for flight **2** : IMMATURE, CALLOW ⟨an *unfledged* writer⟩

un·flinch·ing \-'flin-chiŋ\ *adj* : STEADFAST 1b, 2 — **un·flinch·ing·ly** \-chiŋ-lē\ *adv*

un·fold \-'fōld\ *vb* **1 a** : to spread or cause to spread or straighten out from a folded position or arrangement **b** : UNWRAP **2** : BLOOM 1 **3** : DEVELOP ⟨as the story *unfolds*⟩ **4** : to open out or cause to open out gradually to view or understanding

un·for·get·ta·ble \,ən-fər-'get-ə-bəl\ *adj* : incapable of being forgotten : lasting in memory — **un·for·get·ta·bly** \-blē\ *adv*

un·formed \,ən-'fȯrmd\ *adj* : not arranged in regular shape, order, or relations; *esp* : IMMATURE

¹un·for·tu·nate \-'fȯrch-nət, -ə-nət\ *adj* **1 a** : not fortunate : UNLUCKY **b** : marked or accompanied by or resulting in misfortune **2 a** : INAPPROPRIATE ⟨an *unfortunate* choice of words⟩ **b** : DEPLORABLE ⟨an *unfortunate* lack of taste⟩ — **un·for·tu·nate·ly** *adv*

²unfortunate *n* : an unfortunate person; *esp* : a social outcast

un·found·ed \,ən-'faún-dəd, 'ən-\ *adj* : lacking a sound basis : GROUNDLESS ⟨an *unfounded* accusation⟩

un·fre·quent·ed \,ən-frē-'kwent-əd; ,ən-'frē-kwənt-, 'ən-\ *adj* : not often visited or traveled over

un·friend·ed \,ən-'fren-dəd, 'ən-\ *adj* : having no friends

un·friend·ly \,ən-'fren-dlē, -lē, 'ən-\ *adj* **1 a** : not friendly or social **b** : not kind : HOSTILE ⟨an *unfriendly* greeting⟩ **2** : not favorable ⟨an *unfriendly* environment⟩ — **un·friend·li·ness** *n*

un·frock \-'fräk\ *vt* : to deprive (as a priest) of the right to exercise the functions of office

un·fruit·ful \-'früt-fəl\ *adj* **1** : not bearing fruit or offspring **2** : not producing a desired result ⟨*unfruitful* efforts⟩ — **un·fruit·ful·ly** \-fə-lē\ *adv* — **un·fruit·ful·ness** *n*

un·fund·ed \,ən-'fən-dəd, 'ən-\ *adj* : not funded : FLOATING ⟨an *unfunded* debt⟩

un·furl \-'fərl\ *vb* : to loose from a furled state : UNFOLD ⟨*unfurl* a flag⟩

un·gain·ly \-'gān-lē\ *adj* **1** : AWKWARD 1, CLUMSY **2** : AWKWARD 2b [earlier *gainly* "graceful", from Old English *gēn* "direct, straight", from Old Norse *gegn*] — **un·gain·li·ness** *n*

un·gen·er·ous \-'jen-rəs, -ə-rəs\ *adj* **1** : PETTY 3, MEAN **2** : STINGY 1 — **un·gen·er·ous·ly** *adv*

un·gird \,ən-'gərd, 'ən-\ *vt* : to free from a restraining band or girdle : UNBIND

un·glazed \-'glāzd\ *adj* : not having a glaze ⟨*unglazed* pottery⟩

un·glue \-'glü\ *vt* : to separate by or as if by dissolving an adhesive

un·glued \-'glüd\ *adj, slang* : emotionally upset : DISTRAUGHT

un·god·ly \-'gäd-lē, *also* -'gȯd-\ *adj* **1** : not godly: as **a** : IRRELIGIOUS **b** : WICKED 1, EVIL **2** : UNREASONABLE 2, OUTRAGEOUS ⟨got up at an *ungodly* hour⟩ ⟨an *ungodly* hat⟩ — **un·god·li·ness** *n*

un·gov·ern·able \-'gəv-ər-nə-bəl\ *adj* : not capable of being governed, guided, or restrained SYN see UNRULY — **un·gov·ern·ably** \-blē\ *adv*

un·grace·ful \-'grās-fəl\ *adj* : not graceful : AWKWARD — **un·grace·ful·ly** \-fə-lē\ *adv* — **un·grace·ful·ness** *n*

un·gra·cious \-'grā-shəs\ *adj* **1** : not courteous : RUDE **2** : not pleasing : DISAGREEABLE — **un·gra·cious·ly** *adv* — **un·gra·cious·ness** *n*

un·grate·ful \,ən-'grāt-fəl, 'ən-\ *adj* **1** : not thankful for favors **2** : not pleasing : DISAGREEABLE ⟨an *ungrateful* task⟩ — **un·grate·ful·ly** \-fə-lē\ *adv* — **un·grate·ful·ness** *n*

un·ground·ed \-'graún-dəd\ *adj* **1** : GROUNDLESS, UNFOUNDED **2** : not instructed or informed

un·grudg·ing \-'grəj-iŋ\ *adj* : free from envy or unwillingness

un·guard·ed \-'gärd-əd\ *adj* **1** : vulnerable to attack **2** : free from guile or wariness — **un·guard·ed·ly** *adv*

un·guent \'əŋ-gwənt, 'ən-; 'ən-jənt\ *n* : a soothing or healing salve : OINTMENT [Latin *unguentum,* from *unguere* "to anoint"]

¹un·gu·late \'əŋ-gyə-lət, 'ən-, -,lāt\ *adj* **1** : having hoofs **2** : of or relating to the ungulates [Late Latin *ungulatus,* from Latin *ungula* "hoof", from *unguis* "nail, hoof"]

²ungulate *n* : any of a group (Ungulata) consisting of the hoofed mammals and including the ruminants, swine, horses, tapirs, rhinoceroses, elephants, and hyraxes of which most are plant-eating and many horned

un·hal·lowed \,ən-'hal-ōd, 'ən-\ *adj* **1** : not blessed or holy **2** : IMPIOUS a, PROFANE

un·hand \,ən-'hand, 'ən-\ *vt* : to remove the hand from : let go

un·hand·some \-'han-səm\ *adj* : not handsome: as **a** : not beautiful : HOMELY **b** : lacking in courtesy or taste — **un·hand·some·ly** *adv*

un·handy \-'han-dē\ *adj* **1** : hard to handle : INCONVENIENT ⟨a thick *unhandy* volume⟩ **2** : lacking in skill or dexterity : AWKWARD — **un·handi·ness** *n*

un·hap·py \-'hap-ē\ *adj* **1** : not fortunate : UNLUCKY ⟨an *unhappy* mistake⟩ **2** : not cheerful : SAD, MISERABLE **3** : INAPPROPRIATE — **un·hap·pi·ly** \-'hap-ə-lē\ *adv* — **un·hap·pi·ness** \-'hap-i-nəs\ *n*

un·har·ness \-'här-nəs\ *vt* : to remove a harness from

un·health·ful \-'helth-fəl\ *adj* : UNHEALTHY 1

un·healthy \-'hel-thē\ *adj* **1** : not conducive to health ⟨an *unhealthy* climate⟩ **2** : not in good health : SICKLY **3 a** : DANGEROUS 1, RISKY **b** : causing harm : INJURIOUS **c** : CORRUPT 1, DEPRAVED — **un·health·i·ly** \-thə-lē\ *adv* — **un·health·i·ness** \-thē-nəs\ *n*

un·heard \,ən-'hərd, 'ən-\ *adj* **1** : not perceived by the ear **2** : not given a hearing ⟨*unheard* protests⟩

un·heard-of \-,əv, -,äv\ *adj* : previously unknown : UNPRECEDENTED

un·hinge \,ən-'hinj, 'ən-\ *vt* **1** : to remove (as a door) from the hinges **2** : to make unstable : UNSETTLE, DISRUPT ⟨a mind *unhinged* by grief⟩

un·hitch \-'hich\ *vt* : to free from or as if from being hitched

un·ho·ly \-'hō-lē\ *adj* **1** : not holy : PROFANE, WICKED **2** : SHOCKING, OUTRAGEOUS ⟨an *unholy* noise⟩ — **un·ho·li·ness** *n*

un·ho·mog·e·nized \-hə-'mäj-ə-,nīzd, -hō-\ *adj* : that has not been homogenized

un·hood \-'húd\ *vt* : to remove a hood or covering from

un·hook \-'húk\ *vt* **1** : to remove from a hook **2** : to unfasten by releasing a hook

un·horse \-'hȯrs\ *vt* : to dislodge from or as if from a horse : UNSEAT

un·hou·seled \-'haú-zəld\ *adj, archaic* : not having received the Eucharist especially just before death [derived from earlier *housel* "Eucharist", from Old English *hūsel* "sacrifice, Eucharist"]

un·hur·ried \-'hər-ēd, -'hə-rēd\ *adj* : not hurried : LEISURELY — **un·hur·ried·ly** *adv*

uni- *prefix* : one : single ⟨*uni*cellular⟩ [Latin, from *unus* "one"]

Uni·ate \'ü-nē-,at, 'yü-\ *or* **Uni·at** *n* : a Christian of a church adhering to an Eastern rite but accepting papal authority [Russian *uniyat,* from Polish *uniat,* from *unja* "union", from Late Latin *unio*] — **Uniate** *adj*

uni·ax·i·al \,yü-nē-'ak-sē-əl\ *adj* **1** : having only one axis **2** : of or relating to only one axis — **uni·ax·i·al·ly** \-sē-ə-lē\ *adv*

uni·cam·er·al \,yü-ni-'kam-rəl, -ə-rəl\ *adj* : having or consisting of a single legislative chamber [Late Latin *camera* "chamber"] — **uni·cam·er·al·ly** \-rə-lē\ *adv*

uni·cel·lu·lar \-'sel-yə-lər\ *adj* : having or consisting of a single cell — **uni·cel·lu·lar·i·ty** \-,sel-yə-'lar-ət-ē\ *n*

uni·corn \'yü-nə-,kȯrn\ *n* : a fabulous animal generally depicted with the body and head of a horse, the hind legs of a stag, the tail of a lion, and a single horn on its forehead [Old French *unicorne,* from Late Latin *unicornis,* from Latin *uni-* + *cornu* "horn"]

uni·cy·cle \'yü-ni-ˌsī-kəl\ *n* : a vehicle that has a single wheel and is usually propelled by pedals [*uni-* + *-cycle* (as in *tricycle*)]

uni·di·rec·tion·al \ˌyü-ni-də-'rek-shnəl, -dī-, -shən-l\ *adj* : having, moving in, or responsive in a single direction ⟨a *unidirectional* antenna⟩

¹**uni·form** \'yü-nə-ˌform\ *adj* **1** : having always the same form, manner, or degree : not varying or variable **2** : of the same form with others : conforming to one rule **SYN** see **STEADY** — **uni·for·mi·ty** \ˌyü-nə-'for-mət-ē\ *n* — **uni·form·ly** \'yü-nə-ˌform-lē, ˌyü-nə-'\ *adv* — **uni·form·ness** *n*

²**uniform** *vt* : to clothe with a uniform

³**uniform** *n* : distinctive dress worn by members of a particular group (as an army or a police force)

uni·for·mi·tar·i·an·ism \ˌyü-nə-ˌfor-mə-'ter-ē-ə-ˌniz-əm\ *n* : a geological doctrine that existing processes acting in the same manner as at present are sufficient to account for all geological changes

uni·fy \'yü-nə-ˌfī\ *vt* **-fied; -fy·ing** : to make into a unit or a coherent whole : **UNITE** — **uni·fi·able** \-ˌfī-ə-bəl\ *adj* — **uni·fi·ca·tion** \ˌyü-nə-fə-'kā-shən\ *n* — **uni·fi·er** \'yü-nə-ˌfī-ər, -ˌfīr\ *n*

uni·lat·er·al \ˌyü-ni-'lat-ə-rəl, -'la-trəl\ *adj* : of, relating to, affecting, or done by one side only ⟨*unilateral* paralysis⟩ ⟨*unilateral* disarmament⟩ — **uni·lat·er·al·ly** \-ē\ *adv*

un·im·peach·able \ˌən-im-'pē-chə-bəl\ *adj* : not impeachable : not liable to accusation : **IRREPROACHABLE** — **un·im·peach·ably** \-blē\ *adv*

un·im·proved \-'prüvd\ *adj* : not improved: as **a** : not tilled, built upon, or otherwise prepared for use ⟨*unimproved* land⟩ **b** : not used or employed advantageously **c** : not selectively bred for better quality or productiveness

un·in·hib·it·ed \ˌən-in-'hib-ət-əd\ *adj* : free from inhibition; *esp* : unrestrainedly informal — **un·in·hib·it·ed·ly** *adv*

un·in·tel·li·gent \ˌən-in-'tel-ə-jənt\ *adj* : lacking intelligence : **UNWISE, IGNORANT** — **un·in·tel·li·gent·ly** *adv*

un·in·ter·est·ed \ˌən-'int-ə-ˌres-təd, 'ən-; -'in-trəs-, -ˌtres-; -'int-ərs-, -'int-ə-rəs-\ *adj* **1** : having no interest and especially no property interest **2** : not having the mind or feelings engaged : not having the curiosity or sympathy aroused □ **SYN DISINTERESTED: UNINTERESTED** in discriminating use means having no interest and implies being indifferent through lack of sympathy for or curiosity toward something; **DISINTERESTED** in comparable use suggests a freedom from concern for personal or financial advantage that enables one to judge, advise, or act without bias.

un·in·ter·rupt·ed \ˌən-ˌint-ə-'rəp-təd\ *adj* : not interrupted : **CONTINUOUS** — **un·in·ter·rupt·ed·ly** *adv* — **un·in·ter·rupt·ed·ness** *n*

union \'yün-yən\ *n* **1 a** : an act or instance of uniting two or more things into one: as (1) : the formation of a single political unit from two or more separate and independent units (2) : a uniting in marriage (3) : the growing together of severed parts **b** : a unified condition : **COMBINATION, JUNCTION 2** : something formed by a combining of parts or members: as **a** : a confederation of independent individuals (as nations or persons) for a common purpose **b** : a political unit constituting an organic whole formed from several units that may have been previously independent **c** : **LABOR UNION d** *cap* : an organization on a college or university campus providing recreational, social, cultural, and sometimes dining facilities; *also* : the building housing it **e** : the set of all elements that belong to one or more of a collection of two or more sets **3 a** : a device symbolizing national unity that is borne on a flag **b** : the upper inner corner of a flag **4 a** : a device for con-

necting parts (as of a machine) **b** : a coupling for pipes [Middle French, from Late Latin *unio,* from Latin *unus* "one"] **SYN** see **UNITY**

Union *adj* : of, relating to, or being the side favoring the federal union in the United States Civil War

union card *n* : a card certifying personal membership in good standing in a labor union

union·ism \'yün-yə-ˌniz-əm\ *n* **1** : the principle or policy of forming or adhering to a union **2** *cap* : adherence to the policy of a firm federal union prior to or during the United States Civil War **3** : the principles, theory, or system of trade unions — **union·ist** \-yə-nəst\ *n, often cap*

union·ize \'yün-yə-ˌnīz\ *vt* : to cause to become a member of or subject to the rules of a labor union : form into a labor union — **union·iza·tion** \ˌyün-yə-nə-'zā-shən\ *n*

union jack *n, often cap U & J* **1** : a jack consisting of the part of a national flag that signifies union **2** : the national flag of the United Kingdom

union shop *n* : an establishment in which the employer is free to hire nonunion workers but retains them on the payroll only on condition of their becoming members of the union within a specified time

union suit *n* : an undergarment with shirt and pants in one piece

uni·pa·ren·tal \ˌyü-ni-pə-'rent-l\ *adj* : having or involving a single parent; *also* : **PARTHENOGENETIC** — **uni·pa·ren·tal·ly** \-l-ē\ *adv*

uni·po·lar \ˌyü-ni-'pō-lər\ *adj* : having, produced by, or acting by a single magnetic or electrical pole — **uni·po·lar·i·ty** \-pō-'lar-ət-ē, -pə-\ *n*

unique \yu̇-'nēk\ *adj* **1** : being the only one of its kind **2** : very unusual : **NOTABLE** [French, from Latin *unicus,* from *unus* "one"] **SYN** see **SINGLE** — **unique·ly** *adv* — **unique·ness** *n*

uni·sex \'yü-nə-ˌseks\ *adj* : common to males and females ⟨*unisex* clothing⟩

uni·sex·u·al \ˌyü-ni-'sek-shəl, -shwəl, -shə-wəl\ *adj* : of, relating to, or restricted to one sex : **a** : male or female but not hermaphroditic **b** : **DICLINOUS** ⟨a *unisexual* flower⟩ — **uni·sex·u·al·i·ty** \-ˌsek-shə-'wal-ət-ē\ *n* — **uni·sex·u·al·ly** \-'sek-shə-lē, -shwə-lē, -shə-wə-lē\ *adv*

uni·son \'yü-nə-sən, -zən\ *n* **1 a** : identity in musical pitch **b** : the condition of being tuned or sounded at the same pitch or at an octave **2** : harmonious agreement : **CONCORD** [Middle French, from Medieval Latin *unisonus* "having the same sound", from Latin *uni-* + *sonus* "sound"] — **in unison** : in perfect agreement : so as to harmonize exactly

unit \'yü-nət\ *n* **1 a** : the first and least natural number : **ONE b** : a single quantity regarded as a whole in calculation **2** : a definite quantity (as of length, time, or value) adopted as a standard of measurement; *esp* : an amount of work used in calculating student credits **3 a** : a single thing, person, or group that is a constituent of a whole **b** : a part of a military establishment that has a prescribed organization **c** : a piece or complex of apparatus serving to perform one particular function **d** : a part of a school course focusing on a central theme and making use of resources from numerous subject areas and the pupils' own experience [back-formation from *unity*]

uni·tard \'yü-nə-ˌtärd\ *n* : a close-fitting one-piece garment for the torso, legs, feet, and often the arms [*uni-* + *leotard*]

uni·tar·i·an \ˌyü-nə-'ter-ē-ən\ *n* **1 a** *often cap* : one who believes that the deity exists only in one person **b** *cap* : a member of a Christian denomination that stresses individual freedom of belief, the free use of reason in religion, a united world community, and liberal social action **2** : an advocate of unity or a unitary system — **unitarian** *adj, often cap* — **uni·tar·i·an·ism** \-ē-ə-ˌniz-əm\ *n, often cap*

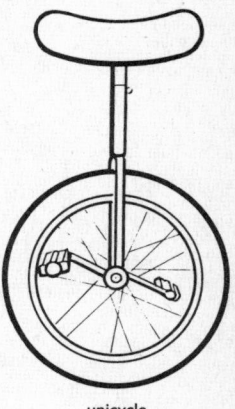

unicycle

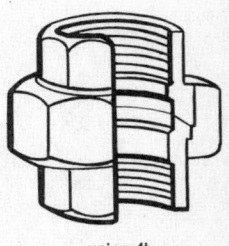

union 4b

\ə\ abut	\ng\ sing
\ər\ **further**	\ō\ bone
\a\ mat	\ȯ\ saw
\ā\ take	\oi\ coin
\ä\ cot, cart	\th\ thin
\au̇\ out	\th\ this
\ch\ chin	\ü\ food
\e\ pet	\u̇\ foot
\ē\ easy	\y\ yet
\g\ go	\yü\ few
\i\ tip	\yu̇\ cure
\ī\ life	\zh\ vision
\j\ job	

uni·tary \'yü-nə-ˌter-ē\ *adj* **1 a** : of or relating to a unit **b** : based on or characterized by unity or units **2** : having the character of a unit : WHOLE

unit circle *n* : a circle with its center at the origin of a coordinate system and its radius one unit of length long

unite \yu̇-'nīt\ *vb* **1 a** : to put or come together to form a single unit **b** : to cause to adhere **c** : to link by a legal or moral bond **2** : to become one or as if one **3** : to join in action : act in concert [Late Latin *unitus,* past participle of *unire* "to unite", from Latin *unus* "one"] SYN see JOIN — **unit·er** *n*

unit·ed \yu̇-'nīt-əd\ *adj* **1** : made one or as if one **2** : relating to or produced by joint action **3** : being in agreement : HARMONIOUS — **unit·ed·ly** *adv*

unit·ize \'yü-nət-ˌīz\ *vt* : to convert into a unit

units digit \'yü-nəts-\ *n* : the numeral (as 6 in 456) occupying the units place in a number expressed in the Arabic system of writing numbers

units place *n* : the place immediately to the left of the decimal point in a number expressed in the Arabic system of writing numbers

uni·ty \'yü-nət-ē\ *n, pl* **-ties** **1** : the quality or state of being one : ONENESS **2** : a condition of harmony : CONCORD **3** : continuity without change (as in purpose or action) **4** : a definite mathematical quantity or combination of quantities taken as one or for which 1 is made to stand in calculation **5** : relevance of all the parts in an artistic or literary work to a single main idea : oneness of effect or style **6** : a totality of related parts [Old French *unité,* from Latin *unitas,* from *unus* "one"] □ SYN UNITY, SOLIDARITY, UNION mean the character of a thing that is a whole composed of many parts. UNITY implies oneness gained by the interdependence of its varied parts; SOLIDARITY implies such unity in a group, class, or community that enables it to show undivided strength as through opinion or influence (working-class *solidarity*) UNION implies a thorough integration of parts and their harmonious cooperation (the *union* of the thirteen states into a nation)

uni·va·lent \ˌyü-ni-'vā-lənt\ *adj* : having a chemical valence of one

¹uni·valve \'yü-ni-ˌvalv\ *adj* : having or consisting of one valve

²univalve *n* : a univalve mollusk shell or a mollusk having such a shell

uni·ver·sal \ˌyü-nə-'vər-səl\ *adj* **1** : including or covering all or a whole without limit or exception **2** : present or occurring everywhere or under all conditions (*universal* cultural patterns) **3 a** : embracing a major part or the greatest portion (*universal* practices) **b** : comprehensively broad and versatile (a *universal* genius) **4** : adapted or adjustable to meet varied requirements (as of use, shape, or size) (a *universal* wrench) — **uni·ver·sal·i·ty** \ˌvər-'sal-ət-ē\ *n* — **uni·ver·sal·ly** \-'vər-sə-lē, -slē\ *adv* — **uni·ver·sal·ness** \-səl-nəs\ *n* □ SYN UNIVERSAL, GENERAL mean of all or of the whole. UNIVERSAL implies reference to each individual without exception in the category considered (*universal* franchise) GENERAL implies reference to all or nearly all (the theory has *general* but not *universal* acceptance)

universal donor *n* : a person with type O blood

uni·ver·sal·ism \ˌyü-nə-'vər-sə-ˌliz-əm\ *n, often cap* **1** : a theological doctrine that all people will eventually be saved **2** : the principles and practices of a liberal Christian denomination founded in the 18th century to uphold belief in universal salvation and now united with Unitarianism — **uni·ver·sal·ist** \-sə-ləst, -sləst\ *n or adj, often cap*

uni·ver·sal·ize \-'vər-sə-ˌlīz\ *vt* : to make universal — **uni·ver·sal·iza·tion** \-ˌvər-sə-lə-'zā-shən\ *n*

universal joint *n* : a shaft coupling capable of transmitting rotation from one shaft to another not in a straight line with it

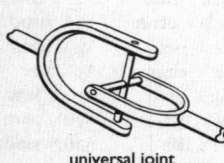
universal joint

uni·verse \'yü-nə-ˌvərs\ *n* **1** : the whole body of things and phenomena observed or postulated : COSMOS **2 a** : a systematic whole held to arise by and persist through the direct intervention of divine power **b** : the world of human experience **3 a** : MILKY WAY GALAXY **b** : an aggregate of stars comparable to the Milky Way galaxy [Latin *universum,* from *universus* "entire, whole", from *uni-* + *versus* "turned toward", from *vertere* "to turn"] SYN see EARTH

uni·ver·si·ty \ˌyü-nə-'vər-sət-ē, -'vər-stē\ *n, pl* **-ties** : an institution of higher learning authorized to grant degrees in various special fields (as law, medicine, and theology) as well as in the arts and sciences

univ·o·cal \yü-'niv-ə-kəl\ *adj* : having one meaning only [Late Latin *univocus,* from Latin *uni-* + *voc-, vox* "voice"] — **univ·o·cal·ly** \-kə-lē, -klē\ *adv*

un·just \ˌən-'jəst, 'ən-\ *adj* : characterized by injustice : deficient in justice and fairness : WRONGFUL (complained of *unjust* treatment by the court) — **un·just·ly** *adv* — **un·just·ness** \-'jəst-nəs, -'jəs-\ *n*

un·kempt \-'kemt, -'kempt\ *adj* **1** : not combed (*unkempt* hair) **2** : being messy and untidy : DISHEVELED [*un-* + Middle English *kempt* "neat, combed", from *kemben* "to comb", from Old English *cemban*]

un·ken·nel \-'ken-l\ *vt* **1 a** : to drive (as a fox) from a hiding place or den **b** : to free (dogs) from a kennel **2** : to bring into the open : DISCLOSE

un·kind \-'kīnd\ *adj* : lacking in kindness or sympathy : HARSH, CRUEL — **un·kind·ly** *adv* — **un·kind·ness** \-'kīnd-nəs, -'kīn-\ *n*

un·kind·ly \-'kīn-dlē\ *adj* : UNKIND — **un·kind·li·ness** *n*

¹un·known \ˌən-'nōn, 'ən-\ *adj* : not known; *also* : having an unknown value (find the *unknown* parts of the triangle)

²unknown *n* : something that is unknown; *esp* : an unknown quantity usually symbolized in mathematics by one of the last letters of the alphabet

Unknown Soldier *n* : an unidentified soldier whose body is selected to receive national honors as a representative of all of that nation who died in a war

un·lace \ˌən-'lās, 'ən-\ *vt* : to loose by undoing a lacing

un·lade \-'lād\ *vb* **1** : to take the load or cargo from **2** : to discharge cargo

un·lash \-'lash\ *vt* : to untie the lashing of : LOOSE, UNDO

un·latch \-'lach\ *vb* **1** : to open or loose by lifting the latch **2** : to become loosed or opened

un·law·ful \-'lȯ-fəl\ *adj* **1** : not lawful : contrary to law : ILLEGAL **2** : not morally right or conventional **3** : ILLEGITIMATE 1 — **un·law·ful·ly** \-fə-lē, -flē\ *adv* — **un·law·ful·ness** \-fəl-nəs\ *n*

un·lay \-'lā\ *vb* **-laid** \-'lād\; **-lay·ing** **1** : to untwist the strands of (as a rope) **2** : UNTWIST 2

un·lead·ed \-'led-əd\ *adj* **1** : stripped of lead **2** : not mixed with lead or lead compounds (*unleaded* fuel)

un·learn \-'lərn\ *vt* : to put out of one's knowledge or memory

un·learned \-'lər-nəd *for 1,* -'lərnd *for 2, 3* \ *adj* **1** : having little formal learning or education **2** : not learned by study : not known (lessons *unlearned* by many) **3** : not learned by previous experience (breathing is *unlearned* behavior)

un·leash \-'lēsh\ *vt* : to free from or as if from a leash : let loose (*unleash* a dog) (the storm *unleashed* its fury)

un·less \ən-'les, ən-, *in some contexts* ᵊn-, ᵊm-, ᵊng-\ *conj* : except on the condition that (will fail *unless* we work harder) [Middle English *onlesse,* from *on* + *lesse* "less"]

un·let·tered \ˌən-'let-ərd, 'ən-\ *adj* **1** : not educated **2** : ILLITERATE

¹un·like \ˌən-'līk, 'ən-\ *adj* : not like: as **a** : marked by dissimilarity : DIFFERENT (the children are quite *unlike*) **b** : UNEQUAL (*unlike* amounts) — **un·like·ness** *n*

²**un·like** *prep* **I** : different from 〈feeling completely *unlike* a hero〉 **2** : not characteristic of 〈it was *unlike* you to be inquisitive〉 **3** : differently from 〈behaving *unlike* your associates〉

un·like·li·hood \ˌən-'līˌklē-ˌhủd, 'ən-\ *n* **I** : the quality or state of being unlikely **2** : something unlikely

un·like·ly \-'lī-klē\ *adj* **I** : not likely : IMPROBABLE **2** : likely to fail : UNPROMISING — **un·like·li·ness** *n*

un·lim·ber \ˌən-'lim-bər, 'ən-\ *vb* : to prepare for action [earlier *unlimber* "to ready a gun for use by removing it from the vehicle to which it is attached", from *limber* "2-wheeled vehicle to which a gun may be attached", from Middle English *lymour* "shaft of a cart"]

un·lim·it·ed \-'lim-ət-əd\ *adj* **I** : lacking any controls **2** : BOUNDLESS, INFINITE **3** : not restricted by exceptions

un·link \-'lingk\ *vt* **I** : to unfasten the links of **2** : to separate by or as if by unlinking a chain

un·list·ed \-'lis-təd\ *adj* : not appearing upon a list: as **a** : not listed on an organized securities exchange 〈*unlisted* stocks〉 **b** : not in the telephone book 〈an *unlisted* number〉

un·liv·able \-'liv-ə-bəl\ *adj* : not fit to live in or with

un·live \-'liv\ *vt* : to live down : ANNUL, REVERSE

un·load \-'lōd\ *vb* **I a** : to take away or off : REMOVE 〈*unload* cargo〉; *also* : to get rid of **b** : to take a load from 〈*unload* a ship〉; *also* : UNBURDEN 〈*unload* your mind of worries〉 **2** : to get rid of a load or burden 〈the ship is *unloading* now〉 **3** : to sell in volume : DUMP 〈*unload* surplus goods〉

un·lock \-'läk\ *vb* **I** : to open or unfasten through release of a lock 〈*unlock* the door〉 〈the chest won't *unlock*〉 **2** : RELEASE 〈*unlock* a flood of emotions〉 **3** : DISCLOSE, REVEAL 〈*unlock* the secrets of nature〉

un·looked–for \-'lủkt-ˌfȯr\ *adj* : not foreseen

un·loose \ˌən-'lüs, 'ən-\ *vt* **I** : to relax the strain of 〈*unloose* a grip〉 **2** : to release from or as if from restraints : set free **3** : to loosen the ties of : UNDO

un·loos·en \-'lüs-n\ *vt* : UNLOOSE

un·love·ly \-'ləv-lē\ *adj* : having no charm or appeal 〈an *unlovely* disposition〉 — **un·love·li·ness** *n*

un·lucky \-'lək-ē\ *adj* **I** : marked by bad luck or failure **2** : likely to bring misfortune **3** : producing dissatisfaction : REGRETTABLE — **un·luck·i·ly** \-'lək-ə-lē\ *adv* — **un·luck·i·ness** \-'lək-ē-nəs\ *n*

un·make \-'māk\ *vt* **-made** \-'mād\; **-mak·ing** **I** : to cause to disappear : DESTROY **2** : to deprive of rank or office : DEPOSE **3** : to change the nature of

un·man \-'man\ *vt* : to deprive of courage, strength, or vigor

un·manned \ˌən-'mand, 'ən-\ *adj* : having no crew aboard

un·man·nered \-'man-ərd\ *adj* **I** : lacking good manners : RUDE **2** : UNAFFECTED 2 — **un·man·nered·ly** *adv*

¹**un·man·ner·ly** \-'man-ər-lē\ *adv* : in an unmannerly fashion

²**unmannerly** *adj* : RUDE 3, IMPOLITE — **un·man·ner·li·ness** *n*

un·mask \ˌən-'mask, 'ən-\ *vb* **I** : to strip of a mask or disguise : EXPOSE 〈*unmask* a traitor〉 **2** : to take off one's own disguise

un·mean·ing \-'mē-ning\ *adj* : having no meaning

un·meant \-'ment\ *adj* : not meant : UNINTENTIONAL

un·meet \-'mēt\ *adj* : not meet : UNSUITABLE, IMPROPER

un·men·tion·able \-'mench-nə-bəl, -ə-nə-\ *adj* : not fit or proper to be talked about — **unmentionable** *n*

un·mer·ci·ful \ˌən-'mər-si-fəl, 'ən-\ *adj* : not merciful : MERCILESS, CRUEL — **un·mer·ci·ful·ly** \-fə-lē, -flē\ *adv*

un·mis·tak·able \ˌən-mə-'stā-kə-bəl\ *adj* : not capable of being mistaken or misunderstood : CLEAR, OBVIOUS — **un·mis·tak·ably** \-blē\ *adv*

un·mit·i·gat·ed \ˌən-'mit-ə-ˌgāt-əd, 'ən-\ *adj* **I** : not softened or lessened **2** : THOROUGH, UTTER 〈an *unmitigated* liar〉 〈*unmitigated* impudence〉 — **un·mit·i·gat·ed·ly** *adv*

un·moor \-'mủr\ *vb* **I** : to loose from or as if from moorings **2** : to cast off moorings

un·mor·al \-'mȯr-əl, -'mär-\ *adj* : having no moral quality or relation : AMORAL — **un·mor·al·ly** \-ə-lē\ *adv*

un·moved \-'müvd\ *adj* **I** : not disturbed emotionally **2 a** : remaining in the same place **b** : firmly set

un·muf·fle \-'məf-əl\ *vt* : to free from something that muffles

un·muz·zle \-'məz-əl\ *vt* : to remove a muzzle from

un·my·elin·at·ed \-'mī-ə-lə-ˌnāt-əd\ *adj* : lacking a myelin sheath

un·nail \ˌən-'nāl, 'ən-\ *vt* : to unfasten by removing nails

un·nat·u·ral \ˌən-'nach-rəl, 'ən-, -ə-rəl\ *adj* **I** : not being in accordance with nature or consistent with a normal course of events **2 a** : not according with normal feelings or behavior : PERVERSE, ABNORMAL **b** : ARTIFICIAL 〈their heartiness was forced and *unnatural*〉 **c** : STRANGE, IRREGULAR 〈an *unnatural* alliance〉 — **un·nat·u·ral·ly** \-'nach-rə-lē, -ə-rə-, -'nach-ər-lē\ *adv* — **un·nat·u·ral·ness** \-'nach-rəl-nəs, -ə-rəl-\ *n*

un·nec·es·sar·i·ly \ˌən-ˌnes-ə-'ser-ə-lē\ *adv* **I** : not by necessity 〈spent money *unnecessarily*〉 **2** : to an unnecessary degree 〈*unnecessarily* harsh〉

un·nec·es·sary \ˌən-'nes-ə-ˌser-ē, 'ən-\ *adj* : not necessary

un·nerve \ˌən-'nərv, 'ən-\ *vt* : to deprive of nerve, courage, or self-control

un·nil·hex·i·um \ˌyün-l-'hek-sē-əm\ *n* : the chemical element of atomic number 106 — see ELEMENT table [New Latin, from *unnil-* (from Latin *unus* "one" + *nil* "zero") + Greek *hex* "six"]

un·nil·pen·ti·um \-ˌpent-ē-əm\ *n* : the chemical element of atomic number 105 — see ELEMENT table [New Latin, from *unnil-* + Greek *pente* "five"]

un·nil·qua·di·um \-ˌkwäd-ē-əm\ *n* : the chemical element of atomic number 104 — see ELEMENT table [New Latin, from *unnil-* + English *quadri-*]

un·num·bered \ˌən-'nəm-bərd, 'ən-\ *adj* **I** : INNUMERABLE 〈*unnumbered* stars〉 **2** : not having an identifying number

un·ob·tru·sive \ˌən-əb-'trü-siv, -ziv\ *adj* : not obtrusive : not blatant or aggressive : INCONSPICUOUS — **un·ob·tru·sive·ly** *adv* — **un·ob·tru·sive·ness** *n*

un·oc·cu·pied \ˌən-'äk-yə-ˌpīd, 'ən-\ *adj* **I** : not busy : UNEMPLOYED **2** : not occupied : EMPTY

un·or·ga·nized \ˌən-'ȯr-gə-ˌnīzd, 'ən-\ *adj* : not subjected to organization: as **a** : not formed or brought into an integrated or ordered whole **b** : not organized into unions

un·pack \ˌən-'pak, 'ən-\ *vb* **I** : to separate and remove things packed **2** : to open and remove the contents of

un·paired \-'paərd, -'peərd\ *adj*; *esp* : not paired **I** : not matched or mated **2** : situated in the median plane of the body 〈an *unpaired* fin〉

un·par·al·leled \-'par-ə-ˌleld\ *adj* : having no parallel; *esp* : having no equal or match

un·par·lia·men·ta·ry \ˌən-ˌpär-lə-'ment-ə-rē, -ˌpärl-yə-, -'men-trē\ *adj* : contrary to parliamentary practice or rules

un·peg \ˌən-'peg, 'ən-\ *vt* : to open by or as if by removing a peg

un·peo·ple \ˌən-'pē-pəl, 'ən-\ *vt* : DEPOPULATE

un·pile \-'pīl\ *vb* : to separate or become separated from a pile

un·pin \-'pin\ *vt* : to undo by or as if by removing a pin

un·pleas·ant \-'plez-nt\ *adj* : not pleasant : not amiable or agreeable — **un·pleas·ant·ly** *adv*

un·pleas·ant·ness \-'plez-nt-nəs\ *n* **I** : the quality or state of being unpleasant **2** : an unpleasant situation, experience, or event

un·plumbed \ˌən-'pləmd, 'ən-\ *adj* **I** : not tested or measured with a plumb line **2** : not thoroughly explored

un·po·lit·i·cal \ˌən-pə-'lit-i-kəl\ *adj* : not interested or engaged in politics

\ə\ abut \ng\ sing
\ər\ further \ō\ bone
\a\ mat \ȯ\ saw
\ā\ take \ȯi\ coin
\ä\ cot, cart \th\ thin
\aủ\ out \th\ this
\ch\ chin \ü\ food
\e\ pet \ủ\ foot
\ē\ easy \y\ yet
\g\ go \yü\ few
\i\ tip \yủ\ cure
\ī\ life \zh\ vision
\j\ job

un·pop·u·lar \ˌən-'päp-yə-lər, 'ən-\ *adj* : not popular : viewed or received unfavorably : disliked by many people — **un·pop·u·lar·i·ty** \ˌən-ˌpäp-yə-'lar-ət-ē\ *n*

un·prec·e·dent·ed \ˌən-'pres-ə-ˌdent-əd, 'ən-\ *adj* : having no precedent : NOVEL — **un·prec·e·dent·ed·ly** *adv*

un·prej·u·diced \ˌən-'prej-əd-əst, 'ən-\ *adj* : not prejudiced : IMPARTIAL

un·pre·ten·tious \ˌən-pri-'ten-chəs\ *adj* : not pretentious : not showy or pompous : SIMPLE, MODEST — **un·pre·ten·tious·ly** *adv* — **un·pre·ten·tious·ness** *n*

un·prin·ci·pled \ˌən-'prin-sə-pəld, 'ən-, -sə-bəld, -spəld\ *adj* : lacking moral principles : UNSCRUPULOUS

un·print·able \-'print-ə-bəl\ *adj* : unfit to be printed

un·pro·fes·sion·al \ˌən-prə-'fesh-nəl, 'ən-, -ən-l\ *adj* : not professional; *esp* : not conforming to the standards of a profession — **un·pro·fes·sion·al·ly** \-ē\ *adv*

un·prof·it·able \ˌən-'präf-ət-ə-bəl, 'ən-, -'präf-tə-bəl\ *adj* : producing no profit, gain, or result — **un·prof·it·able·ness** *n* — **un·prof·it·ably** \-blē\ *adv*

un·prom·is·ing \-'präm-ə-sing\ *adj* : appearing unlikely to prove worthwhile or result favorably — **un·prom·is·ing·ly** \-sing-lē\ *adv*

un·qual·i·fied \-'kwäl-ə-ˌfīd\ *adj* 1 : not fit : lacking necessary qualifications 2 : not modified or restricted by reservations ⟨an *unqualified* denial⟩ — **un·qual·i·fied·ly** \-ˌfī-əd-lē, -ˌfīd-\ *adv*

un·ques·tion·able \-'kwes-chə-nə-bəl, -'kwesh-, *rapid* -'kwesh- nə-\ *adj* 1 : acknowledged as beyond question or doubt ⟨*unquestionable* authority⟩ 2 : not questionable : INDISPUTABLE ⟨*unquestionable* evidence⟩ — **un·ques·tion·ably** \-blē\ *adv*

un·ques·tion·ing \-'kwes-chə-ning, -'kwesh-\ *adj* : not questioning : accepting without hesitation ⟨*unquestioning* trust in God⟩ — **un·ques·tion·ing·ly** \-ning-lē\ *adv*

un·qui·et \-'kwī-ət\ *adj* 1 : not quiet : TURBULENT 2 : physically, emotionally, or mentally restless : UNEASY — **un·qui·et·ly** *adv* — **un·qui·et·ness** *n*

un·quote \'ən-ˌkwōt\ *n* — used orally to indicate the end of a direct quotation

un·rav·el \ˌən-'rav-əl, 'ən-\ *vb* 1 : to separate the threads of : DISENTANGLE ⟨*unravel* a snarl⟩ 2 : SOLVE ⟨*unravel* a mystery⟩ 3 : to become unraveled

un·read \-'red\ *adj* 1 : not read ⟨an *unread* book⟩ 2 : not well informed through reading

un·read·able \-'rēd-ə-bəl\ *adj* 1 : too dull or unattractive to read ⟨a drab *unreadable* dissertation⟩ 2 : not legible or decipherable : ILLEGIBLE — **un·read·abil·i·ty** \ˌən-ˌrēd-ə-'bil-ət-ē\ *n* ☐ SYN UNREADABLE, ILLEGIBLE mean difficult or impossible to read. ILLEGIBLE usually implies a physical impossibility of making out letters or signs ⟨*illegible* handwriting⟩ UNREADABLE more often implies a psychological impossibility of continuing to read with interest or pleasure ⟨a novel now thought *unreadable*⟩

un·ready \ˌən-'red-ē, 'ən-\ *adj* : not ready or qualified ⟨*unready* to deal with a crisis⟩ — **un·read·i·ness** *n*

un·re·al \-'ri-əl, -'ril, -'rē-əl, -'rēl\ *adj* : lacking in reality, substance, or genuineness

un·re·al·is·tic \'ən-ri-ə-'lis-tik, -ˌrē-ə-\ *adj* : not realistic : inappropriate to reality or fact — **un·re·al·is·ti·cal·ly** \-ti-kə-lē, -klē\ *adv*

un·re·al·i·ty \ˌən-rē-'al-ət-ē\ *n* 1 a : the quality or state of being unreal b : something unreal, insubstantial, or visionary 2 : ineptitude in dealing with reality

un·rea·son \ˌən-'rēz-n, 'ən-\ *n* : the absence of reason or sanity

un·rea·son·able \-'rēz-nə-bəl, -n-ə-bəl\ *adj* 1 a : not governed by or acting according to reason ⟨*unreasonable* people⟩ b : not conformable to reason : ABSURD ⟨*unreasonable* arguments⟩ 2 : exceeding the bounds of reason or moderation ⟨*unreasonable* suspicion⟩ SYN see IRRATIONAL — **un·rea·son·able·ness** *n* — **un·rea·son·ably** \-blē\ *adv*

un·rea·son·ing \-'rēz-ning, -n-ing\ *adj* : not reasoning; *esp* : not using or showing the use of reason as a guide or control ⟨*unreasoning* fear⟩ ⟨the *unreasoning* beasts⟩ — **un·rea·son·ing·ly** *adv*

un·re·con·struct·ed \ˌən-ˌrē-kən-'strək-təd\ *adj* : not reconciled to some political, economic, or social change; *esp* : holding stubbornly to principles, beliefs, or views that are held to be outmoded

un·reel \ˌən-'rēl, 'ən-\ *vb* : to unwind from or as if from a reel

un·re·gen·er·ate \ˌən-ri-'jen-rət, -ə-rət\ *adj* : not reborn spiritually : not at peace with God : SINFUL, WICKED

un·re·lent·ing \ˌən-ri-'lent-ing\ *adj* 1 : not softening or yielding in determination : HARD, STERN 2 : not letting up or weakening in vigor or pace — **un·re·lent·ing·ly** \-ing-lē\ *adv*

un·re·mit·ting \ˌən-ri-'mit-ing\ *adj* : not stopping : UNCEASING ⟨hard *unremitting* labor⟩ — **un·re·mit·ting·ly** \-ing-lē\ *adv*

un·re·serve \ˌən-ri-'zərv\ *n* : absence of reserve : FRANKNESS

un·re·served \ˌən-ri-'zərvd\ *adj* 1 : not held in reserve : not kept back 2 : having or showing no reserve in manner or speech — **un·re·serv·ed·ly** \-'zər-vəd-lē\ *adv* — **un·re·served·ness** \-'zər-vəd-nəs, -'zərvd-nəs, -'zərv-nəs\ *n*

un·re·spon·sive \ˌən-ri-'spän-siv\ *adj* : not responsive — **un·re·spon·sive·ly** *adv* — **un·re·spon·sive·ness** *n*

un·rest \ˌən-'rest, 'ən-\ *n* : a disturbed or uneasy state

un·re·strained \ˌən-ri-'strānd\ *adj* 1 : not restrained : IMMODERATE 2 : free of constraint : SPONTANEOUS — **un·re·strain·ed·ly** \-'strā-nəd-lē\ *adv*

un·re·straint \-'strānt\ *n* : lack of restraint

un·rid·dle \ˌən-'rid-l, 'ən-\ *vt* : to find the explanation of : SOLVE

un·righ·teous \-'rī-chəs\ *adj* 1 : not righteous : SINFUL, WICKED 2 : UNJUST, UNCALLED-FOR ⟨*unrighteous* interference⟩ — **un·righ·teous·ly** *adv* — **un·righ·teous·ness** *n*

un·rip \-'rip\ *vt* : to rip or slit up : cut or tear open

un·ripe \-'rīp\ *adj* 1 : not ripe : IMMATURE 2 : UNREADY, UNSEASONABLE — **un·ripe·ness** *n*

un·ri·valed *or* **un·ri·valled** \-'rī-vəld\ *adj* : having no rival : INCOMPARABLE, UNEQUALED

un·robe \ˌən-'rōb, 'ən-\ *vb* : DISROBE, UNDRESS

un·roll \-'rōl\ *vb* 1 : to unwind a roll of : open out ⟨*unroll* a carpet⟩ 2 : to spread out like a scroll for reading or inspection 3 : to be or seem to be unrolled ⟨the scene *unrolled* under the speeding plane⟩

un·roof \-'rüf, -'rùf\ *vt* : to strip off the roof or covering of

un·round \-'raùnd\ *vt* : to pronounce (a sound) without, or with decreased, rounding of the lips — **un·round·ed** \-'raùn-dəd\ *adj*

un·ruf·fled \-'rəf-əld\ *adj* 1 : not upset or agitated 2 : not ruffled : SMOOTH ⟨*unruffled* water⟩

un·ruly \ˌən-'rü-lē, 'ən-\ *adj* : not yielding readily to rule or restraint : hard to handle or manage ⟨an *unruly* temper⟩ ⟨an *unruly* horse⟩ — **un·rul·i·ness** *n* ☐ SYN UNGOVERNABLE, REFRACTORY, RECALCITRANT: UNRULY implies lack of discipline or incapacity for discipline and often connotes waywardness or turbulence of behavior ⟨*unruly* children⟩ UNGOVERNABLE implies either an escape from control or guidance or a state of being unsubdued and incapable of controlling the self or being controlled by others ⟨*ungovernable* rage⟩ ⟨*ungovernable* stampeding cattle⟩ REFRACTORY stresses resistance to attempts to manage or to mold ⟨special schools for *refractory* children⟩ RECALCITRANT suggests determined resistance to or defiance of authority ⟨sabotage by a *recalcitrant* populace⟩

un·sad·dle \ˌən-'sad-l, 'ən-\ *vb* 1 a : to remove the saddle from a horse b : to remove a saddle from 2 : UNHORSE

un·sat·u·rate \-'sach-rət, -ə-rət\ *n* : an unsaturated chemical compound

un·sat·u·rat·ed \-'sach-ə-,rāt-əd\ *adj* **1** : capable of absorbing or dissolving more of something ⟨an *unsaturated* salt solution⟩ **2** : able to form a new product by direct chemical combination with another substance; *esp* : containing double or triple bonds between carbon atoms ⟨an *unsaturated* acid⟩ — **un·sat·u·ra·tion** \,ən-,sach-ə-'rā-shən\ *n*

un·saved \,ən-'sāvd, 'ən-\ *adj* : not saved; *esp* : not rescued from eternal punishment

un·sa·vory \-'sāv-rē, -ə-rē\ *adj* **1** : having little or no taste **2** : having a bad taste or smell **3** : morally offensive ⟨an *unsavory* character⟩ — **un·sa·vor·i·ly** \-'sāv-rə-lē, -ə-rə-\ *adv*

un·say \-'sā\ *vt* **-said** \-'sed\; **-say·ing** \-'sā-ing\ : to take back (something said) : RETRACT, WITHDRAW

un·scathed \,ən-'skāth̪d, 'ən-\ *adj* : wholly unharmed : not injured

un·schooled \-'sküld\ *adj* : not schooled : UNTAUGHT

un·sci·en·tif·ic \,ən-,sī-ən-'tif-ik\ *adj* **1** : not used in scientific work **2** : not according with the principles and methods of science — **un·sci·en·tif·i·cal·ly** \-'tif-i-kə-lē, -klē\ *adv*

un·scram·ble \,ən-'skram-bəl, 'ən-\ *vt* **1** : to separate into original components : RESOLVE, CLARIFY **2** : to restore (as a radio message) to intelligible form

un·screw \-'skrü\ *vb* **1** : to remove the screws from **2** : to loosen or withdraw by turning

un·scru·pu·lous \-'skrü-pyə-ləs\ *adj* : UNPRINCIPLED — **un·scru·pu·lous·ly** *adv* — **un·scru·pu·lous·ness** *n*

un·seal \-'sēl\ *vt* : to break or remove the seal of : OPEN

un·seam \-'sēm\ *vt* : to open the seams of

un·search·able \-'sər-chə-bəl\ *adj* : impossible to explore or examine ⟨the *unsearchable* ways of God⟩ — **un·search·ably** \-blē\ *adv*

un·sea·son·able \-'sēz-nə-bəl, -'sēz-n-ə-\ *adj* : not seasonable : happening or coming at the wrong time : UNTIMELY — **un·sea·son·able·ness** *n* — **un·sea·son·ably** \-blē\ *adv*

un·seat \,ən-'sēt, 'ən-\ *vt* **1** : to dislodge from a seat especially on horseback **2** : to dislodge from a place or position; *esp* : to remove from political office

¹un·seem·ly \-'sēm-lē\ *adj* : not suitable or proper : UNBECOMING ⟨*unseemly* bickering in public⟩ SYN see INDECOROUS

²unseemly *adv* : in an unseemly manner

un·seen \-'sēn\ *adj* : not seen or perceived : INVISIBLE

un·seg·re·gat·ed \-'seg-ri-,gāt-əd\ *adj* : not segregated; *esp* : free from racial segregation

un·self·ish \-'sel-fish\ *adj* : not selfish : GENEROUS — **un·self·ish·ly** *adv* — **un·self·ish·ness** *n*

un·set·tle \,ən-'set-l, 'ən-\ *vb* : to move or loosen from a settled state : make or become displaced or disturbed

un·set·tled \-'set-ld\ *adj* **1** : not settled : not fixed (as in position or character) ⟨*unsettled* weather⟩ **2** : not calm or tranquil ⟨*unsettled* waters⟩ **3** : not decided in mind ⟨*unsettled* what to do⟩ **4** : not paid ⟨an *unsettled* account⟩; *also* : not disposed of according to law ⟨an *unsettled* estate⟩ **5** : not occupied by settlers ⟨an *unsettled* region⟩

un·sew \,ən-'sō, 'ən-\ *vt* **-sewed**; **-sewn** \-'sōn\ *or* **-sewed**; **-sew·ing** : to undo the sewing of

un·sex \-'seks\ *vt* : to deprive of sex or of qualities typical of one's sex

un·shack·le \-'shak-əl\ *vt* : to loose from shackles

un·shaped \-'shāpt\ *adj* : not shaped: as **a** : not dressed or finished to final form ⟨an *unshaped* timber⟩ **b** : imperfect in form or formulation ⟨*unshaped* ideas⟩

un·shap·en \-'shā-pən\ *adj* : UNSHAPED [Middle English, from ¹*un-* + *shapen,* past participle of *shapen* "to shape"]

un·sheathe \-'shēth̪\ *vt* : to draw from or as if from a sheath or scabbard ⟨*unsheathe* a sword⟩

un·ship \,ən-'ship, 'ən-\ *vb* **1** : to remove from a ship **2** : to remove or become removed from position ⟨*unship* an oar⟩

un·shod \-'shäd\ *adj* : lacking shoes

un·sight·ly \-'sīt-lē\ *adj* : unpleasant to the sight : UGLY ⟨an *unsightly* scar⟩ — **un·sight·li·ness** *n*

un·skilled \-'skild\ *adj* **1** : not skilled; *esp* : not skilled in a specified branch of work : lacking technical training **2** : not requiring skill ⟨*unskilled* jobs⟩ **3** : marked by lack of skill ⟨*unskilled* writing⟩

un·skill·ful \-'skil-fəl\ *adj* : lacking in skill or proficiency — **un·skill·ful·ly** \-fə-lē\ *adv* — **un·skill·ful·ness** *n*

un·sling \-'sling\ *vt* **-slung** \-'sləng\; **-sling·ing** \-'sling-ing\ : to remove from being slung

un·snap \-'snap\ *vt* : to loosen or free by or as if by undoing a snap

un·snarl \-'snärl\ *vt* : to straighten out a snarl in

un·so·cia·bil·i·ty \,ən-,sō-shə-'bil-ət-ē\ *n* : the quality or state of being unsociable

un·so·cia·ble \,ən-'sō-shə-bəl, 'ən-\ *adj* **1** : having or showing a preference for avoiding society or conversation : SOLITARY, RESERVED **2** : not conducive to sociability — **un·so·cia·ble·ness** *n* — **un·so·cia·bly** \-blē\ *adv*

un·so·cial \-'sō-shəl\ *adj* **1** : not social : not seeking or given to association **2** : ANTISOCIAL 1 — **un·so·cial·ly** \-'sōsh-lē, -ə-lē\ *adv*

un·so·phis·ti·cat·ed \,ən-sə-'fis-tə-,kāt-əd\ *adj* : not sophisticated: as **a** : not changed or corrupted : GENUINE **b** (1) : not worldly-wise : lacking sophistication (2) : lacking adornment or complexity of structure : PLAIN, SIMPLE

un·so·phis·ti·ca·tion \-,fis-tə-'kā-shən\ *n* : lack of sophistication

un·sought \,ən-'sȯt, 'ən-\ *adj* : not sought : not searched for or asked for ⟨*unsought* honors⟩

un·sound \-'saȯnd\ *adj* : not sound: as **a** : not healthy or whole **b** : not mentally normal : not wholly sane **c** : not firmly made, placed, or fixed **d** : not valid or true — **un·sound·ly** *adv* — **un·sound·ness** \-'saȯnd-nəs, -'saȯn-\ *n*

un·spar·ing \-'spaȯr-ing, -'speȯr-\ *adj* **1** : not merciful : HARD, RUTHLESS **2** : not frugal : LIBERAL — **un·spar·ing·ly** \-ing-lē\ *adv*

un·speak·able \-'spē-kə-bəl\ *adj* **1** : impossible to express in words **2** : extremely bad ⟨*unspeakable* conduct⟩ — **un·speak·ably** \-blē\ *adv*

un·spot·ted \,ən-'spät-əd, 'ən-\ *adj* : not spotted : free from spot or stain; *esp* : free from moral stain

un·sprung \-'sprəng\ *adj* : not sprung; *esp* : not equipped with springs

un·sta·ble \-'stā-bəl\ *adj* : not stable : not firm or fixed : not constant: as **a** : not steady in action or movement **b** : wavering in purpose or intent ⟨*unstable* beliefs⟩; *also* : having defective emotional control ⟨an *unstable* person⟩ **c** : readily changing in chemical composition or physical state or properties ⟨an *unstable* emulsion⟩; *esp* : tending to decompose spontaneously ⟨an *unstable* atomic nucleus⟩ — **un·sta·ble·ness** *n* — **un·sta·bly** \-bə-lē, -blē\ *adv*

un·steady \-'sted-ē\ *adj* : lacking in stability or regularity — **un·stead·i·ly** \-'sted-l-ē\ *adv* — **un·stead·i·ness** \-'sted-ē-nəs\ *n*

un·stick \-'stik\ *vt* **-stuck** \-'stək\; **-stick·ing** : to release from being stuck or bound

un·stint·ing·ly \-'stint-ing-lē\ *adv* : without limit : FREELY ⟨gave *unstintingly* of their time⟩

un·stop \-'stäp\ *vt* **1** : to free from an obstruction : OPEN **2** : to remove a stopper from

un·strap \-'strap\ *vt* : to remove or loose a strap from

un·stressed \-'strest\ *adj* : not stressed; *esp* : not bearing a stress or accent

un·string \-'string\ *vt* **-strung** \-'strəng\; **-string·ing** \-'string-ing\ **1** : to loosen or remove the strings of **2** :

\ə\ abut		\ng\ sing	
\ər\ further		\ō\ bone	
\a\ mat		\ȯ\ saw	
\ā\ take		\ȯi\ coin	
\ä\ cot, cart		\th\ thin	
\aȯ\ out		\th̪\ this	
\ch\ chin		\ü\ food	
\e\ pet		\ȯ\ foot	
\ē\ easy		\y\ yet	
\g\ go		\yü\ few	
\i\ tip		\yȯ\ cure	
\ī\ life		\zh\ vision	
\j\ job			

to remove from a string **3** : to make weak, disordered, or unstable

un·stud·ied \-'stəd-ēd\ *adj* **1** : not acquired by study **2** : not planned with a certain effect in mind : NATURAL

un·sub·stan·tial \,ən-səb-'stan-chəl\ *adj* : lacking substance, firmness, or strength — **un·sub·stan·ti·al·i·ty** \-,stan-chē-'al-ət-ē\ *n* — **un·sub·stan·tial·ly** \-'stanch-lē, -ə-lē\ *adv*

un·suc·cess·ful \,ən-sək-'ses-fəl\ *adj* : not meeting with or producing success — **un·suc·cess·ful·ly** \-fə-lē\ *adv*

un·suit·able \,ən-'süt-ə-bəl, 'ən-\ *adj* : not fitting : UNBECOMING, INAPPROPRIATE — **un·suit·abil·i·ty** \-,süt-ə-'bil-ət-ē\ *n* — **un·suit·ably** \-'süt-ə-blē\ *adv*

un·sung \-'səng\ *adj* **1** : not sung **2** : not praised (as in song or verse) : not publicized (*unsung* heroes)

un·swathe \-'swä͟th, -'swo͟th, -'swä͟th\ *vt* : to free from something that swathes

un·swear \-'swaər, -'sweər\ *vb* **-swore** \-'swōər, -'swȯər\; **-sworn** \-'swōrn -'swȯrn\; **-swear·ing** *archaic* : RECANT, RETRACT

un·swerv·ing \-'swər-ving\ *adj* **1** : not swerving or turning aside **2** : STEADY (*unswerving* loyalty)

un·sym·met·ri·cal \,ən-sə-'me-tri-kəl\ *also* **un·sym·met·ric** \-trik\ *adj* : not symmetrical : ASYMMETRIC — **un·sym·met·ri·cal·ly** \-tri-kə-lē, -klē\ *adv*

un·tan·gle \,ən-'tang-gəl, 'ən-\ *vt* **1** : to remove a tangle from **2** : to straighten (as something complex or confused) out : RESOLVE SYN see EXTRICATE

un·taught \-'tȯt\ *adj* **1** : not instructed or trained : IGNORANT **2** : NATURAL, SPONTANEOUS (*untaught* kindness)

un·teth·er \-'teth-ər\ *vt* : to free from a tether

un·think·able \-'thing-kə-bəl\ *adj* : not to be thought of or considered as possible (*unthinkable* cruelty)

un·think·ing \-'thing-king\ *adj* **1** : not taking thought : HEEDLESS, UNMINDFUL **2** : not indicating thought or reflection **3** : not having the power of thought — **un·think·ing·ly** \-king-lē\ *adv*

un·thought–of \-'thȯt-,əv, -,äv\ *adj* : not thought of : not considered : not imagined

un·thread \-'thred\ *vt* **1** : to draw or take out a thread from **2** : to loosen the threads or connections of **3** : to make one's way through (*unthread* a maze)

un·throne \-'thrōn\ *vt* : to remove from or as if from a throne

un·ti·dy \-'tīd-ē\ *adj* **1** : not neat : CARELESS, SLOVENLY **2 a** : not neatly organized or carried out **b** : tending to cause a lack of neatness — **un·ti·di·ly** \-'tīd-l-ē\ *adv* — **un·ti·di·ness** \-'tīd-ē-nəs\ *n*

un·tie \-'tī\ *vb* **-tied; -ty·ing** *or* **-tie·ing** **1** : to free from something that ties, fastens, or restrains : UNBIND **2 a** : to disengage the knotted parts of **b** : DISENTANGLE, RESOLVE **3** : to become loosened or unbound

¹un·til \ən-,til, -,tl, -,tel, -,ən-, in some contexts ⁿn-, ⁿm-, ⁿng-\ *prep* : up to the time of (stayed *until* morning) [Middle English, from *un-* "to, until" + *til* "till"]

²until *conj* **1** : up to the time that (played *until* it got dark) **2** : to the point or degree that (ran *until* I was breathless)

¹un·time·ly \,ən-'tīm-lē, 'ən-\ *adv* **1** : at an inopportune time : UNSEASONABLY **2** : too soon

²untimely *adj* **1** : occurring or done before the due, natural, or proper time : too early : PREMATURE (*untimely* death) **2** : UNSEASONABLE (an *untimely* joke) (*untimely* frost) — **un·time·li·ness** *n*

un·ti·tled \-'tīt-ld\ *adj* **1** : having no title especially of nobility **2** : not named (an *untitled* painting)

un·to \'ən-tə, -tü\ *prep* : TO [Middle English, from *un-* "to, until" + *to*]

un·told \,ən-'tōld, 'ən-\ *adj* **1** : not told : not revealed (*untold* secrets) (a story yet *untold*) **2** : not counted : VAST, NUMBERLESS (*untold* resources)

¹un·touch·able \-'təch-ə-bəl\ *adj* **1 a** : forbidden to the touch **b** : exempt from criticism or control **2** : being

out of reach **3** : disagreeable or defiling to the touch — **un·touch·abil·i·ty** \-,təch-ə-'bil-ət-ē\ *n*

²untouchable *n* : one that is untouchable; *esp* : a member of a large formerly segregated hereditary group in India having in traditional Hindu belief the quality of defiling by contact a member of a higher caste

un·to·ward \,ən-'tō-ərd, -'tȯ-ərd, -'tōrd, -'tȯrd, 'ən-\ *adj* **1** : difficult to manage : STUBBORN, WILLFUL (an *untoward* child) **2** : INCONVENIENT, TROUBLESOME (an *untoward* encounter) — **un·to·ward·ly** *adv* — **un·to·ward·ness** *n*

un·tread \,ən-'tred, 'ən-\ *vt* **-trod** \-'träd\; **-trod·den** \-'träd-n\; **-tread·ing** *archaic* : to tread back : RETRACE

un·tried \-'trīd\ *adj* **1** : not tested or proved by experience or trial (*untried* soldiers) **2** : not tried in court (a backlog of *untried* cases)

un·true \-'trü\ *adj* **1** : not faithful : DISLOYAL **2** : not according with a standard of correctness : not level or exact **3** : not according with the facts : FALSE — **un·tru·ly** \-'trü-lē\ *adv*

un·truth \-'trüth\ *n* **1** : lack of truthfulness : FALSITY **2** : something that is untrue : FALSEHOOD

un·truth·ful \-'trüth-fəl\ *adj* : not containing or telling the truth : FALSE, INACCURATE (*untruthful* report) — **un·truth·ful·ly** \-fə-lē\ *adv* — **un·truth·ful·ness** *n*

un·tuck \-'tək\ *vt* : to release from a tuck or from being tucked up

un·tune \-'tün, -'tyün\ *vt* **1** : to put out of tune **2** : DISARRANGE, DISCOMPOSE

un·tu·tored \,ən-'tüt-ərd, -'tyüt-, 'ən-\ *adj* **1** : lacking schooling **2** : not gained from instruction : NATIVE (*untutored* shrewdness)

un·twine \-'twīn\ *vb* **1** : to unwind the twisted or tangled parts of **2** : to remove by unwinding **3** : to become disentangled or unwound

un·twist \-'twist\ *vb* **1** : to separate the twisted parts of : UNTWINE **2** : to become untwined

un·used \-'yüzd, *in the phrase "unused to" usually* -'yüs, -'yüst\ *adj* **1** : not habituated : UNACCUSTOMED 2 **2** : not used: as **a** : never yet used : NEW **b** : not now being used **c** : not used up (*unused* vacation)

un·usu·al \-'yüzh-wəl, -ə-wəl, -'yüzh-əl\ *adj* : not usual : UNCOMMON, RARE — **un·usu·al·ly** \-'yüzh-wə-lē, -ə-wə-, -'yüzh-lē, -'yüzh-ə-lē\ *adv* — **un·usu·al·ness** \-'yüzh-wəl-nəs, -ə-wəl-, -'yüzh-əl-\ *n*

un·ut·ter·able \-'ət-ə-rə-bəl\ *adj* : not capable of being put into words : INEXPRESSIBLE — **un·ut·ter·ably** \-blē\ *adv*

un·val·ued \,ən-'val-yüd, 'ən-\ *adj* **1** : not important or prized **2** : not appraised

un·var·nished \-'vär-nisht\ *adj* **1** : not embellished or glossed over : PLAIN, STRAIGHTFORWARD (the *unvarnished* truth) **2** : not covered with or as if with varnish

un·veil \-'vāl\ *vb* **1** : to remove a veil or covering from (*unveil* a statue) **2** : to remove a concealing cover

un·ver·bal·ized \-'vər-bə-,līzd\ *adj* : not put into words or given conscious expression

un·vo·cal \-'vō-kəl\ *adj* : not eloquent or outspoken

un·voiced \-'vȯist\ *adj* **1** : not verbally expressed **2** : VOICELESS 2

un·war·rant·able \-'wȯr-ənt-ə-bəl, -'wär-\ *adj* : not justifiable : INEXCUSABLE — **un·war·rant·ably** \-blē\ *adv*

un·wary \-'waər-ē, -'weər-\ *adj* : easily fooled or surprised : HEEDLESS, GULLIBLE — **un·war·i·ly** \-'war-ə-lē, -'wer-\ *adv* — **un·war·i·ness** \-'war-ē-nəs, -'wer-\ *n*

un·wea·ried \-'wiər-ēd\ *adj* : not tired : FRESH

un·weave \,ən-'wēv, 'ən-\ *vt* **wove** \-'wōv\; **wo·ven** \-'wō-vən\; **weav·ing** : DISENTANGLE, RAVEL

un·well \-'wel\ *adj* **1** : being in poor health : AILING, SICK **2** : undergoing menstruation

un·wept \-'wept\ *adj* : not mourned

un·whole·some \-'hōl-səm\ *adj* : detrimental to physical, mental, or moral well-being : UNHEALTHY

un·wieldy \-'wēl-dē\ *adj* : not easily handled or managed because of size or weight : AWKWARD, CLUMSY, CUMBERSOME (an *unwieldy* tool) — **un·wield·i·ness** *n*

un·willed \-'wild\ *adj* : not willed : INVOLUNTARY

un·wind \-'wīnd\ *vb* **-wound** \-'waunt\ *also* **-wind·ed;
-wind·ing 1 a** : to cause to uncoil : wind off **b** : to become uncoiled or untangled **c** : to free from or as if from a binding or wrapping **2** : to make or become free of tension : RELAX

un·wise \-'wīz\ *adj* : not wise : FOOLISH — **un·wise·ly**
adv

un·wit·ting \-'wit-ing\ *adj* **1** : not intended : INADVERTENT **2** : not knowing : UNAWARE — **un·wit·ting·ly**
\-ing-lē\ *adv*

un·wont·ed \-'wont-əd, -'wont-\ *adj* **1** : being out of the ordinary : RARE, UNUSUAL **2** : not accustomed by experience — **un·wont·ed·ly** *adv* — **un·wont·ed·ness** *n*

un·world·ly \-'wərl-dlē\ *adj* **1** : not of this world; *esp* : SPIRITUAL **2 a** : not wise in the ways of the world : NAIVE **b** : not moved by worldly considerations — **un·world·li·ness** *n*

un·worn \-'wōrn, -'worn\ *adj* **1** : not damaged by use or wear **2** : not worn : NEW

un·wor·thy \,ən-'wər-thē, 'ən-\ *adj* **1** : BASE, DISHONORABLE ⟨*unworthy* duties⟩ **2** : of insufficient merit or worth ⟨*unworthy* to be trusted⟩ — **un·wor·thi·ly** \-thə-lē\ *adv* — **un·wor·thi·ness** \-thē-nəs\ *n*

un·wrap \-'rap\ *vt* : to remove the wrapping from

un·writ·ten \-'rit-n\ *adj* **1** : not put in writing : ORAL, TRADITIONAL **2** : containing no writing : BLANK

unwritten law *n* : law based chiefly on custom rather than legislative enactments

un·yield·ing \,ən-'yēl-ding, 'ən-\ *adj* **1** : marked by lack of softness or flexibility **2** : marked by firmness or stubbornness

un·yoke \-'yōk\ *vt* **1** : to free (as oxen) from a yoke **2** : SEPARATE 1a, DISCONNECT

un·zip \-'zip\ *vb* : to open by means of a zipper

¹up \'əp\ *adv* **1 a** : in or to a higher position or level : away from the center of the earth **b** : from beneath a surface (as ground or water) **c** : from below the horizon **d** : in or into an upright position **e** : out of bed **2** : with greater strength, force, or energy ⟨speak *up*⟩ **3 a** : in or into a better or more advanced state **b** : in or into a state of greater intensity or activity ⟨stir *up* a fire⟩ **4 a** : into existence, evidence, or knowledge ⟨the missing ring turned *up*⟩ **b** : into consideration ⟨brought the matter *up*⟩ **5** : into possession or custody **6 a** : WHOLLY 1, COMPLETELY ⟨eat it *up*⟩ **b** — used for emphasis ⟨clean *up* a room⟩ **7** : ASIDE, BY ⟨lay *up* supplies⟩ ⟨put my car *up* for the winter⟩ **8** : into a state of closure or confinement ⟨button *up*⟩ ⟨seal *up* a package⟩ **9 a** : so as to arrive or approach ⟨came *up* the drive⟩ **b** : in a direction conventionally opposite to down **c** : so as to be even with, overtake, or arrive at ⟨catch *up*⟩ ⟨keep *up* with the times⟩ **10** : in or into parts ⟨tear *up* paper⟩ ⟨blow *up* a bridge⟩ **11** : to a stop ⟨pull *up*⟩ ⟨drew *up* at the curb⟩ **12 a** : AHEAD ⟨went one *up* on their opponent⟩ **b** : for each side ⟨score was 15 *up*⟩ [Old English]

²up *adj* **1 a** : risen above the horizon **b** : being out of bed **c** : relatively high ⟨the river is *up*⟩ ⟨prices are *up*⟩ **d** : raised so as to be open ⟨windows are *up*⟩ **e** : put together ⟨the house is *up* but not finished⟩ **f** : grown above a surface ⟨the corn is *up*⟩ **g** : moving, inclining, or directed upward or in a direction regarded as up ⟨the *up* escalator⟩ **2 a** : marked by agitation, excitement, or activity ⟨was eager to be *up* and doing⟩ **b** : going on : taking place ⟨find out what is *up*⟩ **3** : come to an end ⟨your time is *up*⟩ **4** : well informed ⟨always *up* on the news⟩ **5** : being ahead or in advance of an opponent ⟨was three games *up* in the series⟩ **6 a** : presented for or under consideration ⟨*up* for reelection⟩ **b** : charged before a court ⟨was *up* for robbery⟩ — **up to 1** : capable of performing or dealing with ⟨was fully *up to* the job⟩ **2** : engaged in ⟨what are you *up to*⟩ **3** : being the responsibility of ⟨it's *up to* me⟩

³up \,əp, 'əp\ *prep* **1** : to, toward, or at a higher point of ⟨*up* the hill⟩ **2 a (1)** : toward the source of ⟨*up* the river⟩ **(2)** : toward the northern part of ⟨*up* the coast⟩ **b** : to, toward, or in the inner part of **3** : ALONG ⟨walking *up* the street⟩

⁴up \'əp\ *n* **1** : an upward course or slope **2** : a period or state of prosperity or success ⟨have my *ups* and downs⟩

⁵up *vb* **upped** *or in 1* **up; upped; up·ping; ups** *or in 1* **up 1** : to act abruptly or surprisingly — usually followed by *and* and another verb ⟨they *up* and left⟩ **2** : to rise from a lying or sitting position **3** : to move or cause to move upward : ASCEND, RAISE

up–and–coming \,əp-ən-'kəm-ing, ,əp-m-\ *adj* : alertly active and likely to advance or succeed

up–and–down \,əp-m-'daun, ,əp-ən-\ *adj* **1** : marked by alternate upward and downward movement, action, or surface **2** : very steep : PERPENDICULAR

Upa·ni·shad \ü-'pän-ə-,shäd, yü-'pän-ə-,shad\ *n* : one of a class of Vedic philosophical treatises [Sanskrit *upaniṣad*]

¹up·beat \'əp-,bēt\ *n* : an unaccented beat in a musical measure; *esp* : the last beat of the measure

²upbeat *adj* : marked by optimism : OPTIMISTIC, CHEERFUL

up·braid \,əp-'brād\ *vt* : to criticize or scold severely or vehemently [Old English *ūpbregdan*] — **up·braid·er** *n*

up·bring·ing \'əp-,bring-ing\ *n* : early training; *esp* : a particular way of bringing up a child

up·chuck \'əp-,chək\ *vb* : VOMIT 1

up·com·ing \,əp-kəm-ing\ *adj* : being in the near future : FORTHCOMING

¹up–coun·try \,əp-kən-trē\ *adj* : of or relating to the interior of a country or a region — **up–coun·try** \'əp-\ *n*

²up–coun·try \'əp-'kən-trē\ *adv* : to or in the interior of a country or a region

up·date \,əp-'dāt\ *vt* : to bring up to date — **up·date** \'əp-,dāt\ *n*

up·draft \'əp-,draft, -,dráft\ *n* : an upward movement of gas (as air)

up·end \,ə-'pend\ *vb* : to set, stand, or rise on end

¹up·grade \'əp-,grād\ *n* **1** : an upward grade or slope **2 a** : INCREASE 1 ⟨crime is on the *upgrade*⟩ **b** : a rise toward a better state — **up·grade** \-'grād\ *adv*

²up·grade \-,grād\ *vt* : to raise to a higher grade or position

up·growth \'əp-,grōth\ *n* : the process of increasing (as in height or complexity) : DEVELOPMENT; *also* : a product or result of this

up·heav·al \,əp-'hē-vəl, ə-'pē-\ *n* **1** : the action or an instance of upheaving especially of part of the earth's crust **2** : an instance of violent agitation or change

up·heave \,əp-'hēv, ə-'pēv\ *vb* **-heaved; -heav·ing** : to heave or lift up from beneath — **up·heav·er** *n*

¹up·hill \'əp-'hil\ *adv* **1** : upward on a hill or incline **2** : against difficulties

²up·hill \'əp-,hil\ *adj* **1 a** : situated on elevated ground **b** : going or directed toward higher ground **2** : requiring much effort

up·hold \,əp-'hōld\ *vt* **-held** \-'held\; **-hold·ing 1 a** : to give support to **b** : to support against an opponent **2 a** : to keep elevated **b** : to lift up — **up·hold·er** *n*

up·hol·ster \,əp-'hōl-stər, əp-'hōl-; ə-'pōl-\ *vt* **-stered; -ster·ing** \-stə-ring, -string\ : to furnish with or as if with upholstery [back-formation from *upholstery*] — **up·hol·ster·er** \-stər-ər, -strər\ *n*

up·hol·stery \-stə-rē, -strē\ *n, pl* **-ster·ies** : materials (as fabric, padding, and springs) used to make a soft covering especially for a seat [Middle English *upholdester* "upholsterer", from *upholden* "to uphold, maintain"]

up·keep \'əp-,kēp\ *n* **1** : the act or cost of maintaining in good condition : MAINTENANCE **2** : the state of being maintained

\ə\ abut		\ng\ sing	
\ər\ further		\ō\ bone	
\a\ mat		\o\ saw	
\ā\ take		\oi\ coin	
\ä\ cot, cart		\th\ thin	
\au\ out		\th\ this	
\ch\ chin		\ü\ food	
\e\ pet		\u\ foot	
\ē\ easy		\y\ yet	
\g\ go		\yü\ few	
\i\ tip		\yu\ cure	
\ī\ life		\zh\ vision	
\j\ job			

upland plover

up·land \'əp-lənd, -‚land\ *n* : high land especially at some distance from the sea — **upland** *adj*

upland cotton *n* : any of various usually short-staple cottons cultivated especially in the United States

upland plover *n* : a large sandpiper of eastern North America that frequents fields and uplands

¹up·lift \əp-'lift, ‚əp-\ *vb* **1** : to lift up : ELEVATE **2** : to improve the condition of especially spiritually, socially, or intellectually — **up·lift·er** *n*

²up·lift \'əp-‚lift\ *n* : an act, process, or result of uplifting: as **a** : the uplifting of a part of the earth's surface **b** : moral or social improvement; *also* : a movement to make such improvement **c** : influences intended to uplift

up·load \‚əp-'lōd, 'əp-‚\ *vt* : to transfer (information) from a microcomputer to a remote computer usually with a modem

up·most \'əp-‚mōst\ *adj* : UPPERMOST

up·on \ə-'pȯn, -'pän, -‚pȯn, -pən\ *prep* : ON

¹up·per \'əp-ər\ *adj* **1** : higher in physical position, rank, or order **2** : constituting the smaller and senior branch of a bicameral legislature **3** *cap* : of, relating to, or constituting a later geologic period or formation 〈*Upper* Cretaceous〉 **4** : being toward the interior : further inland 〈the *upper* Amazon〉 **5** : NORTHERN 〈*upper* New York state〉

²upper *n* : one that is upper: as **a** : the parts of a shoe or boot above the sole **b** : an upper tooth or denture **c** : an upper berth

³upper *n* : a stimulant drug; *esp* : AMPHETAMINE

up·per·case \‚əp-ər-'kās\ *adj* : CAPITAL 2 [from the printer's practice of keeping capitals in the upper of two typecases] — **uppercase** *n*

upper class *n* : a social class occupying a position above the middle class and having the highest status in a society — **upper–class** *adj*

up·per·class·man \‚əp-ər-'klas-mən\ *n* : a junior or senior in a college or high school

upper crust *n* : the highest social class or group

up·per·cut \'əp-ər-‚kət\ *n* : a swinging blow (as in boxing) directed upward with a bent arm — **uppercut** *vb*

upper hand *n* : ADVANTAGE 1, BETTER

up·per·most \'əp-ər-‚mōst\ *adv* : in or into the highest or most prominent position — **uppermost** *adj*

up·per·part \-‚pärt\ *n* : a part lying on the upper side (as of a bird)

up·pish \'əp-ish\ *adj* : UPPITY — **up·pish·ness** *n*

up·pi·ty \'əp-ət-ē\ *adj* : putting on airs of superiority : ARROGANT [probably from *up* + *-ity* (as in *persnickity*, variant of *persnickety*)] — **up·pi·ty·ness** *n*

up·raise \‚ə-'prāz, ə-\ *vt* : to raise or lift up : ELEVATE

¹up·right \'əp-‚rīt\ *adj* **1 a** : PERPENDICULAR 2, VERTICAL **b** : erect in carriage or posture **c** : having the main axis or a main part perpendicular **2** : morally correct : HONEST, HONORABLE — **up·right·ly** *adv* — **up·right·ness** *n*

²upright *n* **1** : the state of being upright : PERPENDICULAR 〈a pillar out of *upright*〉 **2** : something upright **3** : UPRIGHT PIANO

upright piano *n* : a piano with vertical frame and strings

upright piano

¹up·rise \‚ə-'prīz\ *vi* **up·rose** \-'prōz\; **up·ris·en** \-'priz-ən\; **up·ris·ing** \-'prī-zing\ **1** : to rise to a higher positon **2** : to get up (as from sleep or a sitting position) — **up·ris·er** *n*

²up·rise \'əp-‚rīz\ *n* **1** : an act or instance of uprising **2** : an upward slope

up·ris·ing \'əp-‚rī-zing\ *n* : an act or instance of rising up; *esp* : a usually localized revolt SYN see REBELLION

up·roar \'əp-‚rōr, -‚rȯr\ *n* : a state of commotion, excitement, or violent disturbance [by folk etymology from Dutch *oproer,* from *op* "up" + *roer* "motion"]

up·roar·i·ous \‚əp-'rōr-ē-əs, -'rȯr-\ *adj* **1** : marked by uproar **2** : extremely funny — **up·roar·i·ous·ly** *adv* — **up·roar·i·ous·ness** *n*

up·root \‚əp-'prüt, -'prüt\ *vt* **1** : to remove by or as if by pulling up by the roots **2** : to displace from a country or traditional habitat — **up·root·er** *n*

¹up·set \‚əp-'set, əp-\ *vb* **-set; -set·ting** **1** : to thicken and shorten (as a heated bar of iron) by hammering on the end : SWAGE **2** : to force or be forced out of the usual upright, level, or proper position : OVERTURN, CAPSIZE **3 a** : to disturb emotionally **b** : to make somewhat ill **4 a** : to throw into disorder : DISARRANGE **b** : INVALIDATE 〈*upset* a will〉 **c** : to defeat unexpectedly — **up·set·ter** *n*

²up·set \'əp-‚set\ *n* **1** : an act or result of upsetting : a state of being upset **2 a** : a minor physical disorder 〈a stomach *upset*〉 **b** : an emotional disturbance **3 a** : a part of a rod (as the head on a bolt) that is upset **b** : a swage used in upsetting

up·shot \'əp-‚shät\ *n* : final result : OUTCOME

up·side \'əp-‚sīd\ *n* : the upper side or part

up·side down \‚əp-‚sīd-'daùn\ *adv* **1** : with the upper and the lower parts reversed in position **2** : in or into great disorder [Middle English *up so doun,* from *up* + *so* + *doun* "down"] — **upside–down** *adv*

up·si·lon \'yüp-sə-‚län, 'əp-, -lən\ *n* : the 20th letter of the Greek alphabet — Y or υ

¹up·stage \'əp-‚stāj\ *adv* : toward or at the rear of a stage

²upstage *adj* **1** : of or relating to the rear of a stage **2** : HAUGHTY

³up·stage \‚əp-'stāj\ *vt* : to steal the show from [earlier *upstage* "to force (an actor) to face away from the audience by staying upstage"]

¹up·stairs \'əp-'staərz, -'steərz\ *adv* **1** : up the stairs : to or on a higher floor **2** : to or at a high altitude or higher position

²up·stairs \-‚staərz, -‚steərz\ *adj* **1** : situated above the stairs **2** : of or relating to the upper floors

³up·stairs \'əp-‚, 'əp-‚\ *n* : the part of a building above the ground floor

up·stand·ing \‚əp-'stan-ding, 'əp-‚\ *adj* **1** : ERECT 1a **2** : marked by integrity : HONEST — **up·stand·ing·ness** *n*

¹up·start \‚əp-'stärt\ *vi* : to jump up suddenly

²up·start \'əp-‚stärt\ *n* : one that has risen suddenly (as from a low position to wealth or power) : PARVENU; *esp* : one that claims more personal importance than is warranted — **up·start** \‚əp-‚\ *adj*

¹up·state \'əp-‚stāt\ *adj* : of, relating to, or characteristic of a part of a state away from a large city and especially to the north — **up·state** \'əp-'stāt\ *adv*

²upstate *n* : an upstate region — **up·stat·er** \-‚stāt-ər\ *n*

up·stream \'əp-'strēm\ *adv* : at or toward the source of a stream — **upstream** *adj*

up·stroke \'əp-‚strōk\ *n* : an upward stroke (as of a pen)

up·surge \'əp-‚sərj\ *n* : a rapid or sudden rise

up·sweep \'əp-‚swēp\ *vb* **-swept** \-‚swept\; **-sweep·ing** : to sweep upward : curve or slope upward — **upsweep** *n*

up·swept \'əp-‚swept\ *adj* : swept upward

up·swing \'əp-‚swing\ *n* : an upward swing; *esp* : a marked increase or rise (as in activity)

up·take \'əp-‚tāk\ *n* **1** : UNDERSTANDING, COMPREHENSION 〈quick on the *uptake*〉 **2** : a flue leading upward **3** : an act or instance of absorbing and incorporating especially into a living organism [Scottish *uptake* "to understand"]

up·throw \'əp-‚thrō\ *n* : an upward displacement (as of a rock stratum) : UPHEAVAL

up·thrust \'əp-‚thrəst\ *n* : an upward thrust; *esp* : an uplift of part of the earth's crust

up·tight \'əp-'tīt, ‚əp-', əp-'; ‚əp-‚\ *adj* **1** : TENSE, UNEASY **2** : ANGRY, INDIGNANT **3** : rigidly conventional

up·tilt \‚əp-'tilt\ *vt* : to tilt upward

up to *prep* **1** : as far as a designated part or place 〈sank *up to* my hips〉 **2** — used as a function word to indicate a limit or boundary 〈save *up to* 15 percent〉

up–to–date *adj* **1** : extending up to the present time **2** : abreast of the times (as in style or technique) : MODERN — **up–to–date·ness** *n*

up·town \'əp-'taùn\ *adv* : toward, to, or in the upper part of a town — **up·town** \,əp-'taùn\ *adj*

up·trend \'əp-,trend\ *n* : a tendency upward

¹**up·turn** \'əp-,tərn, ,əp-'\ *vb* **1** : to turn up or over **2** : to turn or direct upward

²**up·turn** \'əp-,tərn\ *n* : an upward turn (as toward better conditions or higher prices)

¹**up·ward** \'əp-wərd\ *or* **up·wards** \-wərdz\ *adv* **1** : in a direction from lower to higher **2** : toward a higher or better condition **3** : toward a greater amount or higher number, degree, or rate

²**upward** *adj* : directed toward or situated in a higher place or level — **up·ward·ly** *adv* — **up·ward·ness** *n*

upwards of *also* **upward of** *adv* : more than : in excess of

up·well·ing \,əp-'wel-ing\ *n* : the movement of deeper, cooler, and often nutrient-rich layers of ocean water to the surface

up·wind \'əp-'wind\ *adv or adj* : in the direction from which the wind is blowing

ur- *or* **uro-** *combining form* **1** : urine ⟨*uric*⟩ **2** : urinary tract ⟨*uro*logy⟩ **3** : urinary and ⟨*uro*genital⟩ **4** : urea ⟨*ur*acil⟩ [Greek *ouron*]

ura·cil \'yùr-ə-,sil, -səl\ *n* : a pyrimidine base $C_4H_4N_2O_2$ that is one of the four bases coding genetic information in the polynucleotide chain of RNA — compare ADENINE, CYTOSINE, GUANINE [derived from *ur-* + *acetic*]

Ural–Al·ta·ic \,yùr-ə-lal-'tā-ik\ *n* : a language type showing agglutination and occurring especially in languages of Eurasia [*Ural* mountains + *Altai* mountains] — **Ural–Altaic** *adj*

Ural·ic \yù-'ral-ik\ *n* : a language family comprising the Finno-Ugric languages and some languages of northwest Siberia

ura·nic \yù-'ran-ik, -'rā-nik\ *adj* : of, relating to, or containing uranium

ura·ni·nite \yù-'rā-nə-,nīt\ *n* : a mineral that is a black oxide of uranium, contains also various metals (as thorium and lead), and is the chief ore of uranium [German *uranin*, from New Latin *uranium*]

ura·ni·um \yù-'rā-nē-əm\ *n* : a silvery heavy radioactive metallic chemical element that is found especially in pitchblende and uraninite and exists naturally as a mixture of three isotopes of mass number 234, 235, and 238 — see ELEMENT table [New Latin, from *Uranus*]

uranium hexafluoride *n* : a compound of uranium and fluorine that is used in one major process for the separation of uranium 235 from ordinary uranium

uranium 238 *n* : an isotope of uranium of mass number 238 that absorbs neutrons to form a uranium isotope of mass number 239 which then decays through neptunium to form plutonium of mass number 239

uranium 235 *n* : a light isotope of uranium of mass number 235 that when bombarded with low-energy neutrons undergoes rapid fission into smaller atoms with the release of neutrons and atomic energy

ura·nous \yù-'rā-nəs, 'yùr-ə-\ *adj* : of, relating to, or containing uranium especially with a lower valence than in uranic compounds

Ura·nus \'yùr-ə-nəs, yù-'rā-\ *n* : the planet 7th in order from the sun — see PLANET table [*Uranus*, a Greek god]

urate \'yùr-,āt\ *n* : a salt of uric acid

ur·ban \'ər-bən\ *adj* : of, relating to, characteristic of, or constituting a city [Latin *urbanus*, from *urbs* "city"]

ur·bane \,ər-'bān\ *adj* : notably polite or finished in manner : SUAVE [Latin *urbanus* "urban, urbane"] SYN see SUAVE — **ur·bane·ly** *adv* □ ORIGIN The advantages of city over country life (and vice versa) have been debated for many years, and this debate is reflected in our vocabulary. Alongside of *urban*, "relating to or characteristic of a city", we have *urbane*, which de-

veloped the sense of "smoothly courteous or polite" from the belief (encouraged by city dwellers especially) that the social life of the city is more suave and polished than life in the country. Both *urban* and *urbane* come from the Latin *urbanus*, from *urbs*, "city".

ur·ban·ite \'ər-bə-,nīt\ *n* : one living in a city

ur·ban·i·ty \,ər-'ban-ət-ē\ *n, pl* **-ties** **1** : the quality or state of being urbane **2** *pl* : urbane acts or conduct

ur·ban·ize \'ər-bə-,nīz\ *vt* **1** : to cause to take on urban characteristics ⟨*urbanized* areas⟩ **2** : to impart an urban way of life to — **ur·ban·iza·tion** \,ər-bə-nə-'zā-shən\ *n*

urban renewal *n* : a construction program to replace or restore substandard buildings in an urban area

ur·chin \'ər-chən\ *n* **1** : HEDGEHOG 1 **2** : a mischievous youngster **3** : SEA URCHIN [Middle French *herichon*, from Latin *ericius*]

Ur·du \'ùr-dü, 'ər-\ *n* : an Indic language that is an official literary language of Pakistan and is widely used in India [Hindi *urdū-zabān*, literally, "camp language"]

-ure *n suffix* **1** : act : process ⟨expo*sure*⟩ **2 a** : office : function **b** : body performing (such) a function ⟨legisla*ture*⟩ [Latin *-ura*]

urea \yù-'rē-ə\ *n* : a soluble nitrogen-containing compound that is found in mammalian urine and is an end product of protein breakdown [New Latin, from French *urée*, from *urine* "urine"] — **ure·ic** \-'rē-ik\ *adj*

ure·ase \'yùr-ē-,ās, -,āz\ *n* : an enzyme that promotes the hydrolysis of urea

ure·dio·spore \yù-'rēd-ē-ə-,spōr, -,spòr\ *or* **ure·do·spore** \-'rēd-ə-\ *n* : one of the one-celled spores of a rust fungus that spread the disease by infecting new plants [derived from Latin *uredo* "burning, blight", from *urere* "to burn"]

ure·mia \yù-'rē-mē-ə\ *n* : accumulation in the blood usually in severe kidney disease of constituents normally eliminated in the urine resulting in a severe toxic condition — **ure·mic** \-mik\ *adj*

ure·ter \'yùr-ət-ər\ *n* : a duct that carries urine from a kidney to the bladder or cloaca [Greek *ourētēr*, from *ourein* "to urinate"] — **ure·ter·al** \yù-'rēt-ə-rəl\ *or* **ure·ter·ic** \,yùr-ə-'ter-ik\ *adj*

ure·thra \yù-'rē-thrə\ *n, pl* **-thras** *or* **-thrae** \-thrē\ : the canal that in most mammals carries off the urine from the bladder and in the male serves also as a genital duct [Late Latin, from Greek *ourēthra*, from *ourein* "to urinate"] — **ure·thral** \-thrəl\ *adj*

¹**urge** \'ərj\ *vt* **1** : to present, advocate, or demand earnestly ⟨continually *urging* reform⟩ **2 a** : to try to persuade or sway ⟨*urge* a guest to stay longer⟩ **b** : to serve as a motive or reason for **3** : to press or move to some course or activity (as greater speed) ⟨*urge* on a runner⟩ [Latin *urgēre*] — **urg·er** *n*

²**urge** *n* **1** : the act or process of urging **2** : a force or impulse that urges; *esp* : a continuing impulse toward an activity or goal

ur·gent \'ər-jənt\ *adj* **1 a** : calling for immediate attention : PRESSING ⟨*urgent* appeals⟩ **b** : conveying a sense of urgency ⟨an *urgent* manner⟩ **2** : urging insistently [Middle French, from Latin *urgens*, present participle of *urgēre* "to urge"] — **ur·gen·cy** \-jən-sē\ *n* — **ur·gent·ly** *adv*

uric \'yùr-ik\ *adj* : of, relating to, or found in urine

uric acid *n* : a white odorless nearly insoluble nitrogen-containing acid that is present in small quantity in mammalian urine and is the chief nitrogen-containing excretion in birds and lower forms

uri·nal \'yùr-ən-l\ *n* **1** : a receptacle for urine **2** : a place for urinating

uri·nal·y·sis \,yùr-ə-'nal-ə-səs\ *n, pl* **uri·nal·y·ses** \-ə-,sēz\ : the analysis of urine

uri·nary \'yùr-ə-,ner-ē\ *adj* **1** : relating to, occurring in, or constituting the organs concerned with the for-

\ə\	abut	\ng\	sing
\ər\	further	\ō\	bone
\a\	mat	\ò\	saw
\ā\	take	\òi\	coin
\ä\	cot, cart	\th\	thin
\aù\	out	\th\	this
\ch\	chin	\ü\	food
\e\	pet	\ù\	foot
\ē\	easy	\y\	yet
\g\	go	\yü\	few
\i\	tip	\yù\	cure
\ī\	life	\zh\	vision
\j\	job		

urn 2

mation and discharge of urine ⟨*urinary* bladder⟩ **2** : of, relating to, or used for urine **3** : excreted as or in urine

uri·nate \'yùr-ə-ˌnāt\ *vi* : to discharge urine — **uri·na·tion** \ˌyùr-ə-'nā-shən\ *n*

urine \'yùr-ən\ *n* : waste material that is secreted by the kidney, is rich in end products of protein metabolism together with salts and pigments, and is usually a yellowish liquid in mammals but semisolid in birds and reptiles [Middle French, from Latin *urina*]

urn \'ərn\ *n* **1** : a vessel that typically has the form of a vase on a pedestal and often is used for preserving the ashes of the dead **2** : a closed vessel usually with a spigot for serving a hot beverage ⟨coffee urn⟩ [Latin *urna*]

uro- — see UR-

uro·dele \'yùr-ə-ˌdēl\ *n* : any of an order (Caudata) of amphibians (as newts) with a tail throughout life [French *urodèle*, derived from Greek *oura* "tail" + *dēlos* "evident, showing"] — **urodele** *adj*

uro·gen·i·tal \ˌyùr-ō-'jen-ə-tl\ *adj* : of, relating to, or being the organs or functions of excretion and reproduction

urol·o·gy \yù-'räl-ə-jē\ *n* : a branch of medical science dealing with the urinary or urogenital tract and its disorders — **uro·log·ic** \ˌyùr-ə-'läj-ik\ *or* **uro·log·i·cal** \-'läj-i-kəl\ *adj* — **urol·o·gist** \yù-'räl-ə-jəst\ *n*

uro·pod \'yùr-ə-ˌpäd\ *n* : either of the flat lateral appendages of the last abdominal segment of a crustacean [derived from Greek *oura* "tail" + *pod-, pous* "foot"]

uro·style \'yùr-ə-ˌstīl\ *n* : a bony rod made of fused vertebrae that forms the end of the spinal column of a frog or toad [derived from Greek *oura* "tail" + *stylos* "pillar"]

Ur·sa Ma·jor \ˌər-sə-'mā-jər\ *n* : the most conspicuous of the northern constellations that is situated near the north pole of the heavens and contains the stars forming the Big Dipper two of which are in a line indicating the direction of the North Star — called also *Great Bear* [Latin, literally, "greater bear"]

Ursa Mi·nor \-'mī-nər\ *n* : the constellation including the north pole of the heavens and the stars that form the Little Dipper with the North Star at the tip of the handle — called also *Little Bear* [Latin, literally, "lesser bear"]

Ur·su·line \'ər-sə-lən, -ˌlīn, -ˌlēn\ *n* : a member of a teaching order of nuns founded in Italy in 1535 [Saint *Ursula*, legendary Christian martyr] — **Ursuline** *adj*

ur·ti·car·ia \ˌərt-ə-'kar-ē-ə, -'ker-\ *n* : HIVES [New Latin, from Latin *urtica* "nettle"] — **ur·ti·car·i·al** \-ē-əl\ *adj*

urus \'yùr-əs\ *n* : an extinct large long-horned wild ox of the German forests held to be a wild ancestor of domestic cattle [Latin, of Germanic origin]

us \əs, 'əs\ *pron, objective case of* WE [Old English *ūs*]

us·able \'yü-zə-bəl\ *adj* : suitable or fit for use ⟨*usable* waste⟩ — **us·abil·i·ty** \ˌyü-zə-'bil-ət-ē\ *n* — **us·ably** \'yü-zə-blē\ *adv*

us·age \'yü-sij, -zij\ *n* **1 a** : firmly established and generally accepted practice or procedure **b** : the way in which words and phrases are actually used in a language community **2 a** : the action or mode of using : USE **b** : manner of treating : TREATMENT ⟨ill usage⟩ SYN see HABIT

¹use \'yüs\ *n* **1 a** : the act or practice of using something often so as to get an effect or benefit ⟨put knowledge to use⟩ **b** : the fact or state of being used ⟨a dish in daily use⟩ **c** : way of using ⟨the proper *use* of tools⟩ **2 a** : the privilege or benefit of using something ⟨had the *use* of a car⟩ **b** : the ability or power to use something (as a limb or faculty) **3 a** : FUNCTION 2 ⟨what's the *use* of this dial⟩ **b** : the quality of being suitable for employment : USEFULNESS ⟨old clothes that are still of some use⟩ **c** : legitimate employment or application

⟨took only what I had *use* for⟩ **4** : ESTEEM, LIKING ⟨had no use for modern art⟩ [Old French *us*, from Latin *usus*, from *uti* "to use"]

²use \'yüz\ *vb* **used** \'yüzd, *in the phrase* "used to" *usually* 'yüs, 'yüst\; **us·ing** \'yü-zing\ **1** : to put into action or service : EMPLOY **2** : to consume or take (as liquor or drugs) regularly **3** : to carry out a purpose or action by means of : UTILIZE ⟨*use* tact⟩ **4** : to expend or consume by putting to use ⟨the car *uses* a lot of gas⟩ **5** : to behave toward : TREAT ⟨*used* the prisoners cruelly⟩ **6** — used in the past with *to* to indicate a former practice, fact, or state ⟨claims winters *used* to be harder⟩ ⟨how they *used* to quarrel as children⟩ — **us·er** \'yü-zər\ *n* □ SYN EMPLOY, UTILIZE: USE implies availing oneself of something as a means or instrument to an end; EMPLOY suggests the use of a person or thing that is available because idle, inactive, or disengaged; UTILIZE suggests the discovery of a new, profitable, or practical use for something ⟨how to *utilize* scrap metal⟩

used \'yüzd, *in the phrase* "used to" *usually* 'yüs, 'yüst\ *adj* **1** : employed in accomplishing something **2** : that has endured use; *esp* : SECONDHAND ⟨a *used* car⟩ **3** : made familiar by experience : ACCUSTOMED

use·ful \'yüs-fəl\ *adj* : capable of being put to use : USABLE ⟨*useful* scraps of material⟩; *also* : of a kind to be valuable or productive ⟨a *useful* invention⟩ — **use·ful·ly** \-fə-lē\ *adv* — **use·ful·ness** *n*

use·less \'yü-sləs\ *adj* : having or being of no use : WORTHLESS — **use·less·ly** *adv* — **use·less·ness** *n*

¹ush·er \'əsh-ər\ *n* **1** : an officer who walks before a person of rank **2** : one who escorts persons to seats (as in a theater) [Middle French *ussier*, literally, "doorkeeper", derived from Latin *ostium, ustium* "door"]

²usher *vt* **ush·ered; ush·er·ing** \'əsh-ring, -ə-ring\ **1** : to conduct to a place **2** : INAUGURATE, INTRODUCE ⟨*usher* in a new era⟩

usu·al \'yüzh-wəl, -ə-wəl, 'yüzh-əl\ *adj* **1** : accordant with usage, custom, or habit : NORMAL **2** : commonly or ordinarily used ⟨my *usual* route⟩ **3** : found in ordinary practice or in the ordinary course of events : ORDINARY [Late Latin *usualis*, from Latin *usus* "use"] — **usu·al·ly** \'yüzh-wə-lē, -ə-wə-, 'yüzh-lē, 'yüzh-ə-lē, *rapid* 'yüz-lē\ *adv* — **usu·al·ness** \'yüzh-wəl-nəs, -ə-wəl-, 'yüzh-əl-\ *n* □ SYN CUSTOMARY, HABITUAL, ACCUSTOMED: USUAL stresses the absence of strangeness or unexpectedness; CUSTOMARY applies to what accords with the practices, conventions, or usages of an individual or community ⟨their *customary* dress for dinner⟩ HABITUAL suggests a practice settled or established by much repetition ⟨*habitual* frown⟩ ACCUSTOMED is less emphatic than HABITUAL and suggests something that is noticed or expected by others ⟨*accustomed* graciousness⟩

usu·fruct \'yü-zə-ˌfrəkt\ *n* : the legal right of using and enjoying the fruits or profits of something belonging to another [Latin *usufructus*, from *usus et fructus* "use and enjoyment"]

usu·rer \'yü-zhər-ər, 'yüzh-rər\ *n* : one that lends money especially at an excessively high rate of interest

usu·ri·ous \yù-'zhùr-ē-əs, -'zùr-\ *adj* : practicing, involving, or constituting usury ⟨*usurious* interest⟩ — **usu·ri·ous·ly** *adv* — **usu·ri·ous·ness** *n*

usurp \yù-'sərp *also* -'zərp\ *vt* : to seize and hold by force or without right ⟨*usurp* a throne⟩ [Middle French *usurper*, from Latin *usurpare*, from *usu* "by use" + *rapere* "to seize"] — **usur·pa·tion** \ˌyü-sər-'pā-shən *also* ˌyü-zər-\ *n* — **usurp·er** \yù-'sər-pər *also* -'zər-\ *n*

usu·ry \'yüzh-rē, -ə-rē\ *n, pl* **usuries** **1** : the lending of money with an interest charge for its use **2** : an excessive rate or amount of interest charged; *esp* : interest above an established legal rate [Medieval Latin *usuria*, from Latin *usura*, from *usus*, past participle of *uti* "to use"]

Ute \'yüt\ *n, pl* **Ute** *or* **Utes** : a member of a group of Indian peoples of what is now Colorado and Utah having an Aztec-related language [Ute *Yuta*]

uten·sil \yü-'ten-səl\ *n* **1** : an instrument or vessel used in a household and especially a kitchen **2** : an article serving a useful purpose [Middle French *utensile* "vessels for domestic use", from Latin *utensilia,* from *utensilis* "useful", from *uti* "to use"] SYN see IMPLEMENT

uter·us \'yüt-ə-rəs\ *n, pl* **uteri** \-ˌrī, -ˌrē\ *also* **uter·us·es** **1** : an organ of the female mammal for containing and usually for nourishing the young during development previous to birth — called also *womb* **2** : a structure in some lower animals analogous to the uterus of mammals in which eggs or young develop [Latin] — **uter·ine** \-rən, -ˌrīn\ *adj*

utile \'yüt-l, 'yü-ˌtīl\ *adj* : USEFUL [Middle French, from Latin *utilis*]

¹util·i·tar·i·an \yü-ˌtil-ə-'ter-ē-ən\ *n* : an advocate or adherent of utilitarianism

²utilitarian *adj* **1** : of or relating to utilitarianism **2 a** : of or relating to utility **b** : aiming at usefulness rather than beauty **c** : serving a useful purpose

util·i·tar·i·an·ism \-ē-ə-ˌniz-əm\ *n* : a doctrine that one's conduct should be determined by the usefulness of its consequences; *esp* : a theory that the aim of action should be the greatest happiness of the greatest number

¹util·i·ty \yü-'til-ət-ē\ *n, pl* **-ties** **1** : fitness for some purpose or worth to some end **2** : something useful or designed for use **3 a** : PUBLIC UTILITY **b** (1) : a public service or a commodity provided by a public utility (2) : equipment or a piece of equipment (as plumbing in a house) to provide such or a similar service [Middle French *utilité,* from Latin *utilitas,* from *utilis* "useful", from *uti* "to use"]

²utility *adj* **1** : capable of serving as a substitute in various roles or positions 〈*utility* infielder〉 **2** : being of a usable but inferior grade 〈*utility* beef〉 **3** : serving primarily for usefulness rather than beauty : UTILITARIAN 〈*utility* furniture〉 **4** : designed for general use

uti·lize \'yüt-l-ˌīz\ *vt* : to make use of : convert to use SYN see USE — **uti·liz·able** \-ˌī-zə-bəl\ *adj* — **uti·li·za·tion** \ˌyüt-l-ə-'zā-shən\ *n* — **uti·liz·er** *n*

ut·most \'ət-ˌmōst, *especially South* -məst\ *adj* **1** : situated at the farthest or most distant point : EXTREME **2** : of the greatest or highest degree, quantity, number, or amount [Old English *ūtmest,* superlative adj., from *ūt,* adv., "out"] — **utmost** *n*

uto·pia \yü-'tō-pē-ə\ *n* **1** *often cap* : a place of ideal perfection especially in laws, government, and social conditions **2** : an impractical scheme for social improvement [*Utopia,* imaginary ideal country in *Utopia* by Sir Thomas More, from Greek *ou* "not, no" + *topos* "place"] — **uto·pi·an** \-pē-ən\ *adj or n, often cap*

☐ ORIGIN In 1516 Sir Thomas More published his book *Utopia,* in which the social and economic conditions of Europe, outlined in Book I, are compared with those of an ideal society described in Book II, a society established on an imaginary island off the shore of the New World. That such an ideal state is unattainable in reality is implied by the name More gave to this island, *Utopia,* which literally means "no place". In modern English *utopia* has become a generic term for any place of ideal perfection. Less optimistically *utopia* has also come to mean an impractical scheme for social improvement.

utri·cle \'yü-tri-kəl\ *n* : the larger chamber of the membranous labyrinth of the ear into which the semicircular canals open — compare SACCULE [Latin *utriculus* "small leather bag", from *uter* "leather bag"] — **utric·u·lar** \yü-'trik-yə-lər\ *adj*

utric·u·lus \yü-'trik-yə-ləs\ *n* : UTRICLE [Latin, "small bag"]

¹ut·ter \'ət-ər\ *adj* : ABSOLUTE, TOTAL 〈an *utter* impossibility〉 〈*utter* strangers〉 [Old English *ūtera* "outer", comparative adj., from *ūt,* adv., "out"] — **ut·ter·ly** *adv*

²utter *vt* **1** : to send forth as a sound **2** : to express in usually spoken words **3** : PASS 16a [Middle English *uttren* "to put forth, offer for sale", from *utter,* adv., "outside", from Old English *ūtor,* comparative of *ūt* "out"] — **ut·ter·able** \'ət-ə-rə-bəl\ *adj* — **ut·ter·er** \'ət-ər-ər\ *n*

ut·ter·ance \'ət-ə-rəns\ *n* **1** : something uttered; *esp* : an oral or written statement **2** : the action of uttering with the voice : SPEECH **3** : power, style, or manner of speaking

ut·ter·most \'ət-ər-ˌmōst\ *adj* : EXTREME 3, UTMOST — **uttermost** *n*

uvu·la \'yü-vyə-lə\ *n, pl* **-las** *or* **-lae** \-ˌlē, -ˌlī\ : the pendent fleshy lobe in the middle of the rear border of the soft palate [Medieval Latin, from Latin *uva* "grape, uvula"]

uvu·lar \-lər\ *adj* **1** : of or relating to the uvula 〈*uvular* glands〉 **2** : produced with the aid of the uvula 〈*uvular* r〉

ux·o·ri·ous \ˌək-'sōr-ē-əs, -'sȯr-; ˌəg-'zōr-, -'zȯr-\ *adj* : excessively fond of or submissive to a wife [Latin *uxorius,* from *uxor* "wife"] — **ux·o·ri·ous·ly** *adv* — **ux·o·ri·ous·ness** *n*

Uz·bek \'úz-ˌbek, 'əz-\ *n* : a member of a people of Central Asia and especially of Uzbekistan

\ə\ abut	\ng\ sing
\ər\ further	\ō\ bone
\a\ mat	\ȯ\ saw
\ā\ take	\ȯi\ coin
\ä\ cot, cart	\th\ thin
\au̇\ out	\th\ this
\ch\ chin	\ü\ food
\e\ pet	\u̇\ foot
\ē\ easy	\y\ yet
\g\ go	\yü\ few
\i\ tip	\yu̇\ cure
\ī\ life	\zh\ vision
\j\ job	

Vv

v \'vē\ *n, pl* **v's** *or* **vs** \'vēz\ *often cap* **1** : the 22d letter of the English alphabet **2** : five in Roman numerals

va·can·cy \'vā-kən-sē\ *n, pl* **-cies** **1 a** : a vacating of an office, post, or property **b** : the time such office or property is vacant **2** : a vacant office, post, or tenancy ⟨two *vacancies* in a building⟩ **3** : empty space ⟨stare into *vacancy*⟩ **4** : the state of being vacant

va·cant \'vā-kənt\ *adj* **1** : having no occupant : not being used ⟨a *vacant* room⟩ ⟨*vacant* chairs⟩ **2** : free from business or care : LEISURE ⟨a few *vacant* hours⟩ **3** : STUPID **3**, FOOLISH ⟨a *vacant* laugh⟩ [Old French, from Latin *vacans*, present participle of *vacare* "to be empty, be free"] SYN see EMPTY — **va·cant·ly** *adv* — **va·cant·ness** *n*

va·cate \'vā-kāt, vā-'\ *vt* **1** : to make void : ANNUL ⟨*vacate* an agreement⟩ **2** : to make vacant : leave empty ⟨*vacate* a building⟩ ⟨*vacate* a position⟩ [Latin *vacare* "to be empty, be free"]

¹va·ca·tion \vā-'kā-shən, və-\ *n* **1** : a respite or a time of respite from something : INTERMISSION **2 a** : a period during which activity (as of a school) is suspended **b** : a period of freedom from work granted to an employee for rest and relaxation **3** : a period spent away from home or business in travel or recreation ⟨had a restful *vacation* at the beach⟩ **4** : an act or an instance of vacating

²vacation *vi* **-tioned; -tion·ing** \-shə-ning, -shning\ : to take or spend a vacation ⟨*vacation* in July⟩

va·ca·tion·er \-shə-nər, -shnər\ *n* : a person taking a vacation

va·ca·tion·ist \-shə-nəst, -shnəst\ *n* : VACATIONER

va·ca·tion·land \-shən-,land\ *n* : an area with recreational attractions and facilities for vacationers

vac·ci·nate \'vak-sə-,nāt\ *vt* : to inoculate (a person) with cowpox virus in order to produce immunity to smallpox; *also* : to administer a vaccine to usually by injection — **vac·ci·na·tor** \-,nāt-ər\ *n*

vac·ci·na·tion \,vak-sə-'nā-shən\ *n* **1** : the act of vaccinating **2** : the scar left by vaccinating

vac·cine \vak-'sēn, 'vak-,\ *n* : material (as a preparation of killed or modified virus or bacteria) used in vaccinating [Latin *vaccinus* "of cows", from *vacca* "cow"] — **vaccine** *adj* □ ORIGIN Our word *vaccine* was derived from Latin *vacca*, "cow". The Latin adjective *vaccinus*, "of or from cows", was borrowed into English as *vaccine*, which was originally used as an adjective with the same meaning as the Latin. A substance derived from a cow infected with cowpox would be called a *vaccine* substance. In the late 18th century the English physician Edward Jenner discovered that inoculation with a form of cowpox was an effective preventive of smallpox. The substance used in such inoculation came to be called a *vaccine*.

vac·cin·ia \vak-'sin-ē-ə\ *n* : COWPOX [New Latin, from Latin *vaccinus* "of cows"] — **vac·cin·i·al** \-ē-əl\ *adj*

vac·il·late \'vas-ə-,lāt\ *vi* **1** : FLUCTUATE ⟨a *vacillating* stock market⟩ **2** : to incline first to one course or opinion and then to another : WAVER [Latin *vacillare* "to sway, waver"] SYN see HESITATE — **vac·il·la·tion** \,vas-ə-'lā-shən\ *n* — **vac·il·la·tor** \'vas-ə-,lāt-ər\ *n* — **vac·il·la·to·ry** \-lə-,tōr-ē, -,tȯr-\ *adj*

vac·il·lat·ing·ly \'vas-ə-,lāt-ing-lē\ *adv* : in a vacillating manner

va·cu·i·ty \va-'kyü-ət-ē, və-\ *n, pl* **-ties** **1** : an empty space **2 a** : the state, fact, or quality of being vacuous **b** : vacancy of mind **3** : something (as a remark or idea) that is vacuous or inane

vac·u·ole \'vak-yə-,wōl\ *n* : a usually fluid-filled cavity in tissues or in the protoplasm of an individual cell [French, literally, "small vacuum", from Latin *vacuum*] — **vac·u·o·lar** \,vak-yə'wō-lər, -lär\ *adj*

vac·u·ous \'vak-yə-wəs\ *adj* **1** : EMPTY **1** **2** : marked by lack of ideas or intelligence : STUPID ⟨a *vacuous* expression⟩ **3** : having no serious occupation : IDLE [Latin *vacuus*] — **vac·u·ous·ly** *adv* — **vac·u·ous·ness** *n*

¹vac·u·um \'vak-,yüm, -yəm, -yü-əm\ *n, pl* **-u·ums** *or* **-ua** \-yə-wə\ **1 a** : a space absolutely devoid of matter **b** : a space partially exhausted (as to the highest degree possible) by artificial means (as an air pump) **2 a** : a state or condition resembling a vacuum : VOID **b** : a state of isolation from outside influences **3** : a device creating or utilizing a partial vacuum; *esp* : VACUUM CLEANER [Latin, from *vacuus* "empty"]

²vacuum *adj* : of, containing, producing, or making use of a partial vacuum

³vacuum *vt* : to use a vacuum device (as a vacuum cleaner) upon

vacuum bottle *n* : a container with a vacuum between an inner and an outer wall used to keep liquids either hot or cold

vacuum cleaner *n* : an electrical appliance for cleaning (as floors or carpets) by suction

vac·u·um·ize \'vak-yü-,mīz, -yü-ə-,mīz\ *vt* **1** : to produce a vacuum in **2** : to clean, dry or pack by a vacuum mechanism or in a vacuum container

vac·u·um–packed \,vak-yü-əm-'pakt, -yüm-, -yəm-\ *adj* : having much of the air removed before being sealed ⟨a *vacuum-packed* can of coffee⟩

vacuum pump *n* : a pump for exhausting gas from an enclosed space

vacuum tube *n* : an electron tube evacuated to a high degree of vacuum

va·de me·cum \,vād-ē-'mē-kəm, ,vād-ē-'mā-\ *n, pl* **vade mecums** **1** : a book for ready reference : MANUAL **2** : something regularly carried about by a person [Latin, "go with me"]

¹vag·a·bond \'vag-ə-,bänd\ *adj* **1** : moving from place to place without a fixed home ⟨*vagabond* minstrels⟩ **2 a** : of, relating to, or characteristic of a wanderer **b** : leading an unsettled, irresponsible, or disreputable life [Middle French, from Latin *vagabundus*, from *vagari* "to wander"]

²vagabond *n* : one who leads a vagabond life; *esp* : TRAMP — **vag·a·bond·age** \-,bän-dij\ *n* — **vag·a·bond·ism** \-,bän-,diz-əm\ *n*

vag·a·bond·ish \-,bän-dish\ *adj* : of, relating to, or characteristic of a vagabond

va·gar·i·ous \və-'ger-ē-əs, və-, -'gar-\ *adj* : marked by vagaries — **va·gar·i·ous·ly** *adv*

va·ga·ry \'vā-gə-rē; və-'geər-ē, -'gaar-, vā-\ *n, pl* **-ries** : an eccentric or unpredictable manifestation, action, or notion [probably from Latin *vagari* "to wander"] SYN SEE CAPRICE

va·gi·na \və-'jī-nə\ *n, pl* **-nae** \-nē\ *or* **-nas** **I** : a canal that leads from the uterus to the external opening of the genital canal **2** : SHEATH 2; *esp* : an ensheathing leaf base [Latin, literally, "sheath"] — **vag·i·nal** \'vaj-ən-l\ *adj*

va·gran·cy \'vā-grən-sē\ *n, pl* **-cies** **I** : VAGARY **2** : the state, action, or offense of being vagrant or a vagrant

¹va·grant \'vā-grənt\ *n* **I a** : one who wanders idly from place to place without a home or apparent means of support **b** : a person classed as a vagrant by statute **2** : one that leads a wandering life [probably from Middle French *waucrant, wacrant* "wandering", from *waucrer, wacrer* "to roll, wander", of Germanic origin]

²vagrant *adj* **I** : wandering about from place to place usually with no means of support **2 a** : having a fleeting, wayward, or inconstant quality **b** : having no fixed course : RANDOM ⟨*vagrant* thoughts⟩

va·grom \'vā-grəm\ *adj* : VAGRANT ⟨a *vagrom* thought⟩

vague \'vāg\ *adj* **I a** : not clearly expressed : stated in indefinite terms ⟨*vague* accusations⟩ **b** : not having a precise meaning **2** : not clearly felt, grasped, or understood : INDISTINCT ⟨*vague* ideas⟩ ⟨a *vague* longing⟩ **3** : not thinking or expressing one's thoughts clearly or precisely ⟨*vague* about dates and places⟩ **4** : not sharply outlined : HAZY, SHADOWY [Middle French, from Latin *vagus,* literally, "wandering"] SYN SEE OBSCURE — **vague·ly** *adv* — **vague·ness** *n*

va·gus \'vā-gəs\ *n, pl* **va·gi** \'vā-gī, -jī\ : VAGUS NERVE — **va·gal** \'vā-gəl\ *adj*

vagus nerve *n* : either of the 10th pair of cranial nerves that arise from the medulla and supply autonomic sensory and motor fibers mostly to the viscera [New Latin *vagus nervus,* literally, "wandering nerve"]

vail \'vāl\ *vt* : to lower especially as a sign of respect or submission [Middle French *valer,* short for *avaler* "to let fall", from *aval* "downward", from *a* "to" + *val* "valley"]

vain \'vān\ *adj* **I** : WORTHLESS ⟨*vain* promises⟩ **2** : not succeeding : FUTILE ⟨a *vain* attempt⟩ **3** : proud of one's looks or abilities : CONCEITED [Old French, from Latin *vanus* "empty, vain"] — **vain·ly** *adv* — **vain·ness** \'vān-nəs\ *n* □ SYN VAIN, FUTILE mean producing no result. VAIN usually implies simple failure to achieve a purpose or succeed in an attempt ⟨made a *vain* attempt at finishing⟩ FUTILE may suggest completeness of failure or folly of undertaking ⟨a *futile* effort to escape⟩ — **in vain I** : to no purpose : without success **2** : in an irreverent or blasphemous manner

vain·glo·ri·ous \vān-'glōr-ē-əs, 'vān-, -'glȯr-\ *adj* : marked by vainglory : BOASTFUL — **vain·glo·ri·ous·ly** *adv* — **vain·glo·ri·ous·ness** *n*

vain·glo·ry \'vān-,glōr-ē, -,glȯr-\ *n* **I** : excessive or ostentatious pride in onself and one's achievements **2** : vain display or show : VANITY

vair \'vaər, 'veər\ *n* : the bluish gray and white fur of a squirrel prized for ornament during the Middle Ages [Old French, from *vair* "variegated", from Latin *varius* "variegated, various"]

val·ance \'val-əns, 'vāl-\ *n* **I** : a drapery hung along the edge of a bed, table, altar, canopy, or shelf **2** : a short drapery or wood or metal frame used as a decorative heading to conceal the top of curtains and fixtures [Middle English *vallance*]

vale \'vāl\ *n* : VALLEY 1, DALE [Old French *val,* from Latin *valles, vallis*]

val·e·dic·tion \,val-ə-'dik-shən\ *n* : an act or utterance of leave-taking : FAREWELL [Latin *valedicere* "to say farewell", from *vale* "farewell" + *dicere* "to say"]

vale·dic·to·ri·an \,val-ə-,dik-'tōr-ē-ən, -'tȯr-\ *n* : the student usually of the highest rank in a graduating class who delivers the valedictory oration at commencement exercises

¹vale·dic·to·ry \-'dik-tə-rē, -trē\ *adj* : of or relating to leave-taking : FAREWELL; *esp* : given at a leave-taking ceremony (as school commencement exercises)

²valedictory *n, pl* **-ries** : a valedictory oration or statement

va·lence \'vā-ləns\ *n* **I** : the degree of combining power of an element as shown by the number of atomic weights of a univalent element (as hydrogen) with which the atomic weight of the element will combine or for which it can be substituted **2** : relative capacity to unite, react, or interact (as with antigens or a biological substrate) [Late Latin *valentia* "power, capacity", from Latin *valēre* "to be strong"]

Va·len·ci·ennes \və-,len-sē-'en, ,val-ən-sē-, -'enz\ *n* : a fine handmade lace [*Valenciennes,* France]

-va·lent \'vā-lənt\ *adj combining form* : having a (specified) valence or valences ⟨poly*valent*⟩ ⟨uni*valent*⟩

val·en·tine \'val-ən-,tīn\ *n* **I** : a sweetheart chosen or honored (as by a gift) on Saint Valentine's Day **2** : a gift or greeting sent or given on Saint Valentine's Day

Valentine Day *or* **Valentine's Day** *n* : SAINT VALENTINE'S DAY

va·le·ri·an \və-'lir-ē-ən\ *n* **I** : any of a genus of perennial herbs mostly with flat-topped clusters of flowers and with roots and rootstock having medicinal properties **2** : a drug consisting of the dried roots and rootstocks of the garden heliotrope [Medieval Latin *valeriana*]

va·let \'val-ət, 'val-,ā, va-'lā\ *n* : a male servant or hotel employee who takes care of a man's clothes and performs personal services [Middle French *vaslet, varlet, valet* "page, domestic servant", from Medieval Latin *vassus* "servant, vassal"]

val·e·tu·di·nar·i·an \,val-ə-,tüd-n-'er-ē-ən, -,tyüd-\ *n* : a person of a weak or sickly constitution; *esp* : one whose chief concern is his or her invalidism [Latin *valetudinarius* "sickly, infirm", from *valetudo* "state of health, sickness", from *valēre* "to be strong, be well"] — **valetudinarian** *adj* — **val·e·tu·di·nar·i·an·ism** \-,iz-əm\ *n*

Val·hal·la \val-'hal-ə\ *n* : the hall of Odin to which the Valkyries take heroes slain in battle [German *Walhalla,* from Old Norse *Valhöll,* literally, "hall of the slain"]

val·iance \'val-yəns\ *n* : VALOR

val·ian·cy \-yən-sē\ *n* : VALOR

¹val·iant \'val-yənt\ *adj* **I** : boldly brave : COURAGEOUS ⟨a *valiant* leader⟩ **2** : HEROIC ⟨*valiant* fighting⟩ [Middle French *vaillant,* from *valoir* "to be of worth", from Latin *valēre* "to be strong"] — **val·iant·ly** *adv* — **val·iant·ness** *n*

²valiant *n* : a valiant person

val·id \'val-əd\ *adj* **I** : founded on truth or fact : WELL-GROUNDED ⟨*valid* reasons⟩ **2** : binding in law : SOUND ⟨a *valid* contract⟩ [Medieval Latin *validus,* from Latin, "strong", from *valēre* "to be strong"] — **va·lid·i·ty** \və-'lid-ət-ē, va-\ *n* — **val·id·ly** \'val-əd-lē\ *adv* — **val·id·ness** *n* □ SYN VALID, SOUND, COGENT mean having such force as to compel consideration and usually acceptance. VALID implies being supported by objective truth or generally accepted authority; SOUND implies being based on solid fact and reasoning; COGENT stresses soundness or lucidity that makes argument or evidence conclusive.

val·i·date \'val-ə-,dāt\ *vt* **I** : to make valid **2** : to support or confirm on a sound or authoritative basis — **val·i·da·tion** \,val-ə-'dā-shən\ *n*

va·line \'val-,ēn, 'vā-,lēn\ *n* : a crystalline essential amino acid $C_5H_{11}NO_2$ that occurs especially in fibrous

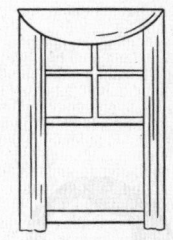

valance 2

\ə\ abut	\ng\ sing
\ər\ further	\ō\ bone
\a\ mat	\ȯ\ saw
\ā\ take	\ȯi\ coin
\ä\ cot, cart	\th\ thin
\au̇\ out	\th\ this
\ch\ chin	\ü\ food
\e\ pet	\u̇\ foot
\ē\ easy	\y\ yet
\g\ go	\yü\ few
\i\ tip	\yu̇\ cure
\ī\ life	\zh\ vision
\j\ job	

proteins [derived from *valeric acid,* an acid that occurs in the roots of valerian, from *valerian*]

va·lise \və-'lēs\ *n* : TRAVELING BAG [French, from Italian *valigia*]

Val·i·um \'val-ē-əm\ *trademark* — used for diazepam

Val·kyr·ie \val-'kir-ē\ *n* : one of the maidens of Odin who in Norse mythology choose the heroes to be slain in battle and conduct them to Valhalla [Old Norse *valkyrja,* literally, "chooser of the slain"]

val·ley \'val-ē\ *n, pl* **valleys** **1** : an elongate depression of the earth's surface usually between ranges of hills or mountains **2 a** : DEPRESSION 2, HOLLOW **b** : the place of meeting of two slopes of a roof forming a drainage channel [Old French *valee,* from *val* "valley, vale"]

val·or \'val-ər\ *n* : personal bravery in combat [Middle French *valour,* from Medieval Latin *valor,* "value, valor", from Latin *valēre* "to be strong"] SYN see COURAGE

val·or·ous \'val-ə-rəs\ *adj* **1** : possessing or showing valor : BRAVE ⟨*valorous* soldiers⟩ **2** : marked by or performed with valor ⟨*valorous* feats⟩ — **val·or·ous·ly** *adv*

valse \väls\ *n* : WALTZ; *esp* : a concert waltz [French, from German *walzer*]

¹valu·able \'val-yə-bəl, -yə-wə-bəl\ *adj* **1 a** : having monetary value **b** : worth a great deal of money **2** : having value : of great use or service ⟨*valuable* information⟩ SYN see COSTLY — **valu·able·ness** *n* — **valu·ably** \-blē\ *adv*

²valuable *n* : a personal possession (as a jewel) of relatively great monetary value ⟨stored *valuables* in the safe⟩

val·u·ate \'val-yə-ˌwāt\ *vt* : to place a value on : APPRAISE — **val·u·a·tor** \-ˌwāt-ər\ *n*

val·u·a·tion \ˌval-yə-'wā-shən\ *n* **1** : the act or process of valuing; *esp* : appraisal of property **2** : the estimated or determined value of a thing **3** : judgement or appreciation of worth or character — **val·u·a·tion·al** \-shnəl, -shən-l\ *adj* — **val·u·a·tion·al·ly** \-ē\ *adj*

¹val·ue \'val-yü\ *n* **1** : a fair return in goods, services, or money for something exchanged **2** : the amount of another commodity for which a given thing can be exchanged; *esp* : the amount of money that something will bring **3** : relative worth, utility or importance : degree of excellence **4 a** : a numerical quantity assigned or computed **b** : the magnitude of a physical quantity **c** : the sound or sounds answering to a letter or orthographic item ⟨the *value* of *a* in ate⟩ **5** : the relative duration of a musical note **6 a** : relative lightness or darkness of a color : LUMINOSITY **b** : the relation of one part in a picture to another with respect to lightness and darkness **7** : something having or held to have real worth or merit ⟨the *values* of the old and young are often very different⟩ **8** : DENOMINATION 4 [Middle French, derived from Latin *valēre* "to be worth, be strong"] SYN see WORTH

²value *vt* **1 a** : to estimate or assign the monetary worth of : APPRAISE ⟨*value* a necklace⟩ **b** : to rate or scale in usefulness, importance, or general worth **2** : to consider or rate highly : PRIZE, ESTEEM ⟨*valued* their friendship⟩ — **valu·er** \-yə-wər\ *n*

val·ued \'val-yüd, -yəd\ *adj* : highly regarded : greatly prized

val·ue·less \'val-yü-ləs, -yə-\ *adj* : of no value : WORTHLESS

valve \'valv\ *n* **1** : a structure especially in a bodily channel (as a vein) that closes temporarily to obstruct passage of material or permits movement of a fluid in one direction only **2 a** : a mechanical device by which the flow of liquid, gas, or loose material in bulk may be started, stopped, or regulated by a movable part; *also* : the movable part of such a device **b** : a device in a brass wind instrument for quickly varying the tube length in order to change the tone by some definite interval **c** *chiefly British* : ELECTRON TUBE **3** : one of the pair of pieces comprising the hinged shell of some

²van 1

Vandyke

shell-bearing animals and especially of bivalve mollusks **4** : one of the segments or pieces into which a ripe seed capsule or pod separates [Latin *valva* "leaf of a double door"] — **valved** \'valvd\ *adj*

val·vu·lar \'val-vyə-lər\ *adj* **1** : resembling or functioning as a valve; *also* : opening by valves **2** : of or relating to a valve especially of the heart

va·moose \və-'müs, va-\ *vi, slang* : to depart quickly : SCRAM [Spanish *vamos* "let us go"]

¹vamp \'vamp\ *n* : the part of a shoe upper or boot upper covering especially the forepart of the foot and sometimes also extending forward over the toe or backward to the back seam of the upper [Old French *avantpié* "sock", from *avant-* "fore-" + *pié* "foot", from Latin *pes*]

²vamp *vt* **1 a** : to provide (a shoe) with a new vamp **b** : to piece (something old) with a new part : PATCH ⟨*vamp* up old sermons⟩ **2** : INVENT ⟨*vamp* up an excuse⟩

³vamp *n* : a woman who uses her charm or wiles to seduce and exploit men [short for *vampire*]

⁴vamp *vt* : to practice seductive wiles on

vam·pire \'vam-ˌpīr\ *n* **1** : the body of a dead person believed to come from the grave at night and suck the blood of persons asleep **2 a** : one who lives by preying on others **b** : a woman who exploits and ruins her lover **3** : VAMPIRE BAT [French, from German *vampir,* of Slavic origin] — **vam·pir·ism** \-ˌpīr-ˌiz-əm\ *n*

vampire bat *n* : any of three South and Central American bats that feed on blood and are dangerous to man and domestic animals especially as vectors of disease (as rabies)

¹van \'van\ *n* : VANGUARD

²van *n* **1** : a usually enclosed wagon or motortruck used for transportation of goods or animals **2** *chiefly British* : an enclosed railroad freight or baggage car [short for *caravan*]

va·na·di·um \və-'nād-ē-əm\ *n* : a grayish malleable metallic chemical element found combined in minerals and used especially to form alloys (as of steel) — see ELEMENT table [New Latin, from Old Norse *Vanadīs* "Freya (goddess of love and beauty)"]

Van Al·len belt \va-'nal-ən-, və-\ *n* : a belt of intense ionizing radiation that surrounds the earth in the magnetosphere [James A. *Van Allen,* born 1914, American physicist]

van·dal \'van-dl\ *n* **1** *cap* : one of a Germanic people overrunning Gaul, Spain, and northern Africa in the 4th and 5th centuries A. D., and in 455 sacking Rome **2** : one who willfully destroys, damages, or defaces public or private property [Latin *Vandalii* "Vandals", of Germanic origin] — **vandal** *adj, often cap*

van·dal·ism \'van-dl-ˌiz-əm\ *n* : willful or malicious destruction or defacement of public or private property

van·dal·is·tic \ˌvan-dl-'is-tik\ *adj* : of, relating to, or committing vandalism

van·dal·ize \'van-dl-ˌiz\ *vt* : to subject to vandalism

Van de Graaff generator \ˌvan-də-ˌgraf-\ *n* : ELECTROSTATIC GENERATOR [Robert J. *Van de Graaff,* died 1967, American physicist]

Van·dyke \van-'dīk\ *n* : a trim pointed beard [Sir Anthony *Vandyke*]

vane \'vān\ *n* **1** : a movable device attached to an elevated object (as a spire) for showing the direction of the wind **2** : a flat or curved object that is rotated about an axis by a flow of fluid (as air or water) or that rotates to cause a fluid to flow or that changes the direction of a flow of fluid **3 a** : the flat expanded part of a feather — called also *web* **b** : a feather fastened to the shaft near the nock of an arrow [Old English *fana* "banner"] — **vaned** \'vānd\ *adj*

van·guard \'van-ˌgärd\ *n* **1** : the troops moving at the head of an army **2** : the forefront of an action or movement or those in the forefront [Middle French *avant-garde,* from *avant-* "fore-" + *garde* "guard"]

va·nil·la \və-'nil-ə, -'nel-\ *n* **1** : any of a genus of tropical American climbing orchids **2 a** : VANILLA BEAN **b** : the flavoring extract from the vanilla bean [Spanish *vainilla,* from *vaina* "sheath", from Latin *vagina*]

vanilla bean *n* : the long pod of a vanilla that is an important article of commerce for the flavoring extract that it yields

va·nil·lin \'van-l-ən\ *n* : a compound that is the chief fragrant component of vanilla

van·ish \'van-ish\ *vi* **1** : to pass quickly from sight : DISAPPEAR **2** : to pass completely from existence [Middle French *evaniss-,* stem of *evanir* "to vanish", from Latin *evanescere,* from *e-* + *vanescere* "to vanish", from *vanus* "empty, vain"] — **van·ish·er** *n*

vanishing cream *n* : a cosmetic preparation that is less oily than cold cream and is used chiefly as a foundation for face powder

vanishing point *n* **1** : a point at which receding parallel lines seem to meet **2** : a point at which something disappears or ceases to exist

van·i·ty \'van-ət-ē\ *n, pl* **-ties 1** : something that is vain **2** : the quality or fact of being vain: as **a** : an empty or worthless state **b** : a state of futility **c** : inflated pride in oneself or one's appearance **3** : a fashionable article or knickknack **4 a** : ³COMPACT 1 **b** : DRESSING TABLE [Old French *vanité,* from Latin *vanitas,* from *vanus* "empty, vain"]

vanity fair *n, often cap V & F* : a scene or place marked by frivolity and pointless show [*Vanity-Fair,* a fair held in the frivolous town of Vanity in John Bunyon's *Pilgrim's Progress*]

van·quish \'vang-kwish, 'van-\ *vt* **1** : to overcome in battle : subdue completely **2** : to gain mastery over (as an emotion or temptation or a competitor) : DEFEAT [Middle French *venquis,* preterit of *veintre* "to conquer", from Latin *vincere*] SYN see CONQUER — **van·quish·able** \-ə-bəl\ *adj* — **van·quish·er** *n*

van·tage \'vant-ij\ *n* **1** : superiority in a contest **2** : a position giving a strategic advantage, commanding perspective, or comprehensive view **3** : ADVANTAGE 3 [Anglo-French, from Middle French *avantage* "advantage"]

van·ward \'van-wərd\ *adj* : located in the vanguard : ADVANCED — **vanward** *adv*

vap·id \'vap-əd\ *adj* : lacking liveliness, tang, briskness, or force : FLAT, UNINTERESTING ⟨*vapid* remark⟩ ⟨*vapid* smile⟩ [Latin *vapidus* "flat tasting"] SYN see INSIPID — **va·pid·i·ty** \va-'pid-ət-ē\ *n* — **vap·id·ly** \'vap-əd-lē\ *adv* — **vap·id·ness** *n*

¹va·por \'vā-pər\ *n* **1** : fine particles of matter (as fog or smoke) floating in the air and clouding it **2** : a substance in a gaseous state; *esp* : such a substance that is liquid under ordinary conditions **3** : something insubstantial or fleeting [Middle French *vapeur,* from Latin *vapor* "steam, vapor"]

²vapor *vi* **va·pored; va·por·ing** \-pə-ring, -pring\ **1 a** : to rise or pass off in vapor **b** : to emit vapor **2** : to indulge in bragging, blustering, or idle talk — **va·por·er** \-pər-ər\ *n*

va·por·ing \'vā-pə-ring, -pring\ *n* : the act or speech of one that vapors; *esp* : an idle, extravagant, or high-flown expression or speech

va·por·ish \'vā-pə-rish, -prish\ *adj* **1** : resembling or suggestive of vapor **2** : given to fits of depression or hysteria — **va·por·ish·ness** *n*

va·por·ize \'vā-pə-ˌrīz\ *vb* : to turn from a liquid or solid into vapor — **va·por·iz·able** \-ˌrī-zə-bəl\ *adj* — **va·por·iza·tion** \ˌvā-pə-rə-'zā-shən\ *n*

va·por·iz·er \'vā-pə-ˌrī-zər\ *n* : a device that vaporizes something (as a fuel oil or a medicated liquid)

vapor lock *n* : a partial or complete interruption of fuel flow in an internal-combustion engine caused by the

formation of bubbles of vapor in the fuel-feeding system

va·por·ous \'vā-pə-rəs, -prəs\ *adj* **1** : consisting or characteristic of vapor **2** : containing or obscured by vapors : MISTY **3** : UNSUBSTANTIAL, VAGUE — **va·por·ous·ly** *adv* — **va·por·ous·ness** *n*

vapor pressure *n* : the pressure exerted by a vapor that is in equilibrium with its solid or liquid form — called also *vapor tension*

vapor trail *n* : CONTRAIL

va·por·ware \'vā-pər-ˌwaər, -ˌweər\ *n* : a new computer-related product that has been widely advertised but is not yet available

va·pory \'vā-pə-rē, -prē\ *adj* : VAPOROUS

va·que·ro \vä-'keər-ō\ *n, pl* **-ros** : a ranch hand : COWBOY [Spanish, from *vaca* "cow", from Latin *vacca*]

var·ia \'ver-ē-ə, 'var-\ *n pl* : MISCELLANY; *esp* : a literary miscellany [Latin, neuter pl. of *varius* "various"]

¹vari·able \'ver-ē-ə-bəl, 'var-\ *adj* **1 a** : able or apt to vary : CHANGEABLE ⟨*variable* winds⟩ **b** : FICKLE, INCONSTANT **2 a** : characterized by variations **b** : not true to type : ABERRANT ⟨a *variable* species of wheat⟩ **3** : having the characteristics of a variable — **vari·abil·i·ty** \ˌver-ē-ə-'bil-ət-ē, ˌvar-\ *n* — **vari·able·ness** \'ver-ē-ə-bəl-nəs, 'var-\ *n* — **vari·ably** \-blē\ *adv*

²variable *n* **1 a** : a quantity that may assume any one of a set of values **b** : a symbol in a mathematical expression representing a variable **2** : something that is variable

variable star *n* : a star whose brightness changes usually in more or less regular periods

vari·ance \'ver-ē-əns, 'var-\ *n* **1** : the fact, quality, or state of being variable or variant : DIFFERENCE ⟨yearly *variance* in crops⟩ **2** : the fact or state of being in disagreement : DISSENSION, DISPUTE — **at variance** : not in harmony or agreement

¹vari·ant \'ver-ē-ənt, 'var-\ *adj* **1** : differing from others of its kind or class and especially from others regarded as representing a norm, standard, or type **2** : being one of two or more similar but not identical forms with the same meaning ⟨a *variant* spelling⟩

²variant *n* : one of two or more individuals exhibiting usually slight differences: as **a** : one that exhibits variation from a type or norm **b** : one of two or more different spellings or pronunciations of the same word

vari·a·tion \ˌver-ē-'ā-shən, ˌvar-\ *n* **1 a** : the act or process of varying : the state or fact of being varied **b** : an instance of varying **c** : the extent to which or range in which a thing varies **2** : DECLINATION 5 **3** : the repetition of a musical theme with modifications in rhythm, tune, harmony, or key **4 a** : divergence in biological characters from those typical or usual to an organism or group **b** : an individual or group exhibiting variation — **vari·a·tion·al** \-shnəl, -shən-l\ *adj* — **vari·a·tion·al·ly** \-ē\ *adv*

vari·col·ored \'ver-i-ˌkəl-ərd, 'var-\ *adj* : having various colors : VARIEGATED ⟨*varicolored* marble⟩

var·i·cose \'var-ə-ˌkōs\ *adj* : abnormally swollen or dilated ⟨*varicose* veins⟩ [Latin *varicosus* "full of dilated veins", from *varic-, varix* "dilated vein"]

var·i·cos·i·ty \ˌvar-ə-'käs-ət-ē\ *n, pl* **-ties 1** : the quality or state of being varicose **2** : a varicose part or lesion (as of a vein)

var·ied \'veər-ēd, 'vaər-\ *adj* **1** : having numerous forms or types : DIVERSE **2** : VARIEGATED 2 — **var·ied·ly** *adv*

var·ie·gate \'ver-ē-ə-ˌgāt, 'ver-i-ˌgāt, 'var-\ *vt* **1** : to diversify in external appearance especially with different colors **2** : to make interesting by variety [Latin *variegare,* from *varius* "various"] — **var·ie·ga·tion** \ˌver-ē-ə-'gā-shən, ˌver-i-'gā-, ˌvar-\ *n* — **var·ie·ga·tor** \'ver-ē-ə-ˌgāt-ər, 'ver-i-ˌgāt-, 'var-\ *n*

var·ie·gat·ed \'ver-ē-ə-ˌgāt-əd, 'ver-i-ˌgāt-, 'var-\ *adj* **1** : VARIED 1 **2** : having patches, stripes, or marks of different colors ⟨*variegated* flowers⟩

vanilla 1: 1 flowering branch, 2 vanilla bean

vanishing point 1

va·ri·ety \və-'rī-ət-ē\ *n, pl* **-eties** **1** : the quality or state of having different forms or types **2** : a number or collection of different things : ASSORTMENT ⟨the store stocks a large *variety* of goods⟩ **3 a** : something differing from others of the same general kind **b** : any of various groups of plants or animals within a species that are distinguished from other groups by characteristics not constant enough or too trivial to distinguish species **4** : entertainment consisting of successive unrelated performances (as dances, skits, or acrobatic feats) [Latin *varietas,* from *varius* "various"] — **va·ri·etal** \-ət-1\ *adj* — **va·ri·etal·ly** \-l-ē\ *adv*

variety store *n* : a retail store that carries a large variety of usually inexpensive merchandise

va·ri·o·la \,ver-ē-'ō-lə, var-; və-'rī-ə-lə\ *n* : any of several virus diseases (as smallpox or cowpox) marked by a pustular eruption [Late Latin, "pustule"]

var·i·o·rum \,ver-ē-'ōr-əm, ,var-, -'ȯr-\ *n* : an edition or text especially of a classical author with notes by different persons and often with variant readings of the text [Latin *cum notis variorum* "with the notes of various persons"]

var·i·ous \'ver-ē-əs, 'var-\ *adj* **1** : marked by variation or variety (as in appearance or properties) : of differing kinds ⟨*various* enterprises use metals⟩ ⟨my *various* responsibilities⟩ **2 a** : differing one from another : UNLIKE ⟨animals as *various* as cat and mouse⟩ **b** : VARIANT ⟨*various* readings are known⟩ **3** : consisting of an indefinite number greater than one ⟨*various* schemes⟩ ⟨stop at *various* towns⟩ [Latin *varius*] — **var·i·ous·ly** *adv* — **var·i·ous·ness** *n*

vari·sized \'ver-i-,sīzd, 'var-\ *adj* : of various sizes

va·ris·tor \və-'ris-tər, ve-\ *n* : an electrical resistor whose resistance depends on the applied voltage [*vari-* "varied" (from Latin *varius*) + re*sistor*]

var·let \'vär-lət\ *n* **1** *archaic* : ²RETAINER 2 **2** : a low fellow [Middle French, "young nobleman, page", from Medieval Latin *vassus* "servant, vassal"]

var·mint \'vär-mənt\ *n* **1** : an animal or bird considered a pest **2** : a contemptible person : RASCAL [alteration of *vermin*]

¹var·nish \'vär-nish\ *n* **1 a** : a liquid preparation that is spread like paint and dries to a hard lustrous typically transparent coating **b** : the covering or glaze given by the application of varnish **2** : deceptive outer appearance [Middle French *vernis*] — **var·nishy** \-ē\ *adj*

²varnish *vt* : to cover with or as if with varnish — **var·nish·er** *n*

var·si·ty \'vär-sət-ē, -stē\ *n, pl* **-ties** : a principal squad representing a university, college, school, or club [from *university*] — **varsity** *adj*

varve \'värv\ *n* : a pair of layers of alternately finer and coarser silt or clay believed to comprise an annual cycle of deposition in a body of still water [Swedish *varv* "turn, layer"]

vary \'veər-ē, 'vaər-\ *vb* **var·ied; vary·ing** : to differ or cause to differ: as **a** : to make a usually minor or partial change in ⟨the rule must not be *varied*⟩ **b** : to give variety to : DIVERSIFY ⟨*vary* a diet⟩ ⟨a program *varied* to avoid monotony⟩ **c** : to exhibit or undergo change ⟨*varying* skies⟩ ⟨the accuracy of the several chapters *varies* greatly⟩; *also* : to be different ⟨laws *vary* from state to state⟩ **d** : to take on increasing or decreasing values from a mathematical set ⟨*y varies* inversely with *x*⟩ **e** : to diverge structurally or physiologically from typical members of a group [Latin *variare,* from *varius* "various"] SYN see CHANGE — **vary·ing·ly** \-ing-lē\ *adv*

varying hare *n* : any of several hares having white fur in winter

va·sa ef·fer·en·tia \'vā-zə-,ef-ə-'ren-chē-ə, -chə\ *n pl* : the 12 to 20 tubes that lead from the testis to the vas deferens and except near their beginning are greatly convoluted and form the compact head of the epididymis [New Latin, literally, "efferent vessels"]

vas·cu·lar \'vas-kyə-lər\ *adj* : of, relating to, or being an anatomical vessel (as a vein, artery, or vascular bundle) or a system of these; *also* : supplied with or made up of such vessels and especially blood vessels ⟨a *vascular* tumor⟩ [Latin *vasculum* "small vessel", from *vas* "vessel"] — **vas·cu·lar·i·ty** \,vas-kyə-'lar-ət-ē\ *n*

vascular bundle *n* : a unit of the vascular system of a higher plant consisting usually of xylem and phloem together with parenchyma cells and fibers

vascular cambium *n* : a ring of meristem between the phloem and xylem of a vascular plant which gives rise to phloem on its outer side and xylem on its inner side

vascular cylinder *n* : STELE

vas·cu·lar·iza·tion \,vas-kyə-lə-rə-'zā-shən\ *n* : the development of vessels in tissue

vascular plant *n* : a plant having a specialized conducting system that includes xylem and phloem : TRACHEOPHYTE

vascular ray *n* : a band of xylem and phloem tissue from the pith through the wood of a woody vascular plant that conducts food and water laterally and looks in a cross section of a stem like a spoke of a wheel

vascular tissue *n* : a specialized conducting tissue of higher plants that consists essentially of phloem and xylem and forms a continuous system throughout the body

vas·cu·lum \'vas-kyə-ləm\ *n, pl* **-la** \-lə\ : a usually metal and commonly cylindrical covered box used in collecting botanical specimens [Latin, "small vessel"]

vas def·er·ens \'vas-'def-ə-rənz, -,renz\ *n, pl* **va·sa def·er·en·tia** \,vas-ə-,def-ə-'ren-chē-ə, -chə\ : a duct conveying sperm especially in a higher vertebrate [New Latin, literally, "vessel that brings down"]

vase *United States* 'vās *also* 'vāz, *Canadian* 'vāz *also* 'vāz, *British* 'väz\ *n* : a usually round vessel of greater depth than width used chiefly for ornament or for flowers

va·sec·to·my \və-'sek-tə-mē, vā-'zek-\ *n, pl* **-mies** : surgical removal of part of the vas deferens especially to induce permanent sterility

Vas·e·line \'vas-ə-,lēn, ,vas-ə-'\ *trademark* — used for petrolatum

va·so·con·stric·tion \,vā-zō-kən-'strik-shən\ *n* : narrowing of the diameter of blood vessels [Latin *vas* "vessel"] — **va·so·con·stric·tive** \-'strik-tiv\ *adj*

va·so·con·stric·tor \-'strik-tər\ *n* : an agent (as a sympathetic nerve fiber or a drug) that induces or initiates vasoconstriction

va·so·di·la·ta·tion \,vā-zō-,dil-ə-'tā-shən, -,dī-lə-\ *or* **vaso·di·la·tion** \-dī-'lā-shən\ *n* : widening of the diameter of blood vessels

va·so·di·la·tor \-dī-'lāt-ər, -'dī-,\ *n* : an agent (as a parasympathetic nerve fiber or a drug) that induces or initiates vasodilatation

va·so·mo·tor \,vā-zə-'mōt-ər\ *adj* : of, relating to, or being nerves or centers controlling the size of blood vessels

va·so·pres·sin \,vā-zō-'pres-n\ *n* : a protein hormone secreted by the pituitary gland that increases blood pressure and decreases urine flow [from *Vasopressin,* a former trademark]

vas·sal \'vas-əl\ *n* **1** : a person under the protection of a feudal lord to whom homage and fealty are vowed : a feudal tenant **2** : one in a subservient or subordinate position [Middle French, from Medieval Latin *vassallus,* from *vassus* "servant, vassal", of Celtic origin] — **vassal** *adj*

vas·sal·age \'vas-ə-lij\ *n* **1** : the condition of being a vassal **2** : homage and loyalty due a lord from his vassal **3** : a position of subordination or submission (as to a political power)

¹vast \'vast\ *adj* : very great in size, amount, degree, intensity, or especially in extent [Latin *vastus*] SYN see ENORMOUS — **vast·ly** *adv* — **vast·ness** \'vast-nəs, 'vas-\ *n*

²vast *n* : a boundless space : **IMMENSITY**

vasty \'vas-tē\ *adj* **vast·i·er; -est** : VAST, IMMENSE

vat \'vat\ *n* : a large vessel (as a cistern, tub, or barrel) especially for liquids [Old English *fæt*]

vat dye *n* : a textile dye in a colorless reduced solution in which material to be dyed is steeped and which on exposure to air is oxidized and deposited in the fibers of the material — **vat-dyed** \'vat-'dīd\ *adj*

vat·ic \'vat-ik\ *adj* : of or relating to a prophet [Latin *vates* "seer, prophet"]

Vat·i·can \'vat-i-kən\ *n* : the headquarters or the government of the Roman Catholic Church [Latin *Vaticanus* "Vatican Hill (in Rome)"]

vau·de·ville \'vòd-vəl, 'väd-, 'vōd-, -ə-vəl, -,vil\ *n* : light theatrical entertainment featuring usually unrelated variety acts (as songs, dances, and sketches) [French, from Middle French *vaudevire, vaudeville* "satirical song", from *vau-de-Vire* "valley of Vire (town in France where such songs were composed)"] — **vau·de·vil·lian** \,vòd-'vil-yən, ,väd-, ,vōd-, -ə-'vil\ *adj or n*

¹vault \'vòlt\ *n* **1 a** : an arched structure of masonry usually forming a ceiling or roof **b** : something suggesting a vault especially in arched or domed structure ⟨the blue *vault* of the sky⟩ **2 a** : a space covered by an arched structure; *esp* : an underground passage or room **b** : an underground storage compartment **c** : a room or compartment for the safekeeping of valuables **3 a** : a burial chamber **b** : a case usually of metal or concrete in which a casket is enclosed at burial [Middle French *voute*]

²vault *vt* : to form or cover with or as if with a vault : ARCH

³vault *vb* : to execute a leap using the hands or a pole to lift and support the body; *also* : to leap over [Middle French *volter*, from Italian *voltare*, derived from Latin *volvere* "to roll"] — **vault·er** \'vòl-tər\ *n*

⁴vault *n* : an act of vaulting; *also* : LEAP

vault·ed \'vòl-təd\ *adj* **1** : built in the form of a vault **2** : covered with a vault

vault·ing \-ting\ *adj* : leaping upwards ⟨*vaulting* sparks⟩ ⟨*vaulting* spirits⟩; *esp* : straining unreasonably or arrogantly toward the heights ⟨a *vaulting* ambition⟩

vaulting horse *n* : a padded rectangular or cylindrical form supported off the floor over which gymnasts vault in competition

¹vaunt \'vònt, 'vänt\ *vb* : BRAG, BOAST [Middle French *vanter*, from Late Latin *vanitare*, from Latin *vanitas* "vanity"] — **vaunt·er** *n* — **vaunt·ing·ly** \-ing-lē\ *adv*

²vaunt *n* **1** : a vainglorious display (as of worth or accomplishment) **2** : a bragging assertive speech

vaunt·ful \-fəl\ *adj* : BOASTFUL, VAINGLORIOUS

VCR \,vē-,sē-'är\ *n* : a videotape recorder that uses videocassettes [*v*ideo*c*assette *r*ecorder]

've \v, əv\ *vb* : HAVE ⟨we*'ve* been there⟩

veal \'vēl\ *n* **1** : CALF 1a; *esp* : VEALER **2** : the flesh of a young calf [Middle French *veel*, from Latin *vitellus* "small calf", from *vitulus* "calf"]

veal·er \'vē-lər\ *n* : a calf grown for or suitable for veal

vec·tor \'vek-tər\ *n* **1** : a quantity that has magnitude, direction, and sense **2** : an organism (as an insect) that transmits a pathogen [Latin, "carrier", from *vectus*, past participle of *vehere* "to carry"] — **vec·to·ri·al** \vek-'tōr-ē-əl, -'tòr-\ *adj* — **vec·to·ri·al·ly** \-ē-ə-lē\ *adv*

Ve·da \'vād-ə\ *n* : any of a primary class of Hindu sacred writings; *esp* : any of four canonical collections of hymns, prayers, and liturgical formulas [Sanskrit, literally, "knowledge"]

Ve·dan·ta \vā-'dänt-ə, və-, -'dant-\ *n* : an orthodox system of Hindu philosophy [Sanskrit *Vedānta*, literally, "end of the Veda"] — **Ve·dan·tic** \-ik\ *adj*

ve·dette *or* **vi·dette** \vi-'det\ *n* : a mounted sentinel stationed in advance of pickets [French, from Italian *veletta, vedetta*]

Ve·dic \'vād-ik\ *adj* : of or relating to the Vedas, the language in which they are written, or Hindu history and culture between 2000 B.C. and 500 B.C.

vee·jay \'vē-jā\ *n* : an announcer of a program (as on television) that features music videos [*v*ideo *j*ockey]

veep \'vēp\ *n* : VICE-PRESIDENT [from *v.p.*, abbreviation for *vice-president*]

¹veer \'viər\ *vb* : to change direction or course : TURN; *esp* : to shift in a clockwise direction ⟨the wind *veered* from northwest to northeast⟩ [Middle French *virer*] SYN see SWERVE — **veer·ing·ly** \-ing-lē\ *adv*

²veer *n* : a change in course or direction

vee·ry \'viər-ē\ *n, pl* **veeries** : a tawny brown thrush common in woodlands of the eastern United States [perhaps imitative]

Ve·ga \'vē-gə, 'vā-\ *n* : a bright star in the constellation Lyra [New Latin, from Arabic (al-Nasr) *al-Wāqi'*, literally, "the falling (vulture)"]

¹veg·e·ta·ble \'vej-tə-bəl, 'vej-ət-ə-bəl\ *adj* **1** : of, relating to, or made up of plants ⟨the *vegetable* kingdom⟩ **2** : obtained from plants ⟨*vegetable* oils⟩ ⟨*vegetable* drugs⟩ **3** : suggesting that of a plant (as in monotony) ⟨a *vegetable* existence⟩ [Medieval Latin *vegetabilis* "vegetative", from *vegetare* "to grow", from Latin, "to animate", from *vegetus* "lively", from *vegēre* "to rouse, excite"] — **veg·e·ta·bly** \-blē\ *adv*

²vegetable *n* **1 a** : PLANT 1 **b** : a usually herbaceous plant grown for an edible part that is usually eaten with the principal course of a meal; *also* : such edible part **2** : a human being having a dull or merely physical existence

vegetable oil *n* : an oil of plant origin

vegetable plate *n* : a main course without meat consisting of several vegetables cooked separately and served on one plate

¹veg·e·tar·i·an \,vej-ə-'ter-ē-ən\ *n* : one who excludes meat from the diet; *esp* : one who believes in or practices living solely on vegetables, fruits, grains, and nuts — **veg·e·tar·i·an·ism** \-ē-ə-,niz-əm\ *n*

²vegetarian *adj* : of, relating to, or suitable for vegetarians

veg·e·tate \'vej-ə-,tāt\ *vb* **1** : to live or grow in the manner of a plant; *esp* : to lead a passive effortless existence **2** : to establish vegetation in or on ⟨richly *vegetated* slopes⟩ [Medieval Latin *vegetare* "to grow"]

veg·e·ta·tion \,vej-ə-'tā-shən\ *n* **1** : the act or process of vegetating **2** : inert existence **3** : plant life or cover (as of an area) — **veg·e·ta·tion·al** \-shnəl, -shən-l\ *adj*

veg·e·ta·tive \'vej-ə-,tāt-iv\ *adj* **1 a** : of, relating to, or functioning in nutrition and growth as contrasted with reproduction ⟨the stem and leaf are *vegetative* organs⟩ **b** : of, relating to, or involving propagation by other than sexual means **2** : VEGETATIONAL ⟨*vegetative* cover⟩ **3** : affecting, arising from, or relating to involuntary bodily functions : AUTONOMIC ⟨*vegetative* nerves⟩ **4** : VEGETABLE 3 — **veg·e·ta·tive·ly** *adv* — **veg·e·ta·tive·ness** *n*

veg·gie *also* **veg·ie** \'vej-ē\ *n* : VEGETABLE

veg out \,vej-'aut, 'vej-\ *vi* **vegged out; veg·ging out** : to spend time idly or passively [short for *vegetate*]

ve·he·ment \'vē-ə-mənt\ *adj* : marked by forceful energy : POWERFUL ⟨a *vehement* wind⟩: as **a** : intensely emotional : IMPASSIONED, FERVID ⟨*vehement* patriotism⟩ ⟨*vehement* denunciations⟩ **b** : deeply felt ⟨*vehement* suspicion⟩ [Middle French, from Latin *vehemens*] — **ve·he·mence** \-məns\ *n* — **ve·he·ment·ly** *adv*

ve·hi·cle \'vē-,ik-əl, -,hik-, 'vē-ə-kəl\ *n* **1** : a medium through which something is administered, transmitted, expressed, achieved, or displayed ⟨movies are *vehicles* of ideas⟩ ⟨turpentine is a common *vehicle* for paint⟩ **2** : something used to transport persons or goods : CONVEYANCE [French *véhicule*, from Latin *vehiculum* "carriage, conveyance", from *vehere* "to carry"]

¹vault 1a

\ə\ abut	\ng\ sing
\ər\ further	\ō\ bone
\a\ mat	\ò\ saw
\ā\ take	\òi\ coin
\ä\ cot, cart	\th\ thin
\au\ out	\th\ this
\ch\ chin	\ü\ food
\e\ pet	\u\ foot
\ē\ easy	\y\ yet
\g\ go	\yü\ few
\i\ tip	\yu\ cure
\ī\ life	\zh\ vision
\j\ job	

ve·hic·u·lar \vē-'hik-yə-lər\ *adj* : of, relating to, or designed for vehicles and especially motor vehicles

V–8 \'vē-'āt\ *n* : an internal-combustion engine having two banks of four cylinders each with the banks at an angle to each other; *also* : an automobile having such an engine [from the resemblance of the angle formed by the two banks to the letter V]

¹veil \'vāl\ *n* **1 a** : a length of cloth or net worn especially by women over the head and shoulders or attached to a hat or headdress and sometimes (as in eastern countries) drawn also over the face **b** : a concealing curtain or cover of cloth **c** : something that covers or obscures like a veil ⟨a *veil* of secrecy⟩ **2** : the vows or life of a nun ⟨take the *veil*⟩ [Old North French *veile*, from Latin *vela*, pl. of *velum* "veil"]

²veil *vt* : to cover, provide, obscure, or conceal with or as if with a veil

veil·ing \'vā-ling\ *n* **1** : VEIL 1a **2** : a light sheer fabric (as net or chiffon) suitable for veils

¹vein \'vān\ *n* **1** : LODE **2 a** : one of the tubular branching vessels that carry blood from the capillaries toward the heart **b** : one of the vascular bundles forming the framework of a leaf **c** : one of the thickened ribs that stiffen the wings of an insect **3** : something like a vein usually in irregular linear form or in forming a channel ⟨underground water *veins*⟩; *esp* : a wavy band or streak (as of a different color or texture) ⟨a marble with greenish *veins*⟩ **4 a** : a distinctive mode of expression : STYLE ⟨writing in a humorous *vein*⟩ **b** : a pervasive element or quality : STRAIN ⟨a *vein* of mysticism in one's character⟩ **c** : ¹MOOD [Old French *veine*, from Latin *vena*] — **vein·al** \'vān-l\ *adj* — **veined** \'vānd\ *adj* — **veiny** \'vā-nē\ *adj*

²vein *vt* : to form veins in or mark with veins

vein·ing \'vā-ning\ *n* : a pattern of veins : VENATION

vein·let \'vān-lət\ *n* : a small vein especially of a leaf

ve·lar \'vē-lər\ *adj* **1** : of, relating to, or forming a velum and especially the soft palate **2** : formed with the back of the tongue touching or near the soft palate ⟨the *velar* \k\ of \'kül\ *cool*⟩ — **velar** *n*

veld *or* **veldt** \'velt, 'felt\ *n* : open grassland especially of southern Africa usually with scattered shrubs or trees [Afrikaans *veld*, from Dutch, "field"]

vel·le·ity \ve-'lē-ət-ē\ *n, pl* **-ities** **1** : the lowest degree of volition **2** : a slight wish or tendency : INCLINATION [Latin *velle* "to wish, will"]

vel·lum \'vel-əm\ *n* **1** : a fine-grained unsplit lambskin, kidskin, or calfskin prepared especially for writing on or for binding books **2** : a strong cream-colored paper resembling vellum [Middle French *veelin*, from *veel* "calf"] — **vellum** *adj*

ve·loc·i·pede \və-'läs-ə-ˌpēd\ *n* : a lightweight wheeled vehicle propelled by the rider; *esp* : TRICYCLE [French *vélocipède*, from Latin *voloc-, velox* "quick" + *ped-, pes* "foot"]

velocipede

ve·loc·i·ty \və-'läs-ət-ē, -'läs-tē\ *n, pl* **-ties** **1** : quickness of motion : SPEED ⟨the *velocity* of sound⟩ **2** : the rate of change of position along a straight line with respect to time **3** : rate of occurrence or action : RAPIDITY [Middle French *velocité*, from Latin *velocitas*, from *veloc-, velox* "quick"]

ve·lour *or* **ve·lours** \və-'lùr\ *n, pl* **velours** \-'lùrz\ : a usually heavy fabric with a pile or napped surface resembling velvet [French *velours*, from Old French *velous*, from Latin *villosus* "shaggy", from *villus*, "shaggy hair"]

ve·lum \'vē-ləm\ *n* : a membrane or anatomical partition likened to a veil or curtain; *esp* : SOFT PALATE [Latin, "curtain, veil"]

¹vel·vet \'vel-vət\ *n* **1** : a usually silk or synthetic fabric with a thick soft short pile **2** : something suggesting velvet (as in softness); *esp* : the soft vascular skin covering the developing antlers of a deer **3** : an unanticipated gain or profit [Middle English *veluet, velvet*,

from Middle French *velu* "shaggy", derived from Latin *villus* "shaggy hair"]

²velvet *adj* **1** : made of or covered with velvet **2** : resembling or suggesting velvet : VELVETY

velvet ant *n* : any of various solitary burrowing usually brightly colored wasps with the females wingless

vel·ve·teen \ˌvel-və-'tēn\ *n* : a cotton fabric made in imitation of velvet

vel·vety \'vel-vət-ē\ *adj* **1** : soft and smooth like velvet ⟨*velvety* fur⟩ **2** : smooth to the taste

ven- *or* **veni-** *combining form* : vein ⟨*ven*ation⟩ ⟨*veni*puncture⟩ [Latin *vena*]

ve·na ca·va \ˌvē-nə-'kā-və\ *n, pl* **ve·nae ca·vae** \ˌvē-ni-'kā-vē\ : one of the large veins by which the blood is returned to the right atrium of the heart in an air-breathing vertebrate [New Latin, literally, "hollow vein"]

ve·nal \'vēn-l\ *adj* **1** : willing to take bribes : open to corrupt influences ⟨*venal* officials⟩ **2** : influenced by bribery : CORRUPT ⟨*venal* conduct⟩ [Latin *venalis* "for sale", from *venus* "sale"] — **ve·nal·i·ty** \vi-'nal-ət-ē\ *n* — **ve·nal·ly** \'vēn-l-lē\ *adv*

ve·na·tion \ve-'nā-shən, vē-\ *n* : an arrangement or system of veins ⟨the *venation* of the hand⟩ ⟨the *venation* of a leaf⟩ — **ve·na·tion·al** \-shnəl, -shən-l\ *adj*

vend \'vend\ *vb* : to sell or offer for sale especially as a hawker or peddler ⟨*vend* fruit⟩ [Latin *vendere* "to sell", from *venum dare* "to give for sale"] — **vend·er** \'ven-dər\ *or* **ven·dor** \'ven-dər, ven-'dór\ *n* — **vend·ible** *or* **vend·able** \'ven-də-bəl\ *adj*

vend·ee \ven-'dē\ *n* : one to whom a thing is sold : BUYER

ven·det·ta \ven-'det-ə\ *n* : a feud marked by bitter hostility and motivated by a desire for revenge [Italian, literally, "revenge", from Latin *vindicta*]

vending machine *n* : a slot machine for vending merchandise

ven·di·tion \ven-'dish-ən\ *n* : the act of selling : SALE

ven·due \ven-'dü, vän-, -'dyü\ *n* : AUCTION [obsolete French, from *vendre* "to sell", from Latin *vendere*]

¹ve·neer \və-'niər\ *n* **1** : a thin sheet of a material: as **a** : a layer of a valuable or beautiful wood to be glued to an inferior wood **b** : any of the thin layers bonded together to form plywood **2** : a protective or ornamental facing (as of brick or stone) **3** : a superficial or deceptively attractive appearance : GLOSS ⟨a *veneer* of courtesy⟩ [German *furnier*, from *furnieren* "to veneer", from French *fournir* "to furnish"]

²veneer *vt* : to overlay with a veneer — **ve·neer·er** *n*

ven·er·a·ble \'ven-ər-bəl, -ər-ə-bəl, 'ven-rə-bəl\ *adj* **1** *often cap* : deserving to be venerated — used as a title usually preceded by *the* before the name of an Episcopal archdeacon or a Roman Catholic in the first stage of canonization ⟨the *Venerable* John M. Doe⟩ ⟨the *Venerable* Mother Ann-Marie⟩ **2** : made sacred by association (as religious or historic) **3 a** : calling forth respect through age, character, and attainments **b** : impressive by reason of age ⟨*venerable* pines⟩ — **ven·er·a·bil·i·ty** \ˌven-rə-'bil-ət-ē, -ə-rə-\ *n* — **ven·er·a·ble·ness** \'ven-ər-bəl-nəs, -ər-ə-bəl-, 'ven-rə-bəl-\ *n* — **ven·er·a·bly** \-blē\ *adv*

ven·er·ate \'ven-ə-ˌrāt\ *vt* : to regard with reverential respect or with admiration and deference [Latin *venerari*, from *vener-, venus* "love, charm"] SYN see REVERE — **ven·er·a·tor** \-ˌrāt-ər\ *n*

ven·er·a·tion \ˌven-ə-'rā-shən\ *n* **1** : a feeling of reverence or deep respect : DEVOTION **2** : the act of venerating : the state of being venerated ⟨*veneration* of saints⟩

ve·ne·re·al \və-'nir-ē-əl\ *adj* : of or relating to sexual intercourse or to diseases transmitted by it ⟨a *venereal* infection⟩ [Latin *venereus*, from *vener-, venus* "love, sexual desire"]

venereal disease *n* : a contagious disease (as syphilis) that is usually transmitted by sexual intercourse with an infected person

¹**ven·ery** \'ven-ə-rē\ *n* **1** : the art, act, or practice of hunting **2** : animals that are hunted : GAME [Middle French *venerie,* from *vener* "to hunt", from Latin *venari*]

²**venery** *n* : the pursuit of or indulgence in sexual pleasure; *also* : SEXUAL INTERCOURSE [Medieval Latin *veneria,* from Latin *vener-, venus* "love, sexual desire"]

vene·sec·tion *or* **veni·sec·tion** \'ven-ə-,sek-shən, 'vēn-\ *n* : the operation of opening a vein to draw off blood [New Latin *venae sectio,* literally, "cutting of a vein"]

ve·ne·tian blind \və-,nē-shən-\ *n* : a blind having thin horizontal slats that can be set at different angles to vary the amount of light admitted [*Venetian* "of Venice, Italy"]

Venetian red *n* : an earthy hematite used as a pigment; *also* : a synthetic iron oxide pigment

ven·geance \'ven-jəns\ *n* : punishment inflicted in return for an injury or offense : RETRIBUTION [Old French, from *vengier* "to avenge", from Latin *vindicare,* from *vindic-, vindex* "avenger"] — **with a vengeance 1** : with great force **2** : to an extreme degree

venge·ful \'venj-fəl\ *adj* **1** : filled with a desire for revenge : VINDICTIVE **2** : serving to gain revenge — **venge·ful·ly** \-fə-lē\ *adv* — **venge·ful·ness** *n*

V-en·gine \'vē-'en-jən\ *n* : an internal-combustion engine whose cylinders are arranged in two banks forming an acute angle

veni- — see VEN-

ve·nial \'vē-nē-əl, -nyəl\ *adj* : of a kind that can be pardoned : FORGIVABLE, EXCUSABLE ⟨*venial* faults⟩ [Old French, from Late Latin *venialis,* from Latin *venia* "indulgence, pardon"] — **ve·ni·al·ly** \-ē\ *adv* — **ve·ni·al·ness** *n*

ven·in \'ven-ən\ *n* : a toxic component of snake venom [*ven*om + *-in*]

ve·ni·punc·ture \'vēn-ə-,pəng-chər, 'ven-, -,pəngk-\ *n* : a puncturing of a vein usually to draw off blood or to introduce medication

ve·ni·re \və-'nī-rē\ *n* : a panel from which a jury is drawn

ve·ni·re fa·ci·as \və-,nī-rē-'fā-shē-əs\ *n* : a writ summoning persons to appear in court to serve as jurors [Medieval Latin, "you should cause to come"]

ven·i·son \'ven-ə-sən *also* -ə-zən\ *n, pl* **venisons** *also* **venison 1** : the edible flesh of a wild animal taken by hunting **2** : the flesh of a deer [Old French *veneison* "hunting, game", from Latin *venatio,* from *venari* "to hunt"]

Venn diagram \'ven-\ *n* : a diagram using circles or ellipses to represent relations between and operations on sets [John *Venn,* died 1923, English logician]

ven·om \'ven-əm\ *n* **1** : poisonous matter normally secreted by an animal (as a snake, scorpion, or bee) and communicated chiefly by biting or stinging **2 a** : a spiteful malicious state of mind **b** : a venomous utterance [Old French *venim,* derived from Latin *venenum* "magic charm, drug, poison"]

ven·om·ous \'ven-ə-məs\ *adj* **1** : filled with venom: as **a** : POISONOUS **b** : SPITEFUL, MALIGNANT ⟨*venomous* words⟩ **2** : secreting and using venom ⟨*venomous* snakes⟩ — **ven·om·ous·ly** *adv* — **ven·om·ous·ness** *n*

ve·nous \'vē-nəs\ *adj* **1** : of, relating to, or full of veins ⟨a *venous* rock⟩ ⟨a *venous* system⟩ **2** : being purplish red oxygen-deficient blood present in most veins — **ve·nous·ly** *adv*

¹**vent** \'vent\ *vt* **1 a** : to provide with an outlet **b** : to serve as an outlet for ⟨chimneys *vent* smoke⟩ **2** : to give forceful or emotional expression to ⟨*vent* one's anger⟩ **3** : to relieve by venting [Middle English *venten*]

²**vent** *n* **1** : a means of release : OUTLET **2** : an opening for the escape or passage of something: as **a** : ANUS **b** : FUMAROLE

³**vent** *n* : a slit in a garment and especially in the lower part of a seam [Middle French *fente* "slit, fissure", from *fendre* "to split", from Latin *findere*]

ven·ter \'vent-ər\ *n* : a protuberant and often hollow anatomical structure [Latin, "belly, womb"]

ven·ti·fact \'vent-ə-,fakt\ *n* : a stone worn, polished, or faceted by windblown sand [Latin *vent*us "wind" + English *-ifact* (as in *artifact*)]

ven·ti·late \'vent-l-,āt\ *vt* **1** : to discuss freely and openly : make public ⟨*ventilate* a complaint⟩ **2 a** : to expose to air and especially to a current of fresh air **b** : to provide with ventilation ⟨*ventilate* a room by fans⟩ [Late Latin *ventilare,* from Latin, "to fan, winnow", derived from *ventus* "wind"] — **ven·ti·la·tive** \-,āt-iv\ *adj*

ven·ti·la·tion \,vent-l-'ā-shən\ *n* **1** : the act or process of ventilating **2** : circulation of air ⟨a room with good *ventilation*⟩ **3** : a system or means of providing fresh air

ven·ti·la·tor \'vent-l-,āt-ər\ *n* : one that ventilates; *esp* : a contrivance for introducing fresh air or expelling foul or stagnant air

ven·tral \'ven-trəl\ *adj* **1** : of or relating to the belly : ABDOMINAL **2** : of or relating to or located on or near the surface of the body that in humans is the front but in most other animals is the lower surface ⟨a fish's *ventral* fins⟩ [French, from Latin *ventralis,* from *venter* "belly"] — **ven·tral·ly** \-trə-lē\ *adv*

ven·tri·cle \'ven-tri-kəl\ *n* : a cavity of a bodily part or organ: as **a** : a chamber of the heart which receives blood from a corresponding atrium and from which blood is forced into the arteries **b** : one of the communicating cavities in the brain that are continuous with the central canal of the spinal cord [Latin *ventriculus,* from *venter* "belly"]

ven·tric·u·lar \ven-'trik-yə-lər, vən-\ *adj* : of, relating to, or being a ventricle

ven·tril·o·quism \ven-'tril-ə-,kwiz-əm\ *n* : the production of the voice in such a manner that the sound appears to come from a source other than the vocal organs of the speaker [Late Latin *ventriloquus* "ventriloquist", from Latin *venter* "belly" + *loqui* "to speak"; from the belief that the voice is produced from the ventriloquist's stomach] — **ven·tri·lo·qui·al** \,ven-trə-'lō-kwē-əl\ *adj* — **ven·tri·lo·qui·al·ly** \-kwē-ə-lē\ *adv*

ven·tril·o·quist \ven-'tril-ə-kwəst\ *n* : one who uses or is skilled in ventriloquism; *esp* : a professional entertainer who holds a dummy and apparently carries on conversation with it — **ven·tril·o·quis·tic** \,ven-,tril-ə-'kwis-tik\ *adj*

ven·tril·o·quize \ven-'tril-ə-,kwīz\ *vb* : to use ventriloquism; *also* : to utter in the manner of a ventriloquist

ven·tril·o·quy \ven-'tril-ə-kwē\ *n* : VENTRILOQUISM

¹**ven·ture** \'ven-chər\ *vb* **ven·tured; ven·tur·ing** \'vench-ring, -ə-ring\ **1** : to expose to hazard : RISK ⟨*ventured* their savings on the stock market⟩ **2** : to face the risks and dangers of : BRAVE ⟨*ventured* the stormy sea⟩ **3** : to offer at the risk of rebuff or censure ⟨*venture* an opinion⟩ ⟨I *venture* to disagree⟩ **4** : to proceed despite danger ⟨*ventured* down the cliff⟩ [Middle English *venteren,* from *aventuren,* from *aventure* "adventure"] — **ven·tur·er** \'vench-rər, -ə-rər\ *n*

²**venture** *n* **1** : an undertaking involving chance, risk, or danger; *esp* : a speculative business enterprise **2** : a venturesome act

ven·ture·some \'ven-chər-səm\ *adj* **1** : inclined to court danger or take risks : DARING ⟨a *venturesome* hunter⟩ **2** : involving risk : HAZARDOUS ⟨a *venturesome* journey⟩ SYN see ADVENTUROUS — **ven·ture·some·ly** *adv* — **ven·ture·some·ness** *n*

ven·tur·ous \'vench-rəs, -ə-rəs\ *adj* **1** : VENTURESOME 1 ⟨*venturous* spirit⟩ **2** : HAZARDOUS ⟨*venturous* enterprises⟩ — **ven·tur·ous·ly** *adv* — **ven·tur·ous·ness** *n*

ven·ue \'ven-,yü\ *n* **1** : the place in which events from which a legal action arises are claimed to take place **2** : the place from which the jury is drawn and in which trial is held in a venue action [Middle French,

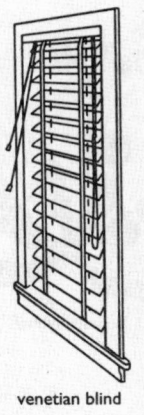

venetian blind

Venus's-flytrap

"action of coming", from *venir* "to come", from Latin *venire*]

ven·ule \'vēn-yül, 'ven-\ *n* : a small vein; *esp* : one of the minute veins connecting blood capillaries with larger veins

Ve·nus \'vē-nəs\ *n* : the planet 2d in order from the sun — see PLANET table [*Venus,* Roman goddess]

Ve·nu·sian \vi-'nü-zhən, -'nyü-\ *adj* : of or relating to the planet Venus — **Venusian** *n*

Venus's–flower–basket \,vē-nəs-əz-'flaú-ər-,bas-kət, ,vē-nəs-'flaú-, -'flaúr-,bas-\ *or* **Venus flower basket** *n* : a tubular or cornucopia-shaped sponge with a delicate glassy silica-containing skeleton

Ve·nus's–fly·trap \,vē-nəs-əz-'flī-,trap, ,vē-nəs-'flī-\ *or* **Venus flytrap** *n* : an insect-eating plant of the sundew family that grows along the Carolina coast and has the leaf apex modified into an insect trap

ve·ra·cious \və-'rā-shəs\ *adj* **1** : TRUTHFUL, HONEST **2** : marked by truth : ACCURATE, TRUE [Latin *verac-, verax,* from *verus* "true"] — **ve·ra·cious·ly** *adv* — **ve·ra·cious·ness** *n*

ve·rac·i·ty \və-'ras-ət-ē\ *n, pl* **-ties 1** : devotion to the truth : TRUTHFULNESS **2** : conformity with truth or fact **3** : something true

ve·ran·da *or* **ve·ran·dah** \və-'ran-də\ *n* : a long roofed gallery extending along one or more sides of a building [Hindi *varanḍā*]

verb \'vərb\ *n* : a word that characteristically is the grammatical center of a predicate and expresses an act, occurrence, or mode of being and that in various languages is inflected (as for agreement with the subject or for tense) — compare ²AUXILIARY 2, COPULA [Middle French *verbe,* from Latin *verbum* "word, verb"]

¹ver·bal \'vər-bəl\ *adj* **1 a** : consisting of or carried on in words (a baby not yet capable of *verbal* communication) **b** : of, relating to, or involving words only rather than meaning or substance or effective action **2** : of, relating to, or formed from a verb (*verbal* adjectives) **3** : spoken rather than written (a *verbal* contract) (*verbal* instructions) **4** : word-for-word : VERBATIM (*verbal* translation) [Late Latin *verbalis,* from Latin *verbum* "word"] SYN see ORAL — **ver·bal·ly** \-bə-lē\ *adv*

²verbal *n* : a word that combines characteristics of a verb with those of a noun or adjective

ver·bal·ism \'vər-bə-,liz-əm\ *n* **1** : a verbal expression : TERM **2** : words used as if they were more important than the realities they represent **3 a** : a wordy expression of little meaning **b** : the quality or state of being wordy

ver·bal·ist \'vər-bə-ləst\ *n* **1** : one who stresses words above substance or reality **2** : a person who uses words skillfully — **ver·bal·is·tic** \,vər-bə-'lis-tik\ *adj*

ver·bal·ize \'vər-bə-,līz\ *vb* **1** : to speak or write in wordy or empty fashion **2** : to express or express something in words : describe verbally **3** : to convert into a verb — **ver·bal·iza·tion** \,vər-bə-lə-'zā-shən\ *n* — **ver·bal·iz·er** \'vər-bə-,lī-zər\ *n*

verbal noun *n* : a noun derived directly from a verb or verb stem and in some uses having the sense and constructions of a verb

ver·ba·tim \,vər-'bāt-əm\ *adv or adj* : word for word : in the same words : LITERAL (a *verbatim* translation) (took down the speech *verbatim*) [Medieval Latin, from Latin *verbum* "word"]

ver·be·na \,vər-'bē-nə\ *n* : VERVAIN; *esp* : any of numerous garden plants of hybrid origin widely grown for their showy spikes of white, pink, red, or blue flowers which are borne in profusion over a long season [New Latin, genus of plants, from Latin *verbenae* "sacred boughs"]

ver·bi·age \'vər-bē-ij\ *n* **1** : excess of words in proportion to sense or content **2** : DICTION 1, WORDING (concise *verbiage*)

ver·bo·ten \vər-'bōt-n, fər-\ *adj* : forbidden usually by authority and often unreasonably [German, "forbidden"]

ver·bose \,vər-'bōs\ *adj* : excessively wordy : PROLIX — **ver·bose·ly** *adv* — **ver·bose·ness** *n* — **ver·bos·i·ty** \-'bäs-ət-ē\ *n*

ver·dant \'vərd-nt\ *adj* **1 a** : green in color (*verdant* grass) **b** : green with growing plants (*verdant* fields) **2** : lacking experience or judgment [Middle French *verdoyant,* from *verdoyer* "to be green", from *verd, vert* "green", from Latin *viridis,* from *virēre* "to be green"] — **ver·dan·cy** \-n-sē\ *n* — **ver·dant·ly** *adv*

ver·dict \'vər-dikt\ *n* **1** : the decision of a jury on the matter submitted to them in trial **2** : an opinion held or expressed [Anglo-French *verdit,* from Old French *ver dit* "true dictum"]

ver·di·gris \'vərd-ə-,grēs, -,gris\ *n* **1** : a green or greenish blue poisonous pigment produced by the action of acetic acid on copper **2** : a green or bluish carbonate of copper formed on copper, bronze, or brass surfaces [Old French *vert de Grice,* literally, "green of Greece"]

ver·dure \'vər-jər\ *n* : the greenness of growing vegetation; *also* : such vegetation itself [Middle French, from *verd* "green"] — **ver·dured** \-jərd\ *adj* — **ver·dur·ous** \'vərj-rəs, -ə-rəs\ *adj* — **ver·dur·ous·ness** *n*

¹verge \'vərj\ *n* **1 a** : a staff carried as an emblem of authority or office **b** : an area around a place or within which jurisdiction is exercised **2 a** : something that borders, limits, or bounds : EDGE, BOUNDARY (the *verge* of the sea) **b** : BRINK, THRESHOLD (on the *verge* of bankruptcy) [Middle French, from Latin *virga* "rod, stripe"]

²verge *vi* **1** : to be contiguous (Canada *verges* on the United States) **2** : to be on the verge (courage that *verged* on recklessness)

³verge *vi* **1** : to move or extend in some direction or toward some condition : INCLINE **2** : to be in transition or change [Latin *vergere* "to bend, incline"]

verg·er \'vər-jər\ *n* **1** *chiefly British* : an attendant who carries a verge (as before a bishop or justice) **2** : a church official who keeps order during services or serves as an usher or a sacristan

ver·i·fi·able \'ver-ə-,fī-ə-bəl\ *adj* : capable of being verified — **ver·i·fi·able·ness** *n* — **ver·i·fi·ably** \-blē\ *adv*

ver·i·fy \'ver-ə-,fī\ *vt* **-fied; -fy·ing 1** : to prove to be true or correct : CONFIRM **2** : to check or test the accuracy of [Middle French *verifier,* from Medieval Latin *verificare,* from Latin *verus* "true"] SYN see CONFIRM — **ver·i·fi·ca·tion** \,ver-ə-fə-'kā-shən\ *n* — **ver·i·fi·er** \'ver-ə-,fī-ər, -,fīr\ *n*

ver·i·ly \'ver-ə-lē\ *adv* : in fact : CERTAINLY [Middle English *verraily,* from *verray* "very"]

veri·sim·i·lar \,ver-ə-'sim-lər, -ə-lər\ *adj* : having the appearance of truth : PROBABLE [Latin *verisimilis,* from *veri similis* "like the truth"] — **veri·sim·i·lar·ly** *adv*

veri·si·mil·i·tude \-sə-'mil-ə-,tüd, -,tyüd\ *n* **1** : the quality or state of being verisimilar **2** : something verisimilar

ver·i·ta·ble \'ver-ət-ə-bəl\ *adj* : ACTUAL, TRUE — **ver·i·ta·ble·ness** *n* — **ver·i·ta·bly** \-blē\ *adv*

ver·i·ty \'ver-ət-ē\ *n, pl* **-ties 1** : the quality or state of being true or real **2** : something true **3** : VERACITY 1 [Middle French *verité,* from Latin *veritas,* from *verus* "true"]

ver·juice \'vər-,jüs\ *n* **1** : the sour juice of crab apples or unripe fruit (as grapes) or an acid liquor made from this **2** : sourness of disposition or manner [Middle French *vert jus,* literally, "green juice"]

ver·meil *n* **1** \'vər-məl, -,māl\ : VERMILION **2** \veər-'mā\ : gilded silver, bronze, or copper [Middle French *vermeil,* adj., "bright red, vermilion"] — **vermeil** *adj*

vermi- *combining form* : worm (*vermi*fuge) [Latin *vermis*]

ver·mi·cel·li \,vər-mə-'chel-ē, -'sel-\ *n* : a food like spaghetti but of smaller diameter [Italian, from pl. of *vermicello* "little worm", from *verme* "worm", from Latin *vermis*]

ver·mic·u·late \,vər-'mik-yə-lət\ *or* **ver·mic·u·lat·ed** \-,lāt-əd\ *adj* : TORTUOUS 2b, INVOLUTE [Latin *vermiculatus*, from *vermiculus* "little worm", from *vermis* "worm"] — **ver·mic·u·la·tion** \-,mik-yə-'lā-shən\ *n*

ver·mic·u·lite \,vər-'mik-yə-,līt\ *n* : any of numerous minerals that are usually altered micas whose granules expand greatly at high temperatures to give a lightweight absorbent heat-resistant material used especially in seedbeds and as insulation [Latin *vermiculus* "little worm", from *vermis* "worm"]

vermiform appendix *n* : APPENDIX 2a

ver·mi·fuge \'vər-mə-,fyüj\ *n* : an agent that expels or destroys parasitic worms [*vermi* + Latin *fugare* "to put to flight"]

ver·mil·ion *or* **ver·mil·lion** \,vər-'mil-yən\ *n* 1 : a bright red pigment; *esp* : one consisting of a sulfide of mercury 2 : a vivid reddish orange color [Old French *vermeillon*, from *vermeil*, adj., "bright red, vermilion", from Late Latin *vermiculus* "kermes", from Latin, "little worm", from *vermis* "worm"]

ver·min \'vər-mən\ *n, pl* **vermin** 1 : small common harmful or objectionable animals (as fleas or mice) that are difficult to control 2 : an offensive person [Middle French, from Latin *vermis* "worm"]

ver·min·ous \'vər-mə-nəs\ *adj* 1 : consisting of or full of vermin ⟨*verminous* houses⟩ 2 : caused by vermin ⟨*verminous* disease⟩ — **ver·min·ous·ly** *adv*

ver·mouth \vər-'müth\ *n* : a fortified wine flavored with aromatic herbs and used as an aperitif or in mixed drinks [French *vermout*, from German *wermut* "wormwood"]

¹ver·nac·u·lar \vər-'nak-yə-lər, və-'nak-\ *adj* 1 : using a language or dialect native to a region or country rather than a literary, cultured, or foreign language 2 : of, relating to, or used in the normal spoken form of a language [Latin *vernaculus* "native", from *verna* "slave born in his master's house, native"] — **ver·nac·u·lar·ly** *adv*

²vernacular *n* 1 : a vernacular language 2 : the mode of expression of a group or class 3 : a common name of a plant or animal as distinguished from the latinized taxonomic name

ver·nal \'vərn-l\ *adj* 1 : of, relating to, or occurring in the spring ⟨the *vernal* equinox⟩ ⟨*vernal* sunshine⟩ 2 : fresh or new like the spring; *also* : YOUTHFUL [Latin *vernalis*, from *vernus* "vernal", from *ver* "spring"] — **ver·nal·ly** \-l-ē\ *adv*

ver·nal·ize \'vərn-l-,īz\ *vt* : to hasten the flowering and fruiting of (plants) by treating seeds, bulbs, or seedlings so as to shorten the vegetative period — **ver·nal·iza·tion** \,vərn-l-ə-'zā-shən\ *n*

ver·na·tion \vər-'nā-shən\ *n* : the arrangement of foliage leaves within the bud [derived from Latin *vernare* "to behave as in spring", from *vernus* "vernal"]

ver·ni·er \'vər-nē-ər\ *n* 1 : a short scale made to slide along the divisions of a graduated instrument for indicating parts of divisions 2 : a small auxiliary device used with a main device to obtain fine adjustment [Pierre *Vernier*, died 1637, French mathematician]

vernier caliper *n* : a caliper gauge with a graduated beam and a sliding jaw having a vernier

ve·ron·i·ca \və-'rän-i-kə\ *n* : SPEEDWELL [New Latin]

ver·ru·cose \və-'rü-,kōs\ *adj* : covered with warty elevations [Latin *verrucosus*, from *verruca* "wart"]

ver·sa·tile \'vər-sət-l\ *adj* 1 : changing or fluctuating readily : VARIABLE 2 : taking in a variety of subjects, fields, or skills; *also* : turning with ease from one thing or position to another 3 : having many uses or applications [Latin *versatilis* "turning easily", from *versare* "to turn", from *versus*, past participle of *vertere* "to turn"] — **ver·sa·tile·ly** \-sət-l-lē, -sət-l-ē\ *adv*

— **ver·sa·tile·ness** \-l-nəs\ *n* — **ver·sa·til·i·ty** \,vər-sə-'til-ət-ē\ *n*

¹verse \'vərs\ *n* 1 : a line of metrical writing 2 a : light or superficial metrical writing b : POETRY ⟨Elizabethan *verse*⟩ c : POEM ⟨read the group some *verses*⟩ 3 : STANZA 4 : one of the short divisions into which a chapter of the Bible is traditionally divided [Old French *vers*, from Latin *versus*, literally, "turning", from *vertere* "to turn"]

²verse *vb* : VERSIFY

³verse *vt* : to familiarize by study or experience ⟨*verse* oneself in history⟩ [back-formation from *versed*, from Latin *versatus*, past participle of *versari* "to be active, be occupied (in)", passive of *versare* "to turn"]

ver·si·cle \'vər-si-kəl\ *n* 1 : a short verse or sentence said or sung in public worship by a leader and followed by a response from the people 2 : a little verse [Latin *versiculus* "small verse", from *versus* "verse"]

ver·si·fi·ca·tion \,vər-sə-fə-'kā-shən\ *n* 1 : the making of verses 2 : metrical arrangement of poetry

ver·si·fy \'vər-sə-,fī\ *vb* **-fied; -fy·ing** 1 : to compose or turn into verse 2 : to relate or describe in verse — **ver·si·fi·er** \-,fī-ər, -,fīr\ *n*

ver·sion \'vər-zhən\ *n* 1 : a translation from another language; *esp* : a translation of the Bible or a part of it 2 a : an account or description from one point of view especially as contrasted with another b : an adaptation of a literary or musical work ⟨a stage *version* of the novel⟩ 3 : a form or variation of an original ⟨an experimental *version* of the plane⟩ 4 : manual turning of the fetus in the uterus to aid delivery [Middle French, from Medieval Latin *versio* "act of turning", from *vertere* "to turn"] — **ver·sion·al** \'vərzh-nəl, -ən-l\ *adj*

ver·so \'vər-sō\ *n, pl* **versos** : a left-hand page — compare RECTO [New Latin *verso folio* "the page being turned"]

verst \'vərst\ *n* : a Russian unit of distance equal to 0.6629 miles (about 1.067 kilometers) [French *verste* and German *werst*, both from Russian *versta*]

ver·sus \'vər-səs, -səz\ *prep* 1 : AGAINST 2a ⟨United States *versus* Doe⟩ 2 : in contrast to or as the alternative of ⟨free trade *versus* protection⟩ [Medieval Latin, "towards, against", derived from Latin *vertere* "to turn"]

vert \'vərt\ *n* : the heraldic color green [Middle French *vert* "green"]

ver·te·bra \'vərt-ə-brə\ *n, pl* **-brae** \-,brē, -,brā\ *or* **-bras** : one of the bony or cartilaginous segments composing the spinal column that in higher vertebrates have a short nearly cylindrical body with ends articulating with adjacent vertebrae and a bony arch enclosing the spinal cord [Latin, "joint, vertebra", from *vertere* "to turn"]

ver·te·bral \vər-'tē-brəl\ *adj* : of, relating to, or made up of vertebrae : SPINAL — **ver·te·bral·ly** \-ē\ *adv*

vertebral column *n* : SPINAL COLUMN

¹ver·te·brate \'vərt-ə-brət, -,brāt\ *adj* 1 a : having a spinal column b : of or relating to the vertebrates 2 : having a strong framework suggesting vertebrae

²vertebrate *n* : any of a primary division (Vertebrata) of chordates comprising animals (as mammals, birds, reptiles, amphibians, or fishes) with a segmented spinal column together with a few primitive forms in which the backbone is represented by a notochord

ver·tex \'vər-,teks\ *n, pl* **ver·ti·ces** \'vərt-ə-,sēz\ *also* **ver·tex·es** 1 a : the point opposite to and farthest from a base of a figure b : the common endpoint of the sides of an angle c : a point where the axis of an ellipse, parabola, or hyperbola intersects the curve itself 2 : the top of the head 3 : the highest point : SUMMIT, APEX [Latin *vertic-, vertex* "whirlpool, top of the head, summit", from *vertere* "to turn"]

ver·ti·cal \'vərt-i-kəl\ *adj* 1 : situated at the highest point : directly overhead or in the zenith 2 : perpendicular to the plane of the horizon or to a primary

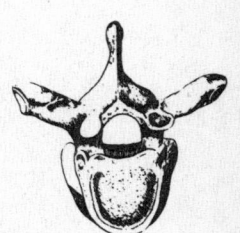

vertebra

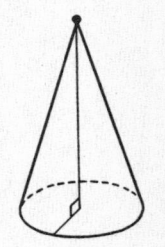

vertex 1a

\ə\ abut		\ng\ sing	
\ər\ further		\ō\ bone	
\a\ mat		\ȯ\ saw	
\ā\ take		\ȯi\ coin	
\ä\ cot, cart		\th\ thin	
\aú\ out		\th\ this	
\ch\ chin		\ü\ food	
\e\ pet		\ú\ foot	
\ē\ easy		\y\ yet	
\g\ go		\yü\ few	
\i\ tip		\yú\ cure	
\ī\ life		\zh\ vision	
\j\ job			

²vest 1a

axis : UPRIGHT **3** : relating to or composed of separate units on different levels ⟨a *vertical* business organization⟩ — **vertical** *n* — **ver·ti·cal·i·ty** \,vərt-ə-'kal-ət-ē\ *n* — **ver·ti·cal·ly** \'vərt-i-kə-lē, -klē\ *adv* — **ver·ti·cal·ness** \-kəl-nəs\ *n* □ SYN VERTICAL, PERPENDICULAR, PLUMB mean being at right angles to a base line. VERTICAL suggests a line or direction rising straight upward toward a zenith; PERPENDICULAR may stress the stiff straightness of a line making a right angle with any other line, not necessarily a horizontal one; PLUMB stresses an exact verticality determined (as with a plumb line) by earth's gravity.

vertical angle *n* : one of two angles that have the same vertex and are on opposite sides of two intersecting straight lines

vertical circle *n* : a great circle of the celestial sphere whose plane is perpendicular to that of the horizon

vertical file *n* : a collection especially of pamphlets and clippings maintained (as in a library) to answer brief questions or to provide information not easily located elsewhere

ver·ti·go \'vərt-i-,gō\ *n, pl* **-goes** *or* **-gos** : a dizzy or giddy state [Latin, from *vertere* "to turn"]

ver·vain \'vər-,vān\ *n* : any of a genus of mostly American herbaceous or shrubby plants with often showy heads or spikes of 5-parted regular flowers — called also *verbena* [Middle French *verveine*, from Latin *verbenae* "sacred boughs"]

verve \'vərv\ *n* **1** : the spirit and enthusiasm that animate artistic composition or performance : VIVACITY **2** : ENERGY 1, VITALITY [French, from Latin *verba*, pl. of *verbum* "word"]

¹very \'ver-ē\ *adj* **ver·i·er; -est 1 a** : properly entitled to the name or designation : TRUE **b** : ACTUAL 1, REAL **2 a** : being exactly as stated ⟨the *very* heart of the city⟩ **b** : exactly suitable or necessary ⟨the *very* thing for the purpose⟩ **3** : ABSOLUTE, UTTER ⟨the *veriest* fool alive⟩ **4** : MERE, BARE ⟨the *very* thought terrified me⟩ **5** : SELF-SAME, IDENTICAL ⟨the *very* person I saw⟩ [Old French *verai*, derived from Latin *verax* "truthful", from *verus* "true"]

²very *adv* **1** : to a high degree ⟨a *very* hot day⟩ ⟨*very* much better⟩ **2** : in actual fact : TRULY — used to give emphasis to a following adjective ⟨the *very* best store in town⟩ ⟨told the *very* same story⟩

very high frequency *n* : a radio frequency in the range between 30 and 300 megahertz — abbreviation VHF

Very light \,ver-ē-, ,viər-ē-\ *n* : a pyrotechnic signal in a system of signaling using white or colored balls of fire shot from a special pistol [Edward W. *Very*, died 1910, American naval officer]

very low frequency *n* : a radio frequency in the range between 3 and 30 kilohertz — abbreviation VLF

Very Reverend — used as a title for various religious officials (as cathedral deans and canons and rectors of Roman Catholic seminaries and colleges)

ves·i·cant \'ves-i-kənt\ *n* : an agent (as a drug or a plant substance) that causes blistering [Latin *vesica* "bladder, blister"] — **vesicant** *adj*

ves·i·cle \'ves-i-kəl\ *n* : a membranous and usually fluid-filled pouch (as a cyst or vacuole) in a plant or animal; *also* : a small abnormal elevation of the outer layer of skin enclosing a watery liquid : BLISTER [Middle French *vesicule*, from Latin *vesicula* "small bladder", from *vesica* "bladder"] — **ve·sic·u·lar** \və-'sik-yə-lər\ *adj* — **ve·sic·u·lar·ly** *adv*

ves·per \'ves-pər\ *adj* : of or relating to vespers or the evening

ves·pers \'ves-pərz\ *n pl, often cap* **1** : the sixth of the canonical hours **2** : a late afternoon or evening worship service

ves·per·tine \'ves-pər-,tīn\ *adj* : of, relating to, or occurring in the evening ⟨*vespertine* shadows⟩ [Latin *vespertinus*, from *vesper* "evening"]

ves·sel \'ves-əl\ *n* **1 a** : a hollow or concave utensil (as a hogshead, bottle, kettle, cup, or bowl) for holding something **b** : a person held to be the recipient of a quality (as grace) **2** : a structure built for transportation on water : BOAT, SHIP; *esp* : one larger than a rowboat **3 a** : a tube or canal (as an artery) in which a body fluid is contained and conveyed or circulated **b** : a conducting tube in a vascular plant [Old French *vaissel*, from Late Latin *vascellum*, from Latin *vas* "vase, vessel"]

¹vest \'vest\ *vb* **1 a** : to place or give (as a right, authority, or title) into the possession or discretion of some person or body ⟨powers *vested* in the presidency⟩ **b** : to become legally vested ⟨the title *vests* in the purchaser⟩ **2 a** : to clothe with or as if with a garment; *esp* : to garb in clerical vestments **b** : to put on garments and especially clerical vestments [Middle French *vestir* "to clothe, invest", from Latin *vestire* "to clothe", from *vestis* "clothing, garment"]

²vest *n* **1 a** : a sleeveless garment typically worn under a suit coat **b** : a protective usually sleeveless garment (as a life preserver) that extends to the waist **2** : a plain or decorative piece used to fill in the front neckline of a woman's outer garment (as a coat, or gown) [French *veste* "robe, jacket", from Italian, from Latin *vestis* "garment"]

ves·tal \'ves-tl\ *n* **1** : a virgin consecrated to the Roman goddess Vesta and to the service of a sacred fire perpetually kept burning on her altar — called also *vestal virgin* **2** : a chaste woman — **vestal** *adj*

vested interest *n* **1** : an interest (as in an existing economic or political arrangement) in which the holder has a strong personal commitment **2** : one having a vested interest in something

vest·ee \ve-'stē\ *n* **1** : DICKEY; *esp* : one made to resemble a vest and worn under a coat **2** : VEST 2

ves·ti·ary \'ves-tē-,er-ē, 'ves-chē-\ *n, pl* **-ar·ies 1** : a room where clothing is kept **2** : CLOTHING; *esp* : clerical vestments [Old French *vestiaire* "vestry"]

ves·tib·u·lar \ve-'stib-yə-lər\ *adj* : of, relating to, or functioning as a vestibule

ves·ti·bule \'ves-tə-,byül\ *n* **1 a** : a passage or room between the outer door and the interior of a building : LOBBY **b** : an enclosed entrance at the end of a railway passenger car **2** : any of various bodily cavities mostly serving as or resembling an entrance to some other cavity or space; *esp* : the central cavity of the labyrinth of the ear [Latin *vestibulum*]

ves·tige \'ves-tij\ *n* **1 a** : a visible sign left by something vanished or lost **b** : a minute remaining amount **2** : a small and imperfectly developed bodily part or organ that remains from one more fully developed in an earlier stage of the individual, in a past generation, or in closely related forms [French, from Latin *vestigium* "footprint, track, vestige"] SYN SEE TRACE — **ves·ti·gial** \ve-'stij-əl, -'stij-ē-əl\ *adj* — **ves·ti·gial·ly** \-ē\ *adv*

vest·ment \'vest-mənt, 'ves-\ *n* **1 a** : an outer garment; *esp* : a ceremonial or official robe **b** *pl* : CLOTHING, GARB **2** : a covering resembling a garment **3** : a ceremonial garment worn by a person officiating at a religious service — **vest·ment·al** \vest-'ment-l, ves-\ *adj*

vest–pock·et \,vest-'päk-ət\ *adj* **1** : adapted to fit into the vest pocket **2** : of very small size or scope

ves·try \'ves-trē\ *n, pl* **vestries 1 a** : SACRISTY **b** : a room used for church meetings and classes **2 a** : the business meeting of an English parish; *also* : the parishioners assembled for it **b** : an elective body administering the business affairs of an Episcopal parish [probably from Middle French *vestiarie*, from Medieval Latin *vestiarium*, from Latin *vestire* "to clothe"]

ves·try·man \-mən\ *n* : a member of a vestry

ves·try·wom·an \-,wùm-ən\ *n* : a woman who is a member of a vestry

ves·ture \'ves-chər\ *n* **1 a** : a covering garment (as a robe or vestment) **b** : CLOTHING, APPAREL **2** : something that covers like a garment

¹vet \'vet\ *n* : VETERINARIAN, VETERINARY

²vet *vt* **vet·ted; vet·ting 1** *chiefly British* : to provide veterinary care for (an animal) or medical care for (a person) **2** : to subject to expert appraisal or correction

³vet *adj or n* : VETERAN

vetch \'vech\ *n* : any of a genus of herbaceous twining plants related to the pea that include valuable fodder and soil-building plants [Old North French *veche*, from Latin *vicia*]

vet·er·an \'vet-ə-rən, 've-trən\ *n* **1** : a person who has had long experience in an occupation or skill and especially in war **2** : a former member of the armed forces [Latin *veteranus* "soldier of long experience", derived from *veter-, vetus* "old"]

Veterans Day *n* : November 11 observed as a legal holiday in commemoration of the end of hostilities in 1918 and 1945

vet·er·i·nar·i·an \,vet-ə-rən-'er-ē-ən, ,ve-trən-, ,vet-n-\ *n* : one qualified and authorized to treat diseases and injuries of animals

¹vet·er·i·nary \'vet-ə-rən-,er-ē, 've-trən-, 'vet-n-\ *adj* : of, relating to, or being the medical care of animals and especially domestic animals [derived from Latin *veterinus* "of beasts of burden"]

²veterinary *n, pl* **-nar·ies** : VETERINARIAN

¹veto \'vēt-ō\ *n, pl* **vetoes 1** : an authoritative rejection or prohibition **2 a** : a power of one branch of a government to forbid or prohibit the carrying out of projects attempted by another department; *esp* : the power of a chief executive to prevent a measure passed by a legislature from becoming law **b** : the exercise of such authority **c** : a power possessed by members of a body (as the United Nations Security Council) to prohibit action by the body [Latin, "I forbid", from *vetare* "to forbid"]

²veto *vt* : to refuse to admit or approve : PROHIBIT; *esp* : to refuse assent to (a legislative bill) so as to prevent enactment or cause reconsideration — **ve·to·er** \'vēt-,ō-ər, -,ōr\ *n*

vex \'veks\ *vt* **vexed** *also* **vext; vex·ing 1 a** : to bring trouble, distress, or agitation to : HARASS **c** : PUZZLE 1, BAFFLE **2** : to debate or discuss at length ⟨a *vexed* question⟩ **3** : to shake or toss about [Middle French *vexer*, from Latin *vexare*]

vex·a·tion \vek-'sā-shən\ *n* **1** : the quality or state of being vexed : IRRITATION **2** : the act of vexing : ANNOYANCE **3** : a cause of trouble or worry

vex·a·tious \-shəs\ *adj* **1 a** : causing vexation ⟨a *vexatious* child⟩ **b** : intended to harass ⟨a *vexatious* lawsuit⟩ **2** : full of disorder or stress — **vex·a·tious·ly** *adv* — **vex·a·tious·ness** *n*

via \,vī-ə, ,vē-ə\ *prep* **1** : by way of **2** : through the medium of; *also* : by means of [Latin, ablative of *via* "way"]

vi·a·ble \'vī-ə-bəl\ *adj* **1** : capable of living; *esp* : born alive with such form and development of organs as to be normally capable of living **2** : capable of growing or developing ⟨*viable* seeds⟩ ⟨*viable* eggs⟩ **3** : WORKABLE ⟨a *viable* plan⟩ [French, from *vie* "life", from Latin *vita*] — **vi·a·bil·i·ty** \,vī-ə-'bil-ət-ē\ *n* — **vi·a·bly** \'vī-ə-blē\ *adv*

vi·a·duct \'vī-ə-,dəkt\ *n* : a bridge with high supporting towers or piers for carrying a road or railroad over something (as a gorge or a highway) [Latin *via* "way, road" + English *-duct* (as in *aqueduct*)]

vi·al \'vī-əl, 'vīl\ *n* : a small vessel for liquids (as medicines or chemicals) [Middle French *fiole*, from Provençal *fiola*, from Latin *phiala*, from Greek *phialē*]

vi·and \'vī-ənd\ *n* **1** : an item of food **2** *pl* : PROVISION 2, FOOD [Middle French *viande*, from Medieval Latin *vivanda* "food", derived from Latin *vivere* "to live"]

vi·at·i·cum \vī-'at-i-kəm, vē-\ *n, pl* **-cums** *or* **-ca** \-kə\ **1** : money or provisions for a journey **2** : Communion given to a person in danger of death [Latin, "traveling money", from *viaticus* "of a journey", from *via* "way"]

vi·brant \'vī-brənt\ *adj* **1 a** (1) : oscillating or pulsating rapidly (2) : pulsating with life, vigor, or activity ⟨a *vibrant* personality⟩ **b** (1) : readily set in vibration (2) : RESPONSIVE 2, SENSITIVE **2** : sounding as a result of vibration : RESONANT — **vi·bran·cy** \-brən-sē\ *n* — **vi·brant·ly** \-brənt-lē\ *adv*

vi·bra·phone \'vī-brə-,fōn\ *n* : a percussion musical instrument resembling the xylophone but having metal bars and motor-driven resonators for sustaining the tone and producing a vibrato — **vi·bra·phon·ist** \-,fō-nəst\ *n*

vi·brate \'vī-,brāt\ *vb* **1** : to swing or move back and forth ⟨a *vibrating* pendulum⟩ **2** : to set in vibration **3** : to oscillate very rapidly so as to produce a quivering effect or sound : SHAKE, QUIVER ⟨guitar strings *vibrate* when plucked⟩ **4** : to respond sympathetically : THRILL **5** : WAVER 1, FLUCTUATE [Latin *vibrare*] SYN see SWAY

vi·bra·tile \'vī-brət-l, -brə-,tīl\ *adj* **1** : characterized by vibration **2** : adapted to or used in vibratory motion ⟨the *vibratile* organs of insects⟩

vi·bra·tion \vī-'brā-shən\ *n* **1 a** : a periodic motion of the particles of an elastic body or medium rapidly to and fro (as when a stretched cord is pulled or struck and produces a musical tone or when molecules in the air transmit sounds to the ear) **b** : the action of vibrating : the state of being vibrated **c** : motion or a movement to and fro : OSCILLATION ⟨the *vibration* of a pendulum⟩ **d** : a quivering or trembling motion ⟨*vibration* of a house caused by a passing truck⟩ **2** : vacillation in opinion or action : WAVERING **3** *pl* : a feeling or impression that someone or something gives off ⟨good *vibrations*⟩ — **vi·bra·tion·al** \-shnəl, -shən-l\ *adj* — **vi·bra·tion·less** \-shən-ləs\ *adj*

vi·bra·to \vi-'brät-ō, vī-\ *n, pl* **-tos 1** : a slightly trembling effect given to vocal or instrumental tone by slight and rapid variations in pitch **2** : TREMOLO 1b [Italian, from *vibrare* "to vibrate", from Latin]

vi·bra·tor \'vī-,brāt-ər\ *n* **1** : one that vibrates or causes vibration **2** : an electromagnetic device that converts low direct current to pulsating direct current or alternating current

vi·bra·to·ry \'vī-brə-,tōr-ē, -,tòr-\ *adj* **1** : consisting in, capable of, or causing vibration **2** : characterized by vibration : VIBRANT

vib·rio \'vib-rē-,ō\ *n, pl* **-ri·os** : any of a genus of short rigid motile bacteria that are typically shaped like a comma or an S and include serious pathogens (as of Asiatic cholera) [New Latin, from Latin *vibrare* "to vibrate"] — **vib·ri·on·ic** \,vib-rē-'än-ik\ *adj*

vi·bris·sa \vī-'bris-ə, və-\ *n, pl* **vi·bris·sae** \vī-'bris-ē; və-'bris-ē, -,ī\ : any of the stiff mostly tactile hairs especially about the face in many mammals [Latin] — **vi·bris·sal** \-'bris-əl\ *adj*

vi·bur·num \vī-'bər-nəm\ *n* : any of a genus of widely distributed shrubs or trees of the honeysuckle family with simple leaves and white or rarely pink flowers in broad clusters [Latin]

vic·ar \'vik-ər\ *n* **1** : AGENT; *esp* : an administrative deputy **2** : an Anglican parish priest who does not hold the right to the tithes **3** : a member of the Episcopal clergy in charge of a mission or a dependent parish [Latin *vicarius*, from *vicarius* "vicarious"] — **vic·ar·ship** \-,ship\ *n*

vic·ar·age \'vik-rij, -ə-rij\ *n* : the benefice or house of a vicar

vicar apostolic *n, pl* **vicars apostolic** : a Roman Catholic titular bishop who administers an ecclesiastical territory not organized as a diocese

vicar–general *n, pl* **vicars–general** : an administrative deputy of a Roman Catholic or Anglican bishop or of the head of a religious order

viaduct

\ə\	abut	\ng\	sing
\ər\	further	\ō\	bone
\a\	mat	\ò\	saw
\ā\	take	\òi\	coin
\ä\	cot, cart	\th\	thin
\aú\	out	\th\	this
\ch\	chin	\ü\	food
\e\	pet	\ù\	foot
\ē\	easy	\y\	yet
\g\	go	\yü\	few
\i\	tip	\yù\	cure
\ī\	life	\zh\	vision
\j\	job		

vi·car·i·al \vī-'ker-ē-əl, və-, -'kar-\ *adj* **1** : VICARIOUS 1 **2** : of or relating to a vicar

vi·car·i·ate \-ē-ət\ *n* : the office, jurisdiction, or tenure of a vicar

vi·car·i·ous \vī-'ker-ē-əs, və-, -'kar-\ *adj* **1** : serving instead of someone or something else **2** : performed or suffered by one person as a substitute for another or to the benefit of another ⟨*vicarious* sacrifice⟩ **3** : experienced or realized through imaginative or sympathetic participation in the experience of another ⟨*vicarious* pleasure⟩ [Latin *vicarius*, from *vicis* "change, alternation, stead"] — **vi·car·i·ous·ly** *adv* — **vi·car·i·ous·ness** *n*

Vicar of Christ : the Roman Catholic pope

¹vice \'vīs\ *n* **1 a** : moral depravity or corruption : WICKEDNESS **b** : a moral fault or failing **c** : a minor fault : FOIBLE **2** : BLEMISH, DEFECT **3** : an undesirable behavior pattern in a domestic animal **4** : sexual immorality; *esp* : PROSTITUTION [Old French, from Latin *vitium* "fault, vice"]

²vice *n, chiefly British* : VISE

³vi·ce \'vī-sē\ *prep* : in the place of [Latin, ablative of *vicis* "change, alternation, stead"]

vice- \vīs, 'vīs, ˌvīs\ *prefix* : one that takes the place of ⟨*vice*-president⟩

vice admiral *n* : an officer rank in the Navy and Coast Guard above rear admiral and below admiral

vice–chan·cel·lor \vīs-'chan-sə-lər, 'vīs-, -slər\ *n* **1** : an officer ranking next below a chancellor and serving as deputy to the chancellor **2** : a judge appointed to act for or to assist a chancellor

vice–con·sul \-'kän-səl\ *n* : a consular officer subordinate to a consul general or to a consul

vi·cen·ni·al \vī-'sen-ē-əl\ *adj* : occurring once every 20 years [Late Latin *vicennium* "period of 20 years", from Latin *vicies* "20 times" + *annus* "year"]

vice–pres·i·dent \vīs-'prez-əd-ənt, 'vīs-, -'prez-dənt *also* -ə-ˌdent\ *n* : an official (as of a government) whose rank is next below that of the president and who takes the place of the president when necessary — **vice–pres·i·den·cy** \-'prez-əd-ən-sē, -'prez-dən-sē *also* -ə-ˌden-sē\ *n* — **vice–pres·i·den·tial** \ˌvīs-ˌprez-ə-'den-chəl\ *adj*

vice–re·gal \-'rē-gəl\ *adj* : of or relating to a viceroy or viceroyalty — **vice–re·gal·ly** \-gə-lē\ *adv*

vice–re·gent \-'rē-jənt\ *n* : a regent's deputy

vice·reine \'vīs-ˌrān\ *n* **1** : the wife of a viceroy **2** : a woman who is a viceroy [French, from *vice*- "vice-" + *reine* "queen", from Latin *regina*, from *reg-, rex* "king"]

vice·roy \'vīs-ˌròi\ *n* **1** : the governor of a country or province who represents a sovereign **2** : a black and orange American butterfly resembling but smaller than the monarch [Middle French *vice-roi*, from *vice*- "vice-" + *roi* "king", from Latin *reg-, rex*] — **vice·roy·ship** \-ˌship\ *n*

vice·roy·al·ty \'vīs-ˌròi-əl-tē, -ˌròil-tē\ *n* : the office, jurisdiction, or term of service of a viceroy

vice ver·sa \ˌvī-si-'vər-sə, vīs-'vər-, 'vīs-'vər-\ *adv* : with the order changed : CONVERSELY [Latin]

vi·chys·soise \ˌvish-ē-'swäz, ˌvē-shē-\ *n* : a soup of pureed leeks or onions and potatoes, cream, and chicken stock that is usually served cold [French, from *vichyssois* "of Vichy", from *Vichy*, France]

Vi·chy water \'vish-ē-\ *n* : a natural sparkling mineral water from Vichy, France; *also* : an imitation of or substitute for this

vic·i·nage \'vis-n-ij, 'vis-nij\ *n* : VICINITY 2

vic·i·nal \'vis-n-əl, 'vis-nəl\ *adj* : of or relating to a limited district : LOCAL

vi·cin·i·ty \və-'sin-ət-ē\ *n, pl* **-ties** **1** : the quality or state of being near : PROXIMITY **2** : a surrounding area or district **3** : NEIGHBORHOOD 2b [Middle French *vicinité*, from Latin *vicinitas*, from *vicinus* "neighboring", from *vicus* "row of houses, village"]

victoria 1

vi·cious \'vish-əs\ *adj* **1 a** : given to vice : WICKED **b** : constituting vice : IMMORAL **2 a** : DEFECTIVE 1, FAULTY **b** : INVALID **3** : IMPURE b, NOXIOUS **4 a** : dangerously aggressive ⟨a *vicious* dog⟩ **b** : extreme in degree, power, or effect : FIERCE ⟨a *vicious* storm⟩ **5** : MALICIOUS, SPITEFUL ⟨*vicious* slander⟩ — **vi·cious·ly** *adv* — **vi·cious·ness** *n*

vicious circle *n* **1** : a chain of events in which the solution of one difficulty creates a new problem that makes the original difficulty worse **2** : an argument or definition that assumes as true something that is to be proved or defined

vi·cis·si·tude \və-'sis-ə-ˌtüd, vī-, -ˌtyüd\ *n* : a change or succession from one thing to another; *esp* : an often unfavorable event or situation that occurs by chance ⟨the *vicissitudes* of the weather⟩ [Middle French, from Latin *vicissitudo*, from *vicissim* "in turn", from *vicis* "change, alternation"] — **vi·cis·si·tu·di·nous** \-ˌsis-ə-'tüd-n-əs, -'tyüd-\ *adj*

vic·tim \'vik-təm\ *n* **1** : a living being offered as a sacrifice in a religious rite **2** : an individual injured or killed (as by disease or accident) **3** : a person cheated, fooled, or damaged by someone else or by an impersonal force ⟨a mugger's *victim*⟩ ⟨a *victim* of circumstance⟩ [Latin *victima*]

vic·tim·ize \'vik-tə-ˌmīz\ *vt* : to make a victim of especially by deception : CHEAT — **vic·tim·iza·tion** \ˌvik-tə-mə-'zā-shən\ *n* — **vic·tim·iz·er** \'vik-tə-ˌmī-zər\ *n*

vic·tor \'vik-tər\ *n* : one that defeats an enemy or opponent : WINNER [Latin, from *victus*, past participle of *vincere* "to conquer, win"] — **victor** *adj*

vic·to·ria \vik-'tōr-ē-ə, -'tòr-\ *n* **1** : a low four-wheeled pleasure carriage for two with a folding top and a raised seat in front for the driver **2** : an old-fashioned automobile with a folding top that usually extends over the rear seat only **3** : any of a genus of very large South American water lilies with immense rose-white flowers [*Victoria*, queen of England]

¹Vic·to·ri·an \vik-'tōr-ē-ən, -'tòr-\ *adj* **1** : of or relating to the reign of Queen Victoria of England or the art, literature, or taste of her time **2** : typical of the moral standards or conduct of the age of Victoria especially when regarded as stuffy or hypocritical — **Vic·to·ri·an·ism** \-ē-ə-ˌniz-əm\ *n*

²Victorian *n* : a person living during Queen Victoria's reign; *esp* : a typical figure of that time

Vic·to·ri·an·ize \-ē-ə-ˌnīz\ *vt* : to make Victorian (as in style or taste)

vic·to·ri·ous \vik-'tōr-ē-əs, -'tòr-\ *adj* : having won a victory ⟨a *victorious* army⟩ ⟨*victorious* strategy⟩ — **vic·to·ri·ous·ly** *adv* — **vic·to·ri·ous·ness** *n*

vic·to·ry \'vik-tə-rē, -trē\ *n, pl* **-ries** **1** : the overcoming of an enemy or opponent **2** : achievement of success in a struggle against odds or difficulties [Middle French *victorie*, from Latin *victoria*, derived from *vincere* "to conquer, win"] □ SYN VICTORY, CONQUEST, TRIUMPH mean a successful outcome in a contest or struggle. VICTORY stresses the fact of winning against an opponent or against odds ⟨the *victory* of good over evil⟩ CONQUEST implies the subjugation of a defeated opponent ⟨the *conquest* of Mexico⟩ TRIUMPH suggests acclaim and personal satisfaction to the victor following a brilliant victory or achievement ⟨the *triumphs* of the space flights⟩

¹vict·ual \'vit-l\ *n* **1** : food usable by humans **2** *pl* **a** : supplies of food **b** : food prepared and served [Middle French *vitaille*, from Late Latin *victualia* "victuals", derived from Latin *victus* "nourishment", from *vivere* "to live"]

²victual *vb* **-ualed** *or* **-ualled; -ual·ing** *or* **-ual·ling** **1** : to supply with food **2** : EAT 1, 2 **3** : to lay in provisions

vict·ual·ler *or* **vict·ual·er** \'vit-l-ər\ *n* **1** : the keeper of a restaurant or tavern **2** : one that furnishes provisions (as to an army or a ship)

vi·cu·ña *or* **vi·cu·na** \vi-'kün-yə, vī-; vī-'kü-nə, və-, -'kyü-\ *n* **1** : a wild ruminant of the Andes that is related to the domesticated llama and alpaca **2 a** : the wool from the vicuña's fine lustrous undercoat **b** : a fabric made of vicuña wool; *also* : a sheep's-wool imitation of this [Spanish *vicuña*, from Quechua *wikúña*]

vi·de \'vīd-ē, 'vē-,dā\ *vb imperative* : SEE — used to direct a reader to another item [Latin, from *vidēre* "to see"]

vi·de·li·cet \və-'del-ə-,set, vī-; vi-'dā-li-,ket\ *adv* : that is to say : NAMELY — abbreviation *viz.* [Latin, from *vidēre* "to see" + *licet* "it is permitted"]

¹vid·eo \'vid-ē-,ō\ *n* : TELEVISION

²video *adj* **1** : relating to or used in the transmission or reception of the television image ⟨*video* channel⟩ — compare AUDIO **2** : being, relating to, or involving images on a television screen or computer display ⟨*video* terminal⟩ [Latin *vidēre* "to see" + English *-o* (as in *audio*)]

vid·eo·cas·sette \,vid-ē-ō-kə-'set\ *n* **1** : a case containing videotape for use with a VCR **2** : a recording (as of movie) on a videocassette

videocassette recorder *n* : VCR

video game *n* : a game played with images on a video screen

vid·e·og·ra·phy \,vid-ē-'äg-rə-fē\ *n* : the practice or art of recording images with a video camera — **vid·e·og·ra·pher** \-fər\ *n*

vid·eo·phile \'vid-ē-ō-,fīl\ *n* : a person fond of video; *esp* : one interested in video equipment or in producing videos

vid·eo·phone \'vid-ē-ə-,fōn\ *n* : a telephone equipped for transmission of a picture as well as sound so that users can see each other

¹vid·eo·tape \'vid-ē-ō-,tāp\ *n* **1** : a recording of visual images and sound (as of a television production) made on magnetic tape **2** : the magnetic tape used for a videotape

²videotape *vt* : to make a videotape of ⟨*videotape* a show⟩

videotape recorder *n* : a device for recording on videotape — called also *video recorder*

vi·dette *variant of* VEDETTE

vie \'vī\ *vi* **vied; vy·ing** \'vī-ing\ : to strive for superiority : CONTEND [Middle French *envier* "to invite, challenge, wager", from Latin *invitare* "to invite"] — **vi·er** \'vī-ər, 'vīr\ *n*

Vi·en·na sausage \vē-,en-ə-\ *n* : a short slender frankfurter [*Vienna*, Austria]

Viet·nam·ese \vē-,et-nə-'mēz, vyet-, ,vē-ət-, ,vēt-, -na-, -nä-, -'mēs\ *n, pl* **Vietnamese 1** : a native or inhabitant of Vietnam **2** : the language of the largest group in Vietnam and the official language of the country — **Vietnamese** *adj*

¹view \'vyü\ *n* **1** : the act of seeing or examining : INSPECTION; *also* : SURVEY **2** : manner of looking at or regarding something : OPINION, JUDGMENT ⟨state one's *views*⟩ **3** : SCENE, PROSPECT ⟨the *view* from my window⟩ **4** : extent or range of vision : SIGHT ⟨the planes passed out of *view*⟩ **5** : something that is looked toward or kept in sight : OBJECT ⟨studied hard with a *view* to getting an A⟩ **6** : the foreseeable future ⟨no hope in *view*⟩ **7** : a pictorial representation [Middle French *veue*, *vue*, from *veeir*, *voir* "to see", from Latin *vidēre*] — **in view of** : in regard to : in consideration of — **on view** : open to public inspection : on exhibition

²view *vt* **1** : SEE, WATCH ⟨*view* a film⟩ **2** : to look at attentively : SCRUTINIZE **3** : to survey or examine mentally : CONSIDER ⟨*view* all sides of a question⟩

view·er \'vyü-ər\ *n* **1** : one that views; *esp* : a person who watches television **2** : an optical device used in viewing

view·find·er \'vyü-,fīn-dər\ *n* : FINDER b

view·less \'vyü-ləs\ *adj* **1** : INVISIBLE, UNSEEN **2** : affording no view **3** : expressing no views or opinions — **view·less·ly** *adv*

view·point \'vyü-,point\ *n* : POINT OF VIEW, STANDPOINT

vi·ges·i·mal \vī-'jes-ə-məl\ *adj* : based on the number 20 [Latin *vicesimus*, *vigesimus* "twentieth"]

vig·il \'vij-əl\ *n* **1 a** : a watch formerly kept on the night before a religious feast with devotions **b** : the day before a religious feast **c** : prayers or devotional services held in the evening or at night — usually used in pl. **2** : the act of keeping awake when sleep is customary; *also* : a period of wakefulness **3** : an act or period of watchful observation : WATCH ⟨the soldiers kept *vigil* all night⟩ [Old French *vigile*, from Latin *vigilia* "wakefulness, watch", from *vigil* "awake, watchful"]

vig·i·lant \'vij-ə-lənt\ *adj* : alertly watchful especially to avoid danger SYN see WATCHFUL — **vig·i·lance** \-ləns\ *n* — **vig·i·lant·ly** \-lənt-lē\ *adv*

vig·i·lan·te \,vij-ə-'lant-ē\ *n* : a member of a local volunteer group organized to suppress and punish crime especially where official law enforcement seems inadequate [Spanish, "watchman, guard", from *vigilante* "vigilant"]

¹vi·gnette \vin-'yet, vēn-\ *n* **1** : a small decorative design or picture put on or just before a title page or at the beginning or end of a chapter **2** : a picture that shades off gradually into the surrounding ground **3** : a brief word picture : SKETCH [French, from *vigne* "vine"] — **vi·gnett·ist** \-'yet-əst\ *n*

²vignette *vt* **1** : to finish (as a photograph) in the manner of a vignette **2** : to describe briefly — **vi·gnett·er** *n*

vig·or \'vig-ər\ *n* **1** : active physical or mental strength or energy ⟨the full *vigor* of youth⟩ **2** : INTENSITY, FORCE ⟨the *vigor* of their quarrel⟩ [Middle French, from Latin, from *vigēre* "to be vigorous"]

vi·go·ro·so \,vig-ə-'rō-sō\ *adj or adv* : energetic in style — used as a direction in music [Italian, literally, "vigorous"]

vig·or·ous \'vig-rəs, -ə-rəs\ *adj* **1** : having vigor : ROBUST ⟨*vigorous* youth⟩ ⟨a *vigorous* plant⟩ **2** : done with force and energy ⟨a *vigorous* protest⟩ ⟨*vigorous* exercise⟩ — **vig·or·ous·ly** *adv* — **vig·or·ous·ness** *n* □ SYN VIGOROUS, ENERGETIC, STRENUOUS mean having great vitality and force. VIGOROUS suggests active strength and implies undiminishing freshness or robustness ⟨still *vigorous* in their old age⟩ ENERGETIC suggests a capacity for intense activity ⟨*energetic* young people⟩ STRENUOUS suggests a preference for coping with the arduous and challenging ⟨*strenuous* objections⟩ ⟨*strenuous* exercise⟩

vig·our \'vig-ər\ *chiefly British variant of* VIGOR

Vi·king \'vī-king\ *n* : any of the Norse plunderers of the European coasts in the 8th to 10th centuries [Old Norse *vikingr*]

vile \'vīl\ *adj* **1** : of little worth or account **2 a** : morally base : WICKED ⟨*vile* deeds⟩ **b** : physically repulsive : FOUL ⟨*vile* living quarters⟩ **3** : tending to degrade ⟨*vile* tasks⟩ **4** : CONTEMPTIBLE, DESPICABLE ⟨a *vile* temper⟩ [Old French *vil*, from Latin *vilis*] — **vile·ly** \'vīl-lē\ *adv* — **vile·ness** *n*

vil·i·fy \'vil-ə-,fī\ *vt* **-fied; -fy·ing 1** : to lower in estimation or importance : DEGRADE **2** : to utter slanderous and abusive statements against : DEFAME — **vil·i·fi·ca·tion** \,vil-ə-fə-'kā-shən\ *n* — **vil·i·fi·er** \'vil-ə-,fī-ər, -,fīr\ *n*

vil·la \'vil-ə\ *n* **1** : a country estate **2** : the rural or suburban residence of a wealthy person [Italian, from Latin]

vil·lage \'vil-ij\ *n* **1** : a settlement usually larger than a hamlet and smaller than a town **2** : the residents of a village ⟨the whole *village* knows about it⟩ [Middle French, from *ville* "farm, village", from Latin *villa* "country estate"]

vil·lag·er \'vil-ij-ər\ *n* : an inhabitant of a village

vil·lain \'vil-ən\ *n* **1** : VILLEIN **2** : an uncouth ill-mannered person : BOOR **3** : a thorough-going scoundrel or

\ə\ abut		\ng\ sing
\ər\ further		\ō\ bone
\a\ mat		\o'\ saw
\ā\ take		\oi\ coin
\ä\ cot, cart		\th\ thin
\au̇\ out		\th\ this
\ch\ chin		\ü\ food
\e\ pet		\u̇\ foot
\ē\ easy		\y\ yet
\g\ go		\yü\ few
\i\ tip		\yu̇\ cure
\ī\ life		\zh\ vision
\j\ job		

criminal **4** : a scoundrel in a story or play **5** : a person or thing blamed for an evil or difficulty [Middle English *vilain, vilein*] ▫ ORIGIN In the feudal society of medieval Europe a *villein* was a member of one of the lower classes, at some times and places a free man and at others fully bound in service to a lord. Because the higher classes often look on the lower as inferior, Middle English *vilein* or *vilain* developed the depreciatory sense of "a person of uncouth mind and manners". This disparaging tendency gained in strength and currency through the common equation of manners and morals, so that the modern *villain* is a scoundrel or criminal or a person or thing blamed for a particular evil or difficulty.

vil·lain·ess \'vil-ə-nəs\ *n* : a girl or woman who is a villain

vil·lain·ous \'vil-ə-nəs\ *adj* **1** : befitting a villain : DEPRAVED **2** : highly objectionable : WRETCHED — **vil·lain·ous·ly** *adv* — **vil·lain·ous·ness** *n*

vil·lainy \'vil-ə-nē\ *n, pl* **-lain·ies 1 a** : villainous conduct **b** : a villainous act **2** : villainous character : WICKEDNESS

vil·la·nelle \,vil-ə-'nel\ *n* : a verse form running on two rhymes and consisting typically of five tercets and a quatrain in which the first and third lines of the opening tercet recur alternately at the end of the other tercets and together as the last two lines of the quatrain [French, from Italian *villanella*]

vil·lein \'vil-ən, 'vil-,ān, vil-'ān\ *n* **1** : a free peasant of any of various feudal classes **2** : an unfree peasant ranking as a slave of his or her feudal lord but as free in legal relations with others [Middle English *vilain, vilein*, from Middle French, from Medieval Latin *villanus*, from Latin *villa* "country estate"]

vil·len·age \'vil-ə-nij\ *n* **1** : tenure of land given by a feudal lord to a villein **2** : the status of a villein

vil·lous \'vil-əs\ *adj* : having soft long hairs ⟨leaves *villous* underneath⟩ [Latin *villosus* "rough, shaggy", from *villus* "shaggy hair"] — **vil·los·i·ty** \vil-'äs-ət-ē\ *n*

vil·lus \'vil-əs\ *n, pl* **vil·li** \'vil-,ī, -ē\ : a small slender usually vascular process; *esp* : one of the tiny finger-shaped processes of the mucous membrane of the small intestine that function in the absorption of nutriments [Latin, "shaggy hair"]

vim \'vim\ *n* : robust energy and enthusiasm : VITALITY [Latin, accusative of *vis* "strength"]

vin·ai·grette \,vin-i-'gret\ *n* : a small ornamental box or bottle with perforated top used for holding an aromatic preparation (as smelling salts) [French, from *vinaigre* "vinegar"]

vin·ca \'ving-kə\ *n* : ¹PERIWINKLE [New Latin, from Latin *pervinca*]

Vin·cen·tian \vin-'sen-chən\ *n* : a member of the Roman Catholic Congregation of the Mission founded in 1625 by St. Vincent de Paul and devoted to missions and seminaries — **Vincentian** *adj*

Vin·cent's angina \,vin-səns-, van-ˌsānᶻ-\ *n* : a contagious disease marked by ulceration of the mucous membrane of the mouth and adjacent parts and caused by a bacterium often in association with a spirochete — compare VINCENT'S INFECTION [Jean Hyacinthe *Vincent*, died 1950, French bacteriologist]

Vincent's infection *n* : a bacterial infection of the respiratory tract and mouth marked by destructive ulceration especially of the mucous membranes — compare VINCENT'S ANGINA

vin·ci·ble \'vin-sə-bəl\ *adj* : capable of being overcome or subdued : SURMOUNTABLE [Latin *vincibilis*, from *vincere* "to conquer"]

vin·cu·lum \'ving-kyə-ləm\ *n, pl* **-lums** *or* **-la** \-lə\ **1** : a unifying bond : LINK, TIE **2** : a straight horizontal mark placed over two or more members of a mathematical expression as a symbol of grouping (as in $a - \overline{b - c} = a - [b - c]$) [Latin, from *vincire* "to bind"]

vin·di·cate \'vin-də-ˌkāt\ *vt* **1 a** : EXONERATE, ABSOLVE **b** (1) : CONFIRM 2, SUBSTANTIATE (2) : to provide defense for : JUSTIFY **c** : to protect from attack or encroachment : DEFEND **2** : to maintain a right to : ASSERT [Latin *vindicare* "to lay claim to, avenge", from *vindic-, vindex* "claimant, avenger"] SYN see MAINTAIN — **vin·di·ca·tor** \-ˌkāt-ər\ *n* — **vin·di·ca·to·ry** \-kə-ˌtōr-ē, -ˌtȯr-\ *adj*

vin·di·ca·tion \,vin-də-'kā-shən\ *n* : the act of vindicating : the state of being vindicated; *esp* : justification against denial or censure

vin·dic·tive \vin-'dik-tiv\ *adj* **1 a** : inclined to seek revenge : VENGEFUL **b** : intended for or involving revenge **2** : intended to cause pain or anguish : SPITEFUL [Latin *vindicta* "revenge", from *vindicare* "to avenge"] — **vin·dic·tive·ly** *adv* — **vin·dic·tive·ness** *n*

¹vine \'vīn\ *n* **1** : GRAPE 2 **2** : a plant whose stem requires support and which climbs by tendrils or twining or creeps along the ground; *also* : the stem of such a plant [Old French *vigne*, from Latin *vinea* "vine, vineyard", derived from *vinum* "wine"]

²vine *vi* : to form or grow in the manner of a vine

vin·eal \'vin-ē-əl, 'vīn-\ *adj* : of or relating to wine [Latin *vinealis* "of vines", from *vinea* "vine"]

vine·dress·er \'vīn-ˌdres-ər\ *n* : one that cultivates and prunes grapevines

vin·e·gar \'vin-i-gər\ *n* **1** : a sour liquid obtained by fermentation of cider, wine, or malt and used to flavor or preserve foods **2** : ill humor : VIM [Old French *vinaigre*, from *vin* "wine" (from Latin *vinum*) + *aigre* "keen, sour", from Latin *acer* "sharp"]

vinegar eel *n* : a tiny roundworm often found in vinegar or acid fermenting vegetable matter

vin·e·gar·ish \'vin-i-gə-rish, -grish\ *adj* : VINEGARY 2

vin·e·gary \-gə-rē, -grē\ *adj* **1** : resembling vinegar : SOUR **2** : disagreeable or bitter in character or manner : CRABBED

vin·ery \'vīn-rē, -ə-rē\ *n, pl* **-er·ies** : an area or building in which vines are grown

vine·yard \'vin-yərd\ *n* : a planting of grapevines — **vine·yard·ist** \-əst\ *n*

vingt–et–un \,van-ˌtā-'ən\ *n* : BLACKJACK 3 [French, literally, "twenty-one"]

vi·ni·cul·ture \'vin-ə-ˌkəl-chər, 'vī-nə-\ *n* : VITICULTURE

vi·nos·i·ty \vī-'näs-ət-ē\ *n* : the characteristic body, flavor, and color of a wine

vi·nous \'vī-nəs\ *adj* **1** : of, relating to, or made with wine ⟨*vinous* medications⟩ **2** : showing the effects of the use of wine [Latin *vinosus*, from *vinum* "wine"]

vin·tage \'vint-ij\ *n* **1 a** (1) : the grapes or wine produced during one season (2) : WINE; *esp* : a wine of a particular type, region, and year and usually of superior quality **b** : a collection or category of comparable persons or things **2** : the act or time of gathering grapes or making wine **3 a** : a period of origin or manufacture ⟨a piano of 1845 *vintage*⟩ **b** : length of existence : AGE [Middle French *vendenge*, from Latin *vindemia*, from *vinum* "wine, grapes" + *demere* "to take off"] — **vintage** *adj*

vint·ner \'vint-nər\ *n* : a wine merchant [Old French *vinetier*, derived from Latin *vinum* "wine"]

viny \'vī-nē\ *adj* **vin·i·er; -est 1** : of, relating to, or resembling vines ⟨*viny* plants⟩ **2** : covered with or abounding in vines

vi·nyl \'vīn-l\ *n* **1** : a univalent radical $CH_2{=}CH$ derived from ethylene by removal of one hydrogen atom **2** : a polymer of a vinyl compound or a product made from such a polymer ⟨*vinyl* upholstery⟩ [Latin *vinum* "wine"]

vinyl resin *n* : any of a group of elastic resins that are resistant to chemical agents and are used for protective coatings and molded articles — called also *vinyl plastic*

vi·ol \'vī-əl, 'vīl\ *n* : an old bowed stringed instrument like the violin but weaker in tone and simpler in construction and playing technique [Middle French *viole,* from Provençal *viola*]

¹**vi·o·la** \vē-'ō-lə\ *n* : a stringed musical instrument similar to a violin but slightly larger and lower in pitch [Italian, from Provençal, "viol"]

²**vi·ola** \vī-'ō-lə, vē-\ *n* : VIOLET 1a; *esp* : any of various garden hybrids with solitary white, yellow, or purple often variegated flowers resembling but smaller than typical pansies [Latin]

vi·o·la·ble \'vī-ə-lə-bəl\ *adj* : that can be violated — **vi·o·la·bil·i·ty** \,vī-ə-lə-'bil-ət-ē\ *n* — **vi·o·la·ble·ness** \'vi-ə-lə-bəl-nəs\ *n* — **vi·o·la·bly** \-blē\ *adv*

vi·o·late \'vī-ə-,lāt\ *vt* 1 : to fail to keep or observe ⟨*violate* the law⟩ 2 : to do harm to the person or the chastity of; *esp* : RAPE 3 : PROFANE, DESECRATE ⟨vandals *violated* the church⟩ 4 : DISTURB 2a, b [Latin *violare*] — **vi·o·la·tor** \-,lāt-ər\ *n*

vi·o·la·tion \,vī-ə-'lā-shən\ *n* : the act of violating : the state of being violated: as **a** : TRANSGRESSION **b** : an act of irreverence or desecration **c** : DISTURBANCE 1, 3 **d** : ³RAPE 2

vi·o·lence \'vī-ə-ləns\ *n* 1 : the use of physical force in a way that harms a person or a person's property 2 : injury especially to something that deserves respect or reverence ⟨does *violence* to our principles⟩ 3 **a** : intense, furious, and often destructive action or force ⟨the *violence* of the storm⟩ **b** : vehement feeling or expression : FERVOR 4 : improper or damaging alteration (as of the wording or the meaning of a text)

vi·o·lent \-lənt\ *adj* 1 : marked by extreme force or sudden intense activity ⟨a *violent* attack⟩ ⟨*violent* storms⟩ 2 **a** : notably furious or vehement ⟨a *violent* denunciation⟩; *also* : excited or mentally disordered to the point of loss of self-control ⟨the patient became *violent* and had to be restrained⟩ **b** : EXTREME, INTENSE ⟨*violent* pain⟩ 3 : caused by force ⟨a *violent* death⟩ [Middle French, from Latin *violentus*] — **vi·o·lent·ly** *adv*

vi·o·let \'vī-ə-lət\ *n* 1 **a** : any of a genus of herbaceous or shrubby plants having alternate leaves with stipules and both aerial and underground flowers; *esp* : one with small usually solid-colored flowers as distinguished from the usually larger-flowered violas and pansies **b** : any of several plants of other genera — compare DOGTOOTH VIOLET 2 : a reddish blue [Middle French *violete,* from *viole* "violet", from Latin *viola*]

vi·o·lin \,vī-ə-'lin\ *n* 1 : a bowed stringed instrument with four strings that has a shallower body and a more curved bridge than the viol 2 : VIOLINIST [Italian *violino,* from *viola* "viola"]

vi·o·lin·ist \-'lin-əst\ *n* : one who plays the violin

vi·o·list \vē-'ō-ləst\ *n* : one who plays the viola

vi·o·lon·cel·list \,vī-ə-lən-'chel-əst, ,vē-\ *n* : CELLIST

vi·o·lon·cel·lo \,vī-ə-lən-'chel-ō, ,vē-\ *n* : CELLO [Italian, from *violone* "double bass", from *viola* "viola, viol"]

VIP \,vē-,ī-'pē\ *n, pl* **VIPs** \-'pēz\ : a person of great influence or prestige [*v*ery *i*mportant *p*erson]

vi·per *n* \'vī-pər\ *n* 1 **a** : any of a family of sluggish heavy-bodied broad-headed Old World venomous snakes with hollow tubular fangs **b** : PIT VIPER **c** : a venomous or reputedly venomous snake 2 : a malicious or treacherous person [Middle French *vipere,* from Latin *vipera*] — **vi·per·ine** \-pə-,rīn\ *adj*

vi·per·ish \'vī-pə-rish, -prish\ *adj* : given to spiteful abusive speech : VENOMOUS

vi·per·ous \'vī-pə-rəs, -prəs\ *adj* 1 : of or relating to vipers 2 : having the qualities attributed to vipers : SPITEFUL, VENOMOUS ⟨a *viperous* treachery⟩ — **vi·per·ous·ly** *adv*

vi·ra·go \və-'räg-ō, -'rāg-; 'vir-ə-,gō\ *n, pl* **-goes** *or* **-gos** 1 : a woman of great stature, strength, and courage 2 : a loud overbearing woman [Latin *viragin-, virago,* from *vir* "man"] — **vi·rag·i·nous** \və-'raj-ə-nəs\ *adj*

vi·ral \'vī-rəl\ *adj* : of, relating to, or caused by a virus

vir·eo \'vir-ē-,ō\ *n, pl* **-e·os** : any of a family of small insect-eating songbirds that are chiefly olive-green or grayish in color [Latin, a small bird, from *virēre* "to be green"]

vir·ga \'vər-gə\ *n* : wisps of precipitation evaporating before reaching the ground [Latin, "branch, streak in the sky suggesting rain"]

¹**vir·gin** \'vər-jən\ *n* 1 : an unmarried woman devoted to religion 2 : a person who has not had sexual intercourse [Old French *virgine,* from Latin *virgin-, virgo* "young woman, virgin"]

²**virgin** *adj* 1 : being, characteristic of, or befitting a virgin : MODEST 2 : not soiled or marred ⟨*virgin* snow⟩; *esp* : not altered by human activity ⟨*virgin* soil⟩ 3 : being used or worked for the first time or produced by a simple extractive process ⟨*virgin* wool⟩ ⟨*virgin* oil⟩

¹**vir·gin·al** \'vər-jən-l\ *adj* : of, relating to, characteristic of, or suitable for a virgin or virginity; *esp* : CHASTE — **vir·gin·al·ly** \-l-ē\ *adv*

²**virginal** *n* : a small rectangular spinet having no legs and only one wire to a note

virgin birth *n* 1 : birth from a virgin 2 *often cap V&B* : the theological doctrine that Jesus was miraculously begotten of God and born of a virgin mother

Vir·gin·ia creeper \vər-,jin-yə-, -,jin-ē-ə-\ *n* : a common North American tendril-climbing vine of the grape family having leaves with five leaflets and bluish black berries — called also *woodbine* [*Virginia,* United States]

Virginia deer *n* : WHITE-TAILED DEER

Virginia reel *n* : a country-dance in which all couples in turn participate in a series of figures

vir·gin·i·ty \vər-'jin-ət-ē\ *n, pl* **-ties** : the quality or state of being virgin; *esp* : MAIDENHOOD

virgin's bower *n* : any of several usually small-flowered and climbing clematises

Vir·go \'vər-gō, 'viər-\ *n* 1 : a zodiacal constellation due south of the handle of the Dipper 2 : the 6th sign of the zodiac; *also* : one born under this sign [Latin, literally, "virgin"]

vir·gule \'vər-gyül\ *n* : DIAGONAL 3 [French, from Latin *virgula* "little rod", from *virga* "branch, rod"]

vir·i·des·cent \,vir-ə-'des-nt\ *adj* : slightly green : GREENISH [Latin *viridis* "green"]

vir·ile \'vir-əl, 'viər-,īl\ *adj* 1 : having the nature, powers, or qualities of a man 2 **a** : ENERGETIC, VIGOROUS **b** : MASTERFUL 1, FORCEFUL [Latin *virilis,* from *vir* "man, male"]

vi·ril·i·ty \və-'ril-ət-ē\ *n* : the quality or state of being virile : **a** : MANHOOD **b** : manly vigor : MASCULINITY

vi·rol·o·gy \vī-'räl-ə-jē\ *n* : a branch of science that deals with viruses — **vi·ro·log·i·cal** \,vī-rə-'läj-i-kəl\ *adj* — **vi·rol·o·gist** \vī-'räl-ə-jəst\ *n*

vir·tu·al \'vərch-wəl, -ə-wəl; 'vər-chəl\ *adj* : being in essence or effect but not in fact or name ⟨the *virtual* ruler of the country⟩ [Medieval Latin *virtualis* "possessed of powers or virtues", from Latin *virtus* "strength, virtue"] — **vir·tu·al·i·ty** \,vər-chə-'wal-ət-ē\ *n* — **vir·tu·al·ly** \'verch-wə-lē, -ə-wə-; 'vərch-lē, -ə-lē\ *adv*

virtual focus *n* : a point from which divergent rays (as of light) seem to originate but do not actually do so (as in the image of a point source seen in a plane mirror)

virtual image *n* : an image formed of virtual foci

vir·tue \'vər-chü\ *n* 1 : conformity to a standard of right : MORALITY 2 : a particular moral excellence ⟨justice and charity are *virtues*⟩ 3 **a** : an active beneficial power ⟨quinine has *virtue* in the treatment of malaria⟩ **b** : a desirable or commendable quality or trait : MERIT ⟨the *virtues* of country life⟩ 4 : chastity especially in a woman [Old French *virtu, vertu,* from Latin *virtus* "manliness, courage, virtue", from *vir* "man"] □ ORIGIN From *vir,* meaning "man", the Romans derived the word *virtus* to denote the sum of the excellent quali-

violin 1

ties of men, including physical strength, valorous conduct, and moral rectitude. The Christian church stressed the moral virtues, and French *virtu* or *vertu*, developed from Latin *virtus*, was used specifically to mean "morality". The French word was borrowed into English in the 13th century. In the 14th century *virtue* came to be applied to any quality, moral or otherwise, felt to be excellent. By the end of the 16th century the sense "chastity, purity" appeared, especially in reference to women. — **by virtue of** *or* **in virtue of** : through the force of : by authority of

vir·tu·os·i·ty \,vər-chə-'wäs-ət-ē\ *n, pl* **-ties** : great technical skill in the practice of the fine arts

vir·tu·o·so \,vər-chə-'wō-sō, -zō\ *n, pl* **-sos** *or* **-si** \-sē, -zē\ **1** : one skilled in or having a taste for the fine arts **2** : one who excels in the technique of an art; *esp* : a highly skilled musical performer [Italian, from *virtuoso* "virtuous, skilled"] — **virtuoso** *adj*

vir·tu·ous \'vər-chə-wəs\ *adj* **1 a** : having or exhibiting virtue **b** : morally excellent **2** : CHASTE 1 — **vir·tu·ous·ly** *adv* — **vir·tu·ous·ness** *n*

vir·u·lent \'vir-ə-lənt, -yə-\ *adj* **1 a** : marked by a rapid, severe, and malignant course ⟨a *virulent* infection⟩ **b** : able to overcome bodily defensive mechanisms ⟨a *virulent* pathogen⟩ **2** : extremely poisonous or venomous : NOXIOUS **3** : full of malice [Latin *virulentus*, from *virus* "poison"] — **vir·u·lence** \-ləns\ *or* **vir·u·len·cy** \-lən-sē\ *n* — **vir·u·lent·ly** *adv*

vi·rus \'vī-rəs\ *n* **1 a** : any of a large group of submicroscopic infective agents that are held by some to be living organisms and by others to be complex protein molecules containing nucleic acids and comparable to genes, that are capable of growth and multiplication only in living cells, and that cause various important diseases in man, lower animals, or plants; *also* : any of various infective agents (as a true virus or a rickettsia) that remain active after passing through a filter too fine for a bacterium to pass — called also *filterable virus* **b** : a disease caused by a virus **2** : something that poisons the mind or spirit [Latin, "slimy liquid, poison"]

¹vi·sa \'vē-zə *also* -sə\ *n* : an endorsement made on a passport by the proper authorities denoting that it has been examined and that the bearer may proceed [French, from Latin *visus*, past participle of *vidēre* "to see"]

²visa *vt* **vi·saed** \-zəd, -səd\; **vi·sa·ing** \-zə-ing, -sə-ing\ : to give a visa to

vis·age \'viz-ij\ *n* **1** : the face or countenance of a person or sometimes a lower animal **2** : ASPECT, APPEARANCE ⟨grimy *visage* of a mining town⟩ [Old French, from *vis* "face", from Latin *visus* "sight", from *vidēre* "to see"] — **vis·aged** \-ijd\ *adj*

¹vis-à-vis \,vēz-ə-'vē, ,vēs- *also* -ä-'vē\ *n, pl* **vis-à-vis** \-'vē, -'vēz\ **1** : one that is face to face with another **2 a** : ESCORT 1b, DATE **b** : COUNTERPART **3** : TÊTE-À-TÊTE 1 [French, literally, "face to face"]

²vis-à-vis *prep* **1** : face to face with : OPPOSITE **2** : in relation to **3** : as compared with

³vis-à-vis *adv* : in company : TOGETHER

viscera *pl of* VISCUS

vis·cer·al \'vis-ə-rəl\ *adj* **1 a** : felt in or as if in the viscera ⟨*visceral* sensation⟩ **b** : of, relating to, or being the viscera : SPLANCHNIC **2** : not intellectual : INSTINCTIVE ⟨a *visceral* reaction⟩ — **vis·cer·al·ly** \-rə-lē\ *adv*

vis·cid \'vis-əd\ *adj* **1** : VISCOUS, STICKY **2** : covered with a sticky layer [Late Latin *viscidus*, from Latin *viscum* "birdlime"] — **vis·cid·i·ty** \vis-'id-ət-ē\ *n* — **vis·cid·ly** \'vis-əd-lē\ *adv*

vis·co·elas·tic \,vis-kō-i-'las-tik\ *adj* : having both viscous and elastic properties in appreciable degree ⟨*viscoelastic* asphalt⟩

vis·com·e·ter \vis-'käm-ət-ər\ *n* : an instrument with which to measure viscosity — **vis·co·met·ric** \,vis-kə-'me-trik\ *adj*

vise

¹vis·cose \'vis-,kōs, -,kōz\ *adj* **1** : VISCOUS **2** : of, relating to, or made from viscose

²viscose *n* **1** : a viscous golden-brown solution made by treating cellulose with caustic alkali solution and carbon disulfide and used in making rayon **2** : viscose rayon

vis·cos·i·ty \vis-'käs-ət-ē\ *n, pl* **-ties** : the quality of being viscous; *esp* : a tendency of a liquid to flow slowly resulting from friction of its molecules ⟨an oil of high *viscosity*⟩

vis·count \'vī-,kaunt\ *n* : a member of the British peerage ranking below an earl and above a baron [Middle French *viscomte*, from Medieval Latin *vicecomes*, from Late Latin *vice-* "vice-" + *comes* "count"] — **vis·count·cy** \-sē\ *n* — **vis·coun·ty** \-,kaunt-ē\ *n*

vis·count·ess \-,kaunt-əs\ *n* **1** : the wife or widow of a viscount **2** : a woman who holds the rank of viscount in her own right

vis·cous \'vis-kəs\ *adj* **1** : somewhat sticky or glutinous : ADHESIVE **2** : having or characterized by viscosity [Late Latin *viscosus*, from Latin *viscum* "birdlime"] — **vis·cous·ly** *adv* — **vis·cous·ness** *n*

vis·cus \'vis-kəs\ *n, pl* **vis·cera** \'vis-ə-rə\ : an internal organ of the body; *esp* : one (as the heart, liver, or intestine) located in the great cavity of the trunk proper [Latin]

vise \'vīs\ *n* : any of various tools having two jaws for holding work that operate usually by a screw, lever, or cam [Middle French *vis* "something winding", from Latin *vitis* "vine"]

vis·i·bil·i·ty \,viz-ə-'bil-ət-ē\ *n* **1** : the quality or state of being visible **2** : the degree of clearness of the atmosphere especially as affording clear vision toward the horizon

vis·i·ble \'viz-ə-bəl\ *adj* **1** : capable of being seen : apparent to the eye ⟨stars *visible* to the naked eye⟩ **2** : APPARENT, DISCOVERABLE ⟨has no *visible* means of support⟩ [Latin *visibilis*, from *vidēre* "to see"] — **vis·i·ble·ness** *n* — **vis·i·bly** \-blē\ *adv*

Visi·goth \'viz-ə-,gäth\ *n* : a member of the western division of the Goths — called also *West Goth*; compare OSTROGOTH [Late Latin *Visigothi* "Visigoths"] — **Visi·goth·ic** \,viz-ə-'gäth-ik\ *adj*

¹vi·sion \'vizh-ən\ *n* **1 a** : something seen in a dream, trance, or ecstasy **b** : an object of imagination **c** : GHOST 2, APPARITION **2 a** : the act or power of imagination **b** : unusual discernment or foresight **3 a** : the act or power of seeing : SIGHT **b** : the special sense by which the qualities of an object (as color, luminosity, texture, or shape and size) constituting its appearance are perceived and which is mediated by the eye **4** : something seen; *esp* : a lovely or charming sight [Old French, from Latin *visio*, from *vidēre* "to see"] — **vi·sion·al** \'vizh-nəl, -ən-l\ *adj* — **vi·sion·al·ly** \-ē\ *adv* — **vi·sion·less** \'vizh-ən-ləs\ *adj*

²vision *vt* **vi·sioned; vi·sion·ing** \'vizh-ning, -ə-ning\ : IMAGINE, ENVISION ⟨couldn't *vision* it happening⟩

¹vi·sion·ary \'vizh-ə-,ner-ē\ *adj* **1** : given to dreaming or imagining **2** : resembling a vision especially in fanciful or impractical quality ⟨*visionary* schemes⟩ — **vi·sion·ar·i·ness** *n*

²visionary *n, pl* **-ar·ies** **1** : one who sees visions : SEER **2** : one whose ideas or projects are impractical : DREAMER

¹vis·it \'viz-ət\ *vb* **vis·it·ed** \'viz-ət-əd, 'viz-təd\; **vis·it·ing** \'viz-ət-ing, 'viz-ting\ **1** : to come to or upon as a reward, affliction, or punishment **2** : to go to see in order to comfort or help **3 a** : to pay a call upon as an act of friendship or courtesy **b** : to go or come to see in an official or professional capacity **c** : to dwell with temporarily as a guest **d** : to go to see or stay at ⟨a place⟩ for a particular purpose (as business or sightseeing) **4** : CHAT, CONVERSE [Old French *visiter*, from Latin *visitare*, from *visere* "to go to see", from *vidēre* "to see"]

²**visit** *n* **1** : a brief stay : CALL **2** : a stay as a guest or nonresident ⟨a weekend *visit*⟩ **3** : an official or professional call

vis·it·able \'viz-ət-ə-bəl, 'viz-tə-\ *adj* **1** : subject to or allowing visitation or inspection **2** : socially eligible to receive visits

Vis·i·tan·dine \ˌviz-ə-'tan-ˌdēn\ *n* : a nun of the Roman Catholic Order of the Visitation of the Blessed Virgin Mary founded in France in 1610 and devoted to contemplation and education [French, derived from Latin *visitare* "to visit"]

vis·i·tant \'viz-ət-ənt, 'viz-tənt\ *n* : VISITOR; *esp* : one thought to come from a spirit world — **visitant** *adj*

vis·i·ta·tion \ˌviz-ə-'tā-shən\ *n* **1** : VISIT; *esp* : an official visit (as for inspection) **2 a** : an instance of divine favor or wrath **b** : a severe trial : AFFLICTION **3** *cap* **a** : the visit of the Virgin Mary to Elizabeth before the birth of Elizabeth's son John the Baptist **b** : a church festival on July 2 commemorating this visit — **vis·i·ta·tion·al** \-shnəl, -shən-l\ *adj*

visiting nurse *n* : a nurse employed to visit sick persons or perform public-health services in a community

vis·i·tor \'viz-ət-ər, 'viz-tər\ *n* : one that visits: as **a** : one that makes formal visits of inspection **b** : GUEST 1a **c** : TOURIST, TRAVELER

vi·sor \'vī-zər\ *n* **1** : the front piece of a helmet; *esp* : a movable upper piece **2** : a projecting part (as on a cap or an automobile windshield) to protect or shade the eyes [Anglo-French *viser,* from Old French *visiere,* from *vis* "face", from Latin *visus* "sight", from *vidēre* "to see"] — **vi·sored** \-zərd\ *adj* — **vi·sor·less** \-zər-ləs\ *adj*

vis·ta \'vis-tə\ *n* **1** : a distant view through or along an avenue or opening : PROSPECT **2** : an extensive mental view (as over a stretch of time or a series of events) [Italian, "sight", from *vedere* "to see", from Latin *vidēre*]

vi·su·al \'vizh-wəl, -ə-wəl; 'vizh-əl\ *adj* **1** : of, relating to, or used in vision ⟨*visual* organs⟩ **2** : attained or maintained by sight ⟨*visual* impressions⟩ **3** : VISIBLE 1 **4** : producing mental images : VIVID **5** : of, relating to, or employing visual aids [Late Latin *visualis,* from Latin *visus* "sight", from *vidēre* "to see"] — **vi·su·al·ly** \-ē\ *adv*

visual acuity *n* : the relative capacity of the visual organ to resolve detail

visual aid *n* : an instructional device (as a chart, map, or model) that appeals chiefly to vision; *esp* : an educational movie or filmstrip

vi·su·al·ize \'vizh-wə-ˌlīz, -ə-wə-; 'vizh-ə-ˌlīz\ *vb* : to make visible; *esp* : to see or form a mental image of : ENVISAGE — **vi·su·al·iz·able** \-ˌlī-zə-bəl\ *adj* — **vi·su·al·iza·tion** \ˌvizh-wə-lə-'zā-shən, -ə-wə-; ˌvizh-ə-lə-\ *n* — **vi·su·al·iz·er** \'vizh-wə-ˌlī-zər, -ə-wə-; 'vizh-ə-ˌlī-\ *n*

visual purple *n* : a photosensitive red or purple pigment in the retinal rods of various vertebrates; *esp* : RHODOPSIN

vi·ta \'vēt-ə, 'vīt-ə\ *n, pl* **vi·tae** \'vē-ˌtī, 'vīt-ē\ : a brief autobiographical sketch [Latin, literally, "life"]

vi·tal \'vīt-l\ *adj* **1** : of, relating to, or characteristic of life : showing the qualities of living things ⟨*vital* activites⟩ **2** : concerned with or necessary to the maintenance of life ⟨*vital* organs⟩ **3** : full of vitality : ANIMATED **4** : of first importance : BASIC [Middle French, from Latin *vitalis* "of life", from *vita* "life"] SYN SEE ESSENTIAL — **vi·tal·ly** \-l-ē\ *adv*

vital capacity *n* : the breathing capacity of the lungs expressed as the number of cubic inches or cubic centimeters of air that can be forcibly exhaled after a full inspiration

vi·tal·ism \'vīt-l-ˌiz-əm\ *n* : the doctrine that the life processes are not wholly explainable by the laws of physics and chemistry and that life is in some part self-determining — compare MECHANISM — **vi·tal·ist** \-l-əst\ *n* — **vi·tal·is·tic** \ˌvīt-l-'is-tik\ *adj*

vi·tal·i·ty \vī-'tal-ət-ē\ *n, pl* **-ties** **1 a** : the peculiarity distinguishing the living from the nonliving **b** : capacity to live and develop; *also* : physical or mental vigor especially when highly developed **2 a** : power of enduring or continuing ⟨the *vitality* of bad habits⟩ **b** : lively and animated character : VIGOR

vi·tal·ize \'vīt-l-ˌīz\ *vt* : to give vitality to : ANIMATE — **vi·tal·iza·tion** \ˌvīt-l-ə-'zā-shən\ *n*

vi·tals \'vīt-lz\ *n pl* **1** : vital organs **2** : essential parts

vital signs *n pl* : the pulse rate, respiratory rate, body temperature, and sometimes blood pressure of a person

vital statistics *n pl* : statistics relating to births, deaths, marriages, health, and disease

vi·ta·min \'vīt-ə-mən\ *n* : any of various organic substances that are essential in minute quantities to the nutrition of most animals and some plants, act in the regulation of metabolic processes but do not provide energy or serve as building units, and are present in natural foodstuffs or sometimes produced within the body [Latin *vita* "life" + English *amine*]

vitamin A *n* : a fat-soluble vitamin or vitamin mixture found especially in animal products (as egg yolk, milk, or fish-liver oils) whose lack causes injury to epithelial tissues (as in the eye with resulting visual defects)

vitamin B *n* **1** : VITAMIN B COMPLEX **2** *or* **vitamin B₁** : THIAMINE

vitamin B complex *n* : a group of water-soluble vitamins found widely in foods that include essential coenzymes and growth factors — called also *B complex*; compare BIOTIN, CHOLINE, NICOTINIC ACID, PANTOTHENIC ACID, THIAMINE

vitamin B₆ \-'bē-'siks\ *n* : pyridoxine or a closely related compound

vitamin B₁₂ \-'bē-'twelv\ *n* : a complex cobalt-containing member of the vitamin B complex that occurs especially in liver, is essential to normal blood formation, neural function, and growth, and is used especially in treating pernicious anemia

vitamin B₂ \-'bē-'tü\ *n* : RIBOFLAVIN

vitamin C *n* : a water-soluble vitamin $C_6H_8O_6$ that is present especially in fruits and leafy vegetables, apparently functions as an enzyme in certain bodily oxidations and syntheses, and is used medicinally in the prevention and treatment of scurvy — called also *ascorbic acid*

vitamin D *n* : any or all of several fat-soluble vitamins that are chemically related to steroids, are essential for normal bone and tooth structure, and are found especially in fish-liver oils, egg yolk, and milk or produced by activation (as by ultraviolet irradiation) of sterols

vitamin E *n* : any of several tocopherols of which the lack in various mammals and birds is associated with infertility, muscular dystrophy, or vascular abnormalities and which occur especially in leaves and in seed-germ oils

vitamin G *n* : RIBOFLAVIN

vitamin H *n* : BIOTIN

vitamin K *n* : any of several fat-soluble vitamins essential for the clotting of blood because of their role in the production of prothrombin [Danish *k*oagulation "coagulation"]

vi·tel·line \vī-'tel-ən, və-\ *adj* : of, relating to, resembling, or producing yolk [derived from Latin *vitellus* "yolk", literally, "small calf"]

vi·ti·ate \'vish-ē-ˌāt\ *vt* **1** : to injure the quality of : SPOIL, DEBASE **2** : to destroy the validity of ⟨fraud *vitiates* a contract⟩ [Latin *vitiare,* from *vitium* "fault, vice"] — **vi·ti·a·tion** \ˌvish-ē-'ā-shən\ *n* — **vi·ti·a·tor** \'vish-ē-ˌāt-ər\ *n*

vi·ti·cul·ture \'vit-ə-ˌkəl-chər, 'vīt-ə-\ *n* : the growing of grapes [Latin *vitis* "vine"] — **vi·ti·cul·tur·al** \ˌvit-ə-'kəlch-rəl, -ə-rəl, ˌvīt-\ *adj* — **vi·ti·cul·tur·ist** \-'kəlch-rəst, -ə-rəst\ *n*

vit·i·li·go \ˌvit-l-ˈī-gō, -ˈē-gō\ *n* : a skin disorder in which smooth white spots appear on the body [Latin, a skin disease]

vit·re·ous \ˈvi-trē-əs\ *adj* **1** : of, relating to, derived from, or resembling glass : GLASSY ⟨*vitreous* rocks⟩ ⟨a *vitreous* luster⟩ **2** : of, relating to, or being the vitreous humor [Latin *vitreus,* from *vitrum* "glass"] — **vit·re·ous·ness** *n*

vitreous humor *n* : the clear colorless transparent jelly that fills the eyeball posterior to the lens

vit·ri·fy \ˈvi-trə-ˌfī\ *vb* **-fied; -fy·ing** : to change into glass or a glassy substance by heat and fusion [French *vitrifier,* from Latin *vitrum* "glass"] — **vit·ri·fi·able** \-ˌfī-ə-bəl\ *adj* — **vit·ri·fi·ca·tion** \ˌvi-trə-fə-ˈkā-shən\ *n*

vit·ri·ol \ˈvi-trē-əl\ *n* **1 a** : a sulfate of any of various metals (as copper, iron, or zinc) **b** : OIL OF VITRIOL **2** : bitter feelings or harsh speech [Middle French, from Medieval Latin *vitriolum,* derived from Latin *vitreus* "vitreous"] — **vit·ri·ol·ic** \ˌvi-trē-ˈäl-ik\ *adj*

vit·tle \ˈvit-l\ *n* : VICTUAL

vi·tu·per·ate \vī-ˈtü-pə-ˌrāt, və-, -ˈtyü-\ *vb* : to abuse or censure severely : use harsh condemning language [Latin *vituperare,* from *vitium* "fault" + *parare* "to make"] — **vi·tu·per·a·tive** \-ˈtü-pə-rət-iv, -pə-ˌrāt-, -prət-iv, -ˈtyü-\ *adj* — **vi·tu·per·a·tive·ly** *adv* — **vi·tu·per·a·tor** \-pə-ˌrāt-ər\ *n* — **vi·tu·per·a·to·ry** \-rə-ˌtōr-ē, -ˌtór-\ *adj*

vi·tu·per·a·tion \-ˌtü-pə-ˈrā-shən, -ˌtyü-\ *n* : sustained and bitter railing and condemnation SYN see ABUSE

vi·va \ˈvē-və, -ˌvä\ *interj* — used to express approval or goodwill [Italian, "long live", from *vivere* "to live", from Latin]

vi·va·ce \vē-ˈväch-ā, vi-, -ē\ *adv or adj* : in a brisk spirited manner — used as a direction in music [Italian, "vivacious"]

vi·va·cious \və-ˈvā-shəs *also* vī-\ *adj* : lively in temper or conduct : SPRIGHTLY [Latin *vivac-, vivax,* literally, "long-lived", from *vivere* "to live"] SYN see LIVELY — **vi·va·cious·ly** *adv* — **vi·va·cious·ness** *n*

vi·vac·i·ty \-ˈvas-ət-ē\ *n* : the quality or state of being vivacious

vi·var·i·um \vī-ˈvar-ē-əm, -ˈver-\ *n, pl* **-ia** \-ē-ə\ *or* **-i·ums** : an enclosure for keeping or raising and observing animals or plants indoors; *esp* : such an enclosure for terrestrial animals — called also *terrarium* [Latin, "park, preserve", from *vivus* "alive"]

¹vi·va vo·ce \ˌvī-və-ˈvō-sē, ˌvē-və-ˈvō-chā\ *adv* : by word of mouth : ORALLY [Medieval Latin, "with the living voice"]

²viva voce *adj* : expressed or conducted by word of mouth : ORAL

viv·id \ˈviv-əd\ *adj* **1** : having the appearance of vigorous life or freshness : very lively ⟨a *vivid* personality⟩ **2** : very strong or intense : of very high saturation ⟨a *vivid* red⟩ **3** : producing a strong or clear impression on the senses : SHARP; *esp* : producing distinct mental images ⟨a *vivid* description⟩ **4** : acting clearly and vigorously ⟨a *vivid* imagination⟩ [Latin *vividus,* from *vivere* "to live"] SYN see GRAPHIC — **viv·id·ly** *adv* — **viv·id·ness** *n*

viv·i·fy \ˈviv-ə-ˌfī\ *vt* **-fied; -fy·ing** **1** : to provide with the quality or appearance of life : ANIMATE **2** : to make vivid [Middle French *vivifier,* from Late Latin *vivificare,* derived from Latin *vivus* "alive"] — **viv·i·fi·ca·tion** \ˌviv-ə-fə-ˈkā-shən\ *n* — **viv·i·fi·er** \ˈviv-ə-ˌfī-ər, -ˌfīr\ *n*

vi·vip·a·rous \vī-ˈvip-rəs, -ə-rəs\ *adj* : producing living young from within the body rather than from eggs [Latin *viviparus,* from *vivus* "alive" + *parere* "to produce"] — **vi·vi·par·i·ty** \ˌvī-və-ˈpar-ət-ē\ *n* — **vi·vip·a·rous·ly** \vī-ˈvip-rəs-lē, -ə-rəs-\ *adv*

vivi·sec·tion \ˌviv-ə-ˈsek-shən\ *n* : the cutting of or operation on a living animal usually for scientific investigation; *also* : animal experimentation especially if considered to cause distress to the subject [Latin *vivus*

"alive" + English *section*] — **vivi·sect** \ˈviv-ə-ˌsekt\ *vb* — **vivi·sec·tion·al** \ˌviv-ə-ˈsek-shnəl, -shən-l\ *adj* — **vivi·sec·tion·al·ly** \-ē\ *adv* — **vivi·sec·tion·ist** \-ˈsek-shə-nəst, -shnəst\ *n* — **vivi·sec·tor** \ˈviv-ə-ˌsek-tər\ *n*

vix·en \ˈvik-sən\ *n* **1** : a female fox **2** : a quick-tempered argumentative woman [Middle English *fixen,* from Old English *fyxe,* feminine of *fox*] — **vix·en·ish** \-sə-nish, -snish\ *adj* — **vix·en·ish·ly** *adv*

viz·ard \ˈviz-ərd, -ˌärd\ *n* : a mask formerly worn especially for disguise [Middle English *viser* "mask, visor"]

vi·zier \və-ˈziər\ *n* : a high executive officer of various Muslim countries and especially of the former Turkish Empire [Turkish *vezir,* from Arabic *wazīr*] — **vi·zier·i·al** \-ˈzir-ē-əl\ *adj* — **vi·zier·ship** \-ˈziər-ˌship\ *n*

vo·ca·ble \ˈvō-kə-bəl\ *n* : a word composed of various sounds or letters without regard to its meaning [Middle French, "term, name", from Latin *vocabulum,* from *vocare* "to call"]

vo·cab·u·lary \vō-ˈkab-yə-ˌler-ē\ *n, pl* **-lar·ies** **1** : a list or collection of words or of words and phrases usually alphabetically arranged and explained or defined **2** : a sum or stock of words employed by a language, group, individual, or work or in a field of knowledge [Middle French *vocabulaire,* probably from Medieval Latin *vocabularium,* derived from Latin *vocabulum* "name, term", from *vocare* "to call"]

vocabulary entry *n* : a word (as the noun *book*), hyphened or open compound (as the adjective *light-headed* or the noun *book review*), word element (as the affix *pro-*), abbreviation (as *agt*), verbalized symbol (as *Na*), or term (as *point of view*) entered alphabetically in a dictionary for the purpose of definition or identification or expressly included as an inflectional form (as the noun *mice* or the verb *saw*) or as a derived form (as the noun *godlessness* or the adverb *globally*) or related phrase (as *one for the book*) run on at its base word and usually set in a type (as boldface) readily distinguishable from that of the lightface text which defines, explains, or identifies the entry

¹vo·cal \ˈvō-kəl\ *adj* **1 a** : uttered by the voice : ORAL **b** : VOICED 2 **2** : relating to, composed or arranged for, or sung by the human voice ⟨*vocal* music⟩ **3** : VOCALIC **4** : given to expressing oneself freely or insistently : OUTSPOKEN **5** : of, relating to, or resembling the voice [Latin *vocalis,* from *voc-, vox* "voice"] — **vo·cal·ly** \-kə-lē\ *adv*

²vocal *n* **1** : a vocal sound **2** : a solo for a singer especially when accompanied by a dance or jazz band

vocal cords *n pl* : either of two pairs of elastic folds of mucous membrane that project into the cavity of the larynx and that play a major role in the production of vocal sounds — called also *vocal folds*

vo·cal·ic \vō-ˈkal-ik\ *adj* **1** : marked by or consisting of vowels **2** : of, relating to, or functioning as a vowel [Latin *vocalis* "vowel", from *vocalis* "vocal"] — **vo·cal·i·cal·ly** \-i-kə-lē, -klē\ *adv*

vo·cal·ist \ˈvō-kə-ləst\ *n* : ¹SINGER

vo·cal·iza·tion \ˌvō-kə-lə-ˈzā-shən\ *n* : an act, process, or instance of vocalizing

vo·cal·ize \ˈvō-kə-ˌlīz\ *vb* **1 a** : to give vocal expression to **b** : SING; *esp* : to sing without words (as in practicing) **2 a** : VOICE 2 **b** : to convert to a vowel — **vo·cal·iz·er** *n*

vo·ca·tion \vō-ˈkā-shən\ *n* **1** : a summons or strong inclination to a particular state or course of action; *esp* : a divine call to the religious life **2 a** : the work in which a person is regularly employed : OCCUPATION **b** : the persons engaged in a particular occupation **3** : the special function of an individual or group : ROLE [Latin *vocatio* "summons", from *vocare* "to call"] □ SYN AVOCATION: VOCATION denotes one's livelihood; AVOCATION denotes a leisure occupation which may or may not bring remuneration.

vo·ca·tion·al \-shnəl, -shən-l\ *adj* **1** : of, relating to, or concerned with a vocation **2** : concerned with choice or of training in a skill or trade to be pursued as a career ⟨*vocational* guidance⟩ ⟨a *vocational* school⟩ — **vo·ca·tion·al·ly** \-ē\ *adv*

vo·ca·tion·al·ism \-,iz-əm\ *n* : emphasis on vocational training in education

voc·a·tive \'väk-ət-iv\ *adj* : of, relating to, or constituting a grammatical case marking the one addressed [Middle French *vocatif*, from Latin *vocativus*, from *vocare* "to call"] — **vocative** *n* — **voc·a·tive·ly** *adv*

vo·cif·er·ant \vō-'sif-ə-rənt\ *adj* : VOCIFEROUS — **vo·cif·er·ance** \-rəns\ *n*

vo·cif·er·ate \vō-'sif-ə-,rāt\ *vb* : to cry out or utter loudly : CLAMOR, SHOUT [Latin *vociferari*, from *voc-*, *vox* "voice" + *ferre* "to carry"] — **vo·cif·er·a·tion** \-,sif-ə-'rā-shən\ *n* — **vo·cif·er·a·tor** \-'sif-ə-,rāt-ər\ *n*

vo·cif·er·ous \vō-'sif-rəs, -ə-rəs\ *adj* : making a loud outcry : NOISY, CLAMOROUS — **vo·cif·er·ous·ly** *adv* — **vo·cif·er·ous·ness** *n*

vod·ka \'väd-kə\ *n* : a colorless and unaged alcoholic liquor distilled fom a mash (as of rye or wheat) [Russian, from *voda* "water"]

vogue \'vōg\ *n* **1 a** : popular approval or favor : POPULARITY **b** : a period of popularity **2** : something or someone in fashion at a particular time [Middle French, "action of rowing, course, fashion", from Italian *voga*, from *vogare* "to row"] SYN SEE FASHION — **vogue** *adj*

vogu·ish \'vō-gish\ *adj* **1** : following the fashion : SMART **2** : suddenly or temporarily popular

¹voice \'vȯis\ *n* **1 a** : sound produced by vertebrates by means of lungs, larynx, or syrinx; *esp* : sound so produced by human beings **b** : musical sound produced by the vocal cords and resonated by the cavities of the head and throat **c** : the quality of the sound produced by the voice ⟨a squeaky *voice*⟩ **2 a** : the ability to produce vocal sound : power of speech **b** : the ability to produce musical tones **c** : the quality of the vocal mechanism with respect to the production of musical tones ⟨in good *voice* today⟩ **d** : the use of the voice in speaking, acting, or singing **3** : something resembling or likened to a vocal utterance ⟨the *voice* of conscience⟩ **4** : distinction of form or a system of inflections of a verb to indicate the relation of the subject of the verb to the action which the verb expresses **5 a** : wish, choice, or opinion openly or formally expressed ⟨the *voice* of the people⟩ **b** : right of expression : SUFFRAGE, SAY **6** : a medium of expression ⟨the newspaper was the *voice* of conservatism⟩ **7 a** : ¹SINGER **b** : one of the melodic parts of a vocal or instrumental composition **8** : expiration of air with the vocal cords drawn close so as to vibrate audibly ⟨consonants pronounced with *voice*⟩ [Old French *vois*, from Latin *voc-*, *vox*] — **with one voice** : UNANIMOUSLY

²voice *vt* **1** : UTTER, EXPRESS ⟨*voiced* serious objections to our proposal⟩ **2** : to pronounce (as a consonant) with voice

voice box *n* : LARYNX

voiced \'vȯist\ *adj* **1 a** : furnished with a voice ⟨soft-*voiced*⟩ **b** : expressed in language ⟨a frequently *voiced* opinion⟩ **2** : uttered with vocal cord vibration ⟨a *voiced* consonant⟩

voice·less \'vȯi-sləs\ *adj* **1** : having no voice : MUTE **2** : not voiced ⟨a *voiceless* consonant⟩ — **voice·less·ly** *adv* — **voice·less·ness** *n*

voice mail *n* : an electronic communication system in which spoken messages are recorded or digitized for later playback to the intended recipient

voice part *n* : VOICE 7b

voice·print \'vȯi-,sprint\ *n* : an individually distinctive pattern of certain voice characteristics that is spectrographically produced [*voice* + *-print* (as in *fingerprint*)]

¹void \'vȯid\ *adj* **1** : containing nothing ⟨*void* space⟩ **2** : not containing or occupied by something usual or normal ⟨hearts *void* of mercy⟩ ⟨a *void* chair⟩ ⟨left the presidency *void*⟩ **3** : of no legal force or effect ⟨a *void* marriage⟩

²void *n* **1 a** : empty space **b** : an unfilled opening **2** : LACK 1, DEFICIENCY **3** : a feeling of want or hollowness **4** : absence of cards of a particular suit in a hand as dealt

³void *vt* **1** : to make empty or vacant : CLEAR **2** : DISCHARGE, EMIT ⟨*void* excrement⟩ **3** : NULLIFY, ANNUL ⟨*void* a contract⟩ — **void·er** *n*

void·able \'vȯid-ə-bəl\ *adj* : capable of being voided

voile \'vȯil\ *n* : a soft sheer fabric of silk, cotton, rayon, or wool used especially for curtains or women's summer clothing [French, "veil", from Latin *velum*]

vo·lan·te \vō-'län-tā\ *adj* : moving with light rapidity — used as a direction in music [Italian, literally, "flying", from Latin *volare* "to fly"]

vo·lar \'vō-lər, -,lär\ *adj* : relating to the palm of the hand or the sole of the foot [Latin *vola* "palm, sole"]

¹vol·a·tile \'väl-ət-l\ *adj* **1** : readily becoming a vapor at a relatively low temperature ⟨a *volatile* solvent⟩ **2 a** : LIGHTHEARTED, LIVELY ⟨a *volatile* mind⟩ **b** : easily aroused ⟨a *volatile* temper⟩ **3 a** : tending or likely to erupt into violent action ⟨a *volatile* situation⟩ **b** : subject to often sudden change ⟨a *volatile* market⟩ [French, "flying, volatile", from Latin *volatilis* "flying", from *volare* "to fly"] — **vol·a·tile·ness** *n* — **vol·a·til·i·ty** \,väl-ə-'til-ət-ē\ *n*

²volatile *n* : a volatile substance

vol·a·til·ize \'väl-ət-l-,īz\ *vb* : to pass off or cause to pass off in vapor — **vol·a·til·iza·tion** \,väl-ət-l-ə-'zā-shən\ *n*

¹vol·ca·nic \väl-'kan-ik, vȯl- *also* -'kän-\ *adj* **1 a** : of or relating to a volcano ⟨a *volcanic* eruption⟩ **b** : having volcanoes ⟨a *volcanic* region⟩ **c** : made of materials from volcanoes ⟨*volcanic* dust⟩ **2** : explosively violent : VOLATILE ⟨*volcanic* passions⟩ — **vol·ca·ni·cal·ly** \-i-kə-lē, -klē\ *adv*

²volcanic *n* : a volcanic rock

volcanic glass *n* : natural glass produced by the cooling of molten lava too rapidly to permit crystallization

vol·ca·nism \'väl-kə-,niz-əm, 'vȯl-\ *n* : volcanic activity

vol·ca·no \väl-'kā-nō, vȯl-\ *n, pl* **-noes** *or* **-nos** **1** : a vent in the earth's crust from which molten or hot rock and steam issue; *also* : a hill or mountain composed wholly or in part of ejected volcanic material [Italian *vulcano*, from Latin *Volcanus, Vulcanus* "Vulcan"]

vol·ca·nol·o·gy \,väl-kə-'näl-ə-jē, ,vȯl-\ *n* : a branch of science that deals with volcanic phenomena — **vol·ca·no·log·i·cal** \-kən-l-'äj-i-kəl\ *adj* — **vol·ca·nol·o·gist** \-kə-'näl-ə-jəst\ *n*

vole \'vōl\ *n* : any of various small rodents closely related to the lemmings and muskrats but in general resembling stocky mice or rats [of Scandinavian origin]

vo·li·tion \vō-'lish-ən, və-\ *n* **1** : the act or power of making one's own choices or decisions ⟨they do not do this of their own *volition*⟩ **2** : the ending of an act or exercise of willing [French, from Medieval Latin *volitio*, from Latin *velle* "to will, wish"] — **vo·li·tion·al** \-'lish-nəl, -ən-l\ *adj*

¹vol·ley \'väl-ē\ *n, pl* **volleys** **1 a** : a flight of missiles (as arrows or bullets) **b** : simultaneous discharge of a number of missile weapons (as rifles) **2 a** : a return of the ball before it touches the ground (as in tennis or volleyball) **b** : a kick of the ball in soccer before it rebounds **c** : the exchange of the shuttlecock in badminton following the serve **3** : a bursting forth of many things at once ⟨a *volley* of bubbles⟩ ⟨a *volley* of curses⟩ [Middle French *volee* "flight", from *voler* "to fly", from Latin *volare*]

²volley *vb* **vol·leyed; vol·ley·ing** **1** : to discharge in a volley **2** : to propel an object (as a ball) while it is in the air before it touches the ground

vole

vol·ley·ball \'väl-ē-ˌbȯl\ *n* : a game played by volleying a large inflated ball over a net

vol·plane \'väl-ˌplān, 'vȯl-\ *vi* : to glide in or as if in an airplane [French *vol plané* "gliding flight"]

volt \'vōlt\ *n* : a unit of electrical potential difference and electromotive force equal to the difference of potential between two points in a conducting wire carrying a constant current of one ampere when the power dissipated between these two points is equal to one watt [Alessandro *Volta,* died 1827, Italian physicist]

volt·age \'vōl-tij\ *n* : potential difference expressed in volts

voltage divider *n* : a resistor or series of resistors provided with taps at certain points and used to provide various potential differences from a single power source

vol·ta·ic \väl-'tā-ik, vōl-, vȯl-\ *adj* : of, relating to, or producing direct electric current by chemical action (as in a battery) [Alessandro *Volta*]

voltaic cell *n* : an apparatus for generating electricity through chemical action on two unlike metals in an electrolyte

volt–am·pere \'vōl-'tam-ˌpiȯr\ *n* : a unit of electric measurement equal to the product of a volt and an ampere that for direct current constitutes a measure of power equivalent to a watt

volte–face \ˌvȯlt-'fäs, ˌvȯlt-ə-\ *n* : reversal of attitude especially in policy : ABOUT-FACE [French, from Italian *voltafaccia,* from *voltare* "to turn" + *faccia* "face"]

volt·me·ter \'vōlt-ˌmēt-ər\ *n* : an instrument for measuring in volts the differences of potential between different points of an electrical circuit

vol·u·ble \'väl-yə-bəl\ *adj* : characterized by ready or rapid speech : GLIB, FLUENT [Latin *volubilis,* from *volvere* "to roll"] SYN see TALKATIVE — **vol·u·bil·i·ty** \ˌväl-yə-'bil-ət-ē\ *n* — **vol·u·bly** \'väl-yə-blē\ *adv*

vol·ume \'väl-yəm, -yüm\ *n* **1** : BOOK (a dozen *volumes* on the shelf) **2** : any of a series of books forming a complete work or collection (the 5th *volume* of an encyclopedia) **3 a** : space occupied **b** : measure of a bounded space especially in cubic units (find the *volume* of the cylinder) **4 a** : a usually shapeless body or mass (a *volume* of gas) **b** : a considerable quantity (*volumes* of smoke) **5** : intensity or quantity of sound (turn up the *volume* on the radio) [Middle French, from Latin *volumen* "roll, book", from *volvere* "to roll] SYN see BULK □ ORIGIN The earliest books were rolls of papyrus. The Romans took their name for such a roll, *volumen,* from the verb *volvere,* "to roll". Later, books were made of parchment, which, unlike papyrus, could be folded and bound. This eliminated the need for rolls. French *volume,* from Latin *volumen,* originally referred to papyrus rolls but was later used for bound books as well. The French word was borrowed into English in the 14th century. By the 16th century *volume* had acquired the additional sense "the size (of a book)", which led to the development of a generalized sense, "quantity, amount, or mass (of anything)". In the 19th century *volume* acquired the meaning "strength" or "intensity" in reference to sound.

vol·u·meter \'väl-yu̇-ˌmēt-ər\ *n* : an instrument for measuring volumes (as of gases or liquids) directly or (as of solids) by displacement of a liquid

vol·u·met·ric \ˌväl-yə-'me-trik\ *adj* : of or relating to the measurement of volume — **vol·u·met·ri·cal·ly** \-tri-kə-lē, -klē\ *adv*

vo·lu·mi·nous \və-'lü-mə-nəs\ *adj* **1** : having many folds, coils, or convolutions **2 a** : filling or capable of filling a large volume or several volumes (a *voluminous* correspondence) **b** : writing or speaking much or at great length (a *voluminous* writer) [Late Latin *voluminosus* "full of folds", from Latin *volumen* "roll, book"] — **vo·lu·mi·nous·ly** *adv* — **vo·lu·mi·nous·ness** *n*

I volva

vol·un·tar·i·ly \ˌväl-ən-'ter-ə-lē\ *adv* : of one's own free will

¹vol·un·tary \'väl-ən-ˌter-ē\ *adj* **1** : done, given, or made in accordance with one's own free will or choice (*voluntary* assistance) **2** : not accidental : INTENTIONAL (*voluntary* manslaughter) **3** : of or relating to the will : controlled by the will (*voluntary* behavior) [Latin *voluntarius,* from *voluntas* "will", from *velle* "to will, wish"] □ SYN VOLUNTARY, INTENTIONAL, DELIBERATE, WILLFULL mean done or brought about of one's own accord. VOLUNTARY implies spontaneousness and freedom from compulsion (*voluntary* contributions) or stresses control of the will (*voluntary* eye movements) INTENTIONAL stresses consciousness of purpose (an *intentional* oversight) DELIBERATE implies full consciousness of the nature of an intended action (a *deliberate* insult) WILLFUL implies an obstinate determination to follow one's own will and a refusal to learn or obey.

²voluntary *n, pl* **-tar·ies** : an organ piece often improvised and played before, during, or after a religious service

voluntary muscle *n* : muscle (as most striated muscle) under voluntary control

¹vol·un·teer \ˌväl-ən-'tier\ *n* **1** : one who enters into a service or offers to serve of his or her own free will; *esp* : one who enters into military service voluntarily **2** : a volunteer plant [French *volontaire,* from *volontaire* "voluntary", from Latin *voluntarius*]

²volunteer *adj* **1** : of, relating to, or consisting of volunteers (a *volunteer* army) **2** : growing spontaneously without direct human care especially from seeds lost from a previous crop

³volunteer *vb* **1** : to offer or bestow voluntarily (*volunteered* one's services) **2** : to offer oneself as a volunteer

vo·lup·tu·ary \və-'ləp-chə-ˌwer-ē\ *n, pl* **-ar·ies** : one whose chief interest is luxury and the gratification of sensual appetites — **voluptuary** *adj*

vo·lup·tu·ous \-chə-wəs, -chəs\ *adj* **1** : giving pleasure to the senses : providing sensual or sensuous gratification (*voluptuous* furnishings) (*voluptuous* dancers) **2** : given to or spent in the enjoyment of pleasure and luxury (a *voluptuous* holiday) **3** : having sensual appeal (*voluptuous* dancing) (a *voluptuous* figure) [Latin *voluptuosus,* from *voluptas* "pleasure"]

vo·lute \və-'lüt\ *n* **1** : a spiral or scroll-shaped form **2** : a spiral scroll-shaped ornament forming the chief feature of the Ionic capital [Latin *voluta,* from *volvere* "to roll"] — **vo·lute** *or* **vo·lut·ed** \-'lüt-əd\ *adj*

vol·va \'väl-və, 'vȯl-\ *n* : a membraneous sac or cup about the base of the stem in many mushrooms [Latin *volva, vulva* "integument"] — **vol·vate** \-ˌvāt\ *adj*

vol·vox \-ˌväks\ *n* : any of a genus of green flagellates that form spherical colonies [New Latin, from Latin *volvere* "to roll"]

vo·mer \'vō-mər\ *n* : a bone of the lower skull of most vertebrates that in human beings forms part of the nasal septum [Latin, "plowshare"] — **vo·mer·ine** \-mə-ˌrīn\ *adj*

¹vom·it \'väm-ət\ *n* : an act or instance of ejecting the contents of the stomach through the mouth; *also* : the matter ejected [Middle French, from Latin *vomitus,* from *vomere* "to vomit"]

²vomit *vb* **1** : to eject the contents of the stomach through the mouth **2** : DISGORGE 2 (lava *vomited* from the volcano) — **vom·it·er** *n*

vom·i·tus \'väm-ət-əs\ *n* : material discharged by vomiting [Latin]

¹voo·doo \'vüd-ü\ *n, pl* **voodoos** **1** : a religion derived from African ancestor worship, practiced chiefly by Negroes of Haiti, and consisting largely of magic and sorcery **2 a** : one who deals in spells and necromancy **b** (1) : a sorcerer's spell (2) : a hexed object [Louisiana French *voudou,* of African origin] — **voodoo** *adj*

²voodoo *vt* : to bewitch by or as if by means of voodoo : HEX

voo·doo·ism \'vüd-ü-ˌiz-əm\ *n* **1** : VOODOO 1 **2** : the practice of witchcraft — **voo·doo·ist** \'vüd-ˌü-əst\ *n* — **voo·doo·is·tic** \ˌvüd-ü-'is-tik\ *adj*

vo·ra·cious \vȯ-'rā-shəs, və-\ *adj* **1** : greedy in eating : RAVENOUS ⟨a *voracious* appetite⟩ **2** : excessively eager : INSATIABLE ⟨a *voracious* reader⟩ [Latin *vorac-, vorax,* from *vorare* "to devour"] — **vo·ra·cious·ly** *adv* — **vo·ra·cious·ness** *n* — **vo·rac·i·ty** \-'ras-ət-ē\ *n*

vor·tex \'vȯr-ˌteks\ *n, pl* **vor·ti·ces** \'vȯrt-ə-ˌsēz\ *also* **vor·tex·es** \'vȯr-ˌtek-səz\ **1** : a mass of fluid and especially of a liquid having a whirling motion that tends to form a cavity in the center and to draw things toward this cavity; *esp* : WHIRLPOOL, EDDY **2** : a whirling mass (as a whirlwind, tornado, or waterspout); *also* : the eye of a cyclone [Latin *vertic-, vertex, vortic-, vortex* "whirlpool", from *vertere* "to turn"]

vor·ti·cal \'vȯrt-i-kəl\ *adj* : of, relating to, or resembling a vortex

vor·ti·cel·la \ˌvȯrt-ə-'sel-ə\ *n, pl* **-cel·lae** \-'sel-ē\ *or* **-cellas** : any of a genus of stalked bell-shaped ciliates [New Latin, from Latin *vortic-, vortex* "whirlpool"]

vor·tic·i·ty \vȯr-'tis-ət-ē\ *n* : the state of a fluid in vortical motion

vo·ta·rist \'vōt-ə-rəst\ *n* : VOTARY

vo·ta·ry \'vōt-ə-rē\ *n, pl* **-ries** **1 a** : ENTHUSIAST, DEVOTEE **b** : a devoted adherent or admirer **2** : a devout or zealous worshiper [Latin *votum* "vow"]

¹vote \'vōt\ *n* **1 a** : a formal expression of opinion or will; *esp* : one given as an indication of approval or disapproval of a proposal or a candidate for office **b** : the total number of such expressions of opinion made known at a single time (as at an election) **c** : BALLOT 1 **2** : the collective opinion of a body of persons expressed by voting **3** : the right to cast a vote : SUFFRAGE **4 a** : the act or process of voting ⟨bring the issue to a *vote*⟩ **b** : a method of voting **5 a** : VOTER **b** : a group of voters with common characteristics ⟨the farm *vote*⟩ [Latin *votum* "vow, wish", from *vovēre* "to vow"]

²vote *vb* **1** : to express one's wish or choice by a vote : cast a vote **2** : to make into law by a vote ⟨*vote* an income tax⟩ **3** : ELECT ⟨*vote* someone into office⟩ **4** : to declare by common consent **5** : PROPOSE 1, SUGGEST

vote·less \'vōt-ləs\ *adj* : having no vote; *esp* : denied the political franchise

vot·er \'vōt-ər\ *n* : one that votes or has the legal right to vote

voting machine *n* : a mechanical device for recording and counting votes cast on it in an election

vo·tive \'vōt-iv\ *adj* **1** : offered or performed in fulfillment of a vow or in gratitude or devotion **2** : consisting of or expressing a vow, wish, or desire ⟨a *votive* prayer⟩ [Latin *votivus,* from *votum* "vow"]

votive mass *n* : a mass celebrated for a special intention (as for a wedding or funeral) in place of the mass of the day

vouch \'vaùch\ *vb* **1** *archaic* **a** : ASSERT 1, AFFIRM **b** : ATTEST **2** : to give a guarantee : become surety ⟨I'll *vouch* for your honesty⟩ **3 a** : to supply supporting evidence or testimony **b** : to give personal assurance ⟨*vouch* for the truth of a story⟩ [Middle French *vocher* "to summon into court to give warranty", from Latin *vocare* "to call, summon", from *voc-, vox* "voice"]

vouch·er \'vaù-chər\ *n* **1** : a person who vouches for another **2** : a document that serves to establish the truth of something; *esp* : a paper (as a receipt) showing payment of a bill or debt

vouch·safe \vaùch-'sāf, 'vaùch-ˌ\ *vt* : to grant in the manner of one doing a favor : condescend to give or grant

vous·soir \vü-'swär\ *n* : one of the wedge-shaped pieces forming an arch or vault [French, derived from Latin *volvere* "to roll"]

¹vow \'vaù\ *n* : a solemn promise or assertion; *esp* : one by which one binds oneself to an act, service, or condition [Old French *vou,* from Latin *votum,* from *vovēre* "to vow"]

²vow *vb* **1** : to make a vow : promise solemnly **2** : to bind or consecrate by a vow

³vow *vt* : AVOW, DECLARE [short for *avow*]

vow·el \'vaù-əl, 'vaùl\ *n* **1** : a speech sound in the articulation of which the oral part of the breath channel is not blocked and is not constricted enough to cause audible friction **2** : a letter representing a vowel; *esp* : any of the letters *a, e, i, o, u,* and sometimes *y* in English [Middle French *vouel,* from Latin *vocalis,* from *vocalis* "vocal"] — **vow·el·like** \'vaù-əl-ˌlīk, 'vaùl-\ *adj*

vox po·pu·li \'väk-'späp-yə-ˌlī, -yə-lē\ *n* : popular sentiment [Latin, "voice of the people"]

¹voy·age \'vȯi-ij, 'vȯ-ij, 'vȯij\ *n* **1** : a journey by water : CRUISE **2** : a journey through air or space [Old French *voiage* "journey", from Latin *viaticum* "traveling money", from *viaticus* "of a journey", from *via* "way"]

²voyage *vb* **1** : to take a trip : TRAVEL **2** : to pass over or cover in traveling ⟨*voyage* the briny deep⟩ — **voy·ag·er** *n*

voya·geur \ˌvȯi-ə-'zhər, ˌvwä-yä-\ *n* : a person employed by a fur company to transport goods and people to and from remote stations in the Northwest [Canadian French, from French, "traveler"]

Vul·ca·ni·an \ˌvəl-'kā-nē-ən\ *adj* : of or relating to Vulcan or to working in metals (as iron)

vul·can·ism \'vəl-kə-ˌniz-əm\ *n* : VOLCANISM

vul·can·ize \'vəl-kə-ˌnīz\ *vt* : to treat (rubber or similar plastic material) chemically in order to give useful properties (as elasticity, strength, or stability) [Latin *Vulcanus* "Vulcan, fire"] — **vul·can·iza·tion** \ˌvəl-kə-nə-'zā-shən\ *n*

vul·gar \'vəl-gər\ *adj* **1** : generally used, applied, or accepted **2** : VERNACULAR **3 a** : of or relating to the common people : PLEBEIAN **b** : of the usual, typical, or ordinary kind **4 a** : lacking in cultivation, perception, or taste : COARSE **b** : ostentatious or excessive in expenditure or display : PRETENTIOUS **5** : offensive in language : OBSCENE, PROFANE [Latin *vulgaris* "of the mob, vulgar", from *vulgus* "mob, common people"] SYN see COARSE — **vul·gar·ly** *adv*

vul·gar·i·an \ˌvəl-'gar-ē-ən, -'ger-\ *n* : a vulgar person

vul·gar·ism \'vəl-gə-ˌriz-əm\ *n* **1 a** : a word or expression originated or used chiefly by illiterate persons **b** : a coarse word or phrase **2** : VULGARITY 1

vul·gar·i·ty \ˌvəl-'gar-ət-ē\ *n, pl* **-ties** **1** : the quality or state of being vulgar **2** : something vulgar

vul·gar·ize \'vəl-gə-ˌrīz\ *vt* **1** : to make generally known or liked : POPULARIZE **2** : to make vulgar : COARSEN — **vul·gar·iza·tion** \ˌvəl-gə-rə-'zā-shən\ *n* — **vul·gar·iz·er** \'vəl-gə-ˌrī-zər\ *n*

Vulgar Latin *n* : the nonliterary Latin of ancient Rome including the speech of plebeians and the informal speech of the educated established by comparative evidence as the chief source of the Romance languages

Vul·gate \'vəl-ˌgāt\ *n* : a Latin version of the Bible authorized and used by the Roman Catholic Church [Late Latin *vulgata editio* "edition in general circulation"]

vul·ner·a·ble \'vəln-rə-bəl, -ə-rə-; 'vəl-nər-bəl\ *adj* **1** : capable of being wounded **2** : open to attack or damage ⟨a *vulnerable* fort⟩ **3** : liable to increased penalties but entitled to increased bonuses in a game of contract bridge [Late Latin *vulnerabilis,* from Latin *vulnerare* "to wound", from *vulner-, vulnus* "wound"] — **vul·ner·a·bil·i·ty** \ˌvəln-rə-'bil-ət-ē, -ə-rə-\ *n* — **vul·ner·a·bly** \'vəln-rə-blē, -ə-rə-; 'vəl-nər-blē\ *adv*

vul·pine \'vəl-ˌpīn\ *adj* : of, relating to, or resembling a fox especially in cunning : CRAFTY [Latin *vulpinus,* from *vulpes* "fox"]

\ə\ abut	\ng\ sing	
\ər\ further	\ō\ bone	
\a\ mat	\ȯ\ saw	
\ā\ take	\ȯi\ coin	
\ä\ cot, cart	\th\ thin	
\aù\ out	\th\ this	
\ch\ chin	\ü\ food	
\e\ pet	\ù\ foot	
\ē\ easy	\y\ yet	
\g\ go	\yü\ few	
\i\ tip	\yù\ cure	
\ī\ life	\zh\ vision	
\j\ job		

vulture 1

vul·ture \ˈvəl-chər\ *n* **1** : any of various large birds that are related to the hawks and eagles but have weaker claws and the head usually naked and that subsist chiefly or entirely on carrion **2** : a greedy or predatory person [Latin *vultur*]

vul·va \ˈvəl-və\ *n, pl* **vul·vae** \-ˌvē, -ˌvī\ : the external parts of the female genital organs; *also* : the opening between their projecting parts [Latin, "integument, womb"] — **vul·val** \ˈvəl-vəl\ *or* **vul·var** \-vər, -ˌvär\ *adj*

vying *present participle of* VIE

waffle iron

w \ˈdəb-əl-ˌyü, -yə, *rapid* ˈdəb-ə-yə, ˈdəb-yə\ *n, pl* **w's** *or* **ws** \-ˌyüz, -yəz\ *often cap* : the 23d letter of the English alphabet

wab·ble \ˈwäb-əl\ *variant of* WOBBLE

Wac \ˈwak\ *n* : a member of the Women's Army Corps [*W*omen's *A*rmy *C*orps]

wacky \ˈwak-ē\ *adj* **wack·i·er; -est** : absurdly or amusingly eccentric or irrational : CRAZY [perhaps from English dialect *whacky* "fool"] — **wack·i·ly** \ˈwak-ə-lē\ *adv* — **wack·i·ness** \ˈwak-ē-nəs\ *n*

¹wad \ˈwäd\ *n* **1** : a small mass, bundle, or tuft ⟨plugged the hole with *wads* of clay⟩: as **a** : a soft mass of usually light fibrous material **b** : a pliable pad or plug (as of felt) used to retain a powder charge in a gun or cartridge **2 a** : a considerable amount (as of money) **b** : a roll of paper money [origin unknown]

²wad *vt* **wad·ded; wad·ding 1** : to form into a wad ⟨*wad* up a handkerchief⟩ **2** : to push a wad into ⟨*wad* a gun⟩ **3** : to hold in by a wad ⟨*wad* a bullet in a gun⟩ **4** : to stuff or line with soft material

wad·ding \ˈwäd-ing\ *n* **1** : wads or material for making wads **2** : a soft mass or sheet of short loose fibers used for stuffing or padding

¹wad·dle \ˈwäd-l\ *vi* **wad·dled; wad·dling** \ˈwäd-ling, -l-ing\ : to walk with short steps swaying from side to side like a duck [derived from *wade*] — **wad·dler** \ˈwäd-lər, -l-ər\ *n*

²waddle *n* : an awkward clumsy swaying gait

¹wade \ˈwäd\ *vb* **1** : to step in or through a medium (as water) offering more resistance than air **2** : to move or proceed with difficulty or labor ⟨*wade* through a dull book⟩ ⟨*wade* into a task⟩ **3** : to pass or cross by wading ⟨*wade* a stream⟩ [Old English *wadan*]

²wade *n* : an act of wading ⟨a *wade* in the brook⟩

wad·er \ˈwäd-ər\ *n* **1** : one that wades **2** : WADING BIRD **3** *pl* : high waterproof boots or trousers for wading

wa·di \ˈwäd-ē\ *n* : a stream bed or valley especially of southwestern Asia and northern Africa that is usually dry except during the rainy season [Arabic *wādiy*]

wading bird *n* : any of many long-legged birds including the shorebirds and various inland water birds (as cranes and herons) that wade in water in search of food

wading pool *n* : a shallow pool of portable or permanent construction used by children for wading

Waf \ˈwaf\ *n* : a member of the women's component of the United States Air Force [*W*omen in the *A*ir *F*orce]

wa·fer \ˈwā-fər\ *n* **1 a** : a thin crisp cake or cracker **b** : a round thin piece of unleavened bread used in the sacrament of Communion **2** : something (as a piece of candy or an adhesive seal) resembling a wafer especially in thin round form [Old North French *waufre*, of Germanic origin]

waf·fle \ˈwäf-əl\ *n* : a crisp cake of batter baked in a waffle iron [Dutch *wafel*]

waffle iron *n* : a cooking utensil with two hinged metal parts that shut upon each other and impress surface projections on waffles being cooked

¹waft \ˈwäft, ˈwaft\ *vb* : to move or cause to move or go lightly by or as if by the impulse of wind or waves [Dutch or Low German *wachten* "to watch, guard"] — **waft·er** *n*

²waft *n* **1** : WHIFF 1a **2** : a slight movement (as of air) : PUFF

¹wag \ˈwag\ *vb* **wagged; wag·ging 1** : to swing to and fro or from side to side ⟨the dog *wagged* its tail⟩ **2** : to move in chatter or gossip ⟨scandal caused tongues to *wag*⟩ [Middle English *waggen*] — **wag·ger** *n*

²wag *n* : an act of wagging : SHAKE

³wag *n* : WIT 4, JOKER [probably from obsolete *waghalter* "person who deserves hanging"]

¹wage \ˈwāj\ *vb* **1** : to engage in or carry on ⟨*wage* war⟩ ⟨*wage* a campaign⟩ **2** : to be waged ⟨the fight *waged* wildly⟩ [Old North French *wagier* "to pledge, give as security", from *wage* "pledge"]

²wage *n* **1** : a payment for labor or services usually according to contract and on an hourly, daily, or piecework basis — often used in pl. **2** *pl* : RECOMPENSE, REWARD [Old North French *wage* "pledge, wage", of Germanic origin] □ SYN WAGE, SALARY, STIPEND, FEE mean the price paid for labor or services. WAGE implies a regular amount paid on an hourly or daily basis and typically at weekly intervals especially for chiefly physical labor; SALARY and STIPEND apply to a fixed amount paid usually at longer intervals for services requiring training or special ability; STIPEND may also imply a grant or allowance rather than direct pay for work done; FEE applies to the sum asked for the services of a doctor, lawyer, artist, or other professional.

wage earner *n* : one that works for wages or salary

¹wa·ger \ˈwā-jər\ *n* **1** : something risked on an uncertain event : STAKE **2** : an act of betting : GAMBLE [Anglo-French *wageure* "pledge, bet", from Old North French *wagier* "to pledge"]

²wager *vb* **wa·gered; wa·ger·ing** \ˈwāj-ring, -ə-ring\ : to risk on an outcome : VENTURE; *esp* : GAMBLE — **wa·ger·er** \ˈwā-jər-ər\ *n*

wag·ery \ˈwag-ə-rē\ *n, pl* **-ger·ies 1** : mischievous fun : PLEASANTRY **2** : JEST 1a; *esp* : PRACTICAL JOKE

wag·gish \ˈwag-ish\ *adj* **1** : resembling or characteristic of a wag : FROLICSOME **2** : done or made in or for sport ⟨a *waggish* trick⟩ — **wag·gish·ly** *adv* — **wag·gish·ness** *n*

wag·gle \ˈwag-əl\ *vb* **wag·gled; wag·gling** \ˈwag-ling, -ə-ling\ : to move backward and forward or from side to side : WAG 1 [derived from ¹*wag*] — **wag·gle** *n* — **wag·gly** \'wag-lē, -ə-lē\ *adj*

wag·on \'wag-ən\ *n* **1** : a four-wheeled vehicle; *esp* : one drawn by animals and used for carrying goods **2** : a child's four-wheeled cart **3** : STATION WAGON **4** : PATROL WAGON [Dutch *wagen*] — **wag·on·er** \'wag-ə-nər\ *n* — **on the wagon** : abstaining from alcoholic liquors

wag·on·ette \,wag-ə-'net\ *n* : a light wagon with two facing seats along the sides in back of a transverse front seat

wa·gon-lit \və-gōⁿ-lē\ *n, pl* **wagons-lits** *or* **wagon-lits** \-gōⁿ-lē\ : a railroad sleeping car [French, from *wagon* "railroad car" + *lit* "bed"]

wagon master *n* : a person in charge of one or more wagons especially for transporting freight

wagon train *n* : a group of wagons (as of pioneers) traveling overland

wag·tail \'wag-,tāl\ *n* : any of numerous slender mostly Old World birds related to the pipits and having a very long tail that is habitually jerked up and down

¹wa·hoo \'wä-,hü, 'wo-\ *n, pl* **wahoos** : a shrubby North American tree having bright autumn foliage and fruit with scarlet capsules which open to expose scarlet seeds [Creek *ûhawhu*]

²wahoo *n, pl* **wahoos** : a large vigorous mackerel that is a common food and sport fish in warm seas [origin unknown]

waif \'wāf\ *n* **1** : something found without an owner and especially by chance **2** : STRAY 2; *esp* : a homeless child [Old North French, "lost, unclaimed"]

¹wail \'wāl\ *vb* **1** : to express sorrow audibly : LAMENT **2** : to make a sound suggestive of a mournful cry **3** : to express dissatisfaction plaintively : COMPLAIN [of Scandinavian origin] — **wail·er** *n*

²wail *n* **1 a** : a usually prolonged cry or sound expressing grief or pain **b** : a sound suggestive of this ⟨the *wail* of an air-raid siren⟩ **2** : an irritable expressing of grievance : COMPLAINT

wail·ful \'wāl-fəl\ *adj* : SORROWFUL, MOURNFUL ⟨the *wailful* sound of distant bagpipes⟩ — **wail·ful·ly** \-fə-lē\ *adv*

wain \'wān\ *n* : a usually large and heavy vehicle for farm use [Old English *wægn*]

¹wain·scot \'wān-skət, -,skōt, -,skät\ *n* **1** : a usually paneled and wooden lining of an interior wall **2** : the lower three or four feet of an interior wall when finished differently from the remainder of the wall [Dutch *wagenschot*]

²wainscot *vt* **-scot·ed** *or* **-scot·ted; -scot·ing** *or* **-scot·ting** : to line with or as if with boards or paneling

wain·scot·ing \-,skōt-ing, -,skät-, -skət-\ *or* **wain·scot·ting** \-,skät-, -skət-\ *n* : material for wainscot; *also* : WAINSCOT

wain·wright \'wān-,rīt\ *n* : a maker and repairer of wagons [Old English *wægnwyrhta*, from *wægn* "wagon" + *wyrhta* "worker, maker"]

waist \'wāst\ *n* **1 a** : the usually narrowed part of the body between the chest and hips **b** : the greatly constricted front part of the abdomen of some insects (as a wasp) **2** : a part resembling the human waist especially in narrowness or central position (the *waist* of a ship) (the *waist* of a violin) **3** : a garment or the part of a garment that covers the body from the neck to the waist [Middle English *wast*]

waist·band \'wāst-,band, 'wās-\ *n* : a band (as of trousers or a skirt) fitting around the waist

waist·coat \'wāst-,kōt, 'wās-; 'wes-kət\ *n, chiefly British* : VEST 1a — **waist·coat·ed** \-əd\ *adj*

waist·line \'wāst-,līn\ *n* **1 a** : WAIST 1a **b** : the circumference of the waist at its narrowest point **2** : the part of a garment surrounding the waist

¹wait \'wāt\ *vb* **1** : to remain inactive in readiness (as for action) or expectation (as of a coming event) : AWAIT ⟨*wait* for sunrise⟩ ⟨*wait* your turn⟩ ⟨*wait* for or-

ders) **2** : POSTPONE, DELAY ⟨*wait* dinner for a guest⟩ **3** : to attend as a waiter or waitress : SERVE ⟨*wait* tables⟩ ⟨*wait* at a luncheon⟩ [Old North French *waitier* "to watch", of Germanic origin] — **wait on** *or* **wait upon** **1 a** : to attend as a servant **b** : to supply the wants of : SERVE ⟨*wait on* a customer⟩ **2** : to make a formal call on — **wait up** : to delay going to bed

²wait *n* **1 a** : a hidden or concealed position — used chiefly in the expression *lie in wait* **b** : a state or attitude of watchfulness and expectancy **2** : an act or period of waiting

wait·er \'wāt-ər\ *n* **1** : one that waits upon another; *esp* : a man who waits on table (as in a restaurant) **2** : a tray on which something is carried

waiting game *n* : a strategy in which one or more participants withhold action temporarily in the hope of having a favorable opportunity for more effective action later

waiting list *n* : a list or roster of those waiting (as for election to a club or appointment to a position)

waiting room *n* : a room (as in a doctor's office) for the use of persons waiting

wait·ress \'wā-trəs\ *n* : a girl or woman who waits on table

waive \'wāv\ *vt* **1** : to give up claim to ⟨*waive* the right to answer⟩ **2** : to put off the consideration of : POSTPONE [Old North French *weyver*, from *waif* "lost, unclaimed"]

waiv·er \'wā-vər\ *n* **1** : the act of waiving a right, claim, or privilege **2** : a document containing the declaration of a waiver [Anglo-French *weyver*, from Old North French *weyver* "to waive"]

¹wake \'wāk\ *vb* **waked** \'wākt\ *or* **woke** \'wōk\; **waked** *or* **wo·ken** \'wō-kən\; **wak·ing** **1** : to be or remain awake **2** : AROUSE 1 — often used with up [Old English *wacan* "to awake" and *wacian* "to be awake"] — **wak·er** *n*

²wake *n* : a watch held over the body of a dead person prior to burial and sometimes accompanied by festivity

³wake *n* : the track left by a moving body (as a ship) in the water; *also* : a track or path left [of Scandinavian origin] — **in the wake of** **1** : close behind and on the same course **2** : as a result of

wake·ful \'wāk-fəl\ *adj* : not sleeping or able to sleep — **wake·ful·ly** \-fə-lē\ *adv* — **wake·ful·ness** *n*

wak·en \'wā-kən\ *vb* **wak·ened; wak·en·ing** \'wāk-ning, -ə-ning\ : AROUSE 1 — often used with *up* — **wak·en·er** \'wāk-nər, -ə-nər\ *n*

wake–rob·in \'wā-,kräb-ən\ *n* : TRILLIUM

Wal·den·ses \wol-'den-,sēz\ *n pl* : a Christian sect arising in southern France in the 12th century, adopting Calvinist doctrines in the 16th century, and later living chiefly in Piedmont [Medieval Latin, from Peter *Waldo*, 12th century French heretic] — **Wal·den·sian** \-'den-chən\ *adj or n*

Wal·dorf salad \,wol-'dorf-\ *n* : a salad made typically of diced apples, celery, and nuts and dressed with mayonnaise [*Waldorf*–Astoria Hotel, New York City]

wale \'wāl\ *n* **1 a** : a streak or ridge made on the skin usually by a rod or whip **b** : a narrow raised surface or ridge (as on corduroy) **2** : one of the extra–strong strakes on the sides of a wooden ship just above the waterline [Old English *walu*]

¹walk \'wok\ *vb* **1 a** : to move or cause to move along on foot usually at a natural unhurried gait ⟨*walk* to town⟩ ⟨*walk* a horse up a hill⟩ **b** : to pass over, through, or along by walking ⟨*walk* the streets⟩ **c** : to perform or affect by walking ⟨*walk* guard⟩ **2** : to follow a course of action or way of life : BEHAVE **3** : to take or cause to take first base with a base on balls **4** : to move or cause to move in a manner suggestive of walking ⟨*walked* my fingers across the table⟩ [Old English *wealcan* "to roll, toss"] — **walk away from** **1** : to outrun or get the better of without difficulty **2** : to

wagon 1

\ə\ abut		\ng\ sing	
\ər\ further		\ō\ bone	
\a\ mat		\o\ saw	
\ā\ take		\oi\ coin	
\ä\ cot, cart		\th\ thin	
\au̇\ out		\th\ this	
\ch\ chin		\ü\ food	
\e\ pet		\u̇\ foot	
\ē\ easy		\y\ yet	
\g\ go		\yü\ few	
\i\ tip		\yu̇\ cure	
\ī\ life		\zh\ vision	
\j\ job			

survive (an accident) with little or no injury — **walk
off with 1** : STEAL 2 **2** : to win or gain especially by
outdoing one's competitors without difficulty — **walk
over** : to disregard the wishes or feelings of

²**walk** *n* **1** : a going on foot ⟨go for a *walk*⟩ **2** : a place,
path, or course for walking **3** : distance to be walked
4 a : manner of living : CONDUCT, BEHAVIOR **b** : social
or economic status ⟨various *walks* of life⟩ **5 a** : manner
of walking **b** : a gait of a four-footed animal in which
there are always at least two feet on the ground; *esp* : a
slow 4-beat gait of a horse in which the feet strike the
ground in the sequence left hind, left fore, right hind,
right fore **6** : BASE ON BALLS

walk·er \ˈwȯ-kər\ *n* **1** : one that walks **2** : something
used in walking; *esp* : a framework designed to support one who walks with difficulty

walk·ie-talk·ie \ˌwȯ-kē-ˈtȯ-kē\ *n* : a small portable radio set for receiving and sending messages

walk-in \ˈwȯ-ˌkin\ *adj* : large enough to be walked into
⟨a *walk-in* refrigerator⟩

walking fern *n* : any of a genus of ferns that form new
plants at the tips of the long fronds

walking papers *n pl* : DISMISSAL, DISCHARGE

walking stick *n* **1** : a stick used in walking **2** *usually*
walk·ing·stick : STICK INSECT

Walk·man \ˈwȯk-mən, -ˌman\ *trademark* — used for a
small portable radio or cassette player listened to by
means of headphones or earphones

walk-on \ˈwȯ-ˌkȯn, -ˌkän\ *n* : a small usually nonspeaking part in a dramatic production

walk·out \ˈwȯ-ˌkaùt\ *n* **1** : STRIKE 2a **2** : the leaving of a
meeting or organization as an expression of disapprov-
al

walk out \wȯ-ˈkaùt, ˈwȯ-\ *vi* **1** : to go on strike **2** : to
leave suddenly often as an expression of disapproval
— **walk out on** : ABANDON 3, DESERT

walk·over \ˈwȯ-ˌkō-vər\ *n* : a one-sided contest or an
easy or uncontested victory

walk-up \ˈwȯ-ˌkəp\ *n* : a building or apartment house
without an elevator — **walk-up** \ˌwȯ-ˌkəp\ *adj*

walk·way \ˈwȯ-ˌkwā\ *n* : a passage for walking : WALK

¹**wall** \ˈwȯl\ *n* **1** : a structure (as of brick or stone)
raised to some height and meant to enclose or shut off
a space; *esp* : a side of a room or building **2** : a material layer enclosing space ⟨the heart *wall*⟩ ⟨the *walls* of a
boiler⟩ **3** : something like a wall; *esp* : something that
acts as a barrier or defense ⟨a *wall* of reserve⟩ [Old English *weall*, from Latin *vallum* "rampart"] — **walled**
\ˈwȯld\ *adj* — **wall-like** \ˈwȯl-ˌlīk\ *adj*

²**wall** *vt* **1** : to provide, separate, or surround with or as
if with a wall ⟨*wall* in the garden⟩ **2** : to close (an
opening) with or as if with a wall ⟨*wall* up a door⟩

wal·la·by \ˈwäl-ə-bē\ *n, pl* **-bies** *also* **-by** : any of various small or medium-sized usually brightly colored
kangaroos [*wolabā*, native name in New South Wales,
Australia]

wall·board \ˈwȯl-ˌbōrd, -ˌbȯrd\ *n* : a structural material
(as of wood pulp, gypsum, or plastic) made in large
rigid sheets and used especially for sheathing interior
walls and ceilings

wal·let \ˈwäl-ət\ *n* **1** : a bag or sack for carrying things
on a journey **2 a** : BILLFOLD **b** : a pocketbook with
compartments (as for change and cards) [Middle English *walet*]

wall·eye \ˈwȯ-ˌlī\ *n* **1 a** : an eye with a whitish iris or an
opaque white cornea **b** : an eye that turns outward
showing more than a normal amount of white; *also* :
the condition of having such eyes **2** : a large vigorous
American freshwater food and sport fish that has
prominent eyes and is related to the perches but resembles the true pike — called also *walleyed pike*
[back-formation from *walleyed*, from Old Norse *vagl-
eygr*, from *vagl* "beam, roost" + *eygr* "eyed"] — **walleyed** \-ˈlīd\ *adj*

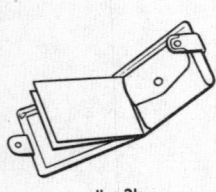

wall·flow·er \ˈwȯl-ˌflaù-ər, -ˌflaùr\ *n* **1** : any of several
Old World perennial plants of the mustard family;
esp : one widely grown for its showy fragrant flowers
2 : a person who from shyness or unpopularity remains
on the sidelines of a social activity (as a dance)

Wal·loon \wä-ˈlün\ *n* : a member of a chiefly Celtic
people of southern and southeastern Belgium and adjacent parts of France [Middle French *Wallon*, of Germanic origin] — **Walloon** *adj*

¹**wal·lop** \ˈwäl-əp\ *n* **1** : a powerful blow or impact
2 : the ability (as of a boxer) to hit hard [Old North
French *walop* "gallop", from *waloper* "to gallop"]

²**wallop** *vt* **1** : to beat soundly : TROUNCE **2** : to hit with
force : SOCK — **wal·lop·er** *n*

wal·lop·ing \ˈwäl-ə-ping\ *adj* **1** : very large **2** : exceptionally fine or impressive

¹**wal·low** \ˈwäl-ō\ *vi* **1** : to roll about in or as if in deep
mud ⟨elephants *wallowing* in the river⟩ **2 a** : to enjoy
or indulge oneself in something without restraint **b** :
to become abundantly supplied ⟨*wallow* in luxury⟩ **3** :
to become or remain helpless ⟨allowed to *wallow* in
ignorance⟩ [Old English *wealwian* "to roll"]

²**wallow** *n* **1** : an act or instance of wallowing **2** : a
muddy or dust-filled area used by animals for wallowing

wall·pa·per \ˈwȯl-ˌpā-pər\ *n* : decorative paper for the
walls of a room — **wallpaper** *vb*

wall plug *n* : an electric receptacle in a wall

Wall Street \ˈwȯl-\ *n* : the influential financial interests of the United States economy [*Wall Street,* New
York City, on which the New York Stock Exchange is
located]

wal·nut \ˈwȯl-ˌnət, -nət\ *n* **1 a** : an edible nut with a
furrowed usually rough shell; *also* : any of a genus of
trees related to the hickories that produce such nuts
b : the usually reddish to dark brown wood of a walnut
widely used for cabinetwork and veneers **c** : a hickory
nut or tree **2** : a moderate reddish brown [Old English
wealhhnutu, literally, "foreign nut", from *wealh*
"Welshman, foreigner" + *hnutu* "nut"] □ ORIGIN
Walnut trees have been cultivated in so many
countries for so many centuries that the early distribution and origin of the walnut cannot now be clearly
discerned. It would appear, however, that the walnut
was known to southern Europe for some time before it
was introduced into England. The walnut's Old English name, *wealhhnutu,* means literally "foreign
nut". It was apparently so called to distinguish the
walnut of southern Europe from the nut native to more northern countries, the hazelnut.

Wal·pur·gis Night \väl-ˈpùr-gəs-\ *n* : the eve of May
Day on which witches are held to ride to a satanic ren-
dezvous [German *Walpurgis* "Saint Walburga (died A.
D. 779, English saint whose feast day falls on May
Day)"]

wal·rus \ˈwȯl-rəs, ˈwäl-\ *n, pl* **walrus** *or* **wal·rus·es** : either of two large mammals of northern seas related to
the seals and hunted especially for the hide, the ivory
tusks of the males, and oil [Dutch, of Scandinavian ori-
gin]

¹**waltz** \ˈwȯls, ˈwȯlts\ *n* **1** : a round dance in ¾ time
with strong accent on the first beat **2** : music for or
suitable for waltzing [German *walzer*, from *walzen*
"to roll, dance"]

²**waltz** *vb* **1 a** : to dance a waltz **b** : to dance a waltz
with **2** : to advance easily or conspicuously — **waltz-
er** *n*

wam·pum \ˈwäm-pəm\ *n* **1** : beads of shells strung in
strands, belts, or sashes and used by North American
Indians as money and ornaments **2** *slang* : MONEY 1 [of
American Indian origin]

wan \ˈwän\ *adj* **1 a** : SICKLY, PALLID ⟨a *wan*
complexion⟩ **b** : lacking vitality : FEEBLE **2** : DIM 1,
FAINT **3** : LANGUID ⟨a *wan* smile⟩ [Old English, "dark,
livid"] — **wan·ly** *adv* — **wan·ness** \ˈwän-nəs\ *n*

wand \'wänd\ *n* **1** : a slender rod used by conjurers or magicians **2** : the rigid tube between nozzle and hose of a vacuum cleaner [Old Norse *vöndr* "slender stick"]

wan·der \'wän-dər\ *vb* **wan·dered; wan·der·ing** \-də-ring, -dring\ **1** : to move about aimlessly or without a fixed course or goal : RAMBLE **2 a** : to deviate (as from a course) : STRAY **b** : to go astray morally : ERR **c** : to lose normal mental contact (as in delirium or madness) [Old English *wandrian*] — **wander** *n* — **wan·der·er** \-dər-ər\ *n*

wandering Jew *n* : any of several mostly creeping plants of the spiderwort family [the *Wandering Jew*, legendary person condemned to wander the earth until Christ's 2d coming for having mocked Him on the day of the crucifixion]

wan·der·lust \'wän-dər-ləst\ *n* : strong longing to travel [German, from *wandern* "to wander" + *lust* "desire, pleasure"]

¹wane \'wān\ *vi* **1** : to grow smaller or less: as **a** : to diminish in phase or intensity — used chiefly of the moon **b** : to become less brilliant or powerful : DIM **2** : to fall gradually from power, prosperity, or influence : DECLINE [Old English *wanian*]

²wane *n* **1** : the act or process of waning **2** : a period or time of waning; *esp* : the period from full phase of the moon to the new moon

wan·gle \'wang-gəl\ *vb* **wan·gled; wan·gling** \-gə-ling, -gling\ **1 a** : to obtain by sly, roundabout, or underhand means **b** : to use trickery or devious means to achieve an end **2 a** : to adjust or manipulate for personal ends **b** : to make or get (one's way) by devious means : FINAGLE [perhaps alteration of *waggle*] — **wan·gler** \-gə-lər, -glər\ *n*

Wan·kel engine \,väng-kəl-, ,wang-\ *n* : an internal-combustion rotary engine that has a rounded triangular rotor functioning as a piston and rotating in a space in the engine and that has only two major moving parts [Felix *Wankel,* born 1902, German engineer]

¹want \'wönt also 'wänt, 'wənt\ *vb* **1** : to be without : LACK ⟨this coat is *wanting* a button⟩ **2** : to fall short by ⟨you *want* one year of being 13⟩ **3 a** : to feel or suffer the need of ⟨cannot get the rest I *want*⟩ **b** : to suffer from a need ⟨never *wanted* for anything⟩ **4** : NEED, REQUIRE ⟨our house *wants* painting⟩ **5** : to desire earnestly : WISH ⟨*wants* to go to college⟩ [Old Norse *vanta*] SYN see DESIRE

²want *n* **1 a** : a lack of a required or usual amount **b** : great need : DESTITUTION **2** : something wanted : NEED, DESIRE

want ad *n* : an advertisement stating that something (as an employee or a specified item) is wanted

¹want·ing *adj* **1** : not present or in evidence : ABSENT **2 a** : falling below standards or expectations **b** : lacking in ability or capacity : DEFICIENT

²wanting *prep* **1** : WITHOUT ⟨a book *wanting* a cover⟩ **2** : LESS, MINUS ⟨a month *wanting* two days⟩

¹wan·ton \'wönt-n, 'wänt-\ *adj* **1** : FROLICSOME ⟨*wanton* play⟩ ⟨a *wanton* breeze⟩ **2** : LEWD 1, BAWDY; *also* : SENSUAL **3 a** : MERCILESS, INHUMANE ⟨*wanton* cruelty⟩ **b** : having no just cause : MALICIOUS ⟨a *wanton* attack⟩ **4** : UNRESTRAINED 1, EXTRAVAGANT ⟨*wanton* luxury⟩ [Middle English, "unruly"] — **wan·ton·ly** *adv* — **wan·ton·ness** \-n-nəs\ *n*

²wanton *n* : a wanton individual; *esp* : a lascivious person

³wanton *vb* **1** : to be wanton or act wantonly **2** : to pass or waste wantonly

wa·pi·ti \'wäp-ət-ē\ *n, pl* **-ti** *or* **-tis** : ELK 1b [of American Indian origin]

¹war \'wör\ *n* **1 a** : a state or period of armed hostile conflict between states or nations **b** : the science of warfare **2 a** : a state of hostility, conflict, or antagonism **b** : a struggle between opposing forces or for a particular end ⟨a *war* against disease⟩ [Old North French *werre*, of Germanic origin]

²war *vi* **warred; war·ring 1** : to engage in warfare **2** : to be in conflict

¹war·ble \'wör-bəl\ *n* **1** : a melodious succession of low pleasing sounds **2** : a musical trill **3** : the action of warbling [Old North French *werble* "tune", of Germanic origin]

²warble *vb* **war·bled; war·bling** \-bə-ling, -bling\ **1** : to sing in a trilling manner or with many turns and variations **2** : to express by or as if by warbling

³warble *n* : a swelling under the hide (as of the back of cattle) caused by the maggot of a warble fly; *also* : such a maggot [perhaps of Scandinavian origin] — **war·bled** \-bəld\ *adj*

warble fly *n* : any of various two-winged flies whose larvae are warbles

war·bler \'wör-blər\ *n* **1** : one that warbles : SINGER **2 a** : any of numerous small Old World singing birds many of which are noted songsters and are closely related to the thrushes **b** : any of numerous small brightly colored American songbirds with a usually weak and unmusical song — called also *wood warbler*

war·bon·net \'wör-,bän-ət\ *n* : an American Indian ceremonial headdress with a feathered extension down the back

war chest *n* : a fund accumulated for a specific purpose, action, or campaign

war crime *n* : a crime (as genocide or maltreatment of prisoners) committed during or in connection with war — usually used in pl. — **war criminal** *n*

war cry *n* **1** : a cry used by a body of fighters in war **2** : a slogan used especially to rally people to a cause

¹ward \'wörd\ *n* **1** : a guarding or being under guard; *esp* : CUSTODY **2 a** : a division (as a cell or block) of a prison **b** : a division in a hospital **3 a** : an electoral or administrative division of a city **b** : a local Mormon congregation **4** : a projecting ridge of metal in a lock casing or keyhole permitting only the insertion of a key with a corresponding notch; *also* : a corresponding notch in a key **5 a** : a person (as a child) who is under the care of a court or a guardian **b** : a person, group, or territory under the protection or tutelage of a government [Old English *weard*] — **ward·ed** \-əd\ *adj*

²ward *vt* **1** : to keep watch over : GUARD **2** : to turn aside : DEFLECT — usually used with *off* ⟨*ward* off a cold⟩ [Old English *weardian*]

¹-ward \wərd\ *also* **-wards** \wərdz\ *adj suffix* **1** : that moves, tends, faces, or is directed toward ⟨wind*ward*⟩ **2** : that occurs or is situated in the direction of ⟨left*ward*⟩ [Old English *-weard*]

²-ward *or* **-wards** *adv suffix* **1** : in a (specified) spatial or temporal direction ⟨after*ward*⟩ ⟨up*wards*⟩ **2** : toward a (specified) point, position, or area ⟨coast*ward*⟩ ⟨heaven*wards*⟩

war dance *n* : a dance performed by primitive peoples as preparation for battle or in celebration of victory

war·den \'wörd-n\ *n* **1** : one having care or charge of something : GUARDIAN **2** : the governor of a town, district, or fortress **3 a** : an official charged with special duties or with the enforcement of specified laws ⟨game *wardens*⟩ ⟨air raid *wardens*⟩ **b** : an official in charge of a prison **4 a** : a lay officer of an Episcopal parish **b** : any of various British college officials [Old North French *wardein*, from *warder* "to guard", of Germanic origin] — **war·den·ship** \-,ship\ *n*

ward·er \'wörd-ər\ *n* : a person who keeps guard [Anglo-French *wardere*, from *warde* "act of guarding", of Germanic origin]

ward heeler *n* : a local worker for a political boss [from his following at the heels of a political boss]

ward·ress \'wör-drəs\ *n* : a woman supervising female prisoners (as in a jail)

\ə\ abut		\ng\ sing	
\ər\ further		\ō\ bone	
\a\ mat		\ó\ saw	
\ā\ take		\ói\ coin	
\ä\ cot, cart		\th\ thin	
\au̇\ out		\th\ this	
\ch\ chin		\ü\ food	
\e\ pet		\u̇\ foot	
\ē\ easy		\y\ yet	
\g\ go		\yü\ few	
\i\ tip		\yu̇\ cure	
\ī\ life		\zh\ vision	
\j\ job			

ward·robe \'wȯr-,drōb\ *n* **1** : a room, closet, or chest where clothes are kept **2** : a collection of wearing apparel (as of one person or for one activity) [Old North French *warderobe,* from *warder* "to guard" + *robe* "robe"]

ward·room \'wȯr-,drüm, -,drům\ *n* : the space in a warship allotted for living quarters to the officers excepting the captain; *esp* : the mess assigned to them

ward·ship \'wȯrd-,ship\ *n* **1** : care and protection of a ward **2** : the state of being under a guardian

¹ware \'waər, 'weər\ *adj* : AWARE, CONSCIOUS [Old English *wær* "careful, aware"]

²ware *vt* : to beware of — used chiefly as a command to hunters [Old English *warian*]

³ware *n* **1 a** : manufactured articles or products of art or craft : GOODS (*ware* whittled from wood) — often used in combination (tin*ware*) **b** : an article of merchandise (peddlers hawking their *wares*) **2** : items (as dishes) of fired clay : POTTERY [Old English *waru*]

¹ware·house \'waər-,haus, 'weər-\ *n* : a place for storing merchandise or commodities — **ware·house·man** \-mən\ *n*

²ware·house \-,haúz, -,haús\ *vt* : to deposit, store, or stock in or as if in a warehouse

ware·room \-,rüm, -,rům\ *n* : a room in which goods are exhibited for sale

war·fare \'wȯr-,faər, -,feər\ *n* **1 a** : military operations between enemies : WAR **b** : an activity undertaken by one country to weaken or destroy another (economic *warfare*) **2** : a struggle between competitors (industrial *warfare*)

war·fa·rin \'wȯr-fə-rən\ *n* : a crystalline compound that deters blood clotting and is used as a rodent poison and in medicine [*W*isconsin *A*lumni *R*esearch *F*oundation (its patentee) + coum*arin,* a chemical]

war footing *n* : the condition of being prepared to undertake or maintain war

war·head \'wȯr-,hed\ *n* : the section of a missile containing the explosive, chemical, or incendiary charge

war–horse \-,hȯrs\ *n* **1** : a horse used in war : CHARGER **2** : a veteran soldier or public person (as a politician)

war·less \'wȯr-ləs\ *adj* : free from war

war·like \-,līk\ *adj* **1** : fit for, disposed to, or fond of war (a *warlike* people) **2** : of, relating to, or useful in war (*warlike* supplies) **3** : befitting or characteristic of war or of soldiers SYN see MARTIAL

war·lock \-,läk\ *n* : a man practicing the black arts : SORCERER — compare WITCH [Old English *wærloga* "one that breaks faith, the Devil", from *wær* "faith" + *lēogan* "to lie"]

war·lord \-,lȯrd\ *n* **1** : a very high military leader **2** : a military commander exercising local civil power by force

¹warm \'wȯrm\ *adj* **1 a** : having or giving out heat to a moderate or adequate degree (*warm* food) (a *warm* stove) **b** : serving to retain heat (as of the body) (*warm* clothes) **c** : feeling or inducing sensations of heat (*warm* from exertion) (a *warm* walk) **2 a** : showing or marked by strong feeling : ARDENT (a *warm* supporter) (a *warm* temperament) **b** : marked by tense excitement or hot anger (a *warm* debate) **3** : marked by or tending toward injury, distress, or pain (gave the enemy a *warm* reception) **4** : newly made : FRESH (a *warm* scent) **5 a** : giving a pleasant impression of warmth or friendliness (a *warm* greeting) **b** : of a color or or tone that suggests warmth (a *warm* red) **6** : near to a goal or answer [Old English *wearm*] — **warm·ly** *adv* — **warm·ness** *n*

²warm *vb* **1** : to make or become warm **2 a** : to give a feeling of warmth or vitality to **b** : to experience feelings of affection or pleasure (*warmed* to the young guests) **3** : to reheat (cooked food) for eating **4 a** : to make or become ready by some preliminary action (*warm* up the car) **b** : to become ardent or interested (a speaker *warming* to the topic)

¹*warp* 1a: *light* warp, *dark* woof

³warm *adv* : WARMLY — usually used in combination (*warm*-clad)

warm–blood·ed \'wȯrm-'bləd-əd\ *adj* **1** : able to maintain a relatively high and constant body temperature that is essentially independent of the environment **2** : warm in feeling : ARDENT — **warm–blood·ed·ness** *n*

warmed–over \'wȯrm-'dō-vər\ *adj* **1** : heated again (*warmed-over* beans) **2** : not fresh or new : STALE

warm·er \'wȯr-mər\ *n* : one that warms; *esp* : a device for keeping something warm (a hand *warmer*)

warm front *n* : an advancing edge of a warm air mass

warm·heart·ed \'wȯrm-'härt-əd\ *adj* : marked by warmth of feeling — **warm·heart·ed·ness** *n*

warming pan *n* : a long-handled covered pan filled with live coals and formerly used to warm a bed

warm·ish \'wȯr-mish\ *adj* : somewhat warm

war·mon·ger \'wȯr-,məng-gər, -,mäng-\ *n* : one who urges or attempts to stir up war : JINGO — **war·mon·ger·ing** \-gə-ring, -gring\ *n*

warmth \'wȯrmth, 'wȯrmpth\ *n* : the quality or state of being warm: as **a** : emotional intensity (as of enthusiasm, anger, or love) **b** : a glowing effect produced by or as if by the use of warm colors

warm–up \'wȯr-,məp\ *n* : the act or an instance of warming up; *also* : a procedure (as a set of exercises) used in warming up

warm up \wȯr-'məp, 'wȯr-\ *vi* **1** : to engage in exercise or practice especially before entering a game or contest **2** : to approach a state of violence, conflict, or danger

warn \'wȯrn\ *vt* **1 a** : to give notice to beforehand especially of danger or evil **b** : ADMONISH 1 **c** : to call to one's attention : INFORM **2** : to order to go or stay away [Old English *warnian*] — **warn·er** *n* □ SYN CAUTION: WARN may range from simple notification of something to be watched for to threats of violence or reprisal; CAUTION stresses giving advice that suggests the need of taking care or watching out.

¹warn·ing \'wȯr-ning\ *n* **1** : the act of warning : the state of being warned **2** : something that warns or serves to warn

²warning *adj* : serving as an alarm, signal, summons, or admonition (a *warning* bell) — **warn·ing·ly** \-ning-lē\ *adv*

war of nerves : a conflict characterized by psychological tactics (as bluff, threats, and intimidation) designed primarily to create confusion, indecision, or breakdown of morale

¹warp \'wȯrp\ *n* **1 a** : a series of yarns extended lengthwise in a loom and crossed by the woof **b** : FOUNDATION 2, BASE **2 a** : a twist or curve that has developed in something originally flat or straight (a *warp* in a door panel) **b** : a mental twist or aberration [Old English *wearp*]

²warp *vb* **1 a** : to turn or twist out of shape; *also* : to become so turned or twisted **b** : to cause to judge, choose, or act wrongly : PERVERT **c** : DISTORT 1, FALSIFY **2** : to arrange (yarns) so as to form a warp **3** : to move (as a ship) by hauling on a line attached to a fixed object [Old English *weorpan* "to throw"] — **warp·er** *n*

war paint *n* **1** : paint put on parts of the body (as the face) by American Indians on going to war **2** : ceremonial dress; *also* : FINERY **3** : MAKEUP 2

war·path \'wȯr-,path, -,påth\ *n* **1** : the route taken by a party of American Indians going on a warlike expedition **2** : a hostile course of action or frame of mind

warp knit *n* : a knit fabric produced by a machine in which the knitting is done with the yarns running in a lengthwise direction — compare WEFT KNIT — **warp knitting** *n*

war·plane \-,plān\ *n* : a military airplane; *esp* : one armed for combat

¹war·rant \'wȯr-ənt, 'wär-\ *n* **1 a** : SANCTION 2, AUTHORIZATION **b** : GROUND 2, JUSTIFICATION **2** : evidence of authority or authorization: as **a** : a legal writ authorizing an officer to make an arrest, seizure, or search **b** : a certificate of appointment issued to a warrant officer [Old North French *warant* "protector, warrant", of Germanic origin]

²**warrant** *vt* **1 a** : to declare or maintain positively : be sure that **b** : to assure (a person) that what is said is true **2** : to guarantee (something) to be as it appears or as it is represented **3** : to guarantee security or immunity to : SECURE **4** : to give sanction to ⟨the law *warrants* this procedure⟩ **5 a** : to give proof of : ATTEST **b** : GUARANTEE 1 **6** : to serve as adequate reason for : JUSTIFY — **war·rant·able** \'wȯr-ənt-ə-bəl, 'wär-\ *adj* — **war·rant·able·ness** *n* — **war·rant·ably** \-blē\ *adv* — **war·ran·tor** \,wȯr-ən-'tȯr, 'wär-; 'wȯr-ənt-ər, 'wär-\ *also* **war·rant·er** \'wȯr-ənt-ər, 'wär-\ *n*

war·ran·tee \,wȯr-ən-'tē, ,wär-\ *n* : the person to whom a warranty is made

warrant officer *n* : an officer in the armed forces holding rank by virtue of a warrant and ranking below a commissioned officer and above a noncommissioned officer

war·ran·ty \'wȯr-ənt-ē, 'wär-\ *n, pl* **-ties** : an explicit or implied statement that a situation or thing is as it appears or is represented to be; *esp* : a usually written guarantee of a product's integrity and of the maker's responsiblity for the repair or replacement of defective parts [Old North French *warantie,* from *warantir* "to guarantee, warrant", from *warant* "warrant"]

war·ren \'wȯr-ən, 'wär-\ *n* **1** : a place for keeping small game (as hare or pheasant) **2** : an area where rabbits breed **3** : a crowded tenement or district [Old North French *warenne*]

war·rior \'wȯr-yər; 'wȯr-ē-ər, 'wär-ē-\ *n* : a person engaged or experienced in warfare [Old North French *werreieur,* from *werreier* "to make war", from *werre* "war"]

war·ship \'wȯr-,ship\ *n* : a government ship used for war purposes; *esp* : one armed for combat

wart \'wȯrt\ *n* **1** : an irregular growth on the skin often caused by a virus **2** : a protuberance (as on a plant) resembling a wart [Old English *wearte*] — **wart·ed** \'wȯrt-əd\ *adj* — **warty** \-ē\ *adj*

wart·hog \'wȯrt-,hȯg, -,häg\ *n* : any of a genus of African wild hogs with two pairs of rough warty protuberances on the face and large protruding tusks

war·time \'wȯr-,tīm\ *n* : a period of war

war whoop *n* : a war cry especially of American Indians

wary \'waər-ē, 'weər-\ *adj* **war·i·er; -est** : very cautious; *esp* : watchfully prudent in detecting and escaping danger [Old English *wær* "careful, aware, wary"] — **war·i·ly** \'war-ə-lē, 'wer-\ *adv* — **war·i·ness** \'war-ē-nəs, 'wer-\ *n*

was *past 1st & 3d sing of* BE [Old English, 1st and 3d singular past indicative of *wesan* "to be"]

¹**wash** \'wȯsh, 'wäsh\ *vb* **1** : to cleanse with or as if with water **2** : to wet thoroughly with liquid **3** : to flow along the border of ⟨waves *wash* the shore⟩ **4** : to pour or flow in a stream or current ⟨the river *washes* against its banks⟩ **5** : to move or carry by the action of water ⟨a passenger *washed* overboard⟩ **6** : to cover or daub lightly with a liquid (as whitewash or varnish) **7** : to run water over in order to separate valuable matter from refuse ⟨*wash* sand for gold⟩ **8** : to undergo laundering ⟨a shirt that *washes* well⟩ **9** : to stand a test for truthfulness ⟨that story won't *wash*⟩ **10** : to wear or be worn by water ⟨heavy rain *washed* away the road⟩ [Old English *wascan*] — **wash one's hands of** : to deny interest in, responsibility for, or further connection with

²**wash** *n* **1 a** : the act or process or an instance of washing or being washed **b** : articles to be or being washed **2** : the surging action of waves or its sound **3 a** : a piece of ground washed by the sea or river **b** : BOG, MARSH **c** : a shallow body of water or creek **d** *West* :

the dry bed of a stream — called also *dry wash* **4** : worthless especially liquid waste : REFUSE **5 a** : a sweep or splash especially of color made by or as if by a long stroke of a brush **b** : a thin coat of paint (as watercolor) **c** : a thin liquid used for coating a surface (as a wall) **6** : LOTION **7** : loose or eroded surface material of the earth (as rock debris) transported and deposited by running water **8 a** : BACKWASH 1 **b** : a disturbance in the air produced by the passage of an airfoil or propeller

³**wash** *adj* : WASHABLE

wash·able \'wȯsh-ə-bəl, 'wäsh-\ *adj* : capable of being washed without damage ⟨a *washable* silk⟩ — **wash·abil·i·ty** \,wȯsh-ə-'bil-ət-ē, ,wäsh-\ *n*

wash and wear *adj* : of, relating to, or being a fabric or garment that needs little or no ironing after washing

wash·ba·sin \'wȯsh-,bās-n, 'wäsh-\ *n* : WASHBOWL

wash·board \-,bȯrd, -,bȯrd\ *n* : a corrugated rectangular surface to scrub clothes on

wash·bowl \-,bōl\ *n* : a large bowl or sink for water especially to wash one's hands and face

wash·cloth \-,klȯth\ *n* : a cloth for washing one's face and body — called also *washrag*

wash drawing *n* : watercolor painting in or chiefly in washes

washed–out \'wȯsh-'taut, 'wäsh-\ *adj* **1** : faded in color **2** : depleted of vigor or animation

washed–up \-'təp\ *adj* **1** : left with no effective power, capacity, or opportunity for recovery **2** *usually* **washed up** : ready to quit especially from disgust : THROUGH

wash·er \'wȯsh-ər, 'wäsh-\ *n* **1** : one that washes; *esp* : WASHING MACHINE **2** : a ring (as of metal or rubber) used to make something fit tightly or to prevent rubbing

wash·er·man \-mən\ *n* : LAUNDRYMAN; *also* : a man operating any of various industrial washing machines

wash·er·wom·an \-,wum-ən\ *n* : LAUNDRESS; *esp* : one who takes in washing

wash·house \'wȯsh-,haus, 'wäsh-\ *n* : a building used or equipped for washing; *esp* : one for washing clothes

wash·ing \'wȯsh-ing, 'wäsh-\ *n* **1** : material obtained by washing **2** : a thin covering or coat ⟨a *washing* of silver⟩ **3** : articles washed or to be washed

washing machine *n* : a machine for washing; *esp* : one for washing clothes and household linen

washing soda *n* : SAL SODA

Wash·ing·ton pie \,wȯsh-ing-tən-, ,wäsh-\ *n* : cake layers put together with a jam or jelly filling [George *Washington*]

Washington's Birthday *n* **1** : February 22 formerly observed as a legal holiday in most of the United States **2** : the third Monday in February observed as a legal holiday in most of the United States — called also *Presidents' Day* [George *Washington*]

wash·out \'wȯsh-,aut, 'wäsh-\ *n* **1** : the washing out or away of earth especially in a roadbed by a freshet; *also* : a place where earth is washed away **2** : one that fails to measure up : FAILURE; *esp* : one who fails in a course of training or study

wash out \wȯsh-'aut, wäsh-, 'wȯsh-, 'wäsh-\ *vb* **1 a** : to cause to fade by laundering **b** : to deplete the strength or vitality of **c** : to eliminate as useless or unsatisfactory : REJECT **2** : to become depleted of color or vitality : FADE **3** : to fail to measure up (as to a standard)

wash·rag \'wȯsh-,rag, 'wäsh-\ *n* : WASHCLOTH

wash·room \-,rüm, -,rum\ *n* : a room equipped with washing and toilet facilities : LAVATORY

wash·stand \-,stand\ *n* **1** : a stand holding articles needed for washing one's face and hands **2** : a washbowl permanently set in place and attached to water pipes and drainpipes

wash·tub \-,təb\ *n* : a tub for washing (as clothes)

wash up *vt* : FINISH 1 ⟨the scandal *washed* them *up*⟩

warthog

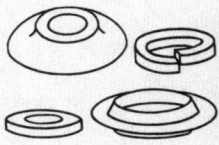

washer 2

\ə\ abut	\ng\ sing
\ər\ further	\ō\ bone
\a\ mat	\ȯ\ saw
\ā\ take	\ȯi\ coin
\ä\ cot, cart	\th\ thin
\au\ out	\t͟h\ this
\ch\ chin	\ü\ food
\e\ pet	\u\ foot
\ē\ easy	\y\ yet
\g\ go	\yü\ few
\i\ tip	\yu\ cure
\ī\ life	\zh\ vision
\j\ job	

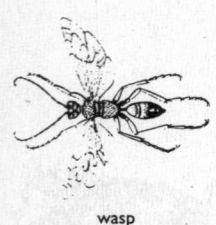

wasp

wash·wom·an \'wȯsh-ˌwu̇m-ən, 'wȧsh-\ *n* : WASHERWOMAN

washy \'wȯsh-ē, 'wȧsh-\ *adj* **wash·i·er; -est** **1** : WEAK, WATERY ⟨*washy* tea⟩ **2** : lacking in color : PALLID **3** : lacking in vigor, individuality, or definiteness

wasn't \'wəz-nt, 'wäz-\ : was not

wasp \'wäsp, 'wȯsp\ *n* : a winged insect related to the bees and ants that has a slender body with the abdomen attached by a narrow stalk and in females and workers a powerful sting [Old English *wæps, wæsp*]

WASP *or* **Wasp** \'wäsp, 'wȯsp\ *n* : an American of North European and especially English Protestant ancestry and background [*w*hite *A*nglo-*S*axon *P*rotestant]

wasp·ish \'wäs-pish, 'wȯs-\ *adj* **1** : SNAPPISH, IRRITABLE ⟨a *waspish* retort⟩ **2** : resembling a wasp in form; *esp* : slightly built — **wasp·ish·ly** *adv* — **wasp·ish·ness** *n*

wasp waist *n* : a very slender waist

¹was·sail \'wäs-əl *also* wä-'sāl\ *n* **1** : an early English toast to someone's health **2** : a liquor that is made of ale or wine, spices, and often baked apples and that is served in a large bowl usually at Christmas **3** : riotous drinking [Old Norse *ves heill* "be well"]

²wassail *vb* **1** : to indulge in wassail : CAROUSE **2** : to drink to the health of

was·sail·er \'wäs-ə-lər *also* wä-'sā-lər\ *n* **1** : one that carouses : REVELER **2** *archaic* : one who goes about singing carols

Was·ser·mann test \'wäs-ər-mən-, 'väs-\ *n* : a test of the blood for the detection of syphilis [August von *Wassermann*, died 1925, German bacteriologist]

wast \wəst, wäst, 'wäst\ *archaic past 2d sing of* BE

wast·age \'wā-stij\ *n* : loss by use, decay, erosion, or leakage or through wastefulness

¹waste \'wāst\ *n* **1 a** : a sparsely settled or barren region : DESERT **b** : uncultivated land **c** : a broad and empty expanse (as of water) **2** : the act or an instance of wasting : the state of being wasted **3** : gradual loss or decrease by use, wear, or decay **4 a** : damaged, defective, or superfluous material produced by a manufacturing process: as (1) : material rejected during a textile manufacturing process (2) : fluid (as steam) allowed to escape without being utilized **b** (1) : refuse (as garbage, sewage, or rubbish) that accumulates about habitations ⟨collection of city *wastes*⟩ (2) : material (as excrement) that is produced by a living body and is of no value to the organism that produces it [Old North French *wast*, from *wast*, adj., "desolate, waste", from Latin *vastus*]

²waste *vb* **1** : to lay waste usually by violence : DEVASTATE ⟨lands *wasted* by war⟩ **2** : to wear away or impair gradually : CONSUME ⟨fields *wasted* by erosion⟩ **3** : to spend or use carelessly : SQUANDER **4** : to lose or cause to lose weight, strength, or vitality — often used with *away* **5 a** : to become diminished in bulk or substance **b** : to become consumed SYN *see* RAVAGE

³waste *adj* **1** : being wild and uninhabited : DESOLATE **2** : being ruined or devastated **3** : discarded as worthless, defective, or useless

waste·bas·ket \'wāst-ˌbas-kət, 'wās-\ *n* : an open receptacle for trash

waste·ful \'wāst-fəl\ *adj* : given to or marked by waste — **waste·ful·ly** \-fə-lē\ *adv* — **waste·ful·ness** *n*

waste·land \'wāst-ˌland\ *n* : barren or uncultivated land

waste·pa·per \'wāst-'pā-pər, 'wās-\ *n* : paper discarded as used, superfluous, or not fit for use

waste pipe *n* : a pipe for carrying off waste fluid

waste product *n* : material resulting from a process (as of metabolism or manufacture) that is of no further use to the system producing it

wast·er \'wā-stər\ *n* : one that wastes or squanders

wast·rel \'wā-strəl\ *n* : WASTER, SPENDTHRIFT [derived from ²*waste*]

¹watch \'wäch, 'wȯch\ *vb* **1** : to stay awake intentionally (as at the bedside of a sick person) **2 a** : to be on the alert or on the lookout **b** : to keep guard ⟨*watch* outside the door⟩ **3** : to keep one's eyes on : keep in view ⟨*watch* a game⟩ **4** : to observe so as to prevent harm or danger ⟨*watch* a brush fire carefully⟩ **5** : to keep oneself informed about ⟨*watch* a competitor's career⟩ **6** : to be on the alert for the chance to make use of ⟨*watched* my opportunity⟩ [Old English *wæccan*] — **watch·er** *n* — **watch it** : to look out : be careful — **watch one's step** : to proceed with great care — **watch over** : to have charge of

²watch *n* **1 a** : the act of keeping awake to guard, protect, or attend **b** : a state of alert and continuous attention **c** : close observation : SURVEILLANCE **2** : one of the indeterminate wakeful intervals marking the passage of night — usually used in pl. **3** : one that watches : LOOKOUT **4 a** : a body of sentinels making up a guard **b** : a watchman or body of watchmen formerly assigned to patrol the streets **5 a** : a portion of time during which a part of a ship's company is on duty **b** : the part of a ship's company on duty during a particular watch **c** : a period of duty : SHIFT **6** : a portable timepiece designed to be worn (as on the wrist) or carried in the pocket

watch·band \-ˌband\ *n* : the bracelet or strap of a wristwatch

watch·case \-ˌkās\ *n* : the outside covering of a watch

watch·dog \-ˌdȯg\ *n* **1** : a dog kept to guard property **2** : a watchful guardian

watch·ful \-fəl\ *adj* : steadily attentive and alert especially to danger — **watch·ful·ly** \-fə-lē\ *adv* — **watchful·ness** *n* □ SYN WATCHFUL, VIGILANT, ALERT mean being on the lookout especially for opportunity or danger. WATCHFUL is the general and least explicit term for this; VIGILANT suggests maintaining a keen, unremitting watchfulness; ALERT stresses readiness or promptness in meeting danger or seizing opportunity.

watch glass *n* **1** : a glass that is usually convex outwardly and used for covering a watch dial **2** : a small circular glass dish used especially in laboratory work

watch·mak·er \'wäch-ˌmā-kər\ *n* : one that makes or repairs watches or clocks — **watch·mak·ing** \-king\ *n*

watch·man \-mən\ *n* : a person who keeps watch : GUARD

watch night *n* : a devotional service lasting until after midnight especially on New Year's Eve

watch out *vi* : to be vigilant — often used with *for*

watch·tow·er \'wäch-ˌtau̇-ər, -ˌtau̇r\ *n* : a tower for a lookout

watch·word \-ˌwərd\ *n* **1** : a secret word used as a signal or sign of recognition **2** : a motto used as a slogan or rallying cry

¹wa·ter \'wȯt-ər, 'wät-\ *n* **1 a** : the liquid that descends from the clouds as rain, forms streams, lakes, and seas, and is a major constituent of all living matter and that is an odorless, tasteless, very slightly compressible oxide of hydrogen H_2O **b** : a natural mineral water — usually used in pl. **2** *pl* : a band of seawater bordering on and under the control of a country ⟨sailing Canadian *waters*⟩ **3** : travel or transportation on water ⟨came by *water*⟩ **4** : the level of water at a particular state of the tide : TIDE **5** : liquid containing or resembling water: as **a** : a pharmaceutical or cosmetic preparation made with water **b** : a watery fluid (as tears, urine, or sap) formed or circulating in a living body **6** : the transparency and luster of a precious stone and especially a diamond ⟨a perfectly clear diamond of the first *water*⟩ [Old English *wætter*] — **above water** : out of difficulty — **in deep water** : in serious difficulties

²water *vb* **1** : to moisten or soak with water **2 a** : to supply with water ⟨*water* horses⟩ **b** : to get or take water **3** : to treat with or as if with water; *esp* : to impart a lustrous appearance and wavy pattern to (cloth) by calendering ⟨*watered* silk⟩ **4 a** : to dilute by or as if by adding water **b** : to increase the total stated value of (stock) without a corresponding addition to capital **5** : to form or secrete water or watery matter (as tears or saliva)

water ballet *n* : a synchronized sequence of movements performed by a group of swimmers

water bed *n* : a bed whose mattress is a plastic bag filled with water

water beetle *n* : any of numerous oval flattened aquatic beetles that swim by means of their fringed hind legs which act together as oars

water bird *n* : a swimming or wading bird — compare WATERFOWL

water blister *n* : a blister with a clear watery content

water bloom *n* : an accumulation of algae and especially of blue-green algae at or near the surface of a body of water; *also* : an alga causing this

water boatman *n* : any of various aquatic bugs with one pair of legs modified into paddles

wa·ter·borne \'wȯt-ər-ˌbȯrn, 'wät-, -ˌbȯrn\ *adj* : supported or carried by water

water boy *n* : one who keeps a group (as of laborers) supplied with drinking water

wa·ter·buck \'wȯt-ər-ˌbək, 'wät-\ *n, pl* **waterbuck** *or* **waterbucks** : any of various Old World antelopes that commonly frequent streams or wetlands

water buffalo *n* : an often domesticated Asian buffalo somewhat resembling a large ox

water chestnut *n* : a whitish crunchy vegetable used especially in Chinese cooking that is the tuber of a sedge; *also* : the tuber or the sedge itself

water clock *n* : an instrument designed to measure time by the fall or flow of water

water closet *n* **1** : a compartment or room for defecation and urination into a toilet bowl : BATHROOM **2** : a toilet bowl along with its accessories

wa·ter·col·or \'wȯt-ər-ˌkəl-ər, 'wät-\ *n* **1** : a paint whose liquid part is water **2** : the art of painting with watercolor **3** : a picture or design painted with watercolor — **wa·ter·col·or·ist** \-ˌkəl-ə-rəst\ *n*

wa·ter·cool \ˌwȯt-ər-ˈkül, ˌwät-\ *vt* : to cool by means of water and especially circulating water (as in a water jacket)

wa·ter·course \'wȯt-ər-ˌkȯrs, 'wät-, -ˌkȯrs\ *n* **1** : a bed over which or channel through which water flows **2** : a stream of water (as a river, brook, or underground stream)

wa·ter·craft \-ˌkraft\ *n* **1** : skill in water activities (as managing boats) **2** : craft for water transport

wa·ter·cress \-ˌkres\ *n* : any of several water-loving cresses; *esp* : a perennial cress found chiefly in springs or running water and used in salads or as a potherb

water dog *n* : a large salamander; *esp* : MUD PUPPY

wa·ter·er \'wȯt-ər-ər, 'wät-\ *n* : one that waters

wa·ter·fall \'wȯt-ər-ˌfȯl, 'wät-\ *n* : a perpendicular or very steep descent of the water of a stream

water flea *n* : any of various small active dark or brightly colored freshwater crustaceans (as a cyclops)

wa·ter·fowl \'wȯt-ər-ˌfau̇l, 'wät-\ *n* **1** : a bird that frequents water; *esp* : a swimming bird **2 waterfowl** *pl* : swimming game birds as distinguished from upland game birds and shorebirds

wa·ter·front \-ˌfrənt\ *n* : land or a section of an urban area bordering on a body of water

water gap *n* : a pass in a mountain ridge through which a stream runs

water gas *n* : a poisonous flammable gaseous mixture that consists chiefly of carbon monoxide and hydrogen, is usually made by blowing air and then steam over red-hot coke or coal, and is used as a fuel

water gate *n* **1** : a gate (as of a building) giving access to a body of water : FLOODGATE 1

water glass *n* **1** : a glass vessel (as a drinking glass) for holding water **2** : an instrument consisting of an open box or tube with a glass bottom used for examining objects in or under water **3** : a water-soluble substance that consists usually of sodium silicate in the form of a glassy mass, a stony powder, or dissolved in water as a syrupy liquid and is used as a protective coating and in preserving eggs

water hemlock *n* : any of a genus of poisonous plants of the carrot family; *esp* : a tall Eurasian perennial herb

water hole *n* **1** : a natural hole or hollow containing water **2** : a hole in a surface of ice

water hyacinth *n* : a showy South American floating aquatic plant that often clogs waterways in the southern United States

water ice *n* : a frozen dessert of water, sugar, and flavoring

watering can *n* : a vessel usually with a perforated spout used to sprinkle water especially on plants

watering place *n* **1** : a place where water may be obtained; *esp* : one where animals and especially livestock come to drink **2** : a health or recreational resort featuring mineral springs or water activities

wa·ter·ish \'wȯt-ə-rish, 'wät-\ *adj* : somewhat watery — **wa·ter·ish·ness** *n*

water jacket *n* : an outer casing which holds water or through which water circulates for cooling something

water jump *n* : an obstacle (as in a steeplechase) consisting of a pool, stream, or ditch of water

wa·ter·less \'wȯt-ər-ləs, 'wät-\ *adj* **1** : lacking water : DRY **2** : not requiring water (as for cooling or cooking) — **wa·ter·less·ly** *adj* — **wa·ter·less·ness** *n*

water lily *n* : any of a family of aquatic plants with rounded floating leaves and usually showy flowers

wa·ter·line \'wȯt-ər-ˌlīn, 'wät-\ *n* : any of several lines that are marked upon the outside of a ship and correspond with the surface of the water when it is afloat on an even keel

wa·ter·logged \-ˌlȯgd, -ˌlägd\ *adj* : so filled or soaked with water as to be heavy or hard to manage ⟨a *water-logged* boat⟩ [*water* + *log* "to accumulate in the hold"]

wa·ter·loo \ˌwȯt-ər-ˈlü, ˌwät-\ *n* : a decisive defeat [*Waterloo*, Belgium, scene of Napoleon's defeat in 1815]

water main *n* : a pipe or conduit for conveying water (as from a reservoir)

¹wa·ter·mark \-ˌmärk\ *n* **1** : a mark that indicates a line to which water has risen **2** : a mark (as the maker's name or trademark) made in paper during manufacture and visible when the paper is held up to the light

²watermark *vt* : to mark (paper) with a watermark

wa·ter·mel·on \'wȯt-ər-ˌmel-ən, 'wät-\ *n* **1** : a large oblong or rounded fruit with a hard green or white rind often striped or variegated, a sweet watery pink, yellowish, or red pulp, and many seeds **2** : a widely grown African vine of the gourd family whose fruits are watermelons

water meter *n* : an instrument for recording the quantity of water passing through a particular outlet

water moccasin *n* : a venomous semiaquatic pit viper of the southern United States closely related to the copperhead

water mold *n* : an aquatic fungus

water nymph *n* : a minor female divinity (as a naiad) associated with a body of water

water oak *n* : any of several American oaks that thrive in wet soil

water of crystallization : water of hydration present in many crystallized substances

water of hydration : water chemically combined with a substance to form a hydrate that can be expelled (as by heating) without essentially altering the composition of the substance

water ouzel *n* : any of several birds related to the thrushes that dive into swift mountain streams and walk on the bottom in search of food — called also *dipper*

water buffalo

water lily

water pipe *n* **1** : a pipe for conveying water **2** : a tobacco-smoking device so arranged that the smoke is drawn through water

water pistol *n* : a toy pistol designed to throw a jet of liquid — called also *squirt gun, water gun*

water plantain *n* : any of a genus of marsh or aquatic herbs with acrid sap and 3-petaled flowers

water polo *n* : a goal game played in water by teams of swimmers using a ball resembling a soccer ball

wa·ter·pow·er \'wȯt-ər-ˌpau̇-ər, 'wät-, -ˌpau̇r\ *n* : the power of moving water used to run machinery (as for generating electricity)

¹wa·ter·proof \ˌwȯt-ər-'prüf, ˌwät-\ *adj* : not letting water through; *esp* : covered or treated with a material (as a solution of rubber) to prevent penetration by water — **wa·ter·proof·ness** *n*

²wa·ter·proof \'wȯt-ər-ˌ, 'wät-\ *n* **1** : a waterproof fabric **2** *chiefly British* : RAINCOAT

³wa·ter·proof \ˌwȯt-ər-', ˌwät-\ *vt* : to make waterproof — **wa·ter·proof·er** *n*

wa·ter·proof·ing \-'prü-fing\ *n* **1 a** : the act or process of making something waterproof **b** : the condition of being made waterproof **2** : something (as a coating) capable of imparting waterproofness

water rat *n* **1** : a rodent that frequents water **2** : a waterfront loafer or petty thief

wa·ter–re·pel·lent \ˌwȯt-ər-ri-'pel-ənt, ˌwȯt-ə-ri-, ˌwät-\ *adj* : treated with a finish that is resistant to penetration by water but not waterproof

wa·ter–re·sis·tant \-ri-'zis-tənt\ *adj* : WATER-REPELLENT

water scorpion *n* : any of various large aquatic bugs with the end of the abdomen prolonged by a long breathing tube

wa·ter·shed \'wȯt-ər-ˌshed, 'wät-\ *n* **1** : a dividing ridge (as a mountain range) separating one drainage area from others **2** : the whole area that drains into a particular river or lake **3** : a crucial or dividing point, line, or factor

wa·ter·side \-ˌsīd\ *n* : the land bordering a body of water

water–ski *vi* : to ski on water while towed by a speedboat

water ski *n* : a ski used on water

water·ski·ing \'wȯt-ər-ˌskē-ing, 'wät-\ *n* : the sport of planing on water skis when towed by a motorboat

water snake *n* : any of numerous snakes frequenting or inhabiting fresh waters and feeding largely on aquatic animals

wa·ter–soak \'wȯt-ər-ˌsōk, 'wät-\ *vt* : to soak in water

water spaniel *n* : a rather large spaniel with a heavy curly coat used especially for retrieving waterfowl

wa·ter·spout \'wȯt-ər-ˌspau̇t, 'wät-\ *n* **1** : a pipe for carrying off water from a roof **2** : a tornado occurring over a body of water

water sprite *n* : a sprite inhabiting or haunting water

water strider *n* : any of various long-legged bugs that move about on the surface of the water

water table *n* : the upper limit of the ground wholly saturated with water

wa·ter·tight \ˌwȯt-ər-'tīt, ˌwät-\ *adj* **1** : of such tight construction or fit as to be waterproof **2** : leaving no possibility of misunderstanding or evasion — **wa·ter·tight·ness** *n*

water tower *n* **1** : a tower or standpipe serving as a reservoir to deliver water **2** : a fire apparatus having a vertical pipe that can be extended to various heights and supplied with water under high pressure

water vapor *n* : the vapor of water especially when below the boiling temperature and in diffused form (as in the atmosphere)

water–vascular system *n* : a system of vessels in echinoderms containing a circulating watery fluid that is used for the movement of tentacles and tube feet and may also function in excretion and respiration

¹wattle 2

water wave *n* : a method or style of setting hair by dampening with water and forming into waves — **wa·ter–waved** \'wȯt-ər-ˌwāvd, 'wät-\ *adj*

wa·ter·way \'wȯt-ər-ˌwā, 'wät-\ *n* : a channel or a body of water by which ships can travel

wa·ter·weed \-ˌwēd\ *n* : a weedy aquatic plant usually with inconspicuous flowers — compare WATER LILY

wa·ter·wheel \-ˌhwēl, -ˌwēl\ *n* : a wheel made to turn by a flow of water against it

water wings *n pl* : an air-filled device to give support to a person learning to swim

wa·ter·works \'wȯt-ər-ˌwərks, 'wät-\ *n pl* : the system of reservoirs, channels, mains, and pumping and purifying equipment by which a water supply is obtained and distributed (as to a city)

wa·ter·worn \-ˌwōrn, -ˌwȯrn\ *adj* : worn, smoothed, or polished by the action of water

wa·tery \'wȯt-ə-rē, 'wät-\ *adj* **1** : of or having to do with water ⟨a *watery* grave⟩ **2** : containing, full of, or giving out water ⟨*watery* clouds⟩ **3** : similar to water : THIN, WEAK ⟨*watery* tea⟩ **4** : being soft and soggy ⟨*watery* turnips⟩ — **wa·ter·i·ness** *n*

Wat·son–Crick model \ˌwät-sən-'krik-\ *n* : a model of DNA structure in which the molecule is a double-stranded helix cross-linked by pairs of purine and pyrimidine bases joined by hydrogen bonds with adenine paired with thymine and cytosine paired with guanine [J. D. *Watson*, born 1928, American biologist and F. H. C. *Crick*, born 1916, English biologist]

watt \'wät\ *n* : a unit of power equal to the work done at the rate of one joule per second [James *Watt*, died 1819, Scottish engineer]

watt·age \-ij\ *n* : amount of power expressed in watts

watt–hour \'wät-'au̇r\ *n* : a unit of work or energy equivalent to the power of one watt operating for one hour

¹wat·tle \'wät-l\ *n* **1 a** : a structure of poles interwoven with slender branches, withes, or reeds and used especially formerly in building **b** : material for such construction **c** *pl* : poles laid on a roof to support thatch **2** : a fleshy process hanging usually about the head or neck (as of a bird) **3** : ACACIA 2 [Old English *watel*] — **wat·tled** \-ld\ *adj*

²wattle *vt* **wat·tled; wat·tling** \'wät-ling, -l-ing\ **1** : to form or build of or with wattle **2 a** : to form into wattle : interlace to form wattle **b** : to unite or make solid by interweaving light flexible material

watt·me·ter \'wät-ˌmēt-ər\ *n* : an instrument for measuring electric power in watts

¹wave \'wāv\ *vb* **1** : to float, play, or shake in an air current : move or cause to move loosely to and fro : FLUTTER **2** : to motion with the hands or with something held in them in signal or salute **3 a** : to become moved or brandished to and fro ⟨a sword *waving* under my nose⟩ **b** : BRANDISH, FLOURISH ⟨*waved* a pistol menacingly⟩ **4** : to move before the wind with a wavelike motion ⟨fields of *waving* grain⟩ **5** : to follow or cause to follow a curving line or take a wavy form [Old English *wafian* "to wave with the hands"]

²wave *n* **1** : a moving swell or crest on the surface of water **2** : a wavelike formation or shape ⟨a *wave* in the hair⟩ **3** : a waving motion (as of the hand or a flag) **4** : FLOW, GUSH ⟨a *wave* of color swept the child's face⟩ **5** : a surge or rapid increase ⟨a *wave* of buying⟩ ⟨a heat *wave*⟩ **6** : a disturbance that transfers energy progressively from point to point and that may take the form of an elastic deformation or of a variation of pressure, electric or magnetic intensity, electric potential, or temperature ⟨a light *wave*⟩ — **wave·like** \-ˌlīk\ *adj*

Wave \'wāv\ *n* : a woman serving in the United States Navy [*W*omen *A*ccepted for *V*olunteer *E*mergency *S*ervice]

waved \'wāvd\ *adj* : having a wavelike form or outline: as **a** : marked by undulations ⟨the *waved* cutting edge of a bread knife) **b** : having wavy lines of color 〈*waved* cloth〉

wave form *n* : a usually graphic representation of the shape of a wave

wave·length \'wāv-ˌlength, -ˌlengkth\ *n* : the distance (as from crest to crest) in the line of advance of a wave from any one point to the next corresponding point

wave·less \-ləs\ *adj* : having no waves : CALM — **wave·less·ly** *adv*

wave·let \-lət\ *n* : a little wave : RIPPLE

wave mechanics *n* : a branch of physics dealing with the wave nature of elementary particles

¹wa·ver \'wā-vər\ *vi* **wa·vered; wa·ver·ing** \'wāv-ring, -ə-ring\ **1** : to swing back and forth uncertainly between choices : fluctuate in opinion, allegiance, or direction **2 a** : to weave or sway unsteadily to and fro : REEL, TOTTER **b** : QUIVER, FLICKER 〈*wavering* flames〉 **c** : FALTER **3 3** : to give an unsteady sound : QUAVER [Middle English *waveren*] SYN see HESITATE, SWAY — **wa·ver·er** \'wā-vər-ər\ *n* — **wa·ver·ing·ly** \'wāv-ring-lē, -ə-ring-\ *adv*

²waver *n* : an act of wavering, quivering, or fluttering

wavy \'wā-vē\ *adj* **wav·i·er; wav·i·est** : having waves : moving in waves 〈*wavy* hair〉 〈a *wavy* surface〉 — **wav·i·ly** \-və-lē\ *adv* — **wav·i·ness** \-vē-nəs\ *n*

¹wax \'waks\ *n* **1** : a yellowish plastic substance secreted by bees and used by them for constructing the honeycomb — called also *beeswax* **2** : any of various substances resembling beeswax in physical or chemical properties: as **a** : a plant or animal product that is harder and less greasy than a typical fat **b** : a solid mixture of higher hydrocarbons **c** : EARWAX **3** : something likened to wax as soft, impressionable, or readily molded [Old English *weax*] — **wax·like** \-ˌlīk\ *adj*

²wax *vt* : to treat or rub with wax

³wax *vi* **1** : to grow larger or greater: as **a** : to grow in volume or duration 〈a stream *waxing* with melting snows〉 **b** : to increase in apparent size and brightness 〈the moon *waxes* toward the full〉 **2** : to pass from one state to another : BECOME 〈the party *waxed* merry〉 [Old English *weaxan*]

⁴wax *n* **1** : INCREASE 1, GROWTH **2** : the period from the new moon to the full phase of the moon

wax bean *n* : a kidney bean with pods that are yellow when fit for use as snap beans

waxed paper *n* : paper treated with wax to make it impervious to water and grease

wax·en \'wak-sən\ *adj* **1** : made of wax **2** : resembling wax (as in pliability, pallor, or lustrous smoothness)

wax myrtle *n* : a shrub of eastern North America having small hairless hard berries with a thick coating of white wax used for candles; *also* : a related shrub of the west coast of the United States

wax·wing \'wak-ˌswing\ *n* : any of several American and Eurasian birds that are mostly brown with a showy crest and velvety plumage

wax·work \'wak-ˌswərk\ *n* **1** : an effigy in wax usually of a person **2** *pl* : an exhibition of wax effigies

waxy \'wak-sē\ *adj* **wax·i·er; -est 1** : covered with wax 〈a *waxy* surface〉 〈*waxy* berries〉 **2** : resembling wax : WAXEN 〈a *waxy* pallor〉 — **wax·i·ness** *n*

¹way \'wā\ *n* **1 a** : a track for travel or passage : PATH, ROAD, STREET **b** : an opening for passage (as through a crowd or a gate) 〈no *way* out〉 **2** : the course traveled from one place to another : ROUTE 〈knew the *way* home〉 **3 a** : a course of action 〈chose the easy *way*〉 **b** : opportunity, capability, or fact of doing as one pleases 〈determined to have our *way*〉 **c** : POSSIBILITY 〈no two *ways* about it〉 **4 a** : method in which something is done or happens 〈a new *way* of painting〉 〈the *way* the mind works〉 **b** : FEATURE, RESPECT 〈a good worker in many *ways*〉 **c** : the usual or characteristic state of affairs 〈as is the *way* with dreams〉 **d** : STATE, CONDITION 〈that's the *way* things are〉 〈was in a bad *way* with rheumatism〉 **5 a** : a particular or characteristic mode

or trick of behavior 〈it's just my *way*〉 **b** : a regular continued course (as of life or action) 〈championing the American *way*〉 〈people met in the *way* of business〉; *also* : a body of ethical or religious practice (as the Christian religion) **6 a** : the length of a course : DISTANCE 〈still a *way* from success〉 **b** : progress along a course 〈earning my *way* through school〉 **7** : something (as a locality) having direction as an attribute 〈come this *way*〉 〈out our *way*〉 〈stroking the fur the wrong *way*〉 **8 a** : room or chance to progress or advance 〈make *way* for the queen〉 **b** : place for something else 〈slums torn down to make *way* for parks〉 **9 a** : a guiding track that eases passage or movement **b** *pl* : an inclined support on which a ship is built and from which it is launched **10** : CATEGORY, KIND 〈get what you need in the *way* of supplies〉 **11** : motion or speed of a boat through the water 〈making slow *way* down the harbor〉 [Old English *weg*] — **by way of 1** : for the purpose of 〈*by way of* illustration〉 **2** : by the route through : VIA — **out of the way 1** : WRONG, IMPROPER **2** : SECLUDED 1, REMOTE — **under way 1** : in motion through the water **2** : in progress

²way *adj* : of, connected with, or constituting an intermediate point on a route 〈*way* station〉

³way *adv* : ¹AWAY 7, FAR 〈*way* back in the woods〉

way·bill \'wā-ˌbil\ *n* : a document prepared by the carrier of a shipment of goods and containing details of the shipment, route, and charges

way·far·er \-ˌfar-ər, -ˌfer-\ *n* : a traveler especially on foot — **way·far·ing** \-ˌfar-ing, -ˌfer-\ *adj*

way·lay \'wā-ˌlā\ *vt* **-laid** \-ˌlād\; **-lay·ing** : to wait for and attack or intercept

Way of the Cross : STATIONS OF THE CROSS

-ways \ˌwāz\ *adv suffix* : in (such) a way, course, direction, or manner 〈side*ways*〉 [Middle English, from *ways*, genitive of *way*]

ways and means *n pl* : methods and resources for accomplishing something and especially for raising money needed by a state; *also* : a legislative committee concerned with this function

way·side \'wā-ˌsīd\ *n* : the side of or land adjacent to a road or path — **wayside** *adj*

way·ward \'wā-wərd\ *adj* **1** : taking an irregular or improper way : DISOBEDIENT 〈*wayward* children〉 **2** : CONTRARY, PERVERSE 〈their *wayward* behavior〉 **3** : following no clear principle : UNPREDICTABLE [Middle English, from *awayward* "turned away"] — **way·ward·ly** *adv* — **way·ward·ness** *n*

way·worn \-ˌwōrn, -ˌwȯrn\ *adj* : wearied by traveling

we \wē, 'wē\ *pron, pl in construction* **1** : I and one or more others — used as pronoun of the 1st person plural; compare I, OUR, OURS, US **2** : I — used by sovereigns; used by writers to keep an impersonal character [Old English *wē*]

weak \'wēk\ *adj* **1** : lacking strength: as **a** : deficient in physical vigor : FEEBLE 〈*weak* as a kitten〉 **b** : not able to sustain or resist much weight, pressure, or strain 〈a *weak* rope〉 **c** : deficient in vigor of mind or character; *also* : resulting from or indicative of such deficiency 〈a *weak* policy〉 **d** : DILUTE 〈*weak* tea〉 **2** : not factually grounded or logically presented 〈a *weak* argument〉 **3 a** : not able to function properly 〈*weak* eyes〉 **b** : lacking skill or proficiency; *also* : indicative of such a lack 〈math's my *weakest* subject〉 **c** : wanting in vigor of expression or effect **4 a** : not having or exerting authority 〈a *weak* government〉 **b** : INEFFECTIVE, IMPOTENT 〈*weak* measures to control crime〉 **5** : of, relating to, or constituting an English verb or verb conjugation that forms the past tense and past participle by adding the suffix *-ed* or *-d* or *-t* **6** : bearing the minimal degree of stress occurring in the language 〈a *weak* syllable〉 [Old Norse *veikr*] — **weak·ly** *adv*

weak·en \'wē-kən\ *vb* **weak·ened; weak·en·ing** \'wēk-ning, -ə-ning\ : to make or become weak or weaker

waxwing

\ə\ abut	\ng\ sing
\ər\ further	\ō\ bone
\a\ mat	\ȯ\ saw
\ā\ take	\ȯi\ coin
\ä\ cot, cart	\th\ thin
\au̇\ out	\th\ this
\ch\ chin	\ü\ food
\e\ pet	\u̇\ foot
\ē\ easy	\y\ yet
\g\ go	\yü\ few
\i\ tip	\yu̇\ cure
\ī\ life	\zh\ vision
\j\ job	

weak·fish \'wēk-ˌfish\ *n* : any of several marine food fishes related to the perches; *esp* : a common sport and market fish of the eastern coast of the United States [Dutch *weekvis,* from *week* "soft" + *vis* "fish"; from its tender flesh]

weak force *n* : a force experienced by elementary particles that causes some forms of radioactivity and also causes some types of particles to break down into other particles

weak·heart·ed \-'härt-əd\ *adj* : lacking courage : FAINT-HEARTED

weak–kneed \'wēk-'nēd\ *adj* : lacking willpower or determination : IRRESOLUTE

weak·ling \'wē-kling\ *n* : one that is weak in body or character — **weakling** *adj*

weak·ly \'wē-klē\ *adj* **weak·li·er; -est** : FEEBLE 1, WEAK — **weak·li·ness** *n*

weak–mind·ed \'wēk-'mīn-dəd\ *adj* **1** : lacking in judgment or good sense : FOOLISH **2** : FEEBLE-MINDED — **weak–mind·ed·ness** *n*

weak·ness \'wēk-nəs\ *n* **1** : the quality or state of being weak; *also* : an instance or period of being weak **2** : DEFECT, FAULT **3** : an object of special desire or fondness

¹**weal** \'wēl\ *n* : WELL-BEING, PROSPERITY [Middle English *wele,* from Old English *wela*]

²**weal** *n* : WELT 2a [alteration of *wale*]

weald \'wēld\ *n* **1** : a heavily wooded area : FOREST **2** : a wild or uncultivated usually upland region [the *Weald,* wooded district in southeastern England]

wealth \'welth\ *n* **1** : abundance of possessions or resources : AFFLUENCE **2** : abundant supply : PROFUSION ⟨a *wealth* of detail⟩ **3 a** : all property that has a money or an exchange value **b** : all material objects that have economic utility; *esp* : those in existence at any one time [Middle English *welthe,* from *wele* "weal"]

wealthy \'wel-thē\ *adj* **wealth·i·er; -est** **1** : having wealth : AFFLUENT **2** : characterized by abundance — **wealth·i·ly** \-thə-lē\ *adv* — **wealth·i·ness** \-thē-nəs\ *n*

wean \'wēn\ *vt* **1** : to accustom (as a child) to take food otherwise than by nursing **2** : to turn (one) away from something long desired or followed ⟨*wean* a child from a bad habit⟩ [Old English *wenian* "to accustom, wean"] — **wean·er** *n*

wean·ling \-ling\ *n* : one newly weaned — **weanling** *adj*

weap·on \'wep-ən\ *n* **1** : something (as a gun, knife, or club) used to injure, defeat, or destroy **2** : a means by which one contends against another ⟨propaganda is a *weapon* of war⟩ [Old English *wǣpen*]

weap·on·less \-ləs\ *adj* : lacking weapons : UNARMED

weap·on·ry \-rē\ *n* **1** : the science of designing and making weapons **2** : aggregate of weapons

¹**wear** \'waər, 'weər\ *vb* **wore** \'wōr, 'wȯr\; **worn** \'wōrn, 'wȯrn\; **wear·ing** **1 a** : to bear on the person or use habitually for clothing or adornment ⟨*wore* a jacket⟩ **b** : to carry on the person ⟨*wear* a watch⟩ **2** : to have or show an appearance of ⟨*wore* a happy smile⟩ **3 a** : to impair, diminish, or decay by use or attrition ⟨the dress finally *wore* to bits⟩ ⟨letters on the stone *worn* away by weathering⟩ **b** : to produce gradually by attrition ⟨*wear* a hole in the rug⟩ **c** : to exhaust or lessen the strength of : WEARY, FATIGUE ⟨*worn* by care and toil⟩ **4** : to stand up under use or the passage of time ⟨a coat that has *worn* well⟩ **5** : to lessen or fail with the passage of time ⟨nagging *wore* my patience away⟩ ⟨the day *wore* on⟩ **6** : to go or cause to go about by turning the stern to the wind [Old English *werian*] — **wear·able** \'war-ə-bəl, 'wer-\ *adj* — **wear·er** \-ər\ *n* — **wear on** : IRRITATE 1, FRAY

²**wear** *n* **1** : the act of wearing : the state of being worn : USE ⟨clothes for everyday *wear*⟩ **2** : clothing or an article of clothing usually of a particular kind or for a special occasion or use ⟨casual *wear*⟩ **3** : wearing

weathercock 1

quality : durability under use **4** : the result of wearing or use : diminution or impairment due to use ⟨*wear*-resistant surface⟩

wear and tear *n* : the loss or injury to which something is subjected by or in the course of use; *esp* : normal depreciation

wear down *vt* : to weary and overcome by persistent effort or pressure

wea·ri·less \'wir-ē-ləs\ *adj* : not subject to fatigue — **wea·ri·less·ly** *adv*

wear·ing \'waər-ing, 'weər-\ *adj* : subjecting to or inflicting wear; *esp* : that fatigues ⟨a *wearing* journey⟩ — **wear·ing·ly** \-ing-lē\ *adv*

wea·ri·some \'wir-ē-səm\ *adj* : causing weariness : TIRESOME — **wea·ri·some·ly** *adv* — **wea·ri·some·ness** *n*

wear off *vt* : to diminish gradually (as in effect)

wear out *vb* **1** : to make or become useless by wear **2** : to weary especially to exhaustion

¹**wea·ry** \'wiər-ē\ *adj* **wea·ri·er; -est** **1** : worn out in strength, endurance, vigor, or freshness **2** : expressing or characteristic of weariness **3** : having one's patience, tolerance, or pleasure exhausted — used with *of* [Old English *wērig*] — **wea·ri·ly** \'wir-ə-lē\ *adv* — **wea·ri·ness** \'wir-ē-nəs\ *n*

²**weary** *vb* **wea·ried; wea·ry·ing** : to become or make weary

wea·sand \'wēz-nd\ *n* : THROAT 1, GULLET; *also* : WINDPIPE [Middle English *wesand*]

¹**wea·sel** \'wē-zəl\ *n, pl* **weasel** *or* **weasels** : any of various small slender active flesh-eating mammals related to the minks [Old English *weosule*]

²**weasel** *vi* **wea·seled; wea·sel·ing** \'wēz-ling, -ə-ling\ **1** : to speak evasively : EQUIVOCATE **2** : to escape from or evade a situation or obligation — often used with *out* [weasel word]

weasel word *n* : a word or statement that is deliberately vague, ambiguous, or misleading [from the weasel's reputed habit of sucking the contents from an egg while leaving the shell superficially intact]

¹**weath·er** \'weth-ər\ *n* **1** : state of the atmosphere with respect to heat or cold, wetness or dryness, calm or storm, clearness or cloudiness **2** : a particular and especially a disagreeable atmospheric state [Old English *weder*] — **under the weather** : somewhat ill or drunk

²**weather** *adj* : WINDWARD — compare LEE

³**weather** *vb* **weath·ered; weath·er·ing** \'weth-ring, -ə-ring\ **1** : to change by exposure to the weather ⟨shingles *weathered* to a silvery gray⟩ **2** : to bear up against and come safely through ⟨*weather* a storm⟩

weath·er·abil·i·ty \ˌweth-rə-'bil-ət-ē, -ə-rə-\ *n* : capability of withstanding weather ⟨*weatherability* of a plastic⟩

weath·er–beat·en \'weth-ər-ˌbēt-n\ *adj* **1** : worn or damaged by the weather **2** : toughened or colored by the weather

weath·er·board \-ˌbōrd, -ˌbȯrd\ *n* : CLAPBOARD, SIDING

weath·er·board·ing \-ˌbōrd-ing, -ˌbȯrd-\ *n* : SIDING 2

weath·er·bound \-ˌbau̇nd\ *adj* : restrained or forced to be inactive by bad weather

weather bureau *n* : a government organization that collects weather reports, formulates weather predictions and storm warnings, and compiles weather statistics

weath·er·cock \-ˌkäk\ *n* **1** : a vane often in the figure of a rooster mounted so as to turn freely with the wind and show the wind's direction **2** : one that changes readily or often especially according to public opinion

weath·er·glass \-ˌglas\ *n* : a simple instrument for showing changes in atmospheric pressure by the changing level of liquid in a spout connected with a closed reservoir

weath·er·ing *n* : alteration of exposed objects by action of the elements; *esp* : physical disintegration and chemical decomposition of earth materials at or near the earth's surface

weath·er·man \'weth-ər-ˌman\ *n* : one who reports and forecasts the weather : METEOROLOGIST

weather map *n* : a chart showing the principal meteorological features at a given hour over an extended region

weath·er·proof \ˌweth-ər-'prüf\ *adj* : able to withstand exposure to weather without damage or loss of function — **weatherproof** *vt* — **weath·er·proof·ness** *n*

weather station *n* : a station for taking, recording, and reporting meteorological observations

weather strip *n* : a strip of material used to make a seal where a door or window joins the sill or casing — **weather–strip** *vt*

weather vane *n* : VANE 1

weath·er·worn \-ˌwōrn, -ˌwȯrn\ *adj* : worn by exposure to the weather

¹**weave** \'wēv\ *vb* **wove** \'wōv\; **wo·ven** \'wō-vən\; **weav·ing** **1 a** : to form by interlacing strands of material; *esp* : to make (cloth) on a loom by interlacing warp and filling threads **b** : to interlace (as threads) into a fabric and especially cloth **2** : SPIN 2b **3 a** : to produce by elaborately combining elements ⟨*weave* a plot⟩ **b** : to unite in a coherent whole **c** : to introduce as an appropriate element : work in ⟨*wove* the episodes into a story⟩ ⟨*weave* a moral into a tale⟩ **4** : to direct or move in a winding or zigzag course especially to avoid obstacles ⟨*weaving* through traffic⟩ [Old English *wefan*] — **weav·er** *n*

²**weave** *n* : a pattern or method of weaving ⟨a coarse loose *weave*⟩

³**weave** *vi* : to move in a wavering manner from side to side : SWAY [Middle English *weven* "to move to and fro, wave"]

weav·er·bird \'wē-vər-ˌbərd\ *n* : any of a family of Old World birds that resemble finches and mostly construct elaborate nests of interlaced vegetation

weaver finch *n* : WEAVERBIRD

¹**web** \'web\ *n* **1** : a fabric on a loom or in process of being removed from a loom **2 a** : COBWEB 1 **b** : SNARE, ENTANGLEMENT ⟨caught in a *web* of fear⟩ **3** : a membrane of an animal or plant; *esp* : one uniting toes (as of many birds) **4** : the plate connecting the upper and lower flanges of a girder or rail **5** : NETWORK ⟨a *web* of highways⟩ **6** : VANE 3a **7** : a continuous sheet of paper manufactured or undergoing manufacture or a reel of this for use in a rotary printing press [Old English] — **web·by** \'web-ē\ *adj* — **web·like** \'web-ˌlīk\ *adj*

²**web** *vb* **webbed; web·bing** **1** : to cover or provide with webs or a network **2** : to form a web

webbed \'webd\ *adj* : having or joined by a web ⟨*webbed* feet⟩

web·bing \'web-ing\ *n* : a strong closely woven tape used especially for straps, harness, or upholstery

web·foot \'web-ˌfut\ *n* : a foot having webbed toes — **web–foot·ed** \-əd\ *adj*

web·worm \'web-ˌwərm\ *n* : any of various mostly gregarious caterpillars that spin large webs

wed \'wed\ *vb* **wed·ded** *also* **wed; wed·ding** **1** : to marry or get married **2** : to unite firmly [Old English *weddian*]

we'd \wēd, ˌwēd\ : we had : we should : we would

wed·ding \'wed-ing\ *n* **1** : a marriage ceremony usually with accompanying festivities **2** : a joining in close association

¹**wedge** \'wej\ *n* **1** : a piece of wood or metal tapered to a thin edge and used especially to split wood or rocks and in lifting heavy weights — compare SIMPLE MACHINE **2** : something (as a piece of pie or land or a formation of wild geese) shaped like a wedge **3** : a thing that serves to make a gradual opening or cause a change in something ⟨use every concession as an entering *wedge*⟩ [Old English *wecg*]

²**wedge** *vt* **1** : to fasten or tighten by or as if by driving in a wedge **2** : to press or force (something) into a narrow space ⟨*wedged* paper around the loose window⟩ **3** : to separate or split with or as if with a wedge

Wedg·wood \'wej-ˌwud\ *trademark* — used for ceramic wares

wed·lock \'wed-ˌläk\ *n* : the state of being married : MARRIAGE [Old English *wedlāc* "marriage bond", from *wedd* "pledge" + *-lāc*, suffix denoting activity] — **out of wedlock** : with the natural parents not legally married to each other

Wednes·day \'wenz-dē\ *n* : the 4th day of the week [Old English *wōdnesdæg*, literally, "day of Odin"]

wee \'wē\ *adj* **1** : very small : TINY **2** : very early ⟨*wee* hours of the morning⟩ [Middle English *we*, from *we* "little bit", from Old English *wǣge* "weight"]

¹**weed** \'wēd\ *n* **1** : a plant of no value and usually of rank growth; *esp* : one that tends to overgrow or choke out more desirable plants **2** : something like a weed [Old English *wēod*] — **weed·less** \-ləs\ *adj*

²**weed** *vb* **1** : to free from or remove weeds or something harmful, inferior, or superfluous **2** : to get rid of — **weed·er** *n*

³**weed** *n* **1** : GARMENT — often used in pl. **2** : dress worn (as by a widow) as a sign of mourning — usually used in pl. [Old English *wǣd*]

weedy \'wēd-ē\ *adj* **weed·i·er; -est** **1** : abounding with or consisting of weeds ⟨a *weedy* field⟩ **2** : resembling a weed especially in rapid growth **3** : noticeably lean and scrawny : LANKY ⟨*weedy* cattle⟩

week \'wēk\ *n* **1 a** : seven successive days ⟨was sick for a *week*⟩ **b** : a calendar period of seven days beginning with Sunday and ending with Saturday ⟨the last *week* of the month⟩ **2** : the working or school days of the calendar week ⟨had a hard *week*⟩ [Old English *wicu*]

week·day \-ˌdā\ *n* : a day of the week except Sunday or sometimes except Saturday and Sunday

week·days \-ˌdāz\ *adv* : on weekdays repeatedly : on any weekday ⟨takes a bus *weekdays*⟩

¹**week·end** \'wē-ˌkend\ *n* : the end of the week; *esp* : the period between the close of one working or school week and the beginning of the next

²**weekend** *vi* : to spend the weekend

week·ends \-ˌendz, -ˌenz\ *adv* : on weekends repeatedly : on any weekend ⟨travels *weekends*⟩

¹**week·ly** \'wē-klē\ *adj* **1** : occurring, done, produced, or issued every week **2** : computed in terms of one week — **weekly** *adv*

²**weekly** *n, pl* **weeklies** : a weekly publication

wee·ny \'wē-nē\ *adj* : exceptionally small [*wee* + ti*ny*]

weep \'wēp\ *vb* **wept** \'wept\; **weep·ing** **1 a** : to express emotion and especially sorrow by shedding tears : CRY **b** : to pour forth (tears) from the eyes **2** : to give off (liquid) slowly or in drops : OOZE [Old English *wēpan*] — **weep·er** \'wē-pər\ *n*

weep·ing \'wē-ping\ *adj* **1** : TEARFUL **2** : RAINY **3** : having slender pendent branches ⟨a *weeping* willow⟩

weepy \'wē-pē\ *adj* **weep·i·er; -est** : inclined to weep

wee·vil \'wē-vəl\ *n* : any of a large group (Rhynchophora) of mostly small beetles having the head long and usually curved downward to form a snout bearing the jaws at the tip and including many very injurious to plants or plant products [Old English *wifel*] — **wee·vily** *or* **wee·vil·ly** \'wēv-lē, -ə-lē\ *adj*

weft \'weft\ *n* **1 a** : WOOF 1 **b** : yard used for the woof **2** : material made by spinning or weaving [Old English]

weft knit *n* : a knit fabric in which the knitting is done with the yarns running in a crosswise or circular direction (as in hand knitting) — compare WARP KNIT — **weft knitting** *n*

wei·ge·la \wī-'jē-lə\ *n* : any of a genus of showy shrubs of the honeysuckle family; *esp* : a Chinese shrub widely grown for its pink or red flowers [Christian E. *Weigel*, died 1831, German physician]

weigh \'wā\ *vb* **1 a** : to ascertain the heaviness of by or as if by a balance **b** : to have weight or a specified weight **2 a** : to consider carefully : PONDER **b** : to merit

weaverbird

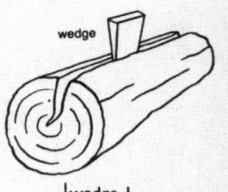

wedge

¹wedge 1

\ə\ abut	\ng\ sing
\ər\ further	\ō\ bone
\a\ mat	\ȯ\ saw
\ā\ take	\ȯi\ coin
\ä\ cot, cart	\th\ thin
\au̇\ out	\t͟h\ this
\ch\ chin	\ü\ food
\e\ pet	\u̇\ foot
\ē\ easy	\y\ yet
\g\ go	\yü\ few
\i\ tip	\yu̇\ cure
\ī\ life	\zh\ vision
\j\ job	

consideration as important : COUNT ⟨evidence will *weigh* heavily against them⟩ **3** : to heave up (an anchor) preparatory to sailing **4** : to measure or apportion (a definite quantity) on or as if on a scale **5 a** : to press down with or as if with a heavy weight **b** : to have a saddening or disheartening effect [Old English *wegan* "to move, carry, weigh"] — **weigh·able** \'wā-ə-bəl\ *adj* — **weigh·er** *n*

weigh down *vt* **1** : OVERBURDEN **2** : OPPRESS 1, DEPRESS

weigh in *vi* : to have something weighed; *esp* : to have oneself weighed preliminary to participation in a sports event

¹weight \'wāt\ *n* **1 a** : the amount that something weighs ⟨worth its *weight* in gold⟩ **b** : the standard or established amount that something should weigh ⟨a coin of full *weight*⟩ **2 a** : a quantity or portion weighing a usually specific amount ⟨add the necessary *weight* of sand⟩ **b** : a heavy object (as a metal ball) thrown, put, or lifted as an athletic exercise or contest **3 a** : a unit (as a pound or kilogram) of weight or mass — see MEASURE table, METRIC SYSTEM table **b** : an object (as a piece of metal) of known specified weight for balancing a scale in weighing other objects **c** : a system of related units of weight **4 a** : something heavy : LOAD **b** : a heavy object used to hold or press something down or to counterbalance **5** : a mental or emotional burden ⟨had a *weight* on my conscience⟩ **6 a** : relative heaviness : MASS **b** : the force with which a body is attracted toward the earth or a celestial body by gravitation and which is equal to the product of the mass and the local gravitational acceleration **7 a** : the relative importance or authority accorded something : NOTE ⟨opinions that carry *weight*⟩ **b** : measurable influence especially on others ⟨throw one's *weight* behind a candidate⟩ **8** : overpowering force ⟨the *weight* of the evidence favors this view⟩ [Old English *wiht*]

²weight *vt* **1** : to load or make heavy with or as if with a weight **2** : to oppress with a burden ⟨*weighted* down with cares⟩ **3** : to assign a relative importance to (as in a statistical study)

weight·less \'wāt-ləs\ *adj* : having little weight : lacking apparent gravitational pull — **weight·less·ly** *adv* — **weight·less·ness** *n*

weight lifter *n* : one that lifts barbells in competition or as an exercise — **weight lifting** *n*

weighty \'wāt-ē\ *adj* **weight·i·er; -est 1** : having much weight : HEAVY **2 a** : of much importance or consequence : SERIOUS ⟨*weighty* problems⟩ **b** : expressing seriousness : SOLEMN ⟨a *weighty* manner⟩ **3** : exerting authority or influence ⟨*weighty* arguments⟩ — **weight·i·ly** \'wāt-l-ē\ *adv* — **weight·i·ness** \'wāt-ē-nəs\ *n*

wei·ma·ra·ner \,vī-mə-'rän-ər, 'wī-mə-,\ *n* : any of a German breed of large gray short-haired sporting dogs [German, from *Weimar*, Germany]

weir \'waər, 'wear, 'wiər\ *n* **1** : a fence set in a stream to catch fish **2** : a dam in a stream to raise the water level or divert its flow [Old English *wer*]

weird \'wiərd\ *adj* **1** : of, relating to, or caused by witchcraft or the supernatural : MAGICAL **2** : of strange or extraordinary character : ODD, FANTASTIC [Middle English *werd* "fate", from Old English *wyrd*] — **weird·ly** *adv* — **weird·ness** *n* □ ORIGIN *Weird* is derived from an Old English noun *wyrd*, meaning "fate". The Middle English form *werd* is found primarily as a noun in Scottish and northern contexts. Not until the 15th century is this word recorded in an attributive or adjectival position, and then only in the combination *weird sister*. The Weird Sisters were the three Fates. Finally in the 18th century *weird* began to appear in other contexts as an adjective meaning "magical", "odd", or "fantastic". □ SYN WEIRD, EERIE, UNCANNY mean mysteriously strange or fantastic. WEIRD may imply unearthliness or simply extreme queerness or oddness; EERIE suggests an uneasy or fearful consciousness of the presence of mysterious and malign spirits; UN-

CANNY applies especially to abilities or perceptions so remarkable as to seem magical.

Weird Sisters *n pl* : the three Fates

Welch \'welch\ *variant of* WELSH

¹wel·come \'wel-kəm\ *interj* — used to express a greeting to a guest or newcomer upon arrival [Old English *wilcume,* from *wilcuma* "desirable guest"]

²welcome *vt* **1** : to greet hospitably and with courtesy **2** : to meet or face with pleasure ⟨*welcomed* criticism of the report⟩ — **wel·com·er** *n*

³welcome *adj* **1** : received gladly into one's presence or companionship ⟨a *welcome* visitor⟩ **2** : giving pleasure : PLEASING ⟨a *welcome* rainfall⟩ ⟨*welcome* news⟩ **3** : willingly permitted to do, have, or enjoy something ⟨anyone is *welcome* to use the swimming pool⟩ **4** — used in the phrase "You're welcome" as a reply to an expression of thanks

⁴welcome *n* : a cordial greeting or reception

¹weld \'weld\ *vb* **1** : to join (pieces of metal or plastic) by heating and allowing the edges to flow together or by hammering or pressing together **2** : to join as if by welding ⟨*welded* together in friendship⟩ **3** : to become or be capable of being welded ⟨not all metals *weld* well⟩ [Middle English *wellen* "to boil, well, weld"] — **weld·er** *n*

²weld *n* **1** : a welded joint **2** : union by welding

weld·ment \'weld-mənt\ *n* : a unit formed by welding together an assembly of pieces

wel·fare \'wel-,faər, -,feər\ *n* **1** : the state of doing well especially in respect to happiness, well-being, or prosperity **2** : WELFARE WORK **3** : RELIEF 1b [Middle English, from *wel faren* "to fare well"] — **welfare** *adj*

welfare state *n* : a nation or state that assumes primary responsibility for the individual and social welfare of its citizens

welfare work *n* : organized efforts for the social betterment of a group in society — **welfare worker** *n*

wel·kin \'wel-kən\ *n* **1** : SKY 1 **2** : AIR 1a [Old English *wolcen* "cloud, sky"]

¹well \'wel\ *n* **1 a** : an issue of water from the earth : a pool fed by a spring **b** : a source of supply : WELLSPRING ⟨was a *well* of information⟩ **2** : a hole sunk into the earth to reach a natural deposit (as of water, oil, or gas) **3** : an enclosure in the middle of a ship's hold around the pumps **4** : an open space extending vertically through floors of a structure (as for a staircase) **5** : something suggesting a well (as in being damp, cool, deep, or dark) [Old English *welle*]

²well *vi* : to rise to the surface and flow forth ⟨tears *welled* from their eyes⟩ [Middle English *wellen*]

³well *adv* **bet·ter** \'bet-ər\; **best** \'best\ **1 a** : in a pleasing or desirable manner ⟨the party turned out *well*⟩ **b** : in a good or proper manner ⟨did the work *well*⟩ **2** : in a full or generous manner ⟨eat *well*⟩ ⟨the orchard bore *well*⟩ **3** : with reason or courtesy : PROPERLY ⟨we could not very *well* refuse⟩ **4** : in all respects ⟨a *well*-deserved ovation⟩ **5** : in an intimate way ⟨know a person *well*⟩ **6** : MUCH 1a, FAR ⟨*well* ahead⟩ ⟨*well* over the quota⟩ **7** : without trouble or difficulty ⟨I could *well* have gone⟩ **8** : EXACTLY 1a ⟨remember it *well*⟩ [Old English *wel*] — **as well 1** : in addition : ALSO ⟨other features *as well*⟩ **2** : without real loss or gain : EQUALLY ⟨might *as well* stop here⟩

⁴well *interj* **1** — used to express surprise or expostulation **2** — used to begin a discourse or to resume one that was interrupted

⁵well *adj* **1** : SATISFACTORY, PLEASING ⟨all's *well* that ends well⟩ **2 a** : PROSPEROUS 2, WELL-OFF **b** : being in satisfactory condition or circumstances **3** : ADVISABLE, DESIRABLE ⟨not *well* to anger them⟩ **4 a** : free or recovered from infirmity or disease : HEALTHY **b** : made sound or whole ⟨the wound is nearly *well*⟩ **5** : being a cause for thankfulness : FORTUNATE ⟨it is *well* that this has happened⟩ SYN see HEALTHY

we'll \wēl, ,wēl\ : we shall : we will

well–ad·vised \ˌwel-əd-'vīzd\ *adj* : acting wisely or properly : based on wise counsel ⟨was *well-advised* to follow the doctor's orders⟩ ⟨*well-advised* restraint⟩

wel·la·way \ˌwel-ə-'wā\ *interj* — used to express sorrow or lamentation [Old English *weilāwei,* from *wā lā wā* "woe! lo! woe!"]

well–be·ing \'wel-'bē-ing\ *n* : the state of being happy, healthy, or prosperous : WELFARE

well–be·loved \ˌwel-bi-'ləvd\ *adj* **1** : sincerely and deeply loved **2** : sincerely respected — used in various ceremonial forms of address

well–born \'wel-'bȯrn\ *adj* : born of good stock either socially or genetically

well–bred \-'bred\ *adj* : having or displaying good breeding : REFINED

well–con·di·tioned \ˌwel-kən-'dish-ənd\ *adj* **1** : characterized by proper disposition, morals, or behavior **2** : having a good physical condition : SOUND ⟨a *well-conditioned* animal⟩

well–de·fined \ˌwel-di-'fīnd\ *adj* : having clearly distinguishable limits or boundaries ⟨a *well-defined* scar⟩ ⟨a *well-defined* collection is a mathematical set⟩

well–dis·posed \-dis-'pōzd\ *adj* : disposed to be friendly, favorable, or sympathetic ⟨*well-disposed* to our plan⟩

well–done \'wel-'dən\ *adj* **1** : rightly or properly performed **2** : cooked thoroughly

well–fa·vored \'wel-'fā-vərd\ *adj* : good-looking : HANDSOME — **well–fa·vored·ness** *n*

well–fixed \-'fikst\ *adj* : well-off financially

well–found \-'faund\ *adj* : fully furnished : properly equipped ⟨a *well-found* ship⟩

well–found·ed \-'faun-dəd\ *adj* : based on sound reasoning, information, judgment, or grounds ⟨your suspicion was *well-founded*: the suspect is wanted for armed robbery⟩

well–groomed \-'grümd, -'grumd\ *adj* **1** : well dressed and extremely neat **2** : made neat, tidy, and attractive down to the smallest details ⟨a *well-groomed* lawn⟩

well–ground·ed \-'graun-dəd\ *adj* : having a firm foundation : WELL-FOUNDED

well·head \'wel-ˌhed\ *n* **1 a** : the source of a spring or a stream **b** : principal source **2** : the top of or a structure built over a well

well–heeled \'wel-'hēld\ *adj* : WELL-FIXED

well–known \-'nōn\ *adj* : fully or widely known

well–mean·ing \-'mē-ning\ *adj* : having or based on good intentions

well·ness \'wel-nəs\ *n* : the quality or state of being in good health especially as an actively sought goal ⟨lifestyles that promote *wellness*⟩

well–nigh \-'nī\ *adv* : ALMOST, NEARLY

well–off \'wel-'ȯf\ *adj* : being in good condition or circumstances; *esp* : well supplied with material possessions

well–or·dered \-'ȯrd-ərd\ *adj* : having an orderly procedure or arrangement ⟨a *well-ordered* household⟩

well–read \-'red\ *adj* : well informed or deeply versed through reading ⟨*well-read* in history⟩

well–spoken \-'spō-kən\ *adj* **1** : having a good command of language : speaking well and especially courteously **2** : spoken with propriety ⟨*well-spoken* words⟩

well·spring \'wel-ˌspring\ *n* **1** : FOUNTAINHEAD 1 **2** : a source of continual supply

well–timed \'wel-'tīmd\ *adj* : occurring opportunely : TIMELY

well–to–do \ˌwel-tə-'dü\ *adj* : having more than adequate material resources : PROSPEROUS

well–turned \'wel-'tərnd\ *adj* **1** : pleasingly shaped : SHAPELY **2** : pleasingly and appropriately expressed ⟨a *well-turned* phrase⟩

well–wish·er \'wel-ˌwish-ər\ *n* : one that wishes well to another — **well–wish·ing** \-ˌwish-ing\ *adj or n*

well–worn \-'wȯrn, -'wȯrn\ *adj* **1 a** : worn by much use ⟨*well-worn* shoes⟩ **b** : made stale by overuse : TRITE ⟨a *well-worn* quotation⟩ **2** : worn well or properly ⟨*well-worn* honors⟩

welsh *or* **welch** \'welsh, 'welch\ *vi* : to cheat by avoiding payment of bets [probably from *Welsh,* adj.] — **welsh·er** *n*

Welsh *also* **Welch** \'welsh *also* 'welch\ *n* **1** *Welsh pl* : the natives or inhabitants of Wales **2** : the Celtic language of the Welsh people [Old English *wælisc* "Celtic, Welsh, foreign", from *Wealh* "Celt, Welshman, foreigner", of Celtic origin] — **Welsh** *adj* — **Welsh·man** \-mən\ — **Welsh–wom·an** \-ˌwum-ən\ *n*

Welsh cor·gi \-'kȯr-gē\ *n* : a short-legged long-backed dog with foxy head occurring in two varieties of Welsh origin : **a** : CARDIGAN **b** : PEMBROKE WELSH CORGI [Welsh *corgi,* from *cor* "dwarf" + *ci* "dog"]

Welsh rabbit *n* : melted often seasoned cheese poured over toast or crackers

Welsh rare·bit \-'raər-bət, -'reər-\ *n* : WELSH RABBIT [by alteration]

¹welt \'welt\ *n* **1** : the narrow strip of leather between a shoe upper and sole to which other parts are stitched **2 a** : a ridge or lump raised on the skin usually by a blow **b** : a heavy blow [Middle English *welte*]

²welt *vt* **1** : to furnish with a welt **2 a** : to raise a welt on ⟨mosquitoes *welted* my arms⟩ **b** : to hit hard

¹wel·ter \'wel-tər\ *vi* **1 a** : to twist or roll one's body about : WALLOW **b** : to rise and fall or toss about in or with waves **2** : to become deeply sunk, soaked, or involved ⟨*weltered* in misery⟩ **3** : to be in turmoil [Middle English *welteren*]

²welter *n* **1** : a state of wild disorder : TURMOIL **2** : a chaotic mass or jumble ⟨a *welter* of conflicting regulations⟩

³welter *n* : WELTERWEIGHT [probably from ¹*welt*]

wel·ter·weight \-ˌwāt\ *n* : a boxer in a weight division having the approximate range of 60 to 67 kilograms [³*welter*]

wen \'wen\ *n* : a cyst formed by obstruction of a skin gland and filled with fatty material [Old English *wenn*]

wench \'wench\ *n* **1** : a young woman : GIRL **2** : a female servant [Middle English *wenchel, wenche* "child", from Old English *wencel*]

wend \'wend\ *vb* : to direct one's course : proceed on (one's way) [Old English *wendan*]

went *past of* GO [Middle English, past of *wenden* "to wend"]

wen·tle·trap \'went-l-ˌtrap\ *n* : any of a family of marine snails with usually tall-spired sculptured white shells; *also* : one of the shells [Dutch *wenteltrap* "winding stair"]

wept *past of* WEEP

were *past 2d sing, past pl, or past subjunctive of* BE [Old English *wæron,* past pl., *wære,* past subjunctive sing., *wæren,* past subjunctive pl. of *wesan* "to be"]

we're \wiər, ˌwiər, wər, ˌwər\ : we are

weren't \wərnt, 'wərnt, 'wər-ənt\ : were not

were·wolf \'wiər-ˌwulf, 'wər-, 'weər-\ *n, pl* **were·wolves** \-ˌwulvz\ : a person held to be transformed or able to transform into a wolf [Old English *werwulf,* from *wer* "man" + *wulf* "wolf"]

wert \wərt, 'wərt\ *archaic past 2d sing of* BE

wes·kit \'wes-kət\ *n* : VEST 1a [alteration of *waistcoat*]

Wes·ley·an \'wes-lē-ən, 'wez-\ *adj* **1** : of or relating to John or Charles Wesley **2** : of or relating to the Methodism taught by John Wesley — **Wesleyan** *n* — **Wes·ley·an·ism** \-lē-ə-ˌniz-əm\ *n*

¹west \'west\ *adv* : to, toward, or in the west [Old English]

²west *adj* **1** : situated toward or at the west **2** : coming from the west

³west *n* **1 a** : the general direction of sunset **b** : the compass point directly opposite to east **2** *cap* : regions or countries west of a specified or implied point **3** : the end of a church opposite the chancel

west·bound \'west-ˌbaund, 'wes-\ *adj* : headed west

west·er \'wes-tər\ *vi* **wes·tered; wes·ter·ing** \-tə-ring, -tring\ : to turn or move westward

¹west·er·ly \'wes-tər-lē\ *adv or adj* **1** : from the west **2** : toward the west

²westerly *n, pl* **-lies** : a wind from the west

¹west·ern \'wes-tərn\ *adj* **1** *often cap* : of, relating to, or characteristic of a region conventionally designated West **2** : lying toward or coming from the west **3** *cap* : of or relating to the Roman Catholic or Protestant segment of Christianity ⟨*Western* liturgies⟩ [Old English *westerne*] — **west·ern·most** \-,mōst\ *adj*

²western *n* **1** : one that is produced in or characteristic of a western region and especially the western United States **2** *often cap* : a novel, story, motion picture, or broadcast dealing with life in the western United States during the latter half of the 19th century

West·ern·er \'wes-tər-nər, -tə-nər\ *n* : a native or inhabitant of the West (as of the United States)

western hemisphere *n* : the half of the earth comprising North and South America and surrounding waters

western hemlock *n* : a commercially important hemlock ranging from Alaska to California and having leaves without pale lines on the underside

west·ern·ize \'wes-tər-,nīz\ *vt* : to give western characteristics to — **west·ern·iza·tion** \,wes-tər-nə'zā-shən\ *n*

western larch *n* : an important timber tree of western North America with pale green sharply pointed leaves and oblong cones; *also* : its wood

western pine beetle *n* : a bark beetle destructive to various pines of the western United States

West Germanic *n* : a subdivision of the Germanic languages including English, Frisian, Dutch, and German

West Goth *n* : VISIGOTH

West Highland white terrier *n* : a small white long-coated dog of a breed developed in Scotland

west·ing \'wes-ting\ *n* **1** : difference in longitude to the west from the last preceding point of reckoning **2** : westerly progress

west–northwest *n* : two points north of west : W 22°30′N

west–southwest *n* : two points south of west : W 22°30′S

¹west·ward \'wes-twərd\ *adv or adj* : toward the west — **west·wards** \-twərdz\ *adv*

²westward *n* : westward direction or part

¹wet \'wet\ *adj* **wet·ter; wet·test** **1 a** : consisting of, containing, covered with, or soaked with liquid (as water) **b** : RAINY **2** : still moist enough to smudge or smear ⟨*wet* paint⟩ **3** : permitting or openly supporting the manufacture and sale of alcoholic liquor **4** : involving the use or presence of liquid ⟨*wet* processes⟩ **5** : perversely wrong (you're all *wet*) [Old English *wǣt*] — **wet·ly** *adv* — **wet·ness** *n* — **wet behind the ears** : lacking experience : IMMATURE

²wet *n* **1** : WATER; *also* : MOISTURE **2** : rainy weather : RAIN **3** : a supporter of a wet liquor policy

³wet *vb* **wet** *or* **wet·ted; wet·ting** **1** : to make or become wet **2** : to urinate or urinate in or on — **wet one's whistle** : to take a drink especially of liquor

wet·back \'wet-,bak\ *n* : a Mexican who enters the United States illegally (as by wading the Rio Grande)

wet blanket *n* : one that quenches or dampens enthusiasm or pleasure — **wet–blanket** *vt*

wet down *vt* : to dampen by sprinkling with water

weth·er \'weth-ər\ *n* : a male sheep castrated before sexual maturity [Old English]

wet·land \'wet-,land\ *n* : land containing much soil moisture : swampy or boggy land

wet–nurse \'wet-'nərs\ *vt* **1** : to tend as a wet nurse **2** : to give constant and often excessive care to

wet nurse *n* : one that cares for and suckles young not her own

wet suit *n* : a close-fitting rubber suit (as for a skin diver) that traps a thin layer of water against the body to hold body heat

whale shark

wet·ta·ble \'wet-ə-bəl\ *adj* : capable of being wetted — **wet·ta·bil·i·ty** \,wet-ə-'bil-ət-ē\ *n*

wetting agent *n* : a substance that when adsorbed on a surface reduces its tendency to repel a liquid

wet·tish \'wet-ish\ *adj* : somewhat wet : MOIST

wet wash *n* : laundry returned damp and not ironed

we've \wēv, ,wēv\ : we have

¹whack \'hwak, 'wak\ *vb* **1** : to strike with a smart or resounding blow **2** : to cut with or as if with a whack : CHOP [probably imitative] — **whack·er** *n*

²whack *n* **1** : a smart or resounding blow; *also* : the sound of or as if of such a blow **2** : PORTION, SHARE ⟨we must each pay our *whack*⟩ **3** : CONDITION; *esp* : proper working order ⟨the machine is out of *whack*⟩ **4 a** : an opportunity or attempt to do something : CHANCE **b** : a single action or occasion : TIME ⟨marked a hundred papers at a *whack*⟩

¹whack·ing \'hwak-ing, 'wak-\ *adj* : very large : WHOPPING

²whacking *adv* : VERY ⟨a *whacking* good story⟩

whack up *vt* : to divide into shares

¹whale \'hwāl, 'wāl\ *n, pl* **whale** *or* **whales** **1** : an aquatic mammal (order Cetacea) that superficially resembles a large fish and is valued commercially for its oil, flesh, and sometimes whalebone; *esp* : one of the larger members of this group **2** : a person or thing impressive in size or qualities ⟨a *whale* of a story⟩ [Old English *hwæl*]

²whale *vt* **1** : THRASH **2** : to strike or hit hard [origin unknown]

whale·boat \-,bōt\ *n* **1** : a long narrow rowboat made with both ends sharp and raking, often steered with an oar, and used by whalers for hunting whales **2** : a long narrow rowboat or motorboat resembling the original whaleboats that is often carried by warships and merchant ships

whale·bone \-,bōn\ *n* : a horny substance found in two rows of long plates attached along the upper jaw of whalebone whales

whalebone whale *n* : any of various usually large whales having whalebone instead of teeth

whal·er \'hwā-lər, 'wā-\ *n* **1** : a person or ship engaged in whale fishing **2** : WHALEBOAT 2

whale shark *n* : a very large harmless shark of tropical seas

whal·ing \'hwā-ling, 'wā-\ *n* : the occupation of catching whales and extracting commercial products from them

¹wham \'hwam, 'wam\ *n* **1** : the loud sound of a hard impact **2** : a solid blow [imitative]

²wham *vb* **whammed; wham·ming** : to propel, strike, or beat so as to produce a loud impact

wham·my \'hwam-ē, 'wam-\ *n, pl* **whammies** **1** : a supernatural power held to bring bad luck **2** : a magic curse or spell [probably from ¹*wham*]

¹whang \'hwang, 'wang\ *vb* **1** : to propel or strike with force **2** : to beat or work with force or violence [Middle English *thong, thwang* "thong"]

²whang *n* : a loud sharp vibrant or resonant sound [imitative]

wharf \'hwȯrf, 'wȯrf\ *n, pl* **wharves** \'hwȯrvz, 'wȯrvz\ *also* **wharfs** : a structure built along or out from the shore of navigable waters so that ships may lie alongside to receive and discharge cargo and passengers [Old English *hwearf*]

wharf·age \'hwȯr-fij, 'wȯr-\ *n* **1** : the provision or the use of a wharf **2** : the charge for the use of a wharf

wharf·in·ger \-fən-jər\ *n* : the operator or manager of a commercial wharf [derived from *wharfage*]

wharf·mas·ter \'hwȯrf-,mas-tər, 'wȯrf-\ *n* : WHARFINGER

¹what \hwät, 'hwät, hwət, 'hwət, wät, 'wät, wət, 'wət\ *pron* **1 a** — used as an interrogative in asking about the identity, nature, or value of a thing ⟨*what* is this⟩ ⟨*what* do they earn⟩ ⟨*what* is wealth without friends⟩ or about the character, occupation, or position of a person ⟨*what* do you think I am, a fool⟩ **b** — used as an exclamation expressing surprise or excitement and frequently introducing a question ⟨*what,* no breakfast⟩ **c** — used in expressions directing attention to a statement that the speaker is about to make ⟨you know *what*⟩ **2** : that which : the one or ones that ⟨no income but *what* I get from my writings⟩ **3** : WHATEVER 1a ⟨say *what* you will⟩ [Old English *hwæt,* neuter of *hwā* "who"]

²**what** *adv* **1 a** : in what respect : HOW **b** : how much ⟨*what* do you care⟩ **2** — used with *with* to introduce a prepositional phrase that expresses cause ⟨kept busy *what with* studies and extracurricular activities⟩

³**what** *adj* **1 a** — used as an interrogative expressing inquiry about the identity or nature of a person, object, or matter ⟨*what* minerals do we export⟩ **b** : how remarkable or surprising ⟨*what* a suggestion⟩ ⟨*what* a charming view⟩ **2** : WHATEVER 1a

¹**what·ev·er** \hwät-'ev-ər, wät-, hwət-, 'hwət-, wət-, ,wət-\ *pron* **1 a** : anything or everything that ⟨take *whatever* is needed⟩ **b** : no matter what ⟨obey orders, *whatever* happens⟩ **2** : ¹WHAT 1a — used to express astonishment or perplexity ⟨*whatever* do you mean by that⟩

²**whatever** *adj* **1 a** : any . . . that : all . . . that ⟨take *whatever* action is needed⟩ **b** : no matter what **2** : of any kind at all ⟨no food *whatever*⟩

what·not \'hwät-,nät, 'hwət-, 'wät-, 'wət-\ *n* : a light open set of shelves for bric-a-brac

what·so·ev·er \,hwät-sə-'wev-ər, ,hwət-, ,wät-, ,wət-\ *pron or adj* : WHATEVER

wheal \'hwēl, 'wēl\ *n* : a suddenly formed elevation of the skin surface: as **a** : WELT 2a **b** : a flat burning or itching eminence on the skin [alteration of *wale*]

wheat \'hwēt, 'wēt\ *n* **1** : a cereal grain that yields a fine white flour, is the chief breadstuff of temperate climates, and is important in animal feeds — compare BRAN, MIDDLINGS **2** : any of a genus of grasses grown in most temperate areas for the wheat they yield; *esp* : an annual cereal grass with long dense flower spikes and white to dark red grains that is the chief source of wheat and is known only in cultivation [Old English *hwǣte*] — **wheat·en** \-n\ *adj*

wheat cake *n* : a pancake made of wheat flour

wheat·ear \'hwēt-,iər, 'wēt-\ *n* : a small white-rumped northern bird related to the whinchat [earlier *wheatears,* probably derived from *white* + Old English *ears* "backside"]

wheat germ *n* : the embryo of the wheat kernel separated in milling and used especially as a source of vitamins

wheat rust *n* : a destructive disease of wheat caused by rust fungi; *also* : a fungus causing a wheat rust

whee \'hwē, 'wē\ *interj* — used to express delight or high spirits [probably imitative]

whee·dle \'hwēd-l, 'wēd-\ *vt* **whee·dled; whee·dling** \'hwēd-ling, 'wēd-, -l-ing\ **1** : to coax or entice by soft words or flattery **2** : to gain or get by wheedling [origin unknown]

¹**wheel** \'hwēl, 'wēl\ *n* **1** : a disk or circular frame capable of turning on a central axis **2** : something that is like a wheel (as in being round or in turning on an axis) **3** : a device the main part of which is a wheel **4** : BICYCLE **5** : a circular frame which when turned controls some apparatus **6 a** : a curving or circular movement **b** : a turning movement of troops or ships in line in which the units preserve alignment and relative positions as they change direction **7 a** : a moving power : MECHANISM ⟨the *wheels* of government⟩ **b** : a person of importance especially in an organization [Old English *hwēol*] — **wheeled** \'hwēld, 'wēld\ *adj* — **wheel·less** \'hwēl-ləs, 'wēl-\ *adj*

²**wheel** *vb* **1** : to carry or move on wheels or in a vehicle with wheels ⟨*wheel* a load into the barn⟩ **2** : to turn or cause to turn on an axis or in a circle : REVOLVE ⟨the earth *wheels* about the sun⟩ **3** : to change direction as if revolving on an axis ⟨*wheeled* about⟩ — **wheel and deal** : to pursue one's interests especially in a shrewd or unscrupulous manner

wheel and axle *n* : a simple machine consisting of a grooved wheel turned by a cord or chain with a rigidly attached axle (as for winding up a weight) together with the supporting standards

wheel animalcule *n* : ROTIFER — called also *wheel animal*

wheel·bar·row \'hwēl-,bar-ō, 'wēl-\ *n* : a small vehicle with handles and one or more wheels for carrying small loads

wheel·base \-,bās\ *n* : the distance in inches between the front and rear axles of an automotive vehicle

wheel·chair \-,cheər, -,chaər\ *n* : a chair on wheels used especially by invalids

wheel·er \'hwē-lər, 'wē-\ *n* **1** : one that wheels **2** : WHEELHORSE 1 **3** : something (as a vehicle or ship) that has wheels — used especially in combinations ⟨side-*wheeler*⟩

wheel·er-deal·er \,hwē-lər-'dē-lər, ,wē-\ *n* : a shrewd operator especially in business or politics [from the phrase *wheel* and *deal*]

wheel·horse \'hwēl-,hórs, 'wēl-\ *n* **1** : a horse in a position nearest the wheels in a tandem or similar arrangement **2** : a steady and effective worker especially in a political body

wheel·house \-,haús\ *n* : PILOTHOUSE

wheels·man \'hwēlz-mən, 'wēlz-\ *n* : one who steers with a wheel; *esp* : HELMSMAN

wheel·wright \'hwēl-,rīt, 'wēl-\ *n* : a man whose occupation is to make or repair wheels and wheeled vehicles

¹**wheeze** \'hwēz, 'wēz\ *vi* **1** : to breathe with difficulty usually with a whistling sound **2** : to make a sound resembling that of wheezing [Middle English *whesen*] — **wheez·i·ly** \'hwē-zə-lē, 'wē-\ *adv* — **wheez·i·ness** \-zē-nəs\ *n* — **wheezy** \-zē\ *adj*

²**wheeze** *n* **1** : a sound of wheezing **2 a** : an old joke **b** : a trite saying

whelk \'hwelk, 'welk, 'wilk\ *n* : any of numerous large marine snails; *esp* : one much used as food in Europe [Old English *weoloc*]

whelm \'hwelm, 'welm\ *vt* : to overcome or engulf completely [Middle English *whelmen*]

¹**whelp** \'hwelp, 'welp\ *n* **1** : one of the young of various flesh-eating mammals and especially of the dog **2** : CUR 2 [Old English *hwelp*]

²**whelp** *vb* **1** : to give birth to (whelps) **2** : to bring forth whelps

¹**when** \hwen, 'hwen, wen, 'wen, hwən, wən\ *adv* **1** : at what time ⟨asked us *when* it happened⟩ **2** : at or during which time ⟨an era *when* the arts decayed⟩ [Old English *hwanne, hwenne*]

²**when** *conj* **1 a** : at or during the time that : WHILE ⟨we go *when* we can⟩ **b** : just after the time that ⟨left *when* the bell rang⟩ **c** : every time that ⟨smile *when* you say that⟩ **2** : in the event that : IF ⟨*when* you cheat you hurt youself⟩ **3** : in spite of the fact that : THOUGH ⟨gave up politics *when* I might have made a great career in it⟩

³**when** \,hwen, ,wen\ *pron* : what or which time ⟨since *when* have you known that⟩

whence \hwens, 'hwens, wens, 'wens\ *adv* **1** : from what place, source, or cause ⟨*whence* come all these doubts⟩ **2** : from or out of which ⟨the stock *whence* I sprang⟩ [Middle English *whenne, whennes,* from Old English *hwanon*]

¹**when·ev·er** \hwe-'nev-ər, we-, hwə-, wə-\ *conj* : at any or every time that ⟨stop *whenever* you wish⟩

²**whenever** *adv* : at whatever time ⟨available *whenever* needed⟩

when·so·ev·er \'hwen-sə-,wev-ər, 'wen-\ *conj* : WHENEVER

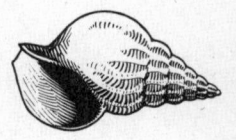

whelk

¹where \'hweər, 'hwaər, 'weər, 'waər, ,hwər, ,wər; or without stress\ *adv* **1** : at, in, or to which place, circumstances, or respect ⟨*where* are we going⟩ ⟨*where* am I wrong⟩ **2** : in, at, or to which ⟨the house *where* I was born⟩ **3** : from what place or source ⟨*where* did you get that idea⟩ [Old English *hwǣr*]

²where *conj* **1 a** : at or in the place at or in which ⟨stay *where* you are⟩ **b** : to the place at, in, or to which ⟨went *where* we had promised to go⟩ **2** : WHEREVER ⟨sit *where* you please⟩ **3** : in a case, situation, or respect in which ⟨outstanding *where* endurance is called for⟩

³where \'hweər, 'hwaər, 'weər, 'waər\ *n* **1** : PLACE, LOCATION ⟨the *where* and the how of the accident⟩ **2** : what place, source, or cause ⟨*where* are you from⟩

¹where·abouts \-ə-,baúts\ *also* **where·about** \-,baút\ *adv* : about where : near what place ⟨*whereabouts* is the house⟩

²whereabouts *n sing or pl* : the place or general locality where a person or thing is

where·as \hwer-'az, hwar-, wer-, war-, hwər-, wər-\ *conj* **1** : in view of the fact that : SINCE — used especially to introduce a preamble **2** : while on the contrary ⟨water puts out fire, *whereas* alcohol burns⟩

where·at \-'at\ *conj* **1** : at or toward which **2** : as a result of which : WHEREUPON

where·by \hweər-'bī, hwaər-, weər-, waər-, hwər-, wər-\ *conj* : by, through, or in accordance with which

¹where·fore \'hweər-,fōr, 'hwaər-, 'weər-, 'waər-, -,fȯr\ *adv* **1** : for what reason or purpose : WHY **2** : THEREFORE 1 [Middle English *wherfor, wherfore*, from *wher* "where" + *for, fore* "for"]

²wherefore *n* : a statement giving an explanation : REASON

where·from \-,frəm, -,främ\ *conj* : from which

¹where·in \hwer-'in, hwar-, wer-, war-, hwər-, wər-\ *adv* : in what : in what particular or respect ⟨*wherein* was I wrong⟩

²wherein *conj* **1** : in which : WHERE ⟨the city *wherein* they live⟩ **2** : during which ⟨the epoch *wherein* feudalism arose⟩

where·of \-'əv, -'äv\ *conj* **1** : of what ⟨I know *whereof* I speak⟩ **2** : of which or whom ⟨books *whereof* the best are lost⟩

where·on \-'ȯn, -'än\ *adv* : on which ⟨the base *whereon* it rests⟩

where·so·ev·er \'hwer-sə-,wev-ər, 'hwar-, 'wer-, 'war-\ *conj, archaic* : WHEREVER 1

¹where·to \-,tü\ *adv* : to what place or purpose

²whereto *conj* : to which

where·un·to \hwer-'ən-tü, hwar-, wer-, war-, hwər-, wər-\ *adv or conj* : WHERETO

where·up·on \'hwer-ə-,pȯn, 'hwar-, 'wer-, 'war-, -,pän\ *conj* **1** : on which **2** : closely following and as a result of which

¹wher·ev·er \hwer-'ev-ər, hwar-, wer-, war-, hwər-, wər-\ *adv* : where in the world ⟨*wherever* did you get that hat⟩

²wherever *conj* **1** : at, in, or to whatever place ⟨thrive *wherever* they go⟩ **2** : in any circumstance in which ⟨*wherever* it is possible, I try to help⟩

¹where·with \'hweər-,with, 'hwaər-, 'weər-, 'waər-, -,with\ *conj* : with or by means of which ⟨we lack tools *wherewith* to repair the damage⟩

²wherewith *adv, obsolete* : with what

where·with·al \'hweər-with-,ȯl, 'hwaər-, 'weər-, 'waər-, -with-\ *n* : MEANS, RESOURCES; *esp* : MONEY

wher·ry \'hwer-ē, 'wer-\ *n, pl* **wherries** : any of various light boats; *esp* : a long light rowboat pointed at both ends [Middle English *whery*]

¹whet \'hwet, 'wet\ *vt* **whet·ted; whet·ting** **1** : to sharpen by rubbing on or with something (as a stone) ⟨*whet* a knife⟩ **2** : to make keen ⟨*whet* the appetite⟩ [Old English *hwettan*]

²whet *n* **1** : GOAD 2 **2** : APPETIZER; *also* : a drink of liquor

wheth·er \'hweth-ər, 'weth-, ,hwəth-ər, ,wəth-, hwəth-, wəth-\ *conj* **1 a** (1) : if it is or was true that ⟨ask *whether* they are going⟩ (2) : if it is or was better ⟨uncertain *whether* to go or stay⟩ **b** : whichever is or was the case, namely, that ⟨*whether* we succeed or fail, we must try⟩ **2** : EITHER ⟨seated us together *whether* by accident or design⟩ [Old English *hwæther, hwether*, from *hwæther, hwether*, pron., "which of two"]

whet·stone \'hwet-,stōn, 'wet-\ *n* : a stone for whetting sharp-edged tools

whew \often read as 'hwü, 'wü, 'hyü; the interjection is a whistle ending with a voiceless ü\ *n* **1** : a whistling sound **2** : a sound like a half-formed whistle uttered as an exclamation — used interjectionally chiefly to express amazement, discomfort, or relief [imitative]

whey \'hwā, 'wā\ *n* : the watery part of milk that separates after the milk sours and thickens [Old English *hwæg*] — **whey·ey** \'hwā-ē\ *adj*

¹which \hwich, wich, 'hwich, 'wich\ *adj* **1** : being what one or ones out of a group — used as an interrogative ⟨*which* coat should I wear⟩ ⟨knew *which* one would win⟩ **2** : WHICHEVER ⟨it will not fit, turn it *which* way you like⟩ [Old English *hwilc* "of what kind, which"]

²which *pron* **1** : what one or ones out of a group — used as an interrogative ⟨*which* of those houses do you live in⟩ ⟨*which* of you want tea and which want lemonade⟩ ⟨they are swimming or canoeing, I don't know *which*⟩ **2** : WHICHEVER ⟨take *which* you like⟩ **3** — used to introduce a relative clause and to serve as a substitute within that clause for the substantive modified by that clause; used in any grammatical relation except that of a possessive; used especially in reference to animals, inanimate objects, groups, or ideas ⟨the records *which* I bought⟩ SYN see WHO

¹which·ev·er \hwich-'ev-ər, wich-\ *pron* : whatever one or ones out of a group ⟨take two of the four elective subjects, *whichever* you prefer⟩

²whichever *adj* : being whatever one or ones out of a group : no matter which ⟨*whichever* way you go⟩

which·so·ev·er \,hwich-sə-'wev-ər, ,wich-\ *pron or adj* : WHICHEVER

whicker \'hwik-ər, 'wik-\ *vi* : WHINNY [imitative] — **whicker** *n*

¹whiff \'hwif, 'wif\ *n* **1 a** : a quick puff or slight gust especially of air, odor, gas, smoke, or spray **b** : an inhalation of odor, gas, or smoke **2** : a slight trace : HINT [imitative]

²whiff *vb* **1 a** : to expel, puff out, or blow away in or as if in whiffs **b** : SMOKE 2 **2** : to inhale an odor

whif·fle·tree \'hwif-əl-,trē, 'wif-\ *or* **whip·ple·tree** \'hwip-əl-, 'wip-\ *n* : the pivoted swinging bar to which the traces of a harness are fastened and by which a vehicle or implement is drawn [perhaps derived from *whip* + *tree*]

Whig \'hwig, 'wig\ *n* **1** : a member or supporter of a British political group of the 18th and early 19th centuries seeking to limit royal authority and increase parliamentary power — compare TORY **2** : an American favoring independence from Great Britain during the American Revolution **3** : a member or supporter of a 19th century American political party formed in opposition to the Jacksonian Democrats [*Whiggamore* "member of a Scottish group that marched to Edinburgh in 1648 to oppose the court party"] — **Whig** *adj* — **Whig·gish** \-ish\ *adj*

¹while \'hwīl, 'wīl\ *n* **1** : a period of time ⟨stay here for a *while*⟩ **2** : the time and effort used (as in the performance of an action) : TROUBLE ⟨worth your *while*⟩ [Old English *hwīl*]

²while *conj* **1 a** : during the time that ⟨take a nap *while* I'm out⟩ **b** : as long as ⟨*while* there's life there's hope⟩ **2** : in spite of the fact that : THOUGH

³while *vt* : to cause to pass especially without boredom or in a pleasant manner — usually used with away ⟨*while* away the time⟩

¹whi·lom \'hwī-ləm, 'wī-\ *adv, archaic* : FORMERLY [Middle English, literally, "at times", from Old English *hwīlum,* from *hwīl* "time, while"]

²whilom *adj* : FORMER ⟨our *whilom* friends⟩

whilst \'hwīlst, 'wīlst\ *conj, chiefly British* : WHILE

whim \'hwim, 'wim\ *n* : a sudden wish, desire, or change of mind : a sudden notion or fancy [earlier *whim-wham,* of unknown origin] SYN see CAPRICE

whim·brel \'hwim-brəl, 'wim-\ *n* : a small European curlew [perhaps imitative]

¹whim·per \'hwim-pər, 'wim-\ *vi* **whim·pered; whim·per·ing** \-pə-ring, -pring\ **1** : to make a low whining or broken sound **2** : to complain with or as if with a whimper [imitative]

²whimper *n* : a low whining or broken sound

whim·si·cal \'hwim-zi-kəl, 'wim-\ *adj* **1** : full of whims : CAPRICIOUS ⟨a *whimsical* person⟩ **2** : resulting from or characterized by whim or caprice : ERRATIC ⟨*whimsical* behavior⟩ — **whim·si·cal·i·ty** \,hwim-zə-'kal-ət-ē, ,wim-\ *n* — **whim·si·cal·ly** \'hwim-zi-kə-lē, 'wim-, -klē\ *adv* — **whim·si·cal·ness** \-kəl-nəs\ *n*

whim·sy *or* **whim·sey** \'hwim-zē, 'wim-\ *n, pl* **whimsies** *or* **whimseys** **1** : WHIM **2** : a fanciful or fantastic device, object, or creation especially in writing or art [derived from *whim-wham* "whim"]

whin \'hwin, 'win\ *n* : FURZE [of Scandinavian origin]

whin·chat \'hwin-,chat, 'win-\ *n* : a small brown and buff European singing bird of grassy meadows

¹whine \'hwīn, 'wīn\ *vi* **1** : to utter a whine or similar sound **2** : to complain with or as if with a whine [Old English *hwīnan* "to whiz"] — **whin·er** *n* — **whin·ing·ly** \'hwī-ning-lē, 'wī-\ *adv*

²whine *n* **1** : a prolonged usually high-pitched plaintive or distressed cry or a similar sound **2** : a complaint uttered with or as if with a whine — **whiny** *or* **whin·ey** \'hwī-nē, 'wī-\ *adj*

¹whin·ny \'hwin-ē, 'win-\ *vi* **whin·nied; whin·ny·ing** : to neigh especially in a low or gentle way [probably imitative]

²whinny *n, pl* **whinnies** **1** : NEIGH **2** : a sound resembling a neigh

¹whip \'hwip, 'wip\ *vb* **whipped; whip·ping** **1** : to move, snatch, or jerk very quickly and forcefully ⟨*whip* out a gun⟩ **2 a** : to strike (as with a lash or rod) especially as a punishment; *also* : SPANK **b** : to drive or urge on by or as if by using a whip **3 a** : to bind or wrap (as a rope) with cord in order to protect, strengthen, or prevent unraveling **b** : to wind or wrap around something **4** : to defeat utterly : TROUNCE **5** : to stir up : AROUSE ⟨*whip* up enthusiasm⟩ **6** : to produce in a hurry ⟨*whip* up a short article⟩ **7** : to beat (as eggs or cream) into a froth **8** : to gather or hold together for united action ⟨*whipped* the doubtful members into line⟩ **9 a** : to move nimbly or briskly **b** : to thrash about flexibly like a whiplash ⟨a flag *whipping* in the wind⟩ [Middle English *whippen*] — **whip·per** *n*

²whip *n* **1** : an instrument consisting usually of a handle and lash forming a flexible rod that is used for whipping **2** : a stroke or cut with or as if with a whip **3 a** : a dessert containing one or more whipped ingredients **b** : a kitchen utensil used in whipping **4** : one that handles a whip; *esp* : a driver of horses **5** : a member of a legislative body appointed by a party to enforce discipline and to secure the attendance of party members at important sessions **6** : a whipping or thrashing motion **7** : a flexible radio antenna — called also *whip antenna* — **whip·like** \'hwip-,līk, 'wip-\ *adj*

whip·cord \'hwip-,kórd, 'wip-\ *n* **1** : a thin tough cord made of braided or twisted hemp or catgut **2** : a cloth of hard-twisted yarns that has fine diagonal cords or ribs

whip hand *n* : positive control : ADVANTAGE

whip·lash \'hwip-,lash, 'wip-\ *n* **1** : the lash of a whip **2** : WHIPLASH INJURY

whiplash injury *n* : injury to the spine often with concussion that is caused by violent flexing of the head and neck (as in an automobile accident)

whip·per·snap·per \'hwip-ər-,snap-ər, 'wip-\ *n* : a small, insignificant, or impertinent person [alteration of earlier *snippersnapper,* of unknown origin]

whip·pet \'hwip-ət, 'wip-\ *n* : a small swift slender dog of greyhound type that is often used for racing [probably from ¹*whip*]

whipping boy *n* : SCAPEGOAT 2 [from the former practice of maintaining a boy to share the education of a prince and be punished in the prince's stead]

whipping post *n* : a post to which offenders are tied to be legally whipped

whip·ple·tree *variant of* WHIFFLETREE

whip·poor·will \,hwip-ər-'wil, ,wip-; 'hwip-ər-,, 'wip-\ *n* : an insect-eating bird of the eastern United States and Canada that is active at night and is often heard at nightfall and just before dawn

whippoorwill

¹whip·saw \'hwip-,só, 'wip-\ *n* **1** : a narrow saw tapering from butt to point and having hook teeth **2** : a crosscut saw operated by two people [²*whip*]

²whipsaw *vt* **whip·sawed; whip·saw·ing** **1** : to saw with a whipsaw **2** : to victimize in two opposite ways at once, by a two-phase operation, or by the combined action of two opponents

whip scorpion *n* : any of an order (Pedipalpida) of arachnids somewhat resembling true scorpions but having a long slender tail process and no sting

whip·worm \'hwip-,wərm, 'wip-\ *n* : any of a family of parasitic roundworms with a body thickened behind and very long and slender in front; *esp* : one of the human intestine

¹whir *also* **whirr** \'hwər, 'wər\ *vb* **whirred; whir·ring** : to fly, revolve, or move rapidly with a whir [Middle English *quirren*]

²whir *also* **whirr** *n* : a continuous fluttering or vibrating sound made by something in rapid motion

¹whirl \'hwərl, 'wərl\ *vb* **1** : to move or drive in a circle or curve especially with force or speed **2 a** : to turn or cause to turn on or around an axis : SPIN **b** : to turn about abruptly : WHEEL **3** : to pass, move, or go quickly **4** : to become giddy or dizzy : REEL [Middle English *whirlen*] — **whirl·er** \'hwər-lər, 'wər-\ *n*

²whirl *n* **1 a** : a rapid whirling movement **b** : something whirling ⟨a *whirl* of dust⟩ **2 a** : COMMOTION 2 **b** : a confused or giddy mental state **3** : an experimental attempt : TRY

whirl·i·gig \'hwər-li-,gig, 'wər-\ *n* **1** : a toy that has a whirling motion **2** : one that continuously whirls or changes; *also* : a whirling course (as of events) [Middle English *whirlegigg,* from *whirlen* "to whirl" + *gigg* "top"]

whirligig beetle *n* : any of a family of swift-moving beetles that live mostly on the surface of water

whirl·pool \'hwərl-,púl, 'wərl-\ *n* : water moving rapidly in a circle so as to produce a depression in the center into which floating objects may be drawn : EDDY, VORTEX

whirl·wind \-,wind\ *n* **1** : a small rotating windstorm marked by an inward and upward spiral motion of the lower air **2** : a confused rush : WHIRL

whirly·bird \'hwər-lē-,bərd, 'wər-\ *n* : HELICOPTER

¹whish \'hwish, 'wish\ *vb* **1** : to urge on or cause to move with a whish **2** : to make a whizzing or swishing sound **3** : to move with a whish especially at high speed : WHIZ [imitative]

²whish *n* : a rushing sound : SWISH

¹whisk \'hwisk, 'wisk\ *n* **1** : a quick light brushing or sweeping motion ⟨a *whisk* of the hand⟩ **2 a** : a usually wire kitchen implement for beating food **b** : WHISK BROOM [Middle English *wisk*]

²whisk *vb* **1** : to move nimbly and quickly ⟨squirrels *whisked* up the trees⟩ **2** : to move or convey briskly ⟨*whisked* the children off to bed⟩ **3** : to mix or fluff up

¹whisk 2a

\ə\ abut	\ng\ sing
\ər\ further	\ō\ bone
\a\ mat	\ò\ saw
\ā\ take	\òi\ coin
\ä\ cot, cart	\th\ thin
\aù\ out	\th\ this
\ch\ chin	\ü\ food
\e\ pet	\ú\ foot
\ē\ easy	\y\ yet
\g\ go	\yü\ few
\i\ tip	\yù\ cure
\ī\ life	\zh\ vision
\j\ job	

by or as if by beating with a whisk ⟨*whisk* eggs⟩ **4** : to brush or wipe off lightly ⟨*whisk* crumbs from a table⟩

whisk broom *n* : a small broom with a short handle

whis·ker \'hwis-kər, 'wis-\ *n* **1 a** : a hair of the beard **b** *pl* : the part of the beard growing on the sides of the face or on the chin **c** : HAIRBREADTH ⟨lost the race by a *whisker*⟩ **2** : one of the long projecting hairs or bristles growing near the mouth of an animal (as a cat or bird) [derived from ²*whisk*] — **whis·kered** \-kərd\ *adj*

whis·key *or* **whis·ky** \'hwis-kē, 'wis-\ *n, pl* **whiskeys** *or* **whiskies** : a distilled alcoholic liquor made from fermented mash of grain (as rye, corn, barley, or wheat) [Irish Gaelic *uisce beathadh* and Scottish Gaelic *uisge beatha,* literally, "water of life"]

¹whis·per \'hwis-pər, 'wis-\ *vb* **whis·pered; whis·per·ing** \-pə-ring, -pring\ **1** : to speak very low or under the breath **2** : to tell or utter by whispering ⟨*whisper* a secret⟩ **3** : to make a low rustling sound ⟨*whispering* leaves⟩ [Old English *hwisperian*] — **whis·per·er** \-pər-ər\ *n*

²whisper *n* **1 a** : an act or instance of whispering; *esp* : speech without vibration of the vocal cords **b** : a sibilant sound that resembles whispered speech **2 a** : RUMOR ⟨*whispers* of a scandal⟩ **b** : HINT 2a, TRACE

whispering campaign *n* : the systematic spreading of derogatory rumors or charges especially against a candidate for public office

whist \'hwist, 'wist\ *n* : a card game for four players from which bridge developed [earlier *whisk,* probably from ³*whisk;* from whisking up the tricks]

¹whis·tle \'hwis-əl, 'wis-\ *n* **1** : a device by which a shrill sound is produced ⟨a tin *whistle*⟩ ⟨a steam *whistle*⟩ **2 a** : a shrill clear sound produced by forcing breath out or air in through puckered lips **b** : the sound or signal produced by a whistle or as if by whistling; *esp* : the shrill clear note of a bird or other animal [Old English *hwistle*]

²whistle *vb* **whis·tled; whis·tling** \'hwis-ling, 'wis-, -ə-ling\ **1 a** : to make a whistle through the puckered lips **b** : to utter a shrill note or call resembling a whistle **c** : to make a shrill clear sound especially by rapid movement ⟨bullets *whistled* by⟩ **d** : to blow or sound a whistle **2** : to signal, order, or summon someone or something by or as if by whistling ⟨*whistle* to a dog⟩ **3** : to send, bring, signal, or call by or as if by whistling ⟨*whistle* the dog back⟩ **4** : to produce, utter, or express by whistling ⟨*whistle* a tune⟩ — **whis·tler** \'hwis-lər, 'wis-, -ə-lər\ *n*

¹whis·tle-stop \'hwis-əl-,stäp, 'wis-\ *n* **1 a** : a small station at which trains stop only on signal **b** : a small community **2** : a brief personal appearance by a political candidate usually on the rear platform of a touring train

²whistle-stop *vi* : to tour especially in a political campaign with many brief personal appearances in small communities

whit \'hwit, 'wit\ *n* : the smallest part imaginable : BIT ⟨cared not a *whit*⟩ [Old English *wiht* "creature, thing, bit"]

¹white \'hwīt, 'wīt\ *adj* **1 a** : free from color **b** : of the color of new snow or milk; *esp* : of the color white **c** : light or pale in color ⟨*white* wine⟩ ⟨lips *white* with fear⟩ **d** : lustrous pale gray : SILVERY; *also* : made of silver **2 a** : of, relating to, or being a member of a group or race characterized by relatively light pigmentation **b** *slang* : FAIR 5a, HONEST **3** : free from spot or blemish: as **a** : free from moral impurity : INNOCENT **b** : unmarked by writing or printing **c** : not intended to cause harm ⟨a *white* lie⟩ ⟨*white* magic⟩ **d** : FAVORABLE, FORTUNATE ⟨a *white* day in my life⟩ **4 a** : wearing or clothed in white **b** : marked by the presence of snow : SNOWY ⟨a *white* Christmas⟩ **5** : very ardent : PASSIONATE ⟨in a *white* fury⟩ **6** : ultraconservative or reactionary in political outlook and action [Old English *hwīt*] — **white·ly** *adv* — **white·ness** *n*

²white *n* **1** : the color of fresh snow **2** : a white or light-colored thing or part: as **a** : a mass of albuminous material surrounding the yolk of an egg **b** : the white part of the ball of the eye **c** : the light-colored pieces in a two-handed board game (as chess) or the player by whom these are played **3** : one that is or approaches the color white **4** : a person belonging to a light-skinned race **5** : a member of a conservative or reactionary political group

white ant *n* : TERMITE

white bass *n* : a North American freshwater food fish

white-beard \'hwīt-,biərd, 'wīt-\ *n* : an old man : GRAY-BEARD

white blood cell *n* : LEUKOCYTE; *esp* : a leukocyte of the blood

white·cap \'hwīt-,kap, 'wīt-\ *n* : a wave crest breaking into white foam

white cedar *n* : any of various North American timber trees: as **a** : a strong-scented evergreen swamp tree that somewhat resembles an arborvitae but has smaller leaves **b** : a common arborvitae

white cell *n* : LEUKOCYTE

white chocolate *n* : a confection of cocoa butter, sugar, milk, lecithin, and flavorings

white clover *n* : a Eurasian clover with round heads of white flowers that is widely used in lawns and pastures and is an important honey plant — called also *Dutch clover, white Dutch clover*

white-col·lar \'hwīt-'käl-ər, 'wīt-\ *adj* : of, relating to, or being the group of salaried employees whose duties do not call for the wearing of work clothes or protective clothing

white corpuscle *n* : LEUKOCYTE

white crappie *n* : a silvery North American sunfish highly esteemed as a panfish and often used for stocking small ponds

white dwarf *n* : a small very dense whitish star of high surface temperature and low luminosity

white elephant *n* **1** : something requiring much care and expense and yielding little profit **2** : an object no longer wanted by its owner though not without value to others [from the fact that in parts of India pale-colored elephants are considered sacred and are maintained without being required to work]

white-faced \'hwīt-'fāst, 'wīt-\ *adj* **1** : having a wan pale face **2** : having the face white in whole or in part ⟨a *white-faced* steer⟩

white feather *n* : a mark or symbol of cowardice ⟨show the *white* feather⟩ [from the superstition that a white feather in the plumage of a gamecock is a mark of a poor fighter]

white-fish \'hwīt-,fish, 'wīt-\ *n* : any of various freshwater food fishes related to the salmons and trouts and mostly greenish above and silvery white below

white flag *n* : a flag of plain white used as a sign of truce or of surrender

white-fly \'hwīt-,flī, 'wīt-\ *n* : any of various small white winged insects related to the scale insects and especially destructive to greenhouse plants

white friar *n, often cap W & F* : CARMELITE [from the white habit]

white gold *n* : a pale alloy of gold especially with nickel or palladium that resembles platinum in appearance

white goods *n pl* **1** : cotton or linen fabrics or articles (as sheets or towels) **2** : major household appliances (as stoves)

white grub *n* : a grub that is the larva of a june beetle and a destructive pest of grass roots

White-hall \'hwīt-,hol, 'wīt-\ *n* : the British government [*Whitehall,* street of London in which are located the chief offices of the British government]

white-head \'hwīt-,hed, 'wīt-\ *n* : a small whitish elevation of the skin caused by accumulation of oil gland secretion when the duct of the gland is blocked by a thin layer of skin cells

white heat *n* **1** : a temperature at which a body (as of metallic or ceramic material) becomes brightly incandescent so as to appear white **2** : a state of intense mental or physical strain, emotion, or activity

White Horde *n* : a Mongolian people powerful in Russia in the 14th century

white–hot \'hwīt-'hät, 'wīt-\ *adj* : being at or radiating white heat

White House *n* : the executive department of the United States goverment [the *White House,* mansion in Washington, D.C. assigned to the use of the president of the United States]

white lead *n* : a heavy white poisonous carbonate of lead chiefly used as a pigment

white–liv·ered \'hwīt-'liv-ərd, 'wīt-\ *adj* : COWARDLY 1, LILY-LIVERED

white matter *n* : whitish nerve tissue that consists largely of nerve fibers sheathed in a fatty material and underlies the gray matter of the brain and spinal cord or forms nerves

whit·en \'hwīt-n, 'wīt-\ *vb* **whit·ened; whit·en·ing** \'hwīt-ning, 'wīt-, -n-ing\ : to make or become white or whiter □ SYN WHITEN, BLANCH, BLEACH mean to make or grow white or whiter. WHITEN implies making white often by the application or addition of a white substance ⟨*whiten* stained linen with a bleach⟩ BLANCH implies the removal or withdrawal of color especially from living tissue ⟨*blanch* plants by growing them in darkness⟩ BLEACH implies the action of sunlight or chemicals in removing color.

whit·en·er \'hwīt-nər, 'wīt-, -n-ər\ *n* : one that whitens; *esp* : an agent (as a bleach) used to impart whiteness to something

white oak *n* : any of various oaks with acorns that mature in one year and leaf veins that never extend beyond the margin of the leaf; *also* : the hard, strong, durable, and moisture-resistant wood of a white oak

white paper *n* : a government report on a subject

white pepper *n* : a pungent seasoning that consists of the fruit of the East Indian pepper ground after the outer husk has been removed

white perch *n* : a small silvery sea bass of the coast and coastal streams of the eastern United States

white pine *n* : a tall-growing pine of eastern North America with needles in clusters of five; *also* : its wood which is much used in building construction

white–pine blister rust *n* : a destructive disease of white pine caused by a rust fungus that passes part of its life on currant or gooseberry bushes; *also* : this fungus

white potato *n* : POTATO 2b

white rust *n* : any of various plant diseases caused by lower fungi and marked by production of masses of white spores that escape through ruptures in the host tissue; *also* : a fungus causing a white rust

white sale *n* : a sale of white goods

white sauce *n* : a sauce consisting essentially of milk, cream, or stock with flour and seasoning

white sea bass *n* : a large Pacific croaker closely related to the Atlantic weakfishes

white shark *n* : GREAT WHITE SHARK

white·tail \'hwīt-,tāl, 'wīt-\ *n* : WHITE-TAILED DEER

white–tailed deer *n* : a North American deer with forward-arching antlers and with a rather long tail white on the underside — called also *Virginia deer*

white tie *n* : formal evening dress for men

white·wall \'hwīt-,wȯl, 'wīt-\ *n* : an automobile tire having a white band on the sidewall

white walnut *n* : BUTTERNUT 2

¹white·wash \'hwīt-,wȯsh, 'wīt-, -,wäsh\ *vt* **1** : to whiten with whitewash **2** : to clear of a charge of wrongdoing by offering excuses, hiding facts, or conducting a superficial investigation — **white·wash·er** *n*

²whitewash *n* **1** : a composition (as of lime and water) for whitening structural surfaces **2** : a covering up or glossing over of something (as wrongdoing)

white·wood \'hwīt-,wùd, 'wīt-\ *n* **1** : any of various trees with pale or white wood: as **a** : COTTONWOOD **b** : TULIP TREE **2** : the wood of a whitewood and especially of the tulip tree

¹whith·er \'hwith-ər, 'with-\ *adv* **1** : to what place ⟨*whither* will they go⟩ **2** : to what situation, position, degree, or end ⟨*whither* will this abuse drive me⟩ [Old English *hwider*]

²whither *conj* **1 a** : to the place at, in, or to which **b** : to which place **2** : to whatever place

whith·er·so·ev·er \,hwith-ər-sə-'wev-ər, ,with-\ *conj* : ²WHITHER 2

whith·er·ward \'hwith-ər-wərd, 'with-\ *adv* : toward what or which place

¹whit·ing \'hwīt-ing, 'wīt-\ *n, pl* **whiting** *or* **whitings** : any of several edible fishes (as the hake) found mostly near seacoasts [Dutch *witinc,* from *wit* "white"]

²whiting *n* : calcium carbonate prepared as fine powder and used especially as a pigment and extender, in putty, and in rubber compounding

whit·ish \'hwīt-ish, 'wīt-\ *adj* : somewhat white

Whit·sun \'hwit-sən, 'wit-\ *adj* : of, relating to, or observed on Whitsunday or at Whitsuntide

Whit·sun·day \'sən-dē, -sən-,dā\ : PENTECOST 2 [Old English *hwīta sunnandæg,* literally, "white Sunday"]

Whit·sun·tide \-sən-,tīd\ *n* : the week beginning with Whitsunday; *esp* : the first three days of this week

whit·tle *vb* **whit·tled; whit·tling** \'hwit-ling, 'wit-, -l-ing\ **1 a** : to pare or cut off chips from the surface of (wood) with a knife **b** : to shape or form by paring or cutting **c** : to cut or shape something by or as if by whittling it **2** : PARE 2 [Middle English *thwitel, whittel* "large knife", from *thwiten* "to whittle", from Old English *thwītan*] — **whit·tler** \'hwit-lər, 'wit-, -l-ər\ *n*

¹whiz *or* **whizz** \'hwiz, 'wiz\ *vb* **whizzed; whiz·zing** **1** : to buzz, whir, or hiss like a speeding object (as an arrow) passing through air **2** : to fly or move swiftly with a whiz **3** : to rotate very rapidly [imitative] — **whiz·zer** *n*

²whiz *or* **whizz** *n, pl* **whiz·zes** **1** : a hissing, buzzing, or whirring sound **2** : a movement or passage of something accompanied by a whizzing sound

³whiz *n, pl* **whiz·zes** : WIZARD 2 [probably from *wizard*]

whiz·bang *or* **whizz·bang** \'hwiz-,bang, 'wiz-\ *n* : one that is conspicuous for noise, speed, or startling effect

whiz–bang *adj* : EXCELLENT, FIRST-CLASS

who \hü, 'hü, ü\ *pron* **1** : what or which person or persons — used as an interrogative ⟨*who* was elected president⟩ ⟨find out *who* they are⟩; used by reputable writers, though disapproved by some grammarians, as the object of a verb or a following preposition ⟨*who* did you meet⟩ ⟨*who* is it for⟩ **2** : the person or persons that : WHOEVER **3** — used as a function word to introduce a relative clause; used especially in reference to persons but also in reference to groups, to animals, or to inanimate objects ⟨my friend, *who* was a lawyer⟩ ⟨a generation *who* has grown up⟩ ⟨dogs *who* bark too much⟩ ⟨earlier sources *who* disagree⟩; used by speakers on all educational levels and by many reputable writers though disapproved by some grammarians, as the object of a verb or a following preposition ⟨a person *who* you all know well⟩ [Old English *hwā*] □ SYN WHO, WHICH, THAT are relative pronouns. WHO is used usually of persons ⟨my friend, *who* is older than I⟩ ⟨those *who* believe in miracles⟩ WHICH refers to animals, to inanimate objects, or to ideas or situations expressed but not named (replacing *and that*) ⟨you are in trouble, *which* is why I am here⟩ THAT may be used of persons, animals, or things in restrictive clauses ⟨the first one *that* spoke to me⟩ ⟨the car *that* just went by⟩ but not in descriptive (nonrestrictive) clauses referring to persons; WHICH is less usual than THAT in re-

white-tailed deer

\ə\ abut		\ng\ sing	
\ər\ further		\ō\ bone	
\a\ mat		\ȯ\ saw	
\ā\ take		\ȯi\ coin	
\ä\ cot, cart		\th\ thin	
\au̇\ out		\th\ this	
\ch\ chin		\ü\ food	
\e\ pet		\u̇\ foot	
\ē\ easy		\y\ yet	
\g\ go		\yü\ few	
\i\ tip		\yu̇\ cure	
\ī\ life		\zh\ vision	
\j\ job			

strictive clauses referring to things except when it follows a preposition (the table on *which* it sat)

whoa \'wō, 'hō, 'hwō\ *imperative verb* — a command (as to a draft animal) to stand still [Middle English *whoo*]

who·dun·it \hü-'dən-ət\ *n* : a detective story or mystery story presented as a novel, play, or motion picture [*who done it?*]

who·ev·er \hü-'ev-ər\ *pron* : whatever person : no matter who — used in any grammatical relation except that of a possessive

¹**whole** \'hōl\ *adj* **1** : being in healthy or sound condition : free from defect or damage : WELL (careful nursing made me *whole* again) **2** : having all its proper parts or elements (*whole* milk) **3 a** : constituting the total sum of : ENTIRE (gave their *whole* time to study) **b** : each or all of the (the *whole* 10 days) **4 a** : constituting an undivided unit (a *whole* roast suckling pig) **b** : directed to one end (give it your *whole* attention) **5 a** : seemingly complete or total (the *whole* sky was red) **b** : very great (feels a *whole* lot better) [Old English *hāl*] — **whole·ness** *n* □ SYN WHOLE, ENTIRE, PERFECT mean not lacking or faulty in any particular. WHOLE suggests a completeness or perfection that is normal and can be sought, gained, or regained (education makes a person *whole*) ENTIRE implies wholeness deriving from integrity, soundness, or completeness with nothing omitted or taken away; PERFECT implies the soundness and excellence of every part or element often as an unattainable or theoretical state (one's idea of the *perfect* novel)

²**whole** *n* **1** : a complete amount or sum : a number, aggregate, or totality lacking no part, member, or element **2** : something constituting a complex unity : an orderly system or organization of parts fitting or working together as one — **whole·ness** *n* — **on the whole 1** : in view of all the circumstances or conditions : all things considered **2** : in general : in most instances : TYPICALLY

whole·heart·ed \'hōl-'härt-əd\ *adj* : undivided in purpose, enthusiasm, or will : HEARTY (*wholehearted* support) — **whole·heart·ed·ly** *adv* — **whole·heart·ed·ness** *n*

whole hog *n* : the whole way or farthest limit : ALL (go the *whole hog*) — **whole–hog** \'hōl-'hòg, -'häg\ *adj or adv* — **whole–hog·ger** \-'hòg-ər, -'häg-\ *n*

whole note *n* : a musical note equal in value to four quarter notes or two half notes to one measure

whole number *n* : INTEGER

¹**whole·sale** \'hōl-,sāl\ *n* : the sale of goods in large quantities usually for resale by a retail merchant

²**wholesale** *adj* **1** : of, relating to, or engaged in wholesaling (a *wholesale* grocer) (*wholesale* prices) **2** : done on a large scale (*wholesale* slaughter) — **wholesale** *adv*

³**wholesale** *vb* : to sell at wholesale — **whole·sal·er** *n*

whole·some \'hōl-səm\ *adj* **1** : promoting mental, spiritual, or bodily health or well-being (*wholesome* advice) (a *wholesome* environment) **2** : sound in body, mind, or morals **3** : based on well-grounded fear : PRUDENT (*wholesome* respect for the law) SYN see HEALTHFUL — **whole·some·ly** *adv* — **whole·some·ness** *n*

whole–souled \-'sōld\ *adj* : WHOLEHEARTED

whole step *n* : a musical interval comprising two half steps — called also *whole tone*

whole wheat *adj* : made of ground entire wheat kernels

whol·ly \'hōl-lē, 'hō-lē\ *adv* **1** : to the full or entire extent : COMPLETELY (*wholly* incompetent) **2** : to the exclusion of other things : SOLELY

whom \hüm, 'hüm, üm\ *pron, objective case of* WHO — used as an interrogative or relative; used as object of a verb or a preceding preposition (to *whom* was it given) or less frequently as the object of a following preposition (the person *whom* you spoke to) though now often considered stilted especially as an interrog-

ative and especially in oral use [Old English *hwām*, dative of *hwā* "who"]

whom·ev·er \hü-'mev-ər\ *pron, objective case of* WHOEVER

whom·so \'hüm-sō\ *pron, objective case of* WHOSO

whom·so·ev·er \,hüm-sə-'wev-ər\ *pron, objective case of* WHOSOEVER

¹**whoop** \'hüp, 'hwüp, 'hùp, 'hwùp, 'wùp\ *vb* **1** : to shout or call loudly and vigorously especially in eagerness, enthusiasm, or enjoyment (the kids *whooped* with joy) **2** : to make the sound that follows an attack of coughing in whooping cough **3** : to go or pass with a loud noise **4 a** : to utter or express with a whoop **b** : to urge, drive, or cheer on with a whoop [Middle French *houpper*] — **whoop it up 1** : to celebrate riotously : CAROUSE **2** : to stir up enthusiasm

²**whoop** *n* **1** : a whooping sound or utterance: as **a** : a shout of hunters or of persons in battle or pursuit **b** : a loud booming cry of a bird (as an owl or crane) **c** : a crowing sound accompanying the intake of breath after a coughing attack in whooping cough **2** : WHIT, BIT (not worth a *whoop*)

¹**whoop·ee** \'hwüp-,ē, 'wùp-; 'hwü-,pē, 'hü-, 'wü-\ *interj* — used to express delight or high spirits [derived from ²*whoop*]

²**whoopee** *n* : boisterous convivial fun

whooping cough *n* : an infectious bacterial disease especially of children marked by a convulsive spasmodic cough sometimes followed by a crowing intake of breath — called also *pertussis*

whooping crane *n* : a large white nearly extinct North American crane

whoop·la \'hüp-,lä, 'hwüp-, 'hùp-, 'hwùp-\ *n* **1** : a noisy commotion **2** : boisterous merrymaking [alteration of *hoopla*]

whoops \'wùps, 'ùps\ *interj* : OOPS

¹**whoosh** \'hwùsh, 'wùsh, 'hwùsh, 'wùsh\ *vb* : to move with an explosive or hissing rush [imitative]

²**whoosh** *n* : a swift or explosive rush

whop \'hwäp, 'wäp\ *vt* **whopped; whop·ping 1** : BEAT, HIT (*whopped* me with a bat) **2** : WHIP 4 [Middle English *wappen, whappen* "to throw, strike"]

whop·per \'hwäp-ər, 'wäp-\ *n* **1** : an unusually large thing **2** : a big lie

whop·ping \'hwäp-ing, 'wäp-\ *adj* : very large or great

¹**whore** \'hōr, 'hòr, 'hùr\ *n* : PROSTITUTE [Old English *hōre*]

²**whore** *vi* : to have unlawful sexual intercourse as or with a whore

whorl \'hwòrl, 'wòrl, 'hwərl, 'wərl\ *n* **1** : a row of parts (as leaves or petals) encircling an axis and especially a stem **2** : something that whirls, coils, or spirals or whose form suggests such movement **3** : one of the turns of a univalve shell [Middle English *wharle, whorle*] — **whorled** \'hwòrld, 'hwərld\ *adj*

whor·tle·ber·ry \'hwərt-l-,ber-ē, 'wərt-\ *n* : a European blueberry with a blackish berry : BILBERRY; *also* : its berry [Middle English *hurtilberye*, from Old English *horte* "whortleberry"]

¹**whose** \hüz, 'hüz, üz\ *adj* : of or relating to whom or which especially as possessor or possessors, agent or agents, or object or objects of an action (asked *whose* cars they were) (*whose* plays are greater than Shakespeare's?) (the book *whose* publication was announced) [Middle English *whos*, genitive of *who, what*]

²**whose** \hüz, 'hüz\ *pron* : that which belongs to whom — used without a following noun as a pronoun equivalent in meaning to the adjective whose

whose·so·ev·er \,hüz-sə-'wev-ər\ *adj* : of or relating to whomsoever

whoso \'hü-,sō\ *pron* : WHOEVER

who·so·ev·er \,hü-sə-'wev-ər\ *pron* : WHOEVER

¹**why** \hwī, 'hwī, wī, 'wī\ *adv* : for what cause, reason, or purpose (*why* did you do it) [Old English *hwy̆*, from *hwæt* "what"]

²why *conj* **1** : the cause, reason, or purpose for which ⟨know *why* you did it⟩ ⟨that is *why* you did it⟩ **2** : for which : on account of which ⟨know the reason *why* you did it⟩

³why \'hwī, 'wī\ *n, pl* **whys** : REASON, CAUSE ⟨the *why* of sexist prejudice⟩

⁴why \wī, ,wī, hwī, ,hwī\ *interj* — used to express mild surprise, hesitation, approval, disapproval, or impatience ⟨*why*, here's what I was looking for⟩

whyd·ah \'hwid-ə, 'wid-\ *n* : any of various mostly black and white African weaverbirds often kept as cage birds [from earlier *widow (bird)*; from its long black tail feathers resembling a widow's veil]

wick \'wik\ *n* : a cord, strip, or ring of loosely woven material through which a liquid (as melted tallow, wax, or oil) is drawn by capillary action to the top in a candle, lamp, or oil stove for burning [Old English *wēoce*]

wick·ed \'wik-əd\ *adj* **1** : morally bad : EVIL **2 a** : FIERCE, VICIOUS ⟨a *wicked* dog⟩ **b** : inclined to mischief : ROGUISH ⟨a *wicked* glance⟩ **3 a** : REPUGNANT, VILE ⟨a *wicked* odor⟩ **b** : causing or likely to cause harm or trouble ⟨a *wicked* storm⟩ [Middle English *wicke*] — **wick·ed·ly** *adv* — **wick·ed·ness** *n*

wick·er \'wik-ər\ *n* **1** : a flexible twig or osier : WITHE **2** : WICKERWORK [of Scandinavian origin] — **wicker** *adj*

wick·er·work \-,wərk\ *n* : work of osiers, twigs or rods : BASKETRY

wick·et \'wik-ət\ *n* **1** : a small gate or door; *esp* : one in or near a larger one **2** : a small window with a grille or grate (as at a ticket office) **3** : either of the 2 sets of 3 rods topped by 2 crosspieces at which the ball is bowled in cricket **4** : an arch or hoop in croquet [Old North French *wiket*, of Germanic origin]

wick·et·keep·er \-,kē-pər\ *n* : the player who plays immediately behind the wicket in cricket

wick·ing \'wik-ing\ *n* : material for wicks

wick·i·up \'wik-ē-,əp\ *n* : a cone-shaped American Indian hut consisting of a rough frame covered with reed mats, grass, or brushwood [of American Indian origin]

¹wide \'wīd\ *adj* **1** : covering a vast area ⟨the *wide* world⟩ **2** : having a specified extent from side to side ⟨cloth 100 centimeters *wide*⟩ **3** : having a generous measure across : BROAD ⟨the road isn't very *wide*⟩ **4** : opened as far as possible ⟨eyes *wide* with wonder⟩ **5** : not limited : EXTENSIVE ⟨*wide* experience⟩ **6** : far from the goal, mark, or truth ⟨a *wide* guess⟩ [Old English *wīd*] SYN see BROAD — **wide·ly** *adv* — **wide·ness** *n*

²wide *adv* **1 a** : over a great distance of extent ⟨searched far and *wide*⟩ **b** : over a specified distance, area, or extent ⟨expanded the business country-*wide*⟩ **2 a** : so as to leave much space or distance between ⟨*wide* apart⟩ **b** : so as to pass at or clear by a considerable distance ⟨ran *wide* around left end⟩ **3** : FULLY 1 ⟨opened my eyes *wide*⟩

wide–awake \,wīd-ə-'wāk\ *adj* : fully awake; *also* : knowingly watchful : ALERT — **wide–awake·ness** *n*

wide–eyed \'wīd-'īd\ *adj* **1** : having the eyes wide open especially with wonder or astonishment **2** : marked by unsophisticated or uncritical acceptance or admiration : NAIVE ⟨*wide-eyed* innocence⟩

wide–mouthed \-'maùthd, -'maùtht\ *adj* **1** : having a wide mouth ⟨*widemouthed* jars⟩ **2** : having one's mouth opened wide (as in awe)

wid·en \'wīd-n\ *vb* **wid·ened; wid·en·ing** \'wīd-ning, -n-ing\ : to make or become wide or wider : BROADEN — **wid·en·er** *n*

wide receiver *n* : an offensive football player principally used to catch passes who lines up several yards wide of the formation

wide·spread \'wīd-'spred\ *adj* **1** : widely extended ⟨*widespread* wings⟩ **2** : widely distributed or prevalent ⟨*widespread* hostility⟩

wid·geon *also* **wi·geon** \'wij-ən\ *n, pl* **widgeon** *or* **widgeons** : any of several freshwater ducks between the teal and the mallard in size [origin unknown]

wid·ish \'wīd-ish\ *adj* : somewhat wide

¹wid·ow \'wid-ō\ *n* **1** : a woman who has lost her husband by death; *esp* : one who has not remarried **2** : GRASS WIDOW [Old English *widuwe*] — **wid·ow·hood** \-,hùd\ *n*

²widow *vt* : to cause to become a widow ⟨*widowed* by war⟩

wid·ow·er \'wid-ə-wər\ *n* : a man who has lost his wife by death and has not married again — **wid·ow·er·hood** \-,hùd\ *n*

widow's peak *n* : a point formed by the hair on the forehead

widow's walk *n* : a railed observation platform atop a usually coastal house

width \'width, 'witth\ *n* **1** : a distance from side to side : the measurement taken at right angles to the length : BREADTH **2** : largeness of extent or scope **3** : a measured and cut piece of material ⟨a *width* of calico⟩ ⟨a *width* of lumber⟩ [¹*wide*]

width·ways \-,wāz\ *adv* : WIDTHWISE

width·wise \-,wīz\ *adv* : in the direction of width

wield \'wēld\ *vt* **1** : to handle effectively ⟨*wield* a broom⟩ **2** : to exert one's authority by means of ⟨*wield* influence⟩ [Old English *wieldan*] — **wield·er** *n*

wieldy \'wēl-dē\ *adj* : capable of wielding or being wielded

wie·ner \'wē-nər, -nē, 'win-ē\ *n* : FRANKFURTER [German *wienerwurst* "Vienna sausage"]

Wie·ner schnit·zel \'vē-nər-,shnit-səl, ,snit-; 'wē-nər-,snit-\ *n* : a thin breaded veal cutlet served with a garnish [German, literally, "Vienna cutlet"]

wife \'wīf\ *n, pl* **wives** \'wīvz\ **1 a** *dialect* : WOMAN 1, 4 **b** : a woman acting in a specified capacity — used in combination ⟨house*wife*⟩ **2** : a married woman [Old English *wīf*] — **wife·hood** \'wīf-,hùd, 'wī-,fùd\ *n* — **wife·less** \'wī-fləs\ *adj*

wife·ly \'wī-flē\ *adj* **wife·li·er; -est** : of, relating to, or befitting a wife — **wife·li·ness** *n*

wig \'wig\ *n* : a manufactured covering of natural or artificial hair for the head; *also* : TOUPEE [short for *periwig*]

wig·gle \'wig-əl\ *vb* **wig·gled; wig·gling** \'wig-ling, -ə-ling\ **1** : to move to and fro with quick jerky or shaking motions : JIGGLE ⟨*wiggled* my toes⟩ **2** : to proceed with twisting and turning movements : WRIGGLE [Middle English *wiglen*] — **wiggle** *n*

wig·gler \'wig-lər, -ə-lər\ *n* **1** : one that wiggles **2** : a larval or pupal mosquito — called also *wriggler*

wig·gly \'wig-lē, -ə-lē\ *adj* **wig·gli·er; -est** **1** : tending to wiggle ⟨a *wiggly* worm⟩ **2** : WAVY ⟨*wiggly* lines⟩

wight \'wīt\ *n* : a living being : CREATURE [Old English *wiht* "creature, thing"]

¹wig·wag \'wig-,wag\ *vb* **wig·wagged; -wag·ging** **1** : to signal by or as if by a flag or light waved according to a code **2** : to make or cause to make a signal (as with the hand or arm) [English dialect *wig* "to move" + English *wag*]

²wigwag *n* **1** : the art or practice of wigwagging **2** : the act of wigwagging

wig·wam \'wig-,wäm\ *n* : an American Indian hut having typically an arched framework of poles overlaid with bark, rush mats, or hides [of American Indian origin]

wil·co \'wil-kō\ *interj* — used especially in radio and signaling to indicate that a message received will be complied with [*wil*l *co*mply]

¹wild \'wīld\ *adj* **1 a** : living in a state of nature and not ordinarily tame or domesticated ⟨*wild* duck⟩ **b** : growing or produced without the aid and care of humans ⟨*wild* honey⟩; *also* : related to or resembling a corresponding cultivated or domesticated organism ⟨*wild* plum⟩ **c** : of or relating to wild organisms ⟨the *wild* state⟩ **2** : not inhabited or cultivated ⟨*wild* land⟩ **3 a** : UNRULY ⟨a *wild* rage⟩ ⟨*wild* mobs⟩ **b** : TURBULENT, STORMY ⟨a *wild* night⟩ **c** : EXTRAVAGANT, FANTASTIC

wickiup

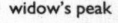

widow's peak

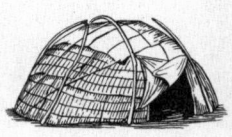

wigwam

⟨*wild* colors⟩ ⟨*wild* ideas⟩ **d** : indicative of strong passion, desire, or emotion ⟨a *wild* stare⟩ **4** : UNCIVILIZED 1, SAVAGE **5 a** : deviating from the natural or expected course ⟨a *wild* price increase⟩ **b** : having no basis in fact ⟨a *wild* guess⟩ **6** : capable of having any value designated by the holder ⟨poker with deuces *wild*⟩ [Old English *wilde*] — **wild·ly** *adv* — **wild·ness** \'wīld-nəs, 'wīl-\ *n*

²**wild** *n* **1** : WILDERNESS **2** : a natural uncultivated or undomesticated state or existence

³**wild** *adv* **1** : in a wild manner **2** : without regulation or control ⟨running *wild*⟩

wild and woolly *adj* : marked by a boisterous and untamed lack of polish and refinement ⟨a *wild and wooly* town⟩

wild boar

wild boar *n* : an Old World wild hog that has contributed to the ancestry of most domestic swine

wild carrot *n* : a widely naturalized white-flowered Eurasian weed that is probably the original of the cultivated carrot — called also *Queen Anne's lace*

¹**wild·cat** \'wīld-,kat, 'wīl-\ *n, pl* **wildcats** *or* **wildcat** **1** : any of various small or medium-sized cats (as the lynx or ocelot) **2** : a savage quick-tempered person

²**wildcat** *adj* **1 a** : financially irresponsible or unreliable ⟨*wildcat* banks⟩ **b** : issued by a wildcat bank ⟨*wildcat* currency⟩ **2** : operating, produced, or carried on outside the bounds of standard or legitimate business practices **3** : of, relating to, or being an oil or gas well drilled in territory not known to be productive **4** : begun by a group of workers without union approval or in violation of a contract ⟨a *wildcat* strike⟩

³**wildcat** *vi* **-cat·ted; -cat·ting** : to prospect and drill an experimental oil or gas well or mine shaft in territory not known to be productive — **wild·cat·ter** *n*

wil·de·beest \'wil-də-,bēst\ *n, pl* **wildebeests** *also* **wildebeest** : GNU [Afrikaans *wildebees,* from *wilde* "wild" + *bees* "beast, ox"]

wil·der·ness \'wil-dər-nəs\ *n* : an uncultivated and uninhabited region : wild or waste land [Middle English, from *wildern* "wild", from Old English *wilddēoren* "of wild beasts"]

wilderness area *n* : an area (as of national forest land) set aside for preservation of natural conditions for scientific or recreational purposes

wild–eyed \'wīl-'dīd\ *adj* **1** : having a wild expression in the eyes **2** : consisting of or favoring extreme measures ⟨*wild-eyed* schemes⟩

wild·fire \'wīld-,fīr, 'wīl-\ *n* **1** : a sweeping and destructive fire **2** : GREEK FIRE

wild flower *n* : the flower of a wild or uncultivated plant; *also* : a plant bearing wild flowers

wild·fowl \'wīld-,faùl, 'wīl-\ *n* : a game bird; *esp* : a game waterfowl (as a wild duck or goose) — **wild·fowl·er** \-,faù-lər\ *n* — **wild·fowl·ing** \-ling\ *n*

wild geranium *n* : a geranium of the eastern United States with rosy purple or white flowers

wild ginger *n* : a North American perennial woodland herb with pungent creeping rhizomes and bluntly heart-shaped leaves

wild–goose chase *n* : a fruitless pursuit or search

wild·ing \'wīl-ding\ *n* : a plant or animal growing or living in the wild — **wilding** *adj*

wild land *n* : WILDERNESS, WASTELAND

wild·life \'wīl-,dlīf, -,līf\ *n* : creatures that are neither human nor domesticated; *esp* : mammals, birds, and fishes hunted by man — **wildlife** *adj*

wild·ling \'wīl-dling, -ling\ *n* : a wild plant or animal

wild marjoram *n* : OREGANO

wild oat *n* **1** : any of several wild grasses closely related to the cultivated oat **2** *pl* : offenses and indiscretions blamed on youthful high spirits — usually used in the phrase *sow one's wild oats*

wild pansy *n* : a common and long-cultivated European viola which has small short-spurred flowers usually blue or purple mixed with white and yellow and from

which most of the garden pansies are derived — called also *heartsease, Johnny-jump-up*

wild parsley *n* : any of various wild plants of the carrot family with finely divided leaves

wild pitch *n* : a pitched ball that cannot be stopped by the catcher and that allows a base runner to advance

wild rice *n* : a tall aquatic North American perennial grass yielding an edible grain

wild type *n* : the typical form of an organism as ordinarily encountered in nature as contrasted with mutant individuals

wild West *n* : the western United States in its frontier period

wild·wood \'wīl-,dwùd, -,wùd\ *n* : a wood unaltered or unfrequented by humans

¹**wile** \'wīl\ *n* **1** : a trick or stratagem intended to tempt or deceive **2** : TRICKERY, GUILE [Middle English *wil*] SYN see TRICK

²**wile** *vt* : LURE, ENTICE ⟨the balmy weather *wiled* them from their work⟩

¹**will** \wəl, l, ᵊl, əl, wil, 'wil\ *vb, past* **would** \wəd, d, əd, wùd, 'wùd\; *present sing & pl* **will 1** : DESIRE, WISH ⟨call it what you *will*⟩ **2** — used as an auxiliary verb (1) to express desire, willingness, or in negative constructions refusal ⟨*will* you have another helping⟩ ⟨no one *would* do it⟩ ⟨they *won't* stop pestering me⟩, (2) to express frequent, customary, or habitual action or natural tendency ⟨*will* get angry over nothing⟩, (3) to express simple futurity ⟨tomorrow we *will* go⟩ (4) to express capability or sufficiency ⟨the back seat *will* hold three⟩, (5) to express probability or recognition and often to serve as the equivalent to the simple verb ⟨that *will* be the mail carrier ringing the doorbell⟩, (6) to express determination or willfulness ⟨I *will* go despite them⟩, and (7) to express a command ⟨you *will* do as I say⟩ [Old English *wille*]

²**will** \'wil\ *n* **1** : wish or desire often combined with determination ⟨the *will* to win⟩ **2** : something desired; *esp* : a choice or determination of one having authority or power **3** : the act, process, or experience of willing : VOLITION **4** : the process or power of wishing, choosing, desiring, or intending **5** : SELF-CONTROL ⟨a person of iron *will*⟩ **6** : a legal declaration in which a person states how his or her property is to be disposed of after death [Old English *willa* "will, desire"] — **at will** : as or whenever one wishes

³**will** \'wil\ *vb* **1** : to dispose of by or as if by a will : BEQUEATH **2 a** : to determine by an act of choice ⟨*willed* myself to sleep⟩ **b** : DECREE, ORDAIN ⟨Providence *wills* it⟩ **c** : INTEND, PURPOSE ⟨I *willed* it so⟩ **3** : to exercise the will

willed \'wild\ *adj* : having a will especially of a specified kind ⟨strong-*willed*⟩

wil·lem·ite \'wil-ə-,mīt\ *n* : a mineral Zn_2SiO_4 of variable color that consists of zinc silicate occurring in prisms and in massive or granular forms [German *willemit,* from *Willem* (William) I, died 1843, king of the Netherlands]

wil·let \'wil-ət\ *n, pl* **willet** : a large shorebird of the eastern and Gulf coasts and the central parts of North America [imitative]

will·ful *or* **wil·ful** \'wil-fəl\ *adj* **1** : stubbornly wanting one's own way : OBSTINATE **2** : done deliberately : INTENTIONAL ⟨*willful* murder⟩ SYN see VOLUNTARY — **willful·ly** \-fə-lē\ *adv* — **will·ful·ness** *n*

wil·lies \'wil-ēz\ *n pl* : a fit of nervousness : JITTERS [origin unknown]

will·ing \'wil-ing\ *adj* **1** : being agreeable and ready ⟨*willing* to go⟩ **2** : prompt to act or respond ⟨*willing* workers⟩ **3** : done, borne, or accepted by choice or without reluctance : VOLUNTARY ⟨*willing* obedience⟩ — **will·ing·ly** \-ing-lē\ *adv* — **will·ing·ness** *n*

wil·li·waw \'wil-i-,wó\ *n* **1** : a sudden violent gust of cold land air common along mountainous coasts of high latitudes **2** : a violent commotion or agitation [origin unknown]

will–less \'wil-ləs\ *adj* **1** : involving no exercise of the will ⟨*will-less* obedience⟩ **2** : not exercising the will

will–o'–the–wisp \,wil-ə-thə-'wisp\ *n* **1** : IGNIS FATUUS 1 **2** : a delusive goal or hope [*Will* (nickname for *William*) + *of* + *the* + *wisp*]

wil·low \'wil-ō\ *n* **1** : any of a large genus of trees and shrubs bearing catkins of flowers without petals and including forms of value for wood, osiers, or tanbark and a few ornamentals **2** : an object made of willow wood; *esp* : a cricket bat [Old English *welig*] — **willow** *adj* — **wil·low·like** \-,līk\ *adj*

willow herb *n* : any of a genus of herbs of the evening= primrose family; *esp* : FIREWEED 1

willow oak *n* : an oak with lance-shaped leaves

wil·low·ware \'wil-ə-,waər, 'wil-ō-, -,weər\ *n* : china that is usually blue and white and that is decorated with a design featuring a large willow tree by a little bridge

wil·lowy \'wil-ə-wē\ *adj* **1** : full of willows **2** : gracefully tall and slender

will·pow·er \'wil-,pau̇-ər, -,pau̇r\ *n* : energetic determination

wil·ly–nil·ly \,wil-ē-'nil-ē\ *adv or adj* : by compulsion : without choice ⟨rushed us along *willy-nilly*⟩ [alteration of *will I nill* (archaic negative of *will*) *I* or *will ye nill ye* or *will be nill he*]

¹wilt \wəlt, wilt, 'wilt\ *archaic present 2d sing of* WILL

²wilt \'wilt\ *vb* **1** : to lose or cause to lose freshness and become limp : DROOP ⟨*wilting* roses⟩ **2** : to grow weak or faint : LANGUISH [Middle English *welken*]

³wilt \'wilt\ *n* **1** : an act or instance of wilting : the state of being wilted **2** : a plant disorder (as various fungus diseases) in which the soft tissues lose their turgor and droop and often shrivel

wily \'wī-lē\ *adj* **wil·i·er; -est** : full of guile : TRICKY SYN see SLY — **wil·i·ness** *n*

wim·ble \'wim-bəl\ *n* : any of various instruments for boring holes [Anglo-French, from Dutch *wimmel* "auger"]

¹wim·ple \'wim-pəl\ *n* : a cloth covering worn over the head and around the neck and chin by women especially in the late medieval period and by some nuns [Old English *wimpel*]

²wimple *vb* **wim·pled; wim·pling** \-pə-ling, -pling\ **1** : to cover with or as if with a wimple **2** : to cause to ripple : RIPPLE **3** : to fall or lie in folds

¹win \'win\ *vb* **won** \'wən\; **win·ning 1** : to be first or best in or as if in a contest : SUCCEED **2** : to get possession of by effort **3 a** : to gain in or as if in battle or contest ⟨*win* land from the sea⟩ **b** : to be the victor in ⟨*won* the war⟩ **4** : to obtain by work : EARN **5** : to seek and gain the favor or support of; *also* : to gain the affections of or a promise of marriage from [Old English *winnan* "to struggle"]

²win *n* : VICTORY; *esp* : first place at the finish of a horse race

wince \'wins\ *vi* : to shrink back involuntarily (as from pain) : FLINCH [Middle English *wenchen* "to be impatient, dart about"] — **wince** *n*

winch \'winch\ *n* : a machine that has a roller on which rope is coiled for hauling or hoisting [Old English *wince*]

¹wind \'wind\ *n* **1** : a movement of the air of any velocity **2** : a force or agency that carries along or influences ⟨the *winds* of change⟩ **3 a** : BREATH **b** : the pit of the stomach : SOLAR PLEXUS **4** : gas generated in the stomach or the intestines **5** : something insubstantial; *esp* : idle words **6 a** : air carrying a scent (as of a hunter or game) **b** : slight information especially about something secret ⟨got *wind* of our plans⟩ **7 a** : wind instruments especially as distinguished from strings and percussion **b** *pl* : players of wind instruments **8 a** : a point of the compass; *esp* : one of the cardinal

points **b** : the direction from which the wind is blowing [Old English] — **get the wind up** : to become excited or alarmed — **have the wind of 1** : to be to windward of **2** : to be on the scent of **3** : to have a superior position to — **in the wind** : about to happen : ASTIR, AFOOT — **near the wind 1** : CLOSE-HAULED **2** : close to a point of danger : near the permissible limit — **off the wind** : away from the direction from which the wind is blowing — **under the wind 1** : to leeward **2** : in a place protected from the wind : under the lee

²wind *vt* **1** : to get a scent of ⟨the dogs *winded* game⟩ **2** : to cause to be out of breath **3** : to allow (as a horse) to rest so as to catch the breath

³wind \'wīnd, 'wind\ *vt* **wind·ed** \'wīn-dəd, 'win-\ *or* **wound** \'wau̇nd\; **wind·ing** : to sound by blowing ⟨*wind* a horn⟩ [¹*wind*]

⁴wind \'wīnd\ *vb* **wound** \'wau̇nd\ *also* **wind·ed; winding 1** : WARP 1a, BEND **2** : to have a curving course or shape ⟨a river *winding* through the valley⟩ **3** : to move or lie so as to encircle ⟨vines *winding* around a tree⟩ **4** : to turn when lying at anchor **5 a** : ENTANGLE 2 **b** : to introduce sinuously or stealthily : INSINUATE **6 a** : to encircle or cover with something pliable **b** : to turn completely or repeatedly about an object : COIL, TWINE ⟨*wind* thread on a spool⟩ **c** : to hoist or haul by means of a rope or chain and a windlass ⟨*wind* up a pail⟩ **d** (1) : to tighten the spring of ⟨*wind* a clock⟩ ⟨*wind* up a toy train⟩ (2) : CRANK ⟨*wound* down the car window⟩ **e** : to raise to a high level (as of excitement or tension) **7 a** : to cause to move in a curving line or path **b** : to traverse on a curving course ⟨the river *winds* the valley⟩ [Old English *windan* "to twist, brandish"]

⁵wind \'wīnd\ *n* : TURN 7c ⟨took a *wind* around the post⟩

wind·age \'win-dij\ *n* **1** : the influence of the wind in turning the course of a projectile **2** : the amount of deflection caused by the wind

wind·bag \'wind-,bag, 'win-\ *n* : a person who talks a lot without saying anything important

wind·blown \-,blōn\ *adj* : blown or looking as if blown by the wind

wind·bound \-,bau̇nd\ *adj* : prevented from sailing by a contrary or a high wind

wind·break \-,brāk\ *n* : something (as a growth of trees or shrubs) serving to break the force of wind

Wind·break·er \-,brā-kər\ *trademark* — used for a wind-resistant outer jacket with fitted cuffs and waistband

wind–bro·ken \-,brō-kən\ *adj* : having an impaired ability to breathe because of disease ⟨*wind-broken* horses⟩

wind·burn \-,bərn\ *n* : skin irritation caused by wind — **wind·burned** \-,bərnd\ *adj*

wind·chill \'wind-,chil, 'win-\ *n* : a still-air temperature that would have the same cooling effect on exposed human flesh as a given combination of temperature and wind speed — called also *windchill factor, windchill index*

wind cone *n* : WIND SOCK

wind·fall \'wind-,fȯl, 'win-\ *n* **1** : something (as a tree or fruit) blown down by the wind **2** : an unexpected or sudden gift, gain, or advantage

wind·flow·er \-,flau̇-ər, -,flau̇r\ *n* : ANEMONE

wind gap *n* : a notch in the crest of a mountain ridge

¹wind·ing \'wīn-ding\ *n* : material (as wire) wound or coiled about an object (as an armature); *also* : a single turn of the wound material

²winding *adj* : marked by winding: as **a** : having a pronounced curve **b** : having a course that winds

wind·ing–sheet \-,shēt\ *n* : a sheet used to wrap a corpse for burial : SHROUD

wind instrument *n* : a musical instrument played by blowing

wind·jam·mer \'wind-,jam-ər, 'win-\ *n* : a sailing ship or one of its crew

winch

\ə\ abut	\ng\ sing
\ər\ further	\ō\ bone
\a\ mat	\ȯ\ saw
\ā\ take	\ȯi\ coin
\ä\ cot, cart	\th\ thin
\au̇\ out	\th\ this
\ch\ chin	\ü\ food
\e\ pet	\u̇\ foot
\ē\ easy	\y\ yet
\g\ go	\yü\ few
\i\ tip	\yu̇\ cure
\ī\ life	\zh\ vision
\j\ job	

¹windmill

wind·lass \'win-dləs\ *n* : a winch used especially on ships for hauling and hoisting [Middle English *wyndas, wyndlas,* from Old Norse *vindāss,* from *vinda* "to wind" + *āss* "pole"]

¹**wind·mill** \'wind-,mil, 'win-\ *n* : a mill or a machine (as for pumping water) worked by the wind turning sails or vanes at the top of a tower

²**windmill** *vb* : to move or cause to move like the vanes of a windmill

win·dow \'win-dō\ *n* **1** : an opening especially in the wall of a building for admission of light and air usually closed by casements or sashes containing glass **2** : WINDOWPANE **3** : something suggestive of or functioning like a window **4** : any of the areas into which a computer display may be divided and on which distinctly different types of information are displayed [Old Norse *vindauga,* from *vindr* "wind" + *auga* "eye"]

window box *n* : a box designed to hold growing plants on a windowsill

window dressing *n* **1** : display of merchandise in a store window **2** : a showing made to create a good but sometimes false impression

window envelope *n* : an envelope having a transparent panel through which the address on the enclosure is visible

win·dow·pane \-,pān\ *n* : a pane in a window

window seat *n* : a seat built into a window recess

window shade *n* : a shade or curtain for a window

win·dow-shop \-,shäp\ *vi* : to look at the displays in store windows without going inside the stores to make purchases — **win·dow-shop·per** *n*

win·dow·sill \-,sil\ *n* : the horizontal member at the bottom of a window opening

wind·pipe \'wind-,pīp, 'win-\ *n* : a firm tubular passage connecting the pharynx and lungs : TRACHEA

wind–pollinated *adj* : pollinated by pollen borne by the wind

wind·proof \'wind-'prüf, 'win-\ *adj* : resistant to the passage of wind ⟨a *windproof* jacket⟩

¹**wind·row** \'win-,drō, -,rō\ *n* **1** : hay raked up into a row to dry **2** : a row of something (as sand or dry leaves) heaped up by or as if by the wind

²**windrow** *vt* : to put into windrows

wind·screen \'wind-,skrēn, 'win-\ *n, British* : an automobile windshield

wind shear *n* : a radical shift in wind speed and direction that occurs over a very short distance

wind·shield \-,shēld\ *n* : a transparent screen (as of glass) in front of the occupants of a vehicle to protect them from the wind

wind sock *n* : a truncated cloth cone open at both ends and mounted in an elevated position to indicate the direction of the wind — called also *wind sleeve*

Wind·sor chair \'win-zər-\ *n* : a wooden chair with spindle back and raking legs [*Windsor,* England]

Windsor knot *n* : a symmetrical knot used for tying neckties

wind sprint *n* : a sprint performed as a training exercise to develop the breathing capacity especially during exertion

wind·storm \'wind-,stȯrm, 'win-\ *n* : a storm marked by high wind with little or no precipitation

wind·swept \-,swept\ *adj* : swept by or as if by wind ⟨*windswept* plains⟩

wind tunnel *n* : an enclosed passage through which air is blown against structures (as airplanes) to test the effect of wind pressure on them

¹**wind·up** \'wīn-,dəp\ *n* **1 a** : the act of bringing to an end **b** : a concluding act or part : FINISH **2** : a preliminary swing of the arms before pitching a baseball

²**windup** *adj* : operated by a spring wound by hand ⟨*windup* toy⟩

wind up \wīn-'dəp, 'wīn-\ *vb* **1** : to bring or come to a conclusion : END **2** : to put in order : SETTLE **3** : to arrive in a place, situation, or condition at the end or as a result of a course of action ⟨and that's how we happened to *wind up* in Baltimore⟩ ⟨*wound up* as millionaires⟩ **4** : to give a preliminary swing to the arm (as before pitching a baseball)

¹**wind·ward** \'win-dwərd, -wərd\ *adj* : moving or situated toward the direction from which the wind is blowing — compare LEEWARD

²**windward** *n* : the side or direction from which the wind is blowing

wind–wing \'win-,dwing, -,wing\ *n* : a small panel in an automobile window that can be turned outward for ventilation

windy \'win-dē\ *adj* **wind·i·er; -est** **1** : having or exposed to wind ⟨a *windy* day⟩ ⟨a *windy* prairie⟩ **2** : given to or marked by useless talk ⟨a *windy* speaker⟩ — **wind·i·ly** \-də-lē\ *adv* — **wind·i·ness** \-dē-nəs\ *n*

¹**wine** \'wīn\ *n* **1 a** : a beverage made from fermented grape juice containing varying percentages of alcohol **b** : a beverage made from the usually fermented juice of other fruits (as peaches or berries) **2** : something that invigorates or intoxicates **3** : a dark red [Old English *wīn,* from Latin *vinum*]

²**wine** *vt* : to treat to wine ⟨*wined* and dined their friends⟩

wine cellar *n* : a room for storing wines; *also* : a stock of wines

wine·grower \'wīn-,grō-ər, -,grȯr\ *n* : one that cultivates a vineyard and makes wine

wine·press \-,pres\ *n* : a vat in which juice is squeezed from grapes

win·ery \'wīn-rē, -ə-rē\ *n, pl* **-er·ies** : a wine-making establishment

wine·shop \'wīn-,shäp\ *n* : a tavern that specializes in serving wine

wine·skin \-,skin\ *n* : a bag made from the skin of an animal and used for holding wine

win·ey *variant of* WINY

¹wing 1: 1 coverts,
2 primary feathers,
3 secondary feathers

¹**wing** \'wing\ *n* **1** : one of the movable feathered or membranous paired appendages by means of which a bird, bat, or insect is able to fly **2** : an appendage or part likened to a wing in shape, appearance, or position: as **a** : a flat or broadly expanded plant or animal part : ALA ⟨the *wings* of the nose⟩ ⟨a stem with woody *wings*⟩; *esp* : either lateral petal of a pealike flower **b** : a sidepiece at the top of an armchair **c** : one of the airfoils that develop a major part of the lift which supports a heavier-than-air aircraft **3** : a means of flight or rapid progress **4** : the act or manner of flying : FLIGHT **5** : a side or outlying region or district **6** : a part or feature projecting from and subordinate to the main or central part ⟨the rear *wing* of the house⟩ **7** *pl* : the area at the side of the stage out of sight **8 a** : a section of an army or fleet **b** : one of the offensive positions or players on each side of a center position in various team sports **9 a** : either of two opposing groups in an organization : FACTION **b** : a section of a legislative chamber representing a distinct group or faction [of Scandinavian origin] — **wing·like** \-,līk\ *adj* — **on the wing** : in flight : FLYING — **under one's wing** : under one's protection : in one's charge or care

²**wing** *vb* **1** : to go with or as if with wings : FLY **2** : to wound in the wing ⟨*wing* a bird⟩; *also* : to wound without killing ⟨*wing* a deer⟩

wing case *n* : ELYTRON

wing chair *n* : an upholstered armchair with high solid back and sides that provide a rest for the head and protection from drafts

wing·ding \'wing-,ding\ *n* : a wild or lively or lavish party [origin unknown]

winged \'wingd *also except for 1b* 'wing-əd\ *adj* **1 a** : having wings **b** : having wings of a specified character — used in combination **2 a** : ELEVATED 2a **b** : SWIFT 1, RAPID

wing·less \'wing-ləs\ *adj* : having no wings or very rudimentary wings — **wing·less·ness** *n*

wing·man \-mən\ *n* : a pilot who flies somewhat behind and to the side of the leader of a flying formation

wing nut *n* : a nut with wings affording a grip for the thumb and finger

wings \'wingz\ *n pl* : insignia consisting of a stylized pair of outspread bird's wings

wing·span \'wing-ˌspan\ *n* : WINGSPREAD; *esp* : the distance between the tips of an airplane's wings

wing·spread \-ˌspred\ *n* : the spread of the wings; *esp* : the distance between the tips of the fully extended wings of a winged animal

¹wink \'wingk\ *vb* **1** : to close and open the eyes quickly : BLINK **2** : to avoid seeing : pretend not to look : pay no attention ⟨*wink* at a violation of the law⟩ **3** : TWINKLE 1, FLICKER **4** : to close and open one eye quickly as a signal or hint [Old English *wincian*] — **wink·er** \'wing-kər\ *n* □ SYN WINK, BLINK mean to close and open one's eyelids. WINK implies light, rapid, usually involuntary motion or the partial closing of an eye in a mischievous or teasing way. BLINK often implies involuntary motion suggesting a dazzled or dazed state or a struggle against drowsiness; in figurative use WINK implies connivance or indulgence, BLINK suggests shirking or evasion.

²wink *n* **1** : a brief period of sleep : NAP **2 a** : a hint or sign given by winking the eye **b** : an act of winking **3** : the time of a wink : INSTANT

win·kle \'wing-kəl\ *n* : ²PERIWINKLE

win·na·ble \'win-ə-bəl\ *adj* : able to be won

Win·ne·ba·go \ˌwin-ə-'bā-gō\ *n, pl* **-go** *or* **-gos** *or* **-goes** : a member of a Siouan people of the western shores of Lake Michigan

win·ner \'win-ər\ *n* : one that wins

winner's circle *n* : an enclosure near the finish line of a racetrack where the winning horse and jockey are brought for photographs and awards

¹win·ning \'win-ing\ *n* **1** : the act of one that wins : VICTORY **2** : something won; *esp* : money won at gambling — often used in pl.

²winning *adj* : ATTRACTIVE, CHARMING ⟨a *winning* smile⟩ — **win·ning·ly** \-ing-lē\ *adv*

win·now \'win-ō\ *vt* **1 a** : to remove (as chaff from grain) by a current of air **b** : to subject (as grain) to a current of air to remove waste **2** : to get rid of (something unwanted) or to sort or separate (something) as if by winnowing [Old English *windwian*]

win·now·er \'win-ə-wər\ *n* : one that winnows; *esp* : a winnowing machine

wino \'wī-nō\ *n, pl* **win·os** : one who is habitually drunk especially on wine

win·some \'win-səm\ *adj* **1** : causing joy or pleasure : WINNING, CHARMING **2** : CHEERFUL 1a, HAPPY [Old English *wynsum*, from *wynn* "joy"] — **win·some·ly** *adv* — **win·some·ness** *n*

¹win·ter \'wint-ər\ *n* **1 a** : the season between autumn and spring comprising in the northern hemisphere usually the months of December, January, and February or as determined astronomically extending from the December solstice to the March equinox **b** : the colder half of the year **2** : YEAR ⟨many *winters* ago⟩ **3** : a time or season of inactivity or decay [Old English]

²winter *vb* **win·tered; win·ter·ing** \'wint-ə-ring, 'win-tring\ **1** : to pass or live through the winter ⟨the cattle *wintered* on the range⟩ **2** : to keep, feed, or manage during the winter ⟨*winter* livestock⟩

³winter *adj* : occurring in or surviving the winter; *esp* : sown in autumn for harvesting in the following spring or summer ⟨*winter* wheat⟩ ⟨*winter* rye⟩

win·ter·ber·ry \'wint-ər-ˌber-ē\ *n* : any of various American hollies with bright red berries persistent through the winter

win·ter·green \'wint-ər-ˌgrēn\ *n* **1** : any of several low=growing evergreen plants related to the heaths; *esp* : one with white bell-shaped flowers followed by spicy red berries **2** : an essential oil from the common wintergreen or its flavor; *also* : something flavored with it

win·ter·ize \'wint-ə-ˌrīz\ *vt* : to make ready for winter — **win·ter·iza·tion** \ˌwint-ə-rə-'zā-shən\ *n*

win·ter·kill \'wint-ər-ˌkil\ *vb* : to kill (as a plant) by exposure to winter conditions; *also* : to die as a result of such exposure — **winterkill** *n*

winter melon *n* : a muskmelon with smooth rind and sweet white or greenish flesh that keeps well

winter quarters *n pl* : a winter residence or station (as of a military unit)

winter squash *n* : any of various squashes or pumpkins that keep well in storage

win·ter·tide \'wint-ər-ˌtīd\ *n* : WINTERTIME

win·ter·time \-ˌtīm\ *n* : the winter season

win through *vi* : to survive difficulties and reach a desired or satisfactory end

win·try \'win-trē\ *adj* **win·tri·er; -est** **1** : of or characteristic of winter : coming in winter : having to do with winter ⟨*wintry* weather⟩ **2** : CHILLY **3**, COLD, CHEERLESS ⟨a *wintry* welcome⟩ — **win·tri·ly** \-trə-lē\ *adv* — **win·tri·ness** \-trē-nəs\ *n*

winy *or* **win·ey** \'wī-nē\ *adj* **1** : having the taste or qualities of wine **2** : crisply fresh ⟨*winy* autumn breezes⟩

¹wipe \'wīp\ *vt* **1** : to clean or dry by rubbing ⟨*wipe* dishes⟩ **2** : to remove by or as if by rubbing ⟨*wipe* away tears⟩ ⟨*wipe* up spilled milk⟩ **3** : to pass or draw over a surface ⟨*wiped* a hand across my face⟩ [Old English *wīpian*]

²wipe *n* **1** : an act or instance of wiping **2** : something used for wiping

wipe·out \'wī-ˌpaut\ *n* : a fall from a surfboard

wipe out \wī-'paut, 'wī-\ *vt* **1** : to destroy completely ⟨the regiment was *wiped out*⟩ **2** : to ruin financially ⟨was *wiped out* by a market crash⟩

wip·er \'wīp-ər\ *n* : one that wipes; *esp* : a device in the form of a rubber squeegee attached to an oscillating arm for wiping a windshield

¹wire \'wīr\ *n* **1 a** : metal in the form of a usually very flexible thread or slender rod **b** : a thread or rod of metal **2** *usually pl* **a** : a system of wires used to operate the puppets in a puppet show **b** : hidden or secret influences on a person or organization **3 a** : a line of wire for conducting electrical current — compare CORD 3b **b** : a telephone or telegraph wire or system **c** : TELEGRAM, CABLEGRAM [Old English *wīr*] — **wire·like** \-ˌlīk\ *adj* — **under the wire** : at the last moment

²wire *vb* **1** : to provide with wire; *also* : to provide with electricity ⟨*wire* a farm⟩ **2** : to send or send word to by telegraph **3** : to send a telegraphic message — **wir·able** \'wī-rə-bəl\ *adj*

wire cloth *n* : a fabric of woven metallic wire (as for strainers)

wired \'wīrd\ *adj* **1** : reinforced or bound with wire ⟨a *wired* container⟩ **2** : having a netting or fence of wire ⟨a *wired* enclosure for chickens⟩

wire gauge *n* : a gauge especially for measuring the diameter of wire or thickness of sheet metal

wire·haired \'wīr-'haərd, -'heərd\ *adj* : having a stiff wiry outer coat of hair

¹wire·less \'wīər-ləs\ *adj* **1** : having no wire **2** *chiefly British* : of or relating to radiotelegraphy, radiotelephony, or radio

²wireless *n* **1** : WIRELESS TELEGRAPHY **2** : RADIOTELEPHONY **3** *chiefly British* : RADIO — **wireless** *vb*

wireless telegraphy *n* : telegraphy carried on by radio waves and without connecting wires

wire·man \'wīr-mən\ *n* : a maker of or worker with wire; *esp* : LINEMAN 1

Wire·pho·to \'wīr-'fōt-ō\ *trademark* — used for a photograph transmitted by electrical signals over telephone wires

wire–pull·er \-ˌpul-ər\ *n* : one who uses secret or underhand means to influence the acts of a person or organization — **wire–pull·ing** \-ˌpul-ing\ *n*

wire recorder *n* : a magnetic recorder using magnetic wire

wire recording *n* : magnetic recording on magnetic wire; *also* : the recording made by this process

wire rope *n* : a rope formed wholly or chiefly of wires

wire service *n* : a news agency that sends out syndicated news copy by wire to subscribers

wire·tap \'wīr-ˌtap\ *vi* : to tap a telephone or telegraph wire to get information — **wiretap** *n* — **wire·tap·per** *n*

wire·worm \-ˌwərm\ *n* : the slender hard-coated larva of various click beetles that is often destructive to roots

wir·ing \'wīr-ing\ *n* **1** : the act of providing or using wire **2** : a system of wires; *esp* : an arrangement of wires used for electric distribution

wiry \'wīr-ē\ *adj* **wir·i·er; wir·i·est** **1** : of, relating to, or resembling wire **2** : being slender yet strong and sinewy — **wir·i·ness** \'wī-rē-nəs\ *n*

wis·dom \'wiz-dəm\ *n* **1 a** : accumulated learning : KNOWLEDGE **b** : ability to discern inner qualities and relationships : INSIGHT **c** : good sense : JUDGMENT **2** : a wise attitude or course of action **3** : the teachings of the ancient sages **4** *cap* — see BIBLE table [Old English *wīsdōm*, from *wīs* "wise"]

Wisdom of Sol·o·mon \-ˈsäl-ə-mən\ — see BIBLE table

wisdom tooth *n* : the last tooth of the full set on each half of each jaw in humans [from its being cut usually in the late teens when children were formerly believed to be approaching wisdom]

¹wise \'wīz\ *n* : WAY 4a, FASHION — used in such phrases *as in any wise, in no wise, in this wise* [Old English *wīse*]

²wise *adj* **1** : having or showing wisdom, good sense, or good judgment : SENSIBLE **2** : aware of what is going on : INFORMED ⟨was *wise* to our plans⟩ **3** : INSOLENT 1, FRESH [Old English *wīs*] — **wise·ly** *adv*

³wise *vb* : to make or become informed or knowledgeable — usually used with *up*

-wise \ˌwīz\ *adv combining form* **1 a** : in the manner of **b** : in the position or direction of ⟨clock*wise*⟩ ⟨length*wise*⟩ **2** : with regard to : in respect of [Old English *-wīsan*, from *wīse* "manner"]

wise·acre \'wī-ˌzā-kər\ *n* : one who pretends to knowledge or cleverness : SMART ALECK [Dutch *wijssegger* "soothsayer", from Old High German *wīzzago*]

¹wise·crack \'wīz-ˌkrak\ *n* : a clever, flippant, or sarcastic remark : QUIP SYN see JEST

²wisecrack *vb* : to make a wisecrack — **wise·crack·er** *n*

wise guy \'wīz-ˌgī\ *n* : SMART ALECK

wi·sen·hei·mer \'wīz-n-ˌhī-mər\ *n* : one who has the air of knowing all about something or everything : WISEACRE [²*wise* + German *-enheimer* (as in German family names such as *Guggenheimer, Oppenheimer*)]

wi·sent \'vē-ˌzent\ *n* : a nearly extinct European bison [German]

¹wish \'wish\ *vb* **1** : to have a desire : long for : WANT ⟨*wish* you were here⟩ ⟨*wish* for a puppy⟩ **2** : to form or express a desire concerning ⟨*wish* you a merry Christmas⟩ **3** : to request by expressing a desire ⟨I *wish* you to go now⟩ [Old English *wȳscan*] SYN see DESIRE — **wish·er** *n*

²wish *n* **1 a** : an act or instance of wishing : WANT, DESIRE **b** : an object of desire : GOAL **2 a** : an expressed will or desire **b** : a request or order expressed as a wish **3** : an invocation of usually good fortune on someone

wish·bone \'wish-ˌbōn\ *n* : a forked bone in front of the breastbone of a bird consisting chiefly of the fused clavicles [from the superstition that when two people pull it apart the one getting the longer fragment will be granted a wish]

wish·ful \'wish-fəl\ *adj* **1** : having a wish : DESIROUS **2** : based on wishes rather than fact ⟨*wishful* thinking⟩ — **wish·ful·ly** \-fə-lē\ *adv* — **wish·ful·ness** *n*

wisent

wisteria

witch hazel 1

wishy–washy \'wish-ē-ˌwȯsh-ē, -ˌwäsh-\ *adj* **1** : INSIPID **2** : weak in character or determination [reduplication of *washy*]

wisp \'wisp\ *n* **1** : a small bunch of hay or straw **2 a** : a thin strip or fragment **b** : a thready streak ⟨a *wisp* of smoke⟩ **c** : something frail, slight, or fleeting ⟨a *wisp* of a smile⟩ [Middle English] — **wispy** \'wis-pē\ *adj*

wist \'wist\ *vt, archaic* : KNOW [earlier *wis,* from *iwis* "certainly", from Old English *gewis* "certain"]

wis·tar·ia \wis-ˈtir-ē-ə *also* -ˈter-\ *n* : WISTERIA

wis·te·ria \wis-ˈtir-ē-ə\ *n* : any of a genus of chiefly Asian mostly woody vines of the pea family having compound leaves and showy blue, white, purple, or rose pealike flowers in long hanging clusters [Caspar *Wistar,* died 1818, American physician]

wist·ful \'wist-fəl\ *adj* : full of unfulfilled longing or desire : YEARNING [blend of *wishful* and obsolete *wistly* "intently"] — **wist·ful·ly** \-fə-lē\ *adv* — **wist·ful·ness** *n*

¹wit \'wit\ *vb* **wist** \'wist\; **wit·ting;** *present 1st & 3d sing* **wot** \'wät\ *archaic* : KNOW, LEARN [Old English *witan*]

²wit *n* **1** : reasoning power : INTELLIGENCE **2** : mental soundness : SANITY — usually used in pl. ⟨scared out of my *wits*⟩ **3 a** : mental capability and resourcefulness — often used in pl. ⟨live by one's *wits*⟩ **b** : the ability to relate seemingly unlike things so as to illuminate or amuse **4** : one noted for making witty remarks [Old English] ▫ SYN WIT, HUMOR mean a mode of expression intended to arouse amusement. WIT is more purely intellectual than HUMOR and depends for its effect chiefly on verbal ingenuity or swift perception, especially of the incongruous; HUMOR implies an ability to perceive the ludicrous, the comical, and the absurd in human life and to express these sympathetically and without bitterness. — **at one's wit's end** *or* **at one's wits' end** : at a loss for a means of solving a problem

wi·tan \'wi-ˌtän\ *n pl* : members of the witenagemot [Old English, pl. of *wita* "sage, adviser"]

¹witch \'wich\ *n* **1** : a person believed to have magic powers **2** : an ugly old woman : HAG [Old English *wicca* (masculine) and *wicce* (feminine)]

²witch *vb* **1** : BEWITCH **2** : DOWSE

witch·craft \'wich-ˌkraft\ *n* : the power or practices of a witch : SORCERY

witch doctor *n* : a professional worker of magic in a primitive society resembling a shaman or medicine man

witch·ery \'wich-rē, -ə-rē\ *n, pl* **-er·ies** **1 a** : the practice of witchcraft : SORCERY **b** : an act of witchcraft **2** : an irresistible fascination : CHARM

witch·es'–broom \'wich-əz-ˌbrüm, -ˌbrum\ *n* : an abnormal tufted growth of small branches on a tree or shrub caused especially by fungi or viruses

¹witch·grass \'wich-ˌgras\ *n* : QUACK GRASS [probably alteration of *quitch* (grass), from Old English *cwice*]

²witchgrass *n* : a North American grass with slender brushy panicles that is often a weed on cultivated land [¹*witch*]

witch ha·zel \'wich-ˌhā-zəl\ *n* **1** : any of a genus of shrubs with slender-petaled yellow flowers borne in late fall or early spring; *esp* : one of eastern North America that blooms in the fall **2** : an alcoholic solution of material from the bark of the common witch hazel used as a soothing and mildly astringent lotion [Old English *wice,* a tree with pliant branches]

witch–hunt \-ˌhənt\ *n* **1** : a searching out and persecution of persons accused of witchcraft **2** : the searching out and deliberate harassment of those (as political opponents) with unpopular views — **witch–hunt·er** *n*

witch·ing \'wich-ing\ *adj* **1** : of, relating to, or suitable for sorcery or supernatural occurrences ⟨the *witching* hour⟩ **2** : very attractive

wi·te·na·ge·mot or **wi·te·na·ge·mote** \'wit-n-ə-gə-,mōt\ n : an Anglo-Saxon council of nobles, prelates, and officials convened to advise the king on administrative and judicial matters [Old English *witena gemōt,* from *wita* "sage, adviser" + *gemōt* "assembly"]

with \with, 'with, with, 'with\ prep 1 a : in opposition to : AGAINST ⟨fought *with* a neighbor⟩ b : so as to be separated from ⟨parting *with* friends⟩ 2 : in mutual relation to ⟨talking *with* a friend⟩ ⟨trade *with* other countries⟩ 3 : as regards : TOWARD ⟨angry *with* me⟩ 4 a : compared to : equal to ⟨on equal terms *with* the others⟩ b : on the side of ⟨voted *with* the majority⟩ c : as well as ⟨can sing *with* the best of them⟩ 5 a : in the judgment or estimation of ⟨in good standing *with* our classmates⟩ b : in the experience or practice of ⟨*with* them a promise is a real obligation⟩ 6 a : by means of ⟨write *with* a pen⟩ b : because of ⟨danced *with* joy⟩ 7 : having or showing as manner of action or attendant circumstance ⟨spoke *with* ease⟩ ⟨stood there *with* hat in hand⟩ 8 a : in possession of ⟨animals *with* horns⟩ ⟨arrived *with* the news⟩ b : characterized or distinguished by ⟨a person *with* a hot temper⟩ 9 a : in the company of ⟨went to the movies *with* me⟩ : in addition to ⟨your money, *with* ours, will be enough⟩ b : inclusive of ⟨costs five dollars *with* the tax⟩ c : that contains ⟨tea *with* sugar⟩ 10 a : at the time of ⟨*with* the outbreak of war they went home⟩ : at the same time as ⟨rose *with* the sun⟩ b : in proportion to ⟨the pressure varies *with* the depth⟩ 11 : in the possession or care of ⟨left the money *with* your cousin⟩ 12 : in spite of ⟨even *with* all the obstacles, you managed to succeed⟩ 13 : in the direction of ⟨drift *with* the current⟩ ⟨easier to run *with* the wind than against it⟩ [Old English, "against, from, with"] SYN see BY

¹with·al \with-'òl, with-\ adv 1 : together with this : BESIDES 2 : on the other hand : NEVERTHELESS [Middle English, from *with* + *all, al* "all"]

²withal prep, archaic : WITH — used with a preceding relative or interrogative pronoun as its object

with·draw \with-'dró, with-\ vb **-drew** \-'drü\; **-drawn** \-'drón\; **-draw·ing** 1 : to take back or away usually from a holder, a place, or a condition : REMOVE ⟨*withdraw* money from the bank⟩ ⟨the troops were *withdrawn* from combat⟩ 2 : to call back (as from consideration or circulation) : RECALL, RESCIND ⟨*withdrew* the nomination⟩ ⟨*withdraw* the product⟩; *also* : RETRACT, RECANT ⟨*withdrew* the remarks and apologized⟩ 3 a : to go away : RETREAT, LEAVE ⟨*withdrew* to the country⟩ b : to end one's participation or involvement in something ⟨ready to *withdraw* from the firm⟩ [Middle English *withdrawen,* from *with* "from" + *drawen* "to draw"] — **with·draw·able** \-'dró-ə-bəl\ adj

with·draw·al \-'dró-əl, -'dról\ n 1 : an act or instance of withdrawing (as a removal, a retreat, or a retraction) 2 a : the discontinuance of administration or use of a drug b : the syndrome of often painful physical and psychological symptoms that follows the discontinuance of an addicting drug ⟨an alcoholic patient in ethanol *withdrawal*⟩

with·drawn \-'drón\ adj 1 : OUT-OF-THE-WAY 1, SECLUDED ⟨*withdrawn* mountain communities⟩ 2 : socially detached and unresponsive ⟨a *withdrawn* manner⟩ — **with·drawn·ness** \-'drón-nəs\ n

withe \'with, 'with, 'wīth\ n : a slender flexible branch or twig; *esp* : one used for tying or binding [Old English *withthe*]

with·er \'with-ər\ vb **with·ered; with·er·ing** \'with-ring, -ə-ring\ 1 : to become dry and sapless; *esp* : to shrivel from or as if from loss of bodily moisture 2 : to lose vitality, force, or freshness — often used with *away* 3 : to cause to wither 4 : to cause to feel shriveled or blighted ⟨*withered* them with a glance⟩ [Middle English *widren*] □ SYN SHRIVEL: WITHER implies the loss of vital moisture with consequent fading, shrinking,

and approaching death and decay; SHRIVEL stresses a wrinkling and shrinking as by drought or intense heat or blight.

with·er·ing adj : acting or serving to destroy ⟨a *withering* fire from the enemy⟩ ⟨*withering* criticism⟩

with·er·ite \'with-ə-,rīt\ n : a mineral $BaCO_3$ consisting of a carbonate of barium occurring as crystals and in masses [German *witherit,* from William *Withering,* died 1799, English physician]

with·ers \'with-ərz\ n pl : the ridge between the shoulder bones of a horse; *also* : the corresponding part in other four-footed animals [probably derived from Old English *wither* "against"]

with·hold \with-'hōld, with-\ vt **-held** \-'held\; **-hold·ing** 1 : to hold back : RESTRAIN ⟨*withhold* an angry answer⟩; *also* : RETAIN 2 : to refrain from granting, giving, or allowing ⟨*withhold* permission⟩ 3 : to deduct (withholding tax) from income [Middle English *withholden,* from *with* "from" + *holden* "to hold"] — **with·hold·er** n

withholding tax n : a tax withheld from income at the source

¹with·in \with-'in, with-\ adv 1 : in or into the interior : INSIDE 2 : inside oneself : INWARDLY ⟨calm without but furious *within*⟩ [Old English *withinnan,* from *with* + *innan* "inwardly, within", from *in*]

²within prep 1 — used to indicate enclosure or containment ⟨*within* the house⟩ ⟨*within* each mind⟩ 2 : falling inside expressed or implied limits: as a : before the end of ⟨left *within* a week⟩ b : inside the limitations of ⟨live *within* one's means⟩ c : in or into the scope, sphere, or range of ⟨*within* reach⟩ ⟨*within* sight⟩

³within n : an inner place or area ⟨revolt from *within*⟩

¹with·out \with-'aut, with-\ prep 1 : OUTSIDE 1, 2 2 a : not having : LACKING ⟨*without* food⟩ b : with absence or omission of ⟨listened *without* answering⟩ [Old English *withūtan,* from *with* + *ūtan* "outside", from *ūt* "out"]

²without adv 1 : on the outside 2 : with something lacking or absent ⟨has learned to do *without*⟩

³without n : an outer place or area ⟨came from *without*⟩

with·stand \with-'stand, with-\ vt **-stood** \-stúd\; **-stand·ing** : to stand against : RESIST; *esp* : to oppose (as an attack or bad influence) successfully [Old English *withstandan,* from *with* "against" + *standan* "to stand"] SYN see OPPOSE

withy \'with-ē\ n, pl **with·ies** : OSIER 1 [Old English *wīthig*]

wit·less \'wit-ləs\ adj : lacking wit or understanding : FOOLISH — **wit·less·ly** adv — **wit·less·ness** n

wit·loof \'wit-,lōf\ n : CHICORY; *also* : ENDIVE 2 [Dutch dialect *witloof* "chicory", from Dutch *wit* "white" + *loof* "foliage"]

¹wit·ness \'wit-nəs\ n 1 a : an attesting of a fact or event : TESTIMONY b : public testimony to a religious faith 2 : one that gives evidence; *esp* : one who testifies in a cause or before a court 3 a : one present at a transaction so as to be able to testify to its having taken place b : one who has personal knowledge or experience of something 4 : something serving as evidence or proof : SIGN 5 cap : JEHOVAH'S WITNESS [Old English *witnes* "knowledge, testimony, witness", from ²*wit*]

²witness vb 1 : to bear witness : ATTEST 2 : to act as legal witness of ⟨*witness* the making of a will⟩ 3 : to furnish proof of 4 : to be a witness of ⟨thousands *witnessed* the parade⟩

witness stand n : an area from which a witness gives evidence in a court

wit·ted \'wit-əd\ adj : having wit or understanding — usually used in combination ⟨dull-*witted*⟩

wit·ti·cism \'wit-ə-,siz-əm\ n : a witty saying [*witty* + *-cism* (as in *criticism*)]

wit·ting·ly \'wit-ing-lē\ adv : with knowledge or awareness of what one is doing : CONSCIOUSLY

\ə\ abut	\ng\ sing
\ər\ further	\ō\ bone
\a\ mat	\ò\ saw
\ā\ take	\òi\ coin
\ä\ cot, cart	\th\ thin
\aú\ out	\th\ this
\ch\ chin	\ü\ food
\e\ pet	\ú\ foot
\ē\ easy	\y\ yet
\g\ go	\yü\ few
\i\ tip	\yú\ cure
\ī\ life	\zh\ vision
\j\ job	

wit·ty \'wit-ē\ *adj* **wit·ti·er; -est** : marked by or full of wit ⟨a *witty* writer⟩ ⟨a *witty* remark⟩ — **wit·ti·ly** \'wit-l-ē\ *adv* — **wit·ti·ness** \'wit-ē-nəs\ *n*

wive \'wīv\ *vb* **I** : to marry a woman **2** : to take for a wife [Old English *wīfian,* from *wīf* "woman, wife"]

wives *pl of* WIFE

wiz·ard \'wiz-ərd\ *n* **I** : MAGICIAN 1, SORCERER **2** : a very clever or skillful person ⟨a *wizard* at chess⟩ [Middle English *wysard,* from *wis, wys* "wise"]

wiz·ard·ry \'wiz-ər-drē\ *n, pl* **-ries I** : the art of practices of a wizard : SORCERY **2** : extraordinary skill or ability

wiz·ened \'wiz-nd\ *also* **wiz·en** \'wiz-n\ *adj* : dried, shriveled, and wrinkled especially with age [Old English *wisnian* "to dry up, wither"]

woad \'wōd\ *n* : a European herb of the mustard family formerly grown for the blue dyestuff yielded by its leaves; *also* : this dyestuff [Old English *wād*]

¹wob·ble *also* **wab·ble** \'wäb-əl\ *vb* **wob·bled; wob·bling** \'wäb-ling, -ə-ling\ **I a** : to move or cause to move with an irregular rocking or side-to-side motion **b** : TREMBLE, QUAVER ⟨a voice that *wobbles*⟩ **2** : WAVER 1 [probably from Low German *wabbeln*] — **wob·bler** \'wäb-lər, -ə-lər\ *n* — **wob·bly** \'wäb-lē, -ə-lē\ *adj*

²wobble *also* **wabble** *n* : a wobbling action or movement ⟨the wheel had a bad *wobble*⟩

¹woe \'wō\ *interj* — used to express grief, regret, or distress [Old English *wā*]

²woe *n* **I** : a condition of deep suffering from misfortune, affliction, or grief **2** : CALAMITY, MISFORTUNE ⟨economic *woes*⟩

woe·be·gone \'wō-bi-,gȯn, -,gän\ *adj* : exhibiting great woe, sorrow, or misery ⟨*woebegone* faces⟩ [Middle English *wo begon,* from *wo* "woe" + *begon,* past participle of *begon* "to go about, beset", from Old English *begān,* from *be-* + *gān* "to go"]

woe·ful *also* **wo·ful** \'wō-fəl\ *adj* **I** : full of woe : WRETCHED **2** : involving or bringing woe ⟨a *woeful* sight⟩ **3** : PALTRY, DEPLORABLE ⟨a *woeful* lack of knowledge⟩ — **woe·ful·ly** \-fə-lē, -flē\ *adv* — **woe·ful·ness** \-fəl-nəs\ *n*

woke *past of* WAKE

woken *past participle of* WAKE

wold \'wōld\ *n* : an upland plain or stretch of rolling country without woods [Old English *weald, wald* "forest"]

¹wolf \'wu̇lf\ *n, pl* **wolves** \'wu̇lvz\ *also* **wolf I** : any of several large erect-eared bushy-tailed predatory mammals that resemble the related dogs and tend to hunt in packs — compare COYOTE, JACKAL **2 a** (1) : a person resembling a wolf (as in ferocity or guile) (2) : a man forward and zealous in attentions to women **b** : dire poverty ⟨trying to keep the *wolf* from the door⟩ [Old English *wulf*] — **wolf·ish** \'wu̇l-fish\ *adj* — **wolf·like** \'wu̇l-,flīk\ *adj* — **wolf in sheep's clothing** : one who hides a hostile intention behind a friendly manner

²wolf *vt* : to eat greedily : DEVOUR

wolf·hound \'wu̇lf-,hau̇nd\ *n* : any of several large dogs used especially formerly in hunting large animals (as wolves)

wol·fram \'wu̇l-frəm\ *n* : TUNGSTEN [German]

wol·fram·ite \'wu̇l-frə-,mīt\ *n* : a brownish or grayish mineral that consists of an iron manganese tungstate, occurs in crystals and masses, and is a source of tungsten

wolf spider *n* : any of various active wandering ground spiders

wol·ver·ine \,wu̇l-və-'rēn\ *n* : a blackish shaggy-furred flesh-eating mammal of northern forests that is related to the martens and sables and is noted especially for its strength [probably derived from *wolv-* (as in *wolves*)]

wom·an \'wu̇m-ən\ *n, pl* **wom·en** \'wim-ən\ **I** : an adult female person **2** : WOMANKIND **3** : a feminine nature : womanly character **4** : a female servant or attendant [Old English *wīfman,* from *wīf* "woman, wife" + *man* "person, man"] — **woman** *adj*

wom·an·hood \'wu̇m-ən-,hu̇d\ *n* **I** : the state of being a woman **2** : womanly qualities **3** : WOMANKIND

wom·an·ish \'wu̇m-ə-nish\ *adj* **I** : characteristic of a woman **2** : suitable to a woman rather than to a man — **wom·an·ish·ly** *adv* — **wom·an·ish·ness** *n*

wom·an·kind \'wu̇m-ən-,kīnd\ *n* : female human beings

wom·an·like \-,līk\ *adj* : resembling or characteristic of a woman : WOMANLY

wom·an·ly \-lē\ *adj* **I** : having qualities held to be appropriate to a woman **2** : befitting an adult woman ⟨*womanly* qualities⟩ — **wom·an·li·ness** *n*

woman suffrage *n* : the possession and exercise of the suffrage by women

womb \'wüm\ *n* **I** : UTERUS 1 **2** : a place where something is generated or developed [Old English] — **wombed** \'wümd\ *adj*

wom·bat \'wäm-,bat\ *n* : any of several stocky burrowing Australian marsupials resembling small bears [native name in New South Wales, Australia]

wom·en·folk \'wim-ən-,fōk\ *or* **wom·en·folks** \-,fōks\ *n pl* : WOMANKIND

¹won \'wən\ *past of* WIN

²won \'wȯn\ *n* **I** : the basic monetary unit of North Korea and South Korea **2** : a coin representing this unit [Korean *wān*]

¹won·der \'wən-dər\ *n* **I a** : a cause of astonishment or surprise : MARVEL **b** : MIRACLE **2 a** : a feeling (as of awed astonishment or of uncertainty) aroused by something extraordinary or affecting **b** : the quality of exciting wonder ⟨the charm and *wonder* of the scene⟩ [Old English *wundor*]

²wonder *vb* **won·dered; won·der·ing** \-də-ring, -dring\ **I** : to feel surprise or amazement **2** : to feel curiosity or doubt ⟨*wondered* about the cost⟩ — **won·der·er** \-dər-ər\ *n*

wonder drug *n* : a medicinal substance of outstanding effectiveness

won·der·ful \'wən-dər-fəl\ *adj* **I** : exciting wonder : MARVELOUS **2** : unusually good : ADMIRABLE — **won·der·ful·ly** \-fə-lē, -flē\ *adv* — **won·der·ful·ness** \-fəl-nəs\ *n*

won·der·land \'wən-dər-,land, -lənd\ *n* **I** : a fairylike imaginary realm **2** : a place that excites admiration or wonder ⟨a scenic *wonderland*⟩

won·der·ment \-mənt\ *n* **I** : a state or feeling of wonder : ASTONISHMENT, SURPRISE **2** : curiosity about something

won·der–work·er \-,wər-kər\ *n* : one that performs wonders

won·drous \'wən-drəs\ *adj* : WONDERFUL 1, MARVELOUS — **wondrous** *adv, archaic* — **won·drous·ly** *adv* — **won·drous·ness** *n*

¹wont \'wȯnt, 'wōnt\ *adj* : ACCUSTOMED 2, USED ⟨as they are *wont* to do⟩ [Middle English, from past participle of *wonen* "to dwell, be used to", from Old English *wunian*]

²wont *n* : CUSTOM, USAGE ⟨according to our *wont*⟩

won't \wōnt, 'wōnt, 'wənt\ : will not

wont·ed \'wȯnt-əd, 'wōnt-\ *adj* : ACCUSTOMED 2, USUAL ⟨took my *wonted* rest⟩ — **wont·ed·ly** *adv* — **wont·ed·ness** *n*

woo \'wü\ *vb* **I a** : to try to gain the love of : make love : COURT **b** : to try to win over ⟨a young author trying to *woo* the reader⟩ **2** : to seek usually urgently to gain or bring about ⟨a clever auctioneer *wooing* dollars from the audience⟩ [Old English *wōgian*]

¹wood \'wu̇d\ *n* **I a** : a dense growth of trees usually greater in extent than a grove and smaller than a forest — often used in pl. ⟨a thick *woods* runs along the ridge⟩ **b** : WOODLAND **2** : a hard fibrous substance that is basically xylem and makes up the greater part of the stems and branches of trees or shrubs beneath the

wolverine

bark; *also* : this material suitable or prepared for some use (as burning or building) **3** : something made of wood; *esp* : a golf club having a wooden head [Old English *wudu*] — **out of the woods** : escaped from peril or difficulty

²**wood** *adj* **1** : WOODEN 1 **2** : suitable for cutting or working wood ⟨*wood* chisels⟩ **3** *or* **woods** \'wu̇dz\ : living or growing in woods

wood alcohol *n* : METHANOL

wood anemone *n* : any of several anemones that grow in open woodlands

wood·bin \'wu̇d-ˌbin\ *n* : a bin for holding firewood

wood·bine \'wu̇d-ˌbīn\ *n* : any of several climbing vines of Europe and America (as a honeysuckle or the Virginia creeper) [Old English *wudubinde,* from *wudu* "wood" + *bindan* "to tie, bind"; from its winding around trees]

wood block *n* : WOODCUT

wood–carv·er \'wu̇d-ˌkär-vər\ *n* : a person who carves usually ornamental objects of wood — **wood carv·ing** \-ving\ *n*

wood·chop·per \-ˌchäp-ər\ *n* : one engaged especially in chopping down trees

wood·chuck \-ˌchək\ *n* : a grizzled thickset marmot of the northeastern United States and Canada; *also* : a related rodent of mountainous western North America [by folk etymology from Ojibwa *otchig* "fisher, marten" or Cree *otcheck* "fisher"]

wood·cock \-ˌkäk\ *n, pl* **woodcocks** *or* **woodcock** : either of two long-billed mottled and usually brown birds related to the snipe; *esp* : an American upland bird prized as a game bird

wood·craft \-ˌkraft\ *n* **1** : knowledge about the woods and how to take care of oneself in them **2** : skill in working with or making things of wood

wood·cut \-ˌkət\ *n* **1** : a printing surface consisting of a wooden block with a usually pictorial design cut with the grain **2** : a print from a woodcut

wood·cut·ter \-ˌkət-ər\ *n* : one that cuts wood especially as an occupation

wood duck *n* : a showy American duck that nests in trees and in the male has a large crest and plumage varied with green, purple, black, white, and chestnut

wood·ed \'wu̇d-əd\ *adj* : covered with trees

wood·en \'wu̇d-n\ *adj* **1** : made of wood **2 a** : lacking flexibility : STIFF ⟨a *wooden* expression⟩ **b** : lacking ease, interest, or zest ⟨written in a *wooden* style⟩ — **wood·en·ly** *adv* — **wood·en·ness** \-n-nəs\ *n*

wood engraving *n* **1** : the art or process of cutting a design upon wood and especially upon the end grain of wood for use as a printing surface; *also* : such a printing surface **2** : a design printed from a wood engraving

wood·en·ware \'wu̇d-n-ˌwa(ə)r, -ˌwe(ə)r\ *n* : articles made of wood for domestic use

wood ibis *n* : a large wading bird closely related to the Old World storks that frequents wooded swamps of South and Central America and the southern United States

¹**wood·land** \'wu̇d-lənd, -ˌland\ *n* : land covered with woody vegetation : FOREST — **wood·land·er** \-ər\ *n*

²**woodland** *adj* **1** : of, relating to, or being woodland **2** : growing or living in woodland

wood·lot \'wu̇d-ˌlät\ *n* : an area of trees kept usually to meet fuel and timber needs

wood louse *n* : a small flat grayish crustacean that lives especially under stones and bark — called also *pill bug, sow bug*

wood·man \'wu̇d-mən\ *n* : WOODSMAN

wood·note \-ˌnōt\ *n* : verbal expression that is natural and artless

wood nymph *n* : a nymph living in the woods or a particular tree — called also *dryad*

wood·peck·er \'wu̇d-ˌpek-ər\ *n* : any of numerous usually brightly marked birds with specialized feet and

stiff spiny tail feathers used in climbing or resting on tree trunks and a very hard bill used to drill into trees for insect food or to excavate nesting cavities

wood·pile \-ˌpīl\ *n* : a pile of wood and especially firewood

wood pulp *n* : pulp from wood used in making cellulose derivatives (as paper or rayon)

wood pussy *n* : SKUNK 1

wood rat *n* : any of numerous native voles of the southern and western United States with soft pale fur, well-furred tails, and large ears

wood ray *n* : XYLEM RAY

woods *variant of* WOOD

wood·shed \'wu̇d-ˌshed\ *n* : a shed for storing wood and especially firewood

woods·man \'wu̇dz-mən\ *n* : one who frequents or works in the woods; *esp* : one skilled in woodcraft

wood sorrel *n* : any of a genus of herbs with acid sap, compound leaves, and regular 5-petaled flowers; *esp* : a stemless herb having leaves with three leaflets that is held to be the original shamrock

woodsy \'wu̇d-zē\ *adj* : relating to or suggestive of woods

wood thrush *n* : a large thrush of eastern North America noted for its loud clear song

wood turning *n* : the art or process of fashioning useful articles from wooden pieces or blocks by means of a lathe

wood turpentine : TURPENTINE 2b

wood warbler *n* : WARBLER 2b

wood·wax·en \'wu̇d-ˌwak-sən\ *n* : a low bushy yellow-flowered Eurasian shrub of the pea family grown for ornament or formerly as the source of a yellow dye [Old English *wuduweaxe*]

wood·wind \'wu̇d-ˌwind\ *n* **1** : one of a group of wind instruments including flutes, clarinets, oboes, bassoons, and sometimes saxophones **2** *pl* : the woodwind section of a band or orchestra — **woodwind** *adj*

wood·work \-ˌwərk\ *n* : work made of wood; *esp* : interior fittings (as moldings or stairways) of wood

wood·work·ing \-ˌwər-kiŋ\ *n* : the act, process, or occupation of working with wood — **wood·work·er** \-kər\ *n* — **woodworking** *adj*

woody \'wu̇d-ē\ *adj* **wood·i·er; -est** **1** : abounding or overgrown with trees **2** : of or containing wood or wood fibers : LIGNEOUS **3** : characteristic of or resembling wood ⟨a *woody* texture⟩ — **wood·i·ness** *n*

woo·er \'wü-ər\ *n* : one that woos : SUITOR

woof \'wu̇f, 'wüf\ *n* **1** : the threads that cross the warp in a woven fabric **2** : a woven fabric or its texture [Old English ō*wef,* from *on* + *wefan* "to weave"]

woof·er \'wu̇f-ər\ *n* : a loudspeaker that is usually larger than a tweeter, is responsive only to the lower acoustic frequencies, and is used for reproducing sounds of low pitch — compare TWEETER [from *woof* "to make a low gruff sound", of imitative origin]

wool \'wu̇l\ *n* **1** : the heavy soft wavy or curly undercoat of various mammals and especially the sheep **2** : a product of wool; *esp* : a woven fabric or garment of such fabric **3 a** : dense hair especially on a plant **b** : material (as of glass or metal) drawn or formed into a thready mass **c** : short thick often crisp curly hair on a human head [Old English *wull*] — **wooled** \'wu̇ld\ *adj*

¹**wool·en** *or* **wool·len** \'wu̇l-ən\ *adj* **1** : made of wool — compare WORSTED **2** : of or relating to the manufacture or sale of woolen products ⟨a *woolen* mill⟩

²**woolen** *or* **woollen** *n* **1** : a fabric made of wool **2** : garments of woolen fabric — usually used in pl.

wool·gath·er·ing \'wu̇l-ˌgath-riŋ, -ə-riŋ\ *n* : idle daydreaming

¹**wool·ly** *also* **wooly** \'wu̇l-ē\ *adj* **wool·li·er; -est** **1 a** : of, relating to, or bearing wool **b** : resembling wool **2** : lacking in clearness : BLURRY ⟨*woolly* thinking⟩ — **wool·li·ness** *n*

woodchuck

woodcock

woodpecker

\ə\ abut	\ŋ\ sing
\ər\ further	\ō\ bone
\a\ mat	\ȯ\ saw
\ā\ take	\ȯi\ coin
\ä\ cot, cart	\th\ thin
\au̇\ out	\th\ this
\ch\ chin	\ü\ food
\e\ pet	\u̇\ foot
\ē\ easy	\y\ yet
\g\ go	\yü\ few
\i\ tip	\yu̇\ cure
\ī\ life	\zh\ vision
\j\ job	

woolly mammoth

²wool·ly *also* **wool·ie** *or* **wooly** \'wùl-ē\ *n, pl* **wool·lies** : a garment made from wool; *esp* : underclothing of knitted wool — usually used in pl.

woolly aphid *n* : any of several plant lice that secrete a dense coating of woolly wax filaments

woolly bear *n* : any of various rather large very hairy moth caterpillars

woolly mammoth *n* : a heavy-coated mammoth of the colder parts of the Northern Hemisphere known from fossil remains, from palaeolithic drawings, and from entire frozen bodies unearthed in Siberia

wool·sack \'wùl-,sak\ *n* **1** : a sack for wool **2** : the official seat of the lord chancellor or his deputy in the House of Lords

woo·zy \'wü-zē\ *adj* **woo·zi·er; -est 1** : having the senses dulled **2** : affected with dizziness, mild nausea, or weakness : SICK [probably alteration of *oozy*] — **woo·zi·ly** \-zə-lē\ *adv* — **woo·zi·ness** \-zē-nəs\ *n*

Worces·ter·shire sauce \,wùs-tər-,shiər-, ,wùs-tə-, -shər\ *n* : a pungent sauce originally made in Worcester, England, of ingredients that include soy, vinegar, and garlic

¹word \'wərd\ *n* **1 a** : something that is said **b** *pl* : TALK, DISCOURSE **c** : a brief remark or conversation **2 a** : a speech sound or series of speech sounds that symbolizes and communicates a meaning without being divisible into smaller units capable of independent use **b** : a written or printed character or combination of characters representing a spoken word **c** : a combination of electrical or magnetic impulses conveying a unit of information in communication and computer work **3** : ORDER, COMMAND (don't advance until you get the *word*) **4** *often cap* **a** : LOGOS **b** : GOSPEL 1a **c** : the expressed or manifested mind and will of God **5** : NEWS 1, INFORMATION (got *word* of the accident) **6** : PROMISE, DECLARATION **7** : a quarrelsome utterance or conversation — usually used in pl. (they had *words* and parted in anger) **8** : a verbal signal : PASSWORD [Old English] — **in a word** : in short — **in so many words** : in precisely these words — **word for word** : in the exact words : VERBATIM

²word *vt* : to express in words : PHRASE

word·age \'wərd-ij\ *n* : a quantity or number of words

word·book \'wərd-,bùk\ *n* : VOCABULARY 1, DICTIONARY

word class *n* : a linguistic form class whose members are words; *esp* : PART OF SPEECH

word·ing \'wərd-ing\ *n* **1** : expression in words **2** : the manner or style of expressing in words : PHRASING

word·less \'wərd-ləs\ *adj* **1** : not expressed in or accompanied by words **2** : SILENT 1a, SPEECHLESS — **word·less·ly** *adv* — **word·less·ness** *n*

word of mouth : oral communication

word order *n* : the order of arrangement of words in a phrase, clause, or sentence

word·play \'wərd-,plā\ *n* : verbal wit

word processing *n* : the production of typewritten documents (as business letters) with automated and usually computerized equipment for preparing text

word processor *n* : a keyboard-operated terminal usually with a video display and a magnetic storage device for use in word processing; *also* : software (as for a computer system) to perform word processing

word stress *n* : the manner in which stresses are distributed on the syllables of a word — called also *word accent*

wordy \'wərd-ē\ *adj* **word·i·er; -est** : using or containing many or too many words : VERBOSE — **word·i·ly** \'wərd-l-ē\ *adv* — **word·i·ness** \'wərd-ē-nəs\ *n*

wore *past of* WEAR

¹work \'wərk\ *n* **1 a** : the use of strength or ability to get something done **b** : the activity engaged in as a means of livelihood : OCCUPATION; *also* : the place of one's employment (didn't go to *work* today) **c** : something that needs to be done : TASK (we've *work* to do) **2** : the energy expended by a force acting over a given distance **3 a** : a particular method or manner of working (careful police *work*) **b** : the manner or quality of working : WORKMANSHIP (careless *work*) **4** *pl* : a place where industrial labor is carried on : PLANT, FACTORY (a locomotive *works*) **5** *pl* : the working or moving parts of a mechanical device (the *works* of a watch) **6** : a product of effort, exertion, or skill (their *work* with retarded children); *esp* : an artistic production **7** *pl* : performance of moral or religious acts (salvation achieved through good *works*) **8** : effective operation : EFFECT **9** : the material that is operated on at some stage in a process (place the *work* to the right of the machine) **10** *pl* : everything possessed, available, or appropriate (ordered a hot dog with the *works*) [Old English *werc, weorc*] — **at work 1** : engaged in working : BUSY; *esp* : engaged in one's regular occupation **2** : having effect — **in the works** : in process of preparation, development, or completion — **out of work** : without regular employment : JOBLESS

²work *adj* **1** : suitable or styled for wear while working (*work* clothes) **2** : used for work (a *work* elephant)

³work *vb* **worked** \'wərkt\ *or* **wrought** \'ròt\; **work·ing 1** : to bring to pass : EFFECT **2** : to fashion or create by expending labor or exertion upon **3 a** : to prepare for use by stirring or kneading **b** : to bring into a desired form by a gradual process of cutting, hammering, scraping, pressing, or stretching (*work* cold steel) **4** : to set or keep in motion or operation (a pump *worked* by hand) **5** : to solve (a problem) by reasoning or calculation **6 a** : to cause to toil or labor : get work out of (*work* horses on the road) **b** : to make use of : EXPLOIT **c** : to control or guide the operation of **7** : to carry on an operation through or in or along (an angler *working* a stream) **8 a** : to get (as oneself or an object) into or out of a condition or position by stages (*work* the nut loose) **b** : CONTRIVE, ARRANGE (if we can *work* it) **9 a** : to practice trickery or deception on for some end (*worked* the management for a free ticket) **b** : EXCITE, PROVOKE (*work* oneself into a rage) **10 a** : to exert oneself physically or mentally especially in sustained effort for a purpose or under compulsion or necessity **b** : to perform a task requiring sustained effort or repeated operations **c** : to perform work regularly for wages **11** : to function or operate according to plan or design **12** : to produce the desired effect : SUCCEED (the oil *worked* well) **13** : to make way slowly and with difficulty **14** : to react in a specified way to being worked (this wood *works* easily) **15 a** : to be in agitation or restless motion **b** : FERMENT **c** : to move slightly in relation to another part **d** : to get into a specific condition by slow or imperceptible movements (the knot *worked* loose) [Old English *wyrcan*] — **work at** : to be engaged or occupied in — **work on 1** : AFFECT (*worked on* our sympathies) **2** : to strive to influence or persuade — **work one's way** : to advance slowly especially against resistance or obstructions

work·able \'wər-kə-bəl\ *adj* **1** : capable of being worked **2** : FEASIBLE 1, PRACTICABLE — **work·abil·i·ty** \,wər-kə-'bil-ət-ē\ *n* — **work·able·ness** \'wər-kə-bəl-nəs\ *n*

work·a·day \'wər-kə-,dā\ *adj* **1** : relating to or suited for working days **2** : ORDINARY [obsolete *workyday* "workday"]

work·bag \'wərk-,bag\ *n* : a bag for implements or materials for work; *esp* : a bag for needlework

work·bas·ket \-,bas-kət\ *n* : a basket for needlework

work·bench \-,bench\ *n* : a bench on which work especially of mechanics, machinists, and carpenters is performed

work·book \-,bùk\ *n* **1** : a booklet outlining a course of study **2** : a workman's manual **3** : a record book of work done **4** : a student's individual book of problems to be solved directly on the pages

work·box \-,bäks\ *n* : a box for work instruments and materials

work·day \-,dā\ *n* **1** : a day on which work is performed as distinguished from Sunday or a holiday **2** : the period of time in a day during which work is performed — **workday** *adj*

worked \'wərkt\ *adj* : that has been subjected to some process of development, treatment, or manufacture

worked up *adj* : emotionally aroused : EXCITED (all *worked up* over the coming wedding)

work·er \'wər-kər\ *n* **1 a** : one that works **b** : a member of the working class **2** : one of the members of a colony of social ants, bees, wasps, or termites that are incompletely developed sexually and usually sterile and that perform most of the labor and protective duties of the colony

work farm *n* : a farm on which persons convicted of minor law violations are confined and put to work

work force *n* **1** : the workers engaged in a specific activity (the factory's *work force*) **2** : the number of workers potentially assignable for any purpose (the nation's *work force*)

work·horse \'wərk-,hórs\ *n* **1** : a horse used chiefly for labor **2 a** : a person who undertakes arduous labor **b** : a markedly useful or durable vehicle, craft, or machine

work·house \-,haús\ *n* **1** *British* : POORHOUSE **2** : an institution where persons who have committed minor law violations are confined

¹work·ing \'wər-king\ *n* : an excavation or group of excavations made in mining, quarrying, or tunneling — usually used in pl.

²working *adj* **1 a** : doing work especially for a living (*working* people) **b** : that functions (a *working* model) **2** : good enough to allow work to be done (a *working* majority) (had a *working* knowledge of French) **3 a** : of, relating to, or occupied with work (*working* hours) **b** : used or fit for use in work (*working* clothes)

working class *n* : the class of people who are employed for wages usually in manual labor — **working–class** *adj*

work·ing·man \'wər-king-,man\ *n* : one who works for wages usually at manual labor or in industry

working papers *n pl* : official documents legalizing the employment of a minor

work·ing·wom·an \'wər-king-,wúm-ən\ *n* : a woman who works for wages

work·less \'wər-kləs\ *adj* : being without work : UNEMPLOYED — **work·less·ness** *n*

work·man \'wərk-mən\ *n* **1** : WORKINGMAN **2** : ARTISAN, CRAFTSMAN

work·man·like \-,līk\ *or* **work·man·ly** \-lē\ *adj* : exhibiting good workmanship : SKILLFUL

work·man·ship \'wərk-mən-,ship\ *n* **1** : the art or skill of an artisan : CRAFTSMANSHIP **2** : the quality or character of a piece of work (the excellent *workmanship* of the desk)

workmen's compensation insurance *n* : insurance that reimburses an employer for damages that are required to be paid to an employee for injury occurring in the scope and course of employment

work of art : a product of one of the fine arts; *esp* : a painting or sculpture of high artistic quality

work off *vt* : to get rid of by work or activity (*work off* anger) (*work off* a debt)

work·out \'wər-,kaút\ *n* : a practice or period of exercise to test or improve one's fitness especially for athletic competition, ability, or performance

work out \wər-'kaút, 'wər-\ *vb* **1** : to bring about by labor and exertion **2 a** : SOLVE **b** : to bring about especially by resolving difficulties (*work out* a compromise) **c** : DEVELOP, ELABORATE (*work out* a plan) **3** : to discharge (as a debt) by labor **4** : to exhaust (as a mine) by working **5 a** : to prove effective, practicable, or suitable **b** : to amount to a total or calculated figure

— usually used with *to* **6** : to go through a training session especially in an athletic specialty

work over *vt* **1** : to do over : REWORK **2** : to beat up (was *worked over* in a dark alley)

work·room \'wər-,krüm, -,krùm\ *n* : a room used especially for manual work

work·shop \'wərk-,shäp\ *n* **1** : a small establishment where manufacturing or handicrafts are carried on **2** : a seminar emphasizing free discussion, exchange of ideas, and practical methods and given mainly for adults already employed in the field

work·ta·ble \-,tā-bəl\ *n* : a table for holding working materials and implements (as for needlework)

work up *vt* **1** : to stir up : ROUSE **2** : to produce by mental or physical work

work·week \'wər-,kwēk\ *n* : the hours or days of work in a calendar week (40-hour *workweek*) (a 5-day *workweek*)

work·wom·an \-,kwùm-ən\ *n* : a woman who works especially at manual labor or in industry

world \'wərld\ *n* **1** : the earth with its inhabitants and all things upon it **2** : people in general : HUMANITY **3** : worldly affairs (withdraw from the *world*) **4** : the system of created things : UNIVERSE **5** : a part or section of the earth or its inhabitants by itself **6** : a state of existence : scene of life and action (the *world* of the future) **7** : a great number or quantity (a *world* of troubles) **8** : a distinctive class of persons or their sphere of interest (the musical *world*) **9** : a heavenly body especially if inhabited [Old English *woruld* "human existence, this world, age", literally, "age of man"] SYN see EARTH — **in the world** : among innumerable possibilities : EVER — used as an intensive (what *in the world* is it) — **out of this world** : of extraordinary excellence : SUPERB

world–beat·er \'wərld-,bēt-ər\ *n* : one that excels all others of its kind : CHAMPION

world·ling \'wərl-dling, -ling\ *n* : a person engrossed in the concerns of this present world

world·ly \'wərl-dlē, -lē\ *adj* **world·li·er; -est** **1** : of, relating to, or devoted to this world and its pursuits rather than to spiritual affairs **2** : WORLDLY-WISE SYN see EARTHLY — **world·li·ness** *n*

world·ly–mind·ed \,wərl-dlē-'mīn-dəd, -lē-\ *adj* : devoted to or engrossed in worldly interests — **world·ly–mind·ed·ness** *n*

world·ly–wise \'wərl-dlē-,wīz, -lē-\ *adj* : having a practical and often shrewd understanding of human affairs

world power *n* : a political unit (as a nation) powerful enough to affect the entire world by its influence or actions

world series *n, often cap W & S* : a series of baseball games played each fall between the pennant winners of the major leagues to decide the professional championship

world war *n* : a war involving all or most of the chief nations of the world; *esp, cap both Ws* : either of two such wars of the 20th century

world–wea·ri·ness \'wərld-,wir-ē-nəs\ *n* : fatigue from or boredom with the life of the world and especially with material pleasures — **world–wea·ry** \-,wiər-ē\ *adj*

world–wide \'wərl-'dwīd\ *adj* : extended throughout the world

¹worm \'wərm\ *n* **1 a** : EARTHWORM; *also* : any annelid worm **b** : any of various small long usually naked and soft-bodied creeping animals (as a maggot or planarian) **2 a** : a human being who is an object of contempt, loathing, or pity : WRETCH **b** : something that inwardly torments or devours **3** *pl* : infestation with or disease caused by parasitic worms **4** : something (as a mechanical device) spiral in form or appearance: as **a** : the thread of a screw **b** : a short revolving screw whose threads gear with the teeth of a worm wheel or rack [Old English *wyrm* "serpent, worm"] — **worm** *adj* — **worm·like** \-,līk\ *adj*

²**worm** *vb* **1** : to move or cause to move or proceed sinuously or insidiously ⟨spies *worm* into important positions⟩ ⟨*wormed* out of the crowd⟩ **2** : to insinuate or introduce (oneself) by devious or subtle means **3** : to rid (as a dog) of worms **4** : to obtain or extract by artful or insidious questioning or by pleading, asking, or persuading ⟨*wormed* the truth out of me⟩ — **worm·er** *n*

worm–eat·en \'wər-ˌmēt-n\ *adj* **1 a** : eaten or burrowed by worms ⟨*worm-eaten* timber⟩ **b** : marked with pits **2** : WORN-OUT, ANTIQUATED

worm fence *n* : a zigzag fence consisting of interlocking rails supported by crossed poles — called also *snake fence*

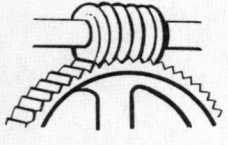

worm gear 2

worm gear *n* **1** : WORM WHEEL **2** : a gear of a worm and a worm wheel working together

worm·hole \'wərm-ˌhōl\ *n* : a hole or passage burrowed by a worm

worm·seed \-ˌsēd\ *n* : any of various plants (as a goosefoot) whose seeds possess vermifuge properties

worm wheel *n* : a toothed wheel that meshes with the thread of a worm

worm·wood \'wərm-ˌwu̇d\ *n* **1** : any of a genus of woody herbs related to the daisies; *esp* : a European plant yielding a bitter slightly aromatic dark green oil used in absinthe **2** : something bitter or grievous [Middle English *wormwode,* from Old English *wermōd*]

wormy \'wər-mē\ *adj* **worm·i·er; -est 1** : containing, infested with, or damaged by worms ⟨*wormy* flour⟩ ⟨*wormy* timbers⟩ **2** : resembling or suggestive of a worm

worn *past participle of* WEAR

worn–out \'wōr-ˈnau̇t, 'wȯr-\ *adj* : exhausted or used up by or as if by wear

wor·ri·ment \'wər-ē-mənt, 'wə-rē-\ *n* : an act or instance of worrying; *also* : TROUBLE, WORRY

wor·ri·some \-səm\ *adj* **1** : causing distress or worry **2** : inclined to worry or fret — **wor·ri·some·ly** *adv*

¹**wor·ry** \'wər-ē, 'wə-rē\ *vb* **wor·ried; wor·ry·ing 1 a** : to shake and tear or mangle with the teeth ⟨a puppy *worrying* an old shoe⟩ **b** : to torment with persistent attacks **2** : to cause to be anxious : FRET ⟨the late hour *worried* my parents⟩ **3** : to feel or express great anxiety [Old English *wyrgan* "to strangle"] SYN see ANNOY — **wor·ri·er** *n*

²**worry** *n, pl* **worries 1** : ANXIETY 1 **2** : a cause of anxiety : TROUBLE

wor·ry·wart \-ˌwȯrt\ *n* : a person who worries without reasonable cause

¹**worse** \'wərs\ *adj* **1** : of more inferior quality, value, or condition **2 a** : more unfavorable, unpleasant, or painful; *esp* : more unwell ⟨I was *worse* the next day⟩ **b** : more faulty, unsuitable, or incorrect **c** : less skillful or efficient **3** : bad, evil, or corrupt in a greater degree : more reprehensible ⟨is failing *worse* than cheating?⟩ [Old English *wyrsa*]

²**worse** *n* : one that is worse

³**worse** *adv* : in a worse manner : to a worse extent or degree

wors·en \'wərs-n\ *vb* **wors·ened; wors·en·ing** \'wərs-ning, -n-ing\ : to make or become worse

¹**wor·ship** \'wər-shəp\ *n* **1** : reverence offered a divine being or supernatural power; *also* : the expression of such reverence **2** : extravagant respect or admiration for or devotion to an object of esteem ⟨*worship* of the dollar⟩ [Old English *weorthscipe* "worthiness, respect, reverence", from *weorth* "worthy, worth" + *-scipe* "-ship"]

²**worship** *vb* **-shiped** *or* **-shipped; -ship·ing** *or* **-ship·ping 1** : to honor or reverence as a divine being or supernatural power **2** : to regard with extravagant respect, honor, or devotion : IDOLIZE **3** : to perform or take part in worship or an act of worship SYN see REVERE — **wor·ship·er** *or* **wor·ship·per** *n*

wor·ship·ful \-fəl\ *adj* **1** *archaic* : EMINENT, NOTABLE **2** : giving worship or veneration — **wor·ship·ful·ly** \-fə-lē\ *adv* — **wor·ship·ful·ness** *n*

¹**worst** \'wərst\ *adj* **1** : most bad, evil, ill, or corrupt **2 a** : most unfavorable, unpleasant, or painful **b** : most unsuitable, faulty, unattractive, or ill-conceived **c** : least skillful or efficient **3** : most wanting in quality, value, or condition [Old English *wyrsta*] — **the worst way** : very much ⟨wanted a car in *the worst way*⟩

²**worst** *n* : one that is worst

³**worst** *adv* **1** : to the extreme degree of badness or inferiority **2** : to the greatest degree

⁴**worst** *vt* : to get the better of : DEFEAT

wor·sted \'wu̇s-təd, 'wərs-\ *n* **1** : a smooth compact yarn from long wool fibers used especially for firm napless fabrics, carpeting, or knitting **2** : a fabric made from worsted yarns [*Worstead,* England] — **worsted** *adj*

¹**wort** \'wərt, 'wȯrt\ *n* : PLANT 1; *esp* : an herbaceous plant — usually used in combination [Old English *wyrt* "root, herb, plant"]

²**wort** *n* : a dilute solution of sugars obtained by infusion from malt and fermented to form beer [Old English *wyrt*]

¹**worth** \'wərth\ *prep* **1 a** : equal in value to **b** : having possessions or income equal to **2** : deserving of ⟨well *worth* the effort⟩ [Old English *weorth* "having value, worthy"]

²**worth** *n* **1 a** : monetary value **b** : the equivalent of a specified amount or figure ⟨a dollar's *worth* of cheese⟩ **2** : the value of something measured by its qualities or by the esteem in which it is held **3 a** : moral or personal value **b** : EXCELLENCE 1, MERIT **4** : the value of one's property □ SYN VALUE, PRICE: WORTH applies to what is intrinsically excellent, admirable, useful, or desirable; VALUE may imply the immediate estimation of the worth of something to an individual or at a particular time or place; PRICE applies to what is actually exchanged for something else and may or may not imply an equivalent intrinsic worth.

worth·ful \'wərth-fəl\ *adj* **1** : full of merit : HONORABLE **2** : having value : VALUABLE — **worth·ful·ness** *n*

worth·less \'wərth-ləs\ *adj* **1 a** : lacking worth : VALUELESS **b** : USELESS **2** : DESPICABLE, LOW — **worth·less·ly** *adv* — **worth·less·ness** *n*

worth·while \'wərth-ˈhwīl, -ˈwīl\ *adj* : being worth the time or effort spent — **worth·while·ness** *n*

¹**wor·thy** \'wər-thē\ *adj* **wor·thi·er; -est 1 a** : having worth or value : ESTIMABLE **b** : MERITORIOUS, HONORABLE **2** : having sufficient worth ⟨you are *worthy* of the honor⟩ — **wor·thi·ly** \-thə-lē\ *adv* — **wor·thi·ness** \-thē-nəs\ *n*

²**worthy** *n, pl* **worthies** : a worthy person

wot *present 1st & 3d sing of* WIT

would \wəd, əd, d, wu̇d, 'wu̇d\ *past of* WILL **1 a** *archaic* : WISHED, DESIRED **b** *archaic* : wish for : WANT **c** : strongly desire : WISH ⟨I *would* I were young again⟩ **2** — used as an auxiliary verb (1) with *rather* or *sooner* to express preference between alternatives ⟨*would* sooner die than face them⟩, (2) to express wish, desire, or intent ⟨those who *would* forbid gambling⟩, (3) to express willingness or preference, (4) to express plan or intention ⟨said they *would* come⟩, (5) to express custom or habitual action ⟨we *would* meet often for lunch⟩, (6) to express consent or choice ⟨*would* put it off if they could⟩, (7) to express contingency or possibility ⟨if they were coming, they *would* be here now⟩, (8) to express completion of a statement of desire, request, or advice ⟨we wish that you *would* go⟩, and (9) to express probability or presumption in past or present time ⟨*would* have won if I had not started late⟩ **3** : COULD ⟨the barrel *would* hold 20 gallons⟩ **4** — used as an auxiliary verb (1) to express a request with which voluntary compliance is expected ⟨*would* you please help us⟩ and (2) to express doubt or uncertainty ⟨the explanation *would* seem satisfactory⟩ **5** : SHOULD ⟨knew I *would* enjoy the trip⟩ ⟨*would* be glad to know the answer⟩ [Old English *wolde*]

would-be \,wůd-,bē\ *adj* : desiring or professing to be ⟨a *would-be* poet⟩

wouldn't \'wůd-nt\ : would not

wouldst \wədst, wůdst, 'wůdst, wətst\ *or* **would·est** \'wůd-əst\ *archaic past 2d sing of* WILL

¹**wound** \'wünd\ *n* **1** : an injury involving cutting or breaking of bodily tissue (as by violence, accident, or surgery) **2** : a mental or emotional hurt or blow [Old English *wund*]

²**wound** *vb* **1** : to cause a wound to or in **2** : to inflict a wound ⟨a *wounding* remark⟩

³**wound** \'waůnd\ *past of* WIND

wove *past of* WEAVE

woven *past participle of* WEAVE

¹**wow** \'waů\ *interj* — used to express strong feeling (as pleasure or surprise) [probably imitative]

²**wow** *n* : a distortion in reproduced sound consisting of a slow rise and fall in pitch caused by speed variation in the reproducing system [imitative]

¹**wrack** \'rak\ *n* **1** : RUIN 1, DESTRUCTION **2** : a remnant of something destroyed [Old English *wræc* "misery, punishment, something driven by the sea"]

²**wrack** *n* **1** : a wrecked ship **2** : a piece of wreckage [Dutch or Low German *wrak*]

³**wrack** *vt* : to utterly ruin : WRECK

⁴**wrack** *vt* : ²RACK 2, 3

⁵**wrack** *n* : ¹RACK 2

wraith \'rāth\ *n, pl* **wraiths** \'rāths *also* 'rāthz\ **1 a** : an apparition of a living person seen usually as an exact likeness and just before death **b** : GHOST 2 **2** : an insubstantial appearance of something : SHADOW [origin unknown]

¹**wran·gle** \'rang-gəl\ *vb* **wran·gled; wran·gling** \-gə-ling, -gling\ **1** : to dispute angrily or peevishly : BICKER **2** : ARGUE 2 **3** : to obtain by persistent arguing **4** : to herd and care for (livestock and especially horses) on the range [Middle English *wranglen*]

²**wrangle** *n* **1** : an angry, noisy, or prolonged dispute or quarrel **2** : the action or process of wrangling

wran·gler \-gə-lər, -glər\ *n* **1** : one that wrangles or bickers **2** : a ranch hand who takes care of the saddle horses

¹**wrap** \'rap\ *vb* **wrapped; wrap·ping 1 a** : to cover especially by winding or folding ⟨*wrap* a baby in a blanket⟩ **b** : to envelop and secure (as for transportation or storage) ⟨*wrap* a gift⟩ **c** : to enclose by grasping or embracing **d** : to coil, fold, draw, or twine about something **2 a** : to envelop closely or completely **b** : to involve completely : ENGROSS ⟨*wrapped* up in a hobby⟩ **3** : to conceal or obscure as if by enveloping ⟨a city *wrapped* in darkness⟩ **4** : to put on clothing : DRESS ⟨*wrapped* up warm⟩ **5** : to be subject to covering, enclosing, or packaging ⟨*wraps* up into a small package⟩ [Middle English *wrappen*]

²**wrap** *n* **1 a** : a covering that encloses something **b** : an article of clothing that may be wrapped round a person; *esp* : an outer garment (as a coat or shawl) **2** : a single turn or convolution of something wound round an object **3** *pl* **a** : RESTRAINT 2 **b** : SECRECY ⟨a plan kept under *wraps*⟩

¹**wrap·around** \,rap-ə-,raůnd\ *adj* **1** : made to be wrapped around the body ⟨a *wraparound* skirt⟩ **2** : shaped to follow a contour ⟨*wraparound* sunglasses⟩

²**wraparound** \'rap-ə-,raůnd\ *n* : a wraparound garment

wrap·per \'rap-ər\ *n* **1** : that in which something is wrapped: as **a** (1) : JACKET 2c (2) : the paper cover of a book not bound in boards **b** : a paper wrapped around a newspaper or magazine in the mail **2** : one that wraps **3** : a wraparound article of clothing

wrap·ping \'rap-ing\ *n* : something used to wrap an object : WRAPPER

wrap-up \'rap-,əp\ *n* : a summarizing report

wrap up \rap-'əp, 'rap-\ *vt* **1** : to bring to a usually successful conclusion : END **2** : to make a single comprehensive report of

wrasse \'ras\ *n* : any of various usually brilliantly colored spiny-finned fishes with a long deep narrow body that include important food fishes especially of warm seas [Cornish *gwragh,* "old woman, hag, wrasse"]

wrath \'rath\ *n* **1** : violent vengeful anger **2** : retributory punishment for sin or crime [Old English *wræththo,* from *wrāth* "wroth"] SYN SEE ANGER — **wrathy** \-ē\ *adj*

wrath·ful \'rath-fəl\ *adj* **1** : filled with wrath : IRATE **2** : arising from, marked by, or indicative of wrath ⟨a *wrathful* expression⟩ — **wrath·ful·ly** \-fə-lē\ *adv* — **wrath·ful·ness** *n*

wreak \'rēk\ *vt* **1** : to exact as a punishment : INFLICT ⟨*wreak* vengeance⟩ **2** : to give free scope or rein to ⟨*wreaked* their wrath⟩ [Old English *wrecan* "to drive, punish, avenge"]

wreath \'rēth\ *n, pl* **wreaths** \'rēthz, 'rēths\ : something (as a garland or chaplet) intertwined into a circular shape ⟨a *wreath* of smoke⟩ ⟨a *wreath* of flowers⟩ [Old English *writha*]

wreathe \'rēth\ *vb* **1** : to twist or contort so as to show folds or creases ⟨a face *wreathed* in smiles⟩ **2 a** : to shape into a wreath **b** : to take on the shape of a wreath : move or extend in circles or spirals ⟨smoke *wreathed* upward⟩ **c** : to cause to coil about something **3** : to encircle or adorn with or as if with a wreath ⟨ivy *wreathed* the pole⟩

¹**wreck** \'rek\ *n* **1** : goods cast upon the land by the sea after a shipwreck **2** : the action of breaking up or destroying something usually by accident ⟨injured in the *wreck* of a train⟩ **3** : the broken remains of something wrecked or otherwise ruined **4** : something disabled or in a state of ruin or dilapidation; *also* : an individual broken in health or strength [Anglo-French *wrek,* of Scandinavian origin]

²**wreck** *vt* **1 a** : SHIPWRECK 2 **b** : to damage or ruin by breaking up ⟨*wreck* a building⟩ ⟨*wreck* a friendship⟩ **c** : to involve in disaster or ruin **2** : WREAK 1

wreck·age \'rek-ij\ *n* **1** : the act of wrecking : the state of being wrecked **2** : the remains of a wreck

wreck·er \'rek-ər\ *n* **1** : one that wrecks **2** : a person who searches for or works on wrecks of ships **3** : a ship used in salvaging wrecks **4** : a truck equipped to remove wrecked or disabled automotive vehicles — called also *tow truck*

wrecking bar *n* : a small crowbar with a claw for pulling nails at one end and a slight bend for prying at the other end

wren \'ren\ *n* **1** : any of a large family of small mostly brown singing birds with short rounded wings and short erect tail **2** : any of various small singing birds resembling the true wrens in size and habits [Old English *wrenna*]

¹**wrench** \'rench\ *vb* **1** : to move with a violent twist **2** : to pull, strain, or tighten with violent twisting **3** : to injure or disable by a violent twisting or straining **4** : to change (as the meaning of a word) violently **5** : to snatch forcibly : WREST **6** : to cause to suffer anguish : RACK [Old English *wrencan*]

²**wrench** *n* **1 a** : a violent twisting or a pull with or as if with twisting **b** : a sharp twist or sudden jerk straining muscles or ligaments; *also* : the resultant injury (as of a joint) **c** : a distorting or perverting alteration **d** : acute emotional distress : sudden violent mental change **2** : a hand or power tool for holding, twisting, or turning an object (as a bolt or nut)

¹**wrest** \'rest\ *vt* **1** : to pull, force, or move by violent wringing or twisting movements **2** : to gain with difficulty by or as if by force or violence ⟨*wrest* a living⟩ ⟨*wrest* the power from the king⟩ **3 a** : to divert to an unnatural or improper use **b** : DISTORT ⟨they *wrest* my every word⟩ [Old English *wræstan*] — **wrest·er** *n*

wrasse

²**wrest** *n* : a forcible twist : WRENCH

¹**wres·tle** \'res-əl\ *vb* **wres·tled; wres·tling** \'res-ling, -ə-ling\ **1** : to grapple with an opponent in an attempt to trip or throw the opponent down **2** : to contend against in wrestling **3** : to struggle for mastery (as with something difficult) ⟨*wrestle* with a problem⟩ [Old English *wrǣstlian,* from *wrǣstan* "to wrest"] — **wres·tler** \'res-lər\ *n*

²**wrestle** *n* : the action or an instance of wrestling : STRUGGLE

wres·tling \'res-ling\ *n* : the sport of hand-to-hand combat between two unarmed contestants who seek to throw each other

wretch \'rech\ *n* **1** : a miserable unhappy person **2** : a base, despicable, or vile person [Old English *wrecca* "outcast"]

wretch·ed \'rech-əd\ *adj* **1** : deeply afflicted, dejected, or distressed : MISERABLE **2** : very or annoyingly bad ⟨a *wretched* accident⟩ **3 a** : being or appearing mean or contemptible ⟨a *wretched* trick⟩ **b** : very poor in quality or ability ⟨*wretched* workmanship⟩ — **wretch·ed·ly** *adv* — **wretch·ed·ness** *n*

wrig·gle \'rig-əl\ *vb* **wrig·gled; wrig·gling** \'rig-ling, -ə-ling\ **1** : to move to and fro with short writhing motions like a worm : SQUIRM ⟨*wriggled* in the chair⟩ ⟨*wriggled* my toes⟩ **2** : to move or progress by wriggling **3** : to extricate or insinuate oneself or reach a goal by maneuvering, ingratiating, or deceiving ⟨*wriggle* out of a difficulty⟩ [Middle English *wrigglen*] — **wriggle** *n* — **wrig·gly** \'rig-lē, -ə-lē\ *adj*

wrig·gler \'rig-lər, -ə-lər\ *n* : one that wriggles; *esp* : WIGGLER 2

wright \'rīt\ *n* : a workman in wood : CARPENTER — usually used in combination ⟨ship*wright*⟩ ⟨wheel*wright*⟩ [Old English *wyrhta, wryhta* "worker, maker"]

wring \'ring\ *vt* **wrung** \'rəng\; **wring·ing** \'ring-ing\ **1** : to squeeze or twist especially so as to make dry or to extract moisture or liquid ⟨*wring* wet clothes⟩ **2** : to get by or as if by twisting or pressing ⟨*wring* the truth out of you⟩ **3 a** : to twist so as to strain or sprain **b** : to twist together (clasped hands) as a sign of anguish **4** : to place or insert by a twisting movement **5** : to affect painfully as if by wringing : TORMENT ⟨a tragedy that *wrung* our hearts⟩ **6** : to shake (a hand) vigorously in greeting [Old English *wringan*] — **wring** *n*

wring·er \'ring-ər\ *n* : one that wrings; *esp* : a machine or device for pressing out liquid or moisture ⟨clothes *wringer*⟩

¹**wrin·kle** \'ring-kəl\ *n* **1** : a crease or small fold on a surface (as in the skin or in cloth) **2 a** : METHOD 1, TECHNIQUE; *also* : information about a method : HINT **b** : an innovation in method, technique, or equipment : NOVELTY ⟨the latest *wrinkle*⟩ [Middle English] — **wrin·kly** \-kə-lē, -klē\ *adj*

²**wrinkle** *vb* **wrin·kled; wrin·kling** \-kə-ling, -kling\ *vb* : to develop or cause to develop wrinkles

wrist \'rist\ *n* : the joint or the region of the joint between the human hand and the arm or a corresponding part on a lower animal [Old English]

wrist·band \'rist-,band, 'ris-\ *n* **1** : the part of a sleeve covering the wrist **2** : a band encircling the wrist

wrist·let \'rist-lət, 'ris-\ *n* : a band encircling the wrist; *esp* : a close-fitting knitted band worn for warmth

wrist pin *n* : a pin by which a connecting rod (as a piston rod) is fastened to another moving part (as of an engine)

wrist·watch \'ris-,twäch\ *n* : a small watch attached to a bracelet or strap to fasten about the wrist

writ \'rit\ *n* **1** : something written : WRITING ⟨Holy *Writ*⟩ **2 a** : a legal order in writing signed by a court or judicial officer **b** : a written order constituting a symbol of the power and authority of the issuer ⟨where the king's *writ* has no force⟩ [Old English]

writ·able \'rīt-ə-bəl\ *adj* : capable of being put in writing

write \'rīt\ *vb* **wrote** \'rōt\; **writ·ten** \'rit-n\ *also* **writ** \'rit\; **writ·ing** \'rīt-ing\ **1** : to form letters or words with pen or pencil ⟨learn to read and *write*⟩ **2** : to form the letters or the words of (as on paper) : IN-SCRIBE ⟨*write* one's name⟩ ⟨*write* a check⟩ **3** : to put down on paper : give expression to in writing ⟨*write* an account of the circus⟩ **4** : to make up and set down for others to read : COMPOSE ⟨*write* a book⟩ ⟨wrote music⟩ **5** : to pen, dictate, or typewrite a letter to ⟨*write* the president⟩ **6** : to communicate by letter : CORRE-SPOND **7** : to be fitted for writing ⟨this pen *writes* easily⟩ **8** : to transfer (as data) from the memory of a computer to an output device ⟨*write* data onto magnetic tape⟩ [Old English *wrītan* "to scratch, draw, inscribe"]

write down *vb* **1** : to record in written form **2 a** : to reduce in status, rank, or value **b** : to play down in writing **3** : to write so as to appeal to a less sophisticated audience ⟨*write down* to meet the needs of children⟩

write in *vt* : to insert (a name not listed on a ballot or voting machine) in an appropriate space — **write-in** \'rīt-,in\ *n*

write off *vt* **1** : to reduce the estimated value of : DEPRE-CIATE **2** : to take off the books : CANCEL ⟨*write off* a bad debt⟩ — **write-off** \'rīt-,óf\ *n*

write out *vt* : to put in writing; *esp* : to put into a full and complete written form

writ·er \'rīt-ər\ *n* **1** : AUTHOR 1 **2** : one that can write

writer's cramp *n* : a painful spasmodic cramp of muscles of the hand or fingers from writing

write-up \'rīt-,əp\ *n* : a written account (as in a newspaper); *esp* : a flattering article

write up \rīt-'əp, 'rīt-\ *vt* **1 a** : to write an account of : DESCRIBE **b** : to put into finished written form **2** : to bring up to date the writing of **3** : to increase the book value of

writhe \'rīth\ *vb* **1** : to twist and turn this way and that ⟨*writhe* in pain⟩ **2** : to suffer with shame or confusion : SQUIRM [Old English *wrīthan*]

writ·ing \'rīt-ing\ *n* **1 a** : the act or process of one that writes : the formation of letters to express words and ideas **b** : HANDWRITING **2 a** : something (as a letter, book, or document) that is written or printed **b** : IN-SCRIPTION 1 **3** : a style or form of composition **4** : the occupation of a writer

writing desk *n* : a desk often with a sloping top for writing on

writing paper *n* : paper intended for writing on with ink

writ of assistance : a writ issued (as by British authorities in the American colonies) to an officer (as a sheriff) to aid in the search for smuggled or illegal goods

¹**wrong** \'róng\ *n* **1 a** : an injurious, unfair, or unjust act **b** : a violation of the legal rights of another; *esp* : TORT **2** : principles, practices, or conduct contrary to justice, goodness, equity, or law ⟨know right from *wrong*⟩ **3 a** : the state, position, or fact of being or doing wrong **b** : the state of being guilty [Old English *wrang,* of Scandinavian origin]

²**wrong** *adj* **wrong·er** \'róng-ər\; **wrong·est** \'róng-əst\ **1** : not according to the moral standard : SINFUL, IMMOR-AL **2** : not right or proper according to a code, standard, or convention : IMPROPER **3** : not according to truth or facts : INCORRECT **4** : not satisfactory (as in condition, results, health, or temper) **5** : not in accordance with one's needs or intent ⟨took the *wrong* bus⟩ **6** : being the side of something opposite to the principal one, naturally turned down, inward, or away, or least finished or polished ⟨the *wrong* side of a fabric⟩ — **wrong** *adv* — **wrong·ly** \'róng-lē\ *adv* — **wrong·ness** *n*

³**wrong** *vt* **wronged; wrong·ing** \'róng-ing\ **1** : to do wrong to : INJURE, HARM **2** : to make unjust remarks about : DISHONOR, MALIGN — **wrong·er** \'róng-ər\ *n*

wrong·do·er \'ròng-'dü-ər\ *n* : a person who does wrong and especially moral wrong — **wrong·do·ing** \-'dü-ing\ *n*

wrong·ful \'ròng-fəl\ *adj* **1** : WRONG, UNJUST ⟨a *wrongful* act⟩ **2** : UNLAWFUL **1** — **wrong·ful·ly** \-fə-lē\ *adv* — **wrong·ful·ness** *n*

wrong·head·ed \'ròng-'hed-əd\ *adj* : stubborn in adherence to wrong opinion or principles : PERVERSE — **wrong·head·ed·ly** *adv* — **wrong·head·ed·ness** *n*

wrote *past of* WRITE

wroth \'ròth *also* 'ròth\ *adj* : filled with wrath : ANGRY [Old English *wrāth*]

¹wrought *past of* WORK

²wrought \'ròt\ *adj* **1** : worked into shape by artistry or effort **2** : elaborately decorated **3** : processed for use **4** : beaten into shape by tools ⟨*wrought* metals⟩ **5** : deeply stirred ⟨gets easily *wrought* up⟩

wrought iron *n* : a commercial form of iron that is tough, malleable, and relatively soft

wrung *past of* WRING

wry \'rī\ *adj* **wri·er** \'rī-ər, 'rīr\; **wri·est** \'rī-əst\ **1 a** : turned abnormally to one side **b** : twisted in expression of disgust or displeasure ⟨*wry* lips⟩ **2** : cleverly and often ironically or grimly humorous [earlier *wry* "to twist", from Old English *wrigian* "to turn"] — **wry·ly** *adv* — **wry·ness** *n*

wry·neck \'rī-,nek\ *n* : a disorder marked by a twisting of the neck and an unnatural position of the head

wurst \'wərst, 'wu̇rst, 'wu̇st, 'wu̇sht\ *n* : SAUSAGE [German]

wy·an·dotte \'wī-ən-,dät\ *n* : any of an American breed of medium-sized domestic fowls [probably from *Wyandot,* member of a group of American Indians]

¹x \'eks\ *n, pl* **x's** *or* **xs** \'ek-səz\ *often cap* **1** : the 24th letter of the English alphabet **2** : 10 in Roman numerals **3** : an unknown quantity □ ORIGIN The standard use of the letter *x* to designate an unknown quantity goes back to the practice of René Descartes, 17th century French mathematician and philosopher. Descartes, in his book *La géométrie* ("Geometry"), used the first letters of the alphabet for known quantities and the final letters, *x, y, z* (and most commonly *x*), for unknowns. Later mathematicians have simply followed Descartes's example.

²x *vt* **x-ed** *also* **x'd** *or* **xed** \'ekst\; **x-ing** *or* **x'ing** \'ek-sing\ **1** : to mark with an x **2** : to cancel or cover over with a series of x's — usually used with *out*

xan·tho·phyll \'zan-thə-,fil\ *n* : any of several neutral yellow carotenoid pigments that are usually oxygen derivatives of carotenes [French *xanthophylle,* from Greek *xanthos* "yellow" + *phyllon* "leaf"] — **xan·tho·phyl·lic** \,zan-thə-'fil-ik\ *adj*

x-ax·is \'ek-,sak-səs\ : the axis in a plane Cartesian coordinate system parallel to which abscissas are measured

X chromosome *n* : a sex chromosome that carries factors for femaleness and usually occurs paired in each female zygote and cell and single in each male zygote and cell in species in which the male typically has two unlike sex chromosomes — compare Y CHROMOSOME

x-co·or·di·nate \,ek-skō-'órd-nət, -n-ət, -n-,āt\ *n* : ABSCISSA

xe·bec \'zē-,bek, zi-'\ *n* : a usually 3-masted Mediterranean sailing ship typically having lateen sails [probably from French *chebec,* from Arabic *shabbāk*]

xe·non \'zē-,nän, 'zen-,än\ *n* : a heavy gaseous chemical element occurring in air in minute quantities — see ELEMENT table [Greek, neuter of *xenos* "strange"]

xe·no·pho·bia \,zen-ə-'fō-bē-ə, ,zēn-\ *n* : fear and hatred of strangers or foreigners or of anything that is strange or foreign [Greek *xenos* "strange, stranger"] — **xe·no·phobe** \'zen-ə-,fōb, 'zēn-\ *n* — **xe·no·pho·bic** \,zen-ə-'fō-bik, ,zēn-\ *adj*

xer- *or* **xero-** *combining form* : dry ⟨*xer*ic⟩ ⟨*xero*phyte⟩ [Greek *xēros*]

xe·ric \'zir-ik, 'zer-\ *adj* **1** : low or deficient in available moisture for the support of life **2** : XEROPHYTIC — **xe·ri·cal·ly** \'zir-i-kə-lē, -klē\ *adv*

xe·rog·ra·phy \zə-'räg-rə-fē, zir-'äg-\ *n* : the formation of pictures or copies of graphic matter by the action of light on an electrically charged surface in which the latent image is developed with powders — **xe·ro·graph·ic** \,zir-ə-'graf-ik\ *adj*

xe·roph·thal·mia \,zir-,äf-'thal-mē-ə, -,äp-'thal-\ *n* : a dry thickened lusterless condition of the eyeball resulting from a severe systemic deficiency of vitamin A — **xe·roph·thal·mic** \-mik\ *adj*

xe·ro·phyte \'zir-ə-,fīt\ *n* : a plant adapted for growth with a limited water supply especially by means of mechanisms that limit transpiration or that provide for the storage of water — **xe·ro·phyt·ic** \,zir-ə-'fit-ik\ *adj*

Xerox *trademark* — used for a xerographic copier

xi \'zī, 'ksī\ *n* : the 14th letter of the Greek alphabet — Ξ or ξ

x-in·ter·cept \'ek-'sint-ər-,sept\ *n* : the x-coordinate of a point where a line, curve, or surface intersects the x-axis

Xmas \'kris-məs *also* 'ek-sməs\ *n* : CHRISTMAS [*X,* symbol for Christ, from the Greek letter chi (X), initial of *Christos* "Christ"] □ ORIGIN Since the 16th century *Xmas* has been used in English as a short form of *Christmas. X* as a symbol for Christ is derived from the Greek, where *chi* (X) is the initial letter of *Christos,* the Greek form of *Christ.* The word *Xmas* is usually pronounced like *Christmas,* although a pronunciation of the letter *x* plus *-mas* as in *Christmas* is also heard.

x-ra·di·a·tion \,eks-,rād-ē-'ā-shən\ *n, often cap X* **1** : exposure to X rays **2** : radiation consisting of X rays

x-ray \'eks-,rā\ *vt, often cap X* : to examine, treat, or photograph with X rays

X ray \'eks-,rā\ *n* **1** : any of the electromagnetic radiations of the same nature as light rays but of very short wavelength that are generated by a stream of electrons striking against a metal surface in vacuum and that are able to penetrate various thicknesses of solids and act on photographic film like light and to cause a fluores-

xebec

\ə\ abut	\ng\ sing
\ər\ further	\ō\ bone
\a\ mat	\ò\ saw
\ā\ take	\òi\ coin
\ä\ cot, cart	\th\ thin
\aù\ out	\th\ this
\ch\ chin	\ü\ food
\e\ pet	\ù\ foot
\ē\ easy	\y\ yet
\g\ go	\yü\ few
\i\ tip	\yù\ cure
\ī\ life	\zh\ vision
\j\ job	

cent screen to emit light **2** : a photograph especially of conditions inside the surface of a body taken by the use of X rays [translation of German *x-strahl*] — **X–ray** *adj* □ ORIGIN In 1895 Wilhelm Conrad Röntgen was conducting experiments on the properties of cathode rays. He noticed that a fluorescent surface in the neighborhood of a cathode-ray tube would become luminous even if shielded. A thick metal object placed before the tube would cast a dark shadow on the fluorescent surface, but an object made of a less dense substance like wood would cast only a weak shadow. Röntgen's explanation was that the tube produced some kind of invisible radiation that could pass through substances not transparent to ordinary light. Because he did not know the nature of this radiation he had discovered, he named it *x-strahl*, which was translated into English as *X ray*.

X–ray therapy *n* : medical treatment (as of a cancer) by controlled application of X rays

X–ray tube *n* : a vacuum tube in which a concentrated stream of electrons strikes a metal target and produces X rays

xyl- *or* **xylo-** *combining form* : wood ⟨*xylo*phone⟩ [Greek *xylon*]

xy·lem \ˈzī-ləm, -ˌlem\ *n* : a complex tissue of higher plants that transports water and dissolved materials upward, functions also in support and storage, lies internal to the phloem, and typically constitutes the woody part (as of a plant stem) [German, from Greek *xylon* "wood"] — **xy·la·ry** \ˈzī-lə-rē\ *adj*

xylem ray *n* : a vascular ray or portion of a vascular ray located in xylem — compare PHLOEM RAY

xy·lene \ˈzī-ˌlēn\ *n* : a colorless flammable liquid obtained from wood tar, coal tar, coke-oven gas, or petroleum and used chiefly as a solvent

xy·lol \ˈzī-ˌlȯl, -ˌlōl\ *n* : XYLENE

xy·lo·phone \ˈzī-lə-ˌfōn\ *n* : a musical instrument consisting of a series of wooden bars graduated in length to sound the musical scale and played by striking with two wooden hammers — **xy·lo·phon·ist** \-ˌfō-nəst\ *n*

Yy

y \ˈwī\ *n, pl* **y's** *or* **ys** \ˈwīz\ *often cap* : the 25th letter of the English alphabet

¹-y *also* **-ey** \ē\ *adj suffix* **-ier; -iest 1 a** : characterized by : full of ⟨clay*y*⟩ ⟨dirt*y*⟩ ⟨mudd*y*⟩ **b** : having the character of : composed of ⟨ic*y*⟩ ⟨wax*y*⟩ **c** : like : like that of ⟨home*y*⟩ ⟨stag*y*⟩ ⟨wintr*y*⟩ **d** : devoted to : addicted to : enthusiastic over ⟨horse*y*⟩ **2 a** : tending or inclined to ⟨chatt*y*⟩ ⟨sleep*y*⟩ **b** : giving occasion for (specified) action ⟨chew*y*⟩ **c** : performing (specified) action ⟨curl*y*⟩ **3 a** : somewhat : rather : -ISH ⟨chill*y*⟩ **b** : having (such) characteristics to a marked degree or in an affected or superficial way [Old English *-ig*]

²-y \ē\ *n suffix, pl* **-ies 1** : state : condition : quality ⟨beggar*y*⟩ **2** : activity, place of business, or goods dealt with ⟨laundr*y*⟩ **3** : whole body or group ⟨soldier*y*⟩ [Old French *-ie*, from Latin *-ia*, from Greek *-ia*, *-eia*]

³-y *n suffix, pl* **-ies** : instance of a (specified) action ⟨entreat*y*⟩ ⟨inquir*y*⟩ [Anglo-French *-ie*, from Latin *-ium*]

⁴-y — see -IE

¹yacht \ˈyät\ *n* : any of various sailing or motor-driven vessels that are used especially for pleasure cruising or racing [obsolete Dutch *jaght*, from Low German *jacht*, short for *jachtschip*, literally, "hunting ship"] □ ORIGIN In the 16th century the Dutch began building light, fast ships designed to chase the ships of pirates and smugglers from the Dutch coast. The Dutch appropriately called this type of vessel *jaght*, which is a derivative of a Low German word for a fast, light sailing vessel, *jachtschip*, meaning literally "hunting ship". The ship was introduced into England in 1660 when the Dutch East India Company presented one to King Charles II, who used it as a pleasure boat. The ship's design was copied by British shipbuilders for those wealthy gentlemen who desired and could afford such pleasure craft.

²yacht *vi* : to race or cruise in a yacht

yacht·ing *n* : the action, fact, or sport of racing or cruising in a yacht

¹yacht

¹yak

yachts·man \ˈyät-smən\ *n* : a person who owns or sails a yacht

ya·hoo \ˈyā-hü, ˈyä-\ *n, pl* **yahoos** : a crude or rowdy person [*Yahoo*, member of a race of brutes in Swift's *Gulliver's Travels* who have the form and the vices of people]

Yah·weh \ˈyä-ˌwā, -ˌvä\ *also* **Yah·veh** \-ˌvā\ *n* : the God of the Hebrews [Hebrew *Yahweh*]

¹yak \ˈyak\ *n, pl* **yaks** *also* **yak** : a large long-haired wild or domesticated ox of Tibet and adjacent elevated parts of central Asia [Tibetan *gyak*]

²yak *n* : persistant or voluble talk [probably imitative] — **yak** *vi*

y'all \ˈyȯl\ *pron, chiefly South* : YOU-ALL

yam \ˈyam\ *n* **1** : an edible starchy tuberous root that is a staple food in tropical areas; *also* : a plant distantly related to the lilies that produces these **2** : a moist-fleshed and usually orange-fleshed sweet potato [Portuguese *inhame* and Spanish *ñame*, of African origin]

yam·mer \ˈyam-ər\ *vi* **yam·mered; yam·mer·ing** \ˈyam-ring, -ə-ring\ **1** : to complain persistently **2** : CHATTER 2 [Old English *gēomrian* "to lament"] — **yammer** *n*

yang \ˈyäng\ *n* : the masculine active principle (as of light, heat, or dryness) in nature that in Chinese cosmic philosophy combines with yin to produce all that comes to be [Chinese (Pekingese dialect) *yang²*]

yank \ˈyangk\ *n* : a strong sudden pull : JERK [origin unknown] — **yank** *vb*

Yank \ˈyangk\ *n* : YANKEE

Yan·kee \ˈyang-kē\ *n* **1 a** : a native or inhabitant of New England **b** : a native or inhabitant of the northern United States **2** : a native or inhabitant of the United States [origin unknown] — **Yankee** *adj*

yan·qui \ˈyäng-kē\ *n, often cap* : a citizen of the United States as distinguished from a Latin American [Spanish, from English *Yankee*]

¹yap \'yap\ *vi* **yapped; yap·ping 1 : YELP 2 :** to talk with shrill insistence : **SCOLD** [imitative]

²yap *n* **1 : YELP 2 :** shrill insistent talk : **CHATTER 3** *slang* : **MOUTH** 1b

¹yard \'yärd\ *n* **1 :** any of various units of measure; *esp* : a unit of length equal in the United States to 0.9144 meter — see **MEASURE** table **2 :** a long spar that supports and spreads the head of a square sail, lateen, or lugsail [Old English *gierd* "twig, measure, yard"]

²yard *n* **1 a :** a small usually enclosed area open to the sky and adjacent to a building **b :** the grounds of a building or group of buildings **2 a :** an enclosure for livestock **b :** an area with its buildings and facilities set aside for a particular business or activity **c :** a system of railroad tracks for storage and maintenance of cars and making up trains **3 :** a locality where deer herd in winter [Old English *geard* "enclosure, yard"]

³yard *vb* : to drive into, gather, or confine in or as if in a yard

yard·age \'yärd-ij\ *n* : a total number of yards; *also* : the length, extent, or volume of something as measured in yards

yard·arm \'yärd-,ärm\ *n* : either end of the yard of a square-rigged ship

yard goods *n pl* : fabrics sold by the yard

yard·man \'yärd-mən, -,man\ *n* **1 :** one who is employed to do outdoor work (as mowing lawns) **2 :** one who works in or about a yard (as a lumberyard or a railroad yard)

yard·mas·ter \-,mas-tər\ *n* : a person in charge of operations in a railroad yard

yard·stick \-,stik\ *n* **1 :** a measuring stick a yard long **2 :** a rule or standard by which something is measured or judged : **CRITERION**

¹yarn \'yärn\ *n* **1 a :** textile fiber (as spun wool, cotton, flax, or silk) for use in weaving, knitting, or the manufacture of thread **b :** a strand of material (as metal, glass, or asbestos) for uses comparable to those of a textile yarn **2 :** an interesting or exciting often made-up story [Old English *gearn*]

²yarn *vi* : to tell a yarn

yarn–dye \-'dī\ *vt* : to dye before weaving or knitting

yar·row \'yar-ō\ *n* : a strong-scented herb related to the daisies that has finely divided leaves and white or rarely pink flowers in flat clusters [Old English *gearwe*]

yat·a·ghan \'yat-ə-,gan\ *n* : a long knife or short saber common among Muslims that is made without a cross guard and usually with a double curve to the edge [Turkish *yatağan*]

yau·pon \'yü-,pän also 'yō-, 'yȯ-\ *n* : a holly of the southern United States with smooth leaves used as a substitute for tea [of American Indian origin]

yaw \'yȯ\ *vi* : to turn abruptly from a straight course : **SWERVE, VEER** ⟨a heavy sea made the ship *yaw*⟩ [origin unknown] — **yaw** *n*

yawl \'yȯl\ *n* : a 2-masted fore-and-aft rigged sailing vessel with a mizzenmast abaft the rudder — compare **KETCH** [Low German *jolle*]

¹yawn \'yȯn, 'yän\ *vb* **1 :** to open wide : **GAPE 2 :** to open the mouth wide usually as an involuntary reaction to fatigue or boredom **3 :** to utter with a yawn [Old English *ginian, geonian*] — **yawn·er** *n*

²yawn *n* : a deep usually involuntary intake of breath through the wide-open mouth

yawn·ing *adj* **1 :** wide open : **CAVERNOUS** ⟨a *yawning* hole⟩ **2 :** showing fatigue or boredom by yawns ⟨a *yawning* audience⟩

¹yawp *or* **yaup** \'yȯp\ *vi* **1 :** to make a raucous noise : **SQUAWK 2 : CLAMOR 2, COMPLAIN** [Middle English *yolpen*] — **yawp·er** *n*

²yawp *also* **yaup** *n* : a raucous noise : **SQUAWK**

yaws \'yȯz\ *n sing or pl* : a tropical disease caused by a spirochete and marked by ulcerating surface lesions with later bone involvement [of American Indian origin]

y–ax·is \'wī-,ak-səs\ *n* : the axis in a plane Cartesian coordinate system parallel to which ordinates are measured

Y chromosome *n* : a sex chromosome occurring in male zygotes and cells in species in which the male typically has two unlike sex chromosomes — compare **X CHROMOSOME**

yclept \i-'klept\ *or* **ycleped** \-'klept, -'klept\ *adj, archaic* : known as : **CALLED** [Middle English, from Old English *geclipod,* past participle of *clipian* to cry out, name]

y–co·or·di·nate \,wī-kō-'ȯrd-nət, -n-ət, -n-,āt\ *n* : **ORDINATE**

¹ye \yē, 'yē\ *pron* : **YOU** 1 — used originally only as a plural pronoun of the 2d person in the subjective case and now used especially in ecclesiastical or literary language and in various English dialects [Old English *gē*]

²ye \yē, yə, *or like* THE\ *definite article, archaic* : **THE** [Middle English *þe* "the"; from the similarity of the handwritten forms of þ (th) and *y*] □ **ORIGIN** The use of *ye* instead of *the* to suggest an earlier time is the result of changes in handwriting styles which took place before the introduction of printing in England. The alphabet used by the Anglo-Saxons included several letters not found in the Latin alphabet but borrowed from the runic alphabet used by several early Germanic peoples. One of these letters was þ, called *thorn,* which represented the sounds now most often indicated by *th* in English. This letter was used in the Middle English period as well, but by the end of the 14th century the written form of the thorn was often indistinguishable from that of *y*. After 1400, the thorn fell into disuse except in a few words such as *the* and *that*. As the thorn was forgotten, the archaic form of *the* came to be written *ye*.

¹yea \'yā\ *adv* **1 : YES** — used in oral voting **2** — used as a function word to introduce a more explicit or emphatic phrase [Old English *gēa*]

²yea *n* **1 : ASSENT, AFFIRMATION 2 a :** an affirmative vote **b :** a person casting a yea vote

yeah \'ye-ə, 'yeȯ, 'ya-ə\ *adv* : **YES**

year \'yiər\ *n* **1 :** the period of one apparent revolution of the sun around the ecliptic or of the earth's revolution around the sun amounting to approximately 365 ¼ days **2 a :** a period of 365 days or in leap year 366 days beginning January 1 **b :** a period of time equal to this but beginning at a different time ⟨a fiscal *year*⟩ **3 :** a continuous period of time that constitutes the period of some event (as revolution of a planet about its sun) or activity whether greater or less than the calendar year ⟨a school *year* of less than six months⟩ [Old English *gēar*]

year·book \-,bùk\ *n* **1 :** a book published yearly especially as a factual report **2 :** a school publication recording the history and activities of a graduating class

year·ling \-ling\ *n* : one that is a year old: **a :** an animal in the second year of its age **b :** a racehorse between January 1st of the year after the year in which it was foaled and the next January 1st — **yearling** *adj*

year·long \-'lȯng\ *adj* : lasting through a year

year·ly \-lē\ *adj* **1 :** computed in terms of one year **2 :** occurring, done, produced, or acted upon every year : **ANNUAL** — **yearly** *adv*

yearn \'yərn\ *vb* **1 :** to feel a longing or craving **2 :** to feel tenderness or compassion [Old English *giernan*] **SYN** see **LONG** — **yearn·er** *n*

yearn·ing *n* : a tender or urgent longing

year of grace : a year of the Christian era ⟨the *year of grace* 1979⟩

year–round \'yiər-'raùnd, 'yiə-'raùnd\ *adj* : effective, employed, or operating for the full year : not seasonal ⟨a *year-round* resort⟩

yeast \'yēst, 'ēst\ *n* **1 a :** a substance that occurs especially in sweet liquids in which it promotes alcoholic

1 ¹yard 2

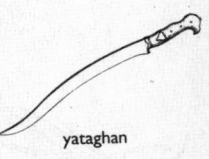

yataghan

yawl

\ə\ abut	\ng\ sing
\ər\ further	\ō\ bone
\a\ mat	\ȯ\ saw
\ā\ take	\ȯi\ coin
\ä\ cot, cart	\th\ thin
\aù\ out	\th\ this
\ch\ chin	\ü\ food
\e\ pet	\ù\ foot
\ē\ easy	\y\ yet
\g\ go	\yü\ few
\i\ tip	\yù\ cure
\ī\ life	\zh\ vision
\j\ job	

fermentation, consists largely of cells of a tiny fungus, and is used especially in the making of alcoholic liquors and as a leaven in baking **b** : a commercial product containing yeast plants in a moist or dry medium **c** : any of various tiny fungi that are usually one-celled and reproduce by budding; *esp* : one present and functionally active in a yeast froth or sediment **2** : foam or froth especially of waves **3** : something that causes ferment or activity [Old English *gist*] — **yeasty** \'yē-stē, 'ē-stē\ *adj*

yegg \'yeg, 'yāg\ *n* : SAFECRACKER; *also* : ROBBER [origin unknown]

¹yell \'yel\ *vb* **1** : to utter a loud cry, scream, or shout **2** : to give a cheer usually in unison **3** : to utter or declare with or as if with a yell : SHOUT [Old English *giellan*] — **yell·er** *n*

²yell *n* **1** : SCREAM 1, SHOUT **2** : a usually rhythmic cheer used especially in schools to encourage athletic teams

¹yel·low \'yel-ō\ *adj* **1 a** : of the color yellow **b** : yellowish from age, disease, or discoloration **c** : having a yellow complexion or skin **2 a** : featuring sensational or scandalous items or ordinary news sensationally distorted ⟨*yellow* journalism⟩ **b** : COWARDLY 1 [Old English *geolu*] — **yel·low·ish** \'yel-ə-wish\ *adj*

²yellow *vb* : to make or turn yellow

³yellow *n* **1 a** : a color whose hue resembles that of ripe lemons or sunflowers or is that of the portion of the spectrum lying between green and orange **b** : a pigment or dye that colors yellow **2** : something yellow or marked by a yellow color **3** *pl* **a** : JAUNDICE **b** : any of several plant virus diseases marked by yellowing of the foliage and stunting

yellow–dog contract *n* : a now illegal employment contract under which a worker agreed not to join a labor union during the period of his or her employment

yellow fever *n* : a destructive infectious disease of warm regions marked by sudden onset, prostration, fever, jaundice, and often hemorrhage and caused by a virus transmitted by a mosquito — called also *yellow jack*

yellow–fever mosquito *n* : a small dark-colored mosquito that is the usual vector of yellow fever

yellow–green alga *n* : any of a division (Chrysophyta) of algae with the chlorophyll masked by brown or yellow pigment

yel·low·ham·mer \'yel-ō-,ham-ər, 'yel-ə-\ *n* **1** : a common European finch having the male largely bright yellow **2** : YELLOW-SHAFTED FLICKER [Old English *amore* "yellowhammer"]

yellow jack *n* : YELLOW FEVER

yellow jacket *n* : any of various small yellow-marked social wasps that commonly nest in the ground

yellow jessamine *n* : a twining evergreen shrub related to the nux vomica and grown in warm regions for its fragrant yellow flowers — called also *yellow jasmine*

yel·low·legs \'yel-ō-,legz, 'yel-ə-, -,lāgz\ *n sing or pl* : either of two American shorebirds with long yellow legs

yellow ocher *n* **1** : a yellow mixture of limonite usually with clay and silica used as a pigment **2** : a moderate orange yellow

yellow perch *n* : a common American perch that is yellowish with broad green bars and is an excellent sport and table fish

yellow pine *n* : the yellowish resinous wood of any of several American pines; *also* : a pine (as the longleaf pine or ponderosa pine) that yields such wood

yel·low–shaft·ed flicker \,yel-ō-,shaf-təd-, ,yel-ə-\ *n* : a common large woodpecker of eastern North America with a black crescent on the breast, red nape, white rump, and yellow shafts to the tail and wing feathers — called also *yellowhammer*

yellow spot *n* : MACULA LUTEA

yel·low·tail \'yel-ō-,tāl, 'yel-ə-\ *n, pl* **-tail** *or* **-tails** : any of various fishes having a yellow or yellowish tail and including several food and sport fishes

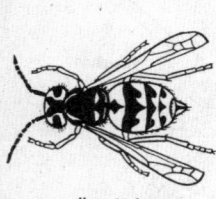

yellow jacket

yel·low·throat \-,thrōt\ *n* : a largely olive American warbler with yellow breast and throat

yel·low·wood \-,wud\ *n* : any of various trees having yellowish wood or yielding a yellow extract; *also* : this wood

¹yelp \'yelp\ *vi* : to utter a yelp or a similar sound [Old English *gielpan* "to boast, exult"]

²yelp *n* : a sharp quick shrill bark or cry

¹yen \'yen\ *n, pl* **yen** **1** : the basic monetary unit of Japan **2** : a coin or note representing one yen [Japanese *en*]

²yen *n* : an intense desire : URGE, LONGING ⟨have a *yen* to travel⟩ [Chinese (Cantonese dialect) *in-yăn* "craving for opium", from *in* "opium" + *yăn* "craving"]

□ ORIGIN During the 18th and 19th centuries China suffered under the encouragement, which amounted to virtual enforcement, of widespread opium addiction by foreign nations whose traders found the drug profitable. In the mid-19th century many Chinese immigrated to the United States, and the word *in-yăn*, "craving for opium", came with them. In English the Chinese syllables became assimilated to *yen-yen*. Eventually the word was shortened to *yen* and generalized from a craving for opium to any strong desire.

yeo·man \'yō-mən\ *n* **1 a** : an attendant or officer in a royal or noble household **b** : a naval petty officer who performs clerical duties **2** : a small farmer who cultivates his own land; *esp* : one of a class of English freeholders below the gentry [Middle English *yoman*]

yeo·man·ly \-lē\ *adj* : becoming to a yeoman : STURDY, SELF-RELIANT, LOYAL

yeoman of the guard : a member of a military corps of the British royal household serving as ceremonial attendants of the sovereign

yeo·man·ry \'yō-mən-rē\ *n* **1** : the body of yeomen and especially of small landed proprietors **2** : a British volunteer cavalry force created from yeomen in 1761 and incorporated in 1907 into the territorial force

yeoman's service *or* **yeoman service** *n* : great and loyal service, assistance, or support

-yer — see -ER

yer·ba ma·té \,yer-bə-'mä-,tā, ,yər-\ *n* : MATÉ [American Spanish *yerba mate*, from *yerba* "herb" + *mate* "maté"]

¹yes \'yes\ *adv* **1** — used to express assent, agreement, or affirmation ⟨are you ready? *Yes*, I am⟩ **2** — used to introduce correction or contradiction of a negative assertion, direction, or request ⟨don't say that! *Yes*, I will⟩ **3** — used to introduce a more emphatic or explicit phrase ⟨we are glad, *yes*, very glad to see you⟩ **4** — used to indicate interest or attentiveness ⟨*yes*, what is it you want⟩ [Old English *gēse*]

²yes *n* : an affirmative reply

ye·shi·va *or* **ye·shi·vah** \yə-'shē-və\ *n, pl* **-shivas** *or* **-shivahs** *or* **-shi·voth** \-,shē-'vōt, -'vōth\ **1** : a school for Talmudic study **2** : an Orthodox Jewish rabbinical seminary **3** : a Jewish day school providing secular and religious instruction [Hebrew *yĕshībbāh*]

yes–man \'yes-,man\ *n* : a person who agrees with everything that is said especially by the boss

¹yes·ter·day \'yes-tərd-ē, -tər-,dā\ *adv* **1** : on the day before today **2** : only a short time ago [Old English *geistran dæg*, from *geistran* "yesterday" + *dæg* "day"]

²yesterday *n* **1** : the day before today **2** : time not long past ⟨*yesterday's* fashions⟩ **3** : past time — usually used in pl.

yes·ter·year \'yes-tər-,yiər\ *n* **1** : last year **2** : the recent past [*yester*day + *year*]

¹yet \'yet, 'yet\ *adv* **1 a** : in addition : BESIDES ⟨gives *yet* another reason⟩ **b** : EVEN 2b ⟨a *yet* higher speed⟩ **2 a** (1) : up to now : so far ⟨hasn't done much *yet*⟩ (2) : at this or that time ⟨not time to go *yet*⟩ **b** : continuously up to the present or a specified time : STILL ⟨is *yet* a new country⟩ **c** : at a future time ⟨may *yet* see the light) **3** : NEVERTHELESS, HOWEVER ⟨led a quiet, *yet* happy life⟩ [Old English *gīet*]

²yet *conj* : despite that fact : BUT

ye·ti \'yet-ē, 'yāt-\ *n* : ABOMINABLE SNOWMAN [Tibetan]

yew \'yü\ *n* **1 a** : any of a genus of evergreen trees and shrubs with stiff poisonous needles and fruits with a fleshy aril **b** : the wood of a yew; *esp* : the heavy fine-grained wood of an Old World yew that is used for bows and small articles **2** *archaic* : an achery bow made of yew [Old English *īw*]

Yid·dish \'yid-ish\ *n* : a High German language spoken by Jews chiefly in eastern Europe and areas to which Jews from eastern Europe have migrated and commonly written in Hebrew characters [Yiddish *yidish*, short for *yidish daytsh,* literally, "Jewish German"] — **Yiddish** *adj*

¹yield \'yēld\ *vb* **1** : to give up possession of on claim or demand : hand over possession of **2** : to give (oneself) up to an inclination, temptation, or habit **3 a** : to bear or bring forth as a natural product especially as a result of cultivation **b** : to furnish as return or result of expended effort **c** : to produce as return from an expenditure or investment : furnish as profit or interest **d** : to produce as revenue : bring in **4** : to be fruitful or productive **5** : to give up and cease resistance or contention **6** : to give way to pressure or influence : submit to urging, persuasion, or entreaty **7** : to give way under physical force so as to bend, stretch, or break **8 a** : to give place or precedence : acknowledge the superiority of someone else **b** : to give way to or become succeeded by someone or something else [Old English *gieldan*] — **yield·er** *n* □ SYN SUBMIT, SUCCUMB: YIELD may apply to any sort or degree of giving way before force, argument, persuasion, or entreaty; SUBMIT suggests full surrendering after resistance or conflict to the will or control of another; SUCCUMB suggests weakness and helplessness on the part of the one giving way or the overwhelming power of the opposing force. SYN see in addition RELINQUISH

²yield *n* : something yielded : PRODUCT; *esp* : the amount or quantity produced or returned ⟨*yield* of wheat per acre⟩

yield·ing *adj* **1** : lacking rigidity or stiffness : FLEXIBLE ⟨a *yielding* mass⟩ **2** : disposed to submit or comply ⟨a cheerful *yielding* nature⟩

yin \'yin\ *n* : the feminine passive principle (as of darkness, cold, or wetness) in nature that in Chinese cosmic philosophy combines with yang to produce all that comes to be [Chinese (Pekingese dialect) *yin*¹]

y–in·ter·cept \,wī-'int-ər-,sept\ *n* : the coordinate of a point where a line, curve, or surface intersects the y-axis

yip \'yip\ *vi* : YELP [imitative] — **yip** *n*

yip·pee \'yip-ē\ *interj* — used to express exuberant delight or triumph

-yl \əl, ᵊl, il, ,il\ *n* combining form : chemical and usually univalent group ⟨eth*yl*⟩ ⟨hydrox*yl*⟩ [Greek *hylē* "matter, material", literally, "wood"]

¹yo·del \'yōd-l\ *vb* **-deled** *or* **-delled; -del·ing** *or* **-del·ling** \'yōd-ling, -l-ing\ : to sing by suddenly changing from the natural voice to falsetto and the reverse; *also* : to shout or call in this manner [German *jodeln*] — **yo·del·er** \'yōd-lər, -l-ər\ *n*

²yodel *n* : a song or refrain sung by yodeling; *also* : a yodeled shout

yo·ga \'yō-gə\ *n* **1** *cap* : a Hindu theistic philosophy **2** : a system of exercises for attaining bodily or mental control and well-being [Sanskrit, literally, "yoking"] — **yo·gic** \-gik\ *adj*

yo·gi \'yō-gē\ *or* **yo·gin** \-gən, -,gin\ *n* **1** : a person who practices yoga **2** *cap* : an adherent of Yoga philosophy [Sanskrit *yogin,* from *yoga*]

yo·gurt *or* **yo·ghurt** \'yō-gərt\ *n* : a slightly acid semifluid milk food made of skimmed cow's milk and milk solids fermented by cultures of bacteria, often flavored (as with fruit), and sometimes frozen [Turkish *yogurt*]

¹yoke \'yōk\ *n, pl* **yokes 1 a** : a wooden bar or frame by which two draft animals (as oxen) are coupled at the heads or necks for working together **b** : a frame fitted to a person's shoulders to carry a load in two equal portions **c** : a clamp or similar piece that embraces two parts to hold or unite them in position **2** *pl usually* **yoke** : two animals yoked together **3 a** : an oppressive agency ⟨freed from the tyrant's *yoke*⟩ **b** : SERVITUDE, BONDAGE **c** : TIE, LINK ⟨the *yoke* of matrimony⟩ **4** : a fitted or shaped piece at the top of a skirt or at the shoulder of various garments [Old English *geoc*]

²yoke *vb* **1 a** : to put a yoke on or couple with a yoke **b** : to attach (a draft animal) to something **2** : to join as if by a yoke **3** : to put to work

yoke·fellow \'yōk-,fel-ō\ *n* : a close companion : MATE

yo·kel \'yō-kəl\ *n* : RUSTIC, BUMPKIN [perhaps from English dialect *yokel,* a kind of woodpecker]

yolk \'yōk, 'yelk also 'yōlk\ *n* **1 a** : the yellow inner mass of the egg of a bird or reptile **b** : the material stored in an ovum that supplies food material to the developing embryo **2** : oily material in raw sheep wool [Old English *geoloca,* from *geolu* "yellow"] — **yolk** *adj* — **yolked** *adj* — **yolky** *adj*

yolk sac *n* : a membranous sac that is attached to many embryos, encloses food yolk, and is continuous with the intestinal cavity

yolk stalk *n* : a narrow tubular stalk connecting the yolk sac with the embryo

Yom Kip·pur \,yōm-ki-'pūr, ,yòm-, ,yäm-, -'kip-ər\ *n* : a Jewish holiday observed in September or October with fasting and prayer as a day of atonement [Hebrew *yōm kippūr,* from *yōm* "day" + *kippūr* "atonement"]

¹yon \'yän\ *adj* : YONDER [Old English *geon*]

²yon *adv* **1** : YONDER **2** : THITHER ⟨ran hither and *yon*⟩

¹yond \'yänd\ *adv, archaic* : YONDER [Old English *geond*]

²yond *adj, dialect* : YONDER

¹yon·der \'yän-dər\ *adv* : at or to that place : over there [Middle English, from *yond* + *-er* (as in *hither*)]

²yonder *adj* **1** : farther removed : more distant ⟨the *yonder* side of the river⟩ **2** : being at a distance within view ⟨*yonder* hills⟩

yore \'yōr, 'yòr\ *n* : time long past — usually used in the phrase of yore [Old English *geāra* "long ago", from *gēar* "year"]

York·ist \'yòr-kəst\ *adj* : of or relating to the English royal house that ruled from 1461 to 1485 — compare LANCASTRIAN [Edward, Duke of *York* (Edward IV of England)] — **Yorkist** *n*

York·shire \'yòrk-,shiər, -shər\ *n* : a white swine of any of several breeds or strains originated in Yorkshire, England

York·shire pudding \,yòrk-,shiər, -shər-\ *n* : a batter of eggs, flour, and milk baked in meat drippings [*Yorkshire,* England]

you \yü, 'yü, yə, yē\ *pron* **1** : the one or ones spoken to — used as the pronoun of the 2d person singular or plural in any grammatical relation except that of a possessive ⟨*you* are my friends⟩ ⟨can I pour *you* a cup of tea⟩; used formerly only as a plural pronoun of the 2d person in the dative or accusative case as direct or indirect object of a verb or as object of a preposition; compare THEE, THOU, YE, YOUR, YOURS **2** : ²ONE 1b [Old English *ēow,* dative and accusative of *gē* "you"]

you–all \yü-'òl, 'yü-,òl, 'yòl\ *pron* : YOU — usually used in addressing two or more persons or sometimes one person as representing also another or others

you'd \yüd, 'yüd, yùd, ,yùd, yəd\ : you had : you would

you'll \yül, 'yül, yùl, ,yùl, yəl\ : you shall : you will

¹young \'yəŋ\ *adj* **youn·ger** \'yəŋ-gər\; **youn·gest** \'yəŋ-gəst\ **1 a** : being in the first or an early stage of life, growth, or development **b** : JUNIOR 1a **2** : having little experience **3 a** : recently come into being : NEW

yew 1a

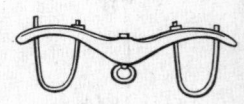

¹yoke 1a

\ə\ **abut**		\ng\ **sing**
\ər\ **further**		\ō\ **bone**
\a\ **mat**		\ò\ **saw**
\ā\ **take**		\òi\ **coin**
\ä\ **cot, cart**		\th\ **thin**
\aù\ **out**		\th\ **this**
\ch\ **chin**		\ü\ **food**
\e\ **pet**		\ù\ **foot**
\ē\ **easy**		\y\ **yet**
\g\ **go**		\yü\ **few**
\i\ **tip**		\yù\ **cure**
\ī\ **life**		\zh\ **vision**
\j\ **job**		

(the *young* democracies) **b** : YOUTHFUL 4 ⟨*young* mountains⟩ **4** : of, relating to, or having the characteristics of youth or a young person [Old English *geong*] — **young·ness** \'yəng-nəs\ *n*

²young *n, pl* **young** **I** *pl* **a** : young persons : YOUTH **b** : immature offspring especially of lower animals **2** : a single recently born or hatched animal — **with young** : PREGNANT — used of animals

young·ber·ry \'yəng-,ber-ē\ *n* : the large sweet reddish black fruit of a hybrid between a trailing blackberry and a southern dewberry grown in the western and southern United States; *also* : the bramble that bears this fruit [B. M. *Young,* 20th century American fruit grower]

youn·ger \'yəng-gər\ *n* : an inferior in age : JUNIOR — usually used with a possessive pronoun ⟨is several years my *younger*⟩

youn·gest \'yəng-gəst\ *n* : one that is the least old

young·ish \'yəng-ish\ *adj* : somewhat young

young·ling \'yəng-ling\ *n* : one that is young : a young person or animal — **youngling** *adj*

young·ster \'yəng-stər\ *n* **I** : a young person : YOUTH **2** : CHILD 2a

Young Turk *n* : an insurgent or a member of an insurgent group in a political party [*Young Turks,* a 20th century revolutionary party in Turkey]

youn·ker \'yəng-kər\ *n* **I** : a young man **2** : CHILD 2a, YOUNGSTER [Dutch *jonker* "young nobleman"]

your \yər, yur, 'yur, yōr, 'yōr, yòr, 'yòr\ *adj* **I** : of or relating to you or yourself or yourselves especially as possessor or possessors, agent or agents, or object or objects of an action ⟨*your* house⟩ ⟨*your* contributions⟩ ⟨*your* discharge⟩ **2** : of or relating to one or oneself ⟨when you face the north, east is at *your* right⟩ [Old English *ēower*]

you're \yər, yur, ,yur, yōr, ,yōr, yòr, ,yòr\ : you are

yours \yurz, 'yōrz, 'yòrz\ *pron, sing or pl in construction* : that which belongs to you : those which belong to you — used without a following noun as an equivalent in meaning to the adjective *your;* often used especially with an adverbial modifier in the complimentary close of a letter ⟨*yours* truly⟩

your·self \yər-'self\ *pron* **I a** : that identical one that is you — used reflexively or for emphasis ⟨don't hurt *yourself*⟩ ⟨do it *yourself*⟩ **b** : your normal, healthy, or sane condition or self **2** : ONESELF

your·selves \-'selvz\ *pron pl* **I** : those identical ones that are you — used reflexively or for emphasis ⟨get *yourselves* a treat⟩ ⟨carry them *yourselves*⟩ **2** : your normal, healthy, or sane conditions or selves

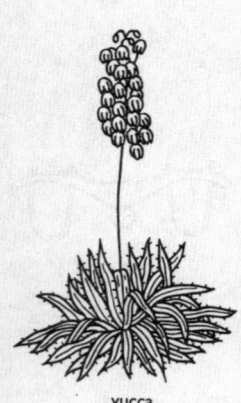

yucca

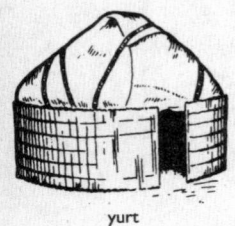

yurt

youth \'yüth\ *n, pl* **youths** \'yüthz, 'yüths\ **I** : the time of life marked by growth and development; *esp* : the period between childhood and maturity **2 a** : a young man **b** : young persons — usually pl. in construction ⟨the *youth* of the nation are a fine lot⟩ **3** : YOUTHFULNESS [Old English *geoguth*]

youth·ful \'yüth-fəl\ *adj* **I** : of, relating to, or appropriate to youth **2** : being young and not yet mature **3** : FRESH 2b (1), VIGOROUS ⟨*youthful* grandparents⟩ **4** : having accomplished or undergone little erosion ⟨a *youthful* valley⟩ ⟨*youthful* streams⟩ — **youth·ful·ly** \-fə-lē\ *adv* — **youth·ful·ness** *n*

youth hostel *n* : HOSTEL 2

you've \yüv, ,yüv, yəv\ : you have

yowl \'yaul\ *vi* : HOWL 1 [Middle English *yowlen*] — **yowl** *n*

yo-yo \'yō-,yō\ *n, pl* **yo-yos** *also* **yo-yoes** : a thick divided disk that is made to fall and rise to the hand by unwinding and rewinding on a string [native name in the Philippines]

yt·ter·bi·um \i-'tər-bē-əm, ə-\ *n* : a metallic chemical element that occurs in several minerals — see ELEMENT table [New Latin, from *Ytterby,* Sweden]

yt·tri·um \'i-trē-əm\ *n* : a metallic chemical element usually included among the rare earth elements with which it occurs in minerals — see ELEMENT table [New Latin, from *yttria* "yttrium oxide", from *Ytterby,* Sweden]

yu·an \'yü-ən, yü-'än\ *n, pl* **yuan** **I** : the basic monetary unit of China **2** : a coin or note representing one yuan [Chinese (Pekingese dialect) *yüan*²]

yuc·ca \'yək-ə\ *n* : any of a genus of plants of the lily family growing in dry regions and having stiff sharp-pointed fibrous leaves mostly in a rosette at the base and whitish flowers usually in erect clusters [Spanish *yuca*]

yule \'yül\ *n, often cap* : the feast of the nativity of Jesus Christ : CHRISTMAS [Old English *geōl*]

yule log *n, often cap* Y : a large log formerly put on the hearth on Christmas Eve as the foundation of the fire

yule·tide \'yül-,tīd\ *n, often cap* : the Christmas season : CHRISTMASTIDE

yum·my \'yəm-ē\ *adj* : highly attractive or pleasing : DELECTABLE [*yum-yum,* interj. expressing pleasure in the taste of food]

yurt \'yurt\ *n* : a light round tent of skins or felt stretched over a lattice framework used by various nomadic tribes in Central Asia [Russian *yurta,* of Turkic origin]

Zz

z \zē, *British & Canadian* 'zed\ *n, pl* **z's** *or* **zs** *often cap* : the 26th and last letter of the English alphabet

¹**za·ny** \'zā-nē\ *n, pl* **zanies** 1 : CLOWN 2a, MERRY-AN-DREW 2 : BUFFOON 1 [Italian *zanni,* from *Zanni,* nickname for *Giovanni* "John"] □ ORIGIN In the 16th century the Italian theater developed a form of comedy improvised from standard situations and stock characters. One of these characters is a subordinate fool, clown, acrobat, or mountebank who mimics ludicrously the tricks of his principal. In Italian the stock name for such a character is *Zanni,* a nickname (in the dialect of Lombardy) for the name *Giovanni,* the Italian form of *John.* Italian *zanni* was soon borrowed into English, and by the early 17th century English *zany* was used for anyone who makes a laughingstock of himself, a buffoon.

²**zany** *adj* **za·ni·er; -est** 1 : being or having the characteristics of a zany 2 : fantastically or irrationally ludicrous : CRAZY — **za·ni·ly** \'zān-l-ē\ *adv* — **za·ni·ness** \'zā-nē-nəs\ *n*

zap \'zap\ *interj* — used to indicate a sudden or instantaneous occurrence [imitative]

zeal \'zēl\ *n* : eagerness and ardent interest in pursuit of something : FERVOR [Late Latin *zelus,* from Greek *zēlos*] □ SYN ENTHUSIASM: ZEAL implies energetic and unflagging pursuit of an aim or devotion to a cause; ENTHUSIASM suggests lively or eager interest in or admiration for a proposal or cause or activity.

zeal·ot \'zel-ət\ *n* 1 *cap* : one of a fanatical sect of ancient Judea bitterly opposing the Roman domination of Palestine 2 : a zealous person; *esp* : a fanatical partisan [Late Latin *zelotes,* from Greek *zēlōtēs,* from *zēlos* "zeal"] — **zeal·ot·ry** \'zel-ə-trē\ *n*

zeal·ous \'zel-əs\ *adj* : filled with, characterized by, or due to zeal ⟨*zealous* missionaries⟩ — **zeal·ous·ly** *adv* — **zeal·ous·ness** *n*

ze·bra \'zē-brə\ *n, pl* **zebras** *also* **zebra** : any of several fleet African mammals related to the horse but distinctively and conspicuously patterned in stripes of black or dark brown and white or buff [Italian, from Spanish *cebra*]

ze·bu \'zē-bü, -byü\ *n* : an Asian ox domesticated and differentiated into many breeds and distinguished from European cattle with which it crosses freely by a large fleshy hump over the shoulders and a loose skin prolonged into dewlap and folds [French *zébu*]

Zech·a·ri·ah \,zek-ə-'rī-ə\ *n* — see BIBLE table

zed \'zed\ *n, chiefly British* : the letter z [Middle French *zede,* from Late Latin *zeta* "zeta", from Greek *zēta*]

ze·in \'zē-ən\ *n* : a protein from Indian corn used especially in making textile fibers, plastics, and adhesives [New Latin *Zea,* genus including Indian corn, from Greek *zea* "wheat"]

zeit·geist \'tsīt-,gīst, 'zīt-\ *n* : the general intellectual, moral, and cultural state of an era [German, from *zeit* "time" + *geist* "spirit"]

zemst·vo \'zemst-vō, 'zempst-, -və\ *n, pl* **zemstvos** : one of the district and provincial assemblies established in Russia in 1864 [Russian]

Zen \'zen\ *n* : a Japanese Buddhist sect that stresses the attainment of enlightenment by direct intuition through meditation rather than through intellectual concepts [Japanese, "religious meditation", from Chinese (Pekingese dialect) *ch'an²,* derived from Sanskrit *dhyāna,* from *dhyāti* "he thinks"]

ze·nith \'zē-nəth\ *n* 1 : the point in the heavens directly overhead 2 : the highest point : PEAK, SUMMIT ⟨the *zenith* of our civilization⟩ [Middle French *cenith,* from Medieval Latin, from Spanish *zenit, cenit,* from Arabic *samt* (ar-ra's) "way (of the head)"]

ze·nith·al \-əl\ *adj* : of, relating to, or located at or near the zenith

ze·o·lite \'zē-ə-,līt\ *n* : any of various silicates chemically related to the feldspars that are used especially in water softening [Swedish *zeolit,* from Greek *zein* "to boil"] — **ze·o·lit·ic** \,zē-ə-'lit-ik\ *adj*

Zeph·a·ni·ah \,zef-ə-'nī-ə\ *n* — see BIBLE table

zeph·yr \'zef-ər\ *n* 1 a : a breeze from the west b : a gentle breeze 2 a : a fine soft wool yarn b : any of various lightweight fabrics and articles of clothing [Latin *Zephyrus,* god of the west wind, west wind, from Greek *Zephyros*]

zep·pe·lin \'zep-lən, -ə-lən\ *n* : a rigid airship consisting of a cylindrical covered frame supported by internal gas cells [Count Ferdinand von *Zeppelin,* died 1917, German airship manufacturer]

¹**ze·ro** \'zē-rō, 'ziər-ō\ *n, pl* **zeros** *also* **zeroes** 1 : a number denoting absence of all quantity; *also* : a symbol representing this number — see NUMBER table 2 a : the point of departure in reckoning; *also* : the point from which the graduation of a scale (as of a speedometer) commences b : a value or reading of zero; *esp* : the temperature represented by the zero mark on a thermometer 3 : a person or thing having no importance or significance : NONENTITY 4 a : a state of total absence or neutrality : NOTHING b : the lowest point : NADIR [Italian, from Medieval Latin *zephirum,* from Arabic *ṣifr*]

²**zero** *adj* 1 a : of, relating to, or being a zero b (1) : amounting to zero ⟨a *zero* growth rate⟩ (2) : having no modified inflectional form ⟨*zero* plurals⟩ 2 a : limiting vision to 50 feet or less ⟨*zero* cloud ceiling⟩ b : limited to 165 feet or less ⟨*zero* visibility⟩

³**zero** *vb* 1 : to determine or adjust the zero of ⟨*zero* a meter⟩ 2 : to concentrate firepower (as of artillery) on the exact range of — usually used with *in* 3 : to adjust fire on a specific target — usually used with *in*

zero hour *n* 1 : the hour at which a planned military movement is scheduled to start 2 : the moment at which something significant, vital, or crucial is to begin or take place [from its being marked by the count of zero in a countdown]

zero–zero *adj* : characterized by or being atmospheric conditions that reduce ceiling and visibility to zero ⟨*zero-zero* weather⟩

zebu

ziggurat

zither

zest \'zest\ *n* **1** : a quality of enhancing enjoyment : PIQUANCY **2** : keen enjoyment : RELISH, GUSTO [French, "orange or lemon peel used as flavoring"] SYN see TASTE — **zest·ful** \-fəl\ *adj* — **zest·ful·ly** \-fə-lē\ *adv* — **zest·ful·ness** *n* — **zesty** \'zes-tē\ *adj* □ ORIGIN *Zest* was borrowed into English in the 17th century from the French *zest* (now spelled *zeste*), meaning "orange or lemon peel". Where the French got the word we do not know. The peels of citrus fruits are still used to add flavoring to food and drinks, and the earliest citations for *zest* in English refer to the peel of such fruit used in this way. By the early 18th century, however, the sense was extended beyond the culinary domain, and *zest* was used to refer to a quality that adds enjoyment or piquancy to something.

ze·ta \'zāt-ə\ *n* : the 6th letter of the Greek alphabet — Z or ζ

zi·do·vu·dine \zi-'dō-vyü-,dēn\ *n* : AZIDOTHYMIDINE

¹zig \'zig\ *n* : one of the sharp turns or changes or a straight section of a zigzag course [*zig*zag]

²zig *vi* **zigged**; **zig·ging** : to execute a turn or follow a section of a zigzag course

zig·gu·rat \'zig-ə-,rat\ *n* : an ancient Mesopotamian temple tower consisting of a lofty pyramidal structure built in successive stages with outside staircases and a shrine at the top [Akkadian *ziggurratu* "pinnacle"]

¹zig·zag \'zig-,zag\ *n* **1** : a line or course made up of sharp opposite angles or turns at short and rather regular intervals; *also* : something (as a road or path) that takes such a course **2** : one of the units making up a zigzag : a sharp angle or turn with the lines enclosing it ⟨the road followed a *zigzag* around the obstruction⟩ [French]

²zigzag *adv* : in or by a zigzag path or course

³zigzag *adj* : having short sharp turns or angles

⁴zigzag *vi* **zig·zagged**; **zig·zag·ging** : to lie in, proceed along, or consist of a zigzag course

zilch \'zilch\ *adj or n* : ZERO [by alteration]

zil·lion \'zil-yən\ *n* : a large indeterminate number [*z* + *-illion* (as in *million*)] — **zillion** *adj*

zinc \'zingk\ *n* : a bluish white metallic chemical element that tarnishes only slightly in moist air at ordinary temperatures and is used especially as a protective coating for iron — see ELEMENT table [German *zink*]

zinc blende *n* : SPHALERITE [German *blende* "sphalerite", from *blenden* "to blind"]

zinc chloride *n* : a poisonous caustic deliquescent salt $ZnCl_2$ used especially as a wood preservative and catalyst

zinc·ic \'zing-kik\ *adj* : relating to, containing, or resembling zinc

zinc·ite \'zing-,kīt\ *n* : a brittle deep-red to orange-yellow mineral consisting of zinc oxide that occurs in massive or granular form

zinc ointment *n* : an ointment containing about 20 percent of zinc oxide used in treating skin diseases

zinc oxide *n* : a white solid ZnO used especially as a pigment, in compounding rubber, and in pharmaceutical and cosmetic preparations

zinc sulfide *n* : a fluorescent compound ZnS used as a white pigment and as the light-producing substance in fluorescent lamps and television tubes

zinc white *n* : a white pigment used especially in house paints and glazes that consists of zinc oxide

¹zing \'zing\ *n* **1** : a shrill humming noise **2** : VITALITY 2b, VIM [imitative]

²zing *vi* : to move with or make a high-pitched hum ⟨tires *zinging* on wet pavement⟩

zinj·an·thro·pus \zin-'jan-thrə-pəs, -'jant-; ,zin-,jan-'thrō-\ *n*, *pl* **-pi** \-,pī, -,pē\ *or* **-pus·es** : any of a genus of fossil hominids based on a skull found in eastern Africa, characterized by very low brow and large molars, and tentatively assigned to the Lower Pleistocene

[New Latin, from Arabic *Zinj* "eastern Africa" + Greek *anthrōpos* "human being"]

zin·nia \'zin-ē-ə, 'zin-yə, 'zēn-\ *n* : any of a small genus of tropical American herbs related to the daisies and having showy flower heads with long-lasting ray flowers [Johann G. *Zinn,* died 1759, German physician]

Zi·on \'zī-ən\ *n* **1 a** : the Jewish people : ISRAEL **b** : the Jewish homeland as a symbol of Judaism or of Jewish national aspiration **c** : the ideal nation or society envisaged by Judaism **2** *also* **Si·on** \'sī-ən\ : HEAVEN 2a **3** : UTOPIA 1 [*Zion,* citadel in Palestine which was the nucleus of Jerusalem, derived from Hebrew *Siyōn*]

Zi·on·ism \'zī-ə-,niz-əm\ *n* : a theory, plan, or movement for setting up a Jewish national or religious community in Palestine; *esp* : one strongly supporting the nation of Israel — **Zi·on·ist** \-nəst\ *adj or n* — **Zi·on·is·tic** \,zī-ə-'nis-tik\ *adj*

¹zip \'zip\ *vb* **zipped**; **zip·ping** **1** : to move or act with speed and vigor **2** : to travel with a sharp hissing or humming sound **3** : to add zest, interest, or life to — often used with *up* [imitative of the sound of a speeding object]

²zip *n* **1** : a sudden sharp hissing or sibilant sound **2** : ENERGY 2, VIM

³zip *vb* **zipped**; **zip·ping** : to close or open or attach by means of a zipper [back-formation from *zipper*]

zip gun *n* : a gun that is made from a toy pistol or a length of pipe, has a firing pin that is usually powered by a rubber band, and fires a .22 caliber bullet

zip·per \'zip-ər\ *n* : a fastener consisting of two rows of metal or plastic teeth on strips of tape and a sliding piece that closes an opening by drawing the teeth together [from *Zipper,* a former trademark]

zip·pered \-ərd\ *adj* : equipped with a zipper

zip·py \'zip-ē\ *adj* **zip·pi·er; -est** : full of zip : BRISK, SNAPPY

zi·ram \'zī-,ram\ *n* : an organic zinc salt used especially as a fungicide [*zinc* + *-ram* (as in *thiram*)]

zir·con \'zər-,kän, -kən\ *n* **1** : a crystalline mineral $ZrSiO_4$ which is a silicate of zirconium and of which several transparent varieties are used as gemstones **2** : a gem cut from zircon [German *zirkon,* from French *jargon,* from Italian *giargone*]

zir·co·nia \,zər-'kō-nē-ə\ *n* : ZIRCONIUM OXIDE

zir·con·ic \,zər-'kän-ik\ *adj* : of, relating to, or containing zirconium

zir·co·ni·um \,zər-'kō-nē-əm\ *n* : a steel-gray strong ductile metallic chemical element with a high melting point that is highly resistant to corrosion and is used especially in alloys — see ELEMENT table [New Latin, from English *zircon*]

zirconium oxide *n* : a white crystalline compound ZrO_2 used especially in refractories, in thermal and electric insulation, in abrasives, and in enamels and glazes

zith·er \'zi th-ər, 'zith-\ *n* : a stringed musical instrument having usually 30 to 40 strings over a flat soundboard played with the tips of the fingers and a plectrum [German, from Latin *cithara* "lyre", from Greek *kithara*] — **zith·er·ist** \-ə-rəst\ *n*

zlo·ty \'zlot-ē, zə-'lot-\ *n, pl* **zlo·tys** \-ēz\ *also* **zloty** **1** : the basic monetary unit of Poland **2** : a coin representing one zloty [Polish *złoty*]

zo- *or* **zoo-** *combining form* : animal : animal kingdom or kind ⟨*zoo*id⟩ ⟨*zoo*logy⟩ [Greek *zōion* "animal"]

zo·di·ac \'zōd-ē-,ak\ *n* **1** : a zone in the heavens that encompasses the apparent paths of all the principal planets except Pluto, that has as its central line the apparent path of the sun, and that is divided into 12 constellations or signs each taken for astrological purposes to extend 30 degrees of longitude **2** : a figure representing the signs of the zodiac and their symbols [Middle French *zodiaque,* from Latin *zodiacus,* from Greek *zōidiakos,* derived from *zōidion* "carved figure, sign of the zodiac", from *zōion* "animal, figure"] — **zo·di·a·cal** \zō-'dī-ə-kəl, zə-\ *adj*

THE SIGNS OF THE ZODIAC

NUMBER	NAME	SYMBOL	SUN ENTERS
1	Aries the Ram	♈	March 21
2	Taurus the Bull	♉	April 20
3	Gemini the Twins	♊	May 21
4	Cancer the Crab	♋	June 22
5	Leo the Lion	♌	July 23
6	Virgo the Virgin	♍	August 23
7	Libra the Balance	♎	September 23
8	Scorpio the Scorpion	♏	October 24
9	Sagittarius the Archer	♐	November 22
10	Capricorn the Goat	♑	December 22
11	Aquarius the Water Bearer	♒	January 20
12	Pisces the Fishes	♓	February 19

-zoic \'zō-ik\ *adj combining form* : of, relating to, or being a (specified) geological era ⟨Archeo*zoic*⟩ [Greek *zōē* "life"]

zom·bie *also* **zom·bi** \'zäm-bē\ *n* : a human in the West Indies without will or the power of speech and capable only of automatic movement who is held to have died and been reanimated but often believed to have been drugged [of African origin] □ ORIGIN Our *zombie* was originally a deity in Africa. In West African voodoo cults, the *zombie* was the python-god. He was later transplanted with African slaves to the West Indies and the southern United States. *Zombie* was also used for a certain power associated with the snake deity, which could enter a corpse and reanimate it. A dead body brought back to life by this power was likewise called a *zombie*.

zon·al \'zōn-l\ *adj* **1** : of, relating to, or having the form of a zone **2** : of, relating to, or being a soil or major soil group marked by well-developed characteristics that are determined primarily by the action of climate and organisms especially vegetation — compare AZONAL, INTRAZONAL

zo·na·tion \zō-'nā-shən\ *n* : distribution or arrangement in zones; *esp* : distribution of organisms in biogeographic zones

¹zone \'zōn\ *n* **1** : any of five great divisions of the earth's surface with respect to latitude and temperature — compare FRIGID ZONE, TEMPERATE ZONE, TORRID ZONE **2** *archaic* : GIRDLE, BELT **3 a** : an encircling anatomical structure **b** : an area that supports a similar flora and fauna throughout its extent **c** : a distinctive belt, layer, or series of layers of earth materials (as rock) **4** : a region or area set off as distinct from surrounding or adjoining parts or created for a particular purpose: as **a** : a zoned section (as of a city) **b** : any of the eight concentric bands of territory centered on a given United States parcel-post shipment point to which mail is charged at a single rate [Latin *zona* "belt, zone", from Greek *zōnē*]

²zone *vt* **1** : to surround with a zone : ENCIRCLE **2** : to arrange in or mark off into zones; *esp* : to divide (as a city) into sections reserved for different purposes

zoo \'zü\ *n, pl* **zoos** : a garden or park where living animals are kept for exhibition [short for *zoological garden*]

zoo- — see ZO-

zoo·ge·og·ra·phy \,zō-ə-jē-'äg-rə-fē\ *n* : a branch of biogeography concerned with the geographical distribution of animals — **zoo·geo·graph·ic** \-jē-ə-'graf-ik\ *or* **zoo·geo·graph·i·cal** \-'graf-i-kəl\ *adj* — **zoo·geo·graph·i·cal·ly** \-i-kə-lē, -klē\ *adv*

zo·oid \'zō-,oid\ *n* : an entity (as a phagocyte) that resembles (as in independent motility) but is not wholly the same as a separate individual organism; *esp* : a more or less independent animal (as a polyp of a colonial coral) produced by other than direct sexual methods

zo·o·log·i·cal \,zō-ə-'läj-i-kəl\ *adj* **1** : of, relating to, or occupied with zoology **2** : of, relating to, or affecting lower animals often as distinguished from man ⟨*zoological* infections⟩ — **zo·o·log·i·cal·ly** \-i-kə-lē, -klē\ *adv*

zoological garden *n* : ZOO

zo·ol·o·gy \zō-'äl-ə-jē, zə-'wäl-\ *n* **1** : a science that deals with animals and is the branch of biology concerned with the animal kingdom and animal life **2 a** : animal life : FAUNA **b** : the properties of vital phenomena exhibited by an animal, animal type, or group — **zo·ol·o·gist** \-jəst\ *n*

¹zoom \'züm\ *vb* **1** : to move with a loud low hum or buzz **2** : to climb for a short time at an angle greater than that which can be maintained in steady flight ⟨the airplane *zoomed* and vanished in the distance⟩ **3** : to focus a camera or microscope using a special lens that permits the apparent distance of the object to be varied **4** : to cause to zoom [imitative]

²zoom *n* **1** : an act or process of zooming **2** : a zooming sound

zoom lens *n* : a camera lens in which the image size can be varied continuously so that the image remains in focus at all times

zoo·par·a·site \,zō-ə-'par-ə-,sīt\ *n* : a parasitic animal

zoo·plank·ton \,zō-ə-'plang-tən, -'plangk-, -,tän\ *n* : animal life of the plankton — **zoo·plank·ton·ic** \-,plang-'tän-ik, -,plangk-\ *adj*

zoo·spo·ran·gi·um \,zō-ə-spə-'ran-jē-əm\ *n* : a spore case or sporangium bearing zoospores

zoo·spore \'zō-ə-,spōr, -,spor\ *n* : a flagellated motile asexual spore of an alga or lower fungus

zoot suit \'züt-,süt\ *n* : a flashy man's suit of the 1940s typically consisting of a thigh-length jacket with wide padded shoulders and trousers tapering to narrow cuffs [coined by Harold C. Fox, born 1910, American clothier and bandmaster] — **zoot–suit·er** \-ər\ *n*

Zo·ro·as·tri·an \,zōr-ə-'was-trē-ən, ,zȯr-\ *adj* : of or relating to the Persian prophet Zoroaster or the religion founded by him and marked by belief in a cosmic war between good and evil — **Zoroastrian** *n* — **Zo·ro·as·tri·an·ism** \-trē-ə-,niz-əm\ *n*

Zou·ave \zu̇-'äv\ *n* **1** : a member of a French infantry unit originally composed of Algerians wearing a colorful uniform and conducting a quick spirited drill **2** : a member of a military unit modeled on the Algerian Zouaves [French, from Berber *Zwāwa*, an Algerian tribe]

zounds \'zau̇nz, 'zwau̇nz, 'zünz, 'zwünz\ *interj* — used as a mild oath [euphemism for *God's wounds*]

zoy·sia \'zȯi-shə, zhə, -sē-ə, -zē-ə\ *n* : any of a genus of creeping perennial grasses having fine wiry leaves and includng some used as lawn grasses [Karl von *Zois*, died 1800, German botanist]

zuc·chet·to \zü-'ket-ō, tsü-\ *n, pl* **-tos** : a small round skullcap worn by Roman Catholic ecclesiastics in colors that vary according to the rank of the wearer [Italian, from *zucca* "gourd, head", from Late Latin *cucutia* "gourd"]

zuc·chi·ni \zü-'kē-nē\ *n, pl* **-ni** *or* **-nis** : a summer squash of bushy growth with smooth slender cylindrical dark green fruits [Italian, pl. of *zucchino* "small gourd, squash", from *zucca* "gourd" from Late Latin *cucutia*]

Zu·lu \'zü-lü\ *n* **1** : a member of a Bantu-speaking people of Natal **2** : a Bantu language of the Zulus — **Zulu** *adj*

Zu·ni \'zü-ne\ *or* **Zu·ñi** \'zün-yē\ *n, pl* **Zuni** *or* **Zunis** *or* **Zuñi** *or* **Zuñis** : a member of an Indian people of the Southwest [American Spanish]

zwie·back \'swē-,bak, 'swī-, 'zwē-, 'zwī-, -,bäk\ *n* : a bread enriched with eggs that is baked and then sliced and toasted until dry and crisp [German, literally, "twice baked"]

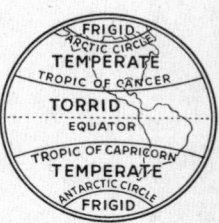

¹zone 1

\ə\ abut	\ng\ sing
\ər\ further	\ō\ bone
\a\ mat	\ȯ\ saw
\ā\ take	\ȯi\ coin
\ä\ cot, cart	\th\ thin
\au̇\ out	\t͟h\ this
\ch\ chin	\ü\ food
\e\ pet	\u̇\ foot
\ē\ easy	\y\ yet
\g\ go	\yü\ few
\i\ tip	\yu̇\ cure
\ī\ life	\zh\ vision
\j\ job	

Zwing·li·an \'zwing-lē-ən, 'swing-, -glē-; 'tsfing-lē-\nē\ *adj* : of or relating to Ulrich Zwingli or his doctrine that in the Lord's Supper there is an influence of Christ upon the soul but that the true body of Christ is present by the contemplation of faith and not in essence or reality — **Zwinglian** *n*

zyg- *or* **zygo-** *combining form* **1** : yoke ⟨*zygo*morphic⟩ **2** : concerned with or produced in sexual reproduction ⟨*zygo*spore⟩ [Greek *zygon*]

zy·go·mat·ic \,zī-gə-'mat-ik\ *adj* : of, relating to, being, or situated in the region of the arched bony support of the part of the cheek below and to the side of the orbit [Greek *zygōmat-, zygōma* "zygomatic arch", from *zygoun* "to yoke", from *zygon* "yoke"]

zy·go·mor·phic \-'mȯr-fik\ *adj* : bilaterally symmetrical in respect to but one axis

zy·go·spore \'zī-gə-,spōr, -,spȯr\ *n* : a plant spore that is formed by conjugation of two similar sexual cells, usually serves as a resting spore, and ultimately produces the sporophyte — compare OOSPORE

zy·gote \'zī-,gōt\ *n* : a cell formed by the union of two gametes; *also* : the developing individual produced from such a cell [Greek *zygōtos* "yoked", from *zygoun* "to yoke", from *zygon* "yoke"] — **zy·got·ic** \zī-'gät-ik\ *adj* — **zy·got·i·cal·ly** \-'gät-i-kə-lē, -klē\ *adv*

-zy·gous \'zī-gəs\ *adj combining form* : having (such) a zygotic constitution ⟨hetero*zygous*⟩

zym- *or* **zymo-** *combining form* **1** : fermentation ⟨*zym*ase⟩ **2** : enzyme ⟨*zymo*gen⟩ [Greek *zymē* "leaven"]

zy·mase \'zī-,mās, -,māz\ *n* : an enzyme or enzyme complex that promotes fermentation of monosaccharides

-zyme \,zīm\ *n combining form* : enzyme ⟨lyso*zyme*⟩

zy·mo·gen \'zī-mə-jən\ *n* : an inactive precursor of an enzyme as secreted by glandular cells and requring activation (as by an acid) before it can function — **zy·mo·gen·ic** \,zī-mə-'jen-ik\ *adj*

Language

Guide to Pronunciation

The English language has, of course, both a written form and a spoken form. Each of these is in a state of continual and inexorable change. The written language, however, is more stable than the spoken. With the rapid spread of printing, particularly from the 16th to the 18th centuries, printers and scholars gradually adopted an increasingly fixed set of spelling conventions. Most of these are adhered to today, though there is still some orthographic variation. Because the spoken language is more susceptible to change, we find ourselves now with spellings that often reveal more about the history of English than about current pronunciation. It has become necessary, therefore, for English dictionaries to indicate pronunciation in order to provide an adequate picture of the English vocabulary.

Just as present-day English is not static, it is also not completely uniform. The pronunciation, vocabulary, and grammar of people living in different areas differ in varying degrees. Similarly, people who have different levels of education, who hold different sorts of jobs, or who, for one reason or another, move only among certain segments of society may have distinct forms of speech. In fact, each person's speech is distinguishable in some ways from that of everyone else; thus, we are able to identify people by the sound of their voices. However, largely because speech is primarily a form of communication, certain patterns in pronunciation, vocabulary, and usage can be discerned among the members of regional or social groups that regularly communicate with one another. The more isolated a particular group is from other speakers of the same language, the greater the differences between the speech of that group and the speech of others will tend to become. As such isolation continues, these differences increase, eventually resulting in distinct dialects. Given a long enough time and sufficiently limited intercommunication, the speech of a particular group may become so incomprehensible to others that it can be classified as a separate language. The evolution of Latin into French, Italian, Portuguese, Romanian, and Spanish is an example of this process.

As geographical and social barriers are overcome, a more widespread mutual comprehensibility becomes possible. Especially as a result of the technological developments in transportation and communication during the past century, many millions of people are crossing or communicating across dialect boundaries. We can therefore be assured that slowly and, for the most part, imperceptibly these boundaries will continue to shift; some may disappear and new ones may develop.

During this century researchers into differences in pronunciation, vocabulary, and grammar have been able to discern patterns that define three major geographical dialect areas in the U.S.—Northern, Southern, and Midland. Each of these areas also has recogniz-

able subdivisions. These dialectal differences began with early settlers from Britain who brought their various dialects to different areas along the eastern coast. With the subsequent isolation from Britain, the speech of the settlers in North America gradually diverged from that of the parts of Britain from which they came. When the population expanded and moved westward, the various dialects were carried westward in an increasingly complex pattern as migration paths crossed and as new lines of communication opened up. However, the pronunciation of English throughout the U.S. is still based on the three major dialects, which are most clearly defined in the eastern states. In Canada, which has had closer contact with and more recent settlement from Britain, greater similarity to British speech can be heard with a mixture of some Northern U.S. features. There are, of course, other aspects of pronunciation, grammar, and vocabulary that arose in or are confined to Canada itself.

There are several broad types or classes of pronunciation variation and these are covered in various ways in a general dictionary. In each dialect area the significant individual sounds (or *phonemes*) of the language may be articulated differently from those in other areas. Many of the features that we perceive as differences in accent fall into this class. In Southern speech, for example, the vowel of *tip* or *bit* is pronounced differently from the same vowel in Northern speech. A Southern speaker seeing the symbol \i\ in the pronunciation respelling of a word in this dictionary can turn to the chart of pronunciation symbols and find there the common words *tip, active,* and *banish* illustrating the pronunciation of that vowel. This speaker knows the sound native to his or her own dialect and can use it in the pronunciation of the word in question. A Northern or Midland speaker will do the same, reproducing the natural and appropriate variety of the sound. It is not necessary, therefore, that a general dictionary indicate these variations for every word. In effect, they are covered implicitly by the set of pronunciation symbols used in the book.

Some dialectal differences are the result not simply of variation in the sounds themselves but in the choice of sounds used. This type of variation is regularly shown in this dictionary. Research has revealed, for example, that south of a line running irregularly westward through Maryland, northern Virginia, and southern West Virginia the word *creek* is usually pronounced \'krēk\. North of this line the more frequent pronunciation is \'krik\, though the spelling pronunciation \'krēk\ is often heard as well. Another such line could be drawn just north of New York City, south along the western boundary of New Jersey, and northwestward through Pennsylvania. To the north of this line the great majority of people pronounce *greasy* as \'grē-sē\, while to the south most people say \'grē-zē\.

Comparison of a large number of such items makes the boundaries of dialect areas apparent. For those cases in which the distribution of variants is restricted to a fairly simple pattern within one or two dialect areas, it is possible to label them appropriately, as the entries for *great* and *help* where a \ *Southern* \ label appears and for *figure* where a \ *Brit* \ label indicates a variant heard most frequently in British speech.

A third type of variation that figures widely in this dictionary may be called unpredictable variation. For many words the distribution of variants is either so widespread (if not random) or so complex in relation to the defined dialect areas that it is impossible to predict accurately which variant or variants a speaker from a particular area might use. This very common variation is represented in the pronunciation of such words as *economic, ration, envelope,* and *temperature,* to name only four out of thousands. Often when a foreign word is borrowed into English, a number of variants will coexist as people attempt either to reproduce its foreign pronunciation or perhaps to pronounce it according to the spelling, as if it were English in origin. Thus we hear a number of pronunciation variants for such well-established words as *junta* and *lingerie.*

A major problem that arises in editing a dictionary is how to determine the incidence and extent of pronunciation variants. Since the middle of the 1930's pronunciation editors have been carrying out an ongoing program of listening to, recording, and transcribing the pronunciation of educated native speakers of English, especially in the United States, Britain, and Canada. The result of this program is a unique and extensive file of transcriptions that provides the data on which decisions regarding pronunciation are based. Along with the transcription are included the name of the speaker, additional identifying information, and the date. These "citations" are collected by listening to radio, television, and live speech, and in these days of network and satellite broadcasting it is possible to hear a wide range of speakers from all over the English-speaking world. It is generally inadvisable, however, to transcribe the pronunciation of actors in performance, since they may not be using their natural speech. The best source of pronunciation is a native speaker of English who can be identified by name and whose geographical and educational background is known. When most people speak, whether privately or publicly, they concentrate more on the content of what they are saying than on the pronunciation of each word. This is ideal for the linguist (or pronunciation editor) who is interested in learning how people speak when communicating with others.

When an entry in the dictionary is written or revised, the pronunciation citations for that word are reviewed to determine whether it has any pronunciation variants that are sufficiently widespread to warrant inclusion. One fact that the evidence in the pronunciation file makes apparent, and that is reflected in the dictionary, is that there is a considerable amount of perfectly acceptable pronunciation variation in the language. Unless restricted by a regional or other usage label, all of the variants shown in this book fall within the range of acceptable variation.

No system of indicating pronunciation is self-explanatory. The following discussion sets out the signification and use of the pronunciation symbols and devices in this book, with special attention to those areas where experience has shown that dictionary users may have questions. The order of symbols discussed below is alphabetical with the exception that the symbols which are not letter characters are here listed first.

\ \ All pronunciation information is printed between reversed virgules. Pronunciation symbols are printed in roman type and all other information, such as labels and notes, is printed in italics.

\' ,\ A high-set stress mark precedes a syllable with primary (strongest) stress; a low-set mark precedes a syllable with secondary (medium) stress; a third level of weak stress requires no mark at all: \ 'pen-mən-,ship \.

Since the nineteenth century the International Phonetics Association has recommended that stress marks precede the stressed syllable, and linguists worldwide have adopted this practice on the basic principle that before a syllable can be uttered the speaker must know what degree of stress to give it.

\ · \ Hyphens are used to separate syllables in pronunciation transcriptions. In actual speech, of course, there is no pause between the syllables of a word. The placement of these hyphens is based on phonetic principles and may not match the end-of-line divisions indicated by centered dots in boldface entry words.

\ ( ) \ Parentheses are used in pronunciations, especially in the section of Common Given Names and Foreign Words and Phrases, to indicate that whatever is symbolized between them is present in some utterances but not in others; thus *Benjamin* \ 'benj-(ə-)mən \ is pronounced both \ 'benj-mən \ and \ 'benj-ə-mən \, *Barbara* \ 'bär-b(ə-)rə \ is pronounced both \ 'bär-bə-rə \ and \ 'bär-brə \, and *Arlo* \ 'är-(,)lō \ is pronounced both \ 'är-lō \ and \ 'är-,lō \. In some phonetic environments, as with the name *Frances* \ 'fran(t)-səs \, it may be difficult to determine whether the sound shown in parentheses is or is not present in a given utterance; even the usage of a single speaker may vary considerably.

\ ,;\ Variant pronunciations are separated by commas; groups of variants are separated by semicolons. The order of variants does not mean that the first is in any way preferable to or more acceptable than the others. All of the variants in this dictionary, except those restricted by a regional or usage label, are widely used in acceptable educated speech. If evidence reveals that a particular variant is used more frequently than another, the former will be given first. This should not, however, prejudice anyone against the second or subsequent variants. In many cases the numerical distribution of variants is equal but one of them, of course, must be printed first.

\ ə \ in stressed and unstressed syllables as in banana, collide, humdrum, abut. This neutral vowel may be represented orthographically by any of the letters *a, e, i, o, u, y,* and by many combinations of letters.

\ ᵊ \ immediately preceding \ l \ and \ n \, especially in pronunciations shown for Common Given Names and Foreign Words and Phrases, as in *Natalie* \ 'nat-ᵊl-ē \, *Quentin* \ 'kwent-ᵊn \ and *gutenTag* \ ,güt-ᵊn-'täk \. The symbol \ ᵊ \ preceding these consonants does not itself represent a sound. It signifies instead that the following consonant is syllabic; that is, the consonant itself forms the nucleus of a syllable that does not contain a vowel.

In the pronunciation of some French or French-derived words \ ᵊ \ is placed immediately after \ l \, \ m \, \ r \ to indicate one nonsyllabic pronunciation of these consonants, as in *coup de maître* \ küd-(ə-)metrᵊ \.

\ ər \ as in **fur**ther, **mer**ger, b**ir**d.

\ 'ər-,'ə-r \ as in two different pronunciations of *hurry*. Most U.S. speakers pronounce \ 'hər-ē \ with the \ ər \ representing the same sounds as in *bird* \ 'bərd \. Usually in metropolitan New York and southern England and frequently in New England and the southeastern U.S. the vowel is much the same as the vowel of *hum* followed by a syllable-initial variety of \ r \. This pronunciation of *hurry* is represented as \ 'hə-rē \ in this dictionary. Both types of pronunciation are shown for words composed of a single meaningful unit (or *morpheme*) as in *current, hurry,* and *worry.* In words such as *furry* and *stirring* in which a vowel or vowel-initial suffix is added to a word ending in *r* or *rr* (as *fur* and *stir*), the second type of pronunciation outlined above is heard only occasionally and is not shown in this dictionary.

\a\ as in **mat, map, mad, gag, snap, patch.** Some variation in this vowel is occasioned by the consonant that follows it; thus, for some speakers *map, mad,* and *gag* have noticeably different vowel sounds. There is a very small number of words otherwise identical in pronunciation that these speakers may distinguish solely by variation of this vowel, as in the two words *can* (put into cans; be able) in the sentence "Let's can what we can." However, this distinction is sufficiently infrequent that the traditional practice of using a single symbol is followed in this dictionary.

\ā\ as in **day, fade, date, aorta, drape, cape.** In most English speech this is actually a diphthong. In lowland South Carolina, in coastal Georgia and Florida, and occasionally elsewhere \ā\ is pronounced as a monophthong. As a diphthong \ā\ has a first element \e\ or monophthongal \ā\ and a second element \i\.

\ä\ as in **bother, cot,** and, with most American speakers, **father, cart.** The symbol \ä\ represents the vowel of *cot, cod,* and the stressed vowel of *collar* in the speech of those who pronounce this vowel differently from the vowel in *caught, cawed,* and *caller,* represented by \ȯ\. In U.S. speech \ä\ is pronounced with little or no rounding of the lips, and it is fairly long in duration, especially before voiced consonants. In southern England \ä\ is usually accompanied by some lip rounding and is relatively short in duration. The vowel \ȯ\ generally has appreciable lip rounding. Some U.S. speakers do not distinguish between *cot—caught, cod—cawed,* and *collar—caller,* usually because they lack or have less lip rounding in the words transcribed with \ȯ\. Though the symbols \ä\ and \ȯ\ are used throughout this dictionary to distinguish the members of the above pairs and similar words, the speakers who rhyme these pairs will automatically reproduce a sound that is consistent with their own speech.

In words such as *card* and *cart* most U.S. speakers have a sequence of sounds that we transcribe as \är\. Most speakers who do not pronounce \r\ before another consonant or a pause, however, do not rhyme *card* with either *cod* or *cawed* and do not rhyme *cart* with either *cot* or *caught.* The pronunciation of *card* and *cart* by such speakers, although not shown in this dictionary, would be transcribed as \'kȧd\ and \'kȧt\. Speakers of r-dropping dialects will automatically substitute \ȧ\ for the transcribed \är\. (See the sections on \ȧ\ and \r\.)

\ȧ\ as in **father** as pronounced by those who do not rhyme it with *bother.* The pronunciation of this vowel varies regionally. In eastern New England and southern England it is generally pronounced farther forward in the mouth than \ä\ but not as far forward as \a\. In New York City and the southeastern U.S. it may have much the same quality as \ä\ but somewhat greater duration.

In areas in which \r\ is not pronounced before another consonant or a pause, \ȧ\ occurs for the sequence transcribed in this book as \är\. (See the sections on \ä\ and \r\.) In these areas \ȧ\ also occurs with varying frequency in a small group of words in which *a* in the spelling is followed by a consonant letter other than *r* and is not preceded by *w* or *wh,* as in *father,* but not in *watch, what,* or *swap.* Especially in southern England and, less consistently, in eastern New England \ȧ\ occurs in certain words in which \a\ is the usual American vowel and in most of which the vowel is followed by \f\, \th\, \s\, or by \n\ and another consonant.

The use of \ȧ\ is to be understood as a variant pronunciation although \ȧ\ is shown only for those few in which it occurs with especially high frequency.

The symbol \ȧ\ is also used in the transcription of some foreign-derived words and names. This vowel, as in French *patte* "paw" and *chat* "cat," is intermediate between \a\ and \ä\ and is similar in quality to the \ȧ\ heard in eastern New England.

\au̇\ as in **now, loud, out.** The initial element of this diphthong may vary from \a\ to \ȧ\ or \ä\, the first being more common in Southern and south Midland speech than elsewhere.

\b\ as in **baby, rib.**

\ch\ as in **chin,** nature \'nā-chər\. Actually, this sound is \t\ + \sh\. The distinction between the phrases *why choose* and *white shoes* is maintained by a difference in the juncture of the \t\ and the \sh\ in each case and the consequent use of different varieties (or *allophones*) of \t\.

\d\ as in **did, adder.**

\e\ as in **bet, bed, peck.**

\'ē, ˌē\ in stressed syllables as in **beat, nosebleed,** **evenly, easy.**

\ē\ in unstressed syllables, as in **easy, mealy.** Though the fact is now shown in this dictionary, some dialects such as southern British and southern U.S. often, if not usually, pronounce \i\ instead of unstressed \ē\.

\f\ as in **fifty, cuff.**

\g\ as in **go, big, gift.**

\h\ as in **hat, ahead.**

\hw\ as in **whale** as pronounced by those who do not have the same pronunciation for both *whale* and *wail.* Most U.S. speakers distinguish these two words as \'hwāl\ and \'wāl\ respectively, though frequently in the U.S. and usually in southern England \'wāl\ is used for both. Some linguists consider \hw\ to be a single sound, a voiceless \w\.

\i\ as in **tip, banish, active.**

\ī\ as in **site, side, buy, tripe.** Actually, this sound is a diphthong, usually composed of \ä\ + \i\ or \ȧ\ + \i\. In Southern speech, especially before a pause or voiced consonant, as in *shy* and *five,* the second element \i\ may not be pronounced. Chiefly in eastern Virginia, coastal South Carolina, and parts of Canada the diphthong is approximately \'ə\ + \i\ before voiceless consonants, as in *nice* and *write.*

\j\ as in **job, gem, edge, join, judge.** Actually, this sound is \d\ + \zh\. Assuming the anglicization of *Jeanne d'Arc* as \zhän-'därk\, the distinction between the sentences *They betray John Dark* and *They betrayed Jeanne d'Arc* is maintained by a difference in the juncture of the \d\ and the \zh\ in each case and the consequent use of different varieties (or *allophones*) of \d\.

\k\ as in **kin, cook, ache.**

\k̠\ as in German *ich* "I," *Buch* "book," and one pronunciation of English *loch.* Actually, there are two distinct sounds in German; the \k̠\ in *ich* is pronounced toward the front of the mouth and the \k̠\ in *Buch* is pronounced toward the back. In English, however, no two words otherwise identical are distinguished by these two varieties of \k̠\, and therefore only a single symbol is necessary. In English speech the front variety of \k̠\ is produced automatically to accompany a front vowel, such as \e\ or \i\, and the back variety to accompany a back vowel, such as \ä\ or \ü\.

\l\ as in **lily, pool.** In words such as *battle* and *fiddle* the \l\ is a syllabic consonant.

\m\ as in murmur, dim, nymph.

\n\ as in no, own. In words such as *cotton* and *sudden*, the \n\ is a syllabic consonant.

\ⁿ\ indicates that a preceding vowel or diphthong is pronounced with the nasal passages open, as in French *un bon vin blanc* \œⁿ-bōⁿ-vaⁿ-blāⁿ\ "a good white wine."

\ng\ in this book is used in Common Given Names and Foreign Words and Phrases to indicate the sound shown elsewhere by \ng\, as in *Ingrid* \ing-grəd\ and *ad unguem* \äd-'ùng.gwem\.

\ō\ as in bone, know, beau. Especially in positions of emphasis, such as when it is word final or when as primary stress, \ō\ tends to become diphthongal, moving from \ō\ toward a second element \ù\. In southern England and in some U.S. speech, particularly in the Philadelphia area and in the Pennsylvania-Ohio-West Virginia border area, the first element is often approximately \ə\. In coastal South Carolina, Georgia, and Florida stressed \ō\ is often monophthongal when final, but when a consonant follows it is often a diphthong moving from \ō\ to \ə\. In this book the symbol \ō\ represents all of the above variants.

\ȯ\ as in saw, all, gnaw, caught. (See the section on \ä\.)

\œ\ as in French boeuf "beef," German Hölle "hell." This vowel, which occurs only in foreign-derived terms and names, can be approximated by attempting to pronounce the vowel \e\ with the lips moderately rounded as for the vowel \ù\.

\œ̄\ as in French feu "fire," German Höhle "hole." This vowel, which occurs primarily in foreign-derived terms and names, can be approximated by attempting to pronounce a monophthongal vowel \ā\ with the lips fully rounded as for the vowel \ü\.

\ȯi\ as in coin, destroy. In some Southern speech, especially before a consonant in the same word, the second element may disappear or be replaced by \ə\.

\p\ as in pepper, lip.

\r\ as in red, rarity, car, beard. In some dialects, especially those of the southeastern U.S., eastern New England, New York City, and southern England, \r\ is not pronounced when another consonant or a pause follows immediately. This is often, if somewhat misleadingly, referred to as r-dropping. In these dialects *r* is pronounced as a nonsyllabic \ə\ when it occurs in these positions or there may be no sound corresponding to the *r*; thus *beard, corn,* and *assured* may be pronounced as \'biəd\, \'kȯən\, and \ə-'shùəd\ or, usually with some lengthening of the vowel sound, as \'bid\, \'kȯn\, and \ə-'shùd\. In *car, card,* and *cart* those who do not pronounce \r\ generally have a vowel which we would transcribe as \ä\, usually pronounced with some lengthening and without a following \ə\. (See the sections on \ä\ and \å\.) The stressed vowel of *bird* and *hurt* in r-dropping speech is similar to the vowel used by r-keepers in the same words but without the simultaneous raising of the center and/or tip of the tongue. In the U.S. most speakers of r-dropping dialects will pronounce \r\ before consonants in some words or in some contexts. Because it is determined by the phonetic context, r-dropping is not explicitly represented in this dictionary; speakers of r-dropping dialects will automatically substitute the sounds appropriate to their own speech.

\s\ as in source, less.

\sh\ as in shy, mission, machine, special. Actually this is a single sound, not two. When the two sounds \s\ and \h\ occur in sequence, they are separated by a hyphen in this book, as in *grasshopper* \'gras-,häp-ər\.

\t\ as in tie, attack, late, later, latter. In some contexts, as when a stressed or unstressed vowel precedes and an unstressed vowel of \ᵊl\ follows, the sound represented by *t* or *tt* is pronounced in much American speech the same as the sound represented by *d* or *dd* in similar contexts. Thus, the pairs *ladder* and *latter*, *leader* and *liter*, *parody* and *parity* are often homophones. In such instances this dictionary shows \d\ at the end of a syllable for those words spelled with *d* or *dd* (\'lad-ər\, \'lēd-ər\, \'par-əd-ē\) and \t\ at the end of a syllable for those with *t* or *tt* (\'lat-ər\, \'lēt-ər\, \'par-ət-ē\).

\th\ as in thin, ether. Actually, this is a single sound, not two. When the two sounds \t\ and \h\ occur in sequence they are separated by a hyphen in this book, as in *knighthood* \'nīt-,hùd\.

\th\ as in then, either, this. Actually, this is a single sound, not two. The basic difference between \th\ and \th\ is that the former is pronounced without and the latter with vibration of the vocal cords.

\ü\ as in rule, youth, union \'yün-yən\, few \'fyü\.

\ù\ as in pull, wood, book, curable \'kyùr-ə-bəl\, fury \'fyùr-ē\.

\ue\ as in German füllen "to fill," hübsch "handsome." This vowel, which occurs only in foreign-derived terms and names, can be approximated by attempting to pronounce the vowel \i\ with the lips moderately rounded as for the vowel \ù\.

\ue̅\ as in French rue "street," German fühlen "to feel." This vowel, which occurs only in foreign-derived terms and names, can be approximated by attempting to pronounce the vowel \ē\ with the lips fully rounded as for the vowel \ü\.

\v\ as in vivid, invite.

\w\ as in we, away.

\y\ as in yard, young, cue \'kyü\, curable \'kyùr-ə-bəl\, few \'fyü\, fury \'fyù(ə)r-ē\, union \'yün-yən\. The sequences \lyü\, \syü\, and \zyü\ in the same syllable, as in *lewd, suit,* and *presume,* are common in southern British speech but are rare in American speech and only \lü\, \sü\, and \zü\ are shown in this dictionary.

In English \y\ does not occur at the end of a syllable after a vowel.

\ʸ\ indicates that during the articulation of the preceding consonant the tongue has substantially the position it has for the articulation of the \y\ of *yard*, as in French *digne* \dēnʸ\ "worthy." Thus \ʸ\ does not itself represent a sound but rather modifies the preceding symbol. It is used in pronunciations in Foreign Words and Phrases.

\z\ as in zone, raise.

\zh\ as in vision, azure \'azh-ər\. Actually, this is a single sound, not two. When the two sounds \z\ and \h\ occur in sequence, they are separated by a hyphen in this book, as in *hogshead* \'hȯgz-,hed, 'hägz-\.

English Spelling
& Sound
Correspondences

The following lists are representative of the more common ways (and some less common ways) of spelling each sound. They are by no means exhaustive, but they should enable the user who is uncertain of the spelling to find most words in this book. In actual practice, knowing the first five letters of almost any word will get the user to within a few inches of the right place in any dictionary.

In these lists, ways of spelling each sound are indicated by boldface letters. Some words may be pronounced in more than one way; any such words on these lists are printed in italics if the relevant portion of the spelling is affected. The pronunciation transcription at the entry for the word will show the variation. If there is no letter in a word representative of a sound heard in that word, the word is given following a dash at the end of the appropriate section, with the pronunciation given in full as in the last two entries at \ə\:

— **chasm** \'kaz-əm\
— **McCoy** \mə-'kȯi\

If it is difficult to tell which letter or letters stand for a particular sound in a word, that word appears at the end of the appropriate section, with the pronunciation given in full as in the last entry at \ch\:

— **nature** \'nā-chər\

VOWELS AND DIPHTHONGS

\ə\	**a**	abut		**oo**	flood
	e	silent		**ou**	rough
	i	maritime	\ər\	**ar**	liar
	o	connect		**er**	batter
	u	circus		**ir**	elixir
	y	physician		**or**	honor
	ah	verandah		**re**	ogre
	ai	*captain*		**ur**	injurer
	ea	ocean		**yr**	martyr
	ei	mullein		**eur**	*chauffeur*
	eo	luncheon		**our**	glamour
	ia	collegiate	\'ər\	**er**	fern, *were*
	io	fashion		**ir**	bird
	oa	*waistcoat*		**or**	world
	oe	Phoenician		**ur**	fur
	oi	porpoise		**yr**	myrtle
	ou	famous		**ear**	earth
	ow	*pillowcase*		**err**	*err*
	ue	guerrilla		**eur**	*chauffeur*
	eau	bureaucrat		**irr**	*squirrel*
	—	chasm \'kaz-əm\		**our**	journal
	—	McCoy \mə-'kȯi\		**urr**	hurry
\'ə, ˌə\	**a**	was		**yrrh**	myrrh
	o	above			colonel \'kərn-l\
	u	humdrum	\a\	**a**	mat, *calf*
	y	*Cymric*		**e**	*there*
	oe	does		**i**	meringue
				ae	*aerial*

	ai	plaid, *air*
	au	*aunt*
	ay	*prayer*
	ea	*bear*
	ei	*their*
	—	*chert* \'chərt, 'chat\
\ā\	a	fade
	e	melee
	ae	maelstrom
	ai	main, straight
	ao	gaol
	au	gauge
	ay	day
	ea	steak
	ee	matinee
	ei	vein, reign, weigh
	ey	prey
	ie	*lingerie*
\ä\	a	farther, *father,* guard
	e	entree, sergeant
	i	*lingerie*
	o	cot
	aa	bazaar
	ah	shah
	au	*nautical*
	ea	heart
	ou	*nought*
	eau	bureaucracy
	—	patois \'pa-ˌtwä, 'pä-\
\à\	a	*father, calf*
	au	*aunt*
\aů\	au	sauerkraut
	ou	loud, bough
	ow	now
	aou	caoutchouc
\e\	a	any
	e	bet, *err,* guess
	i	*vanilla*
	u	bury
	ae	aesthetic, *aerial*
	ai	said, *air*
	ay	says, *prayer*
	ea	bread, *bear*
	ei	heifer, *their*
	eo	leopard
	ie	friend
	oe	*foetid*
\ē\	e	me
	i	ski
	y	pretty
	ae	aeon
	ay	*Monday, quay*
	ea	easy
	ee	see, beet
	ei	receive
	eo	people
	ey	key
	ie	grief
	oe	phoebe
	—	shillelagh, shillalah \shə-'lā-lē\
	—	*chamois* \'sham-ē\
\i\	a	homage, *catercorner*
	e	England, *pretty,* serious
	i	tip
	o	women
	u	busy
	y	myth
	ea	hear
	ee	*been,* beer, *creek*
	ei	counterfeit, weird
	ia	carriage
	ie	sieve
	ui	building
\ī\	i	fine, sigh, guide
	y	sly
	ai	aisle
	ay	bayou, papaya
	ei	heist, height
	ey	geyser
	ie	lie
	oy	coyote
	uy	buy
	ye	dye
	aye	*aye*
	eye	eye
	—	choir \'kwīr\

\ō\	a	*quahog, cupola*
	o	bone, folk
	ao	pharaoh
	au	chauvinist
	eo	yeoman
	ew	sew
	oa	coat
	oe	doe
	oh	oh, Noh
	oo	*brooch*
	ou	boulder, though
	ow	know
	ua	*quahog*
	eau	plateau
	—	burgh \'bər-ō, 'bə-rō\
	—	*ewe* \'yü, 'yō\
\ȯ\	a	ball, talk
	o	soft
	ah	*Utah*
	au	sausage, caught
	aw	saw
	eo	Georgian
	oa	broad
	ou	cough, thought
	ow	toward
\ȯi\	aw	*lawyer*
	eu	Freudian
	oi	coin
	oy	boy
	uoy	*buoy*
	—	*sawing* \'sȯ-ing, 'sȯing\
\ü\	o	do, move, two
	u	flu
	w	crwth, cwm
	eu	rheumatism, maneuver
	ew	crew
	oe	shoe
	oo	school
	ou	youth, through
	ue	blue
	ui	cruise
	eew	*leeward*
	ieu	*lieutenant*
	oeu	manoeuvre
	—	beauty \'byüt-ē\
	—	*ewe* \'yü, 'yō\
	—	*peewit* \'pē-ˌwit, 'pyü-ət\
\ů\	o	woman, wolf
	u	pull
	oo	wood
	ou	*could*

CONSONANTS

\b\	b	baby
	v	*government*
	bb	rubber
	bh	bhang
	pb	cupboard, raspberry
\ch\	c	cello
	ch	chin
	cz	Czech
	si	tension
	te	righteous
	ti	question
	tch	match
	—	nature \'nā-chər\
\d\	d	did
	dd	ladder
	dh	dhow
	ed	seemed
	ld	would (In the speech of most Americans t and tt between vowels are pronounced the same as d and dd.)
\f\	f	fan, safe
	ff	offer
	gh	laugh
	lf	calf
	ph	telephone
\g\	g	go
	gg	egg
	gh	ghost
	gu	guide, plague
	—	example \ig-'zam-pəl\
\h\	g	Gila monster
	h	hat

	j	jai alai
	ch	*Chanukah*
	wh	who
\hw\	**ju**	*marijuana, San Juan*
	wh	*whale, when*
\j\	**g**	gem
	j	joy
	ch	*Greenwich*
	dg	budget, bridge
	di	soldier
	dj	adjective
	gg	exaggerate
	gi	region
	—	graduation \,graj-ə-'wā-shən\
\k\	**c**	catch
	k	kid, take
	q	quit
	cc	account
	ch	chaos, *loch, schism*
	ck	pick
	cq	acquire
	cu	biscuit
	kh	khaki
	kk	chukka, pukka
	lk	talk
	qu	liquor, plaque, quay
	cch	saccharine
	cqu	lacquer
	—	tax \'taks\
\k̲\	**h**	*Hanukkah, Hasid*
	ch	*loch, Chasid*
\l\	**al**	pedal
	el	betel
	l	dirndl
	l	low, sale
	le	battle
	ll	filling, faille
	ln	*kiln*
	yl	phenyl
\m\	**chm**	drachm
	en	*open, happen*
	ernm	*government*
	gm	phlegm
	lm	*calm*
	m	me, come
	mb	comb
	mh	mho
	mm	dummy
	mn	autumn
\n\	**ain**	certain
	en	sudden
	gn	sign, gnat, reign
	kn	knot
	mn	mnemonic
	mp	*comptroller*
	n	no, alone
	nn	banner
	pn	pneumonia
	on	cotton
\ng\	**n**	ink, finger, *orangutan*
	nd	handkerchief
	ng	sing, singer
	ngg	mah-jongg
	ngu	harangue
\p\	**p**	port, stop, ape
	ph	shepherd, *diphthong*
	pp	supper
\r\	**r**	red, care, card, car (Many people usually, some people occasionally, do not pronounce **r** followed by a consonant or a pause)
	rh	rhyme
	rr	merry
	wr	write
	rrh	diarrhea
	—	colonel \'kərn-l\
\s\	**c**	proceed, race
	s	say, loose
	z	pretzel
	ps	psalm
	sc	fascinate, scissors
	ss	mass
	st	listen, Christmas
	ts	*tsar*
	tz	*tzar*
	sch	*schism*

	sth	isthmus
	—	tax \'taks\
\sh\	**c**	oceanic
	s	sugar, sure
	ch	machine
	ci	special
	sc	fascism
	se	*nauseous*
	sh	shy
	si	emulsion
	ss	tissue
	ti	nation
	chi	marchioness
	psh	pshaw
	sch	schist
	sci	conscious
	ssi	mission
	chsi	fuchsia
\t\	**t**	tea, eat, late
	bt	debt
	ct	ctenoid
	ed	walked
	pt	ptomaine, receipt
	th	thyme, Thomas, Thai
	tt	button
	cht	yacht
	ght	night, straight
\th\	**gh**	*trough*
	th	thin, breath
	ght	*drought*
\t̲h\	**th**	this, teething, breathe
\v\	**f**	of
	v	very, save
	ph	Stephen
	vv	savvy
\w\	**u**	persuade, quit
	w	way
	ju	*San Juan, marijuana*
	ou	*bivouac*
	wh	*whale, when*
	—	one \'wən\
	—	choir \'kwīr\
	—	patois \'pa-,twä, 'pä-\
	—	strenuous \'stren-yə-wəs\
\y\	**i**	opinion
	j	hallelujah
	y	yard
	—	beauty \'byüt-ē\
	—	canon \'kan-yən\
	—	cute \'kyüt\
	—	feud \'fyüd\
	—	few \'fyü\
	—	strenuous \'stren-yə-wəs\
	—	tortilla \tȯr-'tē-ə, tȯr-'tē-yə\
	—	unit \'yü-nət\
\z\	**s**	days, was, please
	x	xylophone, *bateaux*
	z	zone, haze
	cz	czar
	sc	*discern*
	ss	scissors
	ts	*tsar*
	tz	*tzar*
	zz	buzz
	—	example \ig-'zam-pəl\
\zh\	**g**	regime, beige
	j	jongleur
	si	vision
	zi	glazier
	ssi	*fission*
	—	azure \'azh-ər\
	—	measure \'mezh-ər, 'māzh-\

SILENT LETTERS

The following letters often appear in the spelling but with no corresponding sound in the pronunciation of some words. Perhaps every letter of the alphabet is "silent" (by which we really mean "unpronounced") in some English word or other. For instance, *nc* is not pronounced in *blancmange*. Many such uncommon or rare instances are not included in this list.

b	comb, debt
c	Connecticut, ctenophore

ch	yacht
e	date, live, battle, seemed, plague
g	gnat, sign, diaphragm
gh	night, straight, though, thought
h	hour, honor, rhyme, thyme
i	business, *parliament*
k	knot, know
l	talk, folk, would, *calm*
m	mnemonic
n	autumn, *government, kiln*
o	sophomore, *opossum*
p	cupboard, pneumonia, psalm, ptomaine, raspberry

r	surprise \sər-ˈprīz, sə-ˈprīz\ (Many people usually, most people occasionally, do not pronounce **r** when followed by a consonant or a pause.)
s	aisle, island, patois, demesne
t	beret, boatswain, Christmas, depot, listen
th	asthma, isthmus, *northeaster*
u	biscuit, build, guest, *pursuivant,* quay
ue	plague, plaque
w	who, write, two, sword, boatswain
x	faux pas, *bateaux*
y	*yeast*
z	rendezvous

Prefixes, Roots, and Suffixes

English words are often amalgams of Latin, Greek, Celtic, Norse, German, and other sources. The basis of the relationship between a word and its source is frequently described in terms of the derived parts that form the origin of that word. These components may include **prefixes,** which are affixed at the beginning of a word, **roots,** which are the bases from which a word is developed, and **suffixes,** which are affixed at the end of a word.

The definition of an unknown word may often be determined by understanding the general meaning of its prefix, root, and/or suffix. The prefixes, roots and suffixes listed in this section are often clues to the origin of a word and its meaning, but are not to be considered absolute and universal building blocks of the English language. The following is a listing of some of the most common.

PREFIXES

PREFIX	MEANING	EXAMPLES
ab, a, abs	away, from, off	abandon, abscond, abnormal
a, an	without, not	apathetic, anarchy, asexual
ad, a, ac, af, ag, al	toward, to	advocate, accommodate, aggregate
amb, ambi	both	ambiguous, ambivalence
amphi	around, on both sides	amphibious, amphitheater
ana	up, throughout, back	anachronism, anagram, analogous
ante	before, prior	anterior, antecedent
anti	against	antinomy, antipathy, antibiotic
apo	away from, off	apocalypse, apology
ap, ar, as, at	to, toward	attack, associate
be	by, around, near	beside, beneath
be	to a greater degree	berate, befuddle
be	to make, treat as	befriend, belittle
bene	good, well	benevolent, benefit
bi	two, twice	bigamy, bilingual, bisexual
cata, cath	down, against	catatonic, catapult, catheter
circum	around, about	circumference, circumstance
com, con, col	together, with	combine, connect
contra, contro	against, in opposition to	contradict, controversial
de	away from, down	descend, depart
de	reduce, remove	devalue, debilitate, dethrone
demi	half	demimonde, demigod
dia	across, through	dialogue, diagonal, diagnosis
dis, di	apart, apart from	digress, dissonant

PREFIX	MEANING	EXAMPLES
dis	opposite, absence of	disinformation, discourage
en, em	in, into	enclose, engage, embroil
endo	inside	endocrine, endoderm
enter, entre	between	entertain, entrepreneur
ex, ef, e	out of, out, away	exegesis, extradite, effort, emit
extra	beyond, outside	extracurricular, extravagant
hemi	half	hemisphere, hemidemisemiquaver
hetero, heter	different	heterosexual, heterogeneous
homo, hom	same, similar	homosexual, homonym
hyper	above, beyond, over	hyperbole, hypersensitive
hypo	beneath, under, down	hypodermic, hypocrisy
in, im, il, ir	in, into, within	intrude, invade
in, im, il, ir	not	invisible, impossible, illegal, irrational
infra	within, below	infrastructure, infrasonic
inter	between, among	intervene, interface, international
int, intra, intro	within	internal, intramural, introduction
juxta	near, beside	juxtapose
mal	bad, inadequate	maladjusted, malpractice
meta, met	after, beyond, more	metaphor, metamorphosis
mis	bad, wrong	misconduct, misspell
mono	one, single	monotony, monologue
multi	many, much	multimedia, multitude
n	not	never, neither, none
non	not	nonsense, noncommittal

PREFIX	MEANING	EXAMPLES
ob	against, opposite	obscure, obliterate
para, par	near, beside, beyond	parable, parallel, paranoid
per	through	perceive, perforate
peri	around, about	periscope, peripatetic
post	after, subsequent	posthumous, postpone, posterior
pre	before, prior to	precede, preface, preview
preter	beyond	preternatural
pro	before, forward	profess, process, promote
re	again, back	recidivist, reconsider, rebel, report
retro	backward	retroactive, retrospect
se	apart	seclude, sequester, segregate
semi	half, almost	semicircle, semiprofessional
stereo, stere	solid	stereophonic, stereotype, cholesterol

PREFIX	MEANING	EXAMPLES
sub, subter	below, under	submarine, subterranean
super, supra, sur	above, over	superficial, superfluous, survive
syn, sym	together, with	sympathetic, synonym, syntax
trans, tra	across, beyond	transubstantiate, transient
ultra	outside, extremely, beyond	ultrasonic, ultraconservative
un	not, reversed	uncouth, undo
uni	single, one	unison, universal
vice	instead, one that takes the place of	viceroy, vice-president
with	against, back	withstand, withhold

ROOTS

ROOT	MEANING	EXAMPLES
acr	sharp, biting	acrimonious, acrid
acro	high, extremity	acrobat, acronym
aero, aer	air	aerodynamics, aerial
ag, act	to do	aggravate, agenda, activate
agogue	leader	demagogue, pedagogue
agon	conflict	agonize, antagonist, protagonist
agr	farm	agriculture, agrarian
al	nourish	alimentary, alimony
alg	pain	analgesic, nostalgic
ali	another	alien, alibi, alias
alter	another, change	alternate, alteration
alti, alto	high	altitude, altar
am	love	amiable, amateur, ambitious
ambul	walk	ambulance, somnambulist
andro	man	android, androgynous
anim	mind, passion, soul	animate, animal
ann, enn	year	annual, perennial
anth	flower	chrysanthemum, anthology
anthro	man	anthropology, misanthrope
aper	open	aperitif, April
apt, ept	adjust, fit	aptitude, adaptation
aqu	water	aquarium, aqueduct
arbor	tree	arboretum, arboreal
arch	chief, rule, first	matriarchy, archetype
archeo, archae	old	archaeology, archaic
arid	burn, dry	arson, arid
arthro	joint	arthritis, arthropod
aster, astro	star	astral, astronomy, astrology
atmo	vapor	atmosphere
aud	hear	audience, audition, auditor
aug	increase	augment, author, auction
auto	self	automobile, autocrat
avi	bird	aviary, aviation
bar, baro	weight, heavy	baritone, barometer
bell	beautiful	belle, embellish
belli	war	belligerent, rebellion, antebellum
bibl, biblio	book	bibliography, Bible
bio	life	biology, biography, biodegradable
brac	arm	embrace, bracelet
brevi	short	abbreviate, brevity

ROOT	MEANING	EXAMPLES
burs	bag, sack	bursitis, reimburse
caco	evil	cacophony
cad, cas	fall	cadence, cascade, casualty
cal	hot	calorie, caldron
calli	beautiful	calligraphy, calisthenics
camer	room	camera, chamber
cand	glowing	candle, incandescent, candor
cant	sing	cantor, incantation, recant, chant
cap, cept, ceive, cip	take	captivate, accept, receive, recipe
capit	head	capital, decapitate
car	dear	caress, cherish, charity
card	heart	cardiac, pericardial
caud	tail	caudal, coward, cue
caust	burn	caustic, holocaust
celer	fast	accelerate
cent	hundred	centipede, century
cern, cert	establish, perceive	certify, ascertain
cess, cede	go, yield	secession, procedure, recede
charg	load	charge, discharge, cargo
charis	favor	charisma, Eucharist
chiro	hand	chiropractic, chiromancy
chloro	green	chlorophyll, chloroform
choreo, chor	dance	choreograph, chorus
chrome	color	chromatic
chrono	time	chronology, chronic
cide, cis	kill, cut	genocide, homicide, incision
cit	summon	citation, incite, recite
civi	citizen, city	civilization, civilian
clam	cry out	exclamatory, clamor
clar	clear	clarify, declaration
clav	key	conclave, clavier, clavicle
clud, clus	close	reclusive, exclude
coct	cook	concoct, precocious
compl, complet	fill out	complex, complicate, complete
copi	abundant	copious, copy
copul	join	copulate, couple
cor, cord	heart	coronary, cordial
corp, corpor	body	corpulence, corporation, corpse
cosmo	universe	cosmology, cosmopolitan
crac, crat	rule, government	democrat, autocracy
cred	believe	credible, creditor, incredulous

ROOT	MEANING	EXAMPLES
cresc, cret	grow	crescent, concrete, decrease
cri	judge	criteria, critic, crisis
crypt	hidden	cryptic, cryptographer
cub, cumb	lie down	incubate, succumb, incumbent
cumul	add to	accumulate, cumulus
cur	care	curate, manicure, sinecure
cur, curse	run	current, concur, excursion
da, don	give	donate, data
dear	precious	endearing, darling
dec	ten	decade, decimal
dem, demo	people	democracy, demography, epidemic
dendr, dendro	tree, plant	rhododendron, dendrite
dent	teeth	indent, dentist
derm	skin	dermatologist, epidermis
dict	say, speak	dictate, interdiction, verdict
digit	finger, toe	digital, digitalis
doc	teach	docile, indoctrinate
dog, dox	opinion, belief	dogma, orthodox, heterodox
dom	home	domain, domestic, kingdom
domin	rule	domineer, predominate
drom	run, course	dromedary, hippodrome, syndrome
duc	lead	induce, deduction
dur	lasting	during, obdurate
dyna	force, power	dynamic, dynasty
dys	difficult, bad	dyslexia, dysfunctional
echino	spiny	echinoderm
eco	home	economy, ecology, ecumenical
ecto	outside	ectoplasm
empt	to buy, to take	redemption, example
entom	insect	entomology
epi, eph	on, over, outside	epicenter, epidermis, ephemeral
equ	equal	equity, equivocate, equation
ethno	race	ethnic, ethnocentric
eu	good	euphoria, euphemism
ev	age, period	primeval, medieval
fac, fic	make, do	facility, manufacture, beneficial
fall, fals	deceive	fallacy, false
fam	report	infamy, famous
fare	to go	farewell, welfare, thoroughfare
fe	property, cattle	feudal, fee, fellow
fer	carry	fertility, transfer, confer
fid	faith	fidelity, confidence, infidel
fin	end	final, infinity, definite
firm	strong	infirmary, confirm
fissi	split	fissile, fission
fix	fasten	fixture, affix
flagr	burn	conflagration, flagrant
flat	blow	flatulent, deflate
flect, flex	bend	flexible, reflect
flict	strike	conflict, afflict
flu	flow	fluid, confluence
foli	leaf	folio, foliage, portfolio
fract, frag, fring	break	fraction, fragment, infringe
fric	rub	friction, dentifrice
frig	cold	frigid, refrigerator
fug	escape from	fugitive, refuge, centrifuge
fum	smoke	fumigate, perfume

ROOT	MEANING	EXAMPLES
funct	perform	function, defunct, perfunctory
fund, fus	pour	effusive, confuse, refund
gamy	marriage	bigamy, monogamy
gast	frighten	ghastly, ghost
ge	earth	geology, geometry, perigee
gen	produce, birth, race, kind	gender, generation, progeny
gest	carry	gesture, suggest, digestion
gloss, glot	language	glossary, polyglot
gluc, glyc	sweet	glucose, glycerine
glypto, glyph	carving	hieroglyph
gnom, gnos	belief	physiognomy, agnostic
gon	angle	diagonal, polygon
gram	written	telegram, diagram, epigram
graph	write	Hagiography, chronograph
gress, grad	step, walk	graduate, degrade, transgress
greg	flock, herd	aggregate, gregarious
gyneco	woman	gynecologist, misogyny
hab	have	habit, exhibition, ability
hedral, hedron	side, sided	tetrahedron, cathedral
helic	spiral	helicopter, helicon, helix
helio	sun	heliocentric, heliograph
hema, hemo	blood	hematology, hemophiliac
her	stick	inherent, coherent, adhesive
hexa	six	hexagon
hilar	merry	hilarious, exhilarate, Hilary
hor	bound	horizon, aphorism
hum	ground	humiliate, exhume
hydro	water	hydrant, hydraulic, hydrogen
hypno	sleep	hypnotize, hypnotherapy
iasis	disease	psoriasis
iatrics, iatry	medical treatment	pediatrics, podiatry
icon	image	iconoclast, iconography
ideo	idea	ideogram, ideology
idio	own, private	idiosyncrasy, idiom
insul	island	insular, insulate, peninsula
integr	whole	integrate, integral, integrity, integer
iso	equal	isotope, isomorphic
itis	inflammation	bronchitis, tonsillitis
jan	doorway	janitor, January
ject	throw	deject, object, interject
joc	joke	jocular, juggler, jewel
journ	day	journal, journey, adjourn
jud	judge	judicial, prejudice, injudicious
junct	join	junction, conjugal
jur	swear	jury, perjure
juv, jun	youth	juvenile, junior, rejuvenate
kine, cine	movement	kinetic, telekinesis, cinema
la	people	laity, layman
lab, lep	take	syllable, epilepsy
labor	work	laborious, belabor, laboratory
lacto	milk	lactic, lactose
lamin	layer	laminate, omelet
lapi	stone	lapidary, dilapidated
lat	carry	translate, ventilate, legislate

ROOT	MEANING	EXAMPLES
lat	wide	latitude, dilate
lav, lu	wash	lavatory, deluge
lef	allow, dear	belief, love
leg, lect	read, choose	legible, legend, elect
leg	law	legal, legislate
lepsy	seizure, fit	epilepsy, narcolepsy
lex	word	lexicon
liber	free	liberty, liberal, libertarian
libr	book	library, libel
lig	bind	ligament, obligate, religion
limin	threshold	eliminate, subliminal
lingu	language	linguistics, bilingual
linqu, lict	leave	relinquish, delinquent, derelict
liter	letter	literature, literal, obliterate
litho	stone	lithograph, monolithic
loft	air	aloft, lift
log, logue	word, speech, discourse	logarithm, epilogue, prologue
logy	study	philology, ethnology
loqu, locut	speak	eloquent, elocution, ventriloquist
luc	light	lucent, elucidate
lud	play	prelude, collusion
lumin	light	luminous, illuminate
lun	moon	lunar, lunette
lys, lyt	to free	analysis, electrolyte
macro	large	macrocosm
magn	large, great	magnify, magnanimous, magnitude
man	hand	manicure, manuscript
man	stay	mansion, permanent, remain
mancy	foretelling	necromancy
mand	order	mandate, reprimand
mania	craving	maniac, kleptomania
manu	hand	manual, manacle, manufacture
mar	sea	marine, maritime, submarine
mater, metr	mother	maternal, matricide, metropolis
med	care for	medicine, mediate, remedy
med	middle	medium, mediate, medieval
mega, megalo	great	megalomania, megadeath, megaphone
mell	honey	mellifluous, molasses, marmalade
melo	song	melodrama, melody
memor	remember	memory, memoranda, commemorate
merc	trade	merchant, mercenary, market
meso	middle	mesosphere, mesoderm, Mesozoic
meter	measure	barometer, thermometer
micro	small	microscope, microfilm
migra	wander	migrate, immigrant
mis, mit	send	mission, submit
miso	hatred	misogyny, misanthrope
mne	remember	amnesia, mnemonic, amnesty
mon	warn, advise	monitor, admonish
mor	stupid	moron, sophomore
mor, mort	death	mortify, mortal, mortician, mortgage
morpho	shape	metamorphosis, amorphous
mors	bite	morsel, remorse, mordant
mov, mot	move	movement, emotion, mobile

ROOT	MEANING	EXAMPLES
mut	change	mutate, immutable, commute
nat	birth	nation, natal
necr	death	necrology, nectar
neo	new	neophyte, neolithic, neoclassic
neth	below	Netherlands, nether, beneath
neuro	nerve	neurosis, neurology
noct	night	nocturnal, nocturne
nom	name	nomination, misnomer, nominal
nomy	system	economy, agronomy
nov	new	novelty, renovate, innovate
nub, nupt	marry	connubial, nubile, nuptial
nunc	announce	enunciate, pronounce, denounce
nym	name	homonym, synonym
oct	eight	octet, octopus, October
oculo	eye	ocular, binoculars
od	road	odometer, method, exodus
odonto	tooth	orthodontist
omni	all	omnipotent, omniscient
oid	like, similar	android, schizoid
oligo	few	oligarchy
onto	being	ontology
op	eye	optical, myopia, ophthalmology
oper	work	operation, opera, cooperate
or, os	mouth	oral, orifice, oracle, osculate
orient	east, rising	oriental, orientation
orn	decorate	ornate, ornament, adorn
ornitho	bird	ornithology
ortho	straight	orthodox, orthopedic
pac	peace	pacifist, pacific
pact	agree	compact, impact
paleo	old	paleolithic
pan	all	pandemic, pantheon, panorama
pan	bread	pantry, company
par	equal	parity, compare, disparage
para	prevent	parachute, parasol, parapet
parl	speech	parley, parlor, parole
past	dough	pasta, pastry, paste, pastel
pat, pass	suffer	patient, passive, passion
pater	father	paternal, patriot
patho	disease, feeling, suffering	pathetic, telepathy, pathos
ped, pod, pus	foot	pedestrian, impede, podiatry, octopus
pedo	child	pediatrician, pedagogue
pel, puls	drive	dispel, repulsion
pen	almost	peninsula, penultimate
pen	punishment	penalize, penance, repent
pend	hang	pendant, dependable
penta	five	pentagram, pentagon
petit	seek	petition, competition, appetite
petro	stone	petroleum, petrify
phan, phen	show	phantom, phenomenon
philo	love	philosophy, philanthropy, Philip
phobia	fear	xenophobia, claustrophobia
phono	sound	phonograph, phonetics, telephone
photo	light	photosynthesis, photograph

ROOT	MEANING	EXAMPLES
phren	mind	phrenology, schizophrenic
physi, physio	nature	physiology, physiognomy
pict	paint	picture, depict, pigment
plac	please	placate, implacable, complacent
plaud	strike, applaud	plausible, explode
plen, plete	full	plenitude, replenish, deplete
plex, plic, ply	fold	complex, explicit, multiply
plumb	lead	plumber, plummet
plus, plur	more	surplus, plural
pluto	riches, wealth	plutocracy
pon, posit	place	postpone, proponent, preposition
porto	bring	report, export, transport
pot, poss	be able	potent, possible
preci	price	precious, appreciate, depreciate
prim	first	primary, primitive
priv	single, separate	private, privilege, deprive
prox	near	proximity, approximate
pseudo	false	pseudonym, pseudodoxy
psycho	mind, spirit, soul	psychology, psychic
put	correct	compute, amputate
pyro	fire	pyromaniac, pyrotechnics
quadr, quart	four	quadrilateral, quadrangle, quarter
qual	nature of	quality, qualify
quant	how much	quantity, quantum
quest, quir	ask, seek	question, inquire
rad	ray	radiate, radius
radic	root	radical, eradicate, radish
rat, ratio	reason, plan	rationalize, irrational
re	thing	republic, real
rect	rule	rector, direct, rectify
reg	rule	regime, regal, region, regulate
rhino	nose	rhinoceros, rhinoplasty
rid, ris	laugh	ridicule, deride
rode, ros	gnaw	rodent, corrosion, erode
rog	ask	interrogate, arrogant
rot	wheel	rotate, rotund
rrhea, rrhage	flow	diarrhea, hemorrhage
rupt	break	rupture, erupt, bankrupt
sacchar	sugar	saccharine
sacr	dedicated, holy	sacrosanct, sacred, sacrifice
sal	salt	saline, salary
sarco	flesh	sarcophagus, sarcastic
saur	lizard	sauropod, dinosaur, brontosaurus
scato	excrement	scatological
schis, schizo	split	schism, schizophrenic, schizoid
sci	knowing	science, conscious
scope	sight, observation	telescope, horoscope
scrip, scrib	write	scripture, describe
sec	cut	section, dissect
sed, sess	remain	sedentary, sediment
semin	seed	seminal, disseminate, seminar
sent, sens	feel	sentiment, sensual
sept	seven	septet, septuagenarian, September
sequ	follow	sequence, consequence
ser	series	serial, insert, dissertation
serv	work	servant, servile, conserve
sign	sign	signal, designation, resign

ROOT	MEANING	EXAMPLES
sist	stand	resist, consist, persistent
soci	companion	society, association, dissociate
solu, solv	loosen, solve	solution, resolve
somn	sleep	somnambulist, insomnia
son	sound	resonant, dissonant, unison
sophy	wisdom	sophistry, sophisticate, philosophy
sort	lot, condition	consort, assortment, sorcerer
spect	watch, look	spectator, inspect, circumspect
sper	hope	desperate, despair, prosper
spher, sphere	sphere	spherical, atmosphere, stratosphere
spin	spin	spinster, spindle, spider
spir	breath	spirit, inspire, perspire
spond, spons	pledge	sponsor, response, spouse
stat	stand	statute, reinstate, constitute
statis, stat	standing	prostate, thermostat
stell	star	stellar, constellation
stip	press together	constipate, stipulate
stor	set up	storage, restoration, restaurant
strict, string	tie	district, constrict, stringent
struct	build	structure, obstruction, instruct
suav	agreeable	suave, assuage, sweet
sum, sumpt	take	sumptuary, consume
surge, surrect	rise	resurrection, insurgence
swer	swear	answer, forswear, sworn
tact, tang	touch	intact, tangible
tail	cut	tailor, detail, retail
tauto	same	tautology, tautomer
taxis	arrangement	taxidermy, tactics
tech	skill, art	technology, technique
tele	distant, far	telepathy, television
tempor	time	temporal, contemporary
ten	hold	tenet, tenacious, detention
tend, tens, tent	stretch	tendency, extensive, attention
termin	limit, end	terminate, determine, exterminate
terr	land	terrain, territory, extraterrestrial
test	witness	testify, protest, testament
theo	god	theology, theosophy, atheist
thermo	heat	thermometer, thermonuclear
tomy	cutting	appendectomy, anatomy
topo	place	topology, topic
tor	twist	torture, contortion, distort
tract	drag, draw	tractor, detract
trop, trope	turning	tropic, heliotrope
tru	faithful	truth, trust, betrothed
typ, type	print, image	typewriter, prototype
ubiqu	everywhere	ubiquitous
ultim	last	ultimate, ultimatum, penultimate
umbr	shade	umbrella, umbrage
urb	city	urbane, suburban
us, ut	use	utensil, utility, abuse
vac	empty	vacuum, vacant, evacuate, vacation
vad, vas	go	invade, evasion, pervasive

ROOT	MEANING	EXAMPLES
vag	wander	vagrancy, extravagant
val	strong, to have worth	valid, valor, valuable
val	valley	vale, valley, avalanche
van	empty	vanish, vanity, evanescence
vap	steam	vapor, vapid, evaporate
vari	different, diverse	variety, various, variorum
vas	vessel	vascular, vasectomy
ven, vent	to come	venture, convenient, revenue
vend	sell	vendor, venal
ver	true	verify, verdict, veracious
verg	learn	converge, divergence
vert, vers	turn	version, revert, controversy
vet	old	veteran, veterinary, inveterate
via	way	viaduct, trivial
vid, vis	sight	video, television, revise

ROOT	MEANING	EXAMPLES
vinc, vict	conquer	victory, victim, invincible
vir	man	virile, virtue, triumvirate
vir	poison	virus, virulent
visc	sticky	viscous, viscid
vita	life	vital, vitamins, revitalize
vitr	glass	vitreous, vitrify
voc	call	vocal, evoke
vol	will	volunteer, volition, benevolent
volv, volu	roll	volume, involve, revolution
vorous	eating	omnivorous, carnivorous
wak	alert	awake, watch, wait
ward	protect	warden, wardrobe, reward
xeno	foreign	xenophobia, xenon
zoo	living, animal	zoology

SUFFIXES

SUFFIX	MEANING	EXAMPLES
able, ible, ble	able to	durable, flexible, portable
ac, ic	pertaining to, relating to	fantastic, historic, maniac
ac, ic	having the character of, quality of	kleptomaniac, alcoholic
acious, aceous	having the quality of	vivacious, pugnacious, herbaceous
acy, cy	having the quality of	legacy, supremacy, accuracy, idiocy
age	aggregate, collection of	marriage, orphanage
al, el, le	relating to, characterized by	fictional, criminal
an, ian	of or belonging to	African, statistician
ance	process or action	performance, appearance
ancy, ency	state or condition	vacancy, dependency, infancy
aneous	having the quality of	instantaneous, spontaneous
ant, ent	one that performs	defendant, transient
ar, ary, ory	of or relating to	aviary, dictionary, directory
ard, art	characterized by	dullard, braggart
ate, ite	possess or being	desolate, propagate, favorite
ate	office or function	sultanate, directorate
ation, ion, tion	action, state of	flirtation, isolation
cle, cule	little	article, molecule
dom	state of being	freedom, wisdom, kingdom
ee	one acted upon, recipient	payee, trainee, employee
en	having quality of, consisting of	wooden, earthen, rotten
ence	action, quality	resurgence, despondence
eous	like	aqueous, igneous
er, or, ar	one who	jogger, doctor, scholar
ese	of, relating to	legalese, Japanese
escent	growing, in state of	obsolescent, adolescent
esque	in the manner of	statuesque, Romanesque
ful	full of, characterized by	masterful, eventful, peaceful
fy, ify	to make or render	mystify

SUFFIX	MEANING	EXAMPLES
hood	condition	childhood, priesthood
ice	act of	prejudice, accomplice
il, ile	pertaining to, capable of	civil, mobile
ine	procedure, art	medicine, discipline
ish	like	foolish, selfish, childish
ism	quality, act	communism, idealism, Protestantism
ist	one who	novelist, orthodontist
ity, ty	state or quality	clarity, liberty
ive	having the nature or quality of	superlative, negative
ize, yze	to make like, form	finalize, analyze
latry	worship	idolatry
less	without	clueless, homeless
let	little	cutlet, booklet
lexia	read	dyslexia
ling	little	sapling, fledgling
ment	result, action	development, fragment
ness	state of being	forgetfulness, sadness
ock	little	shamrock, buttock
oid	resembling	spheroid, asteroid
or	state or quality	stupor, ardor
orama	view	panorama, diorama
ory	place of	factory, dormitory, observatory
ous	full of	dangerous, mysterious, strenuous
ose	full of	morose, verbose
osis, sis	condition of, act	osmosis, analysis
otic	having quality of	narcotic, neurotic
ple	times	triple, multiple
polis	city	metropolis, cosmopolitan
ship	state or quality	friendship, musicianship
some	characterized by	wholesome, awesome
sion, tion	act or state of being	tension, detention
tude	that which is	certitude, exactitude
ulent	having quality of	corpulent, virulent
ulous	having quality of	fabulous, ridiculous
ure	process, being	procedure, departure
ward	direction	backward, heavenward
y	characterized by, full of	sleepy, stinky

Webster's Thesaurus

This thesaurus is a concise guide to the understanding and use of synonyms. It is intended for people who wish to appreciate the shades of difference that exist among English words that have the same or nearly the same essential meaning and who wish to be able to choose the precisely suitable word for a particular purpose.

This section is made up of a collection of main entries consisting of articles in which distinctions are drawn among a group of synonyms. The distinctions usually fall into one of three peripheral areas of meaning: implication, connotation, or application. *Implications* are the usually minor ideas involved in the meaning of a word. *Connotations* are the ideas that color the meaning of a word and are the product of various factors, such as etymology and historical and literary associations. *Applications* are the restrictions on a word's use established by current idiom.

Each main entry begins with a list of the words discussed in that article. The words in the list are set in boldface type for easy recognition, and the entries are alphabetized by the first word in the list. Following the list is a concise statement of the element of meaning that the synonyms have in common:

>   **abandon, desert, forsake** mean to leave without intending to return

After this initial sentence, there is a series of statements describing the differences that distinguish the synonyms from one another. The statements are supplemented and clarified by examples, set in angle brackets, that illustrate typical ways in which the words may be used:

>   **Abandon** suggests that the thing or person may be helpless without protection ⟨they left the house and *abandoned* their cat⟩. **Desert** implies that the object left may be weakened but not destroyed by one's absence ⟨the miners *deserted* once the gold ran out⟩. **Forsake** suggests an action more likely to bring impoverishment or bereavement to that which is forsaken than its exposure to physical dangers ⟨he *forsook* his wife and family for a younger woman⟩.

In addition to main entries, this thesaurus contains thousands of cross-reference entries. By means of these entries, every word discussed in the article at a main entry is entered at its own alphabetical place, followed by a cross-reference in small capital letters to the main entry at which it is discussed:

>   **desert** see ABANDON

When a main-entry word is also discussed as the same part of speech at another main entry, a cross-reference note appears at the end of the main-entry paragraph:

>   **abandon, desert, forsake** mean to leave without intending to return. . . .See in addition to RELINQUISH.

This note indicates that the word *abandon*, which is treated as a verb in this entry, is also discussed as a verb at the main entry for *relinquish*.

When a word that is entered as a cross-reference is discussed at more than one entry and is treated as a different part of speech at each entry, separate cross-reference entries appear:

>   **humor** *vb* see INDULGE
>   **humor** *n* see WIT

Likewise, if a word that is a main entry is also discussed at another entry but as a different part of speech, a separate cross-reference entry appears:

malign *vb* malign, traduce, asperse, vilify, calumniate, defame, slander mean to injure by speaking ill of. . . .
malign *adj* see SINISTER

In the examples for *humor* and *malign,* the entry word is followed by an italic part-of‑speech reference. This label appears whenever the same entry word is listed more than once (whether for a main entry or a cross-reference entry). The meanings of these abbreviations may be found in the section Abbreviations Used in this Dictionary.

A

abandon, desert, forsake mean to leave without intending to return. **Abandon** suggests that the thing or person left may be helpless without protection ⟨they *abandoned* their cat at summer's end⟩. **Desert** implies that the object left may be weakened but not destroyed by one's absence ⟨a town *deserted* once the gold ran out⟩. **Forsake** suggests an action more likely to bring impoverishment or bereavement to that which is forsaken than its exposure to physical dangers ⟨*forsook* his wife and family for a younger woman⟩. See in addition RELINQUISH.

abase, demean, debase, degrade, humiliate mean to lower in one's own estimation or in that of others. **Abase** suggests losing or voluntarily yielding up dignity or prestige ⟨a fine stage actor who *abased* himself by turning to television⟩. **Demean** implies losing or injuring social standing by an unsuitable act or association ⟨commercial endorsements *demean* the Olympics⟩. **Debase** implies a deterioration of moral standards or character ⟨drunkenness has *debased* the Mardi Gras⟩. **Degrade** suggests the taking of a step downward sometimes in rank but more often on the road to moral degeneration ⟨the public altercation *degraded* both candidates⟩. **Humiliate** implies the severe wounding of one's pride and the causing of deep shame ⟨*humiliated* by his suggestive remarks⟩.

abash see EMBARRASS

abate, subside, wane, ebb mean to die down in force or intensity. **Abate** stresses the idea of progressive diminishing ⟨waited until the storm *abated*⟩. **Subside** implies the ceasing of turbulence or agitation ⟨the protests *subsided* after a few days⟩. **Wane** suggests the fading or weakening of something good or impressive ⟨the public's *waning* interest in space flight⟩. **Ebb** suggests the receding of something (as the tide) that commonly comes and goes ⟨her love *ebbs* as regularly and predictably as the tides⟩. See in addition DECREASE.

abbreviate see SHORTEN

abdicate, renounce, resign mean to give up a position with no possibility of resuming it. **Abdicate** implies a giving up of sovereign power or sometimes an evading of responsibility such as that of a parent ⟨by walking out he *abdicated* his rights as a father⟩. **Renounce** may replace it but often implies additionally a sacrifice for a greater end ⟨by this marriage she *renounces* any hope of an inheritance⟩. **Resign** applies to the giving up of an unexpired office or trust ⟨forced to *resign* from office⟩.

aberrant see ABNORMAL
abet see INCITE
abeyant see LATENT
abhor see HATE
abhorrent see HATEFUL, REPUGNANT
abide see BEAR, CONTINUE
abject see MEAN

abjure, renounce, forswear, recant, retract mean to withdraw one's word or professed belief. **Abjure** implies a firm and final rejecting or abandoning often made under oath ⟨candidates for citizenship must *abjure* allegiance to any foreign power⟩. **Renounce** often equals *abjure* but may carry the meaning of disclaim or disown ⟨willing to *renounce* his lifelong friends⟩. **Forswear** may add to *abjure* an implication of perjury or betrayal ⟨I cannot *forswear* my principles to win votes⟩. **Recant** stresses the withdrawing or denying of something professed or taught ⟨the suspect *recanted* his confession and professed his innocence⟩. **Retract** applies to the withdrawing of a promise, an offer, or an accusation ⟨under threat of lawsuit the paper *retracted* the statement⟩.

able, capable, competent, qualified mean having power or fitness for work. **Able** suggests ability above the average as revealed in actual performance ⟨proved that she is an *able* Shakespearean actress⟩. **Capable** stresses the having of qualities fitting one for work but does not imply outstanding ability ⟨*capable* of doing simple tasks under supervision⟩. **Competent** and **qualified** imply having the experience or training for adequate performance ⟨a leap that any *competent* ballet dancer can execute⟩ ⟨seek help from a *qualified* medical professional⟩.

abnormal, atypical, aberrant mean deviating markedly from the rule or standard of its kind. **Abnormal** frequently suggests strangeness and sometimes deformity or monstrosity ⟨a classic study of *abnormal* personalities⟩. **Atypical** stresses divergence upward or downward from some established norm ⟨a markedly *atypical* reaction to a drug⟩. **Aberrant** implies a departure from the usual or natural type ⟨that joyriding incident must be regarded as an *aberrant* episode in his life⟩.

abominable see HATEFUL
abominate see HATE
abomination, anathema, bugbear, bête noire mean a person or thing that arouses intense dislike. **Abomination** suggests the arousal of loathing, disgust, and extreme displeasure ⟨in her opinion all of modern art is an *abomination*⟩. **Anathema** suggests that something is so odious that it is dismissed or rejected out of hand ⟨anything that was Yankee was *anathema* to my Southern aunt⟩. **Bugbear** suggests something so dreaded that one seeks continually to avoid it ⟨the deficit issue became an annual congressional *bugbear*⟩. **Bête noire** suggests a pet aversion that one habitually or especially avoids ⟨his mooching brother-in-law was the *bête noire* of his life⟩.

aboriginal see NATIVE
abridge see SHORTEN
abridgment, abstract, synopsis, conspectus, epitome mean a condensed treatment. **Abridgment** suggests reduction in compass with retention of relative completeness ⟨a desk-size dictionary that is an *abridgment* of a larger work⟩. **Abstract** applies to a summary of points of a treatise, document, or proposed

treatment and usu. has no independent worth ⟨a published *abstract* of a medical paper⟩. **Synopsis** implies a skeletal presentation of an argument or a narrative suitable for rapid examination ⟨read a *synopsis* of the screenplay⟩. **Conspectus** implies a quick overall view of a large detailed subject ⟨the book is a *conspectus* of modern European history⟩. **Epitome** suggests the briefest possible presentation of a complex whole that still has independent value ⟨"know thyself" was the *epitome* of Greek philosophy⟩.

abrogate see NULLIFY

abrupt see PRECIPITATE, STEEP

absolute, autocratic, arbitrary, despotic, tyrannical mean exercising power or authority without restraint. **Absolute** implies that one is not bound by legal constraints or the control of another ⟨King Louis XIV was an *absolute* monarch⟩. **Autocratic** suggests the egotistical, self-conscious use of power or the haughty imposition of one's own will ⟨the flamboyant, *autocratic* director of the ballet company⟩. **Arbitrary** implies the exercise and usu. the abuse of power according to one's momentary inclination ⟨his high-handed, *arbitrary* way of running his department⟩. **Despotic** implies the arbitrary and imperious exercise of absolute power or control ⟨the most decadent and *despotic* of the Roman emperors⟩. **Tyrannical** implies the abuse of absolute power and harsh or oppressive rule ⟨a new regime as *tyrannical* as the one it had deposed⟩.

absolve see EXCULPATE

absorb, imbibe, assimilate mean to take something in so as to become imbued with it. **Absorb** may connote a loss of identity in what is taken in or an enrichment of what takes in ⟨can quickly *absorb* highly technical reports⟩. **Imbibe** implies a drinking in which may be unconscious but whose effect may be significant or profound ⟨children *imbibe* the values of their parents⟩. **Assimilate** stresses an incorporation into the substance of the body or mind ⟨asked to *assimilate* a mass of material in a brief time⟩.

abstract see ABRIDGMENT

abundant see PLENTIFUL

abuse, vituperation, invective, obloquy, scurrility, billingsgate mean vehemently expressed condemnation or disapproval. **Abuse**, the most general term, implies the anger of the speaker and stresses the harshness of the language ⟨charged her husband with verbal *abuse*⟩. **Vituperation** implies fluent and sustained abuse ⟨subjected his aide to a torrent of *vituperation*⟩. **Invective** implies a comparable vehemence but suggests greater verbal and rhetorical skill and may apply to a public denunciation ⟨a politician known for his blistering *invective*⟩. **Obloquy** suggests defamation and consequent shame and disgrace ⟨silently endured the *obloquy* of his former friend⟩. **Scurrility** implies viciousness of attack and coarseness or foulness of language ⟨a debate that was not an exchange of ideas but an exercise in *scurrility*⟩. **Billingsgate** implies practiced fluency and variety of profane or obscene abuse ⟨a *billingsgate* that would make a drunken sailor blush⟩.

accede see ASSENT

acceptation see MEANING

accidental, fortuitous, casual, contingent mean not amenable to planning or prediction. **Accidental** stresses chance ⟨any resemblance to actual persons is entirely *accidental*⟩. **Fortuitous** so strongly suggests chance that it often connotes entire absence of cause ⟨believes that life is more than a series of *fortuitous* events⟩. **Casual** stresses lack of real or apparent premeditation or intent ⟨a *casual* encounter between two acquaintances⟩. **Contingent** suggests possibility of happening but stresses uncertainty and dependence on other future events for existence or occurrence

⟨the *contingent* effects of a proposed amendment to the constitution⟩.

accommodate see ADAPT, CONTAIN

accompany, attend, escort mean to go along with. When referring to persons, **accompany** usu. implies equality of status ⟨*accompanied* his wife to the theater⟩. **Attend** implies a waiting upon in order to serve usu. as a subordinate ⟨will *attend* the President at the summit meeting⟩. **Escort** adds to *accompany* implications of protection, ceremony, or courtesy ⟨a motorcade *escorted* the visiting queen⟩.

accomplish see PERFORM

accomplishment see ACQUIREMENT

accord *vb* see GRANT

accord *n* see HARMONY

accountable see RESPONSIBLE

accoutre see FURNISH

accredit see APPROVE

accumulative see CUMULATIVE

accurate see CORRECT

accuse, charge, indict, impeach mean to declare a person guilty of a fault or offense. **Accuse** implies a direct, personal declaration ⟨*accused* him of trying to steal his wallet⟩. **Charge** usu. implies a formal declaration of a serious offense ⟨an athlete *charged* with taking illegal drugs before the race⟩. **Indict** is usu. used in a legal context and implies a formal consideration of evidence prior to a trial ⟨*indicted* by a grand jury for first-degree murder⟩. **Impeach** technically refers to a formal charge of malfeasance in office on the part of a public official ⟨the House of Representatives *impeached* President Andrew Johnson of high crimes and misdemeanors⟩.

accustomed see USUAL

acerbity see ACRIMONY

achieve see PERFORM

achievement see FEAT

acknowledge, admit, own, avow, confess mean to disclose against one's will or inclination. **Acknowledge** implies the disclosing of something that has been or might be concealed ⟨*acknowledged* an early short-lived marriage⟩. **Admit** implies reluctance to disclose, grant, or concede and refers usu. to facts rather than their implications ⟨*admitted* that the project was over budget⟩. **Own** implies acknowledging something in close relation to oneself ⟨must *own* that I know little about computers⟩. **Avow** implies boldly declaring, often in the face of hostility, what one might be expected to be silent about ⟨*avowed* that he was homosexual⟩. **Confess** may apply to an admission of a weakness, failure, omission, or guilt ⟨*confessed* that she had a weakness for sweets⟩.

acme see SUMMIT

acquaint see INFORM

acquiesce see ASSENT

acquire see GET

acquirement, acquisition, attainment, accomplishment mean a power or skill won through deliberate effort. **Acquirement** suggests the result of constant endeavor to cultivate oneself ⟨an appreciation of good music was not one of his *acquirements*⟩. **Acquisition** stresses the effort involved and the inherent value of what is gained ⟨the ability to concentrate is a valuable *acquisition*⟩. **Attainment** suggests a distinguished achievement ⟨honored as woman of the year for her many *attainments*⟩. **Accomplishment** implies a socially useful skill ⟨wittiness in conversation is an *accomplishment* to be cherished⟩.

acquisition see ACQUIREMENT

acquisitive see COVETOUS

acquit see BEHAVE, EXCULPATE

acrid see CAUSTIC

acrimony, acerbity, asperity mean temper or language marked by angry irritation. **Acrimony** implies feelings of bitterness and a stinging verbal attack (a campaign marked by verbal exchanges of intense *acrimony*). **Acerbity** suggests a morose, embittered, or crabbed temperament (an inbred *acerbity* that pervades even his personal letters). **Asperity** suggests harshness or roughness of expression rather than feelings of bitterness (a certain *asperity* of expression was part of her style).

actuate see MOVE

acumen see DISCERNMENT

acute, critical, crucial mean of uncertain outcome. **Acute** stresses intensification of conditions leading to a culmination or breaking point (the housing shortage is becoming *acute*). **Critical** adds to *acute* implications of imminent change, of attendant suspense, and of decisiveness in the outcome (the war has entered a *critical* phase). **Crucial** suggests a dividing of the ways and often a test or trial involving the determination of a future course or direction (for the campaign, the coming weeks will be *crucial*). See in addition SHARP.

adamant see INFLEXIBLE

adapt, adjust, accommodate, conform, reconcile mean to bring one thing into correspondence with another. **Adapt** implies a modification according to changing circumstances (they *adapted* themselves to the warmer climate). **Adjust** suggests bringing into a close and exact correspondence or harmony as exists between the parts of a mechanism (*adjusted* the budget to allow for inflation). **Accommodate** may suggest yielding or compromising in order to effect a correspondence (*accommodated* his political beliefs in order to win). **Conform** applies to bringing into harmony or accordance with a pattern, example, or principle (refused to *conform* to society's idea of woman's proper role). **Reconcile** implies the demonstration of the underlying consistency or congruity of things that seem to be incompatible (tried to *reconcile* what they said with what I knew).

adaptable see PLASTIC

additive see CUMULATIVE

address see TACT

adept see PROFICIENT

adequate see SUFFICIENT

adhere see STICK

adherent see FOLLOWER

adjacent, adjoining, contiguous, juxtaposed mean being in close proximity. **Adjacent** may or may not imply contact but always implies absence of anything of the same kind in between (the price of the house and the *adjacent* garage). **Adjoining** definitely implies meeting and touching at some point or line (assigned *adjoining* rooms at the hotel). **Contiguous** implies having contact on all or most of one side (offices in all 48 *contiguous* states). **Juxtaposed** means placed side by side esp. so as to permit comparison and contrast (an ultramodern office buiding *juxtaposed* to a Gothic church).

adjoining see ADJACENT

adjure see BEG

adjust see ADAPT

administer see EXECUTE

admire see REGARD

admission see ADMITTANCE

admit see ACKNOWLEDGE

admittance, admission mean permitted entrance. **Admittance** is usu. applied to mere physical entrance to a locality or a building (members must show their cards upon *admittance* to the club). **Admission** applies to entrance or formal acceptance (as into a club) that carries with it rights, privileges, standing, or membership (candidates for *admission* must submit recommendations from two club members).

admonish see REPROVE

adopt, embrace, espouse mean to take an opinion, policy, or practice as one's own. **Adopt** implies accepting something created by another or foreign to one's nature (forced to *adopt* the procedures of the new parent company). **Embrace** implies a ready or happy acceptance (eagerly *embraced* the ways and customs of their new homeland). **Espouse** adds an implication of close attachment to a cause and a sharing of its fortunes (spent her lifetime *espousing* equal rights for women).

adore see REVERE

adorn, decorate, ornament, embellish, beautify, deck, garnish mean to enhance the appearance of something by adding something unessential. **Adorn** implies an enhancing by something beautiful in itself (a diamond necklace *adorned* her neck). **Decorate** suggests relieving plainness or monotony by adding beauty of color or design (*decorate* a birthday cake with colored frosting). **Ornament** and **embellish** imply the adding of something extraneous, *ornament* stressing the heightening or setting off of the original (a white house *ornamented* with green shutters), *embellish* often stressing the adding of superfluous or adventitious ornament (*embellish* a page with floral borders). **Beautify** adds to *embellish* a suggestion of counterbalancing plainnesss or ugliness (will *beautify* the park with flower beds). **Deck** implies the addition of something that contributes to gaiety, splendor, or showiness (a house all *decked* out for Christmas). **Garnish** suggests decorating with a small final touch and is used esp. in referring to the serving of food (airline food is invariably *garnished* with parsley).

adroit see CLEVER, DEXTEROUS

adultery, fornication, incest designate forms of illicit sexual intercourse that are clearly distinguished in legal use. **Adultery** can be applied only to sexual intercourse between a married person and a partner other than his or her wife or husband (listed *adultery* as grounds for divorce). **Fornication** designates sexual intercourse on the part of an unmarried person (religious laws strictly forbidding *fornication*). **Incest** refers to sexual intercourse between persons proscribed from marrying on the basis of kinship ties (*incest* involving father and daughter is the most common).

advance, promote, forward, further mean to help (someone or something) to move ahead. **Advance** stresses effective assisting in hastening a process or bringing about a desired end (a gesture intended to *advance* the cause of peace). **Promote** suggests an encouraging or fostering and may denote an increase in status or rank (a company trying to *promote* better health among employees). **Forward** implies an impetus forcing something ahead (a wage increase would *forward* productivity). **Further** suggests a removing of obstacles in the way of a desired advance (used the marriage to *further* his career).

advantageous see BENEFICIAL

advent see ARRIVAL

adventurous, venturesome, daring, daredevil, rash, reckless, foolhardy mean exposing oneself to danger more than required by good sense. **Adventurous** implies a willingness to accept risks but not necessarily imprudence (*adventurous* pioneers opened the West). **Venturesome** implies a jaunty eagerness for perilous undertakings (*venturesome* pilots became popular heroes). **Daring** heightens the implication of fearlessness in courting danger (mountain climbing attracts the *daring* types). **Daredevil** stresses ostentation in daring (*daredevil* motorcyclists performing stunts). **Rash** suggests imprudence and lack of forethought (a *rash* decision that you will regret later). **Reckless** implies heedlessness of probable consequences (a *reckless* driver who was drunk). **Foolhardy** suggests a recklessness that is inconsistent with good sense (only a *foolhardy* sailor would venture into this storm).

adversary see OPPONENT

adverse, antagonistic, counter, counteractive mean so opposed as to cause often harmful interference. **Adverse** applies to what is unfavorable, harmful, or detrimental (very sensitive to *adverse* criticism). **Antagonistic** usu. implies mutual opposition and either hostility or incompatibility (neighboring countries were *antagonistic* to the new nation). **Counter** applies to forces coming from opposite directions with resulting conflict or tension (the *counter* demands of family and career). **Counteractive** implies an opposition between two things that nullifies the effect of one or both (poor eating habits will have a *counteractive* effect on any gains from exercise).

adversity see MISFORTUNE

advice, counsel denote recommendation as to a decision or a course of conduct. **Advice** implies real or pretended knowledge or experience, often professional or technical, on the part of the one who advises (a book of *advice* for would-be entrepreneurs). **Counsel** often stresses the fruit of wisdom or deliberation and may presuppose a weightier occasion, or more authority, or more personal concern on the part of the one giving counsel (Father would often give me the benefit of his *counsel*).

advisable see EXPEDIENT

advise see CONFER

advocate see SUPPORT

affable see GRACIOUS

affect, influence, touch, impress, strike, sway mean to produce or have an effect upon. **Affect** implies the action of a stimulus that can produce a response or reaction (the sight *affected* her to tears). **Influence** implies a force that brings about a change (as in nature or behavior) (our beliefs are *influenced* by our upbringing) (a drug that *influences* growth rates). **Touch** may carry a vivid suggestion of close contact and may connote stirring, arousing, or harming (plants *touched* by frost) (his emotions were *touched* by her distress). **Impress** stresses the depth and persistence of the effect (only one of the plans *impressed* him). **Strike,** similar to but weaker than *impress,* may convey the notion of sudden sharp perception or appreciation (*struck* by the solemnity of the occasion). **Sway** implies the acting of influences that are not resisted or are irresistible, with resulting change in character or course of action (politicians who are *swayed* by popular opinion). See in addition ASSUME.

affectation see POSE

affecting see MOVING

affection see FEELING

affinity see ATTRACTION, LIKENESS

affirm see ASSERT

affix see FASTEN

afflict, try, torment, torture, rack, grill mean to inflict on a person something that is hard to bear. **Afflict** is a general term and applies to the causing of pain or suffering or of acute annoyance, embarrassment, or any distress (many aged persons who are *afflicted* with blindness). **Try** suggests imposing something that strains the powers of endurance or of self-control (young children often *try* their parents' patience). **Torment** suggests persecution or the repeated inflicting of suffering or annoyance (the horses are *tormented* by flies). **Torture** adds the implication of causing unbearable pain or suffering (*tortured* his wife with charges of infidelity). **Rack** stresses straining or wrenching (a mind *racked* by guilt). **Grill** suggests causing acute discomfort as by long and relent-

less questioning (they *grilled* the prisoner for hours on end).

affluent see RICH

afford see GIVE

affront see OFFEND

afraid see FEARFUL

age see PERIOD

aggravate see INTENSIFY

aggressive, militant, assertive, self-assertive, pushing mean obtrusively energetic esp. in pursuing particular goals. **Aggressive** implies a disposition to dominate often in disregard of others' rights or in determined and energetic pursuit of one's ends (books on how to be *aggressive* in the business world). **Militant** also implies a fighting disposition but suggests not self-seeking but devotion to a cause, movement, or principle (*militant* environmentalists staged a protest). **Assertive** suggests bold self-confidence in expression of opinion (*assertive* speakers dominated the open forum). **Self-assertive** connotes forwardness or brash self-confidence (a *self-assertive* young executive climbing the corporate ladder). **Pushing** may apply to ambition or enterprise or to snobbish and crude intrusiveness or officiousness (*pushing* salespeople using high-pressure tactics).

aggrieve see WRONG

agile, nimble, brisk, spry mean acting or moving with easy quickness. **Agile** implies dexterity and ease in physical or mental actions (very *agile* about distancing himself from unpopular issues). **Nimble** stresses lightness and swiftness of action or thought (a *nimble* tennis player). **Brisk** suggests liveliness, animation, or vigor of movement sometimes with a suggestion of hurry (a *brisk* cleaning-up before the relatives arrived). **Spry** stresses an ability for quick action that is unexpected because of age or known infirmity (*spry* older runners sometimes beat out younger competitors).

agitate see DISCOMPOSE, SHAKE

agony see DISTRESS

agree, concur, coincide mean to come into or be in harmony regarding a matter of opinion. **Agree** implies complete accord usually attained by discussion and adjustment of differences (on some points we all can *agree*). **Concur** tends to suggest cooperative thinking or acting toward an end but sometimes implies no more than approval (as of a decision reached by others) (if my wife *concurs,* then it's a deal). **Coincide,** used more often of opinions, judgments, wishes, or interests than of people, implies an agreement amounting to identity (their wishes *coincide* exactly with my desire). See in addition ASSENT.

aid see HELP

aim see INTENTION

air *vb* see EXPRESS

air *n* see POSE

airs see POSE

alacrity see CELERITY

alarm see FEAR

alert see INTELLIGENT, WATCHFUL

alibi see APOLOGY

alien see EXTRINSIC

alienate see ESTRANGE

alive see AWARE, LIVING

all see WHOLE

allay see RELIEVE

allegiance see FIDELITY

alleviate see RELIEVE

alliance, league, coalition, confederation, federation mean an association to further the common interests of its members. **Alliance** applies to an association formed for the mutual benefit of its members (an *alliance* between feminist and religious groups against pornography). **League** applies to a more formal compact often with a definite goal (the *League* of Nations). **Coalition** applies to a temporary association of parties often of opposing interests (formed a *coalition* government with two other parties). **Confederation** applies to a union of independent states under a central government having powers dealing with common external relations (the *confederation* formed by the American colonies following the revolution). **Federation** specif. applies to a sovereign power formed by a union of states and having a central government and several state and local governments (the United States of America constitutes a *federation*).

allocate see ALLOT

allot, assign, apportion, allocate mean to give as a share, portion, role, or lot. **Allot** may imply haphazard or arbitrary distribution (each student is *alloted* an hour of computer time). **Assign** stresses an authoritative and fixed allotting but carries no clear implication of an even division (each employee is *assigned* a parking space). **Apportion** implies a dividing according to some principle (profits were *apportioned* according to a predetermined ratio). **Allocate** suggests a fixed appropriation usu. of money to a person or group for a particular use (allocated $50,000 for park improvements).

allow see LET

allure see ATTRACT

ally see CONFEDERATE

alone, solitary, lonely, lonesome, lone, forlorn, desolate mean isolated from others. **Alone** suggests the objective fact of being by oneself with slighter notion of emotional involvement than most of the remaining terms (everyone needs to be *alone* sometimes). **Solitary** may indicate isolation as a chosen course (glorying in the calm of her *solitary* life) but more often it suggests sadness and a sense of loss (left *solitary* by the death of his wife). **Lonely** adds to *solitary* a suggestion of longing for companionship (felt *lonely* and forsaken). **Lonesome** heightens the suggestion of sadness and poignancy (an only child often leads a *lonesome* life). **Lone** may replace *lonely* or *lonesome* but typically is as objective as *alone* (a *lone* robin pecking at the lawn). **Forlorn** stresses dejection, woe, and listlessness at separation from one held dear (a *forlorn* lost child). **Desolate** implies inconsolable grief at loss or bereavement (her brother's death now left her totally *desolate*).

aloof see INDIFFERENT

alter see CHANGE

altercation see QUARREL

alternative see CHOICE

altitude see HEIGHT

amalgate see MIX

amateur, dilettante, dabbler, tyro mean a person who follows a pursuit without attaining proficiency or professional status. **Amateur** often applies to one practicing an art without mastery of its essentials (a painting obviously done by an *amateur*), and in sports it may also suggest not so much lack of skill but avoidance of direct remuneration (must remain an *amateur* in order to qualify for the Olympics). **Dilettante** may apply to the lover of an art rather than its skilled practitioner but usu. implies elegant trifling in the arts and an absence of serious commitment (a serious art teacher with no patience for *dilettantes*). **Dabbler** suggests desultory habits of work and lack of persistence (a *dabbler* who never finished a single novel). **Tyro** implies inexperience often combined with audacity with resulting crudeness or blundering (a *tyro* who has yet to master the basics of playwriting).

amaze see SURPRISE

ambiguity, equivocation, tergiversation, double entendre mean an expression capable of more than one interpretation. **Ambiguity** usu. refers to the use of a word or phrase in such a way that it may be taken in either of two senses (the *ambiguity* in the directive's wording caused much confusion). **Equivocation** suggests that the ambiguity is intentional and the intent is to mislead (the government's report on the nuclear accident is filled with *equivocations*). **Tergiversation** stresses the shifting of senses during the course of one's argument and usu. suggests intentional subterfuge (a thesis that resorts to several *tergiversations* of the word "society"). **Double entendre** refers to a word or expression allowing two interpretations, one of them being risqué (the *double entendres* that are de rigueur in any bedroom farce).

ambiguous see OBSCURE

ambition, aspiration, pretension mean strong desire for advancement. **Ambition** applies to the desire for personal advancement or preferment and may suggest equally a praiseworthy or an inordinate desire (driven by the *ambition* to be very rich). **Aspiration** implies a striving after something higher than oneself and usu. implies that the striver is thereby ennobled (an *aspiration* to become President someday). **Pretension** suggests ardent desire for recognition of accomplishment without actual possession of the necessary ability and therefore implies presumption (several people with literary *pretensions* frequent her salon).

ameliorate see IMPROVE

amenable see OBEDIENT, RESPONSIBLE

amend see CORRECT

amiable, good-natured, obliging, complaisant mean having the desire or disposition to please. **Amiable** implies having qualities that make one liked and easy to deal with (a travel club that attracts *amiable* types). **Good-natured** implies cheerfulness or helpfulness and sometimes a willingness to be imposed upon (a *good-natured* boy who was always willing to pitch in). **Obliging** stresses a friendly readiness to be helpful (our *obliging* innkeeper accommodated our request). **Complaisant** often implies passivity or a yielding to others because of weakness (*complaisant* people who only say what others want to hear).

amicable, neighborly, friendly mean exhibiting goodwill and an absence of antagonism. **Amicable** implies a state of peace and a desire on the part of the parties not to quarrel (maintained *amicable* relations even after the divorce). **Neighborly** implies a disposition to live on good terms with others and to be helpful on principle (a *neighborly* concern prompted the inquiry about her health). **Friendly** stresses cordiality and often warmth or intimacy of personal relations (sought his *friendly* advice on this important matter).

ample see PLENTIFUL, SPACIOUS

amplify see EXPAND

amuse, divert, entertain mean to pass or cause to pass the time pleasantly. **Amuse** suggests that one's attention is engaged lightly or frivolously (*amuse* yourselves while I prepare dinner). **Divert** implies the distracting of the attention from worry or routine occupation esp. by something funny (tired businessmen looking for a light comedy to *divert* them). **Entertain** suggests supplying amusement or diversion by specially prepared or contrived methods (comedians and pretty girls *entertained* the troops).

analogous see SIMILAR

analogy see LIKENESS

analyze, dissect, break down mean to divide a complex whole into its parts or elements. **Analyze** suggests separating or distinguishing the component parts of something (as a substance, a process, a situation) so as to discover its true nature or inner relationships (*analyzed* the basis for the current problem of trade imbalances). **Dissect** suggests a searching analysis by laying bare parts or pieces for individual scrutiny ⟨commentators *dissected* every word of the President's statement⟩. **Break down** implies a reducing to simpler parts or divisions ⟨*break down* the budget to see where the money is going⟩.

anathema see ABOMINATION

anathematize see EXECRATE

ancient see OLD

anger, ire, rage, fury, indignation, wrath mean an intense emotional state induced by displeasure. **Anger,** the most general term, names the reaction but in itself conveys nothing about intensity or justification or manifestation of the emotional state ⟨tried to hide his *anger*⟩. **Ire,** more frequent in literary contexts, may suggest greater intensity than *anger,* often with an evident display of feeling ⟨cheeks flushed dark with *ire*⟩. **Rage** suggests loss of self-control from violence of emotion ⟨screaming with *rage*⟩. **Fury** is overmastering destructive rage verging on madness ⟨in her *fury* she started to accuse everyone around her⟩. **Indignation** stresses righteous anger at what one considers unfair, mean, or shameful ⟨behavior that caused general *indignation*⟩. **Wrath** is likely to suggest a desire or intent to revenge or punish ⟨rose in his *wrath* and struck his tormentor to the floor⟩.

angle see PHASE

anguish see SORROW

animal see CARNAL

animate *adj* see LIVING

animate *vb* see QUICKEN

animated see LIVELY, LIVING

animosity see ENMITY

animus see ENMITY

announce see DECLARE

annoy, vex, irk, bother mean to upset a person's composure. **Annoy** implies a wearing on the nerves by persistent petty unpleasantness ⟨her constant complaining *annoys* us⟩. **Vex** implies greater provocation and stronger disturbance and usu. connotes anger but sometimes perplexity or anxiety ⟨a problem that *vexes* cancer researchers⟩. **Irk** stresses difficulty in enduring and the resulting weariness or impatience of spirit ⟨his chronic tardiness *irks* his wife⟩. **Bother** suggests interference with comfort or peace of mind ⟨that discrepancy *bothers* me⟩. See in addition WORRY.

annul see NULLIFY

anomalous see IRREGULAR

answer, respond, reply, rejoin, retort mean to say, write, or do something in return. **Answer** implies the satisfying of a question, demand, call, or need ⟨*answered* all the questions on the form⟩. **Respond** may suggest an immediate or quick reaction ⟨chose not to *respond* to that comment⟩. **Reply** implies making a return commensurate with the original question or demand ⟨an invitation that requires you to *reply* at once⟩. **Rejoin** often implies sharpness or quickness in answering ⟨"who asked you?" she *rejoined*⟩. **Retort** suggests responding to an explicit charge or criticism by way of retaliation ⟨he *retorted* to her every charge with biting sarcasm⟩.

answerable see RESPONSIBLE

antagonism see ENMITY

antagonist see OPPONENT

antagonistic see ADVERSE

antagonize see OPPOSE

antecedent *n* see CAUSE

antecedent *adj* see PRECEDING

anterior see PRECEDING

anticipate see FORESEE, PREVENT

anticipation see PROSPECT

antipathy see ENMITY

antiquated see OLD

antique see OLD

antithetical see OPPOSITE

anxiety see CARE

anxious see EAGER

apathetic see IMPASSIVE

ape see COPY

aperçu see COMPENDIUM

apex see SUMMIT

aplomb see CONFIDENCE

apocryphal see FICTITIOUS

apologia see APOLOGY

apology, apologia, excuse, plea, pretext, alibi mean matter offered in explanation or defense. **Apology** usu. applies to an expression of regret for a mistake or wrong with implied admission of guilt or fault and with or without reference to palliating circumstances ⟨said by way of *apology* that he would have met them if he could⟩. Sometimes *apology,* like **apologia,** implies not admission of guilt or regret but a desire to make clear the grounds for some course, belief, or position ⟨the speech was an effective *apologia* for his foreign policy⟩. **Excuse** implies an intent to avoid or remove blame or censure ⟨used his illness as an *excuse* for missing the meeting⟩. **Plea** stresses argument or appeal for understanding or sympathy or mercy ⟨her usual *plea* that she was nearsighted⟩. **Pretext** suggests subterfuge and the offering of false reasons or motives in excuse or explanation ⟨used any *pretext* to get out of work⟩. **Alibi** implies a desire to shift blame or evade punishment and imputes plausibility rather than truth to the explanation offered ⟨his *alibi* failed to stand scrutiny⟩.

appall see DISMAY

apparent, illusory, seeming, ostensible mean not actually being what appearance indicates. **Apparent** suggests appearance to unaided senses that is not or may not be borne out by more rigorous examination or greater knowledge ⟨the *apparent* cause of the train wreck⟩. **Illusory** implies a false impression based on deceptive resemblance or faulty observation, or influenced by emotions that prevent a clear view ⟨vertical stripes will give an *illusory* height to her figure⟩. **Seeming** implies a character in the thing observed that gives it the appearance, sometimes through intent, of something else ⟨the *seeming* simplicity of the story⟩. **Ostensible** suggests a discrepancy between an openly declared or naturally implied aim or reason and the true one ⟨business was the *ostensible* reason for their visit⟩. See in addition EVIDENT.

appease see PACIFY

appetizing see PALATABLE

appliance see IMPLEMENT

applicable see RELEVANT

appoint see FURNISH

apportion see ALLOT

apposite see RELEVANT

appraise see ESTIMATE

appreciable see PERCEPTIBLE

appreciate, value, prize, treasure, cherish mean to hold in high estimation. **Appreciate** often connotes sufficient understanding to enjoy or admire a thing's excellence ⟨*appreciates* fine wine⟩. **Value** implies rating a thing highly for its intrinsic worth ⟨*values* our friendship⟩. **Prize** implies taking a deep pride in something one possesses ⟨Americans *prize* their freedom⟩. **Treasure** emphasizes jealously safeguarding something considered precious ⟨she *treasures* every momento of her youth⟩. **Cherish** implies a special love and care for something ⟨*cherishes* her children above all⟩. See in addition UNDERSTAND.

apprehend see FORESEE

apprehension, foreboding, misgiving, presentiment mean a feeling that something undesirable will or is about to happen. **Apprehension** implies a mind preoccupied with fear and anxiety ⟨approached the dangerous undertaking with great *apprehension*). **Foreboding** suggests fear that is oppressive, unreasoning, or indefinable (the deserted streets filled me with strange *forebodings*). **Misgiving** suggests uneasiness and mistrust (had my *misgivings* about her from the start). **Presentiment** implies a vague or uncanny sense that something is bound to happen (a *presentiment* that some of our group would not survive).

apprehensive see FEARFUL

apprise see INFORM

appropriate *vb* **Appropriate, preempt, arrogate, usurp, confiscate** mean to seize high-handedly. **Appropriate** suggests making something one's own or converting to one's own use without authority or with questionable right (just *appropriated* the tools meant to be shared by all). **Preempt** implies beforehandedness in taking something desired or needed by others (TV *preempted* much of the programming once broadcast by radio). **Arrogate** implies insolence, presumption, and exclusion of others in seizing rights, powers, or functions (White House staffers *arrogated* powers belonging to cabinet members). **Usurp** implies unlawful or unwarranted intrusion into the place of another and seizure of what is his by custom, right, or law (her new stepmother had *usurped* her status in the household). **Confiscate** always implies seizure through exercise of authority (customs officers *confiscate* all contraband).

appropriate *adj* see FIT

approve, endorse, sanction, accredit, certify mean to have or express a favorable opinion of. **Approve** often implies no more than this but may suggest considerable esteem or admiration (the parents *approve* of the marriage). **Endorse** suggests an explicit statement of support (publicly *endorsed* her for Senator). **Sanction** implies both approval and authorization (the President *sanctioned* covert operations). **Accredit** and **certify** usu. imply official endorsement attesting to conformity to set standards (the board voted to *accredit* the college) (must be *certified* to teach).

apropos see RELEVANT

apt see FIT, QUICK

aptitude see GIFT

arbitrary see ABSOLUTE

archaic see OLD

ardent see IMPASSIONED

ardor see PASSION

arduous see HARD

argot see DIALECT

argue see DISCUSS

arise see SPRING

aristocracy, nobility, gentry, society mean a body of people constituting a socially superior caste. **Aristocracy** usu. refers to those persons of superior birth, breeding, and social station (plantation families constituted the *aristocracy* of the antebellum South). **Nobility** refers to persons of a privileged and titled class that ranks just below royalty (the duke ranks highest in British *nobility*). **Gentry** refers to a class of leisured, well-bred persons who are considered gentlefolk but are without hereditary titles (a private school favored by generations of the *gentry*). **Society** refers to that class of people who are celebrated for their active social life, conspicuous leisure, and fashionable clothes (Newport *society* was famous for its lavish balls).

arm see FURNISH

aroma see SMELL

aromatic see ODOROUS

arrange see ORDER

arrival, advent mean the reaching of a destination. **Arrival** emphasizes the preceding travel or movement (a traffic jam greatly delayed their *arrival*). **Advent** applies to a momentous or conspicuous arrival, an ap-

pearance upon a scene esp. for the first time, or a beginning (the *advent* of a new age in space travel).

arrogant see PROUD

arrogate see APPROPRIATE

art, skill, cunning, artifice, craft mean the faculty of executing well what one has devised. **Art** distinctively implies a personal, unanalyzable creative power (an *art* for saying the right thing). **Skill** stresses technical knowledge and proficiency (the *skills* required of a surgeon). **Cunning** suggests ingenuity and subtlety in devising, inventing, or executing (a mystery thriller written with great *cunning*). **Artifice** suggests mechanical skill esp. in imitating things in nature (a painter with much of the *artifice* of Rubens and none of the art). **Craft** may imply expertness in workmanship (a saltcellar wrought with *craft* worthy of Cellini).

artful see SLY

artifice see ART, TRICK

artificial, factitious, synthetic, ersatz mean brought into being not by nature but by art or effort. **Artificial** is applicable to anything that is not the result of natural processes or conditions (the state is an *artificial* society) but esp. to something that has a counterpart in nature (*artificial* teeth). **Factitious** applies chiefly to emotions or states of mind not naturally caused or spontaneously aroused (created a *factitious* demand for the product). **Synthetic** applies esp. to a manufactured substance or to a natural substance so treated that it acquires the appearance or qualities of another and may substitute for it (*synthetic* furs). **Ersatz** often implies the use of an inferior substitute for a natural product (served *ersatz* cream with the coffee).

artless see NATURAL

ascertain see DISCOVER

ascetic see SEVERE

ascribe, attribute, assign, impute, credit mean to lay something to the account of a person or thing. **Ascribe** suggests an inferring or conjecturing of cause, quality, authorship (none of the frivolity commonly *ascribed* to teenagers). **Attribute** suggests less tentativeness than *ascribe,* less definiteness than *assign* (*attribute* the project's failure to poor planning). **Assign** implies ascribing with certainty or after deliberation (an investigatory panel *assigned* blame to top officials). **Impute** suggests ascribing something that brings discredit by way of accusation or blame (tried to *impute* sinister motives to my actions). **Credit** implies ascribing a thing or esp. an action to a person or other thing as its agent, source, or explanation (*credited* his insecurities to an unhappy childhood).

asinine see SIMPLE

ask *vb* **Ask, question, interrogate, query, inquire** mean to address a person in order to gain information. **Ask** implies no more than the putting of a question (*ask* for directions). **Question** usu. suggests the asking of series of questions (*questioned* them about every detail of the trip). **Interrogate** suggests formal or official systematic questioning (the prosecutor *interrogated* the witness all day). **Query** implies a desire for authoritative information or confirmation (*queried* the reference librarian about the book). **Inquire** implies a searching for facts or for truth often specifically by asking questions (began to *inquire* into the charges of espionage).

ask *vb* **Ask, request, solicit** mean to seek to obtain by making one's wants known. **Ask** implies no more than the statement of the desire (*ask* a favor of a friend). **Request** implies greater formality and courtesy (*requests* the pleasure of your company at the ball). **Solicit** suggests a calling attention to one's wants or desires by public announcement or advertisement (a classified ad that *solicits* a situation as a babysitter).

aspect see PHASE
asperity see ACRIMONY
asperse see MALIGN
aspiration see AMBITION
assail see ATTACK
assassinate see KILL
assault see ATTACK
assemble see GATHER
assent, consent, accede, acquiesce, agree, subscribe mean to concur with what has been proposed. **Assent** implies an act involving the understanding or judgment and applies to propositions or opinions 〈potential members must *assent* to the organization's credo〉. **Consent** involves the will or feelings and indicates compliance with what is requested or desired 〈*consented* to their daughter's going on the trip〉. **Accede** implies a yielding, often under pressure, of assent or consent 〈officials *acceded* to every prisoner demand〉. **Acquiesce** implies tacit acceptance or forbearance of opposition 〈usually *acquiesces* to his wife's wishes〉. **Agree** sometimes implies previous difference of opinion or attempts at persuasion 〈finally *agreed* to give him a raise〉. **Subscribe** implies not only consent or assent but hearty approval and active support 〈totally *subscribed* to the free enterprise system〉.
assert, declare, affirm, protest, avow mean to state positively usu. in anticipation of denial or objection. **Assert** implies stating confidently without need for proof or regard for evidence 〈*asserted* that modern music is just noise〉. **Declare** stresses open or public statement 〈the jury *declared* the defendant guilty〉. **Affirm** implies conviction based on evidence, experience, or faith 〈*affirmed* the existence of an afterlife〉. **Protest** emphasizes affirming in the face of denial or doubt 〈*protested* that he had never had a more splendid meal〉. **Avow** stresses frank declaration and acknowledgment of personal responsibility for what is declared 〈*avowed* that all investors would be repaid in full〉. See in addition MAINTAIN.
assertive see AGGRESSIVE
assess see ESTIMATE
assiduous see BUSY
assign see ALLOT, ASCRIBE
assignment see TASK
assimilate see ABSORB
assist see HELP
associate see JOIN
assuage see RELIEVE
assault see ATTACK
assume, affect, pretend, simulate, feign, counterfeit, sham mean to put on a false or deceptive appearance. **Assume** often implies a justifiable motive rather than an intent to deceive 〈*assumed* an air of cheerfulness for the sake of the patient〉. **Affect** implies making a false show of possessing, using, or feeling 〈willing to *affect* an interest in art in order to impress her〉. **Pretend** implies an overt and sustained false appearance 〈*pretended* not to know about her husband's affair〉. **Simulate** suggests a close imitation of the appearance of something 〈the training chamber *simulates* a weightless atmosphere〉. **Feign** implies more artful invention than *pretend,* less specific mimicry than *simulate* 〈*feigned* sickness in order to stay home from school〉. **Counterfeit** implies achieving the highest degree of verisimilitude of any of these words 〈*counterfeited* drunkenness so perfectly that many forgot he was acting〉. **Sham** implies an obvious falseness that fools only the gullible 〈*shammed* a most unconvincing limp〉.
assurance see CERTAINTY, CONFIDENCE
assure see ENSURE
astonish see SURPRISE
astound see SURPRISE

astute see SHREWD
athirst see EAGER
atmosphere, feeling, aura mean an intangible quality that gives something an individual and distinctly recognizable character. **Atmosphere** implies a quality that accrues to something or that pervades it as a whole and that determines the impression given by that thing 〈a country inn with a warm and friendly *atmosphere*〉. **Feeling** implies that something has distinctive qualities that create a definite if unanalyzable impression 〈a Colorado ski resort with an old-world *feeling*〉. **Aura** suggests an ethereal or mysterious quality that seems to emanate from a person or thing 〈a movie queen with an unmistakable *aura* of glamour〉.
atrocious see OUTRAGEOUS
attach see FASTEN
attack, assail, assault, bombard, storm mean to make an onslaught upon. **Attack** implies taking the initiative in a struggle 〈plan to *attack* at dawn〉. **Assail** implies attempting to break down resistance by repeated blows or shots 〈*assailed* the enemy with artillery fire〉. **Assault** suggests a direct attempt to overpower by suddenness and violence of onslaught 〈commando troops *assaulted* the building from all sides〉. **Bombard** applies to attacking with bombs or shells 〈*bombarded* the city nightly〉. **Storm** implies attempting to break into a defended position 〈a fortress that has never been successfully *stormed*〉.
attainment see ACQUIREMENT
attempt, try, endeavor, essay, strive mean to make an effort to accomplish an end. **Attempt** stresses the initiation or beginning of an effort 〈will *attempt* to photograph the rare bird〉. **Try** stresses effort or experiment made in the hope of testing or proving something 〈*tried* several times to find a solution〉. **Endeavor** heightens the implications of exertion and difficulty 〈*endeavored* to find survivors of the crash〉. **Essay** implies difficulty but also suggests tentative trying or experimenting 〈had *essayed* dramatic roles on two earlier occasions〉. **Strive** implies great exertion against great difficulty and specif. suggests persistent effort 〈continues to *strive* for a lasting peaceful solution〉.
attend see ACCOMPANY
attest see CERTIFY
attract, allure, charm, captivate, fascinate, enchant mean to draw another by exerting a powerful influence. **Attract** applies to any degree or kind of ability to exert influence over another 〈a university that *attracts* students from around the world〉. **Allure** implies an enticing by what is fair, pleasing, or seductive 〈the excitement of the big city *allures* young people〉. **Charm** implies the power of casting a spell over the person or thing affected and so compelling a response 〈*charmed* by the beauty of that serene isle〉, but it may, like **captivate,** suggest no more than evoking delight or admiration 〈her grace and beauty *captivated* us all〉. **Fascinate** suggests a magical influence and tends to stress the ineffectiveness of attempts to resist 〈a story that continues to *fascinate* children〉. **Enchant** is perhaps the strongest of these terms in stressing the appeal of the agent and the degree of delight evoked in the subject 〈hopelessly *enchanted* by his dashing looks and deep voice〉.
attraction, affinity, sympathy mean the relationship existing between things or persons that are naturally or involuntarily drawn together. **Attraction** implies the possession by one thing of a quality that pulls another to it 〈a curious *attraction* between people of opposite temperaments〉. **Affinity** implies a susceptibility or predisposition on the part of the one drawn 〈a student with an *affinity* for mathematics〉. **Sympathy** implies a reciprocal or natural relation between

two things that are both susceptible to the same influence ⟨there is close *sympathy* between the heart and the lungs⟩.

attribute *vb* see ASCRIBE

attribute *n* see QUALITY

atypical see ABNORMAL

audacity see TEMERITY

augment see INCREASE

aura see ATMOSPHERE

auspicious see FAVORABLE

austere see SEVERE

authentic, genuine, veritable, bona fide mean being actually and exactly what is claimed. **Authentic** implies being fully trustworthy as according with fact or actuality ⟨the *authentic* story⟩. **Genuine** implies accordance with an original or a type without counterfeiting, admixture, or adulteration ⟨*genuine* maple syrup⟩ or it may stress sincerity ⟨*genuine* piety⟩. **Veritable** may stress true existence or actual identity ⟨*veritable* offspring⟩ but more commonly merely asserts the suitability of a metaphor ⟨*veritable* hail of questions⟩. **Bona fide** can apply when sincerity of intention is in question ⟨*bona fide* sale of securities⟩.

authenticate see CONFIRM

authority see INFLUENCE, POWER

autocratic see ABSOLUTE

automatic see SPONTANEOUS

autonomous see FREE

avaricious see COVETOUS

average, mean, median, norm mean something that represents a middle point. **Average** is exactly or approximately the quotient obtained by dividing the sum total of a set of figures by the number of figures ⟨scored an *average* of 85 in a series of five tests⟩. **Mean** may be the simple average or it may represent value midway between two extremes ⟨a high of 70° and a low of 50° give a *mean* of 60°⟩. **Median** applies to the value that represents the point at which there are as many instances above as there are below ⟨*average* of a group of persons earning 3, 4, 5, 8, and 10 dollars a day is 6 dollars, whereas the *median* is 5 dollars⟩. **Norm** means the computed or estimated average of performance of a significantly large group, class, or grade ⟨scores about the *norm* for 5th grade arithmetic⟩

averse see DISINCLINED

avert see PREVENT

avid see EAGER

avoid see ESCAPE

avow see ACKNOWLEDGE, ASSERT

awake see AWARE

award see GRANT

aware, cognizant, conscious, sensible, alive, awake mean having knowledge of something. **Aware** implies vigilance in observing or alertness in drawing inferences from what one experiences ⟨*aware* of a greater number of police officers out and about⟩. **Cognizant** implies having special or certain knowledge as from firsthand sources ⟨as yet, not fully *cognizant* of all the facts⟩. **Conscious** implies that one is focusing one's attention on something or is even preoccupied by it ⟨*conscious* that my heart was pounding away⟩. **Sensible** implies direct or intuitive perceiving esp. of intangibles or of emotional states or qualities ⟨a doctor who was *sensible* of the woman's deep depression⟩. **Alive** adds to *sensible* the implication of acute sensitivity to something ⟨we were fully *alive* to the momentousness of the occasion⟩. **Awake** implies that one has become alive to something and is on the alert ⟨a country not *awake* to the dangers of persistent inflation⟩.

awkward, clumsy, maladroit, inept, gauche mean not marked by ease (as of performance or movement). **Awkward** is widely applicable and may suggest unhandiness, inconvenience, lack of muscular control, embarrassment, or lack of tact ⟨a dinner party marked by periods of *awkward* silence⟩. **Clumsy** implies stiffness and heaviness and so may connote inflexibility, unwieldiness, or lack of ordinary skill ⟨a writer with a persistently *clumsy* style⟩. **Maladroit** suggests a tendency to create awkward situations ⟨a *maladroit* handling of a delicate situation⟩. **Inept** often implies complete failure or inadequacy ⟨blamed the conviction on his *inept* defense attorney⟩. **Gauche** implies the effects of shyness, inexperience, or ill breeding ⟨always felt *gauche* and unsophisticated at formal parties⟩.

B

baby see INDULGE

back see RECEDE, SUPPORT

background, setting, environment, milieu, mise-en-scéne mean the place, time, and circumstances in which something occurs. **Background** often refers to the circumstances or events that precede a phenomenon or development ⟨a *background* that prepared her well for the task⟩. **Setting** suggests looking at real-life situations as though they were dramatic or literary representations ⟨a social reformer who was born into the most unlikely social *setting*⟩. **Environment** applies to all the external factors that have a formative influence on one's physical, mental, or moral development ⟨the kind of *environment* that produces juvenile delinquents⟩. **Milieu** applies esp. to the physical and social surroundings of a person or group of persons ⟨an intellectual *milieu* conducive to bold experimentation in the arts⟩. **Mise-en-scéne** strongly suggests the use of properties to achieve a particular atmosphere or theatrical effect ⟨a tale of the occult having a carefully crafted *mise-en-scéne*⟩.

bad, evil, ill, wicked, naughty mean not morally good. **Bad** may apply to any degree of reprehensibility ⟨the *bad* guys in a Western⟩. **Evil** is a stronger term than *bad* and usu. carries a baleful or sinister connotation ⟨*evil* men who would even commit murder⟩. **Ill** is a less emphatic synonym of *evil* and may imply malevolence or vice ⟨paid dearly for his *ill* deeds⟩. **Wicked** usu. connotes malice and malevolence ⟨a *wicked* woman who delighted in the suffering of others⟩. **Naughty** applies either to trivial misdeeds or to matters impolite or amusingly risqué ⟨looked up all the *naughty* words in the dictionary⟩.

badger see BAIT

baffle see FRUSTRATE

bag see CATCH

bait, badger, heckle, hector, chivy, hound mean to harass by efforts to break down. **Bait** implies wanton cruelty or delight in persecuting a helpless victim ⟨teenagers *baited* the chained dog⟩. **Badger** implies pestering so as to drive a person to confusion or frenzy ⟨*badgered* her father for a raise in her allowance⟩. **Heckle** implies persistent interruptive questioning of a speaker in order to confuse or discomfit him ⟨drunks *heckled* the stand-up comic⟩. **Hector** carries an implication of bullying and domineering that breaks the spirit ⟨as a child he had been *hectored* by his father⟩. **Chivy** suggests persecution by teasing or nagging ⟨*chivied* her husband to the breaking point⟩. **Hound** implies unrelenting pursuit and harassing ⟨*hounded* on all sides by creditors⟩.

balance see COMPENSATE

bald see BARE

baleful see SINISTER

balk see FRUSTRATE

balky see CONTRARY

banal see INSIPID

baneful see PERNICIOUS

banish, exile, deport, transport mean to remove by authority from a state or country. **Banish** implies compulsory removal from a country not necessarily one's own ⟨a country that once *banished* the Jesuits⟩. **Exile** may imply compulsory removal or an enforced or voluntary absence from one's own country ⟨a writer who *exiled* himself from South Africa⟩. **Deport** implies sending out of the country an alien who has illegally entered or whose presence is judged inimical to the public welfare ⟨illegal aliens will be *deported*⟩. **Transport** implies sending a convicted criminal to an overseas penal colony ⟨a convict who was *transported* to Australia⟩.

bankrupt see DEPLETE

barbarous see FIERCE

bare, naked, nude, bald, barren mean deprived of naturally or conventionally appropriate covering. **Bare** implies the removal of what is additional, superfluous, ornamental, or dispensable ⟨a bleak apartment with *bare* walls⟩. **Naked** suggests absence of protective or ornamental covering but may imply a state of nature, of destitution, of defenselessness, of simple beauty ⟨poor, half-*naked* children shivering in the cold⟩. **Nude** applies esp. to the unclothed human figure ⟨a *nude* model posing for art students⟩. **Bald** implies actual or seeming absence of natural covering and may suggest a conspicuous bareness ⟨a *bald* mountain peak⟩. **Barren** often suggests aridity or impoverishment or sterility ⟨*barren* plains with few shrubs and no trees⟩.

barren see BARE

base, low, vile mean deserving of contempt because of the absence of higher values. **Base** stresses the ignoble and may suggest cruelty, treachery, greed, or grossness ⟨real estate developers with *base* motives⟩. **Low** may connote crafty cunning, vulgarity, or immorality and regularly implies an outraging of one's sense of decency or propriety ⟨refused to listen to such *low* talk⟩. **Vile,** the strongest of these words, tends to suggest disgusting depravity or filth ⟨a *vile* remark⟩ ⟨matricide, the *vilest* of crimes⟩.

bashful see SHY

batter see MAIM

bear, suffer, endure, abide, tolerate, stand mean to put up with something trying or painful. **Bear** usu. implies the power to sustain without flinching or breaking ⟨forced to *bear* one personal tragedy after another⟩. **Suffer** often suggests acceptance or passivity rather than courage or patience in bearing ⟨never *suffered* a single insult to go unchallenged⟩. **Endure** implies continuing firm or resolute through trials and difficulties ⟨*endured* years of rejection and neglect⟩. **Abide** suggests acceptance without resistance or protest ⟨I cannot *abide* her chronic rudeness⟩. **Tolerate** suggests overcoming or successfully controlling an impulse to resist, avoid, or resent something injurious or distasteful ⟨*tolerated* his affairs for the sake of the children⟩. **Stand** emphasizes even more strongly the ability to bear without discomposure or flinching ⟨she cannot *stand* teasing⟩. See in addition CARRY.

bearing, deportment, demeanor, mien, manner, carriage mean the outward manifestation of personality or attitude. **Bearing** is the most general of these words but now usu. implies characteristic posture ⟨a woman of regal *bearing*⟩. **Deportment** suggests actions or behavior as formed by breeding or training ⟨a child with atrocious *deportment*⟩. **Demeanor** suggests one's attitude toward others as expressed in outward behavior ⟨the haughty *demeanor* of a head waiter⟩. **Mien** is a literary term referring both to bearing and demeanor ⟨a *mien* of supreme self-satisfaction⟩. **Manner** implies characteristic or customary way of moving and gesturing and addressing others ⟨the imperious *manner* of a man used to giving orders⟩. **Carriage** applies chiefly to habitual posture in standing or walking ⟨the kind of *carriage* learned at elite private schools⟩.

beautiful, lovely, handsome, pretty, comely, fair mean exciting sensuous or aesthetic pleasure. **Beautiful** applies to whatever excites the keenest of pleasure to the senses and stirs emotion through the senses ⟨*beautiful* mountain scenery⟩. **Lovely** is close to *beautiful* but applies to a narrower range of emotional excitation in suggesting the graceful, delicate, or exquisite ⟨a *lovely* melody⟩. **Handsome** suggests aesthetic pleasure due to proportion, symmetry, or elegance ⟨a *handsome* Georgian mansion⟩. **Pretty** applies to superficial or insubstantial attractiveness ⟨a painter of conventionally *pretty* scenes⟩. **Comely** is like *handsome* in suggesting what is coolly approved rather than emotionally responded to ⟨the *comely* grace of a dancer⟩. **Fair** suggests beauty because of purity, flawlessness, or freshness ⟨looking for fashion models with *fair* faces⟩.

beautify see ADORN

beg, entreat, beseech, implore, supplicate, adjure, importune mean to ask urgently. **Beg** suggests earnestness or insistence esp. in asking for a favor ⟨children *begging* to stay up later⟩. **Entreat** implies an effort to persuade or to overcome resistance ⟨*entreated* him to change his mind⟩. **Beseech** implies great eagerness or anxiety ⟨I *beseech* you to have mercy⟩. **Implore** adds to *beseech* a suggestion of greater urgency or anguished appeal ⟨*implored* her not to leave him⟩. **Supplicate** suggests a posture of humility ⟨with bowed heads they *supplicated* their Lord⟩. **Adjure** implies advising as well as pleading and suggests the involving of something sacred ⟨in God's name I *adjure* you to cease⟩. **Importune** suggests an annoying persistence in trying to break down resistance to a request ⟨*importuned* Mother nearly every day to buy him a new bike⟩.

begin, commence, start, initiate, inaugurate mean to take the first step in a course, process, or operation. **Begin** and **commence** are practically identical in meaning but the latter suggests greater formality ⟨*began* taking dancing lessons⟩ ⟨let the games *commence*⟩. **Start,** opposed to *stop,* suggests a getting or setting into motion or setting out on a journey ⟨the procession *started* out slowly⟩. **Initiate** implies the taking of a first step of a process or series that is to continue ⟨*initiated* the custom of annual gift giving⟩. **Inaugurate** implies a ceremonious beginning ⟨the discovery of penicillin *inaugurated* a new medical age⟩.

beguile see DECEIVE

behave, conduct, deport, comport, acquit mean to act or to cause oneself to do something in a certain way. **Behave** may apply to the meeting of a standard of what is proper or decorous ⟨*behaved* very badly throughout the affair⟩. **Conduct** implies action or behavior that shows the extent of one's power to control or direct oneself ⟨*conducted* herself with unfailing good humor⟩. **Deport** implies behaving so as to show how far one conforms to conventional rules of discipline or propriety ⟨an ingenue who *deports* herself in the best musical tradition⟩. **Comport** suggests conduct measured by what is expected or required of one in a certain class or position ⟨*comported* themselves as the gentlemen they were⟩. **Acquit** applies to action under stress that deserves praise or meets expectations ⟨*acquitted* himself well in his first battle⟩.

belief, faith, credence, credit mean to assent to the truth of something offered for acceptance. **Belief** may or may not imply certitude in the believer ⟨my *belief* that I had caught all the errors⟩. **Faith** always does even where there is no evidence or proof ⟨an unshakable *faith* in God). **Credence** suggests intellectual assent without implying anything about grounds for assent (a theory given little *credence* by scientists). **Credit** implies assent on grounds other than direct proof (give no *credit* to idle rumors). See in addition OPINION.

belittle see DECRY

bellicose see BELLIGERENT

belligerent, bellicose, pugnacious, quarrelsome, contentious mean having an aggressive or fighting attitude. **Belligerent** implies being actually at war or engaged in hostilities (*belligerent* nations respected the country's neutrality). **Bellicose** suggests a disposition to fight (an intoxicated man in a *bellicose* mood). **Pugnacious** suggests a disposition that takes pleasure in personal combat (a *pugnacious* student always getting into scraps). **Quarrelsome** stresses an ill-natured readiness to fight without good cause (the stifling heat made us all *quarrelsome*). **Contentious** implies perverse and irritating fondness for arguing and quarreling (wearied by her *contentious* disposition).

bemoan see DEPLORE

bend see CURVE

beneficial, advantageous, profitable mean bringing good or gain. **Beneficial** implies esp. promoting health or well- being (legislation that would be *beneficial* to the elderly). **Advantageous** stresses a choice or preference that brings superiority or greater success in attaining an end (a famous surname proved to be *advantageous* in business). **Profitable** implies the yielding of useful or lucrative returns (study of the explanatory notes might be *profitable*).

benign see KIND

benignant see KIND

bent see GIFT

berate see SCOLD

beseech see BEG

bestial see BRUTAL

bestow see GIVE

bête noire see ABOMINATION

betray see REVEAL

better see IMPROVE

bewail see DEPLORE

bewilder see PUZZLE

bias *vb* see INCLINE

bias *n* see PREDILECTION

bid see COMMAND

billingsgate see ABUSE

biting see INCISIVE

bizarre see FANTASTIC

blamable see BLAMEWORTHY

blame see CRITICIZE

blameworthy, blamable, guilty, culpable mean deserving reproach or punishment. **Blameworthy** and **blamable** apply to any degree of reprehensibility (conduct adjudged *blameworthy* by a military court) (an accident for which no one is *blamable*). **Guilty** implies responsibility for or consciousness of crime, sin, or, at the least, grave error or misdoing (the defendant was found *guilty*). **Culpable** is weaker than *guilty* and is likely to connote malfeasance or errors of ignorance, omission, or negligence (a clear case of *culpable* neglect on the part of the landlord).

bland see SUAVE

blandish see COAX

blank see EMPTY

blasé see SOPHISTICATED

blatant see VOCIFEROUS

bleak see DISMAL

blemish, defect, flaw mean an imperfection that mars or damages. **Blemish** suggests something that affects only the surface or appearance (fair skin completely devoid of *blemishes*). **Defect** implies a lack, often hidden, of something that is essential to complete-

ness or perfect functioning (the smoke detector failed because of a mechanical *defect*). **Flaw** suggests a small defect in continuity or cohesion that is likely to cause failure under stress (a *flaw* in a pane of glass).

blench see RECOIL

blend see MIX

blithe see MERRY

block see HINDER

bloody, sanguinary, sanguine, gory mean affected by or involving the shedding of blood. **Bloody** is applied esp. to things that are actually covered with blood or are made up of blood (*bloody* hands). **Sanguinary** applies esp. to something attended by, or someone inclined to, bloodshed (the Civil War was America's most *sanguinary* conflict). **Sanguine** is applied specif. to bleeding, bloodthirstiness, or the color of blood (one of the most *sanguine* of the Jacobean revenge tragedies). **Gory** suggests a profusion of blood and slaughter (exceptionally *gory*, even for a teenage horror movie).

blot out see ERASE

bluff, blunt, brusque, curt, crusty, gruff mean abrupt and unceremonious in speech and manner. **Bluff** connotes good- natured outspokenness and unconventionality (a bartender with a *bluff* manner). **Blunt** suggests directness of expression in disregard of others' feelings (a *blunt* appraisal of the performance). **Brusque** applies to a sharpness or ungraciousness (a *brusque* response to a civil question). **Curt** implies disconcerting shortness or rude conciseness (a *curt* comment about the cause of the foul- up). **Crusty** suggests a harsh or surly manner sometimes concealing an inner kindliness (a *crusty* exterior that conceals a heart of gold). **Gruff** suggests a hoarse or husky speech which may imply bad temper but more often implies embarrassment or shyness (puts on a *gruff* pose in front of strangers).

blunder see ERROR

blunt see BLUFF, DULL

boast, brag, vaunt, crow mean to express pride in oneself or one's accomplishments. **Boast** often suggests ostentation and exaggeration (ready to *boast* of every trivial success), but it may imply acclaiming with proper and justifiable pride (the town *boasts* one of the best hospitals in the area). **Brag** suggests crudity and artlessness in glorifying oneself (boys *bragging* to each other). **Vaunt** usu. connotes more pomp and bombast than *boast* and less crudity or naivete than *brag* (used the occasion to *vaunt* the country's military might). **Crow** usu. implies exultant boasting or bragging (loved to *crow* about his ancestors).

bodily, physical, corporeal, corporal, somatic mean of or relating to the human body. **Bodily** suggests contrasts with *mental* or *spiritual* (an intellectual who also had *bodily* needs). **Physical** suggests more vaguely or less explicitly an organic structure (their ordeal left them at the point of *physical* exhaustion). **Corporeal** suggests the substance of which the body is composed (a divinity who assumed *corporeal* existence). **Corporal** applies chiefly to things that affect or involve the body (a teacher who still used *corporal* punishment). **Somatic** implies contrast with *psychical* and is useful as being free of theological and poetic connotations (*somatic* reactions to the drug).

boisterous see VOCIFEROUS

bombard see ATTACK

bona fide see AUTHENTIC

bon vivant see EPICURE

boorish, churlish, loutish, clownish mean uncouth in manners or appearance. **Boorish** implies rudeness of manner due to insensitiveness to others' feelings and unwillingness to be agreeable (your *boorish* behavior at the wedding reception). **Churlish** suggests surliness, unresponsiveness, and ungraciousness 〈*churlish* remarks made during a television interview〉. **Loutish** implies bodily awkwardness together with stupidity 〈her *loutish* boyfriend spoiled the cocktail party〉. **Clownish** suggests ill-bred awkwardness, ignorance or stupidity, ungainliness, and often a propensity for absurd antics 〈*clownish* conduct that was out of keeping with the solemn occasion〉.

boost see LIFT

booty see SPOIL

border, margin, verge, edge, rim, brim, brink mean a line or outer part that marks the limit of something. **Border** denotes the part of a surface that marks its boundary line 〈the magazine cover's red *border*〉. **Margin** denotes a border of definite width or distinguishing character 〈a *margin* of one inch on the page's left side〉. **Verge** applies to the line marking an extreme limit or termination of something 〈an empire that extended to the *verge* of the known world〉. **Edge** denotes the termination line made by two converging surfaces as of a blade or a box 〈the *edge* of a table〉. **Rim** applies to an edge of something circular or curving 〈the *rim* of a wagon wheel〉. **Brim** applies to the upper inner rim of something hollow 〈fill the cup to the *brim*〉. **Brink** denotes the abrupt edge of something that falls away steeply 〈walked to the *brink* of the cliff〉.

bother see ANNOY

bountiful see LIBERAL

brag see BOAST

brandish see SWING

breach, infraction, violation, trespass, infringement mean the breaking of a law, duty, or obligation. **Breach** implies failure to keep a promise 〈sued for *breech* of contract〉. **Infraction** usu. implies the breaking of a law or promise 〈an *infraction* of the school rules〉. **Violation** implies the flagrant disregard of the law or the rights of others and often suggests the exercise of force or violence 〈the police interference was a *violation* of the right to free assembly〉. **Trespass** implies an encroachment upon the rights, the comfort, or the property of others 〈a would-be burglar who was arrested for *trespass*〉. **Infringement** implies an encroachment upon a legally protected right or privilege 〈any unauthorized reproduction constitutes an *infringement* of the book's copyright〉.

break down see ANALYZE

bridle see RESTRAIN

brief, short mean lacking length. **Brief** applies primarily to duration and may imply condensation, conciseness, or occas. intensity 〈a *brief* speech〉. **Short** may imply sudden stoppage or incompleteness 〈the interview was rather *short*〉.

bright, brilliant, radiant, luminous, lustrous mean shining or glowing with light. **Bright** implies emitting or reflecting a high degree of light 〈one of the *brightest* stars in the sky〉. **Brilliant** implies intense often sparkling brightness 〈*brilliant* diamonds〉. **Radiant** stresses the emission or seeming emission of rays of light 〈an imposing figure in *radiant* armor〉. **Luminous** implies emission of steady, suffused, glowing light by reflection or in surrounding darkness 〈*luminous* white houses dot the shore〉. **Lustrous** stresses an even, rich light from a surface that reflects brightly without sparkling or glittering 〈the *lustrous* sheen of fine satin〉.

brilliant see BRIGHT

brim see BORDER

brink see BORDER

brisk see AGILE

brittle see FRAGILE

broach see EXPRESS

broad, wide, deep mean having horizontal extent. **Broad** and **wide** apply to a surface measured or viewed from side to side 〈a *broad* avenue〉. **Wide** is more common when units of measurement are mentioned 〈rugs eight feet *wide*〉 or applied to unfilled space between limits 〈*wide* doorway〉. **Broad** is preferred when full horizontal extent is considered 〈*broad* shoulders〉. **Deep** may indicate horizontal extent away from the observer or from a front or peripheral point 〈a *deep* cupboard〉 〈*deep* woods〉.

browbeat see INTIMIDATE

brusque see BLUFF

brutal, brutish, bestial, feral mean characteristic of an animal in nature, action, or instinct. **Brutal** applies to people, their acts, or their words and suggests a lack of intelligence, feeling, or humanity 〈a senseless and *brutal* war〉. **Brutish** stresses likeness to an animal in low intelligence, in base appetites, and in behavior based on instinct 〈*brutish* developers were ready to tear down the historic mansion〉. **Bestial** suggests a depravity or state of degradation unworthy of man and fit only for beasts 〈decadent Rome carried sexual indulgence to a *bestial* level〉. **Feral** suggests the savagery or ferocity of wild animals 〈war had unleashed his *feral* impulses〉.

brutish see BRUTAL

bucolic see RURAL

bugbear see ABOMINATION

bulge see PROJECTION

bulk, mass, volume mean the aggregate that forms a body or unit. **Bulk** implies an aggregate that is impressively large, heavy, or numerous 〈the darkened *bulks* of skyscrapers towered over him〉. **Mass** suggests an aggregate made by piling together things of the same kind 〈the cave held a *mass* of weapons〉. **Volume** applies to an aggregate without shape or outline and capable of flowing or fluctuating 〈a tremendous *volume* of water〉.

bulldoze see INTIMIDATE

bully see INTIMIDATE

burdensome see ONEROUS

burlesque see CARICATURE

bury see HIDE

business, commerce, trade, industry, traffic mean activity concerned with the supplying and distribution of commodities. **Business** may be an inclusive term but specif. designates the activities of those engaged in the purchase or sale of commodities or in related financial transactions 〈the *business* section of the newspaper〉. **Commerce** and **trade** imply the exchange and transportation of commodities 〈full power to regulate interstate *commerce*〉 〈seek ways to increase foreign *trade*〉. **Industry** applies to the producing of commodities, esp. by manufacturing or processing, usu. on a large scale 〈*industry* has overtaken agriculture in the South〉. **Traffic** applies to the operation and functioning of public carriers of goods and persons 〈*traffic* managers have rediscovered the railroads〉. See in addition WORK.

busy, industrious, diligent, assiduous, sedulous mean actively engaged or occupied. **Busy** chiefly stresses activity as opposed to idleness or leisure 〈too *busy* to spend time with the children〉. **Industrious** implies characteristic or habitual devotion to work 〈they are by nature an *industrious* people〉. **Diligent** suggests earnest application to some specific object or pursuit 〈very *diligent* in her pursuit of a degree〉. **Assiduous** stresses careful and unremitting application 〈mastered the piano only after *assiduous* practice〉. **Sedulous** implies painstaking and persevering application 〈a *sedulous* reconstruction of the events of that night〉.

butt in see INTRUDE

C

cabal see PLOT

cajole see COAX

calamity see DISASTER

calculate, compute, estimate, reckon mean to determine something mathematically. **Calculate** is usu. preferred in reference to highly intricate processes and problematical rather than exact or definite results ⟨*calculated* when the comet would next appear⟩. **Compute** is the simpler term for reaching an exact result by simpler arithmetic processes ⟨*computed* the interest at a quarterly rate⟩. **Estimate** applies chiefly to the forecasting of costs or trends and suggests a seeking of usable but tentative and approximate results ⟨the mechanic *estimated* the cost of repairs⟩. **Reckon** usu. suggests the simpler arithmetical processes or rough- and-ready methods ⟨*reckoned* the number of yards of fabric needed⟩.

call see SUMMON

calling see WORK

calm, tranquil, serene, placid, peaceful mean quiet and free from disturbance. **Calm** often implies a contrast with a foregoing or nearby state of agitation or violence ⟨the protests ended, and the streets were *calm* again⟩. **Tranquil** suggests a very deep quietude or composure ⟨the *tranquil* beauty of a formal garden⟩. **Serene** stresses an unclouded and lofty tranquility ⟨a woman of *serene* beauty⟩. **Placid** suggests an undisturbed appearance and often implies a degree of complacency ⟨led a very *placid* existence⟩. **Peaceful** implies a state of repose in contrast with or following strife or turmoil ⟨a former firebrand grown *peaceful* in his old age⟩.

calumniate see MALIGN

cancel see ERASE

candid see FRANK

canon see LAW

cant see DIALECT

capable see ABLE

capacious see SPACIOUS

capitulate see YIELD

caprice, whim, vagary, crotchet mean an irrational or unpredictable idea or desire. **Caprice** stresses lack of apparent motivation and suggests willfulness ⟨by sheer *caprice* she quit her job⟩. **Whim** implies a fantastic, capricious turn of mind or inclination ⟨an odd antique that was bought on a *whim*⟩. **Vagary** stresses the erratic, irresponsible character of the notion or desire ⟨recently he had been prone to strange *vagaries*⟩. **Crochet** implies an eccentric opinion or preference ⟨a serious scientist equally known for his bizarre *crotchets*⟩.

capricious see INCONSTANT

captious see CRITICAL

captivate see ATTRACT

capture see CATCH

cardinal see ESSENTIAL

care, concern, solicitude, anxiety, worry mean a troubled or engrossed state of mind or the thing that causes this. **Care** implies oppression of the mind weighed down by responsibility or disquieted by apprehension ⟨a face worn by a host of *cares*⟩. **Concern** implies a troubled state of mind because of personal interest, relation, or affection ⟨your happiness is my only *concern*⟩. **Solicitude** implies great concern and connotes either thoughtful or hovering attentiveness toward another ⟨behaved with typical maternal *solicitude*⟩. **Anxiety** stresses anguished uncertainty or fear of misfortune or failure ⟨plagued by *anxiety* and self-doubt⟩. **Worry** suggests fretting over matters that may or may not be real cause for anxiety ⟨a businessman's endless list of *worries*⟩.

careful, meticulous, scrupulous, punctilious mean showing close attention to detail. **Careful** implies attentiveness and cautiousness in avoiding mistakes ⟨a *careful* worker⟩. **Meticulous** may imply either commendable extreme carefulness or a hampering finicky caution over small points ⟨*meticulous* scholarship⟩. **Scrupulous** applies to what is proper or fitting or ethical ⟨*scrupulous* honesty⟩. **Punctilious** implies minute, even excessive attention to fine points ⟨*punctilious* observance of ritual⟩.

caricature, burlesque, parody, travesty mean a comic or grotesque imitation. **Caricature** implies ludicrous exaggeration of the characteristic features of a subject ⟨the movie is a *caricature* of the novel⟩. **Burlesque** implies mockery either through treating a trivial subject in a mock-heroic style or through giving a serious or lofty subject a frivolous treatment ⟨a *burlesque* that treats a petty quarrel as a great battle⟩. **Parody** applies esp. to treatment of a trivial or ludicrous subject in the exactly imitated style of a well-known author or work ⟨a witty *parody* of a popular soap opera⟩. **Travesty** implies that the subject remains unchanged but that the style is extravagant or absurd ⟨this production is a *travesty* of a classic opera⟩.

carnal, fleshly, sensual, animal mean having a relation to the body. **Carnal** may mean only this but more often connotes derogatorily an action or manifestation of man's lower nature ⟨a woman who was victimized by her own *carnal* appetites⟩. **Fleshly** is somewhat less derogatory than *carnal* ⟨a saint who wrote at length on his *fleshly* temptations⟩. **Sensual** may apply to any gratification of a bodily desire or pleasure but commonly implies sexual appetite with absence of the spiritual or intellectual ⟨a place infamous for providing *sensual* delight⟩. **Animal** stresses a relation to man's physical as distinguished from his rational nature ⟨led a mindless, *animal* existence⟩.

carping see CRITICAL

carriage see BEARING

carry, bear, convey, transport mean to move something from one place to another. **Carry** tends to emphasize the means by which something is moved or the fact of supporting off the ground while moving ⟨*carried* the basket on her head⟩. **Bear** stresses the effort of sustaining or the importance of what is carried ⟨*bear* the banner aloft⟩. **Convey** suggests the continuous movement of something in the mass ⟨the pipeline *conveys* oil for more than a thousand miles⟩. **Transport** implies the moving of something to its destination ⟨trucks *transporting* farm produce to market⟩.

case see INSTANCE

cast see DISCARD, THROW

castigate see PUNISH

casual see ACCIDENTAL, RANDOM

cataclysm see DISASTER

catastrophe see DISASTER

catch, capture, trap, snare, entrap, ensnare, bag mean to come to possess or control by or as if by seizing. **Catch** implies the seizing of something in motion or in flight or in hiding ⟨*caught* the dog as it ran by⟩. **Capture** suggests taking by overcoming resistance or difficulty ⟨*capture* a stronghold of the enemy⟩. **Trap, snare, entrap, ensnare** imply seizing by some device that holds the one caught at the mercy of his captor. *Trap* and *snare* apply more commonly to physical seizing ⟨*trap* animals⟩ ⟨*snared* butterflies with a net⟩. *Entrap* and *ensnare* more often are figurative ⟨*entrapped* the witness with a trick question⟩ ⟨a sting operation that *ensnared* burglars⟩. **Bag** implies shooting down a fleeing or distant prey ⟨*bagged* a brace of pheasants⟩.

cause, determinant, antecedent, reason, occasion mean something that produces an effect. **Cause** applies to any event, circumstance, or condition that brings about or helps bring about a result ⟨an icy road was the *cause* of the accident⟩. **Determinant** applies to a cause that fixes the nature of what results ⟨heredity may be a *determinant* of heart disease⟩. **Antecedent** applies to that which has preceded and may therefore be in some degree responsible for what follows ⟨the *antecedents* of the famine⟩. **Reason** applies to a traceable or explainable cause of a known effect ⟨the *reason* I was late was that my car would not start⟩. **Occasion** applies to a particular time or situation at which underlying causes become effective ⟨the assassination was the *occasion* of the war⟩.

caustic, mordant, acrid, scathing mean stingingly incisive. **Caustic** suggests a biting wit ⟨*caustic* comments about her singing ability⟩. **Mordant** suggests a wit that is used with deadly effectiveness ⟨*mordant* reviews put the play out of its misery⟩. **Acrid** implies bitterness and often malevolence ⟨a speech marked by *acrid* invective⟩. **Scathing** implies indignant attacks delivered with fierce severity ⟨a *scathing* satire of corporate life⟩.

cautious, circumspect, wary, chary mean prudently watchful and discreet in the face of danger or risk. **Cautious** implies the exercise of forethought usu. prompted by fear of danger ⟨a *cautious* driver⟩. **Circumspect** suggests less fear and stresses the surveying of all possible consequences before acting or deciding ⟨the panel must be *circumspect* in assigning blame⟩. **Wary** emphasizes suspiciousness and alertness in watching for danger and cunning in escaping it ⟨be *wary* of those claiming to have all the answers⟩. **Chary** implies a cautious reluctance to give, act, or speak freely ⟨I am *chary* of signing papers I have not read⟩.

cease see STOP

celebrate see KEEP

celebrated see FAMOUS

celerity, alacrity mean quickness in movement or action. **Celerity** implies speed in accomplishing work ⟨got dinner ready with remarkable *celerity*⟩. **Alacrity** stresses promptness in response to suggestion or command ⟨the students volunteered with surprising *alacrity*⟩.

censorious see CRITICAL

censure see CRITICIZE

ceremonial, ceremonious, formal, conventional mean marked by attention to or adhering strictly to prescribed forms. **Ceremonial** and **ceremonious** both imply strict attention to what is prescribed by custom or by ritual, but *ceremonial* applies to things that are associated with ceremonies ⟨a *ceremonial* offering⟩, *ceremonious* to persons given to ceremony or to acts attended by ceremony ⟨a *ceremonious* old man⟩. **Formal** applies both to things prescribed by and to persons obedient to custom and may suggest stiff, restrained, or old-fashioned behavior ⟨a *formal* report on the summit meeting⟩ ⟨a *formal* manner⟩. **Conventional** implies accord with general custom and usage and may suggest a stodgy lack of originality or independence ⟨*conventional* courtesy⟩ ⟨*conventional* standards of beauty⟩.

ceremonious see CEREMONIAL

certain see SURE

certainty, certitude, assurance, conviction mean a state of being free from doubt. **Certainty** and **certitude** are very close; *certainty* may stress the existence of objective proof ⟨claims that cannot be confirmed with any scientific *certainty*⟩, while **certitude** may emphasize a faith in something not needing or not capable of proof ⟨believes with all *certitude* in an afterlife⟩. **Assurance** implies confidence rather than intellectual certainty ⟨as much *assurance* as is ever possible where hurricanes are concerned⟩. **Conviction** applies esp. to belief strongly held by an individual ⟨holds firm *convictions* about everything⟩.

certify, attest, witness, vouch mean to testify to the truth or genuineness of something. **Certify** usu. applies to a written statement, esp. one carrying a signature or seal ⟨*certified* that the candidate had met all requirements⟩. **Attest** applies to oral or written testimony usu. from experts or witnesses ⟨*attested* to the authenticity of the document⟩. **Witness** applies to the subscribing of one's own name to a document as evidence of its genuineness ⟨two persons who *witnessed* the signing of the will⟩. **Vouch** applies to one who testifies as a competent authority or a reliable person and who will defend his affirmation ⟨willing to *vouch* for the woman's integrity⟩. See in addition APPROVE.

certitude see CERTAINTY

champion see SUPPORT

change, alter, vary, modify mean to make or become different. **Change** implies making either an essential difference often amounting to a loss of original identity or a substitution of one thing for another ⟨*changed* the shirt for a larger size⟩. **Alter** implies a difference in some particular respect without suggesting loss of identity ⟨slightly *altered* the original design⟩. **Vary** stresses a breaking away from sameness, duplication, or exact repetition ⟨you can *vary* the speed of the conveyor belt⟩. **Modify** suggests a difference that limits, restricts, or adapts to a new purpose ⟨*modified* the building for use by the handicapped⟩.

character see DISPOSITION, QUALITY, TYPE

characteristic, individual, peculiar, distinctive mean indicating a special quality or identity. **Characteristic** applies to something that distinguishes or identifies a person or thing or class ⟨responded with his *characteristic* wit⟩. **Individual** stresses qualities that distinguish one from all other members of the same kind or class ⟨a highly *individual* writing style⟩. **Peculiar** applies to qualities possessed only by a particular individual or class or kind and stresses rarity or uniqueness ⟨an eccentricity that is *peculiar* to the British⟩. **Distinctive** indicates qualities distinguishing and uncommon and often superior or praiseworthy ⟨her *distinctive* aura of grace and elegance⟩.

charge see ACCUSE, COMMAND

charity see MERCY

charm see ATTRACT

charter see HIRE

chary see CAUTIOUS

chase, pursue, follow, trail mean to go after or on the track of something or someone. **Chase** implies going swiftly after and trying to overtake something fleeing or running ⟨a dog *chasing* a cat⟩. **Pursue** suggests a continuing effort to overtake, reach, attain ⟨*pursued* the criminal through the narrow streets⟩. **Follow** puts less emphasis upon speed or intent to overtake ⟨a stray dog *followed* me home⟩. **Trail** may stress a following of tracks or traces rather than a visible object ⟨*trail* deer through deep snow⟩.

chaste, pure, modest, decent mean free from all taint of what is lewd or salacious. **Chaste** primarily implies a refraining from acts or even thoughts or desires that are not virginal or not sanctioned by marriage vows ⟨maintained *chaste* relations until marriage⟩. **Pure** differs from *chaste* in implying innocence and absence of temptation rather than control of one's impulses and actions ⟨the *pure* of heart⟩. **Modest** and **decent** apply esp. to deportment and dress as outward signs of inward chastity or purity ⟨her dress was always *modest*⟩ ⟨*decent* people didn't go to such movies⟩.

chasten see PUNISH

chastise see PUNISH

cheat, cozen, defraud, swindle mean to get something by dishonesty or deception. **Cheat** suggests using trickery that escapes observation ⟨*cheated* in the written examination⟩. **Cozen** implies artful persuading or flattering to attain a thing or a purpose ⟨always able to *cozen* her doting grandfather out of a few dollars⟩. **Defraud** stresses depriving one of his rights and usu. connotes deliberate perversion of the truth ⟨her own lawyer *defrauded* her of her inheritance⟩. **Swindle** implies large-scale cheating by means of misrepresentation or abuse of confidence ⟨widows were *swindled* of their savings by con artists⟩.

check see RESTRAIN
cheek see TEMERITY
cheerless see DISMAL
cherish see APPRECIATE
chide see REPROVE
chimerical see IMAGINARY
chivalrous see CIVIL
chivy see BAIT

choice *n* Choice, option, alternative, preference, selection, election mean the act or opportunity of choosing or the thing chosen. **Choice** suggests the opportunity or privilege of choosing freely ⟨total freedom of *choice* in the matter⟩. **Option** implies a power to choose that is specif. granted or guaranteed ⟨the *option* of paying now or later⟩. **Alternative** implies a necessity to choose one and reject another possibility ⟨the *alternatives* were peace with dishonor or war⟩. **Preference** suggests the guidance of choice by one's judgment or predilections ⟨stated a *preference* for red-haired women⟩. **Selection** implies a wide range of choice ⟨a store offering a varied *selection* of furniture⟩. **Election** implies an end or purpose which requires exercise of judgment ⟨the careful *election* of college courses⟩.

choice *adj* Choice, exquisite, elegant, rare, dainty, delicate mean having qualities that appeal to a cultivated taste. **Choice** stresses preeminence in quality or kind ⟨a *choice* bit of gossip⟩. **Exquisite** implies a perfection in workmanship or design that appeals only to very sensitive taste ⟨an *exquisite* slender gold bracelet⟩. **Elegant** applies to what is rich and luxurious but restrained by good taste ⟨the *elegant* dining room boasts genuine French antiques⟩. **Rare** suggests an uncommon excellence ⟨refuses to drink any but the *rarest* of wines⟩. **Delicate** implies exquisiteness, subtlety, fragility ⟨the play's *delicate* charm was lost on screen⟩. **Dainty** sometimes also suggests smallness and appeal to the eye or palate ⟨precious, *dainty* food that leaves you hungry⟩.

choleric see IRASCIBLE
chore see TASK
chronic see INVETERATE
churlish see BOORISH
chutzpah see TEMERITY
circumscribe see LIMIT
circumspect see CAUTIOUS
circumstance see OCCURRENCE

circumstantial, minute, particular, detailed mean dealing with a matter fully and usu. point by point. **Circumstantial** implies fullness of detail that fixes something described in time and space ⟨a *circumstantial* account of our visit⟩. **Minute** implies close and searching attention to the smallest details ⟨a *minute* examination of a fossil⟩. **Particular** implies a precise attention to every detail ⟨a *particular* description of the scene of the crime⟩. **Detailed** stresses abundance or completeness of detail ⟨a *detailed* analysis of the event⟩.

circumvent see FRUSTRATE
citation see ENCOMIUM
cite see SUMMON

citizen, subject, national mean a person owing allegiance to and entitled to the protection of a sovereign state. **Citizen** is preferred for one owing allegiance to a state in which sovereign power is retained by the people and sharing in the political rights of those people ⟨the inalienable rights of a free *citizen*⟩. **Subject** implies allegiance to a personal sovereign such as a monarch ⟨the king enjoys the loyalty of his *subjects*⟩. **National** designates one who may claim the protection of a state and applies esp. to one living or traveling outside that state ⟨American *nationals* currently in Libya⟩.

civil, polite, courteous, gallant, chivalrous mean observant of the forms required by good breeding. **Civil** often suggests little more than the avoidance of overt rudeness ⟨a *civil* reply that showed a lack of real enthusiasm⟩. **Polite** commonly implies polish of speech and manners and sometimes suggests an absence of cordiality ⟨the minister's conversation was as *polite* as it was condescending⟩. **Courteous** implies more actively considerate or dignified politeness ⟨clerks who were unfailingly *courteous* to customers⟩. **Gallant** and **chivalrous** imply courteous attentiveness esp. to women. *Gallant* suggests spirited and dashing behavior and ornate expressions of courtesy ⟨a *gallant* suitor of the old school⟩. *Chivalrous* suggests high-minded and self-sacrificing behavior ⟨a *chivalrous* display of duty⟩.

claim see DEMAND
clamorous see VOCIFEROUS
clandestine see SECRET

clear *adj* Clear, transparent, translucent, limpid mean capable of being seen through. **Clear** implies absence of cloudiness, haziness, or muddiness ⟨*clear* water⟩. **Transparent** implies being so clear that objects can be seen distinctly ⟨a *transparent* sheet of film⟩. **Translucent** implies the passage of light but not a clear view of what lies beyond ⟨*translucent* frosted glass⟩. **Limpid** suggests the soft clearness of pure water ⟨pale *limpid* blue eyes⟩.

clear *adj* Clear, perspicuous, lucid mean quickly and easily understood. **Clear** implies freedom from obscurity, ambiguity, or undue complexity ⟨the instructions were perfectly *clear*⟩. **Perspicuous** applies to a style that is simple and elegant as well as clear ⟨the *perspicuous* beauty of Shakespeare's sonnets⟩. **Lucid** suggests a clear logical coherence and evident order of arrangement ⟨an amazingly *lucid* description of nuclear physics⟩. See in addition EVIDENT.

clear-cut see INCISIVE
cleave see STICK, TEAR
clemency see MERCY

clever, adroit, cunning, ingenious mean having or showing practical wit or skill in contriving. **Clever** stresses physical or mental quickness, deftness, or great aptitude ⟨a person *clever* with horses⟩. **Adroit** often implies a skillful use of expedients to achieve one's purpose in spite of difficulties ⟨an *adroit* negotiator of business deals⟩. **Cunning** implies great skill in constructing or creating ⟨a writer who is *cunning* in his manipulation of the reader⟩. **Ingenious** suggests the power of inventing or discovering a new way of accomplishing something ⟨an *ingenious* computer engineer keeping pace with ever-changing technology⟩. See in addition INTELLIGENT.

climax see SUMMIT
cling see STICK
cloak see DISGUISE
clog see HAMPER

close *vb* Close, end, conclude, finish, complete, terminate mean to bring or come to a stopping point or limit. **Close** usu. implies that something has been in some way open as well as unfinished ⟨*close* a debate⟩. **End** conveys a strong sense of finality ⟨*ended* his life⟩.

Conclude may imply a formal closing (as of a meeting) 〈the service *concluded* with a blessing〉. **Finish** may stress completion of a final step in a process (after it is painted, the house will be *finished*). **Complete** implies the removal of all deficiencies or a successful finishing of what has been undertaken 〈the resolving of this last issue *completes* the agreement〉. **Terminate** implies the setting of a limit in time or space 〈your employment *terminates* after three months〉.

close *adj* Close, dense, compact, thick mean massed tightly together. **Close** implies the least possible space or interval between elements without actual pressure or loss of individual identity 〈the paintings are hung *close* together〉. **Dense** implies compression of parts or elements so great as to be almost impenetrable 〈the *dense* growth in a tropical rain forest〉. **Compact** suggests a firm union or consolidation of parts within a small compass 〈a lithe, *compact,* muscular body〉. **Thick** implies a concentrated abundance of parts or units 〈a *thick* head of hair〉. See in addition STINGY.

clownish see BOORISH
cloy see SATIATE
clumsy see AWKWARD
clutch see TAKE
coalesce see MIX
coalition see ALLIANCE
coarse, vulgar, gross, obscene, ribald mean offensive to good taste or morals. **Coarse** implies roughness, rudeness, or crudeness of spirit, behavior, or language 〈found the *coarse* humor of her coworkers offensive〉. **Vulgar** often implies boorishness or ill-breeding 〈a loud *vulgar* laugh〉. **Gross** implies extreme coarseness and insensitiveness 〈*gross* eating habits make others lose their appetites〉. **Obscene** applies to anything strongly repulsive to the sense of decency and propriety esp. in sexual matters 〈*obscene* language that violated the broadcasters' code〉. **Ribald** applies to what is amusingly or picturesquely vulgar or irreverent or mildly indecent 〈entertained the campers with *ribald* folk songs〉.

coax, cajole, wheedle, blandish mean to influence or gently urge by caressing or flattering. **Coax** suggests an artful pleading or teasing in an attempt to gain one's ends 〈*coaxed* their friends into staying for dinner〉. **Cajole** usu. suggests an ingratiating artfulness in attempting to persuade 〈*cajoled* by his wife into trying the exotic dish〉. **Wheedle** stresses the use of soft words, artful flattery, or seductive appeal 〈a pretty young thing *wheedled* the old man out of his money〉. **Blandish** suggests open flattery and the obvious use of charm in an effort to win over 〈a salesclerk not above shameless *blandishing* in order to make a sale〉.

cocksure see SURE
coerce see FORCE
coeval see CONTEMPORARY
cogent see VALID
cogitate see THINK
cognizant see AWARE
cohere see STICK
coincide see AGREE
coincident see CONTEMPORARY
collate see COMPARE
colleague see CONFEDERATE
collect see GATHER
collected see COOL
colossal see ENORMOUS
combat see OPPOSE
combine see JOIN
comely see BEAUTIFUL
comfort, console, solace mean to offer help in relieving suffering or sorrow. **Comfort** implies imparting cheer, strength, or encouragement as well as lessen-

ing pain 〈a message intended to *comfort* the grieving family〉. **Console** emphasizes the alleviating of grief or mitigating the sense of loss rather than distinct or full relief 〈*consoled* herself by remembering the good times〉. **Solace** suggests a lifting of spirits often from loneliness or boredom as well as from pain or grief 〈*solaced* himself by reading books and writing poetry〉.

comfortable, cozy, snug, easy, restful mean enjoying or providing a position of contentment and security. **Comfort able** applies to anything that encourages serenity, well- being, or complacency as well as physical ease 〈began to feel *comfortable* in her new surroundings〉. **Cozy** suggests warmth, shelter, assured ease, and friendliness 〈a *cozy* neighborhood coffee shop〉. **Snug** suggests having just enough space for comfort and safety but no more 〈a *snug* little cottage〉. **Easy** implies relief from or absence of anything likely to cause physical or mental discomfort or constraint 〈our host had a warm, *easy* manner〉. **Restful** applies to whatever induces or contributes to rest or relaxation 〈a quiet *restful* inn where indolence is encouraged〉.

comic see LAUGHABLE
comical see LAUGHABLE
command *vb* Command, order, bid, enjoin, direct, instruct, charge mean to issue orders. **Command** and **order** imply authority and usu. some degree of formality and impersonality. *Command* stresses official exercise of authority 〈when his superior *commands,* a soldier obeys〉. *Order* may suggest peremptory or arbitrary exercise 〈*ordered* his men about like slaves〉. **Bid** suggests giving orders peremptorily (as to children or servants) 〈*bade* her fix a drink for him〉. **Enjoin** implies giving an order or direction authoritatively and urgently and often with admonition or solicitude 〈our guide *enjoined* us to be quiet in the cathedral〉. **Direct** and **instruct** both connote expectation of obedience and usu. concern specific points of procedure or method, *instruct* sometimes implying greater explicitness or formality 〈*directed* her assistant to hold all calls〉 〈the judge *instructed* the jury to ignore the remark〉. **Charge** adds to *enjoin* an implication of imposing as a duty or responsibility 〈*charged* by the President with a covert mission〉.

command *n* see POWER
commemorate see KEEP
commence see BEGIN
commensurable see PROPORTIONAL
commensurate see PROPORTIONAL
commerce see BUSINESS
commingle see MIX
commisseration see PITY
commit, entrust, confide, consign, relegate mean to assign to a person or place esp. for safekeeping. **Commit** may express the general idea of delivering into another's charge or the special sense of transferring to a superior power or to a special place of custody 〈*committed* the person to prison〉. **Entrust** implies committing with trust and confidence 〈the president is *entrusted* with broad powers〉. **Confide** implies entrusting with assurance or reliance 〈*confided* all power over my financial affairs to an attorney〉. **Consign** suggests transferring to remove from one's control with formality or finality 〈*consigned* my paintings to a gallery for sale〉. **Relegate** implies a consigning to a particular class or sphere often with a suggestion of getting rid of 〈*relegated* to an obscure position in the company〉.

commodious see SPACIOUS
common, ordinary, plain, familiar, popular, vulgar mean generally met with and not in any way special, strange, or unusual. **Common** implies usual everyday quality or frequency of occurrence 〈a *common* error〉

⟨lacked *common* honesty⟩ and may additionally suggest inferiority or coarseness ⟨his *common* manners shocked her family⟩. **Ordinary** stresses conformance in quality or kind with the regular order of things ⟨an *ordinary* pleasant summer day⟩ ⟨a very *ordinary* sort of man⟩. **Plain** is likely to suggest homely simplicity ⟨she comes from *plain*, hard-working stock⟩. **Familiar** stresses the fact of being generally known and easily recognized ⟨a *familiar* melody⟩. **Popular** applies to what is accepted by or prevalent among people in general sometimes in contrast to upper classes or special groups ⟨a hero typically found in *popular* fiction⟩. **Vulgar,** otherwise similar to *popular,* is likely to carry derogatory connotations (as of inferiority or coarseness) ⟨goods designed to appeal to the *vulgar* taste⟩. See in addition RECIPROCAL.

common sense see SENSE

commotion, tumult, turmoil, upheaval mean great physical, mental, or emotional excitement. **Commotion** suggests disturbing sometimes violent bustle or hubbub ⟨the unexpected dinner guests caused quite a *commotion*⟩. **Tumult** suggests a shaking up or stirring up that is accompanied by uproar, din, or great disorder ⟨the town was in a *tumult* over the war news⟩. **Turmoil** suggests a state devoid of calm and seething with excitement ⟨a well-ordered life that was suddenly thrown into great *turmoil*⟩. **Upheaval** suggests a violent and forceful thrusting that results in a heaving up or an overthrowing ⟨a nation in need of peace after years of *upheaval*⟩.

compact see CLOSE

compare, contrast, collate mean to set side by side in order to show differences and likenesses. **Compare** implies an aim of showing relative values or excellences by bringing out characteristic qualities whether similar or divergent ⟨wanted to *compare* the convention facilities of the two cities⟩. **Contrast** implies an emphasis on differences ⟨*contrasted* the computerized system with the old filing cards⟩. **Collate** implies minute and critical inspection in order to note points of agreement or divergence ⟨data from police districts across the country will be *collated*⟩.

compass see RANGE

compassion see PITY

compatible see CONSONANT

compel see FORCE

compendious see CONCISE

compendium, syllabus, digest, survey, sketch, précis, aperçu mean a brief treatment of a subject. A **compendium** gathers together and presents in concise or in outline form all the essential facts and details of a subject ⟨a *compendium* of computer technology to date⟩. A **syllabus** gives the material necessary for a comprehensive view of a whole subject often in the form of a series of heads or propositions ⟨a *syllabus* for a college history course⟩. A **digest** presents material gathered from many sources and arranged for ready reference ⟨a *digest* of world opinion on the Central America question⟩. A **survey** is a brief but comprehensive treatment presented often as a preliminary to further study or discussion ⟨a *survey* of current trends in higher education⟩. A **sketch** is a similar but slighter and more tentative treatment ⟨a *sketch* of the president's first year in office⟩. A **précis** is a concise statement of essential facts or points ⟨a *précis* precedes the full medical report⟩. An **aperçu** ignores details and gives a quick impression of the whole ⟨the magazine article is an *aperçu* of current cancer research⟩.

compensate, countervail, balance, offset mean to make up for what is excessive or deficient, helpful or harmful in another. **Compensate** implies making up a lack or making amends for loss or injury ⟨*compensated* for an injury on the job⟩. **Countervail** suggests

counteracting a bad or harmful influence or the damage suffered through it ⟨a compassionate heart *countervails* his short temper⟩. **Balance** implies the equalizing or adjusting of two or more things that are contrary or opposed so that no one outweighs the other or others in effect ⟨in sentencing prisoners, the judge *balanced* justice and mercy⟩. **Offset** implies neutralizing one thing's good or evil effect by something that exerts a contrary effect ⟨overeating will *offset* the benefits of exercise⟩. See in addition PAY.

competent see ABLE, SUFFICIENT

complaisant see AMIABLE

complete see CLOSE

complete see FULL

complex, complicated, intricate, involved, knotty mean having confusingly interrelated parts. **Complex** suggests the unavoidable result of a necessary combining and does not imply a fault or failure ⟨a *complex* problem that calls for a *complex* solution⟩. **Complicated** applies to what offers great difficulty in understanding, solving, or explaining ⟨baffled by the *complicated* budgetary procedures⟩. **Intricate** suggests such interlacing of parts as to make it nearly impossible to follow or grasp them separately ⟨the *intricate* balance of power among nations⟩. **Involved** implies extreme complication and often disorder ⟨an *involved* explanation that clarified nothing⟩. **Knotty** suggests complication and entanglement that make solution or understanding improbable ⟨*knotty* questions concerning free expression and censorship⟩.

complicated see COMPLEX

component see ELEMENT

comport see BEHAVE

composed see COOL

composure see EQUANIMITY

comprehend see INCLUDE, UNDERSTAND

compress see CONTRACT

compunction see PENITENCE, QUALM

compute see CALCULATE

conceal see HIDE

concede see GRANT

conceive see THINK

concept see IDEA

conception see IDEA

concern see CARE

conciliate see PACIFY

concise, terse, succinct, laconic, summary, pithy, compendious mean very brief in statement or expression. **Concise** suggests the removal of all that is superfluous or elaborative ⟨a *concise* study of the situation⟩. **Terse** implies pointed conciseness ⟨a *terse* reply that ended the conversation⟩. **Succinct** implies the greatest possible compression ⟨a *succinct* letter of resignation⟩. **Laconic** implies brevity to the point of seeming rude, indifferent, or mysterious ⟨a *laconic* people who are cold to strangers⟩. **Summary** suggests the statement of main points with no elaboration or explanation ⟨a *summary* listing of the year's main events⟩. **Pithy** adds to *succinct* or *terse* the implication of richness of meaning or substance ⟨the play's dialogue is studded with *pithy* one-liners⟩. **Compendious** applies to a treatment at once full in scope and brief and concise in treatment ⟨a *compendious* report giving all that is known about the disease⟩.

conclude see CLOSE, INFER

conclusive, decisive, determinative, definitive mean bringing to an end. **Conclusive** applies to reasoning or logical proof that puts an end to debate or questioning ⟨*conclusive* evidence of criminal guilt⟩. **Decisive** may apply to something that ends a controversy, a contest, or any uncertainty ⟨the *decisive* battle of the war⟩. **Determinative** adds an implication of giving a fixed course or direction ⟨the *determinative* influence in her life⟩. **Definitive** applies to what is put forth as final and permanent ⟨the *definitive* biography of Jefferson⟩.

concord see HARMONY

concur see AGREE

condemn see CRITICIZE

condense see CONTRACT

condescend see STOOP

condolence see PITY

condone see EXCUSE

conduct, manage, control, direct mean to use one's powers to lead, guide, or dominate. **Conduct** implies taking responsibility for the acts and achievements of a group ⟨in charge of *conducting* the negotiations⟩. **Manage** implies direct handling and manipulating or maneuvering toward a desired result ⟨*manages* the financial affairs of the company⟩. **Control** implies a regulating or restraining in order to keep within bounds or on a course ⟨try to *control* the number of people using the park⟩. **Direct** implies constant guiding and regulating so as to achieve smooth operation ⟨*directs* the day-to-day running of the store⟩. See in addition BEHAVE.

confederate, partner, copartner, colleague, ally mean one who acts in association with another. **Confederate** implies an entering into a close or permanent union esp. for solidarity ⟨*confederates* in crime⟩. **Partner** implies a business association or an association of two ⟨looking for a woman to be his lifelong *partner*⟩. **Copartner** may stress the equality of the partnership ⟨management and labor are *copartners* in this endeavor⟩. **Colleague** implies a professional association ⟨admired by her *colleagues* in the dance world⟩. **Ally** implies an often temporary association in a common cause or in affairs of policy or statecraft ⟨a joint statement by the *allies* condemning the raid⟩.

confederation see ALLIANCE

confer, consult, advise, parley mean to engage in discussion in order to reach a decision or settlement. **Confer** implies comparison of views or opinions and usu. an equality between participants ⟨the executives *confer* weekly about current business problems⟩. **Consult** adds to *confer* the implication of seeking or taking counsel ⟨before acting, the president *consulted* with his aides⟩. **Advise** applies esp. to the seeking of opinions regarding personal matters ⟨before deciding to run, he *advised* with friends⟩. **Parley** implies a conference for the sake of settling differences ⟨the government refusing to *parley* with the rebels⟩.

confer see GIVE

confess see ACKNOWLEDGE

confide see COMMIT

confidence, assurance, self-possession, aplomb mean a state of mind or a manner marked by easy coolness and freedom from uncertainty, diffidence, or embarrassment. **Confidence** stresses faith in oneself and one's powers without any suggestion of conceit or arrogance ⟨had the *confidence* that comes only from long experience⟩. **Assurance** carries a stronger implication of certainty and may suggest arrogance or lack of objectivity in assessing one's own powers ⟨had an exaggerated *assurance* of his own worth⟩. **Self-possession** implies an ease or coolness under stress that reflects perfect self-control and command of one's powers ⟨she answered the insolent question with complete *self-possession*⟩. **Aplomb** implies a manifest self-possession in trying or challenging situations ⟨handled the horde of reporters with great *aplomb*⟩.

configuration see FORM

confine see LIMIT

confirm, corroborate, substantiate, verify, authenticate, validate mean to attest to the truth or validity of something. **Confirm** implies the removing of doubts by an authoritative statement or indisputable fact ⟨*confirmed* reports of troop movments⟩. **Corroborate** suggests the strengthening of what is already partly established ⟨witnesses *corroborated* his story⟩. **Substantiate** implies the offering of evidence that sustains the contention ⟨claims that have yet to be *substantiated*⟩. **Verify** implies the establishing of correspondence of actual facts or details with those proposed or guessed at ⟨all statements of fact in the article have been *verified*⟩. **Authenticate** implies establishing genuineness by adducing legal or official documents or expert opinion ⟨handwriting experts *authenticated* the diaries⟩. **Validate** implies establishing validity by authoritative affirmation or by factual proof ⟨*validate* a passport⟩.

confirmed see INVETERATE

confiscate see APPROPRIATE

conflict see DISCORD

conform see ADAPT

conformation see FORM

confound see PUZZLE

confute see DISPROVE

congenial see CONSONANT

congenital see INNATE

congregate see GATHER

congruous see CONSONANT

conjecture, surmise, guess mean to draw an inference from slight evidence. **Conjecture** implies forming an opinion or judgment upon evidence insufficient for definite knowledge ⟨scientists could only *conjecture* about the animal's breeding cycle⟩. **Surmise** implies even slighter evidence and suggests the influence of imagination or suspicion ⟨*surmised* the real reason for the generous gift⟩. **Guess** stresses a hitting upon a conclusion either wholly at random or from very uncertain evidence ⟨you would never *guess* that they were wealthy⟩.

conjugal see MATRIMONIAL

connect see JOIN

connubial see MATRIMONIAL

conquer, vanquish, defeat, subdue, reduce, overcome, overthrow mean to get the better of by force or strategy. **Conquer** implies gaining mastery of ⟨*conquer* your fear of flying⟩. **Vanquish** implies a complete overpowering ⟨*vanquished* the rebels in a decisive battle⟩. **Defeat** does not imply the finality or completeness of *vanquish* which it otherwise equals ⟨have *defeated* the Miami team on several occasions⟩. **Subdue** implies a defeating and suppression ⟨*subdued* the native tribes after years of fighting⟩. **Reduce** implies a forcing to capitulate or surrender ⟨the city was *reduced* after a month-long siege⟩. **Overcome** suggests getting the better of with difficulty or after hard struggle ⟨*overcame* a host of legal and bureaucratic troubles⟩. **Overthrow** stresses the bringing down or destruction of enemy power ⟨violently *overthrew* the established government⟩.

conscientious see UPRIGHT

conscious see AWARE

consecrate see DEVOTE

consent see ASSENT

consequence see EFFECT, IMPORTANCE

consider, study, contemplate, weigh mean to think about in order to arrive at a judgment or decision. **Consider** may suggest giving thought to in order to reach a suitable conclusion, opinion, or decision ⟨refused to even *consider* my proposal⟩. **Study** implies sustained purposeful concentration and attention to details and minutiae ⟨*study* the budget before making sweeping cuts⟩. **Contemplate** stresses focusing one's thoughts on something but does not imply coming to a conclusion or decision ⟨*contemplate* the consequences of such a decision⟩. **Weigh** implies attempting to reach the truth or arrive at a decision by balancing conflicting claims or evidence ⟨*weigh* the pros and cons of the case⟩.

consign see COMMIT
consistent see CONSONANT
console see COMFORT
consonant, consistent, compatible, congruous, congenial, sympathetic mean being in agreement one with another or agreeable one to another. **Consonant** implies the absence of elements making for discord or difficulty (a spokesperson *consonant* with the company's philosophy). **Consistent** may also imply this or it may stress absence of contradiction between things or between details of the same thing (behavior that is not *consistent* with her general character). **Compatible** suggests having a capacity for existing or functioning together without disagreement, discord, or mutual interference (looking for a *compatible* roommate). **Congruous** is more positive in suggesting a pleasing effect resulting from fitness or appropriateness of component elements (modern furniture is not *congruous* with a colonial house). **Congenial** implies a generally satisfying harmony between personalities or a fitness to one's personal taste (did not find the atmosphere of the bar *congenial*). **Sympathetic** suggests a more subtle or quieter kind of harmony than *congenial* (a music critic not very *sympathetic* to rock).

conspectus see ABRIDGMENT
conspicuous see NOTICEABLE
conspiracy see PLOT
constant see CONTINUAL, FAITHFUL
constituent see ELEMENT
constrain see FORCE
constrict see CONTRACT
consult see CONFER
contain, hold, accommodate mean to have or be capable of having within. **Contain** implies the actual presence of a specified substance or quantity within something (the can *contains* about a quart of oil). **Hold** implies the capacity of containing or the usual or permanent function of containing or keeping (the container will *hold* a gallon of liquid). **Accommodate** stresses holding without crowding or inconvenience (the banquet hall can *accommodate* 500 diners).
contaminate, taint, pollute, defile mean to make impure or unclean. **Contaminate** implies intrusion of or contact with dirt or foulness from an outside source (water *contaminated* by industrial wastes) (the bigotry of elders that may *contaminate* young minds). **Taint** stresses the loss of purity or cleanliness that follows contamination (*tainted* meat) (the scandal *tainted* the rest of his political career). **Pollute,** sometimes interchangeable with *contaminate,* distinctively may imply that the process which begins with contamination is complete and that what was pure or clean has been made foul, poisoned, or filthy (the *polluted* waters of the lake, in parts no better than an open cesspool). **Defile** implies befouling of what could or should have been kept clean and pure or held sacred and commonly suggests violation or desecration (*defile* a hero's memory with slanderous innuendo).
contemn see DESPISE
contemplate see CONSIDER
contemporaneous see CONTEMPORARY
contemporary, contemporaneous, coeval, synchronous, simultaneous, coincident mean existing or occurring at the same time. **Contemporary** is likely to apply to people and what relates to them (Abraham Lincoln was *contemporary* with Charles Darwin). **Contemporaneous** applies to events (Victoria's reign was *contemporaneous* with British hegemony). **Coeval** refers usu. to periods, ages, eras, eons (the rise of the leisure class was *coeval* with the flowering of the arts). **Synchronous** implies exact correspondence in time and esp. in periodic intervals (the movements of

the two pendulums are *synchronous*). **Simultaneous** implies correspondence in a moment of time (a *simultaneous* ringing of church bells miles apart). **Coincident** is applied to events and may be used in order to avoid implication of causal relationship (the end of World War II was *coincident* with a great vintage year).

contemptible, despicable, pitiable, sorry, scurvy mean arousing or deserving scorn. **Contemptible** may imply any quality provoking scorn or a low standing in any scale of values (a *contemptible* bigot and liar). **Despicable** may imply utter worthlessness and usu. suggests arousing an attitude of moral indignation (the *despicable* crime of child abuse). **Pitiable** applies to what inspires mixed contempt and pity (the play is his *pitiable* attempt at tragedy). **Sorry** may stress pitiable inadequacy or may suggest wretchedness or sordidness (the orphanage was the *sorriest* of places). **Scurvy** adds to *despicable* an implication of arousing disgust (the offer of help turned out to be a *scurvy* trick).

contention see DISCORD
contentious see BELLIGERENT
contiguous see ADJACENT
contingency see JUNCTURE
contingent see ACCIDENTAL
continual, continuous, constant, incessant, perpetual, perennial mean characterized by continued occurrence or recurrence. **Continual** implies a close prolonged succession or recurrence (*continual* showers the whole weekend). **Continuous** usu. implies an uninterrupted flow or spatial extension (the *continuous* roar of the falls). **Constant** implies uniform or persistent occurrence or recurrence (lived in *constant* pain). **Incessant** implies ceaseless or uninterrupted activity (the *incessant* quarreling frayed her nerves). **Perpetual** suggests unfailing repetition or lasting duration (the fear of *perpetual* torment after death). **Perennial** implies enduring existence often through constant renewal (a *perennial* source of controversy).
continue, last, endure, abide, persist mean to exist over a period of time or indefinitely. **Continue** applies to a process going on without ending (the stock market will *continue* to rise). **Last,** esp. when unqualified, may stress existing beyond what is normal or expected (buy shoes that will *last*). **Endure** adds an implication of resisting destructive forces or agencies (in spite of everything, her faith *endured*). **Abide** implies stable and constant existing esp. as opposed to mutability (through 40 years of marriage, their love *abided*). **Persist** suggests outlasting the normal or appointed time and often connotes obstinacy or doggedness (the sense of guilt *persisted*).
continuous see CONTINUAL
contort see DEFORM
contour see OUTLINE
contract, shrink, condense, compress, constrict, deflate mean to decrease in bulk or volume. **Contract** applies to a drawing together of surfaces or particles or a reduction of area or length (caused his muscles to *contract*). **Shrink** implies a contracting or a loss of material and stresses a falling short of original dimensions (the sweater will *shrink* if washed improperly). **Condense** implies a reducing of something homogeneous to greater compactness without significant loss of content (*condense* the report to five pages). **Compress** implies a pressing into a small compass and definite shape usu. against resistance (*compressed* the comforter to fit the box). **Constrict** implies a tightening that reduces diameter (the throat is *constricted* by too tight a collar). **Deflate** implies a contracting by reducing the internal pressure of contained air or gas (*deflate* the balloon).

contradict see DENY

contradictory see OPPOSITE

contrary, perverse, restive, balky, wayward mean inclined to resist authority or control. **Contrary** implies a temperamental unwillingness to accept orders or advice ⟨the most *contrary* child in my class⟩. **Perverse** may imply wrongheaded, determined, or cranky opposition to what is reasonable or normal ⟨offered the most *perverse* argument for declaring war⟩. **Restive** suggests unwillingness or inability to submit to discipline or follow orders ⟨*restive* individuals who had no place in the army⟩. **Balky** suggests a refusing to proceed in a desired direction or course of action ⟨workers became *balky* when asked to accept pay cuts⟩. **Wayward** suggests strong-willed capriciousness and irregularity in behavior ⟨*wayward* inmates are isolated from the others⟩. See in addition OPPOSITE.

contrast see COMPARE

contravene see DENY

contrition see PENITENCE

control *vb* see CONDUCT

control *n* see POWER

controvert see DISPROVE

conundrum see MYSTERY

convene see SUMMON

conventional see CEREMONIAL

convert see TRANSFORM

convey see CARRY

conviction see CERTAINTY, OPINION

convincing see VALID

convoke see SUMMON

convulse see SHAKE

convulsive see FITFUL

cool, composed, collected, unruffled, imperturbable, nonchalant mean free from agitation or excitement. **Cool** may imply calmness, deliberateness, or dispassionateness ⟨kept a *cool* head during the emergency⟩. **Composed** implies freedom from agitation as a result of self-discipline or a sedate disposition ⟨the *composed* pianist gave a flawless concert⟩. **Collected** implies a concentration of mind that eliminates distractions esp. in moments of crisis ⟨even in heated debate she remains very *collected*⟩. **Unruffled** suggests apparent serenity and poise in the face of setbacks or in the midst of exitement ⟨his mother remained *unruffled* during the wedding⟩. **Imperturbable** implies coolness or assurance even under severe provocation ⟨a guest speaker who maintained an air of *imperturbable* civility⟩. **Nonchalant** stresses an easy coolness of manner or casualness that suggests indifference or unconcern ⟨*nonchalant* as ever, she was oblivious to the crying baby⟩.

copartner see CONFEDERATE

copious see PLENTIFUL

copy *vb* **Copy, imitate, mimic, ape, mock** mean to make something so that it resembles an existing thing. **Copy** suggests duplicating an original as nearly as possible ⟨*copied* the painting and sold the fake as an original⟩. **Imitate** suggests following a model or a pattern but may allow for some variation ⟨*imitate* a poet's style⟩. **Mimic** implies a close copying (as of voice or mannerism) often for fun, ridicule, or lifelike imitation ⟨pupils *mimicking* their teacher⟩. **Ape** may suggest presumptuous, slavish, or inept imitating of a superior original ⟨American fashion designers *aped* their European colleagues⟩. **Mock** usu. implies imitation with derision ⟨*mocking* a vain man's manner⟩.

copy *n* see REPRODUCTION

coquet see TRIFLE

cordial see GRACIOUS

corporal see BODILY

corporeal see BODILY, MATERIAL

correct *vb* **Correct, rectify, emend, remedy, redress, amend, reform, revise** mean to make right what is wrong. **Correct** implies taking action to remove errors, faults, deviations, defects ⟨*corrected* all her spelling errors⟩. **Rectify** implies a more essential changing to make something right, just, or properly controlled or directed ⟨a major error in judgment that should be *rectified* at once⟩. **Emend** specif. implies correction of a text or manuscript ⟨*emend* the text to match the first edition⟩. **Remedy** implies removing or making harmless a cause of trouble, harm, or evil ⟨set out to *remedy* the evils of the world⟩. **Redress** implies making compensation or reparation for an unfairness, injustice, or imbalance ⟨we must *redress* past social injustices⟩. **Amend, reform, revise** imply an improving by making corrective changes, *amend* usu. suggesting slight changes ⟨a law that needs to be *amended*⟩, *reform* implying drastic change ⟨plans to *reform* the entire court system⟩, and *revise* suggesting a careful examination of something and the making of necessary changes ⟨forced to *revise* the production schedule⟩. See in addition PUNISH.

correct *adj* **Correct, accurate, exact, precise, nice, right** mean conforming to fact, standard, or truth. **Correct** usu. implies freedom from fault or error ⟨*correct* answers⟩ ⟨socially *correct* dress⟩. **Accurate** implies fidelity to fact or truth attained by exercise of care ⟨an *accurate* description of the whole situation⟩. **Exact** stresses a very strict agreement with fact, standard, or truth ⟨a suit tailored to *exact* measurements⟩. **Precise** adds to *exact* an emphasis on sharpness of definition or delimitation ⟨the *precise* terms of the contract⟩. **Nice** stresses great precision and delicacy of adjustment or discrimination ⟨makes *nice* distinctions between freedom and license⟩. **Right** is close to *correct* but has a stronger positive emphasis on conformity to fact or truth rather than mere absence of error or fault ⟨the *right* thing to do⟩.

corroborate see CONFIRM

corrupt *vb* see DEBASE

corrupt *adj* see VICIOUS

costly, expensive, dear, valuable, precious, invaluable, priceless mean having a high esp. monetary value. **Costly** implies high price and may suggest sumptuousness, luxury, or rarity ⟨the *costliest* of delicacies grace her table⟩. **Expensive** may further imply a price beyond the thing's value or the buyer's means ⟨the resort's shops seemed rather *expensive*⟩. **Dear** implies a relatively high or exorbitant price usu. due to factors other than the thing's intrinsic value ⟨coffee was *dear* during the war⟩. **Valuable** may suggest worth measured in usefulness as well as in market value ⟨iron ore was a *valuable* commodity⟩. **Precious** applies to what is of great or even incalculable value because scarce or irreplaceable ⟨our *precious* natural resources⟩. **Invaluable** and **priceless** imply such great worth as to make valuation nearly impossible ⟨a good education is *invaluable*⟩ ⟨a bon mot that was *priceless*⟩.

counsel see ADVICE

countenance see FACE

counter see ADVERSE

counteractive see ADVERSE

counterfeit *vb* see ASSUME

counterfeit *n* see IMPOSTURE

countervail see COMPENSATE

courage, mettle, spirit, resolution, tenacity mean mental or moral strength to resist opposition, danger, or hardship. **Courage** implies firmness of mind and will in the face of danger or extreme difficulty ⟨the *courage* to support unpopular causes⟩. **Mettle** suggests an ingrained capacity for meeting strain or difficulty with fortitude and resilience ⟨a challenge that will test your *mettle*⟩. **Spirit** also suggests a quality of temperament enabling one to hold one's own or keep up one's morale when opposed or threatened (too many failures had broken the *spirit* of the man). **Resolution** stresses firm determination to achieve one's ends (the strong *resolution* of the pioneer women). **Tenacity** adds to *resolution* implications of stubborn persistence and unwillingness to admit defeat (the *tenacity* to continue when all others doubted).

court see INVITE
courteous see CIVIL
covert see SECRET
covet see DESIRE
covetous, greedy, acquisitive, grasping, avaricious mean having or showing a strong desire for material possessions. **Covetous** implies inordinate desire often for another's possessions (*covetous* of his brother's success). **Greedy** stresses lack of restraint and often of discrimination in desire (soldiers *greedy* for glory). **Acquisitive** implies both eagerness to possess and ability to acquire and keep (mansions that were the pride of the *acquisitive* class). **Grasping** adds to *covetous* and *greedy* an implication of selfishness and often suggests unfair or ruthless means (*grasping* developers defrauded the homesteaders). **Avaricious** implies obsessive acquisitiveness esp. of money and strongly suggests stinginess (*avaricious* capitalists detested the social programs).

cow see INTIMIDATE
cowardly, pusillanimous, craven, dastardly mean having or showing a lack of courage. **Cowardly** implies a weak or ignoble lack of courage (the *cowardly* retreat of the army). **Pusillanimous** suggests a contemptible lack of courage (*pusillanimous* politicians feared crossing him). **Craven** suggests extreme defeatism and complete lack of resistance (secretly despised the *craven* toadies around her). **Dastardly** implies behavior that is both cowardly and treacherous or skulking or outrageous (a *dastardly* attack on unarmed civilians).

cower see FAWN
coy see SHY
cozen see CHEAT
cozy see COMFORTABLE
crabbed see SULLEN
craft see ART
crafty see SLY
cranky see IRASCIBLE
crave see DESIRE
craven see COWARDLY
craze see FASHION
create see INVENT
credence see BELIEF
credit *vb* see ASCRIBE
credit *n* see BELIEF, INFLUENCE
crime see OFFENSE
cringe see FAWN
cripple see MAIM, WEAKEN
crisis see JUNCTURE
crisp see FRAGILE, INCISIVE
criterion see STANDARD
critical, hypercritical, faultfinding, captious, carping, censorious mean inclined to look for and point out faults and defects. **Critical** may also imply an effort to see a thing clearly and truly in order to judge it fairly (a *critical* essay on modern drama). **Hypercritical** suggests a tendency to judge by unreasonably strict standards (petty, *hypercritical* disparagement of other people's success). **Faultfinding** implies a querulous or exacting temperament (a *faultfinding* theater reviewer). **Captious** suggests a readiness to detect trivial faults or raise objections on trivial grounds (no point is too minute for this *captious* critic to overlook). **Carping** implies an ill-natured or perverse picking of flaws (the *carping* editorial writer soon wearied read-

ers). **Censorious** implies a disposition to be severely critical and condemnatory (the *censorious* tone of the papal encyclical). See in addition ACUTE.
criticize, reprehend, blame, censure, reprobate, condemn, denounce mean to find fault with openly. **Criticize** implies finding fault esp. with methods or policies or intentions (*criticized* the police for using violence). **Reprehend** implies both criticism and severe rebuking (*reprehends* the self-centeredness of today's students). **Blame** may imply simply the opposite of *praise* but more often suggests the placing of responsibility for something bad or unfortunate (*blames* herself for the accident). **Censure** carries a stronger suggestion of authority and of reprimanding than *blame* (a Senator formally *censured* by his peers). **Reprobate** implies strong disapproval or firm refusal to sanction (*reprobated* his son's adulterous adventures). **Condemn** usu. suggests an unqualified and final unfavorable judgment (*condemn* the government's racial policies). **Denounce** adds to *condemn* the implication of a public declaration (bishops have *denounced* abortion).
cross see IRASCIBLE, STUPID
crotchet see CAPRICE
crow see BOAST
crowd, throng, crush, mob, horde mean an assembled multitude usu. of people. **Crowd** implies a close gathering and pressing together (a small *crowd* greeted the returning athletes). **Throng** strongly suggests movement and pushing (a *throng* of reporters followed the President). **Crush** emphasizes the compactness of the group, the difficulty of individual movement, and the attendant discomfort (a *crush* of fans waited outside the theater). **Mob** implies a disorderly crowd with the potential for violence (heard an angry *mob* outside the jail). **Horde** suggests a rushing or tumultuous crowd (a *horde* of shoppers looking for bargains).
crucial see ACUTE
crude see RUDE
cruel see FIERCE
crush *vb* Crush, quell, extinguish, suppress, quash mean to bring to an end by destroying or defeating. **Crush** implies a force that destroys all opposition or brings an operation to a halt (a rebellion that was brutally *crushed*). **Quell** means to overwhelmn completely and to reduce to submission, inactivity, or passivity (statements intended to *quell* the fears of the people). **Extinguish** suggests ending something as abruptly and completely as putting out a flame (a promising life *extinguished* by a single bullet). **Suppress** implies a conscious determination to subdue (the government *suppressed* all opposition newspapers). **Quash** implies a sudden and summary extinction (the rejection *quashed* all their hopes for a better life).
crush *n* see CROWD
crusty see BLUFF
cryptic see OBSCURE
culmination see SUMMIT
culpable see BLAMEWORTHY
cumbersome see HEAVY
cumbrous see HEAVY
cumulative, accumulative, additive, summative mean increasing or produced by the addition of new material of the same kind. **Cumulative** implies a constant increase (as in amount or power) by a series of additions, accretions, or repetitions (the *cumulative* effect of taking a drug for many months). **Accumulative** may distinctively imply that something has reached its maximum or greatest magnitude through many additions (the *accumulative* impact of a well-ordered sales presentation). **Additive** implies that something is capable of assimilating or incorporating new material (as new art forms arise, we develop an *additive* no-

tion of what is art). **Summative** implies that something is capable of association or combination with others so as to create a total effect ⟨the *summative* effect of the show's music, dancing, and staging⟩.

cunning *n* see ART

cunning *adj* see CLEVER, SLY

curb see RESTRAIN

cure, heal, remedy mean to rectify an unhealthy or undesirable condition. **Cure** implies restoration to health after disease ⟨no *cure* for a disease that inevitably results in death⟩. **Heal** may also apply to this but commonly suggests restoring to soundness after a wound or sore ⟨his wounds were slow to *heal*⟩. **Remedy** suggests correction or relief of a morbid or evil condition ⟨vainly searched for something to *remedy* her arthritis⟩.

curious, inquisitive, prying mean interested in what is not one's personal or proper concern. **Curious**, a neutral term, basically connotes an active desire to learn or to know ⟨children are *curious* about everything⟩. **Inquisitive** suggests impertinent and habitual curiosity and persistent quizzing ⟨dreaded the visits of their *inquisitive* relatives⟩. **Prying** implies busy meddling and officiousness ⟨*prying* neighbors who refuse to mind their own business⟩.

current *adj* see PREVAILING

current *n* see TENDENCY

curse see EXECRATE

cursory see SUPERFICIAL

curt see BLUFF

curtail see SHORTEN

curve, bend, turn, twist mean to swerve or cause to swerve from a straight line. **Curve** implies following or producing a line suggesting the arc of a circle or ellipse ⟨the road *curves* sharply to the left⟩. **Bend** suggests a yielding to force and usu. implies a distortion from normal or desirable straightness ⟨metal rods *bending* under the immense weight⟩. **Turn** implies change of direction essentially by rotation and not usu. as a result of force ⟨the comet will *turn* closer towards the earth⟩. **Twist** implies the influence of irresistible force having a spiral effect throughout the object or course involved ⟨the *twisted* wreckage of the spacecraft⟩.

custom see HABIT

customary see USUAL

cutting see INCISIVE

cynical, misanthropic, pessimistic, misogynistic mean deeply distrustful. **Cynical** implies having a sneering disbelief in sincerity or integrity ⟨always *cynical* about other people's motives⟩. **Misanthropic** suggests a rooted distrust and dislike of human beings and their society ⟨a zoologist who had grown *misanthropic* in recent years⟩. **Pessimistic** implies having a gloomy, distrustful view of life ⟨a philosopher *pessimistic* about the future of the human race⟩. **Misogynistic** applies to a man having a deep-seated distrust of and aversion to women ⟨a *misogynistic* scientist more at home in his laboratory⟩.

D

dabbler see AMATEUR

dainty see CHOICE, NICE

dally see DELAY, TRIFLE

damage see INJURE

damn see EXECRATE

damp see WET

dangerous, hazardous, precarious, perilous, risky mean bringing or involving the chance of loss or injury. **Dangerous** applies to something that may cause harm or loss unless dealt with carefully ⟨soldiers on a *dangerous* mission⟩. **Hazardous** implies great and contin-

uous risk of harm or failure and small chance of successfully avoiding disaster ⟨claims that smoking is *hazardous* to your health⟩. **Precarious** suggests both insecurity and uncertainty ⟨has only a *precarious* hold on reality⟩. **Perilous** strongly implies the immediacy of danger ⟨the situation at the foreign embassy has grown *perilous*⟩. **Risky** often applies to a known and accepted danger ⟨shy away from *risky* investments⟩.

dank see WET

daredevil see ADVENTUROUS

daring see ADVENTUROUS

dark, dim, dusky, murky, gloomy mean more or less deficient in light. **Dark**, the general term, implies utter or virtual lack of illumination ⟨a *dark* cave⟩. **Dim** suggests too weak a light for things to be seen clearly or distinctly ⟨a clandestine meeting in a *dim* bar⟩. **Dusky** suggests deep twilight and close approach to darkness ⟨trudging through *dusky* woods at day's end⟩. **Murky** implies a heavy darkness such as that caused by smoke, fog, or dust in air or mud in water ⟨fish cannot live in the river's *murky* waters⟩. **Gloomy** implies serious interference with normal light and connotes cheerlessness and pessimism ⟨a *gloomy* room in the basement of the house⟩. See in addition OBSCURE.

dastardly see COWARDLY

daunt see DISMAY

dawdle see DELAY

dead, defunct, deceased, departed, late mean devoid of life. **Dead** applies literally to what is deprived of vital force but is used figuratively of anything that has lost any attribute (as energy, activity, radiance) suggesting life ⟨a *dead* engine⟩. **Defunct** stresses cessation of active existence or operation ⟨a *defunct* television series⟩. **Deceased, departed,** and **late** apply to persons who have died recently, *deceased* occurring esp. in legal use ⟨the rights of the *deceased* must be acknowledged⟩, *departed* usu. as a euphemism ⟨pray for our *departed* mother⟩, and *late* esp. with reference to a person in a specific relation or status ⟨the *late* president of the company⟩.

deadly, mortal, fatal, lethal mean causing or capable of causing death. **Deadly** applies to an established or very likely cause of death ⟨a *deadly* disease⟩. **Mortal** implies that death has occurred or is inevitable ⟨a *mortal* wound⟩. **Fatal** stresses the inevitability of what has in fact resulted in death or destruction ⟨*fatal* consequences⟩. **Lethal** applies only to something that is bound to cause death or exists for the destruction of life ⟨*lethal* gas⟩.

deal see DISTRIBUTE

dear see COSTLY

debar see EXCLUDE

debase, vitiate, deprave, corrupt, debauch, pervert mean to cause deterioration or lowering in quality or character. **Debase** implies a loss of position, worth, value, or dignity ⟨commercialism has *debased* the holiday⟩. **Vitiate** implies a destruction of purity, validity, or effectiveness by allowing entrance of a fault or defect ⟨partisanship and factionalism *vitiated* our foreign policy⟩. **Deprave** implies moral deterioration by evil thoughts or influences ⟨accused of *depraving* the children⟩. **Corrupt** implies loss of soundness, purity, or integrity ⟨believes that bureaucratese *corrupts* the language⟩. **Debauch** implies a debasing through sensual indulgence ⟨led a *debauched* life after the divorce⟩. **Pervert** implies a twisting or distorting from what is natural or normal ⟨*perverted* the original goals of the institute⟩. See in addition ABASE.

debate see DISCUSS

debauch see DEBASE

debilitate see WEAKEN

decadence see DETERIORATION

decay, decompose, rot, putrefy, spoil mean to undergo destructive dissolution. **Decay** implies a slow change from a state of soundness or perfection ⟨a *decaying* Southern mansion⟩. **Decompose** stresses a breaking down by chemical change and when applied to organic matter a corruption ⟨the body was badly *decomposed*⟩. **Rot** is a close synonym of *decompose* and often connotes foulness ⟨grain was left to *rot* in warehouses⟩. **Putrefy** implies the rotting of animal matter and offensiveness to sight and smell ⟨corpses *putrefying* on the battlefield⟩. **Spoil** applies chiefly to the decomposition of foods ⟨be on guard against *spoiled* mayonnaise⟩.

deceased see DEAD

deceitful see DISHONEST

deceive, mislead, delude, beguile mean to lead astray or frustrate usu. by underhandedness. **Deceive** implies imposing a false idea or belief that causes ignorance, bewilderment, or helplessness ⟨the salesman tried to *deceive* me about the car⟩. **Mislead** implies a leading astray that may or may not be intentional ⟨I was *mislead* by the confusing sign⟩. **Delude** implies deceiving so thoroughly as to obscure the truth ⟨we were *deluded* into thinking we were safe⟩. **Beguile** stresses the use of charm and persuasion in deceiving ⟨his ingratiating ways *beguiled* us all⟩.

decency see DECORUM

decent see CHASTE

deception, fraud, double-dealing, subterfuge, trickery mean the acts or practices of one who deliberately deceives. **Deception** may or may not imply blameworthiness, since it may suggest cheating or merely tactical resource ⟨magicians are masters of *deception*⟩. **Fraud** always implies guilt and often criminality in act or practice ⟨indicted for *fraud*⟩. **Double-dealing** suggests treachery or at least action contrary to a professed attitude ⟨the guerillas accused the go-between of *double-dealing*⟩. **Subterfuge** suggests the adoption of a stratagem or the telling of a lie in order to escape guilt or to gain an end ⟨obtained the papers by *subterfuge*⟩. **Trickery** implies ingenious acts intended to dupe or cheat ⟨will resort to any *trickery* to gain her ends⟩.

decide, determine, settle, rule, resolve mean to come or cause to come to a conclusion. **Decide** implies previous consideration of a matter causing doubt, wavering, debate, or controversy ⟨will *decide* tonight where to build the school⟩. **Determine** implies fixing the identity, character, scope, or direction of something ⟨*determined* the cause of the problem⟩. **Settle** implies a decision reached by someone with power to end all dispute or uncertainty ⟨the court's decision *settles* the matter⟩. **Rule** implies a determination by judicial or administrative authority ⟨the judge *ruled* that the evidence was inadmissible⟩. **Resolve** implies an expressed or clear decision or determination to do or refrain from doing something ⟨both nations *resolved* to stop terrorism⟩.

declare, announce, publish, proclaim, promulgate mean to make known publicly. **Declare** implies explicitness and usu. formality in making known ⟨the referee *declared* the contest a draw⟩. **Announce** implies the declaration for the first time of something that is of interest or has created speculation ⟨*announced* their engagement at a party⟩. **Publish** implies making public through print ⟨*published* the list of winners in the paper⟩. **Proclaim** implies declaring clearly, forcefully, and authoritatively ⟨the president *proclaimed* a national day of mourning⟩. **Promulgate** implies the proclaiming of a dogma, doctrine, or law ⟨*promulgated* an edict of religious toleration⟩. See in addition ASSERT.

decisive see CONCLUSIVE

deck see ADORN

decline *vb* Decline, refuse, reject, repudiate, spurn mean to turn away by not accepting, receiving, or considering. **Decline** often implies courteous refusal esp. of offers or invitations ⟨*declined the invitation to dinner*⟩. **Refuse** suggests more positiveness or ungraciousness and often implies the denial of something asked for ⟨*refused* them the loan they needed⟩. **Reject** implies a peremptory refusal by sending away or discarding ⟨*rejected* the plan as unworkable⟩. **Repudiate** implies a casting off or disowning as untrue, unauthorized, or unworthy of acceptance ⟨*repudiated* the values of their parents⟩. **Spurn** stresses contempt or disdain in rejection or repudiation ⟨*spurned* his amorous advances⟩.

decline *n* see DETERIORATION

decompose see DECAY

decorate see ADORN

decorum, decency, propriety, dignity, etiquette mean observance of the rules governing proper conduct. **Decorum** suggests conduct according with good taste, often formally prescribed ⟨had violated the *decorum* expected of an army officer⟩. **Decency** implies behavior according with normal self-respect or humane feeling for others, or with what is fitting to a particular profession or condition in life ⟨maintained a strict *decency* in dress⟩. **Propriety** suggests an artificial standard of what is correct in conduct or speech ⟨regarded the *propriety* expected of a society matron as stifling⟩. **Dignity** implies reserve or restraint in conduct prompted less by obedience to a code than by a sense of personal integrity or of social importance ⟨conveyed a quiet *dignity* and sincerity that won him respect⟩. **Etiquette** is the usual term for the detailed rules governing manners and conduct and for the observance of these rules ⟨the *etiquette* peculiar to the U.S. Senate⟩.

decoy see LURE

decrease, lessen, diminish, reduce, abate, dwindle mean to grow or make less. **Decrease** suggests a progressive decline in size, amount, numbers, or intensity ⟨slowly *decreased* the amount of pressure⟩. **Lessen** suggests a decline in amount rather than in number ⟨has been unable to *lessen* her debt at all⟩. **Diminish** emphasizes a perceptible loss and implies its subtraction from a total ⟨his muscular strength has *diminished* with age⟩. **Reduce** implies a bringing down or lowering ⟨*reduce* your caloric intake⟩. **Abate** implies a reducing of something excessive or oppressive in force or amount ⟨the storm *abated* in the afternoon⟩. **Dwindle** implies progressive lessening and is applied to things growing visibly smaller ⟨their provisions *dwindled* slowly but surely⟩.

decree see DICTATE

decrepit see WEAK

decry, depreciate, disparage, belittle, minimize mean to express a low opinion of. **Decry** implies open condemnation with intent to discredit ⟨*decried* their do-nothing attitude⟩. **Depreciate** implies a representing as being of less value than commonly believed ⟨critics *depreciate* his plays for being unabashedly sentimental⟩. **Disparage** implies depreciation by indirect means such as slighting or invidious comparison ⟨*disparaged* golf as recreation for the middle-aged⟩. **Belittle** and **minimize** imply depreciation, *belittle* suggesting usu. a contemptuous or envious attitude ⟨inclined to *belittle* the achievements of others⟩, *minimize* connoting less personal animus ⟨do not try to *minimize* the danger involved⟩.

dedicate see DEVOTE

deduce see INFER

deep see BROAD

deep-rooted see INVETERATE

deep-seated see INVETERATE

defame see MALIGN

defeat see CONQUER

defect see BLEMISH

defend, protect, shield, guard, safeguard mean to keep secure from danger or against attack. **Defend** denotes warding off actual or threatened attack ⟨a large army needed to *defend* the country⟩. **Protect** implies the use of something (as a covering) as a bar to the admission or impact of what may attack or injure ⟨*protect* one's eyes from the sun with dark glasses⟩. **Shield** suggests protective intervention in imminent danger or actual attack ⟨tried to *shield* her child from the real world⟩. **Guard** implies protecting with vigilance and force against expected danger ⟨all White House entrances are well *guarded*⟩. **Safeguard** implies taking precautionary protective measures against merely possible danger ⟨individual rights must be *safeguarded* whatever the cost⟩. See in addition MAINTAIN.

defer, postpone, suspend, stay mean to delay an action or proceeding. **Defer** implies a deliberate putting off to a later time ⟨*deferred* buying a car until next spring⟩. **Postpone** implies an intentional deferring usu. to a definite time ⟨the game was *postponed* until Saturday⟩. **Suspend** implies temporary stoppage with an added suggestion of waiting until some condition is satisfied ⟨all business has been *suspended* while repairs are being made⟩. **Stay** suggests the stopping or checking by an intervening agency or authority ⟨measures intended to *stay* the soaring rate of inflation⟩. See in addition YIELD.

deference see HONOR

defile see CONTAMINATE

definite see EXPLICIT

definitive see CONCLUSIVE

deflate see CONTRACT

deform, distort, contort, warp mean to mar or spoil by or as if by twisting. **Deform** may imply a change of shape through stress, injury, or some accident of growth ⟨relentless winds *deformed* the pines into bizarre shapes⟩. **Distort** and **contort** both imply a wrenching from the natural, normal or justly proportioned, but *contort* suggests a more involved twisting and a more grotesque and painful result ⟨the odd camera angle *distorts* his face in the photograph⟩ ⟨a degenerative bone disease had painfully *contorted* her body⟩. **Warp** indicates physically an uneven shrinking that bends or twists out of a flat plane ⟨*warped* floorboards⟩.

defraud see CHEAT

deft see DEXTEROUS

defunct see DEAD

degenerate see VICIOUS

degeneration see DETERIORATION

degrade see ABASE

deign see STOOP

dejected see DOWNCAST

dejection see SADNESS

delay *vb* Delay, retard, slow, slacken, detain mean to cause to be late or behind in movement or progress. **Delay** implies a holding back, usu. by interference, from completion or arrival ⟨bad weather *delayed* our arrival⟩. **Retard** applies chiefly to motion and suggests reduction of speed without actual stopping ⟨language barriers *retarded* their rate of learning⟩. **Slow** and **slacken** both imply also a reduction of speed, *slow* often suggesting deliberate intention ⟨the engineer *slowed* the train⟩, *slacken* an easing up or relaxing of power or effort ⟨he needs to *slacken* his pace if he intends to finish the race⟩. **Detain** implies a holding back beyond a reasonable or appointed time ⟨unexpected business had *detained* her⟩.

delay *vb* Delay, procrastinate, lag, loiter, dawdle, dally mean to move or act slowly so as to fall behind. **Delay** usu. implies a putting off (as a beginning or departure) ⟨a tight schedule means we cannot *delay* any

longer⟩. **Procrasti nate** implies blameworthy delay esp. through laziness or apathy ⟨*procrastinates* about making every decision⟩. **Lag** implies failure to maintain a speed set by others ⟨we *lag* behind other countries in shoe production⟩. **Loiter** and **dawdle** imply delay while in progress, esp. in walking, but *dawdle* more clearly suggests an aimless wasting of time ⟨*loitered* at several store windows before going to church⟩ ⟨children *dawdling* on their way home from school⟩. **Dally** suggests delay through trifling or vacillation when promptness is necessary ⟨stop *dallying* and get to work⟩.

delete see ERASE

deleterious see PERNICIOUS

deliberate *vb* see THINK

deliberate *adj* see VOLUNTARY

delicate see CHOICE

deliver see RESCUE

delude see DECEIVE

demand, claim, require, exact mean to ask or call for something as due or as necessary. **Demand** implies peremptoriness and insistence and often the right to make requests that are to be regarded as commands ⟨the physician *demanded* payment of her bill⟩. **Claim** implies a demand for the delivery or concession of something due as one's own or one's right ⟨*claimed* to be the first to describe the disease⟩. **Require** suggests the imperativeness that arises from inner necessity, compulsion of law or regulation, or the exigencies of the situation ⟨the patient *requires* constant attention⟩. **Exact** implies not only demanding but getting what one demands ⟨the president *exacts* absolute loyalty from his aides⟩.

demean see ABASE

demeanor see BEARING

demented see INSANE

demonstrate see SHOW

demur see QUALM

denounce see CRITICIZE

dense see CLOSE, STUPID

deny, gainsay, contradict, contravene mean to refuse to accept as true or valid. **Deny** implies a firm refusal to accept as true, to grant or concede, or to acknowledge the existence or claims of ⟨tried to *deny* the charges⟩. **Gainsay** implies disputing the truth of what another has said ⟨no one can *gainsay* that everything I've said is a fact⟩. **Contradict** implies an open or flat denial ⟨her report *contradicts* every point of his statement to the police⟩. **Contravene** implies not so much an intentional opposition as some inherent incompatibility ⟨laws against whaling that *contravene* Eskimo tradition⟩.

depart see SWERVE

departed see DEAD

deplete, drain, exhaust, impoverish, bankrupt mean to deprive of something essential to existence or potency. **Deplete** implies a reduction in number or quantity so as to endanger the ability to function ⟨we cannot afford to *deplete* our natural resources⟩. **Drain** implies a gradual withdrawal and ultimate deprivation of what is necessary to a thing's existence ⟨a series of personal tragedies *drained* him of hope⟩. **Exhaust** stresses a complete emptying or evacuation ⟨a theme that can never be *exhausted*⟩. **Impoverish** suggests a deprivation of something essential to vigorous well-being ⟨without the arts we would lead an *impoverished* existence⟩. **Bankrupt** suggests impoverishment to the point of imminent collapse ⟨war had *bankrupted* the nation of manpower and resources⟩.

deplore, lament, bewail, bemoan mean to express grief or sorrow for something. **Deplore** implies regret for the loss or impairment of something of value ⟨*deplores* the bad manners of today's young people⟩. **Lament** implies a profound or demonstrative expression of sorrow (never stopped *lamenting* the loss of their only son). **Bewail** and **bemoan** imply sorrow, disappointment, or protest finding outlet in words or cries, *bewail* commonly suggesting loudness, and *bemoan* lugubriousness, in uttering complaints or expressing regret (fans *bewailed* the thunderous defeat of the home team) (purists continually *bemoan* the corruption of the language).

deport see BANISH, BEHAVE

deportment see BEARING

deprave see DEBASE

depreciate see DECRY

depreciatory see DEROGATORY

depressed see DOWNCAST

depression see SADNESS

deranged see INSANE

deride see RIDICULE

derive see SPRING

derogatory, depreciatory, disparaging, slighting, pejorative mean designed or tending to belittle. **Derogatory** often applies to expressions or modes of expression that are intended to detract or belittle (does not consider the word "politician" a *derogatory* term). **Depreciatory** is often applied to writing or speech that tends to lower a thing in value or status (her habit of referring to the human body in the most *depreciatory* of ways). **Disparaging** implies an intent to depreciate by the use of oblique or indirect methods (a *disparaging* look at some popular heroes). **Slighting** may imply mild disparagement, indifference, or even scorn (made brief but *slighting* references to the other candidates in the race). **Pejorative** is applied esp. to words whose basic meaning is depreciated either by a suffix or by semantic application or association ("egghead" is a *pejorative* term for an intellectual).

description see TYPE

desert see ABANDON

design see INTENTION, PLAN

desire, wish, want, crave, covet mean to have a longing for. **Desire** stresses the strength of feeling and often implies strong intention or aim (*desires* to start a new life in another state). **Wish** sometimes implies a general or transient longing esp. for the unattainable (she *wished* that there were some way she could help). **Want** specif. suggests a felt need or lack (*want* to have a family). **Crave** stresses the force of physical appetite or emotional need (*crave* constantly for sweets). **Covet** implies strong envious desire (one of the most *coveted* honors in the sports world).

desist see STOP

desolate see ALONE, DISMAL

despairing see DESPONDENT

desperate see DESPONDENT

despicable see CONTEMPTIBLE

despise, contemn, scorn, disdain, scout mean to regard as unworthy of one's notice or consideration. **Despise** may suggest an emotional response ranging from strong dislike to loathing (*despises* those who show any sign of weakness). **Contemn** implies a vehement condemnation of a person or thing as low, vile, feeble, or ignominious (*contemns* the image of women promoted by advertisers). **Scorn** implies a ready or indignant contempt (*scorns* the very thought of retirement). **Disdain** implies an arrogant or supercilious aversion to what is regarded as unworthy (*disdained* all manner of popular music). **Scout** suggests abrupt rejection or dismissal (*scouted* any suggestion that their son was other than angelic).

despoil see RAVAGE

despondent, despairing, desperate, hopeless mean having lost all or nearly all hope. **Despondent** implies a deep dejection arising from a conviction of the uselessness of further effort (*despondent* over the death of her father). **Despairing** suggests the slipping away of all hope and often despondency (*despairing* appeals for the return of the kidnapped boy). **Desperate** implies despair that prompts reckless action or violence in the face of defeat or frustration (one last *desperate* attempt to turn the tide of the war). **Hopeless** suggests despair and the cessation of effort or resistance and often implies acceptance or resignation (the situation of the trapped miners is *hopeless*).

despotic see ABSOLUTE

destiny see FATE

destitution see POVERTY

desultory see RANDOM

detached see INDIFFERENT

detail see ITEM

detailed see CIRCUMSTANTIAL

detain see DELAY, KEEP

deterioration, degeneration, decadence, decline mean the falling from a higher to a lower level in quality, character, or vitality. **Deterioration** implies impairment of vigor, resilience, or usefulness (the *deterioration* of her memory in recent years). **Degeneration** stresses physical, intellectual, or esp. moral retrogression (the *degeneration* of his youthful idealism to cynicism). **Decadence** presupposes a reaching and passing the peak of development and implies a turn downward with a consequent loss in vitality or energy (cited rock music as a sign of cultural *decadence*). **Decline** differs from *decadence* in suggesting a more markedly downward direction and greater momentum as well as more obvious evidence of deterioration (the meteoric rise and *decline* of his career).

determinant see CAUSE

determinative see CONCLUSIVE

determine see DECIDE, DISCOVER

detest see HATE

detestable see HATEFUL

detrimental see PERNICIOUS

devastate see RAVAGE

deviate see SWERVE

devote, dedicate, consecrate, hallow mean to set apart for a special and often higher end. **Devote** is likely to imply compelling motives and often attachment to an objective (*devoted* his evenings to study). **Dedicate** implies solemn and exclusive devotion to a sacred or serious use or purpose (*dedicated* her life to medical research). **Consecrate** stresses investment with a solemn or sacred quality (*consecrate* a church to the worship of God). **Hallow,** often differing little from *dedicate* or *consecrate,* may distinctively imply an attribution of intrinsic sanctity (battleground *hallowed* by the blood of patriots).

devotion see FIDELITY

devout, pious, religious, pietistic, sanctimonious mean showing fervor in the practice of religion. **Devout** stresses a mental attitude that leads to frequent and sincere though not always outwardly evident prayer and worship (a pilgrimage that is the goal of *devout* Christians). **Pious** applies to the faithful performance of religious duties and maintenance of outwardly religious attitudes (a *pious* family that faithfully observes the Sabbath). **Religious** may imply devoutness and piety but it emphasizes faith in a deity and adherence to a way of life in keeping with that faith (a basically *religious* man, although not a regular churchgoer). **Pietistic** implies an insistence on the emotional as opposed to the intellectual aspects of religion (regarded religious articles as *pietistic* excess). **Sanctimonious** implies pretensions to holiness or smug appearance of piety (a *sanctimonious* preacher without mercy or human kindness).

dexterous, adroit, deft mean ready and skilled in physical movement. **Dexterous** implies expertness with consequent facility and quickness in manipulation (a *dexterous* handling of a volatile situation). **Adroit** implies dexterity but may also stress resourcefulness or artfulness or inventiveness (the *adroit* host of a radio call-in show) **Deft** emphasizes lightness, neatness, and sureness of touch or handling (a *deft* interweaving of the novel's several subplots).

dialect, vernacular, lingo, jargon, cant, argot, slang mean a form of language that is not recognized as standard. **Dialect** applies commonly to a form of language found regionally or among the uneducated (the *dialect* of the Cajuns in Louisiana). **Vernacular** applies to the everyday speech of the people in contrast to that of the learned (the doctor used the *vernacular* in describing the disease). **Lingo** is a mildly contemptuous term for any language not readily understood (foreign tourists speaking some strange *lingo*). **Jargon** applies to a technical or esoteric language used by a profession, trade, or cult (educationese is the *jargon* of educational theorists). **Cant** is applied derogatorily to language that is both peculiar to a group or class and marked by hackneyed expressions (the *cant* of TV sportscasters). **Argot** is applied to a peculiar language of a clique or other closely knit group (the *argot* of narcotics smugglers). **Slang** designates a class of mostly recently coined and frequently short-lived terms or usages informally preferred to standard language as being forceful, novel, or voguish (the ever-changing *slang* of college students).

dictate, prescribe, ordain, decree, impose mean to issue something to be followed, observed, obeyed, or accepted. **Dictate** implies an authoritative directive given orally or as if orally (in matters of love, do as the heart *dictates*). **Prescribe** implies an authoritative pronouncement that is clear and definite (the *prescribed* procedure for requesting new supplies). **Ordain** implies institution, establishment, or enactment by a supreme or unquestioned authority (nature has *ordained* that we humans either swelter or shiver). **Decree** implies a formal pronouncement esp. by one of great or absolute authority (the Pope *decreed* that next year will be a Holy Year). **Impose** implies a subjecting to what must be borne, endured, or submitted to (morality cannot be *imposed* by law).

dictatorial, magisterial, dogmatic, doctrinaire, oracular mean imposing one's will or opinions on others. **Dictatorial** stresses autocratic, high-handed methods and a domineering manner (a *dictatorial* manner that alienates her colleagues). **Magisterial** stresses assumption or use of prerogatives appropriate to a magistrate or schoolmaster in forcing acceptance of one's opinions (the *magisterial* tone of his arguments imply that only a fool would disagree). **Dogmatic** implies being unduly and offensively positive in laying down principles and expressing opinions (very *dogmatic* about deciding what is art and what is not). **Doctrinaire** implies a disposition to follow abstract theories in framing laws or policies affecting people (a *doctrinaire* conservative unable to deal with complex realities). **Oracular** implies the manner of one who delivers opinions in cryptic phrases or with pompous dogmatism (for three decades she was the *oracular* voice of fashion).

different, diverse, divergent, disparate, various mean unlike in kind or character. **Different** may imply little more than separateness but it may also imply contrast or contrariness (*different* foods). **Diverse** implies both distinctness and marked contrast (such *diverse* interests as dancing and football). **Divergent** implies movement away from each other and unlikelihood of ultimate meeting or reconciliation (went on to pursue two very *divergent* careers). **Disparate** emphasizes incongruity or incompatibility (*disparate* notions of freedom). **Various** stresses the number of sorts or kinds (*various* methods have been tried).

difficult see HARD

diffident see SHY
diffuse see WORDY
digest see COMPENDIUM
dignity see DECORUM
digress see SWERVE
dilate see EXPAND
dilemma see PREDICAMENT
dilettante see AMATEUR
diligent see BUSY
dim see DARK
diminish see DECREASE
diminutive see SMALL
diplomatic see SUAVE
direct see COMMAND, CONDUCT

dirty, filthy, foul, nasty, squalid mean conspicuously unclean or impure. **Dirty** emphasizes the presence of dirt more than an emotional reaction to it (children *dirty* from play) (a *dirty* littered street). **Filthy** carries a strong suggestion of offensiveness and typically of gradually accumulated dirt that begrimes and besmears (a stained greasy floor, utterly *filthy*). **Foul** implies extreme offensiveness and an accumulation of what is rotten or stinking (a *foul-* smelling open sewer). **Nasty** applies to what is actually foul or is repugnant to one used to or expecting freshness, cleanliness, or sweetness (it's a *nasty* job to clean up after a sick cat). In practice, *nasty* is often weakened to the point of being no more than a synonym of *unpleasant* or *disagreeable* (had a *nasty* fall) (his answer gave her a *nasty* shock). **Squalid** adds to the idea of dirtiness and filth that of slovenly neglect (living in *squalid* poverty) (*squalid* slums). All these terms are applicable to moral uncleanness or baseness or obscenity. **Dirty** then stresses meanness or despicableness (don't ask me to do your *dirty* work), while **filthy** and **foul** describe disgusting obscenity or loathsome behavior (*filthy* language) (a *foul* story of lust and greed), and **nasty** implies a peculiarly offensive unpleasantness (his comedy always has a *nasty* ring to it). Distinctively **squalid** implies sordidness as well as baseness and dirtiness (her life was a series of *squalid* affairs).

disable see WEAKEN
disaffect see ESTRANGE
disallow see DISCLAIM

disaster, catastrophe, calamity, cataclysm mean an event or situation that is a terrible misfortune. **Disaster** is an unforeseen, ruinous, and often sudden misfortune that happens either through lack of foresight or through some hostile external agency (the war proved to be a *disaster* for the country). **Catastrophe** implies a disastrous conclusion emphasizing finality (speculation about the *catastrophe* that befell Atlantis). **Calamity** stresses a great personal or public loss (the father's sudden death was a *calamity* for the family). **Cataclysm,** orig. a deluge or geological convulsion, applies to an event or situation that produces an upheaval or complete reversal (the French Revolution ranks as one of the *cataclysms* of the modern era).

disavow see DISCLAIM

discard, cast, shed, slough, scrap, junk mean to get rid of. **Discard** implies the letting go or throwing away of something that has become useless or superfluous though often not intrinsically valueless (*discard* any clothes you are unlikely to wear again). **Cast,** esp. when used with *off, away,* and *out* implies a forceful rejection or repudiation (*cast* off her friends when they grew tiresome). **Shed** and **slough** imply a throwing off of something both useless and encumbering and often suggest a consequent renewal of vitality or luster (the willpower needed to *shed* a bad habit) (finally *sloughed* her air of jaded worldliness). **Scrap** and **junk** imply throwing away or breaking up as worthless in existent form ⟨all the old ideas of warfare had to be *scrapped*⟩ ⟨those who would *junk* our entire educational system⟩.

discernment, discrimination, perception, penetration, insight, acumen mean a power to see what is not evident to the average mind. **Discernment** stresses accuracy ⟨as in reading character or motives or appreciating art⟩ ⟨had not the *discernment* to know who her friends really were⟩. **Discrimination** stresses the power to distinguish and select what is true or appropriate or excellent ⟨acquire *discrimination* by looking at a lot of art⟩. **Perception** implies quick and often sympathetic discernment ⟨as of shades of feeling⟩ ⟨a novelist of keen *perception*⟩. **Penetration** implies a searching mind that goes beyond what is obvious or superficial ⟨has not the *penetration* to see beneath their deceptive facade⟩. **Insight** suggests depth of discernment coupled with understanding sympathy ⟨a documentary providing *insight* into the plight of the homeless⟩. **Acumen** implies characteristic penetration combined with keen practical judgment ⟨a theater director of reliable critical *acumen*⟩.

discharge see PERFORM

disciple see FOLLOWER

discipline see PUNISH, TEACH

disclaim, disavow, repudiate, disown, disallow mean to refuse to admit, accept, or approve. **Disclaim** implies a refusal to accept either a rightful claim or an imputation made by another ⟨*disclaimed* in equal measure the virtues and vices attributed to her⟩. **Disavow** implies a vigorous denial of personal responsibility, acceptance, or approval ⟨the radical group *disavowed* any responsibility for the bombing⟩. **Repudiate** implies a rejection or denial of something that had been previously acknowledged, recognized, or accepted ⟨*repudiated* the socialist views of his college days⟩. **Disown** implies a vigorous rejection or denial of something with which one formerly had a close relationship ⟨*disowned* his allegiance to the country of his birth⟩. **Disallow** implies the withholding of sanction or approval and sometimes suggests complete rejection or condemnation ⟨IRS auditors *disallowed* that deduction⟩.

disclose see REVEAL

discomfit see EMBARRASS

discompose, disquiet, disturb, perturb, agitate, upset, fluster mean to destroy capacity for collected thought or decisive action. **Discompose** implies some degree of loss of self-control or self-confidence esp. through emotional stress ⟨*discomposed* by the loss of his beloved wife⟩. **Disquiet** suggests loss of sense of security or peace of mind ⟨the *disquieting* news of a tragic accident⟩. **Disturb** implies interference with one's mental processes caused by worry, perplexity, or interruption ⟨the puzzling discrepancy *disturbed* me⟩. **Perturb** implies deep disturbance of mind and emotions ⟨*perturbed* by her husband's strange behavior⟩. **Agitate** suggests obvious external signs of nervous or emotional excitement ⟨in his *agitated* state he was unfit to go to work⟩. **Upset** implies the disturbance of normal or habitual functioning by disappointment, distress, or grief ⟨constant bickering that greatly *upsets* their son⟩. **Fluster** suggests bewildered agitation ⟨his amorous advances completely *flustered* her⟩.

disconcert see EMBARRASS

disconsolate see DOWNCAST

discontinue see STOP

discord, strife, conflict, contention, dissension, variance mean a state or condition marked by a lack of agreement or harmony. **Discord** implies an intrinsic or essential lack of harmony producing quarreling, factiousness, or antagonism ⟨years of *discord* had left its mark on the political party⟩. **Strife** emphasizes a struggle for superiority rather than the incongruity or incompatibility of the persons or things involved ⟨during his reign the empire was free of *strife*⟩. **Conflict** usu. stresses the action of forces in opposition but in static applications implies an irreconcilability as of duties or desires ⟨a *conflict* of professional interests⟩. **Contention** applies to strife or competition that shows itself in quarreling, disputing, or controversy ⟨several points of *contention* between the two sides⟩. **Dissension** implies strife or discord and stresses a division into factions ⟨religious *dissensions* threatened to split the colony⟩. **Variance** implies a clash between persons or things owing to a difference in nature, opinion, or interest ⟨cultural *variances* delayed the process of national unification⟩.

discover, ascertain, determine, unearth, learn mean to find out what one did not previously know. **Discover** may apply to something requiring exploration or investigation or to a chance encounter ⟨*discovered* the source of the river⟩. **Ascertain** implies effort to find the facts or the truth proceeding from awareness of ignorance or uncertainty ⟨will try to *ascertain* the population of the region⟩. **Determine** emphasizes the intent to establish the facts definitely or precisely ⟨unable to *determine* the exact etiology of the disease⟩. **Unearth** implies bringing to light something forgotten or hidden ⟨*unearth* old records⟩. **Learn** may imply acquiring knowledge with little effort or conscious intention ⟨as by simply being told⟩ or it may imply study and practice ⟨I *learned* her name only today⟩ ⟨spent years *learning* Greek⟩. See in addition INVENT, REVEAL.

discrete see DISTINCT

discrimination see DISCERNMENT

discuss, argue, debate, dispute mean to discourse about in order to reach conclusions or to convince. **Discuss** implies a sifting of possibilities esp. by presenting considerations pro and con ⟨*discussed* the need for widening the expressway⟩. **Argue** implies the offering of reasons or evidence in support of convictions already held ⟨*argued* that the project would be too costly⟩. **Debate** suggests formal or public argument between opposing parties ⟨*debated* the merits of the proposed constitutional amendment⟩; it may also apply to deliberation with oneself ⟨I'm *debating* whether I should go⟩. **Dispute** implies contentious or heated argument ⟨scientists *dispute* the reasons for the extinction of the dinosaurs⟩.

disdain see DESPISE

disdainful see PROUD

disembarrass see EXTRICATE

disencumber see EXTRICATE

disentangle see EXTRICATE

disgrace, dishonor, disrepute, infamy, ignominy mean the state or condition of suffering loss of esteem and of enduring reproach. **Disgrace** often implies complete humiliation and sometimes ostracism ⟨his conviction for bribery brought *disgrace* upon his family⟩. **Dishonor** emphasizes the loss of honor that one has enjoyed or the loss of self-esteem ⟨prefer death to life with *dishonor*⟩. **Disrepute** stresses loss of one's good name or the acquiring of a bad reputation ⟨a once-proud name now fallen into *disrepute*⟩. **Infamy** usu. implies notoriety as well as exceeding shame ⟨a gangster whose name retains an enduring *infamy*⟩. **Ignominy** stresses the almost unendurable contemptibility or despicableness of the disgrace ⟨suffered the *ignominy* of being brought back in irons⟩.

disguise, cloak, mask, dissemble mean to alter the dress or appearance so as to conceal the identity or true nature. **Disguise** implies a change in appearance or behavior that misleads by presenting a different apparent identity ⟨*disguised* himself as a peasant to escape detection⟩. **Cloak** suggests a means of hiding a movement or an intention completely ⟨*cloaks* her greed and self-interest in the rhetoric of philosophy). **Mask** suggests some usu. obvious means of preventing recognition and does not always imply deception or pretense (a smiling front that *masks* a will of iron). **Dissemble** stresses simulation for the purpose of deceiving (*dissembled* madness to survive the intrigues at court).

dishonest, deceitful, mendacious, lying, untruthful mean unworthy of trust or belief. **Dishonest** implies a willful perversion of truth in order to deceive, cheat, or defraud (a swindle usually involves two *dishonest* people). **Deceitful** usu. implies an intent to mislead and commonly suggests a false appearance or double-dealing (learned of the secret affairs of his *deceitful* wife). **Mendacious** is less forthright than *lying,* may suggest bland or even harmlessly mischievous deceit, and used of people often suggests a habit of telling untruths (his sea stories became increasingly *mendacious*). **Lying** implies a specific act or instance rather than a habit or tendency (a conviction based upon testimony of a *lying* witness). **Untruthful** is a less brutal term than *lying* and in application to accounts or description stresses a discrepancy between what is said and fact or reality rather than an intent to deceive (the version given in her memoirs is *untruthful* in several respects).

dishonor see DISGRACE

disinclined, hesitant, reluctant, loath, averse mean lacking the will or desire to do something indicated. **Disinclined** implies lack of taste for or inclination toward and often active disapproval of the thing suggested (*disinclined* to believe their story). **Hesitant** implies a holding back through fear, uncertainty, or disinclination (*hesitant* about asking her for a date). **Reluctant** implies a holding back through unwillingness (I'm *reluctant* to blame anyone just now). **Loath** implies hesitancy because of conflict with one's opinions, predilections, or liking (*loath* to believe that he could do anything right). **Averse** implies a holding back from or avoiding because of distaste or repugnance (seems *averse* to anything requiring work).

disinterested see INDIFFERENT

disloyal see FAITHLESS

dismal, dreary, cheerless, dispiriting, bleak, desolate mean devoid of all that is cheerful and comfortable. **Dismal** may imply extreme gloominess or somberness that is utterly depressing (a *dismal* day of unrelenting rain). **Dreary** implies a sustained gloom, dullness, or tiresomeness that discourages or enervates (spent her days alone in a *dreary* apartment). **Cheerless** stresses a pervasive, disheartening joylessness or hopelessness (faced a *cheerless* life as a drudge). **Dispiriting** implies a lessening of morale or determination (problems that made for a *dispiriting* start for their new venture). **Bleak** implies a chilly, dull barrenness (a *bleak,* windswept landscape offering no refuge for the wayward traveler). **Desolate** implies that something disheartens by being utterly barren, lifeless, uninhabitable, or abandoned (the long trek into the country's *desolate* interior).

dismay, appall, horrify, daunt mean to unnerve or deter by arousing fear, apprehension, or aversion. **Dismay** implies that one is balked and perplexed or at a loss as to how to deal with something (*dismayed* to find herself the center of attention). **Appall** implies that one is faced with that which perturbs, confounds, or shocks (*appalled* by your utter lack of concern). **Horrify** stresses a reaction of horror or revulsion (the scope of the famine is quite *horrifying*). **Daunt** suggests a cowing, subduing, disheartening, or frightening in a venture requiring courage (problems that would *daunt* even the most intrepid of reformers).

dismiss see EJECT

disown see DISCLAIM
disparage see DECRY
disparaging see DEROGATORY
disparate see DIFFERENT
dispassionate see FAIR
dispatch *n* see HASTE
dispatch *vb* see KILL
dispel see SCATTER
dispense see DISTRIBUTE
disperse see SCATTER
dispirited see DOWNCAST
dispiriting see DISMAL
displace see REPLACE
display see SHOW
dispose see INCLINE

disposition, temperament, temper, character, personality mean the dominant quality or qualities distinguishing a person or group. **Disposition** implies customary moods and attitude toward the life around one (a boy of cheerful *disposition*). **Temperament** implies a pattern of innate characteristics associated with one's specific physical and nervous organization (an artistic *temperament* inherited from his mother). **Temper** implies the qualities acquired through experience that determine how a person or group meets difficulties or handles situations (the national *temper* has always been one of optimism). **Character** applies to the aggregate of moral qualities by which a person is judged apart from his intelligence, competence, or special talents (a woman of iron-willed *character*). **Personality** applies to an aggregate of qualities that distinguish one as a person (a somber *personality* not to everyone's liking).

disprove, refute, confute, rebut, controvert mean to show or try to show by presenting evidence that something is not true. **Disprove** implies the demonstration by any method of the falseness or invalidness of a claim or argument (the view that one can neither prove nor *disprove* the existence of God). **Refute** stresses a logical method of disproving (*refuted* every piece of his argument). **Confute** implies reducing an opponent to silence by an overwhelming argument (a triumphal flight that *confuted* all of the doubters). **Rebut** suggests formality in the act of answering an argument and does not necessarily imply success in disproving (give the opposing side time to *rebut*). **Controvert** stresses the act of opposing with denial or an answering argument (a thesis that withstood every attempt to *controvert* it).

dispute see DISCUSS
disquiet see DISCOMPOSE
disregard see NEGLECT
disrepute see DISGRACE
dissect see ANALYZE
dissemble see DISGUISE
dissension see DISCORD
dissipate see SCATTER
distasteful see REPUGNANT
distend see EXPAND

distinct, separate, several, discrete mean not being each and every one the same. **Distinct** indicates that something is distinguished by the mind or eye as being apart or different from others (each and every bowl is hand-decorated and *distinct*). **Separate** often stresses lack of connection or a difference in identity between two things (the two schools are *separate* and unequal). **Several** indicates distinctness, difference, or separation from similar items (a survey of the *several* opinions of the new building). **Discrete** strongly emphasizes individuality and lack of physical connection despite apparent similarity or seeming continuity (two *discrete* issues are being confused here). See in addition EVIDENT.

distinctive see CHARACTERISTIC

distinguished see FAMOUS

distort see DEFORM

distract see PUZZLE

distress, suffering, misery, agony mean the state of being in great trouble. **Distress** implies an external and usu. temporary cause of great physical or mental strain and stress ⟨news of the hurricane put everyone in great *distress*⟩. **Suffering** implies conscious endurance of pain or distress ⟨the *suffering* of earthquake victims⟩. **Misery** stresses the unhappiness attending esp. sickness, poverty, or loss ⟨the poor live with *misery* every day⟩. **Agony** suggests pain too intense to be borne ⟨in *agony* over their daughter's suicide⟩.

distribute, dispense, divide, deal, dole mean to give out, usu. in shares, to each member of a group. **Distribute** implies an apportioning by separation of something into parts, units, or amounts ⟨*distributed* the work to all employees⟩. **Dispense** suggests the giving of a carefully weighed or measured portion to each of a group according to due or need ⟨*dispensed* medicine during the epidemic⟩. **Divide** stresses the separation of a whole into parts and implies that the parts are equal ⟨three charitable groups *divided* the proceeds⟩. **Deal** emphasizes the allotment of something piece by piece ⟨*deal* out equipment and supplies to each soldier⟩. **Dole** implies a carefully measured portion that is often scant or niggardly ⟨*doled* out the little food there was⟩.

disturb see DISCOMPOSE

diverge see SWERVE

divergent see DIFFERENT

diverse see DIFFERENT

divert see AMUSE

divide see DISTRIBUTE, SEPARATE

divine see FORESEE

division see PART

divorce see SEPARATE

divulge see REVEAL

docile see OBEDIENT

doctrinaire see DICTATORIAL

dogged see OBSTINATE

dogmatic see DICTATORIAL

dole see DISTRIBUTE

dominant, predominant, paramount, preponderant, sovereign mean superior to all others in power, influence, or importance. **Dominant** applies to something that is uppermost because ruling or controlling ⟨a *dominant* social class⟩. **Predominant** applies to something that exerts, often temporarily, the most marked influence ⟨at the time fear was my *predominant* emotion⟩. **Paramount** implies supremacy in importance, rank, or jurisdiction ⟨inflation was the *paramount* issue in the campaign⟩. **Preponderant** applies to an element or factor that outweighs all others in influence or effect ⟨*preponderant* evidence in his favor⟩. **Sovereign** indicates quality or rank to which everything else is clearly subordinate or inferior ⟨the *sovereign* power resides in the people⟩.

domineering see MASTERFUL

dominion see POWER

donate see GIVE

doom see FATE

dormant see LATENT

double-dealing see DECEPTION

double entendre see AMBIGUITY

doubt see UNCERTAINTY

doubtful, dubious, problematic, questionable mean not affording assurance of the worth, soundness, or certainty of something. **Doubtful** implies little more than a lack of conviction or certainty ⟨still *doubtful* about the cause of the explosion⟩. **Dubious** stresses suspicion, mistrust, or hesitation ⟨*dubious* about the practicality of the scheme⟩. **Problematic** applies esp. to things whose existence, meaning, fulfillment, or realization is highly uncertain ⟨whether the project will ever be finished is *problematic*⟩. **Question able** may imply no more than the existence of doubt but usu. suggests that the suspicions are well-grounded ⟨a real estate agent of *questionable* honesty⟩.

downcast, dispirited, dejected, depressed, disconsolate, woebegone mean affected by or showing very low spirits. **Downcast** implies an overwhelming shame, mortification, or loss of confidence ⟨negative reviews left all of the actors feeling *downcast*⟩. **Dispirited** implies extreme low-spiritedness resulting from failure ⟨*dispirited,* the doomed explorers resigned themselves to failure⟩. **Dejected** implies a sudden but often temporary loss of hope, courage, or vigor ⟨a crushing defeat that left the team in a *dejected* mood⟩. **Depressed** may imply either a temporary or a chronic low- spiritedness ⟨*depressed* by his failures to the point of suicide⟩. **Disconsolate** implies being inconsolable or very uncomfortable ⟨*disconsolate* motorists leaning against their disabled car⟩. **Woebegone** suggests a defeated, spiritless condition ⟨a rundown, *woebegone* motel on an empty back road⟩.

drag see PULL

drain see DEPLETE

dramatic, theatrical, histrionic, melodramatic mean having a character or an effect like that of acted plays. **Dramatic** applies to situations in life and literature that stir the imagination and emotions deeply ⟨a *dramatic* meeting of world leaders⟩. **Theatrical** implies a crude appeal through artificiality or exaggeration in gesture or vocal expression ⟨a *theatrical* oration⟩. **Histrionic** applies to tones, gestures, and motions and suggests a deliberate affectation or staginess ⟨a *histrionic* show of grief⟩. **Melodramatic** suggests an exaggerated emotionalism or an inappropriate theatricalism ⟨making a *melodramatic* scene in public⟩.

draw see PULL

dread see FEAR

dreary see DISMAL

drench see SOAK

drift see TENDENCY

drive see MOVE

drudgery see WORK

drunk, drunken, intoxicated, inebriated, tipsy, tight mean considerably affected by alcohol. **Drunk** and **drunken** are the plainspoken, direct, and inclusive terms ⟨arrived at the party already *drunk*⟩ ⟨a *drunken* man stumbled out of the bar⟩. **Intoxicated** is a more formal term and likely to be used in legal or medical contexts ⟨arrested for driving while *intoxicated*⟩. **Inebriated** stresses the hilarious or noisy aspects of drunkenness ⟨the *inebriated* revelers bellowed out songs⟩. **Tipsy** may imply only slight drunkenness ⟨a *tipsy* patron began making unwelcome amorous advances⟩. **Tight** usu. suggests obvious drunkenness ⟨at midnight he returned, *tight* as a drum⟩.

drunken see DRUNK

dubiety see UNCERTAINTY

dubious see DOUBTFUL

ductile see PLASTIC

dudgeon see OFFENSE

dull, blunt, obtuse mean not sharp, keen, or acute. **Dull** suggests a lack or loss of keenness, zest, or pungency ⟨a *dull* pain⟩ ⟨a *dull* mind⟩. **Blunt** suggests an inherent lack of sharpness or quickness of feeling or perception ⟨even a person of his *blunt* sensibility was moved⟩. **Obtuse** implies such bluntness as makes one insensitive in perception or imagination ⟨too *obtuse* to realize that she had deeply hurt us⟩. See in addition STUPID.

dumb see STUPID

dumbfound see PUZZLE

dupe, gull, trick, hoax mean to deceive by underhanded means. **Dupe** suggests unwariness in the person deluded 〈*duped* us into buying a lemon of a car〉. **Gull** stresses credulousness or readiness to be imposed on (as through greed) on the part of the victim 〈are you so easily *gulled* by these contest promoters〉. **Trick** implies an intent to delude by means of a ruse or fraud but does not always imply a vicious intent 〈special effects can *trick* moviegoers into believing anything〉. **Hoax** implies the contriving of an elaborate or adroit imposture in order to deceive 〈*hoaxed* the public by broadcasting news of a Martian invasion〉.

duplicate see REPRODUCTION

durable see LASTING

dusky see DARK

duty see FUNCTION, TASK

dwindle see DECREASE

E

eager, avid, keen, anxious, athirst mean moved by a strong and urgent desire or interest. **Eager** implies ardor and enthusiasm and sometimes impatience at delay or restraint 〈*eager* to get started on the trip〉. **Avid** adds to *eager* the implication of insatiability or greed 〈young pleasure-seekers *avid* for the next thrill〉. **Keen** suggests intensity of interest and quick responsiveness in action 〈very *keen* on the latest styles and fashions〉. **Anxious** emphasizes fear of frustration or failure or disappointment 〈*anxious* to know that they got home safely〉. **Athirst** stresses yearning but not necessarily readiness for action 〈*athirst* for adventure on her first trip to India〉.

earn see GET

earnest see SERIOUS

earsplitting see LOUD

earthly, mundane, worldly mean belonging to or characteristic of the earth. **Earthly** often implies a contrast with what is heavenly or spiritual 〈abandoned *earthly* concerns and entered a convent〉. **Worldly** and **mundane** both imply a relation to the immediate concerns and activities of human beings, *worldly* suggesting tangible personal gain or gratification 〈a philosopher with no interest in *worldly* goods〉, and *mundane* suggesting reference to the immediate and practical 〈a *mundane* discussion of finances〉.

easy, facile, simple, light, effortless, smooth mean not demanding effort or involving difficulty. **Easy** is applicable either to persons or things imposing tasks or to activity required by such tasks 〈an *easy* college course requiring little work〉. **Facile** often adds to *easy* the connotation of undue haste or shallowness 〈offers only *facile* solutions to complex problems〉. **Simple** stresses ease in understanding or dealing with because complication is absent 〈a *simple* problem in arithmetic〉. **Light** stresses freedom from what is burdensome, and often suggests quickness of movement 〈her novels are pretty *light* stuff〉. **Effortless** stresses the appearance of ease and usu. implies the prior attainment of artistry or expertness 〈a champion figure skater moving with *effortless* grace〉. **Smooth** stresses the absence or removal of all difficulties, hardships, or obstacles 〈appliances make life for working mothers a little *smoother*〉. See in addition COMFORTABLE.

ebb see ABATE

eccentric see STRANGE

economical see SPARING

ecstasy, rapture, transport mean intense exaltation of mind and feelings. **Ecstasy** may apply to any strong emotion (as joy, fear, rage, adoration) 〈the sculptor was in *ecstasy* when his work was unveiled〉. **Rapture** usu. implies intense bliss or beatitude 〈in speechless *rapture* during the entire wedding〉. **Transport** applies to any powerful emotion that lifts one out of oneself and usu. provokes vehement expression or frenzied action 〈in a *transport* of rage after reading the article〉.

edge see BORDER

educate see TEACH

educe, evoke, elicit, extract, extort mean to draw out something hidden, latent, or reserved. **Educe** implies the bringing out of something potential or latent 〈a teacher who can *educe* the best in her students〉. **Evoke** implies a strong stimulus that arouses an emotion or an interest or recalls an image or memory 〈a song that *evokes* many memories〉. **Elicit** usu. implies some effort or skill in drawing forth a response 〈unable to *elicit* a straight answer from the candidate〉. **Extract** implies the use of force or pressure in obtaining answers or information 〈*extract* testimony from a hostile witness〉. **Extort** suggests a wringing or wresting from one who resists strongly 〈*extorted* the money from his father-in-law〉.

eerie see WEIRD

efface see ERASE

effect *n* Effect, consequence, result, issue, outcome mean a condition or occurrence traceable to a cause. **Effect** designates something that necessarily and directly follows or occurs by reason of a cause 〈the *effects* of radiation on the body〉. **Consequence** implies a looser or remoter connection with a cause and usu. implies that the cause is no longer operating 〈a single act that had far-reaching *consequences*〉. **Result** applies often to the last in a series of effects 〈the end *result* was a growth in business〉. **Issue** applies to a result that ends or solves a difficulty 〈a successful *issue* that rendered all the controversy moot〉. **Outcome** suggests the final result of complex or conflicting causes or forces 〈the *outcome* of generations of controlled breeding〉.

effect *vb* see PERFORM

effective, effectual, efficient, efficacious mean producing or capable of producing a result. **Effective** stresses the actual production of or the power to produce an effect 〈an *effective* rebuttal〉. **Effectual** suggests the accomplishment of a desired result esp. as viewed after the fact 〈the measures to halt crime proved *effectual*〉. **Efficient** suggests an acting or a potential for action or use in such a way as to avoid loss or waste of energy in effecting, producing, or functioning 〈an *efficient* small car〉. **Efficacious** suggests possession of a special quality or virtue that gives effective power 〈a detergent that is *efficacious* in removing grease〉.

effectual see EFFECTIVE

efficacious see EFFECTIVE

efficient see EFFECTIVE

effort, exertion, pains, trouble mean the active use of energy in producing a result. **Effort** often suggests a single action or attempt and implies the calling up or directing of energy by the conscious will 〈made the supreme *effort* and crossed the finish line first〉. **Exertion** may describe the bringing into effect of any power of mind or body or it may suggest laborious and exhausting effort 〈a job not requiring much physical *exertion*〉. **Pains** implies toilsome or solicitous effort 〈take *pains* to do the job well〉. **Trouble** implies effort that inconveniences or slows down 〈went through a lot of *trouble* to get the right equipment〉.

effortless see EASY

effrontery see TEMERITY

eject, expel, oust, evict, dismiss mean to drive or force out. **Eject** carries an esp. strong implication of throwing or thrusting out from within as a physical action 〈*ejected* the obnoxious patron from the bar〉. **Expel** stresses a thrusting out or driving away esp. permanently which need not be physical 〈a student *expelled* from college〉. **Oust** implies removal or dispossession by power of the law or by compulsion of ne-

cessity ⟨issued a general order *ousting* all foreigners⟩.
Evict chiefly applies to turning out of house and
home ⟨they were *evicted* for nonpayment of rent⟩.
Dismiss implies a getting rid of something unpleasant
or troublesome simply by refusing to consider it
further ⟨simply *dismissed* the quarrel from her
mind⟩.

elastic, resilient, springy, flexible, supple mean able to
endure strain without being permanently injured.
Elastic implies the property of resisting deformation
by stretching ⟨slacks that come with an *elastic* waist-
band⟩. **Resilient** implies the ability to recover shape
quickly when the deforming force or pressure is removed ⟨a good running shoe has a *resilient* inner-
sole⟩. **Springy** stresses both the ease with which something yields to pressure and the quickness of its return to original shape ⟨the cake is done when the top
is *springy*⟩. **Flexible** applies to something which may
or may not be resilient or elastic but which can be
bent or folded without breaking ⟨*flexible* plastic tub-
ing⟩. **Supple** applies to something that can be readily
bent, twisted, or folded without any sign of injury
⟨shoes made of luxurious, *supple* leather⟩.

election see CHOICE
elegant see CHOICE
element, component, constituent, ingredient, factor
mean one of the parts of a compound or complex
whole. **Element** applies to any such part and often
connotes irreducible simplicity ⟨the basic *elements*
of the gothic novel⟩. **Component** and **constituent** may
designate any of the substances (whether elements or
compounds) or the qualities that enter into the
makeup of a complex product; *component* stresses
its separate entity or distinguishable character ⟨able
to identify every *component* of his firearm⟩; *constituent* stresses its essential and formative character ⟨an-
alyzed the *constituents* of the compound⟩. **Ingredient**
applies to any of the substances which when combined form a particular mixture (as a medicine or
alloy) ⟨the *ingredients* of a cocktail⟩. **Factor** applies
to any constituent or element whose presence helps
actively to perform a certain kind of work or produce
a definite result ⟨price was a *factor* in her decision to
buy⟩.

elevate see LIFT
elevation see HEIGHT
elicit see EDUCE
eliminate see EXCLUDE
elucidate see EXPLAIN
elude see ESCAPE
emanate see SPRING
emancipate see FREE
emasculate see UNNERVE
embarrass, discomfit, abash, disconcert, rattle mean to
distress by confusing or confounding. **Embarrass** implies some influence that impedes thought, speech,
or action ⟨*embarrassed* to admit that she liked the
movie⟩. **Discomfit** implies a hampering or frustrating
accompanied by confusion ⟨persistent heckling *discomfited* the speaker⟩. **Abash** presupposes some initial self-confidence that receives a sudden check by
something that produces shyness, shame, or a conviction of inferiority ⟨completely *abashed* by her swift
and cutting retort⟩. **Disconcert** implies an upsetting of
equanimity or assurance producing uncertainty or
hesitancy ⟨*disconcerted* by the sight of the large au-
dience⟩. **Rattle** implies an agitation that impairs
thought and judgment ⟨a tennis player not at all *rattled* by television cameras⟩.

embellish see ADORN
embolden see ENCOURAGE
embrace see ADOPT, INCLUDE
emend see CORRECT
emergency see JUNCTURE

eminent see FAMOUS
emotion see FEELING
employ see USE
employment see WORK
empty, vacant, blank, void, vacuous mean lacking contents which could or should be present. **Empty** suggests a complete absence of contents ⟨an *empty* buck-
et⟩. **Vacant** suggests an absence of appropriate contents or occupants ⟨a *vacant* apartment⟩. **Blank**
stresses the absence of any significant, relieving, or
intelligible features on a surface ⟨a *blank* wall⟩. **Void**
suggests absolute emptiness as far as the mind or
senses can determine ⟨a statement *void* of meaning⟩.
Vacuous suggests the emptiness of a vacuum and esp.
the lack of intelligence or significance ⟨a *vacuous*
facial expression⟩. See in addition VAIN.

enchant see ATTRACT
encomium, eulogy, panegyric, tribute, citation mean a
formal expression of praise. **Encomium** implies enthusiasm and warmth in praising a person or a thing
⟨the subject of several spirited *encomiums* at the
banquet⟩. **Eulogy** applies to a prepared speech or
writing extolling the virtues and services of a person
⟨delivered the *eulogy* at the funeral⟩. **Panegyric** suggests an elaborate often poetic compliment ⟨corona-
tions once inspired *panegyrics*⟩. **Tribute** implies
deeply felt praise conveyed either through words or
through a significant act ⟨a page of *tributes* marking
his fifty years of service⟩. **Citation** applies to the formal praise accompanying the mention of a person in
a military dispatch or in awarding an honorary degree
⟨a *citation* noting her lasting contribution to biolo-
gy⟩.

encourage, inspirit, hearten, embolden mean to fill
with courage or strength of purpose. **Encourage** suggests the raising of one's confidence esp. by an external agency ⟨the teacher's praise *encouraged* the student to try even harder⟩. **Inspirit** implies instilling
life, energy, courage, or vigor into something ⟨pio-
neers *inspirited* by the stirring accounts of the ex-
plorers⟩. **Hearten** implies a dispiritedness or despondency that is lifted by an infusion of fresh courage or
zeal ⟨a hospital patient *heartened* by the display of
moral support⟩. **Embolden** implies the giving of courage sufficient to overcome timidity or reluctance ⟨a
successful climb *emboldened* her to try more difficult ones⟩.

encroach see TRESPASS
end *n* End, **termination, ending, terminus** mean the
point or line beyond which something does not or
cannot go. **End** is the inclusive term, implying the
final limit in time or space, in extent of influence, or
range of possibility ⟨the report put an *end* to all spec-
ulation⟩. **Termination** and **ending** apply to the end of
something having predetermined limits or being
complete or finished ⟨the *termination* of a lease⟩
⟨the *ending* of a search⟩. *Ending* often includes the
portion leading to the actual final point ⟨a film
marred by a contrived *ending*⟩. **Terminus** applies
commonly to the point to which one moves or progresses ⟨Chicago is the *terminus* for many air routes⟩.
See in addition INTENTION.

end *vb* see CLOSE
endeavor see ATTEMPT
endemic see NATIVE
ending see END
endorse see APPROVE
endure see BEAR, CONTINUE
energetic see VIGOROUS
energy see POWER
enervate see UNNERVE
enfeeble see WEAKEN
engineer see GUIDE
enhance see INTENSIFY

enigma see MYSTERY
enigmatic see OBSCURE
enjoin see COMMAND
enlarge see INCREASE
enliven see QUICKEN

enmity, hostility, antipathy, antagonism, animosity, rancor, animus mean deep-seated dislike or ill will. **Enmity** suggests positive hatred which may be open or concealed ⟨an unspoken *enmity* seethed between the two⟩. **Hostility** suggests an enmity showing itself in attacks or aggression ⟨a history of *hostility* between the two nations⟩. **Antipathy** and **antagonism** imply a natural or logical basis for one's hatred or dislike, *antipathy* suggesting repugnance, a desire to avoid or reject, and *antagonism* suggesting a clash of temperaments leading readily to hostility ⟨a natural *antipathy* for self-important upstarts⟩ ⟨a long-standing *antagonism* between the banker and his prodigal son⟩. **Animosity** suggests intense ill will and vindictiveness that threaten to kindle hostility ⟨*animosity* that eventually led to revenge⟩. **Rancor** esp. is applied to bitter brooding over a wrong ⟨*rancor* filled every line of his letters⟩. **Animus** implies strong prejudice ⟨my objections are devoid of any personal *animus*⟩.

enormous, immense, huge, vast, gigantic, colossal, mammoth mean exceedingly large. **Enormous** and **immense** both suggest an exceeding of all ordinary bounds in size or amount or degree, but *enormous* often adds an implication of abnormality or monstrousness ⟨the *enormous* expense of the program⟩ ⟨the *immense* size of the new shopping mall⟩. **Huge** commonly suggests an immensity of bulk or amount ⟨quickly incurred a *huge* debt⟩. **Vast** usu. suggests immensity of extent ⟨the *vast* Russian steppes⟩. **Gigantic** stresses the contrast with the size of others of the same kind ⟨a *gigantic* sports stadium⟩. **Colossal** applies esp. to a human creation of stupendous or incredible dimensions ⟨a *colossal* statue of Lincoln⟩. **Mammoth** suggests both hugeness and ponderousness of bulk ⟨a *mammoth* boulder⟩.

enough see SUFFICIENT
ensnare see CATCH
ensue see FOLLOW

ensure, insure, assure, secure mean to make a thing or person sure. **Ensure** implies a virtual guarantee ⟨the government has *ensured* the safety of the foreign minister⟩. **Insure** sometimes stresses the taking of necessary measures beforehand ⟨careful planning should *insure* the success of the party⟩. **Assure** distinctively implies the removal of doubt and suspense from a person's mind ⟨I *assure* you that no one will be harmed⟩. **Secure** implies action taken to guard against attack or loss ⟨made a reservation in order to *secure* a table⟩.

enter, penetrate, pierce, probe mean to make way into something. **Enter** is the most general of these and may imply either going in or forcing a way in ⟨*entered* the city in triumph⟩. **Penetrate** carries a strong implication of an impelling force or compelling power that achieves entrance ⟨no bullet has ever *penetrated* a vest of that material⟩. **Pierce** adds to *penetrate* a clear implication of an entering point ⟨a fracture in which the bone *pierces* the skin⟩. **Probe** implies penetration to investigate or explore something hidden from sight or knowledge ⟨*probed* the depths of the sea⟩.

entertain see AMUSE
enthusiasm see PASSION
entice see LURE
entire see PERFECT, WHOLE
entrap see CATCH
entreat see BEG
entrench see TRESPASS
entrust see COMMIT

environment see BACKGROUND
envisage see THINK
envision see THINK
ephemeral see TRANSIENT

epicure, gourmet, gastronome, bon vivant mean one who takes pleasure in eating and drinking. **Epicure** implies fastidiousness and voluptuousness of taste ⟨a delicacy that only an *epicure* would appreciate⟩. **Gourmet** implies being a connoisseur in food and drink and the discriminating enjoyment of them ⟨*gourmets* rate the restaurant highly⟩. **Gastronome** implies that one has studied extensively the history and rituals of haute cuisine ⟨an annual banquet that attracts *gastronomes* from all over⟩. **Bon vivant** stresses the enjoyment of fine food and drink in company ⟨*bon vivants* rang in the New Year in style⟩.

episode see OCCURRENCE
epitome see ABRIDGMENT
epoch see PERIOD
equable see STEADY
equal see SAME

equanimity, composure, sangfroid, phlegm mean evenness of mind under stress. **Equanimity** suggests a habit of mind that is only rarely disturbed under great strain ⟨accepted fortune's slings and arrows with resigned *equanimity*⟩. **Composure** implies the controlling of emotional or mental agitation by an effort of will or as a matter of habit ⟨maintained his *composure* even under hostile questioning⟩. **Sangfroid** implies great coolness and steadiness under strain ⟨an Olympian diver of remarkable *sangfroid*⟩. **Phlegm** implies insensitiveness and suggests apathy rather than self-control ⟨good news and bad news alike had no effect on her *phlegm*⟩.

equip see FURNISH
equitable see FAIR
equivalent see SAME
equivocal see OBSCURE
equivocate see LIE
equivocation see AMBIGUITY
era see PERIOD
eradicate see EXTERMINATE

erase, expunge, cancel, efface, obliterate, blot out, delete mean to remove something so that it no longer has any effect or existence. **Erase** implies the act of rubbing or wiping out (letters or impressions) often in preparation for correction or new matter ⟨*erase* what you wrote and start over⟩. **Expunge** stresses a removal or destruction that leaves no trace ⟨*expunged* all references to the deposed leader⟩. **Cancel** implies an action (as marking, revoking, or neutralizing) that makes a thing no longer effective or usable ⟨a crime that *cancelled* out all her good deeds⟩. **Efface** implies the removal of an impression by damage to or wearing off of the surface ⟨the subway sign had been badly *effaced*⟩. **Obliterate** and **blot out** both imply a covering up or smearing over that removes all traces of a thing's existence ⟨an outdoor mural almost *obliterated* by graffiti⟩ ⟨*blotted* out the offensive passage with black ink⟩. **Delete** implies a deliberate exclusion, or a marking to direct exclusion, of written matter ⟨his editor *deleted* all unflattering references to others⟩.

erratic see STRANGE

error, mistake, slip, blunder, lapse mean a departure from what is true, right, or proper. **Error** suggests the existence of a standard or guide and a straying from the right course through failure to make effective use of this ⟨one *error* in judgment lost the battle⟩. **Mistake** implies misconception or inadvertence and usu. expresses less criticism than *error* ⟨dialed the wrong number by *mistake*⟩. **Blunder** regularly imputes stupidity or ignorance as a cause and connotes some degree of blame ⟨a political campaign noted mostly for its series of *blunders*⟩. **Slip** stresses inadvertence or accident and applies esp. to trivial but embarrassing mistakes ⟨during the speech I made several *slips*⟩. **Lapse** stresses forgetfulness, weakness, or inattention as a cause ⟨apart from a few grammatical *lapses*, the paper is good⟩.

ersatz see ARTIFICIAL

erudition see KNOWLEDGE

escape, avoid, evade, elude, shun, eschew mean to get away or keep away from something. **Escape** stresses the fact of getting away or being passed by not necessarily through effort or by conscious intent ⟨nothing *escapes* her sharp eyes⟩. **Avoid** stresses forethought and caution in keeping clear of danger or difficulty ⟨with careful planning we can *avoid* the fate of previous attempts⟩. **Evade** implies adroitness, ingenuity, or lack of scruple in escaping or avoiding ⟨*evaded* the question by changing the subject⟩. **Elude** implies a slippery or baffling quality in the person or thing that escapes ⟨what she sees in him *eludes* me⟩. **Shun** often implies an avoiding as a matter of habitual practice or policy and may imply repugnance or abhorrence ⟨you have *shunned* your responsibilities⟩. **Eschew** implies an avoiding or abstaining from as unwise or distasteful ⟨a playwright who *eschews* melodrama and claptrap⟩.

eschew see ESCAPE

escort see ACCOMPANY

especial see SPECIAL

espouse see ADOPT

essay see ATTEMPT

essential, fundamental, vital, cardinal mean so important as to be indispensable. **Essential** implies belonging to the very nature of a thing and therefore being incapable of removal without destroying the thing itself or its character ⟨conflict is an *essential* element in drama⟩. **Fundamental** applies to something that is a foundation without which an entire system or complex whole would collapse ⟨the *fundamental* principles of democracy⟩. **Vital** suggests something that is necessary to a thing's continued existence or operation ⟨air bases that are *vital* to our national security⟩. **Cardinal** suggests something on which an outcome turns or depends ⟨one of the *cardinal* events of the Civil War⟩.

esteem see REGARD

estimate, appraise, evaluate, value, rate, assess mean to judge something with respect to its worth or significance. **Estimate** implies a judgment, considered or casual, that precedes or takes the place of actual measuring or counting or testing out ⟨*estimated* that there were a hundred people there⟩. **Appraise** commonly implies the fixing by an expert of the monetary worth of a thing, but it may be used of any critical judgment ⟨a real estate agent *appraised* the house⟩. **Evaluate** suggests an attempt to determine either the relative or intrinsic worth of something in terms other than monetary ⟨instructors will *evaluate* all students' work⟩. **Value** equals *appraise* but without implying expertness of judgment ⟨a watercolor *valued* by the donor at $500⟩. **Rate** adds to *estimate* the notion of placing a thing according to a scale of values ⟨an actress who is *rated* highly by her peers⟩. **Assess** implies a critical appraisal for the purpose of understanding or interpreting, or as a guide in taking action ⟨officials are still trying to *assess* the damage⟩.

estimate see CALCULATE

estrange, alienate, disaffect, wean mean to cause one to break a bond of affection or loyalty. **Estrange** implies the development of indifference or hostility with consequent separation or divorcement ⟨a chance meeting with his *estranged* wife⟩. **Alienate** may or may not suggest separation but always implies loss of affection or interest ⟨managed to *alienate* all her coworkers with her arrogance⟩. **Disaffect** refers esp. to those from whom loyalty is expected and stresses the effects (as rebellion or discontent) of alienation without actual separation ⟨overly strict parents who *disaffect* their children⟩. **Wean** implies separation from something having a strong hold on one ⟨willpower is needed to *wean* yourself from a bad habit⟩.

ethical see MORAL

etiquette see DECORUM

eulogy see ENCOMIUM

evade see ESCAPE

evaluate see ESTIMATE

evanescent see TRANSIENT

even see LEVEL, STEADY

event see OCCURRENCE

eventual see LAST

evict see EJECT

evidence see SHOW

evident, manifest, patent, distinct, obvious, apparent, plain, clear mean readily perceived or apprehended. **Evident** implies presence of visible signs that lead one to a definite conclusion ⟨an *evident* fondness for the company of beautiful women⟩. **Manifest** implies an external display so evident that little or no inference is required ⟨her *manifest* joy upon receiving the award⟩. **Patent** applies to a cause, effect, or significant feature that is clear and unmistakable once attention has been directed to it ⟨*patent* defects in the item when sold⟩. **Distinct** implies such sharpness of outline or definition that no unusual effort to see or hear or comprehend is required ⟨my offer met with a *distinct* refusal⟩. **Obvious** implies such ease in discovering or accounting for that it often suggests conspicuousness or little need for perspicacity in the observer ⟨the motives are *obvious* to all but the most obtuse⟩. **Apparent** is very close to *evident* except that it may imply more conscious exercise of inference ⟨the absurdity of the charge is *apparent* to all who know him⟩. **Plain** implies lack of intricacy, complexity, or elaboration ⟨her feelings about him are quite *plain*⟩. **Clear** implies an absence of anything that confuses the mind or obscures the pattern ⟨it's *clear* now what's been going on⟩.

evil see BAD

evince see SHOW

evoke see EDUCE

exact *adj* see CORRECT

exact *vb* see DEMAND

exacting see ONEROUS

examine see SCRUTINIZE

example see INSTANCE, MODEL

exasperate see IRRITATE

exceed, surpass, transcend, excel, outdo, outstrip mean to go or be beyond a stated or implied limit, measure, or degree. **Exceed** implies going beyond a limit set by authority or established by custom or by prior achievement ⟨*exceed* the speed limit⟩. **Surpass** suggests superiority in quality, merit, or skill ⟨the book *surpassed* our expectations⟩. **Transcend** implies a rising or extending notably above or beyond ordinary limits ⟨*transcended* the values of their culture⟩. **Excel** implies preeminence in achievement or quality and may suggest superiority to all others ⟨*excels* in mathematics⟩. **Outdo** applies to a bettering or exceeding what has been done before ⟨*outdid* herself this time⟩. **Outstrip** suggests surpassing in a race or competition ⟨*outstripped* other firms in selling the new plastic⟩.

excel see EXCEED

excessive, immoderate, inordinate, extravagant, exorbitant, extreme mean going beyond a normal limit. **Excessive** implies an amount or degree too great to be reasonable or acceptable ⟨punishment that was deemed *excessive*⟩. **Immoderate** implies lack of desirable or necessary restraint ⟨an *immoderate* amount of time spent on grooming). **Inordinate** implies an exceeding of the limits dictated by reason or good judgment (an *inordinate* portion of their budget goes to entertainment). **Extravagant** implies an indifference to restraints imposed by truth, prudence, or good taste (*extravagant* claims for the product). **Exorbitant** implies a departure from accepted standards regarding amount or degree (a menu with *exorbitant* prices). **Extreme** may imply an approach to the farthest limit possible or conceivable but commonly means only to a notably high degree (views concerning marriage that are a bit *extreme*).

excite see PROVOKE

exclude, debar, eliminate, suspend mean to shut or put out. **Exclude** implies keeping out what is already outside (children under 17 are *excluded* from seeing the movie). **Debar** implies setting up a barrier that is effectual in excluding a person or class from what is open or accessible to others (arbitrary standards that effectively *debar* most female candidates). **Eliminate** implies the getting rid of what is already within esp. as a constituent part or element (a company's plans to *eliminate* a fourth of its work force). **Suspend** implies temporary and commonly disciplinary removal from membership in a school or organization (a student *suspended* for possession of drugs).

exculpate, absolve, exonerate, acquit, vindicate mean to free from a charge. **Exculpate** implies a clearing from blame or fault often in a matter of small importance (I cannot *exculpate* myself of the charge of overenthusiasm). **Absolve** implies a release either from an obligation that binds the conscience or from the consequences of disobeying the law or committing a sin (*absolved* the subject from his oath of allegiance). **Exonerate** implies a complete clearance from an accusation or charge and from any attendant suspicion of blame or guilt (a committee *exonerated* the governor of bribery). **Acquit** implies a formal decision in one's favor with respect to a definite charge (*acquitted* by a jury of murder). **Vindicate** may refer to things as well as persons that have been subjected to critical attack or imputation of guilt, weakness, or folly, and implies a clearing effected by proving the unfairness of such criticism or blame (an investigation *vindicated* the senator on all counts).

excuse, condone, pardon, forgive mean to exact neither punishment nor redress. **Excuse** may refer to specific acts esp. in social or conventional situations or to the person responsible for these (*excuse* an interruption) (*excused* her for interrupting). Often the term implies extenuating circumstances (injustice *excuses* strong responses). **Condone** implies that one overlooks without censure behavior (as dishonesty or violence) that involves a serious breach of a moral, ethical, or legal code, and the term may refer to the behavior or to the agent responsible f or it (a society that *condones* alcohol but not drugs). **Pardon** implies that one remits a penalty due for an admitted or established offense (*pardon* a criminal) (*pardon* the noisy enthusiasm of a child). **Forgive** implies that one gives up all claim to requital and to resentment or vengeful feelings (*forgave* her husband for his infidelities).

excuse *n* see APOLOGY

execrate, curse, damn, anathematize mean to denounce violently. **Execrate** implies intense loathing and usu. passionate fury (*execrated* the men who had molested his family). **Curse** and **damn** imply angry denunciation by blasphemous oaths or profane imprecations (a drunken wino *cursing* passersby) (*damns* the city council for not anticipating the problem). **Anathematize** implies solemn denunciation of an evil or an injustice (preachers *anathematizing* pornography).

execute, administer mean to carry out the declared intent of another. **Execute** stresses the enforcing of the specific provisions of a law, will, commission, or a command (charged with failing to *execute* the order). **Administer** implies the continuing exercise of delegated authority in pursuance of only generally indicated goals rather than specif. prescribed means of attaining them (the agency in charge of *administering* Indian affairs). See in addition KILL, PERFORM.

exemplar see MODEL
exertion see EFFORT
exhaust see DEPLETE, TIRE
exhibit see SHOW
exigency see JUNCTURE
exile see BANISH
exonerate see EXCULPATE
exorbitant see EXCESSIVE

expand, amplify, swell, distend, inflate, dilate mean to increase in size or volume. **Expand** may apply whether the increase comes from within or without and regardless of manner (as growth, unfolding, addition of parts) (our business has *expanded* with every passing year). **Amplify** implies the extension or enlargement of something inadequate (*amplify* the statement with some details). **Swell** implies gradual expansion beyond a thing's original or normal limits (the bureaucracy *swelled* to unmanageable proportions). **Distend** implies outward extension caused by pressure from within (a stomach *distended* by gas). **Inflate** implies expanding by introduction of air or something insubstantial and suggests a resulting vulnerability and liability to sudden collapse (*inflate* a balloon) (an *inflated* ego). **Dilate** applies esp. to expansion of circumference (dim light causes the pupils of the eyes to *dilate*).

expect, hope, look mean to await some occurrence or outcome. **Expect** implies a high degree of certainty and usu. involves the idea of preparing or envisioning (I *expect* to be finished by Tuesday). **Hope** implies little certainty but suggests confidence or assurance in the possibility that what one desires or longs for will happen (she *hopes* to find a job soon). **Look** suggests a degree of expectancy and watchfulness rather than confidence or certainty (we *look* to the day when peace will be universal).

expedient *adj* **Expedient, politic, advisable** mean dictated by practical or prudent motives. **Expedient** usu. implies what is immediately advantageous without regard for ethics or consistent principles (a truce was the *expedient* answer). **Politic** stresses judiciousness and tactical value but usu. implies some lack of candor or sincerity (converted to Catholicism when it was *politic* to do so). **Advisable** applies to what is practical, prudent, or advantageous but lacks the derogatory implication of *expedient* and *politic* (it's *advisable* to say nothing at all).

expedient *n* see RESOURCE
expedition see HASTE
expeditious see FAST
expel see EJECT
expensive see COSTLY
expert see PROFICIENT

explain, expound, explicate, elucidate, interpret mean to make something clear or understandable. **Explain** implies a making plain or intelligible what is not immediately obvious or entirely known (the doctor *explained* what the operation would entail). **Expound** implies a careful often elaborate explanation (a professor *expounding* the theory of relativity). **Explicate** adds the idea of a developed or detailed analysis (a passage that critics have been inspired to *explicate* at length). **Elucidate** stresses the throwing of light upon as by offering details or motives previously obscure or only implicit (a newspaper report that tries to *elu-*

cidate the reasons for the crime). **Interpret** adds to *explain* the need for imagination or sympathy or special knowledge in dealing with something (*interprets* the play as an allegory about good and evil).

explicate see EXPLAIN

explicit, definite, express, specific mean perfectly clear in meaning. **Explicit** implies such verbal plainness and distinctness that there is no need for inference and no room for difficulty in understanding (the dress code is very *explicit*). **Definite** stresses precise, clear statement or arrangement that leaves no doubt or indecision (the law is *definite* regarding such cases). **Express** implies both explicitness and direct and positive utterance (her *express* wish was to be cremated). **Specific** applies to what is precisely and fully treated in detail or particular (two *specific* criticisms of the proposal).

exploit see FEAT

expose see SHOW

exposed see LIABLE

expostulate see OBJECT

expound see EXPLAIN

express *vb* Express, vent, utter, voice, broach, air mean to make known what one thinks or feels. **Express** suggests an impulse to reveal in words, gestures, or actions, or through what one creates or produces (paintings that *express* the artist's loneliness). **Vent** stresses a strong inner compulsion to express esp. in words (her stories *vent* the frustrations of black women). **Utter** implies the use of the voice not necessarily in articulate speech (would occasionally *utter* words of encouragement). **Voice** does not necessarily imply vocal utterance but does imply expression or formulation in words (an editorial *voicing the concerns of many*). **Broach** adds the implication of disclosing for the first time something long thought over or reserved for a suitable occasion (*broached* the subject of a divorce). **Air** implies an exposing or parading of one's views often in order to gain relief or sympathy or attention (cabinet members publicly *airing* their differences).

express *adj* see EXPLICIT

expunge see ERASE

exquisite see CHOICE

extemporaneous, improvised, impromptu, offhand, unpremeditated mean done or devised on the spur of the moment and not beforehand. **Extemporaneous** stresses the demands imposed by the occasion or situation and may imply a certain sketchiness or roughness (an *extemporaneous* shelter prompted by the sudden storm). **Improvised** implies the constructing or devising of something without advance knowledge, thought, or preparation and often without the proper equipment (*improvised* a barbecue pit at the campground). **Impromptu** stresses the immediacy and the spontaneity of the thing composed or devised (an *impromptu* speech at an awards ceremony). **Offhand** strongly implies casualness, carelessness, or indifference (his *offhand* remarks often got him into trouble). **Unpremeditated** suggests some strong often suddenly provoked emotion that impels one to action (*unpremeditated* murder).

extend, lengthen, prolong, protract mean to draw out or add to so as to increase in length. **Extend** and **lengthen** imply a drawing out in space or time but *extend* may also imply increase in width, scope, area, or range (*extend* a vacation) (*extend* welfare services) (*lengthen* a skirt) (*lengthen* the workweek). **Prolong** suggests chiefly increase in duration esp. beyond usual limits (*prolonged* illness). **Protract** adds to *prolong* implications of needlessness, vexation, or indefiniteness (*protracted* litigation).

exterminate, extirpate, eradicate, uproot mean to effect the destruction or abolition of something. **Exter-**

minate implies complete and immediate extinction by killing off all individuals (failed attempts to *exterminate* the mosquitoes). **Extirpate** implies extinction of a race, family, species, or sometimes an idea or doctrine by destruction or removal of its means of propagation (disease more than anything else *extirpated* the Native Americans). **Eradicate** implies the driving out or elimination of something that has established itself (polio had virtually been *eradicated*). **Uproot** implies a forcible or violent removal and stresses displacement or dislodgment rather than immediate destruction (the war had *uprooted* thousands).

extinguish see CRUSH

extirpate see EXTERMINATE

extort see EDUCE

extract see EDUCE

extraneous see EXTRINSIC

extravagant see EXCESSIVE

extreme see EXCESSIVE

extricate, disentangle, untangle, disencumber, disembarrass mean to free from what binds or holds back. **Extricate** implies the use of care or ingenuity in freeing from a difficult position or situation (a knack for *extricating* himself from damaging political rows). **Disentangle** and **untangle** suggest painstaking separation of a thing from other things (a biography that *disentangles* the myth from the man) (*untangled* a web of deceit). **Disencumber** implies a release from something that clogs or weighs down (a science article *disencumbered* of scientific jargon). **Disembarrass** suggests a release from something that impedes or hinders (*disembarrassed* herself of her frivolous companions).

extrinsic, extraneous, foreign, alien mean external to a thing, its essential nature, or its original character. **Extrinsic** applies to what is distinctly outside the thing in question or is not contained in or derived from its essential nature (sentimental attachment that is *extrinsic* to the house's market value). **Extraneous** applies to what is on or comes from the outside and may or may not be capable of becoming an essential part (*extraneous* arguments that obscure the real issue). **Foreign** applies to what is so different as to be rejected or repelled or, if admitted, to be incapable of becoming identified or assimilated by the thing in question (inflammation resulting from a *foreign* body in the eye). **Alien** is stronger than *foreign* in suggesting opposition, repugnance, or irreconcilability (a practice that is totally *alien* to our democratic principles).

exuberant see PROFUSE

F

fabricate see MAKE

fabulous see FICTITIOUS

face, countenance, visage, physiognomy mean the front part of the head from forehead to chin. **Face** is the simple, direct, and also the inclusive term (a strikingly handsome *face*). **Countenance** applies to a face as seen and as revealing a mood or attitude (the benign *countenance* of my grandmother). **Visage** suggests attention to shape and proportions and sometimes expression (a penetrating gaze and an aquiline nose gave him a birdlike *visage*). **Physiognomy** suggests attention to the contours and characteristic expression as indicative of race, temperament, or qualities of mind or character (a youth with the *physiognomy* of a warrior).

facet see PHASE

facetious see WITTY

facile see EASY

facsimile see REPRODUCTION
factitious see ARTIFICIAL
factor see ELEMENT
faculty see GIFT
fad see FASHION
fag see TIRE
failing see FAULT

fair, just, equitable, impartial, unbiased, dispassionate, objective mean free from favor toward either or any side. **Fair** implies an elimination of one's own feelings, prejudices, and desires so as to achieve a proper balance of conflicting interests ⟨a *fair* decision by a judge⟩. **Just** implies an exact following of a standard of what is right and proper ⟨a *just* settlement of territorial claims⟩. **Equitable** implies a less rigorous standard than *just* and usu. suggests equal treatment of all concerned ⟨provides for the *equitable* distribution of his property⟩. **Impartial** stresses an absence of favor or prejudice ⟨arbitration by an *impartial* third party⟩. **Unbiased** implies even more strongly an absence of all prejudice ⟨your *unbiased* opinion of the whole affair⟩. **Dispassionate** suggests freedom from the influence of strong feeling and often implies cool or even cold judgment ⟨a *dispassionate* summation of the facts⟩. **Objective** stresses a tendency to view events or persons as apart from oneself and one's own interest or feelings ⟨it's impossible for me to be *objective* about my own child⟩. See in addition BEAUTIFUL.

faith see BELIEF

faithful, loyal, constant, staunch, steadfast, resolute mean firm in adherence to whatever one owes allegiance. **Faithful** implies unswerving adherence to a person or thing or to the oath or promise by which a tie was contracted ⟨*faithful* to her marriage vows⟩. **Loyal** implies a firm resistance to any temptation to desert or betray ⟨the army remained *loyal* to the czar⟩. **Constant** stresses continuing firmness of emotional attachment without necessarily implying strict obedience to promises or vows ⟨*constant* lovers⟩. **Staunch** suggests fortitude and resolution in adherence and imperviousness to influences that would weaken it ⟨a *staunch* defender of free speech⟩. **Steadfast** implies a steady and unwavering course in love, allegiance, or conviction ⟨*steadfast* in their support of democratic principles⟩. **Resolute** implies firm determination to adhere to a cause or purpose ⟨*resolute* in his determination to see justice done⟩.

faithless, false, disloyal, traitorous, treacherous, perfidious mean untrue to what should command one's fidelity or allegiance. **Faithless** applies to any failure to keep a promise or pledge or any breach of allegiance or loyalty ⟨*faithless* allies refused to support the sanctions⟩. **False** stresses the fact of failing to be true in any manner ranging from fickleness to cold treachery ⟨betrayed by *false* friends⟩. **Disloyal** implies a lack of complete faithfulness in thought or words or actions to a friend, cause, leader, or country ⟨accused the hostages of being *disloyal* to their country⟩. **Traitorous** implies either actual treason or a serious betrayal of trust ⟨*traitorous* acts punishable by death⟩. **Treacherous** implies readiness to betray trust or confidence ⟨the victim of *treacherous* allies⟩. **Perfidious** adds to *faithless* the implication of an incapacity for fidelity or reliability ⟨repeated and *perfidious* violations of the treaty⟩.

fake see IMPOSTURE
false see FAITHLESS
falter see HESITATE

familiar, intimate mean closely acquainted. **Familiar** suggests the ease, informality, absence of reserve or constraint natural among members of a family or acquaintances of long standing ⟨resent being addressed by strangers in a *familiar* tone⟩. **Intimate** stresses the closeness and intensity rather than the mere frequency of personal association and suggests either deep mutual understanding or the sharing of deeply personal thoughts and feelings ⟨their love letters became increasingly *intimate*⟩. See in addition COMMON.

famous, renowned, celebrated, noted, notorious, distinguished, eminent, illustrious mean known far and wide. **Famous** implies little more than the fact of being, sometimes briefly, widely and popularly known ⟨a *famous* television actress⟩. **Renowned** implies more glory and acclamation ⟨one of the most *renowned* figures in sports history⟩. **Celebrated** implies notice and attention esp. in print ⟨the most *celebrated* beauty of her day⟩. **Noted** suggests well-deserved public attention ⟨the *noted* mystery writer⟩. **Notorious** frequently adds to *famous* an implication of questionableness or evil ⟨a *notorious* gangster⟩. **Distinguished** implies acknowledged excellence or superiority ⟨a *distinguished* scientist who recently won the Nobel Prize⟩. **Eminent** implies even greater conspicuousness for outstanding quality or character ⟨a conference of the country's most *eminent* writers⟩. **Illustrious** stresses enduring honor and glory attached to a deed or person ⟨the *illustrious* deeds of national heroes⟩.

fanciful see IMAGINARY
fancy see THINK

fantastic, bizarre, grotesque mean conceived, made, or carried out without adherence to truth or reality. **Fantastic** may connote unrestrained extravagance in conception or merely ingenuity of decorative invention ⟨*fantastic* theories about the origins of life⟩. **Bizarre** applies to the sensationally queer or strange and implies violence of contrast or incongruity of combination ⟨a *bizarre* pseudo-medieval castle⟩. **Grotesque** may apply to what is conventionally ugly but artistically effective or it may connote ludicrous awkwardness or incongruity often with sinister or tragic overtones ⟨*grotesque* statues adorn the cathedral⟩ ⟨*grotesque* attempts at operatic roles⟩. See in addition IMAGINARY.

fascinate see ATTRACT

fashion *n* Fashion, style, mode, vogue, fad, rage, craze mean the usage accepted by those who want to be up-to-date. **Fashion** is the most general term and applies to any way of dressing, behaving, writing, or performing that is favored at any one time or place ⟨the current *fashion* for Russian ballet dancers⟩. **Style** often implies a distinctive fashion adopted by people of wealth or taste ⟨a media mogul used to traveling in *style*⟩. **Mode** suggests the fashion of the moment among those anxious to appear elegant and sophisticated ⟨sleek, tanned bodies are the *mode* at such resorts⟩. **Vogue** stresses the wide acceptance of a fashion ⟨a novelist who is no longer much in *vogue*⟩. **Fad** suggests caprice in taking up or in dropping a fashion ⟨nothing is more dated than last year's *fad*⟩. **Rage** and **craze** stress intense enthusiasm in adopting a fad ⟨Cajun food was quite the *rage*⟩ ⟨a sport that is more than a passing *craze*⟩. See in addition METHOD.

fashion *vb* see MAKE

fast, rapid, swift, fleet, quick, speedy, hasty, expeditious mean moving, proceeding, or acting with celerity. **Fast** and **rapid** are very close in meaning, but *fast* applies particularly to the thing that moves ⟨*fast* horse⟩ and *rapid* to the movement itself ⟨*rapid* current⟩. **Swift** suggests great rapidity coupled with ease of movement ⟨returned the ball with one *swift* stroke⟩. **Fleet** adds the implication of lightness and nimbleness ⟨*fleet* runners⟩. **Quick** suggests promptness and the taking of little time ⟨a *quick* wit⟩. **Speedy** implies quickness of successful accomplishment ⟨*speedy* delivery of the mail⟩ and may also suggest unusual velocity. **Hasty** suggests hurry and precipitousness and often connotes carelessness ⟨a *hasty* inspection). **Expeditious** suggests efficiency together with rapidity of accomplishment ⟨an *expeditious* processing of a merchandise order⟩.

fasten, fix, attach, affix mean to make something stay firmly in place. **Fasten** implies an action such as tying, buttoning, nailing, locking, or otherwise securing ⟨*fastened* the horse to a post⟩. **Fix** usu. implies a driving in, implanting, or embedding ⟨*fix* the stake so that it remains upright⟩. **Attach** suggests a connecting or uniting by a bond, link, or tie in order to keep things together ⟨*attach* the W-2 form here⟩. **Affix** implies an imposing of one thing on another by gluing, impressing, or nailing ⟨*affix* your address label here⟩.

fastidious see NICE

fatal see DEADLY

fate, destiny, lot, portion, doom mean a predetermined state or end. **Fate** implies an inevitable and usu. an adverse outcome ⟨the *fate* of the mariners remains unknown⟩. **Destiny** implies something foreordained and often suggests a great or noble course or end ⟨our country's *destiny*⟩. **Lot** and **portion** imply a distribution by fate or destiny, *lot* suggesting blind chance ⟨it was her *lot* to die childless⟩, and *portion* implying the apportioning of good and evil ⟨the *portion* that has been meted out to me⟩. **Doom** distinctly implies a grim or calamitous fate ⟨if the rebellion fails, our *doom* is certain⟩.

fateful see OMINOUS

fatigue see TIRE

fatuous see SIMPLE

fault, failing, frailty, foible, vice mean an imperfection or weakness of character. **Fault** implies a failure, not necessarily culpable, to reach some standard of perfection in disposition, action, or habit ⟨a woman of many virtues and few *faults*⟩. **Failing** suggests a minor shortcoming in character ⟨procrastination is one of my *failings*⟩. **Frailty** implies a general or chronic proneness to yield to temptation ⟨a fondness for chocolate is the most human of *frailties*⟩. **Foible** applies to a harmless or endearing weakness or idiosyncrasy ⟨*foibles* that make him all the more lovable⟩. **Vice** can be a general term for any imperfection or weakness, but it often suggests violation of a moral code or the giving of offense to the moral sensibilities of others ⟨gambling and drunkenness were the least of his *vices*⟩.

faultfinding see CRITICAL

favorable, auspicious, propitious mean pointing toward a happy outcome. **Favorable** implies that the persons involved are approving or helpful or that the circumstances are advantageous ⟨*favorable* weather conditions for a rocket launch⟩. **Auspicious** applies to something taken as a sign or omen promising success before or at the beginning of an event ⟨an *auspicious* beginning for a great partnership⟩. **Propitious** may also apply to beginnings but often implies a continuing favorable condition ⟨the time was not *propitious* for starting a new business⟩.

fawn, toady, truckle, cringe, cower mean to behave abjectly before a superior. **Fawn** implies seeking favor by servile flattery or exaggerated attention ⟨waiters *fawning* over a celebrity⟩. **Toady** suggests the attempt to ingratiate oneself by an abjectly menial or subservient attitude ⟨never misses an opportunity to *toady* to his boss⟩. **Truckle** implies the subordination of oneself and one's desires or judgment to those of a superior ⟨the rich are used to seeing others *truckle*⟩. **Cringe** suggests a bowing or shrinking in fear or servility ⟨*cringing* before every supposed superior⟩. **Cower** suggests a display of abject fear in the company of threatening or domineering people ⟨as an adult he still *cowered* before his father⟩.

fealty see FIDELITY

fear, dread, fright, alarm, panic, terror, trepidation mean painful agitation in the presence or anticipation of danger. **Fear** is the most general term and implies anxiety and usu. loss of courage ⟨*fear* of the unknown⟩. **Dread** usu. adds the idea of intense reluctance to face or meet a person or situation and suggests aversion as well as anxiety ⟨the *dread* of having to face her mother⟩. **Fright** implies the shock of sudden, startling fear ⟨imagine our *fright* at being awakened by screams⟩. **Alarm** suggests a sudden and intense awareness of immediate danger ⟨view the situation with *alarm*⟩. **Panic** implies unreasoning and overmastering fear causing hysterical activity ⟨news of the invasion caused great *panic*⟩. **Terror** implies the most extreme degree of fear ⟨immobilized with *terror*⟩. **Trepidation** adds to *dread* the implications of timidity, trembling, and hesitation ⟨raised the subject of marriage with some *trepidation*⟩.

fearful, apprehensive, afraid mean disturbed by fear. **Fearful** implies often a timorous or worrying temperament ⟨the child is *fearful* of loud noises⟩. **Apprehensive** suggests a state of mind and implies a premonition of evil or danger ⟨*apprehensive* that war would break out⟩. **Afraid** often suggests weakness or cowardice and regularly implies inhibition of action or utterance ⟨*afraid* to speak the truth⟩.

feasible see POSSIBLE

feat, exploit, achievement mean a remarkable deed. **Feat** implies strength or dexterity or daring ⟨the *feat* of crossing the Atlantic in a balloon⟩. **Exploit** suggests an adventurous or heroic act ⟨his celebrated *exploits* as a spy⟩. **Achievement** implies hard-won success in the face of difficulty or opposition ⟨honored for her *achievements* as a chemist⟩.

fecund see FERTILE

federation see ALLIANCE

feeble see WEAK

feeling, emotion, affection, sentiment, passion mean a subjective response to a person, thing, or situation. **Feeling** denotes any partly mental, partly physical response marked by pleasure, pain, attraction, or repulsion; it may suggest the mere existence of a response but imply nothing about the nature or intensity of it ⟨whatever *feelings* I had for her are gone⟩. **Emotion** carries a strong implication of excitement or agitation but, like *feeling*, encompasses both positive and negative responses ⟨a play in which the *emotions* are real⟩. **Affection** applies to feelings that are also inclinations or likings ⟨memoirs filled with *affection* and understanding⟩. **Sentiment** implies an emotion inspired by an idea ⟨her feminist *sentiments* are well known⟩. **Passion** suggests a powerful or controlling emotion ⟨revenge became his ruling passion⟩. See in addition ATMOSPHERE.

feign see ASSUME

feint see TRICK

felicitous see FIT

feral see BRUTAL

ferocious see FIERCE

fertile, fecund, fruitful, prolific mean producing or capable of producing offspring or fruit. **Fertile** implies the power to reproduce in kind or to assist in reproduction and growth ⟨*fertile* soil⟩; applied figuratively, it suggests readiness of invention and development ⟨a most *fertile* imagination⟩. **Fecund** emphasizes abundance or rapidity in bearing fruit or offspring ⟨came from a remarkably *fecund* family⟩. **Fruitful** adds to *fertile* and *fecund* the implication of desirable or useful results ⟨undertook *fruitful* research in virology⟩. **Prolific** stresses rapidity of spreading or multiplying by or as if by natural reproduction ⟨one of the most *prolific* writers of science fiction⟩.

fervent see IMPASSIONED

fervid see IMPASSIONED

fervor see PASSION
fetid see MALODOROUS
fetter see HAMPER
fib see LIE
fickle see INCONSTANT

fictitious, fabulous, legendary, mythical, apocryphal mean having the nature of something imagined or invented. **Fictitious** implies fabrication and suggests artificiality or contrivance more than deliberate falsification or deception ⟨all names used in the broadcast are *fictitious*⟩. **Fabulous** stresses the marvelous or incredible character of something without necessarily implying impossibility or actual nonexistence ⟨a land of *fabulous* riches⟩. **Legendary** suggests the elaboration of invented details and distortion of historical facts produced by popular tradition ⟨the *legendary* courtship of Miles Standish⟩. **Mythical** implies a purely fanciful explanation of facts or the creation of beings and events out of the imagination ⟨*mythical* creatures such as centaurs⟩. **Apocryphal** implies an unknown or dubious source or origin or may imply that the thing itself is dubious or inaccurate ⟨a book that repeats many *apocryphal* stories⟩.

fidelity, allegiance, fealty, loyalty, devotion, piety mean faithfulness to something to which one is bound by pledge or duty. **Fidelity** implies strict and continuing faithfulness to an obligation, trust, or duty ⟨*fidelity* in the performance of one's duties⟩. **Allegiance** suggests an adherence like that of a citizen to his country ⟨a politician who owes *allegiance* to no special interest⟩. **Fealty** implies a fidelity acknowledged by the individual and as compelling as a sworn vow ⟨a critic's only *fealty* is to truth⟩. **Loyalty** implies a faithfulness that is steadfast in the face of any temptation to renounce, desert, or betray ⟨valued the *loyalty* of his friends⟩. **Devotion** stresses zeal and service amounting to self-dedication ⟨a painter's *devotion* to her artistic vision⟩. **Piety** stresses fidelity to obligations regarded as natural and fundamental ⟨filial *piety* demands that I visit my parents⟩.

fierce, ferocious, barbarous, savage, cruel mean showing fury or malignity in looks or actions. **Fierce** applies to humans and animals that inspire terror because of their wild and menacing aspect or fury in attack ⟨*fierce* tribes still inhabit the rain forest⟩. **Ferocious** implies extreme fierceness and unrestrained violence and brutality ⟨signs warned of a *ferocious* dog⟩. **Barbarous** implies a ferocity or mercilessness regarded as unworthy of civilized people ⟨the *barbarous* treatment of prisoners⟩. **Savage** implies the absence of inhibitions restraining civilized people filled with rage, lust, or other violent passion ⟨*savage* reviews of the new play⟩. **Cruel** implies indifference to suffering and even positive pleasure in inflicting it ⟨the *cruel* jokes of schoolboys⟩.

figure see FORM
filch see STEAL
filthy see DIRTY
final see LAST

financial, monetary, pecuniary, fiscal mean of or relating to money. **Financial** implies money matters conducted on a large scale or involving some degree of complexity ⟨a business deal secured through a complex *financial* arrangement⟩. **Monetary** refers to money as coined, distributed, or circulating ⟨the country's basic *monetary* unit is the peso⟩. **Pecuniary** implies reference to money matters affecting the individual ⟨a struggling single mother constantly in *pecuniary* difficulties⟩. **Fiscal** refers to money as providing revenue for the state or to the financial affairs of an institution or corporation ⟨the *fiscal* year of the United States ends on June 30⟩.

finicky see NICE
finish see CLOSE

firm, hard, solid mean having a texture or consistency that resists deformation. **Firm** implies such compactness and coherence and often elasticity of substance as to resist pulling, distorting, or pressing ⟨a *firm* mattress with good back support⟩. **Hard** implies impenetrability and nearly complete but inelastic resistance to pressure or tension ⟨a diamond is one of the *hardest* substances known⟩. **Solid** implies a texture of uniform density so as to be not only firm but heavy ⟨*solid* furniture that will last⟩.

fiscal see FINANCIAL

fit, suitable, meet, proper, appropriate, fitting, apt, happy, felicitous mean right with respect to some end, need, use, or circumstance. **Fit** stresses adaptability and sometimes special readiness for use or action ⟨the vessel is now *fit* for service⟩. **Suitable** implies an answering to requirements or demands ⟨shopped for clothes *suitable* for camping⟩. **Meet** suggests a just proportioning ⟨a tip that was *meet* for the services rendered⟩. **Proper** suggests a suitability through essential nature or accordance with custom ⟨the *proper* role of the First Lady⟩. **Appropriate** implies eminent or distinctive fitness ⟨a golf bag is an *appropriate* gift for a golfer⟩. **Fitting** implies harmony of mood or tone ⟨*fitting* subjects for dinner table conversation⟩. **Apt** connotes a fitness marked by nicety and discrimination ⟨a speech laced with some *apt* quotations⟩. **Happy** suggests what is effectively or successfully appropriate ⟨a *happy* choice of words⟩. **Felicitous** suggests an aptness that is opportune, telling, or graceful ⟨a *felicitous* note of apology⟩.

fitful, spasmodic, convulsive mean lacking steadiness or regularity in movement. **Fitful** implies intermittence, a succession of starts and stops or risings and fallings ⟨the *fitful* beginnings of a new enterprise⟩. **Spasmodic** adds to *fitful* the implication of violent activity alternating with inactivity ⟨*spasmodic* trading on the stock exchange⟩. **Convulsive** suggests the breaking of regularity or quiet by uncontrolled movement ⟨the *convulsive* shocks of the earthquake⟩.

fitting see FIT
fix *vb* see FASTEN
fix *n* see PREDICAMENT
flabbergast see SURPRISE

flagrant, glaring, gross, rank mean conspicuously bad or objectionable. **Flagrant** applies usu. to offenses or errors so bad that they can neither escape notice nor be condoned ⟨*flagrant* abuse of the office of president⟩. **Glaring** implies painful or damaging obtrusiveness of something that is conspicuously wrong, faulty, or improper ⟨*glaring* errors in judgment⟩. **Gross** implies the exceeding of reasonable or excusable limits ⟨*gross* carelessness on your part⟩. **Rank** applies to what is openly and extremely objectionable and utterly condemned ⟨it's *rank* heresy to say that⟩.

flash, gleam, glance, glint, sparkle, glitter, glisten, glimmer, shimmer mean to send forth light. **Flash** implies a sudden and transient outburst of bright light ⟨lightning *flashed*⟩. **Gleam** suggests a steady light seen through an obscuring medium or against a dark background ⟨the lights of the town *gleamed* in the valley below⟩. **Glance** suggests a bright darting light relfected from a quickly moving surface ⟨sunlight *glanced* off the hull of the boat⟩. **Glint** implies a cold glancing light ⟨steel bars *glinted* in the moonlight⟩. **Sparkle** suggests innumerable moving points of bright light ⟨the *sparkling* waters of the gulf⟩. **Glitter** connotes a brilliant sparkling or gleaming ⟨*glittering* diamonds⟩. **Glisten** applies to the soft sparkle from a wet or oily surface ⟨rain-drenched sidewalks *glistened* under the street lamps⟩. **Glimmer** suggests a faint or wavering gleam ⟨a lone light *glimmered* in the distance⟩. **Shimmer** implies a soft tremulous gleaming or a blurred reflection ⟨a *shimmering* satin dress⟩.

flashy see GAUDY
flat see INSIPID, LEVEL
flaunt see SHOW
flaw see BLEMISH
fleer see SCOFF
fleet see FAST
fleeting see TRANSIENT
fleshly see CARNAL
flexible see ELASTIC
flightiness see LIGHTNESS
flinch see RECOIL
fling see THROW
flippancy see LIGHTNESS
flirt see TRIFLE
flourish see SWING
flout see SCOFF
flow see SPRING
fluctuate see SWING
fluster see DISCOMPOSE
foible see FAULT
foil see FRUSTRATE

follow, succeed, ensue, supervene mean to come after something or someone. **Follow** may apply to a coming after in time, position, or logical sequence (speeches *followed* the dinner). **Succeed** implies a coming after immediately in a sequence determined by natural order, inheritance, election, or laws of rank (she *succeeded* her father as head of the business). **Ensue** commonly suggests a logical consequence or naturally expected development (after the lecture, a general discussion *ensued*). **Supervene** suggests the following or beginning of something unforeseen or unpredictable (events *supervened* that brought tragedy into his life). See in addition CHASE.

follower, adherent, disciple, partisan mean one who attaches himself to another. **Follower** may apply to a person who attaches himself either to the person or beliefs of another (an evangelist and his *followers*). **Adherent** suggests a close and persistent attachment (*adherents* to Communism). **Disciple** implies a devoted allegiance to the teachings of one chosen as a master (*disciples* of Gandhi). **Partisan** suggests a zealous often prejudiced attachment (*partisans* of the President).

foment see INCITE
foolhardy see ADVENTUROUS
foolish see SIMPLE

forbearing, tolerant, lenient, indulgent mean not inclined to be severe or rigorous. **Forbearing** implies patience under provocation and deliberate abstention from harsh judgment, punishment, or vengeance (the most *forbearing* of music teachers). **Tolerant** implies a freedom from bias or dogmatism and a reluctance to judge others esp. harshly (a very *tolerant* attitude towards drug users). **Lenient** implies softness of temperament and a relaxation of discipline (*lenient* parents pay for it later). **Indulgent** implies compliancy, mercifulness, and a willingness to make concessions (a wife *indulgent* of her husband's shortcomings).

forbid, prohibit, interdict, inhibit mean to debar one from doing something or to order that something not be done. **Forbid** implies that the order is from one in authority and that obedience is expected (smoking is *forbidden* in the building). **Prohibit** suggests the issuing of laws, statutes, or regulations (*prohibited* the manufacture and sale of unapproved drugs). **Interdict** implies prohibition by civil or ecclesiastical authority usu. for a given time or a declared purpose (*interdicted* the administration of the sacraments to proabortionists). **Inhibit** implies the imposition of restraints or restrictions that amount to prohibitions, not only by authority but also by the exigencies of

the time or situation (laws that *inhibit* the growth of free trade).

force *vb* Force, compel, coerce, constrain, oblige mean to make someone or something yield. **Force** is the general term and implies the overcoming of resistance by the exertion of strength, power, weight, stress, or duress (*forced* the prisoner to sign the confession). **Compel** typically requires a personal object and suggests the working of an irresistible force (all workers are *compelled* to pay taxes). **Coerce** suggests overcoming resistance or unwillingness by actual or threatened violence or pressure (*coerced* by gangsters into selling his business). **Constrain** suggests the effect of a force or circumstance that limits freedom of action or choice (*constrained* by my conscience to see that justice was done). **Oblige** implies the constraint of necessity, law, or duty (I am *obliged* to inform you of your rights).

force *n* see POWER
foreboding see APPREHENSION
forecast see FORETELL
foregoing see PRECEDING
foreign see EXTRINSIC
foreknow see FORESEE

forerunner, precursor, harbinger, herald mean one who goes before or announces the coming of another. **Forerunner** is applicable to anything that serves as a sign or presage (the international incident was a *forerunner* to war). **Precursor** applies to a person or thing paving the way for the success or accomplishment of another (18th century poets who were *precursors* of the Romantics). **Harbinger** and **herald** both apply, chiefly figuratively, to one that proclaims or announces the coming or arrival of a notable event (an early victory that was the *harbinger* of a winning season) (the *herald* of a new age in medical science).

foresee, foreknow, divine, apprehend, anticipate mean to know beforehand. **Foresee** implies nothing about how the knowledge is derived and may apply to ordinary reasoning and experience (no one could *foresee* the economic crisis). **Foreknow** usu. implies supernatural assistance, as through revelation (if only we could *foreknow* our own destinies). **Divine** adds to *foresee* the suggestion of exceptional wisdom or discernment (a European traveler who *divined* the course of American destiny). **Apprehend** implies foresight mingled with uncertainly, anxiety, or dread (*apprehended* that his odd behavior was a sign of a troubled soul). **Anticipate** implies taking action about or responding emotionally to something before it happens (the servants *anticipated* our every need).

forestall see PREVENT
foretaste see PROSPECT

foretell, predict, forecast, prophesy, prognosticate mean to tell beforehand. **Foretell** applies to the telling of the coming of a future event by any procedure or any source of information (seers *foretold* of calamitous events). **Predict** commonly implies inference from facts or accepted laws of nature (astronomers *predicted* the return of the comet). **Forecast** adds the implication of anticipating eventualities and differs from *predict* in being usu. concerned with probabilities rather than certainties (*forecasted* a snowfall of six inches). **Prophesy** connotes inspired or mystic knowledge of the future esp. as the fulfilling of divine threats or promises (preachers *prophesying* a day of divine retribution). **Prognosticate** suggests the learned or skilled interpretation of signs or symptoms (economists are *prognosticating* a slow recovery).

forge see MAKE
forget see NEGLECT
forgetful, oblivious, unmindful mean losing one's memory or knowledge of something. **Forgetful** usu. im-

plies a heedless or negligent habit of failing to keep in mind ⟨I had been *forgetful* of my duties as host⟩. **Oblivious** suggests a failure to notice or remember due to external causes or conditions or to a determination to ignore ⟨lost in thought, *oblivious* to the rushing crowd around her⟩. **Unmindful** may suggest inattention and heedlessness or a deliberate ignoring ⟨a crusading reformer who was *unmindful* of his family's needs⟩.

forgive see EXCUSE

forlorn see ALONE

form *n* Form, figure, shape, conformation, configuration mean outward appearance. **Form** usu. suggests reference to both internal structure and external outline and often the principle that gives unity to the whole ⟨an architect who appreciates the interplay of *forms*⟩. **Figure** applies chiefly to the form as determined by bounding or enclosing lines ⟨cutting doll *figures* out of paper⟩. **Shape** like *figure*, suggests an outline but carries a stronger implication of the enclosed body or mass ⟨the *shape* of the monument was pyramidal⟩. **Conformation** implies structure composed of related parts ⟨a body *conformation* that is well-proportioned and symmetrical⟩. **Configuration** refers to the disposition and arrangement of component parts ⟨modular furniture allows for a number of *configurations*⟩.

form *vb* see MAKE

formal see CEREMONIAL

former see PRECEDING

fornication see ADULTERY

forsake see ABANDON

forswear see ABJURE

fortuitous see ACCIDENTAL

fortunate see LUCKY

forward see ADVANCE

foul see DIRTY

foxy see SLY

fragile, frangible, brittle, crisp, friable mean breaking easily. **Fragile** implies extreme delicacy of material or construction and need for careful handling ⟨a *fragile* antique chair⟩. **Frangible** implies susceptibility to being broken without implying weakness or delicacy ⟨*frangible* stone used as paving material⟩. **Brittle** implies hardness together with lack of elasticity or flexibility or toughness ⟨elderly patients with *brittle* bones⟩. **Crisp** implies a firmness and brittleness desirable esp. in some foods ⟨*crisp* lettuce⟩. **Friable** applies to substances that are easily crumbled or pulverized ⟨*friable* soil⟩. See in addition WEAK.

fragment see PART

fragrance, perfume, scent, incense, redolence mean a sweet or pleasant odor. **Fragrance** suggests the odors of flowers or other growing things ⟨household cleansers with the *fragrance* of pine⟩. **Perfume** may suggest a stronger or heavier odor and applies esp. to a prepared or synthetic liquid ⟨the *perfume* of lilacs filled the room⟩. **Scent** is very close to *perfume* but of wider application because more neutral in connotation ⟨furniture polish with a fresh lemon *scent*⟩. **Incense** applies to the smoke from burning spices and gums and suggests an esp. pleasing odor ⟨the odor of *incense* permeated the temple⟩. **Redolence** implies a mixture of fragrant or pungent odors ⟨the *redolence* of a forest after a rain⟩.

fragrant see ODOROUS

frail see WEAK

frailty see FAULT

frangible see FRAGILE

frank, candid, open, plain mean showing willingness to tell what one feels or thinks. **Frank** stresses lack of shyness or secretiveness or of evasiveness from considerations of tact or expedience ⟨*frank* discussions on arms control⟩. **Candid** suggests expression marked by sincerity and honesty esp. in offering unwelcome criticism or opinion ⟨a *candid* appraisal of her singing ability⟩. **Open** implies frankness but suggests more indiscretion than *frank* and less earnestness than *candid*⟨young children are *open* and artless in saying what they think⟩. **Plain** suggests outspokenness and freedom from affectation or subtlety in expression ⟨was very *plain* about telling them to leave⟩.

fraud see DECEPTION, IMPOSTURE

free *adj* Free, independent, sovereign, autonomous mean not subject to the rule or control of another. **Free** stresses the complete absence of external rule and the full right to make all of one's own decisions ⟨you're *free* to do as you like⟩. **Independent** implies a standing alone; applied to a state it implies lack of connection with any other having power to interfere with its citizens, laws, or policies ⟨the struggle for Ireland to become *independent*⟩. **Sovereign** stresses the absence of a superior power and implies supremacy within a thing's own domain or sphere ⟨a *sovereign* nation not subject to the laws of another⟩. **Autonomous** stresses independence in matters pertaining to self-government ⟨a credible investigating committee must be *autonomous*⟩.

free *vb* Free, release, liberate, emancipate, manumit mean to set loose from restraint or constraint. **Free** implies a usu. permanent removal from whatever binds, confines, entangles, or oppresses ⟨*freed* the animals from their cages⟩. **Release** suggests a setting loose from confinement, restraint, or a state of pressure or tension, often without implication of permanent liberation ⟨*released* his anger by exercising⟩. **Liberate** stresses particularly the resulting state of liberty ⟨*liberated* the novel from Victorian inhibitions⟩. **Emancipate** implies the liberation of a person from subjection or domination ⟨labor-saving devices that *emancipated* women from housework⟩. **Manumit** implies emancipation from slavery ⟨the proclamation *manumitted* the slaves⟩.

freedom, liberty, license mean the power or condition of acting without compulsion. **Freedom** has a broad range of application from total absence of restraint to merely a sense of not being unduly hampered or frustrated ⟨*freedom* of the press⟩. **Liberty** suggests release from former restraint or compulsion ⟨the prisoners were willing to fight for their *liberty*⟩. **License** implies freedom specially granted or conceded and may connote an abuse of freedom ⟨the editorial takes considerable *license* with the facts⟩.

fresh see NEW

friable see FRAGILE

friendly see AMICABLE

fright see FEAR

frivolity see LIGHTNESS

frown, scowl, glower, lower mean to put on a dark or threatening face or appearance. **Frown** implies conveying disapproval or displeasure by contracting the brows ⟨the teachers *frowned* on my boyish pranks⟩. **Scowl** suggests a similar facial expression but conveying rather a bad humor, sullenness, or resentful puzzlement ⟨a grumpy old man who *scowled* habitually⟩. **Glower** implies direct staring or glaring as in contempt or defiance ⟨the natives merely *glowered* at the invading tourists⟩. **Lower** suggests a menacing blackness or gloomy anger ⟨*lowered* as he went about his work, never uttering a word⟩.

frugal see SPARING

fruitful see FERTILE

fruitless see FUTILE

frustrate, thwart, foil, baffle, balk, circumvent, outwit mean to check or defeat another's plan or goal. **Frustrate** implies making vain or ineffectual all efforts however vigorous or persistent ⟨*frustrated* all attempts at government reform⟩. **Thwart** suggests frustration or checking by deliberately crossing or opposing (the park department is *thwarted* by public indifference to littering). **Foil** implies checking or defeating so as to discourage further effort (her parents *foiled* my efforts to see her). **Baffle** implies frustration by confusing or puzzling (*baffled* by the maze of rules and regulations). **Balk** suggests the interposing of obstacles or hindrances (legal restrictions *balked* police efforts to control crime). **Circumvent** implies frustration by a particular stratagem (*circumvented* the law by finding loopholes). **Outwit** suggests craft and cunning (the rebels *outwitted* the army repeatedly).

fugitive see TRANSIENT

fulfill see PERFORM

full, complete, plenary, replete mean containing all that is wanted or needed or possible. **Full** implies the presence or inclusion of everything that is wanted or required by something or that can be held, contained, or attained by it (a *full* schedule of appointments). **Complete** applies when all that is needed is present (the report does not give a *complete* picture of the situation). **Plenary** adds to *complete* the implication of fullness without qualification (given *plenary* power as commander in chief). **Replete** implies being filled to the brim or to satiety (a speech *replete* with innuendos and half-truths).

fulsome, oily, unctuous, oleaginous mean too obviously extravagant to be genuine or sincere. **Fulsome** implies that something which is essentially good has been carried to an excessive and tasteless degree (the *fulsome* flattery of a celebrity interviewer). **Oily** implies an offensively ingratiating quality and sometimes suggests a suavity or benevolence that masks a sinister intent (*oily* land developers trying to persuade older residents to sell). **Unctuous** implies the hypocritical adoption of a grave, devout, or spiritual manner (the *unctuous* pleading of the First Amendment by pornographers). **Oleaginous** may be used in place of *oily* to suggest even greater pomposity (an *oleaginous* maître d' fawning over the female diners).

fun, jest, sport, game, play mean action or speech that provides amusement or arouses laughter. **Fun** usu. implies laughter or gaiety but may imply merely a lack of serious or ulterior purpose (played cards just for *fun*). **Jest** implies lack of earnestness in what is said or done and may suggest a hoaxing or teasing (took seriously remarks said only in *jest*). **Sport** applies esp. to the arousing of laughter against someone (teasing begun in *sport* ended in an ugly brawl). **Game** is close to *sport,* and often stresses mischievous or malicious fun (habitually made *game* of their poor relations). **Play** stresses the opposition to *earnest* without implying any element of malice or mischief (pretended to strangle his wife in *play*).

function, office, duty, province mean the acts or operations expected of a person or thing. **Function** implies a definite end or purpose that the one in question serves or a particular kind of work it is intended to perform (the *function* of the stomach is to digest food). **Office** is typically applied to the function or service expected of a person by reason of his trade or profession or his special relationship to others (exercised the *offices* of both attorney and friend). **Duty** applies to a task or responsibility imposed by one's occupation, rank, status, or calling (the lieutenant governor had few official *duties*). **Province** applies to a function, office, or duty that naturally or logically falls to one (it is not the governor's *province* to set foreign policy).

fundamental see ESSENTIAL

furnish, equip, outfit, appoint, accoutre, arm mean to supply one with what is needed. **Furnish** implies the provision of any or all essentials for performing a

function (a sparsely *furnished* apartment). **Equip** suggests the provision of something making for efficiency in action or use (a fully *equipped* kitchen with every modern appliance). **Outfit** implies provision of a complete list or set of articles as for a journey, an expedition, or a special occupation (*outfitted* the whole family for a ski trip). **Appoint** implies provision of complete and usu. elegant or elaborate equipment or furnishings (a lavishly *appointed* penthouse apartment). **Accoutre** suggests the supplying of personal dress or equipment for a special activity (the fully *accoutred* members of a polar expedition). **Arm** implies provision for effective action or operation esp. in war (*armed* to the teeth).

further see ADVANCE

furtive see SECRET

fury see ANGER

fuse see MIX

fusty see MALODOROUS

futile, vain, fruitless mean producing no result. **Futile** may connote completeness of failure or unwisdom of undertaking (a *futile* search for survivors of the crash). **Vain** usu. implies simple failure to achieve a desired result (a *vain* attempt to get the car started). **Fruitless** comes close to *vain* but often suggests long and arduous effort or severe disappointment (*fruitless* efforts to obtain a lasting peace).

G

gain see GET

gainsay see DENY

gall see TEMERITY

gallant see CIVIL

gallantry see HEROISM

game see FUN

gamut see RANGE

gape see GAZE

garish see GAUDY

garnish see ADORN

garrulous see TALKATIVE

gastronome see EPICURE

gather, collect, assemble, congregate mean to come or bring together into a group, mass, or unit. **Gather** is the most general term for bringing or coming together from a spread-out or scattered state (a crowd *gathers* whenever there is excitement). **Collect** often implies careful selection or orderly arrangement (*collected* books on gardening). **Assemble** implies an ordered union or organization of persons or things often for a definite purpose (the country's leading experts on aeronautics *assembled* under one roof). **Congregate** implies a spontaneous flocking together into a crowd or huddle (persons were forbidden to *congregate* under martial law). See in addition INFER.

gauche see AWKWARD

gaudy, tawdry, garish, flashy, meretricious mean vulgarly or cheaply showy. **Gaudy** implies a tasteless use of overly bright, often clashing colors or excessive ornamentation (circus performers in *gaudy* costumes). **Tawdry** applies to what is at once gaudy and cheap and sleazy (*tawdry* saloons along the waterfront). **Garish** describes what is distressingly or offensively bright (*garish* signs along the commercial strip). **Flashy** implies an effect of brilliance quickly and easily seen to be shallow or vulgar (a *flashy* nightclub act with leggy chorus girls). **Meretricious** stresses falsity and may describe a tawdry show that beckons with a false allure or promise (a *meretricious* wasteland of casinos and bars).

gauge see STANDARD

gaunt see LEAN

gay see LIVELY

gaze, gape, stare, glare, peer mean to look (at) long and attentively. **Gaze** implies fixed and prolonged attention (as in wonder, admiration, or abstractedness) ⟨*gazing* at the waves breaking along the shore⟩. **Gape** suggests an openmouthed often stupid wonder ⟨a crowd *gaped* at the man threatening to jump⟩. **Stare** implies a direct open-eyed gazing denoting curiosity, disbelief, or insolence ⟨kept *staring* at them as they tried to eat⟩. **Glare** is a fierce or angry staring ⟨silently *glared* back at her accusers⟩. **Peer** suggests a looking narrowly and curiously as if through a small opening ⟨*peered* at the bird through his binoculars⟩.

general see UNIVERSAL

generic see UNIVERSAL

generous see LIBERAL

genial see GRACIOUS

genius see GIFT

gentry see ARISTOCRACY

genuine see AUTHENTIC

germane see RELEVANT

get, obtain, procure, secure, acquire, gain, win, earn mean to come into possession of. **Get** is a very general term and may or may not imply effort or initiative ⟨*got* a car for my birthday⟩. **Obtain** suggests the attainment of something sought for with some expenditure of time and effort ⟨*obtained* statements from all of the witnesses⟩. **Procure** implies effort in obtaining something for oneself or for another ⟨in charge of *procuring* supplies for the office⟩. **Secure** implies difficulty in obtaining and keeping in possession or under one's control ⟨an ad agency that *secured* many top accounts⟩. **Acquire** often suggests an addition to what is already possessed ⟨*acquired* a greater appreciation of music⟩. **Gain** suggests struggle and usu. value in the thing obtained ⟨gradually *gained* a reputation as a skilled musician⟩. **Win** suggests favoring qualities or circumstances playing a part in the gaining ⟨*won* the admiration of his fellow actors⟩. **Earn** implies a correspondence between the effort and what one gets by effort ⟨a compelling performance that *earned* her many awards⟩.

ghastly, grisly, gruesome, macabre, lurid mean horrifying and repellent in appearance or aspect. **Ghastly** suggests the terrifying aspects of corpses and ghosts ⟨a *ghastly* portrait of life after a nuclear war⟩. **Grisly** and **gruesome** suggest additionally the results of extreme violence or cruelty ⟨the case of an unusually *grisly* murder⟩ ⟨the *gruesome* history of the Nazi death camps⟩. **Macabre** implies a morbid preoccupation with the physical aspects of death ⟨a *macabre* tale of premature burial⟩. **Lurid** adds to *gruesome* the suggestion of shuddering fascination with violent death and esp. with murder ⟨the tabloids wallowed in the crime's *lurid* details⟩.

gibe see SCOFF

gift, faculty, aptitude, bent, talent, genius, knack mean a special ability for doing something. **Gift** often implies special favor by God or nature ⟨the *gift* of a beautiful singing voice⟩. **Faculty** applies to an innate or less often acquired ability for a particular accomplishment or function ⟨a rare *faculty* for remembering people's names⟩. **Aptitude** implies a natural liking for some activity and the likelihood of success in it ⟨a boy with a definite mechanical *aptitude*⟩. **Bent** is nearly equal to *aptitude* but it stresses inclination perhaps more than specific ability ⟨a family that has always had an artistic *bent*⟩. **Talent** suggests a marked natural ability that needs to be developed ⟨allowed her dancing *talent* to go to waste⟩. **Genius** suggests impressive inborn creative ability ⟨the *genius* of Mozart⟩. **Knack** implies a comparatively minor but special ability making for ease and dexterity in performance ⟨has the *knack* for making swift, cutting retorts⟩.

gigantic see ENORMOUS

give, present, donate, bestow, confer, afford mean to convey to another as his possession. **Give**, the general term, is applicable to any passing over of anything by any means ⟨*give* alms⟩ ⟨*give* a boy a ride on a pony⟩ ⟨*give* my love to your mother⟩. **Present** carries a note of formality and ceremony ⟨*present* an award⟩ ⟨*presented* him the keys to the city⟩. **Donate** is likely to imply a publicized giving (as to charity) ⟨*donate* a piano to the orphanage⟩. **Bestow** implies the conveying of something as a gift and may suggest condescension on the part of the giver ⟨*bestow* unwanted advice⟩. **Confer** implies a gracious giving (as of a favor or honor) ⟨the Pope *conferred* the rank of cardinal on three bishops⟩. **Afford** implies a giving or bestowing usu. as a natural or legitimate consequence of the character of the giver ⟨the trees *afforded* us a welcome shade⟩ ⟨a development that *affords* us some hope⟩.

glance see FLASH

glare see GAZE

glaring see FLAGRANT

gleam see FLASH

glee see MIRTH

glimmer see FLASH

glint see FLASH

glisten see FLASH

glitter see FLASH

gloom see SADNESS

gloomy see DARK, SULLEN

glorious see SPLENDID

glossy see SLEEK

glower see FROWN

glum see SULLEN

glut see SATIATE

gluttonous see VORACIOUS

goad see MOTIVE

goal see INTENTION

good-natured see AMIABLE

gorge see SATIATE

gorgeous see SPLENDID

gory see BLOODY

gourmet see EPICURE

govern, rule mean to exercise power or authority in controlling others. **Govern** implies the aim of keeping in a straight course or smooth operation for the good of the individual and the whole ⟨the British monarch reigns, but the prime minister *governs*⟩. **Rule** may imply no more than laying down laws or issuing commands that must be obeyed but often suggests the exercise of despotic or arbitrary power ⟨the emperor *ruled* with an iron hand⟩.

grab see TAKE

grace see MERCY

gracious, cordial, affable, genial, sociable mean markedly pleasant and easy in social intercourse. **Gracious** implies courtesy and kindly consideration ⟨her *gracious* acceptance of the award⟩. **Cordial** stresses warmth and heartiness ⟨our *cordial* host greeted us at the door⟩. **Affable** implies easy approachability and readiness to respond pleasantly to conversation or requests or proposals ⟨the dean of students was surprisingly *affable*⟩. **Genial** stresses cheerfulness and even joviality ⟨the emcee must be a *genial* extrovert⟩. **Sociable** suggests a genuine liking for the companionship of others ⟨*sociable* people enjoying an ocean cruise⟩.

grand, magnificent, imposing, stately, majestic, grandiose mean large and impressive. **Grand** adds to greatness of size the implications of handsomeness and dignity ⟨a mansion with a *grand* staircase⟩. **Magnificent** implies an impressive largeness proportionate to scale without sacrifice of dignity or good taste ⟨*magnificent* paintings and tapestries⟩. **Imposing** implies great size and dignity but esp. stresses impressiveness ⟨large, *imposing* buildings line the avenue⟩. **Stately** may suggest poised dignity, erectness of bearing, handsomeness of proportions, ceremonious deliberation of movement ⟨the *stately* procession proceeded into the cathedral⟩. **Majestic** combines the implications of *imposing* and *stately* and usu. adds a suggestion of solemn grandeur ⟨a *majestic* waterfall⟩. **Grandiose** implies a size or scope exceeding ordinary experience but is most commonly applied derogatorily to inflated pretension or absurd exaggeration ⟨*grandiose* schemes of world conquest⟩.

grandiose see GRAND

grant, concede, vouchsafe, accord, award mean to give as a favor or a right. **Grant** implies giving to a claimant or petitioner something that could be withheld ⟨*granted* them another month to finish the work⟩. **Concede** implies yielding something reluctantly in response to a rightful or compelling claim ⟨even her critics *concede* she can be charming⟩. **Vouchsafe** implies granting something as a courtesy or an act of gracious condescension ⟨the star refused to *vouchsafe* an interview⟩. **Accord** implies giving to another what is due or proper ⟨*accorded* all the honors befitting a head of state⟩. **Award** implies giving what is deserved or merited usu. after a careful weighing of pertinent factors ⟨*awarded* the company a huge defense contract⟩.

graphic, vivid, picturesque, pictorial mean giving a clear visual impression in words. **Graphic** stresses the evoking of a clear lifelike picture ⟨a *graphic* account of his combat experiences⟩. **Vivid** suggests an impressing on the mind the vigorous aliveness of something ⟨a *vivid* re-creation of an exciting period in history⟩. **Picturesque** suggests the presentation of a striking or effective picture composed of features notable for their distinctness and charm ⟨Dickens is famous for his *picturesque* characters⟩. **Pictorial** implies representation in the manner of painting with emphasis upon colors, shapes, and spatial relations ⟨a *pictorial* style of poetry marked by precise, developed imagery⟩.

grasp see TAKE
grasping see COVETOUS
gratuitous see SUPEREROGATORY
grave see SERIOUS
greedy see COVETOUS
grief see SORROW
grievance see INJUSTICE
grill see AFFLICT
grind see WORK
grisly see GHASTLY
gross see COARSE, FLAGRANT
grotesque see FANTASTIC
grudge see MALICE
gruesome see GHASTLY
gruff see BLUFF
guard see DEFEND
guess see CONJECTURE

guide, lead, steer, pilot, engineer mean to direct in a course or show the way to be followed. **Guide** implies intimate knowledge of the way and of all its difficulties and dangers ⟨*guided* the other scouts through the darkened cave⟩. **Lead** implies a going ahead to show the way and often to keep those that follow under control and in order ⟨the flagship *led* the fleet⟩. **Steer** implies an ability to keep to a chosen course and stresses the capacity of maneuvering correctly ⟨*steered* the ship through the narrow channel⟩. **Pilot** suggests guidance over a dangerous, intricate, or complicated course ⟨successfully *piloted* the bill through the Senate⟩. **Engineer** implies guidance by one who finds ways to avoid or overcome difficulties

in achieving an end or carrying out a plan ⟨*engineered* his son's election to the governorship⟩.

guilty see BLAMEWORTHY
gull see DUPE
gumption see SENSE

H

habit, practice, usage, custom, wont mean a way of acting fixed through repetition. **Habit** implies a doing unconsciously and often compulsively ⟨the *habit* of constantly tapping his fingers⟩. **Practice** suggests an act or method followed with regularity and usu. through choice ⟨our *practice* is to honor all major credit cards⟩. **Usage** suggests a customary action so generally followed that it has become a social norm ⟨western-style dress is now common *usage* in international business⟩. **Custom** applies to a practice or usage so steadily associated with an individual or group as to have almost the force of unwritten law ⟨the *custom* of mourners wearing black at funerals⟩. **Wont** usu. applies to an habitual manner, method, or practice distinguishing an individual or group ⟨as was her *wont,* she slept until noon⟩.

habitual see USUAL
hackneyed see TRITE
hale see HEALTHY
hallow see DEVOTE

hamper, trammel, clog, fetter, shackle, manacle mean to hinder or impede in moving, progressing, or acting. **Hamper** may imply the effect of any impeding or restraining influence ⟨*hampered* the investigation by refusing to cooperate⟩. **Trammel** suggests entangling by or confining within a net ⟨rules that serve only to *trammel* the artist's creativity⟩. **Clog** usu. implies a slowing by something extraneous or encumbering ⟨feels that free enterprise is *clogged* by government regulation⟩. **Fetter** suggests a restraining so severe that freedom to move or progress is almost lost ⟨a nation that is *fettered* by an antiquated class system⟩. **Shackle** and **manacle** are stronger than *fetter* and suggest total loss of freedom ⟨a mind *shackled* by stubborn pride and prejudice⟩ ⟨hatred can *manacle* the soul⟩.

handle, manipulate, wield mean to manage dexterously or efficiently. **Handle** implies directing an acquired skill to the accomplishment of immediate ends ⟨*handled* the crisis with cool efficiency⟩. **Manipulate** implies adroit handling and in extended use often suggests the use of craft or of fraud ⟨brutally *manipulates* other people for his own selfish ends⟩. **Wield** implies mastery and vigor in handling a tool or a weapon or in exerting influence, authority, or power ⟨the news media *wield* a tremendous influence on the electorate⟩.

handsome see BEAUTIFUL
hanker see LONG
haphazard see RANDOM
happy see FIT, LUCKY
harass see WORRY
harbinger see FORERUNNER

hard, difficult, arduous mean demanding great exertion or effort. **Hard** implies the opposite of all that is easy ⟨farming is *hard* work⟩. **Difficult** implies the presence of obstacles to be surmounted or puzzles to be resolved and suggests the need of skill, patience, or courage ⟨a *difficult* decision requiring much thought and courage⟩. **Arduous** stresses the need of laborious and persevering exertion ⟨the *arduous* task of rebuilding the town⟩. See in addition FIRM.

hardihood see TEMERITY
harm see INJURE

harmony, accord, concord mean the state resulting when different things come together without clashing or disagreement. **Harmony** implies a beautiful effect achieved by the agreeable blending or arrangement of parts ⟨a resort in splendid *harmony* with its natural setting⟩. **Accord** may imply personal agreement or goodwill or the absence of friction ⟨parents and teachers are in *accord* on this issue⟩. **Concord** adds to *accord* additional implications of peace and amity ⟨a planned utopian community in which all would live in *concord*⟩.

harry see WORRY

harsh see ROUGH

haste, hurry, speed, expedition, dispatch mean quickness in movement or action. **Haste** applies to personal action and implies urgency and precipitancy and often rashness ⟨why this headlong *haste* to get married?⟩. **Hurry** often has a strong suggestion of agitated bustle or confusion ⟨in the *hurry* of departure she forgot her toothbrush⟩. **Speed** suggests swift efficiency in movement or action ⟨exercises to increase your reading *speed*⟩. **Expedition** and **dispatch** both imply speed and efficiency in handling affairs but *expedition* stresses ease or efficiency of performance and *dispatch* carries a stronger suggestion of promptness in bringing matters to a conclusion ⟨with surprising *expedition* the case came to trial⟩ ⟨regularly paid her bills with the greatest possible *dispatch*⟩.

hasty see FAST

hate, detest, abhor, abominate, loathe mean to feel strong aversion or intense dislike for. **Hate** implies an emotional aversion often coupled with enmity or malice ⟨*hated* his former friend with a passion⟩. **Detest** suggests violent antipathy ⟨I *detest* moral cowards⟩. **Abhor** implies a deep often shuddering repugnance ⟨child abuse is a crime *abhorred* by all⟩. **Abominate** suggests strong detestation and often moral condemnation ⟨virtually every society *abominates* incest⟩. **Loathe** implies utter disgust and intolerance ⟨*loathed* self-appointed moral guardians⟩.

hateful, odious, abhorrent, detestable, abominable mean deserving of or arousing intense dislike. **Hateful** applies to something or someone that arouses active hatred and hostility ⟨the *hateful* crime of child abuse⟩. **Odious** applies to that which arouses offense or repugnance ⟨you apparently find the plain truth *odious*⟩. **Abhorrent** characterizes that which outrages a sense of what is right, decent, just, or honorable ⟨the *abhorrent* practice of stereotyping minority groups⟩. **Detestable** suggests something deserving extreme contempt ⟨his *detestable* habit of passing the blame to subordinates⟩. **Abominable** suggests something fiercely condemned as vile or unnatural ⟨the *abominable* living conditions of the plantation slaves⟩.

haughty see PROUD

haul see PULL

have, hold, own, possess mean to keep, control, retain, or experience as one's own. **Have** is a general term carrying no specific implication ⟨they *have* plenty of money⟩. **Hold** suggests stronger control, grasp, or retention ⟨*held* absolute power over the whole country⟩. **Own** implies a natural or legal right to hold as one's property and under one's full control ⟨*own* property in several states⟩. **Possess** is often the preferred term when referring to an intangible ⟨as a characteristic, a power, or a quality⟩ ⟨*possesses* a first-rate intellect⟩.

hazardous see DANGEROUS

headlong see PRECIPITATE

headstrong see UNRULY

heal see CURE

healthful, wholesome, salubrious, salutary mean favorable to the health of mind or body. **Healthful** implies a positive contribution to a healthy condition ⟨a *healthful* diet will provide more energy⟩. **Wholesome** applies to what benefits, builds up, or sustains physically, mentally, or spiritually ⟨*wholesome* foods⟩ ⟨the movie is *wholesome* family entertainment⟩. **Salubrious** applies chiefly to the helpful effects of climate or air ⟨the *salubrious* climate of the American Southwest⟩. **Salutary** describes something corrective or beneficially effective, even though it may in itself be unpleasant ⟨a *salutary* warning that resulted in increased production⟩.

healthy, sound, wholesome, robust, hale, well mean enjoying or indicative of good health. **Healthy** implies full strength and vigor as well as freedom from signs of disease ⟨the doctor pronounced the whole family *healthy*⟩. **Sound** emphasizes the absence of disease, weakness, or malfunction ⟨an examination showed his heart to be *sound*⟩. **Wholesome** implies appearance and behavior indicating soundness and balance ⟨she looks especially *wholesome* in her tennis togs⟩. **Robust** implies the opposite of all that is delicate or sickly ⟨a lively, *robust* little boy⟩. **Hale** applies particularly to robustness in old age ⟨still *hale* at the age of eighty⟩. **Well** implies merely freedom from disease or illness ⟨she has never been a *well* person⟩.

hearten see ENCOURAGE

heartfelt see SINCERE

hearty see SINCERE

heave see LIFT

heavy, weighty, ponderous, cumbrous, cumbersome mean having great weight. **Heavy** implies that something has greater density or thickness than the average of its kind or class ⟨a *heavy* child for his age⟩. **Weighty** suggests having actual and not just relative weight ⟨really *weighty* parcels are shipped by freight⟩. **Ponderous** implies having great weight because of size and massiveness with resulting great inertia ⟨*ponderous* galleons were outmaneuvered by smaller vessels⟩. **Cumbrous** and **cumbersome** imply heaviness and bulkiness that make for difficulty in grasping, moving, carrying, or manipulating ⟨abandoned the *cumbrous* furniture rather than move it⟩ ⟨the old cameras were *cumbersome* and inconvenient⟩.

heckle see BAIT

hector see BAIT

height, altitude, elevation mean vertical distance either between the top and bottom of something or between a base and something above it. **Height** refers to something measured vertically whether high or low ⟨a wall two meters in *height*⟩. **Altitude** and **elevation** apply to height as measured by angular measurement or atmospheric pressure; *altitude* is preferable when referring to vertical distance above the surface of the earth or above sea level; *elevation* i s used esp. in reference to vertical height on land ⟨fly at an *altitude* of 10,000 meters⟩ ⟨Denver is a city with a high *elevation*⟩.

heighten see INTENSIFY

heinous see OUTRAGEOUS

help, aid, assist mean to supply what is needed to accomplish an end. **Help** carries a strong implication of advance toward an objective ⟨*helped* to find a cure for the disease⟩. **Aid** suggests the evident need of help or relief and so imputes weakness to the one aided and strength to the one aiding ⟨an army of volunteers *aided* the flood victims⟩. **Assist** suggests a secondary role in the assistant or a subordinate character in the assistance ⟨*assisted* the chief surgeon during the operation⟩.

help see IMPROVE

herald see FORERUNNER

hereditary see INNATE

heroism, valor, prowess, gallantry mean courageous behavior esp. in conflict. **Heroism** implies superlative courage esp. in fulfilling a high purpose against odds ⟨the boy's outstanding act of *heroism* during the fire⟩. **Valor** implies illustrious bravery and audacity in fighting ⟨awarded the army's highest honor for *valor* in battle⟩. **Prowess** stresses skill as well as bravery ⟨demonstrated his manly *prowess* in hunting⟩. **Gallantry** implies dash and spirit as well as courage and gay indifference to danger or hardship ⟨special forces with a proud tradition of *gallantry*⟩.

hesitant see DISINCLINED

hesitate, waver, vacillate, falter mean to show irresolution or uncertainty. **Hesitate** implies a pause before deciding or acting or choosing ⟨*hesitated* before answering the question⟩. **Waver** implies hesitation after seeming to decide and so connotes weakness or a retreat ⟨*wavered* in his support of the rebels⟩. **Vacillate** implies prolonged hesitation from inability to reach a firm decision ⟨*vacillated* until it was too late and events were out of control⟩. **Falter** implies a wavering or stumbling and often nervousness, lack of courage, or outright fear ⟨never once *faltered* during her testimony⟩.

hide, conceal, screen, secrete, bury mean to withhold or withdraw from sight. **Hide** may or may not suggest intent ⟨*hide* in a closet⟩ ⟨a house *hidden* by trees⟩. **Conceal** usu. does imply intent and often specif. implies a refusal to divulge ⟨*concealed* the weapon in his jacket⟩. **Screen** implies an interposing of something that prevents discovery ⟨*screened* her true identity from her colleagues⟩. **Secrete** suggests a depositing in a place unknown to others ⟨*secreted* the cocaine in the hold of the ship⟩. **Bury** implies covering up so as to hide completely ⟨*buried* the note in a pile of papers⟩.

high, tall, lofty mean above the average in height. **High** implies marked extension upward and is applied chiefly to things which rise from a base or foundation or are placed at a conspicuous height above a lower level ⟨a *high* hill⟩ ⟨a *high* ceiling⟩. **Tall** applies to what grows or rises high by comparison with others of its kind and usu. implies relative narrowness ⟨a *tall* thin man⟩. **Lofty** suggests great or imposing altitude ⟨*lofty* mountain peaks⟩.

hilarity see MIRTH

hinder, impede, obstruct, block mean to interfere with the activity or progress of. **Hinder** stresses causing harmful or annoying delay or interference with progress ⟨the rain *hindered* our climbing⟩. **Impede** implies making forward progress difficult by clogging, hampering, or fettering ⟨too-tight clothing *impeded* my movement⟩. **Obstruct** implies interfering with something in motion or in progress by the sometimes intentional placing of obstacles in the way ⟨the view was *obstructed* by billboards⟩. **Block** implies complete obstruction to passage or progress ⟨boulders *blocked* the road⟩.

hint see SUGGEST

hire, let, lease, rent, charter mean to engage or grant for use at a price. **Hire** and **let,** strictly speaking, are complementary terms, *hire* implying the act of engaging or taking for use and *let* the granting of use ⟨we *hired* a car for the summer⟩ ⟨decided to *let* the cottage to a young couple⟩. **Lease** strictly implies a letting under the terms of a contract but is often applied to hiring on a lease ⟨the diplomat *leased* an apartment for a year⟩. **Rent** stresses the payment of money for the full use of property and may imply either hiring or letting ⟨instead of buying a house, they decided to *rent*⟩ ⟨will not *rent* to families with children⟩. **Charter** applies to the hiring or letting of a vehicle usu. for exclusive use ⟨*charter* a bus to go to the game⟩.

histrionic see DRAMATIC
hoax see DUPE
hoist see LIFT
hold see CONTAIN, HAVE
hollow see VAIN
homage see HONOR
honest see UPRIGHT

honesty, honor, integrity, probity mean uprightness of character or action. **Honesty** implies a refusal to lie, steal, or deceive in any way ⟨a politician of scrupulous *honesty*⟩. **Honor** suggests an active or anxious regard for the standards of one's profession, calling, or position ⟨a keen sense of *honor* in business matters⟩. **Integrity** implies trustworthiness and incorruptibility to a degree that one is incapable of being false to a trust, responsibility, or pledge ⟨her unimpeachable *integrity* as a journalist⟩. **Probity** implies tried and proven honesty or integrity ⟨a judge with a reputation for *probity*⟩.

honor, homage, reverence, deference mean respect and esteem shown to another. **Honor** may apply to the recognition of one's right to great respect or to any expression of such recognition ⟨an *honor* just to be nominated⟩. **Homage** adds the implication of accompanying praise ⟨for centuries dramatists have paid *homage* to Shakespeare⟩. **Reverence** implies profound respect mingled with love, devotion, or awe ⟨have the greatest *reverence* for my father⟩. **Deference** implies a yielding or submitting to another's judgment or preference out of respect or reverence ⟨refused to show any *deference* to senior staffers⟩. See in addition HONESTY.

honorable see UPRIGHT
hope see EXPECT
hopeless see DESPONDENT
horde see CROWD
horrify see DISMAY
hostility see ENMITY
hound see BAIT
huff see OFFENSE
huge see ENORMOUS

humble, meek, modest, lowly mean lacking all signs of pride, aggressiveness, or self-assertiveness. **Humble** may suggest a virtuous absence of pride or vanity or it may suggest undue self-depreciation or humiliation ⟨a quiet life as a simple, *humble* parish priest⟩. **Meek** may suggest mildness or gentleness of temper or it may connote undue submissiveness ⟨the refugees were *meek* and grateful for whatever they got⟩. **Modest** implies a lack of boastfulness or conceit, without any implication of abjectness ⟨sincerely *modest* about her singing talents⟩. **Lowly** may stress lack of pretentiousness ⟨a volunteer willing to accept the *lowliest* hospital duties⟩.

humbug see IMPOSTURE
humid see WET
humiliate see ABASE
humor *vb* see INDULGE
humor *n* see WIT
humorous see WITTY
hunger see LONG
hurl see THROW
hurry see HASTE
hurt see INJURE
hypercritical see CRITICAL

hypothesis, theory, law mean a formula derived by inference from scientific data that explains a principle operating in nature. **Hypothesis** implies insufficient evidence to provide more than a tentative explanation ⟨an *hypothesis* regarding the extinction of the dinosaurs⟩. **Theory** implies a greater range of evidence and greater likelihood of truth ⟨the *theory* of evolution⟩. **Law** implies a statement of order and relation in nature that has been found to be invariable under the same conditions (the *law* of gravitation).

I

idea, concept, conception, thought, notion, impression mean what exists in the mind as a representation (as of something comprehended) or as a formulation (as of a plan). **Idea** may apply to a mental image or formulation of something seen or known or imagined, to a pure abstraction, or to something assumed or vaguely sensed (a mind filled with innovative *ideas*) (my *idea* of paradise). **Concept** may apply to the idea formed by consideration of instances of a species or genus or, more broadly, to any idea of what a thing ought to be (a society with no *concept* of private property). **Conception** is often interchangeable with *concept;* it may stress the process of imagining or formulating rather than the result (our changing *conception* of what constitutes art). **Thought** is likely to suggest the result of reflecting, reasoning, or meditating rather than of imagining (commit your *thoughts* to paper). **Notion** suggests an idea not much resolved by analysis or reflection and may suggest the capricious or accidental (the oddest *notions* fly in and out of her head). **Impression** applies to an idea or notion resulting immediately from some stimulation of the senses (the first *impression* is of soaring height).
ideal see MODEL
identical see SAME
idle see INACTIVE, VAIN
ignoble see MEAN
ignominy see DISGRACE
ignorant, illiterate, unlettered, untutored, unlearned mean not having knowledge. **Ignorant** may imply a general condition or it may apply to lack of knowledge or awareness of a particular thing (an *ignorant* fool) (he's *ignorant* of nuclear physics). **Illiterate** applies to either an absolute or a relative inability to read and write (much of that country's population is still *illiterate*). **Unlettered** implies ignorance of the knowledge gained by reading (a literary reference that is meaningless to the *unlettered*). **Untutored** may imply lack of schooling in the arts and ways of civilization (strange monuments left by an *untutored* people). **Unlearned** suggests ignorance of advanced subjects (a poet who speaks to the *unlearned,* common man).
ignore see NEGLECT
ill see BAD
illiterate see IGNORANT
illusory see APPARENT
illustration see INSTANCE
illustrious see FAMOUS
ill will see MALICE
imaginary, fanciful, visionary, fantastic, chimerical, quixotic mean unreal or unbelievable. **Imaginary** applies to something which is fictitious and purely the product of one's imagination (a chronic sufferer of several *imaginary* illnesses). **Fanciful** suggests the free play of the imagination (the *fanciful* characters created by Lewis Carroll). **Visionary** stresses impracticality or incapability of realization (*visionary* schemes for creating a rural utopia). **Fantastic** implies incredibility or strangeness beyond belief (a *fantastic* world inhabited by prehistoric monsters). **Chimerical** combines the implication of *visionary* and *fantastic* (*chimerical* plans for restoring the British Empire). **Quixotic** implies a devotion to romantic or chivalrous ideals unrestrained by ordinary prudence and common sense (the *quixotic* notion that absolute equality is attainable).
imagine see THINK

imbibe see ABSORB
imbue see INFUSE
imitate see COPY
immense see ENORMOUS
immoderate see EXCESSIVE
impair see INJURE
impartial see FAIR
impassioned, passionate, ardent, fervent, fervid, perfervid mean showing intense feeling. **Impassioned** implies warmth and intensity without violence and suggests fluent verbal expression (an *impassioned* plea for international understanding). **Passionate** implies great vehemence and often violence and wasteful diffusion of emotion (*passion ate* denunciations of American arrogance). **Ardent** implies an intense degree of zeal, devotion, or enthusiasm (an *ardent* admirer of the novels of Jane Austen). **Fervent** stresses sincerity and steadiness of emotional warmth or zeal (*fervent* Christians on a pilgrimage). **Fervid** suggests warmly and spontaneously and often feverishly expressed emotion (*fervid* love letters that suggested mental unbalance). **Perfervid** implies the expression of exaggerated or overwrought feelings (wary of such *perfervid* expressions of selfless patriotism).
impassive, stoic, phlegmatic, apathetic, stolid mean unresponsive to something that might normally excite interest or emotion. **Impassive** stresses the absence of any external sign of emotion in action or facial expression (just sat there with an *impassive* look). **Stoic** implies an apparent indifference to pleasure or esp. to pain often as a matter of principle or self-discipline (remained resolutely *stoic* even in the face of adversity). **Phlegmatic** implies a temperament or constitution hard to arouse (a *phlegmatic* man immune to amorous advances). **Apathetic** may imply a puzzling or deplorable indifference or inertness (charitable appeals met an *apathetic* response). **Stolid** implies an habitual absence of interest, responsiveness, or curiosity (a *stolid* woman, wedded to routine).
impeach see ACCUSE
impede see HINDER
impel see MOVE
imperative see MASTERFUL
imperious see MASTERFUL
impertinent, officious, meddlesome, intrusive, obtrusive mean given to thrusting oneself into the affairs of others. **Impertinent** implies exceeding the bounds of propriety in showing interest or curiosity or in offering advice (a little brat asking *impertinent* questions). **Officious** implies the offering of services or attentions that are unwelcome or annoying (an *officious* salesman followed me outside). **Meddlesome** stresses an annoying and usu. prying interference in others' affairs (*meddlesome* old gossips with nothing to do). **Intrusive** implies a tactless or otherwise objectionable thrusting into others' affairs (an *intrusive* waiter interrupted our conversation). **Obtrusive** stresses improper or offensive conspicuousness of interfering actions (*obtrusive* relatives dictated the wedding arrangements).
imperturbable see COOL
impetuous see PRECIPITATE
implant, inculcate, instill, inseminate, infix mean to introduce into the mind. **Implant** implies teaching that makes for permanence of what is taught (*implanted* an enthusiasm for reading in her students). **Inculcate** implies persistent or repeated efforts to impress on the mind (*inculcated* in him high moral standards). **Instill** stresses gradual, gentle imparting of knowledge over a long period of time (*instill* traditional values in your children). **Inseminate** applies to a sowing of ideas in many minds so that they spread through a class or nation (*inseminated* an unquestioning faith in technology). **Infix** stresses firmly in-

culcating a habit of thought ⟨*infixed* a chronic cynicism⟩.

implement, tool, instrument, appliance, utensil mean a relatively simple device for performing work. **Implement** may apply to anything necessary to perform a task ⟨lawn and gardening *implements*⟩. **Tool** suggests an implement adapted to facilitate a definite kind or stage of work and suggests the need of skill more strongly than *implement* ⟨a carpenter's *tools*⟩. **Instrument** suggests a device capable of delicate or precise work ⟨the surgeon's *instruments*⟩. **Appliance** refers to a tool or instrument utilizing a power source and suggests portability or temporary attachment ⟨modern *appliances* that take the drudgery out of housework⟩. **Utensil** applies to a device used in domestic work or some routine unskilled activity ⟨knives, graters, and other kitchen *utensils*⟩.

implore see BEG

imply see SUGGEST

import see MEANING

importance, consequence, moment, weight, significance mean a quality or aspect having great worth or significance. **Importance** implies a value judgment of the superior worth or influence of something or someone ⟨there are no cities of *importance* in this area⟩. **Consequence** may imply importance in social rank but more generally implies importance because of probable or possible effects ⟨whatever style you choose is of little *consequence*⟩. **Moment** implies conspicuous or self-evident consequence ⟨a decision of very great *moment*⟩. **Weight** implies a judgment of the immediate relative importance of something ⟨idle chitchat of no particular *weight*⟩. **Significance** implies a quality or character that should mark a thing as important but that is not self-evident and may or may not be recognized ⟨time would reveal the *significance* of that casual act⟩.

importune see BEG

impose see DICTATE

imposing see GRAND

imposture, fraud, sham, fake, humbug, counterfeit mean a thing made to seem other than it is. **Imposture** applies to any situation in which a spurious object or performance is passed off as genuine ⟨the movie's claim of social concern is an *imposture*⟩. **Fraud** usu. implies a deliberate perversion of the truth ⟨a diary that was exposed as a *fraud*⟩. **Sham** applies to fraudulent imitation of a real thing or action ⟨condemned the election as a *sham* and a travesty of democracy⟩. **Fake** implies an imitation of or substitution for the genuine but does not necessarily imply dishonesty ⟨these are *fakes,* the real jewels being in the vault⟩. **Humbug** suggests elaborate pretense usu. so flagrant as to be transparent ⟨the diet business is populated with *humbugs*⟩. **Counterfeit** applies esp. to the close imitation of something valuable ⟨20-dollar bills that were *counterfeits*⟩.

impoverish see DEPLETE

impregnate see SOAK

impress see AFFECT

impression see IDEA

impressive see MOVING

impromptu see EXTEMPORANEOUS

improper see INDECOROUS

improve, better, help, ameliorate mean to make more acceptable or bring nearer some standard. **Improve** and **better** are general and interchangeable and apply to what is capable of being made better whether it is good or bad ⟨measures to *improve* the quality of medical care⟩ ⟨immigrants hoping to *better* their lot in life⟩. **Help** implies a bettering that still leaves room for improvement ⟨a coat of paint would *help* that house⟩. **Ameliorate** implies making more tolerable or acceptable conditions that are hard to endure ⟨a can-

cerous condition that cannot be *ameliorated* by chemotherapy⟩.

improvised see EXTEMPORANEOUS

impulse see MOTIVE

impulsive see SPONTANEOUS

impute see ASCRIBE

inactive, idle, inert, passive, supine mean not engaged in work or activity. **Inactive** applies to anyone or anything not in action or in operation or at work ⟨a playwright who's been *inactive* for several years⟩. **Idle** applies to persons that are not busy or occupied or to their powers or their implements ⟨tractors were *idle* in the fields⟩. **Inert** as applied to things implies powerlessness to move or to affect other things; as applied to persons it suggests an inherent or habitual indisposition to activity ⟨*inert* ingredients in drugs⟩ ⟨an *inert* citizenry uninterested in social change⟩. **Passive** implies immobility or lack of normally expected response to an external force or influence and often suggests deliberate submissiveness or self-control ⟨*passive* obedience⟩ ⟨a *passive* individual incapable of strong emotion⟩. **Supine** applies only to persons and commonly implies abjectness or indolence ⟨remained *supine* in the face of his wife's verbal abuse⟩.

inane see INSIPID

inaugurate see BEGIN

inborn see INNATE

inbred see INNATE

incense see FRAGRANCE

incentive see MOTIVE

inception see ORIGIN

incessant see CONTINUAL

incest see ADULTERY

incident see OCCURRENCE

incisive, trenchant, clear-cut, cutting, biting, crisp mean having or showing a keen mind. **Incisive** implies a power to impress the mind by directness and decisiveness ⟨an *incisive* command that left no room for doubt⟩. **Trenchant** implies an energetic cutting or probing deeply into a matter so as to reveal distinctions or to reach the center ⟨a *trenchant* critic of political pretensions⟩. **Clear-cut** suggests the absence of any blurring, ambiguity, or uncertainty of statement or analysis ⟨made a *clear-cut* distinction between the two military actions⟩. **Cutting** implies a ruthless accuracy or directness wounding to the feelings ⟨makes the most *cutting* remarks with that quiet voice⟩. **Biting** adds a greater implication of harsh vehemence or ironic force ⟨a *biting* commentary on the election⟩. **Crisp** suggests both incisiveness and vigorous terseness ⟨jurors were impressed by the witness's *crisp* answers⟩.

incite, instigate, abet, foment mean to spur to action. **Incite** stresses a stirring up and urging on, and may or may not imply initiating ⟨charged with *inciting* a riot⟩. **Instigate** definitely implies responsibility for initiating another's action and often connotes underhandedness or evil intention ⟨*instigated* a conspiracy against the commander⟩. **Abet** implies both assisting and encouraging ⟨accused of aiding and *abetting* the enemy⟩. **Foment** implies persistence in goading ⟨years of *fomenting* kept the flame of rebellion burning⟩.

incline, bias, dispose, predispose mean to influence one to have or take an attitude toward something. **Incline** implies a tendency to favor one of two or more actions or conclusions ⟨*inclined* to do nothing for the moment⟩. **Bias** suggests a settled and predictable leaning in one direction and connotes unfair prejudice ⟨*biased* against young urban professionals⟩. **Dispose** suggests an affecting of one's mood or temper so as to incline one toward something ⟨a naive nature *disposes* her to trust others too much⟩. **Predispose** implies the operation of a disposing influence well in advance of the opportunity to manifest itself ⟨fictional violence *predisposes* them to accept violence in real life).

include, comprehend, embrace, involve mean to contain within as part of the whole. **Include** suggests the containment of something as a constituent, component, or subordinate part of a larger whole ⟨the price of dinner *includes* dessert⟩. **Comprehend** implies that something comes within the scope of a statement or definition ⟨his notion of manners *comprehends* more than just table etiquette⟩. **Embrace** implies a gathering of separate items within a whole ⟨her faith *embraces* both Christian and non-Christian beliefs⟩. **Involve** suggests inclusion by virtue of the nature of the whole, whether by being its natural or inevitable consequence ⟨a procedural change that will *involve* more work for everyone⟩.

inconstant, fickle, capricious, mercurial, unstable mean lacking firmness or steadiness (as in purpose or devotion). **Inconstant** implies an incapacity for steadiness and an inherent tendency to change ⟨the supply of materials was too *inconstant* to depend on⟩. **Fickle** suggests unreliability because of perverse changeability and incapacity for steadfastness ⟨performers discover how *fickle* the public can be⟩. **Capricious** suggests motivation by sudden whim or fancy and stresses unpredictability ⟨an utterly *capricious* manner of selecting candidates⟩. **Mercurial** implies a rapid changeability in mood ⟨so *mercurial* in temperament that one never knew what to expect⟩. **Unstable** implies an incapacity for remaining in a fixed position or steady course and applies esp. to a lack of emotional balance ⟨in love she was impulsive and *unstable*⟩.

increase, enlarge, augment, multiply mean to make or become greater. **Increase** used intransitively implies progressive growth in size, amount, intensity; used transitively it may imply simple not necessarily progressive addition ⟨his waistline *increased* with age⟩ ⟨*increased* her land holdings⟩. **Enlarge** implies expansion or extension that makes greater in size or capacity ⟨*enlarged* the restaurant to its present capacity⟩. **Augment** implies addition to what is already well grown or well developed ⟨an inheritance that only *augmented* his fortune⟩. **Multiply** implies increase in number by natural generation or by indefinite repetition of a process ⟨with each tampering the problems *multiplied*⟩.

inculcate see IMPLANT
incurious see INDIFFERENT
indecent see INDECOROUS

indecorous, improper, unseemly, indecent, unbecoming, indelicate mean not conforming to what is accepted as right, fitting, or in good taste. **Indecorous** suggests a violation of accepted standards of good manners ⟨your *indecorous* manners marred the wedding reception⟩. **Improper** applies to a broader range of transgressions of rules not only of social behavior but of ethical practice or logical procedure or prescribed method ⟨the *improper* use of campaign contributions⟩. **Unseemly** adds a suggestion of special inappropriateness to a situation or an offensiveness to good taste ⟨married again with *unseemly* haste⟩. **Indecent** implies great unseemliness or gross offensiveness esp. in referring to sexual matters ⟨a scene judged by the censors as *indecent*⟩. **Unbecoming** suggests behavior or language that does not suit one's character or status ⟨conduct *unbecoming* an officer⟩. **Indelicate** implies a lack of modesty or of tact or of refined perception of feeling ⟨*indelicate* expressions for bodily functions⟩.

indefatigable, tireless, untiring, unwearied, unflagging mean capable of prolonged and strenuous effort. **Indefatigable** implies persistent and unremitting activity or effort ⟨an *indefatigable* champion of women's

rights⟩. **Tireless** implies a remarkable energy or stamina ⟨honored as a teacher of *tireless* industry and limitless patience⟩. **Untiring** implies the extraordinary ability to go on continuously and without interruption ⟨*untiring* researchers in the fight against the disease⟩. **Unwearied** stresses the apparent absence of any sign of fatigue ⟨detectives remain *unwearied* in their search for the killer⟩. **Unflagging** stresses the absence of any relaxation in one's efforts ⟨an *unflagging* attention to detail⟩.

indelicate see INDECOROUS
indemnify see PAY
independent see FREE
indict see ACCUSE

indifferent, unconcerned, incurious, aloof, detached, disinterested mean not showing or feeling interest. **Indifferent** implies neutrality of attitude from lack of inclination, preference, or prejudice ⟨*indifferent* to the dictates of fashion⟩. **Unconcerned** suggests a lack of sensitivity or regard for others' needs or troubles ⟨*unconcerned* about the problems of the homeless⟩. **Incurious** implies an inability to take a normal interest due to dullness of mind or to self-centeredness ⟨*incurious* about the world beyond their village⟩. **Aloof** suggests a cool reserve arising from a sense of superiority or disdain for inferiors or from shyness ⟨remained *aloof* from the other club members⟩. **Detached** implies an objective attitude achieved through absence of prejudice or selfishness ⟨observed family gatherings with *detached* amusement⟩. **Disinterested** implies a circumstantial freedom from concern for personal or esp. financial advantage that enables one to judge or advise without bias ⟨a panel of *disinterested* observers to act as judges⟩.

indigence see POVERTY
indigenous see NATIVE
indignation see ANGER
individual see CHARACTERISTIC, SPECIAL
indolent see LAZY
inducement see MOTIVE

indulge, pamper, humor, spoil, baby, mollycoddle mean to show undue favor to a person's desires and feelings. **Indulge** implies excessive compliance and weakness in gratifying another's or one's own desires ⟨*indulged* herself with food at the slightest excuse⟩. **Pamper** implies inordinate gratification of desire for luxury and comfort with consequent enervating effect ⟨*pampered* by the conveniences of modern living⟩. **Humor** stresses a yielding to a person's moods or whims ⟨*humored* him by letting him tell the story⟩. **Spoil** stresses the injurious effects on character by indulging or pampering ⟨fond but foolish parents *spoil* their children⟩. **Baby** suggests excessive care, attention, or solicitude ⟨*babying* students by not holding them accountable⟩. **Mollycoddle** suggests an excessive degree of care and attention to another's health or welfare ⟨refused to *mollycoddle* her teenaged patients⟩.

indulgent see FORBEARING
industrious see BUSY
industry see BUSINESS
inebriated see DRUNK
inept see AWKWARD
inerrable see INFALLIBLE
inerrant see INFALLIBLE
inert see INACTIVE
inexorable see INFLEXIBLE

infallible, inerrable, inerrant, unerring mean having or showing the inability to make errors. **Infallible** may imply that one's freedom from error is divinely bestowed ⟨fundamentalists believe in an *infallible* Bible⟩. **Inerrable** may be preferable when one wishes to avoid any association with religious or papal infallibility ⟨no reference source should be considered *in-*

errable). **Inerrant** stresses the fact that no mistakes were made ⟨an *inerrant* interpretation of the most demanding role in drama⟩. **Unerring** stresses reliability, sureness, exactness, or accuracy ⟨a photographer with an *unerring* eye for beauty⟩.

infamy see DISGRACE

infer, deduce, conclude, judge, gather mean to arrive at a mental conclusion. **Infer** implies arriving at a conclusion by reasoning from evidence; if the evidence is slight, the term comes close to *surmise* ⟨from that remark, I *inferred* that they knew each other⟩. **Deduce** adds to *infer* the special implication of drawing a particular inference from a generalization ⟨from that we can *deduce* that man is a mammal⟩. **Conclude** implies arriving at a logically necessary inference at the end of a chain of reasoning ⟨*concluded* that only he could have committed the crime⟩. **Judge** stresses critical examination of the evidence on which a conclusion is based ⟨*judge* people by their actions, not words⟩. **Gather** suggests a direct or intuitive forming of a conclusion from hints or implications ⟨*gathered* that the couple wanted to be alone⟩.

infirm see WEAK

infix see IMPLANT

inflate see EXPAND

inflexible, inexorable, obdurate, adamant mean unwilling to alter a predetermined course or purpose. **Inflexible** implies rigid adherence or even slavish conformity to principle ⟨*inflexible* in her demands⟩. **Inexorable** implies relentlessness of purpose or, esp. when applied to things, inevitableness ⟨the *inexorable* path of progress⟩. **Obdurate** stresses hardness of heart and insensitivity to appeals for mercy or the influence of divine grace ⟨an *obdurate* governor who refused to grant clemency⟩. **Adamant** implies utter immovability in the face of all temptation or entreaty ⟨was *adamant* that the project be completed on time⟩. See in addition STIFF.

influence *n* **Influence, authority, prestige, weight, credit** mean power exerted over the minds or behavior of others. **Influence** may apply to a force exercised and received consciously or unconsciously ⟨used all of her *influence* to get the bill passed⟩. **Authority** implies the power of winning devotion or allegiance or of compelling acceptance and belief ⟨a policy that has the *authority* of the school board behind it⟩. **Prestige** implies the ascendancy given by conspicuous excellence or reputation for superiority ⟨the *prestige* of the newspaper⟩. **Weight** implies measurable or decisive influence in determining acts or choices ⟨the wishes of the President obviously had much *weight*⟩. **Credit** suggests influence that arises from proven merit or favorable reputation ⟨the *credit* that he had built up in the town⟩.

influence *vb* see AFFECT

inform, acquaint, apprise, notify mean to make one aware of something. **Inform** implies the imparting of knowledge esp. of facts or occurrences ⟨*informed* the President of the crisis⟩. **Acquaint** lays stress on introducing to or familiarizing with ⟨*acquainted* myself with the basics of the game⟩. **Apprise** implies communicating something of special interest or importance ⟨*apprise* me of any rallies in the stock market⟩. **Notify** implies sending notice of something requiring attention or demanding action ⟨*notified* them that their mortgage payment was due⟩.

infraction see BREACH

infrequent, uncommon, scarce, rare, sporadic mean not common or abundant. **Infrequent** implies occurrence at wide intervals in space or time ⟨family visits that were *infrequent* and brief⟩. **Uncommon** suggests a frequency below normal expectation ⟨smallpox is now *uncommon* in many countries⟩. **Scarce** implies falling short of a standard or required abundance ⟨jobs

were *scarce* during the Depression⟩. **Rare** suggests extreme scarcity or infrequency and often implies consequent high value ⟨*rare* first editions of classics fetch high prices⟩. **Sporadic** implies occurrence in scattered instances or isolated outbursts ⟨*sporadic* cases of the genetic disorder⟩.

infringe see TRESPASS

infringement see BREACH

infuse, suffuse, imbue, ingrain, inoculate, leaven mean to introduce one thing into another so as to affect it throughout. **Infuse** implies a pouring in of something that gives new life or significance ⟨new members *infused* enthusiasm into the club⟩. **Suffuse** implies a spreading through of something that gives an unusual color or quality ⟨a room *suffused* with light and cheerfulness⟩. **Imbue** implies the introduction of a quality that fills and permeates the whole being ⟨*imbued* her students with intellectual curiosity⟩. **Ingrain** suggests the indelible stamping or deep implanting of a quality or trait ⟨clung to *ingrained* habits and beliefs⟩. **Inoculate** implies an imbuing or implanting with a germinal idea and often suggests surreptitiousness or subtlety ⟨tried to *inoculate* the child with a taste for opera⟩. **Leaven** implies introducing something that enlivens, tempers, or markedly alters the total quality ⟨a serious play *leavened* with comic moments⟩.

ingenious see CLEVER

ingenuous see NATURAL

ingrain see INFUSE

ingredient see ELEMENT

inhibit see FORBID

iniquitous see VICIOUS

initiate see BEGIN

injure, harm, hurt, damage, impair, mar mean to affect injuriously. **Injure** implies the inflicting of anything detrimental to one's looks, comfort, health, or success ⟨an accident that *injured* him physically and emotionally⟩. **Harm** often stresses the inflicting of pain, suffering, or loss ⟨careful not to *harm* the animals⟩. **Hurt** implies inflicting a wound to the body or to the feelings ⟨*hurt* by her callous remarks⟩. **Damage** suggests injury that lowers value or impairs usefulness ⟨a table that was *damaged* in shipping⟩. **Impair** suggests a making less complete or efficient by deterioration or diminution ⟨years of smoking had *impaired* his health⟩. **Mar** applies to injury that spoils perfection (as of a surface) or causes disfigurement ⟨the text is *marred* by numerous typos⟩.

injury see INJUSTICE

injustice, injury, wrong, grievance mean an act that inflicts undeserved hurt. **Injustice** applies to any act that involves unfairness to another or violation of his rights ⟨the *injustices* suffered by the lower classes⟩. **Injury** applies in law specif. to an injustice for which one may sue to recover compensation ⟨a libeled reputation is legally considered an *injury*⟩. **Wrong** applies also in law to any act punishable according to the criminal code; it may apply more generally to any flagrant injustice ⟨a crusading reporter determined to right society's *wrongs*⟩. **Grievance** applies to any circumstance or condition that constitutes an injustice to the sufferer and gives him just ground for complaint ⟨a committee for investigating employee *grievances*⟩.

innate, inborn, inbred, congenital, hereditary mean not acquired after birth. **Innate** applies to qualities or characteristics that are part of one's inner essential nature ⟨a person with an *innate* sense of his own superiority⟩. **Inborn** suggests a quality or tendency either actually present at birth or so marked and deep-seated as to seem so ⟨her *inborn* love of the rugged, outdoorsy life⟩. **Inbred** suggests something acquired from parents either by heredity or early nurture but in any case deeply rooted and ingrained ⟨a person with *inbred* extremist political views⟩. **Congenital** and **hereditary** refer to something acquired before or at birth, *congenital* applying to things acquired during fetal development and *hereditary* applying to things transmitted from one's ancestors ⟨a *congenital* heart condition⟩ ⟨eye color is *hereditary*⟩.

inoculate see INFUSE

inordinate see EXCESSIVE

inquire see ASK

inquisitive see CURIOUS

insane, mad, demented, deranged, lunatic, maniac mean having or showing an unsound mind. **Insane** implies that one is unable to function safely and competently in everyday life and is not responsible for one's actions ⟨adjudged *insane* after a period of observation⟩. **Mad** strongly suggests wildness, rabidness, raving, or complete loss of self-control ⟨drove her husband *mad* with jealousy⟩. **Demented** suggests a clear deterioration into mental unsoundness that manifests itself by an incoherence in thought, speech, or action ⟨years of solitary confinement had left him *demented*⟩. **Deranged** stresses a clear loss of control resulting in erratic behavior ⟨assassinated by a *deranged* anarchist⟩. **Lunatic** may imply no more than extreme folly ⟨invested in one *lunatic* scheme after another⟩. **Maniac** is close to *mad* and often suggests violence, fury, or raving ⟨once behind the wheel, she turns into a *maniac* driver⟩.

inseminate see IMPLANT

insert see INTRODUCE

insight see DISCERNMENT

insinuate see INTRODUCE, SUGGEST

insipid, vapid, flat, jejune, banal, inane mean devoid of qualities that make for spirit and character. **Insipid** implies a lack of sufficient taste or savor to please or interest ⟨*insipid* art and dull prose⟩. **Vapid** suggests a lack of liveliness, force, or spirit ⟨a potentially exciting story given a *vapid* treatment⟩. **Flat** applies to things that have lost their sparkle or zest ⟨although well-regarded in its day, this novel now seems *flat*⟩. **Jejune** suggests a lack of rewarding or satisfying substance ⟨on close reading the poem comes across as *jejune*⟩. **Banal** stresses the complete absence of freshness, novelty, or immediacy ⟨a *banal* tale of unrequited love⟩. **Inane** implies a lack of any significant or convincing quality ⟨an *inane* interpretation of the play⟩.

insolent see PROUD

inspect see SCRUTINIZE

inspirit see ENCOURAGE

instance, case, illustration, example, sample, specimen mean something that exhibits distinguishing characteristics in its category. **Instance** applies to any individual person, act, or thing that may be offered to illustrate or explain ⟨an *instance* of history repeating itself⟩. **Case** is used to direct attention to a real or assumed occurrence or situation that is to be considered, studied, or dealt with ⟨a *case* of mistaken identity⟩. **Illustration** applies to an instance offered as a means of clarifying or illuminating a general statement ⟨an *illustration* of Murphy's law⟩. **Example** applies to a typical, representative, or illustrative instance or case ⟨a typical *example* of bureaucratic waste⟩. **Sample** implies a part or unit taken at random from a larger whole and so presumed to be typical of its qualities ⟨show us a *sample* of your work⟩. **Specimen** applies to any example or sample whether representative or merely existent and available ⟨one of the finest *specimens* of the jeweler's art⟩.

instigate see INCITE

instill see IMPLANT

instinctive see SPONTANEOUS

instruct see COMMAND, TEACH

instrument see IMPLEMENT

insult see OFFEND

insure see ENSURE

insurrection see REBELLION

intact see PERFECT

integrity see HONESTY, UNITY

intelligent, clever, alert, quick-witted mean mentally keen or quick. **Intelligent** stresses success in coping with new situations and solving problems ⟨an *intelligent* person could assemble it in 10 minutes⟩. **Clever** implies native ability or aptness and sometimes suggests a lack of more substantial qualities ⟨a hack writer who was somewhat *clever* with words⟩. **Alert** stresses quickness in perceiving and understanding ⟨*alert* to new developments in technology⟩. **Quick-witted** implies promptness in finding answers in debate or in devising expedients in moments of danger or challenge ⟨no match for her *quick-witted* opponent⟩.

intensify, aggravate, heighten, enhance mean to increase markedly in measure or degree. **Intensify** implies a deepening or strengthening of a thing or of its characteristic quality ⟨police *intensified* their investigation⟩. **Aggravate** implies an increasing in gravity or seriousness, esp. the worsening of something already bad or undesirable ⟨the problem has been *aggravated* by neglect⟩. **Heighten** suggests a lifting above the ordinary or accustomed ⟨special effects *heightened* the sense of terror⟩. **Enhance** implies a raising or strengthening above the normal in desirability, value, or attractiveness ⟨shrubbery *enhanced* the grounds of the estate⟩.

intent see INTENTION

intention, intent, purpose, design, aim, end, object, objective, goal mean what one purposes to accomplish or attain. **Intention** implies little more than what one has in mind to do or bring about ⟨announced his *intention* to marry⟩. **Intent** suggests clearer formulation or greater deliberateness ⟨the clear *intent* of the law⟩. **Purpose** suggests a more settled determination ⟨she stopped for a *purpose,* not an idle chat⟩. **Design** implies a more carefully calculated plan ⟨the order of events was by accident, not *design*⟩. **Aim** adds to these implications of effort directed toward attaining or accomplishing ⟨pursued her *aims* with great courage⟩. **End** stresses the intended effect of action often in distinction or contrast to the action or means as such ⟨will use any means to achieve his *end*⟩. **Object** may equal *end* but more often applies to a more individually determined wish or need ⟨the *object* of the research study⟩. **Objective** implies something tangible and immediately attainable ⟨their *objective* is to seize the oil fields⟩. **Goal** suggests something attained only by prolonged effort and hardship ⟨worked years to achieve her *goal*⟩.

intentional see VOLUNTARY

intercalate see INTRODUCE

intercede see INTERPOSE

interdict see FORBID

interfere see INTERPOSE

interject see INTRODUCE

interlope see INTRUDE

interpolate see INTRODUCE

interpose, interfere, intervene, mediate, intercede mean to come or go between. **Interpose** implies no more than this ⟨a road *interposed* between the house and the beach⟩. **Interfere** implies a getting in the way or otherwise hindering ⟨noise *interfered* with my concentration⟩. **Intervene** may imply an occurring in space or time between two things or a stepping in to halt or settle a quarrel or conflict ⟨family duties *intervened,* and the work came to a halt⟩. **Mediate** implies intervening between hostile factions ⟨chosen to *mediate* between union and management⟩. **Intercede**

implies acting in behalf of an offender in begging mercy or forgiveness ⟨asked to *intercede* on the daughter's behalf⟩. See in addition INTRODUCE.

interpret see EXPLAIN

interrogate see ASK

intervene see INTERPOSE

intimate *adj* see FAMILIAR

intimate *vb* see SUGGEST

intimidate, cow, bulldoze, bully, browbeat mean to frighten into submission. **Intimidate** implies inducing fear or a sense of inferiority into another ⟨*intimidated* by all the other bright young freshmen⟩. **Cow** implies reduction to a state where the spirit is broken or all courage is lost ⟨not at all *cowed* by the odds against making it in show business⟩. **Bulldoze** implies an intimidating or an overcoming of resistance usu. by urgings, demands, or threats ⟨*bulldozed* the city council into approving the plan⟩. **Bully** implies intimidation through swaggering threats or insults ⟨tourists being *bullied* by taxi drivers⟩. **Browbeat** implies a cowing through arrogant, scornful, contemptuous, or insolent treatment ⟨inmates were routinely *browbeaten* by the staff⟩.

intoxicated see DRUNK

intractable see UNRULY

intricate see COMPLEX

intrigue see PLOT

introduce, insert, insinuate, interpolate, intercalate, interpose, interject mean to put between or among others. **Introduce** is a general term for bringing or placing a thing or person into a group or body already in existence ⟨*introduced* a new topic into the conversation⟩. **Insert** implies putting into a fixed or open space between or among ⟨*insert* a clause in the contract⟩. **Insinuate** implies introducing gradually or by gentle pressure ⟨slyly *insinuated* himself into their confidence⟩. **Interpolate** applies to the inserting of something extraneous or spurious ⟨*interpolated* her own comments into the report⟩. **Intercalate** suggests an intrusive inserting of something in an existing series or sequence ⟨a book in which new material is *intercalated* with the old⟩. **Interpose** suggests inserting an obstruction or cause of delay ⟨rules that *interpose* barriers between children and creativity⟩. **Interject** implies an abrupt or forced introduction ⟨quickly *interjected* a question⟩.

intrude, obtrude, interlope, butt in mean to thrust oneself or something in without invitation or authorization. **Intrude** suggests rudeness or officiousness in invading another's property, time, or privacy ⟨didn't mean to *intrude* upon the family's private gathering⟩. **Obtrude** stresses the impropriety or offensiveness of the intrusion ⟨never hesitant about *obtruding* her opinions even when they were least welcome⟩. **Interlope** implies placing oneself in a position leading to adverse consequences ⟨*interloping* nouveaux riches who didn't belong in the club⟩. **Butt in** implies an abrupt or offensive intrusion lacking in propriety or decent restraint ⟨in-laws who *butt in* and tell newlyweds what to do⟩.

intrusive see IMPERTINENT

invade see TRESPASS

invalidate see NULLIFY

invaluable see COSTLY

invective see ABUSE

inveigle see LURE

invent, create, discover mean to bring something new into existence. **Invent** implies fabricating something useful usu. as a result of ingenious thinking or experiment ⟨*invented* numerous energy-saving devices⟩. **Create** implies an evoking of life out of nothing or producing a thing for the sake of its existence rather than its function or use ⟨*created* few lasting works of art⟩. **Discover** presupposes preexistence of something

and implies a finding rather than a making ⟨attempts to *discover* the source of the Nile⟩.

invert see TRANSPOSE

inveterate, confirmed, chronic, deep-seated, deep-rooted mean firmly established. **Inveterate** applies to a habit, attitude, feeling of such long existence as to be practically ineradicable or unalterable ⟨an *inveterate* smoker⟩. **Confirmed** implies a growing stronger and firmer with time so as to resist change or reform ⟨a *confirmed* bachelor⟩. **Chronic** suggests what is persistent or endlessly recurrent and troublesome ⟨sick and tired of his *chronic* complain ing⟩. **Deep-seated** and **deep-rooted** apply to qualities or attitudes so deeply embedded as to become part of the core of character or of lasting endurance ⟨a *deep-seated* fear of heights⟩ ⟨the causes of the problem are *deep-rooted* and cannot be eliminated overnight⟩.

invidious see REPUGNANT

invite, solicit, court mean to request or encourage to respond or act. **Invite** commonly implies a formal or courteous requesting of one's presence or participation, but may also apply to a tacit or unintended attracting or tempting ⟨a movie remake that *invites* comparison with the original⟩. **Solicit** suggests urgency rather than courtesy in encouraging or asking ⟨continually *solicited* our advice⟩. **Court** suggests an endeavoring to win favor or gain love by suitable acts or words ⟨a candidate *courting* the votes of young urban professionals⟩.

involve see INCLUDE

involved see COMPLEX

irascible, choleric, splenetic, testy, touchy, cranky, cross mean easily angered. **Irascible** implies a tendency to be angered on slight provocation ⟨teenagers got a rise out of the *irascible* old man⟩. **Choleric** may suggest impatient excitability and unreasonableness in addition to hot temper ⟨a *choleric* invalid who sorely tried the nurses' patience⟩. **Splenetic** suggests moroseness, and bad rather than hot temper ⟨the *splenetic* type that habored a grudge⟩. **Testy** suggests irascibility over small annoyances ⟨everyone grew *testy* under the emotional strain⟩. **Touchy** implies undue sensitiveness as from jealousy or bad conscience ⟨*touchy* about references to her weight⟩. **Cranky** suggests an habitual fretful irritability ⟨*cranky* neighbors much given to complaining⟩. **Cross** suggests a snappishness or grumpy irritability as from disappointment or discomfort ⟨a squabble that left her feeling *cross* all day⟩.

ire see ANGER

irk see ANNOY

ironic see SARCASTIC

irony see WIT

irregular, anomalous, unnatural mean not conforming to rule, law, or custom. **Irregular** implies not conforming to a law or regulation imposed for the sake of uniformity in methods, practice, or conduct ⟨concerned about her *irregular* behavior⟩. **Anomalous** implies not conforming to what might be expected because of the class or type to which it belongs or the laws that govern its existence ⟨an *anomalous* position of favoring better schools but not wanting to pay for them⟩. **Unnatural** suggests what is contrary to nature or to principles or standards felt to be essential to the well-being of civilized society ⟨treated their prisoners of war with *unnatural* cruelty⟩.

irritate, exasperate, nettle, provoke, rile, peeve mean to excite a feeling of anger or annoyance. **Irritate** implies an often gradual arousing of angry feelings that may range from impatience to rage ⟨her constant nagging *irritated* him to no end⟩. **Exasperate** suggests galling annoyance or vexation and the arousing of extreme impatience ⟨his *exasperating* habit of putting off every decision⟩. **Nettle** suggests a light stinging or piquing ⟨your high-handed attitude *nettled* several people⟩. **Provoke** implies an arousing of strong annoyance or vexation that may excite to action ⟨remarks that were made solely to *provoke* him⟩. **Rile** implies inducing an angry or resentful agitation ⟨the new rules *riled* up the employees⟩. **Peeve** suggests arousing fretful often petty or querulous irritation ⟨she is easily *peeved* after a sleepless night⟩.

isolation see SOLITUDE

issue *n* see EFFECT

issue *vb* see SPRING

item, detail, particular mean one of the distinct parts of a whole. **Item** applies to each thing specified separately in a list or in a group of things that might be listed or enumerated ⟨ordered every *item* on the list⟩. **Detail** applies to one of the small component parts of a larger whole such as a task, building, painting, narration, or process ⟨leave the petty *details* to others⟩. **Particular** stresses the smallness, singleness, and esp. the concreteness of a detail or item ⟨a verbal attack that included few *particulars*⟩.

J

jade see TIRE

jam see PREDICAMENT

jargon see DIALECT

jeer see SCOFF

jejune see INSIPID

jest, joke, quip, witticism, wisecrack mean something said for the purpose of evoking laughter. **Jest** is chiefly literary and applies to any utterance not seriously intended whether sarcastic, ironic, witty, or merely playful ⟨literary *jests* that were lost on her unsophisticated friends⟩. **Joke** may apply to an act as well as an utterance and suggests no intent to hurt feelings ⟨he's very good at taking a *joke*⟩. **Quip** implies lightness and neatness of phrase more definitely than *jest* ⟨whatever the topic, she's ready with a quick *quip*⟩. **Witticism** and **wisecrack** both stress cleverness of phrasing and both may suggest flippancy or unfeelingness ⟨many felt the sting of his *witticisms*⟩ ⟨a comic known for abrasive *wisecracks*⟩. See in addition FUN.

job see TASK

jocose see WITTY

jocular see WITTY

jocund see MERRY

join, combine, unite, connect, link, associate, relate mean to bring or come together into some manner of union. **Join** implies a bringing into contact or conjunction of any degree of closeness ⟨*joined* forces in an effort to win⟩. **Combine** implies some merging or mingling with corresponding loss of identity of each unit ⟨*combine* the ingredients for a cake⟩. **Unite** implies somewhat greater loss of separate identity ⟨the colonies *united* to form a republic⟩. **Connect** suggests a loose or external attachment with little or no loss of identity ⟨a bridge *connects* the island to the mainland⟩. **Link** may imply strong connection or inseparability of elements still retaining identity ⟨a name forever *linked* with liberty⟩. **Associate** stresses the mere fact of frequent occurrence or existence together in space or in logical relation ⟨opera is popularly *associated* with high society⟩. **Relate** suggests the existence of a real or presumed logical connection ⟨the two events were not *related*⟩.

joke see JEST

jollity see MIRTH

jolly see MERRY

jovial see MERRY

judge see INFER

judgment see SENSE

judicious see WISE

juncture, pass, exigency, emergency, contingency, pinch, straits, crisis mean a critical or crucial time or state of affairs. **Juncture** stresses the significant concurrence or convergence of events ⟨at an important *juncture* in our country's history⟩. **Pass** implies a bad or distressing state or situation brought about by a combination of causes ⟨things have come to a sorry *pass* when it's not safe to be on the streets⟩. **Exigency** stresses the pressure of restrictions or urgency of demands created by a special situation ⟨made no effort to provide for *exigencies*⟩. **Emergency** applies to a sudden unforeseen situation requiring prompt action to avoid disaster ⟨the presence of mind needed to deal with *emergencies*⟩. **Contingency** implies an emergency or exigency that is regarded as possible but uncertain of occurrence ⟨*contingency* plans prepared by the Pentagon⟩. **Pinch** implies urgency or pressure for action to a less intense degree than *exigency* or *emergency* ⟨this will do in a *pinch*⟩. **Straits** applies to a troublesome situation from which escape is extremely difficult ⟨in dire *straits* since the death of her husband⟩. **Crisis** applies to a juncture whose outcome will make a decisive difference ⟨the fever broke and the *crisis* passed⟩.

junk see DISCARD

jurisdiction see POWER

just see FAIR, UPRIGHT

justify see MAINTAIN

juxtaposed see ADJACENT

K

keen see EAGER, SHARP

keep *vb* **Keep, observe, celebrate, commemorate** mean to notice or honor a day, occasion, or deed. **Keep** stresses the idea of not neglecting or violating ⟨*keep* the Sabbath⟩. **Observe** suggests marking the occasion by ceremonious performance ⟨not all holidays are *observed* nationally⟩. **Celebrate** suggests acknowledging an occasion by festivity ⟨traditionally *celebrates* Thanksgiving with a huge dinner⟩. **Commemorate** suggests that an occasion is marked by observances that remind one of the origin and significance of the day ⟨*commemorate* Memorial Day with the laying of wreaths⟩.

keep *vb* **Keep, retain, detain, withhold, reserve** mean to hold in one's possession or under one's control. **Keep** may suggest a holding securely in one's possession, custody, or control ⟨*keep* this while I'm gone⟩. **Retain** implies continued keeping, esp. against threatened seizure or forced loss ⟨managed to *retain* their dignity even in poverty⟩. **Detain** suggests a delay in letting go ⟨*detained* them for questioning⟩. **Withhold** implies restraint in letting go or a refusal to let go ⟨*withheld* information from the authorities⟩. **Reserve** suggests a keeping in store for future use ⟨*reserve* some of your energy for the last mile⟩.

kick see OBJECT

kill, slay, murder, assassinate, dispatch, execute mean to deprive of life. **Kill** merely states the fact of death caused by an agency in any manner ⟨routinely *killed* little bugs⟩ ⟨frost *killed* the plants⟩. **Slay** is a chiefly literary term implying deliberateness and violence but not necessarily motive ⟨*slew* thousands of the Philistines⟩. **Murder** specif. implies stealth and motive and premeditation and therefore full moral responsibility ⟨convicted of *murdering* his parents⟩. **Assassinate** applies to deliberate killing openly or secretly often for political motives ⟨terrorists *assassinated* the Senator⟩. **Dispatch** stresses quickness and directness in putting to death ⟨*dispatched* the sentry with a single stab⟩. **Execute** stresses putting to death as a legal penalty ⟨to be *executed* by firing squad at dawn⟩.

kind *adj* Kind, benign, benignant mean showing a gentle, considerate nature. **Kind** stresses a disposition to be helpful ⟨a *kind* heart beneath a gruff exterior⟩. **Kindly** stresses more the expression of a sympathetic nature or impulse ⟨take a *kindly* interest in the poor of the community⟩. **Benign** and **benignant** stress mildness and mercifulness and apply more often to gracious or patronizing acts or utterances of a superior rather than an equal ⟨the belief that a *benign* supreme being controls destiny⟩ ⟨cultural exchange programs have a *benignant* influence in world affairs⟩.

kind *n* see TYPE

kindly see KIND

knack see GIFT

knotty see COMPLEX

knowledge, learning, erudition, scholarship mean what is or can be known by an individual or by mankind. **Knowledge** applies to facts or ideas acquired by study, investigation, observation, or experience ⟨rich in the *knowledge* gained from life⟩. **Learning** applies to knowledge acquired esp. through formal, often advanced, schooling ⟨a book that is evidence of the author's vast *learning*⟩. **Erudition** strongly implies the acquiring of profound, recondite, or bookish learning ⟨an *erudition* unusual even for a classicist⟩. **Scholarship** implies the possession of learning characteristic of the advanced scholar in a specialized field of study or investigation ⟨a work of first-rate literary *scholarship*⟩.

L

labor see WORK

laconic see CONCISE

lag see DELAY

lament see DEPLORE

languor see LETHARGY

lank see LEAN

lanky see LEAN

lapse see ERROR

lassitude see LETHARGY

last *adj* Last, final, terminal, eventual, ultimate mean following all others (as in time, order, or importance). **Last** applies to something that comes at the end of a series but does not always imply that the series is completed or stopped ⟨the *last* page of a book⟩ ⟨the *last* news we had of him⟩. **Final** applies to that which definitely closes a series, process, or progress ⟨the *final* day of school⟩. **Terminal** may indicate a limit of extension, growth, or development ⟨the *terminal* phase of a disease⟩. **Eventual** applies to something that is bound to follow sooner or later as the final effect of causes already operating ⟨the *eventual* defeat of the enemy⟩. **Ultimate** implies the last degree or stage of a long process beyond which further progress or change is impossible ⟨the *ultimate* collapse of civilization⟩.

last *vb* see CONTINUE

lasting, permanent, durable, stable mean enduring for so long as to seem fixed or established. **Lasting** implies a capacity to continue indefinitely ⟨a book that left a *lasting* impression on me⟩. **Permanent** adds usu. the implication of being designed or planned to stand or continue indefinitely ⟨a *permanent* living arrangement⟩. **Durable** implies power to resist destructive agencies ⟨*durable* fabrics⟩. **Stable** implies lastingness because of resistance to being overturned or displaced ⟨a *stable* government⟩.

late see DEAD

latent, dormant, quiescent, potential, abeyant mean not now showing signs of activity or existence. **Latent** applies to a power or quality that has not yet come forth but may emerge and develop ⟨a *latent* sadism that emerged during the war⟩. **Dormant** suggests the inactivity of something (as a feeling or power) as though sleeping ⟨a *dormant* passion existed between them⟩. **Quiescent** suggests a usu. temporary cessation of activity ⟨racial tensions were *quiescent* for the moment⟩. **Potential** applies to what does not yet have existence or effect but is likely soon to have ⟨a toxic waste dump that is a *potential* disaster⟩. **Abeyant** applies to what is for the time being held off or suppressed ⟨an *abeyant* distrust of the neighbors⟩.

laughable, ludicrous, ridiculous, comic, comical mean provoking laughter or mirth. **Laughable** applies to anything occasioning laughter intentionally or unintentionally ⟨her attempts at roller-skating were *laughable*⟩. **Ludicrous** suggests absurdity or preposterousness that excites both laughter and scorn or sometimes pity ⟨a spy thriller with a *ludicrous* plot⟩. **Ridiculous** suggests extreme absurdity, foolishness, or contemptibility ⟨a *ridiculous* portrayal of wartime combat⟩. **Comic** applies esp. to that which arouses thoughtful amusement ⟨Falstaff is one of Shakespeare's great *comic* characters⟩. **Comical** applies to that which arouses unrestrained spontaneous hilarity ⟨his *comical* appearance would have tested a saint⟩.

lavish see PROFUSE

law, rule, regulation, precept, statute, ordinance, canon mean a principle governing action or procedure. **Law** implies imposition by a sovereign authority and the obligation of obedience on the part of all subject to that authority ⟨obey the *law*⟩. **Rule** applies to more restricted or specific situations ⟨the *rules* of a game⟩. **Regulation** implies prescription by authority in order to control an organization or system ⟨*regulations* affecting nuclear power plants⟩. **Precept** commonly suggests something advisory and not obligatory communicated typically through teaching ⟨the *precepts* of effective writing⟩. **Statute** implies a law enacted by a legislative body ⟨a *statute* requiring the use of seat belts⟩. **Ordinance** applies to an order governing some detail of procedure or conduct enforced by a limited authority such as a municipality ⟨a city *ordinance*⟩. **Canon** suggests in nonreligious use a principle or rule of behavior or procedure commonly accepted as a valid guide ⟨a house that violates all the *canons* of good taste⟩. See in addition HYPOTHESIS.

lawful, legal, legitimate, licit mean being in accordance with law. **Lawful** may apply to conformity with law of any sort (as natural, divine, common, or canon) ⟨the *lawful* sovereign⟩. **Legal** applies to what is sanctioned by law or in conformity with the law, esp. as it is written or administered by the courts ⟨*legal* residents of the state⟩. **Legitimate** may apply to a legal right or status but also, in extended use, to a right or status supported by tradition, custom, or accepted standards ⟨a perfectly *legitimate* question about finances⟩. **Licit** applies to a strict conformity to the provisions of the law and applies esp. to what is regulated by law ⟨the *licit* use of the drug by hospitals⟩.

lax see NEGLIGENT

lazy, indolent, slothful mean not easily aroused to activity. **Lazy** suggests a disinclination to work or to take trouble ⟨his habitually *lazy* son⟩. **Indolent** suggests a love of ease and a settled dislike of movement or activity ⟨the summer's heat made us all *indolent*⟩. **Slothful** implies a temperamental inability to act promptly or speedily when action or speed is called for ⟨the agency is usually *slothful* about fulfilling requests⟩.

lead see GUIDE

league see ALLIANCE

lean, spare, lank, lanky, gaunt, rawboned, scrawny, skinny mean thin because of an absence of excess flesh. **Lean** stresses lack of fat and of curving contours ⟨a *lean* racehorse⟩. **Spare** suggests leanness from abstemious living or constant exercise ⟨the *spare* form of a long-distance runner⟩. **Lank** implies tallness as well as leanness ⟨the pale, *lank* limbs of a prisoner of war⟩. **Lanky** suggests awkwardness and loose-jointedness as well as thinness ⟨a *lanky* youth, all arms and legs⟩. **Gaunt** implies marked thinness or emaciation as from overwork or suffering ⟨her *gaunt* face showed the strain of poverty⟩. **Rawboned** suggests a large ungainly build without implying undernourishment ⟨*rawboned* lumberjacks squeezed into the booth⟩. **Scrawny** and **skinny** imply an extreme leanness that suggests deficient strength and vitality ⟨*scrawny* village children⟩ ⟨*skinny* fashion models⟩.

leaning, propensity, proclivity, penchant mean a strong instinct or liking for something. **Leaning** suggests a liking or attraction not strong enough to be decisive or uncontrollable ⟨accused of having socialist *leanings*⟩. **Propensity** implies a deeply ingrained and usu. irresistible longing ⟨the natural *propensity* of in-laws to offer advice⟩. **Proclivity** suggests a strong natural proneness usu. to something objectionable or evil ⟨movies that reinforce viewers' *proclivities* for violence⟩. **Penchant** implies a strongly marked taste in the person or an irresistible attraction in the object ⟨has a *penchant* for overdramatizing his troubles⟩.

learn see DISCOVER
learning see KNOWLEDGE
lease see HIRE
leaven see INFUSE
leech see PARASITE
legal see LAWFUL
legendary see FICTITIOUS
legitimate see LAWFUL
lengthen see EXTEND
lenient see FORBEARING
lenity see MERCY
lessen see DECREASE

let, allow, permit mean not to forbid or prevent. **Let** may imply a positive giving of permission but more often implies failure to prevent either through inadvertence and negligence or through lack of power or effective authority ⟨the goalie *let* the puck get by him⟩. **Allow** implies little more than a forbearing to prohibit ⟨a teacher who *allows* her pupils to do as they like⟩. **Permit** implies willingness or acquiescence ⟨the park *permits* powerboats on the lake⟩. See in addition HIRE.

lethal see DEADLY

lethargy, languor, lassitude, stupor, torpor mean physical or mental inertness. **Lethargy** implies such drowsiness or aversion to activity as is induced by disease, injury, drugs ⟨months of *lethargy* followed my skiing accident⟩. **Languor** suggests inertia induced by an enervating climate or illness or love ⟨*languor* induced by a tropical vacation⟩. **Lassitude** stresses listlessness or indifference resulting from fatigue or poor health ⟨a deepening depression marked by *lassitude*⟩. **Stupor** implies a deadening of the mind and senses by shock, narcotics, or intoxicants ⟨lapsed into a *stupor* following a night of drinking⟩. **Torpor** implies a state of suspended animation as of hibernating animals but may suggest merely extreme sluggishness ⟨a once-alert mind now in a state of *torpor*⟩.

level, flat, plane, even, smooth mean having a surface without bends, curves, or irregularities. **Level** applies to a horizontal surface that lies on a line parallel with the horizon ⟨the vast prairies are nearly *level*⟩. **Flat** applies to a surface devoid of noticeable curvatures, prominences, or depressions ⟨the work surface must be totally *flat*⟩. **Plane** applies to any real or imaginary flat surface in which a straight line between any two points on it lies wholly within that surface ⟨the *plane* sides of a crystal⟩. **Even** applies to a surface that is noticeably flat or level or to a line that is observably straight ⟨trim the hedge so that it is *even*⟩. **Smooth** applies esp. to a polished surface free of irregularities ⟨a *smooth* dance floor⟩.

levity see LIGHTNESS

liable, open, exposed, subject, prone, susceptible, sensitive mean being by nature or through circumstances likely to experience something adverse. **Liable** implies a possibility or probability of incurring something because of position, nature, or particular situation ⟨unless you're careful, you're *liable* to fall⟩. **Open** stresses a lack of barriers preventing incurrence ⟨a claim that is *open* to question⟩. **Exposed** suggests lack of protection or powers of resistance against something actually present or threatening ⟨the town's *exposed* position makes it impossible to defend⟩. **Subject** implies an openness for any reason to something that must be suffered or undergone ⟨all reports are *subject* to editorial revision⟩. **Prone** stresses natural tendency or propensity to incur something ⟨a person who is *prone* to procrastination⟩. **Susceptible** implies conditions existing in one's nature or individual constitution that make incurrence probable ⟨young children are *susceptible* to colds⟩. **Sensitive** implies a readiness to respond to or be influenced by forces or stimuli ⟨her eyes are *sensitive* to light⟩. See in addition RESPONSIBLE.

liberal, generous, bountiful, munificent mean giving freely and unstintingly. **Liberal** suggests openhandedness in the giver and largeness in the thing or amount given ⟨a teacher *liberal* in bestowing praise⟩. **Generous** stresses warmhearted readiness to give more than size or importance of the gift ⟨a friend's *generous* offer of assistance⟩. **Bountiful** suggests lavish, unremitting giving or providing ⟨*bountiful* grandparents spoiling the children⟩. **Munificent** suggests a scale of giving appropriate to lords or princes ⟨the Queen was especially *munificent* to her favorite⟩.

liberate see FREE
liberty see FREEDOM
license see FREEDOM
licit see LAWFUL

lie, prevaricate, equivocate, palter, fib mean to tell an untruth. **Lie** is the blunt term, imputing dishonesty ⟨to *lie* under oath is a serious crime⟩. **Prevaricate** softens the bluntness of *lie* by implying quibbling or confusing the issue ⟨during the hearings the witness did his best to *prevaricate*⟩. **Equivocate** implies using words having more than one sense so as to seem to say one thing but intend another ⟨*equivocated*, dodged questions, and generally misled her inquisitors⟩. **Palter** implies making unreliable statements of fact or intention or insincere promises ⟨a cad *paltering* with a naive, young girl⟩. **Fib** applies to a telling of a trivial untruth ⟨*fibbed* about the price of the suit⟩.

lift, raise, rear, elevate, hoist, heave, boost mean to move from a lower to a higher place or position. **Lift** usu. implies exerting effort to overcome resistance of weight ⟨*lift* the chair while I vacuum⟩. **Raise** carries a stronger implication of bringing up to the vertical or to a high position ⟨soldiers *raising* a flagpole⟩. **Rear** may add an element of suddenness to *raise* ⟨suddenly a flag of truce was *reared*⟩. **Elevate** may replace *lift* or *raise* esp. when exalting or enhancing is implied ⟨*elevated* the musical tastes of the public⟩. **Hoist** implies lifting something heavy esp. by mechanical means ⟨*hoisted* the cargo on board⟩. **Heave** implies lifting with great effort or strain ⟨struggled to *heave* the heavy crate⟩. **Boost** suggests assisting to climb or advance by a push ⟨*boosted* his brother over the fence⟩.

light see EASY

lighten see RELIEVE

lightness, levity, frivolity, flippancy, volatility, flightiness mean gaiety or indifference when seriousness is expected. **Lightness** implies a lack of weight and seriousness in character, mood, or conduct ⟨the only bit of *lightness* in a dreary, ponderous drama⟩. **Levity** suggests trifling or unseasonable gaiety ⟨injected a moment of *levity* in the solemn proceedings⟩. **Frivolity** suggests irresponsible indulgence in gaieties or in idle speech or conduct ⟨a playgirl living a life of uninterrupted *frivolity*⟩. **Flippancy** implies an unbecoming levity esp. in speaking of grave or sacred matters ⟨spoke of the bombing with annoying *flippancy*⟩. **Volatility** implies such fickleness of disposition as prevents long attention to any one thing ⟨the *volatility* of the public interest in foreign aid⟩. **Flightiness** implies extreme volatility that may approach loss of mental balance ⟨the *flightiness* of my grandmother in her old age⟩.

likeness, similarity, resemblance, similitude, analogy, affinity mean agreement or correspondence in details. **Likeness** implies a closer correspondence than **similarity** which often implies that things are merely somewhat alike ⟨a remarkable *likeness* to his late father⟩ ⟨some *similarity* between the two cases⟩. **Resemblance** implies similarity chiefly in appearance or external qualities ⟨statements that bear no *resemblance* to the truth⟩. **Similitude** applies chiefly to correspondence between abstractions ⟨the *similitude* of environments was rigidly maintained⟩. **Analogy** implies likeness or parallelism in relations rather than in appearance or qualities ⟨pointed out the *analogies* to past wars⟩. **Affinity** suggests a cause such as kinship or experiences or influences in common which is accountable for the similarity ⟨a writer with a striking *affinity* for American Indian culture⟩.

limit, restrict, circumscribe, confine mean to set bounds for. **Limit** implies setting a point or line ⟨as in time, space, speed, or degree⟩ beyond which something cannot or is not permitted to go ⟨visits are *limited* to 30 minutes⟩. **Restrict** suggests a narrowing or tightening or restraining within or as if within an encircling boundary ⟨laws intended to *restrict* the freedom of the press⟩. **Circumscribe** stresses a restriction on all sides and by clearly defined boundaries ⟨the work of the investigating committee was carefully *circumscribed*⟩. **Confine** suggests severe restraint and a resulting cramping, fettering, or hampering ⟨our freedom of choice was *confined* by finances⟩.

limpid see CLEAR

lingo see DIALECT

link see JOIN

little see SMALL

lively, animated, vivacious, sprightly, gay mean keenly alive and spirited. **Lively** suggests briskness, alertness, or energy ⟨a *lively* hour of news and information⟩. **Animated** applies to what is spirited, active, and sparkling ⟨an *animated* discussion of current events⟩. **Vivacious** suggests an activeness of gesture and wit, often playful or alluring ⟨a *vivacious* party hostess⟩. **Sprightly** suggests lightness and spirited vigor of manner or of wit ⟨a tuneful, *sprightly* musical revue⟩. **Gay** stresses complete freedom from care and overflowing spirits ⟨the *gay* spirit of Paris in the 1920s⟩.

living, alive, animate, animated, vital mean having or showing life. **Living** and **alive** apply to organic bodies having life as opposed to those from which life has gone ⟨*living* artists⟩ ⟨toss the lobster into the pot while it's still *alive*⟩. **Animate** is used chiefly in direct opposition to *inanimate* to denote things capable of life ⟨a child seemingly afraid of every *animate* ob-

ject⟩. **Animated** is applied to that which comes alive and active or is given motion simulating life ⟨an *animated* cartoon⟩. **Vital** often suggests the opposite of *mechanical* in implying the energy and esp. the power to grow and reproduce characteristic of life ⟨all of his *vital* functions seemed normal⟩.

loath see DISINCLINED

loathe see HATE

lofty see HIGH

loiter see DELAY

lone see ALONE

lonely see ALONE

lonesome see ALONE

long, yearn, hanker, pine, hunger, thirst mean to have a strong desire for something. **Long** implies a wishing with one's whole heart and often a striving to attain ⟨*longed* for some peace and quiet⟩. **Yearn** suggests an eager, restless, or painful longing ⟨*yearned* for a career on the stage⟩. **Hanker** suggests the uneasy promptings of unsatisfied appetite or desire ⟨always *hankering* for more money⟩. **Pine** implies a languishing or a fruitless longing for what is impossible ⟨*pined* for long-lost love⟩. **Hunger** and **thirst** imply an insistent or impatient craving or a compelling need ⟨*hungered* for a business of his own⟩ ⟨*thirsted* for absolute power⟩.

look see EXPECT

loot see SPOIL

loquacious see TALKATIVE

lordly see PROUD

lot see FATE

loud, stentorian, earsplitting, raucous, strident mean marked by intensity or volume of sound. **Loud** applies to any volume above normal and may suggest undue vehemence or obtrusiveness ⟨a *loud* obnoxious person⟩. **Stentorian** implies great power and range ⟨an actor with a *stentorian* voice⟩. **Earsplitting** implies loudness that is physically discomforting ⟨the *earsplitting* sound of a siren⟩. **Raucous** implies a loud harsh grating tone, esp. of voice, and may suggest rowdiness ⟨a barroom filled with the *raucous* shouts of drunken revelers⟩. **Strident** implies a rasping discordant but insistent quality, esp. of voice ⟨the *strident* voices of hecklers⟩.

loutish see BOORISH

lovely see BEAUTIFUL

low see BASE

lower see FROWN

lowly see HUMBLE

loyal see FAITHFUL

loyalty see FIDELITY

lucid see CLEAR

lucky, fortunate, happy, providential mean meeting with unforeseen success. **Lucky** stresses the agency of chance in bringing about a favorable result ⟨the *lucky* day I met my future wife⟩. **Fortunate** suggests being rewarded beyond one's deserts ⟨have been *fortunate* in my business investments⟩. **Happy** combines the implications of *lucky* and *fortunate* with stress on being blessed ⟨a life that has been a series of *happy* accidents⟩. **Providential** more definitely implies the help or intervention of a higher power ⟨it was *providential* that rescuers arrived in the nick of time⟩.

ludicrous see LAUGHABLE

luminous see BRIGHT

lunatic see INSANE

lure, entice, inveigle, decoy, tempt, seduce mean to lead astray from one's true course. **Lure** implies a drawing into danger, evil, or difficulty through attracting and deceiving ⟨*lured* naive investors with get-rich-quick schemes⟩. **Entice** suggests drawing by artful or adroit means ⟨advertising designed to *entice* new customers⟩. **Inveigle** implies enticing by cajoling or flattering

⟨*inveigled* her suitor into proposing marriage⟩. **Decoy** implies a luring away or into entrapment by artifice ⟨the female bird attempted to *decoy* us away from her nest⟩. **Tempt** implies the presenting of an attraction so strong that it overcomes the restraints of conscience or better judgment ⟨*tempted* her to leave her husband and children⟩. **Seduce** implies a leading astray by persuasion or false promises ⟨*seduced* young runaways into the criminal life⟩.

lurid see GHASTLY

lurk, skulk, slink, sneak mean to behave so as to escape attention. **Lurk** implies a lying in wait in a place of concealment and often suggests an evil intent ⟨suspicious men *lurking* in alleyways⟩. **Skulk** suggests more strongly cowardice or fear or sinister intent ⟨spied something *skulking* in the shadows⟩. **Slink** implies moving stealthily often merely to escape attention ⟨during the festivities, I *slunk* away⟩. **Sneak** may add an implication of entering or leaving a place or evading a difficulty by furtive, indirect, or underhanded methods ⟨he *sneaked* out after the others had fallen asleep⟩.

lush see PROFUSE

lustrous see BRIGHT

lusty see VIGOROUS

luxuriant see PROFUSE

luxurious, sumptuous, opulent mean ostentatiously rich or magnificent. **Luxurious** applies to what is choice and costly and suggests gratification of the senses and desire for comfort ⟨a millionaire's *luxurious* penthouse apartment⟩. **Sumptuous** applies to what is extravagantly rich, splendid, or luxurious ⟨an old-fashioned grand hotel with a *sumptuous* lobby⟩. **Opulent** suggests a flaunting of luxuriousness, luxuriance, or costliness ⟨an *opulent* wedding intended to impress the guests⟩. See in addition SENSUOUS.

lying see DISHONEST

M

macabre see GHASTLY

machination see PLOT

mad see INSANE

magisterial see DICTATORIAL

magnificent see GRAND

maim, cripple, mutilate, batter, mangle mean to injure so severely as to cause lasting damage. **Maim** implies the loss or injury of a bodily member through violence ⟨a swimmer *maimed* by a shark⟩. **Cripple** implies the loss or serious impairment of an arm or leg ⟨the fall *crippled* her for life⟩. **Mutilate** implies the cutting off or removal of an essential part of a person or thing thereby impairing its completeness, beauty, or function ⟨a poignant drama *mutilated* by inept acting⟩. **Batter** implies a series of blows that bruise deeply, deform, or mutilate ⟨a ship *battered* by fierce storms at sea⟩. **Mangle** implies a tearing or crushing that leaves deep extensive wounds ⟨thousands are *mangled* every year by auto accidents⟩.

maintain, assert, defend, vindicate, justify mean to uphold as true, right, just, or reasonable. **Maintain** stresses firmness of conviction ⟨steadfastly *maintained* his client's innocence⟩. **Assert** suggests determination to make others accept one's claim ⟨fiercely *asserted* that credit for the discovery belonged to her⟩. **Defend** implies maintaining in the face of attack or criticism ⟨I need not *defend* my wartime record⟩. **Vindicate** implies successfully defending ⟨his success *vindicated* our faith in him⟩. **Justify** implies showing to be true, just, or valid by appeal to a standard or to precedent ⟨threats to public safety *justified* such drastic steps⟩.

majestic see GRAND

make, form, shape, fashion, fabricate, manufacture, forge mean to cause to come into being. **Make** applies to producing or creating whether by an intelligent agency or blind forces and to either material or immaterial existence ⟨*make* a wish⟩ ⟨the factory *makes* furniture⟩. **Form** implies a definite outline, structure, or design in the thing produced ⟨*form* a plan⟩ ⟨*form* a line outside the door⟩. **Shape** suggests impressing a form upon some material ⟨*shaped* shrubbery into animal figures⟩. **Fashion** suggests the use of inventive power or ingenuity ⟨*fashioned* a bicycle out of spare parts⟩. **Fabricate** suggests a uniting of many parts into a whole and often implies an ingenious inventing of something false ⟨*fabricated* an exotic background for her studio biography⟩. **Manufacture** implies making repeatedly by a fixed process and usu. by machinery ⟨*manufacture* shoes⟩. **Forge** implies a making or effecting by great physical or mental effort ⟨*forged* an agreement after months of negotiating⟩.

makeshift see RESOURCE

maladroit see AWKWARD

malevolence see MALICE

malice, malevolence, ill will, spite, malignity, spleen, grudge mean the desire to see another experience pain, injury, or distress. **Malice** implies a deep-seated often unexplainable desire to see another suffer ⟨felt no *malice* for their former enemies⟩. **Malevolence** suggests a bitter persistent hatred that is likely to be expressed in malicious conduct ⟨deep *malevolence* governed his every act⟩. **Ill will** implies a feeling of antipathy of limited duration ⟨a directive that provoked *ill will* among the employees⟩. **Spite** implies petty feelings of envy and resentment that are often expressed in small harassments ⟨petty insults inspired only by *spite*⟩. **Malignity** implies deep passion and relentlessness ⟨never viewed her daughter-in-law with anything but *malignity*⟩. **Spleen** suggests the wrathful release of latent spite or persistent malice ⟨quick to vent his *spleen* at incompetent subordinates⟩. **Grudge** implies a harbored feeling of resentment or ill will that seeks satisfaction ⟨never one to harbor a *grudge*⟩.

malign *vb* Malign, traduce, asperse, vilify, calumniate, defame, slander mean to injure by speaking ill of. **Malign** suggests specific and often subtle misrepresentation but may not always imply deliberate lying ⟨the most *maligned* monarch in British history⟩. **Traduce** stresses the resulting ignominy and distress to the victim ⟨so *traduced* the governor that he was driven from office⟩. **Asperse** implies continued attack on a reputation often by indirect or insinuated detraction ⟨both candidates *aspersed* the other's motives⟩. **Vilify** implies attempting to destroy a reputation by open and direct abuse ⟨no President was more *vilified* in the press⟩. **Calumniate** imputes malice to the speaker and falsity to his assertion ⟨threatened with a lawsuit for publicly *calumniating* the company⟩. **Defame** stresses the actual loss of or injury to one's good name ⟨forced to pay a substantial sum for *defaming* her reputation⟩. **Slander** stresses the suffering of the victim ⟨town gossips carelessly *slandered* their good name⟩.

malign *adj* see SINISTER

malignity see MALICE

malleable see PLASTIC

malodorous, stinking, fetid, noisome, putrid, rank, fusty, musty mean bad-smelling. **Malodorous** may range from the unpleasant to the strongly offensive ⟨*malodorous* unidentifiable substances in the refrigerator⟩. **Stinking** and **fetid** suggest the foul or disgusting ⟨prisoners were held in *stinking* cells⟩ ⟨skunk cabbage is a *fetid* weed⟩. **Noisome** adds a suggestion of being harmful or unwholesome as well as offensive ⟨a *noisome* toxic waste dump⟩. **Putrid** implies particularly the sickening odor of decaying organic matter

⟨the typically *putrid* smell of a fish pier⟩. **Rank** suggests a strong unpleasant smell ⟨rooms filled with the smoke of *rank* cigars⟩. **Fusty** and **musty** suggest lack of fresh air and sunlight, *fusty* also implying prolonged uncleanliness, *musty* stressing the effects of dampness, mildew, or age ⟨the *fusty* rooms of a boarded-up mansion⟩ ⟨the *musty* odor of a damp cellar⟩.

mammoth see ENORMOUS
manacle see HAMPER
manage see CONDUCT
maneuver see TRICK
mangle see MAIM
maniac see INSANE
manifest *adj* see EVIDENT
manifest *vb* see SHOW
manipulate see HANDLE
manner see BEARING, METHOD
mannerism see POSE
manufacture see MAKE
manumit see FREE
mar see INJURE
margin see BORDER
marital see MATRIMONIAL
mark see SIGN
marshal see ORDER
mask see DISGUISE
mass see BULK
masterful, domineering, imperious, peremptory, imperative mean tending to impose one's will on others. **Masterful** implies a strong personality and ability to act authoritatively ⟨her *masterful* personality soon dominated the movement⟩. **Domineering** suggests an overbearing or arbitrary manner and an obstinate determination to enforce one's will ⟨*domineering* mothers refusing to let their sons go⟩. **Imperious** implies a commanding nature or manner and often suggests arrogant assurance ⟨an *imperious* executive used to getting his own way⟩. **Peremptory** implies an abrupt dictatorial manner coupled with an unwillingness to brook disobedience or dissent ⟨his *peremptory* style does not allow for consultation or compromise⟩. **Imperative** implies peremptoriness arising more from the urgency of the situation than from an inherent will to dominate ⟨an *imperative* appeal for assistance⟩.
material, physical, corporeal, phenomenal, sensible, objective mean of or belonging to actuality. **Material** implies formation out of tangible matter; used in contrast with *spiritual* or *ideal* it may connote the mundane, crass, or grasping ⟨*material* possessions⟩. **Physical** applies to what is perceived directly by the senses and may contrast with *mental, spiritual,* or *imaginary* ⟨the *physical* benefits of exercise⟩. **Corporeal** implies having the tangible qualities of a body such as shape, size, or resistance to force ⟨artists have portrayed angels as *corporeal* beings⟩. **Phenomenal** applies to what is known or perceived through the senses rather than by intuition or rational deduction ⟨scientists concerned only with the *phenomenal* world⟩. **Sensible** stresses the capability of readily or forcibly impressing the senses ⟨the earth's rotation is not *sensible* to us⟩. **Objective** may stress material or independent existence apart from a subject perceiving it ⟨tears are the *objective* manifestation of grief⟩. See in addition RELEVANT.
matrimonial, marital, conjugal, connubial, nuptial mean of, relating to, or characteristic of marriage. **Matrimonial** and **marital** apply to whatever has to do with marriage and the married state ⟨enjoyed 40 years of *matrimonial* bliss⟩ ⟨a *marital* relationship built upon mutual trust and understanding⟩. **Conjugal** specif. applies to married persons and their rights ⟨inmates of the prison now have *conjugal* rights⟩. **Connubial**

may refer to the married state itself ⟨a *connubial* contract of no legal standing⟩. **Nuptial** usu. refers to the marriage ceremony ⟨busy all week with the *nuptial* preparations⟩.
meager, scanty, scant, skimpy, spare, sparse mean falling short of what is normal, necessary, or desirable. **Meager** implies the absence of elements, qualities, or numbers necessary to a thing's richness, substance, or potency ⟨a *meager* portion of meat⟩. **Scanty** stresses insufficiency in amount, quantity, or extent ⟨supplies too *scanty* to last the winter⟩. **Scant** suggests a falling short of what is desired or desirable rather than of what is essential ⟨in January the daylight hours are *scant*⟩. **Skimpy** usu. suggests niggardliness or penury as the cause of the deficiency ⟨tacky housing developments on *skimpy* lots⟩. **Spare** may suggest a slight falling short of adequacy or merely an absence of superfluity ⟨a *spare,* concise style of writing⟩. **Sparse** implies a thin scattering of units ⟨a *sparse* population⟩.
mean *adj* **Mean, ignoble, abject, sordid** mean below the normal standards of human decency and dignity. **Mean** suggests having repellent characteristics (as small-mindedness, ill temper, or cupidity) ⟨*mean* and petty characterizations of former colleagues⟩. **Ignoble** suggests a loss or lack of some essential high quality of mind or spirit ⟨*ignoble* collectors who view artworks merely as investments⟩. **Abject** may imply degradation, debasement, or servility ⟨the *abject* poverty of her youth⟩. **Sordid** is stronger than all of these in stressing physical or spiritual degradation and abjectness ⟨a *sordid* story of murder and revenge⟩.
mean *n* see AVERAGE
meander see WANDER
meaning, sense, acceptation, signification, significance, import denote the idea conveyed to the mind. **Meaning** is the general term used of anything (as a word, sign, poem, or action) requiring or allowing of interpretation ⟨the poem's *meaning* has been fiercely debated⟩. **Sense** denotes the meaning or more often a particular meaning of a word or phrase ⟨used "nighthawk" in its figurative *sense*⟩. **Acceptation** is used of a sense of a word or phrase as regularly understood by a large number of speakers and writers ⟨the writer isn't using "sane" in its common *acceptation*⟩. **Signification** denotes the established meaning of a term, symbol, or character ⟨any Christian would immediately know the *signification* of "INRI"⟩. **Significance** applies specif. to a covert as distinguished from the ostensible meaning of an utterance, act, or work of art ⟨an agreement that seemed to have little *significance* at the time⟩. **Import** suggests the meaning a speaker tries to convey esp. through language ⟨failed at first to appreciate the *import* of the news⟩.
mechanical see SPONTANEOUS
meddlesome see IMPERTINENT
median see AVERAGE
mediate see INTERPOSE
meditate see PONDER
meek see HUMBLE
meet see FIT
melancholia see SADNESS
melancholy see SADNESS
melodramatic see DRAMATIC
member see PART
memory, remembrance, recollection, reminiscence mean the capacity for or the act of remembering, or the thing remembered. **Memory** applies both to the power of remembering and to what is remembered ⟨gifted with a remarkable *memory*⟩ ⟨no *memory* of that incident⟩. **Remembrance** applies to the act of remembering or the fact of being remembered ⟨any *remembrance* of his deceased wife was painful⟩. **Recol-**

lection adds an implication of consciously bringing back to mind often with some effort (after a moment's *recollection* he produced the name). **Reminiscence** suggests the recalling of incidents, experience, or feelings from a remote past (recorded my grandmother's *reminiscences* of her Iowa girlhood).

mend, repair, patch, rebuild mean to put into good order something that has been injured, damaged, or defective. **Mend** implies making whole or sound something broken, torn, or injured (the wound *mended* slowly). **Repair** applies to the mending of more extensive damage or dilapidation (the car needs to be *repaired* by a mechanic). **Patch** implies an often temporary mending of a rent or breach with new material (*patch* potholes with asphalt). **Rebuild** suggests making like new without completely replacing (a *rebuilt* telephone is cheaper than a brand-new one).

mendacious see DISHONEST

mercurial see INCONSTANT

mercy, charity, clemency, grace, lenity mean a disposition to show kindness or compassion. **Mercy** implies compassion that forbears punishing even when justice demands it (admitted his guilt and then begged for *mercy*). **Charity** stresses benevolence and goodwill shown in broad understanding and tolerance of others (show a little *charity* for the weak-willed). **Clemency** implies a mild or merciful disposition in one having the power or duty of punishing (a judge little inclined to show *clemency*). **Grace** implies a benign attitude and a willingness to grant favors or make concessions (the victor's *grace* in treating the vanquished). **Lenity** implies lack of severity in punishing (criticized the courts for excessive *lenity*).

meretricious see GAUDY

merge see MIX

merry, blithe, jocund, jovial, jolly mean showing high spirits or lightheartedness. **Merry** suggests cheerful, joyous, uninhibited enjoyment of frolic or festivity (a *merry* group of holiday revelers). **Blithe** suggests carefree, innocent, or even heedless gaiety (arrived late in her usual *blithe* way). **Jocund** stresses elation and exhilaration of spirits (good news had left him in a *jocund* mood). **Jovial** suggests the stimulation of conviviality and good fellowship (grew increasingly *jovial* with every drink). **Jolly** suggests high spirits expressed in laughing, bantering, and jesting (our *jolly* host enlivened the party).

metamorphose see TRANSFORM

method, mode, manner, way, fashion, system mean the means taken or procedure followed in achieving an end. **Method** implies an orderly logical effective arrangement usu. in steps (effective *methods* of birth control). **Mode** implies an order or course followed by custom, tradition, or personal preference (the preferred *mode* of transportation). **Manner** is close to *mode* but may imply a procedure or method that is individual or distinctive (a highly distinctive *manner* of conducting). **Way** is very general and may be used for any of the preceding words (her usual slapdash *way* of doing things). **Fashion** may suggest a peculiar or characteristic way of doing something (rushing about, in typical New Yorker *fashion*). **System** suggests a fully developed or carefully formulated method often emphasizing the idea of rational orderliness (follows no *system* in playing the horses).

methodize see ORDER

meticulous see CAREFUL

métier see WORK

mettle see COURAGE

mien see BEARING

might see POWER

milieu see BACKGROUND

militant see AGGRESSIVE

mimic see COPY

mingle see MIX

miniature see SMALL

minimize see DECRY

minute see CIRCUMSTANTIAL, SMALL

mirth, glee, jollity, hilarity mean a feeling of high spirits that is expressed in laughter, play, or merrymaking. **Mirth** implies generally lightness of heart and love of gaiety (family gatherings that were the occasions of much *mirth*). **Glee** stresses exultation shown in laughter, cries of joy, or sometimes malicious delight (cackled with *glee* at their misfortune). **Jollity** suggests exuberance or lack of restraint in mirth or glee (his endless flow of jokes added to the *jollity*). **Hilarity** suggests loud or irrepressible laughter or high-spirited boisterousness (a dull comedy not likely to inspire much *hilarity*).

misanthropic see CYNICAL

mischance see MISFORTUNE

mise-en-scène see BACKGROUND

miserly see STINGY

misery see DISTRESS

misfortune, mischance, adversity, mishap mean adverse fortune or an instance of this. **Misfortune** may apply to either the incident or conjunction of events that is the cause of an unhappy change of fortune or to the ensuing state of distress (never lost hope even in the depths of *misfortune*). **Mischance** applies esp. to a situation involving no more than slight inconvenience or minor annoyance (took the wrong road by *mischance*). **Adversity** applies to a state of grave or persistent misfortune (had never experienced much *adversity* in life). **Mishap** applies to a trivial instance of bad luck (the usual *mishaps* that are part of a family vacation).

misgiving see APPREHENSION

mishap see MISFORTUNE

mislead see DECEIVE

misogynistic see CYNICAL

mistake see ERROR

mistrust see UNCERTAINTY

mitigate see RELIEVE

mix, mingle, commingle, blend, merge, coalesce, amalgamate, fuse mean to combine into a more or less uniform whole. **Mix** may or may not imply loss of each element's identity (*mix* the salad greens). **Mingle** usu. suggests that the elements are still somewhat distinguishable or separately active (fear *mingled* with anticipation in my mind). **Commingle** implies a closer or more thorough mingling (a sense of duty *commingled* with a fierce pride). **Blend** implies that the elements as such disappear in the resulting mixture (*blended* several teas to create a balanced brew). **Merge** suggests a combining in which one or more elements are lost in the whole (in her mind reality and fantasy *merged*). **Coalesce** implies an affinity in the merging elements and usu. a resulting organic unity (telling details that *coalesce* into a striking portrait). **Amalgamate** implies the forming of a close union without complete loss of individual identities (immigrants that were readily *amalgamated* into the population). **Fuse** stresses oneness and indissolubility of the resulting product (a building in which modernism and classicism are *fused*).

mob see CROWD

mock see COPY, RIDICULE

mode see FASHION, METHOD

model, example, pattern, exemplar, ideal mean someone or something set before one for guidance or imitation. **Model** applies to something taken or proposed as worthy of imitation (a performance that is a *model* of charm and intelligence). **Example** applies to a person to be imitated or in some contexts on no account to be imitated but to be regarded as a warning (for better or worse, children follow the *example* of their parents). **Pattern** suggests a clear and detailed archetype or prototype ⟨American industry set a *pattern* for others to follow⟩. **Exemplar** suggests either a faultless example to be emulated or a perfect typification ⟨cited Hitler as the *exemplar* of power-mad egomania⟩. **Ideal** implies the best possible exemplification either in reality or in conception ⟨never found a suitor who matched her *ideal*⟩.

modern see NEW

modest see CHASTE, HUMBLE, SHY

modify see CHANGE

moist see WET

mollify see PACIFY

mollycoddle see INDULGE

moment see IMPORTANCE

momentary see TRANSIENT

monetary see FINANCIAL

monstrous, prodigious, tremendous, stupendous mean extremely impressive. **Monstrous** implies a departure from the normal (as in size, form, or character) and often carries suggestions of deformity, ugliness, or fabulousness ⟨the *monstrous* waste of the project⟩. **Prodigious** suggests a marvelousness exceeding belief, usu. in something felt as going far beyond a previous maximum (as of goodness, greatness, intensity, or size) ⟨made a *prodigious* effort and rolled the stone aside⟩. **Tremendous** may imply a power to terrify or inspire awe ⟨the *tremendous* roar of the cataract⟩, but in more general and much weakened use it means little more than very large or great or intense ⟨success gave him *tremendous* satisfaction⟩. **Stupendous** implies a power to stun or astound, usu. because of size, numbers, complexity, or greatness beyond one's power to describe ⟨a *stupendous* volcanic eruption that destroyed the city⟩. See in addition OUTRAGEOUS.

moral, ethical, virtuous, righteous, noble mean conforming to a standard of what is right and good. **Moral** implies conformity to established sanctioned codes or accepted notions of right and wrong ⟨the basic *moral* values of a community⟩. **Ethical** may suggest the involvement of more difficult or subtle questions of rightness, fairness, or equity ⟨his strict *ethical* code would not tolerate it⟩. **Virtuous** implies the possession or manifestation of moral excellence in character ⟨a person not conventionally religious, but *virtuous* in all other respects⟩. **Righteous** stresses guiltlessness or blamelessness and often suggests the sanctimonious ⟨responded to the charge with *righteous* indignation⟩. **Noble** implies moral eminence and freedom from anything petty, mean, or dubious in conduct and character ⟨had only the *noblest* of reasons for pursuing the case⟩.

mordant see CAUSTIC

morose see SULLEN

mortal see DEADLY

motive, impulse, incentive, inducement, spur, goad mean a stimulus to action. **Motive** implies an emotion or desire operating on the will and causing it to act ⟨a crime without apparent *motive*⟩. **Impulse** suggests a driving power arising from personal temperament or constitution ⟨my first *impulse* was to hit him⟩. **Incentive** applies to an external influence (as an expected reward) inciting to action ⟨a bonus was offered as an *incentive* for meeting the deadline⟩. **Inducement** suggests a motive prompted by the deliberate enticements or allurements of another ⟨offered a watch as an *inducement* to subscribe⟩. **Spur** applies to a motive that stimulates the faculties or increases energy or ardor ⟨fear was the *spur* that kept me going⟩. **Goad** suggests a motive that keeps one going against one's will or desire ⟨the need to earn a living is the daily *goad*⟩.

move, actuate, drive, impel mean to set or keep in motion. **Move** is very general and implies no more than the fact of changing position ⟨the force that *moves* the moon around the earth⟩. **Actuate** stresses transmission of power so as to work or set in motion ⟨turbines are *actuated* by the force of a current of water⟩. **Drive** implies imparting forward and continuous motion and often stresses the effect rather than the impetus ⟨a ship *driven* aground by hurricane winds⟩. **Impel** suggests a greater impetus producing more headlong action ⟨burning ambition *impelled* her to the seat of power⟩.

moving, impressive, poignant, affecting, touching, pathetic mean having the power to produce deep emotion. **Moving** may apply to any strong emotional effect including thrilling, agitating, saddening, or calling forth pity or sympathy ⟨a *moving* appeal for charitable contributions⟩. **Impressive** implies compelling attention, admiration, wonder, or conviction ⟨an *impressive* list of achievements⟩. **Poignant** applies to what keenly or sharply affects one's sensitivities ⟨a *poignant* documentary on the plight of the homeless⟩. **Affecting** is close to *moving* but most often suggests pathos ⟨an *affecting* reunion of a mother and her child⟩. **Touching** implies arousing tenderness or compassion ⟨the *touching* innocence in a child's eyes⟩. **Pathetic** implies moving to pity or sometimes contempt ⟨*pathetic* attempts to justify gross negligence⟩.

mulish see OBSTINATE

multiply see INCREASE

mundane see EARTHLY

munificent see LIBERAL

murder see KILL

murky see DARK

muse see PONDER

muster see SUMMON

musty see MALODOROUS

mutilate see MAIM

mutiny see REBELLION

mutual see RECIPROCAL

mystery, problem, enigma, riddle, puzzle, conundrum mean something which baffles or perplexes. **Mystery** applies to what cannot be fully understood by human reason or less strictly to whatever resists or defies explanation ⟨the *mystery* of the stone monoliths on Easter Island⟩. **Problem** applies to any question or difficulty calling for a solution or causing concern ⟨the *problems* created by high technology⟩. **Enigma** applies to utterance or behavior that is very difficult to interpret ⟨his suicide was an *enigma* his family never solved⟩. **Riddle** suggests an enigma or problem involving paradox or apparent contradiction ⟨the *riddle* of the reclusive billionaire⟩. **Puzzle** applies to an enigma or problem that challenges ingenuity for its solution ⟨the mechanisms of heredity were long a *puzzle* for scientists⟩. **Conundrum** applies to a question whose answer involves a pun or less often to a problem whose solution can only be speculative ⟨posed *conundrums* to which there are no practical solutions⟩.

mythical see FICTITIOUS

N

naive see NATURAL

naked see BARE

nasty see DIRTY

national see CITIZEN

native, indigenous, endemic, aboriginal mean belonging to a locality. **Native** implies birth or origin in a place or region and may suggest compatibility with it ⟨*native* tribal customs⟩ ⟨a *native* New Yorker⟩. **Indige-**

nous applies to species or races and adds to *native* the implication of not having been introduced from elsewhere ⟨maize is *indigenous* to America⟩. **Endemic** implies being peculiar to a region ⟨edelweiss is *endemic* in the Alps⟩. **Aboriginal** implies having no known race preceding in occupancy of the region ⟨the *aboriginal* peoples of Australia⟩.

natural, ingenuous, naive, unsophisticated, artless mean free from pretension or calculation. **Natural** implies lacking artificiality and self-consciousness and having a spontaneousness suggesting the natural rather than the man-made world ⟨her unaffected, *natural* quality comes across on film⟩. **Ingenuous** implies inability to disguise or conceal one's feelings or intentions ⟨the *ingenuous,* spontaneous utterances of children⟩. **Naive** suggests lack of worldly wisdom often connoting credulousness and unchecked innocence ⟨in money matters she was distressingly *naive*⟩. **Unsophisticated** implies a lack of experience and training necessary for social ease and adroitness ⟨the store intimidates *unsophisticated* customers⟩. **Artless** suggests a naturalness resulting from unawareness of the effect one is producing on others ⟨gave an *artless* impromptu speech at the dinner⟩. See in addition REGULAR.

nature see TYPE
naughty see BAD
nefarious see VICIOUS
negate see NULLIFY

neglect, omit, disregard, ignore, overlook, slight, forget mean to pass over without giving due attention. **Neglect** implies giving insufficient attention to something that has a claim to one's attention ⟨habitually *neglected* his studies⟩. **Omit** implies absence of all attention ⟨*omitted* to remove the telltale fingerprints⟩. **Disregard** suggests voluntary inattention ⟨*disregarded* the wishes of the other members⟩. **Ignore** implies a failure to regard something obvious ⟨*ignored* the snide remarks of passersby⟩. **Overlook** suggests disregarding or ignoring through haste or lack of care ⟨in my rush I *overlooked* some relevant examples⟩. **Slight** implies contemptuous or disdainful disregarding or omitting ⟨*slighted* several worthy authors in her survey⟩. **Forget** may suggest either a willful ignoring or a failure to impress something on one's mind ⟨*forget* what others say and listen to your conscience⟩.

neglectful see NEGLIGENT

negligent, neglectful, lax, slack, remiss mean culpably careless or indicative of such carelessness. **Negligent** implies inattention to one's duty or business ⟨I had been *negligent* in my letter-writing⟩. **Neglectful** adds a more disapproving implication of laziness or deliberate inattention ⟨a society callously *neglectful* of the poor⟩. **Lax** implies a blameworthy lack of strictness, severity, or precision ⟨a reporter who is *lax* about getting the facts straight⟩. **Slack** implies want of due or necessary diligence or care ⟨the *slack* workmanship and slipshod construction⟩. **Remiss** implies blameworthy carelessness shown in slackness, forgetfulness, or neglect ⟨had been *remiss* in her domestic duties⟩.

neighborly see AMICABLE
nerve see TEMERITY
nervous see VIGOROUS
nettle see IRRITATE

new, novel, modern, original, fresh mean having recently come into existence or use. **New** may apply to what is freshly made and unused ⟨*new* brick⟩ or has not been known before ⟨*new* designs⟩ or not experienced before ⟨starts his *new* job⟩. **Novel** applies to what is not only new but strange or unprecedented ⟨a *novel* approach to the problem⟩. **Modern** applies to what belongs to or is characteristic of the present time or

the present era ⟨the lifestyle of the *modern* woman⟩. **Original** applies to what is the first of its kind to exist ⟨a man without one *original* idea⟩. **Fresh** applies to what has not lost its qualities of newness such as liveliness, energy, brightness ⟨*fresh* towels⟩ ⟨a *fresh* start⟩.

nice, dainty, fastidious, finicky, particular, squeamish mean having or showing exacting standards. **Nice** implies fine discrimination in perception and evaluation ⟨makes a *nice* distinction between an artist and a craftsman⟩. **Dainty** suggests a tendency to reject what does not satisfy one's delicate taste or sensibility ⟨when camping, one cannot afford to be *dainty* about food⟩. **Fastidious** implies having very high and often capricious ethical, artistic, or social standards ⟨a woman too *fastidious* to tolerate messy little boys⟩. **Finicky** implies an affected often exasperating fastidiousness ⟨small children are usually *finicky* eaters⟩. **Particular** implies an insistence that one's exacting standards be met ⟨a customer who is very *particular* about his fried eggs⟩. **Squeamish** suggests an oversensitive or prudish readiness to be nauseated, disgusted, or offended ⟨*squeamish* about erotic art⟩. See in addition CORRECT.

niggardly see STINGY
nimble see AGILE
nobility see ARISTOCRACY
noble see MORAL
noisome see MALODOROUS
nonchalant see COOL
nonplus see PUZZLE
norm see AVERAGE
normal see REGULAR
note see SIGN
noted see FAMOUS

noticeable, remarkable, prominent, outstanding, conspicuous, salient, striking mean attracting notice or attention. **Noticeable** applies to something unlikely to escape observation ⟨a piano recital with no *noticeable* errors⟩. **Remarkable** applies to something so extraordinary or exceptional as to invite comment ⟨a film of *remarkable* intelligence and wit⟩. **Prominent** applies to something commanding notice by standing out from its surroundings or background ⟨a doctor who occupies a *prominent* position in the town⟩. **Outstanding** applies to something that rises above and excels others of the same kind ⟨honored for her *outstanding* contributions to science⟩. **Conspicuous** applies to something that is obvious and unavoidable to the sight or mind ⟨the *conspicuous* waste of the corrupt regime⟩. **Salient** applies to something of significance that merits the attention given it ⟨list the *salient* points of the speech⟩. **Striking** applies to something that impresses itself powerfully and deeply upon the observer's mind or vision ⟨the backwardness of the area is *striking* to even casual observers⟩.

notify see INFORM
notion see IDEA
notorious see FAMOUS
novel see NEW
noxious see PERNICIOUS
nude see BARE
nugatory see VAIN

nullify, negate, annul, abrogate, invalidate mean to deprive of effective or continued existence. **Nullify** implies counteracting completely the force, effectiveness, or value of something ⟨his critical insights are *nullified* by tiresome puns⟩. **Negate** implies the destruction or canceling out of each of two things by the other ⟨a relationship *negated* by petty jealousies⟩. **Annul** suggests making ineffective or nonexistent often by legal or official action ⟨the treaty *annuls* all previous agreements⟩. **Abrogate** is like *annul* but more definitely implies a legal or official purposeful act

⟨a law that would *abrogate* certain diplomatic privileges⟩. **Invalidate** implies making something powerless or unacceptable by declaration of its logical or moral or legal unsoundness ⟨the absence of witnesses *invalidates* the will⟩.

nuptial see MATRIMONIAL

O

obdurate see INFLEXIBLE

obedient, docile, tractable, amenable mean submissive to the will of another. **Obedient** implies compliance with the demands or requests of one in authority ⟨cadets must be *obedient* to the honor code⟩. **Docile** implies a predisposition to submit readily to control or guidance ⟨a *docile* child who never caused trouble⟩. **Tractable** suggests having a character that permits easy handling or managing ⟨Indian elephants are more *tractable* than their African cousins⟩. **Amenable** suggests a willingness to yield or to cooperate either because of a desire to be agreeable or because of a natural open-mindedness ⟨he's usually *amenable* to suggestions and new ideas⟩.

object *vb* **Object, protest, remonstrate, expostulate, kick** mean to oppose by arguing against. **Object** stresses dislike or aversions ⟨*objected* to his sweeping generalizations⟩. **Protest** suggests an orderly presentation of objections in speech or writing ⟨an open letter *protesting* the government's foreign policy⟩. **Remonstrate** implies an attempt to convince by warning or reproving ⟨*remonstrated* on his son's free-spending ways at college⟩. **Expostulate** suggests an earnest explanation of one's objection and firm insistence on change ⟨mother *expostulated,* but my room remained a mess⟩. **Kick** suggests more informally a strenuous protesting or complaining ⟨everybody *kicks* when taxes are raised⟩.

object *n* see INTENTION

objective *adj* see FAIR, MATERIAL

objective *n* see INTENTION

oblige see FORCE

obliging see AMIABLE

obliterate see ERASE

oblivious see FORGETFUL

obloquy see ABUSE

obnoxious see REPUGNANT

obscene see COARSE

obscure, dark, vague, enigmatic, cryptic, ambiguous, equivocal mean not clearly understandable. **Obscure** implies a hiding or veiling of meaning through some inadequacy of expression or withholding of full knowledge ⟨the poem is *obscure* to those unlearned in the classics⟩. **Dark** implies an imperfect or clouded revelation often with ominous or sinister suggestion ⟨muttered *dark* hints of revenge⟩. **Vague** implies a lack of clear formulation due to inadequate conception or consideration ⟨*vague* promises of reimbursement were made⟩. **Enigmatic** stresses a puzzling, mystifying quality ⟨left behind *enigmatic* works on alchemy⟩. **Cryptic** implies a purposely concealed meaning ⟨a *cryptic* message only a spy could decode⟩. **Ambiguous** applies to a difficulty of understanding arising from the use of a word or words of multiple meanings ⟨an *ambiguous* directive that could be taken either way⟩. **Equivocal** applies to the deliberate use of language open to differing interpretations with the intention of deceiving or evading ⟨the prisoner would give only *equivocal* answers⟩.

obsequious see SUBSERVIENT

observe see KEEP

obsolete see OLD

obstinate, dogged, stubborn, pertinacious, mulish mean fixed and unyielding in course or purpose. **Obstinate** implies usu. a perverse or unreasonable persistence ⟨a President who was resolute but never *obstinate*⟩. **Dogged** suggests a tenacious unwavering persistence ⟨pursued the story with *dogged* perseverance⟩. **Stubborn** implies sturdiness in resisting attempts to change or abandon a course or opinion ⟨swallow your *stubborn* pride and admit that you are wrong⟩. **Pertinacious** suggests an annoying or irksome persistence ⟨a *pertinacious* salesman who wouldn't take no for an answer⟩. **Mulish** implies a thoroughly unreasonable obstinacy ⟨a *mulish* determination to stick with a lost cause⟩.

obstreperous see VOCIFEROUS

obstruct see HINDER

obtain see GET

obtrude see INTRUDE

obtrusive see IMPERTINENT

obtuse see DULL

obviate see PREVENT

obvious see EVIDENT

occasion see CAUSE

occupation see WORK

occurrence, event, incident, episode, circumstance mean something that happens or takes place. **Occurrence** may apply to a happening without intent, volition, or plan ⟨a meeting that was a chance *occurrence*⟩. **Event** usu. implies an occurrence of some importance and frequently one having antecedent cause ⟨the sequence of *events* following the assassination⟩. **Incident** suggests an occurrence of brief duration or secondary importance ⟨one of the minor *incidents* of the war⟩. **Episode** stresses the distinctiveness or apartness of an incident ⟨recounted some amusing *episodes* from his youth⟩. **Circumstance** implies a specific detail attending an action or event as part of its setting or background ⟨couldn't remember the exact *circumstances*⟩.

odd see STRANGE

odious see HATEFUL

odor see SMELL

odorous, fragrant, redolent, aromatic mean emitting and diffusing scent. **Odorous** applies to whatever has a strong distinctive smell whether pleasant or unpleasant ⟨*odorous* cheeses should be tightly wrapped⟩. **Fragrant** applies to things (as flowers or spices) with sweet or agreeable odors ⟨roses that were especially *fragrant*⟩. **Redolent** applies usu. to a place or thing impregnated with odors ⟨the kitchen was often *redolent* of garlic and tomatoes⟩. **Aromatic** applies to things emitting pungent often fresh odors ⟨an *aromatic* blend of rare tobaccos⟩.

offend, outrage, affront, insult mean to cause hurt feelings or deep resentment. **Offend** need not imply an intentional hurting but it may indicate merely a violation of the victim's sense of what is proper or fitting ⟨hoped that my remarks had not *offended* her⟩. **Outrage** implies offending beyond endurance and calling forth extreme feelings ⟨corruption that *outrages* every citizen⟩. **Affront** implies treating with deliberate rudeness or contemptuous indifference to courtesy ⟨a movie that *affronts* your intelligence⟩. **Insult** suggests deliberately causing humiliation, hurt pride, or shame ⟨managed to *insult* every guest at the party⟩.

offense *n* **Offense, resentment, umbrage, pique, dudgeon, huff** mean an emotional response to a slight or indignity. **Offense** implies hurt displeasure ⟨takes deep *offense* at racial slurs⟩. **Resentment** suggests a longer lasting indignation or smoldering ill will ⟨harbored a life-long *resentment* of his brother⟩. **Umbrage** implies a feeling of being snubbed or ignored ⟨took *umbrage* at a lecturer who debunked American legends⟩. **Pique** applies to a transient feeling of wounded vanity ⟨in a *pique* she foolishly declined the invitation). **Dudgeon** suggests an angry fit of indignation (walked out of the meeting in high *dudgeon*). **Huff** implies a peevish short-lived spell of anger usu. at a petty cause (in a *huff* she threw the ring in his face).

offense *n* Offense, sin, vice, crime, scandal mean a transgression of law. **Offense** applies to the infraction of any law, rule, or code (at that school no *offense* went unpunished). **Sin** implies an offense against the moral law (the *sin* of blasphemy). **Vice** applies to a habit or practice that degrades or corrupts (gambling was traditionally the gentleman's *vice*). **Crime** implies a serious offense punishable by the law of the state (the *crime* of murder). **Scandal** applies to an offense that outrages the public conscience (the woman's affairs were a public *scandal*).

offhand see EXTEMPORANEOUS

office see FUNCTION

officious see IMPERTINENT

offset see COMPENSATE

oily see FULSOME

old, ancient, venerable, antique, antiquated, archaic, obsolete mean having come into existence or use in the more or less distant past. **Old** may apply to either actual or merely relative length of existence (*old* houses) (an *old* sweater of mine). **Ancient** applies to occurrence, existence, or use in or survival from the distant past (*ancient* accounts of dragons). **Venerable** stresses the impressiveness and dignity of great age (the family's *venerable* patriarch). **Antique** applies to what has come down from a former or ancient time (collected *antique* Chippendale furniture). **Antiquated** implies being discredited or outmoded or otherwise inappropriate to the present time (*antiquated* teaching methods). **Archaic** implies having the character or characteristics of a much earlier time (the play used *archaic* language to convey a sense of period). **Obsolete** implies having gone out of currency or habitual practice (this nuclear missile will make all others *obsolete*).

oleaginous see FULSOME

ominous, portentous, fateful mean having a menacing or threatening aspect. **Ominous** implies a menacing, alarming character foreshadowing evil or disaster (*ominous* rumblings from a dormant volcano). **Portentous** suggests being frighteningly big or impressive but now seldom definitely connotes forwarning of calamity (the *portentous* voice of the host of a televised mystery series). **Fateful** suggests being of momentous or decisive importance (the *fateful* conference that led to war).

omit see NEGLECT

omnipresent, ubiquitous mean present or existent everywhere. **Omnipresent** in its strict sense is a divine attribute equivalent to *immanent;* more commonly it implies never being absent (residents of the ghetto have an *omnipresent* sense of fear). **Ubiquitous** implies being so active or so numerous as to seem to be found everywhere (*ubiquitous* tourists toting their *omnipresent* cameras).

onerous, burdensome, oppressive, exacting mean imposing hardship. **Onerous** stresses being laborious and heavy esp. because distasteful (the *onerous* task of informing the family of his death). **Burdensome** suggests causing mental as well as physical strain (*burdensome* government regulations). **Oppressive** implies extreme harshness or severity in what is imposed (found the pressure to conform socially *oppressive*). **Exacting** implies rigor or sternness rather than tyranny or injustice in the demands made or in the one demanding (an *exacting* employer).

open see FRANK, LIABLE

opinion, view, belief, conviction, persuasion, sentiment mean a judgment one holds as true. **Opinion** implies a conclusion thought out yet open to dispute (each expert seemed to be of a different *opinion*). **View** suggests a subjective opinion (very assertive in stating his *views*). **Belief** implies often deliberate acceptance and intellectual assent (a firm *belief* in a supreme being). **Conviction** applies to a firmly and seriously held belief (a *conviction* that animal life is as sacred as human). **Persuasion** suggests a belief grounded on assurance (as by evidence) of its truth (was of the *persuasion* that Republicans were better for business). **Sentiment** suggests a settled opinion reflective of one's feelings (her feminist *sentiments* were well-known).

opponent, antagonist, adversary mean one that takes an opposite position. **Opponent** implies little more than position on the other side as in a debate, election, contest, or conflict (*opponents* of the project cite cost as a factor). **Antagonist** implies sharper opposition in a struggle for supremacy (a formidable *antagonist* in the struggle for corporate control). **Adversary** may carry an additional implication of active hostility (two peoples that have been bitter *adversaries* for centuries).

oppose, combat, resist, withstand, antagonize mean to set oneself against someone or something. **Oppose** can apply to any conflict, from mere objection to bitter hostility or warfare (*opposed* the plan to build a nuclear power plant). **Combat** stresses the forceful or urgent countering of something (*combat* the disease by educating the public). **Resist** implies an overt recognition of a hostile or threatening force and a positive effort to counteract or repel it (struggled valiantly to *resist* the temptation). **Withstand** suggests a more passive resistance (unable to *withstand* peer pressure). **Antagonize** implies an arousing of resistance or hostility in another (statements that *antagonized* even his own supporters).

opposite, contradictory, contrary, antithetical mean being so far apart as to be or seem irreconcilable. **Opposite** applies to things in sharp contrast or in conflict (they held *opposite* views on foreign aid). **Contradictory** applies to two things that completely negate each other so that if one is true or valid the other must be untrue or invalid (made *contradictory* predictions about the stock market). **Contrary** implies extreme divergence or diametrical opposition (*contrary* accounts of the late president's character). **Antithetical** stresses clear and unequivocal diametrical opposition (a law that is *antithetical* to the basic idea of democracy).

oppress see WRONG

oppressive see ONEROUS

option see CHOICE

opulent see LUXURIOUS, RICH

oracular see DICTATORIAL

orbit see RANGE

ordain see DICTATE

order, arrange, marshal, organize, systematize, methodize mean to put persons or things into their proper places in relation to each other. **Order** suggests a straightening out so as to eliminate confusion (*ordered* her business affairs before going on extended leave). **Arrange** implies a setting in sequence, relationship, or adjustment (a bouquet of elaborately *arranged* flowers). **Marshal** suggests gathering and arranging in preparation for a particular operation or effective use (an argument won by carefully *marshalled* facts). **Organize** implies arranging so that the whole aggregate works as a unit with each element having a proper function (*organized* the volunteers into teams). **Systematize** implies arranging according to a predetermined scheme (billing procedures that have yet to be *systematized*). **Methodize** suggests imposing an orderly procedure rather than a fixed

scheme (*methodizes* every aspect of her daily living).
See in addition COMMAND.

ordinance see LAW

ordinary see COMMON

organize see ORDER

origin, source, inception, root mean the point at which
something begins its course or existence. **Origin** applies to the things or persons from which something
is ultimately derived and often to the causes operating before the thing itself comes into being (an investigation into the *origins* of baseball). **Source** applies
more often to the point where something springs into
being (the *source* of the Nile) (the *source* of recurrent trouble). **Inception** stresses the beginning of
something without implying causes (the business has
been a success since its *inception*). **Root** suggests a
first, ultimate, or fundamental source often not easily
discerned (a need to find the real *root* of the violence).

original see NEW

originate see SPRING

ornament see ADORN

oscillate see SWING

ostensible see APPARENT

ostentatious see SHOWY

otiose see VAIN

oust see EJECT

outcome see EFFECT

outdo see EXCEED

outfit see FURNISH

outlandish see STRANGE

outline, contour, profile, silhouette mean the line that
bounds and gives form to something. **Outline** applies
to a line marking the outer limits or edges of a body
or mass (chalk *outlines* of the bodies on the sidewalk). **Contour** stresses the quality of an outline or a
bounding surface as being smooth, jagged, curving,
or sharply angled (a car with smoothly flowing *contours*). **Profile** suggests a varied and sharply defined
outline against a lighter background (her face in *profile* accentuates her patrician beauty). **Silhouette** suggests a shape esp. of a head or figure with all detail
blacked out in shadow leaving only the outline clearly defined (a photograph of two figures in *silhouette*
on a mountain ridge).

outlook see PROSPECT

outrage see OFFEND

outrageous, monstrous, heinous, atrocious mean enormously bad or horrible. **Outrageous** implies exceeding the limits of what is bearable or endurable (*outrageous* terrorist acts against civilians). **Monstrous**
applies to what is abnormally or fantastically wrong,
absurd, or horrible (a *monstrous* waste of the taxpayers' money). **Heinous** implies being so flagrantly evil
as to excite hatred or horror (*heinous* crimes that exceeded normal wartime actions). **Atrocious** implies
merciless cruelty, savagery, or contempt of ordinary
values (decent people cannot condone such *atrocious* treatment of prisoners).

outstanding see NOTICEABLE

outstrip see EXCEED

outwit see FRUSTRATE

overbearing see PROUD

overcome see CONQUER

overlook see NEGLECT

overthrow see CONQUER

own see ACKNOWLEDGE, HAVE

P

pacify, appease, placate, mollify, propitiate, conciliate
mean to ease the anger or disturbance of. **Pacify** suggests a smoothing or calming (a sincere apology

seemed to *pacify* him). **Appease** implies quieting insistent demands by making concessions (nothing
seemed to *appease* their appetite for territorial expansion). **Placate** suggests changing resentment or
bitterness to goodwill (bought flowers to *placate* his
irate wife). **Mollify** implies soothing hurt feelings or
rising anger (a promise of a hearing *mollified* the
demonstrators). **Propitiate** implies averting anger or
malevolence esp. of a superior being (*propitiated* his
mother-in-law by getting the clean-cut look). **Conciliate** suggests ending an estrangement by persuasion,
concession, or settling of differences (America's role
in *conciliating* the nations of the Middle East).

pains see EFFORT

palatable, appetizing, savory, tasty, toothsome mean
agreeable or pleasant esp. to the sense of taste. **Palatable** often applies to something that is unexpectedly
found to be agreeable (surprised to find Indian food
quite *palatable*). **Appetizing** suggests a whetting of
the appetite and applies to aroma and appearance as
well as taste (select from a cart filled with *appetizing*
desserts). **Savory** applies to both taste and aroma and
suggests piquancy and often spiciness (egg rolls variously filled with *savory* fillings). **Tasty** implies a pronounced taste (stale shrimp that were far from *tasty*).
Toothsome stresses the notion of agreeableness and
sometimes implies tenderness or daintiness (a dazzling array of *toothsome* hors d'oeuvres).

pall see SATIATE

palpable see PERCEPTIBLE

palter see LIE

pamper see INDULGE

panegyric see ENCOMIUM

panic see FEAR

parade see SHOW

parallel see SIMILAR

paramount see DOMINANT

parasite, sycophant, toady, leech, sponge mean an obsequious flatterer or self-seeker. **Parasite** applies to
one who clings to a person of wealth, power, or influence or is useless to society (a jet-setter with the
usual entourage of *parasites*). **Sycophant** adds to this
a strong suggestion of fawning, flattery, or adulation
(a religious cult leader surrounded by *sycophants*).
Toady emphasizes the servility and snobbery of the
self-seeker (the president's own *toady* made others
grovel). **Leech** stresses persistence in clinging to or
bleeding another for one's own advantage (*leeches*
who abandoned her when the money ran out). **Sponge**
stresses the parasitic laziness, dependence, and op-
portunism of the cadger (her brother, a shiftless
sponge, often came by for a free meal).

pardon see EXCUSE

parley see CONFER

parody see CARICATURE

parsimonious see STINGY

part *n* Part, portion, piece, member, division, section,
segment, fragment mean something less than the
whole. **Part** is a general term appropriate when indefiniteness is required (they ran only *part* of the
way). **Portion** implies an assigned or allotted part (cut
the pie into six *portions*). **Piece** applies to a separate
or detached part of a whole (a puzzle with 500
pieces). **Member** suggests one of the functional units
composing a body (an arm is a bodily *member*). **Division** applies to a large or diversified part (the manufacturing *division* of the company). **Section** applies to
a relatively small or uniform part (the entertainment
section of the newspaper). **Segment** applies to a part
separated or marked out by or as if by natural lines of
cleavage (the retired *segment* of the population).
Fragment applies to a part produced by or as if by
breaking off or shattering (only a *fragment* of the
play still exists).

part *vb* see SEPARATE
partake see SHARE
participate see SHARE
particular *adj* see CIRCUMSTANTIAL, NICE, SINGLE, SPECIAL
particular *n* see ITEM
partisan see FOLLOWER
partner see CONFEDERATE
pass see JUNCTURE
passion, fervor, ardor, enthusiasm, zeal mean intense emotion compelling action. **Passion** applies to an emotion that is deeply stirring or ungovernable (developed a *passion* for reading). **Fervor** implies a warm and steady emotion (read the poem aloud with great *fervor*). **Ardor** suggests warm and excited feeling likely to be fitful or short-lived (the *ardor* of their honeymoon soon faded). **Enthusiasm** applies to lively or eager interest in or admiration for a proposal or cause or activity (never showed much *enthusiasm* for sports). **Zeal** implies energetic and unflagging pursuit of an aim or devotion to a cause (preaches with the *zeal* of the converted). See in addition FEELING.
passionate see IMPASSIONED
passive see INACTIVE
pastoral see RURAL
patch see MEND
patent see EVIDENT
pathetic see MOVING
pattern see MODEL
pay, compensate, remunerate, satisfy, reimburse, indemnify, repay, recompense mean to give money or its equivalent in return for something. **Pay** implies the discharge of an obligation incurred (we *pay* taxes in exchange for government services). **Compensate** implies a making up for services rendered or help given (an attorney well *compensated* for her services). **Remunerate** more clearly suggests paying for services rendered and may extend to payment that is generous or not contracted for (promised to *remunerate* the searchers handsomely). **Satisfy** implies paying a person what is demanded or required by law (all creditors will be *satisfied* in full). **Reimburse** implies a return of money that has been expended for another's benefit (the company will *reimburse* employees for expenses incurred). **Indemnify** implies making good a loss suffered through accident, disaster, warfare (the government cannot *indemnify* the families of military casualties). **Repay** stresses paying back an equivalent in kind or amount (*repay* a loan). **Recompense** suggests due return in amends, friendly repayment, or reward (the hotel *recompensed* us with a free bottle of champagne).
peaceful see CALM
peak see SUMMIT
peculiar see CHARACTERISTIC, STRANGE
pecuniary see FINANCIAL
peer see GAZE
peeve see IRRITATE
pejorative see DEROGATORY
penchant see LEANING
penetrate see ENTER
penetration see DISCERNMENT
penitence, repentance, contrition, compunction, remorse mean regret for sin or wrongdoing. **Penitence** implies sad and humble realization of and regret for one's misdeeds (absolution is dependent upon sincere *penitence*). **Repentance** adds the implication of a resolve to change (a complete change of character accompanied his *repentance*). **Contrition** stresses the sorrowful regret that constitutes true penitence (the beatings were usually followed by tearful expressions of *contrition*). **Compunction** implies a painful sting of conscience esp. for contemplated wrongdoing (have no *compunctions* about taking back what

is mine). **Remorse** suggests prolonged and insistent self-reproach and mental anguish for past wrongs and esp. for those whose consequences cannot be remedied (swindlers are not usually plagued by feelings of *remorse*).
penurious see STINGY
penury see POVERTY
perceptible, sensible, palpable, tangible, appreciable, ponderable mean apprehensible as real or existent. **Perceptible** applies to what can be discerned by the senses often to a minimal extent (a *perceptible* difference in sound). **Sensible** applies to whatever is clearly apprehended through the senses or impresses itself strongly on the mind (a *sensible* change in the weather). **Palpable** applies either to what has physical substance or to what is obvious and unmistakable (the tension in the air was almost *palpable*). **Tangible** suggests what is capable of being handled or grasped both physically and mentally (submitted the gun as *tangible* evidence). **Appreciable** applies to what is distinctly discernible by the senses or definitely measurable (an *appreciable* increase in temperature). **Ponderable** suggests having definitely measurable weight or importance esp. as distinguished from eluding such determination (exerted a *ponderable* influence on world events).
perception see DISCERNMENT
peremptory see MASTERFUL
perennial see CONTINUAL
perfect, whole, entire, intact mean not lacking or faulty in any particular. **Perfect** implies the soundness and the excellence of every part, element, or quality of a thing frequently as an unattainable or theoretical state (a *perfect* set of teeth) (the *perfect* woman). **Whole** suggests a completeness or perfection that can be sought, gained, or regained (an experience that made him feel a *whole* man again). **Entire** implies perfection deriving from integrity, soundness, or completeness of a thing (recorded the *entire* Beethoven corpus). **Intact** implies retention of perfection of a thing in its natural or original state (somehow the building survived the storm *intact*).
perfervid see IMPASSIONED
perfidious see FAITHLESS
perform, execute, discharge, accomplish, achieve, effect, fulfill mean to carry out or into effect. **Perform** implies action that follows established patterns or procedures or fulfills agreed-upon requirements and often connotes special skill (*performed* gymnastics on the parallel bars). **Execute** stresses the carrying out of what exists in plan or in intent (*executed* the heist exactly as planned). **Discharge** implies execution and completion of appointed duties or tasks (*discharged* his duties promptly and effectively). **Accomplish** stresses the successful completion of a process rather than the means of carrying it out (*accomplished* in a year what had taken others a lifetime). **Achieve** adds to *accomplish* the implication of conquered difficulties (a nation struggling to *achieve* greatness). **Effect** adds to *achieve* an emphasis on the inherent force in the agent capable of surmounting obstacles (a dynamic personality who *effected* sweeping reforms). **Fulfill** implies a complete realization of ends or possibilities (the rare epic that *fulfills* its ambitions).
perfume see FRAGRANCE
perilous see DANGEROUS
period, epoch, era, age mean a division of time. **Period** may designate an extent of time of any length (*periods* of economic prosperity). **Epoch** applies to a period begun or set off by some significant or striking quality, change, or series of events (the steam engine marked a new *epoch* in industry). **Era** suggests a period of history marked by a new or distinct order of things (the *era* of global communications). **Age** is

used frequently of a fairly definite period dominated by a prominent figure or feature ⟨the *age* of Samuel Johnson⟩.

permanent see LASTING

permit see LET

pernicious, baneful, noxious, deleterious, detrimental mean exceedingly harmful. **Pernicious** implies irreparable harm done through evil or insidious corrupting or undermining ⟨the claim that pornography has a *pernicious* effect on society⟩. **Baneful** implies injury through poisoning or destroying ⟨the *baneful* notion that discipline destroys creativity⟩. **Noxious** applies to what is both offensive and injurious to the health of a body or mind ⟨*noxious* fumes emanating from a chemical plant⟩. **Deleterious** applies to what has an often unsuspected harmful effect ⟨megadoses of vitamins can have *deleterious* effects⟩. **Detrimental** implies obvious harmfulness to something specified ⟨the *detrimental* effects of prolonged fasting⟩.

perpendicular see VERTICAL

perpetual see CONTINUAL

perplex see PUZZLE

persecute see WRONG

persist see CONTINUE

personality see DISPOSITION

perspicacious see SHREWD

perspicuous see CLEAR

persuasion see OPINION

pertinacious see OBSTINATE

pertinent see RELEVANT

perturb see DISCOMPOSE

perverse see CONTRARY

pervert see DEBASE

pessimistic see CYNICAL

pester see WORRY

phase, aspect, side, facet, angle mean one of the possible ways of viewing or being presented to view. **Phase** implies a change in appearance often without clear reference to an observer ⟨the second *phase* of the investigation⟩. **Aspect** may stress the point of view of an observer and its limitation of what is seen or considered ⟨an article that considers the financial *aspect* of divorce⟩. **Side** stresses one of several aspects from which something may be viewed ⟨a broadcast that told only one *side* of the story⟩. **Facet** implies one of a multiplicity of sides each of which manifests the central quality of the whole ⟨explores the many *facets* of life in New York City⟩. **Angle** suggests an aspect seen from a very restricted or specific point of view ⟨find a fresh *angle* for covering the political convention⟩.

phenomenal see MATERIAL

phlegm see EQUANIMITY

phlegmatic see IMPASSIVE

physical see BODILY, MATERIAL

physiognomy see FACE

pickle see PREDICAMENT

pictorial see GRAPHIC

picturesque see GRAPHIC

piece see PART

pierce see ENTER

pietistic see DEVOUT

piety see FIDELITY

pilfer see STEAL

pillage *vb* see RAVAGE

pillage *n* see SPOIL

pilot see GUIDE

pinch see JUNCTURE

pine see LONG

pinnacle see SUMMIT

pious see DEVOUT

piquant see PUNGENT

pique *n* see OFFENSE

pique *vb* see PROVOKE

pitch see THROW

pithy see CONCISE

pitiable see CONTEMPTIBLE

pity, compassion, commiseration, ruth, condolence, sympathy mean the act or capacity for sharing the interests of another. **Pity** implies tender or sometimes slightly contemptuous sorrow for one in misery or distress ⟨no *pity* was shown to the captives⟩. **Compassion** implies pity coupled with an urgent desire to aid or to spare ⟨treats alcoholics with great *compassion*⟩. **Commiseration** suggests pity expressed outwardly in exclamations, tears, words of comfort ⟨murmurs of *commiseration* filled the loser's headquarters⟩. **Ruth** implies pity coming from a change of heart or a relenting ⟨not a trace of *ruth* in the judge's sentencing⟩. **Condolence** applies chiefly to formal expression of grief to one who has suffered loss ⟨expressed their *condolences* to the widow⟩. **Sympathy** implies a power to enter into another's emotional experience of any sort ⟨my *sympathies* are with the rebels' cause⟩.

placate see PACIFY

placid see CALM

plague see WORRY

plain see COMMON, EVIDENT, FRANK

plan, design, plot, scheme, project mean a method devised for making or doing something or achieving an end. **Plan** always implies mental formulation and sometimes graphic representation ⟨studied the *plans* for the proposed industrial park⟩. **Design** often suggests a particular pattern and some degree of achieved order or harmony ⟨*designs* for three new gowns⟩. **Plot** implies a laying out in clearly distinguished sections with attention to their relations and proportions ⟨outlined the *plot* of the new play⟩. **Scheme** stresses calculation of the end in view and may apply to a plan motivated by craftiness and self-interest ⟨a *scheme* to swindle senior citizens of their savings⟩. **Project** often stresses imaginative scope and vision ⟨a *project* to develop the waterfront⟩.

plane see LEVEL

plastic, pliable, pliant, ductile, malleable, adaptable mean susceptible of being modified in form or nature. **Plastic** applies to substances soft enough to be molded yet capable of hardening into the desired fixed form ⟨*plastic* materials allow the sculptor greater freedom⟩. **Pliable** suggests something easily bent, folded, twisted, or manipulated ⟨headphones that are *pliable* and can be bent to fit⟩. **Pliant** may stress flexibility and sometimes connote springiness ⟨select an athletic shoe with a *pliant* sole⟩. **Ductile** applies to what can be drawn out or extended with ease ⟨copper is one of the most *ductile* of metals⟩. **Malleable** applies to what may be pressed or beaten into shape ⟨the *malleable* properties of gold enhance its value⟩. **Adaptable** implies the capability of being easily modified to suit other conditions, needs, or uses ⟨computer hardware that is *adaptable*⟩.

play see FUN

plea see APOLOGY

plenary see FULL

plentiful, ample, abundant, copious mean more than sufficient without being excessive. **Plentiful** implies a great or rich supply ⟨peaches are *plentiful* this summer⟩. **Ample** implies a generous sufficiency to satisfy a particular requirement ⟨an *ample* amount of food to last the winter⟩. **Abundant** suggests an even greater or richer supply than does *plentiful* ⟨has surprisingly *abundant* energy for a woman her age⟩. **Copious** stresses largeness of supply rather than fullness or richness ⟨*copious* examples of bureaucratic waste⟩.

pliable see PLASTIC

pliant see PLASTIC

plight see PREDICAMENT

plot, intrigue, machination, conspiracy, cabal mean a plan secretly devised to accomplish an evil or treacherous end. **Plot** implies careful foresight in planning a complex scheme ⟨foiled an assassination *plot*⟩. **Intrigue** suggests secret underhanded maneuvering in an atmosphere of duplicity ⟨finagled the nomination by means of back-room *intrigues*⟩. **Machination** implies a contriving of annoyances, injuries, or evils by indirect means ⟨through *machinations* she pieced together a publishing empire⟩. **Conspiracy** implies a secret agreement among several people usu. involving treason or great treachery ⟨a *conspiracy* of oil companies to set prices⟩. **Cabal** typically applies to political intrigue involving persons of some eminence ⟨the infamous *cabal* against General Washington⟩. See in addition PLAN.

plumb see VERTICAL

plunder see SPOIL

poignant see MOVING, PUNGENT

poise see TACT

polite see CIVIL

politic see EXPEDIENT, SUAVE

pollute see CONTAMINATE

ponder, meditate, muse, ruminate mean to consider or examine attentively or deliberately. **Ponder** implies a careful weighing of a problem or, often, prolonged inconclusive thinking about a matter ⟨*pondered* at length the various recourses open to him⟩. **Meditate** implies a definite focusing of one's thoughts on something so as to understand it deeply ⟨the sight of ruins prompted her to *meditate* upon human vanity⟩. **Muse** suggests a more or less focused daydreaming as in remembrance ⟨*mused* upon the adventures had by heroines of gothic novels⟩. **Ruminate** implies going over the same matter in one's thoughts again and again but suggests little of either purposive thinking or rapt absorption ⟨the product of fifty years of *ruminating* on the meaning of life⟩.

ponderable see PERCEPTIBLE

ponderous see HEAVY

popular see COMMON

portentous see OMINOUS

portion see FATE, PART

pose, air, airs, affectation, mannerism mean an adopted way of speaking or behaving. **Pose** implies an attitude deliberately assumed in order to impress others ⟨her shyness was just a *pose*⟩. **Air** may suggest natural acquirement through environment or way of life ⟨years of living in Europe had given him a sophisticated *air*⟩. **Airs** always implies artificiality and pretentiousness ⟨a snobby couple much given to putting on *airs*⟩. **Affectation** applies to a trick of speech or behavior that strikes the observer as insincere ⟨his foreign accent is an *affectation*⟩. **Mannerism** applies to an acquired eccentricity that has become a habit ⟨gesturing with a cigarette was her most noticeable *mannerism*⟩.

positive see SURE

possess see HAVE

possible, practicable, feasible mean capable of being realized. **Possible** implies that a thing may certainly exist or occur given the proper conditions ⟨contends that life on other planets is *possible*⟩. **Practicable** implies that something may be easily or readily effected by available means or under current conditions ⟨when television became *practicable*⟩. **Feasible** applies to what is likely to work or be useful in attaining the end desired ⟨commercially *feasible* for mass production⟩.

postpone see DEFER

potential see LATENT

poverty, indigence, penury, want, destitution mean the state of one with insufficient resources. **Poverty** may cover a range from extreme want of necessities to an absence of material comforts ⟨the extreme *poverty* of Third World countries⟩. **Indigence** implies seriously straitened circumstances ⟨the *indigence* of her years as a graduate student⟩. **Penury** suggests a cramping or oppressive lack of money ⟨given the *penury* of their lifestyle, few suspected their wealth⟩. **Want** and **destitution** imply extreme poverty that threatens life itself through starvation or exposure ⟨lived in a perpetual state of *want*⟩ ⟨the widespread *destitution* in countries beset by famine⟩.

power *n* Power, authority, jurisdiction, control, command, sway, dominion mean the right to govern or rule or determine. **Power** implies possession of ability to wield force, permissive authority, or substantial influence ⟨the *power* of the President to mold public opinion⟩. **Authority** implies the granting of power for a specific purpose within specified limits ⟨gave her attorney the *authority* to manage her estate⟩. **Jurisdiction** applies to official power exercised within prescribed limits ⟨the bureau that has *jurisdiction* over Indian affairs⟩. **Control** stresses the power to direct and restrain ⟨you are responsible for students under your *control*⟩. **Command** implies the power to make arbitrary decisions and compel obedience ⟨the respect of the men under his *command*⟩. **Sway** suggests the extent or scope of exercised power or influence ⟨an empire that extended its *sway* over the known world⟩. **Dominion** stresses sovereign power or supreme authority ⟨a world government that would have *dominion* over all nations⟩.

power *n* Power, force, energy, strength, might mean the ability to exert effort. **Power** may imply latent or exerted physical, mental, or spiritual ability to act or be acted upon ⟨the incredible *power* of flowing water⟩. **Force** implies the actual effective exercise of power ⟨used enough *force* to push the door open⟩. **Energy** applies to power expended or capable of being transformed into work ⟨a social reformer of untiring *energy*⟩. **Strength** applies to the quality or property of a person or thing that makes possible the exertion of force or the withstanding of strain, pressure, or attack ⟨use weight training to build your *strength*⟩. **Might** implies great or overwhelming power or strength ⟨all of his *might* was needed to budge the boulder⟩.

practicable, practical mean capable of being put to use or put into practice. **Practicable** applies to what has been proposed and seems feasible but has not been actually tested in use ⟨the question of whether colonies in space are *practicable*⟩. **Practical** applies to things and to persons and implies proven success in meeting the demands made by actual living or use ⟨the copier is the most *practical* machine in the office⟩. See in addition POSSIBLE.

practical see PRACTICABLE

practice see HABIT

precarious see DANGEROUS

preceding, antecedent, foregoing, previous, prior, former, anterior mean being before. **Preceding** usu. implies being immediately before in time or in place ⟨the last sentence of the *preceding* paragraph⟩. **Antecedent** applies to order in time and may suggest a causal relation ⟨study the revolution and its *antecedent* economic conditions⟩. **Foregoing** applies chiefly to statements ⟨a restatement of the *foregoing* paragraph⟩. **Previous** and **prior** imply existing or occurring earlier, but *prior* often adds an implication of greater importance ⟨her life in a *previous* marriage⟩ ⟨the prices in this catalogue supersede all *prior* prices⟩. **Former** implies always a definite comparison or contrast with something that is latter ⟨the *former* name of the company⟩. **Anterior** applies to position before or ahead of usu. in space, sometimes in time or order ⟨the *anterior* lobe of the brain⟩.

precept see LAW

precious see COSTLY

precipitate, headlong, abrupt, impetuous, sudden mean showing undue haste or unexpectedness. **Precipitate** stresses lack of due deliberation and implies prematureness of action (the army's *precipitate* withdrawal). **Headlong** stresses rashness and lack of forethought (a *headlong* flight from arrest). **Abrupt** stresses curtness and a lack of warning or ceremony (an *abrupt* refusal). **Impetuous** stresses extreme impatience or impulsiveness (it's a bit *impetuous* to propose on the third date). **Sudden** stresses unexpectedness and sharpness or violence of action (flew into a *sudden* rage).

precipitous see STEEP

précis see COMPENDIUM

precise see CORRECT

preclude see PREVENT

precursor see FORERUNNER

predicament, dilemma, quandary, plight, fix, jam, pickle mean a situation from which escape is difficult. **Predicament** suggests a difficult situation usu. offering no satisfactory solution (the *predicament* posed by increasing automation). **Dilemma** implies a predicament presenting a choice between equally bad alternatives (faced with the *dilemma* of putting him in a nursing home or caring for him ourselves). **Quandary** stresses puzzlement and perplexity (in a *quandary* about how to repair it). **Plight** suggests an unfortunate or trying situation (a study on the *plight* of AIDS victims). **Fix** and **jam** are informal equivalents of *plight* but are more likely to suggest involvement through some fault or wrongdoing (constantly getting their son out of some *fix*) (in a real financial *jam* now that she's lost her job). **Pickle** implies a distressing or embarrassing situation (conflicting commitments that left me in a sorry *pickle*).

predict see FORETELL

predilection, prepossession, prejudice, bias mean an attitude of mind that predisposes one to favor something. **Predilection** implies a strong liking deriving from one's temperament or experience (teenagers with a *predilection* for gory horror movies). **Prepossession** suggests a fixed conception likely to preclude objective judgment of anything counter to it (a slave to his *prepossessions*). **Prejudice** usu. implies an unfavorable prepossession and connotes a feeling rooted in suspicion, fear, or intolerance (strong *prejudices* that are based upon neither reason nor experience). **Bias** implies an unreasoned and unfair distortion of judgment in favor of or against a person or thing (employers show a *bias* against overweight people).

predispose see INCLINE

predominant see DOMINANT

preempt see APPROPRIATE

preference see CHOICE

prejudice see PREDILECTION

preponderant see DOMINANT

prepossession see PREDILECTION

prescribe see DICTATE

present see GIVE

presentiment see APPREHENSION

prestige see INFLUENCE

pretend see ASSUME

pretension see AMBITION

pretentious see SHOWY

pretext see APOLOGY

pretty see BEAUTIFUL

prevailing, prevalent, rife, current mean generally circulated, accepted, or used in a certain time or place. **Prevailing** stresses predominance (the *prevailing* medical opinion regarding smoking). **Prevalent** implies only frequency (dairy farms were once *prevalent* in the area). **Rife** implies a growing prevalence or rapid spread (during the epidemic rumors were *rife*). **Current** applies to what is subject to change and stresses prevalence at the present time (the *current* migration towards the Sunbelt).

prevalent see PREVAILING

prevaricate see LIE

prevent *vb* **Prevent, anticipate, forestall** mean to deal with beforehand. **Prevent** implies taking advance measures against something possible or probable (measures taken to *prevent* an epidemic). **Anticipate** may imply merely getting ahead of another by being a precursor or forerunner or it may imply checking another's intention by acting first (*anticipated* the firing so she decided to quit first). **Forestall** implies a getting ahead so as to stop or interrupt something in its course (a government order that effectively *forestalled* a free election).

prevent *vb* **Prevent, preclude, obviate, avert, ward off** mean to stop something from coming or occurring. **Prevent** implies the existence of or the placing of an insurmountable obstacle (the blizzard *prevented* us from going). **Preclude** implies the shutting out of every possibility of a thing's happening or taking effect (an accident that *precluded* a career in football). **Obviate** suggests the use of forethought to avoid the necessity for unwelcome or disagreeable actions or measures (her quitting *obviated* the task of firing her). **Avert** and **ward off** imply taking immediate and effective measures to avoid, repel, or counteract threatening evil (deftly *averted* a hostile corporate takeover) (a hot drink to *ward off* a chill).

previous see PRECEDING

priceless see COSTLY

prior see PRECEDING

prize *vb* see APPRECIATE

prize *n* see SPOIL

probe see ENTER

probity see HONESTY

problem see MYSTERY

problematic see DOUBTFUL

proceed see SPRING

proclaim see DECLARE

proclivity see LEANING

procrastinate see DELAY

procure see GET

prodigal see PROFUSE

prodigious see MONSTROUS

proficient, adept, skilled, skillful, expert mean having great knowledge and experience in a trade or profession. **Proficient** implies a thorough competence derived from training and practice (a translator thoroughly *proficient* in Russian). **Adept** implies special aptitude as well as proficiency (*adept* at handling large numbers in his head). **Skilled** stresses mastery of technique (a delicate operation requiring a *skilled* surgeon). **Skillful** implies individual dexterity in execution or performance (a shrewd and *skillful* manipulation of public opinion). **Expert** implies extraordinary proficiency and often connotes knowledge as well as technical skill (*expert* in the identification and evaluation of wines).

profile see OUTLINE

profitable see BENEFICIAL

profuse, lavish, prodigal, luxuriant, lush, exuberant mean giving or given out in great abundance. **Profuse** implies pouring forth without restraint (uttered *profuse* apologies). **Lavish** suggests an unstinted or unmeasured profusion (a *lavish* wedding reception of obvious expense). **Prodigal** implies reckless or wasteful lavishness threatening to lead to early exhaustion of resources (*prodigal* spending exhausted the fortune). **Luxuriant** suggests a rich and splendid abundance (the *luxuriant* vegetation of a tropical rain forest). **Lush** suggests rich, soft luxuriance (nude portraits that have a *lush,* sensual quality). **Exuberant** implies marked vitality or vigor in what produces abundantly (a fantasy writer with an *exuberant* imagination).

prognosticate see FORETELL

prohibit see FORBID

project see PLAN

projection, protrusion, protuberance, bulge mean an extension beyond the normal line or surface. **Projection** implies a jutting out esp. at a sharp angle (those *projections* along the wall are safety hazards). **Protrusion** suggests a thrusting out so that the extension seems a deformity (the bizarre *protrusions* of a coral reef). **Protuberance** implies a growing or swelling out in rounded form (a skin disease marked by warty *protuberances*). **Bulge** suggests an expansion caused by internal pressure (*bulges* soon appeared in the tile floor).

prolific see FERTILE

prolix see WORDY

prolong see EXTEND

prominent see NOTICEABLE

promote see ADVANCE

prompt see QUICK

promulgate see DECLARE

prone, supine, prostrate, recumbent mean lying down. **Prone** implies a position with the front of the body turned toward the supporting surface (push-ups require the body to be in a *prone* position). **Supine** implies lying on one's back and suggests inertness or abjectness (lying *supine* upon a couch). **Prostrate** implies lying full-length as in submission, defeat, or physical collapse (a runner fell *prostrate* at the finish line). **Recumbent** implies the posture of one sleeping or resting (he was *recumbent* and relaxed in his hospital bed). See in addition LIABLE.

propel see PUSH

propensity see LEANING

proper see FIT

property see QUALITY

prophesy see FORETELL

propitiate see PACIFY

propitious see FAVORABLE

proportional, proportionate, commensurate, commensurable mean duly proportioned to something else. **Proportional** may apply to several closely related things that change without altering their relations (medical fees are *proportional* to one's income). **Proportionate** applies to one thing that bears a reciprocal relationship to another (a punishment not at all *proportionate* to the offense). **Commensurate** stresses an equality between things different from but in some way dependent on each other (the salary will be *commensurate* with experience). **Commensurable** more strongly implies a common scale by which two quite different things can be shown to be significantly equal or proportionate (equal pay for jobs that are *commensurable* in worth).

proportionate see PROPORTIONAL

propriety see DECORUM

prospect, outlook, anticipation, foretaste mean an advance realization of something to come. **Prospect** implies expectation of a particular event, condition, or development of definite interest or concern (the appealing *prospect* of a quiet weekend). **Outlook** suggests a forecasting of the future (a favorable *outlook* for the state's economy). **Anticipation** implies a prospect or outlook that involves advance suffering or enjoyment of what is foreseen (the *anticipation* of the meeting was the worst of it). **Foretaste** implies an actual though brief or partial experience of something forthcoming (the frost was a *foretaste* of winter).

prostrate see PRONE

protect see DEFEND

protest see ASSERT, OBJECT

protract see EXTEND

protrusion see PROJECTION

protuberance see PROJECTION

proud, arrogant, haughty, lordly, insolent, overbearing, supercilious, disdainful mean showing scorn for inferiors. **Proud** may suggest an assumed superiority or loftiness (a *proud* man, unwilling to admit failure). **Arrogant** implies a claiming for oneself of more consideration or importance than is warranted (an *arrogant* business executive used to being kowtowed to). **Haughty** suggests a consciousness of superior birth or position (a *haughty* manner that barely concealed his scorn). **Lordly** implies pomposity or an arrogant display of power (a *lordly* indifference to the consequences of their carelessness). **Insolent** implies contemptuous haughtiness (suffered the stares of *insolent* waiters). **Overbearing** suggests a tyrannical manner or an intolerable insolence (an *overbearing* society hostess). **Supercilious** implies a cool, patronizing haughtiness (*supercilious* parvenus asserting their position). **Disdainful** suggests a more active and openly scornful superciliousness (*disdainful* of their social inferiors).

providential see LUCKY

province see FUNCTION

provoke, excite, stimulate, pique, quicken mean to arouse as if by pricking. **Provoke** directs attention to the response called forth (my stories usually *provoke* laughter). **Excite** implies a stirring up or moving profoundly (news that *excited* anger and frustration). **Stimulate** suggests a rousing out of lethargy, quiescence, or indifference (*stimulating* conversation). **Pique** suggests stimulating by mild irritation or challenge (that remark *piqued* my interest). **Quicken** implies beneficially stimulating and making active or lively (the high salary *quickened* her desire to have the job). See in addition IRRITATE.

prowess see HEROISM

prudent see WISE

prying see CURIOUS

publish see DECLARE

pugnacious see BELLIGERENT

pull, draw, drag, haul, tug mean to cause to move in the direction determined by an applied force. **Pull** is the general term but may emphasize the force exerted rather than resulting motion (to open the drawer, *pull* hard). **Draw** implies a smoother, steadier motion and generally a lighter force than *pull* (a child *drawing* his sled across the snow). **Drag** suggests great effort overcoming resistance or friction (*dragged* the dead body across the room). **Haul** implies sustained pulling or dragging of heavy or bulky objects (a team of horses *hauling* supplies). **Tug** applies to strenuous often spasmodic efforts to move (the little girl *tugged* at her mother's hand).

punctilious see CAREFUL

pungent, piquant, poignant, racy mean sharp and stimulating to the mind or the senses. **Pungent** implies a sharp, stinging, or biting quality esp. of odors (a cheese with a *pungent* odor). **Piquant** suggests a power to whet the appetite or interest through tartness or mild pungency (grapefruit juice gave the punch its *piquant* taste). **Poignant** suggests something is sharply or piercingly effective in stirring one's consciousness or emotions (upon her departure he felt a *poignant* sense of loss). **Racy** implies having a strongly characteristic natural quality fresh and unimpaired (the spontaneous, *racy* prose of the untutored writer).

punish, chastise, castigate, chasten, discipline, correct mean to inflict a penalty on in requital for wrongdoing. **Punish** implies subjecting to a penalty for wrongdoing (*punished* for stealing). **Chastise** may apply to either the infliction of corporal punishment or to verbal censure or denunciation ⟨*chastised* his son for neglecting his studies⟩. **Castigate** usu. implies a severe, typically public censure ⟨an editorial *castigating* the entire city council⟩. **Chasten** suggests any affliction or trial that leaves one humbled or subdued ⟨a stunning election defeat that left him *chastened*⟩. **Discipline** implies a punishing or chastening in order to bring under control ⟨the duty of parents to *discipline* their children⟩. **Correct** implies punishing aimed at reforming an offender ⟨the function of prison is to *correct* the wrongdoer⟩.

pure see CHASTE
purloin see STEAL
purpose see INTENTION
pursue see CHASE
pursuit see WORK
push, shove, thrust, propel mean to cause to move ahead or aside by force. **Push** implies application of force by a body already in contact with the body to be moved ⟨*push* the door open⟩. **Shove** implies a fast or rough pushing of something usu. along a surface ⟨*shoved* the man out of my way⟩. **Thrust** suggests less steadiness and greater violence than *push* ⟨*thrust* the money in my hand and ran away⟩. **Propel** suggests rapidly driving forward or onward by force applied in any manner ⟨ships *propelled* by steam⟩.
pushing see AGGRESSIVE
pusillanimous see COWARDLY
putrefy see DECAY
putrid see MALODOROUS
puzzle *vb* Puzzle, perplex, bewilder, distract, nonplus, confound, dumbfound mean to baffle and disturb mentally. **Puzzle** implies existence of a problem difficult to solve ⟨a persistent fever which *puzzled* the doctor⟩. **Perplex** adds a suggestion of worry and uncertainty esp. about making a necessary decision ⟨an odd change of personality that *perplexed* her friends⟩. **Bewilder** stresses a confusion of mind that hampers clear and decisive thinking ⟨the number of videotapes available *bewilders* consumers⟩. **Distract** implies agitation or uncertainty induced by conflicting preoccupations or interests ⟨a political scandal that *distracted* the country for two years⟩. **Nonplus** implies a bafflement that makes orderly planning or deciding impossible ⟨she was utterly *nonplussed* by the abrupt change in plans⟩. **Confound** implies temporary mental paralysis caused by astonishment or profound abasement ⟨tragic news that *confounded* us all⟩. **Dumbfound** suggests intense but momentary confounding; often the idea of astonishment is so stressed that it becomes a near synonym of *astound* ⟨*dumbfounded* by her rejection of his marriage proposal⟩.
puzzle *n* see MYSTERY

Q

quail see RECOIL
quaint see STRANGE
qualified see ABLE
quality, property, character, attribute mean an intelligible feature by which a thing may be identified. **Quality** is a general term applicable to any trait or characteristic whether individual or generic ⟨a star whose acting had a persistently amateurish *quality*⟩. **Property** implies a characteristic that belongs to a thing's essential nature and may be used to describe a type or species ⟨name the basic *properties* of mammals⟩. **Character** applies to a peculiar and distinctive quality of a thing or a class ⟨each of the island's villages has a distinctive *character*⟩. **Attribute** implies a

quality ascribed to a thing or a being ⟨a man with none of the traditional *attributes* of a popular hero⟩.
qualm, scruple, compunction, demur mean a misgiving about what one is doing or going to do. **Qualm** implies an uneasy fear that one is not following one's conscience or better judgment ⟨no *qualms* about traveling in the Middle East⟩. **Scruple** implies doubt of the rightness of an act on grounds of principle ⟨a lawyer totally devoid of *scruples*⟩. **Compunction** implies a spontaneous feeling of responsibility or compassion for a potential victim ⟨not likely to have *compunctions* about knocking out his opponent⟩. **Demur** implies hesitation caused by objection to an outside suggestion or influence ⟨accepted her resignation without *demur*⟩.
quandary see PREDICAMENT
quarrel, wrangle, altercation, squabble, spat, tiff mean an angry dispute. **Quarrel** implies a verbal clash followed by strained or severed relations ⟨a bitter *quarrel* that ended their friendship⟩. **Wrangle** suggests a noisy, insistent dispute ⟨an ongoing *wrangle* over the town's finances⟩. **Altercation** suggests determined verbal quarreling often with blows ⟨a violent *altercation* between pro- and anti-abortion groups⟩. **Squabble** implies childish and unseemly wrangling ⟨the children constantly *squabble* over toys⟩. **Spat** implies a lively but brief dispute over a trifle ⟨the couple averages a *spat* a week⟩. **Tiff** suggests a trivial dispute without serious consequence ⟨a *tiff* that was forgotten by dinnertime⟩.
quarrelsome see BELLIGERENT
quash see CRUSH
queer see STRANGE
quell see CRUSH
query see ASK
question see ASK
questionable see DOUBTFUL
quick, prompt, ready, apt mean able to respond without delay or hesitation or indicative of such ability. **Quick** stresses instancy of response and is likely to connote native rather than acquired power ⟨very *quick* in his reflexes⟩ ⟨a keen *quick* mind⟩. **Prompt** is more likely to connote training and discipline that fits one for instant response ⟨the *prompt* response of emergency medical technicians⟩. **Ready** suggests facility or fluency in response ⟨backed by a pair of *ready* assistants⟩. **Apt** stresses the possession of qualities (as intelligence, a particular talent, or a strong bent) that makes quick effective response possible ⟨an *apt* student⟩ ⟨her answer was *apt* and to the point⟩. See in addition FAST.
quicken, animate, enliven, vivify mean to make alive or lively. **Quicken** stresses a sudden renewal of life or activity esp. in something inert ⟨the arrival of spring *quickens* the earth⟩. **Animate** emphasizes the imparting of motion or vitality to what is mechanical or artificial ⟨telling details that *animate* the familiar story⟩. **Enliven** suggests a stimulus that arouses from dullness or torpidity ⟨*enlivened* his lecture with humorous anecdotes⟩. **Vivify** implies a freshening or energizing through renewal of vitality ⟨her appearance *vivifies* a dreary drawing-room drama⟩. See in addition PROVOKE.
quick-witted see INTELLIGENT
quiescent see LATENT
quip see JEST
quit see STOP
quixotic see IMAGINARY

R

rack see AFFLICT
racy see PUNGENT

radiant see BRIGHT
rage see ANGER, FASHION
rail see SCOLD
raise see LIFT
ramble see WANDER
rancor see ENMITY

random, haphazard, casual, desultory mean determined by accident rather than design. **Random** stresses lack of definite aim, fixed goal, or regular procedure ⟨a *random* sampling of public opinion⟩. **Haphazard** applies to what is done without regard for regularity or fitness or ultimate consequence ⟨his selection of college courses was entirely *haphazard*⟩. **Casual** suggests working or acting without deliberation, intention, or purpose ⟨a *casual* tour of the sights⟩. **Desultory** implies a jumping or skipping from one thing to another without method or system ⟨a *desultory* discussion of current events⟩.

range, gamut, compass, sweep, scope, orbit mean the extent that lies within the powers of something (as to cover or control). **Range** is a general term indicating the extent of one's perception or the extent of powers, capacities, or possibilities ⟨the entire *range* of human experience⟩. **Gamut** suggests a graduated series running from one possible extreme to another ⟨a performance that included a *gamut* of emotions⟩. **Compass** implies a sometimes limited extent of perception, knowledge, or activity ⟨your concerns lie beyond the narrow *compass* of this study⟩. **Sweep** suggests extent, often circular or arc-shaped, of motion or activity ⟨the book covers the entire *sweep* of criminal activity⟩. **Scope** is applicable to an area of activity, predetermined and limited, but somewhat flexible ⟨as time went on, the *scope* of the investigation widened⟩. **Orbit** suggests an often circumscribed range of activity or influence within which forces work toward accommodation ⟨within that restricted *orbit* they tried to effect social change⟩.

rank see FLAGRANT, MALODOROUS
ransom see RESCUE
rapacious see VORACIOUS
rapid see FAST
rapture see ECSTASY
rare see CHOICE, INFREQUENT
rash see ADVENTUROUS
rate see ESTIMATE
rattle see EMBARRASS
raucous see LOUD

ravage, devastate, waste, sack, pillage, despoil mean to lay waste by plundering or destroying. **Ravage** implies violent often cumulative depredation and destruction ⟨a hurricane that *ravaged* the Gulf Coast⟩. **Devastate** implies the complete ruin and desolation of a wide area ⟨the atomic bomb that *devastated* Hiroshima⟩. **Waste** may imply producing the same result by a slow process rather than sudden and violent action ⟨years of drought had *wasted* the area⟩. **Sack** implies carrying off all valuable possessions from a place ⟨barbarians *sacked* ancient Rome⟩. **Pillage** implies ruthless plundering at will but without the completeness suggested by *sack* ⟨settlements *pillaged* by Vikings⟩. **Despoil** applies to looting or robbing of a place or person without suggesting accompanying destruction ⟨the Nazis *despoiled* the art museums of Europe⟩.

ravenous see VORACIOUS
raw see RUDE
rawboned see LEAN
ready see QUICK
realize see THINK
rear see LIFT
reason *n* see CAUSE
reason *vb* see THINK

rebellion, revolution, uprising, revolt, insurrection, mutiny mean an armed outbreak against authority. **Rebellion** implies an open formidable resistance that is often unsuccessful ⟨the *rebellion* failed for lack of popular support⟩. **Revolution** applies to a successful rebellion resulting in a major change (as in government) ⟨the American *Revolution*⟩. **Uprising** implies a brief, limited and often immediately ineffective rebellion ⟨quickly put down the *uprising*⟩. **Revolt** and **insurrection** imply an armed uprising that quickly fails or succeeds ⟨a *revolt* by the young Turks that surprised party leaders⟩ ⟨Nat Turner's unsuccessful slave *insurrection*⟩. **Mutiny** applies to group insubordination or insurrection esp. against naval authority ⟨the famous *mutiny* aboard the Bounty⟩.

rebuild see MEND
rebuke see REPROVE
rebut see DISPROVE
recalcitrant see UNRULY
recall see REMEMBER
recant see ABJURE

recede, retreat, retrograde, retract, back mean to move backward. **Recede** implies a gradual withdrawing from a forward or high fixed point in time or space ⟨the flood waters gradually *receded*⟩. **Retreat** implies withdrawal from a point or position reached ⟨under cross-examination he *retreated* from that statement⟩. **Retrograde** implies movement contrary to a normally progressive direction ⟨the social position of women in some areas seems to be *retrograding* instead of advancing⟩. **Retract** implies drawing back from an extended position ⟨a cat *retracting* its claws⟩. **Back** is used with *up, down, out,* or *off,* to refer to any retrograde motion ⟨*backed* off when her claim was challenged⟩.

reciprocal, mutual, common mean shared or experienced by each. **Reciprocal** implies an equal return or counteraction by each of two sides toward or against or in relation to the other ⟨allies with a *reciprocal* defense agreement⟩. **Mutual** applies to feelings or effects shared by two jointly ⟨two people with a *mutual* physical attraction⟩. **Common** does not suggest reciprocity but merely a sharing with others ⟨a couple with many *common* interests⟩.

reciprocate, retaliate, requite, return mean to give back usu. in kind or in quantity. **Reciprocate** implies a mutual or equivalent exchange or a paying back of what one has received ⟨*reciprocated* their hospitality by inviting them for a visit⟩. **Retaliate** usu. implies a paying back of injury in exact kind, often vengefully ⟨the enemy *retaliated* by executing their prisoners⟩. **Requite** implies a paying back according to one's preference and often not equivalently ⟨*requited* her love with cold indifference⟩. **Return** implies a paying back of something usu. in kind but sometimes by way of contrast ⟨*returned* their kindness with ingratitude⟩.

reckless see ADVENTUROUS
reckon see CALCULATE
reclaim see RESCUE

recoil, shrink, flinch, wince, blench, quail mean to draw back in fear or distaste. **Recoil** implies a start or movement away through shock, fear, or disgust ⟨*recoils* at the sight of blood⟩. **Shrink** suggests an instinctive recoil through sensitiveness, scrupulousness, or cowardice ⟨refused to *shrink* from family responsibilities⟩. **Flinch** implies a failure to endure pain or face something dangerous or frightening with resolution ⟨faced her accusers without *flinching*⟩. **Wince** suggests a slight involuntary physical reaction (as a start or recoiling) ⟨*winced* when the new secretary called him by his first name⟩. **Blench** implies fainthearted flinching ⟨never *blenched* even as his head was lowered on the guillotine⟩. **Quail** suggests shrinking and cowering in fear ⟨*quailed* at the appearance of the ghost⟩.

recollect see REMEMBER

recollection see MEMORY

recompense see PAY

reconcile see ADAPT

rectify see CORRECT

recumbent see PRONE

redeem see RESCUE

redolence see FRAGRANCE

redolent see ODOROUS

redress see CORRECT

reduce see CONQUER, DECREASE

reflect see THINK

reform see CORRECT

refractory see UNRULY

refresh see RENEW

refuse see DECLINE

refute see DISPROVE

regard, respect, esteem, admire mean to recognize the worth of a person or thing. **Regard** is a general term that is usu. qualified ⟨he is not highly *regarded* in the profession⟩. **Respect** implies a considered evaluation or estimation ⟨after many years they came to *respect* her views⟩. **Esteem** implies greater warmth of feeling accompanying a high valuation ⟨no citizen of the town was more highly *esteemed*⟩. **Admire** suggests usu. enthusiastic appreciation and often deep affection ⟨a friend that I truly *admire*⟩.

regret see SORROW

regular, normal, typical, natural mean being of the sort or kind that is expected as usual, ordinary, or average. **Regular** stresses conformity to a rule, standard, or pattern ⟨the *regular* monthly meeting of the organization⟩. **Normal** implies lack of deviation from what has been discovered or established as the most usual or expected ⟨*normal* behavior for a two-year-old boy⟩. **Typical** implies showing all important traits of a type, class, or group and may suggest lack of strong individuality ⟨a *typical* small town in America⟩. **Natural** applies to what conforms to a thing's essential nature, function, or mode of being ⟨the *natural* love of a mother for her child⟩.

regulation see LAW

reimburse see PAY

reject see DECLINE

rejoin see ANSWER

rejuvenate see RENEW

relate see JOIN

release see FREE

relegate see COMMIT

relent see YIELD

relevant, germane, material, pertinent, apposite, applicable, apropos mean relating to or bearing upon the matter in hand. **Relevant** implies a traceable, significant, logical connection ⟨use any *relevant* evidence to support your argument⟩. **Germane** may additionally imply a fitness for or appropriateness to the situation or occasion ⟨a topic not *germane* to our discussion⟩. **Material** implies so close a relationship that it cannot be dispensed with without serious alteration of the case ⟨the scene is *material* to the rest of the play⟩. **Pertinent** stresses a clear and decisive relevance ⟨a *pertinent* observation that cut to the heart of the matter⟩. **Apposite** suggests a felicitous relevance ⟨the anecdotes in his sermons are always *apposite*⟩. **Applicable** suggests the fitness of bringing a general rule or principle to bear upon a particular case ⟨a precedent that is not *applicable* in this case⟩. **Apropos** suggests being both relevant and opportune ⟨for your term paper use only *apropos* quotations⟩.

relieve, alleviate, lighten, assuage, mitigate, allay mean to make something less grievous. **Relieve** implies a lifting of enough of a burden to make it tolerable ⟨took drugs to *relieve* the pain⟩. **Alleviate** implies temporary or partial lessening of pain or distress ⟨new buildings that will help to *alleviate* the housing shortage⟩. **Lighten** implies reducing a burdensome or depressing weight ⟨good news that *lightened* his worries⟩. **Assuage** implies softening or sweetening what is harsh or disagreeable ⟨hoped that a vacation would *assuage* the pain of the divorce⟩. **Mitigate** suggests a moderating or countering of the effect of something violent or painful ⟨ocean breezes *mitigated* the intense heat⟩. **Allay** implies an effective calming or soothing of fears or alarms ⟨the encouraging report *allayed* their fears⟩.

religious see DEVOUT

relinquish, yield, resign, surrender, abandon, waive mean to give up completely. **Relinquish** usu. does not imply strong feeling but may suggest some regret, reluctance, or weakness ⟨*relinquished* her crown with bittersweet feelings⟩. **Yield** implies concession or compliance or submission to force ⟨I *yield* to your greater expertise in this matter⟩. **Resign** emphasizes voluntary relinquishment or sacrifice without struggle ⟨the model *resigned* all her rights to the photographs⟩. **Surrender** implies a giving up after a struggle to retain or resist ⟨forced to sign a document *surrendering* all claims to the land⟩. **Abandon** stresses finality and completeness in giving up ⟨*abandon* all hope⟩. **Waive** implies conceding or forgoing with little or no compulsion ⟨*waived* the right to a trial by jury⟩.

reluctant see DISINCLINED

remarkable see NOTICEABLE

remedy see CORRECT, CURE

remember, recollect, recall, remind, reminisce mean to bring an image or idea from the past into the mind. **Remember** implies a keeping in memory that may be effortless or unwilled ⟨*remembers* that day as though it were yesterday⟩. **Recollect** implies a bringing back to mind what is lost or scattered ⟨as near as I can *recollect*⟩. **Recall** suggests an effort to bring back to mind and often to re-create in speech ⟨can't *recall* the words of the song⟩. **Remind** suggests a jogging of one's memory by an association or similarity ⟨that *reminds* me of a story⟩. **Reminisce** implies a casual often nostalgic recalling of experiences long past and gone ⟨old college friends like to *reminisce*⟩.

remembrance see MEMORY

remind see REMEMBER

reminisce see REMEMBER

reminiscence see MEMORY

remiss see NEGLIGENT

remonstrate see OBJECT

remorse see PENITENCE

remunerate see PAY

rend see TEAR

renew, restore, refresh, renovate, rejuvenate mean to make like new. **Renew** implies so extensive a remaking that what had become faded or disintegrated now seems like new ⟨efforts to *renew* a failing marriage⟩. **Restore** implies a return to an original state after depletion or loss ⟨*restored* a fine piece of furniture⟩. **Refresh** implies the supplying of something necessary to restore lost strength, animation, or power ⟨lunch *refreshed* my energy⟩. **Renovate** suggests a renewing by cleansing, repairing, or rebuilding ⟨the apartment has been entirely *renovated*⟩. **Rejuvenate** suggests the restoration of youthful vigor, powers, and appearance ⟨the change in jobs *rejuvenated* her spirits⟩.

renounce see ABDICATE, ABJURE

renovate see RENEW

renowned see FAMOUS

rent see HIRE

repair see MEND

repartee see WIT

repay see PAY

repellent see REPUGNANT

repentance see PENITENCE

replace, displace, supplant, supersede mean to put out of a usual or proper place or into the place of another. **Replace** implies a filling of a place once occupied by something lost, destroyed, or no longer usable or adequate (the broken window will have to be *replaced*). **Displace** implies an ousting or dislodging preceding a replacing (thousands had been *displaced* by the floods). **Supplant** implies either a dispossessing or usurping of another's place, possessions, or privileges or an uprooting of something and its replacement with something else (discovered that he had been *supplanted* in her affections by another). **Supersede** implies replacing a person or thing that has become superannuated, obsolete, or otherwise inferior (the new edition *supersedes* all previous ones).

replete see FULL

replica see REPRODUCTION

reply see ANSWER

reprehend see CRITICIZE

reprimand see REPROVE

reproach see REPROVE

reprobate see CRITICIZE

reproduction, duplicate, copy, facsimile, replica mean a thing made to closely resemble another. **Reproduction** implies an exact or close imitation of an existing thing (*reproductions* from the museum's furniture collection). **Duplicate** implies a double or counterpart exactly corresponding to another thing (make a *duplicate* of the key). **Copy** applies esp. to one of a number of things reproduced mechanically (*copies* of the report were issued to all). **Facsimile** suggests a close reproduction in the same materials that may differ in scale (a *facsimile* of an illuminated medieval manuscript). **Replica** implies the exact reproduction of something in all respects (*replicas* of the ships used by Columbus).

reprove, rebuke, reprimand, admonish, reproach, chide mean to criticize adversely. **Reprove** implies an often kindly intent to correct a fault (gently *reproved* her table manners). **Rebuke** suggests a sharp or stern reproof (the papal letter *rebuked* dissenting church officials). **Reprimand** implies a severe, formal, often public or official rebuke (a general officially *reprimanded* for speaking out of turn). **Admonish** suggest earnest or friendly warning and counsel (*admonished* by my parents to control expenses). **Reproach** and **chide** suggest displeasure or disappointment expressed in mild reproof or scolding (*reproached* him for tardiness) (*chided* by their mother for not keeping their room clean).

repudiate see DECLINE, DISCLAIM

repugnant, repellent, abhorrent, distasteful, obnoxious, invidious mean so unlikable as to arouse antagonism or aversion. **Repugnant** implies being alien to one's ideas, principles, or tastes and arousing resistance or loathing (regards boxing as a *repugnant* sport). **Repellent** suggests a generally forbidding or unpleasant quality that causes one to back away (the public display of grief was *repellent* to her). **Abhorrent** implies a repugnance causing active antagonism (practices that are *abhorrent* to the American system). **Distasteful** implies a contrariness to one's tastes or inclinations (a family to whom displays of affection are *distasteful*). **Obnoxious** suggests an objectionableness too great to tolerate (the colonists found the tea tax especially *obnoxious*). **Invidious** applies to what cannot be used or performed without creating ill will, odium, or envy (the *invidious* task of deciding custody of the child).

request see ASK

require see DEMAND

requite see RECIPROCATE

rescue, deliver, redeem, ransom, reclaim, save mean to set free from confinement or danger. **Rescue** implies freeing from imminent danger by prompt or vigorous action (*rescue* the crew of a sinking ship). **Deliver** implies release usu. of a person from confinement, temptation, slavery, or suffering (*delivered* his people from bondage). **Redeem** implies releasing from bondage or penalties by giving what is demanded or necessary (*redeemed* her from her life as a bored housewife). **Ransom** specif. applies to buying out of captivity (subjects forced to *ransom* their king). **Reclaim** suggests a bringing back to a former state or condition of someone or something abandoned or debased (*reclaimed* long-abandoned farms). **Save** may replace any of the foregoing terms; it may further imply a preserving or maintaining for usefulness or continued existence (a social worker who *saved* youths from life as criminals).

resemblance see LIKENESS

resentment see OFFENSE

reserve see KEEP

reserved see SILENT

resign see ABDICATE, RELINQUISH

resilient see ELASTIC

resist see OPPOSE

resolute see FAITHFUL

resolution see COURAGE

resolve see DECIDE

resort see RESOURCE

resource, resort, expedient, shift, makeshift, stopgap mean something one turns to in the absence of the usual means or source of supply. **Resource** and **resort** apply to anything one falls back upon (haven't exhausted all of my *resources* yet) (favor a sales tax only as a last *resort*). **Expedient** may apply to any device or contrivance used when the usual one is not at hand or not possible (the flimsiest of *expedients* ends the tale). **Shift** implies a tentative or temporary imperfect expedient (her desperate *shifts* satisfied no one). **Makeshift** implies an inferior expedient adopted because of urgent need or countenanced through indifference (the space heater was supposed to be only a *makeshift*). **Stopgap** applies to something used temporarily as an emergency measure (the farm aid bill is no more than a *stopgap*).

respect see REGARD

resplendent see SPLENDID

respond see ANSWER

responsible, answerable, accountable, amenable, liable mean subject to being held to account. **Responsible** implies holding a specific office, duty, or trust (the bureau *responsible* for revenue collection). **Answerable** suggests a relation between one having a moral or legal obligation and a court or other authority charged with oversight of its observance (a fact-finding committee *answerable* only to the President). **Accountable** suggests imminence of retribution for unfulfilled trust or violated obligation (in a democracy the politicians are *accountable* to the voters). **Amenable** and **liable** stress the fact of subjection to review, censure, or control by a designated authority under certain conditions (laws are *amenable* to judicial review) (will not be *liable* for his ex-wife's debts).

restful see COMFORTABLE

restive see CONTRARY

restore see RENEW

restrain, check, curb, bridle mean to hold back from or control in doing something. **Restrain** suggests holding back by force or persuasion from acting or from going to extremes (*restrained* themselves from trading insults). **Check** implies restraining or impeding a progress, activity, or impetus (deep mud *checked* our progress). **Curb** suggests an abrupt or drastic checking ⟨learn to *curb* your appetite⟩. **Bridle** implies keeping under control by subduing or holding in ⟨they could no longer *bridle* their passion⟩.

restrict see LIMIT

result see EFFECT

retain see KEEP

retaliate see RECIPROCATE

retard see DELAY

reticent see SILENT

retort see ANSWER

retract see ABJURE, RECEDE

retreat see RECEDE

retrench see SHORTEN

retrograde see RECEDE

return see RECIPROCATE

reveal, discover, disclose, divulge, tell, betray mean to make known what has been or should be concealed. **Reveal** may apply to supernatural or inspired revelation of truths beyond the range of ordinary human vision or reason ⟨the belief that divine will is *revealed* in the Bible⟩. **Discover** implies an uncovering of matters kept secret and not previously known ⟨a step-by-step comparison that *discovered* a clear case of plagiarism⟩. **Disclose** may also imply a discovering but more often an imparting of information previously kept secret ⟨candidates must *disclose* their financial assets⟩. **Divulge** implies a disclosure involving some impropriety or breach of confidence ⟨refused to *divulge* confidential information⟩. **Tell** implies an imparting of necessary or useful information ⟨never *told* her that he was married⟩. **Betray** implies a divulging that represents a breach of faith or an involuntary or unconscious disclosure ⟨a blush that *betrayed* her embarrassment⟩.

revere, reverence, venerate, worship, adore mean to honor and admire profoundly and respectfully. **Revere** stresses deference and tenderness of feeling ⟨a retiring professor *revered* by generations of students⟩. **Reverence** presupposes an intrinsic merit and inviolability in the one honored and a corresponding depth of feeling in the one honoring ⟨the general *reverenced* the army's code of honor⟩. **Venerate** implies a holding as holy or sacrosanct because of character, association, or age ⟨national heroes who are still *venerated*⟩. **Worship** implies homage usu. expressed in words or ceremony ⟨*worships* the memory of her husband⟩. **Adore** implies love and stresses the notion of an individual and personal attachment ⟨a doctor who is practically *adored* by her patients⟩.

reverence *n* see HONOR

reverence *vb* see REVERE

reverse, transpose, invert mean to change to the opposite position. **Reverse** is the most general term and may imply change in order, side, direction, meaning ⟨*reversed* his position on the arms agreement⟩. **Transpose** implies a change in order or relative position of units often through exchange of position ⟨anagrams are formed by *transposing* the letters of a word or phrase⟩. **Invert** applies chiefly to turning upside down or inside out ⟨a typo consisting of a whole line of *inverted* type⟩.

revile see SCOLD

revise see CORRECT

revolt see REBELLION

revolution see REBELLION

ribald see COARSE

rich, wealthy, affluent, opulent mean having goods, property, and money in abundance. **Rich** implies having more than enough to gratify normal needs or desires ⟨girls looking for *rich* husbands⟩. **Wealthy** stresses the possession of property and intrinsically valuable things ⟨retired from politics a *wealthy* man⟩. **Affluent** suggests prosperity and an increasing wealth ⟨an *affluent* society⟩. **Opulent** suggests lavish expenditure and display of great wealth ⟨*opulent* mansions⟩.

riddle see MYSTERY

ridicule, deride, mock, taunt, twit mean to make an object of laughter of. **Ridicule** implies a deliberate often malicious belittling ⟨consistently *ridiculed* everything she said⟩. **Deride** suggests contemptuous and often bitter ridicule ⟨*derided* their efforts to start their own business⟩. **Mock** implies scorn often ironically expressed as by mimicry or sham deference ⟨youngsters began to *mock* the helpless wino⟩. **Taunt** suggests jeeringly provoking insult or challenge ⟨terrorists *taunted* the hostages⟩. **Twit** usu. suggests mild or good-humored teasing ⟨students *twitted* their teacher about his tardiness⟩.

ridiculous see LAUGHABLE

rife see PREVAILING

right see CORRECT

righteous see MORAL

rigid, rigorous, strict, stringent mean extremely severe or stern. **Rigid** implies uncompromising inflexibility ⟨the school's admission standards are *rigid*⟩. **Rigorous** implies the imposition of hardship and difficulty ⟨the *rigorous* training of recruits⟩. **Strict** emphasizes undeviating conformity to rules, standards, or requirements ⟨her doctor put her on a *strict* diet⟩. **Stringent** suggests restrictions or limitations that curb or coerce ⟨the judge's ruling is a *stringent* interpretation of the law⟩. See in addition STIFF.

rigorous see RIGID

rile see IRRITATE

rim see BORDER

rip see TEAR

rise see SPRING

risky see DANGEROUS

rive see TEAR

roam see WANDER

robust see HEALTHY

rock see SHAKE

root see ORIGIN

rot see DECAY

rough, harsh, uneven, rugged, scabrous mean not smooth or even. **Rough** implies points, bristles, ridges, or projections on the surface ⟨a *rough* wooden board⟩. **Harsh** implies a surface or texture distinctly unpleasant to the touch ⟨the *harsh* fabric chafed his skin⟩. **Uneven** implies a lack of uniformity in height, breadth, or quality ⟨an old house with *uneven* floors⟩. **Rugged** implies irregularity or roughness of land surface and connotes difficulty of travel ⟨follow the *rugged* road up the mountain⟩. **Scabrous** implies scaliness or prickliness of surface ⟨an allergic condition that results in *scabrous* hands⟩. See in addition RUDE.

rove see WANDER

rude, rough, crude, raw mean lacking in social refinement. **Rude** implies ignorance of or indifference to good form; it may suggest intentional discourtesy ⟨consistently *rude* behavior toward her in-laws⟩. **Rough** is likely to stress lack of polish and gentleness ⟨the *rough* manners of a man used to living in the outback⟩. **Crude** may apply to thought or behavior limited to the gross, the obvious, or the primitive and ignorant of civilized amenities ⟨the *crude* antics of college students on spring break⟩. **Raw** suggests being untested, inexperienced, or unfinished ⟨charged with turning *raw* youths into young men⟩.

rugged see ROUGH

rule *vb* see DECIDE, GOVERN

rule *n* see LAW

ruminate see PONDER

rural, rustic, pastoral, bucolic mean relating to or characteristic of the country. **Rural** suggests open country and farming (a diminishing portion of the island remains *rural*). **Rustic** suggests more clearly a contrast with city life and connotes rudeness and lack of polish (a hunting lodge filled with *rustic* furniture and decoration). **Pastoral** implies an idealized simplicity and peacefulness and apartness from the world (the *pastoral* setting of an exclusive health resort). **Bucolic** may refer to either the desirable or undesirable aspects of country life (fed-up city dwellers imagining a *bucolic* bliss).

ruse see TRICK

rustic see RURAL

ruth see PITY

S

sack see RAVAGE

sadness, depression, melancholy, melancholia, dejection, gloom mean the state of mind of one who is unhappy. **Sadness** is a general term that carries no suggestion of the cause, extent, or exact nature of low spirits (a feeling of *sadness* marked the farewell dinner). **Depression** suggests a condition in which one feels let down, disheartened, or enervated (under a doctor's care for severe *depression*). **Melancholy** suggests a mood of sad and serious but not wholly unpleasant pensiveness (old love letters that gave her cause for *melancholy*). **Melancholia** applies to a settled deep depression verging on insanity (fell into a state of *melancholia* after her husband's death). **Dejection** implies a usu. passing mood of being downcast or dispirited from a natural or logical cause (a struggling actor used to periods of *dejection*). **Gloom** applies to the atmosphere or the effect on others created by one afflicted with any of these moods or conditions (a universal *gloom* engulfed the devastated town).

safeguard see DEFEND

sagacious see SHREWD

sage see WISE

salient see NOTICEABLE

salubrious see HEALTHFUL

salutary see HEALTHFUL

same, selfsame, very, identical, equivalent, equal mean not different or not differing from one another. **Same** may imply and **selfsame** always implies that the things under consideration are one thing and not two or more things (we both took the *same* route) (it was the *selfsame* ring I had lost years ago). **Very**, like *selfsame*, may imply identity, or, like *same*, may imply likeness in kind (you're the *very* person I've been looking for). **Identical** may imply self-sameness or suggest absolute agreement in all details (their test answers were *identical*). **Equivalent** implies amounting to the same thing in worth or significance (two houses *equivalent* in market value). **Equal** implies being identical in value, magnitude, or some specified quality (divided it into *equal* shares).

sample see INSTANCE

sanctimonious see DEVOUT

sanction see APPROVE

sane see WISE

sangfroid see EQUANIMITY

sanguinary see BLOODY

sanguine see BLOODY

sap see WEAKEN

sapient see WISE

sarcasm see WIT

sarcastic, satiric, ironic, sardonic mean marked by bitterness and a power or will to cut or sting. **Sarcastic** implies an intentional inflicting of pain by deriding, taunting, or ridiculing (a critic famous mainly for his *sarcastic* remarks). **Satiric** implies that the intent of the ridiculing is censure and reprobation (a *satiric* look at contemporary sexual mores). **Ironic** implies an attempt to be amusing or provocative by saying usu. the opposite of what is meant (made the *ironic* observation that the government could always be trusted). **Sardonic** implies scorn, mockery, or derision that is manifested by either verbal or facial expression (surveyed the scene with a *sardonic* smile).

sardonic see SARCASTIC

sate see SATIATE

satiate, sate, surfeit, cloy, pall, glut, gorge mean to fill to repletion. **Satiate** and **sate** may sometimes imply only complete satisfaction but more often suggest repletion that has destroyed interest or desire (movies that *satiated* their interest in sex) (audiences were *sated* with dizzying visual effects). **Surfeit** implies a nauseating repletion (*surfeited* themselves with junk food). **Cloy** stresses the disgust or boredom resulting from such surfeiting (sentimental pictures that *cloy* after a while). **Pall** emphasizes the loss of ability to stimulate interest or appetite (even a tropical paradise begins to *pall* after ten trips). **Glut** implies excess in feeding or supplying (bookstores *glutted* with diet books). **Gorge** suggests glutting to the point of bursting or choking (*gorged* themselves with chocolate).

satire see WIT

satiric see SARCASTIC

satisfy see PAY

saturate see SOAK

saturnine see SULLEN

savage see FIERCE

save see RESCUE

savoir faire see TACT

savory see PALATABLE

scabrous see ROUGH

scan see SCRUTINIZE

scandal see OFFENSE

scant see MEAGER

scanty see MEAGER

scarce see INFREQUENT

scathing see CAUSTIC

scatter, disperse, dissipate, dispel mean to cause to separate or break up. **Scatter** implies a force that drives parts or units irregularly in many directions (the bowling ball *scattered* the pins). **Disperse** implies a wider separation and a complete breaking up of a mass or group (police *dispersed* the crowd). **Dissipate** stresses complete disintegration or dissolution and final disappearance (the fog was *dissipated* by the morning sun). **Dispel** stresses a driving away or getting rid of as if by scattering (an authoritative statement that *dispelled* all doubt).

scent see FRAGRANCE, SMELL

scheme see PLAN

scholarship see KNOWLEDGE

school see TEACH

scoff, jeer, gibe, fleer, sneer, flout mean to show one's contempt in derision or mockery. **Scoff** stresses insolence, disrespect, or incredulity as motivating the derision (*scoffed* at the religious faith of others). **Jeer** suggests a coarser more undiscriminating derision (the crowd *jeered* the visiting team). **Gibe** implies taunting either good-naturedly or in sarcastic derision (*gibed* at him for repeatedly missing the ball). **Fleer** suggests grinning or grimacing derisively (some freshmen were greeted by *fleering* seniors). **Sneer** stresses insulting by contemptuous facial expression, phrasing, or tone of voice (*sneered* at anything even remotely romantic). **Flout** stresses contempt shown by refusal to heed (*flouted* the conventions of polite society).

scold, upbraid, berate, rail, revile, vituperate mean to reproach angrily and abusively. **Scold** implies rebuking in irritation or ill temper justly or unjustly (relieved her frustrations by *scolding* the children). **Upbraid** implies censuring on definite and usu. justifiable grounds ⟨the governor *upbraided* his aides for poor research⟩. **Berate** suggests prolonged and often abusive scolding ⟨*berated* continually by a violent, abusive father⟩. **Rail** (*at* or *against*) stresses an unrestrained berating ⟨*railed* loudly at the insolent bureaucrat⟩. **Revile** implies a scurrilous, abusive attack prompted by anger or hatred ⟨a President vehemently *reviled* in the press⟩. **Vituperate** suggests a violent reviling ⟨a preacher more given to *vituperating* than to inspiring⟩.

scope see RANGE
scorn see DESPISE
scout see DESPISE
scowl see FROWN
scrap see DISCARD
scrawny see LEAN
screen see HIDE
scruple see QUALM
scrupulous see CAREFUL, UPRIGHT
scrutinize, scan, inspect, examine mean to look at or over carefully and usu. critically. **Scrutinize** stresses close attention to minute detail ⟨closely *scrutinized* the bill from the hospital⟩. **Scan** implies a surveying from point to point often suggesting a cursory overall observation ⟨quickly *scanned* the wine list⟩. **Inspect** implies scrutinizing for errors or defects ⟨*inspected* the restaurant for health-code violations⟩. **Examine** suggests a scrutiny in order to determine the nature, condition, or quality of a thing ⟨*examined* the gems to see whether they were genuine⟩.

scurrility see ABUSE
scurvy see CONTEMPTIBLE
seclusion see SOLITUDE
secret, covert, stealthy, furtive, clandestine, surreptitious, underhanded mean done without attracting observation. **Secret** implies concealment on any grounds for any motive ⟨a *secret* meeting between lovers⟩. **Covert** streses the fact of not being open or declared ⟨*covert* operations against guerrilla forces⟩. **Stealthy** suggests taking pains to avoid being seen or heard esp. in some misdoing ⟨the *stealthy* movements of a cat burglar⟩. **Furtive** implies a sly or cautious stealthiness ⟨exchanged *furtive* smiles across the room⟩. **Clandestine** implies secrecy usu. for an evil or illicit purpose ⟨a *clandestine* drug deal in a back alley⟩. **Surreptitious** applies to action or behavior done secretly often with skillful avoidance of detection and in violation of custom, law, or authority ⟨the *surreptitious* stockpiling of weapons by survivalists⟩. **Underhanded** stresses fraud or deception ⟨a car dealership guilty of *underhanded* practices⟩.

secrete see HIDE
secretive see SILENT
section see PART
secure see ENSURE, GET
sedate see SERIOUS
seduce see LURE
sedulous see BUSY
seeming see APPARENT
segment see PART
seize see TAKE
selection see CHOICE
self-assertive see AGGRESSIVE
self-possession see CONFIDENCE
selfsame see SAME
sense, common sense, gumption, judgment, wisdom mean ability to reach intelligent conclusions. **Sense** implies a reliable ability to judge and decide with soundness, prudence, and intelligence ⟨hasn't the *sense* to come in out of the rain⟩. **Common sense** suggests an average degree of such ability without sophistication or special knowledge ⟨*common sense*

tells me it's wrong⟩. **Gumption** suggests a readiness to use or apply common sense ⟨a shrewd businessman known for his *gumption*⟩. **Judgment** implies sense tempered and refined by experience, training, and maturity ⟨*judgment* is required of a camp counselor⟩. **Wisdom** implies sense and judgment far above average ⟨the *wisdom* that comes from years of living⟩. See in addition MEANING.

sensible see AWARE, MATERIAL, PERCEPTIBLE, WISE
sensitive see LIABLE
sensual see CARNAL, SENSUOUS
sensuous, sensual, luxurious, voluptuous mean relating to or providing pleasure through gratification of the senses. **Sensuous** implies gratification of the senses for the sake of aesthetic pleasure ⟨the *sensuous* delights of a Reubens painting⟩. **Sensual** tends to imply the gratification of the senses or the indulgence of the physical appetites as ends in themselves ⟨a man who indulged his *sensual* appetites⟩. **Luxurious** suggests the providing of or indulgence of sensuous pleasure inducing bodily ease and languor ⟨a vacation devoted to *luxurious* self-indulgence⟩. **Voluptuous** implies more strongly an abandonment esp. to sensual pleasure ⟨promised a variety of *voluptuous* pleasures⟩.

sentiment see FEELING, OPINION
separate *vb* Separate, part, divide, sever, sunder, divorce mean to become or cause to become disunited or disjointed. **Separate** may imply any of several causes such as dispersion, removal of one from others, or presence of an intervening thing ⟨*separated* her personal life from her career⟩. **Part** implies the separating of things or persons in close union or association ⟨an argument that *parted* the friends permanently⟩. **Divide** implies separating into pieces or sections by cutting or breaking ⟨civil war *divided* the nation⟩. **Sever** implies violence esp. in the removal of a part or member ⟨his arm had been *severed* by a chain saw⟩. **Sunder** suggests violent rending or wrenching apart ⟨a province *sundered* by two languages⟩. **Divorce** implies separating two things that commonly interact and belong together ⟨would *divorce* scientific research from moral responsibility⟩.

separate *adj* see DISTINCT, SINGLE
serene see CALM
serious, grave, solemn, sedate, staid, sober, earnest mean not light or frivolous. **Serious** implies a concern for what really matters ⟨prefers gothic romances to *serious* fiction⟩. **Grave** implies both seriousness and dignity in expression or attitude ⟨read the pronouncement in a *grave* voice⟩. **Solemn** suggests an impressive gravity utterly free from levity ⟨the *solemn* occasion of a coronation⟩. **Sedate** implies a composed and decorous seriousness ⟨amidst the frenzy of activity the bride remained *sedate*⟩. **Staid** suggests a settled, accustomed sedateness and prim self-restraint ⟨her dinner parties were *staid* affairs⟩. **Sober** stresses seriousness of purpose and absence of levity or frivolity ⟨an objective and *sober* look at the situation⟩. **Earnest** suggests sincerity or often zealousness of purpose ⟨an *earnest* attempt at dramatizing the Bible⟩.

servile see SUBSERVIENT
setting see BACKGROUND
settle see DECIDE
sever see SEPARATE
several see DISTINCT
severe, stern, austere, ascetic mean given to or marked by strict discipline and firm restraint. **Severe** implies standards enforced without indulgence or laxity and may suggest harshness ⟨the *severe* dress of the Puritans⟩. **Stern** stresses inflexibility and inexorability of temper or character ⟨a *stern* judge who seemed immune to pleas for mercy⟩. **Austere** stresses absence

of warmth, color, or feeling and may apply to rigorous restraint, simplicity, or self-denial (the view that modern architecture is *austere*, brutal, and inhuman). **Ascetic** implies abstention from pleasure and comfort or self-indulgence as spiritual discipline (the *ascetic* life of the monastic orders).

shackle see HAMPER

shake, agitate, rock, convulse mean to move up and down or to and fro with some violence. **Shake** often carries a further implication of a particular purpose (*shake* well before using). **Agitate** suggests a violent and prolonged tossing or stirring (strong winds *agitated* the ship for hours). **Rock** suggests a swinging or swaying motion resulting from violent impact or upheaval (the entire city was *rocked* by the explosion). **Convulse** suggests a violent pulling or wrenching as of a body in a paroxysm (we were *convulsed* with laughter).

shallow see SUPERFICIAL

sham *vb* see ASSUME

sham *n* see IMPOSTURE

shape *n* see FORM

shape *vb* see MAKE

share, participate, partake mean to have, get, or use in common with another or others. **Share** implies that one as the original holder grants to another the partial use, enjoyment, or possession of a thing though it may merely imply a mutual use or possession (*shared* my tools with the others). **Participate** implies a having or taking part in an undertaking, activity, or discussion (students are encouraged to *participate* in outside activities). **Partake** implies accepting or acquiring a share esp. of food or drink (invited everyone to *partake* freely in the refreshments).

sharp, keen, acute mean having or showing alert competence and clear understanding. **Sharp** implies quick perception, clever resourcefulness, or sometimes questionable trickiness (*sharp* enough to know a con job when he saw one). **Keen** suggests quickness, enthusiasm, and a penetrating mind (a *keen* observer of the political scene). **Acute** implies a power to penetrate and may suggest subtlety and sharpness of discrimination (an *acute* sense of what is linguistically effective).

shed see DISCARD

sheer see STEEP

shield see DEFEND

shift see RESOURCE

shimmer see FLASH

short see BRIEF

shorten, curtail, abbreviate, abridge, retrench mean to reduce in extent. **Shorten** implies reduction in length or duration (*shorten* the speech to fit the allotted time). **Curtail** adds an implication of cutting that in some way deprives of completeness or adequacy (the ceremonies were *curtailed* because of the rain). **Abbreviate** implies a making shorter usu. by omitting some part (hostile questioning had the effect of *abbreviating* the interview). **Abridge** implies a reduction in compass or scope with retention of essential elements and a relative completeness in the result (the *abridged* version of the novel). **Retrench** suggests a reduction in extent or costs of something felt to be excessive (falling prices forced the company to *retrench*).

shove see PUSH

show, exhibit, display, expose, parade, flaunt mean to present so as to invite notice or attention. **Show** implies no more than enabling another to see or examine (*showed* her snapshots to the whole group). **Exhibit** stresses putting forward prominently or openly (*exhibit* paintings at a gallery). **Display** emphasizes putting in a position where others may see to advantage (*display* sale items). **Expose** suggests bringing forth from concealment and displaying (sought to *expose* the hypocrisy of the town fathers). **Parade** implies an ostentatious or arrogant displaying (*parading* their piety for all to see). **Flaunt** suggests a shameless, boastful, often offensive parading (nouveaux riches *flaunting* their wealth).

show, manifest, evidence, evince, demonstrate mean to reveal outwardly or make apparent. **Show** is the general term but sometimes implies that what is revealed must be gained by inference from acts, looks, or words (careful not to *show* what he feels). **Manifest** implies a plainer, more immediate revelation (*manifested* musical ability at an early age). **Evidence** suggests serving as proof of the actuality or existence of something (her deep enmity is *evidenced* by her silent glaring). **Evince** implies a showing by outward marks or signs (*evinced* not the slightest grief at the funeral). **Demonstrate** implies showing by action or by display of feeling (*demonstrated* her appreciation in her own way).

showy, pretentious, ostentatious mean given to excessive outward display. **Showy** implies an imposing or striking appearance but usu. suggests cheapness or poor taste (the *showy* costumes of the circus performers). **Pretentious** implies an appearance of importance not justified by the thing's value or the person's standing (for a family-style restaurant, the menu was far too *pretentious*). **Ostentatious** stresses vainglorious display or parade (very *ostentatious,* even for a debutante party).

shrewd, sagacious, perspicacious, astute mean acute in perception and sound in judgment. **Shrewd** stresses practical, hardheaded cleverness and judgment (a *shrewd* judge of character). **Sagacious** suggests wisdom, penetration, and farsightedness (a series of *sagacious* investments tripled her wealth). **Perspicacious** implies unusual power to see through and understand what is puzzling or hidden (a *perspicacious* counselor saw through his facade). **Astute** suggests shrewdness, perspicacity, and diplomatic skill (an *astute* player of party politics).

shrink see CONTRACT, RECOIL

shun see ESCAPE

shy, bashful, diffident, modest, coy mean not inclined to be forward. **Shy** implies a timid reserve and a shrinking from familiarity or contact with others (*shy* in front of total strangers). **Bashful** implies a frightened or hesitant shyness characteristic of childhood and adolescence (the *bashful* boy rarely told us how he felt about anything). **Diffident** stresses a distrust of one's own ability or opinion that causes hesitation in acting or speaking (felt *diffident* about raising an objection). **Modest** suggests absence of undue confidence or conceit (very *modest* about reciting his achievements). **Coy** implies an assumed or affected shyness (don't be misled by her *coy* demeanor).

side see PHASE

sign, mark, token, note, symptom mean a discernible indication of what is not itself directly perceptible. **Sign** applies to any indication to be perceived by the senses or the reason (interpreted her smile as a good *sign*). **Mark** suggests something impressed on or inherently characteristic of a thing often in contrast to general outward appearance (integrity is the *mark* of a gentleman). **Token** applies to something that serves as a proof of something intangible (this gift is a *token* of our esteem). **Note** suggests a distinguishing mark or characteristic (a *note* of despair pervades her poetry). **Symptom** suggests an outward indication of an internal change or condition (rampant violence is a *symptom* of that country's decline).

significance see IMPORTANCE, MEANING

signification see MEANING

silent, taciturn, reticent, reserved, secretive mean showing restraint in speaking. **Silent** implies a habit of saying no more than is needed ⟨her husband was the *silent* type, not given to idle chatter⟩. **Taciturn** implies a temperamental disinclination to speech and usu. connotes unsociability ⟨the locals are *taciturn* and not receptive to outsiders⟩. **Reticent** implies a reluctance to speak out or at length, esp. about one's own affairs ⟨our guest was strangely *reticent* about his plans⟩. **Reserved** implies reticence and suggests the restraining influence of caution or formality in checking easy informal conversational exchange ⟨greetings were brief, formal, and *reserved*⟩. **Secretive,** too, implies reticence but usu. carries a suggestion of deviousness and lack of frankness or of an often ostentatious will to conceal ⟨a *secretive* public official usually stingy with news stories⟩.

silhouette see OUTLINE
silken see SLEEK
silly see SIMPLE
similar, analogous, parallel mean closely resembling each other. **Similar** implies the possibility of being mistaken for each other ⟨all the houses in the development are *similar*⟩. **Analogous** applies to things belonging in essentially different categories but nevertheless having many similarities ⟨*analogous* political systems⟩. **Parallel** suggests a marked likeness in the development of two things ⟨the *parallel* careers of two movie stars⟩.
similarity see LIKENESS
similitude see LIKENESS
simple, foolish, silly, fatuous, asinine mean actually or apparently deficient in intelligence. **Simple** implies a degree of intelligence inadequate to cope with anything complex or involving mental effort ⟨*simple* peasants afraid of revolutionary ideas⟩. **Foolish** implies the character of being or seeming unable to use judgment, discretion, or good sense ⟨*foolish* people believed the ghost story⟩. **Silly** suggests failure to act as a rational being esp. by ridiculous behavior ⟨the *silly* stunts of vacationing college students⟩. **Fatuous** implies foolishness, inanity, and disregard of reality ⟨the *fatuous* conspiracy theories of these extremists⟩. **Asinine** suggests utter and contemptible failure to use normal rationality or perception ⟨a soap opera with an especially *asinine* plot⟩. See in addition EASY.
simulate see ASSUME
simultaneous see CONTEMPORARY
sin see OFFENSE
sincere, wholehearted, heartfelt, hearty, unfeigned mean genuine in feeling. **Sincere** stresses absence of hypocrisy, feigning, or any falsifying embellishment or exaggeration ⟨offered a *sincere* apology⟩. **Wholehearted** suggests sincerity and earnest devotion without reservation or misgiving ⟨promised our *wholehearted* support to the cause⟩. **Heartfelt** suggests depth of genuine feeling outwardly expressed ⟨a gift that expresses our *heartfelt* gratitude⟩. **Hearty** suggests honesty, warmth, and exuberance in displaying feeling ⟨received a *hearty* welcome at the door⟩. **Unfeigned** stresses spontaneity and absence of pretense ⟨her *unfeigned* delight at receiving the award⟩.
single, sole, unique, separate, solitary, particular mean one as distinguished from two or more or all others. **Single** implies being unaccompanied by or unsupported by any other ⟨a *single* example will suffice⟩. **Sole** applies to the one of its kind or character in existence ⟨my *sole* reason for moving there⟩. **Unique** applies to the only one of its kind or character in existence ⟨the medal is *unique,* for no duplicates were made⟩. **Separate** stresses discreteness and disconnection from every other one ⟨a country with a *separate* set of problems⟩. **Solitary** implies being both single and isolated ⟨the television was her *solitary* link to

the outside world⟩. **Particular** implies numerical distinctness from other instances, examples, or members of a class ⟨a *particular* kind of wine⟩.
singular see STRANGE
sinister, baleful, malign mean seriously threatening evil or disaster. **Sinister** suggests a general or vague feeling of fear or apprehension on the part of the observer ⟨a *sinister* aura surrounded the place⟩. **Baleful** imputes perniciousness or destructiveness to something whether working openly or covertly ⟨the *baleful* influence of recreational drugs on our society⟩. **Malign** applies to what is inherently evil or harmful ⟨smoking's *malign* effects on one's health⟩.
skepticism see UNCERTAINTY
sketch see COMPENDIUM
skill see ART
skilled see PROFICIENT
skillful see PROFICIENT
skimpy see MEAGER
skinny see LEAN
skulk see LURK
slack see NEGLIGENT
slacken see DELAY
slander see MALIGN
slang see DIALECT
slavish see SUBSERVIENT
slay see KILL
sleek, slick, glossy, silken mean having a smooth bright surface or appearance. **Sleek** suggests a smoothness or brightness resulting from attentive grooming or physical conditioning ⟨a *sleek* racehorse⟩. **Slick** suggests extreme smoothness that results in a slippery surface ⟨slipped and fell on the *slick* floor⟩. **Glossy** suggests a surface that is smooth and highly polished ⟨photographs having a *glossy* finish⟩. **Silken** implies the smoothness and luster as well as the softness of silk ⟨*silken* hair⟩.
slender see THIN
slick see SLEEK
slight *vb* see NEGLECT
slight *adj* see THIN
slighting see DEROGATORY
slim see THIN
sling see THROW
slink see LURK
slip see ERROR
slothful see LAZY
slough see DISCARD
slow see DELAY
sly, cunning, crafty, tricky, foxy, artful mean attaining or seeking to attain one's ends by devious means. **Sly** implies furtiveness, lack of candor, and skill in concealing one's aims and methods ⟨a *sly* corporate-takeover scheme⟩. **Cunning** suggests the inventive use of sometimes limited intelligence in overreaching or circumventing ⟨relentlessly *cunning* in her pursuit of the governorship⟩. **Crafty** implies cleverness and subtlety of method ⟨a *crafty* trial lawyer⟩. **Tricky** is more likely to suggest shiftiness and unreliability than skill in deception and maneuvering ⟨a *tricky* interviewer who usually got what she wanted from her subject⟩. **Foxy** implies a shrewd and wary craftiness usu. involving devious dealing ⟨a *foxy* thief got away with her jewels⟩. **Artful** implies alluring indirectness in dealing and often connotes sophistication or coquetry or cleverness ⟨an *artful* matchmaker⟩.
small, little, diminutive, minute, tiny, miniature mean noticeably below average in size. **Small** and **little** are often interchangeable, but *small* applies more to relative size determined by capacity, value, number; *little* is more absolute in implication often carrying the idea of petiteness, pettiness, insignificance, or immaturity ⟨the theater was relatively *small*⟩ ⟨your pathetic *little* smile⟩. **Diminutive** implies abnormal

smallness ⟨the *diminutive* gymnast outshone her larger competitors⟩. **Minute** implies extreme smallness ⟨a beverage with only a *minute* amount of caffeine⟩. **Tiny** is an informal equivalent to *minute* ⟨*tiny* cracks have formed in the painting⟩. **Miniature** applies to an exactly proportioned reproduction on a very small scale ⟨a doll house complete with *miniature* furnishings⟩.

smell, scent, odor, aroma mean the quality that makes a thing perceptible to the olfactory sense. **Smell** implies solely the sensation without suggestion of quality or character ⟨an odd *smell* permeated the room⟩. **Scent** applies to the characteristic smell given off by a substance, an animal, or a plant ⟨dogs trained to detect the *scent* of narcotics⟩. **Odor** may imply a stronger or more readily distinguished scent or it may be equivalent to *smell* ⟨a type of cheese with a very pronounced *odor*⟩. **Aroma** suggests a somewhat penetrating usu. pleasant odor ⟨the *aroma* of freshly ground coffee⟩.

smooth see EASY, LEVEL, SUAVE

snare see CATCH

snatch see TAKE

sneak see LURK

sneer see SCOFF

snug see COMFORTABLE

soak, saturate, drench, steep, impregnate mean to permeate or be permeated with a liquid. **Soak** implies usu. prolonged immersion as for softening or cleansing ⟨*soak* the clothes in bleach and water to remove the stains⟩. **Saturate** implies a resulting effect of complete absorption until no more liquid can be held ⟨gym clothes *saturated* with sweat⟩. **Drench** implies a thorough wetting by something that pours down or is poured ⟨the cloudburst *drenched* us to the skin⟩. **Steep** suggests either the extraction of an essence (as of tea leaves) by the liquid or the imparting of a quality (as a color) to the thing immersed ⟨*steep* the tea leaves for exactly five minutes⟩. **Impregnate** implies a thorough interpenetration of one thing by another ⟨a cake strongly *impregnated* with brandy⟩.

sober see SERIOUS

sociable see GRACIOUS

society see ARISTOCRACY

solace see COMFORT

sole see SINGLE

solemn see SERIOUS

solicit see ASK, INVITE

solicitude see CARE

solid see FIRM

solidarity see UNITY

solitary see ALONE, SINGLE

solitude, isolation, seclusion mean the state of one who is alone. **Solitude** may imply a condition of being apart from all human beings or of being cut off by wish or compulsion from one's usual associates ⟨the *solitude* enjoyed by the long-distance trucker⟩. **Isolation** stresses detachment from others often involuntarily ⟨the oppressive *isolation* of the village during winter⟩. **Seclusion** suggests a shutting away or keeping apart from others often connoting deliberate withdrawal from the world or retirement to a quiet life ⟨lived in bucolic *seclusion* surrounded by his art collection⟩.

somatic see BODILY

sophisticated, worldly-wise, blasé mean experienced in the ways of the world. **Sophisticated** often implies refinement, urbanity, cleverness, and cultivation ⟨guests at her salon were usu. rich and *sophisticated*⟩. **Worldly-wise** suggests a close and practical knowledge of the affairs and manners of society and an inclination toward materialism ⟨a *worldly-wise* woman with a philosophy of personal independence⟩. **Blasé** implies a lack of responsiveness to

common joys as a result of a real or affected surfeit of experience and cultivation ⟨*blasé* travelers who claimed to have been everywhere⟩.

sordid see MEAN

sorrow, grief, anguish, woe, regret mean distress of mind. **Sorrow** implies a sense of loss or a sense of guilt and remorse ⟨a nation united in *sorrow* upon the death of the President⟩. **Grief** implies poignant sorrow for an immediate cause ⟨gave his father much *grief*⟩. **Anguish** suggests torturing grief or dread ⟨the *anguish* felt by the hostages⟩. **Woe** is deep or inconsolable grief or misery ⟨cries of *woe* echoed throughout the bombed city⟩. **Regret** implies pain caused by deep disappointment, fruitless longing, or unavailing remorse ⟨never felt a moment of *regret* following the divorce⟩.

sorry see CONTEMPTIBLE

sort see TYPE

sound see HEALTHY, VALID

source see ORIGIN

sovereign see DOMINANT, FREE

spacious, commodious, capacious, ample mean larger in extent or capacity than the average. **Spacious** implies great length and breadth ⟨a mansion with a *spacious* front lawn⟩. **Commodious** stresses roominess and comfortableness ⟨a *commodious* and airy penthouse apartment⟩. **Capacious** stresses the ability to hold, contain, or retain more than the average ⟨a *capacious* suitcase⟩. **Ample** implies having a greater size, expanse, or amount than that deemed adequate ⟨we have *ample* means to buy the house⟩.

spare see LEAN, MEAGER

sparing, frugal, thrifty, economical mean careful in the use of one's money or resources. **Sparing** stresses abstention and restraint ⟨mother was *sparing* in buying luxuries for herself⟩. **Frugal** implies absence of luxury and simplicity of life-style ⟨carried on in the *frugal* tradition of the Yankees⟩. **Thrifty** stresses good management and industry ⟨the store prospered under his *thrifty* management⟩. **Economical** stresses prudent management, lack of wastefulness, and use of things to their best advantage ⟨trucking remains an *economical* means of transport⟩.

sparkle see FLASH

sparse see MEAGER

spasmodic see FITFUL

spat see QUARREL

special, especial, specific, particular, individual mean of or relating to one thing or class. **Special** stresses having a quality, character, identity, or use of its own ⟨airline passengers who require *special* meals⟩. **Especial** may add implications of preeminence or preference ⟨a matter of *especial* importance⟩. **Specific** implies a quality or character distinguishing a kind or a species ⟨children with *specific* nutritional needs⟩. **Particular** stresses the distinctness of something as an individual ⟨an Alpine scene of *particular* beauty⟩. **Individual** implies unequivocal reference to one of a class or group ⟨valued each *individual* opinion⟩.

specific see EXPLICIT, SPECIAL

specimen see INSTANCE

speculate see THINK

speed see HASTE

speedy see FAST

spirit see COURAGE

spite see MALICE

spleen see MALICE

splendid, resplendent, gorgeous, glorious, sublime, superb mean extraordinarily or transcendently impressive. **Splendid** implies outshining the usual or customary ⟨the royal wedding was a *splendid* occasion⟩. **Resplendent** suggests a glowing or blazing splendor ⟨the church was *resplendent* in its Easter decorations⟩. **Gorgeous** implies a rich splendor esp. in display of color ⟨a *gorgeous* red dress⟩. **Glorious** suggests radiance that heightens beauty or distinction ⟨a *glorious* sunset over the ocean⟩. **Sublime** implies an exaltation or elevation almost beyond human comprehension ⟨the *sublime* grandeur of the thunderous falls⟩. **Superb** suggests a magnificence or excellence reaching the highest conceivable degree ⟨a three-star restaurant offering *superb* cuisine⟩.

splenetic see IRASCIBLE

split see TEAR

spoil *n* Spoil, pillage, plunder, booty, prize, loot mean something taken from another by force or craft. **Spoil,** more commonly **spoils,** applies to what belongs by right or custom to the victor in war or political contest ⟨a governor who relished doling out the *spoils* of office⟩. **Pillage** stresses more open violence or lawlessness ⟨filled his capital city with the *pillage* of Europe⟩. **Plunder** applies to what is taken not only in war but in robbery, banditry, grafting, or swindling ⟨a fortune that was the *plunder* of years of political corruption⟩. **Booty** implies plunder to be shared among confederates ⟨the thieves planned to divide their *booty* later⟩. **Prize** applies to spoils captured on the high seas or territorial waters of the enemy ⟨a pirate ship ruthlessly seizing *prizes*⟩. **Loot** applies esp. to what is taken from victims of a catastrophe ⟨prowlers searched the storm-damaged cottages for *loot*⟩.

spoil *vb* see DECAY, INDULGE

sponge see PARASITE

spontaneous, impulsive, instinctive, automatic, mechanical mean acting or activated without deliberation. **Spontaneous** implies lack of prompting and connotes naturalness ⟨a *spontaneous* burst of applause⟩. **Impulsive** implies acting under stress of emotion or spirit of the moment ⟨*impulsive* acts of violence⟩. **Instinctive** stresses spontaneous action involving neither judgment nor will ⟨blinking is an *instinctive* reaction⟩. **Automatic** implies action engaging neither the mind nor the emotions and connotes a predictable response ⟨his denial was *automatic*⟩. **Mechanical** stresses the lifeless, often perfunctory character of the response ⟨over the years her style of teaching became *mechanical*⟩.

sporadic see INFREQUENT

sport see FUN

sprightly see LIVELY

spring, arise, rise, originate, derive, flow, issue, emanate, proceed, stem mean to come up or out of something into existence. **Spring** implies rapid or sudden emerging ⟨a brilliant idea that had *sprung* out of nowhere⟩. **Arise** and **rise** may both convey the fact of coming into existence or notice but *rise* often stresses gradual growth or ascent ⟨a dispute *arose* over the property⟩ ⟨as time passed legends about the house *rose*⟩. **Originate** implies a definite source or starting point ⟨the theory did not *originate* with Darwin⟩. **Derive** implies a prior existence in another form ⟨their system of justice *derives* from British colonial law⟩. **Flow** adds to *spring* a suggestion of abundance or ease of inception ⟨the belief that all good *flows* from God⟩. **Issue** suggests emerging from confinement through an outlet ⟨shouts of joy *issued* from the team's locker room⟩. **Emanate** applies to the coming of something immaterial (as a principle or thought) from a source ⟨serenity *emanated* from her⟩. **Proceed** stresses place of origin, derivation, parentage, or logical cause ⟨bitterness *proceeded* from an unhappy marriage⟩. **Stem** implies originating by dividing or branching off from something as an outgrowth or subordinate development ⟨a whole new industry *stemmed* from the discovery⟩.

springy see ELASTIC

spry see AGILE

spur see MOTIVE

spurn see DECLINE

squabble see QUARREL

squalid see DIRTY

squeamish see NICE

stable see LASTING

staid see SERIOUS

stalwart see STRONG

stand see BEAR

standard, criterion, gauge, yardstick, touchstone mean a means of determining what a thing should be. **Standard** applies to any definite rule, principle, or measure established by authority ⟨the book is a classic by any *standard*⟩. **Criterion** may apply to anything used as a test of quality whether formulated as a rule or principle or not ⟨in art there are no hard-and-fast *criteria*⟩. **Gauge** applies to a means of testing a particular dimension (as thickness, depth, diameter) or figuratively a particular quality or aspect ⟨congressional mail is not always an accurate *gauge* of public opinion⟩. **Yardstick** is an informal substitute for *criterion* that suggests quantity more often than quality ⟨the movie was a flop by most *yardsticks*⟩. **Touchstone** suggests a simple test of the authenticity or value of something intangible ⟨fine service is one *touchstone* of a first-class restaurant⟩.

stare see GAZE

start see BEGIN

stately see GRAND

statute see LAW

staunch see FAITHFUL

stay see DEFER

steadfast see FAITHFUL

steady, even, equable mean not varying throughout a course or extent. **Steady** implies lack of fluctuation or interruption of movement ⟨ran the race at a *steady* pace⟩. **Even** suggests a lack of variation in quality or character ⟨read the statement in an *even* voice⟩. **Equable** implies lack of extremes or of sudden sharp changes ⟨during exercise keep your pulse as *equable* as possible⟩.

steal, pilfer, filch, purloin mean to take from another without right or without detection. **Steal** may apply to any surreptitious taking of something and differs from the other terms by commonly applying to intangibles as well as material things ⟨*steal* jewels⟩ ⟨*stole* a look at her⟩. **Pilfer** implies stealing repeatedly in small amounts ⟨dismissed for *pilfering* from the company⟩. **Filch** adds a suggestion of snatching quickly and surreptitiously ⟨*filched* an apple when the man looked away⟩. **Purloin** stresses removing or carrying off for one's own use or purposes ⟨had *purloined* a typewriter and other office equipment⟩.

stealthy see SECRET

steep *adj* Steep, abrupt, precipitous, sheer mean having an incline approaching the perpendicular. **Steep** implies such sharpness of pitch that ascent or descent is very difficult ⟨a *steep* staircase leading to the attic⟩. **Abrupt** implies a sharper pitch and a sudden break in the level ⟨a beach with an *abrupt* drop-off⟩. **Precipitous** applies to an incline approaching the vertical ⟨the airplane went into a *precipitous* nosedive⟩. **Sheer** suggests an unbroken perpendicular expanse ⟨climbers able to ascend *sheer* cliffs⟩.

steep *vb* see SOAK

steer see GUIDE

stem see SPRING

stentorian see LOUD

stereotyped see TRITE

stern see SEVERE

stick, adhere, cohere, cling, cleave mean to become closely attached. **Stick** implies attachment by affixing or by being glued together ⟨the gummed label will *stick* just by pressing⟩. **Adhere** is often interchangeable with *stick* but sometimes implies a growing together (muscle fibers will *adhere* following surgery). **Cohere** suggests a sticking together of parts so that they form a unified mass (eggs will make the mixture *cohere*). **Cling** implies attachment by hanging on with arms or tendrils (always *cling* to a capsized boat). **Cleave** stresses strength of attachment (barnacles *cleaving* to the hull of a boat).

stiff, rigid, inflexible mean difficult to bend. **Stiff** may apply to any degree of this condition (muscles will become *stiff* if they are not stretched). **Rigid** applies to something so stiff that it cannot be bent without breaking (a *rigid* surfboard). **Inflexible** stresses lack of suppleness or pliability (for adequate support, rock-climbers wear shoes with *inflexible* soles).

stimulate see PROVOKE

stingy, close, niggardly, parsimonious, penurious, miserly mean being unwilling or showing unwillingness to share with others. **Stingy** implies a marked lack of generosity (a *stingy* child, not given to sharing). **Close** suggests keeping a tight grip on one's money and possessions (folks who are very *close* when charity calls). **Niggardly** implies giving or spending the very smallest amount possible (gave his wife a *niggardly* household allowance). **Parsimonious** suggests a frugality so extreme as to lead to stinginess (a *parsimonious* life-style with no room for luxuries). **Penurious** implies niggardliness that gives an appearance of actual poverty (the *penurious* old woman left behind a fortune). **Miserly** suggests a sordid avariciousness and a morbid pleasure in hoarding (a *miserly* man indifferent to the cries of the needy).

stinking see MALODOROUS

stint see TASK

stoic see IMPASSIVE

stolid see IMPASSIVE

stoop, condescend, deign mean to descend from one's level to do something. **Stoop** may imply a descent in dignity or from a relatively high moral plane to a much lower one (how can you *stoop* to such childish name-calling). **Condescend** implies a stooping by one of high rank or position to socialize with social inferiors (the boss's wife *condescending* to mingle with the employees). **Deign** suggests a reluctant condescension of one in a haughty mood (scarcely *deigned* to speak with her poor relations).

stop, cease, quit, discontinue, desist mean to suspend or cause to suspend activity. **Stop** applies to action or progress or to what is operating or progressing and may imply suddenness or definiteness (*stopped* at the red light). **Cease** applies to states, conditions, or existence and may add a suggestion of gradualness and a degree of finality (by nightfall the fighting had *ceased*). **Quit** may stress either finality or abruptness in stopping or ceasing (the engine faltered, sputtered, then *quit* altogether). **Discontinue** applies to the stopping of an accustomed activity or practice (we have *discontinued* the manufacture of that item). **Desist** implies forbearance or restraint as a motive for stopping or ceasing (*desisted* from further efforts to persuade them).

stopgap see RESOURCE

storm see ATTACK

stout see STRONG

straits see JUNCTURE

strange, singular, unique, peculiar, eccentric, erratic, odd, queer, quaint, outlandish mean departing from what is ordinary, usual, or to be expected. **Strange** stresses unfamiliarity and may apply to the foreign, the unnatural, the unaccountable (the *strange* sights of a trip to the Orient). **Singular** suggests individuality or puzzling strangeness (a *singular* feeling of impending disaster). **Unique** implies singularity and the fact of being without a known parallel (a career that is *unique* in the annals of science). **Peculiar** implies a

marked distinctiveness (problems *peculiar* to inner-city areas). **Eccentric** suggests a wide divergence from the usual or normal esp. in behavior (the *eccentric* eating habits of young children). **Erratic** stresses a capricious and unpredictable wandering or deviating (disturbed by his friend's *erratic* behavior). **Odd** applies to a departure from the regular or expected (an *odd* sense of humor). **Queer** suggests a dubious sometimes sinister oddness (puzzled by the *queer* happenings since her arrival). **Quaint** suggests an old-fashioned but pleasant oddness (a *quaint* and remote village in the mountains). **Outlandish** applies to what is uncouth, bizarre, or barbaric (islanders having *outlandish* customs and superstitions).

stratagem see TRICK

strength see POWER

strenuous see VIGOROUS

strict see RIGID

strident see LOUD, VOCIFEROUS

strife see DISCORD

strike see AFFECT

striking see NOTICEABLE

stringent see RIGID

strive see ATTEMPT

strong, stout, sturdy, stalwart, tough, tenacious mean showing power to resist or to endure. **Strong** may imply power derived from muscular vigor, large size, structural soundness, intellectual or spiritual resources (*strong* arms) (a *strong* desire to succeed). **Stout** suggests an ability to endure stress, pain, or hard use without giving way (wear *stout* boots when hiking). **Sturdy** implies strength derived from vigorous growth, determination of spirit, solidity of construction (a *sturdy* table) (people of *sturdy* independence). **Stalwart** suggests an unshakable dependability and connotes great physical strength (*stalwart* supporters of the environmental movement). **Tough** implies great firmness and resiliency (a *tough* political opponent). **Tenacious** suggests strength in seizing, retaining, clinging to, or holding together (*tenacious* of their right to privacy).

stubborn see OBSTINATE

study see CONSIDER

stupendous see MONSTROUS

stupid, dull, dense, crass, dumb mean lacking in power to absorb ideas or impressions. **Stupid** implies a slow-witted or dazed state of mind that may be either congenital or temporary (you're too *stupid* to know what's good for you). **Dull** suggests a slow or sluggish mind such as results from disease, depression, or shock (monotonous work that left his mind *dull*). **Dense** implies a thickheaded imperviousness to ideas (was too *dense* to take a hint). **Crass** suggests a grossness of mind precluding discrimination or delicacy (a *crass*, materialistic people). **Dumb** applies to an exasperating obtuseness or lack of comprehension (too *dumb* to figure out what's going on).

stupor see LETHARGY

sturdy see STRONG

style see FASHION

suave, urbane, diplomatic, bland, smooth, politic mean pleasantly tactful and well-mannered. **Suave** suggests a specific ability to deal with others easily and without friction (a luxury restaurant with an army of *suave* waiters). **Urbane** implies high cultivation and poise coming from wide social experience (the *urbane* host of a televised anthology series). **Diplomatic** stresses an ability to deal with ticklish situations tactfully (be *diplomatic* in asking them to leave). **Bland** emphasizes mildness of manner and absence of irritating qualities (a *bland* manner suitable for early morning radio). **Smooth** suggests often a deliberately assumed suavity (the *smooth* sales pitch of a car dealer). **Politic** implies shrewd as well as tactful and suave handling of people (an ambassador's wife must be *politic* and discreet).

subdue see CONQUER

subject *n* see CITIZEN

subject *adj* see LIABLE

sublime see SPLENDID

submit see YIELD

subscribe see ASSENT

subservient, servile, slavish, obsequious mean showing or characterized by extreme compliance or abject obedience. **Subservient** implies the cringing manner of one very conscious of a subordinate position (domestic help was expected to be properly *subservient*). **Servile** suggests the mean or fawning behavior of a slave (a political boss and his entourage of *servile* hangers-on). **Slavish** suggests abject or debased servility (the *slavish* status of migrant farm workers). **Obsequious** implies fawning or sycophantic compliance and exaggerated deference of manner (waiters who are *obsequious* in the presence of celebrities).

subside see ABATE

substantiate see CONFIRM

subterfuge see DECEPTION

succeed see FOLLOW

succinct see CONCISE

succumb see YIELD

sudden see PRECIPITATE

suffer see BEAR

suffering see DISTRESS

sufficient, enough, adequate, competent mean being what is necessary or desirable. **Sufficient** suggests a close meeting of a need (had supplies *sufficient* to last a month). **Enough** is less exact in suggestion than *sufficient* (do you have *enough* food?). **Adequate** may imply barely meeting a requirement (the room was *adequate,* no more). **Competent** suggests measuring up to all requirements without question or being adequately adapted to an end (a *competent* income for their life-style).

suffuse see INFUSE

suggest, imply, hint, intimate, insinuate mean to convey an idea indirectly. **Suggest** may stress putting into the mind by association of ideas, awakening of a desire, or initiating a train of thought (an actress who can *suggest* a whole character with one gesture). **Imply** is close to *suggest* but may indicate a more definite or logical relation of the unexpressed idea to the expressed (pronouncements that *imply* he has lost touch with reality). **Hint** implies the use of slight or remote suggestion with a minimum of overt statement (*hinted* that she might have a job lined up). **Intimate** stresses delicacy of suggestion without connoting any lack of candor (*intimated* that he was ready to pop the question). **Insinuate** applies to the conveying of a usu. unpleasant idea in a sly underhanded manner (*insinuated* that the neighbors were not what they appeared to be).

suitable see FIT

sulky see SULLEN

sullen, glum, morose, surly, sulky, crabbed, saturnine, gloomy mean showing a forbidding or disagreeable mood. **Sullen** implies a silent ill humor and a refusal to be sociable (remained *sullen* throughout the party). **Glum** suggests a silent dispiritedness (the whole team was *glum* following the defeat). **Morose** adds to *glum* an element of bitterness or misanthropy (became *morose* after the death of his wife). **Surly** implies gruffness and sullenness of speech or manner (a *surly* teenage boy). **Sulky** suggests childish resentment expressed in peevish sullenness (a period of *sulky* behavior followed every argument). **Crabbed** applies to a forbidding morose harshness of manner (his *crabbed* exterior was only a pose). **Saturnine** de-

scribes a heavy forbidding aspect or suggests a bitter disposition (a *saturnine* cynic always finding fault). **Gloomy** implies a depression in mood making for seeming sullenness or glumness (bad news that put everyone in a *gloomy* mood).

summary see CONCISE

summative see CUMULATIVE

summit, peak, pinnacle, climax, apex, acme, culmination mean the highest point attained or attainable. **Summit** implies the topmost level attainable (a singer at the *summit* of his career). **Peak** suggests the highest among other high points (an artist working at the *peak* of his powers). **Pinnacle** suggests a dizzying and often insecure height (the *pinnacle* of success in the entertainment world). **Climax** implies the highest point in an ascending series (the moon landing marked the *climax* of the program). **Apex** implies the point where all ascending lines converge (Dutch culture reached its *apex* in the 17th century). **Acme** implies a level of quality representing the perfection of a thing (a statue that was once deemed the *acme* of beauty). **Culmination** suggests the outcome of a growth or development representing an attained objective (the bill marked the *culmination* of the civil rights movement).

summon, call, cite, convoke, convene, muster mean to demand the presence of. **Summon** implies the exercise of authority (*summoned* by the court to appear as a witness). **Call** may be used less formally for *summon* (the President *called* Congress for a special session). **Cite** implies a summoning to court usu. to answer a charge (*cited* to answer the charge of drunken driving). **Convoke** implies a summons to assemble for deliberative or legislative purposes (*convoked* an assembly of the world's leading scientists). **Convene** is somewhat less formal than *convoke* (*convened* the students in the school auditorium). **Muster** suggests a calling up of a number of things that form a group in order that they may be exhibited, displayed, or utilized as a whole (*muster* the troops for an inspection).

sumptuous see LUXURIOUS

sunder see SEPARATE

superb see SPLENDID

supercilious see PROUD

supererogatory, gratuitous, uncalled-for, wanton mean done without need or compulsion or warrant. **Supererog atory** implies a giving above what is required by rule and may suggest adding something not needed or not wanted (an abrupt man who regarded the usual pleasantries as *supererogatory*). **Gratuitous** usu. applies to something offensive or unpleasant given or done without provocation (my civil question received a *gratuitous* insult). **Uncalled-for** implies impertinence or logical absurdity (resented her *uncalled-for* advice). **Wanton** implies not only a lack of provocation but a malicious or sportive motive (the *wanton* destruction of property by vandals).

superficial, shallow, cursory mean lacking in depth or solidity. **Superficial** implies a concern only with surface aspects (a *superficial* examination of the wound). **Shallow** is more generally derogatory in implying lack of depth in knowledge, reasoning, emotions, or character (a *shallow* interpretation of the character Hamlet). **Cursory** suggests a lack of thoroughness or a neglect of details (even a *cursory* reading of the work will reveal that).

supersede see REPLACE

supervene see FOLLOW

supine see INACTIVE, PRONE

supplant see REPLACE

supple see ELASTIC

supplicate see BEG

support, uphold, advocate, back, champion mean to favor actively one that meets opposition. **Support** is least explicit about the nature of the assistance given ⟨people who *support* the development of the area⟩. **Uphold** implies extended support given to something attacked ⟨*upheld* the legitimacy of the military action⟩. **Advocate** stresses urging or pleading ⟨*advocated* a return to basics in public school education⟩. **Back** suggests supporting by lending assistance to one failing or falling ⟨allies refused to *back* the call for sanctions⟩. **Champion** suggests publicly defending one unjustly attacked or too weak to advocate his own cause ⟨*championed* the rights of pregnant women⟩.

suppress see CRUSH

sure, certain, positive, cocksure mean having no doubt or uncertainty. **Sure** usu. stresses the subjective or intuitive feeling of assurance ⟨felt *sure* that he had forgotten something⟩. **Certain** may apply to a basing of a conclusion or conviction on definite grounds or indubitable evidence ⟨scientists are now *certain* what caused the explosion⟩. **Positive** intensifies sureness or certainty and may imply opinionated conviction or forceful expression of it ⟨she is *positive* that he is the killer⟩. **Cocksure** implies presumptuous or careless positiveness ⟨you're always so *cocksure* about everything⟩.

surfeit see SATIATE

surly see SULLEN

surmise see CONJECTURE

surpass see EXCEED

surprise, astonish, astound, amaze, flabbergast mean to impress forcibly through unexpectedness. **Surprise** stresses causing an effect through being unexpected at a particular time or place rather than by being essentially unusual or novel ⟨*surprised* to find his mother in a bar⟩. **Astonish** implies surprising so greatly as to seem incredible ⟨the young player *astonished* the chess masters⟩. **Astound** stresses the shock of astonishment ⟨news of the atomic bomb *astounded* everyone⟩. **Amaze** suggests an effect of bewilderment ⟨*amazed* by the immense size of the place⟩. **Flabbergast** may suggest thorough astonishment and bewilderment or dismay ⟨*flabbergasted* by his daughter's precocious comments⟩.

surrender see RELINQUISH

surreptitious see SECRET

survey see COMPENDIUM

susceptible see LIABLE

suspend see DEFER, EXCLUDE

suspicion see UNCERTAINTY

sway *vb* see AFFECT, SWING

sway *n* see POWER

sweep see RANGE

swell see EXPAND

swerve, veer, deviate, depart, digress, diverge mean to turn aside from a straight course. **Swerve** may suggest a physical, mental, or moral turning away from a given course, often with abruptness ⟨suddenly *swerved* to avoid hitting an animal⟩. **Veer** implies a major change in direction ⟨at that point the road *veers* to the right⟩. **Deviate** implies a turning from a customary or prescribed course ⟨the witness never *deviated* from her story⟩. **Depart** suggests a deviation from a traditional or conventional course or type ⟨a book that *departs* from the usual memoirs of a film star⟩. **Digress** applies to a departing from the subject of one's discourse ⟨frequently *digressed* during his lecture⟩. **Diverge** may equal *depart* but usu. suggests a branching of a main path into two or more leading in different directions ⟨after medical school their paths *diverged*⟩.

swift see FAST

swindle see CHEAT

swing *vb* Swing, wave, flourish, brandish, thrash mean to wield or cause to move to and fro or up and down. **Swing** implies regular or uniform movement ⟨*swing* the rope back and forth⟩. **Wave** usu. implies smooth or continuous motion ⟨a flag *waving* in the breeze⟩. **Flourish** suggests vigorous, ostentatious, or graceful movement ⟨*flourishing* her racket, she challenged me to a match⟩. **Brandish** implies threatening or menacing motion ⟨*brandishing* his fist, he vowed vengeance⟩. **Thrash** suggests vigorous, abrupt, violent movement ⟨a child *thrashing* his arms about in a tantrum⟩.

swing *vb* Swing, sway, oscillate, vibrate, fluctuate, waver, undulate mean to move from one direction to its opposite. **Swing** implies a movement of something attached at one end or one side ⟨the door suddenly *swung* open⟩. **Sway** implies a slow swinging or teetering movement ⟨the drunk *swayed* a little and then fell⟩. **Oscillate** stresses a usu. rapid alternation of direction ⟨a fan that *oscillates* will cool more effectively⟩. **Vibrate** suggests the rapid oscillation of an elastic body under stress or impact ⟨the *vibrating* strings of a piano⟩. **Fluctuate** suggests constant irregular changes of level, intensity, or value ⟨monetary exchange rates *fluctuate* constantly⟩. **Waver** stresses irregular motion suggestive of reeling or tottering ⟨his whole body *wavered* as he crossed the finish line⟩. **Undulate** suggests a gentle wavelike motion ⟨an *undulating* sea of grass⟩.

sycophant see PARASITE

syllabus see COMPENDIUM

sympathetic see CONSONANT

sympathy see ATTRACTION, PITY

symptom see SIGN

synchronous see CONTEMPORARY

synopsis see ABRIDGMENT

synthetic see ARTIFICIAL

system see METHOD

systematize see ORDER

T

taciturn see SILENT

tact, address, poise, savoir faire mean skill and grace in dealing with others. **Tact** implies delicate and considerate perception of what is appropriate ⟨use *tact* when inquiring about the divorce⟩. **Address** stresses dexterity and grace in dealing with new and trying situations and may imply success in attaining one's ends ⟨brought off her first dinner party with remarkable *address*⟩. **Poise** may imply both tact and address but stresses self-possession and ease in meeting difficult situations ⟨the *poise* of one who has been officiating all his life⟩. **Savoir faire** is likely to stress worldly experience and a sure awareness of what is proper or expedient ⟨has little of the *savoir faire* expected of a Washington hostess⟩.

taint see CONTAMINATE

take, seize, grasp, clutch, snatch, grab mean to get hold of by or as if by catching up with the hand. **Take** is a general term applicable to any manner of getting something into one's possession or control ⟨*take* some salad from the bowl⟩ ⟨*took* control of the company⟩. **Seize** implies a sudden and forcible movement in getting hold of something tangible or an apprehending of something fleeting or elusive when intangible ⟨*seized* the crook as he tried to escape⟩. **Grasp** stresses a laying hold so as to have firmly in possession ⟨firmly *grasp* the handle and pull⟩. **Clutch** suggests avidity or anxiety in seizing or grasping and may imply less success in holding ⟨frantically *clutching* the bush at the edge of the cliff⟩. **Snatch** suggests more suddenness or quickness but less force than seize ⟨*snatched* a doughnut before running out the door⟩. **Grab** implies more roughness or rudeness than ⟨roughly *grabbed* her by the arm⟩.

talent see GIFT

talkative, loquacious, garrulous, voluble mean given to talk or talking. **Talkative** may imply a readiness to engage in talk or a disposition to enjoy conversation ⟨not the *talkative* type who would enjoy a party⟩. **Loquacious** suggests the power of expressing oneself articulately, fluently, or glibly ⟨the corporation needs a spokesperson who is *loquacious* and telegenic⟩. **Garrulous** implies prosy, rambling, or tedious loquacity ⟨forced to endure a *garrulous* companion the whole trip⟩. **Voluble** suggests a free, easy, and unending loquacity ⟨the Italians are a *voluble* people⟩.

tall see HIGH

tangible see PERCEPTIBLE

task, duty, job, chore, stint, assignment mean a piece of work to be done. **Task** implies work imposed by a person in authority or an employer or by circumstance ⟨performed a variety of *tasks* for the company⟩. **Duty** implies an obligation to perform or responsibility for performance ⟨the *duties* of a lifeguard⟩. **Job** applies to a piece of work voluntarily performed; it may sometimes suggest difficulty or importance ⟨took on the *job* of turning the company around⟩. **Chore** implies a minor routine activity necessary for maintaining a household or farm ⟨every child had a list of *chores* to do⟩. **Stint** implies a carefully allotted or measured quantity of assigned work or service ⟨during his *stint* as governor⟩. **Assignment** implies a definite limited task assigned by one in authority ⟨your *assignment* did not include interfering with others⟩.

tasty see PALATABLE

taunt see RIDICULE

tawdry see GAUDY

teach, instruct, educate, train, discipline, school mean to cause to acquire knowledge or skill. **Teach** applies to any manner of imparting information or skill so that others may learn ⟨*teach* French⟩ ⟨*taught* them how to ski⟩. **Instruct** suggests methodical or formal teaching ⟨*instruct* the recruits in calisthenics at boot camp⟩. **Educate** implies attempting to bring out latent capabilities ⟨*educate* students so that they are prepared for the future⟩. **Train** stresses instruction and drill with a specific end in view ⟨*trained* foreign pilots to operate the new aircraft⟩. **Discipline** implies subordinating to a master for the sake of controlling ⟨*disciplined* herself to exercise daily⟩. **School** implies training or disciplining esp. in what is hard to master or to bear ⟨*schooled* myself not to flinch at the sight of blood⟩.

tear, rip, rend, split, cleave, rive mean to separate forcibly. **Tear** implies a pulling apart by force and leaving jagged edges ⟨*tear* up lettuce for a salad⟩. **Rip** implies a pulling apart in one rapid uninterrupted motion often along a seam or joint ⟨*ripped* the jacket along the side seams⟩. **Rend** implies very violent or ruthless severing or sundering ⟨an angry mob *rent* his clothes⟩. **Split** implies a cutting or breaking apart in a continuous, straight, and usu. lengthwise direction or in the direction of grain or layers ⟨*split* logs for firewood⟩. **Cleave** implies very forceful splitting or cutting with a blow ⟨a bolt of lightning *cleaved* the giant oak⟩. **Rive** suggests action rougher and more violent than *split* or *cleave* ⟨a friendship *riven* by jealousy⟩.

tease see WORRY

tell see REVEAL

telling see VALID

temerity, audacity, hardihood, effrontery, nerve, cheek, gall, chutzpah mean conspicuous or flagrant boldness. **Temerity** suggests boldness arising from rashness and contempt of danger ⟨had the *temerity* to ask for a favor after that insult⟩. **Audacity** implies a disregard of restraints commonly imposed by convention or prudence ⟨an entrepreneur with *audacity* and vision⟩. **Hardihood** suggests firmness in daring and defiance ⟨no serious scientist has the *hardihood* to claim that⟩. **Effrontery** implies shameless, insolent disregard of propriety or courtesy ⟨had the *effrontery* to tell me how to do my job⟩. **Nerve, cheek, gall,** and **chutzpah** are informal equivalents for *effrontery* ⟨the *nerve* of that guy⟩ ⟨has the *cheek* to bill herself as a singer⟩ ⟨had the *gall* to demand some evidence⟩ ⟨her *chutzpah* got her into the exclusive party⟩.

temper see DISPOSITION

temperament see DISPOSITION

tempt see LURE

tenacious see STRONG

tenacity see COURAGE

tendency, trend, drift, tenor, current mean movement in a particular direction. **Tendency** implies an inclination sometimes amounting to an impelling force ⟨the *tendency* to expand the limits of what is art⟩. **Trend** applies to the general direction maintained by a winding or irregular course ⟨the long-term *trend* of the stock market is upward⟩. **Drift** may apply to a tendency determined by external forces ⟨the *drift* of the population away from large cities⟩ or it may apply to an underlying or obscure trend of meaning or discourse ⟨a racist *drift* runs through all of his works⟩. **Tenor** stresses a clearly perceptible direction and a continuous, undeviating course ⟨a suburb seeking to maintain its *tenor* of tranquility⟩. **Current** implies a clearly defined but not necessarily unalterable course ⟨an encounter that altered forever the *current* of my life⟩.

tenor see TENDENCY

tenuous see THIN

tergiversation see AMBIGUITY

terminal see LAST

terminate see CLOSE

termination see END

terminus see END

terror see FEAR

terse see CONCISE

testy see IRASCIBLE

theatrical see DRAMATIC

theory see HYPOTHESIS

thick see CLOSE

thin, slender, slim, slight, tenuous mean not thick, broad, abundant, or dense. **Thin** implies comparatively little extension between surfaces or in diameter, or it may imply lack of substance, richness, or abundance ⟨*thin* wire⟩ ⟨soup that was *thin* and tasteless⟩. **Slender** implies leanness or spareness often with grace and good proportion ⟨the *slender* legs of a Sheraton chair⟩. **Slim** applies to slenderness that suggests fragility or scantiness ⟨a *slim* volume of poetry⟩ ⟨a *slim* chance of success⟩. **Slight** implies smallness as well as thinness ⟨the *slight* build of a professional jockey⟩. **Tenuous** implies extreme thinness, sheerness, or lack of substance and firmness ⟨the sword hung by a *tenuous* thread⟩.

think *vb* **Think, conceive, imagine, fancy, realize, envisage, envision** mean to form an idea of. **Think** implies the entrance of an idea into one's mind with or without deliberate consideration or reflection ⟨I just *thought* of a good story⟩. **Conceive** suggests the forming and bringing forth and usu. developing of an idea, plan, or design ⟨*conceive* of a plan to rescue the hostages⟩. **Imagine** stresses a visualization ⟨*imagine* a permanently operating space station⟩. **Fancy** suggests an imagining often unrestrained by reality but spurred by desires ⟨*fancied* himself a super athlete⟩. **Realize** stresses a grasping of the significance of what is conceived or imagined ⟨*realized* the enormity of the task ahead⟩. **Envisage** and **envision** imply a conceiving or imagining that is esp. clear or detailed ⟨*envisaged* a totally computerized operation⟩ ⟨*envisioned* a world free from hunger and want⟩.

think *vb* Think, cogitate, reflect, reason, speculate, deliberate mean to use one's powers of conception, judgment, or inference. **Think** is general and may apply to any mental activity, but used alone often suggests attainment of clear ideas or conclusions ⟨a course that really teaches you to *think*⟩. **Cogitate** implies deep or intent thinking ⟨quietly sitting and *cogitating* on the mysteries of nature⟩. **Reflect** suggests unhurried consideration of something recalled to the mind ⟨*reflected* on fifty years of married life⟩. **Reason** stresses consecutive logical thinking ⟨*reasoned* that the murderer and victim knew each other⟩. **Speculate** implies reasoning about things theoretical or problematic ⟨historians have *speculated* about the fate of the Lost Colony⟩. **Deliberate** suggests slow or careful reasoning before forming an opinion or reaching a conclusion or decision ⟨the jury *deliberated* for five hours⟩.

thirst see LONG

thought see IDEA

thrash see SWING

threadbare see TRITE

thrifty see SPARING

throng see CROWD

throw, cast, toss, fling, hurl, pitch, sling, mean to cause to move swiftly through space by a propulsive movement or a propelling force. **Throw** is general and interchangeable with the other terms but may specif. imply a distinctive motion with bent arm ⟨*throws* the ball with great accuracy⟩. **Cast** usu. implies lightness in the thing thrown and sometimes a scattering ⟨*cast* bread crumbs to the birds⟩. **Toss** suggests a light or careless or aimless throwing and may imply an upward motion ⟨*tossed* her racket on the bed⟩. **Fling** stresses a violent throwing ⟨*flung* the ring back in his face⟩. **Hurl** implies power as in throwing a massive weight ⟨*hurled* the intruder out the window⟩. **Pitch** suggests throwing carefully at a target ⟨*pitch* horseshoes⟩. **Sling** suggests propelling with a sweeping or swinging motion, usu. with force and suddenness ⟨*slung* the bag over his shoulder⟩.

thrust see PUSH

thwart see FRUSTRATE

tiff see QUARREL

tight see DRUNK

tiny see SMALL

tipsy see DRUNK

tire, weary, fatigue, exhaust, jade, fag mean to make or become unable or unwilling to continue. **Tire** implies a draining of one's strength or patience ⟨the long ride *tired* us out⟩. **Weary** stresses tiring until one is unable to endure more of the same thing ⟨*wearied* of the constant arguing⟩. **Fatigue** suggests causing great lassitude through excessive strain or undue effort ⟨*fatigued* by the long, hard climb⟩. **Exhaust** implies complete draining of strength by hard exertion ⟨shoveling snow *exhausted* him⟩. **Jade** suggests the loss of all freshness and eagerness ⟨*jaded* with the endless round of society parties⟩. **Fag** implies a drooping with fatigue ⟨arrived home, all *fagged* out by a day's shopping⟩.

tireless see INDEFATIGABLE

toady *vb* see FAWN

toady *n* see PARASITE

toil see WORK

token see SIGN

tolerant see FORBEARING

tolerate see BEAR

tool see IMPLEMENT

toothsome see PALATABLE

torment see AFFLICT

torpor see LETHARGY

torture see AFFLICT

toss see THROW

total see WHOLE

touch see AFFECT

touching see MOVING

touchstone see STANDARD

touchy see IRASCIBLE

tough see STRONG

toy see TRIFLE

trace, vestige, track mean a perceptible sign made by something that has passed. **Trace** may suggest any line, mark, or discernible effect ⟨an animal species believed to have vanished without a *trace*⟩. **Vestige** applies to a tangible reminder such as a fragment or remnant of what is past and gone ⟨boulders that are *vestiges* of the last ice age⟩. **Track** implies a continuous line that can be followed ⟨the fossilized tracks of dinosaurs⟩.

track see TRACE

tractable see OBEDIENT

trade see BUSINESS

traduce see MALIGN

traffic see BUSINESS

trail see CHASE

train see TEACH

traipse see WANDER

traitorous see FAITHLESS

trammel see HAMPER

tranquil see CALM

transcend see EXCEED

transfigure see TRANSFORM

transform, metamorphose, transmute, convert, transmogrify, transfigure mean to change a thing into a different thing. **Transform** implies a major change in form, nature, or function ⟨*transformed* a small company into a corporate giant⟩. **Metamorphose** suggests an abrupt or startling change induced by or as if by magic or a supernatural power ⟨*metamorphosed* awkward girls into graceful ballerinas⟩. **Transmute** implies transforming into a higher element or thing ⟨*transmuted* a shopworn tale into a psychological masterpiece⟩. **Convert** implies a change fitting something for a new or different use or function ⟨*converted* the boys' room into a guest bedroom⟩. **Transmogrify** suggests a grotesque or preposterous metamorphosis ⟨the prince was *transmogrified* into a frog⟩. **Transfigure** implies a change that exalts or glorifies ⟨ecstasy *transfigured* her face⟩.

transient, transitory, ephemeral, momentary, fugitive, fleeting, evanescent mean lasting or staying only a short time. **Transient** applies to what is actually short in its duration or stay ⟨a hotel catering primarily to *transient* guests⟩. **Transitory** applies to what is by its nature or essence bound to change, pass, or come to an end ⟨fame in the movies is *transitory*⟩. **Ephemeral** implies striking brevity of life or duration ⟨many slang words are *ephemeral*⟩. **Momentary** suggests coming and going quickly and therefore being merely a brief interruption of a more enduring state ⟨my feelings of guilt were only *momentary*⟩. **Fugitive** and **fleeting** imply passing so quickly as to make apprehending difficult ⟨in winter the days are short and sunshine is *fugitive*⟩ ⟨a life with only *fleeting* moments of joy⟩. **Evanescent** suggests a quick vanishing and an airy or fragile quality ⟨the story has an *evanescent* touch of whimsy that is lost on stage⟩.

transitory see TRANSIENT

translucent see CLEAR

transmogrify see TRANSFORM

transmute see TRANSFORM

transparent see CLEAR

transport *vb* see BANISH, CARRY

transport *n* see ECSTASY

transpose see REVERSE

trap see CATCH

travail see WORK

travesty see CARICATURE

treacherous see FAITHLESS

treasure see APPRECIATE

tremendous see MONSTROUS

trenchant see INCISIVE

trend see TENDENCY

trepidation see FEAR

trespass *vb* Trespass, encroach, entrench, infringe, invade mean to make inroads upon the property, territory, or rights of another. **Trespass** implies an unwarranted, unlawful, or offensive intrusion (warned people about *trespassing* on their land). **Encroach** suggests gradual or stealthy entrance upon another's territory or usurpation of his rights or possessions (on guard against laws that *encroach* upon our civil rights). **Entrench** suggests establishing and maintaining oneself in a position of advantage or profit at the expense of others (opposed to regulations that *entrench* upon free enterprise). **Infringe** implies an encroachment clearly violating a right or prerogative (a product that *infringes* upon another's patent). **Invade** implies a hostile and injurious entry into the territory or sphere of another (practices that *invade* our right to privacy).

trespass *n* see BREACH

tribute see ENCOMIUM

trick *n* Trick, ruse, stratagem, maneuver, artifice, wile, feint mean an indirect means to gain an end. **Trick** may imply deception, roguishness, illusion, and either an evil or harmless end (used every *trick* in the book to nail a husband). **Ruse** stresses an attempt to mislead by a false impression (secured a papal audience through a clever *ruse*). **Stratagem** implies a ruse used to entrap, outwit, circumvent, or surprise an opponent or enemy (a series of *stratagems* that convinced both sides he was their agent). **Maneuver** suggests adroit and skillful avoidance of difficulty (a bold *maneuver* that won him the nomination). **Artifice** implies ingenious contrivance or invention (his fawning smile was just an *artifice*). **Wile** suggests an attempt to entrap or deceive with false allurements (used all of his *wiles* to win his uncle's favor). **Feint** implies a diversion or distraction of attention away from one's real intent (ballcarriers use *feints* to draw defensemen out of position).

trick *vb* see DUPE

trickery see DECEPTION

tricky see SLY

trifle, toy, dally, flirt, coquet mean to deal with or act toward without serious purpose. **Trifle** may imply playfulness, unconcern, indulgent contempt (*trifled* with her boyfriend's feelings). **Toy** implies acting without full attention or serious exertion of one's powers (*toying* with the idea of taking a cruise). **Dally** suggests indulging in thoughts or plans merely as an amusement (likes to *dally* with the idea of writing a book someday). **Flirt** implies an interest or attention that soon passes to another object (*flirted* with one college major after another). **Coquet** implies attracting interest or admiration without serious intention (brazenly *coquetted* with the husbands of her friends).

trite, hackneyed, stereotyped, threadbare mean lacking the freshness that evokes attention or interest. **Trite** applies to a once effective phrase or idea spoiled from long familiarity ("you win some, you lose some" is a *trite* expression). **Hackneyed** stresses being worn out by overuse so as to become dull and meaningless (all of the metaphors and images in the poem are *hackneyed*). **Stereotyped** implies falling invariably into the same pattern or form (views of American Indians that are *stereotyped* and out-of-date). **Threadbare** applies to what has been used until its possibilities of interest have been totally exhausted (a mystery novel with a *threadbare* plot).

trouble see EFFORT

truckle see FAWN

truth, veracity, verity, verisimilitude mean the quality of keeping close to fact or reality. **Truth** may apply to an ideal abstraction conforming to a universal or generalized reality or it may represent a quality of statements, acts, or feelings of adhering to reality and avoiding error or falsehood (swore to the *truth* of the statement he had made). **Veracity** implies rigid and unfailing observance of truth (a politician not known for his *veracity*). **Verity** refers to things of lasting, ultimate, or transcendent value (a teacher still believing in the old *verities* of school pride and loyalty). **Verisimilitude** implies the quality of an artistic or literary representation that causes one to accept it as true to life or to human experience (a novel about contemporary marriage that was praised for its *verisimilitude*).

try see AFFLICT, ATTEMPT

tug see PULL

tumult see COMMOTION

turmoil see COMMOTION

turn see CURVE

twist see CURVE

twit see RIDICULE

type, kind, sort, nature, description, character mean a number of individuals thought of as a group because of a common quality or qualities. **Type** may suggest strong and clearly marked similarity throughout the items included so that each is typical of the group (one of three basic body *types*). **Kind** may suggest natural grouping (a zoo with animals of every *kind*). **Sort** often suggests some disparagement (the *sort* of newspaper dealing in sensational stories). **Nature** may imply inherent, essential resemblance rather than obvious or superficial likenesses (two problems of a similar *nature*). **Description** implies a group marked by agreement in all details belonging to a type as described or defined (not all individuals of that *description* are truly psychotic). **Character** implies a group marked by distinctive likenesses peculiar to the type (a society with little of the *character* of an advanced culture).

typical see REGULAR

tyrannical see ABSOLUTE

tyro see AMATEUR

U

ubiquitous see OMNIPRESENT

ultimate see LAST

umbrage see OFFENSE

unbecoming see INDECOROUS

unbiased see FAIR

uncalled-for see SUPEREROGATORY

uncanny see WEIRD

uncertainty, doubt, dubiety, skepticism, suspicion, mistrust mean lack of sureness about someone or something. **Uncertainty** may range from a falling short of certainty to an almost complete lack of definite knowledge esp. about an outcome or result (general *uncertainty* about the program's future). **Doubt** suggests both uncertainty and inability to make a decision (plagued by *doubts* about his upcoming marriage). **Dubiety** stresses a wavering between conclusions (in times of crisis a leader must be free of all *dubiety*). **Skepticism** implies unwillingness to believe without conclusive evidence (an economic forecast that was met with *skepticism*). **Suspicion** stresses lack of faith in the truth, reality, fairness, or reliability of something or someone (viewed the new neighbors with *suspicion*). **Mistrust** implies a genuine doubt based upon suspicion (had a great *mistrust* of all doctors).

uncommon see INFREQUENT

unconcerned see INDIFFERENT

unctuous see FULSOME

underhanded see SECRET

undermine see WEAKEN

understand, comprehend, appreciate mean to have a clear or complete idea of. **Understand** may differ from **comprehend** in implying a result whereas *comprehend* stresses the mental process of arriving at a result (*understood* the instructions without *comprehending* their purpose). **Appreciate** implies a just estimation of a thing's value (failed to *appreciate* the risks involved).

undulate see SWING

unearth see DISCOVER

unerring see INFALLIBLE

uneven see ROUGH

unfeigned see SINCERE

unflagging see INDEFATIGABLE

ungovernable see UNRULY

union see UNITY

unique see SINGLE, STRANGE

unite see JOIN

unity, solidarity, integrity, union mean the quality of a whole made up of closely associated parts. **Unity** implies oneness esp. of what is varied and diverse in its elements or parts (a multiplicity of styles effectively combined into a *unity* of architectural design). **Solidarity** implies a unity in a group or class that enables it to manifest its strength and exert its influence as one (an ethnic minority with a strong sense of *solidarity*). **Integrity** implies unity that indicates interdependence of the parts and completeness and perfection of the whole (a farcical scene that destroys the play's *integrity*). **Union** implies a thorough integration and harmonious cooperation of the parts (the *union* of 13 diverse colonies into one nation).

universal, general, generic mean of or relating to all or the whole. **Universal** implies reference to every one without exception in the class, category, or genus considered; **general** implies reference to all or nearly all (the theory has met *general* but not *universal* acceptance). **Generic** implies reference to every member of a genus (*generic* likenesses among all dogs).

unlearned see IGNORANT

unlettered see IGNORANT

unman see UNNERVE

unmindful see FORGETFUL

unnatural see IRREGULAR

unnerve, enervate, unman, emasculate mean to deprive of strength or vigor and the capacity for effective action. **Unnerve** implies marked often temporary loss of courage, self-control, or power to act (*unnerved* by the near midair collision). **Enervate** suggests a gradual physical or moral weakening (as through luxury or indolence) until one is too feeble to make an effort (totally *enervated* after a week's vacation). **Unman** implies a loss of manly vigor, fortitude, or spirit (the sight of blood usually *unmanned* him). **Emasculate** stresses a depriving of characteristic force by removing something essential (an amendment that *emasculates* existing gun-control laws).

unpremeditated see EXTEMPORANEOUS

unruffled see COOL

unruly, ungovernable, intractable, refractory, recalcitrant, willful, headstrong mean not submissive to government or control. **Unruly** implies lack of dis-

cipline or incapacity for discipline and often connotes waywardness or turbulence of behavior (*unruly* children). **Ungovernable** implies either an escape from control or guidance or a state of being unsubdued and incapable of controlling oneself or being controlled by others (*ungovernable* rage). **Intractable** suggests stubborn resistance to guidance or control (the farmers were *intractable* in their opposition to the hazardous-waste dump). **Refractory** stresses resistance to attempts to manage or to mold (special schools for *refractory* children). **Recalcitrant** suggests determined resistance to or defiance of authority (acts of sabotage by a *recalcitrant* populace). **Willful** implies an obstinate determination to have one's own way (a *willful* disregard for the rights of others). **Headstrong** suggests self-will impatient of restraint, advice, or suggestion (a *headstrong* young cavalry officer).

unseemly see INDECOROUS

unsophisticated see NATURAL

unstable see INCONSTANT

untangle see EXTRICATE

untiring see INDEFATIGABLE

untruthful see DISHONEST

untutored see IGNORANT

unwearied see INDEFATIGABLE

upbraid see SCOLD

upheaval see COMMOTION

uphold see SUPPORT

upright, honest, just, conscientious, scrupulous, honorable mean having or showing a strict regard for what is morally right. **Upright** implies a strict adherence to moral principles (ministers of the church must be *upright* and unimpeachable). **Honest** stresses adherence to such virtues as truthfulness, candor, fairness (doctors must be *honest* with the terminally ill). **Just** stresses conscious choice and regular practice of what is right or equitable (a reputation for being entirely *just* in business dealings). **Conscientious** and **scrupulous** imply an active moral sense governing all one's actions and painstaking efforts to follow one's conscience (*conscientious* in doing all of her chores) (*scrupulous* in carrying out the terms of the will). **Honorable** suggests a firm holding to codes of right behavior and the guidance of a high sense of honor and duty (the *honorable* thing would be to resign my position).

uprising see REBELLION

uproot see EXTERMINATE

upset see DISCOMPOSE

urbane see SUAVE

usage see HABIT

use, employ, utilize mean to put into service esp. to attain an end. **Use** implies availing oneself of something as a means or instrument to an end (willing to *use* any means to achieve her ends). **Employ** suggests the use of a person or thing that is available but idle, inactive, or disengaged (your time might have been better *employed* by reading). **Utilize** may suggest the discovery of a new, profitable, or practical use for something (meat processors *utilize* every part of the animal).

usual, customary, habitual, wonted, accustomed mean familiar through frequent or regular repetition. **Usual** stresses the absence of strangeness or unexpectedness (my *usual* order for lunch). **Customary** applies to what accords with the practices, conventions, or usages of an individual or community (a *customary* waiting period before remarrying). **habitual** suggests a practice settled or established by much repetition (an *habitual* exercise regime that served her well). **Wonted** stresses habituation but usu. applies to what is favored, sought, or purposefully cultivated (his *wonted* pleasures had lost their appeal). **Accustomed**

is less emphatic than *wonted* or *habitual* in suggesting fixed habit or invariable custom (accepted the compliment with her *accustomed* modesty).

usurp see APPROPRIATE
utensil see IMPLEMENT
utilize see USE
utter see EXPRESS

V

vacant see EMPTY
vacillate see HESITATE
vacuous see EMPTY
vagary see CAPRICE
vague see OBSCURE
vain, nugatory, otiose, idle, empty, hollow mean being without worth or significance. **Vain** implies either absolute or relative absence of value (it is *vain* to think that we can alter destiny). **Nugatory** suggests triviality or insignificance (a monarch with *nugatory* powers). **Otiose** suggests that something serves no purpose and is either an encumbrance or a superfluity (not a single scene in the film is *otiose*). **Idle** suggests being incapable of worthwhile use or effect (it is *idle* to speculate on what might have been). **Empty** and **hollow** suggest a deceiving lack of real substance or soundness or genuineness (an *empty* attempt at reconciliation) (a *hollow* victory that benefited no one). See in addition FUTILE.
valid, sound, cogent, convincing, telling mean having such force as to compel serious attention and usu. acceptance. **Valid** implies being supported by objective truth or generally accepted authority (absences will be excused for *valid* reasons). **Sound** implies a basis of flawless reasoning or of solid grounds (a *sound* proposal for combatting terrorism). **Cogent** may stress either weight of sound argument and evidence or lucidity of presentation (the prosecutor's *cogent* summation won over the jury). **Convincing** suggests a power to overcome doubt, opposition, or reluctance to accept (a documentary that makes a *convincing* case for court reform). **Telling** stresses an immediate and crucial effect striking at the heart of a matter (a *telling* example of the bureaucratic mentality).
validate see CONFIRM
valor see HEROISM
valuable see COSTLY
value see APPRECIATE, ESTIMATE
vanquish see CONQUER
vapid see INSIPID
variance see DISCORD
various see DIFFERENT
vary see CHANGE
vast see ENORMOUS
vaunt see BOAST
veer see SWERVE
venerable see OLD
venerate see REVERE
vent see EXPRESS
venturesome see ADVENTUROUS
veracity see TRUTH
verbose see WORDY
verge see BORDER
verify see CONFIRM
verisimilitude see TRUTH
veritable see AUTHENTIC
verity see TRUTH
vernacular see DIALECT
vertical, perpendicular, plumb mean being at right angles to a base line. **Vertical** suggests a line or direction rising straight upward toward a zenith (the side of the cliff is almost *vertical*). **Perpendicular** may

stress the straightness of a line making a right angle with any other line, not necessarily a horizontal one (the parallel bars are *perpendicular* to the support posts). **Plumb** stresses an exact verticality determined (as with a plumb line) by earth's gravity (make sure that the wall is *plumb*).

very see SAME
vestige see TRACE
vex see ANNOY
vibrate see SWING
vice see FAULT, OFFENSE
vicious, villainous, iniquitous, nefarious, corrupt, degenerate mean highly reprehensible or offensive in character, nature, or conduct. **Vicious** may directly oppose *virtuous* in implying moral depravity, or may connote malignancy, cruelty, or destructive violence (a *vicious* gangster wanted for murder). **Villainous** applies to any evil, depraved, or vile conduct or characteristic (*villainous* behavior that must be punished). **Iniquitous** implies absence of all signs of justice or fairness (an *iniquitous* tyrant, ruling by fear and intimidation). **Nefarious** suggests flagrant breaching of time-honored laws and traditions of conduct (pornography, prostitution, and organized crime's other *nefarious* activities). **Corrupt** stresses a loss of moral integrity or probity causing betrayal of principle or sworn obligations (city hall was filled with *corrupt* politicians). **Degenerate** suggests having sunk to an esp. vicious or enervated condition (a *degenerate* regime propped up by foreign support).
view see OPINION
vigilant see WATCHFUL
vigorous, energetic, strenuous, lusty, nervous mean having great vitality and force. **Vigorous** further implies showing no signs of depletion or diminishing of freshness or robustness (still *vigorous* and sharp in her seventieth year). **Energetic** suggests a capacity for intense activity (an *energetic* wife, mother, and career woman). **Strenuous** suggests a preference for coping with the arduous or the challenging (moved to Alaska in search of the *strenuous* life). **Lusty** implies exuberant energy and capacity for enjoyment (a huge meal to satisfy the men's *lusty* appetites). **Nervous** suggests esp. the forcibleness and sustained effectiveness resulting from mental vigor (a *nervous* energy informs his sculptures).
vile see BASE
vilify see MALIGN
villainous see VICIOUS
vindicate see EXCULPATE, MAINTAIN
violation see BREACH
virtuous see MORAL
visage see FACE
visionary see IMAGINARY
vital see ESSENTIAL, LIVING
vitiate see DEBASE
vituperate see SCOLD
vituperation see ABUSE
vivacious see LIVELY
vivid see GRAPHIC
vivify see QUICKEN
vociferous, clamorous, blatant, strident, boisterous, obstreperous mean so loud or insistent as to compel attention. **Vociferous** implies a vehement deafening shouting or calling out (*vociferous* cries of protest and outrage). **Clamorous** may imply insistency as well as vociferousness in demanding or protesting (*clamorous* demands for prison reforms). **Blatant** implies an offensive bellowing or insensitive loudness (a *blatant* and abusive drunkard). **Strident** suggests harsh and discordant noise (heard the *strident* cry of the crow). **Boisterous** suggests a noisiness and turbulence due to high spirits (a *boisterous* crowd of partygoers). **Obstreperous** suggests unruly and aggressive

noisiness and resistance to restraint (the *obstreperous* demonstrators were removed from the hall).

vogue see FASHION

voice see EXPRESS

void see EMPTY

volatility see LIGHTNESS

voluble see TALKATIVE

volume see BULK

voluntary, intentional, deliberate, willing mean done or brought about of one's own will. **Voluntary** implies freedom and spontaneity of choice or action without external compulsion (*voluntary* enlistment in the armed services). **Intentional** stresses an awareness of an end to be achieved (the *intentional* concealment of vital information). **Deliberate** implies full consciousness of the nature of one's act and its consequences (the *deliberate* sabotaging of a nuclear power plant). **Willing** implies a readiness and eagerness to accede to or anticipate the wishes of another (a *willing* accomplice in a bank robbery).

voluptuous see SENSUOUS

voracious, gluttonous, ravenous, rapacious mean excessively greedy. **Voracious** applies esp. to habitual gorging with food or drink (teenagers are often *voracious* eaters). **Gluttonous** applies to one who delights in eating or acquiring things esp. beyond the point of necessity or satiety (an admiral who was *gluttonous* for glory). **Ravenous** implies excessive hunger and suggests violent or grasping methods of dealing with food or with whatever satisfies an appetite (football practice usu. gives them *ravenous* appetites). **Rapacious** often suggests excessive and utterly selfish acquisitiveness or avarice (*rapacious* land developers indifferent to the ruination of the environment).

vouch see CERTIFY

vouchsafe see GRANT

vulgar see COARSE, COMMON

W

waive see RELINQUISH

wander, roam, ramble, rove, traipse, meander mean to move about more or less aimlessly. **Wander** implies an absence of or an indifference to a fixed course (found her *wandering* about the square). **Roam** suggests wandering about freely and often far afield (liked to *roam* through the woods). **Ramble** stresses carelessness and indifference to one's course or objective (the speaker *rambled* on without ever coming to the point). **Rove** suggests vigorous and sometimes purposeful roaming (armed brigands *roved* over the countryside). **Traipse** implies an erratic if purposeful course (*traipsed* all over town looking for the right dress). **Meander** implies a winding or intricate course suggestive of aimless or listless wandering (the river *meanders* for miles through rich farmland).

wane see ABATE

want *vb* see DESIRE

want *n* see POVERTY

wanton see SUPEREROGATORY

ward off see PREVENT

warp see DEFORM

wary see CAUTIOUS

waste see RAVAGE

watchful, vigilant, wide-awake, alert mean being on the lookout esp. for danger or opportunity. **Watchful** is the least explicit term (played under the *watchful* eyes of their mothers). **Vigilant** suggests intense, unremitting, wary watchfulness (*vigilant* taxpayers forestalled all attempts to raise taxes). **Wide-awake** applies to watchfulness for opportunities and developments more often than dangers (*wide-awake* observers will recall other summit meetings). **Alert** stresses readiness or promptness in meeting danger or in seizing opportunity (*alert* traders anticipated the stock market's slide).

wave see SWING

waver see HESITATE, SWING

way see METHOD

wayward see CONTRARY

weak, feeble, frail, fragile, infirm, decrepit mean not strong enough to endure strain, pressure, or strenuous effort. **Weak** applies to deficiency or inferiority in strength or power of any sort (a *weak* government likely to topple soon). **Feeble** suggests extreme weakness inviting pity or contempt (a *feeble* attempt to resist the enemy attack). **Frail** implies delicacy and slightness of constitution or structure (a once-robust man now *frail* with disease). **Fragile** suggest frailty and brittleness unable to resist rough usage (a *fragile* beauty that the camera cannot convey). **Infirm** suggests instability, unsoundness, and insecurity due to old age or crippling illness (an *infirm* old woman confined to her home). **Decrepit** implies being worn-out or broken-down from long use or old age (the *decrepit* butler had been with the family for years).

weaken, enfeeble, debilitate, undermine, sap, cripple, disable mean to lose or cause to lose strength or vigor. **Weaken** may imply loss of physical strength, health, soundness, or stability or of quality, intensity, or effective power (a disease that *weakens* the body's defenses against infection). **Enfeeble** implies an obvious and pitiable condition of weakness and helplessness (so *enfeebled* by arthritis that he requires constant care). **Debilitate** suggests a less marked or more temporary impairment of strength or vitality (the operation has a temporary *debilitating* effect). **Undermine** and **sap** suggest a weakening by something working surreptitiously and insidiously (a poor diet *undermines* your health) (drugs had *sapped* his ability to think). **Cripple** implies causing a serious loss of functioning power through damaging or removing an essential part or element (inflation had *crippled* the economy). **Disable** suggests a usu. sudden crippling or enfeebling (*disabled* soldiers received an immediate discharge).

wealthy see RICH

wean see ESTRANGE

weary see TIRE

weigh see CONSIDER

weight see IMPORTANCE, INFLUENCE

weighty see HEAVY

weird, eerie, uncanny mean mysteriously strange or fantastic. **Weird** may imply an unearthly or supernatural strangeness or it may stress queerness or oddness (*weird* creatures from another world). **Eerie** suggests an uneasy or fearful consciousness that mysterious and malign powers are at work (an *eerie* calm preceded the bombing raid). **Uncanny** implies disquieting strangeness or mysteriousness (bore an *uncanny* resemblance to his dead wife).

well see HEALTHY

wet, damp, dank, moist, humid mean covered or more or less soaked with liquid. **Wet** usu. implies saturation but may suggest a covering of a surface with water or something (as paint) not yet dry (slipped on the *wet* pavement). **Damp** implies a slight or moderate absorption and often connotes an unpleasant degree of moisture (clothes will mildew if stored in a *damp* place). **Dank** implies a more distinctly disagreeable or unwholesome dampness (a prisoner in a cold, *dank* cell). **Moist** applies to what is slightly damp or not felt as dry (treat the injury with *moist* heat). **Humid** applies to the presence of much water vapor in the air (the hot, *humid* conditions brought on heatstroke).

wheedle see COAX

whim see CAPRICE

whole, entire, total, all mean including everything or everyone without exception. **Whole** implies that nothing has been omitted, ignored, abated, or taken away ⟨read the *whole* book⟩. **Entire** may suggest a state of completeness or perfection to which nothing can be added ⟨the *entire* population was wiped out⟩. **Total** implies that everything has been counted, weighed, measured, or considered ⟨the *total* number of people present⟩. **All** may equal *whole, entire,* or *total* ⟨*all* their money went to pay the rent⟩. See in addition PERFECT.

wholehearted see SINCERE

wholesome see HEALTHFUL, HEALTHY

wicked see BAD

wide see BROAD

wide-awake see WATCHFUL

wield see HANDLE

wile see TRICK

willful see UNRULY

willing see VOLUNTARY

win see GET

wince see RECOIL

wisdom see SENSE

wise, sage, sapient, judicious, prudent, sensible, sane mean having or showing sound judgment. **Wise** suggests great understanding of people and of situations and unusual discernment and judgment in dealing with them ⟨*wise* enough to know what really mattered in life⟩. **Sage** suggests wide experience, great learning, and wisdom ⟨sought the *sage* advice of her father in times of crisis⟩. **Sapient** suggests great sagacity and discernment ⟨the *sapient* observations of a veteran foreign correspondent⟩. **Judicious** stresses a capacity for reaching wise decisions or just conclusions ⟨*judicious* parents using kindness and discipline in equal measure⟩. **Prudent** suggests exercise of the restraint of sound practical wisdom and discretion ⟨a *prudent* decision to wait out the storm⟩. **Sensible** applies to action guided and restrained by good sense and rationality ⟨a *sensible* woman who was not fooled by flattery⟩. **Sane** stresses mental soundness, rationality, and levelheadedness ⟨remained *sane* even as the war raged around him⟩.

wisecrack see JEST

wish see DESIRE

wit, humor, irony, sarcasm, satire, repartee mean a mode of expression intended to arouse amusement. **Wit** suggests the power to evoke laughter by remarks showing verbal felicity or ingenuity and swift perception esp. of the incongruous ⟨appreciate the *wit* of Wilde and Shaw⟩. **Humor** implies an ability to perceive the ludicrous, the comical, and the absurd in human life and to express these usu. without bitterness ⟨a person with a finely honed sense of *humor*⟩. **Irony** applies to a manner of expression in which the intended meaning is the opposite of what is seemingly expressed ⟨with wry *irony,* he said to the priest, "Thank God I'm an atheist!"⟩. **Sarcasm** applies to expression frequently in the form of irony that is intended to cut or wound ⟨a cynic much given to heartless *sarcasm*⟩. **Satire** applies to writing that exposes or ridicules conduct, doctrines, or institutions either by direct criticism or more often through irony, parody, or caricature ⟨the play is a *satire* on contemporary living arrangements⟩. **Repartee** implies the power of answering quickly, pointedly, or wittily ⟨a partygoer well known for razor-sharp *repartee*⟩.

withhold see KEEP

withstand see OPPOSE

witness see CERTIFY

witticism see JEST

witty, humorous, facetious, jocular, jocose mean provoking or intended to provoke laughter. **Witty** suggests cleverness and quickness of mind and often a caustic tongue ⟨a film critic remembered for his *witty* reviews⟩. **Humorous** applies broadly to anything that evokes usu. genial laughter and may contrast with *witty* in suggesting whimsicality or eccentricity ⟨laced her lectures with *humorous* anecdotes⟩. **Facetious** stresses a desire to produce laughter and may be derogatory in implying dubious or ill-timed attempts at wit or humor ⟨*facetious* comments that were unappreciated at the funeral⟩. **Jocular** implies a usu. habitual fondness for jesting and joking ⟨a *jocular* fellow whose humor often brightened spirits⟩. **Jocose** is somewhat less derogatory than *facetious* in suggesting habitual waggishness or playfulness ⟨the dim-witted took his *jocose* proposals seriously⟩.

woe see SORROW

woebegone see DOWNCAST

wont see HABIT

wonted see USUAL

wordy, verbose, prolix, diffuse mean using more words than necessary to express thought. **Wordy** may also imply loquaciousness or garrulity ⟨a *wordy* speech that said nothing⟩. **Verbose** suggests a resulting dullness, obscurity, or lack of incisiveness or precision ⟨*verbose* position papers that no one reads⟩. **Prolix** suggests unreasonable and tedious dwelling on details ⟨habitually transformed brief anecdotes into *prolix* sagas⟩. **Diffuse** stresses lack of compactness and pointedness of style ⟨*diffuse* memoirs that are so many shaggy-dog stories⟩.

work *n* Work, labor, travail, toil, drudgery, grind mean activity involving effort or exertion. **Work** may imply activity of body, of mind, of a machine, or of a natural force ⟨too tired to do any *work*⟩. **Labor** applies to physical or intellectual work involving great and often strenuous exertion ⟨believes that farmers are poorly paid for their *labor*⟩. **Travail** is bookish for labor involving pain or suffering ⟨years of *travail* were lost when the building burned⟩. **Toil** implies prolonged and fatiguing labor ⟨his lot would be years of back-breaking *toil*⟩. **Drudgery** suggests dull and irksome labor ⟨a job with a good deal of *drudgery*⟩. **Grind** implies labor exhausting to mind or body ⟨the *grind* of performing the play eight times a week⟩.

work *n* Work, employment, occupation, calling, pursuit, métier, business mean a specific sustained activity engaged in esp. in earning one's living. **Work** may apply to any purposeful activity whether remunerative or not ⟨her *work* as a hospital volunteer⟩. **Employment** implies work for which one has been engaged and is being paid by an employer ⟨*employment* will be terminated in cases of chronic tardiness⟩. **Occupation** implies work in which one engages regularly esp. as a result of training ⟨his *occupation* as a trained auto mechanic⟩. **Calling** applies to an occupation viewed as a vocation or profession ⟨I feel the ministry is my true *calling*⟩. **Pursuit** suggests a trade, profession, or avocation followed with zeal or steady interest ⟨her family considered medicine the only proper *pursuit*⟩. **Métier** implies a calling or pursuit for which one believes oneself to be esp. fitted ⟨from childhood I considered acting my *métier*⟩. **Business** suggests activity in commerce or the management of money and affairs ⟨the *business* of managing a hotel⟩.

worldly see EARTHLY

worldly-wise see SOPHISTICATED

worry *vb* Worry, annoy, harass, harry, plague, pester, tease mean to disturb or irritate by persistent acts. **Worry** implies an incessant goading or attacking that drives one to desperation ⟨pursued a policy of *worrying* the enemy⟩. **Annoy** implies disturbing one's composure or peace of mind by intrusion, interference, or petty attacks ⟨you're doing that just to *annoy* me⟩. **Harass** implies petty persecutions or burdensome de-

mands that exhaust one's nervous or mental power
⟨*harassed* on all sides by creditors⟩. **Harry** may imply
heavy oppression or maltreatment ⟨*harried* mothers
trying to cope with small children⟩. **Plague** implies a
painful and persistent affliction ⟨*plagued* all her life
by poverty⟩. **Pester** stresses the repetition of petty attacks ⟨the bureau was constantly *pestered* with trivial
complaints⟩. **Tease** suggests an attempt to break down
one's resistance or rouse to wrath ⟨malicious children *teased* the dog⟩.

worry *n* see CARE

worship see REVERE

wrangle see QUARREL

wrath see ANGER

wrong *vb* Wrong, oppress, persecute, aggrieve mean to
injure unjustly or outrageously. **Wrong** implies inflicting injury either unmerited or out of proportion
to what one deserves ⟨a penal system that had
wronged him⟩. **Oppress** suggests inhumane imposing
of burdens one cannot endure or exacting more than
one can perform ⟨a people *oppressed* by a warmon-
gering tyrant⟩. **Persecute** implies a relentless and unremitting subjection to annoyance or suffering ⟨a boy
with a clubfoot *persecuted* by his playmates⟩. **Aggrieve** implies suffering caused by an infringement or
denial of rights ⟨a legal aid society representing *ag-
grieved* minority groups⟩.

wrong *n* see INJUSTICE

Y

yardstick see STANDARD

yearn see LONG

yield, submit, capitulate, succumb, relent, defer mean to
give way to someone or something that one can no
longer resist. **Yield** may apply to any sort or degree of
giving way before force, argument, persuasion, or entreaty ⟨*yields* too easily in any argument⟩. **Submit** suggests full surrendering after resistance or conflict to
the will or control of another ⟨voluntarily *submitted*
to an inspection of the premises⟩. **Capitulate** stresses
the fact of ending all resistance and may imply either
a coming to terms (as with an adversary) or hopelessness in the face of an irresistible opposing force ⟨the
college president *capitulated* to the protesters' de-
mands⟩. **Succumb** implies weakness and helplessness
to the one that gives way or an overwhelming power
to the opposing force ⟨a stage actor *succumbing* to
the lure of Hollywood⟩. **Relent** implies a yielding
through pity or mercy by one who holds the upper
hand ⟨finally *relented* and let the children stay up
late⟩. **Defer** implies a voluntary yielding or submitting
out of respect or reverence for or deference and affection toward another ⟨I *defer* to your superior expertise in these matters⟩. See in addition RELINQUISH.

Z

zeal see PASSION

Webster's Style Manual

This section is a concise guide to the basic conventions of English in its written form. Writers and editors generally use the word *style* to refer to these conventions, which includes such matters as punctuating sentences, capitalizing names and terms, using italics or underlining, and deciding when to use abbreviations and numerals.

This guide offers information and advice across this entire range of topics as well as information about writing and styling bibliographical references. The guide offers concise and comprehensive descriptions of the rules and conventions writers and editors have developed for themselves to help them prepare clear and consistent copy. Because different correct styles often coexist, this guide often offers choices rather than a single rule.

There are, of course, limits to the range of acceptable style available to writers. Within that range, most writers and editors try to be consistent in the choices they make. This guide offers information about both the consensus and the variety that are apparent in standard American style.

The consensus is presented with simple descriptive statements, such as "A period terminates a sentence or a sentence fragment that is neither interrogative nor exclamatory." In some cases, these statements are qualified, as in "The abbreviations A.D. and B.C. are usually styled in typeset matter as punctuated, unspaced, small capitals. . . ." The term *usually* is used throughout this guide to indicate that some writers and editors follow a different styling practice from the one described. However, *usually* appears only in statements describing a styling practice that is clearly the prevalent practice. Hence, the writer who prefers AD or AD knows that he or she is departing from the prevalent practice but that such departures are not unprecedented in standard style.

In indicating styling practices that are clearly not prevalent, we have used the word *sometimes* to qualify the descriptive statement, as in "Commas are sometimes used to separate main clauses that are not joined by conjunctions." In most cases, a descriptive statement qualified with *sometimes* is also accompanied by an additional explanation that tells the reader under what circumstances the styling is most likely to occur and what the common alternatives to this styling are. In the example just cited, the reader is told that this styling is likely to be used if the main clauses are short and feature obvious parallelism. The reader is also told that using a comma to join clauses that are not short or obviously parallel is usually considered an error, that most writers avoid it, and that clauses not joined by conjunctions are usually separated by a semicolon.

The qualifiers *often* and *frequently* are used throughout this guide to suggest that the styling is acceptable but not universally followed. For example, "a comma is often used to set off the word *Incorporated* or the abbreviation *Inc.* form the rest of the corporate name; however, many companies elect to omit this comma from their name." This guide is showing that both practices are so well established within standard style that their relative frequency is fundamentally irrelevant.

Finally, some styling practices raise questions demanding explanations that go beyond the use of a simple qualifier. In these cases, a note is appended to the description. Notes are introduced by the all-capitalized designation "NOTE." These serve to explain, in as much detail as needed, variations, exceptions, and fine points that relate to or qualify the descriptive statement that precedes them.

CHAPTER I

Punctuation

Punctuation marks are used in the English writing system to help clarify the structure and meaning of sentences. To some degree, they achieve this end by corresponding to certain elements of the spoken language, such as pitch, volume, pause, and stress. To an even greater degree, however, punctuation marks serve to clarify structure and meaning by virtue of the fact that they conventionally accompany certain grammatical elements in a sentence, no matter how those elements might be spoken. In many cases, the relationship between punctuation and grammatical structure is such that the choice of which mark of punctuation to use in a sentence is clear and unambiguous. In other cases, however, the structure of a sentence may be such that it allows for several patterns of punctuation. In cases like these, varying notions of correctness have grown up, and two writers might, with equal correctness and with equal clarity, punctuate the same sentence quite differently.

This chapter is designed to help writers and editors make decisions about which mark of punctuation to use. In situations where more than one pattern of punctuation may be used, each is explained; if there are reasons to prefer one over another, the reasons are presented. However, even after having read this chapter, writers and editors will find that they still encounter questions requiring them to exercise their judgment and taste.

The descriptions in this chapter focus on the ways in which punctuation marks are used to convey grammatical structure. The chapter does not explain in any detailed way the use of some punctuation marks to style individual words and compounds. Specifically, this chapter does not discuss the use of quotation marks to style titles and other kinds of proper nouns, the use of apostrophes to form plurals and possessives, the use of hyphens to form compounds, or the use of periods to punctuate abbreviations. For a discussion of these topics, see Chapter 2, "Capitals, Italics, and Quotation Marks"; Chapter 3, "Plurals, Possessives, and Compounds"; and Chapter 4, "Abbreviations."

GENERAL PRINCIPLES

In addition to the rules that have been developed for individual marks of punctuation, there are also conventions and principles that apply to marks of punctuation in general, and these are explained in the paragraphs that follow.

OPEN AND CLOSE PUNCTUATION

Two terms frequently used to describe patterns of punctuation, especially in regard to commas, are *open* and *close*. An open punctuation pattern is one in which commas and other marks of punctuation are used sparingly, usually only to separate major syntactical units, such as main clauses, or to prevent misreading. A close punctuation pattern, on the other hand, makes liberal use of punctuation marks, often putting one wherever the grammatical structure of the sentence will allow it. Close punctuation is often considered old-fashioned, and open punctuation more modern; however, contemporary writing displays a wide range of practices in regard to commas, and some grammatical constructions are still punctuated in ways traditionally associated with close punctuation (see paragraphs 8 and 22 under Comma in this chapter).

MULTIPLE PUNCTUATION

The term *multiple punctuation* describes the use of two or more marks of punctuation following the same word in a sentence. A conventional rule says that multiple punctuation is to be avoided except in cases involving brackets, parentheses, quotation marks, and sometimes dashes. Unfortunately, it is not possible to formulate any simple general instructions that would allow writers and editors to apply this rule. This book addresses the question of multiple punctuation by including a section entitled "With Other Marks of Punctuation" at the end of the treatment of each mark of punctuation for which there is a specific convention regarding multiple punctuation.

BOLDFACE AND ITALIC PUNCTUATION

In general, marks of punctuation are set in the same typeface (lightface or boldface, italic or roman) as the word that precedes them, but most writers and editors allow themselves a number of exceptions to this rule. Brackets and parentheses are nearly always set in the font of the surrounding text, usually lightface roman, regardless of the text they enclose. Quotation marks are usually handled in the same manner; however, if the text they enclose is entirely in a contrasting typeface, they are set in a typeface to match. Some writers and editors base decisions regarding the typeface of exclamation points and question marks on the context in which they are used. If the exclamation point or question mark is clearly associated with the word or words that precede it, it is set in a matching typeface. If, on the other hand, it punctuates the sentence as a whole, it is set in the typeface of the sentence.

Summary: Recently completed surveys confirm the theory that . . .

You did *that!*

We were talking with the author of the book *Who Did That?*

Have you seen the latest issue of *Saturday Review?*

SPACING

The conventions regarding the amount of space that precedes or follows a mark of punctuation vary from mark to mark. In general, the usual spacing around each mark of punctuation should be clear from the example sentences included for each mark of punctuation. In cases where additional explanation is needed, it is included at the end of the discussion, often under the heading "Spacing."

AMPERSAND

An ampersand is typically written &, although it has other forms, as &, &, and &. The character represents the word *and*; its function is to replace the word when a shorter form is desirable. However, the ampersand is an acceptable substitute for *and* only in a few constructions.

1. The ampersand is used in the names of companies but not in the names of agencies that are part of the federal government.

> American Telephone & Telegraph Co.
> Gulf & Western Corporation
> Occupational Safety and Health Administration
> Securities and Exchange Commission

NOTE: In styling corporate names, writers and editors often try to reproduce the form of the name preferred by the company (taken from an annual report or company letterhead). However, this information may not be available and, even if it is available, following the different preferences of different companies can lead to apparent inconsistencies in the text. Publications that include very many corporate names usually choose one styling, usually the one with the ampersand, and use it in all corporate names that include *and*.

2. Ampersands are frequently used in abbreviations. Style varies regarding the spacing around the ampersand. Publications that make heavy use of abbreviations, such as business or technical publications, most often omit the spaces. In general-interest publications, both the spaced and the unspaced stylings are common.

> The R&D budget looks adequate for the next fiscal year.
>
> Apply for a loan at your bank or S & L.

3. The ampersand is often used in cases where a condensed text is necessary, as in tabular material. While bibliographies, indexes, and most other listings use *and*, some systems of parenthetical documentation do use the ampersand. For more on parenthetical documentation, see Chapter 6, "Notes and Bibliographies."

> (Carter, Good & Robertson 1984)

4. When an ampersand is used between the last two elements in a series, the comma is omitted.

> the law firm of Shilliday, Fraser & French

APOSTROPHE

1. The apostrophe is used to indicate the possessive case of nouns and indefinite pronouns. For details regarding this use, see the section on Possessives in Chapter 3, "Plurals, Possessives, and Compounds."

2. Apostrophes are sometimes used to form plurals of letters, numerals, abbreviations, symbols, and words referred to as words. For details regarding this use, see the section on Plurals, beginning on page 140 in Chapter 3, "Plurals, Possessives, and Compounds."

3. Apostrophes mark omissions in contractions made of two or more words that are pronounced as one word.

> didn't
> you're

> o'clock
> shouldn't've

4. The apostrophe is used to indicate that letters have been intentionally omitted from the spelling of a word in order to reproduce a perceived pronunciation or to give a highly informal flavor to a piece of writing.

> "Head back to N'Orleans," the man said.
>
> Get 'em while they're hot.
>
> dancin' till three

NOTE: Sometimes words are so consistently spelled with an apostrophe that the spelling with the apostrophe becomes an accepted variant.

> fo'c'sle for *forecastle*
> bos'n for *boatswain*
> rock 'n' roll for *rock and roll*

5. Apostrophes mark the omission of numerals.

> class of '86
> politics in the '80s

NOTE: Writers who use the apostrophe for styling the plurals of words expressed in numerals usually avoid the use of the apostrophe illustrated in the second example above. Either they omit the apostrophe that stands for the missing figures, or they spell the word out.

> 80's *or* eighties *but not* '80's

6. Apostrophes are used to produce the inflected forms of verbs that are made of numerals or individually pronounced letters. Hyphens are sometimes used for this purpose also.

> 86'ed our proposal
> OK'ing the manuscript
> TKO'd his opponent

7. An apostrophe is often used to add an *-er* ending to an abbreviation, especially if some confusion might result from its absence. Hyphens are sometimes used for this purpose also. If no confusion is likely, the apostrophe is usually omitted.

> 4-H'er
> AA'er
> CBer
> DXer

8. The use of apostrophes to form abbreviations (as *ass'n* for *association* or *sec'y* for *secretary*) is avoided in most formal writing.

BRACKETS

Brackets work like parentheses to set off inserted material, but their functions are more specialized. Several of their principal uses occur with quoted material, as illustrated below. For other aspects of styling quotations, see Quotation Marks, Double, and Quotation Marks, Single, in this chapter.

WITH EDITORIAL INSERTIONS

1. Brackets enclose editorial comments, corrections, clarifications, or other material inserted into a text, especially into quoted matter.

> "Remember, this was the first time since it became law that the Twenty-first Amendment [outlining procedures for the replacement of a dead

or incapacitated President or Vice President]
had been invoked.''

"But there's one thing to be said for it [his ap-
prenticeship with Samuels]: it started me thinking about architecture in a new way.''

He wrote, "I am just as cheerful as when you
was [sic] here.''

NOTE: While the text into which such editorial insertions are made is almost always quoted material, they
are sometimes also used in nonquoted material, particularly in cases where an editor wishes to add material
to an author's text without disturbing the author's
original wording.

Furthermore the Committee anticipates additional expenses in the coming fiscal year [Octo-
ber 1985–September 1986] and seeks revenues
to meet these expenses.

2. Brackets set off insertions that supply missing letters.

"If you can't persuade D[israeli], I'm sure no
one can.''

3. Brackets enclose insertions that take the place of
words or phrases that were used in the original version
of a quoted passage.

The report, entitled "A Decade of Progress,''
begins with a short message from President
Stevens in which she notes that "the loving portraits and revealing accounts of [this report] are
not intended to constitute a complete history of
the decade. . . . Rather [they] impart the flavor
of the events, developments, and achievements
of this vibrant period.''

4. Brackets enclose insertions that slightly alter the
form of a word used in an original text.

The magazine reported that thousands of the
country's children were "go[ing] to bed hungry
every night.''

5. Brackets are used to indicate that the capitalization
or typeface of the original passage has been altered in
some way.

As we point out on page 164, "The length of a
quotation usually determines whether it is run
into the text or set as a block quotation . . . .
[L]ength can be assessed in terms of number of
words, the number of typewritten or typeset
lines, or the number of sentences in the passage.''

They agreed with and were encouraged by her
next point: "In the past, many secretaries have
been placed in positions of responsibility *without being delegated enough authority to carry
out the responsibility.* [Italics added.] The current pressures affecting managers have caused
them to rethink the secretarial function and to
delegate more responsibility and authority to
their secretaries.''

NOTE: In situations in which meticulous handling of
original source material is required, a capital M in the
example given above would be placed in brackets to
indicate that it was not capitalized in the original
source.

They agreed with and were encouraged by her
next point: "[M]any secretaries have been
placed in positions of responsibility without be-

ing delegated enough authority to carry out the
responsibility.''

AS A MECHANICAL DEVICE

6. Brackets function as parentheses within parentheses.

The company was incinerating high concentrations of pollutants (such as polychlorinated bi-
phenyls [PCBs]) in a power boiler.

7. Brackets set off phonetic symbols or transcriptions.

[t] in British *duty*

8. Brackets are used in combination with parentheses
(and occasionally braces) to indicate units contained
within larger units in mathematical copy. They are also
used in chemical formulas.

$$x + 5(x + y)(2x - y)]$$
$$NH_4[Cr(NH_3)_2(SCN)_4] \cdot H_2O$$

WITH OTHER MARKS OF PUNCTUATION

9. No punctuation mark (other than a period after an
abbreviation) precedes bracketed material within a
sentence. If punctuation is required, the mark is
placed after the closing bracket.

The report stated, "If we fail to find additional
sources of supply [of oil and gas], our long-term
growth will be limited.''

10. When brackets enclose a complete sentence, the
required punctuation should be placed within the
brackets.

[A paw print photographed last month in the
Quabbin area has finally verified the cougar's
continued existence in the Northeast.]

NOTE: Unlike parentheses, brackets are rarely used to
enclose complete sentences within other sentences.

SPACING

11. No space is left between brackets and the material
they enclose or between brackets and any mark of
punctuation immediately following.

12. In typewritten material, two spaces precede an
opening bracket and follow a closing bracket when the
brackets enclose a complete sentence. In typeset material, one space is used.

We welcome the return of the cougar. [A
paw print photographed last month has
verified its existence locally.] Its
habitation in this area is a good sign
for the whole environment.

We welcome the return of the cougar. [A paw
print photographed last month has verified its
existence locally.] Its habitation in this area is a
good sign for the whole environment.

COLON

The colon is a mark of introduction. It indicates that
what follows it—whether a clause, a phrase, or even a
single word—is linked with some element that precedes it. Many uses of the colon are similar to those of
the dash. Like the dash, the colon gives special emphasis to whatever follows it; lengthy material introduced
by a colon is often further emphasized by indention.

(For information on the question of capitalizing the first word following a colon, see the section on Beginnings in Chapter 2, "Capitals, Italics, and Quotation Marks.")

WITH PHRASES AND CLAUSES

1. A colon introduces a clause or phrase that explains, illustrates, amplifies, or restates what has gone before.

> The sentence was poorly constructed: it lacked both unity and coherence.

> Throughout its history, the organization has combined a tradition of excellence with a dedication to human service: educating the young, caring for the elderly, assisting in community-development programs.

> Disk cartridges provide high-density storage capacity: up to 16 megabytes of information on some cartridges.

> Time was running out: a decision had to be made.

2. A colon directs attention to an appositive.

> The question is this: where will we get the money?

> He had only one pleasure: eating.

3. A colon is used to introduce a series. The introductory statement often includes a phrase such as *the following* or *as follows*.

> The conference was attended by representatives of five nations: England, France, Belgium, Spain, and Portugal.

> Anyone planning to participate should be prepared to do the following: hike five miles with a backpack, sleep on the ground without a tent, and paddle a canoe through rough water.

NOTE: Opinion varies regarding whether a colon should interrupt the grammatical continuity of a clause (as by coming between a verb and its objects). Although most style manuals and composition handbooks advise against this practice and recommend that a full independent clause precede the colon, the interrupting colon is common. It is especially likely to be used before a lengthy and complex list, in which case the colon serves to set the list distinctly apart from the normal flow of running text. With shorter or less complex lists, the colon is usually not used.

> Our programs to increase profitability include: continued modernization of our manufacturing facilities; consolidation of distribution terminals; discontinuation of unprofitable retail outlets; and reorganization of our personnel structure, along with across-the-board staff reductions.

> Our programs to increase profitability include plant modernization, improved distribution and retailing procedures, and staff reductions.

> Our programs to increase profitability include the following: continued modernization of our manufacturing facilities; consolidation of distribution terminals; discontinuation of unprofitable retail outlets; and reorganization of our personnel structure, along with across-the-board staff reductions.

4. A colon is used like a dash to introduce a summary statement following a series.

Physics, biology, sociology, anthropology: he discusses them all.

WITH QUOTATIONS

5. A colon introduces lengthy quoted material that is set off from the rest of a text by indentation but not by quotation marks.

> He took the title for his biography of Thoreau from a passage in *Walden*:
>
>> I long ago lost a hound, a bay horse, and a turtle-dove, and am still on their trail . . . . I have met one or two who had heard the hound, and the tramp of the horse, and even seen the dove disappear behind a cloud, and they seemed as anxious to recover them as if they had lost them themselves.
>
> However, the title *A Hound, a Bay Horse, and a Turtle-Dove* probably puzzled some readers.

6. A colon may be used before a quotation in running text, especially when (1) the quotation is lengthy, (2) the quotation is a formal statement or is being given special emphasis, or (3) the quotation is an appositive.

> Said Murdoch: "The key to the success of this project is good planning. We need to know precisely all of the steps that we will need to go through, what kind of staff we will require to accomplish each step, what the entire project will cost, and when we can expect completion."

> The inscription reads: "Here lies one whose name was writ in water."

> In response, he had this to say: "No one knows better than I do that changes will have to be made soon."

AS A MECHANICAL DEVICE

7. In transcriptions of dialogue, a colon follows the speaker's name.

> Robert: You still haven't heard from her?
> Michael: No, and I'm beginning to worry.

8. A colon follows a brief heading or introductory term.

> NOTE: The library will be closed on the 17th while repairs are being made to the heating system.

> 1977: New developments in microchip technology lead to less-expensive manufacturing.

9. A colon separates elements in page references, bibliographical and biblical citations, and fixed formulas used to express ratios and time.

> *Journal of the American Medical Association* 48:356

> Springfield, Mass.: Merriam-Webster Inc.

> John 4:10

> 8:30 a.m.

> a ratio of 3:5

10. A colon separates titles and subtitles (as of books).

> *The Tragic Dynasty: A History of the Romanovs*

11. A colon is used to join terms that are being contrasted or compared.

Seventeenth-century rhymes include *prayer* : *afar* and *brass* : *was* : *ass*.

12. A colon follows the salutation in formal correspondence.

> Dear General Smith:
> Dear Product Manager:
> Dear Mr. Jiménez:
> Ladies and Gentlemen:

13. A colon punctuates memorandum and government correspondence headings and subject lines in general business letters.

> TO:
> VIA:
> SUBJECT:
> REFERENCE:

14. A colon separates writer/dictator/typist initials in the identification lines of business letters.

> WAL:jml
> WAL:WEB:jml

15. A colon separates carbon-copy or blind carbon-copy abbreviations from the initials or names of copy recipients in business letters.

> cc:RWP
>   JES
> bcc:MWK
>   FCM

WITH OTHER MARKS OF PUNCTUATION

16. A colon is placed outside quotation marks and parentheses.

> There's only one thing wrong with "Harold's Indiscretion": it's not funny.
> I quote from the first edition of *Springtime in Savannah* (published in 1952):

SPACING

17. In typewritten material, two spaces follow a colon used in running text, bibliographical references, publication titles, and letter or memorandum headings. In typeset material, only one space follows.

> The answer is simple: don't go.
> SUBJECT: Project X
> New York: Macmillan, 1980.
> *Typewriting: A Guide*

18. When a colon is being used between two correlated terms (see paragraph 11), it is centered with equal spacing on each side.

> The stature apparent in the two sexes shows the same female : male proportions.

19. No space precedes or follows a colon when it is used between numerals.

> 9:30 a.m.
> ratio of 2:4

20. No space precedes or follows a colon in a business-letter identification line or in a carbon-copy notation that indicates a recipient designated by initials.

> FCM:hg
> cc:FCM

21. Two spaces follow a colon in a carbon-copy notation that indicates a recipient designated by a full name.

cc: Mr. Johnson

COMMA

The comma is the most frequently used punctuation mark in the English writing system. Its most common uses are to separate items in a series and to set off syntactical elements within sentences. Within these two broad categories, there are a great many specific uses to which commas can be put. This section explains the most common aspects of the comma, listed under the following headings.

> Between Main Clauses
> With Compound Predicates
> With Subordinate Clauses and Phrases
> With Appositives
> With Introductory and Interrupting Elements
> With Contrasting Expressions
> With Items in a Series
> With Compound Modifiers
> In Quotations, Questions, and Indirect Discourse
> With Omitted Words
> With Addresses, Dates, and Numbers
> With Names, Degrees, and Titles
> In Correspondence
> Other Uses
> With Other Marks of Punctuation

BETWEEN MAIN CLAUSES

1. A comma separates main clauses joined by a coordinating conjunction (as *and, but, or, nor,* and *for*). For use of commas with clauses joined by correlative conjunctions, see paragraph 24 below.

> She knew very little about him, and he volunteered nothing.
> We will not respond to any more questions on that topic this afternoon, nor will we respond to similar questions at any time in the future.
> His face showed disappointment, for he knew that he had failed.

NOTE: Some reference books still insist that *so* and *yet* are adverbs rather than conjunctions and that therefore they should be preceded by a semicolon when they join main clauses. However, our evidence indicates that the use of *so* and *yet* as conjunctions preceded by a comma is standard.

> The acoustics in this hall are good, so every note is clear.
> We have requested this information many times before, yet we have never gotten a satisfactory reply.

2. When one or both of the clauses are short or when they are closely related in meaning, the comma is often omitted.

> The sun was shining and the birds were singing.
> We didn't realize it at the time but the spot we had picked for our home was the same spot one of our ancestors had picked for his home.
> Six thousand years ago, the top of the volcano blew off in a series of powerful eruptions and the sides collapsed into the middle.
> Many people want to take their vacations in August so it may be difficult for some of them to find good accommodations.

NOTE: In punctuating sentences such as the ones illustrated above, writers have to use their own judgment regarding whether clauses are short enough or closely related enough to warrant omitting the comma. There are no clear-cut rules to follow; however, factors such as the rhythm, parallelism, or logic of the sentence often influence how clearly or smoothly it will read with or without the comma.

3. Commas are sometimes used to separate main clauses that are not joined by conjunctions. This styling is especially likely to be used if the clauses are short and feature obvious parallelism.

> One day you are a successful corporate lawyer, the next day you are out of work.

> The city has suffered terribly in the interim. Bombs have destroyed most of the buildings, disease has ravaged the population.

NOTE: Using a comma to join clauses that are neither short nor obviously parallel is usually called *comma fault* or *comma splice* and most writers and editors avoid such a construction. In general, clauses not joined by conjunctions are separated by semicolons.

4. If a sentence is composed of three or more clauses, the clauses may be separated by either commas or semicolons. Clauses that are short and relatively free of commas can be separated by commas even if they are not joined by a conjunction. If the clauses are long or heavily punctuated, they are separated with semicolons, except for the last two clauses which may be separated by either a comma or a semicolon. Usually a comma will be used between the last two clauses only if those clauses are joined by a conjunction. For more examples of clauses separated with commas and semicolons, see paragraph 5 under Semicolon in this chapter.

> The pace of change seems to have quickened, the economy is uncertain, the technology seems sometimes liberating and sometimes hostile.

> Small fish fed among the marsh weed, ducks paddled along the surface, and a muskrat ate greens along the bank.

> The policy is a complex one to explain; defending it against its critics is not easy, nor is it clear the defense is always necessary.

WITH COMPOUND PREDICATES

5. Commas are not usually used to separate the parts of a compound predicate.

> The firefighter tried to enter the burning building but was turned back by the thick smoke.

NOTE: Despite the fact that most style manuals and composition handbooks warn against separating the parts of compound predicates with commas, many authors and editors use commas in just this way. They are particularly likely to do so if the predicate is especially long and complicated, if they want to stress one part of the predicate, or if the absence of a comma could cause even a momentary misreading of the sentence.

> The board helps to develop the financing, new product planning, and marketing strategies for new corporate divisions, and issues periodic reports on expenditures, revenues, and personnel appointments.

> This is an unworkable plan, and has been from the start.

> I try to explain to him what I want him to do, and get nowhere.

WITH SUBORDINATE CLAUSES AND PHRASES

6. Adverbial clauses and phrases that precede a main clause are usually set off with commas.

> As cars age, they depreciate.

> Having made that decision, we turned our attention to other matters.

> To understand the situation, you must be familiar with the background.

> From the top of this rugged and isolated plateau, I could see the road stretching out for miles across the desert.

> In 1919, his family left Russia and moved to this country.

> In addition, staff members respond to queries, take new orders, and initiate billing.

7. If a sentence begins with an adverbial clause or phrase and can be easily read without a comma following it, writers will often omit the comma. In most cases where the comma is omitted, the phrase will be short—four words or less. But some writers will omit the comma even after a longer phrase if the sentence can be easily read or seems more forceful that way.

> In January the company will introduce a new line of entirely redesigned products.

> On the map the town appeared as a small dot in the midst of vast emptiness.

> If the project cannot be done profitably perhaps it should not be done at all.

8. Adverbial clauses and phrases that introduce a main clause other than the first main clause are usually set off with commas. However, if the adverbial clause or phrase follows a conjunction, style varies regarding how many commas are required to set it off. In most cases, two commas are used: one before the conjunction and one following the clause or phrase. Writers who prefer close punctuation usually use three commas: one before the conjunction and two more to enclose the clause or phrase. If the writer prefers open punctuation, the phrase may not be set off at all. In this case, only one comma that separates the main clauses is used. For more on open and close punctuation, see General Principles above.

> His parents were against the match, and had the couple not eloped, their plans for marriage would have come to nothing.

> They have redecorated the entire store, but, to the delight of their customers, the store retains much of its original flavor. [close]

> We haven't left Springfield yet, but when we get to Boston we'll call you. [open]

9. A comma is not used after an introductory phrase if the phrase immediately precedes the main verb.

> In the road lay a dead rabbit.

10. Subordinate clauses and phrases that follow a main clause or that fall within a main clause are usually not set off by commas if they are restrictive. A clause or phrase is considered restrictive if its removal from the sentence would alter the meaning of the main clause. If the meaning of the main clause would not be altered by removing the subordinate clause or phrase, the clause or phrase is considered nonrestrictive and usually is set off by commas.

We will be delighted if she decides to stay. [restrictive]

Anyone who wants his or her copy of the book autographed by the author should get in line. [restrictive]

Her new book, *Fortune's Passage,* was well received. [nonrestrictive]

That was a good meal, although I didn't particularly like the broccoli in cream sauce. [nonrestrictive]

11. Commas are used to set off an adverbial clause or phrase that falls between the subject and the verb.

The weather, fluctuating from very hot to downright chilly, necessitated a variety of clothing.

12. Commas enclose modifying phrases that do not immediately precede the word or phrase they modify.

Hungry and tired, the soldiers marched back to camp.

We could see the importance, both long-term and short-term, of her proposal.

The two children, equally happy with their lunches, set off for school.

13. Absolute phrases are set off with commas, whether they fall at the beginning, middle, or end of the sentence.

Our business being concluded, we adjourned for refreshments.

We headed southward, the wind freshening behind us, to meet the rest of the fleet in the morning.

I still remember my first car, its bumpers sagging, its tires worn, its body rusting.

WITH APPOSITIVES

14. Commas are used to set off a word, phrase, or clause that is in apposition to a noun and that is nonrestrictive.

My husband, Larry, is in charge of ticket sales for the fair.

The highboy, or tallboy, is a tall chest of drawers typically made between 1690 and 1780.

George Washington, first president of the United States, has been the subject of countless biographies.

We were most impressed by the third candidate, the one who brought a writing sample and asked so many questions.

NOTE: A nonrestrictive appositive sometimes precedes the word with which it is in apposition. It is set off by commas in this position also.

A cherished landmark in the city, the Hotel Sandburg has managed once again to escape the wrecking ball.

15. Restrictive appositives are not set off by commas.

My daughter Andrea had the lead in the school play.

Alfred Hitchcock's thriller "Psycho" will be screened tonight.

WITH INTRODUCTORY AND INTERRUPTING ELEMENTS

16. Commas set off transitional words and phrases (as *finally, meanwhile,* and *after all*).

Indeed, close coordination between departments can minimize confusion during this period of expansion.

We are eager to begin construction; however, the necessary materials have not yet arrived.

The most recent report, on the other hand, makes clear why the management avoids such agreements.

NOTE: Adverbs that can serve as transitional words can often serve in other ways as well. When these adverbs are not used to make a transition, no comma is necessary.

The materials had finally arrived.

17. Commas set off parenthetical elements, such as authorial asides and supplementary information, that are closely related to the rest of the sentence.

All of us, to tell the truth, were completely amazed by his suggestion.

The headmaster, now in his sixth year at the school, was responsible for the changes in the curriculum.

NOTE: When the parenthetical element is digressive or otherwise not closely related to the rest of the sentence, it is often set off by dashes or parentheses. For contrasting examples, see paragraph 3 under Dash and paragraphs 1 and 9 under Parentheses in this chapter.

18. Commas are used to set off words or phrases that introduce examples or explanations.

He expects to visit three countries this summer, namely, France, Spain, and Germany.

I would like to develop a good, workable plan, i.e., one that would outline our goals and set a timetable for their accomplishment.

NOTE: Words and phrases such as *i.e., e.g., namely, for example,* and *that is* are often preceded by a dash, open parenthesis, or semicolon, depending on the magnitude of the break in continuity represented by the examples or explanations that they introduce; however, regardless of the punctuation that precedes the word or phrase, a comma always follows it. For contrasting examples of dashes, parentheses, and semicolons with these words and phrases, see paragraph 6 under Dash, paragraph 2 under Parentheses, and paragraph 6 under Semicolon in this chapter.

19. Commas are used to set off words in direct address.

We would like to discuss your account, Mrs. Reid.

The answer, my friends, lies within us.

20. Commas set off mild interjections or exclamations such as *ah* or *oh*.

Ah, summer—season of sunshine and goodwill.

Oh, what a beautiful baby.

NOTE: The vocative *O* is not set off by commas.

O Time! O Death!

Have mercy, O Lord.

With Contrasting Expressions

21. A comma is used to set off contrasting expressions within a sentence.

> This project will take six months, not six weeks.

> He has merely changed his style, not his ethics.

22. Style varies regarding use of the comma to set off contrasting phrases used to describe a single word that follows immediately. In open punctuation, a comma follows the first modifier but is not used between the final modifier and the word modified. In close punctuation, the contrasting phrase is treated as a nonrestrictive modifier and is both preceded and followed by a comma. For more on open and close punctuation, see General Principles above.

> The harsh, although eminently realistic critique is not going to make you popular. [open]

> The harsh, although eminently realistic, critique is not going to make you popular. [close]

> This street takes you away from, not toward the capitol building. [open]

> This street takes you away from, not toward, the capitol building. [close]

23. Adjectives and adverbs that modify the same word or phrase and that are joined by *but* or some other coordinating conjunction are not separated by a comma.

> a bicycle with a light but sturdy frame
> a multicolored but subdued rag rug
> errors caused by working carelessly or too quickly

24. A comma does not usually separate elements that are contrasted through the use of a pair of correlative conjunctions (as *either . . . or, neither . . . nor,* and *not only . . . but also*).

> The cost is either $69.95 or $79.95.

> Neither my brother nor I noticed the mistake.

> He was given the post not only because of his diplomatic connections but also because of his great tact and charm.

NOTE: Correlative conjunctions are sometimes used to join main clauses. If the clauses are short, a comma is not added; however, if the clauses are long, a comma usually separates them.

> Either you do it my way or we don't do it at all.

> Not only did she have to see three salesmen and a visiting reporter during the course of the day, but she also had to prepare for the next day's meeting with the president.

25. Long parallel contrasting and comparing clauses are separated by commas; short parallel phrases are not.

> The more I heard about this new project, the greater was my desire to volunteer.

> "The sooner the better," I said.

With Items in a Series

26. Words, phrases, and clauses joined in a series are separated by commas. If main clauses are joined in a series, they may be separated by either semicolons or commas. For more on the use of commas and semicolons to separate main clauses, see paragraphs 1, 3, and 4 above and paragraph 5 under Semicolon in this chapter.

> Men, women, and children crowded aboard the train.

> Her job required her to pack quickly, to travel often, and to have no personal life.

> He responded patiently while reporters shouted questions, flashbulbs popped, and the crowd pushed closer.

NOTE: Style varies regarding the use of the comma between the last two items in a series if those items are also joined by a conjunction. In some cases, as in the example below, omitting the final comma (often called the serial comma) can result in ambiguity. Some writers feel that in most sentences the use of the conjunction makes the comma superfluous, and they favor using the comma only when a misreading could result from omitting it. Others feel that it is easier to include the final comma routinely rather than try to consider each sentence separately to decide whether a misreading is possible without the comma. Most reference books, including this one, and most other book-length works of nonfiction use the serial comma. In all other categories of publishing, according to our evidence, usage is evenly or nearly evenly divided on the use or omission of this comma.

> We are looking for a house with a big yard, a view of the harbor, and beach and docking privileges. [with serial comma]

> We are looking for a house with a big yard, a view of the harbor and beach and docking privileges. [without serial comma]

27. A comma is not used to separate items in a series that are joined with conjunctions.

> I don't understand what this policy covers or doesn't cover or only partially covers.

> I have talked to the president and the vice president and three other executives.

28. When the elements in a series are long or complex or consist of clauses that themselves contain commas, the elements are usually separated by semicolons, not commas. For more on this use of the semicolon, see paragraphs 7 and 8 under Semicolon in this chapter.

With Compound Modifiers

29. A comma is used to separate two or more adjectives, adverbs, or phrases that modify the same word or phrase. For the use of commas with contrasting modifiers, see paragraphs 22 and 23 above.

> She spoke in a calm, reflective manner.

> We watched the skier move smoothly, gracefully through the turns.

> His story was too fantastic, too undersupported by facts for us to take seriously.

30. A comma is not used between two adjectives when the first modifies the combination of the second adjective plus the word or phrase it modifies.

> a little brown jug
> a modern concrete-and-glass building

31. A comma is not used to separate an adverb from the adjective or adverb that it modifies.

> a truly distinctive manner
> running very quickly down the street

In Quotations, Questions, and Indirect Discourse

32. A comma separates a direct quotation from a phrase identifying its source or speaker. If the quotation is a question or an exclamation and the identifying phrase follows the quotation, the comma is replaced by a question mark or an exclamation point.

> Mary said, "I am leaving."
>
> "I am leaving," Mary said.
>
> Mary asked, "Where are you going?"
>
> "Where are you going?" Mary asked.
>
> "I am leaving," Mary said, "even if you want me to stay."
>
> "Don't do that!" Mary shouted.

NOTE: In some cases, a colon can replace a comma preceding a quotation. For more on this use of the colon, see paragraph 6 under Colon in this chapter.

33. A comma does not set off a quotation that is tightly incorporated into the sentence in which it appears.

> Throughout the session his only responses were "No comment" and "I don't think so."
>
> Just because he said he was "about to leave this minute" doesn't mean he actually left.

34. Style varies regarding the use of commas to set off shorter sentences that fall within longer sentences and that do not constitute actual dialogue. These shorter sentences may be mottoes or maxims, unspoken or imaginary dialogue, or sentences referred to as sentences; and they may or may not be enclosed in quotation marks. (For more on the use of quotation marks with sentences like these, see paragraph 6 under Quotation Marks, Double, in this chapter.) Typically the shorter sentence functions as a subject, object, or complement within the larger sentence and does not require a comma. Sometimes the structure of the larger sentence will be styled like actual quoted dialogue, and in such cases a comma is used to separate the shorter sentence from the text that introduces or identifies it. In some cases, where an author decides not to use quotation marks, a comma may be inserted simply to mark the beginning of the shorter sentence clearly.

> "The computer is down" was the response she dreaded.
>
> Another confusing idiom is "How do you do?"
>
> He spoke with a candor that seemed to insist, This actually happened to me and in just this way.
>
> The first rule is, When in doubt, spell it out.

When the shorter sentence functions as an appositive in the larger sentence, it is set off with a comma when nonrestrictive and not when restrictive. (For more on restrictive modifiers and appositives, see paragraphs 10, 14, and 15 above.)

> He was fond of the slogan "Every man a king, but no man wears a crown."
>
> We had the club's motto, "We make waves," printed on our T-shirts.

35. A comma introduces a direct question regardless of whether it is enclosed in quotation marks or if its first word is capitalized.

> I wondered, what is going on here?
>
> The question is, How do we get out of here?

What bothered her was, who had eaten all of the cookies?

36. The comma is omitted before quotations that are very short exclamations or representations of sounds.

> He jumped up suddenly and cried "Yow!"
>
> When she was done, she let out a loud "Whew!"

37. A comma is not used to set off indirect discourse or indirect questions introduced by a conjunction (such as *that* or *what*).

> Mary said that she was leaving.
>
> I wondered what was going on there.
>
> The clerk told me that the book I had ordered had just come in.

With Omitted Words

38. A comma indicates the omission of a word or phrase, especially in parallel constructions where the omitted word or phrase appears earlier in the sentence.

> Common stocks are preferred by some investors; bonds, by others.

39. A comma often replaces the conjunction *that*.

> The road was so steep and winding, we thought for sure that we would go over the edge.
>
> The problem is, we don't know how to fix it.

With Addresses, Dates, and Numbers

40. A comma is used to set off the individual elements of an address except for zip codes. In current practice, no punctuation appears between a state name and the zip code that follows it. If prepositions are used between the elements of the address, commas are not needed.

> Mrs. Bryant may be reached at 52 Kiowa Circle, Mesa, Arizona.
>
> Mr. Briscoe was born in Liverpool, England.
>
> The collection will be displayed at the Wilmington, Delaware, Museum of Art.
>
> Write to the Bureau of the Census, Washington, DC 20233.
>
> The White House is located at 1600 Pennsylvania Avenue in Washington, D.C.

NOTE: Some writers omit the comma that follows the name of a state when no other element of an address follows it. This is most likely to happen when a city name and state name are being used in combination to modify a noun that follows; however, our evidence indicates that retaining this comma is still the more common practice.

> We visited their Enid, Oklahoma plant.
> *but more commonly*
> We visited their Enid, Oklahoma, plant.

41. Commas are used to set off the year from the day of the month. When only the month and the year are given, the comma is usually omitted.

> On October 26, 1947, the newly hired employees began work on the project.
>
> In December 1903, the Wright brothers finally succeeded in keeping an airplane aloft for a few seconds.

42. A comma groups numerals into units of three to separate thousands, millions, and so on; however, this comma is generally not used in page numbers, street numbers, or numbers within dates. For more on the styling of numbers, see Chapter 5, "The Treatment of Numbers."

a population of 350,000
the year 1986
4509 South Pleasant Street
page 1419

WITH NAMES, DEGREES, AND TITLES

43. A comma punctuates an inverted name.

Sagan, Deborah J.

44. A comma is used between a surname and *Junior, Senior,* or their abbreviations.

Morton A. Williams, Jr.
Douglas Fairbanks, Senior

45. A comma is often used to set off the word *Incorporated* or the abbreviation *Inc.* from the rest of a corporate name; however, many companies elect to omit this comma from their names.

Leedy Manufacturing Company, Incorporated
Tektronics, Inc.
Merz-Fortunata Inc.

46. A comma separates a surname from a following academic, honorary, military, or religious degree or title.

Amelia P. Artandi, D.V.M.
John L. Farber, Esq.
Sister Mary Catherine, S.C.
Robert Menard, MpA., Ph.D.
Admiral Herman Washington, USN

IN CORRESPONDENCE

47. The comma follows the salutation in informal correspondence and follows the complimentary close in both informal and formal correspondence. In formal correspondence, a colon follows the salutation. For more on this use of the colon, see paragraph 12 under Colon in this chapter.

Dear Rachel,
Affectionately,
Very truly yours,

OTHER USES

48. The comma is used to avoid ambiguity when the juxtaposition of two words or expressions could cause confusion.

Whatever will be, will be.

To John, Marshall was someone special.

I repaired the lamp that my brother had broken, and replaced the bulb.

49. A comma often follows a direct object or a predicate nominative or predicate adjective when they precede the subject and verb in the sentence. If the meaning of the sentence is clear without this comma, it is often omitted.

That we would soon have to raise prices, no one disputed.

Critical about the current state of affairs, we might have been.

A disaster it certainly was.

WITH OTHER MARKS OF PUNCTUATION

50. Commas are used in conjunction with brackets, ellipsis points, parentheses, and quotation marks. Commas are not used in conjunction with colons, dashes, exclamation points, question marks, or semicolons. If one of these latter marks falls at the same point in a sentence at which a comma would fall, the comma is dropped and the other mark is retained. For more on the use of commas with other marks of punctuation, see the heading With Other Marks of Punctuation in the sections of this chapter covering those marks of punctuation.

DASH

In many of its uses, the dash functions like a comma, a colon, or a pair of parentheses. Like commas and parentheses, dashes set off parenthetic material such as examples, supplemental facts, or appositional, explanatory, or descriptive phrases. Like colons, dashes introduce clauses that explain or expand upon some element of the material that precedes them. The dash is sometimes considered to be a less formal equivalent of the colon and parenthesis, and it does frequently take their place in advertising and other informal contexts. However, dashes are prevalent in all kinds of writing, including the most formal, and the choice of which mark to use is usually a matter of personal preference.

The dash exists in a number of different lengths. The dash in most general use is the em dash, which is approximately the width of an uppercase M in typeset material. In typewritten material, it is represented by two hyphens. The en dash and the two- and three-em dashes have more limited uses which are explained in paragraphs 15–18 below.

ABRUPT CHANGE OR SUSPENSION

1. The dash marks an abrupt change in the flow of a writer's thought or in the structure of a sentence.

The mountain that we climbed is higher than—well, never mind how high it is.

The students seemed happy with the change, but the alumni—there was the problem.

2. Dashes mark a suspension in the writer's flow of thought or in the sentence structure. Such suspensions are frequently caused by an authorial aside.

He was—how shall we put it?—a controversial character to say the least.

If I had kept my notes—and I really wish that I had—I would be able to give you the exact date of the sale.

PARENTHETIC AND AMPLIFYING ELEMENTS

3. Dashes are used in place of other punctuation (such as commas or parentheses) to emphasize parenthetic or amplifying material or to make such material stand out more clearly from the rest of the sentence.

She is willing to discuss all problems—those she has solved and those for which there is no immediate solution.

In 1976, they asked for—and received—substantial grants from the federal government.

The privately owned consulting firm—formerly known as Aborjaily and Associates—is now offering many new services.

NOTE: When dashes are used to set off parenthetic elements, they often indicate that the material is more digressive than elements set off with commas but less digressive than elements set off by parentheses. For contrasting examples see paragraph 17 under Comma and paragraphs 1 and 9 under Parentheses in this chapter.

4. Dashes are used to set off or to introduce defining and enumerating phrases.

> The fund sought to acquire controlling positions—a minimum of 25% of outstanding voting securities—in other companies.

> The essay dealt with our problems with waste—cans, bottles, discarded tires, and other trash.

5. A dash is often used in place of a colon or semicolon to link clauses, especially when the clause that follows the dash explains, summarizes, or expands upon the clause that precedes it.

> The test results were surprisingly good—none of the tested models displayed serious problems.

> The deterioration of our bridges and roads has been apparent for many years—parts of the interstate highway system are 30 years old, after all, and most of our bridges are older than that.

6. A dash or a pair of dashes often sets off parenthetic or amplifying material introduced by such phrases as *for example, namely, that is, e.g.,* and *i.e.*

> After some discussion the motion was tabled—that is, it was removed indefinitely from the board's consideration.

> Sports develop two valuable traits—namely, self-control and the ability to make quick decisions.

> Not all "prime" windows—i.e., the ones installed when a house is built—are equal in quality.

NOTE: Commas, parentheses, and semicolons are often used for the same purpose. For contrasting examples, see paragraph 18 under Comma, paragraph 2 under Parentheses, and paragraph 6 under Semicolon in this chapter.

7. A dash introduces a summary statement that follows a series of words or phrases.

> Unemployment, strikes, inflation, stock prices, mortgage rates—all are part of the economy.

> Once into bankruptcy, the company would have to pay cash for its supplies, defer maintenance, and lay off workers—moves that could threaten its long-term profitability.

As a Mechanical Device

8. A dash precedes the name of an author or source at the end of a quoted passage.

> Winter tames man, woman and beast.
> —William Shakespeare

> "A comprehensive, authoritative, and beautifully written biography."—*National Review*

NOTE: This method of attribution is most often used when the quoted material is not part of the main text. Examples of such situations are quotations set as epigraphs and quotations set as extracts. The attribution

may appear immediately after the quotation, or it may appear on the next line.

9. A dash is used to indicate interrupted speech or a speaker's confusion or hesitation.

> "The next point I'd like to bring up—" the speaker started to say. "I'm sorry. I'll have to stop you there," the moderator broke in.

> "Yes," he went on, "yes—that is—I guess I agree."

NOTE: There is some disagreement among style manuals regarding the use of a comma between a quotation ending with a dash and its attribution. Our evidence indicates that the comma is usually omitted in such circumstances. This follows the general practice regarding the use of commas with dashes described in paragraph 11 below.

10. Dashes are used variously as elements in page design. They may, for example, precede items in a vertical enumeration, set off elements in the dateline of a newspaper report, or separate words from their definitions in a glossary. The use of dashes in such circumstances is usually determined by the editor or designer of the publication.

> Required skills are:
> —Shorthand
> —Typing
> —Transcription

With Other Marks of Punctuation

11. If a dash appears at a point in a sentence where a comma could also appear, the dash is retained and the comma is dropped. For one situation in which this practice is not always followed, see paragraph 9 above.

> If we don't succeed—and the critics say we won't—then the whole project is in jeopardy.

> Our lawyer has read the transcript—all 1200 pages of it—and he has decided that an appeal would not be useful.

> Some of the other departments, however—particularly Accounting, Sales, and Credit Collection—have expanded their computer operations.

12. If the second of a pair of dashes appears at a point in a sentence where a period or semicolon would also appear, the period or semicolon is retained and the dash is dropped.

> His conduct has always been exemplary—near-perfect attendance, excellent productivity, a good attitude; nevertheless, his termination cannot be avoided.

13. Dashes are used with exclamation points and question marks. When a pair of dashes sets off parenthetic material calling for either of these marks of punctuation, the exclamation point or the question mark is placed inside the second dash. If the parenthetic material falls at the end of a sentence ending with an exclamation point or question mark, the closing dash is not required.

> His hobby was getting on people's nerves—especially mine!—and he was extremely good at it.

> When the committee meets next week—are you going to be there?—I will present all of the final figures.

Is there any way to predict the future course of this case—one which we really cannot afford to lose?

14. Dashes and parentheses are used in combination to indicate parenthetic material appearing within parenthetic material. Our evidence indicates that dashes within parentheses and parentheses within dashes occur with about equal frequency.

> We were looking for a narrator (or narrators—sometimes a script calls for more than one) who could handle a variety of assignments.

> On our trip south we crossed a number of major rivers—the Hudson, the Delaware, and the Patapsco (which flows through Baltimore)—without paying a single toll.

NOTE: If the inner parenthetic element begins with a dash and its closing dash would fall in the same position as the closing parenthesis, the closing dash is omitted and the parenthesis is retained, as in the first example above. If the inner phrase begins with a parenthesis and its closing parenthesis would coincide with the closing dash, the closing parenthesis and the closing dash are both retained, as in the second example above.

EN DASH

15. En dashes appear only in typeset material. The en dash is shorter than the em dash but slightly longer than the hyphen, and it is used in place of the hyphen in some situations. The most common use of the en dash is as an equivalent to "(up) to and including" when used between numbers, dates, or other notations that indicate range.

> 1984–85
> 8:30 a.m.–4:30 p.m.
> GS 12–14
> $20–$40
> Monday–Friday
> ages 10–15
> levels D–G
> 35–40 years
> pages 128–34

NOTE: The use of the en dash to replace the hyphen in such cases, although urged by most style manuals, is by no means universal. Writers and editors who wish to have en dashes set in their copy need to indicate on their manuscripts which hyphens should be set as en dashes, and this need to mark en dashes can obviously be an inconvenience and an invitation to errors. However, many writers and editors prefer to use en dashes because of the visual clarity they provide between numbers and because of the distinction they make between en dashes used to mean "to" and hyphens used to connect elements in compound words.

16. Publishers make various uses of the en dash, and no one set of rules can be said to be standard. Some common uses of the en dash include using it as a replacement for the hyphen following a prefix that is added to an open compound, as a replacement for the word *to* between capitalized names, and to indicate linkages, such as boundaries, treaties, or oppositions.

> pre–Civil War architecture
> the New York–Connecticut area
> Chicago–Memphis train
> Washington–Moscow diplomacy
> the Dempsey–Tunney fight

LONG DASHES

17. A two-em dash is used to indicate missing letters in a word and, less frequently, to indicate a missing word.

> Mr. P—— of Baltimore
> That's b—— t and you know it.

18. A three-em dash indicates that a word has been left out or that an unknown word or figure is to be supplied. For the use of this dash in bibliography listings, see Chapter 6, "Notes and Bibliographies."

> The study was carried out in ——, a fast-growing Sunbelt city.

> We'll leave New York City on the —— of August.

SPACING

19. Style varies as to spacing around the dash. Some publications insert a space before and after the dash, others do not. Our evidence indicates that the majority of publishers style the dash without spaces.

ELLIPSIS POINTS

Ellipsis points is the name most often given to periods when they are used, usually in groups of three, to signal an omission from quoted material or to indicate a pause or trailing off of speech. Other names for periods used in this way include *ellipses, points of ellipsis,* and *suspension points.* Ellipsis points are often used in conjunction with other marks of punctuation, including periods used to mark the ends of sentences. When ellipsis points are used in this way with a terminal period, the omission is sometimes thought of as being marked by four periods. Most of the conventions described in this section are illustrated with quoted material enclosed in quotation marks. However, the conventions are equally applicable to quoted material set as extracts.

NOTE: The examples given below present passages in which ellipsis points indicate omission of material. In most cases, the full text from which these omissions have been made is some portion of the headnote above.

1. Ellipsis points indicate the omission of one or more words within a quoted sentence.

> One book said, "Other names . . . include *ellipses, points of ellipsis,* and *suspension points.*"

2. Ellipsis points are usually not used to indicate the omission of words that precede the quoted portion. However, style varies on this point, and in some formal contexts, especially those in which the quotation is introduced by a colon, ellipsis points are used.

> The book maintained that "the omission is sometimes thought of as being marked by four periods."

> The book maintained: ". . . the omission is sometimes thought of as being marked by four periods."

3. Punctuation used in the original that falls on either side of the ellipsis points is often omitted; however, it may be retained, especially if such retention helps clarify the sentence.

According to the book, "*Ellipsis points* is the name most often given to periods when they are used . . . to signal an omission from quoted material or to indicate a pause or trailing off of speech."

According to the book, "When ellipsis points are used in this way . . . , the omission is sometimes thought of as being marked by four periods."

According to the book, "*Ellipsis points* is the name most often given to periods when they are used, usually in groups of three, . . . to indicate a pause or trailing off of speech."

4. If an omission comprises an entire sentence within a passage, the last part of a sentence within a passage, or the first part of a sentence other than the first quoted sentence, the end punctuation preceding or following the omission is retained and is followed by three periods.

That book says, "Other names for periods used in this way include *ellipses, points of ellipsis,* and *suspension points* . . . . When ellipsis points are used in this way with a terminal period, the omission is sometimes thought of as being marked by four periods."

That book says, "*Ellipsis points* is the name given to periods when they are used, usually in groups of three, to signal an omission from quoted material. . . . Other names for periods used in this way include *ellipses, points of ellipsis,* and *suspension points.*"

That book says, "Ellipsis points are often used in conjunction with other marks of punctuation, including periods used to mark ends of sentences. . . . The omission is sometimes thought of as being marked by four periods."

NOTE: The capitalization of the word *The* in the third example is acceptable. When the opening words of a quotation act as a sentence within the quotation, the first word is capitalized, even if that word did not begin a sentence in the original version.

5. If the last words of a quoted sentence are omitted and if the original sentence ends with a period, that period is retained and three ellipsis points follow. However, if the original sentence ends with punctuation other than a period, the end punctuation often follows the ellipsis points, especially if it helps clarify the quotation.

Their book said, "Ellipsis points are often used in conjunction with other marks of punctuation. . . ."

He always ends his harangues with some variation on the question, "What could you have been thinking when you . . . ?"

NOTE: Many writers and editors, especially those writing in more informal contexts, choose to ignore the styling considerations presented in paragraphs 4 and 5. They use instead an alternative system in which all omissions are indicated by three periods and all terminal periods that may precede or follow an omission are dropped.

6. Ellipsis points are used to indicate that a quoted sentence has been intentionally left unfinished. In situations such as this the terminal period is not included.

Read the statement beginning "*Ellipsis points* is the name most often given . . . ." and then proceed to the numbered paragraphs.

7. When a full line or several consecutive lines of poetry are omitted from a quotation, the omission is indicated by a line of spaced points. The lines of points extend the length of the preceding line or of the missing line.

Whitman's attitude on the subject is revealed in these lines from "When I Heard the Learned Astronomer":

When I heard the learned astronomer,
. . . .
How soon unaccountable I became tired and sick,
Til rising and gliding out I wandered off by myself,
In the mystical moist night-air, and from time to time,
Looked up in perfect silence at the stars.

NOTE: Style varies regarding the treatment of poetry quotations that do not end in a period. Sometimes authors indicate an omission with ellipsis points, sometimes they prefer not to use ellipsis points but rather to reproduce the text exactly as it appeared in the original version.

Whitman's attitude on the subject is revealed in these lines from "When I Heard the Learned Astronomer":

When I heard the learned astronomer,
. . . .
How soon unaccountable I became tired and sick, . . .

Whitman's attitude on the subject is revealed in these lines from "When I Heard the Learned Astronomer":

When I heard the learned astronomer,
. . . .
How soon unaccountable I became tired and sick,

8. Ellipsis points are used to indicate faltering speech, especially if the faltering involves a long pause between words or a sentence that trails off or is left intentionally unfinished. In these kinds of sentences most writers treat the ellipsis points as terminal punctuation, thus removing the need for any other punctuation; however, style does vary on this point, and some writers routinely use other punctuation in conjunction with ellipsis points.

The speaker seemed uncertain how to answer the question. "Well, that's true . . . but even so . . . I think we can do better."

"Despite these uncertainties, we believe we can do it, but . . ."

"I mean . . ." he said, "like . . . How?"

9. Ellipsis points are sometimes used as a stylistic device to catch and hold a reader's attention.

They think that nothing can go wrong . . . but it does.

10. Each ellipsis point is set off from other ellipsis points, from adjacent punctuation (except for quotation marks, which are closed up to the ellipsis points), and from surrounding text by a space. If a terminal period is used with ellipsis points, it precedes them with no space before it and one space after it.

EXCLAMATION POINT

The exclamation point is used to mark a forceful comment. Writers and editors usually try to avoid using the exclamation point too frequently, because its heavy use can weaken its effect.

1. An exclamation point can punctuate a sentence, phrase, or interjection.

> This is the fourth time in a row he's missed his cue!

> No one that I talked to—not even the accounting department!—seemed to know how the figures were calculated.

> Oh! you startled me.

> Ah, those eyes!

2. The exclamation point replaces the question mark when an ironic or emphatic tone is more important than the actual question.

> Aren't you finished yet!

> Do you realize what you've done!

> Why me!

3. Occasionally the exclamation point is used with a question mark to indicate a very forceful question.

> How much did you say?!

> You did what!?

NOTE: The interrobang, printed ‽, was created to punctuate the types of sentences described in paragraphs 2 and 3 above. However, the character is not available to most typesetters, and it is rarely used.

4. In mathematical expressions, the exclamation point indicates a factorial.

> $n! \cdot m! \geq (n)(m!)$

5. The exclamation point is enclosed within brackets, dashes, parentheses, and quotation marks when it punctuates the material so enclosed rather than the sentence as a whole. It should be placed outside them when it punctuates the entire sentence.

> All of this proves—at long last!—that we were right from the start.

> Somehow the dog got the gate open (for the third time!) and ran into the street.

> He shouted, "Wait!" and sprinted toward the train.

> The correct word is "mousse," not "moose"!

6. Exclamatory phrases that occur within a sentence are set off by dashes or parentheses.

> And now our competition—get this!—wants to start sharing secrets.

> The board accepted most of the recommendations, but ours (alas!) was not even considered.

7. If an exclamation point falls at a place in a sentence where a comma or a terminal period could also go, the comma or period is dropped and the exclamation point is retained.

> "Absolutely not!" he snapped.

> She has written about sixty pages so far—and with no help!

NOTE: If the exclamation point is part of a title, as of a play, book, or movie, it may be followed by a comma.

If the title falls at the end of a sentence, the terminal period is usually dropped.

> Marshall and Susan went to see the musical *Oklahoma!*, and they enjoyed it very much.

> They enjoyed seeing the musical *Oklahoma!*

8. In typewritten material, two spaces follow an exclamation point that ends a sentence. If the exclamation point is followed by a closing bracket, closing parenthesis, or closing quotation marks, the two spaces follow the second mark. In typeset material, only one space follows the exclamation point.

> `The time is now!    Decide what you are`
> `going to do.`

> `She said, The time is now!    That meant`
> `we had to decide what to do.`

> The time is now! Decide what you are going to do.

> She said, "The time is now!" That meant we had to decide what to do.

HYPHEN

1. Hyphens are used to link elements in compound words. For more on the styling of compound words, see the section on Compounds in Chapter 3, "Plurals, Possessives, and Compounds."

2. A hyphen marks an end-of-line division of a word when part of the word is to be carried down to the next line.

> Unemployment, strikes, inflation, stock prices, mortgage rates—all are part of the economy.

3. A hyphen divides letters or syllables to give the effect of stuttering, sobbing, or halting speech.

> S-s-sammy
> ah-ah-ah
> y-y-es

4. Hyphens indicate a word spelled out letter by letter.

> p-r-o-b-a-t-i-o-n

5. A hyphen indicates that a word element is a prefix, suffix, or medial element.

> anti-
> -ship
> -o-

6. A hyphen is used in typewritten material as an equivalent to the phrase "(up) to and including" when placed between numbers and dates. In typeset material this hyphen is very often replaced by an en dash. For more on the use of the en dash, see paragraphs 15 and 16 under Dash in this chapter.

7. Hyphens are sometimes used to produce inflected forms of verbs that are made of individually pronounced letters or to add an *-er* ending to an abbreviation; however, apostrophes are more commonly used for this purpose. For more on these uses of the apostrophe, see paragraphs 6 and 7 under Apostrophe in this chapter.

> D.H.-ing for the White Sox
> a loyal AA-er

PARENTHESES

Parentheses enclose supplementary elements that are inserted into a main statement but that are not intended to be part of the statement; in fact, parenthetic elements often interrupt the main structure of the sentence. For some of the cases described below, especially those listed under the heading "Parenthetic Elements," commas and dashes are frequently used instead of parentheses. (For contrasting examples, see paragraph 17 under Comma and paragraph 3 under Dash in this chapter.) In general, commas tend to be used when the inserted material is closely related, logically or grammatically, to the main clause; parentheses are more often used when the inserted material is incidental or digressive. Some newspapers and news magazines avoid the use of parentheses in straight news reporting and rely instead on the dash. In most cases, however, the choice of dashes or parentheses to enclose parenthetic material is a matter of personal preference.

PARENTHETIC ELEMENTS

1. Parentheses enclose phrases and clauses that provide examples, explanations, or supplementary facts. Supplementary numerical data may also be enclosed in parentheses.

> Nominations for the association's principal officers (president, vice-president, treasurer, and secretary) were heard and approved at the last meeting.

> Although we liked the restaurant (their Italian food was the best), we seldom went there.

> Three old destroyers (all now out of commission) will be scrapped.

> Their first baseman was hitting well that season (.297, 84 RBIs), and their left fielder was doing well also (21 HRs, 78 RBIs).

2. Parentheses enclose phrases and clauses introduced by expressions such as *namely, that is, e.g.,* and *i.e.* Commas, dashes, and semicolons are also used to perform this function. (For contrasting examples, see paragraph 18 under Comma, paragraph 6 under Dash, and paragraph 6 under Semicolon in this chapter.)

> In writing to the manufacturer, be as specific as possible (i.e., list the missing or defective parts, describe the nature of the malfunction, and provide the name and address of the store where the unit was purchased).

3. Parentheses set off definitions, translations, or alternate names for words in the main part of a sentence.

> The company sold off all of its retail outlets and announced plans to sell off its houseware (small appliance) business as well.

> He has followed the fortunes of the modern renaissance (*al-Nahdad*) in the Arab-speaking world.

> The hotel was located just a few blocks from San Antonio's famous Paseo del Rio (river walk).

> They were scheduled to play Beethoven's Trio in B-flat major, Opus 97 ("The Archduke").

4. Parentheses enclose abbreviations synonymous with spelled-out forms and occurring after those forms, or they may enclose the spelled-out form occurring after the abbreviation.

> She referred to a ruling by the Federal Communications Commission (FCC).

> They were involved with a study regarding the manufacture and disposal of PVC (polyvinyl chloride).

5. Parentheses are used in running text to set off bibliographical or historical data about books, articles, or other published or artistic works. For full information regarding the use of parentheses with bibliographical references see the section on Parenthetical References in Chapter 6, "Notes and Bibliographies."

> His work was influenced by several of Freud's essays, including "Some Character Types Met with in Psychoanalytic Work" (1916).

> *Ohio Impromptu* (1981) was written for a special performance at Ohio State University.

> Another book in this category is Alice Schick's *Serengeti Cats* (Lippincott, $10.53).

6. Parentheses often set off cross-references.

> Telephone ordering service is also provided (refer to the list of stores at the end of this catalog).

> Textbooks are available at the bookstore for all on-campus courses. (See page 12 for hours.)

> The diagram (Fig. 3) illustrates the action of the pump.

7. Parentheses enclose Arabic numerals that confirm a spelled-out number in a text.

> Delivery will be made in thirty (30) days.

8. Parentheses enclose the name of a city or state that is inserted into a proper name for identification.

> the Norristown (Pa.) State Hospital
> the *Tulsa* (Okla.) *Tribune*

9. Some writers use parentheses to set off personal asides.

> It was largely as a result of this conference that the committee was formed (its subsequent growth in influence is another story).

10. Parentheses are used to set off quotations, either attributed or unattributed, that illustrate or support a statement made in the main text.

> After he had had a few brushes with the police, his stepfather had him sent to jail as an incorrigible ("It will do him good").

AS A MECHANICAL DEVICE

11. Parentheses enclose unpunctuated numbers or letters in a series within running text.

> We must set forth (1) our long-term goals, (2) our immediate objectives, and (3) the means at our disposal.

NOTE: Some writers and editors use only a single parenthesis following the number; however, most style books advise that parentheses be used both before and after, and most publications do follow that style.

12. Parentheses indicate alternative terms.

> Please indicate the lecture(s) you would like to attend.

13. Parentheses are used in combination with numbers for several mechanical purposes, such as setting off area codes in telephone numbers, indicating losses in accounting, and grouping elements in mathematical expressions.

(413) 256-7899
$3(a + b) + 4(a + b)$

Operating Profits (in millions)	
Cosmetics	26.2
Food products	47.7
Food services	54.3
Transportation	(17.7)
Sporting goods	(11.2)
Total	99.3

WITH OTHER MARKS OF PUNCTUATION

14. If a parenthetic expression is an independent sentence, its first word is capitalized and a period is placed *inside* the last parenthesis. On the other hand, a parenthetic expression that occurs within a sentence—even if it could stand alone as a separate sentence—does not end with a period. It may, however, end with an exclamation point, a question mark, a period after an abbreviation, or a set of quotation marks. A parenthetic expression within a sentence does not require capitalization unless it is a quoted sentence. (For more on the use of capitals with parenthetic expressions, see the section on Beginnings in Chapter 2, "Capitals, Italics, and Quotation Marks.")

> The discussion was held in the boardroom. (The results are still confidential.)

> Although several trade organizations worked actively against the legislation (there were at least three paid lobbyists working on Capitol Hill at any one time), the bill passed easily.

> After waiting in line for an hour (why do we do these things?), we finally left.

> The conference was held in Vancouver (that's in B.C.).

> He was totally confused ("What can we do?") and refused to see anyone.

15. If a parenthetic expression within a sentence is composed of two independent clauses, capitalization and periods are avoided. To separate the clauses within the parentheses, semicolons are usually used. If the parenthetic expression occurs outside of a sentence, normal patterns of capitalization and punctuation prevail.

> We visited several showrooms, looked at the prices (it wasn't a pleasant experience; prices in this area have not gone down), and asked all the questions we could think of.

> We visited several showrooms and looked at the prices. (It wasn't a pleasant experience. Prices in this area have not gone down.) If salespeople were available, we asked all of the questions we could think of.

16. No punctuation mark (other than a period after an abbreviation) is placed before parenthetic material within a sentence; if a break is required, the punctuation is placed after the final parenthesis.

> I'll get back to you tomorrow (Friday), when I have more details.

17. Parentheses sometimes appear within parentheses, although the usual practice is to replace the inner pair of parentheses with a pair of brackets. (For an example of brackets within parentheses, see paragraph 6 under Brackets in this chapter.)

> Checks must be drawn in U.S. dollars. (PLEASE NOTE: In accordance with U.S. Department of Treasury regulations, we cannot accept checks drawn on Canadian banks for amounts less than four U.S. dollars ($4.00). The same regulation applies to Canadian money orders.)

18. Dashes and parentheses are often used together to set off parenthetic material within a larger parenthetic element. For details and examples, see paragraph 14 under Dash in this chapter.

SPACING

19. In typewritten material, a parenthetic expression that is an independent sentence is followed by two spaces. In typeset material, the sentence is followed by one space. In typewritten or typeset material, a parenthetic expression that falls within a sentence is followed by one space.

```
We visited several showrooms and looked
at the prices.   (It wasn't a pleasant
experience.   Prices in this area have
not gone down.)   We asked all the ques-
tions we could think of.
```

> We visited several showrooms and looked at the prices. (It wasn't a pleasant experience. Prices in this area have not gone down.) We asked all the questions we could think of.

NOTE: Paragraphs 14 and 15 above are followed by examples that illustrate the appearance in typeset material of parenthetic expressions that are independent sentences.

PERIOD

This section describes uses of the period in running text. For rules regarding use of the period in bibliographies, see Chapter 6, "Notes and Bibliographies." For the use of three periods to indicate a pause or omission, see the section on Ellipsis Points in this chapter.

1. A period terminates a sentence or a sentence fragment that is neither interrogative nor exclamatory.

> Do your best.

> I did my best.

> Total chaos. Nothing works.

2. A period punctuates some abbreviations. For more on the punctuation of abbreviations, see the section on Punctuation in Chapter 4, "Abbreviations."

> a.k.a.
> fig.
> N.W.
> Assn.
> in.
> U.S.
> Dr.
> No.
> Inc.
> Jr.
> e.g.
> Co.
> Ph.D.
> ibid.
> Corp.

3. A period is used with an individual's initials. If all of the person's initials are used instead of the name, however, the unspaced initials may be written without periods.

> F. Scott Fitzgerald
> Susan B. Anthony
> F.D.R. *or* FDR
> T. S. Eliot

4. A period follows Roman and Arabic numerals and also letters when they are used without parentheses in outlines and vertical enumerations.

> I. Objectives
>   A. Economy
>   1. Low initial cost
>   2. Low maintenance cost
>   B. Ease of operation
>
> Required skills are:
>   1. Shorthand
>   2. Typing
>   3. Transcription

5. A period is placed within quotation marks even when it does not punctuate the quoted material.

> The charismatic leader was known to his followers as "the guiding light."
>
> "I said I wanted to fire him," Henry went on, "but she said, 'I don't think you have the contractual privilege to do that.' "

6. When brackets or parentheses enclose a sentence that is independent of surrounding sentences, the period is placed inside the closing parenthesis or bracket. However, when brackets or parentheses enclose a sentence that is part of a surrounding sentence, the period for the enclosed sentence is omitted.

> On Friday the government ordered a 24-hour curfew and told all journalists and photographers to leave the area. (Authorities later confiscated the film of those who did not comply.)
>
> I took a good look at her (she was standing quite close to me at the time).

7. In typewritten material, two spaces follow a period that ends a sentence. If the period is followed by a closing bracket, closing parenthesis, or quotation marks, the two spaces follow the second mark. In typeset material, only one space follows this period.

> Here is the car.   Do you want to get in?
>
> He said, "Here is the car."   I asked if I should get in.
>
> Here is the car. Do you want to get in?

8. One space follows a period that comes after an initial in a name. If a name is composed entirely of initials, no space is required; however, the usual styling for such names is to omit the periods.

> Mr. H. C. Matthews
> F.D.R. *or* FDR

9. No space follows an internal period within a punctuated abbreviation.

> f.o.b.
> i.e.
> Ph.D.
> A.D.
> p.m.

QUESTION MARK

1. The question mark terminates a direct question.

> What went wrong?
>
> "When do they arrive?" she asked.

NOTE: The intent of the writer, not the word order of the sentence, determines whether or not the sentence is a question. Polite requests that are worded as questions, for instance, usually take periods, because they are not really questions. Similarly, sentences whose word order is that of a statement but whose force is interrogatory are punctuated with question marks.

> Will you please sit down.
>
> He did that?

2. The question mark terminates an interrogative element that is part of a sentence. An indirect question is not followed by a question mark.

> The old arithmetic books were full of How-much-wallpaper-will-it-take-to-cover-a-room? questions.
>
> How did she do it? was the question on everybody's mind.
>
> She wondered, will it work?
>
> She wondered whether it would work.

3. The question mark punctuates each element of an interrogative series that is neither numbered nor lettered. When an interrogative series is numbered or lettered, only one question mark is used, and it is placed at the end of the series.

> Can you give us a reasonable forecast? back up your predictions? compare them with last year's earnings?
>
> Can you (1) give us a reasonable forecast, (2) back up your predictions, (3) compare them with last year's earnings?

4. The question mark indicates a writer's or editor's uncertainty about a fact.

> Geoffrey Chaucer, English poet (1340?–1400)

5. The question mark is placed inside a closing bracket, dash, parenthesis, or pair of quotation marks when it punctuates only the material enclosed by that mark and not the sentence as a whole. It is placed outside that mark when it punctuates the entire sentence.

> What did Andrew mean when he called the project "a fiasco from the start"?
>
> I had a vacation in 1975 (was it really that long ago?), but I haven't had time for one since.
>
> "She thought about it for a moment," Alice continued, "and finally she said, 'Can you guarantee this will work?' "
>
> He asked, "Do you realize the extent of the problem [the housing shortage]?"

6. In typewritten material, two spaces follow a question mark that ends a sentence. If the question mark is followed by a closing bracket, closing parenthesis, or quotation marks, the two spaces follow the second mark. In typeset material, only one space follows the question mark.

> She wondered, will it work?   He said he thought it would.
>
> She asked, "Will it work?"   He said he thought it would.

She wondered, will it work? He said he thought it would.

7. One space follows a question mark that falls within a sentence.

Are you coming today? tomorrow? the day after?

QUOTATION MARKS, DOUBLE

This section describes the use of quotation marks to enclose quoted matter in running text. It also describes the mechanical uses of quotation marks, such as to set off translations of words or to enclose single letters within sentences. For the use of quotation marks to enclose titles of poems, paintings, or other works, see the section on Proper Nouns, Pronouns, and Adjectives in Chapter 2, "Capitals, Italics, and Quotation Marks."

NOTE: Lengthy passages of quoted material are usually indented as separate paragraphs without enclosing quotation marks. These paragraphs are commonly referred to as *extracts, excerpts,* or *block quotations.* Typically, block quotations are preceded by a full sentence ending with a colon, and they begin with a full sentence whose first word is capitalized. For an example of a block quotation, see paragraph 5 under Colon in this chapter.

BASIC USES

1. Quotation marks enclose direct quotations but not indirect quotations.

She said, "I am leaving."

"I am leaving," she said, "and I'm not coming back."

"I am leaving," she said. "This has gone on long enough."

She said that she was leaving.

2. Quotation marks enclose fragments of quoted matter when they are reproduced exactly as originally stated.

The agreement makes it clear that he "will be paid only upon receipt of an acceptable manuscript."

As late as 1754, documents refer to him as "yeoman" and "husbandman."

3. Quotation marks enclose words or phrases borrowed from others, words used in a special way, or words of marked informality when they are introduced into formal writing.

That kind of corporation is referred to as "closed" or "privately held."

Be sure to send a copy of your resume, or as some folks would say, your "biodata summary."

They were afraid the patient had "stroked out"—had had a cerebrovascular accident.

4. Quotation marks are sometimes used to enclose words referred to as words. Italic type is also frequently used for this purpose. For more on this use of italics, see the section on Other Uses of Italics in Chapter 2, "Capitals, Italics, and Quotation Marks."

He went through the manuscript and changed every "he" to "she."

5. Quotation marks enclose short exclamations or representations of sounds. Representations of sounds are also frequently set in italic type. For more on this use of italics, see the section on Other Uses of Italics in Chapter 2, "Capitals, Italics, and Quotation Marks."

"Ssshh!" she hissed.

They never say anything crude like "shaddap."

6. Quotation marks enclose short sentences that fall within longer sentences, especially when the shorter sentence is meant to suggest spoken dialogue. Kinds of sentences that may be treated in this way include mottoes and maxims, unspoken or imaginary dialogue, or sentences referred to as sentences.

Throughout the camp, the spirit was "We can do."

She never could get used to his "That's the way it goes" attitude.

In effect, the voters were saying "You blew it, and you don't get another chance."

Their attitude could only be described as "Kill the messenger."

Another example of a palindrome is "Madam, I'm Adam."

NOTE: Style varies regarding the punctuation of sentences such as these. In general, the force of the quotation marks is to set the shorter sentence off more distinctly from the surrounding sentence and to give the shorter sentence more of the feel of spoken dialogue; omitting the quotation marks diminishes the effect. (For a description of the use of commas in sentences like these, see paragraphs 33 and 34 under Comma in this chapter.)

The first rule is, When in doubt, spell it out.

They weren't happy with the impression she left: "Don't expect favors, because I don't have to give them."

7. Quotation marks are not used to enclose paraphrases.

Build a better mouse trap, Emerson says, and the world will beat a path to your door.

8. Direct questions are usually not enclosed in quotation marks unless they represent quoted dialogue.

The question is, What went wrong?

As we listened to him, we couldn't help wondering, Where's the plan?

She asked, "What went wrong?"

NOTE: As in the sentences presented in paragraph 6 above, style varies regarding the use of quotation marks with direct questions; and in many cases, writers will include the quotation marks.

As we listened to him, we couldn't help wondering, "Where's the plan?"

9. Quotation marks are used to enclose translations of foreign or borrowed terms.

The term *sesquipedalian* comes from the Latin word *sesquipedalis,* meaning "a foot and a half long."

While in Texas, he encountered the armadillo ("little armored one") and developed quite an interest in it.

10. Quotation marks are sometimes used to enclose single letters within a sentence.

The letter "m" is wider than the letter "i."

We started to work on the dictionary, beginning with the letter "A."

Put an "x" in the right spot.

The metal rod was shaped into a "V."

NOTE: Style varies on this point. Sans serif type is most often used when the shape of the letter is being stressed. Letters referred to as letters are commonly set in italic type. (For more on this use of italics, see the section on Other Uses of Italics in Chapter 2, "Capitals, Italics, and Quotation Marks.") Finally, letters often appear in the same typeface as the surrounding text if no confusion would result from the styling.

a V-shaped blade

How many *e*'s are in her name?

He was happy to get a B in the course.

WITH OTHER MARKS OF PUNCTUATION

11. When quotation marks follow a word in a sentence that is also followed by a period or comma, the period or comma is placed within the quotation marks.

He said, "I am leaving."

Her camera was described as "waterproof," but "moisture-resistant" would have been a better description.

NOTE: Some writers draw a distinction between periods and commas that belong logically to the quoted material and those that belong to the whole sentence. If the period or comma belongs to the quoted material, they place it inside the quotation marks; if the period belongs logically to the sentence that surrounds the quoted matter, they place it outside the quotation marks. This distinction was previously observed in a wide range of publications, including U.S. Congressional publications and Merriam-Webster® dictionaries. In current practice, the distinction is made in relatively few publications, although the distinction is routinely made for dashes, exclamation points, and question marks used with quotation marks, as described in paragraph 13 below.

The package was labeled "Handle with Care".

The act was referred to as the "Army-Navy Medical Services Corps Act of 1947".

Her camera was described as "waterproof", but "moisture-resistant" would have been a better description.

He said, "I am leaving."

12. When quotation marks follow a word in a sentence that is also followed by a colon or semicolon, the colon or semicolon is placed outside the quotation marks.

There was only one thing to do when he said, "I may not run": promise him a larger campaign contribution.

She spoke of her "little cottage in the country"; she might better have called it a mansion.

13. The dash, question mark, and exclamation point are placed inside quotation marks when they punctuate the quoted matter only. They are placed outside the quotation marks when they punctuate the whole sentence.

He asked, "When did she leave?"

What is the meaning of "the open door"?

Save us from his "mercy"!

"I can't see how—" he started to say.

He thought he knew where he was going—he remembered her saying, "Take two lefts, then stay to the right"—but the streets didn't look familiar.

14. One space follows a quotation mark that is followed by the rest of a sentence.

"I am leaving," she said.

15. In typewritten material, two spaces follow a quotation mark that ends a sentence. In typeset material one space follows.

```
He said, "Here is the car."    I asked if
I should get in.
```

He said, "Here is the car." I asked if I should get in.

QUOTATION MARKS, SINGLE

1. Single quotation marks enclose a quotation within a quotation in conventional English.

The witness said, "I distinctly heard him say, 'Don't be late,' and then I heard the door close."

The witness said, "I distinctly heard him say, 'Don't be late.' "

NOTE: When both single and double quotation marks occur at the end of a sentence, the period typically falls *within* both sets of marks.

2. Single quotation marks are sometimes used in place of double quotation marks especially in British usage.

The witness said, 'I distinctly heard him say, "Don't be late," and then I heard the door close.'

3. On rare occasions, authors face the question of how to style a quotation within a quotation within a quotation. Standard styling practice would be to enclose the innermost quotation in double marks; however, this construction can be confusing, and in many cases rewriting the sentence can remove the need for it.

The witness said, "I distinctly heard him say, 'Don't you say "Shut up" to me.' "

The witness said that she distinctly heard him say, "Don't you say 'Shut up' to me."

4. In some specialized fields, such as theology, philosophy, and linguistics, special terminology or words referred to as words are enclosed within single quotation marks. When single quotation marks are used in this way, any other punctuation following the word enclosed is placed outside the quotation marks.

She was interested in the development of the word 'humongous', especially during the 1960s.

SEMICOLON

The semicolon is used in ways that are similar to those in which periods and commas are used. Because of these similarities, the semicolon is often thought of as either a weak period or a strong comma. As a weak period, the semicolon marks the end of a complete clause and signals that the clause that follows it is closely related to the clause that precedes it. As a strong comma, the semicolon clarifies meaning usually by distinguishing major sentence divisions from the minor pauses that are represented by commas.

BETWEEN CLAUSES

1. A semicolon separates independent clauses that are joined together in one sentence without a coordinating conjunction.

> He hemmed and hawed for over an hour; he couldn't make up his mind.

> The river rose and overflowed its banks; roads became flooded and impassable; freshly plowed fields disappeared from sight.

> Cream the shortening and sugar; add the eggs and beat well.

2. Ordinarily a comma separates main clauses joined with a coordinating conjunction. However, if the sentence might be confusing with a comma in this position, a semicolon is used in its place. Potentially confusing sentences include those with other commas in them or with particularly long clauses.

> We fear that this situation may, in fact, occur; but we don't know when.

> In a society that seeks to promote social goals, government will play a powerful role; and taxation, once simply a means of raising money, becomes, in addition, a way of furthering those goals.

> As recently as 1978 the company felt the operation could be a successful one that would generate significant profits in several different markets; but in 1981 the management changed its mind and began a program of shutting down plants and reducing its product line.

3. A semicolon joins two statements when the grammatical construction of the second clause is elliptical and depends on that of the first.

> The veal dishes were very good; the desserts, too.

> In many cases the conference sessions, which were designed to allow for full discussions of topics, were much too long and tedious; the breaks between them, much too short.

4. A semicolon joins two clauses when the second begins with a conjunctive adverb, as *accordingly, also, besides, consequently, furthermore, hence, however, indeed, likewise, moreover, namely, nevertheless, otherwise, still, then, therefore,* and *thus.* Phrases such as *by the same token, in that case, as a result, on the other hand,* and *all the same* can also act as conjunctive adverbs.

> Most people are covered by insurance of one kind or another; indeed, many people don't even see their medical bills.

> It won't be easy to sort out the facts of this confusing situation; however, a decision must be made.

> The case could take years to work its way through the court system; as a result, many plaintiffs will accept out-of-court settlements.

NOTE: Style varies regarding the treatment of clauses introduced by *so* and *yet.* Although many writers continue to treat *so* and *yet* as adverbs, it has become stan-

dard to treat these words as coordinating conjunctions that join clauses. In this treatment, a comma precedes *so* and *yet* and no punctuation follows them. (For examples, see paragraph 1 under Comma in this chapter.)

5. When three or more clauses are separated by semicolons, a coordinating conjunction may or may not precede the final clause. If a coordinating conjunction does precede the final clause, the final semicolon is often replaced with a comma. (For the use of commas to separate three or more clauses without conjunctions, see paragraph 4 under Comma in this chapter.)

> Their report was one-sided and partial; it did not reflect the facts; it distorted them.

> They don't understand; they grow bored; and they stop learning.

> The report recounted events leading up to the incident; it included observations of eyewitnesses, but it drew no conclusions.

NOTE: The choices of whether to use a conjunction and whether to use a semicolon or comma with the conjunction are matters of personal preference. In general, the force of the semicolon is to make the transition to the final clause more abrupt, which often serves to place more emphasis on that clause. The comma and conjunction ease the transition and make the sentence seem less choppy.

WITH PHRASES AND CLAUSES INTRODUCED BY *FOR EXAMPLE, I.E.,* ETC.

6. A semicolon is sometimes used before expressions (as *for example, for instance, that is, namely, e.g.,* or *i.e.*) that introduce expansions or series. Commas, dashes, and parentheses are also used in sentences like these. For contrasting examples, see paragraph 18 under Comma, paragraph 6 under Dash, and paragraph 2 under Parentheses in this chapter.

> On one point only did everyone agree; namely, that too much money had been spent already.

> We were fairly successful on that project; that is, we made our deadlines and met our budget.

> Most of the contestants had traveled great distances to participate; for example, three had come from Australia, one from Japan, and two from China.

IN A SERIES

7. A semicolon is used in place of a comma to separate phrases in a series when the phrases themselves contain commas. A comma may replace the semicolon before the last item in a series if the last item is introduced with a conjunction.

> She flung open the door; raced up the stairs, taking them two at a time; locked herself in the bathroom; and, holding her sides, started to laugh uncontrollably.

> The visitor to Barndale was offered three sources of overnight accommodation: The Rose and Anchor, which housed Barndale's oldest pub; The Crawford, an American-style luxury hotel; and Ellen's Bed and Breakfast on Peabody Lane.

> We studied mathematics and geography in the morning; English, French, and Spanish right after lunch, and science in the late afternoon.

8. When the individual items in an enumeration or series are long or are sentences themselves, they are usually separated by semicolons.

> Among the committee's recommendations: more hospital beds in urban areas where there are waiting lists for elective surgery; smaller staff size in half-empty rural hospitals; review procedures for all major purchases.

> There is a difference between them: she is cross and irritable; he is merely moody.

As a Mechanical Device

9. A semicolon separates items in a list in cases where a comma alone would not clearly separate the items or references.

> (Friedlander 1957; Ballas 1962)
> (Genesis 3:1-19; 4:1-16)

With Other Marks of Punctuation

10. A semicolon is placed outside quotation marks and parentheses.

> They referred to each other as "Mother" and "Father"; they were the archetypal happily married elderly couple.

> She accepted the situation with every appearance of equanimity (but with some inward qualms); however, all of that changed the next day.

VIRGULE

The virgule is known by many names, including *diagonal, solidus, oblique, slant, slash,* and *slash mark.* Most commonly, the virgule is used to represent a word that is not written out or to separate or set off certain adjacent elements of text.

In Place of Missing Words

1. A virgule represents the word *per* or *to* when used with units of measure or when used to indicate the terms of a ratio.

> 40,000 tons/year
> 9 ft./sec.
> a 50/50 split
> 14 gm/100 cc
> price/earnings ratio
> risk/reward tradeoff

2. A virgule separates alternatives. In this context, the virgule usually represents the words *or* or *and/or*.

> alumni/ae
> his/her
> introductory/refresher courses
> oral/written tests

3. A virgule replaces the word *and* in some compound terms.

> molybdenum/vanadium steel
> in the May/June issue
> 1973/74
> in the Falls Church/McLean, Va., area
> an innovative classroom/laboratory

4. A virgule is used, although less commonly, to replace a number of prepositions, such as *at, versus, with,* and *for.*

> U.C./Berkeley
> parent/child issues
> table/mirror
> Vice President/Editorial

With Abbreviations

5. A virgule punctuates some abbreviations.

> c/o
> A/V
> d/b/a
> A/R
> A/1C
> S/Sgt
> w/
> V/STOL

NOTE: In some cases the virgule may stand for a word that is not represented in the abbreviation (e.g., *in* in *W/O,* the abbreviation for *water in oil*).

To Separate Elements

6. The virgule is used in a number of mechanical ways to separate groups of numbers, such as elements in a date, numerators and denominators in fractions, and area codes in telephone numbers. For more on the use of virgules with numbers, see Chapter 5, "The Treatment of Numbers."

7. The virgule serves as a divider between lines of poetry that are run in with the text around them. This method of quoting poetry is usually limited to passages of no more than three or four lines. Longer passages are usually set off from the text as extract quotations, with the lines set exactly as in the original, and without virgules separating them.

> When Samuel Taylor Coleridge wrote in "Christabel" that "'Tis a month before the month of May,/And the Spring comes slowly up this way," he could have been describing New England.

8. The virgule sets off certain elements—such as the parts of an address that are normally placed on separate lines—when they appear run in with the surrounding text.

> Mlle Christine Lagache/20, Passage des Écoliers/75051 Paris/France

9. The virgule sets off phonemes and phonemic transcriptions.

> /b/ as in *but*
> pronounced /ˌekəˈnämik/ or /ˌēkəˈnämik/

Spacing

10. In general, no space is used between the virgule and the words, letters, or figures separated by it. Some authors and editors prefer to place spaces around a virgule used to separate lines of poetry, but most omit the space. In the case of virgules used to set off phonemes and phonemic transcriptions, however, a space precedes the first virgule and follows the second virgule.

CHAPTER 2

Capitals, Italics, and Quotation Marks

Words and phrases are capitalized, italicized, or enclosed in quotation marks in order to indicate that they have a special significance in a particular context. Some rules regarding capitals, italics, and quotation marks are backed by long tradition and are quite easy to apply ("The first word of a sentence or sentence fragment is capitalized"); others require arbitrary decisions or personal judgment ("Foreign words and phrases that have not been fully adopted into the English language are italicized"). Careful writers and editors usually make notes or keep a style sheet to record the decisions that they make so they can be consistent in their use of capitals, italics, and quotation marks.

This chapter is divided into four sections. The first section explains the use of capitalized words to begin sentences and phrases. The second section explains the use of capitals, italics, and quotation marks to indicate that a word or phrase is a proper noun, pronoun, or adjective. The third and fourth sections explain other uses of capital letters and italics. For other uses of quotation marks, see the section on Quotation Marks in Chapter 1, "Punctuation."

BEGINNINGS

1. The first word of a sentence or sentence fragment is capitalized.

> The meeting was postponed.
>
> No! I cannot do it.
>
> Will you go?
>
> Total chaos. Nothing works.

2. The first word of a sentence contained within parentheses is capitalized; however, a parenthetical sentence occurring inside another sentence is not capitalized unless it is a complete quoted sentence.

> The discussion was held in the boardroom. (The results are still confidential.)
>
> Although we liked the restaurant (their Italian food was the best), we could not afford to eat there often.
>
> After waiting in line for an hour (why do we do these things?), we finally left.
>
> He was totally demoralized ("There is just nothing we can do") and was contemplating resignation.

3. The first word of a direct quotation is capitalized; however, if the quotation is interrupted in midsentence, the second part does not begin with a capital.

> The President said, "We have rejected this report entirely."
>
> "We have rejected this report entirely," the President said, "and we will not comment on it further."

4. When a quotation, whether a sentence fragment or a complete sentence, is syntactically dependent on the sentence in which it occurs, the quotation does not begin with a capital.

> The President made it clear that "there is no room for compromise."

5. The first word of a sentence within a sentence is usually capitalized. Examples of sentences within sentences include mottoes and rules, unspoken or imaginary dialogue, sentences referred to as sentences, and direct questions. (For an explanation of the use of commas and quotation marks with sentences such as these, see paragraphs 34 and 35 in the section on Comma and paragraph 6 in the section on Quotation Marks, Double in Chapter 1, "Punctuation.")

> You know the saying, "A stitch in time saves nine."
>
> The first rule is, When in doubt, spell it out.
>
> The clear message coming back from the audience was "We don't care."
>
> My question is, When can we go?
>
> She kept wondering, how did they get here so soon?

NOTE: In the cases of unspoken or imaginary dialogue and of direct questions, it is a matter of individual preference whether or not to capitalize the first word; however, the most common practice is to capitalize it.

6. The first word of a line of poetry is conventionally capitalized.

> The best lack all conviction, while the worst
> Are full of passionate intensity.
> —W. B. Yeats

7. The first word following a colon may be either lowercased or capitalized if it introduces a complete sentence. While the former is the usual styling, the latter is also quite common, especially when the sentence introduced by the colon is fairly lengthy and distinctly separate from the preceding clause.

> The advantage of this particular system is clear: it's inexpensive.
>
> The situation is critical: This company cannot hope to recoup the fourth-quarter losses that were sustained in five operating divisions.

NOTE: For the sake of consistency, many authors and editors prefer to use one style or the other in all cases, regardless of sentence length. The capitalized style is more common in newspapers, but overall the lowercased styling is more frequently used.

8. If a colon introduces a series of sentences, the first word of each sentence is capitalized.

> Consider the following steps that we have taken: A subcommittee has been formed to evaluate our past performance and to report its findings to the full organization. New sources of revenue are being explored, and relevant or-

ganizations are being contacted. And several candidates have been interviewed for the new post of executive director.

9. The first words of run-in enumerations that form complete sentences are capitalized, as are the first words of phrasal lists and enumerations arranged vertically beneath running texts. Phrasal enumerations run in with the introductory text, however, are lowercased.

> Do the following tasks at the end of the day: 1. Clean your typewriter. 2. Clear your desktop of papers. 3. Cover office machines. 4. Straighten the contents of your desk drawers, cabinets, and bookcases.

> This is the agenda:
> Call to order
> Roll call
> Minutes of the previous meeting
> Treasurer's report

> On the agenda will be (1) call to order, (2) roll call, (3) minutes of the previous meeting, (4) treasurer's report . . .

10. The introductory words *Whereas* and *Resolved* are capitalized in minutes and legislation, as is the word *That* or an alternative word or expression which immediately follows either.

> Resolved, That . . .
> Whereas, Substantial benefits . . .

11. The first word in an outline heading is capitalized.

> I. Editorial tasks
> II. Production responsibilities
> A. Cost estimates
> B. Bids

12. The first word of the salutation of a letter and the first word of a complimentary close are capitalized.

> Dear Mary,
> Dear Sir or Madam:
> Ladies and Gentlemen:
> Gentlemen:
> Sincerely yours,
> Very truly yours,

13. The first word and each subsequent major word following a SUBJECT or TO heading (as in a memorandum) are capitalized.

> SUBJECT: Pension Plans
> TO: All Department Heads and Editors

PROPER NOUNS, PRONOUNS, AND ADJECTIVES

This section describes the ways in which a broad range of proper nouns, pronouns, and adjectives are styled—with capitals, italics, quotation marks, or some combination of these devices. In almost all cases, proper nouns, pronouns, and adjectives are capitalized. The essential distinction in the use of capitals and lowercase letters lies in the particularizing or individualizing significance of capitals as against the generalizing significance of lowercase. A capital is used with a proper noun because it distinguishes some individual person, place, or thing from others of the same class. A capital is used with a proper adjective because it takes its descriptive meaning from a proper noun.

In many cases, proper nouns are italicized or enclosed in quotation marks in addition to being capitalized. No clear distinctions can be drawn between the

kinds of words that are capitalized and italicized, capitalized and enclosed in quotation marks, or simply capitalized, as styling on these points is governed almost wholly by tradition.

The paragraphs in this section are grouped under the following alphabetically arranged headings:

> Abbreviations
> Abstractions and Personifications
> Academic Degrees
> Animals and Plants
> Awards, Honors, and Prizes
> Derivatives of Proper Names
> Geographical and Topographical References
> Governmental, Judicial, and Political Bodies
> Historical Periods and Events
> Hyphenated Compounds
> Legal Material
> Medical Terms
> Military Terms
> Numerical Designations
> Organizations
> People
> Pronouns
> Religious Terms
> Scientific Terms
> Time Periods and Zones
> Titles
> Trademarks
> Transportation

ABBREVIATIONS

1. Abbreviated forms of proper nouns and adjectives are capitalized, just as the spelled-out forms would be. For more on the capitalization of abbreviations, see the section on Capitalization in Chapter 4, "Abbreviations."

> Dec. for *December*
> Wed. for *Wednesday*
> Col. for *Colonel*
> Brit. for *British*

ABSTRACTIONS AND PERSONIFICATIONS

2. Abstract terms, such as names of concepts or qualities, are usually not capitalized unless the concept or quality is being presented as if it were a person. If the term is simply being used in conjunction with other words that allude to human characteristics or qualities, it is usually not capitalized. For more on the capitalization of abstract terms, see the section on Other Uses of Capitals in this chapter.

> a time when Peace walked among us
> as Autumn paints each leaf in fiery colors
> an economy gripped by inflation
> hoping that fate would lend a hand

3. Fictitious names used as personifications are capitalized.

> Uncle Sam
> Ma Bell
> John Bull
> Jack Frost
> Big Oil squirmed under the new regulations.

ACADEMIC DEGREES

4. The names of academic degrees are capitalized when they follow a person's name. The names of specific academic degrees not following a person's name are capitalized or not capitalized according to individual preference. General terms referring to degrees, such as *doctorate, master's degree,* or *bachelor's* are not capitalized. Abbreviations for academic degrees are always capitalized.

> Martin Bonkowski, Doctor of Divinity
> earned her Doctor of Laws degree   *or*
>   earned her doctor of laws degree
> working for a bachelor's degree
> Susan Wycliff, M.S.W.
> received her Ph.D.

ANIMALS AND PLANTS

5. The common names of animals and plants are not capitalized unless they contain a proper noun as a separate element, in which case the proper noun is capitalized, but any element of the name following the proper noun is lowercased. Elements of the name preceding the proper noun are usually but not always capitalized. In some cases, the common name of the plant or animal contains a word that was once a proper noun but is no longer thought of as such. In these cases, the word is usually not capitalized. When in doubt about the capitalization of a plant or animal name, consult a dictionary. (For an explanation of the capitalization of genus names in binomial nomenclature or of New Latin names for groups above genera in zoology and botany, see paragraphs 67 and 68 below.)

> cocker spaniel
> lily of the valley
> ponderosa pine
> great white shark
> Hampshire hog
> Kentucky bluegrass
> Steller's jay
> Bengal tiger
> Japanese beetle
> Rhode Island red
> Great Dane
> Brown Swiss
> black-eyed Susan
> wandering Jew
> holstein

NOTE: In references to specific breeds, as distinguished from the animals that belong to the breed, all elements of the name are capitalized.

> Gordon Setter
> Rhode Island Red
> Holstein

AWARDS, HONORS, AND PRIZES

6. Names of awards, honors, and prizes are capitalized. Descriptive words and phrases that are not actually part of the award's name are lowercased. (For an explanation of capitalizing the names of military decorations, see paragraph 44 below.)

> Academy Award
> Emmy
> New York Drama Critics' Circle Award
> Nobel Prize
> Nobel Prize in medicine
> Nobel Prize winner
> Nobel Peace Prize
> Rhodes Scholarship
> Rhodes scholar

BRAND NAMES—See **TRADEMARKS** below.

COMPUTER TERMS—See **SCIENTIFIC TERMS** below.

DERIVATIVES OF PROPER NAMES

7. Derivatives of proper names are capitalized when they are used in their primary sense. However, if the derived term has taken on a specialized meaning, it is usually not capitalized.

> Roman architecture
> Victorian customs
> Keynesian economics
> an Americanism
> an Egyptologist
> french fries
> manila envelope
> pasteurized milk
> a quixotic undertaking

GEOGRAPHICAL AND TOPOGRAPHICAL REFERENCES

8. Terms that identify divisions of the earth's surface and distinct areas, regions, places, or districts are capitalized, as are derivative nouns and adjectives.

> Chicago, Illinois
> Tropic of Capricorn
> the Middle Eastern situation
> Western Hemisphere
> the Southwest
> the Sunbelt

9. Popular names of localities are capitalized.

> the Big Apple
> the Loop
> Hell's Kitchen
> the Village
> the Twin Cities
> the Valley

10. Compass points are capitalized when they refer to a geographical region or when they are part of a street name. They are lowercased when they refer to a simple direction.

> back East
> West Columbus Avenue
> up North
> South Pleasant Street
> out West
> down South
> east of the Mississippi
> traveling north on I-91

11. Nouns and adjectives that are derived from compass points and that designate or refer to a specific geographical region are usually capitalized.

> a Southern accent
> a Western crop
> Northerners
> part of the Eastern establishment

12. Words designating global, national, regional, or local political divisions are capitalized when they are essential elements of specific names. However, they are usually lowercased when they precede a proper name or when they are not part of a specific name.

> the British Empire
> New York City
> Washington State
> Ward 1
> Hampden County

Ohio's Ninth Congressional District
the fall of the empire
the city of New York
the state of Washington
fires in three wards
the county of Hampden
carried her district

NOTE: In legal documents, these words are often capitalized regardless of position.

the State of Washington
the County of Hampden
the City of New York

13. Generic geographical terms (as *lake, mountain, river, valley*) are capitalized if they are part of a specific proper name.

Crater Lake
Lake Como
Rocky Mountains
Columbia River
Ohio Valley
Long Island
Great Barrier Reef
Atlantic Ocean
Niagara Falls
Hudson Bay
Strait of Gibraltar
Bering Strait

14. Generic geographical terms preceding names are usually capitalized.

Lakes Mead and Powell
Mounts Whitney and Shasta

NOTE: When *the* precedes the generic term, the generic term is lowercased.

the river Thames

15. Generic geographical terms that are not used as part of a proper name are not capitalized. These include plural generic geographical terms that follow two or more proper names and generic terms that are used descriptively or alone.

the Himalaya and Andes mountains
the Missouri and Platte rivers
the Atlantic coast of Labrador
the Arizona desert
the Mississippi delta
the Caribbean islands
the river valley
the valley

16. The names of streets, monuments, parks, landmarks, well-known buildings, and other public places are capitalized. However, generic terms that are part of these names (as *avenue, bridge,* or *tower*) are lowercased when they occur after multiple names or are used alone (but see paragraph 17 below).

Golden Gate Bridge
the Capitol
Rock Creek Park
Eddystone Lighthouse
the Dorset Hotel
Fanueil Hall
the San Diego Zoo
Coit Tower
the Mall
the Pyramids
the Statue of Liberty
Peachtree Street
the Dorset and Drake hotels

Fifth and Park avenues
on the bridge
walking through the park

17. Well-known informal or shortened forms of place-names are capitalized.

the Avenue for *Fifth Avenue*
the Street for *Wall Street*
the Exchange for the *New York Stock Exchange*

GOVERNMENTAL, JUDICIAL, AND POLITICAL BODIES

18. Full names of legislative, deliberative, executive, and administrative bodies are capitalized, as are easily recognizable short forms of these names. However, nonspecific noun and adjective references to them are usually lowercased.

United States Congress
the Federal Reserve Board
the Congress
the House
the Federal Bureau of Investigation
the Fed
congressional hearings
a federal agency

NOTE: Style varies regarding the capitalization of words such as *department, committee,* or *agency* when they are being used in place of the full name of a specific body. They are most often capitalized when the department or agency is referring to itself in print. In most other cases, these words are lowercased.

The Connecticut Department of Transportation is pleased to offer this new booklet on traffic safety. The Department hopes that it will be of use to all drivers.

We received a new booklet from the Connecticut Department of Transportation. This is the second pamphlet the department has issued this month.

19. The U.S. Supreme Court and the short forms *Supreme Court* and *Court* referring to it are capitalized.

the Supreme Court of the United States
the United States Supreme Court
the Supreme Court
the Court

20. Official and full names of higher courts and names of international courts are capitalized. Short forms of official higher court names are often capitalized in legal documents but lowercased in general writing.

The International Court of Arbitration
the United States Court of Appeals for the Second Circuit
the Virginia Supreme Court
the Court of Queen's Bench
a ruling by the court of appeals
the state supreme court

21. Names of city and county courts are usually lowercased.

the Lawton municipal court
police court
the Owensville night court
the county court
small claims court
juvenile court

22. The single designation *court,* when specifically applicable to a judge or a presiding officer, is capitalized.

It is the opinion of this Court that . . .
The Court found that . . .

23. The terms *federal* and *national* are capitalized only when they are essential elements of a name or title.

Federal Trade Commission
National Security Council
federal court
national security

24. The word *administration* is capitalized in some publications when it refers to the administration of a specific United States president; however, the word is more commonly lowercased in this situation. If the word does not refer to a specific presidential administration, it is not capitalized except when it is a part of an official name of a government agency.

the Truman administration   *or*   the Truman Administration
the administration   *or*   the Administration
the Farmers Home Loan Administration

The running of the White House varies considerably from one administration to another.

25. Names of political organizations and their adherents are capitalized, but the word *party* may or may not be capitalized, depending on the writer's or publication's preference.

the Democratic National Committee
the Republican platform
Tories
Nazis
the Democratic party   *or*   the Democratic Party
the Communist party   *or*   the Communist Party

26. Names of political groups other than parties are usually lowercased, as are their derivative forms.

rightist
right wing
left winger
but usually
the Left
the Right

27. Terms describing political and economic philosophies and their derivative forms are usually capitalized only if they are derived from proper names.

authoritarianism
nationalism
isolationist
democracy
supply-side economics
civil libertarian
fascism   *or*   Fascism
social Darwinism
Marxist

HISTORICAL PERIODS AND EVENTS

28. The names of conferences, councils, expositions, and specific sporting, historical, and cultural events are capitalized.

the Yalta Conference
the Congress of Vienna
the Minnesota State Fair
the Games of the XXIII Olympiad
the World Series
the Series
the Boston Tea Party

the San Francisco Earthquake
the Bonus March of 1932
the Philadelphia Folk Festival
the Golden Gate International Exposition

29. The names of some historical and cultural periods and movements are capitalized. When in doubt about such a name, consult a dictionary or encyclopedia.

Augustan Age
Renaissance
Stone Age
Prohibition
the Enlightenment
the Great Depression
fin de siècle
space age
cold war   *or*   Cold War

30. Numerical designations of historical time periods are capitalized only when they are part of a proper name; otherwise they are lowercased.

the Third Reich
Roaring Twenties
seventeenth century
eighties

31. Full names of treaties, laws, and acts are capitalized.

Treaty of Versailles
The Controlled Substances Act of 1970

32. The full names of wars are capitalized; however, words such as *war, revolution, battle,* and *campaign* are capitalized only when they are part of a proper name. Descriptive terms such as *assault, seige,* and *engagement* are usually lowercased even when used in conjunction with the name of the place where the action occurred.

the French and Indian War
the Spanish American War
the War of the Roses
the Six-Day War
the War of the Spanish Succession
the American Revolution
the Whiskey Rebellion
the Revolution of 1688
the Battle of the Coral Sea
the Battle of the Bulge
the naval battle of Guadalcanal
the Peninsular Campaign
the American and French revolutions
the second battle of Manassas
the seige of Yorktown
the Meuse-Argonne offensive
the winter campaign
the assault on Iwo Jima
was in action throughout most of the war

HYPHENATED COMPOUNDS

33. Elements of hyphenated compounds are capitalized if they are proper nouns or adjectives.

Arab-Israeli negotiations
Tay-Sachs disease
East-West trade agreements
U.S.-U.S.S.R. détente
an eighteenth-century poet
American-plan rates

NOTE: If the second element in a two-word compound is not a proper noun or adjective, it is lowercased.

French-speaking peoples
an A-frame house
Thirty-second Street

34. Word elements (as prefixes and combining forms) may or may not be capitalized when joined to a proper noun or adjective. Common prefixes (as *pre-* or *anti-*) are usually not capitalized when so attached. Geographical and ethnic combining forms (as *Anglo-* or *Afro-*) are capitalized; *pan-* is usually capitalized when attached to a proper noun or adjective.

the pro-Soviet faction
post-Civil War politics
un-American activities
Afro-Americans
Sino-Soviet relations
Greco-Roman architecture
Pan-Slavic nationalism
the Pan-African Congress

LANGUAGES—See also PEOPLE below.

LEGAL MATERIAL—See also GOVERNMENTAL, JUDICIAL, AND POLITICAL BODIES above.

35. The names of both plaintiff and defendant in legal case titles are italicized. The *v.* for *versus* may be roman or italic. Cases that do not involve two opposing parties have titles such as *In re Watson* or *In the matter of John Watson*; these case titles are also italicized. When the person involved rather than the case itself is being discussed, the reference is not italicized.

Jones v. *Massachusetts*
In re Jones
Smith et al. v. Jones

She covered the Jones trial for the newspaper.

NOTE: In running text a case name involving two opposing parties may be shortened.

The judge based his ruling on a precedent set in the *Jones* decision.

MEDICAL TERMS

36. Proper names that are elements in terms designating diseases, symptoms, syndromes, and tests are capitalized. Common nouns are lowercased.

Down's syndrome
Parkinson's disease
Duchenne-Erb paralysis
Rorschach test
German measles
syndrome of Weber
acquired immunodeficiency syndrome
mumps
measles
herpes simplex

37. Taxonomic names of disease-causing organisms follow the rules established for binomial nomenclature discussed in paragraph 67 below. The names of diseases or pathological conditions derived from taxonomic names of organisms are lowercased and not italicized.

a neurotoxin produced by *Clostridium botulinum*
nearly died of botulism

38. Generic names of drugs are lowercased; trade names should be capitalized.

a prescription for chlorpromazine
had been taking Thorazine

MILITARY TERMS

39. The full titles of branches of the armed forces are capitalized, as are easily recognized short forms of full branch designations.

U.S. Air Force
the Air Force
U.S. Navy
the Navy
U.S. Army
the Army
U.S. Coast Guard
the Coast Guard
U.S. Marine Corps
the Marine Corps
the Marines
the Corps

40. The terms *air force, army, coast guard, marine* (*s*), and *navy* are lowercased unless they form a part of an official name or refer back to a specific branch of the armed forces previously named. They are also lowercased when they are used collectively or in the plural.

the combined air forces of the NATO nations
the navies of the world
the American army

In some countries the duty of the coast guard may include icebreaking in inland waterways.

41. The adjectives *naval* and *marine* are lowercased unless they are part of a proper name.

naval battle
marine barracks
Naval Reserves

42. The full titles of units and organizations of the armed forces are capitalized. Elements of full titles are lowercased when they stand alone.

U.S. Army Corps of Engineers
the corps
the Reserves
a reserve commission
First Battalion
the battalion
4th Marine Regiment
the regiment
Eighth Fleet
the fleet
Cruiser Division
the division
Fifth Army
the army

43. Military ranks are capitalized when they precede the names of their holders, and when they take the place of a person's name (as in direct address). Otherwise they are lowercased.

Admiral Nimitz
General Creighton W. Abrams

I can't get this rifle any cleaner, Sergeant.

The major arrived precisely on time.

44. The specific names of decorations, citations, and medals are capitalized.

Medal of Honor
Purple Heart
Silver Star
Navy Cross
Distinguished Service Medal

NICKNAMES—See paragraphs 49, 51, and 52 below.

NUMERICAL DESIGNATIONS

45. A noun introducing a reference number is usually capitalized.

> Order 704
> Flight 409
> Form 2E
> Policy 118-4-Y

46. Nouns used with numbers or letters to designate major reference headings (as in a literary work) are capitalized. However, nouns designating minor reference headings are typically lowercased.

> Book II
> Table 3
> paragraph 6.1
> Volume V
> page 101
> item 16
> Division 4
> line 8
> question 21
> Figure 1
> note 10

ORGANIZATIONS

47. Names of firms, corporations, schools, and organizations and terms derived from those names to designate their members are capitalized. However, common nouns used descriptively or occurring after the names of two or more organizations are lowercased.

> Merriam-Webster Inc.
> Rotary International
> University of Michigan
> Kiwanians
> Smith College
> American and United airlines
> Washington Huskies
> Minnesota North Stars
> played as a Pirate last year

NOTE: The word *the* at the beginning of such names is capitalized only when the full legal name is used.

48. Words such as *agency, department, division, group,* or *office* that designate corporate and organizational units are capitalized only when they are used with a specific name.

> while working for the Criminal Division in the Department of Justice
> a notice to all department heads

NOTE: Style varies regarding the capitalization of these words when they are used in place of the full name of a specific body. For more on this aspect of styling, see the note following paragraph 18 above.

49. Nicknames, epithets, or other alternate terms for organizations are capitalized.

> referred to IBM as Big Blue
> the Big Three automakers
> trading stocks on the Big Board

PEOPLE

50. The names and initials of persons are capitalized. If a name is hyphenated, both elements are capitalized. Particles forming the initial elements of surnames (as *de, della, der, du, la, ten, ter, van,* and *von*) may or may not be capitalized, depending on the styling of the individual name. However, if a name with a lowercase initial particle begins a sentence, the particle is capitalized.

> Thomas de Quincey
> E. I. du Pont de Nemours
> Sir Arthur Thomas Quiller-Couch
> Gerald ter Hoerst
> James Van Allen
> Heinrich Wilhelm Von Kleist
> the paintings of de Kooning
> De Kooning's paintings are . . .

51. The name of a person or thing can be added to or replaced entirely by a nickname or epithet, a characterizing word or phrase. Nicknames and epithets are capitalized.

> Calamity Jane
> the Golden Bear
> Doctor J.
> Buffalo Bill
> Wilt the Stilt
> Attila the Hun
> Louis the Fat
> Murph the Surf
> Dizzy Gillespie
> Bubba Smith
> Dusty Rhodes
> Rusty Staub
> Goose Gossage
> Bird Parker
> Meadowlark Lemon
> Big Mama Thornton
> Night Train Lane
> Lefty Grove

52. Nicknames and epithets are frequently used in conjunction with both the first and last names of a person. If the nickname or epithet is placed between the first and last name, it will often be enclosed in quotation marks or parentheses; however, if the nickname is expected to be very well known to readers, the quotation marks or parentheses are often omitted. If the nickname precedes the first name, it is sometimes enclosed in quotation marks, but more often it is not.

> Thomas P. "Tip" O'Neill
> Joanne "Big Mama" Carner
> Earl ("Fatha") Hines
> Dennis (Oil Can) Boyd
> Mary Harris ("Mother") Jones
> Anna Mary Robertson "Grandma" Moses
> Kissin' Jim Folsom
> Blind Lemon Jefferson
> Slammin' Sammy Snead
> Mother Maybelle Carter

53. Words of family relationship preceding or used in place of a person's name are capitalized. However, these words are lowercased if they are part of a noun phrase that is being used in place of a name.

> Cousin Mercy
> Grandfather Barnes
> I know when Mother's birthday is.
> I know when my mother's birthday is.

54. Words designating languages, nationalities, peoples, races, religious groups, and tribes are capitalized. Descriptive terms used to refer to groups of people are variously capitalized or lowercased. Designations based on color are usually lowercased.

> Latin
> Canadians

Ibo
Afro-American
Caucasians
Muslims
Christians
Navajo
Bushman (for a nomadic hunter of southern Africa)
bushman (for an inhabitant of the Australian bush)
the red man in America
black, brown, and white people

55. Corporate, professional, and governmental titles are capitalized when they immediately precede a person's name, unless the name is being used as an appositive.

President Clinton
Queen Elizabeth
Senator Carol Moseley-Braun
Doctor Malatesta
Professor Greenbaum
Pastor Linda Jones

They wanted to meet the new pastor, Linda Jones.

Almost everyone has heard of Chrysler's president, Lee Iacocca.

56. When corporate or governmental titles are used as part of a descriptive phrase to identify a person rather than as a person's official title, the title is lowercased.

Senator Ted Stevens of Alaska *but* Ted Stevens, senator from Alaska
Lee Iacocca, president of Chrysler Corporation

NOTE: Style varies when governmental titles are used in descriptive phrases that precede a name.

Alaska senator Ted Stevens *or* Alaska Senator Ted Stevens

57. Specific governmental titles may be capitalized when they are used in place of particular individuals' names. In minutes and official records of proceedings, corporate titles are capitalized when they are used in place of individuals' names.

The Secretary of State gave a news conference.

The Judge will respond to questions in her chambers.

The Treasurer then stated his misgivings about the project.

58. Some publications always capitalize the word *president* when it refers to the United States presidency. However, the more common practice is to capitalize the word *president* only when it refers to a specific individual.

It is one of the duties of the President to submit a budget to Congress.

It is one of the duties of the president to submit a budget to Congress.

59. Titles are capitalized when they are used in direct address.

Tell me the truth, Doctor.
Where are we headed, Captain?

PERSONIFICATIONS—See **ABSTRACTIONS AND PERSONIFICATIONS** above.

PREFIXES—See **HYPHENATED COMPOUNDS** above.

PRONOUNS

60. The pronoun *I* is capitalized. For pronouns referring to the Deity, see rule 62 below.

He and I will attend the meeting.

RELIGIOUS TERMS

61. Words designating the Deity are capitalized.

Allah
God Almighty
Christ
Jehovah
Yahweh
the Holy Spirit

62. Personal pronouns referring to the Deity are usually capitalized. Relative pronouns (as *who, whom,* and *whose*) usually are not.

God in His mercy when God asks us to do His bidding believing that it was God who created the universe

NOTE: Some style manuals maintain that the pronoun does not need to be capitalized if it is closely preceded by its antecedent; however, in current practice, most writers capitalize the pronoun regardless of its position.

63. Traditional designations of apostles, prophets, and saints are capitalized.

our Lady
the Prophet
the Lawgiver

64. Names of religions, denominations, creeds and confessions, and religious orders are capitalized, as are adjectives derived from these names. The word *church* is capitalized only when it is used as part of the name of a specific body or edifice or, in some publications, when it refers to organized Christianity in general.

Judaism
Catholicism
the Church of Christ
the Southern Baptist Convention
Apostles' Creed
the Society of Jesus
the Poor Clares
Franciscans
Hunt Memorial Church
a Buddhist monastery
Islamic
the Baptist church on the corner
the Thirty-nine Articles of the Church of England

65. Names of the Bible or its books, parts, versions, or editions of it and other sacred books are capitalized but not italicized. Adjectives derived from the names of sacred books are variously capitalized and lowercased. When in doubt, consult a dictionary.

Authorized Version
Old Testament
Apocrypha
Talmud
Genesis
Pentateuch

Gospel of Saint Mark
Koran
biblical
talmudic
Koranic
Vedic

66. The names of prayers and well-known passages of the Bible are capitalized.

Ave Maria
the Sermon on the Mount
Ten Commandments
the Beatitudes
the Lord's Prayer
the Our Father

SCIENTIFIC TERMS

67. Genus names in biological binomial nomenclature are capitalized; species names are lowercased, even when derived from a proper name. Both genus and species names are italicized.

Both the wolf and the domestic dog are included in the genus *Canis.*

The California condor (*Gymnogyps californianus*) is facing extinction.

Trailing arbutus (*Epigaea repens*) and rue anemone (*Anemonella thalictroides*) are among the earliest wildflowers to bloom in the spring.

NOTE: When used, the names of races, varieties, or subspecies are lowercased. Like genus and species names, they are italicized.

Hyla versicolor chrysoscelis
Otis asio naevius

68. The New Latin names of classes, families, and all groups above the genus level in zoology and botany are capitalized but not italicized. Their derivative adjectives and nouns in English are neither capitalized nor italicized.

Gastropoda
gastropod
Thallophyta
thallophyte

69. The names, both scientific and informal, of planets and their satellites, asteroids, stars, constellations, groups of stars, and other unique celestial objects are capitalized. However, the words *sun, earth,* and *moon* are usually lowercased unless they occur with other astronomical names. Generic terms that are the final element in the name of a celestial object are usually lowercased.

Ganymede
Sirius
Great Bear
the Milky Way
Venus
Ursa Major
Pleiades
Big Dipper
Barnard's star
probes heading for the Moon and Mars

70. Names of meteorological phenomena are lowercased.

aurora australis
northern lights

aurora borealis
parhelic circle

71. Terms that identify geological eras, periods, epochs, and strata are capitalized. The generic terms that follow them are lowercased. The words *upper, middle,* and *lower* are capitalized when they are used to designate an epoch or series within a period; in most other cases, they are lowercased. The word *age* is capitalized in names such as *Age of Reptiles* or *Age of Fishes.*

Mesozoic era
Quaternary period
Oligocene epoch
Upper Cretaceous
Middle Ordovician
Lower Silurian

72. Proper names forming essential elements of scientific laws, theorems, and principles are capitalized. However, the common nouns *law, theorem, theory,* and the like are lowercased.

Boyle's law
Planck's constant
the Pythagorean theorem
Einstein's theory of relativity

NOTE: In terms referring to popular or fanciful theories or observations, descriptive words are usually capitalized as well.

Murphy's Law
the Peter Principle

73. The names of chemical elements and compounds are lowercased.

hydrogen fluoride
ferric ammonium citrate

74. The names of computer services and data bases are usually trademarks and should always be capitalized. The names of computer languages are irregularly styled either with an initial capital letter or with all letters capitalized. The names of some computer languages are commonly written either way. When in doubt, consult a dictionary.

CompuServe
TeleTransfer
Dow Jones News Retrieval Service
Atek
Pascal
BASIC
COBOL *or* Cobol
APL
PENTA
PL/1
FORTRAN *or* Fortran

TIME PERIODS AND ZONES

75. The names of days of the week, months of the year, and holidays and holy days are capitalized.

Easter
Independence Day
June
Passover
Memorial Day
Thanksgiving
Tuesday
Yom Kippur
Ramadan

76. The names of time zones are capitalized when abbreviated but usually lowercased when written out except for words that are themselves proper names.

> CST
> central standard time
> mountain time
> Pacific standard time

77. Names of the seasons are lowercased if they simply declare the time of year; however, they are capitalized if they are personified.

> My new book is scheduled to appear this
> spring.
> the sweet breath of Spring

TITLES—For titles of people, see **PEOPLE** above.

78. Words in titles of books, long poems, magazines, newspapers, plays, movies, novellas that are separately published, and works of art such as paintings and sculpture are capitalized except for internal articles, conjunctions, prepositions, and the *to* of infinitives. The entire title is italicized. For the styling of the Bible and other sacred works, see paragraph 65 above.

> *The Lives of a Cell*
> *Of Mice and Men*
> *Saturday Review*
> *Christian Science Monitor*
> Shakespeare's *Othello*
> *The Old Man and the Sea*
> Gainsborough's *Blue Boy*
> the movie *Wait until Dark*

NOTE: Some publications also capitalize prepositions of five or more letters (as *about* or *toward*).

79. An initial article that is part of a title is often omitted if it would be awkward in context. However, when it is included it is capitalized and italicized. A common exception to this style regards books that are referred to by an abbreviation. In this case, the initial article is neither capitalized nor italicized.

> *The Oxford English Dictionary*
> the 13-volume *Oxford English Dictionary*
> the *OED*

80. Style varies widely regarding the capitalization and italicization of initial articles and city names in the titles of newspapers. One style rule that can be followed is to capitalize and italicize any word that is part of the official title of the paper as shown on its masthead. However, this information is not always available, and even if it is available it can lead to apparent inconsistencies in styling. Because of this, many publications choose one way of styling newspaper titles regardless of their official titles. The most common styling is to italicize the city name but not to capitalize or italicize the initial article.

> the *New York Times*
> the *Wall Street Journal*
> the *Des Moines Register*
> the *Washington Post*

81. Many publications, especially newspapers, do not use italics to style titles. They either simply capitalize the words of the title or capitalize the words and enclose them in quotation marks.

> the Heard on the Street column in the Wall
> Street Journal
> our review of "The Lives of a Cell" in last
> week's column

82. The first word following a colon in a title is capitalized.

> John Crowe Ransom: An Annotated Bibliography

83. The titles of short poems, short stories, essays, lectures, dissertations, chapters of books, articles in periodicals, radio and television programs, and novellas that are published in a collection are capitalized and enclosed in quotation marks. The capitalization of articles, conjunctions, and prepositions is the same as it is for italicized titles, as explained in paragraph 78 above.

> Robert Frost's "Dust of Snow"
> Katherine Anne Porter's "That Tree"
> John Barth's "The Literature of Exhaustion"
> The talk, "Labor's Power: A View for the Eighties," will be given next week.
> the third chapter of *Treasure Island,* entitled "The Black Spot"
> Her article, "Computer Art on a Micro," was in last month's *Popular Computing.*
> listening to "A Prairie Home Companion"
> watching "The Tonight Show"
> D. H. Lawrence's "The Woman Who Rode Away"

84. Common titles of sections of books (as a preface, introduction, or index) are capitalized but not enclosed in quotation marks when they refer to a section of the same book in which the reference is made. If they refer to another book, they are usually lowercased.

> See the Appendix for further information.
> In the introduction to her book, the author explains her goals.

85. Style varies regarding the capitalization of the word *chapter* when it is used with a cardinal number to identify a specific chapter in a book. In some publications the word is lowercased, but more commonly it is capitalized.

> See Chapter 3 for more details.
> is discussed further in Chapter Four
> *but* in the third chapter

86. The titles of long musical compositions such as operas and symphonies are capitalized and italicized; the titles of short compositions are capitalized and enclosed in quotation marks. The titles of musical compositions identified by the nature of the musical form in which they were written are capitalized only.

> Verdi's *Don Carlos*
> "America the Beautiful"
> Ravel's "Bolero"
> Serenade No. 12 in C Minor

TRADEMARKS

87. Registered trademarks, service marks, collective marks, and brand names are capitalized.

> Band-Aid
> Jacuzzi
> Kleenex
> Grammy
> Realtor
> Kellogg's All-Bran

Diet Pepsi
Lay's potato chips

TRANSPORTATION

88. The names of individual ships, submarines, airplanes, satellites, and space vehicles are capitalized and italicized. The designations *U.S.S., S.S., M.V.,* and *H.M.S.* are not italicized.

Apollo 11
Enola Gay
Mariner 5
Explorer 10
Spirit of Saint Louis
M.V. *West Star*

OTHER USES OF CAPITALS

1. Full capitalization of a word is sometimes used for emphasis or to indicate that a speaker is talking very loudly. Both of these uses of capitals are usually avoided or at least used very sparingly in formal prose. Italicization of words for emphasis is more common. For examples of this use of italics, see paragraph 8 of the section on Other Uses of Italics in this chapter.

Results are not the only criteria for judging performance. HOW we achieve results is important also.

All applications must be submitted IN WRITING before January 31.

The waiter rushed by yelling "HOT PLATE! HOT PLATE!"

2. A word is sometimes capitalized to indicate that it is being used as a philosophical concept or to indicate that it stands for an important concept in a discussion. Style manuals generally discourage this practice, but it is still in common use today even in formal writing.

Many people seek Truth, but few find it.

the three M's of advertising, Message, Media, and Management

3. Full capitals or a mixture of capitals and lowercase letters or sometimes even small capitals are used to reproduce the text of signs, labels, or inscriptions.

a poster reading SPECIAL THRILLS COMING SOON

a Do Not Disturb sign

a barn with CHEW MAIL POUCH on the side

a truck with WASH ME written in the dust

4. A letter used to indicate a shape is usually capitalized. If sans serif type is available, it is often used for such a letter, because it usually best approximates the shape that is being referred to.

an A-frame house
a J-bar
V-shaped

OTHER USES OF ITALICS

Italic type is used to indicate that there is something out of the ordinary about a word or phrase or about the way in which it is being used. For some of the uses listed below, quotation marks can be substituted. For more on this use of quotation marks, see the section on

Quotation Marks, Double, in Chapter 1, "Punctuation," beginning on page 74. For each of the uses listed below, underlining is used in place of italicizing when the text is typewritten instead of typeset.

1. Foreign words and phrases that have not been fully adopted into the English language are italicized. The decision whether or not to italicize a word will vary according to the context of the writing and the audience for which the writing is intended. In general, however, any word that appears in the main A-Z vocabulary section of *Webster's Ninth New Collegiate Dictionary* does not need to be italicized.

These accomplishments will serve as a monument, *aere perennius,* to the group's skill and dedication.

They looked upon this area as a *cordon sanitaire* around the city.

"The cooking here is *wunderbar,*" he said.

After the concert, the crowd headed en masse for the parking lot.

The committee meets on an ad hoc basis.

NOTE: A complete sentence (such as a motto) can also be italicized. However, passages that comprise more than one sentence, or even a single sentence if it is particularly long, are usually treated as quotations; i.e., they are set in roman type and enclosed in quotation marks.

2. Unfamiliar words or words that have a specialized meaning are set in italics, especially when they are accompanied by a short definition. Once these words have been introduced and defined, they do not need to be italicized in subsequent references.

Vitiligo is a condition in which skin pigment cells stop making pigment.

Another method is the *direct-to-consumer* transaction in which the publisher markets directly to the individual by mail or door-to-door.

3. Style varies somewhat regarding the italicization of Latin abbreviations. During the first half of this century, these abbreviations were most commonly set in italic type. Some authors and publishers still italicize them, either by tradition or on the grounds that they should be treated like foreign words. However, most authors and publishers now set these abbreviations in roman type. (For an explanation of the use of *ibid., op. cit.,* and other Latin bibliographical abbreviations, see Chapter 6, "Notes and Bibliographies.")

et al.   cf   e.g.   i.e.   viz.

4. Italic type is used to indicate words referred to as words, letters referred to as letters, or numerals referred to as numerals. However, if the word referred to as a word was actually spoken, it is often enclosed in quotation marks. If the letter is being used to refer to its sound and not its printed form, virgules or brackets can be used instead of italics. And if there is no chance of confusion, numerals referred to as numerals are often not italicized. (For an explanation of the ways in which to form the plurals of words, letters, and numerals referred to as such, see the section on Plurals, beginning on page 140, in Chapter 3, "Plurals, Possessives, and Compounds.")

The panel could not decide whether *data* was a singular or plural noun.

Only can be an adverb modifying a verb, as in the case of "I *only* tried to help."

We heard his warning, but we weren't sure what "other repercussions" meant in that context.

You should dot your *i*'s and cross your *t*'s.

She couldn't pronounce her *s*'s.

He was still having trouble with the /p/ sound.

The first *2* and the last *1* are barely legible.

5. A letter used to indicate a shape is usually capitalized but not set in italics. For more on this use of capital letters, see the section on Other Uses of Capitals in this chapter.

6. Individual letters are sometimes set in italic type to provide additional typographical contrast. This use of italics is common when letters are used in run-in enumerations or when they are used to identify elements in an illustration.

> providing information about (*a*) typing, (*b*) transcribing, (*c*) formatting, and (*d*) graphics

> located at point *A* on the diagram

7. Italics are used to indicate a word created to suggest a sound.

> From the nest came a high-pitched *whee* from one of the young birds.

> We sat listening to the *chat-chat-chat* of the sonar.

8. Italics are used to emphasize or draw attention to a word or words in a sentence.

> Students must notify the dean's office *in writing* of all courses added or dropped from their original list.

> She had become *the* hero, the one everyone else looked up to.

NOTE: Italics serve to draw attention to words in large part because they are used so infrequently. Writers who overuse italics for giving emphasis may find that the italics lose their effectiveness.

Plurals, Possessives, and Compounds

This chapter describes the ways in which plurals, possessives, and compound words are most commonly formed. In doing so, it treats some of the simplest and some of the most problematic kinds of questions that are faced by writers and editors. For some of the questions raised in this chapter, various solutions have been developed over the years, but no single solution has come to be universally accepted. This chapter describes the range of solutions that are available; however, many of the questions raised in this chapter inevitably require arbitrary decisions and personal judgments. In cases like these, careful writers and editors usually make notes or keep a style sheet so that they can be consistent in the way that they form plurals, possessives, and compounds for certain specific words or categories of words.

Writers and editors are frequently told that consulting a good dictionary will solve many of the problems that are discussed in this chapter. To some extent this is true, and this chapter does recommend consulting a dictionary at a number of points. In this regard, the best dictionary to consult is an unabridged dictionary, such as *Webster's Third New International Dictionary*. In the absence of such a comprehensive reference book, writers and editors should consult a good desk dictionary, such as *Webster's Ninth New Collegiate Dictionary*. Any dictionary that is much smaller than the *Ninth Collegiate* will often be more frustrating in what it fails to show than helpful in what it shows.

In giving examples of plurals, possessives, and compounds, this chapter uses both *or* and *also* to separate variant forms of the same word. The word *or* is used when both forms of the word are used with approximately equal frequency in standard prose; the form that precedes the *or* is probably slightly more common than the form that follows it. The word *also* is used when one form of the word is much more common than the other; the more common precedes the less common.

PLURALS

The plurals of most English words are formed by adding -*s* to the singular. If the noun ends in -*s*, -*x*, -*z*, -*ch*, or -*sh*, so that an extra syllable must be added in order to pronounce the plural, -es is added to the singular. If the noun ends in a -y preceded by a consonant, the -y is changed to -i- and -es is added. Most proper nouns ending in -y (as *Mary* or *January*), however, simply add -s to the singular.

Many English nouns do not follow the general pattern for forming plurals. Most good dictionaries give thorough coverage to irregular and variant plurals, so they are often the best place to start to answer questions about the plural form of a specific word. The paragraphs that follow describe the ways in which plurals are formed for a number of categories of words whose plural forms are most apt to raise questions.

The symbol → is used throughout this section of the chapter. In each case, the element that follows the arrow is the plural form of the element that precedes the arrow.

ABBREVIATIONS

1. The plurals of abbreviations are commonly formed by adding -s or an apostrophe plus -s to the abbreviation; however, there are some significant exceptions to this pattern. For more on the formation of plurals of abbreviations, see the section on Plurals, Possessives, and Compounds, beginning on page 192, in Chapter 4, "Abbreviations."

COLA → COLA's
CPU → CPUs
bldg. → bldgs.
f.o.b. → f.o.b.'s
Ph.D. → Ph.D.'s
p. → pp.

ANIMALS

2. The names of many fishes, birds, and mammals have both a plural formed with a suffix and one that is identical with the singular. Some have only the -s plural; others have only an uninflected plural.

flounder → flounder *or* flounders
mink → mink *or* minks
quail → quail *or* quails
buffalo → buffalo *or* buffalos
cow → cows
hen → hens
rat → rats
monkey → monkeys
bison → bison
sheep → sheep
shad → shad
moose → moose

3. Many of the animals that have both plural forms are ones that are hunted, fished, or trapped, and those who hunt, fish for, and trap them are most likely to use the uninflected form. The -s form is especially likely to be used to emphasize diversity of kinds.

caught four trout
   but
trouts of the Rocky Mountains

a place where fish gather
   but
the fishes of the Pacific Ocean

COMPOUNDS AND PHRASES

4. Most compounds composed of two nouns, whether styled as one word or two words or as hyphenated words, are pluralized by pluralizing the final element.

matchbox → matchboxes
spokeswoman → spokeswomen

judge advocate → judge advocates
tree house → tree houses
city-state → city-states
crow's-foot → crow's-feet
face-lift → face-lifts
battle-ax → battle-axes

5. The plural form of a compound consisting of an -er agent noun and an adverb is made by pluralizing the noun element.

hanger-on → hangers-on
looker-on → lookers-on
onlooker → onlookers
passerby → passersby

6. Nouns made up of words that are not nouns form their plurals on the terminal element.

also-ran → also-rans
ne'er-do-well → ne'er-do-wells
put-down → put-downs
set-to → set-tos
changeover → changeovers
blowup → blowups

7. Plurals of compounds that are phrases consisting of two nouns separated by a preposition are regularly formed by pluralizing the first noun.

aide-de-camp → aides-de-camp
base on balls → bases on balls
auto-da-fe → autos-da-fe
mother-in-law → mothers-in-law
man-of-war → men-of-war
coup d'état → coups d'etat
attorney-at-law → attorneys-at-law
lady-in-waiting → ladies-in-waiting
power of attorney → powers of attorney

8. Compounds that are phrases consisting of two nouns separated by a preposition and a modifier form their plurals in various ways.

flash in the pan → flashes in the pan
jack-in-the-box → jack-in-the-boxes *or*
jacks-in-the-box
jack-of-all-trades → jacks-of-all-trades
son of a gun → sons of guns
stick-in-the-mud → stick-in-the-muds

9. Compounds consisting of a noun followed by an adjective are regularly pluralized by adding a suffix to the noun.

cousin-german → cousins-german
heir apparent → heirs apparent
knight-errant → knights-errant

NOTE: If the adjective in such a compound tends to be construed as a noun, the compound may have more than one plural form.

attorney general → attorneys general *or* attorney generals
sergeant major → sergeants major *or* sergeant majors
poet laureate → poets laureate *or* poet laureates

FOREIGN WORDS AND PHRASES

10. Many nouns of foreign origin retain the foreign plural; most of them also have a regular English plural.

alumnus → alumni
beau → beaux *or* beaus
crisis → crises

emporium → emporiums *or* emporia
index → indexes *or* indices
larynx → larynges *or* larynxes
phenomenon → phenomena *or* phenomenons
schema → schemata *also* schemas
seraph → seraphim *or* seraphs
series → series
tempo → tempi *or* tempos

NOTE: A foreign plural may not be used for all senses of
a word or may be more commonly used for some
senses than for others.

antenna (on an insect) → antennae
antenna (on a radio) → antennas

11. Phrases of foreign origin may have a foreign plural,
an English plural, or both.

beau monde → beau mondes *or* beaux
mondes
carte blanche → cartes blanches
charlotte russe → charlottes russe
felo-de-se → felones-de-se *or* felos-de-se
hors d'oeuvre → hors d'oeuvres

-FUL WORDS

12. A plural *-fuls* can be used for any noun ending in
-ful, but some of these nouns also have an alternative,
usually less common plural with *-s-* preceding the suffix.

eyeful → eyefuls
mouthful → mouthfuls
barnful → barnfuls
worldful → worldfuls
barrelful → barrelfuls *or* barrelsful
bucketful → bucketfuls *or* bucketsful
cupful → cupfuls *also* cupsful
tablespoonful → tablespoonfuls *also* table-
spoonsful

IRREGULAR PLURALS

13. A small group of English nouns form their plurals
by changing one or more of their vowels.

foot → feet
man → men
woman → women
goose → geese
mouse → mice
tooth → teeth
louse → lice

14. A few nouns have *-en* or *-ren* plurals.

ox → oxen
child → children
brother → brethren

15. Some nouns ending in *-f*, *-fe*, and *-ff* have plurals
that end in *-ves*. Some of these also have regularly
formed plurals.

elf → elves
beef → beefs *or* beeves
knife → knives
staff → staffs *or* staves
life → lives
wharf → wharves *also* wharfs
loaf → loaves
dwarf → dwarfs *or* dwarves

ITALIC ELEMENTS

16. Italicized words, phrases, abbreviations, and letters
in roman context are variously pluralized with either
an italic or roman *s*. Most stylebooks urge use of a roman *s*, and our evidence indicates that that is the form
used most commonly. If the plural is formed with an
apostrophe and an *-s*, the *-s* is almost always roman.

fifteen *Newsweek*s on the shelf
answered with a series of *uh-huh*s
a row of *x*'s

LETTERS

17. The plurals of letters are usually formed by the addition of an apostrophe and an *-s*, although uppercase
letters are sometimes pluralized by the addition of an
-s alone.

p's and q's
V's of geese flying overhead
dot your *i*'s
straight As

NUMBERS

18. Numerals are pluralized by adding an *-s*, or, less
commonly, an apostrophe and an *-s*.

two par 5s
1960's
1970s
the mid-$20,000s
in the 80s
DC-10's

19. Spelled-out numbers are usually pluralized without an apostrophe.

in twos and threes
scored two sixes

-O WORDS

20. Most words ending in an *-o* are pluralized by adding an *-s*; however, some words ending in an *-o* preceded by a consonant have *-s* plurals, some have *-es*
plurals, and some have both. When you are in doubt
about such a word, consult a dictionary.

alto → altos
echo → echoes
motto → mottoes *also* mottos
tornado → tornadoes *or* tornados

PROPER NOUNS

21. The plurals of proper nouns are usually formed
with *-s* or *-es*.

Bruce → Bruces
Charles → Charleses
John Harris → John Harrises
Hastings → Hastingses
Velasquez → Velasquezes

22. Proper nouns ending in *-y* usually retain the *-y* and
add *-s*.

February → Februarys
Mary → Marys
Mercury → Mercurys
but
Ptolemy → Ptolemies
Sicily → The Two Sicilies
The Rockies

NOTE: Words that were originally proper nouns and that end in -y are usually pluralized by changing -y to -i- and adding -es, but a few retain the -y.

bobby → bobbies
johnny → johnnies
Jerry → Jerries
Tommy → Tommies
Bloody Mary → Bloody Marys
Typhoid Mary → Typhoid Marys

QUOTED ELEMENTS

23. Style varies regarding the plural form of words in quotation marks. Some writers form the plural by adding an -s or an apostrophe plus -s within the quotation marks; others add an -s outside the quotation marks. Both arrangements look awkward, and writers generally try to avoid this construction.

too many "probably's" in the statement
didn't hear any "nays"
One "you" among millions of "you"s
a response characterized by its "yes, but"s

SYMBOLS

24. Although symbols are not usually pluralized, when a symbol is being referred to as a character in itself without regard to meaning, the plural is formed by adding an -s or an apostrophe plus -s.

used &'s instead of *and*'s
his π's are hard to read
printed three *s

WORDS USED AS WORDS

25. Words used as words without regard to meaning usually form their plurals by adding an apostrophe and an -s.

five *and*'s in one sentence
all those *wherefore*'s and *howsoever*'s

NOTE: When a word used as a word has become part of a fixed phrase, the plural is usually formed by adding a roman -s without the apostrophe.

oohs and aahs
dos and don'ts

POSSESSIVES

The possessive case of most nouns is formed by adding an apostrophe or an apostrophe plus -s to the end of the word. For most other uses of the apostrophe, such as to form contractions, see the section on Apostrophe, beginning on page 7, in Chapter 1, "Punctuation." For the use of the apostrophe to form plurals, see the section on Plurals in this chapter.

COMMON NOUNS

1. The possessive case of singular and plural common nouns that do not end in an *s* or *z* sound is formed by adding an apostrophe plus -s to the end of the word.

the boy's mother
at her wit's end
the potato's skin
men's clothing
children's books
the symposia's themes

2. The possessive case of singular nouns ending in an *s* or *z* sound is usually formed by adding an apostrophe plus -s to the end of the word. Style varies somewhat on this point, as some writers prefer to add an apostrophe plus -s to the word only when the added -s is pronounced; if it isn't pronounced, they add just an apostrophe. According to our evidence, both approaches are common in contemporary prose, although always adding an apostrophe plus -s is the much more widely accepted approach.

the press's books
the index's arrangement
the boss's desk
the horse's saddle
the audience's reaction   *also*   the audience' reaction
the waitress's duties   *also*   the waitress' duties
the conference's outcome   *also*   the conference' outcome

NOTE: Even writers who follow the pattern of adding an apostrophe plus -s to all singular nouns will often make an exception for a multisyllabic word that ends in an *s* or *z* sound if it is followed by a word beginning with an *s* or *z* sound.

for convenience' sake
for conscience' sake
the illness' symptoms   *or*   the illness's symptoms
to the princess' surprise   *or*   to the princess's surprise

3. The possessive case of plural nouns ending in an *s* or *z* sound is formed by adding only an apostrophe to the end of the word. One exception to this rule is that the possessive case of one-syllable irregular plurals is usually formed by adding an apostrophe plus -s.

horses' stalls
consumers' confidence
geese's calls
mice's habits

PROPER NAMES

4. The possessive forms of proper names are generally made in the same way as they are for common nouns. The possessive form of singular proper names not ending in an *s* or *z* sound is made by adding an apostrophe plus -s to the name. The possessive form of plural proper names is made by adding just an apostrophe.

Mrs. Wilson's store
Utah's capital
Canada's rivers
the Wattses' daughter
the Cohens' house
Niagara Falls' location

5. As is the case for the possessive form of singular common nouns (see paragraph 2 above), the possessive form of singular proper names ending in an *s* or *z* sound may be formed either by adding an apostrophe plus -s or by adding just an apostrophe to the name. For the sake of consistency, most writers choose one pattern for forming the possessive of all singular names ending in an *s* or *z* sound, regardless of the pronunciation of individual names (for exceptions see paragraphs 6 and 7 below). According to our evidence, adding an apostrophe plus -s to all such names is more common than adding just the apostrophe.

Jones's car *also* Jones' car
Bliss's statue *also* Bliss' statue
Dickens's novels *also* Dickens' novels

6. The possessive form of classical and biblical names of two or more syllables ending in *-s* or *-es* is usually made by adding an apostrophe without an *-s*. If the name has only one syllable, the possessive form is made by adding an apostrophe and an *-s*.

Aristophanes' plays
Achilles' heel
Odysseus' journey
Judas' betrayal
Zeus's anger
Mars's help

7. The possessive forms of the names *Jesus* and *Moses* are always formed with just an apostrophe.

Jesus' time
Moses' law

8. The possessive forms of names ending in a silent *-s*, *-z,* or *-x* usually include the apostrophe and the *-s*.

Arkansas's capital
Camus's *The Stranger*
Delacroix's paintings
Josquin des Prez's work

9. For the sake of convenience and appearance, some writers will italicize the possessive ending when adding it to a name that is in italics; however, most frequently the possessive ending is in roman.

the U.S.S. *Constitution*'s cannons
the *Mona Lisa*'s somber hues
Gone With the Wind's ending
High Noon's plot

PRONOUNS

10. The possessive case of indefinite pronouns such as *anyone, everybody,* and *someone* is formed by adding an apostrophe and an *-s*.

everyone's
anybody's
everyone's
everybody's
someone's somebody's

NOTE: Some indefinite pronouns usually require an *of* phrase rather than inflection to indicate possession.

the rights of each
the satisfaction of all
the inclination of many

11. Possessive pronouns include no apostrophes.

mine
yours
his
hers
its
ours
theirs

PHRASES

12. The possessive form of a phrase is made by adding an apostrophe or an apostrophe plus *-s* to the last word in the phrase.

board of directors' meeting
his brother-in-law's sidecar

from the student of politics' point of view
a moment or so's thought

NOTE: Constructions such as these can become awkward, and it is often better to rephrase the sentence to eliminate the need for the possessive ending. For instance, the last two examples above could be rephrased as follows:

from the point of view of the student of politics
thinking for a moment or so

WORDS IN QUOTATION MARKS

13. Style varies regarding the possessive form of words in quotation marks. Some writers place the apostrophe and *-s* inside the quotation marks; others place them outside the quotation marks. Either arrangement will look awkward, and writers usually try to avoid this construction.

the "Today Show"'s cohosts
the "Grande Dame's" escort
but more commonly
the cohosts of the "Today Show"
escort to the "Grande Dame"

ABBREVIATIONS

14. Possessives of abbreviations are formed in the same way as those of nouns that are spelled out. The singular possessive is formed by adding an apostrophe plus *-s* to the abbreviation; the plural possessive, by adding an apostrophe only.

the AMA's executive committee
Itek Corp.'s Applied Technology Division
the Burns Bros.' stores
the MPs' decisions

NUMERALS

15. The possessive form of nouns composed of or including numerals is made in the same way as for nouns composed wholly of words. The possessive of singular nouns is formed by adding an apostrophe plus *-s*; the possessive form of plural nouns, by adding an apostrophe only.

1985's most popular model
Louis XIV's court
the 1980s' most colorful figure

INDIVIDUAL AND JOINT POSSESSION

16. Individual possession is indicated when an apostrophe plus *-s* is added to each noun in a sequence. Joint possession is most commonly indicated by adding an apostrophe or an apostrophe plus *-s* to the last noun in the sequence. In some cases, joint possession is also indicated by adding a possessive ending to each name.

Kepler's and Clark's respective clients
John's, Bill's, and Larry's boats
Kepler and Clark's law firm
Christine and James's vacation home *or*
   Christine's and James's vacation home

COMPOUNDS

A compound is a word or word group that consists of two or more parts working together as a unit to express a specific concept. Compounds can be formed by combining two or more words (as in *eye shadow, graphic* equalizer, *farmhouse, cost-effective, blue-pencil, around-the-clock,* or *son of a gun*), by combining word elements (as prefixes or suffixes) with words (as in *ex-president, shoeless, presorted, uninterruptedly,* or *meaningless*), or by combining two or more word elements (as in *supermicro* or *photomicrograph*). Compounds are written in one of three ways: solid (as *cottonmouth*), hyphenated (as *player-manager*), or open (as *field day*).

Some of the explanations in this section make reference to permanent and temporary compounds. Permanent compounds are those that are so commonly used that they have become established as permanent parts of the language; many of them can be found in dictionaries. Temporary compounds are those made up to fit the writer's need at the particular moment. Temporary compounds, of course, cannot be found in dictionaries and therefore present the writer with styling problems.

Presenting styling problems similar to those of temporary compounds are self-evident compounds. These are compounds (as *baseball game* or *economic policy*) that are readily understood from the meanings of the words that make them up. Self-evident compounds, like temporary compounds, are not to be found in dictionaries.

In other words, writers faced with having to use compounds such as *farm stand* (*farm-stand? farmstand?*), *wide body* (*wide-body? widebody?*), or *picture framing* (*picture-framing? pictureframing?*) cannot rely wholly on dictionaries to guide them in their styling of compounds. They need, in addition, to develop an approach for dealing with compounds that are not in the dictionary. A few of those approaches are explained below.

One approach is simply to leave open any compound that is not in the dictionary. Many writers do this, but there are drawbacks to this approach. A temporary compound may not be as easily recognized as a compound by the reader when it is left open. For instance if you need to use *wide body* as a term for a kind of jet airplane, a phrase like "the operation of wide bodies" may catch the reader unawares. And if you use the open style for a compound modifier, you may create momentary confusion (or even unintended amusement) with a phrase like "the operation of wide body jets."

Another possibility would be to hyphenate all compounds that aren't in the dictionary. Hyphenation would give your compound immediate recognition as a compound. But hyphenating all such compounds runs counter to some well-established American practice. Thus you would be calling too much attention to the compound and momentarily distracting the reader.

A third approach is to use analogy to pattern your temporary compound after some other similar compound. This approach is likely to be more complicated than simply picking an open or hyphenated form, and will not free you from the need to make your own decisions in most instances. But it does have the advantage of making your compound less distracting or confusing by making it look as much like other more familiar compounds as possible.

The rest of this section is aimed at helping you to use the analogical approach to styling compounds. You will find compounds listed according to the elements that make them up and the way that they function in a sentence.

This section deals first with compounds formed from whole English words, then compounds formed with word elements, and finally with a small collection of miscellaneous styling conventions relating to compounds. The symbol + in the following paragraphs can be interpreted as "followed immediately by."

COMPOUND NOUNS

Compound nouns are combinations of words that function in a sentence as nouns. They may consist of two or more nouns, a noun and a modifier, or two or more elements that are not nouns.

1. noun + noun Compounds composed of two nouns that are short, commonly used, and pronounced with falling stress—that is, with the most stress on the first noun and less or no stress on the second—are usually styled solid.

> teapot
> cottonmouth
> birdbath
> handmaiden
> catfish
> sweatband
> handsaw
> farmyard
> football
> handlebar
> railroad
> bandwagon

2. When a noun + noun compound is short and common but pronounced with equal stress on both nouns, the styling is more likely to be open.

> bean sprouts
> beach buggy
> head louse
> fuel oil
> duffel bag
> dart board
> fuel cell
> fire drill
> rose fever

3. Many short noun + noun compounds begin as temporary compounds styled open. As they become more familiar and better established, there is a tendency for them to become solid.

> data base   *is becoming*   database
> chain saw   *is becoming*   chainsaw
> lawn mower   *is becoming*   lawnmower

4. Noun + noun compounds that consist of longer nouns, are self-evident, or are temporary are usually styled open.

> wildlife sanctuary
> reunion committee
> football game
> television camera

5. When the nouns in a noun + noun compound describe a double title or double function, the compound is hyphenated.

> city-state
> dinner-dance
> player-manager
> decree-law
> secretary-treasurer
> author-critic

6. Compounds formed from a noun or adjective followed by *man, woman, person,* or *people* and denoting an occupation are regularly solid.

> salesman
> saleswoman
> salesperson
> salespeople
> congresswoman

handyman
spokesperson
policewoman

7. Compounds that are units of measurement are hyphenated.

foot-pound
man-hour
light-year
kilowatt-hour
column-inch
board-foot

8. adjective + noun Most temporary or self-evident adjective + noun compounds are styled open. Permanent compounds formed from relatively long adjectives or nouns are also open.

automatic weapons
modal auxiliary
modular arithmetic
religious freedom
automatic pilot
graphic equalizer
pancreatic juice
minor seminary
white lightning

9. Adjective + noun compounds consisting of two short words may be styled solid when pronounced with falling stress. Just as often, however, short adjective + noun compounds are styled open; a few are hyphenated.

bigfoot
blueprint
drywall
highland
longboat
longhand
redline
shortcake
shortcut
shorthand
sickbed
wetland
yellowhammer
big deal
dry cleaner
dry rot
dry run
dry well
high gear
long haul
red tape
short run
short story
sick leave
wet nurse
yellow jacket
red-eye
red-hot

10. participle + noun Most participle + noun compounds are styled open, whether permanent, temporary, or self-evident.

frying pan
furnished apartment
shredded wheat
whipped cream
nagging backache
whipping boy

11. noun's + noun Compounds consisting of a possessive noun followed by another noun are usually styled hyphenated or open.

crow's-feet
lion's share
fool's gold
cat's cradle
cat's-eye
cat's-paw
stirred up a hornet's nest

NOTE: Compounds of this type that have become solid have lost the apostrophe.

foolscap
menswear
sheepshead

12. noun + verb + -er; noun + verb + -ing Temporary compounds in which the first noun is the object of the verb to which the suffix has been added are most often styled open; however, many writers use a hyphen to make the relationships of the words immediately apparent. Permanent compounds like these are sometimes styled solid as well.

temporary
fact checker
risk-taking
opinion maker
career planning
cost-cutting
English-speakers
permanent
lifesaver
data processing
lawn mower
copyediting
bird-watcher
penny-pinching
flyswatter
fund-raising
bookkeeper

13. object + verb Noun compounds consisting of a verb preceded by a noun that is its object are variously styled.

clambake
car wash
face-lift
turkey shoot

14. verb + object A few compounds are formed from a verb followed by a noun that is its object. These are mostly older words, and they are solid.

tosspot
breakwater
pinchpenny
cutthroat
carryall
pickpocket

15. noun + adjective Compounds composed of a noun followed by an adjective are styled open or hyphenated.

battle royal
consul general
secretary-general
governor-designate
heir apparent
letters patent
sum total
mayor-elect
president-elect

16. particle + noun Compounds consisting of a particle (usually a preposition or adverb having prepositional, adverbial, or adjectival force in the compound) and a noun are usually styled solid, especially when they are short and pronounced with falling stress.

downpour
inpatient
outpatient
input
output
throughput
aftershock
overskirt
offshoot
undershirt
crossbones
upkeep

17. A few particle + noun compounds, especially when composed of longer elements or having equal stress on both elements, may be hyphenated or open.

off-season
down payment
off year
cross-fertilization

18. verb + particle; verb + adverb These compounds may be hyphenated or solid. Compounds with two-letter particles (*by, to, in, up, on*) are most frequently hyphenated, since the hyphen aids quick comprehension. Compounds with three-letter particles (*off, out*) are hyphenated or solid with about equal frequency. Those with longer particles or adverbs are more often but not always solid.

call-up
lay-up
lead-in
run-on
set-to
sign-on
sit-in
trade-in
turn-on
warm-up
wrap-up
write-in
flyby
letup
pileup
brush-off
shoot-out
show-off
sick-out
write-off
dropout
layout
strikeout
tryout
turnoff
follow-through
get-together
breakdown
breakthrough
gadabout
giveaway
rollback
takeover

19. verb + -er + particle; verb + -ing + particle Except for *passerby*, these compounds are hyphenated.

hanger-on
diner-out
falling-out
runner-up

summing-up
talking-to
goings-on
looker-on

20. compounds of three or four elements Compounds of three or four elements are styled either hyphenated or open. Those consisting of noun + prepositional phrase are generally open, although some are hyphenated. Those formed from other combinations are usually hyphenated.

base on balls
justice of the peace
lady of the house
lily of the valley
lord of misrule
son of a gun
good-for-nothing
jack-of-all-trades
lady-in-waiting
love-in-a-mist
by-your-leave
Johnny-jump-up
know-it-all
pick-me-up
stick-to-itiveness

21. letter + noun Compounds formed from a single letter (or sometimes a combination of them) followed by a noun are either open or hyphenated.

A-frame
B-girl
H-bomb
T-shirt
C ration
D day
I beam
T square
ABO system
J-bar lift
Rh factor
H and L hinge

COMPOUNDS THAT FUNCTION AS ADJECTIVES

Compound adjectives are combinations of words that work together to modify a noun—that is, they work as unit modifiers. As unit modifiers they should be distinguished from other strings of adjectives that may also precede a noun. For instance, in "a low, level tract of land" or "that long, lonesome road" the two adjectives each modify the noun separately. We are talking about a tract of land that is both low and level and about a road that is both long and lonesome. These are coordinate modifiers.

In "a low monthly fee" or "a wrinkled red necktie" the first adjective modifies the noun plus the second adjective. In other words, we mean a monthly fee that is low and a red necktie that is wrinkled. These are noncoordinate modifiers. But in "low-level radiation" we do not mean radiation that is low and level or level radiation that is low; we mean radiation that is at a low level. Both words work as a unit to modify the noun.

Unit modifiers are usually hyphenated. The hyphens not only make it easier for the reader to grasp the relationship of the words but also avoid confusion. The hyphen in "a call for more-specialized controls" removes any ambiguity as to which word *more* modifies. A phrase like "graphic arts exhibition" may seem clear to its author, but may have an unintended meaning for some readers.

22. Before the Noun (attributive position) Most two-word permanent or temporary compound adjectives are hyphenated when placed before the noun.

tree-lined streets
fast-acting medication
an iron-clad guarantee
a tough-minded negotiator
class-conscious persons
Spanish-American relations
well-intended advice
the red-carpet treatment
a profit-loss statement
an input-output device
arrested on a trumped-up charge
a risk-free investment

23. Temporary compounds formed of an adverb (as *well, more, less, still*) followed by a participle (or sometimes an adjective) are usually hyphenated when placed before a noun.

more-specialized controls
a just-completed survey
a still-growing company
a well-funded project
these fast-moving times
a now-vulnerable politician

24. Temporary compounds formed from an adverb ending in *-ly* followed by a participle may sometimes be hyphenated but are more commonly open, because adverb + adjective + noun is a normal word order.

a widely-read feature
internationally-known authors
but more often
generally recognized categories
a beautifully illustrated book
publicly supported universities
our rapidly changing plans

25. The combination of *very* + adjective is not a unit modifier.

a very satisfied smile

26. Many temporary compound adjectives are formed by using a compound noun—either permanent or temporary—to modify another noun. If the compound noun is an open compound, it is usually hyphenated so that the relationship of the words is more immediately apparent to the reader.

the farm-bloc vote
a picture-framing shop
a short-run printing press
a secret-compartment ring
a tax-law case
ocean-floor hydrophones

27. Some open compound nouns are considered so readily recognizable that they are frequently placed before a noun without a hyphen.

a high school diploma   *or*   a high-school diploma
a data processing course   *or*   a data-processing course
dry goods store   *or*   a dry-goods store

28. A proper name placed before a noun to modify it is not hyphenated.

a Thames River marina
a Huck Finn life
a Korean War veteran
a General Motors car

29. Compound adjectives of three or more words are hyphenated when they precede the noun. Many temporary compounds are formed by taking a phrase, hyphenating it, and placing it before a noun.

spur-of-the-moment decisions
higher-than-anticipated costs
her soon-to-be-released movie

30. Compound adjectives composed of foreign words are not hyphenated when placed before a noun unless they are always hyphenated.

the per capita cost
an a priori argument
a cordon bleu restaurant
a ci-devant professor

31. Chemical names used as modifiers before a noun are not hyphenated.

a sodium hypochlorite bleach
a citric acid solution

32. Following the Noun (as a complement or predicate adjective) When the words that make up a compound adjective follow the noun they modify, they tend to fall in normal word order and are no longer unit modifiers. They are therefore no longer hyphenated.

Controls have become more specialized.

The company is still growing.

a device for both input and output

a statement of profit and loss

arrested on charges that had been trumped up

decisions made on the spur of the moment

They were ill prepared for the journey.

33. Many permanent and temporary compounds keep their hyphens after the noun in a sentence if they continue to function as unit modifiers. Compounds consisting of adjective or noun + participle, adjective or noun + noun + -ed (which looks like a participle), or noun + adjective are most likely to remain hyphenated.

Your ideas are high-minded but impractical.

streets that are tree-lined

You were just as nice-looking then.

metals that are corrosion-resistant

tends to be accident-prone

34. Permanent compound adjectives that are entered in dictionaries are usually styled in the way that they appear in the dictionary whether they precede or follow the noun they modify.

The group was public-spirited.

The problems are mind-boggling.

is well-read in economics

35. Compound adjectives of three or more words are normally not hyphenated when they follow the noun they modify.

These remarks are off the record.

36. Permanent compounds of three or more words may be entered as hyphenated adjectives in dictionaries. In such cases the hyphens are retained as long as the phrase is being used as a unit modifier.

the plan is still pay-as-you-go
but   a plan in which you pay as you go

37. It is possible that a permanent hyphenated adjective from the dictionary may appear alongside a temporary compound in a position where it would normally be open (as "one who is both ill-humored and ill prepared"). Editors usually try to resolve these inconsistencies, either by hyphenating both compounds or leaving both compounds open.

38. When an adverb modifies another adverb that is the first element of a compound modifier, the compound may lose its hyphen. If the first adverb modifies the whole compound, however, the hyphen should be retained.

> a very well developed idea
> a delightfully well-written book
> a most ill-humored remark

39. Adjective compounds that are names of colors may be styled open or hyphenated. Color names in which each element can function as a noun (as *blue green* or *chrome yellow*) are almost always hyphenated when they precede a noun; they are sometimes open when they follow the noun. Color names in which the first element can only be an adjective are less consistently treated; they are often not hyphenated before a noun and are usually not hyphenated after.

> blue-gray paint
> paint that is blue-gray   *also*   paint that is blue gray
> bluish gray paint   *or*   bluish-gray paint
> paint that is bluish gray

40. Compound modifiers that include a number followed by a noun are hyphenated when they precede the noun they modify. When the modifier follows the noun, it is usually not hyphenated. For more on the styling of numbers, see Chapter 5, "The Treatment of Numbers."

> five-card stud
> ten-foot pole
> twelve-year-old girl
> an 18-inch rule
> *but*
> a 10 percent raise
> an essay that is one page
> a child who is ten years old

41. An adjective that is composed of a number followed by a noun in the possessive is not hyphenated.

> a two weeks' wait
> a four blocks' walk

Compounds That Function as Adverbs

42. Adverb compounds consisting of preposition + noun are almost always written solid; however, there are a few well-known exceptions.

> downtown
> downwind
> onstage
> overseas
> upstairs
> upfield
> offhand
> underhand
> *but*
> in-house
> off-line
> on-line

43. Compound adverbs of more than two words are usually styled open, and they usually follow the words they modify.

> every which way
> high and dry
> off and on
> little by little
> hook, line, and sinker
> over and over

44. A few three-word adverbs are homographs of hyphenated adjectives and are therefore styled with hyphens. But many adverbs are styled open even if an adjective formed from the same phrase is hyphenated.

> back-to-back (adverb or adjective)
> face-to-face (adverb or adjective)
> *but*
> hand-to-hand combat
> fought hand to hand
> off-the-cuff remarks
> spoke off the cuff

Compound Verbs

45. Two-word verbs consisting of a verb followed by an adverb or a preposition are styled open.

> get together
> run around
> run across
> set to
> run wild
> put down
> break through
> strike out
> print out

46. A compound composed of a particle followed by a verb is styled solid.

> upgrade
> outflank
> overcome
> bypass

47. A verb derived from an open or hyphenated compound noun—permanent, temporary, or self-evident—is hyphenated.

> blue-pencil
> double-check
> poor-mouth
> sweet-talk
> tap-dance
> water-ski

48. A verb derived from a solid noun is styled solid.

> bankroll
> roughhouse
> mainstream

Compounds Formed with Word Elements

Many new and temporary compounds are formed by adding word elements to existing words or by combining word elements. There are three basic word elements: prefixes (as *anti-*, *re-*, *non-*, *super-*), suffixes (as *-er*, *-ly*, *-ness*, *-ism*), and what the dictionaries call combining forms (as *mini-*, *macro-*, *pseud-*, *ortho-*, *-ped*, *-graphy*, *-gamic*, *-plasty*). Prefixes and suffixes are usually attached to existing words; combining forms are usually combined to form new words.

49. prefix + word Except as specified below, compounds formed from a prefix and a word are usually styled solid.

> precondition
> refurnish

suborder
postwar
interagency
misshapen
overfond
unhelpful

50. If the prefix ends with a vowel and the word it is attached to begins with the same vowel, the compound is usually hyphenated.

anti-inflation
co-owner
de-emphasize
multi-institutional

NOTE: Many exceptions to this styling (as *cooperate* and *reentry*) can be found by checking a dictionary.

51. If the base word to which a prefix is added is capitalized, the compound is hyphenated.

anti-American
post-Victorian
pro-Soviet
inter-Caribbean

NOTE: The prefix is usually not capitalized in such compounds. But if the prefix and the base word together form a new proper name, the compound may be solid with the prefix capitalized (as *Postimpressionist, Precambrian*). Such exceptions can be found in a dictionary.

52. Compounds made with *self-* and *ex-* meaning "former" are hyphenated.

self-pity
ex-wife

53. If a prefix is added to a hyphenated compound, it may be either followed by a hyphen or closed up solid to the next element. Permanent compounds of this kind should be checked in a dictionary.

unair-conditioned
non-self-governing
ultra-up-to-date
unself-conscious

54. If a prefix is added to an open compound, the prefix is followed by a hyphen in typewritten material. In typeset material, this hyphen is often represented by an en dash. (For more on this use of the en dash, see paragraph 16 in the section on Dash, beginning on page 42, in Chapter 1, "Punctuation.")

ex–Boy Scout
post–coup d'etat

55. A compound that would be identical with another word if styled solid is usually hyphenated to prevent misreading.

a multi-ply fabric
re-collect the money
un-ionized particles

56. Some writers and editors like to hyphenate a compound that might otherwise be solid if they think the reader might be momentarily puzzled (as by consecutive vowels, doubled consonants, or simply an odd combination of letters.)

coed   *or*   co-ed
overreact   *or*   over-react
coworker   *or*   co-worker
interrow   *or*   inter-row

57. Temporary compounds formed from *vice-* are usually hyphenated; however, some permanent compounds (as *vice president* and *vice admiral*) are open.

58. When prefixes are attached to numerals, the compounds are hyphenated.

pre-1982 expenses
post-1975 vintages
non-20th-century ideas

59. Compounds formed from combining forms like *Anglo-*, *Judeo-*, or *Sino-* are hyphenated when the second element is an independent word and solid when it is a combining form.

Judeo-Christian
Austro-Hungarian
Sino-Soviet
Italophile
Francophone
Anglophobe

60. Prefixes that are repeated in the same compound are separated by a hyphen.

sub-subheading

61. Some prefixes and initial combining forms have related independent adjectives or adverbs that may be used where the prefix might be expected. A temporary compound with *quasi(-)* or *pseudo(-)* therefore may be written open as modifier + noun or hyphenated as combining form + noun. A writer or editor must thus decide which style to follow.

quasi intellectual   *or*   quasi-intellectual
pseudo liberal   *or*   pseudo-liberal

NOTE: in some cases (as *super*, *super-*), the independent modifier may not mean quite the same as the prefix.

62. Compounds consisting of different prefixes with the same base word and joined by *and* or *or* are sometimes shortened by pruning the first compound back to the prefix. The missing base word is indicated by a hyphen on the prefix.

pre- and postoperative care
anti- or pro-Revolutionary sympathies

63. word + suffix Except as noted below, compounds formed by adding a suffix to a word are styled solid.

Darwinist
fortyish
landscaper
powerlessness

64. Permanent or temporary compounds formed with a suffix are hyphenated if the addition of the suffix would create a sequence of three like letters.

bell-like
will-less
a coffee-er coffee

65. Temporary compounds made with a suffix are often hyphenated if the base word is more than three syllables long, if the base word ends with the same letter the suffix begins with, or if the suffix creates a confusing sequence of letters.

tunnel-like
Mexican-ness
jaw-wards
umbrella-like
industry-wide
battle-worthy

66. Compounds made from a number + *odd* are hyphenated whether the number is spelled out or in numerals; a number + *-fold* is solid if the number is spelled out but hyphenated if it is in numerals.

    20-odd
    twenty-odd
    12-fold
    twelvefold

67. Most compounds formed from an open or hyphenated compound + a suffix do not separate the suffix by a hyphen. But such suffixes as *-like*, *-wide*, *-worthy*, and *-proof*, all of which are homographs of independent adjectives, are attached by a hyphen.

    good-humoredness
    dollar-a-yearism
    do-it-yourselfer
    a United Nations-like agency

NOTE: Open compounds often become hyphenated when a suffix is added unless they are proper nouns.

    middle age   *but*   middle-ager
    New Englandism
    tough guy   *but*   tough-guyese
    Wall Streeter

68. combining form + combining form Many new terms in technical fields are created by adding combining form to combining form or combining form to a word or a word part. Such compounds are generally intended to be permanent, even though many never get into the dictionary. They are regularly styled solid.

MISCELLANEOUS STYLING CONVENTIONS

69. Compounds that would otherwise be styled solid according to the principles described above are written open or hyphenated to avoid ambiguity, to make sure of rapid comprehension, or to make the pronunciation more obvious.

    meat-ax   *or*   meat ax
    bi-level
    tri-city
    re-utter
    umbrella-like
    un-iced

70. When typographical features such as capitals or italics make word relationships in a sentence clear, it is not necessary to hyphenate an open compound (as when it precedes a noun it modifies).

    a *Chicago Tribune* story
    an "eyes only" memo
    I've been Super Bowled to death.
    a *noblesse oblige* attitude

71. Publications (as technical journals) aimed at a specialized readership likely to recognize the elements of a compound and their relationship tend to use open and solid stylings more frequently than more general publications would.

    electrooculogram
    radiofrequency
    rapid eye movement

72. Words that are formed by reduplication and so consist of two similar-sounding elements (as *hush-hush*, *razzle-dazzle*, or *hugger-mugger*) present styling questions like those of compounds. Words like these are hyphenated if each of the elements is made up of more than one syllable. If each element has only one syllable, the words are variously styled solid or hy-

phenated. The solid styling is slightly more common overall; however, for very short words (as *no-no*, *go-go*, and *so-so*), for words in which both elements may have primary stress (as *tip-top* and *sci-fi*), and for words coined in the twentieth century (as *ack-ack* and *hush-hush*), the hyphenated styling is more common.

    goody-goody
    palsy-walsy
    teeter-totter
    topsy-turvy
    agar-agar
    ack-ack
    boo-boo
    tip-top
    crisscross
    peewee
    knickknack
    singsong

CHAPTER 4

Abbreviations

Punctuation, 1368 Capitalization, 1368
Plurals, Possessives, and Compounds, 1369
Specific Styling Conventions, 1369

Abbreviations are used for a variety of reasons. They serve to save space, to avoid repetition of long words and phrases that may distract the reader, and to reduce keystrokes for typists and thereby increase their output. In addition, abbreviations are used simply to conform to conventional usage.

The frequency of abbreviations in typewritten or printed material is directly related to the nature of the material itself. For example, technical literature (as in the military and in the fields of aerospace, engineering, data processing, and medicine) features many abbreviations, but formal literary writing has relatively few. By the same token, the number of abbreviations in a piece of business writing depends on the nature of the business, as do the particular abbreviations employed. A person working in a university English department will often see *ibid., ll.,* and *TESOL,* while the employee of an electronics firm will instead see *CAD, CPU,* and *mm* from day to day.

Unfortunately, the contemporary styling of abbreviations is to a large extent inconsistent and arbitrary. No set of rules can hope to cover all the possible variations, exceptions, and peculiarities actually encountered in print. The styling of abbreviations—whether capitalized or lowercased, closed up or spaced, punctuated or unpunctuated—depends most often on the writer's preference or the organization's policy. For example, some companies style the abbreviation for *cash on delivery* as *COD,* while others prefer *C.O.D.,* and still others, *c.o.d.*

All is not confusion, however, and general patterns can be discerned. Some abbreviations (as *a.k.a., e.g., etc., i.e., No.,* and *viz.*) are governed by a strong tradition of punctuation, while others (as *NATO, NASA, NOW, OPEC,* and *SALT*) that are pronounced as words tend to be all—capitalized and unpunctuated. Styling problems can be dealt with by consulting a good general dictionary such as *Webster's Ninth New Collegiate Dictionary,* especially for capitalization guidance, and by following the guidelines of one's own organization or the dictates of one's own preference. An abbreviations dictionary such as *Webster's Guide to Abbreviations* may also be consulted.

PUNCTUATION

The paragraphs that follow describe a few broad principles that apply to abbreviations in general; however, there are many specific situations in which these principles will not apply. For instance, U.S. Postal Service abbreviations for names of states are always unpunctuated, as are the abbreviations used within most branches of the armed forces for the names of ranks. The section on Specific Styling Conventions in this chapter contains more information on particular kinds of abbreviations.

1. A period follows most abbreviations that are formed by omitting all but the first few letters of a word.

> bull. for *bulletin*
> fig. for *figure*
> bro. for *brother*
> Fr. for *French*

2. A period follows most abbreviations that are formed by omitting letters from the middle of a word.

> secy. for *secretary*
> agcy. for *agency*
> mfg. for *manufacturing*
> Mr. for *Mister*

3. Punctuation is usually omitted from abbreviations that are made up of initial letters of words that constitute a phrase or compound word. However, for some of these abbreviations, especially ones that are not capitalized, the punctuation is retained.

> GNP for *gross national product*
> PC for *personal computer*
> EFT for *electronic funds transfer*
> f.o.b. for *free on board*

4. Terms in which a suffix is added to a numeral, such as *1st, 2nd, 3d, 8vo,* and *12mo,* are not abbreviations and do not require a period.

5. Isolated letters of the alphabet used to designate a shape or position in a sequence are not punctuated.

> T square
> A 1
> I beam
> V sign

6. Some abbreviations are punctuated with one or more virgules in place of periods.

> c/o for *care of*
> w/o for *without*
> d/b/a for *doing business as*
> w/w for *wall to wall*

CAPITALIZATION

1. Abbreviations are capitalized if the words they represent are proper nouns or adjectives.

> F for *Fahrenheit*
> Nov. for *November*
> NFL for *National Football League*
> Brit. for *British*

2. Abbreviations are usually capitalized when formed from the initial letters of the words or word elements that make up what is being abbreviated. There are, however, some very common abbreviations formed in this way that are not capitalized.

> TM for *trademark*
> EEG for *electroencephalogram*
> ETA for *estimated time of arrival*
> FY for *fiscal year*
> CATV for *community antenna television*
> a.k.a. for *also known as*
> d/b/a for *doing business as*

3. Most abbreviations that are pronounced as words, rather than as a series of letters, are capitalized. If they have been assimilated into the language as words in their own right, however, they are most often lowercased.

OPEC
NATO
MIRV
NOW account
quasar
laser
sonar
scuba

PLURALS, POSSESSIVES, AND COMPOUNDS

1. Punctuated abbreviations of single words are pluralized by adding *-s* before the period.

bldgs.
bros.
figs.
mts.

2. Punctuated abbreviations that stand for phrases or compounds are pluralized by adding *-'s* after the last period.

Ph.D.'s
f.o.b.'s
J.P.'s
M.B.A.'s

3. Unpunctuated abbreviations that stand for phrases or compound words are usually pluralized by adding *-s* to the end of the abbreviation.

COLAs
CPUs
PCs
DOSs

NOTE: Some writers pluralize such abbreviations by adding *-'s* to the abbreviation; however, this styling is far less common than the one described above.

4. The plural form of most lowercase single-letter abbreviations is made by repeating the letter. For the plural form of single-letter abbreviations that are abbreviations for units of measure, see paragraph 5 below.

cc. for *copies*
ff. for *and the following ones*
ll. for *lines*
nn. for *notes*
pp. for *pages*
vv. for *verses*

5. The plural form of abbreviations of units of measure is the same as the singular form.

30 sec.
24 ml
20 min.
200 bbl.
30 d.
24 h.
50 m
10 mi.

6. Possessives of abbreviations are formed in the same way as those of spelled-out nouns: the singular possessive is formed by the addition of *-'s*, the plural possessive simply by the addition of an apostrophe.

the CPU's memory
most CPUs' memories
Brody Corp.'s earnings
Bay Bros.' annual sale

7. Compounds that consist of an abbreviation added to another word are formed in the same way as compounds that consist of spelled-out nouns.

a Kalamazoo, Mich.-based company
an AMA-approved medical school

8. Compounds formed by adding a prefix or suffix to an abbreviation are usually styled with a hyphen.

an IBM-like organization
non-DNA molecules
pre-HEW years

SPECIFIC STYLING CONVENTIONS

The following paragraphs describe styling practices commonly followed for specific kinds of situations involving abbreviations. The paragraphs are arranged under the following alphabetical headings.

A and An
A.D. and B.C.
Agencies, Associations, and Organizations
Beginning a Sentence
Books of the Bible
Company Names
Compass Points
Contractions
Dates
Degrees
Division of Abbreviations
Footnotes
Full Forms
Geographical and Topographical Names
Latin Words and Phrases
Latitude and Longitude
Laws and Bylaws
Military Ranks and Units
Number
Personal Names
Saint
Scientific Terms
Time
Titles
Units of Measure
Versus

A AND AN

1. The choice of the article *a* or *an* before abbreviations depends on the *sound* with which the abbreviation begins. If an abbreviation begins with a consonant sound, *a* is normally used. If an abbreviation begins with a vowel sound, *an* is used.

a B.A. degree
a YMCA club
a UN agency
an FCC report
an SAT score
an IRS agent

A.D. AND B.C.

2. The abbreviations A.D. or C.E. and B.C. or B.C.E. are usually styled in typeset matter as punctuated, unspaced small capitals; in typed material they usually appear as punctuated, unspaced capitals.

in printed material
41 B.C.
A.D. 185

in typed material
41 B.C.
A.D. 185

3. The abbreviation A.D. usually precedes the date; the abbreviation B.C. usually follows the date. However, many writers and editors place A.D. after the date, thus making their placement of A.D. consistent with their placement of B.C. In references to whole centuries, the usual practice is to place A.D. after the century. The only alternative is not to use the abbreviation at all in such references.

A.D. 185   *but also*   185 A.D.
the fourth century A.D.

AGENCIES, ASSOCIATIONS, AND ORGANIZATIONS

4. The names of agencies, associations, and organizations are usually abbreviated after they have been spelled out on their first occurrence in a text. The abbreviations are usually all capitalized and unpunctuated.

EPA
SEC
NAACP
NCAA
USO
NOW

NOTE: In contexts where the abbreviation is expected to be instantly recognizable, it will generally be used without having its full form spelled out on its first occurrence.

BEGINNING A SENTENCE

5. Most writers and editors avoid beginning a sentence with an abbreviation that is ordinarily not capitalized. Abbreviations that are ordinarily capitalized, on the other hand, are commonly used to begin sentences.

Page 22 contains . . .   *not*   P. 22 contains . . .
Doctor Smith believes . . .   *or*   Dr. Smith believes . . .
OSHA regulations require . . .
PCB concentrations that were measured at . . .

BOOKS OF THE BIBLE

6. Books of the Bible are generally spelled out in running text but abbreviated in references to chapter and verse.

The minister based his sermon on Genesis.

In the beginning God created the heavens and the earth.—Gen. 1:1

CAPITALIZATION—See section on Capitalization in this chapter.

CHEMICAL ELEMENTS AND COMPOUNDS—See **SCIENTIFIC TERMS** below.

COMPANY NAMES

7. The styling of company names varies widely. Many published style manuals say that the name of a company should not be abbreviated unless the abbreviation is part of its official name; however, many publications routinely abbreviate words such as *Corporation, Company,* and *Incorporated* when they appear in company names. Words such as *Airlines, Associates, Fabricators, Manufacturing,* and *Railroad,* however, are spelled out.

Ginn and Company   *or*   Ginn and Co.
The Bailey Banks and Biddle Company   *or*
    The Bailey Banks and Biddle Co.
Cross & Trecker Corp.
Canon, U.S.A., Inc.

NOTE: An ampersand frequently replaces the word *and* in official company names. For more on this use of the ampersand, see paragraph 1 in the section on Ampersand, beginning on page 5, in Chapter 1, "Punctuation."

8. If a company is easily recognizable from its initials, its name is usually spelled out for the first mention and abbreviated in all subsequent references. Some companies have made their initials part of their official name, and in those cases the initials appear in all references.

first reference   General Motors Corp. released figures today . . .
subsequent reference   A GM spokesperson said . . .

MCM Electronics, an Ohio-based electronics company . . .

COMPASS POINTS

9. Compass points are abbreviated when occurring after street names, though styling varies regarding whether these abbreviations are punctuated and whether they are preceded by a comma. When compass points form essential internal elements of street names, they are usually spelled out in full.

2122 Fourteenth Street, NW *or* 2122 Fourteenth Street NW *or* 2122 Fourteenth Street, N.W.
192 East 49th Street
1282 North Avenue

COMPOUNDS—See **SECTION ON PLURALS, POSSESSIVES, AND COMPOUNDS ABOVE.**

COMPUTER TERMS—See **SCIENTIFIC TERMS** below.

CONTRACTIONS

10. Some abbreviations resemble contractions by including an apostrophe in place of omitted letters. These abbreviations are not punctuated with a period.

sec'y   for   *secretary*
ass'n   for   *association*
dep't   for   *department*

NOTE: This style of abbreviation is usually avoided in formal writing.

COURTESY TITLES—See **TITLES** below.

DATES

11. The names of days and months are usually not abbreviated in running text, although some publications do abbreviate names of months when they appear in dates that refer to a specific day or days. The names of months are not abbreviated in date lines of business letters, but they may be abbreviated in government or military correspondence.

the December issue of *Scientific American*
going to camp in August
a report due on Tuesday
a meeting held on August 1, 1985   *or*   a meeting held on Aug. 1, 1985

general business date line   November 1, 1985
military date line   1 Nov 1985

DEGREES

12. Except for a few academic degrees with highly recognizable abbreviations (as *A.B., M.S.,* and *Ph.D.*), the names of degrees and professional ratings are spelled out in full when first mentioned in running text. Often the name of the degree is followed by its abbreviation enclosed in parentheses, so that the abbreviation may be used alone later in running text. When a degree or professional rating follows a person's name it is usually abbreviated.

> Special attention is devoted to the master of arts in teaching (M.A.T.) degree.
>
> Julia Ramirez, P.E.

13. Like other abbreviations, abbreviations of degrees and professional ratings are often unpunctuated. In general, punctuated abbreviations are more common for academic degrees, and unpunctuated abbreviations are slightly more common for professional ratings, especially if the latter comprise three or more capitalized letters.

> R.Ph.
> P.E.
> CLA
> CMET
> Ph.D.
> B.Sc.
> M.B.A.
> BGS

14. The initial letter of each element in abbreviations of all degrees and professional ratings is capitalized. Letters other than the initial letter are usually not capitalized.

> D.Ch.E.
> Litt.D.
> M.F.A.
> D.Th.

DIVISION OF ABBREVIATIONS

15. Division of abbreviations at the end of lines or between pages is usually avoided.

> received an M.B.A.   *not*   received an M.B.-
> degree   A. degree

EXPANSIONS—See FULL FORMS below.

FOOTNOTES

16. Footnotes sometimes incorporate abbreviations.

> ibid.
> op. cit.
> loc. cit.

NOTE: In current practice these abbreviations are usually not italicized.

FULL FORMS

17. When using an abbreviation that may be unfamiliar or confusing to the reader, many publications give the full form first, followed by the abbreviation in parentheses; in subsequent references just the abbreviation is used.

> *first reference*   At the American Bar Association (ABA) meeting in June . . .

> *subsequent reference*   At that particular ABA meeting . . .

GEOGRAPHICAL AND TOPOGRAPHICAL NAMES

18. U.S. Postal Service abbreviations for states, possessions, and Canadian provinces are all-capitalized and unpunctuated, as are Postal Service abbreviations for streets and other geographical features when these abbreviations are used on envelopes addressed for automated mass handling.

> *addressed for automated handling*
> 1234 SMITH BLVD
> SMITHVILLE, MN 56789

> *regular address styling*
> 1234 Smith Blvd.
> Smithville, MN 56789

19. Abbreviations of states are often used in running text to identify the location of a city or county. In this context they are set off with commas, and punctuated, upper- and lowercase state abbreviations are usually used. In other situations within running text, the names of states are usually not abbreviated.

> John Smith of 15 Chestnut St., Sarasota, Fla., has won . . .
> the Louisville, Ky., public library system
> Boston, the largest city in Massachusetts, . . .

20. Terms such as *street* and *parkway* are variously abbreviated or unabbreviated in running text. When they are abbreviated, they are usually punctuated.

> our office at 1234 Smith Blvd. (*or* Boulevard)
> an accident on Windward Road (*or* Rd.)

21. Names of countries are typically abbreviated in tabular data, but they are usually spelled in full in running text. The most common exceptions to this pattern are the abbreviations *U.S.S.R.* and *U.S.* (see paragraph 23 below).

> *in a table*
> Gt. Brit. *or* U.K. *or* UK

> *in text*
> Great Britain and the U.S.S.R. announced the agreement.

22. Abbreviations for the names of most countries are punctuated. Abbreviations for countries whose names include more than one word are often not punctuated if the abbreviations are formed from only the initial letters of the individual words.

> Mex.
> Can.
> Scot.
> Ger.
> Gt. Brit.
> U.S. *or* US
> U.S.S.R. *or* USSR
> U.K. *or* UK
> U.A.E. *or* UAE

23. *United States* is often abbreviated when it is being used as an adjective, such as when it modifies the name of a federal agency, policy, or program. When *United States* is used as a noun in running text, it is usually spelled out, or it is spelled on its initial use and then abbreviated in subsequent references.

> U.S. Department of Justice
> U.S. foreign policy
> The United States has offered to . . .

24. *Saint* is usually abbreviated when it is part of the
name of a geographical or topographical feature.
Mount, Point, and *Fort* are variously spelled out or
abbreviated according to individual preference. *Saint,
Mount,* and *Point* are routinely abbreviated when
space is at a premium. (For more on the abbreviation
of *Saint,* see paragraph 36 below.)

> St. Louis, Missouri
> St. Kitts
> Mount McKinley
> Mount St. Helens
> Fort Sumter
> Point Pelee

LATIN WORDS AND PHRASES—See also FOOTNOTES above.

25. Words and phrases derived from Latin are commonly abbreviated in contexts where readers can reasonably be expected to recognize them. They are punctuated, not capitalized, and usually not italicized.

> etc.
> i.e.
> e.g.
> viz.
> et al.
> pro tem.

LATITUDE AND LONGITUDE

26. Latitude and longitude are abbreviated in tabular
data but written out in running text.

> *in a table*
> lat. 10°20′N *or* lat. 10–20N
>
> *in text*
> from 10°20′ north latitude to 10°30′ south lati-
> tude

LAWS AND BYLAWS

27. Laws and bylaws, when first mentioned, are spelled
in full; however, subsequent references to them in a
text may be abbreviated.

> *first reference*   Article I, Section 1
> *subsequent reference* Art. I, Sec. 1

MILITARY RANKS AND UNITS

28. Military ranks are usually given in full when used
with a surname only but are abbreviated when used
with a full name.

> Colonel Howe
> Col. John P. Howe

29. In nonmilitary publications, abbreviations for
military ranks are punctuated and set in capital and
lowercase letters. Within the military (with the exception of the Marine Corps) these abbreviations are all-
capitalized and unpunctuated. The Marine Corps follows the punctuated, capital and lowercase styling.

> *in the military*   BG John T. Dow, USA
>   LCDR Mary I. Lee, USN
>   Col. S. J. Smith, USMC
> *outside the military* Brig. Gen. John T. Dow,
>   USA
>   Lt. Comdr. Mary I. Lee,
>   USN
>   Col. S. J. Smith, USMC

30. Abbreviations for military units are capitalized and
unpunctuated.

> USA
> USAF
> SAC
> NORAD

NUMBER

31. The word *number,* when used with figures such as
1 or *2* to indicate a rank or rating, is usually abbreviated. When it is, the *N* is capitalized, and the abbreviation is punctuated.

> The No. 1 priority is to promote profitability.

32. The word *number* is usually abbreviated when it is
part of a set unit (as a contract number), when it is
used in tabular data, or when it is used in bibliograph-
ic references.

> Contract No. N-1234-76-57
> Publ. Nos. 12 and 13
> Policy No. 123-5-X
> Index No. 7855

PERIOD WITH ABBREVIATIONS—See section on PUNCTUATION above.

PERSONAL NAMES

33. First names are not usually abbreviated.

> George S. Patterson   *not*   Geo. S. Patterson

34. Unspaced initials of famous persons are sometimes
used in place of their full names. The initials may or
may not be punctuated.

> FDR   *or*   F.D.R.

35. When initials are used with a surname, they are
spaced and punctuated.

> F. D. Roosevelt

PLURALS—See section on PLURALS, POSSESSIVES, AND COMPOUNDS above.

POSSESSIVES—See section on PLURALS, POSSESSIVES, AND COMPOUNDS above.

SAINT

36. The word *Saint* is often abbreviated when used before the name of a saint or when it is the first element
of the name of a city or institution named after a saint.
However, when it forms part of a surname, it may or
may not be abbreviated. In the case of surnames and
names of institutions, the styling should be the one
used by the person or the institution.

> St. Peter   *or*   Saint Peter
> St. Cloud, Minnesota
> St. John's University
> Saint Joseph College
> Ruth St. Denis
> Louis St. Laurent
> Augustus Saint-Gaudens

SCIENTIFIC TERMS—See also UNITS OF MEASURE below.

37. In binomial nomenclature, a genus name is usually
abbreviated with its initial letter after the first reference to it is spelled out. The abbreviation is always
punctuated.

first reference   *Escherichia coli*
subsequent reference   *E. coli*

38. Abbreviations for the names of chemical compounds or mechanical or electronic equipment or processes are usually not punctuated.

OCR
PCB
CPU
PBX

39. The symbols for chemical elements are not punctuated.

H
C1
Pb
Na

TIME—See also A.D. AND B.C. and DATES above and UNITS OF MEASURE below.

40. When time is expressed in figures, the abbreviations that follow are most often styled as punctuated lowercase letters; punctuated small capital letters are also common.

8:30 a.m.
10:00 p.m.
8:30 A.M.
10:00 P.M.

41. In transportation schedules *a.m.* and *p.m.* are generally styled in capitalized, unpunctuated, unspaced letters.

8:30 AM
10:00 PM

42. Time zone designations are usually styled in capitalized, unpunctuated, unspaced letters.

EST
PST
CDT

TITLES—See also DEGREES and MILITARY RANKS AND UNITS above.

43. The only courtesy titles that are invariably abbreviated in written references are *Mr., Ms., Mrs.,* and *Messrs.* Other titles, such as *Doctor, Representative,* or *Senator,* may be either written out or abbreviated.

Ms. Lee A. Downs
Messrs. Lake, Mason, and Nambeth
Doctor Howe   *or*   Dr. Howe
Senator Long   *or*   Sen. Long

44. Despite some traditional injunctions against the practice, the titles *Honorable* and *Reverend* are often abbreviated when used with *the.*

the Honorable Samuel I. O'Leary   *or*   the Hon.
 Samuel I. O'Leary
the Reverend Samuel I. O'Leary   *or*   the Rev.
 Samuel I. O'Leary

NOTE: There is also a traditional injunction against using the titles *Honorable* and *Reverend* without *the* preceding them. However, in current practice, *Reverend* and *Rev.* are commonly used without *the.*

the Reverend Samuel I. O'Leary   *or*   Rev. Samuel
 I. O'Leary

45. The designations *Jr.* and *Sr.* may be used in conjunction with courtesy titles, with abbreviations for academic degrees, and with professional rating abbreviations. They may or may not be preceded by a comma according to the writer's preference. They are terminated with a period, and they are commonly only used with a full name.

Mr. John K. Walker, Jr.
Dr. John K. Walker, Jr.
General John K. Walker Jr.
The Honorable John K. Walker, Jr.
John K. Walker Jr., M.D.

46. When an abbreviation for an academic degree, professional certification, or association membership follows a name, it is usually preceded by a comma. No courtesy title should precede the name.

Dr. John Smith   *or*   John Smith, M.D.
  but not Dr. John Smith, M.D.
Katherine Derwinski, CLU
Carol Manning, M.D., FACPS

47. The abbreviation *Esq.* for *Esquire* is used in the United States after the surname of professional persons such as attorneys, architects, consuls, clerks of the court, and justices of the peace. It is not used, however, if *the Honorable* precedes the first name. If a courtesy title such as *Dr., Hon., Miss, Mr., Mrs.,* or *Ms.* is used in correspondence, *Esq.* is omitted. *Esquire* or *Esq.* is frequently used in the United States after the surname of a woman lawyer, although the practice has not yet gained acceptance in all law offices or among all state bar associations.

Carolyn B. West, Esq.

UNITS OF MEASURE

48. Measures and weights may be abbreviated in figure plus unit combinations; however, if the numeral is written out, the unit should also be written out.

15 cu ft   *or*   15 cu. ft.   *but* fifteen cubic feet
How many cubic feet does the refrigerator
hold?

49. Abbreviations for metric units are usually not punctuated. In many scientific and technical publications, abbreviations for traditional nonmetric units are also unpunctuated. However, in most general-interest publications, abbreviations for traditional units are punctuated.

14 ml
12 km
22 mi.
8 ft.
4 sec.
20 min.

VERSUS

50. *Versus* is abbreviated as the lowercase roman letter *v.* in legal contexts; it is either spelled out or abbreviated as lowercase roman letters *vs.* in general contexts.

in a legal context   *Smith* v. *Vermont*
in a general context   honesty versus dishonesty
                         or
                      honesty vs. dishonesty

CHAPTER 5

The Treatment of Numbers

The styling of numbers presents special difficulties to writers and editors because there are so many conventions to follow, some of which may conflict when applied to particular passages. The writer's major decision is whether to write out numbers in running text or to express them in figures. Usage varies considerably, in part because no single neat formula covers all the categories in which numbers are used. In general, the more formal the writing the more likely that numbers will be spelled out. In scientific, technical, or statistical contexts, however, numbers are likely to be expressed as figures. This chapter explains most of the conventions used in the styling of numbers. A discussion of general principles is followed by detailed information on specific situations involving numbers.

NUMBERS AS WORDS OR FIGURES

At one extreme of styling, all numbers, sometimes even including dates, are written out. This usage is uncommon and is usually limited to proclamations, legal documents, and some other types of very formal writing. This styling is space-consuming and time-consuming; it can also be ungainly or, worse, unclear. At the other extreme, some types of technical writing, such as statistical reports, contain no written-out numbers except at the beginning of a sentence.

In general, figures are easier to read than the spelled-out forms of numbers; however, the spelled-out forms are helpful in certain circumstances, such as in distinguishing different categories of numbers or in providing relief from an overwhelming cluster of numerals. Most writers follow one or the other of two common conventions combining numerals and written-out numbers. The conventions are described in this section, along with the situations that provide exceptions to the general rules.

BASIC CONVENTIONS

1. The first system requires that a writer use figures for exact numbers that are greater than nine and words for numbers nine and below (a variation of this system sets the number ten as the dividing point). In this system, numbers that consist of a whole number between one and nine followed by *hundred, thousand, million,* etc. may be spelled out or expressed in figures.

> She has performed in 22 plays on Broadway, seven of which won Pulitzer prizes.

> The new edition will consist of 25 volumes which will be issued at a rate of approximately four volumes per year.

> The cat show attracted an unexpected two thousand entries.

> They sold more than 2,000 units in the first year.

2. The second system requires that a writer use figures for all exact numbers 100 and above (or 101 and above) and words for numbers from one to ninety-nine (or one to one hundred) and for numbers that consist of a whole number between one and ninety-nine followed by *hundred, thousand, million,* etc.

> The artist spent nearly twelve years completing these four volumes, which comprise 435 hand-colored engravings.

> The 145 participants in the seminar toured the area's eighteen period houses.

> In the course of four hours, the popular author signed twenty-five hundred copies of her new book.

SENTENCE BEGINNINGS

3. Numbers that begin a sentence are written out, although some make an exception for the use of figures for dates that begin a sentence. Most writers, however, try to avoid spelled-out numbers that are lengthy and awkward by restructuring the sentence so that the number appears elsewhere than at the beginning and may then be styled as a figure.

> Sixty-two species of Delphinidae inhabit the world's oceans.
> *or*
> The Delphinidae consist of 62 ocean-dwelling species.

> Twelve fifteen was the year King John of England signed the Magna Carta.
> *or*
> 1215 was the year King John of England signed the Magna Carta.
> *or*
> In 1215 King John of England signed the Magna Carta.

> One hundred fifty-seven illustrations, including 86 color plates, are contained in the book.
> *or*
> The book contains 157 illustrations, including 86 color plates.

ADJACENT NUMBERS AND NUMBERS IN SERIES

4. Generally, two separate sets of figures should not be written adjacent to one another in running text unless they form a series. So that the juxtaposition of unrelated figures will not confuse the reader, either the sentence is restructured or one of the figures is spelled out. Usually the figure with the written form that is shorter and more easily read is converted. When one of two adjacent numbers is an element of a compound modifier, the first of the two numbers is often expressed in words, the second in figures. But if the second number is the shorter, the styling is often reversed.

original	change to
16 ½-inch dowels	sixteen ½-inch dowels
25 11-inch platters	twenty-five 11-inch platters
20 100-point games	twenty 100-point games
78 20-point games	78 twenty-point games
By 1997, 300 more of the state's schools will have closed their doors.	By 1997, three hundred more of the state's schools will have closed their doors.

5. Numbers paired at the beginning of a sentence are usually styled alike. If the first word of the sentence is a spelled-out number, the second, related number is also spelled out. However, some writers and editors prefer that each number be styled independently, even if that results in an inconsistent pairing.

> Sixty to seventy-five acres were destroyed.
> Sixty to 75 acres were destroyed.

6. Numbers that form a pair or a series referring to comparable quantities within a sentence or a paragraph should be treated consistently. The style of the largest number usually determines the style of the other numbers. Thus, a series of numbers including some which would ordinarily be spelled out might all be styled as figures. Similarly, figures are used to express all the numbers in a series if one of those numbers is a mixed or simple fraction.

> Graduating from the obedience class were 3 corgis, 20 Doberman pinschers, 19 German shepherds, 9 golden retrievers, 10 Labrador retrievers, and 1 Rottweiler.

> The three jobs took 5, 12, and 4½ hours, respectively.

ROUND NUMBERS

7. Approximate or round numbers, particularly those that can be expressed in one or two words, are often written out in general writing; in technical and scientific writing they are more likely to be expressed as numerals.

> seven hundred people
> five thousand years
> four hundred thousand volumes
> seventeen thousand metric tons
> four hundred million dollars

> *but in technical writing*
> 50,000 people per year
> 20,000 species of fish

8. For easier reading, numbers of one million and above may be expressed as figures followed by the word *million, billion,* and so forth. The figure may include a decimal fraction, but the fraction is not usually carried past the first digit to the right of the decimal point, and it is never carried past the third digit. If a more exact number is required, the whole amount should be written in figures.

> about 4.6 billion years old
> 1.2 million metric tons of grain
> the last 600 million years
> $7.25 million
> $3,456,000,000

> *but* 200,000 years *not* 200 thousand years

NOTE: In the United Kingdom, the word *billion* refers to an amount that in the United States is called *trillion.* In the American system each of the denominations above 1,000 millions (the American billion) is one thousand times the one preceding (thus, one trillion equals 1,000 billions; one quadrillion equals 1,000 trillions). In the British system the first denomination above 1,000 millions (the British milliard) is one thousand times the preceding one, but each of the denominations above 1,000 milliards (the British billion) is one million times the preceding one (thus, one trillion equals 1,000,000 billions; one quadrillion equals 1,000,000 trillions).

ORDINAL NUMBERS

1. Ordinal numbers generally follow the styling rules for cardinal numbers that are listed above in the section on Numbers as Words or Figures: if a figure would be required for the cardinal form of a number, it should also be used for the ordinal form; if conventions call for a written-out form, it should be used for both cardinal and ordinal numbers. In technical writing, however, as well as in footnotes and tables, all ordinal numbers are written as figure-plus-suffix combinations. In addition, certain ordinal numbers—those specifying percentiles and latitudinal lines are common ones—are conventionally set as figures in both general and technical writing.

> the sixth Robert de Bruce
> the 20th century
> the ninth grade
> the 98th Congress
> the 9th and 14th chapters
> the 12th percentile
> his twenty-third try
> the 40th parallel

2. The forms *second* and *third* may be written with figures as *2d* or *2nd, 3d* or *3rd, 22d* or *22nd, 93d* or *93rd, 102d* or *102nd.* A period does not follow the suffix.

ROMAN NUMERALS

Roman numerals, which may be written either in capital or lowercase letters, are conventional in the specific situations described below. Roman numerals are formed by adding the numerical values of letters as they are arranged in descending order going from left to right. If a letter with a smaller numerical value is placed to the left of a letter with a greater numerical value, the value of the smaller is subtracted from the value of the larger. A bar placed over a numeral $(\overline{V})$ multiplies its value by one thousand. A list of Roman numerals and their Arabic equivalents is given in the table on page 1795.

1. Roman numerals are traditionally used to differentiate rulers and popes that have identical names.

> Elizabeth II
> Innocent X
> Henry VIII
> Louis XIV

2. Roman numerals are used to differentiate related males who have the same name. The numerals are used only with a person's full name and, unlike the similar forms *Junior* and *Senior,* they are placed after the surname with no intervening comma. Ordinals are sometimes used instead of Roman numerals.

> James R. Watson II
> James R. Watson 2nd *or* 2d

James R. Watson III
James R. Watson 3rd *or* 3d
James R. Watson IV
James R. Watson 4th

NOTE: Possessive patterns for these names are the following:

singular
James R. Watson III's (*or* 3rd's *or* 3d's) house
plural
the James R. Watson IIIs' (*or* 3rds' *or* 3ds') house

3. Roman numerals are used to differentiate certain vehicles and vessels, such as yachts, that have the same name. If the name is italicized, the numeral is italicized also. Names of American spacecraft formerly bore Roman numerals, but Arabic numerals are now used.

Shamrock V

The U.S. spacecraft *Rangers VII, VIII,* and *IX* took pictures of the moon.

On July 20, 1969, *Apollo 11* landed on the moon.

4. Lowercase Roman numerals are often used to number book pages that precede the regular Arabic sequence, as in a foreword, preface, or introduction.

5. Roman numerals are often used in enumerations to list major headings. An example of an outline with Roman-numeral headings is shown on page 240.

6. Roman numerals are sometimes used to specify a particular act and scene of a play or a particular volume in a collection. In this system, capitalized Roman numerals are used for the number of the act, and lowercase Roman numerals for the number of the scene. Arabic numerals are increasingly used for these purposes, however.

Roman style
Richard II, Act II, scene i
Hamlet, I.i.63
II, iii, 13-20
Arabic style
Act 2, scene 1
Act 1, scene 1, line 63 *or* 1.1.63
2, 3, 13-20

7. Roman numerals are found as part of a few established technical terms such as blood-clotting factors, quadrant numbers, and designations of cranial nerves. Also, chords in the study of music harmony are designated by capital and lowercase Roman numerals. For the most part, however, technical terms that include numbers express them in Arabic form.

blood-clotting factor VII
quadrant III
the cranial nerves II, IV, and IX
Population II stars
type I error
but
adenosine 3', 5'-monophosphate
cesium 137
PL/1 programming language

PUNCTUATION, SPACING, AND INFLECTION

This section explains general rules for the use of commas, hyphens, and spacing in compound and large

numbers, as well as the plural forms of numbers. For the styling of specific categories of numbers, such as dates, money, and decimal fractions, see the section on Specific Styling Conventions in this chapter.

COMMAS AND SPACES IN LARGE NUMBERS

1. In general writing, with the exceptions explained in paragraph 3 below, figures of four digits may be styled with or without a comma; the punctuated form is more common. In scientific writing, these numerals are usually styled with a comma (but see paragraph 4 below). If the numerals form part of a tabulation, commas are necessary so that four-digit numerals can align with numerals of five or more digits.

2,000 case histories   *or less commonly*   1253 people

2. Whole numbers of five digits or more (but not decimal fractions) use a comma or a space to separate three-digit groups, counting from the right. Commas are used in general writing; either spaces or commas are used in technical writing.

a fee of $12,500
15,000 units   *or*   15 000 units
a population of 1,500,000   *or*   1 500 000

3. Certain types of numbers do not conform to these conventions. Decimal fractions and serial and multidigit numbers in set combinations, such as the numbers of policies, contracts, checks, streets, rooms, suites, telephones, pages, military hours, and years, do not contain commas. Numerals used in binary notation are also written without commas or spaces.

check 34567
the year 1929
page 209
Policy No. 33442
Room 606
10011
1650 hours
111010

NOTE: Year numbers of five or more digits (as geological or archeological dates) do contain a comma.

The Wisconsin glaciation lasted from approximately 70,000 to 10,000 years B.P.

4. In technical and scientific writing, lengthy figures are usually avoided by the use of special units of measure and by the use of multipliers and powers of ten. When long figures are written, however, each group of three digits may be separated by a space counting from the decimal point to the left and the right. If the digits are separated by a comma instead of a space, neither commas nor spaces are placed to the right of the decimal point. Whichever system is used should be applied consistently to all numbers with four or more digits.

27 483 241
27,483,241
23.000 003
23.000003
27 483.241 755
27,483.241755

HYPHENS

5. Hyphens are used with written-out numbers between 21 and 99.

forty-one
forty-first

four hundred twenty-two
the twenty-fifth day

6. A hyphen is used between the numerator and the denominator of a fraction that is written out when that fraction is used as a modifier. A written-out fraction consisting of two words only (as *two thirds*) is usually styled open, although the hyphenated form is common also. Multiword numerators and denominators are usually hyphenated. If either the numerator or the denominator is hyphenated, no hyphen is used between them. For more on fractions, see page 1380.

a two-thirds majority of the staff
three fifths of her paycheck
seven and four fifths
forty-five hundredths
four five-hundredths

7. Numbers that form the first part of a compound modifier expressing measurement are followed by a hyphen. An exception to this practice is that numbers are not followed by a hyphen when the second part of the modifier is the word *percent*.

a 5-foot board
an eight-pound baby
a 28-mile trip
a 680-acre ranch
a 10-pound weight
a 75 percent reduction

8. An adjective or adverb made from a numeral plus the suffix *-fold* contains a hyphen, while a similar term made from a written-out number is styled solid. (For more on the use of suffixes with numbers, see page 184 in Chapter 3, "Plurals, Possessives, and Compounds.")

a fourfold increase
increased 20-fold

9. Serial numbers, such as social security or engine numbers, often contain hyphens that make lengthy numerals more readable.

020-42-1691

10. Numbers are usually not divided at the end of a line. If division is unavoidable, the break occurs only after a comma. End-of-line breaks do not occur at decimal points, and a name with a numerical suffix (as *Elizabeth II*) is not divided between the name and the numeral.

INCLUSIVE NUMBERS

11. Inclusive numbers—those which express a range—are separated either by the word *to* or by an en dash, which serves as an arbitrary equivalent of the phrase "(up) to and including" when used between dates and other inclusive numbers. (The en dash is explained further in the section on Dash in Chapter 1, "Punctuation.") En dashes are used in tables, parenthetical references, and footnotes to save space. In running text, however, the word *to* is more often used.

pages 40 to 98
the years 1960–1965
pages 40–98
spanning the years 1915 to 1941
pp. 40–98
the decade 1920–1930
14–18 months
the fiscal year 1984–1985

NOTE: Inclusive numbers separated by an en dash are not used in combination with the words *from* or *be-*

tween, as in "from 1955–60" or "between 1970–90." Instead, phrases like these are written as "from 1955 to 1960" or "between 1970 and 1990."

12. Units of measurement expressed in words or abbreviations are usually used only after the second element of an inclusive number. Symbols, however, are repeated.

an increase in dosage from 200 to 500 mg
running 50 to 75 miles every week
ten to fifteen dollars
30 to 35 degrees Celsius
but
$50 to $60 million
45° to 48° F
45°–48°
3′–5′ long

13. Numbers that are part of an inclusive set or range are usually styled alike: figures with figures, spelled-out words with other spelled-out words. Similarly, approximate numbers are usually not paired with exact numbers.

from 8 to 108 absences
five to twenty guests
300,000 to 305,000 *not* 300 thousand to 305,000

14. Inclusive page numbers and dates that use the en dash may be written in full (1981–1982) or elided (1981–82). Both stylings are widely used. However, inclusive dates that appear in titles and other headings are almost never elided. Dates that appear with era designations are also not elided.

NOTE: Elided numbers are commonly used because they save space, but the principles governing their use must be understood and followed consistently. The most frequently used style for the elision of inclusive numbers is based on the following rules:

1. Never elide inclusive numbers that have only two digits: 33–37, *not* 33–7.

2. Never elide inclusive numbers when the first number ends in 00: 100–108, *not* 100–08 *and not* 100–8.

3. In other numbers, omit *only* the hundreds digit from the higher number: 232–34, *not* 232–4.

4. Where the next-to-last digit of both numbers is zero, write only one digit for the higher number: 103–4, *not* 103–04.

467–68   *or*   467–468
1724–27   *or*   1724–1727
550–602
1463–1510
203–4   *or*   203–204
1800–1801
552–549 B.C.

PLURALS

15. The plurals of written-out numbers are formed by the addition of *-s* or *-es*.

Back in the thirties these roads were unpaved.

Christmas shoppers bought the popular toy in twos and threes.

16. The plurals of figures are formed by adding *-s*. Some writers and publications prefer to add an apostrophe before the *-s*. For more on the plurals of figures, see the section on Plurals, in Chapter 3, "Plurals, Possessives, and Compounds," and the section on Apostrophe, in Chapter 1, "Punctuation."

> This ghost town was booming back in the 1840s.

> The first two artificial hearts to be implanted in human patients were Jarvik-7s.

> *but also*
> linen manufacture in France in the 1700's
> *1*'s and *7*'s that looked alike

SPECIFIC STYLING CONVENTIONS

The following paragraphs describe styling practices commonly followed for specific types of situations involving numbers. The paragraphs are arranged under the following alphabetical headings:

> Addresses
> Dates
> Degrees of Temperature and Arc
> Enumerations and Outlines
> Fractions and Decimal Fractions
> Money
> Percentages
> Proper Names
> Ratios
> Serial Numbers and Miscellaneous Numbers
> Time of Day
> Units of Measurement

ADDRESSES

1. Arabic numerals are used for all building, house, apartment, room, and suite numbers except for *one*, which is written out.

> 6 Lincoln Road
> 1436 Fremont Street
> Apt. 281, Regency Park Drive
> Room 617, McClaskey Building
>   *but*
> One Bayside Drive
> One World Trade Center

NOTE: When the address of a building is used as its name, the number in the address is written out.

> Fifty Maple Street

2. Numbered streets have their numbers written as ordinals. There are two distinct conventions for the styling of numbered street names. The first, useful where space is limited, calls for Arabic numerals to denote all numbered streets above Twelfth; numbered street names from First through Twelfth are written out. A second, more formal, convention calls for the writing out of all numbered street names up to and including One Hundredth.

> 19 South 22nd Street
> 145 East 145th Street
> 167 West Second Avenue
> 122 East Forty-second Street
> One East Ninth Street
> 36 East Fiftieth
> in the Sixties (streets from 60th to 69th)
> in the 120s (streets from 120th to 129th)

NOTE: A disadvantage of the first convention is that the direct juxtaposition of the house or building number and the street number may occur when there is no intervening word such as a compass direction. In these cases, a spaced hyphen or en dash may be inserted to distinguish the two numbers, or the second convention may be used and the street number written out.

> 2018–14th Street
> 2018 Fourteenth Street

3. Arabic numerals are used to designate interstate, federal, and state highways and, in some states, county roads.

> U.S. Route 1   *or*   U.S. 1
> Interstate 91   *or*   I-91
> Massachusetts 57
> Indiana 60
> County 213

DATES

4. Year numbers are styled as figures. However, if a number representing a year begins a sentence, it may be written in full or the sentence rewritten to avoid beginning it with a figure. (For additional examples, see paragraph 3 in the section on Numbers as Words or Figures in this chapter.)

> in 323 B.C.
> before A.D. 40
> 1888–96

> Fifteen eighty-eight marked the end to Spanish ambitions for the control of England.
>   *or*
> Spanish ambitions for the control of England ended in 1588 with the destruction of their "Invincible Armada."

5. A year number may be abbreviated, or cut back to its last two digits, in informal writing or when an event is so well-known that it needs no century designation. In these cases an apostrophe precedes the numerals. For more on this use of the apostrophe, see the section on Apostrophe, in Chapter 1, "Punctuation."

> He always maintained that he'd graduated from Korea, Clash of '52.

> the blizzard of '88

6. Full dates (month, day, and year) may be styled in one of two distinct patterns. The traditional styling is the month-day-year sequence, with the year set off by commas that precede and follow it. An alternate styling is the inverted date, or day-month-year sequence, which does not require commas. This sequence is used in Great Britain, in U.S. government publications, and in the military.

> *traditional style*
> July 8, 1776, was a warm, sunny day in Philadelphia.
> the explosion on July 16, 1945, at Alamogordo

> *military style*
> the explosion on 16 July 1945 at Alamogordo
> Lee's surrender to Grant on 9 April 1865 at Appomattox

7. Ordinal numbers are not used in expressions of full dates. Even though the numbers may be pronounced as ordinals, they are written as cardinal numbers. Ordinals may be used, however, to express a date without an accompanying year, and they are always used when preceded in a date by the word *the*.

> December 4, 1829
> on December 4th   *or*   on December 4
> on the 4th of December
> on the 4th

8. Commas are usually omitted from dates that include the month and year but not the day. Alternatively, writers sometimes insert the word *of* between month and year.

> in November 1805
> back in January of 1981

9. Once a numerical date has been given, a reference to a related date may be written out.

> After the rioting of August 3 the town was quiet, and by the seventh most troops had been pulled out.

10. All-figure dating (as 6-8-85 or 6/8/85) is inappropriate except in the most informal writing. It also creates a problem of ambiguity, as it may mean either June 8, 1985, or August 6, 1985.

11. References to specific centuries are often written out, although they may be expressed in figures, especially when they form the first element of a compound modifier.

> the nineteenth century
> a sixteenth-century painting
> *but also*
> a 12th-century illuminated manuscript
> 20th-century revolutions

12. In general writing, the name of a specific decade often takes a short form. Although many writers place an apostrophe before the shortened word and a few capitalize it, both the apostrophe and the capitalization are often omitted when the context clearly indicates that a date is being referred to.

> in the turbulent seventies
> growing up in the thirties
> *but also*
> back in the 'forties
> in the early Fifties

13. The name of a specific decade is often expressed in numerals, usually in plural form. (For more on the formation of plural numbers, see paragraphs 1 and 2 in the section on Punctuation, Spacing, and Inflection in this chapter.) The figure may be shortened with an apostrophe to indicate the missing numerals, but any sequence of such numbers should be styled consistently. (For more on this use of the apostrophe, see the section on Apostrophe, in Chapter 1, "Punctuation.")

> during the 1920s *or* during the 1920's
> the 1950s and 1960s *or* the '50s and '60s
> *but not*
> the 1950s and '60s
> the 1930s and forties
> *and not*
> the '50's and '60's

14. Era designations precede or follow words that specify centuries or numerals that specify years. Era designations are unspaced and are nearly always abbreviated; they are usually printed as small capitals and typed as regular capitals, and they may or may not be punctuated with periods. Any date that is given without an era designation or context is understood to mean A.D. The two most commonly used abbreviations are B.C. (before Christ) and A.D. (*anno Domini,* "in the year of our Lord"). The abbreviation B.C. is placed after the date, while A.D. is usually placed before the date but after a century designation. (For more on the use of these abbreviations, see pages 195–196 of Chapter 4, "Abbreviations.")

> 1792–1750 B.C.
> between 600 and 400 B.C.

> from the fifth or fourth millennium to c. 250 B.C.
> 35,000 B.C.
> between 7 B.C. and A.D. 22
> c. A.D. 1100
> the second century A.D.
> the seventeenth century

15. Less commonly used era designations include A.H. (*anno Hegirae,* "in the year of [Muhammad's] Hegira," or *anno Hebraico,* "in the Hebrew year"); B.C.E. (before the common era; a synonym for B.C.); C.E. (of the common era; a synonym for A.D.); and B.P. (before the present; often used by geologists and archaeologists, with or without the word *year*). The abbreviation A.H. in both its meanings is usually placed before the year number, while B.C.E., C.E., and B.P. are placed after it.

> the tenth of Muharram, A.H. 61 (October 10, A.D. 680)
> the first century A.H.
> from the first century B.C.E. to the fourth century C.E.
> 63 B.C.E.
> the year 200 C.E.
> 5,000 years B.P.
> two million years B.P.

DEGREES OF TEMPERATURE AND ARC

16. In technical writing, figures are generally used for quantities expressed in degrees. In addition, the degree symbol (°) rather than the word *degree* is used with the figure. With the Kelvin scale, however, neither the word *degree* nor the symbol is used with the figure.

> a 45° angle
> 6°40'10"N
> 32° F
> 0° C
> Absolute zero is zero kelvins or 0 K.

NOTE: In some technical and scientific publications, the degree symbol and the *F* or *C* that may follow it are always written without any space between them. Another style followed in some scientific publications is to omit the degree symbol in expressions of temperature.

> 100°F *or* 100F
> 39°C *or* 39C

17. In general writing the quantity expressed in degrees may or may not be written out, depending upon the styling conventions being followed. In general, a figure is followed by the degree symbol or the word *degree*; a written-out number is always followed by the word *degree*.

> latitude 43°19' N
> latitude 43 degrees N
> a difference of 43 degrees latitude

> The temperature has risen thirty degrees since this morning.

ENUMERATIONS AND OUTLINES

18. Both run-in and vertical enumerations are often numbered. In run-in enumerations, each item is preceded by a number (or an italicized letter) enclosed in parentheses. The items in the list are separated by commas if the items are brief and have little or no internal punctuation; if the items are complex, they are separated by semicolons. The entire run-in enumeration is introduced by a colon if it is preceded by a full clause.

> We feel that she should (1) increase her administrative skills, (2) pursue additional professional education, and (3) increase her production.

> The oldest and most basic word-processing systems consist of the following: (1) a typewriter for keyboarding information, (2) a console to house the storage medium, and (3) the medium itself.

> The vendor of your system should (1) instruct you in the care and maintenance of your system; (2) offer regularly scheduled maintenance to ensure that the system is clean, with lubrication and replacement of parts as necessary; and (3) respond promptly to service calls.

19. In vertical enumerations, the numbers are usually not enclosed in parentheses but are followed by a period. Each item in the enumeration begins its own line, which is either flush left or indented. Runover lines are usually aligned with the first word that follows the number, and figures are aligned on the periods that follow them. Each item on the list is usually capitalized if the items on the list are syntactically independent of the words that introduce them; however, style varies on this point, and use of a lowercase style for such items is fairly common. There is no terminal punctuation following the items unless at least one of the items is a complete sentence, in which case a period follows each item. Items that are syntactically dependent on the words that introduce them begin with a lowercase letter and carry the same punctuation marks that they would if they were a run-in series in a sentence.

> Required skills include the following:
> 1. Shorthand
> 2. Typing
> 3. Transcription

> To type a three-column table, follow this procedure:
> 1. Clear tab stops.
> 2. Remove margin stops.
> 3. Determine precise center of the page. Set a tab stop at center.

> The vendor of your system should
> 1. instruct you in the care and maintenance of your system;
> 2. offer regularly scheduled maintenance to ensure that the system is clean, with lubrication and replacement parts as necessary; and
> 3. respond promptly to service calls.

20. Outlines make use of Roman numerals, Arabic numerals, and letters.

> I. Editorial tasks
>   A. Manuscript editing
>   B. Author contact
>   1. Authors already under contract
>   2. New authors
> II. Production responsibilities
>   A. Scheduling
>   1. Composition
>   2. Printing and binding
>   B. Cost estimates and bids
>   1. Composition
>   2. Printing and binding

FRACTIONS AND DECIMAL FRACTIONS

21. In running text, fractions standing alone are usually written out. Common fractions used as nouns are usually styled as open compounds, but when they are used as modifiers they are usually hyphenated. For more on written-out fractions, see the section on treatment of numbers in this chapter.

> two thirds of the paint
> a two-thirds majority
> three thirty-seconds
> seventy-two hundredths
> one one-hundredth

NOTE: Most writers try to find ways to avoid the necessity of writing out complicated fractions (as *forty-two seventy-fifths*).

22. Mixed fractions (fractions with a whole number, such as 3½) and fractions that form part of a unit modifier are expressed in figures in running text. A *-th* is not added to a figure fraction.

> waiting 2½ hours
> a ⅞-mile course
> 1¼ million population
> a 2½-kilometer race

NOTE: When mixed fractions are typewritten, the typist leaves a space between the whole number and the fraction. The space is closed up when the number is set in print. Fractions that are not on the typewriter keyboard may be made up by typing the numerator, a virgule, and the denominator in succession without spacing.

23. Fractions used with units of measurement are expressed in figures.

> $\frac{1}{10}$ km
> ¼ mile

24. Decimal fractions are always set as figures. In technical writing, a zero is placed to the left of the decimal point when the fraction is less than a whole number. In general writing, the zero is usually omitted.

> An example of a pure decimal fraction is 0.375, while 1.402 is classified as a mixed decimal fraction.
> 0.142857
> 0.2 gm
> received 0.1 mg/kg diazepam i.v.
>   *but*
> a .40 gauge shotgun

25. A comma is never inserted in the numbers following a decimal point, although spaces may be inserted as described and illustrated in paragraph 4 in the section on Punctuation, Spacing, and Inflection in this chapter.

26. Fractions and decimal fractions are usually not mixed in a text.

> 5½ lb. 2⅕ oz.
> 5.5 lb. 2.2 oz.
>   *but not*
> 5½ lb. 2.2 oz.

MONEY

27. Sums of money are expressed in words or figures, according to the conventions described in the first section of this chapter. If the sum can be expressed in one or two words, it is usually written out in running text. But if several sums are mentioned in the sentence or paragraph, all are usually expressed as figures. When the amount is written out, the unit of currency is also written out. If the sum is expressed in figures, the symbol of the currency unit is used, with no space between it and the numerals.

> We paid $175,000 for the house.
>
> My change came to 87¢.
>
> The shop charged $67.50 for hand-knit sweaters.
>
> The price of a nickel candy bar seems to have risen to more like forty cents.
>
> Fifty dollars was stolen from my wallet.
>
> forty thousand dollars
> fifty-two dollars

28. Monetary units of mixed dollars-and-cents amounts are expressed in figures.

> $16.75
> $307.02
> $1.95

29. Even-dollar amounts are often expressed in figures without a decimal point and zeros. But when even-dollar amounts are used in a series with or are near to amounts that include dollars and cents, the decimal point and zeros are usually added for consistency. The dollar sign is repeated before each amount in a series or inclusive range; the word *dollar* may or may not be repeated.

> The price of the book rose from $7.95 in 1970 to $8.00 in 1971 and then to $8.50 in 1972.
>
> The bids were eighty, ninety, and one hundred dollars.
> *or*
> The bids were eighty dollars, one hundred dollars, and three hundred dollars.

30. Sums of money given in round units of millions or above are usually expressed in a combination of figures and words, either with a dollar sign or with the word *dollars*. For more on the handling of round numbers, see paragraphs 7 and 8 in the section on Numbers as Words or Figures in this chapter.

> 60 million dollars
> a $10 million building program
> $4.5 billion

31. In legal documents a sum of money is usually written out fully, with the corresponding figures in parentheses immediately following.

> twenty-five thousand dollars ($25,000)

PERCENTAGES

32. In technical writing and in tables and footnotes, specific percentages are styled as figure plus unspaced percent sign (%). In general writing, the percentage number may be expressed as a figure or spelled out, depending upon the conventions that apply to it. The word *percent* rather than the symbol is used in non-scientific texts.

> *technical*
> 15%
> 13.5%
>
> *general*
> 15 percent
> 87.2 percent
> Twenty-five percent of the office staff was out with the flu.
> a four percent increase

33. The word *percentage* or *percent*, used as a noun without an adjacent numeral, should never be replaced by a percent sign.

> Only a small percentage of the test animals exhibited a growth change.
>
> The clinic treated a greater percentage of outpatients this year.

34. In a series or unit combination the percent sign should be included with all numbers, even if one of the numbers is zero.

> a variation of 0% to 10%

PROPER NAMES

35. Numbers in the names of religious organizations and of churches are usually written out in ordinal form. Names of specific ruling houses and governmental bodies may include ordinals, and these are written out if they are one hundred or below. A few ruling houses, however, are traditionally designated by Roman numerals that follow the name.

> First Church of Christ, Scientist
> Third Congregational Church
> Seventh-Day Adventists
> Fifth Republic
> Third Reich
> First Continental Congress
> *but*
> Egyptian tombs from Dynasty XI

36. Names of electoral, judicial, and military units may include ordinal numbers that precede the noun. Numbers of one hundred or below may either be written out or styled as numerals.

> First Congressional District
>
> Twelfth Precinct
>
> Ninety-eighth Congress   *or*   98th Congress
>
> Circuit Court of Appeals for the Third Circuit
>
> United States Eighth Army   *or*   8th United States Army
>
> At H hour, the 32d would drive forward to seize the 77th Division's position southeast of Maeda.
>
> The assault was led by the 54th Massachusetts, the first black regiment recruited in a free state.

37. Specific branches of labor unions and fraternal organizations are conventionally identified by an Arabic numeral usually placed after the name.

> International Brotherhood of Electrical Workers Local 42
>
> Elks Lodge No. 61
>
> Local 98 Operating Engineers

RATIOS

38. Ratios expressed in figures use a colon, a hyphen, a virgule, or the word *to* as a means of comparison. Ratios expressed in words use a hyphen, or the word *to*.

> a 3:1 chance
> odds of 100 to 1
> a 6-1 vote
> 22.4 mi/gal
> a ratio of ten to four
> a fifty-fifty chance

SERIAL NUMBERS AND MISCELLANEOUS NUMERALS

39. Figures are used to refer to things that are numbered serially, such as chapter and page numbers, addresses, years, policy and contract numbers, and so forth.

> Serial No. 5274
> vol. 5, p. 202
> Permit No. 63709
> 1636 Freemont Street
> paragraphs 5–7
> Table 16
> pages 420–515

40. Figures are also used to express stock market quotations, mathematical calculations, scores, and tabulations.

> won by a score of 8 to 2
> 3⅛ percent bonds
> the tally: 322 ayes, 80 nays
> $3 \times 15 = 45$

TIME OF DAY

41. In running text the time of day is usually spelled out when expressed in even, half, or quarter hours.

> Quitting time is four-thirty.
>
> By half past eleven we were all getting hungry.
>
> We should arrive at a quarter past five.

42. The time of day is also usually spelled out when it is followed by the contraction *o'clock* or when *o'clock* is understood.

> I plan to leave here at eight o'clock.
>
> He should be here by four at the latest.
>
> My appointment is at eleven o'clock.
> *or*
> My appointment is at 11 o'clock.

43. Figures are used to delineate a precise time.

> The patient was discharged at 9:15 in the morning.
>
> Her plane is due in at 3:05 this afternoon.
>
> The program starts at 8:30 in the evening.

44. Figures are also written when the time of day is used in conjunction with the abbreviations *a.m. (ante meridiem)* and *p.m. (post meridiem)*. The punctuated lowercase styling for these abbreviations is most common, but punctuated small capital letters are also frequently used. These abbreviations should not be used in conjunction with the words *morning* or *evening*; and the word *o'clock* should not be combined with either *a.m.* or *p.m.*

> 8:30 a.m.   *or*   8:30 A.M.
> 10:30 p.m.   *or*   10:30 P.M.
> 8 a.m.   *or*   8 A.M.
>   *but*
> 9:15 in the morning
> 11:00 in the evening
> nine o'clock

NOTE: When twelve o'clock is written, it is often helpful to add the designation *midnight* or *noon*, as *a.m.* and *p.m.* sometimes cause confusion.

> twelve o'clock (midnight)
> twelve o'clock (noon)

45. For consistency, even-hour times should be expressed with a colon and two zeros, when used in a series or pairing with any odd-hour times.

> He came at 7:00 and left at 9:45.

46. The 24-hour clock system—also called military time—uses no punctuation and is expressed without the use of *a.m., p.m.,* or *o'clock*.

> from 0930 to 1100
> at 1600 hours

UNITS OF MEASUREMENT

47. In technical writing, numbers used with units of measurement—even numbers below ten—are expressed as numerals.

> 2 liters
> 12 miles
> 55 pounds
> 6 hectares
> 60 watts
> 15 cubic centimeters
> 20 kilometers
> 35 milligrams

48. General writing, on the other hand, usually treats these numbers according to the basic conventions explained in the first section of this chapter. However, in some cases writers achieve greater clarity by styling all numbers—even those below ten—that express quantities of physical measurement as numerals.

> The car was traveling in excess of 80 miles an hour.
>
> The old volume weighed three pounds and was difficult to hold in a reading position.
>
> *but also in some general texts*
> 3 hours, 25 minutes
> saw 18 eagles in 12 minutes
> a 6-pound hammer
> weighed 3 pounds, 5 ounces

49. When units of measurement are written as abbreviations or symbols, the adjacent numbers are always figures, in both general and technical texts.

> 6 cm
> 67.6 fl oz
> 1 mm
> 4'
> 10 cm³
> 98.6°
> 3 kg
> $4.25

50. When two or more quantities are expressed, as in ranges or dimensions or series, an accompanying symbol is usually repeated with each figure.

> 2' x 4'
> 4" by 6" cards
> temperature on successive days of 30°, 55°, 43°, and 58°
> $400–$500

CHAPTER 6

Notes and Bibliographies

Footnotes and Endnotes, 1383
Parenthetical References, 1387
Bibliographies and Lists of References, 1390

Writers and editors often need to provide readers with documentation of the source of a quotation or a piece of information. Authors may also wish to provide additional information and commentary or cross-references. This type of information is usually included in a note, which may take the form of a footnote at the bottom of a page, an endnote at the end of a chapter or at the end of a work, or a note in parentheses.

This chapter describes both the footnote or endnote system and the system of parenthetical references. For both of these systems, the examples in this chapter illustrate generally acceptable ways of styling references; however, writers and editors should be aware that many professions and academic disciplines have developed their own systems for documenting sources, and some of these systems differ from the stylings illustrated in this chapter.

FOOTNOTES AND ENDNOTES

A footnote or an endnote links full bibliographical information about a source, including author, title, place of publication, publisher, date, and page number, to a specific text passage making use of that source. The text passage is marked with a number, and all such notes are set aside from the rest of the text. Notes that appear at the bottom of the page are called *footnotes*. Notes that appear at the end of the chapter or at the end of an entire work are called *endnotes*.

PLACEMENT OF THE ELEMENTS

Footnotes and endnotes to a text are indicated by unpunctuated superior Arabic numerals (or reference symbols) placed immediately after the quotation or information with no space in between. The notes should be numbered consecutively, starting with 1, throughout the paper, article, or chapter. The number is usually placed at the end of a sentence or clause, or at some other natural break in the sentence when the reference material is not a quotation. The number follows all marks of punctuation except the dash. If a terminal quotation mark appears (as at the end of a short quotation that is included in the running text), the numeral is placed outside the final quotation mark with no space intervening (see the sample in figure 6.1).

The text of the note itself is introduced with the corresponding Arabic numeral or reference symbol. The numeral may be superior, unpunctuated, and separated from the first word of the footnote by one space, or it may be set on the line and followed by a period and one or two spaces. The latter styling has

become more popular recently and is much easier to type.

traditional styling
[7] Ibid., p. 223.

newer styling
7. Ibid., p. 223.

According to Lesikar, if a "quoted passage is four lines or less in length, it is typed with the report text and is distinguished from the normal text by quotation marks."[17] However, a different procedure is used for longer quotations:

But if a longer quotation (five lines or more) is used, the conventional practice is to set it in from both left and right margins (about five spaces) but without quotation marks. . . . The quoted passage is further distinguished from the report writer's work by single spacing. . . .[18]

A series of usually three periods called ellipsis is used to indicate omissions of material from a passage.[19]

Footnotes may be placed "at the bottom of the page . . . separated from the text by a horizontal line. If a line is used, it is typed a single space below the text and followed by one blank line."[20] Lesikar prefers the separation line to be one and one-half or two inches.[21] Generally, typewriting textbooks state that a two-inch line is adequate (20 pica strokes; 24 elite strokes). The line is constructed by striking the underscore key.

From a typing standpoint, reserve three lines of blank typing space per footnote at the bottom of the page.

17. <u>Report</u> <u>Writing</u> <u>for</u> <u>Business</u> (Homewood, Ill.: Richard D. Irwin, Inc., 1981), p. 187.
18. Ibid.
19. Ibid., p. 188.
20. Ruth I. Anderson et al., <u>The</u> <u>Administrative</u> <u>Secretary:</u> <u>Resource</u> (New York: McGraw-Hill Book Company, 1970), p. 391.
21. Lesikar, op. cit., p. 189.

Figure 6.1 A typewritten page with footnotes

Footnotes and endnotes are usually indented like a paragraph. The first line is indented and all other lines are set flush left (as shown in figures 6.2 and 6.3). Other common stylings are the flush-left and flush-and-hang stylings, in which the first line is set flush left and succeeding lines are indented. The following examples reproduce the first three footnotes in figure 6.2. In these examples, the reference number is set on the line in the flush-left styling and is raised in the flush-and-hang styling; however, either of the positions for reference numbers may be used with any of the indention styles.

flush left
1. John E. Warriner and Francis Griffith, *English Grammar and Composition* (New York: Harcourt Brace Jovanovich, 1977), p. 208.
2. Ruth I. Anderson et al., *The Administrative Secretary: Resource* (New York: McGraw-Hill, 1970), p. 357.
3. Simone de Beauvoir, *The Second Sex,* trans. and ed. H. M. Parshley (New York: Alfred A. Knopf, 1953), p. 600.

flush and hang
[1] John E. Warriner and Francis Griffith, *English Grammar and Composition* (New York: Harcourt Brace Jovanovich, 1977), p. 208.

[2] Ruth I. Anderson et al., *The Administrative Secretary: Resource* (New York: McGraw-Hill, 1970), p. 357.

[3] Simone de Beauvoir, *The Second Sex,* trans. and ed. H. M. Parshley (New York: Alfred A. Knopf, 1953), p. 600.

In typewritten publications, the notes themselves are usually single-spaced, but double spacing is used between notes. When a manuscript is being typed prior to typesetting, however, the notes should be double-spaced, with triple spacing between the notes. In typeset material, footnotes and endnotes are usually set in type that is one or two points smaller than the text type. Extra space may or may not be placed between the notes according to individual preference.

When endnotes rather than footnotes are used, all of the notes are gathered together in a single list (as shown in figure 6.3) either at the end of a chapter or other section or at the end of an entire work. When a book uses a single list of notes at the end of the entire work, the section is usually divided with chapter headings to show where the notes of a particular chapter begin and end. An endnote may be styled in any of the ways that a footnote is styled.

CONTENT AND STYLING FOR FIRST REFERENCES

Both footnotes and endnotes provide full bibliographical information for a source the first time it is cited. However, in subsequent references, this information is provided in a shortened form. The following paragraphs describe the content and style used for first references. Subsequent references are discussed later in this section. Examples of the stylings described in figures 6.2 and 6.3. (The content and style for entries in bibliographies and lists of references are given in the section on Bibliographies and Lists of References later in this chapter.)

Books A footnote or endnote that refers to a book contains as many of the following elements as are relevant. Examples of each of the elements described below can be found in the references in Figure 6.2.

1. *Author's name* In footnotes and endnotes, the author's first name comes first and the last name after. If a book has more than three authors, the first author's name is followed by the phrase *et al.,* which is an abbreviation for the phrase *et alii* or *et aliae,* meaning "and others." (For examples of notes referring to books with multiple authors, see notes 1 and 2 in figure 6.2.) If a publication is issued by a group or organization and no individual is mentioned on the title page, the name of the group or organization may be used in place of an author's name. In this case, the group or organization is thought of as being the corporate author. (For an example of a note describing a work with a corporate author, see note 5 in figue 6.2.) In footnotes and endnotes, the author's name is followed by a comma.

2. *Title of the work* The title is underlined in typewritten manuscript and italicized in type. Each word of the title is capitalized except for articles and short prepositions other than the first word. When no author's name is used in the note, the title comes first. This is commonly the styling for well-known reference books and for publications that have

NOTES

1. John E. Warriner and Francis Griffith, *English Grammar and Composition* (New York: Harcourt Brace Jovanovich, 1977), p. 208.

2. Ruth I. Anderson et al., *The Administrative Secretary: Resource* (New York: McGraw-Hill, 1970), p. 357.

3. Simone de Beauvoir, *The Second Sex,* trans. and ed. H. M. Parshley (New York: Alfred A. Knopf, 1953), p. 600.

4. Martha L. Manheimer, *Style Manual: A Guide for the Preparation of Reports and Dissertations,* Books in Library and Information Science, vol. 5 (New York: Marcel Dekker, 1973), p. 14.

5. National Micrographics Association, *An Introduction to Micrographics,* rev. ed. (Silver Spring, Md.: National Micrographics Association, 1980), p. 42.

6. *Rules for Alphabetical Filing as Standardized by ARMA* (Prairie Village, Kans.: Association of Records Managers and Administrators, 1981), p. 14.

7. Peggy F. Bradbury, ed., *Transcriber's Guide to Medical Terminology* (New Hyde Park, N.Y.: Medical Examination Publishing Co., 1973), p. 446.

8. Kemp Malone, "The Phonemes of Current English," *Studies for William A. Read,* ed. Nathaniel M. Caffee and Thomas A. Kirby (Baton Rouge: Louisiana State University Press, 1940), p. 133–165.

9. Robert Chambers, *Cyclopaedia of English Literature,* 2 vols. (New York: World Publishing House, 1875), vol. 1, p. 45.

Figure 6.2. A page of endnotes illustrating footnote and endnote style for references to books

corporate authors but are more likely to be known by their titles. (For an example of a note in which the title comes first, see note 6 in figure 6.2.)

3. *Portion of the book* If a reference is to one portion of a book (as an essay within a collection), the name of the portion should be included. The titles of chapters within nonfiction works by a single author are usually not part of a footnote reference. The titles of parts of books, such as short poems, short stories, and essays, are enclosed in quotation marks. (For an example of a reference to a work within a collection, see note 8 in figure 6.2.)

4. *Editor, compiler, or translator* The name of an editor, compiler, or translator is preceded by the abbreviation *ed., comp.,* or *trans.* or some combination of them joined by *and.* The abbreviation is separated from the title that precedes it by a comma. (For examples of notes referring to a book with a translator or editor, see notes 3 and 8 in figure 6.2.) If there is no author mentioned on the title page of the book, the name of the editor, compiler, or translator is placed first in the note, followed by the abbreviation *ed., comp.,* or *trans.* (For an example of a note in which the editor's name comes first, see note 7 in figure 6.2.)

5. *Name of the series* If a book is part of a series, the name of the series should be included. If the book corresponds to a specific volume in that series, the volume number is also included. The volume number is separated

from the title by a comma. The name of the series is separated from the title of the volume by a comma and is capitalized as a title, although it is not underlined or italicized. (For an example of a note referring to a book that is part of a series, see note 4 in figure 6.2.)

6. *Edition* If a work is other than the first edition, the number or the nature of the edition should be indicated. (For an example of a note referring to a book that is not a first edition, see note 5 in figure 6.2.)

7. *Volume number* If a work has more than one volume, the total number of volumes is given after the title and edition data. In addition, the number of the particular volume cited should precede the page number. In traditional footnote styling, a *vol.* or *vols.* precedes the volume number, but many authors now omit these abbreviations. (For an example of a note referring to a multivolume work, see note 9 in figure 6.2.)

8. *Publishing data* The city of publication, the name of the publisher, and the year of publication should all be included. These items are usually placed within parentheses; a colon separates the city from the publisher's name. Names of states may be abbreviated, but not names of cities. A comma separates the publisher's name from the year of issue.

9. *Page number* The number of the page on which the quotation or piece of information can be found should be included. In traditional footnote styling, a *p.* or *pp.* precedes the page number or numbers; however, many authors now omit those abbreviations.

Periodicals A footnote or endnote referring to an article in a periodical should include all of the following information that is relevant. Examples of each of the elements described below can be found in the sample references in figure 6.3.

1. *Author's name* The author's name is treated in the same way as described above for a reference to a book. The names of writers of letters to a periodical and contributors of signed book reviews are treated like names of authors. (For examples of references to a letter and to a signed review, see notes 6 and 7 in the sample below).

2. *Title of the article* The title of the article is enclosed in quotation marks. The words of the title are capitalized as in a book title. The title of the article is followed by a comma that is placed inside the quotation marks.

3. *Name of the periodical* The name of the periodical is treated in the way described above for the title of a book.

4. *Volume and number of the periodical* If a periodical uses both volume and number designations to identify an issue, both should be used. If a periodical uses some other system for identifying issues (as the month and year of issue), that system should be used. Note 1 in figure 6.3 illustrates a reference to a periodical in which pages are numbered consecutively through a volume, and therefore only a volume number is required. Note

NOTES

1. John Heil, ''Seeing is Believing,'' *American Philosophical Quarterly* 19 (1982): 229–239.

2. Donald K. Ourecky, ''Cane and Bush Fruits,'' *Plants & Gardens* 27, No. 3 (Autumn 1971): pp. 13–15.

3. Xan Smiley, ''Misunderstanding Africa,'' *Atlantic* (Sept. 1982): pp. 70–79.

4. Shiva Naipaul, ''A Trinidad Childhood,'' *New Yorker* (17 Sept. 1984): pp. 63–64.

5. Gail Pitts, ''Money Funds Holding Own,'' *Morning Union* [Springfield, Mass.] (Aug. 23, 1982): p. 6.

6. Jeremy C. Rosenberg, ''Letters,'' *Advertising Age* (7 June, 1982): p. M–1.

7. M. O. Vassell, rev. of *Applied Charged Particle Optics,* ed. A. Septier, *American Scientist* 70 (1982): 229.

8. Joyce A. Velasquez, ''The Format of Formal Reports,'' report prepared for the Southern Engineering Company, Johnson City, Miss. (May 29, 1985).

9. Clive Johnson, letter to Elizabeth O'Hara, 9 Nov. 1916, Johnson Collection, item 5298, California State Historical Society, San Marino, Calif.

Figure 6.3 Sample notes showing footnote and endnote styling for references to periodicals and unpublished sources

2 illustrates a reference to a periodical that uses a seasonal designation as well as volume and number designations for each issue, and which paginates each issue independently of the volume. Note 3 illustrates a reference to a monthly magazine. Most monthly magazines have a volume and number designation somewhere in them, but they are more commonly referred to by month and year.

5. *Issue date* Periodicals variously use months, days, and years to identify issues. The date is written in whatever form the periodical uses, but the names of the months may be abbreviated.

6. *Page number* The number of the page on which the quotation or piece of information can be found is included. The varying use and omission of the abbreviation *p.* or *pp.* as described above for books hold true for references to periodicals as well. One situation in which the abbreviation is almost always dropped occurs when the reference is to a volume number and page number only. In that case, the volume number and page number are separated by a colon, and neither is identified with an abbreviation. Notes 1 and 7 in figure 6.3 illustrate this styling. NOTE: In making the decision of whether or not to include the abbreviation, writers and editors should keep in mind the needs of their readers. If most of the readers are well acquainted with footnote style, the abbreviation can be safely dropped. However, if a significant number of the readers of a text are unfamiliar with footnote styling, including the identifying abbreviation will help lessen the chances of confusion.

Unpublished materials A footnote referring to a work that is unpublished should include as many of the following elements as are known or are relevant. The elements described below are illustrated in notes 8 and 9 in figure 6.3.

1. *Author's name* The author's name is treated in the same way as described above for a book.

2. *Title of the work* The title is enclosed in quotation marks and capitalized like a book title.

3. *The nature of the material* The reference should include a description of the document (as "letter" or "dissertation").

4. *Date* Include the date of the material if it is known.

5. *Folio number or other identification number* Include whatever kind of identification number is conventionally used with the material.

6. *Geographical location of the material* Include the name of the institution where the material can be found and the city where the institution is located.

STYLE AND CONTENT FOR SUBSEQUENT REFERENCES

There are two systems that are currently used to refer to a source that has already been cited. One makes use of a shortened footnote styling; the other uses Latin abbreviations. Both systems are described below.

Shortened footnotes When the same source is cited repeatedly with intervening footnotes, shortened footnotes may be used as space-saving devices. The following styling is generally acceptable for most publications.

1. If the author's name occurs in the running text, it need not be repeated in footnote references to the work after the first one.

first reference
1. Albert H. Marckwardt, *American English* (New York: Oxford University Press, 1980), p. 94.

repeated reference
2. *American English,* p. 95.

2. If the author's name does not appear in the running text prior to a repeated reference, either of the following stylings may be used. The styling of footnote 3 should be followed if more than one work by the same author is cited within the text.

repeated reference
3. Marckwardt, *American English,* p. 95.
    or
4. Marckwardt, p. 95.

3. In repeated references to books by more than one author, the authors' names may be shortened. The styling of footnote 6 should be followed if more than one work by the same authors is cited within the text.

first reference
5. De Witt T. Starnes and Gertrude E. Noyes, *The English Dictionary from Cawdrey to Johnson 1604–1775* (Chapel Hill: University of North Carolina Press, 1946), p. 120.

repeated reference
6. Starnes and Noyes, *The English Dictionary*

from Cawdrey to Johnson 1604–1775, p. 126.
    or
7. Starnes and Noyes, p. 126.

4. A long title may be shortened if it has already been given in full in an earlier footnote.

8. Starnes and Noyes, *The English Dictionary,* p. 126.

5. A shortened reference to an article in a periodical that has been cited earlier should include the author's last name; the title of the article, which can be shortened if it is a long one, and if no similar title by the same author is being cited; and the page number.

9. Goldman, "Warren G. Harding," p. 45.

Latin abbreviations While the simplified and shortened footnote stylings described above have gained wide currency, some writers still prefer to use the traditional Latin abbreviations *ibid., loc. cit.,* and *op. cit.* as space-savers in repeated references to sources cited earlier. Current usage indicates that these abbreviations need no longer be typed with underscoring or italicized in type; however, some writers still prefer this traditional styling. When a page reference follows one of these abbreviations, it may or may not be set off with a comma.

10. Ibid. pp. 95–98.
    or
11. Ibid., pp. 95–98.

These Latin abbreviations are capitalized when they appear at the beginning of a footnote or endnote, but not otherwise.

The abbreviation *ibid.* (for *ibidem,* "in the same place") is used when the writer is referring to the work cited in the immediately preceding footnote. The abbreviation may be used several times in succession.

first reference
12. Simone de Beauvoir, *The Second Sex,* trans. and ed. H. M. Parshley (New York: Alfred A. Knopf, 1953), p. 600.

repeated reference (immediately following note 12)
13. Ibid., p. 609.

repeated reference (immediately following note 13)
14. Ibid.

When *ibid.* is used without a page number, it indicates that the same page of the same source is being cited as in the footnote immediately preceding. Thus, note 14 above cites page 609 of *The Second Sex.*

The abbreviations *loc. cit.* (for *loco citato,* "in the place cited") and *op. cit.* (for *opere citato,* "in the work cited") may be used only in conjunction with the author's name, which may occur in the running text or at the beginning of the first reference. When the writer cites a book or periodical, its complete title should be included the first time it is referred to in a footnote. In subsequent references, *loc. cit.* or *op. cit.* with or without page numbers may be substituted for the title, depending on the type of citation.

The difference between *loc. cit.* and *op. cit.* is that *loc. cit.* is used only when referring to the same page or pages of the same source cited earlier with footnotes intervening, while *op. cit.* is used to refer to a source cited earlier but not to the same page or pages of that source.

first reference
15. De Witt T. Starnes and Gertrude E. Noyes, *The English Dictionary from Cawdrey to John-*

son 1604–1775 (Chapel Hill: University of North Carolina Press, 1946), pp. 119–133.

repeated reference (with other footnotes intervening)

    18. Starnes and Noyes, loc. cit.
    21. Starnes and Noyes, loc. cit., p. 119.

The note without a page number indicates that pages 119–133 are being cited again.

Examples of the use of *op. cit.* are as follows:

first reference

    22. Albert H. Marckwardt, *American English* (New York: Oxford University Press, 1980), p. 94.

repeated reference

    24. Marckwardt, op. cit., p. 98.

The title of the work rather than the Latin abbreviation should be used if the writer is using material from more than one work by the same author.

NONBIBLIOGRAPHICAL FOOTNOTES AND ENDNOTES

Nonbibliographical notes provide additional information, commentary, or cross-references that the author does not want to include in the main text. They are keyed to the text in the same way as bibliographical notes. In texts in which bibliographical notes are keyed with superior numerals, nonbibliographical notes are included in the same sequence, as in the examples below. In some cases, authors will use numbered endnotes for bibliographical notes and footnotes keyed with reference marks for nonbibliographical notes; however, this system is not very common.

    1. Lyon Richardson, *A History of Early American Magazines* (New York: Thomas Nelson and Sons, 1931), p. 8.

    2. Total average circulation per issue of magazines reporting to the Bureau of Circulation rose from 96.8 million in 1939 to 147.8 million in 1945.

    3. For a particularly compelling account of this episode, see James P. Wood, *Magazines in the United States* (New York: The Ronald Press Company, 1949), pp. 92–108.

    4. Richardson, op. cit., p. 42.

    5. For more details, see Appendix.

Texts that rely on parenthetical references for bibliographical notes can still include footnotes or endnotes for other notes. When a nonbibliographical note mentions the name of a book or article that is not the source of a quotation or piece of information in the text, footnote styling is used to describe the reference.

In some publications, there are certain nonbibliographical notes that are not keyed to the text with any kind of symbol. These include notes that an editor places at the beginning of each part of a collection of works by different authors and that identify each author. They also include notes that an author uses to acknowledge those who gave assistance or contributed to the writing of the work. One reason that these notes are not keyed is that the only logical place to put the reference mark (described below) or number would be following the title of the work or the name of the author (both of which are often set in a larger distinctive type style), and some editors and designers are reluctant to use footnote symbols in this position. These unnumbered notes are conventionally placed in the footnote position on the first page.

List of References

Anderson, Ruth I., et al. *The Administrative Secretary: Resource*. New York: McGraw-Hill, 1970.

"Aristotle." *Webster's New Biographical Dictionary*. Springfield, Mass.: Merriam-Webster Inc., 1983.

Brushaw, Charles T., Gerald J. Alred, and Walter E. Oliu. *Handbook of Technical Writing*. 2d ed. New York: St. Martin's Press, 1982.

Chambers, Robert. *Cyclopaedia of English Literature*. 2 vols. New York: World Publishing House, 1875.

Lesikar, Raymond V. *Report Writing For Business*. Homewood, Ill.: Richard D. Irwin, Inc., 1981.

National Micrographics Association. *An Introduction to Micrographics*. Rev. ed. Silver Spring, Md.: National Micrographics Association, 1980.

Rules for Alphabetical Filing as Standardized by ARMA. Prairie Village, Kans.: Association of Record Managers and Administrators, 1981.

Figure 6.4 A sample list of references

REFERENCE MARKS

In texts that have only a limited number of footnotes or endnotes, writers sometimes substitute reference marks for reference numbers. The traditional footnote reference symbols are listed below in the order in which they are usually used.

    * asterisk
    † dagger
    ‡ double dagger
    § section mark
    / parallels
    ¶ paragraph mark
    # number sign

The sequence of these symbols can begin anew with each page or with each chapter. If more than seven notes are needed in a sequence, the reference marks are doubled, as **, ‡, etc.; however, if such a large number of footnotes is needed, reference numbers rather than reference symbols should probably be used. A common alternative to using the full set of symbols when only a few footnotes are needed is to use an asterisk for the first note, a double asterisk for the second, and so on without using the dagger or other marks. A variation on this that works for up to four footnotes in a sequence is to use the asterisk and dagger in the following order: *, **, †, ‡.

PARENTHETICAL REFERENCES

Parenthetical references present very abbreviated bibliographical information (typically the name of the author, followed by a page number, but sometimes just a page number) enclosed in parentheses. They are placed in the main body of the text, and they refer readers to a fuller bibliographical description included in a list of references that is found at the end of the article, chapter, or book. A list of references is simply a bibliography, and details regarding its content and styling are presented in the section on Bibliographies and Lists of References, later in this chapter. For purposes of convenience, a sample list of references is included in figure 6.4 and all parenthetical references in this section refer to it.

Most systems of parenthetical references are similar, but differences in details of styling do exist among the systems used by various academic disciplines and pro-

According to Lesikar, if a "quoted passage is four lines or less in length, it is typed with the report text and is distinguished from the normal text by quotation marks" (187). However, a different procedure is used for longer quotations:

> But if a longer quotation (five lines or more) is used, the conventional practice is to set it in from both left and right margins (about five spaces) but without quotation marks. . . . The quoted passage is further distinguished from the report writer's work by single spacing. . . . (187)

A series of usually three periods called ellipsis is used to indicate omissions of material from a passage (Lesikar 188).

Footnotes may be placed "at the bottom of the page . . . separated from the text by a horizontal line. If a line is used, it is typed a single space below the text and followed by one blank line" (Anderson et al. 391). Lesikar prefers the separation line to be one and one-half or two inches (189). Generally, typewriting textbooks state that a two-inch line is adequate (20 pica strokes; 24 elite strokes). The line is constructed by striking the underscore key.

From a typing standpoint, reserve three lines of blank typing space per footnote at the bottom of the page.

The first line of a footnote is indented from one to six (but usually two or five) spaces from the left margin, depending on the writer's preference or the style manual being followed. The footnote may be introduced with the applicable superscript Arabic numeral, unpunctuated and separated from the first letter of the author's first name by one space; or it may be introduced by the

Figure 6.5 A typewritten page with parenthetical references.

fessional organizations. The examples in this section of the book are styled in accordance with the precepts of the *MLA Handbook for Writers of Research Papers,* second edition, to which readers of this book are referred for more details regarding parenthetical references. A discussion of two different parenthetical reference systems that are used in the sciences follows at the end of this section.

PLACEMENT OF THE REFERENCE

Parenthetical references are placed immediately after the quotation or piece of information whose source they refer to. The sample in figure 6.5 reproduces the text of the sample in figure 6.1 and shows how the same text would appear using parenthetical references instead of footnotes. Note especially that sentence punctuation (that is, punctuation not associated with a quotation) is placed after the reference. This means that periods and commas are placed outside of quotation marks and that run-in quoted sentences that end in an omission are styled with three spaced ellipsis points before the reference and a terminal period closed-up after the reference. If the final sentence of the extract quotation in figure 6.5 had been set as a run-in quotation, it would appear as follows:

Lesikar says, "The quoted passage is further distinguished from the report writer's work by single spacing . . ." (187).

CONTENT AND STYLE OF PARENTHETICAL REFERENCES

The content and style are determined by two factors: (1) the style and content of the first element of the entry in the list of references to which it refers and (2) the bibliographical information that is included in the text around it.

These general principles are illustrated in the example in figure 6.5. For instance, in the third paragraph, the parenthetical reference "(Anderson et al. 391)" is given because, in the list of references, the full reference to this source begins "Anderson, Ruth I., et al."

The way that bibliographical information in the text determines the styling of the parenthetical reference is illustrated in the first sentence of the first paragraph. The parenthetical reference "(187)" is sufficient, because it is clear that Lesikar is the author of the source that is being quoted. In the second paragraph, the full parenthetical reference "(Lesikar 188)" is required because it is not clear from the sentence who is the source of the information being provided.

Sometimes a reference is supported by citations to two separate sources; the two citations are enclosed in the same parentheses but are separated by a semicolon, as "(Lesikar 189; Anderson et al. 390)." Lengthy parenthetical references should be avoided because they interrupt the flow of text. Authors can avoid unwieldy parenthetical references by incorporating as much of the bibliographical information within the text as can be smoothly absorbed.

Matching the list of references The name in a parenthetical reference must correspond to a name that begins an entry in the list of references. In general, the last name of the author is usually sufficient within a parenthetical reference, as it was in the case of the references to Lesikar's book in the sample in figure 6.5. However, if there had been another author with the last name Lesikar in the list of references, it would have been necessary to include both first and last name, as "(Lesikar, Raymond, 188)." Alternatively, if the list of references had included two different books, both of which were by Raymond Lesikar, it would have been necessary to include both the author's name and the book's title (which may be shortened) in the parenthetical reference, as "(Lesikar, *Report Writing* 188)." The following paragraphs explain some other special cases.

1. *A work with two or three authors* The list of references in figure 6.4 includes an entry for a book by Charles T. Brushaw, Gerald J. Alred, and Walter E. Oliu. A parenthetical reference to that work would take the following form:

   (Brushaw, Alred, and Oliu 182–184)

2. *A work with more than three authors* A work with more than three authors is listed in the list of references under the name of the first author, followed by the phrase *et al.* The reference to Anderson et al. in the third paragraph of the sample in figure 6.5 illustrates this style.

3. *A work by a corporate author* The list of references in figure 6.4 includes an entry in which National Micrographics Association is given as the author. A parenthetical reference to that work would also use National Micrographics Association as its author, although the name may be abbreviated.

(National Micrographics 42)
or
(Natl. Micrographics 42)

4. *A work listed by its title* The list of references in figure 6.4 includes an entry for a book *Rules for Alphabetical Filing as Standardized by ARMA*. A parenthetical reference to that work should also refer to it by its title, which may be shortened for convenience.

(*Rules for Alphabetical Filing* 14)
or
(*Rules* 14)

Locators Usually the only locator that is required in a parenthetical reference is a page number. However, sometimes additional or alternate information is needed to help the reader find the original source. The following paragraphs describe some of these special situations. Note that in all cases no punctuation separates the author's name or the title from the locator and that no abbreviation is used to identify the nature of the locator unless confusion would result from its omission (but see the note following paragraph 1 below).

1. *A multivolume work* The list of references in figure 6.4 includes a reference to Robert Chambers's two-volume *Cyclopaedia of English Literature*. A reference to that work would have to include a volume designation as well as a page number. The volume number and the page number are separated by an unspaced colon.

(Chambers 1:45)
NOTE: If an entire volume of a multivolume work is being referred to, the abbreviation *vol.* is used to make it clear that the number is a volume number and not a page number.

(Chambers, vol. 1)

2. *A reference book* A reference to an entry in a reference book often begins with the name of the entry being cited, as in the entry for "Aristotle" in figure 6.4. A parenthetic reference need only mention the name of the entry, as no page number is included in the list of references. The name of the reference book should be mentioned in the text preceding such a reference; otherwise, the reader must consult the list of references to know what source is being cited.

("Aristotle")

3. *Literary works* Parenthetical references to literary works often include references to stanzas, lines, verses, chapters, books, parts, and the like. This is often very useful to readers trying to find a particular passage, because they may be using an edition of the work whose pagination differs from that of the edition used by the author of the note.

References to unpublished sources Parenthetical references are also used to cite unpublished sources that are not listed in a bibliography, such as letters to the author or telephone interviews. The following information should be included: the name of the person providing the information, the type of source, and the date, as "(Paul Roberts, letter to the author, Sept. 1986)." Any of these elements may be omitted from the parenthetical reference if included in the text.

PARENTHETICAL REFERENCE SYSTEMS USED IN THE SCIENCES

Two other systems of parenthetical citation that are used mostly in the social and natural sciences are the author-date system (also called the name-year system) and the number system.

Author-date system In the author-date system the parenthetical reference contains the author's last name and the date of publication with no intervening punctuation. A third element, a page number, is optional. If the author's name is mentioned in the introductory text, only the date and possibly the page number are needed within the parentheses. By referring to the list of references, the reader can find complete bibliographical information about the work. However, lists of references written in connection with the author-date system must also follow the scientific styling of placing the date after the author's name in each entry.

A book or article by two or more authors would be represented by the following stylings:

(Martin and Zim 1951)

(Martin, Zim, and Nelson 1951)

(Martin et al. 1951)

A corporate author name or a title may be substituted when there are no individual authors. An editor's last name may also be substituted, but the name is not followed by the abbreviation *ed*.

A page number or other number indicating a division of the work is often added to the date with a comma (a colon in some stylings) between date and page numbers. For citations to the short articles so prevalent in the scientific literature, page numbers are unnecessary, but for books, page references are certainly helpful to the reader.

(Martin et al. 1951, 147–149) *or* (Martin et al. 1951:147–149)

Volumes are indicated by Arabic numerals. Thus, "(1.147–149)" denotes volume 1, pages 147–149.

More than one work by the same author can be readily shown with the listing of a second date that follows the first with a comma between them, as "(Martin et al. 1951, 1958)." Two or more separate citations can also be included within one parenthesis if they are separated by a semicolon.

More than one work published in the same year by the same author can be indicated by adding an *a, b,* or *c* to the date. The same letters should be added to the dates in the entries in the list of references.

(Martin and Zim 1952a)

Number system In the number system, the parenthetical references consist only of numerals that are keyed to numbered entries in a list of references. Sometimes the numerals are italicized to show that they represent a title. In most variations on this system, a comma and a page number may follow the key numeral, as "(*3*, 259)."

A list of references developed in connection with this system is usually arranged not in alphabetical order but in order of the first citation of each entry in the text, since this arrangement is easier for the reader who wants to locate an entry on the list. Also, the year is usually written toward the end of the entry; it does not need to appear as the second element, as it would in the author-date system. Since the list is not alphabetized, it is unnecessary to use flush-and-hang indention.

The number system is not widely used. Although it takes up less space in the text, it can be no more satisfying to the reader than the system of footnote reference numbers. Furthermore, it is difficult for the editor and author to make last-minute revisions in the text where repositioning of the numbers might be involved.

BIBLIOGRAPHIES AND LISTS OF REFERENCES

A bibliography differs from a list of references in that it lists all of the works that a writer has found relevant in writing the text. A list of references, on the other hand, includes only those works that are specifically mentioned in the text or from which a particular quotation or piece of information was taken. In all other respects, however, bibliographies and lists of references are quite similar. They both appear at the end of an article, chapter, or book, where they list sources of information that are relevant to the text. They differ from a section of bibliographical endnotes in that their entries are arranged alphabetically (as in the sample in figure 6.4), and they use different patterns of indention, punctuation, and capitalization, as explained in the paragraphs that follow. Bibliographies and lists of references are punctuated and capitalized in the same way, and hereafter in this chapter, references to bibliographies should be understood to be inclusive of lists of references as well.

Additional detail regarding the styling of bibliographical entries is provided in the following paragraphs. For each of the kinds of entries that are described below, two examples are given. The first example is in a style used in the humanities, which is also the style used in most general writing and the style that is familiar to most writers. The second example is in a style that is representative of the social and natural sciences.

In general, bibliographical stylings used in the sciences differ from those used in general writing in that (1) the author's first and middle names are expressed with initials only, (2) the date, which is important in scientific writings, is often placed near the beginning instead of at the end of the entry, (3) less capitalization is used, (4) titles of articles are not enclosed in quotation marks, (5) book titles are not underlined or italicized, (6) dates are usually written as day-month-year, which results in less punctuation, and (7) more abbreviations are used. In content, however, the two stylings are much the same, and both rely on periods to separate each element of the bibliographical entry.

The examples used in this section by no means exhaust the possible variations on these two basic stylings. Different combinations of the styles illustrated here, as well as other alternatives, are found in print. Several of these variations are recommended by various professional organizations and academic disciplines within the social and natural sciences. The entries in this section that illustrate scientific style are based on the style described in the *CBE Style Manual*, fifth edition, published by the Council of Biology Editors. (NOTE: Some entries in this section may differ somewhat from preferred CBE style. Writers who need to style their bibliographies in strict accordance with CBE style should consult that manual.) Similar style manuals that give details of bibliographical styling used in specialized fields within the social and natural sciences are published by professional organizations in those fields.

BOOKS

Style and content of entries A bibliographical entry that refers to a book includes as many of the following ele-

ments as are relevant. The order of elements listed here is the order in which they appear in entries written in the styling of the humanities. Each of these elements is illustrated in the examples that begin on page 285.

1. *Author's name* The author's name or authors' names come first, whether the author is a single individual, or a group of individuals, or an organization. Names of coauthors are arranged in the order in which they are found on the title page. A work without an author but with an editor is styled with the editor's name first, followed by a comma and *ed.* (see paragraph 4 below). The name of the first author is inverted so that the surname comes first and can be alphabetized. In bibliographies that follow the style of the humanities, the author's name is written as it appears on the title page. In many stylings used in the social and natural sciences, the last name and first two initials are always used, regardless of how the author's name is printed on the title page. This is the style followed in this section for examples of bibliographical entries in the social and natural sciences; however, authors should remember that some confusion can result if more than one writer in the relevant subject area has the same initials and last name. The best way to avoid this difficulty is to include first names whenever there is a chance of confusion.

   In the humanities and in some stylings in the social and natural sciences, if there are more than three authors, the first author's name is followed by *et al.,* which is an abbreviation for the Latin phrase *et alii* or *et aliae,* meaning "and others." In other stylings, the names of all the authors are included.

2. *Title of the work* In the humanities, the title is underlined in typewritten manuscript and italicized in type. In the social and natural sciences, the title may follow this styling or it may be left without underlining or italicization. Capitalization is either headline-style (that is, all words are capitalized except for internal articles and prepositions) or sentence-style (that is, only the first word and proper nouns and adjectives are capitalized). In the humanities, headline-style capitalization is used; in the social and natural sciences, both styles of capitalization are used. The titles of references in the sciences that appear as examples in this chapter are unitalicized and use sentence-style capitalization. Another difference between the two stylings is that titles in the humanities include any subtitles, whereas subtitles are often omitted in bibliographies for the sciences. Subtitles are italicized and capitalized to match the styling of the titles that precede them.

3. *Portion of the book* Some bibliography entries cite only one portion of a book, as an essay within a collection or an article within a symposium. For these entries, the name of that portion is given first as a title. It is either italicized or enclosed in quotation marks, depending on its nature, or it is left alone as in stylings for the sciences. The title of the book is given next. The titles of chapters within nonfiction works by a single author are usually not included in the entry.

4. *Editor, compiler, or translator* In entries for books that have an author, the name of an editor, compiler, or translator comes after the title and is preceded or followed by the abbreviation *ed., comp.,* or *trans.* or some combination of these. If no author is listed, the name of the editor, compiler, or translator is placed first in the entry—styled like an author's name but followed by a comma and the lowercase abbreviation *ed., comp.,* or *trans.*

5. *Edition* If a book is other than the first edition, the number (as "2d ed." or "1986 ed.") or other description of the edition is written after the title. If the edition is identified by a word instead of a numeral, the first letter in that word is capitalized, as "Rev. ed."

6. *Volume number or number of volumes* In a bibliography entry that cites a multivolume work, the total number of volumes in that work is written before the publication information, as, for example, "9 vols." There is no need to cite the volumes actually used, since this information will be in a note or in a parenthetical reference. On the other hand, if only one volume of a multivolume work was consulted, that volume alone is listed as an entry, so that the text references need cite only page numbers, not volume numbers as well.

7. *Name of the series* If the book is part of a series, the name of the series should be included, as well as the book or volume number if the book represents a specific numbered volume in that series. The series name is not italicized.

8. *Publication data* The city of publication (with the state abbreviation if the city is not well known), the name of the publisher, and the year of publication of the particular edition used—together these form the grouping called the publication data. A colon usually follows the city name, a comma follows the name of the publisher, and a period after the date ends the bibliographical entry if the styling is that used in the humanities. In stylings used in the sciences, the date often appears after the author's name.

All of this information comes from the title page and the copyright page. If the title page lists more than one city, only the first is mentioned in the bibliography. Some books are published under a special imprint name, which is usually printed on the title page above the publisher's name. In a bibliographical entry, the imprint name is joined to the publisher's name with a hyphen, as *Golden Press-Western Publishing Co.* Short forms of publisher's names are often used in bibliographies. This usage is acceptable if consistently applied. Also the word *and* and the ampersand are equally acceptable within a publisher's name if they are used consistently.

For a multivolume work that is published over a period of several years, inclusive numbers are given for those years. The phrase *in press* is substituted for the date in works that are about to be published.

9. *Locators* Page numbers are added to book entries in a bibliography only when the entry cites a portion of a book such as a story or essay in an anthology or an article in a collection. If that portion is in a volume of a multivolume work, both volume and page number are given.

Examples The following examples illustrate how each of the elements described above is styled in a number of different situations. In each case, the first example illustrates a typical style in the humanities and general publications; the second illustrates a representative style used in the social and natural sciences.

1. *Book with a single author*

Chapman, R. F. *The Insects.* New York: American Elsevier, 1969.

Chapman, R. F. 1969. The insects. New York: American Elsevier.

2. *Book with two or three authors*

Starnes, De Witt T., and Gertrude E. Noyes. *The English Dictionary from Cawdrey to Johnson 1604–1775.* Chapel Hill: University of North Carolina Press, 1946.

Starnes, D. T.; Noyes, G. E. 1946. The English dictionary from Cawdrey to Johnson 1604–1775. Chapel Hill: University of North Carolina Press.

3. *Book with more than three authors*

Allee, W. C., et al. *Principles of Animal Ecology.* Philadelphia: W. B. Saunders Co., 1949.

Allee, W. C.; Emerson, A. E.; Park, O.; Park, S.; Schmidt, K. D. 1949. Principles of animal ecology. Philadelphia: W. B. Saunders Co.

4. *Book with a corporate author*

National Micrographics Association. *An Introduction to Micrographics.* Rev. ed. Silver Spring, Md.: National Micrographics Association, 1980.

National Micrographics Association. 1980. An introduction to micrographics. Rev. ed. Silver Spring, Md.: National Micrographics Association.

5. *Book without an author listed*

The World Almanac & Book of Facts. New York: Newspaper Enterprises Association, Inc., 1985.

The world almanac & book of facts. 1985. New York: Newspaper Enterprises Association.

6. *Book with editor listed and no author*

Bradbury, Peggy F., ed. *Transcriber's Guide to Medical Terminology.* New Hyde Park, N.Y.: Medical Examination Publishing Co., 1973.

Bradbury, P. F., editor. 1973. Transcriber's guide to medical terminology. New Hyde Park, N.Y.: Medical Examination Publishing Co.

7. *Book with author and editor-translator*

Beauvoir, Simone de. *The Second Sex.* Trans. and ed. H. M. Parshley. New York: Alfred A. Knopf, 1953.

Beauvoir, S. 1953. The second sex. Parshley, H. M., translator and editor. New York: Alfred A. Knopf.

8. *Multivolume book*

Farrand, John Jr., ed. *The Audubon Society Master Guide to Birding.* 3 vols. New York: Alfred A. Knopf, 1983.

Farrand, J. Jr., editor. 1983. The Audubon Society master guide to birding. New York: Alfred A. Knopf, 3 vol.

9. *Multivolume book only one volume of which was consulted*

Chambers, Robert. Vol. 1 of *Cyclopaedia of English Literature.* 2 vols. New York: World Publishing House, 1875.

Chambers, R. 1875. Cyclopaedia of English literature. Vol. 1. New York: World Publishing House.

10. *Portion of a book*

Malone, Kemp. "The Phonemes of Current English." *Studies for William A. Read.* Ed. Nathaniel M. Caffee and Thomas A. Kirby. Baton Rouge: Louisiana State University Press, 1940. pp. 133–165.

Malone, K. 1940. The phonemes of current English. In: Caffee, N. M.; Kirby, T. A., eds. Studies for William A. Read. Baton Rouge: Louisiana State University Press: p. 133–165.

11. *Book in a series*

Manheimer, Martha L. *Style Manual: A Guide for the Preparation of Reports and Dissertations.* Vol. 5 of Books in Library and Information Science. New York: Marcel Dekker, 1973.

Manheimer, M. L. 1973. Style manual. New York: Marcel Dekker. (Books in library and information science; vol. 5.)

ARTICLES IN JOURNALS OR OTHER PERIODICALS

Style and Content of Entries A bibliography entry for an article in a journal or other periodical or in a newspaper includes as many of the following elements as are relevant. Examples of each of these elements can be found in the reference samples beginning on page 291. The elements are listed here in the order in which they appear in entries styled on the humanities pattern.

1. *Author's name* The author's name is written as it appears on the printed page and is styled in the way described above for an entry that refers to a book. Names of people who write letters to a periodical or who contribute signed reviews are treated like names of authors.

2. *Title of the article* The title of the article is written in full as it appears in the printed article. In most bibliography stylings used in the humanities, the title and subtitle are enclosed in quotation marks (with a period before the closing quotation mark) and capitalized headline-style. Titles of articles styled for use in the social and natural sciences tend to omit the quotation marks, use sentence-style capitalization, and omit subtitles.

3. *Name of the periodical* The name of the periodical is treated in the same way as described above for a book: underlined to indicate italics in bibliographies for the humanities, but not italicized in bibliographies for

the sciences. However, unlike book titles, periodical titles are fully capitalized in bibliographies in both the humanities and the sciences. In addition, there are special principles for the styling of periodical names in both categories. One is the omission of an initial article. Whereas the initial article is included in a book title but ignored in alphabetizing, the initial article of a journal title is dropped completely. Another is the use of abbreviations for journal titles of more than one word. These abbreviations are widely used in technical writing. Each discipline has its own set of abbreviations for the journals that tend to be used in that discipline. For general writing, however, these titles are written in full for the reader's convenience, and the examples that follow show journal titles in unabbreviated form. Journal titles that begin with the words *Transactions, Proceedings,* and *Annals* are often reversed for the purpose of alphabetizing so that these words come last.

Names of newspapers are treated as they appear on the masthead, except that initial articles are omitted. Also, a place name is added in brackets after the newspaper's name if it is necessary to distinguish that particular paper.

4. *Volume and number of the periodical* This information comes after the name of the periodical and identifies the particular issue cited. An issue that is identified by both volume and number should be identified in that way in a bibliography entry, as "3(2):25–37" for volume 3, number 2, pages 25–37. If the issue is identified in some other manner, as by a full date, that method is used in the bibliography entry. Issue numbers are not commonly used, however, unless the issue is paginated independently of the volume as a whole and the number is needed to identify the issue. Examples 1 and 5 below illustrate entries for a periodical in which pages are numbered consecutively through a volume and which therefore needs only a volume number. If the volume number corresponds to a particular year, as in the examples, the year in parentheses follows the volume number—but not, of course, in the scientific stylings, where the year is placed after the author's name.

Example 2 below illustrates a reference to a periodical that uses a seasonal designation in addition to a volume and number designation; the pages in this issue are numbered independently of the volume as a whole. Example 3 illustrates a popular monthly magazine, issues of which are commonly referred to by date rather than by volume or issue number. Newspapers are always identified by date.

5. *Issue date* Periodicals issued daily, weekly, monthly, and bimonthly are usually designated by date of issue. The date follows the unpunctuated day-month-year order (27 May 1984) rather than the punctuated month-day-year order (May 27, 1984). Names of months that are spelled with more than four letters are usually abbreviated.

6. *Page numbers* Inclusive pages for the whole article are written at the end of the entry. For newspaper entries, it may be necessary to add

a section number or edition identification number as well, as "p. B6." Articles that are continued on later pages are styled thus: "38–41, 159–160." The use of the abbreviations *p.* or *pp.* in bibliographies is the same as it is in footnotes.

Examples The following examples illustrate how each of the elements described above is styled in a number of different situations. The first example of each group illustrates a style used in the humanities and in general publications; the second illustrates a style used in the social and natural sciences.

1. *Article in journal with continuous pagination of volume*

Heil, John. "Seeing is Believing." *American Philosophical Quarterly* 19 (1982): 229–239.

Heil, J. 1982. Seeing is believing. American Philosophical Quarterly 19:229–239.

2. *Article in journal that paginates each issue separately*

Ourecky, Donald K. "Cane and Bush Fruits." *Plants & Gardens* 27, No. 3 (Autumn 1971): pp. 13–15.

Ourecky, D. K. 1971. Cane and bush fruits. Plants & Gardens 27(3):13–15.

3. *Articles in periodicals issued by date*

Smiley, Xan. "Misunderstanding Africa." *Atlantic,* Sept. 1982, pp. 70–79.
Smiley, X. 1982. Misunderstanding Africa. Atlantic, Sept.:70–79.

Rosenberg, Jeremy C. "Letters." *Advertising Age,* 7 June 1982, p. M–1.
Rosenberg, J. C. 1982. Letters. Advertising Age, 7 June: M–1.

4. *Article in newspaper*

Pitts, Gail. "Money Funds Holding Own." *Morning Union* [Springfield, Mass.], 23 Aug. 1982, p. 6.

Pitts, G. 1982. Money funds holding own. Morning Union [Springfield, Mass.] 23 Aug.:6.

5. *Signed review*

Vassell, M. O. Rev. of *Applied Charge Particle Optics,* ed. A. Septier. *American Scientist* 70 (1982): 229.

Vassell, M. O. 1982. Rev. of A. Septier, ed., Applied charge particle optics. American Scientist 70:229.

6. *Anonymous article*

"Education at Home: A Showdown in Texas." *Newsweek,* 25 March 1985, p. 87.

Anonymous. 1985. Education at home. Newsweek 25 March:87.

UNPUBLISHED MATERIALS

Bibliography entries for unpublished materials include as many of the following elements as are known or are relevant.

1. *Author's name* The author's name is treated in the same way as described above for a book.

2. *Title of the work* If there is an official title, it is copied as it appears on the work. It is enclosed in quotation marks and capitalized like a book title in a bibliography using a styling

from the humanities. If the work has no official title, a descriptive title is used, as in example 2 below, but it is not enclosed in quotation marks.

3. *The nature of the material* The entry should include a description of the document, such as "letter to the author" or "doctoral dissertation." For works without official author or title, this element is the first part of the entry.

4. *Date* The date must be included if it is known. If the date is known but is not written on the document, it is enclosed in brackets.

5. *Name of collection and identification number* Whatever information is necessary to completely identify the document is included.

6. *Geographical location* The name of the institution and the city where the materials can be located are often listed last in this kind of bibliographical entry.

EXAMPLES

1. *Unpublished report*

Velasquez, Joyce A. "The Format of Formal Reports." Report prepared for the Southern Engineering Company. Johnson City, Miss., May 29, 1985.

Velasquez, J. A. 1985. The format of formal reports. Report prepared for the Southern Engineering Company. 29 May. Johnson City, Miss.

2. *Letter in a collection*

Johnson, Clive. Letter to Elizabeth O'Hara. 9 Nov. 1916. Johnson Collection, item 5298. California State Historical Society, San Marino, Calif.

Johnson, C. 1916. Letter to Elizabeth O'Hara. 9 Nov. Located at California State Historical Society, San Marino, Calif.

FORMAT OF A BIBLIOGRAPHY

Bibliographies are always typed beginning on a new page. Most are alphabetically arranged and indented flush-and-hang to set off the alphabetical sequence. Initial articles that are included in a title that begins an entry are ignored in determining the alphabetical order. All the entries are usually listed together in a single alphabetical arrangement, whether the first word is an author's surname or the title of an anonymous work. It is possible to divide a bibliography into categories by date of publication or by subject matter, but such divisions are not recommended unless the single-list form proves unmanageable.

More than one work by an author After the first listing of an entry by an author or group of coauthors who have more than one work listed in the bibliography, that person's name is replaced in succeeding, adjacent entries by a dash. In typewritten bibliographies, the dash is usually represented by three typed hyphens. The author is not usually expected to type this dash or its equivalent in hyphens; instead, the editor substitutes the dash for the author's names as needed on the copyedited page. The dash is followed by a period, just as a name would be, or by a comma and an abbreviation such as *ed.*

The dash substitutes for the author's full name (or the full names of the set of coauthors) but no more. Thus, the dash may be used only when the names are exactly the same in adjacent entries. For example, if an entry for a work by Kemp Malone is followed by an entry for a work coauthored by Malone and someone else, the second entry would be spelled out. But if Malone and his coauthor wrote more than one book together, the dash would be used to replace both names in the second reference. A work by a single author precedes a work by that author and another; and works edited by an author usually follow works written by the same person.

In the general bibliographical stylings, the various works by a single author or group of coauthors are arranged alphabetically by title. In bibliographies in the social and natural sciences, however, where the date appears after the author's name, these multiple entries are arranged by date of publication. Occasionally an author publishes more than one article during a year. In these cases, the work is identified by a letter (often italicized) that follows the year. Thus, an author's works may be listed as 1977, 1979a, 1979b, 1980, and so on.

Headings Depending on their scope as explained at the beginning of this section, bibliographies may be headed *Bibliography* or *List of References*. Writings in the sciences often list bibliographical entries under the heading *Literature Cited*. If this heading is used, then only "literature"—that is, published works—and only works actually cited can be included on the list. Unpublished works that are referred to in the text must carry information such as the author's name and the title and where the work can be located, as well as the word *unpublished,* within the text or within parentheses. To avoid having to refer to an unwieldy number of unpublished works in the text, the author or editor may head the reference list *References Cited,* which allows the inclusion of unpublished works. Works in press are usually listed under *Literature Cited* heads even though they are not yet published. In lieu of the date, the entry contains the phrase *in press*.

Annotated bibliographies Annotated bibliographies are those in which the entries are written as for a regular bibliography but are then followed by a sentence or paragraph of description. Annotated bibliographies are designed to lead the reader to the most useful works for further study. Comments may be added to all or just some of the entries. The descriptive part may be run in with the bibliographical entry, or it may be set off typographically by lines of space, indention, italics, or smaller type.

ARABIC AND ROMAN NUMERALS

NAME	ARABIC NUMERAL	ROMAN NUMERAL	NAME	ARABIC NUMERAL	ROMAN NUMERAL
zero	0		thirty-one	30	XXXI
one	1	I	thirty-two	30	XXXII
two	2	II	forty	40	XL
three	3	III	forty-one	41	XLI
four	4	IV	fifty	50	L
five	5	V	sixty	60	LX
six	6	VI	70	70	LXX
seven	7	VII	eighty	80	LXXX
eight	8	VIII	ninety	90	XC
nine	9	IX	one hundred	100	C
ten	10	X	one hundred one	101	CI
eleven	11	XI	*or* one hundred and one		
twelve	12	XII	one hundred two	102	CII
thirteen	13	XIII	*or* one hundred and two	102	CII
fourteen	14	XIV	two hundred	200	CC
fifteen	15	XV	three hundred	300	CCC
sixteen	16	XVI	four hundred	400	CD
seventeen	17	XVII	five hundred	500	D
eighteen	18	XVIII	six hundred	600	DC
nineteen	19	XIX	seven hundred	700	DCC
twenty	20	XX	eight hundred	800	DCCC
twenty-one	21	XXI	nine hundred	900	CM
twenty-two	22	XXII	one thousand	1,000	M
twenty-three	23	XXIII	two thousand	2,000	MM
twenty-four	24	XXIV	five thousand	5,000	$\overline{V}$
twenty-five	25	XXV	ten thousand	10,000	$\overline{X}$
twenty-six	26	XXVI	one hundred thousand	100,000	$\overline{C}$
twenty-nine	29	XXIX	one million	1,000,000	$\overline{M}$
thirty	30	XXX			

PROOFREADERS' MARKS

Mark	Meaning
ℐ or ϒ or ⌀	delete; take it out
⌒	close up; print as one word
ℨ	delete and close up
∧ or > or h	caret; insert here ⟨ something
#	insert a space
eq#	space evenly where indicated
stet	let marked ~~text~~ stand as set
tr	transpose; change order the
/	used to separate two or more marks and often as a concluding stroke at the end of an insertion
⌐	set farther to the left
⌐ set	farther to the right
⌢	set æ or fl as ligatures æ or fl
⹀	straighten alignment
‖	straighten or align
X	imperfect or broken character
□	indent or insert em quad space
¶	begin a new paragraph
(sp)	spell out (set ⑤ lbs. as five pounds)
cap	set in capitals (CAPITALS)
sm cap or s.c.	set in small capitals (SMALL CAPITALS)
lc	set in lowercase (lowercase)
ital	set in italic (*italic*)
rom	set in roman (roman)
bf	set in boldface (**boldface**)
= or -/ or ⌄ or /H/	hyphen
$\frac{1}{N}$ or en or /N/	en dash (1965–72)
$\frac{1}{M}$ or em or /M/	em — or long — dash
∨	superscript or superior (as in πr^2)
∧	subscript or inferior (as in H_2O)
◇	centered (for a centered dot in $p \cdot q$)
⋀	comma
⋁	apostrophe
⊙	period
;/	semicolon
⊙	colon
⟨⟨ ⟩⟩ or ⟨⟩	quotation marks
(/)	parentheses
[/]	brackets

Forms of Address

This table contains the most common formal ways of address styling and salutation in American English. The wide array of personal, regional, and stylistic preferences makes it unfeasible to provide a complete listing of all the possible variations.

When a person holds several titles, his or her highest title is the preferred choice.

ADDRESS STYLING	SALUTATION STYLING
CLERICAL AND RELIGIOUS ORDERS	
abbot	
The Right Reverend John R. Smith, O.S.B. Abbot of _____	Right Reverend and dear Father Dear Father Abbot Dear Father
archbishop	
The Most Reverend Archbishop of _____	Your Excellency
or	
The Most Reverend John R. Smith Archbishop of _____	Your Excellency Dear Archbishop Smith
bishop, Catholic	
The Most Reverend John R. Smith Bishop of _____	Your Excellency Dear Bishop Smith
bishop, Episcopal	
The Right Reverend The Bishop of _____	Right Reverend Sir
or	
The Right Reverend John R. Smith Bishop of _____	Right Reverend Sir Dear Bishop Smith
bishop, Protestant (excluding Episcopal)	
The Reverend John R. Smith	Reverend Sir Dear Bishop Smith
brotherhood, member of	
Brother John, S.J. *(or other initials for the order)*	Dear Brother John
cardinal	
His Eminence John Cardinal Smith	Your Eminence Dear Cardinal Smith
or	
His Eminence Cardinal Smith	(same)
clergyman, Protestant	
The Reverend Amelia R. Smith	Dear Ms. Smith
or if having a doctorate	
The Reverend Dr. Amelia R. Smith	Dear Dr. Smith
monsignor, domestic prelate	
The Right Reverend Monsignor John R. Smith	Right Reverend and dear Monsignor Smith
or	
The Rt. Rev. Msgr. John R. Smith	Dear Monsignor Smith
mother superior (of a sisterhood)	
The Reverend Mother Superior Convent of _____	Reverend Mother Dear Reverend Mother My dear Reverend Mother Mary Angelica
or	
Reverend Mother Mary Angelica, O.S.D. *(or other initials of the order)* Convent of _____	(same)
patriarch (of an Eastern Orthodox Church)	
His Beatitude the Patriarch of _____	Most Reverend Lord

pope

His Holiness the Pope

Your Holiness
Most Holy Father

or

His Holiness Pope John

(same)

president, Mormon

The President
Church of Jesus Christ of Latter-day Saints

My dear President
Dear President Smith

priest, Catholic

The Reverend Father Smith

Dear Father Smith

or

The Reverend John R. Smith

(same)

rabbi

Rabbi John R. Smith

Dear Rabbi Smith

or if having a doctorate

Rabbi John R. Smith, D.D.

Dear Dr. Smith

sisterhood, member of

Sister Mary Angelica, S.C. *(or other initials of the order)*

Dear Sister
Dear Sister Mary Angelica

COLLEGE AND UNIVERSITY FACULTY AND OFFICIALS

chancellor (of a university)

Dr. Amelia R. Smith
Chancellor

Dear Dr. Smith

dean (of a college or university)

Dean Amelia R. Smith

Dear Dr. Smith
Dear Dean Smith

or

Dr. Amelia R. Smith
Dean

(same)

president

Dr. Amelia R. Smith
President

Dear Dr. Smith

or

President Amelia R. Smith

Dear President Smith

president, priest

The Very Reverend John R. Smith
President

Dear Father Smith

professor, assistant (or **associate**)

Dr. Dale R. Smith
Assistant (or Associate) Professor of _____

Dear Dr. Smith
Dear Professor Smith
Dear Mr. Smith
Dear Ms. Smith

professor, full

Professor John R. Smith

Dear Professor Smith

or

Dr. John R. Smith
Professor of _____

Dear Dr. Smith

CONSULAR OFFICERS

consul, American (covers all consular grades such as *Consul, Consul General, Vice-
Consul,* and *Consular Agent*)

The American Consul
(foreign city, country)

Sir
Sir or Madam

or if in Latin America or Canada

The Consul of the United States of America

(same)

or if individual name is known

Amelia R. Smith, Esq.
American Consul

Madam
Dear Ms. Smith

or if in Latin America or Canada

Amelia R. Smith, Esq.
Consul of the United States of America

(same)

consuls, foreign (covers all consular grades)

The _____ Consul
(U.S. city, state, zip code)

Sir
Sir or Madame

or

The Consul of _____   (same)
(U.S. city, state, zip code)
  or if individual name is known
The Honorable John R. Smith   Sir
_____ Consul   Dear Mr. Smith

DIPLOMATS

ambassador, American

The Honorable Dale R. Smith   Sir (or Madam)
American Ambassador   Dear Mr. (or Madam)
                                             Ambassador

  or if in Latin America or Canada
The Honorable Dale R. Smith   (same)
Ambassador of the United States of America

ambassador, foreign

His Excellency John R. Smith   Excellency
Ambassador of _____   Dear Mr. Ambassador
  or
Her Excellency Amelia R. Smith   Excellency
Ambassador of _____   Dear Madame Ambassador

chargé d'affaires, American

Dale R. Smith, Esq.   Sir (or Madam)
American Chargé d'Affaires   Dear Mr. (or Ms.) Smith
  or if in Latin America or Canada
Dale R. Smith, Esq.   (same)
United States Chargé d'Affaires

chargé d'affaires, foreign

Mr. John R. Smith   Sir
Chargé d'Affaires of _____   Dear Mr. Smith
  or
Ms. Amelia R. Smith   Madame
Chargé d'Affaires of _____   Dear Ms. Smith

minister, American

The Honorable Dale R. Smith   Sir (or Madam)
American Minister   Dear Mr. Minister
                                             Dear Madam Minister

  or if in Latin America or Canada
The Honorable Dale R. Smith   (same)
Minister of the United States of America

minister, foreign

The Honorable Dale R. Smith   Sir (or Madame)
Minister of _____   Dear Mr. Minister
                                             Dear Madame Minister

FOREIGN HEADS OF STATE: A BRIEF SAMPLING

premier

His Excellency John R. Smith   Excellency
Premier of _____   Dear Mr. Premier
  or
Her Excellency Amelia R. Smith   Excellency
Premier of _____   Dear Madame Premier

president of a republic

Her Excellency Amelia R. Smith   Excellency
President of _____   Dear Madame President
  or
His Excellency John R. Smith   Excellency
President of _____   Dear Mr. President

prime minister

His Excellency John R. Smith   Excellency
                                             Dear Mr. Prime Minister

  or

Her Excellency Amelia R. Smith   Excellency
                                             Dear Madame Prime Minister

GOVERNMENT OFFICIALS—FEDERAL

attorney general

The Honorable Amelia R. Smith   Dear Madam Attorney General
The Attorney General

cabinet officer (other than attorney general)

The Honorable Dale R. Smith   Sir (or Madam)
Secretary of _____   Dear Mr. (or Madam) Secretary

   or

The Secretary of _____   (same)

chairman of a (sub) committee, U.S. Congress (stylings shown apply to House of Representatives & Senate)

The Honorable Dale R. Smith   Dear Mr. (or Madam) Chairman
Chairman   Dear Senator Smith
Committee on _____
United States Senate

chief justice—see SUPREME COURT, FEDERAL; STATE

commissioner

The Honorable Amelia R. Smith   Dear Mr. (or Madam)
Commissioner   Commissioner
                                                   Dear Mr. (or Ms.) Smith

congressman—see REPRESENTATIVE, U.S. CONGRESS

director (as of an independent federal agency)

The Honorable John R. Smith   Dear Mr. Smith
Director
_____ Agency

district attorney

The Honorable Amelia R. Smith   Dear Ms. Smith
District Attorney

federal judge

The Honorable John R. Smith   Sir
Judge of the United States District Court of   My dear Judge Smith
the _____ District of _____   Dear Judge Smith

justice—see SUPREME COURT, FEDERAL; STATE

librarian of congress

The Honorable Amelia R. Smith   Madam
Librarian of Congress   Dear Ms. Smith

postmaster general

The Honorable John R. Smith   Sir
The Postmaster General   Dear Mr. Postmaster General

president of the United States

The President   Mr. President
The White House   My dear Mr. President
                                                   Dear Mr. President

   or

The Honorable Amelia R. Smith   Madam President
President of the United States   My dear Madam President
The White House   Dear Madam President

representative, United States Congress

The Honorable Amelia R. Smith   Madam
United States House of Representatives   Dear Representative Smith
  or for local address
The Honorable Amelia R. Smith   Dear Ms. Smith
Representative in Congress

senator, United States Senate

The Honorable Amelia R. Smith   Madam
United States Senate   Dear Senator Smith

speaker, United States House of Representatives

The Honorable   Sir (or Madam)
The Speaker of the House of Representatives
  or
The Honorable Speaker of the House of Representatives   (same)
  or
The Honorable Dale R. Smith   Sir (or Madam)
Speaker of the House of Representatives   Dear Mr. (or Madam) Speaker
                                                   Dear Mr. (or Ms.) Smith

supreme court, associate justice

Mr. (or Ms.) Justice Smith   Sir (or Madam)
The Supreme Court of the United States   Mr. (or Madam) Justice
                                                   My dear Mr. (or Madam) Justice
                                                   Dear Mr. (or Madam) Justice
                                                   Smith

supreme court, chief justice

The Chief Justice of the United States
The Supreme Court of the United States

Sir (or Madam)
My dear Mr. (or Madam) Chief
Justice
Dear Mr. (or Madam) Chief
Justice

or

The Chief Justice
The Supreme Court

Sir (or Madam)
My dear Mr. (or Madam) Chief
Justice
Dear Mr. (or Madam) Chief
Justice

vice president of the United States

The Vice President of the United States
United States Senate

Sir (or Madam)
My dear Mr. (or Madam) Vice
President
Dear Mr. (or Madam) Vice
President

or

The Honorable Dale R. Smith
Vice President of the United States
Washington, DC (zip code)

(same)

GOVERNMENT OFFICIALS—LOCAL

alderman (or councilman or selectman)

The Honorable Dale R. Smith

Dear Mr. (or Ms.) Smith
Dear Alderman Smith

or

Alderman Dale R. Smith

(same)

city attorney (includes city counsel, corporation counsel)

The Honorable Amelia R. Smith

Dear Ms. Smith

councilman—see ALDERMAN

county clerk

The Honorable John R. Smith
Clerk of _____ County

Dear Mr. Smith

county treasurer—see COUNTY CLERK

judge

The Honorable Amelia R. Smith
Judge of the _____ Court of _____

Dear Judge Smith

mayor

The Honorable Dale R. Smith
Mayor of _____

Sir (or Madam)
Dear Mayor Smith

selectman—see ALDERMAN

GOVERNMENT OFFICIALS—STATE

assemblyman—see REPRESENTATIVE, STATE

attorney (as commonwealth's attorney, state's attorney)

The Honorable Amelia R. Smith
(title)

Dear Ms. Smith

attorney general

The Honorable John R. Smith
Attorney General of the State of _____

Sir
Dear Mr. Attorney General

clerk of a court

Amelia R. Smith, Esq.
Clerk of the Court of _____

Dear Ms. Smith

delegate—see REPRESENTATIVE, STATE

governor

The Honorable Dale R. Smith
Governor of _____
   or in some states
His Excellency, the Governor of _____
Her Excellency, the Governor of _____

Sir (or Madam)
Dear Governor Smith

(same)

judge, state court

The Honorable John R. Smith
Judge of the _____ Court

Dear Judge Smith

ADDRESS STYLING	SALUTATION STYLING

judge/justice, state supreme court—see SUPREME COURT, STATE

lieutenant governor

The Honorable Lieutenant Governor of _____	Madam
or	
The Honorable Amelia R. Smith	Madam
Lieutenant Governor of _____	Dear Ms. Smith

representative, state (includes assemblyman, delegate)

The Honorable John R. Smith	Sir
House of Representatives (or The State Assembly or The	Dear Mr. Smith
House of Delegates)	

secretary of state

The Honorable Secretary of State of _____	Sir (or Madam)
or	
The Honorable Dale R. Smith	Sir (or Madam)
Secretary of State of _____	Dear Mr. (or Madam) Secretary

senate, state, president of

The Honorable John R. Smith	Sir
President of the Senate of the State (or the Commonwealth)	Dear Mr. Smith
of _____	Senator

senator, state

| The Honorable Amelia R. Smith | Madam |
| The Senate of _____ | Dear Senator Smith |

speaker, state assembly, house of delegates, or house of representatives

| The Honorable John R. Smith | Sir |
| Speaker of _____ | Dear Mr. Smith |

supreme court, state, associate justice

| The Honorable Amelia R. Smith | Madam |
| Associate Justice of the Supreme Court of _____ | Dear Justice Smith |

supreme court, state, chief justice

| The Honorable Dale R. Smith | Sir (or Madam) |
| Chief Justice of the Supreme Court of _____ | Dear Mr. (or Madam) Chief Justice |

MILITARY RANKS

for any rank

full rank + full name + comma + abbreviation of the branch of service	Dear *+ full rank + surname*
or	
abbreviation of rank + full name + comma + abbreviation of branch of service	*(same)*

(A small sampling of address formats for military ranks is shown here. Abbreviations for each rank and the branches of service using them are shown at individual entries.)

admiral [coast guard, navy (ADM)]

Admiral Amelia R. Smith, USCG (etc)	Dear Admiral Smith
or	
ADM Amelia R. Smith, USCG (etc)	*(same)*

a similar pattern is used for **rear admiral** *(RADM) and* **vice admiral** *(VADM) with the full rank given in the salutation line.*

airman [air force (AMN)]

Airman John R. Smith, USAF	Dear Airman Smith
or	
AMN John R. Smith, USAF	*(same)*

a similar pattern is used for **airman basic** *(AB) and* **airman first class** *(A1C) with the full rank given in the salutation line.*

captain [air force, army (CPT); coast guard, navy (CAPT); marine corps (Capt.)]

Captain John R. Smith, USAF (etc)	Dear Captain Smith
or	
CPT John R. Smith, USAF (etc)	*(same)*

chief petty officer [coast guard, navy (CPO)]

Chief Petty Officer Dale R. Smith, USN (etc)	Dear Chief Smith
or	
CPO Dale R. Smith, USN (etc)	*(same)*

chief warrant officer [army, navy, marine corps] (covers all grades of chief warrant officers, CWO2-CWO4)

Chief Warrant Officer Dale R. Smith, USA (etc)	Dear Mr. Smith Dear Ms. Smith Dear Chief Warrant Officer Smith

or

CWO4 Dale R. Smith, USA (etc)	(same)

colonel [air force, army (COL); marine corps (Col.)]

Colonel Amelia R. Smith, USMC (etc)	Dear Colonel Smith

or

Col. Amelia R. Smith, USMC (etc)	(same)

commander [coast guard, navy (CDR)]

Commander John R. Smith, USN (etc)	Dear Commander Smith

or

CDR John R. Smith, USCG (etc)	(same)

corporal [army (CPL); marine corps (Cpl.)]

Corporal Amelia R. Smith, USA (etc)	Dear Corporal Smith

or

CPL Amelia R. Smith, USA (etc)	(same)

*a similar pattern is used for **lance corporal** [marine corps (L/Cpl.)] with the full rank given in the salutation line.*

ensign [coast guard, navy (ENS)]

Ensign Dale R. Smith, USN (etc)	Dear Ensign Smith Dear Mr. Smith Dear Ms. Smith

or

ENS Dale R. Smith, USN (etc)	(same)

first lieutenant [air force, army (1LT); marine corps (1st Lt.)]

First Lieutenant Amelia R. Smith, USMC (etc)	Dear Lieutenant Smith

or

1st Lt. Amelia R. Smith, USMC (etc)	(same)

general [air force, army (GEN); marine corps (Gen.)]

General Amelia R. Smith, USAF (etc)	Dear General Smith

or

GEN Amelia R. Smith, USAF (etc)	(same)

*a similar pattern is used for **brigadier general** [air force, army (BG); marine corps (Brig. Gen.)], **major general** [air force, army (MG); marine corps (Maj. Gen.)], and **lieutenant general** [air force, army (LTG); marine corps (Lt. Gen.)] with the full rank given in the salutation line.*

lieutenant [coast guard, navy (LT)]—see also FIRST LIEUTENANT, SECOND LIEUTENANT; LIEUTENANT JUNIOR GRADE

Lieutenant Dale R. Smith, USN (etc)	Dear Lieutenant Smith Dear Mr. Smith Dear Ms. Smith

or

LT Dale R. Smith, USN (etc)	(same)

lieutenant junior grade [coast guard, navy (LTJG)]—see also LIEUTENANT

Lieutenant (j.g.) Dale R. Smith, USCG (etc)	Dear Lieutenant Smith Dear Mr. Smith Dear Ms. Smith

or

LTJG Dale R. Smith, USCG (etc)	(same)

major [air force, army (MAJ); marine corps (Maj.)]

Major John R. Smith, USAF (etc)	Dear Major Smith

or

MAJ John R. Smith, USAF (etc)	(same)

master chief petty officer [coast guard, navy (MCPO)]

Master Chief Petty Officer Amelia R. Smith, USN (etc)	Dear Master Chief Smith

or

MCPO Amelia R. Smith, USN (etc)	(same)

petty officer first class [coast guard, navy (PO1)]

Petty Officer First Class John R. Smith, USN (etc)	Dear Petty Officer Smith

or

PO1 John R. Smith, USN (etc)	(same)

similar pattern is used for **petty officer second class** *(PO2) and* **petty officer third class** *(PO3).*

private [army (PVT); marine corps (Pvt.)]

Private John R. Smith, USMC (etc)   Dear Private Smith

or

Pvt. John R. Smith, USCM (etc)   (same)

a similar pattern is used for **private first class** *[army (PFC)].*

seaman [coast guard, navy (SMN)]

Seaman Amelia R. Smith, USCG (etc)   Dear Seaman Smith

or

SMN Amelia R. Smith, USCG (etc)   (same)

a similar pattern is used for **seaman apprentice** *and* **seaman recruit** *[coast guard, navy].*

second lieutenant [air force, army (2LT); marine corps (2nd Lt.)]

Second Lieutenant John R. Smith, USA (etc)   Dear Lieutenant Smith

or

2LT John R. Smith, USA (etc)   (same)

senior chief petty officer [coast guard, navy (SCPO)]

Senior Chief Petty Officer John R. Smith, USCG (etc)   Dear Senior Chief Smith

or

SCPO John R. Smith, USCG (etc)   (same)

sergeant [air force, army (SGT)]

Sergeant Amelia R. Smith, USAF (etc)   Dear Sergeant Smith

or

SGT Amelia R. Smith, USAF (etc)   (same)

a similar pattern is used for other sergeant ranks, including **first sergeant** *[army (1SG); marine corps (1st Sgt.)];* **gunnery sergeant** *[marine corps (Gy. Sgt.)];* **master sergeant** *[air force (MSGT); army (MSG)];* **sergeant first class** *[army (SFC)];* **staff sergeant** *[air force (SSGT); army (SSG); marine corps (SSgt.)]; and* **technical sergeant** *[air force (TSGT)] with the full rank given in the salutation line.*

sergeant major [army (SGM); marine corps (Sgt. Maj.)]

Sergeant Major Amelia R. Smith, USMC (etc)   Dear Sergeant Major Smith

or

Sgt. Maj. Amelia R. Smith, USMC (etc)   (same)

warrant officer [army, coast guard, navy (WO1)]—see also CHIEF WARRANT OFFICER

Warrant Officer Dale R. Smith, USA (etc)   Dear Warrant Officer Smith
Dear Mr. Smith
Dear Ms. Smith

or

WO1 Dale R. Smith, USA (etc)   (same)

UNITED NATIONS OFFICIALS

representative, American (with ambassadorial rank)

The Honorable Dale R. Smith   Sir (or Madam)
United States Permanent Representative to the United Nations   Dear Mr. (or Madam)
Ambassador

representative, foreign (with ambassadorial rank)

His Excellency John R. Smith   Excellency
Representative of _____ to the United Nations   My dear Mr. Ambassador
Dear Mr. Ambassador

or

Her Excellency Amelia R. Smith   Excellency
Representative of _____ to the United Nations   My dear Madam Ambassador
Dear Madam Ambassador

secretary-general

Her Excellency Amelia R. Smith   Excellency
Secretary-General of the United Nations   My dear Madam (or Madame)
Secretary-General
Dear Madam (or Madame)
Secretary-General

or

His Excellency John R. Smith   Excellency
Secretary-General of the United Nations   My dear Mr. Secretary-General
Dear Mr. Secretary-General

undersecretary

The Honorable John R. Smith   Sir
Undersecretary of the United Nations   Dear Mr. Smith

Common Abbreviations

Most of the following abbreviations have been normalized to one form. In practice, however, there is considerable variation in the use of periods and in capitalization (such as in *mph, m.p.h.,* and *MPH*), and stylings other than those given in this dictionary are often acceptable.

For a list of special signs and symbols that cannnot be readily alphabetized, see the section Signs and Symbols.

a absent, acre, answer, are, atto-
A ace, ampere, argon
Å angstrom unit
AA administrative assistant, Alcoholics Anonymous, associate in arts, author's alterations
A and M agricultural and mechanical
AAR against all risks
AB able-bodied seaman, Alberta, bachelor of arts [New Latin *artium baccalaureus*]
abbr abbreviation
ABC American Broadcasting Company
abl ablative
abp archbishop
abs absolute, abstract
abstr abstract
ac account, acre
Ac actinium, altocumulus
AC air conditioning, alternating current, before Christ [Latin *ante Christum*], area code
acad academic, academy
acc, accus accusative
accel accelerando
acct account, accountant
ack acknowledge, acknowledgment
ACLU American Civil Liberties Union
act active, actor, actual
ACT American College Test, Australian Capital Territory
actg acting
AD after date, anno Domini
ADC aide-de-camp, Aid to Dependent Children
addn addition
ad int ad interim
adj adjective, adjunct, adjustment, adjutant
ad loc to or at the place [Latin *ad locum*]
ADM admiral
admin administration
adv adverb, advertisement, advertising
ad val ad valorem
advt advertisement
AEC Atomic Energy Commission
AEF American Expeditionary Force
aet, aetat of age, aged [Latin *aetatis*]
AF air force, audio frequency
AFB air force base
AFDC Aid to Families with Dependent Children
afft affidavit

AFL-CIO American Federation of Labor and Congress of Industrial Organizations
Afr Africa, African
Ag silver [Latin *argentum*]
agcy agency
agric agricultural, agriculture
agt agent
AK Alaska
aka also known as
Al aluminum
AL Alabama, American Legion
Ala Alabama
Alb Albania, Albanian
alc alcohol
ald alderman
alg algebra
alk alkaline
alt alternate, altitude
Alta Alberta
a.m., AM ante meridiem
Am America, American, americium
AM master of arts [New Latin *artium magister*]
amb ambassador
amdt amendment
Amer America, American
amp ampere
amt amount
AMU atomic mass unit
anal analogy, analysis, analytic
anat anatomical, anatomy
anc ancient
ANC African National Congress
ann annals, annual
anon anonymous, anonymously
ans answer
ant antenna, antonym
Ant Antarctica, Antrim
anthrop anthropology
antilog antilogarithm
AO account of
ap apostle, apothecaries'
AP additional premium, American plan, arithmetic progression, Associated Press
APB all points bulletin
APO army post office
app apparatus, appendix

appl applied
approx approximate, approximately
Apr April
apt apartment, aptitude
aq aqua, aqueous
ar arrival, arrive
Ar Arabic, argon
AR accounts receivable, Arkansas
Arab Arabian, Arabic
arch architect, architecture
archeol archeology
arith arithmetic
Ariz Arizona
Ark Arkansas
arr arranged, arrival, arrive
art article, artificial
As altostratus, arsenic
AS Anglo-Saxon
ASAP as soon as possible
ASPCA American Society for the Prevention of Cruelty to Animals
assn association
assoc associate, association
asst assistant
astrol astrologer, astrology
astron astronomer, astronomy
ASV American Standard Version
At astatine
Atl Atlantic
atm atmosphere, atmospheric
ATM automated teller machine, automatic teller machine
at no atomic number
att attached, attention, attorney
attn attention
attrib attributive, attributively
atty attorney
ATV all-terrain vehicle
at wt atomic weight
Au gold [Latin *aurum*]
Aug August
AUS Army of the United States
Austral Australian
auth authentic, author, authorized
aux, auxil auxiliary
av avenue, average, avoirdupois
AV ad valorem, audiovisual, Authorized Version
avdp avoirdupois
ave avenue
avg average
avn aviation
AZ Arizona
b back, before, book, born
B bachelor, Bible, bishop, boron
Ba barium
BA bachelor of arts
bal balance
bar barometer, barometric, barrel
Bart baronet
BBC British Broadcasting Corporation
bbl barrel, barrels
BBQ barbeque
BC before Christ, British Columbia
BCS bachelor of commercial science
bd board, bound
BD bachelor of divinity, bank draft, bills discounted, brought down
bd ft board foot
bdl, bdle bundle
Be beryllium
BE bill of exchange
Belg Belgian, Belgium
bet between
BeV billion electron volts

bf boldface
BF board foot, brought forward
bg background, bag
Bi bismuth
bib Bible, biblical
bid twice a day [Latin *bis in die*]
biog biographer, biographical, biography
biol biologic, biological, biologist, biology
bk bank, book, break
Bk berkelium
bkg banking, bookkeeping
bkt basket, bracket
bl bale, barrel, black, blue
BL bill of lading
bldg building
blvd boulevard
BM basal metabolism, board measure, bowel movement
BMR basal metabolic rate
BO back order, best offer, body odor, box office, branch office, buyer's option
BOQ bachelor officers' quarters
bor borough
bot botanical, botanist, botany, bottle, bottom, bought
bp baptized, birthplace, bishop
BP bills payable, blood pressure, blueprint, boiling point
bpl birthplace
BPW Board of Public Works
br branch, brown
Br Britain, British, bromine
BR bills receivable
Braz Brazil, Brazilian
brig brigade, brigadier
Brit Britain, British
bro brother, brothers
bros brothers
BS bachelor of science, balance sheet, bill of sale
BSA Boy Scouts of America
BSc bachelor of science
bskt basket
btry battery
Btu British thermal unit
bu bureau, bushel
bull bulletin
bur bureau
bus business
BV Blessed Virgin
BWI British West Indies
bx box
c carat, cent, centi-, centimeter, century, chapter, circa, circumference, copyright
C capacitance, carbon, Celsius, centigrade
ca circa
Ca calcium
CA California, chartered accountant, chief accountant, chronological age
CAF, C and F cost and freight
cal calendar, caliber, calorie (small)
Cal California, calorie (large)
Calif California
Can, Canad Canada, Canadian
canc canceled
cap capacity, capital, capitalize, capitalized
CAP Civil Air Patrol
caps capitals, capsule
Capt captain
card cardinal
CARE Cooperative for American Relief to Everywhere
cat catalog
CATV community antenna television
Cb columbium, cumulonimbus
CB citizens band
CBC Canadian Broadcasting Corporation
CBD cash before delivery

CBS Columbia Broadcasting System
cc cubic centimeter
CC carbon copy, common carrier, community college
cd candela, candle, cord
Cd cadmium
CD carried down, civil defense
CDR commander
CDT Central daylight time
Ce cerium
CE chemical engineer, civil engineer
cent centigrade, central, century
cert certificate, certification, certified, certify
cf compare [Latin *confer*]
Cf californium
CF carried forward
CFI cost, freight, and insurance
cg centigram
CG coast guard
cgs centimeter-gram-second
ch chain, chapter, church
CH clearinghouse, courthouse, customhouse
chap chapter
chem chemical, chemist, chemistry
chg change, charge
Chin Chinese
chm chairman, checkmate
chron chronicle, chronology
CI cost and insurance
CIA Central Intelligence Agency
CIF cost, insurance, and freight
C in C commander in chief
cir circle, circuit, circular, circumference
circ circular
cit citation, cited, citizen
civ civil, civilian
ck cask, check
cl centiliter, class
Cl chlorine
CL carload
clk clerk
clo clothing
cm centimeter
Cm curium
cml commercial
CN credit note
CNO chief of naval operations
CNS central nervous system
co company, county
Co cobalt
CO cash order, Colorado, commanding officer, conscientious objector
c/o care of
COD cash on delivery, collect on delivery
C of C Chamber of Commerce
C of S chief of staff
cog cognate
col colonial, colony, color, colored, column, counsel
Col colonel, Colorado
coll college
collat collateral
colloq colloquial
Colo Colorado
colog cologarithm
com comedy, comic, comma
comb combination, combined, combining
comdg commanding
comdr commander
comdt commandant
coml commercial
comm commission, commonwealth
comp comparative, compensation, compiled, compiler, composition, compound
comr commissioner
con consolidated, consul

conc concentrated
cond conductivity
conf conference, confidential
Confed Confederate
cong congress, congressional
conj conjunction
Conn Connecticut
cons conservative, consonant
consol consolidated
const constant, constitution, constitutional
constr construction
cont containing, contents, continent, continental, continued, control
contd continued
contg containing
contr contract, contraction
contrib contribution, contributor
corp corporal, corporation
corr corrected, correction, correspondence, corresponding
cos companies, cosine, counties
COS cash on shipment, chief of staff
cosec cosecant
cot cotangent
cp compare, coupon
CP candlepower, chemically pure, communist party
CPA certified public accountant
cpd compound
Cpl corporal
CPO chief petty officer
CPS cycles per second
CQ charge of quarters
cr credit, creditor
Cr chromium
cresc crescendo
crit critical, criticism, criticized
cryst crystalline, crystallized
cs case, cases
Cs cesium, cirrostratus
CS civil service
CSA Confederate States of America
csc cosecant
CSF cerebrospinal fluid
CST Central standard time
ct carat, cent, count, court
CT Central time, certified teacher, Connecticut
ctn carton
ctr center, counter
cu cubic
Cu copper [Latin *cuprum*]
cur currency, current
CV cardiovascular
CW continuous waves
CWO cash with order, chief warrant officer
cwt hundredweight
cyl cylinder
CZ Canal Zone
d date, daughter, day, dead, deceased, deci-, degree, penny, pence [Latin *denarius, denarii*]
D Democrat, deuterium, diameter
da deka-
DA days after acceptance, deposit account, district attorney
dag dekagram
dal dekaliter
dam dekameter
Dan Danish
DAR Daughters of the American Revolution
dat dative
db debenture
dB decibel
DBH diameter at breast height
dbl double

DC da capo, direct current, District of Columbia, doctor of chiropractic, double crochet

DD days after date, demand draft, doctor of divinity

DDD direct distance dialing

DDS doctor of dental science, doctor of dental surgery

DE Delaware

deb debenture

dec deceased, decrease, decrescendo

Dec December

def defendant, definite, definition

deg degree

del delegate, delegation

Del Delaware

dely delivery

Dem Democrat, Democratic

Den Denmark

dent dental, dentist, dentistry

dep depart, departure, deposit, deputy

dept department

der, deriv derivation, derivative

det detached, detachment, detail, determine

DEW distant early warning

DF damage free

DFC Distinguished Flying Cross

dg decigram

DG by the grace of God [Late Latin *Dei gratia*], director general

DH designated hitter

dia, diam diameter

diag diagonal, diagram

dial dialect

dict dictionary

dif, diff difference

dig digest

dil dilute

dim dimension, diminished, diminuendo, diminutive

dir director

disc discount

dist distance, district

distn distillation

distr distribute, distribution

div divided, dividend, division, divorced

dk dark, deck, dock

dl deciliter

DLitt, DLit doctor of letters, doctor of literature

DLO dead letter office

dm decimeter

DMD doctor of dental medicine

DMZ demilitarized zone

dn down

do ditto

DOA dead on arrival

DOB date of birth

doc document

DOD Department of Defense

dol dollar

dom domestic, dominion

DOS disk operating system

doz dozen

DP data processing, dew point, double play

dpt department

dr debtor, dram, drive, drum

Dr doctor

DS days after sight, dal segno

DSC Distinguished Service Cross

DSM Distinguished Service Medal

DSO Distinguished Service Order

DSP died without issue [Latin *decessit sine prole*]

DST daylight saving time

Du Dutch

dup duplex, duplicate

DUI driving under the influence

DV Deo volente, Douay Version

DVM doctor of veterinary medicine

DWI driving while intoxicated

dwt pennyweight

DX distance

Dy dysprosium

dz dozen

E east, eastern, energy, English, error, excellent

ea each

E and OE errors and omissions excepted

EB eastbound

eccl ecclesiastic, ecclesiastical

ECG electrocardiogram

ecol ecological, ecology

econ economics, economist, economy

Ecua Ecuador

ed edited, edition, editor, education

EDT Eastern daylight time

educ education, educational

EEG electroencephalogram, electroencephalograph

EEO equal employment opportunity

e.g. for example [Latin *exempli gratia*]

Eg Egypt, Egyptian

EHF extremely high frequency

EKG electrocardiogram, electrocardiograph [German *elektrokardiogramm*]

el, elev elevation

elec electric, electrical, electricity

elem elementary

emer emeritus

emp emperor, empress

emu electromagnetic unit

enc, encl enclosure

ency, encyc encyclopedia

eng engine, engineer, engineering

Eng England, English

engr engineer, engraved, engraver, engraving

enl enlarged, enlisted

ENS ensign

entom, entomol entomological, entomology

env envelope

EOM end of month

EP European plan, extended play

EPA Environmental Protection Agency

eq equal, equation

equip equipment

equiv equivalency, equivalent

Er erbium

Es einsteinium

Esk Eskimo

ESL English as a second language

esp especially

Esq, Esqr esquire

est established, estimate, estimated

EST Eastern standard time

ET eastern time

ETA estimated time of arrival

et al and others [Latin *et alii*]

etc et cetera

ETD estimated time of departure

et seq and the following one [Latin *et sequens*], and the following ones [Latin *et sequentes* or *et sequentia*]

Eu europium

Eur Europe, European

eV electron volt

evap evaporate

ex example, exchange, executive, express, extra

exc excellent, except

exch exchange, exchanged

exec executive

exp expense, experiment, experimental, export, express

expt experiment

exptl experimental

ext extension, exterior, external, externally, extra, extract

f and the following one, faraday, female, feminine, femto-, focal length, folio, force, forte, frequency

F Fahrenheit, farad, fluorine, French, Friday

FAA Federal Aviation Administration

fac facsimile, faculty

FADM fleet admiral

Fah, Fahr Fahrenheit

FAO Food and Agricultural Organization of the United Nations

FAS free alongside ship

fath fathom

FB freight bill

FBI Federal Bureau of Investigation

FCC Federal Communications Commission

fcp foolscap

fcy fancy

FDA Food and Drug Administration

FDIC Federal Deposit Insurance Corporation

Fe iron [Latin *ferrum*]

Feb February

fed federal, federation

fem female, feminine

FEPC Fair Employment Practices Commission

ff and the following ones, folios, fortissimo

FHA Federal Housing Administration

FICA Federal Insurance Contributions Act

FIFO first in, first out

fig figurative, figuratively, figure

fin finance, financial, finish

Finn Finnish

fl flanker, floor, flourished [Latin *floruit*], fluid

FL, Fla Florida

fl dr fluidram

Flem Flemish

fl oz fluidounce

fm fathom

Fm fermium

fn footnote

fo, fol folio

FOB free on board

FOC free of charge

for foreign, forestry

FOR free on rail

FOS free on steamer

FOT free on truck

fp freezing point

fpm feet per minute

FPO fleet post office

fps feet per second, foot-pound-second

fr father, franc, friar, from

Fr francium, French, Friday

freq frequency, frequent, frequently

Fri Friday

front frontispiece

FRS Federal Reserve System

frt freight

frwy freeway

FSH follicle-stimulating hormone

ft feet, foot, fort

ft lb foot-pound

fur furlong

fut future

fwd foreword, forward

FYI for your information

g acceleration of gravity, gauge, gram, gravity

G German, giga-, good

ga gauge

Ga gallium, Georgia

GA general agent, general assembly, general average, Georgia

gal gallery, gallon

galv galvanized

gar garage

gaz gazette, gazetteer

GB Great Britain

GCA ground-controlled approach

GCD greatest common divisor

GCF greatest common factor

Gd gadolinium

Ge germanium

gen general, genitive, genus

genl general

geog geographic, geographical, geography

geol geologic, geological, geology

geom geometric, geometrical, geometry

ger gerund

Ger German, Germany

GHQ general headquarters

gi gill

GI gastrointestinal, general issue, government issue

Gib, Gibr Gibraltar

Gk Greek

gm gram

GM general manager, grand master, guided missile

GMT Greenwich mean time

GNP gross national product

GOP Grand Old Party (Republican)

Goth Gothic

gov government, governor

govt government

gp group

GP general practice, general practitioner, geometric progression

GPA grade point average

GPO general post office, Government Printing Office

GQ general quarters

gr grade, grain, gram, gravity, gross

Gr Greece, Greek

grad graduate, graduated

gram grammar, grammatical

GRAS generally recognized as safe

gro gross

GSA Girl Scouts of America

gt great

Gt Brit Great Britain

GU genitourinary, Guam

h hard, hardness, hecto-, high, hit, hour, husband

H heroin, hydrogen

ha hectare

Hb hemoglobin

HBM Her Britannic Majesty, His Britannic Majesty

HC House of Commons

HCF highest common factor

hd head

HD heavy-duty

hdbk handbook

hdkf handkerchief

hdwe hardware

He helium

HE Her Excellency, high explosive, His Eminence, His Excellency

Heb Hebrew

HEW Department of Health, Education, and Welfare

hf half

Hf hafnium

HF high frequency

hg hectogram, hemoglobin

Hg mercury [Latin *hydrargyrum*]

hgt height

HH Her Highness, His Highness, His Holiness

HI Hawaii, high intensity

hist historian, historical, history

hl hectoliter

HL House of Lords

hm hectometer

HM Her Majesty, Her Majesty's, His Majesty, His Majesty's

HMS Her Majesty's ship, His Majesty's ship

Ho holmium

hon honor, honorable, honorary
hor horizontal
hort horticultural, horticulture
hosp hospital
HP high pressure, horsepower
HQ headquarters
hr here, hour
HR House of Representatives
HRH Her Royal Highness, His Royal Highness
HS high school
ht height
HT Hawaiian time, high-tension
Hung Hungarian, Hungary
hwy highway
hyp hypothesis, hypothetical
Hz hertz
I interstate, intransitive, iodine, island, isle
Ia, IA Iowa
IAA indoleacetic acid
ib, ibid ibidem
ICBM intercontinental ballistic missile
ICC Interstate Commerce Commission
ICJ International Court of Justice
id idem
ID Idaho, identification
i.e. that is [Latin *id est*]
IF intermediate frequency
IL Illinois
ill, illus, illust illustrated, illustration
Ill Illinois
ILS instrument landing system
imit imitative
imp imperative, imperfect, imperial, import, imported
imperf imperfect
in inch, inlet
In indium
IN Indiana
inc incomplete, incorporated, increase
incl including, inclusive
incog incognito
ind independent, index, industrial, industry
Ind Indian, Indiana
indef indefinite
indic indicative
inf infantry, infinitive
infl influenced
INP International News Photo
INRI Jesus of Nazareth, King of the Jews [Latin *Iesus Nazarenus Rex Iudaeorum*]
ins inches, insurance
insol insoluble
inst instant, institute, institution, institutional
instr instructor, instrument, instrumental
int interest, interior, intermediate, internal, international, intransitive
interj interjection
interrog interrogative
intl, intnl international
intrans intransitive
introd introduction
inv inventor, invoice
iq the same as [Latin *idem quod*]
Ir iridium, Irish
IRBM intermediate range ballistic missile
Ire Ireland
irreg irregular
is island, isle
ISBN International Standard Book Number
Isr Israel, Israeli
ISV International Scientific Vocabulary
It Italian, Italy
ital italic, italicized
Ital Italian
IU international unit

IV intravenous, intravenously
IWW Industrial Workers of the World
J jack, joule
Jam Jamaica
Jan January
Jap Japan, Japanese
JC junior college
JCS joint chiefs of staff
jct junction
JD justice department, juvenile delinquent
jg junior grade
jour journal, journeyman
JP jet propulsion, justice of the peace
Jpn Japan, Japanese
jr, jun junior
jt, jnt joint
junc junction
juv juvenile
JV junior varsity
k karat, kindergarten, king, knit, knot
K Kelvin, kilometer, potassium [Latin *kalium*]
Kan, Kans Kansas
kc kilocycle
KC Kansas City, King's Counsel
kcal kilocalorie
kc/s kilocycles per second
KD knocked down
kg kilogram, king
KG knight of the Order of the Garter
KIA killed in action
KJV King James Version
KKK Ku Klux Klan
kl kiloliter
km kilometer
KP kitchen police
Kr krypton
KS Kansas
kt karat, knight, knot
kV kilovolt
kW kilowatt
kWh kilowatt-hour
Ky, KY Kentucky
l late, left, liter, long
L lake, large, Latin, pound [Latin *libra*]
La lanthanum, Louisiana
LA law agent, Los Angeles, Louisiana
Lab Labrador
lang language
lat latitude
Lat Latin
lb pound [Latin *libra*]
lc lowercase
LC landing craft, Library of Congress
LCD least common denominator, lowest common denominator
LCM least common multiple
ld load, lord
LD lethal dose
ldg landing, loading
lect lecture, lecturer
leg legal, legato, legislative, legislature
legis legislation, legislative, legislature
LEM lunar excursion module
lf lightface
LF low frequency
lg large, long
LH left hand, luteinizing hormone
li link
Li lithium
LI Long Island
lib liberal, librarian, library
lieut lieutenant
LIFO last in, first out
lin lineal, linear

liq liquid, liquor
lit liter, literal, literally, literary, literature
lith, litho lithographic, lithography
Litt D, Lit D doctor of letters, doctor of literature
ll lines
LLD doctor of laws
LM lunar module
loc cit in the place cited [Latin *loco citato*]
log logarithm, logic
Lond London
long longitude
loq he speaks, she speaks [Latin *loquitur*]
LP low pressure
LPN licensed practical nurse
Lr lawrencium
LS left side, letter signed, place of the seal [Latin *locus sigilli*]
lt light
Lt lieutenant
LT long ton, low-tension
LTC, Lt Col lieutenant colonel
ltd limited
ltr letter, lighter
Lu lutetium
lub lubricant, lubricating
lv leave
LVN licensed vocational nurse
m male, married, masculine, mass, meridian, meter, mile, milli-, minute, molal, molality, molar, molarity, month, moon, noon [Latin *meridies*], thousand [Latin *mille*]
M Mach, medium, mega-, million, monsieur
mA milliampere
MA Massachusetts, master of arts, mental age, Middle Ages
mach machine, machining, machinist
mag magazine, magnesium, magnetism, magneto, magnitude
Maj major
man manual
Man Manitoba
manuf manufacture, manufacturing
mar maritime
Mar March
masc masculine
Mass Massachusetts
math mathematical, mathematician
max maximum
mb millibar
mc megacycle
MC member of Congress
Md Maryland, mendelevium
MD doctor of medicine, Maryland, months after date, muscular dystrophy
mdse merchandise
MDT Mountain daylight time
Me Maine, methyl
ME Maine, mechanical engineer, medical examiner, Middle English
meas measure
mech mechanical, mechanics
med medical, medicine, medieval, medium
meg megohm
mem member, memoir, memorial
mer meridian
met meteorological, meteorology, metropolitan
MeV million electron volts
Mex Mexican, Mexico
mf mezzo forte
MF medium frequency, microfiche
mfd manufactured
mfg manufacturing
mfr manufacture, manufacturer
mg milligram
Mg magnesium

mgr manager, monseigneur, monsignor
mgt management
mi mile, mileage, mill
MI, Mich Michigan
MIA missing in action
mid middle
mil military, million
min minim, minimum, mining, minor, minute
Minn Minnesota
misc miscellaneous
Miss Mississippi
mixt mixture
mk mark
mks meter-kilogram-second
ml milliliter
MLD median lethal dose, minimum lethal dose
Mlle mademoiselle
mm millimeter
MM messieurs
Mme madame
Mn manganese
MN magnetic north, Minnesota
mo month
Mo Missouri, molybdenum, Monday
MO mail order, medical officer, Missouri, modus operandi, money order
mod moderate, modern, modulo, modulus
modif modification
mol mole, molecular, molecule
mol wt molecular weight
MOM middle of month
Mon Monday
Mont Montana
mos months
MP melting point, member of parliament, metropolitan police, military police, military policeman
mpg miles per gallon
mph miles per hour
MRI magnetic resonance imaging
mRNA messenger RNA
MS manuscript, master of science, Mississippi, motor ship, multiple sclerosis
MSc master of science
msec millisecond
MSG, MSgt master sergeant
msgr monseigneur, monsignor
MSS manuscripts
MST Mountain standard time
mt mount, mountain
MT metric ton, Montana, Mountain time
mtg meeting, mortgage
mtge mortgage
mtn mountain
mun, munic municipal
mus museum, music, musical, musician
mV millivolt
n nano-, net, neuter, noon, note, noun, number
N nitrogen, normal, north, northern
Na sodium [Latin *natrium*]
NA no account, North America, not applicable
NAACP National Association for the Advancement of Colored People
NAS naval air station
NASA National Aeronautics and Space Administration
nat national, native, natural
natl national
NATO North Atlantic Treaty Organization
naut nautical
nav naval, navigable, navigation
Nb niobium
NB New Brunswick, northbound, nota bene
NBC National Broadcasting Company
NBS National Bureau of Standards
NC no charge, North Carolina

NCE   New Catholic Edition
NCO   noncommissioned officer
Nd   neodymium
ND   no date, North Dakota
N Dak   North Dakota
Ne   neon
NE   Nebraska, New England, northeast
Neb, Nebr   Nebraska
NEB   New English Bible
NED   New English Dictionary
neg   negative
Neth   Netherlands
neurol   neurological, neurology
neut   neuter
Nev   Nevada
NF   no funds, Newfoundland
Nfld   Newfoundland
NG   National Guard, no good
NH   New Hampshire
Ni   nickel
NJ   New Jersey
NL   night letter
NM, N Mex   New Mexico
no   north, number
No   nobelium
nom   nominative
non seq   non sequitur
Nor, Norw   Norway, Norwegian
NOS   not otherwise specified
Nov   November
Np   neptunium
NP   no protest, notary public
NPN   nonprotein nitrogen
NS   New Style, not specified, Nova Scotia
NSF   not sufficient funds
NSW   New South Wales
NT   New Testament, Northern Territory
NTP   normal temperature and pressure
nt wt, n wt   net weight
numis   numismatic, numismatics
NV   Nevada
NW   northwest
NWT   Northwest Territories
NY   New York
NYC   New York City
NZ   New Zealand
o   ocean, ohm
O   Ohio, oxygen
o/a   on or about
OAS   Organization of American States
ob   he died, she died [Latin *obiit*], obstetrical, obstetrician
obj   object, objective
obl   oblique, oblong
obs   obsolete
obv   obverse
oc   ocean
OC   officer candidate
occas   occasionally
OCS   officer candidate school
oct   octavo
Oct   October
OD   officer of the day, olive drab, on demand, overdose, overdraft, overdrawn
OE   Old English
OED   Oxford English Dictionary
off   office, officer, official
OG   original gum
OH   Ohio
OJ   orange juice
OK, Okla   Oklahoma
ON, Ont   Ontario
op   opus
OP   out of print

op cit   in the work cited [Latin *opere citato*]
opp   opposite
opt   optical, optician, optics, optional
OR   operating room, Oregon, owner's risk
orch   orchestra
ord   order, ordnance
Ore, Oreg   Oregon
org   organic, organization, organized
orig   original, originally, originator
ornith   ornithology
Os   osmium
OS   Old Style, ordinary seaman, out of stock
OT   occupational therapy, Old Testament, overtime
OTS   officers' training school
oz   ounce, ounces
p   page, participle, past, pawn, pence, penny, per, piano, pico-, pint, proton, purl
P   phosphorus, pressure
Pa   Pennsylvania, protactinium
PA   passenger agent, Pennsylvania, per annum, power of attorney, press agent, private account, public address, purchasing agent
Pac   Pacific
paleon   paleontology
pam   pamphlet
Pan   Panama
P & L   profit and loss
par   paragraph, parallel, parish
part   participial, participle, particular
pass   passenger, passive
pat   patent
path, pathol   pathological, pathology
payt   payment
Pb   lead [Latin *plumbum*]
PBS   Public Broadcasting Service
PC   Peace Corps, percent, politically correct, postcard
pct   percent, percentage
pd   paid
Pd   palladium
PD   per diem, police department, potential difference
PDT   Pacific daylight time
PE   physical education, printer's error
PEI   Prince Edward Island
pen   peninsula
Penn, Penna   Pennsylvania
per   period, person
perf   perfect, perforated, performance
perh   perhaps
perm   permanent
perp   perpendicular
pers   person, personal, personnel
Pers   Persia, Persian
pert   pertaining
pf, pfd   preferred
PFC   private first class
pg   page
PG   postgraduate
pharm   pharmaceutical, pharmacist, pharmacy
PhD   doctor of philosophy [Latin *philosophiae doctor*]
philos   philosopher, philosophy
phon   phonetics
photog   photographic, photography
phr   phrase
phys   physical, physician, physics
physiol   physiologist, physiology
PI   Philippine Islands, private investigator, programmed instruction
pizz   pizzicato
pk   park, peak, peck, pike
pkg   package
pkt   packet, pocket
PKU   phenylketonuria
pkwy   parkway
pl   place, plate, plural

PLO Palestine Liberation Organization

pm premium

p.m., PM post meridiem

Pm promethium

PM paymaster, police magistrate, postmaster, postmortem, prime minister, provost marshal

pmk postmark

PMS premenstrual syndrome

pmt payment

PN promissory note

Po polonium

PO petty officer, post office

POC port of call

POD pay on delivery

POE port of embarkation, port of entry

Pol Poland, Polish

polit political, politician

poly polytechnic

pop popular, population

POR pay on return

Port Portugal, Portuguese

pos position, positive

poss possessive

POW prisoner of war

pp pages, pianissimo

PP parcel post, past participle, postpaid, prepaid

ppd postpaid, prepaid

PPS an additional postscript [Latin *post postscriptum*]

ppt precipitate

pptn precipitation

PQ Province of Quebec

pr pair, price, printed

Pr praseodymium

PR payroll, public relations, Puerto Rico

prec preceding

pred predicate

pref preface, preference, preferred, prefix

prem premium

prep preparatory, preposition

pres present, president

prev previous, previously

prf proof

prim primary, primitive

prin principal, principle

PRO public relations officer

prob probable, probably, problem

proc proceedings

prod production

prof professional, professor

prom promontory

pron pronoun, pronounced, pronunciation

prop property, proposition, proprietor

pros prosody

Prot Protestant

prov province, provincial, provisional

PS postscript [Latin *postscriptum*], public school

pseud pseudonym, pseudonymous

psf pounds per square foot

psi pounds per square inch

PST Pacific standard time

psych psychology

psychol psychologist, psychology

pt part, payment, pint, point, port

Pt platinum

PT Pacific time, part-time, physical therapy, physical training

PTA Parent-Teacher Association

pte private (British)

ptg printing

PTO Parent-Teacher Organization, please turn over

PTV public television

Pu plutonium

pub public, publication, published, publisher, publishing

publ publication, published, publisher

pvt private

PW prisoner of war

pwt pennyweight

PX please exchange, post exchange

q quart, quarto, query, question, quetzal, quire

Q quartile, queen

QC Queen's Counsel

QED which was to be demonstrated [Latin *quod erat demonstrandum*]

QEF which was to be done [Latin *quod erat faciendum*]

QEI which was to be found out [Latin *quod erat inveniendum*]

qid four times a day [Latin *quater in die*]

Qld Queensland

QM quartermaster

QMC quartermaster corps

QMG quartermaster general

qq v which see [Latin pl. *quae vide*]

qr quarter, quire

qt quantity, quart

qto quarto

qty quantity

qu, ques question

quad quadrant

Que Quebec

quot quotation

qv which see [Latin *quod vide*]

qy query

r rare, resistance, right, river, roentgen, rook, run

R rabbi, radical — used especially of a univalent hydrocarbon radical, radius, regular, Republican

Ra radium

RA regular army, royal academy

RAAF Royal Australian Air Force

rad radian, radiator, radical, radio, radius

RADM rear admiral

RAF Royal Air Force

Rb rubidium

RBC red blood cells, red blood count

RBI run batted in

RC Red Cross, Roman Catholic

RCAF Royal Canadian Air Force

RCMP Royal Canadian Mounted Police

rd road, rod, round

RD rural delivery

RDA Recommended Daily Allowance

Re rhenium

rec receipt, record, recording, recreation

recd received

recip reciprocal, reciprocity

rec sec recording secretary

rect receipt, rectangle, rectangular, rectified

ref reference, referred, reformed, refunding

refl reflex, reflexive

refrig refrigerating, refrigeration

reg region, register, registered, regular, regulation

regt regiment

rel relating, relative, released, religion, religious

relig religion

rep report, reporter, representative, republic

Rep Republican

repl replace, replacement

rept report

req require, required, requisition

res research, reserve, residence, resolution

resp respective, respectively

ret retain, retired, return

retd retained, retired, returned

rev revenue, reverse, review, reviewed, revised, revision, revolution

Rev reverend

RF radio frequency

RFD rural free delivery
Rh rhodium
RH right hand
RI Rhode Island
RIP may he [she] rest in peace [Latin *requiescat in pace*]
rit ritardando
riv river
rm ream, room
Rn radon
RN registered nurse, Royal Navy
rnd round
RNZAF Royal New Zealand Air Force
ROG receipt of goods
Rom Roman, Romance, Romania, Romanian
ROTC Reserve Officers' Training Corps
rpm revolutions per minute
RPO railway post office
rps revolutions per second
rpt repeat, report
RQ respiratory quotient
RR railroad, rural route
RS recording secretary, revised statutes, right side, Royal Society
RSFSR Russian Soviet Federated Socialist Republic
RSV Revised Standard Version
RSVP please reply [French *répondez s'il vous plaît*]
RSWC right side up with care
rt right
rte route
Ru ruthenium
Rum Rumania, Rumanian
Russ Russia, Russian
RW right worshipful, right worthy
rwy, ry railway
s saint, scruple, second, secondary, section, senate, series, shilling, signor, sine, singular, small, son
S satisfactory, short, south, southern, sulfur
SA Salvation Army, sex appeal, South Africa, South America, South Australia, subject to approval, without date [Latin *sine anno*]
SAC Strategic Air Command
SAM surface-to-air missile
sanit sanitary, sanitation
Sask Saskatchewan
sat saturate, saturated, saturation
Sat Saturday
S Aust South Australia
sb substantive
Sb antimony [Latin *stibium*]
SB bachelor of science [New Latin *scientiae baccalaureus*], southbound
SBN Standard Book Number
sc scale, scene, science, scilicet
Sc scandium, Scots
SC small capitals, South Carolina, supreme court
Scand Scandinavia, Scandinavian
sch school
sci science, scientific
scil scilicet
Scot Scotland, Scottish
script scripture
SD sea-damaged, sine die, South Dakota, special delivery, stage direction
S Dak South Dakota
Se selenium
SE southeast, Standard English
SEATO Southeast Asia Treaty Organization
sec according to [Latin *secundum*], secant, second, secondary, secretary, section
sect section, sectional
secy secretary
sel select, selected, selection
sem semicolon, seminar, seminary
sen senate, senator, senior
sep separate, separated

sepn separation
Sept, Sep September
seq the following one [Latin *sequens*]
seqq the following ones [Latin pl. *sequentia*]
ser serial, series, service
serg, sergt sergeant
serv service
sf, sfz sforzando
SF science fiction, sinking fund, square feet, square foot
SFC sergeant first class
sg specific gravity
SG senior grade, sergeant, solicitor general, surgeon general
Sgt sergeant
sh share
Shak Shakespeare
SHF superhigh frequency
shpt, shipt shipment
sht sheet
shtg shortage
Si silicon
SI International System of Units [French *Système International d'Unités*]
SIDS sudden infant death syndrome
sig signal, signature, signor
sin sine
sing singular
SJ Society of Jesus
Skt Sanskrit
SL salvage loss, sea level
sm small
Sm samarium
SM master of science [New Latin *scientiae magister*], sergeant major
Sn tin [Late Latin *stannum*]
so south, southern
SO seller's option
soc social, society
sociol sociologist, sociology
sol solicitor, soluble, solution
soln solution
SOP standard operating procedure, standing operating procedure
soph sophomore
sp special, species, specific, specimen, spelling, spirit
Sp Spain, Spanish
SP shore patrol, shore patrolman, shore police, without issue [Latin *sine prole*]
Span Spanish
SPCA Society for the Prevention of Cruelty to Animals
SPCC Society for the Prevention of Cruelty to Children
spec special, specifically
specif specific, specifically
SPF sun protection factor
sp gr specific gravity
spp species
sq squadron, square
Sr senior, senor, señor, sister, strontium
SR seaman recruit
Sra senora, señora
SRO standing room only
Srta senorita, señorita
SS saints, Social Security, steamship, sworn statement
SSG, SSgt staff sergeant
ssp subspecies
SSR Soviet Socialist Republic
SSS Selective Service System
SST supersonic transport
st stanza, state, stitch, stone, street
St saint
ST short ton
sta station, stationary
stat immediately [Latin *statim*], statute
stbd starboard

std standard

STD doctor of sacred theology [Latin *sacrae theologiae doctor*]

Ste saint (female) [French *sainte*]

ster, stg sterling

STP standard temperature and pressure

stud student

Su, Sun Sunday

sub subtract, suburb

subj subject, subjunctive

suff sufficient, suffix

sup above [Latin *supra*], superior, supplement, supplementary, supply

supp, suppl supplement, supplementary

supt superintendent

surg surgeon, surgery, surgical

surv survey, surveying, surveyor

SV under the word [Latin *sub verbo* or *sub voce*]

Sw, Swed Sweden, Swedish

SW shortwave, southwest

Switz Switzerland

syl, syll syllable

sym symbol, symmetrical

syn synonym, synonymous, synonymy

syst system

t teaspoon, temperature, ton, transitive, troy, true

T tablespoon, tritium

Ta tantalum

tan tangent

taxon taxonomic, taxonomy

tb tablespoon, tablespoonful

Tb terbium

TB trial balance

tbs, tbsp tablespoon, tablespoonful

Tc technetium

tchr teacher

TD touchdown

TDN total digestible nutrients

Te tellurium

tech technical, technically, technician, technological, technology

tel telegram, telegraph, telephone

teleg telegraphy

temp in the time of [Latin *tempore*], temperature, temporary

Tenn Tennessee

ter terrace, territory

terr territory

Tex Texas

TGIF thank God it's Friday

Th thorium, Thursday

ThD doctor of theology [New Latin *theologiae doctor*]

theat theater, theatrical

theol theological, theology

therm thermometer

Thurs, Thu Thursday

Ti titanium

tid three times a day [Latin *ter in die*]

tinc tincture

TKO technical knockout

tkt ticket

Tl thallium

TL total loss

TLC tender loving care

Tm thulium

TM trademark

tn ton, town, train

TN Tennessee, true north

tnpk turnpike

TO telegraph office, turn over

topog topography

tot total

tp title page, township

tpk, tpke turnpike

tr translated, translation, translator, transpose

trans transaction, transitive, translated, translation, translator, transportation

transl translated, translation

transp transportation

treas treasurer, treasury

trib tributary

TSgt technical sergeant

TSH thyroid-stimulating hormone

tsp teaspoon, teaspoonful

TT telegraphic transfer, teletypewriter

Tues, Tue Tuesday

Turk Turkey, Turkish

TVA Tennessee Valley Authority

TX Texas

u unit

U university, unsatisfactory, uranium

UAR United Arab Republic

UC uppercase

ugt urgent

UHF ultrahigh frequency

UK United Kingdom

ult ultimate, ultimo

UN United Nations

UNESCO United Nations Educational, Scientific, and Cultural Organization

UNICEF United Nations Children's Fund

univ universal, university

UNRWA United Nations Relief and Works Agency

UPI United Press International

US United States

USA United States Army, United States of America

USAF United States Air Force

USCG United States Coast Guard

USDA United States Department of Agriculture

USMC United States Marine Corps

USN United States Navy

USO United Service Organizations

USP United States Pharmacopeia

USPS United States Postal Service

USS United States ship

USSR Union of Soviet Socialist Republics

usu usual, usually

UT Utah

UV ultraviolet

UW underwriter

v vector, velocity, verb, verse, versus, vice, victory, vide, voice, volume, vowel

V vanadium, volt, voltage

Va Virginia

VA Veterans Administration, vice admiral, Virginia, visual aid

VADM vice admiral

val value, valued

var variable, variant, variation, variety, various

vb verb, verbal

VC vice-chancellor, vice-consul, Victoria Cross

VD venereal disease

veg vegetable

vel vellum, velocity

Ven venerable

vert vertebrate, vertical

VFD volunteer fire department

VFW Veterans of Foreign Wars

VG very good

VHF very high frequency

vi see below [Latin *vide infra*], verb intransitive

VI Virgin Islands

vic vicinity

Vic Victoria

vil village

vis visibility, visible, visual

VISTA Volunteers in Service to America

viz videlicet

VLF   very low frequency
VNA   Visiting Nurse Association
voc   vocative
vocab   vocabulary
vol   volcano, volume, volunteer
VOR   very-high-frequency omnidirectional radio range
vou   voucher
VP   vice president
vs   see above [Latin *vide supra*], verse, versus
vss   verses, versions
vt   verb transitive
Vt, VT   Vermont.
VTR   videotape recorder
Vulg   Vulgate
vv   verses, vice versa
w   water, week, weight, wide, width, wife, with
W   tungsten [German *wolfram*], watt, west, western, work
WA   Washington, Western Australia
WAC   Women's Army Corps
WAF   Women in the Air Force
war   warrant
Wash   Washington
W Aust   Western Australia
WAVES   Women Accepted for Volunteer Emergency Service
WB   water ballast, waybill, westbound
WBC   white blood cells
WC   water closet, without charge
WCTU   Women's Christian Temperance Union
wd   wood, word, would
We, Wed   Wednesday
wh   which, white
WH   watt-hour
whf   wharf
WHO   World Health Organization
whr   watt-hour
whs, whse   warehouse
whsle   wholesale

WI   West Indies, Wisconsin
WIA   wounded in action
wid   widow, widower
Wis, Wisc   Wisconsin
wk   week, work
WL   wavelength
wmk   watermark
WO   warrant officer
w/o   without
WPM   words per minute
wrnt   warrant
wt   weight
WV, W Va   West Virginia
WW   world war
WY, Wyo   Wyoming
Xe   xenon
XL   extra large, extra long
Xn   Christian
y   yard, year
Y   YMCA, yttrium
Yb   ytterbium
YB   yearbook
yd   yard
YMCA   Young Men's Christian Association
YMHA   Young Men's Hebrew Association
YOB   year of birth
yr   year, younger, your
yrbk   yearbook
yrs   years, yours
YT   Yukon Territory
Yug   Yugoslavia
YWCA   Young Women's Christian Association
YWHA   Young Women's Hebrew Association
z   zero, zone
Zn   zinc
zool   zoological, zoology
ZPG   zero population growth
Zr   zirconium

Languages of the World

This section shows the major languages of the world in use today. This is not an exhaustive list of the many variances in regional dialects; rather, it is a catalog of languages that are spoken by at least one million people. This list also includes the language group from which each language originates, the primary locale in which it is spoken, and the approximate number, in millions, of people who use it. For a listing of the principal languages spoken in each country, see the section Nations of the World.

LANGUAGE	LANGUAGE GROUP	PRIMARY LOCALES	MILLIONS OF SPEAKERS
Achinese	Austronesian (West Malayo-Polynesian)	Indonesia	3
Afar	Afro-Asiatic (Cushitic)	Ethiopia	1
Afrikaans	Indo-European (Germanic)	South Africa	10
Albanian	Indo-European (Albanian)	Balkan Europe	5
Amharic	Afro-Asiatic (Semitic)	Ethiopia	18
Arabic	Afro-Asiatic (Semitic)	N. Africa, Mid-East	208
Armenian	Indo-European (Armenian)	Armenia	5
Assamese	Indo-European (Indo-Iranian)	India, Bangladesh	23
Aymara	Quechumaran (Andean)	Bolivia, Peru	2
Azerbaijani	Altaic (Turkik)	Azerbaijan, Iran	15
Bagri	Indo-Aryan (Central Indo-Aryan)	India	1
Balinese	Austronesian (West Malayo-Polynesian)	Indonesia	3
Baluchi	Indo-European (Indo-Iranian)	Pakistan, Iran	4
Basque	Isolate	Spain, France	1
Batak	Austronesian (West Malayo-Polynesian)	Indonesia	4
Bemba	Niger-Congo (Benue-Bantu)	Zambia	2
Bengali	Indo-European (Indo-Iranian)	Bangladesh, India	189
Beti	Niger-Congo (Benue-Bantu)	Cameroon, Gabon	2
Bhili	Indo-European (Indo-Iranian)	India	4
Bhojpuri	Indo-Aryan (East Indo-Aryan)	India, Nepal	41
Bihari	Indo-European (Indo-Iranian)	India	17
Bikol	Austronesian (West Malayo-Polynesian)	Philippines	4
Braj Bhasha	Indo-Aryan (Central Indo-Aryan)	India	11
Bugis	Austronesian (West Malayo-Polynesian)	Indonesia	4
Bulgarian	Indo-European (Slavic)	Bulgaria	9
Bundeli	Indo-Aryan (Central Indo-Aryan)	India	8
Burmese	Sino-Tibetan (Tibeto-Burman)	Myanmar	31
Byelorussian	Indo-European (Slavic)	Belarus	10
Cameroon Pidgin	English-based creole	Cameroon	2
Cantonese	Sino-Tibetan (Sinitic)	China, Hong Kong	65
Catalán	Indo-European (Romance)	Spain, France, Andorra	9
Cebuano	Austronesian (West Malayo-Polynesian)	Philippines	13
Chuvash	Altaic (Turkik)	Russia	2
Czech	Indo-European (Slavic)	Czech Republic	12
Danish	Indo-European (Germanic)	Denmark	5
Dayak	Austronesian (West Malayo-Polynesian)	Borneo, Indonesia	1
Dong	Sino-Tibetan (Sinitic)	China	2
Dutch (Flemish)	Indo-European (Germanic)	Netherlands, Belgium	21
Dyerma	Nilo-Saharan (Songhai)	Niger	2
Edo	Niger-Congo (Benue-Congo)	Nigeria	1
Efik (Ibibio)	Niger-Congo (Benue-Congo)	Nigeria	6
English	Indo-European (Germanic)	USA, UK, Canada, Australia	456

LANGUAGE	LANGUAGE GROUP	PRIMARY LOCALES	MILLIONS OF SPEAKERS
Estonian	Uralic (Finno-Ugric)	Estonia	1
Ewe	Niger-Congo (Kwa)	Ghana, Togo	3
Fang-Bulu	Niger-Congo (Benue-Bantu)	West Africa	2
Filipino (see Tagalog)			
Finnish	Uralic (Finno-Ugric)	Finland	6
Fon	Niger-Congo (Kwa)	Benin, Togo	1
French	Indo-European (Romance)	France, Canada, Africa, Switzerland	123
Fula (Fulani)	Niger-Congo (West Atlantic)	Cameroon, Nigeria	13
Fulakunda	Niger-Congo (West Atlantic)	Guinea	2
Futa Jalon	Niger-Congo (West Atlantic)	Guinea	3
Ga-Adangme	Niger-Congo (Kwa)	Ghana	1
Galician	Indo-European (Romance)	Spain	3
Ganda (Luganda)	Niger-Congo (Benue-Congo)	Uganda	3
Georgian	Caucasian (Northeastern Caucasian)	Georgia	4
German	Indo-European (Germanic)	Germany, Austria, Switzerland	119
Gilaki	Indo-European (Indo-Iranian)	Iran	2
Gondi	Dravidian (South-Central Dravidian)	India	2
Greek	Indo-European (Greek)	Greece, Albania, Cyprus	11
Guarani	South American (Tupian)	Paraguay	4
Gujarti	Indo-European (Indo-Iranian)	India, Pakistan	39
Gusii	Niger-Congo (Benue-Congo)	Kenya	2
Hadiyya	Afro-Asiatic (Cushitic)	Ethiopia	2
Haitian Creole	French-based creole	Haiti	3
Hakka	Sino-Tibetan (Sinitic)	China	33
Hausa	Afro-Asiatic (Chadic)	Nigeria, Niger, Cameroon	36
Hebrew	Afro-Asiatic (Semitic)	Israel	4
Hindi	Indo-European (Indo-Iranian)	India	383
Ibo (Ibgo)	Niger-Congo (Kwa)	Niger, Nigeria, Equatorial Guinea	17
Ijaw	Niger-Congo (Kwa)	Nigeria	2
Ilocano (Iloka)	Austronesian (West Malayo-Polynesian)	Philippines	7
Italian	Indo-European (Romance)	Italy, Switzerland	63
Japanese	Isolate	Japan	126
Javanese	Austronesian (West Malayo-Polynesian)	Indonesia	61
Kabyle	Afro-Asiatic (Berber)	Algeria	3
Kamba	Niger-Congo (Benue-Bantu)	Kenya	3
Kannada (Kanarese)	Dravidian (South Dravidan)	India	43
Kanauji	Indo-Aryan (Central Indo-Aryan)	India	6
Kanuri	Nilo-Saharan (Saharan)	Central & West Africa	4
Kashmiri	Indo-European (Indo-Iraninan)	India, Pakistan	4
Kazakh	Altaic (Turkik)	Kazakhstan	8
Khalkha	Altaic (Mongolian)	Mongolia, China	5
Khmer	Austro-Asiatic (Mon Khmer)	Cambodia, Vietnam	7
Kikuyu (Gekoya)	Niger-Congo (Benue-Congo)	Kenya	5
Kituba	Niger-Congo (Benue-Bantu)	Zaire	4
Kongo (Kikongo)	Niger-Congo (Benue-Congo)	Zaire, Congo	3
Konkani	Indo-European (Indo-Iranian)	India	4
Korean	Isolate	Korea, China	73
Kurdish	Indo-European (Indo-Iranian)	Iran, Iraq, Turkey	10
Kurux (Oraon)	Dravidian (North Dravidian)	India	1
Kyrgyz	Altaic (Turkik)	Kyrgyzstan	2
Lao	Sino-Tibetan (Tai)	Laos	4
Latvian	Indo-European (Baltic)	Latvia	2
Lithuanian	Indo-European (Baltic)	Lithuania	3
Luba-Lulua	Niger-Congo (Benue-Bantu)	Zaire	6
Luhya	Niger-Congo (Benue-Congo)	Kenya	1
Luo	Nilo-Saharan (Nilotic)	Kenya, Tanzania	3
Luri	Indo-European (Indo-Iranian)	Iran, Iraq	2
Macedonian	Indo-European (Slavic)	Macedonia	2
Madurese	Austronesian (West Malayo-Polynesian)	Indonesia	10
Magyar	Uralic (Finno-Ugric)	Hungary	14
Makua	Niger-Congo (Kwa)	Tanzania, Mozambique	3
Malagasay	Austronesian (West Malayo-Polynesian)	Madagascar, Comoros	12

LANGUAGE	LANGUAGE GROUP	PRIMARY LOCALES	MILLIONS OF SPEAKERS
Malay-Indonesian	Austronesian (West Malayo-Polynesian)	Indonesia, Malaysia, Brunei	148
Malayalam	Dravidian (South Dravidian)	India	35
Malinke-Bambara-Dyula	Niger-Congo (Mande)	West Africa	9
Mandarin	Sino-Tibetan (Sinitic)	China	907
Marathi	Indo-European (Indo-Iranian)	India	67
Marwari	Indo-Aryan (Central Indo-Aryan)	India	6
Mazandarani	Indo-European (Indo-Iranian)	Iran	2
Mbundu (Umbundu)	Niger-Congo (Benue-Bantu)	Angola	4
Mbundu (Kimbundu)	Niger-Congo (Benue-Bantu)	Angola	3
Mende	Niger-Congo (Mande)	Sierra Leone	2
Miao (Meo)	Sino-Tibetan (Sinitic)	Southeast Asia	5
Min	Sino-Tibetan (Sinitic)	China, Taiwan, Malaysia	50
Minankabau	Austronesian (West Malayo-Polynesian)	Indonesia	6
Mongolian	Altaic (Mongolian)	Mongolia	2
Mordvin	Uralic (Finno-Ugric)	Russia	1
More (Mossi)	Niger-Congo (Voltaic)	Burkina Faso	4
Nepali (Gurhali)	Indo-European (Indo-Iranian)	Nepal, India, Bhutan	14
Ngala (Lingala)	Niger-Congo (Benue-Congo)	Zaire	6
Norwegian	Indo-European (Germanic)	Norway	5
Nyamwezi-Sukuma	Niger-Congo (Benue-Bantu)	Tanzania	4
Nyanja	Niger-Congo (Benue-Congo)	Malawi, Zambia, Zimbabwe	4
Oriya	Indo-European (Indo-Iranian)	India	31
Oromo (Galla)	Afro-Asiatic (Cushitic)	Ethiopia	10
Panay-Hiligaynon	Austronesian (West Malayo-Polynesian)	Philippines	6
Persian (Farsi)	Indo-European (Indo-Iranian)	Iran, Afghanistan	37
Polish	Indo-European (Slavic)	Poland	44
Portuguese	Indo-European (Romance)	Brazil, Portugal, Angola	177
Provençal	Indo-European (Romance)	France	4
Punjabi	Indo-European (Indo-Iranian)	India, Pakistan	89
Pushto (Pashto)	Indo-European (Indo-Iranian)	Afghanistan, Pakistan, Iran	21
Quechua	South American (Andean-Equatorial)	Peru, Bolivia, Ecuador	8
Rajasthani	Indo-European (Indo-Iranian)	India	16
Romanian (Moldovan)	Indo-European (Romance)	Romania, Moldova	26
Ruanda	Niger-Congo (Benue-Congo)	Rwanda, Uganda, Zaire	8
Rundi	Niger-Congo (Benue-Congo)	Burundi	6
Russian	Indo-European (Slavic)	Russia, Commonwealth of Independent States	293
Samar-Leyte (Waray-Waray)	Austronesian (West Malayo-Polynesian)	Philippines	3
Sango	Niger-Congo (Ngbardi)	Central African Rep.	3
Santali	Afro-Asiatic (Munda)	India, Nepal	5
Serbo-Croatian	Indo-European (Slavic)	Balkan Europe	20
Sgaw	Sino-Tibetan (Karen)	Myanmar	2
Shan	Sino-Tibetan (Burmic)	Myanmar	2
Shona	Niger-Congo (Benue-Bantu)	Zimbabwe	8
Sindhi	Indo-European (Indo-Iranian)	India, Pakistan	17
Sinhalese	Indo-European (Indo-Iranian)	Sri Lanka	13
Slovak	Indo-European (Balto-Slavic)	Slovakia	5
Slovene	Indo-European (Balto-Slavic)	Slovenia	2
Somali	Afro-Asiatic (Cushitic)	Somalia, Ethiopia, Kenya	7
Sotho (Northern)	Niger-Congo (Benue-Congo)	South Africa	3
Sotho (Southern)	Niger-Congo (Benue-Congo)	South Africa, Lesotho	4
Spanish	Indo-European (Romance)	Latin America, Spain	362
Sundanese	Austronesian (West Malayo-Polynesian)	Indonesia	25
Swahili	Niger-Congo (Benue-Bantu)	East Africa	46
Swazi (Swati)	Niger-Congo (Niger-Bantu)	Swaziland, South Africa	1
Swedish	Indo-European (Germanic)	Sweden, Finland	9
Sylhetti	Indo-Arayan (East Indo-Arayan)	Bangladesh	5
Tachelhit	Afro-Asiatic (Berber)	Morocco, Algeria	3
Tagalog	Austronesian (West Malayo-Polynesian)	Philippines	43
Tajiki	Indo-European (Indo-Iranian)	Tajikistan, Uzbekistan	4
Tamazight	Afro-Asiatic (Berber)	Morocco, Algeria	3
Tamil	Dravidian (South Dravidian)	India, Sri Lanka, Malaysia	67
Tarifit	Afro-Asiatic (Berber)	Morocco, Algeria	1
Tatar (Kazan Turkik)	Altaic (Turkik)	Russia	8

LANGUAGE	LANGUAGE GROUP	PRIMARY LOCALES	MILLIONS OF SPEAKERS
Telugu	Dravidian (South-Central Dravidian)	India	71
Teso	Nilo-Saharan (Nilotic)	Uganda, Kenya	1
Thai (Siamese)	Sino-Tibetan (Tai)	Thailand	59
Thonga (Tonga)	Niger-Congo (Benue-Congo)	Mozambique, South Africa	3
Tibetan	Sino-Tibetan (Tibeto-Burman)	Tibet, China, Nepal	6
Tigrinya	Afro-Asiatic (Semitic)	Ethiopia	4
Tiv	Niger-Congo (Benue-Congo)	Nigeria, Cameroon	2
Tswana	Niger-Congo (Benue-Congo)	Botswana, S. Africa	4
Tukolor (Toucouleur)	Niger-Congo (West Atlantic)	Senegal	2
Tulu	Dravidian (South Dravidian)	India	2
Turkish	Altaic (Turkik)	Turkey	57
Turkoman	Altaic (Turkik)	Turkmenistan, Afghanistan	3
Twi-Fante (Akan)	Niger-Congo (Kwa)	Ghana, Côte d'Ivoire	3
Uighur	Altaic (Turkik)	China	7
Ukrainian	Indo-European (Balto-Slavic)	Ukraine, Russia, Poland	46
Urdu	Indo-European (Indo-Iranian)	Pakistan, India	96
Uzbek	Altaic (Turkik)	Uzbekistan	13
Vietnamese	Austro-Asiatic (Mon Khmer)	Vietnam	61
Wolof	Niger-Congo (West Atlantic)	Senegal, Gambia	6
Wu	Sino-Tibetan (Sinitic)	China	64
Xhosa	Niger-Congo (Benue-Bantu)	South Africa	7
Yi	Sino-Tibetan (Tibeto-Burman)	China	6
Yiddish	Indo-European (Germanic)	Israel, Central Europe, USA	3
Yoruba	Niger-Congo (Kwa)	Nigeria, Benin	19
Zhuang	Sino-Tibetan (Tai)	China	15
Zulu	Niger-Congo (Benue-Bantu)	South Africa	7

Foreign Words and Phrases

The following entries include commonly encountered foreign words and phrases that have not been assimilated into English.

---

ab•eunt stu•dia in mo•res \'äb-e-ˌu̇nt-'stüd-ē-ˌä-ˌin-'mō-ˌräs\ [L] : practices zealously pursued pass into habits

à bien•tôt \ȧ-byaⁿ-tō\ [F] : so long : farewell

ab in•cu•na•bu•lis \ˌäb-ˌing-kə-'näb-ə-ˌlēs\ [L] : from the cradle : from infancy

à bon chat, bon rat \ȧ-bōⁿ-'shȧ-bōⁿ-'rȧ\ [F] : to a good cat, a good rat : retaliation in kind

à bouche ou•verte \ȧ-bü-shü-vert\ [F] : with open mouth : eagerly : uncritically

ab ovo us•que ad ma•la \äb-ˌō-vō-ˌu̇s-kwe-ˌäd-'mäl-ä\ [L] : from egg to apples : from soup to nuts : from beginning to end

à bras ou•verts \ȧ-brȧ-zü-ver\ [F] : with open arms : cordially

ab•sit in•vi•dia \'äb-ˌsit-in-'wid-ē-ˌä\ [L] : let there be no envy or ill will

ab uno dis•ce om•nes \äb-'ü-nō-ˌdis-ke-'ȯm-ˌnäs\ [L] : from one learn to know all

ab ur•be con•di•ta \äb-'u̇r-be-'kȯn-də-ˌtä\ [L] : from the founding of the city (Rome, founded 753 B.C.) — used by the Romans in reckoning dates

ab•usus non tol•lit usum \'äb-ˌü-səs-ˌnōn-ˌtȯ-lət-'ü-səm\ [L] : abuse does not take away use, i.e., is not an argument against proper use

à compte \ȧ-kōⁿt\ [F] : on account

à coup sûr \ȧ-kü-su̅e̅r̅\ [F] : with sure stroke : surely

acte gra•tuit \ȧk-tə-grȧ-twⁱē\ [F] : gratuitous impulsive act

ad ar•bi•tri•um \ˌad-är-'bit-rē-əm\ [L] : at will : arbitrarily

ad as•tra per as•pe•ra \ad-'as-trə-ˌpər-'as-pə-rə\ [L] : to the stars by hard ways — motto of Kansas

ad ex•tre•mum \ˌad-ik-'strē-məm\ [L] : to the extreme : at last

ad ka•len•das Grae•cas \ˌäd-kə-'len-dəs-'grī-ˌkäs\ [L] : at the Greek calends : never (since the Greeks had no calends)

ad ma•jo•rem Dei glo•ri•am \ˌäd-mä-'yȯr-ˌem-'de-ē-'glȯr-ē-ˌäm\ [L] : to the greater glory of God — motto of the Society of Jesus

ad pa•tres \ˌäd-'pä-ˌträs\ [L] : (gathered) to his fathers : deceased

à droite \ȧ-drwȧt\ [F] : to or on the right hand

ad un•guem \ˌäd-'u̇ng-ˌgwem\ [L] : to the fingernail : to a nicety : exactly (from the use of the fingernail to test the smoothness of marble)

ad utrum•que pa•ra•tus \ˌäd-u̇-'trum-kwe-pə-'rät-əs\ [L] : prepared for either (event)

ad vi•vum \ˌäd-'wē-ˌwu̇m\ [L] : to the life

ae•gri som•nia \'ī-grē-'sȯm-nē-ˌä\ [L] : a sick man's dreams

ae•quam ser•va•re men•tem \'ī-ˌkwäm-sər-ˌwä-rä-'men-ˌtem\ [L] : to preserve a calm mind

ae•quo ani•mo \'ī-ˌkwō-'än-ə-ˌmō\ [L] : with even mind : calmly

ae•re per•en•ni•us \'ī-rä-pə-'ren-ē-ˌu̇s\ [L] : more lasting than bronze

à gauche \ȧ-gōsh\ [F] : to or on the left hand

age quod agis \'äg-e-ˌkwȯd-'äg-is\ [L] : do what you are doing : to the business at hand

à grands frais \ȧ-grän-fre\ [F] : at great expense

à huis clos \ȧ-wⁱē-klō\ [F] : with closed doors

aide–toi, le ciel t'ai•dera \ed-twȧ, lə-'syel-te-drȧ\ [F] : help yourself (and) heaven will help you

ai•né \e-nā\ [F] : elder : senior (masc.)

ai•née \e-nā\ [F] : elder : senior (fem.)

à l'aban•don \ȧ-lȧ-bän-dōⁿ\ [F] : carelessly : in disorder

à la belle étoile \ȧ-lȧ-bel-ā-twȧl\ [F] : under the beautiful star : in the open air at night

à la bonne heure \ȧ-lȧ-bȯ-nœr\ [F] : at a good time : well and good : all right

à la fran•çaise \ȧ-lȧ-frän-sez\ [F] : in the French style

à l'an•glaise \ȧ-läⁿ-glez\ [F] : in the English style

alea jac•ta est \'äl-ē-ˌä-ˌyäk-tə-'est\ [L] : the die is cast

à l'im•pro•viste \ȧ-laⁿ-prȯ-vēst\ [F] : unexpectedly

ali•quan•do bo•nus dor•mi•tat Ho•me•rus \ˌäl-i-ˌkwän-dō-'bȯ-nəs-dȯr-'mē-tät-hō-'mer-əs\ [L] : sometimes (even) good Homer nods

alis vo•lat pro•pri•is \'äl-ˌēs-'wȯ-ˌlät-'prō-prē-ˌēs\ [L] : she flies with her own wings — motto of Oregon

al–ki \'al-ˌkī\ [Chinook Jargon] : by and by — motto of Washington

alo•ha oe \ä-ˌlō-hä-'ȯi,-'ō-ē\ [Hawaiian] : love to you : greetings : farewell

al•ter idem \ˌȯl-tər-'ī-ˌdem, ˌäl-tər-ē-\ [L] : second self

a max•i•mis ad mi•ni•ma \ä-'mäk-sə-ˌmēs-ˌäd-'min-ə-ˌmä\ [L] : from the greatest to the least

ami•cus hu•ma•ni ge•ne•ris \ä-'mē-kəs-hū-ˌmän-ē-'gen-ə-rəs\ [L] : friend of the human race

ami•cus us•que ad aras \-ˌu̇s-kwe-ˌäd-'är-ˌäs\ [L] : a friend as far as to the altars, i.e., except in what is contrary to one's religion; *also* : a friend to the last extremity

ami de cour \ȧ-ˌmēd-ə-'ku̇r\ [F] : court friend : insincere friend

amor pa•tri•ae \ˌäm-ˌȯr-'pä-trē-ˌī\ [L] : love of one's country

amor vin•cit om•nia \'ä-ˌmȯr-ˌwing-kət-'ȯm-nē-ə\ [L] : love conquers all things

an•cienne no•blesse \äⁿ-syen-nȯ-bles\ [F] : old-time nobility : the French nobility before the Revolution of 1789

an•guis in her•ba \ˌäng-gwis-in-'her-ˌbä\ [L] : snake in the grass

ani•mal bi•pes im•plu•me \'än-i-ˌmäl-ˌbip-ˌäs-im-'plü-me\ [L] : two-legged animal without feathers (i.e., man)

an·i·mis opi·bus·que pa·ra·ti \'än-ə-ˌmēs-ˌȯ-pi-ˈbu̇s-kwe- pə-ˈrät-ē\ [L] : prepared in mind and resources — one of the mottoes of South Carolina

an·no ae·ta·tis su·ae \'än-ō-ī-ˌtät-is-ˈsü-ˌī\ [L] : in the (specified) year of his (or her) age

an·no mun·di \ˌän-ō-ˈmu̇n-dē\ [L] : in the year of the world — used in reckoning dates from the supposed period of the creation of the world, esp. as fixed by James Ussher at 4004 B.C. or by the Jews at 3761 B.C.

an·no ur·bis con·di·tae \ˌän-ō-ˌu̇r-bis-ˈkȯn-də-ˌtī\ [L] : in the year of the founded city (Rome, founded 753 B.C.)

an·nu·it coep·tis \ˌän-ə-ˌwit-ˈkȯip-ˌtēs\ [L] : He (God) has smiled on our undertakings — motto on the reverse of the Great Seal of the United States

à peu près \å-pœ-pre\ [F] : nearly : approximately

à pied \å-pyä\ [F] : on foot

après moi le dé·luge \å-pre-mwȧ-lə-dä-lüĕzh\ [F] : after me the deluge (at·tributed to Louis XV)

à pro·pos de bottes \å-prə-pōd-ə-bȯt\ [F] : apropos of boots — used to change the subject

à pro·pos de rien \-ryäⁿ\ [F] : apropos of nothing

aqua et ig·ni in·ter·dic·tus \ˌäk-wä-et-ˈig-nē-ˌint-ər-ˈdik-təs\ [L] : forbidden to be furnished with water and fire : outlawed

Ar·ca·des am·bo \ˌär-kə-ˌdes-ˈäm-bō\ [L] : both Arcadians : two persons of like occupations or tastes; *also* : two rascals

ar·rec·tis au·ri·bus \ä-ˈrek-ˌtēs-ˈau̇-ri-ˌbu̇s\ [L] : with ears pricked up : attentively

ar·ri·ve·der·ci \ä-ˌrē-ve-ˈder-chē\ [It] : till we meet again : farewell

ars est ce·la·re ar·tem \ˌärs-ˌest-kä-ˌlär-ē-ˈär-ˌtem\ [L] : it is (true) art to conceal art

ars lon·ga, vi·ta bre·vis \ˌärs-ˈlȯng-ˌgä-ˌwē-tä-ˈbre-wis\ [L] : art is long, life is short

a ter·go \ä-ˈter-(ˌ)gō\ [L] : from behind

à tort et à tra·vers \å-tȯr-ā-å-trȧ-ver\ [F] : wrong and crosswise : at random : without rhyme or reason

au bout de son la·tin \ō-büd-(ə-)sōⁿ-lȧ-taⁿ\ [F] : at the end of one's Latin : at the end of one's mental resources

au con·traire \ō-kōⁿ-trer\ [F] : on the contrary

au·de·mus ju·ra nos·tra de·fen·de·re \au̇-ˈdā-məs-ˌyu̇r-ə-ˈnȯ-strə-dā-ˈfen-də-rā\ [L] : we dare defend our rights — motto of Alabama

au·den·tes for·tu·na ju·vat \au̇-ˈden-ˌtäs-fȯr-ˌtü-nə-ˈyu̇-ˌwät\ [L] : fortune favors the bold

au·di al·ter·am par·tem \'au̇-ˌdē-ˌäl-tə-ˌräm-ˈpär-ˌtem\ [L] : hear the other side

au fait \ō-fet, -fe\ [F] : to the point : fully competent : fully informed : socially correct

au fond \ō-fōⁿ\ [F] : at bottom : fundamentally

au grand sé·rieux \ō-grän-sā-ryœ\ [F] : in all seriousness

au pays des aveugles les borgnes sont rois \ō-pā-ē-dä-zà-vœglə-lä-bȯrnʸ-ə- sōⁿ-rwä\ [F] : in the country of the blind the one-eyed men are kings

au pied de la lettre \ō-pyäd-lȧ-letrᵉ\ [F] : literally

au·rea me·di·o·cri·tas \'au̇-rē-ə-ˌmed-ē-ˈȯ-krə-ˌtäs\ [L] : the golden mean

au reste \ō-rest\ [F] : for the rest : besides

aus·si·tôt dit, aus·si·tôt fait \ō-sē-tō-dē ō-sē-tō-fe\ [F] : no sooner said than done

aut Cae·sar aut ni·hil \au̇t-ˈkī-sär-ˌau̇t-ˈni-ˌhil\ [L] : either a Caesar or nothing

aut Caesar aut nul·lus \-ˈnu̇l-əs\ [L] : either a Caesar or a nobody

au·tres temps, au·tres mœurs \ō-trə-täⁿ ō-trə-mœrs\ [F] : other times, other customs

aut vin·ce·re aut mo·ri \au̇t-ˈwing-kə-rē-ˌau̇t-ˈmȯ-ˌrē\ [L] : either to conquer or to die

aux armes \ō-zȧrm\ [F] : to arms

ave at·que va·le \ˈä-ˌwā-ˌät-kwe-ˈwä-ˌlā\ [L] : hail and farewell

à vo·tre san·té \ȧ-vȯt-säⁿ-tā, -vȯ-trə-\ [F] : to your health — used as a toast

beaux yeux \bō-zyœ̄\ [F] : beautiful eyes : beauty of face

bien en·ten·du \byaⁿ-näⁿ-täⁿ-du̇ĕ\ [F] : well understood : of course

bien–pen·sant \byaⁿ-päⁿ-säⁿ\ [F] : right-minded : one who holds orthodox views

bien·sé·ance \byaⁿ-sā-äⁿs\ [F] : propriety

bis dat qui ci·to dat \ˌbis-ˌdät-kwē-ˈki-tō-ˌdät\ [L] : he gives twice who gives promptly

bon ap·pé·tit \bȯ-nȧ-pā-tē\ [F] : good appetite : enjoy your meal

bon gré, mal gré \ˈbōⁿ-ˌgrä ˈmȧl-ˌgrä\ [F] : whether with good grace or bad : willy-nilly

bo·nis avi·bus \ˌbȯ-ˌnēs-ˈä-wi-ˌbu̇s\ [L] : under good auspices

bon jour \bōⁿ-zhu̇r\ [F] : good day : good morning

bonne foi \bȯn-fwä\ [F] : good faith

bon soir \bōⁿ-swȧr\ [F] : good evening

bru·tum ful·men \ˌbrüt-əm-ˈfu̇l-men\ [L] : insensible thunderbolt : a futile threat or display of force

buon gior·no \bwȯn-ˈjȯr-nō\ [It] : good day

ca·dit quae·stio \ˌkäd-ət-ˈkwī-stē-ˌō\ [L] : the question drops : the argument collapses

cau·sa si·ne qua non \ˈkau̇-ˌsä-ˌsin-ē-kwä-ˈnōn\ [L] : an indispensable cause or condition

ca·ve ca·nem \ˌkä-wā-ˈkän-ˌem\ [L] : beware the dog

ce·dant ar·ma to·gae \ˈkä-ˌdänt-ˌär-mə-ˈtō-ˌgī\ [L] : let arms yield to the toga : let military power give way to civil power — motto of Wyoming

ce n'est que le pre·mier pas qui coûte \snek-lə-prə-myä- pä-kē-küt\ [F] : it is only the first step that costs

c'est a dire \se-tȧ-dēr\ [F] : that is to say : namely

c'est au·tre chose \se-tōt-shōz, -tō-trə-\ [F] : that's a different thing

c'est la guerre \se-lȧ-ger\ [F] : that's war : it cannot be helped

c'est la vie \se-lȧ-vē\ [F] : that's life : that's how things happen

c'est plus qu'un crime, c'est une faute \se-plüĕ-kœⁿ-krēm se-tüĕn-fōt\ [F] : it is worse than a crime, it is a blunder

ce·te·ra de·sunt \ˌkät-ə-ˌrä-ˈdā-ˌsu̇nt\ [L] : the rest is missing

cha·cun à son goût \shȧ-kœⁿ- nȧ-sōⁿ-gü\ [F] : everyone to his taste

châ·teau en Es·pagne \shä-tō-äⁿ-nes-pȧnʸ\ [F] : castle in Spain : a visionary project

cher·chez la femme \sher-shā-lȧ-fȧm\ [F] : look for the woman

che sa·rà, sa·rà \ˌkā-sä-ˌrä sä-ˈrä\ [It] : what will be, will be

che·val de ba·taille \shə-vȧl-də-bȧ-täʸ\ [F] : war-horse : argument constantly relied on : favorite subject

co·gi·to, er·go sum \ˈkō-gi-ˌtō ˌer-gō-ˈsu̇m\ [L] : I think, therefore I exist

co·mé·die hu·maine \kȯ-mä-dē-üĕ-men\ [F] : human comedy : the whole variety of human life

comme ci, comme ça \kȯm-sē-kȯm-sä\ [F] : so-so

com·pa·gnon de voy·age \kōⁿ-pȧ-nʸōⁿ-də-vwȧ-yȧzh\ [F] : traveling companion

compte ren·du \kōⁿt-räⁿ-du̇ĕ\ [F] : report (as of proceedings in an investigation)

con·cor·dia dis·cors \kän-kȯrd-ē-ä-ˈdis-ˌkȯrs\ [L] : discordant harmony

cor·rup·tio op·ti·mi pes·si·ma \kə-ˈru̇p-tē-ˌō-ˈäp-tə-ˌmē- ˈpes-ə-ˌmä\ [L] : the corruption of the best is the worst of all

coup de maî·tre \küd-(ə-)metrᵉ\ [F] : masterstroke

coup d'es·sai \kü-dä-se\ [F] : experiment : trial

coûte que coûte \küt-kə-küt\ [F] : cost what it may

cre·do quia ab·sur·dum est \ˌkräd-ō-ˈkwē-ä-ˌäp-ˌsu̇rd-əm-ˈest\ [L] : I believe it because it is absurd

cres·cit eun·do \,kres-kət-'eún·dō\ [L] : it grows as it goes — motto of New Mexico

crise de nerfs *or* **crise des nerfs** \krēz-də-ner\ [F] : crisis of nerves : nervous collapse : hysterical fit

crux cri·ti·co·rum \'krùks-,krit-ə-'kòr-əm\ [L] : crux of critics

cum gra·no sa·lis \kùm-,grän-ō-'säl-is\ [L] : with a grain of salt

cus·tos mo·rum \,kùs-tōs-'mòr-əm\ [L] : guardian of manners or morals : censor

d'ac·cord \dá-kór\ [F] : in accord : agreed

dame d'hon·neur \dàm-dò-nœr\ [F] : lady-in-waiting

dam·nant quod non in·tel·li·gunt \'däm-,nänt-,kwòd-,nòn-in-'tel-ə-,gùnt\ [L] : they condemn what they do not understand

de bonne grâce \də-bòn-gräs\ [F] : with good grace : willingly

de gus·ti·bus non est dis·pu·tan·dum \dā-'gùs-tə-,bùs,nōn-,est-,dis-pù-'tän-,dùm\ [L] : there is no disputing about tastes

Dei gra·tia \'de-,ē-'grät-ē-,ä\ [L] : by the grace of God

de in·te·gro \dā-'int-ə-,grō\ [L] : anew : afresh

de l'au·dace, en·core de l'au·dace, et tou·joursde l'au·dace \də-lō-'dás än-'kór-də-lō-dás ā-tü- 'zhùr-də-lō-dás\ [F] : audacity, more audacity, and ever more audacity

de·len·da est Car·tha·go \dā-'len-dä-,est-kär-'täg-ō\ [L] : Carthage must be destroyed

de·li·ne·a·vit \dā-,lē-nā-'ä-wit\ [L] : he (or she) drew it

de mal en pis \də-má-län-pē\ [F] : from bad to worse

de mi·ni·mis non cu·rat lex \dā-'min-ə-,mēs,nōn-,kü-,rät-'leks\ [L] : the law takes no account of trifles

de mor·tu·is nil ni·si bo·num \dā-'mòrt-ə-,wēs,nēl-,nis- ē-'bò-,nùm\ [L] : of the dead (say) nothing but good

de nos jours \də-nō-zhùr\ [F] : of our time : contemporary — used postpositively esp. after a proper name

Deo fa·ven·te \,dā-ō-fä-'vent-ā\ [L] : with God's favor

Deo gra·ti·as \,dā-ō-'grät-ē-,äs\ [L] : thanks (be) to God

de pro·fun·dis \,dā-prō-'fùn-dēs\ [L] : out of the depths

der Geist der stets ver·neint \dər-'gīst-dər-,shtāts-fer- 'nīnt\ [G] : the spirit that ever denies — applied originally to Mephistopheles

de·si·pe·re in lo·co \dā-'sip-ə-rē-in-'lò-kō\ [L] : to indulge in trifling at the proper time

Deus vult \,dā-əs-'wùlt\ [L] : God wills it — rallying cry of the First Crusade

di·es fau·stus \,dē-,äs-'faù-stəs\ [L] : lucky day

dies in·fau·stus \-'in-,faù-stəs\ [L] : unlucky day

dies irae \-'ē-,rī\ [L] : day of wrath — used of the Judgment Day

Dieu et mon droit \dyœ̃-ā-mòn-drwä\ [F] : God and my right — motto on the British royal arms

Dieu vous garde \dyœ̃-vü-gárd\ [F] : God keep you

di·ri·go \'dē-ri-,gō\ [L] : I direct — motto of Maine

dis ali·ter vi·sum \,dēs-,äl-ə-,ter-'wē-,sùm\ [L] : the Gods decreed otherwise

di·tat De·us \,dē-,tät-'dā-,ùs\ [L] : God enriches — motto of Arizona

di·vi·de et im·pe·ra \'dē-wi-,de-,et-'im-pə-,rä\ [L] : divide and rule

do·cen·do dis·ci·mus \dò-,ken-dō-'dis-ki-,mùs\ [L] : we learn by teaching

Do·mi·ne di·ri·ge nos \'dò-mi-,ne-,dē-ri-ge-'nōs\ [L] : Lord, direct us — motto of the City of London

Do·mi·nus vo·bis·cum \,dò-mi-,nùs-wō-'bēs-,kùm\ [L] : the Lord be with you

dul·ce et de·co·rum est pro pa·tria mo·ri \,dùl-,ket-de-'kòr-,est-prō-,pä-trē-,ä-'mò,rē\ [L] : it is sweet and seemly to die for one's country

dum spi·ro, spe·ro \,dùm-'spē-rō-'spä-rō\ [L] : while I breathe I hope — one of the mottoes of South Carolina

dum vi·vi·mus vi·va·mus \,dùm-'wē-wē-,mùs-wē-'wäm-ùs\ [L] : while we live, let us live

dux fe·mi·na fac·ti \,dùks-,fā-mi-nä-'fäk-,tē\ [L] : a woman was leader of the exploit

ec·ce sig·num \,ek-e-'sig-,nùm\ [L] : behold the sign : look at the proof

e con·tra·rio \,ā-kòn-'trär-ē-,ō\ [L] : on the contrary

écra·sez l'in·fâme \ā-krä-zā-lan-'fäm\ [F] : crush the infamous thing

eheu fu·ga·ces la·bun·tur an·ni \ā-,heú-fù-'gä-,käs-lä-,bún-,tùr-'än-,ē\ [L] : alas! the fleeting years glide on

ein' fes·te Burg ist un·ser Gott \īn-,fes-tə-'bùrk-ist-,ùn-zər-'gòt\ [G] : a mighty fortress is our God

em·bar·ras de ri·chesses \än-bá-räd-(ə)rē-shes\ [F] : embarrassing surplus of riches : confusing abundance

em·bar·ras du choix \än-bá-rä-duē-shwä\ [F] : embarrassing variety of choice

en ami \än-ná-mē\ [F] : as a friend

en ef·fet \än-ná-fe\ [F] : in fact : indeed

en fa·mille \än-fä-mēy\ [F] : in or with one's family : at home : informally

en·fant gâ·té \än-fän-gä-tā\ [F] : spoiled child

en·fants per·dus \än-fän-per-duē\ [F] : lost children : soldiers sent to a dangerous post

en·fin \än-faⁿ\ [F] : in conclusion : in a word

en gar·çon \än-gár-sōⁿ\ [F] : as or like a bachelor

en pan·tou·fles \än-pän-tüflə\ [F] : in slippers : at ease : informally

en plein air \än-plen-er\ [F] : in the open air

en plein jour \än-plan-zhür\ [F] : in broad day

en règle \än-reglə\ [F] : in order : in due form

en re·tard \änr-(ə)tár\ [F] : behind time : late

en re·traite \än-rə-tret\ [F] : in retreat : in retirement

en re·vanche \änr-(ə)vänsh\ [F] : in return : in compensation

en se·condes noces \äns-(ə)gōnd-nòs\ [F] : in a second marriage

en·se pe·tit pla·ci·dam sub li·ber·ta·tequi·e·tem \'en-se-,pet-ət-'pläk-i-,däm-sùb-,lē-ber-,tä-te-kwē-'ä-,tem\ [L] : with the sword she seeks calm repose under liberty — motto of Massachusetts

épa·ter les bour·geois \ä-pá-tā-lä-bür-zhwà\ [F] : to shock the middle classes

e plu·ri·bus unum \,ē-,plùr-ə-bəs-'(y)ü-nəm, ,ā-,plùr-\ [L] : one out of many — used on the seal of the U.S. and on several U.S. coins

ep·pur si muo·ve \äp-,pür-sē-'mwò-vā\ [It] : and yet it does move — attributed to Galileo after recanting his assertion ofthe earth's motion

Erin go bragh \,er-ən-gə-'brò, -gō-'brä\ [IrGael *go brāth*, lit., till doomsday] : Ireland forever

er·ra·re hu·ma·num est \e-'rär-e-hü-,män-əm-'est\ [L] : to err is human

es·prit de l'es·ca·lier \es-prēd-les-ká-lyä\ *or* **es·prit d'es·ca·lier** \-prē-des-,ká-lyä\ [F] : staircase wit : repartee thought of only too late

es·se quam vi·de·ri \'es-ē-,kwäm-wi-'dā-rē\ [L] : to be rather than to seem — motto of North Carolina

est mo·dus in re·bus \est-'mó-,dùs-in-'rä-,bùs\ [L] : there is a proper measure in things, i.e., the goldenmean should always be observed

es·to per·pe·tua \'es-,tō-pər-'pet-ə-,wä\ [L] : may she endure forever — motto of Idaho

et hoc ge·nus om·ne \et-,hōk-,gen-əs-'óm-ne\ *or* **et id genus omne** \et-,id-\ [L] : and everything of this kind

et in Ar·ca·dia ego \,et-in-är-,kăd-ē-ə-'eg-ō\ [L] : I too (lived) in Arcadia

et sic de si·mi·li·bus \et-,sēk-dā-si-'mil-ə-,bùs\ [L] : and so of like things

et tu Bru·te \et-'tü-'brü-te\ [L] : thou too, Brutus — exclamation attributed toJulius Caesar on seeing his friend Brutus among his assassins

eu·re·ka \yù-'rē-kə\ [Gk] : I have found it — motto of California

Ewig–Weib•li•che \‚ā-vik-'vīp-li-kə\ [G] : eternal feminine

ex ani•mo \ek-'sän-ə-‚mō\ [L] : from the heart : sincerely

ex•cel•si•or \ik-'sel-sē-ər, eks-'kel-sē-‚ȯr\ [L] : still higher — motto of New York

ex•cep•tio pro•bat re•gu•lam de re•bus nonex•cep•tis \eks-'kep-tē-‚ō-‚prō-bät-'rā-gə-‚läm-dā-'rā-‚bùs-‚nōn-eks-'kep-‚tēs\ [L] : an exception establishes the rule as to things notexcepted

ex•cep•tis ex•ci•pi•en•dis \eks-'kep-‚tēs-eks-‚kip-ē-'en-‚dēs\ [L] : with the proper or necessary exceptions

ex•i•tus ac•ta pro•bat \'ek-sə-‚tùs-‚äk-tə-'prȯ-‚bät\ [L] : the event justifies the deed

ex li•bris \eks-'lē-bris\ [L] : from the books of — used on bookplates

ex me•ro mo•tu \‚eks-‚mer-ō-'mō-tü\ [L] : out of mere impulse : of one's own accord

ex ne•ces•si•ta•te rei \‚eks-ne-‚kes-i-'tä-te-'rā(-‚ē)\ [L] : from the necessity of the case

ex ni•hi•lo ni•hil fit \eks-'ni-hi-‚lō-‚ni-‚hil-'fit\ [L] : from nothing nothing is produced

ex pe•de Her•cu•lem \eks-‚ped-e-'her-kə-‚lem\ [L] : from the foot (we may judge of the size of) Hercules : from a part we may judge of the whole

ex•per•to cre•di•te \eks-‚pert-ō-'krād-ə-‚te\ [L] : believe one who has had experience

ex un•gue le•o•nem \eks-'ùng-gwe-le-'ō-‚nem\ [L] : from the claw (we may judge of) the lion : from a part we may judge of the whole

ex vi ter•mi•ni \eks-‚wē-'ter-mə-‚nē\ [L] : from the force of the term

fa•ci•le prin•ceps \‚fäk-i-le-'pring-‚keps\ [L] : easily first

fa•ci•lis de•scen•sus Aver•no \'fäk-i-‚lis-dā-‚skän-‚sùs-ä-'wer-nō\ or **facilis descensus Aver•ni** \-(‚)nē\ [L] : the descent to Avernus is easy : the road to evil is easy

fa•çon de par•ler \fa-sōⁿ-də-pár-lā\ [F] : manner of speaking : figurative or conventional expression

faire suivre \fer-swēvrᵊ\ [F] : have forwarded : please forward

fas est et ab ho•stedo•ce•ri \fäs-'est-et-‚äb-'hȯ-ste-dȯ-'kā-(‚)rē\ [L] : it is right to learn even from an enemy

Fa•ta vi•am in•ve•ni•ent \‚fä-tä-'wē-‚äm-in-'wen-ē-‚ent\ [L] : the Fates will find a way

fat•ti mas•chii, pa•ro•le fe•mi•ne \‚fät-tē-'mäs-‚kē pä-‚rȯ-lā-'fä-mē-‚nā\ [It] : deeds are males, words are females : deeds are more effective than words — motto of Maryland, where it is generally interpreted as meaning "manly deeds, womanly words"

faux bon•homme \fō-bȯ-nȯm\ [F] : pretended good fellow

faux–naïf \fō-nà-ēf\ [F] : pretending to be childlike

femme de cham•bre \fäm-də-shäⁿbrᵊ\ [F] : chambermaid : lady's maid

fe•sti•na len•te \fe-‚stē-nə-'len-‚tā\ [L] : make haste slowly

feux d'ar•ti•fice \fœ-dár-tē-fēs\ [F] : fireworks : display of wit

fi•at ex•pe•ri•men•tum in cor•po•revi•li \'fē-‚ät-ek-‚sper-ē-'men-‚tùm-in-‚kȯr-pə-re-'wē-lē\ [L] : let experiment be made on a worthless body

fi•at ju•sti•tia, ru•at cae•lum \‚fē-ät-yùs-'tit-ē-ä ‚rù-‚ät-'kī-‚lùm\ [L] : let justice be done though the heavens fall

fi•at lux \fē-‚ät-'lùks\ [L] : let there be light

Fi•dei De•fen•sor \‚fid-e-‚ē-dā-'fän-‚sȯr\ [L] : Defender of the Faith — a title of the sovereigns of England

fi•dus Acha•tes \‚fēd-əs-ä-'kä-‚tās\ [L] : faithful Achates : trusty friend

fille de cham•bre \fēy-də-shäⁿbrᵊ\ [F] : lady's maid

fille d'hon•neur \fēy-dȯ-nœr\ [F] : maid of honor

fils \fēs\ [F] : son — used after French proper names to distinguish a son fromhis father

fi•nem re•spi•ce \‚fē-‚nem-'rā-spi-‚ke\ [L] : consider the end

fi•nis co•ro•nat opus \‚fē-nəs-kə-'rō-‚nät-'ō-‚pùs\ [L] : the end crowns the work

fluc•tu•at nec mer•gi•tur \'flùk-tə-‚wät-‚nek-'mer-gə-‚tùr\ [L] : it is tossed by the waves but does not sink — motto of Paris

fo•lie de gran•deur or **folie des gran•deurs** \fȯ-lē-də-grän-dœr\ [F] : delusion of greatness : megalomania

fors•an et haecolim me•mi•nis•se ju•va•bit \‚fȯr-‚sän-‚et-'hīk-‚ō-lim-‚mem-ə-'nis-e-‚yù-'wä-bit\ [L] : perhaps this too will be a pleasure to look back onone day

for•tes for•tu•na ju•vat \'fȯr-‚tās-fȯr-‚tü-nə-'yù-‚wät\ [L] : fortune favors the brave

fron•ti nul•la fi•des \'frȯn-‚tē-‚nùl-ə-'fid-‚ās\ [L] : no reliance can be placed on appearance

fu•it Ili•um \'fü-ət-'il-ē-əm\ [L] : Troy has been (i.e., is no more)

fu•ror lo•quen•di \‚fùr-‚ȯr-lȯ-'kwen-(‚)dē\ [L] : rage for speaking

furor po•e•ti•cus \-pȯ-'ät-i-kùs\ [L] : poetic frenzy

furor scri•ben•di \-skrē-'ben-(‚)dē\ [L] : rage for writing

Gal•li•ce \'gäl-ə-‚ke\ [L] : in French : after the French manner

gar•çon d'hon•neur \gàr-sōⁿ-dȯ-nœr\ [F] : bridegroom's attendant

garde du corps \gárd-duē-kȯr\ [F] : bodyguard

gar•dez la foi \gàr-dā-là-fwà\ [F] : keep faith

gau•de•a•mus igi•tur \‚gaùd-ē-'äm-əs-'ig-ə-‚tùr\ [L] : let us then be merry

gens d'é•glise \zhäⁿ-dā-glēz\ [F] : church people : clergy

gens de guerre \zhäⁿ-də-ger\ [F] : military people : soldiery

gens du monde \zhäⁿ-duē-mōⁿd\ [F] : people of the world : fashionable people

gno•thi se•au•ton \gə-'nō-thē-‚se-aù-'tȯn\ [Gk] : know thyself

grand monde \gräⁿ-mōⁿd\ [F] : great world : high society

guerre à ou•trance \ger-à-ü-träⁿs\ [F] : war to the uttermost

gu•ten Tag \‚güt-ᵊn-'täk\ [G] : good day

has•ta la vis•ta \‚äs-tä-lä-'vēs-tä\ [Sp] : good-bye

haut goût \ō-gü\ [F] : high flavor : slight taint of decay

hic et ubi•que \‚hēk-et-ù-'bē-kwe\ [L] : here and everywhere

hic ja•cet \hik-'jā-sət‚hēk-'yäk-ət\ [L] : here lies — used preceding a name on a tombstone

hinc il•lae la•cri•mae \‚hingk-‚il-‚ī-'läk-ri-‚mī\ [L] : hence those tears

hoc age \hōk-'äg-e\ [L] : do this : apply yourself to what you are about

hoc opus, hic la•bor est \hōk-'ȯ-‚pùs-‚hēk-‚lä-‚bȯr-'est\ [L] : this is the hard work, this is the toil

homme d'af•faires \ȯm-dà-fer\ [F] : man of business : business agent

homme d'es•prit \-des-prē\ [F] : man of wit

homme moyen sen•suel \ȯm-mwà-yaⁿ-sän-swᵛel\ [F] : the average nonintellectual man

ho•mo sum: hu•ma•ni nil a me ali•e•numpu•to \'hȯ-mō-‚sùmhü-‚män-ē-'nēl-ä-‚mā-‚äl-ē-'ä-nəm-'pù-‚tō\ [L] : I am a man: I regard nothing that concerns man asforeign to my interests

ho•ni soit qui mal y pense \ȯ-nē-swà-kē-màl-ē-päⁿs\ [F] : shamed be he who thinks evil of it — motto of the Order of the Garter

hu•ma•num est er•ra•re \hü-‚män-əm-‚est-e-'rär-e\ [L] : to err is human

ich dien \iḵ-'dēn\ [G] : I serve — motto of the Prince of Wales

ici on parle fran•çais \ē-sē-ōⁿ-párl-(-ə)-fräⁿ-se\ [F] : French is spoken here

id est \id-'est\ [L] : that is

ig·no·ran·tia ju·ris ne·mi·nemex·cu·sat \,ig-nə-,ränt-ē-ä-'yùr-əs-'nā-mə-,nem-eks-'kü-,sät\ [L] : ignorance of the law excuses no one

ig·no·tum per ig·no·ti·us \ig-'nōt-əm-,per-ig-'nōt-ē-,ùs\ [L] : (explaining) the unknown by means of the more unknown

il faut cul·ti·ver no·tre jar·din \ēl-fō-kuĕl-tē-vā-nótzhár-daⁿ, -nò-trə-zhàr-\ [F] : we must cultivate our garden : we must tend to our own affairs

in ae·ter·num\,in-ī-'ter-,nùm\ [L] : forever

in du·bio \in-'dùb-ē-,ō\ [L] : in doubt : undetermined

in fu·tu·ro \,in-fə-'tùr-ō\ [L] : in the future

in hoc sig·no vin·ces \in-hōk-'sig-nō-'ving-,kās\ [L] : by this sign (the Cross) you will conquer

in li·mi·ne \in-'lē-mə-,ne\ [L] : on the threshold : at the beginning

in om·nia pa·ra·tus \in-'òm-nē-ə-pə-'rä-,tùs\ [L] : ready for all things

in par·ti·bus in·fi·de·li·um \in-'pärt-ə-,bùs,in-fə-'dā-lē-,ùm\ [L] : in the regions of the infidels — used of a titular bishop having no diocesan jurisdiction, usu. in non-Christian countries

in prae·sen·ti \,in-prī-'sen-,tē\ [L] : at the present time

in sae·cu·la sae·cu·lo·rum \in-'sī-kù-,lä-,sī-kə-'lòr-əm, -'sā-kù-,lä-,sā-\ [L] : for ages of ages : forever and ever

insh·al·lah \,in-shä-'lä\ [Ar] : if Allah wills : God willing

in sta·tu quo an·tebel·lum \in-,stä-,tü-kwō-,änt-ē-'bel-əm\ [L] : in the same state as before the war

in·te·ger vi·tae sce·le·ris·que pu·rus \,in-tə-,ger-'wē-,tī-,skel-ə-'ris-kwe-'pü-rəs\ [L] : upright of life and free from wickedness

in·ter nos \,int-ər-'nōs\ [L] : between ourselves

in·tra mu·ros \,in-trä-'mü-,rōs\ [L] : within the walls

in usum Del·phi·ni \in-'ü-səm-del-'fē-nē\ [L] : for the use of the Dauphin : expurgated

in utrum·que pa·ra·tus \in-ü-'trùm-kwe-pə-'rä-,tùs\ [L] : prepared for either (event)

in·ve·nit \in-'wā-nit\ [L] : he (or she) devised it

in vi·no ve·ri·tas\in-'wē-nō-'wā-rə-,täs\ [L] : there is truth in wine

in·vi·ta Mi·ner·va \in-,wē-,tä-mi-'ner-,wä\ [L] : Minerva being unwilling : without natural talent or inspiration

ip·sis·si·ma ver·ba \ip-,sis-ə-,mä-'wer-,bä\ [L] : the very words

ira fu·ror bre·vis est \,ē-rä-'fùr-,òr-'bre-wis-,est\ [L] : anger is a brief madness

j'ac·cuse \zhá-kuĕz\ [F] : I accuse

jac·ta alea est \'yäk-,tä-,ä-lē-,ä-'est\ [L] : the die is cast

j'adoube \zhá-düb\ [F] : I adjust — used in chess when touching a piece without intending tomove it

ja·nu·is clau·sis \,yän-ə-,wēs-'klaù-,sēs\ [L] : behind closed doors

je main·tien·drai \zhə-maⁿ-tyaⁿ-drā\ [F] : I will maintain — motto of the Netherlands

jeu de mots \zhœd-(ə-)mō\ [F] : play on words : pun

jo·an·nes est no·men eius \yō-'än-ās-,est-,nō-men-ā-yùs\ [L] : John is his name — motto of Puerto Rico

jo·lie laide \zhó-lē-led\ [F] : good-looking ugly woman : woman who is attractive though not conventionally pretty

jour·nal in·time \zhür-nál-aⁿ-tēm\ [F] : intimate journal : private diary

jus di·vi·num \,yüs-di-'wē-,nùm\ [L] : divine law

jus·ti·tia om·ni·bus \yùs-,tit-ē-,ä-'òm-ni-,bùs\ [L] : justice for all — motto of the District of Columbia

j'y suis, j'y reste \zhē-swēⁱ-zhē-rest\ [F] : here I am, here I remain

la belle dame sans mer·ci \lá-bel-dàm-sä̈ⁿ-mer-sē\ [F] : the beautiful lady without mercy

la·bo·ra·re est ora·re \'läb-ō-,rär-ā-,est-'ō-,rär-ā\ [L] : to work is to pray

la·bor om·nia vin·cit \'lä-,bòr-,òm-nē-,ä-'wing-kit\ [L] : labor conquers all things — motto of Oklahoma

la·cri·mae re·rum \,läk-ri-,mī-'rā-,rùm\ [L] : tears for things : pity for misfortune; *also* : tears in things : tragedy in life

lais·sez–al·ler *or* **lais·ser–al·ler** \le-sā-á-lā\ [F] : letting go : lack of restraint

lap·sus ca·la·mi \,läp-sùs-'käl-ə-,mē\ [L] : slip of the pen

lap·sus lin·guae \-'ling-,gwī\ [L] : slip of the tongue

la reine le veut \lá-ren-lə-vœ\ [F] : the queen wills it

la·scia·te ogni spe·ran·za, voich'en·tra·te \läsh-'shä-tä-,ō-nᵞē-spä-'rän-tsä-,vō-ē-kän-'trä-tä\ [It] : abandon all hope, ye who enter

lau·da·tor tem·po·ris ac·ti \laù-'dä-,tór,tem-pə-ris-'äk-,tē\ [L] : one who praises past times

laus Deo \laùs-'dā-ō\ [L] : praise (be) to God

le cœur a ses rai·sons que la rai·son ne con·naitpoint \lə-kœr-á-sā-re-zōⁿk-lá-re-zōⁿn-(ə-)kò-ne-pwaⁿ\ [F] : the heart has its reasons that reason knows nothing of

le roi est mort, vive le roi \lə-rwä-e-mór vēv-lə-rwä\ [F] : the king is dead, long live the king

le roi le veut \-lə-vœ\ [F] : the king wills it

le roi s'avi·se·ra \-sá-vēz-rá\ [F] : the king will consider

le style, c'est l'homme \lə-stēl-se-lóm\ [F] : the style is the man

l'état, c'est moi \lā-tà-se-mwà\ [F] : the state, it is I

l'étoile du nord \lā-twál-düē-nór\ [F] : the star of the north — motto of Minnesota

Lie·der·kranz \'lēd-ər-,kräns\ [G] : wreath of songs : German singing society

lit·tera scrip·ta ma·net \,lit-ə-,rä-,skrip-tə-'män-et\ [L] : the written letter abides

lo·cus in quo \,lò-kəs-in-'kwō\ [L] : place in which

l'union fait la force \luē-nyōⁿ-fe-lá-fórs\ [F] : union makes strength — motto of Belgium

lu·sus na·tu·rae \,lü-səs-nə-'tùr-ē, -'tùr-,ī\ [L] : freak of nature

ma foi \má-fwä\ [F] : my faith! : indeed

mag·na est ve·ri·tas et prae·va·le·bit \,mäg-nä-,est-'wā-ri-,täs-et-,prī-wä-'lā-bit\ [L] : truth is mighty and will prevail

mag·ni no·mi·nis um·bra \,mäg-nē-,nō-mə-nis-'ùm-brä\ [L] : the shadow of a great name

mai·son de san·té \má-zōⁿd-(ə-)sän-tā\ [F] : private hospital : asylum

ma·lade ima·gi·naire \má-lád-ē-má-zhē-ner\ [F] : imaginary invalid : hypochondriac

ma·lis avi·bus\,mäl-,ēs-'ä-wi-,bùs\ [L] : under evil auspices

ma·no a ma·no \,män-ō-ä-'män-ō\ [Sp] : hand to hand : in direct competition or confrontation

man spricht Deutsch \män-shprikt-'dòich\ [G] : German spoken

ma·riage de con·ve·nance \má-ryàzh-də-kōⁿv-näⁿs\ [F] : marriage of convenience

mau·vaise honte \mó-vez-ōⁿt\ [F] : bad shame : bashfulness

mau·vais quart d'heure \mó-ve-kàr-dœr\ [F] : bad quarter hour : an uncomfortable though brief experience

me·dio tu·tis·si·mus ibis \'med-ē-,ō-tü-,tis-ə-mùs-'ē-bis\ [L] : you will go most safely by the middle course

me ju·di·ce \mā-'yüd-ə-ķe\ [L] : I being judge : in my judgment

mens sa·na in cor·po·re sa·no \mäns-'sän-ə-in-,kòr-pə-re-'sän-ō\ [L] : a sound mind in a sound body

me·um et tu·um \,mē-əm-,et-'tü-əm, ,mä-əm-\ [L] : mine and thine : distinction of private property

mi·ra·bi·le vi·su \mi-,räb-ə-lā-'wē-sü\ [L] : wonderful to behold

mi·ra·bi·lia \,mir-ə-'bil-ē-ə\ [L] : wonders : miracles

mœurs \mœr(s)\ [F] : mores : attitudes, customs, and manners of a society

mo·le ru·it sua \'mō-le-,rù-it-'sù-ä\ [L] : it collapses from its own bigness

monde \mōⁿd\ [F] : world : fashionable world : society

mon·ta·ni sem·per li·be·ri \mȯn-ˈtän-ē-ˌsem-pər-ˈlē-bə-ˌrē\ [L] : mountaineers are always free men — motto of West Virginia

mo·nu·men·tum ae·re per·en·ni·us \ˌmȯ-nə-ˈmen-tùm-ˌī-re-pə-ˈren-ē-ús\ [L] : a monument more lasting than bronze — used of an immortal work of art or literature

mo·ri·tu·ri te sa·lu·ta·mus \ˌmȯr-ə-ˈtúr-ē-ˌtā-ˌsäl-ə-ˈtäm-ús\ or **morituri te sa·lu·tant** \-ˈsäl-ə-ˌtänt\ [L] : we (or those) who are about to die salute thee

mul·tum in par·vo \ˌmúl-təm-in-ˈpär-vō\ [L] : much in little

mu·ta·to no·mi·ne de te fa·bu·lanar·ra·tur \mü-ˌtät-ō-ˈnō-mə-ne-dā-ˈtä-ˌfäb-ə-lä-nä-ˈrä-ˌtúr\ [L] : with the name changed the story applies to you

na·tu·ram ex·pel·las fur·ca, ta·menus·que re·cur·ret \nä-ˈtü-ˌräm-ek-ˌspel-äs-ˈfúr-ˌkä-ˌtäən-ˈús-kwe-re-ˈkúr-et\ [L] : you may drive nature out with a pitchfork, but she will keep coming back

na·tu·ra non fa·cit sal·tum \nä-ˈtü-rä-ˌnōn-ˌfäk-ət-ˈsäl-ˌtúm\ [L] : nature makes no leap

ne ce·de ma·lis \nā-ˌkā-de-ˈmäl-ˌēs\ [L] : yield not to misfortunes

ne·mo me im·pu·ne la·ces·sit \ˈnä-mō-ˌmā-im-ˌpü-nä-lä-ˈkes-ət\ [L] : no one attacks me with impunity — motto of Scotland and of the Order of the Thistle

ne quid ni·mis \ˌnā-ˌkwid-ˈnim-əs\ [L] : not anything in excess

n'est–ce pas? \nes-ˈpä\ [F] : isn't it so?

nicht wahr? \nikt-ˈvär\ [G] : not true? : isn't it so?

nil ad·mi·ra·ri \ˈnēl-ˌäd-mə-ˈrär-ē\ [L] : to be excited by nothing : equanimity

nil de·spe·ran·dum \ˈnēl-ˌdā-spā-ˈrän-dùm\ [L] : never despair

nil si·ne nu·mi·ne \ˈnēl-ˌsin-e-ˈnü-mə-ne\ [L] : nothing without the divine will — motto of Colorado

n'im·porte \naⁿ-ˈpȯrt\ [F] : it's no matter

no·lens vo·lens \ˌnō-ˌlenz-ˈvō-ˌlenz\ [L] : unwilling (or) willing : willy-nilly

non om·nia pos·su·mus om·nes \nōn-ˈȯm-nē-ä-ˌpȯ-sə-mús-ˈȯm-ˌnās\ [L] : we can't all (do) all things

non om·nis mo·ri·ar \nōn-ˈȯm-nis-ˈmȯr-ē-ˌär\ [L] : I shall not wholly die

non sans droict \nōⁿ-ˌsäⁿ-ˈdrwä\ [OF] : not without right — motto on Shakespeare's coat of arms

non sum qua·lis eram \ˌnōn-ˌsúm-ˌkwäl-əs-ˈer-ˌäm\ [L] : I am not what I used to be

nos·ce te ip·sum \ˌnȯs-ke-ˌtā-ˈip-ˌsúm\ [L] : know thyself

nos·tal·gie de la boue \nȯs-ˌtäl-zhēd-(ə-)lä-bü\ [F] : nostalgia for the mud : homesickness for the gutter

nous avons chan·gé tout ce·la \nü-zȧ-vōⁿ-shäⁿ-zhā-tü-slä\ [F] : we have changed all that

nous ver·rons ce que nous ver·rons \nü-ve-rōⁿs-(ə-)kə-nü-ve-rōⁿ\ [F] : we shall see what we shall see

no·vus ho·mo \ˌnȯ-wəs-ˈhȯ-mō\ [L] : new man : man newly ennobled : upstart

no·vus or·do se·clo·rum \-ˈȯr-ˌdō-sā-ˈklȯr-əm\ [L] : a new cycle of the ages — motto on the reverse of the Great Seal of the United States

nu·gae \ˈnü-ˌgī\ [L] : trifles

nuit blanche \nwē-blänsh\ [F] : white night : a sleepless night

nyet \ˈnyet\ [Russ] : no

ob·iit \ˈȯ-bē-ˌit\ [L] : he (or she) died

ob·scu·rum per ob·scu·ri·us \əb-ˈskyúr-əm-ˌper-əb-ˈskyúr-ē-əs\ [L] : (explaining) the obscure by means of the more obscure

ode·rint dum me·tu·ant \ˈȯd-ə-ˌrint-ˌdúm-ˈmet-ə-ˌwänt\ [L] : let them hate, so long as they fear

odi et amo \ˈȯ-ˌdē-et-ˈäm-(ˌ)ō\ [L] : I hate and I love

om·ne ig·no·tum pro mag·ni·fi·co \ˌȯm-ne-ig-ˈnō-ˌtùm-prō-mäg-ˈnif-i-ˌkō\ [L] : everything unknown (is taken) as grand : the unknown tends to be exaggerated in importance or difficulty

om·nia mu·tan·tur, nos et mu·ta·mur inil·lis \ˌȯm-nē-ä-mü-ˈtän-ˌtúr-ˌnȯs-et-mü-ˌtäm-ər-in-ˈil-ˌēs\ [L] : all things are changing, and we are changing with them

om·nia vin·cit amor \ˈȯm-nē-ä-ˈwing-kət-ˈäm-ˌȯr\ [L] : love conquers all

onus pro·ban·di \ˌō-nəs-prō-ˈban-ˌdī-ˌdē\ [L] : burden of proof

ora pro no·bis \ˌō-rä-prō-ˈnō-ˌbēs\ [L] : pray for us

ore ro·tun·do \ˌōr-ä-rō-ˈtùn-dō\ [L] : with round mouth : eloquently

oro y pla·ta \ˌōr-ō-ē-ˈplät-ə\ [Sp] : gold and silver — motto of Montana

o tem·po·ra! o mo·res! \ō-ˈtem-pə-rä-ō-ˈmō-ˌräs\ [L] : oh the times! oh the manners!

oti·um cum dig·ni·ta·te \ˈōt-ē-ˌùm-kùm-ˌdig-nə-ˈtä-te\ [L] : leisure with dignity

où sont les neiges d'an·tan? \ü-sōⁿ-lā-nezh-däⁿ-täⁿ\ [F] : where are the snows of yesteryear?

pal·li·da Mors \ˌpal-id-ə-ˈmȯrz\ [L] : pale Death

pa·nem et cir·cen·ses \ˈpän-ˌem-et-kir-ˈkän-ˌsäs\ [L] : bread and circuses : provision of the means of life and recreation by government to appease discontent

pan·ta rhei \ˌpän-tä-ˈ(h)rä\ [Gk] : all things are in flux

par avance \pär-ä-väⁿs\ [F] : in advance : by anticipation

par avion \pär-ä-vyōⁿ\ [F] : by airplane — used on airmail

par ex·em·ple \pär-āg-zäⁿplə\ [F] : for example

par·tu·ri·unt mon·tes, nas·ce·turri·di·cu·lus mus \pär-ˌtúr-ē-ˌùnt-ˈmȯn-ˌtäs-näs-ˈkä-ˌtúr-ri-ˌdik-ə-lùs-ˈmüs\ [L] : the mountains are in labor, and a ridiculous mouse will be brought forth

pa·ter pa·tri·ae \ˈpä-ˌter-ˈpä-trē-ˌī\ [L] : father of his country

pau·cis ver·bis \ˌpaú-ˌkēs-ˈwer-ˌbēs\ [L] : in a few words

pax vo·bis·cum \ˌpäks-vō-ˈbēs-ˌkùm\ [L] : peace (be) with you

peine forte et dure \pen-ˌfȯr-tā-düēr\ [F] : strong and hard punishment : torture

per an·gus·ta ad au·gus·ta \per-ˈän-ˌgús-tə-äd-ˈaú-ˌgús-tə\ [L] : through difficulties to honors

père \per\ [F] : father — used after French proper names to distinguish a father from his son

per·eant qui an·te nos nos·tra dix·e·runt \ˈper-e-ˌänt-kwē-ˌän-te-ˈnȯs-ˈnȯs-trä-dēk-ˈsä-ˌrùnt\ [L] : may they perish who have expressed our bright ideas before us

per·fide Al·bion \per-fēd-ál-byōⁿ\ [F] : perfidious Albion (England)

peu a peu \pœ-ä-pœ\ [F] : little by little

peu de chose \pœd-(ə-)shōz\ [F] : a trifle

pièce d'oc·ca·sion \pyes-dȯ-kä-zyōⁿ\ [F] : piece for a special occasion

pinx·it \ˈpingk-sət\ [L] : he (or she) painted it

place aux dames \plȧs-ō-däm\ [F] : (make) room for the ladies

ple·no ju·re \ˌplā-nō-ˈyùr-e\ [L] : with full right

plus ça change, plus c'est la même chose \plœ-sȧ-shäⁿzh-plœ-se-lä-mem-shōz\ [F] : the more that changes, the more it's the same thing

plus roy·a·liste que le roi \plœ-rwȧ-yȧ-lēst-kəl-rwä\ [F] : more royalist than the king

po·cas pa·la·bras \ˌpō-käs-pä-ˈläb-räs\ [Sp] : few words

po·eta nas·ci·tur, non fit \pȯ-ˌā-tä-ˈnäs-kə-ˌtùr-nōn-ˈfit\ [L] : a poet is born, not made

pol·li·ce ver·so \ˌpȯ-li-ke-ˈver-sō\ [L] : with thumb turned : with a gesture or expression of condemnation

post hoc, er·go prop·ter hoc \ˈpȯst-ˌhōk-ˌer-gō-ˈprȯp-ter-ˌhōk\ [L] : after this, therefore on account of it (a fallacy of argument)

post ob·itum \ˌpȯst-ˈȯ-bə-ˌtúm\ [L] : after death

pour ac·quit \pür-ä-kē\ [F] : received payment

pour le mé•rite \pür-lə-mā-rēt\ [F] : for merit

pro aris et fo•cis \prō-ä-rēs-et-'fō-kēs\ [L] : for altars and firesides

pro bo•no pu•bli•co \prō-bȯ-nō-'pü-bli-kō\ [L] : for the public good

pro hac vi•ce \prō-häk-'wik-e\ [L] : for this occasion

pro pa•tria \prō-'pä-trē-ä\ [L] : for one's country

pro re•ge, le•ge, et gre•ge \prō-'rā-ge-'lā-ge-et-'greg-,e\ [L] : for the king, the law, and the people

pro re na•ta \,prō-,rā-'nät-ə\ [L] : for an occasion that has arisen : as needed — used in medical prescriptions

quand même \kän-'mem\ [F] : even though : whatever may happen

quan•tum mu•ta•tus ab il•lo \,kwänt-əm-mü-'tät-əs-äb-'il-ō\ [L] : how changed from what he once was

quan•tum suf•fi•cit \kwänt-əm-'səf-ə-,kit\ [L] : as much as suffices : a sufficient quantity — used in medical prescriptions

☆**quién sa•be?** \kyän-'sä-bā\ [Sp] : who knows?

qui fa•cit per ali•um fa•cit per se \kwē-,fäk-it-,per-'äl-ē-,um-,fäk-it-,per-'sā\ [L] : he who does (anything) through another does it through himself ipsos custodes?

quis cus•to•di•et ip•sos cus•to•des? \,kwis-kus-'tōd-ē-,et-ip-,sōs-kus-'tō-,dās\ [L] : who will keep the keepers themselves?

qui s'ex•cuse s'ac•cuse \kē-'sek-,skuĕz-'sà-,kuĕz\ [F] : he who excuses himself accuses himself

quis se•pa•ra•bit? \,kwis-,sā-pə-'räb-it\ [L] : who shall separate (us)? — motto of the Order of St. Patrick

qui trans•tu•lit sus•ti•net \kwē-'träns-tə-,lit-'sus-tə-,net\ [L] : He who transplanted sustains (us) — motto of Connecticut

qui va là? \kē-vá-là\ [F] : who goes there?

quo•ad hoc \,kwō-,äd-'hōk\ [L] : as far as this : to this extent

quod erat de•mon•stran•dum \kwȯd-'er-,ät-,dem-ən-'strän-dəm\ [L] : which was to be proved

quod erat fa•ci•en•dum \-,fäk-ē-'en-,dùm\ [L] : which was to be done

quod sem•per, quod ubi•que, quod ab om•ni•bus \kwȯd-'sem-,per kwȯd-'ub-i-,kwā,kwȯd-äb-'ȯm-ni-,bùs\ [L] : what (has been held) always, everywhere, by everybody

quod vi•de \kwȯd-'wid-,e\ [L] : which see

quo•rum pars mag•na fui \'kwȯr-əm-,pärs-,mäg-nə-'fù-ē\ [L] : in which I played a great part

quos de•us vult per•de•re pri•us de•men•tat \kwōs-'de-ùs-,wùlt-'perd-ə-,re-,prē-ùs-dā-'men-,tät\ [L] : those whom a god wishes to destroy he first drives mad

quot ho•mi•nes, tot sen•ten•ti•ae \kwȯt-'hȯ-mə-,nās-,tȯt-sen-'ten-tē-,ī\ [L] : there are as many opinions as there are men

quo va•dis? \kwō-'väd-is, -'wäd-\ [L] : whither are you going?

rai•son d'état \re-zōⁿ-dā-tá\ [F] : reason of state

re•cu•ler pour mieux sau•ter \rə-kuĕ-lā-pür-myœ̃-sō-tā\ [F] : to draw back in order to make a better jump

reg•nat po•pu•lus \'reg-,nät-'pȯ-pə-,lùs\ [L] : the people rule — motto of Arkansas

re in•fec•ta \,rā-in-'fek-,tä\ [L] : the business being unfinished : without accomplishing one's purpose

re•li•gio lo•ci \re-,lig-ē-,ō-'lȯ-,kē\ [L] : religious sanctity of a place

rem acu te•ti•gis•ti \rem-'ä-,kü-,tet-ə-'gis-tē\ [L] : you have touched the point with a needle : you have hit the nail on the head

ré•pon•dez s'il vous plait \rā-pōⁿ-dā-sēl-vü-ple\ [F] : reply, if you please

re•qui•es•cat in pa•ce \,rek-wē-'es-,kät-in-'päk-,e, ,rā-kwē-'es-,kät-in-'päch-,ā\ [L] : may he (or she) rest in peace — used on tombstones

re•spi•ce fi•nem \,rā-spi-,ke-'fē-,nem\ [L] : look to the end : consider the outcome

re•sur•gam \re-'sùr-,gäm\ [L] : I shall rise again

re•te•nue \rət-nuĕ\ [F] : self-restraint : reserve

re•ve•nons à nos mou•tons \rəv-nōⁿ-ä-nō-mü-tōⁿ\ [F] : let us return to our sheep : let us get back to the subject

ruse de guerre \ruĕz-də-ger\ [F] : war stratagem

rus in ur•be \,rüs-in-'ùr-,be\ [L] : country in the city

sae•va in•dig•na•tio \,sī-wä-,in-dig-'nät-ē-ō\ [L] : fierce indignation

sal At•ti•cum \,sal-'at-i-kəm\ [L] : Attic salt : wit

salle à man•ger \sál-á-mäⁿ-zhā\ [F] : dining room

sa•lus po•pu•li su•pre•ma lex es•to \,säl-,üs-'pȯ-pə-,lē-sù-,prā-mə-,leks-'es-tō\ [L] : let the welfare of the people be the supreme law — motto of Missouri

sans doute \säⁿ-düt\ [F] : without doubt

sans gêne \säⁿ-zhen\ [F] : without embarrassment or constraint

sans peur et sans re•proche \säⁿ-pœr-ā-säⁿ-rə-'prȯsh\ [F] : without fear and without reproach

sans sou•ci \säⁿ-sü-sē\ [F] : without worry

sa•yo•na•ra \,sä-yə-'när-ə\ [Jp] : good-bye

sculp•sit \'skülp-,sit\ [L] : he (or she) carved it

scu•to bo•nae vo•lun•ta•tis tu•aeco•ro•nas•ti nos \'skü-tō-'bȯ-,nī-,vȯ-lùn-,tät-əs-,tù-,ī-,kȯr-ə-,näs-tē-'nȯs\ [L] : Thou hast crowned us with the shield of Thy good will — a motto on the Great Seal of Maryland

se•cun•dum ar•tem \se-,kùn-dəm-'är-,tem\ [L] : according to the art : according to the accepted practice of a profession ortarde

secundum na•tu•ram \-,nä-'tü-,räm\ [L] : according to nature : naturally

se de•fen•den•do\'sä-,dā-,fen-'den-dō\ [L] : in self-defense

se ha•bla es•pa•ñol \sā-,äb-lä-,äs-pä-'nʸȯl\ [Sp] : Spanish spoken

sem•per ea•dem \,sem-,per-'e-ä-,dem\ [L] : always the same (fem.) — motto of Queen Elizabeth I

sem•per fi•de•lis \,sem-pər-fi-'dā-lis\ [L] : always faithful — motto of the U.S. Marine Corps

sem•per idem \,sem-,per-'ē-,dem\ [L] : always the same (masc.)

sem•per pa•ra•tus \,sem-pər-pä-'rät-əs\ [L] : always prepared — motto of the U.S. Coast Guard

se non è ve•ro, è ben tro•va•to \sā-,nōn-e-'vā-rō-e-,ben-trō-'vä-tō\ [It] : even if it is not true, it is well conceived

sic itur ad as•tra \sēk-'i-,tùr-,äd-'äs-,trə\ [L] : thus one goes to the stars : such is the way to immortality

sic sem•per ty•ran•nis \,sik-,sem-pər-ti-'ran-is\ [L] : thus ever to tyrants — motto of Virginia

sic trans•it glo•ria mun•di \sēk-'trän-sət-,glōr-ē-ä-'mún-dē\ [L] : so passes away the glory of the world

si jeu•nesse sa•vait, si vieil•lesse pou•vait! \sē-'zhœ-nes-'sá-ve sē-'vye-yes-'pü-ve\ [F] : if youth only knew, if age only could!

si•lent le•ges in•ter ar•ma \,sil-,ent-'lā-,gäs-,int-ər-'är-mä\ [L] : the laws are silent in the midst of arms

s'il vous plait \sēl-vü-ple\ [F] : if you please

si•mi•lia si•mi•li•bus cu•ran•tur \sim-,il-ē-ä-sim-'il-ə-,bùs-kü-'rän-,tùr\ [L] : like is cured by like

si•mi•lis si•mi•ligau•det \'sim-ə-lis-'sim-ə-lē-'gaù-,det\ [L] : like takes pleasure in like

si mo•nu•men•tum re•qui•ris,cir•cum•spi•ce \,sē-,mȯ-nə-,ment-əm-re-'kwē-rəs kir-'kùm-spi-ke\ [L] : if you seek his monument, look around — epitaph of Sir Christopher Wren in St. Paul's, London, of which he was architect

si quae•ris pen•in•su•lam amoe•nam,cir•cum•spi•ce \sē-,kwī-rəs-pä-,nin-sə-,läm-ə-'mȯi-,näm kir-'kùm-spi-ke\ [L] : if you seek a beautiful peninsula, look around — motto of Michigan

sis•te vi•a•tor \,sis-te-wē-'ä-,tȯr\ [L] : stop, traveler — used on Roman roadside tombs

si vis pa·cem, pa·ra bel·lum \sē-,wēs-'pä-,kem ,pä-rä-'bel-,úm\ [L] : if you wish peace, prepare for war

sol·vi·tur am·bu·lan·do \'sól-wi-,túr-,äm-bə-'län-dō\ [L] : it is solved by walking : the problem is solved by a practical experiment

splen·di·de men·dax\'splen-də-,dā-'men-,däks\ [L] : nobly untruthful

spo·lia opi·ma \'spò-lē-ə-ō-'pē-mə\ [L] : rich spoils : the arms taken by the victorious from the vanquished-general

sta·tus in quo \'stät-əs-,in-'kwō\ [L] : state in which : the existing state

status quo an·te bel·lum \-,kwō-,änt-ə-'bel-úm\ [L] : the state existing before the war

sua·vi·ter in mo·do, for·ti·ter in re \'swä-wə-,ter-in-'mód-ō 'fórt-ə-,ter-in-'rā\ [L] : gently in manner, strongly in deed

sub ver·bo \sùb-'wer-bō\ *or* **sub vo·ce** \sùb-'wō-ke\ [L] : under the word — introducing a cross-reference in a dictionary or index

sunt la·cri·mae re·rum \sùnt-,läk-ri-,mī-'rā-rùm\ [L] : there are tears for things

suo ju·re \,sú-ō-'yúr-e\ [L] : in his (or her) own right

suo lo·co \-'lō-kō\ [L] : in its proper place

suo Mar·te \-'mär-te\ [L] : by one's own exertions

su·um cui·que \,sú-əm-'kwik-we\ [L] : to each his own

tant mieux \täⁿ-myœ\ [F] : so much the better

tant pis \-'pē\ [F] : so much the worse

tem·po·ra mu·tan·tur, nos et mu·ta·mur inil·lis \,tem-pə-rä-mü-'tän-,túr ,nōs,et-mü-,täm-ər-in-'il-,ēs\ [L] : the times are changing, and we are changing with them

tem·pus edax re·rum \'tem-pùs,ed-,äks-'rā-rùm\ [L] : time, that devours all things

tem·pus fu·git \,tem-pəs-'fyü-jət, -'fü-git\ [L] : time flies

ti·meo Da·na·os et do·na fe·ren·tes \,tim-ē-,ō-'dän-ä-,ōs,-et,dō-nä-fe-'ren,-tās\ [L] : I fear the Greeks even when they bring gifts

to·ti·dem ver·bis \,tót-ə-,dem-'wer-,bēs\ [L] : in so many words

to·tis vi·ri·bus \,tō-,tēs-'wē-ri-,bùs\ [L] : with all one's might

to·to cae·lo \,tō-tō-'kī-lō\ *or* **toto coe·lo** \-'kói-lō\ [L] : by the whole extent of the heavens : diametrically

tou·jours per·drix \tü-zhür-per-drē\ [F] : always partridge : too much of a good thing

tour d'ho·ri·zon \tür-dò-rē-zōⁿ\ [F] : circuit of the horizon : general survey

tous frais faits \tü-fre-fe\ [F] : all expenses defrayed

tout à fait \tü-tà-fe\ [F] : altogether : quite

tout au con·traire \tü-tō-kōⁿ-trer\ [F] : quite the contrary

tout à vous \tü-tà-vü\ [F] : wholly yours : at your service

tout bien ou rien \tü-'byaⁿ-nü-'ryaⁿ\ [F] : everything well (done) or nothing (attempted)

tout com·pren·dre c'est tout par·don·ner \'tü-kōⁿ-prän-drə se-'tü-pár-dò-nä\ [F] : to understand all is to forgive all

tout court \tü-kür\ [F] : quite short : simply; *also* : brusquely

tout de même \tüt-mem\ [F] : all the same : nevertheless

tout de suite \tüt-swēt\ [F] : immediately; *also* : all at once : consecutively

tout en·sem·ble \tü-täⁿ-säⁿblə\ [F] : all together : general effect

tout est per·du fors l'hon·neur \tü-te-per-düē-fòr-lò-nœr\ *or* **tout est perdu hors l'honneur** \-düē-òr-\ [F] : all is lost save honor

tout le monde \tül-mōⁿd\ [F] : all the world : everybody

tranche de vie \träⁿsh-də-'vē\ [F] : slice of life

trist·esse \trē-'stes\ [F] : melancholy

tru·di·tur di·es die \'trüd-ə-,túr,-di-,äs-'di-,ä\ [L] : day is pushed forth by day : one day hurries on another

tu·e·bor \tù-'ā-,bór\ [L] : I will defend — a motto on the Great Seal of Michigan

ua mau ke ea o ka ai·na i ka po·no \,ù-ä-'mä-ù-ke-'e-ä-ō-kä-'ä-ē-nä-,ē-kä-'pō-nō\ [Hawaiian] : the life of the land is established in righteousness — motto of Hawaii

ue·ber·mensch \'ūē-bər-,mensh\ [G] : superman

ul·ti·ma ra·tio re·gum \'úl-ti-mä-,rät-ē-ō-'rā-gùm\ [L] : the final argument of kings, i.e., war

und so wei·ter \únt-zō-'vī-tər\ [G] : and so on

uno ani·mo \,ü-nō-'än-ə-,mō\ [L] : with one mind : unanimously

ur·bi et or·bi \,úr-bē-,et-'òr-bē\ [L] : to the city (Rome) and the world

uti·le dul·ci \,üt-^əl-e-'dúl-,kē\ [L] : the useful with the agreeable

ut in·fra \út-'in-frä\ [L] : as below

ut su·pra \út-'sü-prä\ [L] : as above

va·de re·tro me, Sa·ta·na \,wä-de-'rā-trō-,mä-'sä-tə-,nä\ [L] : get thee behind me, Satan

vae vic·tis \wī-'wik-,tēs\ [L] : woe to the vanquished

va·ria lec·tio \,wär-ē-ä-'lek-tē-,ō\ *pl* **va·ri·ae lec·ti·o·nes** \,wär-ē-,ī-,lek-tē-'ō-,nās\ [L] : variant reading

va·ri·um et mu·ta·bi·le sem·perfe·mi·na \,wär-ē-,et-,mü-'tä-bə-le-,sem-,per-'fä-mə-nä\ [L] : woman is ever a fickle and changeable thing

ve·di Na·po·li e poi mo·ri \,vä-dē-'nä-pō-lē-ā-,pò-ē-'mò-rē\ [It] : see Naples, and then die

ve·ni, vi·di, vi·ci \,wä-nē-,wēd-ē-'wē-kē\ [L] : I came, I saw, I conquered

ven·tre à terre \väⁿ-trà-ter\ [F] : belly to the ground : at very great speed

ver·ba·tim ac lit·te·ra·tim \wer-'bä-tim,-äk,-lit-ə-'rā-tim\ [L] : word for word and letter for letter

ver·bum sat sa·pi·en·ti est \,wer-bùm-'sät-,säp-ē-'ent-ē-,est\ [L] : a word to the wise is sufficient

vin·cit om·nia ve·ri·tas \,wing-ket-'òm-nē-ä-'wā-rə-,täs\ [L] : truth conquers all things

vin·cu·lum ma·tri·mo·nii \,wing-kə-lùm,-mä-trə-'mō-nē-,ē\ [L] : bond of marriage

vir·gi·ni·bus pu·e·ris·que \wir-'gin-ə-bùs,-pù-ə-'rēs-kwe\ [L] : for girls and boys

vir·tu·te et ar·mis \wir-'tü-te-,et-'är-mēs\ [L] : by valor and arms — motto of Mississippi

vis me·di·ca·trixna·tu·rae \'wēs-,med-i-'kä-triks-nä-'tü-,rī\ [L] : the healing power of nature

vive la dif·fé·rence \vēv(-ə)-lä-dē-fā-räⁿs\ [F] : long live the difference (between the sexes)

vive la reine \vēv-là-ren\ [F] : long live the queen

vive le roi \vēv-lə-rwä\ [F] : long live the king

vix·e·re for·tes an·te Aga·mem·no·na \wik,-sä-re-'fòr-,tās,-änt-,äg-ə-'mem-nə-,nä\ [L] : brave men lived before Agamemnon

vogue la ga·lère \vòg-là-gà-ler\ [F] : let the galley be kept rowing : keep on, whatever may happen

voi·là \vwà-là\ [F] : there you are : there you see (it)

voi·là tout \vwä-là-tü\ [F] : that's all

vox et prae·te·rea ni·hil \'wōks-et-prī-,ter-e-ä-'ni-,hil\ [L] : voice and nothing more

vox po·pu·li vox Dei \wōks-'pò-pə-,lē-,wōks-'de-ē\ [L] : the voice of the people is the voice of God

Wan·der·jahr \'vän-dər-,yär\ [G] : year of wandering

wie geht's? \vē-'gäts\ [G] : how goes it?

Common English Given Names

The following vocabulary presents given names that are most frequent in English use. The list is not exhaustive of either the names themselves or the variant spellings of those names which are entered. Compound or double names and surnames used as given names are not entered except in cases where long-continued or common use gives them an independent character.

Besides the pronunciations of the names, the list usually provides at least one of the following kinds of information at each entry: (1) etymology, indicating the language source but not the original form of the name, and (2) meaning where known or ascertainable with reasonable certainty.

NAMES OF MEN

Aar•on \'ar-rən, 'er-\ [Heb]
Abra•ham \'ā-brə-,ham\ [Heb]
Ad•am \'ad-əm\ [Heb] man
Ad•di•son \'ad-ə-sən\ [fr. a surname]
Adolph \'ad-,älf, 'ā-,dälf\ [Gmc] noble wolf, *i.e.,* noble hero
Adri•an \'ā-drē-ən\ [L] of Hadria, ancient town in central Italy
Al \al\ *dim of* ALAN, ALBERT, *etc.*
Al•an \'al-ən\ [Celt]
Al•bert \'al-bərt\ [Gmc] illustrious through nobility
Al•den \'ȯl-dən\ [OE] old friend
Al•ex \'al-iks\ *or* **Al•ec** \'al-ik\ *dim of* ALEXANDER
Al•ex•an•der \,al-ig-'zan-dər\ [Gk] a defender of men
Al•fred \'al-frəd, -fərd\ [OE] elf counsel, *i.e.,* good counsel
Al•len *or* **Al•lan** *or* **Al•lyn** \'al-ən\ *var of* ALAN
Al•ton \'ȯlt-ᵊn, 'alt-\ [prob. fr. a surname]
Al•va *or* **Al•vah** \'al-və\ [Heb]
Al•vin \'al-vən\ [Gmc]
Amos \'ā-məs\ [Heb]
An•dre \'än-(,)drā\ [F] *var of* ANDREW
An•drew \'an-(,)drü\ [Gk] manly
An•dy \'an-dē\ *dim of* ANDREW
An•ge•lo \'an-jə-,lō\ [It, fr. Gk] angel, messenger
An•gus \'ang-gəs\ [Celt]
An•tho•ny \'an(t)-thə-nē, *chiefly Brit* 'an-tə-\ [L]
An•ton \'ant-ᵊn, 'an-,tän\ [G & Slav] *var of* ANTHONY
An•to•nio \an-'tō-nē-,ō\ [It] *var of* ANTHONY
Ar•chi•bald \'är-chə-,bȯld, -bəld\ [Gmc]
Ar•chie \'är-chē\ *dim of* ARCHIBALD
Ar•den \'ärd-ᵊn\ [prob. fr. a surname]
Ar•len *or* **Ar•lin** \'är-lən\ [prob. fr. a surname]
Ar•lo \'är-(,)lō\
Ar•mand \'är-,mänd, -mənd\ [F] *var of* HERMAN
Arne \'ärn\ [Scand] eagle
Ar•nold \'ärn-ᵊld\ [Gmc] power of an eagle
Art \'ärt\ *dim of* ARTHUR
Ar•thur \'är-thər\ [prob.L]

Au•brey \'ȯ-brē\ [Gmc] elf ruler
Au•gust \'ȯ-gəst\ [L] August, majestic
Aus•tin \'ȯs-tən, 'äs-\ *alter of* Augustine
Bai•ley \'bā-lē\ [fr. a surname]
Bar•clay \'bär-klē\ [fr. a surname]
Bar•net *or* **Bar•nett** \bär-'net\ [fr. a surname]
Bar•ney \'bär-nē\ *dim of* BERNARD
Bar•rett \'bar-ət\ [fr. a surname]
Bar•ry *or* **Bar•rie** \'bar-ē\ [Ir]
Bart \'bärt\ *dim of* Bartholomew
Bar•ton \'bärt-ᵊn\ [fr. a surname]
Ba•sil \'baz-əl, 'bäs-, 'bās-, 'bāz-\ [Gk] kingly, royal
Ben \'ben\ *or* **Ben•nie** *or* **Ben•ny** \'ben-ē\ *dim of* BENJAMIN
Ben•e•dict \'ben-ə-,dikt\ [L] blessed
Ben•ja•min \'benj-(ə-)mən\ [Heb] son of the right hand
Ben•nett \'ben-ət\ [OF] *var of* BENEDICT
Ben•ton \'bent-ᵊn\ [fr. a surname]
Ber•nard \'bər-nərd, (,)bər-'närd\ *or* **Bern•hard** \'bərn-,härd\ [Gmc] bold as a bear
Ber•nie \'bər-nē\ *dim of* BERNARD
Bert *or* **Burt** \'bərt\ *dim of* BERTRAM, ALBERT, *etc.*
Ber•tram \'bər-trəm\ [Gmc] bright raven
Bill \'bil\ *or* **Bil•ly** *or* **Bil•lie** \'bil-ē\ *dim of* WILLIAM
Blaine \'blān\ [fr. a surname]
Blair \'bla(ə)r, 'ble(ə)r\ [fr. a surname]
Bob•by \'bäb-ē\ *or* **Bob** \'bäb\ *dim of* ROBERT
Bo•ris \'bōr-əs, 'bȯr-, 'bär-\ [Russ]
Boyd \'bȯid\ [fr. a surname]
Brad•ford \'brad-fərd\ [fr. a surname]
Brad•ley \'brad-lē\ [fr. a surname]
Bran•don \'bran-dən\ [fr. a surname]
Bren•dan \'bren-dən\ [Celt]
Brent \'brent\ [fr. a surname]
Brett *or* **Bret** \'bret\ [IrGael]
Bri•an *or* **Bry•an** \'brī-ən\ [Celt]
Brooks \'brüks\ [fr. a surname]
Bruce \'brüs\ [fr. a surname]
Bru•no \'brü-(,)nō\ [It, fr. Gmc] brown
Bryce *or* **Brice** \'brīs\ [fr. a surname]
Bud•dy \'bəd-ē\ [prob. alter. of *brother*]

Bu·ford \'byü-fərd\ [fr. a surname]
Burke \'bərk\ [fr. a surname]
Bur·ton \'bərt-ᵊn\ [fr. a surname]
By·ron \'bī-rən\ [fr. a surname]
Cal·vin \'kal-vən\ [fr. a surname]
Cam·er·on \'kam-(ə-)rən\ [fr. a surname]
Carl \'kär(-ə)l\ *var of* KARL
Car·los \'kär-ləs, -,lōs\ [Sp] *var of* CHARLES
Carl·ton *or* **Carle·ton** \'kär(-ə)l-tən, 'kärlt-ᵊn\ [fr. a surname]
Car·lyle \kär-'lī(ə)l, 'kär-,\ [fr. a surname]
Car·men \'kär-mən\ [Sp, fr. L] song
Car·roll \'kar-əl\ [fr. a surname]
Car·son \'kärs-ᵊn\ [fr. a surname]
Car·ter \'kärt-ər\ [fr. a surname]
Cary *or* **Car·ey** \'ka(ə)r-ē, 'ke(ə)r-ē\ [fr. a surname]
Ce·cil \'sē-səl, 'ses-əl\ [L]
Chad \'chad\ [Gmc]
Charles \'chär(-ə)lz\ [Gmc] man of the common people
Ches·ter \'ches-tər\ [fr. a surname]
Chris \'kris\ *dim of* CHRISTOPHER
Chris·tian \'kris(h)-chən\ [Gk] Christian (the believer)
Chris·to·pher \'kris-tə-fər\ [Gk] Christ bearer
Clar·ence \'klar-ən(t)s\ [fr. the English dukedom]
Clark *or* **Clarke** \'klärk\ [fr. a surname]
Claude *or* **Claud** \'klȯd\ [L]
Clay \'klā\ *dim of* CLAYTON
Clay·ton \'klāt-ᵊn\ [fr. a surname]
Clem \'klem\ *dim of* CLEMENT
Clem·ent \'klem-ənt\ [L] mild, merciful
Clif·ford \'klif-ərd\ [fr. a surname]
Clif·ton \'klif-tən\ [fr. a surname]
Clint \'klint\ *dim of* CLINTON
Clin·ton \'klint-ᵊn\ [fr. a surname]
Clyde \'klīd\ [fr. a surname]
Cole \'kōl\ [fr. a surname]
Co·lin \'käl-ən, 'kō-lən\ *or* **Col·lin** \'käl-ən\ *dim of* NICHOLAS
Con·rad \'kän-,rad, -rəd\ [Gmc] bold counsel
Con·stan·tine \'kän(t)-stən-,tēn, -,tīn\ [L]
Cor·ey \'kȯr-ē\ [fr. a surname]
Cor·ne·lius \kȯr-'nēl-yəs\ [L]
Craig \'krāg\ [fr. a surname]
Cur·tis \'kərt-əs\ [OF] courteous
Cyr·il \'sir-əl\ [Gk] lordly
Cy·rus \'sī-rəs\ [OPer]
Dale \'dā(ə)l\ [fr. a surname]
Dal·las \'dal-əs\ [fr. a surname]
Dal·ton \'dȯlt-ᵊn\ [fr. a surname]
Dan \'dan\ [Heb] judge
Da·na \'dā-nə\ [fr. a surname]
Dan·iel \'dan-yəl *also* 'dan-ᵊl\ [Heb] God has judged
Dan·ny \'dan-ē\ *dim of* DANIEL
Dar·old \'dar-əld\ *perh alter of* DARRELL
Dar·rell *or* **Dar·rel** *or* **Dar·ryl** *or* **Dar·yl** \'dar-əl\ [fr. a surname]
Dar·win \'där-wən\ [fr. a surname]
Dave \'dāv\ *dim of* DAVID
Da·vid \'dā-vəd\ [Heb] beloved
Da·vis \'dā-vəs\ [fr. a surname]
Dean *or* **Deane** \'dēn\ [fr. a surname]
Del·a·no \'del-ə-,nō\ [fr. a surname]
Del·bert \'del-bərt\ *dim of* Adalbert
Del·mar \'del-mər, -,mär\ *or* **Del·mer** \-mər\ [fr. a surname]
Den·nis *or* **Den·is** \'den-əs\ [OF, fr. Gk] belonging to Dionysus, god of wine
Den·ny \'den-ē\ *dim of* DENNIS
Den·ton \'dent-ᵊn\ [fr. a surname]
Der·ek \'der-ik\ [Middle Dutch, fr. Gmc] ruler of the people
Dew·ey \'d(y)ü-ē\ [fr. a surname]
De·witt \di-'wit\ [fr. a surname]
Dex·ter \'dek-stər\ [L] on the right hand, fortunate
Dick \'dik\ *dim of* RICHARD

Dirk \'dərk\ [Dutch] *var of* DEREK
Dom·i·nic *or* **Dom·i·nick** \'däm-ə-(,)nik\ [L] belonging to the Lord
Don *or* **Donn** \'dän\ *dim of* DONALD
Don·al \'dän-ᵊl\ *var of* DONALD
Don·ald \'dän-ᵊld\ [ScGael] world ruler
Don·nie \'dän-ē\ *dim of* DON
Don·o·van \'dän-ə-vən, 'dən-\ [fr. a surname]
Doug \'dəg\ *dim of* DOUGLAS
Doug·las *or* **Doug·lass** \'dəg-ləs\ [fr. a surname]
Duane \du̇-'ān, 'dwān\ [fr. a surname]
Dud·ley \'dəd-lē\ [fr. a surname]
Dun·can \'dəng-kən\ [ScGael] brown head
Dur·ward \'dər-wərd\ [fr. a surname]
Dwayne *or* **Dwaine** \'dwān\ [fr. a surname]
Dwight \'dwīt\ [fr. a surname]
Dy·lan \'dil-ən\ [W]
Earl *or* **Earle** \'ər(-ə)l\ [OE] warrior, noble
Ed \'ed\ *dim of* EDWARD, EDGAR, etc.
Ed·die *or* **Ed·dy** \'ed-ē\ *dim of* ED
Ed·gar \'ed-gər\ [OE] spear of wealth
Ed·mund *or* **Ed·mond** \'ed-mənd\ [OE] protector of wealth
Ed·son \'ed-sən\ [fr. a surname]
Ed·ward \'ed-wərd\ [OE] guardian of wealth
Ed·win \'ed-wən\ [OE] friend of wealth
El·bert \'el-bərt\ *var of* ALBERT
Eli \'ē-,lī\ [Heb] high
E·li·as \i-'lī-əs\ [Gk] *var of* Elijah
El·liott *or* **El·liot** *or* **El·iot** \'el-ē-ət, 'el-yət\ [fr. a surname]
El·lis \'el-əs\ *var of* ELIAS
Ells·worth \'elz-(,)wərth\ [fr. a surname]
El·mer \'el-mər\ [fr. a surname]
El·mo \'el-(,)mō\ [It, fr. Gk] lovable
El·ton \'elt-ᵊn\ [fr. a surname]
El·vin \'el-vən\ [fr. a surname]
El·wood *or* **Ell·wood** \'el-,wu̇d\ [fr. a surname]
Em·man·u·el *or* **Eman·u·el** \i-'man-yə(-wə)l\ [Heb] God with us
Em·er·son \'em-ər-sən\ [fr. a surname]
Emil \'ā-məl\ *or* **Emile** \ā-'mē(ə)l\ [L]
Em·mett \'em-ət\ [fr. a surname]
Em·o·ry *or* **Em·ery** \'em-(ə-)rē\ [Gmc]
Er·ic *or* **Er·ich** *or* **Er·ik** \'er-ik\ [Scand]
Er·nest *or* **Ear·nest** \'ər-nəst\ [G] earnestness
Er·nie \'ər-nē\ *dim of* ERNEST
Ernst \'ərn(t)st, 'e(ə)rn(t)st\ [G] *var of* ERNEST
Er·rol \'er-əl\ [prob. fr. a surname]
Ethan \'ē-thən\ [Heb] strength
Eu·gene \yu̇-'jēn, 'yü-,\ [Gk] wellborn
Ev·an \'ev-ən\ [W] *var of* JOHN
Ev·er·ett \'ev-(ə-)rət\ [fr. a surname]
Fe·lix \'fē-liks\ [L] happy, prosperous
Fer·di·nand \'fərd-ᵊn-,and\ [Gmc]
Fer·nan·do \fər-'nan-(,)dō\ [Sp] *var of* FERDINAND
Fletch·er \'flech-ər\ [fr. a surname]
Floyd \'flȯid\ [fr. a surname]
For·rest *or* **For·est** \'fȯr-əst, 'fär-\ [fr. a surname]
Fos·ter \'fȯs-tər, 'fäs-\ [fr. a surname]
Fran·cis \'fran(t)-səs\ [OIt & OF] Frenchman
Fran·cis·co \fran-'sis-(,)kō\ [Sp] *var of* FRANCIS
Frank \'frangk\ [Gmc] freeman, Frank
Frank·lin *or* **Frank·lyn** \'frang-klən\ [fr. a surname]
Fred \'fred\ *dim of* FREDERICK, ALFRED
Fred·die \'fred-ē\ *dim of* FREDERICK
Fred·er·ick *or* **Fred·er·ic** *or* **Fred·rick** *or* **Fred·ric** \'fred-(ə-)rik\ [Gmc] peaceful ruler
Free·man \'frē-mən\ [fr. a surname]
Fritz \'frits\ [G] *dim of* Friedrich
Ga·bri·el \'gā-brē-əl\ [Heb] man of God
Gar·land \'gär-lənd\ [fr. a surname]
Gar·rett \'gar-ət\ [fr. a surname]
Garth \'gärth\ [fr. a surname]

Gary \\'gar-ē, 'ger-ē\\ or Gar•ry \\'gar-\\ [prob. fr. a sur-
name]
Gay•lord \\'gā-‚lò(ə)rd\\ [fr. a surname]
Gene \\'jēn\\ dim of EUGENE
Geof•frey \\'jef-rē\\ [OF, fr. Gmc]
George \\'jò(ə)rj\\ [Gk] of or relating to a farmer
Ger•ald \\'jer-əld\\ [Gmc] spear dominion
Ge•rard \\jə-'rärd, chiefly Brit 'jer-‚ärd, -ərd\\ or Ger-
hard \\'ge(ə)r-‚härd\\ [Gmc] strong with the spear
Ger•ry \\'jer-ē\\ var of JERRY
Gil•bert \\'gil-bərt\\ [Gmc] prob illustrious through hos-
tages
Giles \\'jī(ə)lz\\ [OF, fr. LL]
Glenn or Glen \\'glen\\ [fr. a surname]
Gor•don \\'gòrd-ᵊn\\ [fr. a surname]
Gra•ham \\'grā-əm, 'gra(-ə)m\\ [fr. a surname]
Grant \\'grant\\ [fr. a surname]
Gran•ville \\'gran-‚vil\\ [fr. a surname]
Gray \\'grā\\ [fr. a surname]
Gregg or Greg \\'greg\\ dim of GREGORY
Greg•o•ry \\'greg-(ə-)rē\\ [LGk] vigilant
Gro•ver \\'grō-vər\\ [fr. a surname]
Gus \\'gəs\\ dim of Gustav or Augustus
Guy \\'gī\\ [OF, fr. Gmc]
Hal \\'hal\\ dim of HENRY
Hall \\'hòl\\ [fr. a surname]
Ham•il•ton \\'ham-əl-tən, -əlt-ᵊn\\ [fr. a surname]
Hans \\'hanz, 'hän(t)s\\ [G] dim of Johannes
Har•lan \\'här-lən\\ or Har•land \\-lənd\\ [fr. a surname]
Har•ley \\'här-lē\\ [fr. a surname]
Har•low \\'här-‚lō\\ [fr. a surname]
Har•mon \\'här-mən\\ [fr. a surname]
Har•old \\'har-əld\\ [OE] army dominion
Har•ris \\'har-əs\\ [fr. a surname]
Har•ri•son \\'har-ə-sən\\ [fr. a surname]
Har•ry \\'har-ē\\ dim of HENRY
Har•vey \\'här-vē\\ [fr. a surname]
Hec•tor \\'hek-tər\\ [Gk] holding fast
Hel•mut \\'hel-mət, -‚müt\\ [G] helmet courage
Hen•ry \\'hen-rē\\ [Gmc] ruler of the home
Her•bert \\'hər-bərt\\ [Gmc] illustrious by reason of an
army
Her•man or Her•mann \\'hər-mən\\ [Gmc] warrior
Her•schel or Her•shel \\'hər-shəl\\ [fr. a surname]
Hi•ram \\'hī-rəm\\ [Phoenician]
Ho•bart \\'hō-bərt, -‚bärt\\ [fr. a surname]
Hol•lis \\'häl-əs\\ [fr. a surname]
Ho•mer \\'hō-mər\\ [Gk]
Hor•ace \\'hòr-əs, 'här-\\ [L]
How•ard \\'haù(-ə)rd\\ [fr. a surname]
How•ell \\'haù(-ə)l\\ [W]
Hu•bert \\'hyü-bərt\\ [Gmc] bright in spirit
Hud•son \\'həd-sən\\ [fr. a surname]
Hugh \\'hyü\\ or Hu•go \\'hyü-(‚)gō\\ [Gmc] prob mind,
spirit
Ian \\'ē-ən\\ [ScGael] var of JOHN
Ira \\'ī-rə\\ [Heb]
Ir•ving \\'ər-ving\\ or Ir•vin \\-vən\\ [fr. a surname]
Ir•win \\'ər-wən\\ [fr. a surname]
Isaac \\'ī-zik, -zək\\ [Heb] he laughs
Ivan \\'ī-vən\\ [Russ] var of JOHN
Jack \\'jak\\ dim of JOHN
Jack•son \\'jak-sən\\ [fr. a surname]
Ja•cob \\'jā-kəb, -‚kəp\\ [Heb] one who supplants
Jacques or Jacque \\'zhäk\\ [F] var of JAMES
Jake \\'jāk\\ dim of JACOB
James \\'jāmz\\ [OF, fr. LL Jacobus] var of JACOB
Ja•mie \\'jā-mē\\ dim of JAMES
Jan \\'jan\\ [Dutch & LG] var of JOHN
Jar•ed \\'jar-əd, 'jer-\\ [Heb] descent
Ja•son \\'jās-ᵊn\\ [Gk]
Jay \\'jā\\ [prob. fr. a surname]
Jed \\'jed\\ dim of Jedidiah
Jef•frey or Jeff•ery or Jef•fry \\'jef-(ə-)rē\\ var of GEOF-
FREY

Jer•ald or Jer•old or Jer•rold \\'jer-əld\\ var of GERALD
Jer•e•my \\'jer-ə-mē\\ or Jer•e•mi•ah \\‚jer-ə-'mī-ə\\ [Heb]
prob Yahweh exalts
Je•rome \\jə-'rōm, Brit also 'jer-əm\\ [Gk] bearing a holy
name
Jer•ry or Jere \\'jer-ē\\ dim of GERALD
Jes•se \\'jes-ē\\ [Heb]
Jim \\'jim\\ or Jim•my or Jim•mie \\'jim-ē\\ dim of JAMES
Jo•dy \\'jō-dē\\ perh alter of JOSEPH
Joe \\'jō\\ dim of JOSEPH
Jo•el \\'jō-əl\\ [Heb] Yahweh is God
John \\'jän\\ [Heb] Yahweh is gracious
Jon \\'jän\\ var of JOHN
Jo•nah \\'jō-nə\\ [Heb]
Jon•a•than \\'jän-ə-thən\\ [Heb] Yahweh has given
Jor•dan \\'jòrd-ᵊn\\ [fr. a surname]
Jo•seph or Jo•sef \\'jō-zəf also -səf\\ [Heb] he shall add
Josh•u•a \\'jäsh-(ə-)wə\\ [Heb] Yahweh saves
Judd \\'jəd\\ [fr. a surname]
Jud•son \\'jəd-sən\\ [fr. a surname]
Jules \\'jülz\\ [F] var of JULIUS
Ju•lian or Ju•lien \\'jül-yən\\ [L] sprung from or belong-
ing to Julius
Ju•lius \\'jül-yəs\\ or Ju•lio \\-(‚)yō\\ [L]
Jus•tin \\'jəs-tən\\ or Jus•tus \\-təs\\ [L] just
Karl \\'kär(-ə)l\\ [G & Scand] var of CHARLES
Keith \\'kēth\\ [fr. a surname]
Kel•ly \\'kel-ē\\ [fr. a surname]
Ken \\'ken\\ dim of KENNETH
Ken•dall \\'ken-dᵊl\\ [fr. a surname]
Ken•neth \\'ken-əth\\ [ScGael]
Kent \\'kent\\ [prob. fr. a surname]
Ken•ton \\'kent-ᵊn\\ [fr. a surname]
Ker•mit \\'kər-mət\\ [prob. fr. a surname]
Ker•ry \\'ker-ē\\ [prob. fr. the county of Ireland]
Kev•in \\'kev-ən\\ [OIr]
Kir•by \\'kər-bē\\ [fr. a surname]
Kirk \\'kərk\\ [fr. a surname]
Klaus \\'klaùs, 'klòs\\ [G] dim of Nikolaus
Kurt \\'kərt, 'kù(ə)rt\\ [G] dim of CONRAD
Kyle \\'kī(ə)l\\ [Celt]
La•mar \\lə-'mär\\ [fr. a surname]
Lance \\'lan(t)s\\ dim of Lancelot
Lane \\'lān\\ [fr. a surname]
Lan•ny \\'lan-ē\\ prob dim of LAWRENCE
Lar•ry \\'lar-ē\\ dim of LAWRENCE
Lars \\'lärz\\ [Sw] var of LAWRENCE
Law•rence or Lau•rence \\'lòr-ən(t)s, 'lär-\\ [L] of Lau-
rentum, ancient city in central Italy
Lee or Leigh \\'lē\\ [fr. a surname]
Leigh•ton or Lay•ton \\'lāt-ᵊn\\ [fr. a surname]
Le•land \\'lē-lənd\\ [fr. a surname]
Len \\'len\\ dim of LEONARD
Leo \\'le-(‚)ō\\ [L] lion
Le•on \\'lē-‚än, -ən\\ [Sp] var of LEO
Leon•ard \\'len-ərd\\ [G] strong or brave as a lion
Le•roy \\li-'ròi, 'lē-‚\\ [OF] royal
Les•lie \\'les-lē, 'lez-\\ [fr. a surname]
Les•ter \\'les-tər\\ [fr. a surname]
Lew•is \\'lü-əs\\ var of LOUIS
Li•am \\'lē-əm\\ [Ir]
Lin•coln \\'ling-kən\\ [fr. a surname]
Li•o•nel \\'lī-ən-ᵊl, -ə-‚nel\\ [OF] young lion
Lloyd or Loyd \\'lòid\\ [W] gray
Lo•gan \\'lō-gən\\ [fr. a surname]
Lon \\'län\\ dim of Alonzo
Lon•nie or Lon•ny \\'län-ē\\ dim of LON
Lo•ren \\'lōr-ən, 'lòr-\\ dim of Lorenzo
Lou•ie \\'lü-ē\\ var of LOUIS
Lou•is or Lu•is \\'lü-əs, 'lü-ē\\ [Gmc] famous warrior
Low•ell \\'lō-əl\\ [fr. a surname]
Lu•cian \\'lü-shən\\ [Gk]
Lud•wig \\'ləd-(‚)wig, 'lüd-\\ [G] var of LOUIS
Luke \\'lük\\ [Gk] prob dim of Lucius
Lu•ther \\'lü-thər\\ [fr. a surname]

Lyle \'lī(ə)l\ [fr. a surname]
Ly·man \'lī-mən\ [fr. a surname]
Lynn \'lin\ [fr. a surname]
Mack *or* **Mac** \'mak\ [fr. surnames beginning with *Mc* or *Mac*, fr. Gael *mac* son]
Mal·colm \'mal-kəm\ [ScGael] servant of (St.) Columba
Man·fred \'man-frəd\ [Gmc] peace among men
Man·u·el \'man-yə(-wə)l\ [Sp & Pg] *var of* EMMANUEL
Mar·cus \'mär-kəs\ [L]
Ma·rio \'mär-ē-ˌō\ [It] *var of* Marius
Mar·i·on \'mer-ē-ən, 'mar-\ [fr. a surname]
Mark *or* **Marc** \'märk\ *var of* MARCUS
Mar·lin \'mär-lən\ [prob. fr. a surname]
Mar·shall *or* **Mar·shal** \'mär-shəl\ [fr. a surname]
Mar·tin \'märt-ᵊn\ [LL] of Mars
Mar·vin \'mär-vən\ [prob. fr. a surname]
Ma·son \'mās-ᵊn\ [fr. a surname]
Matt \'mat\ *dim of* MATTHEW
Mat·thew \'math-(ˌ)yü *also* 'math-(ˌ)ü\ [Heb] gift of Yahweh
Mau·rice \'mȯr-əs, 'mär-; mȯ-'rēs\ [LL] *prob* Moorish
Max \'maks\ *dim of* Maximilian
Max·well \'mak-ˌswel, -swəl\ [fr. a surname]
May·nard \'mā-nərd\ [Gmc] bold in strength
Mel·ville \'mel-ˌvil\ [fr. a surname]
Mel·vin *or* **Mel·vyn** \'mel-vən\ [prob. fr. a surname]
Mer·e·dith \'mer-əd-əth\ [W]
Merle \'mər(-ə)l\ [F] blackbird
Mer·lin *or* **Mer·lyn** \'mər-lən\ [Celt]
Mer·rill \'mer-əl\ [fr. a surname]
Mi·chael \'mī-kəl\ [Heb] who is like God?
Mick·ey \'mik-ē\ *dim of* MICHAEL
Mike \'mīk\ *dim of* MICHAEL
Mi·lan \'mī-lən\ [prob. fr. the city in Italy]
Miles *or* **Myles** \'mī(ə)lz\ [Gmc]
Mil·ford \'mil-fərd\ [fr. a surname]
Mil·lard \'mil-ərd, mil-'ärd\ [fr. a surname]
Mi·lo \'mī-(ˌ)lō\ [prob.L]
Mil·ton \'milt-ᵊn\ [fr. a surname]
Mitch·ell \'mich-əl\ [fr. a surname]
Mon·roe \mən-'rō, 'mən-ˌ\ [fr. a surname]
Mon·te *or* **Mon·ty** \'mänt-ē\ *dim of* Montague
Mor·gan \'mȯr-gən\ [W] *prob* dweller on the sea
Mor·ris \'mȯr-əs, 'mär-\ *var of* MAURICE
Mor·ton \'mȯrt-ᵊn\ [fr. a surname]
Mur·ray \'mər-ē, 'mə-rē\ [fr. a surname]
My·ron \'mī-rən\ [Gk]
Na·than \'nā-thən\ [Heb] given, gift
Na·than·iel \'nə-'than-yəl\ [Heb] gift of God
Ned \'ned\ *dim of* EDWARD, EDWIN
Neil *or* **Neal** \'nē(ə)l\ [Celt]
Nel·son \'nel-sən\ [fr. a surname]
Nev·ille \'nev-əl\ [fr. a surname]
Nev·in \'nev-ən\ [fr. a surname]
New·ell \'n(y)ü-əl\ [fr. a surname]
New·ton \'n(y)üt-ᵊn\ [fr. a surname]
Nich·o·las \'nik-(ə-)ləs\ [Gk] victorious among the people
Nick \'nik\ *dim of* NICHOLAS
Niles \'nī(ə)lz\ [fr. a surname]
Nils \'nils, 'nē(ə)ls\ [Scand]
No·ah \'nō-ə\ [Heb] rest
No·el \'nō-əl\ [F, fr. L] Christmas
No·lan \'nō-lən\ [fr. a surname]
Nor·man \'nȯr-mən\ [Gmc] Norseman, Norman
Nor·ris \'nȯr-əs, 'när-\ [fr. a surname]
Nor·ton \'nȯrt-ᵊn\ [fr. a surname]
Ol·i·ver \'äl-ə-vər\ [OF]
Ol·lie \'äl-ē\ *dim of* OLIVER
Or·lan·do \ȯr-'lan-(ˌ)dō\ [It] *var of* ROLAND
Or·rin \'ȯr-ən, 'är-\ *or* **Orin** *or* **Oren** \'ȯr-, 'är-, 'ōr-\ [prob. fr. a surname]
Or·ville *or* **Or·val** \'ȯr-vəl\ [prob. fr. a surname]
Os·car \'äs-kər\ [OE] spear of a deity
Otis \'ōt-əs\ [fr. a surname]

Ot·to \'ät-(ˌ)ō\ [Gmc]
Ow·en \'ō-ən\ [OW]
Palm·er \'päm-ər, 'päl-mər\ [fr. a surname]
Par·ker \'pär-kər\ [fr. a surname]
Pat \'pat\ *dim of* PATRICK
Pat·rick \'pa-trik\ [L] patrician
Paul \'pȯl\ [L] little
Pe·dro \'pē-(ˌ)drō, 'pā-\ [Sp] *var of* PETER
Per·cy \'pər-sē\ [fr. a surname]
Per·ry \'per-ē\ [fr. a surname]
Pete \'pēt\ *dim of* PETER
Pe·ter \'pēt-ər\ [Gk] rock
Phil \'fil\ *dim of* PHILIP
Phil·ip *or* **Phil·lip** \'fil-əp\ [Gk] lover of horses
Pierre \pē-'e(ə)r\ [F] *var of* PETER
Por·ter \'pōrt-ər, 'pȯrt-\ [fr. a surname]
Pres·ton \'pres-tən\ [fr. a surname]
Quen·tin \'kwent-ᵊn\ [LL] of or relating to the fifth
Ra·fa·el *or* **Ra·pha·el** \'raf-ē-əl, 'rä-fē-\ [Heb] God has healed
Ra·leigh \'rȯl-ē, 'räl-\ [fr. a surname]
Ralph \'ralf, *Brit also* 'rāf\ [Gmc] wolf in counsel
Ra·mon \rä-'mōn, 'rā-mən\ [Sp] *var of* RAYMOND
Ran·dall *or* **Ran·dal** \'ran-dᵊl\ *var of* RANDOLPH
Ran·dolph \'ran-ˌdälf\ [Gmc] shield wolf
Ran·dy \'ran-dē\ *dim of* RANDOLPH
Ray \'rā\ *dim of* RAYMOND
Ray·mond \'rā-mənd\ [Gmc] wise protection
Reed *or* **Reid** \'rēd\ [fr. a surname]
Reg·gie \'rej-ē\ *dim of* REGINALD
Reg·i·nald \'rej-ən-ᵊld\ [Gmc] wise dominion
Re·gis \'rē-jəs\ [fr. a proper name]
Re·ne \'ren-(ˌ)ā, rə-'nā, 'rā-nē, 'rē-nē\ [F, fr. L] reborn
Reu·ben *or* **Ru·ben** \'rü-bən\ [Heb]
Rex \'reks\ [L] king
Reyn·old \'ren-ᵊld\ *var of* REGINALD
Rich·ard \'rich-ərd\ [Gmc] strong in rule
Rob·ert \'räb-ərt\ [Gmc] bright in fame
Ro·ber·to \rə-'bərt-(ˌ)ō, rō-, -'bert-\ [Sp & It] *var of* ROBERT
Rob·in \'räb-ən\ *dim of* ROBERT
Rod·er·ick \'räd-(ə-)rik\ [Gmc] famous ruler
Rod·ney \'räd-nē\ [fr. a surname]
Rog·er *or* **Rod·ger** \'räj-ər\ [Gmc] famous spear
Rog·ers \'räj-ərz\ [fr. a surname]
Ro·land \'rō-lənd\ *or* **Rol·land** \'räl-ənd\ *or* **Row·land** \'rō-lənd\ [Gmc] famous land
Rolf \'rälf\ *var of* RUDOLPH
Rol·lin \'räl-ən\ *var of* ROLAND
Ron \'rän\ *dim of* RONALD
Ron·al \'rän-ᵊl\ *var of* RONALD
Ron·ald \'rän-ᵊld\ [ON] *var of* REGINALD
Ron·nie *or* **Ron·ny** \'rän-ē\ *dim of* RONALD
Ros·coe \'räs-(ˌ)kō, 'rȯs-\ [fr. a surname]
Ross \'rȯs\ [fr. a surname]
Roy \'rȯi\ [ScGael]
Roy·al \'rȯi(-ə)l\ [prob. fr. a surname]
Royce \'rȯis\ [fr. a surname]
Ru·dolph *or* **Ru·dolf** \'rü-ˌdälf\ [Gmc] famous wolf
Ru·dy \'rüd-ē\ *dim of* RUDOLPH
Ru·fus \'rü-fəs\ [L] red, red-haired
Ru·pert \'rü-pərt\ *var of* ROBERT
Rus·sell *or* **Rus·sel** \'rəs-əl\ [fr. a surname]
Ry·an \'rī-ən\ [IrGael]
Sal·va·tore \'sal-və-ˌtō(ə)r, -ˌtȯ(ə)r; ˌsal-və-'tōr-ē, -'tȯr-\ [It] savior
Sam \'sam\ *dim of* SAMUEL
Sam·my *or* **Sam·mie** \'sam-ē\ *dim of* SAM
Sam·u·el \'sam-yə(-wə)l\ [Heb] name of God
San·ford \'san-fərd\ [fr. a surname]
Saul \'sȯl\ [Heb] asked for
Scott \'skät\ [fr. a surname]
Sean \'shȯn\ [Ir] *var of* JOHN
Seth \'seth\ [Heb]
Sey·mour \'sē-ˌmō(ə)r, -ˌmȯ(ə)r\ [fr. a surname]

Shel·by \'shel-bē\ [fr. a surname]
Shel·don \'shel-dən\ [fr. a surname]
Sher·i·dan \'sher-əd-ᵊn\ [fr. a surname]
Sher·man \'shər-mən\ [fr. a surname]
Sher·win \'shər-wən\ [fr. a surname]
Sher·wood \'shər-,wùd, 'she(ə)r-\ [fr. a surname]
Sid·ney or **Syd·ney** \'sid-nē\ [fr. a surname]
Sieg·fried \'sig-,frēd, 'sēg-\ [Gmc] victorious peace
Sig·mund \'sig-mənd\ [Gmc] victorious protection
Si·mon \'sī-mən\ [Heb]
Sol·o·mon \'säl-ə-mən\ [Heb] peaceable
Spen·cer \'spen(t)-sər\ [fr. a surname]
Sta·cy or **Sta·cey** \'stā-sē\ [ML]
Stan \'stan\ dim of STANLEY
Stan·ford \'stan-fərd\ [fr. a surname]
Stan·ley \'stan-lē\ [fr. a surname]
Stan·ton \'stant-ᵊn\ [fr. a surname]
Ste·fan \'stef-ən, -,än\ [Pol] var of STEPHEN
Ste·phen or **Ste·ven** or **Ste·phan** \'stē-vən\ [Gk] crown
Ster·ling \'stər-liŋ\ [fr. a surname]
Steve \'stēv\ dim of STEVEN
Stu·art or **Stew·art** \'st(y)ü-ərt, 'st(y)ü-(ə)rt\ [fr. a surname]
Syl·ves·ter \sil-'ves-tər\ [L] woodsy, of the woods
Tay·lor \'tā-lər\ [fr. a surname]
Ted \'ted\ or **Ted·dy** \'ted-ē\ dim of EDWARD, THEODORE
Ter·ence or **Ter·rance** or **Ter·rence** \'ter-ən(t)s\ [L]
Ter·rell or **Ter·rill** \'ter-əl\ [fr. a surname]
Ter·ry \'ter-ē\ dim of TERENCE
Thad \'thad\ dim of THADDEUS
Thad·de·us \'thad-ē-əs\ [Gk]
The·o·dore \'thē-ə-,dō(ə)r, -,dȯ(ə)r, -əd-ər\ [Gk] gift of God
Thom·as \'täm-əs\ [Aram] twin
Thur·man \'thər-mən\ [fr. a surname]
Tim \'tim\ dim of TIMOTHY
Tim·o·thy \'tim-ə-thē\ [Gk] revering God
To·by \'tō-bē\ dim of Tobias
Todd \'täd\ [prob. fr. a surname]
Tom \'täm\ or **Tom·my** or **Tom·mie** \'täm-ē\ dim of THOMAS
To·ny \'tō-nē\ dim of ANTHONY
Tra·cy \'trā-sē\ [fr. a surname]
Trav·is \'trav-əs\ [fr. a surname]
Trent \'trent\ [fr. a surname]
Tre·vor \'trev-ər\ [Celt]
Troy \'trȯi\ [prob. fr. a surname]
Tru·man \'trü-mən\ [fr. a surname]
Ty·ler \'tī-lər\ [fr. a surname]
Ty·rone \'tī-,rōn, tī-'; tir-'ōn\ [prob. fr. the county in Ireland]
Val \'val\ dim of Valentine
Van \'van\ [fr. surnames beginning with Van, fr. Dutch van of]
Vance \'van(t)s\ [fr. a surname]
Vaughn \'vȯn, 'vän\ [fr. a surname]
Verne or **Vern** \'vərn\ prob alter of VERNON
Ver·non \'vər-nən\ [prob. fr. a surname]
Vic·tor \'vik-tər\ [L] conqueror
Vin·cent \'vin(t)-sənt\ [LL] of or relating to the conquering one
Vir·gil \'vər-jəl\ [L]
Wade \'wād\ [fr. a surname]
Wal·lace or **Wal·lis** \'wäl-əs\ [fr. a surname]
Walt \'wȯlt\ dim of WALTER
Wal·ter \'wȯl-tər\ [Gmc] army of dominion
Wal·ton \'wȯlt-ᵊn\ [fr. a surname]
Ward \'wȯ(ə)rd\ [fr. a surname]
War·ner \'wȯr-nər\ [fr. a surname]
War·ren \'wȯr-ən, 'wär-\ [fr. a surname]
Wayne \'wān\ [fr. a surname]
Wel·don \'wel-dən\ [fr. a surname]
Wen·dell \'wen-dᵊl\ [fr. a surname]
Wer·ner \'wər-nər, 'we(ə)r-\ [Gmc] army of the Varini, a Germanic people

Wes·ley \'wes-lē also 'wez-\ [fr. a surname]
Wil·bur or **Wil·ber** \'wil-bər\ [fr. a surname]
Wi·ley or **Wy·lie** \'wī-lē\ [fr. a surname]
Wil·ford \'wil-fərd\ [fr. a surname]
Wil·fred \'wil-frəd\ [OE] desired peace
Will \'wil\ or **Wil·lie** -ē\ dim of WILLIAM
Wil·lard \'wil-ərd\ [fr. a surname]
Wil·liam \'wil-yəm\ [Gmc] desired helmet
Wil·lis \'wil-əs\ [fr. a surname]
Wil·mer \'wil-mər\ [fr. a surname]
Wil·son \'wil-sən\ [fr. a surname]
Wil·ton \'wilt-ᵊn\ [fr. a surname]
Win·field \'win-,fēld\ [fr. a surname]
Win·fred \'win-frəd\ [OE] prob joyous peace
Win·ston \'win(t)-stən\ [fr. a surname]
Win·ton \'wint-ᵊn\ [fr. a surname]
Wood·row \'wùd-(,)rō\ [fr. a surname]
Wy·att \'wī-ət\ [fr. a surname]
Yale \'yā(ə)l\ [fr. a surname]
Zach·a·ry \'zak-ə-rē\ dim of Zachariah
Zane \'zān\ [fr. a surname]

NAMES OF WOMEN

Ab·by \'ab-ē\ dim of ABIGAIL
Ab·i·gail \'ab-ə-,gāl\ [Heb] prob source of joy
Ada \'ād-ə\ [Heb] prob ornament
Ad·di·son \'ad-ə-sən\ [fr. a surname]
Ad·e·laide \'ad-ᵊl-,ād\ [Gmc] of noble rank
Adele \ə-'del\ [Gmc] noble
Adri·enne \'ā-drē-,en, -ən\ [F] fem of Adrien
Ag·nes \'ag-nəs\ [LL]
Ai·leen \ī-'lēn\ [IrGael] var of HELEN
Al·ber·ta \al-'bərt-ə\ fem of ALBERT
Al·ex·an·dra \,al-ig-'zan-drə\ [Gk] fem of ALEXANDER
Alex·is \ə-'lek-səs\ [Gk]
Al·ice or **Al·yce** \'al-əs\ [OF] var of ADELAIDE
Ali·cia \ə-'lish-ə\ [ML] var of ADELAIDE
Al·i·son or **Al·li·son** \'al-ə-sən\ [OF] dim of ALICE
Al·ma \'al-mə\ [L] nourishing, cherishing
Al·va \'al-və\ [Sp, fr. L] white
Aman·da \ə-'man-də\ [L] worthy to be loved
Am·ber \'am-bər\ [E]
Ame·lia \ə-'mēl-yə\ [Gmc]
Amy \'ā-mē\ [L] beloved
An·as·ta·sia \,an-ə-'stā-zh(ē-)ə\ [LGk] of the resurrection
An·drea \'an-drē-ə, an-'drā-ə\ fem of ANDREW
An·ge·la \'an-jə-lə\ [It, fr. Gk] angel
An·gel·i·ca \an-'jel-i-kə\ var of ANGELA
An·ge·line \'an-jə-,līn, -,lēn\ dim of ANGELA
Ani·ta \ə-'nēt-ə\ [Sp] dim of ANN
Ann or **Anne** \'an\ or **An·na** \'an-ə\ [Heb] grace
An·na·belle \'an-ə-,bel\ prob var of MABEL
An·nette \a-'net, ə-\ or **An·net·ta** \-'net-ə\ [F] dim of ANN
An·nie \'an-ē\ dim of ANN
An·toi·nette \,an-t(w)ə-'net\ [F] dim of Antonia
April \'ā-prəl\ [E] April (the month)
Ar·dell or **Ar·delle** \är-'del\ var of ADELE
Ar·lene or **Ar·leen** or **Ar·line** \är-'lēn\
Ash·ley \'ash-lē\ [OE] ash-tree meadow
As·trid \'as-trəd\ [Scand] beautiful as a deity
Au·dra \'ȯ-drə\ var of AUDREY
Au·drey \'ȯ-drē\ [OE] noble strength
Ba·bette \ba-'bet\ [F] dim of ELIZABETH
Bar·ba·ra \'bär-b(ə-)rə\ [Gk] foreign
Be·atrice \'bē-ə-trəs\ [It, fr. ML] she that makes happy
Becky \'bek-ē\ dim of REBECCA
Ber·na·dette \,bər-nə-'det\ [F] fem of BERNARD
Ber·na·dine \'bər-nə-,dēn\ fem of BERNARD
Ber·nice \(,)bər-'nēs, 'bər-nəs\ [Gk] bringing victory
Ber·tha \'bər-thə\ [Gmc] bright

Ber•yl \'ber-əl\ [Gk] beryl (the mineral)
Bes•sie \'bes-ē\ *dim of* ELIZABETH
Beth \'beth\ *dim of* ELIZABETH
Bet•sy *or* **Bet•sey** \'bet-sē\ *dim of* ELIZABETH
Bet•ty *or* **Bet•te** *or* **Bet•tye** *or* **Bet•tie** \'bet-ē\ *dim of* ELIZABETH
Beu•lah \'byü-lə\ [Heb] married
Bev•er•ly *or* **Bev•er•ley** \'bev-ər-lē\ [prob. fr. a surname]
Bil•lie \'bil-ē\ *fem of* BILLY
Blair \'ble(ə)r\ [fr. a surname]
Blake \'blāk\ [fr. a surname]
Blanche \'blanch\ [OF, fr. Gmc] white
Bob•bie \'bäb-ē\ *dim of* ROBERTA
Bo•ni•ta \bə-'nēt-ə\ [Sp] pretty
Bon•nie \'bän-ē\ [ME] pretty
Bran•dy \'bran-dē\ [E]
Bren•da \'bren-də\ [Scand]
Bri•gitte \'brij-ət, brə-'jit\ [G] *var of* Bridget
Brit•tany \'brit-ᵊn-ē\ [E]
Brooke \'brúk\ [OE] brook
Cait•lin \'kāt-lin\ [Ir] *var of* CATHERINE
Ca•mil•la \kə-'mil-ə\ [L] freeborn girl attendant at a sacrifice
Ca•mille \kə-'mē(ə)l\ [F] *var of* CAMILLA
Can•da•ce \'kan-dəs, kan-'dā-sē\ [Gk]
Car•la \'kär-lə\ [It] *fem of* Carlo
Car•lene \kär-'lēn\ *var of* CARLA
Car•lot•ta \kär-'lät-ə\ [It] *var of* CHARLOTTE
Car•men \'kär-mən\ *or* **Car•mine** \kär-'mēn, 'kär-mən\ [Sp, fr. L] song
Car•ol *or* **Car•ole** *or* **Car•yl** \'kar-əl\ *dim of* CAROLYN
Car•o•lyn \'kar-ə-lən\ *or* **Car•o•line** \-lən, -,līn\ [It] *fem of* CHARLES
Car•rie \'kar-ē\ *dim of* CAROLINE
Cath•er•ine *or* **Cath•a•rine** \'kath-(ə-)rən\ [LGk]
Cath•leen \kath-'lēn\ [IrGael] *var of* CATHERINE
Cath•ryn \'kath-rən\ *var of* CATHERINE
Cathy *or* **Cath•ie** \'kath-ē\ *dim of* CATHERINE
Ce•cile \sə-'sē(ə)l\ *var of* CECILIA
Ce•ci•lia \sə-'sēl-yə, -'sil-\ *or* **Ce•ce•lia** \-'sēl-\ [L] *fem of* CECIL
Ce•leste \sə-'lest\ [L] heavenly
Ce•lia \'sēl-yə\ *dim of* CECILIA
Char•lene \shär-'lēn\ *fem of* CHARLES
Char•lotte \'shär-lət\ [F] *fem dim of* CHARLES
Cher•ie \'sher-ē\ [F] dear
Cher•ry \'cher-ē\ [E] cherry
Cher•yl \'cher-əl, 'sher-\ *prob var of* CHERRY
Chloe \'klō-ē\ [Gk] young verdure
Chris•tie \'kris-tē\ *dim of* CHRISTINE
Chris•tine \kris-'tēn\ *or* **Chris•ti•na** \-'tē-nə\ [Gk] Christian
Cin•dy \'sin-dē\ *dim of* LUCINDA
Claire *or* **Clare** \'kla(ə)r, 'kle(ə)r\ *var of* CLARA
Clara \'klar-ə\ [L] bright
Cla•rice \'klar-əs, klə-'rēs\ *dim of* CLARA
Clau•dette \klò-'det\ [F] *fem of* CLAUDE
Clau•dia \'klòd-ē-ə\ [L] *fem of* CLAUDE
Clau•dine \klò-'dēn\ [F] *fem of* CLAUDE
Cleo \'klē-(,)ō\ *dim of* Cleopatra
Co•lette \kä-'let\ [OF] *fem dim of* NICHOLAS
Col•leen \kä-'lēn\ [IrGael] girl
Con•nie \'kän-ē\ *dim of* CONSTANCE
Con•stance \'kän(t)-stən(t)s\ [L] constancy
Co•ra \'kōr-ə, 'kòr-\ [Gk] maiden
Cor•ey \'kòr-ē\ [Ir]
Co•rinne *or* **Cor•rine** \kə-'rin, -'rēn\ [Gk] *dim of* CORA
Cor•ne•lia \kòr-'nēl-yə\ [L] *fem of* CORNELIUS
Court•ney \'kō(ə)rt-nē, 'kò(ə)rt-\ [OE] of the court
Crys•tal \'kris-tᵊl\ [E]
Cyn•thia \'sin(t)-thē-ə\ [Gk] she of Mount Cynthus on the island of Delos
Dai•sy \'dā-zē\ [E] daisy
Dale \'dā(ə)l\ [E] valley

Da•na \'dā-nə\ [fr. a surname]
Dan•ielle \dán-'yel\ [F] *fem of* DANIEL
Daph•ne \'daf-nē\ [Gk] laurel
Dar•la \'där-lə\ [deriv. of *darling*]
Dar•lene \där-'lēn\ [deriv. of *darling*]
Dawn \'dòn, 'dän\ [E] dawn
De•an•na \dē-'an-ə\ *or* **De•anne** \-'an\ *var of* DIANA
Deb•bie *or* **Deb•by** \'deb-ē\ *dim of* DEBORAH
Deb•o•rah *or* **Deb•o•ra** \'deb-(ə-)rə\ [Heb] bee
Deb•ra \'deb-rə\ *var of* DEBORAH
Dee \'dē\ *prob dim of* EDITH
Deir•dre \'di(ə)r-drē, 'de(ə)r-\ [IrGael]
De•lia \'dēl-yə\ [Gk] she of Delos (i.e. the goddess Artemis)
Del•la \'del-ə\ *dim of* ADELAIDE, DELIA
De•lo•res \də-'lòr-əs, -'lòr-\ *var of* DOLORES
Dee•na *or* **Dee•na** \'dē-nə\ *dim of* GERALDINE
De•nise \də-'nēz, -'nēs\ [F] *fem of* DENIS
Di•ana *or* **Di•an•na** \dī-'an-ə\ [L]
Di•ane *or* **Di•anne** *or* **Di•an** *or* **Di•ann** \dī-'an\ [F] *var of* DIANA
Di•na *or* **Di•nah** \'dī-nə\ [Heb] judged
Dix•ie \'dik-sē\ [E] *prob* Dixie (nickname for the southern states of the U.S.)
Do•lo•res \də-'lòr-əs, -'lòr-\ [Sp, fr. L] sorrows (i.e. those of the Virgin Mary)
Don•na \'dän-ə\ *or* **Do•na** \'dän-ə, 'dō-nə\ [It, fr. L] lady
Do•ra \'dōr-ə, 'dòr-\ *dim of* THEODORA, Eudora
Do•reen \dò-'rēn, də-\ [IrGael]
Dor•is \'dòr-əs, 'där-\ [Gk] *prob* Dorian (a member of an ancient Hellenic race)
Dor•o•thy \'dòr-ə-thē, 'där-\ *or* **Dor•o•thea** \,dòr-ə-'thē-ə, ,där-\ [LGk] goddess of gifts
Dot•tie *or* **Dot•ty** \'dät-ē\ *dim of* DOROTHY
Edith *or* **Edythe** \'ēd-əth\ [OE]
Ed•na \'ed-nə\ [Aram]
Ed•wi•na \e-'dwē-nə, -'dwin-ə\ *fem of* EDWIN
Ef•fie \'ef-ē\ *dim of* Euphemia
Ei•leen \ī-'lēn\ [IrGael] *var of* HELEN
Elaine \i-'lān\ [OF] *var of* HELEN
El•ea•nor *or* **El•i•nor** *or* **El•ea•nore** \'el-ə-nər, -,nò(ə)r, -,nō(ə)r\ [OProv] *var of* HELEN
Ele•na \'el-ə-nə, ə-'lē-nə\ [It] *var of* HELEN
Elise \ə-'lēz, -'lēs\ [F] *var of* ELIZABETH
Eliz•a•beth *or* **Elis•a•beth** \i-'liz-ə-bəth\ [Heb] God has sworn
El•la \'el-ə\ [OF]
El•len *or* **El•lyn** \'el-ən\ *var of* HELEN
El•o•ise \'el-ə-,wēz, ,el-ə-'\ [OF, fr. Gmc]
El•sa \'el-sə\ [G] *dim of* ELIZABETH
El•sie \'el-sē\ *dim of* ELIZABETH
El•va \'el-və\ [Gmc] elf
Em•i•ly *or* **Em•i•lie** \'em-(ə-)lē\ [L] *fem of* EMIL
Em•ma \'em-ə\ [Gmc] *var of* ERMA
Enid \'ē-nəd\ [W]
Er•i•ka \'er-i-kə\ *fem of* ERIC
Er•in \'er-ən\ [IrGael]
Er•ma \'ər-mə\ [Gmc]
Er•nes•tine \'ər-nə-,stēn\ *fem of* ERNEST
Es•telle \e-'stel\ *or* **Es•tel•la** \e-'stel-ə\ [OProv, fr. L] star
Es•ther \'es-tər\ [prob. fr. Per] *prob* star
Eth•el \'eth-əl\ [OE] noble
Et•ta \'et-ə\ *dim of* HENRIETTA
Eu•ge•nia \yú-'jēn-yə\ *or* **Eu•ge•nie** \-'jē-nē\ *fem of* EUGENE
Eu•nice \'yü-nəs\ [Gk] having (i.e. bringing) happy victory
Eva \'ē-və\ *var of* EVE
Evan•ge•line \i-'van-jə-lən, -,lēn, -,līn\ [Gk] bringing good news
Eve \'ēv\ [Heb] life, living
Ev•e•lyn \'ev-(ə-)lən, *chiefly Brit* 'ēv-\ [OF, fr. Gmc]
Faith \'fāth\ [E] faith
Faye *or* **Fay** \'fā\ *dim of* FAITH

Fe•lice \fə-'lēs\ [L] happiness
Fern or Ferne \'fərn\ [E] fern
Flo•ra \'flōr-ə, 'flȯr-\ [L] goddess of flowers
Flor•ence \'flȯr-ən(t)s, 'flär-\ [L] bloom, prosperity
Fran•ces \'fran(t)-səs, -səz\ fem of FRANCIS
Fran•cine \fran-'sēn\ [F] prob dim of FRANCES
Fre•da or Frie•da \'frēd-ə\ dim of WINIFRED
Fred•er•ic•ka or Fred•er•i•ca \,fred-(ə-)'rē-kə, -'rik-ə\
  fem of FREDERICK
Gail or Gayle or Gale \'gā(ə)l\ dim of ABIGAIL
Gay \'gā\ [E] gay
Ge•ne•va \jə-'nē-və\ var of GENEVIEVE
Gen•e•vieve \'jen-ə-,vēv\ [prob. fr. Celt]
George•ann \jȯr-'jan\ [George + Ann]
Geor•gette \jȯr-'jet\ fem of GEORGE
Geor•gia \'jȯr-jə\ fem of GEORGE
Geor•gi•na \jȯr-'jē-nə\ fem of GEORGE
Ger•al•dine \'jer-əl-,dēn\ fem of GERALD
Ger•trude \'gər-,trüd\ [Gmc] spear strength
Gil•li•an \'jil-ē-ən\ var of JULIANA
Gin•ger \'jin-jər\ [E] ginger
Gi•sela \jə-'sel-ə, -'zel-\ [Gmc] pledge
Gi•selle \jə-'zel\ var of GISELA
Glad•ys \'glad-əs\ [W]
Glen•da \'glen-də\ prob var of GLENNA
Glen•na \'glen-ə\ fem of GLENN
Glo•ria \'glōr-ē-ə, 'glȯr-\ [L] glory
Grace \'grās\ [L] favor, grace
Gre•ta \'grēt-ə, 'gret-\ dim of MARGARET
Gretch•en \'grech-ən\ [G] dim of MARGARET
Gwen \'gwen\ dim of GWENDOLYN
Gwen•do•lyn \'gwen-də-lən\ [W]
Han•nah \'han-ə\ [Heb] var of ANN
Har•ri•et or Har•ri•ett or Har•ri•ette \'har-ē-ət\ var
  of HENRIETTA
Hat•tie \'hat-ē\ dim of HARRIET
Ha•zel \'hā-zəl\ [E] hazel
Heath•er \'heth-ər\ [ME] heather (the shrub)
Hei•di \'hīd-ē\ [G] dim of ADELAIDE
He•laine \hə-'lān\ var of HELEN
Hel•en \'hel-ən\ or He•le•na \'hel-ə-nə, hə-'lē-nə\ [Gk]
He•lene \hə-'lēn\ [F] var of HELEN
Hel•ga \'hel-gə\ [Scand] holy
Hen•ri•et•ta \,hen-rē-'et-ə\ [MF] fem of HENRY
Her•mine \'hər-,mēn\ [G] prob fem of HERMAN
Hes•ter \'hes-tər\ var of ESTHER
Hil•ary or Hil•la•ry \'hil-ə-rē\ [L] cheerful
Hil•da \'hil-də\ [OE] battle
Hil•de•gard or Hil•de•garde \'hil-də-,gärd\ [Gmc]
  prob battle enclosure
Hol•ly \'häl-ē\ [E] holly
Hope \'hōp\ [E] hope
Ida \'īd-ə\ [Gmc]
Ilene \ī-'lēn\ var of EILEEN
Imo•gene \'im-ə-,jēn, 'ī-mə-\
Ina \'ī-nə\
Inez \ī-'nez, 'ī-nəz\ [Sp] var of AGNES
In•grid \'ing-grəd\ [Scand] beautiful as Ing (an ancient
  Germanic god)
Irene \ī-'rēn\ [Gk] peace
Iris \'ī-rəs\ [Gk] rainbow
Ir•ma \'ər-mə\ var of ERMA
Is•a•bel or Is•a•belle \'iz-ə-,bel\ [OProv] var of ELIZA-
  BETH
Jack•ie or Jacky \'jak-ē\ dim of JACQUELINE
Jac•que•line or Jac•que•lyn or Jac•que•lin \'jak-(w)ə-
  lən, -,lēn\ fem of JACOB
Ja•mie \'jā-mē\ fem of JAMES
Jan \'jan\ dim of JANET
Jane or Jayne \'jān\ [OF] var of JOAN
Ja•net or Ja•nette \'jan-ət, jə-'net\ dim of JANE
Ja•nice \'jan-əs, jə-'nēs\ or Jan•is \'jan-əs\ prob dim of
  JANE
Ja•nie \'jā-nē\ dim of JANE
Jean or Jeanne \'jēn\ [OF] var of JOAN

Jea•nette or Jean•nette \jə-'net\ [F] dim of JEANNE
Jean•nie or Jean•ie \'jē-nē\ dim of JEAN
Jean•nine or Jea•nine \jə-'nēn\ [F] dim of JEANNE
Jen•nie or Jen•ny \'jen-ē\ dim of JANE
Jen•ni•fer \'jen-ə-fər\ [Celt]
Jer•al•dine \'jer-əl-,dēn\ var of GERALDINE
Jer•i•lyn \'jer-ə-lən\ var of GERALDINE
Jer•ry or Jeri or Jer•rie \'jer-ē\ dim of GERALDINE
Jes•si•ca \'jes-i-kə\ [prob. Heb]
Jes•sie \'jes-ē\ [Sc] dim of JANET
Jew•el or Jew•ell \'jü(-ə)l, 'jú(-ə)l\ [E] jewel
Jill \'jil\ dim of JULIANA
Jo \'jō\ dim of JOSEPHINE
Joan or Joann or Joanne \'jō(-ə)n, jō-'an\ [Gk] fem of
  JOHN
Jo•an•na \jō-'an-ə\ or Jo•han•na \-'(h)an-ə\ var of
  JOAN
Joc•e•lyn \'jäs-(ə-)lən\ [OF, fr. Gmc]
Jo•dy or Jo•die \'jō-dē\ alter of JUDITH
Jo•lene \jō-'lēn\ prob dim of JO
Jo•se•phine \'jō-zə-,fēn also 'jō-sə-\ fem of JOSEPH
Joy \'jȯi\ [E] joy
Joyce \'jȯis\ [OF]
Jua•ni•ta \wä-'nēt-ə\ [Sp] fem dim of JOHN
Ju•dith \'jüd-əth\ [Heb] Jewess
Ju•dy or Ju•di or Ju•die \'jüd-ē\ dim of JUDITH
Ju•lia \'jül-yə\ [L] fem of JULIUS
Ju•li•ana \,jü-lē-'an-ə\ [LL] fem of JULIAN
Ju•li•anne or Ju•li•ann \,jü-lē-'an, jül-'yan\ var of JULIA-
  NA
Ju•lie \'jü-lē\ [MF] var of JULIA
Ju•liet \'jül-yət, -ē-,et, -ē-ət; ,jül-ē-'et, jül-'yet, 'jül-,yet\
  [It] dim of JULIA
June \'jün\ [E] June (the month)
Jus•tine \,jəs-'tēn\ [F] fem of JUSTIN
Ka•ra \'kär-ə, 'kar-ə\ var of CATHERINE
Kar•en or Kar•in or Kaa•ren \'kar-ən, 'kär-\ [Scand]
  var of CATHERINE
Kar•la \'kär-lə\ var of CARLA
Kar•ol \'kar-əl\ var of CAROL
Kar•o•lyn \'kar-ə-lən\ var of CAROLYN
Kate \'kāt\ dim of CATHERINE
Kath•er•ine or Kath•a•rine or Kath•ryn \'kath-
  (ə-)rən\ var of CATHERINE
Kath•leen \kath-'lēn\ [IrGael] var of CATHERINE
Kathy \'kath-ē\ dim of CATHERINE
Ka•tie \'kāt-ē\ dim of KATE
Kay or Kaye \'kā\ dim of CATHERINE
Kel•ly \'kel-ē\ [fr. a surname]
Ker•ry \'ker-ē\ [prob. fr. the county of Ireland]
Kim \'kim\ prob dim of KIMBERLY
Kim•ber•ly \'kim-bər-lē\ [OE]
Kit•ty \'kit-ē\ dim of CATHERINE
Kris•tin \'kris-tən\ [Scand] var of CHRISTINE
Kris•tine \kris-'tēn\ var of CHRISTINE
La•na \'lan-ə, 'län-ə, 'lā-nə\
Lau•ra \'lȯr-ə, 'lär-\ [ML] prob fem dim of LAWRENCE
Lau•rel \'lȯr-əl, 'lär-\ [E] laurel
Lau•ren \'lȯr-ən, 'lär-\ var of LAURA
Lau•rie \'lȯr-ē, 'lär-\ dim of LAURA
La•verne or La•vern \lə-'vərn\
Le•ah \'lē-ə\ [Heb] prob wild cow
Le•anne \lē-'an\ [prob. fr. Lee + Ann]
Lee \'lē\ [fr. a surname]
Leigh \'lē\ var of LEE
Lei•la or Le•la \'lē-lə\ [Per] dark as night
Le•lia \'lēl-yə\ [L]
Le•na \'lē-nə\ [G] dim of HELENA, Magdalena
Le•nore \lə-'nō(ə)r, -'nȯ(ə)r\ or Le•no•ra \lə-'nȯ-ə,
  -'ȯr-\ var of LEONORA
Le•o•na \lē-'ō-nə\ fem of LEON
Le•o•no•ra \,lē-ə-'nōr-ə, -'nȯr-\ var of ELEANOR
Les•lie or Les•ley \'les-lē also 'lez-\ [fr. a surname]
Le•ti•tia \li-'tish-ə, -'tē-shə\ [L] gladness
Lib•by \'lib-ē\ dim of ELIZABETH

Li•la \'lī-lə\ *var of* LEILA
Lil•lian \'lil-yən, 'lil-ē-ən\ *prob dim of* ELIZABETH
Lil•lie \'lil-ē\ *dim of* LILLIAN
Lily \'lil-ē\ [E] lily
Lin•da *or* Lyn•da \'lin-də\ *dim of* MELINDA, Belinda
Lind•sey *or* Lind•say \'lin-zē\ [OE] linden isle
Li•sa \'lī-zə, 'lē-\ *dim of* ELIZABETH
Lo•is \'lō-əs\ [Gk]
Lo•la \'lō-lə\ [Sp] *dim of* DOLORES
Lon•na \'län-ə\ *fem of* LON
Lo•ra \'lōr-ə, 'lȯr-\ *var of* LAURA
Lo•re•lei \'lōr-ə-,lī, 'lȯr-\ [G]
Lo•rene \lȯ-'rēn\ *dim of* LORA
Lo•ret•ta \lə-'ret-ə, lȯ-\ [ML] *var of* Lauretta
Lo•ri \'lōr-ē, 'lȯr-\ *var of* LAURA
Lor•na \'lȯr-nə\
Lor•raine *or* Lo•raine \lə-'rān, lȯ-\ [prob. fr. *Lorraine*, region in northeast France]
Lou \'lü\ *dim of* LOUISE
Lou•ise \lü-'ēz\ *or* Lou•i•sa \-'ē-zə\ *fem of* LOUIS
Lu•anne \lü-'an\ [*Lu* - *Anne*]
Lu•cille *or* Lu•cile \lü-'sē(ə)l\ [L] *prob dim of* LUCIA
Lu•cin•da \lü-'sin-də\ [L] *var of* LUCY
Lu•cre•tia \lü-'krē-shə\ [L]
Lu•cy \'lü-sē\ *or* Lu•cia \'lü-shə\ [L] *fem of* Lucius
Lu•el•la \lü-'el-ə\ [prob. fr. *Lou* (dim. of *Louise*) + *Ella*]
Lyd•ia \'lid-ē-ə\ [Gk] woman of Lydia, ancient country in Asia Minor
Ly•nette \lə-'net\ [W]
Lynne *or* Lynn \'lin\ *dim of* CAROLYN, JACQUELYN, etc.
Ma•bel \'mā-bəl\ [L] lovable
Mac•ken•zie \mə-'ken-zē\ [fr. a surname]
Mad•e•line *or* Mad•e•leine *or* Mad•e•lyn \'mad-ᵊl-ən\ [Gk] woman of Magdala, ancient town in northern Palestine
Madge \'maj\ *dim of* MARGARET
Mal•lory \'mal-(ə-)rē\ [fr. a surname]
Ma•mie \'mā-mē\ *dim of* MARGARET
Ma•ra \'mär-ə\ *var of* MARY
Mar•cel•la \mär-'sel-ə\ [L] *fem of* Marcellus
Mar•cia \'mär-shə\ [L] *fem of* MARCUS
Mar•ga•ret \'mär-g(ə-)rət\ [Gk] pearl
Mar•gery \'märj-(ə-)rē\ [OF] *var of* MARGARET
Mar•gie \'mär-jē\ *dim of* MARGARET
Mar•go \'mär-(,)gō\ *var of* MARGOT
Mar•got \'mär-(,)gō, -gət\ *dim of* MARGARET
Mar•gue•rite \,mär-g(y)ə-'rēt\ [OF] *var of* MARGARET
Ma•ria \mə-'rē-ə *also* -'rī-\ *var of* MARY
Mar•i•an \'mer-ē-ən, 'mar-\ *var of* MARIANNE
Mar•i•anne \,mer-ē-'an, ,mar-\ *or* Mar•i•an•na \-'an-ə\ [F] *dim of* MARY
Ma•rie \mə-'rē\ [OF] *var of* MARY
Mar•i•et•ta \,mer-ē-'et-ə, ,mar-\ *dim of* MARY
Mar•i•lee \'mer-ə-(,)lē, 'mar-\ [prob. fr. *Mary + Lee*]
Mar•i•lyn *or* Mar•i•lynn *or* Mar•y•lyn \'mer-ə-lən, 'mar-\ [prob. fr. *Mary + -lyn*]
Ma•ri•na \mə-'rē-nə\ [LGk]
Mar•i•on \'mer-ē-ən, 'mar-\ *dim of* MARY
Mar•jo•rie *or* Mar•jo•ry \'märj-(ə-)rē\ *var of* MARGERY
Mar•la \'mär-lə\ *prob dim of* MARLENE
Mar•lene \mär-'lēn(-ə), -'lā-nə\ [G] *dim of* Magdalene
Mar•lyn \'mär-lən\ *prob var of* MARLENE
Mar•sha \'mär-shə\ *var of* MARCIA
Mar•ta \'märt-ə\ [It] *var of* MARTHA
Mar•tha \'mär-thə\ [Aram] lady
Mar•va \'mär-və\ *prob fem of* MARVIN
Mary \'me(ə)r-ē, 'mā-rē\ [Gk, fr. Heb]
Mary•ann *or* Mary•anne \,mer-ē-'an, ,mā-rē-\ [*Mary + Ann*]
Mary•el•len \,mer-ē-'el-ən, ,mā-rē-\ [*Mary + Ellen*]
Mar•y•lon \'mer-ə-lən, 'mar-\ *var of* MARILYN
Maude \'mȯd\ [OF] *var of* Matilda
Mau•reen *or* Mau•rine \mȯ-'rēn\ [Ir] *dim of* MARY
Max•ine \mak-'sēn\ [F] *fem dim of* Maximilian

May *or* Mae \'mā\ *dim of* MARY
Me•gan \'meg-ən, 'mē-gən\ [Ir]
Mel•a•nie \'mel-ə-nē\ [Gk] blackness
Mel•ba \'mel-bə\ [E] woman of Melbourne, Australia
Me•lin•da \mə-'lin-də\ *prob alter of* Belinda
Me•lis•sa \mə-'lis-ə\ [Gk] bee
Mel•va \'mel-və\ *prob fem of* MELVIN
Mer•e•dith \'mer-əd-əth\ [W]
Merle \'mər(-ə)l\ [F] blackbird
Mer•ri•ly \'mer-ə-lē\ *alter of* MARILEE
Mer•ry \'mer-ē\ [E] merry
Mia \'mē-ə\ [It]
Mi•chele *or* Mi•chelle \mi-'shel\ [F] *fem of* MICHAEL
Mil•dred \'mil-drəd\ [OE] gentle strength
Mil•li•cent \'mil-ə-sənt\ [Gmc]
Mil•lie \'mil-ē\ *dim of* MILDRED
Min•nie \'min-ē\ [Sc] *dim of* MARY
Mir•an•da \mə-'ran-də\ [L] admirable
Mir•i•am \'mir-ē-əm\ [Heb] *var of* MARY
Mit•zi \'mit-sē\ *prob dim of* MARGARET
Mol•ly *or* Mol•lie \'mäl-ē\ *dim of* MARY
Mo•na \'mō-nə\ [IrGael]
Mon•i•ca \'män-i-kə\ [LL]
Mu•ri•el \'myùr-ē-əl\ [prob. Celt]
My•ra \'mī-rə\
Myr•na \'mər-nə\
Myr•tle \'mərt-ᵊl\ [Gk] myrtle
Na•dine \nä-'dēn, nə-\ [F, fr. Russ] hope
Nan \'nan\ *dim of* ANN
Nan•cy \'nan(t)-sē\ *dim of* ANN
Nan•nette *or* Na•nette \na-'net, nə-\ [F] *dim of* ANN
Na•o•mi \nā-'ō-mē\ [Heb] pleasant
Nat•a•lie \'nat-ᵊl-ē\ [LL] of or relating to Christmas
Nel•lie \'nel-ē\ *or* Nell \'nel\ *dim of* ELLEN, HELEN, ELEANOR
Net•tie \'net-ē\ [Sc] *dim of* JANET
Ni•cole \nē-'kōl\ [F] *fem of* NICHOLAS
Ni•na \'nē-nə\ [Russ] *dim of* ANN
Ni•ta \'nēt-ə\ [Sp] *dim of* JUANITA
No•na \'nō-nə\ [L] ninth
No•ra \'nōr-ə, 'nȯr-\ *dim of* LEONORA, ELEANOR, Honora
No•reen \nȯ-'rēn\ [IrGael] *dim of* NORA
Nor•ma \'nȯr-mə\ [It]
Ol•ga \'äl-gə, 'ȯl-\ [Russ] *var of* HELGA
Ol•ive \'äl-iv, -əv\ *or* O•liv•ia \ə-'liv-ē-ə, ō-\ [L] olive
Opal \'ō-pəl\ [E] opal
Pam \'pam\ *dim of* PAMELA
Pa•me•la \'pam-ə-lə; pə-'mē-lə, pa-\
Pa•tri•cia \pə-'trish-ə, -'trē-shə\ [L] *fem of* PATRICK
Pat•sy \'pat-sē\ *dim of* PATRICIA
Pat•ty *or* Pat•ti *or* Pat•tie \'pat-ē\ *dim of* PATRICIA
Pau•la \'pȯ-lə\ [L] *fem of* PAUL
Pau•lette \pȯ-'let\ *fem dim of* PAUL
Pau•line \pȯ-'lēn\ *fem dim of* PAUL
Pearl \'pər(-ə)l\ [E] pearl
Peg•gy \'peg-ē\ *dim of* MARGARET
Pe•nel•o•pe \pə-'nel-ə-pē\ [Gk]
Pen•ny \'pen-ē\ *dim of* PENELOPE
Phoe•be \'fē-bē\ [Gk] shining
Phyl•lis \'fil-əs\ [Gk] greenleaf
Pol•ly \'päl-ē\ *dim of* MARY
Por•tia \'pōr-shə, 'pȯr-\ [L]
Pris•cil•la \prə-'sil-ə\ [L]
Pru•dence \'prüd-ᵊn(t)s\ [E] prudence
Ra•chel \'rā-chəl\ [Heb] ewe
Rae \'rā\ *dim of* RACHEL
Ra•mo•na \rə-'mō-nə\ [Sp] *fem of* RAMON
Re•ba \'rē-bə\ *dim of* REBECCA
Re•bec•ca \ri-'bek-ə\ [Heb]
Re•gi•na \ri-'jē-nə, -'jī-\ [L] queen
Re•nee \rə-'nā, ren-(,)ā, 'rä-nē, 'rē-nē\ [F] reborn
Rhea \'rē-ə\ [Gk]
Rho•da \'rōd-ə\ [Gk] rose
Ri•ta \'rēt-ə\ [It] *dim of* MARGARET
Ro•ber•ta \rə-'bərt-ə, rō-\ *fem of* ROBERT

Rob•in or **Rob•yn** \'räb-ən\ [E] robin
Ro•chelle \rō-'shel\ [prob. fr. a surname]
Ro•na or **Rho•na** \'rō-nə\
Ron•da \'rän-də\ var of Rhonda
Ron•nie \'rän-ē\ dim of VERONICA
Ro•sa•lie \'rō-zə-(,)lē, 'räz-ə-\ [L] festival of roses
Ro•sa•lind \'räz-(ə-)lənd, 'rō-zə-lənd\ [Sp]
Rose \'rōz\ or **Ro•sa** \'rō-zə\ [L] rose
Rose•anne \rō-'zan\ [Rose + Anne]
Rose•mary \'rōz-,mer-ē\ or **Rose•ma•rie** \,rōz-mə-'rē\ [E] rosemary
Ro•set•ta \rō-'zet-ə\ dim of ROSE
Ros•lyn \'räz-lən\ or **Ro•sa•lyn** or **Ro•se•lyn** \'räz-(ə-)lən, 'rō-zə-lən\ var of ROSALIND
Ro•we•na \rə-'wē-nə\ [perh. fr. OE]
Rox•anne \räk-'san\ [OPer]
Ru•by \'rü-bē\ [E] ruby
Ruth \'rüth\ [Heb]
Ruth•ann \rü-'than\ [Ruth + Ann]
Sa•bra \'sā-brə\ dim of Sabrina
Sa•die \'sād-ē\ dim of SARA
Sal•ly or **Sal•lie** \'sal-ē\ dim of SARA
Sa•man•tha \sə-'man-thə\ [Aram]
San•dra \'san-drə, 'sän-\ dim of ALEXANDRA
San•dy \'san-dē\ dim of ALEXANDRA
Sar•ah or **Sara** \'ser-ə, 'sar-ə, 'sā-rə\ [Heb] princess
Sara•lee \'ser-ə-(,)lē, 'sar-\ [prob. fr. Sara + Lee]
Saun•dra \'són-drə, 'sän-\ var of SANDRA
Sel•ma \'sel-mə\ [Sw] fem dim of Anselm
Shari \'sha(ə)r-ē, 'she(ə)r-\ dim of SHARON
Shar•lene \shär-'lēn\ var of CHARLENE
Shar•on or **Shar•ron** \'shar-ən, 'sher-\ [Heb]
Shei•la \'shē-lə\ [IrGael] var of CECILIA
She•lia \'shēl-yə\ var of SHEILA
Shel•ley \'shel-ē\ [fr. a surname]
Sher•rill or **Sher•yl** \'sher-əl\ [prob. fr. a surname]
Sher•ry or **Sher•rie** or **Sheri** \'sher-ē\
Shir•ley \'shər-lē\ [fr. a surname]
Sig•rid \'sig-rəd\ [Scand] beautiful as victory
Son•dra \'sän-drə\ var of SANDRA
So•nia or **So•nya** or **So•nja** \'sō-nyə, 'só-\ [Russ] dim of SOPHIA
So•phia \sə-'fē-ə, -'fī-\ or **So•phie** \'sō-fē\ [Gk] wisdom
Sta•cy or **Sta•cey** \'stā-sē\ dim of ANASTASIA
Stel•la \'stel-ə\ [L] star
Steph•a•nie \'stef-ə-nē\ fem of STEPHEN
Sue \'sü\ or **Su•sie** \'sü-zē\ dim of SUSAN
Su•el•len \sü-'el-ən\ [Sue + Ellen]
Su•san or **Su•zan** \'süz-ᵊn\ dim of SUSANNA

Su•san•na or **Su•san•nah** \sü-'zan-ə-\ [Heb] lily
Su•zanne or **Su•sanne** or **Su•zann** \sü-'zan\ [F] var of SUSAN
Syb•il \'sib-əl\ [Gk] sibyl
Syl•via \'sil-vē-ə\ [L] she of the forest
Ta•mara \tə-'mar-ə\ [prob. fr. Georgian (language of the republic of Georgia)]
Tan•ya \'tan-yə\ [Russ] dim of TATIANA
Ta•ra \'tár-ə\ [IrGael]
Tat•i•ana \,tät-ē-'än-ə\ [Russ]
Te•re•sa \tə-'rē-sə\ var of THERESA
Ter•ry or **Ter•ri** \'ter-ē\ dim of THERESA
Thel•ma \'thel-mə\
The•o•do•ra \,thē-ə-'dōr-ə, -'dór-\ [LGk] fem of THEODORE
The•re•sa or **Te•re•sa** \tə-'rē-sə\ [LL]
The•rese \tə-'rēs\ var of THERESA
Tif•fa•ny \'tif-ə-nē\ [Gk]
Ti•na \'tē-nə\ dim of CHRISTINA
To•by \'tō-bē\
To•ni \'tō-nē\ dim of Antonia
Tra•cy \'trā-sē\ [fr. a surname]
Tru•dy \'trüd-ē\ dim of GERTRUDE
Ur•su•la \'ər-sə-lə\ [LL] little she-bear
Val•er•ie \'val-ə-rē\ [L] prob strong
Van•es•sa \və-'nes-ə\
Vel•ma \'vel-mə\
Ve•ra \'vir-ə\ [Russ] faith
Ver•na \'vər-nə\ prob fem of VERNON
Ve•ron•i•ca \və-'rän-i-kə\ [LL]
Vicki or **Vicky** or **Vick•ie** \'vik-ē\ dim of VICTORIA
Vic•to•ria \vik-'tōr-ē-ə, -'tór-\ [L] victory
Vi•da \'vēd-ə, 'vīd-\ fem dim of DAVID
Vi•o•la \vī-'ō-lə, vē-'ō-, 'vī-ə-, 'vē-ə-\ [L] violet
Vi•o•let \'vī-ə-lət\ [OF, fr. L] violet
Vir•gin•ia \vər-'jin-yə, -'jin-ē-ə\ [L]
Viv•i•an \'viv-ē-ən\ [LL]
Wan•da \'wän-də\ [Pol]
Wen•dy \'wen-dē\
Whit•ney \'hwit-nē, 'wit-\ [OE]
Wil•da \'wil-də\ var of WILLA
Wil•la \'wil-ə\ or **Wil•lie** \'wil-ē\ prob fem dim of WILLIAM
Wil•ma \'wil-mə\ prob fem dim of WILLIAM
Win•i•fred \'win-ə-frəd\ [W]
Yvette \i-'vet\ [F]
Yvonne \i-'vän\ [F]
Zel•da \'zel-də\ dim of Griselda

Signs and Symbols

ALPHABET TABLE

HEBREW[1,4]

Letter	Name	Translit.
א	aleph	' [2]
ב	beth	b, bh
ג	gimel	g, gh
ד	daleth	d, dh
ה	he	h
ו	waw	w
ז	zayin	z
ח	heth	ḥ
ט	teth	ṭ
י	yodh	y
כ ך	kaph	k, kh
ל	lamedh	l
מ ם	mem	m
נ ן	nun	n
ס	samekh	s
ע	ayin	'
פ ף	pe	p, ph
צ ץ	sadhe	ṣ
ק	qoph	q
ר	resh	r
ש	sin	ś
ש	shin	sh
ת	taw	t, th

ARABIC[3,4]

(Forms: alone / joined to preceding / joined to both / joined to following)

Name	Translit.
alif	[5]
bā	b
tā	t
thā	th
jīm	j
ḥā	ḥ
khā	kh
dāl	d
dhāl	dh
rā	r
zāy	z
sīn	s
shīn	sh
ṣād	ṣ
ḍād	ḍ
ṭā	ṭ
ẓā	ẓ
'ayn	'
ghayn	gh
fā	f
qāf	q
kāf	k
lām	l
mīm	m
nūn	n
hā	h[6]
wāw	w
yā	y

GREEK[7]

Letter	Name	Translit.
A α	alpha	a
B β	beta	b
Γ γ	gamma	g, n
Δ δ	delta	d
E ε	epsilon	e
Z ζ	zeta	z
H η	eta	ē
Θ θ	theta	th
I ι	iota	i
K κ	kappa	k
Λ λ	lambda	l
M μ	mu	m
N ν	nu	n
Ξ ξ	xi	x
O o	omicron	o
Π π	pi	p
P ρ	rho	r, rh
Σ σ ς	sigma	s
T τ	tau	t
Υ υ	upsilon	y, u
Φ φ	phi	ph
X χ	chi	ch
Ψ ψ	psi	ps
Ω ω	omega	ō

RUSSIAN[8]

Letter	Translit.
А а	a
Б б	b
В в	v
Г г	g
Д д	d
Е е	e
Ж ж	zh
З з	z
И и Й й	i, ĭ
К к	k
Л л	l
М м	m
Н н	n
О о	o
П п	p
Р р	r
С с	s
Т т	t
У у	u
Ф ф	f
Х х	kh
Ц ц	ts
Ч ч	ch
Ш ш	sh
Щ щ	shch
Ъ ъ[9]	"
Ы ы	y
Ь ь[10]	'
Э э	e
Ю ю	yu
Я я	ya

SANSKRIT[11]

Letter	Translit.	Letter	Translit.
अ	a	ञ	ñ
आ	ā	ट	ṭ
इ	i	ठ	ṭh
ई	ī	ड	ḍ
उ	u	ढ	ḍh
ऊ	ū	ण	ṇ
ऋ	r̥	त	t
ॠ	r̥̄	थ	th
ऌ	l̥	द	d
ॡ	l̥̄	ध	dh
ए	e	न	n
ऐ	ai	प	p
ओ	o	फ	ph
औ	au	ब	b
ं[12]	ṁ	भ	bh
ः[13]	ḥ	म	m
क	k	य	y
ख	kh	र	r
ग	g	ल	l
घ	gh	व	v
ङ	ṅ	श	ś
च	c	ष	ṣ
छ	ch	स	s
ज	j	ह	h
झ	jh		

1 See HEBREW ALPHABET and ALEPH, BETH, etc., in Vocab. Where two forms of a letter are given, the second one is the form used at the end of a word. 2 Not repre-sented in transliteration when initial. 3 See ARABIC ALPHABET. In this table the first form given for each letter is used when it stands alone, the second when it is join[ed] to the preceding letter, the third when it is joined to both the preceding and the following letter, and the fourth when it is joined to the following letter only. Many of th[e] letters also have other forms which are used only in certain combinations; the number and nature of these differ from one style of handwriting or font of type to anothe[r] 4 The Hebrew and Arabic letters are all primarily consonants; a few of them are also used secondarily to represent certain vowels, but full indication of vowels, whe[n] provided at all, is by means of a system of dots or strokes adjacent to the consonantal characters. 5 Alif represents no sound in itself, but is used principally as a bear[er] of the hamza (transliterated ' medially and finally; not represented in transliteration when initial) and as the sign of a long a. 6 When ة has two dots above it (ة), is called tā marbūta and, if it immediately precedes a vowel, is transliterated t instead of h. 7 See ALPHA, BETA, GAMMA, etc., in Vocab. The letter gamma is transliterate[d] n only before velars; the letter upsilon is transliterated u only as the final element in diphthongs. 8 See CYRILLIC ALPHABET in Vocab. 9 This sign indicates that the im-mediately preceding consonant is not palatalized even though immediately followed by a palatal vowel. 10 This sign indicates that the immediately preceding consona[nt] is palatalized even though not immediately followed by a palatal vowel. 11 The alphabet shown here is the Devanagari. When vowels are combined with precedi[ng] consonants they are indicated by various strokes or hooks instead of by the signs here given, or, in the case of short a, not written at all. Thus the character क represen[ts] ka; the character का, kā; the character कि, ki; the character की, kī; the character कु, ku; the character कू, kū; the character कृ, kr; the character कॄ, kr̄; the charact[er] के, ke; the character कै, kai; the character को, ko; the character कौ, kau; and the character क्, k without any following vowel. There are also many compound cha[r]acters representing combinations of two or more consonants. 12 See ANUSVARA. 13 See VISARGA.

☊	ascending node
①,②,③	asteroids in order of discovery
⊖	center
⚷	comet
☌	conjunction
☋	descending node
♁, ⊖, or ♁	the earth
♃	Jupiter, Thursday
♂	Mars, Tuesday
☿	Mercury, Wednesday
☽, ☾, or ☽	the moon, Monday
●	moon, new
☽, ◐, ☽, ☽	moon, first quarter
○ or ☺	moon, full
☾, ◑, ☾, ☾	moon, last quarter
♆, ♆, or ♆	Neptune
☍	opposition
♇, ♇	Pluto
□	quadrature
♄ or ♄	Saturn, Saturday
☉	the sun, Sunday
* or ✳	star
α, β, γ, etc.	stars in a constellation in order of brightness
♅, ♅, or ♅	Uranus
♀	Venus, Friday

SIGNS OF THE ZODIAC

♒	Aquarius
♓	Pisces
♈	Aries
♉	Taurus
♊	Gemini
♋	Cancer
♌	Leo
♍	Virgo
♎	Libra
♏	Scorpio
♐	Sagittarius
♑	Capricorn

BIOLOGY

○	an individual, specifically, a female—used chiefly in inheritance charts
□	an individual, specifically, a male—used chiefly in inheritance charts
♀	female
♂	male
⚥	perfect or hermaphroditic plant or flower
X	crossed with a hybrid
+	wild type
F_1	offspring of the first generation
F_2	offspring of the second generation
F_3, F_4, F_5 ...	offspring of the third, fourth, fifth, etc., generation
P	parental herb
∞	indefinite number

BRAILLE

⠁	A or 1	⠓	H or 8	⠕	O	⠧	V
⠃	B or 2	⠊	I or 9	⠏	P	⠺	W
⠉	C or 3	⠚	J or 0	⠟	Q	⠭	X
⠙	D or 4	⠅	K	⠗	R	⠽	Y
⠑	E or 5	⠇	L	⠎	S	⠵	Z
⠋	F or 6	⠍	M	⠞	T	⠠	capital sign
⠛	G or 7	⠝	N	⠥	U	⠼	number sign

BUSINESS TERMS AND SYMBOLS

A/C, a/c	account in or with	lb	pound, pounds
@	at; each (4 apples @ 10¢ = 40¢)	%	percent
/	per	‰	per thousand
c/o	care of	$	dollars
#	number if it precedes a numeral (track #3); pounds if it follows (a 5# sack of sugar)	¢	cents
		©	copyright

B/D	bank draft	L/C, l/c	letter of credit
B/E	bill of exchange	N/S	insufficient funds
B/L	bill of lading	o/c	overcharge
B/P	bills payable	®	registered trademark
B/R	bills receivable	TM	trademark
A/R	accounts receivable	A/O, a/o	account of
A/P	accounts payable	O/S	out of stock
B/V	book value	O/S/C	out of stock cancel
C/D	certificate of deposit, carried down	O/S/F	out of stock follow with reorder
d/d	delivered	P/A	power of attorney
D/O	delivery order	P/N	promissory note
G/A	general average	W/B	waybill

CHEMISTRY

+ signifies "plus," "and," "together with" and is used between the symbols of substances brought together for, or produced by, a reaction; placed to the right of a symbol above the line, it signifies a unit charge of positive electricity: Ca^{++} denotes the ion of calcium, which carries two positive charges

− signifies a single "bond" or unit of attractive force or affinity and is used between the symbols of elements or groups which unite to form a compound: H−Cl for HCl, H−O−H for H_2O; placed to the right of a symbol above the line, it signifies a unit charge of negative electricity: Cl^- denotes a chlorine ion carrying a negative charge

● is often used: (1) to indicate a single bond (as H·Cl for H-Cl) or (2) to denote the presence of a single unpaired electron (as H·) or (3) to separate parts of a compound regarded as loosely joined (as $CuSO_4·5H_2O$)

◯ or ◎ denotes the benzene ring

= indicates a double bond; placed to the right of a symbol above the line, it signifies two unit charges of negative electricity (as $SO_4^=$, the negative ion of sulfuric acid, carrying two negative charges)

: indicates a double bond (as $H_2C{:}CH_2$) or an unshared pair of electrons (as $:NH_3$)

≡ indicates a triple bond or a triple negative charge

( ) mark groups within a compound [as in $C_6H_4(CH_3)_2$ the formula for xylene, which contains two methyl groups CH_3]

= gives or forms

→ gives, leads to, or is converted to

⇄ forms and is from; is in equilibrium with

↓ indicates precipitation of the substance

↑ indicates that the substance passes off a gas

pH negative logarithm of hydrogen-ion concentration

< bivalent element

> bivalent radical

β^- electron

β^+ positron

β proton

α alpha particle

n neutron

γ gamma radiation

ELECTRICITY

A	ampere	Z	impedance
⊖	alternating current source	⁛	inductor
Ⓐ	ammeter	—⊙—	neon lamp
⊽	antenna	—⊛—	filament lamp
⊣⊢	battery, single cell	Φ	magnetic flux
⊣⊩⊢	battery, multicell	–	negative charge
cd/m^2	candela per square meter	Ω	ohm
⊣⊢	capacitor, fixed	+	positive charge
⊣⊬	capacitor, variable	⋎⋎⋎	resistor, fixed
⊓⊓	connected	⋎⋎	resistor, variable
⊣	not connected	→←	spark gap
⇆	current	Ⓧ	transistor
→	current direction	V	volts
—◀—	diode	Ⓥ	voltmeter
⏚	ground	——	wire
		λ	wavelength

´	acute accent (étranger)	~	tilde (São Paulo)
‿	breve signifies a short vowel	¨	umlaut (Grösse)
¸	cedilla (façade)	¿	begins a question in Spanish
^	circumflex (fête)	«	guillmets open quotation marks
`	grave accent (à la carte)	»	guillmets close quotation marks
-	macron signifies a long vowel		

MATHEMATICS

+   plus; positive—used also to indicate omitted figures or an approximation (3.141+)

−   minus; negative

±   plus or minus (the square root of $4a^2$ is ± 2a); more or less than (a deviation of $2a$)

×   multiplied by; times (6 x 4 = 24)—also indicated by placing a dot between the factors (6 · 4 = 24) or by writing factors other than numerals without signs

÷ or : or / or $\overset{x}{\overset{}{v}}$ divided by (24 ÷ 6 = 4)—also indicated by writing the divisor under the dividend with a line between or by writing the divisor after the dividend with a diagonal between (3/8)

=   equals (6 + 2 = 8)

≠   is not equal to

>   is greater than (6>5)

>>   is much greater than

<   is less than (3<4)

<<   is much less than

≥   is greater than or equal to

≤   is less than or equal to

≯   is not greater than

≮   is not less than

≈   is approximately equal to

≡   is identical to

~   equivalent, similar

≅   is congruent to

∝   varies directly as; is proportional to

:   is to; the ratio of

∴   therefore

∵   because

::   proportion

н   geometric proportion

∞   infinity

∠   angle

∟   right angle

⊥   perpendicular

○   circle

⌒   arc of a circle

△   triangle

□   square

▭   rectangle

0   zero

√   radical or root—used without a figure to indicate a square root (as in √4 = 2) or with an index above the sign to indicate another degree (as in $\sqrt[3]{3}$, $\sqrt[7]{7}$); also denoted by a fractional index to the right of a number whose denominator expresses the degree of the root ($3^{1/3} = \sqrt[3]{3}$)

( )   parentheses   the quantities enclosed are to be taken together

[ ]   brackets   the quantities enclosed are to be taken together

{ }   braces   the quantities enclosed are to be taken together

π   pi; the number is 3.14159+; the ratio of the circumference of a circle to its diameter

e or ε   (1) the number 2.7182818+; the base of the natural system of logarithms (2) the eccentricity of a conic section

°   degree (60°)

′   minute (1/60th of a degree); foot (30′)

″   second (1/60th of a second); inch (30″)

!   factorial—used to indicate the product of all the whole numbers up to and including a given preceding number

∪   union of two sets

∩   intersection of two sets

⊂   is included in, is a subset of

⊃   contains a subset

∈ or ε   is an element of

∉   is not an element of

Λ or 0 or φ or {}   empty set, null set

MEDICINE AND PHARMACOLOGY

A, Ā, or āā   of each

℞   take—used on prescriptions; prescription; treatment

☠   poison

APOTHECARIES' MEASURES

℥   ounce

ƒ℥   fluidounce

ƒℨ   fluidram

♏, ♏, ♏ or min   minim

APOTHECARIES' WEIGHTS

℔   pound

℥   ounce (as ℥ i or ℥ j, one ounce; ℥ ss, half an ounce; ℥ iss or ℥ jss, one ounce and a half; ℥ ij, two ounces)

ℨ   dram

Э   scruple

MORSE CODE

A	.—	M	——	Y	—.——	,	——..——
B	—...	N	—.	Z	——..		
C	—.—.	O	———	1	.————	?	..——..
D	—..	P	.——.	2	..———	;	—.—.—.
E	.	Q	——.—	3	...——	:	———...
F	..—.	R	.—.	4	....—		
G	——.	S	...	5	.....	'	.————.
H	....	T	—	6	—....	/	—..—.
I	..	U	..—	7	——...	( )	—.——.—
J	.———	V	...—	8	———..		
K	—.—	W	.——	9	————.		
L	.—..	X	—..—	0	—————		

MUSIC

o	whole note	▬	whole rest	
♩ (half)	half note	▬	half rest	
♩	quarter note	𝄽	quarter rest	
♪	eighth note	𝄾	eighth rest	
♬	sixteenth note	𝄿	sixteenth rest	

G clef; treble clef—used to indicate that the second line represents the first G above middle C

triplet—three notes grouped together under a curved line or bracket; the three notes have a total duration that two of those notes would ordinarily receive

F clef; bass clef—used to indicate that the second line represents the first F below middle C.

2/4 two counts per measure; quarter note = one count

C clef; alto clef

3/4 three counts per measure; quarter note = one count

measure

4/4 four counts per measure; quarter note = one count

final bar

6/8 six counts per measure; eighth note = one count

repeat—used to indicate the beginning and end respectively of a passage to be played or sung twice.

common time; same as 4/4

repeat measure

cut time

sharp

dal segno (D.S.)—repeat from the sign

♭ flat

hold, pause

♮ natural—used to annul the effect of a previous # or ♭; the *sharps* or *flats* placed at the beginning of a composition or section are called collectively the *key signature*.

sforzando—strong accent

staccato—shorten value of note and substitute a rest

𝄪 double sharp—used to raise a note two half steps

p piano (soft)

♭♭ double flat—used to lower a note two half steps

pp pianissimo (very soft)

< crescendo

f forte (loud)

> decrescendo, diminuendo

ff fortissimo (very loud)

<> swell

~ trill

NUMBERS

MODERN	EGYPTIAN (HIEROGLYPHIC)	EGYPTIAN (HIERATIC)	BABYLONIAN	GREEK (ATTIC)	ROMAN	HEBREW	CHINESE (CIPHERED)	HINDU (DEVANAGARI)	ARABIC (MODERN)
1	I	ı	▼	I	I	א	一	१	١
2	II	ıı	▼▼	II	II	ב	二	२	٢
3	III	ııı	▼▼▼	III	III	ג	三	३	٣
4	IIII	ч	▼▼/▼▼	IIII	IIII	ד	四	४	٤
5	III/II	ๅ	▼▼▼/▼▼	Γ	V	ה	五	५	٥
6	III/III	ใ	▼▼▼/▼▼▼	ΓI	VI	ו	六	६	٦
7	IIII/III	ว	▼▼▼▼/▼▼▼	ΓII	VII	ז	七	७	٧
8	IIII/IIII	=	▼▼▼▼/▼▼▼▼	ΓIII	VIII	ח	八	८	٨
9	IIIII/IIII	ใ	▼▼▼▼▼/▼▼▼▼	ΓIIII	IX	ט	九	९	٩
10	∩	λ	◄	Δ	X	י	十	10	١٠
20	∩∩	⌐	◄◄	ΔΔ	XX	כ	二十	20	٢٠
30	∩∩∩	⋌	◄◄◄	ΔΔΔ	XXX	ל	三十	30	٣٠
40	∩∩∩∩	⌐	◄◄/◄◄	ΔΔΔΔ	XL	מ	四十	80	٤٠
50	∩∩∩∩∩	⌐	◄◄◄/◄◄	ΓΔ	L	נ	五十	90	٥٠
60	∩∩∩/∩∩∩	ᴗᴗ	▼	ΓΔΔ	LX	ס	六十	50	٦٠
70	∩∩∩∩/∩∩∩	3	▼◄	ΓΔΔΔ	LXX	ע	七十	70	٧٠
80	∩∩∩∩/∩∩∩∩	ᴗᴗᴗ	▼◄◄	ΓΔΔΔΔ	LXXX	פ	八十	80	٨٠
90	∩∩∩∩∩/∩∩∩∩	ᴗᴗᴗ	▼◄◄◄	ΓΔΔΔΔΔ	XC	צ	九十	90	٩٠
100	ᡡ	ノ	▼◄◄◄	H	C	ק	百	100	١٠٠

PHYSICS

T	absolute temperature	Φ	flux
α	alpha particle	υ	frequency
Å	angstrom	γ	gamma ray
β	beta ray	Z	impedance
G	conductance	L	inductance
Λ	conductivity	n	index of refraction
ρ	density	μ	magnetic moment
E	electric field	X	magnification
V	electrical potential	B	magnetic field or induction
e	electron, electronic charge	Ω	ohm
W	energy or work	p	particle momentum
H	enthalpy	h	Planck's constant
S	entropy	c	speed of light
ψ	fluidity	R	universal constant of gas
		λ	wavelength

POSTAL ABBREVIATIONS AND SYMBOLS

AL	Alabama	HA	Hawaii	PA	Pennsylvania
AK	Alaska	Hts	Heights	Pl	Place
Aly	Alley	Hwy	Highway	Plz	Plaza
AS	American Samoa	ID	Idaho	Pt	Point
Arc	Arcade	IL	Illinois	PO	Post Office
AZ	Arizona	IN	Indiana	PR	Puerto Rico
AR	Arkansas	IA	Iowa	RI	Rhode Island
Ave	Avenue	KS	Kansas	Rd	Road
Blvd	Boulevard	KY	Kentucky	R	Rural
Br	Branch	Ln	Lane	RR	Rural Route
Byp	Bypass	LA	Louisiana	SC	South Carolina
CA	California	ME	Maine	SD	South Dakota
Cswy	Causeway	Mnr	Manor	Sq	Square
Ctr	Center	MD	Maryland	St	Street
Cir	Circle	MA	Massachusetts	TN	Tennessee
CO	Colorado	MI	Michigan	Ter	Terrace
CT	Connecticut	MN	Minnesota	TX	Texas
Ct	Court	MS	Mississippi	Trl	Trail
Cts	Courts	MO	Missouri	Tpke	Turnpike
Cres	Crescent	MT	Montana	UT	Utah
DC	District of Columbia	NE	Nebraska	VT	Vermont
Dr	Drive	NV	Nevada	Via	Viaduct
Expy	Expressway	NH	New Hampshire	VA	Virginia
Ext	Extension	NJ	New Jersey	VI	Virgin Islands
FL	Florida	NM	New Mexico	Vis	Vista
Fwy	Freeway	NY	New York	WA	Washington
Gdns	Gardens	NC	North Carolina	WV	West Virginia
GA	Georgia	ND	North Dakota	WI	Wisconsin
Grv	Grove	OH	Ohio	WY	Wyoming
GU	Guam	OK	Oklahoma		

RADIO CODE

A	alpha	N	november
B	bravo	O	oscar
C	charlie	P	papa
D	delta	Q	quebec
E	echo	R	romeo
F	foxtrot	S	sierra
G	golf	T	tango
H	hotel	U	uniform
I	india	V	victor
J	juliet	W	whiskey
K	kilo	X	x-ray
L	lima	Y	yankee
M	mike	Z	zulu

REFERENCE MARKS

*	asterisk or star	§	section or numbered clause
†	dagger	‖	parallels
‡	double dagger	¶	paragraph

WARNINGS

Stop Ahead

Stop

Curve

Main Road Ahead

Road Bends Right

Road Bends Left

Traffic Merges from Left

Traffic Merges from Right

Road Narrows

Divided Highway Ends

Two Way Traffic

Intersection

T Junction

Staggered Intersection

Steep Hill Downwards

Steep Hill Upwards

Draw Bridge

People Working

Tunnel

Pedestrian Crossing

Watch Out for Children

Animal Crossing

Slippery Road

Danger

Falling Rocks

Height Limit

Traffic Light Ahead

Hilly Road

COMMANDS

No Entry

Road Closed

No Vehicles

No Motorcycles

No Pedestrians

Trucks Prohibited

No Left Turn

No Right Turn

No U Turns

No Passing

Keep Left

Pass Either Side

Ahead Only

Turn Left Ahead

Turn Left

No Waiting

No Stopping

Speed Limit

Resume Speed

Minimum Speed Limit

Yield

Stop and Yield Right of Way

Vehicle Total Weight Limit

Width Limit

INFORMATION

One Way Traffic

No Through Street

Traffic Circle

Parking

Hospital

Mechanic

Telephone

Gas Station

Camp Site

Trailer Camp

Hostel

SEMAPHORE

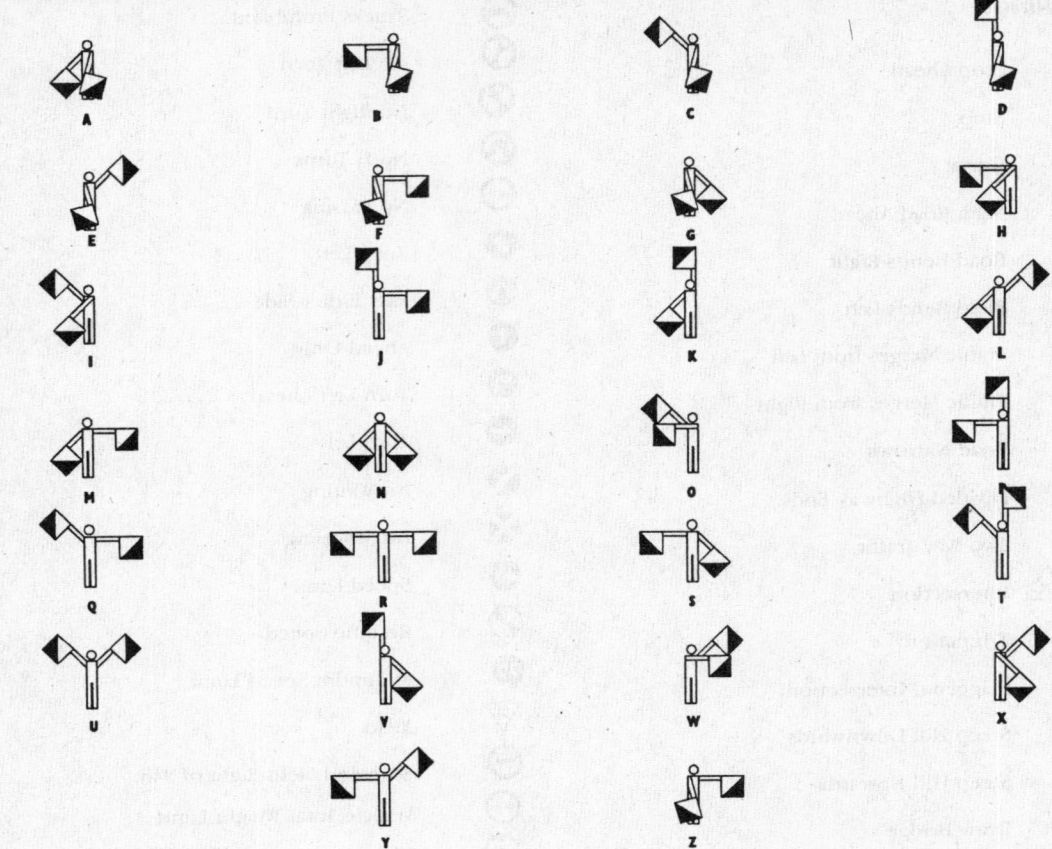

SIGN LANGUAGE (DACTYLOLOGY)

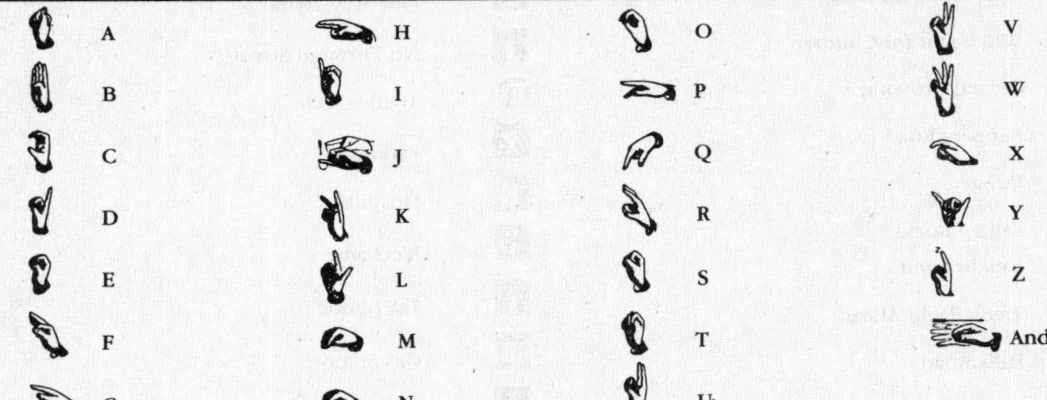

WEATHER

BAROMETER

		—	steady, same as three hours ago
⌃	rising, then falling	∨	falling, then rising, same or lower than three hours ago
⌐	rising, then steady; or rising, then rising more slowly	＼	falling, then steady; or falling, then falling more slowly
/	rising steadily, or unsteadily	＼	falling steadily, or unsteadily
∨	falling or steady, then rising; or rising, then rising more quickly	⌃	steady or rising, then falling; or falling, then falling more quickly

OUD TYPES

⌒	cumulus
∿	stratocumulus
—	stratus
∠	thin altostratus
⦜	thick altostratus
∽	thin altocumulus
∾	thin but increasing altocumulus
∾∾	dense altocumulus
⌐	thin cirrus
⟩	thickening cirrus
⌐₋	dense cirrus
⌐	cirrostratus
∠	thickening cirrostratus
⌐	thick cirrostratus

IND SPEED

⎯o	1–2 knots
⎯o	3–7 knots
⎯o	8–12 knots
⎯o	13–17 knots
⎯o	18–22 knots
⎯o	23–27 knots

MISCELLANEOUS

◎	calm
○	clear
◑	cloudy (partly)
●	cloudy (completely overcast)
+	drifting or blowing snow
⟩	drizzle
=	fog
∾	freezing rain
▴▴▴▴	cold front
⌒⌒⌒	warm front
▴⌒▴⌒	occluded front
⌒▾⌒	stationary front
)(	funnel clouds
∞	haze
◉	hurricane
↻	tropical storm
•	rain
⁚	rain and snow
⧣	rime or frost
⌇	sandstorm or dust storm
▽	shower(s)
⟁̇	shower of rain
⟁̇	shower of hail
△	sleet
∗	snow
ↆ	thunderstorm
⌒⌒⌒	visibility reduced by smoke

ISCELLANEOUS

&	and
&c	et cetera, and so forth
" or ")	ditto marks
/	virgule: used to mean "or" (as in *and/or*), "and/or" (as in *dead/wounded*), "per" (as in *feet/second*); indicates end of a line of verse; separates the figures of a date (1/17/71)
☞	index *or* first
<	derived from—sometimes used in etymologies
>	whence derived—sometimes used in etymologies
+	and—sometimes used in etymologies
*	assumed—used in etymologies
†	died—used esp. in genealogies
✚	cross—can be represented in various recognized forms as a symbol of the crucifixion of Jesus Christ and of the Christian religion
✶	monogram from Greek XP signifying Jesus
✡	Star of David, Judaism
☥	ankh—a symbol of life in ancient Egypt

卐	swastika—an ancient mystical symbol adopted by the Fascists in Germany in the 20th century as the symbol of the Nazi party
℣	versicle—a short verse in a church service
℟	response—the response of the congregation or a choir in a church service
*	used in Roman Catholic and Anglican service books to divide each verse of a psalm, indicating where the response begins
✠ *or* +	used in some service books to indicate where the sign of the cross is to be made; also used by certain Roman Catholic and Anglican prelates as a sign of the cross preceding their signatures
LXX	Septuagint
f/ or *f:*	relative aperture of a photographic lens
⚙	civil defense
☮	peace
☪	Star and crescent (Islamic)
☯	Yin-yang (Taoist)
☭	hammer and sickle (Communist party)
⊕	world
☢	radioactive
🔥	flammable

History and the World Today

Chronology of World History

Human history is often described in terms of events, seemingly unconnected, that have significantly changed our world. Wars and famines have obvious and immediate impact; the relevance of other events—the invention of the telephone and the camera, or the polio vaccines—often become apparent only decades, even centuries, after their occurrence. This Chronology includes both the momentous and the minute changes that have altered, transformed, or destroyed civilizations throughout history.

70,000,000 B.C.E. First primates appear.

4,000,000 B.C.E. Upright-walking australopithecine appears in southern and eastern Africa.

2,000,000 B.C.E. Appearance of *Homo habilis,* who becomes the first to use stone tools.

1,600,000 B.C.E. Emergence of *Homo erectus* as the human species continues to develop. Use of fire becomes widespread.

200,000 B.C.E. *Homo sapiens* present in Africa.

130,000 B.C.E. *Homo sapiens* splits into two lines, *Homo sapiens neanderthalis* and *Homo sapiens sapiens*. Neanderthal becomes a skilled hunter and is the first to communicate by speech.

40,000 B.C.E. *Homo sapiens sapiens* (modern humanity) begins to dominate as Neanderthals die out. The species spreads to Asia and Europe; their skill in making tools allows them to obtain food easily; beginnings of paleolithic art and religious ceremonies.

20,000 B.C.E. Modern humans migrate to North America.

19,000 B.C.E. Cave painting begins in South America. Cave paintings at Lascaux, France, represent attempts at realistic portrayal and the use of symbolism.

18,000 B.C.E. Culmination of last ice age; height of paleolithic art and development of arrowhead.

14,000 B.C.E. Free-standing cabins built for the first time.

12,000 B.C.E. Dog is domesticated.

11,000 B.C.E. First permanent settlements with systematic hunting and gathering begin to develop in the Middle East.

9000 B.C.E. Neolithic Age begins in Egypt and Mesopotamia.

8000 B.C.E. Agriculture begins at end of Pleistocene period in Near East.

6500 B.C.E. Wheel invented by Sumerians in Tigris-Euphrates Basin.

6000 B.C.E. Pottery evolves, producing decorative works and new possibilities for cookery.

5500 B.C.E. Copper, first metal to be molded and shaped, smelted in Persia; alloys developed c. 3600 B.C.E.

5000 B.C.E. Earliest cities develop in Mesopotamia.

5000 B.C.E. Egyptian calendar developed, based on movements of sun and moon.

5000 B.C.E. First centers of population established in Mexico.

5000 B.C.E. Eskimos begin migration to North America.

4350 B.C.E. Domesticated horses provide new source of power in transportation and agriculture.

4000 B.C.E. Sumerian writing on clay tablets, using pictographs, begins.

4000 B.C.E. Cretan ships begin to dominate Mediterranean.

4000 B.C.E. Assyrians begin to produce richly decorated painted pottery.

4000 B.C.E. Mesopotamians begin to use mortar to bind bricks.

3760 B.C.E. First year according to Jewish calendar.

3700 B.C.E. Sumerian language develops, with symbols representing specific words rather than just ideas. A script using phonetic elements is in use in the Sumerian city of Uruk.

3600 B.C.E. Bronze, first metal hard enough to hold an edge, produced in southwest Asia.

3500 B.C.E. Babylonian influence dominates in Mediterranean areas of Asia, until c. 2000 B.C.E.

3500 B.C.E. Neolithic period begins in western Europe, lasting until c. 1700 B.C.E.

3500 B.C.E. Sumerians develop oar-powered ships, wheeled vehicles, and animal-drawn plows, irrigate desert lands and establish cities of Ur and Eridu.

3400 B.C.E. Egypt's 1st Dynasty, under Menes, unites northern and southern kingdoms, as Nile-valley civilization begins to flourish.

3400 B.C.E. Kilns introduced in Sumer.

3200 B.C.E. Earliest known examples of pottery in North America.

3000 B.C.E. Beginning of "Sage Kings" period in China leads to development of Chinese agriculture.

3000 B.C.E. Forked plows first used in Mesopotamia and Egypt.

3000 B.C.E. Development of Minoan civilization in Crete; cities of Knossos and Phestus founded.

3000 B.C.E. Inhabitants of the Indus valley in India begin weaving cotton.

2900 B.C.E. Great Pyramid of Pharaoh Cheops (Khufu) built at Giza.

2850 B.C.E. Great Sphinx carved at Giza.

2800 B.C.E. First known written epic, *Gilgamesh*, written in Sumerian cuneiform. Use of hieroglyphics begins in Egypt.

2800 B.C.E. Sickle developed by Sumerian farmers for harvesting grain.

2800 B.C.E. Chinese emperor Fu Hsi introduces the Yin and Yang philosophy.

2700 B.C.E. Principles of herbal medicine and acupuncture developed by Chinese emperor Shen Nung.

2640 B.C.E. Silk manufacturing begins in China.

2600 B.C.E. Egyptians sail to Phoenician city of Byblos in first recorded seagoing voyage.

2500 B.C.E. Iron Age begins in Middle East; Bronze Age continues in Near East; British Isles and central Europe enter the Stone Age.

2500 B.C.E. Indus civilization develops in India, lasting until c. 1500 B.C.E.

2500 B.C.E. Egyptians discover use of papyrus.

2500 B.C.E. Native American communities begin in South America.

2400 B.C.E. Mesopotamian builders begin using arch-and-vault construction.

2350 B.C.E. Akkadian Empire founded by Sargon, establishing vast Semitic empire over Mesopotamia, lasting until c. 2100 B.C.E.

2000 B.C.E. Indo-European tribes of Asia Minor unite in single kingdom of the Hittites.

1849 B.C.E. Vast irrigation system developed in Egypt under Pharaoh Amenemhet III.

1800 B.C.E. Stonehenge, an arrangement of stones, constructed in England; the arrangement of the stones indicates a possible use in religious ritual.

1766 B.C.E. Shang Dynasty rises to power in China; rules until 1122 B.C.E. Beginnings of Chinese script.

1750 B.C.E. Hammurabi, king of Babylon, reunites Mesopotamia and establishes first legal system based on the principle of "an eye for an eye."

1700 B.C.E. Judaism founded by Abraham of Mesopotamia.

1700 B.C.E. Bronze Age begins in Europe.

1700 B.C.E. Cretans build Great Palace at Knossos employing an elaborate design and a system of water pipes and baths.

1600 B.C.E. Linear B script, an ancestor of Ancient Greek, develops in Minoan civilization.

1570 B.C.E. Beginning of New Kingdom in Egypt; 18th Dynasty rules until c. 330 B.C.E.

1525 B.C.E. Pharaoh Thutmose expands Egyptian empire to include Palestine and Syria.

1500 B.C.E. Indus civilization falls after Aryan invasion; the mixture of Aryans and native Dravidian cultures results in the beginnings of Hinduism.

1360 B.C.E. Monotheism introduced to Egypt when Aton, the Sun disc, is the only god recognized by the pharaoh Amenhotep IV (Akhenaton) and his wife Nefertiti.

1349 B.C.E. Tutankhamen buried in Thebes in a tomb filled with works of art and other treasures including a gold coffin.

1275 B.C.E. Moses and Aaron lead the Israelites out of Egypt to escape the oppressive rule of Ramses II. The Jews wander the desert for the next 40 years.

1200 B.C.E. Mycenaeans destroy Troy.

1170 B.C.E. First recorded labor strike occurs as Theban laborers stop working on a new pyramid when their pay is delayed.

1122 B.C.E. Zhou (Chou) Dynasty founded in China; it lasts until c. 220 B.C.E.

1100 B.C.E. Assyrian Empire establishes its dominance in Mesopotamia.

1100 B.C.E. Greeks develop simple linear patterns for decorating pottery and small sculptures.

1025 B.C.E. Saul becomes first king of the Jews.

1005 B.C.E. David becomes king (ruling until c. 960 B.C.E.) of united Judea and Israel, with its center at Jerusalem.

1000 B.C.E. Beginning of Hebrew Bible (Old Testament) in the Torah, five books of Moses; text compiled over next ten centuries

1000 B.C.E. Iron Age begins in Europe.

1000 B.C.E. Chavin culture on Peruvian coast begins to develop agriculture and metallurgy.

930 B.C.E. Hebrew Kingdom divides into kingdoms of Israel and Judea following death of King Solomon.

900 B.C.E. Etruscans become the first settlers on the Italian peninsula and establish towns built on hillside terraces.

850 B.C.E. Greek epics *Iliad* and *Odyssey* written by poet Homer.

814 B.C.E. Phoenicians, led by Princess Dido, found city of Carthage.

800 B.C.E. Phoenicians begin to colonize North Africa.

776 B.C.E. First recorded Olympic games in Greece.

753 B.C.E. City of Rome founded.

750 B.C.E. Nubians conquer Egypt.

750 B.C.E. Chinese cities and industries flourish during period.

720 B.C.E. Sargon II of Assyria conquers kingdom of Israel, deports 10 northern tribes ("lost tribes of Israel") to Central Asia.

705 B.C.E. Assyria, having established control over most of southwest Asia, enters period of achievement in the arts and literature based in the city of Nineveh.

700 B.C.E. Aqueducts provide water for developing cities in the Near East.

700 B.C.E. Athenians adopt black-figure style for vase painting.

658 B.C.E. Byzantium, later Constantinople, founded by Greek colonists.

630 B.C.E. Zoroaster born; his teachings dominate Persian religion for centuries.

621 B.C.E. Draco, Athenian ruler, issues a severe code of laws making almost all offenses punishable by death.

605 B.C.E. Nebuchadnezzar II of Babylon begins reign in which he extends his empire to Syria and Palestine. His ambitious building program includes the construction of the Hanging Gardens of Babylon.

600 B.C.E. The Greek poet Sappho begins writing lyric poetry in the woman's colony of Lesbos. Her poetry, surviving only in fragments, will later influence poets such as H. D. and the Imagists.

600 B.C.E. Influenced by Oriental art, Greek art takes on a more fluid style as straight lines are replaced by curvilinear forms.

594 B.C.E. King Solon of Athens introduces a new constitution and set of laws and establishes the beginnings of Athenian democracy.

587 B.C.E. Babylonian King Nebuchadnezzar II conquers Jerusalem, exiles Jews in Babylonian Captivity.

570 B.C.E. Aesop, a Greek, writes popular fables about morality.

565 B.C.E. Lao-tse founds Chinese philosophy of Taoism; principles set down in the *Tao Te Ching*.

538 B.C.E. Cyrus the Great of Persia conquers Babylon, creating vast Persian Empire.

536 B.C.E. Cyrus allows Jews to return to Jerusalem; the Jews rebuild Great Temple destroyed by Nebuchadnezzar.

525 B.C.E. Gautama Siddhartha originates Buddhist religious thought in India.

525 B.C.E. Persian forces under Cambyses defeat Egypt and add the Nile Delta to Persian Empire.

525 B.C.E. Red-figure style of Greek vase painting begins, introducing the depiction of spatial depth.

522 B.C.E. Darius I becomes king of Persia, institutes vast reforms, including common currency and regular taxes.

509 B.C.E. Rome becomes a republic as last Tarquin king is expelled.

500 B.C.E. Confucius (Kung Fu-tzu) begins teaching philosophy of moral beliefs and practices across China. His views on morality, customs, and statecraft influence Chinese thought and society for the next two thousand years.

490 B.C.E. Athenian forces defeat Persians at Battle of Marathon.

480 B.C.E. Early classical period begins in Greek art, emphasizing naturalism in painting and sculpture. Works include Myron's *The Discus Thrower* and Polykleitos's *The Spear Carrier*.

479 B.C.E. Greeks defeat Persian forces at the Battle of Platae, marking further decline of Persian Empire.

478 B.C.E. Athens takes control of the Delian League and begins to dominate Greece.

475 B.C.E. Pindar's famous odes and songs celebrating the accomplishments of athletes shape the development of Greek lyrical poetry.

468 B.C.E. Sophocles bests Aeschylus in Athenian prize for drama; with Euripides and Aristophanes, they embody classical age of Greek drama for next century.

460 B.C.E. Beginning of Golden Age of Athenian power and culture; high classical period of Greek Art; Pericles begins rebuilding of the Acropolis.

460 B.C.E. Hippocrates, Greek physician and Father of Medicine, born.

460 B.C.E. Greeks build Temple of Zeus, which epitomizes the Doric style in architecture.

450 B.C.E. Celtic peoples settle in British Isles; development of Celtic La Tene art style characterized by abstract design and patterning; style combines Greek, Celtic, and Etruscan influences.

449 B.C.E. *History* by Greek historian Herodotus (Father of History) describes the wars between the Greeks and Persians. His works, combining legend and anecdote, are the first to critically assess historical material.

437 B.C.E. The Parthenon built under the supervision of the sculptor Phidias. The architecture and friezes epitomize the Golden Age in Greek art.

431 B.C.E. Beginning of Peloponnesian Wars between Athens and Sparta; Athens falls c. 404 B.C.E.

422 B.C.E. Aristophanes's *The Wasps* is performed; his other works include *The Clouds*, *The Birds*, and *The Frogs*. His plays satirize contemporary figures and issues.

401 B.C.E. Greek historian Thucydides dies after chronicling the Golden Age of Pericles. Later considered the father of scientific history, he tried to give an objective account of events.

399 B.C.E. Greek philosopher Socrates, inventor of Socratic dialogue, condemned to death for impiety and corrupting youth.

396 B.C.E. Romans conquer Etruscan city of Veil after a ten-year struggle; decline of Etruscan civilization in Italy begins.

387 B.C.E. Plato, follower of Socrates, founds Academy in Athens; works and concepts such as the philosopher-king and the existence of ideal forms establish the basis of Western philosophy.

382 B.C.E. Demosthenes's *Phillipics Concerning the Crown* embody the traditions of Greek oratory.

343 B.C.E. Aristotle, student of Plato, becomes teacher of Alexander of Macedonia. His works shape varied fields of thought including ethics, drama, metaphysics, and science and become central to the doctrine of the Christian Church.

338 B.C.E. Philip of Macedonia conquers Greece at the Battle of Chaironeia.

336 B.C.E. Alexander the Great becomes king of Macedonia; by the time of his death in 323 B.C.E., Alexander has expanded his Empire to occupy the Persian Empire, Egypt, and all of Greece; also during his reign, the culture and philosophy of Athenian Greece spread over much of the Near East and Middle East.

321 B.C.E. Civil wars begin among Alexander's successors over empire; empire ultimately divided, but Hellenistic culture continues to spread to Egypt and the Middle East.

307 B.C.E. Ptolemy Soter of Egypt begins foundations of museum and builds first library at Alexandria.

305 B.C.E. Epicurus begins teaching system of philosophy, arguing that human happiness is the highest good and its rational pursuit should be adopted. Epicurean philosophy continued by Roman philosopher Lucretius.

300 B.C.E. Euclid's *Elements* lays out principles of geometry.

300 B.C.E. Mencius, a follower of Confucius, argues that human nature is inherently good but must be properly cultivated.

272 B.C.E. Rome secures control of southern Italy with victory at Tarentum.

264 B.C.E. First Punic War (until 241 B.C.E.) between Rome and Carthage begins; in Second (219–210 B.C.E.) and Third (149–146 B.C.E.) Punic Wars, Rome gains control over Carthage and its Mediterranean and Iberian possessions.

222 B.C.E. Rome conquers northern Italy with defeat of Mediolanum (Milan).

219 B.C.E. In Second Punic War, Hannibal of Carthage invades northern Italy across Alps.

215 B.C.E. Great Wall of China built to keep out Mongol invaders.

206 B.C.E. Han Dynasty begins expansion of Chinese empire and increases contact with the West. During the Han Dynasty, China establishes the first civil service.

200 B.C.E. *Venus de Milo*, modeled on the work of the Greek sculptor Praxiteles, begins the tradition of free-standing nudes in Classical sculpture.

172 B.C.E. Rome-Macedon War; Macedonia falls into Roman control in 168 B.C.E.

168 B.C.E. Captured Macedonians sold into slavery following defeat by Rome.

167 B.C.E. Jewish Maccabees revolt against Syrian control of Judea.

147 B.C.E. Rome annexes remainder of Greece.

146 B.C.E. Carthage destroyed in Third Punic War.

142 B.C.E. Judea achieves independence from Syria; Jerusalem liberated.

140 B.C.E. Roman empire continues to expand; Rome conquers Asia Minor (133 B.C.E.), Southern Gaul (121), and Cyrrenaica (96).

100 B.C.E. Teotihuacán becomes first major city in Mexico and dominates central part of the country for the next 600 years.

100 B.C.E. Roman architect Vitruvius writes *De Architectura* outlining the Classical rules of architecture. His work will greatly influence architects of the Italian Renaissance.

91 B.C.E. Italian cities revolt against Roman rule; as a result, all Italians are given the vote.

73 B.C.E. Spartacus leads a slave insurrection and captures Mt. Vesuvius before the rebellion is crushed by Roman armies.

63 B.C.E. Pompey conquers Palestine, expanding Roman province of Syria.

63 B.C.E. Cicero exposes the Cataline conspiracy. A politician, writer, and orator, Cicero influences the culture and politics of the Roman republic; his writings and speeches serve as models for rhetoric and Latin literature.

60 B.C.E. Julius Caesar begins rise as head of Rome; expands republic into Gaul, Britain, and Africa; first triumvirate of Pompey, Caesar, and Crassus established.

55 B.C.E. Lucretius, Roman poet and philosopher, dies. His *De rerum Natura* is one of the first Latin treatments of Greek philosophy

54 B.C.E. Catullus, Roman poet, dies. His most famous lyrical poems are expressions of his devotion to Lesbia.

48 B.C.E. After leading his troops across the Rubicon, defeating the forces of Pompey and the Senate, Caesar takes power in Rome.

46 B.C.E. Julian calendar of 365.25 days adopted

44 B.C.E. Julius Caesar assassinated by Roman Senate.

43 B.C.E. Mark Antony, Octavian, and Lepidus form the Second Triumvirate to rule Rome.

38 B.C.E. *Laocoön* sculpted by Greek sculptors Agesander, Athendorus, and Poludorus. The work embodies the dramatic Hellenistic style.

31 B.C.E. Octavian defeats Mark Antony and Cleopatra, Queen of Egypt, at the Battle of Actium and becomes leader of the Roman world.

27 B.C.E. Octavian, Julius Caesar's nephew, proclaimed Augustus Caesar as the Roman republic becomes an empire. Under Augustus the empire expands and literature and the arts flourish.

25 B.C.E. Architectural style of Roman painting, in which scenes are framed by architectural details, develops.

19 B.C.E. Virgil's epic poem *The Aeneid* dramatizes the founding of Rome. *The Aeneid* and Virgil's pastoral works *The Ecologues* and *Georgics* will later influence the development of European literature.

9 B.C.E. Livy, one of the most important prose writers of the Augustan Age, writes *The History of Rome*.

8 B.C.E. Horace, Roman lyric poet, dies. Under the patronage of Augustus he became one of the leading poets of the Roman Empire.

4 B.C.E. Birth of Jesus Christ (probable date).

8 Roman poet Ovid banished from Rome for his erotic verse, particularly *Metamorphoses* and *Art of Love*.

30 Crucifixion of Christ (probable date).

43 Emperor Claudius leads invasion to extend Roman control over England.

50 St. Paul spreads the teachings of Christ and establishes churches; gospels of Mark, Luke, Peter, Matthew, and John transcribed.

50 Architectural style of painting declines and is replaced by the style of wall painting at Pompeii characterized by use of brilliant color, landscapes, and illusionistic architecture.

60 Buddhism becomes official religion of China.

64 Emperor Nero launches persecution of Christians and Jews; persecution of Christians increases during 2nd century C.E.

70 Jewish religious revolt defeated by Romans; Jerusalem destroyed, with only the Wailing Wall remaining.

70 Construction begins on Roman Colosseum.

98 Roman Empire attains largest geographical extent, under Emperor Trajan.

100 Paper invented in China; paper use becomes more widespread at start of 3rd century C.E.

100 Marble sculpture of Trajan's bust exemplifies Roman interest in portraying the character and personality of the subject and glorifying the image of the emperors.

120 Plutarch, Greek biographer, dies; his *Lives* documents the history of famous Greek and Roman soldiers and leaders and later becomes source material for some Shakespeare plays.

120 Roman Pantheon built, incorporating a massive concrete dome.

122 Roman Emperor Hadrian builds Hadrian's Wall in Britain as a defensive barrier.

124 First imperial university is established in China for the study of the Five Confucian Classics. Extensive knowledge of Confucian philosophy will be required for Chinese civil servant examination until 1905.

133 Trajan's column in Rome completed; the column celebrates the military campaign of Trajan and is noted for its great height and relief sculpture.

165 Plague brought by returning armies spreads across Roman Empire and continues for decades.

200 Huns from Central Asia invade Afghanistan.

212 Emperor Carcalla grants Roman citizenship to all free subjects in Roman Empire.

220 Han Dynasty of China falls; three centuries of division among various kingdoms follow. During this period Confucianism is superseded by Taoism and Buddhism.

250 Persecution of Christians becomes official policy under Roman Emperor Decius; martyrs will become revered as saints.

260 Plotinus founds Neoplatonism; his argument for the superiority of ideas over reality influences the Christian concept of heaven, and Islamic thought.

271 Compass believed to be in use in China.

276 Mani, founder of Manichaean religion in Persia, crucified. Mani combined the teachings of Zoroaster, Jesus, Buddha, and Gnostics and argued that only knowledge of God and oneself can bring liberation from one's present state of darkness. Despite widespread persecution the religion continues until the 10th century.

284 Diocletian establishes College of Emperors and begins program of reforms in Rome.

313 In Edict of Milan, Emperor Constantine establishes religious toleration for Christianity.

315 The Arch of Constantine in Rome integrates elements of Christian art with the Classical style.

320 Northern India united under Gupta Dynasty; beginning classical period of art and culture in India; Sanskrit literature thrives.

325 Ecumenical Council of Nicaea under Constantine condemns Arianist view that Christ was not divine.

330 City of Constantinople, rebuilt on ancient Byzantium, becomes capital of Roman Empire.

360 Japan conquers Korea.

360 Huns invade Europe.

371 New Persian Empire reaches its peak under Shapur II (309–379).

395 Roman Empire divided into separate eastern and western empires, setting the stage for further division of eastern and western Christianity.

399 St. Augustine's *Confessions* tells of his conversion to Christianity. In *City of God*, written in 411, Augustine synthesizes classical thought with church doctrine. His works shape Christian thought in the following centuries.

400 Christian basilicas are built using designs from Roman public buildings. The basilica incorporates the nave, atrium, transept, and apse.

410 Visigoths sack Rome, after having waged war on Roman Empire since 3rd century C.E.

451 Huns under Attila thwarted in invasions of Gaul and Italy after having ravaged much of Europe; Huns leave Europe c. 470.

455 Vandals attack Rome from North Africa, where they settled after Visigoths invaded Spain in 416.

476 Roman Empire in the west falls as various barbarian kingdoms are established; warfare continues across former empire over the next centuries.

500 T'ien-t'ai and Mahayana Amitabha become dominant sects of Buddhism during this period.

500 Sudanic kingships in Africa grow over the next five hundred years; empire eventually stretches from the Nile to Zimbabwe and from Senegal to the Red Sea.

500 Native Americans begin settlement and cultivation of the Mississippi Basin.

517 Emperor Wu Ti converts to Buddhism, brings new religion to central China.

517 Indian astronomer Aryabhata compiles his work into a manual.

519 Temporary end of first schism between eastern and western Catholicism that began in 484.

524 Boethius writes *The Consolation of Philosophy* while in prison, bringing Aristotelian thought into Latin culture.

529 St. Benedict founds Benedictine Order and establishes the first monastery. The order has a strong influence over medieval learning.

529 Byzantine Emperor Justinian closes Academy in Athens founded by Plato on charges of un-Christian paganism.

529 Justinian codifies Roman Law; Byzantine Empire expands under his rule; Byzantine art and architecture—a combination of Classical, Oriental, and Middle Eastern traditions and characterized by heavy stylization, linear emphasis, and the use of gold coloring and mosaic work—enters a golden age. Achievements in architecture include the church of St. Sophia in Constantinople.

537 According to legend, Arthur, king of the Britons, is killed at Battle of Camlan.

542 Great Plague begins in Constantinople, spreads across Europe over next fifty years, killing about half of Europe's population.

552 Buddhism introduced to Japan (date also recorded as 538).

552 Silk industry becomes state monopoly in Byzantine Empire following smuggling of silkworms out of China and Ceylon.

568 Lombard Kingdom of north and central Italy established; endures until 774.

570 Prophet Muhammad, founder of Islam, born.

581 Sui Dynasty ascends to the throne in north China; reunifies China in 589.

587 First Buddhist monastery in Japan founded; Chinese influence in Japan increases over the next decades, ultimately resulting in a Japanese envoy to China in 607.

590 St. Gregory becomes pope; during his papacy he asserts papal absolutism, leads war against Lombards in Italy, and the Gregorian chant is developed.

598 First school in England founded at Canterbury.

600 Barbarian invasions, which plagued Europe since fall of Roman Empire, come to an end during the 7th century.

601 St. Augustine named archbishop of Canterbury, Britain; St. Andrew's Church of Rochester and first St. Paul's Church of London built 603.

610 Muhammad's vision on Mt. Hira tells him he is the prophet of Allah; begins teaching new faith publicly; preaches Muslim brotherhood.

612 Harsha of northern India takes title Emperor of the Five Indies.

618 T'ang Dynasty comes to power in China; under the dynasty (lasting until 907) Chinese culture and literature enjoy a Golden Age. China establishes trade relations with the Islamic and Byzantine world.

620 Persian Empire extends over Egypt, Jerusalem, and Damascus, restoring old Empire of Darius I.

620 Porcelain production in China advances under T'ang Dynasty.

622 Muhammad and followers migrate to Medina to escape persecution in Mecca; this Hegira (flight, or exile) marks year one in Muslim calendar.

630 Muhammad and followers conquer Mecca in jihad (holy war); Mecca becomes spiritual center of Islam; Muhammad dies in 632.

632 Muhammad's successor becomes major issue of conflict between Sunni and Shi'ite Muslim factions.

636 Differences between French and German languages appear in Frankish Empire.

642 Rapid expansion of Islam signified with final victory over Persian Empire; Muslim rule in Persia, Egypt, Syria, Jerusalem, Mesopotamia, and Armenia; by end of century Islam dominates North Africa.

645 Reform of Japanese state and nobility to conform to Chinese system begins.

650 Official version of Qur'an (Koran) lays down principles of Islam, stating that Allah is the only God and Muhammad is his messenger.

669 Archbishop of Canterbury Theodore of Tarsus introduces a system that becomes the model for a secular state and includes the concept of kingship; gradual unification of British Isles follows.

687 Pepin the Younger unites Frankish Kingdom.

700 Mombassa (modern Kenya) establishes itself as the economic center for African- Arab trade.

700 Composition of *Beowulf*; the epic poem is the oldest complete surviving example of the Germanic folk epic.

701 Codification of political law in Japan makes Mikado sole proprietor of all lands.

711 Moors, North African Arabs, invade Iberian Peninsula, establish Muslim state; Muslim state established in India; Arab merchants introduce oriental spices into Mediterranean markets.

717 Byzantine Emperor Leo III repels Arab attack on Constantinople; Arab conquest of Constantinople never achieved, although Muslim empire soon extends from the Pyrenees to China.

726 Byzantine Emperor Leo III bans use of religious images, creating conflict with pope in Rome; Leo III is soon excommunicated by Pope Gregory II.

730 English theologian the Venerable Bede writes *History of the English Church and People*, which becomes an important source for early English history.

730 In Central America, Mayan study of astronomy and mathematics reaches its peak.

732 At Battle of Tours, Frankish leader Charles Martel defeats invading Moorish troops, stemming Arab western advance.

739 Pope Gregory III asks Charles Martel to help fight Arabs, Greeks, and Lombards.

750 The Golden Age of Chinese poetry thrives with the works of Li Po, Wang Wei, and Tu Fu.

750 The Abbasids defeat the Umayyads in the Near East and North Africa to take over Muslim Caliphate; they will rule Muslim world for over three centuries.

751 Arabs learn process of making paper from the Chinese.

756 Pepin III, Frankish King, grants Italian lands to Pope, establishing papal states.

768 Charlemagne succeeds Pepin as Frankish king; under Charlemagne, France will be united and expand into northern Spain, Italy, Saxony, and Bavaria; Frankish culture and learning revives in Carolingian Renaissance.

775 Tibet conquers Himalayan neighbors and concludes border agreement with China.

786 Harun al-Rashid becomes Caliph; under his leadership, Arab trade and contact with Europe increases and Arabic culture thrives.

790 Beginning of long period of Norse invasions into British Isles, France, Germany, and Russia; from Kiev (founded 850) the Norse establish contact with Byzantine commerce, culture, and religion.

794 Japanese capital moves to Heian (Kyoto); during Heian period feudalism supersedes the Chinese-based social order.

800 Charlemagne crowned Holy Roman Emperor by Pope Leo III on Christmas day, reviving idea of western Roman Empire; Byzantium recognizes it in 812.

800 The construction of Islamic mosques comes under the influence of Persian and Byzantine styles. Columns and cupolas are added and minarets and lofty towers take the place of bell towers.

810 Under King Krum, Bulgarian Kingdom expands at the expense of Byzantine Empire; Bulgaria fights Byzantium and other European peoples for several centuries.

813 Al-Mamun becomes Muslim Caliph; his reign is characterized by continuing growth of Arab science and literature.

843 Treaty of Verdun divides Frankish Empire among the three sons of Holy Roman Emperor Louis the Pious; Lothair is given the title of emperor and control of Italy and the valley of the Rhone. The treaty breaks the unity of the Carolingian Empire.

850 Jews settling in Germany develop the Yiddish language, a combination of German and Hebrew.

850 Kaldi, Arabian goatherd, said to have discovered coffee.

863 Cyrillic alphabet invented by Macedonian missionaries in Moravia.

867 Schism between Roman and Eastern Orthodox forms of Christianity begins.

868 *The Diamond Sutra*, made in China, is the first printed book.

890 King Alfred the Great of England establishes regular militia and navy and extends powers of king's court; he also forces Danish presence out of England.

895 Magyar people expelled from Russia and settle in Hungary, where they soon establish strong dynasty under the leadership of Arpad.

900 Romanesque architecture begins to develop in European churches. The style is characterized by massive size, round arches, emphasis on perpendicular elements, and relative simplicity.

900 Construction of European castles during this time reflects the need for strong defense and protection.

907 T'ang Dynasty falls in China; five different dynasties assert imperial authority, creating a half century of weak imperial power.

911 Dukedom of Normandy established by Treaty of St. Clair-sur-Epte under Rollo (Robert I).

912 Abd-al-Rahman III becomes Caliph in Spain, beginning rise of Umayyad culture and rule.

919 Henry I becomes king of Germany, extending German power and unity during his 17-year reign.

955 Magyar invasion of West halted by Otto I, who later becomes Holy Roman Emperor.

960 Sung Dynasty founded in China; under its rule China is unified and governmental reforms are initiated.

960 Mieczyslav becomes first ruler of Poland; converts Poles to Christianity.

975 Modern arithmetical notation brought to Europe by the Arabs.

982 Vikings under Eric the Red establish colonies in Greenland; Viking attacks on British Isles resume.

986 Muslims under Sultan of Ghazni invade India.

987 Hugh Capet becomes king of France, instituting Capetian Dynasty; his reign sees reassertion of monarchical authority over nobility, papacy, and the Holy Roman Emperor.

992 Venice is granted trading privileges in Byzantine Empire and begins its rise as a major trading and economic power.

1000 Norseman Leif Ericsson believed to have landed in Nova Scotia, first European exploration of America.

1000 Rise of Kanem Empire in modern-day northern Nigeria.

1008 Mahmud, Muslim ruler of Ghaznavid Kingdom in Afghanistan, extends his realm to the Ganges with defeat of Hindus; Muslims continue raids of west India.

1010 *The Tale of Gengi*, a classic Japanese novel, written around this time by the court lady Murasaki Shikibu.

1012 Heretics persecuted for first time in German states.

1014 Byzantine forces conquer Bulgaria; Basil II orders Bulgarian armies be blinded; under Basil, Byzantine Empire briefly expands in the Mediterranean.

1020 Prince Jaroslav the Wise of Kiev codifies Russian law and promotes building of churches, schools, and cities.

1022 Synod of Pavia orders celibacy for higher Catholic clergy.

1026 Benedictine monk Guido d'Arezzo introduces solmization to music, defining relative pitches of notes and pioneering modern musical notation.

1030 Arab physician Avicenna's (Ibn Sina) work on medicine will influence medical theory and practice in Europe for centuries.

1054 Schism between Eastern Orthodox and Roman (Western) churches becomes permanent.

1060 Arabs of Almoravud Dynasty of Algeria and Morocco conquer West Africa, defeating Ghana Kingdom that had ruled over the region since the 4th century.

1066 William the Conqueror leads Norman forces in conquest of England; fully feudal society introduced to England under William. Bayeaux Tapestry depicts Norman conquest.

1068 Chinese Emperor Shen Tsung introduces radical reforms in agriculture and state finances.

1071 Beginnings of Ottoman Empire and end of Byzantine rule in Asia Minor marked by victories of Seljuk Turks, who soon capture Syria and Palestine.

1075 Conflict between Emperor Henry IV and Pope Gregory VII over respective powers of papacy and Holy Roman Emperor; Henry's German forces wage attacks on papal allies in Italy.

1085 *Domesday Book* compiled, listing assets of all British landowners for taxation and administrative purposes.

1096 First Crusade against "infidels" in Near East launched by Europeans with attack on Constantinople; many knights join crusade with hopes of acquiring land.

1097 Muslim Turks defeated by crusade forces and crusaders take Jerusalem in 1099, ending First Crusade; as a result of disease and starvation, only some 60,000 of original 300,000 forces survive.

1099 Frankish and Norman kingdoms set up in Near East following crusade.

1100 The age of the Troubadours begins to develop in music. The Troubadours in France and the Minnesingers in Germany sing secular hymns dedicated to such things as spring and the beauty of women.

1110 First miracle play performed; this form, based on both the scriptures and legends of saints, is representative of medieval drama.

1122 Conflict between the papacy and Holy Roman Emperor Henry V achieves a partial compromise with Concordat of Worms, which restores church property and provides for the free election of the clergy.

1122 Omar Khayyám, prominent Persian mathematician, scientist, poet, and author of the *Rubáiyát*, dies.

1145 The construction of Chartres Cathedral and the Abbey of St. Denis signal the beginning of Gothic architecture. The buildings use pointed arches and are noted for their stained-glass windows and use of the flying buttress.

1145 Pope Eugene III calls for crusade; by 1147 the Second Crusade will have proved a failure.

1145 Silk manufacturing begins in Italy.

1156 Civil war rages in Japan between clans over succession to the throne; by 1186 the emperor is a virtual puppet of the shoguns and for the next three centuries conflicts between the feudal lords dominate the country.

1162 Thomas Beckett is named archbishop of Canterbury by King Henry II; intense feud between Henry and Beckett over issues of papal vs. secular authority ends in Beckett's murder.

1163 Maimonides, Jewish philosopher and physician, works for Sultan Saladin in Egypt, where he writes on medicine, theology, law, and philosophy.

1167 Oxford University in England founded.

1173 Bela III becomes King of Hungary, introducing Byzantine culture and customs to Hungary.

1182 Jews banished from France.

1187 Saladin of Egypt conquers Jerusalem; under Saladin, the Muslim world is briefly united and western advances in the East are stymied as Muslim learning and culture flourish.

1187 Muhammad of Ghor conquers Punjab; he completes conquest of Upper India by 1203 and Muslim kingdom is established in India following his death.

1189 English Jews are massacred at coronation of Richard I (Richard the Lion-Hearted).

1189 Third Crusade begins, led by Holy Roman Emperor Frederick Barbarossa with Richard I of England and Philip II of France; ends in 1192. The crusades bring Arab learning that influences European culture and thought.

1191 Zen Buddhism is introduced to Japan, emphasizing personal instruction for enlightenment.

1197 German civil wars over succession to Holy Roman Emperor; Declaration of Speyer in 1199 confirms right of German princes to elect a king.

1200 Peace of Le Goulet ends long period of hostilities between England and France.

1200 Manco Capac establishes the Inca dynasty in South America; Cuzco becomes the capital.

1202 Fourth Crusade called by Pope Innocent III in hope of reuniting Roman and Eastern Orthodox Churches; Crusaders take Constantinople in 1204 and establish Latin empire; bubonic plague ends Crusade in 1204.

1204 Independent Greek empire founded under Emperor Michael.

1204 Venice, the leader of the Fourth Crusade, greatly expands its power following conquest of Constantinople;

Venice has become the leading commercial center in Europe by this time.

1206 Genghis Khan becomes ruler of Mongols; leads Mongol invasion of China in 1211 and invades Near East in 1216, causing widespread destruction; conquers Persia in 1218.

1209 Franciscan Order of monks founded by Francis of Assisi. The order pledges poverty and an intense personal devotion to God and distinguishes itself through its interaction with laypeople rather than maintaining a monastic lifestyle.

1212 Children's Crusade is launched; most of the children end up sold into slavery by Egyptian slave dealers.

1215 King John signs Magna Carta subjecting power of English monarchy to traditional feudal law; the Magna Carta also reaffirms human rights.

1215 Dominican Order of monks founded by St. Dominic.

1222 Mongols under Genghis Khan invade Russia.

1225 Cotton manufactured in Spain.

1228 Emperor Frederick II leads Sixth Crusade until 1229; crowns himself king of Jerusalem.

1230 Leprosy introduced into Europe by returning crusaders.

1233 Coal mined for the first time in Newcastle, England.

1235 Mongols annex the Qin (Chin) Empire; rockets used by Chinese in battle.

1241 Navigational inventions including the rudder and bowsprit are introduced in Europe.

1244 Muslims retake Jerusalem.

1248 France's Louis IX leads Seventh Crusade; fails to conquer Egypt or recapture Jerusalem.

1250 Crusaders introduce Arabic numerals and decimal system into Europe.

1250 Cannons first employed by the Moors.

1252 Golden florins first minted in Florence; introduction of gold currencies in Florence and Genoa.

1253 Sorbonne founded in Paris.

1256 Thomas Aquinas (1224–1274) receives degree in theology; a scholastic philosopher, he integrates Aristotelian thought with Christian doctrine, arguing the compatibility of reason and faith.

1259 China's Sung army makes first known use of firearms to propel bullets.

1260 Kublai Khan establishes Yuan Dynasty, which rules China until 1368; during his reign construction begins on Peking (Beijing) and China undertakes many technological and civil reforms.

1273 Rudolf of Hapsburg elected King of Germany and founds Hapsburg Empire.

1275 Moses de Leon, Jewish theologian, writes *Zohar*, the central text in Jewish mysticism.

1277 Roger Bacon imprisoned in England for heresy. Bacon introduced several new scientific concepts and invented the magnifying glass.

1280 Cimabue, considered the Father of Italian Painting, active during this time; his *Madonna and Child* prefigures the works of Giotto and the style of the Renaissance.

1290 Osman begins the Ottoman Empire, which rules much of the Mediterranean region for the next six centuries.

1291 The Mamelukes conquer Acre, ending Christian rule in the East and bringing an end to the crusades.

1292 Venice develops the "great galley" allowing for longer voyages and larger cargoes. The development leads to an expansion of European trade in the East.

1295 Marco Polo returns to Italy from India and Far East after serving under Kublai Khan and introduces Far Eastern thought and customs to Europe.

1298 Invention of the spinning wheel in Germany.

1300 Gunpowder introduced into Europe during the early 14th century.

1300 The manufacturing of paper in the West ends the monastery's monopoly over manuscripts and written communication.

1305 Giotto completes Padua's Arena chapel; frescoes break away from earlier painting in their use of naturalistic detail, narrative, perspective, and solidity of forms.

1307 Dante begins *The Divine Comedy*; Dante's epic poem describes a journey through hell, purgatory, and heaven. His influential works are some of the first to be written in a modern language rather than Latin.

1307 Edward II crowned king of England; his reign is filled with dissension and conflict with barons, culminating with his murder in 1327.

1309 Papacy moves to Avignon as "Babylonian Exile" begins; it lasts until 1377.

1309 Venice begins building of Doge's Palace, completed in 1483.

1310 Giovanni Pisano completes pulpit in Pisa cathedral begun by his father; the pulpit introduces to sculpture elements of naturalism and classical simplicity and the portrayal of figures in perspectival space.

1310 The style of the Sienese school, characterized by linear harmony and gold detail, develops with the works of Simone Martini and Duccio. Their works fused elements of Byzantine art with recent developments in Italian painting.

1325 Aztecs found Tenochtitlán and begin colonization of Central America.

1333 Death of Takatoki Hojo ends the Kamakura period in Japan and begins Muromachi era, which lasts until 1568 and is characterized by conflict among independent warlords.

1337 Hundred Years' War begins between England and France over claims for the French crown.

1340 First known use of double-entry bookkeeping used by the Masari family in Florence.

1340 Francisco Petrarch, Italian poet and scholar, revives the classical tradition in literature. His sonnets become a model for later poetry.

1343 Genoese merchant infected with bubonic plague through contact with Tartars spreads the disease to other port cities such as Constantinople and Venice.

1343 William of Ockham writes *Dialogues*, challenging many of the church's traditional assumptions about separation of church and state and influencing later secular philosophy.

1344 Fall of Florentine banking houses of Bardi and Peruzzi leads to attempts by the Florentine lower class to overthrow the merchant-dominated oligarchy.

1348 The Black Death begins to spread in Europe and lasts until 1351, killing half of Europe's population and crippling industry and agriculture for the next century.

1353 Italian writer Giovanni Boccaccio's *Decameron*; set during the Black Plague, the novella will have tremendous influence on Renaissance literature.

1354 The Alhambra palace is completed during the height of Arab influence in Granada.

1356 Holy Roman Emperor Charles IV issues the Golden Bull changing the empire from a monarchy to an aristocratic federation.

1361 Reappearance of the Black Death in England and France.

1368 Overthrow of the Mongols leads to the establishment of the Ming Dynasty in China, which lasts until 1644.

1370 Steel crossbow first used in warfare.

1376 John Wycliffe's Reform party wins control of English Parliament; attacks the authority of the church in government

1377 Pope Gregory IX enters Rome, ending the "Babylonian Exile" of the Church.

1378 "Great Schism" begins, creating rival popes in Avignon and Rome after failure to reform the papacy.

1380 Tamerlane, descendent of Genghis Khan, invades Persia and begins campaign to conquer much of Central Asia.

1381 Wat Tyler leads rebellion of English peasants against the government, calling for the abolition of serfdom, which is accepted but later repealed.

1383 Motokio Zeami develops Noh drama in Japan.

1385 Portugal wins its independence after defeating Castile in the Battle of Alujubarrota.

1392 Northern and southern dynasties end 56 years of civil war in Japan; the Ashikagas become Shoguns of Muromachi.

1392 I Songgye proclaims himself king; Yi Dynasty will rule in Korea until 1910.

1400 Geoffrey Chaucer dies, leaving *The Canterbury Tales* unfinished. Chaucer employed a variety of styles in

the poem and confirmed the domination of southern English as the language of literature throughout England.

1402 Tamerlane's victory over the sultan Bayazid I threatens the stability of the Ottoman Empire.

1403 Chinese emperor Yung-lo sponsors compilation of an 11,095-volume encyclopedia.

1405 Tamerlane dies; his empire dissolves after his death.

1412 Filippo Brunelleschi writes *Rules of Perspective*, which strongly influences the development of Italian painting and architecture; later designs the Foundling Hospital in Florence.

1415 Limbourg brothers commissioned by the Duc de Berry to work on *The Very Rich Book of Hours*. The manuscript epitomizes the International Gothic style with its combination of naturalism and Gothic stylization.

1417 The "Great Schism" of the Catholic Church ends; Pope Martin V elected and papacy returns to Rome.

1424 Italian sculptor Lorenzo Ghiberti's bronze doors for San Giovanni baptistry at Florence installed; known as the *Gates of Paradise*, the doors are completed in 1452.

1425 Henry the Navigator of Portugal captures the Canary Islands; Henry develops a more sophisticated method of navigation and introduces many shipbuilding innovations.

1425 Tommaso Masaccio begins work on his frescoes for the Brancacci Chapel in Florence. His earlier work, *The Trinity*, is the first known work of a painter to employ one-point perspective; his frescoes mark a breaking away from Gothic style and shape the development of Italian painting.

1428 Itzcoatl leads the Aztecs in a series of battles lasting until 1440 and expands the empire throughout Mexico and Guatemala.

1431 Joan of Arc, who believed she was on a divine mission to expel the British from France, is burned at the stake after liberating Orleans.

1434 African slaves introduced into Portugal.

1434 Dutch painter Jan Van Eyck's *Giovanni Arnolfini and His Bride*; his works exemplify northern Renaissance painting with its innovative use of color, subtle lighting effects, and careful attention to detail.

1434 Florence's duomo completed with the installation of Brunelleschi's 350-foot dome.

1435 Florentine sculptor Donatello completes his bronze *David* statue; his other famous works include *The Feast of Herod* and *St. George*; Donatello's varied work leads to the classical revival in sculpture and prefigures later artistic developments.

1435 Rogier Van Der Weyden's *Descent from the Cross*; his paintings incorporate boldly defined gestures and expressions and introduce a more dramatic style to the Gothic tradition.

1436 Leon Battista Alberti's *Della Pittura*, a treatise on aesthetic and scientific theories, embodies the principles and style of Italian Renaissance art.

1436 Fra Angelico begins work at the San Marco Monastery in Florence. His works exemplify the early Renaissance style of simple composition employing classical harmony.

1438 Inca dynasty founded by Pachacutec; dynasty rules Peru until 1553 and expands throughout South America.

1440 During this period patronage of the arts is increasingly viewed as essential to a ruler's prestige in Italy and leads to an expansion of cultural activity in Italy.

1441 Slave trade begins in Portugal.

1445 Charles VII of France creates the first French army independent of feudal ties.

1450 Francesco Sforza overthrows Ambrosian Republic in Milan and assumes title of Duke; establishes prolific court of scholars and artists.

1450 Growth of the Kongo and Ndongo empires in Angola and Zaire.

1450 Alliance between Venice, Florence, and Milan provides a balance of power among Italian states.

1453 Constantinople falls to Ottoman Empire, ending nearly 1,000 years of Byzantine rule.

1454 Italian painter Paolo Uccello's *Battles*; his works along with those of Piero della Francesca reflect early experimentation with perspective in painting.

1455 War of the Roses begins in England between houses of York and Lancaster.

1456 Ottoman Turks conquer Athens; maintain rule over Greece and the Balkans for the next four centuries.

1456 Johann Gutenberg publishes the Bible using movable type, signaling the advent of printing in the West.

1461 Edward of the House of York defeats the Lancasterians and is crowned king of England; however, the civil war soon revives.

1461 French poet François Villon completes *Le Grand Testament*.

1463 Venetians and Turks begin war over control of the Mediterranean.

1464 Cosimo de' Medici dies; as head of a major banking family he was the patron to many artists and during his life Florence became a major center for European art and Humanistic thought.

1465 Andrea Mantegna's *Crucifixion* and the works of Jacopo Bellini exemplify the early Renaissance emphasis on perspective, motifs from classical architecture, naturalistic landscape, and idealized figures; Bellini's work helped to shape the Venetian school of painting.

1465 First printed music.

1467 Senshu, Japanese Zen priest and painter, travels to Peking and synthesizes the Japanese and Chinese styles of painting.

1472 Ivan the Great (Ivan III) marries Sophia Palaeologus, niece of the last Byzantine emperor; Muscovy returns to the church and Ivan takes the title of tsar.

1474 Emperor Topa extends Inca Empire into southern Peru and Ecuador and begins extensive road-building program.

1476 Incas complete conquest of South America after capturing parts of Bolivia, Argentina, and Chile.

1479 Italian sculptor Andrea del Verrocchio is commissioned to work on the equestrian monument to Bartolomeo Colleone in Venice.

1480 Ivan III defeats the Tartars, ending the Tartar threat to Russia.

1481 Bayazid II becomes sultan of the Turks; during his 31-year reign, Turkish power strengthens in Europe through campaigns against Hungary, Poland, and Venice.

1482 Spanish Inquisition begins under the joint control of church and state and leads to the persecution of converted Jews, Muslims, Catholic intellectuals, and "heretics."

1484 Botticelli paints his *Birth of Venus*; other works include *Primavera*, *The Annunciation*, and *The Magnificat*. His religious and mythological paintings commissioned by the Medicis epitomize the Renaissance spirit of humanism and classical ideals.

1484 Netherlandish painter Hieronymus Bosch completes *Garden of Delights*; his other works include *Earthly Paradise* and *Ship of Fools*. Painted in the style of late Gothic art, his works depict fantastic visions and employ complex imagery.

1484 Ashikaga Shogun Yoshimasa introduces tea ceremony, which becomes an integral part of Japanese culture.

1485 Henry, earl of Richmond, defeats Richard III at Battle of Bosworth and is crowned Henry VII, beginning the 117-year reign of the Tudors.

1487 Portuguese navigator Bartolomeu Diaz rounds the Cape of Good Hope, southernmost point in Africa.

1489 African slaves, led by former slave Yasuf Adil Shah, revolt in Bijapur, India, but are defeated.

1490 Portuguese explorers convert the king of the Congo Empire to Christianity. They establish a post at São Salvador and maintain Portuguese influence in the region for the next century.

1490 Development of ballet begins at Italian courts.

1492 Spain seizes Granada, the last Moorish foothold, further strengthening the monarchy's control of the Iberian peninsula.

1492 King Ferdinand V and Queen Isabella I of Spain finance the voyage of Christopher Columbus to the East Indies. However, he lands in the Bahamas and subsequently sails to Haiti and Cuba. In subsequent years, Columbus sails to Jamaica, Puerto Rico, and Santo Domingo.

1493 After Columbus's return to Spain, Isabella sends him back with 1,500 men and names him governor of the New World. Columbus's voyages begin the age of European colonization of the Americas and the slaughter of Native American peoples.

1493 Pope Alexander VI issues a papal bull dividing the lands of the New World between Spain and Portugal.

1495 First recorded outbreak of syphilis strikes Naples; spreads throughout Europe for the next 25 years and plagues Europe for over three centuries.

1495 Charles VIII of France is crowned king of Naples but is eventually driven out by an alliance of Venice and the papacy, who join together to protect Italy from foreign influence.

1495 Emanuel I ascends to the throne of Portugal; during his reign Portugal continues its ambitious program of exploration.

1497 John Cabot, under commission from Henry VII of England, reaches Cape Breton Island and Nova Scotia and later Newfoundland; the voyages signal an end to Spanish and Portuguese domination of the New World.

1498 Vasco da Gama reaches India via the Cape of Good Hope; he establishes a trade route between Portugal and India and ends Venetian domination of the spice trade.

1498 200 Spanish colonists settle in Hispaniola.

1501 Spanish colonists bring slaves to Hispaniola and introduce slavery to the colonies.

1502 Amerigo Vespucci returns to Europe and expresses his conviction that the Americas are not part of Asia but a separate continent.

1502 Montezuma II becomes emperor of the Aztec Empire at Tenochtitlán.

1502 Shah Ismail founds the Safavid Dynasty, which rules Persia until 1736.

1502 Peter Henlein of Nuremberg makes the first watch.

1504 German artist Albrecht Dürer engraves *Adam and Eve*; Dürer's *The Apocalypse* (1498) becomes the first book published by an artist of his own works and influences the development of woodcut and engraving.

1504 Louis XII cedes Naples to Ferdinand II of Aragon; Spanish control of southern Italy and Sicily lasts until 1707.

1504 Michelangelo completes his *David* statue and sets a new standard for nude sculpture.

1505 Portuguese establish factories on east coast of Africa; during this period, Portugal expands its influence in Africa, establishing footholds in Zanzibar and Mozambique.

1506 Spanish begin to cultivate sugar in the Caribbean's Great Antilles; sugar soon becomes a vital crop in the world's economy.

1507 Leonardo da Vinci's *Mona Lisa*; his other works include *The Last Supper* and *Madonna of the Rocks*. Leonardo's works and writings revolutionize painting. His studies of human anatomy and the principle of flight were of great influence.

1508 Maximilian I assumes title of Holy Roman Emperor; Pope Julius II establishes that the German king automatically becomes Holy Roman Emperor.

1508 Pope Julius II, France's Louis XII, and Ferdinand of Aragon join the League of Cambrai in order to weaken Venice. Over the next several years, battles on the Italian peninsula bring about a decline in the power of Italian cities and change the political makeup of Europe.

1509 Desiderius Erasmus writes *Praise of Folly*, poking fun at church corruption and scholastic philosophy.

1510 Portuguese conquer the Indian island of Goa; it becomes Europe's first foothold in India and remains in Portuguese hands for four and a half centuries.

1511 Pope Julius II forms Holy League with Aragon and Venice to force the French out of Italy.

1512 Pope Julius II convenes the Fifth Lateran council (1512–1517) to begin reforms of Church abuses.

1513 Allied forces of Henry VIII of England and the Holy Roman Emperor Maximilian defeat Louis XII and begin to drive the French out of Italy.

1513 Florentine thinker and politician Niccolo Machiavelli analyzes the nature and struggle for power in his work *The Prince*. He argues that a ruler must be cunning and manipulative to further his interests and those of his people.

1513 Spanish explorer and governor of Puerto Rico Ponce de León sails to Florida and subsequently begins the cultivation of orange and lemon trees.

1513 Spanish explorer Vasco Núñez de Balboa crosses the Panamanian isthmus and is first European known to see the Pacific Ocean.

1514 Portuguese expedition lands in Canton on the first European ships to land in China.

1514 Slave trade continues to grow despite Pope Leo X's papal bull condemning slavery.

1514 Ottoman sultan Selim the Grim (Selim I) attacks Persia in effort to convert the region to his Sunnite faith; the war lasts until 1555.

1514 Henry VIII charters the Trinity House, which helps to bolster the emerging shipping industry in England.

1514 Florentine painter Raffaelo Santi Raphael completes the Stanza Frescoes for the Vatican; his other works include *Julius II* and *Madonna and Child Enthroned with Saints*. Raphael's paintings embody the high Renaissance style of classical composition and harmonious design.

1515 English author Thomas More writes *Utopia*, depicting an ideal commonwealth.

1515 France opens first nationalized factories; they are used to manufacture tapestry and weapons.

1516 Carlos I becomes king of Spain and later creates the Hapsburg Empire that rules Spain until 1700; in 1519 he becomes Holy Roman Emperor.

1517 Martin Luther nails his 95 Theses to the door of Wittenberg Cathedral; his criticism of church corruption and abuses sparks the Protestant Reformation, which spreads throughout Europe. Early Protestantism was characterized by an emphasis on the Bible as the source of God's word and minimizing the priesthood and liturgical aspects of the church.

1517 Ottoman Empire begins rule of Egypt that lasts over three centuries.

1519 Spanish conquistador Hernando Cortez lands in Tenochtitlán, capital of Mexico; he takes Montezuma II prisoner and eventually conquers the Aztec Empire in 1521.

1519 Ferdinand Magellan leaves Europe to circumnavigate the world; on his journey he sails to the Pacific Ocean and lands in the Philippine Islands.

1519 Indian guru Nanak founds Sikhism, a combination of Hinduism and Islam.

1520 Coal increasingly comes into use as a source of fuel; in the following years, coal mines open in Newcastle, England, and Liege, Belgium.

1521 Martin Luther appears before the Diet of Worms after being excommunicated the previous year; refusing to retract his earlier teachings, Luther is imprisoned in the Wartburg, where he begins to translate the Bible into the German vernacular.

1522 Large-scale slave rebellion in Hispaniola sets off discord lasting for the next thirty years.

1525 German Anabaptist Thomas Münzer overthrows town government of Muhlhausen and establishes communistic theocracy, but it is soon ended and Münzer is executed. Peasant revolts in Central Europe and Germany (1524–26), often in support of Luther, lead to 150,000 deaths.

1525 Germans and Spanish defeat the French and Swiss at the Battle of Pavia; Holy Roman Emperor Charles V becomes ruler of Italy, extending the power of the Hapsburg Empire.

1525 Blast furnaces develop in the following years in Europe, allowing for production of cast iron, essential in the production of weapons.

1525 After a civil war over the right of succession, the Inca Empire is split between the brothers Huascar and Atahualpa.

1526 Congolese king Mbemba Nzinga protests Portuguese exploitation of his kingdom for the purpose of the slave trade in Brazil.

1526 Babar, a descendant of Genghis Kahn and Tamerlane, founds the Mogul Dynasty, which rules India until 1761.

1527 Soldiers of the Holy Roman Empire overrun Rome, pillaging the city and imprisoning Pope Clement VII.

1527 Conte Baldassare Castiglione's *The Courtier* provides a guide for manners and behavior for courtly life; the work embodies the humanistic spirit of the Renaissance.

1530 Portuguese begin to colonize Brazil.

1530 Use of the spinning wheel becomes widespread in Europe.

1530 Spanish conquistador Jiménez de Quesada discovers the potato in the South American Andes. The potato later becomes a cheap source of food and a staple in the European diet.

1531 Civil war begins in Switzerland between Catholic and Protestant cantons; Protestants defeated later that year.

1531 Spanish colonists in the West Indies begin tobacco cultivation.

1532 Lodovico Ariosto writes "Orlando Furioso," a romantic poem of chivalry typifying Italian Renaissance poetry.

1533 Spanish conquistador Francisco Pizarro ends the Peruvian empire by executing Atahualpa, the last Inca ruler.

1533 Henry VIII secretly marries Anne Boleyn after the archbishop of Canterbury declares the marriage with Catherine of Aragon null and void; the pope excommunicates Henry for divorce.

1533 Hans Holbein, who later becomes court painter for Henry VIII, completes *The Ambassadors*. Other northern painters of the time, including Matthias Grünewald, Pieter Breughel, and Dürer, revive Classical elements in German art.

1534 Act of Supremacy gives Henry VIII authority over the church in England; Henry dissolves the monasteries, causing a radical change in the country's ownership of property.

1534 Ignatius of Loyola founds the Jesuit order, which receives papal recognition in 1540. Jesuits become critical instruments in church efforts during the Counter-Reformation. Over the next two centuries they begin missionary work in China and Japan and among Native Americans.

1535 Jacques Cartier sails up the St. Lawrence River, beginning French exploration of North America; in 1541 he establishes a short-lived colony in Quebec.

1536 The Anabaptist theocracy in Münster is suppressed after two years in power. The Anabaptists seek to establish utopian communities and they spawn sects such as the Mennonites and Amish.

1536 Spanish explorer Hernando Cortez sails to lower California.

1537 First conservatories of music are established, in Venice for girls and in Naples for boys.

1541 Michelangelo completes *The Last Judgment* on the altar wall of the Sistine Chapel; he had earlier painted the chapel's ceiling with scenes from the Hebrew Bible.

1541 John Calvin forms a theocratic government in Geneva. Calvin's rigorous form of Protestantism emphasizes the doctrine of predestination.

1542 Portuguese Jesuits become the first Europeans to land in Japan; they introduce muskets and Christianity to the Japanese.

1542 Pope Paul III establishes the Universal Inquisition at Rome in an effort to stop the Reformation's momentum.

1543 *On the Revolutions of the Celestial Orbs* by Nikolaus Copernicus argues that the planets revolve around the sun, opposing church doctrine that the earth was the center of the universe.

1543 Andreas Vesalius, Belgian anatomist, goes against church rules and dissects human bodies; his *De Corporis Humani Fabrica* is the first accurate book on human anatomy.

1545 Pope Paul III calls the Council of Trent to respond to the Reformation and initiate the Counter-Reformation.

1545 Discovery of silver in Peru and importation into Spain helps stimulate the growth of the European middle and commercial classes.

1546 Charles V goes to war against the rebellious German Protestant states who have formed the Schmalkaldic League; although Charles is victorious, the German princes retain some independence.

1547 Ivan IV (Ivan the Terrible) crowned Tsar of Russia. During his reign Russia extends its empire eastward and establishes trade with western nations.

1548 Sigusmund I of Poland dies after 42-year reign; his son Sigusmund II takes power; during his 24-year reign Protestant Reformation spreads to Poland.

1549 Archbishop of Canterbury Thomas Cranmer issues *The Book of Common Prayer*; written in English, it serves as the model for English Protestant services.

1550 Venetian painter Titian active during this period. Titian's work broke from the High Renaissance style and its emphasis on linear harmony; his use of free brushwork created highly sensuous works leading to the development of Mannerism.

1550 The next 50 years witness the decline of Native American population in Spanish America from 7 million to 1 million.

1550 Giorgio Vasari's *Lives of the Artists* published in Florence; the book celebrates the genius of Renaissance artists and establishes many of the traditional assumptions underlying art historiography.

1550 *Odes*, by Pierre de Ronsard, published; along with the La Pleiade group of poets he helped shape French poetry by turning to classical themes.

1550 Vicenzan architect Andrea Palladio designs Palazzo Chiericati and Villa Rotunda. His style emphasizes order and balance and is pivotal in the development of European architecture.

1550 Corn, peanuts, and sweet potatoes first cultivated in China; the production of large harvests contributes to population growth in China.

1551 Alehouses in England and Wales licensed for the first time.

1553 French writer François Rabelais completes *Gargantua* and *Pantagruel*. His use of a bawdy style satirizes and attacks established institutions and thought.

1555 The Peace of Augsburg ends religious wars in Germany, permits German princes to determine the religion of their subjects, and allows Lutheran states the same rights as Catholic states.

1555 Queen Mary I of England reestablishes Catholicism in England and begins persecution of Protestants.

1555 Richard Chancellor forms the Muscovy Company, the first English trading company.

1556 Charles V abdicates the throne, leaving Spain, the Netherlands, Milan, and the Spanish colonies in his son Philip's power while giving the title of Emperor and Hapsburg lands to his brother Ferdinand.

1556 Akbar defeats the Hindus at the battle of Panipat and becomes Mogul Emperor of India for the next 49 years; under his reign Mogul power extends and consolidates over most of India and Afghanistan.

1556 Bohemian doctor and mine owner Georg Bauer's *De Re Metallica* (Agricola) is published in Basel; the book introduces the study of mineralogy.

1556 An earthquake hits the Shansi province in China, killing 830,000.

1557 Portuguese establish colony off the Chinese coast in Macao and develop trade with China.

1558 Queen Mary of England dies; Elizabeth I ascends to the throne.

1560 Puritanism, a stricter and more ascetic form of Protestantism, begins to develop in England.

1560 Hsu Wei writes *Ching P'ing mei*, the first classic Chinese novel.

1561 Thomas Norton and Thomas Sackville write the first known English tragedy, *Gorboduc, or Ferrex and Porrex*.

1562 Religious wars begin in France between the Protestant Huguenots and Roman Catholics after a massacre of Huguenots at Massy; fighting lasts until 1598.

1562 John Hawkins, English navigator, hijacks Portuguese ship carrying African slaves to Brazil and begins England's involvement in the slave trade.

1563 Church of England established after the adoption of the 39 Articles. The articles combine Protestant doctrine with the hierarchical structure of the Catholic church. Puritans, Separatists, and Presbyterians all dissent.

1564 The Peace of Troyes ends the war between France and England; Calais is returned to the French.

1564 Disease wipes out the Aztecs of New Spain.

1564 The Boyars (Russian nobles) force Tsar Ivan IV to withdraw from Moscow.

1565 A Spanish expedition led by Pedro Menéndez de Avilés settles in St. Augustine, Florida, establishing the first permanent European colony in North America.

1565 Knights of St. John, led by Jean de La Vallete, with the help of the Spanish defeat the Turks' attempt to seize Malta.

1565 John Hawkins introduces tobacco into England.

1565 Sir Thomas Gresham founds the London Royal Exchange.

1566 Suleiman the Magnificent (Suleiman II) dies. During his reign the Ottoman Empire expanded into eastern Europe and Persia; he oversaw the reform of the empire's legal and administrative systems and the buildup of the navy.

1567 Typhoid fever spreads in South America, killing two million Native Americans.

1568 The Calvinist and mercantile Dutch provinces begin to revolt against Spanish rule.

1568 Nobunaga takes power from the feudal lords, centralizes the Japanese government, and unifies the empire; during his reign, Nobunaga reduces the power of the Buddhist clergy.

1569 Flemish cartographer Gerhardus Mercator publishes the Mercator projection map of the world. His map improves the accuracy of navigation.

1570 Ivan the Terrible (Ivan IV) enters Novgorod and begins five-week reign of terror, sacking the city and killing many of its citizens in retribution for their alleged sympathy for the Poles.

1570 The Mohawk, Oneida, Onondaga, Cayuga, and Seneca form the Iroquois League.

1570 Crops such as corn, peanuts, sweet potatoes, and beans introduced into Africa by slave ships from Brazil. The new crops lead to a population growth in Africa, which in turn bolsters the slave trade.

1571 Venetian and Spanish navies defeat the Turks at the battle of Lepanto, ensuring that complete control of the Mediterranean is kept out of Turkish hands.

1571 Bornu Empire in the Sudan reaches its apex under Idris III.

1572 Massacre of St. Bartholomew kills 50,000 Huguenots in France.

1572 All the Dutch provinces unite in revolt against Spanish rule. The revolt reflects the growing economic strength and prestige of the Dutch in Europe.

1572 Wan-li (Shen Zong) begins 48-year reign of China, sees the growth of Ming culture and power.

1572 Tycho Brahe discovers new star in the milky way; his discovery disproves Aristotelian notion that no changes were possible in the celestial regions.

1573 Nobunaga Oda defeats the shogun Yoshiake and ends the Ashikaga shogunate, which had ruled Japan since 1336.

1574 Portuguese begin to settle in Angola.

1574 Giorgio Vasari completes the Florentine Uffizi Palace after 14 years of construction.

1575 The erotic Chinese novel *The Golden Lotus* published.

1576 First playhouse built in England in Shoreditch, London.

1576 French political theorist Jean Bodin argues for a constitutional monarchy and states that the basis of society is the family.

1577 Sir Francis Drake begins voyage to circumnavigate the globe.

1577 Mogul emperor Akbar the Great unifies and annexes northern India.

1577 Javanese reach Bali, resist the spread of Islam, and preserve traditional Indonesian music.

1579 The Union of Utrecht joins seven Protestant Netherlands provinces against the Spanish and becomes the foundation for the Dutch republic.

1580 Portugal and Spain unite under Philip II of Spain after the defeat of the Portuguese at the battle of Alcantara.

1580 French author and theorist Michel de Montaigne writes *Essais*; his skeptical works develop the essay form.

1581 First dramatic ballet, *Ballet Comique de la Reyne*, performed at Versailles.

1581 Union of Utrecht declares its independence from Spain and forms the Dutch Republic, electing William of Orange as leader.

1582 War between Russia, Poland, and Sweden ends with Russia losing access to the Baltic; Tsar Ivan the Terrible gives up claims to Estonia and Livonia.

1583 Italian sculptor Giovanni da Bologna completes his work *Rape of the Sabine Women*.

1583 Italian botanist Andrea Cesalpino publishes the first modern classification of plant life.

1584 Venetian Banco di Rialto forms the first public banking system in Europe.

1584 English explorer Walter Raleigh establishes a colony on Roanoke Island near Virginia.

1585 England sends aid and troops to the Netherlands in their effort against the Spanish.

1585 Dutch mathematician Simon Stevin introduces decimals into mathematics and physics.

1585 Hideyoshi establishes a dictatorship in Japan.

1586 Akbar attempts to establish universal religion for India; his effort collapses during the 18th-century Muslim revival.

1587 Pope Sixtus V calls for a Catholic crusade against England; Sir Francis Drake defeats the Spanish at the Bay of Cádiz.

1587 Christopher Marlowe's *Tamburlaine the Great* first performed, introducing blank verse in the dramatic form. His other works include *Dr. Faustus*.

1587 Mary Queen of Scots executed under orders of Queen Elizabeth I.

1588 The English defeat the Spanish Armada; the victory helps establish English power over worldwide trade and colonization.

1589 Henri of Navarre succeeds to the throne as Henri IV of France and establishes the Bourbon Dynasty, which rules France until 1792.

1589 Boris Godunov declares the Russian Orthodox Church independent from Constantinople.

1590 Caravaggio's "realistic" paintings break away from the erudite style of the Renaissance and convey an immediate and emotional appeal; his works are some of the earliest examples of Baroque art.

1590 During this period Spanish power gradually declines due to a weak middle class and a sluggish economy.

1590 English poet Edmund Spenser begins his allegorical romance *The Faerie Queen*.

1590 William Shakespeare begins his work as a playwright, producing comedies and historical dramas such as *Romeo and Juliet*, *As You Like It*, and *Julius Caesar*. The Elizabethan period produces many noted works in English drama.

1590 Spanish painter El Greco paints *St Jerome*; his work, distinguished by its distorted figures and eerie coloring, is characteristic of the mannerist style of the period.

1591 Songhai Empire in North Africa destroyed by Spanish and Portuguese mercenaries in the service of Morocco.

1591 First running of the bulls at Pamplona, Spain.

1592 Galileo Galilei writes *Della Scienza Mechanica* arguing, against accepted doctrine, that objects fall at the same rate despite their weight. Galileo breaks from traditional science by relying on experimentation rather than theological assumptions.

1592 Windmills in Holland used to power mechanical saws.

1593 Chu-tsai-ya of China discovers the 12 semitones in an octave.

1595 Dutch East India Company takes over Indian spice trade from Portugal, signaling the beginning of Dutch efforts at colonization.

1595 War continues between Spain and England as the Spanish navy sacks Penzance and Mousehole.

1597 English suppress Irish revolt led by Hugh O'Neill.

1597 *Dafne*, by Italian composer Jacopo Peri, is first opera performed. The opera is based on musical forms used in Greek tragedies.

1597 Galileo invents the sector, allowing algebraic problems to be solved mechanically.

1598 Henri IV issues the Edict of Nantes ending the French wars of religion and granting French Huguenots (Protestants) equal rights.

1598 Peace of Verins ends war between France and Spain; all Spanish conquests of French lands are returned and France is united under Henri IV.

1598 Korean admiral Visunsin develops the ironclad warship.

1598 Spanish begin to settle in Pueblo territory in the American Southwest.

1599 High prices in Europe during this period hurt the nobility and force many to sell their land to the emerging middle and merchant classes.

1600 Elizabeth grants charter to English East India Company, establishing a challenge to Dutch supremacy in the spice trade.

1601 England's Poor Law forces parishes to provide for the needy.

1602 Dutch East India Company becomes the first public company.

1603 After a power struggle following the death of Hideyoshi, the Tokugawa Dynasty establishes itself under Ieyasu and brings economic and educational reform to Japan. Dynasty remains in power until 1868.

1603 Queen Elizabeth I dies and is succeeded by James VI of Scotland, who rules England, Scotland, and Ireland as James I.

1603 Japanese kabuki theater has its beginnings.

1604 Tsar Boris Godunov dies during revolt led by the "False Dmitri," a pretender to the throne; during this period, Russia is plagued by power struggles and conflict.

1604 Samuel de Champlain makes second voyage to North America; he establishes a colony in Nova Scotia and explores the North American Atlantic coast.

1605 Officials expose the Gunpowder Plot led by Guy Fawkes protesting harsh measures against Catholics in England; Fawkes and the other conspirators are arrested and sentenced to death.

1605 The first part of *Don Quixote* by Miguel de Cervantes published.

1605 The world's first newspaper begins in Antwerp.

1606 Shakespeare's *Macbeth* is performed; the latter part of Shakespeare's career produces many of his famous tragedies and tragicomedies, including *King Lear*, *Hamlet*, and *The Tempest*.

1606 James I charters the Plymouth Company and the London Company to settle colonies in North America.

1606 Dutch become the first Europeans to sail to Australia.

1607 Founded by John Smith, Jamestown becomes the first English settlement in North America. Four years later private property is established on the colony but the colony faces many hardships during its first years.

1607 Spain declares national bankruptcy.

1607 Monteverdi's *Orfeo*, the oldest existing opera, first performed in Europe.

1608 The telescope invented by Dutch scientist Johann Lippershey.

1608 Protestant Union formed in Germany under the leadership of Frederick IV.

1608 Champlain founds the French colony of Quebec.

1609 Spain recognizes Dutch independence and signs a truce ending warfare with the northern provinces.

1609 Catholic League is formed in Germany in response to the Protestant Union.

1609 Hostility begins between French settlers and the Iroquois after Champlain kills member of the Mohawk tribe at the request of the Huron tribe.

1609 English explorer Henry Hudson sails to the Delaware Bay and to what is later called the Hudson River.

1609 Johannes Kepler's *Astronomia Nova* argues that the universe is heliocentric. His *Three Laws of Planetary Motion* revolutionizes conceptions about the nature of the universe.

1610 English playwright Ben Jonson writes *The Alchemist*; his satirical works introduce classical forms and rules of drama to the English theater.

1610 Henri IV assassinated; nine-year-old Louis XIII ascends to the French throne. The king's mother, Marie de' Medici, acts as regent and influences French policy for many years.

1610 Tea introduced to Europe.

1611 King James I authorizes his version of the Bible.

1612 Japanese begin persecution of Christians and end friendly relations with missionaries but continue trade with Europeans.

1612 John Rolfe begins cultivation of tobacco in the Virginia colony; tobacco provides the economic base for the colony.

1613 Michael Romanov crowned tsar of Russia; Romanov Dynasty rules until 1917.

1614 Scottish mathematician John Napier introduces logarithms.

1614 The Estates-General, the representative body of the French people, meets for the last time until 1789.

1615 Manchus, led by Nurachi, begin to organize themselves in northern China. The following year they begin invasions of China.

1616 Inigo Jones's Greenwich House introduces Palladian architecture to England. His designs shape the direction of English architecture in the following years.

1618 "The Defenestration of Prague" sets off Thirty Years' War after a nationalist and Protestant uprising begins in Bohemia; conflict between Catholics and Protestants spreads throughout Europe.

1619 First African slaves arrive in Virginia.

1619 First American legislature meets in Jamestown.

1620 Pilgrims aboard the *Mayflower* land in Cape Cod, Massachusetts, establish New Plymouth. The Mayflower Compact establishes a government based on the wishes of the colonists rather than the crown.

1620 English philosopher Francis Bacon's *Novum Organum* argues that observation and experience are the basis for scientific theory. Bacon's writings help initiate the empirical school in science and philiosophy.

1621 John Donne, considered a "metaphysical" poet, named Dean of St. Paul's and begins his famous sermons; his love and devotional poems seek to combine passion and reason.

1622 Louis XIII names Richelieu cardinal and in the following year Richelieu is made chief minister. Richelieu's tremendous influence over political affairs helps esablish monarchical control over France.

1622 Flemish painter Peter Paul Rubens begins *The Medici Cycle*; his most famous allegorical work is characterized by the use of lush colors and dramatic composition. Rubens is also responsible for introducing the Baroque style to northern Europe.

1624 First part of the Louvre palace is completed by French architect Jacques Lemercier.

1625 French settlement begins in the Caribbean.

1625 The musical form of the fugue comes into use.

1626 The Dutch buy Manhattan Island from the chiefs of the Wappinger confederacy and establish the New Amsterdam colony.

1626 Nicolas Poussin's *Triumph of David* demonstrates the classical style popular in French painting of the time. The landscapes of Claude Lorrain also reflect classical ideals and influence 17th- and 18th-century taste in painting.

1626 French colonists settle in Madagascar and expel the native Hovas from their land.

1627 The Manchus overrun Korea.

1628 English physician William Harvey discovers the circulation of blood.

1629 English king Charles I dissolves Parliament and rules alone until 1640.

1630 Swedish king Gustavus Adolphus, "The Lion of the North," invades the Holy Roman Empire in support of the Protestant cause in the Thirty Years' War.

1630 War disrupts trade in Europe and intensifies the search for colonial wealth.

1630 Bel canto, a lyrical style of singing, develops in Italy and is popularized by the castrati.

1630 "Great Migration" begins and brings thousands of Puritan settlers to the Massachusetts colony during the next twelve years.

1633 Galileo put on trial; under threat of the Inquisition he retracts his defense of Copernicus's argument for heliocentrism.

1634 The Oberammergau Passion Play performed for the first time in Bavaria; the play, which commemorates the end of the Black Plague, has since been performed every ten years.

1635 Peace of Prague creates truce between Holy Roman Empire and Saxony; Thirty Years' War becomes a conflict between the House of Hapsburg and a French-Swedish alliance.

1636 Roger Williams founds Providence, Rhode Island, establishes a democratic government, and declares religious toleration.

1637 Revolt in Japan by Christian peasants suppressed by Tokugawa shogun Iemitsu; all cultural and trade contacts with the West are ended.

1637 French philosopher and mathematician René Descartes argues that the material world can be explained by mathematics and that the truth of ideas is established

independent of experience; introduces the phrase *Cogito ergo sum* ("I think, therefore I am").

1637 Pierre Corneille's *Le Cid* employs classical themes and dramatic rules that set the dominant style in French drama.

1637 Teatro San Cassiano, the first opera house, opens in Venice.

1640 Portugal wins its independence from Spain; loss further weakens the power of Spain.

1641 English Parliament abolishes Star Chamber and High Commission as tensions mount between Parliament and the king.

1641 Irish peasants revolt against landlords; Catholics kill Protestants in Ulster.

1641 Dutch capture Malacca from the Portuguese and strengthen their control over the East Indies.

1642 Power struggle in England leads to a civil war between Royalists and Parliamentarians. The gentry and high Anglican clergy support the king while the middle class and nobility support Parliament.

1642 Dutch sailor Abel Tasman becomes first European to sight New Zealand and Tasmania.

1642 Rembrandt van Rijn paints his group portrait *Night Watch*; his works, including his self-portraits, are noted for their innovative and dramatic use of chiaroscuro.

1644 The Manchus establish the Qing (Ch'ing) Dynasty, ending the reign of the Ming which had ruled since 1368. The Qing Dynasty lasts until 1912.

1645 Italian artist Giovanni Lorenzo Bernini begins work on *The Ecstasy of St. Theresa*; the statue exemplifies the highly dramatic and emotive style of his work and of Baroque sculpture. Bernini also creates several fountains in Rome and the Colonnade Piazza in St. Peter's.

1645 Turkey goes to war with Venice in an effort to seize Crete; the nineteen-year war further weakens Venetian power.

1646 King Charles I surrenders to Parlimentarian forces, ending the English Civil War.

1648 George Fox organizes the Religious Society of Friends (Quakers) in England; the society has no priests and encourages open participation in services. Many members of the society migrate to Pennsylvania after being persecuted in England.

1648 Treaty of Westphalia ends the Thirty Years' War; Dutch and Swiss independence recognized and German states are left in shambles.

1648 The Fronde, an uprising of French nobility and peasants, calls for a government by law rather than royal power.

1648 Taj Mahal completed at Agra; Mogul emperor Shah Jahan has had it built in memory of his wife Mumtaz Mahal.

1649 King Charles I is executed; commonwealth is established in England under the leadership of Oliver Cromwell, who begins a bloody supression of an Irish uprising.

1649 Serfdom firmly established in Russia.

1650 Modulation begins to develop in music as does the modern conception of harmony.

1650 The works of Jan Steen and Jan Vermeer exemplify the popularity of genre paintings in Dutch art of the time. Their paintings depict everyday subjects and scenes from peasant life.

1651 Charles II crowned king of Scotland. In an effort to restore the crown, he invades England but is defeated by Cromwell and flees to France.

1651 Thomas Hobbes publishes *Leviathan*, which articulates his theory that political absolutism is the best guarantee to maintain order and security in society.

1651 Itsuna begins 29-year shogunate of Japan; during his reign Japan's treasury is depleted.

1652 Fronde War continues in France; the Fronde army led by the Conde sets up a provisional government in Paris but is later defeated by Louis XIV.

1652 Catalán revolt ends as Barcelona surrenders to Philip IV.

1652 The musical form of the minuet develops at the French court.

1654 Treaty of Westminster ends two-year war between England and the Dutch; the Dutch agree to recognize England's Navigation Act, a bill that contributes to greater English naval power.

1654 French philosopher and mathematician Blaise Pascal articulates the theory of probability.

1654 Queen Christina of Sweden abdicates and flees the country after converting to Roman Catholicism.

1655 Charles X of Sweden invades Poland and begins the Northern Wars.

1655 England seizes Jamaica from the Spanish, beginning a three-year war between the two countries.

1656 Dutch astronomer Christian Huygens invents the pendulum clock. He is also credited with proposing the wave theory of light and observing Saturn's rings.

1656 Velázquez, court painter for the Spanish monarchy, completes *Las Meninas*. His portraits are characterized by their realism, sense of dignity, and intimate view of their subjects.

1656 Venetians drive the Turks from the Dardanelles after period of anarchy among the Ottomans.

1657 Northern War expands as Denmark and the Holy Roman Empire join forces with Poland, Austria, and Russia against Sweden.

1658 Mogul Emperor Shah Jahan becomes ill and is imprisoned by his son Aurangzeb, who seizes power and begins his 49-year reign. Shah Jahan's reign had brought great wealth and power to India.

1659 English army forces Richard Cromwell to resign as lord protector.

1659 Treaty of Pyrenées establishes peace between France and Spain. The conditions of the treaty reflect French power and the decline of Spain's fortunes.

1660 Charles II restored to the English throne.

1660 Treaty of Oliva ends five-year Northern War, with Poland ceding Livonia to Sweden and giving up its Baltic territories. Treaty of Copenhagen ends war between Denmark and Sweden with Danish surrender of territory.

1660 First female actor appears on the British stage.

1661 Louis XIV begins personal rule of France; during his reign the power of the monarchy becomes absolute and French culture flourishes.

1661 English acquire Bombay from the Portuguese.

1662 Kangxi (K'ang-hsi) becomes emperor of China; under his rule China undergoes a period of extensive cultural activity; Jesuit missionaries introduce western scientific knowledge to China.

1662 Robert Boyle, often considered the Father of Modern Chemistry, states Boyle's Law—the volume of gas varies inversely with pressure.

1664 England takes New Amsterdam from the Dutch and rename it New York.

1664 Austrians defeat the Turks at the battle of St. Gotthard; Truce of Vasvar ends the war between the Turks and the Holy Roman Empire and allows Turkey to retain its newly won territories.

1664 First performance of Molière's *Tartuffe*; Molière's comedies satirize contemporary society and break from a reliance on classical themes in French drama.

1665 Great Plague breaks out in London, killing 70,000.

1666 Great Fire of London ravages the city, destroying most buildings and churches.

1666 Isaac Newton states the laws of gravity and invents integral calculus. Newton's work lays the foundations for the modern study of physics and calculus.

1667 Treaty of Andrussov ends war between Russia and Poland; Russia gains Kiev and Smolensk.

1667 John Milton publishes his epic poem *Paradise Lost*.

1668 Enlargement of Versailles begins; the building project takes more than 100 years.

1668 Jean de La Fontaine's *Fables* published.

1668 English author Aphra Behn's *Oroonoko* is published; Behn was one of the first women to earn a living as a writer.

1669 Famine in Bengal kills 3 million.

1669 Mogul emperor Aurangzeb prohibits Hinduism in India, provoking massive Hindu resistance and protest.

1669 Stradivarius violin created by violin maker Antonio Stradivari in Cremona, Italy.

1672 English Royal African Company granted monopoly of the slave trade.

1673 Jacques Marquette and Louis Joliet explore the Great Lakes region and travel down the Mississippi River as far as Arkansas.

1674 Spain and the Holy Roman Empire join the Dutch in an effort to stop French invasions in Europe.

1675 English architect Christopher Wren oversees the construction of St. Paul's Cathedral in London. Wren's designs for churches, which combine Baroque and Classical influences, are built throughout London.

1675 King Philip's War begins in North America as hostilities erupt between the Narragansett and Wampanoag tribes and colonists in New England. The war ends the following year with the defeat of Chief Metacum but leaves many New England towns devastated.

1676 Treaty of Zuravno ends the war between Turkey and Poland with much of the Polish Ukraine seized by the Turks.

1677 Dutch philosopher Baruch Spinoza's *Ethics* published shortly after his death.

1677 Jean Baptiste Racine's *Phedre* performed; his work displays the neo-classical style dominating the French theater throughout the reign of Louis XIV.

1677 Using microscopes of his own invention, Dutch scientist Anton van Leeuwenhoek discovers protozoa and later discovers bacteria (1681).

1678 "Popish Plot" falsely alleges a plot by Catholics to massacre Protestants and overtake the English throne. The story leads to turmoil in London and the persecution of Catholics.

1678 *The Pilgrim's Progress*, a religious allegory by John Bunyan, becomes immensely popular in England soon after its publication.

1678 Treaty of Nimwegen ends war between France and the Netherlands; territories lost during the war are returned to the Dutch.

1679 England passes Act of Habeas Corpus, preventing imprisonment without trial.

1680 Sweden's King Charles XI seizes land from the nobility and further asserts the absolute power of the crown.

1680 Pueblos in Santa Fe and Taos rebel against the Spanish colonization and drive 2,500 colonists from the territory.

1681 Treaty of Radzin gives Russia most of the Turkish Ukraine.

1681 English poet Andrew Marvell's works are published posthumously; the collection includes "To His Coy Mistress."

1681 William Penn granted land in North America by King Charles II; the land later becomes Pennsylvania and is settled chiefly by Quakers and other Non-Conformists.

1682 Louis XIV moves the royal court to Versailles, further asserting his independence from Paris and the nobility.

1682 Edmund Halley observes the comet that is later to bear his name.

1682 The Sieur de la Salle claims the Louisiana Territory for the French.

1683 Chinese conquer Formosa (Taiwan).

1684 Pope Innocent XI forms the Holy League of Linz; Venice, Austria, and the Holy Roman Empire unite against the Turks.

1684 Japanese Prime Minister Hotta Masatoshi assassinated, leaving Shogun Sunayoshi with no able adviser; the subsequent years bring financial and political difficulties to Japan.

1685 Louis XIV revokes the Edict of Nantes; all religions except Roman Catholicism are outlawed. Huguenots begin mass migration from France, crippling the French shipping industry and economy.

1685 Chinese ports opened to overseas trade.

1686 League of Augsburg formed among the Holy Roman Empire, Spain, Sweden, Saxony, Bavaria, and the Palatinate against France and Louis XIV.

1687 Isaac Newton publishes the *Principia*; Newton postulates the law of gravity and universal laws of motion.

1687 John Dryden's poem *St. Cecilia's Day* is published; Dryden's poetry reflects the rational climate of ideas during the late 17th century and seeks to achieve clarity and precision in verse; his satirical poems are noted for their use of argument.

1688 The Glorious Revolution ends the reign of James II in England; fearing the likelihood of a succession of Catholic kings, Whig leaders invite William III of Orange to take the throne. James flees to France.

1689 English Parliament issues a declaration of rights and establishes a constitutional monarchy; William and Mary named king and queen for life, subject to parliamentary restrictions.

1689 War of the League of Augsburg expands as England and the Netherlands join the alliance against France. The Dutch, under invasion from France, neglect their navy and allow English naval superiority to grow.

1689 Peter the Great (Peter I) becomes tsar of Russia; he expands the Russian empire and attempts to westernize the country.

1690 England builds a factory in Calcutta, strengthening its position in India.

1690 John Locke's *On Human Understanding* denies the existence of innate knowledge and asserts the importance of experience as the basis of knowledge. His *Two Treatises on Government* asserts that governments derive their authority from popular consent and can righthfully be overthrown if they violate fundamental rights. His political theories influence political thought during the period of the American and French revolutions.

1692 Salem witchcraft trials begin in Salem, Massachusetts; during the next 20 years 20 women are executed.

1694 Bank of England chartered.

1696 English engineer Thomas Savery invents the first practical steam engine.

1696 Peter the Great strengthens the Russian Empire by taking Azov from the Turks, enabling Russia to control the Black Sea.

1697 Treaty of Ryswick ends the 11-year-old War of the League of Augsburg; France returns all territory conquered after 1679 to Spain and recognizes William III as King of England; Spain gives Haiti to the French.

1697 *Mother Goose Tales*, a collection of fairy tales by Charles Perrault, published in France.

1698 English Parliament opens up the slave trade to all merchants, breaking the monopoly of the Royal African Company. The move intensifies the "triangular trade" between Africa, the colonies, and England.

1699 Treaty of Karlowitz ends the war between the Holy League and the Turks. Turks cede almost all of Hungary, Transylvania, Slavonia, and Croatia to Austria; Podolia and Turkish Ukraine to Poland; Morea and most of Dalmatia to Venice.

1699 France establishes a settlement in the Illinois wilderness and a fort in Louisiana in an effort to strengthen their foothold in the Mississippi Valley.

1699 English explorer William Dampier explores Australia and New Guinea.

1699 Govind Singh leads Sikh rebellion in India against Mogul persecution.

1700 English restoration theater is exemplified in the production of William Congreve's *Way of the World*. Restoration comedies satirize contemporary morality, particularly in regard to sex. Other Restoration playwrights include William Wycherley and George Farquhar.

1700 Charles II of Spain dies; dispute over his successor leads to the War of Succession.

1700 Great Northern War begins; Russia and Denmark fight Sweden for control of the Baltic.

1700 Samuel Sewall's *The Selling of Joseph* becomes first American protest against slavery.

1700 Asante Empire begins its rise to power in Ghana.

1701 Frederick III, elector of Brandenburg, becomes the first king of Prussia, crowning himself King Frederick I.

1702 Fighting widens in the War of Spanish Succession; the Grand Alliance composed of England, the Netherlands, Holy Roman Empire, and Savoy declares war against France.

1703 The Grand Alliance proclaims Austria's Archduke Charles king of Spain in opposition to the French choice of Louis XIV's grandson Philip, duke of Anjou. Portugal joins the Grand Alliance.

1704 Allied army led by the duke of Marlborough and Prince Eugene of Savoy score a major victory over the French, Prussian, and Bavarian forces in the Battle of Blenheim. French losses continue the following year and their forces are driven completely out of Italy.

1705 Rebellion in Astrakhan protests Peter's attempt to westernize Russia.

1707 England and Scotland united as Great Britain by the Act of Union.

1707 Death of Aurangzeb begins the disintegration of the Mogul Empire as local princes begin to assert their independence and seek assistance from western traders in the midst of foreign invasions.

1708 Sikhs assert the independence of Punjab from the Mogul Empire.

1709 The pianoforte invented by Bartolomeo Cristofori in Italy.

1709 Russian victory in the Battle of Poltava asserts their dominance in northern Europe.

1709 Iron is produced using coke; this discovery makes iron production less expensive and is instrumental in stimulating the Industrial Revolution.

1710 Irish philosopher George Berkely's *The Principles of Human Knowledge* asserts that nothing exists apart from that which is perceived; his ideas shape Empiricist philosophy.

1711 Peter the Great forced to return Azov and to destroy Russian forts in Turkey after being defeated by the Turks.

1711 Afghanistan, led by Ghilzai chieftan Mir Vais, establishes itself as an independent state after defeating the Persians.

1712 First piston-operated steam engine is invented by Thomas Newcomen in England.

1712 War of succession erupts in India among Shah Bahadur's four sons.

1712 Protestant cantons defeat the Catholics and establish their supremacy in Switzerland.

1712 Uprising of African Americans is suppressed in New York; 21 blacks are convicted and executed.

1713 The Treaty of Utrecht ends the War of Spanish Succession; France recognizes Protestant succession in England, cedes Newfoundland and Nova Scotia to the English.

1713 The Pragmatic Sanction affirms females' right to the succession of the Hapsburg kingdom. The order is recognized in 1720.

1713 Frederick William becomes king of Prussia; he improves the state's organization and establishes Prussian military power by creating a standing army.

1714 German mathematician and philosopher Baron Gottfried von Leibniz, in such works as *Monadology*, attempts to provide a rational explanation of the nature of the universe and argues that Christian faith and scientific reason are compatible; he also helps to develop the study of calculus.

1714 English poet and critic Alexander Pope publishes *Rape of the Lock*, a parody of the heroic epic. Pope's satirical works employ the heroic couplet and rely on economical expression; his poems and criticisms are central to the neo-classical style.

1714 House of Hanover begins reign in England, which lasts for the next two centuries; George I crowned king of England.

1714 Treaty of Rastatt and Baden ends the war between France and the Holy Roman Empire.

1714 German physicist Daniel Fahrenheit invents the mercury thermometer.

1716 Yoshimune becomes ruler of Japan; he opens trade with the West and improves the country's agricultural system by building irrigation projects.

1717 French artist Antoine Watteau completes *L'Embarquement pour l'Ille de Cythere*; his paintings epitomize the popular genre of the *fêtes galantes*, which portray pastoral scenes of pleasure and leisure.

1717 Baroque composer George Frederick Handel composes the *Water Music*.

1718 Quadruple alliance between England, France, the Holy Roman Emperor, and the Netherlands forms against Spain; Spain's invasion of Sicily raises the possibility of a new European war.

1718 Mexico Cathedral, the country's largest and most impressive church, designed by Jerónimo Balbas.

1718 Inoculation method against smallpox (existing in the East since ancient times) is described by Lady Mary Wortley. It is later used in England, as an epidemic spreads.

1718 Charles XII of Sweden shot; his sister Ulrika Elenora succeeds him but abdicates the following year and is replaced by her husband, Frederick of Hesse. During his reign, the nobility curtails the power of the monarchy.

1718 French explorers found New Orleans. The following years witness further French activity in the Mississippi Valley as more forts are built in the area.

1719 *Robinson Crusoe* by Daniel Defoe published; his work helps to establish the genre of the novel.

1720 The tangano, an ancestor to the modern tango, is introduced to Central America by African slaves.

1721 Great Northern War between Russia and Sweden comes to an end with the Treaty of Nystadt; Russia gains territory from the Swedes and becomes a formidable power throughout Europe; Peter declares himself tsar of all the Russias.

1721 Bach's *Brandenburg Concertos* performed for the first time; Bach's compositions epitomize the Baroque style of polyphonic sound; his use of counterpoint and works for keyboard instruments revolutionizes music.

1723 The following years witness the development of the French Rococo style in design emphasizing S-curves and scroll-like forms. The elegant and decorative style spreads throughout Europe.

1724 Russia and Turkey form an alliance to conquer Persian lands; Persian ruler Shah Mahmud goes insane and begins a reign of terror.

1725 The Spanish Steps in Rome designed by Francesco de Sanctis is completed; the steps embody the ornate and decorative style of Baroque design.

1726 The ministry of Cardinal Fleury begins to exert its influence over French affairs; his administration maintains peace and helps bring economic growth to France.

1726 *Gulliver's Travels* by Jonathan Swift published; his work satirizes English attitudes and politics.

1728 John Gay's immensely popular *Beggars Opera* employs traditional songs and elements of Italian opera to create a new kind of political satire.

1730 Charles Townshend introduces scientific methods to husbandry and farming; his system cuts down on the need for spices for preserving meat and makes farming more efficient.

1731 English mathematician John Hadley invents the reflecting quadrant, improving navigation for ships. His quadrant prefigures the sextant.

1732 British colony of Georgia is founded by James Oglethorpe; the colony is established primarily for English debtors.

1732 Benjamin Franklin publishes his first *Poor Richard's Almanack*. In the same year, Franklin reforms the colonial postal system, increasing its efficiency and revenue.

1732 Herman Boerhaave's *Elements of Chemistry* establishes the foundation for modern organic chemistry.

1733 War of Polish Succession begins with Russia and Austria recognizing Frederick Augustus, the elector of Saxony, and France and Spain supporting Polish noble Stanislaus Leszczynski. The war ends two years later with Frederick Augustus being crowned.

1733 John Kay invents the flying shuttle; this invention improves the hand loom and quickens the development of cotton weaving as a cottage industry.

1734 War of Polish Succession spreads as Spain captures Naples and Sicily.

1734 Jonathan Edwards's sermons spur the Great Awakening, a religious revival, throughout New England.

1734 Voltaire publishes his *Lettres Philiosophiques*, which supports the empiricism of Newton and Locke. Voltaire's works and advocacy of religious and political tolerance shape the ideas behind the French Enlightenment.

1735 Carolus Linnaeus publishes *Systema Naturae*; the book establishes the modern system of classification for plants and animals. In 1737 his *Genera Pantarum* lays the foundation for the study of botany.

1735 The trial of Peter Zenger establishes the principle of freedom of the press in the colonies.

1735 *Gil Blas* by Alain René Lesage popularizes the picaresque novel in Europe.

1736 Afghan Nadir Kuli becomes ruler of the Persian Empire, ending the Safavid Dynasty that has ruled since 1502; he will reign as Nadir Shah until 1747.

1736 The ship's chronometer invented by John Harrison further improves the accuracy of navigation.

1739 Methodism, a form of Protestantism, founded by John Wesley.

1739 War of Jenkins's Ear begins in the North American colonies between England and Spain. England declares war after mistreatment of English smugglers by the Spaniards.

1739 Persian forces led by Nadir Khan defeat the Mogul army and shatter the empire.

1739 Treaty of Belgrade ends three-year war between Austria and Turkey; Austria cedes Belgrade and northern Serbia.

1739 Cato Conspiracy, a slave uprising in Stono, South Carolina, leads to the deaths of 30 whites and 44 blacks.

1739 Scottish philosopher David Hume's *Treatise on Human Nature* underscores many ideas behind British empiricist philosophy. Hume's works argue that true knowledge is unattainable and limited to the subjective experience of ideas and impressions.

1740 Frederick the Great (Frederick II) ascends to the Prussian throne; his reign introduces religious tolerance, agricultural reform, and military improvements. The Prussian occupation of Silesia sets off the War of Austrian Succession.

1741 In his effort to discover if North America and Asia are connected by land, Danish navigator Vitus Bering becomes first European to sail to Alaska.

1741 Handel composes *Messiah*, his most famous choral piece.

1741 War of Austrian Succession spreads as Frederick II of Prussia forms an alliance with France, Bavaria, and Spain against Austria.

1741 Elizabeth Petrovna seizes power from the infant Tsar Ivan VI and his regent Count Biron in Russia. During her rule she gives new powers to the Senate.

1742 The Celsius system of measuring temperature is devised by Swedish scientist Anders Celsius.

1742 Peace of Berlin ends first Silesian War between Austria and Prussia. Maria Theresa gives the coal-rich regions of upper and lower Silesia to Prussia.

1742 English cotton factories established in Birmingham and Northampton help to set the stage for the Industrial Revolution.

1742 Color printing developed by Japanese painter Kitagawa Utamaro.

1743 English artist William Hogarth engraves his *Marriage á la Mode*; the work employs many of the elements of Rococo style, particularly the serpentine line.

1743 Pogroms in Russia kill thousands of Jews.

1744 Frederick II starts the second Silesian War by invading Saxony and Bohemia; the invasion is halted by Hapsburg troops fighting for Maria Theresa.

1744 The Wahhabi movement spreads throughout the Muslim world; Muhammed ibn Abd al-Wahhab calls for a return to the original principles of Islam.

1745 Bonny Prince Charles organizes Scottish clans in Jacobite Rebellion to restore the Stuart family to the throne of England. The rebellion advances into England but is defeated the following year at the Battle of Culloden.

1745 The study of electricity begins with the introduction of the Leyden jar.

1745 The symphony orchestra begins to develop in its present form at the Mannheim court in Bavaria.

1746 The Netherlands are freed from Austrian rule after French victory in the Battle of Rocoux.

1747 Samuel Richardson's *Clarissa* is published and gains popularity throughout Europe. Richardson's works help to develop the modern novel through its exploration of characters' psychology.

1747 Nadir Shah assassinated, leading to disorder within the Persian Empire. One of Nadir's generals, Ahmad Shah, seizes control of the Afghan provinces and founds the Barkzai Dynasty, which rules until 1929.

1747 Building-trade workers organize in New York, forming the first labor organization in the colonies.

1748 War of the Austrian Succession comes to an end with the Peace of Aix-la-Chappelle. The House of Hanover maintains right to succession in Britain and the German states; the Pragmatic Sanction is confirmed in Austria; Prussia retains Silesia.

1748 *The Spirit of the Laws* by French theorist Montesquieu analyzes the workings of government and proposes the separation of powers. His work helps to shape the discipline of sociology.

1749 *Tom Jones*, a "comic epic in prose" by Henry Fielding, further develops the genre of the novel.

1749 Sign language invented by Giacobbo Rodriguez Pereire.

1749 The first volume of *Histoire Naturelle*, a massive study of nature and biology by George Louis Clerc, published.

1750 José Manuel ascends to the Portuguese throne following the death of his father João V, who had ruled for 44 years. José Manuel and chief minister, the marquess of Pombal, undermine Jesuit influence and introduce reforms and Enlightenment ideas to Portugal.

1751 Robert Clive captures Arcot and establishes English authority over India, ending a French threat; three years later England has firm control over all of India.

1751 China invades and conquers Tibet.

1752 Benjamin Franklin's experiments with a kite during a thunderstorm lead him to discover the electrical nature of lightning and subsequently invent the lightning rod.

1752 Austrian composer Franz Joseph Haydn's work over the next ten years changes the nature and sound of the symphony and marks the development of the sonata form. He is later the teacher of Mozart and Beethoven.

1752 French naturalist René de Reaumur discovers the chemical nature of the digestive process.

1753 The British Museum is founded; one of the first museums in Europe, it goes on to collect treasures from all over the world.

1754 Britain and France go to war in North America. The Albany Congress convenes to develop a strategy against the French; Benjamin Franklin's suggestion to unite the colonies is rejected.

1754 The Winter Palace is completed in St. Petersburg; it will later house the Hermitage Museum.

1754 First female doctor graduates in Germany.

1755 Earthquake in Lisbon destroys the city and kills 30,000.

1755 Rangoon founded by Burmese King Aloung P'Houra.

1756 Prussia invades Saxony and the Seven Years' War begins in Europe after Frederick the Great learns of plot by Austria and Saxony to challenge Prussian power. Britain declares war on France and allies itself with Prussia.

1756 Siraj-ud-Daulah Nawab of Bengal invades Calcutta and imprisons 146 British in the "Black Hole of Calcutta"; only 23 survive. The following year Robert Clive reconquers the city and goes on to establish British sovereignty in India.

1758 France suffers defeats in the European Seven Years' War at the hands of Prince Ferdinand of Brunswick; in North America the French lose forts at Duquesne, Frontenac, and Louisburg.

1758 The sextant, invented by John Bird, improves navigational accuracy.

1758 The first blast furnace is put into use in England for production of iron.

1758 François Quensay's *Tableau Economique* provides a scientific approach to economics. Leader of the Physiocrat school of thought, Quensay argues for a laissez-faire approach to the economy rather than the dominant mercantilist policy, and sees agriculture as the basis of a nation's wealth.

1759 British success in war with France in North America continues as they capture Quebec and score a series of naval victories.

1759 Austrian and Russian forces are victorious over Frederick the Great at the Battle of Kunersdorf.

1760 The first volumes of *The Life and Opinions of Tristam Shandy* by Laurence Sterne published. The work radically departs from the traditional conventions of the novel, and many of Sterne's techniques will influence 20th-century modernist novelists such as James Joyce and Henry James.

1762 Jean-Jacques Rousseau's *Social Contract* argues that government should act on the general will of the people. His ideas play a significant role in developing political theory of the American and French revolutions; his theories also influence the direction of the Romantic movement.

1762 Catherine the Great (Catherine II) becomes tsarina of Russia, beginning 34-year reign of "benevolent despotism" in which she seizes church lands, reforms Russian law, and establishes religious tolerance.

1763 Treaty of Paris ends Seven Years' War between England and France and Spain. The provisions of the treaty strengthen British control over North America.

1763 Frederick the Great signs treaty with Austria ending Seven Years' War in Europe.

1763 Pontiac's Rebellion, a Native American protest against westward colonial expansion, is defeated.

1764 Spinning Jenny invented by James Hargreaves.

1764 The advent of realism in Chinese literature is exemplified in Tsao Chan's *The Dream of the Red Chamber*, which describes the decline of a Chinese family.

1764 Horace Walpole's *The Castle of Otranto* develops the genre of the Gothic novel and influences elements of Romanticism.

1765 The Stamp Act, imposed to create revenue for England, draws fierce criticism from the American colonies; the act stimulates colonial opposition to British rule, specifically taxation without representation, and is repealed the following year.

1765 Robert Clive reforms British rule in India, maintaining a puppet government.

1766 Ali Bey declares Egyptian independence from the Turks.

1766 Henry Cavendish discovers hydrogen; he also makes several discoveries concerning the nature of electricity.

1767 Reform Judaism begins to develop with the writings of Moses Mendelssohn. His works attempt to integrate Judaism with modern metaphysics and scientific thought.

1767 The Townshend Act arouses colonial opposition to British taxes and leads to nonimportation agreements among the colonies.

1768 The treaties of Hard Labor and Stanwix provide the cession of Iroquois and Cherokee land to the British.

1768 English explorer James Cook embarks on journey in which he explores Tahiti, New Zealand, and Australia.

1768 Cotton manufacturing is immensely improved by Richard Arkwright's invention of the water frame.

1768 Gurkhas conquer Nepal.

1769 James Watt patents the steam engine; his invention enables power to be produced more quickly and efficiently than ever and is pivotal to the Industrial Revolution.

1769 Famine in Bengal kills 10 million Indians.

1770 Five colonists are killed in the Boston Massacre after a disturbance between English soldiers and colonists; the Townshend Acts are repealed, but a tax on tea is maintained.

1771 Russia conquers the Crimea, increasing its power in Europe.

1772 Poland is partitioned among Russia, Prussia, and Austria.

1772 The French *Encyclopedie*, supervised by Denis Diderot, published; the volumes illustrate the Enlightenment's quest for knowledge.

1772 Absolute monarchy returns to Sweden under the rule of Gustavus III. During his reign, Gustavus ends the practice of torture, establishes religious toleration, reforms Sweden's poor laws, and encourages trade.

1773 The Boston Tea Party, protesting the tax on tea, is led by radical colonists disguised as Native Americans.

1773 Pope Clement XIV dissolves the Jesuits.

1773 Cossack Pugachev leads a peasant revolt in Russia. The rebellion is suppressed two years later but leads to a reform of provincial administration.

1774 Treaty of Kuchuk Kainarji between Russia and Turkey gives Russia ports on the Black Sea and the right to represent the Greek Orthodox Church in Turkey.

1774 "Intolerable Acts" passed by British Parliament to suppress rebellious activities in Boston; First Continental Congress meets in Philadelphia to protest the measures.

1774 *The Sorrows of Young Werther* by Johann Wolfgang von Goethe published; Goethe's works, including the play *Faust*, help to shape the style and ideas behind European romanticism.

1774 Oxygen is discovered by English chemist Joseph Priestly.

1774 String quartets become the dominant form in classical music.

1775 American War of Independence begins with battles at Lexington, Concord, and Bunker Hill. George Washington appointed commander-in-chief of the Continental army.

1776 The Declaration of Independence drafted by Thomas Jefferson is adopted by the Continental Congress on July 4. Jefferson greatly influences political thought in America, arguing for a republic based on independent farmers.

1776 *The Wealth of Nations* by Scottish economist Adam Smith published. Smith's work defines the Classical school of economics, arguing for free-market competition and limited government intervention.

1776 The submarine, invented by American engineer David Bushnell, first used in warfare during the American Revolution.

1776 Thomas Paine's pamphlet "Common Sense," supporting the revolutionary cause, becomes an immediate best-seller in the colonies. A leading radical thinker of the time, Paine advocates republicanism, abolition of slavery, and greater freedom for women.

1777 American troops under General Gates defeat the British at Saratoga but suffer other losses as the British take Philadelphia.

1778 France signs a treaty of alliance in support of the American colonists; the following year Spain pledges its support for the colonies.

1778 The opera house La Scala opens in Milan.

1779 The spinning mule invented by Samuel Crompton increases the productivity and efficiency of the nascent textile industry.

1779 The American navy led by John Paul Jones scores a series of victories against the British.

1780 Peruvian Indians, led by Inca Tupac Amaru, rebel against Spanish rule; two years later the revolt is quelled.

1780 Britain goes to war with the Dutch in the East Indies, resulting in a further loss of Dutch influence in the area.

1780 Serfdom is abolished in Hungary and Bohemia.

1781 Americans defeat the British as General Cornwallis surrenders at Yorktown.

1781 In *Critique of Pure Reason*, Immanuel Kant argues that the organizational principle behind human perception is innate and develops before experience.

1781 Uranus is discovered by English scientist William Herschel; it is the first planet discovered that was not known to the ancients.

1782 War between England and Marathas, the people of western India, ends after seven years with the Treaty of Salabi.

1782 Steam engine first introduced into a manufacturer's factory by Josiah Wedgwood.

1783 Treaty of Versailles formally ends American War of Independence; Britain recognizes American independence.

1783 First human flight takes place in a hot-air balloon, flown and invented by two French brothers, Joseph and Jacques Montgolfier.

1784 French Painter Jacques David's *Oath of the Horati* epitomizes the dominant neo-classical style of the time. His later work, including *Death of Marat* (1793), contributes to the visual propaganda of the French Revolution.

1784 William Pitt the Younger establishes government control over political affairs in India, taking power away from the East India Company.

1784 Economic depression begins in America.

1785 The power loom, which mechanizes weaving, invented by Edmund Cartwright.

1785 The dollar becomes the official currency of America.

1786 Shays's Rebellion begins in Massachusetts to protest against further foreclosing of farms. The rebellion brings attention to the need for a strong central government for America.

1786 The folk traditions of Scotland are explored in Robert Burns's *Poems Chiefly in the Scottish Dialect*.

1787 The Constitution of the United States is drawn up in Philadelphia; the document defines the role and nature of government, and establishes a balance of power among the various branches and between the states and the federal government.

1787 The Northwest Ordinance provides for the Northwest Territory's ultimate statehood as free states. The ordinance signals the beginning of westward expansion by the United States.

1787 The African Methodist Episcopal Church is founded by Richard Allen and Absalom Jones. Along with the Free African Society, the church becomes an important institution for African American attempts to improve their social and economic conditions.

1787 In an effort to reach a compromise between northern and southern states over representation in Congress, the Constitution establishes black slaves as three-fifths of an individual.

1787 Britain establishes Sierra Leone in Africa as a settlement for ex-slaves and poor blacks.

1788 Australia established as a convict settlement by Britain.

1788 A list of grievances is submitted to Louis XVI of France. National bankruptcy is announced and the king assembles the Estates-General as pressure on the monarchy mounts.

1788 The United States Constitution gains support from nine states and is ratified.

1788 First practical steamboat invented by James Symington.

1789 The French Revolution begins; the Paris mob storms the Bastille; the National Assembly, composed of the bourgeoisie and some of the clergy and nobility, takes power under the leadership of Count Mirabeau; the assembly adopts the Declaration of the Rights of Man. The revolution leads to the abolition of the feudal system in France and the nationalization of church property.

1789 George Washington becomes the first president of the United States.

1789 The Austrian Netherlands declares its independence under the name of Belgium; Austria refuses to recognize the independence of Belgium and the rebellion is suppressed the following year.

1789 The study of modern chemistry is developed by French scientist Antoine Lavoisier in his *Traité Élémentaire de Chimie*.

1789 American factory system begins following Samuel Slater's visit to English industries; the following year Slater opens the first cotton mill in the United States.

1789 Jeremy Bentham's *An Introduction to the Principles of Morals and Legislation* receives immediate attention; it establishes the doctrine of "the greatest happiness of the greatest number" and the theory of utilitarianism. Bentham's writings develop liberalism and argue for the protection of individuals' rights from the state.

1790 Indian Nonintercourse Act forbids the seizing of land from Native Americans; however, the practice continues in New England.

1791 Louis XVI fails to escape from France and is returned to Paris; the National Assembly votes for a constitutional monarchy; King Louis XVI accepts the new constitution.

1791 Canada Act divides the territory into French- and English-speaking provinces.

1791 The Bill of Rights is amended to the United States Constitution.

1791 Toussaint l'Ouverture leads a slave rebellion against the French in Haiti.

1791 Wolfgang Amadeus Mozart's *The Magic Flute* is first performed as the composer's career comes to an end. His work includes over 50 symphonies and several operas and marks the apex of the Classical age in its purity of melody and form.

1791 First Bank of the United States opens; Secretary of Treasury Alexander Hamilton's fiscal plan calls for a strong central government and the encouragement of manufacturing.

1792 Parisian mob led by Georges Jacques Danton storms the Tuileries Palace and establishes the Revolutionary Commune; the royal family is imprisoned and Louis XVI is put on trial; France is declared a republic.

1792 France is invaded by Prussian and Austrian armies; France scores a major victory over the Prussians at the battle of Valmy.

1792 Mary Wollstonecraft publishes *Vindication of the Rights of Women*; her book is one of the earliest examples of feminist thought.

1793 Eli Whitney invents the cotton gin, leading to the rapid growth of cotton planting in the southern United States and the textile industry in the north; the development of the cotton industry leads to an increased demand for slave labor.

1793 Louis XVI is executed; Reign of Terror begins by the Committee on Public Safety under the leadership of Robespierre and Danton.

1793 France goes to war against Britain, Holland, Austria, Prussia, and Spain.

1794 Reign of Terror reaches its height and then comes to an end in France with the execution of Robespierre; Commune of Paris is abolished.

1794 Tadeusz Kosciuzko leads uprising against Russian occupation in Poland; the rebellion is crushed by Prussian and Russian forces.

1794 The Kajar Dynasty is founded in Persia by Aga Muhammad; lasts until 1925.

1794 Legislative Assembly in France abolishes slavery in the Caribbean colonies.

1794 Poet and artist William Blake publishes his *Songs of Experience*. Blake's mystical poetry explores the imaginative possibilities of humans and the decline of the modern individual. His engravings break from the dominant style of the British Academy.

1795 The Directory, a five-man executive, comes to power in France after the establishment of the third constitution.

1795 France makes peace with several countries including Prussia and Spain.

1795 The third partition of Poland further divides the country between Russia, Prussia, and Austria; Poland does not exist as a single entity again until 1918.

1795 The British take Ceylon from the Dutch.

1795 Metric system of measurement is adopted in France.

1796 Napoleon Bonaparte leads French army; he defeats Austrian troops in several battles and conquers most of Italy.

1796 Vaccination for smallpox is discovered by British physician Edward Jenner.

1796 Qian Long (Ch'ien Lung), emperor of China, abdicates; his sixty-year reign witnessed the expansion of the Chinese Empire, establishment of trade with the United States, and encouragement of the arts and literature.

1797 Marquis de Sade publishes his novel *Juliette*. His controversial works deal with explicit sexual situations and practices.

1797 Treaty of Campo Formio ends war between France and Austria; the terms of the treaty further strengthen French military power in Italy; Napoleon founds the Ligurian Republic in Genoa and unites Cisalpine with the Cispadane Republic.

1798 French armies occupy Rome and establish Roman Republic; they overtake Switzerland and set up the Helvetic Republic; Napoleon gains control of Egypt in the battle of the Pyramids, but the French navy is defeated by the British under Admiral Horatio Nelson.

1798 Romantic movement begins to define itself in Britain; lyrical ballads including Wordsworth's "Tintern Abbey" and Coleridge's "Rime of the Ancient Mariner" published. Wordsworth's conception of poetry as an intensely subjective expression is a crucial element of Romantic poetry.

1798 English economist Thomas Malthus publishes his *Essays on the Principles of Population*; his work explores the problems of overpopulation and hunger.

1799 Napoleon invades Syria; a coalition of England, Austria, Portugal, Russia, Naples, and Turkey forms and drives the French out of Italy, but Napoleon reconquers it the next year.

1799 Napoleon returns to France, overthrows the Directory, establishes a consulate and becomes First Consul.

1799 Discovery of the Rosetta Stone leads to the deciphering of Egyptian hieroglyphics.

1800 First electric battery invented by Italian physicist Alessandro Volta.

1800 Robert Owen takes over New Lanark mills in Scotland and begins to implement social reforms; his actions are some of the first to counter the effects of industrialization on workers and society. His later attempt to establish a workers' commune in New Harmony, Indiana, fails.

1801 United Kingdom of Britain and Ireland is formed in the Act of Union.

1801 Treaty of Luneville between Austria and France leads to the breakup of the Holy Roman Empire; France gains left bank of the Rhine and retains most of Italy.

1802 Napoleon names himself consul for life; he begins improvements in education, establishes the Prefecture, makes compromises with the church, and reintroduces slavery into Haiti.

1803 President Thomas Jefferson buys the Louisiana Purchase territory from the French, doubling the size of the United States.

1803 Judicial review is established by the United States Supreme Court in the case of *Marbury* v. *Madison*. Chief Justice John Marshall's decision gives the court ultimate power in interpreting the law and constitution.

1803 Atomic theory first proposed by English chemist-physicist John Dalton.

1803 Robert Fulton propels boat using steam power. In 1807 first regular steamboat service begins along the Hudson River.

1804 Napoleon crowns himself emperor of France and imposes the Napoleonic Code on France and the conquered lands; the code reforms French law and influences the legal codes of other European countries.

1804 Haiti gains its independence after defeating the French and establishes a republican government.

1804 Serbian nationalists revolt against Turkish rule but are suppressed by 1813.

1804 English engineer Richard Trevithick builds the first steam locomotive.

1804 Lewis and Clark begin exploration of the Louisiana Purchase and eventually reach the Pacific Ocean.

1804 Johann Schiller's *Wilhelm Tell* establishes Schiller as a preeminent German playwright.

1805 Austria joins third coalition with Russia and England to stop Napoleonic invasions; Napoleon wins a major victory over the Austrians at Austerlitz; Admiral Nelson triumphs at Trafalgar ending the French naval threat.

1805 Egypt is granted independence from the Ottomans; Muhammad Ali is named governor.

1806 Holy Roman Empire formally ends with the Confederation of the Rhine organized by France. Confederation places most German states under French control, leading to renewed hostilities between France and Prussia.

1806 Napoleon imposes Continental System to prevent English access to continental ports.

1807 Slave trade abolished in Britain but slavery remains legal.

1808 French armies invade and occupy Spain.

1808 French utopian Charles Fourier publishes *The Social Destiny of Man*; his work influences later socialist and utopian thought.

1808 United States Congress prohibits the importation of African slaves, but illegal imports continue and slavery continues to be the basis of the southern economy.

1808 Ludwig van Beethoven's Fifth Symphony first performed; his works, including nine symphonies, help to bring music from the Classical to the Romantic era.

1809 Napoleon defeats Austrians at Wagram; Treaty of Schonbrunn forces Austrian concessions of territory and acceptance of the Continental System.

1810 Napoleon annexes Holland, Hanover, Bremen, and Hamburg.

1811 Venezuela breaks away from Spanish rule; Simón Bolívar emerges as a leader in the South American struggle for independence from Spain and Portugal.

1811 "Luddites" riot in Britain protesting mechanization and the textile manufacturers.

1811 The Mamelukes, a powerful family in Egypt, are massacred by Ottoman Viceroy Muhammad Ali for plotting against him. Muhammad Ali rules supreme for the next 38 years.

1811 Jane Austen's *Sense and Sensibility* is published; her other novels, including *Pride and Prejudice* and *Emma*, explore the manners and morals of English country society.

1812 Britain and the United States go to war over shipping and territorial disputes; the war ends two years later with neither side making substantial gains; however, the inability to purchase manufactured goods from England encourages the growth of American industry.

1812 Napoleon invades Russia and occupies Moscow but is later forced to retreat and suffers tremendous losses; Napoleonic empire begins to collapse.

1812 British Romantic poet Lord Byron publishes the first cantos of *Childe Harold's Pilgrimage*. Byron's dramatic life, filled with love affairs and fighting for the revolutionary cause in Greece, contributes to his fame.

1813 King Frederick William III of Prussia leads forces in the War of Liberation against France; Britain, Austria, Russia, and Sweden join Prussia and form fourth coalition against Napoleon; allied forces achieve major victory at the Battle of Leipzig.

1814 Allied forces move into Paris; Napoleon abdicates and is exiled to Elba; Louis XVIII ascends to the throne.

1815 Napoleon escapes from Elba and marches on Paris beginning the "One Hundred Days," but he is defeated at Waterloo in Belgium by Lord Wellington and is banished to St. Helena; second Treaty of Paris restores France's boundaries to those of 1790.

1815 American general Andrew Jackson scores decisive victory over the British in the Battle of New Orleans, but the War of 1812 has already ended with the Treaty of Ghent.

1815 Congress of Vienna convenes to work out peace settlement in Europe; the congress restores the monarchy to Prussia and Austria and confirms the kingdom of the Netherlands. Congresses continue to convene to settle international disputes through the 1830s.

1815 Grimm brothers Jacob and Wilhelm publish their collection of fairy tales.

1816 Colonial rule continues to break down in South America as Brazil declares its independence from Portugal and Argentina from Spain.

1816 Gioacchino Antonio Rossini's *Barber of Seville* opens, gaining immediate popularity and establishing the Italian operatic style of the 19th century.

1817 The Obrenovic Dynasty, which rules Serbia from 1858 to 1903, is founded; Serbia granted partial autonomy by Turkey.

1817 David Ricardo's *Principles of Political Economy* contributes to Adam Smith's free-trade doctrines; Ricardo asserts a growing antagonism between the landlords of the English establishment and the rising industrial capitalists.

1817 Georg Wilhelm Friedrich Hegel's *Science of Logic* published; Hegel's influential dialectical method of reasoning will shape Marx's conception of the inevitability of radical change in history and society.

1818 Zulu Empire in Africa is founded by military chieftain Chaka.

1818 Mary Shelley publishes *Frankenstein*; the novel combines the style of Gothic horror with Romantic theories about human perversion of nature.

1819 Percy Bysshe Shelley's poem "Ode to the West Wind" published. Shelley's works, including "Ode to a Skylark" and "Ozymandias," often explore neo-Platonic and Romantic themes and express a love for freedom and idealism.

1819 Seminole War ends in southeastern United States; Spain cedes Florida to the United States and gives up all claims to land north of 42nd parallel. Native Americans subsequently driven out of the region by the American government.

1819 Singapore founded by East India Company.

1819 John Keats writes many of his odes, including "To a Nightingale" and "On a Grecian Urn," exploring the implications of beauty and art. Keats seeks to express a spontaneous apprehension of experience as suggested in his conception of "negative capability."

1819 German philosopher Arthur Schopenhauer's *The World as Will and Idea* published; its pessimistic philosophy departs from the Enlightenment's confidence in human capability for rational progress and will have great influence in the late 19th century.

1820 The Missouri Compromise prohibits slavery in the new territories north of 36°30′. The compromise acts only as a temporary settlement and is disregarded in subsequent years.

1820 Liberal revolutions break out in Spain, Portugal, and Italy, demanding governmental reforms.

1820 French poet Lamartine publishes *Méditations Poétiques*, which helps to develop the Romantic movement in French literature.

1820 French physicist André Ampère founds the study of electrodynamics.

1821 Mexico, Peru, Panama, and Guatemala gain independence from Spain.

1821 Greek war for independence from the Ottoman Empire begins.

1822 Liberia is founded by Washington Colonization Society for the repatriation of African Americans.

1822 Haiti conquers Santo Domingo and wins complete control of Hispaniola.

1822 Slave rebellion in South Carolina led by Denmark Vesey is crushed. The rebellion sends shock waves throughout the South as even tighter controls are placed on slaves.

1822 First permanent photograph produced by French physicist J. N. Niepce.

1823 Spanish revolt protesting the need for a constitution and political reform is ended with the help of the French. Ferdinand VII restored to the throne.

1823 President James Monroe issues the Monroe Doctrine asserting that European influence and colonization will no longer be allowed on the American continent. In later years the doctrine will allow for United States to increase its influence in the hemisphere.

1823 Japanese painter Hokusai begins his *Thirty-six Views of Mount Fuji*.

1823 Guatemala, San Salvador, Nicaragua, Honduras, and Costa Rica form Confederation of United Provinces of Central America; union dissolves in 1840.

1824 Anglo-Burmese war leads to English annexation of Burma.

1824 U.S. Corps of Army Engineers begins to build canals and other projects; this improves the country's transportation system and fuels the growing manufacturing industries.

1824 British trade unions form as Parliament repeals the Combination Acts and allows workers to organize.

1824 Eugène Delacroix paints *Massacre at Chois*; his works epitomize French Romantic painting in their expressive use of color and dramatic subjects.

1825 World's first steam locomotive passenger system opens in England.

1825 United States begins removal of Native Americans to the western lands.

1825 Erie Canal opens connecting the Great Lakes with the Atlantic and the Hudson River; the Great Lakes region booms as cities such as Cleveland, Chicago, and Buffalo play a more vital role in the nation's economy.

1825 Egyptian forces land in Greece in support of the Ottomans.

1825 New York Stock Exchange opens.

1826 Portugal's João VI dies; his son Dom Pedro succeeds to the throne and draws up a constitution providing for a parliamentary government.

1826 *Last of the Mohicans*, by James Fenimore Cooper, published; considered one of the first major American novels.

1827 Treaty of London signed by Britain, Russia, and France in support of Greek independence.

1827 Ohm's law relating current, voltage, and resistance formulated by German physicist Georg Ohm.

1828 Miguelite wars break out in Portugal and civil war continues for six years after Regent Dom Miguel names himself king of Portugal after a successful coup d'etat.

1828 "Tariff of Abominations" passed by the United States Congress; southern states protest against the tariff on imported manufactured and raw goods; South Carolina Senator John Calhoun's protest shapes the southern theory of states' rights.

1828 Madagascar's Queen Ranavaloana begins 33-year reign that resists British and French influence.

1829 Turkey recognizes Greek independence.

1829 Andrew Jackson takes office; he is the first president to use the "spoils system" and patronage for government appointments; he attacks the Bank of the United States in an effort to decentralize the nation's economy.

1829 African American David Walker publishes his *An Appeal . . . to the Colored Citizens of the World*, condemning American slavery and calling for its abolition by any means, including insurrection and violent force if necessary; the controversial document is banned by state legislatures across the South.

1830 Liberal opposition in France overthrows Charles X and replaces him with Louis-Phillippe. Inspired by the events in France, Belgians revolt against Dutch rule and win their independence.

1830 President Jackson signs Indian Removal Act providing for the removal of Native Americans to lands west of the Mississippi.

1830 France establishes colonial rule in Algiers.

1830 Church of Jesus Christ of Latter-Day Saints (Mormons) founded by Joseph Smith in Fayette, New York.

1830 Stendhal's novel *The Scarlet and the Black* published; the novel helps to develop the style of social realism.

1830 Romantic movement in music becomes the dominant form in Europe. Romanticism breaks away from the Classical concern with form, emphasizes content, and seeks new means of expression. Composers include Hector Berlioz, Franz Schubert, Franz von Listz, and Felix Mendelssohn-Bartholdy.

1831 Polish diet declares Poland's independence, but the revolt is suppressed by Russian forces who occupy Warsaw.

1831 Giuseppe Mazzini starts the Young Italy group dedicated to achieving Italian national independence. His group influences similar movements throughout Europe.

1831 Movements for Italian unification in Modena, Parma, and the papal states reflect the revolutionary mood in Europe; uprising is suppressed by the Austrians.

1831 Victor Hugo publishes *Hunchback of Notre-Dame*.

1831 Alexander Pushkin completes verse novel *Eugene Onegin*. Pushkin's works introduce a more realistic language to Russian literature, and his willingness to experiment breaks literary conventions.

1831 Nat Turner leads a slave revolt in Virginia; the uprising is put down and thirteen blacks are executed. Samuel Sharp leads a slave rebellion in Jamaica that is also suppressed.

1831 English chemist and physicist Michael Faraday discovers electromagnetic induction.

1831 William Lloyd Garrison starts the abolitionist paper *The Liberator* in Boston, Massachusetts. His moral crusade against slavery, at first rejected by a majority of Northerners, would later influence northern opinion about slavery.

1832 Reform Act in Britain extends the vote to the middle class.

1832 Egypt and Turkey go to war. The Turks are badly defeated at Battle of Koniah; the following year they recognize Egyptian independence.

1832 Frederic Chopin, a Polish muscian working in Paris, begins to write short pieces for the piano and develops forms such as the nocturne, mazurka, and polonaise; his works are characterized by volatile moods and fluid rhythms.

1832 Unification movements in Germany and Italy are abandoned.

1832 First party conventions held in the United States to nominate presidential candidates.

1833 Slavery abolished in the British Empire.

1834 Civil War begins in Spain; Don Carlos claims the throne with the support of the church and regional elements in Spain; the movement against Queen Isabella's liberal regime is opposed by England, France, and Portugal.

1834 Dom Miguel abdicates the Portuguese throne, ending 6-year civil war.

1834 The Braille system is devised by Louis Braille enabling the blind to read.

1834 South and west Australia colonized by English settlers.

1834 French novelist Honoré de Balzac publishes *Le Père Goriot*; Balzac's novel depicts contemporary French life by combining new techniques of realism with elements of fantasy.

1835 "Great Trek" begins in South Africa as Dutch settlers migrate to the Transvaal to escape British rule.

1835 Hans Christian Andersen publishes his first collection of fairy tales.

1835 Samuel Colt patents the Colt pistol, the first repeating firearm. The gun becomes an icon of the American West.

1836 Chartist movement begins in Britain; it is the first national working-class movement and calls for universal suffrage.

1836 Texas wins its independence from Mexico at the Battle of San Jacinto after suffering a loss at the Alamo. The Republic of Texas is founded with Sam Houston as president.

1836 Ralph Waldo Emerson publishes his essay "Nature"; Emerson becomes one of the leading figures of the American Transcendental movement and his works shape the direction of American literature and thought.

1837 Republic of Natal founded by Dutch settlers in South Africa.

1837 Major advances in the development of communication technology; the Morse code is invented by Samuel Morse and the electrical telegraph is patented by Charles Wheatstone and William Fothergil Cooke.

1837 Panic of 1837 leads to a depression in the United States, causing bankruptcy and starvation for thousands.

1837 Seminole tribe loses to United States in battle over territory in Florida; over the next few years the tribe is exterminated. Florida becomes a state in 1845.

1838 Boers defeat Zulus at the Battle of Blood River.

1838 First transatlantic steamboat crossings made between the United States and Britain.

1838 The Underground Railroad, helping southern slaves to escape to the North, continues operation despite northern opposition to the abolition movement.

1838 The Trail of Tears takes more than 14,000 members of the Cherokee Nation away from their land in the southeast and transports them west of the Red River at the Texas-Oklahoma border; over 4,000 die on the journey.

1838 Charles Dickens's *Oliver Twist* is serialized. Dickens's works, including *A Tale of Two Cities* and *Great Expectations*, are immensely popular in Victorian England and are noted for their vivid characterization and portrayal of social evils.

1838 English painter J. M. W. Turner's *The Fighting Temeraire* displays his unconventional style of depicting light and atmosphere. His later seascapes and landscapes tend toward abstraction, and his works introduce many elements of Impressionist painting.

1839 Opium Wars begin between China and England after Chinese officials burn illegal opium imported from India and stored by foreign merchants. The war illustrates Britain's concern with maintaining the profitable opium trade in China.

1839 Photography is invented by French painter Louis Daguerre.

1839 British war with Afghanistan, begun in 1838, continues; British forces restore the unpopular Shah Shuja to power; Afghan patriots protest British influence but are defeated the following year.

1839 Vulcanization of rubber is invented by Charles Goodyear, leading to increased commercial uses for rubber.

1839 Edgar Allen Poe's "Fall of the House Usher" published. Poe's works reflect a "darker" vision than much of the Transcendental writing of the time; Poe also helps to pioneer the genre of the detective story.

1840 New Zealand becomes a British Crown Colony as Maori chiefs cede authority to the British under the terms of the Treaty of Waitangi.

1840 Union Act unites Lower and Upper Canada.

1840 Pierre Joseph Proudhon challenges the notion of property in *What is Property?*; his work adds to the increasing body of socialist and radical literature in Europe reacting to expanding industrialism and capitalism.

1840 English physicist James Prescot Joule formulates the first law of thermodynamics, which states that energy can be converted from one form to another but cannot be destroyed.

1841 Convention of Alexandria confirms Muhammad Ali's right to hereditary rule of Egypt in exchange for giving up Crete and Syria amid pressure from Britain, Russia, Prussia, and Austria.

1841 Hong Kong comes under British sovereignty during the Opium Wars.

1841 Louis Kossuth becomes nationalist leader of Hungary.

1842 Treaty of Nanking ends the Opium Wars; Chinese ports are opened to Britain and westerners are granted special privileges, beginning a period of increased foreign influence in China.

1842 Britain surrenders to Afghani forces at Kabul and suffer heavy losses during their retreat to India; Dost Muhammad is restored to the throne.

1842 The Boers establish Orange Free State in South Africa.

1842 *Dead Souls* by Nikolai Gogol combines satire with elements of fantasy and the picaresque in its depiction of Russian provincial life.

1842 Positivism and the study of sociology are founded by French philosopher Auguste Comte in his *Course of Positive Philosophy*.

1842 The use of anesthesia is pioneered by American physician Crawford Williamson Long.

1843 The dictatorship of General Baldomero Espertero is overthrown in Spain and Isabella II ascends to the throne.

1843 Maoris rise up against the British in New Zealand beginning a five-year war.

1843 Danish philosopher Sören Kierkegaard publishes *Either/Or*. His writings establish existentialism and argue against rationalism, proposing that no system of thought can adequately explain the unique experience of the individual.

1843 India's Emirs of Sind refuse to relinquish their independence to the East India Company, provoking a war with Great Britain; they are defeated by British forces led by Charles Napier.

1843 Hawaii gains its independence from Britain.

1844 Utopian socialism becomes popular among French intellectuals and the working class, setting the stage for the revolutionary fervor of 1848.

1844 Telegraph developed by Samuel Morse transmits messages between Baltimore and Washington, D.C.

1844 Santo Domingo gains its independence from Haiti and establishes the Dominican Republic.

1845 Anglo-Sikh wars; Britain annexes Punjab.

1845 Polk Doctrine views U.S. acquisition of the Oregon Territory as its "Manifest Destiny." This belief in the unique greatness of the United States leads to increased American imperialism and expansion throughout the western hemisphere during the 19th century.

1845 Potato crop fails throughout Europe; Ireland is the hardest hit, leading to a massive wave of migration to the United States.

1846 United States declares war on Mexico over disputed territory on the Mexican-American border.

1846 First act of segregation established in South Africa after separate Zulu reserves are established in Natal.

1847 Liberia becomes first African colony to declare its independence.

1847 *Wuthering Heights* by Emily Brontë published; the novel employs varying narrators and time shifts in its depiction of two British families and the love affair of Heathcliff and Catherine. Her sister Charlotte Brontë writes the novel *Jane Eyre* the same year.

1847 Mormons establish independent republic in Utah with Brigham Young as president.

1848 *The Communist Manifesto* by Karl Marx and Friedrich Engels published; the pamphlet calls for the abolition of property and collective ownership of the means of production. Their critique of capitalism contributes to the revolutionary movements of 1848.

1848 Urban radicalism in Paris leads to Louis-Phillippe's abdication and the establishment of the Second Republic with Louis-Napoleon as president. Revolutions spread in Berlin, Budapest, Vienna, Rome, and much of Europe, but are quickly suppressed.

1848 Revolution in Austria leads to the resignation of Prince Metternich and to the abdication of Emperor Ferdinand I in favor of his nephew Franz Joseph.

1848 Treaty of Guadalupe Hidalgo ends Mexican-American War; the United States gains California and New Mexico as Mexico loses more than one-third of its territory.

1848 Gold rush in California leads to wave of westward migration the following year.

1848 The first Convention of Women's Rights is held in Seneca Falls, New York, under the leadership of Elizabeth Cady Stanton and Lucretia Coffin Mott.

1848 British novelist W. M. Thackeray completes *Vanity Fair* and is established as a major literary figure.

1848 The Pre-Raphaelite brotherhood of painters is founded in England, returning to the style of 15th-century Italian painting. Pre-Raphaelite artists include Dante Gabriel Rossetti, John Millais, and Holman Hunt.

1849 Rome proclaimed a republic under the leadership of Mazzini and Giuseppe Garibaldi. Later in the year, French troops return Pope Pius IX to power.

1849 John Ruskin's *Seven Lamps of Architecture* develops the modern study of architecture. His *Modern Painters* helps unorthodox painters such as Turner and the Pre-Raphaelites gain wider acceptance, and his other works reveal his concern with the moral implications of art and society.

1849 Hungarian struggle for independence crushed by Austrians with the help of Russian troops; Hungarian leader Louis Kossuth flees to Turkey.

1849 American writer and theorist Henry David Thoreau's "On the Duty of Civil Disobedience" is published; the essay advocates the individual's resistance to unjust laws through the means of passive resistance. Thoreau's other works, including *Walden*, explore the desire of the individual to break off from society.

1849 Harriet Tubman escapes from slavery and begins working for the Underground Railroad.

1850 German confederation restored under Austrian leadership by the Treaty of Olmutz.

1850 Taiping rebellion in China protests the Qing (Ch'ing) Dynasty; it is led by Xong Xiuquan (Hung Hsiu-ch'uan) who believes himself to be the younger brother of Jesus Christ. The rebellion lasts 14 years and results in some 20 or 30 million deaths.

1850 Nathaniel Hawthorne's *The Scarlet Letter* published; the novel depicts Hester Prynne's struggle to break free from the morality and hyprocrisy of Puritan society. This struggle of the individual is a central theme in the works of the "American Renaissance" during the mid-19th century.

1850 California admitted to the United States as a free state, renewing the controversial question of slavery in the territories. The issue is addressed by the Compromise of 1850, calling for the abolition of slavery in Washington, D.C., and establishing a tougher fugitive-slave act, but the Compromise only adds to the growing sectional hostilities over slavery and states' rights.

1850 Emperor Theodore consolidates independent Ethiopia.

1851 *Moby Dick*, by Herman Melville, completed; the novel's unusual form combines dramatic and symbolic elements with vast detail concerning whaling. It explores the "darker" side of individuals and the American experience.

1851 First world's fair opens at London's Crystal Palace, displaying the industrial achievements of the century. The radical glass design of the palace influences the construction of European railway stations.

1851 Siam's Rama III dies after 27-year reign that established contact with the West; he is succeded by his half-brother, who reigns as Rama IV and implements educational, economic, and governmental reforms during his 17-year rule.

1852 Louis-Napoleon establishes Second Empire and is named Emperor of the French.

1852 Sand River Convention establishes the South African Republic (Transvaal), which is recognized by Britain.

1852 Harriet Beecher Stowe's *Uncle Tom's Cabin* published. The novel's depiction of slavery sparks northern sympathy to the antislavery cause and becomes the most popular book in American history.

1852 The elevator is invented by American engineer Elisha Graves Otis.

1853 Scottish explorer David Livingstone begins crossing Africa. His discovery of Victoria Falls leads to an increased European exploration and colonization of the African continent.

1853 Russia and Turkey go to war after a dispute over the status of holy lands in Palestine; the conflict brings the French to the side of the Turks and leads to the Crimean War the following year.

1853 Giuseppe Verdi's *La Traviata* performed. Verdi's works, often celebrating the Italian nationalist movement, will bring opera to new heights of dramatic expression.

1854 Crimean War begins in Europe as the allied forces of England, France, and Turkey declare war on Russia. The war is sparked by French and English mistrust of Russian intentions in the Balkans.

1854 U.S. naval officer Matthew Perry forces Japan into a commercial treaty and ends Japan's isolation from the West.

1854 Kansas-Nebraska Act refuels slavery controversy in the United States; the bill invalidates the Missouri Compromise and establishes popular sovereignty in the territories, allowing each new state to vote whether to allow slavery. The act further galvanizes antislavery and antisouthern sentiment in the North, and leads to bloody confrontations between pro- and anti-slavery forces in Kansas the following year.

1854 Symbolic logic is founded by British mathematician George Boole in his *Laws of Thought*.

1854 Alfred Tennyson's "Charge of the Light Brigade" glorifies British heroism in the Crimean War. Tennyson epitomizes the Victorian age of poetry, which contains a strong element of morality while maintaining Romantic themes.

1855 Settlement of Kansas territory breaks treaty that had reserved the land for Native Americans.

1855 Florence Nightingale establishes nursing as a profession during the Crimean War. Her nurses were able to reduce the war's hospital death rate from 42% to 2%.

1855 *Leaves of Grass* by Walt Whitman first published; the poem, using the unconventional form of free verse, celebrates a particularly American vision of individual freedom and kinship.

1855 First plastic material patented by British chemist Alexander Parkes.

1856 Treaty of Paris ends the Crimean War; independence of Turkey guaranteed by the French, British, and Austrians; Black Sea declared neutral and Serbia formally recognized.

1856 Steel produced cheaply with the invention of Henry Bessemer's converter. Bessemer's invention leads to a reduction in the price of steel and is pivotal to the development of industrialization.

1856 Arrow War (Second Opium War) begins between England, France, and China, after a British ship is seized by the Chinese. Two years later the Treaty of Tientsin forces the opening of Chinese ports to Britain, France, Russia, and the United States.

1857 Sepoys in Bengal army revolt against British rule in India but are brutally suppressed.

1857 Emancipation of Russian serfs begins under Tsar Alexander II.

1857 *Madame Bovary*, by Gustave Flaubert, published; the novel introduces many innovations in narrative and influences the development of the modernist novel.

1857 French poet Charles Baudelaire publishes *Les Fleurs du Mal (Flowers of Evil)*. Baudelaire's works help establish the Symbolist movement in poetry and emphasize the power of the human imagination, but also suggest a darker side.

1857 The Dred Scott decision by the United States Supreme Court rules that blacks are not citizens and that the Missouri Compromise of 1820, which banned slavery in the territories, is unconstitutional.

1858 *Gray's Anatomy* is published for the first time and becomes the standard for over 100 years.

1859 Charles Darwin's *On the Origin of Species by Means of Natural Selection* is published. Its revolutionary theory of human evolution and natural selection and its denial of the biblical understanding of creation is extremely controversial and has profound effects on both the scientific world and the society at large.

1859 American abolitionist John Brown leads a raid on the Harpers Ferry arsenal in Virginia hoping to incite a slave rebellion, but his attempt fails and he is executed; the action, though radical in comparison to mainstream northern opinion, reflects the growing sectional tension over the slavery issue.

1859 First oil well drilled in Titusville, Pennsylvania, and production of petroleum as a source of energy begins.

1859 In the war for independence, the Italian states of Parma, Modena, Tuscany, and Romagna defeat Austria and unite with Piedmont. Garibaldi and his Thousand Redshirts overthrow the Neapolitan monarchy in southern Italy.

1860 Abraham Lincoln is elected president of the United States, precipitating South Carolina's secession from the Union.

1860 George Eliot's *Mill on the Floss* published; it and her other works, *Silas Marner* and *Middlemarch*, explore contemporary social and moral issues.

1860 First internal-combustion engine invented by French engineer Étienne Lenoir.

1861 Italy, with the exception of Rome and Venice, formally unites under the rule of Victor Emmanuel of Piedmont.

1861 Southern states secede from the United States and form the Confederate States. The Confederacy fires on Fort Sumter, a federal military base in South Carolina, beginning the American Civil War, which lasts until 1865.

1861 Tsar Alexander II officially decrees the freedom of serfs in Russia.

1861 Open-hearth process for making steel is developed by William Siemens and Pierre Emile Martin, improving the production of steel.

1862 Zanzibar's independence recognized by Britain and France.

1862 Christina Rossetti publishes her first major collection of poetry, which includes "The Goblin Market." Rossetti's poetry differs from contemporary Victorian works in its emphasis on beauty of form and expression instead of ideas of morality.

1862 *Fathers and Sons*, by Ivan Turgenev, published; the novel introduces the term *nihilism* and underscores his support for westernizing Russia. Turgenev's works are noted for their pessimism and poetic realism.

1862 President Lincoln issues the Emancipation Proclamation, freeing all the slaves in the rebel states; the document signals a shift in northern war aims away from simply unionism to the complete abolition of slavery, something Lincoln had not previously publicly supported.

1862 First black unit composed of ex-slaves is formed in the Union army.

1862 Homestead Act provides western lands for settlers, encouraging westward migration and leading to an increase in European immigration to the United States.

1863 French troops occupy Mexico City and set up puppet government with Austria's Archduke Maximilian as head of state. French imperialism also spreads to Cambodia, which becomes a French protectorate.

1863 Edouard Manet's *Olympia* takes the classical subject of the female nude and places it in a contemporary setting. The painting is highly controversial for its unconventional portrayal of a female subject, signaling a shift away from the academic style of painting.

1863 The Confederate army suffers a serious defeat at Gettysburg, Pennsylvania. Lincoln delivers his famous Gettysburg Address, which proclaims the Union's cause and the principles of the U.S. Constitution.

1863 Draft riots break out in New York City protesting the Civil War; African Americans are terrorized by the rioters.

1863 Japanese Ukiyoe paintings become popular in London, influencing painters such as James Whistler, who introduces them in Paris, shaping the work of later artists such as Toulouse-Lautrec.

1864 Karl Marx founds the First International in London.

1864 Louis Pasteur develops process of pasteurization to kill bacteria.

1864 Ulysses S. Grant becomes Union commander; Georgia falls to Union troops as General William T.

Sherman terrorizes the state and sets fire to most of Atlanta.

1864 Tsar Alexander II reforms Russia's judicial and legislative institutions; trial by jury is enacted and local governments are formed in which all classes are equally represented.

1864 Kit Carson forces Navajo and Apache tribes onto reservations and hundreds die from disease and maltreatment. Cheyenne and Arapahoe are massacred at Sand Creek, Colorado.

1865 The Confederate army under General Robert E. Lee surrenders, ending the American Civil War. President Lincoln is assassinated by John Wilkes Booth.

1865 13th Amendment to the Constitution abolishes slavery in the United States.

1865 Natural laws of heredity formulated by Austrian botanist Gregor Johann Mendel.

1865 Lewis Carroll's *Alice's Adventures in Wonderland* published.

1865 German composer Johannes Brahms's formalism, as opposed to the passion and sensuality of Wagner, creates works that fuse the contemporary style of Romanticism with Classical ideals.

1866 Dynamite invented by Swedish chemist Alfred Nobel.

1866 Reconstruction begins in the southern United States; the 14th Amendment is passed establishing citizenship and equal protection under the law for African Americans; congressional elections bring Radical Republicans and blacks to office in the South.

1866 Prussian military victories strengthen control over northern Germany and weaken Austrian power.

1866 *Crime and Punishment*, by Fedor Dostoyevski, published; Dostoyevski's writings dramatize life in tsarist Russia and greatly influence Russian and Western literature. Other works include *The House of the Dead*, *Notes from the Underground*, and *The Brothers Karamazov*.

1867 Dominion of Canada unites Ontario, Quebec, New Brunswick, and Nova Scotia as a federation.

1867 Austro-Hungarian dual monarchy established with Austrian emperor Franz Josef as ruler.

1867 Mexican troops overthrow and execute Emperor Maximilian, ending the hopes of Napoloeon III for a French empire in Latin American.

1867 Otto von Bismarck organizes Northern German Confederation under Prussian rule.

1867 Volume one of Karl Marx's *Das Kapital* published.

1867 Reconstruction Act divides the American South into five districts under military rule; white southern reaction against Reconstruction leads to the formation of racist groups such as the Ku Klux Klan.

1868 The Tokugawa shogunate is abolished and feudalism ends in Japan; it is replaced by the Meiji Dynasty led by Emperor Mutsuhito. Japan begins period of industrialization.

1868 Uprising in Spain forces Queen Isabella II to abdicate. The new government led by Francisco Serrano y Domínguez annuls reactionary laws, eliminates the Jesuit and other religous orders, and establishes universal suffrage and freedom of the press.

1868 Cuba begins 10-year war with Spain to gain its independence.

1868 Ethiopian emperor Theodore is defeated by British forces led by Robert Napier. After the withdrawl of British troops, the country undergoes anarchy until Johannes IV takes power in 1872.

1868 Somdeth Phra Paraminda Maha Chullalongkorn ascends to the Siamese throne after the death of his father, Rama IV. He will reign until 1910, implementing reforms such as the abolition of slavery and the feudal system and the introduction of the telegraph.

1869 Suez Canal opens, linking the Mediterranean with the Gulf of Suez at the head of the Red Sea; the canal substantially minimizes traveling distances.

1869 Leo Tolstoy completes *War and Peace*, a novel combining realism with philosophical issues.

1869 The first form of the periodic table of the elements is devised by Russian chemist Dmitri Mendeleyev.

1869 First transcontinental railway is built in United States.

1870 Prussian forces defeat France at the battle of Sedan, sparking a popular revolt in Paris and leading to the collapse of the Second Empire.

1870 Kingdom of Italy annexes the papal states and Rome becomes Italian capital.

1870 The first Vatican council declares the infallibility of the Pope.

1870 French poet Paul Verlaine publishes *La Bonne Chanson*. Verlaine is part of the Parnassian movement, which breaks away from the emotionalism of Romanticism and replaces it with a detached and disciplined style of poetry.

1870 John D. Rockefeller founds Standard Oil; the rapid and tremendous success of the company reflects the monopolistic tendencies and excesses of big business during the Gilded Age of the late 19th century.

1870 15th amendment to the U.S. Constitution ratified, ensuring African Americans the right to vote. In subsequent years southern states implement "Jim Crow" laws making it virtually impossible for blacks to vote and enforcing the caste system of racial segregation.

1871 United German empire declared under the leadership of King William I of Prussia marks the unification of Germany and the beginning of the Second Reich.

1871 The Peace of Frankfurt ends the war between Prussia and France; France cedes Alsace to Germany and is forced to pay a heavy indemnity.

1871 Revolutionary Paris commune established in opposition to the government after the surrender to Prussia; the commune is suppressed by the army after ruling Paris for two months, resulting in 20,000 to 30,000 deaths.

1872 First railway is built in Japan.

1873 French poet Arthur Rimbaud publishes *Season in Hell*; his symbolist poetry emphasizes the subjective, visionary imagination of the poet.

1873 Herbert Spencer publishes *The Study of Sociology*, in which he applies Darwinian theories to sociology. His popular work advocates a laissez-faire policy for government, theorizing that "survival of the fittest" will lead to the progress of society.

1874 Works by Claude Monet, Pierre Auguste Renoir, Edgar Degas, Paul Cézanne, and Camille Pissaro are exhibted in Paris, signaling the advent of Impressionism. Their paintings attempt to capture fleeting moments of light and color and employ quick and distinct brushstrokes.

1874 Thomas Hardy completes his novel *Far from the Madding Crowd*. Hardy's novels, which also include *Tess of the D'Urbervilles* and *Jude the Obscure*, portray human relations in a doomed and indifferent world.

1874 Russian composer Modest Mussorgsky's *Pictures at an Exhibition* is performed. His works and those of Nikolai Rimsky-Korsakov combine traditional Russian music with elements of conventional composition.

1875 Gerard Manley Hopkins writes the sonnet "The Windhover"; his influential poems break from the Victorian style with their original use of language and rhythm.

1875 The Civil Rights Act, passed by the U.S. Congress, grants equal rights for African Americans. In reality, however, the condition of African Americans in the South barely improves as northern support for Reconstruction begins to wane; the advent of the system of share cropping ensures the economic subjugation of African Americans to white landlords.

1875 British prime minister Benjamin Disraeli obtains a share of control in the Suez canal, ensuring European control.

1876 In the Battle of Little Big Horn the Sioux, led by Chief Sitting Bull, defeat U.S. forces led by General George Custer; it is the last major Native American military victory.

1876 Japan recognizes Korea's independence from China in a treaty that allows Japanese access to Korean ports. The Chinese do not protest the treaty, signaling increased Japanese power in the region.

1876 Alexander Graham Bell invents the telephone, beginning a new era in communication.

1876 Thomas Edison invents the phonograph.

1876 The president of Mexico is overthrown by General Porfirio Díaz, who brings stability to the country, promotes public works, develops industry, and attracts foreign capital.

1876 Richard Wagner's *Ring of the Nibelungs* performed. Wagner's works change the concept of opera, envisioning it as unifying drama, music, and painting; he develops such devices as the leitmotif, and his work anticipates many elements of 20th-century composition.

1877 Russia declares war on Turkey in attempt to gain further control over the Balkans and in support of rebellions against Turkish rule; uprisings in Bulgaria, Serbia, and Montenegro against the Turks are all brutally suppressed.

1877 The conservative Satsuma rebellion in Japan fails and the country continues its policy of reform and modernization.

1877 First performance of Russian composer Pyotr Tchaikovsky's *Swan Lake*. Tchaikovsky's works are characterized by their melodies and sentimentality. He is the first Russian composer to establish a reputation in western Europe.

1877 U.S. Government regulation of business given legal backing with the Supreme Court's ruling in *Munn v. Illinois*; the decision allows the government to implement reforms to protect workers and to curb monopolitistic tendencies in business.

1878 Treaty of San Stefano ends war between Russia and Turkey; the Congress of Berlin dismembers the Ottoman Empire as Montenegro, Serbia, Bulgaria, and Romania are granted formal independence; various other parts of the empire are divided among Russia, France, and Britain.

1878 Gilbert and Sullivan's *H.M.S. Pinafore* is performed; their operettas become immensely popular in England during this period.

1878 Jehovah's Witnesses founded under the leadership of Charles T. Russell; the group believes in the establishment of Christ's kingdom on earth.

1878 Famine in China kills 10 million.

1878 Knights of Labor becomes a national organization composed of both skilled and nonskilled workers and is the first sucessful national labor union in the United States.

1879 Britain declares war on the Zulus under the leadership of Cetewayo; the British triumph and firmly establish their control in Africa allowing for further colonization of the continent.

1879 Norwegian playwright Henrik Ibsen writes *A Doll's House*. His concern with social and contemporary issues influences the development European drama.

1879 Thomas Edison patents the incandescent lightbulb.

1879 African Americans begin mass migration to Kansas as Jim Crow laws increase in the South.

1879 The Church of Christ, Scientist, is chartered in Boston by Mary Baker Eddy, advocating prayer rather than medicine as a cure for illness.

1880 French sculptor Auguste Rodin completes *The Thinker*. Rodin's works break from the idealizing conventions of the time and employ a bolder, more expressionistic treatment of the human figure.

1880 France expands its colonial empire in Africa, establishing a French protectorate in Equatorial Africa. The following year it establishes a protectorate in Tunis.

1881 South African independence recognized after the Boers defeat the British at the Battle of Majuba Hill, but the republic remains under British suzerainty.

1881 Egyptian nationalists revolt against European rule; the following year the revolt is suppressed as Britain bombards Alexandria and occupies Cairo, leading to French withdrawal and full English control of Egypt.

1881 American author Henry James completes *Portrait of a Lady*; his concern with narrative, form, and portrayal of character influence the development of the modern novel.

1882 Germany, Austria, and Italy form the Triple Alliance, reflecting the desire of German leader Bismarck to build a strong power in Europe.

1882 Commercialization of electricity begins in London; in New York the Consolidated Edison Company forms and begins to light public houses and businesses.

1882 Irish resistance to British rule continues after a boycott against landowners. British officials are murdered in Dublin and Irish bomb public buildings in England; these acts are disavowed by Charles Parnell, one of the movement's leaders.

1882 Psychoanalysis has its beginnings as Viennese physician Josef Breuer uses hypnosis to treat hysteria.

1883 French forces begin conquest of Upper Niger region; Anman and Tonkin become French protectorates in Indochina.

1883 Antonio Gaudi begins building Church of the Sagrada Familia in Barcelona, a quasi-Gothic structure of enormous size.

1883 Brooklyn Bridge is built, designed by John Augustus Roebling.

1883 The Spoils System in American government is undermined by the Pendleton Civil Service Act, which calls for exams as part of the hiring process.

1884 The Treaty of Berlin divides Africa into spheres of influence among European nations; the partition of Africa is virtually complete by 1895. The treaty signifies the height of European imperialism.

1884 The machine gun is invented by American gunsmith Hiram Maxim.

1884 Steam turbine invented by British engineer Charles Parsons.

1884 Social reform continues in Germany under Bismarck; he extends accident insurance to workers in an effort to quell the growing socialist movement in Germany.

1884 Mark Twain's *Huckleberry Finn* published; the hero of Twain's satirical view of society's conventions travels along the Mississippi River and escapes from "civilization." The book is noted for its use of dialect and distinctive humor.

1884 The Zionist movement holds its first conference in Prussia as anti-Semitism grows in Europe.

1884 Anarchism is developed by Peter Kropotkin in *Words of a Rebel*. Kropotkin argues that cooperation and nonviolence lead to progress rather than conflict; his ideas shape later revolutionary movements in Russia.

1885 European imperialism continues as New Guinea is annexed by Germany and England, and Congo Free State comes under Belgian rule.

1885 Karl Benz invents the automobile; the gasoline engine is patented by Gottlieb Daimler, who uses it to power the first motorcycle; both inventions begin a new era in transportation.

1885 First skyscraper built in United States, pioneering the use of an iron frame.

1885 Khartoum falls to the forces of the Mahdi Muhammad Ahmed, who defeats the British and forces them to retreat from the Sudan.

1885 English critic Walter Pater completes *Marius the Epicurean*; Pater's works celebrate the aesthetic life and influence the modernist movement of the early 20th century.

1886 American labor movement grows; in the Haymarket massacre in Chicago, police fire on striking workers and kill four. Strikes break out throughout the country in support of better working conditions; American Federation of Labor (AF of L) founded by Samuel Gompers.

1886 The final exhibition of French Impressionists includes Georges Seurat's work *La Grande Jatte*. Seurat's painting employs the pointillist technique and initiates the Neo-Impressionist movement.

1886 Fredrich Nietzsche publishes *Beyond Good and Evil*, challenging conventional assumptions about knowledge and values. His work influences later philosophical movements with its emphasis on subjectivity and the denial of truth as a fixed value.

1886 Symbolist art begins to develop in Europe; these works appeal to the senses and imagination and create ideal worlds rejecting realistic or naturalistic treatment of subject matter. Artists include Paul Gaugin and Edvard Munch.

1887 Radio waves are produced by German physicist Heinrich Hertz.

1887 Interstate Commerce Commission, created to regulate railroad companies, becomes the first U.S. government regulatory agency.

1887 Sherlock Holmes makes his literary debut in Sir Arthur Conan Doyle's "A Study in Scarlet."

1888 Kodak develops a camera for mass consumption making it possible for the general public to take photographs.

1888 Chicago's Tacoma Building, with a steel skeleton and load-bearing metal throughout its structure, revolutionizes building techniques and ushers in the age of the modern skyscraper.

1888 Alternating-current electric motor constructed by Croatian engineer Nikola Tesla.

1889 Ethiopia becomes an Italian protectorate.

1889 Eiffel Tower built in Paris; the structure is a testament to French progress and exemplifies the advent of steel construction.

1889 Brazil becomes a republic.

1890 First elections held in Japan.

1890 The Sherman Anti-Trust Act gives Congress the right to curtail the abuses of monopolies; the act has little initial effect but in later years is used more effectively.

1890 United States cavalry defeats the last Native American resistance at Wounded Knee, South Dakota.

1890 Scottish anthropologist James Frazer compiles myths and customs from throughout history in the first volume of *Golden Bough*; the book becomes a landmark in anthropology and argues that belief systems evolved from a magical to a scientific basis.

1890 The poems of Emily Dickinson are published four years after her death.

1890 Oscar Wilde publishes *The Picture of Dorian Gray*; the novel epitomizes the Decadent Movement in English art. Wilde's work and attitudes break away from Victorian conventions and celebrate art for art's sake.

1890 The works of French painter Paul Cézanne represent an important link between the Impressionists and later Cubist and Abstract painters in their attempt to capture not only light but the structure of natural forms.

1891 Louis Sullivan's Wainwright Building is built in St. Louis. Sullivan influences later architects and helps to develop modern American architecture.

1891 First old-age pension goes into effect in Germany, providing a pension for retired workers over 70.

1892 Toulouse-Lautrec's posters for music halls become popular throughout Paris. Lautrec's works depict scenes of Parisian venues, an increasingly common subject for the Neo-Impressionists.

1892 Paul Gaugin begins his paintings of Tahitian subjects; his work develops the style of synthetism, incorporating strong flat colors in well-defined areas. Gaugin's work and life criticize modern society and help to shape the myth of the alienated artist.

1893 Art Nouveau gains prominence throughout Europe; mostly employed in the decorative arts, the new style reflects the belief that design and aesthetics have positive social and psychological effects. Artists include Beardsley, Horta, and Mucha.

1894 Alfred Dreyfus, a French officer of Jewish descent, is convicted of treason but is later proved innocent; the trial produces a wave of anti-Semitism in France.

1894 Sun Yat-sen begins to form revolutionary societies in China; his efforts help to bring about the decline of imperial rule in the early 20th century.

1894 Pullman strike led by Eugene V. Debs paralyzes American railroads. Coxey's army marches to Washington, D.C., demanding public works to provide employment. This period sees a rise in labor and populist activity in support of workers and small farmers.

1894 Republic of Hawaii is formed with Sanford Ballard Dole as president; three years later it agrees to be annexed by the United States under pressure from Hawaiian sugar planters.

1894 French composer Claude Debussy's *Afternoon of a Faun* is performed for the first time. His music epitomizes the Impressionist style in music.

1895 The X-ray is discovered by Bavarian physicist Wilhelm Conrad Roentgen.

1895 Cuban rebels revolt against Spanish rule; though the uprising is put down, the island undergoes a period of turmoil for the next three years.

1895 Treaty of Shimonoseki ends war between China and Japan; the war ends in a terrible defeat for the Chinese as they are forced to pay heavy reparations and cede land to the Japanese; the treaty also forces the Chinese to open more of their ports to the West.

1895 The first theatrical exhibition of motion pictures is presented in France. The movie is by the Lumière brothers, who invented the motion picture camera. Movies become the dominant form of popular entertainment in the following decades.

1895 Modernismo dominates South American literature as epitomized by the work of Rubén Darío.

1895 Ragtime, with its lively syncopation, becomes a popular musical style during this period. Led by pianist Scott Joplin, the music represents an African-American art form influencing mainstream American culture.

1896 Ethiopian troops defeat the Italians; the Treaty of Addis Ababa ends the Italian protectorate and Italy recognizes Ethiopia's independence.

1896 Anglo-Egyptian troops begin reconquest of Sudan.

1896 Radioactivity is discovered by French physicist Antoine Becquerel.

1896 The United States Supreme Court upholds Jim Crow segregation in public facilities, confirming the doctrine of separate but equal in *Plessy v. Ferguson*.

1896 The Olympic games of ancient Greece are revived by Baron de Coubertin. The event will be held every four years and grows to include over one hundred countries.

1897 The electron is discovered by British physicist J. J. Thomson.

1897 First Zionist Congress is held in Basel, Switzerland, as Theodor Herzl proclaims his hopes for a Jewish homeland.

1897 German forces occupy Qingdao (Tsingtao) as Chinese power begins to wane in the face of European exploitation; the following year Russia obtains lease of Port Arthur and Britain obtains lease of Kowloon. Western power over China strengthened by Open Door policy.

1897 Émile Durkheim pioneers French sociology with his work *Suicide*; Durkheim links positivist social ideas with issues of morality.

1897 American philosopher William James develops philosophical pragmatism in *Will to Believe*. His works also contribute to the growing study of psychology.

1897 Austrian Secession established to promote the Art Nouveau style in Austria. Led by Gustav Klimt, the movement incorporates many of the intellectual and artistic trends in fin-de-siècle Vienna, including many of Freud's theories.

1897 A large collection of art from Benin is brought to France; these works influence the artistic and formal concerns of modern artists, especially Pablo Picasso and the Cubists.

1898 Britain successfully reconquers Sudan at the Battle of Omdurman.

1898 United States defeats Spain in war over Cuba; Cuba gains its independence and the United States receives Puerto Rico, Guam, and the Philippines from Spain.

1898 Group of Spanish intellectuals led by philosopher and novelist Miguel de Unamuno form the Generation of '98 in an effort to revive Spanish culture.

1898 The theoretical basis for space travel is provided by the work of Russian scientist Konstantin Tsiolkovsky.

1899 War between Britain and the Boers begins in South Africa as Boer president Paul Kruger acts to block suspected British attempts to acquire the gold-rich Transvaal.

1899 The Ashanti of West Africa revolt against the British for the last time; their siege of the colonial governor's fortress ends in two months.

1899 American philosopher and reformer John Dewey publishes *The School and Society*. His writings, emphasizing a more progressive approach to learning rather than simple memorization and drilling, change the American educational system.

1899 American economist and social critic Thorstein Veblen publishes *The Theory of the Leisure Class*; Veblen's concept of conspicuous consumption argues that social attitudes and behavior are influenced and determined by the wealthy.

1900 Sigmund Freud publishes *The Interpretation of Dreams*, pioneering psychoanalysis and revolutionizing Western thought; he emphsizes the importance of the unconscious and sexuality in determining human behavior.

1900 The so-called Boxer Rebellion encouraged by the Empress Dowager leads to attacks on Westerners in China;

a six-nation force ends the rebellion, killing thousands of Chinese and increasing western presence in China.

1900 26,000 women and children are killed in British concentration camps set up during the Boer War.

1900 Max Planck develops his quantum theory of light; his work revolutionizes scientific though and influences the work of Einstein.

1900 Russian playwright Anton Chekov's *Uncle Vanya* is performed. Chekov's plays focus on the creation of mood and internal development rather than external action; his "naturalistic" plays dramatize the alienation and stagnancy of Russian provincial life.

1901 Guglielmo Marconi sends the first transatlantic radio signal; he later invents the radio.

1901 Oil drilling begins in Persia; in subsequent years, the Middle East becomes a focus of western interest because of its oil-rich fields.

1902 Treaty of Vereeniging ends the Boer war; the Transvaal and Orange Free State accept British sovereignty.

1902 V. I. Lenin publishes his pamphlet *What is to be Done?* The pamphlet outlines Lenin's concept of the revolutionary leadership of the proletariat and contributes to the growing revolutionary fervor in Russia.

1902 American photographer Alfred Stieglitz founds the Photo-Secession group in New York. Stieglitz's work and ideas help to establish photography as an art form.

1902 Five-month strike of American coal workers demanding a pay raise ends; the workers gain a wage increase but fail to win recognition for their union.

1903 United States acquires perpetual control over the Panama canal. The United States supports a separatist movement struggling to achieve Panamanian independence from Colombia thus ensuring the U.S. the opportunity to continue building and controlling the Panama Canal.

1903 American aviators Orville and Wilbur Wright make first successful flight of powered airplane.

1904 Japanese attack Russian fleet at Port Arthur, precipitating the Russo-Japanese War. The war is the first to use modern weapons such as the machine gun and the armored battleship.

1904 Giacomo Puccini's *Madame Butterfly* first performed, bringing to an end the age of the Italian grand opera.

1904 The Roosevelt Corollary to the Monroe Doctrine rationalizes United States intervention in South and Central American affairs.

1904 Max Weber's work *The Protestant Work Ethic and the Spirit of Capitalism* challenges the Marxist materialistic view of history. Weber emphasizes the role of ideas, rather than just economic factors, in shaping history.

1905 Japan defeats Russia in Russo-Japanese War; Russia is forced to recognize Japanese interests in Korea and cedes territory to the Japanese. The war establishes Japan as a major military power.

1905 The end of the Russo-Japanese War brings widespread discontent and uprisings in Russia. After troops fire on a peaceful protest, sailors stage a mutiny on the battleship *Potemkin* and Russian workers call a general strike. Tsar Nicholas yields to popular demands and creates a parliament.

1905 German artists form the Die Brücke organization, beginning the German Expressionist movement. Artists include Kirchner, Ernst Nolde, and Wassily Kandinsky.

1905 Albert Einstein's Theory of Relativity challenges Newtonian views of space and time. He postulates that light has a fixed velocity that can never be exceeded.

1905 Industrial Workers of the World (IWW) forms. Popularly known as the Wobblies, the IWW views itself as more radical than the AF of L and opens membership to all workers.

1905 Blues becomes an increasingly popular musical form in the United States during this period. Created primarily by African American muscians, the style is characterized by varying intonation, frequently melancholy lyrics, and a 12-bar construction.

1906 An earthquake strikes San Francisco causing massive damage and leading to an outbreak of fires throughout the city.

1906 Britain revolutionizes battleship design with the launching of HMS *Dreadnought*. In response, Germany begins upgrading its navy, starting a naval arms race.

1906 Algeciras Conference gives France and Spain control over Morocco.

1906 Modern Japanese fiction with an emphasis on naturalism begins during this period; writers include Shimazaki Toson and Tayama Katai.

1907 Anglo-Russian treaty defines their respective spheres of influence in Persia and Afghanistan. The treaty reflects a further distancing of Germany from the rest of the European powers.

1907 The helicopter, designed by Paul Cornu, has its first flight.

1907 French philosopher Henri Bergson's *Creative Evolution* stresses the importance of a creative life, influencing the modernist movement in literature.

1907 An exhibition of Cubist paintings marks a radical departure from the imitation of reality, as subjects are reduced to their geometric elements, beginning the movement towards abstraction in European painting. Cubist artists include Pablo Picasso and Georges Braque.

1907 Picasso's *Les Demoiselles d'Avignon* is exhibited in Paris; the painting becomes a landmark in modern art in its use of African styles and rejection of western artistic assumptions.

1908 Futurism, a movement primarily in Italy, attempts to integrate the sense of energy and speed of modern life into paintings through the use of shifting geometric planes and vibrant colors; artists include Severini, Boccioni, and Balla.

1908 Frank Lloyd Wright's Robie House exemplifies his prairie houses, in which he seeks to integrate buildings with their natural surroundings; Wright's organic style and rejection of Neo-Classicism spawn a new direction in architecture.

1908 Austria annexes Bosnia and Herzegovina, causing consternation and dissension in Europe.

1908 The Haber process for synthesizing ammonia enables the production of high explosives.

1908 New Orleans becomes the center of jazz during this period. A new style of music emerging from ragtime and popular African American music, jazz emphasizes instrumental and vocal improvisation and a syncopated polyphonic sound.

1909 Henry Ford begins assembly-line production of the Model T; this method of production lowers the price of automobiles, making them affordable to more consumers, and begins the age of the automobile in the United States.

1909 American explorer Robert Peary reaches the North Pole.

1909 The National Association for the Advancement of Colored People is formed to promote equal rights for African Americans and to end Jim Crow segregation. The new organization is headed by writer and political theorist W. E. B. Dubois.

1909 Dissension and internal strife in Turkey lead to the overthrow of Sultan Abdul Hamid of the Ottoman Empire by the Young Turks.

1909 William Carlos Williams publishes his first collection of poetry. Williams's poems employ spare images and language and influence the development of objectivist poetry.

1910 Kandinsky begins painting the first truly abstract works; his paintings, such as *Battles and Cossacks*, and his theoretical writings are a tremendous influence in the development of abstract art.

1910 Revolution in Portugal leads to the overthrow of the monarchy that has ruled since 1143; a republican government is formed and introduces a liberal constitution and anticlerical laws.

1910 Japan formally annexes Korea.

1910 South Africa becomes a dominion within the British Empire.

1911 Henri Matisse paints *The Red Studio*; his work concentrates on designs that emphasize curvaceous surface patterns, linear arabesques, and brilliant color. Matisse's varied career led him from Fauvism to his own invention of the paper cut-out technique.

1911 The Qing dynasty, which has ruled China since 1644, is overthrown by the Kuomintang led by Sun Yat-sen. The following year China becomes a republic and begins social and political reform.

1911 Mexico's president, Porfirio Díaz, is overthrown by revolutionary forces led by Francisco Madero, who becomes the new president; the following year peasants begin redistributing the land previously held by white landowners.

1911 Italy goes to war with Turkey; the Italians annex Tripoli and Cyrenaica as they defeat the Turks; Italy becomes the first to use aircraft in battle.

1911 Robert La Follette founds the National Progressive Republican League. The works of "muckrakers" like Upton Sinclair contribute to the spreading of the progressives' message; Sinclair's novels depict the squalid conditions of the working class.

1911 A nuclear model of the atom is presented by New Zealand-born British physicist Ernest Rutherford.

1912 The *Titanic*, the largest ocean liner ever built, sinks, leaving 2,200 dead.

1912 United States marines land in Honduras and later in Cuba and Nicaragua to protect American interests. The marines remain in Nicaragua until 1933.

1912 Georges Braque's *Fruit Dish and Glass* is the first use of the collage in painting; his technique introduces synthetic cubism, which further challenges traditional assumptions of representation, and it is later taken up by Juan Gris and Picasso.

1912 The imagist poets, including Ezra Pound, H. D., and Richard Aldington, begin their work. This influential movement, shaped by Classical Greek and Oriental poetry, emphasizes a direct representation of images, poetic impersonality, and clear hard diction.

1913 Treaty of London ends the war between Greece, Bulgaria, Serbia, and Turkey; a second war breaks out when Turkey, Romania, and Serbia react against Bulgarian attacks on Serbo-Greek positions; Bulgaria is defeated but the region remains unstable.

1913 Marcus Garvey founds the Universal Negro Improvement Association. Garvey's organization, promoting black pride, economic self-sufficiency, and a return to Africa, influences later black-nationalist movements and Rastafarianism.

1913 Marcel Duchamp exhibits his *Bicycle Wheel*; Duchamp's "ready-made" works undermine traditonal assumptions about the values and aims of art and influence the Dada movement.

1913 The Vorticist movement begins with the paintings of Wyndham Lewis, which are characterized by a harsh, angular semiabstract style. Lewis also writes several influential but controversial modernist novels including *Tarr* and *Apes of Gods*.

1913 The peformance of Igor Stravinsky's ballet *The Rite of Spring*, choreographed by Waslaw Nijinsky, causes a riot in Paris. Stravinsky's work emphasizes the use of rhythm in classical music and employs dissonance, ushering in a new era of music.

1913 Federal income tax established in the United States.

1913 The Armory Show displays European and American modernist works in New York and Chicago. Though very controversial, the exhibition brings some acceptance for Cubist and Post-Impressionist art in the United States.

1914 World War I begins in Europe. The assassination of Archduke Ferdinand of Austria by a Serbian nationalist leads to the Austrian invasion of Serbia; the invasion precipitates the involvement of most of Europe because of a complex web of alliances and pacts.

1914 Alliance of Germany, Austria, and the Ottoman Empire fight against France and England on the western front and Russia on the eastern; trench warfare characterizes much of the war, and there is extensive use of airplanes and chemical weapons.

1914 The Clayton Antitrust Act strengthens the Sherman Act; the bill culminates many of the progressive movement's efforts to limit the economic power of monopolies.

1914 United States forces occupy Vera Cruz, Mexico, after a series of disturbances and acts against American interests; Mexican president Huerta resigns and is replaced by Venustiano Carranza.

1915 Stalemate continues on the western front in Europe; Italy enters the war on the side of the Allies; German U-boat sinks the *Lusitania*, killing British and American civilians and leading to anti-German sentiment in the United States.

1915 The controversial *Birth of a Nation* by D. W. Griffith becomes one of the first major feature-length films. Griffith's works introduce many cinematic innovations including flashback, closeup, and cross-cut and help develop cinema as an art form. The film's subject matter, however, is quite controversial, as its heavily racist tone glorifies the rise of the Ku Klux Klan in the post-bellum South, resulting in the boycott of the film by the NAACP.

1915 Einstein expands upon his theories in his General Theory of Relativity, revolutionizing the science of physics.

1915 United States marines land in Santo Domingo, where they remain in control until 1924.

1915 Charlie Chaplin's "Tramp" character gains international popularity; Chaplin becomes one of the first major film stars and his silent comedies contribute to making motion pictures a dominant form of popular entertainment.

1915 Tractors, invented by Henry Ford, are introduced and greatly improve agricultural productivity and efficiency.

1915 Charles Ives becomes one of the first major American composers. Ives's highly experimental music incorporates polytonality and polyrhythms and uses quotations from popular and American folk music; his works include *Holidays Symphony* and *Concord Sonata*.

1916 Battle of Verdun leaves hundreds of thousands dead as the war continues with little advance for either side; tanks, invented by Ernest Dunlap, are first used in battle.

1916 Mexican revolutionary Pancho Villa leads raid against Colombus, New Mexico; U.S. forces led by General Pershing cross the border in an attempt to find Villa but are unsuccessful.

1916 First birth-control clinic in the United States is established by Margaret Sanger in New York City; Sanger is imprisoned for thirty days but later continues her efforts.

1916 Dadaist movement begins in Switzerland; the movement takes an irreverent attitude toward art and seeks to upset the complacency in society and the arts. Artists included Tristan Tzara and Hans Arp.

1916 Easter Rebellion in Ireland protests British rule; the revolt is supressed after a few days but fuels Irish nationalism.

1917 Arab revolt against the Ottoman Empire leads to the formation of an independent state under the leadership of the grand sherif of Mecca, Husein Ibn-Ali. Husein is politically advised by his son Faisal and British soldier-archeologist T. E. Lawrence ("Lawrence of Arabia").

1917 Losses in the war with Germany and workers' strikes lead to Tsar Nicholas II's abdication in Russia; Alexander Kerensky's provisional government, which takes power after the tsar's fall, is overthrown by the Bolsheviks in October.

1917 Lenin, escorted back to Russia by the Germans, arranges a cease-fire ending Russian involvement in the war. Lenin begins to centralize the government and collectivize land and industry and in subsequent years tightens Bolshevik control of Russia.

1917 British army officer T. E. Lawrence takes control of the Arab revolt against the Turks.

1917 British Foreign Secretary Alfred Balfour issues the Balfour Declaration declaring British support for a Jewish national homeland in Palestine.

1917 The United States declares war against Germany, joining the Allied cause.

1917 Piet Mondrian leads the De Stijl movement. The De Stijl artists emphasize geometric abstraction and a harmony of spatial relationships; the movement influences the development of Modernist architecture.

1918 Allied troops repel a major German offensive, launch a counter-offensive, and seriously weaken the German army; later in the year Germany sues for peace, ending the war.

1918 American President Woodrow Wilson introduces his fourteen-point plan for a peace settlement, including the formation of the League of Nations. Wilson's plan, never implemented, calls for "open covenants openly arrived at" and self-determination for European peoples.

1918 United States troops sent to occupy the Russian port of Vladivostok as western nations begin attempt to undermine the Bolsheviks.

1918 Women over thirty given the vote in England.

1918 Oswald Spengler's *The Decline of the West* claims western civilization has become overly concerned with materialism and is no longer "creative"; the book influences European thought.

1918 Poetry of the First World War dramatizes the effects and conditions of combat. Poets included Wilfred Owen, Siegfried Sasson, and Isaac Rosenberg.

1919 Treaty of Versailles sets the terms for peace; Germany is forced to pay heavy reparations, return Alsace-Lorraine to France, and limit its armed forces. The terms are seen as being too harsh on Germany, eventually contributing to the outbreak of the Second World War.

1919 League of Nations founded to settle international disputes; the United States does not join the league despite Wilson's urgings, and the organization is subsequently not truly effective.

1919 Hapsburg monarchy comes to an end with the Treaty of Saint-Germain; Austria recognizes the independence of Czechoslovakia, Poland, Yugoslavia, and Hungary.

1919 Mahatma Gandhi begins movement of passive resistance against British rule in India; British troops open fire on Indian protesters at Amritsar in the Punjab, killing 379.

1919 Uprising of German Communists in Berlin suppressed; socialist leader Rosa Luxembourg murdered; Weimar republic established in Germany.

1919 Prohibition introduced to the United States with the 18th amendment. Prohibition curtails drinking among the lower classes but ushers in an age of speakeasies and the growth of organized crime; the amendment is repealed in 1933.

1919 Civil war in Russia pits the Bolsheviks against the White army, which is supported by Allied troops.

1919 Race riots break out in American cities; the next several years see a growth in racial tensions as lynchings and Ku Klux Klan activities spread throughout the South with no retribution. President Wilson's administration is later seen by many to be extremely insensitive to African Americans.

1919 Oliver Wendell Holmes formulates the doctrine of "clear and present danger" to define the limits of free speech. During his stay on the court, Holmes has a tremendous role in ensuring the rights of individuals and creating a more active government.

1919 Bauhaus Movement founded by architect Walter Gropius in Germany; the movement, seeking to combine artistic design with technolgy, pioneers functionalism in design and influences architects and designers such as Le Courbusier.

1919 The first transatlantic flight completed by British aviators Alcock and Brown.

1920 *The Cabinet of Dr. Caligari* establishes German expressionism in film; other directors of the movement include Fritz Lang, who later directs *Metropolis*.

1920 Palestine established as a Jewish state under British rule.

1920 Soviet Russia in turmoil as civil war, peasant uprisings, and famines continue; Poland encroaches on Russian land; nationalist revolts in Lithuania, Latvia, and Estonia lead to Bolshevik recognition of their independence, undermining the young U.S.S.R.

1920 Women given the vote in the United States as the 19th amendment is ratified; the amendment culminates years of protest and struggle on the part of women activists.

1920 Composer Béla Bartók begins to create his style of dissonance and elegant melody; his use of Hungarian folk music combined with mathematical concepts of tone and rhythmic proportions create a unique style that influences 20th-century compostition.

1921 After years of violence and dissension, the Irish Free State is established in southern Ireland; northern Ireland remains part of Great Britain as the Catholic Irish Republican Army continues opposition throughout the century.

1921 Hermann Rorschach develops his ink-blot test for testing psychological states and probing the unconscious.

1921 Persia obtains independence from Russia after a coup expels all Russian officers; Riza Khan Pahlevi gains power.

1921 Ludwig Wittgenstein publishes his *Tractus Logico-Philosophicus*; Wittgenstein's works examine the function and use of language and challenge traditional assumptions about the aims and concerns of philosophy.

1921 Marcel Proust pioneers the technique of stream of consciousness in the novel *Remembrance of Things Past*. This technique influences writers such as James Joyce and Virginia Woolf.

1921 Ferdinand Leger's paintings, including *Three Women*, reflect contemporary artistic interest in technology and the machine.

1921 Rudolph Valentino's role in the film *The Sheik* makes him one of film's first major stars. His death in 1927 causes hysteria, and mobs attend his funeral.

1922 Defeats by the Rifs in Morocco lead to turmoil in Spain as the prime minister is assassinated.

1922 Lenin begins a New Economic Policy in Russia as a response to declining industrial and agricultural production; the plan ends grain levies in order to help the peasants and allow for a degree of free trade.

1922 Fascists march on Rome; King Victor Emmanuel invites Benito Mussolini to become prime minister.

1922 *Ulysses* by James Joyce is published in Paris; Joyce's highly influential Modernist novel depicts a single day in the lives of two Dubliners. The novel experiments with language and is unique in its combination of forms and narrative structures.

1922 Kingdom of Egypt is declared independent of French and English influence.

1922 *The Waste Land* by T. S. Eliot is published; Eliot's work pioneers a style of intricate metrics and clear, hard diction. His poetry and criticism help to make modernism and new criticism the dominant trends in literature.

1922 Washington Armament Conference leads to a pledge by the Allies and Japan to curtail the buildup of naval armaments.

1922 Stock market boom begins in United States bringing years of prosperity.

1923 French and Belgian troops occupy the Ruhr valley after Germany fails to meet reparation payments; inflation soars in Germany; National Socialist (Nazi) leader Adolf Hitler attempts to overthrow Bavarian government and is imprisoned.

1923 Earthquake in Tokyo destroys city and leaves more than 100,000 dead.

1923 German poet Rainer Maria Rilke completes the *Duino Elegies*.

1923 Le Courbusier formulates his conception of functionalism in architecture in his *Towards a New Architecture*. Le Courbusier's ideas assert the primacy of architecture in shaping industrial society and his designs revolutionize architecture and town planning.

1923 The Union of Soviet Socialist Republics is officially formed.

1923 Jordan becomes an autonomous state under the protectorate of the British.

1923 Turkey becomes a republic, ending centuries of Ottoman rule. General Mustafa Kemal becomes president and begins a program of reform, declaring Turkey a secular state.

1923 President Warren Harding dies as the Teapot Dome scandal begins to break.

1923 Wallace Stevens publishes *Harmonium*. Stevens's poetry combines sensual imagery and language with philosophical meditations.

1924 Lenin dies and Josef Stalin assumes power in the U.S.S.R. Stalin's leadership is challenged by his rival Leon Trotsky, who advocates the spread of revolutionary movements and communism throughout the world.

1924 Chinese government established under Sun Yat-sen; the new government includes members of the Communist party.

1924 The surrealist manifesto is published by André Breton. Surrealism attempts to express the unconscious and is influenced by Freudian theories; many of the works embody dreamlike images. Surrealist artists include Salvador Dali, Giorgio De Chirico, René Magritte, and Joan Miró.

1924 Arnold Schoenberg creates the twelve-tone, or serial, method of composition using all notes on the chromatic scale and denying a tonal center. His music challenges traditional musical forms and ideas and influences composers such as Berg and Weber.

1924 Marianne Moore publishes her first collection of poetry. Moore's writing is characterized by its careful observation of detail and its complexity; her works include "The Octopus."

1925 Chiang Kai-shek takes over the Kuomintang party in China after the death of Sun Yat-sen.

1925 Czech writer Franz Kafka's *The Trial* is published; Kafka's highly imaginative, nightmarish works depict the alienated individual trapped in an impersonal world.

1925 F. Scott Fitzgerald publishes *The Great Gatsby*; his most famous work depicts the jazz age of the 1920s. Fitzgerald explores and questions the myth of the American dream.

1925 Sergei Eisenstein's *The Battleship Potemkin* epitomizes the style of Soviet experimental cinema.

1925 John Scopes is prosecuted in Tennessee for teaching the theory of evolution; the trial attracts nationwide attention and reflects the growing tension in America between the rise of urban culture and traditional rural culture.

1925 *Mein Kampf* by Adolf Hitler is published; the work defines many of the ideas and philosophies of the Nazi party.

1925 A. Philip Randolph forms the Brotherhood of Sleeping Car Porters; the union is unique in that it is primarily composed of African Americans who were previously excluded from most unions.

1925 Ezra Pound publishes the first volume of the *Cantos*, which he works on for the rest of his life; Pound's *Cantos* become part of the Modernist canon and his earlier work helped to develop Imagism and introduce Asian forms into western poetry.

1925 The British novelists Ford Maddox Ford, Joseph Conrad, E. M. Forester, and D. H. Lawrence break away from Victorian morality, sensibilities, and style, and along with James Joyce and Virginia Woolf begin to experiment with form in their works.

1925 The Harlem Renaissance, a movement of African American writers using black life as subject matter, begins to flourish. Writers and thinkers associated with the movement include W. E. B Dubois, Langston Hughes, Zora Neale Hurston, and James Weldon Johnson, among others.

1925 The Lost Generation of writers begin to publish their work. Works include the experimental novels of Gertrude Stein and the minimal and direct novels of Ernest Hemingway.

1926 United States marines land in Nicaragua to protect U.S. interests threatened by a popular revolt.

1926 Martha Graham, a pioneer in modern dance who introduces a distinctive vocabulary of dance, debuts in New York City. Her works include *Appalachian Spring* and *Clytemnestra*.

1926 A television system developed by Scottish inventor John Logie is demonstrated.

1927 Stalin tightens his control over the Soviet Union with the expulsion of his two chief foes, Leon Trotsky and Grigori Zinoviev.

1927 Chiang Kai-shek strengthens his control of China as he purges Communists from the Kuomintang.

1927 Charles Lindbergh makes first solo transatlantic flight in his monoplane *The Spirit of St. Louis*. Lindbergh's flight makes him an international celebrity.

1927 German philosopher Martin Heidegger develops existentialist philosophy in his work *Being and Time* and argues that western philosophy has ignored the question of meaning in human existence.

1927 The sound motion picture gains popularity with *The Jazz Singer* starring Al Jolson.

1927 Duke Ellington begins an orchestral sound in jazz by introducing more formal compositions and arrangements. His works help to found big-band jazz.

1927 Louis Armstrong develops an innovative solo style with his trumpet improvisations; Armstrong later develops the singing style of scat.

1927 Virginia Woolf publishes *To the Lighthouse*. Woolf's experimental, interior novels employ the technique of stream of consciousness to explore the thoughts and emotions of characters; her other works include *Mrs. Dalloway* and *Jacob's Room*.

1928 Penicillin is discovered by Scottish scientist Alexander Fleming.

1928 Stalin initiates his five-year plan to develop heavy industry and collectivize farming; the plan leads to the suppression and liquidation of the kulaks (rich peasants). Stalin's regime is characterized by severe brutality and leads to the death of millions in an effort to rid the country of perceived enemies.

1928 Margaret Mead publishes her pioneering study in anthropology, *Coming of Age in Samoa*.

1928 Luis Buñuel and Salvador Dali direct *Un Chien Andalou*; it introduces surrealist techniques and images in film.

1928 The Kellogg-Briand Pact signed by 63 countries denounces war.

1928 Walt Disney introduces Mickey Mouse, who becomes the basis for the growth of the popular Walt Disney movies.

1928 Gandhi begins a new campaign of civil disobedience in India against British rule.

1928 W. B. Yeats publishes *The Tower*. Yeats's works vary from his romantic poems of the 1890s to the more modern works of the teens and 1920s; his poetry combines an imaginative, often mystic vision with directness and immediacy of language.

1929 U.S. stock market crash leads to worldwide depression and unemployment. The Great Depression lasts throughout the 1930s.

1929 William Faulkner publishes *The Sound and the Fury*; Faulkner's fiction employs experimental techniques such as stream of consciousness in depicting southern life.

1929 First major dispute between Jews and Arabs over the status of Palestine.

1930 Haile Selassi ascends to the throne in Ethiopia. He becomes a hero of many blacks throughout the world, especially Rastafarians, who view him as a savior.

1930 Ortega y Gasset publishes *The Revolt of the Masses*; the book critiques democracy and warns against the threat of majority suppression of minorities.

1930 The Chrysler Building designed by William Van Alan exemplifies the Art Deco style in American architecture.

1930 *The Bridge* by poet Hart Crane describes a mystical connection between humanity's present and past, using the Brooklyn Bridge as a symbol.

1930 Social unrest in Argentina and Brazil leads to the establishment of right-wing dictatorships.

1931 King Alfonso flees Spain and a republic is established dominated by liberals and socialists.

1931 Japanese occupy Manchuria and begin to assert their military dominance of the Far East.

1931 Austrian and German banks close, causing a financial crisis in central Europe, as the Depression continues.

1931 The case of the Scottsboro Boys, in which nine black youths are charged with rape, demonstrates the inequalities of the southern justice system. The case leads to a Supreme Court decision ruling that all defendants must have adequate legal representation.

1932 War between Bolivia and Paraguay begins over the Chaco region; the war lasts three years and causes 100,000 deaths.

1932 Elections in Germany lead to major gains for the Nazi party.

1932 17,000 World War I veterans march on Washington demanding their bonuses; the group is dispersed by troops led by Douglas MacArthur.

1933 Adolf Hitler is named chancellor of Germany by President Hindenburg; Hitler consolidates his power by eliminating opposition parties and begins to establish the first concentration camps for "political and racial enemies."

1933 The Neo-Classical movement, integrating classical forms with modern music, develops in the works of Igor Stravinsky, Paul Hindemith, and Sergei Prokofiev.

1933 Franklin Delano Roosevelt is inaugurated president of the United States and initiates New Deal Program to end the Depression. His plan calls for the creation of government agencies and programs to regulate and

stimulate the economy and provide relief and
employment.

1933 Antonio de Oliveira Salazar creates a new
constitution ensuring his dictatorship and control of
Portugal; lasting for 37 years, his rule is characterized by
repression and fascism.

1933 Prohibition is repealed in the United States.

1934 Hitler becomes führer of Germany; he eliminates
his opponents in the Nazi party (Night of the Long
Knives).

1934 Chinese Communists led by Mao Zedong begin the
Long March to escape Chiang Kai-shek's armies.

1934 Stalin begins a series of show trials and initiates
purge of the Communist party.

1935 Hitler passes the Nuremburg laws making Jews
second-class citizens of Germany. He begins the
rearmament of Germany, denouncing the Treaty of
Versailles.

1935 Italy invades Ethiopia as Mussolini tries to establish
an east African empire; sanctions imposed by the League
of Nations against Mussolini are ineffective.

1935 George Gershwin's opera *Porgy and Bess* integrates
jazz rhythms and popular song styles in an operatic
format. His other works, written in collaboration with his
brother Ira, include *Rhapsody in Blue* and such popular
songs as *I Got Rhythm* and *Embraceable You*.

1935 The Works Progress Administration is established to
create jobs through public works; Social Security Act is
passed providing unemployment and old-age insurance in
the United States.

1935 Radar is developed by the British.

1936 Civil war begins in Spain as General Francisco
Franco leads the army in a revolt against the republican
government; the war lasts three years, bringing Germany
and Italy to the side of Franco and the Soviet Union to the
aid of the republican forces.

1936 Italy and Germany form an alliance.

1936 German troops enter the Rhineland, violating the
Treaty of Versailles.

1936 British economist John Maynard Keynes writes *The
General Theory of Employment, Interest, and Money*.
Keynes advocates government intervention and spending
for economic growth; his theories provide the theoretical
framework for the New Deal.

1936 Italy takes Addis Ababa and annexes Ethiopia.

1936 The BBC becomes the first broadcasting service to
air television.

1937 Japan invades China, capturing Beijing (Peking),
Shanghai, and Tianjin (Tientsin) and killing over 200,000
citizens.

1937 German air force bombs Guernica, Spain, in
support of Franco and destroys the Basque stronghold.
Civil war spreads as an international brigade of English,
French, and Americans comes to the aid of republican
forces.

1937 Russian composer Dmitri Shostakovich's Fifth
Symphony first performed. Shostakovich creates a
dramatic, expressive, and often highly personal style; his
work is constantly scrutinized for its ideological content
during Stalin's regime and underlines the difficulty of
creative and artistic endeavor in the Soviet Union.

1938 The Anschluss unites Germany and Austria as Nazi
troops march into Austria.

1938 With Germany threatening Czechoslovakia, an
agreement between England, France, and Germany is
reached at Munich. The Sudentenland is returned to
Germany with a guarantee that Germany will not invade
Czechloslovakia. The pact is seen as appeasing the Nazis.

1938 Jean-Paul Sartre publishes his first novel, *Nausea*,
describing his existential struggle and repudiation of
bourgeois values. Sartre's works become central to
existential philosophy of the postwar period.

1938 Mexico nationalizes its oil fields, ending British and
American domination of the commodity.

1938 Mao Zedong applies Marxist-Leninist doctrine to
China during this period; he argues that both the
industrial proletariat and country peasantry can succeed
in creating a socialist revolution. His ideas influence later
Third World revolutions.

1938 Anton von Webern and Alban Berg develop serial
music, ultimately making all notes conform to a
mathematical pattern.

1939 Spanish Civil War ends with the victory of Franco
and the Fascists.

1939 Germany breaks Munich Pact and annexes
Czechoslovakia; Germans invade Poland; England and
France declare war on Germany.

1939 Germany and Russia sign secret nonaggression pact;
Russia invades Poland and partitions it with Germany.
Russo-Finnish War ends with the defeat of Finland.

1939 John Steinbeck publishes his novel *The Grapes of
Wrath*, depicting the struggle of a family of migrant
farmers during the Great Depression.

1939 Two American film classics, *Gone with the Wind*
and *The Wizard of Oz*, released. The movies cap off a
decade in which Hollywood's influence on popular
culture is at its peak.

1939 America begins to get out of the Depression as
economy is stimulated by European orders for weapons;
America declares its neutrality.

1939 Nuclear fission as an energy source is first
discovered.

1939 German playwright Bertolt Brecht writes *Mother
Courage*; Brecht's plays aim to destroy the suspension of
belief common in the theater and develop drama as a
social and political forum to express leftist ideals. His
ideas shape postwar European theater.

1940 Germany conquers France, Belgium, the
Netherlands, Luxembourg, Denmark, Norway, and
Romania; Italy declares war on England. Dunkirk is
evacuated as Germany overruns France; Battle of Britain;
British air force stops German bombing of Britain;
Winston Churchill becomes British prime minister.

1940 Leon Trotsky murdered in Mexico by Stalinist
agents.

1940 Soviet troops move into Estonia, Latvia, and
Lithuania, incorporating them into the U.S.S.R.

1940 Big Band swingtime jazz dominates popular music.
Bands like Benny Goodman's play arranged jazz music
with a highly charged sound.

1941 Germany invades Russia and begins long siege of
Leningrad; Russia begins counter-offensive in the Ukraine;
Germany conquers Greece; Italy and Germany invade
Egypt.

1941 Japanese bomb Pearl Harbor; United States declares
war on Japan and Germany.

1941 *Citizen Kane*, directed by Orson Welles, departs
from traditional filmmaking and introduces many
innovations in lighting and camera work.

1941 The first jet-powered airplane flies using an engine
invented by Frank Whittle.

1942 German army under Erwin Rommel suffers losses in
North Africa.

1942 Japan captures Manila, Singapore, Rangoon,
Mandalay, and the Philippines; the United States navy
stops a Japanese advance in the Pacific in the Battle of
Midway.

1942 *Casablanca*, starring Humphrey Bogart and Ingrid
Bergman, epitomizes classical Hollywood filmmaking.
The film reflects American anxiety about its involvement
in the war.

1942 The United States begins policy of internment; over
100,000 Japanese-Americans are forcibly placed into
camps on the West Coast.

1942 German V-2 rockets set the foundation for further
development of rockets in war.

1942 The first nuclear reactor built in Chicago, leading to
the development of the atomic bomb.

1943 German forces at Stalingrad surrender, a major
turning point in the war; German and Italian troops retreat
from North Africa; Italy surrenders. The Axis powers
further weakened by American victories in the Pacific.

1944 Allied armies continue to gain in Europe. Allies
enter Rome behind German lines; D-Day, June 6, Allied
troops led by General Dwight D. Eisenhower land in
Normandy and begin liberation of France and Belgium.

1944 First V-2 rockets hit England.

1944 Plot by German generals to kill Hitler fails.

1944 IBM creates first mechanical calculating machine.

1945 Allied bombing of Dresden decimates the city and
kills thousands of civilians; Russians enter Berlin in April
and Hitler kills himself in next few days; Germany
surrenders.

1945 Concentration camps are liberated. Nazi extermination policies have led to the death of 14 million, primarily Jews, Gypsies, and Slavs.

1945 Stalin, Churchill, and Roosevelt meet in Yalta to discuss postwar Europe; the leaders divide Europe into spheres of influence. Roosevelt is later accused of failing to recognize the Soviet threat in Eastern Europe.

1945 Americans drop the first atomic bomb on Hiroshima, Japan; three days later another bomb is dropped on Nagasaki; both cities are devastated and Japan surrenders, ending World War II. The bombs kill 200,000, and many die later from radiation.

1945 Roberto Rossellini's *Rome, Open City* introduces the Neo-Realist style in film. Neo-Realism is characterized by its naturalism, location filming, and interest in social themes; directors include Rossellini, Vittorio de Sica, and Visconti.

1945 Internal fighting resumes between nationalists and communists in China; a truce is reached the following year.

1945 United Nations is established as a forum to mediate international disputes.

1945 The works of Leonard Bernstein and Aaron Copland begin to shape both American classical and popular music. Copland's works include the ballet *Appalachian Spring* along with several film scores. Bernstein later writes the music for *West Side Story*.

1946 Former Nazi leaders are tried for war crimes at Nuremburg; ten are executed and many are sentenced to prison.

1946 Civil war begins in Indochina between Vietnam nationalists led by Ho Chi Minh and the French.

1946 Juan Perón elected president of Argentina. He organizes a government based on Spanish fascism.

1946 Churchill gives his "Iron Curtain" speech warning against the Soviet threat in Eastern Europe. Relationships between the Soviet Union and the West begin to deteriorate.

1946 Albania, Hungary, Jordan, and Bulgaria become independent states.

1947 The Marshall Plan, initiated by the United States, begins a massive effort to rebuild Western Europe. Similar efforts begin in Japan.

1947 India gains its independence from England; two states are created—India (Hindu) and Pakistan (Muslim).

1947 Truman Doctrine promises economic and military aid to countries fighting communism. The doctrine reflects the policy of containment as articulated by George Kennan.

1947 The Central Intelligence Agency is formed to counter Moscow's attempts to spread communism throughout Europe and the world.

1947 Jackie Robinson joins the Brooklyn Dodgers, becoming the first African American to break baseball's color line.

1947 After years of ascendancy the labor movement suffers a defeat with the passage of the Taft-Hartley Act; the bill restricts unions' power to strike, prohibits their right to contribute to political causes, and eliminates the closed shop.

1947 Albert Camus publishes *The Plague*. Camus's novels and the works of Jean-Paul Sartre and Simone de Beauvoir create a literary forum for existentialist philosophy; these intellectuals and their works dominate French intellectual life in the immediate postwar period.

1948 The Cold War intensifies as Communist coup takes over Czechoslovakia. The Soviet Union blockades Berlin, cutting the city off from West Germany; American airlift sends food and supplies to the city.

1948 Israel declared a Jewish state, precipitating an Arab invasion that is later repelled. Israel opens itself to Jews from all over the world. The existence of Israel continues to be a source of intense conflict between Arabs and Israelis.

1948 Gandhi is assassinated by a Hindu extremist.

1948 Korea is divided into two independent states—North Korea (communist) and South Korea.

1948 The first transistor is invented at Bell Laboratories by John Bardeen. It allows for the miniaturization of electronic devices such as radios, computers, and calculators.

1948 Norbert Wiener, MIT mathematician, publishes his study *Cybernetics*. Wiener explores the advent of communication and information-control by technology such as computers; his work is among the first to recognize the influence of computers on society.

1949 South African government establishes apartheid, the separation of blacks and whites, as official policy; the following year blacks riot in protest.

1949 NATO formed as a defensive alliance by western nations. The organization becomes the foundation for western military strategy amid tensions with the Soviet Union.

1949 The Communists led by Mao Zedong defeat nationalist forces. The Chinese People's Republic is established; Chiang Kai-shek and the Nationalists escape to Taiwan to form the Republic of China.

1949 Germany is divided into two states as the area under Soviet control proclaims itself the German Democratic Republic.

1949 The Soviet Union breaks the U.S. monopoly on the atomic bomb as they explode their first atomic device.

1949 Simone de Beauvoir publishes *The Second Sex*, which explores the role of women in society. Her study influences the feminist movement in the postwar era.

1949 France recognizes the independence of Vietnam and Cambodia but maintains a military presence.

1949 The Dutch grant independence to Indonesia after four years of hostility. Sukarno is elected president and remains in power until 1967.

1949 Abstract Expressionism develops in the United States led by artists such as Jackson Pollack, Willem de Kooning, and Mark Rothko.

1950 Korean War begins as North Korea invades South Korea. United Nations forces (mostly American), led by General Douglas MacArthur, come to the aid of South Korea and launch a counter-attack that is eventually repelled by the Chinese army.

1950 Senator Joseph McCarthy begins his 4-year investigation of suspected Communists in the United States. McCarthy's investigations often rely on scanty evidence and take advantage of American paranoia about communism; many lives and careers are ruined as a result of McCarthy's "witch hunt."

1950 Charlie Parker's saxophone playing introduces be-bop style to jazz, incorporating solo improvisation and complex rhythms; the style is a reaction against the popular big-band sound dominated by white band leaders. Other popular be-bop artists include Thelonious Monk and Dizzy Gillespie.

1950 Arab nations form an alliance and begin a blockade of Israel.

1951 Korean War reaches a stalemate; President Truman fires MacArthur for his public call for bombing China.

1951 Japanese film director Akira Kurosawa's work reaches the United States. The influx of foreign films creates a distinction between popular Hollywood films and the more serious "art" films.

1952 Mau Mau freedom fighters, led by Jomo Kenyatta, begin efforts to end British colonization in Kenya.

1952 Irish playwright Samuel Beckett's *Waiting for Godot* performed; the play establishes the Theater of the Absurd as a dominant style in avant-garde theater. The works often explore existential themes and the fate of humanity in modern society; playwrights include Jean Genet, Eugene Ionesco and Luigi Pirandello.

1952 Military coup in Egypt ends the reign of the monarchy and a republic is established the following year.

1952 Korean War continues; China accuses the United States of using germ warfare.

1952 Britain produces its first atomic bomb; the United States tests the hydrogen bomb for the first time.

1952 Frantz Fanon's *Black Skin, White Masks* examines the psychological and societal oppression of blacks. His advocacy of an independent and socialist Third World reflects the growing nationalistic sentiment in oppressed nations.

1952 John Cage's composition *4′ 3″*, which is completely silent, performed. Cage's work challenges traditional western assumptions about musical forms and composition; his compositions allow for randomness and give musicians greater freedom to improvise from the score.

1952 17 million American homes have television sets as the medium becomes the dominant form of entertainment in the country. Television forever changes American life and introduces new patterns of family and social life, popular entertainment, consumerism, and politics.

1953 Sir Edmund Hilary becomes the first to climb Mt. Everest.

1953 Josef Stalin dies and is replaced by G. M. Malenkov; Nikita Khrushchev later rises to power. Stalin's totalitarian rule has made the Soviet Union a world power but has also contributed to the failure of Communism to develop a more equal distribution of wealth and ownership.

1953 The Korean War ends with the signing of the Treaty of Panmunjom. The war ends with neither side achieving major gains and leaves two million Korean civilians dead.

1953 Communist leader Marshal Tito comes to power in Yugoslavia. Tito resists Soviet domination, and Yugoslavia enjoys a greater degree of economic and personal freedom than the rest of the eastern-bloc nations.

1953 The double-helix structure of DNA is discovered by Frances Crick and James Watson.

1953 Norodom Sihanouk takes over all Cambodian government buildings in an effort to win independence from France; the French grant Cambodia full sovereignty in economic, military, and judicial matters.

1953 Iranian leader Muhammad Mossadegh nationalizes the country's oil fields, disrupting British and American interests; the CIA engineers a coup to reinstate Muhammad Reza Pahlevi as shah and prevent a feared Soviet takeover.

1953 French novelist Alain Robbe Grillet publishes *The Erasers*; along with Nathalie Sarraute, he pioneers the "new novel," which disregards traditional forms of plot structure and characterization.

1953 Ralph Ellison's *Invisible Man* and James Baldwin's *Go Tell It on the Mountain* depict the conditions of African Americans in the United States. The novels help to establish an African-American literary voice, which continues.

1953 Fears of a Communist conspiracy persist in the United States as blacklisting of suspected party members continues. In a highly charged and controversial case, Julius and Ethel Rosenberg are executed for allegedly passing atomic secrets to the Soviet Union.

1954 Viet Minh defeat the French at Dien Bien Phu; the Geneva conference divides Vietnam into North Vietnam under the leadership of Ho Chi Minh and South Vietnam, which is supported by the United States and Great Britain. The convention calls for free elections to decide leadership for all of Vietnam, but the results are disregarded by the South and the United States after Communist leader Ho Chi Minh wins, and the country remains divided.

1954 General Abdel Nasser becomes prime minister of Egypt and leader of the Arab nationalist movement.

1954 General Alfredo Stroessner is elected president of Uruguay. He retains power until 1989, heading a repressive right-wing dictatorship that grants refuge to Nazi war criminals.

1954 American microbiologist Jonas Salk develops a vaccine for polio.

1954 The United States Supreme Court rules in *Brown v. Board of Education of Topeka* that segregation in public schools is unconstitutional, and overturns the doctrine of "separate but equal."

1954 Joseph McCarthy's televised hearings against suspected Communists in the army contribute to his growing unpopularity, leading to a Senate vote to formally censure him.

1954 The Oxford School of Language Philosophy, including J. L. Austin and Gilbert Ryle, influenced by Wittengenstein's later works, explore the uses and function of language. Ryle's work challenges traditional Cartesian philosophical paradigms.

1955 The Warsaw Pact unites the eastern bloc nations in a mutual defense treaty.

1955 Armed revolts and a general strike in Argentina force Juan Perón into exile after he suffers a loss of popularity as a result of his suppression of the newspaper *La Prensa* and the death of his popular wife, Eva. During his dictatorship, Perón has created South America's first

labor movement and nationalized the British-owned railroads.

1955 Rosa Parks's refusal to give up her seat on a bus to a white man spurs the Montgomery, Alabama, bus boycott; the Montgomery boycott vaults Atlanta minister Dr. Martin Luther King, Jr., into the leadership of the growing civil rights movement.

1955 Russian novelist Vladimir Nabokov publishes his most famous novel, *Lolita*. His other works include *Pale Fire* and *Laughter in the Dark*.

1955 Allen Ginsberg reads his poem "Howl"; the poem becomes central to the "Beat" movement, which challenges societal norms and literary conventions. Other "Beat" works include Jack Kerouac's *On the Road* and William Burroughs's *Junky*.

1955 American film *Rebel Without a Cause* released; the leading character, played by James Dean, popularizes the myth of the disaffected youth of prosperous white America. Dean along with Elvis Presley and Marlon Brando are viewed as challenging mainstream values and become idols to American and British youth.

1956 Soviet premier Nikita Khrushchev denounces Stalinist policies.

1956 Russian troops crush Hungarian revolt against the Communist regime; Hungarian leader Imre Nagy, who proposed free elections and the end of one-party rule, is ousted from office.

1956 Nasser nationalizes the Suez Canal, provoking attacks on Egypt by Israeli, French, and English troops seeking to restore international control. The attacks end under pressure from the U.N.; the canal comes under U.N. control.

1956 France recognizes independence of Tunisia and Morocco as the movement for African independence grows.

1956 Polish workers in Pozan protest social and economic conditions under Communism and Soviet domination; revolts spread to other parts of Poland, but the movement is crushed by Soviet troops.

1956 Liquidation of Chinese peasants resisting communization continues; by 1960 it is estimated that over 26 million have been killed.

1956 Elvis Presley's "Hound Dog" is released. Presley's works integrate country music with African American blues music and helps to shape the direction of rock 'n' roll; Presley's music and image continue to grow in popularity as does rock 'n' roll, which becomes the focal point of a burgeoning youth culture.

1956 Great Britain employs first large-scale use of nuclear energy to produce electricity.

1957 The Treaty of Rome, signed by Belgium, France, West Germany, Italy, Luxembourg, and the Netherlands, establishes the European Economic Community (EEC). The countries remove mutual tariffs in an effort to spur economic growth in Europe.

1957 The U.S.S.R. launches *Sputnik*, the first human-made satellite. The launching begins the space race between the United States and the Soviet Union.

1957 Federal troops are sent into Little Rock, Arkansas, to ensure the enforcement of *Brown* v. *Board of Education*. President Eisenhower orders the troops in after Governor Orval Faubus leads an effort to prevent integration of Arkansas schools.

1957 The Eisenhower Doctrine promises aid to any Middle Eastern country resisting communist aggression and authorizes the president to send troops if necessary. The doctrine reflects the growing importance of the region in Cold War politics; earlier in the year, Chinese and Russian leaders met announcing support of Middle Eastern nations against western aggression.

1957 Ghana, under the leadership of Kwame N. Nkrumah, becomes first sub-Saharan African country to declare its independence. Terrorist activitiy spreads in Algeria against French colonial rule.

1957 Berry Gordy establishes Motown corporation, which helps to popularize African American singers and groups. The Motown sound has a tremendous influence in the development of pop music and rhythm and blues.

1957 American linguist Noam Chomsky's *Syntactic Structures* explores the structure of language, arguing that grammatical speech is too complex to learn by example. His works have tremendous influence on both linguistics and philosophy. He later becomes a leading critic of American foreign policy and the media's role in support of government policies.

1958 Fidel Castro begins his guerrilla campaign in Cuba against the dictatorship of Fulgencio Batista.

1958 Mao begins a second five-year plan (the Great Leap Forward) in China to strengthen the economy by placing people in large communes; the communes promise food, clothing, shelter, child care, and collectivized agricultural and industrial production. The plan eventually ends in failure and economic chaos after the loss of Soviet aid in 1960.

1958 The United States begins its space program and creates NASA and launches its first satellite.

1958 President Eisenhower sends U.S. troops to Lebanon to quell riots instigated by Arab nationalists.

1958 Charles de Gaulle elected president of France and he begins policy of loosening French rule in Africa. Most colonies become autonomous states within the French community, but Guinea, under the leadership of Sekou Toure, rejects any connection with France.

1958 Pop Art begins in the United States with the work of Robert Rauschenberg. The movement integrates elements of popular and consumer culture into artistic works; Andy Warhol's *Soup Can* becomes one of the movement's most important works.

1958 French anthropologist Claude Levi-Strauss's *Structural Anthropology* develops structuralist thought, an attempt to reveal basic patterns and structures in various societies. Structuralism is later extended to the study of literature and the history of ideas by such thinkers as French philosopher Michel Foucault.

1959 Guerrilla troops, led by Fidel Castro, overthrow the dictatorship of Batista; Castro becomes Cuban premier and nationalizes United States-owned sugar mills. Later in the year, Castro visits the United States, proclaiming the Cuban revolution "humanistic" not Communist.

1959 Uprising begins in Tibet opposing Chinese rule; the rebellion is suppressed and Tibet's Dalai Lama escapes to India.

1959 President Sukarno dissolves Indonesia's assembly, calling for a "guided democracy." Sukarno's rule becomes progressively more authoritarian as the Communist party asserts greater power.

1959 American vice-president Richard Nixon and Soviet premier Khrushchev engage in famous "kitchen debate." Nixon extols the United States' economic progress and abundance of material goods, reflecting the rise of consumerism in American society.

1959 American engineers Jack Kilby and Robert N. Noyce invent the semiconductor, which eventually leads to the personal computer.

1959 Anti-European riots break out in the Belgian Congo as the country demands independence.

1959 The films of directors Jean-Luc Godard and François Truffaut begin the New Wave movement in French cinema; the films take a self-conscious approach to film and narrative.

1959 Miles Davis's album *Kind of Blue* epitomizes the style of cool jazz. Davis's trumpet playing helped develop be-bop, and he later pioneers fusion jazz.

1959 American author William Burroughs publishes *Naked Lunch*; Burroughs's work uses a variety of narrative techniques and employs hallucinatory images to describe heroin addiction and withdrawal. His controversial works and theories of conspiracy in society influence American literature and culture.

1959 American rock 'n' roll singer Buddy Holly, along with Richie Valens and the Big Bopper, dies in an airplane crash. Holly's innovative music will influence such rock 'n' roll performers as the Beatles.

1960 Seventeen African nations are granted independence from France and Belgium.

1960 Protests against the policy of apartheid leads to the death of 56 blacks in Sharpeville, South Africa.

1960 American U-2 reconnaissance flight is shot down over the Soviet Union. It is later revealed that the flight was on a spy mission, causing a worsening of Soviet-American relations.

1960 Organization of Petroleum Exporting Countries is formed; OPEC's control over a significant amount of the world's oil gives it enormous power.

1960 The Civil Rights Act is passed protecting the right to vote for African Americans; the measure is largely ineffective, however, and denial of the vote continues in the South. As the civil rights movement grows, the sit-in movement is intiated in Greensboro, North Carolina, in an effort to desegregate lunch counters.

1960 Cuba begins to establish ties with the Soviet Union, causing a strong reaction from the United States, which fears the spread of Communism in the Western Hemisphere; Castro nationalizes all banks and major industries.

1960 John F. Kennedy defeats Richard Nixon to become the first Catholic president of the U.S. The televised debates between the two candidates contribute to Kennedy's victory and exemplify television's power to influence elections and public opinion.

1960 Italian filmmaker Federico Fellini releases *La Dolce Vita*. The advent of directors such as Fellini and Ingmar Bergman reveal the growing emphasis placed on the director or "auteur" in films.

1960 The laser is developed in the United States.

1961 An invasion by U.S.-backed Cuban rebels fails to overthrow Fidel Castro. The so-called Bay of Pigs invasion leads to Cuba's continued reliance on the Soviet Union for aid and defense; the U.S. continues covert efforts to overthrow and assassinate Castro throughout the decade.

1961 Soviet and East German troops erect the Berlin Wall to stop the flow of East Germans to the West. The wall becomes a symbol of the Cold War and heightens the tensions between the superpowers.

1961 Chaos and violence continue in the Belgian Congo as ex-premier Patrice Lumumba is murdered; Lumumba, who was suspected of having communist leanings, is rumored to have been killed with assistance from the West.

1961 A military junta overthrows the democratic government in South Korea. General Chung Hee Park becomes dictator and heads a repressive government that continues after his death in 1979.

1961 Soviet cosmonaut Yuri Gagarin becomes the first person in space; President Kennedy announces Apollo project to land a person on the moon before the end of the decade.

1961 President Kennedy establishes the Alliance for Progress, a joint project between the U.S. and South America, to begin agrarian and tax reform in Latin America. The program has little success, and repressive dictatorships continue to dominate the region.

1961 Post-colonial literature explores the effects of European rule on African culture in the works of Chinua Achebe and the plays of Wole Soyinka.

1961 American musician Bob Dylan releases his debut album. Influenced by Woody Guthrie and other folk-singers, Dylan helps initiate a revival of folk music and writes songs responding to the growing protest movements in the United States; Dylan's career is characterized by several musical and stylistic changes and experimentation.

1962 Discovery of Russian missiles in Cuba leads to the Cuban missile crisis. The U.S.S.R. eventually agrees to U.S. demands for their removal; the conflict has brought the two nations to the brink of war.

1962 Algeria gains its independence from France after 8-year conflict.

1962 African National Congress leader Nelson Mandela begins his 29-year imprisonment in South Africa.

1962 United States military presence grows in Vietnam in support of South Vietnam against the Viet Cong.

1962 President Kennedy sends Federal troops to Mississippi to ensure African American student James Meredith's enrollment at the University of Mississippi.

1962 Marshall McLuhan's *Understanding Media* becomes a highly influential study of the impact of electronic media on society and human sensibilities.

1962 Michael Harrington's *The Other America: Poverty in the United States* describes the "underclass" of employed people who live below the poverty line in America and are ignored by society.

1962 Russian author Aleksandr Isayevich Solzhenitsyn describes life in a Soviet labor camp in his novel *One Day in the Life of Ivan Denisovitch*.

1962 The Beach Boys release "Surfin' Safari"; the Beach Boys' songs incorporate the myth of California as a place of sunshine, surfing, and pleasure. *Pet Sounds*, released in 1966, influences rock and pop music's growing emphasis on studio production.

1963 President Kennedy assassinated in Dallas; Lee Harvey Oswald is arrested and charged with the murder; Vice-president Lyndon Baines Johnson becomes president. Johnson will initiate major civil rights acts, increase government programs for the needy, and drastically escalate America's involvement in the Vietnam War during his tenure in office.

1963 Martin Luther King, Jr., leads a major civil rights march on Washington and gives his famous "I have a dream" speech. The march becomes a central event in the struggle for African American rights and freedoms.

1963 Betty Friedan's *The Feminine Mystique* argues that American middle-class women are suppressed by societal expectations and denied opportunities for personal growth and fulfillment; the work lays an important foundation for the modern feminist movement in the United States.

1963 A U.S.-backed military coup ousts Diem from office in South Vietnam, increasing U.S. involvement in the region.

1963 Britain grants independence to Kenya, and Jomo Kenyatta becomes president of the new republic.

1963 Great Britain, Russia, and the United States sign a nuclear-test-ban treaty; China explodes its first atomic weapon the following year.

1964 North Vietnamese attack U.S. navy in the Gulf of Tonkin; Congress authorizes the president to use American forces in Vietnam. It is later suspected that Americans provoked the attack as an excuse to enter the conflict.

1964 Congress passes the Civil Rights Act, guaranteeing equal treatment in public accommodation, education, voting, and employment. The newly-ratified 24th Amendment abolishes the poll tax.

1964 French thinker Roland Barthes's *Elements of Semiology* views language and literature as a system of linguistic and social signs; his influential work challenges traditional assumptions of literary criticism, dismissing notions of a fixed meaning or truth behind a work.

1964 Brazilian president João Goulart is overthrown by a military coup after he announces his plan of land redistribution. U.S. navy is dispatched to prevent a leftist takeover.

1964 The Free Speech Movement at the University of California's Berkeley campus signals the beginning of campus activism and protest that will continue throughout the decade.

1964 The Student Non-Violent Coordinating Committee, an organization of African American and white college students, launches a voter registration drive to help register blacks to vote in the Deep South in the face of violence and intimidation from white southerners. Three civil rights workers, Chaney, Goodman, and Schwerner, are murdered in Mississippi; northern Freedom Riders face increasing violence.

1964 Zanzibar, after banishing the sultan, declares itself a republic and joins with Tanganyika to form Tanzania.

1964 Herbert Marcuse's *One Dimensional Man* explores the repressive and totalitarian nature of modern democratic technological society. His work influences leftist thought in the United States and the antiwar movement.

1965 First American marines land in South Vietnam, and by the end of the year 125,000 U.S. troops are in the country; United States begins bombing raids of North Vietnam.

1965 India and Pakistan go to war over Kashmir.

1965 Rhodesia declares its independence from Britain but maintains white-only rule; England declares the move toward independence illegal and places economic sanctions on Rhodesia.

1965 Martin Luther King leads civil rights march in Selma, Alabama, that is attacked by state police; a second march from Selma to Montgomery, Alabama, is conducted. Shortly after the march the U.S. Congress passes the Voting Rights Act and federal marshals are sent to the South to help register and protect African American voters.

1965 Race riots break out in the predominantly black Watts district of Los Angeles; the riots result in the deaths of 35 people. Watts reflects an increasing racial tension in areas outside the South, and, together with the emerging black power movement, signals the growing frustration of African Americans, particularly in urban areas.

1965 Muslim and black Nationalist leader Malcolm X is shot in New York City. Malcolm X called for greater African American self-reliance and self-empowerment, challenging many of the integrationist notions of the civil rights movement.

1965 Indonesian army puts down an attempted communist takeover; the government's crackdown on communists leads to the deaths of 400,000.

1965 U.S. marines land in the Dominican Republic to prevent a suspected communist takeover and protect American citizens and interests.

1965 Timothy Leary's *The Psychedelic Reader* promotes the use of psychedelic drugs such as LSD and "dropping out" of society; many of Leary's ideas reflect the burgeoning counter-culture movement in the United States, which challenges mainstream American values and goals.

1965 The Rolling Stones release "(I Can't Get No) Satisfaction" and gain huge popularity as the song reaches #1 on the music charts; the Rolling Stones, who are influenced heavily by Blues music, write and perform songs reflecting a more rebellious and often more cynical sentiment than most musicians of the time.

1966 Mao Zedong initiates the Cultural Revolution in China. Mao attempts to weaken the party's bureaucracy and increase participation among the people; the effort to stimulate the party leads to further repression and millions of deaths.

1966 *Quotations from Chairman Mao* (the Red Book), a collection of Mao's ideas and thoughts, circulates throughout the world and influences revolutionary movements, especially in the Third World.

1966 The Black Panther Party is founded in Oakland, California, by Huey P. Newton and Bobby Seale. Advocating black power and community self-determination and armed self-defense, the party reflects a shift from the mainstream civil rights movement; the Black Panthers are active in sponsoring social programs for African-American communities across the country.

1966 American architect Robert Venturi publishes *Complexity and Contradiction in Architecture*. Venturi's writings and designs help to develop Post-Modern architecture; the movement breaks away from Modernist concerns with purity of form and integrates varying styles.

1967 Israel launches a preemptive attack against its Arab neighbors after months of hostilities with Syria. The war lasts only six days, and Israel's success leads to its occupation of the Golan Heights, the West Bank of the Jordan River, and Jerusalem.

1967 Civil war breaks out in Nigeria after the Ibo of the eastern region declare their independence in the nation of Biafra. The war lasts three years and results in widespread destruction, death, and famine.

1967 Che Guevara, Castro's chief adviser, who assisted revolutionary movements in the West, is killed in Bolivia.

1967 Thurgood Marshall becomes the first African American to sit on the U.S. Supreme Court. Marshall had successfully argued the case of *Brown v. Board of Education* as chief lawyer for the NAACP.

1967 American popular sentiment against involvement in Vietnam grows and a major protest is held at the Pentagon.

1967 Race riots break out in 127 cities across the U.S.; Federal troops are called into Detroit, Michigan, and Newark, New Jersey, to quell the riots. The following year a study headed by Illinois governor Otto Kerner asserts, "[America] is moving towards two societies, one black, one white, separate and unequal."

1967 The counter-culture movement spreads as thousands descend on San Francisco for the summer. The movement, consisting largely of young whites from middle-class families, tries to build a community based on tolerance and cooperation; the movement affects larger society by loosening social conventions, particularly regarding drug use and sexual norms.

1967 Gabriel García Márquez publishes *One Hundred Years of Solitude*, exemplifying the magical-realist style in literature.

1968 Martin Luther King is assassinated in Memphis; riots break out in American cities. Two months later Senator Robert F. Kennedy is killed during his presidential campaign. The assassinations reflect the growing turmoil and violence in American society.

1968 The student movement in Paris is joined by factory workers and intellectuals as demonstrations and riots convulse Paris; students take over universities and a general strike is called.

1968 Soviet troops enter Czechoslovakia to crush popular demonstrations and the growing reform movement of Czech leader Alexander Dubcek. The Soviets force Dubcek out of office and dismantle his reforms.

1968 North Vietnam launches the Tet Offensive, scoring major victories; the success of the offensive displays the military strength of the Viet Cong and further weakens American support for the war. Later in the year Johnson halts bombing of the North and announces he will not seek reelection.

1968 Demonstrations at the Democratic party convention in Chicago turn violent as police, acting under the orders of Mayor Richard Daley, force demonstrators to disperse.

1968 A police raid of the Stonewall Inn, a gay bar in New York, leads to rioting; the incident sparks the gay rights movement, protesting discrimination and violence against gays.

1969 American astronaut Neil Armstrong becomes the first person to walk on the moon.

1969 A concert near Woodstock, New York, attracts over 200,000 as the counter-culture reaches its apex. The movement begins to dissipate in the following years.

1969 Chicago police raid the local Black Panther office, killing two of the group's leaders; the raid exemplifies the intense harassment of the party by local and federal law enforcement agencies that has led to the arrest and murder of most of the party's top leadership. Under Richard Nixon's presidency the efforts to disrupt the party are stepped up, and the FBI's Counterintelligence Program (COINTELPRO) is extremely effective in fomenting internal dissension; by the end of the decade the Black Panther party is almost completely decimated.

1969 Revelation of a U.S. army massacre of Vietnamese civilians in My Lai leads to the trial of two officers.

1970 Despite campaign promises, President Nixon expands U.S. involvement in Vietnam by secretly invading Cambodia and renewing bombing of North Vietnam. A subsequent antiwar demonstration at Kent State University in Ohio results in four protesters' being killed by the national guard.

1970 Hostilities are renewed in the Middle East as Israel attacks Arab and Syrian guerrillas in the Golan Heights.

1970 Salvador Allende is elected President of Chile, becoming the first Marxist elected head of state in the West; Allende begins a program of nationalizing the economy and extends recognition to Cuba.

1970 French composer Pierre Boulez forms an institute for electronic music, reflecting the growth of technology in music. The works of Varese and Stockhausen (c. 1950) were among the first to make use of electronic music.

1971 Pakistani civil war ends with East Pakistan declaring its independence under the name of Bangladesh.

1971 Idi Amin heads a military coup in Uganda; Amin seizes control, abolishes parliament, and begins mass killings of his political enemies.

1971 The first computer microchip is produced in California's "Silicon Valley." The microchip initiates a new age of technology and information and increases the capabilities of computers.

1971 The U.S. Supreme Court upholds busing of children to integrate public schools; busing continues to be a divisive issue throughout the decade, often resulting in violence and revealing continued racial tensions in America.

1972 The Olympic games in Munich are disrupted after Palestinian terrorists take Israeli athletes hostage. The hostages and five terrorists are killed during a rescue attempt by German police.

1972 The Strategic Arms Limitation Treaty (SALT I) reflects Nixon's policy of détente with the Soviet Union.

1972 President Nixon normalizes relations with China.

1972 Congress passes the Equal Rights Amendment prohibiting discrimination on the basis of sex; despite numerous campaigns the measure is never amended to the constitution.

1972 Nixon renews large-scale bombing of major North Vietnamese cities as the Viet Cong continue to gain in the South.

1972 Britain declares direct rule over Northern Ireland after years of violence between Catholics and Protestants; following a civil rights march in Northern Ireland, rioting leads to the killing of 13 Roman Catholics by British troops.

1972 FBI director J. Edgar Hoover dies after heading the organization for the past four decades. Hoover's FBI reflected his conservative and anti-communist outlook, keeping files and spying on all suspected leftists and civil rights leaders including Martin Luther King; Hoover's files extended to personal details about presidents and ensured his power and influence over law enforcement.

1973 A ceasefire in Vietnam is reached as American troops end direct involvement in the war, but the United States continues bombing the North and maintains an advisory role in South Vietnam.

1973 Syria and Egypt launch a surprise attack on Israel; Israeli forces launch a counter-attack regaining their position and moving within 60 miles of Cairo. A U.N. cease-fire is reached after a few weeks of fighting.

1973 A military coup overthrows President Allende of Chile; General Pinochet is named the new president and begins a regime characterized by severe political repression. It is later revealed that the CIA supported the coup to protect the interests of ITT.

1973 The Watergate scandal grows as congressional hearings are held to investigate the Nixon administration's involvement in the 1972 burglary of Democratic party headquarters and subsequent cover-up; the Supreme Court forces Nixon to release taped conversations regarding the incident; impeachment proceedings begin.

1973 OPEC's oil embargo causes a worldwide energy crisis and economic recession; the embargo is a response to western European and American support of Israel.

1973 Native Americans occupy South Dakota hamlet of Wounded Knee to protest U.S. policies toward Native Americans.

1973 U.S. Supreme Court ruling in *Roe v. Wade* legalizes a woman's right to an abortion. Abortion remains a volitile and divisive issue.

1974 President Richard Nixon resigns from office rather than face impeachment proceedings concerning his role in the Watergate scandal; the new president, Gerald Ford, pardons Nixon for any possible criminal acts. Several members of the Nixon administration are tried and convicted.

1974 Turkey invades Cyprus, seizes half the island, and establishes a Turkish federated state.

1974 A coup in Portugal ends President Caetano's repressive right-wing dictatorship; two years later, Portugal holds its first free election in 50 years.

1974 Thomas Pynchon's *Gravity's Rainbow* further establishes him as one of America's premier novelists.

1975 The Vietnam War ends as Saigon falls and the South surrenders to Communist North Vietnam. A unified communist Vietnam is formed.

1975 Spanish dictator Franco dies, ending over 30 years of fascist rule. King Juan Carlos becomes head of state; two years later Spain will hold its first free elections since the Spanish Civil War.

1975 Portugal grants independence to Angola, Mozambique, and its other African colonies; civil war begins in Angola, lasting until 1988.

1975 Christian and Muslim forces begin fighting in Lebanon; the civil war ravages the country and destroys Beirut.

1975 The Khmer Rouge seize power in Cambodia; Pol Pot's Communist regime initiates a brutal campaign of terror against political opponents, killing a reported 3.5 million. Communists seize control in Laos. Political unrest in Southeast Asia over 15 years leaves hundreds of thousand of refugees.

1975 Minimalism in music develops in the works of composers Steve Reich, Terry Riley, and Philip Glass; the works employ alternating repetitive patterns and limited pitch, rhythm, and timbres.

1976 Major riots break out in Soweto, protesting South Africa's apartheid policies; an estimated 600 people die, almost all of them black.

1976 Chinese Communist leader Mao Zedong dies; China slowly begins to shift away from Maoist policies and liberalize the economy under the leadership of Deng Xiaoping.

1976 Led by groups such as the Sex Pistols and The Clash, punk music challenges the staid and commercial nature of contemporary rock and pop music. Punk stresses three-chord music performed in an aggressive style.

1976 The worst earthquake in modern history strikes China, killing 655,000.

1977 President Jimmy Carter signs treaty giving up U.S. control of the Panama Canal by the year 2000 and giving administrative powers to Panama.

1977 South African activist Steven Biko is beaten to death while in police custody.

1977 George Lucas's *Star Wars* is released and is called the most popular American film ever.

1977 President Carter calls for major actions to curb the energy crisis. The high price of fuel contributes to the weakening American economy of the late 1970s.

1978 John Paul II of Poland becomes the first non-Italian Pope in 450 years.

1978 Egypt and Israel normalize relations after meetings at Camp David organized by Jimmy Carter. Israel agrees to withdraw from the Sinai and promises to establish autonomous territory for the Palestinians; the agreements are the first between an Arab nation and Israel.

1978 Acting under the orders of cult leader Jim Jones, 900 people commit suicide in Guyana.

1979 The Sandinistas overthrow the repressive Somoza dictatorship that has ruled Nicaragua for 46 years; Sandinistas begin program of reform and nationalize business.

1979 Muslim fundamentalists overthrow the shah of Iran; an Islamic theocracy is established under the leadership of Ayatollah Ruholla Khomeini; Iranian students seize the United States embassy and hold Americans hostage, demanding the shah's return to face trial. Khomeini begins brutal repression of political enemies and supporters of the shah.

1979 Soviet troops enter Afghanistan in support of the Communist regime against rebel insurgents; U.S.-backed Afghan guerrillas resist Soviet troops for the next nine years.

1979 Expatriate Ugandan and Tanzanian forces invade Uganda, forcing Idi Amin to relinquish power and flee the country.

1979 Vietnam invades Kampuchea (Cambodia) and deposes Pol Pot.

1979 The Israeli army responds to Arab terrorist attacks by attacking Palestinian sanctuaries in Lebanon.

1979 Margaret Thatcher becomes the first female prime minister of Great Britain. Thatcher's Conservative government cuts social spending, reduces the welfare state, and limits the power of unions in England; Thatcher retains her post for the next 11 years.

1979 Blacks are granted the vote in Rhodesia, establish a majority in the Senate and Assembly, and rename the country Zimbabwe. The following year Marxist Robert Mugabe takes power.

1980 Polish labor union Solidarity, led by Lech Walesa, challenges the Communist government, demanding better social, political, and economic conditions.

1980 Border disputes lead to war between Iran and Iraq, which lasts for the next 8 years.

1980 Civil war spreads in El Salvador between leftist guerrillas and the right-wing dictatorship. The death squads of the Salvadoran government kill thousands of political enemies; Archbishop Oscar Romero, supporter of human rights, is killed by a sniper during mass services.

1980 The Soviet Union banishes Andrei Sakharov and increases efforts to suppress dissent.

1980 United States auto companies suffer the worst losses in their history. The decline in profits reflects the growing dominance of Japanese companies in the American market.

1981 First flight of the U.S. space shuttle begins new era of space exploration.

1981 Civil unrest spurred on by Solidarity's activities leads to a declaration of martial law in Poland.

1981 American hostages in Iran are released after 444 days of captivity on the same day Ronald Reagan is inaugurated president. The Reagan administration cuts social spending, increases the defense budget, and is characterized by strident anti-Communism and a conservative social agenda.

1981 President Reagan names Sandra Day O'Connor as the first woman on the Supreme Court.

1981 The AIDS virus begins to spread worldwide; Africans, homosexual men, intravenous-drug users, and American minorities are the hardest hit by the virus. The origins of the disease and a cure are still unknown.

1981 Italo Calvino publishes *If on a Winter's Night a Traveller*; his works and the novels and stories of Borges, Márquez, and Umberto Eco examine issues of narrative and literary theory.

1982 Argentina invades Britain's Falkland Islands, causing a war that takes Britain little over 2 months to reclaim the islands.

1982 Israel invades Lebanon in an effort to drive out Palestinian terrorists. U.S. marines enter the country as a peace-keeping force; the following year the marines' barracks are destroyed by terrorists, killing 63.

1983 U.S. marines invade Grenada, overthrowing the country's Cuban-backed regime.

1983 Soviet fighter planes down a Korean passenger jet that had flown into Soviet air space; the incident adds to growing tensions between the Soviet Union and the United States. Earlier in the year, President Reagan had called the Soviet Union a "focus of evil in the modern world" and an "evil empire."

1983 President Reagan escalates the arms race by proposing a Strategic Defense Initiative ("Star Wars"), which would place arms in space.

1983 European protests against United States deployment of nuclear missiles on the continent become more widespread.

1983 The wide use of junk bonds leads to increased corporate takeovers. The 1980s are characterized by risky speculation and furious activity on Wall Street.

1983 The use of crack cocaine spreads, especially in urban areas; the highly addictive drug leads to the further deterioration of inner cities and an increased crime rate.

1984 Indian troops kill 600–1,200 Sikhs after recapturing the Golden Temple in Amritsar. Violence spreads as Sikhs demand their independence; later in the year Sikh extremists assassinate Prime Minister Indira Gandhi.

1984 Toxic gas from Union Carbide leaks and kills 2,500 in Bhopal, India.

1984 Famine spreads in Ethiopia killing hundreds of thousands. The government prevents food and aid from being transported to areas occupied by rebel factions.

1985 Mikhail Gorbachev becomes Soviet leader and general secretary of the Communist party; Gorbachev initiates a policy of reforms to liberalize the economy and increase personal freedom in the Soviet Union. Relations between the Soviet Union and the United States slowly improve as Gorbachev meets with Reagan.

1985 Palestinian and fanatic Muslim terrorism spreads; terrorists seize the cruise ship *Achille Lauro* and open fire in airports in Vienna and Rome.

1985 Civilian rule returns to Brazil after 21 years of military rule.

1985 South Africa declares a state of emergency, giving the military almost complete control of black townships.

1986 A nuclear accident at the power plant in Chernobyl kills thousands in the Ukraine and spreads radioactive fallout across much of Europe.

1986 In response to terrorist attacks believed to have been supported by Libyan leader Muammar Qadaffi, the United States bombs Tripoli, Benghazi, and Libyan weapon centers.

1986 A popular revolt in the Philippines overthrows the repressive and corrupt regime of Ferdinand Marcos; Corazon Aquino is elected new leader.

1986 The Iran-Contra scandal shakes the Reagan administration when it is revealed that the administration had arranged with Iran to trade arms for hostages; funds from weapon sales were illegally diverted to support the Nicaraguan Contras.

1986 Jean-Claude Duvalier resigns as president of Haiti amid popular protest; his regime was characterized by corruption and brutal repression. Conditions in Haiti fail to improve after his departure.

1986 Black protests of apartheid continue in South Africa as workers call for a massive strike; U.S. imposes economic sanctions on South Africa.

1987 Gorbachev and Reagan meet in Washington and agree on major arms reductions. Gorbachev's economic and social policies of glasnost and perestroika slowly begin to influence Soviet society.

1987 Stock market suffers a major collapse. The crash is blamed on computerized trading, the U.S trade deficit, and the massive budget deficit.

1987 Congressional hearings on the Iran-Contra scandal reveal constitutional abuses, confusion, and intrigue within the upper echelons of the Reagan administration. The death of former CIA director William Casey leaves many questions surrounding Iran-Contra unanswered.

1987 Palestinians in the West Bank and Gaza Strip protest and riot in opposition to Israeli occupation. The uprising, or Intifada, continues; hundreds of Arabs are killed by the Israeli army.

1987 African American author Toni Morrison publishes *Beloved*. Morrison's novels depicting black southern life win both critical and popular success.

1988 Moscow begins to withdraw troops from Afghanistan. Soviet efforts are considered largely unsuccessful and have drained the economy.

1988 A ceasefire is reached between Iran and Iraq after the death of 105,000 Iraqis and 1 million Iranians; the war ends with neither side making significant gains. The war saw the use of chemical weapons by the Iraqis on Kurdish rebels.

1988 A truce is reached between South Africa, Cuba, and rival factions in Angola, ending years of hostilities in the country.

1989 Communist control begins to collapse in Eastern Europe; opposition candidates win elections in Poland and the Soviet Union; the Berlin Wall is torn down and East Germans begin to leave for the West.

1989 Hungary declares itself a democratic republic as the Communists relinquish control of the government; the "Velvet Revolution" ends Communist rule in Czechoslovakia as popular protests lead to its collapse.

1989 Vietnamese troops withdraw from Cambodia, but civil war continues as the Khmer Rouge and other factions struggle to gain power.

1989 Carlos Saul Menem is elected president of Argentina as the country has its first peaceful transition of power since 1927. Menem promises to reform the tax system and curb inflation.

1989 Augusto Pinochet's right-wing dictatorship in Chile ends as elections oust him from office and democracy returns to the country; Pinochet retains position as military chief of staff.

1989 Free elections are held in Brazil for the first time in 29 years. The elections reflect the move towards democracy and the decline of right-wing dictatorships in Latin America.

1989 American troops invade Panama in an attempt to capture Manuel Noriega, who has retained power despite being defeated in elections. The U.N. denounces the invasion as a "flagrant violation of international law"; Noriega eludes American troops but eventually surrenders and is sent to the U.S. to face trial on drug charges. It is later revealed that Noriega was an ally and informant for the United States and the CIA.

1989 Chinese students occupy Beijing's Tiananmen Square protesting government corruption and demanding greater democracy and political reform; Chinese leader Deng Xiaoping sends in troops to crush the movement, leaving hundreds dead.

1989 Nicolae Ceausescu is deposed as leader of Romania, ending one of the most brutal communist regimes.

1989 F. W. de Klerk becomes president of South Africa; he permits antiapartheid marches, releases political prisoners, and meets with imprisoned ANC leader Nelson Mandela. The moves signal de Klerk's intention to end the apartheid system.

1989 Soviet republics demand independence and greater autonomy; ethnic rivalries begin to flare in the Soviet states.

1990 Iraqi president Saddam Hussein invades and annexes Kuwait. The invasion is condemned by the U.N. and President George Bush sends U.S. troops to protect Saudi Arabia from an Iraqi attack.

1990 Lebanon's 15-year civil war ends as Christian forces surrender.

1990 The Communist party relinquishes sole power of the Soviet Union after 72 years; Gorbachev is granted wide powers as the Soviet economy worsens.

1990 Lithuania declares its independence from the Soviet Union; Gorbachev sends troops to Vilnius.

1990 East and West Germany reunite; U.S. and U.S.S.R. agree to troop and weapon reductions in Europe; the events signal the ending of the Cold War.

1990 Lech Walesa, Solidarity leader, elected president in Poland's first free elections since before World War II.

1990 Elections in Nicaragua end the Sandinista regime of Daniel Ortega as Violeta Chamorro becomes president. The Sandinista government and the Nicaraguan economy have been crippled by the civil war with the American-backed Contras.

1990 Nelson Mandela is released from prison and de Klerk grants amnesty to ANC exiles; talks begin regarding creating a new constitution giving blacks equal power in South Africa. Fighting breaks out between Zulu tribes and supporters of the ANC.

1990 Civil war ends in El Salvador as leftist guerrillas and the government negotiate a ceasefire.

1991 A coup against Mikhal Gorbachev, engineered by hardliners in the Soviet Union, ends under popular pressure led by Russian president Boris Yeltsin.

1991 Gorbachev suspends the Communist party; in the face of political and economic collapse, Gorbachev arranges for the dissolution of the Soviet Union as the Baltic republics gain independence and the other republics are granted greater autonomy.

1991 United States begins air attacks on Iraq and a subsequent ground invasion forces Iraq out of Kuwait, but allied troops are unable to capture Hussein. It is later revealed that the U.S. had previously supported Hussein and knew of his invasion plans.

1991 Iraqi missiles hit Israel; Israel does not retaliate lest they disrupt the allied coalition of western and Arab nations.

1991 President Aristide takes office in Haiti but is soon deposed by the military after trying to limit their power; the military regime begins to implement repressive measures as thousands attempt to flee.

1991 Slovenia and Croatia declare their independence from Yugoslavia. The declaration of a Croatian republic leads to increased Serbian nationalism as fighting breaks out between Serbs and Croats.

1992 Rioting breaks out in many areas of Los Angeles after a jury finds four white police officers innocent in the of beating Rodney King, an African American. Thousands are arrested as violence and looting convulse the city.

1992 Violence and warfare intensify in Bosnia; Serbs bomb Sarajevo in an effort to dismantle the government of the newly established Bosnia and Herzegovina; Serbs intiate a brutal program of "ethnic cleansing" against Bosnian Muslims and establish prison camps for Muslims. The United Nations sends peace-keeping troops as protests mount against Serbian actions.

1992 Major famine in Somalia deprives millions of food as warring factions prevent the distribution of the food; the United States sends peacekeeping troops.

1993 Carol Moseley-Braun is sworn into the U.S. Senate. She is the first female African American to serve in that body.

1993 United States President George Bush and Russian President Boris Yeltsin sign the START II treaty calling for the elimination of 3/4 of nuclear warheads by the year 2003.

1993 Arkansas governor Bill Clinton is inaugurated president of the United States. His defeat of George Bush in the election ends 12 years of Republican rule; a sluggish U.S. economy contributes to Bush's defeat.

1993 Cease-fire accord reached in Somali civil war. U.S. troops withdraw after helping to disarm warring factions and are replaced by a U.N. peacekeeping force; Pakistani soldiers are killed later in the year by Somali warlord General Muhammad Aidid as fighting and violence continues.

1993 Iraqi leader Saddam Hussein's refusal to allow U.N. officials to inspect Iraqi missile sites and violations of no-flight zones leads to allied bombings. The allied forces of the United States, France, and Britain attack missile sites in southern Iraq and a major industrial complex just outside of Baghdad.

1993 The failure of reform and problems caused by the conversion to a free-market economy in Russia intensifies the conflict between President Boris Yeltsin and the congress consisting of many former Communists. Yeltsin survives a vote in the congress to overthrow him and wins a popular referendum on his economic policies.

1993 Evidence of bribery, graft, and connections with the Mafia reveal widespread corruption in Italian politics and industry, prompting the resignation of several key politicians. A popular referendum calls for massive changes in the political system and represents a serious challenge to the ruling parties of Italy.

1993 Violence in India between Hindus and Muslims causes hundreds of deaths; Indian forces quash a riot of Muslim separatists in the Kashmir region; the growing sense of Hindu pride and nationalism threatens the delicate balance between the two religions in India

1993 Chris Hani, leader of the South African Communist party, is assassinated, causing riots among blacks.

1993 Violence and uncertainty continue to plague the countries of the former Soviet Union. Armenia and Azerbaijan battle over the Nagorno-Kaabakh region; Georgian leader Shevardnadze calls for citizens to donate arms to fight separatists in Abkhazia, whom he claims are supported by the Russians; fighting continues in Tajikistan as resurgent Communists try to suppress growing Islamic power.

1993 Fighting between the Khmer Rouge and the Cambodian army resumes as the U.N. cease-fire and plans for elections are jeopardized; the Khmer Rouge is responsible for the killing of ethnic Vietnamese.

1993 Attempts to end the fighting in Bosnia continue to fail as various peace plans are rejected by all sides; Serbs continue their attacks on Muslims in Bosnia and reports of systematic rape of Muslim women by Serbian troops are revealed. Violence continues in Croatia as Croat forces attack Serbian nationalists.

1993 A U.N. human rights organization reports the El Salvadoran death squads supported by the right-wing government were responsible for the death of thousands during the 1980s including Archbishop Oscar Romero. The Salvadoran government votes to grant amnesty to those responsible; it is also revealed that the U.S., which had supported the government in their fight against leftist guerillas, had extensive knowledge of the death squads' activities.

1993 Rebel forces led by Jonas Savambi break the cease-fire in Angola, renewing political strife in the area.

1993 Zairian president Mobutu retains power despite calls for him to step down by the prime minister and the West; the dispute leads to rioting and fighting between rival political factions, resulting in 1,000 deaths.

1993 Islamic fundamentalists plant a bomb in one of the buildings of New York City's World Trade Center, causing massive damage and scores of injuries. It is later revealed that fanatic Muslim terrorists had been planning more bomb attacks, targeting two major New York City tunnels, the Federal building that houses the FBI in New York, and the United Nations building.

1993 President Kim Young Sam becomes the first non-military president in South Korea since the Korean war. Kim's appointment represents an effort to limit the role of the military in government, which had been responsible for the repressive regime in past decades.

1993 President Clinton orders a bombing raid on Iraq's intelligence center in Baghdad in retribution for an alleged assassination plot against President Bush during his 1992 visit to Kuwait.

1993 Devastating floods ravage the Mississippi and Missouri River Valleys covering millions of acres of farmland and scores of towns and cities.

1993 Forty years of rule by the Liberal Democratic Party ends in Japan as Morihiro Hosokawa, leader of the New Party, forms a coalition government.

Biographical, Biblical, and Mythological Names

This section constitutes a pronouncing dictionary of the names of important figures from contemporary life, history, biblical tradition, legend, and myth. Names containing connectives like *d', de, di, van,* or *von* are alphabetized generally under the part of the name following the connective. When two sets of dates are given, the first set indicates the dates of the person's birth and death, and the second pertains only to the particular office, honor, or achievement that it immediately follows. If a person has a commonly encountered second name, a nickname, or an epithet, it is given in italics, usually immediately after the birth and death dates.

Aar·on \'ar-ən, 'er-\ brother of Moses; 1st high priest of the Hebrews

Abel \'ā-bəl\ son of Adam and Eve; killed by his brother Cain

Abra·ham \'ā-brə-,ham\ Old Testament patriarch; founder of the Hebrew people

Achil·les \ə-'kil-ēz\ Greek warrior in the Trojan War

Ad·am \'ad-əm\ the first man in biblical tradition

Ad·ams \'ad-əmz\ Ansel Easton 1902–84 American photographer

Adams John 1735–1826 2d president of the United States (1797–1801)

Adams John Quin·cy \'kwin-zē, -sē\ 1767–1848 6th president of the United States (1825–29); son of John Adams

Adams Samuel 1722–1803 American patriot

Ad·dams \'ad-əmz\ Jane 1860–1935 American social worker; Nobel prize winner (1931)

Ad·di·son \'ad-ə-sən\ Joseph 1672–1719 English essayist

Ado·nis \ə-'dän-əs, -'dō-nəs\ beautiful youth in Greek mythology who is loved by Aphrodite

Ae·ne·as \i-'nē-əs\ Trojan hero in classical mythology

Ae·o·lus \'ē-ə-ləs\ god of the winds in classical mythology

Aes·chy·lus \'es-kə-ləs, 'ēs-\ 525–456 B.C. Greek dramatist

Aes·cu·la·pi·us \'es-kyə-'lā-pē-əs\ — see ASCLEPIUS

Ae·sop \'ē-,säp, -səp\ Greek writer of fables; probably legendary

Ag·a·mem·non \,ag-ə-'mem-,nän, -nən\ legendary king of Mycenae; leader of the Greeks in the Trojan War

Aggeus — see HAGGAI

Ag·nes \'ag-nəs\ Saint *died* 304 A.D. Christian martyr

Ag·rip·pi·na \,ag-rə-'pī-nə, -'pē-\ *about* 14 B.C.–33 A.D. mother of Caligula

Ahab \'ā-,hab\ king of Israel in the 9th century B.C.; husband of Jezebel

Ajax \'ā-,jaks\ Greek hero in the Trojan War who kills himself because the armor of Achilles is awarded to Odysseus

Alad·din \ə-'lad-n\ youth in the *Arabian Nights' Entertainments* who comes into possession of a magic lamp and ring

Al·a·ric \'al-ə-rik\ *about* 370–410 A.D. king of the Visigoths

Al·ber·tus Mag·nus \al-'bərt-ə-'smag-nəs\ Saint *about* 1200–1280 *Albert* Count *von Boll·städt* \-'bȯl-,shtet\ German philosopher and theologian

Al·ci·bi·a·des \,al-sə-'bī-ə-,dēz\ *about* 450–404 B.C. Athenian general

Al·cott \'ȯl-kət\ Louisa May 1832–88 American author

Al·ex·an·der \,al-ig-'zan-der, ,el-\ name of 8 popes: especially **VI** (*Rodrigo Lanzol y Borja*) 1431–1503 (pope 1492–1503)

Alexander name of 3 emperors of Russia: **I** 1777–1825 (reigned 1801–25); **II** 1818–81 (reigned 1855–81); **III** 1845–94 (reigned 1881–94)

Alexander III of Macedon 356–323 B.C. *the Great* king (336–323)

Al·fred \'al-frəd, -fərd\ 849–899 *the Great* king of the West Saxons (871–899)

Al·len \'al-ən\ Ethan 1738–89 American Revolutionary soldier

Am·brose \'am-,brōz\ Saint 339–397 A.D. bishop of Milan and church father

Amerigo Vespucci — see VESPUCCI

\ə\	abut	\ng\	sing
\ər\	further	\ō\	bone
\a\	mat	\ȯ\	saw
\ā\	take	\ȯi\	coin
\ä\	cot, cart	\th\	thin
\au̇\	out	\th\	this
\ch\	chin	\ü\	food
\e\	pet	\u̇\	foot
\ē\	easy	\y\	yet
\g\	go	\yü\	few
\i\	tip	\yu̇\	cure
\ī\	life	\zh\	vision
\j\	job		

Am·herst \'am-ərst, -ˌərst\ Baron Jeffrey *or* Jeffery 1717–97 British general in America

Amon \'äm-ən\ ancient Egyptian god often worshiped as a supreme deity identified with the sun-god Ra

Amos \'ā-məs\ Hebrew prophet of the 8th century B.C.

Amund·sen \'äm-ən-sən\ Roald 1872–1928 Norwegian explorer

An·a·ni·as \ˌan-ə-'nī-əs\ early Christian struck dead for lying

An·chi·ses \an-'kī-sēz, ang-\ father of Aeneas

An·der·sen \'an-dər-sən\ Hans Christian 1805–75 Danish writer of fairy tales

An·der·son \'an-dər-sən\ Marian 1902– American contralto

An·drea del Sar·to \än-ˌdrä-ə-ˌdel-'särt-ō\ 1486–1530 Florentine painter

An·dro·cles \'an-drə-ˌklēz\ legendary Roman slave spared in the arena by a lion from whose foot he had years before taken a thorn

An·drom·a·che \an-'dräm-ə-kē\ wife of Hector

An·drom·e·da \an-'dräm-ə-də\ Ethiopian princess rescued from a monster by her future husband Perseus

Angelico Fra — see FIESOLE

Anne \'an\ 1665–1714 daughter of James II; queen of Great Britain (1702–14)

An·tho·ny \'an-thə-nē, *chiefly British* 'an-tə-nē\ Saint *about* 250–355 A.D. Egyptian monk

Anthony Mark — see ANTONIUS

Anthony Susan Brownell 1820–1906 American suffragist

Anthony of Padua Saint 1195–1231 Franciscan monk

An·tig·o·ne \an-'tig-ə-nē\ daughter of Oedipus and Jocasta

An·to·ni·nus \ˌan-tə-'nī-nəs\ Marcus Au·re·lius \ò-'rēl-yəs, -'rē-lē-əs\ 121–180 A.D. Roman emperor (161–180); philosopher

An·to·ni·us \an-'tō-nē-əs\ Marcus *about* 82–30 B.C. *Mark or Marc* An·to·ny *or* An·tho·ny \'an-thə-nē, *chiefly British* 'an-tə-nē\ Roman general

Aph·ro·di·te \ˌaf-rə-'dīt-ē\ Greek goddess of love and beauty whose Roman counterpart is Venus

Apol·lo \ə-'päl-ō\ *or* **Phoe·bus** \'fē-bəs\ god of sunlight, prophecy, music, and poetry in classical mythology

Apol·lyon \ə-'päl-yən, -'päl-ē-ən\ the angel of hell in the book of Revelation

Aqui·nas \ə-'kwī-nəs\ Saint Thomas 1224 (or 1225)–1274 Italian theologian

Arach·ne \ə-'rak-nē\ Lydian girl who is changed into a spider for challenging Athena to a contest in weaving

Ar·chi·me·des \ˌär-kə-'mēd-ēz\ *about* 287–212 B.C. Greek mathematician

Ares \'aər-ēz, 'eər-; 'ā-ˌrēz\ Greek god of war whose Roman counterpart is Mars

Ar·gus \'är-gəs\ hundred-eyed monster in Greek mythology

Ar·i·ad·ne \ˌar-ē-'ad-nē\ daughter of Minos who gives Theseus the thread whereby he escapes from the labyrinth

Ar·is·ti·des *or* **Ar·is·tei·des** \ˌar-ə-'stīd-ēz\ *about* 530–*about* 468 B.C. *the Just* Athenian statesman and general

Ar·is·toph·a·nes \ˌar-ə-'stäf-ə-ˌnēz\ *about* 450–*about* 388 B.C. Greek dramatist

Ar·is·tot·le \'ar-ə-ˌstät-l\ 384–322 B.C. Greek philosopher

Ari·us \ə-'rī-əs; 'ar-ē-əs, 'er-\ *about* 250–336 A.D. Greek theologian

Arm·strong \'ärm-ˌstrong\ Louis 1901–1971 *Satch·mo* \'sach-ˌmō\ American jazz musician

Armstrong Neil Alden 1930– American astronaut; first man on the moon (1969)

Ar·nold \'ärn-ld\ Benedict 1741–1801 American Revolutionary general and traitor

Arnold Matthew 1822–88 English poet, essayist, and critic

Ar·te·mis \'ärt-ə-məs\ *or* **Phoe·be** \'fē-bē\ Greek goddess of the moon, wild animals, and hunting whose Roman counterpart is Diana

Ar·thur \'är-thər\ legendary king of the Britons whose story is based on traditions of a 6th century military leader — **Ar·thu·ri·an** \är-'thur-ē-ən, -'thyur-\ *adj*

Arthur Chester Alan 1829–86 21st president of the United States (1881–85)

As·cle·pi·us \ə-'sklē-pē-əs\ Greek god of medicine whose Roman counterpart is Aesculapius

As·tar·te \ə-'stärt-ē\ Phoenician goddess of love and fertility

As·tor \'as-tər\ John Jacob 1763–1848 American (German-born) fur trader and capitalist

At·a·lan·ta \ˌat-l-'ant-ə\ beautiful fleet-footed heroine of Greek legend who challenges her suitors to a race and is defeated when she stops to pick up three golden apples dropped by one of the suitors

Ath·el·stan \'ath-əl-ˌstan\ *died* 939 Anglo-Saxon ruler

Athe·ne \ə-'thē-nē\ *or* **Athe·na** \-nə\ *or* **Pal·las** \'pal-əs\ Greek goddess of wisdom whose Roman counterpart is Minerva

At·las \'at-ləs\ Titan forced to bear the heavens on his shoulders

Atreus \'ā-ˌtrüs, -trē-əs\ legendary king of Mycenae; father of Agamemnon and Menelaus

At·ti·la \'at-l-ə, ə-'til-ə\ 406?–453 A.D. *the Scourge of God* king of the Huns

Au·du·bon \'od-ə-bən, -ˌbän\ John James 1785–1851 American (Haitian-born) artist and naturalist

Au·gus·tine \'o-gə-ˌstēn; o-'gəs-tən, ə-\ Saint 354–430 A.D. church father; bishop of Hippo (396–430)

Augustine Saint *died* 604 A.D. *Apostle of the English* 1st archbishop of Canterbury (601–604)

Au·gus·tus \o-'gəs-təs, ə-\ *or* **Augustus Caesar** *or* **Oc·ta·vi·an** \äk-'tā-vē-ən\ 63 B.C.–14 A.D. *Gaius Julius Caesar Octavianus* 1st Roman emperor 27 B.C.–14 A.D.

Au·ro·ra \ə-'rōr-ə, o-, -'ror-\ — see EOS

Aus·ten \'os-tən, 'äs-\ Jane 1775–1817 English author

Bac·chus \'bak-əs\ — see DIONYSUS

Bach \'bäk, 'bák\ Johann Sebastian 1685–1750 German composer and organist

Ba·con \'bā-kən\ Francis 1561–1626 1st Baron *Ver·u·lam* \'ver-ə-ləm, -yə-\ Viscount *Saint Al·bans* \sänt-'ol-bənz, sənt-\ English philosopher and author

Bacon Roger, Friar *about* 1220–92 English philosopher

Ba·den–Pow·ell \ˌbād-n-'pō-əl\ Robert Stephenson Smyth 1857–1941 English founder of Boy Scout movement

Bal·boa, de \bal-'bō-ə\ Vasco Núñez 1475–1519 Spanish explorer; discovered Pacific Ocean (1513)

Baltimore Lord — see George CALVERT

Bal·zac, de \'bol-ˌzak, 'bal-, *French* bál-zák\ Honoré 1799–1850 French author

Baptist — see JOHN *the Baptist*

Ba·rab·bas \bə-'rab-əs\ prisoner released in preference to Christ at the demand of the multitude

Barbarossa — see FREDERICK 1

Bar·num \'bär-nəm\ Phineas Taylor 1810–91 American showman

Bar·rie \'bar-ē\ Sir James Matthew 1860–1937 Scottish author

Bar·ry·more \'bar-i-ˌmōr, -ˌmor\ family of American actors: Maurice 1847–1905; his wife Georgiana Emma 1854–93; their children Lionel 1878–1954, Ethel 1879–1959, and John Blythe 1882–1942

Bar·thol·di \bär-'täl-dē, -'tol-, -'thäl-, -'thol-\ Frédéric Auguste 1834–1904 French sculptor; works include Statue of Liberty

Bar·tók \'bar-ˌtäk, -ˌtok\ Bé·la \'bā-lə\ 1881–1945 Hungarian composer

Bar·ton \'bärt-ᵊn\ Clara 1821–1912 founder of American Red Cross Society

Ba·sie \'bā-sē\ William 1904–84 *Count* American bandleader and composer

Ba·sil \'baz-əl, 'bās-, 'bas-, 'bāz-\ Saint *about* 329–379 A.D. *the Great* church father; bishop of Caesarea

Bau·de·laire \bōd-'laər, -'leər\ Charles Pierre 1821–67 French poet

Beau·re·gard \'bōr-ə-,gärd, 'bȯr-\ Pierre Gustave Toutant 1818–93 American Confederate general

Beck·et, à \ə-'bek-ət, ä-\ Saint Thomas *about* 1118–70 archbishop of Canterbury (1162–70)

Bede \'bēd\ Saint *about* 672–735 A.D. *the Venerable Bede* English historian and theologian

Beel·ze·bub \bē-'el-zi-,bəb, 'bēl-zi-, 'bel-\ prince of the demons identified with Satan in the New Testament

Bee·tho·ven, van \'bā-,tō-vən\ Ludwig 1770–1827 German composer

Bell \'bel\ Alexander Graham 1847–1922 American (Scottish-born) inventor of the telephone

Bel·ler·o·phon \bə-'ler-ə-fən, -,fän\ hero in Greek mythology who slays the monster Chimera with the help of his horse Pegasus

Bel·li·ni \bə-'lē-nē\ Vincenzo 1801–35 Italian composer

Bel·low \'bel-ō\ Saul 1915– American (Canadian-born) author; Nobel prize winner (1976)

Ben·e·dict \'ben-ə-dikt\ name of 15 popes: especially **XIV** (*Prospero Lambertini*) 1675–1758 (pope 1740–58); **XV** (*Giacomo della Chiesa*) 1854–1922 (pope 1914–22)

Benedict of Nur·sia \'nər-shə, -shē-ə\ Saint *about* 480–*about* 547 A.D. Italian founder of Benedictine order

Be·nét \bə-'nā\ Stephen Vincent 1898–1943 American author

Ben·ja·min \'benj-mən, -ə-mən\ Jacob's youngest son; ancestor of one of the 12 tribes of Israel

Ben·tham \'ben-thəm\ Jeremy 1748–1832 English jurist and philosopher

Ben·ton \'bent-ᵊn\ Thomas Hart 1889–1975 American painter

Be·o·wulf \'bā-ə-,wulf\ legendary Geatish warrior and hero of the Old English poem *Beowulf*

Be·ring \'biər-ing, 'beər-\ Vitus 1681–1741 Danish navigator; discovered Bering Strait and Bering Sea

Ber·lin \bər-'lin, ,bər-\ Irving 1888–1989 American (Russian-born) composer and songwriter

Ber·li·oz \'ber-lē-,ōz\ (Louis) Hector 1803–69 French composer

Ber·ni·ni \bər-'nē-nē\ Giovanni Lorenzo 1598–1680 Italian sculptor, architect, and painter

Bern·stein \'bərn-,stīn *also* -,stēn\ Leonard 1918–90 American conductor and composer

Bes·se·mer \'bes-ə-mər\ Sir Henry 1813–98 English engineer

Beyle Marie Henri — see STENDHAL

Bierce \'biərs\ Ambrose (Gwinnett) 1842–?1914 American author

Bis·marck, von \'biz-,märk\ Prince Otto Eduard Leopold 1815–98 1st chancellor of German Empire (1871–90)

Bi·zet \bē-'zā\ Alexandre César Léopold 1838–75 *Georges* French composer

Black Hawk \'blak-,hȯk\ 1767–1838 American Indian chief

Black·stone \'blak-,stōn, *chiefly British* -stən\ Sir William 1723–80 English jurist

Black·well \'blak-,wel, -wəl\ Elizabeth 1821–1910 American (English-born) physician

Blake \'blāk\ William 1757–1827 English poet and artist

Bloom·er \'blü-mər\ Amelia Jenks 1818–94 American social reformer

Boc·cac·cio \bō-'käch-ē-,ō, -'käch-ō\ Giovanni 1313–75 Italian author

Bohr \'bōr, 'bȯr\ Niels 1885–1962 Danish physicist

Bo·leyn \bu̇-'lin, 'bu̇l-ən\ Anne 1507?–36 2d wife of Henry VIII of England; mother of Elizabeth I

Bo·lí·var Si·món \sē-,mōn-bə-'lē-,vär, ,sī-mən-'bäl-ə-vər\ 1783–1830 South American liberator

Bo·na·parte \'bō-nə-,pärt\ *or Italian* **Buo·na·par·te** \,bwȯn-ə-'pärt-ē\ Corsican family: Jérôme 1784–1860 king of Westphalia; Joseph 1768–1844 king of Naples and Spain; Louis 1778–1846 king of Holland; Lucien 1775–1840 prince of Canino *all brothers of Napoleon I*

Bon·i·face \'bän-ə-fəs, -,fās\ Saint *about* 675–754 A.D. *Winfrid* or *Wynfrith* English missionary in Germany

Boniface name of 9 popes: especially **VIII** (*Benedetto Caetani*) *about* 1235 (or 1240)–1303 (pope 1294–1303)

Boone \'bün\ Daniel 1734–1820 American pioneer

Booth \'büth\ John Wilkes 1838–65 assassin of Abraham Lincoln

Booth \'büth, *chiefly British* 'bu̇th\ William 1829–1912 English founder of Salvation Army

Bo·re·as \'bōr-ē-əs, 'bȯr-\ Greek god of the north wind

Bor·gia \'bȯr-jä, -jə, -zhə\ Cesare 1475 (or 1476)–1507 Italian cardinal and military leader; son of Rodrigo Borgia

Borgia Lucrezia 1480–1519 duchess of Ferrara; daughter of Rodrigo Borgia

Borgia Rodrigo —— see Pope ALEXANDER VI

Bo·ro·din \,bȯr-ə-'dēn, ,bär-\ Aleksandr Porfirevich 1833–87 Russian composer

Bosch \'bäsh, 'bȯsh, *Dutch* 'bäs, 'bȯs\ Hieronymus *about* 1450–*about* 1516 Dutch painter

Bos·co \'bäs-kō, 'bȯs-\ Saint John 1815–88 Italian priest; founder of the Salesians

Bos·well \'bäz-,wel, -wəl\ James 1740–95 Scottish biographer of Samuel Johnson

Bot·ti·cel·li \,bät-ə-'chel-ē\ Sandro 1445–1510 Italian painter

Boyle \'bȯil\ Robert 1627–91 British physicist and chemist

Brad·bury \'brad-,ber-ē, -bə-rē, -brē\ Ray Douglas 1920– American author

Brad·dock \'brad-ək\ Edward 1695–1755 British general in America

Brad·ford \'brad-fərd\ William 1590–1657 Pilgrim father; 2d governor of Plymouth colony

Brad·street \'brad-,strēt\ Anne *about* 1612–72 American poet

Brah·ma \'bräm-ə\ creator god of the Hindu sacred triad — compare SIVA, VISHNU

Brahms \'brämz\ Johannes 1833–97 German composer

Braille \'brāl, 'brī\ Louis 1809–52 French blind teacher of the blind

Bran·deis \'bran-,dīs, -,dīz\ Louis Dembitz 1856–1941 American jurist

Brezh·nev \'brezh-,nef\ Leonid Ilyich 1906–82 Russian politician; 1st secretary of Communist party (1964–82); president of the U.S.S.R. (1960–64; 1977–82)

Bri·an Bo·ru \,brī-ən-bə-'rü\ 941–1014 king of Ireland (1002–14)

Brig·id \'brij-əd, 'brē-əd\ Saint *died about* 524–28 A.D. a patron saint of Ireland

Brit·ten \'brit-ᵊn\ (Edward) Benjamin 1913–76 English composer

Bron·të \'bränt-ē, 'brän-,tā\ family of English writers: Charlotte 1816–55 *and her sisters* Emily 1818–48 *and* Anne 1820–49

Brooks \'bru̇ks\ Gwendolyn Elizabeth 1917– American poet

Brown \'braun\ John *Old Brown of Osa·wat·o·mie* \,ō-sə-'wät-ə-mē\ 1800–59 American abolitionist

Brow·ning \'brau̇-ning\ Elizabeth Barrett 1806–61 English poet

Browning Robert 1812–89 English poet; husband of Elizabeth

\ə\ abut	\ng\ sing
\ər\ further	\ō\ bone
\a\ mat	\ȯ\ saw
\ā\ take	\ȯi\ coin
\ä\ cot, cart	\th\ thin
\au̇\ out	\t͟h\ this
\ch\ chin	\ü\ food
\e\ pet	\u̇\ foot
\ē\ easy	\y\ yet
\g\ go	\yü\ few
\i\ tip	\yu̇\ cure
\ī\ life	\zh\ vision
\j\ job	

Broz \'brōz, 'bròz\ *or* **Bro·zo·vitch** \'brō-zə-ˌvich, 'brò-\ Josip 1892–1980 *Ti·to* \'tēt-ō\ Yugoslav marshal; prime minister (1945–53); president (1953–80)

Bruce \'brüs\ Robert 1274–1329 liberator and king of Scotland (1306–29)

Bruck·ner \'brùk-nər\ Anton 1824–96 Austrian composer

Brue·ghel *or* **Breu·ghel** \'brü-gəl, 'bròi-\ Pieter *the Elder about* 1525 (or 1530)–69 Flemish painter

Brun·hild \'brün-ˌhilt\ legendary Germanic queen won by Siegfried for Gunther

Bru·tus \'brüt-əs\ Marcus Junius 85–42 B.C. Roman politician; one of Julius Caesar's assassins

Bry·an \'brī-ən\ William Jennings 1860–1925 American lawyer and politician

Bry·ant \'brī-ənt\ William Cul·len \'kəl-ən\ 1794–1878 American poet

Bu·chan·an \byü-'kan-ən, bə-\ James 1791–1868 15th president of the United States (1857–61)

Buck \'bək\ Pearl 1892–1973 American author; Nobel prize winner (1938)

Buddha — see GAUTAMA BUDDHA

Buffalo Bill — see William Frederick CODY

Bunche \'bench\ Ralph Johnson 1904–71 American diplomat

Bun·yan \'bən-yən\ John 1628–88 English preacher and author

Bur·bank \'bər-ˌbangk\ Luther 1849–1926 American horticulturist

Bur·ger \'bər-gər\ Warren Earl 1907–   Am. jurist; chief justice U.S. Supreme Court (1969–86)

Bur·goyne \'bər-ˌgòin, ˌbər-'\ John 1722–92 British general in America

Burke \'bərk\ Edmund 1729–97 British statesman and writer

Burns \'bərnz\ Robert 1759–96 Scottish poet

Burn·side \'bərn-ˌsīd\ Ambrose Everett 1824–81 American general

Burr \'bər\ Aaron 1756–1836 vice-president of the United States (1801–05)

Bur·roughs \'bər-ˌōz, 'bə-ˌrōz\ Edgar Rice 1875–1950 American author

Bush \'bùsh\ George Herbert Walker 1924–   41st president of the United States (1989–93)

But·ler \'bət-lər\ Samuel 1835–1902 English author

By·ron \'bī-rən\ 6th Baron 1788–1824 *George Gordon Byron* English poet

Cab·ot \'kab-ət\ John *about* 1450–*about* 1499 Italian navigator; explored coast of North America for England

Ca·bri·ni \kə-'brē-nē\ Saint Frances Xavier 1850–1917 *Mother Cabrini* 1st American (Italian-born) to be canonized (1946)

Cad·mus \'kad-məs\ founder of Thebes in Greek mythology

Caed·mon \'kad-mən\ *flourished* 658–680 A.D. English poet

Cae·sar \'sē-zər\ Gaius Julius 100–44 B.C. Roman general, statesman, and writer

Cain \'kān\ son of Adam and Eve; brother and murderer of Abel

Cal·houn \kal-'hün\ John Caldwell 1782–1850 vice-president of the United States (1825–32)

Ca·lig·u·la \kə-'lig-yə-lə\ 12–41 A.D. *Gaius Caesar* Roman emperor (37–41)

Cal·li·o·pe \kə-'lī-ə-pē\ Greek Muse of heroic poetry

Cal·vert \'kal-vərt\ George 1580?–1632 1st Baron *Baltimore* English proprietary in America

Cal·vin \'kal-vən\ John 1509–64 French theologian and reformer

Ca·lyp·so \kə-'lip-sō\ sea nymph who keeps Odysseus for seven years on an island

Ca·mus \kà-'mūē\ Albert 1913–60 French author

Ca·nute \kə-'nüt, -'nyüt\ *died* 1035 king of England (1016–35); of Denmark (1018–35); of Norway (1028–35)

Ča·pek \'chäp-ˌek\ Karel 1890–1938 Czech author

Capet Hugh — see HUGH CAPET

Car·lyle \kär-'līl, 'kär-ˌ\ Thomas 1795–1881 Scottish essayist and historian

Car·ne·gie \'kär-nə-gē, kär-'neg-ē\ Andrew 1835–1919 American (Scottish-born) industrialist and philanthropist

Carroll Lewis — see DODGSON

Car·son \'kärs-n\ Christopher 1809–68 *Kit* American frontiersman

Carson Rachel Louise 1907–1964 American biologist and environmentalist

Car·ter \'kärt-ər\ James Earl, Jr. 1924–   *Jimmy* 39th president of the United States (1977–81)

Car·tier \kär-'tyā, 'kärt-ē-ˌā\ Jacques 1491–1557 French navigator; discovered Saint Lawrence river

Ca·ru·so \kə-'rü-sō, -zō\ En·ri·co \en-'rē-kō\ 1873–1921 Italian tenor

Car·ver \'kär-vər\ George Washington 1864–1943 American botanist

Ca·sals \kə-'sälz, -'zälz\ Pablo 1876–1973 Spanish-born cellist, conductor, and composer

Ca·sa·no·va \ˌkaz-ə-'nō-və, ˌkas-\ Giacomo Girolamo 1725–98 Italian adventurer

Cas·san·dra \kə-'san-drə\ daughter of Priam endowed with the gift of prophecy but fated never to be believed

Cas·satt \kə-'sat\ Mary 1845–1926 American painter

Cas·tor \'kas-tər\ the mortal twin of Pollux in mythology

Cas·tro \'kas-trō, 'käs-\ Fi·del \fē-'del\ 1926–   Cuban premier (1959–   )

Cath·er \'kath-ər\ Willa Sibert 1873–1947 American author

Cath·er·ine \'kath-rən, -ə-rən\ name of 1st, 5th, and 6th wives of Henry VIII of England: Catherine of Aragon 1485–1536; Catherine Howard 1520?–42; Catherine Parr 1512–48

Catherine I 1684–1727 wife of Peter the Great; empress of Russia (1725–27)

Catherine II 1729–96 *the Great* empress of Russia (1762–96)

Cat·i·line \'kat-l-ˌīn\ *about* 108–62 B.C. Roman politician; conspired against Rome

Ca·to \'kāt-ō\ Marcus Porcius 234–149 B.C. *the Elder; the Censor* Roman statesman

Cato Marcus Porcius 95–46 B.C. *the Younger* Roman Stoic philosopher; great-grandson of the preceding

Ca·tul·lus \kə-'təl-əs\ Gaius Valerius *about* 84–*about* 54 B.C. Roman poet

Cax·ton \'kak-stən\ William *about* 1422–91 first English printer

Ce·ci·lia \sə-'sēl-yə, -'sil-\ Saint 2d or 3d century A.D. Roman martyr; patron saint of music

Cel·li·ni \chə-'lē-nē\ Benvenuto 1500–71 Italian goldsmith and sculptor

Cer·ber·us \'sər-bə-rəs, -brəs\ 3-headed dog in classical mythology who guards the entrance to Hades

Ce·res \'siər-ˌēz\ — see DEMETER

Cer·van·tes Saa·ve·dra, de \sər-'van-ˌtēz-ˌsä-ə-'vā-drə\ Miguel 1547–1616 Spanish author

Cé·zanne \sā-'zan\ Paul 1839–1906 French painter

Cha·gall \shə-'gäl, -'gal\ Marc 1887–1985 Russian painter in France

Cham·ber·lain \'chām-bər-lən\ (Arthur) Neville 1869–1940 British prime minister (1937–40)

Cham·plain, de \sham-'plān, shäⁿ-'plaⁿ\ Samuel *about* 1567–1635 French explorer in America; founder of Quebec

Chap·lin \'chap-lən\ Sir Charles Spencer 1889–1977 British film actor and producer

Char·le·magne \'shär-lə-ˌmān\ 742–814 A.D. *Charles the Great* or *Charles I* Frankish king (768–814); emperor of the West (800–814)

Charles \'chärlz\ name of 10 kings of France: especially **I** 823–877 A.D. (reigned 840–877) *the Bald;* Holy

Roman emperor as *Charles II* (875–877); **IV** 1294–1328 (reigned 1322–28) *the Fair;* **V** 1337–80 (reigned 1364–80) *the Wise;* **VI** 1368–1422 (reigned 1380–1422) *the Mad* or *the Beloved;* **VII** 1403–61 (reigned 1422–61) *the Victorious;* **IX** 1550–74 (reigned 1560–74); **X** 1757–1836 (reigned 1824–30)

Charles name of 2 kings of Great Britain: **I** 1600–49 (reigned 1625–49) *Charles Stuart;* **II** 1630–85 (reigned 1660–85) son of Charles I

Charles 1948– son of Elizabeth II; prince of Wales

Charles I 1887–1922 *Charles Francis Joseph* emperor of Austria and (as *Charles IV*) king of Hungary (1916–18)

Charles V 1500–58 Holy Roman emperor (1519–56); king of Spain as *Charles I* (1516–56)

Charles XII 1682–1718 king of Sweden (1697–1718)

Charles Edward Stuart 1720–88 *the Young Pretender; (Bonnie) Prince Charlie* British prince

Charles Mar·tel \mär-'tel\ *about* 688–741 A.D. grandfather of Charlemagne; Frankish ruler (715–741)

Char·on \'kar-ən, 'ker-\ boatman in Greek mythology who ferries the souls of the dead across the river Styx to Hades

Cha·teau·bri·and, de \sha-₁tō-brē-'äⁿ\ Vi·comte \vē-kōⁿt\ François René 1768–1848 French author

Chau·cer \'chȯ-sər\ Geoffrey *about* 1342–1400 English poet

Che·khov \'chek-₁ȯf, -ȯv\ Anton Pavlovich 1860–1904 Russian author

Cheops — see KHUFU

Ches·ter·field \'ches-tər-₁fēld\ 4th Earl of 1694–1773 English statesman and author

Ches·ter·ton \'ches-tərt-n\ Gilbert Keith 1874–1936 English author

Chiang Kai-shek \jē-'äng-'kī-'shek, 'chang-\ 1887–1975 Chinese general and statesman; president of China (1948–49; Taiwan, 1950–75)

Chi·ron \'kīr-ən, 'kī-₁rän\ wise centaur and tutor to many heroes in Greek mythology

Cho·pin \'shō-₁pan, -₁paⁿ\ Frédéric François 1810–49 Polish pianist and composer

Chou En-lai \'jō-'en-'lī\ 1898–1976 Chinese Communist politician; premier (1949–76)

Christ Jesus — see JESUS

Chris·tie \'kris-tē\ Agatha 1890–1976 English author

Chry·sos·tom \'kris-əs-təm, kris-'äs-təm\ Saint John *about* 347–407 A.D. church father; patriarch of Constantinople

Chur·chill \'chər-₁chil, 'chərch-₁hil\ Randolph Henry Spencer 1849–95 *Lord Randolph Churchill* British statesman

Churchill Sir Winston Leonard Spencer 1874–1965 British prime minister (1940–45; 1951–55); son of Lord Randolph Churchill

Cic·ero \'sis-ə-₁rō\ Marcus Tullius 106–43 B.C. Roman statesman, orator, and writer

Cid, El \'sid\ *about* 1043–99 *Rodrigo* (or *Ruy*) *Díaz de Bi·var* \bē-'vär\ Spanish soldier and hero

Cir·ce \'sər-sē\ enchantress in Greek mythology who turns her victims into swine

Clark \'klärk\ George Rogers 1752–1818 American soldier and frontiersman

Clark William 1770–1838 American explorer (with Meriwether Lewis)

Clay \'klā\ Henry 1777–1852 American statesman and orator

Cle·men·ceau \₁klem-ən-'sō, klā-mäⁿ-'sō\ Georges 1841–1929 French statesman

Clem·ens \'klem-ənz\ Samuel Langhorne 1835–1910 pseudonym *Mark Twain* \'twān\ American author

Clem·ent \'klem-ənt\ name of 14 popes

Cle·o·pa·tra \₁klē-ə-'pa-trə, -'pä-, -'pā-\ 69–30 B.C. queen of Egypt (51–49; 48–30)

Cleve·land \'klēv-lənd\ (Stephen) Grover 1837–1908 22d and 24th president of the United States (1885–89; 1893–97)

Clin·ton \'klint-n\ William Jefferson 1946– 42d president of the United States (1993–)

Clio \'klī-ō, 'klē-\ Greek Muse of history

Clo·vis I \'klō-vəs\ *about* 466–511 A.D. Frankish king (481–511)

Cly·tem·nes·tra \₁klīt-əm-'nes-trə\ wife of Agamemnon

Co·chise \kō-'chēs\ 1812?–74 Apache Indian chief

Co·dy \'kōd-ē\ William Frederick 1846–1917 *Buffalo Bill* American frontiersman and entertainer

Co·han \'kō-₁han\ George Michael 1878–1942 American actor and composer

Cole·ridge \'kōl-rij, 'kō-lə-rij\ Samuel Taylor 1772–1834 English poet

Co·lette \kȯ-'let\ Sidonie Gabrielle Claudine 1873–1954 French author

Co·lum·bus \kə-'ləm-bəs\ Christopher 1451–1506 Italian navigator; explored America (1492)

Con·fu·cius \kən-'fyü-shəs\ *about* 551–479 B.C. Chinese philosopher

Con·rad \'kän-₁rad\ Joseph 1857–1924 British (Ukrainian-born of Polish parents) author

Con·stan·tine \'kän-stən-₁tēn, -₁tīn\ *died* 337 A.D. *the Great* Roman emperor (306-337)

Cook \'kȯk\ Captain James 1728–79 English navigator

Coo·lidge \'kü-lij\ (John) Calvin 1872–1933 30th president of the United States (1923–29)

Coo·per \'kü-pər, 'kȯp-ər\ James Fen·i·more \'fen-ə-₁mȯr, -₁mȯr\ 1789–1851 American author

Co·per·ni·cus \kō-'pər-ni-kəs\ Nicolaus 1473–1543 Polish astronomer

Cop·land \'kō-plənd\ Aaron 1900–90 American composer

Corn·wal·lis \kȯrn-'wäl-əs\ Charles 1st Marquis 1738–1805 British general and statesman

Co·ro·na·do, de \₁kȯr-ə-'näd-ō, ₁kär-\ Francisco Vásquez *about* 1510–54 Spanish explorer of southwestern United States

Cor·tes *or* **Cor·tez** \kȯr-'tez, 'kȯr-,\ Hernando 1485–1547 Spanish conqueror of Mexico

Cow·per \'kü-pər, 'kȯp-ər, 'kaȯ-pər\ William 1731–1800 English poet

Crane \'krān\ Stephen 1871–1900 American author

Crazy Horse \'krā-zē-₁hȯrs\ 1842–77 Sioux Indian chief

Cres·si·da \'kres-əd-ə\ Trojan woman who in medieval legend is unfaithful to her lover Troilus

Crock·ett \'kräk-ət\ David 1786–1836 *Davy* American frontiersman

Croe·sus \'krē-səs\ *died* 546 B.C. king of Lydia (560–546)

Crom·well \'kräm-₁wel, 'krəm-, -wəl\ Oliver 1599–1658 English general and statesman; lord protector of England (1653–58)

Cro·nus \'krō-nəs\ Titan dethroned by his son Zeus

Cu·pid \'kyü-pəd\ — see EROS

Cu·rie \kyu̇-'rē, 'kyu̇r-ē\ Marie 1867–1934 French (Polish-born) chemist; Nobel prize winner (1903, 1911)

Curie Pierre 1859–1906 French chemist; husband of Marie; Nobel prize winner (1903)

Cus·ter \'kəs-tər\ George Armstrong 1839–76 American general

Cyb·e·le \'sib-ə-lē\ nature goddess of ancient Asia Minor incorporated into classical mythology

Cy·ra·no de Ber·ge·rac, de \₁sir-ə-₁nō-də-'ber-zhə-₁rak\ Savinieu 1619–55 French poet and soldier

Cyr·il \'sir-əl\ Saint *about* 827–869 A.D. Apostle to the Slavs; brother of Methodius

Cy·rus \'sī-rəs\ *about* 585–*about* 529 B.C. *the Great* or *the Elder* king of Persia (550–529)

Cyrus 424?–401 B.C. *the Younger* Persian prince and satrap

\ə\ abut		\ng\ sing	
\ər\ further		\ō\ bone	
\a\ mat		\ȯ\ saw	
\ā\ take		\ȯi\ coin	
\ä\ cot, cart		\th\ thin	
\aȯ\ out		\th\ this	
\ch\ chin		\ü\ food	
\e\ pet		\u̇\ foot	
\ē\ easy		\y\ yet	
\g\ go		\yü\ few	
\i\ tip		\yu̇\ cure	
\ī\ life		\zh\ vision	
\j\ job			

Dae·da·lus \\'ded-l-əs, 'dēd-\\ builder in Greek mythology of the Cretan labyrinth and inventor of wings by which he and his son Icarus escape from it

Dal·ton \\'dȯlt-n\\ John 1766–1844 English chemist and physicist

Dam·o·cles \\'dam-ə-‚klēz\\ courtier of ancient Syracuse said to have been seated at a banquet beneath a sword hung by a single hair

Da·mon \\'dā-mən\\ a Sicilian said to have pledged his life for his condemned friend Pythias

Da·na \\'dā-nə\\ Richard Henry 1815–82 American author

Dan·aë \\'dan-ə-‚ē\\ mother of Perseus; visited by Zeus as a shower of gold during her imprisonment

Dan·iel \\'dan-yəl\\ Hebrew prophet captive in Babylon who was saved from death in a lions' den by his faith in God

Dan·te \\'dän-tā, 'dan-, -tē\\ 1265–1321 Italian poet

Daph·ne \\'daf-nē\\ nymph transformed into a laurel tree to escape the pursuing Apollo

Dare \\'daər, 'deər\\ Virginia 1587–? first child born in America of English parents

Da·ri·us I \\də-'rī-əs\\ 550–486 B.C. *the Great* king of Persia (522–486)

Dar·row \\'dar-ō\\ Clarence Seward 1857–1938 American lawyer

Dar·win \\'där-wən\\ Charles Robert 1809–82 English naturalist

Da·vid \\'dā-vəd\\ the 2d king of Israel who in his youth killed Goliath; successor to Saul and father of Solomon

David Saint 6th century A.D. patron saint of Wales

Da·vid \\dä-'vēd\\ Jacques Louis 1748–1825 French painter

Da·vis \\'dā-vəs\\ Jefferson 1808–89 president of the Confederate States of America (1861–65)

Da·vy \\'dā-vē\\ Sir Humphry 1778–1829 English chemist

Debs \\'debz\\ Eugene Victor 1855–1926 American socialist

De·bus·sy \\‚deb-yu̇-'sē, ‚dāb-; də-'byü-sē\\ Claude Achille 1862–1918 French composer

De·ca·tur \\di-'kāt-ər\\ Stephen 1779–1820 American naval officer

De·foe \\di-'fō\\ Daniel 1660–1731 English author

De·gas \\də-'gä\\ (Hilaire Germain) Edgar 1834–1917 French painter

de Gaulle \\di-'gōl, -'gȯl\\ Charles André Joseph Marie 1890–1970 French general; president of Fifth Republic (1959–69)

de Klerk \\də-'klərk\\ Frederik Willem 1936–   president of Republic of South Africa (1989–   )

De·la·croix \\‚del-ə-'krwä, -'kwä\\ (Ferdinand Victor) Eugène 1798–1863 French painter

de la Mare \\‚del-ə-'maər, -'meər\\ Walter John 1873–1956 English author

De·li·lah \\di-'lī-lə\\ mistress and betrayer of Samson

De·me·ter \\di-'mēt-ər\\ Greek goddess of agriculture whose Roman counterpart is Ceres

de Mille \\də-'mil\\ Agnes George 1905–   American choreographer

de·Mille Cec·il \\'ses-əl\\ Blount \\'blənt\\ 1881–1959 American movie producer

De·mos·the·nes \\di-'mäs-thə-‚nēz\\ 384–322 B.C. Athenian orator and statesman

De·nis *or* **De·nys** \\'den-əs, də-'nē\\ Saint *died* 258? A.D. 1st bishop of Paris; patron saint of France

De Quin·cey \\di-'kwin-sē, -'kwin zē\\ Thomas 1785–1859 English author

Des·cartes \\dā-'kärt\\ René 1596–1650 French mathematician and philosopher

de So·to \\di-'sōt-ō\\ Hernando *or* Fernando 1496 (or 1499 or 1500)–1542 Spanish explorer in America; discovered Mississippi River (1541)

Dew·ey \\'dü-ē, 'dyü-\\ George 1837–1917 American admiral

Dewey John 1859–1952 American philosopher and educator

Di·ana \\dī-'an-ə\\ — see ARTEMIS

Di·as *or* **Di·az** \\'dē-‚äsh\\ Bartholomeu *about* 1450–1500 Portuguese navigator; 1st to sail around the southern tip of Africa

Dick·ens \\'dik-ənz\\ Charles John Huffam 1812–1870 *Boz* \\'bäz, 'bōz\\ English author

Dick·in·son \\'dik-ən-sən\\ Emily Elizabeth 1830–86 American poet

Di·de·rot \\dē-'drō, 'dēd-ə-‚rō\\ Denis 1713–84 French philosopher and author

Di·do \\'dīd-ō\\ legendary queen of Carthage who entertains and falls in love with Aeneas and kills herself upon his departure

Di·o·cle·tian \\‚dī-ə-'klē-shən\\ 245 (or 248)–313 (or 316) A.D. Roman emperor (284–305)

Di·og·e·nes \\dī-'äj-ə-‚nēz\\ *died about* 320 B.C. Greek Cynic philosopher

Di·o·me·des \\‚dī-ə-'mēd-ēz\\ Greek warrior in the Trojan War

Di·o·ny·sus \\‚dī-ə-'nī-səs, -'nē-\\ Greek god of wine and fertility whose Roman counterpart is Bacchus

Dis \\'dis\\ — see PLUTO

Dis·ney \\'diz-nē\\ Walter Elias 1901–66 American animated-film producer

Dis·rae·li \\diz-'rā-lē\\ Benjamin 1804–81 1st Earl of *Bea·cons·field* \\'bē-kənz-‚fēld\\ British prime minister (1868; 1874–80)

Dix \\'diks\\ Dorothea Lynde 1802–87 American social reformer

Dodg·son \\'däj-sən, 'dȧd-\\ Charles Lut·widge \\'lət-wij\\ 1832–98 pseudonym *Lewis Car·roll* \\'kar-əl\\ English mathematician and author

Dom·i·nic \\'däm-ə-nik\\ Saint *about* 1170–1221 Spanish-born founder of the Dominican order of friars

Do·mi·tian \\də-'mish-ən\\ 51–96 A.D. Roman emperor (81–96)

Don·i·zet·ti \\‚dän-əd-'zet-ē, ‚dōn-, -ə-'zet-\\ Gaetano 1797–1848 Italian composer

Donne \\'dən\\ John *about* 1572–1631 English poet and clergyman

Dos·to·ev·ski \\‚däs-tə-'yef-skē, -'yev-\\ Fëdor Mikhailovich 1821–81 Russian author

Doug·las \\'dəg-ləs\\ Stephen Arnold 1813–61 American statesman

Doug·lass \\'dəg-ləs\\ Frederick 1817–95 American abolitionist

Doyle \\'dȯil\\ Sir Arthur Co·nan \\'kō-nən, 'kȯ-\\ 1859–1930 British author and physician

Dra·co \\'drā-kō\\ late 7th century B.C. Athenian lawgiver

Drake \\'drāk\\ Sir Francis 1540 (or 1543)–96 English navigator and admiral

Drei·ser \\'drī-sər, -zər\\ Theodore 1871–1945 American author

Drey·fus \\'drī-fəs, 'drā-\\ Alfred 1859–1935 French army officer

Dry·den \\'drīd-n\\ John 1631–1700 English author

Du Bois \\dü-'bȯis, dyü-\\ William Edward Burghardt 1868–1963 American educator

Du·mas \\dü-'mä, dyü-; 'dü-‚mä, 'dyü-\\ Alexandre 1802–70 *Dumas père* \\'peər\\ French author

Dumas Alexandre 1824–95 *Dumas fils* \\'fēs\\ French author

Dun·bar \\'dən-‚bär\\ Paul Laurence 1872–1906 American poet

Dun·can \\'dəng-kən\\ Isadora 1877–1927 American dancer

Dü·rer \\'dur-ər, 'dyur-, 'du̅r-\\ Albrecht 1471–1528 German painter and engraver

Du·se \\'dü-zā\\ Eleanora 1858–1924 Italian actress

Dvo·řák \\də-'vȯr-‚zhäk, 'vȯr-‚zhäk\\ Anton 1841–1904 Czech composer

Ea·kins \\'ā-kənz\\ Thomas 1844–1916 American artist

Ear·hart \\'eər-,härt, 'iər-\\ Amelia 1897–1937 American aviator

Ed·dy \\'ed-ē\\ Mary Baker 1821–1910 American founder of the Christian Science Church

Ed·i·son \\'ed-ə-sən\\ Thomas Alva 1847–1931 American inventor

Ed·ward \\'ed-wərd\\ name of 8 post-Norman kings of England: **I** 1239–1307 (reigned 1272–1307) *Longshanks;* **II** 1284–1327 (reigned 1307–27); **III** 1312–77 (reigned 1327–77); **IV** 1442–83 (reigned 1461–70; 1471–83); **V** 1470–83 (reigned 1483); **VI** 1537–53 (reigned 1547–53) son of Henry VIII and Jane Seymour; **VII** 1841–1910 (reigned 1901–10) *Albert Edward* son of Queen Victoria; **VIII** 1894–1972 (reigned 1936; abdicated) *Duke of Windsor* son of George V

Edward 1330–76 *the Black Prince* son of Edward III; prince of Wales

Edward 1003?–66 *the Confessor* king of the English (1042–66)

Ed·wards \\'ed-wərdz\\ Jonathan 1703–58 American theologian

Ein·stein \\'īn-,stīn\\ Albert 1879–1955 American (German-born) physicist; Nobel prize winner (1921)

Ei·sen·how·er \\'īz-n-,haù-ər, -,haùr\\ Dwight David 1890–1969 American general; 34th president of the United States (1953–61)

Elec·tra \\i-'lek-trə\\ sister of Orestes who aids him in avenging their father's murder

El·gar \\'el-,gär, -gər\\ Sir Edward 1857–1934 English composer

Eli \\'ē-,lī\\ early Hebrew judge and priest

Eli·jah \\i-'lī-jə\\ *or* **Eli·as** \\i-'lī-əs\\ Hebrew prophet of the 9th century B.C.

El·iot \\'el-ē-ət, 'el-yət\\ George 1819–80 pseudonym of *Mary Ann Evans* English author

Eliot Thomas Stearns 1888–1965 British (American-born) poet and critic

Elis·a·beth \\i-'liz-ə-bəth\\ mother of John the Baptist

Eli·sha \\i-'lī-shə\\ Hebrew prophet; disciple and successor of Elijah

Eliz·a·beth I \\i-'liz-ə-bəth\\ 1533–1603 daughter of Henry VIII and Anne Boleyn; queen of England (1558–1603)

Elizabeth II 1926– daughter of George VI; queen of Great Britain (1952–   )

El·ling·ton \\'el-ing-tən\\ Edward Kennedy 1899–1974 *Duke* American bandleader and composer

Em·er·son \\'em-ər-sən\\ Ralph Waldo 1803–82 American essayist and poet

En·dym·i·on \\en-'dim-ē-ən\\ beautiful youth loved by the moon goddess Selene in classical mythology

Eos \\'ē-,äs\\ Greek goddess of dawn whose Roman counterpart is Aurora

Ep·i·cu·rus \\,ep-i-'kyùr-əs\\ 341–270 B.C. Greek philosopher

Eras·mus \\i-'raz-məs\\ Desiderius 1466?–1536 Dutch scholar

Er·a·to \\'er-ə-,tō\\ Greek Muse of lyric and especially love poetry

Er·ic \\'er-ik\\ 10th century *the Red* Norwegian navigator

Ericsson, Leif — see LEIF ERICSSON

Erin·y·es \\i-'rin-ē-,ēz\\ *or* **Eu·men·i·des** \\yü-'men-ə-,dēz\\ the Furies in Greek mythology

Eris \\'ir-əs, 'er-\\ Greek goddess of discord

Ernst \\'eərnst, 'ərnst\\ Max 1891–1976 German painter

Eros \\'eər-,äs, 'iər-\\ Greek god of love whose Roman counterpart is Cupid

Esau \\'ē-,sò\\ son of Isaac and Rebekah; elder twin brother of Jacob to whom he sold his birthright

Es·ther \\'es-tər\\ Hebrew woman who became Xerxes' queen during the Babylonian captivity and delivered her people from destruction

Eu·clid \\'yü-kləd\\ *flourished about* 300 B.C. Greek mathematician

Eumenides — see ERINYES

Eu·rip·i·des \\yù-'rip-ə-,dēz\\ *about* 484–406 B.C. Greek dramatist

Eu·ro·pa \\yù-'rō-pə\\ Phoenician princess abducted by Zeus disguised as a white bull

Eu·ryd·i·ce \\yù-'rid-ə-sē\\ wife of Orpheus

Eu·ter·pe \\yù-'tər-pē\\ Greek Muse of music

Eve \\'ēv\\ the first woman in biblical tradition; wife of Adam

Eze·kiel \\i-'zē-kyəl, -kē-əl\\ Hebrew prophet of the 6th century B.C.

Ez·ra \\'ez-rə\\ Hebrew priest, scribe, and reformer of the 5th century B.C.

Fa·bi·us \\'fā-bē-əs\\ *died* 203 B.C. *Quintus Fabius Maximus Verrucosus Cunc·ta·tor* \\'kəngk-tāt-ər\\ Roman general against Hannibal

Fahd \\'fäd\\ 1922– king of Saudi Arabia (1982–   )

Fahr·en·heit \\'far-ən-,hīt, 'fär-\\ Gabriel Daniel 1686–1736 German physicist

Far·a·day \\'far-ə-,dā, -əd-ē\\ Michael 1791–1867 English chemist and physicist

Far·ra·gut \\'far-ə-gət\\ David Glasgow 1801–70 American admiral

Faulk·ner \\'fòk-nər\\ William 1897–1962 American author; Nobel prize winner (1949)

Faust \\'faùst\\ Doctor Johann *about* 1480–*about* 1540 German magician and astrologer; basis of legend of Faust

Faust *or* **Fau·stus** \\'faù-stəs, 'fò-\\ magician and astrologer in legend and literature who sells his soul to the devil for worldly experience and power

Fawkes \\'fòks\\ Guy 1570–1606 English conspirator

Fer·ber \\'fər-bər\\ Edna 1887–1968 American writer

Fer·di·nand I \\'fərd-n-,and\\ 1016 (or 1018)–1065 *the Great* king of Castile (1035–65); of Navarre and León (1037–65); emperor of Spain (1056–65)

Ferdinand V of Castile or **II** of Aragon 1452–1516 *the Catholic* king of Castile (1474–1504); of Aragon (1479–1516); of Naples (1504–16); founder of the Spanish monarchy

Fer·mi \\'feər-mē\\ Enrico 1901–54 American (Italian-born) physicist; Nobel prize winner (1938)

Fiel·ding \\'fēl-ding\\ Henry 1707–54 English author

Fie·so·le, da \\fē-'ā-zə-,lā, -lē\\ Giovanni *about* 1400–1455 *Fra An·ge·li·co* \\an-'jel-i-,kō\\ Italian painter

Fill·more \\'fil-,mōr, -,mòr\\ Millard 1800–74 13th president of the United States (1850–53)

Fitz·ger·ald \\fits-'jer-əld\\ Francis Scott Key 1896–1940 American author

Fitz·Ger·ald \\fits-'jer-əld\\ Edward 1809–83 English poet

Flau·bert \\flō-'beər\\ Gustave 1821–80 French author

Flem·ing \\'flem-ing\\ Sir Alexander 1881–1955 British bacteriologist; Nobel prize winner (1945)

Flo·ra \\'flōr-ə, 'flòr-\\ Roman goddess of flowers

Flying Dutchman legendary Dutch mariner condemned to sail the seas until Judgment Day

Foch \\'fòsh, 'fäsh\\ Ferdinand 1851–1929 French general; marshal of France (1918)

Ford \\'fōrd, 'fòrd\\ Gerald Rudolph 1913–   38th president of the United States (1974–77)

Ford Henry 1863–1947 American automobile manufacturer

Fos·ter \\'fòs-tər, 'fäs-\\ Stephen Collins 1826–64 American songwriter

Fox \\'fäks\\ George 1624–91 English founder of Society of Friends

Fran·cis I \\'fran-səs\\ 1494–1547 King of France (1515–47)

Francis II 1768–1835 last Holy Roman emperor (1792–1806); emperor of Austria (as *Francis I*) (1804–35)

Francis Ferdinand 1863–1914 archduke of Austria; assassinated

Francis Joseph I 1830–1916 emperor of Austria (1848–1916)

\ə\ abut		\ng\ sing	
\ər\ further		\ō\ bone	
\a\ mat		\ò\ saw	
\ā\ take		\òi\ coin	
\ä\ cot, cart		\th\ thin	
\aù\ out		\th\ this	
\ch\ chin		\ü\ food	
\e\ pet		\ù\ foot	
\ē\ easy		\y\ yet	
\g\ go		\yü\ few	
\i\ tip		\yù\ cure	
\ī\ life		\zh\ vision	
\j\ job			

Francis of As•si•si \ə-'sē-sē, -zē, -'sis-ē\ Saint 1181 (or 1182)–1226 Italian friar; founder of Franciscan order

Franck \'frängk\ César Auguste 1822–90 Belgian=French organist and composer

Fran•co \'fräng-kō, 'fräng-\ Francisco 1892–1975 Spanish general and dictator

Frank \'frangk\ Anne 1929–1945 Jewish diarist during the Holocaust

Frank•lin \'frang-klən\ Benjamin 1706–90 American statesman, philosopher, and inventor

Fred•er•ick I \'fred-rik, -ə-rik\ *about* 1123–90 *Frederick Bar•ba•ros•sa* \,bär-bə-'räs-ə, -'ros-\ Holy Roman emperor (1152–90)

Frederick II 1194–1250 Holy Roman emperor (1215–50); king of Sicily (1198–1250)

Frederick IX 1899–1972 king of Denmark (1947–72)

Frederick I 1657–1713 king of Prussia (1701–13)

Frederick II 1712–86 *the Great* king of Prussia (1740–86)

Frè•mont \'frē-,mänt\ John Charles 1813–90 American general and explorer

Freud \'froid\ Sigmund 1856–1939 Austrian neurologist; founder of psychoanalysis

Fron•te•nac, de \'fränt-n-,ak\ Comte *de Pal•lu•au* \pà-lw'ō\ *et* 1622–98 French general and colonial administrator

Frost \'frost\ Robert Lee 1874–1963 American poet

Ful•ton \'fult-n\ Robert 1765–1815 American inventor

Ga•bri•el \'gā-brē-əl\ one of the four archangels named in Hebrew tradition — compare MICHAEL, RAPHAEL, URIEL

Ga•ga•rin \gə-'gär-ən\ Yu•ri \'yur-ē\ Alekseyevich 1934–68 Russian cosmonaut; 1st man in space (1961)

Gage \'gāj\ Thomas 1721–87 British general in America

Gains•bor•ough \'gānz-,bər-ə, -bə-rə, -brə\ Thomas 1727–88 English painter

Gal•a•had \'gal-ə-,had\ knight of the Round Table who finds the Holy Grail

Gal•a•tea \,gal-ə-'tē-ə\ an ivory statue of a maiden carved by Pygmalion in Greek myth and given life by Aphrodite in response to the sculptor's prayer

Ga•len \'gā-lən\ 129–*about* 199 A.D. Greek physician and writer

Ga•li•lei \,gal-ə-'lā-,ē\ Ga•li•leo \,gal-ə-'lē-ō, -'lā-\ 1564–1642 *Galileo* Italian astronomer and physicist

Gall \'gol\ 1840?–94 Sioux Indian leader

Ga•lois \gal-'wä\ Évariste 1811–32 French mathematician

Gals•wor•thy \'golz-,wər-thē\ John 1867–1933 English author; Nobel prize winner (1932)

Ga•ma, da \'gam-ə, 'gäm-\ Vasco *about* 1460–1524 Portuguese navigator

Gan•y•mede \'gan-i-,mēd\ cupbearer of Zeus

Gar•field \'gär-,fēld\ James Abram 1831–81 20th president of the United States (1881)

Gar•i•bal•di \,gar-ə-'bol-dē\ Giuseppe 1807–82 Italian patriot

Gar•ri•son \'gar-ə-sən\ William Lloyd 1805–79 American abolitionist

Gau•guin \gō-'ga^n\ (Eugène Henri) Paul 1848–1903 French painter

Gauss \'gaus\ Karl Friedrich 1777–1855 German mathematician and astronomer

Gau•ta•ma Bud•dha \,gaut-ə-mə-'büd-ə, -'bud-\ *about* 563–*about* 483 B.C. Indian founder of Buddhism

Ga•wain \gə-'wān, 'gä-,wän, 'gau-ən\ nephew of King Arthur; knight of the Round Table

Gay \'gā\ John 1685–1732 English author

Gei•sel \'gī-zəl\ Theodor Seuss 1904–91 pseudonym *Dr. Seuss* \'süs\ American writer and illustrator

Gen•ghis Khan \,jeng-gə-'skän, ,geng-\ *about* 1162–1227 Mongol conqueror

George \'jorj\ Saint *about* 3d century Christian martyr; patron saint of England

George name of 6 kings of Great Britain: **I** 1660–1727 (reigned 1714–27); **II** 1683–1760 (reigned 1727–60); **III** 1738–1820 (reigned 1760–1820); **IV** 1762–1830 (reigned 1820–30); **V** 1865–1936 (reigned 1910–36); **VI** 1895–1952 (reigned 1936–52)

George I 1845–1913 king of Greece (1863–1913)

George II 1890–1947 king of Greece (1922–23; 1935–47)

George David Lloyd — see LLOYD GEORGE

Ge•ron•i•mo \jə-'rän-ə-,mō\ 1829–1909 Apache Indian leader

Gersh•win \'gərsh-wən\ George 1898–1937 American composer

Gib•bon \'gib-ən\ Edward 1737–94 English historian

Gide \'zhēd\ André 1869–1951 French author; Nobel prize winner (1947)

Gid•e•on \'gid-ē-ən\ Hebrew hero noted for his defeat of the Midianites

Gil•bert \'gil-bərt\ Sir William Schwenck 1836–1911 English librettist and poet; collaborated with Sir Arthur S. Sullivan

Giot•to \'jot-tō, 'jo-tō, jē-'ät-ō\ 1266/67 (or 1276)–1337 *Giotto di Bondone* Florentine painter, architect, and sculptor

Glad•stone \'glad-,stōn, *chiefly British* -stən\ William Ewart 1809–98 British prime minister (1868–74; 1880–85; 1886; 1892–94)

Glenn \'glen\ John Herschel 1921– American astronaut; 1st American to orbit the earth (1962)

God•dard \'gäd-ərd\ Robert Hutchings 1882–1945 American physicist

Go•di•va \gə-'dī-və\ Saxon lady noted in legend for riding naked through the streets of Coventry to relieve the town of a burdensome tax levied by her husband

Goeb•bels \'gərb-əlz, 'gœb-əls\ Joseph Paul 1897–1945 German Nazi propagandist

Goe•thals \'gō-thəlz\ George Washington 1858–1928 American general and engineer

Goe•the, von \'gər-tə, 'gœ-tə\ Johann Wolfgang 1749–1832 German author

Gogh, van \van-'gō, -'gäk, -kōk\ Vincent 1853–90 Dutch painter

Go•gol \'go-gəl, 'gō-,gol\ Nikolai Vasilievich 1809–52 Russian author

Gold•smith \'gōld-,smith, 'gōl-\ Oliver 1730–74 British author

Go•li•ath \gə-'lī-əth\ Philistine giant held in the Old Testament to have been killed by David with a sling

Gom•pers \'gäm-pərz\ Samuel 1850–1924 American (British-born) labor leader

Good•year \'gud-,yiər, 'guj-,iər\ Charles 1800–60 American inventor

Gor•ba•chev \,gor-bə-'chof\ Mikhail Sergeyevich 1931– Soviet politician; 1st secretary of communist party (1985–91); president of the U.S.S.R. (1990–91)

Gore \'gōr, 'gor\ Albert, Jr. 1948– vice-president of the United States (1993–)

Gor•gas \'gor-gəs\ William Crawford 1854–1920 American army surgeon

Gor•ky \'gor-kē\ Maksim 1868–1936 pseudonym of *Aleksei Maksimovich Pesh•kov* \'pesh-,kof, -,kov\ Russian author

Gou•nod \'gü-,nō\ Charles François 1818–93 French composer

Go•ya y Lu•cien•tes, de \'goi-ə-,ē-,lü-sē-,en-,täs\ Francisco José 1746–1828 Spanish painter

Grac•chus \'grak-əs\ Gaius Sempronius 153–121 B.C. and his brother Tiberius Sempronius 163–133 B.C. *the Grac•chi* \'grak-,ī\ Roman statesmen

Gra•ham \'grā-əm, 'gra-əm, 'gram\ Martha 1893–1991 American dancer

Grant \\'grant\\ Ulysses Simpson 1822–85 *Ulysses Hiram* (baptized *Hiram Ulysses*) *Grant* American general; 18th president of the United States (1869–77)

Gray \\'grā\\ Thomas 1716–71 English poet

Gre·co, El \\'grek-ō, 'grāk-, 'grēk-\\ 1541–1614 *Doménikos Theotokópoulos* Spanish (Cretan-born) painter

Gree·ley \\'grē-lē\\ Horace 1811–72 American journalist and politician

Greene \\'grēn\\ Graham 1904–91 British author

Greene Nathanael 1742–86 American Revolutionary general

Greg·o·ry \\'greg-rē, -ə-rē\\ name of 16 popes: especially **I** Saint *about* 540–604 A.D. *the Great* (pope 590–604); **VII** Saint (*Hil·debrand* \\'hil-də-,brand\\) 1020–85 (pope 1073–85); **XIII** 1502–85 (pope 1572–85)

Grey \\'grā\\ Lady Jane 1537–54 English noblewoman beheaded as a possible rival for the throne

Grey (Pearl) Zane 1875–1939 American author

Grieg \\'grēg, 'grig\\ Edvard Hagerup 1843–1907 Norwegian composer

Grimm \\'grim\\ Jacob 1785–1863 and his brother Wilhelm 1786–1859 German philologists and fairy tale writers

Guin·e·vere \\'gwin-ə-,viər, 'gwen-\\ wife of King Arthur and mistress of Lancelot in Arthurian legend

Gun·ther \\'günt-ər\\ Burgundian king and husband of Brunhild in Germanic legend

Gu·ten·berg \\'güt-n-,bərg\\ Johann *about* 1390–1468 *Johann Gensfleisch* German inventor of printing from movable type

Ha·dri·an \\'hā-drē-ən\\ 76–138 A.D. Roman emperor (117–138)

Ha·gar \\'hā-,gär, -gər\\ concubine of Abraham driven into the desert with her son Ishmael because of Sarah's jealousy

Hag·gai \\'hag-ē-,ī, 'hag-,ī\\ *or* **Ag·ge·us** \\a-'gē-əs\\ Hebrew prophet of the 6th century B.C.

Hai·le Se·las·sie \\,hī-lē-sə-'las-ē, -'läs-\\ 1892–1975 emperor of Ethiopia (1930–36; 1941–74); dethroned

Hale \\'hāl\\ Edward Everett 1822–1909 American clergyman and author

Hale Nathan 1755–76 American Revolutionary hero

Hal·sey \\'hȯl-sē, -zē\\ William Frederick 1882–1959 American admiral

Ham \\'ham\\ son of Noah; ancestor of the Hamitic peoples in biblical tradition

Ha·man \\'hā-mən\\ Old Testament enemy of the Jews hanged for plotting their destruction

Ha·mil·car Bar·ca \\hə-'mil-,kär-'bär-kə, 'ham-əl-\\ 270?–229 (or 228) B.C. Carthaginian general; father of Hannibal

Ham·il·ton \\'ham-əl-tən, -əlt-n\\ Alexander 1755–1804 American statesman

Hamilton Edith 1867–1963 American classicist

Ham·mu·ra·bi \\,ham-ə-'räb-ē\\ *died* 1750 B.C. king of Babylon (1792–50)

Ham·sun \\'häm-sən\\ Knut 1859–1952 pseudonym of *Knut Pedersen* Norwegian author; Nobel prize winner (1920)

Han·cock \\'han-,käk\\ John 1737–93 American statesman; 1st signer of Declaration of Independence

Han·del \\'han-dl\\ George Frederick 1685–1759 British (German-born) composer

Han·dy \\'han-dē\\ William Christopher 1873–1958 *W. C.* American blues musician

Han·ni·bal \\'han-ə-bəl\\ 247–183 B.C. Carthaginian general

Har·de·ca·nute \\,härd-i-kə-'nüt, -'nyüt\\ *about* 1019–42 king of the English (1040–42); king of Denmark (1028–42)

Har·ding \\'härd-ing\\ Warren Gamaliel 1865–1923 29th president of the United States (1921–23)

Har·dy \\'härd-ē\\ Thomas 1840–1928 English author

Har·old I \\'har-əld\\ *died* 1040 *Harold Hare·foot* \\'haər-,fút, 'heər-\\ king of the English (1035–40)

Harold II *about* 1022–66 king of the English (1066)

Har·ris \\'har-əs\\ Joel Chandler 1848–1908 American author

Har·ri·son \\'har-ə-sən\\ Benjamin 1833–1901 23d president of the United States (1889–93); grandson of William Henry Harrison

Harrison William Henry 1773–1841 American general; 9th president of the United States (1841)

Harte \\'härt\\ Francis Brett 1836–1902 *Bret* American author

Har·vey \\'här-vē\\ William 1578–1657 English physician and anatomist

Haw·thorne \\'hȯ-,thȯrn\\ Nathaniel 1804–64 American author

Haydn \\'hīd-n\\ (Franz) Joseph 1732–1809 Austrian composer

Hayes \\'hāz\\ Rutherford Birchard 1822–93 19th president of the United States (1877–81)

Haz·litt \\'haz-lət, 'hāz-\\ William 1778–1830 English essayist

Hearst \\'hərst\\ William Randolph 1863–1951 American newspaper publisher

He·be \\'hē-bē\\ Greek goddess of youth; cupbearer of the gods

Hec·ate \\'hek-ət-ē\\ Greek goddess associated especially with the underworld, the moon, and witchcraft

Hec·tor \\'hek-tər\\ son of Priam and bravest of the Trojans in the Trojan War; slain by Achilles

Hec·u·ba \\'hek-yə-bə\\ wife of Priam and mother of Hector and Paris

He·gel \\'hā-gəl\\ Georg Wilhelm Friedrich 1770–1831 German philosopher

Hei·deg·ger \\'hī-,deg-ər, 'hīd-i-gər\\ Martin 1889–1976 German philosopher

Hei·ne \\'hī-nə *also* -nē\\ Heinrich 1797–1856 German author

Hel·en of Troy \\,hel-ə-nəv-'trȯi\\ wife of Menelaus whose abduction by Paris caused the Trojan War

He·li·os \\'hē-lē-,ōs, -əs\\ Greek sun-god whose Roman counterpart is Sol

Hell·man \\'hel-mən\\ Lillian 1905–84 American dramatist

Hem·ing·way \\'hem-ing-,wā\\ Ernest Miller 1899–1961 American author; Nobel prize winner (1954)

Hen·ry \\'hen-rē\\ name of 8 kings of England: **I** 1068–1135 (reigned 1100–35); **II** 1133–89 (reigned 1154–89); **III** 1207–72 (reigned 1216–72); **IV** 1366–1413 (reigned 1399–1413); **V** 1387–1422 (reigned 1413–22); **VI** 1421–71 (reigned 1422–61; 1470–71); **VII** 1457–1509 (reigned 1485–1509); **VIII** 1491–1547 (reigned 1509–47)

Henry name of 4 kings of France: **I** 1008–60 (reigned 1031–60); **II** 1519–59 (reigned 1547–59); **III** 1551–89 (reigned 1574–89); **IV** 1553–1610 *Henry of Navarre* (reigned 1589–1610)

Henry O. — see William Sydney PORTER

Henry Patrick 1736–99 American statesman and orator

He·phaes·tus \\hi-'fes-təs, -'fēs-\\ Greek god of fire and of metalworking whose Roman counterpart is Vulcan

He·ra \\'hir-ə, 'hē-rə\\ Greek goddess of women and marriage whose Roman counterpart is Juno; sister and wife of Zeus

Her·bert \\'hər-bərt\\ Victor 1859–1924 American (Irish-born) composer and conductor

Her·cu·les \\'hər-kyə-,lēz\\ *or* **Her·a·cles** *also* **Her·a·kles** \\'her-ə-,klēz\\ hero in classical mythology noted for his strength and for performing 12 labors imposed on him by Hera

Her·maph·ro·di·tus \\hər-,maf-rə-'dīt-əs\\ son of Hermes and Aphrodite who is joined with a nymph into one body

Her·mes \\'hər-,mēz, -mēz\\ Greek god whose Roman counterpart is Mercury; herald and messenger for the other gods and protector of travelers

\\ə\\ abut	\\ng\\ sing
\\ər\\ further	\\ō\\ bone
\\a\\ mat	\\ȯ\\ saw
\\ā\\ take	\\ȯi\\ coin
\\ä\\ cot, cart	\\th\\ thin
\\aú\\ out	\\th\\ this
\\ch\\ chin	\\ü\\ food
\\e\\ pet	\\ú\\ foot
\\ē\\ easy	\\y\\ yet
\\g\\ go	\\yü\\ few
\\i\\ tip	\\yú\\ cure
\\ī\\ life	\\zh\\ vision
\\j\\ job	

He·ro \ 'hē-rō, 'hiər-ō \ priestess of Aphrodite loved by Leander

Her·od \ 'her-əd \ 73–4 B.C. *the Great* Roman king of Judea (37–4)

Herod An·ti·pas \ 'ant-ə-,pas, -pəs \ 21 B.C.–39 A.D. Roman tetrarch of Galilee (4 B.C.–39 A.D.); son of Herod the Great

He·rod·o·tus \ hi-'räd-ə-təs \ *about* 484–between 430 and 420 B.C. Greek historian

Her·rick \ 'her-ik \ Robert 1591–1674 English poet

He·si·od \ 'hē-sē-əd, 'hes-ē- \ *flourished about* 800 B.C. Greek poet

Hes·se \ 'hes-ə \ Hermann 1877–1962 German author

Hes·tia \ 'hes-tē-ə; 'hes-chə, 'hesh- \ Greek goddess of the hearth and domestic activity whose Roman counterpart is Vesta

Hey·er·dahl \ 'hā-ər-,däl, 'hī- \ Thor 1914– Norwegian explorer and author

Hi·a·wa·tha \ ,hī-ə-'wò-thə, ,hē-ə-, -'wäth-ə \ 16th century Mohawk chieftain and hero of Iroquoian legend

Hick·ok \ 'hik-,äk \ James Butler 1837–76 *Wild Bill* American scout and United States marshal

Hildebrand — see GREGORY VII

Hil·la·ry \ 'hil-ə-rē \ Sir Edmund Percival 1919– New Zealand mountaineer and explorer

Hil·ton \ 'hilt-n \ James 1900–54 English novelist

Hin·den·burg, von \ 'hin-dən-,bərg, -,bùrg \ Paul 1847–1934 German field marshal; president of Germany (1925–34)

Hip·poc·ra·tes \ hip-'äk-rə-,tēz \ *about* 460–*about* 377 B.C. *father of medicine* Greek physician

Hi·ro·hi·to \ ,hir-ō-'hē-tō \ 1901–89 emperor of Japan (1926–89)

Hit·ler \ 'hit-lər \ Adolf 1889–1945 German (Austrian-born) chancellor and führer (1933–45)

Hobbes \ 'häbz \ Thomas 1588–1679 English philosopher

Ho·garth \ 'hō-,gärth \ William 1697–1764 English painter and engraver

Hol·bein \ 'hōl-,bīn, 'hòl- \ Hans *father* 1465?–1524 *and son* 1497?–1543 German painters

Holmes \ 'hōmz, 'hōlmz \ Oliver Wendell 1809–94 American physician and author

Holmes Oliver Wendell 1841–1935 American jurist; son of the preceding

Ho·mer \ 'hō-mər \ 9th-8th? century B.C. Greek epic poet

Homer Winslow 1836–1910 American painter

Hook·er \ 'hùk-ər \ Thomas 1586?–1647 English puritan clergyman; a founder of Connecticut

Hoo·ver \ 'hü-vər \ Herbert Clark 1874–1964 31st president of the United States (1929–33)

Hoover John Edgar 1895–1972 American criminologist; director of the Federal Bureau of Investigation (1924–72)

Hop·kins \ 'häp-kənz \ Gerard Manley 1844–89 English poet

Hor·ace \ 'hòr-əs, 'här- \ 65–8 B.C. Roman poet

Ho·rae \ 'hōr-,ē, 'hòr-, -,ī \ Greek goddesses of the seasons

Ho·ra·tius \ hə-'rā-shē-əs, -shəs \ hero in Roman legend noted for his defense of a bridge over the Tiber against the Etruscans

Ho·sea \ hō-'zē-ə, -'zā- \ *or* **Osee** \ 'ō-zē, ō-'zā-ə \ Hebrew prophet of the 8th century B.C.

Hous·man \ 'haù-smən \ Alfred Edward 1859–1936 English classical scholar and poet

Hous·ton \ 'hyü-stən, 'yü- \ Samuel 1793–1863 *Sam* American general; president of the Republic of Texas (1836–38; 1841–44)

Howe \ 'haù \ Elias 1819–67 American inventor

Howe Julia 1819–1910 née *Ward* American suffragist and reformer

How·ells \ 'haù-əlz \ William Dean 1837–1920 American author

Hud·son \ 'həd-sən \ Henry *died* 1611 English navigator

Hudson William Henry 1841–1922 English naturalist and author

Hugh Ca·pet \ 'kā-pət, 'kap-ət, ka-'pā \ *about* 938–996 A.D. king of France (987–996)

Hughes \ 'hyüz *also* 'yüz \ Charles Evans 1862–1948 chief justice of the United States Supreme Court (1930–41)

Hughes (James) Langston 1902–67 American author

Hu·go \ 'hyü-gō, yü- \ Victor Marie 1802–85 French author

Hume \ 'hyüm *also* 'yüm \ David 1711–76 Scottish philosopher and historian

Huss *or* **Hus** \ 'həs, 'hùs \ John *or* Jan 1372 (or 1373)–1415 Bohemian religious reformer

Hus·sein I \ hü-'sān \ 1935– king of Jordan (1953–

Hussein Saddam al-Tikriti 1937– leader of Iraq (1979–)

Hux·ley \ 'hək-slē \ Aldous Leonard 1894–1963 English author

Hy·ge·ia \ hī-'jē-ə, -yə \ Greek goddess of health

Hy·men \ 'hī-mən \ Greek god of marriage

Hy·pe·ri·on \ hī-'pir-ē-ən \ Titan; father of Eos, Selene, and Helios

Ib·sen \ 'ib-sən, 'ip- \ Henrik 1828–1906 Norwegian author

Ic·a·rus \ 'ik-ə-rəs \ son of Daedalus who falls into the sea when the wax of his artificial wings melts as he flies too near the sun

Ig·na·tius \ ig-'nā-shē-əs, -shəs \ *Saint Ignatius of Loyo·la* \ lòi-'ō-lə \ 1491–1556 Spanish founder of the Society of Jesus

In·no·cent \ 'in-ə-sənt \ name of 13 popes: especially **II** died 1143 (pope 1130–43); **III** 1160 (or 1161)–1216 (pope 1198–1216); **IV** died 1254 (pope 1243–54); **XI** 1611–89 (pope 1676–89)

Iph·i·ge·nia \ ,if-ə-jə-'nī-ə \ daughter of Agamemnon offered by him as a sacrifice but saved and made a priestess of Artemis

Iris \ 'ī-rəs \ goddess of the rainbow and a messenger of the gods in Greek mythology

Ir·ving \ 'ər-ving \ Washington 1783–1859 American author

Isaac \ 'ī-zik, -zək \ Hebrew patriarch; son of Abraham and father of Jacob

Is·a·bel·la I \ ,iz-ə-'bel-ə \ 1451–1504 queen of Castile (1474–1504); wife of Ferdinand V of Castile

Isa·iah \ ī-'zā-ə \ Hebrew prophet of the 8th century B.C.

Iseult — see ISOLDE

Ish·ma·el \ 'ish-mē-əl, -mā- \ outcast son of Abraham and Hagar

Ish·tar \ 'ish-,tär \ chief goddess of the Babylonian and Assyrian pantheons

Isis \ 'ī-səs \ Egyptian goddess of motherhood and fertility

Isol·de \ i-'zōl-də \ *or* **Iseult** \ is-'ült, iz- \ Irish princess married to King Mark of Cornwall and loved by Tristram

Ivan III \ ē-'vän, 'ī-vən \ **Va·si·lie·vich** \ və-'sil-yə-,vich \ 1440–1505 *Ivan the Great* grand duke of Russia (1462–1505)

Ivan IV Vasilievich 1530–84 *Ivan the Terrible* ruler of Russia (1533–84)

Ives \ 'īvz \ Charles Edward 1874–1954 American composer

Jack·son \ 'jak-sən \ Andrew 1767–1845 American general; 7th president of the United States (1829–37)

Jackson Jesse Louis 1941– American clergyman and civil rights leader

Jackson Thomas Jonathan 1824–63 *Stonewall* American Confederate general

Ja·cob \ 'jā-kəb \ Hebrew patriarch; son of Isaac and Rebekah and younger twin brother of Esau

James \ 'jāmz \ one of the 12 apostles; son of Zebedee and brother of the apostle John

James *the Less* one of the 12 apostles; son of Alphaeus

James name of 2 kings of Great Britain: **I** 1566–1625 (reigned 1603–25); king of Scotland as *James VI* (reigned 1567–1603); **II** 1633–1701 (reigned 1685–88)

James Henry 1843–1916 British (American-born) author

James William 1842–1910 American psychologist and philosopher; brother of Henry James

Ja·nus \'jā-nəs\ Roman god of gates and doors and of beginnings and endings conventionally portrayed as having two opposite faces

Ja·pheth \'jā-fəth\ son of Noah; ancestor of the Medes and Greeks in biblical tradition

Ja·son \'jās-n\ hero in Greek mythology noted for his successful quest of the Golden Fleece

Jay \'jā\ John 1745–1829 American jurist and statesman; 1st chief justice of the United States Supreme Court (1789–95)

Jef·fer·son \'jef-ər-sən\ Thomas 1743–1826 3d president of the United States (1801–09)

Jen·ner \'jen-ər\ Edward 1749–1823 English physician

Jer·e·mi·ah \,jer-ə-'mī-ə\ Hebrew prophet of the 6th and 7th centuries B.C.

Je·rome \jə-'rōm\ Saint *about* 347–419 (or 420) A.D. church father and biblical translator

Je·sus \'je-zəs, -zəz\ *about* 6 B.C.–*about* 30 A.D. *Jesus Christ* founder of the Christian religion

Jez·e·bel \'jez-ə-,bel\ queen of Israel noted for her wickedness; wife of Ahab

Joan of Arc \,jō-nə-'värk\ Saint 1412–1431 *the Maid of Orleans* French national heroine

Job \'jōb\ Old Testament patriarch who endured afflictions with fortitude and faith

Jo·cas·ta \jō-'kas-tə\ queen of Thebes who unknowingly marries her son Oedipus

Jo·el \'jō-əl\ Hebrew prophet of the Old Testament

John \'jän\ *the Baptist* forerunner and baptizer of Jesus

John one of the 12 apostles held to be the author of the fourth Gospel, three Epistles, and the Book of Revelation

John name of 21 popes: especially **XXIII** (*Angelo Giuseppe Roncalli*) 1881–1963 (pope 1958–63)

John 1167–1216 *John Lack·land* \'lak-,land\ king of England (1199–1216)

John of Gaunt \-'gȯnt, -'gänt\ 1340–99 Duke of Lancaster; son of Edward III of England

John·son \'jän-sən\ Andrew 1808–75 17th president of the United States (1865–69)

Johnson Lyndon Baines 1908–73 36th president of the United States (1963–69)

Johnson Philip Cortelyou 1906– American architect

Johnson Samuel 1709–84 *Dr. Johnson* English lexicographer and author

Jo·liet *or* **Jol·liet** \zhȯl-'yā\ Louis 1645–1700 French-Canadian explorer

Jo·nah \'jō-nə\ Hebrew prophet who in biblical tradition is cast overboard during a storm, is swallowed by a great fish, and is vomited up after three days in its belly

Jon·a·than \'jän-ə-thən\ son of Saul and friend of David

Jones \'jōnz\ John Paul 1747–92 American (Scottish-born) naval officer

Jon·son \'jän-sən\ Benjamin 1572–1637 *Ben* English author

Jo·seph \'jō-zəf *also* -səf\ Hebrew patriarch who was sold into slavery by his jealous brothers, and became a ruler in Egypt and saved his father Jacob and his brothers in time of famine

Joseph *about* 1840–1904 Nez Percé Indian chief

Joseph Saint husband of Mary, the mother of Jesus

Jo·se·phine \'jō-zə-,fēn *also* -sə-\ 1763–1814 1st wife of Napoleon I; empress of France (1804–09)

Joseph of Ar·i·ma·thea \-,ar-ə-mə-'thē-ə\ *Saint* wealthy member of the Sanhedrin who placed the body of Jesus in his own tomb

Jo·se·phus \jō-'sē-fəs\ Flavius *about* 37–*about* 100 A.D. Jewish historian

Josh·ua \'jäsh-wə, -ə-wə\ Hebrew leader and successor of Moses during the settlement of the Israelites in Canaan

Jove \'jōv\ — see ZEUS

Joyce \'jȯis\ James 1882–1941 Irish author

Ju·dah \'jüd-ə\ son of Jacob; ancestor of one of the 12 tribes of Israel

Ju·das \'jüd-əs *or* **Judas Is·car·i·ot** \-is-'kar-ē-ət\ one of the 12 apostles; betrayer of Jesus

Ju·das Mac·ca·bae·us \'jud-ə-,smak-ə-'bē-əs\ *died* 161 B.C. Jewish patriot

Ju·lian \'jül-yən\ *about* 331–363 A.D. *the Apostate* Roman emperor (361–363)

Jung \'yùng\ Carl Gustav 1875–1961 Swiss psychologist

Ju·no \'jü-nō\ — see HERA

Ju·pi·ter \'jü-pət-ər\ — see ZEUS

Jus·tin·i·an I \,jə-'stin-ē-ən\ 483–565 A.D. *the Great* Byzantine emperor (527–565)

Ju·ve·nal \'jü-vən-l\ 55 to 60–*about* 127 A.D. Roman satirist

Kaf·ka \'käf-kə, 'kaf-\ Franz 1883–1924 Austrian author

Kalb \'kälp, 'kalb\ Johann 1721–80 Baron *de Kalb* \di-'kalb\ German general in American Revolutionary army

Kant \'kant, 'känt\ Immanuel 1724–1804 German philosopher

Keats \'kēts\ John 1795–1821 English poet

Kel·ler \'kel-ər\ Helen Adams 1880–1968 American deaf and blind lecturer

Kel·vin \'kel-vən\ 1st Baron 1824–1907 *William Thomson* British mathematician and physicist

Kempis Thomas a — see THOMAS A KEMPIS

Ken·ne·dy \'ken-əd-ē\ John Fitzgerald 1917–63 35th president of the United States (1961–63)

Kennedy Robert Francis 1925–68 attorney general of the United States (1961–64); brother of John F. Kennedy

Ke·o·kuk \'kē-ə-,kək\ 1788–?1848 American Indian chief

Kep·ler \'kep-lər\ Johannes 1571–1630 German astronomer

Ke·ren·ski \'ker-ən-skē\ Aleksandr Feodorovich 1881–1970 Russian revolutionist

Key \'kē\ Francis Scott 1779–1843 American lawyer; author of "The Star-Spangled Banner"

Keynes \'kānz\ 1st Baron 1883–1946 *John Maynard Keynes* English economist — **Keynes·ian** \'kān-zē-ən\ *adj or n*

Khayyám Omar — see OMAR KHAYYÁM

Khru·shchev \krùsh-'chȯf, -'ȯf, -'chȯv, -'ȯv, -'chef, -'ef, 'krüsh-\ Ni·ki·ta \nə-'kēt-ə\ Sergeevich 1894–1971 premier of U.S.S.R. (1958–64)

Khu·fu \'kü-,fü\ *or Greek* **Che·ops** \'kē-,äps\ 26th century B.C. king of Egypt and pyramid builder

Kidd \'kid\ William *about* 1645–1701 *Captain Kidd* Scottish pirate

Kier·ke·gaard \'kir-kə-,gärd, -,gär, -,gȯr\ Sören Aabye 1813–55 Danish philosopher and theologian

King \'king\ Ernest Joseph 1878–1956 American admiral

King Martin Luther, Jr. 1929–68 American clergyman and civil rights leader; Nobel prize winner (1964)

Kip·ling \'kip-ling\ Rud·yard \'rəd-yərd, 'rȧj-ərd\ 1865–1936 English author

Kis·sin·ger \'kis-n-jər\ Henry Alfred 1923– American (German-born) scholar and government official; United States secretary of state (1973–77); Nobel prize winner (1973)

Klee \'klā\ Paul 1879–1940 Swiss painter

Knox \'näks\ John *about* 1514–72 Scottish religious reformer

Koch \'kȯk, 'kȯk, 'kōk, 'kōk, 'käk, 'käk\ Robert 1843–1910 German bacteriologist; Nobel prize winner (1905)

\ə\ abut		\ng\ sing	
\ər\ further		\ō\ bone	
\a\ mat		\ȯ\ saw	
\ā\ take		\ȯi\ coin	
\ä\ cot, cart		\th\ thin	
\aù\ out		\th\ this	
\ch\ chin		\ü\ food	
\e\ pet		\ù\ foot	
\ē\ easy		\y\ yet	
\g\ go		\yù\ few	
\i\ tip		\yù\ cure	
\ī\ life		\zh\ vision	
\j\ job			

Kohl \\'kōl\\ Helmut 1930– chancellor of Germany (1990–)

Kos·ciusz·ko \\,käs-ē-'əs-,kō, kȯsh-'chúsh-kō\\ Thaddeus 1746–1817 Polish general in American Revolutionary army

Krish·na \\'krish-nə\\ deity or deified hero of later Hinduism worshiped as an incarnation of Vishnu

Kriss Kringle — see SANTA CLAUS

Ku·blai Khan \\,kü-blə-'kän, -,blī-\\ 1215–94 founder of Mongol dynasty in China; grandson of Genghis Khan

La·fa·yette, de \\,läf-ē-'et, ,laf-\\ Marquis 1757–1834 French general in American Revolutionary army

La Fon·taine, de \\lə-,fän-'tän, -,fōⁿ-'ten\\ Jean 1621–95 French writer of fables

La·ius \\'lā-əs, 'lī-\\ king of Thebes slain by his son Oedipus

La·marck, de \\lə-'märk\\ Chevalier 1744–1829 French naturalist

Lamb \\'lam\\ Charles 1775–1834 English author

Lan·ce·lot \\'lan-sə-,lät\\ knight of the Round Table and lover of Queen Guinevere in Arthurian legend

Lang·land \\'lang-lənd\\ William *about* 1330–*about* 1400 English poet

Lang·ley \\'lang-lē\\ Samuel Pierpont 1834–1906 American astronomer and airplane pioneer

La·oc·o·ön \\lā-'äk-ə-,wän\\ Trojan priest killed with his two sons by sea serpents after warning the Trojans against the wooden horse

Lao-tzu *or* **Lao-tse** *or* **Lao-tze** \\'laúd-'zə\\ 6th century B.C. Chinese philosopher; founder of Taoism

La·place, de \\lə-'pläs\\ Marquis Pierre Simon 1749–1827 French astronomer and mathematician

La Roche·fou·cauld, de \\lä-,rȯsh-,fü-'kō, -,rȯsh-\\ Duc François 1613–80 French author and moralist

La Salle, de \\lə-'sal\\ Sieur 1643–87 French explorer in North America

La·voi·sier \\ləv-'wäz-ē-,ā\\ Antoine Laurent 1743–94 French chemist

Law·rence \\'lȯr-əns, 'lär-\\ David Herbert 1885–1930 English author

Lawrence Sir Thomas 1769–1830 English painter

Lawrence Thomas Edward 1888–1935 *Lawrence of Arabia* British archaeologist, soldier, and author

Laz·a·rus \\'laz-rəs, -ə-rəs\\ brother of Mary and Martha raised by Jesus from the dead

Lazarus beggar in the biblical parable of the rich man and the beggar

Le·an·der \\lē-'an-dər\\ youth in Greek mythology who swims the Hellespont nightly to visit his lover Hero

Le·da \\'lēd-ə\\ Spartan princess in Greek mythology who is visited by Zeus in the form of a swan

Lee \\'lē\\ Ann 1736–84 English mystic; founder of Shaker society in the United States

Lee Henry 1756–1818 *Light-Horse Harry* American general

Lee Robert Edward 1807–70 American Confederate general; son of Henry Lee

Leeu·wen·hoek *or* **Leu·wen·hoek, van** \\'lā-vən-,húk\\ Anton 1632–1723 Dutch naturalist

Leib·niz *or* **Leib·nitz, von** \\'līb-nəts, 'līp-nits\\ Baron Gottfried Wilhelm 1646–1716 German philosopher and mathematician

Leif Er·ic·son \\'lā-,ver-ik-sən, 'lē-'fer-\\ *flourished* 1000 Norwegian mariner; son of Eric the Red

Le·nin \\'len-ən\\ V. I. 1870–1924 *Vladimir Ilyich Ul·ya·nov* \\úl-'yän-əf, -,ȯf, -,ȯv\\ Russian Communist leader

Leo \\'lē-ō\\ name of 13 popes: especially I Saint *died* 461 A.D. (pope 440–461); III Saint *died* 816 A.D. (pope 795–816); XIII 1810–1903 (pope 1878–1903)

Leonardo da Vinci — see VINCI

Le·on·ca·val·lo \\,lā-,ōn-kə-'väl-ō\\ Ruggiero 1858–1919 Italian composer and librettist

Le·on·i·das \\lē-'än-əd-əs\\ *died* 480 B.C. Greek hero; king of Sparta (490?–480)

Lep·i·dus \\'lep-əd-əs\\ Marcus Aemilius *died* 13 (or 12) B.C. Roman triumvir

Le·to \\'lēt-ō\\ mother of Apollo and Artemis by Zeus

Le·vi \\'lē-,vī\\ son of Jacob; ancestor of one of the 12 tribes of Israel

Lew·is \\'lü-əs\\ John Llewellyn 1880–1969 American labor leader

Lewis Meriwether 1774–1809 American explorer (with William Clark)

Lewis (Harry) Sinclair 1885–1951 American author; Nobel prize winner (1930)

Lin·coln \\'ling-kən\\ Abraham 1809–65 16th president of the United States (1861–65)

Lind·bergh \\'lind-,bərg, 'lin-\\ Charles Augustus 1902–74 American aviator

Lin·nae·us \\lə-'nē-əs, -'nā-\\ Carolus 1707–78 *Carl von Lin·né* \\lə-'nā\\ Swedish botanist

Lip·pi \\'lip-ē\\ Fra Fi·lip·po \\fə-'lip-ō\\ *or* Lip·po \\'lip-ō\\ *about* 1406–69 Florentine painter

Lis·ter \\'lis-tər\\ Joseph 1827–1912 English surgeon

Liszt \\'list\\ Franz 1811–86 Hungarian pianist and composer

Liv·ing·stone \\'liv-ing-stən\\ David 1813–73 Scottish explorer in Africa

Livy \\'liv-ē\\ 59 B.C.–17 A.D. Roman historian

Lloyd George \\'lȯid-'jȯrj\\ David 1863–1945 1st Earl of *Dwy·for* \\'dü-ē-,vȯr\\ British prime minister (1916–22)

Locke \\'läk\\ John 1632–1704 English philosopher

Lo·hen·grin \\'lō-ən-,grin\\ son of Parsifal and knight of the Holy Grail in German legend

Long·fel·low \\'lȯng-,fel-ō\\ Henry Wads·worth \\'wädz-wərth, -,wərth\\ 1807–82 American poet

Lo·re·lei \\'lōr-ə-,lī, 'lȯr-\\ siren in German legend whose beauty and song lured sailors to destruction on a reef in the Rhine

Lot \\'lät\\ nephew of Abraham in biblical tradition whose wife was turned into a pillar of salt for looking back during their flight from Sodom

Lou·is \\'lü-ē, 'lü-əs\\ name of 18 kings of France: especially IX Saint 1214–70 (reigned 1226–70); XI 1423–83 (reigned 1461–83); XII 1462–1515; (reigned 1498–1515); XIII 1601–43 (reigned 1610–43); XIV 1638–1715 (reigned 1643–1715); XV 1710–74 (reigned 1715–74); XVI 1754–93 (reigned 1774–92; guillotined); XVII 1785–95 (nominally reigned 1793–95); XVIII 1755–1824 (reigned 1814–15; 1815–24)

Louis Napoleon — see NAPOLEON III

Louis Phi·lippe \\fi-'lēp\\ 1773–1850 *the Citizen King* king of the French (1830–48)

Low·ell \\'lō-əl\\ Amy 1874–1925 American poet

Lowell James Russell 1819–91 American author

Loyola — see IGNATIUS

Lu·cre·tius \\lü-'krē-shē-əs, -shəs\\ *about* 96–*about* 55 B.C. Roman poet and philosopher

Luke \\'lük\\ physician and companion of the apostle Paul held to be the author of the third Gospel and of the Book of Acts

Lu·na \\'lü-nə\\ — see SELENE

Lu·ther \\'lü-thər\\ Martin 1483–1546 German Reformation leader

Ly·on \\'lī-ən\\ Mary 1797–1849 American educator

Lyt·ton \\'lit-n\\ 1st Baron 1803–73 *Edward George Earle Lytton Bul·wer-Lytton* \\,búl-wər-\\ English author

Mac·Ar·thur \\mə-'kär-thər\\ Douglas 1880–1964 American general

Ma·cau·lay \\mə-'kȯ-lē\\ Thomas Babington 1st Baron 1800–59 English author and statesman

Mc·Car·thy \\mə-'kärth-ē\\ Joseph Raymond 1908–57 American politician

Mc·Clel·lan \\mə-'klel-ən\\ George Brinton 1826–85 American general

Mc·Cor·mick \\mə-'kȯr-mik\\ Cyrus Hall 1809–84 American inventor of a mechanical reaper

Mc·Cul·lers \mə-'kəl-ərz\ Carson 1917–67 née *Smith* American writer

Ma·chi·a·vel·li \,mak-ē-ə-'vel-ē\ Niccolò 1469–1527 Italian political philosopher

Mc·Kin·ley \mə-'kin-lē\ William 1843–1901 25th president of the United States (1897–1901)

Mad·i·son \'mad-ə-sen\ James 1751–1836 4th president of the United States (1809–17)

Mae·ter·linck \'māt-ər-,lingk *also* 'met-, 'mat-\ Count Maurice 1862–1949 Belgian author

Ma·gel·lan \mə-'jel-ən\ Ferdinand *about* 1480–1521 Portuguese navigator

Mah·ler \'mäl-ər\ Gustav 1860–1911 Austrian composer

Mahomet *or* **Mahomed** — see MUHAMMAD

Ma·jor \'mā-jər\ John 1943–   prime minister of Great Britain (1990–   )

Mal·a·chi \'mal-ə-,kī\ Hebrew prophet of the 5th century B.C.

Malcolm X \,mal-kə-'meks\ 1925–65 American civil rights leader

Mal·o·ry \'mal-rē, -ə-rē\ Sir Thomas *flourished* 1470 English author

Mal·thus \'mal-thəs\ Thomas Robert 1766–1834 English economist

Man·dela \man-'del-ə\ Nelson Rolihlahla 1918– South African black political leader

Ma·net \ma-'nā, mä-\ Édouard 1832–83 French painter

Mann \'man\ Horace 1796–1859 American educator

Mann \'män, 'man\ Thomas 1875–1955 American (German-born) author; Nobel prize winner (1929)

Mao Tse-tung \,maud-zə-'dung, ,maù-zə-, ,maùt-sə-\ 1893–1976 Chinese Communist leader

Ma·rat \mə-'rä\ Jean Paul 1743–93 French (Swiss-born) revolutionist; assassinated

Mar·co·ni \mär-'kō-nē\ Marchese Guglielmo 1874–1937 Italian electrical engineer and inventor; Nobel prize winner (1909)

Marcus Aurelius — see ANTONINUS

Ma·ria The·re·sa \mə-,rē-ə-tə-'rā-sə, -'rā-zə\ 1717–80 wife of Emperor Francis I; queen of Hungary and Bohemia

Ma·rie An·toi·nette \mə-'rē-,an-twə-'net, -tə-'net\ 1755–93 daughter of Maria Theresa and wife of Louis XVI of France

Mark \'märk\ evangelist held to be the author of the 2d Gospel

Mar·lowe \'mär-,lō\ Christopher 1564–93 English dramatist

Mar·quette \mär-'ket\ Jacques 1637–75 *Père* \,piər, ,pear\ *Marquette* Jesuit missionary and explorer in America

Mars \'märz\ — see ARES

Mar·shall \'mär-shəl\ George Catlett 1880–1959 American general and diplomat

Marshall John 1755–1835 American jurist; chief justice of the United States Supreme Court (1801–35)

Marshall Thurgood 1908–93 American jurist

Martel Charles — see CHARLES MARTEL

Mar·tha \'mär-thə\ sister of Lazarus and Mary and friend of Jesus

Mar·tial \'mär-shəl\ *about* 40–*about* 103 A.D. Roman epigrammatist

Mar·tin \'märt-n, mär·'ta\ Saint *about* 316–397 A.D. *Martin of Tours* \-'túr\ a patron saint of France

Marx \'märks\ Karl 1818–83 German political philosopher and socialist

Mary \'meər-ē, 'maər-ē, 'mā-rē\ mother of Jesus

Mary sister of Lazarus and Martha

Mary I 1516–58 *Mary Tudor; Bloody Mary* queen of England (1553–58)

Mary II 1662–94 joint British sovereign with William III (1689–94)

Mary Mag·da·lene \,-'mag-də-,lēn, -,mag-də-'lē-nē\ woman healed of evil spirits by Jesus; identified with the repentant sinner who anointed Jesus' feet

Mary Stuart 1542–87 *Mary, Queen of Scots* queen of Scotland (1542–67; beheaded)

Ma·sca·gni \mä-'skän-yē, ma-\ Pietro 1863–1945 Italian composer

Mase·field \'mās-,fēld\ John 1878–1967 English author

Mason \'mās-n\ George 1725–1792 American statesman

Mas·sa·soit \,mas-ə-'sóit\ *died* 1661 Indian chief in eastern Massachusetts

Mas·se·net \,mas-n-'ā, ma-'snā\ Jules Émile Frédéric 1842–1912 French composer

Math·er \'math-ər, 'math-\ Cotton 1663–1728 American clergyman and author

Mather Increase 1639–1723 American clergyman and author; father of Cotton Mather

Ma·tisse \ma-'tēs, mə-\ Henri 1869–1954 French painter

Mat·thew \'math-yü\ one of the 12 apostles; held to be the author of the first gospel

Maugham \'móm\ William Somerset 1874–1965 English author

Mau·pas·sant, de \,mō-pə-'sä\ (Henri René Albert) Guy 1850–93 French author

Max·i·mil·ian \,mak-sə-'mil-yən\ 1832–67 emperor of Mexico (1864–67); brother of Francis Joseph I

Maximilian I 1459–1519 Holy Roman emperor (1493–1519)

Maximilian II 1527–76 Holy Roman emperor (1564–76)

Max·well \'mak-,swel, -swəl\ James Clerk \'klärk\ 1831–79 Scottish physicist

Ma·za·rin \,maz-ə-'ra\ Jules 1602–61 French cardinal and statesman

Maz·zi·ni \mät-'sē-nē, mäd-'zē-\ Giuseppe 1805–72 Italian patriot and revolutionist

Mead Margaret 1901–78 American anthropologist

Mea·ny \'mē-nē\ George 1894–1980 American labor leader

Me·dea \mə-'dē-ə\ enchantress in Greek mythology who helps Jason to win the Golden Fleece and kills her children when he deserts her

Me·di·ci, de' \'med-ə-chē\ Catherine 1519–89 *Catherine de Médicis* \,mād-ə-'sē, -'sēs\ queen of Henry II of France

Medici, de' Lorenzo 1449–92 *Lorenzo the Magnificent* Florentine ruler, statesman, and patron of the arts

Me·du·sa \mi-'dü-sə, -'dyü-, -zə\ a Gorgon slain by Perseus

Mel·pom·e·ne \mel-'päm-ə-nē\ Greek Muse of tragedy

Mel·ville \'mel-,vil\ Herman 1819–91 American author

Men·del \'men-dl\ Gregor Johann 1822–84 Austrian botanist and monk

Men·de·le·ev \,men-də-'lā-əf\ Dmitri Ivanovich 1834–1907 Russian chemist

Men·dels·sohn–Bar·thol·dy \'men-dl-sən-bär-'tòl-dē, -'thòl-\ Ludwig Felix 1809–47 German composer, pianist, and conductor

Men·e·la·us \,men-l-'ā-əs\ king of Sparta, brother of Agamemnon, and husband of Helen of Troy

Meph·is·toph·e·les \,mef-ə-'stäf-ə-,lēz\ a chief devil in the Faust legend

Mer·ca·tor \,mər-'kāt-ər\ Gerhardus 1512–94 Flemish geographer

Mer·cu·ry \'mər-kyə-rē, -kə-rē, -krē\ — see HERMES

Mere·e·dith \'mer-əd-əth\ George 1828–1909 English author

Mer·lin \'mər-lən\ prophet and magician in Arthurian legend

Me·tho·di·us \mə-'thōd-ē-əs\ Saint *about* 825–884 A.D. Apostle to the Slavs; brother of Cyril

Me·thu·se·lah \mə-'thüz-lə, -'thyüz-, -ə-lə\ Old Testament patriarch held to have lived 969 years

Met·ter·nich, von \'met-ər-nik, -nik\ Prince Klemens Wenzel Nepomuk Lothar 1773–1859 Austrian statesman

\ə\	abut	\ng\	sing
\ər\	further	\ō\	bone
\a\	mat	\ó\	saw
\ā\	take	\ói\	coin
\ä\	cot, cart	\th\	thin
\aù\	out	\th̲\	this
\ch\	chin	\ü\	food
\e\	pet	\ù\	foot
\ē\	easy	\y\	yet
\g\	go	\yü\	few
\i\	tip	\yù\	cure
\ī\	life	\zh\	vision
\j\	job		

Mey•er•beer \'mī-ər-ˌbiər, -ˌbeər\ Giacomo 1791–1864 German composer

Mi•cah \'mī-kə\ Hebrew prophet of the 8th century B.C.

Mi•chael \'mī-kəl\ one of the four archangels named in Hebrew tradition; cast Satan and his followers out of heaven — compare GABRIEL, RAPHAEL, URIEL

Mi•chel•an•ge•lo Buo•nar•ro•ti \ˌmī-kə-'lan-jə-ˌlō-ˌbwȯn-ə-'rȯt-ē, ˌmik-ə-'lan-, ˌmē-kə-'län-\ 1475–1564 Italian sculptor, painter, architect, and poet

Mich•e•ner \'mich-nər, -ə-nər\ James Albert 1907– American author

Mi•das \'mīd-əs\ legendary king of Phrygia having the power to turn everything he touched into gold

Mil•lay \mil-'ā\ Edna St. Vincent 1892–1950 American poet

Mil•ler \'mil-ər\ Arthur 1915– American author

Mil•let \mē-'yā, mi-'lā\ Jean François 1814–75 French painter

Mil•li•kan \'mil-i-kən\ Robert Andrew 1868–1953 American physicist; Nobel prize winner (1923)

Milne \'miln, 'mil\ Alan Alexander 1882–1956 English author

Mil•ti•ades \mil-'tī-ə-ˌdēz\ *about* 544–?489 B.C. Athenian general

Mil•ton \'milt-n\ John 1608–74 English poet

Mi•ner•va \mə-'nər-və\ — see ATHENE

Mi•nos \'mī-nəs\ king and lawgiver of Crete; son of Zeus and Europa; after death a judge in Hades

Min•o•taur \'min-ə-ˌtȯr, 'mī-nə-\ monster of Greek mythology shaped half like a man and half like a bull

Min•u•it \'min-yə-wət\ Peter 1580–1638 Dutch colonial administrator in America

Mi•ró \mē-'rō\ Joan \zhu̇-'än\ 1893–1983 Spanish painter

Mitch•ell \'mich-əl\ Maria 1818–89 American astronomer

Mith•ras \'mith-rəs\ Persian god of light who was the savior hero of an oriental mystery cult for men flourishing in the late Roman empire — **Mith•ra•ic** \mith-'rā-ik\ *adj* — **Mith•ra•ism** \'mith-rə-ˌiz-əm\ *n* — **Mith•ra•ist** \mith-'rā-əst, 'mith-rā-ˌist\ *n*

Mit•ter•rand \ˌmē-ter-'äⁿ\ François-Maurice 1916– president of France (1981–)

Mne•mos•y•ne \ni-'mäs-n-ē\ Greek goddess of memory and mother of the Muses by Zeus

Mo•dred \'mō-drəd, 'mäd-rəd\ knight of the Round Table and rebellious nephew of King Arthur

Mohammed — see MUHAMMAD

Mo•lière \mōl-'yeər, 'mōl-ˌ\ 1622–73 pseudonym of *Jean Baptist Poque•lin* \pō-'klaⁿ, -kə-'laⁿ\ French actor and dramatist

Mol•och \'mäl-ək, 'mō-ˌläk\ *or* **Mol•ech** \'mäl-ək, 'mō-ˌlek\ a Semitic deity worshiped through the sacrifice of children

Mo•lo•tov \'mäl-ə-ˌtȯf, 'mȯl-, 'mōl-, -ˌtȯv\ Vyacheslav Mikhailovich 1890–1986 Russian statesman

Mo•net \mō-'nā\ Claude 1840–1926 French painter

Mon•roe \mən-'rō\ James 1758–1831 5th president of the United States (1817–25)

Mon•taigne, de \män-'tān, mōⁿ-'tenʸ\ Michel Eyquem 1533–92 French essayist

Mont•calm de Saint–Véran, de \mänt-'käm-də-ˌsaⁿ-vā-'räⁿ, -'kälm-\ Marquis Louis Joseph 1712–59 French field marshal in Canada

Mon•tes•quieu, de \ˌmänt-əs-'kyü, -'kyər, -'kyœ̄\ Baron de La Brède et 1689–1755 French political philosopher

Mon•tes•so•ri \ˌmänt-ə-'sōr-ē, -'sȯr-\ Maria 1870–1952 Italian physician and educator

Mon•te•ver•di \ˌmänt-ə-'veərd-ē, -'vərd-\ Claudio Giovanni Antonio 1567–1643 Italian composer

Mon•te•zu•ma II \ˌmänt-ə-'zü-mə\ 1466–1520 last Aztec emperor of Mexico (1502–20)

Moore \'mōr, 'mȯr, 'mu̇r\ Marianne Craig 1887–1972 American poet

Moore Thomas 1779–1852 Irish poet

Mor•de•cai \'mȯrd-i-ˌkī\ cousin of Esther who saved the Jews from the destruction planned by Haman

More \'mōr, 'mȯr\ Sir Thomas 1478–1535 *Saint* English statesman and author

Mor•gan \'mȯr-gən\ Sir Henry 1635–88 English buccaneer

Morgan John Pierpont 1837–1913 American financier

Mor•pheus \'mȯr-fē-əs, -ˌfyüs, -ˌfüs\ Greek god of dreams

Mor•ris \'mȯr-əs, 'mär-\ William 1834–1896 English poet, artist, and socialist

Morse \'mȯrs\ Samuel Finley Breese 1791–1872 American artist and inventor of the electrical telegraph

Mo•ses \'mō-zəz *also* -zəs\ Hebrew prophet and lawgiver and liberator of the Israelites from Egypt

Moses Anna Mary 1860–1961 *Grandma Moses* American painter

Mo•zart \'mōt-ˌsärt\ Wolfgang Amadeus 1756–91 Austrian composer

Mu•bar•ak \mu̇-'bär-ək\ Muhammad Hosni 1929– president of Egypt (1981–)

Mu•ham•mad \mō-'ham-əd, -'häm- *also* mü-\ *or* **Mo•ham•med** \mō-'häm-əd\ *also* **Ma•ho•met** \mə-'häm-ət, 'mä-ə-mət\ *or* **Ma•hom•ed** \mə-'häm-əd\ *about* 570–632 A.D. Arab prophet and founder of Islam

Muir \'myu̇r\ John 1838–1914 American (Scottish-born) naturalist

Mul•ro•ney \məl-'rü-nē\ (Martin) Brian 1939– prime minister of Canada (1984–)

Mus•so•li•ni \ˌmü-sə-'lē-nē, ˌmu̇s-ə-\ Be•ni•to \bə-'nēt-ō\ 1883–1945 *Il Du•ce* \ēl-'dü-chā\ Italian premier (1922–43)

My•ron \'mī-rən\ *flourished about* 480–440 B.C. Greek sculptor

Na•bo•kov \nə-'bȯ-kəf, -ˌkȯf\ Vladimir Vladimirovich 1899–1977 American (Russian-born) author

Na•hum \'nā-əm, -həm\ Hebrew prophet of the 7th century B.C.

Na•o•mi \nā-'ō-mē\ mother-in-law of the Old Testament heroine Ruth

Na•pier \'nā-pē-ər, -ˌpiər; nə-'piər\ John 1550–1617 *Laird of Mer•chis•ton* \'mər-kə-stən\ Scottish mathematician

Na•po•leon I \nə-'pōl-yən, -'pō-lē-ən\ *or* **Napoleon Bo•na•parte** \'bō-nə-ˌpärt\ 1769–1821 emperor of the French (1804–15) — **Na•po•le•on•ic** \nə-ˌpō-lē-'än-ik\ *adj*

Napoleon III 1808–73 *Louis Napoleon* emperor of the French (1852–71); son of Louis Bonaparte and nephew of Napoleon I

Nar•cis•sus \när-'sis-əs\ beautiful youth in Greek legend punished by being made to pine away for love of his own image and transformed into the narcissus

Nas•ser \'näs-ər, 'nas-\ Ga•mal \gə-'mäl\ Ab•del \'ab-dl\ 1918–70 Egyptian politician; president of Egypt (1956–70)

Na•tion \'nā-shən\ Car•ry \'kar-ē\ Amelia 1846–1911 American social reformer

Neb•u•chad•nez•zar \ˌneb-yə-kəd-'nez-ər, ˌneb-ə-kəd-\ *also* **Neb•u•cha•drez•zar** \-kə-'drez-\ *about* 630–562 B.C. king of Babylon (605–562) B.C.; conqueror of Jerusalem

Ne•he•mi•ah \ˌnē-ə-'mī-ə, ˌnē-hə-\ Hebrew leader of the 5th century B.C.

Neh•ru \'neər-ˌü, 'nā-ˌrü\ Ja•wa•har•lal \jə-'wä-hər-ˌläl\ 1889–1964 Indian nationalist; 1st prime minister (1947–64)

Nel•son \'nel-sən\ Horatio Viscount 1758–1805 British admiral

Nem•e•sis \'nem-ə-səs\ Greek goddess of retributive justice

Nep•tune \'nep-ˌtün, -ˌtyün\ — see POSEIDON

Ne•ro \'nē-ˌrō, 'niər-ˌō\ 37–68 A.D. Roman emperor (54–68)

Nes·tor \'nes-tər\ aged and wise counselor of the Greeks in the Trojan War

New·man \'nü-mən, 'nyü-\ John Henry 1801–90 English cardinal and author

New·ton \'nüt-n, 'nyüt-\ Sir Isaac 1642–1727 English mathematician and physicist

Nich·o·las \'nik-ləs, -ə-ləs\ Saint 4th century A.D. bishop of Myra, Asia Minor; patron saint of children — see SANTA CLAUS

Nicholas I 1796–1855 czar of Russia (1825–55)

Nicholas II 1868–1918 czar of Russia (1894–1917)

Nietz·sche \'nē-chə, -chē\ Friedrich Wilhelm 1844–1900 German philosopher

Night·in·gale \'nīt-n-,gāl, -ing-\ Florence 1820–1910 English nurse and philanthropist

Ni·jin·sky \nə-'zhin-skē, -'jin-\ Was·law \'vät-släf\ 1890–1950 Russian dancer

Ni·ke \'nī-kē\ Greek goddess of victory usually represented as winged and as carrying a wreath and a palm branch

Nim·itz \'nim-əts\ Chester William 1885–1966 American admiral

Nim·rod \'nim-,räd\ mighty hunter and ruler described in the Old Testament

Ni·o·be \'nī-ə-bē, nī-'ō-bē\ legendary Theban queen whose boasting impels the gods to slay her children and who is turned into a stone from which her tears continue to flow

Nix·on \'nik-sən\ Richard Mil·hous \'mil-,haús\ 1913– 37th president of the United States (1969–74)

No·ah \'nō-ə\ Old Testament patriarch and builder of the ark in which he, his family, and living creatures of every kind survived the Flood

No·bel \nō-'bel\ Alfred Bernhard 1833–96 Swedish manufacturer, inventor, and philanthropist

Nos·tra·da·mus \,näs-trə-'dā-məs, ,nōs-trə-'däm-əs\ 1503–66 French physician and astrologer

Noyes \'noiz\ Alfred 1880–1958 English poet

Oba·di·ah \,ō-bə-'dī-ə\ Hebrew prophet of Old Testament times

Ober·on \'ō-bə-,rän, -rən\ king of the fairies in medieval legend and in Shakespeare's *A Midsummer Night's Dream*

O'·Ca·sey \ō-'kā-sē\ Sean 1880–1964 Irish dramatist

Oce·anus \ō-'sē-ə-nəs\ god of the great outer sea that in Greek mythology encircles the earth

O'·Con·nor \ō-'kän-ər\ Sandra Day 1930– American jurist

Octavian — see AUGUSTUS

Odin \'ōd-n\ chief god in Norse mythology identified with Woden

Odys·seus \ō-'dish-,üs, -'dis-,yüs, -'dis-ē-əs\ *or* **Ulys·ses** \yü-'lis-ēz\ king of Ithaca and Greek leader in the Trojan War who after the war wanders 10 years before reaching home

Oe·di·pus \'ed-ə-pəs, 'ēd-\ son of the king and queen of Thebes who according to Greek legend unknowingly kills his father and marries his mother as foretold by an oracle

Of·fen·bach \'óf-ən-,bäk, -,bäk\ Jacques 1819–80 French composer

Ogle·thorpe \'ō-gəl-,thórp\ James Edward 1696–1785 English general and philanthropist; founder of Georgia

O'·Keeffe \ō-'kēf\ Georgia 1887–1986 American painter

Olaf I \'ō-ləf, -ləv\ *about* 964–1000 king of Norway (995–1000)

Olaf II 995?–1030 *Saint Olaf* king of Norway (1016–28)

Olav V 1903–91 king of Norway (1957–91)

Omar Khay·yám \,ō-,mär-,kī-'äm, -'yäm, -'am, -'yam\ 1048?–1122 Persian poet and astronomer

O'·Neill \ō-'nēl\ Eugene Gladstone 1888–1953 American dramatist; Nobel prize winner (1936)

Ores·tes \ə-'res-tēz, ò-\ son of Agamemnon and Clytemnestra who avenges his father's murder by slaying his mother and her lover

Or·pheus \'ór-,fyüs, -fē-əs\ poet and musician of Greek mythology who almost rescues his wife Eurydice from Hades by charming Pluto and Persephone with his lyre

Or·well \'ór-,wel, -wəl\ George 1903–50 pseudonym of *Eric Blair* English author — **Or·well·ian** \òr-'wel-ē-ən\ *adj*

Osce·o·la \,äs-ē-'ō-lə, ,ō-sē-\ *about* 1800–38 Seminole Indian chief

Osee \'ō-zē, ō-'zā-ə\ — see HOSEA

Osi·ris \ō-'sī-rəs\ great god of the underworld and judge of the dead in ancient Egyptian mythology

Otis \'ōt-əs\ James 1725–83 American Revolutionary statesman

Ot·to \'ät-ō\ 912–973 A.D. *the Great* Holy Roman emperor (936–973)

Ov·id \'äv-əd\ 43 B.C.–? 17 A.D. Roman poet

Ow·en \'ō-ən\ Robert 1771–1858 Welsh social reformer

Paine \'pān\ Thomas 1737–1809 American (English-born) political philosopher and author

Pa·le·stri·na \,pal-ə-'strē-nə\ Giovanni Pierluigi da *about* 1525–94 Italian composer

Pal·las \'pal-əs\ *or* **Pallas Athene** — see ATHENE

Pan \'pan\ Greek god of forests, pastures, flocks, and shepherds represented as having the legs and sometimes the ears and horns of a goat

Pan·da·rus \'pan-də-rəs\ procurer of Cressida for Troilus in medieval legend

Pan·do·ra \pan-'dōr-ə, -'dòr-\ woman to whom Zeus gave a box enclosing all human ills which escaped when she opened it

Par·a·cel·sus \,par-ə-'sel-səs\ Philippus Aureolus 1493–1541 Swiss-born alchemist and physician

Par·is \'par-əs\ son of Priam whose abduction of Helen of Troy led to the Trojan War

Park \'pärk\ Mungo 1771–1806 Scottish explorer of the Niger

Park·man \'pärk-mən\ Francis 1823–93 American historian

Parks \'pärks\ Rosa Lee 1913– American civil rights activist

Par·nell \pär-'nel\ Charles Stewart 1846–91 Irish nationalist

Par·si·fal \'pär-zi-,fäl, -sə-,fól\ knight of the Holy Grail

Pas·cal \pas-'kal, päs-kál\ Blaise 1623–62 French mathematician and philosopher

Pas·ter·nak \'pas-tər-,nak\ Boris Leonidovich 1890–1960 Russian author; Nobel prize winner (1958)

Pas·teur \pas-'tər\ Louis 1822–95 French chemist and microbiologist

Pat·rick \'pa-trik\ Saint 5th century A.D. bishop and patron saint of Ireland

Pa·tro·clus \pə-'trō-kləs, -'träk-ləs\ Greek slain in the Trojan War by Hector and avenged by his friend Achilles

Pat·ton \'pat-n\ George Smith 1885–1945 American general

Paul \'pól\ Saint *died between* 62 *and* 68 A.D. *apostle to the Gentiles* author of several New Testament epistles — **Paul·ine** \'pó-,līn\ *adj*

Paul name of 6 popes: especially **III** 1468–1549 (pope 1534–49); **V** 1552–1621 (pope 1605–21); **VI** (*Giovanni Battista Montini*) 1897–1978 (pope 1963–1978)

Paul Bun·yan \'pól-'bən-yən\ giant lumberjack in American folklore

Pau·ling \'pó-ling\ Linus Carl 1901– American chemist; Nobel prize winner (1954, 1962)

Pav·lov \'päv-,lóf, 'pav-, -,lòv\ Ivan Petrovich 1849–1936 Russian physiologist; Nobel prize winner (1904)

Pa·vlo·va \'pav-lə-və, pav-'lō-və\ Anna 1882–1931 Russian ballerina

Pea·ry \'piər-ē\ Robert Edwin 1856–1920 American explorer

Peg·a·sus \'peg-ə-səs\ winged horse in Greek mythology

\ə\ abut		\ng\ sing	
\ər\ further		\ō\ bone	
\a\ mat		\ò\ saw	
\ā\ take		\òi\ coin	
\ä\ cot, cart		\th\ thin	
\aú\ out		\th\ this	
\ch\ chin		\ü\ food	
\e\ pet		\ú\ foot	
\ē\ easy		\y\ yet	
\g\ go		\yü\ few	
\i\ tip		\yú\ cure	
\ī\ life		\zh\ vision	
\j\ job			

Pe·nel·o·pe \pə-'nel-ə-pē\ wife of Odysseus who waits faithfully for him during his 20 years' absence

Penn \'pen\ William 1644–1718 English Quaker; founder of Pennsylvania

Pepys \'pēps\ Samuel 1633–1703 English diarist

Per·ce·val \'pər-sə-vəl\ Arthurian knight who wins a sight of the Holy Grail

Per·i·cles \'per-ə-,klēz\ about 495–429 B.C. Athenian statesman

Per·ry \'per-ē\ Matthew Calbraith 1794–1858 American commodore

Perry Oliver Hazard 1785–1819 American naval officer; brother of Matthew Perry

Per·seph·o·ne \pər-'sef-ə-nē\ or **Pro·ser·pi·na** \prə-'sər-pə-nə\ or **Pros·er·pine** \'präs-ər-,pīn\ daughter of Zeus and Demeter; abducted by Pluto and made his wife and queen

Per·seus \'pər-,süs, -sē-əs\ son of Zeus and Danaë; slayer of Medusa

Per·shing \'pər-shing, -zhing\ John Joseph 1860–1948 American general

Pé·tain \pā-'taⁿ\ Henri Philippe 1856–1951 French general; marshal of France; premier of Vichy France (1940–44)

Pe·ter \'pēt-ər\ Saint died about 64 A.D. Si·mon Peter \'sī-mən-\ fisherman chosen to become one of the 12 apostles

Peter I 1672–1725 the Great czar of Russia (1682–1725)

Peter the Hermit about 1050–1115 French preacher of the 1st Crusade

Pe·trarch \'pē-,trärk, 'pe-\ Francesco Pe·trar·ca \pā-'trär-kə\ 1304–74 Italian poet — **Pe·trarch·an** \pē-'trär-kən, pe-\ adj

Phae·dra \'fē-drə\ daughter of Minos and wife of Theseus; hanged herself after her stepson Hippolytus resisted her advances

Pha·ë·thon \'fā-ət-n; 'fā-ə-tən, -,thän\ son of Helios permitted for a day to drive the chariot of the sun and struck down with a thunderbolt by Zeus to keep the world from being set on fire

Phid·i·as \'fid-ē-əs\ flourished about 490–430 B.C. Greek sculptor

Phil·ip \'fil-əp\ Saint; one of the 12 apostles

Philip 1639?–1676 American Indian chief

Philip name of 6 kings of France: especially **II** or **Philip Augustus** 1165–1223 (reigned 1179–1223); **IV** 1268–1314 (reigned 1285–1314) the Fair; **VI** 1293–1350 (reigned 1328–50)

Philip name of 5 kings of Spain: especially **II** 1527–98 (reigned 1556–98); **V** 1683–1746 (reigned 1700–24; 1724–46)

Philip II 382–336 B.C. king of Macedon (359–336); father of Alexander the Great

Philip Prince 1921–   consort of Elizabeth II of Great Britain; 3d Duke of Edinburgh (from 1947)

Phoebe — see ARTEMIS

Phoebus — see APOLLO

Pi·cas·so \pi-'käs-ō, -'kas-\ Pablo 1881–1973 Spanish painter and sculptor in France

Pick·ett \'pik-ət\ George Edward 1825–75 American Confederate general

Pierce \'piərs\ Franklin 1804–69 14th president of the United States (1853–57)

Pilate — see PONTIUS PILATE

Pin·dar \'pin-dər, -,där\ about 522–438 B.C. Greek poet

Pi·ran·del·lo \,pir-ən-'del-ō\ Luigi 1867–1936 Italian author; Nobel prize winner (1934)

Pi·sis·tra·tus or **Pei·sis·tra·tus** \pī-'sis-trət-əs, pə-\ died 527 B.C. tyrant of Athens

Pitt \'pit\ William 1708–78 Earl of Chatham; English statesman

Pitt William 1759–1806 English prime minister (1783–1801; 1804–06); son of the preceding

Pi·us \'pī-əs\ name of 12 popes: especially **VII** 1742–1823 (pope 1800–23); **IX** 1792–1878 (pope 1846–78); **X** 1835–1914 (pope 1903–14); **XI** 1857–1939 (pope 1922–39); **XII** 1876–1958 (pope 1939–58)

Pi·zar·ro \pə-'zär-ō\ Francisco about 1475–1541 Spanish conqueror of Peru

Planck \'plängk\ Max Karl Ernst Ludwig 1858–1947 German physicist; Nobel prize winner (1918)

Pla·to \'plāt-ō\ about 428–348 (or 347) B.C. Greek philosopher

Plau·tus \'plot-əs\ Titus Maccius about 254–184 B.C. Roman dramatist

Pliny \'plin-ē\ 23–79 A.D. the Elder Roman scholar

Pliny 61 (or 62)–about 113 A.D. the Younger Roman author; nephew of the preceding

Plu·tarch \'plü-,tärk\ about 46–after 119 A.D. Greek biographer

Plu·to \'plüt-ō\ god of the dead and the lower world in Greek mythology whose Roman counterpart is Dis

Po·ca·hon·tas \,pō-kə-'hänt-əs\ about 1595–1617 American Indian princess reputed to have saved the life of Captain John Smith; daughter of Powhatan

Poe \'pō\ Edgar Allan 1809–49 American author

Polk \'pōk\ James Knox 1795–1849 11th president of the United States (1845–49)

Pol·lux \'päl-əks\ immortal twin of Castor in classical mythology

Po·lo \'pō-lō\ Mar·co \'mär-kō\ 1254–1324 Italian merchant who traveled to Asia

Pol·y·hym·nia \,päl-i-'him-nē-ə\ Greek Muse of sacred song and later of learning

Poly·phe·mus \,päl-ə-'fē-məs\ Cyclops whom Odysseus blinded in order to escape from his cave

Pom·pa·dour, de \'päm-pə-,dōr, -,dȯr, -,dūr\ Marquise 1721–64 mistress of Louis XV of France

Pom·pey \'päm-pē\ 106–48 B.C. the Great Roman general and statesman

Ponce de Le·ón \,päns-də-'lē-ən, ,pän-sə-,dā-lē-'ōn\ Juan 1460–1521 Spanish explorer; discovered Florida (1513)

Pon·ti·ac \'pänt-ē-,ak\ about 1720–1769 Ottawa Indian chief

Pon·tius Pi·late \,pän-chəs-'pī-lət, ,pən-\ died after 36 A.D. Roman procurator of Judea; tried and condemned Jesus

Pope \'pōp\ Alexander 1688–1744 English poet

Por·ter \'pōrt-ər, 'pȯrt-\ Cole Albert 1891–1964 American composer and songwriter

Porter David Dixon 1813–1891 American admiral

Porter Katherine Anne 1890–1980 American author

Porter William Sydney 1862–1910 pseudonym O. Hen·ry \ō-'hen-rē, 'ō-\ American author

Po·sei·don \pə-'sīd-n\ Greek god of the sea whose Roman counterpart is Neptune

Pot·ter \'pät-ər\ Beatrix 1866–1943 British author and illustrator

Pound \'paund\ Ezra Loomis 1885–1972 American poet

Pow·ha·tan \,pau-ə-'tan, pau-'hat-n\ 1550?–1618 American Indian chief; father of Pocahontas

Prax·it·e·les \prak-'sit-l-,ēz\ flourished 370–330 B.C. Athenian sculptor

Pri·am \'prī-əm, -,am\ king of Troy during the Trojan War; father of Hector and Paris

Priest·ley \'prēst-lē\ Joseph 1733–1804 English clergyman and chemist

Pro·crus·tes \prə-'krəs-tēz, pə-, prō-\ robber in Greek mythology who forces travelers to fit one of two unequally long beds by stretching their bodies or cutting off their legs

Pro·kof·iev \prə-'kȯf-yəf, -,yef, -,yev\ Sergei Sergeevich 1891–1953 Russian composer

Pro·me·theus \prə-'mē-thyüs, -,thüs, -thē-əs\ Titan tortured by Zeus for stealing fire from heaven as a gift to the human race

Proserpina or **Proserpine** — see PERSEPHONE

Pro·tag·o·ras \prō-'tag-ə-rəs\ *about* 485–410 B.C. Greek philosopher and teacher

Pro·teus \'prō-,tyüs, -,tüs; 'prōt-ē-əs\ Greek sea god capable of assuming different forms

Proust \'prüst\ Marcel 1871–1922 French novelist

Psy·che \'sī-kē\ beautiful princess in classical mythology loved by Cupid

Ptol·e·my \'täl-ə-mē\ name of 15 kings of Egypt: especially **I** 367 (or 366 or 364)–283 (or 282) B.C. (reigned 323–285); **II** 308–246 B.C. (reigned 285–246)

Ptolemy 2d century A.D. Alexandrian astronomer, geographer, and mathematician

Puc·ci·ni \pü-'chē-nē\ Giacomo 1858–1924 Italian composer

Puck — see ROBIN GOODFELLOW

Pu·las·ki \pə-'las-kē, pyü-\ Casimir 1747–79 Polish soldier in American Revolution

Pu·lit·zer \'pùl-ət-sər, 'pyü-lət-sər\ Joseph 1847–1911 American (Hungarian-born) journalist

Push·kin \'pùsh-kən\ Aleksander Sergeevich 1799–1837 Russian author

Pyg·ma·lion \pig-'māl-yən, -'mā-lē-ən\ sculptor and king of Cyprus — see GALATEA

Pyr·a·mus \'pir-ə-məs\ legendary Babylonian youth who dies for the love of Thisbe

Py·thag·o·ras \pə-'thag-ə-rəs, pī-\ *about* 580–*about* 500 B.C. Greek philosopher and mathematician

Pyth·i·as \'pith-ē-əs\ condemned man for whom Damon stands as hostage and who is granted freedom because of his friend's devotion

Quayle \'kwāl\ James Danforth 1947–   vice-president of the United States (1989–93)

Quin·til·ian \kwin-'til-yən\ *about* 35–*about* 100 A.D. Roman rhetorician

Ra \'rä, 'rò\ god of the sun and chief deity of ancient Egypt

Ra·be·lais \'rab-ə-,lā, ,rab-ə-'lā\ François *about* 1483–1553 French author

Ra·bin \rä-'bēn\ Yitzhak 1922–   prime minister of Israel (1974–77; 92–   )

Ra·chel \'rā-chəl\ one of the wives of Jacob

Rach·ma·ni·noff \räk-'män-ə-,nóf, rak-'man-, -,nòv\ Sergei Wassilievitch 1873–1943 Russian composer, pianist, and conductor

Ra·cine \ra-'sēn, rə-\ Jean Baptiste 1639–99 French dramatist

Ra·leigh *or* **Ra·legh** \'ról-ē, 'räl- *also* 'ral-\ Sir Walter 1554–1618 English navigator and historian

Ra·ma \'räm-ə\ deity or deified hero of later Hinduism worshiped as an incarnation of Vishnu

Ram·say \'ram-zē\ Sir William 1852–1916 British chemist; Nobel prize winner (1904)

Ram·ses \'ram-,sēz\ *or* **Ram·e·ses** \'ram-ə-,sēz\ name of 11 kings of Egypt: especially **II** (reigned 1304–1237 B.C.); **III** (reigned 1198–1166 B.C.)

Ra·pha·el \'raf-ē-əl, 'rā-fē-\ one of the four archangels named in Hebrew tradition — compare GABRIEL, MICHAEL, URIEL

Ra·pha·el \'raf-ē-əl, 'rā-fē-, 'räf-ē-\ 1483–1520 Italian painter

Ras·pu·tin \ra-'spyüt-n, -'spüt-, -'spüt-\ Grigori Efimovich 1872–1916 Russian monk

Ra·vel \rə-'vel, ra-\ Mau·rice \mò-'rēs\ Joseph 1875–1937 French composer

Rea·gan \'rā-gən, 'rē-\ Ronald Wilson 1911–   40th president of the United States (1981–89)

Re·bek·ah *or* **Re·bec·ca** \ri-'bek-ə\ wife of Isaac

Red Cloud \'red-,klaùd\ 1822–1909 Sioux Indian chief

Reed \'rēd\ Walter 1851–1902 American army surgeon

Rehn·quist \'ren-,kwist\ William Hubbs 1924–   Am. jurist; chief justice U.S. Supreme Court (1986–   )

Re·marque \rə-'märk\ Erich Maria 1898–1970 American (German-born) author

Rem·brandt van Rijn *or* **Ryn** \'rem-,brant-vän-'rīn\ 1606–69 Dutch painter

Re·mus \'rē-məs\ son of Mars slain by his brother Romulus

Re·noir \ren-'wär, 'ren-,wär\ Pierre Auguste 1841–1919 French painter

Re·vere \ri-'viər\ Paul 1735–1818 American patriot and silversmith

Reyn·olds \'ren-ldz, -lz\ Sir Joshua 1723–92 English painter

Rhodes \'rōdz\ Cecil John 1853–1902 British administrator and financier in South Africa

Rich·ard \'rich-ərd\ name of 3 kings of England: **I** 1157–99 (reigned 1189–99) *the Lion-Hearted;* **II** 1367–1400 (reigned 1377–99); **III** 1452–85 (reigned 1483–85)

Rich·ard·son \'rich-ərd-sən\ Samuel 1689–1761 English author

Ri·che·lieu \'rish-əl-,ü, -,yü; rē-shə-'lyœ̄\ Duc de 1585–1642 French cardinal and statesman

Rim·ski-Kor·sa·kov \,rim-skē-'kòr-sə-,kóf, ,rimp-, -,kóv, -,kòr-sə-'\ Nikolai Andreevich 1844–1908 Russian composer

Ri·ve·ra \ri-'ver-ə\ Diego 1886–1957 Mexican painter

Robes·pierre \'rōbz-,piər, -,pyeər; ,rō-,bes-'pyeər\ Maximilién François Marie Isidore de 1758–94 French revolutionist

Rob·in Good·fel·low \,räb-ən-'gùd-,fel-ō\ *or* **Puck** \'pək\ mischievous sprite in English folklore

Rob·in Hood \,räb-ən-'hùd\ legendary English outlaw noted for his skill in archery and for his robbing the rich to help the poor

Rob·in·son \'räb-ən-sən\ Edwin Arlington 1869–1935 American poet

Ro·cham·beau \,rō-sham-'bō\ Comte de 1725–1807 French general in American Revolution

Rocke·fel·ler \'räk-i-,fel-ər, 'räk-,fel-\ John Davison father 1839–1937 and son 1874–1960 American oil magnates and philanthropists

Ro·din \'rō-,daⁿ, -,daⁿ\ François Auguste René 1840–1917 French sculptor

Roent·gen *or* **Rönt·gen** \'rent-gən, 'rənt-, -jən\ Wilhelm Conrad 1845–1923 German physicist; Nobel prize winner (1901)

Ro·land \'rō-lənd\ stalwart defender of the Christians against the Saracens in the Charlemagne legends who was killed at Roncesvalles in 778 A.D.

Röl·vaag \'ról-,väg\ Ole \'ō-lə\ Ed·vart \'ed-,värt\ 1876–1931 Norwegian-born educator and author in America

Ro·ma·nov *or* **Ro·ma·noff** \rō-'män-əf, 'rō-mə-,näf\ Mikhail Feodorovich 1596–1645 1st czar of Russia (1613–45)

Rom·mel \'räm-əl\ Erwin 1891–1944 German field marshal

Rom·u·lus \'räm-yə-ləs\ son of Mars and twin brother of Remus; legendary founder of Rome

Roo·se·velt \'rō-zə-vəlt *(Roosevelts' usual pronunciation),* -,velt *also* 'rü-\ (Anna) Eleanor 1884–1962 American humanitarian and writer; wife of Franklin Delano Roosevelt

Roosevelt Franklin Del·a·no \'del-ə-,nō\ 1882–1945 32d president of the United States (1933–45)

Roosevelt Theodore 1858–1919 26th president of the United States (1901–09); Nobel prize winner (1906)

Root \'rüt, 'rùt\ Elihu 1845–1937 American lawyer and statesman; Nobel prize winner (1912)

Ross \'ròs\ Betsy 1752–1836 reputed maker of first American flag

Ros·set·ti \rō-'zet-ē, -'set-\ Christina Georgina 1830–94 English poet; sister of Dante Gabriel Rossetti

Rossetti Dante Gabriel 1828–82 English painter and poet

\ə\ abut		\ng\ sing	
\ər\ further		\ō\ bone	
\a\ mat		\ò\ saw	
\ā\ take		\òi\ coin	
\ä\ cot, cart		\th\ thin	
\aù\ out		\t͟h\ this	
\ch\ chin		\ü\ food	
\e\ pet		\ù\ foot	
\ē\ easy		\y\ yet	
\g\ go		\yü\ few	
\i\ tip		\yù\ cure	
\ī\ life		\zh\ vision	
\j\ job			

Ros•si•ni \rȯ-'sē-nē, rə-\ Gioacchino Antonio 1792–1868 Italian composer

Ros•tand \rȯ-'stäⁿ, 'räs-,tand\ Edmond 1868–1918 French author

Roth•schild \'rȯths-,chīld, 'rȯth-, 'rȯs-; *German* 'rōt-,shilt\ Mayer Amschel 1744–1812 German financier

Rothschild Nathan Mayer 1777–1836 financier in London; son of the preceding

Rous•seau \rü-'sō, 'rü-,\ Jean Jacques 1712–78 French (Swiss-born) philosopher and author

Ru•bens \'rü-bənz\ Peter Paul 1577–1640 Flemish painter

Ru•bin•stein \'rü-bən-,stīn\ An•ton \än-'tȯn\ 1829–94 Russian pianist and composer

Rumford, Count — see THOMPSON

Ru•pert \'rü-pərt\ Prince 1619–82 nephew of Charles I of England; German-English general and admiral

Rus•kin \'rəs-kən\ John 1819–1900 English author

Rus•sell \'rəs-əl\ Bertrand Arthur William 3d Earl 1872–1970 English mathematician and philosopher; Nobel prize winner (1950)

Ruth \'rüth\ Moabite woman who became the wife of Boaz and ancestress of David

Ruth•er•ford \'rəth-ər-fərd, 'rəth-ə-, 'rəth-\ Ernest 1st Baron 1871–1937 British physicist; Nobel prize winner (1908)

Sa•dat, \sə-'dat, -'dät\ Anwar as- 1918–81 president of Egypt (1970–81)

Saint–Gau•dens \sānt-'gȯd-nz, sənt-\ Augustus 1848–1907 American (Irish-born) sculptor

Saint Nicholas — see NICHOLAS, SANTA CLAUS

Saint–Saëns \saⁿ-'säⁿs\ (Charles) Camille 1835–1921 French composer

Sal•a•din \'sal-əd-ən, ,sal-ə-'dēn\ 1137 (or 1138)–93 sultan of Egypt and Syria

Sal•in•ger \'sal-ən-jər\ Jerome David 1919–   American author

Salk \'sȯk, 'sȯlk\ Jonas Edward 1914–   American physician

Sa•lo•me \sə-'lō-mē\ niece of Herod Antipas given the head of John the Baptist as a reward for her dancing

Sa•mo•set \'sam-ə-,set, sə-'mäs-ət\ *died about* 1653 Indian leader; friend of the Pilgrims

Sam•son \'sam-sən, 'samp-\ Hebrew hero of great physical strength who wreaked havoc among the Philistines

Sam•u•el \'sam-yəl, -yə-wəl\ Hebrew judge; 1st of the great prophets

Sand \'sand, 'säⁿd, 'säⁿnd, 'säⁿ\ George 1804–76 pseudonym of *Amandine Aurore Lucie* French author

Sand•burg \'sand-,bərg, 'san-\ Carl 1878–1967 American author

Sang•er \'sang-ər\ Margaret 1883–1966 née *Higgins* American birth-control leader

San•ta Claus \'sant-ə-,klȯz, 'sant-ē-\ *or* **Saint Nich•o•las** \sänt-'nik-ləs, sənt-, -'nik-ə-ləs\ *or* **Kriss Krin•gle** \'kris-'kring-gəl\ a jolly old man of modern folklore who developed from the legends and traditions associated with Saint Nicholas of Myra and who delivers presents to good children at Christmastime

Sap•pho \'saf-ō\ *flourished about* 610–*about* 580 B.C. Greek poet

Sa•rah \'ser-ə, 'sar-ə, 'sā-rə\ wife of Abraham and mother of Isaac

Sar•gent \'sär-jənt\ John Singer 1856–1925 American painter

Sar•tre \'särtr\ Jean-Paul 1905–80 French philosopher and author

Sat•urn \'sat-ərn\ Roman god of agriculture

Saul \'sȯl\ 1st king of Israel

Saul *or* **Saul of Tarsus** the apostle Paul

Sa•vo•na•ro•la \,sav-ə-nə-'rō-lə, sə-,vän-ə-'rō-\ Gi•ro•la•mo \ji-'rȯl-ə-,mō\ 1452–98 Italian friar and reformer; executed

Scar•lat•ti \skär-'lät-ē\ Alessandro 1660–1725 and his son Domenico 1685–1757 Italian composers

Sche•her•a•zade \shə-,her-ə-'zäd, -'zäd-ə, -'zäd-ē\ fictional wife of the sultan of India and narrator of the tales in the *Arabian Nights' Entertainments*

Schil•ler, von \'shil-ər\ Johann Christoph Friedrich 1759–1805 German author

Scho•pen•hau•er \'shō-pən-,haú-ər, -,haúr\ Arthur 1788–1860 German philosopher

Schu•bert \'shü-bərt, -,bert\ Franz Peter 1797–1828 Austrian composer

Schu•mann \'shü-,män, -mən\ Robert 1810–56 German composer

Schweit•zer \'shwīt-sər, 'swīt-, 'shvīt-\ Albert 1875–1965 French Protestant clergyman, philosopher, physician, and music scholar; Nobel prize winner (1952)

Scip•io \'sip-ē-,ō, 'skip-\ **Aemilianus Af•ri•ca•nus** \,af-rə-'kan-əs\ **Numantinus** Publius Cornelius 185 (or 184)–129 B.C. *Scipio the Younger* Roman general; adopted grandson of Scipio the Elder

Scipio Africanus Publius Cornelius 236–184 (or 183) B.C. *Scipio the Elder* Roman general

Scott \'skät\ Dred \'dred\ 1795?–1858 American slave

Scott Sir Walter 1771–1832 Scottish author

Scott Winfield 1786–1866 American general

Se•le•ne \sə-'lē-nē, -nə\ goddess of the moon in Greek mythology whose Roman counterpart is Luna

Se•leu•cus I \sə-'lü-kəs\ 358 (to 354)–281 B.C. ruler (306–281) of a Greek dynasty in Syria

Sen•e•ca \'sen-i-kə\ 4 B.C.?–A.D. 65 Roman philosopher and dramatist

Sen•nach•er•ib \sə-'nak-ə-rəb\ *died* 681 B.C. king of Assyria (704–681); son of Sargon II

Se•quoya \si-'kwȯi-ə\ *about* 1760–1843 Cherokee Indian scholar

Se•ton \'sēt-n\ Saint Elizabeth Ann Bayley 1774–1821 *Mother Seton* American religious leader

Sew•ard \'sü-ərd, 'sú-ərd, 'súrd\ William Henry 1801–72 American statesman; secretary of state (1861–69)

Shake•speare \'shāk-,spiər\ William 1564–1616 English dramatist and poet

Shaw \'shȯ\ George Bernard 1856–1950 British author

Shel•ley \'shel-ē\ Mary Woll•stone•craft \'wúl-stən-,kraft\ 1797–1851 English novelist; wife of Percy Bysshe Shelley

Shelley Percy Bysshe \'bish\ 1792–1822 English poet

Shem \'shem\ eldest son of Noah; ancestor of the Semitic peoples in biblical tradition

Shep•ard \'shep-ərd\ Alan Bartlett 1923–   American astronaut; 1st American in space (1961)

Sher•i•dan \'sher-əd-n\ Philip Henry 1831–88 American general

Sheridan Richard Brins•ley \'brinz-lē\ 1751–1816 Irish dramatist

Sher•man \'shər-mən\ John 1823–1900 American statesman; brother of William Tecumseh Sherman

Sherman William Tecumseh 1820–91 American general

Shiva — see SIVA

Si•be•lius \sə-'bāl-yəs, -'bā-lē-əs\ Jean 1865–1957 Finnish composer

Sid•ney \'sid-nē\ Sir Philip 1554–86 English poet

Sieg•fried \'sig-,frēd, 'sēg-\ hero in Germanic legend noted for winning the hoard of the Nibelungs and for slaying a dragon

Sig•urd \'sig-,úrd, 'sig-ərd\ a dragon slayer in Norse mythology

Si•kor•sky \sə-'kȯr-skē\ Igor Ivan 1889–1972 American (Russian-born) aeronautical engineer

Si•mon \'sī-mən\ — see PETER

Simon *or* **Simon the Zealot** one of the 12 apostles

Sind•bad the Sailor \'sin-,bad-\ citizen of Baghdad whose adventures are narrated in the *Arabian Nights' Entertainments*

Sis•y•phus \'sis-i-fəs\ legendary king of Corinth condemned to roll a heavy stone up a hill in Hades only to have it roll down again as it nears the top — **Sis•y•phe•an** \,sis-i-'fē-ən\ *adj*

Sit•ting Bull \,sit-ing-'bùl\ *about* 1831–90 Sioux leader

Si•va \'shiv-ə, 'siv-; 'shē-və, 'sē-\ *or* **Shi•va** \'shiv-ə, 'shē-və\ god of destruction in the Hindu sacred triad — compare BRAHMA, VISHNU — **Si•va•ism** \-,iz-əm\ *n*

Smith \'smith\ Adam 1723–90 Scottish economist

Smith John *about* 1580–1631 English colonist in America

Smith Joseph 1805–44 American founder of the Mormon Church

Smol•lett \'smäl-ət\ Tobias George 1721–71 British author

Soc•ra•tes \'säk-rə-,tēz\ *about* 470–399 B.C. Greek philosopher

Sol \'säl\ — see HELIOS

Sol•o•mon \'säl-ə-mən\ son of David and 10th-century B.C. king of Israel noted for his wisdom

Soph•o•cles \'säf-ə-,klēz\ *about* 496–406 B.C. Greek dramatist

Sou•sa \'sü-zə, 'sü-sə\ John Philip 1854–1932 American bandmaster and composer

Sou•they \'saù-<u>th</u>ē, 'səth-ē\ Robert 1774–1843 English author

Spaatz \'späts\ Carl 1891–1974 American general

Spar•ta•cus \'spärt-ə-kəs\ *died* 71 B.C. Roman slave and gladiator from Thrace; leader of a slave rebellion

Spen•ser \'spen-sər\ Edmund 1552–99 English poet

Spi•no•za \spin-'ō-zə\ Baruch *or* Benedict 1632–77 Dutch philosopher

Squan•to \'skwän-tō, 'skwòn-\ *died* 1622 Indian friend of the Pilgrims

Sta•lin \'stäl-ən, 'stal-, -,ēn\ Joseph 1879–1953 *Iosif Vissarionovich Dzhu•gash•vi•li* \,jü-gəsh-'vē-lē\ Soviet leader

Stan•dish \'stan-dish\ Myles *or* Miles 1584?–1656 English colonist in America

Stan•ley \'stan-lē\ Sir Henry Morton 1841–1904 British explorer in Africa

Stan•ton \'stant-n\ Elizabeth Cady 1815–1902 American suffragist

Steele \'stēl\ Sir Richard 1672–1729 British author

Stein \'stīn\ Gertrude 1874–1946 American author

Stein•beck \'stīn-,bek\ John Ernst 1902–1968 American author; Nobel prize winner (1962)

Stein•metz \'stīn-,mets, 'shtīn-\ Charles Proteus 1865–1923 American (German-born) electrical engineer and inventor

Sten•dhal \sten-'däl, stan-, *French* staⁿ-'dâl\ 1783–1842 pseudonym of *Marie Henri Beyle* \'bel\ French author

Ste•phen \'stē-vən\ Saint *died about* 36 A.D. Christian martyr; stoned to death

Stephen *about* 1097–1154 *Stephen of Blois* king of England (1135–54)

Sterne \'stərn\ Laurence 1713–68 British author

Steu•ben, von \'stü-bən, 'styü-, 'shtöi-\ Baron Friedrich Wilhelm Ludolf Gerhard Augustin 1730–94 Prussianborn general in American Revolution

Ste•ven•son \'stē-vən-sən\ Adlai Ewing 1900–65 American statesman

Stevenson Robert Louis Balfour 1850–94 Scottish author

Stowe \'stō\ Harriet Elizabeth 1811–96 née *Beecher* American author

Stra•di•va•ri \,strad-ə-'vär-ē, -'var-, -'ver-\ Antonio 1644–1737 *Antonius Strad•i•var•i•us* \,strad-ə-'var-ē-əs, -'ver-\ Italian violin maker

Strauss \'straùs, 'shtraùs\ Johann father 1804–49 and his sons Johann 1825–99 and Josef 1827–70 Austrian composers

Strauss Ri•chard \'rik-,ärt, 'rik-\ 1864–1949 German composer

Stra•vin•sky \strə-'vin-skē\ Igor \'ē-,gòr\ Fēdorovich 1882–1971 American (Russian-born) composer

Stu•art \'stü-ərt, 'styü-, 'styú-, 'styùrt\ — see CHARLES I, MARY STUART

Stuart Charles — see CHARLES EDWARD STUART

Stuart Gilbert Charles 1755–1828 American painter

Stuart James Ewell Brown 1833–64 *Jeb* American Confederate general

Stuy•ve•sant \'stī-və-sənt\ Peter *about* 1610–1672 Dutch administrator in America

Sue•to•ni•us \swē-'tō-nē-əs, sù-ə-'tō-\ *about* 69–*after* 122 A.D. Roman biographer and historian

Su•lei•man I \'sü-lā-,män, -li-\ 1494 (or 1495)–1566 *the Magnificent* Ottoman sultan (1520–66)

Sul•la \'səl-ə\ 138–78 B.C. Roman general and statesman

Sul•li•van \'səl-ə-vən\ Sir Arthur Seymour 1842–1900 English composer; collaborated with Sir William S. Gilbert

Sullivan Louis Henri 1856–1924 American architect

Sum•ner \'səm-nər\ Charles 1811–74 American statesman

Sun Yat-sen \'sùn-'yät-'sen\ 1866–1925 Chinese statesman

Swift \'swift\ Jonathan 1667–1745 English (Irish-born) author

Swin•burne \'swin-,bərn, -bərn\ Algernon Charles 1837–1909 English poet

Tac•i•tus \'tas-ət-əs\ Cornelius *about* 56–*about* 120 A.D. Roman historian

Taft \'taft\ William Howard 1857–1930 27th president of the United States (1909–13); chief justice of the United States Supreme Court (1921–30)

Tal•ley•rand–Pé•ri•gord, de \'tal-ē-,rand-,per-ə-'gòr, -,ran-, *French* tȧl-ē-'räⁿ, tȧl-'rän\ Charles Maurice 1754–1838 French statesman

Tam•er•lane \'tam-ər-,lān\ *or* **Tam•bur•laine** \'tam-bər-,lān\ 1336–1405 *Timur Lenk* Mongol conqueror

Tan•cred \'tang-krəd\ 1078?–1112 Norman leader in first crusade

Ta•ney \'tò-nē\ Roger Brooke 1777–1864 American jurist; chief justice of the United States Supreme Court (1836–64)

Tann•häu•ser \'tän-,hòi-zər\ knight and minnesinger of Germanic legend noted for his stay with Venus in the Venusberg cavern and his subsequent repentance

Tan•ta•lus \'tant-l-əs\ legendary king of Lydia condemned to stand up to his chin in a pool of water in Hades and beneath fruit-laden boughs only to have the water or fruit recede at each attempt to eat or drink

Tay•lor \'tā-lər\ Zachary 1784–1850 American general; 12th president of the United States (1849–50)

Tchai•kov•sky \chī-'kòf-skē, chə-, -'kòv-\ Pyotr Ilich 1840–93 Russian composer

Te•cum•seh \tə-'kəm-sə, -'kəmp-, -sē\ 1768–1813 Shawnee Indian chief

Te•lem•a•chus \tə-'lem-ə-kəs\ son of Odysseus and Penelope who aids his father in the slaying of his mother's suitors

Ten•ny•son \'ten-ə-sən\ Alfred 1st Baron 1809–92 English poet

Ter•ence \'ter-əns\ 186 (or 185)–?159 B.C. Roman dramatist

Terp•sich•o•re \,tərp-'sik-ə-rē\ Greek Muse of dancing and choral song

Thack•er•ay \'thak-rē, -ə-rē\ William Makepeace 1811–63 English author

Tha•les \'thā-,lēz\ 625?–?547 B.C. Greek philosopher

Tha•lia \thə-'lī-ə\ Greek Muse of comedy and pastoral poetry

The•mis•to•cles \thə-'mis-tə-,klēz\ *about* 524–*about* 460 B.C. Athenian general and statesman

The•oc•ri•tus \thē-'äk-rət-əs\ *about* 310–250 B.C. Greek poet

The•od•o•ric \thē-'äd-ə-rik\ 454?–526 A.D. *the Great* king of the Ostrogoths (493–526)

The·o·do·sius I \,thē-ə-'dō-shəs, -shē-əs\ 347–395 A.D. *the Great* Roman general and emperor (379–395)

The·re·sa *or* **Te·re·sa** \tə-'rē-sə, -'rā-sə, -'rā-zə\ Saint 1515–82 Spanish Carmelite nun, mystic, and author

The·seus \'thē-,süs, -sē-əs\ hero in Greek mythology who slays Procrustes and the Minotaur and conquers the Amazons

Thes·pis \'thes-pəs\ 6th century B.C. Greek poet

The·tis \'thēt-əs\ sea goddess and mother of Achilles

This·be \'thiz-bē\ legendary Babylonian maiden who dies for the love of Pyramus

Thom·as \'täm-əs\ Saint; one of the 12 apostles; demanded proof of Christ's resurrection

Thomas Clarence 1948– American jurist

Thomas Dyl·an \'dil-ən\ 1914–53 British poet

Thomas à Becket — *see* BECKET

Thomas a Kem·pis \ə-'kem-pəs, ä-'kem-\ 1379 (or 1380)–1471 German priest and author

Thomp·son \'täm-sən, 'tämp-\ Benjamin 1753–1814 Count *Rum·ford* \'rəm-fərd, 'rəmp-\ British (American-born) physicist and statesman

Thor \'thor\ Norse god of thunder, weather, and crops

Tho·reau \thə-'rō, thȯ-; 'thȯr-ō\ Henry David 1817–62 American author

Thu·cyd·i·des \thü-'sid-ə-,dēz, thyü-\ *died about* 401 B.C. Greek historian

Thur·ber \'thər-bər\ James Grover 1894–1961 American author

Ti·be·ri·us \tī-'bir-ē-əs\ 42 B.C.–37 A.D. Roman emperor (14-37)

Tim·o·thy \'tim-ə-thē\ disciple of the apostle Paul

Tin·to·ret·to, Il \,tin-tə-'ret-ō\ *about* 1518-94 *Jacopo Robusti* Italian painter

Ti·re·si·as \tī-'rē-sē-əs, -zē-əs\ legendary blind soothsayer of Thebes who predicts the doom of Oedipus

Ti·ta·nia \tə-'tän-yə, -'tän-, tī-'tän-\ queen of the fairies and wife of Oberon in Shakespeare's *A Midsummer Night's Dream*

Ti·tian \'tish-ən\ *about* 1488–1576 Italian painter

Tito — *see* BROZ

Ti·tus \'tīt-əs\ associate of the apostle Paul

Titus 39–81 A.D. Roman emperor (79–81)

Tocque·ville, de \'tōk-,vil, 'tȯk-, 'täk-, -,vēl, -vəl\ Alexis Charles 1805–59 French statesman and author

Tol·kien \'tȯl-,kēn, 'tōl-, 'täl-\ John Ronald Reuel 1892–1973 English author

Tol·stoy *or* **Tol·stoi** \tȯl-'stȯi, tōl-', täl-', 'tȯl-,, 'tōl-,, 'täl-,\ Count Lev Nikolaevich 1828–1910 Russian author

Tou·louse–Lau·trec, de \tü-,lüz-lō-'trek\ Henri 1864–1901 French painter

Tra·jan \'trā-jən\ 53–117 A.D. Roman emperor (98–117)

Tris·tram \'tris-trəm\ *or* **Tris·tan** \'tris-tən, -,tän, -,tan\ hero of medieval romance who drinks a love potion and falls in love with the Irish princess Isolde

Tri·ton \'trīt-n\ son of Poseidon who is half man and half fish

Troi·lus \'trȯi-ləs, 'trō-ə-ləs\ son of Priam who in medieval legend loves Cressida but loses her to Diomedes

Trots·ky *or* **Trots·ki** \'trät-skē, 'trȯt-\ Leon 1879–1940 *Leib* or *Lev Davydovich Bronstein* Russian Communist leader

Tru·deau \'trü-dō, trü-'\ Pierre Elliott 1919– prime minister of Canada (1968–79; 1980–84)

Tru·man \'trü-mən\ Harry S. 1884–1972 33d president of the United States (1945–53)

Truth \'trüth\ Sojourner *about* 1797–1883 American evangelist and reformer

Tub·man \'təb-mən\ Harriet *about* 1820–1913 American abolitionist

Tur·ner \'tər-nər\ Joseph Mallord William 1775–1851 English painter

Turner Nat 1800–31 American slave leader

Tut·ankh·a·men \,tü-,tang-'käm-ən, -,täng-\ *or* **Tut·enkh·a·mon** \-,teng-'käm-ən\ *about* 1370–1352 B.C. king of Egypt (1361–1352 B.C.)

Twain, Mark — *see* CLEMENS

Tweed \'twēd\ William Marcy 1823–78 *Boss Tweed* American politician

Ty·ler \'tī-lər\ John 1790–1862 10th president of the United States (1841–45)

Ulysses — *see* ODYSSEUS

Up·dike \'əp-,dīk\ John 1932– American author

Ura·nia \yu̇-'rā-nē-ə, -nyə\ Greek Muse of astronomy

Ura·nus \'yu̇r-ə-nəs, yu̇-'rā-nəs\ the heavens personified in Greek mythology as the father of the Titans and ruler of the universe until overthrown by his son Cronus

Ur·ban \'ər-bən\ name of 8 popes: especially II 1035–99 (pope 1088–99)

Urey \'yu̇r-ē\ Harold Clayton 1893–1981 American chemist; Nobel prize winner (1934)

Uri·el \'yu̇r-ē-əl\ one of the four archangels named in Hebrew tradition — compare GABRIEL, MICHAEL, RAPHAEL

Uther \'ü-thər, 'yü-, -ə-\ *or* **Uther Pen·drag·on** \-pen-'drag-ən, -'pen-,\ father of Arthur in Arthurian legend

Va·le·ri·an \və-'lir-ē-ən\ died 260 A.D. Roman emperor (253–260)

Van Bu·ren \van-'byu̇r-ən, vən-\ Martin 1782–1862 8th president of the United States (1837–41)

Van·dyke *or* **Van Dyck** \van-'dīk, vən-\ Sir Anthony 1599–1641 Flemish-born painter in England

Ve·ga, de \'vā-gə\ Lo·pe \'lō-pā\ 1562–1635 Spanish dramatist

Ve·láz·quez *or* **Ve·lás·quez** \və-'las-kəs\ Diego Rodriguez de Silva y 1599–1660 Spanish painter

Ve·nus \'vē-nəs\ — *see* APHRODITE

Ver·di \'veərd-ē\ Giuseppe 1813–1901 Italian composer

Ver·gil *or* **Vir·gil** \'vər-jəl\ 70–19 B.C. Roman poet — **Ver·gil·i·an** *or* **Vir·gil·i·an** \,vər-'jil-ē-ən\ *adj*

Verne Jules \'jülz-'vərn, 'zhu̅el-'veərn\ 1828–1905 French author

Ve·ro·ne·se \,ver-ə-'nā-sē, -'nā-zē\ Paolo 1528–88 Italian painter

Ves·puc·ci \ve-'spü-chē\ Ame·ri·go \,äm-ə-'rē-gō\ 1454–1512 *Amer·i·cus Ves·pu·cius* \ə-'mer-ə-kəs, ,ves-'pyü-shəs,-shē-əs\ Italian navigator for whom America was named

Ves·ta \'ves-tə\ — *see* HESTIA

Vic·tor Em·man·u·el I \'vik-tər-i-'man-yə-wəl, -'man-yəl\ 1759–1824 king of Sardinia (1802–21)

Victor Emmanuel II 1820–78 king of Sardinia (1849–61); 1st king of Italy (1861–78)

Victor Emmanuel III 1869–1947 king of Italy (1900–46)

Vic·to·ria \vik-tōr-ē-ə, -'tȯr-\ Alexandrina 1819–1901 queen of Great Britain (1837–1901)

Vil·lon \vē-'ōⁿ, -'yōⁿ\ François 1431–*after* 1463 French poet

Vin·cent de Paul \,vin-sənt-də-'pȯl\ Saint 1581–1660 French priest; founder of the Vincentians

Vin·ci, da \'vin-chē, 'vēn-\ Le·o·nar·do \,lē-ə-'närd-ō, ,lā-\ 1452–1519 Florentine painter, sculptor, architect, and engineer

Vish·nu \'vish-nü\ god of preservation in the Hindu sacred triad — compare BRAHMA, SIVA

Vi·val·di \vi-'väl-dē, -'vȯl-\ Antonio 1678–1741 Italian violinist and composer

Vol·taire \vōl-'taer, vȯl-, väl-, -'teər\ 1694–1778 *François Marie Arouet* French author

Von Braun \vän-'braun, fən-, vən-\ Wern·her \'veər-nər\ 1912–1977 American (German-born) rocket scientist

Vul·can \'vəl-kən\ — *see* HEPHAESTUS

Wag·ner \'väg-nər\ (Wilhelm) Ri·chard \'rik-,ärt, 'riḵ-\ 1813–83 German composer

Wal·len·berg \'wäl-ən-,bərg\ Raoul 1912–1947? Swedish diplomat and hero of the Holocaust

Wal·pole \'wȯl-,pōl, 'wäl-\ Horace 1717–97 4th Earl of *Or·ford* \'ȯr-fərd\ English author

Wal·ton \'wȯlt-n\ Izaak \'ī-zik, -zək\ 1593–1683 English author

War·ren \'wȯr-ən, 'wär-\ Earl 1891–1974 American lawyer and politician; chief justice of the United States Supreme Court (1953–69)

Wash·ing·ton \'wȯsh-ing-tən, 'wäsh-\ Book·er \'bùk-ər\ Tal·ia·ferro \'tǎl-ə-vər\ 1856–1915 American educator

Washington George 1732–99 American general; 1st president of the United States (1789–97)

Watt \'wät\ James 1736–1819 Scottish inventor

Wayne \'wān\ Anthony 1745–96 *Mad Anthony* American Revolutionary general

We·ber, von \'vā-bər\ Baron Karl Maria Friedrich Ernst 1786–1826 German composer and conductor

Web·ster \'web-stər\ Daniel 1782–1852 American statesman

Webster Noah 1758–1843 American lexicographer

Welles \'welz\ (George) Orson 1915–1985 American film director and producer

Wel·ling·ton \'wel-ing-tən\ 1st Duke of 1769–1852 *Arthur Wellesley; the Iron Duke* British general and statesman

Wells \'welz\ Herbert George 1866–1946 English author

Wes·ley \'wes-lē, 'wez-\ John 1703–91 English founder of Methodism

West \'west\ Benjamin 1738–1820 American painter in England

Wes·ting·house \'wes-ting-,haús\ George 1846–1914 American inventor

Whar·ton \'hwȯrt-n, 'wȯrt-\ Edith Newbold 1862–1937 American author

Whis·tler \'hwis-lər, 'wis-\ James Abbott McNeill 1834–1903 American artist

Whit·man \'hwit-mən, 'wit-\ Walt 1819–92 American poet

Whit·ney \'hwit-nē, 'wit-\ Eli 1765–1825 American inventor of the cotton gin

Whit·ti·er \'hwit-ē-ər, 'wit-\ John Greenleaf 1807–92 American poet

Wilde \'wīld\ Oscar Fingal O'Flahertie Wills 1854–1900 Irish author

Wil·der \'wīl-dər\ Thornton Niven 1897–1975 American author

Wil·hel·mi·na \,wil-,hel·'mē-nə, ,wil-ə-'mē-\ 1880–1962 queen of the Netherlands (1890–1948)

Wil·lard \'wil-ərd\ Emma 1787–1870 née *Hart* American educator

Wil·liam \'wil-yəm\ name of 4 kings of England: **I** *about* 1028–87 (reigned 1066–87) *the Conqueror;* **II** *about* 1056–1100 (reigned 1087–1100) *Ru·fus* \'rü-fəs\; **III** 1650–1702 (reigned 1689–1702); **IV** 1765–1837 (reigned 1830–37)

William I 1533–84 *the Silent* prince of Orange and founder of the Dutch Republic

William I 1797–1888 king of Prussia (1861–88) and emperor of Germany (1871–88)

William II 1859–1941 emperor of Germany and king of Prussia (1888–1918; abdicated)

Wil·liam Tell \,wil-yəm-'tel\ legendary Swiss patriot sentenced to shoot an apple from his son's head

Wil·liams \'wil-yəmz\ Roger 1603?–1683 English-born clergyman; founder of Rhode Island

Williams Tennessee 1911–83 *Thomas Lanier Williams* American dramatist

Williams William Carlos 1883–1963 American author

Wil·son \'wil-sən\ (Thomas) Wood·row \'wùd-rō\ 1856–1924 28th president of the United States (1913–21); Nobel prize winner (1919)

Windsor, Duke of — see EDWARD VIII

Win·throp \'win-thrəp, 'wint-\ John 1588–1649 English colonist in America; 1st governor of Massachusetts Bay Colony

Wo·den \'wōd-n\ chief god in Anglo-Saxon mythology identified with Odin

Wolfe \'wùlf\ James 1727–59 British general

Wolfe Thomas Clayton 1900–38 American author

Wol·sey \'wùl-zē\ Thomas *about* 1475–1530 English cardinal and statesman

Woolf \'wùlf\ Virginia 1882–1941 née *Stephen* English author

Words·worth \'wərdz-wərth, -,wərth\ William 1770–1850 English poet

Wren \'ren\ Sir Christopher 1632–1723 English architect

Wright \'rīt\ Frank Lloyd 1867–1959 American architect

Wright Or·ville \'ȯr-vəl\ 1871–1948 and his brother Wilbur 1867–1912 American pioneers in aviation

Wyc·liffe \'wik-,lif, -ləf\ John *about* 1330–84 English reformer and Bible translator

Wy·eth \'wī-əth\ Andrew Newell 1917– American painter

Xa·vi·er \'zāv-yər, 'zā-vē-ər, ig-'zā-\ Saint Francis 1506–52 *Apostle of the Indies* Spanish Jesuit missionary

Xen·o·phon \'zen-ə-fən\ *about* 431–*about* 352 B.C. Greek historian and soldier

Xer·xes I \'zərk-,sēz\ *about* 519–465 B.C. *the Great* son of Darius I; king of Persia (486–465); assassinated

Yeats \'yāts\ William Butler 1865–1939 Irish author

Yelt·sin \'yelt-sən, 'yel-sin\ Boris Nikolayevich 1931– president of Russia (1991–)

Young \'yəng\ Brig·ham \'brig-əm\ 1801–77 American Mormon leader

Zech·a·ri·ah \,zek-ə-'rī-ə\ Hebrew prophet of the 6th century B.C.

Zeng·er \'zeng-ər, 'zeng-gər\ John Peter 1697–1746 American (German-born) journalist and printer

Ze·no \'zē-nō\ *about* 335–*about* 263 B.C. Greek philosopher; founder of Stoic school

Zeph·a·ni·ah \,zef-ə-'nī-ə\ Hebrew prophet of the 7th century B.C.

Zeph·y·rus \'zef-ə-rəs\ Greek god of the west wind

Zeus \'züs\ chief Greek god, ruler of the elements, and husband of Hera; Roman counterpart is Jupiter or Jove

Zo·la \'zō-lə, 'zō-,lä, zō-'lä\ Émile 1840–1902 French author

Zo·ro·as·ter \'zōr-ə-,was-tər, 'zȯr-\ *or* **Za·ra·thus·tra** \,zar-ə-'thüs-trə, -'thəs-\ *about* 628–*about* 551 B.C. founder of Persian religion

Zwing·li \'zwing-lē, 'swing-, -glē; 'tsfing-lē\ Huldreich *or* Ulrich 1484–1531 Swiss Reformation leader

\ə\ abut	\ng\ sing
\ər\ **further**	\ō\ **bone**
\a\ **mat**	\ȯ\ **saw**
\ā\ **take**	\ȯi\ **coin**
\ä\ **cot, cart**	\th\ **thin**
\aù\ **out**	\th\ **this**
\ch\ **chin**	\ü\ **food**
\e\ **pet**	\ù\ **foot**
\ē\ **easy**	\y\ **yet**
\g\ **go**	\yü\ **few**
\i\ **tip**	\yù\ **cure**
\ī\ **life**	\zh\ **vision**
\j\ **job**	

World Leaders and Rulers

This section includes the names of noted leaders of the world throughout history and today and provides the dates during which they were in power. It covers the leaders of ancient civilizations and features complete listings of the leaders of many European and North American nation-states. For other geographic areas—Africa, Asia, and South America—the listing highlights the most familiar names or those most likely to be encountered in books on the history and culture of the area.

EUROPE

LEADERS	YEARS IN POWER	PARTY
England		
SAXON KINGS		
Egbert	828–839	
Ethelwulf	839–858	
Ethelbald	858–860	
Ethelbert	860–866	
Ethelred I	866–871	
Alfred the Great	877–899	
Edward the Elder	899–925	
Athelstan	925–940	
Edmund	940–946	
Edred	946–955	
Edwy	955–959	
Edgar	959–975	
Edward the Martyr	975–978	
Ethelred II	978–1016	
Edmund II Ironside	1016	
DANISH KINGS		
Canute	1016–1040	
Hardicanute	1040–1042	
Harold I	1035–1040	
WEST SAXON KINGS (restored)		
Edward the Confessor	1042–1066	
Harold II	1066	
NORMAN KINGS		
William I the Conqueror	1066–1087	
William II	1087–1100	
Henry I	1100–1135	
Stephen	1135–1154	
HOUSE OF PLANTAGENET		
Henry II	1154–1189	
Richard I	1189–1199	
John	1199–1216	
Henry III	1216–1272	
Edward I	1272–1307	
Edward II	1307–1327	
Edward III	1327–1377	
Richard II	1377–1399	

LEADERS	YEARS IN POWER	PARTY
HOUSE OF LANCASTER		
Henry IV	1399–1413	
Henry V	1413–1422	
Henry VI	1422–1461	
HOUSE OF YORK		
Edward IV	1461–1470	
HOUSE OF LANCASTER		
Henry VI	1470–1471	
HOUSE OF YORK		
Edward IV (restored)	1471–1483	
Edward V	1483	
Richard III	1483–1485	
HOUSE OF TUDOR		
Henry VII	1485–1509	
Henry VIII	1509–1547	
Edward VI	1547–1553	
Mary I	1553–1558	
Elizabeth I	1558–1603	
HOUSE OF STUART		
James I	1603–1625	
Charles I	1625–1649	
THE COMMONWEALTH		
Oliver Cromwell (Lord Protector)	1649–1658	
Richard Cromwell (Lord Protector)	1658–1659	
HOUSE OF STUART (restored)		
Charles II	1660–1685	
James II	1685–1689	
William and Mary	1689–1702	
Anne	1702–1714	
HOUSE OF HANOVER		
George I	1714–1727	
George II	1727–1760	
George III	1760–1820	
George IV	1820–1830	
William IV	1830–1837	
Victoria	1837–1901	

LEADERS	YEARS IN POWER	PARTY
HOUSE OF SAXE COBURG		
Edward VII	1901–1910	
HOUSE OF WINSDOR		
George V	1910–1936	
Edward VIII	1936	
George VI	1936–1952	
Elizabeth II	1952–	
PRIME MINISTERS		
Robert Walpole	1721–1742	Whig
Spencer Compton	1742–1743	Whig
Henry Pelham	1743–1754	Whig
Thomas Pelham-Holles	1754–1756	Whig
William Cavendish	1756–1757	Whig
Thomas Pelham-Holles	1757–1762	Whig
John Stuart	1762–1763	Tory
George Grenville	1763–1765	Whig
Charles Watson-Wentworth	1765–1766	Whig
William Pitt	1766–1768	Whig
Augustus Henry Fitzroy	1768–1770	Whig
Frederick North	1770–1782	Tory
Charles Watson-Wentworth	1782	Whig
William Petty	1782–1783	Whig
William Henry Bentinck	1783	Whig
William Pitt the Younger	1783–1801	Tory
Henry Addington	1801–1804	Tory
William Pitt the Younger	1801–1804	Tory
William Wyndham Grenville	1806–1807	Whig
William Henry Bentinck	1807–1809	Tory
Spencer Perceval	1809–1812	Tory
Robert Banks Jenkinson	1812–1827	Tory
George Canning	1827	Tory
Frederick John Robinson	1827–1828	Tory
Arthur Wellesley	1828–1830	Tory
Charles Grey	1830–1834	Whig
William Lamb	1834	Whig
Robert Peel	1834–1835	Tory
William Lamb	1835–1841	Whig
Robert Peel	1841–1846	Tory
John Russel	1846–1852	Liberal
Edward Stanley	1852	Tory
George Hamilton Gordon	1852–1855	Tory
Henry John Temple	1855–1858	Liberal
Edward Stanley	1858	Conservative
Henry John Temple	1858–1865	Liberal
John Russel	1865–1866	Liberal
Edward Stanley	1866–1868	Conservative
Benjamin Disraeli	1868	Conservative
William Ewart Gladstone	1868–1874	Liberal
Benjamin Disraeli	1874–1880	Conservative
William Ewart Gladstone	1880–1885	Liberal
Robert Gascoyne-Cecil	1885–1886	Conservative
William Ewart Gladstone	1886	Liberal
Robert Gascoyne-Cecil	1886–1892	Conservative
William Ewart Gladstone	1892–1894	Liberal
Archibald Philip Primrose	1894–1895	Liberal
Robert Gascoyne-Cecil	1895–1902	Conservative
Arthur James Balfour	1902–1905	Conservative
Henry Campbell-Bannerman	1905–1908	Liberal
Herbert Henry Asquith	1908–1916	Liberal
David Lloyd George	1916–1922	Liberal
Andrew Bonar Law	1922–1923	Conservative
Stanley Baldwin	1923–1924	Conservative
Ramsay MacDonald	1924	Labor
Stanley Baldwin	1924–1929	Conservative
Ramsay MacDonald	1929–1935	Labor
Ramsay MacDonald	1931–1935	Coalition Government
Stanley Baldwin	1935–1937	Coalition Government

LEADERS	YEARS IN POWER	PARTY
Neville Chamberlain	1937–1940	Coalition Government
Winston Churchill	1940–1945	Coalition Government
Clement Atlee	1945–1951	Labor
Winston Churchill	1951–1955	Conservative
Anthony Eden	1955–1957	Conservative
Harold Macmillan	1957–1963	Conservative
Alec Douglas-Home	1963–1964	Conservative
Harold Wilson	1964–1970	Labor
Edward Heath	1970–1974	Conservative
Harold Wilson	1974–1976	Labor
James Callaghan	1976–1979	Labor
Margaret Thatcher	1979–1990	Conservative
John Major	1990–	Conservative

Ireland

LEADERS	YEARS IN POWER	PARTY
PRIME MINISTERS		
Eamon de Valera	1919–1922	Sinn Fein
Arthur Griffith	1922	Sinn Fein
William Cosgrave	1922–1932	United Ireland
Eamon de Valera	1932–1948	Fianna Fail
John Costello	1948–1951	Fine Gael
Eamon de Valera	1951–1954	Fianna Fail
John Costello	1954–1957	Fine Gael
Eamon de Valera	1957–1959	Fianna Fail
Sean Lemass	1959–1966	Fianna Fail
Jack Lynch	1966–1973	Fianna Fail
Liam Cosgrave	1973–1977	Fine Gael-Labor
Jack Lynch	1977–1979	Fianna Fail
Charles Haughey	1979–1981	Fianna Fail
Garret Fitzgerald	1981–1982	Fine Gael-Labor
Charles Haughey	1982	Fianna Fail
Garret Fitzgerald	1982–1987	Fine Gael-Labor
Charles Haughey	1987–1992	Fianna Fail
Albert Reynolds	1992–	Fianna Fail

France

LEADERS	YEARS IN POWER	PARTY
CAROLINGIAN DYNASTY		
KINGDOM OF THE FRANKS		
Pepin the Elder	628–639	
Pepin II the Younger	687–714	
Charles Martel	714–741	
Pepin III the Short	741–768	
Charlemagne	768–814	
Louis I	814–840	
KINGS OF FRANCE		
Charles II the Bald	840–877	
Louis II	877–879	
Louis III (ruled with Carloman)	879–882	
Carloman	879–884	
Charles III the Fat	882–887	
Eudes	888–898	
Charles III the Simple	893–923	
Robert I	922–923	
Rudolf, duke of Burgundy	923–936	
Louis IV	936–954	
Lothair	954–986	
Louis V	986–987	
CAPETIAN DYNASTY		
Hugues Capet	987–996	
Robert II	996–1031	
Henri I	1031–1060	
Philippe I	1060–1108	
Louis VI	1108–1137	
Louis VII	1137–1180	

LEADERS	YEARS IN POWER	PARTY
Philippe II	1180–1223	
Louis VIII	1223–1226	
Louis IX	1226–1270	
Philippe III	1270–1285	
Philippe IV	1285–1314	
Louis X	1314–1316	
Jean I	1316	
Philippe V	1316–1322	
Charles IV	1322–1328	

VALOIS DYNASTY

LEADERS	YEARS IN POWER	PARTY
Philippe VI	1328–1350	
Jean II	1350–1364	
Charles V	1364–1380	
Charles VI	1380–1422	
Charles VII	1422–1461	
Louis XI	1461–1483	
Charles VIII	1483–1498	
Louis XII	1498–1515	
Francois I	1515–1547	
Henri II	1547–1559	
Francois II	1559–1560	
Charles IX	1560–1574	
Henri III	1574–1589	

BOURBON DYNASTY

LEADERS	YEARS IN POWER	PARTY
Henri IV	1589–1610	
Louis XIII	1610–1643	
Louis XIV	1643–1715	
Louis XV	1715–1774	
Louis XVI	1774–1792	

FIRST REPUBLIC

LEADERS	YEARS IN POWER	PARTY
The Convention (Robespierre)	1792–1795	
Directorate (Five Members)	1795–1799	
Consulate (First Consul Napoleon Bonaparte)	1799–1804	

FIRST EMPIRE

LEADERS	YEARS IN POWER	PARTY
Emperor Napoleon	1804–1814	

RESTORED BOURBON DYNASTY

LEADERS	YEARS IN POWER	PARTY
Louis XVIII	1814–1815	

FIRST EMPIRE

LEADERS	YEARS IN POWER	PARTY
Emperor Napoleon	1815	

RESTORED BOURBON DYNASTY

LEADERS	YEARS IN POWER	PARTY
Louis XVIII	1815–1824	
Charles X	1824–1830	
Louis-Philippe	1830–1848	

SECOND REPUBLIC

LEADERS	YEARS IN POWER	PARTY
Louis-Napoleon Bonaparte	1848–1852	

SECOND EMPIRE

LEADERS	YEARS IN POWER	PARTY
Napoleon III (Louis-Napoleon Bonaparte)	1852–1870	

PRESIDENTS OF THIRD REPUBLIC

LEADERS	YEARS IN POWER	PARTY
Louis A. Theirs	1871–1873	
Patrice Maurice de MacMahon	1873–1879	
Jules Grévy	1879–1887	
Sadi Carnot	1887–1894	
Jean-Paul Casmir Périer	1894–1895	
François Félix Faure	1895–1899	
Émile Loubet	1899–1906	
Armand Fallierer	1906–1913	
Raymond Poincaré	1913–1920	
Paul Deschanel	1920	
Alexandre Millerand	1920–1924	
Gaston Doumergue	1924–1931	
Paul Doumer	1931–1932	
Albert Lebrun	1932–1940	

CHIEF OF STATE OF THE VICHY GOVERNMENT

LEADERS	YEARS IN POWER	PARTY
Philippe Pétain	1940–1944	

HEADS OF PROVISIONAL GOVERNMENT

LEADERS	YEARS IN POWER	PARTY
Charles de Gaulle	1944–1946	
Félix Gouin	1946	
Georges Bidault	1946	
Léon Blum	1946	

PRESIDENTS OF THE FOURTH REPUBLIC

LEADERS	YEARS IN POWER	PARTY
Vincent Auriol	1947–1954	Socialist
René Coty	1954–1959	Independent Republican Party

PRESIDENTS OF THE FIFTH REPUBLIC

LEADERS	YEARS IN POWER	PARTY
Charles de Gaulle	1959–1969	Union for the New Republic Democratic
Georges Pompidou	1969–1974	Democratic Union for Fifth Republic
Valéry Giscard d'Estaing	1974–1981	Independent Republican Party
François Mitterand	1981–	Socialist

Germany

KINGS OF PRUSSIA

LEADERS	YEARS IN POWER	PARTY
Frederick I	1701–1713	
Frederick William I	1713–1740	
Frederick II the Great	1740–1786	
Frederick William II	1786–1797	
Frederick William III	1797–1840	
Frederick William IV	1840–1861	
William I	1861–1871	

EMPERORS OF GERMANY

LEADERS	YEARS IN POWER	PARTY
William I	1871–1888	
Frederick III	1888	
William II	1888–1918	

PROVISIONAL GOVERNMENT

LEADERS	YEARS IN POWER	PARTY
Six man ruling council	1918–1919	

PRESIDENTS OF THE WEIMAR REPUBLIC

LEADERS	YEARS IN POWER	PARTY
Friedrich Ebert	1919–1925	Socialist Party
Marshal Paul von Hindenburg	1925–1934	

FÜHRERS OF THE NATIONAL SOCIALIST REGIME (THIRD REICH)

LEADERS	YEARS IN POWER	PARTY
Adolf Hitler	1934–1945	National Socialist
Admiral Karl Dönitz	1945	National Socialist

ALLIED OCCUPATION 1945–1949

CHANCELLORS OF THE FEDERAL GERMAN REPUBLIC (WEST GERMANY)

LEADERS	YEARS IN POWER	PARTY
Konrad Adenauer	1949–1963	Christian Democrat
Prof. Ludwig Erhard	1963–1966	Christian Democrat
Dr. Kurt Georg Kiesinger	1966–1969	Christian Democrat
Dr. Willy Brandt	1969–1974	Social Democrat
Walter Scheel	1974	Free Democratic Party
Helmut Schmidt	1974–1982	Social Democrat
Helmut Kohl	1982–	Christian Democrat

LEADERS OF THE GERMAN DEMOCRATIC REPUBLIC (EAST GERMANY)

LEADERS	YEARS IN POWER	PARTY
Wilhelm Pieck	1949–1960	Communist
Walter Ulbricht	1960–1973	Communist
Willy Stoph	1973–1976	Communist
Erich Honecker	1976–1989	Communist
Egon Krenz	1989	Communist
Manfred Gerlach	1989–1990	Communist
Sabine Bergman-Pohl	1990	Communist

CHANCELLORS OF THE GERMAN FEDERAL REPUBLIC (UNIFIED GERMANY)

LEADERS	YEARS IN POWER	PARTY
Helmut Kohl	1991–	Christian Democrat

1513

LEADERS	YEARS IN POWER	PARTY
Emanuel I	1495–1521	
John III	1521–1557	
Sebastian	1557–1578	
Henry	1578–1580	
Antonio	1580	
SPANISH RULE	1580–1640	

HOUSE OF BRAGANZA

LEADERS	YEARS IN POWER	PARTY
John IV	1640–1656	
Alfonso VI	1656–1667	
Pedro II (regent)	1667–1683	
Pedro II	1683–1706	
John V	1706–1750	
Joseph Emanuel	1750–1777	
Maria I (joint ruler)	1777–1816	
Pedro III (joint ruler)	1777–1786	
John VI	1816–1826	
Pedro IV	1826	
Maria II	1826–1828	
Miguel (usurper)	1828–1834	
Maria II	1834–1853	
Pedro V	1853–1861	
Louis I	1861–1889	
Carlos I	1889–1908	
Emanuel II	1908–1910	

PRESIDENTS

LEADERS	YEARS IN POWER	PARTY
Dr. Teófilo Braga	1910–1911	
Dr. Manuel José de Arriaga	1911–1915	
Dr. Teófilo Braga	1915	
Dr. Bernardino Luis Machado Guimaraes	1915–1917	
Maj. Cardoso da Silva Pais	1917–1918	
Adm. Joao da Canto e Castro	1918–1919	
Dr. Antonio José de Almeida	1919–1923	
Manoel Teixeira Gomes	1923–1925	
Dr. Bernardino Luis Machado Guimaraes	1925–1926	

MILITARY RULE

LEADERS	YEARS IN POWER	PARTY
Dr. Antonio de Oliveira Salazar	1926–1968	National Union
Prof. Marcelo Caetano	1968–1974	National Union
Gen. Antonio Sebastiao de Spinola	1974	Armed Forces Movement
Gen. Francisco da Costa Gomes	1974–1976	Socialist-Communist

PRIME MINISTERS

LEADERS	YEARS IN POWER	PARTY
Dr. Mario Lopes Soares	1976–1978	Socialist
Alfredo da Costa	1978	Coalition
Prof. Carlos Mota Pinto	1978–1979	Coalition
Dr. Maria de Lourdes Pintasilgo	1979–1980	Coalition
Dr. Francisco sa Carneiro	1980	Democratic Alliance
Prof. Diogo Freitas do Amaral	1980–1981	Coalition
Dr. Francisco Pinto Balsemao	1981–1983	Democratic Alliance
Dr. Mario Lopes Soares	1983–1985	Socialist
Anibal Cavaco Silva	1985–	Social Democrat: still retains position but no longer head of government

PRESIDENT

LEADERS	YEARS IN POWER	PARTY
Dr. Mario Lopes Soares	1986–	Social Democrat

Greece

PRESIDENTS

LEADERS	YEARS IN POWER	PARTY
Ioannis Capodistrias	1828–1831	
Agostino Capodistrias	1831–1832	

KINGS

LEADERS	YEARS IN POWER	PARTY
Othon	1832–1862	
Giorgios I	1862–1913	
Konstantinos	1913–1917	
Alexandros	1917–1920	
Konstantinos (restored)	1920–1922	
Giorgios II	1922–1924	

PRESIDENTS OF THE HELLENIC EMPIRE

LEADERS	YEARS IN POWER	PARTY
Admiral Pavlos Kondoriotis	1924–1926	
Gen. Theodoros Pangalos	1926	
Admiral Pavlos Kondoriotis	1926–1929	
Alexandros Zaimis	1929–1935	

KINGS

LEADERS	YEARS IN POWER	PARTY
Giorgios II (restored)	1935–1941	
GERMAN OCCUPATION	1941–1944	

MONARCHS

LEADERS	YEARS IN POWER	PARTY
Archbishop Damaskinos (regent)	1944–1946	
Pavlos	1946–1964	
Konstantinos II	1964–1973	

MILITARY RULE

LEADERS	YEARS IN POWER	PARTY
Giorgios Papadopoulos	1967–1973	
Spyros Markezinis	1973	
Adamantios Androutsopoulos	1973–1974	

PRIME MINISTERS

LEADERS	YEARS IN POWER	PARTY
Konstantinos Karamanlis	1974–1980	New Democracy Party
Giorgios Rallis	1980–1984	New Democracy Party
Andreas Papandreou	1984–1989	Panhellic Socialist Movement
Tzannis Tzannetakis	1989	Coalition Government
Yannis Grivas	1989–1990	Coalition Government
Xenefon Zolotas	1990	Coalition Government
Konstantinos Mitsotakis	1990–	New Democracy Party

Austria

EMPERORS

LEADERS	YEARS IN POWER	PARTY
Franz I	1804–1835	
Ferdinand I	1835–1848	
Franz Joseph I	1848–1916	
Karl I	1916–1918	

PRESIDENTS

LEADERS	YEARS IN POWER	PARTY
Dr. Karl Seitz	1918–1920	
Dr. Michael Hainisch	1920–1928	
Dr. Wilhelm Miklas	1928–1938	
GERMAN THIRD REICH (ANCHLUSS)	1938–1945	
ALLIED OCCUPATION	1945–1955	

CHANCELLORS

LEADERS	YEARS IN POWER	PARTY
Leopold Figl	1945–1953	Austria's People Party
Julius Raab	1953–1961	Austria's People Party
Alfons Gorbach	1961–1964	Austria's People Party
Josef Klaus	1964–1970	Austrian People's Party
Bruno Kreisky	1970–1983	Socialist Party of Austria
Dr. Fred Sinowatz	1983–1986	Coalition
Fraz Vranitzky	1986–	Coalition

LEADERS	YEARS IN POWER	PARTY

Belgium

KINGS

Leopold I	1831–1865	
Leopold II	1865–1909	
Albert I	1909–1934	
Leopold III	1934–1951	
Prince Charles (regent)	1944–1950	
Baudouin	1951– 1993	
Albert II	1993	

PRIME MINISTERS

Charles Rogier	1830–1831	
Erasme Surlet de Chokier	1831	
Charles de Brouckere	1831–1832	
Charles Rogier	1832–1834	
Barthelemy Theux de Meylandt	1834–1840	
Joseph Lebeau	1840–1841	
Jean-Baptiste Nothomb	1841–1845	
Sylvain van de Weyer	1845–1846	
Barthelemy Theux de Meylandt	1846–1847	
Charles Rogier	1847–1852	
Henri de Brouckere	1852–1855	
Pierre de Decker	1855–1857	
Charles Rogier	1857–1868	
Hubert Frere-Orban	1868–1870	
Jules d'Anethan	1870–1871	
Barthelemy Theux de Meylandt	1871–1874	
Jules Malou	1874–1878	
Hubert Frere-Orban	1878–1884	
Jules Malou	1884	
Auguste Beernaert	1884–1894	
Paul de Smet de Nayer	1896–1899	
Julius vanden Peereboom	1899	
Paul de Smet de Nayer	1899–1907	
Jules de Trooz	1907–1908	
Francois Schollaert	1908–1911	
Charles de Broqueville	1911–1914	
GERMAN OCCUPATION	1914–1918	

PRIME MINISTERS

Gerhard Cooreman	1918	
Leon Delacroix	1918–1920	
Henri Carton de Wiart	1920–1921	
Georges Theunis	1921–1925	
Alois van der Vyvere	1925	
Prosper Poullet	1925–1926	
Henri Jaspar	1926–1931	
Jules Renkin	1931–1932	
Charles de Broqueville	1932–1934	
George Theunis	1934–1935	
Paul Van Zeeland	1935–1937	
Paul Janson	1937–1938	
Paul-Henri Spaak	1938–1939	
Hubert Pierlot	1939–1940	
GERMAN OCCUPATION	1940–1945	

PRIME MINISTERS

Hubert Pierlot	1944–1945	Catholic
Achille Van Acker	1945–1946	Socialist
Paul-Henri Spaak	1946	Socialist
Achille Van Acker	1946	Socialist
Camille Huysmans	1946–1947	Socialist
Paul-Henri Spaak	1947–1949	Socialist
Gaston Eyskens	1949–1950	Social Christian
Jean Duvieusart	1950	Social Christian
Joseph Pholien	1950–1952	Social Christian
Jean van Houtte	1952–1954	Social Christian
Achille Van Acker	1954–1958	Socialist
Gaston Eyskens	1958–1961	Social Christian

LEADERS	YEARS IN POWER	PARTY
Theo Lefevre	1961–1965	Social Christian
Pierre Harmel	1965–1966	Social Christian
Paul vanden Boeynants	1966–1968	Social Christian
Gaston Eyskens	1968–1972	Social Christian
Edmond Leburton	1972–1974	Socialist
Leo Tindeman	1974–1978	Social Christian
Paul vanden Boeynants	1978–1979	Social Christian
Wilfried Martens	1979–1981	Social Christian
Mark Eyskens	1981	Social Christian
Wilfried Martens	1981–1992	Social Christian
Jean-Luc Dehaene	1992–	Social Christian

The Netherlands

STADHOLDERS OF THE DUTCH REPUBLIC

William I	1579–1584	
Maurice	1584–1625	
Frederick Henry	1625–1647	
William II	1647–1659	
STADHOLDER SUSPENDED	1650–1672	
STADHOLDER		
William III	1672–1702	
REPUBLIC	1702–1747	
STADHOLDERS		
William IV	1747–1751	
William V	1751–1795	
FRENCH RULE	1795–1813	
MONARCHS		
Willem I	1815–1840	
Willem II	1840–1849	
Willem III	1849–1890	
Wilhelmina	1890–1948	
Juliana	1948–1980	
Beatrix	1980–	

PRIME MINISTERS

Gerrit Schimmelpenninck	1848	
Jacob de Kempenaer/ Dirk Donker Curtius	1848–1849	
Jan Thorbecke	1849–1853	
Floris van Hall/ Dirk Donker Curtius	1853–1856	
Justinius van der Brugghen	1856–1858	
Jacob Rochussen/ Pieter van Bosse	1858–1860	
Floris van Hall/ Schelte van Heemstra	1860–1861	
Julius van Zuylen van Nijevelt/ James Louden	1861–1862	
Jan Thorbecke	1862–1866	
Isaac Fransen van de Putte	1866	
Julius van Zuylen van Nijevelt/ Jan Heemskerk	1866–1868	
Pieter van Bosse	1868–1871	
Jan Thorbecke	1871–1872	
Isaac Fransen van de Putte/ Gerrit de Vries	1872–1874	
Constantinius van Lynden van Sandenburg/Jan Heemskerk	1874–1877	
Johannes Kappeyne van de Coppello	1877–1879	
Constantinjus van Lynden van Sandenburg	1879–1883	
Jan Heemskerk	1883–1888	
Aeneas Mackay	1888–1891	
Cornelius van Tienhoven	1891–1894	
Johan Roell	1894–1897	
Nicolaas Pierson	1897–1901	

LEADERS	YEARS IN POWER	PARTY
Abraham Kuyper	1901–1905	
Theodor de Meester	1905–1908	
Theodor Heemskerk	1908–1913	
Pieter Cort van der Linden	1913–1918	
Charles Ruys de Beerenbrouck	1918–1925	
Hendrickus Colijn	1925–1929	
Dirk de Geer	1929	
Charles Ruys de Beernbrouck	1929–1933	
Hendrickus Colijn	1933–1939	
Dirk de Geer	1939–1940	
GERMAN OCCUPATION	1940–1945	

PRIME MINISTERS

LEADERS	YEARS IN POWER	PARTY
Pieter Sjoerd Gerbrandy	1945	
Prof. Willem Schermerhorn	1945–1946	Labor-Catholic
Dr. Louis Beel	1946–1948	Catholic-Labor
Dr. Willem Drees	1948–1958	Catholic
Dr. Louis Beel	1958–1959	Catholic
Prof. Jan de Quay	1959	Catholic
Dr. Louis Beel	1959	Catholic
Prof. Jan de Quay	1959–1963	Catholic
Dr. Victor Marijnen	1963–1965	Catholic
Dr. Joseph Cals	1965–1966	Catholic
Prof. Jelle Zijstra	1966–1967	Catholic
Petrus de Jong	1967–1971	Catholic
Barend Biesheuvel	1971–1973	Catholic
Dr. Johannes den Uyl	1973–1977	Labor
Andreas van Agt	1977–1982	Christian Democratic Appeal
Rudolph Lubbers	1982–	Christian Democratic Appeal

Denmark

MONARCHS

Harold Bluetooth	950–985
Sweyn I	985–1014
Harold	1014–1018
Canute	1019–1035
Canute III	1035–1042
Magnus the Good	1042–1047
Sweyn II	1047–1074
Harold Hen	1074–1080
Canute IV	1080–1086
Oluf I	1086–1095
Eric I Evergood	1095–1103
Niels	1103–1134
Eric II	1134–1137
Eric III	1137–1146
Sweyn	1146–1157
Knud	1157
Valdemar I the Great	1157–1182
Canute VI	1182–1202
Valdemar II	1202–1241
Eric IV	1241–1250
Abel	1250–1252
Christopher	1252–1259
Eric V	1259–1286
Eric VI	1286–1319
Christopher II	1319–1332
Valdemar IV	1340–1375
Oluf II	1375–1387
Margrethe	1387–1412
Eric VII	1412–1439
Christopher III	1439–1448
Christian I	1448–1481
Hans	1481–1513
Christian II	1513–1523
Frederik I	1523–1533
Christian III	1533–1559
Frederik II	1559–1588

LEADERS	YEARS IN POWER	PARTY
Christian IV	1588–1648	
Frederik III	1648–1670	
Christian V	1670–1699	
Frederik V	1699–1730	
Christian VI	1730–1746	
Frederik V	1746–1766	
Christian VII	1766–1808	
Frederik VI	1808–1839	
Christian VIII	1839–1848	
Frederik VII	1848–1863	
Christian IX	1863–1906	
Frederik VIII	1906–1912	
Christian X	1912–1947	
Frederik IX	1947–1972	
Margrethe II	1972–	

PRIME MINISTERS

LEADERS	YEARS IN POWER	PARTY
Adam Vilhelm Moltke	1848–1852	
Christian Albrecht Bluhme	1852–1853	
Andreas Sando Orsted	1853–1854	
Peter Georg Bang	1854–1856	
Carl C. G. Andrae	1856–1857	
Carl Christian Hall	1857–1863	
Ditlev Gothard Monrad	1863–1864	
Christian Albrecht Bluhme	1864–1865	
Christian Emil Frijs	1865–1870	
Ludwig Henrik C. H. Holstein	1870–1874	
Christian Andreas Fonnerbech	1874–1875	
Jacob B.S. Estrup	1875–1894	
K. T. Tage Reedtz-Thott	1894–1897	
Hugo Egmont Horring	1897–1900	
Hannibal Sehested	1900–1901	
Johan Henrik Deuntzer	1901–1905	
Jens Christian Christensen	1905–1908	
Niels T. Neergaard	1908–1909	
Johan Ludwig Holstein	1909	
Carl Theodor Zahle	1909–1910	
Klaus Bernsten	1910–1913	
Carl Theodor Zahle	1913–1920	
C.J. Otto Liebe	1920	
Michael Petersen Friis	1920	
Niels T. Neergaard	1920–1924	
Thorvald A.M. Stauning	1924–1926	
Thomas Madsen-Mygdal	1926–1929	
Thorvald A.M. Stauning	1929–1942	
Vilhelm Buhl	1942	
Erik Scavenius	1942–1945	
Vilhelm Buhl	1945	Coalition
Knud Kristensen	1945–1947	Liberal
Hans Hedtoft	1947–1950	Social Democrat
Erik Eriksen	1950–1953	Liberal-Conservative
Hans Hedtoft	1953–1955	Social Democrat
Hans Christian Hansen	1955–1960	Social Democrat
Viggo Kampmann	1960	Social Democrat
Jens Otto Krag	1960–1968	Social Democrat
Hilmar Baunsgaard	1968–1971	Radical
Jens Otto Krag	1971–1972	Social Democrat
Anker Jorgensen	1972–1973	Social Democrat
Poul Hartling	1973–1975	Liberal
Anker Jorgensen	1975–1982	Social Democrat
Poul Schluter	1982–	Liberal-Conservative

Sweden

KINGS

Olof Sköttkonung	994–1022
Anund Jakob	1022–1050
Edmund the Old	1050–1060
Steinkel	1060–1066
Halstan	1080–1110
Philip	1112–1118

LEADERS	YEARS IN POWER	PARTY
SVERKER AND ERIC DYNASTIES		
Sverker	1133–1156	
Eric IX (rival king)	1150–1160	
Magnus Henriksson	1160–1161	
Charles VII	1161–1167	
Knut Eriksson	1167–1195	
Sverker Karlsson	1195–1208	
Eric X	1208–1216	
John I Sverkersson	1216–1222	
Eric XI	1222–1250	
Knut Lange (rival king)	1229–1234	
FOLKUNG DYNASTY		
Waldemar I	1250–1275	
Magnus I	1275–1290	
Birger II	1290–1318	
Magnus Eriksson	1319–1365	
Albert	1365–1389	
Eric XIII	1396–1439	
Christopher	1439–1448	
Charles VIII	1448–1457	
Christian I	1457–1464	
Charles VIII	1464–1470	
Sten Sure (regent)	1470–1497	
John	1497–1501	
Sten II (regent)	1501–1503	
Svante Nilsson II (regent)	1503–1512	
Sten the Younger (regent)	1512–1520	
Christian II	1520–1521	
Gustaf I Adolf	1523–1560	
Eric XIV	1560–1568	
Johan III	1568–1592	
Sigismund	1592–1599	
Carl IX	1599–1611	
Gustavus Adolphus	1611–1632	
Christina	1632–1654	
Carl X Gustaf	1654–1660	
Carl XI	1660–1697	
Carl XII	1697–1718	
Ulrika Elenora	1718–1726	
Fredrik	1726–1751	
Adolf Fredrik	1751–1771	
Gustaf III	1771–1792	
Gustaf IV Adolf	1792–1809	
Carl XIII	1809–1818	
Carl XIV	1818–1844	
Oscar I	1844–1859	
Carl XV	1859–1872	
Oscar II	1872–1907	
Gustaf V	1907–1950	
Gustaf VI	1950–1973	
Carl XVI Gustaf	1973–	
PRIME MINISTERS		
Bernhard Horn	1710–1719	
Gustav Cronhjelm	1719–1720	
Arvid Bernhard Horn	1720–1738	
Carl Gyllenborg	1739–1746	
Karl Gustav Tessin	1747–1752	
Anders Johan von Hopken	1752–1761	
Klas Ekeblad	1761–1765	
Karl Gustav Lowenheim	1765–1768	
Klas Ekeblad	1769–1771	
Joachim von Duben	1772	
Ulrik Scheffer	1772–1783	
Gustav Philip Creutz	1783–1785	
Emanuel De Geer	1785–1787	
Johan Gabriel Oxenstierna	1787–1789	
Carl Wilhelm von Duben	1789–1790	
CHANCELLOR		
Frederick Sparre	1792–1797	

LEADERS	YEARS IN POWER	PARTY
COUNSELLOR		
Gustav Adolf Reuterholm	1792–1796	
CHANCELLOR PRESIDENT		
Fredrik Vilhelm von Ehrenheim	1801–1809	
EARL MARSHALL		
Hans Axel von Fersen	1801–1810	
Magnus Brahe	1834–1844	
CHANCELLOR		
Louis Gerhard de Geer	1858–1870	
Axel Gustav Adlercreutz	1870–1874	
Edvard Henrik	1874–1875	
Louis Gerhard de Geer	1875–1876	
PRIME MINISTERS		
Louis Gerhard de Geer	1876–1880	
Arvid Rutger F. Posse	1880–1883	
Carl Johan Thyselius	1883–1884	
Oskar Robert Themptander	1884–1888	
Didrik A.G. Bildt	1888–1889	
Joh. Gustav N.S. Åkerhielm	1889–1891	
Erik Gustav Bostrm	1891–1900	
Fredrik Wilhelm von Otter	1900–1902	
Erik Gustav Boström	1902–1905	
Johan Olof Ramstedt	1905	
Christian Lundeberg	1905	
Karl Albert Staaff	1905–1906	
Salomon Arvid Achates Lindman	1906–1911	
Per Albin Hansson	1932–1946	Social Democrat
Tage Erlander	1946–1969	Social Democrat
Olof Palme	1969–1976	Social Democrat
Nils Olof Thorbjorn Falldin	1976–1978	Center
Ola Ullster	1978–1979	Liberal
Nils Olof Thorbjorn Falldin	1979–1982	Center
Olof Palme	1982–1986	Social Democrat
Ingvar Carlsson	1986–1991	Social Democrat
Carl Bildt	1991–	Moderate Union Party

Norway

LEADERS	YEARS IN POWER	PARTY
DANISH RULE	1380–1814	
SWEDISH RULE	1814–1905	
KINGS		
Haakon VII	1905–1951	
Olav V	1951–1991	
Harald	1991–	
PRIME MINISTERS		
Christian Michelsen	1905–1907	
J. Lövland	1907–1908	
Gunnar Knudsen	1908–1910	
Wollert Konow	1910–1912	
Jens Bratlie	1912–1913	
Gunnar Knudsen	1913–1920	
Otto B. Halvorsen	1920–1921	
Otto Blehr	1921–1923	
Otto B. Halverson	1923	
Abraham Berge	1923–1924	
Johan Ludwig Mowinckel	1924–1926	
Ivar Lykke	1926–1928	
Christopher Hornsrud	1928	
Johan Ludwig Mowinckel	1928–1931	
Peder Kolstad	1931–1932	
Jens Hundseid	1932–1933	
Johan Ludwig Mowinckel	1933–1935	
Johan Nygaardvold	1935–1945	
Einar Gehardsen	1945–1951	Labor

LEADERS	YEARS IN POWER	PARTY
Oscar Torp	1951–1955	Labor
Einar Gerhardsen	1955–1963	Labor
Johan Lyng	1963	Coalition
Einar Gehardsen	1963–1965	Labor
Per Borten	1965–1971	Center Party
Trygve Bratteli	1971–1972	Labor
Lars Korvald	1972–1973	Coalition Government
Trygve Bratteli	1973–1976	Labor
Odvar Nordli	1976–1981	Labor
Gro Harlem Bruntland	1981	Labor
Kare Willoch	1981–1986	Conservative
Gro Harlem Bruntland	1986–1989	Labor
Jan Syse	1989–1990	Conservative
Gro Harlem Brundtland	1990–	Labor

Russia and the Soviet Union

TSARS

RIURIKID DYNASTY (MOSCOW)

Daniel	1283–1303
Yuri	1303–1325
Ivan I	1325–1341
Semeon	1341–1353
Ivan II	1353–1359
Dimitri Donskoi	1359–1389
Vasili I	1389–1425
Vasili II	1425–1462
Ivan III the Great	1462–1505
Ivan IV the Terrible	1533–1584
Feodor I	1584–1598
Boris Godunov	1598–1605
Feodor II	1605
Dimitri (usurper)	1605–1606
Vasily V	1606–1610
Dimitri II (usurper)	1607–1610

POLISH OCCUPATION   1610–1612

HOUSE OF ROMANOV

Michael III	1613–1645
Alexis	1645–1676
Feodor III	1676–1682
Ivan V (co-tsar)	1682–1689
Peter I the Great	1689–1725
Catherine I	1725–1727
Peter II	1727–1730
Anna Ivanovna	1730–1740
Ivan VI	1740–1741
Elizabeth Petrovna	1741–1762
Peter III	1762
Catherine II the Great	1762–1796
Paul I	1796–1801
Alexander I	1801–1825
Nicholas I	1825–1855
Alexander II	1855–1881
Alexander III	1881–1894
Nicholas II	1894–1917

PROVISIONAL GOVERNMENT PREMIERS

Prince Georgi Lvov	1917
Alexander Kerensky	1917

PRIME MINISTER OF THE USSR

Vladimir Ilyich Lenin	1917–1924

USSR COMMUNIST PARTY LEADERS

Josef Stalin	1922–1953
Georgi Malenkov	1953–1955
Nikolai Bulganin	1955–1958
Nikita Khrushchev	1958–1964

LEADERS	YEARS IN POWER	PARTY
Leonid Brezhnev	1964–1982	
Yuri Andropov	1982–1984	
Konstantin Chernenko	1984–1985	
Mikhail Gorbachev	1985–1991	

PRESIDENT OF RUSSIAN REPUBLIC

Boris Yeltsin	1991–	Democratic Russia

Poland

KINGS

Mieszko I (Mieczyslav)	c. 960–992
Boleslaus I	992–1025
Mieszko II	1025–1034
Casimir I	1034–1058
Boleslaus II	1058–1079
Ladislaus I	1079–1102
Tbigniew	1102–1107
Boleslaus III	1107–1138
Ladislaus II	1138–1146
Boleslaus IV	1146–1173
Mieszko III	1173–1177
Casimir II	1177–1194
Mieszko III	1194–1202
Ladislaus Spindleshanks	1202
Lesek the White	1202–1210
Mieszko the Stumbling	1210–1211
Lesek the White	1211–1227
Ladislaus Spindleshanks	1227–1229
Conrad of Mazovia	1229–1232
Henry I	1232–1238
Henry II	1238–1241
Konrad I	1241–1243
Boleslaus V the Chaste	1241–1279
Lesek the Black	1279–1288
Henry III	1288–1290
Przemyslav II	1295–1296
Wenceslaus II	1300–1305
Wenceslaus III	1305–1306
Ladislaus I	1306–1333
Casimir III	1333–1370
Louis of Hungary	1370–1382

HOUSE OF JAGIELLO

Jadwiga	1382–1399
Ladislaus II	1399–1434
Ladislaus III	1434–1444
Casimir IV	1444–1492
John I	1492–1501
Alexander	1501–1506
Sigusmund I	1506–1548
Sigusmund II	1548–1572

ELECTIVE KING

Henry IV	1573–1574

ARISTOCRATIC REPUBLIC   1574–1576

Stephen Batory	1576–1586
Sigusmund III	1587–1632
Ladislaus IV	1632–1648
John II	1648–1668
Michael Winiowiecki	1669–1673
Jan III Sobieski	1674–1696
Augustus II	1697–1706
Stanislaus Leszczynski	1706–1709
Augustus II	1709–1733
Augustus III	1733–1763
Stanislaus Augustus Poniatowski	1764–1795

POLAND PARTITIONED   1795–1918

PRESIDENTS OF THE POLISH REPUBLIC

Marshal Jósef Pilsudski	1918–1922	
Gabriel Narutowicz	1922	
Stanislaw Wojciechowski	1922–1926	

MILITARY DICTATOR

Marshal Josef Pilsudski	1926–1935	

PRESIDENT

Prof. Ignacy Moscicki	1926–1939	

GERMAN OCCUPATION

	1939–1945	

LEADERS OF THE POLISH COMMUNIST PARTY

Boleslaw Bierut	1945–1956	
Wladyslaw Gomulka	1956–1970	
Edward Gierek	1970–1981	
General Wojciech Jaruzelski	1981–1985	
Zbigniew Messner	1985–1988	
Mieczyslay F Rakowski	1989–1988	

PRESIDENTS AND PRIME MINISTERS

Gen. Wojciech Jaruzelski	1989–1990	
Lech Walesa	1990–1993	Communist Solidarity
Hanna Suchocka	1993–	

Czechoslovkia and Czech Republic

KINGS OF BOHEMIA

PREMYSLID DYNASTY

Ladislas II	1158–1173	
Ottokar I	1197–1230	
Wenceslaus I	1230–1253	
Ottokar II	1253–1278	
Wencelaus II	1278–1305	
Wencelaus III	1305–1306	
Rudolph	1306–1307	
Henry	1307–1310	

LUXEMBURG DYNASTY

John the Blind	1310–1346	
Charles	1346–1373	
Wencelaus IV	1373–1419	
Sigismund of Hungary	1419–1437	

HABSBURG (AND OTHER) DYNASTIES

Albert of Austria	1437–1439	
Ladislaus Posthumus	1440–1457	
George of Podebrad	1458–1471	
Matthias of Hungary (rival king)	1469	
Ladislas II	1471–1516	
Louis	1516–1526	

CZECHOSLOVAKIA UNITED WITH AUSTRIA

UNDER THE HABSBURGS

	1526–1918	

PRESIDENTS

Tomás Garrigue Masaryk	1918–1935	
Edvard Benes	1935–1938	
Gen. Jan Sirovy	1938	
Dr. Emil Hácha	1938–1939	

GERMAN OCCUPATION

	1939–1945	

LEADERS OF THE COMMUNIST PARTY

Edvard Benes	1945–1948	
Rudolf Slansky	1948–1952	
Antonin Novotny	1953–1968	
Alexander Dubcek	1968–1969	
Gustav Husak	1969–1989	

PRESIDENTS

Vaclav Havel	1989–1992	Civic Forum
Jan Strasky	1992–	Civic Democratic Party

Hungary

ARAPAD MONARCHS

Stephen I	997–1038	
Peter Orseolo	1038–1041	
Aba Samuel	1041–1044	
Peter Orseolo	1044–1046	
Andrew I	1046–1060	
Bela I	1060–1063	
Salomon I	1063–1074	
Geza I	1074–1077	
Ladislaus	1077–1095	
Salomon II	1095–1116	
Stephen II	1116–1131	
Bela II	1131–1141	
Geza II	1141–1161	
Stephen III	1161–1162	
Ladislaus II	1162–1163	
Stephen IV	1163–1165	
Stephen III	1165–1172	
Bela III	1173–1196	
Emeric	1196–1204	
Ladislaus III	1204–1205	
Andrew II	1205–1235	
Bela IV	1235–1270	
Stephen V	1270–1272	
Ladislaus IV	1272–1290	
Andrew III	1290–1301	
Wenceslaus of Bohemia	1301–1305	
Otto of Bavaria	1305–1307	
Charles I	1308–1342	
Louis the Great	1342–1382	
Mary	1382–1387	
Sigismund	1387–1437	
Albert	1437–1439	
Elizabeth	1439–1440	
Ladislaus of Poland	1440–1444	
Ladislaus V	1444–1457	
Matthias Corvinus	1458–1490	
Ladislaus of Bohemia	1490–1516	
Louis II	1516–1526	

HUNGARY DIVIDED BETWEEN TURKEY AND AUSTRIA

	1526–1711	

AUSTRIAN RULE

	1711–1918	

PRESIDENT

Mihaly Karolyi	1919	

HEAD OF BOLSHEVIK GOVERNMENT

Bela Kun	1919	

REGENTS

Joseph of Austria	1919	
Admiral Miklos von Horthy	1920–1944	
Ferenc Szalasi	1944–1945	
Bela Miklos (opposition government)	1944–1945	

PRESIDENTS

Zoltan Tildy	1946–1948	

LEADERS OF THE COMMUNIST PARTY

Matyas Rakosi	1946–1953	
Imre Nagy	1953–1956	
Janos Kadar	1956–1989	
Karoly Grosz	1989–1990	

LEADERS	YEARS IN POWER	PARTY
PREMIER		
Joszsef Antall	1990–	Hungarian Democratic Forum

Romania

MONARCHS		
Carol I	1881–1914	
Ferdinand I	1914–1927	
Michael	1927–1930	
Carol II	1930–1940	
Michael	1940–1947	

LEADERS OF THE COMMUNIST PARTY		
Constantin I. Parhon	1948–1952	
Petru Groza	1952–1958	
Ion Gheorghe Maurer	1958–1961	
Nicolas Ceausescu	1961–1989	

PRESIDENTS		
Ion Illiescu	1990–	National Salvation Front

Yugoslavia

KINGS		
Peter I (of Serbia)	1919–1921	
Alexander I	1921–1934	
Peter II	1934–1945	

LEADERS OF THE COMMUNIST PARTY		
Josip Broz Tito	1945–1980	
Collective leadership	1980–1990	

PRIME MINISTER		
Milan Panic	1992–	

Turkey

OTTOMAN EMPIRE (1300–1918)

EMIRS	
Osman I	1300–1326

SULTANS	
Orkhan	1326–1359
Murad I	1359–1389
Bayazid (Bajazet)	1389–1403
Suleiman	1403–1411
Prince Musa	1411–1413
Muhammad I	1413–1421
Murad II	1421–1451
Muhammad II	1451–1481
Bayazid II	1481–1512
Selim I	1512–1520
Suleiman II	1520–1566
Selim II	1566–1574
Murad III	1574–1595
Muhammad III	1595–1603
Ahmed I	1603–1617
Mustafa	1617–1618
Osman II	1618–1622
Mustafa I	1622–1623
Murad IV	1623–1640
Ibrahim	1640–1648
Muhammad IV	1648–1687
Suleiman III	1687–1691
Ahmed II	1691–1695
Mustafa II	1695–1703

LEADERS	YEARS IN POWER	PARTY
Ahmed III	1703–1730	
Mahmud I	1730–1754	
Osman III	1754–1757	
Mustafa III	1757–1773	
Abdul-Hamid	1773–1789	
Selim III	1789–1807	
Mustafa IV	1807–1808	
Mahmud II	1808–1839	
Abdul Medjid I	1839–1861	
Abdul-Aziz	1861–1876	
Murad V	1876	
Abdul-Hamid II	1876–1909	
Muhammad V	1909–1918	
Muhammad VI	1918–1922	

PRESIDENTS OF TURKISH REPUBLIC		
Kemal Ataturk	1923–1938	
Ismet Inonu	1938–1950	
Celal Bayar	1950–1960	
Cemal Gursel	1960–1966	
Cevdet Sunay	1966–1973	
Fahri Koruturk	1973–1980	
Kenan Evren	1980–1989	
Turgut Ozal	1989–1993	Motherland Party

ASIA

Israel

PRIME MINISTERS		
David Ben Gurion	1948–1953	Mapai
Moshe Sharett	1953–1955	Mapai
David Ben Gurion	1955–1963	Mapai
Levi Eshkol	1963–1969	Mapai
Gen. Yigal Allon	1969	Labor
Golda Meir	1969–1974	Labor
Itzhak Rabin	1974–1977	Labor
Menahem Begin	1977–1983	Likud
Itzhak Shamir	1983–1984	Likud
Shimon Peres	1984–1986	Labor
Itzhak Shamir	1986–1992	Likud
Itzhak Rabin	1992–	Labor

India

Asoka	c. 269–232 B.C.E. Maurya Dynasty	

MOGUL EMPERORS		
Babar	1526–1530	
Humayan	1530–1540	

SURI DYNASTY OF AFGHANISTAN	1540–1555	
Sher Shah	1540–1545	
Islam Shah	1545–1553	
Muhammad Adil	1553–1555	

MOGUL EMPERORS		
Humayan (restored)	1555–1556	
Akbar the Great	1556–1605	
Jahangir and Empress Nur Jahan	1605–1627	
Davar Bakhsh	1627–1628	
Shah Jahan I	1628–1657	
Murad Bakhsh	1657–1658	Gujarat
Shah Shuja	1657–1660	Bengal
Aurangzeb Alamgir I	1658–1707	
Bahadur Shah I	1707–1712	
Jahandar Shah	1712–1713	
Farrukhsiyar (Farruk-Siar)	1713–1719	
Rafi-ud-Darajat	1719	
Shah Jahan II	1719	

LEADERS	YEARS IN POWER	PARTY
Nikusiyar	1719	
Muhammad Shah	1719–1720	
Muhammad Ibrahaim	1720	
Muhammad Shah (restored)	1720–1748	
Ahmad Shah	1748–1754	
Alamgir II	1754–1759	
Shah Alam II	1759–1806	
Akbar II	1806–1837	
Bahadur Shah II	1837–1858	
BRITISH RULE	1858–1947	

PRIME MINISTERS OF INDIA

LEADERS	YEARS IN POWER	PARTY
Jawaharlal Nehru	1950–1964	Congress
Gulzarilal Nanda	1964	Congress
Lal Bahadur Shastri	1964–1966	Congress
Gulzarilal Nanda	1966	Congress
Indira Gandhi	1966–1977	Congress
Morarji Desai	1977–1979	Janata
Charan Singh	1979–1980	Janata
Indira Gandhi	1980–1984	Congress
Rajiv Gandhi	1984–1989	Congress
Vishwanath Pratap Singh	1989–1990	Coalition
Chandra Shekhar	1990–1991	Coalition
P.V. Narasimha Rao	1991–	Congress

China

HSIA DYNASTY (LEGENDARY)	c. 2000–1766 B.C.E.
SHANG (YIN) DYNASTY	c. 1766–1122 B.C.E
ZHOU (CHOU) DYNASTY	1122–221 B.C.E.
QIN (CH'IN) DYNASTY	221–206 B.C.E.
HAN DYNASTY	206 B.C.E.–220 C.E.
SIX DYNASTIES PERIOD	220–589
SUI DYNASTY	581–618
Emperor Wen Ti	581–604
T'ANG DYNASTY	618–907
FIVE DYNASTIES PERIOD	907–960
SUNG DYNASTY	960–1279
YUAN (MONGOL) DYNASTY	1260–1368
Kublai Khan	1260–1294

MING DYNASTY

Hung-wu	1368–1398
Chien-wen	1398–1402
Yung-lo	1402–1424
Hung-hsi	1424–1425
Hsuan-te	1425–1435
Cheng-t'ung	1435–1449
Qind Di (Ching-t'ai)	1449–1457
T'ien-shun	1457–1464
Ch'eng-hua	1464–1487
Hung-chih	1487–1505
Cheng-te	1505–1521
Jia Qing (Chia-ching)	1521–1566
Lung-ch'ing	1566–1572
Wan-li	1572–1620
T'ai-ch'ang	1620
T'ien-ch'i	1620–1627
Chongzhen (Ch'ung-chen)	1627–1644

QING (CHING) DYNASTY (MANCHU)

Shun-chih	1644–1661
Kangxi (K'ang-hsi)	1661–1722

LEADERS	YEARS IN POWER	PARTY
Yangzheng (Yung-cheng)	1722–1735	
Qian Long (Ch'ien-lung)	1735–1796	
Jia Qing (Chia-ch'ing)	1796–1820	
Daoguang (Tao-kuang)	1821–1850	
Xian Feng (Hsien-feng)	1851–1861	
Tongzhi (T'ung-chih)	1862–1875	
Guangxu (Kwang-hsu)	1875–1908	
Xuan Zong (Hsuen-t'ung)	1908–1912	

PRESIDENTS OF THE REPUBLIC OF CHINA

Sun Yat-sen	1911–1912
Yuan Shi-kai	1912–1916
Li Yuan-hung	1916–1917
Feng Kuo-chang	1917–1918
Hsu Shih-chang	1918–1922
Li Yuan-hung	1922–1923
Ts'ao K'un	1923–1924
Tuan Ch'i-jui	1924–1926
Chang Tso-lin	1927–1928
Chiang Kai-shek	1928–1932
Lin Sen	1932–1943
Chiang Kai-Shek	1943–1949

LEADERS OF THE COMMUNIST PARTY OF THE PEOPLE'S REPUBLIC OF CHINA

Mao Zedong	1949–1976	
Deng Xiaoping	1977–	Deng has held no official title but is considered the effective ruler.

Japan

EMPERORS AND EMPRESSES

Sukio Tenno	592–628
Jomei	629– ?
Kogyoku	642–645
Kotoku	645–655
Saimei	655
Tenchi	662?–672
Kobun	672
Temmu	672–686
Jito	686–697
Mommu	697–708
Gemmyo	708–724
Shomu	724–749
Koken	749–758
Junnin	758–764
Shotoku	764–770
Konin	770–781
Kammu	781–806

POWER PASSED TO NOBLE FAMILIES	806–1017
Yorimichi (regent)	1017–1067

EMPERORS

Sanjo II	1068–1072
Shirakawa	1072–1129
Toba	1129–1156
Shirakawa	1156–1158
Taira Kiyomori (regent)	1160–1181
Antoku	1180–1185

SHOGUNATE OR KAMAKURA PERIOD

Minamoto Yoritomo	1185–1199
Minamoto Yorii	1199–1203
Minamoto Sanetomo	1203–1219
Hojo Yasutok (Shogunal regent)	1224–1242
Emperor Daigo	1318–1336

ASHIKAGA SHOGUNATE OR MUROMACHI SHOGUNATE

Takauji	1336–1358
Yoshimitsu	1358–1394
Yoshimochi	1394–1423
Yoshikazu	1423–1429

LEADERS	YEARS IN POWER	PARTY
Yoshinon	1429–1441	
Yoshikatsu	1441–1443	
Yoshimasa	1443–1474	
Yoshihisa	1474–1490	
Yoshitane	1490–1493	
Yoshizumi	1493	

FEUDAL DISCORD 1493–1568

ODA SHOGUNATE

Oda Nobunaga	1568–1582	
Toyotomi Hideyoshi	1585–1598	

TOKUGAWA SHOGUNATE

Tokugawa Ieyasu	1603–1605	
Tokugawa Hidetada	1605–1623	
Tokugawa Iemitsu	1623–1651	
Tokugawa Ietsuna	1651–1680	
Tokugawa Sunayoshi	1680–1709	
Tokugawa Ineobu	1709–1712	
Tokugawa Ietsugu	1712	
Yoshimune	1716–1745	
Tokugawa Ieshige	1745–1760	
Tokugawa Ieharu	1760–1786	
Tokugawa Ienari	1786–1837	
Tokugawa Ieyoshi	1837–1853	
Tokugawa Iesada	1853–1858	
Tokugawa Iemochi	1858–1866	
Tokugawa Keiki	1866–1867	

MEIJI EMPERORS

Mutsuhito	1867–1912	
Taisho	1912–1926	
Hirohito	1926–1989	
Akihito	1989–	

PRIME MINISTERS

Hirobumi Ito	1885–1888	
Kiyotaka Kuroda	1888–1889	
Aritomo Yamagata	1889–1891	
Masayoshi Matsukata	1891–1892	
Hirobumi Ito	1892–1896	
Masayoshi Matsukata	1896–1898	
Hirobumi Ito	1898	
Shigenobu Okuma	1898	
Aritomo Yamagata	1898–1900	
Hirobumi Ito	1900–1901	
Kimmochi Saionji	1901	
Taro Katsura	1901–1906	
Kimmochi Saionji	1906–1908	
Taro Katsura	1908–1911	
Kimmochi Sainoji	1911–1912	
Taro Katsura	1912–1913	
Gombei Yamamoto	1913–1914	
Shigenobu Okuma	1914–1916	
Masatake Terauchi	1916–1918	
Takashi Hara	1918–1921	
Korekiyo Takahashi	1921–1922	
Tomosaburo Kato	1922–1923	
Gombei Yamamoto	1923–1924	
Keigo Kiyoura	1924	
Takaakira Kato	1924–1926	
Reijiro Wakatsuki	1926–1927	
Giichi Tanaka	1927–1929	
Osachi Hamaguchi	1929–1931	
Reijiro Wakatsuki	1931	
Ki Tsuyoshi Inukai	1931–1932	
Korekiyo Takahashi	1932	
Makoto Saito	1932–1934	
Keisuki Okada	1934–1936	
Koki Hirota	1936–1937	
Senjuro Hayashi	1937	
Fumimaro Konoye	1937–1939	

LEADERS	YEARS IN POWER	PARTY
Kiichiro Hiranuma	1939	
Nobuyuki Abe	1939–1940	
Mitumasa Yonai	1940	
Fumimaro Konoye	1940–1941	
Hideki Tojo	1941–1944	
Kuniaki Kosio	1944–1945	
Kantaro Suzuki	1945	
Haruhiko Higashikuma	1945	

UNITED STATES OCCUPATION 1945–1951

PRIME MINISTERS

Shigeru Yoshida	1948–1955	Liberal
Ichiro Hatoyama	1955–1956	Liberal Democrat
Tanzan Ishibashi	1956–1957	Liberal Democrat
Nobusuke Kishi	1957–1960	Liberal Democrat
Hayeto Ikeda	1960–1964	Liberal Democrat
Eisaku Sato	1964–1972	Liberal Democrat
Kakeui Tanaka	1972–1974	Liberal Democrat
Takeo Miki	1974–1976	Liberal Democrat
Takeo Fukuda	1976–1978	Liberal Democrat
Masayoshi Ohira	1978–1980	Liberal Democrat
Zenko Suzuki	1980–1982	Liberal Democrat
Yashiro Nakasone	1982–1987	Liberal Democrat
Noboru Takeshita	1987–1989	Liberal Democrat
Sosuke Uno	1989	Liberal Democrat
Toshiki Kaifu	1989–1991	Liberal Democrat
Kiichi Miyazawa	1991–	Liberal Democrat

NOTABLE ASIAN RULERS AND HEADS OF STATE

AFGHANISTAN

Mahmud	998–1030	Ghaznavid Dynas
Ahmad Shah	1747–1773	Barkzai Dynasty

CAMBODIA

Norodom Sihanouk	1941–1970 (King 1941–55; premier 1955–69; chief of state 1960–1970)	
Pol Pot	1976–1978	Khmer Rouge

INDONESIA

Muhammad Achmed Sukarno	1949–1967	
Gen. Raden Soeharto	1967–	

IRAN (PERSIA)

Shah Ismail	1502–1524	Safavid Dynasty
Shah Mahmud	1722–1725	Safavid Dynasty
Nadir Shah	1736–1747	
Aga Muhammad	1794–1797	Kajar Dynasty
Shah Riza Pahlevi	1921–1941	
Muhammad Mossadegh	1950–1953	
Shah Muhammad Riza Pahlevi	1953–1978	
Ayatollah Ruhollah Khomeini	1979–1989	

IRAQ

Faisal I	1921–1933	
Saddam Hussein	1979–	

JORDAN

King Abdullah ibn Hussein	1923–1951	
King Hussein I	1952–	

KOREA

I Songgye (Yi Song-gye)	1392–1408	Yi Dynasty

SOUTH KOREA

Syngman Rhee	1948–1960	
Gen. Park Chung Hee	1962–1979	

NORTH KOREA

Kim Il Sung	1948–1993	

LEADERS	YEARS IN POWER	PARTY
MONGOL EMPIRE		
Genghis Khan	1206–1227	
Tamerlane	c. 1369–1405	
MYANMAR (BURMA)		
King Aloung P'Houra (Alaungpaya)	1752–1760	
PAKISTAN		
Zulfiqar Ali Bhutto	1971–1978	
Gen. Muhammad Zia ul-Haq	1978–1988	
Benazir Bhutto	1988–1990	
PHILIPPINES		
Ramon Magsaysay	1954–1957	
Ferdinand Marcos	1965–1986	
Corazon Aquino	1986–1992	
SAUDI ARABIA		
King Ibn Saud	1882–1953	
SYRIA		
Hafez al-Assad	1971–	
TAIWAN		
Chaing Kai-shek	1949–1975	
THAILAND (SIAM)		
Rama III (Phra Nang Klao)	1824–1851	Chakri Dynasty
Rama IV (Phra Chom Klao)	1851–1868	Chakri Dynasty
Rama V (Phra Maha Chulalongkorn)	1868–1910	Chakri Dynasty
VIETNAM (NORTH)		
Ho Chi Minh	1945–1969	

AFRICA

Egypt

ANCIENT EGYPT

OLD KINGDOM		
1st and 2nd Thinite Dynasty	3400–2980 B.C.E	
3rd Memphite Dynasty	2980–2900 B.C.E	
4th Memphite Dynasty	2900–2750 B.C.E	
5th Memphite Dynasty	2750–2625 B.C.E	
6th Memphite Dynasty	2625–2475 B.C.E	
7th and 8th Memphite Dynasty	2575–2445 B.C.E	
MIDDLE KINGDOM		
9th and 10th Heraclepolitan Dynasty	2445–2160 B.C.E	
11th Theban Dynasty	2160–2000 B.C.E	
12th Theban Dynasty	2000–1788 B.C.E	
13th–17th Sheperd Kings Dynasty	1788–1580 B.C.E	
NEW KINGDOM		
18th Diospolite Dynasty	1580–1350 B.C.E	
19th Diospolite Dynasty	1350–1215 B.C.E	
20th Diospolite Dynasty	1198–1150 B.C.E.	
21st Farite Dynasty	1090–945 B.C.E	
22nd Bubastite Dynasty	945–745 B.C.E	
23rd Tanite Dynasty	745–718 B.C.E	
24th Saite Dynasty	718–712 B.C.E	
25th Ethiopian Dynasty	712–663 B.C.E	
26th Saite Dynasty	663–525 B.C.E	
PERSIAN RULE	523–332 B.C.E	
GREEK RULE	323–30 B.C.E	
ROMAN RULE	30 B.C.E– 640 C.E.	

LEADERS	YEARS IN POWER	PARTY
ARAB RULE	640–868	
TULUNID DYNASTY	868–884	
FATIMIDIES DYNASTY	969–1171	
AYUBID DYNASTY	1171–1250	
BAHRI MAMELUKE FAMILY	1260–1382	
BURJI MAMELUKE FAMILY	1382–1517	
OTTOMAN RULE	1517–1914	
BRITISH RULE	1914–1922	
KINGS		
Fuad I	1922–1936	
Faruq	1936–1952	
Fuad ii	1952–1953	
PRESIDENTS		
Gen. Muhammad Neguib	1952–1954	Military
Col. Gamal Abdel Nasser	1954–1970	Military
Anwar Sadat	1970–1981	National Democratic Party
Gen. Muhammad Hosni Mubarak	1981–	National Democratic Party

South Africa

PRIME MINISTERS		
Gen. Louis Botha	1910–1919	South African Party
Jan Christiaan Smuts	1919–1924	South African Party
James Barry Munnik Hertzog	1924–1939	Nationalist Party
Jan Christiaan Smuts	1939–1948	South African Party
Daniel Fancois Malan	1948–1954	Nationalist Party
Johannes Strijdom	1954–1958	Nationalist Party
Charles Swart	1958	Nationalist Party
Hendrik Verwoerd	1958–1966	Nationalist Party
Balthazar John Vorster	1966–1978	Nationalist Party
Pieter Willem Botha	1978–1984	Nationalist Party
PRESIDENTS		
Pieter Willem Botha	1984–1989	Nationalist Party
Frederick Willem de Klerk	1989–	Nationalist Party

NOTABLE AFRICAN RULERS AND HEADS OF STATE

ALGERIA		
Ahmed Ben Bella	1963–1965	
Col. Houari Boumediene	1965–1978	
ANGOLA		
Jose Eduardo Santos	1979–	
CENTRAL AFRICAN REPUBLIC		
Jean-Bedel Bokassa	1965–1979	
David Dacko	1960–1965, 1979–1981	
CHAD		
Ngarta Tombalbaye	1960–1975	
CONGO KINGDOM		
Mbemba Nzinga	1506–1543	
COTE D'IVOIRE (IVORY COAST)		
Felix Houphouet-Boigny	1960–	
ETHIOPIA		
King Theodore	1855–1868	
Emperor Menelik II	1889–1911	

LEADERS	YEARS IN POWER	PARTY
Emperor Haile Selassie I	1930–1936, 1941–1974	
Lt. Col Mengistu Haile Mariam	1977–1991	

GHANA

Kwame Nkrumah	1960–1966	

GUINEA

Sekou Toure	1958–1984	

KENYA

Jomo Kenyatta	1963–1978	
Daniel arap Moi	1978–	

LIBERIA

Joseph Roberts	1847–1856	
William V.S. Tubman	1944–1971	
Samuel K. Doe	1980–1990	

LIBYA

Col. Muammar el-Qadaffi	1969–	

MADAGASCAR

King Radama	1810–1828	Merina Dynasty
Queen Ranavaloana	1828–1861	Merina Dynasty
Philibert Tsiranana	1959–1972	
Didier Ratsiraka	1975–	

MALAWI

Hastings Kamuzu Banda	1966–	

MOROCCO

King Hassan II	1961–	

NIGER

Hamani Diori	1960–1974	

NIGERIA

Gen. Yakubu Gowon	1966–1975	

SUDAN

Gaafar Mohamed Nimeiri	1969–1985	

TANZANIA

Julius Kambarage Nyerere	1964-1985	

TUNISIA

Habib Bourguiba	1957–1987	

UGANDA

Idi Amin	1971–1979	

ZAIRE

Patrice Lumumba	1960	
Mobutu Sese Seko	1965–	

ZAMBIA

Kenneth Kaunda	1964–1990	

ZIMBABWE

Ian Smith	1965–1976	
Robert Mugabe	1980–	

ZULU EMPIRE

Chaka	1818–1828	

OCEANIA

Australia

Sir Edmund Barton	1901–1903	Coalition
Alfred Deakin	1903–1904	Liberal-Labor
John Christian Watson	1904	Labor
George Houston Reid	1904–1905	Coalition
Alfred Deakin	1905–1908	Liberal-Conservative

LEADERS	YEARS IN POWER	PARTY
Andrew Fisher	1908–1909	Labor
Alfred Deakin	1909–1910	Liberal-Conservative
Andrew Fisher	1910–1913	Labor
Joseph Cook	1913–1914	
Andrew Fisher	1914–1915	Labor
William Morris Hughes	1915–1923	Labor-Nationalist
Stanley Melbourne Bruce	1923–1929	Nationalist-Country
James Henry Scullin	1929–1932	Labor
Joseph Aloysius Lyons	1932–1939	United Australia
Earle Christmas Grafton Page	1939	Country-United Australia
Robert Gordon Menzies	1939–1941	Country-United Australia
Arthur William Fadden	1941	Country-United Australia
John Joseph Curtin	1941–1945	Labor
Francis Michael Forde	1945	Labor
Joseph Benedict Chifley	1945–1949	Labor
Robert Gordon Menzies	1949–1966	Liberal-Country
Harold Edward Holt	1966–1967	Liberal-Country
John McEwen	1967–1968	Liberal-Country
John Grey Gorton	1968–1971	Liberal-Country
William McMahon	1971–1972	Liberal-Country
Edward Gough Whitlam	1972–1975	Labor
John Malcolm Fraser	1975–1983	Liberal-Country
Robert James Lee Hawke	1983–1991	Labor
Paul Keating	1991–	Labor

New Zealand

PRIME MINISTERS OF THE DOMINION

Joseph Ward	1906–1912	Liberal
William Fergusson Massey	1912–1925	Reform
Francis Bell	1925	Reform
Joseph Gordon Coates	1925–1928	Reform
Joseph Ward	1928–1930	United Party
George Forbes	1930–1935	Reform-United Party
Michael Jospeh Savage	1935–1940	Labor
Peter Fraser	1940–1949	Labor
Sidney George Holland	1949–1957	National Party
Keith Jacka Holyoake	1957	National Party
Walter Nash	1957–1960	Labor
Keith Jacka Holyoake	1960–1972	Labor
John Ross Marshall	1972	National Party
Norman Eric Kirk	1972–1974	Labor
Hugh Watt	1974	Labor
Wallace Rowling	1974–1975	Labor
Robert David Muldoon	1975–1984	National Party
David Lange	1984–1989	Labor
Geoffrey Palmer	1989–1990	Labor
Michael Moore	1990	Labor
Jim Bolger	1990–	National Party

NORTH AND SOUTH AMERICA

United States of America

George Washington	1789–1797	Federalist
John Adams	1797–1801	Federalist
Thomas Jefferson	1801–1809	Democratic Republican
James Madison	1809–1817	Democratic Republican
James Monroe	1817–1825	Democratic Republican
John Quincy Adams	1825–1829	Democratic Republican
Andrew Jackson	1829–1837	Democrat
Martin Van Buren	1837–1841	Democrat
William H. Harrison	1841	Whig

LEADERS	YEARS IN POWER	PARTY
John Tyler	1841–1845	Whig
James K. Polk	1845–1849	Democrat
Zachary Taylor	1849–1850	Whig
Millard Fillmore	1850–1853	Whig
Franklin Pierce	1853–1857	Democrat
James Buchanan	1857–1861	Democrat
Abraham Lincoln	1861–1865	Republican
Andrew Johnson	1865–1869	Democrat Union
Ulysses S. Grant	1869–1877	Republican
Rutheford B. Hayes	1877–1881	Republican
James A. Garfield	1881	Republican
Chester A. Arthur	1881–1885	Republican
Grover Cleveland	1885–1889	Democrat
Benjamin Harrison	1889–1893	Republican
Grover Cleveland	1893–1897	Democrat
William McKinley	1897–1901	Republican
Theodore Roosevelt	1901–1909	Republican
William H. Taft	1909–1913	Republican
Woodrow Wilson	1913–1921	Democrat
Warren Harding	1921–1923	Republican
Calvin Coolidge	1923–1929	Republican
Herbert Hoover	1929–1933	Republican
Franklin Delano Roosevelt	1933–1945	Democrat
Harry S. Truman	1945–1953	Democrat
Dwight D. Eisenhower	1953–1961	Republican
John F. Kennedy	1961–1963	Democrat
Lyndon B. Johnson	1963–1969	Democrat
Richard M. Nixon	1969–1974	Republican
Gerald Ford	1974–1977	Republican
Jimmy Carter	1977–1981	Democrat
Ronald Reagan	1981–1989	Republican
George Bush	1989–1993	Republican
Bill Clinton	1993–	Democrat

Canada

PRIME MINISTERS

John Alexander MacDonald	1867–1873	Liberal Conservative
Alexander Mackenzie	1873–1878	Conservative
John Alexander MacDonald	1878–1891	Liberal-Conservative
John Caldwell Abbot	1891–1892	Liberal-Conservative
John Thompson	1892–1894	Liberal-Conservative
Mackenzie Bowell	1894–1896	Liberal-Conservative
Charles Tupper	1896	Liberal-Conservative
Wilfred Laurier	1896–1911	Liberal
Robert Borden	1911–1920	Conservative
Arthur Meighen	1920–1921	Conservative
William Lyon MacKenzie King	1921–1926	Liberal
Arthur Meighen	1926	Conservative
William Lyon MacKenzie King	1926–1930	Liberal
Richard Bedford Bennett	1930–1935	Conservative
William Lyon MacKenzie King	1935–1948	Liberal
Louis Stephen St. Laurent	1948–1957	Liberal
John George Diefenbaker	1957–1963	Progressive-Conservative
Lester Bowles Pearson	1963–1968	Liberal
Pierre Elliot Trudeau	1968–1979	Liberal
Charles Joseph Clark	1979–1980	Progressive-Conservative
Pierre Elliot Trudeau	1980–1984	Liberal
John Napier Turner	1984	Liberal
Brian Mulroney	1984–1993	Progressive-Conservative
Kim Campbell	1993	Progressive-Conservative
Jean Chrétien	1993–	Liberal

Mexico

AZTEC CIVILIZATION — c. 1200–1524

Chimalpopoca	1414–1428
Itzcoatl	1428–1440

LEADERS	YEARS IN POWER	PARTY
Montezuma	1440–1469	
Axayacatl	1469–1481	
Tizoc	1481–1486	
Ahuitzotl	1486–1503	
Montezuma II	1503–1520	
Cuitlahuac	1520	
Cuauhtmoc	1520–1522	

SPANISH COLONIAL RULE — 1524–1823

PRESIDENTS

Guadalupe Victoria	1824–1829
Vicente Guerrero	1829
José María de Bocangera	1829
Anastasio Bustamante	1829–1832
Melchor Múzquiz	1832
Manuel Gómez Pedraza	1832–1833
Gen. Antonio López de Santa Anna	1833–1835
Miguel Barragán	1835–1836
José Justo Corro	1836–1837
Anastasio Bustamante	1837–1841
Javier Echeverra	1841
Gen. Antonio López de Santa Anna	1841–1842
Nicolás Bravo	1842–1843
Gen. Antonio López de Santa Anna	1843
Valentín Canalizo	1843–1844
José Joaquín Herrera	1844–1845
Mariano Paredes y Arrillaga	1846
Nicolás Bravo	1846
José Mariano Salas	1846
Valentín Gómes Farías	1846–1847
Gen. Antonio López de Santa Anna	1847
Pedro María Anaya	1847
Gen. Antonio López de Santa Anna	1847
Manuel de la Peña y Peña	1847
Pedro María Anaya	1847–1848
Manuel de la Peña y Peña	1848
José Joaquín Herrera	1848–1851
Mariano Arista	1851–1853
Juan Bautista Ceballos	1853
Manuel M. Lombardine	1853
Gen. Antonio López de Santa Anna	1853–1855
Martín Carrera	1855
Juan Alvarez	1855
Ignacio Comonfort	1855–1857
Benito Pablo Juárez	1857–1861

FRENCH OCCUPATION — 1861–1867

Emperor Maximilian	1864–1867
Josef of Austria	1867

PRESIDENTS

Benito Pablo Jurez	1867–1872
Sebastin Lerdo de Tejada	1872–1876
Porfirio Díaz	1876
Juan N. Méndez	1876–1877
Gen. Porfirio Díaz	1877–1880
Manuel González	1880–1884
Gen. Porfirio Díaz	1884–1911
Francisco León De la Barra	1911
Francisco Indalecio Madero	1911–1913
Pedro Lascurain	1913
Vicoriano Huerta	1913–1914
Francisco Carbajal	1914
Venustiano Carranza	1914
Eulalio Martin Gutiérrez	1914–1915
Roque González Garza	1915
Francisco Lagos Chzaro	1915

LEADERS	YEARS IN POWER	PARTY
Venustiano Carranza	1915–1920	
Gen. Plutarco Elas Calles	1924–1928	Institutional Revolutionary Party
Emilio Portes Gil	1928–1930	Institutional Revolutionary Party
Pascual Ortiz Rubio	1930–1932	Institutional Revolutionary Party
Gen. Abelardo Rodríguez	1932–1934	Institutional Revolutionary Party
Gen. Lazardo Cárdenas	1934–1940	Institutional Revolutionary Party
Gen. Manuel Avila Camacho	1940–1946	Institutional Revolutionary Party
Miguel Aleman Valdès	1946–1952	Institutional Revolutionary Party
Adolfo Ruiz Cortines	1952–1958	Institutional Revolutionary Party
Adolfo López Mateos	1958–1964	Institutional Revolutionary Party
Dr. Gustavo Díaz Ordaz	1964–1970	Institutional Revolutionary Party
Luis Echeverría Alvárez	1970–1976	Institutional Revolutionary Party
José López Portillo	1976–1982	Institutional Revolutionary Party
Miguel de la Madrid Hurtado	1982–1988	Institutional Revolutionary Party
Carlos Salinas	1988–	Institutional Revolutionary Party

Chile

SPANISH RULE	1541–1818	
DICTATOR		
Bernardo O'Higgins	1818–1823	
PRESIDENTS		
Ramon Freire	1823–1826	
Manuel Blanco Encalada	1826–1828	
Francisco A. Pinto	1828–1831	
Joaquin Prieto	1831–1841	
Manuel Bulnes	1841–1851	
Manuel Montt	1851–1861	
Jose Joaquin Perez	1861–1871	
Federico Errazuriz Zanartu	1871–1876	
Anibal Pinto	1876–1881	
Domingo Santa Maria	1881–1886	
Jose Manuel Balmaceda	1886–1891	
Jorge Montt	1891–1896	
Federico Errazuriz Echaurren	1896–1901	
German Riesco	1901–1906	
Pedro Montt	1906–1910	
Ramon Barros Luco	1910–1915	
Juan Luis Sanfuentes	1915–1920	
Arturo Alessandri Palma	1920–1925	
Luis Altamirano	1925	
Emiliano Figueroa Larrain	1925–1927	
Carlos Ibanez del Campo	1927–1931	
Juan Estaban Montero	1931–1932	
Carlos Davila Espinoza	1932	
Arturo Alessandri Palma	1932–1938	
Pedro Aguirre Cerda	1938–1942	
Juan Antonio Rios	1942–1946	
Gabriel Gonzalez Videla	1946–1952	
Carlos Ibanez del Campo	1952–1958	
Jorge Alessandri Rodriguez	1958–1964	
Eduardo Frei	1964–1970	Christian Democratic
Salvador Allende	1970–1973	Marxist
Augusto Pinochet Ugarte	1973–1989	Military Dictatorship
Patricio Aylwin	1989–	Christian Democratic

Brazil

PORTUGUESE RULE	1500–1822	
EMPERORS		
Pedro I	1822–1831	
Pedro II	1831–1889	
PRESIDENTS		
Manuel Deodoro da Fonseca	1889–1891	
Floriano Peixoto	1891–1894	
Prudente Jose de Moraeis Barros	1894–1896	
Manuel Vitorino Pereira	1896–1897	
Manuel Ferraz de Campos Salles	1898–1900	
Francisco de Assis Rosa e Silva	1900–	
Manuel Ferraz de Campos Salles	1900–1902	
Francisco de Paula Rodrigues Alves	1902–1906	
Affonso Augusto Moreira Penna	1906–1909	
Nilo Pecanha	1909–1910	
Hermes Rodrigues da Fonseca	1910–1914	
Wenceslao Braz Pereira Gomes	1914–1917	
Urbano Santos da Costa Araujo	1917	
Wenceslao Braz Pereira Gomes	1917–1918	
Delfim Moreira da Costa Ribeiro	1918–1919	
Epitacio da Silva Pessoa	1919–1922	
Arthur da Silva Bernardes	1922–1926	
Washington Luiz Pereira de Souza	1926–1930	
MILITARY JUNTA	1930	
PRESIDENTS		
Getulio Dornelles Vargas	1930–1945	
Jose Linhares	1945–1946	
Enrico Gaspar Dutra	1946–1951	
Getulio Dornelles Vargas	1951–1954	
Joao Cafe Filho	1954–1955	
Carlos Coimbra da Luz	1955	
Nereu Ramos	1955–1956	
Juscelino Kubitschek de Oliveira	1956–1961	
Janio (da Silva) Quadros	1961	
Joao (Belchoir Marques) Goulart	1961–1964	
Pascoal Ranieri Mazzilli	1964	
Humberto de Alencar Castelo Branco	1964–1967	
Arturo da Costa e Silva	1967–1969	
MILITARY JUNTA	1969	
PRESIDENTS		
Emilio Garrastazu Medici	1969–1971	
Ernesto Geisel	1971–1979	
Joao Baptista de Oliveira Figueiredo	1979–1985	
Tancredo Neves	1985	
Jose Sarney Costa	1985–1989	
Fernando Collor	1989–1993	National Reconstruction Party
Itamar Franco	1993–	National Reconstruction Party

Argentina

SPANISH RULE	1553–1816	
PRESIDENTS		
Bernardino Rivadavia	1826–1827	
Vicente Lopez y Planes	1827–1828	

PERIOD OF ANARCHY	1828–1835	
DICTATOR		
Juan Manuel de Rosas	1835–1852	
PERIOD OF ANARCHY	1852–1854	
PRESIDENTS		
Justo Jose de Urquiza	1854–1860	
Santiago Derqui	1860–1861	
Juan Esteban Pedernera	1861	
Bartolome Mitre	1862–1868	
Domingo Faustino Sarmiento	1868–1874	
Nicoas Avellaneda	1874–1880	
Julio A. Roca	1880–1886	
Miguel Juarez Celman	1886–1890	
Carlos Pellegrini	1890–1892	
Luis Saenz Pena	1892–1895	
Jose Evaristo Uriburu	1895–1898	
Julio A. Roca	1898–1904	
Manuel Quintana	1904–1906	
Jose Figueroa Alcorta	1906–1910	
Roque Saenz Pena	1910–1914	
Victorino de la Plaza	1914–1916	
Hipolito Irigoyen	1916–1922	
Marcelo Torcuato de Alvear	1922–1928	
Hipolito Irigoyen	1928–1930	
Jose Felix Uriburu	1930–1932	
Augustin P. Justo	1932–1938	
Roberto M. Ortiz	1938–1941	
Ramon S. Castillo	1941–1943	
Pedro Ramirez	1943–1944	
Edelmiro J. Farrel	1944–1946	
Juan Domingo Peron	1946–1955	
Eduardo Lonardi	1955	
Pedro Eugenio Aramburu	1955–1958	
Arturo Frondizi	1958–1962	
Jose Maria Guido	1962–1963	
Arturo Umberto Illia	1963–1966	
MILITARY RULE		
Alejandro Agustin Lanuss	1966–1970	
Roberto Marcelo Levingston	1970–1971	
CHIEFS OF STAFF (MILiTARY)	1971	
Alejandro Agustin Lanusse	1971–1973	
Hector J. Campora	1973	
Raul Alberto Lastiri	1973	
PRESIDENTS		
Juan Domingo Peron	1973–1975	
Italo Argentino Luder	1975	
Maria Estela Martinez Peron	1975–1976	
MILITARY RULE		
Jorge Rafeal Videla	1976–1981	
Gen. Roberto Viola	1981	
Gen. Leopoldo Galtieri	1981–1982	
Reynaldo Bignone	1982–1983	
PRESIDENTS		
Raul Alfonsin	1983–1989	Radical Civic Union
Carlos Menem	1989–	Justicialist

NOTABLE LATIN AMERICAN AND CARRIBEAN RULERS AND HEADS OF STATE

BOLIVIA		
Simón Bolívar	1825–1826	
COLOMBIA		
Simón Bolívar	1810–1821	

COSTA RICA		
Oscar Arias	1986–1990	
CUBA		
Fulgencio Batista	1933–1944, 1952–1959	
Fidel Castro	1959–	
DOMINICAN REPUBLIC		
Rafael Trujillo	1930–1961	
ECUADOR		
Gabriel Garcia Marcho	1861–1865, 1869–1875	
Eoy Alfaro	1897–1901, 1907–1911	
EL SALVADOR		
José Napoleon Duarte	1972, 1980–1982, 1984–1988	
GUATEMALA		
Rafael Carrera	1844–1848, 1851–1868	
HAITI		
Toussaint l'Ouverture	1794–1802	
François Duvalier	1957–1971	
Jean-Claude Duvalier	1971–1986	
NICARAGUA		
Gen. Anastasio Somoza	1934–1956	
Gen. Anastasio Somoza Jr.	1967–1979	
Daniel Ortega	1979–1990	
PANAMA		
Gen. Manuel Noriega	1984–1989	
PERU		
Manco Capac	c. 1200	Inca Empire
Pachacutec	1438–1471	Inca
Atahualpa	1525–1533	Inca
José de San Martin	1821–1822	

ANCIENT EMPIRES

Roman Empire

CLAUDIAN EMPERORS		
Augustus	27 B.C.E-14 C.E.	
Tiberius	14–37	
Caligula	37–41	
Claudius	41–54	
Nero	54–68	
Galba	68–69	
Otho	69	
Vitellius	69	
FLAVIAN EMPERORS		
Vespasianus	69–79	
Titus	79–81	
Domitianus	81–96	
ANTONINE EMPERORS		
Nerva	96–98	
Trajanus	98–117	
Hadrianus	117–138	
Antoninus Pius	138–161	
Lucius Verus	161–169	
Marcus Aurelius	169–180	
Commodus	180–192	

LEADERS	YEARS IN POWER	PARTY

EMPERORS OF AFRICAN AND ASIAN ORIGIN
(including co-emperors)

Pertinax	193
Didius Julianus	193
Septimus Severus	193–211
Caracalla	211–217
Geta	209–212
Macrinus	217–219
Elagabalus	218–222
Severus Alexander	222–235
Maximinus	235–238
Gordianus I	238
Gordianus II	238
Pupienus Maximus	238
Balbinus	238
Gordianus III	238–244
Philippus	244–249
Decius	249–251
Gallius	251–253
Hostilianus	251
Aemilianus	253
Valerianus	253–260
Gallienus	260–268

ILLYRIAN EMPERORS

Claudius II	268–270
Quintillus	270
Aurelianus	270–275
Ulpia Severina	275
Tacitus	275–276
Florianus	276
Probus	276–282
Carus	282–283
Carinus	283–285
Numerianus	283–284

COLLEGIATE EMPERORS (More than one emperor ruled at a time under the collegiate system)

Diocletianus	284–305
Maximianus	286–305
Chlorus	305–306
Galerius	305–311
Severus	306–307
Maximianus (restored)	307–308
Maximinus Daia	308–313
Constantine the Great	312–337
Maxentius	306–312
Licinius	308–324
Constantinus II	337–340
Constans I	337–350
Constantius II	337–361
Magnus Magnentius	350–353
Julianus (Julian the Apostate)	361–363
Jovianus	363–364
Valentinianus (Emperor in the West)	364–375
Gratianus (Emperor in the West)	367–383
Valens (Emperor in the East)	364–378
Procopius (Emperor in the East)	365–366
Valentinianus (Emperor in the West)	375–385

LEADERS	YEARS IN POWER	PARTY
Magnus Maximus (Emperor in the West)	383–388	
Flavius Victor (Emperor in the West)	386–388	
Theodosius I (Emperor in the East 379–388; in the East and West 388–395)	379–395	
Valentinianus (Emperor in the West)	388–392	
Eugenius (Emperor in the West)	392–394	
Honorius (Emperor in the West)	393–395	

EMPERORS OF THE WESTERN EMPIRE

Honorius	395–423
Constantius III	421
Valentinianus III	425–455
Petronius Maximus	455
Avitus	455–456
Majorianus	457–461
Libius Severus	461–465
Anthemius	467–472
Olybrius	472
Glycerius	473–474
Julius Nepos	474–475
Romulus Augustus	475–476

NOTABLE RULERS OF ANCIENT EMPIRES

AKKADIA

Sargon the Great	c. 2334–2279 B.C.E	

ASSYRIA

Sargon II	c. 722–705 B.C.E.

BABYLONIA

Hammurabi	c. 1792–1749 B.C.E
Nebuchadnezzar	c. 1125–1103 B.C.E
Nebuchadnezzar II	605–562 B.C.E

KINGS OF THE JEWS

Saul	1025–1005 B.C.E
David	1005–960 B.C.E

PERSIA

Cyrus the Great	550–529 B.C.E	
Darius	521–486 B.C.E	
Xerxes	486–465 B.C.E	
Seleucus	312–281 B.C.E	
Shapur II	309–371 C.E.	Neo-Persian Empire

ATHENS

Draco	c. 621 B.C.E
Archon Solon	594–570 B.C.E
Pericles	460–429 B.C.E

CARTHAGE

Hannibal	440–406 B.C.E.

MACEDONIA

Philip of Macedon	359–336 B.C.E
Alexander the Great	336–323 B.C.E

Religions of the World

This section is a general introduction to the more established or better-known religions in existence today. It does not include religions no longer known to be influential, nor does it include every sect of the religions in the world. An effort has been made to present these religions in a clear, brief, and general manner and, more importantly, without preference. Religions not listed are by no means more or less valid than those included.

Adventism At the core of Adventist belief is a conviction that the second coming of Jesus Christ is near at hand. All Adventist sects hold that believers are guaranteed salvation, but they differ over what effect the second coming will have on unrepentant sinners. The most prominent of the Christian Adventist sects is the Seventh-Day Adventists, who derive their name from the belief that Saturday is the true Sabbath.

Agnosticism The idea that a complete understanding of God and the universe is unattainable and that faith alone is an inadequate reason to follow a religion.

Amish See *Mennonite*.

Anglican or Anglican Communion See *Church of England* and *Episcopalianism*.

Animism A set of beliefs, common in many African countries, holding that the spirits of the dead, as well as gods, inhabit lifeless natural features such as mountains, rivers, oceans, and forests.

Assemblies of God See *Pentecostalism*.

Atheism A belief that no god exists.

Baha'i Faith A belief that originated in Iran in the nineteenth century based on the teachings of the Bab (Mirza Ali Muhammad) and the Bahá u'lláh (Mirza Husain Ali), who were thought to be manifestations of God. Although its origins are Islamic, Baha'i's basic belief is in the unity of all religions and of all humankind, emphasizing an individual's responsibility of service to others.

Baptist An evangelical Protestant Christian denomination centered on the belief that religion is a personal relationship between the human soul and God. Baptists sum up this belief in the concept that their church is the "priesthood of all believers." Baptists hold that baptism should be by total immersion, administered only to those old enough to confess their sins and express their faith. Many Baptists believe that the Bible should be interpreted literally. The modern Baptist church is an outgrowth of early Anabaptist sects founded in Amsterdam by a Church of England minister, John Smyth, who established his first church in London in 1612. The church was established in the United States in 1639 in Providence, Rhode Island, by Roger Williams, who had been exiled from Massachusetts for his insistence on religious liberty.

Buddhism Founded by Gautama Buddha, who is believed to have lived from 563 to 483 B.C.E., Buddhism teaches that although suffering is inherent in life, one may alleviate or overcome it through mental and moral self-purification. The origin of suffering, he taught, is craving, which may be transcended through the "Noble Eightfold Way," a set of guidelines that lead a soul to a state of redemption known as nirvana. Buddhism teaches that such a state, achieved through a complete extinction of individual consciousness, can free a human from reincarnation, which is also central to Buddhist belief. The major schools of Buddhism include: Mahayana Buddhism, which includes Zen and is practiced primarily in Cambodia, China, Laos, Japan, and Tibet; Therevada Buddhism, common to Myanmar, Sri Lanka, and Thailand; and Vajrayana, or Tantric, Buddhism, which is most prominent in Tibet.

Calvinism A Protestant Christian doctrine founded in the sixteenth century by Jean Chauvin, remembered as John Calvin for the anglicized version of his name. Calvin's teaching centered on the idea of predestination, the belief that God preselected some souls for salvation and others for damnation. His beliefs became central to Reformed and Presbyterian churches and were at the heart of the early Protestant movement in France and Holland as well as the inspiration for the English Puritans who migrated to America. The Puritan belief that gave America its so-called "work ethic" also comes directly from John Calvin, who preached that industriousness is God's greatest commandment. Contrary to the belief that poverty is a sign of blessedness, Calvin taught that financial success can be a sign of God's favor.

Christianity Based primarily upon the writings that make up the New Testament in the Bible, Christians profess their faith that Jesus, a Jew from Roman-occupied Israel, is the son of God, both human and divine. Christians believe that Jesus, crucified and killed by the Romans, rose from the dead to become Christ, or the anointed one. Central to Christian faith is the belief in an afterlife for human souls, typically described in terms of heaven and hell. Christians believe that actions against religious or moral laws during this life will prevent a soul from entering heaven unless one repents to Jesus Christ, who has the power to forgive sins. Early Christians were converted Jews who saw Jesus as the messiah who fulfilled prophesies of the Hebrew Scriptures. When Jesus was rejected by the Jewish Sanhedrin as one of many false messiahs, early Christians began to allow non-Jews into their religion, spreading Christianity all over the world. Hundreds of sects of Christianity exist today, but most can be classified as either Protestant, Eastern Orthodox, or Roman Catholic.

Christian Science Founded in Boston, Massachusetts, in 1879 by Mary Baker Eddy, the Church of Christ, Scientist claims to be based directly on the works and words of Jesus Christ. Mrs. Eddy taught that her purpose was to bring back the form of Christianity practiced by the earliest Christians and to restore their belief in healing by faith. Her followers believe that it is possible to dispel both physical diseases and sin through spiritual means.

Church of Christ See *Disciples of Christ*.

Church of England The official Christian church of the United Kingdom traces its origins back to a mission founded in Britain in 597 C.E. by St. Augustine. During the Reformation, the English church repudiated the papacy in favor of the monarchy. Among its other reforms were the translation of the Mass from Latin into English and the extension of communion to include the laity as well as the clergy. England's monarch has been the head of the church since King Henry VIII declared his own authority in 1534, but the Archbishop of Canterbury has remained the spiritual head of the Church of England. The Church of England is affiliated with similar churches throughout the world, including the Episcopal Church in the United States and the Anglican Church.

Church of God A Protestant Christian religion similar to the Pentecostal churches. Church of God worshipers typically believe in baptism by immersion, in foot washing, and in the celebration of the Lord's Supper. The church teaches the unity of all Christians through shared spiritual experience rather than through creeds and religious doctrine. Closely related to the Church of God is the Church of God in Christ. See *Pentecostalism*.

Church of Jesus Christ of Latter-Day Saints See *Mormonism*.

Church of Scotland Founded by John Knox. See *Presbyterianism*.

Confucianism The Chinese philosopher K'ung Fu-tzu, known in the West as Confucius, established his code of ethics in the fifth century B.C.E. He codified the teachings of writers and philosophers who preceded him, incorporating them into a new set of values. Central to Confucianism is ancestor worship, which Confucius interpreted to be the highest expression of filial piety. He deliberated "five relations," describing each as the levels of respect: king to subject, father to son, man to wife, older brother to younger brother, and friend to friend.

Congregationalism A Protestant Christian denomination that believes that each individual church should be completely independent of any authority outside its own walls. Originally known as nonconformism, its adherents were persecuted in England, where the movement began, and many moved to Holland looking for religious freedom. Some joined the Pilgrims who sailed for America aboard the *Mayflower* in 1620. In the 1970s, some Congregational churches in England and Wales combined with the Presbyterian Church to form the United Reformed Church.

Coptic Church Common in Ethiopia, the Coptic Church traces its origins to the early Christians in Egypt. Their refusal to accept the dual nature of Jesus Christ as God and man has caused them to be labeled as heretical by many other Christian denominations.

Disciples of Christ Also called Church of Christ, the Disciples of Christ is a Protestant Christian religion that holds that every person has the right to pray directly to God for guidance and that he or she may do so without any human intermediary. A follower need only confess faith that Christ is Lord and Savior and be baptized by immersion. Disciples have no creed but Christ and no doctrines other than those found in the Bible, especially in the New Testament.

Daoism See *Taoism*.

Dutch Reformed Church See *Presbyterianism*.

Eastern Orthodox See *Orthodox Church*.

Episcopalianism A common designation for the Protestant Episcopal Church in the United States (see *Church of England*) which applies to other denominations and signifies that the church is governed by bishops. Although a Protestant denomination, the Episcopal Church is often regarded as a bridge between Protestantism and Catholicism because it preserves many of the Catholic sacraments and uses old Catholic creeds.

Evangelicalism A belief among many Christians that salvation is gained either primarily or wholly through faith in the resurrection and divinity of Jesus Christ rather than through good works. Evangelicals also believe that many established church rituals are based on superstitions and therefore prefer their worship to be free of sacraments and traditional form. They often believe that the Bible should be interpreted literally and that Christians have a responsibility to encourage others to convert and to accept Jesus as Lord and savior.

Greek Orthodox See *Orthodox Church*.

Hinduism The origin of Hinduism is unknown, but most experts agree that it dates back to prehistory. As a religion, it has no common creed, no special doctrine, and no binding rules. A Hindu can believe in several gods, one god, or no god at all. But Hinduism is unique as a social system because each Hindu believes that he or she has been born into a specific social caste. Hinduism's religious tenets date back to the sacred Vedic books, believed to have been written about 1000 B.C.E., which describe the creation of the universe. Central to Hindu belief is the idea of reincarnation, which holds that all living things—trees, plants, animals, even gods—are caught in an everlasting cycle. All life is determined, in the Hindu view, by karma, through which one's next life is determined by one's moral behavior in preceding ones. The ultimate goal of a Hindu is release from the cycle and the attainment of a state of peace marked by a complete absence of passion.

Islam Islam was founded in the seventh century C.E. by the prophet Muhammad. Muhammad spent many years in contemplation in the desert and became convinced, through revelations, that he had been appointed by God, or Allah, to lead his people away from idolatry. In 622 C.E. he left Mecca in an exile, called the Hegira, to Medina, where he established a new religion as the prophet of Allah. Eight years later he led an army to attack Mecca and conquered it in the name of Islam. Although Muhammad died only ten years after the Hegira, he managed to set the stage for a uniting of the Arab world, which had been hopelessly divided, with a basic law of brotherhood. Islam makes five basic demands on its followers: confession of the oneness of God and his prophet Muhammad, prayer five times each day, giving of alms to the poor and to the house of worship called a mosque, fasting during the daylight hours during the month of Ramadan, and at least one lifetime pilgrimage to Mecca. Not long after Muhammad's death, disagreements over the succession of the prophet divided Islam into two main groups: Sunni and Shi'ite. Followers of Islam are called Muslims, from an Arab word meaning "one who submits."

Jainism A religion common in India, especially among merchants and professionals, founded in the sixth century C.E. as an alternative to Hinduism. Jainism eliminates the Hindu deities, replacing them with twenty-four immortal saints. It also rejects the caste system and alters the Hindu idea of karma. Basic to Jainism is *ahisma,* a belief that all life is sacred. A Jain refuses to kill any living thing, from the smallest insect to the biggest predator.

Jehovah's Witnesses Followers of this movement, founded in Pittsburgh, Pennsylvania, by Charles T. Russell in 1881, strive to follow the examples of figures in the Bible beginning with Abel, who offered a sacrifice to the Lord by which "he obtained witness that he was righteous." Among the Biblical witnesses was Jesus Christ, who is described as "the faithful and true witness." Jehovah's Witnesses do not accept Christ as divine. The movement, a part of the Watchtower Bible and Tract Society, believes that the second coming of Christ has already occurred and that Armageddon, the ultimate war between the forces of good and evil, is imminent.

Judaism Judaism is perhaps the earliest monotheistic religion. Early Jews lived in small tribes that inhabited what is now Israel and Jordan. Tradition holds that the first Jew was Abraham, who embraced the idea that one God created and rules the universe. Abraham's descendants, often called the Children of Israel (named after Abraham's son Jacob, who changed his name to Israel), established kingdoms in the region, until they were exiled by the Babylonians and finally the Romans into scattered colonies throughout the world. This scattering is often called the Diaspora. Jewish religious life once centered around the Temple in Jerusalem, but it is currently based upon a rabbinical tradition, with various written interpretations of of the Torah (the first five books of the Bible) and what Christians refer to as the Old Testament serving as guidelines for living and for serving humanity.

Lamaism An outgrowth of Buddhism that is most prominent in Mongolia and Tibet. It is characterized by tantric and shamanistic rituals and a dominant monastic hierarchy headed by the Dalai Lama, whose followers believe he is the reincarnated Buddha.

Lutheranism Lutheranism is the first Protestant denomination, being the first major Christian group to break from the Roman Catholic Church. Lutherans base their belief on Christian faith described in the New Testament and in the Apostles' Creed. They believe that faith is the essential element for salvation. The Lutheran Church traces its origins to October 31, 1517, when Martin Luther protested elements of Roman Catholicism, most notably the Church's selling of indulgences. Because Luther was a devout Catholic before beginning the Reformation, the Lutheran Church retains many elements of Roman Catholic ritual.

Mahayana Buddhism See *Buddhism.*

Mennonites A Protestant Christian movement founded in Holland in the fourteenth century by Anabaptist reformer Menno Simons. Mennonites accept only adult baptism as a profession of their faith. They reject military service, the taking of oaths, and membership in secret societies. The Mennonites found religious asylum in Pennsylvania in 1683, moving there in direct response to an invitation from William Penn. An offshoot of the Mennonite tradition is the Amish, whose beliefs stem from the teachings of a seventeenth-century Mennonite bishop, Jacob Amman. Amman charged his followers to follow the Bible literally and with complete simplicity.

Methodism A Protestant Christian movement founded in 1783 by Church of England minister John Wesley. Wesley organized a movement based upon personal and social morality, and the denomination came to be called Methodist for its stressing of the importance of living one's life according to a strict, methodical schedule.

Moravian Church A Protestant Christian movement originated by the followers of Jan Hus in 1457, calling for reform of the established Christian Church in Moravia, now the Czech Republic. The Moravian Church predates Luther's Protestant Reformation. From the beginning, the religion has been marked by a refusal to take oaths, by its rejection of the use of force, and by its lack of submission to any authority other than divinity. Moravians believe that faith comes directly from God and is not influenced by good works or piety, and that only those who accept Jesus Christ are guaranteed salvation.

Mormonism Founded in the mid-nineteenth century by Joseph Smith, the Church of Jesus Christ of Latter-Day Saints is also known as the Mormon Church. It teaches that Smith found golden tablets, which he translated into the Book of Mormon. This book suggests that Native Americans are descendants of the ancient Israelites and that Jesus Christ visited North America. Today's believers regard the book as sacred, but only as a supplement to the Bible and not as its replacement. The church practices baptism by immersion and extends the sacrament to the dead, who are baptized symbolically with a living person as a stand-in. Mormons also believe that marriage vows extend beyond death and that family relationships continue throughout eternity. The name *Latter-Day Saints* comes from Joseph Smith's belief that he was living in "the latter days" and that the end of the world would take place in his lifetime.

Nation of Islam Popularly known as the Black Muslims, the Nation of Islam was founded in the 1930s by W. D. Fard, or Wali Farad, and greatly expanded under the leadership of Elijah Muhammad (born Elijah Poole) from the late 1930s until the mid-1970s. Followers of the Nation believe that both Fard and Elijah Muhammad are "Holy Prophets and Messengers of Allah." The Black Muslim doctrine advocated hard work, economic prudence, and personal morality for African Americans, and its separatist teachings and rejection of racial integration set the Nation of Islam apart from the traditional Islamic faith. The Nation underwent substantial growth during the late 1950s and early 1960s with the work of Malcolm X, but Malcolm X eventually split with the Nation of Islam in 1964. The so-called Black Muslims have moved closer to traditional Islam in recent years. The primary groups today are the American Muslim Mission, under the leadership of Wallace Muhammad, a son of Elijah Muhammad, and the Nation of Islam, led by the Rev. Louis Farrakhan.

Netherlands Reformed Church See *Presbyterianism.*

Orthodox Church Also known as the Eastern Orthodox Church. A family of churches reflecting the beliefs and practices of the early Christian churches in what was once the Byzantine Empire. Orthodox churches are similar to the Roman Catholic Church in that they adhere to the tenets of the first seven ecumenical councils. But unlike the Roman Catholics, they do not accept the primacy of the pope. The Orthodox churches are well-known for their use of religious icons, sacred pictures of the saints that are an important part of their worship. Modern Orthodoxy is most prominent in Eastern Europe and in the former Soviet republics in Europe. The most prominent churches include the Armenian Orthodox Church, the Bulgarian Orthodox Church, the Ethiopian Orthodox Church, the Georgian Orthodox Church, the Greek Orthodox Church, the Romanian Orthodox Church, and the Russian Orthodox Church.

Pantheism The belief that equates God or gods with everything that exists in the universe.

Pentecostalism A belief among some Protestants that true Christianity is the result of a strong spiritual or mystical experience, usually accompanying conversion. Pentecostalist belief often emphasizes revivalistic worship, baptism, faith healing, and glossolalia (speaking in tongues). Pentecostal churches cover a broad spectrum of churches, many with roots in the Baptist or Methodist traditions. There are more than two hundred different Pentecostal denominations in the United States, the largest of which is the Assemblies of God.

Presbyterianism A Protestant Christian denomination that stresses the Old and New Testaments of the Bible as the basis of faith and as a rule of life. John Knox founded the Church of Scotland on the teachings of John Calvin (see *Calvinism*). Its ministry consists of presbyters, who all share equal rank in the church hierarchy. Ministers in each individual church are elected by its members, as are lay leaders known as elders, who assist the minister in the government of the church.

Protestantism Any of hundreds of Christian denominations that broke from Roman Catholicism during the sixteenth century Reformation, or that developed after the Reformation, may be called Protestant. The term originally referred to the followers of Martin Luther, who joined with him in protesting a 1517 decree from the Pope forbidding ecclesiastic reform. In time, Protestantism became the definition of a belief that personal interpretation of the Bible should be the only authority in matters of faith, rejecting papal direction. Protestants believe that faith is the ultimate road to salvation and that all believers are part of the priesthood in fellowship with God.

Quakerism Another name for the Religious Society of Friends founded by George Fox in seventeenth-century England. The basis of Quakerism is that every believer has the power of direct communication with God in a search for truth. Quakers believe in an "inner light," which is the light of Christ that shines in every human heart. Many Quaker meetings are held without any form of ritual or any guidance from a minister. Members sit in silence until one of their number is moved by the Holy Spirit to make a statement. In the early days of the church, many of these statements took the form of loud outbursts and violent trembling, from which the name Quaker is derived.

Rastafarianism A religious group taking its name from Ras Tafari, a common name for former Emperor Haile Selassie of Ethiopia, considered a messiah and a champion of blacks. The religion developed in Jamaica in the 1920s and now claims adherents throughout the Caribbean and in the United States and western Europe. Rastifarians consider marijuana a sacrament.

Reformed Christian See *Presbyterianism*.

Roman Catholicism Roman Catholics believe that the bishop of Rome, the pope, is the vicar of Christ and successor of Peter, whose power was granted directly by Christ. All bishops of the Roman Church are also regarded as direct successors of Peter and the apostles. The faith of the church is considered to be exactly the same as the original teachings of Christ and is considered virtually unchangeable. The centerpiece of its worship is the mass, a symbolic reenactment of Christ's death and resurrection. The mass, or eucharist, is one of seven sacraments of the Roman Catholic Church, along with baptism, confirmation, confession, marriage, ordination of priests and bishops, and the anointing of the sick. The church also venerates the Virgin Mary and the saints, and prayers are made to them to intercede with God. More than half of all the Christians in the world belong to the Roman Catholic Church.

Russian Orthodox Church See *Orthodox Church*.

Shamanism A religion of the Ural-Altaic peoples in which shamans, or priests, call upon the aid of gods, demons, and spirits for healing, divining the future, and magic.

Shi'itism See *Islam*.

Shintoism An indigenous religion of Japan, characterized by veneration of ancestors and nature. The Japanese words for the idea are *Kami no Michi*, the Way of the Gods. Kami, the gods, are forces of nature that are to be worshipped; they inhabit natural features such as rivers, trees, some animals, the sun, and the moon. In the ninth century C.E., Buddhism came to Japan by way of Korea and threatened to replace Shintoism. The two religions were merged for a time, with Buddhist priests ensconced in Shinto shrines and Buddhist gods replacing the traditional Kami. But in the Meiji Restoration of the late nineteenth century, Shintoism became the state religion of Japan. Its centers of worship are shrines that are believed to be the homes of deities. Many Japanese homes have small Shinto shrines, usually dedicated to the family's ancestors.

Sikhism Established by the Guru Nanak in the Indian state of Punjab in the fifteenth century C.E., Sikhism holds that there is basic truth in all religions. Nanak intended to eliminate the counterproductive conflicts between religions, pointing out that if there is only one God, then the many different names humanity gives God are irrelevant. After a Muslim emperor ordered the execution of the father of the Govind Singh, the last guru, for not embracing Islam, the Sikhs became a cult of warriors, with Govind Singh establishing new rules for them. Among other things, he eliminated caste distinctions, and commanded his followers to wear their hair long and to take the name Singh, which means lion. Eventually, the group ruled a greater part of Punjab, but it lost its independence, after two wars, when Punjab was annexed by the British in 1849. Since the creation of Pakistani and Indian independence in 1947, the Sikhs have been divided between the two countries, representing a militant minority in both.

Society of Friends See *Quakerism*.

Sunniism See *Islam*.

Tantric Buddhism See *Buddhism*.

Taoism A religion prominent in China, Taoism was founded in the sixth century B.C.E. by the philosopher Lao tse. The word *Tao* means "the way," and the religion teaches that its followers can resist change in the world by following the principles outlined in Lao tse's book *Tao Te Ching*, "The Way and Its Power." The power comes from an avoidance of striving through submitting to the forces of the universe, yin and yang, negative and positive. As a religion, Taoism often involves magic and supernatural prophecy as well as worship of a host of deities and spirits.

Therevada Buddhism See *Buddhism*.

Unification Church Founded in the 1950s by the Rev. Sun Myung Moon, the Unification Church teaches that both Jesus Christ and Rev. Moon are messiahs. Also known as the Moonies, the Unification Church is most prominent in South Korea, where it originated, and in Japan.

Unitarianism Most Christians believe in the concept of the Trinity, but Unitarians hold that God is a single entity. Unitarians base their outlook on the concept of simple morality and the kinship of all humanity. Unitarians stress the free use of reason, as opposed to faith, in religion. They stress the importance of freedom of belief, of a united community, and of social action.

Universalism A Protestant Christian religion founded upon the belief that all humans will find salvation. It is united with the Unitarian movement.

Vajrayana Buddhism See *Buddhism*.

Zen or Zen Buddhism See *Buddhism*.

Nations of the World

With the dramatic changes that have occurred across the globe in recent years, the political, social, economic, and geographical make-up of the nations of the world has been altered in many ways. The former Soviet Union broke apart to form some fifteen new sovereign nations; the former Yugoslavian nation now exists as the independent sovereign nations of Slovenia, Croatia, Bosnia and Herzegovina, Macedonia, and Yugoslavia (Serbia and Montenegro); East and West Germany are unified, as are North and South Yemen. What follows is the most up-to-date listing of the nations of the world, including area and recent population figures as well as over a dozen other vital statistics for the 190 sovereign nations of the world.

AFGHANISTAN
Islamic State of Afghanistan
De Afghanistan Jamhuriat

Area: 251,773 sq. mi. (647,500 sq. km.)
Population: 16,450,000
Language: Pashto 52%, Persian 32%, Uzbek 9%, other 7%
Capital: Kabul
Currency: Afghani
Religion: Muslim (Sunni 84%, Shi'ite 15%), other 1%
Ethnic Groups: Pushtun 50%, Tajik 25%, Uzbek 9%, Hazara 9%, other 7%
Government: Ruling council, awaiting free elections
Literacy (1990): 29%
Life Expectancy at Birth (1991): 43 years female, 44 years male
Infant Mortality (per 1,000 live births 1991): 164
Gross National Product (1989): $3 billion
GNP per Capita (1989): $200
Principal Industries: Textiles, furniture, cement
Principal Crops: Nuts, wheat, fruits

ALBANIA
The Republic of Albania
Republika e Shqipërisë

Area: 11,110 sq. mi. (28,748 sq. km.)
Population: 3,335,000
Language: Albanian 98%, Greek 2%
Capital: Tirana
Currency: Lek
Religion: Muslim (Sunni) 90%, Roman Catholic 5%, Orthodox 4%, other 1%
Ethnic Groups: Albanian 90%, Greek 8%, other 2%
Government: Democracy
Literacy (1990): 75%
Life Expectancy at Birth (1991): 79 years female, 72 years male
Infant Mortality (per 1,000 live births 1991): 50
Gross National Product (1990): $4.1 billion
GNP per Capita: $1,250
Principal Industries: Cement, textiles
Principal Crops: Corn, wheat, cotton, potatoes, tobacco, fruits

ALGERIA
Democratic and Popular Republic of Algeria
El Djemhouria El Djazariria Demokratika Echaabia

Area: 918,500 sq. mi. (2,381,751 sq. km.)
Population: 26,022,000
Language: Arabic (official) 83%, French (official), Kabyle 8%, Tamazight 5%, other Berber dialects 4%
Capital: Algiers
Currency: Dinar
Religion: Muslim (Sunni)
Ethnic Groups: Arab 75%, Berber 25%
Government: Military
Literacy (1991): 52%
Life Expectancy at Birth (1991): 68 years female, 66 years male
Infant Mortality (per 1,000 live births 1991): 57
Gross Domestic Product (1993): $47.2 billion
GDP per Capita: $1,696
Principal Industries: Petrochemicals, steel, textiles, fertilizers, plastics
Principal Crops: Wheat, barley, grapes, fruits, olives

ANDORRA
Principality of Andorra
Principat d'Andorra

Area: 175 sq. mi. (453 sq. km.)
Population: 53,000
Language: Catalan (official) 28%, Spanish 56%, French 8%, other 8%
Capital: Andorra la Vella
Currency: French franc and Spanish peseta
Religion: Roman Catholic
Ethnic Groups: Catalan 61%, Spanish 30%, Andorran 6%, French 3%
Government: General council
Literacy (1991): 99%
Gross National Product (1990 est.): $727 million
GNP per Capita: $14,000
Principal Industries: Tobacco products, tourism
Principal Crops: Tobacco, fruits

ANGOLA
People's Republic of Angola
República Popular de Angola

Area: 481,350 sq. mi. (1,246,700 sq. km.)
Population: 8,668,000
Language: Ovimbundu 37%, Kimbundu 22%, Kongo 13%, Other African languages 27%
Capital: Luanda
Currency: Kwanza
Religion: Indigenous 47%, Roman Catholic 38%, Protestant 15%
Ethnic Groups: Ovimbundu 38%, Kimbundu 25%, Bakongo 13%, other 22%
Government: Democratic socialism
Literacy (1991): 40%
Life Expectancy at Birth (1991): 46 years female, 42 years male
Infant Mortality (per 1,000 live births 1991): 151
Gross Domestic Product (1990): $7.9 billion
GDP per Capita: $620
Principal Industries: Oil, diamond mining, fish processing, cement
Principal Crops: Coffee, sisal, bananas

ANTIGUA AND BARBUDA
Area: 170 sq. mi. (442 sq. km.)

ANTIGUA AND BARBUDA (continued)

Population: 64,000
Language: English (official), Creole English 96%, other 4%
Capital: St. John's
Currency: East Caribbean dollar
Religion: Anglican and Roman Catholic
Ethnic Groups: Mostly African
Government: Parliamentary
Literacy (1990): 90%
Infant Mortality (per 1,000 live births 1989): 11
Gross Domestic Product (1990): $350 million
GDP per Capita: $5,000
Principal Industries: Tourism, sugar refining
Principal Crops: Cotton, fruit, vegetables

ARGENTINA

Argentine Republic
República Argentina

Area: 1,072,067 sq. mi. (2,776,654 sq. km.)
Population: 32,664,000
Language: Spanish (official) 96%, other 4%
Capital: Buenos Aires
Currency: Peso
Religion: Roman Catholic 92%, other 8%
Ethnic Groups: European descent 85% (Spanish, Italian), Native American and mestizo 5%
Government: Republic
Literacy (1991): 92%
Life Expectancy at Birth (1990): 74 years female, 67 years male
Infant Mortality (per 1,000 live births 1991): 31
Gross Domestic Product (1993): $273 billion
GNP per Capita: $8,142
Principal Industries: Meat processing, cement, motor vehicles, textiles, chemicals
Principal Crops: Wheat, corn, cotton, beef cattle, grapes, sugar, tobacco, rice

ARMENIA

Republic of Armenia
Haikakan Hanrapetoutioun

Area: 11,500 sq. mi. (29,800 sq. km.)
Population: 3,300,000
Language: Armenian 90%, Azerbaijani 5%, other 5%
Capital: Yerevan
Currency: Ruble
Religion: Christian
Ethnic Groups: Armenian 88%, Azerbaijani 6%, Kurd and Russian 6%
Government: Constitutional republic
Literacy (1991): 98%
Life Expectancy at Birth (1990): 74 years female, 65 years male
Infant Mortality (per 1,000 live births 1991): 20
Principal Industries: Mining, chemicals
Principal Crops: Cotton, figs, grain

AUSTRALIA

Commonwealth of Australia

Area: 2,966,150 sq. mi. (7,682,300 sq. km.)
Population: 17,228,000
Language: English 89%, aboriginal languages 1%, other 10%
Capital: Canberra
Currency: Australian dollar
Religion: Protestant 55%, Roman Catholic 31%, other 14%
Ethnic Groups: White 95%, Asian 4%, aboriginal 1%
Government: Democracy
Literacy: 89%
Life Expectancy at Birth (1991): 80 years female, 73 years male
Infant Mortality (per 1,000 live births 1991): 9
Gross Domestic Product (1993): $308.7 billion
GDP per Capita: $17,320
Principal Industries: Iron, steel, textiles, electrical equip., chemicals, automobiles, aircraft, ships, machinery
Principal Crops: Wheat, barley, oats, corn, hay, sugar, wine, fruit, vegetables

AUSTRIA

Republic of Austria
Republik Österreich

Area: 32,375 sq. mi. (83,851 sq. km.)
Population: 7,666,000
Language: German 99%, other 1%
Capital: Vienna
Currency: Schilling
Religion: Roman Catholic 89%, other 11%
Ethnic Groups: German 99%, Slovene, Croatian 1%
Government: Federal republic
Literacy (1991): 99%
Life Expectancy at Birth (1991): 81 years female, 74 years male
Infant Mortality (per 1,000 live births 1991): 12
Gross Domestic Product (1993): $190 billion
GDP per Capita: $23,800
Principal Industries: Steel, machinery, autos, electrical and optical equip., glassware, cement, paper, textiles, chemicals
Principal Crops: Grains, potatoes, beets

AZERBAIJAN

Republic of Azerbaijan
Azerbaijachan Respublikasy

Area: 33,400 sq. mi. (86,600 sq. km.)
Population: 7,000,000
Language: Azerbaijani 78%, Russian 12%, Armenian 6%, other 4%
Capital: Baku
Currency: Ruble
Religion: Muslim
Ethnic Groups: Azerbaijani 78%, Russian 8%, Armenian 8%, other 6%
Government: Constitutional republic
Literacy: 98%
Life Expectancy at Birth (1991): 74 years female, 65 years male
Infant Mortality (per 1,000 live births 1991): 26
Principal Industries: Oil refining
Principal Crops: Grain, cotton, rice, silk

BAHAMAS

Commonwealth of the Bahamas

Area: 5,380 sq. mi. (13,939 sq. km.)
Population: 252,685
Language: English (official), English Creole 85%, French Creole 15%
Capital: Nassau
Currency: Bahamian dollar
Religion: Baptist 29%, Anglican 23%, Roman Catholic 22%, other 26%
Ethnic Groups: Black 85%, white (British, Canadian, U.S.) 15%
Government: Independent commonwealth
Literacy: 95%
Life Expectancy at Birth (1991): 76 years female, 69 years male
Infant Mortality (per 1,000 live births 1991): 17
Gross Domestic Product (1990): $2.8 billion
GDP per Capita: $11,055
Principal Industries: Tourism, rum, pharmaceuticals
Principal Crops: Fruits, vegetables

BAHRAIN

State of Bahrain
Dawlat al-Bahrayan

Area: 240 sq. mi. (620 sq. km.)
Population: 537,000
Language: Arabic (official) 80%, Farsi 12%, Urdu 3%, other 5%
Capital: Manama
Currency: Dinar
Religion: Muslim (Shi'ite 50%, Sunni 40%), Christian 7%, other 3%
Ethnic Groups: Bahraini 63%, Asian 13%, other Arab 10%, Iranian 6%, other 8%
Government: Monarchy
Literacy (1990): 77%
Life Expectancy at Birth (1991): 76 years female, 71 years male
Infant Mortality (per 1,000 live births 1991): 17

Gross Domestic Product (1989): $3.4 billion
GDP per Capita: $7,500
Principal Industries: Oil refining, aluminum processing
Principal Crops: Fruits, vegetables

BANGLADESH

People's Republic of Bangladesh
Gama Prajätantri Bangladesh

Area: 55,600 sq. mi. (143,998 sq. km.)
Population: 116,601,000
Language: Bengali (official) 98%, other 2%, Assamese widely spoken
Capital: Dhaka
Currency: Taka
Religion: Muslim 85%, Hindu 14%, other 1%
Ethnic Groups: Bengali 98%, Bihari tribes 2%
Government: Parliamentary
Literacy (1991): 35%
Life Expectancy at Birth (1991): 53 years female, 54 years male
Infant Mortality (per 1,000 live births 1991): 118
Gross Domestic Product (1990): $20.2 billion
GDP per Capita: $180
Principal Industries: Jute, textiles, leather goods manufacture, cement, fertilizers
Principal Crops: Rice, jute, tea, sugar, grains

BARBADOS

Area: 166 sq. mi. (431 sq. km.)
Population: 295,000
Language: English (official) 98%, other 2%
Capital: Bridgetown
Currency: Barbados dollar
Religion: Protestant 67%, Roman Catholic 4%, other 29%
Ethnic Groups: Black 80%, mixed 16%, white 4%
Government: Democracy
Literacy (1991): 99%
Life Expectancy at Birth (1991): 77 years female, 73 years male
Infant Mortality (per 1,000 live births 1991): 23
Gross Domestic Product: $1.7 billion
GDP per Capita: $6,500
Principal Industries: Light manufacturing, sugar milling, tourism
Principal Crops: Sugarcane, foods

BELARUS

Republic of Belarus
Respublika Belarus

Area: 80,150 sq. mi. (207,600 sq. km.)
Population: 10,250,000
Language: Byelorussian (white Russian) 78%, Russian 20%, other 2%
Capital: Minsk
Currency: Ruble
Religion: Orthodox
Ethnic Groups: Byelorussian 80%, Polish 12%, other 8%
Government: Constitutional republic
Literacy (1991): 98%
Life Expectancy at Birth (1991): 74 years female, 65 years male
Infant Mortality (per 1,000 live births 1991): 12
Principal Industries: Food processing, chemicals, machine tool and agricultural machinery
Principal Crops: Grain, flax, potatoes, sugar beets

BELGIUM

Kingdom of Belgium
Koninkrijk België

Area: 11,780 sq. mi. (30,510 sq. km.)
Population: 9,922,000
Language: Flemish 58%, French (Walloon) 39%, other 3%
Capital: Brussels
Currency: Belgian franc
Religion: Roman Catholic 90%, Muslim 3%, other 7%
Ethnic Groups: Flemish 55%, Walloon 33%, other 12%

Government: Parliamentary democracy
Literacy (1991): 98%
Life Expectancy at Birth (1991): 81 years female, 74 years male
Infant Mortality (per 1,000 live births 1991): 6
Gross Domestic Product (1993): $225 billion
GDP per Capita: $22,600
Principal Industries: Steel, glassware, diamond cutting, textiles, chemicals
Principal Crops: Wheat, potatoes, sugar beets

BELIZE

Area: 8,865 sq. mi. (22,965 sq. km.)
Population: 228,000
Language: English (official) 60%, Spanish 25%, Maya 8%, Caribe 7%
Capital: Belmopan
Currency: Belize dollar
Religion: Roman Catholic 62%, Protestant 30%, other 8%
Ethnic Groups: Creole 40%, Mestizo 33%, Maya 10%, Garifuna 8%, white 4%, other 5%
Government: Parliamentary democracy
Literacy (1991): 93%
Life Expectancy at Birth (1991): 52 years female, 49 years male
Infant Mortality (per 1,000 live births 1991): 35
Gross Domestic Product (1990 est): $290 million
GDP per Capita: $1,320
Principal Industries: Processed foods, timber products, rum
Principal Crops: Sugarcane, fruits, corn, rice

BENIN

Republic of Benin
République de Benin

Area: 43,480 sq. mi. (112,620 sq. km.)
Population: 4,832,000
Language: French (official), Fon, Yoruba, Somba
Capital: Porto-Novo
Currency: Franc CFA
Religion: Indigenous animist 61%, Roman Catholic 19%, Muslim 15%, other 4%
Ethnic Groups: Fon, Adja, Bariba, Yoruba
Government: Democracy
Literacy (1991): 28%
Life Expectancy at Birth (1991): 52 years female, 49 years male
Infant Mortality (per 1,000 live births 1991): 119
Gross Domestic Product (1989 est.): $1.7 billion
GDP per Capita: $400
Principal Industries: Palm oil processing
Principal Crops: Oil palms, peanuts, coffee, cotton, tobacco

BHUTAN

Kingdom of Bhutan
Druk-Yul

Area: 18,000 sq. mi. (46,620 sq. km.)
Population: 1,598,000
Language: Dzongkha (official) 30%, Kebumtamp 25%, Sarchagpakha 25%, Nepali 19%, other 1%
Capital: Thimphu
Currency: Ngultrum
Religion: Buddhist 75%, Hindu 25%
Ethnic Groups: Bhote 60%, Napalese 30%, other 10%
Government: Constitutional monarchy
Literacy (1989): 15%
Life Expectancy at Birth (1991): 48 years female, 50 years male
Infant Mortality (per 1,000 live births 1991): 139
Gross Domestic Product (1989): $273 million
GDP per Capita: $199
Principal Industries: Mining, cement manufacture
Principal Crops: Rice, corn, wheat, barley

BOLIVIA
Republic of Bolivia
República de Bolivia

Area: 424,160 sq. mi. (1,098,580 sq. km.)
Population: 7,157,000
Language: Spanish 34%, Quechua 32%, Aymara 29% (all official), other 5%
Capital: La Paz
Currency: Boliviano
Religion: Roman Catholic 95%, other 5%
Ethnic Groups: Quechua 30%, mestizo 30%, Aymara 25%, white 14%, other 1%
Government: Democracy
Literacy (1991): 78%
Life Expectancy at Birth (1991): 64 years female, 59 years male
Infant Mortality (per 1,000 live births 1991): 34
Gross National Product (1990): $4.85 billion
GNP per Capita: $690
Principal Industries: Textiles, food processing, mining, clothing
Principal Crops: Potatoes, sugar, coffee, corn, coca

BOSNIA AND HERZEGOVINA
Republic of Bosnia and Herzegovina

Area: 19,741 sq. mi. (51,129 sq. km.)
Population: 4,200,000
Language: Serbo-Croatian
Capital: Sarajevo
Currency: Dinar
Religion: Roman Catholic, Eastern Orthodox, Muslim
Ethnic Groups: Muslim Slav 43%, Serbian 31%, Croatian 17%, other 9%
Government: Republic
Literacy: 90%
Principal Industries: Textiles, rugs, timber
Principal Crops: Corn, wheat, oats, barley

BOTSWANA
Republic of Botswana

Area: 231,804 sq. mi. (600,360 sq. km.)
Population: 1,258,000
Language: English (official), Setswana (Tswana) 75%, Shona 12%, other 13%
Capital: Gaborone
Currency: Pula
Religion: Christian and local animist
Ethnic Groups: Tswana, Kalanga, other
Government: Parliamentary republic
Literacy (1989): 80%
Life Expectancy at Birth (1991): 65 years female, 59 years male
Infant Mortality (per 1,000 live births 1991): 67
Gross Domestic Product (1991): $3.1 billion
GDP per Capita: $2,385
Principal Industries: Livestock processing, mining
Principal Crops: Corn, sorghum, beans

BRAZIL
Federative Republic of Brazil
República Federativa do Brasil

Area: 3,286,470 sq. mi. (8,511,957 sq. km.)
Population: 155,356,000
Language: Portuguese (official)
Capital: Brasilia
Currency: Novo cruzado
Religion: Roman Catholic 90%, Protestant 6%, other 4%
Ethnic Groups: White (primarily Portuguese descent) 53%, mulatto 22%, mestizo 12%, black 11%
Government: Federal republic
Literacy (1991): 81%
Life Expectancy at Birth (1991): 68 years female, 62 years male
Infant Mortality (per 1,000 live births): 67
Gross Domestic Product (1993): $393 billion
GDP per Capita: $2,466

Principal Industries: Steel, automobiles, ships, appliances, petrochemicals, machinery
Principal Crops: Coffee, cotton, soybeans, sugar, cocoa, rice, corn, fruits

BRUNEI DARUSSALAM
State of Brunei Darussalam
Negara Brunei Darussalam

Area: 2,226 sq. mi. (5,765 sq. km.)
Population: 398,000
Language: Malay (official) 69%, Chinese 13%, English 3%, other 15%
Capital: Bandar Seri Begawan
Currency: Brunei dollar
Religion: Muslim 63%, indigenous 15%, Buddhist 14%, Christian 8%
Ethnic Groups: Malay 64%, Chinese 20%, Indian 8%, other 8%
Government: Sultanate
Literacy: 77%
Life Expectancy at Birth (1991): 77 years female, 74 years male
Infant Mortality (per 1,000 live births 1991): 10
Gross Domestic Product (1989): $3.1 billion
GDP per Capita: $9,600
Principal Industries: Oil
Principal Crops: Rice, bananas, cassava

BULGARIA
Republic of Bulgaria
Republika Bulgaria

Area: 42,820 sq. mi. (110,910 sq. km.)
Population: 8,911,000
Language: Bulgarian (official) 85%, Turkish 8%, other 7%
Capital: Sofia
Currency: Lev
Religion: Bulgarian Orthodox 85%, Muslim 15%
Ethnic Groups: Bulgarian 85%, Turk 8.5%, Gypsy 3%, other 3.5%
Government: Republic
Literacy (1990): 95%
Life Expectancy at Birth (1991): 76 years female, 69 years male
Infant Mortality (per 1,000 live births 1991): 13
Gross Domestic Product (1993): $8.8 billion
GDP per Capita: $1,021
Principal Industries: Chemicals, machinery, metals, textiles
Principal Crops: Grains, fruit, corn, potatoes, tobacco

BURKINA FASO

Area: 105,870 sq. mi. (274,200 sq. km.)
Population: 9,360,000
Language: French (official), Mossi 52%, local tribal languages 48%
Capital: Ouagadougou
Currency: Franc CFA
Religion: Local animist 65%, Muslim 25%, Christian 10%
Ethnic Groups: Voltaic Groups (Mossi, Bobo, Lobi), Mande groups (Samo, Marka, Boussance, Dioula)
Government: Military
Literacy (1991): 26.9%
Life Expectancy at Birth (1991): 53 years female, 52 years male
Infant Mortality (per 1,000 live births 1991): 119
Gross Domestic Product (1989): $1.7 billion
GDP per Capita: $205
Principal Industries: Agriculture, forestry, lumbering, manufacturing
Principal Crops: Millet, sorghum, rice, peanuts

BURMA See Myanmar

BURUNDI
Republic of Burundi
Republika y'Uburundi

Area: 10,750 sq. mi. (27,835 sq. km.)
Population: 5,831,000
Language: French (official), Rundi 97%, other 3%,
Capital: Bujumbura

Currency: Burundi franc

Religion: Roman Catholic 62%, local animist 32%, Protestant 5%

Ethnic Groups: Hutu 85%, Tutsi 14%, Twa (pygmy) 1%

Government: Republic

Literacy (1991): 40%

Life Expectancy at Birth (1991): 54 years female, 50 years male

Infant Mortality (per 1,000 live births 1991): 114

Gross Domestic Product (1989): $1.2 billion

GDP per Capita: $220

Principal Industries: Agriculture, fishing

Principal Crops: Coffee, cotton, tea

CAMBODIA
State of Cambodia

Area: 69,880 sq. mi. (181,000 sq. km.)

Population: 7,146,000

Language: Khmer (official) 80%, Kuy 9%, Chinese 4%, Vietnamese 4%, other 3%

Capital: Phnom Penh

Currency: Riel

Religion: Theravada Buddhist 95%

Ethnic Groups: Cambodian 90%, Chinese 5%, Vietnamese 4%, other 1%

Government: Coalition

Literacy (1990): 50%

Life Expectancy at Birth (1991): 51 years female, 48 years male

Infant Mortality (per 1,000 live births 1991): 125

Gross Domestic Product (1989): $890 million

GDP per Capita: $130

Principal Industries: Agriculture, forestry, textiles, cement

Principal Crops: Rice, rubber, corn, sugar

CAMEROON
Republic of Cameroon
République du Cameroun

Area: 183,570 sq. mi. (475,440 sq. km.)

Population: 11,390,000

Language: French, English (both official), Beti, Fula, Hausa, Tiv, Cameroon Pidgin, over 20 other African languages

Capital: Yaoundé

Currency: Franc CFA

Religion: Local animist 51%, Christian 33%, Muslim 16%

Ethnic Groups: Around 200 tribes largest of which are Bamileke and Fulani

Government: Democracy

Literacy (1991): 65%

Life Expectancy at Birth (1991): 53 years female, 40 years male

Infant Mortality (per 1,000 live births 1991): 118

Gross Domestic Product (1991): $11.6 billion

GDP per Capita: $1,010

Principal Industries: Aluminum processing, oil production, palm products

Principal Crops: Cocoa, coffee, cotton

CANADA

Area: 3,851,810 sq. mi. (9,976,185 sq. km.)

Population: 26,835,000

Language: English 62%, French 25%, other 13%

Capital: Ottawa

Currency: Canadian dollar

Religion: Roman Catholic 46%, Protestant 41%, other 13%

Ethnic Groups: British 25%, French 24%, other European descent 16%, mixed 28%, Native American 7%

Government: Democracy

Literacy (1991): 99%

Life Expectancy at Birth (1991): 80 years female, 73 years female

Infant Mortality (per 1,000 live births 1991): 7.3

Gross Domestic Product (1993): $516 billion

GDP per Capita: $19,500

Principal Industries: Manufacturing, mining, agriculture, forestry

Principal Crops: Beef cattle, wheat, milk, barley, corn, vegetables, fruits

CAPE VERDE
Republic of Cape Verde
República de Cabo Verde

Area: 1,555 sq. mi. (4,035 sq. km.)

Population: 387,000

Language: Portuguese (official), Criuolo 70%, Mandyak 30%

Capital: Praia

Currency: Cape Verdean escudo

Religion: Roman Catholic 98%, Protestant 2%

Ethnic Groups: Creole (mulatto) 71%, African 28%, European 1%

Government: Republic

Life Expectancy at Birth (1989): 63 years female, 59 years male

Infant Mortality (per 1,000 live births 1991): 66

Gross Domestic Product (1989): $281 million

GDP per Capita: $760

Principal Industries: Agriculture, salt mining

Principal Crops: Bananas, coffee, sugarcane, corn, beans

CENTRAL AFRICAN REPUBLIC
République Centrafricaine

Area: 241,310 sq. mi. (625,000 sq. km.)

Population: 2,952,000

Language: French (official), Banda, Gbaya, Sango, Manja, other

Capital: Bangui

Currency: Franc CFA

Religion: Protestant 25%, Roman Catholic 25%, local animist 24%, Muslim 15%, other 11%

Ethnic Groups: Baya 34%, Banda 27%, Mandja 21%, Sara 10%, other 8%

Government: Military

Literacy (1989): 40%

Life Expectancy at Birth (1989): 48 years female, 45 years male

Infant Mortality (per 1,000 live births 1991): 138

Gross Domestic Product (1990): $1.3 billion

GDP per Capita: $440

Principal Industries: Agriculture, mining, light manufacturing, forestry, textiles

Principal Crops: Cotton, coffee, peanuts, corn, sorghum

CHAD
Republic of Chad
République du Tchad

Area: 495,750 sq. mi. (1,284,000 sq. km.)

Population: 5,122,000

Language: French, Arabic 30% (both official), Ngambai 12%, other African languages 58%

Capital: N'Djamena

Currency: Franc CFA

Religion: Muslim 44%, Christian 33%, animist 23%

Ethnic Groups: Sudanese Arab 30%, Sudanic tribes 25%, Nilotic, Saharan tribes, over 200 other African tribes

Government: Military

Literacy (1991): 17%

Life Expectancy at Birth (1991): 41 years female, 39 years male

Infant Mortality (per 1,000 live births 1991): 134

Gross Domestic Product (1989): $1.0 billion

GDP per Capita: $190

Principal Industries: Agriculture

Principal Crops: Cotton, sugar, peanuts, livestock

CHILE
Republic of Chile
República de Chile

Area: 292,130 sq. mi. (756,620 sq. km.)

Population: 13,287,000

Language: Spanish (official) 92%, Mapundungun 4%, other 4%

Capital: Santiago

Currency: Peso

Religion: Roman Catholic 89%, Protestant 11%

Ethnic Groups: Mestizo 66%, Spanish 25%, Native American 5%, other 4%

Government: Democracy

CHILE (continued)

Literacy (1991): 93%
Life Expectancy at Birth (1991): 77 years female, 70 years male
Infant Mortality (per 1,000 live births 1991): 18
Gross Domestic Product (1993): $43 billion
GDP per Capita: $3,074
Principal Industries: Steel, textiles, wood products, mining
Principal Crops: Grains, sugar beets, potatoes, beans, fruits

PEOPLE'S REPUBLIC OF CHINA
Zhonghua Renmin Gonghe Guo

Area: 3,691,520 sq. mi. (9,561,000 sq. km.)
Population: 1,151,487,000
Language: Mandarin, Cantonese, Dong, Hakka, Khalkha, Min, Tibetan, Uighur, Wu, Zhuang, other languages
Capital: Beijing
Currency: Yuan
Religion: Atheist (official), Confucianist, Buddhist, Taoist
Ethnic Groups: Han Chinese 94%, Mongol, Manchu, Korean 6%
Government: Communist
Literacy: 73%
Life Expectancy at Birth (1991): 72 years female, 68 years male
Infant Mortality (per 1,000 live births 1991): 33
Gross Domestic Product (1993): $475.9 billion
GDP per Capita: $399
Principal Industries: Iron and steel, textiles, agricultural implements, trucks
Principal Crops: Grain, rice, cotton, tea

TAIWAN
Republic of China
Chung-hua Min-kuo

Area: 13,895 sq. mi. (35,988 sq. km.)
Population: 20,659,000
Language: Chinese (Mandarin) (official), Min, Yi, Hakka dialects
Capital: Taipei
Currency: New Taiwan dollar
Religion: Chinese folk 49%, Buddhist 43%, Christian 7%, other 1%
Ethnic Groups: Taiwanese 86%, Chinese 14%
Government: Republic
Literacy (1991): 90%
Life Expectancy at Birth (1991): 78 years female, 72 years male
Infant Mortality (per 1,000 live births 1991): 6
Gross National Product (1990): $241 billion
GNP per Capita: $11,500
Principal Industries: Textiles, clothing, electronics, processed foods, chemicals, plastics
Principal Crops: Rice, bananas, pineapples, sugarcane, sweet potatoes, peanuts

COLOMBIA
Republic of Colombia
República de Colombia

Area: 439,735 sq. mi. (114,400 sq. km.)
Population: 33,778,000
Language: Spanish (official)
Capital: Bogotá
Currency: Peso
Religion: Roman Catholic 95%, other 5%
Ethnic Groups: Mestizo 58%, European descent 20%, mulatto 14%, black 4%, Native American 1%, other 3%
Government: Republic
Literacy (1990): 80%
Life Expectancy at Birth (1991): 74 years female, 68 years male
Infant Mortality (per 1,000 live births 1991): 37
Gross Domestic Product (1990): $43 billion
GDP per Capita: $1,300
Principal Industries: Textiles, steel, hides, chemicals
Principal Crops: Coffee, rice, tobacco, cotton, sugar, bananas

COMOROS
Federal Islamic Republic of the Comoros
Jumhurïyat al-Qumar al-Itthädïyah al-Islämïyah

Area: 690 sq. mi. (1,787 sq. km.)
Population: 477,000
Language: French, Arabic (both official), Swahili 100%
Capital: Moroni
Currency: Franc CFA
Religion: Muslim (Sunni) 86%, Roman Catholic 14%
Ethnic Groups: Arab, African, East Indian
Government: Republic
Literacy (1989): 15%
Life Expectancy at Birth (1991): 58 years female, 54 years male
Infant Mortality (per 1,000 live births 1991): 91
Gross Domestic Product (1990): $245 million
GDP per Capita: $530
Principal Industries: Perfume distillation
Principal Crops: Vanilla, copra, perfume, plants, fruits

CONGO
Republic of the Congo
République Populaire du Congo

Area: 132,000 sq. mi. (342,000 sq. km.)
Population: 2,309,000
Language: French (official), Kikongo 47%, Teke 20%, Mbosi 11%, Mbere 7%, other 15%
Capital: Brazzaville
Currency: Franc CFA
Religion: Christian 50%, local animist 48%, Muslim 2%
Ethnic Groups: Bakongo 45%, Bateke 20%, other including M'Bochi, Sangha 35%
Government: Republic
Literacy (1991): 57%
Life Expectancy at Birth (1991): 56 years female, 52 years male
Infant Mortality (per 1,000 live births 1991): 110
Gross Domestic Product (1989): $2.0 billion
GDP per Capita: $930
Principal Industries: Agriculture, forestry, mining
Principal Crops: Palm kernels, coffee, corn, bananas, rice, cassava, peanuts, tobacco

COSTA RICA
Republic of Costa Rica
República de Costa Rica

Area: 19,650 sq. mi. (50,900 sq. km.)
Population: 3,111,000
Language: Spanish 97%, other 3%
Capital: San José
Currency: Colón
Religion: Roman Catholic 88%, other 12%
Ethnic Groups: Spanish descent 87%, mestizo 7%, other 6%
Government: Republic
Literacy (1991): 93%
Life Expectancy at Birth (1991): 78 years female, 74 years male
Infant Mortality (per 1,000 live births 1991): 15
Gross Domestic Product (1990): $5.5 billion
GDP per Capita: $1,810
Principal Industries: Processed foods, textiles, fertilizers
Principal Crops: Coffee, bananas, sugarcane, rice, cacao

CÔTE D'IVOIRE (Ivory Coast)
Republic of Côte d'Ivoire
République de la Côte d'Ivoire

Area: 124,500 sq. mi. (322,460 sq. km.)
Population: 12,978,000
Language: French (official), many African languages including Twi-Fante (Akan), Kru, Voltaic, Malinke
Capital: Yamoussoukro
Currency: Franc CFA
Religion: Indigenous 63%, Muslim 25%, Christian 12%

Ethnic Groups: Akan 41%, Kru 17%, Voltaic 16%, Malinke 15%, Mande 10%, other 1%
Government: Republic
Literacy (1990): 45%
Life Expectancy at Birth (1991): 55 years female, 52 years male
Infant Mortality (per 1,000 live births 1991): 97
Gross Domestic Product: $9.3 billion
GDP per Capita: $820
Principal Industries: Agriculture, food processing, cement
Principal Crops: Coffee, cocoa, sugar, corn

CROATIA
Republic of Croatia
Hrvatska

Area: 21,830 sq. mi. (56,8540 sq. km.)
Population: 4,600,000
Language: Serbo-Croatian
Capital: Zagreb
Currency: Dinar
Religion: Roman Catholic
Ethnic Groups: Croatian, Serbian
Government: Parliamentary democracy
Literacy (1990): 90%
Life Expectancy at Birth (1991): 76 years female, 70 years male
Infant Mortality (per 1,000 live births 1989): 11.3
Principal Industries: Textiles, chemicals, aluminum products, paper
Principal Crops: Olives, wine

CUBA
Republic of Cuba
República de Cuba

Area: 44,215 sq. mi. (114,525 sq. km.)
Population: 10,732,000
Language: Spanish
Capital: Havana
Currency: Peso
Religion: Roman Catholic
Ethnic Groups: Spanish descent 66%, mulatto 22%, black 12%
Government: Communist
Literacy (1990): 98%
Life Expectancy at Birth (1991): 78 years female, 73 years male
Infant Mortality (per 1,000 live births 1991): 12
Gross National Product (1990 est.): $20.9 billion
GNP per Capita: $2,000
Principal Industries: Oil refining, textiles, chemicals, food processing
Principal Crops: Sugar, tobacco, coffee, pineapples, citrus fruits, rice

CYPRUS
Republic of Cyprus
Kypriaki Demokratia

Area: 3,570 sq. mi. (9,250 sq. km.)
Population: 709,000
Language: Greek 73%, Turkish 23% (both official), other 4%
Capital: Nicosia
Currency: Cyprus pound
Religion: Greek Orthodox 78%, Muslim (Sunni) 18%, other 4%
Ethnic Groups: Greek 78%, Turk 18.7%, Armenian, Maronite 4.3%
Government: Republic
Literacy (1991): 95%
Life Expectancy at Birth (1991): 80 years female, 74 years male
Infant Mortality (per 1,000 live births 1991): 10
Gross Domestic Product (1990): $5.3 billion
GDP per Capita: $7,585
Principal Industries: Wine, clothing, chemicals
Principal Crops: Grains, grapes, citrus fruits, potatoes

CZECH REPUBLIC
Ceská Federativni Republika

Area: 30,440 sq. mi. (78,700 sq. km.)

Population: 10,314,000
Language: Czech
Capital: Prague
Currency: Koruna
Religion: Roman Catholic, Protestant
Government: Republic
Gross Domestic Product (1993): $26.6 billion
GDP per Capita: $2,562

DENMARK
Kingdom of Denmark
Kongeriget Danmark

Area: 16,630 sq. mi. (43,000 sq. km.)
Population: 5,133,000
Language: Danish 97%, other 3%
Capital: Copenhagen
Currency: Krone
Religion: Lutheran 90%, other Christian 7%, other 3%
Ethnic Groups: Danish 97%, other 3%
Government: Constitutional monarchy
Literacy (1991): 99%
Life Expectancy at Birth (1991): 79 years female, 73 years male
Infant Mortality (per 1,000 live births 1991): 6
Gross Domestic Product (1993): $145 billion
GDP per Capita: $28,200
Principal Industries: Machinery, textiles, electronics, furniture
Principal Crops: Barley, beef and dairy cattle, oats, potatoes, wheat

DJIBOUTI
Republic of Djibouti
Jumhouriyya Djibouti

Area: 8,500 sq. mi. (22,000 sq. km.)
Population: 346,000
Language: Arabic 12%, French 4% (both official), Somali 47%, Afar 37%
Capital: Djibouti
Currency: Djibouti Franc
Religion: Muslim (Sunni) 94%, Christian 6%
Ethnic Groups: Somali 60%, Afar 35%, European, Arab 5%
Government: Republic
Literacy (1988): 20%
Life Expectancy at Birth (1991): 49 years female, 45 years male
Infant Mortality (per 1,000 live births): 121
Gross Domestic Product (1989): $340 million
GDP per Capita: $1,030
Principal Industries: Dairy, dock work, livestock

DOMINICA
Commonwealth of Dominica

Area: 290 sq. mi. (750 sq. km.)
Population: 86,000
Language: English (official), French patois 100%
Capital: Roseau
Currency: East Caribbean dollar
Religion: Roman Catholic 77%, other 23%
Ethnic Groups: African descent 91%, mulatto 6%, Native American 2%, other 1%
Government: Republic
Literacy: 94%
Life Expectancy at Birth: 79 years female, 73 years male
Infant Mortality (per 1,000 live births 1991): 13
Gross Domestic Product (1989): $153 million
GDP per Capita: $ 1,840
Principal Industries: Agriculture, tourism
Principal Crops: Bananas, citrus fruits, coconuts

DOMINICAN REPUBLIC
República Dominicana

Area: 18,700 sq. mi. (48,440 sq. km.)
Population: 7,385,000

DOMINICAN REPUBLIC (continued)

Language: Spanish 98%, Creole French 2%
Capital: Santo Domingo
Currency: Peso
Religion: Roman Catholic 92%, other 8%
Ethnic Groups: Mulatto 73%, white 16%, black 11%
Government: Democracy
Literacy (1991): 83%
Life Expectancy at Birth (1991): 69 years female, 65 years male
Infant Mortality (per 1,000 live births 1991): 60
Gross Domestic Product (1990): $7.1 billion
GDP per Capita: $998
Principal Industries: Sugar refining, cement, textiles
Principal Crops: Sugarcane, coffee, cocoa, tobacco, rice

ECUADOR

Republic of Ecuador
República del Ecuador

Area: 106,925 sq. mi. (276,840 sq. km.)
Population: 10,752,000
Language: Spanish 93%, Quechua 7%
Capital: Quito
Currency: Sucre
Religion: Roman Catholic 94%, other 6%
Ethnic Groups: Quechua 50%, mestizo 40%, Spanish descent 9%, Native American 1%
Government: Republic
Literacy (1991): 88%
Life Expectancy at Birth (1989): 68 years female, 64 years male
Infant Mortality (per 1,000 live births 1991): 60
Gross Domestic Product (1990): $10.9 billion
GDP per Capita: $1,040
Principal Industries: Processed foods, textiles, fishing
Principal Crops: Bananas, coffee, rice, sugar, corn

EGYPT

Arab Republic of Egypt
Jumhüriyah Misr al-Arabiya

Area: 386,900 sq. mi. (1,002,000 sq. km.)
Population: 54,452,000
Language: Arabic
Capital: Cairo
Currency: Egyptian pound
Religion: Muslim (Sunni) 94%, Christian (mostly Coptic) 6%
Ethnic Groups: Eastern Hamitic stock 90%, Bedouin, Nubian 10%
Government: Republic
Literacy (1990): 44%
Life Expectancy at Birth (1991): 61 years female, 60 years male
Infant Mortality (per 1,000 live births 1991): 82
Gross Domestic Product (1993): $42.7 billion
GDP per Capita: $751
Principal Industries: Textiles, chemicals, cement
Principal Crops: Cotton, rice, grains, vegetables, sugar, corn, beans

EL SALVADOR

Republic of El Salvador
República de El Salvador

Area: 8,260 sq. mi. (21,990 sq. km.)
Population: 5,419,000
Language: Spanish (official)
Capital: San Salvador
Currency: Colón
Religion: Roman Catholic 93%, other 7%
Ethnic Groups: Mestizo 89%, Native American 10%, other 1%
Government: Republic
Literacy (1991): 75%
Life Expectancy at Birth (1985): 66 years female, 63 years male
Infant Mortality (per 1,000 live births 1991): 47
Gross Domestic Product (1990): $5.1 billion
GDP per Capita: $940

Principal Industries: Food processing, textiles, oil refining
Principal Crops: Coffee, cotton, sugar, corn

EQUATORIAL GUINEA

Republic of Equatorial Guinea
República de Guinea Ecuatorial

Area: 10,830 sq. mi. (28,051 sq. km.)
Population: 379,000
Language: Spanish (official), Fang 75%, Krio 10%, Bubi 5%, other 10%
Capital: Malabo
Currency: Franc CFA
Religion: Predominantly Roman Catholic
Ethnic Groups: Fang 80%, Bubi 15%, other 5%
Government: Republic
Literacy (1989): 55%
Life Expectancy at Birth (1990): 52 years female, 48 years male
Infant Mortality (per 1,000 live births 1990): 127
Gross Domestic Product (1988): $144 million
GDP per Capita: $411
Principal Industries: Agriculture, timber
Principal Crops: Cocoa, wood, coffee, bananas

ESTONIA

Republic of Estonia
Eesti Vabariik

Area: 18,000 sq. mi. (47,530 sq. km.)
Population: 1,600,000
Language: Estonian (official) 65%, Russian 32%, other 3%
Capital: Tallin
Currency: Ruble
Religion: Lutheran 78%, Russian Orthodox 19%, other 3%
Ethnic Groups: Estonian 62%, Russian 30%, Ukrainian 3%, Byelorussian 2%, Finn 1%, other 2%
Government: Republic
Life Expectancy at Birth (1989): 75 years female, 65 years male
Infant Mortality (per 1,000 live births 1989): 14.7
Gross Domestic Product (1993): $968 million
GDP per Capita: $613
Principal Industries: Oil shale processing, mineral fertilizers, wood processing, pulp, peat
Principal Crops: Grains, vegetables

ETHIOPIA

People's Democratic Republic of Ethiopia
Ye Etiyop'iya Hezbawi Dimokrasiyawi Republek

Area: 472,000 sq. mi. (1,223,000 sq. km.)
Population: 53,191,000
Language: Amharic (official) 31%, Oromo (Galla) 27%, Tigrinya 14%, Hadiyya 3%, Somali, Afar, other African languages 25%
Capital: Addis Ababa
Currency: Birr
Religion: Orthodox Christian 40%, Muslim 40%, animist 15%, other 5%
Ethnic Groups: Oromo 40%, Amhara 25%, Tigre 12%, Sidama 9%, other 14%
Government: Provisional
Literacy (1991): 62%
Life Expectancy at Birth (1991): 53 years female, 50 years male
Infant Mortality (per 1,000 live births 1991): 113
Gross Domestic Product (1991): $6.6 billion
GDP per Capita: $130
Principal Industries: Cement, textiles, sugar refining
Principal Crops: Coffee, grains, sugarcane, cotton

FIJI

Republic of Fiji

Area: 7,000 sq. mi. (18,300 sq. km.)
Population: 744,000
Language: English (official), Hindi 49%, Fijian 46%, other 5%
Capital: Suva
Currency: Fiji dollar

Religion: Christian 52%, Hindu 38%, Muslim 8%, other 2%
Ethnic Groups: Indian 48%, Melanesian-Polynesian 46%, European 2%, other 4%
Government: Republic
Literacy (1990): 80%
Life Expectancy at Birth (1991): 67 years female, 62 years male
Infant Mortality (per 1,000 live births 1991): 19
Gross Domestic Product (1990): $ 1.3 billion
GDP per Capita: $1,840
Principal Industries: Sugar refining, tourism
Principal Crops: Sugar, bananas, ginger

FINLAND

Republic of Finland
Suomen Tasavalta

Area: 130,119 sq. mi. (337,000 sq. km.)
Population: 4,991,000
Language: Finnish 94%, Swedish 6% (both official)
Capital: Helsinki
Currency: Markka
Religion: Lutheran 97%, other 3%
Ethnic Groups: Finn 94%, Swede, Lapp 6%
Government: Republic
Literacy (1991): 99%
Life Expectancy at Birth (1991): 80 years female, 71 years male
Infant Mortality (per 1,000 live births 1991): 6
Gross Domestic Product (1993): $105 billion
GDP per Capita: $21,000
Principal Industries: Machinery, metals, shipbuilding, textiles
Principal Crops: Grains, potatoes, dairy products

FRANCE

French Republic
République Française

Area: 212,900 sq. mi. (547,025 sq. km.)
Population: 56,596,000
Language: French 87%, Basque 7%, Provençal 3%, other 3%
Capital: Paris
Currency: French franc
Religion: Roman Catholic 92%, Muslim 3%, other 5%
Ethnic Groups: French 87%, Arab 3%, other 10%
Government: Republic
Literacy (1991): 99%
Life Expectancy at Birth (1991): 82 years female, 74 years male
Infant Mortality (per 1,000 live births 1991): 6
Gross Domestic Product (1990): $1.36 trillion
GDP per Capita: $23,900
Principal Industries: Chemicals, automobiles, iron and steel, aircraft, textiles, wine, perfume
Principal Crops: Grains, grapes, other fruits and vegetables

GABON

Gabonese Republic
République Gabonaise

Area: 103,346 sq. mi. (267,667 sq. km.)
Population: 1,080,000
Language: French (official) 6%, Fang 29%, Sira-Pumu 19%, Mbere 15%, Myene 5%, Beti and other 26%
Capital: Libreville
Currency: Franc CFA
Religion: Local animist, Christian minority
Ethnic Groups: Fang 25%, Bapounon 10%, other 65%
Government: Republic
Literacy (1991): 70%
Life Expectancy at Birth (1991): 56 years female, 51 years male
Infant Mortality (per 1,000 live births 1991): 104
Gross Domestic Product (1991): $5.3 billion
GDP per Capita: $4,400
Principal Industries: Agriculture, mining
Principal Crops: Sugarcane, wood, palm, rice, cocoa, coffee, peanuts

GAMBIA

Republic of The Gambia

Area: 4,100 sq. mi. (10,600 sq. km.)
Population: 875,000
Language: English (official), Mandingo 40%, Fulani 13%, Wolof 12%, Tukolor 8%, other African languages 27%
Capital: Banjul
Currency: Dalasi
Religion: Muslim 90%, Christian 9%, traditional 1%
Ethnic Groups: Mandinka 42%, Fula 16%, Wolof 16%, other 26%
Government: Republic
Literacy (1989) 12%
Life Expectancy at Birth (1991): 51 years female, 47 years male
Infant Mortality (per 1,000 live births 1991): 138
Gross Domestic Product (1990): $196 million
GDP per Capita: $230
Principal Industries: Agriculture
Principal Crops: Peanuts, rice, palm kernels, bananas, cassava, corn

GEORGIA

Republic of Georgia
Sakartvelos Respublica

Area: 26,900 sq. mi. (167,700 sq. km.)
Population: 5,500,000
Language: Georgian 69% (official), Russian 11%, Armenian 7%, other 13%
Capital: Tbilisi
Currency: Ruble
Religion: Eastern Orthodox
Ethnic Groups: Georgian 70%, Armenian 7%, Russian 6%, other 17%
Government: In transition
Literacy (1991): 98%
Life Expectancy at Birth (1991): 74 years female, 65 years male
Infant Mortality (per 1,000 live births 1991): 20
Principal Industries: Manganese mining
Principal Crops: Citrus fruits, wheat, grapes

GERMANY

Federal Republic of Germany
Bundesrepublik Deutschland

Area: 137,838 sq. mi. (357,000 sq. km.)
Population: 79,548,000
Language: German 98%, Turkish 2%
Capital: Berlin (seat of government, Bonn)
Currency: Deutsche Mark
Religion: Protestant 49%, Roman Catholic 45%, other 6%
Ethnic Groups: German 93%, other 7%
Government: Republic
Literacy (1991): 99%
Life Expectancy at Birth: 79 years female, 73 years male
Infant Mortality (per 1,000 live births 1991): 7
Gross Domestic Product (1993): $1.95 trillion
GDP per Capita: $24,120
Principal Industries: Steel, ships, vehicles, machinery, coal, chemicals
Principal Crops: Grains, potatoes, sugar beets

GHANA

Republic of Ghana

Area: 92,100 sq. mi. (238,537 sq. km.)
Population: 15,617,000
Language: English (official), Akan 44%, Ewe 13%, Ga-Adangme 6%, Twi-Fante (Akan) and other African languages 37%
Capital: Accra
Currency: Cedi
Religion: Traditional 46%, Muslim 30%, Christian 24%
Ethnic Groups: Akan 44%, Moshi-Dagomba 16%, Ewe 13%, Ga 8%, other 19%
Government: Military
Literacy (1991): 60%
Life Expectancy at Birth: 56 years female, 53 years male
Infant Mortality (per 1,000 live births 1991): 86

GHANA (continued)
Gross National Product (1990): $5.8 billion
GNP per Capita: $380
Principal Industries: Agriculture, mining
Principal Crops: Cocoa, coffee, coconuts, cassava, rice, palm kernels

GREECE
Hellenic Republic
Elliniki Dimokratia

Area: 50,960 sq. mi. (131,990 sq. km.)
Population: 10,043,000
Language: Greek 95%, other 5%
Capital: Athens
Currency: Drachma
Religion: Greek Orthodox 97%, other 3%
Ethnic Groups: Greek 98.5%, other 1.5%
Government: Parliamentary republic
Literacy (1991): 96% (men), 89% (women)
Life Expectancy at Birth: 80 years female, 75 years male
Infant Mortality (per 1,000 live births 1991): 11
Gross Domestic Product (1993) 80 billion
GDP per Capita: $7,600
Principal Industries: Textiles, chemicals, metals, wine, processed foods
Principal Crops: Grains, rice, corn, cotton, olives, citrus fruits, tobacco, grapes

GRENADA

Area: 133 sq. mi. (344 sq. km.)
Population: 84,000
Language: English (official), Creole English 97%, other 3%
Capital: St. George's
Currency: East Caribbean dollar
Religion: Roman Catholic 64%, Anglican 22%, other 22%
Ethnic Groups: African descent 84%, mulatto 12%, other 4%
Government: Independent state within the commonwealth
Literacy (1991): 95%
Life Expectancy at Birth (1991): 74 years female, 69 years male
Infant Mortality (per 1,000 live births 1991): 30
Gross National Product (1989): $179 million
GNP per Capita: $1,900
Principal Industries: Agriculture, tourism, fishing
Principal Crops: Spices, cocoa, bananas

GUATEMALA
Republic of Guatemala
República de Guatemala

Area: 42,042 sq. mi. (108,889 sq. km.)
Population: 9,266,000
Language: Spanish 65%, Quiche 12%, Mayan languages 7%, Kekchi 6%, Cakchiquel 6%, Mam 4%
Capital: Guatemala City
Currency: Quetzal
Religion: Roman Catholic
Ethnic Groups: Native American 54%, mestizo 42%, white or European descent 4%
Government: Republic
Literacy (1991): 55%
Life Expectancy at Birth (1989): 63 years female, 59 years male
Infant Mortality (per 1,000 live births 1991): 58
Gross Domestic Product (1990): $11.1 billion
GDP per Capita (1990): $1,180
Principal Industries: Agriculture, textiles, chemicals, tires, plastics
Principal Crops: Coffee, cotton, sugar, bananas

GUINEA
Republic of Guinea
République de Guinée

Area: 94,925 sq. mi. (245,857 sq. km.)
Population: 7,456,000
Language: French (official), Fulakunda 40%, Malinke 25%, Futa Jalon 10%, Susu 10%, Kissi 6%, Kpelle 6%, Toma 3%

Capital: Conakry
Currency: Guinean franc
Religion: Muslim 85%, Christian 8%, indigenous 7%
Ethnic Groups: Fulani 35%, Malinke 30%, Soussous 20%, other 15%
Government: Military
Literacy (1991): 24% in French, 48% in local languages
Life Expectancy at Birth (1991): 45 years female, 41 years male
Infant Mortality (per 1,000 live births 1991): 144
Gross Domestic Product (1989): $2.7 billion
GDP per Capita: $380
Principal Industries: Agriculture, mining
Principal Crops: Rice, coffee, bananas, pineapples, corn, palm nuts

GUINEA-BISSAU
Republic of Guinea-Bissau
República da Guiné-Bissau

Area: 13,948 sq. mi. (36,125 sq. km.)
Population: 1,024,000
Language: Portuguese (official), Balanta 44%, Fulani 20%, Mandyak 14%, Mandinka 12%, Papel 7%, Mankanya 3%
Capital: Bissau
Currency: Guinea-Bissau peso
Religion: Traditional 65%, Muslim 30%, Christian 4%
Ethnic Groups: Balanta 27%, Fula 23%, Mandinka 12%, Manjaca 11%, other 27%
Government: Republic
Literacy (1991): 36%
Life Expectancy at Birth (1991): 48 years female, 45 years male
Infant Mortality (per 1,000 live births 1991): 125
Gross Domestic Product: $154 million
GDP per Capita: $160
Principal Industries: Agriculture
Principal Crops: Peanuts, cotton, rice

GUYANA
Cooperative Republic of Guyana

Area: 83,000 sq. mi. (214,969 sq. km.)
Population: 750,000
Language: English (official), English Creole 78%, indigenous dialects 22%
Capital: Georgetown
Currency: Guyana dollar
Religion: Christian 50%, Hindu 39%, Muslim 11%
Ethnic Groups: East Indian 51%, African 30%, mixed 14%
Government: Republic
Literacy (1991): 95%
Life Expectancy at Birth (1991): 68 years female, 61 years male
Infant Mortality (per 1,000 live births 1991): 51
Gross Domestic Product (1989): $248 million
GDP per Capita: $380
Principal Industries: Mining, textiles
Principal Crops: Sugar, rice, citrus and other fruits

HAITI
Republic of Haiti
République d'Haiti

Area: 10,715 sq. mi. (27,750 sq. km.)
Population: 6,287,000
Language: French (official) 1%, Creole 99%
Capital: Port-au-Prince
Currency: Gourde
Religion: Roman Catholic 80%, Baptist 10%, Voodoo 10%
Ethnic Groups: African descent
Government: Military
Literacy (1991): 53%
Life Expectancy at Birth (1991): 55 years female, 52 years male
Infant Mortality (per 1,000 live births 1991): 106
Gross Domestic Product (1990): $2.7 billion
GDP per Capita: $440
Principal Industries: Sugar refining, textiles
Principal Crops: Coffee, sugar, bananas, cocoa, tobacco, rice

HONDURAS

Republic of Honduras
República de Honduras

Area: 43,277 sq. mi. (12,088 sq. km.)
Population: 4,949,000
Language: Spanish 97%, other 3%
Capital: Tegucigalpa
Currency: Lempira
Religion: Roman Catholic 94%, other 6%
Ethnic Groups: Mestizo 90%, Native American 7%, other 3%
Government: Republic
Literacy (1991): 73%
Life Expectancy at Birth (1991): 68 years female, 64 years male
Infant Mortality (per 1,000 live births 1991): 56
Gross Domestic Product (1990): $4.9 billion
GDP per Capita: $960
Principal Industries: Agriculture, clothing, textiles, forest products
Principal Crops: Bananas, coffee, corn, beans, sugarcane

HUNGARY

Republic of Hungary
Magyar Köztársaság

Area: 35,913 sq. mi. (93,030 sq. km.)
Population: 10,558,000
Language: Magyar (Hungarian) 98%, other 2%
Capital: Budapest
Currency: Forint
Religion: Roman Catholic 67%, Protestant 25%, other 8%
Ethnic Groups: Magyar 92%, Gypsy 3%, German 2.5%, other 2.5%
Government: Republic
Literacy (1989): 98%
Life Expectancy at Birth (1991): 76 years female, 68 years male
Infant Mortality (per 1,000 live births 1991): 14
Gross Domestic Product (1993): $40.2 billion
GDP per Capita: $3,896
Principal Industries: Steel, chemicals, machinery, pharmaceuticals, textiles, vehicles
Principal Crops: Grains, potatoes, beets, vegetables, grapes

ICELAND

Republic of Iceland
Lyoveldio Island

Area: 39,700 sq. mi. (102,845 sq. km.)
Population: 260,000
Language: Icelandic
Capital: Reykjavik
Currency: M.N. krona
Religion: Lutheran 93%, other 7%
Ethnic Groups: Icelandic 97%, other 3%
Government: Republic
Literacy (1991): 99%
Life Expectancy at Birth (1991): 81 years female, 75 years male
Infant Mortality (per 1,000 live births 1991): 7
Gross Domestic Product (1990): $4.2 billion
GDP per Capita (1990): $16,300
Principal Industries: Fishing, agriculture, mining
Principal Crops: Hay, fodder

INDIA

Republic of India
Bharat

Area: 1,266,595 sq. mi. (3,185,025 sq. km.)
Population: 869,515,000
Language: Hindi, English, Assamese, Bengali, Bhili, Bihari, Bhojpuri, Braj Bhasha, Bundeli, Gondi, Gujarti, Kannada (Kanarese), Kashmiri, Konkani, Kurux (Oraon), Malayalam, Marathi, Nepali, Oriya, Rajasthani, Santali, Sindhi, Tamil, Telugu, Urdu, other
Capital: New Delhi
Currency: Rupee
Religion: Hindu 83%, Muslim 11%, Christian 3%, Sikh 2%
Ethnic Groups: Indo-Aryan 72%, Dravidian 25%, Mongoloid 3%
Government: Republic
Literacy (1991): 48%
Life Expectancy at Birth (1991): 58 years female, 57 years male
Infant Mortality (per 1,000 live births 1991): 87
Gross Domestic Product (1993): $236 billion
GDP per Capita: $269
Principal Industries: Textiles, steel, cement, machinery, chemicals, fertilizer
Principal Crops: Rice, grains, cotton, jute, tea, sugarcane, spices

INDONESIA

Republic of Indonesia
Republik Indonesia

Area: 735,265 sq. mi. (1,904,345 sq. km.)
Population: 193,560,000
Language: Javanese 42%, Sundanese 15%, Bahasa Indonesian (Malay) 6%, Minankabau 4%, Achinese, Balinese, Batak, Bugis, Dayak, Madurese, other Austronesian 33%
Capital: Djakarta
Currency: Rupiah
Religion: Muslim 88%, Christian 9%, Hindu 3%
Ethnic Groups: Javanese 40%, Sundanese 15%, Malay 8%, Madurese 8%, other 29%
Government: Republic
Literacy (1990): 85%
Life Expectancy at Birth (1991): 63 years female, 59 years male
Infant Mortality (per 1,000 live births 1991): 73
Gross Domestic Product (1993): $140 billion
GDP per Capita: $740
Principal Industries: Agriculture, food processing, textiles, mining
Principal Crops: Rice, cassava, sugarcane, coffee, peanuts, spices

IRAN

Islamic Republic of Iran
Jamhori-e-Islami-e-Irän

Area: 636,295 sq. mi. (1,648,000 sq. km.)
Population: 59,051,000
Language: Farsi (Persian) (official) 50%, Azerbaijani 17%, Kurdish 8%, Luri 7%, Mazandarani 5%, Gilaki 4%, other 9%
Capital: Teheran
Currency: Rial
Religion: Muslim (Shi'ite 95%, Sunni 5%)
Ethnic Groups: Persian 51%, Azerbaijani 25%, Kurd 9%, other 15%
Government: Islamic republic
Literacy (1990): 54%
Life Expectancy at Birth (1991): 65 years male, 64 years female
Infant Mortality (per 1,000 live births 1991): 66
Gross Domestic Product (1993): $60.3 billion
GDP per Capita: $957
Principal Industries: Cement, sugar refining, carpets
Principal Crops: Grains, rice, fruits, sugar beets, cotton, grapes

IRAQ

Republic of Iraq
al Jumhouriya al 'Iraqia

Area: 167,925 sq. mi. (434,915 sq. km.)
Population: 19,525,000
Language: Arabic 78%, Kurdish 18%, Luri 4%
Capital: Baghdad
Currency: Iraqi dinar
Religion: Muslim 95% (Shi'ite 60%, Sunni 35%) Christian 5%
Ethnic Groups: Arab 75%, Kurd 15%, Turk and other 10%
Government: Republic
Literacy (1990): 54%
Life Expectancy at Birth (1991): 68 years female, 66 years male
Infant Mortality (per 1,000 live births 1991): 66
Gross Domestic Product (1993): $20.8 billion
GNP per Capita: $1,000
Principal Industries: Oil refining, petrochemicals, textiles
Principal Crops: Grains, sugarcane, rice, cotton, dates

IRELAND

Republic of Ireland
Eire

Area: 27,135 sq. mi. (70,280 sq. km.)
Population: 3,489,000
Language: English 95%, Irish (Gaelic) 5%
Capital: Dublin
Currency: Irish pound (punt)
Religion: Roman Catholic 94%, Anglican 4%, other 2%
Ethnic Groups: Irish 94%, other 6%
Government: Parliamentary republic
Literacy (1991): 99%
Life Expectancy at Birth: 79 years female, 73 years male
Infant Mortality (per 1,000 live births 1991): 6
Gross Domestic Product (1993): $50 billion
GDP per Capita: $14,700
Principal Industries: Agriculture, food processing, metals, electronics, beverages, machinery, tourism
Principal Crops: Barley, sugar beets, potatoes

ISRAEL

State of Israel
Medinat Israel

Area: 8,020 sq. mi. (20,772 sq. km.)
Population: 4,558,000
Language: Hebrew 69%, Arabic 18% (both official), Yiddish 2%, Russian 2%, other 9%
Capital: Jerusalem (U.S. recognizes Tel Aviv)
Currency: Shekel
Religion: Judaism 83%, Muslim 14%, Christian 2%
Ethnic Groups: Jewish 83%, Arab 16%, other 1%
Government: Democracy
Literacy (1991): 92% (Jewish), 70% (Arab)
Life Expectancy at Birth (1991): (Jewish population only) 79 years female, 76 years male
Infant Mortality (per 1,000 live births 1991): 9
Gross Domestic Product (1993): $71.0 Billion
GDP per Capita: $12,241
Principal Industries: Diamond cutting, textiles, processed foods, chemicals, plastics, agriculture
Principal Crops: Citrus fruits, grains, olives

ITALY

Italian Republic
Repubblica Italiana

Area: 116,300 sq. mi (310,275 sq. km.)
Population: 57,772,000
Language: Italian 94%, other 6%
Capital: Rome
Currency: Lira
Religion: Roman Catholic
Ethnic Groups: Italian 98%, other 2%
Government: Republic
Literacy (1991): 98%
Life Expectancy at Birth (1991): 82 years female, 75 years male
Infant Mortality (per 1,000 live births 1991): 6
Gross Domestic Product (1990): $1.17 trillion
GDP per Capita: $20,200
Principal Industries: Steel, machinery, autos, textiles, shoes, machine tools
Principal Crops: Grapes, olives, citrus fruits, vegetables, wheat, rice

JAMAICA

Area: 4,410 sq. mi. (11,424 sq. km.)
Population: 2,489,000
Language: English 27% (official), English Creole 70%, other 3%
Capital: Kingston
Currency: Jamaican dollar
Religion: Protestant 56%, Roman Catholic 5%, other 39%
Ethnic Groups: African 76%, mixed 15%, Native American and Afro-Indian 4%, white or European descent 3%, other 2%

Government: Democracy
Literacy (1990): 98%
Life Expectancy at Birth (1991): 76 years female, 72 years male
Infant Mortality (per 1,000 live births 1991): 17
Gross Domestic Product (1990): $3.9 billion dollars
GDP per Capita: $1,580
Principal Industries: Tourism, rum, molasses
Principal Crops: Sugarcane, coffee, bananas, citrus fruits

JAPAN

Nippon

Area: 145,860 sq. mi. (377,810 sq. km.)
Population: 124,017,000
Language: Japanese
Capital: Tokyo
Currency: Yen
Religion: Shinto Buddhist 87%, other 13%
Ethnic Groups: Japanese 99.5%, Korean 0.5%
Government: Parliamentary democracy
Literacy (1991): 99%
Life Expectancy at Birth: 82 years female, 76 years male
Infant Mortality (per 1,000 live births 1991): 4
Gross Domestic Product (1993): $4 trillion
GDP per Capita: $32,018
Principal Industries: Electrical and electronic equipment, automobiles, machinery, chemicals
Principal Crops: Rice, grains, vegetables, fruits

JORDAN

Hashemite Kingdom of Jordan
al Mamlaka al Urduniya al Hashemiyah

Area: 35,000 sq. mi. (89,500 sq. km.)
Population: 3,413,000
Language: Arabic (official)
Capital: Amman
Currency: Jordanian dinar
Religion: Muslim (Sunni) 92%, Christian 8%
Ethnic Groups: Arab 98%, other 2%
Government: Constitutional monarchy
Literacy (1989): 71%
Life Expectancy at Birth (1991): 73 years female, 70 years male
Infant Mortality (per 1,000 live births 1991): 38
Gross National Product (1990): $4.6 billion
GNP per Capita: $1,400
Principal Industries: Textiles, cement, food processing
Principal Crops: Grains, olives, vegetables, fruits

KAZAKHSTAN

Republic of Kazakhstan
Kazak Respublikasy

Area: 1,049,000 sq. mi. (2,717,300 sq. km.)
Population: 16,700,000
Language: Kazakh (official) 36%, Russian 50%, German 4%, Ukrainian 3%, other 7%
Capital: Alma-Ata
Currency: Ruble
Religion: Muslim
Ethnic Groups: Kazakh 40%, Russian 37%, German 6%, Ukrainian 5%, other 12%
Government: Republic
Literacy (1991): 98%
Life Expectancy at Birth (1991): 74 years female, 65 years male
Infant Mortality (per 1,000 live births 1991): 26
Gross Domestic Product (1993): $2.6 billion
GDP per Capita: $155
Principal Industries: Steel, cement, footwear, textiles
Principal Crops: Grain, cotton

KENYA

Republic of Kenya
Jamhuri ya Kenya

Area: 224,960 sq. mi. (582,645 sq. km.)
Population: 25,242,000
Language: English, Swahili (official), Gusii, Kamba, Kikuyu, Luhya, Luo, Somali, Teso, several other African
Capital: Nairobi
Currency: Kenyan shilling
Religion: Protestant 38%, Roman Catholic 28%, traditional 27%, Muslim 6%
Ethnic Groups: Kikuyu 21%, Luhya 14%, Luo 13%, Kelenjin 11%, Kamba 11%, other 30%
Government: Republic
Literacy (1989): 50%
Life Expectancy at Birth (1989): 63 years female, 59 years male
Infant Mortality (per 1,000 live births 1989): 70
Gross Domestic Product (1990): $8.1 billion
GDP per Capita: $320
Principal Industries: Agriculture, textiles, food processing, tourism
Principal Crops: Coffee, corn, tea, cereals, cotton, sisal

KIRIBATI

Republic of Kiribati

Area: 275 sq. mi. (725 sq. km.)
Population: 71,000
Language: Ikiribati 97%, other 3%
Capital: Tarawa
Currency: Australian dollar
Religion: Roman Catholic 53%, Protestant 41%, other 5%
Ethnic Groups: Gilbertese 96%, mixed 3%, other 1%
Government: Republic
Literacy (1985): 90%
Gross Domestic Product (1990): $36.8 million
GDP per Capita: $525
Principal Industries: Agriculture, fishing
Principal Crops: Copra, vegetables

NORTH KOREA

Democratic People's Republic of Korea
Chosun Minchu-chui Immin Kongwa-guk

Area: 46,750 sq. mi. (121,125 sq. km.)
Population: 21,185,000
Language: Korean
Capital: Pyongyang
Currency: Won
Religion: Buddhist, Confucian, Chondokyo (religious activity virtually nonexistent)
Ethnic Groups: Korean
Government: Communist
Literacy (1989): 99%
Life Expectancy at Birth (1991): 73 years female, 69 years male
Infant Mortality (per 1,000 live births 1991): 32
Gross National Product (1990): $29 billion
GNP per Capita: $1,390
Principal Industries: Textiles, petrochemicals, food processing
Principal Crops: Corn, potatoes, fruits, vegetables, rice

SOUTH KOREA

Republic of Korea
Taehan Min'guk

Area: 38,030 sq. mi. (98,500 sq. km.)
Population: 43,134,000
Language: Korean
Capital: Seoul
Currency: Won
Religion: Confucian, Christian, Buddhist
Ethnic Groups: Korean
Government: Republic
Literacy (1991): 96%

Life Expectancy at Birth (1991): 73 years female, 67 years male
Infant Mortality (per 1,000 live births 1991): 23
Gross Domestic Product (1993): $354 billion
GDP per Capita: $8,040
Principal Industries: Electronics, ships, textiles, clothing, motor vehicles
Principal Crops: Rice, barley, vegetables, wheat

KUWAIT

State of Kuwait
Dowlat al-Kuwait

Area: 6,880 sq. mi. (17,820 sq. km.)
Population: 2,204,000
Language: Arabic (official) 85%, other 15%
Capital: Kuwait
Currency: Kuwait dinar
Religion: Muslim 85% (Sunni 45%, Sh'ite 30%, other 10%), other 15%
Ethnic Groups: Kuwaiti 40%, other Arab 30%, Asian 21%, other 9%
Government: Constitutional monarchy
Literacy (1989): 71%
Life Expectancy at Birth (1991): 76 years female, 72 years male
Infant Mortality (per 1,000 live births 1991): 15
Gross Domestic Product (1989): $19.9 billion
GDP per Capita: $19,700
Principal Industries: Oil products
Principal Crops: Wheat, dates, vegetables

KYRGYZSTAN

Republic of Kyrgyzstan
Kyrgyz Respublikasy

Area: 76,000 sq. mi. (198,500 sq. km.)
Population: 4,500,000
Language: Kyrgyz (official) 48%, Russian 30%, Uzbek 13%, other 9%
Capital: Bishkek
Currency: Ruble
Religion: Muslim
Ethnic Groups: Kyrgyz 52%, Russian 22%, Uzbec 13%, other 13%
Government: Republic
Literacy (1991): 98%
Life Expectancy at Birth (1991): 74 years female, 65 years male
Infant Mortality (per 1,000 live births 1991): 32
Principal Industries: Tanning, tobacco, textiles, mining
Principal Crops: Wheat, sugar beets, tobacco

LAOS

Lao People's Democratic Republic
Sathalanalat Paxathipatai Paxoxön Lao

Area: 91,430 sq. mi. (236,000 sq. km.)
Population: 4,113,000
Language: Lao (official) 79%, Khmu 8%, Hmong 3%, Tai 3%, other 7%
Capital: Vientiane
Currency: Kip
Religion: Buddhism 85%, tribal 15%
Ethnic Groups: Lao 48%, Mon Khmer tribes 25%, Thai 14%, Meo and Yao 13%
Government: Communist
Literacy (1991): 45%
Life Expectancy at Birth (1991): 52 years female, 49 years male
Infant Mortality (per 1,000 live births): 124
Gross Domestic Product (1990): $600 million
GDP per Capita: $150
Principal Industries: Agriculture, forestry, mining
Principal Crops: Rice, corn, tobacco, cotton

LATVIA

The Republic of Latvia
Latvijas Republika

Area: 25,400 sq. mi. (65,785 sq. km.)
Population: 2,700,000
Language: Latvian (official) 54%, Russian 40%, other 6%

LATVIA (continued)

Capital: Riga

Currency: Ruble

Religion: Predominantly Lutheran, also Roman Catholic and Russian Orthodox

Ethnic Groups: Latvian 54%, Russian 33%, Ukrainian, Byelorussian 13%

Government: Republic

Life Expectancy at Birth (1990): 75 years female, 64 years male

Infant Mortality (per 1,000 live births 1989): 11

Gross Domestic Product (1993): $744 million

GDP per Capita: $279

Principal Industries: Machinery and metalworking, electrical equipment, agricultural engineering, paper

Principal Crops: Oats, barley, potatoes

LEBANON

Republic of Lebanon
al-Jumhouriya al-Lubnaniya

Area: 4,000 sq. mi. (10,400 sq. km.)

Population: 3,385,000

Language: Arabic (official) 93%, Armenian 6%, other 1%

Capital: Beirut

Currency: Lebanese pound

Religion: Muslim 60%, Christian 40%

Ethnic Groups: Arab 85%, Palestinian 9%, Armenian 5%

Government: Republic

Literacy (1991): 75%

Life Expectancy at Birth (1991): 71 years female, 66 years male

Infant Mortality (per 1,000 live births 1991): 50

Gross Domestic Product (1990): $3.3 billion

GDP per Capita: $1,000

Principal Industries: Trade, food products, textiles, cement, oil products

Principal Crops: Fruits, olives, tobacco, grapes, vegetables, grains

LESOTHO

Kingdom of Lesotho

Area: 11,700 sq. mi. (30,355 sq. km.)

Population: 1,801,000

Language: English, Sotho 85% (both official), Zulu 15%

Capital: Maseru

Currency: Loti

Religion: Protestant 42%, Roman Catholic 38%, local religions 20%

Ethnic Groups: Sotho

Government: Military

Literacy (1990): 50%

Life Expectancy at Birth (1991): 62 years female, 59 years male

Infant Mortality (per 1,000 live births 1991): 81

Gross Domestic Product (1990): $420 million

GDP per Capita: $420

Principal Industries: Diamond polishing, food processing

Principal Crops: Grains, sorghum, corn, beans

LIBERIA

Republic of Liberia

Area: 43,000 sq. mi. (111,370 sq. km.)

Population: 2,730,000

Language: English (official), Kpelle 23%, Bassa 16%, Grebo-Krahn 15%, Klao 7%, Loma 7%, Dan 6%, other African 26%

Currency: Liberian dollar

Religion: Traditional 70%, Muslim 20%, Christian 10%

Ethnic Groups: Indigenous tribes 95%, African-American descent 5%

Government: Republic

Literacy (1989): 25%

Life Expectancy at Birth (1991): 59 years female, 54 years male

Infant Mortality (per 1,000 live births 1991): 124

Gross National Product (1989): $1 billion

GNP per Capita: $440

Principal Industries: Rubber processing, food processing, agriculture, mining

Principal Crops: Rice, cassava, coffee, cocoa, sugar

LIBYA

Socialist People's Libyan Jamahiriyah
al-Jamahiriyah al-Arabiya al-Libya al-Shabiya al-Ishti-rakiya

Area: 679,535 sq. mi. (1,759,995 sq. km.)

Population: 4,353,000

Language: Arabic 95%, Tuareg 3%, other 2%

Capital: Tripoli

Currency: Libyan dinar

Religion: Muslim (Sunni) 97%, other 3%

Ethnic Groups: Arab-Berber 97%, other 3%

Government: Socialist military dictatorship

Literacy: (1989) 60%

Life Expectancy at Birth (1991): 71 years female, 66 years male

Infant Mortality (per 1,000 live births 1991): 62

Gross National Product (1989): $24 billion

GNP per Capita: $5,680

Principal Industries: Oil refining, textiles, agriculture

Principal Crops: Dates, olives, citrus fruits, grapes

LIECHTENSTEIN

Principality of Liechtenstein
Fürstentum Liechtenstein

Area: 61 sq. mi. (157 sq. km.)

Population: 28,000

Language: German (official)

Capital: Vaduz

Currency: Swiss franc

Religion: Roman Catholic 87%, Protestant 8%, other 5%

Ethnic Groups: Alemannic 95%, Italian 5%

Government: Constitutional monarchy

Literacy (1991): 100%

Infant Mortality (per 1,000 live births 1991): 5

Gross Domestic Product (1990): $630 million

GDP per Capita: $22,300

Principal Industries: Manufacturing of machinery and chemicals, ceramics, forestry, banking

Principal Crops: Grains, vegetables

LITHUANIA

Republic of Lithuania
Lietuvos Respublika

Area: 25,175 sq. mi. (64,445 sq. km.)

Population (1992): 3,700,000

Language: Lithuanian (official) 80%, Russian 11%, Polish 6%, other 3%

Capital: Vilnius

Currency: Ruble

Religion: Predominantly Roman Catholic

Ethnic Groups: Lithuanian 80%, Russian 9%, Polish 7%, other 4%

Government: Republic

Life Expectancy at Birth (1989): 76 years female, 67 years male

Infant Mortality (per 1,000 live births): 10

Gross Domestic Product (1993): $996 million

GDP per Capita: $265

Principal Industries: Engineering, shipbuilding

Principal Crops: Grain, potatoes, vegetables

LUXEMBOURG

Grand Duchy of Luxembourg
Grand-Duché de Luxembourg

Area: 999 sq. mi. (2,586 sq. km.)

Population: 388,000

Language: French, German (both official), Luxembourgish

Capital: Luxembourg

Currency: Luxembourg franc

Religion: Roman Catholic 93%, other 7%

Ethnic Groups: Luxembourger 70%, Portuguese 9%, Italian 6%, French 4%, German 3%, other 8%

Government: Constitutional monarchy

Literacy (1989): 100%
Life Expectancy at Birth (1991): 80 years female, 73 years male
Gross Domestic Product (1990): $6.9 billion
GDP per Capita: $18,000
Principal Industries: Steel, chemicals, beer, tires, tobacco, metal products, cement
Principal Crops: Corn, grapes

MACEDONIA
Republic of Macedonia

Area: 9,925 sq. mi. (25,710 sq. km.)
Population: 1,900,000
Language: Macedonian
Capital: Skopje
Currency: Denar
Religion: Eastern Orthodox
Ethnic Groups: Macedonians 71%, Albanians 21%, Turkish 5%, other 3%
Government: Republic
Principal Industries: Agriculture
Principal Crops: Tobacco, cotton, fruits and vegetables, wheat, rye, corn

MADAGASCAR
Democratic Republic of Madagascar
Repoblika Demokratika Malagasy

Area: 226,600 sq. mi. (587,050 sq. km.)
Population: 12,185,000
Language: Malagasy 99%, French (official) 1%
Capital: Antananarivo
Currency: Malagasy Franc
Religion: Animist 52%, Christian 41%, Muslim 7%
Ethnic Groups: Merina 27%, Malagasy 27% Betsimisaraka 15%, Betsileo 12%, Tsimihety 7%, Sakalava 6%, Antandray 5%, other 1%
Government: Republic
Literacy (1987): 53%
Life Expectancy at Birth (1991): 54 years female, 51 years male
Infant Mortality (per 1,000 live births 1991): 95
Gross Domestic Product (1990): $2.5 billion
GDP per Capita: $200
Principal Industries: Agriculture, textiles, processed foods, fishing
Principal Crops: Coffee, cloves, vanilla, chromite

MALAWI
Republic of Malawi

Area: 45,750 sq. mi. (118,485 sq. km.)
Population: 9,438,000
Language: Chewa, English (both official), Nyanja and African languages 50%
Capital: Lilongwe
Currency: Kwacha
Religion: Christian 75%, Muslim 20%, other 5%
Ethnic Groups: Chewa 90%, Nyanja, Lomwe, other Bantu tribes 10%
Government: Single party
Literacy (1989): 25%
Life Expectancy at Birth (1991): 51 years female, 48 years male
Infant Mortality (per 1,000 live births 1991): 136
Gross Domestic Product (1990): $1.6 billion
GDP per Capita: $175
Principal Industries: Agriculture, fishing, sugar refining
Principal Crops: Tea, tobacco, coffee, sugar

MALAYSIA

Area: 128,330 sq. mi. (332,370 sq. km.)
Population: 17,982,000
Language: Malay (official) 47%, Chinese 28%, Tamil 2%, other 23%
Capital: Kuala Lumpur
Currency: Ringgit
Religion: Muslim 53%, Buddhist 17%, Chinese folk 12%, Hindu 7%, Christian 6%, other 5%
Ethnic Groups: Malays 59%, Chinese 32%, Indian 9%
Government: Parliamentary democracy

Literacy (1991): 80%
Life Expectancy at Birth (1991): 70 years female, 65 years male
Infant Mortality (per 1,000 live births 1991): 29
Gross Domestic Product (1993): $66 billion
GDP per Capita: $3,468
Principal Industries: Rubber processing, mining, forestry
Principal Crops: Rubber, palm oil, rice, lumber, copra, pepper

MALDIVES
Republic of Maldives
Divehi Jumhuriya

Area: 115 sq. mi. (298 sq. km.)
Population: 226,000
Language: Divehi (Sinhalese dialect)
Capital: Male
Currency: Maldivian rufiyaa
Religion: Muslim (Sunni)
Ethnic Groups: Sinhalese 40%, Dravidian 30%, Arab and black 30%
Government: Republic
Literacy (1989): 93%
Life Expectancy at Birth (1991): 65 years female, 61 years male
Infant Mortality (per 1,000 live births 1991): 72
Gross Domestic Product (1989): $136 million
GDP per Capita: $670
Principal Industries: Fish and coconut processing, tourism
Principal Crops: Coconuts, fruit, millet

MALI
Republic of Mali
République du Mali

Area: 478,765 sq. mi. (1,240,140 sq. km.)
Population: 8,339,000
Language: French (official), African languages
Capital: Bamako
Currency: Franc CFA
Religion: Muslim 90%, other 10%
Ethnic Groups: Mande Groups 50%, Peul 17%, Voltaic Groups 12%, Songhai 6%, Tuareg and Moor 5%, other 10%
Government: Military
Literacy (1991): 25%
Life Expectancy at Birth (1991): 47 years female, 45 years male
Infant Mortality (per 1,000 live births 1991): 114
Gross Domestic Product (1989): $2.0 billion
GDP per Capita: $250
Principal Industries: Agriculture, mining
Principal Crops: Millet, rice, peanuts, cotton

MALTA
Repubblika Ta' Malta

Area: 122 sq. mi. (316 sq. km.)
Population: 356,000
Language: Maltese 96%, English 2% (both official), Italian 2%
Capital: Valletta
Currency: Maltese lira
Religion: Roman Catholic 97%, other 3%
Ethnic Groups: Maltese 96%, other 4%
Government: Democracy
Literacy (1988): 90%
Life Expectancy at Birth (1991): 79 years female, 74 years male
Infant Mortality (per 1,000 live births 1991): 7
Gross National Product (1989): $2.3 billion
GNP per Capita: $6,564
Principal Industries: Agriculture, textiles, plastics, electronic equipment manufacture
Principal Crops: Fruits and vegetables

MARSHALL ISLANDS
Republic of the Marshall Islands

Area: 70 sq. mi. (181.3 sq. km.)

The World

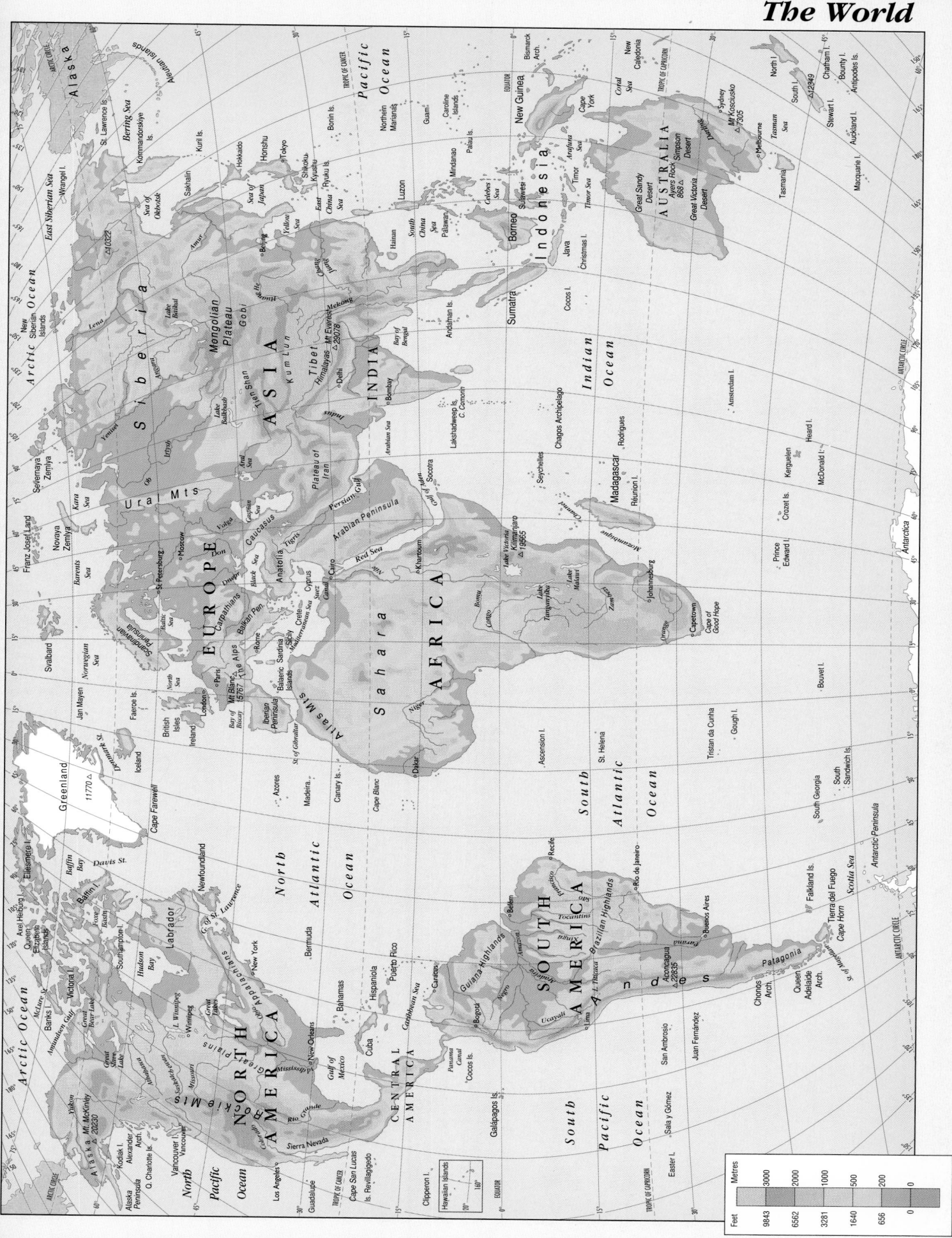

Metres 3000 2000 1000 500 200 0

Feet 9843 6562 3281 1640 656 0

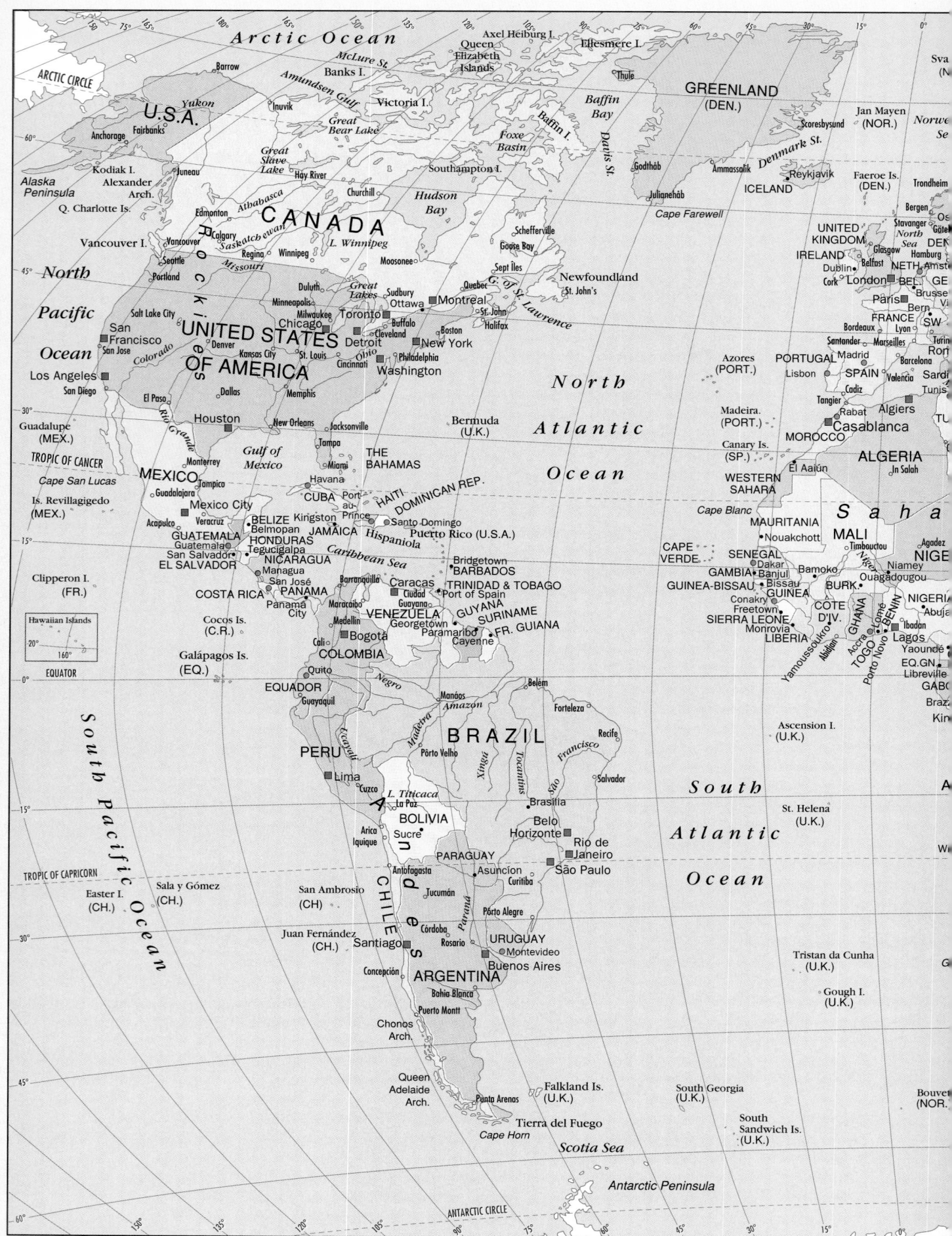

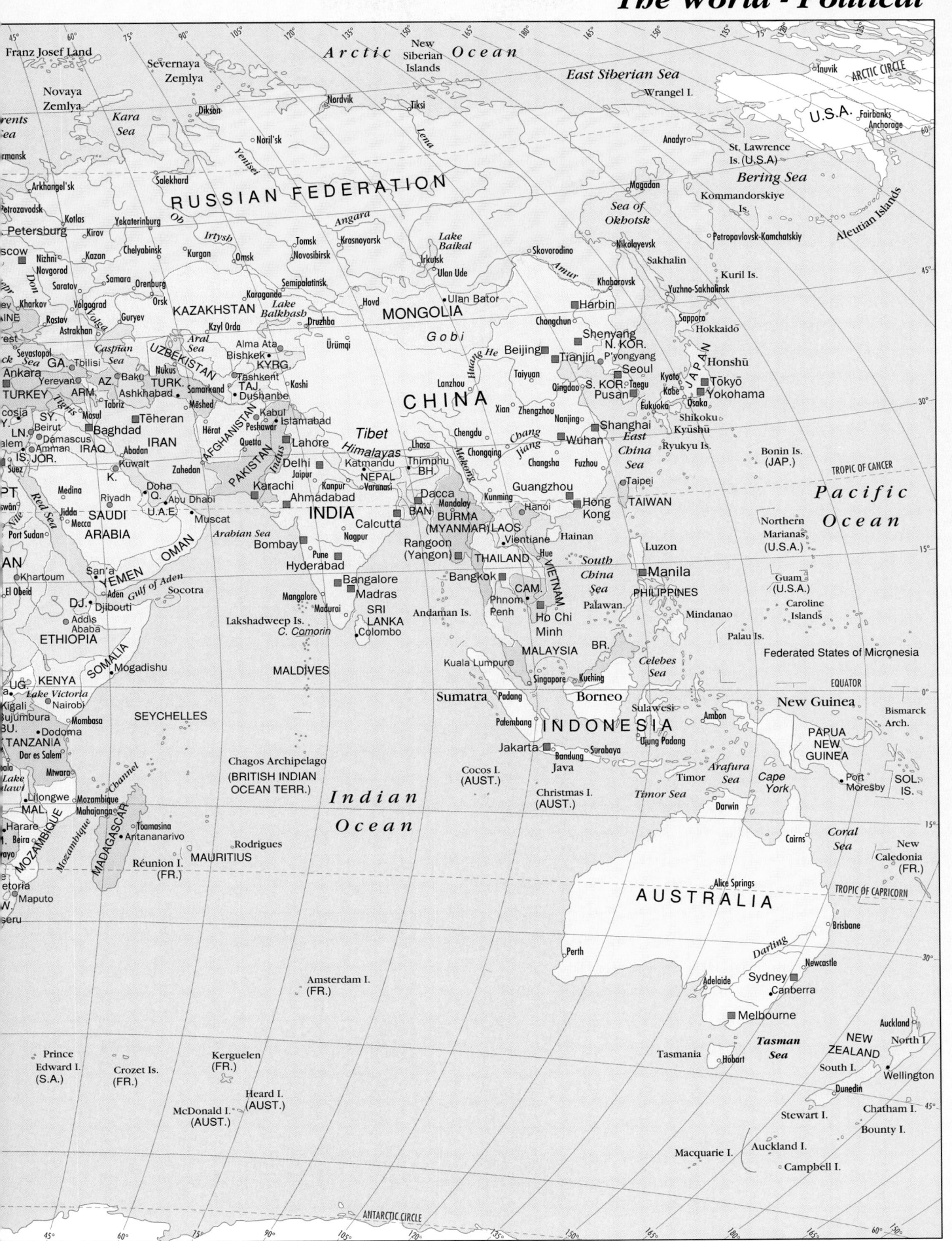

Canada

Davis Strait

Bylot I.
Pond Inlet
Clyde
Baffin I.
Penny Highland 8500△
Broughton Island
ARCTIC CIRCLE

Greenland (Den.)
Holsteinsborg
Saondre Strømfjord
Sukkertoppen
Godthåb
Friskenæsset

Hall Beach
Prince Charles I.
Netilling Lake
Pangnirtung
Cumberland Sound

Foxe Basin
Foxe Peninsula
Frobisher Bay
Lake Harbour
Frobisher Bay

Atlantic Ocean

Hampton I.
Coral Harbour
Hudson Strait
Cape Chidley

Coats I.
Mansel I.
Salluit
Ivujivik
Kangiqsujuaq
Kangiqsuk

Ungava Peninsula
Ungava Bay
Kangiqsualujjuaq
Kuujjuaq
R. Aux Feuilles
George
Nain
Hopedale
Indian Harbour
Labrador

Hudson Bay
Inukjuac (Port Harrison)
Schefferville
Newfoundland and Labrador
Cartwright
Battle Harbour
Cape Bauld
St. Anthony

Les Îles Belcher
Kuujjuarapik
Québec
Labrador City
Wabush City
Smallwood Reservoir
Churchill
Strait of Belle Isle
Gander
Bonavista
Grand Falls
Newfoundland
St. Johns
Buchans
Harbour Grace
Corner Brook
Cape Race

La Grande
Fort George
3700△
Gagnon
Natashquan
Mingan
Île d'Anticosti
Channel Port aux Basques

James Bay
Winisk
Eastmain
Perihonca
Sept-Îles
Port Cartier
Gaspé
Gulf of St. Lawrence

Winisk
Akimiski Island
Eastmain
Lake Mistassini
Baie-Comeau
Matane
Sydney
Cape Breton Island

Fort Albany
Fort Rupert
Chibougamau
Dolbeau
Chicoutimi
Tadoussac
Riviere Du-Loup
Campbellton
Bathurst
Chatham
Charlottetown
Port Hawkesbury

Ontario
Moosonee
Réservoir Gouin
Prince Edward Is.
New Brunswick
Nova Scotia

Nakina
Albany
Amos
Senneterre
Edmundston
Moncton
Dartmouth
Halifax

Lake Nipigon
Longlac
Hearst
Cochrane
Rouyn
Val D'Or
Réservoir Cabonga
Québec
Lévis
St. John
Fredericton
Saint John
Bridgewater

Nipigon
Oba
Timmins
Kirkland Lake
Trois-Rivières
Maine
Liverpool

Thunder Bay
Michipicoten
Cobalt
Ottawa
Joliette
St. Hyacinthe
Sherbrooke
Bangor
Shelborne

Lake Superior
Sault Sainte Marie
Blind River
Sudbury
North Bay
Pembroke
Hull
Montréal
Granby
Augusta
Bay of Fundy
Yarmouth
Cape Sable

TRANS CANADA HIGHWAY
Brockville
OTTAWA
Burlington
Montpelier
Portland

Ironwood
Marquette
Kingston
New York
Vermont
N.H.
Manchester
Lawrence

Rhinelander
Michigan
Peterborough
Wiarton
Oshawa
Albany
Worcester
Boston
Cape Cod

Wisconsin
Sheboygan
Green Bay
Ludington
Cadillac
Traverse City
L. Huron
Toronto
Kitchener
Hamilton
London
St. Catharines
Niagara Falls
Rochester
Syracuse
Utica
Hartford
Providence
Rhode Island
Conn.
New Haven

Milwaukee
Madison
Waterloo
Rapids
Chicago
Rockford
Gary
Grand Rapids
Flint
Lansing
Kalamazoo
Bay City
L. Michigan
Detroit
L. Erie
Erie
Buffalo
Williamsport
Scranton
Newark
Long I.
New York
New Jersey

Illinois
Indiana
Toledo
Fort Wayne
Lima
Cleveland
Ohio
Pittsburgh
Youngstown
Pennsylvania
Reading
Harrisburg
Philadelphia
Baltimore
Md.
Del.

Atlantic Ocean

Northwest Territories

Beaufort Sea
Prince Patrick I.
Queen Elizabeth Islands
Ellesmere I.
Eureka
Axel Heiberg I.
Nares Strait

McClure Strait
Melville I.
Bathurst I.
Devon I.
Resolute
Banks I.
Parry Islands

Feet	Metres
16409	5000
9843	3000
6562	2000
3281	1000
1640	500
656	200
0	0

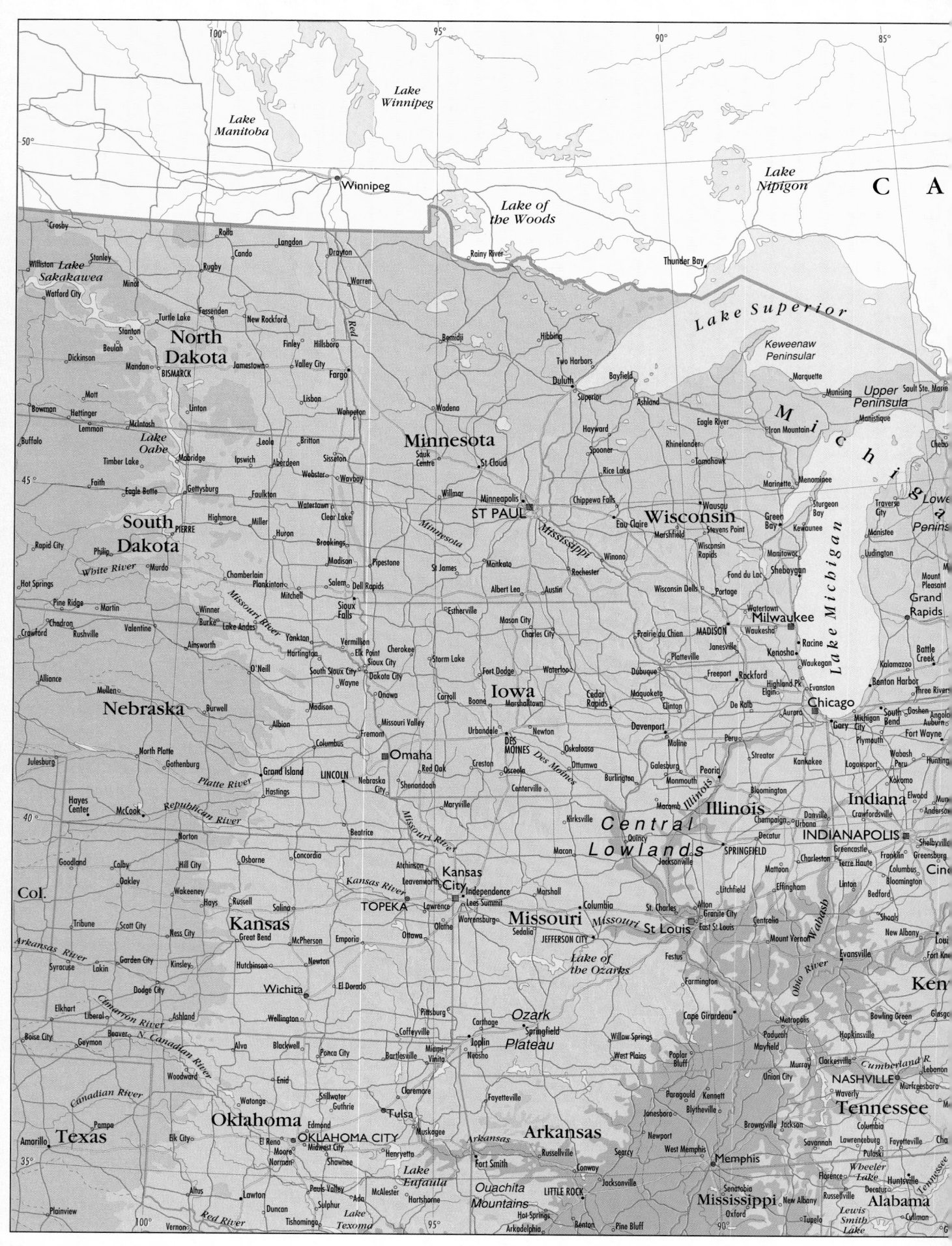

Northeast U.S.A.

Gulf of St. Lawrence

Laurentian Highlands

CANADA

Saguenay

Rimouski

Jonquière Chicoutimi

St John River

Presque Isle

Moncton

Fredericton

Québec

Sherbrooke

Halifax

45°

Maine

Bangor

Rockland

Ellsworth

Cape Sable

North Bay

Sudbury

Montreal

Hull OTTAWA

Saint Albans

Plattsburgh

Ogdensburg

Burlington

Mt. Washington 6 288

MONTPELIER

Vermont

Waterville

AUGUSTA

Portland

Biddeford

New Hampshire

Portsmouth

Dover

Manchester

CONCORD

Nashua

Peterborough

Watertown

Adirondack Mountains

Glens Falls

Rutland

Bennington

Keene

Lowell

Fitchburg

BOSTON

Cape Cod

Toronto

Lake Ontario

Oswego

Rome

Utica

Johnstown

Schenectady

Troy

ALBANY

Worcester

Brockton

Fall River

Appalachian Mountains

Rochester

Syracuse

New York

Ithaca

Binghamton

Hudson

Pittsfield

Holyoke

Springfield

PROVIDENCE

New Bedford

Nantucket I.

Lockport

Niagara Falls

Buffalo

Elmira

HARTFORD

Conn.

Waterbury

West Warwick

Newport

R.I.

Martha's Vineyard

London

Dunkirk

Jamestown

Warren

Erie

Williamsport

Scranton

White Plains

Bridgeport

New Haven

Stamford

New London

Westerley

40°

65°

Ashtabula

Oil City

Wilkes-Barre

Hazleton

Paterson

New York

Newark

Long Island

Cleveland

Warren

Sharon

Youngstown

Pennsylvania

Altoona

Allentown

Easton

Elizabeth

N.J.

New Brunswick

Asbury Park

Elyria

Akron

East Liverpool

Canton

Steubenville

Johnstown

Lewistown

Reading

TRENTON

Lorain

Newark

Zanesville

Wheeling

Moundsville

Pittsburgh

Juniata River

HARRISBURG

Lancaster

York

Philadelphia

Camden

Athens

New Martinsville

Morgantown

Fairmont

Hagerstown

Cumberland

Martinsburg

Aberdeen

Wilmington

Bridgeton

Atlantic City

Chillicothe

Marietta

Parkersburg

Buckhannon

Clarksburg

Susquehanna R.

Potomac River

Frederick

Md.

Baltimore

DOVER

Delaware Bay

Point Pleasant

St Albans

CHARLESTON

Huntington

W. Virginia

Winchester

Rockville

Shenandoah River

ANNAPOLIS

WASHINGTON

Alexandria

Easton

Del.

Milford

Cambridge

Salisbury

ATLANTIC OCEAN

Prestonburg

Beckley

Bluefield

Staunton

Charlottesville

Virginia

RICHMOND

Fredericksburg

Chesapeake Bay

Cape Charles

Hazard

Wytheville

Roanoke

Salem

James River

Petersburg

Newport News

Hampton

Virginia Beach

Cape Hatteras

Mt. Mitchell △ 6 684

New River

Roanoke River

Lynchburg

Norfolk

Elizabeth City

Johnson City

Elizabethton

Boone

Danville

Henderson

Roanoke Rapids

greeneville

Asheville

Blue Ridge

Lenoir

Winston Salem

Burlington

Durham

Rocky Mt

Wilson

Greenville

Pamlico Sd.

Seneca

Hickory

Statesville

Salisbury

RALEIGH

Smithfield

Goldsboro

Morehead City

Beaufort

Cape Lookout

Franklin

Kannapolis

Concord

North Carolina

Sanford

Clinton

Jacksonville

Onslow Bay

Gastonia

Albemarle

Fayetteville

Spartanburg

Greenville

Union

Chester

Bennettsville

Whiteville

Wilmington

Anderson

Shelby

Charlotte

Gainesville

Greenwood

Newberry

South Carolina

Florence

Conway

Myrtle Beach

Cape Fear

Athens

North Augusta

Augusta

Aiken

Orangeburg

COLUMBIA

Santee R.

Kingstree

Savannah R.

ATLANTA

Covington

Feet	Metres
12000	3658
9000	2743
5000	1524
2000	610
1000	305
500	152
0	0

Lake Erie

Connecticut River

Hudson River

Delaware River

Allegheny R.

Muskingum R.

Ohio River

Allegheny Mountains

0 200 400 kms

0 125 250 miles

80° 75° 70° 65° 60°

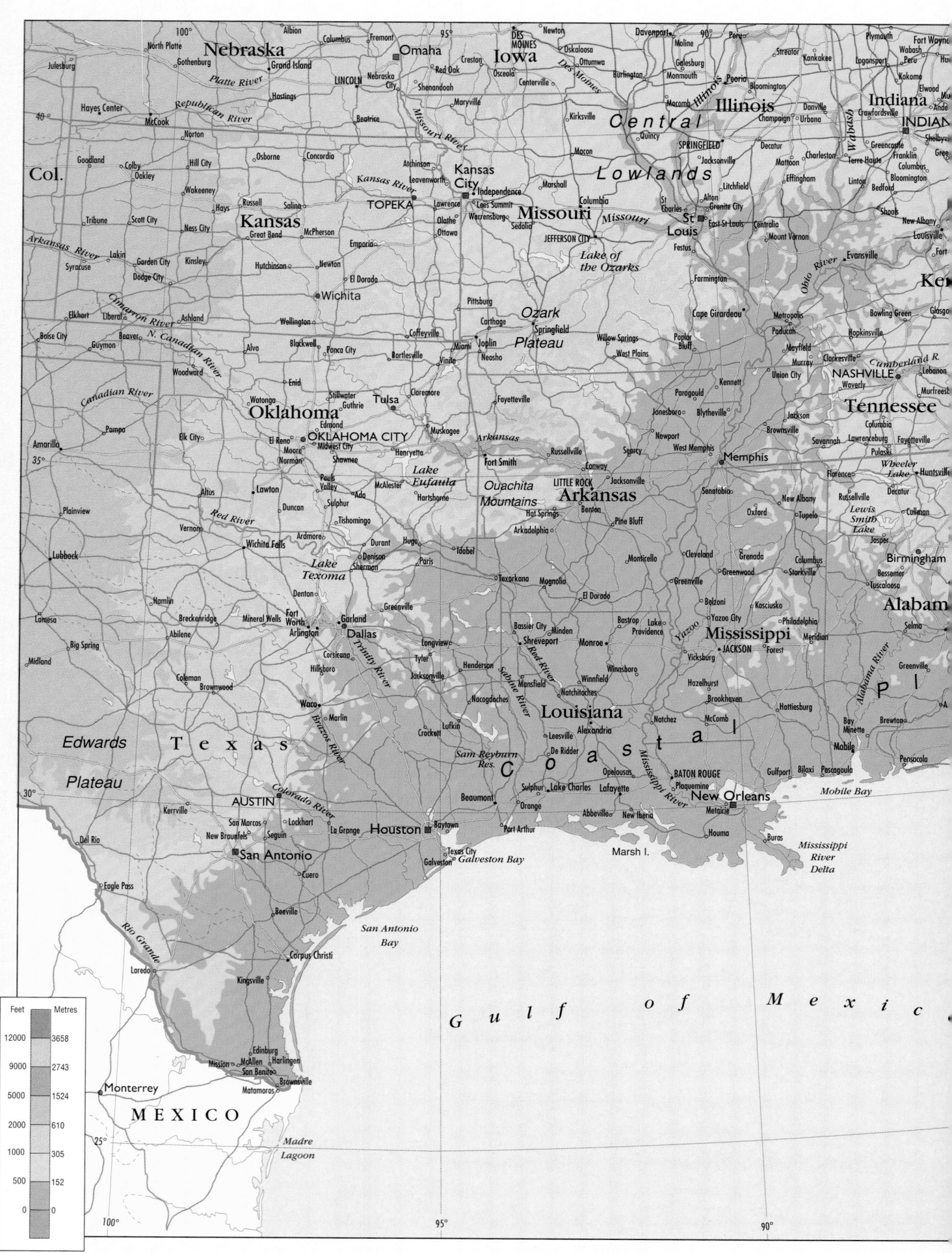

Southeast U.S.A.

Population density

Natural vegetation

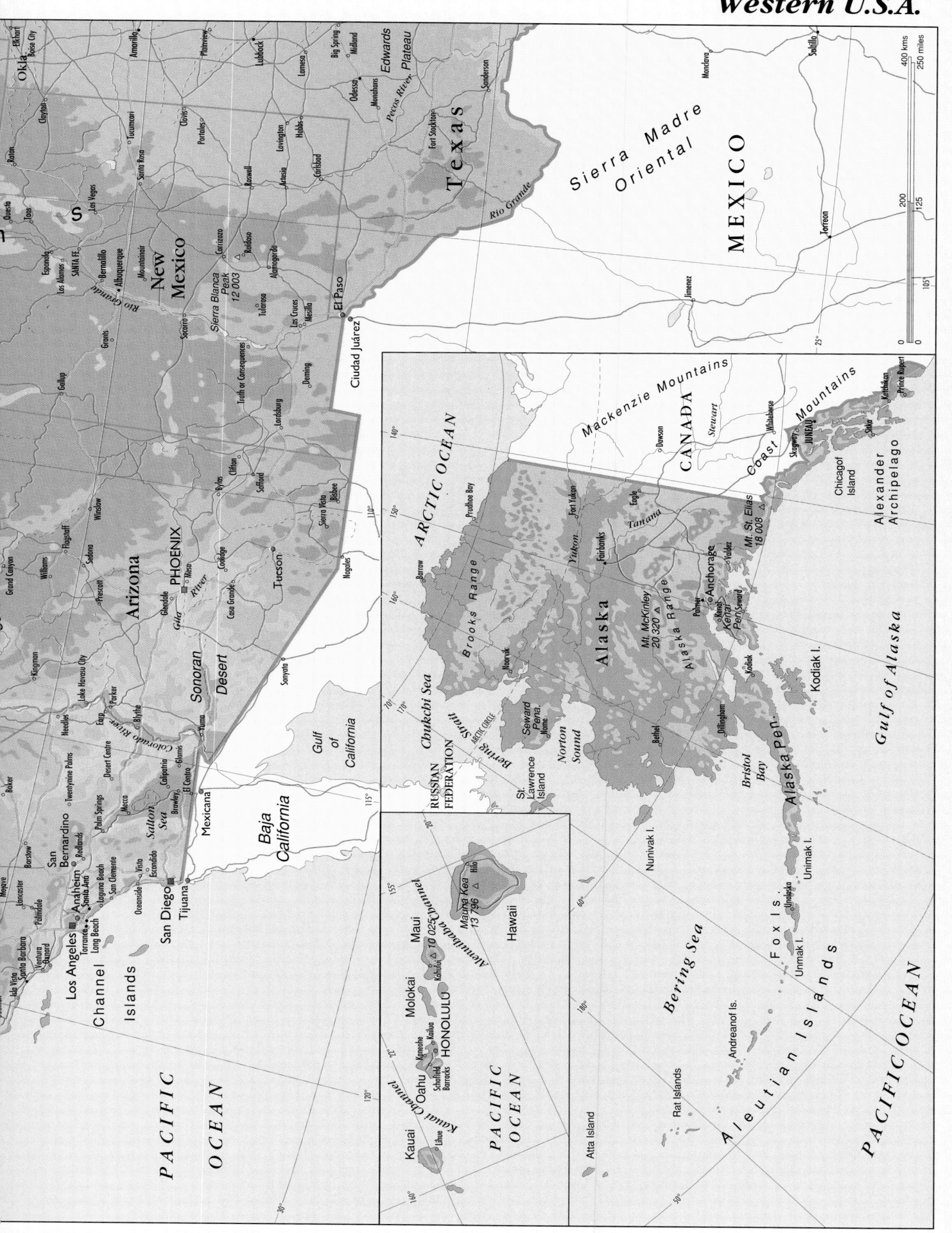

400 kms
250 miles

MEXICO

Sierra Madre
Oriental

Monclova

Saltillo

Jimenez

Torreon

Texas

Edwards
Pecos River Plateau

Sanderson

Fort Stockton

Midland

Big Spring

Lamesa

Odessa

Monahans

Plainview

Lubbock

Amarillo

Clayton

Raton

Cuesta

Taos

Elkhart
Boise City
Okla.

T **S**

Las Vegas

Tucumcari

Santa Rosa

Clovis

Portales

Espanola
Los Alamos
SANTA FE
Bernalillo
Mountainair
Albuquerque

New Mexico

Carrizozo
Ruidoso
Alamogordo
Sierra Blanca
Peak △
12 003

Tularosa

Roswell

Lovington

Hobbs

Artesia

Carlsbad

Socorro

Truth or Consequences

Las Cruces

Mesilla

El Paso

Ciudad Juárez

Rio Grande

Grants

Gallup

Grand Canyon

Williams

Flagstaff

Sedona

Prescott

Arizona

Winslow

Clifton

Safford

Lordsburg

Deming

Sierra Vista
Bisbee

Kingman

Lake Havasu City

Parker

PHOENIX
Glendale
Mesa
Gila River
Coolidge
Casa Grande

Tucson

Nogales

Sonoyta

Sonoran

Desert

Sonoita

Gulf
of
California

Baja
California

Mexicana

MEXICO

Needles

Blythe

Fargo

Mecca

Indio

Calipatria

Brawley

Glamis

El Centro

Salton
Sea

ARCTIC OCEAN

Barrow

Prudhoe Bay

Mackenzie Mountains

CANADA

Dawson

Stewart

Whitehorse

Coast Mountains

Skagway

JUNEAU

Sitka

Chicagof Island

Ketchikan

Prince Rupert

Alexander
Archipelago

Fort Yukon

Eagle

Tanana

Yukon

Fairbanks

Brooks Range

Noorvik

Chukchi Sea

RUSSIAN
FEDERATION

St. Lawrence Island

ARCTIC CIRCLE

Bering Strait

Seward
Pena.
Nome

Norton
Sound

Alaska

Mt. McKinley
20 320 △

Mt. St. Elias △
18 008

Alaska Range

Valdez
Palmer
Anchorage
Seward
Kenai
Pen.

Bethel

Dillingham

Bingham

Bristol
Bay

Alaska Pen.

Kodiak

Kodiak I.

Gulf of Alaska

Nunivak I.

Unalaska

Unimak I.

F o x I s.

Unalaska
Umnak I.

Bering Sea

Andreanof Is.

Rat Islands

Atta Island

A l e u t i a n I s l a n d s

PACIFIC OCEAN

Kauai
Lihue

PACIFIC
OCEAN

Kauai Channel

Oahu
Schofield Barracks
Kaneohe
Kailua
HONOLULU

Molokai

Maui
Kahului

Auau Channel

Mauna Kea △
13 796

Hawaii
Hilo

PACIFIC

OCEAN

Los Angeles
Torrance
Long Beach
Anaheim
Santa Ana
Laguna Beach
San Clemente

San Bernardino
Redlands

Palm Springs

Oceanside

Vista
Escondido

San Diego

Tijuana

Channel

Islands

PACIFIC

OCEAN

Ventura
Oxnard

Santa Barbara

Lancaster
Palmdale

Mojave

Baker

Barstow

Twentynine Palms

Desert Centre

Isla Vista

Colorado River

Yuma

Somerton

Yuma

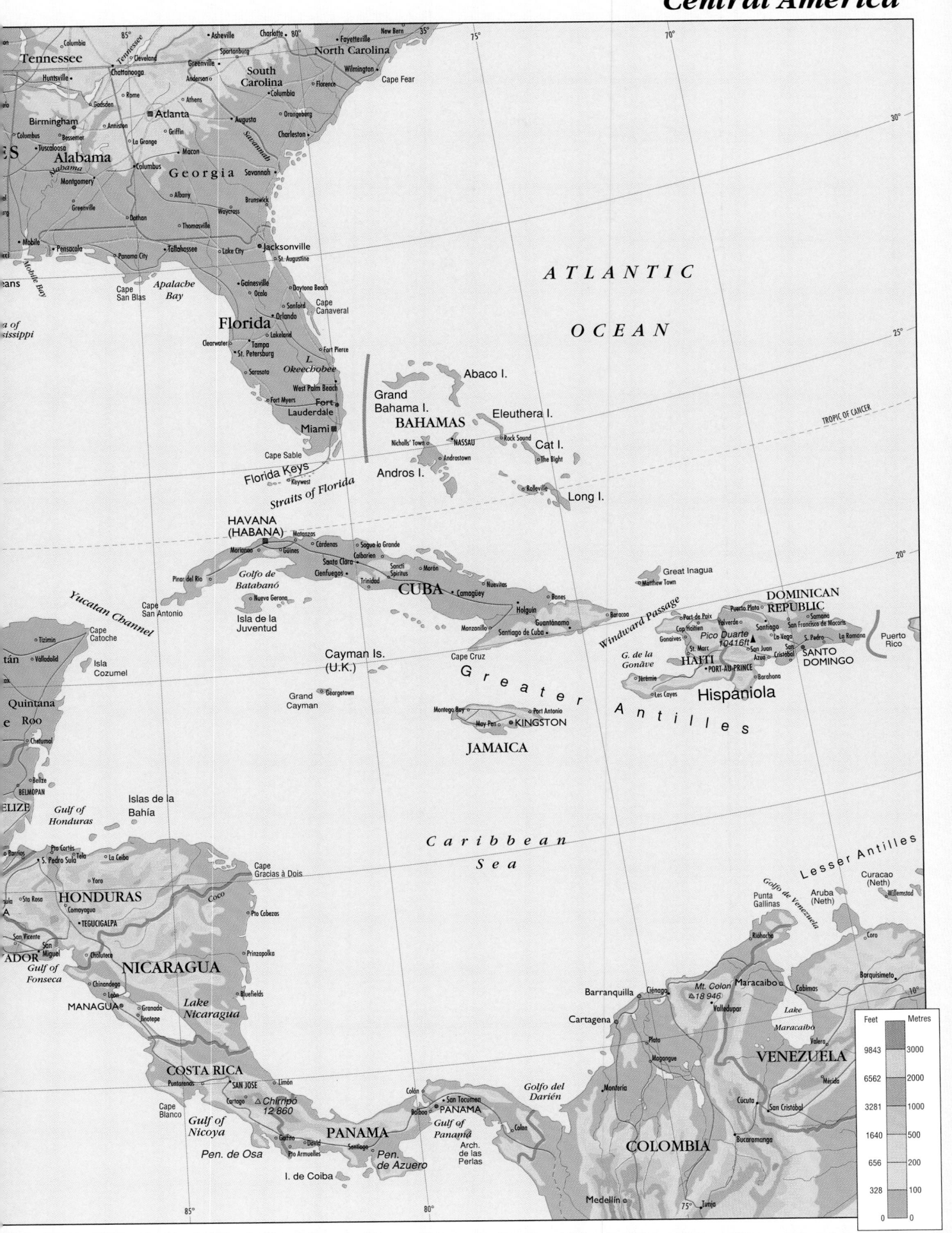

Central America

ATLANTIC

OCEAN

Tennessee

Columbia · · Asheville · Charlotte · 80° · Fayetteville · New Bern
Huntsville · Cleveland · Spartanburg · · **North Carolina**
· Chattanooga · Greenville · Anderson · · Wilmington
Birmingham · Rome · Athens · **South** · Florence · Cape Fear
· Columbus · Bessemer · Gadsden · Anniston · **Carolina** · Columbia
· Tuscaloosa · ■ **Atlanta** · Augusta · Orangeburg
Alabama · · Griffin · · Charleston
· Montgomery · **Georgia** · Savannah
· Greenville · Albany · Brunswick
· Dothan · Thomasville · Waycross
Mobile · Pensacola · · Panama City · Tallahassee · Lake City · Jacksonville
· · · St. Augustine
Cape San Blas · **Apalache Bay** · Gainesville · Ocala · Daytona Beach
a of ssippi · · Sanford · Cape Canaveral
Florida · Orlando
· Clearwater · · Lakeland · Fort Pierce
· Tampa · St. Petersburg
· Sarasota · L. Okeechobee · West Palm Beach
· Fort Myers · **Fort Lauderdale**
Miami
Cape Sable
Florida Keys · Keywest
Straits of Florida

Grand Bahama I. · Abaco I.
Eleuthera I.
BAHAMAS · Rock Sound · Cat I.
Nicholls' Town · **NASSAU** · The Bight
Androstown
Andros I. · Rolleville · Long I.

TROPIC OF CANCER

HAVANA (HABANA) · Matanzas
Marianao · Cárdenas · Sagua la Grande
· Guines · Santa Clara · Caibarién
Pinar del Río · **Golfo de Batabanó** · Cienfuegos · Sancti Spíritus · Morón
· Nueva Gerona · Trinidad · **CUBA** · Nuevitas
Cape San Antonio · Isla de la Juventud · Camagüey
Holguín
Manzanillo · Santiago de Cuba
Cape Cruz
Bánes
Baracoa

Great Inagua
Matthew Town
Port-de-Paix · **DOMINICAN**
Cap Haitien · Valverde · Puerto Plata · **REPUBLIC** · Samaná
Gonaïves · Santiago · San Francisco de Macorís
Pico Duarte · La Vega · S. Pedro · La Romana
G. de la Gonâve · St. Marc · 10416ft▲ · San Juan · San Cristóbal · **SANTO DOMINGO** · Puerto Rico
HAITI · Azua
· Jérémie · **PORT-AU-PRINCE** · Barahona
Les Cayes · **Hispaniola**

Windward Passage

G r e a t e r   A n t i l l e s

Cayman Is. (U.K.)
Grand Cayman · Georgetown
Montego Bay · Port Antonio
May Pen · **KINGSTON**
JAMAICA

Lesser Antilles

Yucatan Channel
Cape Catoche
· Tizimín
· Valladolid · Isla Cozumel
tán
Quintana Roo
· Chetumal
· Belize
BELMOPAN
ELIZE
Gulf of Honduras
Islas de la Bahía
· Barrios · Pto Cortés · Tela
· S. Pedro Sula · La Ceiba
ula · Sta Rosa · Yoro
HONDURAS
· Comayagua
· **TEGUCIGALPA** · Coco
· Pto Cabezas
DOR · San Vicente
San Miguel · Choluteca
· Prinzapolka
Gulf of Fonseca
· Chinandega · Bluefields
NICARAGUA
· León
MANAGUA · Granada · **Lake Nicaragua**
· Jinotepe

Cape Gracias à Dois

C a r i b b e a n   S e a

Golfo de Venezuela
Punta Gallinas
Curacao (Neth)
Aruba (Neth) · Willemstad
· Riohacha · Coro
· Barquisimeto
· Barranquilla · Ciénaga · **Mt. Colon** · Maracaibo · Cabimas
· Cartagena · Plato · △18 946 · Valledupar · **Lake Maracaibo** · Valera
· Magangue · **VENEZUELA**
· Montería · Cúcuta · San Cristóbal

COSTA RICA
Cape Blanco · **SAN JOSE** · Limón
· Cartago · △**Chirripó** · Colón · **Gulf del Darién**
· Puntarenas · 12 860 · San Tocumen
Gulf of Nicoya · Balboa · **PANAMA** · Colon
· Golfito · Santiago · **Gulf of Panama**
Pen. de Osa · David · Pto Armuelles · **PANAMA** · **Arch. de las Perlas**
Pen. de Azuero
I. de Coiba

COLOMBIA
· Bucaramanga
· Medellín · Tunja

Feet		Metres
9843		3000
6562		2000
3281		1000
1640		500
656		200
328		100
0		0

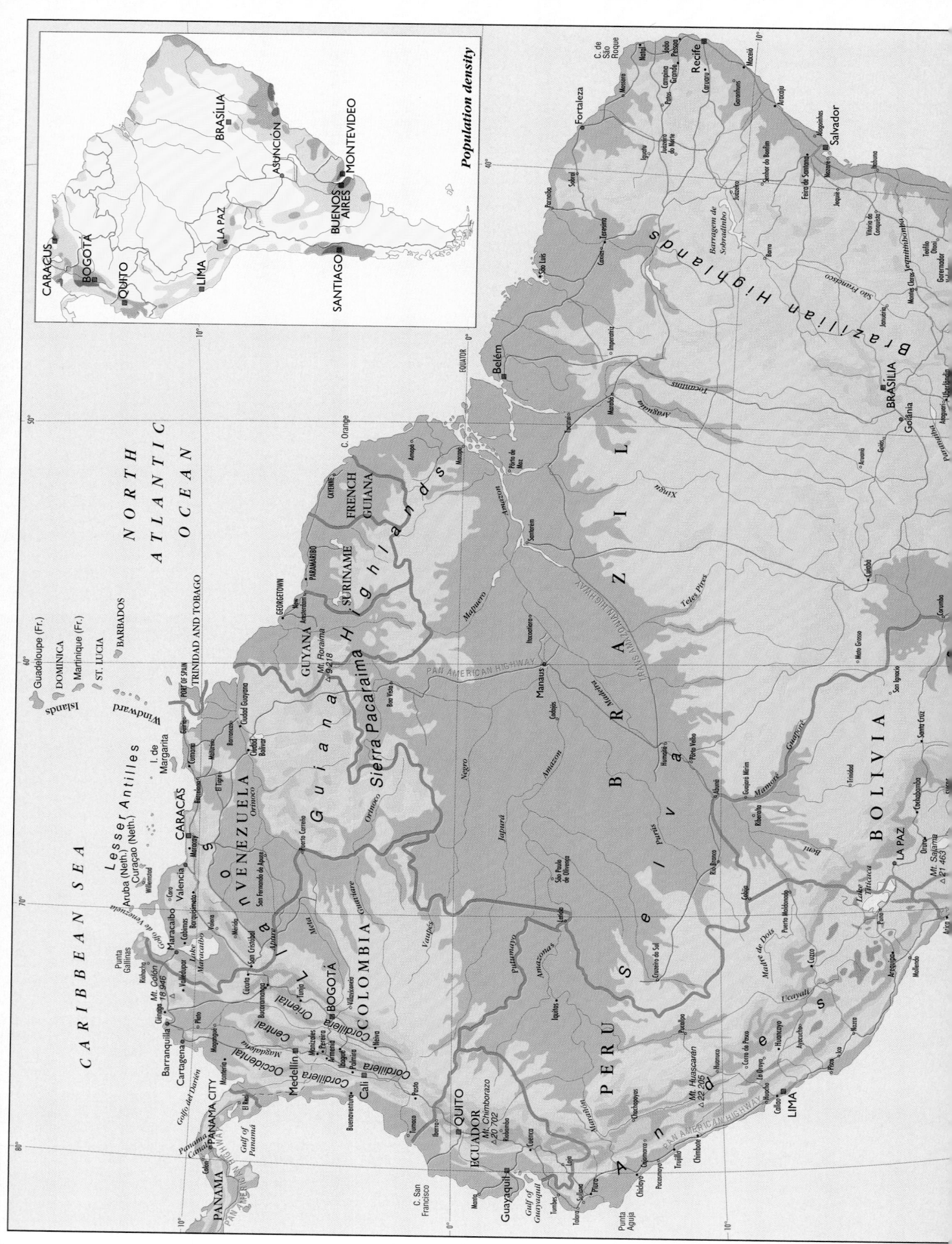

Population density

CARACAS
BOGOTÁ
QUITO
LIMA
LA PAZ
BRASÍLIA
ASUNCIÓN
SANTIAGO
BUENOS AIRES
MONTEVIDEO

CARIBBEAN SEA

NORTH ATLANTIC OCEAN

Lesser Antilles

Guadeloupe (Fr.)
DOMINICA
Martinique (Fr.)
ST. LUCIA
BARBADOS

Windward Islands

Aruba (Neth.)
Curaçao (Neth.)
Willemstad
I. de Margarita
TRINIDAD AND TOBAGO
PORT OF SPAIN

Punta Gallinas
Barranquilla
Cartagena
Ciénaga
Mt. Colón 18,946
Maracaibo
Lago de Maracaibo
Valledupar
Valencia
Barquisimeto
Ciudad Guayana
Coro
Maracay
CARACAS
Barcelona
Cumaná
Carúpano
Maturín
El Tigre

VENEZUELA
San Fernando de Apure
Ciudad Bolívar
Orinoco
GEORGETOWN
GUYANA
Mt. Roraima 9,218
PARAMARIBO
SURINAME
CAYENNE
FRENCH GUIANA
C. Orange
Amapá
Macapá

Guiana Highlands

Sierra Pacaraima

PANAMA
PANAMA CITY
Gulf of Panamá
Colón
Gulf of Darién
El Real
Quibdó
Montería
Magangué
Medellín
Manizales
Pereira
Armenia
Ibagué
Cali
Palmira
Buenaventura
Pasto
Tumaco

COLOMBIA
BOGOTÁ
Cúcuta
Bucaramanga
San Cristóbal
Mérida
Tunja
Villavicencio
Neiva

Cordillera Occidental
Cordillera Central
Cordillera Oriental
Magdalena
Cauca
Meta
Arauca
Vaupés
Guaviare
Vichada

ECUADOR
QUITO
Mt. Chimborazo 20,702
Riobamba
Cuenca
Loja
Ambato
Guayaquil
Gulf of Guayaquil
Manta
C. San Francisco

Tumbes
Talara
Punta Aguja
Chiclayo
Chimbote
Trujillo
Cajamarca
Mt. Huascarán 22,205
Chachapoyas
Cerro de Pasco
Huánuco
La Oroya
Callao
LIMA
Pisco
Ica
Ayacucho
Cuzco
Juliaca
Arequipa
Moquegua
Mollendo

PERU
Iquitos
Pucallpa
Moyobamba

Marañón
Ucayali
Amazonas
Madre de Dios
Purús

Andes

PAN AMERICAN HIGHWAY

BOLIVIA
LA PAZ
Lake Titicaca
Oruro
Cochabamba
Mt. Sajama 21,463
Sucre
Santa Cruz
Potosí
Puerto Maldonado
Riberalta
Guayaramerín
Trinidad
Cobija

Beni
Mamoré
Guaporé

Belém
Pôrto de Móz
Macapá
EQUATOR
Manaus
Manacapuru
Codajás
São Paulo de Olivença
Tefé
Tabatinga
Leticia
Benjamin Constant

Amazon
Negro
Japurá
Içá
Putumayo
Javari

BRAZIL
BRASÍLIA
GOIÂNIA
Goiás
Anápolis
Uberlândia
Araguari

Brazilian Highlands

TRANSNATIONAL HIGHWAY
PAN AMERICAN HIGHWAY

Santarém
Óbidos
Itacoatiara
Boa Vista
Imperatriz
Marabá
Tucuruí
São Luís
Sobral
Fortaleza
Crateús
Teresina
Parnaíba
Caxias

Xingu
Tapajós
Teles Pires
Tocantins
Araguaia

Humaitá
Pôrto Velho
Guajará-Mirim
Abunã

Madeira
Purús

Mato Grosso
Cuiabá
Corumbá
San Ignacio

C. de São Roque
Natal
Mossoró
João Pessoa
Campina Grande
Recife
Caruaru
Maceió
Aracaju
Salvador
Garanhuns
Propriá
Feira de Santana
Senhor do Bonfim
Juàzeiro
Barra
Barragem de Sobradinho
Montes Claros
Januária
Januária
Janaúba

São Francisco
Vitória da Conquista
Jequié
Jequitinhonha

Nazaré
Itabuna
Ilhéus

B R A Z I L

South America

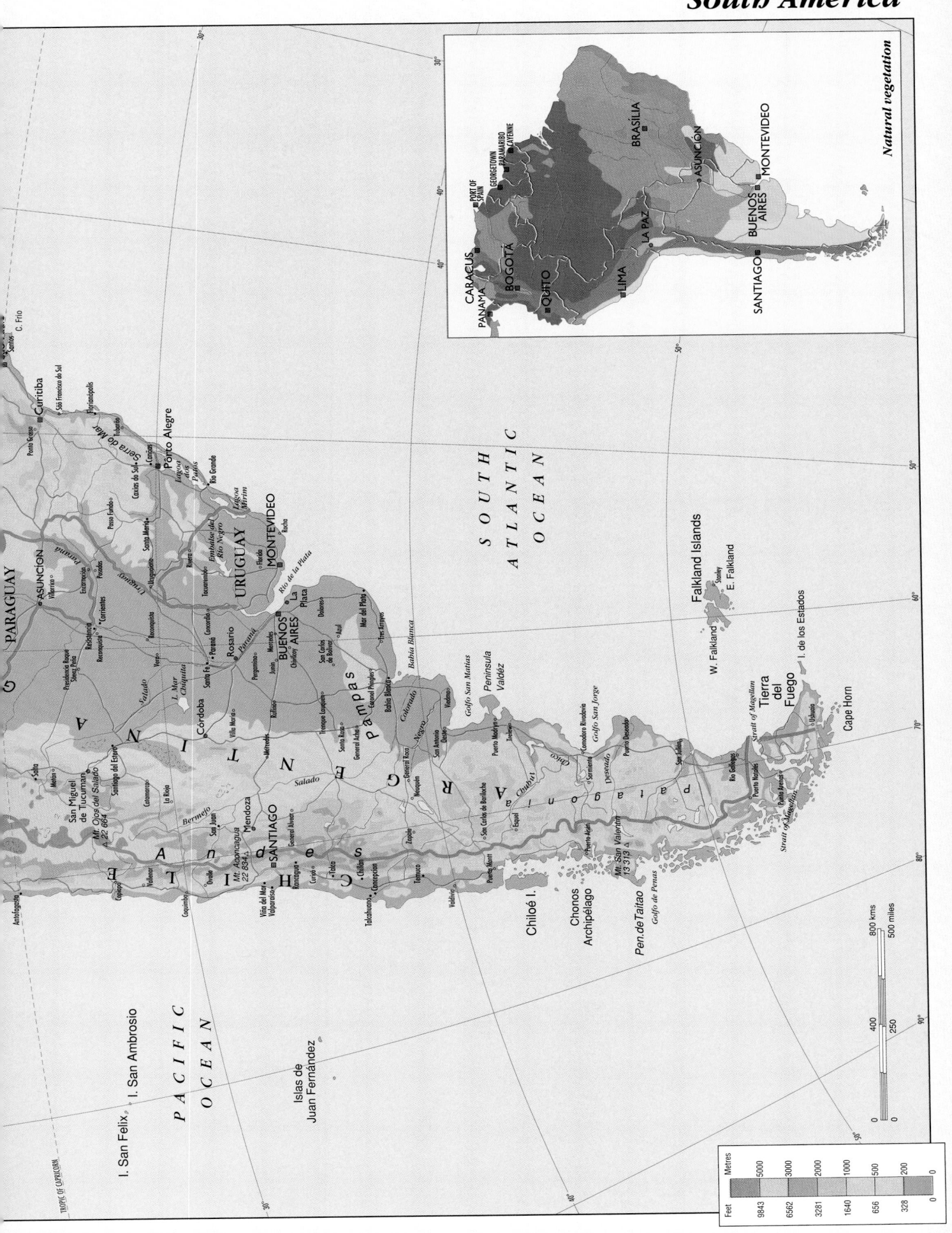

Natural vegetation

PACIFIC OCEAN

SOUTH ATLANTIC OCEAN

PARAGUAY

URUGUAY

ASUNCIÓN
MONTEVIDEO
BUENOS AIRES
SANTIAGO

Curitiba
Porto Alegre
Rosario
Córdoba
Mendoza
SANTIAGO
Valparaíso
Concepción
Valdivia

Pampas

ANDES
Andes

PATAGONIA

Tierra del Fuego
Cape Horn
Strait of Magellan

Falkland Islands
W. Falkland
E. Falkland
Stanley

Chiloé I.
Chonos Archipélago
Pen. de Taitao
Golfo de Penas

I. San Félix   I. San Ambrosio

Islas de Juan Fernández

TROPIC OF CAPRICORN

Mt Aconcagua 22 834

Mt San Valentín 13 313

Península Valdéz
Golfo San Matías
Golfo San Jorge
Bahía Blanca

San Miguel de Tucuman
Mt Ojos del Salado 22 664

800 kms
500 miles
400
250
0

Metres
5000
3000
2000
1000
500
200
0

Feet
9843
6562
3281
1640
656
328
0

CARACAS
PANAMA
BOGOTÁ
QUITO
LIMA
LA PAZ
BRASÍLIA
ASUNCIÓN
BUENOS AIRES
MONTEVIDEO
SANTIAGO
PORT OF SPAIN
GEORGETOWN
PARAMARIBO
CAYENNE

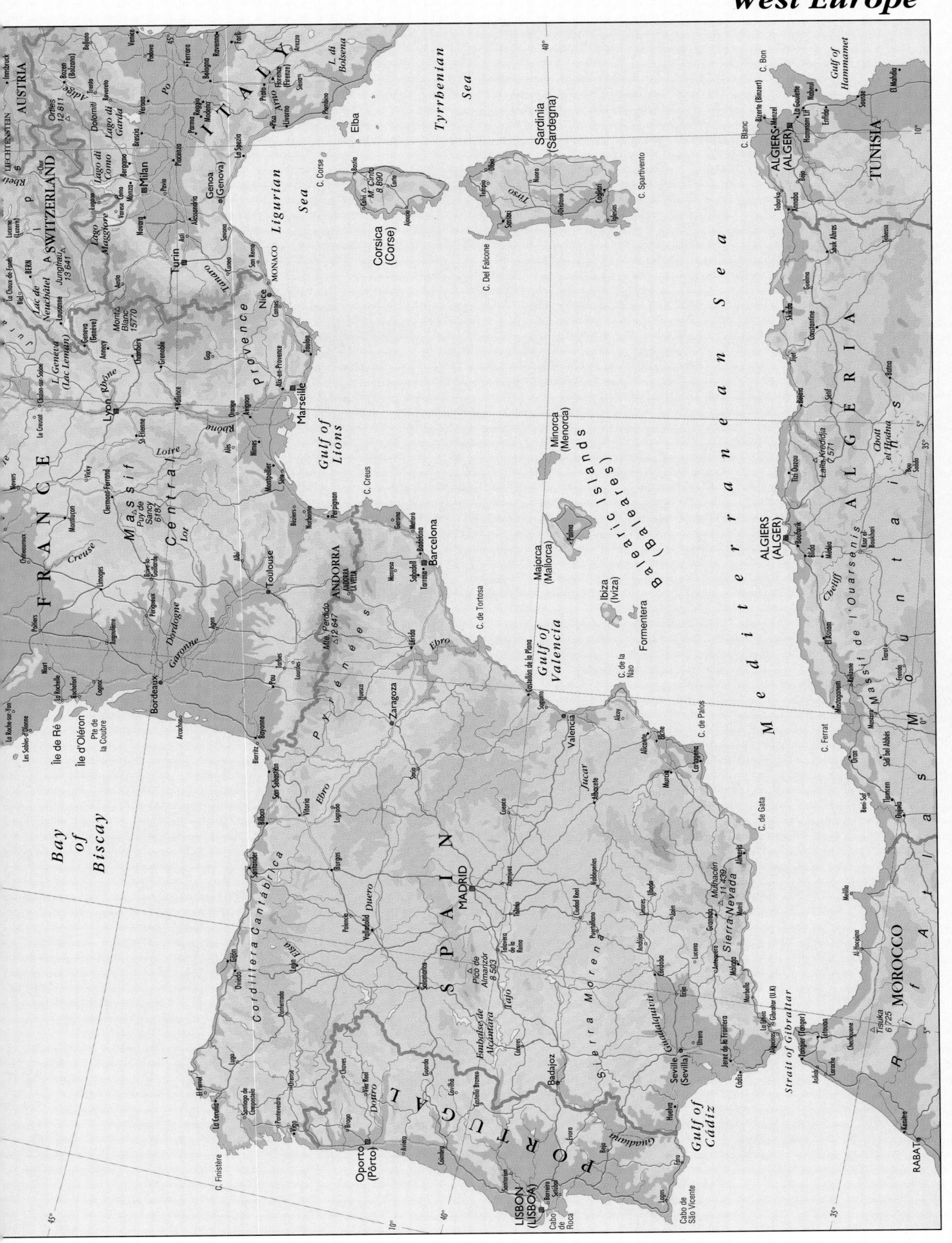

West Europe

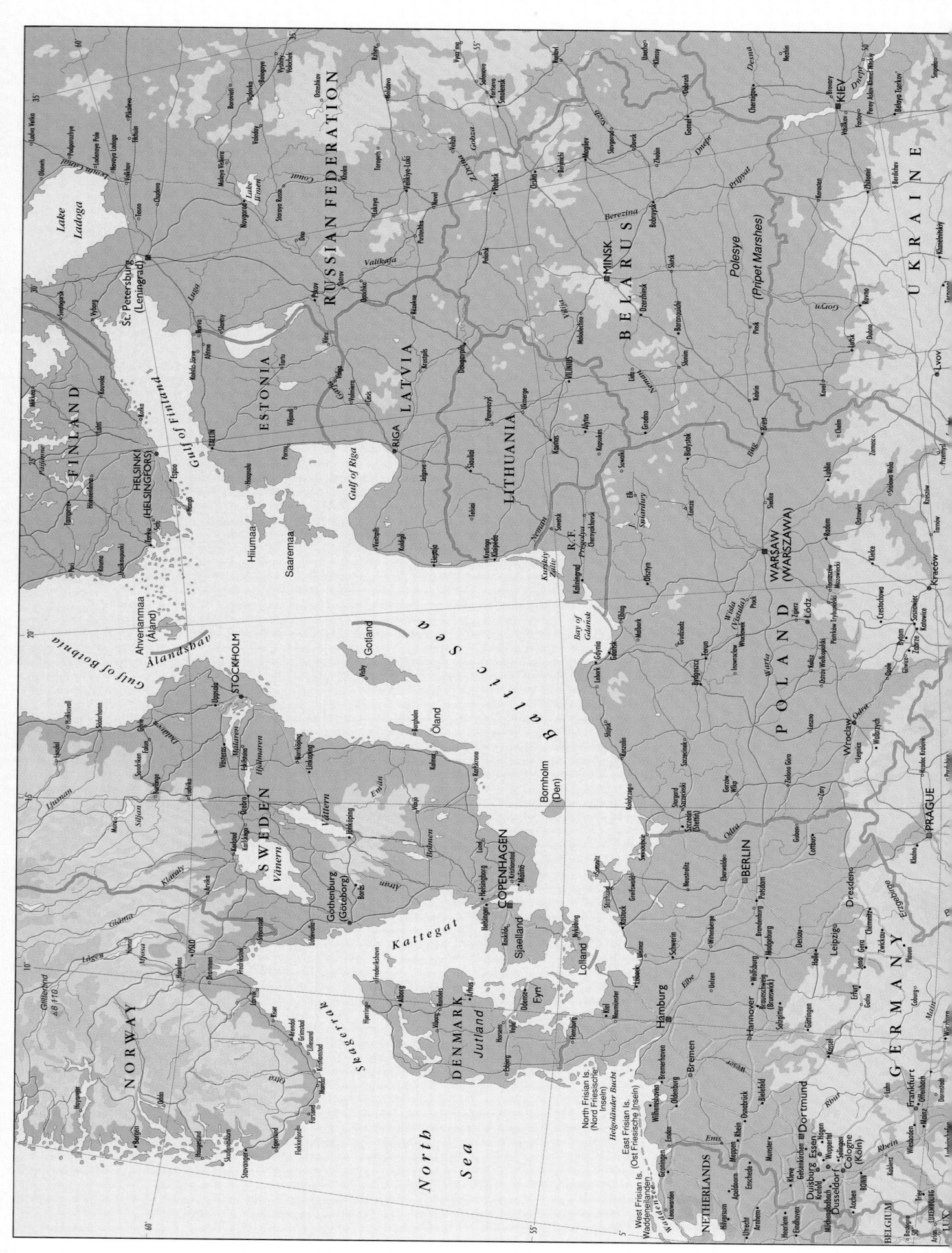

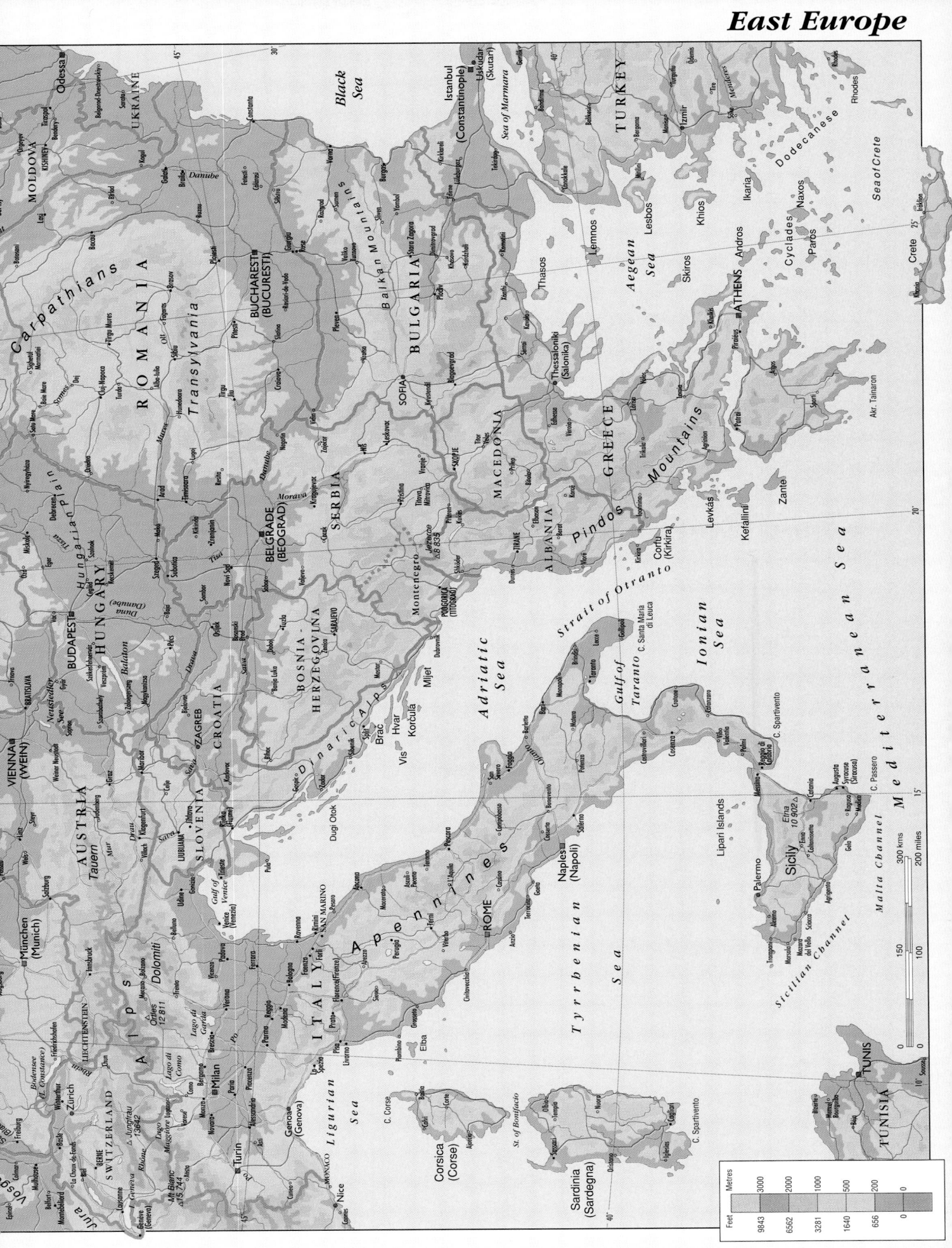

East Europe

Natural vegetation

Population density

HELSINKI

COPENHAGEN

LONDON
AMSTERDAM
BERLIN
MINSK
WARSAW
PARIS
PRAGUE
VIENNA
KIEV
BUDAPEST
ZAGREB
BUCHAREST
LISBON
MADRID
ROME
ALGIERS
(ALGER)
ATHENS
TUNIS

ARCTIC CIRCLE
Ísafjöður
Hùnaflói
Húsavík
Akureyri
Breiðafjörður
Egilsstaðir
I C E L A N D
Öræfajökull
6 950
Höfn
REYKJAVIK
Þjórsá

A T L A N T I C

O C E A N

0   150   300 kms
0   100   200 miles

Torshavn
Faroe Is.
(DEN)

Shetland Is.

Lerwick

Cape Wrath
Kirkwall
Orkney Is
Duncansby Head
Wick

Hebrides

Skye

Inverness
Moray Firth

Kinnairds Head

Loch Ness

Mull

Ben Nevis
4406
Grampian Mountains
Aberdeen

Perth
Loch Lomond
Dundee

Malin Head

Islay

Glasgow
Dunfermline Kirkcaldy
Kilmarnock
Ayr
Edinburgh
Tweed

N o r t

S e a

Donegal
Londonderry
(Derry)
Omagh
Sligo
Belfast
Lough Neagh

N. Ireland
Scotland

UNITED
KINGDOM

Lough Ree

Central Plains
Dundalk

Carlisle
Newcastle-upon-Tyne
Sunderland
Hartlepool

The Pennines

I. of
Man
Douglas

Middlesbrough

Galway
DUBLIN
Irish Sea
England

Blackpool

Leeds

Humber

REP. OF
IRELAND
Wicklow Mountains

Carrauntoohil
3415
Bantry
Cork
Waterford

Holyhead
Liverpool
Chester
Manchester
Sheffield

Wales

Flamborough Head
Kingston-upon-Hull

Feet	Metres
13124	4000
9843	3000
6562	2000
3281	1000
1640	500
656	200
0	0

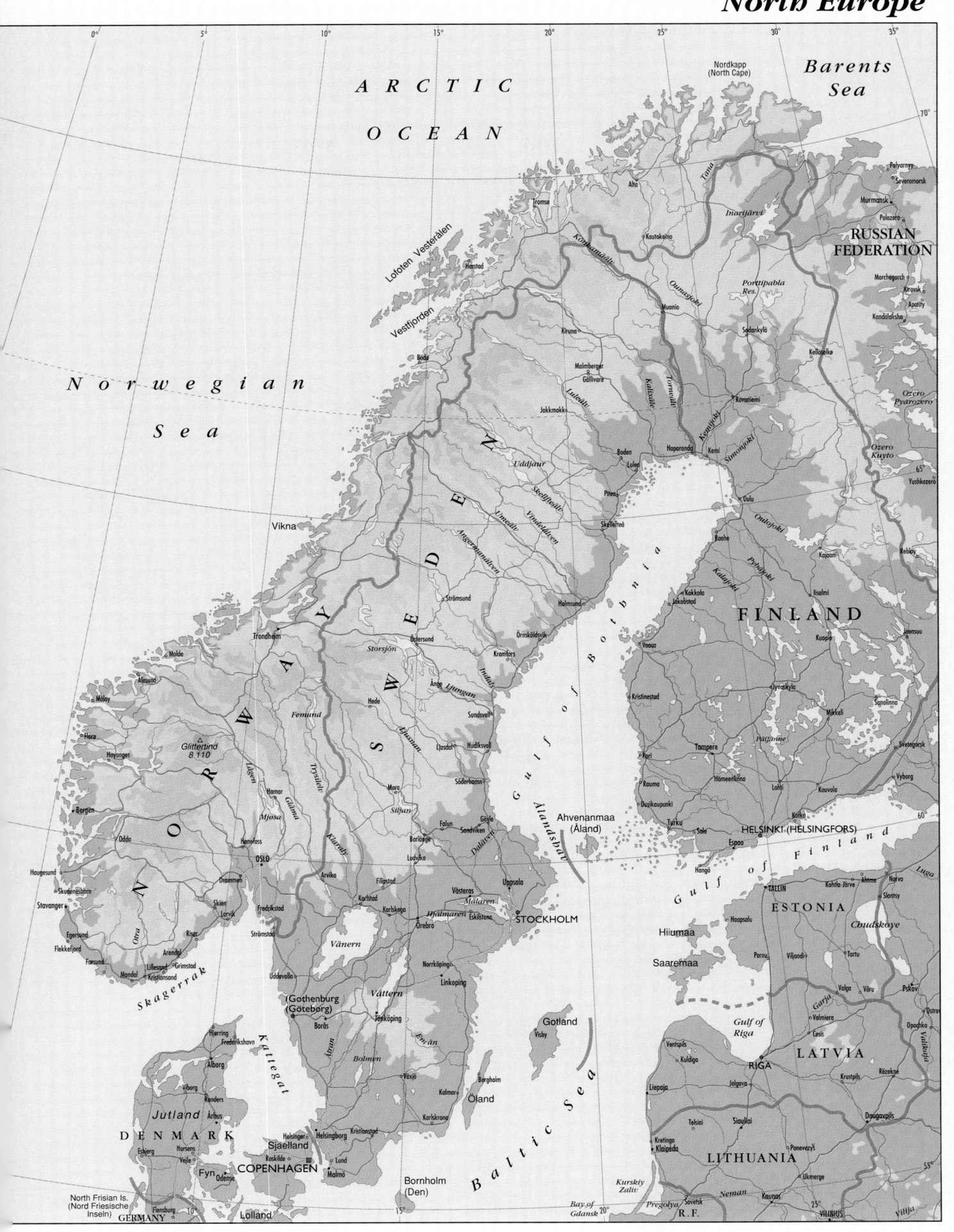

North Europe

ARCTIC

OCEAN

Barents Sea

Nordkapp
(North Cape)

Norwegian

Sea

RUSSIAN
FEDERATION

Polyarnyy
Severomorsk
Murmansk
Kirovsk
Apatity
Morchegorch
Kandalaksha

Alta
Kautokeino
Tromsø
Harstad
Lofoten Vesterålen
Vestfjorden
Bodø

Karasjokka
Inarijärvi
Porttipahla
Res.
Ounasjoki
Muonio
Sodankylä
Kelloselkä
Ozero
Pyarozero
Ozero
Kuyto
Yushkozero

Kiruna
Malmberget
Gällivare
Jokkmokk
Luleälv
Kalixälv
Tornëälv
Kemijoki
Rovaniemi

Vikna
Uddjaur
Skellytälv
Umeälv
Vindelälven
Ångermanälven
Boden
Haparanda
Kemi
Simonjoki
Oulu
Oulujoki
Kajaani
Rebløy

Trondheim
Molde
Ålesund
Måløy
Flora
Hoyanger
Bergen
Odda
Haugesund
Skudenishavn
Stavanger
Egersund
Flekkefjord
Forsund
Mandal
Kristiansand
Lillesand
Grimstad
Arendal
Risør
Skien
Larvik
Fredrikstad
Strömstad
Uddevalla
(Gothenburg
(Göteborg)
Borås

Glittertind
8 110
Femund
Trysilelv
Lågen
Gløma
Klarälv
Mjøsa
Hamar
OSLO
Drammen
Arvika
Karlstad
Karlskoga
Örebro
Vänern

Strömsund
Storsjön
Östersund
Åre
Ljungan
Hede
Sundsvall
Ljusdal
Hudiksvall
Mora
Siljan
Falun
Sandviken
Gävle
Borlänge
Ludvika
Filipstad
Västerås
Hjälmaren
Eskilstuna
Uppsala
Mälaren
STOCKHOLM

S W E D E N
N O R W A Y

Ängermanälven
Indalsälv
Ånge
Kramfors
Örnsköldsvik
Holmsund
Piteå
Skellefteå

Gulf of Bothnia

Råhe
Pyhäjoki
Kalajoki
Kokkola
Jakobstad
Iisalmi
Kuopio
Joensuu
Jyväskylä
Savonlinna
Mikkeli
Svetogorsk
Vyborg
Kotka
Kouvola
Lahti
Tampere
Hämeenlinna
Pori
Rauma
Uusikaupunki
Naantali
Turku
Salo
Espoo
HELSINKI (HELSINGFORS)
Hangö

F I N L A N D

Kristinestad
Vaasa

Ahvenanmaa
(Åland)
Ålandshav

Gulf of Finland

TALLIN
Kohtla-Järve
Ahtme
Narva
Slantsy
ESTONIA
Haapsalu
Hiiumaa
Saaremaa
Pärnu
Viljandi
Chudskoye
Tartu
Võru
Pskov
Ostrov

Norrköping
Linköping
Jönköping
Emån
Gotland
Visby
Vättern
Bolmen
Växjö
Borgholm
Kalmar
Öland
Karlskrona
Kristianstad

Baltic Sea

Gulf of
Riga
Ventspils
Kuldiga
RIGA
Gauja
Valmiera
Cēsis
Krustpils
Rēzekne
Daugavpils
LATVIA
Valka
Valga
Ostrov

Hjørring
Frederikshavn
Ålborg
Viborg
Randers
Jutland
Århus
DENMARK
Esbjerg
Horsens
Vejle
Fyn
Odense
Sjælland
Roskilde
COPENHAGEN
Helsingør
Helsingborg
Lund
Malmö
Bornholm
(Den)

Kattegat
Skagerrak
Göta
Nissan
Lagan

Liepaja
Teksiai
Šiauliai
Panevežys
Ukmerge
Kretinga
Klaipeda
Kaunas
LITHUANIA
VILNIUS
Vilija

North Frisian Is.
(Nord Friesische
Inseln)
GERMANY
Flensburg
Lolland

Bay of
Gdansk

Kurskiy
Zaliv
Pregolya
R.F.
Sovetsk
Neman

Luga

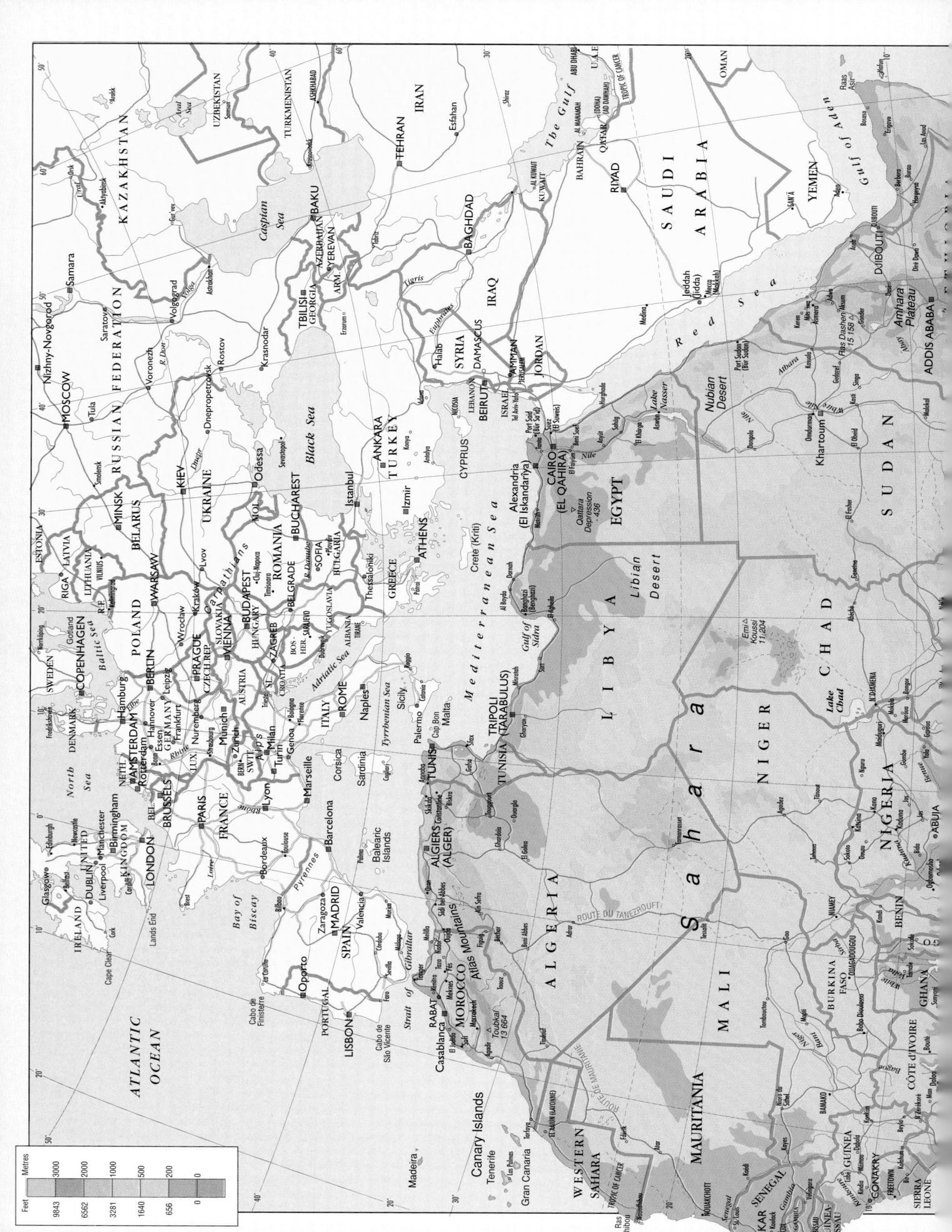

Africa

INDIAN OCEAN

OCEAN

Gulf of Guinea

Population density

Natural vegetation

Russia and Central Asia

Population density - Asia

MOSCOW
TEHERAN
BEIJING
TŌKYŌ
TAIPEI
HANOI
MANILA
YANGON
(RANGOON)
BANGKOK

Natural vegetation - Asia

80°   70°   60°

U. S. A.
Cape Prince
of Wales
C. Deshnev
Bering Strait
Nunivak
Is.

**Chukchi
Sea**
Wrangel Island
Chukchi
Peninsula
Saint Lawrence
Is.
Egrekinot

**East
Siberian
Sea**
Perek
Anadyr
Gulf
**Bering
Sea**
Beringovski
Mys Navarin

New Siberian Islands
New Siberia
Ambarchik
Bilibino
Markovo
Kotelny
Cherski
Lyakhov
Islands
Evensk
Mys Olyutorski

*Laptev
Sea*
Tiksi
Ust-Kuiga

Gora Pobeda
△ 10 324
Susuman
Ust-Nera
Omolun

Polana
Ust-Kamchatsk

Verkhoyansk Mountains
Lena
Sangar
Amur
Handyga
Shelikhov
Gulf

*Kamchatka
Peninsula*

Yakutsk
Ust-Maya
Petropavlosk
-Kamchatski

160°

TION
Njurba
Lena
Amga
Aldan
**Sea of
Okhotsk**
Mys Lopatka
50°

Mirny
Olëkminsk
Chulman
Okha

Lensk
Tynda
Nikolayevsk-na-Amure
Sakhalin

Bodaybo
Stoyba
Aleksandrovsk-Sakhalinsk

Kirensk
Zeja
Chegdomyn
Poronaysk

-Kut
Nizhneangarsk
Mogocha
Maha
Skovorodino
Amur
Belogorsk
Sovetskaya-Gavan
Yuzhno-Sakhalinsk

Lake
Baikal
Chita
Sretensk
Blagoveshchensk
Tatar Strait
Khabarovsk
Wakkanai

Ulan-Ude
Borzja
Ergun Zuoqi
Aihui
Dalnerechensk
La Perouse Strait
Asahikawa

Petrovsk-Zabaykalski
Manzhouli
Haitar
Nenjiang
Bel'an
Hegang
Dalnegorsk
Sapporo
Hokkaido

Chaybalsan
Manchuria
Shuang Yashan
Vladivostok
Hakodate

ULAN-BATOR
(ULAANBAATAR)
Qiqihar
Dalnerechensk
Aomori
Hachinohe

Arxan
Baicheng
Harbin
Chŏngjin
Morioka

Saynshand
Horqin-Youyi Qianqi
Mudanjiang
Akita

IA
Jilin
Z
Sendai

Dalan-Dzadgad
Abagnar Qi
Changchun
Niigata
Nagano

oi Desert
Erenhot
Tongliao
Siping
Chŏngjin
Honshū
Toyama

Wuyan
Zhangjiakou
Jining
Funshun
**Sea of
Japan**
TŌKYŌ
Yokohama

Hohhot
Shenyang
Hamhung
Nagoya

Dengkou
Huang He
Baotou
BEIJING
Anshan
Dandong
Sinŭiju
NORTH
KOREA
Wŏnsan
Kobe
Kyōto
Osakā

Pingluo
Tangshan
PYONGYANG
Koesŏng
Okayama
Hiroshima
Shikoku

Zhongwei
Yulin
Shiziazhuang
Luda
*Korea
Bay*
SEOUL
Taegu
Kitakyushu
Fukuoka
Kyūshū

CHINA
Taiyuan
Jinan
Wei-fang
Qingdao
Inch'on
Taejŏn
Chŏnju
SOUTH
KOREA
Pusan
Masan
Kwangju
Kagoshima

Lanzhou
Yan'an
Xuzhou
Cheju
*Korea
Strait*
**East
China
Sea**

Tianshui
Xian
Luoyang
Zhengzhou
**Yellow
Sea**

Hanzhong
Huainan
Hefei
Wuxi
Suzhou

Ankang
Nanjing
Shanghai
110°
120°
130°
140°
150°

**PACIFIC
OCEAN**

0   500   1000 kms
0   250   500 miles

40°
30°

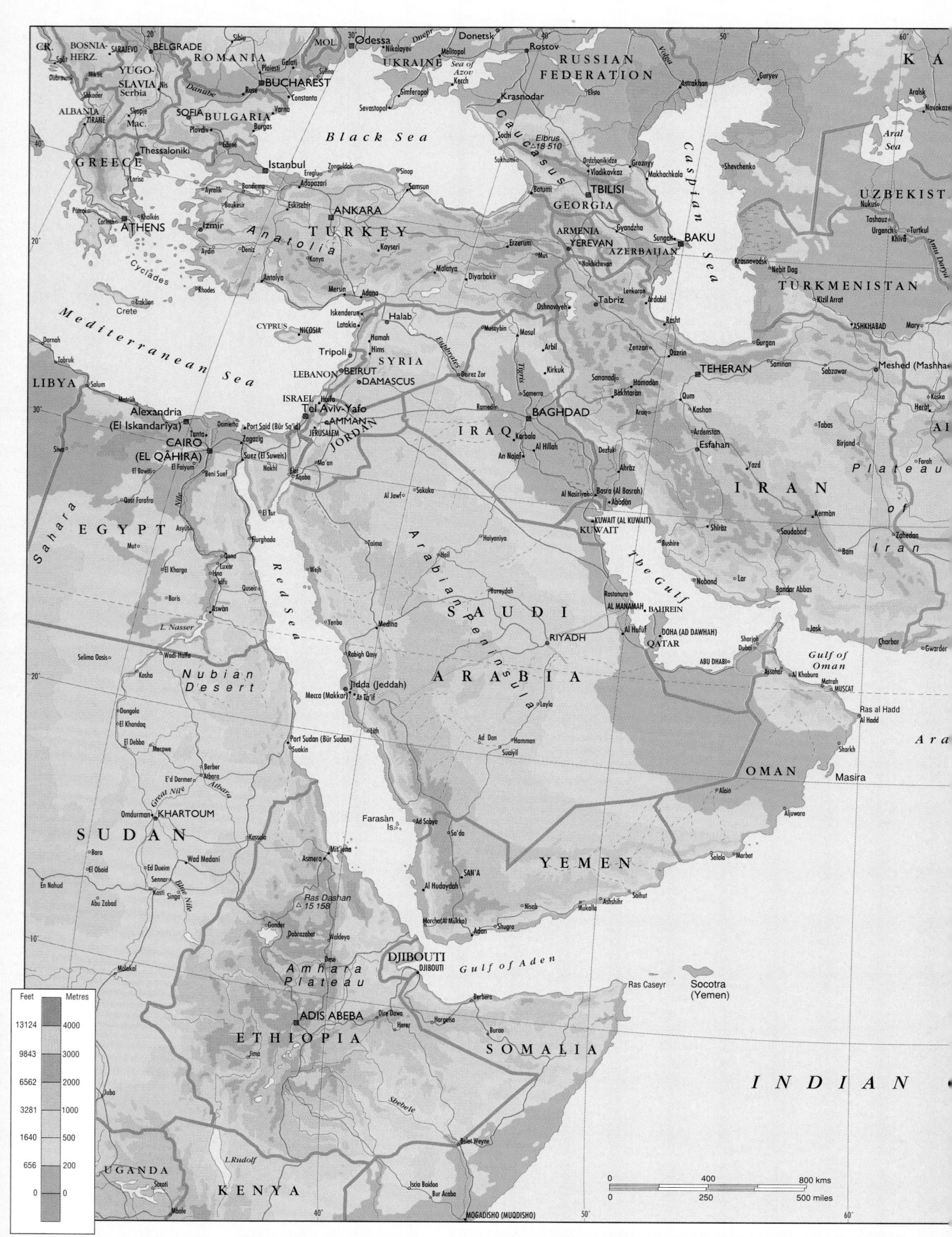

CR. BOSNIA-
Split HERZ.
Dubrovnik
ALBANIA
SHKODER
TIRANE
GREECE
Larisa
ATHENS
Corinthus
Patros
Khalkis
Crete
Iraklion

SARAJEVO
BELGRADE
YUGO-
SLAVIA
Serbia
Nis
Skopje
Mac.
SOFIA
Plovdiv
BULGARIA
Burgas
Edirne

ROMANIA
Sibiu
Ploiesti
BUCHAREST
Danube
Ruse
Constanta
Varna

Odessa
Nikolayev
MOL.
Dnepr
UKRAINE
Sea of
Azov
Kerch
Sevastopol
Simferopol
Melitopol

Donetsk
Rostov

RUSSIAN
FEDERATION
Volga
Astrakhan
Guryev

KA
Aralsk
Novokazalinsk

Black Sea

Mediterranean Sea

Istanbul
Eregli
Zonguldak
Sinop
Samsun
Adapazari
Bandirma
Ayvalik
ANKARA
TURKEY
Anatolia
Izmir
Deniz
Aydin
Rhodes
Cyclades

Krasnodar
Sochi
Elbrus
△18 510
Caucasus
Sukhumi
Batumi
TBILISI
GEORGIA
Erzurum
ARMENIA
YEREVAN
Mus
Nakhichevan
AZERBAIJAN

Ordzhonikidze
Vladikavkaz
Grozzny
Makhachkala
Shevchenko

Elista

Caspian Sea

Aral
Sea

UZBEKIST
Nukus
Tashauz
Urgench
Khiva
Turtkul
Amu Darya

Antalya
Konya
Kayseri
Mersin
Adana
Iskenderun
Latakia
Eskisehir
Baukesir

Malatya
Diyarbakir
Gyandzha
Sungait
BAKU

Tabriz
Lenkoran
Ardabil
Krasnovodsk
Nebit Dag
Kizil Arvat
TURKMENISTAN
ASHKHABAD
Mary

LIBYA
Darnah
Tobruk
Salum
Matruh

CYPRUS
NICOSIA
Tripoli
Halab
Hamah
Hims
SYRIA
BEIRUT
DAMASCUS
LEBANON
ISRAEL
Haifa
Tel Aviv-Yafo
JERUSALEM
AMMAN
JORDAN

Mosayn
Mosul
Arbil
Kirkuk
Deirez Zor
Euphrates
Tigris
Samerra
Ramadin
BAGHDAD
Kūrbala
Al Hillah
An Najaf
IRAQ

Sananadja
Bakhtaran
Hamadan
Araq
Qum
Kashan
Ardenstan
Dezful
Ahrāz
Abādān

Zenzan
Qazvin
Resht
Gurgan
TEHERAN
Samnan
Sabzawar

Meshed (Mashha

Herät

AI

Alexandria
(El Iskandariya)
Damietta
Port Said (Bür Sa'id)
Zagazig
CAIRO
(EL QÂHIRA)
Tanta
Suez (El Suweis)
Nokhl
El Faiyum
Beni Suef
Siwa
El Bawiti

Al Jawf
Sakaka
Ma'an
El Aqaba
El Tur

SAUDI

Basra (Al Basrah)
Al Nasiriyah
KUWAIT (AL KUWAIT)
KUWAIT
Bushire
Shīrāz
Saudabad
Kermän
Zahedan

Yazd
Esfahan
IRAN
Plateau
of
Iran
Tabas
Birjand
Farah

EGYPT
Qasr Farafra
Asyūta
Qena
Luxor
Isna
Idfu
Quseir

Sahara
El Kharga
Baris
Aswān
Mut

L. Nasser
Wadi-Halfa
Selima Oasis
Kosha
Dongola
El Khandaq
El Debba
Merowe

Nubian
Desert

Rabigh Qasy
Jidda (Jeddah)
Mecca (Makkar)
At Ta'if
Lith
Medina
Yenbo
Wejh

Hail
Haiyaniya
Taima
Bureydah
ARABIA
RIYADH
Layla

Rastanna
AL MANAMAH
BAHREIN
Al Hufuf
DOHA (AD DAWHAH)
QATAR
ABU DHABI

Lar
Noband
Bushire
Bandar Abbas
Jask
Charbar
Gwarder

Arabian Peninsula

Gulf of
Oman
Sharjah
Dubai
Assohar
Al Khabura
Matrah
MUSCAT
Ras al Hadd
Al Hadd

The Gulf

SUDAN
Omdurman
KHARTOUM
Bara
El Obaid
Ed Dueim
Sennar
Kosti
Singa
En Nahud
Abu Zabad

Farasān
Is.
Ad Sabya
Sa'da
Mit'jena
Asmera
Kassala
Wad Medani

Port Sudan (Bür Sudan)
Suakin
Berber
E'd Darmer
Atbara
Great Nile
Blue Nile

Ad Dan
Hamman
Suaiyil

OMAN
Masira
Alain
Aljuwara

Sharkh

Ara

Ras Dashan
△15 158
Gonder
Dabrazobat
Waldeya
Dese

YEMEN
Al Hudaydah
SAN'A
Nisab
Morcha (Al Mukka)
Adan
Shugra
Mukalla
Ashshihr
Saihut
Salala
Marbat

Red Sea

Amhara
Plateau
DJIBOUTI
DJIBOUTI
Gulf of Aden

Ras Caseyr
Socotra
(Yemen)

ADIS ABEBA
Dire Dawa
Jima
Harer
Hargeisa
Burao
ETHIOPIA
SOMALIA
Berbera

INDIAN

Malakal
Juba
L. Rudolf
Sbebele

Belet Weyne
Iscia Baidon
Bur Acaba

UGANDA
Soroti
Mbale
KENYA

MOGADISHO (MUQDISHO)

Feet   Metres
13124   4000
9843   3000
6562   2000
3281   1000
1640   500
656   200
0   0

0   400   800 kms
0   250   500 miles

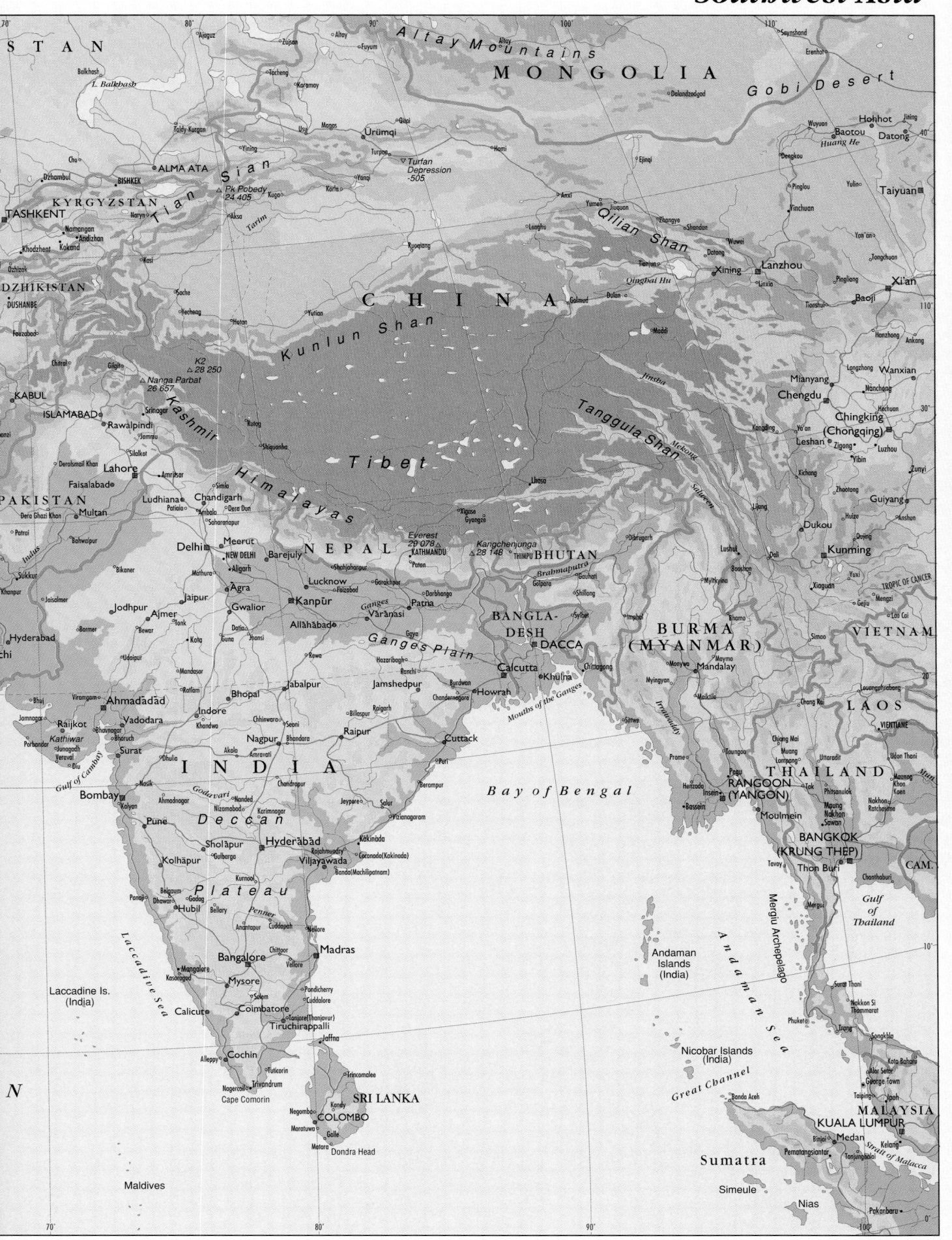

S T A N

L. Balkhash

Balkhash

Dzhambul

ALMA ATA

BISHKEK

KYRGYZSTAN

TASHKENT

Namangan Andizhan

Khodzhent Kokand

Ozhizek

DZHIKISTAN

DUSHANBE

Fouzabad

Chitral

KABUL

ISLAMABAD

Rawalpindi

Derailsmail Khan

PAKISTAN

Dera Ghazi Khan Multan

Patrai

Bahwalpur

Sukkur

Khanpur

Hyderabad

chi

Jamnagar

Porbandar Junagadh

Diu

Bhuj

Viramgam

Rajkot Bhavnagar

Kathiwar Junagadh

Yeraval

Gulf of Cambay

Bombay

Kalyan Nasik

Pune Ahmadnagar

Deccan

Sholapur Gulbarga

Kolhapur

Panaji Dhawar

Plateau

Hubil

Belgaum Godag

Bellary

Mangalore Anantapur

Kasorgad

Calicut

Laccadive Is.
(India)

Laccadive Sea

Maldives

Chu

Taldy-Kurgan

Naryn

Kasi

Gigit

Srinagar

Kashmir

Gagit

Nanga Parbat
26 657

K2
△ 28 250

Kunlun Shan

Himalayas

Simla

Ludhiana Patiala Ambala

Chandigarh Dera Dun

Saharanpur

Delhi Meerut

NEW DELHI

Mathura Aligarh

Bikaner

Agra

Jaipur

Gwalior

Jodhpur Ajmer

Barmer

Bewar Kota

Udaipur

Mandasar

Ratlam

Ahmadabad Indore

Dhulia

Vadodara Khandwa

Bharuch

Surat

I N D I A

Akola

Nagpur

Aurangabad

Chandrapur

Karimnagar

Nanded

Godavari

Hyderabad

Vijayawada

Kurnool

Cuddapah

Nellore

Chittoor

Bangalore Vellore

Mysore Salem

Coimbatore

Tanjore(Thanjavur)

Tiruchirappalli

Cochin Alleppy

Tuticorin

Nagercoil Trivandrum

Cape Comorin

Zujsan

Ajaguz

Tacheng

Karamay

Yining

Aksa

Sache

Yecheng

Hotan

Rutog

Shiquanhe

Kuga

Korla

Yutian

Mandsor

Jabalpur

Bhopal

Raipur

Chhindwara

Seoni

Billaspur

Rajgarh

Raigarh

Bilaspur

Sironj

Guna

Datia

Jhansi

Rewa

Kota

Allahabad

Gaya

Hazaribagh

Ranchi

Burdwan

Jamshedpur

Tacheng

Altay Mountains

M O N G O L I A

Gobi Desert

Fuyum

Usu

Qitai

Ürümqi

Turfan
Depression
-505

Turpan

Yanqi

Hami

Magas

C H I N A

Tibet

Golmud

Dulan

Maddi

Jinsha

Lhasa

Xigase
Gyangze

Everest
29 078 △
KATHMANDU
Patan

Kangchenjunga
△ 28 148 THIMPU BHUTAN

NEPAL

Barejuly

Shahjahanpur

Lucknow

Gorakhpur

Kanpur

Faizabad

Darbhanga

Patna

Ganges

Varanasi

Gya

Ganges Plain

Dalandzadgad

Ejinqi

Anxi

Yumen Jiuquan Zhangye

Longhuy

Qilian Shan

Qinghai Hu

Xining

Linxia

Tianshui

Kangding

Ya'an

Leshan

Zigong

Xichang

Dukou

Huize

Dali

Kunming

Gejiu

Mengzi

Lao Cai

Yuxi

Simao

Jinsha

Tanggula Shan

Mekong

Salween

Lijiang

Anshun

Zunyi

Guiyang

TROPIC OF CANCER

Saynshand

Erenhot

Wuyuan Baotou Hohhot Jining

Huang He Datong

Dengkou

Pinglou

Yulin

Yan'an

Yinchuan

Lanzhou

Xining Linxia

Tongchuan

Hanzhong Ankang

Mianyang

Chengdu

Nanchong

Hechuan

Chingking
(Chongqing)

Luzhou

Zhaotong

Langzhong Wanxian

Taiyuan

Baoji

Xi'an

Tianshui

Pingliang

VIETNAM

BANGLA-
DESH DACCA

Gauhati

Shillong

Gopara

Brahmaputra

Sylhet

Imphal

Calcutta

Howrah

Khulna

Chandernagore

Chittagong

Mouths of the Ganges

Sittwe

BURMA
(MYANMAR)

Myitkyina

Mymyo
Mandalay

Myingyan

Monywa

Meiktila

Bhamo

Lashui

Baoshan

Dibrugarh

LAOS

VIENTIANE

Chang Rai

Louangphrabang

Chiang Mai

Muang Udon Thani

Lampang

Uttaradit

THAILAND

Tak Khon
Kaen

Phitsanulok

Maung
Nakhon Nakhon
Sawan Ratchasima

Mun

Prome

Youngoo

Pegu

Henzada

RANGOON
(YANGON)

Insein

Bassein

Moulmein

Tavoy

BANGKOK
(KRUNG THEP)

Thon Buri

Chanthaburi

CAM.

Gulf
of
Thailand

Mergu

Mergui Archepelago

Andaman
Islands
(India)

A n d a m a n

S e a

Nicobar Islands
(India)

Great Channel

Banda Aceh

Surat Thani

Nakkon Si
Thammarat

Phuket

Trang

Songkhla

Kota Baharu

Alor Setar

George Town

Taiping Ipoh

MALAYSIA
KUALA LUMPUR

Kelang

Binjai

Medan

Pematangsiantar

Sumatra

Tanjungbalai

Strait of Malacca

Simeule

Nias

Pakanbaru

Bay of Bengal

Cuttack

Puri

Berampur

Jeypore

Salur

Vizianagaram

Visakhapatnam

Kakinada

Rajahmundry

Coconada(Kakinada)

Banda(Machilipatnam)

Madras

Pondicherry

Cuddalore

Jaffna

Trincomalee

Kandy

SRI LANKA

Negombo

COLOMBO

Moratuwa

Galle

Matara Dondra Head

Indus

N

70° 80° 90° 100°

110°

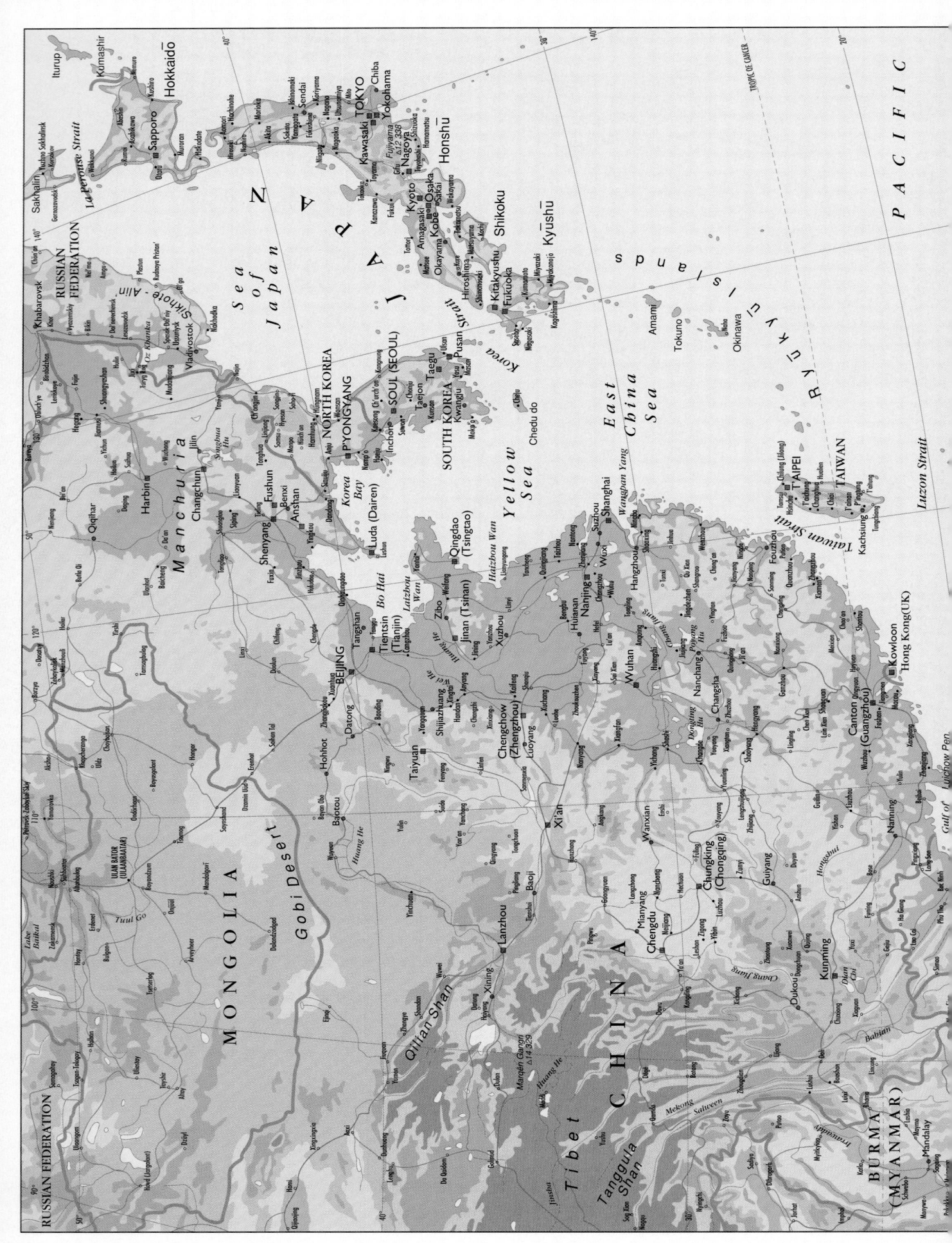

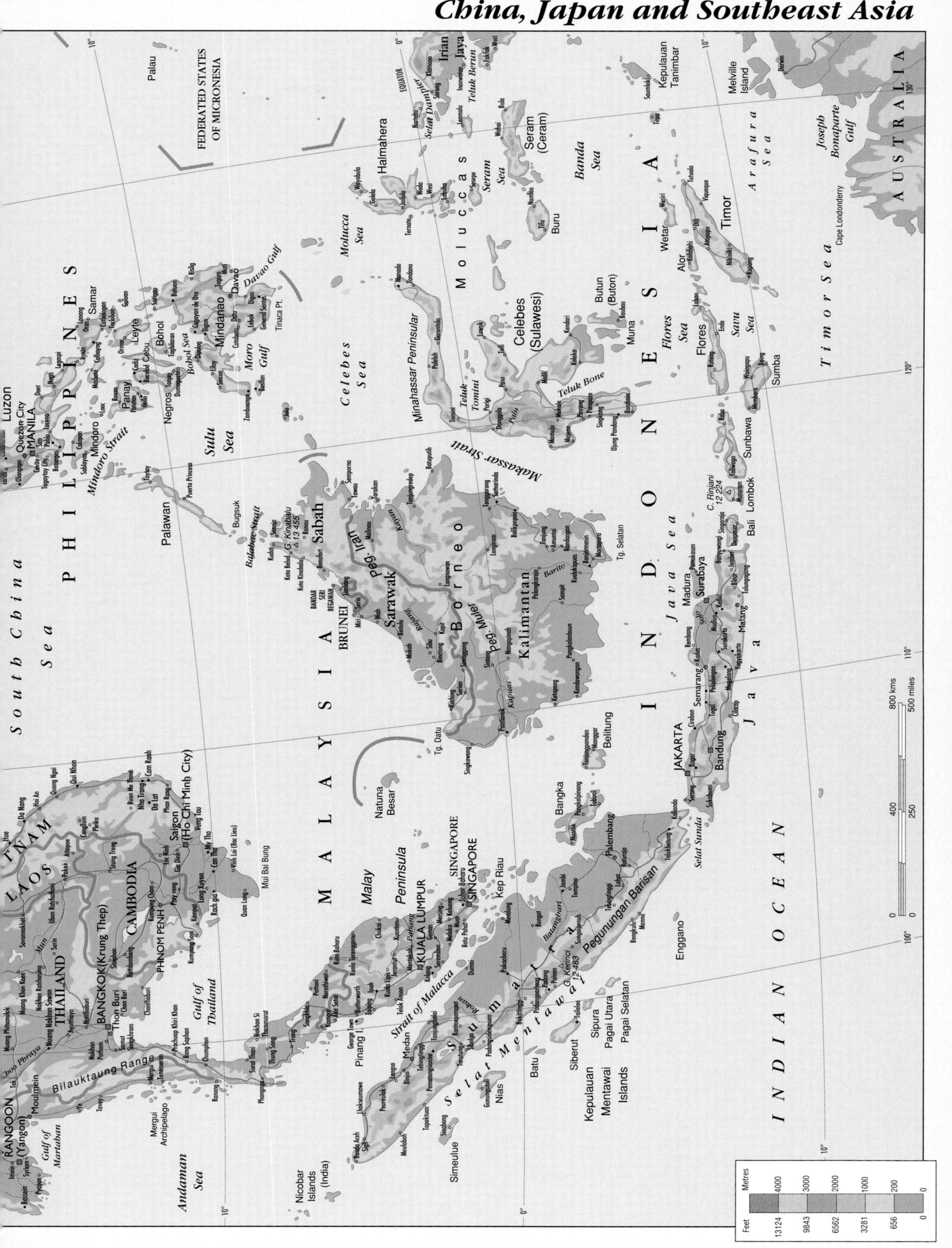

AUSTRALIA

FEDERATED STATES OF MICRONESIA

Palau

Irian Jaya

Java

Kepulauan Tanimbar

Melville Island

Darwin

Halmahera

Seram (Ceram)

Banda Sea

Joseph Bonaparte Gulf

M O L U C C A S

Molucca Sea

Seram Sea

Buru

Timor

Arafura Sea

Cape Londonderry

Moluccas

Alor

Wetar

PHILIPPINES

Samar

Leyte

Bohol

Davao Gulf

Mindanao

Tinaca Pt.

Davao

Celebes (Sulawesi)

Butun (Buton)

Flores Sea

Timor Sea

Muna

LUZON

Quezon City

MANILA

Minahassar Peninsular

Celebes Sea

Teluk Bone

Flores

Savu Sea

Sumba

Mindoro Strait

Sulu Sea

Teluk Tomini

Makassar Strait

Sunbawa

Lombok

C. Rinjani 12 224

Bali

S O U T H   C H I N A   S E A

Palawan

Bugsuk

Balabac Strait

Sabah

G. Kinabalu 13 455

BRUNEI BANDAR SERI BEGAWAN

Sarawak

Peg. Iran

Borneo

Peg. Muler

Kalimantan

Barito

Tg. Selatan

Surabaya

Madura

Semarang

J a v a   S e a

Tg. Datu

Natuna Besar

I N D O N E S I A

JAKARTA Bogor Bandung

J a v a

Kep. Riau

Belitung

Bangka

Palembang

Selat Sunda

Puerto Princesa

LAOS

VIETNAM

Saigon (Ho Chi Minh City)

Mui Bai Bung

CAMBODIA

PHNOM PENH

THAILAND

BANGKOK (Krung Thep)

Thon Buri

Gulf of Thailand

M A L A Y S I A

Malay Peninsula

SINGAPORE

Johor Baharu

KUALA LUMPUR

Strait of Malacca

Pinang

George Town

Medan

S u m a t r a

Pegunungan Barisan

G. Kerinci 12 483

Enggano

Bilauktaung Range

Moulmein

RANGOON (Yangon)

Gulf of Martaban

Mergui Archipelago

A n d a m a n   S e a

Nicobar Islands (India)

Simeulue

Nias

Siberut

Sipura

Kepulauan Mentawai Islands

Pagai Utara

Pagai Selatan

Batu

Selat Mentawai

I N D I A N   O C E A N

Metres					
4000	3000	2000	1000	200	0
Feet					
13124	9843	6552	3281	656	0

800 kms
500 miles
400
250

EQUATOR

10°

0°

10°

100°

110°

120°

130°

Middle East - detail

The Balkans - detai

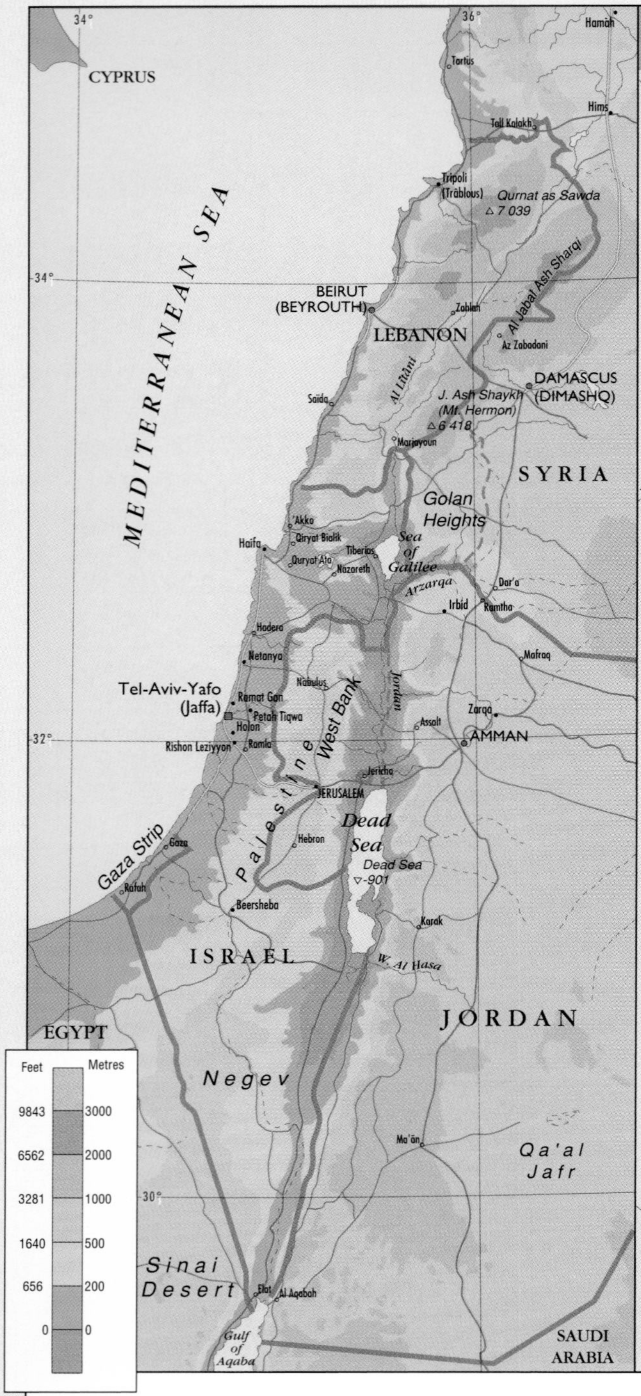

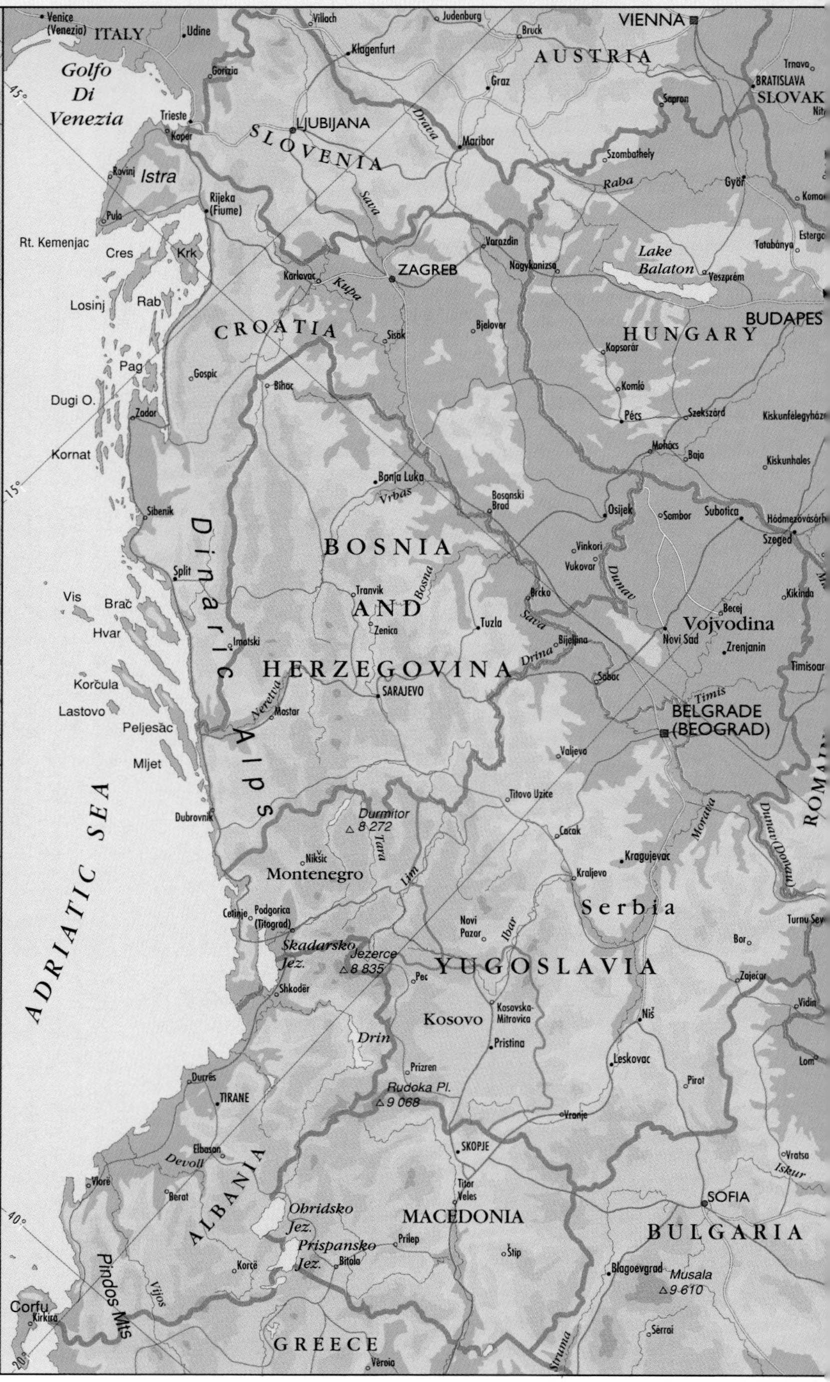

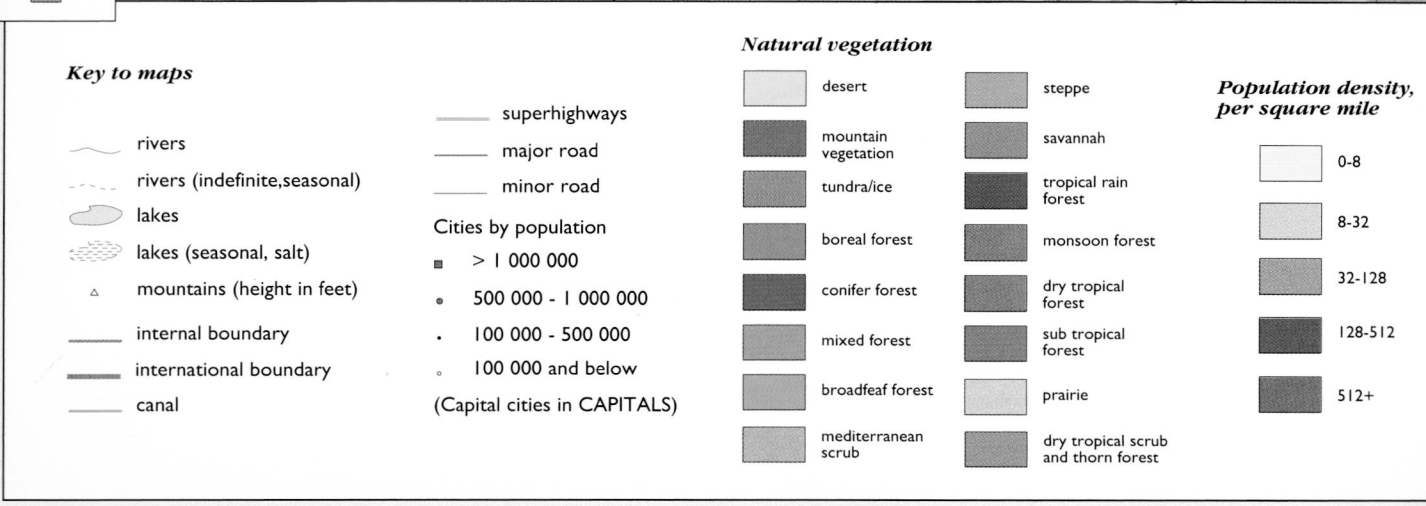

Key to maps

- rivers
- rivers (indefinite,seasonal)
- lakes
- lakes (seasonal, salt)
- △ mountains (height in feet)
- internal boundary
- international boundary
- canal
- superhighways
- major road
- minor road

Cities by population

- ▪ > 1 000 000
- ● 500 000 - 1 000 000
- • 100 000 - 500 000
- ∘ 100 000 and below

(Capital cities in CAPITALS)

Natural vegetation

- desert
- mountain vegetation
- tundra/ice
- boreal forest
- conifer forest
- mixed forest
- broadfeaf forest
- mediterranean scrub
- steppe
- savannah
- tropical rain forest
- monsoon forest
- dry tropical forest
- sub tropical forest
- prairie
- dry tropical scrub and thorn forest

Population density, per square mile

- 0-8
- 8-32
- 32-128
- 128-512
- 512+

MARSHALL ISLANDS (continued)

Population: 48,000
Language: Marshallese, English (both official)
Capital: Majuro
Currency: U.S. dollar
Religion: Christian
Ethnic Groups: Micronesian
Government: Republic
Literacy (1990): 86%
Life Expectancy at Birth (1991): 64 years female, 61 years male
Infant Mortality (per 1,000 live births 1991): 53
Gross Domestic Product (1989): $63 million
GDP per Capita: $1,500
Principal Industries: Fishing, agriculture
Principal Crops: Coconut palms, fruits, vegetables

MAURITANIA

Islamic Republic of Mauritania
République Islamique de Mauritanie

Area: 397,950 sq. mi. (1,030,700 sq. km.)
Population: 1,996,000
Language: Arabic 80%, French (both official), Wolof 8%, Tukolor 6%, Soninke 3%, other 3%
Capital: Nouakchott
Currency: Ouguiya
Religion: Muslim (Sunni)
Ethnic Groups: Arab-Berber 80%, African 20%
Government: In transition
Literacy (1991): 30%
Life Expectancy at Birth (1991): 50 years female, 44 years male
Infant Mortality (per 1,000 live births 1991): 94
Gross Domestic Product (1989): $953 million
GDP per Capita: $490
Principal Industries: Agriculture, fish processing
Principal Crops: Millet, corn, rice, dates

MAURITIUS

Area: 787 sq. mi. (2,040 sq. km.)
Population: 1,081,000
Language: English (official), French Creole 54%, Bhojpuri 20%, Hindi 11%, French 4%, Tamil 4%, Urdu 2%, other 5%
Capital: Port Louis
Currency: Mauritian rupee
Religion: Hindu 51%, Christian 30%, Muslim 16%, other 3%
Ethnic Groups: Indo-Mauritian 68%, Creole 27%, other 5%
Government: Democracy
Literacy (1989): 94%
Life Expectancy at Birth (1991): 74 years female, 66 years male
Infant Mortality (per 1,000 live births 1991): 20
Gross Domestic Product (1989): $2 billion
GDP per Capita: $1,950
Principal Industries: Agriculture, sugar processing, rum
Principal Crops: Sugarcane, tea

MEXICO

United Mexican States
Estados Unidos Mexicanos

Area: 761,600 sq. mi. (1,972,547 sq. km.)
Population: 90,007,000
Language: Spanish 91% (official), various indigenous 6%, other 1%
Capital: Mexico City
Currency: Peso
Religion: Roman Catholic 97% other 3%
Ethnic Groups: Mestizo 60%, Native American 29%, white or European descent 9%, other 2%
Government: Republic
Literacy (1989): 88%
Life Expectancy at Birth (1991): 76 years female, 68 years male
Infant Mortality (per 1,000 live births 1991): 29
Gross Domestic Product (1993): $382 billion
GDP per Capita: $4,186

Principal Industries: Agriculture, mining, food processing, chemicals, textiles, petroleum
Principal Crops: Cotton, coffee, wheat, rice, sugar cane, vegetables, corn

MICRONESIA

Federated States of Micronesia

Area: 270 sq. mi. (702 sq. km.)
Population: 108,000
Language: English (official), Micronesian dialects
Capital: Kolonia
Currency: U.S. dollar
Religion: Predominantly Christian
Ethnic Groups: Trukese, Pohnpeian
Government: Republic
Literacy (1991): 90%
Life Expectancy at Birth (1991): 73 years female, 68 years male
Infant Mortality (per 1,000 live births 1991): 65
Gross National Product (1989): $150 million
GNP per Capita: $150
Principal Industries: Fishing, agriculture, mining
Principal Crops: Tropical fruits, vegetables, coconuts

MOLDOVA

Republic of Moldova
Republica Moldoveneasca

Area: 13,000 sq. mi. (33,700 sq. km.)
Population: 4,400,000
Language: Moldovan 62%, Russian 22%, Ukrainian 10%, other 6%
Capital: Kishinev
Currency: Ruble
Religion: Primarily Orthodox
Ethnic Groups: Moldovian 65%, Ukrainian 14%, Russian 13%, other 8%
Government: Republic
Literacy (1991): 98%
Life Expectancy at Birth (1991): 74 years female, 65 years male
Infant Mortality (per 1,000 live births 1991): 20
Principal Industries: Agriculture, food processing, canning, wine making, textiles
Principal Crops: Wheat, corn, barley, sugar beets, fruits and wine grapes

MONACO

Principality of Monaco

Area: 0.73 sq. mi. (465 acres)
Population: 30,000
Language: French 58% (official), Italian 17%, Provençal 15%, other 10%
Capital: Monaco-Ville
Currency: French franc
Religion: Roman Catholic 95%, other 5%
Ethnic Groups: French 47%, Italian 16%, Monégasque 16%, other 11%
Government: Constitutional monarchy
Literacy (1989): 99%
Life Expectancy at Birth: 80 years female, 72 years male
Infant Mortality (per 1,000 live births 1991): 7
Gross Domestic Product: $234 million
GDP per Capita: $11,000
Principal Industries: Tourism, gambling, chemicals, precision instruments, plastics

MONGOLIA

Mongolian People's Republic
Bügd Nayramdakh Mongol Ard Uls

Area: 604,245 sq. mi. (1,565,000 sq. km.)
Population: 2,247,000
Language: Mongolian (official) 90%, Kazakh 7%, Khalkha 3%
Capital: Ulan Bator
Currency: Tugrik
Religion: Predominantly Tibetan Buddhist, Muslim, traditional beliefs
Ethnic Groups: Mongol 85%, Kazakh 5%, other 10%
Government: Republic

Literacy (1985): 89%
Life Expectancy at Birth (1991): 67 years female, 63 years male
Infant Mortality (per 1,000 live births 1991): 49
Gross Domestic Product (1990): $2.2 billion
GDP per Capita: $1,000
Principal Industries: Agriculture, food processing, textiles, chemicals, cement
Principal Crops: Grain

MOROCCO

Kingdom of Morocco
al-Mamlaka al-Maghrebia

Area: 172,415 sq. mi. (446,550 sq. km.)
Population: 26,182,000
Language: Arabic 65% (official), Tamazight 15%, other Berber dialects 19%, other 1%, French and Spanish widely spoken in north
Capital: Rabat
Currency: Dirham
Religion: Muslim (Sunni)
Ethnic Groups: Arab-Berber 99%, other 1%
Government: Constitutional monarchy
Literacy (1985): 35%
Life Expectancy at Birth (1991): 66 years female, 63 years male
Infant Mortality (per 1,000 live births 1991): 76
Gross Domestic Product (1990): $25.4 billion
GDP per Capita: $990
Principal Industries: Agriculture, carpet, clothing, leather goods, mining, tourism
Principal Crops: Grains, fruits, dates, grapes

MOZAMBIQUE

Republic of Mozambique
República de Mocambique

Area: 303,075 sq. mi. (799,380 sq. km.)
Population: 15,113,000
Language: Portuguese (official), Makua 38%, Tsonga (Thonga) 24%, other Bantu dialects 38%
Capital: Maputo
Currency: Metical
Religion: Traditional 60%, Christian 30%, Muslim 10%
Ethnic Groups: Makua 47%, Tsonga 23%, Malawi 12%, Shona 11%, Yao 4%, other 3%
Government: Socialist
Literacy (1989): 14%
Life Expectancy at Birth (1991): 49 years female, 46 years male
Infant Mortality (per 1,000 live births 1991): 134
Gross Domestic Product (1989): $1.6 billion
GDP per Capita: $110
Principal Industries: Agriculture, processed foods, petroleum products, textiles, cement, alcohol
Principal Crops: Cashews, cotton, sugar, copra, tea

MYANMAR (Formerly Burma)

Union of Myanmar
Pyeidaungzu Myanmar Naingngandaw

Area: 261,220 sq. mi. (676,560 sq. km.)
Population: 45,112,000
Language: Burmese 69% (official), Karen 10%, Shan 8%, Tibeto-Burman 5%, other 8%
Capital: Yangon
Currency: Kyat
Religion: Buddhist 85%, animist, Christian 15%
Ethnic Groups: Burman 68%, Shan 7%, Karen 4%, Rakhine 3%, other 18%
Government: Military
Literacy (1989): 66%
Life Expectancy at Birth (1991): 56 years female, 53 years male
Infant Mortality (per 1,000 live births 1991): 95
Gross Domestic Product (1990): $16.8 billion
GDP per Capita: $408
Principal Industries: Agriculture, forestry, mining
Principal Crops: Rice, sugarcane, peanuts, beans

NAMIBIA

Republic of Namibia

Area: 318,260 sq. mi. (824,295 sq. km.)
Population: 1,521,000
Language: English (official), Kwanyama 47%, Afrikaans 14%, Nama 13%, Hevero 7%, Kwangali 7%, other African 12%
Capital: Windhoek
Currency: South African rand
Religion: Lutheran 51%, Roman Catholic 20%, other 29%
Ethnic Groups: Ovambo 50%, Kavango 10%, Herero 7%, Damara 7%, other African 26%
Government: Democracy
Literacy (1989): 58%
Life Expectancy at Birth (1991): 63 years female, 58 years male
Infant Mortality (per 1,000 live births 1991): 72
Gross National Product (1990): $1.8 billion
GNP per Capita: $1,240
Principal Industries: Mining, canned meat, textiles
Principal Crops: Corn, millet, sorghum, livestock

NAURU

Republic of Nauru
Naoero

Area: 8 sq. mi. (20 sq. km.)
Population: 9,000
Language: Nauruan 58% (official), Ikiribati 17%, Tuvalu 9%, Chinese 9%, English 7%
Capital: Yaren
Currency: Australian dollar
Religion: Congregational 54%, other 46%
Ethnic Groups: Nauruan 57%, Pacific Islander 26%, Chinese 8%, European 8%
Government: Republic
Literacy (1988): 99%
Infant Mortality (per 1,000 live births 1991): 41
Gross National Product (1989): $90 million
GNP per Capita: $10,000
Principal Industries: Phosphates

NEPAL

Kingdom of Nepal
Sri Nepala Sarkar

Area: 54,463 sq. mi. (141,059 sq. km.)
Population: 19,612,000
Language: Nepali 58% (official), Santali, Tibetan, Bhojpuri, several other Indian languages 42%
Capital: Kathmandu
Currency: Nepalese rupee
Religion: Hindu 90%, Buddhist 7%, other 3%
Ethnic Groups: Nepalese 58%, Bihari 19%, Tharu 4%, Tamdag 4%, Newar 3%, other 12%
Government: Democracy
Literacy (1989): 29%
Life Expectancy at Birth (1989): 49 years female, 50 years male
Infant Mortality (per 1,000 live births 1991): 98
Gross Domestic Product (1990): $3.1 billion
GDP per Capita: $160
Principal Industries: Agriculture, sugar, jute mills, tourism
Principal Crops: Jute, rice, grain

THE NETHERLANDS

Kingdom of the Netherlands
Koninkrijk der Nederlanden

Area: 16,000 sq. mi. (41,545 sq. km.)
Population: 15,022,000
Language: Dutch 93%, Frisan 5%, other 2%
Capital: Amsterdam (seat of government, The Hague)
Currency: Guilder
Religion: Roman Catholic 36%, Protestant 27%, other 4%, unaffiliated 33%
Ethnic Groups: Dutch 97%, other 3%

THE NETHERLANDS (continued)

Government: Constitutional monarchy

Literacy (1991): 99%

Life Expectancy at Birth (1991): 81 years female, 74 years male

Infant Mortality (per 1,000 live births 1991): 7

Gross Domestic Product (1993): $330 billion

GDP per Capita: $21,400

Principal Industries: Metals, machinery, chemicals, oil refinery, diamond cutting, electronics, tourism

Principal Crops: Grains, potatoes, sugar beets, vegetables, fruits, flowers

NEW ZEALAND

Area: 103,880 sq. mi. (269,060 sq. km.)

Population: 3,309,000

Language: English 93%, Maori 3% (both official), other 4%

Capital: Wellington

Currency: New Zealand dollar

Religion: Protestant, Roman Catholic

Ethnic Groups: European (mostly British) 87%, Polynesian (mostly Maori) 9%, other 4%

Government: Democracy

Literacy (1991): 99%

Life Expectancy at Birth (1991): 78 years female, 72 years male

Infant Mortality (per 1,000 live births 1991): 10

Gross Domestic Product (1993): $43 billion

GDP per Capita: $12,300

Principal Industries: Livestock, food processing, textiles, forestry

Principal Crops: Grains

NICARAGUA

Republic of Nicaragua
República de Nicaragua

Area: 50,180 sq. mi. (130,000 sq. km.)

Population: 3,752,000

Language: Spanish 95%, Miskito 4%, English 1%

Capital: Managua

Currency: Cordoba

Religion: Roman Catholic 88%, other 12%

Ethnic Groups: Mestizo 69%, white or European descent 17%, black 9%, Native American 5%

Government: Republic

Literacy (1991): 57%

Life Expectancy at Birth (1991): 65 years female, 61 years male

Infant Mortality (per 1,000 live births 1991): 60

Gross Domestic Product (1990): $1.7 billion

GDP per Capita: $470

Principal Industries: Oil refining, food processing, chemicals, textiles

Principal Crops: Bananas, cotton, fruit, yucca, coffee, sugar, corn, beans, cocoa, tobacco

NIGER

Republic of Niger
République du Niger

Area: 489,205 sq. mi. (1,267,040 sq. km.)

Population: 8,154,000

Language: French (official), Hausa 46%, Songhai 21%, Fulani 14%, Tamasheq 11%, Kanuri 8%, Ibo widely spoken

Capital: Niamey

Currency: Franc CFA

Religion: Muslim (Sunni) 80%, traditional 20%

Ethnic Groups: Hausa 56%, Dyerma 22%, Fulani 8%, Tuareg 8%, Ijaw 6%

Government: Military

Literacy (1991): 21%

Life Expectancy at Birth (1991): 53 years female, 49 years male

Infant Mortality (per 1,000 live births 1991): 129

Gross Domestic Product (1989): $2.1 billion

GDP per Capita: $290

Principal Industries: Agriculture, mining

Principal Crops: Peanuts, cotton

NIGERIA

Federal Republic of Nigeria

Area: 356,700 sq. mi. (923,850 sq. km.)

Population: 122,471,000

Language: English (official), Hausa 21%, Yoruba 20%, Ibo 17%, Fulani 9%, Efik (Ibibio) 5%, Kanuri 4%, Edo, Fula, Ijaw, Tiv 24%

Capital: Abuja

Currency: Naira

Religion: Muslim (mostly in north) 50%, Christian (mostly in South) 40%, indigenous 10%

Ethnic Groups: Hausa 21%, Yoruba 20%, Ibo 17%, Fulani 9%, other 33%

Government: Military

Literacy (1991): 51%

Life Expectancy at Birth (1991): 50 years female, 48 years male

Infant Mortality (per 1,000 live births 1991): 118

Gross Domestic Product (1993): $27.8 billion

GDP per Capita: $301

Principal Industries: Oil, food processing, assembly of vehicles, textiles

Principal Crops: Cocoa, peanuts, cotton, tobacco

NORWAY

Kingdom of Norway
Kongeriket Norge

Area: 125,050 sq. mi. (323,875 sq. km.)

Population: 4,273,000

Language: Norwegian 99%, other 1%

Capital: Oslo

Currency: Krone

Religion: Lutheran 94%, other 6%

Ethnic Groups: Norwegian 97%, other 3%

Government: Constitutional monarchy

Literacy (1991): 99%

Life Expectancy at Birth (1991): 81 years female, 74 years male

Infant Mortality (per 1,000 live births 1991): 7.1

Gross Domestic Product (1990): $120 billion

GDP per Capita: $28,200

Principal Industries: Fishing, forestry, shipbuilding, engineering, metals, chemicals, oil, gas

Principal Crops: Grains, potatoes

OMAN

Sultanate of Oman
Saltanat 'Uman

Area: 82,030 sq. mi. (212,458 sq. km.)

Population: 1,534,000

Language: Arabic 68%, Baluchi 19%, Mehri 6%, Farsi 3%, other 4%

Capital: Muscat

Currency: Omani rial

Religion: Muslim 95%, other 5%

Ethnic Groups: Omani Arab 74%, Pakistani 21%, other 5%

Government: Absolute monarchy

Literacy (1989): 20%

Life Expectancy at Birth (1991): 68 years female, 65 years male

Infant Mortality (per 1,000 live births 1991): 40

Gross Domestic Product (1989): $10.6 billion

GDP per Capita: $5,131

Principal Industries: Oil, agriculture, fishing

Principal Crops: Dates, fruits, vegetables, wheat, bananas

PAKISTAN

Islamic Republic of Pakistan
Islam-i Jamhuriya-e Pakistan

Area: 310,400 sq. mi. (803,935 sq. km.)

Population: 117,490,000

Language: Urdu (national) 8%, English (official), Punjabi 48%, Sindhi 12%, Pasht 8%, Baluchi 3%, Gujarti, Kashmiri, and other 21%

Capital: Islamabad

Currency: Pakistani rupee

Religion: Muslim 97%, other 3%

Ethnic Groups: Punjabi 66%, Sindhi 13%, Pushtun 8.5%, Urdu 7.6%, Baluchi 2.5%, other 8.4%
Government: Republic
Literacy (1991): 35%
Life Expectancy at Birth (1991): 57 years female, 56 years male
Infant Mortality (per 1,000 live births 1991): 109
Gross Domestic Product (1993): $53 billion
GDP per Capita: $430
Principal Industries: Textiles, food processing, chemicals, petroleum products
Principal Crops: Rice, wheat

PANAMA
Republic of Panama
República de Panamá

Area: 29,760 sq. mi. (77,080 sq. km.)
Population: 2,476,000
Language: Spanish 81%, English Creole 14%, other 5%
Capital: Panama City
Currency: Balboa
Religion: Roman Catholic 93%, Protestant 6%, other 1%
Ethnic Groups: Mestizo 70%, West Indian 14%, white or European descent 10%, Native American 6%
Government: Republic
Literacy (1991): 87%
Life Expectancy at Birth (1991): 76 years female, 72 years male
Infant Mortality (per 1,000 live births 1991): 21
Gross Domestic Product (1990): $4.8 billion
GDP per Capita: $380
Principal Industries: Oil refining, sugar refining, cement, paper products
Principal Crops: Bananas, pineapples, cocoa, corn, coconuts, sugar

PAPUA NEW GUINEA

Area: 178,700 sq. mi. (462,840 sq. km.)
Population: 3,913,000
Language: English (official), Papuan 73%, Melanesian 20%, other 7%
Capital: Port Moresby
Currency: Kina
Religion: Protestant 63%, Roman Catholic 31%, local religions 6%
Ethnic Groups: Papuan 84%, Melanesian 15%, pygmy 1%
Government: Democracy
Literacy (1991): 52%
Life Expectancy at Birth (1991): 56 years female, 55 years male
Infant Mortality (per 1,000 live births 1991): 66
Gross Domestic Product (1989): $2.7 billion
GDP per Capita: $725
Principal Industries: Agriculture, fishing, mining, forestry
Principal Crops: Coffee, coconuts, tea, copra

PARAGUAY
Republic of Paraguay
República del Paraguay

Area: 157,050 sq. mi. (406,755 sq. km.)
Population: 4,799,000
Language: Spanish 6%, Guarani 89% (both official), Portuguese 3%, other 2%
Capital: Asunción
Currency: Guarani
Religion: Roman Catholic 97%, other 3%
Ethnic Groups: Mestizo 95%, small white, Native American, black minorities
Government: Republic
Literacy (1989): 81%
Life Expectancy at Birth (1991): 72 years female, 67 years male
Infant Mortality (per 1,000 live births 1991): 47
Gross Domestic Product (1990): $4.7 billion
GDP per Capita (1990): $1,100
Principal Industries: Food processing, wood products, textiles, cement
Principal Crops: Corn, cotton, beans, sugarcane

PERU
Republic of Peru
República del Peru

Area: 496,220 sq. mi. (1,285,215 sq. km.)
Population: 22,362,000
Language: Spanish 68%, Quechua 27% (both official), Aymara 3%, other 2%
Capital: Lima
Currency: Nuevo sol
Religion: Roman Catholic 90%, other 10%
Ethnic Groups: Quechua 45%, mestizo 37%, white or European descent 15%, black and Asian 3%
Government: Military
Literacy (1991): 85%
Life Expectancy at Birth (1991): 67 years female, 62 years male
Infant Mortality (per 1,000 live births 1991): 66
Gross Domestic Product (1989): $19.3 billion
GDP per Capita: $898
Principal Industries: Fish meal, mineral processing, light industry, textiles
Principal Crops: Cotton, sugar, coffee, corn

THE PHILIPPINES
Republic of the Philippines

Area: 115,830 sq. mi. (300,000 sq. km.)
Population: 65,759,000
Language: Filipino (based on Tagalog) 24%, English (both official), Cebuano 24%, Ilocano 11%, Bikol 7%, Samar-Leyte (Waray-Waray) 5%, other including Panay-Hiligayon 29%
Capital: Manila
Currency: Peso
Religion: Roman Catholics 83%, Protestant 9%, Muslim 5%, other 3%
Ethnic Groups: Malay 96%, Chinese 2%, other 2%
Government: Republic
Literacy (1989): 88%
Life Expectancy at Birth (1991): 67 years female, 62 years male
Infant Mortality (per 1,000 live births 1991): 54
Gross National Product (1993): $54 billion
GNP per Capita: $823
Principal Industries: Food processing, textiles, clothing, drugs, wood products, appliances
Principal Crops: Sugar, rice, corn, pineapple, coconut

POLAND
Republic of Poland
Rzeczpospolita Polska

Area: 120,725 sq. mi. (312,680 sq. km.)
Population: 37,800,000
Language: Polish 98%, Ukrainian 1%, other 1%
Capital: Warsaw
Currency: Zloty
Religion: Roman Catholic 94%, other 6%
Ethnic Groups: Polish 98%, small minorities of German, Byelorussian, and Ukrainian
Government: Republic
Literacy (1991): 98%
Life Expectancy at Birth (1991): 77 years female, 69 years male
Infant Mortality (per 1,000 live births 1991): 14
Gross Domestic Product (1993): $63.7 billion
GDP per Capita: $1,660
Principal Industries: Shipbuilding, chemicals, metals, autos, food processing
Principal Crops: Grains, potatoes, sugar beets, tobacco, flax

PORTUGAL
Republic of Portugal
República Portuguesa

Area: 35,550 sq. mi. (92,075 sq. km.)
Population: 10,388,000
Language: Portuguese
Capital: Lisbon

PORTUGAL (continued)

Currency: Escudo
Religion: Roman Catholic 97%, other 3%
Ethnic Groups: Portuguese with small African minority
Government: Democracy
Literacy (1990): 83%
Life Expectancy at Birth (1991): 78 years female, 71 years male
Infant Mortality (per 1,000 live births 1991): 13
Gross Domestic Product (1993): $80 billion
GDP per Capita: $7,600
Principal Industries: Textiles, footwear, cork, chemicals, fish, canning, wine, paper
Principal Crops: Grains, potatoes, rice, grapes, olives, fruits

QATAR

State of Qatar
Dawlet al-Qatar

Area: 4,000 sq. mi. (11,435 sq. km.)
Population: 518,000
Language: Arabic 56% (official), Farsi 23%, Urdu 7%, other 14%
Capital: Doha
Currency: Qatari riyal
Religion: Muslim (Sunni) 93%, other 7%
Ethnic Groups: Arab 40%, Pakistani 18%, Iranian 14%, Indian 10%, other 18%
Government: Emirate
Literacy (1991): 76%
Life Expectancy at Birth (1991): 74 years female, 69 years male
Infant Mortality (per 1,000 live births 1990): 24
Gross Domestic Product (1988): $6.6 billion
GDP per Capita: $12,500
Principal Industries: Oil

ROMANIA

Republic of Romania
Republica Socialista România

Area: 91,700 sq. mi. (237,500 sq. km.)
Population: 23,397,000
Language: Romanian 87% (official), Magyar 9%, German 2%, other 2%
Capital: Bucharest
Currency: Leu
Religion: Romanian Orthodox 86.8%, Roman Catholic, Protestant 13.2%
Ethnic Groups: Romanian 89%, Hungarian 8%, German 3%
Government: Republic
Literacy (1991): 96%
Life Expectancy at Birth (1991): 75 years female, 69 years male
Infant Mortality (per 1,000 live births): 18
Gross Domestic Product (1993): $15.8 billion
GDP per Capita: $680
Principal Industries: Steel, metals, machinery, oil products, chemicals, textiles, shoes
Principal Crops: Grains, sunflowers, vegetables, potatoes

RUSSIA

Russian Federation

Area: 6,592,800 sq. mi. (17,075,400 sq. km.)
Population: 148,542,700
Language: Russian (official) 87%, other including Chuvash, Ukrainian, Byelorussian, Uzbek, Armenian, Azerbaijani, Georgian, Mordvin 13%
Capital: Moscow
Currency: Ruble
Religion: Russian Orthodox
Ethnic Groups: Russian 82%, Tatar 3%, other 15%
Government: Republic
Literacy (1991): 99%
Life Expectancy at Birth (1991): 74 years female, 64 years male
Infant Mortality (per 1,000 live births): 25.2
Gross Domestic Product (1993): $137.8 billion
GDP per Capita: $929
Principal Industries: Steel, machinery, machine tools, vehicles, chemicals, cement, textiles, appliances, paper

Principal Crops: Grain, cotton, sugar beets, potatoes, vegetables, sunflowers

RWANDA

Republic of Rwanda
Republika y'u Rwanda

Area: 10,170 sq. mi. (26,338 sq. km.)
Population: 7,903,000
Language: Ruanda 100%, French (both official)
Capital: Kigali
Currency: Rwanda franc
Religion: Roman Catholic 56%, traditional 25%, Protestant 18%, Muslim 1%
Ethnic Groups: Hutu 90%, Tutsi 9%, Twa (pygmy) 1%
Government: Republic
Literacy (1991): 50%
Life Expectancy at Birth (1991): 54 years female, 51 years male
Infant Mortality (per 1,000 live births): 110
Gross Domestic Product (1989): $2.1 billion
GDP per Capita: $310
Principal Industries: Agriculture, mining
Principal Crops: Coffee, tea

ST. KITTS AND NEVIS

Federation of St. Kitts and Nevis

Area: 100 sq. mi. (262 sq. km.)
Population: 40,000
Language: English (official), English Creole 100%
Capital: Basseterre (on St. Kitts)
Currency: East Caribbean dollar
Religion: Protestant 76%, other 24%
Ethnic Groups: Black 91%, mixed 5%, Native American 3%, white or European descent 1%
Government: Constitutional monarchy
Literacy (1991): 98%
Gross Domestic Product (1988): $97.5 million
GDP per Capita: $2,400
Principal Industries: Tourism, sugar processing
Principal Crops: Sugar, cotton

ST. LUCIA

Area: 238 sq. mi. (616 sq. km.)
Population: 153,000
Language: English (official), French Creole 100%
Capital: Castries
Currency: East Caribbean dollar
Religion: Roman Catholic 90%, Protestant 7%, Anglican 3%
Ethnic Groups: Black 90%, mixed 6%, Native American 3%, other 1%
Government: Democracy
Literacy (1989): 78%
Life Expectancy at Birth (1991): 74 years female, 69 years male
Infant Mortality (per 1,000 live births): 18
Gross Domestic Product (1989): $267 million
GDP per Capita: $1,180
Principal Industries: Agriculture, tourism, manufacturing
Principal Crops: Bananas, coconuts, cocoa, citrus fruits

ST. VINCENT AND THE GRENADINES

Area: 150 sq. mi. (389 sq. km.)
Population: 114,000
Language: English (official), English Creole
Capital: Kingstown
Currency: East Caribbean dollar
Religion: Anglican 47%, Methodist 28%, Roman Catholic 13%, other 12%
Ethnic Groups: Black 74%, mulatto 19%, white or European descent 3%, Native American 4%
Government: Constitutional monarchy
Literacy (1989): 85%
Life Expectancy at Birth (1991): 74 years female, 69 years male
Infant Mortality (per 1,000 live births): 31
Gross Domestic Product (1989): $146 million
GDP per Capita (1989): $1,315

Principal Industries: Agriculture, tourism
Principal Crops: Bananas, arrowroot, coconuts

SAN MARINO

Most Serene Republic of San Marino
Serenissima Republica di San Marino

Area: 23.6 sq. mi. (62 sq. km.)
Population: 23,000
Language: Italian
Capital: San Marino
Currency: Lira
Religion: Roman Catholic 95%, other 5%
Ethnic Groups: San Marinese 84%, Italian 15%
Government: Republic
Literacy (1991): 97%
Infant Mortality (per 1,000 live births 1991): 8
Gross Domestic Product (1990): $393 million
GDP per Capita: $17,000
Principal Industries: Postage stamps, tourism, woolen goods, paper, cement, ceramics

SAO TOMÉ AND PRINCIPE

Democratic Republic of Sao Tomé and Principe
República Democrática de Sao Tomé e Principe

Area: 370 sq. mi. (958 sq. km.)
Population: 128,000
Language: Portuguese (official), Criulo
Capital: Sao Tomé
Currency: Dobra
Religion: Roman Catholic 83%, Protestant 17%
Ethnic Groups: Servicais (Tonga) 60%, Farros 26%, Angolares 7%, mestizo 6%, other 1%
Government: Republic
Literacy (1988): 50%
Infant Mortality (per 1,000 live births 1991): 60
Gross Domestic Product (1989): $46 million
GDP per Capita: $384
Principal Industries: Agriculture, fishing
Principal Crops: Cocoa, coconuts, copra, coffee

SAUDI ARABIA

Kingdom of Saudi Arabia
al-Mamlaka al-'Arabiya as-Sa'udiya

Area: 840,000 sq. mi. (2,200,000 sq. km.)
Population: 17,870,000
Language: Arabic
Capital: Riyadh
Currency: Riyal
Religion: Muslim 99%, other 1%
Ethnic Groups: Arab 95%, other 5%
Government: Monarchy
Literacy (1990): 62%
Life Expectancy at Birth: 68 years female, 65 years male
Infant Mortality (per 1,000 live births 1991): 69
Gross Domestic Product (1993): $122.4 billion
GDP per Capita: $7,463
Principal Industries: Oil products, plastic products, steel, packaged goods
Principal Crops: Dates, wheat, barley, fruit

SENEGAL

Republic of Senegal
République du Sénégal

Area: 75,750 sq. mi. (196,700 sq. km.)
Population: 7,953,000
Language: French (official), Wolof 44%, Tukulor 21%, Serer 16%, Mandinka 6%, Malinke 3%, other 10%
Capital: Dakar
Currency: Franc CFA
Religion: Muslim (Sunni) 92%, indigenous 6%, Christian 2%

Ethnic Groups: Wolof 36%, Serer 17%, Fulani 17%, Diola 9%, Toucouleur 9%, Mandingo 6%, other 6%
Government: Republic
Literacy (1988): 38%
Life Expectancy at Birth: 56 years female, 54 years male
Infant Mortality (per 1,000 live births 1991): 86
Gross Domestic Product (1989): $4.7 billion
GDP per Capita: $615
Principal Industries: Processed foods, phosphates, refined petroleum, cement, fishing
Principal Crops: Peanuts, grains, sorghum

SEYCHELLES

Republic of Seychelles

Area: 175 sq. mi. (453 sq. km.)
Population: 69,000
Language: French 3%, English 2% (both official), French Creole 94%, other 1%
Capital: Victoria
Currency: Seychelles rupee
Religion: Roman Catholic 90%, other 10%
Ethnic Groups: Creole (mixture of Asian, African, and French) 89%, Indian 5%, Malagasy 3%, other 3%
Government: Republic
Literacy (1989): 80%
Life Expectancy at Birth (1991): 71 years female, 65 years male
Infant Mortality (per 1,000 live births 1991): 15
Gross Domestic Product (1989): $285 million
GDP per Capita: $4,1790
Principal Industries: Processed coconut and vanilla, coir rope
Principal Crops: Coconuts, cinnamon, vanilla, patchouli

SIERRA LEONE

Republic of Sierra Leone

Area: 27,700 sq. mi. (71,740 sq. km.)
Population: 4,275,000
Language: English (official), Mende 31%, Temne 30%, Limba 9%, Kono 5%, Kuranko 4%, Sherbro 3%, Susu 3%, Loko 3%, other 12%
Capital: Freetown
Currency: Leone
Religion: Traditional 50%, Muslim 31%, Christian 10%, other 9%
Ethnic Groups: Temne 30%, Mende 29%, other 41%
Government: Military
Literacy (1991): 21%
Life Expectancy at Birth (1991): 48 years female, 42 years male
Infant Mortality (per 1,000 live births 1991): 151
Gross Domestic Product (1989): $1.3 billion
GDP per Capita: $325
Principal Industries: Mining, tourism
Principal Crops: coffee, cocoa, palm kernels, rice

SINGAPORE

Republic of Singapore

Area: 246.7 sq. mi. (639 sq. km.)
Population: 2,756,000
Language: Chinese (Mandarin) 56%, Malay 15%, English 9%, Tamil 4%, (all official), other 16%
Capital: Singapore
Currency: Singapore dollar
Religion: Buddhism 29%, Christian 19%, Muslim 16%, Taoist 13%, other 23%
Ethnic Groups: Chinese 77%, Malay 15%, Indian 6%, other 2%
Government: Republic
Literacy (1990): 87%
Life Expectancy at Birth (1991): 77 years female, 72 years male
Infant Mortality (per 1,000 live births 1991): 8
Gross Domestic Product (1990): $34.6 billion
GDP per Capita: $12,700
Principal Industries: Petroleum refining, ship repair, electronics, financial and business services
Principal Crops: Vegetables and fruits

SLOVAKIA

Slovak Republic
Slovenská Republika

Area: 18,919 sq. mi. (48,951 sq. km.)
Population: 5,297,000
Language: Slovak
Capital: Bratislava
Currency: Koruna
Religion: Christian
Government: Republic
Gross Domestic Product (1993): $10 billion
GDP per Capita: $1,900

SLOVENIA

Republic of Slovenia
Slovenija

Area: 7,820 sq. mi. (20,250 sq. km.)
Population: 1,962,600
Language: Predominantly Slovene (official) , Serbo-Croatian
Capital: Ljubljana
Currency: Tolar
Religion: Roman Catholic
Ethnic Groups: Slovene majority, Serbian, Croatian, Hungarian minorities
Government: Democracy
Literacy (1991): 90%
Life Expectancy at Birth (1991): 76 years female, 70 years male
Infant Mortality (per 1,000 live births 1991): 22
Principal Industries: Agriculture, automobiles, iron, steel, cement, textiles
Principal Crops: Corn, rye, oats, potatoes, fruit

SOLOMON ISLANDS

Area: 11,500 sq. mi. (29,785 sq. km.)
Population: 347,000
Language: English (official), Melanesian 67%, Papuan 33%
Capital: Honiara
Currency: Solomon dollar
Religion: Anglican 34%, Evangelical 24%, local 23%, Roman Catholic 19%
Ethnic Groups: Melanesian 93%, Polynesian 4%, other 3%
Government: Democracy
Literacy (1989): 60%
Life Expectancy at Birth (1991): 67 years male, 72 years female
Infant Mortality (per 1,000 live births): 39
Gross Domestic Product (1989): $156 million
GDP per Capita: $570
Principal Industries: Fish canning, copra
Principal Crops: Coconuts, rice, bananas

SOMALIA

Somali Democratic Republic
al-Jimhouriya as-Somalya al-Dimocradia

Area: 246,200 sq. mi. (637,655 sq. km)
Population: 6,709,000
Language: Somali 97% Arabic 1% (both official), other 2%
Capital: Mogadishu
Currency: Somali shilling
Religion: Muslim (Sunni)
Ethnic Groups: Somali 98%, other 2%
Government: Anarchy
Literacy (1990): 24%
Life Expectancy at Birth (1991): 56 years female, 56 years male
Infant Mortality (per 1,000 live births): 116
Gross Domestic Product (1989): $1.7 billion
GDP per Capita: $210
Principal Industries: Agriculture
Principal Crops: Incense, sugar, bananas, sorghum, corn, gum

SOUTH AFRICA

Republic of South Africa
Republiek van Suid-Afrika

Area: 471,440 sq. mi. (1,221,000 sq. km.)
Population: 40,601,000
Language: Afrikaans 16%, English 9% (both official), Xhosa 25%, Zulu 20%, Sotho 15%, Tswana 8%, Tsonga (Thonga) 3%, other 4%
Capital: Pretoria (legislative capital, Cape Town)
Currency: Rand
Religion: Mostly Christian, Muslim, and Hindu
Ethnic Groups: Black 75%, white 14%, colored 8%, Asian 3%
Government: Republic
Literacy: 76% (total), 99% (white), 69% (Asian), 62% (colored)
Life Expectancy at Birth (1991): 67 years female, 61 years male
Infant Mortality (per 1,000 live births 1991): 51
Gross Domestic Product (1993): $123.3 billion
GDP per Capita: $3,312
Principal Industries: Mining, steel, tires, motors, textiles, plastics
Principal Crops: Corn, wool, dairy products, grain, tobacco, sugar, fruit, peanuts, grapes

SPAIN

Kingdom of Spain
España

Area: 194,884 sq. mi. (504,750 sq. km.)
Population: 39,385,000
Language: Spanish 70% (official), Catalán 21%, Galician 7%, Basque 1%, other 1%
Capital: Madrid
Currency: Peseta
Religion: Roman Catholic 90%, other 10%
Ethnic Groups: Spanish 72.8%, Catalán 16.4%, Galician 8.2%, Basque 2.3%
Government: Constitutional monarchy
Literacy (1991): 97%
Life Expectancy at Birth (1991): 82 years female, 75 years male
Infant Mortality (per 1,000 live births): 6
Gross Domestic Product (1990): $540 billion
GDP per Capita: $13,600
Principal Industries: Machinery, steel, textiles, shoes, autos, processed foods
Principal Crops: Grains, olives, grapes, citrus fruits, vegetables, olives

SRI LANKA

Democratic Socialist Republic of Sri Lanka
Sri Lanka Prajathanthrika Samajavadi Janarajaya

Area: 25,330 sq. mi. (65,610 sq. km.)
Population: 17,424,000
Language: Sinhalese 67%, Tamil 33% (both official)
Capital: Colombo (Sri Jeyewardenepura Kotte)
Currency: Sri Lanka rupee
Religion: Buddhist 69%, Hindu 15%, Muslim 8%, Christian 8%
Ethnic Groups: Sinhalese 74%, Tamil 17%, Moor 7%, other 2%
Government: Republic
Literacy (1990): 90%
Life Expectancy at Birth (1991): 74 years female, 69 years male
Infant Mortality (per 1,000 live births): 21
Gross Domestic Product (1990): $6.6 billion
GDP per Capita: $380
Principal Industries: Plywood, paper, milling, chemicals, textiles
Principal Crops: Tea, coconuts, rice

SUDAN

Republic of the Sudan
Jamhuryat as-Sudan

Area: 967,490 sq. mi. (2,505,802 sq. km.)
Population: 27,220, 000
Language: Arabic 51% (official), Dinka 10%, other African 39%
Capital: Khartoum
Currency: Sudanese pound

Religion: Muslim (Sunni) 70%, animist 18%, Christian 5%, other 7%
Ethnic Groups: Black 52%, Arab 39%, Beja 6%, other 3%
Government: Military
Literacy (1991): 27%
Life Expectancy at Birth (1991): 54 years female, 52 years male
Infant Mortality (per 1,000 live births 1991): 85
Gross Domestic Product: $8.5 billion
GDP per Capita: $380
Principal Industries: Agriculture, textiles, food processing
Principal Crops: Gum arabic, durra, cotton, sesame, peanuts, rice, coffee, sugarcane, wheat, dates

SURINAME
Republic of Suriname

Area: 63,250 sq. mi. (163,820 sq. km.)
Population: 402,000
Language: Dutch (official), Surinamese 33%, Hindi 33%, Javanese 13%, English Creole 11%, other 10%
Capital: Paramaribo
Currency: Suriname guilder
Religion: Christian 47%, Hindu 27%, Muslim 19%, other 7%
Ethnic Groups: Hindustani 37%, Creole 31%, Javanese 15%, other 17%
Government: Republic
Literacy (1989): 65%
Life Expectancy at Birth (1991): 71 years female, 66 years male
Infant Mortality (per 1,000 live births 1991): 40
Gross Domestic Product (1989): $1.3 billion
GDP per Capita: $3,400
Principal Industries: Aluminum
Principal Crops: Rice, sugar, fruits

SWAZILAND
Kingdom of Swaziland

Area: 6,700 sq. mi. (17,360 sq. km.)
Population: 859,000
Language: Swazi 91%, English 9% (both official)
Capital: Mbabane
Currency: Lilangeni
Religion: Christian 60%, local 40%
Ethnic Groups: Swazi 90%, Zulu 2.3%, European 2.1%, other 3.3%
Government: Monarchy
Literacy (1990): 65%
Life Expectancy at Birth: 59 years female, 51 years male
Infant Mortality (per 1,000 live births 1991): 101
Gross National Product (1990): $563 billion
GNP per Capita: $670
Principal Industries: Wood pulp
Principal Crops: Sugar, corn, cotton, rice, pineapples, sugar, citrus fruits

SWEDEN
Kingdom of Sweden
Konungariket Sverige

Area: 173,800 sq. mi. (449,965 sq. km.)
Population: 8,564,000
Language: Swedish 93%, Finn 3%, other 4%
Capital: Stockholm
Currency: Krona
Religion: Lutheran 95%, other 5%
Ethnic Groups: Swedish 91%, Finnish 3%, Lapp, European immigrants 6%
Government: Constitutional monarchy
Literacy (1991): 99%
Life Expectancy at Birth: 81 years female, 75 years male
Infant Mortality (per 1,000 live births 1991): 6
Gross Domestic Product (1993): $260 billion
GDP per Capita: $29,600
Principal Industries: Steel, machinery, instruments, autos, shipbuilding, shipping, paper
Principal Crops: Grains, potatoes, sugar beets

SWITZERLAND
Swiss Confederation
Suisse

Area: 15,940 sq. mi. (41,285 sq. km.)
Population: 6,784,000
Language: German, French, Italian (all official)
Capital: Bern
Currency: Swiss franc
Religion: Roman Catholic 49%, Protestant 48%, other 3%
Ethnic Groups: Mixed European stock
Government: Republic
Literacy (1991): 99%
Life Expectancy at Birth (1991): 83 years female, 75 years male
Infant Mortality (per 1,000 live births 1991): 5
Gross Domestic Product (1993): $240 billion
GDP per Capita: $35,500
Principal Industries: Watches and clocks, precision instruments, machinery, foodstuffs, banking, tourism
Principal Crops: Grains, potatoes, sugar beets, vegetables, tobacco

SYRIA
Syrian Arab Republic
al-Jamhouriya al-Arabia as-Souriya

Area: 71,500 sq. mi. (185,180 sq. km.)
Population: 12,966,000
Language: Arabic 88% (official), Kurdish 6%, Armenian 3%, other 3%
Capital: Damascus
Currency: Syrian pound
Religion: Muslim 90% (Sunni 74%), Christian 10%
Ethnic Groups: Arab 90%, Kurd, Armenian, other 10%
Government: Military
Literacy (1990): 64%
Life Expectancy at Birth (1991): 71 years female, 68 years male
Infant Mortality (per 1,000 live births 1991): 37
Gross Domestic Product (1990): $20 billion
GDP per Capita: $1,600
Principal Industries: Textiles, phosphates, oil products, tobacco, glassware, brassware
Principal Crops: Cotton, grain, olives, fruits, vegetables

TAJIKISTAN
Republic of Tajikistan
Respubliki i Tojikiston

Area: 55,300 sq. mi. (143,100 sq. km.)
Population: 5,500,000
Language: Tajiki 59%, Uzbek 22%, Russian 13%, other 6%
Capital: Dushanbe
Currency: Ruble
Religion: Muslim (predominantly Sunni)
Ethnic Groups: Tajik 55%, Uzbek 23%, Russian 13%, other 9%
Government: Republic
Literacy (1991): 98%
Life Expectancy at Birth: 74 years female, 65 years male
Infant Mortality (per 1,000 live births 1991): 43
Principal Industries: Cement, knitwear, footwear
Principal Crops: Barley, cotton, wheat, vegetables

TANZANIA
United Republic of Tanzania
Jamhuri ya Mwungano wa Tanzania

Area: 364,875 sq. mi. (945,035 sq. km.)
Population: 26,869,000
Language: Swahili 9%, English (both official), Nyamwezi-Sukuma 21%, Luo, Makua, several other African 70%
Capital: Dar es Salaam
Currency: Tanzanian shilling
Religion: Christian 34%, Muslim 33%, local 33%
Ethnic Groups: Nyamwezi-Sukuma 21%, Swahili 9%, Hehet 7%, Makonde 6%, Haya 6%, other 51%
Government: Republic

TANZANIA (continued)

Literacy (1987): 85%
Life Expectancy at Birth (1991): 55 years female, 50 years male
Infant Mortality (per 1,000 live births): 105
Gross Domestic Product: $5.9 billion
GDP per Capita: $240
Principal Industries: Textiles, wood products, refined oil, processed agricultural products, diamonds, cement
Principal Crops: Sisal, cotton, coffee, tea, tobacco

THAILAND

Kingdom of Thailand
Muang Thai

Area: 198,455 sq. mi. (514,000 sq. km.)
Population: 56,814,000
Language: Thai 92% (official), Chinese 2%, Malay 2%, Khmer 2%, other 2%
Capital: Bangkok
Currency: Baht
Religion: Buddhist 96%, Muslim 4%
Ethnic Groups: Siamese 53%, Lao 27%, Chinese 12%, Malay 4%, Khmer 2%, other 2%
Government: Military
Literacy (1991): 89%
Life Expectancy at Birth (1991): 71 years female, 66 years male
Infant Mortality (per 1,000 live births 1991): 37
Gross National Product (1993): $117 billion
GNP per Capita: $1,605
Principal Industries: Textiles, mining, wood products, tourism
Principal Crops: Rice, corn tapioca, sugarcane

TOGO

Republic of Togo
République Togolaise

Area: 21,925 sq. mi. (56,785 sq. km.)
Population: 3,811,000
Language: French (official), Ewe 22%, Mina, Gur, Kwa dialects, Fon and other African 78%
Capital: Lomé
Currency: Franc CFA
Religion: Local 70%, Christian 20%, Muslim 10%
Ethnic Groups: Ewe 35%, Kabye 22%, Mina 6%, other 37%
Government: Republic
Literacy (1990): 45% (male)
Life Expectancy at Birth (1991): 58 years female, 54 years male
Infant Mortality (per 1,000 live births 1991): 110
Gross Domestic Product (1989): $1.4 billion
GDP per Capita: $395
Principal Industries: Textiles, shoes
Principal Crops: Coffee, cocoa, yams, manioc, millet, rice

TONGA

Kingdom of Tonga
Pule 'anga Tonga

Area: 290 sq. mi. (751 sq. km.)
Population: 102,000
Language: Tongan 98%, English (both official), other 2%
Capital: Nuku'alofa
Currency: Pa'anga
Religion: Free Wesleyan 47%, Roman Catholic 14%, Free Church of Tonga 14% Mormons 9%, Church of Tonga 9%, other 7%
Ethnic Groups: Tongan 98%, other 2%
Government: Constitutional monarchy
Literacy (1988): 99%
Life Expectancy at Birth (1991): 70 years female, 65 years male
Infant Mortality (per 1,000 live births 1991): 23
Gross Domestic Product (1989): $86 million
GDP per Capita: $850
Principal Industries: Tourism, agriculture, fishing
Principal Crops: Coconut products, bananas

TRINIDAD AND TOBAGO

Republic of Trinidad and Tobago

Area: 1,980 sq. mi. (5,128 sq. km.)
Population: 1,285,000
Language: English 53% (official), English Creole 43%, Hindi 4%
Capital: Port-of-Spain
Currency: Trinidad and Tobago dollar
Religion: Roman Catholic 32%, Protestant 29%, Hindu 25%, Muslim 6%, other 18%
Ethnic Groups: Black 43%, East Indian 40%, mixed 14%, other 3%
Government: Constitutional monarchy
Literacy (1988): 97%
Life Expectancy at Birth (1991): 72 years female, 68 years male
Infant Mortality (per 1,000 live births): 18
Gross Domestic Product (1989): $4.05 billion
GDP per Capita: $3,363
Principal Industries: Oil products, processed food, cement, tourism
Principal Crops: Sugar, cocoa, coffee, citrus fruits, bananas

TUNISIA

Republic of Tunisia
al-Jumhuriyah at-Tunisiyah

Area: 63,380 sq. mi. (164,150 sq. km.)
Population: 8,276,000
Language: Arabic 99% (official), other, French widely spoken
Capital: Tunis
Currency: Tunisian dinar
Religion: Muslim (Sunni)
Ethnic Groups: Arab 98%, other 2%
Government: Republic
Literacy (1990): 62%
Life Expectancy at Birth (1991): 74 years female, 70 years male
Infant Mortality (per 1,000 live births 1991): 38
Gross Domestic Product (1990): $10 billion
GDP per Capita: $1,253
Principal Industries: Food processing, textiles, oil products, mining, construction materials
Principal Crops: Grains, dates, olives, citrus fruits, figs, vegetables, grapes

TURKEY

Republic of Turkey
Turkiye Cumhuriyeti

Area: 300,945 sq. mi. (779,450 sq. km.)
Population: 58,581,000
Language: Turkish 90% (official), Kurdish 9%, other 1%
Capital: Ankara
Currency: Turkish lira
Religion: Muslim (Sunni)
Ethnic Groups: Turk 80%, Kurd 17%, other 3%
Government: Republic
Literacy (1990): 81%
Life Expectancy at Birth: 72 years female, 68 years male
Infant Mortality (per 1,000 live births 1991): 54
Gross Domestic Product (1993): $130 billion
GDP per Capita: $2,170
Principal Industries: Textiles, coal, minerals, processed foods, steel, petroleum
Principal Crops: Tobacco, cereals, cotton, barley, corn, fruits, potatoes, sugar beets

TURKMENISTAN

Republic of Turkmenistan

Area: 188,500 sq. mi. (488,100 sq. km.)
Population: 3,900,000
Language: Turkoman 68% (official), Russian 15%, Uzbek 8%, Kazakh 3%, other 6%
Capital: Ashkhabad
Currency: Ruble
Religion: Muslim
Ethnic Groups: Turkoman 68%, Russian 13%, Uzbek 9%, other 10%

Government: Republic
Literacy (1991): 98%
Life Expectancy at Birth (1991): 74 years female, 65 years male
Infant Mortality (per 1,000 live births 1991): 55
Principal Industries: Mining, textiles
Principal Crops: Grain, cotton, grapes

TUVALU

Area: 10 sq. mi. (26 sq. km.)
Population: 9,250
Language: English (official), Tuvaluan 97%, Ikiribati 3%
Capital: Funafuti
Currency: Australian dollar
Religion: Congregationalist 97%, other 3%
Ethnic Groups: Tuvaluan 91%, mixed 7%, other 2%
Government: Constitutional monarchy
Literacy (1990): 96%
Life Expectancy at Birth (1991): 63 years female, 60 years male
Infant Mortality (per 1,000 live births 1991): 33
Gross National Product (1989): $4.6 million
GNP per Capita: $530
Principal Industries: Copra
Principal Crops: Coconuts

UGANDA

Republic of Uganda

Area: 93,000 sq. mi. (237,000 sq. km.)
Population: 18,690,000
Language: English (official), Luganda 16%, Teso 8%, Ruanda and other African 76%
Capital: Kampala
Currency: Ugandan shilling
Religion: Roman Catholic 46%, Protestant 26%, traditional 13%, Muslim 7%, other 7%
Ethnic Groups: Ganda 18%, Teso 9%, Nkole 8%, Soga 8%, Gisu 7%, Chiga 7%, Lango 6%, Ruanda 6%, Acholi 5%, other 26%
Government: Military
Literacy (1989): 52%
Life Expectancy at Birth (1991): 52 years female, 50 years male
Infant Mortality (per 1,000 live births 1991): 94
Gross Domestic Product (1989): $4.9 billion
GDP per Capita: $300
Principal Industries: Sugar refining, beer, tobacco, cotton, textiles, cement
Principal Crops: Coffee, cotton, tea, corn, bananas, sugar

UKRAINE

Ukrayina

Area: 233,000 sq. mi. (603,700 sq. km.)
Population: 52,100,000
Language: Ukrainian 66% (official), Russian 31%, other 3%
Capital: Kiev
Currency: Coupon
Religion: Orthodox 76%, Ukrainian Catholic 13.5%, Muslim 8.2%, other 2.3%
Ethnic Groups: Ukrainian 73%, Russian 21%, other 6%
Government: Republic
Literacy (1992): 99%
Life Expectancy at Birth (1991): 75 years female, 66 years male
Infant Mortality (per 1,000 live births 1991): 13
Gross Domestic Product (1993): $9.7 billion
GDP per Capita: $188
Principal Industries: Steel, chemicals, machinery, vehicles, cement
Principal Crops: Grains, sugar beets, potatoes

UNITED ARAB EMIRATES

Ittihäd al-Imarat al-Arabiyah

Area: 32,00 sq. mi. (82,880 sq. km.)
Population: 2,390,000
Language: Arabic 48% (official), Maylayalam 19%, Baluchi 6%, Pashto 6%, Farsi, Bengali 4%, Tagalog 3%, Sinhalese 2%, Somali 2%, other 5%

Capital: Abu Dhabi
Currency: Dirham
Religion: Muslim 96% (Sunni 80%, Shi'ite 16%) other 4%
Ethnic Groups: Arab 87%, Iranian and Pakistani 9%, other 4%
Government: Emirate federation
Literacy (1989): 68%
Life Expectancy at Birth (1991): 74 years female, 69 years male
Infant Mortality (per 1,000 live births): 23
Gross Domestic Product (1989): $28.4 billion
GDP per Capita: $12,100
Principal Industries: Oil, light manufacturing, construction materials
Principal Crops: Vegetables, dates, limes

UNITED KINGDOM

United Kingdom of Great Britain and Northern Ireland

Area: 94,247 sq. mi. (244,100 sq. km.)
Population: 57,515,000
Language: English 98%, Welsh (spoken in western Wales), Scots, Gaelic 2%
Capital: London
Currency: Pound sterling
Religion: Anglican 57%, other Protestant 15%, Roman Catholic 13%, other 15%
Ethnic Groups: English 81.5%, Scottish 9.6%, Irish 2.4%, Welsh 1.9%, Ulster 1.8%, West Indian, Indian, Pakistani 2%, other 2.6%
Government: Constitutional monarchy
Literacy (1991): 97%
Life Expectancy at Birth (1991): 79 years female, 73 years male
Infant Mortality (per 1,000 live births 1991): 7
Gross Domestic Product (1993): $1 trillion
GDP per Capita: $17,300
Principal Industries: Steel, metals, vehicles, shipbuilding, banking, textiles, chemicals, electronics, aircraft, machinery, distilling
Principal Crops: Grains, sugar beets, fruits, vegetables

UNITED STATES

The United States of America

Area: 3,536,341 sq. mi. (9,159,123 sq. km.)
Population: 252,502,000
Language: English 89%, Spanish 6%, other 5%
Capital: Washington, D.C.
Currency: Dollar
Religion: Protestant 61%, Roman Catholic 25%, Jewish 2%, other 12%
Ethnic Groups: White or European descent 71.3%, African-American 12%, Latino/Chicano 9%, Asian 3%, Native American and Eskimo 1%, other 3.7%
Government: Democracy
Literacy (1991): 97%
Life Expectancy at Birth (1991): 79 years female, 72 years male
Infant Mortality (per 1,000 live births 1991): 10
Gross National Product (1993): $5.6 trillion
GNP per Capita: $22,520
Principal Industries: Petroleum products, cement, iron and steel, plastics, newsprint, motor vehicles, machinery
Principal Crops: Grains, sugar, potatoes, soybeans, fruit

URUGUAY

Republic of Uruguay
República del Uruguay

Area: 68,040 sq. mi. (176,224 sq. km.)
Population: 3,121,000
Language: Spanish
Capital: Montevideo
Currency: Peso
Religion: Roman Catholic 66%, other 34%
Ethnic Groups: Hispanic 86%, mestizo 3%, Italian 3%, Jewish 2%, other 6%
Government: Republic
Literacy (1990): 96%
Life Expectancy at Birth (1991): 76 years female, 69 years male
Infant Mortality (per 1,000 live births 1991): 22
Gross Domestic Product (1990): $9.2 billion

URUGUAY (continued)

GDP per Capita: $2,970
Principal Industries: Meatpacking, textiles, wine, cement, oil products
Principal Crops: Corn, wheat, citrus fruits, rice, oats, linseed

UZBEKISTAN
Ozbekiston Republikasy

Area: 172,700 sq. mi. (447,400 sq. km.)
Population: 21,300,000
Language: Uzbek 69% (official), Russian 13%, Kazakh 4%, Tajik 4%, Tatar 3%, other 7%
Capital: Tashkent
Currency: Ruble
Religion: Predominantly Muslim (Sunni)
Ethnic Groups: Uzbek 70%, Russian 11%, other 19%
Government: Republic
Literacy (1991): 98%
Life Expectancy at Birth (1991): 74 years female, 65 years male
Infant Mortality (per 1,000 live births 1991): 38
Principal Industries: Steel, tractors, cars, textiles
Principal Crops: Cotton, rice

VANUATU
Republic of Vanuatu
Ripablik Blong Vanuatu

Area: 5,700 sq. mi. (14,765 sq. km.)
Population: 170,000
Language: French, English (both official), Melanesian 94%, other 6%
Capital: Port Vila
Currency: Vatu
Religion: Presbyterian 40%, Roman Catholic 16%, animist 15%, Anglican 14%, other 15%
Ethnic Groups: Vanuatuan 97%, other 3%
Government: Republic
Literacy: 90%
Life Expectancy at Birth (1991): 72 years female, 67 years male
Infant Mortality (per 1,000 live births 1991): 37
Gross Domestic Product (1989): $131 million
GDP per Capita: $860
Principal Industries: Fish-freezing, meat canneries, tourism
Principal Crops: Copra, cocoa, coffee

VATICAN CITY
The Holy See

Area: 0.17 sq. mi. (0.44 sq. km.)
Population: 778
Language: Latin and Italian
Currency: Lira
Religion: Roman Catholic
Ethnic Groups: Italian, Swiss
Government: Papal

VENEZUELA
Republic of Venezuela
Republica de Venezuela

Area: 352,145 sq. mi. (912,050 sq. km.)
Population: 20,189,000
Language: Spanish 97% (official), various indigenous 2%, other 1%
Capital: Caracas
Currency: Bolívar
Religion: Roman Catholic 92%, other 8%
Ethnic Groups: Mestizo 69%, white (Spanish, Portuguese, Italian descent) 20%, black 9%, Native American 2%
Government: Republic
Literacy (1991): 88%
Life Expectancy at Birth (1991): 78 years female, 71 years male
Infant Mortality (per 1,000 live births 1991): 26
Gross Domestic Product (1990): $42.4 billion
GDP per Capita: $2,150

Principal Industries: Steel, oil, aluminum, cement, textiles, transport equipment
Principal Crops: Coffee, rice, fruits, sugar

VIETNAM
Socialist Republic of Vietnam
Cong Hoa Xa Hoi Chu Nghia Viet Nam

Area: 127,245 sq. mi. (329,565 sq. km.)
Population: 67,568,000
Language: Vietnamese 90% (official), Tai 3%, other 7%
Capital: Ho Chi Minh City
Currency: Dong
Religion: Buddhist 55%, Roman Catholic 7%, Taoist 3%, Hoa Hao 2%, other 33%
Ethnic Groups: Vietnamese 84%, Chinese 2%, Muong, Thai, Khmer, Man, Cham 14%
Government: Communist
Literacy (1989): 88%
Life Expectancy at Birth (1991): 67 years female, 63 years male
Infant Mortality (per 1,000 live births 1991): 48
Gross National Product (1990): $15.2 billion
GNP per Capita: $230
Principal Industries: Food processing, textiles, cement, chemical fertilizers
Principal Crops: Rice, rubber, fruits and vegetables, corn, manioc, sugarcane

WESTERN SAMOA
Independent State of Western Samoa
Malotuto'atasi o Samoa i Sisifo

Area: 1,093 sq. mi. (2,831 sq. km.)
Population: 190,000
Language: Samoan 99%, English (both official), other 1%
Capital: Apia
Currency: Tala
Religion: Protestant 70%, Roman Catholic 20%, other 10%
Ethnic Groups: Samoan (Polynesian) 88%, Euronesian (mixed) 10%, other 2%
Government: Constitutional monarchy
Literacy (1989): 90%
Life Expectancy at Birth (1991): 69 years female, 64 years male
Infant Mortality (per 1,000 live births 1991): 48
Gross Domestic Product (1989): $114 million
GDP per Capita: $620
Principal Industries: Agriculture, timber, processed foods, fishing
Principal Crops: Copra, coconuts, cocoa, bananas, taro, yams

YEMEN
Republic of Yemen
al-Jumhurïyah al-Yamanïyah

Area: 303,850 sq. mi. (527,970 sq. km.)
Population: 10,063,000
Language: Arabic 93%, Hindi 3%, Somali 3%, other 1%
Capital: Sanaa
Currency: Dinar and Rial
Religion: Muslim (Sunni 53%, Shi'ite 47%)
Ethnic Groups: Arab 86%, Indian 3%, other 11%
Government: Republic
Literacy (1990): 38%
Life Expectancy at Birth (1991): 51 years female, 49 years male
Infant Mortality (per 1,000 live births 1991): 121
Gross Domestic Product (1990): $5.3 billion
GDP per Capita: $545
Principal Industries: Oil, textiles, leather goods, handicrafts, fish
Principal Crops: Wheat, sorghum, fruits, coffee, cotton

YUGOSLAVIA (SERBIA AND MONTENEGRO)
Federal Republic of Yugoslavia
Federativna Republika Jugoslavija

Area: 26,940 sq. mi. (69,775 sq. km.)
Population: 10,528,000

Language: Serbo-Croatian
Capital: Belgrade
Currency: New dinar
Religion: Orthodox majority, Roman Catholic and Muslim minorities
Ethnic Groups: Predominantly Bosian and Serbian, many ethnic minorities
Government: Republic

ZAIRE
Republic of Zaire
République du Zaire

Area: 905,365 sq. mi. (2,344,885 sq. km.)
Population: 37,832,00
Language: French (official), English, Ruanda, Luba-Lulua, Kituba, Kongo, Ngala, other African languages and Bantu dialects
Capital: Kinshasha
Currency: Zaire
Religion: Roman Catholic 50%, Protestant 20%, Kimbanguist 10%, Muslim 10%, traditional 10%
Ethnic Groups: Bantu 80%, over 200 other tribes 20%
Government: Republic
Literacy (1990): 72%
Life Expectancy at Birth (1991): 56 years female, 52 years male
Infant Mortality (per 1,000 live births 1991): 99
Gross Domestic Product (1990): $6.6 billion
GDP per Capita: $180
Principal Industries: Agriculture, mining, forestry, light manufacturing
Principal Crops: Rubber, coffee, tea, cocoa, cotton, sugarcane

ZAMBIA
Republic of Zambia

Area: 290,585 sq. mi. (752,618 sq. km.)
Population: 8,446,000
Language: English (official), Bemba 25%, Nyanja 12%, Tonga 12%, Lozi 6%, other African languages and Bantu dialects 45%

Capital: Lusaka
Currency: Kwacha
Religion: Christian 72%, traditional 27%, other 1%
Ethnic Groups: Mostly Bantu tribes
Government: Republic
Literacy (1991): 54%
Life Expectancy at Birth (1991): 56 years female, 52 years male
Infant Mortality (per 1,000 live births 1991): 79
Gross Domestic Product (1990): $4.7 billion
GDP per Capita: $580
Principal Industries: Copper, textiles, chemicals, zinc, lead, cobalt, coal
Principal Crops: Corn, tobacco, peanuts, cotton, sugar

ZIMBABWE
Republic of Zimbabwe

Area: 150,700 sq. mi. (390,310 sq. km.)
Population: 10,720,000
Language: English 7% (official), Shona 55%, Ndeble 15%, Nyanja 5%, other African 18%
Capital: Harare
Currency: Zimbabwean dollar
Religion: Predominantly traditional, Christian
Ethnic Groups: Shona 80%, Ndebele 19%, other 1%
Government: Republic
Literacy (1990): 67%
Life Expectancy at Birth (1991): 64 years female, 60 years male
Infant Mortality (per 1,000 live births 1991): 61
Gross Domestic Product (1993): $4.1 billion
GDP per Capita: $412
Principal Industries: Steel, textiles, chemicals, vehicles, gold, copper
Principal Crops: Tobacco, sugar, cotton, corn, wheat

World Census Information

This section includes the most recent census figures for the nations and sovereign territories of the world. Also included is a listing of the world's 94 largest cities according to census population figures.

POPULATION BY COUNTRY

COUNTRY	POPULATION (1,000's) MOST CURRENT ESTIMATES	2000 PROJ.	2010 PROJ.	POP. RANK	ANNUAL RATE OF GROWTH (PERCENT)	POP. PER SQ MILE
World Total	**5,422,908**	**6,284,643**	**7,239,935**	**(X)**	**1.6**	**107**
Afghanistan	16,450	24,935	32,358	52	4.7	66
Albania	3,335	3,824	4,265	123	1.6	315
Algeria	26,022	32,024	39,106	36	2.3	28
Andorra	53	63	72	204	2	305
Angola	8,668	11,424	14,887	76	3	18
Antigua and Barbuda	64	69	76	198	0.7	376
Argentina	32,664	36,036	39,884	31	1.1	31
Armenia	3,300	3,552	3,685	125	0.6	287
Australia	17,288	19,511	21,689	50	1.4	6
Austria	7,666	7,762	7,660	84	0.2	240
Azerbaijan	7,000	8,177	8,911	89	1.3	213
Bahamas	252	283	313	175	1.3	65
Bahrain	537	694	863	159	2.9	2,247
Bangladesh	116,601	143,226	176,562	10	2.3	2,255
Barbados	255	260	272	174	0.2	1,534
Belarus	10,250	10,629	10,901	68	0.4	126
Belgium	9,922	9,989	9,889	71	0.1	850
Belize	228	301	377	176	3.2	26
Benin	4,832	6,509	8,939	103	3.3	113
Bhutan	1,598	1,909	2,277	143	2	88
Bolivia	7,157	8,721	10,574	87	2.2	17
Bosnia and Herzegovina	4,200	4,828	5,039	104	0.7	212
Botswana	1,258	1,554	1,869	147	2.4	6
Brazil	155,356	180,536	207,462	5	1.7	48
Brunei Darussalam	398	562	660	164	4.1	195
Bulgaria	8,911	9,004	9,072	75	0.1	209
Burkina Faso	9,360	12,464	17,158	73	3.2	89
Burundi	5,831	7,731	10,423	94	3.1	589
Cambodia	7,146	8,498	10,023	88	2	105
Cameroon	11,390	14,453	18,625	60	2.6	63
Canada	26,835	29,301	31,464	34	1	8
Cape Verde	387	504	649	166	3	248
Central African Republic	2,952	3,702	4,712	118	2.5	12
Chad	5,122	6,204	7,652	100	2.1	11
Chile	13,287	15,025	16,817	56	1.4	46
People's Republic of China (Mainland)	1,151,487	1,303,342	1,420,312	1	1.4	320
Republic of China (Taiwan)	20,659	22,441	24,065	42	0.9	1,659
Colombia	33,778	39,745	45,603	30	1.8	84

COUNTRY	POPULATION (1,000's)			POP. RANK	ANNUAL RATE OF GROWTH (PERCENT)	POP. PER SQ MILE
	MOST CURRENT ESTIMATES	2000 PROJ.	2010 PROJ.			
Comoros*	477	656	920	161	3.5	569
Congo	2,309	2,995	3,908	135	2.9	18
Costa Rica	3,111	3,803	4,546	128	2.3	159
Côte d'Ivoire	12,978	18,144	25,263	57	3.7	106
Croatia	4,600	4,717	4,729	106	0.1	211
Cuba	10,732	11,613	12,277	62	0.9	251
Cyprus	709	768	830	156	0.9	199
Czechoslavkia (former)	15,725	16,303	16,824	(NA)	0.4	325
Czech Republic	10,428	(NA)	(NA)	67	(NA)	339
Slovakia	5,297	(NA)	(NA)	98	(NA)	280
Denmark	5,133	5,147	5,095	99	(Z)	314
Dijibouti	346	440	571	170	2.7	41
Dominica	86	101	118	192	1.7	298
Dominican Republic	7,385	8,676	10,080	86	1.8	395
Ecuador	10,752	12,997	15,543	61	2.1	101
Egypt	54,452	66,498	81,750	21	2.2	142
El Salvador	5,419	6,471	7,628	97	2	677
Equatorial Guinea	379	477	615	167	2.6	35
Estonia	1,600	1,675	1,770	142	0.6	96
Ethiopia	53,191	69,374	93,593	22	3	125
Fiji	744	823	932	155	1.1	105
Finland	4,991	5,075	5,088	101	0.2	42
France	56,596	58,548	59,708	20	0.4	269
Gabon	1,080	1,231	1,423	150	1.4	11
Gambia	875	1,151	1,553	152	3.1	227
Georgia	5,500	5,865	6,184	95	0.7	201
Germany	79,548	81,532	82,189	12	0.3	588
Ghana	15,617	20,527	27,141	54	3.1	176
Greece	10,043	10,166	10,160	69	0.1	199
Grenada	84	83	96	193	−0.1	640
Guatemala	9,266	11,315	13,537	74	2.2	221
Guinea	7,456	9,232	11,562	85	2.4	79
Guinea-Bissau	1,024	1,265	1,579	151	2.4	95
Guyana	750	728	807	154	−0.3	10
Haiti	6,287	7,649	9,421	92	2.2	591
Honduras	4,949	6,243	7,660	102	2.6	115
Hungary	10,558	10,604	10,602	64	(Z)	296
Iceland	260	280	296	173	0.9	7
India†	869,515	1,018,092	1,172,101	2	1.8	757
Indonesia	193,560	223,820	256,818	4	1.6	274
Iran	59,051	78,246	107,406	15	3.2	93
Iraq	19,525	27,205	38,047	45	3.7	117
Ireland	3,489	3,509	3,685	120	(Z)	131
Israel	4,558	5,321	6,103	107	1.8	581
Italy	57,772	58,592	58,011	17	0.2	509
Jamaica	2,489	2,762	3,155	132	1.1	595
Japan	124,017	128,144	130,480	7	0.4	814
Jordan	3,413	4,880	6,810	121	4	97
Kazakhstan	16,700	18,272	19,718	51	0.9	16†
Kenya	25,242	34,259	45,498	37	3.4	115
Kiribati	71	81	90	196	1.5	257
North Korea	21,815	25,491	28,491	40	1.7	469
South Korea	43,134	45,962	48,063	24	0.7	1,138
Kuwait	2,204	2,879	3,635	137	3	320
Kyrgyzstan	4,500	5,207	6,029	108	1.7	57
Laos	4,113	4,964	5,951	113	2.1	46
Latvia	2,700	2,840	3,008	131	0.5	107
Lebanon	3,385	4,058	4,934	122	1.9	857
Lesotho	1,801	2,242	2,776	141	2.4	154
Liberia	2,730	3,674	4,977	130	3.3	73
Libya	4,353	5,599	7,067	110	2.8	6
Liechtenstein	28	30	31	211	0.5	458
Lithuania	3,700	4,589	4,726	119	0.4	147
Luxembourg	388	410	409	165	0.7	389
Macedonia	1,900	2,324	2,478	140	0.9	191
Madagascar	12,185	16,185	21,954	60	3.2	54
Malawi	9,438	11,892	16,450	72	2.6	260
Malaysia	17,982	21,950	26,562	47	2.2	142

COUNTRY	POPULATION (1,000'S)			POP. RANK	ANNUAL RATE OF GROWTH (PERCENT)	POP. PER SQ MILE
	MOST CURRENT ESTIMATES	2000 PROJ.	2010 PROJ.			
Maldives	226	312	427	177	3.6	1,953
Mali	8,339	10,667	14,398	79	2.7	18
Malta	356	377	393	168	0.6	2,876
Marshall Islands	48	68	100	205	3.9	688
Mauritania	1,996	2,652	3,624	138	3.2	5
Mauritius	1,081	1,168	1,270	149	0.9	1,514
Mexico	90,007	108,754	129,017	11	2.1	121
Micronesia	108	125	130	188	1.8	397
Moldova	4,400	4,589	4,726	109	0.4	331
Monaco	30	32	34	209	0.7	38,477
Mongolia	2,247	2,836	3,579	136	2.6	4
Morocco	26,182	31,392	37,349	35	2	152
Mozambique	15,113	20,936	27,494	54	3.6	50
Myanmar	42,112	49,787	58,601	25	1.9	166
Namibia	1,521	2,081	2,895	145	3.6	5
Nauru	9	10	11	221	1.3	1,151
Nepal	19,612	24,340	30,622	44	2.4	371
The Netherlands	15,022	15,642	15,814	55	0.5	1,146
New Zealand	3,309	3,400	3,441	124	0.3	32
Nicaragua	3,752	4,729	5,858	117	2.7	81
Niger	8,154	11,056	15,323	81	3.4	17
Nigeria	122,471	160,751	213,042	8	3	348
Norway	4,273	4,411	4,463	112	0.4	36
Oman	1,534	2,099	2,990	144	3.5	19
Pakistan†	117,490	149,147	195,215	9	2.6	391
Panama	2,476	2,937	3,433	133	1.9	84
Papua New Guinea	3,913	4,806	5,924	114	2.3	22
Paraguay	4,799	6,023	7,381	105	2.6	31
Peru	22,362	26,435	30,880	39	1.9	45
The Philippines	65,759	77,734	90,261	14	1.9	571
Poland	37,800	38,889	40,599	29	0.3	322
Portugal	10,388	10,652	10,764	66	0.3	294
Qatar	518	743	954	160	4.1	122
Romania	23,397	24,534	25,417	38	0.5	263
Russia	148,542	152,910	157,946	6	0.3	22
Rwanda	7,903	11,047	15,787	83	3.7	820
St. Kitts and Nevis	40	44	51	208	0.9	290
St. Lucia	153	186	226	184	2.2	649
St. Vincent & the Grenadines	114	132	156	187	1.6	873
San Marino	23	24	26	213	0.6	1,004
São Tomé and Principe	128	166	211	186	2.9	347
Saudi Arabia	17,870	25,003	34,134	48	3.8	22
Senegal	7,953	10,482	14,090	82	3.1	107
Seychelles	69	74	80	197	0.8	392
Sierra Leone	4,275	5,399	6,980	111	2.6	155
Singapore	2,756	3,021	3,233	129	1	11,441
Slovenia	1,962	1,998	2,025	139	0.2	251
Solomon Islands	347	469	620	169	3.4	33
Somalia	6,709	9,409	12,849	91	3.5	28
South Africa	40,601	51,375	66,005	26	2.6	86
Spain	39,385	40,456	40,998	27	0.3	204
Sri Lanka	17,424	19,296	21,435	49	1.2	697
Sudan	27,220	35,870	46,980	32	3.1	30
Suriname	402	463	535	163	1.5	6
Swaziland	859	1,124	1,545	153	3	129
Sweden	8,564	8,761	8,728	77	0.3	54
Switzerland	6,784	7,018	6,989	90	0.4	442
Syria	12,966	18,212	25,947	58	3.8	182
Tajikistan	5,500	6,967	8,577	96	2.7	96
Tanzania	26,869	36,489	50,795	33	3.4	79
Thailand	56,814	63,832	70,740	19	1.3	288
Togo	3,811	5,248	7,336	116	3.6	181
Tonga	102	110	119	189	0.8	369
Trinidad and Tobago	1,285	1,425	1,601	146	1.1	649
Tunisia	8,276	9,713	11,203	80	1.8	138
Turkey	58,581	70,368	83,494	16	2.1	197
Turkmenistan	3,900	4,428	5,118	115	1.9	19

COUNTRY	POPULATION (1,000'S)			POP. RANK	ANNUAL RATE OF GROWTH (PERCENT)	POP. PER SQ MILE
	MOST CURRENT ESTIMATES	2000 PROJ.	2010 PROJ.			
Tuvalu	9	11	12	222	1.6	928
Uganda	18,690	25,802	35,002	46	3.6	242
Ukraine	52,100	32,361	52,949	23	0.1	220†
United Arab Emirates	2,390	3,598	4,920	134	4.7	74
United Kingdom	57,515	58,719	59,178	18	0.2	617
United States	252,502	268,266	282,575	3	0.7	71
Uruguay	3,121	3,289	3,469	127	0.6	47
Uzbekistan	21,300	24,988	29,034	42	1.9	118
Vanuatu	170	221	279	183	2.9	30
Vatican City	0.778	(NA)	(NA)	226	(NA)	778
Venezuela	20,189	24,596	29,518	43	2.2	59
Vietnam	67,568	79,801	92,027	13	1.9	538
Western Samoa	190	235	289	180	2.3	173
Yemen	10,063	13,603	18,985	69	3.3	49
Yugoslavia	10,528	11,121	11,625	65	0.7	371
Montenegro	645	696	733	(X)	0.8	(X)
Serbia	9,883	10,425	10,892	(X)	0.5	(X)
Zaire	37,832	50,043	67,540	28	3.1	43
Zambia	8,446	11,572	16,181	78	3.5	30
Zimbabwe	10,720	13,806	17,559	64	2.8	72

AREAS OF SPECIAL SOVEREIGNTY AND DEPENDENCIES

COUNTRY	MOST CURRENT ESTIMATES	2000 PROJ.	2010 PROJ.	POP. RANK	ANNUAL RATE OF GROWTH (PERCENT)	POP. PER SQ MILE
American Samoa	43	52	57	207	2.1	560
Anguilla	7	7	8	223	0.7	197
Aruba	64	67	70	199	0.6	860
Bermuda	58	59	60	201	0.1	3,089
British Virgin Islands	12	14	16	219	1.2	214
Cayman Islands	27	36	46	212	3.1	274
Cook Islands	18	19	20	215	0.5	192
Faroe Islands	48	52	55	206	0.8	89
French Guiana	102	132	163	190	2.9	3
French Polynesia	195	242	296	179	2.4	138
Gaza Strip	642	838	1,060	157	3	4,366
Gibraltar	30	30	30	210	0.1	12,783
Greenland	57	62	66	203	1	(Z)
Guadeloupe	345	376	406	169	1	507
Guam	145	179	209	185	2.4	694
Guernsey	58	60	62	202	0.5	769
Hong Kong	5,856	6,146	6,370	93	0.5	15,335
Isle of Man	64	66	66	200	0.1	282
Jersey	84	90	93	194	0.7	1,867
Macau	446	474	487	162	0.7	72,239
Martinique	345	374	396	172	0.9	844
Mayotte	75	106	153	195	3.9	517
Montserrat	13	13	13	218	0.2	324
Netherlands Antilles	184	192	204	181	0.5	496
New Caledonia	172	200	229	182	1.7	24
Northern Mariana Islands	23	29	32	214	2.4	128
Pacific Islands, Trust Territory of the	14	15	16	217	0.7	81
Puerto Rico	3,295	3,406	3,688	126	0.3	953
Reunion	607	708	808	158	1.7	629
St. Helena	7	7	7	224	0.6	42
St. Pierre and Miquelon	6	7	7	225	0.3	68
Turkes and Caicos Islands	10	12	13	220	1.7	60
Virgin Islands	99	110	127	191	1	736
Wallis and Futuna	17	22	28	216	2.9	157
West Bank	1,105	1,380	1,697	148	2.5	507
Western Sahara	197	246	304	178	2.5	2

NA Not available.   X Not applicable.   Z Less than .05 percent or .5.   †Indian-held part of Jammu and Kashmir included in India population figures, not Pakistan.   * Excludes Mayotte, area subject to dispute over sovereignty.

POPULATION AND AVERAGE ANNUAL RATES OF GROWTH FOR WORLD'S LARGEST CITIES

CITY AND COUNTRY	RANK	POPULATION (1,000'S)			ANNUAL RATE OF GROWTH (PERCENT)		POP. PER SQ MILE
		1991	1995	2000	1991-1995	1995-2000	
Tokyo-Yokohama, Japan	1	27,245	28,447	29,971	0.9	1	25,018
Mexico City, Mexico	2	20,899	23,913	27,872	2.7	3.1	40,037
São Paulo, Brazil	3	18,701	21,539	25,354	2.8	3.3	41,466
Seoul, South Korea	4	16,792	19,065	21,976	2.5	2.8	49,101
New York, United States	5	14,625	14,638	14,648	(Z)	(Z)	11,480
Osaka-Kobe-Kyoto, Japan	6	13,872	14,060	14,287	0.3	0.3	28,025
Bombay, India	7	12,109	13,532	15,357	2.2	2.5	127,461
Calcutta, India	8	11,898	12,885	14,088	1.6	1.8	56,927
Rio de Janeiro, Brazil	9	11,688	12,786	14,169	1.8	2.1	44,952
Buenos Aires, Argentina	10	11,657	12,232	12,911	1	1.1	21,790
Moscow, Russia	11	10,446	10,769	11,121	0.6	0.6	27,562
Manilla, Philippines	12	10,156	11,342	12,846	2.2	2.5	54,024
Los Angeles, United States	13	10,130	10,414	10,714	0.6	0.6	9,126
Cairo, Egypt	14	10,099	11,155	12,512	2	2.3	97,106
Djakarta, Indonesia	15	9,882	11,151	12,804	2.4	2.8	130,026
Tehran, Iran	16	9,779	11,681	14,251	3.6	4	87,312
London, United Kingdom	17	9,115	8,897	8,574	-0.5	-0.7	10,429
Dehli, India	18	8,778	10,105	11,849	2.8	3.2	63,612
Paris, France	19	8,720	8,764	8,803	0.1	0.1	20,185
Karachi, Pakistan	20	8,014	8,350	11,299	3.1	3.8	42,179
Lagos, Nigeria	21	7,998	9,799	12,528	4.1	4.9	142,821
Essen, Germany	22	7,452	7,364	7,239	-0.2	-0.3	10,585
Shanghai, China	23	6,936	7,194	7,540	0.7	0.9	88,924
Lima, Peru	24	6,815	7,853	9,241	2.8	3.3	56,794
Taipei, Taiwan	25	6,695	7,477	8,516	2.2	2.6	48,517
Istanbul, Turkey	26	6,678	7,624	8,875	2.6	3	40,476
Chicago, United States	27	6,529	6,541	6,568	(Z)	0.1	8,568
Bangkok, Thailand	28	5,955	6,657	7,587	2.2	2.6	58,379
Bogotá, Columbia	29	5,913	6,801	7,935	2.8	3.1	74,851
Madras, India	30	5,896	6,550	7,384	2.1	2.4	51,270
Beijing, China	31	5,762	5,865	5,993	0.4	0.4	38,156
Hong Kong, Hong Kong	32	5,693	5,841	5,956	0.5	0.4	247,501
Santiago, Chile	33	5,378	5,812	6,294	1.6	1.6	42,018
Pusan, South Korea	34	5,008	5,748	6,700	2.8	3.1	92,735
Tianjin, China	35	4,850	5,041	5,298	0.8	1	98,990
Bangalore, India	36	4,802	5,644	6,754	3.2	3.6	96,041
Nagoya, Japan	37	4,791	5,017	5,303	0.9	1.1	15,606
Milan, Italy	38	4,749	4,795	4,839	0.2	0.2	13,806
St. Petersburg, Russia	39	4,672	4,694	4,738	0.1	0.2	33,614
Madrid, Spain	40	4,513	4,772	5,104	1.1	1.4	68,385
Dhaka, Bangladesh	41	4,419	5,296	6,492	3.6	4.1	138,108
Lahore, Pakistan	42	4,376	4,986	5,864	2.6	3.2	76,779
Shenyang, China	43	4,289	4,457	4,684	0.8	1	109,974
Barcelona, Spain	44	4,227	4,492	4,834	1.2	1.5	48,584
Baghdad, Iraq	45	4,059	4,566	5,239	2.4	2.8	41,843
Manchester, United Kingdom	46	4,030	3,949	3,827	-0.4	-0.6	11,287
Philadelphia, United States	47	4,003	3,988	3,979	-0.1	-0.1	8,499
San Francisco, United States	48	3,987	4,104	4,214	0.6	0.5	9,315
Belo Horizonte, Brazil	49	3,812	4,373	5,125	2.7	3.2	48,249
Kinshasa, Zaire	50	3,747	4,520	5,646	3.8	4.5	65,732
Ho Chi Minh City, Vietnam	51	3,725	4,064	4,481	1.7	2	120,168
Ahmadabad, India	52	3,709	4,200	4,837	2.5	2.8	115,893
Hyderabad, India	53	3,673	4,149	4,765	2.4	2.8	41,741
Sydney, Australia	54	3,536	3,619	3,708	0.5	0.5	10,460
Athens, Greece	55	3,507	3,670	3,866	0.9	1	30,237
Miami, United States	56	3,471	3,679	3,894	1.2	1.1	7,748
Guadalajara, Mexico	57	3,370	3,839	4,451	2.6	3	43,205
Guangzhou, China	58	3,360	3,485	3,652	0.7	0.9	42,537
Surabaya, Indonesia	59	3,248	3,428	3,632	1.1	1.2	75,544
Caracas, Venezuela	60	3,217	3,338	3,435	0.7	0.6	59,582
Wuhan, China	61	3,200	3,325	3,495	0.8	1	49,225
Toronto, Canada	62	3,145	3,296	3,296	0.9	–	20,420
Porto Alegre, Brazil	63	3,114	3,541	4,109	2.6	3	13,479
Rome, Italy	64	3,033	3,079	3,129	0.3	0.3	43,949
Greater Berlin, Germany	65	3,021	3,018	3,006	(Z)	-0.1	11,026

POPULATION AND AVERAGE ANNUAL RATES OF GROWTH FOR WORLD'S LARGEST CITIES

CITY AND COUNTRY	RANK	POPULATION (1,000'S)			ANNUAL RATE OF GROWTH (PERCENT)		POP. PER SQ MILE
		1991	1995	2000	1991-1995	1995-2000	
Naples, Italy	66	2,978	3,051	3,134	0.5	0.5	48,032
Casablanca, Morocco	67	2,973	3,327	3,795	2.2	2.6	84,953
Detroit, United States†	68	2,969	2,865	2,735	−0.7	−0.9	6,343
Alexandria, Egypt	69	2,941	3,114	3,304	1.1	1.2	84,022
Monterrey, Mexico	70	2,939	3,385	3,974	2.8	3.2	38,169
Montreal, Canada	71	2,916	2,996	3,071	0.5	0.5	17,779
Melbourne, Australia	72	2,915	2,946	2,968	0.2	0.2	8,914
Ankara, Turkey	73	2,872	3,263	3,777	2.6	2.9	52,221
Rangoon, Myanmar	74	2,864	3,075	3,332	1.4	1.6	60,927
Kiev, Ukraine	75	2,796	2,983	3,237	1.3	1.6	45,095
Dallas, United States	76	2,787	2,972	3,257	1.3	1.8	6,652
Singapore, Singapore	77	2,719	2,816	2,913	0.7	0.7	34,856
Taegu, South Korea	78	2,651	3,201	4,051	3.8	4.7	(NA)
Harbin, China	79	2,643	2,747	2,887	0.8	1	88,110
Washington, United States	80	2,565	2,637	2,707	0.6	0.5	7,184
Poona, India	81	2,547	2,987	3,647	3.2	4	(NA)
Boston, United States	82	2,436	2,480	2,485	(Z)	(Z)	8,172
Lisbon, Portugal	83	2,426	2,551	2,717	1	1.3	(NA)
Tashkent, Uzbekistan	84	2,418	2,640	2,947	1.8	2.2	(NA)
Chongqing, China	85	2,395	2,632	2,962	1.9	2.4	(NA)
Chengdu, China	86	2,372	2,465	2,591	0.8	1	94,870
Vienna, Austria	87	2,344	2,474	2,647	1.1	1.4	(NA)
Houston, United States	88	2,329	2,456	2,651	1.1	1.5	7,512
Budapest, Hungary	89	2,303	2,313	2,335	0.1	0.2	16,691
Salvador, Brazil	90	2,298	2,694	3,286	3.2	4	(NA)
Bucharest, Romania	91	2,163	2,214	2,271	0.5	0.5	41,589
Birmingham, United Kingdom	92	2,162	2,130	2,078	−0.3	−0.5	9,695
Havana, Cuba	93	2,130	2,218	2,333	0.8	1	(NA)
Kanpur, India	94	2,129	2,356	2,673	2	2.5	(NA)

−Represents zero.   NA Not available.   Z Less than .05 percent.   †Includes Windsor, Canada

World Economic and Social Data

The following section shows geographical areas that lead in various categories. The first listing in each category is the most prominent of that section, followed by the others in descending order of prominence. This section is based upon general statistics and figures, some of which will change. For a more detailed look at the geographical areas mentioned, see the section Nations of the World.

Largest Countries in Area
- Russia
- Canada
- China
- United States
- Brazil
- Australia
- India

Most Populous Countries in 1993
- China
- India
- United States
- Indonesia
- Brazil
- Russia
- Japan

Most Populous Countries in 2000
- China
- India
- United States
- Indonesia
- Brazil
- Nigeria
- Russia

Most Populous Countries in 2025
- China
- India
- United States
- Pakistan
- Indonesia
- Nigeria
- Brazil

Fastest-Growing Countries
- United Arab Emirates
- Afghanistan
- Qatar
- Brunei
- Jordan
- Saudi Arabia
- Syria

Most Urbanized Countries
- Singapore
- Monaco
- Belgium
- Kuwait
- United Kingdom
- Israel
- Spain

Most Densely Populated Countries
- Bangladesh
- Taiwan
- Netherlands
- South Korea
- Belgium
- Rwanda
- Japan

Most Populous Cities in 1993
- Tokyo, Japan
- Mexico City, Mexico
- São Paulo, Brazil
- Seoul, Korea
- New York, United States
- Osaka-Kyoto-Kobe, Japan
- Bombay, India

Most Populous Cities in 2000
- Tokyo, Japan
- Mexico City, Mexico
- São Paulo, Brazil
- Seoul, Korea
- Bombay, India
- New York, United States
- Osaka-Kyoto-Kobe, Japan

Most Populous Cities in 2010
- Mexico City, Mexico
- São Paulo, Brazil
- Bombay, India
- Seoul, Korea
- Tehran, Iran
- Karachi, Pakistan
- Lagos, Nigeria

World's Refugees (sources)
- Afghanistan
- Israel
- countries within the former state of Yugoslavia (incl. Bosnia and Herzegovina, Croatia, Serbia, etc.)
- Mozambique
- Ethiopia
- Somalia
- Liberia

World's Refugees (places of asylum)
- Pakistan
- Iran
- Jordan
- Sudan
- Malawi
- Ethiopia
- Zaire

Continents (by area)
- Asia
- Africa
- North America
- South America
- Antarctica
- Europe
- Australia

Continents (by population)
- Asia
- Africa
- Europe
- South America
- North America
- Australia
- Antarctica

WORLD HEALTH

Health Expenditures (per capita)
United States
Canada
Switzerland
Sweden
France
Iceland
Luxembourg

Life Expectancy (female)
Switzerland
France
Italy
Japan
Spain
Austria
Sweden

Life Expectancy (male)
Japan
Israel
Greece
Iceland
Italy
Spain
Switzerland

Birth Rate
Malawi
Rwanda
Mali
Uganda
Yemen
Burkina Faso
Niger

Death Rate
Western Sahara
Chad

Guinea
Mali
Afghanistan
Angola
Sierra Leone

Calorie Consumption (highest)
Belgium
Luxembourg
Germany
United Arab Emirates
Greece
United States
Bulgaria

Calorie Consumption (lowest)
Mozambique
Ghana
Guinea
Sierra Leone
Rwanda
Haiti
Bangladesh

Protein Consumption (highest)
Iceland
Greece
Germany
France
New Zealand
United Arab Emirates
Italy

Protein Consumption (lowest)
Mozambique
Zaire
Ghana
Guinea
Bangladesh

Sierra Leone
Liberia

Infant Mortality
Afghanistan
Angola
Sierra Leone
Guinea
Bhutan
Central African Republic
Gambia

Suicide
Austria
Denmark
France
Sweden
Germany
Hungary
Japan

Number of People per Available Hospital Bed
Nepal
Ethiopia
Bangladesh
Lesotho
Niger
Afghanistan
Guinea

Number of People per Doctor
Equatorial Guinea
Chad
Niger
Mozambique
Rwanda
Ethiopia
Malawi

WEALTH OF NATIONS

Largest Countries in GNP
United States
Japan
Germany
France
Italy
United Kingdom
Russia

GNP per Capita (highest)
Switzerland
Luxembourg
Japan
Finland
Norway
Sweden
United States

GNP per Capita (lowest)
Mozambique
Cambodia
Ethiopia
Tanzania
Laos
Madagascar
Chad

Exports
United States
Germany
Japan
France
United Kingdom
Italy
Netherlands

Imports
United States
Germany
Japan
France
United Kingdom
Italy
Netherlands

Concentration of World's Largest Corporations
United States
Japan
United Kingdom
Germany
France
Sweden
Canada

Number of Inventions per Annum
Japan
United States
Germany
France
United Kingdom
Italy
Canada

Number of Tourists per Annum
France
United States
Spain
Italy
Austria
Germany
United Kingdom

National External Public Debt
Brazil
Mexico
India
Argentina
China
Indonesia
Poland

Telephones per Capita
Sweden
Denmark
Switzerland
Canada
United States
New Zealand
Netherlands

Newspapers per Capita
Japan
Norway
Finland
Sweden
Switzerland

Iceland
Russia

Television Sets per Capita
United States
Canada
Japan
Germany
Denmark
Finland
Australia

Radio Receivers per Capita
United States
Australia

United Kingdom
Canada
Denmark
South Korea
Finland

Private Automobiles per Capita
United States
Canada
Australia
New Zealand
Sweden
France
Italy

EDUCATION

Literacy
Liechtenstein
Luxembourg
Andorra
Finland
Japan
Iceland
Tonga

Proficiency Test in Mathematics
South Korea
Taiwan
Switzerland
Russia
Hungary
France
Italy

Proficiency Test in Science
South Korea
Taiwan
Switzerland
Hungary
Russia
Slovenia
Italy

Primary School Teachers
China
Russia
India
United States

Indonesia
Brazil
Mexico

Most Students per Teacher (primary school)
Burundi
Chad
Malawi
Bangladesh
Equatorial Guinea
Central African Republic
Congo

Secondary School Teachers
China
India
United States
Japan
Germany
Mexico
France

Most Students per Teacher (secondary school)
Namibia
Zaire
Central African Republic
Afghanistan
Dominican Republic
Ethiopia
Liberia

University and Graduate School Teachers
United States
China
Germany
Japan
Russia
Brazil
Mexico

Most Students per Teacher (university and graduate school)
Chad
Madagascar
North Korea
Hong Kong
Syria
Bahamas
South Korea

Number of Books Published per Year
Germany
United Kingdom
Russia
United States
Japan
France
South Korea

MINING AND MINERAL PRODUCTION

Bauxite
Australia
Guinea
Brazil
Jamaica
India
Suriname
China

Copper
Chile
United States
Canada
Zambia

Zaire
Poland
Peru

Diamonds
Australia
Zaire
Botswana
Russia
South Africa
Angola
China

Gold
South Africa
United States
Australia
Canada
Russia
Brazil
Philippines

Iron Ore
China
Brazil
Ukraine
Australia

Iron Ore continued
Russia
United States
India

Lead
Australia
United States
Canada
China
Peru
Mexico
Bulgaria

Magnesium
United States
Norway
France
Japan
Canada
China
Italy

Phosphate
United States
Russia

Morocco
China
Tunisia
Jordan
Brazil

Salt
United States
China
Germany
Canada
India
France
United Kingdom

Silver
Mexico
United States
Peru
Russia
Canada
Australia
Poland

Tin
Malaysia

Brazil
Indonesia
China
Thailand
Russia
Bolivia

Uranium
Canada
United States
Australia
South Africa
France
Namibia
Niger

Zinc
Canada
Russia
Australia
Peru
China
United States
Mexico

AGRICULTURAL PRODUCTION

Apples
China
Russia
United States
Germany
France
Italy
Canada

Bananas
Brazil
India
China
Philippines
Ecuador
Indonesia
Thailand

Barley
Germany
Canada
France
Ukraine
Spain
United States
Russia

Cocoa
Côte d'Ivoire
Brazil
Ghana
Malaysia
Cameroon
Nigeria
Togo

Coffee
Brazil
Colombia

Indonesia
Mexico
Côte d'Ivoire
Guatemala
Ethiopia

Corn (Maize)
United States
China
Brazil
France
South Africa
Mexico
Russia

Oats
Russia
Ukraine
United States
Canada
Poland
Belarus
Germany

Potatoes
Russia
Poland
China
United States
Ukraine
Germany
India

Rice
China
India
Indonesia
Thailand
Vietnam

Bangladesh
Myanmar

Soybeans
United States
Brazil
China
Argentina
Italy
Paraguay
India

Sugar
India
Cuba
Brazil
United States
China
France
Germany

Tea
India
Turkey
China
Georgia
Sri Lanka
Kenya
Indonesia

Wheat
China
United States
India
Russia
France
Canada
Ukraine

ANIMAL AND ANIMAL PRODUCT PRODUCTION

Beef and Veal Consumption (per capita)
Argentina
Uruguay
United States
Australia
Canada
New Zealand
France

Butter
India
Germany
United States
France
Pakistan
Poland
New Zealand

Cattle
India
Brazil
United States
Russia
China
Argentina
Ukraine

Cheese
United States
Germany
France
Italy
Netherlands
Poland
Egypt

Chicken Eggs
China
United States

Russia
Japan
Brazil
India
Germany

Cow's Milk
United States
Russia
Germany
France
Ukraine
India
Poland

Fishing Catch
Japan
China
Russia
United States
Chile
Peru
Norway

Goats
India
China
Pakistan
Nigeria
Somalia
Ethiopia
Egypt

Meat and Meat Products
China
United States
Germany
France
Argentina
Russia
Ukraine

Pigs
China
United States
Germany
Russia
Brazil
Poland
Ukraine

Pork and Pork Product Consumption (per capita)
Hungary
Denmark
Germany
Czech Republic
Austria
Poland
Slovakia

Poultry Consumption (per capita)
United States
Israel
Hong Kong
Singapore
Canada
Saudi Arabia
Australia

Sheep
Australia
Russia
China
India
New Zealand
Turkey
Iran

NONFOOD AGRICULTURAL PRODUCTS

Cotton Lint
China
United States
Pakistan
India
Brazil
Turkey
Egypt

Hardwood Production
India
United States
Brazil
Indonesia
China
Nigeria
Russia

Softwood Production
United States
Russia
Canada
China
Sweden
Brazil
Finland

Natural Rubber
Malaysia
Indonesia
Thailand
China
India
Philippines
Sri Lanka

Tobacco
China
United States
India
Brazil
Turkey
Italy
Indonesia

Cigarettes
United States
Japan
Germany
Brazil
Indonesia
United Kingdom
South Korea

Wine
France
Italy
Spain
Argentina
United States
Portugal
Germany

Beer
United States
Germany
United Kingdom
Japan
Mexico
China
Brazil

Wool
Australia
New Zealand
China
Argentina
Kazakhstan
South Africa
Uruguay

MISCELLANEOUS INDUSTRIAL PRODUCTION

Aluminum
United States
Canada
Australia
Japan
Brazil
Russia
Norway

Automobiles
Japan
United States
Germany
France
Italy
Spain
United Kingdom

Cement
China
United States
Japan
Russia
India
Germany
Italy

Commercial Vehicles
Japan
United States

Canada
France
Brazil
United Kingdom
Germany

Merchant Ships Produced
Japan
South Korea
Germany
Italy
Denmark
China
Finland

Merchant Fleets
Liberia
Panama
Japan
Greece
Russia
Cyprus
United States

Paper and Paper Products
United States
Japan
China
Germany
Finland

Canada
France

Radios
Hong Kong
United States
China
Malaysia
Singapore
Japan
Taiwan

Steel
Japan
United States
China
Russia
Germany
Brazil
Italy

Television Sets
China
United States
South Korea
Japan
Taiwan
Germany
United Kingdom

ENERGY

Coal Reserves
China
United States
Russia
Australia
Germany
India
South Africa

Coal Production
China
United States
Germany
Russia
Poland
India
South Africa

Coal Consumption
China
United States
Germany
Russia
Poland
India
South Africa

Natural Gas Reserves
Russia
Iran

United Arab Emirates
Saudi Arabia
United States
Qatar
Algeria

Natural Gas Production
Russia
United States
Canada
Netherlands
Algeria
United Kingdom
Uzbekistan

Natural Gas Consumption
United States
Russia
Germany
Canada
United Kingdom
Japan
Romania

Crude Oil Reserves
Saudi Arabia
Iraq
Kuwait
Iran
Venezuela

United Arab Emirates
Mexico

Crude Oil Production
Russia
United States
Saudi Arabia
Iran
Iraq
China
Mexico

Crude Oil Consumption
United States
Russia
Japan
Germany
United Kingdom
France
Canada

Electricity Consumption
United States
Japan
Germany
China
Canada
France
United Kingdom

World Monetary Systems

This section lists the monetary units of the nations of the world, including the currency subunits and symbols. The value, or exchange rate, of currencies fluctuate from time to time, and the values listed here in United States dollars are the most recent figures prior to press time.

WORLD MONETARY UNITS

COUNTRY	CURRENCY	SUBDIVISIONS	SYMBOL	VALUE (U.S. $)
Afghanistan	Afghani	100 puls	Af	1050
Albania	Lek	100 qintar	L	110
Algeria	Dinar	100 centimes	DA	20.98
Andorra	French franc	100 centimes	Fr or F	5.9693
	Spanish peseta	100 centimes	Pta or P	144.30
Angola	Kwanza	100 lwei	NKz	4000.2
Antigua and Barbuda	East Caribbean dollar	100 cents	$	2.7
Argentina	Peso	100 centavos	$	0.9999
Armenia	Ruble	100 kopecks	R or Rub	1066.00 †
Australia	Australian dollar	100 cents	$A	1.45
Austria	Schilling	100 groschen	S or Sch	11.9645
Azerbaijan	Ruble	100 kopecks	R or Rub	1066.00 †
Bahamas	Bahamian dollar	100 cents	B$	1
Bahrain	Bahrainian dinar	1000 fils	BD	0.377
Bangladesh	Taka	100 paisa	Tk	39.809
Barbados	Barbados dollar	100 cents	Bda $	2.0113
Belarus	Ruble	100 kopecks	R or Rub	1066.00
Belgium	Belgian franc	100 centimes	Fr, F or BF	34.94
Belize	Belize dollar	100 cents	$	2
Benin	Franc CFA	100 centimes	Fr or F	278.625
Bhutan	Ngultrum	100 chetrums	N	31.35
Bolivia	Boliviano	100 centavos	$b	4.255
Bosnia and Herzegovina	Dinar			*
Botswana	Pula	100 thebe	P	2.4328
Brazil	Novo cruzeiro	100 centavos	Cz$	51735.5
Brunei Darussalam	Brunei dollar	100 sen	B$	1.6247
Bulgaria	Lev	100 stotinki	Lv	26.697
Burkina Faso	Franc CFA	100 centimes	F or Fr	278.625
Burundi	Burundi franc	100 centimes	FBu	231.9224
Cambodia	Riel	100 sen	CR	3500
Cameroon	Franc CFA	100 centimes	Fr or F	278.625
Canada	Canadian dollar	100 cents	$	1.2842
Cape Verde	Cape Verdean escudo	100 centavos	Esc	74.2
Central African Republic	Franc CFA	100 centimes	Fr or F	278.625
Chad	Franc CFA	100 centimes	Fr or F	278.625
Chile	Peso	100 centavos	$	429.09
China, Peoples Republic of	Yuan	100 cents	¥	5.76
Republic of China (Taiwan)	New Taiwan dollar	100 cents	NT$	26.44
Colombia	Peso	100 centavos	$	786.42
Commonwealth of Independent States	Ruble	100 kopecks	R or Rub	1066.00 †
Comoros	Franc CFA	100 centimes	Fr or F	278.625
Congo	Franc CFA	100 centimes	Fr or F	278.625
Costa Rica	Colón	100 centimos		140.56
Côte d'Ivoire	Franc CFA	100 centimes	Fr or F	278.625

COUNTRY	CURRENCY	SUBDIVISIONS	SYMBOL	VALUE (U.S. $)
Croatia	Croatian dinar		Hrd	*
Cuba	Peso	100 centavos	$	1.3203
Cyprus	Cyprus pound	1000 mils	£	1.9852 ‡
Czech Republic	Koruna	100 halers	Kcs	29.789
Denmark	Krone	100 re	Kr	6.5085
Djibouti	Djibouti franc	100 centimes	DjFr	177.72
Dominica	East Caribbean dollar	100 cents	$	2.7
Dominican Republic	Peso	100 centavos	RD$	13
Ecuador	Sucre	100 centavos	S/	1910
Egypt	Egyptian pound	100 piasters	£E	3.3405
El Salvador	Colón	100 centavos	¢	8.77
Equatorial Guinea	Franc CFA	100 centimos	E	278.625
Estonia	Ruble	100 kopecks	R or Rub	13.668
Ethiopia	Birr	100 cents	E$ or EB	5
Fiji	Fiji dollar	100 cents	$F	1.549
Finland	Markka	100 pennia	Mk or Fmk	5.6525
France	French franc	100 centimes	Fr or F	5.9693
Gabon	Franc CFA	100 centimes	Fr or F	278.625
Gambia	Dalasi	100 bututs	D	8.9
Georgia	Ruble	100 kopecks	R or Rub	1066.00 †
Germany	Deutsche Mark	100 pfennigs	DM	1.7405
Ghana	Cedi	100 pesewas	¢	615
Greece	Drachma	100 lepta	Dr	231.235
Grenada	East Caribbean dollar	100 cents	$	2.7
Guatemala	Quetzal	100 centavos	Q	5.6721
Guinea	Guinean franc	100 cauris	GF	812.29
Guinea-Bissau	Guinea-Bissau peso	100 centavos	Esc	5000
Guyana	Guyana dollar	100 cents	$	126
Haiti	Gourde	100 centimes	G or GDE	12
Honduras	Lempira	100 centavos	L	6.32
Hong Kong	Dollar	100 cents	HK$	7.758
Hungary	Forint	100 filler	F or Ft	92.1
Iceland	M.N. krona	100 aurur	Kr	66.13
India	Rupee	100 paise	Re (pl, Rs)	31.35
Indonesia	Rupiah	100 sen	Rp	2093.5
Iran	Rial	100 dinars	R or Rl	1612
Iraq	Iraqi dinar	1000 fils	ID	0.3108
Ireland	Irish pound (punt)	100 pence	£	1.4332 ‡
Israel	Shekel	100 agorot	IS	2.8125
Italy	Lira	100 centesimi	L	1611.71
Jamaica	Jamaican dollar	100 cents	J$	22.5
Japan	Yen	100 sen	¥	104.80
Jordan	Jordanian dinar	1000 fils	JD	0.697
Kazakhstan	Ruble	100 kopecks	R or Rub	1066.00 †
Kenya	Kenyan shilling	100 cents	Ksh	65.284
Kiribati	Australian dollar	100 cents	$A	1.45
North Korea	Won	100 jun	W	2.15
South Korea	Won	100 chon	W	802.6
Kuwait	Kuwait dinar	1000 fils	KD	0.3014
Kyrgyzstan	Ruble	100 kopecks	R or Rub	1066.00 †
Laos	Kip	100 at	K	720
Latvia	Ruble	100 kopecks	R or Rub	1066.00 †
Lebanon	Lebanese pound	100 piasters	£ or LL	1731.5
Lesotho	Loti	100 licente	M	3.3022
Liberia	Liberian dollar	100 cents	$	1
Libya	Libyan dinar	1000 dirhams	LD	0.2979
Liechtenstein	Swiss franc	100 centimes	SFr	1.5320
Lithuania	Ruble	100 kopecks	R or Rub	1066.00 †
Luxembourg	Luxembourg franc	100 centimes	Fr or F	34.94
Madagascar	Malagasy franc	100 centimes	Fr or F	1922.41
Malawi	Kwacha	100 tambala	K	4.477
Malaysia	Ringgit	100 sen	$	2.554
Maldives	Maldivian rufiyaa	100 cents	Rf	11.975
Mali	Franc CFA	100 centimes	Fr or F	278.625
Malta	Maltese lira	100 pence	£ or Lm	2.5783 ‡
Mauritania	Ouguiya	5 khoums	UM	113.81
Mauritius	Mauritain rupee	100 cents	Re (pl. Rs)	17.642
Mexico	Peso	100 centavos	$	3.115
Micronesia	U.S. dollar	100 cents	$	1
Moldova	Ruble	100 kopecks	R or Rub	1066.00 †
Monaco	French franc	100 centimes	F or Fr	5.9693

COUNTRY	CURRENCY	SUBDIVISIONS	SYMBOL	VALUE (U.S. $)
Mongolia	Tugrik	100 mongo	Tug	400
Morocco	Dirham	100 centimes or francs	DH	9.2569
Mozambique	Metical	100 centavos	Mt	3521.063
Myanmar	Kyat	100 pyas	K	6.1177
Namibia	South African rand	100 cents	R	3.3022
Nauru	Australian dollar	100 cents	$A	1.45
Nepal	Nepalese rupee	100 paisa	Re (pl Rs.)	46.3125
The Netherlands	Guilder	100 cents	G	1.9055
New Zealand	New Zealand dollar	100 cents	NZ$	1.858
Nicaragua	Cordoba	100 centavos	C$	6.1338
Niger	Franc CFA	100 centimes	Fr or F	278.625
Nigeria	Naira	100 kobo	N	25
Norway	Krone	100 re	Nkr	7.164
Oman	Omani rial	1000 baizas	R	0.385
Pakistan	Pakistani rupee	100 paisa	Re (pl. Rs)	27.3028
Panama	Balboa	100 centesimos	B	1
Papua New Guinea	Kina	100 toea	K	0.9833
Paraguay	Guarani	100 centimos	G	1733
Peru	Nuevo sol	100 centavos	S/ or $	1.995
The Philippines	Peso	100 sentimos or centavos	P	26.75
Poland	Zloty	100 groszy	Zl or Z	17730
Portugal	Escudo	100 centavos	$ or Esc	161.2
Qatar	Qatari riyal	100 dirhams	Qr	3.64
Romania	Leu	100 bani	L	713
Russia	Ruble	100 kopecks	R or Rub	1066.00 †
Rwanda	Rwanda franc	100 centimes	Fr or F	144.8005
St. Kitts and Nevis	East Caribbean dollar	100 cents	$	2.7
St. Lucia	East Caribbean dollar	100 cents	$	2.7
St. Vincent & the Grenadines	East Caribbean dollar	100 cents	$	2.7
San Marino	Lira	100 centesimi	L	1536
São Tomé and Príncipe	Dobra	100 centimos	Dn	240
Saudi Arabia	Riyal	100 halala	R	3.7503
Senegal	Franc CFA	100 centimes	Fr or F	278.625
Seychelles	Seychelles rupee	100 cents	Re (pl. Rs)	5.2017
Sierra Leone	Leone	100 cents	Le	550
Singapore	Singapore dollar	100 cents	S$	1.6247
Slovakia	Koruna	100 halers		29.789
Slovenia	Tolar		SIT	119.411
Solomon Islands	Solomon dollar	100 cents	$	3.1211
Somalia	Somali shilling	100 cents	SomSh	2620
South Africa	Rand	100 cents	R	3.3022
Spain	Peseta	100 centimos	Pta or P (pl. Pts)	144.30
Sri Lanka	Sri Lanka rupee	100 cents	Re (pl. Rs)	48.105
Sudan	Sudanese pound	100 piasters	£S or LSd	130
Suriname	Suriname guilder	100 cents	F or Fl or G	1.785
Swaziland	Lilangeni	100 cents	E or L	3.3022
Sweden	Krona	100 re	SKr	7.7625
Switzerland	Swiss franc	100 centimes or rappen	SFr	1.5230
Syria	Syrian pound	100 piasters	£S or LS	21.5
Tajikistan	Ruble	100 kopecks	R or Rub	1066.00 †
Tanzania	Tanzanian shilling	100 cents or centi	TSh	396.0019
Thailand	Baht	100 satang	B or Tc	25.315
Togo	Franc CFA	100 centimes	Fr or F	278.625
Tonga	Pa'anga	100 seniti	T$	1.49
Trinidad and Tobago	Trinidad and Tobago dollar	100 cents	TT$	5.45
Tunisia	Tunisian dinar	1000 millimes	D	0.99
Turkey	Turkish lira	100 kurus or piasters	Lt	10946.38
Turkmenistan	Ruble	100 kopecks	R or Rub	1066.00 †
Tuvalu	Australian dollar	100 cents	$A	1.45
Uganda	Ugandan shilling	100 cents	Ush	1201.837
Ukraine	Karbovanet	100 karbonetf		5760.00
United Arab Emirates	Dirham	1000 fils	UD	3.671
United Kingdom	Pound sterling	100 pence	£	1.4930 ‡
United States	Dollar	100 cents	$	1
Uruguay	Peso	100 centesimios	$	3.92
Uzbekistan	Ruble	100 kopecks	R or Rub	1066.00 †
Vanuatu	Vatu		V	122.09
Vatican City State	Lira	100 centesimi	L	1536
Venezuela	Bolivar	100 centimos	B	89.8
Vietnam	Dong	100 xu	D	10575

COUNTRY	CURRENCY	SUBDIVISIONS	SYMBOL	VALUE (U.S. $)
Western Samoa	Tala	100 sene	WS$	2.5582
Yemen	Dinar	1000 fils	£SY	0.4609
	Rial	40 buqshas	YR	18
Yugoslavia	New dinar	100 paras	Din	1565492
Zaire	Zaire	100 makuta (sing likuta)	Z	4101000
Zambia	Kwacha	100 ngwee	K	555.973

* Exchange rates not available at press time.
† The C.I.S. ruble exchange rate applies for all former Soviet Republics.
‡ US$ per unit of currency (£).

Business Terms

Designed as both an introduction for the novice and a quick reference for the more experienced, this section covers a wide range of business terms. In addition to defining basic terms in accounting, marketing, management, production, etc., it clarifies concepts of importance in national and international trade and economics.

abatement the amount deducted from a full tax amount. Also the reduction of an expenditure, charge, or tax.

accounts payable the balance due to a creditor.

actuary a person who calculates the premiums, reserves, and dividends on insurance plans and annuities.

added value or value added the sales revenue from selling a product less the cost of the materials or purchases used in those products. It is increasingly used as an indicator of relative efficiency within and between firms, although in the latter case it is open to distortion where mark-up varies between standard and premium-priced segments of a market.

adverse variance difference between actual and budgeted spending or income that results in the organization having less money than planned.

aid, development money given or lent on concessional terms to developing countries or spent on maintaining agencies for this purpose. In the late 1980s official aid from governments of wealthy nations amounted to $45–60 billion annually and voluntary organizations in the West received about $2.4 billion a year for the Third World. The World Bank is the largest dispenser of aid. In 1990 it transferred $467 billion to developing countries. All industrialized United Nations (U.N.) member countries devote a portion of their gross national product to aid, ranging from 0.20% of GNP (Ireland) to 1.10% (Norway) (1988 figures). Each country spends more than half this contribution on direct bilateral assistance to countries with which they have historical or military links or hope to encourage trade. The rest goes to international organizations such as U.N. and World Bank agencies, which distribute aid multilaterally.

amortization the ending of a debt by paying it off gradually, over a period of time. The term is used to describe either the paying off of a cash debt or the accounting procedure by which the value of an asset is progressively reduced (depreciated) over a number of years.

annual accounts summary of the records of a company's financial activities, and in most countries made available for public inspection. Annual accounts include a balance sheet and profit/loss or income/expenditure account.

annual general meeting (AGM) yearly meeting of the stockholders of a company or the members of an organization, at which business, including consideration of the annual report and accounts, the election of officers, and the appointment of auditors, is normally carried out.

annual percentage rate (APR) charge (including interest) for granting consumer credit, expressed as an equivalent once-a-year percentage figure of the amount of the credit granted.

annuity a sum of money payable at regular intervals, usually every year. Also, the contract or agreement that stipulates the payment of an annuity.

antitrust laws statutes that seek to protect free trade and commerce by prohibiting certain restraints, such as monopolies or other combinations, and unfair business practices. See trust.

appraisal the valuation of property or assets as estimated by an authorized appraiser.

arbitrageur a person who buys securities (such as currency or commodities) in one country or market for immediate resale in another market, to take advantage of different prices.

arrears an unpaid and overdue amount, which may be subject to interest or other penalties.

assembly line the arrangement of equipment and workers in a manner such that the work passes in a direct line from a succession of work stations until a finished product is assembled.

asset the land or property of a company or individual, payments due from bills, investments, and anything else owned that can be turned into cash. On a company's balance sheet, total assets must be equal to liabilities (money and services owed). A *fixed asset* is normally not for sale and is intended for use within a business; for example, machinery, land, buildings, plant, and equipment. A *liquid asset* refers to cash or any asset that can easily be converted into cash, for example stock-exchange investments. Compare liability.

asset stripping sale, or exploitation by other means, of assets of a business taken over usually because the parts of the business may be potentially more valuable separately than together.

audit the official inspection of a company's accounts by a qualified accountant as required each year by law to ensure that the company balance sheet reflects the true state of its affairs. An *internal audit* is an independent in-house inspection of accounts.

balance of payments an account of a country's debit and credit transactions with other countries. Items are divided into the *current account*, which includes both visible trade (imports and exports of goods) and invisible trade (services such as transport, tourism, interest, and dividends), and the *capital account*, which includes investment in and out of the country, international grants, and loans. Deficits or surpluses on these accounts are brought into balance by buying and selling reserves of foreign currencies.

balance sheet a statement of the financial position of a company or individual on a specific date, showing assets, liabilities, and capital.

balloon loan a loan, often short term, in which the full balance is due at the end of a term, usually at a fixed interest rate. This type of loan generally has lower monthly payments of interest with little or no principle payments and a sustantial final payment of principle at the end of the term of the loan.

bank draft a check drawn by a bank from funds deposited to an account in another bank.

bankruptcy the process by which the property of a person (in legal terms, an individual or corporation) unable to pay debts is taken away under a court order and divided fairly among the person's creditors, after preferential payments such as taxes and wages. Proceedings may be instituted either by the debtor (voluntary bankruptcy) or by any creditor for a substantial sum (involuntary bankruptcy). Until discharged, a bankrupt person is severely restricted in financial activities.

barter the direct exchange of commodities or services without the use of money or credit.

base lending rate the rate of interest to which most bank lending is linked, with the actual rate determined by the status of the borrower. For example, a prestigious company might command a rate only 1% above base rate while an individual would be charged several points above.

bear a speculator who sells stocks or shares on the stock exchange expecting a fall in the price in order to buy them back at a profit. In a bear market, prices fall and bears prosper. Compare bull.

bill of exchange a written order from one person to another requiring a specified sum of money to be paid to a third designated person. Also, a form of commercial credit instrument, or IOU, used in international trade.

blue chip a stock that is considered strong and reliable in terms of the dividend yield and capital value. Blue chip companies are favored by stock market investors more interested in security than in risk taking.

bond a security issued by a government, company, bank, or other institution, on fixed interest. Usually regarded as a long-term security, a bond may be irredeemable, secured, or unsecured. Property bonds are non-fixed securities with the yield fixed to property investment.

bond rating the evaluation of a company's or a government's ability to honor the bonds it issues.

boom a sudden and rapid economic growth and expansion, usually accompanied by an increase in prices. Compare bust.

bottom line the net financial profit or loss. Also, the final result or outcome of something.

breakeven point situation where income equals expenditure so that neither a profit nor a loss is made.

broker intermediary who arranges the sale of financial products (shares, insurance, mortgages, etc.) to the public for a commission or brokerage fee.

budget financial plan for an organization, usually drawn up for a future 12-month period. A *capital budget* is a financial plan for tangible items whose benefits and/or costs may extend over a period longer than one year. A *cash budget* or *cash-flow projection* is a statement drawn up to show the net inflows and outflows of cash, with the resulting balance identified at the end of each period. Its purpose is to identify when surpluses or deficits of cash are expected, in order to allow for appropriate action.

bull a speculator who buys stocks or shares on the stock exchange expecting a rise in the price in order to sell them later at a profit. In a bull market, prices rise and bulls profit. Compare bear.

business plan document that analyzes the activities of a business in detail and predicts its objectives for at least the coming year. It is usually presented to the bank in support of a request for a loan or investments.

bust a sudden and severe decrease in economic activity. Compare boom.

call a demand for money, usually installments of part-paid securities.

capital accumulated or inherited wealth held in the form of assets (such as stocks and shares, property, and bank deposits). In stricter terms, capital is defined as the stock of goods used in the production of other goods, and may be *fixed capital* (such as buildings, plant, and machinery) that is durable, or *circulating capital* (raw materials and components) that is used up quickly.

capital employed total assets (excluding intangibles, such as good will) less current liabilities (including overdrafts, short-term loans, trade and other creditors).

capital expenditure spending on fixed assets such as plant and equipment, trade investments, or the purchase of other businesses.

capital flight transfer of funds from a particular national economy or out of a particular currency in anticipation of less attractive investment conditions.

capital gain the increase in the value of an asset from the time it was bought to the time it was sold. The term most often refers to the taxation of such an income.

capital intensive requiring a high expenditure for capital assets, particularly regarding the higher cost of capital in relation to the cost of labor.

capital investment the investment of funds in capital goods.

cartel association of firms that remain independent but which enter into agreement to set mutually acceptable prices for their products. A cartel may restrict output or raise prices in order to prevent entrants to the market and increase member profits.

cash flow the input of cash required to cover all expenses of a business, whether revenue or capital. Alternatively, the actual or prospective balance between the various outgoing and incoming movements, which is designated negative or positive according to whether outflow or inflow is greater.

closed shop a business enterprise which hires only members of a union by agreement with the union. The Taft-Hartley Act of 1947 made the closed shop illegal in the United States. Compare open shop, union shop.

collective bargaining process whereby management, representing an employer, and organized employees, negotiate terms and conditions of employment.

commodity something produced for sale. Commodities may be consumer goods, such as radios, or producer goods, such as copper bars. *Commodity markets* deal in raw materials that are amenable to grading and that can be stored for considerable periods without deterioration.

common stock a share in a corporation for which the stockholder has the right to vote on company matters but for which there is no guarantee of payment of dividends. Compare preferred stock.

company a number of people grouped together as a business enterprise. Types of companies include public limited companies, partnerships, joint ventures, sole proprietorships, and branches of foreign companies.

comparative advantage observation of international trade whereby differences in the cost of production of a particular item gives one country a competitive advantage over another.

consumption the purchase of goods and services for final use, as opposed to spending by firms on capital goods, known as capital formation.

corporate raider an individual, group, or company that tries to take over another company by buying up the company's stock, usually through clandestine means.

corporate strategy the way an organization intends to meet its objectives. This may be set out in a document of its principles, its situation, and the environment in which it expects to operate.

corporation a business organization, authorized by a state or federal government, in which there is transfer of ownership through stock sales and in which there is limited liability. See limited liability. Compare partnership, proprietorship.

cost-benefit analysis technique used in business decision-making that assesses all relevant costs and compares them with estimated returns. It is often used to take into account factors that are difficult to quantify and therefore might be overlooked.

cost of living the cost of purchasing goods and services which are considered necessary according to an accepted standard level of consumption, such as the consumer price index.

cost-of-living-adjustment the adjustment of wages and payments in order to reflect and offset the changes in the cost of living and protect the real purchasing power of wages.

cost of sales cost incurred directly in making sales. This could include the cost of raw materials or goods bought for resale and labor costs incurred in producing goods. It does not include overhead costs.

credit means by which goods or services are obtained without immediate payment, usually by agreeing to pay interest. The three main forms are *consumer credit* (usually extended to individuals by retailers), *bank credit* (such as overdrafts or personal loans), and *trade credit* (common in the commercial world both within countries and internationally). Also, the balance in a person's account, as in credits and debits. Compare debit.

critical path analysis procedure used in the management of complex business projects, which indicates the project's minimum duration and those subprojects critical to reduction in execution time, by identifying the duration and the relationship between them.

cumulative preference share preference share whose entitlement to dividend is carried forward to a subsequent year whenever the dividend is not paid.

current asset or *circulating* or *floating asset* any asset of a business that could be turned into cash in a limited period of time, generally less than a year. Current assets include stocks, accounts receivable or billings, short-term investments, and cash.

current liability any debt of a business that falls due within one year. Current liabilities include creditors (including employees), bank overdrafts, and interest.

current ratio in a company, the ratio of current assets to current liabilities. It is a general indication of the adequacy of an organization's working capital and its ability to meet day-to-day calls upon it.

debenture loan raised by a company using its assets as security for repayment.

debit a record of indebtedness. It is the entry on an account which records an addition to the expenses or costs of the account or a reduction in revenue or net worth. Compare credit.

debt crisis any situation in which an individual, company, or country owes more to others than it can repay or pay interest on; more specifically, the massive indebtedness of many Third World countries that became acute in the 1980s, threatening the stability of the international banking system as many debtor countries became unable to service their debts.

decision theory mathematical technique for analyzing decision-making problems, especially over unpredictable factors, seeking to minimize error; it includes game theory, risk analysis, and utility theory.

deferred share a share that typically warrants a dividend only after a specified dividend has been paid on the ordinary shares; it may, however, be entitled to a dividend on all the profits after that point.

deficit financing in economics, a planned excess of expenditure over income, dictated by government policy, creating a shortfall of public revenue which is met by borrowing. The decision to create a deficit is made to stimulate an economy by increasing consumer purchasing and at the same time to create more jobs.

deflation an actual decline in the prices of goods and services due to a decrease in the amount of available money or credit. Compare inflation.

demand the desire for goods and services as expressed by the willingness and ability to pay for them.

depreciation the decline of a currency's value in relation to other currencies. Depreciation also describes the fall in value of an asset (such as factory machinery) resulting from age, wear and tear, or other circumstances. It is an important factor in assessing company profits and tax liabilities.

depression an economic condition in which business activity is severely diminished, usually resulting in high unemployment and business failures, as in a severe recession. See recession.

deregulation action to abolish or reduce government controls and supervision over private economic activities, as with the deregulation of the US airline industry in 1978. Its purpose is to improve competition and lower prices. Increased competition has the effect, in some areas, of driving smaller companies out of business. A tremendous increase in mergers, acquisitions, and bankruptcies follows deregulation as the stronger companies consumed the weaker.

devaluation the lowering of the official value of a currency against other currencies, so that exports become cheaper and imports more expensive. Used when a country is badly in deficit in its balance of trade, it results in the goods the country produces being cheaper abroad, so that the economy is stimulated by increased foreign demand.

director person appointed to participate in decisions relating to the everyday running of a company, who may or may not have executive powers. A director is usually elected by the stockholders of a company. A *board of directors* (comprising all of the directors of a company) meets regularly to decide company policy and may elect one of its members to act as *managing director*, with responsibility for the overall running of the company.

diversification a corporate strategy of entering distinctly new products or markets as opposed to simply adding to an existing product range. A company may diversify in order to spread its risks or because its original area of operation is becoming less profitable.

dividend the amount of money that company directors decide should be taken out of profits for distribution to stockholders. It is usually declared as a percentage or fixed amount per share. Most companies pay dividends once or twice a year.

Dow Jones Index (*Dow Jones Industrial Share 30 Index*) scale for measuring the average share price and percentage change of 30 major US industrial companies. It has been calculated and published since 1897 by the financial news publisher Dow Jones and Co.

economic growth rate of growth of output of all goods and services in an economy, usually measured as the percentage increase in gross domestic product or gross national product from one year to the next. It is regarded as an indicator of the rate of increase or decrease (if economic growth is negative) in the standard of living.

economies of scale increase in production capacity at a financial cost that is more than compensated for by the greater volume of output. In a dress factory, for example, a reduction in the unit cost may be possible only by the addition of new machinery, which would be worthwhile only if the volume of dresses produced were increased and there was sufficient market demand for them.

electronic funds transfer (EFT) method of transferring funds automatically from one account to another by electronic means.

electronic funds transfer at point of sale (EFT-POS) the transfer of funds from one bank account to another by electronic means. For example, a bank customer's plastic card is inserted in a point-of-sale computer terminal in a supermarket, and telephone lines are used to make an automatic debit from the customer's bank account to settle the bill.

enterprise a business organization or any unit of economic organization or activity.

equal-opportunity policy plan of action that spells out what constitutes discrimination in order to guide employment practices and to ensure proper prevention against sexism, racism and other forms of discrimination.

equity a company's assets, less its liabilities, which are the property of the owner or stockholders. Popularly, equities are stocks and shares which, unlike debenture and preference shares, do not pay interest at fixed rates but pay dividends based on the company's performance. The value of equities tends to rise over the long term, but in the short term they are a risk investment because of fluctuating values.

exchange rate the price at which one currency is bought or sold in terms of other currencies, gold, or accounting units such as the special drawing right (SDR) of the International Monetary Fund. Exchange rates may be fixed by international agreement or by government policy; or they may be wholly or partly allowed to "float" (that is, find their own level) in world currency markets.

exemption the state of being free from some liability or requirement. Also, the amount of money free from taxation.

experience curve the observed effect of improved performance of individuals and organizations as experience of a repeated task increases.

export goods or service produced in one country and sold to another. Exports may be visible (goods physically exported) or invisible (services provided in the exporting country but paid for by residents of another country).

face value the stated value or significance of an instrument such as a bond or insurance policy.

favorable variance difference between actual and budgeted spending or income that results in the organization having more money than planned.

Federal Reserve System the system established to regulate the United States banking and monetary system. Established in 1913, the Federal Reserve System is made up of twelve regional banks and all commercial banks that have chosen to be a part of the system; the Federal Reserve Board is the governing body of the system.

fiduciary an individual granted the legal power to act on behalf of another in financial affairs.

Financial Times Index (FT Index) indicator measuring the daily movement of 30 major industrial share prices on the London Stock Exchange (1935 = 100), issued by the UK *Financial Times* newspaper.

fiscal policy that part of government policy devoted to achieving the desired level of revenue, notably through taxation, and deciding the priorities and purposes governing its expenditure.

fiscal year a continuous twelve-month accounting period.

fixed asset a tangible asset used in running a business and usually not converted into cash.

fixed costs or *indirect costs* or *overheads* the costs of a business that do not vary in proportion to changes in sales or output; for example rent and administrative expenses.

float quantity of money represented by checks issued but not yet collected. Also, the time period between the writing of a check or a purchase on credit and the actual withdrawal of funds to pay for it.

Fordism type of mass production characterized by a high degree of job specialization, as typified by Ford motor company's early use of assembly lines. *Post-Fordism* management theory and practice emphasizes flexibility and autonomy of decision-making for nonmanagerial staff. It is concerned more with facilitating and coordinating tasks than with control.

foreclosure the barring or extinguishing of a mortgagor's right to own a mortgaged property because of failure to pay by the date the mortgage was due.

franchise the right to use the name of another company and to market its products and/or services in exchange for a royalty. The franchisee agrees to abide by the conditions set out in the franchise agreement.

fraud the intentional perversion and misrepresentation of truth for the purpose of gaining an unfair advantage.

free enterprise the organizing and conducting of business free from direct government interference. A free enterprise system is to be regulated only by the laws of supply and demand and free competition.

free market an economic market that operates free from the control or interference of the government or any other powerful economic force or body, such as monopolies.

free trade the trading of goods and services based on unrestricted international exchange. In a free trade system tariffs are nonexistent or are employed only for the purpose of creating revenue. See tariff.

frozen asset an asset that cannot be converted into cash because of certain restrictions or only with heavy losses.

fund an available amount of money or resources, often set apart for a specific objective.

future a contract to buy or sell a specific quantity of a particular commodity or currency (or even a purely notional sum, such as the value of a particular stock index) at a particular date in the future. There is usually no physical exchange between buyer and seller. It is only the difference between the ground value and the market value that changes hands. The *futures market* trades in financial futures.

gearing, financial the relationship between fixed-interest debt and stockholders' equity used to finance a company. The additional profit made by borrowing at fixed interest and earning a greater return on those funds than the interest payable accrues to the stockholders. A high proportion of fixed-interest funding, known as "high gearing" can leave the firm more vulnerable in poorer trading conditions.

golden share a share, often with overriding voting powers, issued by governments to control privatized companies.

gray market dealing in shares using methods that are legal but perhaps officially frowned upon—for example, before issue and flotation.

greenmail payment made by a target company to avoid a bid—for example, buying back a stake in its own shares (where permitted) from a potential predator at an inflated price.

gross of a particular figure or price, calculated before the deduction of specific items such as commission, discounts, interest, and taxes. Compare net.

gross domestic product (GDP) value of the output of all goods and services produced within a nation's borders, normally given as a total for the year. It thus includes the production of foreign-owned firms within the country, but excludes the income from domestically owned firms located abroad.

gross national product (GNP) the most commonly used measurement of the wealth of a country. GNP is defined as the total value of all goods and services produced by firms owned by the country concerned. It is measured as the gross domestic product plus income from abroad, minus income earned during the same period by foreign investors within the country.

holding company a company whose primary business is holding a controlling interest in other companies, usually without direct participation in the other companies' operation. Compare investment company.

horizontal merger the combination of two or more companies that sell similar products into a single company. Such mergers can work to create monopolies and are thus often closely regulated by government agencies. See merger. Compare vertical merger.

hostile takeover the taking over of a company by buying enough stock to achieve a controlling interest in that company often through clandestine means. See takeover.

human-resource management or *personnel management* recruitment, selection, and training of staff, and efforts to involve them in the company.

hyperinflation rapid and uncontrolled inflation, or increases in prices, usually associated with political and/or social instability (as in Germany in the 1920s).

import product or service that one country purchases from another for domestic consumption, or for processing and reexporting (Hong Kong, for example, is heavily dependent on imports for its export business). Imports may be visible (goods) or invisible (services). If an importing country does not have a counterbalancing value of exports, it may experience balance-of-payments difficulties and accordingly consider restricting imports by some form of protectionism (such as an import tariff or import quotas).

income tax a direct tax levied on corporate profits and on personal income, mainly wages and salaries, but which may include dividends, interests, rents, royalties, and the value of receipts other than in cash.

industrial tribunal independent judicial body whose principal role is to deal with individual employment rights in cases such as unfair dismissal. Industrial tribunals are more flexible and less formal and expensive than ordinary courts of law.

inflation a rise in the general level of prices. The many causes include *cost-push inflation* that occurred 1974 as a result of the world price increase in oil, thus increasing production costs. *Demand-pull inflation* results when overall demand exceeds supply. *Supressed inflation* occurs in controlled economies and is reflected in rationing, shortages, and black market prices. Compare deflation.

inflation accounting a method of accounting that allows for the changing purchasing power of money due to inflation.

insider trading or *insider dealing* illegal use of privileged information in dealing on the stock exchanges, for example when a company takeover bid is imminent. Insider trading is in theory detected by the Securities and Exchange Commission (SEC) in the US. This, however, has no legal powers other than public disclosure and does not bring prosecution.

insolvent unable to pay debts.

insurance the contractual guarantee against loss by a specified contingency or danger.

interest a sum of money paid by a borrower to a lender in return for the loan, usually expressed as a percentage per annum. *Simple interest* is interest calculated as a straight percentage of the amount loaned or invested. In *compound interest*, the interest earned over a period of time (for example, per annum) is added to the investment, so that at the end of the next period interest is paid on that total.

International Monetary Fund (IMF) organization set up in 1944 that works to lower trade barriers and stabilize foreign exchange rates. The IMF can also aid developing countries to pay their international debts.

investment the purchase of any asset with the potential to yield future financial benefit to the purchaser.

investment company a company whose primary business is holding securities of other companies strictly for investment purposes. Compare holding company.

investment trust public company that makes investments in other companies on behalf of its stockholders. It may issue shares to raise capital and issue fixed interest securities.

issued capital the nominal value of those shares in a company that have been allotted. The issued capital is equivalent to the amount invested, provided the issue has not been at a premium price.

joint venture an undertaking in which an individual or legal entity of one company or country forms a company with those of another, with risks being shared.

junk bond slang term for a security, officially rated as "below investment grade." It is issued in order to raise capital quickly, typically to finance a takeover to be paid for by the sale of assets once the company is acquired. Junk bonds have a high yield, but are a high-risk investment.

just-in-time (JIT) production management practice requiring that incoming supplies arrive at the time when they are needed by the customer, most typically in a manufacturer's assembly operations. JIT requires considerable cooperation between supplier and customer, but can reduce expenses and improve efficiency.

Keynesian economics theory of macroeconomics developed by British economist John Maynard Keynes in the 1930s and '40s. This body of thought believes that active government intervention in monetary and fiscal policy will ensure economic growth and stability. See macroeconomics.

key-results analysis management procedure involving the identification of performance components critical to a particular process or event, the necessary level of performance required from them, and the methods of monitoring to be used.

labor union an association of workers formed for the purpose of bargaining with employers in order to improve and advance general working conditions, especially with regards to wages, benefits, and physical working conditions.

laissez faire theory that the state should not intervene in economic affairs, except to break up a monopoly. The degree to which intervention should take place is still one of the chief problems of economics.

law of diminishing returns economic principle that beyond a certain point the rate of yield no longer increases in proportion to additional expenditures of labor and capital input.

law of supply and demand economic principle that, all other things being equal, the amount of a product supplied and the amount demanded, and the interaction between the forces of supply and demand, are directly related to the price of the product.

learning curve graphical representation of the improvement in performance of a person executing a new task.

leveraged buyout the purchase of a controlling proportion of the shares of a company by its own management, financed almost exclusively by borrowing. It is so called because the ratio of a company's long-term debt to its equity (capital assets) is known as its "leverage."

liability the amount that is owed by an individual or company, whether money, products, or services, to others. Compare asset.

limited liability a stipulation whereby the shareholders of a corporation are responsible for the corporation's liabilities only to a certain point, usually not beyond the amount invested by the individual in the company.

liquidation the termination of a company by converting all its assets into money to pay off its liabilities.

macroeconomics the study of economics in terms of the entire system and the forces which shape a nation's economy, focusing on broad issues such as monetary flow, gross national product, and government fiscal policies. Compare microeconomics.

management buyout purchase of control of a company by its management, generally with debt funding, making it a leveraged buyout.

management information system (MIS) computer system for converting company data from internal and external sources into appropriate information and communicating it to managers at all levels.

margin the difference between net sales and costs. Also, the part of an equity investment purchased with credit from a broker.

market capitalization the market value of a company, based on the market price of all its issued securities— price that would be unlikely to apply, however, if a bid were actually made for control of them.

market forces the forces of demand (a want backed by the ability to pay) and supply (the willingness and ability to supply).

market segment portion of a market characterized by such similarity of customers, their requirements, and/or buying behavior that those who sell the products or services bought by these customers can aim their marketing effort specifically at this segment.

market share the percentage of total market sales in a given period that is attributable to one business.

marketing mix the blending of the four key elements of all marketing activity—product or service, price, promotion, and distribution—in such a way that the combination is likely to prove attractive to chosen sectors of the customer market.

maturity the date specified for redemption of a bond, bill, etc., after which no further interest is payable.

merger the combination of two or more companies, either by creating a new organization by consolidating the original companies or by the absorption of one company by another. Unlike a takeover, a merger is the result of an agreement. See horizontal merger, vertical merger.

microeconomics the study of economics in terms of individual economic units or areas of activity, such as households, companies, or industries. Compare macroeconomics.

minority interest an item in the consolidated accounts of a holding company that represents the value of any shares in its subsidiaries that it does not itself own.

mixed economy an economy in which market forces and nonmarket forces, usually governmental intervention, both determine the economic system.

monetarism economic policy, advocated by the economist Milton Friedman and the Chicago school of economists, that proposes control of a country's money supply to keep it in step with the country's ability to produce goods, with the aim of curbing inflation. Cutting government spending is advocated, and the long-term aim is to return as much of the economy as possible to the private sector, allegedly in the interests of efficiency.

monetary policy economic policy aimed at controlling the amount of money in circulation, usually through controlling the level of lending or credit. Increasing interest rates is an example of a contractionary monetary policy, which aims to reduce inflation by reducing the rate of growth of spending in the economy.

money supply the quantity of money present in an economy at a given moment. Monetarists hold that a rapid increase in money supply inevitably provokes an increase in the rate of inflation.

monopoly the domination of a market for a particular product or service by a single company, which therefore has no competition and can keep prices high. In practice, a company can be said to have a monopoly when it controls a significant proportion of the market (see oligopoly). Compare monopsony.

monopsony a situation in which a product is purchased by a single consumer. Compare monopoly.

mortgage a long-term loan backed by real estate or valuable property, usually the item purchased with the loan. The creditor can claim that property if all payments are not made by the borrower when they are due.

multinational corporation company or enterprise operating in several countries, usually defined as one that has 25% or more of its output capacity located outside its country of origin.

multiplier the theoretical concept, formulated by John Maynard Keynes, of the effect on national income or employment by an adjustment in overall demand. For example, investment by a company in a new plant will stimulate new income and expenditure, which will in turn generate new investment, and so on, so that the actual increase in national income may be several times greater than the original investment.

national debt debt incurred by the central government of a country to its own people and institutions and also to overseas creditors. A government can borrow either from the public by means of selling interest-bearing bonds, for example, or from abroad.

net of a particular figure or price, calculated after the deduction of specific items such as commission, discounts, interest, and taxes. Compare gross.

net assets either the total assets of a company less its current liabilities (that is, the capital employed) or the total assets less current liabilities, debt capital, long-term loans and provisions.

net worth the total assets of a company less its total liabilities, equivalent to the interest of the ordinary stockholders in the company.

nominal wage the measurement of wages according to units of currency rather than actual purchasing power. Compare real wage.

nonprofit organization an organization that functions for the purpose of providing a public service without regard to economic gain and profit. Such organizations are exempt from paying income taxes.

oligopoly a situation in which a few companies control the major part of a particular market and concert their actions to perpetuate such control. This may include an agreement to fix prices (a cartel). See cartel, monopoly.

open shop a business enterprise in which the hiring of employees is not determined by membership in a labor union. Compare closed shop, union shop.

option a contract giving the owner the right (as opposed to the obligation, as with futures contracts) to buy or sell a specific quantity of a particular commodity or currency at a future date and at an agreed price, in return for a premium. The buyer or seller can decide not to exercise the option if it would prove disadvantageous.

overhead fixed costs in a business that do not vary in the short term. These might include property rental, heating and lighting, insurance, and administration costs.

par value the monetary value of a stock or bond.

partnership a business organization in which two or more individuals have a contractual agreement to share in the profits and the risks and losses of the business. There is no limited liability for partners of a company. See limited liability. Compare corporation, proprietorship.

pension a fixed gratuity guaranteed to an individual for past services to be paid at regular intervals upon that individual's retirement.

performance-related pay element of a wage or salary that is linked to the working performance of an individual or working group, according to a prior arrangement.

piggy-back export scheme a firm already established in the export field making its services available without charge to a small firm just entering the market. The small firm thus obtains the assistance of the large firm's good will, experience, and know-how, and is saved the trouble and expense of setting up its own export department.

poison pill a tactic to avoid hostile takeover by making the target unattractive. For example, a company may give a certain class of stockholders the right to have their shares redeemed at a very good price in the event of the company being taken over, thus involving the potential predator in considerable extra cost.

preference share a share in a company with rights in various ways superior to those of ordinary shares; for example, priority to a fixed dividend and priority over ordinary shares in the event of the company being wound up.

preferred stock a share of a corporation that entitles the holder of the stock to a fixed dividend to be paid before any of the dividends on common stocks are paid. Compare common stock.

premium price difference between the current market price of a security and its issue price (where the current price is the greater).

price/earnings ratio or *p/e ratio* a company's share price divided by its earnings per share after tax.

price elasticity of demand/supply a measurement of the responsiveness of the demand and supply of a product, respectively, to a change in price.

price war a period of commercial competition during which competitors repeatedly cut their prices below those of their competition.

prime rate the rate charged by commercial banks to their best customers. It is the base rate on which other rates are calculated according to the risk involved. Only borrowers who have the highest credit rating qualify for the prime rate.

principal the original sum of money or capital, not including interest.

privatization policy or process of selling or transferring state-owned or public assets and services (notably nationalized industries) to private investors. Privatization of services involves the government contracting private firms to supply services previously supplied by public authorities.

productivity the output produced by a given quantity of labor, usually measured as output per person employed in the firm, industry, sector, or economy concerned. Productivity is determined by the quality and quantity of the fixed capital used by labor, and the effort of the workers concerned.

profit also called net income or net earnings, it is the amount that revenues exceed expenditures or the earnings that remain after all expenses and taxes are deducted from the gross income.

profit-sharing scheme in a company, arrangements for some or all the employees to receive cash or shares on a basis generally related to the performance of the company.

promissory note a written promise to pay a specified amount of money at a fixed future date.

property something owned or possessed that has value.

proprietorship a business organization owned by a single individual. That individual has sole right to the profits and also sole responsibility for the liabilities of that company. Compare corporation, partnership.

protectionism an economic policy designed to protect domestic industries against foreign competition. High tariffs and restrictions on imports are common protectionist tactics. See tariff.

proxy the authority to act on behalf of another, such as in voting corporate stock. Also, the document authorizing such a relationship.

public domain land and property owned by the government as opposed to private individuals. Also, information or properties which have no protection by copyright or patent and which may be appropriated by anyone.

public relations deliberate, planned, and sustained effort of an organization to establish and maintain mutual understanding between itself and its employees, customers, stockholders, relevant labor unions, and local communities.

public sector borrowing requirement (PSBR) amount of money needed by a government to cover any deficit in financing its own activities.

public sector debt repayment (PSDR) amount left over when government expenditure (public spending) is subtracted from government receipts. This occurs only when government spending is less than government receipts. A PSDR enables a government to repay some of the national debt.

put option the right to sell a specific number of shares at a specific price on or before a specific date.

quality circle small group of production workers concerned with problems relating to the quality, safety, and efficiency of their product. Key characteristics of quality circles are size (8–12 members); voluntary membership; autonomy in setting their own agenda; access to the senior managers; and a relatively permanent existence. Quality circles were popularized in Japan.

quality control inspection of a product at various stages of completion. It usually involves an *input stage* when components and materials purchased from suppliers are inspected; a *process stage* when production processes are observed; and an *output stage* when the finished product is checked against the design specification. Typically, although not universally, quality control involves the use of sampling.

quantity theory of money economic theory claiming that an increase in the amount of money in circulation causes a proportionate increase in prices.

quota a quantitative amount of goods that a worker is expected to produce within a certain time frame. Also, a limit on the amount of goods that can be imported during a specific time frame, as imposed by the government.

quotation the highest bid offered and the lowest price asked for a particular stock or security.

rate of return the income from an investment expressed as a percentage of the cost of that investment.

real earnings the value of all earnings as adjusted for inflation or currency devaluation to reflect actual purchasing power.

real wage the wage paid to a worker after being adjusted for inflation to reflect actual purchasing power of the wage. Compare nominal wage.

recession a fall in business activity lasting more than a few months, causing stagnation in a country's output. See depression.

redeemable preference share a share in a company that the company has a right to buy back at a specific price.

reserve currency a country's holding of internationally acceptable means of payment (major foreign currencies or gold); central banks also hold the ultimate reserve of money for their domestic banking sector. On the asset side of company balance sheets, undistributed profits are listed as reserves.

residual income the income that is distributed as dividends to holders of common stock after the payments have been made to holders of bonds and preferred stock.

revenue the gross income produced by a given source, such as from sales of a product or service or returns from investments.

reverse takeover a takeover where a company sells to another to avoid being the target of a purchase by an unwelcome predator.

revolving credit credit which may be used repeatedly up to a specified limit after partial or total repayments have been made. Also called open-end credit.

rights issue new shares offered to existing stockholders to raise new capital. Shareholders receive a discount on the market price while the company benefits from not having the costs of a re-launch of the new issue.

risk capital or *venture capital* finance provided by venture capital companies, individuals, and merchant banks for medium or long-term business ventures that are not their own and in which there is a strong element of risk.

salary a fixed payment for services or labor paid at a weekly, monthly, or annual rate.

sales promotion any marketing activity intended to sell a product or service, especially activities that exclude advertising and public relations. Examples of sales promotion are free samples, price reductions, and sponsorship of sporting events.

savings the amount of current income that is not spent on consumption. Distinct from investments, which are considered expenditures for the production of goods for future consumption, savings usually take the form of bank time deposits. The savings rate depends on many factors, such as interest rates, inflation rates, unemployment rates, and expectations for future earnings.

Say's law the "law of markets" formulated by Jean-Baptiste Say (1767–1832) to the effect that supply creates its own demand and that resources can never be underused.

scrip issue or *subscription certificate* a free issue of new shares to existing stockholders based on their holdings. It does not involve the raising of new capital as in a rights issue.

secondary stock an inexpensive stock issued by a smaller company, which is traded on the major exchanges but is generally less risky.

secured loan a loan for which repayment is guaranteed by a promise of something of value.

Securities and Exchange Commission (SEC) official US agency created in 1934 to ensure full disclosure to the investing public and protection against malpractice in the securities (stocks and shares) and financial markets (such as insider trading).

security an evidence of ownership or debt, such as a stock certificate or a bond. Also, something given or pledged as guarantee for the fulfillment of an obligation, such as payment of a debt.

sequestrator person or organization appointed by a court of law to control the assets of another person or organization within the jurisdiction of that court.

share any of the equal portions into which the entire capital stock of a corporation is divided. See stock.

silent partner a partner who is known by the public to be a partner but who takes no role in the operation of the business.

sinking fund a fund set up, usually accumulated by regular installments, for the paying off of a debt.

social costs and benefits the costs and benefits to society as a whole that result from economic decisions. These include private costs (the financial cost of production incurred by firms) and benefits (the profits made by firms and the value to people of consuming goods and services) and external costs and benefits (affecting those not directly involved in production or consumption); pollution is one of the external costs.

spreadsheet matrix format on a computer that can provide a basis for numerical manipulation; it is used in financial planning.

stagflation economic condition (experienced in the US in the 1970s) in which rapid inflation is accompanied by stagnating, even declining, output and by increasing unemployment. It is a recently coined term to explain a condition that violates many of the suppositions of classical economics. Under the Carter administration, interest rates skyrocketed, prices rose dramatically, and a deep recession occurred. The increase in OPEC petroleum prices was a major contributing factor.

Standard and Poor's Stock Price Index or *S & P 500* index of the US stock market covering 500 stocks broken down into sectors.

stock ownership of a corporation as represented by shares. See share, common stock, preferred stock.

stock exchange institution for the buying and selling of stock in publicly held corporations. An exchange trades in stocks that are already issued. Trading is done only by members who have purchased or inherited a "seat" on the exchange. They can act as brokers for nonmembers, on a commission basis, or as floor brokers, acting for other members. Registered traders have no contact with the public but trade only their private accounts. The world's largest exchanges are in New York, London, and Tokyo, and stock prices are watched carefully as indicators of confidence in the economy.

strategic alliance joining forces with a major competitor for business advantages.

strike a work stoppage by a body of workers for the purpose of forcing the employer to comply with certain demands of the workforce.

strikebreaker also called a scab, a person hired to replace a striking worker.

subsidiary a company in which a majority or all of the stocks are held by another company and is thus controlled by that other company.

supply-side economics a macroeconomic theory which holds that drastic reductions in personal and corporate tax rates will encourage productive investment in industry and thus stimulate prosperity for the overall national economy. Contrasts directly with Keynesian economics.

SWOT analysis breakdown of an organization into its *s*trengths and *w*eaknesses (the internal analysis), with an assessment of the *o*pportunities open to it and the *t*hreats confronting it. SWOT analysis is commonly used in marketing and strategic studies.

takeover the acquisition by a company of a sufficient number of shares in another company to have effective control of that company—usually 51%, although a controlling stake may be as little as 30%. See hostile takeover.

tariff a duty or custom imposed by a government on imports or exports for the purpose of protecting domestic businesses from foreign competition and also to raise revenue. See free trade, protectionism.

tax shelter a strategy or investment by which a taxpayer legally reduces her/his tax liability.

trade cycle or *business cycle* period of time that includes a peak and trough of economic activity, as measured by a country's national income. In Keynesian economics, one of the main roles of the government is to smooth out the peaks and troughs of the trade cycle by intervening in the economy, thus mini-

mizing "overheating" and "stagnation." This is accomplished by regulating interest rates and government spending.

trade deficit an imbalance in trade resulting from an excess of imports over exports. See balance of payments.

trading account summary of a company's sales for a period, usually a year, together with the cost of sales for the same period, showing the resulting gross profit or loss.

treasury bill (T-bill) a short-term investment issued by the United States treasury with a maturity of less than one year.

treasury note (T-note) a note issued by the U.S. treasury usually with a maturity of between one and seven years.

trickle-down theory an economic theory which holds that financial benefits granted to big businesses and investors will eventually "trickle down" and lead to greater prosperity for smaller businesses and the middle and lower classes.

trust a fiduciary relationship in which the property interests of an individual (the beneficiary) are held by another (the trustee). Also, a combination of companies that seeks to reduce competition and control prices. See antitrust laws.

unemployment lack of paid employment. The unemployed are usually defined as those out of work who are available for and actively seeking work. Unemployment is measured either as a total or as a percentage of those who are available for work, known as the working population or labor force.

union shop a business enterprise in which an employer is free to hire any worker without regard to membership or nonmembership in a union, but in which nonunion employees are hired under condition that she/he must join the union within a specified time. Compare closed shop, open shop.

unit trust a company that invests its clients' funds in other companies. The units it issues represent holdings of shares, which means unit stockholders have a wider spread of capital than if they bought shares on the stock market.

value-added tax (VAT) a tax levied on a commodity at each stage in its manufacturing and distribution. The cost of the taxes is ultimately passed on to the consumer.

vertical merger the combination of one or more businesses involved in different stages of production into a single company. See merger. Compare horizontal merger.

wage the payment, usually of money, for labor or services based either on an hourly, daily, or piecework rate. See nominal wage, real wage.

white knight a company invited by the target of a takeover bid to make a rival bid.

working capital the capital required to finance the short-term activities of a business, principally the investment in stock and debtors.

yield the annual percentage return from an investment; on ordinary shares it is the dividend expressed as a percentage.

zero-based budgeting management technique requiring that no resources for a new period of a program are approved and/or released unless their justification can be

zoning ordinance a local ordinance that regulates the types of businesses or buildings that can be established at a specific location.

Business Tables

WAGE COMPUTATION TABLE

This table assumes an eight-hour workday, a five-day workweek, and a 52-week year.

HOURLY	DAILY	WEEKLY	MONTHLY	QUARTERLY	YEARLY
$2.50	$20.00	$100.00	$433.33	$1,300.00	$5,200.00
$3.00	$24.00	$120.00	$520.00	$1,560.00	$6,240.00
$3.50	$28.00	$140.00	$606.67	$1,820.00	$7,280.00
$4.00	$32.00	$160.00	$693.33	$2,080.00	$8,320.00
$4.50	$36.00	$180.00	$780.00	$2,340.00	$9,360.00
$5.00	$40.00	$200.00	$866.67	$2,600.00	$10,400.00
$5.50	$44.00	$220.00	$953.33	$2,860.00	$11,440.00
$6.00	$48.00	$240.00	$1,040.00	$3,120.00	$12,480.00
$6.50	$52.00	$260.00	$1,126.67	$3,380.00	$13,520.00
$7.00	$56.00	$280.00	$1,213.33	$3,640.00	$14,560.00
$7.50	$60.00	$300.00	$1,300.00	$3,900.00	$15,600.00
$8.00	$64.00	$320.00	$1,386.67	$4,160.00	$16,640.00
$8.50	$68.00	$340.00	$1,473.33	$4,420.00	$17,680.00
$9.00	$72.00	$360.00	$1,560.00	$4,680.00	$18,720.00
$9.50	$76.00	$380.00	$1,646.67	$4,940.00	$19,760.00
$10.00	$80.00	$400.00	$1,733.33	$5,200.00	$20,800.00
$10.50	$84.00	$420.00	$1,820.00	$5,460.00	$21,840.00
$11.00	$88.00	$440.00	$1,906.67	$5,720.00	$22,880.00
$11.50	$92.00	$460.00	$1,993.33	$5,980.00	$23,920.00
$12.00	$96.00	$480.00	$2,080.00	$6,240.00	$24,960.00
$12.50	$100.00	$500.00	$2,166.67	$6,500.00	$26,000.00
$13.00	$104.00	$520.00	$2,253.33	$6,760.00	$27,040.00
$13.50	$108.00	$540.00	$2,340.00	$7,020.00	$28,080.00
$14.00	$112.00	$560.00	$2,426.67	$7,280.00	$29,120.00
$14.50	$116.00	$580.00	$2,513.33	$7,540.00	$30,160.00
$15.00	$120.00	$600.00	$2,600.00	$7,800.00	$31,200.00
$16.00	$128.00	$640.00	$2,773.33	$8,320.00	$33,280.00
$17.00	$136.00	$680.00	$2,946.67	$8,840.00	$35,360.00
$18.00	$144.00	$720.00	$3,120.00	$9,360.00	$37,440.00
$19.00	$152.00	$760.00	$3,293.33	$9,880.00	$39,520.00
$20.00	$160.00	$800.00	$3,466.67	$10,400.00	$41,600.00
$21.00	$168.00	$840.00	$3,640.00	$10,920.00	$43,680.00
$22.00	$176.00	$880.00	$3,813.33	$11,440.00	$45,760.00
$23.00	$184.00	$920.00	$3,986.67	$11,960.00	$47,840.00
$24.00	$192.00	$960.00	$4,160.00	$12,480.00	$49,920.00
$25.00	$200.00	$1,000.00	$4,333.33	$13,000.00	$52,000.00
$30.00	$240.00	$1,200.00	$5,200.00	$15,600.00	$62,400.00
$35.00	$280.00	$1,400.00	$6,066.67	$18,200.00	$72,800.00
$40.00	$320.00	$1,600.00	$6,933.33	$20,800.00	$83,200.00
$45.00	$360.00	$1,800.00	$7,800.00	$23,400.00	$93,600.00
$50.00	$400.00	$2,000.00	$8,666.67	$26,000.00	$104,000.00

MONTHLY MORTGAGE PAYMENT TABLES

The Monthly Mortgage Payment Tables assume a fixed rate of interest. Each payment is the sum of that month's share of the principal and interest owed.

MONTHLY MORTGAGE PAYMENTS AT 6.00% INTEREST

FINANCED AMOUNT	1 YEAR	5 YEARS	10 YEARS	15 YEARS	20 YEARS	25 YEARS	30 YEARS
$5,000	$430.33	$96.66	$55.51	$42.19	$35.82	$32.22	$29.98
$10,000	$860.66	$193.33	$111.02	$84.39	$71.64	$64.43	$59.96
$15,000	$1,291.00	$289.99	$166.53	$126.58	$107.46	$96.65	$89.93
$20,000	$1,721.33	$386.66	$222.04	$168.77	$143.29	$128.86	$119.91
$25,000	$2,151.66	$483.32	$277.55	$210.96	$179.11	$161.08	$149.89
$30,000	$2,581.99	$579.98	$333.06	$253.16	$214.93	$193.29	$179.87
$35,000	$3,012.33	$676.65	$388.57	$295.35	$250.75	$225.51	$209.84
$40,000	$3,442.66	$773.31	$444.08	$337.54	$286.57	$257.72	$239.82
$45,000	$3,872.99	$869.98	$499.59	$379.74	$322.39	$289.94	$269.80
$50,000	$4,303.32	$966.64	$555.10	$421.93	$358.22	$322.15	$299.78
$55,000	$4,733.65	$1,063.30	$610.61	$464.12	$394.04	$354.37	$329.75
$60,000	$5,163.99	$1,159.97	$666.12	$506.31	$429.86	$386.58	$359.73
$65,000	$5,594.32	$1,256.63	$721.63	$548.51	$465.68	$418.80	$389.71
$70,000	$6,024.65	$1,353.30	$777.14	$590.70	$501.50	$451.01	$419.69
$75,000	$6,454.98	$1,449.96	$832.65	$632.89	$537.32	$483.23	$449.66
$80,000	$6,885.31	$1,546.62	$888.16	$675.09	$573.14	$515.44	$479.64
$85,000	$7,315.65	$1,643.29	$943.67	$717.28	$608.97	$547.66	$509.62
$90,000	$7,745.98	$1,739.95	$999.18	$759.47	$644.79	$579.87	$539.60
$95,000	$8,176.31	$1,836.62	$1,054.69	$801.66	$680.61	$612.09	$569.57
$100,000	$8,606.64	$1,933.28	$1,110.21	$843.86	$716.43	$644.30	$599.55
$150,000	$12,909.96	$2,899.92	$1,665.31	$1,265.79	$1,074.65	$966.45	$899.33
$200,000	$17,213.29	$3,866.56	$2,220.41	$1,687.71	$1,432.86	$1,288.60	$1,199.10
$250,000	$21,516.61	$4,833.20	$2,775.51	$2,109.64	$1,791.08	$1,610.75	$1,498.88
$300,000	$25,819.93	$5,799.84	$3,330.62	$2,531.57	$2,149.29	$1,932.90	$1,798.65
$350,000	$30,123.25	$6,766.48	$3,885.72	$2,953.50	$2,507.51	$2,255.05	$2,098.43
$400,000	$34,426.57	$7,733.12	$4,440.82	$3,375.43	$2,865.72	$2,577.21	$2,398.20
$450,000	$38,729.89	$8,699.76	$4,995.92	$3,797.36	$3,223.94	$2,899.36	$2,697.98
$500,000	$43,033.22	$9,666.40	$5,551.03	$4,219.28	$3,582.16	$3,221.51	$2,997.75
$1,000,000	$86,066.43	$19,332.80	$11,102.05	$8,438.57	$7,164.31	$6,443.01	$5,995.51

MONTHLY MORTGAGE PAYMENTS AT 7.00% INTEREST

FINANCED AMOUNT	1 YEAR	5 YEARS	10 YEARS	15 YEARS	20 YEARS	25 YEARS	30 YEARS
$5,000	$432.63	$99.01	$58.05	$44.94	$38.76	$35.34	$33.27
$10,000	$865.27	$198.01	$116.11	$89.88	$77.53	$70.68	$66.53
$15,000	$1,297.90	$297.02	$174.16	$134.82	$116.29	$106.02	$99.80
$20,000	$1,730.53	$396.02	$232.22	$179.77	$155.06	$141.36	$133.06
$25,000	$2,163.17	$495.03	$290.27	$224.71	$193.82	$176.69	$166.33
$30,000	$2,595.80	$594.04	$348.33	$269.65	$232.59	$212.03	$199.59
$35,000	$3,028.44	$693.04	$406.38	$314.59	$271.35	$247.37	$232.86
$40,000	$3,461.07	$792.05	$464.43	$359.53	$310.12	$282.71	$266.12
$45,000	$3,893.70	$891.05	$522.49	$404.47	$348.88	$318.05	$299.39
$50,000	$4,326.34	$990.06	$580.54	$449.41	$387.65	$353.39	$332.65
$55,000	$4,758.97	$1,089.07	$638.60	$494.36	$426.41	$388.73	$365.92
$60,000	$5,191.60	$1,188.07	$696.65	$539.30	$465.18	$424.07	$399.18
$65,000	$5,624.24	$1,287.08	$754.71	$584.24	$503.94	$459.41	$432.45
$70,000	$6,056.87	$1,386.08	$812.76	$629.18	$542.71	$494.75	$465.71
$75,000	$6,489.51	$1,485.09	$870.81	$674.12	$581.47	$530.08	$498.98
$80,000	$6,922.14	$1,584.10	$928.87	$719.06	$620.24	$565.42	$532.24
$85,000	$7,354.77	$1,683.10	$986.92	$764.00	$659.00	$600.76	$565.51
$90,000	$7,787.41	$1,782.11	$1,044.98	$808.95	$697.77	$636.10	$598.77
$95,000	$8,220.04	$1,881.11	$1,103.03	$853.89	$736.53	$671.44	$632.04
$100,000	$8,652.67	$1,980.12	$1,161.08	$898.83	$775.30	$706.78	$665.30
$150,000	$12,979.01	$2,970.18	$1,741.63	$1,348.24	$1,162.95	$1,060.17	$997.95
$200,000	$17,305.35	$3,960.24	$2,322.17	$1,797.66	$1,550.60	$1,413.56	$1,330.61
$250,000	$21,631.69	$4,950.30	$2,902.71	$2,247.07	$1,938.25	$1,766.95	$1,663.26
$300,000	$25,958.02	$5,940.36	$3,483.25	$2,696.48	$2,325.90	$2,120.34	$1,995.91
$350,000	$30,284.36	$6,930.42	$4,063.80	$3,145.90	$2,713.55	$2,473.73	$2,328.56
$400,000	$34,610.70	$7,920.48	$4,644.34	$3,595.31	$3,101.20	$2,827.11	$2,661.21
$450,000	$38,937.03	$8,910.54	$5,224.88	$4,044.73	$3,488.85	$3,180.51	$2,993.86
$500,000	$43,263.37	$9,900.60	$5,805.42	$4,494.14	$3,876.49	$3,533.90	$3,326.51
$1,000,000	$86,526.74	$19,801.20	$11,610.85	$8,988.28	$7,752.99	$7,067.79	$6,653.03

MONTHLY MORTGAGE PAYMENTS AT 8.00% INTEREST

FINANCED AMOUNT	1 YEAR	5 YEARS	10 YEARS	15 YEARS	20 YEARS	25 YEARS	30 YEARS
$5,000	$434.94	$101.38	$60.66	$47.78	$41.82	$38.59	$36.69
$10,000	$869.88	$202.76	$121.33	$95.57	$83.64	$77.18	$73.38
$15,000	$1,304.83	$304.15	$181.99	$143.35	$125.47	$115.77	$110.06
$20,000	$1,739.77	$405.53	$242.66	$191.13	$167.29	$154.36	$146.75
$25,000	$2,174.71	$506.91	$303.32	$238.91	$209.11	$192.95	$183.44
$30,000	$2,609.65	$608.29	$363.98	$286.70	$250.93	$231.54	$220.13
$35,000	$3,044.60	$709.67	$424.65	$334.48	$292.75	$270.14	$256.82
$40,000	$3,479.54	$811.06	$485.31	$382.26	$334.58	$308.73	$293.51
$45,000	$3,914.48	$912.44	$545.97	$430.04	$376.40	$347.32	$330.19
$50,000	$4,349.42	$1,013.82	$606.64	$477.83	$418.22	$385.91	$366.88
$55,000	$4,784.36	$1,115.20	$667.30	$525.61	$460.04	$424.50	$403.57
$60,000	$5,219.31	$1,216.58	$727.97	$573.39	$501.86	$463.09	$440.26
$65,000	$5,654.25	$1,317.97	$788.63	$621.17	$543.69	$501.68	$476.95
$70,000	$6,089.19	$1,419.35	$849.29	$668.96	$585.51	$540.27	$513.64
$75,000	$6,524.13	$1,520.73	$909.96	$716.74	$627.33	$578.86	$550.32
$80,000	$6,959.07	$1,622.11	$970.62	$764.52	$669.15	$617.45	$587.01
$85,000	$7,394.02	$1,723.49	$1,031.28	$812.30	$710.97	$656.04	$623.70
$90,000	$7,828.96	$1,824.88	$1,091.95	$860.09	$752.80	$694.63	$660.39
$95,000	$8,263.90	$1,926.26	$1,152.61	$907.87	$794.62	$733.23	$697.08
$100,000	$8,698.84	$2,027.64	$1,213.28	$955.65	$836.44	$771.82	$733.76
$150,000	$13,048.26	$3,041.46	$1,819.91	$1,433.48	$1,254.66	$1,157.72	$1,100.65
$200,000	$17,397.69	$4,055.28	$2,426.55	$1,911.30	$1,672.88	$1,543.63	$1,467.53
$250,000	$21,747.11	$5,069.10	$3,033.19	$2,389.13	$2,091.10	$1,929.54	$1,834.41
$300,000	$26,096.53	$6,082.92	$3,639.83	$2,866.96	$2,509.32	$2,315.45	$2,201.29
$350,000	$30,445.95	$7,096.74	$4,246.47	$3,344.78	$2,927.54	$2,701.36	$2,568.18
$400,000	$34,795.37	$8,110.56	$4,853.10	$3,822.61	$3,345.76	$3,087.26	$2,935.06
$450,000	$39,144.79	$9,124.38	$5,459.74	$4,300.43	$3,763.98	$3,473.17	$3,301.94
$500,000	$43,494.21	$10,138.20	$6,066.38	$4,778.26	$4,182.20	$3,859.08	$3,668.82
$1,000,000	$86,988.43	$20,276.39	$12,132.76	$9,556.52	$8,364.40	$7,718.16	$7,337.65

MONTHLY MORTGAGE PAYMENTS AT 9.00% INTEREST

FINANCED AMOUNT	1 YEAR	5 YEARS	10 YEARS	15 YEARS	20 YEARS	25 YEARS	30 YEARS
$5,000	$437.26	$103.79	$63.34	$50.71	$44.99	$41.96	$40.23
$10,000	$874.51	$207.58	$126.68	$101.43	$89.97	$83.92	$80.46
$15,000	$1,311.77	$311.38	$190.01	$152.14	$134.96	$125.88	$120.69
$20,000	$1,749.03	$415.17	$253.35	$202.85	$179.95	$167.84	$160.92
$25,000	$2,186.29	$518.96	$316.69	$253.57	$224.93	$209.80	$201.16
$30,000	$2,623.54	$622.75	$380.03	$304.28	$269.92	$251.76	$241.39
$35,000	$3,060.80	$726.54	$443.37	$354.99	$314.90	$293.72	$281.62
$40,000	$3,498.06	$830.33	$506.70	$405.71	$359.89	$335.68	$321.85
$45,000	$3,935.32	$934.13	$570.04	$456.42	$404.88	$377.64	$362.08
$50,000	$4,372.57	$1,037.92	$633.38	$507.13	$449.86	$419.60	$402.31
$55,000	$4,809.83	$1,141.71	$696.72	$557.85	$494.85	$461.56	$442.54
$60,000	$5,247.09	$1,245.50	$760.05	$608.56	$539.84	$503.52	$482.77
$65,000	$5,684.35	$1,349.29	$823.39	$659.27	$584.82	$545.48	$523.00
$70,000	$6,121.60	$1,453.08	$886.73	$709.99	$629.81	$587.44	$563.24
$75,000	$6,558.86	$1,556.88	$950.07	$760.70	$674.79	$629.40	$603.47
$80,000	$6,996.12	$1,660.67	$1,013.41	$811.41	$719.78	$671.36	$643.70
$85,000	$7,433.38	$1,764.46	$1,076.74	$862.13	$764.77	$713.32	$683.93
$90,000	$7,870.63	$1,868.25	$1,140.08	$912.84	$809.75	$755.28	$724.16
$95,000	$8,307.89	$1,972.04	$1,203.42	$963.55	$854.74	$797.24	$764.39
$100,000	$8,745.15	$2,075.84	$1,266.76	$1,014.27	$899.73	$839.20	$804.62
$150,000	$13,117.72	$3,113.75	$1,900.14	$1,521.40	$1,349.59	$1,258.79	$1,206.93
$200,000	$17,490.30	$4,151.67	$2,533.52	$2,028.53	$1,799.45	$1,678.39	$1,609.25
$250,000	$21,862.87	$5,189.59	$3,166.89	$2,535.67	$2,249.32	$2,097.99	$2,011.56
$300,000	$26,235.44	$6,227.51	$3,800.27	$3,042.80	$2,699.18	$2,517.59	$2,413.87
$350,000	$30,608.02	$7,265.42	$4,433.65	$3,549.93	$3,149.04	$2,937.19	$2,816.18
$400,000	$34,980.59	$8,303.34	$5,067.03	$4,057.07	$3,598.90	$3,356.79	$3,218.49
$450,000	$39,353.17	$9,341.26	$5,700.41	$4,564.20	$4,048.77	$3,776.38	$3,620.80
$500,000	$43,725.74	$10,379.18	$6,333.79	$5,071.33	$4,498.63	$4,195.98	$4,023.11
$1,000,000	$87,451.48	$20,758.36	$12,667.58	$10,142.67	$8,997.26	$8,391.96	$8,046.23

MONTHLY MORTGAGE PAYMENTS AT 10.00% INTEREST

FINANCED AMOUNT	1 YEAR	5 YEARS	10 YEARS	15 YEARS	20 YEARS	25 YEARS	30 YEARS
$5,000	$439.58	$106.24	$66.08	$53.73	$48.25	$45.44	$43.88
$10,000	$879.16	$212.47	$132.15	$107.46	$96.50	$90.87	$87.76
$15,000	$1,318.74	$318.71	$198.23	$161.19	$144.75	$136.31	$131.64
$20,000	$1,758.32	$424.94	$264.30	$214.92	$193.00	$181.74	$175.51
$25,000	$2,197.90	$531.18	$330.38	$268.65	$241.26	$227.18	$219.39
$30,000	$2,637.48	$637.41	$396.45	$322.38	$289.51	$272.61	$263.27
$35,000	$3,077.06	$743.65	$462.53	$376.11	$337.76	$318.05	$307.15
$40,000	$3,516.64	$849.88	$528.60	$429.84	$386.01	$363.48	$351.03
$45,000	$3,956.21	$956.12	$594.68	$483.57	$434.26	$408.92	$394.91
$50,000	$4,395.79	$1,062.35	$660.75	$537.30	$482.51	$454.35	$438.79
$55,000	$4,835.37	$1,168.59	$726.83	$591.03	$530.76	$499.79	$482.66
$60,000	$5,274.95	$1,274.82	$792.90	$644.76	$579.01	$545.22	$526.54
$65,000	$5,714.53	$1,381.06	$858.98	$698.49	$627.26	$590.66	$570.42
$70,000	$6,154.11	$1,487.29	$925.06	$752.22	$675.52	$636.09	$614.30
$75,000	$6,593.69	$1,593.53	$991.13	$805.95	$723.77	$681.53	$658.18
$80,000	$7,033.27	$1,699.76	$1,057.21	$859.68	$772.02	$726.96	$702.06
$85,000	$7,472.85	$1,806.00	$1,123.28	$913.41	$820.27	$772.40	$745.94
$90,000	$7,912.43	$1,912.23	$1,189.36	$967.14	$868.52	$817.83	$789.81
$95,000	$8,352.01	$2,018.47	$1,255.43	$1,020.87	$916.77	$863.27	$833.69
$100,000	$8,791.59	$2,124.70	$1,321.51	$1,074.61	$965.02	$908.70	$877.57
$150,000	$13,187.38	$3,187.06	$1,982.26	$1,611.91	$1,447.53	$1,363.05	$1,316.36
$200,000	$17,583.18	$4,249.41	$2,643.01	$2,149.21	$1,930.04	$1,817.40	$1,755.14
$250,000	$21,978.97	$5,311.76	$3,303.77	$2,686.51	$2,412.55	$2,271.75	$2,193.93
$300,000	$26,374.77	$6,374.11	$3,964.52	$3,223.82	$2,895.06	$2,726.10	$2,632.71
$350,000	$30,770.56	$7,436.47	$4,625.28	$3,761.12	$3,377.58	$3,180.45	$3,071.50
$400,000	$35,166.36	$8,498.82	$5,286.03	$4,298.42	$3,860.09	$3,634.80	$3,510.29
$450,000	$39,562.15	$9,561.17	$5,946.78	$4,835.72	$4,342.60	$4,089.15	$3,949.07
$500,000	$43,957.94	$10,623.52	$6,607.54	$5,373.03	$4,825.11	$4,543.50	$4,387.86
$1,000,000	$87,915.89	$21,247.05	$13,215.07	$10,746.05	$9,650.22	$9,087.01	$8,775.72

MONTHLY MORTGAGE PAYMENTS AT 11.00% INTEREST

FINANCED AMOUNT	1 YEAR	5 YEARS	10 YEARS	15 YEARS	20 YEARS	25 YEARS	30 YEARS
$5,000	$441.91	$108.71	$68.88	$56.83	$51.61	$49.01	$47.62
$10,000	$883.82	$217.42	$137.75	$113.66	$103.22	$98.01	$95.23
$15,000	$1,325.72	$326.14	$206.63	$170.49	$154.83	$147.02	$142.85
$20,000	$1,767.63	$434.85	$275.50	$227.32	$206.44	$196.02	$190.46
$25,000	$2,209.54	$543.56	$344.38	$284.15	$258.05	$245.03	$238.08
$30,000	$2,651.45	$652.27	$413.25	$340.98	$309.66	$294.03	$285.70
$35,000	$3,093.36	$760.98	$482.13	$397.81	$361.27	$343.04	$333.31
$40,000	$3,535.27	$869.70	$551.00	$454.64	$412.88	$392.05	$380.93
$45,000	$3,977.17	$978.41	$619.88	$511.47	$464.48	$441.05	$428.55
$50,000	$4,419.08	$1,087.12	$688.75	$568.30	$516.09	$490.06	$476.16
$55,000	$4,860.99	$1,195.83	$757.63	$625.13	$567.70	$539.06	$523.78
$60,000	$5,302.90	$1,304.55	$826.50	$681.96	$619.31	$588.07	$571.39
$65,000	$5,744.81	$1,413.26	$895.38	$738.79	$670.92	$637.07	$619.01
$70,000	$6,186.72	$1,521.97	$964.25	$795.62	$722.53	$686.08	$666.63
$75,000	$6,628.62	$1,630.68	$1,033.13	$852.45	$774.14	$735.08	$714.24
$80,000	$7,070.53	$1,739.39	$1,102.00	$909.28	$825.75	$784.09	$761.86
$85,000	$7,512.44	$1,848.11	$1,170.88	$966.11	$877.36	$833.10	$809.47
$90,000	$7,954.35	$1,956.82	$1,239.75	$1,022.94	$928.97	$882.10	$857.09
$95,000	$8,396.26	$2,065.53	$1,308.63	$1,079.77	$980.58	$931.11	$904.71
$100,000	$8,838.17	$2,174.24	$1,377.50	$1,136.60	$1,032.19	$980.11	$952.32
$150,000	$13,257.25	$3,261.36	$2,066.25	$1,704.90	$1,548.28	$1,470.17	$1,428.49
$200,000	$17,676.33	$4,348.48	$2,755.00	$2,273.19	$2,064.38	$1,960.23	$1,904.65
$250,000	$22,095.42	$5,435.61	$3,443.75	$2,841.49	$2,580.47	$2,450.28	$2,380.81
$300,000	$26,514.50	$6,522.73	$4,132.50	$3,409.79	$3,096.57	$2,940.34	$2,856.97
$350,000	$30,933.58	$7,609.85	$4,821.25	$3,978.09	$3,612.66	$3,430.40	$3,333.13
$400,000	$35,352.66	$8,696.97	$5,510.00	$4,546.39	$4,128.75	$3,920.45	$3,809.29
$450,000	$39,771.75	$9,784.09	$6,198.75	$5,114.69	$4,644.85	$4,410.51	$4,285.46
$500,000	$44,190.83	$10,871.21	$6,887.50	$5,682.98	$5,160.94	$4,900.57	$4,761.62
$1,000,000	$88,381.66	$21,742.42	$13,775.00	$11,365.97	$10,321.88	$9,801.13	$9,523.23

MONTHLY MORTGAGE PAYMENTS AT 12.00% INTEREST

FINANCED AMOUNT	1 YEAR	5 YEARS	10 YEARS	15 YEARS	20 YEARS	25 YEARS	30 YEARS
$5,000	$444.24	$111.22	$71.74	$60.01	$55.05	$52.66	$52.66
$10,000	$888.49	$222.44	$143.47	$120.02	$110.11	$105.32	$105.32
$15,000	$1,332.73	$333.67	$215.21	$180.03	$165.16	$157.98	$157.98
$20,000	$1,776.98	$444.89	$286.94	$240.03	$220.22	$210.64	$210.64
$25,000	$2,221.22	$556.11	$358.68	$300.04	$275.27	$263.31	$263.31
$30,000	$2,665.46	$667.33	$430.41	$360.05	$330.33	$315.97	$315.97
$35,000	$3,109.71	$778.56	$502.15	$420.06	$385.38	$368.63	$368.63
$40,000	$3,553.95	$889.78	$573.88	$480.07	$440.43	$421.29	$421.29
$45,000	$3,998.20	$1,001.00	$645.62	$540.08	$495.49	$473.95	$473.95
$50,000	$4,442.44	$1,112.22	$717.35	$600.08	$550.54	$526.61	$526.61
$55,000	$4,886.68	$1,223.44	$789.09	$660.09	$605.60	$579.27	$579.27
$60,000	$5,330.93	$1,334.67	$860.83	$720.10	$660.65	$631.93	$631.93
$65,000	$5,775.17	$1,445.89	$932.56	$780.11	$715.71	$684.60	$684.60
$70,000	$6,219.42	$1,557.11	$1,004.30	$840.12	$770.76	$737.26	$737.26
$75,000	$6,663.66	$1,668.33	$1,076.03	$900.13	$825.81	$789.92	$789.92
$80,000	$7,107.90	$1,779.56	$1,147.77	$960.13	$880.87	$842.58	$842.58
$85,000	$7,552.15	$1,890.78	$1,219.50	$1,020.14	$935.92	$895.24	$895.24
$90,000	$7,996.39	$2,002.00	$1,291.24	$1,080.15	$990.98	$947.90	$947.90
$95,000	$8,440.63	$2,113.22	$1,362.97	$1,140.16	$1,046.03	$1,000.56	$1,000.56
$100,000	$8,884.88	$2,224.44	$1,434.71	$1,200.17	$1,101.09	$1,053.22	$1,053.22
$150,000	$13,327.32	$3,336.67	$2,152.06	$1,800.25	$1,651.63	$1,579.84	$1,579.84
$200,000	$17,769.76	$4,448.89	$2,869.42	$2,400.34	$2,202.17	$2,106.45	$2,106.45
$250,000	$22,212.20	$5,561.11	$3,586.77	$3,000.42	$2,752.72	$2,633.06	$2,633.06
$300,000	$26,654.64	$6,673.33	$4,304.13	$3,600.50	$3,303.26	$3,159.67	$3,159.67
$350,000	$31,097.08	$7,785.56	$5,021.48	$4,200.59	$3,853.80	$3,686.28	$3,686.28
$400,000	$35,539.51	$8,897.78	$5,738.84	$4,800.67	$4,404.34	$4,212.90	$4,212.90
$450,000	$39,981.95	$10,010.00	$6,456.19	$5,400.76	$4,954.89	$4,739.51	$4,739.51
$500,000	$44,424.39	$11,122.22	$7,173.55	$6,000.84	$5,505.43	$5,266.12	$5,266.12
$1,000,000	$88,848.79	$22,244.45	$14,347.10	$12,001.68	$11,010.86	$10,532.24	$10,532.24

MONTHLY MORTGAGE PAYMENTS AT 13.00% INTEREST

FINANCED AMOUNT	1 YEAR	5 YEARS	10 YEARS	15 YEARS	20 YEARS	25 YEARS	30 YEARS
$5,000	$446.59	$113.77	$74.66	$63.26	$58.58	$56.39	$55.31
$10,000	$893.17	$227.53	$149.31	$126.52	$117.16	$112.78	$110.62
$15,000	$1,339.76	$341.30	$223.97	$189.79	$175.74	$169.18	$165.93
$20,000	$1,786.35	$455.06	$298.62	$253.05	$234.32	$225.57	$221.24
$25,000	$2,232.93	$568.83	$373.28	$316.31	$292.89	$281.96	$276.55
$30,000	$2,679.52	$682.59	$447.93	$379.57	$351.47	$338.35	$331.86
$35,000	$3,126.10	$796.36	$522.59	$442.83	$410.05	$394.74	$387.17
$40,000	$3,572.69	$910.12	$597.24	$506.10	$468.63	$451.13	$442.48
$45,000	$4,019.28	$1,023.89	$671.90	$569.36	$527.21	$507.53	$497.79
$50,000	$4,465.86	$1,137.65	$746.55	$632.62	$585.79	$563.92	$553.10
$55,000	$4,912.45	$1,251.42	$821.21	$695.88	$644.37	$620.31	$608.41
$60,000	$5,359.04	$1,365.18	$895.86	$759.15	$702.95	$676.70	$663.72
$65,000	$5,805.62	$1,478.95	$970.52	$822.41	$761.52	$733.09	$719.03
$70,000	$6,252.21	$1,592.72	$1,045.18	$885.67	$820.10	$789.48	$774.34
$75,000	$6,698.80	$1,706.48	$1,119.83	$948.93	$878.68	$845.88	$829.65
$80,000	$7,145.38	$1,820.25	$1,194.49	$1,012.19	$937.26	$902.27	$884.96
$85,000	$7,591.97	$1,934.01	$1,269.14	$1,075.46	$995.84	$958.66	$940.27
$90,000	$8,038.56	$2,047.78	$1,343.80	$1,138.72	$1,054.42	$1,015.05	$995.58
$95,000	$8,485.14	$2,161.54	$1,418.45	$1,201.98	$1,113.00	$1,071.44	$1,050.89
$100,000	$8,931.73	$2,275.31	$1,493.11	$1,265.24	$1,171.58	$1,127.84	$1,106.20
$150,000	$13,397.59	$3,412.96	$2,239.66	$1,897.86	$1,757.36	$1,691.75	$1,659.30
$200,000	$17,863.46	$4,550.61	$2,986.21	$2,530.48	$2,343.15	$2,255.67	$2,212.40
$250,000	$22,329.32	$5,688.27	$3,732.77	$3,163.11	$2,928.94	$2,819.59	$2,765.50
$300,000	$26,795.18	$6,825.92	$4,479.32	$3,795.73	$3,514.73	$3,383.51	$3,318.60
$350,000	$31,261.05	$7,963.58	$5,225.88	$4,428.35	$4,100.51	$3,947.42	$3,871.70
$400,000	$35,726.91	$9,101.23	$5,972.43	$5,060.97	$4,686.30	$4,511.34	$4,424.80
$450,000	$40,192.78	$10,238.88	$6,718.98	$5,693.59	$5,272.09	$5,075.26	$4,977.90
$500,000	$44,658.64	$11,376.54	$7,465.54	$6,326.21	$5,857.88	$5,639.18	$5,531.00
$1,000,000	$89,317.28	$22,753.07	$14,931.07	$12,652.42	$11,715.76	$11,278.35	$11,062.00

MONTHLY MORTGAGE PAYMENTS AT 14.00% INTEREST

FINANCED AMOUNT	1 YEAR	5 YEARS	10 YEARS	15 YEARS	20 YEARS	25 YEARS	30 YEARS
$5,000	$448.94	$116.34	$77.63	$66.59	$62.18	$60.19	$59.24
$10,000	$897.87	$232.68	$155.27	$133.17	$124.35	$120.38	$118.49
$15,000	$1,346.81	$349.02	$232.90	$199.76	$186.53	$180.56	$177.73
$20,000	$1,795.74	$465.37	$310.53	$266.35	$248.70	$240.75	$236.97
$25,000	$2,244.68	$581.71	$388.17	$332.94	$310.88	$300.94	$296.22
$30,000	$2,693.61	$698.05	$465.80	$399.52	$373.06	$361.13	$355.46
$35,000	$3,142.55	$814.39	$543.43	$466.11	$435.23	$421.32	$414.71
$40,000	$3,591.48	$930.73	$621.07	$532.70	$497.41	$481.50	$473.95
$45,000	$4,040.42	$1,047.07	$698.70	$599.28	$559.58	$541.69	$533.19
$50,000	$4,489.36	$1,163.41	$776.33	$665.87	$621.76	$601.88	$592.44
$55,000	$4,938.29	$1,279.75	$853.97	$732.46	$683.94	$662.07	$651.68
$60,000	$5,387.23	$1,396.10	$931.60	$799.04	$746.11	$722.26	$710.92
$65,000	$5,836.16	$1,512.44	$1,009.23	$865.63	$808.29	$782.44	$770.17
$70,000	$6,285.10	$1,628.78	$1,086.87	$932.22	$870.46	$842.63	$829.41
$75,000	$6,734.03	$1,745.12	$1,164.50	$998.81	$932.64	$902.82	$888.65
$80,000	$7,182.97	$1,861.46	$1,242.13	$1,065.39	$994.82	$963.01	$947.90
$85,000	$7,631.90	$1,977.80	$1,319.76	$1,131.98	$1,056.99	$1,023.20	$1,007.14
$90,000	$8,080.84	$2,094.14	$1,397.40	$1,198.57	$1,119.17	$1,083.38	$1,066.38
$95,000	$8,529.78	$2,210.48	$1,475.03	$1,265.15	$1,181.34	$1,143.57	$1,125.63
$100,000	$8,978.71	$2,326.83	$1,552.66	$1,331.74	$1,243.52	$1,203.76	$1,184.87
$150,000	$13,468.07	$3,490.24	$2,329.00	$1,997.61	$1,865.28	$1,805.64	$1,777.31
$200,000	$17,957.42	$4,653.65	$3,105.33	$2,663.48	$2,487.04	$2,407.52	$2,369.74
$250,000	$22,446.78	$5,817.06	$3,881.66	$3,329.35	$3,108.80	$3,009.40	$2,962.18
$300,000	$26,936.13	$6,980.48	$4,657.99	$3,995.22	$3,730.56	$3,611.28	$3,554.62
$350,000	$31,425.49	$8,143.89	$5,434.33	$4,661.09	$4,352.32	$4,213.16	$4,147.05
$400,000	$35,914.85	$9,307.30	$6,210.66	$5,326.97	$4,974.08	$4,815.04	$4,739.49
$450,000	$40,404.20	$10,470.71	$6,986.99	$5,992.84	$5,595.84	$5,416.92	$5,331.92
$500,000	$44,893.56	$11,634.13	$7,763.32	$6,658.71	$6,217.60	$6,018.81	$5,924.36
$1,000,000	$89,787.12	$23,268.25	$15,526.64	$13,317.41	$12,435.21	$12,037.61	$11,848.72

MONTHLY MORTGAGE PAYMENTS AT 15.00% INTEREST

FINANCED AMOUNT	1 YEAR	5 YEARS	10 YEARS	15 YEARS	20 YEARS	25 YEARS	30 YEARS
$5,000	$451.29	$118.95	$80.67	$69.98	$65.84	$64.04	$63.22
$10,000	$902.58	$237.90	$161.33	$139.96	$131.68	$128.08	$126.44
$15,000	$1,353.87	$356.85	$242.00	$209.94	$197.52	$192.12	$189.67
$20,000	$1,805.17	$475.80	$322.67	$279.92	$263.36	$256.17	$252.89
$25,000	$2,256.46	$594.75	$403.34	$349.90	$329.20	$320.21	$316.11
$30,000	$2,707.75	$713.70	$484.00	$419.88	$395.04	$384.25	$379.33
$35,000	$3,159.04	$832.65	$564.67	$489.86	$460.88	$448.29	$442.56
$40,000	$3,610.33	$951.60	$645.34	$559.83	$526.72	$512.33	$505.78
$45,000	$4,061.62	$1,070.55	$726.01	$629.81	$592.56	$576.37	$569.00
$50,000	$4,512.92	$1,189.50	$806.67	$699.79	$658.39	$640.42	$632.22
$55,000	$4,964.21	$1,308.45	$887.34	$769.77	$724.23	$704.46	$695.44
$60,000	$5,415.50	$1,427.40	$968.01	$839.75	$790.07	$768.50	$758.67
$65,000	$5,866.79	$1,546.35	$1,048.68	$909.73	$855.91	$832.54	$821.89
$70,000	$6,318.08	$1,665.30	$1,129.34	$979.71	$921.75	$896.58	$885.11
$75,000	$6,769.37	$1,784.24	$1,210.01	$1,049.69	$987.59	$960.62	$948.33
$80,000	$7,220.67	$1,903.19	$1,290.68	$1,119.67	$1,053.43	$1,024.66	$1,011.56
$85,000	$7,671.96	$2,022.14	$1,371.35	$1,189.65	$1,119.27	$1,088.71	$1,074.78
$90,000	$8,123.25	$2,141.09	$1,452.01	$1,259.63	$1,185.11	$1,152.75	$1,138.00
$95,000	$8,574.54	$2,260.04	$1,532.68	$1,329.61	$1,250.95	$1,216.79	$1,201.22
$100,000	$9,025.83	$2,378.99	$1,613.35	$1,399.59	$1,316.79	$1,280.83	$1,264.44
$150,000	$13,538.75	$3,568.49	$2,420.02	$2,099.38	$1,975.18	$1,921.25	$1,896.67
$200,000	$18,051.66	$4,757.99	$3,226.70	$2,799.17	$2,633.58	$2,561.66	$2,528.89
$250,000	$22,564.58	$5,947.48	$4,033.37	$3,498.97	$3,291.97	$3,202.08	$3,161.11
$300,000	$27,077.50	$7,136.98	$4,840.05	$4,198.76	$3,950.37	$3,842.49	$3,793.33
$350,000	$31,590.41	$8,326.48	$5,646.72	$4,898.55	$4,608.76	$4,482.91	$4,425.55
$400,000	$36,103.33	$9,515.97	$6,453.40	$5,598.35	$5,267.16	$5,123.32	$5,057.78
$450,000	$40,616.24	$10,705.47	$7,260.07	$6,298.14	$5,925.55	$5,763.74	$5,690.00
$500,000	$45,129.16	$11,894.97	$8,066.75	$6,997.94	$6,583.95	$6,404.15	$6,322.22
$1,000,000	$90,258.32	$23,789.93	$16,133.50	$13,995.87	$13,167.90	$12,808.31	$12,644.44

MONTHLY MORTGAGE PAYMENTS AT 16.00% INTEREST

FINANCED AMOUNT	1 YEAR	5 YEARS	10 YEARS	15 YEARS	20 YEARS	25 YEARS	30 YEARS
$5,000	$453.65	$121.59	$83.76	$73.44	$69.56	$67.94	$67.24
$10,000	$907.31	$243.18	$167.51	$146.87	$139.13	$135.89	$134.48
$15,000	$1,360.96	$364.77	$251.27	$220.31	$208.69	$203.83	$201.71
$20,000	$1,814.62	$486.36	$335.03	$293.74	$278.25	$271.78	$268.95
$25,000	$2,268.27	$607.95	$418.78	$367.18	$347.81	$339.72	$336.19
$30,000	$2,721.93	$729.54	$502.54	$440.61	$417.38	$407.67	$403.43
$35,000	$3,175.58	$851.13	$586.30	$514.05	$486.94	$475.61	$470.66
$40,000	$3,629.23	$972.72	$670.05	$587.48	$556.50	$543.56	$537.90
$45,000	$4,082.89	$1,094.31	$753.81	$660.92	$626.07	$611.50	$605.14
$50,000	$4,536.54	$1,215.90	$837.57	$734.35	$695.63	$679.44	$672.38
$55,000	$4,990.20	$1,337.49	$921.32	$807.79	$765.19	$747.39	$739.62
$60,000	$5,443.85	$1,459.08	$1,005.08	$881.22	$834.75	$815.33	$806.85
$65,000	$5,897.51	$1,580.67	$1,088.84	$954.66	$904.32	$883.28	$874.09
$70,000	$6,351.16	$1,702.26	$1,172.59	$1,028.09	$973.88	$951.22	$941.33
$75,000	$6,804.81	$1,823.85	$1,256.35	$1,101.53	$1,043.44	$1,019.17	$1,008.57
$80,000	$7,258.47	$1,945.44	$1,340.10	$1,174.96	$1,113.00	$1,087.11	$1,075.81
$85,000	$7,712.12	$2,067.03	$1,423.86	$1,248.40	$1,182.57	$1,155.06	$1,143.04
$90,000	$8,165.78	$2,188.63	$1,507.62	$1,321.83	$1,252.13	$1,223.00	$1,210.28
$95,000	$8,619.43	$2,310.22	$1,591.37	$1,395.27	$1,321.69	$1,290.94	$1,277.52
$100,000	$9,073.09	$2,431.81	$1,675.13	$1,468.70	$1,391.26	$1,358.89	$1,344.76
$150,000	$13,609.63	$3,647.71	$2,512.70	$2,203.05	$2,086.88	$2,038.33	$2,017.14
$200,000	$18,146.17	$4,863.61	$3,350.26	$2,937.40	$2,782.51	$2,717.78	$2,689.51
$250,000	$22,682.72	$6,079.51	$4,187.83	$3,671.75	$3,478.14	$3,397.22	$3,361.89
$300,000	$27,219.26	$7,295.42	$5,025.39	$4,406.10	$4,173.77	$4,076.67	$4,034.27
$350,000	$31,755.80	$8,511.32	$5,862.96	$5,140.45	$4,869.40	$4,756.11	$4,706.65
$400,000	$36,292.35	$9,727.22	$6,700.52	$5,874.80	$5,565.02	$5,435.56	$5,379.03
$450,000	$40,828.89	$10,943.13	$7,538.09	$6,609.15	$6,260.65	$6,115.00	$6,051.41
$500,000	$45,365.43	$12,159.03	$8,375.66	$7,343.50	$6,956.28	$6,794.44	$6,723.79
$1,000,000	$90,730.86	$24,318.06	$16,751.31	$14,687.01	$13,912.56	$13,588.89	$13,447.57

SIMPLE INTEREST TABLE—Future Value of $1.00 at a fixed rate of interest

Simple interest is the amount of interest earned on a principal (in this case, $1.00) in a given period. For example: $1.00 invested for five years at 4.00% interest will be worth $1.20—$1.00 + 4.00% x 5.

The future value of an invested amount may be determined by multiplying that principal by the table's computed value of a dollar. For example: $5,053.00 at 12% interest for five years (periods) will be worth $8,084.00 at maturity—$5,053.00 x $1.60.

PERIOD†	4%	6%	8%	10%	12%	14%	16%	18%	20%
1	$1.04	$1.06	$1.08	$1.10	$1.12	$1.14	$1.16	$1.18	$1.20
2	$1.08	$1.12	$1.16	$1.20	$1.24	$1.28	$1.32	$1.36	$1.40
3	$1.12	$1.18	$1.24	$1.30	$1.36	$1.42	$1.48	$1.54	$1.60
4	$1.16	$1.24	$1.32	$1.40	$1.48	$1.56	$1.64	$1.72	$1.80
5	$1.20	$1.30	$1.40	$1.50	$1.60	$1.70	$1.80	$1.90	$2.00
6	$1.24	$1.36	$1.48	$1.60	$1.72	$1.84	$1.96	$2.08	$2.20
7	$1.28	$1.42	$1.56	$1.70	$1.84	$1.98	$2.12	$2.26	$2.40
8	$1.32	$1.48	$1.64	$1.80	$1.96	$2.12	$2.28	$2.44	$2.60
9	$1.36	$1.54	$1.72	$1.90	$2.08	$2.26	$2.44	$2.62	$2.80
10	$1.40	$1.60	$1.80	$2.00	$2.20	$2.40	$2.60	$2.80	$3.00
11	$1.44	$1.66	$1.88	$2.10	$2.32	$2.54	$2.76	$2.98	$3.20
12	$1.48	$1.72	$1.96	$2.20	$2.44	$2.68	$2.92	$3.16	$3.40
13	$1.52	$1.78	$2.04	$2.30	$2.56	$2.82	$3.08	$3.34	$3.60
14	$1.56	$1.84	$2.12	$2.40	$2.68	$2.96	$3.24	$3.52	$3.80
15	$1.60	$1.90	$2.20	$2.50	$2.80	$3.10	$3.40	$3.70	$4.00
16	$1.64	$1.96	$2.28	$2.60	$2.92	$3.24	$3.56	$3.88	$4.20
17	$1.68	$2.02	$2.36	$2.70	$3.04	$3.38	$3.72	$4.06	$4.40
18	$1.72	$2.08	$2.44	$2.80	$3.16	$3.52	$3.88	$4.24	$4.60
19	$1.76	$2.14	$2.52	$2.90	$3.28	$3.66	$4.04	$4.42	$4.80
20	$1.80	$2.20	$2.60	$3.00	$3.40	$3.80	$4.20	$4.60	$5.00
30	$2.20	$2.80	$3.40	$4.00	$4.60	$5.20	$5.80	$6.40	$7.00
40	$2.60	$3.40	$4.20	$5.00	$5.80	$6.60	$7.40	$8.20	$9.00

COMPOUND INTEREST TABLE—Future Value of $1.00

Compound interest is the amount of interest earned on the original principal (in this case, $1.00) in a given period, with the sum of principal and interest combining to become the new principal for the next period. For example: $1.00, invested for one year at 4.00% interest, will be worth $1.04 at the end of that period—$1.00 + 4.00%; $1.04 becomes the new principal. At the end of two years, the original dollar will be worth $1.08—$1.04 + 4.00% or ($1.00 + 4.00%)^2.

The future value of an invested amount may be determined by multiplying that principal with the table's computed value of a dollar. For example: $5,053.00, if compounded annually for five years (periods) at 12% interest, will be worth $8,893.00 at maturity—$5,053.00 x $1.76.

PERIOD†	4%	6%	8%	10%	12%	14%	16%	18%	20%
1	$1.04	$1.06	$1.08	$1.10	$1.12	$1.14	$1.16	$1.18	$1.20
2	$1.08	$1.12	$1.17	$1.21	$1.25	$1.30	$1.35	$1.39	$1.44
3	$1.12	$1.19	$1.26	$1.33	$1.40	$1.48	$1.56	$1.64	$1.73
4	$1.17	$1.26	$1.36	$1.46	$1.57	$1.69	$1.81	$1.94	$2.07
5	$1.22	$1.34	$1.47	$1.61	$1.76	$1.93	$2.10	$2.29	$2.49
6	$1.27	$1.42	$1.59	$1.77	$1.97	$2.19	$2.44	$2.70	$2.99
7	$1.32	$1.50	$1.71	$1.95	$2.21	$2.50	$2.83	$3.19	$3.58
8	$1.37	$1.59	$1.85	$2.14	$2.48	$2.85	$3.28	$3.76	$4.30
9	$1.42	$1.69	$2.00	$2.36	$2.77	$3.25	$3.80	$4.44	$5.16
10	$1.48	$1.79	$2.16	$2.59	$3.11	$3.71	$4.41	$5.23	$6.19
11	$1.54	$1.90	$2.33	$2.85	$3.48	$4.23	$5.12	$6.18	$7.43
12	$1.60	$2.01	$2.52	$3.14	$3.90	$4.82	$5.94	$7.29	$8.92
13	$1.67	$2.13	$2.72	$3.45	$4.36	$5.49	$6.89	$8.60	$10.70
14	$1.73	$2.26	$2.94	$3.80	$4.89	$6.26	$7.99	$10.15	$12.84
15	$1.80	$2.40	$3.17	$4.18	$5.47	$7.14	$9.27	$11.97	$15.41
16	$1.87	$2.54	$3.43	$4.59	$6.13	$8.14	$10.75	$14.13	$18.49
17	$1.95	$2.69	$3.70	$5.05	$6.87	$9.28	$12.47	$16.67	$22.19
18	$2.03	$2.85	$4.00	$5.56	$7.69	$10.58	$14.46	$19.67	$26.62
19	$2.11	$3.03	$4.32	$6.12	$8.61	$12.06	$16.78	$23.21	$31.95
20	$2.19	$3.21	$4.66	$6.73	$9.65	$13.74	$19.46	$27.39	$38.34
30	$3.24	$5.74	$10.06	$17.45	$29.96	$50.95	$85.85	$143.37	$237.38
40	$4.80	$10.29	$21.72	$45.26	$93.05	$188.88	$378.72	$750.38	$1,469.77

†A period may be a day, a month, a quarter, a year, etc.

Computer Terms

The impact of the computer and computer technology on every aspect of our lives cannot be underestimated; moreover, their influence promises to grow rapidly as multi-media endeavors of all kinds continue to expand. With the increasing use of computers in the home and school as well as in business, understanding computer vocabulary, the terms used in describing hardware and software and the relationships among them, is vital for today's world. The following section provides clear explanations of words pertaining to the engineering and operation of computers, from personal computers to large computer networks.

artificial intelligence (AI) branch of science concerned with creating computer programs that can perform actions comparable with those of an intelligent human. Current AI research covers such areas as planning (for robot behavior), language understanding, pattern recognition, and knowledge representation.

ASCII (acronym for *American standard code for information interchange*) a coding system in which numbers are assigned to letters, digits, and punctuation symbols. Although computers work in binary number code, ASCII numbers are usually quoted as decimal or hexadecimal numbers. For example, the decimal number 45 (binary 0101101) represents a hyphen, and 65 (binary 1000001) a capital A. The first 32 codes are used for control functions, such as carriage return and backspace.

binary number system or *binary number code* system of numbers to base two, using combinations of the digits 1 and 0. Codes based on binary numbers are used to represent instructions and data in all modern digital computers, the values of the binary digits (contracted to "bits") being represented as the on/off states of switches and high/low voltages in circuits.

bit (contraction of *binary digit*) a single binary digit, either 0 or 1. A bit is the smallest unit of data stored in a computer; all other data must be coded into a pattern of individual bits.

boot or *bootstrap* the process of starting up a computer. Most computers have a small, built-in boot program that starts automatically when the computer is switched on—its only task is to load a slightly larger program, usually from a disk, which in turn loads the main operating system.

buffer a part of the memory used to store data temporarily while it is waiting to be used. For example, a program might store data in a printer buffer until the printer is ready to print it.

byte sufficient computer memory to store a single character of data. The character is stored in the byte of memory as a pattern of bits (binary digits), using a code such as ASCII. A byte usually contains eight bits.

CAD (acronym for *computer-aided design*) the use of computers in creating and editing design drawings.

CAD also allows such things as automatic testing of designs and multiple or animated three-dimensional views of designs. CAD systems are widely used in architecture, electronics, and engineering; for example in the motor-vehicle industry, where CAD is used to design automobiles.

CAL (acronym for *computer-assisted learning*) or CAI (acronym for *computer-aided instruction*) the use of computers in education and training: the computer displays instructional material to a student and asks questions about the information given; the student's answers determine the sequence of the lessons.

CAM (acronym for *computer-aided manufacturing*) the use of computers to control production processes; in particular, the control of machine tools and robots in factories.

chip or *silicon chip* another name for an integrated circuit, a complete electronic circuit on a slice of silicon (or other semiconductor) crystal only a few millimeters square.

computer graphics use of computers to display and manipulate information in pictorial form. The output may be as simple as a pie chart, or a seemingly three-dimensional engineering blueprint. Input may be achieved by scanning an image, by drawing with a mouse or stylus on a graphics tablet, or by drawing directly on the screen with a light pen. The drawing is stored in the computer as raster graphics or vector graphics. Computer graphics are increasingly used in computer-aided design (CAD), and to generate models and simulations in engineering, meteorology, medicine and surgery, and other fields of science.

data facts, figures, and symbols, especially as stored in computers. The term is often used to mean raw, unprocessed facts, as distinct from information, to which a meaning or interpretation has been applied.

database a structured collection of data, which may be manipulated to select and sort desired items of information. For example, an accounting system might be built around a database containing details of customers and suppliers. In larger computers, the database makes data available to the various programs that need it, without the need for those programs to be aware of how the data are stored. The term is also sometimes used for simple record-keeping systems, such as mailing lists, in which there are facilities for searching, sorting, and producing records.

data compression techniques for reducing the amount of storage needed for a given amount of data. They include word tokenization (in which frequently used words are stored as shorter codes), variable bit lengths (in which common characters are represented by fewer bits than less common ones), and run-length encoding (in which a repeated value is stored once along with a count).

desktop publishing (DTP) use of microcomputers for small-scale typesetting and page makeup. DTP systems are capable of producing camera-ready pages (pages ready for photographing and printing), made up of text and graphics, with text set in different typefaces and sizes. The page can be previewed on the screen before final printing on a laser printer.

disk or *disc* in computing, a common medium for storing large volumes of data. A *magnetic disk* is rotated at high speed in a disk-drive unit as a read-write (playback or record) head passes over its surfaces to record or read the magnetic variations that encode the data. Recently, *optical disks*, such as CD-ROM (compact-disc read-only memory) and WORM (write once, read many times), have been used to store computer data. Data are recorded on the disk surface as etched microscopic pits and are read by a laser-scanning device. Optical disks have an enormous capacity—about 550 megabytes (million bytes) on a compact disc, and thousands of megabytes on a full-size optical disk.

DOS (acronym for *d*isk *o*perating *s*ystem) computer operating system specifically designed for use with disk storage; also used as an alternate name for a particular operating system, MS-DOS.

electronic mail or *E-mail* system that enables the users of a computer network to send messages to other users. Passwords are frequently used to prevent unauthorized access to stored messages.

expert system computer program for giving advice (such as diagnosing an illness or interpreting the law) that incorporates knowledge derived from human expertise. It is a kind of knowledge-based system containing rules that can be applied to find the solution to a problem. It is a form of artificial intelligence.

function a small part of a program that supplies a specific value—for example, the square root of a specified number, or the current date. Most programming languages incorporate a number of built-in functions; some allow programmers to write their own. A function may have one or more arguments (the values on which the function operates). A *function key* on a keyboard is one that, when pressed, performs a designated task, such as ending a program.

fuzzy logic in mathematics and computing, a form of knowledge representation suitable for notions (such as "hot" or "loud") that cannot be defined precisely but which depend on their context. For example, a jug of water may be described as too hot or too cold, depending on whether it is to be used to wash one's face or to make tea. The central idea of fuzzy logic is probability of set membership. For instance, referring to someone 5 ft 9 in tall, the statement "this person is tall" (or "this person is a member of the set of tall people") might be about 70% true if that person is a man, and about 85% true if that person is a woman. Fuzzy logic enables computerized devices to reason more like humans, responding effectively to complex messages from their control panels and sensors.

gigabyte a measure of memory capacity, equal to one billion bytes. It is also used, less precisely, to mean 1,000 megabytes.

hacking unauthorized access to a computer, either for fun or for malicious or fraudulent purposes. Hackers generally use microcomputers and telephone lines to obtain access.

hardware the mechanical, electrical, and electronic components of a computer system, as opposed to the various programs, which constitute software.

hexadecimal number system number system to the base 16, used in computing. In hex (as it is commonly known) the decimal numbers 0–15 are represented by the characters 0, 1, 2, 3, 4, 5, 6, 7, 8, 9, A, B, C, D, E, F. Hexadecimal numbers are easy to convert to the computer's internal binary code and are more compact than binary numbers.

image compression in computing, one of a number of methods used to reduce the amount of information required to represent an image, so that it takes up less computer memory and can be transmitted more rapidly and economically via telecommunications systems. It plays a major role in fax transmission and in videophone and multi-media systems.

integrated circuit (IC), popularly called *silicon chip*, a miniaturized electronic circuit produced on a single crystal, or chip, of a semiconducting material—usually silicon. It may contain many thousands of components and yet measure only 0.2 in/5 mm square and 0.04 in/1 mm thick.

interface the point of contact between two programs or pieces of equipment. The term is most often used for the physical connection between the computer and a peripheral device. For example, a *printer interface* is the cabling and circuitry used to transfer data from a computer to a printer, and to compensate for differences in speed and coding.

joystick an input device that signals to a computer the direction and extent of displacement of a hand-held lever. It is similar to the joystick used to control the flight of some aircraft.

keyboard an input device resembling a typewriter keyboard, used to enter instructions and data. There are many variations on the layout and labeling keys. Extra numeric keys may be added, as may special-purpose function keys, whose effects can be defined by programs in the computer.

kilobyte (K or KB) a unit of memory equal to 1,024 bytes. It is sometimes used, less precisely, to mean 1,000 bytes.

laptop computer portable microcomputer, small enough to be used on the operator's lap. It consists of a single unit, incorporating a keyboard, floppy disc or hard disc drives, and a screen. The screen often forms a lid that folds back in use. It uses a liquid-crystal or gas-plasma display, rather than the bulkier and heavier cathode-ray tubes found in most display terminals. A typical laptop computer measures about 8.3–11.7 in/210–297 mm, is 2 in/5 cm thick, and weighs less than 6 lb 9 oz/3 kg.

light pen a device resembling an ordinary pen, used to indicate locations on a computer screen. With certain computer-aided design (CAD) programs, the light pen can be used to instruct the computer to change the shape, size, position, and colors of sections of a screen image.

macro a new command created by combining a number of existing ones. For example, if a programming language has separate commands for obtaining data from the keyboard and for displaying data on the screen, the programmer might create a macro that performs both these tasks with one command. A *macro key* on the keyboard combines the effects of pressing several individual keys.

megabyte (MB) a unit of memory equal to 1,024 kilobytes. It is sometimes used, less precisely, to mean 1 million bytes.

memory the part of a system used to store data and programs either permanently or temporarily. There are two main types: immediate access memory and backing storage. Memory capacity is measured in bytes or, more conveniently, in kilobytes (units of 1,024 bytes) or megabytes (units of 1,024 kilobytes).

microprocessor complete computer central processing unit contained on a single integrated circuit, or chip. The appearance of the first microprocessors in 1971 heralded the introduction of the microcomputer. The microprocessor has led to a dramatic fall in the size and cost of computers.

modem (acronym for *mo*dulator/*dem*odulator) device for transmitting computer data over telephone lines. It converts digital signals to analog, and back again. Modems enable computers to communicate with each other anywhere in the world.

mouse an input device used to control a pointer on a computer screen. Moving the mouse across a flat surface causes a corresponding movement of the pointer. In this way, the operator can manipulate objects on the screen and make menu selections.

MS-DOS (abbreviation for *Microsoft Disk Operating System*) computer operating system produced by Microsoft Corporation, widely used on microcomputers with 16-bit microprocessors. A version called PC-DOS is sold by IBM specifically for its personal computers. MS-DOS and PC-DOS are usually referred to as DOS.

multitasking or *multiprogramming* a system in which one processor appears to run several different programs (or different parts of the same program) at the same time. All the programs are held in memory together and each is allowed to run for a certain period.

neural network artificial network of processors that attempts to mimic the connections between nerve cells (neurons) in the human brain. Neural networks may be electronic, optical, or simulated by computer software.

operating system (OS) a program that controls the basic operation of a computer. A typical OS controls the peripheral devices, organizes the filing system, provides a means of communicating with the operator, and runs other programs.

pixel (abbreviation for picture element) single dot on a computer screen. All screen images are made up of a collection of pixels, with each pixel being either off (dark) or on (illuminated, possibly in color). The number of pixels available determines the screen's resolution. Typical resolutions of microcomputer screens vary from 320–200 pixels to 640–480 pixels, but screens with over 1,000–1,000 pixels are now quite common for high- quality graphic (pictorial) displays.

printer an output device for producing printed copies of text or graphics. Types include the *daisywheel printer*, which produces good-quality text but no graphics; the *dot-matrix printer*, which produces text and graphics by printing a pattern of small dots; the *ink-jet printer*, which creates text and graphics by spraying a fine jet of quick-drying ink onto the paper; and the *laser printer*, which uses electrostatic technology very similar to that used by a photocopier to produce high-quality text and graphics.

procedure a small part of a computer program that performs a specific task, such as clearing the screen or sorting a file. In some programming languages there is an overlap between procedures, functions, and subroutines. Careful use of procedures is an element of structured programming. A procedural language, such as BASIC, is one in which the programmer describes a task in terms of how it is to be done, as opposed to a declarative language, such as PROLOG, in which it is described in terms of the required result.

RISC (acronym for *reduced instruction-set computer*) a microprocessor that carries out fewer instructions than other microprocessors in common use. Because of the low number of machine-code instructions, the processor carries out those instructions very quickly.

screen or monitor output device on which the computer displays information for the benefit of the operator. The most common type is the cathode-ray tube (CRT), which is similar to a television screen. Portable computers often use liquid crystal display (LCD) screens. These are harder to read than CRTs, but require less power, making them suitable for battery operation.

software a collection of programs and procedures for making a computer perform a specific task, as opposed to hardware, the physical components of a computer system. Software is created by programmers and is either distributed on a suitable medium, such as the floppy disk, or built into the computer in the form of firmware. Examples of software include operating systems, compilers, and applications programs. No computer can function without some form of software.

speech recognition or *voice input* any technique by which a computer can understand ordinary speech. Spoken words are divided into "frames," each lasting about one-thirtieth of a second, which are converted to a wave form. These are then compared with a series of stored frames to determine the most likely word.

spreadsheet a program that mimics a sheet of ruled paper, divided into columns and rows. The user enters values in the sheet, then instructs the program to perform some operation on them, such as totaling a column or finding the average of a series of numbers. Highly complex numerical analyses may be built up from these simple steps.

touch screen an input device allowing the user to communicate with the computer by touching a display screen with a finger. In this way, the user can point to a required menu option or item of data. Touch screens are used less widely than other pointing devices such as the mouse or joystick.

Unix multiuser operating system designed for minicomputers but becoming increasingly popular on large microcomputers, workstations, mainframes, and supercomputers. It was developed by AT&T's Bell Laboratories in the US during the late 1960s, using the programming language C. It could therefore run on any machine with a C compiler. Its wide range of functions and flexibility have made it widely used by universities and in commercial software.

video display terminal (VDT) computer terminal consisting of a keyboard for input data and a screen for displaying output.

virtual memory a technique whereby a portion of the computer-backing storage memory is used as an extension of its immediate-access memory. For instance, the contents of an area of the immediate-access memory are stored on a hard disk while they are not needed, and brought back into main memory when required.

virtual reality advanced form of computer simulation, in which a participant has the illusion of being part of an artificial environment. The participant views the environment through two tiny television screens (one for each eye) built into a visor. Sensors detect movements of the participant's head or body, causing the apparent viewing position to change. Gloves (datagloves) fitted with sensors may be worn, which allow the participant seemingly to pick up and move objects in the environment.

virus a piece of software that can replicate itself and transfer itself from one computer to another, without the user being aware of it. Some viruses are relatively harmless, but others can damage or destroy data. They are written by anonymous programmers, often maliciously, and are spread along telephone lines or on floppy discs. Antivirus software can be used to detect and destroy well-known viruses, but new viruses continually appear and these may bypass existing antivirus programs.

word a group of bits (binary digits) that a computer's central processing unit treats as a single working unit. The size of a word varies from one computer to another and, in general, increasing the word length leads to a faster and more powerful computer. In a popular microcomputer it is16 bits but 32-bit microcomputers are now available.

word processing storage and retrieval of written text by computer. Word-processing software packages enable the writer to key in text and amend it in a number of ways. A print-out can be obtained or the text can be sent to another person or organization on disk or via electronic mail.

workstation high-performance desktop computer with strong graphics capabilities, traditionally used for engineering (CAD and CAM), scientific research, and desktop publishing. Frequently based on fast RISC (reduced instruction-set computer) chips, workstations generally offer more processing power than microcomputers.

WYSIWYG (acronym for *what you see is what you get*) a program that attempts to display on the screen a faithful representation of the final printed output. For example, a WYSIWYG word processor would show actual line widths, page breaks, and the sizes and styles of type.

Legal Terms

This glossary offers plain English definitions of common legal terms that appear in legal documents, court proceedings, and general writings concerning the laws of the land. The words and phrases defined here encompass terms derived from American and English legal traditions, the Napoleonic Code, as well as concepts used in International Law. General definitions of various fields of law—for example, maritime and martial law—are also given.

abscond to depart secretly and/or hide out in order to avoid legal proceedings.

absolve to set free from an obligation or from the consequences of guilt.

accessory an accessory is a criminal accomplice who aids in commission of a crime that is actually committed by someone else. An accomplice may be either "before the fact" (assisting, ordering, or procuring another to commit a crime) or "after the fact" (giving assistance after the crime). An accomplice present when the crime is committed is an "abettor."

accomplice a person who acts with another in the commission or attempted commission of a crime, either as a principal or as an accessory.

acquittal the setting free of someone charged with a crime after a trial. It follows a verdict of "not guilty" and prevents retrial of a defendant on the same charges under the US Constitution. See double jeopardy.

action one of the proceedings whereby a person or agency seeks to enforce rights in a civil court. Actions fall into three principal categories, namely civil (such as the enforcement of a debt), criminal (in which a government agency prosecutes a defendant accused of violation of a criminal law), and penal (violation of a law enacted to preserve public order).

act of Congress in the US, a bill or resolution passed by both houses of Congress, the Senate and the House of Representatives, which becomes law with the signature of the president. If vetoed by the president, it may still become law if it returns to Congress again and is passed by a majority of two-thirds in each house.

adoption permanent legal transfer of parental rights and duties in respect of a child from one person to another. State laws determine processes for adoption, rights of adoptees (such as access to information about natural parents), and inheritance rights.

adultery voluntary sexual intercourse between a married person and someone other than his or her legal partner.

advisory opinion the formal opinion of a legal body or law officer regarding a question of law is submitted by a government body. The opinion is not presented in an actual legal proceeding and is not binding by law.

affidavit legal document, used in court applications and proceedings, in which a person swears that certain facts are true.

alibi in law, a provable assertion that the accused was at some other place when a crime was committed.

alimony an allowance to be paid to a spouse for support, as ordered by the court in the case of divorce or separation.

allegation an assertion made by a party in a legal proceeding. It is a statement of what each party is intending to prove as truth.

amnesty release of political prisoners under a general pardon, or a person or group of people from criminal liability for a particular action.

annul to declare something void, invalidate, as in marriage.

a posteriori application of a particular experience or observation to a general law or principle, not achieved or proven by logical conclusions. In Latin, literally "from the latter, or most recent." Compare *a priori*.

appeal in law, an application for a rehearing of all or part of an issue that has already been dealt with by a lower court or tribunal. The outcome can be a new decision on all or part of the points raised, or the previous decision may be upheld. In criminal cases, an appeal may be against conviction and either the prosecution or the defense may appeal against sentence.

appellate court a court that treats appeals from cases of a lower court to review the decision.

a priori application of a general law or principle to a particular instance, not achieved or proven by actual experience or observation. In Latin, literally "from the one before." Compare *a posteriori*.

arbitrator an individual empowered to settle a dispute or differences. The arbitrator is chosen by both parties involved in the controversy and is not subject to appeal.

arraign to bring a person before a court to answer an indictment.

arrest deprivation of personal liberty by legal authority to stop commission of a crime or to charge someone with violation of a criminal or civil law.

arson malicious and willful setting fire to property. Often arson is a crime committed to claim insurance benefits fraudulently.

assault intentional act or threat of physical violence against a person. The kinds of criminal assault are common (ordinary); aggravated (more serious, such as causing actual bodily harm); or indecent (of a sexual nature).

Attorney General principal law officer. In the US, the principal officer of the federal government or of a state. Attorneys general act as chief officers for criminal and civil law and as chief legal representatives of their governments in government operations.

bail a security, bonds, or money deposited with the court to obtain the temporary release of an arrested person, on the assurance that the person will obey the court, as by attending a legal proceeding at a stated time and place. If the person does not attend, the bail may be forfeited.

beneficiary an individual designated to receive funds or other property, as named in a will or trust.

bequeath to dispose of or give through a will.

bigamy in law, the offense of marrying a person while already lawfully married to another. In some countries marriage to more than one wife or husband is lawful.

blackmail criminal offense of extorting money with menaces or threats of detrimental action, such as exposure of some misconduct on the part of the victim.

blasphemy written or spoken insult directed against religious belief or sacred things with deliberate intent to outrage believers. There are numerous laws in the US against blasphemy, but they are rarely, if ever, enforced.

blue laws a law that prohibits certain practices or activities to preserve observance of the sabbath. Most often applies to business activity being conducted on Sundays.

breach of contract the wrongful violation of a contractual obligation, or the failure to perform such actions. It can also apply to the prevention or hindrance of the performance of such obligations.

brief a written argument of points of law relevant to a lawyer's case. This will often include precedents, the questions of law relevant to the case, and a statement of how the law should be applied for the lawyer's arguments.

burden of proof in court proceedings, the duty of a party to produce sufficient evidence to prove that his case is true. In the US, the burden of proof is on the government, prosecution or plaintiff, since the accused is presumed innocent; in many other countries, the accused is presumed guilty until cleared, thus putting the burden or proof on the defense.

capital punishment punishment by death. Capital punishment is retained in 92 countries and territories (1990), including the US (37 states), China, and Islamic countries. In the US, the Supreme Court declared capital punishment unconstitutional in 1972 (as a cruel and unusual punishment) but decided in 1976 that this was not so in all circumstances. It was therefore reintroduced in some states, and in 1990 there were more than 2,000 prisoners on death row (awaiting execution) in the US.

certiorari a writ from a higher court to a lower court requesting further review.

child abuse the molesting of children by parents and other adults. It can give rise to various criminal charges and has become a growing concern since the early 1980s.

circuit court part of the federal court system, circuit courts hold sessions at various sections within a jurisdiction.

circumstantial evidence also called indirect evidence, it is evidence presented from which other facts or evidence is to be inferred.

civil disobedience deliberate breaking of laws considered unjust, a form of nonviolent direct action; the term was coined by the US writer Henry Thoreau in an essay of that name 1849. It was advocated by Mahatma Gandhi to prompt peaceful withdrawal of British power from India.

civil law legal system based on Roman law. It is one of the two main European legal systems, English (common) law being the other. Civil law may also mean the law relating to matters other than criminal law, such as contract and tort.

collusion a conspiracy or secret agreement for fraudulent or illegal activity.

common law that part of the English law not embodied in legislation. It consists of rules of law based on common custom and usage and on judicial decisions. English common law became the basis of law in the US and many other English-speaking countries.

concurrent sentence a sentence ordered by the court that overlaps and runs simultaneously with another sentence. See sentence. Compare consecutive sentence.

consecutive sentence a sentence that runs separately from other sentences facing an individual and that ends before or begins after the completion of another sentence. See sentence. Compare concurrent sentence.

conspiracy the joining of individuals in agreement to commit unlawful acts or to use unlawful means to accomplish a lawful end.

constitutional right rights and liberties guaranteed by federal or state constitutions which are protected from government interference.

consumer protection laws and measures designed to ensure fair trading for buyers. Responsibility for checking goods and services for quality, safety, and suitability has in the past few years moved increasingly away from the consumer to the producer.

contempt of court behavior that shows lack of respect for the authority of a court of law, such as disobeying a court order, breach of an injunction, or improper use of legal documents. Behavior that disrupts, prejudices, or interferes with court proceedings either inside or outside the courtroom may also be contempt. The court may punish contempt with a fine or imprisonment.

continuance the adjournment of a legal proceeding until a specified later date.

contract a binding agreement between two or more persons which is enforceable by law.

copyright law applying to literary, musical, and artistic works (including plays, recordings, films, photographs, radio and television broadcasts, and, in the US and the UK, computer programs), which prevents the reproduction of the work, in whole or in part, without the author's consent.

coroner official who investigates the deaths of persons who have died suddenly by acts of violence or under suspicious circumstances, by holding an inquest or ordering a postmortem examination (autopsy).

corporal punishment physical punishment of wrongdoers—for example, by whipping. It is still used as a punishment for criminals in many countries, especially under Islamic law. Corporal punishment of children by parents is illegal in some countries, including Sweden, Finland, Denmark, and Norway.

court martial court convened for the trial of persons subject to military discipline who are accused of violations of military laws.

criminal law body of law that defines the public wrongs (crimes) that are punishable by the state and establishes methods of prosecution and punishment. It is distinct from civil law, which deals with legal relationships between individuals (including organizations), such as contract law. Criminal offenses are either felonies or misdemeanors. Felonies are more likely to require a formal charge, called an indictment, by a grand jury. Punishments include imprisonment, fines, suspended terms of imprisonment, probation, and community service.

cross-examination the process of questioning a witness called by the opposing party for the purpose of checking, clarifying, or discrediting the testimony given by that witness. Compare direct examination.

damages in law, compensation for a tort (such as personal injuries caused by negligence) or breach of contract. In the case of breach of contract the complainant can claim all the financial loss he or she has suffered. Damages for personal injuries include compensation for loss of earnings, as well as for the injury itself. The court might reduce the damages if the claimant was partly to blame. In the majority of cases, the parties involved reach an out-of-court settlement (a compromise without going to court).

decree nisi conditional order of divorce. A *decree absolute* is normally granted six weeks after the decree nisi, and from the date of the decree absolute the parties cease to be husband and wife.

deed legal document that passes an interest in property or binds a person to perform or abstain from some action.

defamation in law, an attack on a person's reputation by libel or slander.

de facto existing in reality or practice, often without lawful authority, such as de facto segregation. Compare *de jure*.

defendant the party against whom a legal action or suit is brought in court. Also called the accused, particularly in criminal cases. Compare plaintiff.

de jure according to law or lawful. Compare *de facto*.

deposition a statement by witness made under oath before a trial in the presence of both attorneys. Can take the form of a written or an oral deposition.

dictum a judicial assertion or pronouncement of a principle.

direct examination the initial questioning of a witness by the attorney or party who called the witness for the purpose of presenting the factual arguments of the party. Compare cross-examination.

disbar to expel an attorney from the legal profession by rescinding the license to practice law. It is most often the result of illegal or unethical actions.

disorderly conduct various petty misdemeanors. Most often disturbing the peace or public indecency.

district attorney the prosecuting attorney acting on behalf of the people or the government of a particular jurisdiction.

district court a federal trial court having jurisdiction over a particular district of the United States. District courts have original jurisdiction in all cases involving offenses against United States laws, and has general jurisdiction in cases involving parties from two or more different states. Established by the United States Constitution.

divorce legal dissolution of a lawful marriage. It is distinct from an annulment, which is a legal declaration that the marriage was invalid. The ease with which a divorce can be obtained in different countries varies considerably and is also affected by different religious practices.

double jeopardy the act of prosecuting an individual a second time for the same offense. Prohibited by the Fifth Amendment to the United States Constitution.

due process of law the normal administration of the law, which must conform to basic legal principles and must be applied to all citizens without favor or prejudice. Established in the American legal system by the Fifth and Fourteenth Amendments to the U.S. Constitution, it is the principle that the government

may not deprive anyone of "life, liberty, and the pursuit of happiness" without the full and fair application of certain rules and procedures established by law.

easement rights that a person may have over the land of another. A common example is a right of way; others are the right to bring water over another's land and the right to a sufficient quantity of light.

embezzle to appropriate fraudulently to one's own use money or property lawfully in one's possession.

eminent domain the power of the state to take private property for public use, with due compensation to the property owner.

employment law law covering the rights and duties of employers and employees. During the 20th century, statute law rather than common law has increasingly been used to give new rights to employees. Industrial tribunals are statutory bodies that adjudicate in disputes between employers and employees or labor unions and deal with complaints concerning unfair dismissal, sex or race discrimination, and equal pay.

encroachment trespassing on the rights, property, or domain of another.

English law one of the major European legal systems, Roman law being the other. English law has spread to many other countries, including the US, Australia, and New Zealand.

enjoin to prohibit or restrain by legal injunction; or to order to do something with authority.

entrapment the luring of an individual by law enforcement or government agents into making an illegal or compromising act or statement. This excuses the defendant for any crimes committed as a result of such action.

equal opportunity the right to be employed or considered for employment without discrimination on the grounds of race, gender, religion, sexual orientation, physical or mental handicap.

equity system of law supplementing the ordinary rules of law where the application of these would operate harshly in a particular case; sometimes it is regarded as an attempt to achieve "natural justice." So understood, equity appears as an element in most legal systems, and in a number of legal codes judges are instructed to apply both the rules of strict law and the principles of equity in reaching their decisions.

escrow a document sealed and delivered to a third party and not released or coming into effect until some condition has been fulfilled or performed, whereupon the document takes full effect.

evidence information presented to a court or jury for the purpose of substantiating claims and allegations. Includes testimony, records, and other documents and objects used to support an assertion of fact.

executor in law, a person appointed in a will to carry out the instructions of the deceased. A person so named has the right to refuse to act.

extradition surrender, by one state or country to another, of a person accused of a criminal offense in the state or country to which that person is extradited.

ex post facto in Latin, literally "after the fact," it refers to a law that makes punishable as a crime an act committed that was legal before the passage of the law. Such laws are prohibited by the United States Constitution.

eyewitness a individual who actually sees an act or occurrence and can testify as to a first-hand account of the event.

false arrest the unlawful arrest of an individual, or the unlawful restraint of an individual's rights or liberties.

felony an offense characterized as a high crime and usually punishable by imprisonment for more than one year. Compared to a misdemeanor, or minor offense.

finding a decision or verdict reached by a court after judicial action and inquiry.

foreclosure in law, the transfer of title of a mortgaged property from the mortgagor (borrower, usually a home owner) to the mortgagee (loaner, for example a bank) if the mortgagor is in breach of the mortgage agreement, usually by failing to make a number of payments on the mortgage (loan).

forensic pertaining to or applied in judicial courts.

forgery the making of a false document, painting, or object with deliberate intention to deceive or defraud. The most common forgeries involve financial instruments such as checks or credit-card transactions or money (counterfeiting).

frame-up fraudulent incrimination of an innocent person.

fraud an act of deception resulting in injury to another. To establish fraud it has to be demonstrated that (1) a false representation (for example, a factually untrue statement) has been made, with the intention that it should be acted upon; (2) the person making the representation knows it is false or does not attempt to find out whether it is true or not; and (3) the person to whom the representation is made acts upon it to his or her detriment.

gag order a court-imposed order prohibiting the public discussion of a case.

good faith the observance of honest and fair standards in dealings, or the absence of intention to take unfair advantage of another party.

grandfather clause a legal provision which grants exemption to all persons engaged in a particular activity from new regulations or restrictions.

grand jury a jury designated to determine if a law has been violated and whether the facts and evidence warrant prosecution.

grand larceny larceny in which the value of the goods taken is above a certain amount as specified by law. See larceny. Compare petit (petty) larceny.

grievance an allegation that an illegal or unjust action has been imposed on oneself or that a legal right has been denied.

habeas corpus a writ requiring that an individual must be brought before a court, especially to determine whether that individual has been justly detained. The suspension of the writ means that an individual can be detained without judicial determination, and is allowable only in extreme cases of national security. In Latin, literally "have the body."

hearing a preliminary legal proceeding to examine evidence and issues of fact. Such proceedings take place before a magistrate granted judicial authority without a jury.

hearsay evidence evidence given by a witness based on information passed to that person by others rather than evidence experienced at first hand by the witness. It is usually not admissible as evidence in criminal proceedings.

homicide the killing of a human being. This may be unlawful, lawful, or excusable, depending on the circumstances. Unlawful homicides include murder, manslaughter, infanticide, and causing death by dangerous driving (vehicular homicide). Lawful homicide occurs where, for example, a police officer is justified in killing a criminal in the course of apprehension. Excusable homicide occurs when a person is killed in self-defense or by accident.

hostile witness an individual in an adversarial relationship with a party such that her/his testimony may be prejudiced.

hung jury a jury whose members cannot come to a required agreement (whether unanimous, or, in some cases, substantial majority) on a verdict.

immaterial facts or statements which have no relevance or significance to a case.

immunity exemption from a duty or penalty, such as diplomatic immunity.

indemnity an undertaking to compensate another for damage, loss, trouble, or expenses, or the money paid by way of such compensation—for example, under fire insurance agreements.

indict to formally charge with a criminal offense. Indictments are written under oath and submitted to a grand jury.

injunction court order that forbids a person from doing something, or orders him or her to take certain action. Breach of an injunction is contempt of court.

in loco parentis in Latin, literally in the place or role of a parent. A person or body granted *in loco parentis* has parental authority.

inquest inquiry held by a coroner into an unexplained death. At an inquest, a coroner is assisted by a jury of between 7 and 11 people. Evidence is on oath, and medical and other witnesses may be summoned.

interdiction a prohibitory decree of a court or law officer.

international law body of rules generally accepted as governing the relations between countries, pioneered by Hugo Grotius, especially in matters of human rights, territory, and war.

judge person invested with power to hear and determine legal disputes. In the US, the federal judiciary is chosen by executive appointments. It consists of Supreme Court justices, judges of the US district courts, magistrates, and administrative law judges. Similar offices exist at the state level with judges elected or appointed. There are also county and municipal judges elected to office.

judicial review in the US, the power of a court to decide whether legislative acts or executive actions are constitutional. The ultimate authority for judicial review is the Supreme Court, which established its right to review executive and legislative actions in *Marbury* v. *Madison* (1803.)

jurisdiction the power or authority to hear a case and administer justice.

jurisprudence the science of law in the abstract—that is, not the study of any particular laws or legal system, but of the principles upon which legal systems are founded.

jury body of lay people (usually 12, sometimes 6) sworn to decide the facts of a case and reach a verdict in a court of law. Juries, used mainly in English-speaking countries, are implemented primarily in criminal cases, but also sometimes in civil cases. The members of the jury are carefully selected by both prosecution and defense attorneys.

justice of the peace a judicial officer with limited jurisdiction having authority to hear minor criminal or civil cases, administer oaths, perform marriage ceremonies, etc.

justifiable homicide the killing of a person under the legal justification of executing the law or public justice, or justified in the name of self-defense or defending lives, home, and property.

kidnapping the carrying off of a person against her/his will by force or fraud, especially for the purpose of extracting ransom or keeping the person hostage.

larceny the unlawful taking of personal property with intent to deprive the rightful owner of it permanently. Often classified as either *petit* or *grand* depending on the value of the property taken and the method employed. See grand larceny, petit (petty) larceny.

lawsuit a case before a court.

leasehold in law, land or property held by a tenant (lessee) for a specified period, (unlike freehold, outright ownership) usually at a rent from the landlord (lessor).

legacy in law, a gift of personal property made by a testator in a will and transferred on the testator's death to the legatee. *Specific legacies* are definite named objects; a *general legacy* is a sum of money or item not specially identified; a *residuary legacy* is all the remainder of the deceased's personal estate after debts have been paid and the other legacies have been distributed.

legal tender money that is legally valid for the payment of debts and that must be accepted for that purpose when offered.

liability assumption of responsibility for one's actions. A duty to either do or refrain from doing something such as pay money owed.

libel in law, defamation published in a permanent form, such as in a newspaper, book, or broadcast. A libel may be directed to a living or a dead person; either may be actionable. A person is defamed when publication of false and malicious statements hold the person up to public scorn, hatred, contempt, or ridicule, or impugn a person's capacity to perform a job. Truth of a published statement is a defense against an action for libel. With respect to public officials and public figures, the press has some protection against actions for libel in that malice and reckless disregard for the truth must be shown.

license the legal permission to do a particular thing or exercise a certain privilege. May be granted by either the government or private persons.

licensing laws laws governing the sale of alcoholic drinks. Most countries have some restrictions on the sale of alcoholic drinks, if not an outright ban, as in the case of Islamic countries.

lien in law, the right to retain goods owned by another until the owner has satisfied a claim against him by the person in possession of the goods. For example, the goods may have been provided as security for a debt.

maintenance in law, payments to support children or a spouse, under the terms of an agreement, or by a court order.

malfeasance wrongdoing or misconduct which interferes with a public official's duty and is often conducted by the official himself.

malicious mischief willful, wanton, or reckless damage to or destruction of another's property.

malpractice in law, negligence by a professional person, usually a doctor, that may lead to an action for damages by the client. Such legal actions result in doctors having high insurance costs that are reflected in higher fees charged to their patients.

manslaughter the unlawful killing of a human being in circumstances less culpable than murder—for example, when the killer suffers extreme provocation, is in some way mentally ill (diminished responsibility), did not intend to kill but did so accidentally in the course of another crime or by behaving with criminal recklessness, or is the survivor of a genuine suicide pact that involved killing the other person.

maritime law that part of the law dealing with the sea: in particular, fishing areas, ships, and navigation. Seas are divided into *internal waters* governed by a state's internal laws (such as harbors, inlets); *territorial waters* (the area of sea adjoining the coast over

which a state claims rights); the *continental shelf* (the seabed and subsoil that the coastal state is entitled to exploit beyond the territorial waters); and the *high seas*, where international law applies.

martial law replacement of civilian by military authorities in the maintenance of order. In the US martial law is usually proclaimed by the president or the government of a state in areas of the country where the civil authorities have been rendered unable to act, or to act with safety. The legal position of martial law is neither well defined in the constitution nor laid down in statutes. In effect, when war or rebellion is in progress in an area, the military authorities are recognized as having the powers to maintain order by summary means.

minor legal term for those under the age of majority, which varies from country to country but is usually between 18 and 21. In the US (from 1971 for voting, and in some states for nearly all other purposes) and certain European countries (in Britain since 1970) the age of majority is 18.

miranda rule the requirement to make it known to a person their legal right against self-incrimination and to make it known that one has the option of having a retained or appointed lawyer present for advice before questioning by law enforcement authorities. Additionally, it must be made known to the suspect that anything the suspect says during the questioning by legal authorities can be used as evidence against the suspect.

miscarriage of justice the impairment of one's rights made by legal officials during one's trial that require reversal.

misdemeanor a crime less serious than a felony and which carries a lesser penalty.

moratorium a legally authorized period of delay in the performance of a legal obligation or the payment of a debt.

motoring law law affecting the use of vehicles on public roads. It covers the licensing of vehicles and drivers, and the criminal offenses that can be committed by the owners and drivers of vehicles.

murder unlawful killing of one person by another. In the US, first-degree murder requires proof of premeditation; second-degree murder falls between first-degree murder and manslaughter. If the killer can show provocation by the victim (action or words hat would make a reasonable person lose self-control) or diminished responsibility (an abnormal state of mind caused by illness, injury, or mental subnormality), the charge may be reduced to a less serious one.

naturalization to become established as a native and admission to citizenship.

negligence in law, doing some act that a "prudent and reasonable" person would not do, or omitting to do some act that such a person would do. Negligence may arise in respect of a person's duty toward an individual or toward other people in general. Breach of the duty of care that results in reasonably foreseeable damage is a tort.

nolo contendere a plea by the defendant in a criminal prosecution that without admitting guilt subjects him to conviction but does not preclude him from denying the truth of the charges in a collateral proceeding.

notary public a public officer, or authorized lawyers or citizens, who attest or certify documents to make them authentic and take affidavits, depositions, and protests of negotiable paper.

oath solemn promise to tell the truth or perform some duty, combined with a declaration naming a deity or something held sacred. In the US witnesses raise their right hand in taking the oath.

objection made during a trial by a party claiming that a certain aspect of the trial is improper and asks the court to rule on its illegality.

obscenity law law prohibiting the publishing of any material that tends to deprave or corrupt. Publication of any books, films, etc., that, when judged by contemporary standards, are found to have a prurient interest in sex, be patently offensive, and have no serious artistic, scientific, or social value is an offense.

obstruction of justice the hindrance of those who seek justice through the legal system. Often pertaining to actions which interfere with the delegated duties of those within the judicial process, as well as law enforcement and administrative officials.

ordinance a law made at the local level which is applied to those subject to the local jurisdiction.

pardon the relaxation of one's punishment of a crime, in which he or she had been convicted, by a sovereign prerogative which results in the absolution of one's punishment and guilty conviction to the extent that in the eyes of the law the offender is innocent and was never convicted.

parole conditional release of a prisoner from jail. The prisoner remains on license until the date release would have been granted, and may be recalled if the authorities deem it necessary.

party either a person directly interested in a judicial proceeding such as a litigant who asserts a claim, makes a defense, examines witnesses, makes an appeal, etc. or a person or entity that enters into a contract, deed, lease, etc.

patent or *letters patent* documents conferring the exclusive right to make, use, and sell an invention for a limited period. Ideas are not eligible; neither is anything not new.

perjury the offense of deliberately making a false statement on oath (or affirmation) when appearing as a witness in legal proceedings, on a point material to the question at issue. In the US it is punishable by a fine, imprisonment, or both.

petition a formal written request addressed to a court or judge asking for judicial action necessary to provide legal relief to the circumstances formally stated in the request.

petit (petty) larceny larceny in which the value of the goods taken is below a certain amount as specified by law. See larceny. Compare grand larceny.

plaintiff one who initiates a suit as a means of being granted a remedy from injury to his or her rights. Compare defendant.

plea the defendant's answer denoting his or her response to the plaintiff's petition or complaint. In a criminal proceeding the plea is stated at the arraignment in the form of guilty, not guilty, and occasionally nolo contendere or non vult.

plea bargain the procedure in which the defendant seeks a lower sentence by agreeing to plea guilty in return for a lesser charge.

power of attorney in law, legal authority to act on behalf of another, for a specific transaction, or for a particular period.

precedent the common law principle that, in deciding a particular case, an earlier case is recognized as the basis for rendering a decision.

premeditation denoting distinct intention and conscious purpose. Used as a requirement for first-degree murder.

presumption of innocence the status of innocence until guilt is proved beyond a reasonable doubt in a court of law. This procedure requires the government to bear the burden of proof.

privileged communication authorizing that certain forms of communication be deemed confidential, so that any breach by one party can result in a concurrent civil suit by the damaged party. Examples of privileged communication are communication between physicians or psychological counselor and their patients, between an attorney and client, and communications within a marriage.

probable cause an assessment which concludes that there is significant and reasonable cause to believe that a crime has been committed. It is a necessary element to establish as a means of obtaining a warrant for either arrest or search and seizure of property.

probate system for the administration of inheritance. Generally the function of probate (sometimes surrogate's) courts, probate determines the validity of wills, and the the satisfaction of requirements of inheritance law. In the cases of persons dying without wills (intestacy), probate courts appoint administrators of estates.

probation in law, the placing of offenders under supervision of probation officers in the community, as an alternative to prison.

prosecute to bring legal action against either a civil or criminal party.

prosecuting attorney an employee of the government who conducts proceedings in the court on its behalf.

proviso the introduction of a condition within a contract in the form of an article or clause.

proxy in law, a person authorized to stand in another's place; also the document conferring this right. The term usually refers to voting at meetings, but marriages by proxy are possible.

quitclaim to release a legal claim.

rape sexual intercourse without the consent of the subject. Most cases of rape are of women by men. In Islamic law a rape accusation requires the support of four independent male witnesses. Some jurisdictions allow charges of rape to be brought against husbands replacing older legal doctrine asserting a wife's duty to submit to sex with her spouse. Sexual intercourse (consensual or nonconsensual) with a minor, not necessarily involving penetration, is defined as statutory rape.

reasonable doubt the term referring to the amount of certainty that a juror must have before deciding on the guilt of a criminal defendant. These words are used to instruct jurors in a criminal case and to explain that defendants are to be presumed innocent until all doubt regarding the defendant's guilt has been removed.

receiver in law, a person appointed by a court to collect and manage the assets of an individual, company, or partnership in serious financial difficulties. In the case of bankruptcy, the assets may be sold and distributed by a receiver to creditors.

recidivist an habitual criminal.

recognizance an obligation of record entered in a court requiring the performance of a particular act, such as appearing in court.

remand the committing of an accused but not convicted person into custody or to release on bail pending a court hearing.

repeal to rescind or reverse a previous law through subsequent authoritative action.

reprieve legal temporary suspension of the execution of a sentence of a criminal court. It is usually associated with the death penalty. It is distinct from a pardon (extinguishing the sentence) and commutation (alteration) of a sentence (for example, from death to life imprisonment).

restitution a legal action calling for the return of something to its previous state.

restraining order a legal order to keep a situation in its existing state temporarily until further legal action determines the application for injunction.

retainer the fee paid to an attorney for services in a particular case.

robbery the taking of another's property either by force or threat of force. It is considered *armed robbery* if the robber is armed with a dangerous weapon, regardless of whether the weapon is actually used in the course of the robbery.

rule of law doctrine that no individual, however powerful, is above the law. The principle had a significant influence on attempts to restrain the arbitrary use of power by rulers and on the growth of legally enforceable human rights in many Western countries. It is often used as a justification for separating legislative from judicial power.

search warrant an order authorizing the search of specified premises by law enforcement agents for the purpose of finding stolen goods or unlawful possessions or for specified objects or individuals.

sentence a judgment ordered by a court specifying the punishment to be inflicted on a convicted criminal. The sentence can take the form of a fine or probation, or imprisonment. See concurrent sentence, consecutive sentence, suspended sentence.

settlement the resolution of a legal matter, often a compromise established before the final judgment of the court. See settlement out of court.

settlement out of court a compromise reached between the parties to a legal dispute. Most civil legal actions are settled out of court, reducing legal costs and avoiding the uncertainty of the outcome of a trial.

slander spoken defamatory statement; if written, or broadcast on radio or television, it constitutes libel.

small-claims court a court specifically delegated to handle small claims on debts.

solicitor a chief law officer of a municipality or other government department. Also, a British lawyer who advises clients, handles cases in lower courts, and prepares cases for barristers in the higher courts.

stare decisis a policy whereby courts follow rules or principles laid down in previous decisions and rely on precedent to decide cases similar to previous cases. In Latin, literally "to stand by decided matters."

stay the suspension of judicial proceedings by judicial or executive order. See stay of execution.

stay of execution the suspension of the execution of a judgment for a specified period.

subpoena an order requiring someone who might not otherwise come forward of his or her own volition to give evidence before a court or judicial official at a specific time and place. A witness who fails to comply with a subpoena is in contempt of court.

summons a court order officially delivered, requiring someone to appear in court on a certain date.

suspended sentence a sentence whose execution is withheld or delayed, by order of the court, according to certain terms and conditions.

tagging, electronic long-distance monitoring of the movements of people charged with or convicted of a crime, thus enabling them to be detained in their homes rather than in prison. The system is in use in the US.

testify to make a statement in court, under oath, for the purpose of establishing facts relating to a case based on personal knowledge.

testimony the statement made by a witness, under oath, giving evidence relating to a case.

title legal ownership, or the facts surrounding the legal right of possession of property.

tort a wrongful act for which someone can be sued for damages in a civil court. It includes such acts as libel, trespass, injury done to someone (whether intentionally or by negligence), and inducement to break a contract (although breach of contract itself is not a tort).

treason act of betrayal, in particular against the sovereign or the state to which the offender owes allegiance.

trespass going on to the land of another without authority. In law, a landowner has the right to eject a trespasser by the use of reasonable force and can sue for any damage caused.

trial the formal examination before a competent tribunal for the purpose of determining the matter in issue in a criminal or civil cause.

trial by jury the formal examination of a case whereby the final decision is determined by a preselected jury. See jury.

tribunal strictly, a court of justice, but used in English law for a body appointed by the government to arbitrate in disputes, or investigate certain matters.

trust arrangement whereby a person or group of people (the trustee or trustees) hold property for others (the beneficiaries) entitled to the beneficial interest. A trust can be a legal arrangement under which A is empowered to administer property belonging to B for the benefit of C. A and B may be the same person; B and C may not.

unconstitutional not consistent with a provision of the constitution. Such laws or statutes found to be unconstitutional are not considered valid.

verdict a jury's decision, usually a finding of 'guilty' or 'not guilty.'

vested interest a fixed and absolute legal right or interest to a particular right or title.

voluntary manslaughter the intentional killing of a person, but with a reduced evil intent, such as homicide committed under rage or terror.

will declaration of how a person wishes his or her property to be disposed of after death. It also appoints administrators of the estate (executors) and may contain wishes on other matters, such as place of burial or use of organs for transplant. Wills must comply with formal legal requirements of the local jurisdiction.

wiretapping listening in on a telephone conversation, without the knowledge of the participants; in the US and the UK a criminal offense if done without a warrant or the consent of the person concerned.

witness a person who was present at some event (such as an accident, a crime, or the signing of a document) or has relevant special knowledge (such as a medical expert) and can be called on to give evidence in a court of law.

writ a document issued by a court requiring performance of certain actions. Examples include a writ of habeas corpus, a writ of certiorari by which the US Supreme Court calls up cases from inferior courts for futher review.

Earth and Science

Geographical Names

This section constitutes a pronouncing dictionary of current and historical place names. In the entries the letters **N**, **E**, **S**, and **W**, singly or in combination, indicate direction and are not part of a place name. They may represent either the name of the direction (as *north*) or the adjective derived from it (as *northern*); thus, west-northwest of Santiago appears as **WNW** of Santiago and southern California appears as **S** California. The only other special abbreviations used in this section are U.S. for United States and U.S.S.R. indicating the former Union of Soviet Socialist Republics. All heights and distances are given in metric units.

Aa·chen \'äk-ən\ *or French* **Aix-la-Cha·pelle** \,äk-,slä-shə-'pel, ,ek-\ city W Germany WSW of Cologne

Aarhus — see ÅRHUS

Aba·dan \,äb-ə-'dän, ,ab-ə-'dan\ city W Iran on Abadan Island in delta of Shatt-al-Arab

Abe·o·ku·ta \,ab-ē-'ō-kət-ə\ city SW Nigeria S of Ibadan

Ab·er·deen \,ab-ər-'dēn\ **1** *or* **Ab·er·deen·shire** \-,shiər, -shər\ former country NE Scotland **2** city NE Scotland — **Ab·er·do·ni·an** \-'dō-nē-ən\ *adj or n*

Ab·i·djan \,ab-i-'jän\ city Côte d'Ivoire

Abu·Dha·bi \,äb-ü-'däb-ē\ city, capital of Abu Dhabi sheikdom & of United Arab Emirates

Abruz·zi \ä-'brüt-sē\ region central Italy on the Adriatic E of Latium; capital L'Aquila

Ab·ys·sin·ia \,ab-ə-'sin-ē-ə, -'sin-yə\ — SEE ETHIOPIA — **Ab·ys·sin·i·an** \-ē-ən, -yən\ *adj or n*

Aca·dia \ə-'kād-ē-ə\ *or French* **Aca·die** \,à-kà-'dē\ NOVA SCOTIA — an early name

Acadia National Park section of coast of Maine including areason Mount Desert Island & Isle au Haut

Aca·pul·co \,äk-ə-'pül-kō, ,ak-\ city S Mexico on the Pacific

Ac·ar·na·nia \,ak-ər-'nā-nē-ə, -'nā-nyə\ district W Greece on Ionian sea

Accad — SEE AKKAD

Ac·cra \ə-'krä\ city, capital of Ghana

Achaea \ə-'kē-ə\ *or* **Acha·ia** *or Greek* **Akhaï·a** \ə-'kī-ə, -'kā-ə, -'kā-yə\ district S Greece in N Peloponnesus

Ach·er·on \'ak-ə-,rän, -rən\ a river of Hades in Greek mythology

Acon·ca·gua \,ak-ən-'käg-wə, ,äk-, -əng-\ mountain 6960 meters W Argentina; highest in the Andes & western hemisphere

Açores — SEE AZORES

Ac·ti·um \'ak-shē-əm, 'ak-tē-\ promotory & ancient town W Greece in NW Acarnania

Ada·na \'äd-ə-nə, -,nä; ə-'dän-ə\ city S Turkey

Ad·dis Aba·ba \,ad-ə-'sab-ə-bə\ city, capital of Ethiopia

Ad·e·laide \'ad-l-,ād\ city, capital of South Australia

Aden \'äd-n, 'äd-, 'ad-\ **1** former British Protectorate S Arabia E of Yemen **2** former British colony in SW Aden Protectorate **3** city & port S Yemen; formerly capital of People's Democratic Republic of Yemen

Aden, Gulf of arm of Indian ocean between Yemen (Arabia) & Somalia (Africa)

Adi·ge \'äd-ə-,jā\ river 354 kilometers long N Italy flowing SE into the Adriatic

Ad·i·ron·dack \,ad-ə-'rän-,dak\ mountains NE New York; highest Mount Marcy 1629 meters

Ad·mi·ral·ty \'ad-mrəl-tē, -mə-rəl-\ **1** island SE Alaska in N Alexander archipelago **2** islands W Pacific N of New Guinea in Bismark archipelago; belong to Papua New Guinea

Adri·at·ic \,ā-drē-'at-ik, ,ad-rē-\ sea arm of Mediterranean between Italy & Balkan peninsula

Ae·ge·an \i-'jē-ən\ sea arm of Mediterranean between Asia Minor & Greece

Ae·gi·na \i-'jī-nə\ *or Greek* **Aí·yi·na** \'ā-yē-,nä\ island & ancient state SE Greece in Saronic gulf

Ae·o·lis \'ē-ə-ləs\ *or* **Ae·o·lia** \ē-'ō-lē-ə, -'ōl-yə\ ancient country NW Asia Minor

Afars and the Issas, French Territory of the — SEE DJIBOUTI 1

Af·ghan·i·stan \af-'gan-ə-,stan\ country W Asia E of Iran; capital, Kabul

Af·ri·ca \'af-ri-kə\ continent of eastern hemisphere S of Mediterranean

Aga·na \ə-'gän-yə\ town, capital of Guam

Ag·as·siz Lake \'ag-ə-sē\ prehistoric lake 1130 kilometers long in region comprising present S Manitoba, E Saskatchewan, NW Minnesota, & E North Dakota

Agra \'äg-rə\ city N India in W Uttar Pradesh

Agri Dagi *or* **Aghri Dagh** — SEE ARARAT

Aguas·ca·lien·tes \,äg-wə-,skäl-yen-,tās\ **1** state central Mexico **2** city, its capital, NE of Guadalajara

Agul·has, Cape \ə-'gəl-əs\ headland Republic of South Africa in S Cape Province; most southerly point of Africa, at 34° 50′ S latitude

Agulhas Current warm current of the Indian Ocean flowing SW along SE coast of Africa

Ahag·gar \ə-'häg-ər, ,ä-hə-'gär\ *or* **Hog·gar** \'häg-ər, hə-'gär\ mountains S Algeria in W central Sahara; highest Tahat 3000 meters

Ah·mad·abad *or* **Ah·med·abad** \'äm-əd-ə,bäd\ city W India in Gujarat

Ah·ven·an·maa \'äk-və-,nän-,mä, 'ä-və-\ *or Swedish* **Åland** \'ō-,länd\ archipelago SW Finland in Baltic sea

Ah·waz \ä-'wäz\ city SW Iran

Aisne \'ān\ river 282 kilometers long N France flowing from Argonne Forest into the Oise

Aix-la-Chapelle — see AACHEN

Aj·mer \,əj-'miər, -'meər\ city NW India in central Rajasthan SW of Delhi

\ə\	abut	\ng\	sing
\ər\	further	\ō\	bone
\a\	mat	\ȯ\	saw
\ā\	take	\ȯi\	coin
\ä\	cot, cart	\th\	thin
\au̇\	out	\th\	this
\ch\	chin	\ū\	food
\e\	pet	\u̇\	foot
\ē\	easy	\y\	yet
\g\	go	\yü\	few
\i\	tip	\yu̇\	cure
\ī\	life	\zh\	vision
\j\	job		

Aki•ta \ä-'kēt-ə, 'äk-i-,tä\ city Japan in N Honshu on Sea of Japan

Ak•kad or **Ac•cad** \'ak-,ad, 'äk-,äd\ **1** N division of ancient Babylonia **2** or **Aga•de** \ə-'gäd-ə\ ancient city, its capital

Ak•ron \'ak-rən\ city NE Ohio

Al•a•bama \,al-ə-'bam-ə\ state SE U.S.; capital, Montgomery — **Al•a•bam•i•an** \-'bam-ē-ən\ or **Al•a•bam•an** \-'bam-ən\ adj or n

Alas•ka \ə-'las-kə\ **1** peninsula SW Alaska SW of Cook inlet **2** state of U.S. in NW North America; capital, Juneau **3** mountain range S Alaska extending from Alaska peninsula to Yukon boundary — **Alas•kan** \-kən\ adj or n

Alaska, Gulf of inlet of Pacific off S Alaska between Alaska peninsula on W & Alexander archipelago on E

Al•ba Lon•ga \,al-bə-'lòng-gə\ ancient city central Italy in Latiun SE of Rome

Al•ba•nia \al-'bā-nē-ə, -nyə\ country S Europe in Balkan peninsula on Adriatic; capital, Tirana

Al•ba•ny \'òl-bə-nē\ city, capital of New York

Al•be•marle \'al-bə-,märl\ sound inlet of Atlantic in NE North Carolina

Al•bert, Lake \'al-bərt\ lake E Africa between Uganda & Zaire in course of Nile

Al•ber•ta \al-'bərt-ə\ province W Canada; capital, Edmonton — **Al•ber•tan** \-bərt-n\ adj or n

Albert Nile — see NILE

Al•bi•on \'al-bē-ən\ **1** island of Great Britain **2** ENGLAND

Al•bu•quer•que \'al-bə-,kər-kē, -byə-\ city central New Mexico

Al•da•bra \'al-də-brə\ island (atoll) Seychelles, in NW Indian ocean N of Madagascar

Al•der•ney \'òl-dər-nē\ island in English channel — see CHANNEL

Alep•po \ə-'lep-ō\ or **Alep** \ä-'lep\ city N Syria

Aleu•tian \ə-'lü-shən\ islands SW Alaska extending in an arc 1930 kilometers W from Alaska peninsula

Al•ex•an•der \,al-ig-'zan-dər, ,el-\ archipelago SE Alaska

Al•ex•an•dria \,al-ig-'zan-drē-ə, ,el-\ **1** city N Virginia **2** city N Egypt on Mediterranean — **Al•ex•an•dri•an** \-drē-ən\ adj or n

Al•ge•ria \al-'jir-ē-ə\ country NW Africa on Mediterranean; capital, Algiers — **Al•ge•ri•an** \-ē-ən\ adj or n

Al•giers \al-'jiərz\ **1** Algeria especially as one of former Barbary States **2** city, capital of Algeria — **Al•ge•rine** \,al-jə-'rēn\ adj or n

Al•i•garh \,al-i-'gär\ city N India in NW Uttar Pradesh N of Agra

Al•lah•abad \'al-ə-hə-,bad, -,bäd\ city N India in S Uttar Pradesh W of Banaras

Al•le•ghe•ny \,al-ə-'gā-nē\ mountains of Applachian system E U.S. in Pennsylvania, Maryland, Virginia, & West Virginia

Al•len•town \'al-ən-,taùn\ city E Pennsylvania

Al•ma–Ata \,al-mə-ə-'tä\ city, capital of Kazakhstan

Alps \'alps\ mountain system central Europe — see MONT BLANC

Al•sace \al-'sas, -sās, 'al-,\ or German **El•sass** \'el-,zäs\ or ancient **Al•sa•tia** \al-'sā-shē-ə, -shə\ region & former province NE France between Rhine river & Vosges mountains — **Al•sa•tian** \al-'sā-shən\ adj or n

Al•sace–Lor•raine \-lə-'rän, -lò-'rän\ region N France W of the Rhine including Alsace & part of Lorraine

Al•tai \'al-,tī\ mountain system central Asia between Outer Mongolia & W China & between Kazakhstan & Russia in Asia; highest peak Tabun Bogdo 4653 meters

Al•ta•mi•ra \,al-tə-'mir-ə\ caverns N Spain WSW of Santander

Al•to Adi•ge \,äl-tō-'äd-i-,jā\ or **South Ti•rol** \-tə-'ròl, -'tī-,ròl, -,tī-'; -'tir-əl\ district N Italy in S Tirol in N Trentino-Alto Adige region

Al•to Pa•ra•ná \,al-tō-,par-ə-'nä\ upper course of the Paraná

Ama•ga•sa•ki \,am-ə-gə-'säk-ē\ city Japan in W central Honshu on Osaka Bay

Am•a•ril•lo \,am-ə-'ril-ō, -'ril-ə\ city NW Texas

Am•a•zon \'am-ə-,zän, -zən\ or Portuguese and Spanish **Ama•zo•nas** \,am-ə-'zō-nəs\ river about 6275 kilometers long N South America flowing from Peruvian Andes into Atlantic in N Brazil

Am•a•zo•nia \,am-ə-'zō-nē-ə\ region N South America; basin of the Amazon

Amer•i•ca \ə-'mer-ə-kə\ **1** either continent (North America or South America) of western hemisphere **2** or **the Amer•i•cas** \-kəz\ lands of western hemisphere including North, Central & South America & West Indies **3** UNITED STATES OF AMERICA

American Samoa or **Eastern Samoa** islands SW central Pacific; capital, Pago Pago (on Tutuila Island)

Am•man \a-'män, -'man\ city, capital of Jordan

Amoy — see XIAMEN

Am•rit•sar \,əm-'rit-sər\ city N India in NW Punjab

Am•ster•dam \'am-stər-,dam, 'amp-\ city, official capital of the Netherlands

Amu Dar•ya \,äm-ü-'där-yə\ or ancient **Ox•us** \'äk-səs\ river 2575 kilometers long in central & W Asia flowing from the Pamirs into Aral sea

Amur \ä-'mùr\ river 2865 kilometers long E Asia formed by junction of Shilka & Argun rivers flowing into the Pacific at N end of Tatar strait & forming part of boundary between China & Russia in Asia

An•a•heim \'an-ə-,hīm\ city SW California E of Long Beach

Aná•huac \ə-'nä-,wäk\ the central plateau of Mexico

An•a•to•lia \,an-ə-'tō-lē-ə, -'tòl-yə\ — see ASIA MINOR — **An•a•to•li•an** \-ən, -yən\ adj or n

An•chor•age \'ang-kə-rij, -krij\ city S central Alaska; largest in state

An•co•hu•ma \,ang-kə-'hü-mə, -'hyü-\ mountain peak 6388 meters W Bolivia; highest in Illampu massif

An•co•na \ang-'kō-nə, an-\ city central Italy, capital of the Marches

An•da•lu•sia \,an-də-'lü-zhē-ə, -zhə\ or Spanish **An•da•lu•cía** \,an-də-'lü-'sē-ə\ region S Spain including Sierra Nevada & valley of the Guadalquivir — **An•da•lu•sian** \,an-də-'lü-zhən\ adj or n

An•da•man \'an-də-mən, -,man\ **1** islands India in Bay of Bengal S of Myanmar & N of Nicobar islands; in **Andaman and Nic•o•bar** \'nik-ə-,bär\ territory **2** sea arm of Bay of Bengal S of Myanmar — **An•da•man•ese** \,an-də-ə-'nēz, -'nēs\ adj or n

An•des \'an-dēz, -,dēz\ mountain system W South America extending from Panama to Tierra del Fuego — see ACONCAGUA — **An•de•an** \'an-dē-ən, an-'\ — **An•dine** \'an-,dēn, -,dīn\ adj

An•dhra Pra•desh \,än-drə-prə-'däsh, -'desh\ state S India N of Tamil Nadu bordering on Bay of Bengal; capital, Hyderabad

An•dor•ra \an-'dòr-ə, -'där-ə\ country SW Europe in E Pyrenees between France & Spain; capital, Andorra la Vella — **An•dor•ran** \-ən\ adj or n

An•dros **1** \'an-drəs\ island, largest of Bahamas **2** \'an-drəs, -,dräs\ island Greece in N Cyclades SE of Euboea

An•gel Falls \,än-jəl-\ waterfall 979 meters SE Venezuela on Auyán-tepuí Mountain

An•gers \äⁿ-'zhā\ city W France ENE of Nantes

Ang•kor \'ang-,kòr\ ruins of ancient city NW Cambodia

An•gle•sey \'ang-gəl-sē\ island & former county NW Wales

An•glo–Egyp•tian Sudan \,ang-glō-i-,jip-shən-\ former territory NE Africa under joint British & Egyptian rule; since 1956 has formed republic of Sudan

An•go•la \ang-'gō-lə, an-\ or formerly **Portuguese West Africa** country SW Africa S of mouth of Congo river; until 1975 a dependency of Portugal; capital, Luanda — **An•go•lan** \-lən\ adj or n

An•gus \'ang-gəs\ former county E Scotland

An·hui _or_ **An·hwei** \'än-'hwā, -'wā\ province E China W of Jiangsu; capital, Hefei

An·i·ak·chak Crater \,an-ē-'ak-,chak\ volcano 1347 meters SW Alaska on Alaska peninsula; crater 10 kilometers in diameter

An·jou \'an-,jü, än-'zhü\ region & former province NW France in Loire valley SE of Brittany; chief city Angers

An·ka·ra \'ang-kə-rə, 'äng\ _or formerly_ **An·go·ra** \ang-'gōr-ə, an-, -'gȯr-\ city, capital of Turkey in N central Anatolia

An·na·ba \ə-'näb-ə\ _or formerly_ **Bône** \'bōn\ city NE Algeria

An·nam \a-'nam, ə-; 'an-,am\ region & former kingdom E Indochina in central Vietnam; capital, Hue

An·nap·o·lis \ə-'nap-ləs, -'ə-ləs\ city, capital of Maryland

An·shan \'än-'shän\ city NE China in E central Liaoning

An·ta·nan·a·ri·vo \,an-tə-,nan-ə-'rē-vō\ _or formerly_ **Ta·nan·a·rive** \tə-'nan-ə-,rēv\ city, capital of Madagascar

Ant·arc·ti·ca \ant-'ärk-ti-kə, 'ant-, -'ärt-i-\ _or_ **Ant·arc·tic Continent** \-'ärk-tik, -ärt-ik\ body of land around the South Pole; plateau covered by great ice cap

Antarctic Peninsula _or formerly_ **Palm·er Peninsula** \,päm-ər-, ,päl-mər-\ peninsula 1930 kilometers long W Antarctica S of S end of South America

An·ti·gua \an-'tē-gə\ island British West Indies in the Leewards; with Barbuda constitutes independent country of **Antigua and Barbuda**; capital, Saint Johns

Anti–Leb·a·non \'ant-i-'leb-ə-nən, -,nän\ mountains SW Asia on Lebanon-Syria border — see HERMON

An·til·les \an-'til-ēz\ the West Indies excluding the Bahamas — see GREATER ANTILLES, LESSER ANTILLES — **An·til·le·an** \-'til-ē-ən\ _adj_

An·ti·och \'ant-ē-,äk\ city of ancient Syria on the Orontes; site at modern Antakya, Turkey

An·trim \'an-trəm\ traditional county E Northern Ireland; includes Belfast

Antung — see DANDONG

Ant·werp \'ant-wərp\ city N Belgium on the Scheldt

An·yang \'än-'yäng\ city E China in N Henan

An·zio \'an-zē-ō, 'än-\ _or ancient_ **An·ti·um** \'an-shē-əm\ Mediterranean seaport Italy in Latium SSE of Rome

Ao·mo·ri \'au̇-mə-rē\ city N Japan in NE Honshu on Mutsu Bay

Aorangi — see COOK (Mount)

Aos·ta \ä-'ȯs-tə\ city NW Italy

Ap·en·nines \'ap-ə-,nīz\ mountain chain Italy extending length of the peninsula; highest point Monte Corno (NE of Rome) 2914 meters — **Ap·en·nine** \-,nīn\ _adj_

Apia \ə-'pē-ə\ town, capital of Western Samoa on Upolu Island

Apo, Mount \'äp-ō\ volcano Phillipines in SE Mindanao 2594 meters; highest peak in the Phillipines

Ap·pa·la·chia \,ap-ə-'lā-chə, -'lach-ə, -'lā-shə\ region E U.S. including Appalachian mountains from S central New York to central Alabama

Ap·pa·la·chian \,ap-ə-'lā-chən, -'lach-ən, -'lā-shən\ mountain system E North America extending from S Quebec to central Alabama — see MITCHELL (Mount)

Apu·lia \ə-'pyül-yə, -'pyü-lē-ə\ _or Italian_ **Pu·glia** \'pül-yä\ _or_ **Le Pu·glie** \lä-'pül-yä\ region SE Italy bordering on the Adriatic & Gulf of Taranto; capital, Bari — **Apu·lian** \ə-'pyül-yən, -'pyü-lē-ən\ _adj_

'Aqu·ba, Gulf of \'äk-ə-bə, 'ak-\ arm of Red sea E of Sinai peninsula

Aquid·neck Island \ə-'kwid-,nek\ _or_ **Rhode Island** \'rōd\ island SE Rhose Island in Narragansett Bay

Aq·ui·taine \'ak-wə-,tān\ old region of SW France comprising later Guienne; chief city, Toulouse

Aq·ui·ta·nia \,ak-wə-'tā-nyə, -nē-ə\ a Roman division of SW Gaul

Ara·bia \ə-'rā-bē-ə\ peninsula of SW Asia including Saudi Arabia, Yemen, Oman, & Persian Gulf States

Ara·bi·an \ə-'rā-bē-ən\ 1 desert E Egypt between Red sea & the Nile 2 sea NW section of Indian ocean between Arabia & India

Ara·ca·ju \,ar-ə-kə-'zhü\ city E Brazil NE of Salvador

Arad \ä-'räd\ city W Romania

Ar·a·fu·ra \,ar-ə-'für-ə\ sea between N Australia & W New Guinea

Ar·a·gon \'ar-ə-,gän, -gən\ region NE Spain bordering on France — **Ar·a·go·nese** \,ar-ə-gə-'nēz, -'nēs\ _adj or n_

Arak \är-'äk, ə-'rak\ city W Iran SW of Tehran

Ar·al sea \'ar-əl\ _or Russian_ **Aral·sko·ye Mo·re** \ə-,ral-skə-yə-'mȯr-ə, yə\ _or formerly_ **Lake Aral** lake W Asia between Kazakhstan & Uzbekistan

Ar·a·rat \'ar-ə-,rat\ _or Turkish_ **Ag·ri Da·gi** _or_ **Agh·ri Dagh** \,ä-rē-dä-'ē, ,äg-rē-däg-'e\ mountain 5165 meters E Turkey near border of Iran

Ar·bil _or_ **Ir·bil** _or_ **Er·bil** \ər-'bēl\ city N Iraq

Ar·ca·dia \ä-'kād-ē-ə\ mountain region S Greece in central Peloponnesus

Arch·es National Park \'är-chəz\ reservation E Utah

Arc·tic \'ärk-tik, 'ärt-ik\ 1 ocean N of Arctic circle 2 Arctic regions 3 archipelago N Canada in N & E Northwest Territories

Ar·da·bil _or_ **Ar·de·bil** \,är-də-'bēl\ city NW Iran

Ar·dennes \är-'den\ wooded plateau NE France, W Luxemburg, & SE Belgium E of the Meuse

Are·qui·pa \,ar-ə-'kē-pə\ city S Peru

Ar·gen·ti·na \,är-jən-'tēn-ə\ country S South America between the Andes & the Atlantic S of the Pilcomayo; a republic; capital, Buenos Aires — **Argentine** \'är-jən-,tēn\ _adj or n_ — **Argen·tin·ean** _or_ **Ar·gen·tin·i·an** \,är-jən-'tin-ē-ən\ _adj or n_

Ar·go·lis \,är-gə-lis\ district S Greece in E Peloponnesus

Ar·gonne \är-'gän, 'är-,\ _or_ **Argonne Forest** wooded plateau NE France S of the Ardennes between Meuse & Aisne rivers

Ar·gos \,är-,gäs, -gəs\ ancient Greek city & state S Greece in Argolis; site at present town of Argos

Ar·gyll \är-'gīl, 'är-,\ _or_ **Ar·gyll·shire** \-,shiər, -shər\ former county W Scotland

Är·hus _or_ **Aar·hus** \'ȯr-,hüs\ city & port Denmark in E Jutland

Ar·i·zo·na \,ar-ə-'zō-nə\ state SW U.S.; capital, Phoenix — **Ar·i·zo·nan** \-nən\ _or_ **Ar·i·zo·nian** \-nē-ən, -nyən\ _adj or n_

Ar·kan·sas \'är-kən-,sȯ; 1 is also är-'kan-zəs\ 1 river 2335 kilometers long SW central U.S. flowing SE into the Mississippi 2 state S central U.S.; capital, Little Rock — **Ar·kan·san** \är-'kan-zən\ _adj or n_

Ar·khan·gelsk \är-'kan-,gelsk\ _or_ **Arch·an·gel** \'är-,kān-jəl\ city N Russia in Europe, on the Northern Dvina

Ar·ling·ton \'är-ling-tən\ city N Texas E or Fort Worth

Ar·magh \är-'mä, 'är-,\ traditional county S Northern Ireland

Ar·me·nia \är-'mē-nē-ə, -nyə\ 1 region W Asia in mountainous area SE of Black sea & SW of Caspian sea divided between Iran, Turkey, Armenia (country) & Azerbaijan 2 country E Europe, capital Yerevan; a constituent republic of U.S.S.R. 1936–91 — see LESSER ARMENIA — **Ar·me·ni·an** \-nē-ən, -nyən\ _adj or n_

Arn·hem Land \'ärn-,hem, 'är-nəm\ region N Australia on N coast of Northern Territory

Ar·no \'är-nō\ river 225 kilometers long central Italy flowing through Florence into Ligurian sea

Aru·ba \ə-'rü-bə\ island Netherlands Antilles off coast of NW Venezuela NW of Curacao; chief town, Oranjestad

Arun·a·chal Pra·desh \,är-ə-,näch-əl-prə-'däsh, -desh\ _or formerly_ **North East Frontier Agency** state NE India N of Assam; capital, Itanagar

Asa·hi·ka·wa \,äs-ə-hē-'kä-wə\ _or_ **Asa·hi·ga·wa** \-'gä-wə\ city Japan in central Hokkaido

Ashan·ti \ə-'shant-ē, -'shänt-\ _or_ **Asan·te** \ə-'sänt-ē\ region central Ghana

Ashkh·a·bad \'ash-kə-,bad, -,bäd\ city, capital of Turkmenistan

Asia \'ā-zhə, -shə\ continent eastern hemisphere N of equator — see EURASIA

\ə\ abut		\ng\ sing	
\ər\ further		\ō\ bone	
\a\ mat		\ȯ\ saw	
\ā\ take		\ȯi\ coin	
\ä\ cot, cart		\th\ thin	
\au̇\ out		\th\ this	
\ch\ chin		\ü\ food	
\e\ pet		\u̇\ foot	
\ē\ easy		\y\ yet	
\g\ go		\yü\ few	
\i\ tip		\yu̇\ cure	
\ī\ life		\zh\ vision	
\j\ job			

Asia Mi·nor \-'mī-nər\ *or* **An·a·to·lia** \,an-ə-'tō-lē-ə, -'tōl-yə\ peninsula in modern Turkey between Black sea on N & the Mediterranean on S

Asir \a-'siər\ province S Saudi Arabia on Red sea SE of Hejaz

As·ma·ra \az-'mär-ə, -'mar-ə\ city N Ethiopia, capital of Eritrea

As·sam \ə-'sam, a-; 'as-,am\ state NE India on edge of the Himalayas NW of Myanmar; capital, Dispur — **As·sam·ese** \,as-ə-'mēz, -'mēs\ *adj or n*

As·syr·ia \ə-'sir-ē-ə\ ancient empire W Asia extending along the middle Tigris & over foothills to the E; early capital Calah, later capital Nineveh — **As·syr·i·an** \-ən\ *adj or n*

As·tra·khan \'as-trə-,kan, -kən\ city Russia in Europe, on the Volga at head of its delta

Asun·ción \ə-,sün-sē-'ōn, ä-\ city, capital of Paraguay

As·wân \a-'swän, ä-\ city S Egypt on the Nile near site of **Aswân High Dam** which forms Lake Nasser

As·yût \,as-ē-'üt, äs-\ city central Egypt on the Nile

Ata·ca·ma \,at-ə-'käm-ə\ **1** desert N Chile between Copiapó & Peru border **2** — see PUNA DE ATACAMA

Atchaf·a·laya \ə-,chaf-ə-'lī-ə, ,chaf-\ river 362 kilometers long S Louisiana flowing S into Gulf of Mexico; receives waters of Red & Mississippi rivers

Ath·a·bas·ca *or* **Ath·a·bas·ka** \,ath-ə-'bas-kə\ river 1231 kilometers long NE Alberta flowing into Lake Athabasca

Athabasca, Lake lake W central Canada on Alberta-Saskatchewan border

Ath·ens \'ath-ənz\ city, capital of Greece — **Athe·nian** \ə-'thē-nē-ən, -nyən\ *adj or n*

At·lan·ta \ət-'lant-ə, at-\ city, capital of Georgia

At·lan·tic \ət-'lant-ik, at-\ ocean separating North America & South America from Europe & Africa

At·lan·tis \ət-'lant-əs, at-\ fabled island that was traditionally placed W of Strait of Gibraltar and that sank into sea

At·las \'at-ləs\ mountains NW Africa extending from SW Morocco to N Tunisia

At·ti·ca \'at-i-kə\ region E Greece; chief city, Athens

Auck·land \'ò-klənd\ city N New Zealand on NW North Island

Augs·burg \'ògz-,bərg, 'aùgz-,bùrg\ city S Germany in S Bavaria NW of Munich

Au·gus·ta \ò-'gəst-ə, ə-\ city, capital of Maine

Aus·tin \'òs-tən, 'äs-\ city, capital of Texas

Austral — see TUBUAI

Aus·tral·asia \,òs-trə-'lā-shə, ,äs-, -'lā-shə\ Australia, Tasmania, New Zealand, & Melanesia — **Aus·tral·asian** \-zhən, -shən\ *adj or n*

Aus·tra·lia \ò-'strāl-yə, ä-, ə-\ **1** continent of eastern hemisphere SE of Asia **2** *or in full* **Commonwealth of Australia** dominion of the Commonwealth including continent of Australia & island of Tasmania; capital, Canberra — **Aus·tra·lian** \-yən\ *adj or n*

Australian Alps mountain range SE Australia in E Victoria & SE New South Wales; part of Great Dividing range

Australian Capital Territory district SE Australia including two areas, one containing Canberra (capital of Australia) & the other on Jervis Bay; surrounded by New South Wales

Aus·tria \'òs-trē-ə, 'äs-\ country central Europe; capital, Vienna — **Aus·tri·an** \-ən\ *adj or n*

Aus·tria–Hun·ga·ry \-'həng-gə-rē\ dual monarchy 1867–1918 central Europe including what is now Austria, Hungary, the Czech Republic, Bukovina & Transylvania in Romania, Slovenia, Croatia, Galicia in Poland, & part of NE Italy — **Aus·tro·Hun·gar·i·an** \'òs-trō-,həng-'gar-ē-ən, 'äs-, -'ger-\ *adj or n*

Aus·tro·ne·sia \,òs-trə-'nē-zhə, ,äs-, -'nē-shə\ **1** islands of the S Pacific **2** area extending from Madagascar through Malay peninsula & archipelago to Hawaii & Easter Island — **Aus·tro·ne·sian** \-zhən, -shən\ *adj or n*

Au·vergne \ō-'vearn, -'vearn-yə, -'vərn\ **1** region & former province S central France; capital, Clermont (now Clermont-Ferrand) **2** mountains S central France in Massif Central; highest Puy de Sancy 1886 meters

Ave·lla·ne·da \,av-ə-zhə-'nä-də\ city E Argentina on Río de la Plata E of Buenos Aires

Avon \'ā-vən, 'av-ən, *in the United States also* 'ā-,vän\ **1** river 155 kilometers long central England rising in Northamptonshire & flowing WSW past Stratford-upon-Avon into the Severn **2** county SW England including Bristol

Ayers Rock \'aərz-, 'eərz-\ outcrop central Australia in SW Northern Territory SW of Alice Springs

Ayr \'aər, 'eər\ *or* **Ayr·shire** \-,shiər, -shər\ former county SW Scotland

Azer·bai·jan \,az-ər-,bī-'jän, ,äz-\ country SE Europe, capital Baku; a constituent republic of U.S.S.R. 1936–91

Azores \'ā-,zōrz, -,zòrz, ə-'\ *or Portuguese* **Aço·res** \ə-'sōr-ēsh\ islands N Atlantic belonging to Portugal & lying 1290 kilometers W of Portuguese coast — **Azor·e·an** *or* **Azor·i·an** \ā-'zōr-ē-ən, ə-, -'zòr-\ *adj or n*

Az·ov, Sea of \'az-,òf, 'āz-, -,äv\ gulf of Black sea between Ukraine & Russia

Baalbek — see HELIOPOLIS

Ba·bel·thu·ap \,bäb-əl-'tü-,äp\ island W Pacific; chief of Belau islands

Bab·y·lon \'bab-ə-lən, -,län\ ancient city, capital of Babylonia; site about 80 kilometers S of Baghdad near the Euphrates — **Bab·y·lo·nian** \,bab-ə-'lō-nyən, -nē-ən\ *adj or n*

Bab·y·lo·nia \,bab-ə-'lō-nyə, -nē-ə\ ancient country W Asia in valley of lower Euphrates and Tigris rivers; capital, Babylon — **Bab·y·lo·nian** \-nyən, -nē-ən\ *adj or n*

Ba·co·lod \bäk-'ō-,lód\ city Philippines on Negros

Bac·tria \'bak-trē-ə\ ancient country W Asia between the Hindu Kush & upper Oxus in present NE Afghanistan — **Bac·tri·an** \-ən\ *adj or n*

Ba·den-Würt·tem·berg \,bäd-n-'wərt-əm-,bərg, -'wùrt-; 'vuert-əm-,berk\ state SW Germany W of Bavaria; capital, Stuttgart

Bad·lands National Park \'bad-,landz-, -,lanz-\ reservation SW South Dakota E of Black hills

Baf·fin \'baf-ən\ island NE Canada in Arctic archipelago N of Hudson strait

Baffin Bay inlet of the Atlantic between W Greenland & E Baffin Island

Bagh·dad *or* **Bag·dad** \'bag-,dad\ city, capital of Iraq on the middle Tigris

Ba·guio \,bäg-ē-'ō\ city, summer capital of the Philippines in NW central Luzon

Ba·ha·ma \bə-'häm-ə, *by outsiders also* -'hä-mə\ islands in N Atlantic SE of Florida; an independent member of the Commonwealth; capital, Nassau — **Ba·ha·mi·an** \-'hä-mē-ən, -'häm-ē-ən\ *or* **Ba·ha·man** \-'hä-mən, -'häm-ən\ *adj or n*

Bahia — see SALVADOR

Bah·rain *or* **Bah·rein** \bä-'rān\ islands in Persian gulf off coast of Arabia; capital, Manama

Bai·kal *or* **Bay·kal** \bī-'kòl, -'käl\ lake Russia in Asia, in mountains N of Mongolia

Baile Atha Cliath — see DUBLIN

Ba·ja \'bä-hä\ BAJA CALIFORNIA

Ba·ja California \,bä-hä-\ **1** peninsula NW Mexico W of Gulf of California **2** state NW Mexico in N Baja California Peninsula; capital, Mexicali

Baja California Sur \'sùr\ state NW Mexico in S Baja California Peninsula; capital, La Paz

Bakh·ta·ran \,bäk-tə-'rän\ city W Iran

Ba·ku \bä-'kü\ city, capital of Azerbaijan on W coast of Caspian sea

Bakwanga — see MBUJI–MAYI

Bal·a·ton \'bal-ə-,tän, 'ból-ə-,tōn\ lake W Hungary

Balboa Heights \bal-,bō-ə-\ town Panama; former administrative center for Canal Zone

Bâle — see BASEL

Bal•e•ar•ic \,bal-ē-'ar-ik\ islands ᴇ Spain in the ᴡ Mediterranean — see MAJORCA, MINORCA, IBIZA

Ba•li \'bäl-ē\ island Indonesia off ᴇ end of Java; chief town, Singaradja — **Ba•li•nese** \,bäl-i-'nēz, ,bal-, -'nēs\ adj or n

Bal•kan \'ból-kən\ 1 mountains ɴ Bulgaria extending from Yugoslavia border to Black sea; highest about 2380 meters 2 peninsula sᴇ Europe between Adriatic & Ionian seas on the ᴡ & Aegean & Black seas on the ᴇ

Balkan States or **Bal•kans** \'ból-kənz\ countries occupying the Balkan peninsula: Slovenia, Croatia, Bosnia and Herzegovina, Macedonia, Yugoslavia, Romania, Bulgaria, Albania, Greece, Turkey (in Europe)

Bal•khash or **Bal•kash** \bal-'kash, bäl-'käsh\ lake ᴇ Kazakhstan

Bal•tic \'ból-tik\ sea arm of the Atlantic ɴ Europe ᴇ of Scandinavian peninsula

Bal•ti•more \'ból-tə-,mōr, -,mór; 'ból-tə-mər, 'ból-mər\ city ɴ central Maryland

Ba•lu•chi•stan \bə-,lü-chə-'stan\ arid region s Asia bordering on Arabian sea in sᴡ Pakistan & sᴇ Iran — **Ba•lu•chi** \bə-'lü-chē\ n

Ba•ma•ko \,bäm-ə-'kō\ city, capital of Mali on the Niger

Ba•na•ras or **Be•na•res** \bə-'när-əs, -ēz\ or **Va•ra•na•si** \və-'rän-ə-sē\ city ɴ India in sᴇ Uttar Pradesh

Ban•dar — see MACHILIPATNAM

Ban•dar Lam•pung \,bən-dər-'läm-pùng\ city & port Indonesia in s Sumatra

Ban•dar Se•ri Be•ga•wan \,bən-dər-,ser-ē-bə-'gä-wən\ town, capital of Brunei

Ban•dung \'bän-,dùng\ city Indonesia in ᴡ Java sᴇ of Djakarta

Banff \'bamf, 'bampf\ or **Banff•shire** \-,shiər, -shər\ former county ɴᴇ Scotland

Ban•ga•lore \'bang-gə-,lōr, -,lór\ city s India ᴡ of Madras, capital of Karnataka

Bang•kok \'bang-,käk, bang-'\ city, capital of Thailand on Chao Phraya river

Ban•gla•desh \,bäng-glə-'desh, ,bang-, -'däsh\ country s Asia ᴇ of India; formerly part of Pakistan; an independent republic since 1971; capital, Dacca — see EAST PAKISTAN

Ban•gui \bän-'gē\ city, capital of Central African Republic

Ban•jul \'bän-,jül\ or formerly **Bath•urst** \'bath-,ərst, -ərst\ city, capital of Gambia

Bao•ding or **Pao•ting** \'baù-'ding\ city ɴᴇ China in Hebei sᴡ of Beijing

Bao•tou or **Pao•t'ou** \'baù-'tō\ city ɴ China in sᴡ Inner Mongolia

Bar•ba•dos \bär-'bād-əs, -ōz, -äs, -ōs\ island British West Indies in Lesser Antilles ᴇ of Windward islands; an independent dominion of the Commonwealth since 1966; capital, Bridgetown — **Bar•ba•di•an** \-'bād-ē-ən\ adj or n

Bar•ba•ry States \'bär-bə-rē, -brē\ the states of Morocco, Algeria, Tunisia, & Tripolitania while under Turkish flag

Bar•bu•da \bär-'büd-ə\ island British West Indies in the Leewards — see ANTIGUA

Bar•ce•lo•na \,bär-sə-'lō-nə\ city ɴᴇ Spain on the Mediterranean; chief city of Catalonia

Ba•reil•ly or **Ba•re•li** \bə-'rā-lē\ city ɴ India in ɴᴡ central Uttar Pradesh

Ba•rents \'bar-əns, 'bär-\ sea comprising part of Arctic ocean between Spitsbergen & Novaya Zemlya

Ba•ri \'bär-ē\ city sᴇ Italy, capital of Apulia on the Adriatic

Bar•king \'bär-king\ borough of ᴇ Greater London, England

Bar•na•ul \,bär-nə-'ül\ city s Russia in Asia, on the Ob

Bar•net \'bär-nət\ borough of ɴ Greater London, England

Ba•ro•da \bə-'rōd-ə\ city ᴡ India in sᴇ Gujarat

Bar•qui•si•me•to \,bär-kə-sə-'mät-ō\ city ɴᴡ Venezuela

Ban•ran•qui•lla \,bar-ən-'kē-ə, -'kē-yə\ city ɴ Colombia on the Magdalena

Barren Grounds treeless plains ɴ Canada ᴡ of Hudson Bay

Bar•row, Point \'bar-ō\ most northerly point of Alaska & of United States at about 71°25′N latitude

Ba•sel \'bäz-əl\ or French **Bâle** \'bäl\ city ɴᴡ Switzerland

Ba•si•lan \bä-'sē-,län\ 1 island s Philippines 2 city on the island

Bas•il•don \'baz-əl-dən\ town sᴇ England in Essex

Ba•si•li•ca•ta \bə-,zil-ə-'kät-ə, -,sil-\ region s Italy on Gulf of Taranto; capital Potenza

Basque Provinces \'bask\ region ɴ Spain on Bay of Biscay including Álava, Guipúzcoa, & Vizcaya provinces

Bas•ra \'bäs-rə, 'bəs-, 'bas-\ city s Iraq on Shatt-al-Arab

Bass \'bas\ strait separating Tasmania & continent of Australia

Bas•sein \bə-'sān\ city s Myanmar

Basse•terre \bäs-'ter\ town, capital of Saint Kitts and Nevis

Bas•tille \ba-'stēl\ medieval fortress, Paris; used as prison until destroyed by mobs on July 14, 1789

Basutoland — see LESOTHO

Ba•taan \bə-'tan, -'tän\ peninsula Philippines in ᴡ Luzon on ᴡ side of Manila Bay

Batavia — see DJAKARTA

Bathurst — see BANJUL

Bat•on Rouge \,bat-n-'rüzh\ city, capital of Louisiana

Ba•var•ia \bə-'ver-ē-ə, -'var-\ or German **Bay•ern** \'bī-ərn\ state sᴇ Germany bordering on the Czech Republic & Austria; capital, Munich — **Ba•var•i•an** \bə-'ver-ē-ən, -'var-\ adj or n

Ba•ya•mon \,bī-ə-'mōn\ city ɴᴇ central Puerto Rico

Baykal — see BAIKAL

Beard•more \'biərd-,mōr, -,mór\ glacier Antarctica, world's largest

Beau•fort \'bō-fərt\ sea comprising part of Arctic ocean ɴᴇ of Alaska & ɴᴡ of Canada

Beau•mont \'bō-,mänt, bō-'\ city sᴇ Texas

Bech•u•a•na•land \,bech-'wän-ə-,land, -ə-'wän-\ 1 region s Africa ɴ of Orange river 2 — see BOTSWANA — **Bech•u•a•na** \,bech-'wän-ə, -ə-'wän-\ adj or n

Bed•ford•shire \'bed-fərd-,shiər, -shər\ or **Bedford** county sᴇ England

Bedloe's — see LIBERTY

Bei•jing \'bā-'jing\ or **Pe•king** \'pē-'king, 'pā-\ city, capital of China

Bei•rut \bā-'rüt\ or ancient **Be•ry•tus** \bə-'rīt-əs\ city, capital of Lebanon

Be•la•rus \,bē-lə-'rüs, 'byel-ə\ country central Europe; capital, Minsk

Be•lau \bə-'laù\ or **Pa•lau** \pə-'laù\ islands ᴡ Pacific; a trust territory in association with the U.S.

Be•lém \bə-'lem\ or **Pa•rá** \pə-'rä\ city ɴ Brazil on Pará river

Bel•fast \'bel-,fast, bel-'\ city, capital of Northern Ireland

Belgian Congo — see ZAIRE

Bel•gium \'bel-jəm\ or French **Bel•gique** \bel-zhēk\ or Flemish **Bel•gië** \'bel-gē-ə\ country ᴡ Europe; capital, Brussels — **Bel•gian** \'bel-jən\ adj or n

Bel•grade \'bel-,grād, -,gräd, -,grad, bel-'\ or **Be•o•grad** \'beù-,gräd\ city, capital of Yugoslavia on the Danube

Be•lize \bə-'lēz\ or Spanish **Be•li•ce** \bā-'lē-sā\ 1 or formerly **British Hon•du•ras** \hän-'dùr-əs, -'dyùr-\ country Central America on the Caribbean; capital, Belmopan 2 city ᴇ Belize on the Caribbean

Bel•mo•pan \,bel-mō-'pan\ city, capital of Belize

Be•lo Ho•ri•zon•te \'bā-lō-,hór-ə-'zänt-ē, 'bel-ō-, -,här-\ city ᴇ Brazil ɴ of Rio de Janeiro

Be•lo•rus•sian Soviet Socialist Republic \,bel-ō-'rəsh-ən\ or **Bye•lo•rus•sian Soviet Socialist Republic** \bē-

\ə\ abut		\ng\ sing
\ər\ further		\ō\ bone
\a\ mat		\ó\ saw
\ā\ take		\ói\ coin
\ä\ cot, cart		\th\ thin
\aú\ out		\th\ this
\ch\ chin		\ū̄\ food
\e\ pet		\ú\ foot
\ē\ easy		\y\ yet
\g\ go		\yü\ few
\i\ tip		\yù\ cure
\ī\ life		\zh\ vision
\j\ job		

,el-ō-\ former constituent republic of U.S.S.R.; became independent Belarus 1991 — **Belorussian** *adj or n*

Beloye More — see WHITE SEA

Benarea — see BANARAS

Be·ne·lux \'ben-l-,aks\ economic union comprising Belgium, Luxembourg, & the Netherlands formed 1947

Ben·gal \ben-'gól, beng-\ region s Asia including delta of Ganges & Brahmaputra rivers; divided between West Bengal, India, & Bangladesh — see EAST BENGAL, WEST BENGAL — **Ben·gal·ese** \,beng-gə-'lēz, ,ben-, -'lēs\ *adj or n*

Bengal, Bay of arm of Indian ocean between India & Myanmar

Ben·gha·zi \ben-'gäz-ē, beng-, -'gaz-\ city NE Libya; formerly a capital of Libya

Ben·guela Current \ben-'gwel-ə, 'beng-, -'gel-\ cold current of the Atlantic Ocean flowing N along SW coast of Africa

Be·nin \bə-'nin, -'nēn; 'ben-ən\ **1** *or formerly* **Da·ho·mey** \də-'hō-mē\ country w Africa on Gulf of Guinea; a republic; capital, Porto-Novo **2** city SW Nigeria — **Ben·i·nese** \bə-,nin-'ēz, -,nēn-; ,ben-i-'nēz, -'nēs\ *adj or n*

Benin, Bight of the N section of Gulf of Guinea

Ben Nev·is \ben-'nev-əs\ mountain 1343 meters w Scotland in the Grampians; highest in Great Britain

Be·no·ni \bə-'nō-nē\ city NE Republic of South Africa in s Transvaal

Ber·ga·mo \'beər-gə-,mō, 'bər-\ city N Italy in Lombardy NE of Milan

Ber·gen \'bər-gən, 'beər-\ city SW Norway

Be·ring \'biər-ing, 'beər-\ **1** sea arm of the N Pacific between Alaska & NE Siberia **2** strait about 90 kilometers wide between North America (Alaska) and Asia (Russia)

Berke·ley \'bər-klē\ city w California on San Francisco Bay N of Oakland

Berk·shire \'bərk-,shiər, -shər, *for 2 British usually* 'bärk-\ **1** hills w Massachusetts; highest point Mount Greylock 1064 meters **2** county s England w of London

Ber·lin \bər-'lin, ,bər-\ city, capital of Germany; divided 1945–90 into East Berlin & West Berlin — **Ber·lin·er** \-'lin-ər\ *n*

Berlin, East former city, capital of East Germany 1945–1990

Berlin, West former city, West Germany; an enclave lying wholly within East Germany

Ber·mu·da \bər-'myüd-ə, ,bər-\ islands w Atlantic ESE of Cape Hatteras; a British colony; capital, Hamilton — **Ber·mu·dan** \-'myüd-n\ *or* **Ber·mu·di·an** \-'myüd-ē-ən\ *adj or n*

Bern \'bərn, 'beərn\ city, capital of Switzerland — **Ber·nese** \bər-'nēz, ,bər-, -'nēs\ *adj or n*

Ber·wick \'ber-ik\ *or* **Ber·wick·shire** \-,shiər, -shər\ former county SE Scotland

Berytus — see BEIRUT

Bes·kids \'bes-,kidz, be-'skēdz\ mountain ranges central Europe in the w Carpathians including West Beskids (in Poland, NW Slovakia, & E Czech Republic w of Tatra mountains) & East Beskids (in NE Slovakia)

Bes·sa·ra·bia \,bes-ə-'rā-bē-ə\ region SE Europe between Dniester & Prut rivers now chiefly in Moldova — **Bes·sa·ra·bi·an** \-bē-ən\ *adj or n*

Beth·le·hem \'beth-li-,hem, -lē-həm, -lē-əm\ town of ancient Palestine in Judea SW of Jerusalem in area occupied by Israel since 1967

Bex·ley \'bek-slē\ borough of E Greater London, England

Bezwada — see VIJAYAWADA

Bhav·na·gar \faù-'nəg-ər\ city w India in s Gujarat

Bho·pal \bō-'päl\ city N central India NW of Nagpur, capital of Madhya Pradesh

Bhu·tan \bü-'tan, -'tän\ country s Asia in the Himalayas on NE border of India; a protectorate of India; capital, Thimbu — **Bhu·ta·nese** \,büt-n-'ēz, -'ēs\ *adj or n*

Bi·af·ra, Bight of \bē-'af-rə, bī-, -'äf-\ the E section of Gulf of Guinea in w Africa

Bia·ly·stok \bē-,äl-i-,stók\ city NE Poland

Bie·le·feld \'bē-lə-,felt\ city NW central Germany E of Münster

Big Bend National Park reservation SW Texas on Rio Grande

Big Thicket wilderness area E Texas NE of Houston

Bi·har \bi-'här\ state E India bordering on Nepal; capital, Patna

Bi·ki·ni \bə-'kē-nē\ island (atoll) w Pacific in Marshall islands

Bil·bao \bil-'bä-,ō, -'baù, -'bä-ō\ city N Spain

Bil·lings \'bil-ingz\ city s central Montana; largest in state

Bio·ko \bē-'ō-(,)kō\ *or formerly* **Fer·nan·do Po** \fər-,nan-(,)dō-'pō\ island Equatorial Guinea in Bight of Biafra

Bir·ken·head \'bər-kən-,hed, ,bər-kən-'\ borough NW England in Merseyside

Bir·ming·ham \'bər-ming-,ham, *British usually* -ming-əm\ **1** city N central Alabama **2** city w central England in Warwickshire

Bisayas — see VISAYAN

Bis·cay, Bay of \'bis-,kā, -kē\ inlet of the Atlantic between w coast of France & N coast of Spain

Bis·cayne National Park \bis-'kān-, 'bis-,\ reservation s Florida

Bish·kek \bish-'kek\ *or formerly* **Frun·ze** \'frün-zə\ city, capital of Kyrgyzstan

Bis·marck \'biz-,märk\ **1** city, capital of North Dakota **2** archipelago w Pacific N of E end of New Guinea

Bis·sau \bis-'aù\ city, capital of Guinea-Bissau

Bi·thyn·ia \bə-'thin-ē-ə\ ancient country NW Asia Minor bordering on Sea of Marmara and Black sea — **Bi·thyn·i·an** \-ē-ən\ *adj or n*

Black·burn \'blak-bərn, -,bərn\ borough NW England in Lancashire

Black Forest *or German* **Schwarz·wald** \'shfärts-,vält, 'shwórt-,swóld\ forested mountain region SW Germany along E bank of the upper Rhine

Black Hills mountains w South Dakota & NE Wyoming; highest Harney Peak 2207 meters

Black·pool \'blak-,pül\ borough NW England in Lancashire

Black Sea *or ancient* **Pon·tus Eux·i·nus** \,pän-təs-yük-'sī-nəs\ *or* **Pon·tus** \'pän-təs\ sea between Europe & Asia connected with Aegean sea through the Bosporus, Sea of Marmara, & Dardanelles

Blan·tyre \'blan-,tīr\ city s Malawi

Bloem·fon·tein \'blüm-fən-,tān, -,fän-\ city, judicial capital of the Republic of South Africa & capital of Orange Free State

Blue Nile river 1375 kilometers long Ethiopia & Sudan flowing NNW into the Nile at Khartoum

Blue Ridge E range of the Appalachians E U.S. extending from s Pennsylvania to N Georgia

Bo·bo-Diou·las·so \'bō-,bō-dyù-,las-ō\ town w Burkina Faso

Bo·chum \'bō-kəm\ city w Germany in Ruhr valley

Boe·o·tia \bē-'ō-shē-ə, -shə\ district E central Greece NW of Attica; chief ancient city, Thebes — **Boe·o·tian** \-shē-ən, -shən\ *adj or n*

Bo·go·tá \,bō-gə-'tó, -'tä\ city, capital of Colombia

Bo Hai *or* **Po Hai** \'bō-'hī\ *or* **Gulf of Chih·li** \'chē-lē, 'jiər-'lē\ arm of Yellow sea NE China N of Shandong peninsula

Bo·he·mia \bō-'hē-mē-ə\ region w Czech Republic; once a kingdom & later a province; chief city, Prague

Boi·se \'bói-sē, -zē\ city, capital of Idaho

Bokhara — see BUKHARA

Boks·burg \'bäks-,bərg\ city NE Republic of South Africa in s Transvaal

Bo·liv·ia \bə-'liv-ē-ə\ country w central South America; administrative capital, La Paz; constitutional capital, Sucre — **Bo·liv·i·an** \-ē-ən\ *adj or n*

Bo·lo·gna \bə-'lōn-yə, -'lōn-ə\ city N Italy N of Florence, capital of Emilia-Romagna

Bol·ton \'bōlt-n\ *or in full* **Bolton-le-Moors** \,bōlt-n-lə-'mu̇drz\ borough NW England in Greater Manchester

Bom·bay \bäm-'bā\ **1** former state W India; divided 1960 into Gujarat & Maharashtra states **2** city, capital of Maharashtra

Bône — see ANNABA

Bo·nin \'bō-nən\ *or* **Oga·sa·wa·ra** \ō-,gäs-ə-'wär-ə\ islands Japan in W Pacific SE of Honshu

Bonn \'bän, 'bȯn\ city W Germany on the Rhine SSE of Cologne; formerly capital of West Germany

Boo·thia \'bü-thē-ə\ peninsula N Canada W of Baffin Island; its N tip is most northerly point on North American mainland

Bor·deaux \bȯr-'dō\ city SW France on the Garonne

Bor·ders \'bȯrd-ərz\ region SE Scotland; established 1975

Bor·neo \'bȯr-nē-,ō\ island Malay archipelago SW of the Philippines — see BRUNEI, KALIMANTAN, SABAH, SARAWAK

Bos·nia \'bäz-nē-ə\ region S Europe; with Herzegovina constitutes country of **Bosnia and Herzegovina**; capital, Sarajevo (in Bosnia) — **Bos·ni·an** \-nē-ən\ *adj or n*

Bos·po·rus \'bäs-pə-rəs, -prəs\ *or ancient* **Bosporus Thra·ci·us** \-'thrā-shē-əs, -shəs\ strait about 29 kilometers long between Turkey in Europe & Turkey in Asia connecting Sea of Marmara & Black sea

Bos·ton \'bȯs-tən\ city, capital of Massachusetts — **Bos·to·nian** \bȯ-'stō-nē-ən, -nyən\ *adj or n*

Bot·a·ny Bay \'bät-n-ē, 'bät-nē\ inlet of S Pacific SE Australia in New South Wales S of Sydney

Both·nia, Gulf of \'bäth-nē-ə\ arm of Baltic sea between Sweden & Finland

Bo·tswa·na \bät-'swän-ə\ country S Africa N of Molopo river; formerly British protectorate of Bechuanaland; now an independent republic; capital, Gaborone

Boulder Dam — see HOOVER DAM

Bourgogne — see BURGUNDY

Bourne·mouth \'bōrn-məth, 'bȯrn-, 'bu̇rn-\ town S England in Dorset on English channel

Brad·ford \'brad-fərd\ city N England in West Yorkshire

Brah·ma·pu·tra \,bräm-ə-'pü-trə, -'pyü-\ river 2705 kilometers long S Asia flowing from the Himalayas in Tibet to Ganges delta

Bra·ila \brə-'ē-lə\ city E Romania

Bra·sí·lia \brə-'zil-yə\ city, capital of Brazil in Federal District in E Goiás state

Bra·sov \bräsh-'ȯv\ city central Romania

Bra·ti·sla·va \,brat-ə-'släv-ə, ,brät-\ city, capital of Slovakia

Bratsk \'brätsk\ city S central Russia in Asia, NNE of Irkutsk

Braunschweig — see BRUNSWICK

Bra·zil \brə-'zil\ country E & central South America; a federal republic; capital, Brasília — **Bra·zil·ian** \brə-'zil-yən\ *adj or n*

Brazil Current warm current of the Atlantic Ocean flowing S along coast of Brazil

Braz·za·ville \'braz-ə-,vil, 'bräz-ə-,vēl\ city, capital of Congo Republic on W bank of Stanley Pool in lower Congo river

Brec·on \'brek-ən\ *or* **Breck·nock** \'brek-,näk, -nək\ *or* **Brec·on·shire** *or* **Breck·nock·shire** \-,shiər, -shər\ former county SE Wales

Bre·men \'brem-ən, 'brā-mən\ **1** state NW Germany **2** city, its capital

Bren·ner \'bren-ər\ pass 1397 meters in the Alps between Austria & Italy

Brent \'brent\ borough of W Greater London, England

Bre·scia \'bresh-ə, 'brā-shə\ city N Italy in Lombardy ENE of Milan

Breslau — see WROCLAW

Brest \'brest\ **1** city NW France in Brittany **2** city SW Belarus

Bret·on, Cape \kāp-'bret-n, kə-'bret-, -'brit-\ headland Canada; most easterly point of Cape Breton Island & of Nova Scotia

Bridge·port \'brij-,pōrt, -,pȯrt\ city SW Connecticut

Bridge·town \'brij-,tau̇n\ city, capital of Barbados

Brigh·ton \'brīt-n\ county borough S England in East Sussex on English channel

Bris·bane \'briz-bən, -,bān\ city E Australia, capital of Queensland

Bris·tol \'bris-tl\ **1** city SW England in Avon **2** channel between S Wales & SW England

Brit·ain \'brit-n\ **1** the island of Great Britain **2** UNITED KINGDOM

British Columbia province W Canada on Pacific coast; capital, Victoria

British Commonwealth — see COMMONWEALTH OF NATIONS

British Guiana — see GUYANA

British Honduras — see BELIZE

British India the part of India formerly under direct British administration

British Indian Ocean Territory British colony in Indian ocean comprising Chagos archipelago & formerly Aldabra, Farquhar, & Desroches islands (returned to Seychelles 1976)

British Isles island group W Europe comprising Great Britain, Ireland, & adjacent islands

British Solomon Islands former British protectorate comprising the Solomon islands (except Bougainville, Buka, & adjacent small islands) & Santa Cruz islands; capital, Honiara

British Somaliland former British protectorate E Africa bordering on Gulf of Aden; capital, Hargeisa; since 1960 part of Somalia

British Virgin Islands E islands of Virgin islands group; a British dependency; capital, Road Town (on Tortola Island)

British West Indies islands of the West Indies belonging to the Commonwealth & including Jamaica, Trinidad and Tobago, & the Bahama, Cayman, Windward, Leeward, & British Virgin islands

Brit·ta·ny \'brit-n-ē\ *or French* **Bre·tagne** \brə-'tàny\ region & former province NW France SW of Normandy

Brno \'bər-nō\ city SE Czech Republic chief city of Moravia

Brom·ley \'bräm-lē\ borough of SE Greater London, England

Bronx \'brängs, 'brängks\ *or* **The Bronx** borough of New York City on mainland NE of Manhattan Island

Brook·lyn \'bru̇k-lən\ borough of New York City at SW end of Long Island

Brooks Range \'bru̇ks\ mountains N Alaska

Bruges \'brüzh, 'brüēzh\ *or Flemish* **Brug·ge** \'brüēg-ə\ city NW Belgium

Bru·nei \brün-'ī, 'brü-,nī\ sultanate NE Borneo; formerly a British protectorate; capital, Bandar Seri Begawan

Bruns·wick \'brənz-wik\ *or German* **Braun·schweig** \'brau̇n-,shwīg, -,shfīk\ city central Germany W of Berlin

Brus·sels \'brəs-əlz\ city, capital of Belgium

Bryansk \brē-'änsk\ city W Russia in Europe, SW of Moscow

Bryce Canyon National Park \'brīs\ reservation S Utah NE of Zion National Park

Bu·ca·ra·man·ga \,bü-kə-rə-'mäng-gə\ city N Colombia NNE of Bogotá

Bu·cha·rest \'bü-kə-,rest, 'byü-\ city, capital of Romania

Buck·ing·ham·shire \'bək-ing-əm-,shiər, -shər, *in the United States also* -ing-,ham-\ *or* **Buckingham** county SE central England

Bu·da·pest \'büd-ə-,pest *also* 'byüd-, 'bu̇d-, -,pesht\ city, capital of Hungary

Bue·nos Ai·res \,bwā-nə-'saər-ēz, ,bō-nə-, -'seər-, -'sīr-\ city, capital of Argentina on Rio de la Plata

Buf·fa·lo \'bəf-ə-,lō\ city W New York on Lake Erie

\ə\ abut	\ng\ sing
\ər\ further	\ō\ bone
\a\ mat	\ȯ\ saw
\ā\ take	\ȯi\ coin
\ä\ cot, cart	\th\ thin
\au̇\ out	\th\ this
\ch\ chin	\ü\ food
\e\ pet	\u̇\ foot
\ē\ easy	\y\ yet
\g\ go	\yü\ few
\i\ tip	\yu̇\ cure
\ī\ life	\zh\ vision
\j\ job	

Bu·jum·bu·ra \,bü-jəm-'bùr-ə\ *or formerly* **Usum·bu-ra** \,ü-səm-'bùr-ə\ city, capital of Burundi

Bu·ka·vu \bü-'käv-ü\ city E Zaire

Bu·kha·ra \bü-'kär-ə, -'kar-, -'här-, -'har-\ *or* **Bo·khara** \bō-\ city Uzbekistan, E of the Amu Darya

Bu·la·wayo \,bùl-ə-'wā-ō, -'wī-\ city SW Zimbabwe

Bul·gar·ia \,bəl-'gar-ē-ə, bùl-, -'ger-\ country SE Europe on Black sea; capital, Sofia

Bur·gun·dy \'bər-gən-dē\ *or French* **Bour·gogne** \bür-'gòn^y\ region E France; a former kingdom, duchy, & province — **Bur·gun·di·an** \bər-'gən-dē-ən, ,bər-\ *adj or n*

Bur·ki·na Fa·so \bùr-'kē-nə-'fäs-ò, bər-\ *or formerly* **Upper Vol·ta** \'vōl-tə, 'vòl-, 'väl-\ country W Africa N of Côte d'Ivoire, Ghana, & Togo; a republic; capital, Ouagadougou

Bur·ling·ton \'bər-ling-tən\ city NW Vermont; largest in state

Bur·ma — see MYANMAR

Bur·sa \bùr-'sä, 'bər-sə\ city NW Turkey in Asia near Sea of Marmara

Bu·run·di \bù-'rün-dē\ *or formerly* **Urun·di** \ù-'rün-dē\ country E central Africa; capital, Bujumbura — see RUANDA-URUNDI

Bute \'byüt\ **1** island SW Scotland in Firth of Clyde **2** *or* **Bute·shire** \-,shiər, -shər\ former county SW Scotland

Byd·goszcz \'bid-,góshch, -,gósh\ *or German* **Brom·berg** \'bräm-,bərg, 'bròm-,berk\ city NW central Poland

Byelorussian Soviet Socialist Republic — see BELORUS-SIAN SOVIET SOCIALIST REPUBLIC

Byzantium — see ISTANBUL

Caen \'kän\ city NW France

Caer·nar·von·shire \kär-'när-vən-,shiər, -shər\ *or* **Caer-narvon** former county NW Wales

Cae·sa·rea \,sē-zə-'rē-ə; ,ses-ə-, ,sez-ə-\ ancient city W Palestine in Samaria on the Mediterranean; Roman capital of Palestine

Ca·glia·ri \'käl-yə-rē\ city Italy, capital of Sardinia

Cai·ro \'kī-rō\ city, capital of Egypt — **Cai·rene** \kī-'rēn\ *adj or n*

Caith·ness \'kāth-nəs\ *or* **Caith·ness·shire** \-nəs-,shiər, -nəsh-, -shər\ former county N Scotland

Ca·la·bria \kə-'lā-brē-ə, -'läb-rē-\ **1** district of ancient Italy comprising area forming heel of Italian peninsula; now S part of Apulia **2** *or ancient* **Brut·ti·um** \'brüt-ē-əm, 'brət-\ region S Italy occupying toe of Italian peninsula; capital, Catanzaro — **Ca·la·ri·an** \kə-'lā-brē-ən, -'läb-rē-\ *adj or n*

Cal·cut·ta \kal-'kət-ə\ city E India on Hooghly river, capital of West Bengal — **Cal·cut·tan** \-'kət-n\ *adj or n*

Cal·e·do·nia \,kal-ə-'dō-nyə, -nē-ə\ — see SCOTLAND — **Cal·e·do·nian** \-nyən, -nē-ən\ *adj or n*

Cal·ga·ry \'kal-gə-rē\ city SW Alberta

Ca·li \'käl-ē\ city W Colombia

Cal·i·cut \'kal-i-kət\ *also* **Ko·zhi·kode** \'kō-zhə-,kōd\ city SW India

Cal·i·for·nia \,kal-ə-'fòr-nyə\ state SW U. S.; capital, Sacramento — **Cal·i·for·nian** \-nyən\ *adj or n*

California, Gulf of arm of the Pacific NW Mexico

California Current cold current of the Pacific Ocean flowing SE along W coast of North America

Ca·llao \kə-'yä-ō, kə-'yaù\ city W Peru W of Lima

Cal·va·ry \'kalv-rē, -ə-rē\ *or Hebrew* **Gol·go·tha** \'gäl-gə-thə, gäl-'gäth-ə\ place outside ancient Jerusalem where Christ was crucified

Ca·ma·güey \,kam-ə-'gwā\ city E central Cuba

Cam·bay, Gulf of \kam-'bā\ inlet of Arabian sea India N of Bombay

Cam·ber·well \'kam-bər-,wel, -wəl\ city SE Australia in S Victoria E of Melbourne

Cam·bo·dia \kam-'bōd-ē-ə\ *or officially* **Democratic Kam·pu·chea** \-,kam-pù-'chē-ə\ country SE Asia bordering on Gulf of Siam; capital Phnom Penh — **Cam·bo·di·an** \-ē-ən\ *adj or n*

Cam·bria \'kam-brē-ə\ WALES — an old name

Cam·bridge \'kām-brij\ **1** city E Massachusetts W of Boston **2** city E England in Cambridgeshire

Cam·bridge·shire \'kām-brij-,shiər, -shər\ *or* **Cambridge** *or formerly* **Cambridgeshire and Isle of Ely** \'ē-lē\ county E England

Cam·den \'kam-dən\ **1** city SW New Jersey **2** borough of N Greater London, England

Cam·er·oon *or French* **Cam·er·oun** \,kam-ə-'rün\ country W equatorial Africa; capital, Yaoundé — **Cam·er·oo·nian** \-'rü-nē-ən, -'rü-nyən\ *adj or n*

Cam·er·oons \,kam-ə-'rünz\ region W Africa on NE Gulf of Guinea formerly belonging to the British and French but now divided between Nigeria & Cameroon

Cam·pa·nia \kam-'pā-nyə, -nē-ə\ region S Italy bordering on Tyrrhenian sea; capital, Naples — **Cam·pa·nian** \-nyən, -nē-ən\ *adj or n*

Cam·pe·che \kam-'pē-chē, käm-'pā-chā\ state SE Mexico in W Yucatán peninsula; capital, Campeche

Cam·pi·nas \kam-'pē-nəs\ city SE Brazil N of São Paulo

Cam·po·bas·so \,käm-pō-'bäs-,ō\ city central Italy

Cam·po Gran·de \,kam-pü-'gran-də, -dē\ city SW Brazil

Cam·pos \'kam-pəs\ city SE Brazil NE of Rio de Janeiro

Ca·naan \'kā-nən\ ancient region corresponding vaguely to later Palestine — **Ca·naan·ite** \'kā-nə-,nīt\ *adj or n*

Can·a·da \'kan-ə-də\ country N North America; dominion of the Commonwealth; capital, Ottawa — **Ca·na·di·an** \kə-'nād-ē-ən\ *adj or n*

Canadian Shield plateau region E Canada & NE U.S. extending from Mackenzie basin E to Davis strait & S to S Quebec, S central Ontario, NE Minnesota, N Wisconsin, NW Michigan, and NE New York including the Adirondacks

Canal Zone *or* **Panama Canal Zone** strip of territory Panama; under U.S. control through 1999 for administration of the Panama Canal

Ca·nary \kə-'neər-ē\ islands in the Atlantic off NW coast of Africa belonging to Spain; capital, Las Palmas

Ca·nav·er·al, Cape \kə-'nav-rəl, -ə-rəl\ *or 1963–1973 officially* **Cape Ken·ne·dy** \-'ken-ə-dē\ headland E Florida in the Atlantic on Canaveral peninsula E of Indian river

Can·ber·ra \'kan-bə-rə, -brə, -,ber-ə\ city, capital of Australia in Australian Capital Territory

Can·ter·bury \'kant-ər-,ber-ē, 'kant-ə-, -bə-rē, -brē\ **1** city SE Australia in E New South Wales **2** city SE England in Kent

Can·ton \'kant-n\ city NE Ohio

Canton — see GUANGZHOU

Can·yon·lands National Park \'kan-yən-,landz, -,lanz\ reservation SE Utah

Cape Bret·on Island \kāp-,bret-n-, kə-,bret-, -,brit-\ island NE Nova Scotia

Cape of Good Hope 1 — see GOOD HOPE **2** *or* **Cape Province** *or formerly* **Cape Colony** province S Republic of South Africa; capital, Cape Town

Ca·per·na·um \kə-'pər-nē-əm\ city of ancient Palestine on NW shore of Sea of Galilee

Cape Town *or* **Cape·town** \'kāp-,taùn\ city Republic of South Africa, capital of Cape of Good Hope & legislative capital of Republic

Cape Verde \'vərd\ **1** islands in the N Atlantic off W Africa; a republic; capital, Praia; until 1975 belonged to Portugal **2** — see VERT

Cape York Peninsula \'yòrk-\ peninsula NE Australia in N Queensland

Capitol Reef National Park reservation S central Utah

Cap·pa·do·cia \,kap-ə-'dō-shə, -shē-ə\ ancient country & Roman province E Asia Minor; capital, Caesarea Mazaca

Ca·pri \ka-'prē, kə-; 'käp-rē, 'kap-\ island Italy S of Bay of Naples

Ca·ra·cas \kə-'rak-əs, -'räk-\ city, capital of Venezuela

Car·diff \'kärd-əf\ city, capital of Wales in South Glamorgan

Car·di·gan·shire \'kärd-i-gən-,shiər, -shər\ *or* **Cardigan** former county W Wales on Cardigan Bay

Ca·rib·be·an \,kar-ə-'bē-ən, kə-'rib-ē-ən\ sea arm of the Atlantic bounded on N & E by West Indies, on S by South America, & on W by Central America

Ca·rin·thia \kə-'rin-thē-ə, -'rint-\ **1** region central Europe in E Alps in S Austria & Slovenia **2** region S Austria; capital, Klagenfurt

Car·low \'kär-,lō\ county SE Ireland in Leinster

Carls·bad Caverns \'kärlz-,bad-\ limestone caves SE New Mexico in **Carlsbad Caverns National Park**

Car·mar·then·shire \kär-'mär-thən-,shiər, kər-, kə-, -shər\ or **Carmarthen** former county S Wales

Carmel, Mount \'kär-məl\ mountain ridge N Israel; highest point about 550 meters

Car·o·li·na \,kar-ə-'lī-nə\ English colony on E coast of North America founded 1663 & divided 1729 into North Carolina & South Carolina (the **Carolinas**) — **Car·o·lin·i·an** \-'lin-ē-ən\ adj or n

Ca·ro·li·na \,kär-ə-'lē-nə\ city NE central Puerto Rico

Car·o·line \'kar-ə-,līn, -lən\ islands W Pacific E of S Philippines; formerly part of Trust Territory of the Pacific Islands

Car·pa·thi·an \kär-'pā-thē-ən\ mountains E central Europe along boundary between Czechoslovakia & Poland & in N & central Romania; highest Gerlachovka 2663 meters

Carpathian Ruthenia — see RUTHENIA

Car·pen·tar·ia, Gulf of \,kär-pən-'ter-ē-ə, -tar-\ inlet of Arafura sea N of Australia

Car·son City \'kärs-n\ city, capital of Nevada

Car·ta·ge·na \,kärt-ə-'gā-nə, -'hā-\ **1** city NW Colombia **2** city SE Spain

Car·thage \'kär-thij\ ancient city N Africa NE of modern Tunis; capital of an empire that included at greatest extent much of NW Africa, E Spain, & Sicily — **Car·tha·gin·ian** \,kär-thə-'jin-yən, -'jin-ē-ən\ adj or n

Ca·sa·blan·ca \,kas-ə-'blang-kə, ,kaz-\ or Arabic **Dar el Bei·da** \,där-,el-bā-'dä\ city W Morocco on the Atlantic

Cas·cade Range \kas-'kād, 'kas-'kād\ mountains NW U.S. in Washington, Oregon, & N California — see RAINIER (Mount)

Cas·pi·an Sea \'kas-pē-ən\ salt lake between Europe & Asia about 27 meters below sea level

Cas·tile \kas-'tēl\ or Spanish **Cas·ti·lla** \kä-'stē-lyä, -'stē-yä\ region & ancient kingdom central & N Spain

Cas·tries \kas-'strē, 'kas-,trēz\ city, capital of St. Lucia

Cat·a·lo·nia \,kat-l-'ō-nyə, -nē-ə\ or Spanish **Ca·ta·lu·ña** \,kät-l-'ü-nyə\ region NE Spain bordering on France & the Mediterranean; chief city, Barcelona — **Cat·a·lo·nian** \-'ō-nyən, -nē-ən\ adj or n

Ca·ta·nia \kə-'tān-yə, -'tän-\ city Italy in E Sicily at foot of Mount Etna

Ca·tan·za·ro \,kät-,än-'zär-,ō, -,änd-\ city S Italy

Ca·thay \kə-'thā, ka-\ — an old name for CHINA

Cats·kill \'kat-,skil\ mountains in Appalachian system SE New York W of the Hudson

Cau·ca·sus \'kȯ-kə-səs\ **1** or **Cau·ca·sia** \kȯ-'kā-zhə, -shə\ region SE Europe between Black & Caspian seas **2** mountain system in Caucasia — see ELBRUS

Cav·an \'kav-ən\ county NE Republic of Ireland in Ulster

Cay·enne \kī-'en, kā-\ city, capital of French Guiana

Cay·man \kā-'man, 'kā-, attributively 'kā-mən\ islands British West Indies NW of Jamaica; a British colony; capital, Georgetown (on Grand Cayman Island)

Ce·bu \sā-'bü\ **1** island E central Philippines in Visayan islands **2** city on E coast of Cebu Island

Ce·dar Rapids \'sēd-ər\ city E Iowa

Celebes — see SULAWESI

Celestial Empire the former Chinese Empire

Cel·le \'tsel-ə, 'sel-ə\ city N central Germany NE of Hannover

Cel·tic \'kel-tik, 'sel-\ sea inlet of the Atlantic in British Isles SE of Ireland, SW of Wales, & W of Cornwall

Central region central Scotland; established 1975

Central African Republic country N central Africa; formerly the French territory of **Uban·gi–Sha·ri** \ü-'bang-gē-'shär-ē, yü-, -'bang-ē-\; capital, Bangui

Central America narrow portion of North America from S border of Mexico to South America — **Central American** adj or n

Ce·ram or **Se·ram** \'sā-,räm\ island E Indonesia in central Moluccas

Cé·vennes \sā-'ven\ mountain range S France W of the Rhone in SE Massif Central; highest peak Mount Mézenc 1754 meters

Cey·lon \si-'län, sā-\ **1** island in Indian ocean off S India **2** — see SRI LANKA — **Cey·lon·ese** \,sā-lə-'nēz, ,sē-lə-, ,sel-ə-, -'nēs\ adj or n

Chad or French **Tchad** \'chad\ country N central Africa; a republic; capital, N'Djamana — **Chad·ian** \'chad-ē-ən\ adj or n

Chad, Lake shallow lake N central Africa at junction of boundaries of Chad, Niger, & Nigeria

Cha·gos \'chä-gəs\ archipelago central Indian ocean; comprises British Indian Ocean Territory — see DIEGO GARCIA

Chal·cid·i·ce \kal-'sid-ə-sē\ peninsula NE Greece in E Macedonia

Chal·dea \kal-'dē-ə\ ancient region SW Asia on Euphrates river & Persian gulf — **Chal·de·an** \-'dē-ən\ adj or n — **Chal·dee** \'kal-,dē\ n

Champlain, Lake \sham-'plān\ lake between New York & Vermont extending N into Quebec

Chan·di·garh \'chən-dē-gər\ city N India N of Delhi in Chandigarh Territory, capital of Punjab (Punjabi Suba) & of Haryana

Chang \'chäng\ or **Yang·tze** \'yang-'sē; 'yangt-sē, 'yangkt-\ river 4990 kilometers long central China flowing into East China sea

Changan — see XI'AN

Ch'ang–chia–k'ou — see ZHANGJIAKOU

Ch'ang–chou — see ZHANGZHOU

Chang–chun \'chäng-'chùn\ city NE China, capital of Jilin

Chang·de or **Chang·te** \'chäng-'də\ city SE central China in N Hunan

Chang·sha \'chäng-'shä\ city SE central China, capital of Hunan

Channel Islands National Park reservation SW California

Channel 1 — see SANTA BARBARA **2** islands in English channel including Jersey, Guernsey, & Alderney & belonging to Great Britain; capital, Saint Helier

Cha·pa·la \chə-'päl-ə\ lake W central Mexico SE of Guadalajara

Charles \'chärlz\ river 76 kilometers long E Massachusetts flowing into Boston harbor

Charles, Cape cape E Virginia N of entrance to Chesapeake Bay

Charles·ton \'chärl-stən\ city, capital of West Virginia

Char·lotte \'shär-lət\ city S North Carolina

Charlotte Ama·lie \ə-'mäl-yə\ city, capital of Virgin Islands of the U.S.; on Saint Thomas Island

Char·lotte·town \'shär-lət-,taùn\ city, capital of Prince Edward Island, Canada

Chat·ta·noo·ga \,chat-ə-'nü-gə, ,chat-n-'ü-\ city SE Tennessee

Che·bok·sa·ry \,cheb-,äk-'sär-ē\ city central Russia in Europe on the Volga W of Kazan

Chekiang — see ZHEJIANG

Chelsea — see KENSINGTON AND CHELSEA

Che·lya·binsk \chel-'yä-bənsk\ city W Russia in Asia S of Sverdlovsk

Chemnitz \'kem-,nits, -nəts\ or 1953–90 **Karl–Marx–Stadt** \,kärl-'märk-,shtät, -,stät\ city E Germany SE of Leipzig

Chen–chiang — see ZHENJIANG

Cheng–chou — see ZHENGZHOU

Cheng·du or **Ch'eng–tu** \'chəng-'dü\ city SW central China, capital of Sichuan

Cher·so·nese \'kər-sə-,nēz, -,nēs\ any of several peninsulas (as the Gallipoli & Crimea peninsulas)

Ches·a·peake Bay \'ches-,pēk, -ə-,pēk\ inlet of the Atlantic in Virginia & Maryland

\ə\ abut | \ng\ sing
\ər\ further | \ō\ bone
\a\ mat | \ȯ\ saw
\ā\ take | \ȯi\ coin
\ä\ cot, cart | \th\ thin
\aù\ out | \th\ this
\ch\ chin | \ü\ food
\e\ pet | \ù\ foot
\ē\ easy | \y\ yet
\g\ go | \yü\ few
\i\ tip | \yù\ cure
\ī\ life | \zh\ vision
\j\ job

Chesh·ire \'chesh-ər, 'chesh-,iər\ *or* **Ches·ter** \'ches-tər\ county w England bordering on Wales

Chev·i·ot \'chev-ē-ət, 'chē-vē-ət\ hills along English-Scottish border

Chey·enne \shī-'an, -'en\ city, capital of Wyoming

Chia–mu–ssu — see JIAMUSI

Chia·pas \chē-'äp-əs\ state SE Mexico; capital, Tuxtla Gutiérrez

Chi·ba \'chē-bə\ city E Japan in Honshu on Tokyo Bay E of Tokyo

Chi·ca·go \shə-'käg-ō, -'kòg-\ city NE Illinois — **Chi·ca·go·an** \-'käg-ə-wən, -'kòg-\ *n*

Chi·chén It·zá \chə-,chen-ət-'sä\ ruined Mayan city SE Mexico in Yucatán ESE of Mérida

Ch'i–ch'i–ha–erh — see QIQIHAR

Chihli, Gulf of — see BO HAI

Chi·hua·hua \chə-'wä-wä, shə-, -wə\ **1** state N Mexico bordering on U.S. **2** city, its capital

Chile \'chil-ē\ country SW South America; capital, Santiago — **Chil·ean** \'chil-ē-ən, chə-'lā-ən\ *adj or n*

Chim·bo·ra·zo \,chim-bə-'räz-ō, ,shim-\ mountain 6267 meters w central Ecuador

Chim·kent \chim-'kent\ city S Kazakhstan N of Tashkent

Chi·na \'chī-nə\ **1** country E Asia; capital, Beijing — see TAIWAN **2** sea section of the w Pacific E & SE of China; divided at Taiwan strait into **East China** & **South China** seas

Chinan — see JINAN

Chin–chou *or* **Chinchow** — see JINZHOU

Chi·os \'kī-,äs\ island Greece in the Aegean off w coast of Turkey

Chisinau — see KISHINEV

Chi·ta \chit-'ä\ city S Russia in Asia, E of Lake Baikal

Chit·ta·gong \'chit-ə-,gäng, -,gòng\ city SE Bangladesh on Bay of Bengal

Chkalov — see ORENBURG

Chong·jin \'chòng-,jin\ city & port NE North Korea on Sea of Japan

Chong·ju \'chòng-,jü\ city central South Korea

Chong·qing *or* **Ch'ung–ch'ing** \'chùng-'ching\ *or* **Chung·king** \'chùng-'king\ city SW central China in SE Sichuan

Chon·ju \'jən-,jü\ city w South Korea

Cho·sen \'chō-'sen\ KOREA — an old name

Christ·church \'krīs-,chərch, 'krīst-\ city New Zealand on E coast of South Island

Christ·mas \'kris-məs\ **1** island E Indian ocean SW of Java administered by Australia **2** — see KIRITIMATI

Ch'üan–chou *or* **Chuanchow** — see QUANZHOU

Chu–chou *or* **Chuchow** — see ZHUZHOU

Ci·li·cia \sə-'lish-ə, -'lish-ē-ə\ ancient country SE Asia Minor on coast S of Taurus mountains

Cin·cin·na·ti \,sin-sə-'nat-ē, -'nat-ə\ city SW Ohio

Cis·al·pine Gaul \sis-'al-,pīn-\ the part of Gaul lying S & E of the Alps

Ci·tlal·te·petl \sē-,tläl-'tä-,pet-l\ *or* **Pi·co de Ori·za·ba** \'pē-kō-dā-,ōr-ə-'zäb-ə, -,òr-\ inactive volcano 5700 meters SE Mexico on Puebla-Veracruz border; highest point in Mexico & third highest in North America

Città del Vaticano — see VATICAN CITY

Ci·u·dad Gua·ya·na \,sē-ù-,thä-gwə-'yän-ə, -,thäth-\ city E Venezuela

Ci·u·dad Juá·rez \,sē-ù-,thä-'hwär-əs, -ù-,dad-, -'wär-\ *or* **Juárez** \'hwär-əs, 'wär-\ city N Mexico in Chihuahua on Rio Grande opposite El Paso, Texas

Ciudad Trujillo — see SANTO DOMINGO

Clack·man·nan \klak-'man-ən\ *or* **Clack·man·nan·shire** \-,shiər, -shər\ former county central Scotland

Clare \'klaər, 'kleər\ county w Ireland in Munster

Cler·mont–Fer·rand \,kler-,mōⁿ-fə-'räⁿ\ city S central France

Cleve·land \'klēv-lənd\ **1** city NE Ohio **2** county N England N of North Yorkshire

Cluj–Na·po·ca \'klüzh-'näp-ō-kə\ city NW central Romania

Clwyd \'klüid\ county NE Wales; established 1974

Clyde \'klīd\ river 171 kilometers long SW Scotland flowing into **Firth of Clyde** (estuary)

Clydes·dale \'klīdz-,dāl\ valley of upper Clyde, Scotland

Cnossus — see KNOSSOS

Coa·hui·la \,kō-ə-'wē-lə, kwä-'wē-\ state N Mexico bordering on U.S.; capital, Saltillo

Coast Mountains mountain range w British Columbia; the N continuation of Cascade range

Coast Ranges chain of mountain ranges w North America extending along Pacific coast w of Sierra Nevada & Cascade Range & through Vancouver Island into S Alaska to Kenai peninsula & Kodiak Island

Co·cha·bam·ba \,kō-chə-'bäm-bə\ city w central Bolivia

Co·chin China \,kō-chən-\ region S Vietnam

Cod, Cape \'käd\ peninsula SE Massachusetts

Coim·ba·tore \,kòim-bə-'tōr, -'tòr\ city S India in w Tamil Nadu

Col·chis \'käl-kəs\ ancient country bordering on Black sea S of Caucasus mountains; district now in w Republic of Georgia

Co·li·ma \kə-'lē-mə\ **1** state SW Mexico **2** city, its capital

Co·logne \kə-'lōn\ *or German* **Köln** \'kœln\ city w Germany on the Rhine

Co·lom·bia \kə-'ləm-bē-ə\ country NW South America; capital, Bogotá — **Co·lom·bi·an** \-bē-ən\ *adj or n*

Co·lom·bo \kə-'ləm-bō\ city, capital of Sri Lanka

Co·lón \kə-'lōn\ city Panama on the Caribbean

Colón Archipelago — see GALAPAGOS ISLANDS

Col·o·ra·do \,käl-ə-'rad-ō, -'räd-\ **1** river 2335 kilometers long SW U.S. & NW Mexico flowing from N Colorado into Gulf of California **2** desert SE California **3** plateau region SW U.S. w of Rocky Mountains **4** state w U.S.; capital, Denver — **Col·o·rad·an** \-'rad-n, -'räd-n\ *or* **Co·lo·ra·do·an** \-'rad-ə-wən, -'räd-\ *adj or n*

Colorado Springs city central Colorado

Co·lum·bia \kə-'ləm-bē-ə\ **1** river 2045 kilometers long SW Canada & NW U.S. rising in SE British Columbia & flowing S & w into the Pacific **2** plateau in Columbia river basin in E Washington, E Oregon, & SW Idaho **3** city, capital of South Carolina **4** — see UNITED STATES OF AMERICA

Co·lum·bus \kə-'ləm-bəs\ **1** city w Georgia **2** city, capital of Ohio

Commonwealth of Independent States association of the former constituent republics of the U.S.S.R. except for Georgia, Lithuania, Latvia, & Estonia; formed 1991

Commonwealth of Nations *or* **Commonwealth** *or formerly* **British Commonwealth** political organization consisting of nations loyal to the British monarch

Co·mo, Lake \'kō-mō\ lake N Italy in Lombardy

Com·o·ro \'käm-ə-,rō\ islands off SE Africa NW of Madagascar; formerly a French possession; a republic (except for Mayotte Island remaining French) since 1975; capital, Moroni

Com·stock Lode \,käm-,stäk-\ gold & silver deposit at Virginia City, Nevada, discovered 1859

Con·a·kry *or* **Kon·a·kry** \'kän-ə-krē\ city, capital of Guinea

Con·cep·ción \kən-,sep-sē-'ōn, -'sep-shən\ city S central Chile

Con·cord \'käng-kərd\ **1** city, capital of New Hampshire **2** town E Massachusetts NW of Boston

Con·go \'käng-gō\ **1** *or* **Zaire** \zä-'iər\ river 4830 kilometers long w equatorial Africa flowing into the Atlantic **2** — see ZAIRE **3** *or formerly* **Middle Congo** country w central Africa w of lower Congo river; capital, Brazzaville — **Con·go·lese** \,käng-gə-'lēz, -'lēs\ *adj or n*

Con·nacht \'kän-,òt\ province w Ireland

Con·nect·i·cut \kə-'net-i-kət\ **1** river 655 kilometers long NE U.S. flowing S from N New Hampshire into Long Island Sound **2** state NE U.S.; capital, Hartford

Con·stan·tine \'kän-stən-,tēn\ city NE Algeria

Constantinople — see ISTANBUL

Con·stan·tsa \kən-'stän-sə, -'stänt-\ city SE Romania

Cook \'kůk\ **1** inlet of the Pacific s Alaska w of Kenai peninsula **2** islands s Pacific sw of Society islands belonging to New Zealand; capital, Avarua (on Rarotonga Island) **3** strait New Zealand between North Island & South Island

Cook, Mount *or formerly* **Ao•rangi** \aů-'räng-ē\ mountain 3764 meters New Zealand in w central South Island in Southern Alps; highest in New Zealand

Co•pen•ha•gen \ˌkō-pən-'hā-gən, -'häg-ən\ city, capital of Denmark

Coquilhatville — see MBANDAKA

Cor•al \'kòr-əl, 'kär-\ sea arm of the w Pacific NE of Australia

Cór•do•ba \'kòrd-ə-bə, -ə-və\ **1** *or* **Cor•do•va** \'kòrd-ə-və\ *or ancient* **Cor•du•ba** \'kòrd-yə-bə, 'kòrd-ů-bə\ city s Spain on the Guadalquivir **2** city N central Argentina

Cor•fu \kòr-'fü; 'kòr-ˌfü, -ˌfyü\ island NW Greece in Ionian islands

Cor•inth \'kòr-ənth, 'kär-, -ǝntth\ **1** region of ancient Greece occupying most of Isthmus of Corinth & part of NE Peloponnesus **2** ancient city, its capital; site sw of present city of Corinth — **Co•rin•thi•an** \kə-'rinthē-ən, -'rint-\ *adj or n*

Corinth, Gulf of inlet of Ionian sea central Greece N of the Peloponnesus

Corinth, Isthmus of neck of land connecting the Peloponnesus with rest of Greece

Cork \'kòrk\ **1** county s Ireland in Munster **2** city s Ireland in County Cork

Corn•wall \'kòrn-ˌwòl, -wəl\ *or since 1974* **Cornwall and Isles of Scil•ly** \'sil-ē\ county sw England

Cor•o•man•del \ˌkòr-ə-'man-dl, ˌkär-\ coast region SE India on Bay of Bengal

Cor•pus Chris•ti \ˌkòr-pə-'skris-tē\ city s Texas

Cor•reg•i•dor \kə-'reg-ə-ˌdòr\ island Philippines at entrance to Manila Bay

Cor•si•ca \'kòr-si-kə\ *or French* **Corse** \kòrs\ island France in the Mediterranean N of Sardinia — **Cor•si•can** \'kòr-si-kən\ *adj or n*

Cos•ta Bra•va \ˌkäs-tə-'bräv-ə, ˌkòs-, ˌkōs-\ coast region NE Spain on the Mediterranean extending NE from Barcelona

Costa del Sol \-del-'sòl, -'sōl\ coast region s Spain on the Mediterranean extending E from Gibraltar

Cos•ta Ri•ca \ˌkäs-tə-'rē-kə, ˌkòs-, ˌkōs-\ country Central America between Nicaragua & Panama; a republic; capital, San José — **Cos•ta Ri•can** \-'rē-kən\ *adj or n*

Côte d'A•zur \ˌkōt-də-'zůr\ region SE France on Mediterranean coast; part of the Riviera

Côte d'Ivoire — see IVORY COAST

Co•to•nou \ˌkōt-ə-'nü\ city s Benin

Cots•wold \'kät-ˌswōld\ hills sw central England in Gloucestershire

Cov•en•try \'käv-ən-trē, 'kəv-\ city central England in West Midlands

Co•zu•mel \ˌkō-zə-'mel\ island SE Mexico off NE coast of Quintana Roo

Cracow — see KRAKOW

Cra•io•va \krä-'yō-və\ city s Romania

Cra•ter \'krāt-ər\ lake sw Oregon in Cascade range; main feature of **Crater Lake National Park** — see MAZAMA (Mount)

Crete \'krēt\ island Greece in E Mediterranean; capital, Canea — **Cre•tan** \'krēt-n\ *adj or n*

Cri•mea \krī-'mē-ə, krə-\ peninsula E Europe, extending into Black sea — **Cri•me•an** \krī-'mē-ən, krə-\ *adj*

Cro•atia \krō-'ā-shə, -shē-ə\ country s Europe; formerly a constituent republic of Yugoslavia; capital, Zagreb

Croy•don \'kròid-n\ borough of s Greater London, England

Cu•ba \'kyü-bə\ island in the West Indies; a republic; capital, Havana — **Cu•ban** \-bən\ *adj or n*

Cú•cu•ta \'kü-kət-ə\ city N Colombia

Cu•lia•cán \ˌkül-yə-'kän\ city NW Mexico, capital of Sinaloa

Cu•ma•ná \ˌkü-mə-'nä\ city NE Venezuela

Cum•ber•land \'kəm-bər-lənd\ former county NW England — see CUMBRIA

Cumberland Plateau *or* **Cumberland Mountains** mountain region E U.S.; part of s Appalachian mountains w of Tennessee river extending from s West Virginia to NE Alabama

Cum•bria \'kəm-brē-ə\ county NW England including former counties of Cumberland & Westmorland — **Cum•bri•an** \-ən\ *adj or n*

Cumbrian mountains NW England chiefly in Cumbria

Cu•ra•çao \'kůr-ə-ˌsō, 'kyůr-, -ˌsaů\ island Netherlands Antilles in the s Caribbean; chief town, Willemstad

Cu•ri•ti•ba \ˌkůr-ə-'tē-bə\ city s Brazil sw of São Paulo

Cush \'kəsh, 'kůsh\ ancient country NE Africa in upper Nile valley s of Egypt — **Cush•ite** \-ˌīt\ *n* — **Cush•it•ic** \ˌkəsh-'it-ik, kůsh-\ *adj*

Cut•tack \'kət-ək\ city E India in Orissa

Cyc•la•des \'sik-lə-ˌdēz\ islands Greece in s Aegean

Cymru — see WALES

Cy•prus \'sī-prəs\ island E Mediterranean s of Turkey; a republic of the Commonwealth; capital, Nicosia — **Cyp•ri•ot** \'sip-rē-ət, -rē-ˌät\ *or* **Cyp•ri•ote** \-ˌōt, -ət\ *adj or n*

Cy•re•na•ica \ˌsir-ə-'nā-ə-kə, ˌsī-rə-\ **1** ancient region N Africa on coast w of Egypt; capital, Cyrene **2** region E Libya; formerly a province — **Cy•re•na•i•can** \-kən\ *adj or n*

Czecho•slo•va•kia \ˌchek-ə-slō-'väk-ē-ə, -'vak-\ former country central Europe; capital, Prague; divided 1993 into Czech Republic & Slovakia — **Czecho•slo•vak** \-'slō-ˌväk, -ˌvak\ *adj or n* — **Czecho•slo•va•ki•an** \-slō-'väk-ē-ən, -'vak-\ *adj or n*

Czech Republic country central Europe; capital Prague

Cze•sto•cho•wa \ˌchen-stə-'kō-və\ city s Poland

Dac•ca *or* **Dha•ka** \'dak-ə, 'däk-ə\ city, capital of Bangladesh

Da•cia \'dā-shə, -shē-ə\ ancient country & Roman province SE Europe roughly equivalent to Romania & Bessarabia

Da•dra and Na•gar Ha•ve•li \də-'drä-ən-ˌnag-ər-ə-ˌvel-ē\ territory India bordering on Gujarat & Maharashtra

Da•ho•mey \də-'hō-mē\ — see BENIN — **Da•ho•man** \-mən\ *or* **Da•ho•me•an** *or* **Da•ho•mey•an** \-mē-ən\ *adj or n*

Dairen — see LÜDA

Da•kar \'dak-ˌär, də-'kär\ city, capital of Senegal

Da•ko•ta Territory \də-'kōt-ə\ territory 1861–89 NW U.S. divided 1889 into states of North Dakota & South Dakota (the **Da•ko•tas**)

Dal•las \'dal-əs, 'da-lis\ city NE Texas

Dal•ma•tia \dal-'mā-shə, -shē-ə\ region w Balkan Peninsula on the Adriatic — **Dal•ma•tian** \-shən\ *adj or n*

Da•man and Diu \də-ˌmän-ən-'dē-ˌü, -'man-\ territory w India on Gulf of Cambay

Da•mas•cus \də-'mas-kəs\ city, capital of Syria

Da•ma•vand \'dam-ə-ˌvand\ *or* **Dem•a•vend** \'dem-ə-ˌvend\ mountain 5771 meters N Iran NE of Tehran

Da Nang \dä-'näng, 'dä-\ *or formerly* **Tou•rane** \tü-'rän\ city s Vietnam in Annam SE of Hue

Dan•dong \'dän-'dùng\ *or* **An•tung** \'än-'dùng\ *or* **Tan•tung** \'dän-'dùng\ city NE China in SE Liaoning at mouth of the Yalu

Dan•ube \'dan-ˌyüb\ *or German* **Do•nau** \'dō-ˌnaů\ river 2776 kilometers long s Europe flowing from s Germany into Black sea — **Da•nu•bi•an** \da-'nyü-bē-ən\ *adj*

Danzig — see GDANSK

Dar•da•nelles \ˌdärd-n-'elz\ *or* **Hel•les•pont** \'hel-ə-ˌspänt\ strait NW Turkey connecting Sea of Marmara & the Aegean

Dar el Beida — see CASABLANCA

Dar es Sa•laam \ˌdär-ˌes-sə-'läm\ city, capital of Tanzania

Darien, Isthmus of — see PANAMA (Isthmus of)

Dar·ling \'där-ling\ river 1865 kilometers long SE Australia in Queensland & New South Wales flowing SW into the Murray

Dar·win \'där-wən\ city Australia, capital of Northern Territory

Da·tong or **Ta·tung** \'dä-'tung\ city NE China in N Shanxi

Da·vao \'däv-,aú, dä-'vaú\ city S Philippines in E Mindanao on Davao Gulf

Da·vis \'dā-vəs\ strait between SW Greenland & E Baffin Island connecting Baffin Bay & the Atlantic

Day·ton \'dāt-n\ city SW Ohio

Dead Sea \'ded\ salt lake between Israel & Jordan; 397 meters below sea level

Dear·born \'diər-,bórn, -bərn\ city SE Michigan SW of Detroit

Death Valley \'deth\ arid valley E California & S Nevada containing lowest point in U.S. (86 meters below sea level); most of area included in **Death Valley National Monument**

De·bre·cen \'deb-rət-,sen\ city E Hungary

Dec·can \'dek-ən, -,an\ plateau region S India

Del·a·ware \'del-ə-,waər, -,weər, -wər\ **1** river 476 kilometers long E U.S. flowing S from S New York into Delaware Bay **2** state E U.S.; capital, Dover — **Del·a·war·ean** or **Del·a·war·ian** \,del-ə-'war-ē-ən, -'wer-\ adj or n

Delaware Bay inlet of the Atlantic between SW New Jersey & E Delaware

Del·hi \'del-ē\ **1** territory N India W of Uttar Pradesh **2** city, its capital — see NEW DELHI

De·los \'dē-,läs\ island Greece in central Cyclades — **De·lian** \'dē-lē-ən, 'dēl-yən\ adj or n

Del·phi \'del-,fī\ ancient town central Greece in Phocis on S slope of Mount Parnassus

Denali, Denali National Park — see MCKINLEY (Mount)

Den·bigh·shire \'den-bē-,shiər, -shər\ or **Denbigh** former county N Wales

Den·mark \'den-,märk\ country N Europe occupying most of Jutland & adjacent islands; capital, Copenhagen

Den·ver \'den-vər\ city, capital of Colorado

Der·by \'där-bē, chiefly in the United States 'dər-bē\ borough N central England in Derbyshire

Der·by·shire \'där-bē-,shiər, -shər, United States also 'dər-\ or **Derby** county N central England

Der·ry \'der-ē\ or **Lon·don·der·ry** \,lən-dən-'der-ē, 'lən-dən-,\ traditional county NW Northern Ireland

Des Moines \di-'móin\ city, capital of Iowa

De·troit \di-'tróit\ **1** river 50 kilometers long between SE Michigan & Ontario connecting Lakes Saint Clair & Erie **2** city SE Michigan

Dev·on \'dev-ən\ or **De·von·shire** \-,shiər, -shər\ county SW England

Dhaka — see DACCA

Dhau·la·gi·ri, Mount \,daú-lə-'giər-ē\ mountain 8172 meters W central Nepal in the Himalayas

Di·e·go Gar·cia \dē-,ā-gō-,gär-'sē-ə\ island in Indian ocean; chief island of Chagos archipelago

Di·jon \dē-'zhōⁿ\ city E France N of Lyons

Di·nar·ic Alps \də-,nar-ik-\ range of the E Alps in W Balkan Peninsula

Diospolis — see THEBES

District of Co·lum·bia \kə-'ləm-bē-ə\ federal district E U.S. coextensive with city of Washington

Djakarta or **Ja·kar·ta** \jə-'kär-tə\ or formerly **Ba·ta·via** \bə-'tā-vē-ə\ city, capital of Indonesia in NW Java

Dji·bou·ti or **Ji·bu·ti** \jə-'büt-ē\ **1** or formerly **French Somaliland** or later **French Territory of the Afars** \'äf-,är, -,ärz\ **and the Is·sas** \ē-'sä, -'säz\ republic E Africa on Gulf of Aden **2** city, its capital

Dne·pro·pe·trovsk \,nep-rō-pə-'trófsk\ city E Ukraine

Dnie·per \'nē-pər\ river 2255 kilometers long flowing from Valdai Hills, Russia through Belarus & Ukraine into Black Sea

Dnies·ter \'nēs-tər\ river 1365 kilometers long W Ukraine & E Moldova flowing SE from the Carpathians into Black sea

Do·dec·a·nese \dō-'dek-ə-,nēz, 'dō-di-kə-, -,nēs\ islands Greece in the SE Aegean — see RHODES

Do·ha \'dō-hä\ city & port, capital of Qatar on Persian Gulf

Do·lo·mites \'dō-lə-,mīts, 'däl-ə-\ or Italian **Do·lo·mi·ti** \,dó-lə-'mēt-ē\ range of the E Alps in NE Italy

Dom·i·ni·ca \,däm-ə-'nē-kə\ island British West Indies in the Leewards; capital, Roseau

Do·min·i·can Republic \də-,min-i-kən-\ or formerly **San·to Do·min·go** \,sant-əd-ə-'ming-gō\ country West Indies in E Hispaniola; a republic; capital, Santo Domingo — **Do·min·i·can** \də-'min-i-kən\ adj or n

Don \'dän\ river 1930 kilometers long S Russia in Europe flowing into Sea of Azov

Donau — see DANUBE

Don·e·gal \,dän-i-'gól, ,dən-\ county NW Republic of Ireland in Ulster

Do·nets Basin \də-,nets-\ or Russian **Do·net·ski Bas·sein** \dən-,yet-skē-bäs-'yän\ or **Don·bass** or **Don·bas** \'dän-,bas\ region E Ukraine SW of Donets river

Do·netsk \də-'netsk\ city E Ukraine in Donets Basin

Dor·set \'dór-sət\ or **Dor·set·shire** \-,shiər, -shər\ county S England on English channel

Dort·mund \'dórt-,münt, -mənd\ city W Germany in the Ruhr

Dou·a·la or **Du·a·la** \dü-'äl-ə\ city SW Cameroon

Doug·las \'dəg-ləs\ town Great Britain, capital of Isle of Man

Dou·ro \'dōr-ü, 'dór-\ or Spanish **Due·ro** \'dweər-ō\ or ancient **Du·ri·us** \'dúr-ē-əs, 'dyúr-\ river 780 kilometers long N Spain & N Portugal flowing into the Atlantic

Do·ver \'dō-vər\ **1** city, capital of Delaware **2** borough SE England in Kent on Strait of Dover

Dover, Strait of channel between SE England & N France; the most easterly section of English channel

Down \'daún\ traditional county SE Northern Ireland

Dra·kens·berg \'dräk-ənz-,bərg\ mountain range E Republic of South Africa & Lesotho; highest peak Thabana Ntlenyana 3482 meters

Dres·den \'drez-dən\ city E Germany in Saxony

Du·bai \dü-'bī\ city United Arab Emirates on Persian Gulf

Dub·lin \'dəb-lən\ or Gaelic **Bai·le Atha Cli·ath** \blä-'klē-ə\ **1** county E Ireland in Leinster **2** city, capital of Republic of Ireland in County Dublin

Dud·ley \'dəd-lē\ borough W central England in West Midlands

Duis·burg \'dü-əs-,bərg; 'düz-,bərg, 'dyüz-; German 'dūes-,búrk\ city W Germany at junction of Rhine & Ruhr rivers

Du·luth \də-'lüth\ city NE Minnesota

Dum·fries \,dəm-'frēs\ or **Dum·fries·shire** \-'frēs-,shiər, -'frēsh-, -shər\ former county S Scotland; incorporated 1975 in **Dumfries and Gal·lo·way** \-'gal-ə-,wā\ region

Dun·bar·ton \,dən-'bärt-n\ or **Dun·bar·ton·shire** \-,shiər, -shər\ or **Dum·bar·ton** \,dəm-\ or **Dum·bar·ton·shire** \,dəm-\ former county W central Scotland

Dun·dee \,dən-'dē\ city E Scotland in Tayside

Dun·e·din \,də-'nēd-n\ city New Zealand in SE South Island

Du·que de Ca·xi·as \,dü-kə-də-kə-'shē-əs\ city SE Brazil NW of Rio de Janeiro

Du·ran·go \dú-'rang-gō, dyú-\ **1** state NW central Mexico **2** city, its capital

Dur·ban \'dər-bən\ city E Republic of South Africa in E Natal

Dur·ham \'dər-əm, 'də-rəm, 'dúr-əm\ county N England on North Sea

Du·shan·be \dü-'sham-bē, dyü-, -'shäm-\ city, capital of Tajikistan

Düs·sel·dorf \'düs-əl-,dórf, 'dyüs-, 'dúes-\ city W Germany, capital of North Rhine-Westphalia

Dutch Borneo — see KALIMANTAN

Dutch Guiana — see SURINAME

Dy·fed \'dəv-ed, -əd\ county SW Wales; established 1974

Dzaudzhikau — see VLADIKAVKAZ

Dzer·zhinsk \dər-'zhinsk\ city central Russia in Europe, ENE of Moscow

Ea·ling \'ē-ling\ borough of W Greater London, England

East An·glia \'ang-glē-ə\ region E England including Norfolk & Suffolk

East Bengal the part of Bengal now in Bangladesh

East China sea — see CHINA

Eas·ter \'ē-stər\ island SE Pacific 3220 kilometers W of Chilean coast; belongs to Chile

Eastern Ghats \'gȯts\ chain of low mountains SE India along coast

Eastern Samoa — see AMERICAN SAMOA

East Germany the German Democratic Republic — see GERMANY

East Indies the Malay archipelago — **East Indian** adj or n

East London city S Republic of South Africa in SE Cape of Good Hope province

East Lo·thi·an \'lō-thē-ən\ former county SE Scotland — see LOTHIAN

East Pakistan the former E division of Pakistan comprising E portion of Bengal; now the independent republic of Bangladesh

East Prussia region N Europe on the Baltic; formerly a part of Germany; divided 1945 between Poland & U.S.S.R. (Russia & Lithuania)

East Ri·ding \'rīd-ing\ former administrative county N England in SE Yorkshire

East River strait SE New York connecting upper New York Bay & Long Island Sound & separating Manhattan Island and Long Island

East Sus·sex \'səs-iks, *United States also* -,eks\ county SE England

Ebro \'ā-brō\ river 775 kilometers long NE Spain flowing into the Mediterranean

Ec·ua·dor \'ek-wə-,dȯr\ country W South America; a republic; capital, Quito — **Ec·ua·dor·an** \,ek-wə-'dȯr-ən, -'dōr-\ or **Ec·ua·dor·ean** or **Ec·ua·dor·ian** \-ē-ən\ adj or n

Ede \'ā-,dā\ city SW Nigeria

Ed·in·burgh \'ed-n-,bər-ə, -,bə-rə, -bə-rə, -brə\ city, capital of Scotland

Ed·mon·ton \'ed-mən-tən\ city, capital of Alberta

Edom \'ēd-əm\ or **Id·u·maea** or **Id·u·mea** \,ij-ə-'mē-ə\ ancient country SW Asia S of Judea & Dead sea — **Edomite** \'ēd-ə-,mīt\ n

Egypt \'ē-jəpt\ country NE Africa & Sinai peninsula of SW Asia bordering on Mediterranean & Red seas; capital, Cairo

Eire — see IRELAND

Elam \'ē-ləm\ ancient country SW Asia at head of Persian gulf E of Babylonia; capital, Susa (Shushan) — **Elam·ite** \'ē-lə-,mīt\ n

El·ba \'el-bə\ island Italy E of N Corsica off coast of Tuscany; chief town, Portoferraio

Elbe \'el-bə, 'elb\ or *Czech* **La·be** \'lä-be\ or *ancient* **Albis** \'al-bəs\ river 1160 kilometers long N Czech Republic & N Germany flowing NW into North sea

El·bert, Mount \'el-bərt\ mountain 4399 meters W central Colorado; highest in Colorado & the Rocky mountains

El·brus \el-'brüz\ mountain 5633 meters S Russia in Europe in NW Caucasus mountains

El·burz \el-'bùrz\ mountains N Iran — see DAMAVEND

Elis \'ē-ləs\ ancient country in NW Peloponnesus, Greece

Elisabethville — see LUBUMBASHI

Eliz·a·beth \i-'liz-ə-bəth\ city NE New Jersey on Newark Bay

Ellás — see GREECE

Elles·mere \'elz-,miər\ island N Canada in N Northwest Territories

Ellice — see TUVALU

El Paso \el-'pas-ō\ city W Texas on Rio Grande

El Sal·va·dor \el-'sal-və-,dȯr, -,sal-və-'\ country Central America bordering on the Pacific; capital, San Salvador

Elsass — see ALSACE

Ely, Isle of \'ē-lē\ district E England in Cambridgeshire — see CAMBRIDGE 2

Emi·lia-Ro·ma·gna \ā-,mēl-yə-rō-'män-yə\ region N Italy on the Adriatic S of the Po; capital, Bologna

En·field \'en-,fēld\ borough of N Greater London, England

En·gland \'ing-glənd *also* ing-lənd\ country S Great Britain; a division of United Kingdom; capital, London

English Channel arm of the Atlantic between S England & N France

En·se·na·da \,en-sə-'näd-ə\ city NW Mexico in Baja California

Ephra·im \'ē-frē-əm\ 1 hilly region N Jordan E of River Jordan 2 — see ISRAEL — **Ephra·im·ite** \'ē-frē-ə-,mīt\ n

Epi·rus \i-'pī-rəs\ region NW Greece on Ionian sea

Equatorial Guinea or *formerly* **Spanish Guinea** country W Africa on Bight of Biafra including Mbini & Bioko; capital, Malabo

Erbil — see ARBIL

Ere·bus, Mount \'er-ə-bəs\ volcano 3795 meters Antarctica on Ross Island in SW Ross sea

Er·furt \'eər-fərt, -,fùrt\ city central Germany WSW of Leipzig

Erie \'iər-ē\ 1 city NW Pennsylvania 2 canal New York between Hudson river at Albany & Lake Erie at Buffalo; built 1817–25; now superseded by New York State Barge Canal

Erie, Lake lake E central North America in U.S. & Canada; one of the Great Lakes

Er·in \'er-ən\ IRELAND

Er·i·trea \,er-ə-'trē-ə, -'trā-\ region N Ethiopia on Red sea; capital, Asmara

Er Rif or **Er Riff** \er-'rif\ mountain region N Morocco on Mediterranean coast E of Strait of Gibraltar

Erz·ge·bir·ge \'erts-gə-,bir-gə\ mountains E central Germany & NW Czech Republic

Escaut — see SCHELDT

Esfahan — see ISFAHAN

Es·ki·se·hir \,es-ki-shə-'hiər\ city W central Turkey

España — see SPAIN

Española — see HISPANIOLA

Es·sen \'es-n\ city W Germany in the Ruhr

Es·sex \'es-iks\ county SE England on North sea

Es·to·nia \e-'stō-nē-ə, -nyə\ country E Europe on Baltic sea; a constituent republic (**Estonian Republic**) of U.S.S.R. 1940–91; capital, Tallinn

Ethi·o·pia \,ē-thē-'ō-pē-ə\ 1 ancient country NE Africa S of Egypt 2 or **Ab·ys·sin·ia** \,ab-ə-'sin-yə, -'sin-ē-ə\ country E Africa; a republic since 1975; capital, Addis Ababa

Et·na \'et-nə\ volcano 3323 meters Italy in NE Sicily

Eto·bi·coke \et-'ō-bik-,ō\ city Canada in SE Ontario

Etru·ria \i-'trùr-ē-ə\ ancient country central Italy coextensive with modern Tuscany & part of Umbria

Eu·boea \yủ-'bē-ə\ island E Greece NE of Attica & Boeotia

Eu·phra·tes \yủ-'frāt-ēz\ river 2735 kilometers long SW Asia flowing from E Turkey & uniting with the Tigris to form the Shatt-al-Arab

Eur·asia \yủ-'rā-zhə, -shə\ landmass comprising Europe & Asia — **Eur·asian** \-zhən, -shən\ adj or n

Eu·rope \'yùr-əp\ continent of the eastern hemisphere between Asia & the Atlantic

European Communities or **European Community** economic, scientific, & political organization consisting of Belgium, France, Italy, Luxembourg, Netherlands, Germany, Denmark, Greece, Ireland, United Kingdom, Spain, & Portugal

Ev·ans·ville \'ev-ənz-,vil\ city SW Indiana

Ev·er·est, Mount \'ev-rəst, -ə-rəst\ mountain 8848 meters S Asia in the Himalayas on border between Nepal & Tibet; highest in the world

\ə\ abut		\ng\ sing	
\ər\ further		\ō\ bone	
\a\ mat		\ȯ\ saw	
\ā\ take		\ȯi\ coin	
\ä\ cot, cart		\th\ thin	
\aủ\ out		\th\ this	
\ch\ chin		\ü\ food	
\e\ pet		\ủ\ foot	
\ē\ easy		\y\ yet	
\g\ go		\yü\ few	
\i\ tip		\yủ\ cure	
\ī\ life		\zh\ vision	
\j\ job			

Ev·er·glades \'ev-ər-ˌglādz\ swamp region s Florida now partly drained; sw part forms **Everglades National Park**

Eyre, Lake \'aər, 'eər\ intermittent lake central Australia in N South Australia

Faer·oe or **Far·oe** \'faər-ō, 'feər-\ islands NE Atlantic NW of the Shetlands belonging to Denmark; capital, Thorshavn — **Faero·ese** \ˌfar-ə-'wēz, ˌfer-, -'wēs\ adj or n

Fai·sa·la·bad \ˌfī-ˌsäl-ə-'bäd, -ˌsal-ə-'bad\ or formerly **Ly·all·pur** \lē-ˌäl-'pur\ city NE Pakistan w of Lahore

Falk·land \'fò-klənd, 'fòl-\ or Spanish **Is·las Mal·vi·nas** \ˌēz-läz-mäl-'vē-näs\ islands sw Atlantic E of s end of Argentina; a British colony; capital, Stanley

Far East the countries of E Asia & the Malay archipelago — usually considered as comprising the Asian countries bordering on the Pacific but sometimes as including also India, Sri Lanka, Bangladesh, Tibet, & Myanmar — **Far Eastern** adj

Far·go \'fär-gō\ city E North Dakota; largest in state

Fear, Cape \'fiər\ cape SE North Carolina at mouth of Cape Fear river

Federated Malay States former British protectorate (1895–1945) comprising states of Negri Sembilan, Pahang, Perak, and Selangor; now part of Federation of Malaysia

Fengtien — see SHENYANG

Fer·man·agh \fər-'man-ə\ traditional county sw Northern Ireland

Fernando Po — see BIOKO

Fer·ra·ra \fə-'rär-ə\ city N Italy NE of Bologna

Fez \'fez\ or **Fès** \'fes\ city N central Morocco

Fife \'fīf\ or **Fife·shire** \-ˌshiər, -shər\ region E Scotland; until 1975 a county

Fi·ji \'fē-jē\ islands sw Pacific; a dominion of the Commonwealth; capital, Suva — **Fi·ji·an** \-jē-ən\ adj or n

Fin·is·terre, Cape \ˌfin-ə-'stear, -'ster-ē\ cape NW Spain

Fin·land \'fin-lənd\ or Finnish **Suo·mi** \'swò-mē\ or **Suo·men Ta·sa·val·ta** \'swò-mən-'tas-ə-ˌval-tə\ country NE Europe on gulfs of Bothnia and Finland; a republic; capital, Helsinki — **Fin·land·er** \'fin-lənd-ər\ n

Finland, Gulf of arm of the Baltic between Finland & Estonia

Fiume — see RIJEKA

Flan·ders \'flan-dərz\ region w Belgium & N France on North sea

Flat·tery, Cape \'flat-ə-rē\ cape NW Washington at entrance to Juan de Fuca strait

Flint \'flint\ city SE Michigan

Flint·shire \'flint-ˌshiər, -shər\ or **Flint** former county NE Wales

Flor·ence \'flòr-əns, 'flär-\ or Italian **Fi·ren·ze** \fē-'rent-sā\ or ancient **Flo·ren·tia** \flə-'ren-chə, -chē-ə\ city central Italy, capital of Tuscany — **Flor·en·tine** \'flòr-ən-ˌtēn, 'flär-, -ˌtīn\ adj or n

Flo·res \'flòr-əs, 'flòr-\ island Indonesia in Lesser Sunda islands

Flo·ri·a·nó·po·lis \ˌflòr-ē-ə-'näp-ə-ləs, ˌflòr-\ city s Brazil on an island NE of Pôrto Alegre

Flor·i·da \'flòr-əd-ə, 'flär-\ state SE U.S.; capital, Tallahassee — **Flo·rid·i·an** \flə-'rid-ē-ən\ or **Flor·i·dan** \'flòr-əd-n, 'flär-\ adj or n

Florida, Straits of channel between Florida Keys on NW & Cuba & Bahamas on s & E connecting Gulf of Mexico & the Atlantic

Florida Keys chain of islands off s tip of Florida

Fog·gia \'fò-jə, -jä\ city SE Italy in Apulia

Foochow — see FUZHOU

For·a·ker, Mount \'fòr-i-kər, 'fär-\ mountain 5304 meters s central Alaska in Alaska range

For·mo·sa \fòr-'mō-sə, fər-, -zə\ — see TAIWAN — **For·mo·san** \-sən, -zən\ adj or n

For·ta·le·za \ˌfòrt-l-'ā-zə\ city NE Brazil NW of Recife

Fort-de-France \ˌfòrd-ə-'fräns\ city French West Indies, capital of Martinique on w coast

Forth \'fòrth, 'fòrth\ river 183 kilometers long s central Scotland flowing E into North sea through **Firth of Forth** (estuary)

Fort Knox \'näks\ military reservation N central Kentucky ssw of Louisville; location of U.S. Gold Bullion Depository

Fort–Lamy — see N'DJAMENA

Fort Lau·der·dale \'lòd-ər-ˌdāl\ city SE Florida

Fort Wayne \'wān\ city NE Indiana

Fort Worth \'wərth\ city NE Texas

Foxe Basin \'fäks\ inlet of the Atlantic N Canada w of Baffin Island

France \'frans\ country w Europe between the English channel & the Mediterranean; a republic; capital, Paris

Frank·fort \'frangk-fərt\ city, capital of Kentucky

Frank·furt \'frangk-fərt, 'frängk-ˌfurt\ or in full **Frankfurt am Main** \-ˌäm-'mīn\ or **Frankfort on the Main** city sw central Germany on Main river

Frank·lin \'frang-klən\ former district N Canada in Northwest Territories including Arctic islands & Boothia & Melville peninsulas

Fra·ser \'frā-zər, -zhər\ river 1370 kilometers long Canada in s central British Columbia flowing into the Pacific

Fred·er·ic·ton \'fred-rik-tən, -ə-rik-\ city, capital of New Brunswick

Free·town \'frē-ˌtaun\ city, capital of Sierra Leone

Fre·mont \'frē-ˌmänt\ city w California

French Equatorial Africa former country w central Africa N of Congo river comprising a federation of Chad, Gabon, Middle Congo, & Ubangi-Shari territories

French Guiana country N South America on the Atlantic; a dependency of France; capital, Cayenne

French Guinea — see GUINEA

French Indochina — see INDOCHINA

French Morocco — see MOROCCO

French Polynesia islands in s Pacific belonging to France & including Society, Marquesas, Tuamotu, Gambier, & Tubuai groups; capital, Papeete

French Somaliland — see DJIBOUTI

French Sudan — see MALI

French Territory of the Afars and the Issas — see DJIBOUTI

French Togo — see TOGO

French West Indies islands of the West Indies belonging to France & including Guadeloupe, Martinique, Désirade, Les Saintes, Marie Galante, Saint Barthélemy, & part of Saint Martin

Fres·no \'frez-nō\ city s central California

Fri·sian \'frizh-ən, 'frē-zhən\ islands N Europe in North sea including **West Frisian** islands off N Netherlands, **East Frisian** islands off NW Germany, & **North Frisian** islands off N Germany and w Denmark

Fri·u·li-Ve·ne·zia Giu·lia \frē-ˌü-lē-və-ˌnet-sē-ə-'jü-yə\ region N Italy; capital Udine

Frunze — see BISHKEK

Fu·ji·sa·wa \ˌfü-jē-'sä-wə\ city Japan in SE Honshu

Fu·ji \'fü-jē, 'fyü-\ or **Fu·ji·ya·ma** \ˌfü-jē-'äm-ə, ˌfyü-, -'yäm-\ or **Fu·ji-no-ya·ma** \-jē-nō-'yäm-ə\ or **Fu·ji·san** \-jē-'sän\ mountain 3776 meters Japan in s central Honshu; highest in Japan

Fu·jian \'fü-'jän, -jē-'än\ or **Fu·kien** \'fü-'kyen, -kē-'en\ province SE China on Formosa strait; capital, Fuzhou

Fu·ku·o·ka \ˌfü-kə-'wō-kə\ city Japan in N Kyushu

Fu·ku·ya·ma \ˌfü-kə-'yäm-ə\ city Japan in sw Honshu

Fu·na·ba·shi \ˌfü-nə-'bäsh-ē\ city Japan in SE Honshu on Tokyo Bay

Fu·na·fu·ti \ˌfü-nə-'füt-ē, ˌfyü-, -'fyüt-\ city, capital of Tuvalu

Fun·dy, Bay of \'fən-dē\ inlet of the Atlantic SE Canada between New Brunswick & Nova Scotia

Fu·shun \'fü-'shùn\ city NE China in NE Liaoning

Fu·zhou \'fü-'jō\ or **Foo·chow** \'fü-'jō, -'chaù\ or formerly **Min·how** \'min-'hō\ city SE China, capital of Fujian

Ga·bon \ga-'bōn\ country w equatorial Africa; capital, Libreville — **Gab·o·nese** \ˌgab-ə-'nēz, -'nēs\ adj or n

Ga·bo·rone \ˌgäb-ə-'rōn\ city, capital of Botswana

Gads•den Purchase \'gadz-dən\ tract of land s of Gila river in present Arizona & New Mexico purchased 1853 by the U.S. from Mexico

Ga•lá•pa•gos Islands \gə-'läp-ə-gəs, -'lap-\ or **Co•lón Archipelago** \kə-'lōn\ island group Ecuador in the Pacific 965 kilometers w of mainland

Ga•lati \gə-'läts, -'lät-sē\ city E Romania on the Danube

Ga•la•tia \gə-'lā-shə, -shē-ə\ ancient country & Roman province central Asia Minor in region centering on modern Ankara, Turkey — **Ga•la•tian** \-shən\ adj or n

Ga•li•cia \gə-'lish-ə, -'lish-ē-ə\ 1 region E central Europe now divided between Poland & Ukraine 2 region NW Spain on the Atlantic — **Ga•li•cian** \-shən\ adj or n

Gal•i•lee \'gal-ə-,lē\ hilly region N Israel — **Gal•i•le•an** \,gal-ə-'lē-ən\ adj or n

Galilee, Sea of or **Lake of Gen•nes•a•ret** \gə-'nes-ə-,ret, -rət\ or **Sea of Ti•be•ri•as** \tī-'bir-ē-əs\ lake N Israel on Syrian border traversed by Jordan river

Gal•lip•o•li \gə-'lip-ə-lē\ or Turkish **Ge•li•bo•lu Ya•ri•ma•da•si** \,gel-ə-bə-'lü-,yär-ə-,mäd-ə-'sē\ peninsula Turkey in Europe between the Dardanelles & Saros gulf

Gal•lo•way \'gal-ə-,wā\ district SW Scotland — see DUMFRIES

Gal•way \'gol-,wā\ county W Ireland in Connacht

Gam•bia \'gam-bē-ə\ country W Africa; a republic; capital, Banjul — **Gam•bi•an** \-ən\ adj or n

Gand — see GHENT

Gan•ges \'gan-,jēz\ river 2495 kilometers long N India flowing from the Himalayas SE & E to unite with the Brahmaputra & empty into Bay of Bengal through a vast delta — **Gan•get•ic** \gan-'jet-ik\ adj

Gan•su or **Kan•su** \'gän-'sü\ province NW China; capital, Lanzhou

Gar•da, Lake \'gärd-ə\ lake N Italy NW of Verona

Garden Grove city SW California

Ga•ronne \gə-'rän, -'rōn\ river 571 kilometers long SE France flowing into Gironde estuary

Gary \'gaər-ē, 'geər-ē\ city NW Indiana on Lake Michigan

Gas•co•ny \'gas-kə-nē\ or French **Gas•cogne** \gȧ-'skōnʸ\ region and former province SW France

Gas•pé \gas-'pā, 'gas-,\ peninsula SE Quebec E of mouth of the Saint Lawrence — **Gas•pe•sian** \ga-'spē-zhən\ adj or n

Gates•head \'gāts-,hed\ borough N England in Tyne and Wear county

Gates of the Arctic National Park reservation N central Alaska in Brooks Range

Gaul \'gol\ or Latin **Gal•lia** \'gal-ē-ə\ ancient country W Europe chiefly comprising region occupied by modern France & Belgium but at one time including also Po valley in N Italy — see CISALPINE GAUL, TRANSALPINE GAUL

Ga•za Strip \'gäz-ə, 'gaz-, 'gāz-\ district S Palestine on the Mediterranean; administered 1949–67 by Egypt & since 1967 by Israel; chief town, Gaza

Ga•zi•an•tep \,gäz-ē-,än-'tep, -än-\ city S Turkey

Gdansk \gə-'dänsk, -'dansk\ or German **Dan•zig** \'dan-sig, 'dän-\ city N Poland on Gulf of Danzig

Gdyn•ia \gə-'din-ē-ə\ city N Poland

Gee•long \jə-'loŋ\ city SE Australia in S Victoria

Gel•sen•kir•chen \,gel-zən-'kir-kən\ city W Germany in the Ruhr W of Dortmund

Ge•ne•ral San Mar•tín \,hā-nä-,räl-,san-mär-'tēn\ also **San Mar•tín** \,san-mär-'tēn\ city E Argentina NW of Buenos Aires

Ge•ne•va \jə-'nē-və\ city SW Switzerland on Lake of Geneva — **Ge•ne•van** \-vən\ adj or n

Geneva, Lake of or **Lake Le•man** \'lē-mən, 'lem-ən, lə-'man\; ancient **Le•man•nus** \li-'man-əs\ or **Le•ma•nus** \li-'mān-əs\ lake on border between SW Switzerland & E France traversed by the Rhone

Gen•oa \'jen-ə-wə\ or Italian **Ge•no•va** \'je-nō-vä\ city NW Italy, capital of Liguria — **Gen•o•ese** \,jen-ə-'wēz, -'wēs\ or **Gen•o•vese** \-ə-'vēz, -'vēs\ adj or n

George•town \'jorj-,taun\ 1 a W section of Washington, District of Columbia 2 city, capital of Guyana

George Town or **Pi•nang** \pi-'nang\ or **Pe•nang** \pə-'nang\ city Malaysia, on an island in Peninsular Malaysia

Geor•gia \'jor-jə\ 1 state SE U.S.; capital, Atlanta 2 country SE Europe on Black sea S of Caucasus mountains; a constituent republic of U.S.S.R. 1936–91; capital, Tbilisi — **Geor•gian** \'jor-jən\ adj or n

Georgia, Strait of channel Canada & U.S. between Vancouver Island & mainland NW of Puget Sound

Georgian Bay inlet of Lake Huron in S Ontario

Ger•man•town \'jər-mən-,taun\ a NW section of Philadelphia, Pennsylvania

Ger•ma•ny \'jərm-nē, -ə-nē\ country central Europe bordering on North & Baltic seas; divided into two republics 1940–90: the Federal Republic of Germany (capital, Bonn) & the German Democratic Republic (capital, East Berlin); capital, Berlin

Ger•mis•ton \'jər-mə-stən\ city NE Republic of South Africa in S Transvaal E of Johannesburg

Gha•na \'gän-ə, 'gan-ə\ or formerly **Gold Coast** country W Africa on Gulf of Guinea; a republic of the Commonwealth; capital, Accra — **Gha•na•ian** \gä-'nā-ən, ga-, -yən; -'nī-ən\ or **Gha•ni•an** \'gän-ē-ən, 'gän-yən, 'gan-\ adj or n

Ghats \'gots\ two mountain chains S India — see EASTERN GHATS, WESTERN GHATS

Ghent \'gent\ or Flemish **Gent** \'gent\ or French **Gand** \'gänⁿ\ city NW central Belgium

Gi•bral•tar \jə-'brol-tər\ British colony & fortress on S coast of Spain including Rock of Gibraltar

Gibraltar, Rock of headland on S coast of Spain in Gibraltar colony at E end of Strait of Gibraltar; highest point 426 meters — see PILLARS OF HERCULES

Gibraltar, Strait of passage between Spain & Africa connecting the Atlantic & the Mediterranean

Gi•fu \'gē-,fü\ city Japan in central Honshu

Gi•jón \hē-'hōn\ city & port NW Spain on Bay of Biscay

Gi•la \'hē-lə\ river 1015 kilometers long SW New Mexico and S Arizona flowing W into the Colorado

Gil•bert \'gil-bərt\ islands Kiribati in W Pacific; until 1975 formed with Ellice islands the British colony of **Gilbert and El•lice Islands** \'el-əs\ — see KIRIBATI

Gil•e•ad \'gil-ē-əd\ mountain region NE Palestine E of Jordan river; now in NW Jordan — **Gil•e•ad•ite** \-ē-ə-,dīt\ n

Gi•ronde \jə-'rän d, zhə-; zhē-'rōⁿd\ estuary W France formed by junction of Garonne & Dordogne rivers

Gi•za \'gē-zə\ or **Al-Gi•zeh** \al-\ or **Al-Ji•zah** \-'jē-zə\ city N Egypt on the Nile SW of Cairo

Gla•cier Bay \,glā-shər-\ inlet SE Alaska at S end of Saint Elias range in **Glacier Bay National Park**

Glacier National Park 1 mountain area NW Montana adjoining Waterton Lakes National Park, Canada, & with it forming Waterton-Glacier International Peace Park 2 mountain area SE British Columbia

Glades \'glādz\ EVERGLADES

Gla•mor•gan \glə-'mor-gən\ or **Gla•mor•gan•shire** \-,shiər, ər\ former county SE Wales — see MID GLAMORGAN, SOUTH GLAMORGAN, WEST GLAMORGAN

Glas•gow \'glas-kō, 'glas-gō, 'glaz-gō\ city S central Scotland On the Clyde — **Glas•we•gian** \glas-'wē-jən\ adj or n

Glen•dale \'glen-,dal\ city S California NE of Los Angeles

Glouces•ter•shire \'gläs-tər-,shiər, 'glos-, -shər\ or **Gloucester** county SW central England

Gnossus — see KNOSSOS

Goa \'gō-ə\ state W India on Malabar coast belonging before 1962 to Portugal; capital, Panaji

Go•bi \'gō-bē\ desert E central Asia in Mongolia & N China

Godt•haab \'got-,hob, 'gät-\ town, capital of Greenland on SW coast

God•win Aus•ten \,gäd-wə-'no-stən, -'näs-tən\ or **K2** \'kā-'tü\ mountain 8611 meters N Kashmir in Karakoram range; second highest in the world

\ə\	abut	\ng\	sing
\ər\	further	\ō\	bone
\a\	mat	\o\	saw
\ā\	take	\oi\	coin
\ä\	cot, cart	\th\	thin
\au\	out	\th\	this
\ch\	chin	\ü\	food
\e\	pet	\u\	foot
\ē\	easy	\y\	yet
\g\	go	\yü\	few
\i\	tip	\yu\	cure
\ī\	life	\zh\	vision
\j\	job		

Goi·â·nia \gói-'an-ē-ə\ city SE central Brazil SW of Brasília

Go·lan Heights \,gō-,län-, -lən-\ hilly region between NE Israel & SW Syria

Gol·con·da \gäl-'kän-də\ ruined city central India W of Hyderabad

Gold Coast 1 coast region W Africa on N shore of Gulf of Guinea E of Ivory Coast 2 — see GHANA

Golden Gate strait W California connecting San Francisco Bay and the Pacific

Golden Horn inlet of the Bosporus, Turkey in Europe; harbor of Istanbul

Golgotha — see CALVARY

Go·mel \'gō-məl, 'gȯ-\ city SE Belarus

Go·mor·rah \gə-'mär-ə, -'mȯr-\ city, ancient Palestine in plain of Jordan

Good Hope, Cape of \,gu̇d-'hōp\ cape S Republic of South Africa in SW Cape Province — see CAPE OF GOOD HOPE

Go·rakh·pur \'gȯr-ək-,pu̇r, 'gȯr-\ city NE India in E Uttar Pradesh N of Banaras

Gor'kiy or **Gorki** — see NIZHNI NOVGOROD

Gor·lov·ka \gȯr-'lȯf-kə, -'lȯv-\ city E Ukraine in Donets basin

Go·shen \'gō-shən\ district of ancient Egypt E of Nile delta

Gö·te·borg \,yərt-ə-'bȯr-ē, Swedish ,yȫ-tə-'bȯry\ or **Goth·en·burg** \'gäth-ən-,bərg\ city SW Sweden

Got·land \'gät-,land, -lənd\ island Sweden in the Baltic; capital, Visby

Göt·ting·en \'gərt-ing-ən, 'get-, 'gœt-\ city central Germany SSW of Brunswick

Gram·pi·an \'gram-pē-ən\ 1 hills N central Scotland — see BEN NEVIS 2 region NE central Scotland; established 1975

Gra·na·da \grə-'näd-ə\ city S Spain in Andalusia

Grand Banks shoal area in the W Atlantic SE of Newfoundland

Grand Canyon gorge of Colorado river NW Arizona; area largely in **Grand Canyon National Park**

Grand Canyon of the Snake — see HELLS CANYON

Grande, Rio — see RIO GRANDE

Grand Rapids city SW Michigan

Grand Te·ton National Park \'tē-,tän\ reservation NW Wyoming S of Yellowstone National Park

Grau·bün·den \grau̇-'bin-dən, -'bün-, -'bu̇en-\ or French **Gri·sons** \grē-'zōⁿ\ canton E Switzerland

Gravenhage, 's — see HAGUE (The)

Graz \'gräts\ city S Austria, capital of Styria

Great Australian Bight wide bay on S coast of Australia

Great Barrier Reef coral reef Australia off NE coast of Queensland

Great Basin region W U.S. between Sierra Nevada & Wasatch mountains including most of Nevada & parts of California, Idaho, Utah, Wyoming, and Oregon; has no drainage to ocean

Great Basin National Park reservation E Nevada

Great Bear lake Canada in W Northwest Territories draining through Great Bear river into Mackenzie river

Great Brit·ain \'brit-n\ 1 island W Europe NW of France comprising England, Scotland, & Wales 2 UNITED KINGDOM

Great Dividing Range mountain system E Australia & Tasmania extending S from Cape York peninsula — see KOSCIUSKO (Mount)

Greater An·til·les \an-'til-ēz\ group of islands of the West Indies including Cuba, Hispaniola, Jamaica, & Puerto Rico — see LESSER ANTILLES

Greater London metropolitan county SE England comprising City of London & 32 surrounding boroughs

Greater Manchester metropolitan county NW England including city of Manchester

Greater Sunda — see SUNDA

Great Lakes 1 chain of five lakes (Superior, Michigan, Huron, Erie, & Ontario) central North America in U.S.

& Canada 2 group of lakes E central Africa including Rudolf, Albert, Victoria, Tanganyika, & Nyasa

Great Plains elevated plains region W central U.S. & W Canada E of the Rockies; chiefly W of the 100th meridian extending from W Texas to NE British Columbia & NW Alberta

Great Rift Valley \'rift\ depression SW Asia & E Africa extending with several breaks from valley of the Jordan S to central Mozambique

Great Salt lake N Utah having strongly saline waters & no outlet

Great Slave lake NW Canada in S Northwest Territories drained by Mackenzie river

Great Smoky mountains between W North Carolina & E Tennessee partly in **Great Smoky Mountains National Park**; highest Clingmans Dome 2024 meters

Greece \'grēs\ or ancient **Hel·las** \'hel-əs\ or Greek **El·lás** \e-'läs\ country S Europe at S end of Balkan peninsula; a republic; capital, Athens

Green \'grēn\ 1 mountains E North America in the Appalachians extending from S Quebec S through Vermont into W Massachusetts 2 river 1175 kilometers long W U.S. flowing from Wind River Range in W Wyoming S into the Colorado in SE Utah

Green Bay 1 inlet of NW Lake Michigan 193 kilometers long in NW Michigan & NE Wisconsin 2 city NE Wisconsin

Green·land \'grēn-lənd, -,land\ island in the N Atlantic off NE North America belonging to Denmark; capital, Godthaab

Greens·boro \'grēnz-,bər-ə, -,bə-rə\ city N central North Carolina

Green·wich \'grin-ij, 'gren-, -ich\ SE borough of Greater London, England

Green·wich Village \,gren-ich-, ,grin-, -ij\ section of New York City in Manhattan on lower W side

Gre·na·da \grə-'näd-ə\ island British West Indies in S Windwards; an independent country since 1974; capital, Saint George's

Gren·a·dines \,gren-ə-'dēnz\ islands British West Indies; divided between Grenada & Saint Vincent and the Grenadines

Gre·no·ble \grə-'nō-bəl\ city SE France

Grisons — see GRAUBÜNDEN

Gro·ning·en \'grō-ning-ən\ city NE Netherlands

Groz·ny \'grȯz-nē, 'gräz-\ city S Russia in Europe, N of Caucasus mountains

Gua·da·la·ja·ra \,gwäd-ə-lə-'här-ə\ city W central Mexico, capital of Jalisco

Gua·dal·ca·nal \,gwäd-l-kə-'nal, ,gwäd-ə-kə-\ island W Pacific in the SE Solomons

Gua·dal·qui·vir \,gwäd-l-'kwiv-ər, -ki-'viər\ river 602 kilometers long S Spain flowing into the Atlantic

Gua·da·lupe Mountains National Park \'gwäd-l-,üp\ reservation W Texas

Gua·de·loupe \'gwäd-l-,üp\ two islands, Basse-Terre (or Guadeloupe proper) & Grande-Terre, separated by a narrow channel in French West Indies in central Leewards; capital, Basse-Terre (on Basse-Terre Island)

Gua·di·a·na \,gwäd-ē-'än-ə, -'an-\ river 829 kilometers long S Spain & SE Portugal flowing into the Atlantic

Guaira — see SETE QUEDAS

Guam \'gwäm\ island W Pacific in S Marianas belonging to U.S.; capital, Agana — **Gua·ma·ni·an** \gwä-'mä-nē-ən\ adj or n

Gua·na·ba·coa \,gwän-ə-bə-'kō-ə\ city W Cuba

Gua·na·ba·ra Bay \,gwän-ə-'bar-ə, -'bär-\ inlet of the Atlantic SE Brazil on which city of Rio de Janeiro is situated

Gua·na·jua·to \,gwän-ə-'hwät-ō, -'wät-\ 1 state central Mexico 2 city, its capital

Guang·xi Zhuang·zu \'gwäng-'shē-je-'wäng-'zü\ or **Kwang·si-Chuang** \'gwäng-se-chə-'wäng\ region & former province S China; capital, Nanning

Guang·zhou or **Kuang-chou** \'gwäng-'jō\ or **Can·ton** \'kan-,tän, kan-'\ city SE China, capital of Guangdong

Guan·ta·na·mo Bay \gwän-'tän-ə-ˌmō\ inlet of the Caribbean in SE Cuba; site of U.S. naval station

Gua·te·ma·la \ˌgwät-ə-'mä-lə\ 1 country Central America; a republic 2 or Guatemala City city, its capital — Gua·te·ma·lan \-lən\ adj or n

Gua·ya·quil \ˌgwī-ə-'kēl, -'kil\ city W Ecuador

Guern·sey \'gərn-zē\ island in English channel — see CHANNEL

Guer·re·ro \gə-'reər-ō\ state S Mexico on the Pacific; capital, Chilpancingo

Gui·a·na \gē-'an-ə, -'än-ə; gī-'an-ə\ region N South America on the Atlantic bounded on W & S by Orinoco, Negro, & Amazon rivers; includes Guyana, French Guiana, Suriname, & adjacent parts of Brazil & Venezuela — Gui·a·nan \-ən\ adj or n

Gui·lin \'gwē-'lin\ or Kwei·lin or Kuei–lin \'gwā-'lin\ city S China in NE Guangxi Zhuangzu

Guin·ea \'gin-ē\ 1 region W Africa on the Atlantic extending along coast from Gambia to Angola 2 or formerly French Guinea country W Africa N of Sierra Leone & Liberia; a republic; capital, Conakry — Guin·ean \'gin-ē-ən\ adj or n

Guinea, Gulf of arm of the Atlantic W central Africa

Guin·ea–Bis·sau \ˌgin-ē-bis-'aù\ or formerly Portuguese Guinea country W Africa; a republic since 1974; capital, Bissau

Gui·yang \'gwē-'yäng\ or Kuei–yang \'gwā-'yäng\ city S China, capital of Guizhou

Gu·ja·rat or Gu·je·rat \ˌgü-jə-'rät, ˌgùj-ə-\ state W India N & E of Gulf of Cambay; capital, Gandhinagar

Guj·ran·wa·la \ˌgüj-rən-'wäl-ə, ˌgùj-\ city NE Pakistan

Gulf States states of U.S. bordering on Gulf of Mexico: Florida, Alabama, Mississippi, Louisiana, and Texas

Gulf Stream warm current of the Atlantic Ocean flowing from Gulf of Mexico NE along coast of U.S. to Nantucket Island and thence eastward

Gun·tur \gùn-'tùr\ city E India in central Andhra Pradesh

Gus·ta·vo A. Ma·de·ro \gùs-ˌtäv-ō-ˌä-mə-'der-ō\ city central Mexico N of Mexico City

Guy·ana \gī-'an-ə\ or formerly British Guiana country N South America on the Atlantic; a republic in the Commonwealth since 1970; capital, Georgetown

Gwa·li·or \'gwäl-ē-ˌór\ city N central India in NW Andhra Pradesh SSE of Agra

Gwent \'gwent\ county SE Wales; established 1974

Gwyn·edd \'gwin-eth\ county NW Wales; established 1974

Habana, La — see HAVANA

Ha·chi·ō·je \ˌhäch-ē-'ō-jē\ city Japan in SE central Honshu W of Tokyo

Hack·ney \'hak-nē\ borough of N Greater London, England

Hague, The \thə-'hāg\ or Dutch 's Gra·ven·ha·ge \ˌskräv-ən-'häg-ə, ˌskräv-\ city SW Netherlands; a capital of the Netherlands

Haidarabad — see HYDERABAD

Hai·fa \'hī-fə\ city NW Israel

Hai·kou \'hī-'kaù, -'kō\ city SE China, capital of Hainan

Hai·nan \'hī-'nän\ island SE China in South China sea; a province; capital, Haikou

Hai·phong \'hī-'fóng\ city N Vietnam in Tonkin

Hai·ti \'hāt-ē\ 1 — see HISPANIOLA 2 country West Indies in W Hispaniola; a republic; capital, Port-au-Prince — Hai·tian \'hā-shən\ adj or n

Ha·ko·da·te \ˌhäk-ə-'dät-ē\ city & port Japan in SW Hokkaido

Ha·le·a·ka·la Crater \ˌhäl-ē-ˌäk-ə-'lä\ crater 829 meters deep & 32 kilometers in circumference Hawaii in E Maui Island in Haleakala National Park

Hal·i·car·nas·sus \ˌhal-ə-kär-'nas-əs\ ancient city SW Asia Minor in SW Caria on Aegean sea

Hal·i·fax \'hal-ə-ˌfaks\ 1 city, capital of Nova Scotia 2 city N England in West Yorkshire

Hal·le \'häl-ə\ city E central Germany NW of Leipzig

Hal·ma·hera \ˌhal-mə-'her-ə, ˌhäl-\ island E Indonesia; largest of the Moluccas

Ha·ma \'ham-ˌä\ city W Syria

Ha·ma·dan \ˌham-ə-'dan, -'dän\ city W Iran

Ha·ma·ma·tsu \ˌhäm-ə-'mät-sü\ city Japan in S Honshu

Ham·burg \'ham-bərg, 'häm-ˌbùrg\ city N Germany on the Elbe — Ham·burg·er \-ˌbər-gər, -ˌbùr-\ n

Ham·hung \'häm-ˌhùng\ city E central North Korea

Ham·il·ton \'ham-əl-tən, -əlt-n\ 1 city S Ontario 2 town, capital of Bermuda

Ham·mer·smith \'ham-ər-ˌsmith\ borough of SW Greater London, England

Ham·mond \'ham-ənd\ city NW Indiana

Hamp·shire \'hamp-ˌshiər, 'ham-, -shər\ 1 former county S England comprising present counties of Hampshire & Isle of Wight 2 county S England on English channel

Hamp·ton \'hamp-tən, 'ham-\ city SE Virginia

Hampton Roads channel SE Virginia through which James & Elizabeth rivers flow into Chesapeake Bay

Hang·zhou \'häng-'jō\ or Hang–chou \-'jō\ or Hang·chow \'hang-'chaù, 'häng-jò\ city E China, capital of Zhejiang

Han·kow \'hang-ˌkaù, -'kō; 'häng-'kō\ former city E central China — see WUHAN

Han·no·ver or Han·o·ver \'han-ˌō-vər, 'han-ə-vər; German hä-'nō-vər\ city N central Germany, capital of Lower Saxony

Ha·noi \ha-'nói, hə-, hä-\ city, capital of Vietnam in Tonkin

Han·yang \'hän-'yäng\ former city E central China — see WUHAN

Ha·ra·re \hə-'rä-ˌrä\ or formerly Salis·bury \'sólz-ˌber-ē, 'salz-, -bə-rē, -brē\ city, capital of Zimbabwe

Har·bin \'här-bən, här-'bin\ or Ha–erh–pin \'hä-'er-'bin\ or formerly Pin·kiang \'bin-jē-'äng\ city NE China, capital of Heilongjiang

Har·in·gey \'har-ing-gā\ borough of N Greater London, England

Har·lem \'här-ləm\ section of New York City in N Manhattan

Har·ris·burg \'har-əs-ˌbərg\ city, capital of Pennsylvania

Har·row \'har-ō\ borough of NW Greater London, England

Hart·ford \'härt-fərd\ city, capital of Connecticut

Hart·le·pool \'härt-lē-ˌpül\ borough N England in Cleveland

Ha·ry·a·na or Ha·ri·a·na \ˌhə-rē-'än-ə\ state N India formed 1966 from S part of state of Punjab; capital, Chandigarh

Harz \'härts\ mountains central Germany between Elbe & Leine rivers

Hat·ter·as, Cape \'hat-ə-rəs, 'ha-trəs\ cape, North Carolina on Cape Hatteras Island

Haute–Volta French name for Upper Volta

Ha·vana \hə-'van-ə\ or Spanish La Ha·ba·na \ˌlä-ä-'vän-ə, ˌlä-'vän-ə\ city, capital of Cuba

Hav·ant and Water·loo \'hav-ənt-n-ˌwòt-ər-'lü, -ˌwät-\ town S England in Hampshire

Ha·ver·ing \'hāv-ring, -ə-ring\ borough of NE Greater London, England

Ha·waii \hə-'wä-ē, -'wī-, -'wó-, -yē\ 1 or formerly Sandwich Islands \ˌsan-wich-, ˌsand-\ group of islands central Pacific belonging to U.S. 2 island, largest of the group 3 state of U.S. comprising Hawaiian islands except Midway; capital, Honolulu

Hawaii Volcanoes National Park reservation Hawaii on Hawaii Island including Mauna Loa & Kilauea

He·bei \'həb-'ā\ or Hopeh or Hopei \'hō-'bā\ province NE China; capital, Shijiazhuang

Heb·ri·des \'heb-rə-ˌdēz\ islands W Scotland in the Atlantic comprising Outer Hebrides (to W) and Inner Hebrides (to E) — see WESTERN ISLES — Heb·ri·de·an \ˌheb-rə-'dē-ən\ adj or n

\ə\	abut	\ng\	sing
\ər\	further	\ō\	bone
\a\	mat	\ó\	saw
\ā\	take	\ói\	coin
\ä\	cot, cart	\th\	thin
\aù\	out	\th\	this
\ch\	chin	\ü\	food
\e\	pet	\ù\	foot
\ē\	easy	\y\	yet
\g\	go	\yü\	few
\i\	tip	\yù\	cure
\ī\	life	\zh\	vision
\j\	job		

He·fei or **Ho·fei** \'həf-'ā\ or formerly **Lu·chow** \'lü'jō\ city E China, capital of Anhui W of Nanjing

Hei·long·jiang \'hā-'lùng-jē-'äng\ province NE China in N Manchuria; capital, Harbin

He·jaz \hej-'az, hij-\ province W Saudi Arabia on Red sea; capital, Mecca

Hel·e·na \'hel-ə-nə\ city, capital of Montana

He·li·op·o·lis \,hē-lē-'äp-ə-ləs\ 1 either of two cities of ancient Egypt near modern Cairo 2 city of ancient Syria; site at modern town of **Baal·bek** \'bä-əl-,bek, 'bäl-,bek\ in E Lebanon N of Damascus

Hellas — see GREECE

Hellespont — see DARDANELLES

Hells Canyon \'helz\ or **Grand Canyon of the Snake** canyon of Snake river on Idaho-Oregon boundary

Hel·sin·ki \'hel-,sing-kē, hel-'\ or Swedish **Hel·sing·fors** \'hel-sing-,fôrz\ city, capital of Finland

Helvetia — see SWITZERLAND

He·nan \'hən-'än\ or **Ho·nan** \'hō-'nän\ province E central China; capital, Zhengzhou

Heng·yang \'həng-'yäng\ city SE central China in SE Hunan

Henry, Cape \'hen-rē\ headland E Virginia S of entrance to Chesapeake Bay

Her·e·ford and Wor·ces·ter \'her-ə-fərd-n-'wús-tər, in the United States also 'hər-fərd-\ county W England bordering on Wales

Her·e·ford·shire \'her-ə-fərd-,shiər, -shər, in the United States also 'hər-fərd-\ or **Hereford** former county W England — see HEREFORD AND WORCHESTER

Her·mon, Mount \'hər-mən\ mountain 2814 meters on Lebanon-Syria border; highest in Anti-Lebanon mountains

Her·mo·si·llo \,er-mə-'sē-ō, -yō\ city NW Mexico, capital of Sonora

Hert·ford·shire \'här-fərd-,shiər, also 'härt-, in the United States also 'härt-\ or **Hertford** county SE England

Her·ze·go·vi·na \,hert-sə-gō-'vē-nə, ,härt-\ region S Europe S of Bosnia; now part of Bosnia and Herzegovina

Hesse \'hes, 'hes-ē\ or German **Hes·sen** \'hes-n\ state central Germany E of the Rhine & N of the Main; capital, Wiesbaden

Hi·a·le·ah \,hī-ə-'lē-ə\ city SE Florida

Hi·ber·nia \hī-'bər-nē-ə\ — see IRELAND — **Hi·ber·ni·an** \-ən\ adj or n

Hi·dal·go \hid-'al-gō\ state central Mexico; capital, Pachuca

Hi·ga·shi·osa·ka \hē-,gä-shē-ō-'säk-ə\ city Japan in S Honshu E of Osaka

High·land \'hī-lənd\ region NW Scotland; established 1975

High·lands \'hī-ləndz, -lənz\ the mountainous N part of Scotland lying N & W of the Lowlands

High Plains the Great Plains especially from Nebraska southward

High Tatra — see TATRA

Hil·ling·don \'hil-ing-dən\ borough of W Greater London, England

Hi·ma·chal Pra·desh \hi-,mäch-əl-prə-'desh, -'däsh\ state NW India comprising two areas NW of Uttar Pradesh; capital, Simla

Hi·ma·la·ya \,him-ə-'lā-ə; hə-'mäl-yə, -'mäl-ə-yə\ mountain system S Asia on border between India & Tibet & in Kashmir, Nepal, & Bhutan — see EVEREST (Mount) — **Hi·ma·la·yan** \,him-ə-'lā-ən; hə-'mäl-yən, -'mäl-ə-yən\ adj

Hi·me·ji \hi-'mej-ē\ city Japan in W Honshu WNW of Kobe

Hin·du Kush \,hin-dú-'kúsh, -'kəsh\ mountain range central Asia SW of the Pamirs on border of Kashmir & in Afghanistan

Hin·du·stan \,hin-dú-'stan, -də-, -'stän\ 1 region N India N of the Deccan 2 the subcontinent of India 3 the Republic of India

Hip·po \'hip-ō\ ancient city N Africa; chief town of Numidia

Hi·ra·ka·ta \,hir-ə-'kät-ə\ city Japan on Honshu

Hi·ro·shi·ma \,hir-ə-'shē-mə, hə-'rō-shə-mə\ city Japan in SW Honshu on Inland sea

Hispalis — see SEVILLE

His·pa·nia \his-'pān-ē-ə, -'pān-yə, -'pan-\ 1 the Iberian peninsula 2 — see SPAIN

His·pan·io·la \,his-pən-'yō-lə\ or Spanish **Es·pa·ño·la** \,es-,pän-'yō-lə\ or formerly **Hai·ti** \'hät-ē\ or **San·to Do·min·go** \,sant-əd-ə-'ming-gō\ island West Indies in Greater Antilles divided between Haiti on W & Dominican Republic on E

Ho·bart \'hō-,bärt\ city Australia, capital of Tasmania

Ho Chi Minh City \,hō-,chē-,min-, -,shē-\ or formerly **Sai·gon** \sī-'gän, 'sī-,\ city S Vietnam

Hofei — see HEFEI

Hoggar — see AHAGGAR

Hoh·hot \'hō-'hôt\ or **Hu·he·hot** \'hü-,hä-'hôt\ or **Hu·ho-hao-t'e** \'hü-'hō-'haú-'tə\ city N China, capital of Inner Mongolia

Hok·kai·do \hä-'kīd-ō\ or formerly **Ye·zo** \'yez-ō\ island N Japan N of Honshu

Hol·land \'häl-ənd\ 1 medieval county of Holy Roman Empire bordering on North sea & comprising area now forming North & South Holland provinces of the Netherlands 2 — see NETHERLANDS — **Hol·land·er** \-ən-dər\ n

Holland, Parts of district & former administrative county E England in SE Lincolnshire

Hol·ly·wood \'häl-ē-,wúd\ 1 section of Los Angeles, California, NW of downtown district 2 city SE Florida

Hol·stein \'hōl-,stīn, -,stēn\ region NW Germany S of Jutland peninsula adjoining Schleswig — see SCHLESWIG-HOLSTEIN

Holy Land PALESTINE

Homs \'hòmz, 'hùms\ city W Syria

Honan — see HENAN

Hon·du·ras \hän-'dùr-əs, -'dyúr-\ country Central America; a republic; capital, Tegucigalpa — **Hon·du·ran** \-ən\ or **Hon·du·ra·ne·an** or **Hon·du·ra·ni·an** \,hän-dù-'rä-nē-ən, -dyú-\ adj or n

Hong Kong \'häng-,käng, -'käng; 'hòng-,kòng, -'kòng\ British colony on coast of SE China including Hong Kong Island & Kowloon peninsula; capital, Victoria

Ho·no·lu·lu \,hän-l-'ü-lü, ,hōn-l-\ city, capital of Hawaii on Oahu Island

Hon·shu \'hän-shü\ or **Hon·do** \'hän-dō\ island Japan; largest of the four chief islands

Hood, Mount \'hùd\ mountain 3424 meters NW Oregon in Cascade range

Hoo·ghly or **Hu·gli** \'hü-glē\ river 193 kilometers long E India flowing S into Bay of Bengal; most westerly channel of the Ganges in its delta

Hoo·ver Dam \,hü-vər-\ or **Boul·der Dam** \,bōl-dər-\ dam 221 meters high in Colorado river between Arizona & Nevada — see MEAD (Lake)

Hopeh or **Hopei** — see HEBEI

Ho·reb \'hōr-,eb, 'hòr-\ or **Si·nai** \'sī-,nī also -nē-,ī\ mountain where according to the Bible the Law was given to Moses; generally thought to be in Musa on Sinai peninsula

Horn, Cape \'hòrn\ headland S Chile on Horn Island in Tierra del Fuego; the most southerly point of South America at 55°59′ S latitude

Hos·pi·ta·let \,äs-,pit-l-'et, ,häs-\ city NE Spain

Hot Springs National Park reservation SW central Arkansas adjoining city of Hot Springs

Houns·low \'haúnz-,lō\ borough of SW Greater London, England

Hous·ton \'hyü-stən, 'yü-\ city SE Texas

How·rah \'haú-rə\ city E India in West Bengal on Hooghly river opposite Calcutta

Hsia–men — see XI'AMEN

Hsiang–t'an — see XIANGTAN

Huai·nan \hü-ī-'nän, 'hwī-\ city E China in N central
Anhui

Huang or **Hwang** \'hwäng\ or **Yellow** river 4830 kilometers long N China flowing into Bohai

Huas·ca·rán \,wäs-kə-'rän\ mountain 6768 meters W
Peru

Hu·bei \'hü-'bā\ or **Hu·peh** \'hü-'bē\ or **Hu·pei** \'hü-'bā,
-'pā\ province E central China; capital, Wuhan

Hu·bli-Dhar·war \,húb-lē-'där-'wär\ city SW India in W
Karnataka

Hud·ders·field \'həd-ərz-,fēld\ county borough N England in West Yorkshire NE of Manchester

Hud·son \'həd-sən\ **1** river 492 kilometers long E New
York flowing S into New York Bay **2** bay inlet of the
Atlantic in N Canada **3** strait NE Canada connecting
Hudson Bay & the Atlantic

Hue \'hwā, 'wā, hü-'ā, hyü-'ā\ city central Vietnam in
Annam

Huhehot or **Hu-ho-hao-t'e** — see HOHHOT

Hull \'həl\ or **Kings·ton upon Hull** \'king-stən, 'kingk-\
city N England in Humberside

Hum·ber \'həm-bər\ estuary E England formed by the
Ouse & the Trent & flowing into North sea

Hum·ber·side \'həm-bər-,sīd\ county E England; area
formerly in Yorkshire

Hum·boldt \'həm-,bōlt\ glacier NW Greenland

Humboldt Current — see PERU CURRENT

Hu·nan \'hü-'nän\ province SE central China; capital,
Changsha

Hun·ga·ry \'həng-grē, -gə-rē\ country central Europe;
capital, Budapest

Hun·ting·don \'hənt-ing-dən\ or **Hun·ting·don·shire**
\-,shiər, -shər\ or **Huntingdon and Pe·ter·bor·ough**
\'pēt-ər-,bər-ə, -,bə-rə, -bə-rə, -brə\ former county E
central England; since 1974 part of Cambridgeshire

Hunt·ing·ton Beach city SW California

Hunts·ville \'həns-,vil, -vəl\ city N Alabama

Hu·ron, Lake \'hyúr-ən, 'yúr-, -,än\ lake E central North
America in U.S. & Canada; one of the Great Lakes

Hy·der·abad \'hīd-rə-,bad, -ə-rə-, -,bäd\ **1** or **Hai·dar·**
abad \same\ city S central India; capital of Andhra
Pradesh **2** city SE Pakistan on the Indus

Hy·met·tus \hī-'met-əs\ mountain ridge 1026 meters
central Greece E & SE of Athens

Ia·si \'yäsh, 'yäsh-ē\ city NE Romania

Iba·dan \i-'bäd-n, -'bad-\ city SW Nigeria

Ibe·ri·an \ī-'bir-ē-ən\ peninsula SW Europe occupied by
Spain & Portugal

Ibi·za \ē-'vē-thə, -'bē-\ island Spain in Balearic islands
SW of Majorca

Ice·land \'ī-slənd, -,sland\ island SE of Greenland between Arctic & Atlantic oceans; a republic; capital,
Reykjavik — **Ice·land·er** \-slən-dər, -,slan-dər\ n

Ichi·ka·wa \i-'chē-,kä-wə\ city Japan in SE Honshu E of
Tokyo

Ida \'īd-ə\ **1** mountain 2498 meters Greece in central
Crete **2** mountain 1771 meters NW Turkey in Asia SE of
ancient Troy

Ida·ho \'īd-ə-,hō\ state NW U.S.; capital, Boise — **Ida·ho·**
an \,īd-ə-'hō-ən\ adj or n

Idumaea or **Idumea** — see EDOM

If·ni \'if-nē\ former territory SW Morocco on the Atlantic; administered by Spain 1934–69; capital, Sidi Ifni

Igua·çu or **Spanish Igua·zú** \,ē-gwə-'sü\ river 612 kilometers long S Brazil flowing W into the Alto Paraná;
contains Iguaçu Falls (waterfall over 3 kilometers
wide composed of numerous cataracts averaging 61
meters in height)

IJs·sel or **Ijs·sel** or **Ys·sel** \'ī-səl\ river 113 kilometers
long E Netherlands flowing out of Rhine N into IJsselmeer

Ijs·sel·meer \,ī-səl-'meər\ or **Lake Ijs·sel** \'ī-səl\ freshwater lake N Netherlands separated from North sea by a
dike; part of former Zuider Zee (inlet of North sea)

Ika·ria \,ē-kə-'rē-ə\ or ancient **Icar·ia** \ī-'ker-ē-ə,
-'kar-; ik-'er-, -'ar-\ island Greece central Aegean W of
Samos

Ilium or **Ilion** — see TROY

Illam·pu \ē-'äm-pü, -'yäm-\ or **So·ra·ta** \sə-'rät-ə\
mountain W Bolivia in the Andes E of Lake Titicaca —
see ANCOHUMA

Il·li·nois \,il-ə-'nói also -'nóiz\ state N central U.S.; capital, Springfield — **Il·li·nois·an** \-'nói-ən, -'nóiz-\ adj
or n

Il·lyr·ia \il-'ir-ē-ə\ ancient country S Europe and Balkan
peninsula on the Adriatic — **Il·lyr·i·an** \-ē-ən\ adj or n

Ilo·ilo \,ē-lə-'wē-lō\ city central Philippines on S coast
of Panay Island

In·chon \'in-,chän\ city South Korea on Yellow sea

In·de·pen·dence \,in-də-'pen-dəns\ city W Missouri E of
Kansas City

In·dia \'in-dē-ə\ **1** peninsula region S Asia S of the Himalayas between Bay of Bengal & Arabian sea **2** or **Bha-**
rat \'bər-ət, 'bə-rət\ country comprising major portion of the peninsula; a republic of the Commonwealth; capital, New Delhi **3** or **Indian Empire** before
1947 those parts of the Indian subcontinent under
British rule or protection

In·di·an \'in-dē-ən\ **1** ocean E of Africa, S of Asia, W of
Australia, & N of Antarctica **2** — see THAR

In·di·ana \,in-dē-'an-ə\ state E central U.S.; capital, In-
dianapolis — **In·di·an·an** \-'an-ən\ or **In·di·an·i·an**
\-'an-ē-ən\ adj or n

In·di·a·nap·o·lis \,in-dē-ə-'nap-ləs, -ə-ləs\ city, capital
of Indiana

Indian river lagoon 266 kilometers long E Florida between mainland & coastal islands

Indian Territory former territory S U.S. in present state
of Oklahoma

In·dies \'in-dēz\ **1** EAST INDIES **2** WEST INDIES

In·do·chi·na \'in-dō-'chī-nə\ **1** peninsula SE Asia including Myanmar, Malay peninsula, Thailand, Cambodia, Laos, & Vietnam **2** or **French Indochina** former
country SE Asia comprising area now forming Cambodia, Laos, & Vietnam — **In·do–Chi·nese** \-chī-'nēz,
-'nēs\ adj or n

In·do·ne·sia \,in-də-'nē-zhə, -shə\ country SE Asia in
Malay archipelago comprising Sumatra, Java, S & E Borneo, Sulawesi, W New Guinea, & many smaller islands;
a republic; capital, Djakarta — see NETHERLANDS EAST
INDIES — **In·do·ne·sian** \-zhən, -shən\ adj or n

In·dore \in-'dōr, -'dòr\ city W central India in W Madhya
Pradesh

In·dus \'in-dəs\ river 2900 kilometers long S Asia flowing from Tibet NW & SSW through Pakistan into Arabian
sea

In·land \'in-,land, -lənd\ sea inlet of the Pacific in SW
Japan between Honshu Island on N and Shikoku Island
and Kyushu Island on S

Inner Hebrides — see HEBRIDES

Inner Mongolia region N China in SE Mongolia & W Manchuria; capital, Huhhot

Inns·bruck \'inz-,brúk, 'ins-\ city W Austria in Tirol

Inside Passage or **Inland Passage** protected shipping
route between Puget Sound, Washington, & Skagway,
Alaska

In·ver·ness \,in-vər-'nes\ or **In·ver·ness·shire** \-'nes-
,shiər, -'nesh-, -shər\ former county NW Scotland

Io·ni·an \ī-'ō-nē-ən\ **1** sea arm of the Mediterranean
between SE Italy & W Greece **2** islands W Greece in Ionian sea

Io·wa \'ī-ə-wə\ state N central U.S.; capital, Des Moines
— **Io·wan** \-wən\ adj or n

I-pin — see YIBIN

Ipoh \'ē-pō\ city Malaysia NNW of Kuala Lumpur

Ips·wich \'ip-swich\ borough SE England in Suffolk

Iran \i-'ran, -'rän; ī-'ran\ or formerly **Per·sia** \'pər-zhə\
country SW Asia S of Caspian sea; capital, Tehran —

\ə\ abut	\ng\ sing
\ər\ further	\ō\ bone
\a\ mat	\ò\ saw
\ā\ take	\òi\ coin
\ä\ cot, cart	\th\ thin
\au̇\ out	\t͟h\ this
\ch\ chin	\ü\ food
\e\ pet	\ù\ foot
\ē\ easy	\y\ yet
\g\ go	\yü\ few
\i\ tip	\yu̇\ cure
\ī\ life	\zh\ vision
\j\ job	

Irani \i-'ran-ē, -'rän-\ *adj or n* — **Ira·nian** \i-'ran-ē-ən, -'rän-, -'rān-\ *adj or n*

Iraq \i-'räk, -'rak\ country sw Asia in Mesopotamia; a republic; capital, Baghdad — **Iraqi** \-'räk-ē, -'rak-\ *adj or n*

Irbil — see ARBIL

Ire·land \'īr-lənd\ **1** *or Latin* **Hi·ber·nia** \hī-'bər-nē-ə\ island w Europe in the Atlantic; one of the British Isles **2** *or* **Irish Republic** *or* **Ei·re** \'er-ə\ country w Europe occupying major portion of the island; a republic; capital, Dublin

Irian — see NEW GUINEA

Irish \'īr-ish\ sea arm of the Atlantic between Great Britain & Ireland

Ir·kutsk \iər-'kütsk, ,ər-\ city s Russia in Asia, near Lake Baikal

Ir·ra·wad·dy \,ir-ə-'wäd-ē\ river 2175 kilometers long Myanmar flowing s into Bay of Bengal

Ir·tysh \iər-'tish, ,ər-\ river 3540 kilometers long central Asia flowing NW & N from Altai mountains in China, through Kazakhstan, and into the Ob in Russia

Is·fa·han \,is-fə-'hän, -'han\ *or* **Es·fa·han** \,es-\ *or formerly* **Is·pa·han** \,is-pə-\ city w central Iran

Is·lam·abad \is-'läm-ə-,bäd, iz-'lam-ə-,bad\ city, capital of Pakistan in NE Pakistan

Isle of Man — see MAN (Isle of)

Isle Roy·ale \'īl-'rȯi-əl, -'rȯil\ island Michigan in Lake Superior in **Isle Royale National Park**

Is·ling·ton \'iz-ling-tən\ borough of N Greater London, England

Is·ma·ilia \,iz-mā-ə-'lē-ə\ city NE Egypt on Suez canal

Is·ra·el \'iz-rē-əl\ **1** ancient kingdom Palestine comprising lands occupied by the Hebrew people **2** *or* **Northern Kingdom** *or* **Ephra·im** \'ē-frē-əm\ the N part of the Hebrew kingdom after about 933 B.C. — see JUDAH **3** country sw Asia in Palestine; a republic established 1948; capital, Jerusalem — **Is·rae·li** \iz-'rā-lē\ *adj or n*

Is·tan·bul \,is-təm-'bül, -,täm-, -,tam-, -,tän-\ *or formerly* **Con·stan·ti·no·ple** \,kän,stant-n-'ō-pəl\ *or ancient* **By·zan·tium** \bə-'zan-shəm, -shē-əm; -'zant-ē-əm\ city NW Turkey on the Bosporus & Sea of Marmara; former capital of Turkey

Is·tria \'is-trē-ə\ peninsula s central Europe extending into the N Adriatic; belongs to Croatia & Slovenia except for Trieste (to Italy) — **Is·tri·an** \-trē-ən\ *adj or n*

Italian Somaliland former country E Africa now part of Somalia

It·a·ly \'it-l-ē\ **1** peninsula 1225 kilometers long s Europe extending into the Mediterranean between Adriatic & Tyrrhenian seas **2** country including the peninsula of Italy, Sicily, & Sardinia; a republic; capital, Rome

Itas·ca, Lake \ī-'tas-kə\ lake NW central Minnesota; source of the Mississippi

Ith·a·ca \'ith-i-kə\ island w Greece in Ionian islands

Iva·no·vo \i-'vän-ə-və\ city central Russia in Europe, WNW of Nizhni Novgorod

Ivory Coast *or French* **Côte d'Ivoire** \,kȯt-dēv-'wär\ country w Africa on Gulf of Guinea; a republic; capital, Abidjan

Iwo \'ē-wō\ city sw Nigeria NE of Ibadan

Iwo Ji·ma \,ē-wō-'jē-mə\ island Japan in w Pacific in Volcano islands about 1130 kilometers SSE of Tokyo

Izhevsk \'ē-,zhefsk\ city E central Russia in Europe NE of Kazan

Iz·mir \iz-'miər\ *or formerly* **Smyr·na** \'smər-nə\ city w Turkey

Ja·bal·pur \'jəb-əl-,pür\ city central India in central Madhya Pradesh

Jack·son \'jak-sən\ city, capital of Mississippi

Jack·son·ville \'jak-sən-,vil\ city NE Florida

Jadotville — see LIKASI

Jaf·fa \'jaf-ə, 'yaf-ə\ *or ancient* **Jop·pa** \'jäp-ə\ former city, now part of Tel Aviv, Israel

Jai·pur \'jī-,pür\ city NW India, capital of Rajasthan

Ja·kar·ta — see DJAKARTA

Ja·la·pa \hə-'läp-ə\ city E Mexico, capital of Veracruz

Ja·lis·co \hə-'lis-kō\ state w central Mexico; capital, Guadalajara

Ja·mai·ca \jə-'mā-kə\ island West Indies in Greater Antilles; a dominion of the Commonwealth; capital, Kingston — **Ja·mai·can** \-kən\ *adj or n*

James \'jāmz\ **1** river 1145 kilometers long North and South Dakota flowing s into the Missouri **2** river 550 kilometers long Virginia flowing E into Chesapeake Bay

James Bay the s extension of Hudson Bay between NE Ontario & w Quebec

James·town \'jām-,staȯn\ ruined village E Virginia on James river; first permanent English settlement in America (1607)

Jammu and Kashmir — see KASHMIR

Jam·na·gar \jäm-'nəg-ər\ *or* **Na·va·na·gar** \,näv-ə-'nəg-ər\ city w India in w Gujarat

Jam·shed·pur \'jäm-,shed-,pür\ city E India in s Bihar

Ja·pan \jə-'pan, ji-, ja-\ *or Japanese* **Nip·pon** \nip-'än\ *or* **Ni·hon** \'nē-'hȯn\ country E Asia comprising Honshu, Hokkaido, Kyushu, Shikoku, & other islands in the w Pacific; an empire; capital, Tokyo

Japan, Sea of arm of the Pacific between Japan & Asian mainland

Japan current *or Japanese* **Ku·ro·shio** \,kür-ō-'shē-,ō\ warm current of the Pacific ocean flowing from E coast of Philippines N along E coast of Japan and thence eastward

Jas·per National Park \'jas-pər\ reservation w Alberta on E slope of Rocky mountains

Ja·va \'jäv-ə, 'jav-ə\ island Indonesia sw of Borneo; chief city, Djakarta — **Ja·van** \-ən\ *adj or n*

Jef·fer·son City \'jef-ər-sən\ city, capital of Missouri

Je·rez \hə-'rās\ *or in full* **Je·rez de la Fron·te·ra** \hə-'rez-də-lə-,frən-'ter-ə\ city sw Spain

Jer·i·cho \'jer-i-,kō\ ancient city E Palestine N of Dead sea

Jer·sey \'jər-zē\ **1** island in English channel — see CHANNEL **2** NEW JERSEY — **Jer·sey·ite** \-zē-,īt\ *n*

Jersey City city NE New Jersey on Hudson river

Je·ru·sa·lem \jə-'rü-sə-ləm, -sləm; -'rüz-ə-ləm, -'rüz-ləm\ city NW of Dead sea divided 1948-67 between Israel & Jordan; capital of Israel since 1950 & formerly of ancient kingdoms of Israel & Judah

Jhan·si \'jän-sē\ city N India in SE Uttar Pradesh sw of Kanpur

Jia·mu·si \jē-'ä-'mü-'sē\ *or* **Chia-mu-ssu** \jē-'ä-'mü-'sü\ *or* **Kia·mu·sze** \jē-'ä-'mü-'sə\ city NE China in E Heilongjiang

Jiang·su *or* **Kiang·su** \jē-'äng-'sü\ province E China; capital, Nanjing

Jiang·xi *or* **Kiang·si** \jē-'äng-shē\ province SE China; capital, Nanzhang

Jibuti — see DJIBOUTI

Jid·da \'jid-ə\ *or* **Jed·da** \'jed-ə\ city w Saudi Arabia in Hejaz on Red sea; port for Mecca

Ji·lin \'jē-'lin\ *or* **Ki·rin** \'kē-'rin\ **1** province NE China; capital Changchun **2** city in Jilin province

Ji·nan *or* **Chi·nan** *or* **Tsi·nan** \'jē-'nän\ city E China, capital of Shandong

Jin·zhou *or* **Chin-chou** *or* **Chin·chow** \'jin-'jō\ city NE China in sw Liaoning

João Pes·soa \,zhaȯⁿ-pə-'sō-ə, ,zhaȯⁿm-\ city NE Brazil N of Recife

Jodh·pur \'jäd-pər, -,pür\ city NW India in central Rajasthan

Jo·han·nes·burg \jō-'han-əs-,bərg, -'hän-\ city NE Republic of South Africa in s Transvaal

Jo·hore Bah·ru \jə-'hȯr-'bär-ü, -'hȯr-\ city Malaysia in s Peninsular Malaysia opposite Singapore Island

Jor·dan \'jȯrd-n\ **1** river 320 kilometers long Israel & Jordan rising in Syria & flowing s from Anti-Lebanon mountains into Dead sea **2** *or formerly* **Trans·jor·dan**

\trans-, tranz-, 'trans-, 'tranz-\ country **SW** Asia in **NW** Arabia; capital, Amman — **Jor•da•ni•an** \jȯr-'dā-nē-ən\ *adj or n*

Juan de Fu•ca \ˌhwän-də-'fyü-kə, ˌwän-\ strait 160 kilometers long between Vancouver Island, British Columbia, & Olympic peninsula, Washington

Juan Fer•nán•dez \ˌhwän-fər-'nan-dəs, ˌwän-\ group of three islands **SE** Pacific 645 kilometers **W** of Chile; belongs to Chile

Juárez — see CIUDAD JUÁREZ

Ju•dah \'jüd-ə\ ancient kingdom **S** Palestine; capital, Jerusalem — see ISRAEL

Ju•dea *or* **Ju•daea** \jù-'dē-ə, -'dā-\ ancient region Palestine constituting the **S** division (Judah) of the country under Persian, Greek, & Roman rule — **Ju•de•an** \-ən\ *adj or n*

Ju•go•sla•via \ˌyü-gō-'släv-ē-ə\ — see YUGOSLAVIA — **Ju•go•slav** \ˌyü-gō-'släv, -'slav\ *or* **Ju•go•sla•vi•an** \-'släv-ē-ən\ *adj or n*

Juiz de Fo•ra \ˌzhwēzh-də-'fōr-ə, -'fȯr-\ city **E** Brazil **N** of Rio de Janeiro

Jul•lun•dur \'jəl-ən-dər\ city **N** India in Punjab **SE** of Amritsar

Ju•neau \'jü-nō, jù-'\ city, capital of Alaska

Jung•frau \'yùng-ˌfraù\ mountain 4158 meters **SW** central Switzerland in Bernese Alps

Ju•ra \'jùr-ə\ mountain range extending along boundary between France & Switzerland **N** of Lake Geneva

Jut•land \'jət-lənd\ **1** peninsula **N** Europe extending into North sea & comprising mainland of Denmark & **N** portion of Schleswig-Holstein, Germany **2** the mainland of Denmark

Ka•bul \'käb-əl, kä-'bül\ city, capital of Afghanistan

Ka•di•yev•ka \kə-'dē-əf-kə, -yəf-\ city **E** Ukraine in Donets basin

Kae•song \'kā-ˌsȯng\ city North Korea **SE** of Pyongyang

Ka•go•shi•ma \ˌkäg-ə-'shē-mə, kä-'gō-shə-mə\ city Japan in **S** Kyushu

Kai•feng \'kī-'fəng\ city **E** central China in **NE** Henan

Ka Lae \kä-'lä-ā\ *or* **South Cape** *or* **South Point** most southerly point of Hawaii & of U.S.

Ka•la•ha•ri \ˌkal-ə-'här-ē\ desert region **S** Africa **N** of Orange river in **S** Botswana & **NW** Republic of South Africa

Kalgan — see ZHANGJIAKOU

Ka•li•man•tan \ˌkal-ə-'man-ˌtan, ˌkäl-ə-'män-ˌtän\ **1** BORNEO — its Indonesian name **2** the **S** & **E** portion of Borneo belonging to Indonesia; formerly (as **Dutch Borneo**) part of Netherlands East Indies

Ka•li•nin \kə-'lē-nən, -'lēn-ˌyēn\ city Russia in Europe on the Volga

Ka•li•nin•grad \kə-'lē-nən-ˌgrad, -nyən-\ *or German* **Kö•nigs•berg** \'kā-nigz-ˌbərg, 'kərn-igz-, -ˌbeərg, *German* 'kȫ-niks-ˌberk\ city Russia in small area between Poland and Lithuania

Ka•lu•ga \kə-'lü-gə\ city Russia in Europe **WNW** of Oka

Kam•chat•ka \kam-'chat-kə\ peninsula 1205 kilometers long **NE** Russia in Asia between Sea of Okhotsk & Bering sea

Kam•pa•la \käm-'päl-ə\ city, capital of Uganda

Kampuchea, Democratic — see CAMBODIA

Ka•nan•ga \kə-'näng-gə\ *or formerly* **Lu•lua•bourg** \lü-'lü-ə-ˌbùrg, -ˌbùr\ city **S** central Zaire

Ka•na•za•wa \kə-'näz-ə-wə, ˌkan-ə-'zä-wə\ city Japan in **W** Honshu **N** of Nagoya near Sea of Japan

Kan•chen•jun•ga \ˌkan-chən-'jəng-gə, -'jùng-\ mountain 8598 meters Nepal & Sikkim (India) in the Himalayas; third highest in the world

Kan•da•har \'kan-də-ˌhär\ city **SE** Afghanistan

Ka•no \'kän-ō\ city **N** central Nigeria

Kan•pur \'kän-ˌpùr\ city **N** India in **S** Uttar Pradesh on the Ganges

Kan•sas \'kan-zəs\ state **W** central U.S.; capital, Topeka — **Kan•san** \-zən\ *adj or n*

Kansas City 1 city **NE** Kansas adjoining Kansas City, Missouri **2** city **W** Missouri

Kansu — see GANSU

Kao•hsiung \'kaù-shē-'ùng, 'gaù-\ city China in **SW** Taiwan

Ka•ra \'kär-ə\ sea arm of Arctic ocean off **N** coast of Russia **E** of Novaya Zemlya

Ka•ra•chi \kə-'räch-ē\ city **S** Pakistan on Arabian sea

Karafuto — see SAKHALIN

Ka•ra•gan•da \ˌkar-ə-gən-'dä\ city central Kazakhstan

Ka•raj \kə-'räj\ city **N** Iran **NW** of Tehran

Kar•a•ko•ram \ˌkar-ə-'kōr-əm, -'kȯr-\ mountain system **S** central Asia in **N** Kashmir & **NW** Tibet connecting the Himalayas & the Pamirs

Ka•re•lia \kə-'rē-lē-ə, -'rēl-yə\ region **NE** Europe between Gulf of Finland & White sea; now chiefly in Russia — **Ka•re•lian** \-'rē-lē-ən, -'rēl-yən\ *adj or n*

Karl–Marx–Stadt — see CHEMNITZ

Karls•ru•he \'kärlz-ˌrü-ə\ city **SW** Germany

Kar•na•ta•ka \kär-'nät-ə-kə\ *or formerly* **My•sore** \mī-'sōr, -'sȯr\ state **S** India; capital, Bangalore

Kar•roo \kə-'rü\ plateau region **W** Republic of South Africa **W** of Drakensberg mountains; divided into **Little**, or **Southern**, **Karroo** (in **S** Cape Province), **Great**, or **Central**, **Karroo** (in **S** central Cape Province), & **Northern**, or **Upper**, **Karroo** (in **N** Cape Province, Orange Free State, & **W** Transvaal)

Kashi \'kash-ē, 'käsh-\ *or* **Kash•gar** \'kash-ˌgär, 'käsh-\ city **W** China in **SW** Xinjiang Uygur

Ka•shi•wa \'kä-shē-ˌwä\ city Japan on Honshu

Kash•mir \'kash-ˌmiər, 'kazh-, kash-', kazh-'\ **1** mountain region **N** Indian subcontinent **NW** of Tibet & **SW** of Xinjiang Uygur **2** *or* **Jam•mu and Kashmir** \'jəm-ü\ state comprising Kashmir & Jammu regions; claimed by India & Pakistan; capital, Srinagar; winter capital, Jammu — **Kash•miri** \kash-'miər-ē, kazh-\ *adj or n*

Kas•sel \'kas-əl, 'käs-\ city central Germany **WNW** of Erfurt

Ka•thi•a•war \ˌkät-ē-ə-'wär\ peninsula **W** India in Gujarat **N** of Gulf of Cambay

Kath•man•du *or* **Kat•man•du** \ˌkat-man-'dü, ˌkät-ˌmän-\ city, capital of Nepal

Kat•mai, Mount \'kat-ˌmī\ volcano 2047 meters **S** Alaska in **Katmai National Park**

Ka•to•wi•ce \ˌkät-ə-'vēt-sə\ city **S** Poland **WNW** of Krakow

Kat•te•gat \'kat-i-ˌgat\ arm of North sea between Sweden & **E** coast of Jutland peninsula of Denmark

Kau•ai \'kaù-ˌī\ island Hawaii **NW** of Oahu

Kau•nas \'kaù-nəs, -ˌnäs\ *or Russian* **Kov•no** \'kȯv-nō\ city central Lithuania

Ka•wa•goe \kə-'wäg-ˌói\ city Japan on **SE** central Honshu

Ka•wa•gu•chi \ˌkä-wə-'gü-chē, kä-'wäg-ù-chē\ city Japan in **E** Honshu **N** of Tokyo

Ka•wa•sa•ki \ˌkä-wə-'säk-ē\ city Japan in **E** Honshu **S** of Tokyo

Kay•se•ri \ˌkī-zə-'rē\ city central Turkey

Ka•zakh•stan \kə-ˌzak-'stan; kə-ˌzäk-'stän, ˌkä-\ country **NW** central Asia; capital, Alma-Ata; a constituent republic of U.S.S.R. 1936–91

Ka•zan \kə-'zan, -'zän, -'zän-yə\ city **E** central Russia in Europe

Kazan Retto — see VOLCANO ISLANDS

Kee•lung \'kē-'lùg\ city & port **N** Taiwan

Kee•wa•tin \kē-'wāt-n\ former district **N** Canada in **E** Northwest Territories **NW** of Hudson Bay

Kej•im•ku•jik National Park \ˌkej-mə-'kü-jik, -ə-mə-\ reservation **E** Canada in **SW** Nova Scotia

Ke•me•ro•vo \'kem-ə-rə-və, -ˌrō-və, -rə-ˌvō\ city **S** Russia in Asia in Kuznetsk basin

Ke•nai \'kē-ˌnī\ peninsula **S** Alaska **E** of Cook inlet; site of **Kenai Fjords National Park**

Ke•ni•tra \kə-'nē-trə\ *or formerly* **Port Lyau•tey** \ˌpȯr-lē-ō-'tā, -'ō-, \ city **N** Morocco

Kennedy, Cape — see CANAVERAL

Ken•sing•ton and Chel•sea \'ken-zing-tən-ən-'chel-sē, 'ken-sing-\ royal borough of **W** Greater London, England

\ə\ abut		\ng\ sing	
\ər\ further		\ō\ bone	
\a\ mat		\ȯ\ saw	
\ā\ take		\ȯi\ coin	
\ä\ cot, cart		\th\ thin	
\aù\ out		\th\ this	
\ch\ chin		\ü\ food	
\e\ pet		\ù\ foot	
\ē\ easy		\y\ yet	
\g\ go		\yü\ few	
\i\ tip		\yù\ cure	
\ī\ life		\zh\ vision	
\j\ job			

Kent \'kent\ county SE England — **Kent·ish** \'kent-ish\ *adj*

Ken·tucky \kən-'tək-ē\ state E central U.S.; capital, Frankfort — **Ken·tuck·i·an** \-ē-ən\ *adj or n*

Ken·ya \'ken-yə, 'kēn-\ **1** mountain 5194 meters central Kenya **2** country E Africa S of Ethiopia; a republic; capital, Nairobi — **Ken·yan** \-yən\ *adj or n*

Ker·a·la \'ker-ə-lə\ state SW India bordering on Arabian sea; capital, Trivandrum

Ker·gue·len \'kər-gə-lən, ‚kər-gə-'len\ **1** archipelago S Indian ocean belonging to France **2** chief island of the archipelago

Ker·man \kər-'män, ker-\ city SE central Iran

Ker·ry \'ker-ē\ county SW Ireland in Munster

Kes·te·ven, Parts of \ke-'stē-vən\ district & former administrative county E England in SW Lincolnshire

Kha·ba·rovsk \kə-'bär-əfsk\ city SE Russia in Asia on the Amur

Khan·ka \'kang-kə\ lake E Asia between Russia & China

Khar·kov \'kär-‚kóf, -‚kóv -kəf\ city NE Ukraine

Khar·toum \kär-'tüm\ city, capital of Sudan

Kher·son \keər-'són\ city S Ukraine

Khy·ber \'kī-bər\ pass 53 kilometers long on border between Afghanistan & Pakistan WNW of Peshawar

Kiamusze — see JIAMUSI

Kiangsi — see JIANGXI

Kiangsu — see JIANGSU

Ki·bo \'kē-bō\ mountain peak 5888 meters NE Tanzania; highest peak of Kilimanjaro & highest point in Africa

Kiel \'kēl\ **1** city N Germany, capital of Schleswig-Holstein **2** ship canal 98 kilometers long N Germany connecting Baltic & North seas

Kiel·ce \kē-'elt-sā\ city S Poland S of Warsaw

Ki·ev *or Russian* **Ki·yev** \'kē-‚ef, -‚ev, -əf, -‚yef, -‚yev, -yəf\ city, capital of Ukraine

Ki·ga·li \ki-'gäl-ē\ city, capital of Rwanda

Ki·lau·ea \‚kē-‚laù-'ā-ə\ volcanic crater Hawaii on Hawaii Island on E slope of Mauna Loa in Hawaii Volcanoes National Park

Kil·dare \kil-'daər, -'deər\ county E Ireland in Leinster

Kil·i·man·ja·ro \‚kil-ə-mən-'jär-ō, -'jar-\ mountain NE Tanzania; highest in Africa — see KIBO

Kil·ken·ny \kil-'ken-ē\ county SE Ireland in Leinster

Kil·lar·ney, Lakes of \kil-'är-nē\ three lakes SW Ireland in Kerry

Kim·ber·ley \'kim-bər-lē\ city Republic of South Africa in N Cape of Good Hope

Kin·car·dine \kin-'kärd-n\ *or* **Kin·car·dine·shire** \-‚shiər, -shər\ former county E Scotland

Kings Canyon National Park \'kingz-\ reservation SE central California in Sierra Nevada N of Sequoia National Park

Kings·ton \'king-stən\ city, capital of Jamaica

Kingston upon Hull — see HULL

Kingston upon Thames \'temz\ royal borough of SW Greater London, England

Kin·ross \kin-'rós\ *or* **Kin·ross–shire** \-'rós-‚shiər, -shər, -'rósh-\ former county E central Scotland

Kin·sha·sa \kin-'shäs-ə\ *or formerly* **Lé·o·pold·ville** \'lē-ə-‚póld-‚vil, 'lā-\ city, capital of Zaire

Kirghizia *or* **Kirghiz Republic** *or* **Kirgiz Republic** — see KYRGYZSTAN

Kir·i·bati \'kir-ə-‚bas\ islands W Pacific including the Gilberts; an independent member of British Commonwealth; capital Tarawa

Kirin — see JILIN

Ki·riti·mati \kə-'ris-məs\ *or formerly* **Christ·mas** \'kris-məs\ island in Line Islands; largest atoll in the Pacific

Kirk·cud·bright \kər-'kü-brē\ *or* **Kirk·cud·bright·shire** \-‚shiər, -shər\ former county S Scotland

Kir·kuk \kiər-'kük\ city NE Iraq

Ki·rov \'kē-‚róf, -‚róv, -rəf\ city central Russia in Europe N of Kazan

Ki·ro·vo·grad \ki-'rō-və-‚grad\ city S central Ukraine

Ki·san·ga·ni \‚kē-sən-'gän-ē\ *or formerly* **Stan·ley·ville** \'stan-lē-‚vil\ city NE Zaire

Ki·shi·nev \'kish-ə-‚nef, -‚nev\ *or Romanian* **Chi·si·nau** \‚kē-shi-'naù\ city, capital of Moldova

Ki·ta·kyu·shu \kē-‚tä-kē-'ü-shü\ city Japan in N Kyushu

Kitch·e·ner \'kich-nər, -ə-nər\ city Canada in SE Ontario

Klon·dike \'klän-‚dīk\ region NW Canada in central Yukon Territory in valley of Klondike river E of Dawson

Knos·sos *or* **Cnos·sus** \kə-'näs-əs, 'näs-əs\ *or* **Gnos·sus** \gə-'näs-əs, 'näs-əs\ ruined city, capital of ancient Crete near N coast

Knox·ville \'näks-‚vil, -vəl\ city E Tennessee

Ko·be \'kō-bē, -‚bā\ city Japan in S Honshu

Ko·buk Valley National Park \kō-'bùk-\ reservation NW Alaska N of Arctic circle

Ko·chi \'kō-chē\ city Japan on S coast of Shikoku

Ko·di·ak \'kōd-ē-‚ak\ island S Alaska E of Alaska peninsula

Ko·kand \kō-'kand\ city E Uzbekistan SE of Tashkent

Ko·la \'kō-lə\ peninsula NW Russia in Europe between Barents & White seas

Ko·lar Gold Fields \kō-'lär\ city S India in SE Karnataka NE of Bangalore

Kol·ha·pur \'kō-lə-‚pùr\ city W India in SW Maharashtra SSE of Bombay

Köln — see COLOGNE

Ko·mo·do \kə-'mōd-ō\ island Indonesia in the Lesser Sundas W of Flores Island

Konakry — see CONAKRY

Königsberg — see KALININGRAD

Kon·ya \kón-'yä\ city SW central Turkey

Koo·te·nay National Park \'küt-n-‚ā, -n-ē\ reservation SE British Columbia

Ko·rea \kə-'rē-ə, *especially South* kō-\ country E Asia between Yellow sea & Sea of Japan; capital, Seoul; divided after World War II at 38th parallel into republics of **North Korea** (capital, Pyongyang) & **South Korea** (capital, Seoul)

Kos·ci·us·ko, Mount \‚käz-ē-'əs-kō\ mountain 2230 meters SE Australia in SE New South Wales; highest in Great Dividing range & in Australia

Ko·shi·ga·ya \kō-'shē-gä-yə; ‚kō-shig-'ä-yə\ city Japan on Honshu

Kos·tro·ma \‚käs-trə-'mä\ city central Russia in Europe on the Volga

Ko·ta Bha·ru \‚kōt-ə-'bär-‚ü, -‚ü\ city Malaysia in N Peninsular Malaysia

Kovno — see KAUNAS

Kow·loon \'kaù-'lün\ city Hong Kong colony on Kowloon peninsula opposite Hong Kong Island

Kozhikode — see CALICUT

Krak·a·toa \‚krak-ə-'tō-ə\ *or* **Krak·a·tau** \-'taù\ island & volcano Indonesia between Sumatra & Java

Kra·kow *or* **Cra·cow** \'kräk-‚aù, 'krak-, 'kräk-, -ō, *Polish* 'kräk-‚üf\ city S Poland

Kras·no·dar \'kräs-nə-‚där\ city S Russia in Europe in N Caucasus

Kras·no·yarsk \‚kras-nə-'yärsk\ city S central Russia in Asia on the upper Yenisei

Kre·feld \'krā-‚felt\ city W Germany on the Rhine WSW of Essen

Kri·voy Rog \‚kri-‚vói-'rōg, -'rók\ city SE central Ukraine

Kru·ger National Park \'krü-gər\ game reserve NE Republic of South Africa in E Transvaal on Mozambique border

Kru·gers·dorp \'krü-gərz-‚dórp, 'krüē-ərz-\ city NE Republic of South Africa in S Transvaal

K2 — see GODWIN AUSTEN

Kua·la Lum·pur \‚kwäl-ə-'lùm-‚pùr, -'ləm-\ city, capital of Federation of Malaysia in Peninsular Malaysia

Kuang–chou — see GUANGZHOU

Kuei–yang — see GUIYANG

Ku·ma·mo·to \‚küm-ə-'mōt-ō\ city Japan in W Kyushu

Ku·ma·si \kü-'mäs-ē, -'mas-\ city S central Ghana

Kun·lun \'kün-'lün\ mountain system w China extending ᴇ from the Pamirs to sᴇ Qinghai; highest peak Muztag 7724 meters

Kun·ming \'kùn-'ming\ or formerly **Yun·nan** \yü-'nän\ or **Yun·nan·fu** \-'fü\ city s China, capital of Yunnan

Ku·ra·shi·ki \kü-'rä-shē-kē, ,kür-ə-'shē-kē\ city Japan in w Honshu wsw of Okayama

Kur·di·stan \,kùrd-ə-'stan, ,kərd-\ region sw Asia chiefly in ᴇ Turkey, ɴw Iran, and ɴ Iraq

Ku·re \'kùr-ē, 'kyùr-ē, 'kü-rä\ city Japan in sw Honshu on Inland sea sᴇ of Hiroshima

Kur·gan \kùr-'gan, -'gän\ city w Russia in Asia, sᴇ of Yekaterinburg

Ku·ril or **Ku·rile** \'kyùr-,ēl, kyù-'rēl\ islands Russia in the Pacific between s Kamchatka peninsula & ɴᴇ Hokkaido Island

Kur·nool \kər-'nül\ city s India in w Andhra Pradesh ssw of Hyderabad

Kuroshio — see ᴊᴀᴘᴀɴ ᴄᴜʀʀᴇɴᴛ

Kursk \'kùrsk\ city sw Russia in Europe, ɴ of Kharkov

Ku·wait \kù-'wāt\ **1** country sw Asia in Arabia at head of Persian gulf **2** city, its capital — **Ku·wai·ti** \-'wāt-ē\ adj or n

Kuybyshev — see sᴀᴍᴀʀᴀ

Kuz·netsk Basin \kùz-'netsk\ or **Kuz·bass** or **Kuz·bas** \'kùz-,bas\ basin of Tom river s Russia in Asia, extending from Tomsk to Novokuznetsk

Kwa·ja·lein \'kwäj-ə-lən, -,lān\ island (atoll) w Pacific in Ralik chain of Marshall islands

Kwang·ju \'gwäng-,jü, 'kwäng-\ city sw South Korea

Kwangsi–Chuang — see ɢᴜᴀɴɢxɪ ᴢʜᴜᴀɴɢᴢᴜ

Kwang·tung \'gwäng-'dùng, 'kwäng-, -'tùng\ province sᴇ China bordering on South China sea & Gulf of Tonkin; capital, Canton

Kwei·chow \'gwā-'jō, 'kwä-\ province s China s of Szechwan; capital, Kweiyang

Kweilin or **Kuei–lin** — see ɢᴜɪʟɪɴ

Kyo·to \kē-'ōt-ō\ city Japan in w central Honshu; formerly capital of Japan

Kyr·gyz·stan \,kir-gi-'stan, -'stän; 'kir-gi-,\ country w central Asia; capital, Bishkek; a constituent republic (**Kir·giz Republic** or **Kir·ghiz Republic** \kiər-'gēz-\ or **Kir·ghi·zia** \kiər-'gē-zē-ə, -zhə, -zhē-ə\) of U.S.S.R. 1936–91

Kyu·shu \kē-'ü-shü\ island Japan s of w end of Honshu

Labe — see ᴇʟʙᴇ

Lab·ra·dor \'lab-rə-,dòr\ **1** peninsula ᴇ Canada between Hudson Bay & the Atlantic divided between Quebec & Newfoundland **2** the part of the peninsula belonging to Newfoundland — **Lab·ra·dor·ean** or **Labra·dor·ian** \,lab-rə-'dòr-ē-ən, -'dòr-\ adj or n

Labrador Current cold current flowing s from Baffin Bay through Davis strait to Newfoundland

Lac·ca·dive \'lak-ə-,dēv, -,dīv\ islands India in Arabian sea ɴ of Maldive islands

Lac·e·dae·mon \,las-ə-'dē-mən\ — see sᴘᴀʀᴛᴀ — **Lac·e·dae·mo·nian** \,las-əd-i-'mō-nē-ən, -nyən\ adj or n

La·co·nia \lə-'kō-nē-ə, -nyə\ ancient country s Greece in sᴇ Peloponnesus; capital, Sparta — **La·co·nian** \-nē-ən, -nyən\ adj or n

Lad·o·ga \'lad-ə-gə, 'läd-\ lake w Russia, near Finland border

La·gos \'lä-,gäs\ city, capital of Nigeria

La Habana — see ʜᴀᴠᴀɴᴀ

La·hon·tan, Lake \lə-'hänt-n\ prehistoric lake ɴw Nevada & ɴᴇ California

La·hore \lə-'hōr, -'hòr\ city Pakistan in ᴇ Punjab province

Lake Clark National Park \läk-'klärk-\ reservation s central Alaska wsw of Anchorage

Lake District region ɴw England in Cumbria & ɴw Lancashire containing many lakes & mountains

Lak·shad·weep \lək-'shäd-,wēp, ,lək-shəd-'\ territory India comprising the Laccadive islands

Lam·beth \'lam-bəth, -,beth\ borough of s Greater London, England

La·nai \lə-'nī\ island Hawaii w of Maui

Lan·ark \'lan-ərk\ or **Lan·ark·shire** \-,shiər, -shər\ former county s central Scotland; chief city, Glasgow

Lan·ca·shire \'lang-kə-,shiər, -shər\ or **Lan·cas·ter** \'lang-kə-stər\ county ɴw England — **Lan·cas·tri·an** \lang-'kas-trē-ən, lan-\ adj or n

Lands End or **Land's End** \'land-'zend, 'lan-\ or ancient **Bo·le·ri·um** \bə-'lir-ē-əm\ cape sw England at sw tip of Cornwall

Lan·gue·doc \,lang-gə-'däk; 'läⁿ-gə-'dók, 'läⁿng-\ region & former province s France on the Mediterranean w of Provence

Lan·sing \'lan-sing\ city, capital of Michigan

La·nús \lə-'nüs\ city ᴇ Argentina s of Buenos Aires

Lan·zhou or **Lan–chou** \'län-'jō\ city w central China, capital of Gansu

Laoighis \'lāsh, 'lēsh\ or **Leix** \'lāsh, 'lēsh\ or formerly **Queen's** \'kwēnz\ county central Ireland in Leinster

Laos \'laús, 'lā-,äs, 'lä-ōs\ country sᴇ Asia in Indochina ɴᴇ of Thailand; a republic; capital, Vientiane

La Paz \lə-'paz, -'päz, -'päs\ city, administrative capital of Bolivia

Lap·land \'lap-,land, -lənd\ region ɴ Europe above the arctic circle in ɴ Norway, ɴ Sweden, ɴ Finland, & Kola peninsula of Russia — **Lap·land·er** \-,lan-dər, -lən-\ n

La Pla·ta \lə-'plät-ə\ city ᴇ Argentina sᴇ of Buenos Aires

L'Aqui·la \'läk-wi-lə, 'lak-\ city central Italy ɴᴇ of Rome

Las Pal·mas \lä-'späl-məs\ city Spain in the Canary islands on Grand Canary Island

La Spe·zia \lä-'spet-sē-ə\ city ɴw Italy in Liguria sᴇ of Genoa

Las·sen Peak \'las-n\ volcano 3187 meters ɴ California at s end of Cascade range in **Lassen Volcanic National Park**

Las Ve·gas \läs-'vā-gəs\ city sᴇ Nevada

Lat·a·kia \,lat-ə-'kē-ə\ city ɴw Syria

Latin America 1 Spanish America and Brazil **2** all of the Americas s of the U.S. — **Latin–American** adj — **Latin American** n

La·tium \'lā-shē-əm, -shəm\ or Italian **La·zio** \'lät-sē-ō\ region central Italy on Tyrrhenian sea; capital, Rome

Lat·via \'lat-vē-ə\ country ᴇ Europe on Baltic sea; capital, Riga; a constituent republic (**Latvian Republic**) of U.S.S.R. 1940–91

Lau·ren·tian \lò-'ren-chən\ hills ᴇ Canada in s Quebec ɴ of the Saint Lawrence on s edge of Canadian Shield

La·val \lə-'val\ city s Quebec ɴw of Montreal

Leb·a·non \'leb-ə-nən, -,nän\ **1** or ancient **Lib·a·nus** \'lib-ə-nəs\ mountains Lebanon running parallel to coast; highest Dahr el Qadib 3088 meters **2** country sw Asia on the Mediterranean; a republic; capital, Beirut — **Leb·a·nese** \,leb-ə-'nēz, -'nēs\ adj or n

Leeds \'lēdz\ city ɴ England in West Yorkshire

Lee·ward \'lē-wərd\ **1** islands Hawaii extending wɴw from main islands of the group **2** islands s Pacific in w Society islands **3** islands West Indies in ɴ Lesser Antilles

Le Ha·vre \lə-'hävr\ city ɴ France on English channel

Leices·ter \'les-tər\ city central England in Leicestershire ᴇɴᴇ of Birmingham

Leices·ter·shire \'les-tər-,shiər, -shər\ or **Leicester** county central England

Lein·ster \'len-stər\ province ᴇ Ireland

Leip·zig \'līp-sig, -sik\ city ᴇ central Germany in Saxony

Lei·trim \'lē-trəm\ county ɴw Ireland in Connacht

Leix — see ʟᴀᴏɪɢʜɪs

Leman, Lake or ancient **Lemannus** or **Lemanus** — see ɢᴇɴᴇᴠᴀ

Lemberg — see ʟᴠᴏᴠ

Lem·nos \'lem-,näs, -nəs\ or Greek **Lím·nos** \'lēm-,nòs\ island Greece in the ɴ Aegean

\ə\ abut
\ər\ further
\a\ mat
\ā\ take
\ä\ cot, cart
\aú\ out
\ch\ chin
\e\ pet
\ē\ easy
\g\ go
\i\ tip
\ī\ life
\j\ job

\ng\ sing
\ō\ bone
\ò\ saw
\òi\ coin
\th\ thin
\th\ this
\ü\ food
\ù\ foot
\y\ yet
\yü\ few
\yù\ cure
\zh\ vision

Le•na \\'lē-nə, 'lā-\\ river 4830 kilometers long **E** central Russia in Asia, flowing **NE & N** into Arctic ocean

Leningrad — see SAINT PETERSBURG

Le•ón \\lā-'ōn\\ **1** city central Mexico in Guanajuato **2** region & ancient kingdom **NW** Spain

Léopoldville — see KINSHASA

Le Puglie — see APULIA

Les•bos \\'lez-,bäs, -bəs\\ or **Myt•i•le•ne** \\,mit-l-'ē-nē\\ island Greece in the Aegean off **NW** coast of Asia Minor

Le•so•tho \\lə-'sō-tō, 'sü-,tü\\ country **S** Africa surrounded by Republic of South Africa; formerly British territory of **Ba•su•to•land** \\bə-'süt-ə-,land\\, now an independent monarchy in the Commonwealth; capital, Maseru

Lesser An•til•les \\an-'til-ēz\\ islands in the West Indies including Virgin, Leeward, & Windward islands, Barbados, Trinidad, Tobago, & islands in the **S** Caribbean **N** of Venezuela — see GREATER ANTILLES

Lesser Armenia region **S** Turkey corresponding to ancient Cilicia

Lesser Sunda — see SUNDA

Le•vant \\lə-'vant\\ the countries bordering on the **E** Mediterranean — **Lev•an•tine** \\'lev-ən-,tīn, -,tēn, lə-'van-\\ adj or n

Lew•i•sham \\'lü-ə-shəm\\ borough of **SE** Greater London, England

Lew•is with Har•ris \\,lü-ə-swəth-'har-əs, -swəth-\\ island **NW** Scotland in Outer Hebrides

Lex•ing•ton \\'lek-sing-tən\\ city **N** central Kentucky

Ley•te \\'lāt-ē\\ island Philippines in Visayan islands **S** of Samar

Lha•sa \\'läs-ə, 'las-\\ city **SW** China, capital of Tibet

Liao•ning \\lē-'aú-'ning\\ province **NE** China in **S** Manchuria; capital, Shenyang

Liao•yang \\lē-'aú-'yäng\\ city **NE** China in central Liaoning **NE** of Anshan

Libanus — see LEBANON

Li•be•ria \\lī-'bir-ē-ə\\ country **W** Africa on the Atlantic; a republic; capital, Monrovia — **Li•be•ri•an** \\-ē-ən\\ adj or n

Lib•er•ty \\'lib-ərt-ē\\ or formerly **Bed•loe's** \\'bed-,lōz\\ or **Bed•loe** \\-lō\\ island **SE** New York in Upper New York Bay; the Statue of Liberty is on it

Li•bre•ville \\'lē-brə-,vil, -,vēl\\ city, capital of Gabon

Lib•ya \\'lib-ē-ə\\ **1** the part of Africa **N** of the Sahara between Egypt & Gulf of Sidra — an ancient name **2** northern Africa **W** of Egypt — an ancient name **3** or **Libyan Arab Republic** country **N** Africa on the Mediterranean **W** of Egypt; a republic; capital, Tripoli — **Lib•y•an** \\'lib-ē-ən\\ adj or n

Libyan desert **N** Africa **W** of the Nile in Libya, Egypt, & Sudan

Li•do \\'lēd-ō\\ island Italy in Adriatic sea

Liech•ten•stein \\'lik-tən-,stīn, -,shtīn\\ country **W** Europe between Austria & Switzerland; a principality; capital, Vaduz — **Liech•ten•stein•er** \\-,stī-nər, -,shtī-\\ n

Li•ège \\lē-'ezh, -'āzh\\ or Flemish **Luik** \\'līk\\ city **E** Belgium

Lif•fey \\'lif-ē\\ river 80 kilometers long **E** Ireland flowing into Dublin Bay

Li•gu•ria \\lə-'gyùr-ē-ə\\ region **NW** Italy; capital, Genoa — **Li•gu•ri•an** \\-ē-ən\\ adj or n

Ligurian sea arm of the Mediterranean **N** of Corsica

Li•ka•si \\li-'käs-ē\\ or formerly **Ja•dot•ville** \\,zhad-ō-'vēl\\ city **SE** Zaire

Lille \\'lēl\\ city **N** France

Li•lon•gwe \\li-'lóng-wā\\ city, capital of Malawi

Li•ma \\'lē-mə\\ city, capital of Peru

Lim•burg \\'lim-,bərg\\ or French **Lim•bourg** \\'lim-,bərg, laⁿ-'búr\\ province **NE** Belgium

Lim•er•ick \\'lim-rik, -ə-rik\\ county **SW** Ireland in Munster

Límnos — see LEMNOS

Lim•po•po \\lim-'pō-pō\\ river 1610 kilometers long Africa flowing from Transvaal into Indian ocean in Mozambique

Lin•coln \\'ling-kən\\ city, capital of Nebraska

Lin•coln•shire \\'ling-kən,shiər, -shər\\ or **Lincoln** county **E** England

Lind•sey, Parts of \\'lin-zē\\ district & former administrative county **E** England in **N** Lincolnshire

Line \\'līn\\ islands Kiribati **S** of Hawaii, formerly divided between U.S. & Great Britain

Lip•a•ri \\'lip-ə-rē\\ islands Italy off **NE** Sicily

Li•petsk \\'lē-,petsk\\ city **S** central Russia in Europe, **N** of Voronezh

Lis•bon \\'liz-bən\\ or Portuguese **Lis•boa** \\lēzh-'vō-ə\\ city, capital of Portugal

Lith•u•a•nia \\,lith-ə-'wā-nē-ə, ,lith-yə-, -nyə\\ country **E** Europe; capital, Vilnius; a constituent republic (**Lithuanian Republic**) of U.S.S.R. 1940–91

Lit•tle Rock \\'lit-l-,räk\\ city, capital of Arkansas

Liv•er•pool \\'liv-ər-,púl\\ city **NW** England in Merseyside

Li•vo•nia \\lə-'vō-nē-ə, -nyə\\ **1** city **SE** Michigan **2** region **E** Europe on Baltic sea in Latvia & Estonia

Lju•blja•na \\lē-,ü-blē-'än-ə\\ city central Slovenia on Sava river

Lla•no Es•ta•ca•do \\'lan-ō-,es-tə-'käd-ō, 'län-\\ or **Staked Plain** \\'stākt-, 'stāk-\\ plateau region **SE** New Mexico & **NW** Texas

Lodz \\'lúj, 'lädz\\ city central Poland **WSW** of Warsaw

Lo•fo•ten \\'lō-,fōt-n\\ islands **NW** Norway

Lo•gan, Mount \\'lō-gən\\ mountain 6050 meters **NW** Canada in Saint Elias range; highest in Canada & second highest in North America

Loire \\lə-'wär\\ river 1005 kilometers long central France flowing **NW** & **W** into Bay of Biscay

Lo•mas de Za•mo•ra \\'lō-,mäz-də-zə-'mōr-ə, -'mór-\\ city **E** Argentina **SW** of Buenos Aires

Lom•bar•dy \\'läm-,bärd-ē, -bərd-\\ region **N** Italy **N** of Po river; capital, Milan

Lo•mé \\lō-'mā\\ city, capital of Togo

Lo•mond, Loch \\'lō-mənd\\ lake **S** central Scotland

Lon•don \\'lən-dən\\ **1** city **S** Ontario, Canada **2** city, capital of England & of United Kingdom on the Thames; comprises **City of London** & 12 inner boroughs of Greater London — **Lon•don•er** \\-də-nər\\ n

Londonderry — see DERRY

Long Beach city **SW** California **S** of Los Angeles

Long•ford \\'lóng-fərd\\ county **E** central Ireland in Leinster

Long Island island 190 kilometers long **SE** New York **S** of Connecticut

Long Island Sound inlet of the Atlantic between Connecticut & Long Island, New York

Lon•gueuil \\lóng-'gāl\\ city Canada in **S** Quebec **E** of Montreal

Lor•raine \\lə-'rān, ló-\\ region **NE** France around upper Moselle & Meuse rivers — see ALSACE- LORRAINE

Los An•ge•les \\lō-'san-jə-ləs also -'sang-gə-ləs\\ city **SW** California

Lo•thi•an \\'lō-thē-ən\\ region **SE** Scotland **S** of Firth of Forth; established 1975; includes Edinburgh

Lou•ise, Lake \\lú-'ēz\\ lake **SW** Alberta in Banff National Park

Lou•i•si•ana \\lú-,ē-zē-'an-ə, ,lü-ə-zē-, ,lü-zē-\\ state **S** U.S.; capital, Baton Rouge — **Lou•i•si•an•ian** \\-'an-ē-ən, -'an-yən\\ or **Lou•i•si•an•an** \\-'an-ən\\ adj or n

Louisiana Purchase area **W** central U.S. between Rocky mountains & the Mississippi purchased 1803 from France

Lou•is•ville \\'lü-i-,vil, -vəl\\ city **N** Kentucky on the Ohio river

Lourenço Marques — see MAPUTO

Louth \\'laúth\\ county **E** Ireland in Leinster

Low Countries region **W** Europe comprising modern Belgium, Luxembourg, & the Netherlands

Lower California — see BAJA CALIFORNIA

Lower Canada former province, Canada in **S** part of present-day Quebec

Lower Saxony *or German* **Nie·der·sach·sen** \,nēd-ər-'zäk-sən\ state NW Germany; capital, Hannover

Low·lands \'lō-ləndz, -lənz, -,landz, -,lanz\ the central & E part of Scotland lying between the Highlands & the Southern Uplands

Lu·an·da \lü-'an-də\ city, capital of Angola

Lub·bock \'ləb-ək\ city NW Texas

Lü·beck \'lü-,bek, 'lue-\ city N Germany NE of Hamburg

Lu·blin \'lü-blən, -,blēn\ city E Poland SE of Warsaw

Lu·bum·ba·shi \,lü-büm-'bäsh-ē\ *or formerly* **Elis·a·beth·ville** \i-'liz-ə-bəth-,vil\ city SE Zaire

Lu·cerne, Lake of \lü-'sərn\ lake central Switzerland

Luchow — see HEFEI

Luck·now \'lək-,naú\ city N India, capital of Uttar Pradesh

Lü·da *or* **Lü–ta** \'lü-'dä\ *or* **Dai–ren** \'dī-'ren\ city NE China in S Liaoning

Lu·dhi·a·na \,lüd-ē-'än-ə\ city NW India in Punjab SE of Amritsar

Luik — see LIÈGE

Luluabourg — see KANANGA

Lu·sa·ka \lü-'säk-ə\ city, capital of Zambia

Lü·shun \'lü-'shün\ *or* **Port Ar·thur** \'är-thər\ city NE China in S Liaoning

Lusitania — see PORTUGAL

Lu·ton \'lüt-n\ borough SE central England in Bedfordshire

Lux·em·bourg *or* **Lux·em·burg** \'lək-səm-,bərg, 'lük-səm-,bürg\ **1** country W Europe bordered by Belgium, France, & Germany; a grand duchy **2** city, its capital — **Lux·em·bourg·er** \-,bər-gər, -,bür-\ *n* — **Lux·em·bourg·ian** \,lək-səm-'bər-gē-ən, ,lük-səm-'bür-\ *adj*

Lu·zon \lü-'zän\ island N Philippines

Lvov \lə-'vóf, -'vóv\ *or Polish* **Lwów** \lə-'vüf, -'vüv\ *or German* **Lem·berg** \'lem-,bərg, -,berg\ *or Ukrainian* **Lwiw** \lə-'vēf\ city W Ukraine

Lyallpur — see FAISALABAD

Ly·cia \'lish-ə, 'lish-ē-ə\ ancient district & Roman province SW Asia Minor

Lyd·ia \'lid-ē-ə\ ancient country W Asia Minor on the Aegean; capital, Sardis — **Lyd·i·an** \-ē-ən\ *adj or n*

Ly·ons \lē-'ōⁿ, 'lī-ənz\ *or* **Lyon** \'lyōⁿ\ *or ancient* **Lug·du·num** \lúg-'dü-nəm, ,ləg-\ city SE central France

Maas — see MEUSE

Ma·cao *or Portuguese* **Ma·cau** \mə-'kaú\ **1** Portuguese territory on coast of SE China W of Hong Kong **2** city, its capital — **Mac·a·nese** \,mak-ə-'nēz, -'nēs\ *n*

Macassar — see UJUNG PANDANG

Mac·e·do·nia \,mas-ə-'dō-nyə, -nē-ə\ region S Europe in Balkan peninsula in NE Greece, S Yugoslavia, and SW Bulgaria including territory of ancient kingdom of Macedonia (**Mac·e·don** \'mas-əd-ən, -ə-,dän\) — **Mac·e·do·nian** \,mas-ə-'dō-nyən, -nē-ən\ *adj or n*

Ma·ceió \,mas-ā-'ō\ city NE Brazil

Mac·gil·li·cud·dy's Reeks \mə-,gil-ə-,kəd-ēz-'rēks\ mountains SW Ireland in Kerry; highest Carrantuohill 1041 meters

Ma·chi·da \mə-'chē-də, 'mä-chi-,dä\ city Japan on Honshu

Ma·chi·li·pat·nam \,məch-ə-lə-'pət-nəm\ *or* **Ban·dar** \'bənd-ər\ city SE India in E Andhra Pradesh

Ma·chu Pic·chu \,mäch-ü-'pēk-chü\ site SE Peru of ancient Inca city NW of Cuzco

Mac·ken·zie \mə-'ken-zē\ **1** river 1800 kilometers long NW Canada flowing from Great Slave Lake NW into Beaufort sea **2** former district NW Canada in W Northwest Territories in basin of Mackenzie river

Ma·khach·ka·la \mə-,käch-kə-'lä\ city S Russia in Europe, on the Caspian

Mack·i·nac, Straits of \'mak-ə-,nó\ channel N Michigan connecting Lakes Huron & Michigan

McKinley, Mount \mə-'kin-lē\ *or* **De·na·li** \də-'näl-ē\ mountain 6194 meters S central Alaska in Alaska range; highest in U.S. & North America; in **Denali National Park**

Ma·con \'mā-kən\ city central Georgia

Mad·a·gas·car \,mad-ə-'gas-kər\ *or formerly* **Mal·a·gasy Republic** \,mal-ə-,gas-ē\ island W Indian ocean off SE Africa; a republic; capital, Antananarivo — **Mad·a·gas·can** \,mad-ə-'gas-kən\ *adj or n*

Ma·dei·ra \mə-'dir-ə, -'der-\ **1** river 3380 kilometers long W Brazil flowing NE into the Amazon **2** islands in the N Atlantic N of the Canaries belonging to Portugal; capital, Funchal **3** island; chief of the Madeira group — **Ma·dei·ran** \-ən\ *adj or n*

Ma·dhya Pra·desh \,mäd-yə-prə-'desh, -'däsh\ state central India; capital, Bhopal

Mad·i·son \'mad-ə-sən\ city, capital of Wisconsin

Ma·dras \mə-'dras, -'dräs\ **1** — see TAMIL NADU **2** city SE India, capital of Tamil Nadu

Ma·drid \mə-'drid\ city, capital of Spain

Ma·du·ra \mə-'dúr-ə\ island Indonesia NE of Java

Ma·du·rai \,mäd-ə-'rī\ *or* **Ma·du·ra** \'maj-ə-rə\ city S India in S Tamil Nadu

Mag·de·burg \'mäg-də-,bùrg, 'mag-də-,bərg\ city central Germany WSW of Berlin

Magellan, Strait of \mə-'jel-ən\ strait at S end of South America between mainland & Tierra del Fuego archipelago

Mageröy — see NORTH CAPE

Mag·gio·re, Lake \mə-'jōr-ē, -'jòr-\ lake N Italy & S Switzerland

Mag·ni·to·gorsk \mag-'nēt-ə-,górsk\ city SW Russia in Asia, on Ural river

Ma·hal·la el Ku·bra \mə-,hal-ə-el-'kü-brə\ city N Egypt in Nile delta

Ma·ha·rash·tra \,mä-hə-'räsh-trə\ state W India on Arabian sea; capital, Bombay

Main \'mīn, 'mān\ river 490 kilometers long S central Germany flowing W into the Rhine

Maine \'mān\ state NE U.S.; capital, Augusta

Mainz \'mīns\ city W Germany on the Rhine, capital of Rhineland-Palatinate

Ma·jor·ca \mə-'jór-kə, -'yòr-\ *or Spanish* **Ma·llor·ca** \mə-'yòr-kə\ island Spain; largest of the Balearic islands — **Ma·jor·can** \-'jòr-kən, -'yòr-\ *adj or n*

Ma·ka·lu \'mək-ə-,lü\ mountain 8481 meters NE Nepal in the Himalayas

Makasar *or* **Makassar** — see UJUNG PANDANG

Ma·ke·yev·ka \mə-'kā-əf-kə, -yəf-\ city E Ukraine in Donets basin

Mal·a·bar \'mal-ə-,bär\ coast region SW India on Arabian sea in Karnataka & Kerala states

Ma·la·bo \mä-'läb-ō\ *or formerly* **San·ta Isa·bel** \,san-tə-'iz-ə-bel\ city, capital of Equatorial Guinea

Ma·lac·ca, Strait of \mə-'lak-ə, -'läk-\ channel between S Malay peninsula & island of Sumatra

Má·la·ga \'mal-ə-gə\ city S Spain in Andalusia

Ma·lang \mə-'läng\ city Indonesia in E Java

Ma·la·wi \mə-'lä-wē, -'laù-ē\ *or formerly* **Ny·asa·land** \nī-'as-ə-,land, nē-\ country SE Africa on Lake Nyasa; a former British protectorate; independent republic since 1964; capital, Lilongwe

Malawi, Lake — see NYASA

Ma·lay \mə-'lā, 'mā-lā\ **1** archipelago SE Asia including Sumatra, Java, Borneo, Sulawesi, Moluccas, & Timor; usually considered as including the Philippines & sometimes New Guinea **2** peninsula about 1100 kilometers long SE Asia divided between Thailand & Federation of Malaysia

Ma·laya \mə-'lā-ə, mā-\ **1** the Malay peninsula **2** *or* **Federation of Malaya** former country SE Asia on Malay peninsula; since 1963 part of Federation of Malaysia — see PENINSULAR MALAYSIA

Ma·lay·sia \mə-'lā-zhə, -shə, -zhē-ə, -shē-ə\ **1** the Malay archipelago **2** the Malay peninsula & Malay archipelago **3** *or* **Federation of Malaysia** country SE Asia, a union of Malaya, Sabah (North Borneo), Sarawak, & (until 1965) Singapore; a limited constitutional

\ə\ abut	\ng\ sing	
\ər\ further	\ō\ bone	
\a\ mat	\ó\ saw	
\ā\ take	\ói\ coin	
\ä\ cot, cart	\th\ thin	
\aú\ out	\th\ this	
\ch\ chin	\ü\ food	
\e\ pet	\ú\ foot	
\ē\ easy	\y\ yet	
\g\ go	\yü\ few	
\i\ tip	\yù\ cure	
\ī\ life	\zh\ vision	
\j\ job		

monarchy; capital, Kuala Lumpur — **Ma·lay·sian** \mə-'lā-zhən, -shən\ *adj or n*

Mal·dive \'mȯl-,dēv, -,dīv\ islands in Indian ocean s of the Laccadives; formerly a sultanate under British protection; since 1965 **Republic of Maldives**; capital, Male — **Mal·div·i·an** \mȯl-'div-ē-ən\ *adj or n*

Ma·li \'mäl-ē, 'mal-ē\ *or formerly* **French Sudan** country w Africa; a republic; capital, Bamako — **Ma·li·an** \-ē-ən\ *adj or n*

Malmö \'mal-,mər, 'mal-,mœ̄\ city sw Sweden

Mal·ta \'mȯl-tə\ **1** islands in the Mediterranean s of Sicily; a former British colony; an independent republic since 1964; capital, Valletta **2** island, chief of the group

Maluku — see MOLUCCAS

Malvinas, Islas — see FALKLAND

Mam·moth Cave \,mam-əth-\ limestone caverns sw central Kentucky in **Mammoth Cave National Park**

Man, Isle of \'man\ island British Isles in Irish sea; capital, Douglas; has own legislature & laws

Ma·na·do \mə-'näd-,ō\ city & port Indonesia on NE Sulawesi

Ma·na·gua \mə-'näg-wə\ city, capital of Nicaragua

Ma·na·ma \mə-'nam-ə\ city, capital of Bahrain

Ma·naus \mə-'naus\ city w Brazil on Rio Negro 20 kilometers above its junction with the Amazon

Man·ches·ter \'man-,ches-tər, -chə-stər\ city NW England in Lancashire — see GREATER MANCHESTER

Man·chu·kuo \'man-'chü-'kwō, man-'chü-,\ former country (1931–45) E Asia in Manchuria & E Inner Mongolia; capital, Changchun

Man·chu·ria \man-'chur-ē-ə\ region NE China s of the Amur — **Man·chu·ri·an** \man-'chur-ē-ən\ *adj or n*

Man·da·lay \,man-də-'lā\ city central Myanmar

Man·hat·tan \man-'hat-n, mən-\ **1** island sE New York in New York City **2** borough of New York City comprising chiefly Manhattan Island

Manihiki — see NORTHERN COOK

Ma·nila \mə-'nil-ə\ city, capital of Philippines

Ma·ni·pur \,man-ə-'pur, ,mən-\ state NE India between Assam & Myanmar; capital, Imphal

Man·i·to·ba \,man-ə-'tō-bə\ province central Canada; capital, Winnipeg — **Man·i·to·ban** \-'tō-bən\ *adj or n*

Man·i·tou·lin \,man-ə-'tü-lən\ island 130 kilometers long s Ontario in Lake Huron

Ma·ni·za·les \,man-ə-'zäl-əs, -'zal-\ city w central Colombia

Man·nar, Gulf of \mə-'när\ inlet of Indian ocean between Sri Lanka & s tip of India

Mann·heim \'man-,hīm, 'män-\ city sw Germany on the Rhine NW of Stuttgart

Man·za·ni·llo \,man-zə-'nē-ō, -yō\ city sw Mexico in Colima on the Pacific

Ma·pu·to \mä-'pü-tō\ *or formerly* **Lou·ren·ço Marquez** \lə-,ren-sō-,mär-'kes, -'märks, -'märk\ city, capital of Mozambique

Mar·a·cai·bo \,mar-ə-'kī-bō\ city NW Venezuela

Maracaibo, Lake the s extension of Gulf of Venezuela in NW Venezuela

Ma·ra·cay \,mär-ə-'kī\ city N Venezuela

Mar·a·thon \'mar-ə-,thän, -thən\ plain E Greece in Attica NE of Athens

March·es \'mär-chəz\ region central Italy on the Adriatic; capital, Ancona

Mar del Pla·ta \,mär-del-'plät-ə\ city & port E Argentina

Mar·i·ana \,mar-ē-'an-ə, ,mer-\ islands w Pacific N of Caroline islands including the Northern Marianas and Guam

Ma·ri·a·nao \,mär-ē-ə-'naù\ city w Cuba w of Havana

Mariana Trench ocean trench w Pacific extending from sE of Guam to NW of Mariana islands; deepest in world

Maritime Alps section of the w Alps sE France & NW Italy extending N from Mediterranean coast

Maritime Provinces the Canadian provinces of New Brunswick, Nova Scotia, & Prince Edward Island and sometimes thought to include Newfoundland

Ma·ri·u·pol \,mar-ē-'ü-,pȯl\ *or 1949–89* **Zhda·nov** \zhe-'dä-nəf, 'shtä-\ city E Ukraine on Sea of Azov

Mark·ham, Mount \'mär-kəm\ mountain 4351 meters Antarctica E of Ross Ice Shelf

Mar·ma·ra, Sea of *or* **Sea of Mar·mo·ra** \'mär-mə-rə\ *or ancient* **Pro·pon·tis** \prə-'pänt-əs\ sea NW Turkey connected with Black sea by the Bosporus & with Aegean sea by the Dardanelles

Marne \'märn\ river 523 kilometers long NE France flowing w into the Seine

Mar·que·sas \mär-'kā-zəz, -zəs, -səz, -səs\ islands s Pacific N of Tuamotu archipelago in French Polynesia — **Mar·que·san** \-zən, -sən\ *adj or n*

Mar·ra·kech \mə-'räk-ish, ,mar-ə-'kesh\ *or formerly* **Mo·roc·co** \mə-'räk-ō\ city central Morocco

Mar·seilles \mär-'sā, -'sālz\ *or* **Mar·seille** \mär-'sā\ *or ancient* **Mas·sil·ia** \mə-'sil-ē-ə\ city sE France

Mar·shall \'mär-shəl\ islands w Pacific E of the Carolines in Trust Territory of the Pacific Islands

Mar·tha's Vineyard \,mär-thəz-\ island sE Massachusetts off sw coast of Cape Cod WNW of Nantucket

Mar·ti·nique \,märt-n-'ēk\ island West Indies in the Windwards; an overseas department of France; capital, Fort-de-France

Mary·land \'mer-ə-lənd\ state E U.S.; capital, Annapolis — **Mary·land·er** \-lən-dər, -,lan-\ *n*

Ma·san \'mäs-,än\ city South Korea E of Pusan

Mas·e·ru \'maz-ə-,rü\ city, capital of Lesotho

Mash·had \mə-'shad\ city NE Iran

Ma·son–Dix·on Line \,mās-n-'dik-sən-\ boundary between Maryland & Pennsylvania; was in part boundary between free & slave states

Mas·sa·chu·setts \,mas-ə-'chü-səts, ,mas-'chü-, -zəts\ state NE U.S.; capital, Boston

Mas·sif Cen·tral \ma-,sēf-,sen-'träl, -,sän-'träl\ plateau central France w of the Rhone-Saône valley — see AUVERGNE, CÉVENNES

Mat·a·be·le·land \,mat-ə-'bē-lē-,land\ region sw Zimbabwe; chief town, Bulawayo

Ma·to Gros·so \,mat-ə-'grō-sō\ plateau region sw Brazil in E central Mato Grosso state

Mat·su·do \mät-'sü-dō\ city Japan in sE Honshu NE of Tokyo

Ma·tsu·shi·ma \,mät-sü-'shē-mə, mät-'sü-shi-mə\ group of islets Japan off N Honshu NE of Sendai

Ma·tsu·ya·ma \,mät-sə-'yäm-ə\ city Japan in w Shikoku

Mat·ter·horn \'mat-ər-,hȯrn, 'mät-\ mountain 4478 meters in Pennine Alps on border between Switzerland & Italy

Maui \'maù-ē\ island Hawaii NW of Hawaii Island

Mau·na Kea \,maù-nə-'kā-ə\ extinct volcano 4205 meters Hawaii in N central Hawaii Island

Mau·na Loa \,maù-nə-'lō-ə\ volcano 4170 meters Hawaii in s central Hawaii Island in Hawaii Volcanoes National Park

Mau·re·ta·nia *or* **Mau·ri·ta·nia** \,mȯr-ə-'tā-nē-ə, ,mär-, -nyə\ ancient country NW Africa in modern Morocco & w Algeria — **Mau·re·ta·ni·an** \-nē-ən, -nyən\ *adj or n*

Mauritania country NW Africa on the Atlantic N of Senegal river; a republic; capital, Nouakchott — **Mauritanian** *adj or n*

Mau·ri·tius \mȯ-'rish-əs, -'rish-ē-əs\ island in Indian ocean E of Madagascar; a dominion of the Commonwealth; capital, Port Louis — **Mau·ri·tian** \-'rish-ən\ *adj or n*

May, Cape \'mā\ cape s New Jersey at entrance to Delaware Bay

Mayo \'mā-ō\ county NW Ireland in Connacht

Ma·yon, Mount \mä-'yōn\ volcano 2525 meters Philippines in sE Luzon

Ma·za·ma, Mount \mə-'zäm-ə\ prehistoric mountain sw Oregon the collapse of whose summit formed Crater Lake in Crater Lake National Park

Ma·za·tlán \,mäz-ə-'tlän, ,mäs-\ city w Mexico in Sinaloa on the Pacific

Mba·bane \,em-bə-'bän\ city, capital of Swaziland

Mban·da·ka \,em-,bän-'däk-ə\ *or formerly* **Co·qui·lhat·ville** \,kō-kē-'at-,vil\ city w Zaire

Mbi·ni \em-'bē-nē\ *or formerly* **Río Mu·ni** \,rē-ō-'mü-nē\ mainland portion of Equatorial Guinea on Gulf of Guinea

Mbuji–Mayi \em-,bü-jē-'mī-,ē\ *or formerly* **Ba·kwan·ga** \bə-'kwäng-gə\ city s Zaire

Mead, Lake \'mēd\ reservoir nw Arizona & se Nevada formed by Hoover Dam in Colorado river

Meath \'mēth, 'mēth\ county e Ireland in Leinster

Mec·ca \'mek-ə\ city w Saudi Arabia, capital of Hejaz

Me·dan \mä-'dän\ city Indonesia in ne Sumatra

Me·de·llín \,med-l-'ēn, ,mä-thə-'yēn\ city nw Colombia

Me·dia \'mēd-ē-ə\ ancient country & province of Persian Empire

Me·di·na \mə-'dē-nə\ city w Saudi Arabia

Mediolanum — see MILAN

Med·i·ter·ra·nean \,med-ə-tə-'rā-nē-ən, -nyən\ sea 3750 kilometers long between Europe & Africa connecting with the Atlantic through Strait of Gibraltar

Mee·rut \'mā-rət, 'mir-ət\ city n India in nw Uttar Pradesh

Me·gha·la·ya \,mä-gə-'lā-ə\ state ne India; created 1972 out of sw part of Assam; capital, Shillong

Méjico — see MEXICO

Mek·nes \mek-'nes\ city n Morocco

Me·kong \'mā-'kòng, -'käng\ river 4185 kilometers long se Asia flowing from e Tibet s & se into South China sea in s Vietnam

Mel·a·ne·sia \,mel-ə-'nē-zhə, -shə\ islands of the Pacific ne of Australia & s of Micronesia including Bismarck archipelago, the Solomons, Vanuatu, New Caledonia, & the Fijis

Mel·bourne \'mel-bərn\ city se Australia, capital of Victoria

Me·los *or Greek* **Mí·los** \'mē-,läs\ island Greece in sw Cyclades — **Me·li·an** \'mē-lē-ən\ *adj or n*

Mel·ville \'mel-,vil\ island n Canada in n Northwest Territories in Parry islands

Me·mel \'mā-məl\ city w Lithuania

Mem·phis \'mem-fəs, 'memp-\ **1** city sw Tennessee **2** ancient city n Egypt s of modern Cairo

Men·do·ci·no, Cape \,men-də-'sē-nō\ headland nw California

Menorca — see MINORCA

Mer·cia \'mər-shə, -shē-ə\ ancient Anglo-Saxon kingdom central England — **Mer·cian** \'mər-shən\ *adj or n*

Mé·ri·da \'mer-əd-ə\ city se Mexico, capital of Yucatán

Mer·i·on·eth·shire \,mer-ē-'än-əth-,shiər, -shər\ *or* **Merioneth** former county nw Wales

Mer·sey \'mər-zē\ river 110 kilometers long nw England flowing nw & w into Irish sea through a large estuary

Mer·sey·side \'mər-zē-,sīd\ metropolitan county nw England; includes Liverpool

Mer·ton \'mərt-n\ borough of sw Greater London, England

Me·sa \'mā-sə\ city sw central Arizona e of Phoenix

Me·sa·bi range \mə-'säb-ē\ region ne Minnesota that contains iron ore

Me·sa Verde National Park \,mä-sə-'vərd-ē, -'vərd\ reservation sw Colorado containing prehistoric cliff dwellings

Mes·o·po·ta·mia \,mes-ə-pə-'tā-mē-ə, -myə\ **1** region sw Asia between Euphrates & Tigris rivers **2** the entire Tigris-Euphrates valley — **Mes·o·po·ta·mian** \-mē-ən, -myən\ *adj or n*

Mes·si·na \mə-'sē-nə\ city Italy in ne Sicily

Messina, Strait of channel between ne Sicily & sw tip of Italian peninsula

Meuse \'myüz, 'myərz, French mœz\ *or Dutch* **Maas** \'mäs\ river 925 kilometers long w Europe flowing from ne France into North sea in the Netherlands

Mex·i·cali \,mek-si-'kal-ē\ city nw Mexico, capital of Baja California

Mex·i·co \'mek-si-,kō\ *or Spanish* **Mé·ji·co** \'me-hē-kō\ **1** country s North America; a republic **2** *or* **Mexico City** city, its capital, in Federal District **3** state s central Mexico; capital, Toluca

Mexico, Gulf of inlet of the Atlantic se North America

Mi·ami \mī-'am-ē, -'am-ə\ city se Florida

Mich·i·gan \'mish-i-gən\ state n central U.S.; capital, Lansing — **Mich·i·gan·der** \,mish-i-'gan-dər\ *n* — **Mich·i·gan·ite** \'mish-i-gə-,nīt\ *n*

Michigan, Lake lake n central U.S.; one of the Great Lakes

Mi·cho·acán \,mē-chə-wä-'kän\ state sw Mexico on the Pacific; capital, Morelia

Mi·cro·ne·sia \,mī-krə-'nē-zhə, -shə\ islands of the w Pacific e of the Philippines & n of Melanesia including Caroline, Kiribati, Mariana, & Marshall groups — **Mi·cro·ne·sian** \-zhən, -shən\ *adj or n*

Middle Congo — see CONGO

Middle East the countries of sw Asia & n Africa — usually considered as including the countries extending from Libya on the w to Afghanistan on the e — **Middle Eastern** *or* **Mid·east·ern** \'mid-'ē-stərn\ *adj*

Mid·dles·brough \'mid-lz-brə\ town n England in Cleveland; formerly a county borough in North Riding, Yorkshire

Mid·dle·sex \'mid-l-,seks\ former county se England including nw part of present Greater London

Mid Gla·mor·gan \'mid-glə-'mòr-gən\ county se Wales; established 1974

Mi·di \mē-'dē\ the south of France

Mid·i·an \'mid-ē-ən\ ancient region nw Arabia e of Gulf of Aqaba — **Mid·i·an·ite** \-ē-ə-,nīt\ *n*

Mid·lands \'mid-ləndz, -lənz\ the central counties of England — see WEST MIDLANDS

Mid·lo·thi·an \mid-'lō-thē-ən\ former county se Scotland; chief city, Edinburgh

Mid·way \'mid-,wā\ islands (atoll) central Pacific in Hawaiian group 2090 kilometers wnw of Honolulu belonging to U.S.; not included in state of Hawaii

Mid·west *or* **Middle West** \'mid-'west\ region n central U.S. including area around Great Lakes & in upper Mississippi valley from Ohio on the e to North & South Dakota, Nebraska, & Kansas on the w — **Mid·west·ern** \'mid-'wes-tərn\ *or* **Middle Western** *adj* — **Mid·west·ern·er** \'mid-'wes-tər-nər, -tə-nər\ *or* **Middle Western·er** *n*

Mi·lan \mə-'lan, -'län\ *or Italian* **Mi·la·no** \mi-'län-ō\ *or ancient* **Me·di·o·la·num** \,med-ē-ō-'lā-nəm\ city nw Italy, capital of Lombardy — **Mil·a·nese** \,mil-ə-'nēz, -'nēs\ *adj or n*

Mílos — see MELOS

Mil·wau·kee \mil-'wò-kē\ city se Wisconsin

Mi·nas Basin \,mī-nəs-\ landlocked bay central Nova Scotia; ne extension of Bay of Fundy

Min·da·nao \,min-də-'nä-ō, -'naù\ island s Philippines

Min·do·ro \min-'dōr-ō, -'dòr-\ island central Philippines

Minhow — see FUZHOU

Min·ne·ap·o·lis \,min-ē-'ap-ləs, -ə-ləs\ city se Minnesota

Min·ne·so·ta \,min-ə-'sōt-ə\ state n central U.S.; capital, Saint Paul — **Min·ne·so·tan** \-'sōt-n\ *adj or n*

Mi·nor·ca \mə-'nòr-kə\ *or Spanish* **Me·nor·ca** \mā-\ island Spain in Balearic islands — **Mi·nor·can** \mə-'nòr-kən\ *adj or n*

Minsk \'minsk\ city, capital of Belarus

Mi·que·lon \'mik-ə-,län, French mēk-lō^n, mēk-ə-\ island off s coast of Newfoundland belonging to France — see SAINT PIERRE

Mis·sis·sau·ga \,mis-ə-'sòg-ə\ city Canada in s Ontario

Mis·sis·sip·pi \,mis-ə-'sip-ē, mis-'sip-ē\ **1** river 3975 kilometers long central U.S. flowing into Gulf of Mexico — see ITASCA (Lake) **2** state s U.S.; capital, Jackson

Mis·sou·ri \mə-'zùr-ē, -'zùr-ə\ **1** river 4345 kilometers long w U.S. flowing from sw Montana to the Mississip-

\ə\ abut		\ng\ sing
\ər\ further		\ō\ bone
\a\ mat		\ò\ saw
\ā\ take		\òi\ coin
\ä\ cot, cart		\th\ thin
\aù\ out		\th\ this
\ch\ chin		\ü\ food
\e\ pet		\ù\ foot
\ē\ easy		\y\ yet
\g\ go		\yü\ few
\i\ tip		\yù\ cure
\ī\ life		\zh\ vision
\j\ job		

pi in **E** Missouri **2** state central U.S.; capital, Jefferson City — **Mis·sou·ri·an** \-'zùr-ē-ən\ *adj or n*

Mitch·ell, Mount \'mich-əl\ mountain 2037 meters **w** North Carolina in Black mountains of the Appalachians; highest in U.S. **E** of the Mississippi

Mi·ya·za·ki \mē-,äz-'äk-ē, -,yäz-; mē-'äz-ə-kē, -'yäz-\ city Japan in **SE** Kyushu

Mi·zo·ram \mi-'zór-əm\ state **NE** India

Mo·ab \'mō-,ab\ region Jordan **E** of Dead sea; in biblical times a kingdom

Mo·bile \mō-'bēl, 'mō-,bēl\ city **sw** Alabama on Mobile Bay

Moçambique — see MOZAMBIQUE

Mo·de·na \'mòd-n-ə, -n-,ä\ city **N** Italy **sw** of Venice

Moe·sia \'mē-shə, -shē-ə\ ancient country & Roman province **s** of the Danube in modern Bulgaria & Serbia

Mog·a·di·shu \,mäg-ə-'dish-ü, -'dēsh-\ *or* **Mog·a·di·scio** \-ō\ city, capital of Somalia

Mo·hen·jo–Da·ro \mō-,hen-jō-'där-ō\ prehistoric city Pakistan in Indus valley **NE** of modern Karachi

Mo·ja·ve *or* **Mo·ha·ve** \mə-'häv-ē\ desert **s** California **SE** of **s** end of Sierra Nevada

Mo·ji \'mō-jē\ city Japan in **N** Kyushu

Mol·do·va \mäl-'dō-və, mòl-\ country **E** Moldavia region; capital, Kishinev; formerly a constituent republic of U.S.S.R.

Mol·da·via \mäl-'dāv-ē-ə, -vyə\ **1** region **E** Europe in **NE** Romania & Moldova **w** of the Dniester **2** — see MOLDOVA — **Mol·da·vian** \-vē-ən, -vyən\ *adj or n*

Mo·li·se \'mò-li-,zā\ region central Italy on the Adriatic; capital, Campobasso

Mol·o·kai \,mäl-ə-'kī, ,mō-lə-\ island Hawaii **ESE** of Oahu

Molotov — see PERM

Mo·luc·cas \mə-'lək-əz\ *or* **Spice Islands** \'spīs\ *or Indonesian* **Ma·lu·ku** \mə-'lü-kü\ islands Indonesia **E** of Sulawesi — **Mo·luc·ca** \mə-'lək-ə\ *adj* — **Mo·luc·can** \-ən\ *adj or n*

Mom·ba·sa \mäm-'bäs-ə\ city **s** Kenya on Mombasa Island

Mo·na·co \'män-ə-,kō *also* mə-'näk-ō\ country **w** Europe on Mediterranean coast of France; a principality; capital, Monaco — **Mo·na·can** \'mä-ə-kən, mə-'näk-ən\ *adj or n* — **Mon·e·gasque** \,män-i-'gask\ *n*

Mon·a·ghan \'män-ə-hən, -,han\ county **NE** Republic of Ireland in Ulster

Mön·chen·glad·bach \,mœn-kən-'glät-,bäḵ\ city **w** Germany

Mon·go·lia \män-'gōl-yə, mäng-, -'gō-lē-ə\ **1** region **E** Asia **E** of Altai mountains; includes Gobi desert **2** INNER MONGOLIA **3** *or* **Outer Mongolia** country **E** Asia comprising major portion of Mongolia; capital, Ulan Bator

Mon·mouth·shire \'män-məth-,shiər, 'mən-, -,shər\ *or* **Monmouth** former county **SE** Wales bordering on England

Mon·ro·via \mən-'rō-vē-ə, ,mən-\ city, capital of Liberia

Mon·tana \män-'tan-ə\ state **NW** U.S.; capital, Helena — **Mon·tan·an** \-ən\ *adj or n*

Mont Blanc \mōⁿ-'bläⁿ\ mountain 4807 meters **SE** France on Italian border; highest in the Alps

Mon·te·ne·gro \,mänt-ə-'nē-grō, -'nā-\ federated republic **w** Yugoslavia on the Adriatic; capital, Titograd — **Mon·te·ne·grin** \-grən\ *adj or n*

Mon·ter·rey \,mänt-ə-'rā\ city **NE** Mexico, capital of Nuevo León

Mon·te·vi·deo \,mänt-ə-və-'dā-ō, -'vid-ē-,ō\ city, capital of Uruguay

Mont·gom·ery \mənt-'gəm-rē, mänt-, mən-, män-, -'gäm-, -ə-rē\ city, capital of Alabama

Mont·gom·ery·shire \-,shiər, -,shər\ *or* **Montgomery** former county **E** Wales

Mont·pe·lier \mänt-'pēl-yər, -'pil-\ city, capital of Vermont

Mon·tre·al \,män-trē-'ól, ,mən-\ city **s** Quebec on Montreal Island in the Saint Lawrence

Mont–Saint–Mi·chel \mōⁿ-saⁿ-mē-'shel\ islet **NW** France off coast of Brittany in Gulf of Saint-Malo

Mont·ser·rat \,män-sə-'rat\ island British West Indies in the Leewards; capital, Plymouth

Mo·ra·via \mə-'rä-vē-ə\ region **E** Czech Republic; chief city, Brno

Mor·ay \'mər-ē, 'mə-rē\ *or* **Mor·ay·shire** \-,shiər, -,shər\ former county **NE** Scotland

Mo·rea \mə-'rē-ə\ PELOPONNESUS — an old name — **Mo·re·an** \-'rē-ən\ *adj or n*

Mo·re·los \mə-'rä-ləs\ state **s** central Mexico; capital, Cuernavaca

Mo·roc·co \mə-'räk-ō\ **1** country **NW** Africa; a kingdom; capital, Rabat; formerly divided into **French Morocco** (capital, Rabat), **Spanish Morocco** (capital, Tetuán) & **International Zone** of Tangier **2** — see MARRAKECH — **Mo·roc·can** \-'räk-ən\ *adj or n*

Mo·ro·ni \mò-'rō-nē\ city, capital of Comoro

Morris Jes·up, Cape \,mòr-əs-'jes-əp, ,mär-\ headland **N** Greenland in Arctic ocean

Mos·cow \'mäs-,kaù, -kō\ *or Russian* **Mos·kva** \mäsk-'vä\ city, capital of Russia, on Moskva river

Mo·selle \mō-'zel\ *or German* **Mo·sel** \'mō-zəl\ river 515 kilometers long **E** France & **w** Germany flowing from Vosges mountains into the Rhine at Koblenz

Mo·sul \mō-'sül, 'mō-səl\ city **N** Iraq on the Tigris

Moul·mein \mül-'mān, mōl-, -'mīn\ city **s** Myanmar at mouth of the Salween

Mount Rainier National Park — see RAINIER (Mount)

Mount Rev·el·stoke National Park \'rev-əl-,stōk\ reservation **SE** British Columbia

Mo·zam·bique \,mō-zəm-'bēk\ *or Portuguese* **Mo·çam·bi·que** \,mü-səm-'bē-kə\ **1** channel **SE** Africa between Mozambique & Madagascar **2** *or formerly* **Portuguese East Africa** country **SE** Africa; formerly a dependency of Portugal; capital, Maputo

Mukden — see SHENYANG

Mul·tan \mùl-'tän\ city **NE** Pakistan **sw** of Lahore

Mu·nich \'myü-nik\ *or German* **Mün·chen** \'muen-kən\ city **s** Germany, capital of Bavaria

Mun·ster \'mən-stər\ province **s** Ireland

Mün·ster \'mən-stər, 'mün-, 'myün-, 'muen-\ city **w** Germany **NNE** of Dortmund

Mur·cia \'mər-shə, -shē-ə\ **1** region, province, & ancient kingdom **SE** Spain **2** city, its capital, **NE** of Granada — **Mur·cian** \-shən\ *adj or n*

Mur·mansk \mùr-'mansk, -'mänsk\ city **NW** Russia in Europe, on Barents sea

Mur·ray \'mər-ē, 'mə-rē\ river 1930 kilometers long **SE** Australia flowing **w** from **E** Victoria into Indian ocean in South Australia — see DARLING

Mur·rum·bidg·ee \,mər-əm-'bij-ē, ,mə-rəm-\ river 1610 kilometers long **SE** Australia in New South Wales flowing **w** into the Murray

Mu·sa, Ge·bel \,jeb-əl-'mü-sə\ mountain group **NE** Egypt in **s** Sinai peninsula; highest Gebel Katherina 2737 meters — see HOREB

Mu·sa, Je·bel \,jeb-əl-'mü-sə\ mountain 846 meters **N** Morocco opposite Rock of Gibraltar — see PILLARS OF HERCULES

Mus·cat \'məs-,kat, -kət\ town **E** Arabia, capital of Oman

Muscat and Oman — see OMAN

Mus·co·vy \mə-'skō-vē; 'məs-kə-vē, -,kō-\ **1** the principality of Moscow (founded 1295) which in 15th century came to dominate Russia **2** RUSSIA — an old name

Myan·mar \'myän-,mär\ *or formerly* **Bur·ma** \'bər-mə\ country **SE** Asia; capital, Yangon

My·ce·nae \mī-'sē-nē\ ancient city **s** Greece in **NE** Peloponnesus **N** of Argos

My·sia \'mish-ə, 'mish-ē-ə\ ancient country **NW** Asia Minor bordering on the Propontis

My·sore \mī-'sōr, -'sòr\ **1** — see KARNATAKA **2** city in **s** Karnataka

Myt•i•le•ne \‚mit-l-'ē-nē\ **1** ancient city Greece on E coast of Lesbos Island; site at modern town of Mytilene **2** — see LESBOS

Nab•a•taea or **Nab•a•tea** \‚nab-ə-'tē-ə\ ancient Arab kingdom SE of Palestine — **Nab•a•tae•an** or **Nab•a•te•an** \-'tē-ən\ adj or n

Na•be•rezh•nye Chel•ny \‚näb-ə-'rezh-nə-'chel-nē, -nyə-\ city E Russia in Europe

Na•ga•land \'näg-ə-‚land\ state E India N of Manipur in Naga hills; capital, Kohima

Na•ga•no \nä-'gän-ō\ city Japan in SE Honshu NW of Tokyo

Na•ga•sa•ki \‚näg-ə-'säk-ē, ‚nag-ə-'sak-ē\ city Japan in W Kyushu

Na•goya \nə-'gȯi-ə, 'näg-ə-‚yä\ city Japan in S central Honshu

Nag•pur \'näg-‚pu̇r\ city E central India in NE Maharashtra

Na•ha \'nä-hä\ city Japan in Ryukyu islands, capital of Okinawa

Na•huel Hua•pí \nä-‚wel-wä-'pē\ lake SW Argentina in the Andes

Nairn \'naərn, 'neərn\ or **Nairn•shire** \-‚shiər, -shər\ former county NE Scotland

Nai•ro•bi \nī-'rō-bē\ city, capital of Kenya

Najd — see NEJD

Na•mib•ia \nə-'mib-ē-ə\ or formerly **South–West Africa** country SW Africa, on the Atlantic; administered by South Africa 1919–90; capital, Windhoeck

Nan•chang \'nän-'chäng\ city SE China, capital of Jiangxi

Nan•cy \'nan-sē, näⁿ-sē\ city NE France

Nanjing or **Nan•king** \'nan-'king, 'nän-\ city E China on the Chang, capital of Jiangsu

Nan•ning \'nän-'ning\ city S China, capital of Guangxi Zhuangzu

Nantes \'nants\ city NW France

Nan•tuck•et \nan-'tək-ət\ island SE Massachusetts S of Cape Cod

Na•ples \'nā-pəlz\ or Italian **Na•po•li** \'näp-ə-lē\ or ancient **Ne•ap•o•lis** \nē-'ap-ə-ləs\ city S Italy on Bay of Naples — **Ne•a•pol•i•tan** \‚nē-ə-'päl-ət-n\ adj or n

Na•ra \'när-ə\ city Japan in W central Honshu E of Osaka

Nar•ra•gan•sett Bay \‚nar-ə-'gan-sət\ inlet of the Atlantic SE Rhode Island

Nash•ville \'nash-‚vil, -vəl\ city, capital of Tennessee

Nas•sau \'nas-‚ȯ\ city, capital of Bahamas on New Providence Island

Na•tal \nə-'tal, -'täl\ **1** city NE Brazil **2** province E Republic of South Africa; capital, Pietermaritzburg

Na•u•ru \nä-'ü-rü\ island (atoll) W Pacific; formerly a joint British, New Zealand, & Australian trust territory; an independent republic in the Commonwealth since 1968

Na•varre \nə-'vär\ or Spanish **Na•var•ra** \nə-'vär-ə\ **1** region & former kingdom N Spain & SW France in W Pyrenees **2** province N Spain W of Aragon; capital, Pamplona

Nax•os \'nak-səs, -‚säs\ island Greece in the Aegean; largest of the Cyclades

Na•ya•rit \‚nī-ə-'rēt\ state W Mexico on the Pacific; capital, Tepic

Naz•a•reth \'naz-rəth, -ə-rəth\ town of ancient Palestine in central Galilee; now a city of N Israel

N'Dja•me•na \en-'jäm-ə-nə\ or formerly **Fort–La•my** \‚fȯr-lə-'mē\ city, capital of Chad

Neagh, Lough \'nä\ lake Northern Ireland; largest in British Isles

Near East the countries of NE Africa & SW Asia — **Near Eastern** adj

Ne•bras•ka \nə-'bras-kə\ state central U.S.; capital, Lincoln — **Ne•bras•kan** \-kən\ adj or n

Neg•ev \'neg-‚ev\ or **Neg•eb** \-‚eb\ desert region S Israel

Ne•gros \'nā-grōs\ island S central Philippines in Visayan islands

Neis•se \'nī-sə\ river 225 kilometers long N Europe flowing from N Czech Republic N into the Oder; forms part of boundary between Poland & Germany — see ODER

Nejd \'nejd, 'nezhd\ or **Najd** \'najd, 'nazhd\ region central & E Saudi Arabia; capital, Riyadh

Ne•pal \nə-'pȯl, -'päl, -'pal\ country Asia on NE border of India in the Himalayas; a kingdom; capital, Kathmandu — **Nep•a•lese** \‚nep-ə-'lēz, -'lēs\ adj or n — **Ne•pali** \nə-'pȯl-ē, -'päl-, -'pal-\ adj or n

Neth•er•lands \'neth-ər-lənz, -ləndz\ **1** or Dutch **Ne•der•land** \'nād-ər-‚länt\ also **Holland** country NW Europe on North sea; a kingdom; official capital, Amsterdam, de facto capital, The Hague **2** LOW COUNTRIES — an historical usage — **Neth•er•land** \'neth-ər-lənd\ adj — **Neth•er•land•er** \-‚lan-dər, -lən-\ n — **Neth•er•land•ish** \-dish\ adj

Netherlands An•til•les \an-'til-ēz\ islands of the West Indies belonging to the Netherlands: Aruba, Bonaire, Curaçao, Saba, Saint Eustatius, & S part of Saint Martin; capital, Willemstad (on Curaçao)

Netherlands East Indies or **Netherlands India** or **Dutch East Indies** former Dutch possessions in the East Indies including Indonesia

Netherlands New Guinea — see WEST IRIAN

Ne•va \'nē-və, 'nā-\ river 65 kilometers long W Russia in Europe, flowing from lake Ladoga into Gulf of Finland at St. Petersburg

Ne•vada \nə-'vad-ə, -'väd-ə\ state W U.S.; capital, Carson City — **Ne•vad•an** \-'vad-n, -'väd-n\ or **Ne•vad•i•an** \-'vad-ē-ən, -'väd-\ adj or n

Ne•vis \'nē-vəs\ island British West Indies in the Leewards — see SAINT KITTS

Nevis, Ben — see BEN NEVIS

New Am•ster•dam \'am-stər-'dam, 'amp-\ town founded 1625 on Manhattan Island by the Dutch; renamed New York 1664 by the British

New•ark \'nü-ərk, 'nu̇-, 'nyü-, 'nyu̇-\ city NE New Jersey

New Bed•ford \'bed-fərd\ city SE Massachusetts

New Brit•ain \'brit-n\ island W Pacific, largest in Bismarck archipelago

New Bruns•wick \'brənz-wik\ province SE Canada; capital, Fredericton

New Cal•e•do•nia \‚kal-ə-'dō-nyə, -nē-ə\ island SW Pacific SW of Vanuatu; an overseas department of France; capital, Nouméa

New•cas•tle \'nü-‚kas-əl, 'nyü-\ city SE Australia in E New South Wales

New•cas•tle up•on Tyne \nü-'kas-əl-ə-‚pȯn-'tīn, nyü-, -‚pän-, -pən-, 'nü-‚, 'nyü-, \ city N England in Tyne and Wear

New Del•hi \-'del-ē\ city, capital of India S of city of (Old) Delhi

New England section of U.S. comprising states of Maine, New Hampshire, Vermont, Massachusetts, Rhode Island, & Connecticut — **New En•gland•er** \-'ing-glən-dər also -'ing-lən-\ n

New•found•land \'nü-fən-dlənd, 'nyü-, -lənd, -‚dland, -‚land; ‚nü-fən-'dland, ‚nyü-, -'land\ **1** island Canada in the Atlantic E of Gulf of Saint Lawrence **2** province E Canada comprising Newfoundland Island & Labrador; capital, Saint John's — **New•found•land•er** \-ər\ n

New France the possessions of France in North America before 1763

New Guin•ea \'gin-ē\ or Indonesian **Iri•an** \‚ir-ē-'än\ **1** island W Pacific N of E Australia divided between West Irian & Papua New Guinea **2** the NE portion of the island of New Guinea together with Bismarck archipelago, Bougainville, Buka, & adjacent small islands; now part of Papua New Guinea — **New Guin•ean** \'gin-ē-ən\ adj or n

New•ham \'nü-əm, 'nyü-\ borough of E Greater London, England

New Hamp•shire \'ham-shər, 'hamp-, -‚shiər\ state NE U.S.; capital, Concord — **New Hamp•shire•man** \-mən\ n — **New Hamp•shir•ite** \-‚īt\ n

New Ha•ven \'hā-vən\ city S Connecticut

\ə\ abut		\ng\ sing	
\ər\ further		\ō\ bone	
\a\ mat		\ȯ\ saw	
\ā\ take		\ȯi\ coin	
\ä\ cot, cart		\th\ thin	
\au̇\ out		\th\ this	
\ch\ chin		\ü\ food	
\e\ pet		\u̇\ foot	
\ē\ easy		\y\ yet	
\g\ go		\yü\ few	
\i\ tip		\yu̇\ cure	
\ī\ life		\zh\ vision	
\j\ job			

New Hebrides — see VANUATU

New Jer·sey \'jər-zē\ state E U.S.; capital, Trenton — **New Jer·sey·ite** \-,īt\ n

New Mex·i·co \'mek-si-,kō\ state SW U.S.; capital, Santa Fe — **New Mex·i·can** \-si-kən\ adj or n

New Neth·er·land \'neth-ər-lənd\ former Dutch colony (1613–64) North America along Hudson & lower Delaware rivers; capital, New Amsterdam

New Or·leans \'or-lē-ənz; 'orl-ənz, -yənz; or-'lēnz\ city SE Louisiana

New·port \'nü-,pōrt, 'nyü-, -,pört\ city SE Wales

New·port News \,nü-,pōrt-'nüz, -,pört-, -pərt-, ,nyü. . .'nyüz\ city SE Virginia

New Prov·i·dence \'präv-əd-əns, -ə-,dens\ island NW central Bahamas; chief town, Nassau

New South Wales state SE Australia; capital, Sydney

New Spain former Spanish possessions in North America, Central America, West Indies, & the Philippines; capital, Mexico City

New Sweden former Swedish colony (1638–55) North America on W bank of Delaware river

New York \'york\ 1 state NE U.S.; capital, Albany 2 or **New York City** city SE New York; includes Bronx, Brooklyn, Manhattan, Queens, & Staten Island — **New York·er** \'yor-kər\ n

New Zea·land \'zē-lənd\ country SW Pacific ESE of Australia; a dominion of the Commonwealth; capital, Wellington — **New Zea·land·er** \lən-dər\ n

Ni·ag·a·ra Falls \nī-'ag-rə, -ə-rə\ falls New York & Ontario in **Niagara River** (58 kilometers long flowing N from Lake Erie into Lake Ontario); divided by Goat Island into Horseshoe, or Canadian, Falls (48 meters high, 917 meters wide at crest) & American Falls (51 meters high, 323 meters wide)

Nia·mey \nē-'äm-ā, nyä-'mā\ city, capital of Niger

Ni·caea \nī-'sē-ə\ or **Nice** \'nīs\ ancient city W Bithynia; site at modern village of Iznik in NW Turkey — **Ni·cae·an** \nī-'sē-ən\ adj or n — **Ni·cene** \'nī-,sēn, nī-'sēn\ adj

Ni·ca·ra·gua \,nik-ə-'räg-wə\ 1 lake 160 kilometers long S Nicaragua 2 country Central America; capital, Managua — **Ni·ca·ra·guan** \-wən\ adj or n

Nice \'nēs\ or ancient **Ni·caea** \nī-'sē-ə\ city SE France

Nic·o·bar \'nik-ə-,bär\ islands India in Bay of Bengal S of the Andamans — see ANDAMAN

Nic·o·sia \,nik-ə-'sē-ə\ city, capital of Cyprus

Niedersachsen — see LOWER SAXONY

Ni·ger \'nī-jər\ 1 river 4185 kilometers long W Africa flowing into Gulf of Guinea 2 country W Africa N of Nigeria; a republic; capital, Niamey

Ni·ge·ria \nī-'jir-ē-ə\ country W Africa on Gulf of Guinea; a republic in the Commonwealth; capital, Lagos — **Ni·ge·ri·an** \-ē-ən\ adj or n

Nihon — see JAPAN

Nii·ga·ta \nē-'gät-ə, 'nē-gə-,tä\ city Japan in N Honshu on Sea of Japan

Nii·hau \'nē-,haù\ island Hawaii WSW of Kauai

Ni·ko·la·yev \,nik-ə-'lī-əf\ city S Ukraine

Nile \'nīl\ river 6497 kilometers long E Africa flowing from Lake Victoria in Uganda N into the Mediterranean in Egypt; in various sections called specifically **Vic·to·ria** \vik-'tōr-ē-ə, -'tòr-\, or **Som·er·set** \'səm-ər-sət, -,set\, **Nile** between Lake Victoria & Lake Albert, **Al·bert** \'al-bərt\ **Nile** between Lake Albert & Lake No, & **White Nile** from Lake No to Khartoum — see BLUE NILE

Nil·gi·ri \'nil-gə-rē\ hills S India in W Tamil Nadu

Nîmes \'nēm\ city S France NW of Marseilles

Nin·e·veh \'nin-ə-və\ ancient city, capital of Assyria; ruins in Iraq

Ning·xia Hui·zu \'ning-shē-'ä-'hwēd-'zü\ or **Ning·sia Hui** \'ning-shē-'ä-'hwē\ region N China; before 1954 part of former province of **Ningsia**

Nip·i·gon, Lake \'nip-ə-,gän\ lake Canada in W Ontario N of Lake Superior

Nip·pon \nip-'än\ — see JAPAN — **Nip·pon·ese** \,nip-ə-'nēz, -'nēs\ adj or n

Nis or **Nish** \'nish\ city E Yugoslavia in E Serbia

Ni·shi·no·mi·ya \,nish-ə-'nō-mē-,ä, -,yä\ city Japan in central Honshu E of Kobe

Ni·te·rói \,nēt-ə-'roi\ city SE Brazil on Guanabara Bay opposite Rio de Janeiro

Nizh·ni Nov·go·rod \,nizh-nē-'näv-gə-,räd, -'nov-gə-rət\ or **Gor'·kiy** or **Gor·ki** \'gor-kē\ city central Russia in Europe, on the Volga E of Moscow

Nizh·ni Ta·gil \,nizh-nē-tə-'gil\ city W Russia, in the Urals

Nor·folk \'nor-fək, in the United States also -,fòk\ 1 city SE Virginia 2 county E England on North sea

Nor·i·cum \'nor-i-kəm, 'när-\ ancient country & Roman province S central Europe S of the Danube in modern Austria & Germany

Nor·man·dy \'nor-mən-dē\ or French **Nor·man·die** \nor-mä͟n-'dē\ region & former province NW France NE of Brittany; capital, Rouen

North 1 river estuary of the Hudson between NE New Jersey & SE New York 2 sea arm of the Atlantic E of Great Britain 3 island N New Zealand

North America continent of western hemisphere NW of South America & N of the equator — **North American** adj or n

North·amp·ton \north-'am-tən, -'ham-, 'amp-, 'hamp-\ borough central England in Northamptonshire

North·amp·ton·shire \-,shiər, -shər\ or **Northampton** county central England

North Borneo — see SABAH

North Cape 1 headland New Zealand at N end of North Island 2 headland NE Norway on **Ma·ger·öy** \,mäg-ə-'roi\ island

North Car·o·li·na \,kar-ə-'lī-nə\ state E U.S.; capital, Raleigh — **North Car·o·lin·ian** \-'lin-ē-ən, -'lin-yən\ adj or n

North Cas·cades National Park \kas-'kādz, 'kas-,\ reservation N Washington

North Da·ko·ta \də-'kōt-ə\ state N U.S.; capital, Bismarck — **North Da·ko·tan** \-'kōt-n\ adj or n

North East Frontier Agency — see ARUNACHAL PRADESH

North–East New Guinea the NE section of Papua New Guinea on New Guinea mainland

Northern Cook \'kúk\ or **Ma·ni·hi·ki** \,män-ə-'hē-kē\ islands S central Pacific N of Cook islands

Northern Ireland region N Ireland; a division of United Kingdom; capital, Belfast

Northern Kingdom — see ISRAEL

Northern Mariana the Mariana islands except for Guam; a U.S. commonwealth

Northern Rhodesia — see ZAMBIA

Northern Territory territory N & central Australia; capital, Darwin

North Korea — see KOREA

North Rhine–Westphalia or German **Nord·rhein–West·fa·len** \'nort-,rīn-,vest-'fä-lən\ state W Germany; capital, Düsseldorf

North Ri·ding \'rī-ding\ former administrative county N England in N Yorkshire

North Slope region N Alaska between Brooks Range & Arctic ocean

North·um·ber·land \nor-'thəm-bər-lənd\ county N England — **North·um·bri·an** \-'thəm-brē-ən\ adj or n

North·um·bria \nor-'thəm-brē-ə\ ancient country Great Britain between the Humber & Firth of Forth — **North·um·bri·an** \-brē-ən\ adj or n

North Vietnam — see VIETNAM

Northwest Territories territory N Canada comprising the arctic islands, the mainland N of 60° between Yukon Territory & Hudson Bay, & the islands in Hudson Bay

North York \'york\ city Canada in SE Ontario

North York·shire \'york-,shiər, -shər\ county N England

Nor·way \'nȯr-ˌwā\ country N Europe in Scandinavia; a kingdom; capital, Oslo

Nor·we·gian \nȯr-'wē-jən\ sea between Atlantic & Arctic oceans W of Norway

Nor·wich \'nȯr-wich; 'nȯr-ich, 'när-\ city E England in Norfolk

Not·ting·ham \'nät-ing-əm, *in the United States also* -ˌham\ city N central England in Nottinghamshire

Not·ting·ham·shire \-ˌshiər, -shər\ *or* **Nottingham** county N central England

Nouak·chott \nu̇-'äk-ˌshät\ city, capital of Mauritania

Nou·méa \nü-'mā-ə\ city, capital of New Caledonia

No·va Igua·çu \ˌnȯ-və-ˌē-gwə-'sü\ city SE Brazil NW of Rio de Janeiro

No·va Sco·tia \ˌnō-və-'skō-shə\ province SE Canada; capital, Halifax — **No·va Sco·tian** \-'skō-shən\ *adj or n*

No·va·ya Zem·lya \ˌnō-və-yə-ˌzem-lē-'ä\ two islands N of Russia in Europe, in Arctic ocean between Barents & Kara seas

Nov·go·rod \'näv-gə-ˌräd, 'nȯv-gə-rət\ city W Russia in Europe, SSE of St. Petersburg

No·vi Sad \ˌnō-vē-'säd\ city N Yugoslavia

No·vo·kuz·netsk \ˌnō-vō-ku̇z-'netsk\ city S Russia in Asia at S end of Kuznetsk basin

No·vo·si·birsk \ˌnō-vō-sə-'biərsk\ city S Russia in Asia, on the Ob

Nu·bia \'nü-bē-ə, 'nyü-\ region NE Africa in Nile valley in S Egypt & N Sudan — **Nu·bi·an** \-bē-ən\ *adj or n*

Nubian desert NE Sudan E of the Nile

Nue·vo Le·ón \nu̇-ˌā-vō-lā-'ōn\ state N Mexico; capital, Monterrey

Nu·ku·a·lo·fa \ˌnü-kə-wə-'lȯ-fə\ seaport, capital of Tonga

Nu·mid·ia \nu̇-'mid-ē-ə, nyu̇-\ ancient country N Africa E of Mauretania in modern Algeria; chief city, Hippo — **Nu·mid·i·an** \-ē-ən\ *adj or n*

Nu·rem·berg \'nu̇r-əm-ˌbərg, 'nyu̇r-\ *or German* **Nürn·berg** \'nu̇ern-ˌberk\ city S central Germany in N Bavaria

Ny·asa, Lake \nī-'as-ə, nē-\ *or* **Lake Ma·la·wi** \mə-'lä-wē, -'lau̇-ē\ lake SE Africa in Malawi, Mozambique, & Tanzania

Nyasaland — see MALAWI

Oa·hu \ə-'wä-hü\ island Hawaii; site of Honolulu

Oak·land \'ō-klənd\ city W California on San Francisco Bay E of San Francisco

Oa·xa·ca \wə-'hä-kə\ 1 state SE Mexico 2 city, its capital

Ob \'äb, 'ȯb\ river 4025 kilometers long W central Russia in Asia flowing NW & N into **Gulf of Ob** (inlet of Arctic ocean)

Oce·a·nia \ˌō-shē-'an-ē-ə, -'ä-nē-ə\ lands of the central & S Pacific: Micronesia, Melanesia, Polynesia including New Zealand, & sometimes Australia & Malay archipelago — **Oce·a·ni·an** \-'an-ē-ən, -'ä-nē-\ *adj or n*

Oden·se \'ōd-n-sə, 'u̇-ən-zə\ city central Denmark on Fyn Island

Oder \'ōd-ər\ *or* **Odra** \'ȯ-drə\ river 906 kilometers long central Europe flowing from E Czech Republic NW into Baltic sea; forms part of boundary between Poland & Germany — see NEISSE

Odes·sa \ō-'des-ə\ city S Ukraine on Black sea

Of·fa·ly \'ȯf-ə-lē, 'äf-\ county central Ireland in Leinster

Ogasawara — see BONIN

Og·bo·mo·sho \ˌäg-bə-'mō-shō\ city W Nigeria

Ohio \ō-'hī-ō\ 1 river 1579 kilometers long E U.S. flowing from W Pennsylvania into the Mississippi 2 state E central U.S.; capital, Columbus — **Ohio·an** \ō-'hī-ə-wən\ *adj or n*

Oi·ta \'ȯi-ˌtä, ō-'ēt-ə\ city Japan in NE Kyushu

Oka·ya·ma \ˌō-kə-'yäm-ə\ city Japan in W Honshu on Inland sea

Oka·za·ki \ˌō-kə-'zäk-ē\ city Japan in S central Honshu

Okee·cho·bee, Lake \ˌō-kē-'chō-bē\ lake S central Florida

Oke·fe·no·kee \ˌō-kē-fə-'nō-kē\ swamp SE Georgia & NE Florida

Okhotsk, Sea of \ō-'kätsk\ inlet of the Pacific E Russia in Asia, W of Kamchatka peninsula & Kuril islands

Oki·na·wa \ˌō-kə-'nä-wə, -'nau̇-ə\ 1 islands Japan in central Ryukyus; capital, Naha 2 island, chief of group — **Oki·na·wan** \-'nä-wən, -'nau̇-ən\ *adj or n*

Okla·ho·ma \ˌō-klə-'hō-mə\ state S U.S.; capital, Oklahoma City — **Okla·ho·man** \-mən\ *adj or n*

Oklahoma City city, capital of Oklahoma

Old·ham \'ōl-dəm\ city NW England in Greater Manchester

Old Point Comfort cape SE Virginia N of entrance to Hampton Roads

Ol·du·vai Gorge \'ōl-də-ˌvī\ canyon N Tanzania SE of Serengeti Plain; site of fossil beds

Olives, Mount of *or* **Ol·i·vet** \'äl-ə-ˌvet, ˌäl-ə-'\ mountain ridge W Jordan on E side of Jerusalem

Olym·pia \ə-'lim-pē-ə, ō-\ 1 city, capital of Washington 2 plain S Greece in NW Peloponnesus

Olym·pic \ə-'lim-pik, ō-\ mountains NW Washington on Olympic peninsula, partly in **Olympic National Park**; highest Mt. Olympus 2428 meters

Olym·pus \ə-'lim-pəs, ō-\ mountains NE Greece in Thessaly; home of the gods in Greek mythology

Oma·ha \'ō-mə-ˌhȯ, -ˌhä\ city E Nebraska

Oman \ō-'män, -'man\ *or formerly* **Mus·cat and Oman** \'məs-ˌkat, -kət\ country SW Asia in SE Arabia; a sultanate; capital, Muscat — see UNITED ARAB EMIRATES

Oman, Gulf of arm of Arabian sea between Oman & SE Iran

Om·dur·man \ˌäm-dər-'man, -'män\ city central Sudan on left bank of the Nile opposite Khartoum

Omi·ya \ō-'mē-ə, 'ō-mē-ˌä\ city Japan in SE Honshu NW of Tokyo

Omsk \'ȯmsk, 'ȯmpsk, 'ämsk, 'ämpsk\ city S Russia in Asia, at confluence of Irtysh & Om rivers

On·ta·ke \ōn-'täk-ē\ mountain 3063 meters Japan in central Honshu NNW of Nagoya

On·tar·io \än-'ter-ē-ˌō\ province E Canada; capital, Toronto — **On·tar·i·an** \-ē-ən\ *adj or n*

Ontario, Lake lake E central North America in U.S. & Canada; one of the Great Lakes

Ophir \'ō-fər\ a biblical land rich in gold; probably in Arabia

Opor·to \ō-'pȯrt-ō, -'pȯrt-\ *or Portuguese* **Pôr·to** \'pȯr-tü\ city NW Portugal

Ora·dea \ȯ-'räd-ē-ə\ city NW Romania

Oran \ȯ-'rän\ city NW Algeria

Or·ange \'ȯr-inj, 'är-, -ənj\ river 2090 kilometers long S Africa flowing W from Drakensberg mountains into the Atlantic

Orange Free State province E central Republic of South Africa; capital, Bloemfontein

Ordzhonikidze — see VLADIKAVKAZ

Or·e·gon \'ȯr-i-gən, 'är-, -ˌgän\ state NW U.S.; capital, Salem — **Or·e·go·nian** \ˌȯr-i-'gō-nē-ən, ˌär-, -nyən\ *adj or n*

Oregon Trail pioneer route to the Pacific Northwest about 3220 kilometers long from vicinity of Independence, Missouri, to Vancouver, Washington

Orel \ȯ-'rel, ȯr-'yȯl\ city SW Russia in Europe, S of Moscow

Oren·burg \'ȯr-ən-ˌbərg, 'ȯr-, -ˌbu̇rg\ *or formerly* **Chka·lov** \chə-'käl-əf\ city E Russia in Europe, on Ural river

Ori·no·co \ˌȯr-ə-'nō-kō, ˌȯr-\ river 2575 kilometers long Venezuela flowing into the Atlantic

Oris·sa \ȯ-'ris-ə\ state E India; capital, Bhubaneswar

Ori·za·ba \ˌȯr-ə-'zäb-ə, ˌȯr-\ city E Mexico in Veracruz state

Orizaba, Pico de — see CITLALTEPETL

Ork·ney \'ȯrk-nē\ islands N Scotland; a county

Or·lan·do \ȯr-'lan-dō\ city central Florida

Or·léans \ȯr-'lā-'ä[n]\ city N central France

Osa·ka \ō-'säk-ə\ city Japan in S Honshu

Osh·a·wa \'äsh-ə-ˌwä\ city Canada in SE Ontario on lake Ontario ENE of Toronto

Os·lo \'äz-lō, 'äs-\ city, capital of Norway

\ə\ abut		\ng\ sing	
\ər\ further		\ō\ bone	
\a\ mat		\ȯ\ saw	
\ā\ take		\ȯi\ coin	
\ä\ cot, cart		\th\ thin	
\au̇\ out		\th\ this	
\ch\ chin		\ü\ food	
\e\ pet		\u̇\ foot	
\ē\ easy		\y\ yet	
\g\ go		\yü\ few	
\i\ tip		\yu̇\ cure	
\ī\ life		\zh\ vision	
\j\ job			

Os•sa \'äs-ə\ mountain 1978 meters NE Greece in E Thessaly near Mount Pelion

Ostra•va \'ȯ-strə-və\ city E Czech Republic in Moravia

Otran•to, Strait of \ō-'tran-tō, 'ō-trən-,tō\ strait between SE Italy & Albania

Ot•ta•wa \'ät-ə-,wä, -wə, -,wȯ\ city, capital of Canada in SE Ontario on Ottawa river

Oua•ga•dou•gou \,wäg-ə-'dü-,gü\ city, capital of Burkina Faso

Ouj•da \uzh-'dä\ city NE Morocco near Algerian border

Outer Hebrides — see HEBRIDES

Outer Mongolia — see MONGOLIA

Ovie•do \,ō-vē-'ä-thō\ city NW Spain

Ox•ford \'äks-fərd\ city central England in Oxfordshire

Ox•ford•shire \'äks-fərd-,shiər, -shər\ or **Oxford** county central England

Oxus — see AMU DARYA

Ozark Plateau \'ō-,zärk\ eroded tableland N Arkansas, S Missouri, & NE Oklahoma

Pa•cif•ic \pə-'sif-ik\ ocean extending from arctic circle to antarctic regions & from W North America & W South America to E Asia & Australia

Pacific Islands, Trust Territory of the islands in W Pacific in association with the U.S.: the Carolines, the Marshalls, & until 1978 the Northern Marianas

Pa•dang \'pä-,däng\ city & port Indonesia in W Sumatra

Pa•dre \'päd-rē, 'pad-\ island about 160 kilometers long S Texas in Gulf of Mexico

Padus — see PO

Pa•go Pa•go \,päng-gō-'päng-gō, ,päng-ō-'päng-ō, ,päg-ō-'päg-ō\ town, capital of American Samoa on Tutuila Island

Pa•kan•ba•ru \,päk-ən-'bär-ü\ city Indonesia in central Sumatra

Pak•i•stan \'pak-i-,stan, ,päk-i-'stän\ country S Asia in Indian subcontinent NW of India; until 1971 included also an eastern division E of India; a republic; capital, Islamabad — see EAST PAKISTAN — **Pak•i•stani** \-'stan-ē, -'stän-ē\ adj or n

Pal•at•i•nate \pə-'lat-n-ət\ or German **Pfalz** \'pfälts, 'fälts\ either of two districts SW Germany once ruled by counts palatine of the Holy Roman Empire: **Rhenish Palatinate** or **Rhine Palatinate** or German **Rhein•pfalz** \'rīn-,pfälts, -,fälts\ (on the Rhine E of Saarland) & **Upper Palatinate** (on the Danube around Regensburg) — see RHINELAND-PALATINATE

Palau — see BELAU

Pa•la•wan \pə-'lä-wən, -,wän\ island W Philippines between South China & Sulu seas

Pa•lem•bang \,päl-əm-'bäng\ city Indonesia in SE Sumatra

Pa•ler•mo \pə-'lər-mō, -'leər-\ city Italy, capital of Sicily

Pal•es•tine \'pal-ə-,stīn, -,stēn\ region SW Asia between Syrian desert & the Mediterranean now divided between Israel & Jordan — **Pal•es•tin•ian** \,pal-ə-'stin-ē-ən, -'stin-yən\ adj or n

Pal•ma \'päl-mə\ or **Palma de Ma•llor•ca** \-,dä-mə-'yȯr-kə, -məl-\ city Spain on Majorca

Palmer Peninsula — see ANTARCTIC PENINSULA

Pa•mirs \pə-'miərz\ or **Pa•mir** \pə-'miər\ elevated mountainous region central Asia in E Tajikistan & on borders of Xinjiang Uygur, Kashmir, & Afghanistan; many peaks over 6000 meters

Pam•li•co \'pam-li-,kō\ sound inlet of the Atlantic E North Carolina between mainland & offshore islands

Pam•plo•na \pam-'plō-nə\ city N Spain in Navarre

Pan•a•ma \'pan-ə-,mä, -,mȯ, ,pan-ə-'\ 1 country S Central America; a republic 2 or **Panama City** city, its capital on the Pacific 3 canal 82 kilometers long Panama connecting Atlantic & Pacific oceans — **Pan•a•ma•ni•an** \,pan-ə-'mā-nē-ən\ adj or n

Panama, Isthmus of or formerly **Isthmus of Dar•i•en** \-,dar-ē-'en\ strip of land central Panama connecting North America & South America

Panama Canal Zone — see CANAL ZONE

Pa•nay \pə-'nī\ island Philippines in Visayan islands; chief city, Iloilo

Pan•de•mo•ni•um \,pan-də-'mō-nē-əm\ the capital of Hell in John Milton's Paradise Lost

Panjab — see PUNJAB

Paoting — see BAODING

Pao-t'ou — see BAOTOU

Papal States — see STATES OF THE CHURCH

Pa•pee•te \,päp-ē-'āt-ē; pə-'pāt-ē, -'pēt-\ city Society islands on Tahiti, capital of French Polynesia

Pap•ua, Territory of \'pap-yə-wə, 'päp-ə-wə\ former British territory comprising SE New Guinea & offshore islands; now part of Papua New Guinea

Papua New Guinea country combining former territories of Papua & New Guinea; formerly a United Nations trust territory administered by Australia; independent since 1975; capital, Port Moresby

Pará — see BELEM

Par•a•guay \'par-ə-,gwī, -,gwä\ 1 river 2415 kilometers long central South America flowing from Brazil S into the Paraná in Paraguay 2 country central South America; a republic; capital, Asunción — **Par•a•guay•an** \,par-ə-'gwī-ən, -'gwä-ən\ adj or n

Par•a•mar•i•bo \,par-ə-'mar-ə-,bō\ city, capital of Suriname

Pa•ra•ná \,par-ə-'nä\ 1 river 3285 kilometers long central South America flowing S from Brazil into Rio de la Plata in Argentina 2 city NE Argentina

Par•is \'par-əs\ city, capital of France — **Pa•ri•sian** \pə-'rizh-ən, -'rēzh-\ adj or n

Par•ma \'pär-mə\ 1 city NE Ohio 2 city N Italy in Emilia-Romagna SE of Milan

Par•nas•sus \pär-'nas-əs\ massif central Greece N of Gulf of Corinth; highest point 2457 meters

Par•os \'par-,äs, 'per-\ island Greece in central Cyclades — **Par•i•an** \'par-ē-ən, 'per-\ adj

Par•ra•mat•ta \,par-ə-'mat-ə\ city SE Australia in New South Wales NW of Sydney

Par•thia \'pär-thē-ə\ ancient country SW Asia in NE modern Iran — **Par•thi•an** \-thē-ən\ adj or n

Pas•a•de•na \,pas-ə-'dē-nə\ city SW California E of Glendale

Pat•a•go•nia \,pat-ə-'gō-nyə, -nē-ə\ barren region South America S of about 40° S latitude in S Argentina & S tip of Chile; sometimes considered to include Tierra del Fuego — **Pat•a•go•nian** \-nyən, -nē-ən\ adj or n

Pat•er•son \'pat-ər-sən\ city NE New Jersey

Pat•mos \'pat-məs\ island Greece in the Dodecanese SSW of Samos

Pat•na \'pət-nə\ city NE India on the Ganges, capital of Bihar

Pat•ras \pə-'tras, 'pa-trəs\ city W Greece in N Peloponnesus on Gulf of Patras

Pearl Harbor inlet Hawaii on S coast of Oahu W of Honolulu

Pee•bles \'pē-bəlz\ or **Pee•bles•shire** \'pē-bəl-,shiər, -shər\ former county SE Scotland

Peking — see BEIJING

Pe•li•on \'pē-lē-ən\ mountain 1618 meters NE Greece in E Thessaly near Mount Ossa

Pel•o•pon•ne•sus \,pel-ə-pə-'nē-səs\ or **Pel•o•pon•ne•sos** \-'ne-səs\ or **Pel•o•pon•nese** \'pel-ə-pə-,nēz, -,nēs\ peninsula forming S part of mainland of Greece — **Pel•o•pon•ne•sian** \,pel-ə-pə-'nē-zhən, -shən\ adj or n

Pe•lo•tas \pə-'lōt-əs\ city S Brazil SW of Pôrto Alegre

Pem•broke•shire \'pem-brúk-,shiər, -shər\ or **Pembroke** former county SW Wales

Penang — see GEORGE TOWN

Peninsular Malaysia or **West Malaysia** territory W Malaysia comprising that part of Malaysia contained on Malay peninsula

Pen•nine Chain \'pen-,īn\ mountains N England; highest Cross Fell 893 meters

Penn·syl·va·nia \,pen-səl-'vā-nyə, -nē-ə\ state E U.S.; capital, Harrisburg

Pen·tel·i·cus \pen-'tel-i-kəs\ *or* **Pen·del·i·kon** \,pen-,del-ē-'kón\ mountain 1109 meters E Greece NE of Athens

Pen·za \'pen-zə\ city S central Russia in Europe

People's Democratic Republic of Yemen — see YEMEN

Pe·o·ria \pē-'ór-ē-ə, -'ōr-\ city N central Illinois

Per·ga·mum \'pər-gə-məm\ *or* **Per·ga·mus** \-məs\ ancient Greek kingdom including most of Asia Minor; at its height 263–133 B.C.; capital, Pergamum (in what is now W Turkey)

Perm \'pərm, 'peərm\ *or formerly* **Mo·lo·tov** \'mäl-ə-,tóf, 'mól-, 'mōl-, -,tōv\ city E Russia in Europe

Pernambuco — see RECIFE

Per·pi·gnan \per-pē-'nyäⁿ\ city S France SE of Toulouse

Per·sep·o·lis \pər-'sep-ə-ləs\ city of ancient Persia; site in SW Iran NE of Shiraz

Persia — see IRAN

Per·sian \'pər-zhən\ gulf arm of Arabian sea between Iran & Arabia

Persian Gulf States Kuwait, Bahrain, Qatar, & United Arab Emirates

Perth \'pərth\ **1** city, capital of Western Australia **2** *or* **Perth·shire** \-,shiər, -shər\ former county central Scotland

Pe·ru \pə-'rü\ country W South America; a republic; capital, Lima — **Pe·ru·vi·an** \pə-'rü-vē-ən\ *adj or n*

Peru Current *or* **Hum·boldt Current** \'həm-,bōlt\ cold current of the S Pacific flowing N & NW along coast of N Chile, Peru, & Ecuador

Pe·ru·gia \pə-'rü-jə, -jē-ə\ city central Italy SE of Florence

Pe·sha·war \pə-'shä-wər, -'shaủ-ər\ city N Pakistan ESE of Khyber pass

Pe·ta·re \pet-'är-,ā\ city N Venezuela

Pe·ter·bor·ough, Soke of \,sō-kəv-'pēt-ər-,bər-ə, -,bə-rə, -brə\ former administrative county E central England in Northamptonshire and later in Huntingdonshire; since 1974 part of Cambridgeshire

Pe·tra \'pē-trə, 'pe-trə\ ancient city NW Arabia; site in SW Jordan

Petrified Forest National Park reservation E Arizona

Petrograd — see SAINT PETERSBURG

Pe·tro·pav·lovsk \,pe-trə-'pav-,lófsk\ city N Kazakhstan

Pe·tro·za·vodsk \,pe-trə-zə-'vätsk\ city NW Russia in Europe, on Lake Onega

Pfalz — see PALATINATE

Phil·a·del·phia \,fil-ə-'del-fyə, -fē-ə\ city SE Pennsylvania — **Phil·a·del·phian** \-fyən, -fē-ən\ *adj or n*

Phi·lae \'fī-lē\ island S Egypt in the Nile above Aswân; now submerged in Lake Nasser

Phil·ip·pines \,fil-ə-'pēnz, 'fil-ə-,\ *or* **Republic of the Philippines** republic, an archipelago approximately 800 kilometers off SE coast of Asia; capital, Manila — **Philip·pine** \-'pēn, -,pēn\ *adj*

Phi·lis·tia \fə-'lis-tē-ə\ ancient country SW Palestine on the coast; the land of the Philistines

Phnom Penh \pə-'nóm-'pen, 'nóm-, pə-'näm-, 'näm-\ city, capital of Cambodia

Phoe·ni·cia \fi-'nish-ə, -'nēsh-, -ē-ə\ ancient country SW Asia on the Mediterranean in modern Syria & Lebanon

Phoe·nix \'fē-niks\ city, capital of Arizona

Phry·gia \'frij-ə, 'frij-ē-ə\ ancient country W central Asia Minor

Pia·cen·za \pyä-'chen-sə, ,pē-ə-'chen-\ city N Italy SE of Milan

Pic·ar·dy \'pik-ərd-ē\ *or French* **Pi·car·die** \pē-kär-dē\ region & former province N France N of Normandy; capital, Amiens

Pico de Orizaba — see CITLALTEPETL

Pied·mont \'pēd-,mänt\ **1** plateau region E U.S. E of the Appalachians between SE New York & NE Alabama **2** *or Italian* **Pie·mon·te** \pyä-'mōn-tā\ region NW Italy W of Lombardy; capital, Turin — **Pied·mon·tese** \,pēd-mən-'tēz, -,män-, -'tēs\ *adj or n*

Pierre \'piər\ city, capital of South Dakota

Pie·ter·mar·itz·burg \,pēt-ər-'mar-əts-,bərg\ city E Republic of South Africa, capital of Natal

Pikes Peak \'pīks\ mountain 4301 meters E central Colorado in a range of the Rockies

Pillars of Her·cu·les \'hər-kyə-,lēz\ two promontories at E end of Strait of Gibraltar: Rock of Gibraltar (in Europe) & Jebel Musa (in Africa)

Pinang — see GEORGE TOWN

Pin·dus \'pin-dəs\ mountains W Greece W of Thessaly; highest point 2480 meters

Pinkiang — see HARBIN

Pi·rae·us \pī-'rē-əs\ *or Greek* **Pi·rai·évs** \,pē-rē-'efs\ city E Greece on Saronic gulf; port for Athens

Pi·sa \'pē-zə, *Italian* 'pē-sä\ city W central Italy W of Florence

Pit·cairn \'pit-,kaərn, -,keərn\ island S Pacific SE of Tuamotu archipelago; a British colony

Pitts·burgh \'pits-,bərg\ city SW Pennsylvania

Pla·ta, Río de la \,rē-ō-,del-ə-'plät-ə\ estuary of Paraná & Uruguay rivers between Uruguay & Argentina

Plov·div \'plóv-,dif, -,div\ city S Bulgaria

Plym·outh \'plim-əth\ city SW England in Devonshire

Po \'pō\ *or ancient* **Pa·dus** \'päd-əs\ river 673 kilometers N Italy flowing into the Adriatic

Po Hai — see BO HAI

Po·land \'pō-lənd\ country central Europe on Baltic sea; a republic; capital, Warsaw

Pol·y·ne·sia \,päl-ə-'nē-zhə, -shə\ islands of the central & S Pacific including Hawaii, the Line, Tuvala, Phoenix, Tonga, Cook, & Samoa islands, French Polynesia, & often New Zealand

Pom·er·a·nia \,päm-ə-'rā-nē-ə, -'rā-nyə\ region N Europe on Baltic sea; formerly in Germany, now mostly in Poland

Pom·peii \päm-'pā, -'pā-,ē\ ancient city S Italy SE of Naples destroyed 79 A.D. by eruption of Vesuvius — **Pompe·ian** \-'pā-ən\ *adj or n*

Po·na·pe \'pō-nə-,pā\ island W Pacific in the E Carolines

Pon·ce \'pón-sā\ city S Puerto Rico

Pon·di·cher·ry \,pän-də-'cher-ē, -'sher-\ territory SE India SSW of Madras; a settlement of French India before 1954

Pon·ta Del·ga·da \,pänt-ə-del-'gäd-ə, -'gad-\ city Portugal in the Azores on São Miguel Island

Pont·char·train, Lake \'pän-chər-,trān, ,pän-chər-'\ lake SE Louisiana E of the Mississippi & N of New Orleans

Pon·ti·a·nak \,pän-tē-'ä-,näk\ city Indonesia on SW coast of Borneo

Pon·tine Marshes \'pän-,tīn, -,tēn\ district central Italy in SW Latium; marshes now reclaimed

Pon·tus \'pänt-əs\ **1** ancient country & Roman province NE Asia Minor **2** *or* **Pontus Euxinus** — see BLACK SEA — **Pon·tic** \'pänt-ik\ *adj or n*

Poole \'pül\ borough S England in Dorset on English Channel

Poo·na \'pü-nə\ city W India in Maharashtra ESE of Bombay

Po·po·ca·te·petl \,pō-pə-,kat-ə-'pet-l\ volcano 5452 meters SE central Mexico in Puebla

Port Arthur — see LÜSHUN

Port–au–Prince \,pōrt-ō-'prins, ,port-, -'prans, -'praⁿs\ city, capital of Haiti

Port Eliz·a·beth \-l-'iz-ə-bəth, i-'liz-\ city S Republic of South Africa in SE Cape Province

Port Jack·son \'jak-sən\ inlet of S Pacific SE Australia in New South Wales; harbor of Sydney

Port·land \'pōrt-lənd, 'pórt-\ city NW Oregon

Port Lou·is \'lü-əs, 'lü-ē, lü-'ē\ city, capital of Mauritius

Port Lyautey — see KENITRA

Port Mores·by \'mōrz-bē, 'mórz-\ city, capital of Papua New Guinea

Pôrto — see OPORTO

\ə\ abut		\ng\ sing	
\ər\ further		\ō\ bone	
\a\ mat		\ó\ saw	
\ā\ take		\oi\ coin	
\ä\ cot, cart		\th\ thin	
\aủ\ out		\th\ this	
\ch\ chin		\ü\ food	
\e\ pet		\ủ\ foot	
\ē\ easy		\y\ yet	
\g\ go		\yü\ few	
\i\ tip		\yủ\ cure	
\ī\ life		\zh\ vision	
\j\ job			

Pôr·to Ale·gre \,pōrt-ō-ə-'leg-rə, ,pórt-\ city s Brazil

Port of Spain city NW Trinidad, capital of Trinidad and Tobago

Por·to–No·vo \,pōrt-ə-'nō-vō, ,pórt-\ city, capital of Benin

Porto Rico — see PUERTO RICO

Port Phil·lip Bay \'fil-əp\ inlet of s Pacific SE Australia in Victoria; harbor of Melbourne

Port Said \sä-'ēd, 'sīd\ city NE Egypt on the Mediterranean at N end of Suez canal

Ports·mouth \'pōrt-sməth, 'pórt-\ **1** city SE Virginia **2** city s England in Hampshire

Port Su·dan \sü-'dan, -'dän\ city NE Sudan

Por·tu·gal \'pōr-chi-gəl, 'pór-\ or ancient **Lu·si·ta·nia** \,lü-sə-'tā-nē-ə, -nyə\ country SW Europe; a republic; capital, Lisbon

Portuguese East Africa — see MOZAMBIQUE

Portuguese Guinea — see GUINEA-BISSAU

Portuguese India former Portuguese possession on w coast of India including Goa, Daman, & Diu; annexed to India 1962

Portuguese West Africa — see ANGOLA

Po·ten·za \pə-'tent-sə; -'ten-sə, -zə\ city s Italy

Po·to·mac \pə-'tō-mək, -mik\ river 462 kilometers long flowing from West Virginia into Chesapeake Bay & forming boundary between Maryland & Virginia

Po·wys \'pō-əs\ county E central Wales; established 1974

Poz·nan \'pōz-,nan-yə, 'póz-, -,nän-yə, -,nan, -,nän\ city w central Poland

Prague \'präg\ or Czech **Pra·ha** \'prä-hä\ city, capital of Czech Republic and formerly of Czechoslovakia

Praia \'prī-ə\ town, capital of Cape Verde

Prairie Provinces the Canadian provinces of Alberta, Manitoba, & Saskatchewan

Pres·ton \'pres-tən\ borough NW England in Lancashire

Pre·to·ria \pri-'tōr-ē-ə, -'tór-\ city Republic of South Africa, capital of Transvaal & administrative capital of the Republic

Prib·i·lof \'prib-ə-,lóf\ islands Alaska in Bering sea

Prince Al·bert National Park \'al-bərt\ reservation Canada in central Saskatchewan

Prince Ed·ward Island \,ed-wərd\ island SE Canada in Gulf of Saint Lawrence; a province; capital, Charlottetown

Prince Ru·pert's Land \'rü-pərts\ historical region N & w Canada comprising drainage basin of Hudson Bay granted 1670 by King Charles II to Hudson's Bay Company

Prin·cí·pe \'prin-sə-pə\ island w Africa in Gulf of Guinea — see SÃO TOMÉ

Pro·ko·pyevsk \prə-'kóp-yəfsk\ city s Russia in Asia, NW of Novokuznetsk

Propontis — see MARMARA

Pro·vence \prə-'väⁿs\ region & former province SE France on the Mediterranean

Prov·i·dence \'präv-əd-əns, -ə-,dens\ city, capital of Rhode Island

Prus·sia \'prəsh-ə\ former kingdom &, later, state Germany; capital, Berlin — **Prus·sian** \-ən\ adj or n

Pu·chon \'pü-,chón\ city NW South Korea

Pu·eb·la \pü-'eb-lə, 'pweb-, pyü-'eb-\ **1** state SE central Mexico **2** city, its capital

Puer·to Ri·co \,pōrt-ə-'rē-kō, ,pórt-, -, pwert-\ or formerly **Por·to Ri·co** \,pōrt-, ,pórt-\ island West Indies E of Hispaniola; a self-governing commonwealth associated with U.S.; capital, San Juan — **Puer·to Ri·can** \-'rē-kən\ adj or n

Pu·get Sound \,pyü-jət-\ arm of the Pacific w Washington

Puglia — see APULIA

Pu·na de Ata·ca·ma \'pü-nə-,dā-,at-ə-'käm-ə, -,ät-\ plateau region NW Argentina NW of San Miguel de Tucumán

Pun·jab or **Pan·jab** \,pən-'jäb, -'jab, 'pən-,\ **1** region NW Indian subcontinent in Pakistan & NW India in valley of the Indus **2** or **Pun·jabi Su·ba** \,pən-,jäb-ē-'sü-bə, -,jab-\ state NW India in E Punjab region; capital, Chandigarh — see HARYANA **3** or formerly **West Punjab** province NE Pakistan

Pu·rus \pə-'rüs\ river 3220 kilometers long NW central South America in SE Peru & NW Brazil flowing into the Amazon

Pu·san \'pü-,sän\ city South Korea on Korea strait

Pyong·yang \pē-'óng-,yäng, pē-'əng-, -,yang\ city, capital of North Korea

Pyr·e·nees \'pir-ə-,nēz\ mountains on French-Spanish border extending from Bay of Biscay to the Mediterranean; highest Pico de Aneto (Pic de Néthou) 3404 meters

Qa·tar \'kät-ər, 'gät-, -'gət-\ country E Arabia on peninsula extending into Persian gulf; an independent emirate; capital, Doha

Qing·dao \'ching-'daù\ or **Tsing·tao** \'ching-'daù, 'tsing-, 'sing-\ city E China in E Shandong

Qing·hai or **Tsing·hai** \'ching-'hī\ province w China w of Gansu; capital, Xining

Qi·qi·har \'chē-'chē-'här\ or **Ch'i–ch'i–ha–erh** \'chē-'chē-'hä-'ər\ city NE China in w Heilongjiang

Qom \'küm\ city NW central Iran

Quan·zhou or **Ch'üan–chou** or **Chuan·chow** \chə-'wän-'jō\ city SE China in Fujian on Taiwan strait

Que·bec \kwi-'bek, ki-\ or French **Qué·bec** \kā-bek\ **1** province E Canada **2** city, its capital, on the Saint Lawrence

Queens \'kwēnz\ borough of New York City on Long Island E of borough of Brooklyn

Queen's — see LAOIGHIS

Queens·land \'kwēnz-,land, -lənd\ state NE Australia; capital, Brisbane — **Queens·land·er** \-ər\ n

Que·moy \kwi-'mói, ki-, 'kwē-, \ island E China in Taiwan strait

Que·ré·ta·ro \kə-'ret-ə-,rō\ **1** state central Mexico **2** city, its capital

Quet·ta \'kwet-ə\ city Pakistan in N Baluchistan

Que·zon City \'kā-,sòn\ city Philippines in Luzon NE of Manila; former (1948–76) official capital of the Philippines

Quil·mes \'kēl-,mäs, -,mes\ city E Argentina SE of Buenos Aires

Quin·ta·na Roo \kēn-,tän-ə-'rō\ state SE Mexico in E Yucatán; capital, Chetumal

Qui·to \'kē-tō\ city, capital of Ecuador

Ra·bat \rə-'bät\ city, capital of Morocco

Rad·nor·shire \'rad-nər-,shiər, -,nór-, -shər\ or **Radnor** former county E Wales

Ra·dom \'räd-,óm\ city E central Poland

Rai·nier, Mount \rə-'niər, rā-\ mountain 4392 meters w central Washington in **Mount Rainier National Park**; highest in Cascade mountains

Ra·ja·sthan \'räj-ə-,stän\ **1** state NW India bordering on Pakistan; capital, Jaipur **2** RAJPUTANA

Raj·kot \'räj-,kōt\ city w India in Gujarat

Raj·pu·ta·na \,räj-pə-'tän-ə\ region NW India s of Punjab now largely included in Rajasthan state

Ra·leigh \'ró-lē, 'räl-ē\ city, capital of North Carolina

Ran·chi \'rän-chē\ city E India NW of Calcutta

Rand — see WITWATERSRAND

Range·ley Lakes \'rānj-lē-\ chain of lakes w Maine & N New Hampshire

Rangoon — see YANGON

Rasht \'rasht\ city NW Iran

Rat islands SW Alaska in w Aleutians

Ra·wal·pin·di \,rä-wəl-'pin-dē, raúl-'pin-, ról-'pin-\ city NE Pakistan NNW of Lahore

Read·ing \'red-ing\ borough s England in Berkshire

Re·ci·fe \rə-'sē-fə\ or formerly **Per·nam·bu·co** \,pər-nəm-'bü-kō, -'byü-, ,per-nəm-'bü-\ city NE Brazil

Red \'red\ **1** river 1638 kilometers long flowing E on Oklahoma-Texas boundary & into the Atchafalaya & the Mississippi in Louisiana **2** sea between Arabia & NE Africa

Red·bridge \'red-brij\ borough of NE Greater London, England

Redwood National Park reservation NW California

Reg·gio \'rej-ō, 'rej-ē-,ō\ **1** or **Reggio di Ca·la·bria** \-,dē-kə-'läb-rē-ə\ city S Italy on Strait of Messina **2** or **Reggio nel·l'Emi·lia** \-,nel-ə-'mēl-yə\ city N Italy NW of Bologna

Re·gi·na \ri-'jī-nə\ city, capital of Saskatchewan

Reims or **Rheims** \'rēmz, French 'raⁿs\ city NE France

Ren·frew \'ren-,frü\ or **Ren·frew·shire** \-,shiər, -shər\ former county SW Scotland

Rennes \'ren\ city NW France

Ré·union \rē-'yün-yən\ island W Indian ocean E of Madagascar; an overseas department of France; capital, Saint-Denis

Revel — see TALLINN

Rey·kja·vik \'rāk-yə-,vik, 'rāk-ə-,,-,vēk\ city, capital of Iceland

Rey·no·sa \rā-'nōs-ə\ city NE Mexico in Tamaulipas

Rheinpfalz — see PALATINATE

Rhine or German **Rhein** \'rīn\ or French **Rhin** \'raⁿ\ or Dutch **Rijn** \'rīn\ or ancient **Rhe·nus** \'rē-nəs\ river 1320 kilometers long W Europe flowing from SE Switzerland to North sea in the Netherlands — **Rhen·ish** \'ren-ish, 'rē-nish\ adj or n

Rhine·land \'rīn-,land, -lənd\ or German **Rhein·land** \'rīn-,länt\ the part of Germany W of the Rhine — **Rhine·land·er** \'rīn-'lan-dər, -lən-\ n

Rhineland–Palatinate or German **Rhein·land–Pfalz** \-'pfälts, -'fälts\ state W Germany chiefly W of the Rhine; capital, Mainz

Rhode Is·land \rō-'dī-lənd\ **1** or officially **Rhode Island and Providence Plantations** state NE U.S.; capital, Providence **2** — see AQUIDNECK — **Rhode Is·land·er** \-lən-dər\ n

Rhodes \'rōdz\ **1** island Greece in the SE Aegean; chief island of the Dodecanese **2** city, its capital

Rhodesia — see ZIMBABWE — **Rho·de·sian** \-zhən, -zhē-ən\ adj or n

Rhon·dda \'rän-də, 'rän-thə, 'hrän-thə\ municipal borough SE Wales

Rhone or French **Rhône** \'rōn\ or ancient **Rhod·a·nus** \'räd-n-əs\ river 800 kilometers long Switzerland & SE France

Ri·bei·rão Prê·to \,rē-və-'rauⁿ-'prā-tü\ city SE Brazil NNW of São Paulo

Rich·mond \'rich-mənd\ **1** — see STATEN ISLAND **2** city, capital of Virginia **3** or **Richmond upon Thames** royal borough of SW Greater London, England

Rid·ing Mountain National Park \,rīd-ing-\ reservation Canada in SW Manitoba

Rift Valley GREAT RIFT VALLEY

Ri·ga \'rē-gə\ city, capital of Latvia

Ri·je·ka or **Ri·e·ka** \rē-'ek-ə, -'yek-\ or Italian **Fiu·me** \'fyü-,mā, fē-'ü-\ city W Croatia

Rio \'rē-ō\ RIO DE JANEIRO

Rio de Ja·nei·ro \'rē-ō-,dā-zhə-'neər-ō, -,dē-, -də-, -jə-'neər-\ city SE Brazil on Guanabara Bay

Río de Oro \,rē-ōd-ē-'ōr-ō, -'òr-\ territory NW Africa comprising S zone of Western Sahara

Rio Grande \,rē-ō-'grand, -'grand-ē\ or Mexican **Río Bra·vo** \-'bräv-ō\ river 3035 kilometers long SW U.S. forming part of U.S.-Mexico boundary & flowing into Gulf of Mexico

Río Muni — see MBINI

Riv·er·side \'riv-ər-,sīd\ city S California

Riv·i·era \,riv-ē-'er-ə\ coast region SE France & NW Italy

Ri·yadh \rē-'äd, -'yäd\ city, capital of Saudi Arabia

Ro·a·noke \'rō-ə-,nōk, 'rō-,nōk\ island North Carolina S of entrance to Albemarle sound

Rob·son, Mount \'räb-sən\ mountain 3954 meters W Canada in E British Columbia; highest in the Canadian Rockies

Roch·es·ter \'räch-ə-stər, 'räch-,es-tər\ city W New York

Rock·ford \'räk-fərd\ city N Illinois

Rocky \'räk-ē\ mountains W North America extending SE from N Alaska to central New Mexico — see ELBERT (Mount), ROBSON (Mount)

Rocky Mountain National Park reservation N Colorado

Ro·ma·nia \rù-'mā-nē-ə, rō-\ or **Ru·ma·nia** \rù-'mā-nē-ə\ country SE Europe on Black sea; capital, Bucharest

Rome \'rōm\ **1** or Italian **Ro·ma** \'rō-mä\ city, capital of Italy **2** the Roman Empire

Ron·ces·va·lles \,ròn-səs-'vī-əs\ commune N Spain

Roo·de·poort–Ma·rais·burg \'rōd-ə-,pòrt-mə-'rā-,bərg, 'rō-i-,pòrt-, -,pòrt-\ city Republic of South Africa in Transvaal

Ro·sa·rio \rō-'zär-ē-,ō, -'sär-\ city E central Argentina

Ros·com·mon \rä-'skäm-ən\ county central Ireland in Connacht

Ro·seau \rō-'zō\ seaport, capital of Dominica

Ross \'ròs\ sea arm of S Pacific extending into Antarctica E of Victoria Land

Ross and Crom·ar·ty \'kräm-ərt-ē\ former county N Scotland

Ros·tock \'räs-,täk, 'rò-,stòk\ city NE Germany near Baltic coast

Ros·tov \rə-'stòf, -'stòv\ city S Russia in Europe, on the Don

Rot·ter·dam \'rät-ər-,dam\ city SW Netherlands

Rou·baix \rü-'bā\ city N France NE of Lille

Rou·en \rü-'äⁿ, rü-'äⁿ\ city N France on the Seine

Rox·burgh \'räks-,bər-ə, -,bə-rə, -brə\ or **Rox·burgh·shire** \-,shiər, -shər\ former county SE Scotland

Ru·an·da–Urun·di \rù-,än-də-ù-'rün-dē\ former trust territory E central Africa bordering on Lake Tanganyika & administered by Belgium; divided 1962 into independent nations of Burundi (formerly Urundi) & Rwanda (formerly Ruanda) — see BURUNDI, RWANDA

Ru·dolf, Lake \'rü-,dälf\ lake N Kenya in Great Rift valley

Ruhr \'rùr\ industrial district W Germany E of the Rhine in valley of Ruhr river

Ru·me·lia \rü-'mēl-yə, -'mē-lē-ə\ a division of the old Ottoman Empire including Albania, Macedonia, & Thrace

Run·ny·mede \'rən-ē-,mēd\ meadow S England in Surrey on S bank of the Thames where Magna Charta was signed 1215

Rupert's Land PRINCE RUPERT'S LAND

Ru·se \'rü-sā\ city NE Bulgaria

Rush·more, Mount \'rəsh-,mōr, -,mòr\ mountain 1890 meters W South Dakota in Black hills SW of Rapid City

Rus·sia \'rəsh-ə\ **1** former empire largely coextensive with present U.S.S.R.; capital, Petrograd (Saint Petersburg) **2** UNION OF SOVIET SOCIALIST REPUBLICS **3** country N Asia (**Russia in Asia**) & E Europe (**Russia in Europe**) bordering on Arctic & Pacific oceans & Baltic & Black seas; capital, Moscow; a constituent republic (**Russian Soviet Federated Socialist Republic** or **Soviet Russia**) of U.S.S.R. 1922–91

Ru·the·nia \rü-'thē-nyə, -nē-ə\ or **Car·pa·thi·an Ruthe·nia** \kär-,pā-thē-ən\ region W Ukraine W of the N Carpathians — **Ru·the·nian** \rü-'thē-nyən, -nē-ən\ adj or n

Rut·land \'rət-lənd\ or **Rut·land·shire** \-,shiər, -shər\ former county E central England

Ru·wen·zo·ri \,rü-ən-'zōr-ē, -'zòr-\ mountain group E central Africa between Uganda & Zaire; highest Mount Margherita (highest peak of Mount Stanley) 5019 meters

Rwan·da or formerly **Ru·an·da** \rü-'än-də\ country E central Africa, until 1962 part of Ruanda-Urundi trust territory; a republic; capital, Kigali — **Rwan·dan** \rü-'än-dən\ adj or n

Rya·zan \,rē-ə-'zan-yə, -'zan\ city W Russia in Europe, SE of Moscow

Ry·binsk \'rib-,ənsk\ or formerly **Shcher·ba·kov** \,shcher-bə-'kòf, ,sher-, -'kòv\ city central Russia in Europe, NNE of Moscow

\ə\ abut \ng\ sing
\ər\ further \ō\ bone
\a\ mat \ò\ saw
\ā\ take \òi\ coin
\ä\ cot, cart \th\ thin
\au̇\ out \th\ this
\ch\ chin \ü\ food
\e\ pet \u̇\ foot
\ē\ easy \y\ yet
\g\ go \yü\ few
\i\ tip \yu̇\ cure
\ī\ life \zh\ vision
\j\ job

Ryu•kyu \rē-'ü-kyü, -'yü-, -kü\ islands w Pacific extending in an arc from Kyushu, Japan, to Taiwan, China; belong to Japan — **Ryu•kyu•an** \-kyü-ən, -kü-ən\ *adj or n*

Saar \'sär, 'zär\ **1** river 135 kilometers long Europe flowing from Vosges mountains in E France into the Moselle in Germany **2** *or* **Saar•land** \'sär-,land, 'zär-\ district w Europe in valley of Saar river; a state of w Germany; capital, Saarbrücken

Sa•ba \'säb-ə\ island West Indies in Netherlands Antilles; capital, The Bottom

Sa•bah \'säb-ə\ *or formerly* **North Borneo** state Federation of Malaysia in NE Borneo; capital, Kota Kinabalu

Sachsen — see SAXONY

Sac•ra•men•to \,sak-rə-'ment-ō\ **1** river 615 kilometers long N California flowing s into Suisun Bay **2** city, capital of California

Sa•ga•mi \sə-'gäm-ē\ sea inlet of Pacific in central Honshu, Japan

Sa•ga•mi•ha•ra \sə-,gäm-ē-'här-ə\ city Japan on Honshu

Sag•ue•nay \'sag-ə-,nā, ,sag-ə-'\ river 200 kilometers long Canada in s Quebec flowing from Lake Saint John E into the Saint Lawrence

Sa•hara \sə-'har-ə, -'her-, -'här-\ desert region N Africa N of Sudan region extending from Atlantic coast to Red sea or, as sometimes considered, to the Nile — **Sa•har•an** \-ən\ *adj*

Saigon — see HO CHI MINH CITY

Saint Ber•nard \,sānt-bər-'närd, -bə-\ either of two mountain passes in the Alps: the **Great Saint Bernard** (2472 meters between Italy & Switzerland E of Mont Blanc) & the **Little Saint Bernard** (2188 meters between France & Italy s of Mont Blanc)

Saint Cath•a•rines \'kath-rənz, -ə-rənz\ city Canada in SE Ontario

Saint Clair, Lake \'klaər, 'kleər\ lake SE Michigan & SE Ontario connected by **Saint Clair River** (64 kilometers long) with Lake Huron & draining by Detroit river into Lake Erie

Saint Croix \sānt-'kroi, sənt-\ **1** river 120 kilometers long Canada & U.S. on border between New Brunswick & Maine **2** island West Indies; largest of Virgin Islands of the U.S.

Saint Eli•as, Mount \,sānt-l-'ī-əs\ mountain 5489 meters on Alaska-Canada boundary in **Saint Elias Range**

Saint George's \'jor-jəz\ **1** channel British Isles between sw Wales & Ireland **2** town, capital of Grenada

Saint Gott•hard \sānt-'gät-ərd, -'gäth-, sənt-, ,san-gə-'tär\ **1** pass s central Switzerland in Saint Gotthard range of the Alps **2** tunnel 15 kilometers long near the pass

Saint He•le•na \,sānt-l-'ē-nə, ,sānt-hə-'lē-\ island s Atlantic; a British colony; capital, Jamestown

Saint Hel•ens \sānt-'hel-ənz, sənt-\ borough NW England in Merseyside ENE of Liverpool

Saint Helens, Mount volcano about 2560 meters sw Washington

Saint John \sānt-'jän, sənt-\ city Canada in s New Brunswick

Saint John's \sānt-'jänz, sənt-\ city Canada, capital of Newfoundland

Saint Kitts \'kits\ *or* **Saint Chris•to•pher** \'kris-tə-fər\ island British West Indies in the Leewards; with Nevis constitutes country of **Saint Kitts and Nevis**; capital, Basseterre (on Saint Kitts)

Saint Law•rence \sānt-'lor-əns, sənt-, -'lär-\ **1** river 1225 kilometers long E Canada in Ontario & Quebec bordering on U.S. in New York & flowing from Lake Ontario NE into the **Gulf of Saint Lawrence** (inlet of the Atlantic) **2** seaway Canada & U.S. in & along the Saint Lawrence between Lake Ontario & Montreal

Saint Lou•is \sānt-'lü-əs, sənt-\ city E Missouri on the Mississippi

Saint Lu•cia \sānt-'lü-shə, sənt-\ island British West Indies in the Windwards s of Martinique; capital, Castries

Saint Paul \'pol\ city, capital of Minnesota

Saint Pe•ters•burg \'pēt-ərz-,bərg\ **1** city w Florida **2** *or* 1914–24 **Pet•ro•grad** \'pe-trə-,grad\ *or* 1924–91 **Le•nin•grad** \'len-ən-,grad\ city w Russia, on Gulf of Finland

Saint Pierre \sānt-'piər, sənt-, -pē-'eər, *French* san-'pyer\ **1** island in the Atlantic off s Newfoundland; with nearby island of Miquelon constitutes French territory of **Saint Pierre and Miquelon 2** town, capital of Saint Pierre and Miquelon

Saint Thom•as \'täm-əs\ **1** island West Indies, one of Virgin Islands of the U.S.; chief town, Charlotte Amalie **2** — see SÃO TOMÉ

Saint Vin•cent \sānt-'vin-sənt, sənt-\ island British West Indies in the central Windwards; with N Grenadines constitutes independent country of **Saint Vincent and the Grenadines**; capital, Kingstown (on Saint Vincent)

Sai•pan \sī-'pan, -'pän, 'sī-,\ island w Pacific in s central Marianas

Sa•kai \sä-'kī, 'sä-\ city Japan in s Honshu on Osaka Bay

Sa•kha•lin \'sak-ə-,lēn, -lən; ,sak-ə-'lēn\ *or formerly* **Sa•ghal•ien** \'sag-ə-,lēn, ,sag-ə-'\ *or Japanese* **Ka•ra•fu•to** \kə-'räf-ə-,tō\ island Russia in w Pacific N of Hokkaido, Japan; until 1945 divided between Japan & U.S.S.R.

Sal•a•man•ca \,sal-ə-'mang-kə, ,säl-ə-'mäng-\ city w Spain

Sal•a•mis \'sal-ə-məs\ **1** ancient city Cyprus on E coast **2** island Greece in Saronic gulf off Attica

Sa•lé \sal-'ā\ city & port NW Morocco

Sa•lem \'sā-ləm\ **1** city, capital of Oregon **2** city s India in N Tamil Nadu sw of Madras

Sa•ler•no \sə-'lər-nō, -'leər-\ city s Italy on Gulf of Salerno

Sal•ford \'sol-fərd\ urban area NW England in Greater Manchester

Salisbury — see HARARE

Sa•lon•i•ka \sə-'län-i-kə, ,sal-ə-'nē-kə\ *or* **Sal•o•ni•ki** \,sal-ə-'nē-kē\ *or* **Thes•sa•lo•ni•ca** \,thes-ə-lə-'nī-kə, -'län-i-kə\ city N Greece in Macedonia

Sal•op \'sal-əp\ *or* **Shrop•shire** \'shräp-,shiər, -shər\ county w England bordering on Wales

Sal•ta \'säl-tə\ city NW Argentina

Salt Lake City city, capital of Utah

Sal•va•dor \'sal-və-,dor, ,sal-və-'\ *or formerly* **São Salvador** \saun-\ *or* **Ba•hia** \bä-'ē-ə\ city NE Brazil on the Atlantic — **Sal•va•dor•an** \,sal-və-'dor-ən, -'dor-\ *or* **Sal•va•do•re•an** *or* **Sal•va•do•ri•an** \-ē-ən\ *adj or n*

Sal•ween \'sal-,wēn\ river 2815 kilometers long SE Asia flowing s into Gulf of Martaban in Myanmar

Salz•burg \'solz-,bərg, 'sälz-, 'salz-, 'solts-, -,burg, *German* 'zälts-,burk\ city w Austria

Sa•mar \'säm-,är\ island central Philippines in Visayan islands

Sa•ma•ra \sə-'mär-ə\ *or* 1935–91 **Kuy•by•shev** \'kwē-bə-,shef, 'kü-ē-, -,shev\ city w Russia, on the Volga

Sa•mar•ia \sə-'mer-ē-ə, -'mar-\ **1** district of ancient Palestine w of the Jordan between Galilee & Judea **2** ancient city, its capital & capital of the Northern Kingdom (Israel)

Sam•a•rin•da \,sam-ə-'rin-də\ city Indonesia in E Borneo

Sam•ar•kand \'sam-ər-,kand\ city E Uzbekistan

Sam•ni•um \'sam-nē-əm\ ancient country s central Italy SE of Latium — **Sam•nite** \'sam-,nīt\ *adj or n*

Sa•moa \sə-'mō-ə\ islands sw central Pacific N of Tonga islands; divided at longitude 171° w into American, or Eastern, Samoa & Western Samoa — **Sa•mo•an** \-ən\ *adj or n*

Sa•mos \'sā-,mäs\ island Greece in the Aegean off coast of Turkey N of the Dodecanese — **Sa•mi•an** \-mē-ən\ *adj or n*

Sam•o•thrace \'sam-ə-,thrās\ island Greece in the NE Aegean

San•'a \'san-ˌä, san-'ä\ city SW Arabia, capital of Yemen & formerly of Yemen Arab Republic

San An•to•nio \ˌsan-ən-'tō-nē-ˌō\ city S Texas

San Ber•nar•di•no \ˌsan-ˌbər-nə-'dē-nō, -nər-'dē-\ city S California

San Cris•tó•bal \ˌsan-kris-'tō-bəl\ city W Venezuela

Sanc•ti Spi•ri•tus \ˌsäng-tē-'spir-ə-ˌtüs, ˌsängk-\ city W central Cuba

San Di•ego \ˌsan-dē-'ā-gō\ city SW California

Sandwich Islands — see HAWAII

San Fran•cis•co \ˌsan-frən-'sis-kō\ city W California

San Isi•dro \ˌsan-ə-'sē-drō\ city E Argentina NW of Buenos Aires

San Joa•quin \ˌsan-wä-'kēn, -wȯ-\ river 563 kilometers long central California flowing NW into the Sacramento

San Jo•se \ˌsan-ə-'zā\ city W California SE of San Francisco

San Jo•sé \ˌsan-ə-'zā, -ō-'zā, -hō-'zā\ city, capital of Costa Rica

San Juan \san-'hwän, -'wän\ city, capital of Puerto Rico

San Lu•is Po•to•sí \ˌsän-lü-ˌē-ˌspōt-ə-'sē\ 1 state central Mexico 2 city, its capital

San Ma•ri•no \ˌsan-mə-'rē-nō\ 1 country S Europe on Italian peninsula ENE of Florence near Adriatic sea; a republic 2 town, its capital

San Martín — see GENERAL SAN MARTÍN

San Mi•guel de Tu•cu•mán \ˌsan-mig-ˌel-də-ˌtü-kə-'män\ or **Tu•cu•mán** \ˌtü-kə-'män\ city NW Argentina

San Pe•dro Su•la \san-ˌpā-ˌdrō-'sü-lə\ city NW Honduras

San Sal•va•dor \san-'sal-və-ˌdȯr\ 1 or formerly **Wat•lings** \'wät-lingz\ island central Bahama islands 2 city, capital of El Salvador

San•ta Ana \ˌsant-ə-'an-ə\ 1 city SW California ESE of Long Beach 2 city NW El Salvador

San•ta Bar•ba•ra \-'bär-brə, -bə-rə\ or **Channel** islands California in the Pacific off SW coast

San•ta Clara \-'klar-ə, -'kler-ə\ city W central Cuba

San•ta Cruz \-'krüz\ city E Bolivia

San•ta Cruz de Te•ne•rife \-də-ˌten-ə-'rēf-ˌā, -'rēf, -'rif\ city Spain in W Canary islands on Tenerife Island

San•ta Fe \ˌsant-ə-'fā\ 1 city, capital of New Mexico 2 city central Argentina

Santa Fe Trail pioneer route to the Southwest 1290 kilometers long used especially 1821–80 from vicinity of Kansas City, Missouri, to Santa Fe, New Mexico

Santa Isabel — see MALABO

San•ta Mar•ta \ˌsant-ə-'märt-ə\ city N Colombia

San•tan•der \ˌsän-ˌtän-'deər, ˌsan-ˌtan-\ city N Spain WNW of Bilbao

San•ti•a•go \ˌsant-ē-'äg-ō, ˌsänt-\ 1 city, capital of Chile 2 or **Santiago de los Ca•ba•lle•ros** \-də-ˌlȯs-ˌkäb-ə-'yeər-ōs\ city N central Dominican Republic

Santiago de Cu•ba \-də-'kyü-bə\ city SE Cuba

San•to Do•min•go \ˌsant-əd-ə-'ming-gō\ 1 — see HISPANIOLA 2 — see DOMINICAN REPUBLIC 3 or formerly **Ci•u•dad Tru•ji•llo** \sē-ü-ˌt͟hä-trü-'hē-ō, sē-ù-ˌdad-\ city, capital of Dominican Republic

San•tos \'sant-əs\ city SE Brazil

São Lu•ís \ˌsaùⁿ-lü-'ēs\ city NE Brazil on Maranhão Island

Saône \'sōn\ river E France flowing into the Rhone

São Pau•lo \ˌsaùⁿ-'paù-lü, saùm-, -lō\ city SE Brazil

São Salvador — see SALVADOR

São To•mé or **São Tho•mé** \ˌsaùⁿt-ə-'mä, ˌsaùⁿnt-\ or **Saint Thom•as** \ˌsänt-'täm-əs\ island W Africa in Gulf of Guinea; with Príncipe Island, forms republic of **São Tomé and Príncipe** capital, São Tomé; until 1975 a Portuguese colony

Sap•po•ro \'säp-ə-ˌrō; sə-'pōr-ō, -'pȯr-\ city Japan on W Hokkaido

Saragossa — see ZARAGOZA

Sa•ra•je•vo \'sär-ə-ye-ˌvȯ\ city, capital of Bosnia and Herzegovina

Sa•ransk \sə-'ränsk, -'ransk\ city central Russia in Europe

Sa•ra•tov \sə-'rät-əf\ city S central Russia in Europe, on the Volga

Sa•ra•wak \sə-'rä-wä, -wäk, -ˌwak\ state Federation of Malaysia in N Borneo on South China sea; capital, Kuching

Sar•din•ia \sär-'din-ē-ə, -'din-yə\ island Italy in the Mediterranean S of Corsica; a region; capital, Cagliari — **Sar•din•ian** \-'din-ē-ən, -'din-yən\ adj or n

Sar•dis \'särd-əs\ ancient city W Asia Minor, capital of Lydia

Sar•gas•so Sea \ˌsär-ˌgas-ō-\ area of comparatively still water in the N Atlantic lying chiefly between 25° & 35° N latitude & 40° & 70° W longitude

Sa•ron•ic Gulf \sə-ˌrän-ik-\ inlet of the Aegean SE Greece between Attica & the Peloponnesus

Sas•katch•e•wan \sə-'skach-ə-wən, sa-, -ˌwän\ province W Canada; capital, Regina

Sas•ka•toon \ˌsas-kə-'tün\ city Canada in central Saskatchewan

Sas•sa•ri \'säs-ə-rē\ city Italy in NW Sardinia

Sau•di Arabia \ˌsaùd-ē-ə-'rä-bē-ə, ˌsȯd-ē-, ˌsä-ˌüd-ē-\ country SW Asia occupying largest part of Arabian peninsula; a kingdom; capital, Riyadh — **Saudi** adj or n — **Saudi Arabian** adj or n

Sault Sainte Ma•rie Canals \ˌsü-ˌsänt-mə-'rē\ or **Soo Canals** \ˌsü-\ three ship canals, two in U.S. (Michigan) & one in Canada (Ontario), at rapids in Saint Marys river connecting Lakes Superior & Huron

Sa•vaii \sə-'vī-ˌē\ island, largest in Western Samoa

Sa•van•nah \sə-'van-ə\ city E Georgia

Sa•voy \sə-'vȯi\ or French **Sa•voie** \sa-'vwä\ region SE France SW of Switzerland bordering on Italy — **Sa•voy•ard** \sə-'vȯi-ˌärd, ˌsav-ˌȯi-'ärd; ˌsav-ˌwä-'yär, -'yärd\ adj or n

Sax•o•ny \'sak-sə-nē, 'sak-snē\ or German **Sach•sen** \'zäk-sən\ region & former state E Germany N of the Erzgebirge — see LOWER SAXONY

Sca•fell Pike \ˌskȯ-'fel\ mountain 978 meters NW England in Cumbria; highest in Cumbrian mountains & in England

Scan•di•na•via \ˌskan-də-'nā-vē-ə, -vyə\ 1 peninsula N Europe occupied by Norway & Sweden 2 Denmark, Norway, Sweden, & sometimes also Iceland & Finland

Scar•bor•ough \'skär-ˌbər-ə, -ˌbə-rə, -bər-ə, -brə\ city Canada in SE Ontario

Scheldt \'skelt\ or **Schel•de** \'skel-də\ or French **Escaut** \es-kō\ or ancient **Scal•dis** \'skal-dəs\ river 435 kilometers long W Europe flowing from N France through Belgium into North sea in Netherlands

Schleswig–Hol•stein \'shles-wig-'hōl-ˌstīn, 'sles-, -vik-'hōl-\ state N Germany consisting of Holstein & part of Schleswig; capital, Kiel

Schwarzwald — see BLACK FOREST

Schweiz — see SWITZERLAND

Scil•ly \'sil-ē\ islands SW England off Lands End in county of Cornwall and Isles of Scilly

Sco•tia \'skō-shə\ SCOTLAND — the Medieval Latin name

Scot•land \'skät-lənd\ or Latin **Cal•e•do•nia** \ˌkal-ə-'dō-nyə, -nē-ə\ country N Great Britain; a division of United Kingdom of Great Britain and Northern Ireland; capital, Edinburgh

Scran•ton \'skrant-n\ city NE Pennsylvania

Scyth•ia \'sith-ē-ə, 'sit͟h-\ country of the ancient Scythians comprising parts of Europe & Asia in regions N & NE of Black sea & E of Aral sea — **Scyth•i•an** \-ē-ən\ adj or n

Se•at•tle \sē-'at-l\ city W Washington

Seine \'sān, 'sen\ river 773 kilometers long N France flowing NW into English channel

Sel•kirk \'sel-kərk\ 1 range of the Rocky mountains SE British Columbia; highest peak, Mount Sir Donald 3390 meters 2 or **Sel•kirk•shire** \-ˌshiər, -shər\ former county SE Scotland

Se•ma•rang \sə-'mär-ˌäng\ city Indonesia in central Java

Sem•i•pa•la•tinsk \ˌsem-i-pə-'lä-ˌtinsk\ city NE Kazakhstan

Sen•dai \sen-'dī, 'sen-\ city Japan in NE Honshu

\ə\ abut	\ng\ sing
\ər\ further	\ō\ bone
\a\ mat	\ȯ\ saw
\ā\ take	\ȯi\ coin
\ä\ cot, cart	\th\ thin
\aù\ out	\t͟h\ this
\ch\ chin	\ü\ food
\e\ pet	\ù\ foot
\ē\ easy	\y\ yet
\g\ go	\yü\ few
\i\ tip	\yù\ cure
\ī\ life	\zh\ vision
\j\ job	

Sen·e·gal \\,sen-i-'gȯl\\ **1** river 1690 kilometers long **w** Africa flowing **w** into the Atlantic **2** country **w** Africa; a republic; capital, Dakar — **Sen·e·ga·lese** \\,sen-i-gə-'lēz, -'lēs\\ *adj or n*

Seoul \\'sōl\\ city, capital of South Korea

Se·quoia National Park \\si-'kwȯi-ə\\ reservation **se** central California; includes Mount Whitney

Seram — see CERAM

Ser·bia \\'sər-bē-ə\\ region Balkan peninsula; capital, Belgrade; with Montenegro constitutes Yugoslavia

Ser·en·ge·ti Plain \\,ser-ən-'get-ē\\ area **n** Tanzania including **Serengeti National Park**

Se·te Que·das \\,sāt-ə-'kā-<u>th</u>əsh\\ *or formerly* **Guaí·ra** *or* **Guay·ra** \\gwī-'rä\\ former cataract 114 meters high in Alto Paraná on Brazil-Paraguay boundary; now submerged in dam-created lake

Se·vas·to·pol \\sə-'vas-tə-,pōl, -,pȯl, -pəl; ,sev-ə-'stȯ-pəl, -'stō-\\ *or formerly* **Se·bas·to·pol** \\-'bas-; ,seb-ə-\\ city **sw** Crimea

Sev·ern \\'sev-ərn\\ river 338 kilometers long Wales & England flowing from **e** central Wales into Bristol channel

Se·ville \\sə-'vil\\ *or Spanish* **Se·vi·lla** \\sā-'vē-ä, -yä\\ *or ancient* **His·pa·lis** \\'his-pə-ləs\\ city **sw** Spain

Sey·chelles \\sā-'shel, -'shelz\\ islands **w** Indian ocean **ne** of Madagascar; formerly a British colony; became independent 1976; capital, Victoria (on Mahé Island)

's Gravenhage — see HAGUE

Shaan·xi \\'shän-'shē\\ *or* **Shen·si** \\'shen-'sē, 'shən-'shē\\ province **n** central China; capital, Xi'an

Shan·dong \\'shän-'dȯng\\ *or* **Shan·tung** \\'shan-'təng\\ **1** peninsula **e** China extending into Yellow sea **2** province **e** China including Shandong peninsula; capital, Jinan

Shang·hai \\shang-'hī\\ city **e** China in **se** Jiangsu

Shan·non \\'shan-ən\\ river 386 kilometers long **w** Ireland flowing **s** & **w** into the Atlantic

Shan·tou \\'shän-'tō\\ *or* **Swa·tow** \\'swä-'taù\\ city **se** China in **e** Guangdong

Shan·xi \\'shän-'shē\\ *or* **Shan·si** \\'shän-'sē, -'shē\\ province **n** China bordering on Yellow river; capital, Taiyuan

Shas·ta, Mount \\'shas-tə\\ mountain 4317 meters **n** California in Cascade range

Shatt-al-Ar·ab \\,shat-,al-'ar-əb\\ river 193 kilometers long **se** Iraq formed by confluence of Euphrates & Tigris rivers & flowing **se** into Persian gulf

Shcherbakov — see RYBINSK

She·ba \\'shē-bə\\ ancient country **s** Arabia

She·chem \\'shē-kəm, -,kem\\ ancient city central Palestine in Samaria; site at present city of Nablus in Jordan

Shef·field \\'shef-,ēld\\ city **n** England in South Yorkshire

Shen·an·do·ah National Park \\,shen-ən-'dō-ə, ,shan-ə-'dō-ə\\ reservation **n** Virginia in Blue Ridge mountains

Shen·yang \\'shən-'yäng\\ *or* **Muk·den** \\'mùk-dən, 'mək-; 'mùk-'den\\ *or formerly* **Feng·tien** \\'fəng-tē-'en\\ city **ne** China, capital of Liaoning

Sher·wood Forest \\,shər-,wùd-\\ ancient royal forest central England chiefly in Nottinghamshire

Shet·land \\'shet-lənd\\ **1** islands **n** Scotland **ne** of the Orkneys **2** *or* **Zet·land** \\'zet-\\ county comprising the Shetland islands

Shi·jia·zhuang *or* **Shih–chia–chuang** *or* **Shih·kia·chwang** \\'shiər-jē-'äj-'wäng, 'shē-jē-\\ city **ne** China, capital of Hebei

Shi·ko·ku \\shi-'kō-kü\\ island **s** Japan **e** of Kyushu

Shi·mo·no·se·ki \\,shim-ə-nō-'sek-ē\\ city Japan in **sw** Honshu opposite Kitakyushu

Shi·raz \\shi-'räz\\ city **sw** Iran

Shi·zu·o·ka \\,shiz-ə-'wō-kə, ,shē-zə-'ō-kə\\ city Japan in central Honshu **sw** of Tokyo

Sho·la·pur \\'shō-lə-,pùr\\ city **w** India in **se** Maharashtra **se** of Bombay

Shreve·port \\'shrēv-,pōrt, -,pȯrt\\ city **nw** Louisiana

Shropshire — see SALOP

Shushan — see SUSA

Si·al·kot \\sē-'äl-,kōt\\ city **ne** Pakistan **nne** of Lahore

Siam — see THAILAND

Siam, Gulf of *or* **Gulf of Thailand** arm of South China sea between Indochina & Malay peninsula

Sian — see XI'AN

Siangtan — see XIANGTAN

Si·be·ria \\sī-'bir-ē-ə\\ region **n** Asia in Russia between the Urals & the Pacific — **Si·be·ri·an** \\-ē-ən\\ *adj or n*

Sic·i·ly \\'sis-ə-lē, 'sis-lē\\ *or Italian* **Si·ci·lia** \\sē-'chēl-yä\\ island **s** Italy **sw** of toe of Italian peninsula; a region; capital, Palermo — **Si·cil·ian** \\sə-'sil-yən\\ *adj or n*

Si·er·ra Le·one \\sē-,er-ə-lē-'ōn, ,sir-ə-\\ country **w** Africa on the Atlantic; a dominion of the Commonwealth; capital, Freetown — **Si·er·ra Le·on·ean** \\-'ō-nē-ən\\ *adj or n*

Si·er·ra Ma·dre \\sē-,er-ə-'mäd-rē\\ mountain system Mexico including **Sierra Madre Oc·ci·den·tal** \\-,äk-sə-,den-'täl\\ range **w** of the central plateau, **Sierra Madre Ori·en·tal** \\-,ȯr-ē-,en-täl, -,ȯr-\\ range **e** of the plateau, & **Sierra del Sur** \\sē-,er-ə-,del-'sùr\\ range to the **s**

Sierra Ne·va·da \\-nə-'vad-ə, -'väd-\\ **1** mountain range **e** California & **w** Nevada — see WHITNEY (Mount) **2** mountain range **s** Spain; highest peak Mulhacén 3477 meters, highest in Spain

Sik·kim \\'sik-əm, -,im\\ region **se** Asia on **s** slope of the Himalayas between Nepal & Bhutan; a state of Republic of India since 1975; capital, Gangtok

Si·le·sia \\sī-'lē-zhə, sə-, -zhē-ə, -sha, -shē-ə\\ region **e** central Europe in valley of the upper Oder bordering on Sudeten mountains; formerly chiefly in Germany now chiefly in **ne** Czech Republic & **sw** Poland — **Si·le·sian** \\-zhən, -shən\\ *adj or n*

Simbirsk — see ULYANOVSK

Sim·coe, Lake \\'sim-kō\\ lake Canada in **se** Ontario

Sim·fe·ro·pol \\,sim-fə-'rȯ-pəl, ,simp-, -'rō-\\ city **s** central Crimea peninsula

Sim·la \\'sim-lə\\ city **n** India, capital of Himachal Pradesh

Sim·plon \\'sim-,plän\\ **1** pass between Italy & Switzerland in Lepontine Alps **2** tunnel 19.8 kilometers long near the pass

Si·nai \\'sī-,nī\\ **1** — see HOREB **2** peninsula extension of continent of Asia **ne** Egypt between Red sea & the Mediterranean

Si·na·loa \\,sē-nə-'lō-ə, ,sin-ə-\\ state **w** Mexico on Gulf of California; capital, Culiacán

Sind \\'sind\\ province **s** Pakistan in lower Indus river valley; chief city Karachi

Sin·ga·pore \\'sing-ə-,pōr, -gə-, -,pȯr\\ **1** island off **s** end of Malay peninsula; a republic in the Commonwealth **2** city, its capital — **Sin·ga·por·ean** \\,sing-ə-'pōr-ē-ən, -gə-, -'pȯr-\\ *adj or n*

Sining — see XINING

Sinkiang–Uighur — see XINJIANG UYGUR

Sion — see ZION

Siracusa — see SYRACUSE

Sjæl·land \\'shel-,än\\ *or* **Zea·land** \\'zē-lənd\\ island, largest of islands of Denmark; site of Copenhagen

Skag·ge·rak \\'skag-ə-,rak\\ arm of North sea between **s** Norway & **n** Denmark

Skop·je \\'skȯp-,yä\\ city **n** Macedonia

Sky·ros \\'skī-rəs, -,räs\\ *or Greek* **Skí·ros** \\'skē-,rȯs\\ island Greece in Northern Sporades **e** of Euboea

Sla·vo·nia \\slə-'vō-nē-ə, -nyə\\ region **e** Croatia between Sava, Drava, & Danube rivers — **Sla·vo·nian** \\-ne-ən, -nyən\\ *adj or n*

Sli·go \\'slī-gō\\ county **n** Republic of Ireland in Connacht

Slo·va·kia \\slō-'väk-ē-ə, -'vak-\\ country central Europe; capital, Bratislava

Slo·ve·nia \\slō-'vē-nē-ə, -nyə\\ country **s** Europe **n** & **w** of Croatia; formerly a constituent republic of Yugoslavia; capital, Ljubljana — **Slo·ve·nian** \\-nē-ən, -nyən\\ *adj or n*

Smo•lensk \smō-'lensk\ city w Russia in Europe, wsw of Moscow

Smyrna — see IZMIR

Snow•don \'snōd-n\ massif 1085 meters NW Wales; highest point in Wales

Snow•do•nia \snō-'dō-nē-ə, -nyə\ mountainous district NW Wales centering around Snowdon

So•chi \'sō-chē\ city s Russia in Europe, on Black sea

So•ci•e•ty \sə-'sī-ət-ē\ islands s Pacific in French Polynesia; capital Papeete (on Tahiti)

So•co•tra \sə-'kō-trə\ island Yemen in Indian ocean E of Gulf of Aden; capital, Tamrida

So•fia \'sō-fē-ə, 'sò-, sō-'\ city, capital of Bulgaria

So•ho \'sō-,hō\ district of central London, England, in Westminster

So•li•hull \,sō-li-'həl\ county borough central England in West Midlands

Sol•o•mon \'säl-ə-mən\ 1 islands w Pacific E of New Guinea divided between Papua New Guinea & British Solomon Islands 2 sea arm of Coral sea w of the Solomons

So•ma•lia \sō-'mäl-ē-ə, sə-, -'mäl-yə\ or **So•ma•li Re•public** \-'mäl-ē\ country E Africa on Gulf of Aden & Indian ocean; a republic; capital, Mogadishu — **So•ma•li•an** \-'mäl-ē-ən, -'mäl-yən\ adj or n

So•ma•li•land \sō-'mäl-ē-,land, sə-\ region E Africa comprising Somalia, Djibouti, & part of E Ethiopia

Som•er•set \'səm-ər-,set, -sət\ or **Som•er•set•shire** \-,shiər, -shər\ county sw England

Somerset Nile — see NILE

Song•nam \'sòng-'näm\ city NW South Korea

So•no•ra \sə-'nōr-ə, -'nòr-\ state NW Mexico bordering on U.S.; capital, Hermosillo

So•nor•an \sə-'nōr-ən, -'nòr-\ or **Sonora** desert sw U.S. & NW Mexico in s Arizona, SE California, & N Sonora

Soo Canals — see SAULT SAINTE MARIE CANALS

Soochow — see SUZHOU

Sorata — see ILLAMPU

So•ro•ca•ba \,sōr-ə-'kab-ə, ,sòr-\ city SE Brazil w of São Paulo

Sos•no•wiec \säs-'nō-,vyets\ city sw Poland

South \'saùth\ island s New Zealand

South Africa, Republic of country s Africa; an independent republic; until 1961 (as **Union of South Africa**) a British dominion; administrative capital, Pretoria; legislative capital, Cape Town; judicial capital, Bloemfontein

South America continent of western hemisphere SE of North America & chiefly s of the equator — **South American** adj or n

South•amp•ton \saùth-'am-tən, -'ham-, -'amp-, -'hamp-\ city s England in Hampshire

South Australia state s Australia; capital, Adelaide — **South Australian** adj or n

South Bend \'bend\ city N Indiana

South Cape or **South Point** — see KA LAE

South Car•o•li•na \,kar-ə-'lī-nə\ state SE U.S.; capital, Columbia — **South Car•o•lin•i•an** \-'lin-ē-ən, -'lin-yən\ adj or n

South China sea — see CHINA

South Da•ko•ta \də-'kōt-ə\ state NW central U.S.; capital, Pierre — **South Da•ko•tan** \-'kōt-n\ adj or n

South•end on Sea \,saù-,thend-\ borough SE England in Essex E of London

Southern Alps mountain range New Zealand in w South Island extending almost the length of the island

Southern Rhodesia — see ZIMBABWE

Southern Yemen — see YEMEN

South Gla•mor•gan \glə-'mòr-gən\ county SE Wales; established 1974; includes Cardiff

South Korea — see KOREA

South Seas the areas of the Atlantic, Indian, & Pacific oceans in the southern hemisphere; especially, the s Pacific

South Shields \'shēldz, 'shēlz\ city N England in Tyne and Wear

South Tirol — see ALTO ADIGE

South Vietnam — see VIETNAM

South•wark \'səth-ərk, 'saùth-wərk\ borough of s London, England

South–West Africa — see NAMIBIA

South York•shire \'yòrk-,shiər, -shər\ metropolitan county N England

Soviet Central Asia former name for the portion of central & sw Asia belonging to U.S.S.R. & comprising the Kazakh, Kirgiz, Tadzhik, Turkmen, & Uzbek republics

Soviet Russia 1 — see RUSSIA **2** — see UNION OF SOVIET SOCIALIST REPUBLICS

Soviet Union — see UNION OF SOVIET SOCIALIST REPUBLICS

Spain \'spän\ or Spanish **Es•pa•ña** \ā-'spän-yä\ or ancient **His•pa•nia** \his-'pān-ē-ə, -'pān-yə, -'pan-\ country sw Europe in Iberian peninsula; a kingdom; capital, Madrid

Spanish America 1 the Spanish-speaking countries of America **2** the parts of America settled & formerly governed by the Spanish

Spanish Guinea — see EQUATORIAL GUINEA

Spanish Main \'mān\ **1** the mainland of Spanish America especially along N coast of South America **2** the Caribbean sea & adjacent waters especially when region was infested with pirates

Spanish Morocco — see MOROCCO

Spanish Sahara former Spanish territory NW Africa sw of Morocco comprising Río de Oro & Saguia el Hamra — see WESTERN SAHARA

Spar•ta \'spärt-ə\ or **Lac•e•dae•mon** \,las-ə-'dē-mən\ ancient city s Greece in Peloponnesus, capital of Laconia

Spey•er \'shpī-ər, 'spī-; 'shpīr, 'spīr\ or **Spires** \'spīrz\ city sw Germany on Rhine N of Karlsruhe

Spice Islands — see MOLUCCAS

Spits•ber•gen \'spits-,bər-gən\ islands in Arcitc ocean N of Norway; chief island, West Spitsbergen — see SVALBARD

Split \'split\ or **Spljet** \'splʸet, splē-'et\ or Italian **Spa•la•to** \'späl-ə-,tō\ city s Croatia

Spo•kane \spō-'kan\ city E Washington

Spor•a•des \'spòr-ə-,dēz, 'spär-\ two island groups Greece in the Aegean: the **Northern Sporades** (chief island, Skyros, E of Euboea) & **Southern Sporades** (including Samos, Icaria, & the Dodecanese, off sw Turkey)

Spring•field \'spring-,fēld\ **1** city, capital of Illinois **2** city sw Massachusetts **3** city sw Missouri

Springs \'springz\ city NE Republic of South Africa in s Transvaal

Sri Lan•ka \srē-'läng-kə, 'srē-\ or formerly **Cey•lon** \si-'län, sā-\ country coextensive with island of Ceylon; an independent republic in the Commonwealth; capital, Colombo

Sri•na•gar \sri-'nəg-ər\ city, summer capital of Jammu and Kashmir, in w Kashmir on Jhelum river

Staf•ford•shire \'staf-ərd-,shiər, -shər\ or **Stafford** county w central England

Staked Plain — see LLANO ESTACADO

Stalingrad — see VOLGOGRAD

Stam•ford \'stam-fərd, 'stamp-\ city sw Connecticut

Stan•ley \'stan-lē\ town, capital of Falkland Islands

Stanley, Mount — see RUWENZORI

Stanleyville — see KISANGANI

Stat•en Island \'stat-n\ **1** island SE New York sw of mouth of the Hudson **2** or formerly **Rich•mond** \'rich-mənd\ borough of New York City including Staten Island

States of the Church or **Papal States** temporal domain of the popes in central Italy 755–1870

Stavropol — see TOL'YATTI

\ə\ abut		\ng\ sing	
\ər\ further		\ō\ bone	
\a\ mat		\ò\ saw	
\ā\ take		\òi\ coin	
\ä\ cot, cart		\th\ thin	
\aù\ out		\th\ this	
\ch\ chin		\ū\ food	
\e\ pet		\ù\ foot	
\ē\ easy		\y\ yet	
\g\ go		\yū\ few	
\i\ tip		\yù\ cure	
\ī\ life		\zh\ vision	
\j\ job			

Stir·ling \'stər-ling\ *or* **Stir·ling·shire** \-,shiər, -shər\ former county central Scotland

Stock·holm \'stäk-,hōlm, -,hōm\ city, capital of Sweden

Stock·port \'stäk-,pōrt, -,pȯrt\ borough NW England in Greater Manchester

Stock·ton \'stäk-tən\ city central California

Stoke on Trent \,stō-,kȯn-'trent, -,kän-\ city central England in Staffordshire

Stone·henge \'stōn-,henj, stōn-'henj\ assemblage of megaliths S England in Wiltshire on Salisbury Plain; erected by a prehistoric people

Stone Mountain mountain 514 meters NW Georgia E of Atlanta

Straits Settlements former British crown colony SE Asia on Strait of Malacca comprising Singapore Island & George Town & Malacca settlements on Malay peninsula

Stras·bourg \'sträs-,bûrg, 'sträz-, -,bərg\ city NE France

Strat·ford–upon–Avon \'strat-fərd\ borough central England in Warwickshire

Strath·clyde \strath-'klīd\ region SW Scotland; established 1975; includes Glasgow

Strom·bo·li \'sträm-bə-lē\ volcano 927 meters Italy in Lipari islands on Stromboli Island

Stutt·gart \'shtút-,gärt, 'stút-, 'stət-\ city SW Germany, capital of Baden-Württemberg

Styr·ia \'stir-ē-ə\ region central & SE Austria; capital, Graz

Styx \'stiks\ chief river of Hades in Greek mythology

Süchow 1 — see XUZHOU 2 — see YIBIN

Su·cre \'sü-krā\ city, constitutional capital of Bolivia

Su·dan \sü-'dan, -'dän\ 1 region N Africa S of the Sahara between the Atlantic & the upper Nile 2 country NE Africa S of Egypt; a republic; capital, Khartoum — see ANGLO-EGYPTIAN SUDAN — **Su·da·nese** \,süd-n-'ēz, -'ēs\ *adj or n*

Su·de·ten \sü-'dāt-n\ 1 mountains central Europe between Czech Republic & Poland 2 *or* **Su·de·ten·land** \sü-'dāt-n-,land\ region NE Czech Republic in Sudeten mountains

Su·ez \sü-'ez, 'sü-,ez\ 1 city NE Egypt at S end of Suez canal on **Gulf of Suez** (arm of Red sea) 2 canal 148 kilometers long NE Egypt across Isthmus of Suez

Suez, Isthmus of neck of land NE Egypt between Mediterranean & Red seas connecting Africa & Asia

Suf·folk \'səf-ək\ county E England on North sea

Su·i·ta \sü-'ēt-ə\ city Japan in S Honshu N of Osaka

Su·la·we·si \,sü-lə-'wā-sē\ *or* **Ce·le·bes** \'sel-ə-,bēz, sə-'lē-bēz\ island Indonesia E of Borneo

Su·lu \'sü-lü\ archipelago SW Philippines SW of Mindanao — see BASILAN

Su·ma·tra \sü-'mä-trə\ island W Indonesia S of Malay peninsula — **Su·ma·tran** \-trən\ *adj or n*

Su·mer \'sü-mər\ the S division of ancient Babylonia — **Su·me·ri·an** \sü-'mer-ē-ən, -'mir-\ *adj or n*

Sun·da \'sün-də\ 1 islands Malay archipelago comprising the **Greater Sunda** islands (Sumatra, Borneo, Java, Sulawesi, & adjacent islands) & the **Lesser Sunda** islands (extending from Bali to Timor); with exception of N Borneo belongs to Indonesia 2 strait between Java & Sumatra

Sun·der·land \'sən-dər-lənd\ borough N England in Tyne and Wear

Suomi *or* **Suomen Tasavalta** — see FINLAND

Su·pe·ri·or, Lake \sù-'pir-ē-ər\ lake E central North America in U.S. & Canada; largest of the Great Lakes

Su·ra·ba·ja \,sùr-ə-'bī-ə\ city Indonesia in NE Java

Su·ra·kar·ta \,sùr-ə-'kärt-ə\ city Indonesia in central Java

Su·rat \'sùr-ət, sə-'rat\ city W India in SE Gujarat

Su·ri·na·me \,sùr-ə-'näm-ə\ *or* **Su·ri·nam** \'sùr-ə-,nam, ,sùr-ə-'näm\ *or formerly* **Dutch Guiana** country N South America between Guyana & French Guiana; capital, Paramaribo

Sur·rey \'sər-ē, 'sə-rē\ 1 county SE England SW of London 2 city Canada in SW British Columbia

Su·sa \'sü-zə\ *or biblical* **Shu·shan** \'shü-shən, -,shan\ ancient city, capital of Elam; ruins in SW Iran

Sus·sex \'səs-iks\ former county SE England on English channel — see EAST SUSSEX, WEST SUSSEX

Suth·er·land \'səth-ər-lənd\ *or* **Suth·er·land·shire** \-,shiər, -shər\ former county N Scotland

Sut·ton \'sət-n\ borough of S Greater London, England

Su·va \'sü-və\ city, capital of Fiji on Viti Levu Island

Su·won \'sü-,wän\ city SW South Korea S of Seoul

Su·zhou \'sü-'jō\ *or* **Soo·chow** \'sü-'jō, -'chaù\ *or formerly* **Wu·hsien** \'wü-shē-'en\ city E China in Jiangsu W of Shanghai

Sval·bard \'sfäl-,bär\ islands in Arctic ocean including Spitsbergen & Bear Island; under Norwegian administration

Sverdlovsk — see YEKATERINBURG

Swan·sea \'swän-zē\ city SE Wales

Swatow — see SHANTOU

Swa·zi·land \'swäz-ē-,land\ country SE Africa between Transvaal & Mozambique; an independent kingdom; capital, Mbabane — **Swa·zi** \'swäz-ē\ *adj or n*

Swe·den \'swēd-n\ country N Europe on Scandinavian peninsula bordering on Baltic sea; a kingdom; capital, Stockholm

Swit·zer·land \'swit-sər-lənd\ *or Latin* **Hel·ve·tia** \hel-'vē-shə, -shē-ə\ *or French* **Suisse** \'swÿēs\ *or German* **Schweiz** \'shfīts\ *or Italian* **Sviz·ze·ra** \'zvēt-sä-rä\ country W Europe in the Alps; a republic; capital, Bern

Syd·ney \'sid-nē\ city SE Australia, capital of New South Wales

Syr·a·cuse \'sir-ə-,kyūs, -kyúz\ 1 city central New York 2 ancient city Italy in SE Sicily; site at modern city of **Si·ra·cu·sa** \,sē-rä-'kü-zə\

Syr·ia \'sir-ē-ə\ 1 ancient region SW Asia bordering on the Mediterranean 2 former French mandate (1920–44) including present Syria & Lebanon 3 country S of Turkey; a republic; capital, Damascus — **Syr·i·an** \'sir-ē-ən\ *adj or n*

Syrian Desert desert region N Saudi Arabia, SE Syria, W Iraq, & NE Jordan

Szcze·cin \'shchet-,sēn\ city NW Poland on the Oder

Sze·chwan \'sech-'wän\ *or* **Si·chuan** \'sēch-'wän\ province SW China; capital, Chengdu

Ta·bas·co \tə-'bas-kō\ state SE Mexico SW of Yucatán peninsula; capital, Villahermosa

Ta·ble Bay \,tā-bəl-\ harbor of Cape Town, Republic of South Africa

Ta·briz \tə-'brēz\ city NW Iran

Ta·co·ma \tə-'kō-mə\ city W Washington

Tae·gu \ta-'gü, tī-\ city South Korea NNW of Pusan

Tae·jon \ta-'jȯn, tī-\ city South Korea NW of Taegu

Ta·gan·rog \'tag-ən-,räg\ city SW Russia in Europe, W of Rostov

Ta·gus \'tā-gəs\ *or Spanish* **Ta·jo** \'tä-hō\ *or Portuguese* **Te·jo** \'tā-zhü\ river 911 kilometers long Spain & Portugal flowing W into the Atlantic

Ta·hi·ti \tə-'hēt-ē\ island S Pacific in French Polynesia in Society islands; chief town, Papeete — **Ta·hi·tian** \-'hē-shən\ *adj or n*

Tai·chung \'tī-'chùng\ city China in W Taiwan

Tai·nan \'tī-'nän\ city China in SW Taiwan

Tai·pei \'tī-'pā, -'bā\ *or formerly* **Dai·ho·ku** \'dī-'hō-,kü\ city, capital of (Nationalist) Republic of China in N Taiwan

Tai·wan \'tī-'wän\ *or* **For·mo·sa** \fȯr-'mō-sə, fər-, -zə\ 1 island China off SE coast; since 1949 seat of government of (Nationalist) Republic of China; capital, Taipei 2 strait between Taiwan & China mainland connecting East China & South China seas — **Tai·wan·ese** \,tī-wə-'nēz, -'nēs\ *adj or n*

Tai·yuan \'tī-yü-'än\ *or formerly* **Yang·ku** \'yäng-'kü\ city N China, capital of Shanxi

Tai·zhou or **T'ai-chou** \'tī-'jō\ city E China in central Jiangsu NW of Shanghai

Ta·jik·i·stan \tä-'jik-i-,stan, -'jēk-\ country W central Asia; capital, Dushanbe; a constituent republic (**Ta·dzhik·i·stan** \same \ or **Ta·dzhik Republic** \tä-'jik, -'jēk\) of U.S.S.R. 1929–91

Ta·ka·ma·tsu \,täk-ə-'mät-sū, tä-'käm-ət-,sū\ city Japan in NE Shikoku

Ta·kat·su·ki \tə-'kät-sú-kē\ city Japan in S Honshu NNE of Osaka

Ta·kli·ma·kan or **Ta·kla Ma·kan** \,täk-lə-mə-'kän\ desert W China in Xinjiang Uygur

Tal·la·has·see \,tal-ə-'has-ē\ city, capital of Florida

Tal·linn \'tal-ən, 'täl-\ or formerly **Re·val** \'rä-vəl\ city, capital of Estonia

Ta·mau·li·pas \,täm-aú-'lē-pəs, təm-\ state NE Mexico; capital, Ciudad Victoria

Tam·bov \täm-'bóf, -'bóv\ city S central Russia in Europe, SE of Moscow

Tam·il Na·du \,tam-əl-'näd-ü\ or formerly **Ma·dras** \mə-'dras, -'dräs\ state S India on Bay of Bengal; capital, Madras

Tam·pa \'tam-pə\ city W Florida on Tampa Bay

Tam·pe·re \'tam-pə-,rä, 'täm-\ city SW Finland

Tam·pi·co \tam-'pē-kō\ city E Mexico in S Tamaulipas

Tananarive — see ANTANANARIVO

Tan·gan·yi·ka \,tan-gən-'yē-kə, ,tang-gən-, -gə-'nē-\ former country E Africa S of Kenya; became part of Tanzania 1964

Tanganyika, Lake lake E Africa between Tanzania & Zaire

Tang·shan \'täng-'shäng\ city NE China in E Hebei

Tan·ta \'tänt-ə\ city N Egypt in central Nile delta

Tan-tung — see DANDONG

Tan·za·nia \,tan-zə-'nē-ə, ,tän-\ country E Africa on Indian ocean; a republic formed 1964 by union of Tanganyika & Zanzibar; capital, Dar es Salaam — **Tan·za·ni·an** \-'nē-ən\ adj or n

Taor·mi·na \taúr-'mē-nə\ city Italy in NE Sicily

Ta·ran·to \'tär-ən-,tō, tə-'rant-ō\ or ancient **Ta·ren·tum** \tə-'rent-əm\ city SE Italy on Gulf of Taranto

Ta·ra·wa \tə-'rä-wə\ island, capital of Kiribati

Ta·rim \dä-'rēm, 'tä-\ river 2010 kilometers long W China in Xinjiang Uygur flowing into a marshy depression

Tar·lac \'tär-,läk\ city Philippines in central Luzon

Tar·shish \'tär-shish\ ancient maritime country referred to in the Bible & often identified with Tartessus

Tar·sus \'tär-səs\ ancient city of S Asia Minor, capital of Cilicia; now a city of S Turkey

Tar·tes·sus or **Tar·tes·sos** \tär-'tes-əs\ ancient kingdom on SW coast of Spain near mouth of the Guadalquivir — see TARSHISH

Tash·kent \tash-'kent\ city, capital of Uzbekistan

Tas·man \'taz-mən\ sea comprising the part of the S Pacific between SE Australia & New Zealand

Tas·ma·nia \taz-'mā-nē-ə, -nyə\ or earlier **Van Diemen's Land** \van-'dē-mənz\ island SE Australia S of Victoria; a state; capital, Hobart — **Tas·ma·nian** \-nē-ən, -nyən\ adj or n

Ta·ta·ry \'tät-ə-rē\ or **Tar·ta·ry** \'tärt-ə-rē\ indefinite historical region in Asia & Europe extending from Sea of Japan to the Dnieper

Ta·tra \'tä-trə\ or **High Tatra** or Czech **Vy·so·ké Ta·try** \,vis-ə-,kā-'tä-trē\ mountains N Slovakia & S Poland in central Carpathian mountains

Tatung — see DATONG

Tau·rus \'tór-əs\ mountains S Turkey parallel to Mediterranean coast; highest 3734 meters

Tay·side \'tā-,sīd\ region E central Scotland; established 1975

Tbi·li·si \tə-'bē-lə-sē, tə-bə-'lē-sē\ or **Tif·lis** \'tif-ləs, tə-'flēs\ city, capital of Republic of Georgia

Te·gu·ci·gal·pa \tə-,gü-si-'gal-pə\ city, capital of Honduras

Teh·ran or **Te·he·ran** \,tā-ə-'ran, -'rän\ city, capital of Iran

Tel·a·nai·pura \,tel-ə-'nī-,pùr-ə\ city & port Indonesia in Sumatra

Tel Aviv \,tel-ə-'vēv\ city W Israel on the Mediterranean

Ten·nes·see \,ten-ə-'sē, 'ten-ə-,\ state E central U.S.; capital, Nashville — **Ten·nes·se·an** or **Ten·nes·see·an** \,ten-ə-'sē-ən\ adj or n

Te·re·si·na \,ter-ə-'zē-nə\ city NE Brazil

Té·tou·an \tā-twän\ or **Te·tuán** \te-'twän, ,tet-ə-'wän\ city N Morocco

Tex·as \'tek-səs, -siz\ state S U.S.; capital, Austin — **Tex·an** \-sən\ adj or n

Thai·land \'tī-,land, -lənd\ or formerly **Si·am** \sī-'am\ country SE Asia on Gulf of Siam; capital, Bangkok — **Thai·land·er** \'tī-,lan-dər, -lən-dər\ n

Thailand, Gulf of — see SIAM

Thames \'temz\ river 338 kilometers long S England flowing E from the Cotswolds in Gloucestershire into the North sea

Thar \'tär\ or **Indian** desert E Pakistan & NW Republic of India E of Indus river

Thebes \'thēbz\ 1 or ancient **The·bae** \'thē-bē\ or later **Di·os·po·lis** \dī-'äs-pə-ləs\ ancient city S Egypt, capital of Upper Egypt on the Nile on site including modern towns of Karnak & Luxor 2 ancient city E Greece NNW of Athens on site of modern village of Thivai — **The·ban** \'thē-bən\ adj or n

Theodore Roosevelt National Park reservation W North Dakota

Thes·sa·lo·ni·ca \,thes-ə-lə-'nī-kə, -'län-i-kə\ — see SALONIKA — **Thes·sa·lo·nian** \-'lō-nē-ən, -'lō-nyən\ adj or n

Thes·sa·ly \'thes-ə-lē\ region central Greece between Pindus mountains & the Aegean — **Thes·sa·lian** \thə-'sā-lē-ən, -'säl-yən\ adj or n

Thim·bu \'thim-bü\ city, capital of Bhutan

Thousand islands Canada & U.S. in the Saint Lawrence in Ontario & New York

Thrace \'thrās\ or ancient **Thra·cia** \'thrā-shə, -shē-ə\ region SE Europe in Balkan peninsula N of the Aegean now divided between Greece & Turkey; in ancient times extended N to the Danube — **Thra·cian** \'thrā-shən\ adj or n

Thunder Bay city Canada in SW Ontario

Thur·rock \'thər-ək, 'thə-rək\ district SE England in Essex

Tian·jin \tē-'än-'jin\ or **Tien·tsin** \tē-'ent-'sin, 'tint-\ city NE China in Hebei

Tian Shan \tē-'än-'shän\ or **Tien Shan** \tē-'en-'shän\ mountain system central Asia extending NE from Pamirs into Xinjiang Uygur; highest Pobeda Peak (in Kyrgyzstan) 7439 meters

Ti·ber \'tī-bər\ or Italian **Te·ve·re** \'tā-vā-rā\ or ancient **Ti·ber·is** \'tī-bə-rəs\ river 360 kilometers long central Italy flowing through Rome into Tyrrhenian sea

Tiberias, Sea of — see GALILEE

Ti·bes·ti \tə-'bes-tē\ mountains N central Africa in central Sahara in NW Chad; highest 3415 meters

Ti·bet \tə-'bet\ or **Xi·zang** \'shēd-'zäng\ autonomous region SW China on high plateau N of the Himalayas; capital, Lhasa

Tier·ra del Fue·go \tē-'er-ə-,del-fù-'ā-gō, -fyü-\ 1 archipelago off S South America S of Strait of Magellan 2 chief island of the group; divided between Argentina & Chile

Tiflis — see TBILISI

Ti·gris \'tī-grəs\ river 1850 kilometers long Turkey & Iraq flowing SSE & uniting with the Euphrates to form the Shatt-al-Arab

Ti·jua·na \,tē-ə-'wän-ə, tē-'wän-\ city NW Mexico on U.S. border in Baja California

Til·burg \'til-,bərg\ city S Netherlands

Tim·buk·tu or **Tim·buc·too** \,tim-,bək-'tü, tim-'bək-tü\ or **Tom·bouc·tou** \tōⁿ-bük-'tü\ town W Africa in Mali near Niger river

\ə\ abut \ng\ sing
\ər\ further \ō\ bone
\a\ mat \ó\ saw
\ā\ take \ói\ coin
\ä\ cot, cart \th\ thin
\aú\ out \th\ this
\ch\ chin \ü\ food
\e\ pet \ú\ foot
\ē\ easy \y\ yet
\g\ go \yü\ few
\i\ tip \yú\ cure
\ī\ life \zh\ vision
\j\ job

Ti·mi·soa·ra \,tē-mish-ə-'wär-ə, -mish-'wär-\ city **sw** Romania

Ti·mor \'tē-,mȯr, tē-'\ island Indonesia **se** of Sulawesi; **w** half formerly belonged to Netherlands, **e** half to Portugal

Tip·pe·rary \,tip-ə-'reər-ē\ county **s** Ireland in Munster

Ti·ra·ne or **Ti·ra·na** \ti-'rän-ə\ city, capital of Albania

Ti·rol or **Ty·rol** \tə-'rōl; 'tī-,rōl, tī-'; 'tir-əl\ or Italian **Ti·ro·lo** \tē-'rȯ-lō\ region in **e** Alps in **w** Austria & **ne** Italy — **Ti·ro·le·an** \tə-'rō-lē-ən, tī-; ,tir-ə-', ,tī-rə-'\ or **Tir·o·lese** \,tir-ə-'lēz, ,tī-rə-, -'lēs\ adj or n

Ti·ruch·chi·rap·pal·li \,tir-ə-chə-'räp-ə-lē\ city **s** India in Tamil Nadu

Ti·ti·ca·ca, Lake \,tit-i-'käk-ə\ lake on Bolivia-Peru boundary at altitude of 3810 meters

Tlax·ca·la \tlä-'skäl-ə\ state **se** central Mexico; capital, Tlaxcala

To·ba·go \tə-'bā-gō\ island West Indies **ne** of Trinidad; a territory of Trinidad and Tobago

To·go \'tō-gō\ or **To·go·land** \-,land\ region **w** Africa on Gulf of Guinea between Benin & Ghana; until 1918 a German protectorate; then divided into two trust territories: **British Togoland** (in **w**, since 1957 part of Ghana) & **French Togo** (in **e**, since 1958 the **Republic of Togo**; capital, Lomé) — **To·go·land·er** \-,lan-dər\ n — **To·go·lese** \,tō-gō-'lēz, -'lēs\ adj or n

To·ko·ro·za·wa \,tō-kə-'rō-zə-,wä\ city Japan on Honshu

To·ku·shi·ma \,tō-kə-'shē-mə\ city Japan in **e** Shikoku

To·kyo \'tō-kē-,ō\ city, capital of Japan in **se** Honshu on Tokyo Bay — **To·kyo·ite** \'tō-kē-,ō-,īt\ n

To·le·do \tə-'lēd-ō, -'lēd-ə\ **1** city **nw** Ohio **2** city central Spain **sw** of Madrid

To·lu·ca \tə-'lü-kə\ city central Mexico, capital of Mexico state

Tol'·yat·ti or **To·gliat·ti** \tȯl-'yät-ē\ or formerly **Stav·ro·pol** \stav-'rȯ-pəl, -'rō-\ city Russia in Europe, **nw** of Samara

Tombouctou — see TIMBUKTU

Tomsk \'tämsk, 'tämpsk, 'tȯmsk, 'tȯmpsk\ city **s** central Russia in Asia

Ton·ga \'täŋ-gə, 'täŋ-ə\ or **Friendly** islands **sw** Pacific **e** of Fiji islands; a kingdom in the Commonwealth; capital, Nukualofa — **Ton·gan** \-gən, -ən\ adj or n

Tong·hua or **T'ung-hua** \'tȯŋ-'hwä, -'wä\ city **ne** China in **sw** Jilin

To·pe·ka \tə-'pē-kə\ city, capital of Kansas

Tor·bay \tȯr-'bā, 'tȯr-\ town **sw** England in Devonshire

To·ron·to \tə-'ränt-ō, -'ränt-ə\ city, capital of Ontario

Tor·rance \'tȯr-əns, 'tär-\ city **sw** California

Tor·re·ón \,tȯr-ē-'ōn\ city **n** Mexico in **sw** Coahuila

Tor·res \'tȯr-əs\ strait between New Guinea & Cape York peninsula, Australia

Tor·tu·ga \tȯr-'tü-gə\ island Haiti off **n** coast; a resort of pirates in 17th century

To·run \'tȯr-,ün-yə, -,ün\ city **n** Poland on the Vistula

Toscana — see TUSCANY

Tou·lon \tü-'lōⁿ\ city **se** France **ese** of Marseilles

Tou·louse \tü-'lüz\ city **s** France on the Garonne

Tou·raine \tù-'rän, -'ren\ region **nw** central France; chief city Tours

Tourane — see DA NANG

Tours \'tùr\ city **nw** central France

Tow·er Hamlets \'taủ-ər-, 'taủr-\ borough of **e** Greater London, England

To·ya·ma \tō-'yäm-ə\ city Japan in **w** central Honshu

To·yo·ha·shi \,tȯi-ə-'häsh-ē\ city Japan in **s** Honshu

To·yo·na·ka \,tȯi-ə-'nä-kə\ city Japan on Honshu

To·yo·ta \tȯi-'ōt-ə\ city Japan on Honshu

Tra·fal·gar, Cape \trə-'fal-gər, Spanish ,trä-fäl-'gär\ headland **sw** Spain at **w** end of Strait of Gibraltar

Trans·al·pine Gaul \trans-,al-,pīn-, tranz-\ the part of Gaul included in modern France & Belgium

Transjordan — see JORDAN

Trans·vaal \trans-'väl, tranz-\ province **ne** Republic of South Africa between Vaal & Limpopo rivers; capital, Pretoria

Tran·syl·va·nia \,trans-əl-'vā-nyə, -nē-ə\ region **w** Romania — **Tran·syl·va·nian** \-nyən, -nē-ən\ adj or n

Transylvanian Alps a **s** extension of Carpathian mountains in central Romania

Treb·i·zond \'treb-ə-,zänd\ Greek empire 1204–1461, an offshoot of Byzantine Empire; at greatest extent included Crimea, Georgia, & **n** coast of Black sea **e** of Sakarya river; capital, Trebizond (modern Trabon, in Turkey)

Tren·ti·no-Al·to Adi·ge \tren-'tē-,nō-,äl-,tō-'äd-i-,jā\ region **n** Italy; capital, Trento

Tren·to \'tren-,tō\ city **ne** Italy

Tren·ton \'trent-n\ city, capital of New Jersey

Trier \'triər\ or **Treves** \'trēvz\ city **sw** Germany on the Moselle

Tri·este \trē-'est, trē-'es-tē\ city **ne** Italy on the Adriatic

Trin·i·dad \'trin-ə-,dad\ island West Indies off **ne** coast of Venezuela; with Tobago forms (since 1962) the country of **Trinidad and Tobago**; capital, Port of Spain — **Trin·i·da·di·an** \,trin-ə-'däd-ē-ən, -'dad-\ adj or n

Trip·o·li \'trip-ə-lē\ **1** city, capital of Libya **2** city **nw** Lebanon **3** Tripolitania when it was one of the Barbary States

Trip·ol·i·ta·nia \trip-,äl-ə-'tān-yə, ,trip-ə-lə-\ region **nw** Libya; chief city, Tripoli

Tri·pu·ra \'trip-ə-rə\ state **e** India between Bangladesh & Assam; capital, Agartala

Tris·tan da Cu·nha \,tris-tən-də-'kü-nə\ island **s** Atlantic, chief of the Tristan da Cunha islands belonging to British colony of Saint Helena

Tri·van·drum \triv-'an-drəm\ city **s** India **nw** of Cape Comorin, capital of Kerala

Tro·as \'trō-,as\ or **Tro·ad** \-,ad\ territory surrounding ancient city of Troy in **nw** Mysia

Tro·bri·and \'trō-brē-,änd\ islands **sw** Pacific in Solomon sea belonging to Papua New Guinea

Troy \'trȯi\ or **Il·i·um** \'il-ē-əm\ or **Il·i·on** \'il-ē-,än, -ē-ən\ or ancient **Troia** \'trȯi-ə, 'trō-yə\ or **Tro·ja** \'trō-jə, -yə\ ancient city **nw** Asia Minor **sw** of the Dardanelles

Trucial States or **Trucial Oman** — see UNITED ARAB EMIRATES

Tru·ji·llo \trü-'hē-ō, -yō\ city **nw** Peru

Truk \'trək, 'trük\ islands **w** Pacific in central Carolines; chief town, Moen (on Moen Island)

Tsaritsyn — see VOLGOGRAD

Tsinan — see JINAN

Tsinghai — see QINGHAI

Tsingtao — see QINGDAO

Tu·a·mo·tu \,tü-ə-'mō-tü\ archipelago **s** Pacific in French Polynesia **e** of Society islands

Tu·buai \tüb-'wä-ē\ or **Aus·tral** \'ȯs-trəl, 'äs-\ islands **s** Pacific in French Polynesia **s** of Tahiti

Tuc·son \tü-'sän, 'tü-,\ city **se** Arizona

Tucumán — see SAN MIGUEL DE TUCUMÁN

Tu·la \'tü-lə\ city **w** Russia in Europe, **s** of Moscow

Tul·sa \'təl-sə\ city **ne** Oklahoma

T'ung-hua — see TONGHUA

Tu·nis \'tü-nəs, 'tyü-\ **1** city, capital of Tunisia **2** Tunisia especially as one of the former Barbary States — **Tu·ni·sian** \tü-'nē-zhən, tyü-, -zhē-ən; -'nizh-ən, -ē-ən\ adj or n

Tu·ni·sia \tü-'nē-zhə, tyü-, -zhē-ə; -'nizh-ə, -ē-ə\ country **n** Africa on the Mediterranean **e** of Algeria; a republic; capital, Tunis — **Tu·ni·sian** \-zhən, -zhē-ən; -ən, -ē-ən\ adj or n

Tu·rin \'tùr-ən, 'tyùr-; tù-'rin, tyü-\ or Italian **To·ri·no** \tō-'rē-nō\ city **nw** Italy on the Po, capital of Piedmont

Tur·key \'tər-kē\ country **w** Asia (**Turkey in Asia**) & **se** Europe (**Turkey in Europe**) between Mediterranean & Black seas; a republic; capital, Ankara

Turk·men·i·stan \,tərk-'men-ə-,stan\ country central Asia bordering on Afghanistan, Iran, & Caspian sea; a constituent republic (or **Turk·men Republic** \,tərk-mən-\ ) of U.S.S.R. 1925–91; capital, Ashkhabad — **Turk·me·ni·an** \ˌtərk-'mē-nē-ən\ *adj*

Turks and Cai·cos \ˌtərk-sən-'kā-kəs\ two groups of islands (Turks islands & Caicos islands) British West Indies at SE end of the Bahamas; a British colony

Tur·ku \'tùr-kü\ city SW Finland

Tus·ca·ny \'təs-kə-nē\ *or Italian* **To·sca·na** \tō-'skän-ə\ region NW central Italy; capital, Florence

Tu·tu·i·la \ˌtüt-ə-'wē-lə\ island S Pacific, chief of American Samoa group

Tu·va·lu \tü-'väl-ü, -'vär-\ *or formerly* **El·lice** \'el-əs\ islands W Pacific N of Fiji; an independent member of the Commonwealth; capital, Funafuti — see GILBERT

Tyne and Wear \'tī-nən-'dwiər, -'wiər\ metropolitan county N England; includes Newcastle upon Tyne

Tyre \'tīər\ ancient city, capital of Phoenicia; now a town of S Lebanon — **Tyr·i·an** \'tir-ē-ən\ *adj or n*

Tyrol — see TIROL — **Tyrolean** *adj or n* — **Tyrolese** *adj or n*

Ty·rone \tir-'ōn\ traditional county W central Northern Ireland

Tyr·rhe·ni·an \tə-'rē-nē-ən\ sea, part of the Mediterranean SW of Italy, N of Sicily, & E of Sardinia & Corsica

Tyu·men \tyü-'men\ city W Russia in Asia, ENE of Sverdlovsk

Tzu–kung — see ZIGONG

Tzu–po — see ZIBO

Ubangi–Shari — see CENTRAL AFRICAN REPUBLIC

Udi·ne \'üd-i-ˌnā\ city NE Italy NE of Venice

Ufa \ü-'fä\ city E Russia in Europe, NE of Samara

Ugan·da \yü-'gan-də, -'gàn-, -'gän-\ country E Africa N of Lake Victoria; a republic in the Commonwealth; capital, Kampala — **Ugan·dan** \-dən\ *adj or n*

Ujung Pan·dang \ü-ˌjùng-pän-'däng\ *or formerly* **Ma·cas·sar** *or* **Ma·kas·sar** *or* **Ma·kas·sar** \mə-'kas-ər\ city Indonesia in SW Celebes

Ukraine \yü-'krān, 'yü-ˌ\ country E Europe on N coast of Black sea; capital, Kiev; a constituent republic of U.S.S.R. 1923–91

Ulan Ba·tor \ˌü-ˌlän-'bä-ˌtòr\ *or formerly* **Ur·ga** \'ùr-gə\ city, capital of Mongolia

Ulan–Ude \ˌü-ˌlän-ù-'dä\ city S Russia in Asia, E of Lake Baikal

Ul·san \'ül-ˌsän\ city SE South Korea

Ul·ster \'əl-stər\ **1** region N Ireland comprising Northern Ireland & N Republic of Ireland; a province until 1921 **2** province N Republic of Ireland comprising counties Donegal, Cavan, & Monaghan **3** NORTHERN IRELAND

Ul·ya·novsk \ül-'yän-əfsk\ *or formerly* **Sim·birsk** \sim-'biərsk\ city central Russia in Europe

Um·bria \'əm-brē-ə\ region central Italy in the Apennines; capital, Perugia — **Um·bri·an** \-brē-ən\ *adj or n*

Un·ga·va \ˌən-'gav-ə\ **1** bay inlet of Hudson strait NE Canada **2** peninsula region NE Canada in N Quebec

Union of South Africa — see SOUTH AFRICA (Republic of)

Union of Soviet Socialist Republics *or* **Soviet Union** *or* **Soviet Russia** country (1922–91) E Europe & N Asia; a union of 15 constituent republics; capital, Moscow

United Arab Emir·ates \i-'mir-əts, ā-, -'miər-ˌāts\ *or formerly* **Tru·cial States** \'trü-shəl-\ *or* **Trucial Oman** country E Arabia on Persian Gulf; a republic composed of seven emirates; capital, Abu Dhabi

United Arab Republic former name (1961–71) of Arab Republic of Egypt & previously (1958–61) of union of Egypt & Syria

United Kingdom *or in full* **United Kingdom of Great Britain and Northern Ireland** country W Europe in British Isles comprising England, Scotland, Wales, Northern Ireland, Channel islands, & Isle of Man; capital, London

United Nations international territory; a small area in New York City in E central Manhattan; seat of permanent headquarters of the United Nations

United States of America *or* **United States** country North America bordering on Atlantic, Pacific, & Arctic oceans & including Hawaii; a federal republic; capital, Washington

Upper Canada former province, Canada in S part of present-day Ontario

Upper Volta — see BURKINA FASO — **Upper Vol·tan** \'vält-n, 'vōlt-, 'vòlt-\ *adj or n*

Ural \'yùr-əl\ **1** mountains W central Russia extending about 2575 kilometers S from point near Kara sea; usually considered dividing line between Europe & Asia; highest about 1830 meters **2** river 2255 kilometers long Russia flowing from S end of Ural mountains into Caspian sea

Uralsk \yù-'ralsk\ city W Kazakhstan

Ura·wa \ù-'rä-wə\ city Japan in central Honshu N of Tokyo

Ur·mia \'ùr-mē-ə\ city NW Iran

Uru·guay \'ùr-ə-ˌgwī, 'yùr-; 'yùr-ə-ˌgwä\ **1** river 1577 kilometers long SE South America rising in Brazil & flowing into Río de la Plata **2** country SE South America; a republic; capital, Montevideo — **Uru·guay·an** \ˌùr-ə-'gwī-ən, ˌyùr-; ˌyùr-ə-'gwä-\ *adj or n*

Ürüm·qi \ˈüē-'rüem-ˈchē\ *or* **Urum·chi** \ù-'rùm-chē, ˌùr-əm-'chē\ *or* **Wu·lu·mu·ch'i** \'wü-'lü-'mü-'chē\ city NW China, capital of Xinjiang Uygur

Urundi — see BURUNDI

Us·pa·lla·ta \ˌü-spə-'yät-ə, -'zhät-\ mountain pass 3840 meters S South America in the Andes between Argentina & Chile

Usumbura — see BUJUMBURA

Utah \'yü-ˌtò, -ˌtä\ state W U.S.; capital, Salt Lake City — **Utah·an** \'yü-ˌtò-ən, -ˌtòn, -ˌtä-ən, -ˌtän\ *adj or n* — **Utahn** \-ˌtò-ən, -ˌtòn, -ˌtä-ən, -ˌtän\ *n*

Utrecht \'yü-ˌtrekt\ city central Netherlands

Utsu·no·mi·ya \ˌüt-sə-'nō-mē-ˌä, -ˌyä\ city Japan in central Honshu N of Tokyo

Ut·tar Pra·desh \ˌüt-ər-prə-'desh, -'däsh\ state N India bordering on Tibet & Nepal; capital, Lucknow

Uz·bek·i·stan \ùz-ˌbek-i-'stan, ˌəz-, -'stän\ country W central Asia between Aral sea & Afghanistan; capital, Tashkent; a constituent republic (**Uz·bek Soviet Socialist Republic** \'ùz-ˌbek, 'əz-, ùz-'\) of U.S.S.R. 1924–91

Va·duz \vä-'düts\ town, capital of Liechtenstein

Va·len·cia \və-'len-chə, -chē-ə, -'len-sē-ə\ **1** region & ancient kingdom E Spain between Andalusia & Catalonia **2** city, its capital, on the Mediterranean **3** city N Venezuela WSW of Caracas

Val·la·do·lid \ˌval-əd-ə-'lid, -'lē\ city NW central Spain

Val·le d'Ao·sta \ˌväl-ā-dä-'òs-tə\ region NW Italy bordering on France & Switzerland; capital Aosta

Val·let·ta \və-'let-ə\ city, capital of Malta

Val·pa·rai·so \ˌval-pə-'rī-zō, -'rā-\ *or Spanish* **Val·pa·ra·í·so** \ˌväl-pä-rä-'ē-sō\ city central Chile on the Pacific WNW of Santiago

Van·cou·ver \van-'kü-vər\ **1** island W Canada in SW British Columbia **2** city SW British Columbia

Van Diemen's Land — see TASMANIA

Va·nu·a·tu \ˌvä-nü-'ä-ˌtü\ *or formerly* **New Heb·ri·des** \-'heb-rə-ˌdēz\ islands SW Pacific W of Fiji; an independent member of the Commonwealth; capital, Vila

Varanasi — see BANARAS

Var·na \'vär-nə\ city & port E Bulgaria on Black sea

Vat·i·can City \ˌvat-i-kən-\ *or Italian* **Cit·tà del Va·ti·ca·no** \chēt-'tä-del-ˌvä-tē-'kä-nō\ independent papal state within commune of Rome, Italy; created 1929

Ve·ne·to \'ven-ə-ˌtō, 'vā-nə-\ region NE Italy; capital, Venice

Ven·e·zu·e·la \ˌven-əz-ə-'wā-lə, -əz-'wā-, -'wē-\ country N South America; capital, Caracas — **Ven·e·zu·e·lan** \-lən\ *adj or n*

Ven·ice \'ven-əs\ *or Italian* **Ve·ne·zia** \vä-'net-sē-ə\ city N Italy on islands in Lagoon of Venice — **Ve·ne·tian** \və-'nē-shən\ *adj or n*

\ə\	abut	\ng\	sing
\ər\	further	\ō\	bone
\a\	mat	\ò\	saw
\ā\	take	\òi\	coin
\ä\	cot, cart	\th\	thin
\aù\	out	\th\	this
\ch\	chin	\ü\	food
\e\	pet	\ù\	foot
\ē\	easy	\y\	yet
\g\	go	\yü\	few
\i\	tip	\yù\	cure
\ī\	life	\zh\	vision
\j\	job		

Ve·ra·cruz \,ver-ə-'krüz, -'krüs\ **1** state E Mexico; capital, Jalapa **2** city E Mexico in Veracruz state on Gulf of Mexico

Ver·ee·ni·ging \fə-'rā-nə-ging, -nək-əng\ city NE Republic of South Africa in S Transvaal S of Johannesburg

Ver·mont \vər-'mänt\ state NE U.S.; capital, Montpelier — **Ver·mont·er** \-ər\ n

Ve·ro·na \və-'rō-nə\ city N Italy W of Venice

Ver·sailles \vər-'sī, ver-\ city N France; suburb of Paris

Vert, Cape \'vərt\ or **Cape Verde** \'vərd\ promontory W Africa in Senegal; most westerly point of Africa

Ve·su·vi·us \və-'sü-vē-əs\ volcano about 1220 meters S Italy near Bay of Naples

Vi·cen·te Ló·pez \vē-,sent-ə-'lō-,pez\ city E Argentina N of Buenos Aires

Vi·cen·za \vi-'chen-sə\ city NE Italy W of Venice

Vic·to·ria \vik-'tōr-ē-ə, -'tór-\ **1** city, capital of British Columbia on Vancouver Island **2** island N Canada in Arctic archipelago S of Melville Sound **3** state SE Australia; capital, Melbourne **4** city, capital of Hong Kong colony — **Vic·to·ri·an** \-ē-ən\ adj or n

Victoria, Lake lake E Africa in Tanzania, Kenya, & Uganda

Victoria Falls waterfall 107 meters high S Africa in the Zambezi on border between Zambia & Zimbabwe

Victoria Nile — see NILE

Vi·en·na \vē-'en-ə\ or German **Wien** \'vēn\ or ancient **Vin·dob·o·na** \vin-'däb-ə-nə\ or **Vin·dob·na** \-'däb-nə\ city, capital of Austria on the Danube — **Vi·en·nese** \,vē-ə-'nēz, -'nēs\ adj or n

Vien·tiane \vyen-'tyän\ city, capital of Laos

Viet·nam \vē-'et-näm, vyet-, vē-ət-, vēt-, -'nam\ country SE Asia in Indochina; capital, Hanoi; established 1945–46 & divided 1954–75 at 17th parallel into republics of **North Vietnam** (capital, Hanoi) & **South Vietnam** (capital, Saigon)

Vi·go \'vē-,gō\ city & port NW Spain

Vi·ja·ya·wa·da \,vij-ə-yə-'wäd-ə\ or formerly **Bez·wa·da** \bez-'wäd-ə\ city SE India in E Andhra Pradesh

Vi·la \'vē-lə\ city, capital of Vanuatu

Vil·ni·us \'vil-nē-əs\ or Polish **Wil·no** \'vil-nō\ or Russian **Vil·na** \'vil-nə\ or **Vil·no** \-nō\ city, capital of Lithuania

Vin·land \'vin-lənd\ a portion of the coast of North America visited and so called by Norse voyagers about 1000 A.D.; perhaps Newfoundland

Vin·ni·tsa \'vin-ət-sə\ city W central Ukraine

Vin·son Massif \'vin-sən\ mountain 5139 meters W Antarctica in Sentinel range of Ellsworth mountains; highest in Antarctica

Vir·gin·ia \vər-'jin-yə, -'jin-ē-ə\ state E U.S.; capital, Richmond — **Vir·gin·ian** \-yən, -ē-ən\ adj or n

Virginia Beach city SE Virginia

Vir·gin Islands \,vər-jən-\ island group West Indies E of Puerto Rico — see BRITISH VIRGIN ISLANDS, VIRGIN ISLANDS OF THE UNITED STATES

Virgin Islands National Park reservation Saint John, Virgin Islands of the United States

Virgin Islands of the United States the W islands of the Virgin islands group including Saint Croix, Saint John, & Saint Thomas; capital, Charlotte Amalie (on Saint Thomas)

Vi·sa·yan \və-'sī-ən\ or **Bi·sa·yas** \bə-'sī-əz\ islands central Philippines including Bohol, Cebu, Leyte, Masbate, Negros, Panay, & Samar

Vish·a·kha·pat·nam \vish-,äk-ə-'pət-nəm\ city & port E India in Andhra Pradesh

Vis·tu·la \'vis-chə-lə, 'vish-; 'vis-tə-lə\ or Polish **Wis·la** \'vē-slä\ river 1015 kilometers long Poland flowing N from the Carpathians into Gulf of Danzig

Vi·tebsk \'vē-,tepsk, -,tebsk, və-'\ city NE Belarus

Vi·ti Le·vu \vēt-ē-'lev-ü\ island SW Pacific; largest of the Fiji group

Vi·to·ria \vi-'tōr-ē-ə, -'tór-\ city N Spain

Vi·tó·ria \vi-'tōr-ē-ə, -'tór-\ city E Brazil NE of Rio de Janeiro

Vlad·i·kav·kaz \,vlad-ə-,käf-'käz, -'kaz\ or 1932–43 & 1955–91 **Or·dzho·ni·kid·ze** \,ór-,jän-ə-'kid-zə\ or 1944–54 **Dzau·dzhi·kau** \dzau-'jē-,kau̇, zau̇-\ city S Russia, in the Caucasus

Vlad·i·vos·tok \,vlad-ə-və-'stäk, -'väs-,täk\ city SE Russia in Asia, on Sea of Japan

Volcano islands or **Ka·zan Ret·to** \,käz-,än-'ret-ō\ island chain Japan in W Pacific S of Bonin islands — see IWO JIMA

Vol·ga \'väl-gə, 'vól-, 'vōl-\ river 3742 kilometers long W Russia flowing into Caspian sea

Vol·go·grad \'väl-gə-,grad, 'vól-, 'vōl-\ or formerly **Sta·lin·grad** \'stäl-ən-,grad, 'stal-\ or earlier **Tsa·ri·tsyn** \tsə-'rēt-sən, sə-\ city S Russia in Europe, on the Volga

Vol·ta \'väl-tə, 'vōl-, 'vól-\ river 160 kilometers long Ghana flowing from Lake Volta (reservoir) into Bight of Benin

Vo·ro·nezh \və-'rō-nish\ city SW Russia in Europe, near Don river

Vo·ro·shi·lov·grad \,vór-ə-'shē-ləf-,grad, ,vär-, -ləv-\ city E Ukraine in Donets basin

Vosges \'vōzh\ mountains NE France on W side of Rhine valley; highest 1423 meters

Voy·a·geurs National Park \,vói-ə-'zhərz\ reservation N Minnesota on Rainy Lake

Vysoké Tatry — see TATRA

Wa·ka·ya·ma \,wäk-ə-'yäm-ə\ city Japan in SW Honshu SW of Osaka

Wake \'wāk\ island N Pacific N of Marshall islands; belongs to U.S.

Wa·la·chia or **Wal·la·chia** \wä-'lä-kē-ə\ region S Romania between Transylvanian Alps & the Danube

Wales \'wālz\ or **Welsh Cym·ru** \'kəm-rē\ principality SW Great Britain; a division of United Kingdom; capital, Cardiff

Wal·la·sey \'wäl-ə-sē\ borough NW England in Merseyside

Wal·lis \'wäl-əs\ islands SW Pacific NE of Fiji; with Futuna islands constituting a French overseas territory (**Wallis and Futuna Islands**)

Wal·sall \'wól-,sól, -səl\ borough W central England in West Midlands

Wal·tham Forest \,wól-thəm-\ borough of NE Greater London, England

Wands·worth \'wändz-wərth, 'wänz-\ borough of SW Greater London, England

Wan·ne-Eick·el \,vän-ə-'ī-kəl\ city W Germany in the Ruhr

War·ley \'wór-lē\ county borough W central England in Worcestershire

War·ren \'wór-ən, 'wär-\ city SE Michigan

War·saw \'wór-,só\ or Polish **War·sza·wa** \vär-'shäv-ə\ city, capital of Poland

War·wick·shire \'wär-ik-,shiər, -shər\ or **Warwick** county central England

Wa·satch \'wó-,sach\ range of the Rockies SE Idaho & N central Utah; highest Mount Timpanogos 3660 meters (in Utah)

Wash·ing·ton \'wósh-ing-tən, 'wäsh-\ **1** state NW U.S.; capital, Olympia **2** city, capital of U.S.; coextensive with District of Columbia — **Wash·ing·to·nian** \,wósh-ing-'tō-nē-ən, ,wäsh-, -nyən\ adj or n

Washington, Mount mountain 1917 meters N New Hampshire; highest in White mountains

Wa·ter·bury \'wót-ər-,ber-ē, 'wót-ə-, 'wät-\ city W central Connecticut

Wa·ter·ford \'wót-ər-fərd, 'wät-\ county S Ireland in Munster

Wa·ter·ton Lakes National Park \'wót-ərt-n, 'wät-\ mountain area W Canada in S Alberta adjoining Glacier National Park, Montana, & with it forming **Waterton-Glacier International Peace Park**

Watlings — see SAN SALVADOR

Wed·dell \wə-'del, 'wed-l\ sea arm of the S Atlantic E of Antarctic peninsula

Wei·mar Republic \'vī-,mär, 'wī-\ the German republic 1919–33

Wel·land \'wel-ənd\ canal 45 kilometers long SE Ontario connecting Lakes Erie & Ontario

Wel·ling·ton \'wel-ing-tən\ city, capital of New Zealand

Wes·sex \'wes-iks\ ancient Anglian kingdom S England; capital, Winchester

West Australian Current warm current flowing N off W coast of Australia

West Bengal state E India; capital, Calcutta

West Brom·wich \'brəm-ij, 'bräm-, -ich\ borough W central England in West Midlands

Western Australia state W Australia; capital, Perth

Western Ghats \'gȯts\ chain of low mountains SW India

Western Isles the Outer Hebrides constituting since 1975 a regional division of W Scotland

Western Sahara or formerly **Spanish Sahara** region NW Africa divided 1975 between Mauritania which gave up its claim in 1979 & Morocco which thereafter occupied the entire territory

Western Samoa islands Samoa W of 171° W ; an independent state in the Commonwealth since 1962; capital, Apia

West Germany — see GERMANY

West Gla·mor·gan \glə-'mȯr-gən\ county S Wales; established 1974

West Indies islands lying between SE North America & N South America & comprising the Greater Antilles, Lesser Antilles, & Bahamas — **West Indian** adj or n

West Iri·an \,ir-ē-'än\ or **West New Guinea** or formerly **Netherlands New Guinea** territory of Indonesia comprising W half of New Guinea; capital, Djajapura

West Lo·thi·an \'lō-t͟hē-ən\ former county SE Scotland — see LOTHIAN

West Malaysia — see PENINSULAR MALAYSIA

West·meath \west-'mēt͟h, wes-, -'mēth\ county E central Ireland in Leinster

West Midlands metropolitan county W central England

West·min·ster \'west-,min-stər, 'wes-\ or **City of Westminster** borough of W central Greater London, England

West·mor·land \'west-mər-lənd, 'wes-\ former county NW England

West Pakistan the former W division of Pakistan now coextensive with Pakistan

West·pha·lia \west-'fāl-yə, -'fā-lē-ə, wes-\ region NW Germany E of the Rhine; now part of North Rhine-Westphalia — **West·pha·lian** \-'fāl-yən, -'fā-lē-ən\ adj or n

West Punjab — see PUNJAB 3

West Quod·dy Head \,kwäd-ē-\ cape; most easterly point of Maine & of U.S.

West Ri·ding \'rīd-ing\ former administrative county N England in W & SW Yorkshire

West Sus·sex \'səs-iks\ county SE England

West Virginia state E U.S.; capital, Charleston — **West Virginian** adj or n

West York·shire \'yȯrk-,shiər, -shər\ metropolitan county NW England

Wex·ford \'weks-fərd\ county SE Ireland in Leinster

White mountains N New Hampshire in the Appalachians — see WASHINGTON

White·horse \'hwīt-,hȯrs, 'wīt-\ city NW Canada, capital of Yukon Territory

White Nile — see NILE

White Sea or **Be·lo·ye Mo·re** \,bel-ə-yə-'mȯr-yə\ sea inlet of Barents sea NW Russia

Whit·ney, Mount \'hwit-nē, 'wit-\ mountain 4418 meters SE central California in Sierra Nevada in Sequoia National Park; highest in U.S. outside of Alaska

Wich·i·ta \'wich-ə-,tȯ\ city S Kansas

Wick·low \'wik-lō\ county E Ireland in Leinster

Wien — see VIENNA

Wies·ba·den \'vēs-,bäd-n, 'vis-\ city W Germany on the Rhine W of Frankfurt, capital of Hesse

Wight, Isle of \'wīt\ island & county S England in English channel

Wig·town \'wig-tən, -,taůn\ or **Wig·town·shire** \-,shiər, -shər\ former county SW Scotland

Wil·helms·ha·ven \,vil-,helmz-'häf-ən, 'vil-əmz-,\ city NW Germany NW of Bremen

Wil·lem·stad \'vil-əm-,stät\ city, capital of Netherlands Antilles on Curaçao Island

Wil·ming·ton \'wil-ming-tən\ city N Delaware; largest in state

Wilno — see VILNIUS

Wilt·shire \'wilt-,shiər, 'wil-chər, 'wilt-shər\ county S England

Wind Cave National Park reservation SW South Dakota in Black Hills

Win·der·mere \'win-dər-,miər, -də-\ lake NW England in Lake District

Wind·hoek \'vint-,hůk\ city, capital of Namibia

Wind·sor \'win-zər\ city S Ontario on Detroit river

Wind·ward \'win-dwərd\ islands West Indies in the S Lesser Antilles extending S from Martinique but not including Barbados, Tobago, or Trinidad

Win·ni·peg \'win-ə-,peg\ city, capital of Manitoba

Winnipeg, Lake lake S central Manitoba

Win·ni·pe·sau·kee, Lake \,win-ə-pə-'sȯ-kē\ lake central New Hampshire

Win·ston–Sa·lem \,win-stən-'sā-ləm\ city N central North Carolina

Wis·con·sin \wis-'kän-sən\ state N central U.S.; capital, Madison — **Wis·con·sin·ite** \-sə-,nīt\ n

Wisla — see VISTULA

Wit·wa·ters·rand \'wit-,wȯt-ərz-,rand, -,wät-, -,ränd, -,ränt\ or **Rand** \'rand, 'ränd, 'ränt\ ridge of gold-bearing rock NE Republic of South Africa in S Transvaal

Wol·lon·gong \'wůl-ən-,gäng, -,gȯng\ city SE Australia in E New South Wales S of Sydney

Wol·ver·hamp·ton \'wůl-vər-,ham-tən, -,hamp-\ borough W central England in West Midlands NW of Birmingham

Won·san \'wən-,sän\ city North Korea on E coast

Worces·ter \'wůs-tər\ city E central Massachusetts

Worces·ter·shire \'wůs-tər-,shiər, -tə-, -shər\ or **Worcester** former county W central England — see HEREFORD AND WORCESTER

Wran·gell, Mount \'rang-gəl\ volcano 4317 meters S Alaska in Wrangell range; highest volcano in U.S.

Wrangell–Saint Eli·as National Park \-,sänt-i-'lī-əs-\ reservation S central Alaska E of Anchorage

Wro·claw \'vrȯt-,släf, -,släv\ or German **Bres·lau** \'bres-,laů\ city SW Poland in Silesia

Wu·chang \'wü-'chäng\ former city E central China — see WUHAN

Wu·han \'wü-'hän\ city S China, capital of Hubei; formed from former separate cities of Hankow, Hanyang, & Wuchang

Wuhsien — see SUZHOU

Wu–lu–mu–ch'i — see ÜRÜMQI

Wup·per·tal \'vůp-ər-,täl\ city W Germany in Ruhr valley ENE of Düsseldorf

Würt·tem·berg \'wərt-əm-,bərg, 'wůrt-; 'vuert-əm-,berk\ region SW Germany between Baden & Bavaria; chief city, Stuttgart; now part of Baden-Württemberg

Wy·o·ming \wī-'ō-ming\ state NW U.S.; capital, Cheyenne — **Wy·o·ming·ite** \-ming-,īt\ n

Xia·men or **Hsia–men** \shē-'ä-'mən\ or **Amoy** \ä-'mȯi\ city SE China in S Fujian on two islands

Xi'·an or **Si·an** \'shē-'än\ or formerly **Chang·an** \'chäng-'än\ city E central China, capital of Shaanxi

Xiang·tan or **Hsiang-t'an** or **Siang·tan** \shē-'äng-'tän\ city SE China in Hunan

Xi·ning or **Si·ning** \'shē-'ning\ city NW China, capital of Qinghai

\ə\ abut		\ng\ sing	
\ər\ further		\ō\ bone	
\a\ mat		\ȯ\ saw	
\ā\ take		\ȯi\ coin	
\ä\ cot, cart		\th\ thin	
\aů\ out		\t͟h\ this	
\ch\ chin		\ü\ food	
\e\ pet		\ů\ foot	
\ē\ easy		\y\ yet	
\g\ go		\yü\ few	
\i\ tip		\yů\ cure	
\ī\ life		\zh\ vision	
\j\ job			

Xin·jiang Uy·gur or **Sin·kiang–Ui·ghur** \'shin-jē-'āng-'wē-gər\ region & former province w China; capital, Ürümqi

Xizang — see TIBET

Xu·zhou \'shü-'jō\ or **Hsü–chou** or **Süchow** \'shü-'jō, 'sü-; 'sü-'chaù\ city E China in NW Jiangsu

Ya·kutsk \yə-'kütsk\ city E central Russia in Asia

Ya·lu \'yäl-ü\ or **Am·nok** \'am-,näk\ river 480 kilometers long SE Manchuria & North Korea flowing into Korea Bay

Yan·gon \,yän-'gōn\ or formerly **Ran·goon** \ran-'gün, rang-\ city, capital of Myanmar

Yangku — see TAIYUAN

Yangtze — see CHANG

Yao \'yaù\ city Japan in S Honshu E of Osaka

Yaoun·dé \yaùn-'dā\ city, capital of Cameroon

Yap \'yap, 'yäp\ island W Pacific in the W Carolines

Ya·ro·slavl \,yär-ə-'släv-əl\ city central Russia in Europe, NE of Moscow

Ye·ka·te·rin·burg \yi-'kat-ə-rən-,bərg, yi-,kät-ə-rən-'bùrk\ or 1924–91 **Sverd·lovsk** \sverd-'lòfsk\ city W Russia, in central Ural mountains

Yellow 1 — see HUANG 2 sea section of East China sea between N China & Korea

Yel·low·knife \'yel-ə-,nīf\ town Canada, capital of Northwest Territories

Yel·low·stone National Park \'yel-ə-,stōn\ reservation NW Wyoming, E Idaho, & S Montana

Ye·men \'yem-ən\ country S Arabia bordering on Red sea & Gulf of Aden; a republic formed 1990 by merger of **Yemen Arab Republic** (capital, San'a) with **People's Democratic Republic of Yemen** or **Southern Yemen** (capital, Aden); capital, San'a — **Ye·me·ni** \'yem-ə-nē\ adj or n — **Ye·men·ite** \-ə-,nīt\ n

Yen·i·sey or **Yen·i·sei** \,yen-ə-'sā\ river 4505 kilometers long central Russia, flowing N into Arctic ocean

Ye·re·van \,yer-ə-'vän\ city, capital of Armenia

Yezo — see HOKKAIDO

Yi·bin \'yē-'bēn\ or **I–pin** \'ē-'bēn, -'pin\ or formerly **Süchow** \'shü-'jō, 'sü-; 'sü-'chaù\ city central China in S Szechwan

Yog·ya·kar·ta \,yōg-yə-'kär-tə\ city Indonesia in S Java

Yo·ho National Park \'yō-hō\ reservation W Canada in SE British Columbia on Alberta boundary

Yo·ko·ha·ma \,yō-kə-'häm-ə\ city Japan in SE Honshu on Tokyo Bay S of Tokyo

Yo·ko·su·ka \yō-'kò-sə-kə, -'kò-skə\ city Japan in E Honshu W of entrance to Tokyo Bay

Yon·kers \'yäng-kərz\ city SE New York N of New York City

York \'yòrk\ city N England in North Yorkshire

York·shire \'yòrk-,shiər, -shər\ or **York** former county N England comprising city of York & administrative counties of East Riding, North Riding, & West Riding — see CLEVELAND, HUMBERSIDE, NORTH YORKSHIRE, SOUTH YORKSHIRE, WEST YORKSHIRE

York, Cape cape NE Australia in Queensland at N tip of Cape York peninsula

Yo·sem·i·te Falls \yō-'sem-ət-ē\ waterfall E California in Yosemite valley in Yosemite National Park; includes two falls, the upper 436 meters & the lower 98 meters, connected by a cascade 248 meters high

Yosemite National Park reservation E central California in Sierra Nevada

Youngs·town \'yəng-,staùn\ city NE Ohio

Yssel — see IJSSEL

Yu·ca·tán \,yü-kə-'tan, -'tän\ 1 peninsula SE Mexico & N Central America including Belize & N Guatemala 2 state SE Mexico; capital, Mérida

Yu·go·sla·via or **Ju·go·sla·via** \,yü-gō-'släv-ē-ə\ country S Europe on the Adriatic consisting of Serbia & Montenegro and formerly also of Slovenia, Croatia, Bosnia and Herzegovina, & N Macedonia; capital, Belgrade — **Yu·go·slav** \,yü-gō-'släv, -'slav\ or **Yu·go·sla·vi·an** \-'släv-ē-ən\ adj or n

Yu·kon \'yü-,kän\ 1 river 3185 kilometers long NW Canada & Alaska flowing into Bering sea 2 or **Yukon Territory** territory NW Canada; capital, Whitehorse

Yun·nan \yü-'nän\ 1 province SW China bordering on Myanmar & Indochina; capital, Kunming 2 — see KUNMING

Yunnanfu — see KUNMING

Zab·rze \'zäb-zhā\ city SW Poland in Silesia

Za·ca·te·cas \,zak-ə-'tā-kəs, -'tek-əs\ 1 state N central Mexico 2 city; its capital

Zag·a·zig \'zag-ə-,zig\ city N Egypt NNE of Cairo

Za·greb \'zäg-,reb\ city, capital of Croatia

Za·he·dan \,zä-hi-'dän\ city E Iran

Zaire \zä-'iər\ 1 river in Africa — see CONGO 2 or formerly **Democratic Republic of the Congo** or earlier **Belgian Congo** country central Africa comprising most of Congo river basin E of lower Congo river; a republic; capital, Kinshasa

Zam·be·zi or **Zam·be·si** \zam-'bē-zē\ river 2655 kilometers long SE Africa flowing from NW Zambia into Mozambique channel

Zam·bia \'zam-bē-ə\ country S Africa N of the Zambezi; formerly the British protectorate of **Northern Rhodesia**; an independent republic since 1964; capital, Lusaka

Zam·bo·an·ga \,zam-bə-'wäng-gə\ city S Philippines in SW Mindanao

Zan·zi·bar \'zan-zə-,bär\ island Tanzania off NE Tanganyika coast; formerly a sultanate & British protectorate including also Pemba & other islands; became independent 1963; united 1964 with Tanganyika forming Tanzania

Za·po·ro·zhye \,zäp-ə-'rò-zhə\ city SE Ukraine

Za·ra·go·za \,zar-ə-'gō-zə\ or **Sar·a·gos·sa** \,sar-ə-'gäs-ə\ city NE Spain in W Aragon

Zealand — see SJÆLLAND

Zetland — see SHETLAND

Zhang·jia·kou \'jäng-jē'ä-'kō\ or **Ch'ang–chia–k'ou** \'chäng-jē-'ä-'kō\ or **Kal·gan** \'kal-'gan\ city NE China in NW Hebei NW of Beijing

Zhang·zhou or **Chang–chou** \'jäng-'jō\ city SE China in S Fujian

Zhdanov — see MARIUPOL

Zhe·jiang or **Che·kiang** \'jəj-ē-'äng\ province E China bordering on East China Sea; capital, Hangzhou

Zheng·zhou or **Cheng–chou** \'jəng-'jō\ city NE central China, capital of Henan

Zhen·jiang or **Chen–chiang** \'jən-jē-'äng\ city E China in NW central Jiangsu

Zhi·to·mir \zhi-'tò-,miər\ city W Ukraine

Zhu·zhou or **Chu–chou** or **Chu·chow** \'jü-'jō\ city SE China in E Hunan

Zi·bo or **Tzu–po** \'dzə-'bō, 'zə-\ city E China in central Shandong

Zi·gong or **Tzu–kung** or **Tze·kung** \'dzə-'gùng, 'zə-\ city S central China in S Szechwan

Zim·ba·bwe \zim-'bäb-wā, -wē\ or formerly **Southern Rhodesia** or 1970-79 **Rho·de·sia** \rō-'dē-zhə, -zhē-ə\ country S Africa S of Zambezi river; an independent member of the Commonwealth; capital Harare — **Zim·ba·bwe·an** \-ən\ adj or n

Zi•on \'zī-ən\ *or* **Si•on** \'sī-ən\ **1** the stronghold of Jerusalem conquered by David **2** a hill in Jerusalem occupied in ancient times by the Jewish Temple **3** JERUSALEM **4** ISRAEL

Zion National Park reservation sw Utah

Zla•to•ust \,zlät-ə-'üst\ city w Russia in Asia in the s Urals

Zom•ba \'zäm-bə\ city s Malawi

Zui•der Zee \,zīd-ər-'zā, -'zē\ former inlet of North sea N Netherlands now (as IJsselmeer) partly reclaimed — see IJSSELMEER

Zu•lu•land \'zü-lü-,land\ territory E Republic of South Africa in NE Natal on Indian ocean; capital, Eshowe

Zu•rich \'zür-ik\ city N Switzerland on Lake of Zurich

Zwick•au \'tsfik-,aù, 'zwik-\ city E Germany s of Leipzig

\ə\ abut	\ng\ sing
\ər\ **further**	\ō\ **bone**
\a\ **mat**	\ȯ\ **saw**
\ā\ **take**	\ȯi\ **coin**
\ä\ **cot, cart**	\th\ **thin**
\aù\ **out**	\th\ **this**
\ch\ **chin**	\ü\ **food**
\e\ **pet**	\ù\ **foot**
\ē\ **easy**	\y\ **yet**
\g\ **go**	\yü\ **few**
\i\ **tip**	\yù\ **cure**
\ī\ **life**	\zh\ **vision**
\j\ **job**	

World Geography

The following topographical survey offers a concise overview of the earth's physical characteristics. Included are charts of major mountain peaks, oceans and seas, lakes, and rivers. Each chart provides relevant statistics—location, altitude, depth, area, etc.—in both standard English and metric measurements and is designed to facilitate making comparisons among the various entries.

OCEANS AND SEAS

NAME	SQ. MI.	SQ. KM.	AVERAGE DEPTH FEET	AVERAGE DEPTH METERS
Pacific Ocean	64,186,300	166,242,510	12,925	3,928
Atlantic Ocean	33,420,000	86,557,800	11,730	3,566
Indian Ocean	28,350,000	73,427,795	12,598	3,830
Arctic Ocean	5,105,700	13,223,763	3,407	1,036
South China Sea	1,148,500	2,974,615	4,802	1,460
Caribbean Sea	971,400	2,515,926	8,448	2,568
Mediterranean Sea	969,100	2,509,969	4,926	1,498
Bering Sea	873,000	2,261,070	4,893	1,487
Gulf of Mexico	582,100	1,507,639	5,297	1,610
Sea of Okhotsk	537,500	1,392,125	3,192	970
Sea of Japan	391,100	1,012,949	5,468	1,622
Hudson Bay	281,900	730,121	305	93
East China Sea	256,600	664,594	620	188
Andaman Sea	218,100	564,879	3,667	1,115
Black Sea	196,100	507,899	3,906	1,187
Red Sea	174,900	452,990	1,764	536
North Sea	164,900	427,090	308	94
Baltic Sea	147,500	382,025	180	55

LARGEST NATURAL LAKES OF THE WORLD

NAME	LOCATION	SQ MI.	KM.	DEPTH FEET	DEPTH METERS	ELEVATION FEET	ELEVATION METERS
Caspian Sea	Azerbaijan-Iran	152,239	394,299	3,104	946	92	34
Superior	U.S.-Canada	31,820	82,414	1,333	406	600	183
Victoria	Tanzania-Uganda	26,828	69,485	270	82	3,720	1,134
Aral	Kazakhstan-Uzbekistan	25,659	66,457	223	68	174	53
Huron	U.S.-Canada	23,010	59,596	750	229	579	177
Michigan	U.S.	22,400	58,016	923	281	579	177
Tanganyika	Tanzania-Zaire	12,700	32,893	4,708	1,435	2,534	773
Baikal	Russia	12,162	31,500	5,712	1,741	1,493	455
Great Bear	Canada	12,000	31,080	270	82	512	156
Nyasa	Malawi-Tanzania-Mozambique	11,600	30,044	2,316	706	1,550	473
Great Slave	Canada	11,170	28,930	2,015	614	513	156
Chad	Chad-Niger-Nigeria	9,946	25,670	23	7	787	240
Erie	U.S.-Canada	9,930	25,719	210	64	570	174
Winnipeg	Canada	9,094	23,553	204	62	713	217
Ontario	U.S.-Canada	7,520	19,477	778	237	245	75
Balkhash	Kazakhstan	7,115	18,428	87	27	1,115	340
Ladoga	Russia	7,000	18,130	738	225	13	4
Onega	Russia	3,819	9,891	361	110	108	33
Titicaca	Bolivia-Peru	3,141	8,135	1,214	370	12,500	3,811
Nicaragua	Nicaragua	3,089	8,001	230	70	102	31

MAJOR MOUNTAIN PEAKS OF THE WORLD

MOUNTAIN PEAK	RANGE	LOCATION	FEET	METERS
Everest	Himalayas	Nepal-Tibet	29,028	8,848
K-2	Karakoram	India	28,250	8,611
Kanchenjunga	Himalayas	Nepal-India	28,208	8,598
Lhtose	Himalayas	Nepal-Tibet	27,890	8,501
Makulu	Himalayas	Tibet-Nepal	27,790	8,470
Dhaulagiri I	Himalayas	Nepal	26,810	8,172
Manaslu	Himalayas	Nepal	26,760	8,156
Cho Oyu	Himalayas	Nepal	26,750	8,153
Nanga Parbat	Himalayas	India	26,660	8,126
Annapurna I	Himalayas	Nepal	26,504	8,078
Aconcagua	Andes	Argentina	23,034	7,021
Ojos de Salado	Andes	Argentina-Chile	22,588	6,895
McKinley	Alaska	United States	20,320	6,194
Logan	Canadian Rockies	Canada	19,524	5,951
Kilimanjaro		Tanzania	19,340	5,879
El'brus	Caucasus	Georgia	18,510	5,627
Citlaltepetl	Sierra Madre	Mexico	18,405	5,610
Kenya		Kenya	17,058	5,199
Vinson	Trans-Antarctic	Antarctica	16,863	5,140
Djaja	Central New Guinea	New Guinea	16,500	5,016
Mont Blanc	Alps	France-Italy	15,771	4,794
Monte Rosa	Alps	Switzerland	15,203	4,634
Fujiyama		Japan	12,385	3,755
Elbert	Rockies	U.S.	14,433	4,400
Rainier	Cascades	U.S.	14,410	4,392
Jebel Toubkal	Atlas	Morocco	13,665	4,165
Pico de Aneto	Pyrenees	Spain	11,178	3,407
Monte Corno	Apennines	Italy	9,617	2,931
Jotunheimen	Scandanavian	Norway	8,098	2,469
Kosciusko	Great Dividing	Australia	7,316	2,230
Mitchell	Appalachians	U.S.	6,684	2,037
Gora Belukha	Urals	Russia-Kazakhstan	6,214	1,894

HIGHEST AND LOWEST CONTINENTAL ALTITUDES

CONTINENT	HIGHEST POINT	FEET	METERS	LOWEST POINT	FEET BELOW SEA LEVEL	METERS BELOW SEA LEVEL
Africa	Kilimanjaro, Tanzania	19,340	5,879	Lake Assal, Djibouti	282	89
Antarctica	Vinson Massif	16,863	5,140	Unknown		
Asia	Mount Everest, Nepal-Tibet	29,028	8,848	Dead Sea, Israel-Jordan	1,312	400
Australia	Mount Kosciusko	7,316	2,230	Lake Eyre	52	16
Europe	Mount El'brus, Turkmenistan-Kazakhstan	18,510	5,627	Caspian Sea, Azerbaijan	512	157
North America	Mount McKinley, U.S.	20,320	6,194	Death Valley, U.S.	282	89
South America	Mount Acancagua, Argentina	23,034	7,021	Valdes Peninsula, Argentina	131	40

MAJOR RIVERS OF THE WORLD

NAME	APPROX. LENGTH MI.	APPROX. LENGTH KM.	SOURCE	OUTFLOW
Nile	4,180	6,690	Tributaries of Lake Victoria	Mediterranean Sea
Amazon	3,912	6,296	Glacier-fed lakes, Peru	Atlantic Ocean
Mississippi-Missouri-Red Rock	3,880	6,240	Source of Red Rock, Montana	Gulf of Mexico
Yangtze Kiang	3,602	5,797	Tibetan Plateau, China	China Sea
Ob	3,459	5,567	Altai Mts., Russia	Gulf of Ob
Huang Ho (Yellow)	2,900	4,667	E. Kunlun Mts., China	Gulf of Chihli
Yenisei	2,800	4,506	Tannu-Ola Mts., Tuva, Russia	Arctic Ocean
Parana	2,795	4,498	Confluence Paranaiba & Grande Rivers	Rio de la Plata
Irtish	2,758	4,438	Altai Mts., Russia	Ob River
Zaire (Congo)	2,716	4,371	Confluence Lualaba & Luapula rivers, Zaire	Atlantic Ocean
Heilong (Amur)	2,704	4,352	Confluence Shilka (Russia) & Argun (Manchuria) rivers	Tatar Strait
Lena	2,652	4,268	Baikal Mts, Russia	Arctic Ocean
Mackenzie	2,635	4,241	Head of Finlay River, Canada	Beaufort Sea
Niger	2,600	4,184	Guinea	Gulf of Guinea
Mekong	2,500	4,023	Tibetan Highlands	South China Sea
Volga	2,291	3,687	Valdai Plateau, Russia	Caspian Sea
Madeira	2,012	3,238	Confluence Beni & Maumore rivers, Bolivia-Brazil border	Amazon River
Purus	1,993	3,207	Peruvian Andes	Amazon River
Sao Francisco	1,987	3,198	Southwest Minas Gerais, Brazil	Atlantic Ocean
Yukon	1,979	3,185	Confluence Lewes & Pelly rivers, Canada	Bering Sea
St. Lawrence	1,900	3,058	Lake Ontario	Gulf of St. Lawrence
Rio Grande	1,885	3,034	San Juan Mts., Colorado	Gulf of Mexico
Brahmaputra	1,800	2,897	Himalayas	Bay of Bengal
Indus	1,800	2,897	Himalayas	Arabian Sea
Danube	1,766	2,842	Black Forest, Germany	Black Sea

SELECTED WATERFALLS OF THE WORLD

NAME	HEIGHT FEET	HEIGHT METERS	LOCATION	RIVER
Angel	3,281	1,000	Venezuela	Tributary of Caroni
Tugela	3,000	914	South Africa	Tugela
Utigard	2,625	800	Norway	Jostedal Glacier
Mardalfossen	2,149	653	Norway	Mardals
Cuquenan	2,000	610	Venezuela	Cuquenan
Sutherland	1,904	580	New Zealand	Arthur
Takkakaw	1,605	503	Canada	Tributary of Yoho
Ribbon (Yosemite)	1,612	491	U.S.	Creek flowing into Yosemite
Upper Yosemite	1,430	436	U.S.	Yosemite Creek, tributary of Merced
Gavarnie	1,348	422	France	Gave de Pau
Vettisfoss	1,200	366	Norway	Morkedola
Widows' Tears	1,170	357	U.S.	Tributary of Merced (Yosemite)
Victoria	343	104	Zambia	Zambezi River
American	182	55	U.S.	Niagara River (Niagara Falls)
Horseshoe	173	53	Canada	Niagara River (Niagara Falls)

MAJOR DESERTS OF THE WORLD

NAME	LOCATION	SQ. MI.	SQ. KM.
Arabian	Egypt and North Sudan	70,000	181,300
Atacama	North Chile	*	
Chihuahuan	Southwestern U.S. and Mexico	140,000	362,600
Gobi	Mongolia and China	500,000	1,295,000
Great Sandy	Western Australia	150,000	388,500
Great Victoria	Western and southern Australia	150,000	388,500
Kalahari	Southern Africa	225,000	582,700
Libyan	Libya, Egypt, Sudan	450,000	1,165,500
Mojave	Southern California, U.S.	15,000	39,000
Nubian	Northeast Sudan	100,000	259,000
Sahara	North Africa	3,500,000	9,065,000
Taklimakan	China	140,000	362,600
Thar (Great Indian)	India and Pakistan	100,000	259,000

* Approx. 600 mi. (966 km.) long.

LARGEST ISLANDS OF THE WORLD

NAME	LOCATION	SQ. MI.	SQ. KM.
Greenland	North Atlantic	839,999	2,175,587
New Guinea	Southwest Pacific	316,615	820,033
Borneo	West Mid-Pacific	286,914	743,107
Madagascar	Indian Ocean	226,657	587,042
Baffin	North Atlantic	183,310	476,078
Sumatra	Northeast Indian Ocean	182,859	473,605
Honshu	Sea of Japan	88,925	230,316
Great Britain	North Atlantic	88,758	229,883
Ellesmere	Arctic Ocean	82,119	212,688
Victoria	Arctic Ocean	81,930	212,199
Celebes (Sulawesi)	West Mid-Pacific	72,986	189,034
South Island	South Pacific	58,093	150,461
Java	Indian Ocean	48,990	126,884
North Island	South Pacific	44,281	114,688
Cuba	Caribbean Sea	44,218	114,525
Newfoundland	North Atlantic	42,734	110,681
Luzon	West Mid-Pacific	40,420	104,688
Iceland	North Atlantic	39,768	102,999
Mindanao	West Mid-Pacific	36,537	94,631
Ireland	North Atlantic	32,597	84,426
Hokkaido	Sea of Japan	30,372	78,663
Hispaniola	Caribbean Sea	29,355	76,029
Tasmania	Indian Ocean	26,215	67,897
Sri Lanka (Ceylon)	Indian Ocean	25,332	65,610
Sakhalin (Karafuto)	Sea of Okhotsk	24,560	63,610

PRINCIPAL ACTIVE VOLCANOES OF THE WORLD

NAME	LATEST ACTIVITY	LOCATION	HEIGHT	
			FEET	METERS
Cameroon	1982	Cameroon	13,354	4,060
Colima	1991	Mexico	14,003	4,257
Erebus	1991	Antarctica	12,450	4,233
Etna	1992	Italy	11,053	3,360
Fuego	1991	Guatemala	12,582	3,825
Guallatiri	1987	Chile	19,882	6,044
Kelud	1990	Indonesia	5,679	1,726
Kerintji	1987	Indonesia	12,467	3,790
Kliuchevskol	1991	Russia	15,584	4,738
Lascar	1991	Chile	19,652	5,974
Mauna Loa	1987	United States	13,680	4,159
Mt. St. Helens	1991	United States	8,300	2,523
Mt. Vesuvius	1944	Italy	4,200	1,280
Ruiz	1992	Colombia	17,716	5,386
Semeru	1991	Indonesia	12,060	3,666

Stars, Planets, and Astronomy

Since the beginning of time, the heavens have fascinated and intrigued humankind. With the development of sophisticated instruments over the centuries, more and more precise information about celestial bodies and phenomena has become accessible. The following section presents basic data on all the planets of the solar system, the sun, the moon, and the Milky Way. Also included is information on the brightest and nearest stars and largest moons, as well as definitions of astronomical constants.

PLANETS

	MERCURY	VENUS	EARTH	MARS	JUPITER	SATURN	URANUS	NEPTUNE	PLUTO
Mean dist. from sun (millions of km)	58	108	150	228	778	1,427	2,870	4,497	5,890
Mean dist. from sun (millions of miles)	36	68	93	142	484	887	1784	2797	3666
Mean surface temp. [°C]	172	464	15	−53	−108	−139	−197	−193	−220
Orbits sun in	90d	225d	365.2d	687d	11.9yr	29.5yr	84yr	165yr	248yr
Rotation period	59d	243d	23h56m	24h37m	9h55m	10h40m	16h48m	16h11m	6.4d
Equatorial diameter (km)	4,880	12,100	12,756	6,794	142,800	120,660	51,810	49,528	2,290(?)
Equatorial diameter (mi)	3,032.4	7,519	7,926.2	4,194	88,736	74,978	32,193	30,775	1,423(?)
Gravity (% of Earth's)	37	88	100	38	264	120	110	140	?
Velocity in orbit (km/sec)	47.9	35	29.8	24.1	13.1	9.6	6.8	5.4	4.7
Velocity in orbit (m/sec)	29.8	21.7	18.5	15	8.1	6	4.2	3.4	2.9
Mass (kg)	3.30×10^{23}	4.86×10^{24}	5.97×10^{24}	6.41×10^{23}	1.89×10^{27}	5.68×10^{26}	8.68×10^{25}	1.02×10^{26}	1.2×10^{23}
Atmosphere	Trace	CO_2	N & O_2	CO_2	H, He & CH_4	H & He	He & H	H & He	?
Known satellites	0	0	1	2	16	18	15	8	1
Rings	0	0	0	0	1	1,000 (?)	11	4	?

BRIGHTEST STARS

NAME	CONSTELLATION	MAGNITUDE (APPARENT)	DISTANCE (LIGHT YEARS)
Sun		−26.74	
Sirius	Canis Majoris	−1.45	8.7
Canopus	Carinae	−0.72	1200
Rigel Kentaurus	Centauri	−0.27	4.3
Arcturus	Bootis	−0.04	34
Vega	Lyrae	0.03	26
Capella	Aurigae	0.08	45
Rigel	Orionis	0.12	900
Procyon	Canis Minoris	0.38	11.4
Achernar	Eridani	0.46	85
Betelgeuse	Orionis	0.5	310

NEAREST STARS

NAME	DISTANCE (LIGHTYEARS)	MAGNITUDE
Proxima Centauri	4.28	11.05
Alpha Centauri A	4.37	−0.01
Alpha Centauri B	4.37	1.33
Barnard's Star	5.8	9.54
Wolf 359	7.6	13.53
Lalande 21185	8.13	7.5
Sirius A	8.7	−1.45
Sirius B	8.7	8.68
Luyten 726-8A	8.88	12.45
Ross 154	9.44	10.6
Ross 248	10.28	12.3

CONSTELLATIONS AND STARS — NORTHERN HEMISPHERE

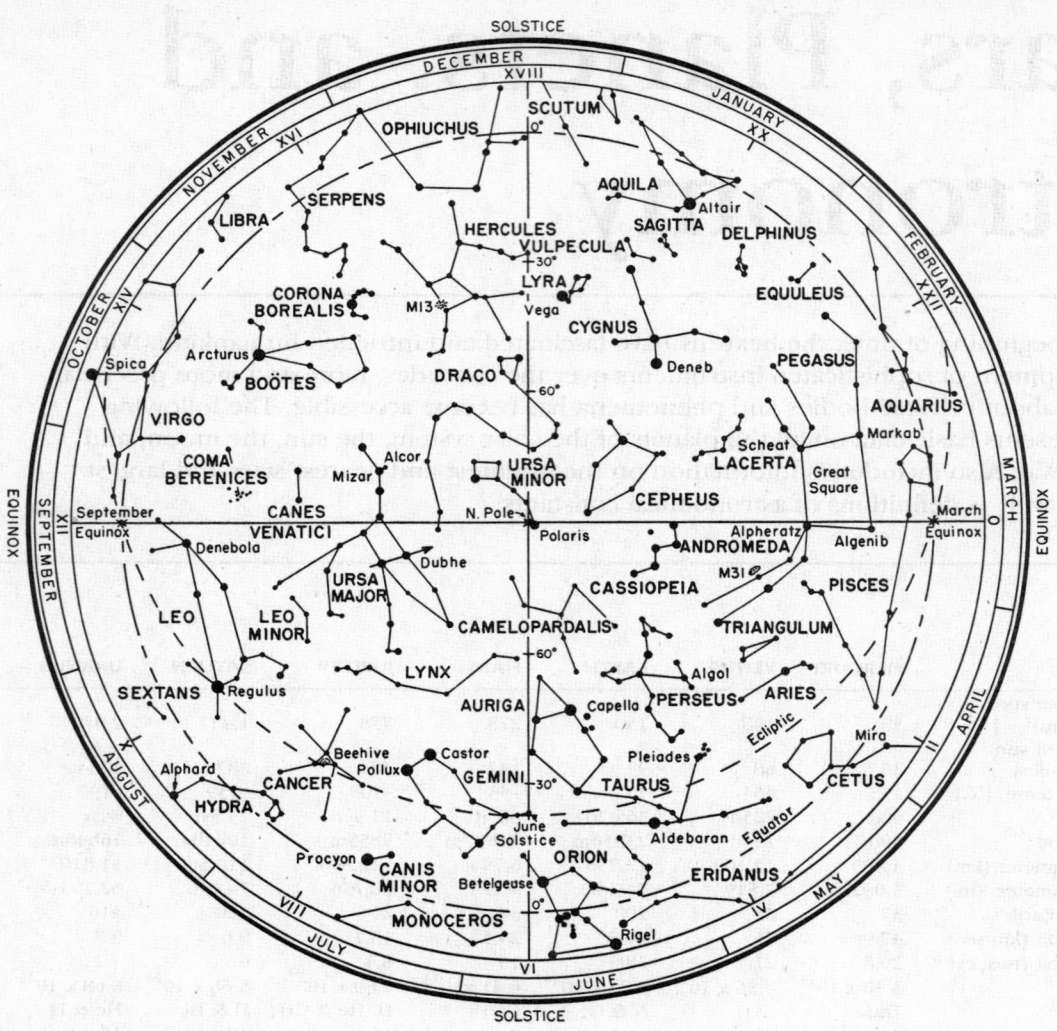

TABLE OF CONSTELLATIONS

NAME AND PRONUNCIATION	[3]GENITIVE AND PRONUNCIATION	MEANING	DECLINATION
[1]Andromeda \an'drämədə\	Andromedae \-,dē\	Andromeda, the Chained Lady	40° N
Antlia (Antlia Pneumatica) \'antlēən(y)ü'mad·ika\	Antliae \-ē,ē\	Pump (Air Pump)	35° S
Apus \'āpəs\	Apodis \'apədás\	Bird of Paradise	75° S
Aquarius \ə'kwa(a)rēəs\	Aquarii \-rē,ī\	Water Carrier	10° S
Aquila \'akwələ\	Aquilae \-,lē\	Eagle	5° N
Ara \'a(a)rə\	Arae \'a(a),rē\	Altar	55° S
Aries \'a(a)rē,ēz, 'er-,'ār, -rēz\	Arietis \ə'rīəd·əs\	Ram	20° N
Auriga \ȯ'rīgə\	Aurigae \-ī,jē\	Charioteer	40° N
[1]Boötes \bō'ōd·ēz\	Boötis \-'ōd·əs\	Herdsman	30° N
Caelum (Caela Sculptoris) \'sēləm (-lə ,skəlp'tōrəs\	Caeli \-,lī\	Graving Tool	40° S
Camelopardalis \kə,melə'pärd·ləs, ,kam∧(,)lō'-\	Camelopardalis \"\	Giraffe	70° N
[1]Cancer \'kan(t)sər\	Cancri \'kaŋ,krī\	Crab	20° N
[1]Canes Venatici \'kā,nēzvə'nad·ə,sī\	Canum Venaticorum \'kānəmvə,nad·ə-'kōrəm\	Hunting Dogs	40° N
[1]Canis Major \'kānə'smäjər, -'a-\	Canis Majoris \-,smə'jōrəs\	Larger Dog	20° S
[1]Canis Minor \-'smīnər\	Canis Minoris \-,smī'nōrəs\	Lesser Dog	5° N
[1]Capricornus \,kaprə'kórnəs\	Capricorni \,₊₊'₊,nī\	Horned Goat	20° S
[2]Carina \kə'rīnə\	Carinae \-,nē\	Keel	60° S
[1]Cassiopeia \,kasēə'pē(y)ə\	Cassiopeiae \-pē,(y)ē, -,(y)ī\	Cassiopeia, the Lady in the Chair	60° N
[1]Centaurus \sen'tórəs\	Centauri \-,rī\	Centaur	45° S
[1]Cepheus \'sē,fyüs, -,fēəs\	Cephei \-,fē,ī\	Cepheus, the Monarch	70° N
[1]Cetus \'sēd·əs\	Ceti \-ē,tī\	Whale	5° S
Chamaeleon \kə'mēlyən, -lēən\	Chamaeleontis \-,mēlē'äntəs\	Chameleon	80° S
Circinus \'sərs∧nəs\	Circini \-,n,ī\	Pair of Compasses	65° S
Columba (Columba Noae) \kə'ləmbə'nō,ē\	Columbae \-m,bē\	Dove (Noah's Dove)	35° S
Coma Berenices \'kōmə,berə'nī(,),sēz\	Comae Berenices \-(,)mē,b-\	Berenice's Hair	25° N
Corona Australis \kə'rōnə,ó'strāləs, -al-\	Coronae Australis \-(,)nē,ó-\	Southern Crown	40° S
[1]Corona Borealis \-,bōrē'aləs, -'ā-\	Coronae Borealis \-(,)nē,b-\	Northern Crown	30° N
[1]Corvus \'kórvəs\	Corvi \-,vī\	Crow	20° S
[1]Crater \'krād·ər\	Crateris \krā'ti(ə)rəs\	Cup	15° S
Crux \'krəks\	Crucis \'krüsəs\	Southern Cross	60° S
Cygnus \'signəs\	Cygni \-,nī\	Swan	40° N
[1]Delphinus \del'fīnəs\	Delphini \-,nī\	Dolphin	15° N
Dorado \də'rü(,)dō\	Doradus \-,dəs\	Dorado [a fish]	60° S
[1]Draco \'drā,kō\	Draconis \drā'kōnəs\	Dragon	65° N
Equuleus \e'kwüleəs\	Equulei \-lē,ī\	Colt	5° N
[1]Eridanus \ə'rid∧nəs\	Eridani \-n,ī\	Eridanus, the River Po	20° S
Fornax \'fór,naks\	Fornacis \fór'nasəs, -'ā-\	Furnace	30° S
[1]Gemini \'jemə,nī\	Geminorum \,jemə'nōrəm\	Twins	25° N
Grus \'grəs, -üs\	Gruis \'grüəs\	Crane	45° S
[1]Hercules \'hərkyə,lēz\	Herculis \-yələs\	Hercules	30° N
Horologium \,hórə'lōjēəm\	Horologii \-,ōjē,ī\	Clock	50° S
[1]Hydra \'hīdrə\	Hydrae \-,drē\	Water Monster	10° S
Hydrus \'hīdrəs\	Hydri \-,drī\	Water Snake	70° S
Indus \'indəs\	Indi \-,dī\	Indian	55° S

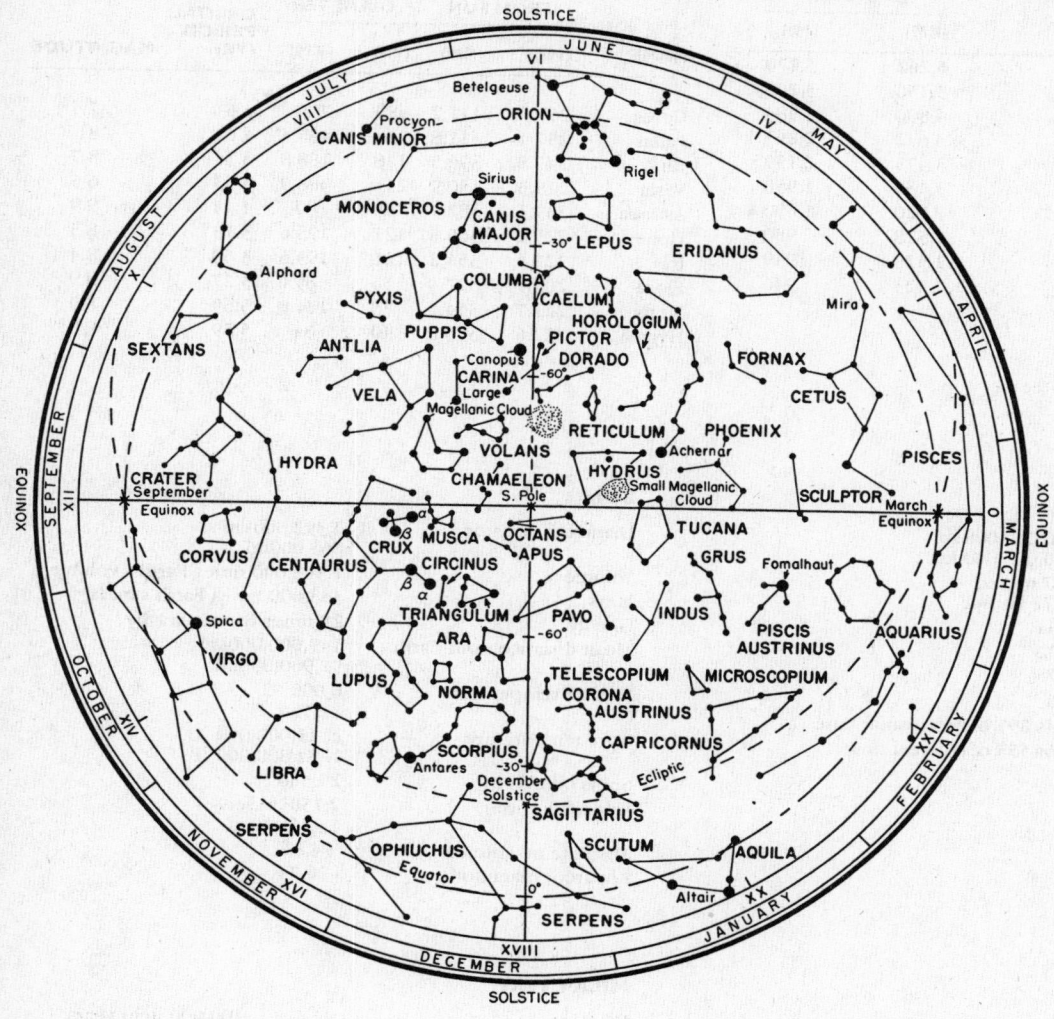

Lacerta \lə'sərd·ə\	Lacertae \-r,tē\	Lizard	45° N
¹Leo \'lē(,)ō\	Leonis \lē'ōnəs\	Lion	15° N
Leo Minor \-'mīnər\	Leonis Minoris \-nə,smī'nōrəs\	Smaller Lion	25° N
¹Lepus \'lēpəs, -'e-\	Leporis \'lepərəs\	Hare	20° S
¹Libra \'lībrə\	Librae \-,brē\	Balance	15° S
¹Lupus \'lüpəs\	Lupi \-,pī\	Wolf	40° S
Lynx \'liŋks\	Lyncis \'linsəs\	Lynx	45° N
¹Lyra \'līrə\	Lyrae \-,rē\	Lyre	35° N
Mensa (Mons Mensae) \'men(t)sə ('mänz'men,sē)\	Mensae \'men,sē\	Table (Table Mountain)	75° S
Microscopium \,mīkrə'skōpēəm\	Microscopii \-pē,ī\	Microscope	35° S
Monoceros \mə'näsərəs\	Monocerotis \-,näsə'rōd·əs\	Unicorn	5° S
Musca \'məskə\	Muscae \'ma,sē\	Fly	70° S
Norma \'nórmə\	Normae \-,mē\	Square (and Rule)	50° S
Octans \'äk,tanz\	Octantis \äk'tantəs\	Octant	85° S
Ophiuchus \,äfē'(y)ükəs\	Ophiuchi \-ü,kī\	Serpent Holder	0°
¹Orion \ə'rīən\	Orionis \ə'rīənəs, ,órē'ōnəs\	Orion, the Hunter	0°
Pavo \'pā(,)vō, -'ä-\	Pavonis \pə'vōnəs\	Peacock	65° S
¹Pegasus \'pegəsəs\	Pegasi \-ə,sī\	Pegasus, the Winged Horse	20° N
¹Perseus \'pər,süs\	Persei \-rsē,ī\	Perseus, the Rescuer or Champion	45° N
Phoenix \'fēniks\	Phoenicis \fē'nīsəs\	Phoenix	50° S
Pictor \'piktər\	Pictoris \pik'tōrəs\	Painter's Easel	55° S
¹Pisces \'pi,sēz\	Piscium \'pis(h)ēəm\	Fishes	10° N
Piscis Austrinus \'pisə,sò'strīnəs\	Piscis Austrini \-,nī\	Southern Fish	30° S
²Puppis \'pəpəs\	Puppis \"\	Stern	30° S
²Pyxis \'piksəs\	Pyxidis \-ksadəs\	Mariner's Compass	30° S
Reticulum \rə'tikyələm\	Reticuli \-,lī\	Net	60° S
Sagitta \sə'jid·ə\	Sagittae \-i,tē\	Arrow	20° N
Sagittarius \,sajə'terēəs\	Sagittarii \-,rē,ī\	Archer	30° S
Scorpius \'skórpēəs\	Scorpii \-pē,ī\	Scorpion	30° S
Sculptor \'skəlptər\	Sculptoris \,skəlp'tōrəs\	Sculptor's Workshop	30° S
Scutum \'sk(y)üd·əm\	Scuti \-ü,tī\	Shield	10° S
Serpens \'sərpənz, -,penz\	Serpentis \(,)sər'pentəs\	Serpent	
Sextans \'sek,stanz\	Sextantis \sek'stantəs\	Sextans	0°
¹Taurus \'tórəs\	Tauri \-,rī\	Bull	5° S
Telescopium \,telə'skōpēəm\	Telescopii \-pē,ī\	Telescope	20° S
Triangulum \trī'aŋgyələm\	Trianguli \-,lī\	Triangle	50° S
Triangulum Australe \-,ò'strā̇(,)lē\	Trianguli Australis \-,lī,ò'strāləs\	Southern Triangle	30° N
Tucana \tü'kanə, -'kä-\	Tucanae \-,nē\	Toucan	65° S
¹Ursa Major \'ərsə'mājər\	Ursae Majoris \'ər,sēmə'jōrəs\	Larger Bear	65° S
¹Ursa Minor \'ərsə'mīnər\	Ursae Minoris \'ər,sēmi'nōrəs\	Smaller Bear	50° N
²Vela \'vēlə\	Velorum \vē'lōrəm\	Sails	80° N
¹Virgo \'vər,gō\	Virginis \-rjənəs\	Virgin	0°
Volans (Piscis Volans) \'pisəs'vō,lanz\	Volantis \vō'lantəs\	Flying Fish	70° S
Vulpecula \,vəl'pekyələ\	Vulpeculae \-,lē\	Little Fox	25° N

¹One of the 48 constellations of Ptolemy. ²One of the subdivisions of the Ptolemaic constellation Argo or Argo Navis \,är(,)gō-'nāvəs\ the Ship Argo, which included Carina, Puppis, Pyxis, and Vela. ³The genitive is used in referring to the individual stars of a constellation (as α Aurigae for the star Capella).

LARGEST MOONS

NAME	PLANET	DIAMETER (KM)	(MI)
Ganymede	Jupiter	5,262	3,270
Titan	Saturn	5,150	3,200
Callisto	Jupiter	4,800	2,983
Io	Jupiter	3,642	2,263
Moon	Earth	3,475	2,159
Europa	Jupiter	3,138	1,950
Triton	Neptune	2,720	1,690
Titania	Uranus	1,578	980
Rhea	Saturn	1,528	949
Oberon	Uranus	1,523	946

FIRST TEN MINOR PLANETS (ASTEROIDS)

NAME	MEAN DIST FROM SUN (MI)	(KM)	DIAMETER (MI)	(KM)	ORBITAL PERIOD (YR)	MAGNITUDE
Ceres	257	411.2	485	776	4.6	7.4
Pallas	257.4	411.8	304	486.4	4.61	8
Juno	247.8	396.5	118	188.8	4.36	8.7
Vesta	219.3	350.9	243	388.9	3.63	6.5
Astraea	239.3	382.9	50	80	4.14	9.9
Hebe	225.2	360.3	121	193.6	3.78	8.5
Iris	221.4	354.2	121	193.6	3.68	8.4
Flora	204.4	327	56	89.6	3.27	8.9
Metis	221.7	354.7	78	124.8	3.69	8.9
Hygeia	222.6	356.2	40	64	5.59	9.5

ASTRONOMICAL CONSTANTS

Light-year (distance traveled by light in one year)	5,880,000,000,000 mi 9,460,000,000,000 km
Velocity of light	186,281.7 mi/sec 298,050.72 km/sec
Sidereal year	365d.2564
Tropical year	365d.2422
Sidereal month	27d.3217
Synodic month	29d.5306
Mean sidereal day	23h56m4s.091 of mean solar time
Mean solar day	24h3m56s.555 of sidereal time

SUN

Diameter, equator	1,392,000km 865,000mi
Volume	1,303,600 times Earth's volume
Mass	333,000 times Earth's mass
Gravity	28 times Earth's gravity
Mean distance from Earth	149,600,000km 92,960,000mi.
Surface temperature	6,000 °C 12,720 °F
Core temperature	c. 15,000,000 °C c. 31,800,000 °F
Spins on axis in	25.38d
Velocity in orbit	2,150km/sec 1,336mi/sec
Absolute magnitude	+4.83
Apparent magnitude	−26.74

MOON

Diameter, equator	3,476km 2,160mi
Volume	1/49 Earth's
Mass	1/81 Earth's
Gravity	1/6Earth's
Mean distance from Earth	384,400km 238,860mi
Spins on axis in	27 1/3 days
Orbits earth in	27 1/3 days
Synodic month (new moon to new moon)	29 1/2 days

MILKY WAY

Diameter	100,000 light years
Thickness at center	20,000 light years
Thickness at edge	7000 light years
Total mass of the system	100,000 solar masses
Absolute magnitude	−20.5 (from above galactic pole)
Total number of stars	100 billion
Total number of globular clusters	500
Total number of open clusters	18,000
Total number of stellar associations	800
Distance of sun from galactic center	32,000 light-years
Rotational velocity near the Sun	155 mi/sec 250 km/sec
Rotational period near the Sun	225 million years
Age of Galaxy	12,000 million years

Calendars and Time Systems

Many of the devices for charting, acknowledging, or celebrating the passage of time are presented in this section, from calendars developed by various civilizations to a listing of religious and secular holidays observed worldwide. Symbols traditionally associated with each month and with notable anniversaries are given, and an easy-to-use perpetual calendar beginning in 1801 pinpoints the day of the week of dates in the past, present, and future.

SIGNS OF THE ZODIAC

The circular path of the sun through the stars, as viewed from Earth, is called ecliptic. In the first century B.C.E. the Greek astronomer Hipparchus divided the ecliptic into the twelve signs of the zodiac naming each sign for a constellation along the ecliptic. During the year the sun appears to move eastward through the zodiac. In the time of Hipparchus the vernal equinox occurred when the sun was in the constellation Aries. However in the 2,000 years since then, owing to what scientists call precession, the vernal equinox has moved to the last part of the constellation Pisces. By definition, the zodiac begins at 0 degrees Aries, at the point of the vernal equinox; therefore, the zodiac no longer coincides with the astronomical constellations.

The signs are:

Aries (the Ram)	March 21—April 19
Taurus (the Bull)	April 20—May 20
Gemini (the Twins)	May 21—June 20
Cancer (the Crab)	June 21—July 22
Leo (the Lion)	July 23—August 22
Virgo (the Virgin)	August 23—Sept. 22
Libra (the Balance)	Sept. 23—October 22
Scorpio (the Scorpion)	Oct. 23—November 21
Sagittarius (the Archer)	Nov. 22—December 21
Capricorn (the Goat)	Dec. 22—January 19
Aquarius (Water Bearer)	Jan. 20—February 18
Pisces (the Fishes)	February 19—March 20

HOLIDAYS — RELIGIOUS AND SECULAR

January 1	New Year's Day (most of world)
January 6	Epiphany (Christian holy day)
Third Monday in January	Martin Luther King Day (U.S.)
January 26	Australia Day
January 26	Republic Day (India)
January or February	Chinese New Year
February 2	Groundhog Day (U.S.)
February 6	New Zealand Day
February 12	Lincoln's Birthday (U.S.)
February 14	Valentines Day (U.S., Canada, U.K.)
Third Monday in February	President's Day (George Washington's birthday) U.S.
February (ninth month of Islamic calendar year)*	1st Day of Ramadan (Muslim holy day)
February or March (day before Ash Wednesday)	Mardi Gras (Christian Celebration)
February or March (40 days before Easter)	Ash Wednesday (Christian holy day)
February or March	Purim (Jewish holy day)
February or March	Holi (Hindu festival)
March 3	Hina Matsuri (Japan)
March 8	International Women's Day (China and Russia)
March 17	St. Patrick's Day (Ireland)
March 21	Juárez's Birthday (Mexico)
March or April	1st Day of Passover (Jewish holy day)
March or April (Sunday before Easter)	Palm Sunday (Christian holy day)
March or April (Friday before Easter)	Good Friday (Christian holy day)
March or April (first Sunday after the first full moon after the spring equinox)	Easter Sunday (Christian holy day)
March (tenth month of Islamic calendar year)*	1st Day of Id al-Fitr (Muslim holy day)
April 8	Kambutsue — Buddha's Birthday (Japan, Korea, & SE Asia)
April 14	Pan American Day
April or May	Baisakhi (Hindu new year)
April or May	Vesak — Buddhist holy day (Japan and SE Asia)

April or May	Israeli Independence Day
May 1	May Day (U.K. and Socialist countries)
May 5	Tango-no-sekku (Japan)
May 5	Cinco de Mayo (Mexico)
May 9	Victory Day (Russia)
Second Sunday in May	Mother's Day (U.S.)
First Monday before May 25	Victoria Day (Canada)
Last Monday in May	Memorial Day (U.S.)
May 25	African Freedom Day
May 31	South African Republic Day
May or June (40 days after Easter)	Ascension (Christian holy day)
May or June (50 days after Easter)	Pentecost (Christian holy day)
May or June	Shavouth (Jewish holy day)
May (twelfth month of Islamic calendar year)*	1st Day of Id al-Adha (Muslim holy day)
May or June	Tuan Wu Chieh (China)
June 2	Italian Republic Day
June 12	Philippine Independence Day
Third Sunday in June	Father's Day (U.S.)
July 1	Canada (Dominion) Day
July 4	American Independence Day
July 13–15	Bon (Japan)
July 14	Bastille Day (France)
July 17	Korean Constitution Day
July 24	Simón Bolívar's Birthday (Venezuela)
July	Gion Matsuri (Shinto Festival)
August 1	Swiss Confederation Day
August or September	Birthday of Krishna (Hindu celebration)
First Monday in September	Labor Day (U.S. and Canada)
Sepember 16	Mexican Independence Day
Sepember 28	Confucius' Birthday (China and Taiwan)
September or October	1st Day of Rosh Hashanah (Jewish holy day)
September or October	Yom Kippur (Jewish holy day)
September or October	Sukkoth (Jewish holy day)
September or October	Durga-Puja (Hindu festival)
September or October	Chung Ch'iu Chieh (China)
Second Monday in October	Columbus Day (U.S.)
October 1	Chinese National Day
October 2	Mahatma Gandhi's Birthday (India)
October 3	German Unity Day
October 10	Taiwanese National Day
October 24	United Nations Day
October 31	Halloween (U.S., Canada, Australia, N. Europe)
October 31	Reformation Day (Germany & Scandinavia)
October or November	Divali (India)
November 1	All Saints Day (Christian holy day)
First Tuesday after first Monday in November	Election Day (U.S.)
November 5	Guy Fawkes Day (U.K.)
November 7–8	Russian National Day
November 11	Veterans' (Armistice or Remembrance) Day (U.S. & Europe)
Fourth Thursday in November	Thanksgiving Day (U.S.)
Sunday nearest November 30	Advent (Christian)
November or December	1st Day of Hanukkah (Jewish holy day)
December 25	Christmas Day
December 26	Boxing Day (U.K., Canada)

* These holy days, based on the Islamic calendar, which is lunar, retrogress approximately ten days each Gregorian year.

GREGORIAN CALENDAR

Begins with the traditional date for the birth of Jesus Christ. B.C. (Before Christ) or B.C.E. (Before Common Era) refers to dates before the year 1 A.D. (Anno Domini) or C.E. (Common Era).

There are 365 days in the normal year and 366 days in a leap year which occurs every four years. The year begins 10 days after the winter solstice.

Month	Number of Days
January	31
February	28 or 29*
March	31
April	30
May	31
June	30
July	31
August	31
September	30
October	31
November	30
December	31

*29 days in leap years.

MUSLIM CALENDAR

Begins with 622 C.E. the year of the Hejiraho when Muhammad traveled from Mecca to Medina. There are 354 days in the year and 355 days in the leap year which occurs every 2nd, 5th, 7th, 10th, 13th, 16th, 18th, 21st, 24th, 26th, and 29th year in a 30-year cycle.

Month	Number of Days
Muharram	30
Safar	29
Rabi I	30
Rabi II	29
Jumada I	30
Jumada II	29
Rajab	30
Sha' ban	29
Ramadan	30
Shawwal	29
Dhu'l-Qa'dah	30
Dhu'l-Hijja	29 or 30 *

* 30 days in leap years.

JEWISH CALENDAR

Begins with 3761 B.C.E. calculated to be the Biblical year of creation. There are 353 to 355 days in normal years and 383 to 385 days in leap years.

Month	Number of Days
Tishri	30
Heshvan	29 or 30*
Kislev	29 or 30*
Tebet	29
Shebat	30
Adar	29 or 30*
Ve-Adar†	30
Nisan	30
Iyar	29
Sivan	30
Tammuz	29
Ab	30
Elul	29

* Depending on year can be 29 or 30 days
†Every 3rd, 6th, 8th, 11th, 14th, 17th, and 19th year in a 19-year cycle Ve-Adar (the 13th month) occurs.

HINDU CALENDAR

Month	
Chait	(March–April)
Baisakh	(April–May)
Jeth	(May–June)
Asarh	(June–July)
Sawan	(July–August)
Bhadon	(August–September)
Asin	(September–October)
Kartik	(October–November)
Aghan	(November–December)
Pus	(December–January)
Magh	(January–February)
Phagun	(February–March)

JAPANESE CALENDAR

Similar in many respects to the Gregorian Calendar but the months in the traditional Japanese calendar are unnamed and there are epochs that begin with the accession of each emperor. Thus the current epoch, Heisei, commences with the beginning of the reign of Emperor Akihito in 1989. Traditional Japanese calendar begins in 660 B.C.E.

CHINESE CALENDAR

Ancient Chinese astronomers developed their calendars on the movement of the moon. To calculate their lunar year, simply add 2698 to the current year in the Gregorian calendar. But there is another designation more interesting than numbers. The Chinese give the names of animals to their years, repeating them in twelve-year cycles. For what we regard as the 20th century, these are the designations:

The lunar year begins in China with a four-day festival known as Hsin Nien, and in Southeast Asia with a three-day celebration called Tet. Both mark the start of the new year at the first new moon after the sun enters the constellation of Aquarius, which in Western calendars falls in the period between January 21 and February 19. There are 354 days in the year consisting of 12 months of alternately 29 or 30 days. The years follow the following sequence in the traditional calendar:

Rat	Ox	Tiger	Rabbit	Dragon	Snake	Horse	Goat	Monkey	Rooster	Dog	Pig
1900	1901	1902	1903	1904	1905	1906	1907	1908	1909	1910	1911
1912	1913	1914	1915	1916	1917	1918	1919	1920	1921	1922	1923
1924	1925	1926	1927	1928	1929	1930	1931	1932	1933	1934	1935
1936	1937	1938	1939	1940	1941	1942	1943	1944	1945	1946	1947
1948	1949	1950	1951	1952	1953	1954	1955	1956	1957	1958	1959
1960	1961	1962	1963	1964	1965	1966	1967	1968	1969	1970	1971
1972	1973	1974	1975	1976	1977	1978	1979	1980	1981	1982	1983
1984	1985	1986	1987	1988	1989	1990	1991	1992	1993	1994	1995
1996	1997	1998	1999	2000	2001	2002	2003	2004	2005	2006	2007
2008	2009	2010	2011	2012	2013	2014	2015	2016	2017	2018	2019
2020	2021	2022	2023	2024	2025	2026	2027	2028	2029	2030	2031

The modern Chinese calendar begins with 1911 C.E. the year of the founding of the Chinese Republic.

FLOWERS

Month	Flower
January	Carnation or Snowdrop
February	Violet or Primrose
March	Jonquil or Violet
April	Sweet Pea or Daisy
May	Lily of the Valley or Hawthorn
June	Rose
July	Larkspur or Water Lily
August	Gladiola or Poppy
September	Aster or Morning Glory
October	Calendula or Hops
November	Chrysanthemum
December	Narcissus or Holly

BIRTHSTONES OF THE MONTH

Month	Stone
January	Garnet
February	Amethyst
March	Aquamarine or Bloodstone
April	Diamond
May	Emerald
June	Pearl or Moonstone
July	Ruby
August	Sardonyx or Peridot
September	Sapphire
October	Opal or Tourmaline
November	Topaz
December	Turquoise, Zircon, or Lapus Lazuli

ANNIVERSARIES

Year	Gift
First	Paper
Second	Cotton, Straw, Calico
Third	Leather
Fourth	Flowers, Fruit, Books
Fifth	Wood
Sixth	Sugar and Sweets
Seventh	Copper, Brass or Wool
Eighth	Bronze or Rubber
Ninth	Pottery
Tenth	Aluminum, Tin or Pewter
Eleventh	Steel
Twelfth	Silk or Linen
Thirteenth	Lace
Fourteenth	Ivory
Fifteenth	Crystal or Glass
Twentieth	China or Porcelain
Twenty-fifth	Silver
Thirtieth	Pearl
Thirty-Fifth	Coral
Fortieth	Ruby or Garnet
Forty-fifth	Sapphire
Fiftieth	Gold
Fifty-fifth	Emerald or Turquoise
Sixtieth	Diamond
Seventy-fifth	Diamond or Platinum

SHIP'S BELLS

BELLS	HOURS (A.M. or P.M.)		
1	12:30	4:30	8:30
2	1:00	5:00	9:00
3	1:30	5:30	9:30
4	2:00	6:00	10:00
5	2:30	6:30	10:30
6	3:00	7:00	11:00
7	3:30	7:30	11:30
8	4:00	8:00	12:00

GEOLOGICAL TIME CHART

Years Ago	Era	Period	Epoch	Mountains Formed	Life Appeared
10,000	CENOZOIC	QUATERNARY	Holocene		Homo sapiens sapiens
2,000,000	CENOZOIC	QUATERNARY	Pleistocene	Cascadian	Mammoths
5,000,000	CENOZOIC	TERTIARY	Pliocene		Mammals spread
25,000,000	CENOZOIC	TERTIARY	Miocene	Alpine	Whales and apes
38,000,000	CENOZOIC	TERTIARY	Oligocene		
55,000,000	CENOZOIC	TERTIARY	Eocene		Horses and elephants
65,000,000	CENOZOIC	TERTIARY	Paleocene		
145,000,000	MESOZOIC	CRETACEOUS	Laramie	Rockies	Placental mammals
	MESOZOIC	CRETACEOUS	Montana		
	MESOZOIC	CRETACEOUS	Colorado		
	MESOZOIC	CRETACEOUS	Dakota		
	MESOZOIC	CRETACEOUS	Washita		
	MESOZOIC	CRETACEOUS	Fredericksburg		Flowering plants
	MESOZOIC	CRETACEOUS	Trinity		
	MESOZOIC	CRETACEOUS	Arundel		Grasses and cereals
	MESOZOIC	CRETACEOUS	Petuxent		First birds
215,000,000	MESOZOIC	JURASSIC		Nevadas	First mammals
250,000,000	MESOZOIC	TRIASSIC			Ginkos and dinosaurs
285,000,000	PALAEOZOIC	PERMIAN		Apppalacian	Conifers
360,000,000	PALAEOZOIC	CARBONIFEROUS		Acadian	Insects and reptiles
410,000,000	PALAEOZOIC	DEVONIAN		Caledonian	Amphibians and ferns
440,000,000	PALAEOZOIC	SILURIAN		Taconic	Vascular plants
500,000,000	PALAEOZOIC	ORDOVICIAN			Fishes
600,000,000	PALAEOZOIC	CAMBRIAN		Killarney	Invertebrates
1,000,000,000	PRECAMBRIAN	PROTEROZOIC		Algoman	Marine algae
4,600,000,000	PRECAMBRIAN	ARCHEOZOIC		Laurentian	Earth formed

PERPETUAL CALENDAR

TO DETERMINE THE CALENDAR FOR A PARTICULAR YEAR MATCH THE LETTER WITH THE YEAR AND REFER TO THE CORRESPONDING CALENDAR ON PAGES 1702–1706.

1801 .....E	1833 C	1865 .....A	1897 .....F	1929 C	1961 .....A	1993 .....F	2025 .....D
1802 .....F	1834 .....D	1866 .....B	1898 .....G	1930 .....D	1962 .....B	1994 .....G	2026 .....E
1803 .....G	1835 .....E	1867 C	1899 .....A	1931 .....E	1963 C	1995 .....A	2027 .....F
1804 .....H	1836 .....M	1868 .....K	1900 .....B	1932 .....M	1964 .....K	1996 I	2028 .....N
1805 C	1837 .....A	1869 .....F	1901 C	1933 .....A	1965 .....F	1997 .....D	2029 .....B
1806 .....D	1838 .....B	1870 .....G	1902 .....D	1934 .....B	1966 .....G	1998 .....E	2030 C
1807 .....E	1839 C	1871 .....A	1903 .....E	1935 C	1967 .....A	1999 .....F	2031 .....D
1808 .....M	1840 .....K	1872 I	1904 .....M	1936 .....K	1968 I	2000 .....N	2032 L
1809 .....A	1841 .....F	1873 .....D	1905 .....A	1937 .....F	1969 .....D	2001 .....B	2033 .....G
1810 .....B	1842 .....G	1874 .....E	1906 .....B	1938 .....G	1970 .....E	2002 C	2034 .....A
1811 C	1843 .....A	1875 .....F	1907 C	1939 .....A	1971 .....F	2003 .....D	2035 .....B
1812 .....K	1844 I	1876 .....N	1908 .....K	1940 I	1972 .....N	2004 L	2036 .....J
1813 .....F	1845 .....D	1877 .....B	1909 .....F	1941 .....D	1973 .....B	2005 .....G	2037 .....E
1814 .....G	1846 .....E	1878 C	1910 .....G	1942 .....E	1974 C	2006 .....A	2038 .....F
1815 .....A	1847 .....F	1879 .....D	1911 .....A	1943 .....F	1975 .....D	2007 .....B	2039 .....G
1816 I	1848 .....N	1880 L	1912 I	1944 .....N	1976 L	2008 .....J	2040 .....H
1817 .....D	1849 .....B	1881 .....G	1913 .....D	1945 .....B	1977 .....G	2009 .....E	2041 C
1818 .....E	1850 C	1882 .....A	1914 .....E	1946 C	1978 .....A	2010 .....F	2042 .....D
1819 .....F	1851 .....D	1883 .....B	1915 .....F	1947 .....D	1979 .....B	2011 .....G	2043 .....E
1820 .....N	1852 L	1884 .....J	1916 .....N	1948 L	1980 .....J	2012 .....H	2044 .....M
1821 .....B	1853 .....G	1885 .....E	1917 .....G	1949 .....G	1981 .....E	2013 C	2045 .....A
1822 C	1854 .....A	1886 .....F	1918 C	1950 .....A	1982 .....F	2014 .....D	2046 .....B
1823 .....D	1855 .....B	1887 .....G	1919 .....D	1951 .....B	1983 .....G	2015 .....E	2047 C
1824 L	1856 .....J	1888 .....H	1920 L	1952 .....J	1984 .....H	2016 .....M	2048 .....K
1825 .....G	1857 .....E	1889 C	1921 .....G	1953 .....E	1985 C	2017 .....A	2049 .....F
1826 .....A	1858 .....F	1890 .....D	1922 .....A	1954 .....F	1986 .....D	2018 .....B	2050 .....G
1827 .....B	1859 .....G	1891 .....E	1923 .....B	1955 .....G	1987 .....E	2019 C	
1828 .....J	1860 .....H	1892 .....M	1924 .....J	1956 .....H	1988 .....M	2020 .....K	
1829 .....E	1861 C	1893 .....A	1925 .....A	1957 .....A	1989 .....A	2021 .....F	
1830 .....F	1862 .....D	1894 .....B	1926 .....F	1958 .....D	1990 .....B	2022 .....G	
1831 .....G	1863 .....E	1895 C	1927 .....G	1959 .....E	1991 C	2023 .....A	
1832 .....H	1864 .....M	1896 .....K	1928 .....H	1960 .....M	1992 .....K	2024 I	

A

JANUARY
S	M	T	W	T	F	S
1	2	3	4	5	6	7
8	9	10	11	12	13	14
15	16	17	18	19	20	21
22	23	24	25	26	27	28
29	30	31				

FEBRUARY
S	M	T	W	T	F	S
				1	2	3	4
5	6	7	8	9	10	11
12	13	14	15	16	17	18
19	20	21	22	23	24	25
26	27	28				

MARCH
S	M	T	W	T	F	S
			1	2	3	4
5	6	7	8	9	10	11
12	13	14	15	16	17	18
19	20	21	22	23	24	25
26	27	28	29	30	31	

APRIL
S	M	T	W	T	F	S
						1
2	3	4	5	6	7	8
9	10	11	12	13	14	15
16	17	18	19	20	21	22
23	24	25	26	27	28	29
30						

MAY
S	M	T	W	T	F	S
	1	2	3	4	5	6
7	8	9	10	11	12	13
14	15	16	17	18	19	20
21	22	23	24	25	26	27
28	29	30	31			

JUNE
S	M	T	W	T	F	S
				1	2	3
4	5	6	7	8	9	10
11	12	13	14	15	16	17
18	19	20	21	22	23	24
25	26	27	28	29	30	

JULY
S	M	T	W	T	F	S
						1
2	3	4	5	6	7	8
9	10	11	12	13	14	15
16	17	18	19	20	21	22
23	24	25	26	27	28	29
30	31					

AUGUST
S	M	T	W	T	F	S
		1	2	3	4	5
6	7	8	9	10	11	12
13	14	15	16	17	18	19
20	21	22	23	24	25	26
27	28	29	30	31		

SEPTEMBER
S	M	T	W	T	F	S
					1	2
3	4	5	6	7	8	9
10	11	12	13	14	15	16
17	18	19	20	21	22	23
24	25	26	27	28	29	30

OCTOBER
S	M	T	W	T	F	S
1	2	3	4	5	6	7
8	9	10	11	12	13	14
15	16	17	18	19	20	21
22	23	24	25	26	27	28
29	30	31				

NOVEMBER
S	M	T	W	T	F	S
			1	2	3	4
5	6	7	8	9	10	11
12	13	14	15	16	17	18
19	20	21	22	23	24	25
26	27	28	29	30		

DECEMBER
S	M	T	W	T	F	S
					1	2
3	4	5	6	7	8	9
10	11	12	13	14	15	16
17	18	19	20	21	22	23
24	25	26	27	28	29	30
31						

B

JANUARY
S	M	T	W	T	F	S
	1	2	3	4	5	6
7	8	9	10	11	12	13
14	15	16	17	18	19	20
21	22	23	24	25	26	27
28	29	30	31			

FEBRUARY
S	M	T	W	T	F	S
					1	2	3
4	5	6	7	8	9	10
11	12	13	14	15	16	17
18	19	20	21	22	23	24
25	26	27	28			

MARCH
S	M	T	W	T	F	S
				1	2	3
4	5	6	7	8	9	10
11	12	13	14	15	16	17
18	19	20	21	22	23	24
25	26	27	28	29	30	31

APRIL
S	M	T	W	T	F	S
1	2	3	4	5	6	7
8	9	10	11	12	13	14
15	16	17	18	19	20	21
22	23	24	25	26	27	28
29	30					

MAY
S	M	T	W	T	F	S
		1	2	3	4	5
6	7	8	9	10	11	12
13	14	15	16	17	18	19
20	21	22	23	24	25	26
27	28	29	30	31		

JUNE
S	M	T	W	T	F	S
					1	2
3	4	5	6	7	8	9
10	11	12	13	14	15	16
17	18	19	20	21	22	23
24	25	26	27	28	29	30

JULY
S	M	T	W	T	F	S
1	2	3	4	5	6	7
8	9	10	11	12	13	14
15	16	17	18	19	20	21
22	23	24	25	26	27	28
29	30	31				

AUGUST
S	M	T	W	T	F	S
				1	2	3	4
5	6	7	8	9	10	11
12	13	14	15	16	17	18
19	20	21	22	23	24	25
26	27	28	29	30	31	

SEPTEMBER
S	M	T	W	T	F	S
						1
2	3	4	5	6	7	8
9	10	11	12	13	14	15
16	17	18	19	20	21	22
23	24	25	26	27	28	29
30						

OCTOBER
S	M	T	W	T	F	S
	1	2	3	4	5	6
7	8	9	10	11	12	13
14	15	16	17	18	19	20
21	22	23	24	25	26	27
28	29	30	31			

NOVEMBER
S	M	T	W	T	F	S
				1	2	3
4	5	6	7	8	9	10
11	12	13	14	15	16	17
18	19	20	21	22	23	24
25	26	27	28	29	30	

DECEMBER
S	M	T	W	T	F	S
						1
2	3	4	5	6	7	8
9	10	11	12	13	14	15
16	17	18	19	20	21	22
23	24	25	26	27	28	29
30	31					

C

JANUARY
S	M	T	W	T	F	S
		1	2	3	4	5
6	7	8	9	10	11	12
13	14	15	16	17	18	19
20	21	22	23	24	25	26
27	28	29	30	31		

FEBRUARY
S	M	T	W	T	F	S
					1	2
3	4	5	6	7	8	9
10	11	12	13	14	15	16
17	18	19	20	21	22	23
24	25	26	27	28		

MARCH
S	M	T	W	T	F	S
					1	2
3	4	5	6	7	8	9
10	11	12	13	14	15	16
17	18	19	20	21	22	23
24	25	26	27	28	29	30
31						

APRIL
S	M	T	W	T	F	S
	1	2	3	4	5	6
7	8	9	10	11	12	13
14	15	16	17	18	19	20
21	22	23	24	25	26	27
28	29	30				

MAY
S	M	T	W	T	F	S
			1	2	3	4
5	6	7	8	9	10	11
12	13	14	15	16	17	18
19	20	21	22	23	24	25
26	27	28	29	30	31	

JUNE
S	M	T	W	T	F	S
						1
2	3	4	5	6	7	8
9	10	11	12	13	14	15
16	17	18	19	20	21	22
23	24	25	26	27	28	29
30						

JULY
S	M	T	W	T	F	S
	1	2	3	4	5	6
7	8	9	10	11	12	13
14	15	16	17	18	19	20
21	22	23	24	25	26	27
28	29	30	31			

AUGUST
S	M	T	W	T	F	S
				1	2	3
4	5	6	7	8	9	10
11	12	13	14	15	16	17
18	19	20	21	22	23	24
25	26	27	28	29	30	31

SEPTEMBER
S	M	T	W	T	F	S
1	2	3	4	5	6	7
8	9	10	11	12	13	14
15	16	17	18	19	20	21
22	23	24	25	26	27	28
29	30					

OCTOBER
S	M	T	W	T	F	S
		1	2	3	4	5
6	7	8	9	10	11	12
13	14	15	16	17	18	19
20	21	22	23	24	25	26
27	28	29	30	31		

NOVEMBER
S	M	T	W	T	F	S
					1	2
3	4	5	6	7	8	9
10	11	12	13	14	15	16
17	18	19	20	21	22	23
24	25	26	27	28	29	30

DECEMBER
S	M	T	W	T	F	S
1	2	3	4	5	6	7
8	9	10	11	12	13	14
15	16	17	18	19	20	21
22	23	24	25	26	27	28
29	30	31				

D

```
JANUARY                 FEBRUARY                MARCH                   APRIL
S  M  T  W  T  F  S      S  M  T  W  T  F  S     S  M  T  W  T  F  S     S  M  T  W  T  F  S
         1  2  3  4                        1                       1            1  2  3  4  5
5  6  7  8  9 10 11      2  3  4  5  6  7  8     2  3  4  5  6  7  8     6  7  8  9 10 11 12
12 13 14 15 16 17 18     9 10 11 12 13 14 15     9 10 11 12 13 14 15    13 14 15 16 17 18 19
19 20 21 22 23 24 25    16 17 18 19 20 21 22    16 17 18 19 20 21 22    20 21 22 23 24 25 26
26 27 28 29 30 31       23 24 25 26 27 28       23 24 25 26 27 28 29    27 28 29 30
                                                30 31

MAY                     JUNE                    JULY                    AUGUST
S  M  T  W  T  F  S      S  M  T  W  T  F  S     S  M  T  W  T  F  S     S  M  T  W  T  F  S
            1  2  3      1  2  3  4  5  6  7              1  2  3  4  5                  1  2
4  5  6  7  8  9 10      8  9 10 11 12 13 14     6  7  8  9 10 11 12     3  4  5  6  7  8  9
11 12 13 14 15 16 17    15 16 17 18 19 20 21    13 14 15 16 17 18 19    10 11 12 13 14 15 16
18 19 20 21 22 23 24    22 23 24 25 26 27 28    20 21 22 23 24 25 26    17 18 19 20 21 22 23
25 26 27 28 29 30 31    29 30                   27 28 29 30 31          24 25 26 27 28 29 30
                                                                        31

SEPTEMBER               OCTOBER                 NOVEMBER                DECEMBER
S  M  T  W  T  F  S      S  M  T  W  T  F  S     S  M  T  W  T  F  S     S  M  T  W  T  F  S
   1  2  3  4  5  6               1  2  3  4                       1        1  2  3  4  5  6
7  8  9 10 11 12 13     5  6  7  8  9 10 11     2  3  4  5  6  7  8     7  8  9 10 11 12 13
14 15 16 17 18 19 20    12 13 14 15 16 17 18     9 10 11 12 13 14 15    14 15 16 17 18 19 20
21 22 23 24 25 26 27    19 20 21 22 23 24 25    16 17 18 19 20 21 22    21 22 23 24 25 26 27
28 29 30 31             26 27 28 29 30 31       23 24 25 26 27 28 29    28 29 30 31
                                                30
```

E

```
JANUARY                 FEBRUARY                MARCH                   APRIL
S  M  T  W  T  F  S      S  M  T  W  T  F  S     S  M  T  W  T  F  S     S  M  T  W  T  F  S
            1  2  3      1  2  3  4  5  6  7     1  2  3  4  5  6  7                 1  2  3  4
4  5  6  7  8  9 10      8  9 10 11 12 13 14     8  9 10 11 12 13 14     5  6  7  8  9 10 11
11 12 13 14 15 16 17    15 16 17 18 19 20 21    15 16 17 18 19 20 21    12 13 14 15 16 17 18
18 19 20 21 22 23 24    22 23 24 25 26 27 28    22 23 24 25 26 27 28    19 20 21 22 23 24 25
25 26 27 28 29 30 31                            29 30 31                26 27 28 29 30

MAY                     JUNE                    JULY                    AUGUST
S  M  T  W  T  F  S      S  M  T  W  T  F  S     S  M  T  W  T  F  S     S  M  T  W  T  F  S
               1  2         1  2  3  4  5  6              1  2  3  4                        1
3  4  5  6  7  8  9      7  8  9 10 11 12 13     5  6  7  8  9 10 11     2  3  4  5  6  7  8
10 11 12 13 14 15 16    14 15 16 17 18 19 20    12 13 14 15 16 17 18     9 10 11 12 13 14 15
17 18 19 20 21 22 23    21 22 23 24 25 26 27    19 20 21 22 23 24 25    16 17 18 19 20 21 22
24 25 26 27 28 29 30    28 29 30               26 27 28 29 30 31       23 24 25 26 27 28 29
31                                                                      30 31

SEPTEMBER               OCTOBER                 NOVEMBER                DECEMBER
S  M  T  W  T  F  S      S  M  T  W  T  F  S     S  M  T  W  T  F  S     S  M  T  W  T  F  S
      1  2  3  4  5                  1  2  3    1  2  3  4  5  6  7            1  2  3  4  5
6  7  8  9 10 11 12     4  5  6  7  8  9 10     8  9 10 11 12 13 14     6  7  8  9 10 11 12
13 14 15 16 17 18 19    11 12 13 14 15 16 17    15 16 17 18 19 20 21    13 14 15 16 17 18 19
20 21 22 23 24 25 26    18 19 20 21 22 23 24    22 23 24 25 26 27 28    20 21 22 23 24 25 26
27 28 29 30             25 26 27 28 29 30 31    29 30                   27 28 29 30 31
```

F

```
JANUARY                 FEBRUARY                MARCH                   APRIL
S  M  T  W  T  F  S      S  M  T  W  T  F  S     S  M  T  W  T  F  S     S  M  T  W  T  F  S
               1  2         1  2  3  4  5  6        1  2  3  4  5  6                  1  2  3
3  4  5  6  7  8  9      7  8  9 10 11 12 13     7  8  9 10 11 12 13     4  5  6  7  8  9 10
10 11 12 13 14 15 16    14 15 16 17 18 19 20    14 15 16 17 18 19 20    11 12 13 14 15 16 17
17 18 19 20 21 22 23    21 22 23 24 25 26 27    21 22 23 24 25 26 27    18 19 20 21 22 23 24
24 25 26 27 28 29 30    28                      28 29 30 31             25 26 27 28 29 30
31

MAY                     JUNE                    JULY                    AUGUST
S  M  T  W  T  F  S      S  M  T  W  T  F  S     S  M  T  W  T  F  S     S  M  T  W  T  F  S
                  1         1  2  3  4  5                  1  2  3      1  2  3  4  5  6  7
2  3  4  5  6  7  8      6  7  8  9 10 11 12     4  5  6  7  8  9 10     8  9 10 11 12 13 14
9 10 11 12 13 14 15     13 14 15 16 17 18 19    11 12 13 14 15 16 17    15 16 17 18 19 20 21
16 17 18 19 20 21 22    20 21 22 23 24 25 26    18 19 20 21 22 23 24    22 23 24 25 26 27 28
23 24 25 26 27 28 29    27 28 29 30            25 26 27 28 29 30 31    29 30 31
30 31

SEPTEMBER               OCTOBER                 NOVEMBER                DECEMBER
S  M  T  W  T  F  S      S  M  T  W  T  F  S     S  M  T  W  T  F  S     S  M  T  W  T  F  S
         1  2  3  4                     1  2       1  2  3  4  5  6            1  2  3  4
5  6  7  8  9 10 11     3  4  5  6  7  8  9     7  8  9 10 11 12 13     5  6  7  8  9 10 11
12 13 14 15 16 17 18    10 11 12 13 14 15 16    14 15 16 17 18 19 20    12 13 14 15 16 17 18
19 20 21 22 23 24 25    17 18 19 20 21 22 23    21 22 23 24 25 26 27    19 20 21 22 23 24 25
26 27 28 29 30          24 25 26 27 28 29 30    28 29 30                26 27 28 29 30 31
                        31
```

G

JANUARY
S	M	T	W	T	F	S
						1
2	3	4	5	6	7	8
9	10	11	12	13	14	15
16	17	18	19	20	21	22
23	24	25	26	27	28	29
30	31					

FEBRUARY
S	M	T	W	T	F	S
	1	2	3	4	5	
6	7	8	9	10	11	12
13	14	15	16	17	18	19
20	21	22	23	24	25	26
27	28					

MARCH
S	M	T	W	T	F	S
	1	2	3	4	5	
6	7	8	9	10	11	12
13	14	15	16	17	18	19
20	21	22	23	24	25	26
27	28	29	30	31		

APRIL
S	M	T	W	T	F	S
					1	2
3	4	5	6	7	8	9
10	11	12	13	14	15	16
17	18	19	20	21	22	23
24	25	26	27	28	29	30

MAY
S	M	T	W	T	F	S
1	2	3	4	5	6	7
8	9	10	11	12	13	14
15	16	17	18	19	20	21
22	23	24	25	26	27	28
29	30	31				

JUNE
S	M	T	W	T	F	S
			1	2	3	4
5	6	7	8	9	10	11
12	13	14	15	16	17	18
19	20	21	22	23	24	25
26	27	28	29	30		

JULY
S	M	T	W	T	F	S
					1	2
3	4	5	6	7	8	9
10	11	12	13	14	15	16
17	18	19	20	21	22	23
24	25	26	27	28	29	30
31						

AUGUST
S	M	T	W	T	F	S
	1	2	3	4	5	6
7	8	9	10	11	12	13
14	15	16	17	18	19	20
21	22	23	24	25	26	27
28	29	30	31			

SEPTEMBER
S	M	T	W	T	F	S
				1	2	3
4	5	6	7	8	9	10
11	12	13	14	15	16	17
18	19	20	21	22	23	24
25	26	27	28	29	30	

OCTOBER
S	M	T	W	T	F	S
						1
2	3	4	5	6	7	8
9	10	11	12	13	14	15
16	17	18	19	20	21	22
23	24	25	26	27	28	29
30	31					

NOVEMBER
S	M	T	W	T	F	S
		1	2	3	4	5
6	7	8	9	10	11	12
13	14	15	16	17	18	19
20	21	22	23	24	25	26
27	28	29	30			

DECEMBER
S	M	T	W	T	F	S
				1	2	3
4	5	6	7	8	9	10
11	12	13	14	15	16	17
18	19	20	21	22	23	24
25	26	27	28	29	30	31

H

JANUARY
S	M	T	W	T	F	S
1	2	3	4	5	6	7
8	9	10	11	12	13	14
15	16	17	18	19	20	21
22	23	24	25	26	27	28
29	30	31	32	33	34	35

FEBRUARY
S	M	T	W	T	F	S
		1	2	3	4	
5	6	7	8	9	10	11
12	13	14	15	16	17	18
19	20	21	22	23	24	25
26	27	28	29			

MARCH
S	M	T	W	T	F	S
			1	2	3	
4	5	6	7	8	9	10
11	12	13	14	15	16	17
18	19	20	21	22	23	24
25	26	27	28	29	30	31

APRIL
S	M	T	W	T	F	S
1	2	3	4	5	6	7
8	9	10	11	12	13	14
15	16	17	18	19	20	21
22	23	24	25	26	27	28
29	30					

MAY
S	M	T	W	T	F	S
		1	2	3	4	5
6	7	8	9	10	11	12
13	14	15	16	17	18	19
20	21	22	23	24	25	26
27	28	29	30	31		

JUNE
S	M	T	W	T	F	S
				1	2	
3	4	5	6	7	8	9
10	11	12	13	14	15	16
17	18	19	20	21	22	23
24	25	26	27	28	29	30

JULY
S	M	T	W	T	F	S
1	2	3	4	5	6	7
8	9	10	11	12	13	14
15	16	17	18	19	20	21
22	23	24	25	26	27	28
29	30	31				

AUGUST
S	M	T	W	T	F	S
	1	2	3	4		
5	6	7	8	9	10	11
12	13	14	15	16	17	18
19	20	21	22	23	24	25
26	27	28	29	30	31	

SEPTEMBER
S	M	T	W	T	F	S
						1
2	3	4	5	6	7	8
9	10	11	12	13	14	15
16	17	18	19	20	21	22
23	24	25	26	27	28	29
30						

OCTOBER
S	M	T	W	T	F	S
	1	2	3	4	5	6
7	8	9	10	11	12	13
14	15	16	17	18	19	20
21	22	23	24	25	26	27
28	29	30	31			

NOVEMBER
S	M	T	W	T	F	S
			1	2	3	
4	5	6	7	8	9	10
11	12	13	14	15	16	17
18	19	20	21	22	23	24
25	26	27	28	29	30	

DECEMBER
S	M	T	W	T	F	S
						1
2	3	4	5	6	7	8
9	10	11	12	13	14	15
16	17	18	19	20	21	22
23	24	25	26	27	28	29
30	31					

I

JANUARY
S	M	T	W	T	F	S
	1	2	3	4	5	6
7	8	9	10	11	12	13
14	15	16	17	18	19	20
21	22	23	24	25	26	27
28	29	30	31			

FEBRUARY
S	M	T	W	T	F	S
				1	2	3
4	5	6	7	8	9	10
11	12	13	14	15	16	17
18	19	20	21	22	23	24
25	26	27	28	29		

MARCH
S	M	T	W	T	F	S
					1	2
3	4	5	6	7	8	9
10	11	12	13	14	15	16
17	18	19	20	21	22	23
24	25	26	27	28	29	30
31						

APRIL
S	M	T	W	T	F	S
	1	2	3	4	5	6
7	8	9	10	11	12	13
14	15	16	17	18	19	20
21	22	23	24	25	26	27
28	29	30				

MAY
S	M	T	W	T	F	S
			1	2	3	4
5	6	7	8	9	10	11
12	13	14	15	16	17	18
19	20	21	22	23	24	25
26	27	28	29	30	31	

JUNE
S	M	T	W	T	F	S
						1
2	3	4	5	6	7	8
9	10	11	12	13	14	15
16	17	18	19	20	21	22
23	24	25	26	27	28	29
30						

JULY
S	M	T	W	T	F	S
	1	2	3	4	5	6
7	8	9	10	11	12	13
14	15	16	17	18	19	20
21	22	23	24	25	26	27
28	29	30	31			

AUGUST
S	M	T	W	T	F	S
				1	2	3
4	5	6	7	8	9	10
11	12	13	14	15	16	17
18	19	20	21	22	23	24
25	26	27	28	29	30	31

SEPTEMBER
S	M	T	W	T	F	S
1	2	3	4	5	6	7
8	9	10	11	12	13	14
15	16	17	18	19	20	21
22	23	24	25	26	27	28
29	30					

OCTOBER
S	M	T	W	T	F	S
		1	2	3	4	5
6	7	8	9	10	11	12
13	14	15	16	17	18	19
20	21	22	23	24	25	26
27	28	29	30	31		

NOVEMBER
S	M	T	W	T	F	S
					1	2
3	4	5	6	7	8	9
10	11	12	13	14	15	16
17	18	19	20	21	22	23
24	25	26	27	28	29	30

DECEMBER
S	M	T	W	T	F	S
1	2	3	4	5	6	7
8	9	10	11	12	13	14
15	16	17	18	19	20	21
22	23	24	25	26	27	28
29	30	31				

J

JANUARY
```
S  M  T  W  T  F  S
         1  2  3  4  5
 6  7  8  9 10 11 12
13 14 15 16 17 18 19
20 21 22 23 24 25 26
27 28 29 30 31
```

FEBRUARY
```
S  M  T  W  T  F  S
                  1  2
 3  4  5  6  7  8  9
10 11 12 13 14 15 16
17 18 19 20 21 22 23
24 25 26 27 28 29
```

MARCH
```
S  M  T  W  T  F  S
                     1
 2  3  4  5  6  7  8
 9 10 11 12 13 14 15
16 17 18 19 20 21 22
23 24 25 26 27 28 29
30 31
```

APRIL
```
S  M  T  W  T  F  S
      1  2  3  4  5
 6  7  8  9 10 11 12
13 14 15 16 17 18 19
20 21 22 23 24 25 26
27 28 29 30
```

MAY
```
S  M  T  W  T  F  S
            1  2  3
 4  5  6  7  8  9 10
11 12 13 14 15 16 17
18 19 20 21 22 23 24
25 26 27 28 29 30 31
```

JUNE
```
S  M  T  W  T  F  S
 1  2  3  4  5  6  7
 8  9 10 11 12 13 14
15 16 17 18 19 20 21
22 23 24 25 26 27 28
29 30
```

JULY
```
S  M  T  W  T  F  S
         1  2  3  4  5
 6  7  8  9 10 11 12
13 14 15 16 17 18 19
20 21 22 23 24 25 26
27 28 29 30 31
```

AUGUST
```
S  M  T  W  T  F  S
                  1  2
 3  4  5  6  7  8  9
10 11 12 13 14 15 16
17 18 19 20 21 22 23
24 25 26 27 28 29 30
31
```

SEPTEMBER
```
S  M  T  W  T  F  S
      1  2  3  4  5  6
 7  8  9 10 11 12 13
14 15 16 17 18 19 20
21 22 23 24 25 26 27
28 29 30
```

OCTOBER
```
S  M  T  W  T  F  S
            1  2  3  4
 5  6  7  8  9 10 11
12 13 14 15 16 17 18
19 20 21 22 23 24 25
26 27 28 29 30 31
```

NOVEMBER
```
S  M  T  W  T  F  S
                     1
 2  3  4  5  6  7  8
 9 10 11 12 13 14 15
16 17 18 19 20 21 22
23 24 25 26 27 28 29
30
```

DECEMBER
```
S  M  T  W  T  F  S
      1  2  3  4  5  6
 7  8  9 10 11 12 13
14 15 16 17 18 19 20
21 22 23 24 25 26 27
28 29 30 31
```

K

JANUARY
```
S  M  T  W  T  F  S
            1  2  3  4
 5  6  7  8  9 10 11
12 13 14 15 16 17 18
19 20 21 22 23 24 25
26 27 28 29 30 31
```

FEBRUARY
```
S  M  T  W  T  F  S
                     1
 2  3  4  5  6  7  8
 9 10 11 12 13 14 15
16 17 18 19 20 21 22
23 24 25 26 27 28 29
```

MARCH
```
S  M  T  W  T  F  S
 1  2  3  4  5  6  7
 8  9 10 11 12 13 14
15 16 17 18 19 20 21
22 23 24 25 26 27 28
29 30 31
```

APRIL
```
S  M  T  W  T  F  S
         1  2  3  4
 5  6  7  8  9 10 11
12 13 14 15 16 17 18
19 20 21 22 23 24 25
26 27 28 29 30
```

MAY
```
S  M  T  W  T  F  S
                  1  2
 3  4  5  6  7  8  9
10 11 12 13 14 15 16
17 18 19 20 21 22 23
24 25 26 27 28 29 30
31
```

JUNE
```
S  M  T  W  T  F  S
      1  2  3  4  5  6
 7  8  9 10 11 12 13
14 15 16 17 18 19 20
21 22 23 24 25 26 27
28 29 30
```

JULY
```
S  M  T  W  T  F  S
            1  2  3  4
 5  6  7  8  9 10 11
12 13 14 15 16 17 18
19 20 21 22 23 24 25
26 27 28 29 30 31
```

AUGUST
```
S  M  T  W  T  F  S
                     1
 2  3  4  5  6  7  8
 9 10 11 12 13 14 15
16 17 18 19 20 21 22
23 24 25 26 27 28 29
30 31
```

SEPTEMBER
```
S  M  T  W  T  F  S
         1  2  3  4  5
 6  7  8  9 10 11 12
13 14 15 16 17 18 19
20 21 22 23 24 25 26
27 28 29 30
```

OCTOBER
```
S  M  T  W  T  F  S
                  1  2  3
 4  5  6  7  8  9 10
11 12 13 14 15 16 17
18 19 20 21 22 23 24
25 26 27 28 29 30 31
```

NOVEMBER
```
S  M  T  W  T  F  S
 1  2  3  4  5  6  7
 8  9 10 11 12 13 14
15 16 17 18 19 20 21
22 23 24 25 26 27 28
29 30
```

DECEMBER
```
S  M  T  W  T  F  S
         1  2  3  4  5
 6  7  8  9 10 11 12
13 14 15 16 17 18 19
20 21 22 23 24 25 26
27 28 29 30 31
```

L

JANUARY
```
S  M  T  W  T  F  S
            1  2  3
 4  5  6  7  8  9 10
11 12 13 14 15 16 17
18 19 20 21 22 23 24
25 26 27 28 29 30 31
```

FEBRUARY
```
S  M  T  W  T  F  S
 1  2  3  4  5  6  7
 8  9 10 11 12 13 14
15 16 17 18 19 20 21
22 23 24 25 26 27 28
29
```

MARCH
```
S  M  T  W  T  F  S
      1  2  3  4  5  6
 7  8  9 10 11 12 13
14 15 16 17 18 19 20
21 22 23 24 25 26 27
28 29 30 31
```

APRIL
```
S  M  T  W  T  F  S
                  1  2  3
 4  5  6  7  8  9 10
11 12 13 14 15 16 17
18 19 20 21 22 23 24
25 26 27 28 29 30
```

MAY
```
S  M  T  W  T  F  S
                     1
 2  3  4  5  6  7  8
 9 10 11 12 13 14 15
16 17 18 19 20 21 22
23 24 25 26 27 28 29
30 31
```

JUNE
```
S  M  T  W  T  F  S
         1  2  3  4  5
 6  7  8  9 10 11 12
13 14 15 16 17 18 19
20 21 22 23 24 25 26
27 28 29 30
```

JULY
```
S  M  T  W  T  F  S
                  1  2  3
 4  5  6  7  8  9 10
11 12 13 14 15 16 17
18 19 20 21 22 23 24
25 26 27 28 29 30 31
```

AUGUST
```
S  M  T  W  T  F  S
 1  2  3  4  5  6  7
 8  9 10 11 12 13 14
15 16 17 18 19 20 21
22 23 24 25 26 27 28
29 30 31
```

SEPTEMBER
```
S  M  T  W  T  F  S
         1  2  3  4
 5  6  7  8  9 10 11
12 13 14 15 16 17 18
19 20 21 22 23 24 25
26 27 28 29 30
```

OCTOBER
```
S  M  T  W  T  F  S
                  1  2
 3  4  5  6  7  8  9
10 11 12 13 14 15 16
17 18 19 20 21 22 23
24 25 26 27 28 29 30
31
```

NOVEMBER
```
S  M  T  W  T  F  S
      1  2  3  4  5  6
 7  8  9 10 11 12 13
14 15 16 17 18 19 20
21 22 23 24 25 26 27
28 29 30
```

DECEMBER
```
S  M  T  W  T  F  S
            1  2  3  4
 5  6  7  8  9 10 11
12 13 14 15 16 17 18
19 20 21 22 23 24 25
26 27 28 29 30 31
```

M

JANUARY

S	M	T	W	T	F	S
					1	2
3	4	5	6	7	8	9
10	11	12	13	14	15	16
17	18	19	20	21	22	23
24	25	26	27	28	29	30
31						

FEBRUARY

S	M	T	W	T	F	S
	1	2	3	4	5	6
7	8	9	10	11	12	13
14	15	16	17	18	19	20
21	22	23	24	25	26	27
28	29					

MARCH

S	M	T	W	T	F	S
	1	2	3	4	5	
6	7	8	9	10	11	12
13	14	15	16	17	18	19
20	21	22	23	24	25	26
27	28	29	30			

APRIL

S	M	T	W	T	F	S
					1	2
3	4	5	6	7	8	9
10	11	12	13	14	15	16
17	18	19	20	21	22	23
24	25	26	27	28	29	30

MAY

S	M	T	W	T	F	S
1	2	3	4	5	6	7
8	9	10	11	12	13	14
15	16	17	18	19	20	21
22	23	24	25	26	27	28
29	30	31				

JUNE

S	M	T	W	T	F	S
			1	2	3	4
5	6	7	8	9	10	11
12	13	14	15	16	17	18
19	20	21	22	23	24	25
26	27	28	29	30		

JULY

S	M	T	W	T	F	S
					1	2
3	4	5	6	7	8	9
10	11	12	13	14	15	16
17	18	19	20	21	22	23
24	25	26	27	28	29	30
31						

AUGUST

S	M	T	W	T	F	S
1	2	3	4	5	6	
7	8	9	10	11	12	13
14	15	16	17	18	19	20
21	22	23	24	25	26	27
28	29	30	31			

SEPTEMBER

S	M	T	W	T	F	S
				1	2	3
4	5	6	7	8	9	10
11	12	13	14	15	16	17
18	19	20	21	22	23	24
25	26	27	28	29	30	

OCTOBER

S	M	T	W	T	F	S
						1
2	3	4	5	6	7	8
9	10	11	12	13	14	15
16	17	18	19	20	21	22
23	24	25	26	27	28	29
30	31					

NOVEMBER

S	M	T	W	T	F	S
		1	2	3	4	5
6	7	8	9	10	11	12
13	14	15	16	17	18	19
20	21	22	23	24	25	26
27	28	29	30			

DECEMBER

S	M	T	W	T	F	S
				1	2	3
4	5	6	7	8	9	10
11	12	13	14	15	16	17
18	19	20	21	22	23	24
25	26	27	28	29	30	31

N

JANUARY

S	M	T	W	T	F	S
						1
2	3	4	5	6	7	8
9	10	11	12	13	14	15
16	17	18	19	20	21	22
23	24	25	26	27	28	29
30	31					

FEBRUARY

S	M	T	W	T	F	S
		1	2	3	4	5
6	7	8	9	10	11	12
13	14	15	16	17	18	19
20	21	22	23	24	25	26
27	28	29				

MARCH

S	M	T	W	T	F	S
			1	2	3	4
5	6	7	8	9	10	11
12	13	14	15	16	17	18
19	20	21	22	23	24	25
26	27	28	29	30	31	

APRIL

S	M	T	W	T	F	S
						1
2	3	4	5	6	7	8
9	10	11	12	13	14	15
16	17	18	19	20	21	22
23	24	25	26	27	28	29
30						

MAY

S	M	T	W	T	F	S
	1	2	3	4	5	6
7	8	9	10	11	12	13
14	15	16	17	18	19	20
21	22	23	24	25	26	27
28	29	30	31			

JUNE

S	M	T	W	T	F	S
				1	2	3
4	5	6	7	8	9	10
11	12	13	14	15	16	17
18	19	20	21	22	23	24
25	26	27	28	29	30	

JULY

S	M	T	W	T	F	S
						1
2	3	4	5	6	7	8
9	10	11	12	13	14	15
16	17	18	19	20	21	22
23	24	25	26	27	28	29
30	31					

AUGUST

S	M	T	W	T	F	S
		1	2	3	4	5
6	7	8	9	10	11	12
13	14	15	16	17	18	19
20	21	22	23	24	25	26
27	28	29	30	31		

SEPTEMBER

S	M	T	W	T	F	S
					1	2
3	4	5	6	7	8	9
10	11	12	13	14	15	16
17	18	19	20	21	22	23
24	25	26	27	28	29	30

OCTOBER

S	M	T	W	T	F	S
1	2	3	4	5	6	7
8	9	10	11	12	13	14
15	16	17	18	19	20	21
22	23	24	25	26	27	28
29	30	31				

NOVEMBER

S	M	T	W	T	F	S
		1	2	3	4	
5	6	7	8	9	10	11
12	13	14	15	16	17	18
19	20	21	22	23	24	25
26	27	28	29	30		

DECEMBER

S	M	T	W	T	F	S
					1	2
3	4	5	6	7	8	9
10	11	12	13	14	15	16
17	18	19	20	21	22	23
24	25	26	27	28	29	30
31						

Scientific Terms

Groundbreaking developments in scientific inquiry and discovery, concern about the environment, and an urgent interest in the future of the planet and humankind have brought the scientific world to the front pages of newspapers all over the world. The following section of concise descriptions and definitions of scientific phenomena, laws, and terms provides the basic vocabulary and knowledge needed to understand both physical and natural sciences.

abacus method of calculating with a handful of stones on "a flat surface" (Latin *abacus*), familiar to the Greeks and Romans, and used by earlier peoples, possibly even in ancient Babylon; it still survives in the more sophisticated bead-frame form.

aberration of starlight apparent displacement of a star from its true position, due to the combined effects of the speed of light and the speed of the Earth in orbit around the Sun (about 18.5 mi per second/30 km per second).

abscissa in coordinate geometry, the x-coordinate of a point—that is, the horizontal distance of that point from the vertical or y-axis. For example, a point with the coordinates (4, 3) has an abscissa of 3. The y-coordinate of a point is known as the ordinate.

absolute zero lowest temperature theoretically possible, zero degrees Kelvin (0K), equivalent to -459.67°F / -273.15°C at which molecules are motionless. Near absolute zero, the physical properties of some materials change substantially; for example, some metals lose their electrical resistance and become superconductive.

abyssal zone dark ocean region 6,500–19,500 ft/ 2,000–6,000 m deep; temperature 39°F/4°C. Three-quarters of the area of the deep ocean floor lies in the abyssal zone, which is too far from the surface for photosynthesis to take place. Some fish and crustaceans living there are blind or have their own light sources. The region above is the bathyal zone; the region below, the hadal zone.

acid compound that, in solution in an ionizing solvent (usually water), gives rise to hydrogen ions (H^+ or protons). In modern chemistry, acids are defined as substances that are proton donors and accept electrons to form ionic bonds. Acids react with bases to form salts, and they act as solvents. Strong acids are corrosive; dilute acids have a sour or sharp taste, although in some organic acids this may be partially masked by other flavor characteristics.

acoustics in general, the experimental and theoretical science of sound and its transmission; in particular, that branch of the science that has to do with the phenomena of sound in a particular space such as a room or theater.

activation energy in chemistry, the energy required in order to start a chemical reaction. Some elements and compounds will react together merely by bringing them into contact (spontaneous reaction). For others it is necessary to supply energy in order to start the reaction, even if there is ultimately a net output of energy. This initial energy is the activation energy.

adaptation any change in the structure or function of an organism that allows it to survive and reproduce more effectively in its environment.

additive in food, any natural or artificial chemical added to prolong the shelf life of processed foods (salt or nitrates), alter the color or flavor of food, or improve its food value (vitamins or minerals). Many chemical additives are used and they are subject to regulation, since individuals may be affected by constant exposure even to traces of certain additives and may suffer side effects ranging from headaches and hyperactivity to cancer. They must be listed on labels of foods sold in the US so consumers may be aware of those they cannot tolerate.

adhesive substance that sticks two surfaces together. Natural adhesives (glues) include gelatin in its crude industrial form (made from bones, hide fragments, and fish offal) and vegetable gums. Synthetic adhesives include thermoplastic and thermosetting resins, which are often stronger than the substances they join; mixtures of epoxy resin and hardener that set by chemical reaction; and elastomeric (stretching) adhesives for flexible joints. Superglues are fast-setting adhesives used in very small quantities.

aerobic a description of those living organisms that require oxygen (usually dissolved in water) for the efficient release of energy contained in food molecules, such as glucose. They include almost all living organisms (plants as well as animals) with the exception of certain bacteria.

aerosol particles of liquid or solid suspended in a gas. Fog is a common natural example. Aerosol cans contain a substance such as scent or cleaner packed under pressure with a device for releasing it as a fine spray. Most aerosols used chlorofluorocarbons (CFCs) as propellants until these were found to cause destruction of the ozone layer in the stratosphere.

air pollution contamination of the atmosphere caused by the discharge, accidental or deliberate, of a wide range of toxic airborne substances. Often the amount of the released substance is relatively high in a certain locality, so the harmful effects become more noticeable. The cost of preventing any discharge of pollutants into the air is prohibitive, so attempts are more usually made to reduce gradually the amount of discharge and to disperse this as quickly as possible by using a very tall chimney, or by intermittent release.

albedo the fraction of the incoming light reflected by a body such as a planet. A body with a high albedo, near 1, is very bright, while a body with a low albedo, near 0, is dark. The Moon has an average albedo of 0.12, Venus 0.65, Earth 0.37.

alcohol any member of a group of organic chemical compounds characterized by the presence of one or more aliphatic OH (hydroxyl) groups in the molecule, and which form esters with acids. The main uses of alcohols are as solvents for gums, resins, lacquers, and varnishes; in the making of dyes; for essential oils in perfumery; and for medical substances in pharmacy. Alcohol (ethanol) is produced naturally in the fermentation process and is consumed as part of alcoholic beverages.

aldehyde any of a group of organic chemical compounds prepared by oxidation of primary alcohols, so that the OH (hydroxyl) group loses its hydrogen to give an oxygen joined by a double bond to a carbon atom (the aldehyde group, with the formula CHO). The name is made up from alcohol dehydrogenation—that is, alcohol from which hydrogen has been removed. Aldehydes are usually liquids and include methanol or formaldehyde, ethanal, benzaldehyde, and citral.

algae (singular alga) diverse group of organisms (including those commonly called seaweeds) that shows great variety of form, ranging from single-celled forms to multicellular seaweeds of considerable size and complexity.

algebra system of arithmetic applying to any set of nonnumerical symbols (usually letters), and the axioms and rules by which they are combined or operated upon; sometimes known as generalized arithmetic.

Algol or Beta Persei eclipsing binary, a pair of rotating stars in the constellation Perseus, one of which eclipses the other every 69 hours, causing its brightness to drop by two-thirds.

aliphatic compound any organic chemical compound in which the carbon atoms are joined in straight chains, as in hexane (C_6H_{14}), or in branched chains, as in 2methylpentane ($CH_3CH(CH_3)CH_2CH_2CH_3$).

alkali a compound classed as a base that is soluble in water. Alkalis neutralize acids and are soapy to the touch. The hydroxides of metals are alkalis; those of sodium (sodium hydroxide, NaOH) and of potassium (potassium hydroxide, KOH) being chemically powerful; both were derived from the ashes of plants.

alkane member of a group of hydrocarbons having the general formula C_nH_{2n+2}, commonly known as paraffins. Lighter alkanes, such as methane, ethane, propane, and butane, are colorless gases; heavier ones are liquids or solids. In nature they are found in natural gas and petroleum. As alkanes contain only single covalent bonds, they are said to be saturated.

alkene member of the group of hydrocarbons having the general formula C_nH_{2n}, formerly known as olefins. Lighter alkenes, such as ethene and propene, are gases, obtained from the cracking of oil fractions. Alkenes are unsaturated compounds, characterized by one or more double bonds between adjacent carbon atoms. They react by addition, and many useful compounds, such as poly(ethene) and bromoethane, are made from them.

alkyne member of the group of hydrocarbons with the general formula C_nH_{2n-2}, formerly known as the acetylenes. They are unsaturated compounds, characterized by one or more triple bonds between adjacent carbon atoms. Lighter alkynes, such as ethyne, are gases; heavier ones are liquids or solids.

allele one of two or more alternate forms of a gene at a given position (locus) on a chromosome, caused by a difference in the DNA. Blue and brown eyes in hu-

mans are determined by different alleles of the gene for eye color.

alloy metal blended with some other metallic or nonmetallic substance to give it special qualities, such as resistance to corrosion, greater hardness, or tensile strength. Useful alloys include bronze, brass, cupronickel, duralumin, pewter, solder, steel, and stainless steel.

alluvial deposit layer of broken rocky matter, or sediment, formed from material that has been carried in suspension by a river or stream and dropped as the velocity of the current changes. River plains and deltas are made entirely of alluvial deposits, but smaller pockets can be found in the beds of upland torrents.

Alpha Centauri or *Rigil Kent* brightest star in the constellation Centaurus and the third brightest star in the sky. It is actually a triple star; the two brighter stars orbit each other every 80 years, and the third, Proxima Centauri, is the closest star to the Sun, 4.2 light-years away, 0.1 light-years closer than the other two.

alternate angles a pair of angles that lie on opposite sides and at opposite ends of a transversal (a line that cuts two or more lines in the same plane). The alternate angles formed by a transversal of two parallel lines are equal.

altitude in geometry, the perpendicular distance from a vertex (corner) of a figure, such as a triangle, to the base (the side opposite the vertex).

amino acid water-soluble organic molecule, mainly composed of carbon, oxygen, hydrogen, and nitrogen, containing both a basic amino group (NH_2) and an acidic carboxyl (COOH) group. When two or more amino acids are joined together, they are known as peptides; proteins are made up of interacting polypeptides (peptide chains consisting of more than three amino acids) and are folded or twisted in characteristic shapes.

ammonia NH_3 colorless pungent-smelling gas, lighter than air and very soluble in water. It is made on an industrial scale by the Haber process, and used mainly to produce nitrogenous fertilizers, some explosives, and nitric acid.

amphibian member of the vertebrate class Amphibia, which generally spend their larval (tadpole) stage in fresh water, transferring to land at maturity (after metamorphosis) and generally returning to water to breed. Like fish and reptiles, they continue to grow throughout life, and cannot maintain a temperature greatly differing from that of their environment. The class includes caecilians (wormlike in appearance), salamanders, frogs, and toads.

amylase one of a group of enzymes that break down starches into their component molecules (sugars) for use in the body. It occurs widely in both plants and animals. In humans, it is found in saliva and in pancreatic juices.

anaerobic (of living organisms) not requiring oxygen for the release of energy from food molecules such as glucose. Anaerobic organisms include many bacteria, yeasts, and internal parasites.

analog signal in electronics, current or voltage that conveys or stores information, and varies continuously in the same way as the information it represents (compare digital signal). Analog signals are prone to interference and distortion.

analytical chemistry branch of chemistry that deals with the determination of the chemical composition of substances.

Andromeda galaxy galaxy 2.2 million light-years away from Earth in the constellation Andromeda, and the most distant object visible to the naked eye.

It is the largest member of the Local Group of galaxies. Like the Milky Way, it is a spiral orbited by several companion galaxies but contains about twice as many stars. It is about 200,000 light-years across.

angiosperm flowering plant in which the seeds are enclosed within an ovary, which ripens to a fruit. Angiosperms are divided into monocotyledons (single seed leaf in the embryo) and dicotyledons (two seed leaves in the embryo). They include the majority of flowers, herbs, grasses, and trees except conifers.

angle in mathematics, the amount of turn or rotation; it may be defined by a pair of rays (half-lines) that share a common endpoint but do not lie on the same line. Angles are measured in degrees (°) or radians (rads) - a complete turn or circle being 360° or 2 rads. Angles are classified generally by their degree measures: acute angles are less than 90°; right angles are exactly 90° (a quarter turn); obtuse angles are greater than 90° but less than 180°; reflex angles are greater than 180° but less than 360°.

animal or metazoan member of the kingdom Animalia, one of the major categories of living things, the science of which is zoology. Animals are all heterotrophs (they obtain their energy from organic substances produced by other organisms); they have eukaryotic cells (the genetic material is contained within a distinct nucleus) bounded by a thin cell membrane rather than the thick cell wall of plants. Most animals are capable of moving around for at least part of their life cycle.

anode the positive electrode toward which negative particles (anions, electrons) move within a device such as the cells of a battery, electrolytic cells, and diodes.

Antarctic Circle imaginary line that encircles the South Pole at latitude 66° 32′ S. The line encompasses the continent of Antarctica and the Antarctic Ocean.

anticline in geology, a fold in the rocks of the Earth's crust in which the layers or beds bulge upward to form an arch (seldom preserved intact).

antimatter a form of matter in which most of the attributes (such as electrical charge, magnetic moment, and spin) of elementary particles are reversed.

apex the highest point of a triangle, cone, or pyramid—that is, the vertex (corner) opposite a given base.

aphelion the point at which an object, traveling in an elliptical orbit around the Sun, is at its furthest from the Sun.

apogee the point at which an object, traveling in an elliptical orbit around the Earth, is at its furthest from the Earth.

Apollo asteroid member of a group of asteroids whose orbits cross that of the Earth. They are so small and faint that they are difficult to see except when close to Earth (Apollo is about 1.2 mi/2 km across).

aquifer any rock formation containing water. The rock of an aquifer must be porous and permeable (full of interconnected holes) so that it can absorb water.

Arabic numerals or *Hindu-Arabic numerals* the symbols 0, 1, 2, 3, 4, 5, 6, 7, 8, 9, early forms of which were in use among the Arabs before being adopted by the peoples of Europe during the Middle Ages. The symbols appear to have originated in India and probably reached Europe by way of Spain.

arc in geometry, a section of a curved line or circle. A circle has three types of arc: a semicircle, which is exactly half of the circle; minor arcs, which are less than the semicircle; and major arcs, which are greater than the semicircle.

Archean or Archeozoic the earliest eon of geological time; the first part of the Precambrian era, from the formation of Earth up to about 2,500 million years ago. It was a time when no life existed, and with every new discovery of ancient life its upper boundary is being pushed further back.

archipelago group of islands, or an area of sea containing a group of islands. The islands of an archipelago are usually volcanic in origin, and they sometimes represent the tops of peaks in areas around continental margins flooded by the sea.

Arctic Circle imaginary line that encircles the North Pole at latitude 66° 32′ N. Within this line there is at least one day in the summer during which the Sun never sets, and at least one day in the winter during which the Sun never rises.

area the size of a surface. It is measured in square units, usually square inches (in^2), square feet (ft^2), or square miles (mi^2). Surface area is the area of the outer surface of a solid.

arithmetic branch of mathematics concerned with the study of numbers and their properties. The fundamental operations of arithmetic are addition, subtraction, multiplication, and division. Raising to powers (for example, squaring or cubing a number), the extraction of roots (for example, square roots), percentages, fractions, and ratios are developed from these operations.

aromatic compound organic chemical compound in which some of the bonding electrons are delocalized (shared among several atoms within the molecule and not localized in the vicinity of the atoms involved in bonding). The commonest aromatic compounds have ring structures, the atoms comprising the ring being either all carbon or containing one or more different atoms (usually nitrogen, sulfur, or oxygen). Typical examples are benzene (C_6H_6) and pyridine (C_6H_5N).

arsenic brittle, grayish-white, semimetallic element (a metalloid), symbol As, atomic number 33, atomic weight 74.92. It occurs in many ores and occasionally in its elemental state, and is widely distributed, being present in minute quantities in the soil, the sea, and the human body. In larger quantities, it is poisonous.

artesian well well that is supplied with water rising from an underground water-saturated rock layer (aquifer).

arthropod member of the phylum Arthropoda; an invertebrate animal with jointed legs and a segmented body with a horny or chitinous casing (exoskeleton), which is shed periodically and replaced as the animal grows. Included are arachnids such as spiders and mites, as well as crustaceans, millipedes, centipedes, and insects.

artificial selection selective breeding of individuals that exhibit particular characteristics that a plant or animal breeder wishes to develop.

asexual reproduction reproduction that does not involve the manufacture and fusion of sex cells, nor the necessity for two parents. The process carries a clear advantage in that there is no need to search for a mate nor to develop complex pollinating mechanisms; every asexual organism can reproduce on its own. Asexual reproduction can therefore lead to a rapid population build-up.

associative operation in mathematics, an operation in which the outcome is independent of the grouping of the numbers or symbols concerned. For example, multiplication is associative, as $4 \times (3 \times 2) = (4 \times 3) \times 2 = 24$; however, division is not, as $12 \div (4 \div 2) = 6$, but $(12 \div 4) \div 2 = 1.5$.

asteroid or *minor planet* any of many thousands of small bodies, composed of rock and iron, that orbit the Sun. Most lie in a belt between the orbits of Mars and Jupiter, and are thought to be fragments left over from the formation of the Solar System. About 100,000 may exist, but their total mass is only a few hundredths the mass of the Moon.

asthenosphere division of the Earth's structure lying beneath the lithosphere, at a depth of approximately 45 mi/70 km to 160 mi/260 km. It is thought to be the soft, partially molten layer of the mantle on which the rigid plates of the Earth's surface move to produce the motions of plate tectonics.

astrometry measurement of the precise positions of stars, planets, and other bodies in space. Such information is needed for practical purposes including accurate timekeeping, surveying and navigation, calculating orbits and measuring distances in space.

astronomical unit unit (symbol AU) equal to the mean distance of the Earth from the Sun: 92,955,800 mi/149,597,870 km. It is used to describe planetary distances. Light travels this distance in approximately 8.3 minutes.

atom smallest unit of matter that can take part in a chemical reaction, and which cannot be broken down chemically into anything simpler. An atom is made up of protons and neutrons in a central nucleus surrounded by electrons. The atoms of the various elements differ in atomic number, atomic weight, and chemical behavior. There are 109 different types of atom, corresponding with the 109 known elements as listed in the periodic table of the elements.

atomic number or *proton number* the number (symbol Z) of protons in the nucleus of an atom. It is equal to the positive charge on the nucleus. In a neutral atom, it is also equal to the number of electrons surrounding the nucleus. The 109 elements are arranged in the periodic table of the elements according to their atomic number.

atomic weight the mass of an atom relative to one-twelfth the mass of an atom of carbon-12. It depends on the number of protons and neutrons in the atom, the electrons having negligible mass. If more than one isotope of the element is present, the atomic weight is calculated by taking an average that takes account of the relative proportions of each isotope, resulting in values that are not whole numbers.

aurora colored light in the night sky near the Earth's magnetic poles, called aurora borealis, "northern lights", in the northern hemisphere and aurora australis in the southern hemisphere. Auroras are caused at heights of over 60 mi/100 km by a fast stream of charged particles from solar flares and low-density "holes" in the Sun's corona. These are guided by the Earth's magnetic field toward the north and south magnetic poles, where they enter the upper atmosphere and bombard the gases in the atmosphere, causing them to emit visible light.

autotroph any living organism that synthesizes organic substances from inorganic molecules by using light or chemical energy. Autotrophs are the primary producers in all food chains since the materials they synthesize and store are the energy sources of all other organisms. All green plants and many planktonic organisms are autotrophs, using sunlight to convert carbon dioxide and water into sugars by photosynthesis.

bacillus member of a group of rodlike bacteria that occur everywhere in the soil and air. Some are responsible for diseases such as anthrax or for causing food spoilage.

bacteria (singular *bacterium*) microscopic unicellular organisms with prokaryotic cells (see prokaryote). They usually reproduce by binary fission (dividing into two equal parts), and since this may occur approximately every 20 minutes, a single bacterium is potentially capable of producing 16 million copies of itself in a day.

bacteriophage virus that attacks bacteria. Such viruses are now of use in genetic engineering.

Barnard's star second closest star to the Sun, six light-years away in the constellation Ophiuchus. It is a faint red dwarf of 10th magnitude, visible only through a telescope. It is named after the US astronomer Edward E. Barnard (1857–1923).

barometer instrument that measures atmospheric pressure as an indication of weather. Most often used are the *mercury barometer* and the *aneroid barometer*.

baryon in nuclear physics, a heavy subatomic particle made up of three indivisible elementary particles called quarks. The baryons form a subclass of the hadrons, and comprise the nucleons (protons and neutrons) and hyperons.

basal metabolic rate (BMR) amount of energy needed by an animal just to stay alive. It is measured when the animal is awake but resting, and includes the energy required to keep the heart beating, sustain breathing, repair tissues, and keep the brain and nerves functioning. Measuring the animal's consumption of oxygen gives an accurate value for BMR, because oxygen is needed to release energy from food.

base in chemistry, a substance that accepts protons, such as the hydroxide ion (OH_-) and ammonia (NH_3). Bases react with acids to give a salt. Those that dissolve in water are called alkalis.

base in mathematics, the number of different single-digit symbols used in a particular number system. In our usual (decimal) counting system of numbers (with symbols 0, 1, 2, 3, 4, 5, 6, 7, 8, 9) the base is 10. In the binary number system, which has only the symbols 1 and 0, the base is two. A base is also a number that, when raised to a particular power (that is, when multiplied by itself a particular number of times as in $10^2 = 10 \times 10 = 100$), has a logarithm equal to the power. For example, the logarithm of 100 to the base ten is 2. In geometry, the term is used to denote the line or area on which a polygon or solid stands.

base pair the linkage of two base (purine or pyrimidine) molecules in DNA. They are found in nucleotides, and form the basis of the genetic code.

bathyal zone upper part of the ocean, which lies on the continental shelf at a depth of between 650 ft/200 m and 6,500 ft/2,000 m.

battery any energy-storage device allowing release of electricity on demand. It is made up of one or more electrical cells. Primary-cell batteries are disposable; secondary-cell batteries, or accumulators, are rechargeable. Primary-cell batteries are an extremely uneconomical form of energy, since they produce only 2% of the power used in their manufacture. The lead–acid car battery is a secondary-cell battery. The car's generator continually recharges the battery. It consists of sets of lead (positive) and lead peroxide (negative) plates in an electrolyte of sulfuric acid (battery acid). The introduction of rechargeable nickel–cadmium batteries has revolutionized portable electronic newsgathering (sound recording, video) and information processing (computing). These batteries offer a stable, short-term source of power free of noise and other electrical hazards.

bearing the direction of a fixed point, or the path of a moving object, from a point of observation on the

Earth's surface, expressed as an angle from the north. Bearings are taken by compass and are measured in degrees (°), given as three-digit numbers increasing clockwise. For instance, north is 000°, northeast is 045°, south is 180°, and southwest is 225°.

Beaufort scale system of recording wind velocity. It is a numerical scale ranging from 0 to 17, calm being indicated by 0 and a hurricane by 12; 13–17 indicate degrees of hurricane force.

bed in geology, a single sedimentary rock unit with a distinct set of physical characteristics or contained fossils, readily distinguishable from those of beds above and below.

bicarbonate of soda or *baking soda* (technical name *sodium hydrogencarbonate*) $NaHCO_3$ white crystalline solid that neutralizes acids and is used in medicine to treat acid indigestion. It is also used in baking powders and effervescent drinks.

Big Bang the hypothetical "explosive" event that marked the origin of the universe as we know it. At the time of the Big Bang, the entire universe was squeezed into a hot, superdense state. The Big Bang explosion threw this compacted material outwards, producing the expanding universe. The cause of the Big Bang is unknown; observations of the current rate of expansion of the universe suggest that it took place about 10 to 20 billion years ago. The Big Bang theory began modern cosmology.

binary fission in biology, a form of asexual reproduction, whereby a single-celled organism, such as the ameba, divides into two smaller "daughter" cells. It can also occur in a few simple multicellular organisms, such as sea anemones, producing two smaller sea anemones of equal size.

binary star pair of stars moving in orbit around their common center of mass. Observations show that most stars are binary, or even multiple—for example, the nearest star system to the Sun, Alpha Centauri.

binomial in mathematics, an expression consisting of two terms, such as $a + b$ or $a - b$.

biochemistry science concerned with the chemistry of living organisms: the structure and reactions of proteins (such as enzymes), nucleic acids, carbohydrates, and lipids.

biodegradable capable of being broken down by living organisms, principally bacteria and fungi.

biodiversity (contraction of *biological diversity*) measure of the variety of the Earth's animal, plant, and microbial species; of genetic differences within species; and of the ecosystems that support those species.

biosensor device based on microelectronic circuits that can directly measure medically significant variables for the purpose of diagnosis or monitoring treatment.

biosynthesis synthesis of organic chemicals from simple inorganic ones by living cells–for example, the conversion of carbon dioxide and water to glucose by plants during photosynthesis.

biotechnology industrial use of living organisms to manufacture food, drugs, or other products. The brewing and baking industries have long relied on the yeast microorganism for fermentation purposes, while the dairy industry employs a range of bacteria and fungi to convert milk into cheeses and yogurts. Enzymes, whether extracted from cells or produced artificially, are central to most biotechnological applications.

bird backboned animal of the class *Aves*, the biggest group of land vertebrates, characterized by warm blood, feathers, wings, breathing through lungs, and egglaying by the female. There are nearly 8,500 species of birds.

birth act of producing live young from within the body of female animals. Both viviparous and ovoviviparous animals give birth to young. In viviparous animals, embryos obtain nourishment from the mother via a placenta or other means. In ovoviviparous animals, fertilized eggs develop and hatch in the oviduct of the mother and gain little or no nourishment from maternal tissues.

black hole object in space whose gravity is so great that nothing can escape from it, not even light. Thought to form when massive stars shrink at the ends of their lives, a black hole sucks in more matter, including other stars, from the space around it. Matter that falls into a black hole is squeezed to infinite density at the center of the hole. Black holes can be detected because gas falling toward them becomes so hot that it emits X-rays.

boiling point for any given liquid, the temperature at which the application of heat raises the temperature of the liquid no further, but converts it into vapor.

bond in chemistry, the result of the forces of attraction that hold together atoms of an element or elements to form a molecule. The principal types of bonding are ionic, covalent, metallic, and intermolecular (such as hydrogen bonding).

boson in physics, an elementary particle whose spin can only take values that are whole numbers or zero. Bosons may be classified as gauge bosons (carriers of the four fundamental forces) or mesons. All elementary particles are either bosons or fermions.

bryophyte member of the Bryophyta, a division of the plant kingdom containing three classes: the Hepaticae (liverwort), Musci (moss), and Anthocerotae (hornwort). Bryophytes are generally small, low–growing, terrestrial plants with no vascular (water-conducting) system as in higher plants. Their life cycle shows a marked alternation of generations. Bryophytes chiefly occur in damp habitats and require water for the dispersal of the male gametes (antherozoids).

budding type of asexual reproduction in which an outgrowth develops from a cell to form a new individual. Most yeasts reproduce in this way.

buffer mixture of chemical compounds chosen to maintain a steady pH. The commonest buffers consist of a mixture of a weak organic acid and one of its salts or a mixture of acid salts of phosphoric acid. The addition of either an acid or a base causes a shift in the chemical equilibrium, thus keeping the pH constant.

calculus branch of mathematics that permits the manipulation of continuously varying quantities, used in practical problems involving such matters as changing speeds, problems of flight, varying stresses in the framework of a bridge, and alternating current theory. Integral calculus deals with the method of summation or adding together the effects of continuously varying quantities. Differential calculus deals in a similar way with rates of change. Many of its applications arose from the study of the gradients of the tangents to curves.

caldera in geology, a very large basin-shaped crater. Calderas are found at the tops of volcanoes, where the original peak has collapsed into an empty chamber beneath.

Callisto second largest moon of Jupiter, 3,000 mi/4,800 km in diameter, orbiting every 16.7 days at a distance of 1.2 million mi/1.9 million km from the planet. Its surface is covered with large craters.

Cambrian period of geological time 570–510 million

years ago; the first period of the Paleozoic era. All invertebrate animal life appeared, and marine algae were widespread. The earliest fossils with hard shells, such as trilobites, date from this period.

canal artificial waterway constructed for drainage, irrigation, or navigation.

carbohydrate chemical compound composed of carbon, hydrogen, and oxygen, with the basic formula $C_m(H_2O)_n$, and related compounds with the same basic structure but modified functional groups. As sugar and starch, carbohydrates form a major energy-providing part of the human diet.

carbon nonmetallic element, symbol C, atomic number 6, atomic weight 12.011. It is one of the most widely distributed elements, both inorganically and organically, and occurs in combination with other elements in all plants and animals. The atoms of carbon can link with one another in rings or chains, giving rise to innumerable complex compounds. It occurs in nature (1) in the pure state in three crystalline forms of graphite, diamond and various fullerenes; (2) as calcium carbonate ($CaCO_3$) in carbonaceous rocks such as chalk and limestone; (3) as carbon dioxide (CO_2) in the atmosphere; and (4) as hydrocarbons in the fossil fuels petroleum, coal, and natural gas. Noncrystalline forms of pure carbon include charcoal and coal.

carbon cycle the sequence by which carbon circulates and is recycled through the natural world. The carbon element from carbon dioxide in the atmosphere is taken up during the process of photosynthesis, and the oxygen component is released back into the atmosphere. Some of this carbon becomes locked up in coal and petroleum and other sediments. Carbon (as carbon dioxide) is released during aerobic respiration of plants and animals. New carbon also enters the atmosphere during volcanic eruptions. Today, the carbon cycle is being altered by the increased consumption of fossil fuels and the burning of large tracts of tropical forests, as a result of which levels of carbon dioxide are building up in the atmosphere and probably contributing to the greenhouse effect.

carbon dioxide CO^2 colorless, odorless gas, slightly soluble in water and denser than air. It is formed by the complete oxidation of carbon.

Carboniferous period of geological time 363–290 million years ago, the fifth period of the Paleozoic era. It is divided into two periods: the Mississippian (lower) and the Pennsylvanian (upper). Typical of the lower-Carboniferous rocks are shallow-water limestones, while upper-Carboniferous rocks have delta deposits with coal (hence the name). Amphibians were abundant, and reptiles evolved during this period.

carbon monoxide CO colorless, odorless gas formed when carbon is oxidized in a limited supply of air. It is a poisonous constituent of car exhaust fumes, forming a stable compound with haemoglobin in the blood, thus preventing the haemoglobin from transporting oxygen to the body tissues.

cardinal number in mathematics, one of the series of numbers 0, 1, 2, 3, 4, ... Cardinal numbers relate to quantity, whereas ordinal numbers (first, second, third, fourth, ...) relate to order.

carnivore animal that eats other animals. Although the term is sometimes confined to those that eat the flesh of vertebrate prey, it is often used more broadly to include any animal that eats other animals, even microscopic ones. The mammalian order Carnivora includes civet cats, raccoons, cats, dogs, and bears.

catalyst substance that alters the speed of, or makes possible, a chemical or biochemical reaction but remains unchanged at the end of the reaction. Enzymes are natural biochemical catalysts. In practice most catalysts are used to speed up reactions.

catalytic converter device fitted to the exhaust system of a motor vehicle in order to reduce toxic emissions from the engine. It converts harmful exhaust products to relatively harmless ones by passing the exhaust gases over a mixture of catalysts. *Oxidation catalysts* (small amounts of precious palladium and platinum metals) convert hydrocarbons (unburnt fuel) and carbon monoxide into carbon dioxide and water, while *three-way catalysts* (platinum and rhodium metals) convert nitrogen oxide gases into nitrogen and oxygen.

cathode in chemistry, the negative electrode of an electrolytic cell, toward which positive particles (cations), usually in solution, are attracted.

celestial mechanics the branch of astronomy that deals with the calculation of the orbits of celestial bodies, their gravitational attractions (such as those that produce the Earth's tides), and also the orbits of artificial satellites and space probes. It is based on the laws of motion and gravity laid down by Isaac Newton.

celestial sphere imaginary sphere surrounding the Earth, on which the celestial bodies seem to lie. The positions of bodies such as stars, planets, and galaxies are specified by their coordinates on the celestial sphere. The equivalents of latitude and longitude on the celestial sphere are called declination and right ascension (which is measured in hours from 0 to 24). The celestial poles lie directly above the Earth's poles, and the celestial equator lies over the Earth's equator. The celestial sphere appears to rotate once around the Earth each day, actually a result of the rotation of the Earth on its axis.

cell in biology, a discrete, membrane-bound portion of living matter, the smallest unit capable of an independent existence. All living organisms consist of one or more cells, with the exception of viruses. Bacteria, protozoa, and many other microorganisms consist of single cells, whereas a human is made up of billions of cells. Essential features of a cell are the membrane, which encloses it and restricts the flow of substances in and out; the jellylike material within, often known as protoplasm; the ribosomes, which carry out protein synthesis; and the DNA, which forms the hereditary material.

cellular phone or cellphone mobile radio telephone, one of a network connected to the telephone system by a computer-controlled communication system. Service areas are divided into small "cells", about 3 mi/5 km across, each with a separate low-power transmitter.

center of mass or *center of gravity* point in or near an object from which its total weight appears to originate and can be assumed to act. A symmetrical homogeneous object such as a sphere or cube has its center of mass at its physical centre; a hollow shape (such as a cup) may have its center of mass in space inside the hollow.

Cepheid variable yellow supergiant star that varies regularly in brightness every few days or weeks as a result of pulsations. The time that a Cepheid variable takes to pulsate is directly related to its average brightness; the longer the pulsation period, the brighter the star.

Ceres the largest asteroid, 584 mi/940 km in diameter, and the first to be discovered. Ceres orbits the Sun every 4.6 years at an average distance of 257 million mi/414 million km. Its mass is about one-seventieth of that of the Moon.

chain reaction in chemistry, mechanism that produces very fast, exothermic reactions, as in the formation of flames and explosions.

chain reaction in nuclear physics, a fission reaction that is maintained because neutrons released by the splitting of some atomic nuclei themselves go on to split others, releasing even more neutrons. Such a reaction can be controlled (as in a nuclear reactor) by using moderators to absorb excess neutrons. Uncontrolled, a chain reaction produces a nuclear explosion (as in an atomic bomb).

chemical equation method of indicating the reactants and products of a chemical reaction by using chemical symbols and formulae. A chemical equation gives two basic pieces of information: (1) the reactants (on the left-hand side) and products (right-hand side); and (2) the reacting proportions (stoichiometry)—that is, how many units of each reactant and product are involved. The equation must balance; that is, the total number of atoms of a particular element on the left-hand side must be the same as the number of atoms of that element on the right-hand side.

chemical equilibrium condition in which the products of a reversible chemical reaction are formed at the same rate at which they decompose back into the reactants, so that the concentration of each reactant and product remains constant.

chemosynthesis method of making protoplasm (contents of a cell) using the energy from chemical reactions, in contrast to the use of light energy employed for the same purpose in photosynthesis. The process is used by certain bacteria, which can synthesize organic compounds from carbon dioxide and water using the energy from special methods of respiration.

chlorofluorocarbon (CFC) synthetic chemical that is odorless, nontoxic, nonflammable, and chemically inert. CFCs have been used as propellants in aerosol cans, as refrigerants in refrigerators and air conditioners, and in the manufacture of foam packaging. They are partly responsible for the destruction of the ozone layer.

chlorophyll green pigment present in most plants; it is responsible for the absorption of light energy during photosynthesis. The pigment absorbs the red and blue-violet parts of sunlight but reflects the green, thus giving plants their characteristic color.

chloroplast structure (organelle) within a plant cell containing the green pigment chlorophyll. Chloroplasts occur in most cells of the green plant that are exposed to light, often in large numbers. Typically, they are flattened and disklike, with a double membrane enclosing the stroma, a gellike matrix. Within the stroma are stacks of fluid-containing cavities, or vesicles, where photosynthesis occurs.

chord in geometry, a straight line joining any two points on a curve. The chord that passes through the center of a circle (its longest chord) is the diameter. The longest and shortest chords of an ellipse (a regular oval) are called the major and minor axes respectively.

chromatography technique for separating or analyzing a mixture of gases, liquids, or dissolved substances. This is brought about by means of two immiscible substances, one of which (the mobile phase) transports the sample mixture through the other (the stationary phase). The mobile phase may be a gas or a liquid; the stationary phase may be a liquid or a solid, and may be in a column, on paper, or in a thin layer on a glass or plastic support. The components of the mixture are absorbed or impeded by the stationary phase to different extents and therefore become separated. The technique is used for both qualitative and quantitive analyses in biology and chemistry.

chromosome structure in a cell nucleus that carries the genes. Each chromosome consists of one very long strand of DNA, coiled and folded to produce a compact body. The point on a chromosome where a particular gene occurs is known as its locus. Most higher organisms have two copies of each chromosome (they are diploid) but some have only one (they are haploid). There are 46 chromosomes in a normal human cell.

chromosphere layer of mostly hydrogen gas about 6,000 mi/10,000 km deep above the visible surface of the Sun (the photosphere). It appears pinkish red during eclipses of the Sun.

circle perfectly round shape, the path of a point that moves so as to keep a constant distance from a fixed point (the center). Each circle has a *radius* (the distance from any point on the circle to the center), a *circumference* (the boundary of the circle), *diameters* (straight lines crossing the circle through the center), *chords* (lines joining two points on the circumference), *tangents* (lines that touch the circumference at one point only), *sectors* (regions inside the circle between two radii), and *segments* (regions between a chord and the circumference).

circulatory system system of vessels in an animal's body that transports essential substances (blood or other circulatory fluid) to and from the different parts of the body. Except for simple animals such as sponges and coelenterates (jellyfishes, sea anemones, corals), all animals have a circulatory system.

circumference in geometry, the curved line that encloses a curved plane figure, for example a circle or an ellipse. Its length varies according to the nature of the curve, and may be ascertained by the appropriate formula. The circumference of a circle is πd or $2\pi\rho$, where d is the diameter of the circle, r is its radius and is the constant π, *approximately equal to 3.1416*.

cladistics method of biological classification (taxonomy) that uses a formal step-by-step procedure for objectively assessing the extent to which organisms share particular characters, and for assigning them to taxonomic groups. Taxonomic groups (for example, species, genus, family) are termed *clades*.

climate weather conditions at a particular place over a period of time. Climate encompasses all the meteorological elements and the factors that influence them. The primary factors that determine the variations of climate over the surface of the Earth are: (a) the effect of latitude and the tilt of the Earth's axis to the plane of the orbit about the Sun (66.5°); (b) the large-scale movements of different wind belts over the Earth's surface; (c) the temperature difference between land and sea; (d) contours of the ground; and (e) location of the area in relation to ocean currents. Catastrophic variations to climate may be caused by the impact of another planetary body, or by clouds resulting from volcanic activity. The most important local or global meteorological changes brought about by human activity are those linked with ozone depleters and the greenhouse effect.

cloud water vapor condensed into minute water particles that float in masses in the atmosphere. Clouds, like fogs or mists, which occur at lower levels, are formed by the cooling of air containing water vapor, which generally condenses around tiny dust particles.

codon in genetics, a triplet of bases in a molecule of DNA or RNA that directs the placement of a particular amino acid during the process of protein (polypeptide) synthesis. There are 64 codons in the genetic code.

coefficient the number part in front of an algebraic term, signifying multiplication. For example, in the expression $4x^2 + 2xy - x$, the coefficient of x^2 is 4 (because $4x^2$ means $4 \times x^2$), that of xy is 2, and that of x is -1 (because $-1 \times x = -x$).

colloid substance composed of extremely small particles of one material (the dispersed phase) evenly and stably distributed in another material (the continuous phase). The size of the dispersed particles (1–1,000 nanometers across) is less than that of particles in suspension but greater than that of molecules in true solution. Colloids involving gases include *aerosols* (dispersions of liquid or solid particles in a gas, as in fog or smoke) and *foams* (dispersions of gases in liquids). Those involving liquids include *emulsions* (in which both the dispersed and the continuous phases are liquids) and *sols* (solid particles dispersed in a liquid). Sols in which both phases contribute to a molecular three-dimensional network have a jellylike form and are known as gels; gelatin, starch "solution", and silica gel are common examples.

comet small, icy body orbiting the Sun, usually on a highly elliptical path. A comet consists of a central nucleus a few miles across, and has been likened to a dirty snowball because it consists mostly of ice mixed with dust. As the comet approaches the Sun the nucleus heats up, releasing gas and dust which form a tenuous coma, up to 60,000 mi/100,000 km wide, around the nucleus. Gas and dust stream away from the coma to form one or more tails, which may extend for millions of miles.

commutative operation in mathematics, an operation that is independent of the order of the numbers or symbols concerned. For example, addition is commutative: the result of adding $4 + 2$ is the same as that of adding $2 + 4$; subtraction is not as $4 - 2 = 2$, but $2 - 4 = -2$.

competition in ecology, the interaction between two or more organisms, or groups of organisms (for example, species), that use a common resource which is in short supply. Competition invariably results in a reduction in the numbers of one or both competitors, and in evolution contributes both to the decline of certain species and to the evolution of adaptations.

complement the set of the elements within the universal set that are not contained in the designated set. For example, if the universal set is the set of all positive whole numbers and the designated set S is the set of all even numbers, then the complement of S (denoted S') is the set of all odd numbers.

compound chemical substance made up of two or more elements bonded together, so that they cannot be separated by physical means. Compounds are held together by ionic or covalent bonds.

concave of a surface, curving inwards, or away from the eye. For example, a bowl appears concave when viewed from above. In geometry, a concave polygon is one that has an interior angle greater than 180°. Concave is the opposite of convex.

concentric circles two or more circles that share the same centre.

cone in geometry, a solid or surface consisting of the set of all straight lines passing through a fixed point (the vertex) and the points of a circle or ellipse whose plane does not contain the vertex.

conic section curve obtained when a conical surface is intersected by a plane. If the intersecting plane cuts both extensions of the cone, it yields a hyperbola; if it is parallel to the side of the cone, it produces a parabola. Other intersecting planes produce circles or ellipses.

conjunction in astronomy, the alignment of two celestial bodies as seen from Earth. A superior planet (or other object) is in conjunction when it lies behind the Sun. An inferior planet (or other object) comes to *inferior conjunction* when it passes between the Earth and the Sun; it is at *superior conjunction* when it passes behind the Sun. *Planetary conjunction* takes place when a planet is closely aligned with another celestial object, such as the Moon, a star, or another planet.

constant in mathematics, a fixed quantity or one that does not change its value in relation to variables. For example, in the algebraic expression $y^2 = 5x - 3$, the numbers 3 and 5 are constants. In physics, certain quantities are regarded as universal constants, such as the speed of light in a vacuum.

constellation one of the 88 areas into which the sky is divided for the purposes of identifying and naming celestial objects. The first constellations were simple, arbitrary patterns of stars in which early civilizations visualized gods, sacred beasts, and mythical heroes.

continent any one of the seven large land masses of the Earth, as distinct from the oceans. They are Asia, Africa, North America, South America, Europe, Australia, and Antarctica. Continents are constantly moving and evolving. A continent does not end at the coastline; its boundary is the edge of the shallow continental shelf, which may extend several hundred miles out to sea.

continental drift the theory that, about 250—200 million years ago, the Earth consisted of a single large continent (Pangaea), which subsequently broke apart to form the continents known today.

convergent evolution the independent evolution of similar structures in species (or other taxonomic groups) that are not closely related, as a result of living in a similar way. Thus, birds and bats have wings, not because they are descended from a common winged ancestor, but because their respective ancestors independently evolved flight.

converse in mathematics, the reversed order of a conditional statement; the converse of the statement "if a, then b" is "if b, then a". The converse does not always hold true; for example, the converse of "if $x = 3$, then $x^2 = 9$" is "if $x^2 = 9$, then $x = 3$", which is not true, as x could also be -3.

convex of a surface, curving outwards, or toward the eye. For example, the outer surface of a ball appears convex. In geometry, the term is used to describe any polygon possessing no interior angle greater than 180°. Convex is the opposite of concave.

coordinate geometry or *analytical geometry* system of geometry in which points, lines, shapes, and surfaces are represented by algebraic expressions. In plane (two-dimensional) coordinate geometry, the plane is usually defined by two axes at right angles to each other, the horizontal x-axis and the vertical y-axis, meeting at O, the origin. A point on the plane can be represented by a pair of Cartesian coordinates, which define its position in terms of its distance along the x-axis and along the y-axis from O. These distances are respectively the x and y coordinates of the point.

core in earth science, the innermost part of the Earth. It is divided into an inner core, the upper boundary of which is 1,060 mi/1,700 km from the center, and an outer core, 1,130 mi/1,820 km thick. Both parts are thought to consist of iron-nickel alloy, with the inner core being solid and the outer core being semisolid. The temperature may be 5,400°F/3,000°C.

corona faint halo of hot (about 3,600,000°F/2,000,000°C) and tenuous gas around the Sun, which boils from the surface. It is visible at solar eclipses or through a coronagraph, an instrument that blocks light from the Sun's brilliant disk. Gas flows away from the corona to form the solar wind.

cosine in trigonometry, a function of an angle in a right-angled triangle found by dividing the length of the side adjacent to the angle by the length of the hypotenuse (the longest side). It is usually shortened to cos.

cosmic background radiation or 3° radiation electromagnetic radiation left over from the original formation of the universe in the Big Bang around 15 billion years ago. It corresponds to an overall background temperature of 3K (−454°F/−270°C), or 5°C above absolute zero. In 1992 the Cosmic Background Explorer satellite, COBE, detected slight "ripples" in the strength of the background radiation that are believed to mark the first stage in the formation of galaxies.

cosmid fragment of DNA from the human genome inserted into a bacterial cell. The bacterium replicates the fragment along with its own DNA. In this way the fragments are copied for a gene library. Cosmids are characteristically 40,000 base pairs in length. The most commonly used bacterium is *Escherichia coli*.

cosmology study of the structure of the universe. Modern cosmology began in the 1920s with the discovery that the universe is expanding, which suggested that it began in an explosion, the Big Bang.

covalent bond chemical bond produced when two atoms share one or more pairs of electrons (usually each atom contributes an electron). The bond is often represented by a single line drawn between the two atoms. Covalently bonded substances include hydrogen (H_2), water (H_2O), and most organic substances.

Crab nebula cloud of gas 6,000 light-years from Earth, in the constellation Taurus. It is the remains of a star that exploded as a supernova (observed as a brilliant point of light on Earth 1054). At its center is a pulsar that flashes 30 times a second. The name comes from its crablike shape.

cracking reaction in which a large alkane molecule is broken down by heat into a smaller alkane and a small alkene molecule. The reaction is carried out at a high temperature (1,100°C or higher) and often in the presence of a catalyst. Cracking is a commonly used process in the petrochemical industry.

crater bowl-shaped depression, usually round and with steep sides. Craters are formed by explosive events such as the eruption of a volcano or by the impact of a meteorite.

Cretaceous period of geological time 146–65 million years ago. It is the last period of the Mesozoic era, during which angiosperm (seed-bearing) plants evolved, and dinosaurs reached a peak before their almost complete extinction at the end of the period. Chalk is a typical rock type of the second half of the period.

critical mass in nuclear physics, the minimum mass of fissile material that can undergo a continuous chain reaction. Below this mass, too many neutrons escape from the surface for a chain reaction to carry on; above the critical mass, the reaction may accelerate into a nuclear explosion.

crust the outermost part of the structure of Earth, consisting of two distinct parts, the oceanic crust and the continental crust. The oceanic crust is on average about 6.2 mi/10 km thick and consists mostly of basaltic types of rock. By contrast, the continental crust is largely made of granite and is more complex in its structure. Because of the movements of plate tectonics, the oceanic crust is in no place older than about 200 million years. However, parts of the continental crust are over 3 billion years old.

cryogenics science of very low temperatures (approach-

ing absolute zero), including the production of very low temperatures and the exploitation of special properties associated with them, such as the disappearance of electrical resistance (superconductivity).

cube in geometry, a regular solid figure whose faces are all squares. It has six equal-area faces and 12 equal-length edges. If the length of one edge is l, the volume V of the cube is given by $V = l^3$ and its surface area A by $A = 6l^2$.

cuboid six-sided three-dimensional prism whose faces are all rectangles. A brick is a cuboid.

current flow of a body of water or air, or of heat, moving in a definite direction. Ocean currents are fast flowing currents of seawater generated by the wind or by variations in water density between two areas. They are partly responsible for transferring heat from the equator to the poles and thereby evening out the global heat imbalance.

curve in geometry, the locus of a point moving according to specified conditions. The circle is the locus of all points equidistant from a given point (the centre). Other common geometrical curves are the ellipse, parabola, and hyperbola, which are also produced when a cone is cut by a plane at different angles.

cybernetics science concerned with how systems organize, regulate, and reproduce themselves, and also how they evolve and learn. In the laboratory, inanimate objects are created that behave like living systems. Applications range from the creation of electronic artificial limbs to the running of the fully automated factory where decision-making machines operate up to managerial level.

cycloid in geometry, a curve resembling a series of arches traced out by a point on the circumference of a circle that rolls along a straight line. Its applications include the study of the motion of wheeled vehicles along roads and tracks.

cylinder in geometry, a tubular solid figure with a circular base. In everyday use, the term applies to a *right cylinder*, the curved surface of which is at right angles to the base.

cytochrome one of a number of iron-containing, red proteins responsible for part of the process of respiration by which food molecules are broken down in aerobic organisms. Cytochromes are also used for the part of the process of photosynthesis by which molecules of water are oxidized to oxygen gas. Cytochromes are part of the electron transport chain, by which energized electrons are passed along to release energy and to make ATP.

cytoplasm the part of the cell outside the nucleus. Strictly speaking, this includes all the organelles (mitochondria, chloroplasts, and so on), but often cytoplasm refers to the jellylike matter in which the organelles are embedded (correctly termed the cytosol).

dam structure built to hold back water in order to prevent flooding, provide water for irrigation and storage, and to provide hydroelectric power.

dating science of determining the age of geological structures, rocks, and fossils, and placing them in the context of geological time. The techniques are of two types: relative dating and absolute dating. *Relative dating* can be carried out by identifying fossils of creatures that lived only at certain times (marker fossils), and by looking at the physical relationships of rocks to other rocks of a known age. *Absolute dating* is achieved by measuring how much of a rock's radioactive elements have changed since the rock was formed, using the process of radiometric dating.

day time taken for the Earth to rotate once on its axis.

The *solar day* is the time that the Earth takes to rotate once relative to the Sun. It is divided into 24 hours, and is the basis of our civil day. The sidereal day is the time that the Earth takes to rotate once relative to the stars. It is 3 minutes 56 seconds shorter than the solar day, because the Sun's position against the background of stars as seen from Earth changes as the Earth orbits it.

DDT abbreviation for dichloro-diphenyltrichloroethane ($ClC_6H_5)_2CHCHCl_2$), an insecticide useful in the control of insects that spread malaria, but resistant strains develop. DDT is highly toxic and persists in the environment and in living tissue. Its use is now banned in most countries, but it continues to be used on food plants in Latin America.

death the cessation of all life functions, so that the molecules and structures associated with living things become disorganized and indistinguishable from similar molecules found in non-living things.

decimal fraction a fraction in which the denominator is any higher power of 10. Thus 3/10, 51/100, and 23/1,000 are decimal fractions and are normally expressed as 0.3, 0.51, 0.023. The use of decimals greatly simplifies addition and multiplication of fractions, though not all fractions can be expressed exactly as decimal fractions.

decomposer any organism that breaks down dead matter. Decomposers play a vital role in the ecosystem by freeing important chemical substances, such as nitrogen compounds, locked up in dead organisms or excrement. They feed on some of the released organic matter, but leave the rest to filter back into the soil or pass in gas form into the atmosphere. The principal decomposers are bacteria and fungi, but earthworms and many other invertebrates are often included in this group. The nitrogen cycle relies on the actions of decomposers.

decomposition process whereby a chemical compound is reduced to its component substances. In biology, it is the destruction of dead organisms either by chemical reduction or by the action of decomposers.

degree in mathematics, a unit (symbol °) of measurement of an angle or arc. A circle or complete rotation is divided into 360°. A degree may be subdivided into 60 minutes (symbol ′), and each minute may be subdivided in turn into 60 seconds (symbol ″). Temperature is also measured in degrees, which are divided on a decimal scale.

Deimos one of the two moons of Mars. It is irregularly shaped, $9 \times 7.5 \times /15 \times 12 \times 11$ km 7 mi, orbits at a height of 15,000 mi/24,000 km every 1.26 days, and is not as heavily cratered as the other moon, Phobos. Deimos was discovered 1877 by US astronomer Asaph Hall (1829–1907), and is thought to be an asteroid captured by Mars's gravity.

delta tract of land at a river's mouth, composed of silt deposited as the water slows on entering the sea.

denominator the bottom number of a fraction, so called because it names the family of the fraction. The top number, or numerator, specifies how many unit fractions are to be taken.

desert arid area without sufficient rainfall and, consequently, vegetation to support human life. The term includes the ice areas of the polar regions (known as cold deserts). Almost 33% of the Earth's land surface is desert, and this proportion is increasing.

desertification creation of deserts by changes in climate, or by human-aided processes. Desertification can sometimes be reversed by special planting (marram grass, trees) and by the use of water-absorbent plastic grains, which, added to the soil, enable crops to be grown.

detergent surface-active cleansing agent. The common detergents are made from fats (hydrocarbons) and sulfuric acid, and their long-chain molecules have a type of structure similar to that of soap molecules: a salt group at one end attached to a long hydrocarbon "tail". They have the advantage over soap in that they do not produce scum by forming insoluble salts with the calcium and magnesium ions present in hard water.

Devonian period of geological time 408–360 million years ago, the fourth period of the Paleozoic era. Many desert sandstones from North America and Europe date from this time. The first land plants flourished in the Devonian period, corals were abundant in the seas, amphibians evolved from air-breathing fish, and insects developed on land.

dextrose or *grapesugar* dextrorotatory form of glucose, occurring in fruits and in animal tissues. It is commercially obtainable from starch by acid hydrolysis.

diagenesis or *lithification* in geology, the physical and chemical changes by which a sediment becomes a sedimentary rock. The main processes involved include compaction of the grains, and the cementing of the grains together by the growth of new minerals deposited by percolating groundwater.

differentiation in mathematics, a procedure for determining the gradient of the tangent to a curve f(x) at any point x. It may be regarded as the limit of the expression $[f(x + ax) \cdot f(x)]/ax$ as ax tends to zero. Graphically, this is equivalent to the gradient (slope) of the curve represented by $y = f(x)$ at any point x.

diffraction the slight spreading of a light beam into a pattern of light and dark bands when it passes through a narrow slit or past the edge of an obstruction. A diffraction grating is a plate of glass or metal ruled with close, equidistant parallel lines used for separating a wave train such as a beam of incident light into its component frequencies (white light results in a spectrum).

diffusion spontaneous and random movement of molecules or particles in a fluid (gas or liquid) from a region in which they are at a high concentration to a region in which they are at a low concentration, until a uniform concentration is achieved throughout. No mechanical mixing or stirring is involved. For instance, if a drop of ink is added to water, its molecules will diffuse until their color becomes evenly distributed throughout.

digital in electronics and computing, a term meaning "coded as numbers". A digital system uses two-state, either on/off or high/low voltage pulses, to encode, receive, and transmit information. A digital display shows discrete values as numbers (as opposed to an analog signal, such as the continuous sweep of a pointer on a dial).

dioxin any of a family of over 200 organic chemicals, all of which are heterocyclic hydrocarbons. The term is commonly applied, however, to only one member of the family, 2,3,7,8-tetrachlorodibenzo-*p*-dioxin (2,3,7,8-TCDD), a highly toxic chemical that occurs, for example, as an impurity in the defoliant Agent Orange, used in the Vietnam War, and sometimes in the weedkiller 2,4,5-T. It has been associated with a disfiguring skin complaint (chloracne), birth defects, miscarriages, and cancer.

diploid having two sets of chromosomes in each cell. In sexually reproducing species, one set is derived from each parent, the gametes, or sex cells, of each parent being haploid (having only one set of chromosomes) due to meiosis (reduction cell division).

dipole the uneven distribution of magnetic or electrical characteristics within a molecule or substance so that it behaves as though it possesses two equal but opposite poles or charges, a finite distance apart.

dissociation in chemistry, the process whereby a single compound splits into two or more smaller products, which may be capable of recombining to form the reactant.

distillation technique used to purify liquids or to separate mixtures of liquids possessing different boiling points. Simple distillation is used in the purification of liquids (or the separation of substances in solution from their solvents)—for example, in the production of pure water from a salt solution.

distributive operation in mathematics, an operation, such as multiplication, that bears a relationship to another operation, such as addition, such that $a \times (b + c) = (a \times b) + (a \times c)$. For example, $3 \times (2 + 4) = (3 \times 2) + (3 \times 4) = 18$. Multiplication may be said to be distributive over addition. Addition is not, however, distributive over multiplication because $3 + (2 \times 4) \neq (3 + 2) \times (3 + 4)$

DNA (*deoxyribonucleic acid*) complex giant molecule that contains, in chemically coded form, all the information needed to build, control, and maintain a living organism. DNA is a ladderlike double-stranded nucleic acid that forms the basis of genetic inheritance in all organisms, except for a few viruses that have only RNA. In organisms other than bacteria it is organized into chromosomes and contained in the cell nucleus.

doldrums area of low atmospheric pressure along the equator, in the intertropical convergence zone where the NE and SE trade winds converge. The doldrums are characterized by calm or very light winds, during which there may be sudden squalls and stormy weather. For this reason the areas are avoided as far as possible by sailing ships.

double star two stars that appear close together. Most double stars attract each other due to gravity, and orbit each other, forming a genuine binary star, but other double stars are at different distances from Earth, and lie in the same line of sight only by chance. Through a telescope both types of double star look the same.

drought period of prolonged dry weather. The area of the world subject to serious droughts, such as the Sahara, is increasing because of destruction of forests, overgrazing, and poor agricultural practices.

dune mound or ridge of wind-drifted sand. Loose sand is blown and bounced along by the wind, up the windward side of a dune. The sand particles then fall to rest on the lee side, while more are blown up from the windward side. In this way a dune moves gradually downwind.

dynamics or kinetics in mechanics, the mathematical and physical study of the behavior of bodies under the action of forces that produce changes of motion in them.

Earth third planet from the Sun. It is almost spherical, flattened slightly at the poles. 70% of the surface (including the north and south polar icecaps) is covered with water. The Earth is surrounded by a life supporting atmosphere and is the only planet on which life is known to exist. It is composed of three concentric layers: the core, the mantle, and the crust.

earthquake shaking of the Earth's surface as a result of the sudden release of stresses built up in the Earth's crust. The study of earthquakes is called seismology. Most earthquakes occur along faults (fractures or breaks) in the crust. Plate tectonic move-

ments generate the major proportion: as two plates move past each other they can become jammed and deformed, and a series of shock waves (seismic waves) occur when they spring free.

eclipse passage of an astronomical body through the shadow of another. The term is usually employed for solar and lunar eclipses, which may be either partial or total, but also, for example, for eclipses by Jupiter of its satellites. An eclipse of a star by a body in the Solar System is called an occultation.

eclipsing binary binary (double) star in which the two stars periodically pass in front of each other as seen from Earth.

ecliptic path, against the background of stars, that the Sun appears to follow each year as the Earth orbits the Sun. It can be thought of as the plane of the Earth's orbit projected on to the celestial sphere (imaginary sphere around the Earth).

ecology study of the relationship among organisms and the environments in which they live, including all living and nonliving components.

efficiency output of a machine (work done by the machine) divided by the input (work put into the machine), usually expressed as a percentage. Because of losses caused by friction, efficiency is always less than 100%, although it can approach this for electrical machines with no moving parts (such as a transformer).

elasticity in physics, the ability of a solid to recover its shape once deforming forces (stresses modifying its dimensions or shape) are removed. An elastic material obeys Hooke's law: that is, its deformation is proportional to the applied stress up to a certain point, called the *elastic limit*, beyond which additional stress will deform it permanently. Elastic materials include metals and rubber; however, all materials have some degree of elasticity.

electric current the flow of electrically charged particles through a conducting circuit due to the presence of a potential difference. The current at any point in a circuit is the amount of charge flowing per second; its SI unit is the ampere (coulomb per second).

electricity all phenomena caused by electric charge, whether static or in motion. Electric charge is caused by an excess or deficit of electrons in the charged substance, and an electric current by the movement of electrons around a circuit. Substances may be electrical conductors, such as metals, which allow the passage of electricity through them, or insulators, such as rubber, which are extremely poor conductors.

electrodynamics the branch of physics dealing with electric currents and associated magnetic forces. Quantum electrodynamics (QED) studies the interaction between charged particles and their emission and absorption of electromagnetic radiation. This field combines quantum theory and relativity theory, making accurate predictions about subatomic processes involving charged particles such as electrons and protons.

electromagnetic waves oscillating electric and magnetic fields traveling together through space at a speed of nearly 186,000 mi/300,000 km per second. The (limitless) range of possible wavelengths or frequencies of electromagnetic waves, which can be thought of as making up the *electromagnetic spectrum*, includes radio waves, infrared radiation, visible light, ultraviolet radiation, X-rays, and gamma rays.

electron stable, negatively charged elementary particle; it is a constituent of all atoms, and a member of the class of particles known as leptons. The electrons in each atom surround the nucleus in groupings called shells; in a neutral atom the number of electrons is equal to the number of protons in the nucleus. This electron structure is responsible for the chemical properties of the atom .

electronegativity the ease with which an atom can attract electrons to itself. Electronegative elements attract electrons, so forming negative ions.

electronics branch of science that deals with the emission of electrons from conductors and semiconductors, with the subsequent manipulation of these electrons, and with the construction of electronic devices. The first electronic device was the thermionic valve, or vacuum tube, in which electrons moved in a vacuum, and led to such inventions as radio, television, radar, and the digital computer. Replacement of valves with the comparatively tiny and reliable transistor in 1948 revolutionized electronic development. Modern electronic devices are based on minute integrated circuits (silicon chips), wafer-thin crystal slices holding tens of thousands of electronic components.

electron microscope instrument that produces a magnified image by using a beam of electrons instead of light rays, as in an optical microscope. An *electron lens* is an arrangement of electromagnetic coils that control and focus the beam. Electrons are not visible to the eye, so instead of an eyepiece there is a fluorescent screen or a photographic plate on which the electrons form an image. The wavelength of the electron beam is much shorter than that of light, so much greater magnification and resolution (ability to distinguish detail) can be achieved. The development of the electron microscope has made possible the observation of very minute organisms, viruses, and even large molecules.

electrophoresis the diffusion of charged particles through a fluid under the influence of an electric field. It can be used in the biological sciences to separate molecules of different sizes, which diffuse at different rates. In industry, electrophoresis is used in paint-dipping operations to ensure that paint reaches awkward corners.

element substance that cannot be split chemically into simpler substances. The atoms of a particular element all have the same number of protons in their nuclei (their atomic number). Elements are classified in the periodic table. Of the 109 known elements, 95 are known to occur in nature (those with atomic numbers 1–95). Those from 96 to 109 do not occur in nature and are synthesized only, produced in particle accelerators. Eighty-one of the elements are stable; all the others, which include atomic numbers 43, 61, and from 84 up, are radioactive.

ellipse curve joining all points (loci) around two fixed points (foci) such that the sum of the distances from those points is always constant. The diameter passing through the foci is the major axis, and the diameter bisecting this at right angles is the minor axis. An ellipse is one of a series of curves known as conic sections. A slice across a cone that is not made parallel to, and does not pass through, the base will produce an ellipse.

elongation in astronomy, the angular distance between the Sun and a planet or other solar-system object. This angle is 0° at conjunction, 90° at quadrature, and 180° at opposition.

embryo early development stage of an animal or a plant following fertilization of an ovum (egg cell), or activation of an ovum by parthenogenesis. In humans, the term embryo describes the fertilized egg during its first seven weeks of existence; from the eighth week onwards it is referred to as a fetus.

emulsion a stable dispersion of a liquid in another liquid —for example, oil and water in some cosmetic lotions.

Encke's comet comet with the shortest known orbital period, 3.3 years. It is named after German mathematician and astronomer Johann Franz Encke (1791–1865), who calculated its orbit in 1819 from earlier sightings.

energy capacity for doing work. Potential energy (PE) is energy deriving from position; thus a stretched spring has elastic PE, and an object raised to a height above the Earth's surface, or the water in an elevated reservoir, has gravitational PE. A lump of coal and a tank of gasoline, together with the oxygen needed for their combustion, have chemical energy. Other sorts of energy include electrical and nuclear energy, and light and sound. Moving bodies possess kinetic energy (KE). Energy can be converted from one form to another, but the total quantity stays the same (in accordance with the conservation of energy principle). For example, as an apple falls, it loses gravitational PE but gains KE. Although energy is never lost, after a number of conversions it tends to finish up as the kinetic energy of random motion of molecules (of the air, for example) at relatively low temperatures. This is "degraded" energy in that it is difficult to convert it back to other forms.

energy conservation methods of reducing energy use through insulation, increasing energy efficiency, and changes in patterns of use. Profligate energy use by industrialized countries contributes greatly to air pollution and the greenhouse effect when it draws on nonrenewable energy sources.

energy of reaction energy released or absorbed during a chemical reaction, also called enthalpy of reaction or heat of reaction. In a chemical reaction, the energy stored in the reacting molecules is rarely the same as that stored in the product molecules. Depending on which is the greater, energy is either released (an exothermic reaction) or absorbed (an endothermic reaction) from the surroundings. The amount of energy released or absorbed by the quantities of substances represented by the chemical equation is the energy of reaction.

engine device for converting stored energy into useful work or movement. Most engines use a fuel as their energy store. The fuel is burned to produce heat energy—hence the name "heat engine"—which is then converted into movement. Heat engines can be classified according to the fuel they use (gasoline engine or diesel engine), or according to whether the fuel is burned inside (internal combustion engine) or outside (steam engine) the engine, or according to whether they produce a reciprocating or rotary motion (turbine or Wankel engine).

entropy in thermodynamics, a parameter representing the state of disorder of a system at the atomic, ionic, or molecular level; the greater the disorder, the higher the entropy. Thus the fast-moving disordered molecules of water vapor have higher entropy than those of more ordered liquid water, which in turn have more entropy than the molecules in solid crystalline ice.

enzyme biological catalyst produced in cells, and capable of speeding up the chemical reactions necessary for life by converting one molecule (substrate) into another. Enzymes are not themselves destroyed by this process. They are large, complex proteins, and are highly specific, each chemical reaction requiring its own particular enzyme. The enzyme fits into a "slot" (active site) in the substrate molecule, forming an enzyme–substrate complex that lasts until the substrate is altered or split, after which the enzyme can fall away. The substrate may therefore be compared to a lock, and the enzyme to the key required to open it.

epicycloid in geometry, a curve resembling a series of arches traced out by a point on the circumference of a circle that rolls around another circle of a different diameter. If the two circles have the same diameter, the curve is a cardioid.

epoch subdivision of a geological period in the geological time scale. Epochs are sometimes given their own names (such as the Paleocene, Eocene, Oligocene, Miocene, and Pliocene epochs comprising the Tertiary period), or they are referred to as the late, early, or middle portions of a given period (as the Late Cretaceous or the Middle Triassic epoch).

equation in mathematics, expression that represents the equality of two expressions involving constants and/or variables, and thus usually includes an equals sign (=). For example, the equation $A = r^2$ equates the area A of a circle of radius r to the product r^2. The algebraic equation $y = mx + c$ is the general one in coordinate geometry for a straight line.

equator the *terrestrial equator* is the great circle whose plane is perpendicular to the Earth's axis (the line joining the poles). Its length is 24,901.8 mi/40,092 km, divided into 360 degrees of longitude. The equator encircles the broadest part of the Earth, and represents 0° latitude. It divides the Earth into two halves, called the northern and the southern hemispheres.

equilateral of a geometrical figure, having all sides of equal length. For example, a rhombus is an equilateral parallelogram. An equilateral triangle is also equiangular, which means that all three angles are equal as well.

equilibrium in physics, an unchanging condition in which the forces acting on a particle or system of particles (a body) cancel out, or in which energy is distributed among the particles of a system in the most probable way; or the state in which a body is at rest or moving at constant velocity. A body is in *thermal equilibrium* with its surroundings if no heat enters or leaves it, so that all its parts are at the same temperature as the surroundings.

equinox the points in spring and autumn at which the Sun's path, the ecliptic, crosses the celestial equator, so that the day and night are of approximately equal length. The *vernal equinox* occurs about 21 March and the *autumnal equinox*, 23 Sept.

era any of the major divisions of geological time, each including several periods, but smaller than an eon. The currently recognized eras all fall within the Phanerozoic eon—or the vast span of time, starting about 570 million years ago, when fossils are found to become abundant. The eras in ascending order are the Paleozoic, Mesozoic, and Cenozoic. We are living in the Recent epoch of the Quaternary period of the Cenozoic era.

erosion wearing away of the Earth's surface, caused by the breakdown and transportation of particles of rock or soil. Agents of erosion include the sea, rivers, glaciers, and wind. People also contribute to erosion by bad farming practices and the cutting down of forests, which can lead to the formation of dust bowls.

escape velocity minimum velocity with which an object must be projected for it to escape from the gravitational pull of a planetary body. In the case of the Earth, the escape velocity is 6.9 mps/11.2 kps; the Moon 1.5 mps/2.4 kps; Mars 3.1 mps/5 kps; and Jupiter 37 mps/59.6 kps.

ester organic compound formed by the reaction between an alcohol and an acid, with the elimination of water. Unlike salts, esters are covalent compounds.

estuary river mouth widening into the sea, where fresh water mixes with salt water and tidal effects are felt. Estuaries are extremely rich in life forms and are breeding grounds for thousands of species. Water pollution threatens these ecosystems.

ethanoic acid common name acetic acid CH_3CO_2H one of the simplest fatty acids (a series of organic acids). In the pure state it is a colorless liquid with an unpleasant pungent odor; it solidifies to an icelike mass of crystals at 62.4°F/16.7°C, and hence is often called glacial ethanoic acid. Vinegar contains 5% or more ethanoic acid, produced by fermentation.

ether any of a series of organic chemical compounds having an oxygen atom linking the carbon atoms of two hydrocarbon radical groups (general formula R-O-R×6); also the common name for ethoxyethane $C_2H_5OC_2H_5$ (also called diethyl ether). This is used as an anesthetic and as an external cleansing agent before surgical operations. It is also used as a solvent, and in the extraction of oils, fats, waxes, resins, and alkaloids.

eukaryote one of the two major groupings into which all organisms are divided. Included are all organisms, except bacteria and cyanobacteria (blue-green algae), which belong to the prokaryote grouping.

Europa the fourth largest moon of the planet Jupiter, diameter 1,950 mi/3,140 km, orbiting 417,000 mi/671,000 km from the planet every 3.55 days. It is covered by ice and criss-crossed by thousands of thin cracks, each some 30,000 mi/50,000 km long.

eutrophication excessive enrichment of rivers, lakes, and shallow sea areas, primarily by nitrate fertilizers washed from the soil by rain, by phosphates from fertilizers and detergents in municipal sewage, and by sewage itself. These encourage the growth of algae and bacteria which use up the oxygen in the water, thereby making it uninhabitable for fishes and other animal life.

evolution slow process of change from one form to another, as in the evolution of the universe from its formation in the Big Bang to its present state, or in the evolution of life on Earth. The idea did not gain wide acceptance until the 19th century, following the work of Scottish geologist Charles Lyell, French naturalist Jean Baptiste Lamarck, English naturalist Charles Darwin, and English biologist Thomas Henry Huxley. Darwin assigned the major role in evolutionary change to natural selection acting on randomly occurring variations. Natural selection occurs because those individuals better adapted to their particular environments reproduce more effectively, thus contributing their characteristics to future generations. The current theory of evolution, called Neo-Darwinism, combines Darwin's theory with Gregor Mendel's theories on genetics and Hugo de Vries' discovery of genetic mutation. Although neither the general concept of evolution nor the importance of natural selection is doubted by the vast majority of biologists, there remains dispute over other possible processes involved in evolutionary change. Besides natural selection and sexual selection, chance may play a large part in deciding which genes become characteristic of a population, a phenomenon called "genetic drift". It is now also clear that evolutionary change does not always occur at a constant rate, but that the process can have long periods of relative stability interspersed with periods of rapid change. This has led to new theories, such as the punctuated equilibrium model.

exosphere the uppermost layer of the atmosphere. It is an ill-defined zone above the thermosphere, beginning at about 435 mi/700 km and fading off into the vacuum of space. The gases are extremely thin, with hydrogen as the main constituent.

exponent or *index* in mathematics, a number that indicates the number of times a term is multiplied by itself; for example $x^2 = x \, x \, x$, $4^3 = 4 \times 4 \times 4$.

exponential in mathematics, descriptive of a function in which the variable quantity is an exponent (a number indicating the power to which another number or expression is raised). *Exponential growth* is not constant. It applies, for example, to population growth, where the population doubles in a short time period. A graph of population number against time is an exponential growth function and produces a curve that is characteristically rather flat at first but then shoots almost directly upward.

extinction the complete disappearance of a species. In the past, extinctions are believed to have occurred because species were unable to adapt quickly enough to a naturally changing environment. Today, most extinctions are due to human activity.

factor a number that divides into another number exactly. For example, the factors of 64 are 1, 2, 4, 8, 16, 32, and 64. In algebra, certain kinds of polynomials (expressions consisting of several or many terms) can be factorized. For example, the factors of $x^2 + 3x + 2$ are $x + 1$ and $x + 2$, since $x^2 + 3x + 2 = (x + 1)(x + 2)$. This is called factorization.

factorial of a positive number, the product of all the whole numbers (integers) inclusive between 1 and the number itself. A factorial is indicated by the symbol "!". Thus $6! = 1 \times 2 \times 3 \times 4 \times 5 \times 6 = 720$. Factorial zero, $0!$, is defined as 1.

fat in the broadest sense, a mixture of lipids – chiefly triglycerides (lipids containing three fatty acid molecules linked to a molecule of glycerol). More specifically, the term refers to a lipid mixture that is solid at room temperature (20°C); lipid mixtures that are liquid at room temperature are called *oils*. The higher the proportion of saturated fatty acids in a mixture, the harder the fat.

fatty acid or *carboxylic acid* organic compound consisting of a hydrocarbon chain, up to 24 carbon atoms long, with a carboxyl group (–COOH) at one end. The covalent bonds between the carbon atoms may be single or double; where a double bond occurs the carbon atoms concerned carry one instead of two hydrogen atoms. Chains with only single bonds have all the hydrogen they can carry, so they are said to be *saturated* with hydrogen. Chains with one or more double bonds are said to be *unsaturated*.

fault in geology, a fracture in the Earth's crust along which the two sides have moved as a result of differing strains in the adjacent rock bodies. Displacement of rock masses horizontally or vertically along a fault may be microscopic, or it may be massive, causing major earthquakes.

fax (common name for *facsimile transmission* or telefax) the transmission of images over a telecommunications link, usually the telephone network. When placed on a fax machine, the original image is scanned by a transmitting device and converted into coded signals, which travel via the telephone lines to the receiving fax machine, where an image is created that is a copy of the original. Photographs as well as printed text and drawings can be sent. The standard transmission takes place at 4,800 or 9,600 bits of information per second.

fermentation the breakdown of sugars by bacteria and yeasts using a method of respiration without oxygen (anaerobic). Fermentation processes have long been utilized in baking bread, making beer and wine, and producing cheese, yogurt, soy sauce, and many other foodstuffs.

fermion a subatomic particle whose spin can only take values that are half-integers, such as 1/2 or 3/2. Fermions may be classified as leptons, such as the electron, and baryons, such as the proton and neutron. All elementary particles are either fermions or bosons.

fertilization in sexual reproduction, the union of two gametes (sex cells, often called egg and sperm) to produce a zygote, which combines the genetic material contributed by each parent. In self-fertilization the male and female gametes come from the same plant; in cross-fertilization they come from different plants. Self-fertilization rarely occurs in animals; usually even hermaphrodite animals cross-fertilize each other.

field in physics, a region of space in which an object exerts a force on another separate object because of certain properties they both possess. For example, there is a force of attraction between any two objects that have mass when one is in the gravitational field of the other.

fish aquatic vertebrate that uses gills for obtaining oxygen from fresh or sea water. There are three main groups, not closely related: the bony fishes or Osteichthyes (goldfish, cod, tuna); the cartilaginous fishes or Chondrichthyes (sharks, rays); and the jawless fishes or Agnatha (hagfishes, lampreys).

fjord or *fiord* narrow sea inlet enclosed by high cliffs. Fjords are found in Norway, New Zealand, and western parts of Scotland. They are formed when an over-deepened U-shaped glacial valley is drowned by a rise in sea-level. At the mouth of the fjord there is a characteristic lip causing a shallowing of the water. This is due to reduced glacial erosion and the deposition of moraine at this point.

flare, solar brilliant eruption on the Sun above a sunspot, thought to be caused by release of magnetic energy. Flares reach maximum brightness within a few minutes, then fade away over about an hour. They eject a burst of atomic particles into space at up to 600 mps/1,000 kps. When these particles reach Earth they can cause radio blackouts, disruptions of the Earth's magnetic field, and auroras.

flood plain area of periodic flooding along the course of river valleys. When river discharge exceeds the capacity of the channel, water rises over the channel banks and floods the adjacent low-lying lands. As water spills out of the channel some alluvium (silty material) will be deposited on the banks to form levees (raised river banks). This water will slowly seep into the flood plain, depositing a new layer of rich fertile alluvium as it does so. Many important floodplains, such as the inner Niger delta in Mali, occur in arid areas where their exceptional productivity has great importance for the local economy.

flower the reproductive unit of an angiosperm or flowering plant, typically consisting of four whorls of modified leaves: sepals, petals, stamens, and carpels. These are borne on a central axis or receptacle. The many variations in size, color, number, and arrangement of parts are closely related to the method of pollination. Flowers adapted for wind pollination typically have reduced or absent petals and sepals and long, feathery stigmas that hang outside the flower to trap airborne pollen. In contrast, the petals of insect-pollinated flowers are usually conspicuous and brightly colored.

fluorescence microscopy technique for examining samples under a microscope without slicing them into thin sections. Instead, fluorescent dyes are introduced into the tissue and used as a light source for imaging purposes. Fluorescent dyes can also be bonded to monoclonal antibodies and used to highlight areas where particular cell proteins occur.

fog cloud that collects at the surface of the Earth, composed of water vapor that has condensed on particles of dust in the atmosphere.

fold in geology, a bend in beds or layers of rock. If the bend is arched in the middle it is called an *anticline*; if it sags downward in the middle it is called a *syncline*. The line along which a bed of rock folds is called its axis. The axial plane is the plane joining the axes of successive beds.

food chain in ecology, a sequence showing the feeding relationships between organisms in a particular ecosystem. Each organism depends on the next lowest member of the chain for its food.

force any influence that tends to change the state of rest or the uniform motion in a straight line of a body. The action of an unbalanced or resultant force results in the acceleration of a body in the direction of action of the force or it may, if the body is unable to move freely, result in its deformation (see Hooke's law). Force is a vector quantity, possessing both magnitude and direction; its SI unit is the newton.

formula in chemistry, a representation of a molecule, radical, or ion, in which the component chemical elements are represented by their symbols. An *empirical formula* indicates the simplest ratio of the elements in a compound, without indicating how many of them there are or how they are combined. A *molecular formula* gives the number of each type of element present in one molecule. A *structural formula* shows the relative positions of the atoms and the bonds between them. For example, for ethanoic acid, the empirical formula is CH_2O, the molecular formula is $C_2H_4O_2$, and the structural formula is CH_3COOH. Formula is also another name for chemical equation.

fossil fuel fuel, such as coal, oil, and natural gas, formed from the fossilized remains of plants that lived hundreds of millions of years ago. Fossil fuels are a nonrenewable resource and will eventually run out. Extraction of coal and oil causes considerable environmental pollution, and burning coal contributes to problems of acid rain and the greenhouse effect.

fractal an irregular shape or surface produced by a procedure of repeated subdivision. Generated on a computer screen, fractals are used in creating models for geographical or biological processes (for example, the creation of a coastline by erosion or accretion, or the growth of plants).

fraction in mathematics, a number that indicates one or more equal parts of a whole. Usually, the number of equal parts into which the unit is divided (denominator) is written below a horizontal line, and the number of parts comprising the fraction (numerator) is written above; thus 2/3 or 3/4. Such fractions are called vulgar or simple fractions. The denominator can never be zero.

free radical an atom or molecule that has an unpaired electron and is therefore highly reactive. Most free radicals are very short-lived. If free radicals are produced in living organisms they can be very damaging.

freezing change from liquid to solid state, as when water becomes ice. For a given substance, freezing occurs at a definite temperature, known as the *freezing point*, that is invariable under similar conditions of pressure, and the temperature remains at this point until all the liquid is frozen. The amount of heat per unit mass that has to be removed to freeze a substance is a constant for any given substance, and is known as the latent heat of fusion.

frequency the number of periodic oscillations, vibrations, or waves occurring per unit of time. The unit of frequency is the hertz (Hz), one hertz being equivalent to one cycle per second.

friction the force that opposes the relative motion of two bodies in contact. The *coefficient of friction* is the ratio of the force required to achieve this relative motion to the force pressing the two bodies together.

front in meteorology, the boundary between two air masses of different temperature or humidity. A *cold front* marks the line of advance of a cold air mass from below, as it displaces a warm air mass; a *warm front* marks the advance of a warm air mass as it rises up over a cold one. Frontal systems define the weather of the midlatitudes, where warm tropical air is constantly meeting cold air from the poles.

frost condition of the weather that occurs when the air temperature is below freezing, 32°F/0°C. Water in the atmosphere is deposited as ice crystals on the ground or exposed objects.

fructose $C_6H_{12}O_6$ a sugar that occurs naturally in honey, the nectar of flowers, and many sweet fruits; it is commercially prepared from glucose.

function in mathematics, a function f is a non-empty set of ordered pairs $(x, f(x))$ of which no two can have the same first element. Hence, if $f(x) = x^2$, two ordered pairs are $(-2, 4)$ and $(2, 4)$. The set of all first elements in a function's ordered pairs is called the *domain*; the set of all second elements is the *range*. In the algebraic expression $y = 4x^3 + 2$, the dependent variable y is a function of the independent variable x, generally written as $f(x)$.

functional group in chemistry, a small number of atoms in an arrangement that determines the chemical properties of the group and of the molecule to which it is attached (for example, the carboxyl group COOH, or the amine group NH2). Organic compounds can be considered as structural skeletons, with a high carbon content, with functional groups attached.

fundamental constant physical quantity that is constant in all circumstances throughout the whole universe. Examples are the electric charge of an electron and the speed of light.

fundamental forces in physics, the four fundamental interactions believed to be at work in the physical universe. There are two long-range forces: *gravity*, which keeps the planets in orbit around the Sun, and acts between all particles that have mass; and the *electromagnetic force*, which stops solids from falling apart, and acts between all particles with electric charge. There are two very short-range forces: the *weak force*, responsible for radioactive decay and for other subatomic reactions; and the *strong force*, which binds together the protons and neutrons in the nuclei of atoms.

Gaia hypothesis theory that the Earth's living and nonliving systems form an inseparable whole that is regulated and kept adapted for life by living organisms themselves. The planet therefore functions as a single organism, or a giant cell. Since life and environment are so closely linked, there is a need for humans to understand and maintain the physical environment and living things around them. The Gaia hypothesis was elaborated by British scientist James (Ephraim) Lovelock (1919–) in the 1970s.

galaxy congregation of millions or billions of stars, held together by gravity. *Spiral galaxies*, such as the Milky Way, are flattened in shape, with a central bulge of old stars surrounded by a disk of younger stars, arranged in spiral arms like a Catherine wheel. *Barred spirals* are spiral galaxies that have a straight bar of stars across their centre, from the ends of which the spiral arms emerge. The arms of spiral galaxies contain gas and dust from which new stars are still forming. *Elliptical galaxies* contain old stars and very little gas. They include the most massive galaxies known, containing a trillion stars. At least some elliptical galaxies are thought to be formed by mergers between spiral galaxies. There are also irregular galaxies. Most galaxies occur in clusters, containing anything from a few to thousands of members.

gamete cell that functions in sexual reproduction by merging with another gamete to form a zygote. Examples of gametes include sperm and egg cells. In most organisms, the gametes are haploid (they contain half the number of chromosomes of the parent), owing to reduction division or meiosis.

Ganymede in astronomy, the largest moon of the planet Jupiter, and the largest moon in the Solar System, 3,270 mi/5,260 km in diameter (larger than the planet Mercury). It orbits Jupiter every 7.2 days at a distance of 700,000 mi/1.1 million km. Its surface is a mixture of cratered and grooved terrain.

gas exchange in biology, the exchange of gases between living organisms and the atmosphere, principally oxygen and carbon dioxide. In animals, gas exchange is only respiratory (or using oxygen to convert food to energy). In plants, gas exchange is photosynthetic (or using carbon dioxide to make food) as well as respiratory. In humans and other tetrapods (four-limbed vertebrates), gas exchange or respiration is the absorption of oxygen into the blood when air meets blood vessels in the lungs, and the exhalation of carbon dioxide with water and small quantities of ammonia and waste matter. Many adult amphibia and terrestrial invertebrates can absorb oxygen directly through the skin. The bodies of insects and some spiders contain a system of air-filled tubes known as tracheae. Fish and most other aquatic organisms have gills, which exchange gases with the surrounding water. In plants, gas exchange necessary for photosynthesis and respiration generally takes place via the stomata.

gauge boson or *field particle* any of the particles that carry the four fundamental forces of nature. Gauge bosons are elementary particles that cannot be subdivided, and include the photon, the graviton, the gluons, and the weakons.

gene unit of inherited material, encoded by a strand of DNA, and transcribed by RNA. In higher organisms, genes are located on the chromosomes. The term "gene" refers to the inherited factor that consistently affects a particular character in an individual—for example, the gene for eye color. It occurs at a particular point or locus on a particular chromosome and may have several variants or alleles, each specifying a particular form of that character—for example, the alleles for blue or brown eyes. Some alleles show dominance. These mask the effect of other alleles known as recessive.

gene therapy proposed medical technique for curing or alleviating inherited diseases or defects. In 1990 a genetically engineered gene was used for the first time to treat a patient.

genetic code the way in which instructions for building proteins, the basic structural molecules of living matter, are "written" in the genetic material DNA. This relationship between the sequence of bases (the subunits of a DNA molecule) and the sequence of amino acids (the subunits of a protein molecule) is the basis of heredity. The code employs codons of three bases each; it is the same in almost all organisms, except for a few minor differences recently discovered in some protozoa.

genetic engineering deliberate manipulation of genetic material by biochemical techniques. It is often achieved by the introduction of new DNA, usually by means of a virus or plasmid. This can be for pure research or to breed functionally specific plants, animals, or bacteria. These organisms with a foreign gene added are said to be transgenic.

genome the full complement of genes carried by a single (haploid) set of chromosomes. The term may be applied to the genetic information carried by an individual or to the range of genes found in a given species.

genotype the particular set of alleles (variants of genes) possessed by a given organism. The term is usually used in conjunction with phenotype, which is the product of the genotype and all environmental effects.

geochemistry science of chemistry as it applies to geology. It deals with the relative and absolute abundances of the chemical elements and their isotopes in the Earth, and also with the chemical changes that accompany geological processes.

geological time time scale embracing the history of the Earth from its physical origin to the present day. Geological time is traditionally divided into eras (Precambrian, Paleozoic, Mesozoic, Cenozoic), which in turn are divided into periods, epochs, ages, and finally chrons.

geometry branch of mathematics concerned with the properties of space, usually in terms of plane (two-dimensional) and solid (three-dimensional) figures. The subject is usually divided into *pure geometry*, which embraces roughly the plane and *solid geometry* dealt with in Euclid's *Elements*, and *analytical* or *coordinate geometry*, in which problems are solved using algebraic methods. A third, quite distinct, type includes the non-Euclidean geometries.

geophysics branch of earth science using physics to study the Earth's surface, interior, and atmosphere. Studies also include winds, weather, tides, earthquakes, volcanoes, and their effects.

geostationary orbit circular path 22,300 mi/35,900 km above the Earth's equator on which a satellite takes 24 hours, moving from west to east, to complete an orbit, thus appearing to hang stationary over one place on the Earth's surface. Geostationary orbits are particularly used for communications satellites and weather satellites.

geothermal energy energy extracted for heating and electricity generation from natural steam, hot water, or hot dry rocks in the Earth's crust.

geyser natural spring that intermittently discharges an explosive column of steam and hot water into the air due to the build-up of steam in underground chambers.

glacier tongue of ice, originating in mountains in snowfields above the snowline, which moves slowly downhill and is constantly replenished from its source. The scenery produced by the erosive action of glaciers is characteristic and includes glacial troughs (U-shaped valleys), corries, and arêtes. In lowlands, the laying down of moraine (rocky debris once carried by glaciers) produces a variety of landscape features.

global warming projected imminent climate change attributed to the greenhouse effect.

globular cluster spherical or near-spherical star cluster containing from approximately 10,000 to millions of stars. More than a hundred globular clusters are distributed in a spherical halo around our Galaxy. They consist of old stars, formed early in the Galaxy's history. Globular clusters are also found around other galaxies.

glucose $C_6H_{12}O_6$ sugar present in the blood, and

found also in honey and fruit juices. It is a source of energy for the body, being produced from other sugars and starches to form the "energy currency" of many biochemical reactions also involving ATP.

gluon in physics, a gauge boson that carries the strong nuclear force, responsible for binding quarks together to form the strongly interacting subatomic particles known as hadrons. There are eight kinds of gluon.

Gondwanaland or *Gondwana* southern land mass formed 200 million years ago by the splitting of the single world continent Pangaea. (The northern land mass was Laurasia.) It later fragmented into the continents of South America, Africa, Australia, and Antarctica, which then drifted slowly to their present positions. The baobab tree found in both Africa and Australia is a relic of this ancient land mass.

grand unified theory (GUT) in physics, a sought-for theory that would combine the theory of the strong nuclear force (called quantum chromodynamics) with the theory of the weak nuclear and electromagnetic forces. The search for the grand unified theory is part of a larger program seeking a unified field theory, which would combine all the forces of nature (including gravity) within one framework.

graviton in physics, the gauge boson that is the postulated carrier of gravity.

gravity force of attraction that arises between objects by virtue of their masses. On Earth, gravity is the force of attraction between any object in the Earth's gravitational field and the Earth itself. It is regarded as one of the four fundamental forces of nature, the other three being the electromagnetic force, the strong nuclear force, and the weak nuclear force. The gravitational force is the weakest of the four forces, but it acts over great distances. The particle that is postulated as the carrier of the gravitational force is the graviton.

gravitational lensing bending of light by a gravitational field, predicted by Einstein's general theory of relativity. The effect was first detected 1917 when the light from stars was found to be bent as it passed the totally eclipsed Sun. More remarkable is the splitting of light from distant quasars into two or more images by intervening galaxies. In 1979 the first double image of a quasar produced by gravitational lensing was discovered and a quadruple image of another quasar was later found.

greenhouse effect phenomenon of the Earth's atmosphere by which solar radiation, trapped by the Earth and re-emitted from the surface, is prevented from escaping by various gases in the air. The result is a rise in the Earth's temperature. The main greenhouse gases are carbon dioxide, methane, and chlorofluorocarbons (CFCs). Fossil-fuel consumption and forest fires are the main causes of carbon-dioxide buildup; methane is a byproduct of agriculture (rice, cattle, sheep). Water vapor is another greenhouse gas.

ground water water collected underground in porous rock strata and soils; it emerges at the surface as springs and streams. The groundwater's upper level is called the *water table*. Sandy or other kinds of beds that are filled with groundwater are called *aquifers*.

group in mathematics, a finite or infinite set of elements that can be combined by an operation; formally, a group must satisfy certain conditions. For example, the set of all integers (positive or negative whole numbers) forms a group with regard to addition because: (1) addition is associative, that is, the sum of two or more integers is the same regardless of the order in which the integers are added; (2) adding two integers gives another integer; (3) the set includes an identity element 0, which has no effect on any integer to which it is added (for example, $0 + 3 = 3$); and (4) each integer has an inverse (for instance, 7 has the inverse -7), such that the sum of an integer and its inverse is 0. *Group* theory is the study of the properties of groups.

gymnosperm in botany, any plant whose seeds are exposed, as opposed to the structurally more advanced angiosperms, where they are inside an ovary. The group includes conifers and related plants such as cycads and ginkgos, whose seeds develop in cones. Fossil gymnosperms have been found in rocks about 350 million years old.

habitat in ecology, the localized environment in which an organism lives. Habitats are often described by the dominant plant type or physical feature, such as a grassland habitat or rocky seashore habitat.

hadron in physics, a subatomic particle that experiences the strong nuclear force. Each is made up of two or three indivisible particles called quarks. The hadrons are grouped into the baryons (protons, neutrons, and hyperons) and the mesons (particles with masses between those of electrons and protons).

hail precipitation in the form of pellets of ice (hailstones). It is caused by the circulation of moisture in strong convection currents, usually within cumulonimbus clouds.

half-life during radioactive decay, the time in which the strength of a radioactive source decays to half its original value. In theory, the decay process is never complete and there is always some residual radioactivity. For this reason, the half-life (the time taken for 50% of the isotope to decay) is measured, rather than the total decay time. It may vary from millionths of a second to billions of years.

Halley's comet comet that orbits the Sun about every 76 years, named after Edmond Halley who calculated its orbit. It is the brightest and most conspicuous of the periodic comets. Recorded sightings go back over 2,000 years. It travels around the Sun in the opposite direction to the planets. Its orbit is inclined at almost 20° to the main plane of the Solar System and ranges between the orbits of Venus and Neptune. It will next reappear 2061.

halogen any of a group of five nonmetallic elements with similar chemical bonding properties: fluorine, chlorine, bromine, iodine, and astatine. They form a linked group in the periodic table of the elements, descending from fluorine, the most reactive, to astatine, the least reactive. They combine directly with most metals to form salts, such as common salt (NaCl). Each halogen has seven electrons in its valence shell, which accounts for the chemical similarities displayed by the group.

halon organic chemical compound containing one or two carbon atoms, together with bromine and other halogens. The most commonly used are halon 1211 (bromochlorodifluoromethane) and halon 1301 (bromotrifluoromethane). The halons are gases and are widely used in fire extinguishers. As destroyers of the ozone layer, they are up to ten times more effective than chlorofluorocarbons (CFCs), to which they are chemically related.

haploid having a single set of chromosomes in each cell. Most higher organisms are diploid – that is, they have two sets—but their gametes (sex cells) are haploid. Some plants, such as mosses, liverworts, and many seaweeds, are haploid, and male honey bees are haploid because they develop from eggs that have not been fertilized.

heat form of internal energy possessed by a substance by virtue of the kinetic energy in the motion of its molecules or atoms. Heat energy is transferred by conduction, convection, and radiation. It always flows from a region of higher temperature (heat intensity) to one of lower temperature. Its effect on a substance may be simply to raise its temperature, or to cause it to expand, melt (if a solid), vaporize (if a liquid), or increase its pressure (if a confined gas).

heat storage any means of storing heat for release later. It is usually achieved by using materials that undergo phase changes, for example, Glauber's salt and sodium pyrophosphate, which melts at 158°F/70°C. The latter is used to store off-peak heat in the home: the salt is liquefied by cheap heat during the night and then freezes to give off heat during the day.

helix in mathematics, a three-dimensional curve resembling a spring, corkscrew, or screw thread. It is generated by a line that encircles a cylinder or cone at a constant angle.

herbivore animal that feeds on green plants (or photosynthetic single-celled organisms) or their products, including seeds, fruit, and nectar. Herbivores are more numerous than other animals because their food is the most abundant. They form a vital link in the food chain between plants and carnivores.

hermaphrodite organism that has both male and female sex organs. Hermaphroditism is the norm in species such as earthworms and snails, and is common in flowering plants. Cross-fertilization is the rule among hermaphrodites, with the parents functioning as male and female simultaneously, or as one or the other sex at different stages in their development.

Hertzsprung–Russell diagram in astronomy, a graph on which the surface temperatures of stars are plotted against their luminosities. Most stars, including the Sun, fall into a narrow band called the main sequence. When a star grows old it moves from the *main sequence* to the upper right part of the graph, into the area of the giants and supergiants. At the end of its life, as the star shrinks to become a white dwarf, it moves again, to the bottom left area.

heterotroph any living organism that obtains its energy from organic substances produced by other organisms. All animals and fungi are heterotrophs, and they include herbivores, carnivores, and saprotrophs (those that feed on dead animal and plant material).

heterozygous in a living organism, having two different alleles for a given trait.

Holocene epoch of geological time that began 10,000 years ago, the second and current epoch of the Quaternary period. The glaciers retreated, the climate became warmer, and humans developed significantly.

homologous series any of a number of series of organic chemicals with similar chemical properties in which members differ by a constant molecular weight.

homozygous in a living organism, having two identical alleles for a given trait.

Hubble's constant in astronomy, a measure of the rate at which the universe is expanding, named after Edwin Hubble. Observations suggest that galaxies are moving apart at a rate of 30–60 mps/50–100 kps for every million parsecs of distance. This means that the universe, which began at one point according to the Big Bang theory, is between 10 billion and 20 billion years old (probably closer to 20).

Hubble's law the law that relates a galaxy's distance from us to its speed of recession as the universe expands, announced in 1929 by Edwin Hubble. He found that galaxies are moving apart at speeds that increase in direct proportion to their distance apart.

human species, origins of evolution of humans from ancestral primates. The African apes (gorilla and chimpanzee) are shown by anatomical and molecular comparisons to be the closest living relatives of humans. Humans are distinguished from apes by the size of their brain and jaw, their bipedalism, and their elaborate culture. Molecular studies put the date of the split between the human and African ape lines at 5–10 million years ago. There are only fragmentary remains of ape and *hominid* (of the human group) fossils from this period; the oldest known hominids, found in Ethiopia and Tanzania, date from 3.5 to 4 million years ago. These creatures are known as *Australopithecus afarensis*, and they walked upright. They were either direct ancestors or an offshoot of the line that led to modern humans. They may have been the ancestors of *Homo habilis* (considered by some to be a species of *Australopithecus*), who appeared about a million years later, had slightly larger bodies and brains, and were probably the first to use stone tools. *Australopithecus robustus* and *A. africanus* also lived in Africa at the same time, but these are not generally considered to be our ancestors. Over 1.5 million years ago, *Homo erectus*, believed by some to be descended from *H. habilis*, appeared in Africa. The *erectus* people had much larger brains, and were probably the first to use fire and the first to move out of Africa. Their remains are found as far afield as China, Java, western Asia, Spain, Germany, and England. Modern humans, *H. sapiens sapiens*, and the Neanderthals, *H. sapiens neanderthalensis*, are probably descended from *H. erectus*. Analysis of DNA in recent human populations shows that *H. sapiens* originated about 200,000 years ago in Africa. The oldest known fossils of *H. sapiens* also come from Africa, between 150,000 and 100,000 years ago. Separation of human populations occurred later, with separation of Asian, European, and Australian populations between 100,000 and 50,000 years ago. Neanderthals were large-brained and heavily built, probably adapted to the cold conditions of the ice ages. They lived in Europe and the Middle East, and died out about 40,000 years ago, leaving *H. sapiens sapiens* as the only remaining species of the hominid group.

hurricane revolving storm in tropical regions, called *typhoon* in the N Pacific. It originates between 5° and 20° N or S of the equator, when the surface temperature of the ocean is above 80°F/27°C. A central calm area, called the eye, is surrounded by inwardly spiraling winds (counterclockwise in the northern hemisphere) of up to 200 mph/320 kph. A hurricane is accompanied by lightning and torrential rain, and can cause extensive damage. In meteorology, a hurricane is a wind of force 12 or more on the Beaufort scale.

hydrocarbon any of a class of chemical compounds containing only hydrogen and carbon (for example, the alkanes and alkenes). Hydrocarbons are obtained industrially principally from petroleum and coal tar.

hydrochloric acid highly corrosive aqueous solution of hydrogen chloride (HCl, a colorless, corrosive gas). It has many industrial uses, including recovery of zinc from galvanized scrap iron and the production of chlorides and chlorine. It is also produced in the stomachs of animals for the purposes of digestion.

hydrodynamics science of nonviscous liquids (for example water, alcohol, ether) in motion.

hydroelectric power (HEP) electricity generated by moving water. In a typical HEP scheme, water stored in a reservoir, often created by damming a river, is piped into water turbines, coupled to electricity generators. In pumped storage plants, water flowing through the turbines is recycled. A tidal power station exploits the rise and fall of the tides. About one-fifth of the world's electricity comes from HEP.

hydrogen colorless, odorless, gaseous, nonmetallic element, symbol H, atomic number 1, atomic weight 1.00797. It is the lightest of all the elements and occurs on Earth chiefly in combination with oxygen as water. Hydrogen is the most abundant element in the universe, where it accounts for 93% of the total number of atoms and 76% of the total mass. It is a component of most stars, including the Sun, whose heat and light are produced through the nuclear-fusion process that converts hydrogen into helium. When subjected to a pressure 500,000 times greater than that of the Earth's atmosphere, hydrogen becomes a solid with metallic properties, as in one of the inner zones of Jupiter. Hydrogen's common and industrial uses include the hardening of oils and fats by hydrogenation, the creation of high-temperature flames for welding, and as rocket fuel.

hydrostatics in physics, the branch of statics dealing with the mechanical problems of liquids in equilibrium, that is, in a static condition. Practical applications include shipbuilding and dam design.

hyperbola in geometry, a curve formed by cutting a right circular cone with a plane so that the angle between the plane and the base is greater than the angle between the base and the side of the cone. All hyperbolae are bounded by two asymptotes (straight lines which the hyperbola moves closer and closer to but never reaches). A hyperbola is a member of the family of curves known as conic sections.

hyperon in physics, a hadron; any of a group of highly unstable elementary particles that includes all the baryons with a mass greater than the neutron. They are all composed of three quarks. The lambda, xi, sigma, and omega particles are hyperons.

hypotenuse the longest side of a right triangle, opposite the right angle.

ice age any period of glaciation occurring in the Earth's history, but particularly that in the Pleistocene epoch, immediately preceding historic times. On the North American continent, glaciers reached as far south as the Great Lakes, and an ice sheet spread over N Europe, leaving its remains as far south as Switzerland. There were several glacial advances separated by interglacial stages during which the ice melted and temperatures were higher than today.

immiscible term describing liquids that will not mix with each other, such as oil and water. When two immiscible liquids are shaken together, a turbid mixture is produced. This normally forms separate layers on being left to stand.

inclination angle between the ecliptic and the plane of the orbit of a planet, asteroid, or comet. In the case of satellites orbiting a planet, it is the angle between the plane of orbit of the satellite and the equator of the planet.

indicator in chemistry, a compound that changes its structure and color in response to its environment. The commonest chemical indicators detect changes in pH (for example, litmus), or in the oxidation state of a system (redox indicators).

inertia in physics, the tendency of an object to remain in a state of rest or uniform motion until an external force is applied, as stated by Isaac Newton's first law of motion (see Newton's laws of motion).

inferior planet a planet (Mercury or Venus) whose orbit lies between that of the Earth and the Sun.

infinity mathematical quantity that is larger than any fixed assignable quantity; symbol ∞. By convention, the result of dividing any number by zero is regarded as infinity.

inorganic chemistry branch of chemistry dealing with the chemical properties of the elements and their compounds, excluding the more complex covalent compounds of carbon, which are considered in organic chemistry.

integer any whole number. Integers may be positive or negative; 0 is an integer, and is often considered positive. Formally, integers are members of the set $Z = \{... -3, -2, -1, 0, 1, 2, 3,... \}$. Fractions, such as 1/2 and 0.35, are known as nonintegral numbers ("not integers").

integration in mathematics, a method in calculus of determining the solutions of definite or indefinite integrals. An example of a definite integral can be thought of as finding the area under a curve (as represented by an algebraic expression or function) between particular values of the function's variable. In practice, integral calculus provides scientists with a powerful tool for doing calculations that involve a continually varying quantity (such as determining the position at any given instant of a space rocket that is accelerating away from Earth).

interference in physics, the phenomenon of two or more wave motions interacting and combining to produce a resultant wave of larger or smaller amplitude (depending on whether the combining waves are in or out of phase with each other).

interplanetary matter gas and dust thinly spread through the Solar System. The gas flows outwards from the Sun as the solar wind. Fine dust lies in the plane of the Solar System, scattering sunlight to cause the zodiacal light. Swarms of dust shed by comets enter the Earth's atmosphere to cause meteor showers.

interstellar molecules over 50 different types of molecule existing in gas clouds in our Galaxy. Most have been detected by their radio emissions, but some have been found by the absorption lines they produce in the spectra of starlight. The most complex molecules, many of them based on carbon, are found in the dense clouds where stars are forming. They may be significant for the origin of life elsewhere in space.

intrusion mass of igneous rock that has formed by "injection" of molten rock, or magma, into existing cracks beneath the surface of the Earth.

invertebrate an animal without a backbone. The invertebrates form all of the major divisions of the animal kingdom called phyla, with the exception of vertebrates. Invertebrates include the sponges, coelenterates, flatworms, nematodes, annelids, arthropods, mollusks, and echinoderms.

Io in astronomy, the third largest moon of the planet Jupiter, 2,260 mi/3,630 km in diameter, orbiting in 1.77 days at a distance of 262,000 mi/422,000 km. It is the most volcanically active body in the Solar System, covered by hundreds of vents that erupt not lava but sulfur, giving Io an orange-colored surface.

ion atom, or group of atoms, which is either positively charged (cation) or negatively charged (anion), as a result of the loss or gain of electrons during chemical reactions or exposure to certain forms of radiation.

ion exchange process whereby an ion in one compound is replaced by a different ion, of the same charge, from another compound. It is the basis of a type of chromatography in which the components of a mixture of ions in solution are separated according to the ease with which they will replace the ions on the polymer matrix through which they flow. The exchange of positively charged ions is called cation exchange; that of negatively charged ions is called anion exchange.

ionic bond or *electrovalent bond* bond produced when atoms of one element donate electrons to atoms of another element, forming positively and negatively charged ions respectively. The electrostatic attraction between the oppositely charged ions constitutes the bond. Sodium chloride (Na^+Cl^-) is a typical ionic compound.

island area of land surrounded entirely by water. Australia is classed as a continent rather than an island, because of its size.

isobar line drawn on maps and weather charts linking all places with the same atmospheric pressure (usually measured in millibars). When used in weather forecasting, the distance between the isobars is an indication of the barometric gradient.

isomer chemical compound having the same molecular composition and mass as another, but with different physical or chemical properties owing to the different structural arrangement of its constituent atoms. For example, the organic compounds butane (CH3(CH2)2 CH3) and methyl propane (CH3CH(CH3) CH3) are isomers, each possessing four carbon atoms and ten hydrogen atoms but differing in the way that these are arranged with respect to each other.

isotope one of two or more atoms that have the same atomic number (same number of protons), but which contain a different number of neutrons, thus differing in their atomic masses. They may be stable or radioactive, naturally occurring or synthesized.

jet stream narrow band of very fast wind (velocities of over 95 mph/150 kph) found at altitudes of 6–10 mi/10–16 km in the upper troposphere or lower stratosphere. Jet streams usually occur about the latitudes of the Westerlies (35°–60°).

Jupiter the fifth planet from the Sun, and the largest in the Solar System (equatorial diameter 88,700 mi/142,800 km), with a mass more than twice that of all the other planets combined, 318 times that of the Earth's. It takes 11.86 years to orbit the Sun, at an average distance of 484 million mi/778 million km, and has at least 16 moons. It is largely composed of hydrogen and helium, liquefied by pressure in its interior, and probably with a rocky core larger than the Earth. Its main feature is the Great Red Spot, a cloud of rising gases, revolving counterclockwise, 8,500 mi/14,000 km wide and some 20,000 mi/30,000 km long.

K-T boundary geologists' shorthand for the boundary between the rocks of the Cretaceous and the Tertiary periods 65 million years ago. It marks the extinction of the dinosaurs and in many places reveals a layer of iridium, possibly deposited by a meteorite that may have caused the extinction by its impact.

karyotype in biology, the set of chromosomes characteristic of a given species. It is described as the number, shape, and size of the chromosomes in a single cell of an organism. In humans for example, the karyotype consists of 46 chromosomes, in mice 40, crayfish 200, and in fruit flies 8.

ketone member of the group of organic compounds containing the carbonyl group (C=O) bonded to two atoms of carbon (instead of one carbon and one hydrogen as in aldehydes). Ketones are liquids or low-melting-point solids, slightly soluble in water.

kinetic theory theory describing the physical properties of matter in terms of the behavior—principally movement—of its component atoms or molecules. The temperature of a substance is dependent on the velocity of movement of its constituent particles, increased temperature being accompanied by increased movement. A gas consists of rapidly moving atoms or molecules and, according to kinetic theory, it is their continual impact on the walls of the containing vessel that accounts for the pressure of the gas. The slowing of molecular motion as temperature falls, according to kinetic theory, accounts for the physical properties of liquids and solids, culminating in the concept of no molecular motion at absolute zero (0K/−460°F).

lactic acid or *2-hydroxypropanoic acid* CH3CHOHCOOH organic acid, a colorless, almost odorless liquid, produced by certain bacteria during fermentation and by active muscle cells when they are exercised hard and are experiencing oxygen debt.

lagoon coastal body of shallow salt water, usually with limited access to the sea. The term is normally used to describe the shallow sea area cut off by a coral reef or barrier islands.

landslide sudden downward movement of a mass of soil or rocks from a cliff or steep slope. Landslides happen when a slope becomes unstable, usually because the base has been undercut or because materials within the mass have become wet and slippery.

larva stage between hatching and adulthood in those species in which the young have a different appearance and way of life from the adults. Examples include tadpoles (frogs) and caterpillars (butterflies and moths).

laser (acronym for *light amplification by stimulated emission of radiation*) a device for producing a narrow beam of light, capable of traveling over vast distances without dispersion, and of being focused to give enormous power densities (10^8 watts per cm^2 for high-energy lasers). The laser operates on a principle similar to that of the maser (a high-frequency microwave amplifier or oscillator). The uses of lasers include communications (a laser beam can carry much more information than can radio waves), cutting, drilling, welding, satellite tracking, medical and biological research, and surgery.

latitude and longitude imaginary lines used to locate position on the globe. Lines of latitude are drawn parallel to the equator, with 0° at the equator and 90° at the north and south poles. Lines of longitude are drawn at right angles to these, with 0° (the Prime Meridian) passing through Greenwich, England.

Laurasia northern land mass formed 200 million years ago by the splitting of the single world continent Pangaea. (The southern land mass was Gondwanaland.) It consisted of what was to become North America, Greenland, Europe, and Asia, and is believed to have broken up about 100 million years ago with the separation of North America from Europe.

lava molten rock that erupts from a volcano and cools to form extrusive igneous rock. It differs from magma in that it is molten rock on the surface; magma is molten rock below the surface. Lava that is high in silica is viscous and sticky and does not flow far; it forms a steep-sided conical volcano. Low-silica lava can flow for long distances and forms a broad flat volcano.

leaching process by which substances are washed out of the soil. Fertilizers leached out of the soil drain into rivers, lakes, and ponds and cause water pollution. In tropical areas, leaching of the soil after the destruction of forests removes scarce nutrients and can lead to a dramatic loss of soil fertility. The leaching of soluble minerals in soils can lead to the formation of distinct soil horizons as different minerals are deposited at successively lower levels.

leaf lateral outgrowth on the stem of a plant, and in

most species the primary organ of photosynthesis. The chief leaf types are cotyledons (seed leaves), scale leaves (on underground stems), foliage leaves, and bracts (in the axil of which a flower is produced). A simple leaf is undivided, as in the maple or oak. A compound leaf is composed of several leaflets, as in the blackberry, horse chestnut, or ash (the latter being a pinnate leaf). Leaves that fall in the autumn are termed deciduous, while evergreen leaves are persistent.

lens in optics, a piece of a transparent material, such as glass, with two polished surfaces—one concave or convex, and the other plane, concave, or convex—that modifies rays of light. A convex lens brings rays of light together; a concave lens makes the rays diverge. Lenses are essential to glasses, microscopes, telescopes, cameras, and almost all optical instruments.

lepton any of a class of light elementary particles that are not affected by the strong nuclear force; they do not interact strongly with other particles or nuclei. The leptons are comprised of the electron, muon, and tau, and their neutrinos (the electron neutrino, muon neutrino, and tau neutrino), plus their six antiparticles.

lever simple machine consisting of a rigid rod pivoted at a fixed point called the fulcrum, used for shifting or raising a heavy load or applying force in a similar way. Levers are classified into orders according to where the effort is applied, and the load-moving force developed, in relation to the position of the fulcrum.

life cycle in biology, the sequence of developmental stages through which members of a given species pass. Most vertebrates have a simple life cycle consisting of fertilization of sex cells or gametes, a period of development as an embryo, a period of juvenile growth after hatching or birth, an adulthood including sexual reproduction, and finally death. Invertebrate life cycles are generally more complex and may involve major reconstitution of the individual's appearance (metamorphosis) and completely different styles of life. Plants have a special type of life cycle with two distinct phases, known as alternation of generations. Many insects such as cicadas, dragonflies, and mayflies have a long larvae or pupae phase and a short adult phase. Dragonflies live an aquatic life as larvae and an aerial life during the adult phase. In many invertebrates and protozoa there is a sequence of stages in the life cycle, and in parasites different stages often occur in different host organisms.

light electromagnetic waves in the visible range, having a wavelength from about 400 nanometers in the extreme violet to about 770 nanometers in the extreme red. Light is considered to exhibit particle and wave properties, and the fundamental particle, or quantum, of light is called the photon. The speed of light (and of all electromagnetic radiation) in a vacuum is approximately 186,000 mi/300,000 km per second, and is a universal constant denoted by c.

light-year in astronomy, the distance traveled by a beam of light in a vacuum in one year, approximately 9.46 trillion (million million) km/5.88 trillion miles.

linear equation in mathematics, a relationship between two variables that, when plotted on Cartesian axes produces a straight-line graph; the equation has the general form $y = mx + c$, where m is the slope of the line represented by the equation and c is the y-intercept, or the value of y where the line crosses the y-axis in the Cartesian coordinate system. Sets of linear equations can be used to describe the behavior of buildings, bridges, trusses, and other static structures.

lipid any of a large number of esters of fatty acids, commonly formed by the reaction of a fatty acid with glycerol (see glycerides). They are soluble in alcohol but not in water. Lipids are the chief constituents of plant and animal waxes, fats, and oils.

lithosphere topmost layer of the Earth's structure, forming the jigsaw of plates that take part in the movements of plate tectonics. The lithosphere comprises the crust and a portion of the upper mantle. It is regarded as being rigid and moves about on the semimolten asthenosphere. The lithosphere is about 47 mi/75 km thick.

litmus dye obtained from various lichens and used in chemistry as an indicator to test the acidic or alkaline nature of aqueous solutions; it turns red in the presence of acid, and blue in the presence of alkali.

Local Group in astronomy, a cluster of about 30 galaxies that includes our own, the Milky Way. Like other groups of galaxies, the Local Group is held together by the gravitational attraction among its members, and does not expand with the expanding universe. Its two largest galaxies are the Milky Way and the Andromeda galaxy; most of the others are small and faint.

locus in mathematics, traditionally the path traced out by a moving point, but now defined as the set of all points on a curve satisfying given conditions. For example, the locus of a point that moves so that it is always at the same distance from another fixed point is a circle; the locus of a point that is always at the same distance from two fixed points is a straight line that perpendicularly bisects the line joining them.

logarithm or log the exponent or index of a number to a specified base—usually 10. For example, the logarithm to the base 10 of 1,000 is 3 because $10^3 = 1,000$; the logarithm of 2 is 0.3010 because $2 = 10^{0.3010}$. Before the advent of cheap electronic calculators, multiplication and division could be simplified by being replaced with the addition and subtraction of logarithms.

lone pair in chemistry, a pair of electrons in the outermost shell of an atom that are not used in bonding. In certain circumstances, they will allow the atom to bond with atoms, ions, or molecules (such as boron trifluoride, BF3) that are deficient in electrons, forming coordinate covalent (dative) bonds in which they provide both of the bonding electrons.

luminescence emission of light from a body when its atoms are excited by means other than raising its temperature. Short-lived luminescence is called fluorescence.

Magellanic Clouds in astronomy, the two galaxies nearest to our own galaxy. They are irregularly shaped, and appear as detached parts of the Milky Way, in the southern constellations Dorado and Tucana.

magma molten rock material beneath the Earth's surface from which igneous rocks are formed. Lava is magma that has reached the surface and solidified, losing some of its components on the way.

magnetosphere volume of space, surrounding a planet, controlled by the planet's magnetic field, and acting as a magnetic "shell". The Earth's magnetosphere extends 40,000 mi/64,000 km toward the Sun, but many times this distance on the side away from the Sun.

magnetism phenomena associated with magnetic fields. Magnetic fields are produced by moving charged particles: in electromagnets, electrons flow through a coil of wire connected to a battery; in permanent magnets, spinning electrons within the atoms generate the field.

magnetic storm in meteorology, a sudden disturbance affecting the Earth's magnetic field, causing anomalies in radio transmissions and magnetic compasses. It is probably caused by sunspot activity.

magnitude in astronomy, measure of the brightness of a star or other celestial object. The larger the number denoting the magnitude, the fainter the object. Zero or first magnitude indicates some of the brightest stars. Still brighter are those of negative magnitude, such as Sirius, whose magnitude is −1.46. *Apparent magnitude* is the brightness of an object as seen from Earth; *absolute magnitude* is the brightness at a standard distance of 10 parsecs (32.6 light-years).

mammal animal characterized by having mammary glands in the female; these are used for suckling the young. Other features of mammals are hair (very reduced in some species, such as whales); a middle ear formed of three small bones (ossicles); a lower jaw consisting of two bones only; seven vertebrae in the neck; and no nucleus in the red blood cells.

mantle intermediate zone of the Earth between the crust and the core, accounting for 82% of the Earth's volume. It is thought to consist of silicate minerals such as olivine.

Mars fourth planet from the Sun, average distance 141.6 million mi/227.9 million km. It revolves around the Sun in 687 Earth days, and has a rotation period of 24 hr 37 min. It is much smaller than Venus or Earth, with a diameter 4,210 mi/6,780 km, and mass 0.11 that of Earth. Mars is slightly pearshaped, with a low, level northern hemisphere, which is comparatively uncratered and geologically "young", and a heavily cratered "ancient" southern hemisphere.

mass in physics, the quantity of matter in a body as measured by its inertia. Mass determines the acceleration produced in a body by a given force acting on it, the acceleration being inversely proportional to the mass of the body. The mass also determines the force exerted on a body by gravity on Earth, although this attraction varies slightly from place to place. In the SI system, the base unit of mass is the kilogram.

mass extinction an event that produced the extinction of many species at about the same time. One notable example is the boundary between the Cretaceous and Tertiary periods (known as the K-T boundary) that saw the extinction of the dinosaurs and other big reptiles, and many of the marine invertebrates as well. Mass extinctions have taken place several times during Earth's history.

matrix in mathematics, a square ($n \times n$) or rectangular ($m \times n$) array of elements (numbers or algebraic variables). They are a means of condensing information about mathematical systems and can be used for, among other things, solving simultaneous linear equations and transformations.

maximum and minimum in coordinate geometry, points at which the slope of a curve representing a function changes from positive to negative (maximum), or from negative to positive (minimum). A tangent to the curve at a maximum or minimum has zero gradient.

mean in mathematics, a measure of the average of a number of terms or quantities. The simple *arithmetic mean* is the average value of the quantities, that is, the sum of the quantities divided by their number. The weighted mean takes into account the frequency of the terms that are summed; it is calculated by multiplying each term by the number of times it occurs, summing the results and dividing this total by the total number of occurrences. The *geometric mean* of n quantities is the *n*th root of their product. In statistics, it is a measure of central tendency of a set of data.

meander loop-shaped curve in a river flowing across flat country. As a river flows, any curve in its course is accentuated by the current. The current is fastest on the outside of the curve where it cuts into the bank; on the curve's inside the current is slow and deposits any transported material.

mechanics branch of physics dealing with the motions of bodies and the forces causing these motions, and also with the forces acting on bodies in equilibrium. It is usually divided into dynamics and statics.

meiosis a process of cell division in which the number of chromosomes in the cell is halved. It only occurs in eukaryotic cells, and is part of a life cycle that involves sexual reproduction because it allows the genes of two parents to be combined without the total number of chromosomes increasing.

Mercury in astronomy, the closest planet to the Sun, at an average distance of 36 million mi/58 million km. Its diameter is 3,030 mi/4,880 km, its mass 0.056 that of Earth. Mercury orbits the Sun every 88 days, and spins on its axis every 59 days. On its sunward side the surface temperature reaches over 752°F/400°C, but on the "night" side it falls to -274°F/-170°C. Mercury has an atmosphere with minute traces of argon and helium. In 1974 the US space probe *Mariner 10* discovered that its surface is cratered by meteorite impacts. Mercury has no moons. Its largest known feature is the Caloris Basin, 870 mi/1,400 km wide. There are also cliffs hundreds of miles long and up to 2.5 mi/4 km high, thought to have been formed by the cooling of the planet billions of years ago. Inside is an iron core three-quarters of the planet's diameter, which produces a magnetic field 1% the strength of the Earth's.

meridian half a great circle drawn on the Earth's surface passing through both poles and thus through all places with the same longitude. Terrestrial longitudes are usually measured from the Greenwich Meridian.

meson in physics, an unstable subatomic particle made up of two indivisible elementary particles called quarks. It has a mass intermediate between that of the electron and that of the proton, is found in cosmic radiation, and is emitted by nuclei under bombardment by very high-energy particles.

mesosphere layer in the Earth's atmosphere above the stratosphere and below the thermosphere. It lies between about 31 mi/50 km and 50 mi/80 km above the ground.

Mesozoic era of geological time 245–65 million years ago, consisting of the Triassic, Jurassic, and Cretaceous periods. At the beginning of the era, the continents were joined together as Pangaea; dinosaurs and other giant reptiles dominated the sea and air; and ferns, horsetails, and cycads thrived in a warm climate worldwide. By the end of the Mesozoic era, the continents had begun to assume their present positions, flowering plants were dominant, and many of the large reptiles and marine fauna were becoming extinct.

metal any of a class of chemical elements with certain chemical characteristics (metallic character) and physical properties: they are good conductors of heat and electricity; opaque but reflect light well; malleable, which enables them to be coldworked and rolled into sheets; and ductile, which permits them to be drawn into thin wires.

metamorphism geological term referring to the changes in rocks of the Earth's crust caused by increasing pressure and temperature. The resulting rocks are metamorphic rocks. All metamorphic changes take place in solid rocks. If the rocks melt and then harden, they become igneous rocks.

metamorphosis period during the life cycle of many invertebrates, most amphibians, and some fish, during which the individual's body changes from one form to another through a major reconstitution of its tissues. For example, adult frogs are produced by metamorphosis from tadpoles, and butterflies are produced from caterpillars following metamorphosis within a pupa.

meteor flash of light in the sky, popularly known as a *shooting* or *falling star*, caused by a particle of dust, a meteoroid, entering the atmosphere at speeds up to 45 mps/70 kps and burning up by friction at a height of around 60 mi/100 km. On any clear night, several *sporadic meteors* can be seen each hour.

meteorite piece of rock or metal from space that reaches the surface of the Earth, Moon, or other body. Most meteorites are thought to be fragments from asteroids, although some may be pieces from the heads of comets. Most are stony, although some are made of iron and a few have a mixed rock-iron composition. Meteorites provide evidence for the nature of the Solar System and may be similar to the Earth's core and mantle, neither of which can be observed directly. Thousands of meteorites hit the Earth each year, but most fall in the sea or in remote areas and are never recovered. Meteorites are slowed down by the Earth's atmosphere, but if they are moving fast enough they can form a crater on impact. Meteor Crater in Arizona, about 4,000 ft/1,200 m in diameter and 650 ft/200 m deep, is the site of a meteorite impact about 50,000 years ago.

meteorology scientific observation and study of the atmosphere, so that weather can be accurately forecast. Data from meteorological stations and weather satellites are collated by computer at central agencies, and forecast and weather maps based on current readings are issued at regular intervals. Modern analysis can give useful forecasts for up to six days ahead.

microorganism or *microbe* living organism invisible to the naked eye but visible under a microscope. Microorganisms include viruses and single-celled organisms such as bacteria, protozoa, yeasts, and some algae. The study of microorganisms is known as microbiology.

Milky Way faint band of light crossing the night sky, consisting of stars in the plane of our Galaxy. The name Milky Way is often used for the Galaxy itself. It is a spiral galaxy, about 100,000 light-years in diameter, containing at least 100 billion stars. The Sun is in one of its spiral arms, about 25,000 light-years from the center.

Mira or *Omicron Ceti* brightest long-period pulsating variable star, located in the constellation Cetus. Mira was the first star discovered to vary periodically in brightness.

mirror any polished surface that reflects light; often made from "silvered" glass (in practice, a mercury-alloy coating of glass). A plane (flat) mirror produces a same-size, erect "virtual" image located behind the mirror at the same distance from it as the object is in front of it. A spherical concave mirror produces a reduced, inverted real image in front or an enlarged, erect virtual image behind it (as in a shaving mirror), depending on how close the object is to the mirror. A spherical convex mirror produces a reduced, erect virtual image behind it (as in a car's rear-view mirror).

mitochondria (singular *mitochondrion*) membrane-enclosed organelles within eukaryotic cells, containing enzymes responsible for energy production during aerobic respiration. These rodlike or spherical bodies are thought to be derived from free-living bacteria that, at a very early stage in the history of life, invaded larger cells and took up a symbiotic way of life inside. Each still contains its own small loop of DNA called mitochondrial DNA, and new mitochondria arise by division of existing ones.

mixture in chemistry, a substance containing two or more compounds that still retain their separate physical and chemical properties. There is no chemical bonding between them and they can be separated from each other by physical means.

modulus a number that divides exactly into the difference between two given numbers. Also, the multiplication factor used to convert a logarithm of one base to a logarithm of another base. Also, another name for absolute value.

Mohorovičić discontinuity also *Moho* or *M-discontinuity* boundary that separates the Earth's crust and mantle, marked by a rapid increase in the speed of earthquake waves. It follows the variations in the thickness of the crust and is found approximately 20 mi/ 32 km below the continents and about 6 mi/10 km below the oceans.

molecular biology study of the molecular basis of life, including the biochemistry of molecules such as DNA, RNA, and proteins, and the molecular structure and function of the various parts of living cells.

molecular clock use of rates of mutation in genetic material to calculate the length of time elapsed since two related species diverged from each other during evolution. The method can be based on comparisons of the DNA or of widely occurring proteins, such as hemoglobin.

molecule group of two or more atoms bonded together. A molecule of an element consists of one or more like atoms; a molecule of a compound consists of two or more different atoms bonded together. Molecules vary in size and complexity from the hydrogen molecule (H_2) to the large macromolecules of proteins. They are held together by ionic bonds, in which the atoms gain or lose electrons to form ions, or by covalent bonds, where electrons from each atom are shared in a new molecular orbital. The symbolic representation of a molecule is known as its formula. The presence of more than one atom is denoted by a subscript figure—for example, one molecule of the compound water, having two atoms of hydrogen and one atom of oxygen, is shown as H_2O.

monsoon wind pattern that brings seasonally heavy rain to S Asia; it blows toward the sea in winter and toward the land in summer. The monsoon may cause destructive flooding all over India and SE Asia from April to Sept.

month unit of time based on the motion of the Moon around the Earth. The time from one new or full Moon to the next (the *synodic* or *lunar* month) is 29.53 days. The time for the Moon to complete one orbit around the Earth relative to the stars (the *sidereal* month) is 27.32 days. The *solar* month equals 30.44 days, and is exactly one-twelfth of the solar or tropical year, the time taken for the Earth to orbit the Sun.

Moon natural satellite of Earth, 2,160 mi/3,476 km in diameter, with a mass 0.012 (approximately one-eightieth) that of Earth. Its surface gravity is only 0.16 (one-sixth) that of Earth. Its average distance from Earth is 238,855 mi/384,400 km, and it orbits in a west-to-east direction every 27.32 days (the *sidereal* month). It spins on its axis with one side permanently turned toward Earth. The Moon has no atmosphere or water.

moon in astronomy, any natural satellite that orbits a planet. Mercury and Venus are the only planets in the Solar System that do not have moons.

moraine rocky debris or till carried along and deposited by a glacier. Material eroded from the side of a glaciated valley and carried along the glacier's edge is called lateral moraine; that worn from the valley floor and carried along the base of the glacier is called ground moraine. Rubble dropped at the foot of a melting glacier is called terminal moraine.

muscle contractile animal tissue that produces locomotion and maintains the movement of body substances. Muscle is made of long cells that can contract to between one-half and one-third of their relaxed length.

mutation in biology, a change in the genes produced by a change in the DNA that makes up the hereditary material of all living organisms. Mutations, the raw material of evolution, result from mistakes during replication (copying) of DNA molecules. Only a few improve the organism's performance and are therefore favored by natural selection. Mutation rates are increased by certain chemicals and by radiation.

nadir the point on the celestial sphere vertically below the observer and hence diametrically opposite the zenith.

natural gas mixture of flammable gases found in the Earth's crust (often in association with petroleum), now one of the world's three main fossil fuels (with coal and oil). Natural gas is a mixture of hydrocarbons, chiefly methane, with ethane, butane, and propane.

natural selection the process whereby gene frequencies in a population change through certain individuals producing more descendants than others because they are better able to survive and reproduce in their environment. The accumulated effect of natural selection is to produce adaptations such as the insulating coat of a polar bear or the spadelike forelimbs of a mole. The process is slow, relying firstly on random variation in the genes of an organism being produced by mutation and secondly on the genetic recombination of sexual reproduction. It was recognized by Charles Darwin and Alfred Russel Wallace as the main process driving evolution.

nebula cloud of gas and dust in space. Nebulae are the birthplaces of stars, but some nebulae are produced by gas thrown off from dying stars (see planetary nebula; supernova). Nebulae are classified depending on whether they emit, reflect, or absorb light.

neo-Darwinism the modern theory of evolution, built up since the 1930s by integrating Darwin's theory of evolution through natural selection with the theory of genetic inheritance founded on the work of Gregor Mendel.

Neptune the eighth planet in average distance from the Sun. Neptune orbits the Sun every 164.8 years at an average distance of 2.794 billion mi/4.497 billion km. It is a giant gas (hydrogen, helium, methane) planet, with a diameter of 30,200 mi/48,600 km and a mass 17.2 times that of Earth. Its rotation period is 16 hours 7 minutes. The methane in its atmosphere absorbs red light and gives the planet a blue coloring. It is believed to have a central rocky core covered by a layer of ice. Neptune has eight known moons.

nervous system the system of interconnected nerve cells of most invertebrates and all vertebrates. It is composed of the central and autonomic nervous systems. It may be as simple as the nerve net of coelenterates (for example, jellyfishes) or as complex as the mammalian nervous system, with a central nervous system comprising brain and spinal cord, and a peripheral nervous system connecting up with sensory organs, muscles, and glands.

neutralization in chemistry, a process occurring when the excess acid (or excess base) in a substance is reacted with added base (or added acid) so that the resulting substance is neither acidic nor basic.

neutrino in physics, any of three uncharged elementary particles (and their antiparticles) of the lepton class, having a mass too close to zero to be measured. The most familiar type, the antiparticle of the electron neutrino, is emitted in the beta decay of a nucleus. The other two are the muon neutrino and the tau neutrino.

neutron one of the three chief subatomic particles (the others being the proton and the electron). Neutrons have about the same mass as protons but no electric charge, and occur in the nuclei of all atoms except hydrogen. They contribute to the mass of atoms but do not affect their chemistry, which depends on the proton or electron numbers. For instance, isotopes of a single element (with different masses) differ only in the number of neutrons in their nuclei and have identical chemical properties.

neutron star very small, "superdense" star composed mostly of neutrons. They are thought to form when massive stars explode as supernovae, during which the protons and electrons of the star's atoms merge, owing to intense gravitational collapse, to make neutrons. A neutron star may have the mass of up to three Suns, compressed into a globe only 12 mi/20 km in diameter.

Newton's laws of motion in physics, three laws that form the basis of Newtonian mechanics. (1) Unless acted upon by a net force, a body at rest stays at rest, and a moving body continues moving at the same speed in the same straight line. (2) A net force applied to a body gives it a rate of change of momentum proportional to the force and in the direction of the force. (3) When a body A exerts a force on a body B, B exerts an equal and opposite force on A; that is, to every action there is an equal and opposite reaction.

niche in ecology, the "place" occupied by a species in its habitat, including all chemical, physical, and biological components, such as what it eats, the time of day at which the species feeds, temperature, moisture, the parts of the habitat that it uses (for example, trees or open grassland), the way it reproduces, and how it behaves.

nitrate any salt of nitric acid, containing the $NO_3=$ ion. Nitrates are used as inorganic fertilizers. They are the most water-soluble salts known.

nitric acid or *aqua fortis* HNO_3 fuming acid obtained by the oxidation of ammonia or the action of sulfuric acid on potassium nitrate. It is a highly corrosive acid, dissolving most metals, and a strong oxidizing agent. It is used in the nitration and esterification of organic substances, and in the making of sulfuric acid, nitrates, explosives, plastics, and dyes.

nitrogen colorless, odorless, tasteless, gaseous, nonmetallic element, symbol N, atomic number 7, atomic weight 14.0067. It forms almost 80% of the Earth's atmosphere by volume and is a constituent of all plant and animal tissues (in proteins and nucleic acids). Nitrogen is obtained for industrial use by the liquefaction and fractional distillation of air. Its compounds are used in the manufacture of foods, drugs, fertilizers, dyes, and explosives.

nitrogen cycle the process of nitrogen passing through the ecosystem. Nitrogen, in the form of inorganic compounds (such as nitrates) in the soil, is absorbed by plants and turned into organic compounds (such as proteins) in plant tissue. A proportion of this nitrogen is eaten by herbivores, with some of this in turn being passed on to the carnivores, which feed on the herbivores. The nitrogen is ultimately returned to the soil as excrement and when organisms die and are converted back to inorganic form by decomposers.

nonmetal one of a set of elements (around 20 in total) with certain physical and chemical properties opposite to those of metals. Nonmetals accept electrons and are sometimes called electronegative elements.

nova (plural *novae*) faint star that suddenly erupts in brightness by 10,000 times or more. Novae are believed to occur in close binary star systems, where gas from one star flows to a companion white dwarf. The gas ignites and is thrown off in an explosion at speeds of 930 mps/1,500 kps or more. Unlike a supernova, the star is not completely disrupted by the outburst. After a few weeks or months it subsides to its previous state; it may erupt many more times.

nuclear energy energy from the inner core or nucleus of the atom, as opposed to energy released in chemical processes, which is derived from the electrons surrounding the nucleus. *Nuclear fusion* is the release of thermonuclear energy by the conversion of hydrogen nuclei to helium nuclei, a continuing reaction in the Sun and other stars. Nuclear fusion is the principle behind thermonuclear weapons (the hydrogen bomb). Attempts to harness fusion for commercial power production have so far not succeeded.

nuclear fission process whereby an atomic nucleus breaks up into two or more major fragments with the emission of two or three neutrons. It is accompanied by the release of energy in the form of gamma radiation and the kinetic energy of the emitted particles.

nuclear fusion process whereby two atomic nuclei are fused, with the release of a large amount of energy. Very high temperatures and pressures are thought to be required in order for the process to happen. Under these conditions the atoms involved are stripped of all their electrons so that the remaining particles, which together make up plasma, can come close together at very high speeds and overcome the mutual repulsion of the positive charges on the atomic nuclei. At very close range another nuclear force will come into play, fusing the particles together to form a larger nucleus. As fusion is accompanied by the release of large amounts of energy, the process might one day be harnessed to form the basis of commercial energy production. Methods of achieving controlled fusion are therefore the subject of research around the world.

nuclear waste the radioactive and toxic byproducts of the nuclear-energy and nuclear-weapons industries. Nuclear waste may have an active life of several thousand years. Disposal, by burial on land or at sea, has raised problems of safety, environmental pollution, and security. In absolute terms, nuclear waste cannot be safely relocated or disposed of.

nucleotide organic compound consisting of a purine (adenine or guanine) or a pyrimidine (thymine, uracil, or cytosine) base linked to a sugar (deoxyribose or ribose) and a phosphate group. DNA and RNA are made up of long chains of nucleotides.

nucleus in biology, the central, membrane-enclosed part of a eukaryotic cell, containing the chromosomes.

nucleus in physics, the positively charged central part of an atom, which constitutes almost all its mass. Except for hydrogen nuclei, which have only protons, nuclei are composed of both protons and neutrons. Surrounding the nuclei are electrons, which contain a negative charge equal to the protons, thus giving the atom a neutral charge.

number symbol used in counting or measuring. In mathematics, there are various kinds of numbers. The everyday number system is the decimal ("proceeding by tens") system, using the base ten. *Real numbers* include all rational numbers (integers, or whole numbers, and fractions) and irrational numbers (those not expressible as fractions). *Complex numbers* include the real and unreal numbers (real-number multiples of the square root of –1). The binary number system, used in computers, has two as its base. The ordinary numerals, 0, 1, 2, 3, 4, 5, 6, 7, 8, and 9, give a counting system that, in the decimal system, continues 10, 11, 12, 13, and so on. These are whole numbers (integers), with fractions represented as, for example, $\frac{1}{4}$, $\frac{1}{2}$, $\frac{3}{4}$, or as decimal fractions (0.25, 0.5, 0.75). They are also rational numbers. Irrational numbers cannot be represented in this way and require symbols, such as $\sqrt{2}$, and e. They can be expressed numerically only as the (inexact) approximations 1.414, 3.142 and 2.718 (to three places of decimals) respectively. The symbols and e are also examples of transcendental numbers, because they (unlike $\sqrt{2}$) cannot be derived by solving a polynomial equation (an equation with one variable quantity) with rational coefficients (multiplying factors). Complex numbers take the general form $a + bi$, where $i = \sqrt{1}$ (that is, $i^2 = -1$), and a is the real part and bi the unreal part.

nutation in astronomy, a slight "nodding" of the Earth in space, caused by the varying gravitational pulls of the Sun and Moon. Nutation changes the angle of the Earth's axial tilt (average 23.5°) by about 9 seconds of arc to either side of its mean position, a complete cycle taking just over 18.5 years.

occultation in astronomy, the temporary obscuring of a star by a body in the Solar System. Occultations are used to provide information about changes in an orbit, and the structure of objects in space, such as radio sources.

oceanography study of the oceans, their origin, composition, structure, history, and wildlife (seabirds, fish, plankton, and other organisms).

ocean ridge mountain range on the seabed indicating the presence of a constructive plate margin (where tectonic plates are moving apart and magma rises to the surface). Ocean ridges, such as the Mid-Atlantic Ridge, consist of many segments offset along faults, and can rise thousands of meters above the surrounding seabed.

ocean trench deep trench in the seabed indicating the presence of a destructive margin (produced by the movements of plate tectonics). The subduction or dragging downward of one plate of the lithosphere beneath another means that the ocean floor is pulled down. Ocean trenches are found around the edge of the Pacific Ocean and the NE Indian Ocean; minor ones occur in the Caribbean and near the Falkland Islands.

oil flammable substance, usually insoluble in water, and composed chiefly of carbon and hydrogen. Oils may be solids (fats and waxes) or liquids. The three main types are: *essential oils*, obtained from plants; *fixed oils*, obtained from animals and plants; and *mineral oils*, obtained chiefly from the refining of petroleum.

omnivore animal that feeds on both plant and animal material. Omnivores have digestive adaptations intermediate between those of herbivores and carnivores, with relatively unspecialized digestive systems and gut microorganisms that can digest a variety of foodstuffs.

Oort cloud spherical cloud of comets beyond Pluto, extending out to about 100,000 astronomical units (1.5 light-years) from the Sun. The gravitational effect of passing stars and the rest of our Galaxy disturbs comets from the cloud so that they fall in toward the Sun on highly elongated orbits, becoming visible from Earth. As many as 10 trillion comets may reside in the Oort cloud, named after Dutch astronomer Jan Oort who postulated it in 1950.

ooze sediment of fine texture consisting mainly of organic matter found on the ocean floor at depths greater than 6,600 ft/2,000 m. Several kinds of ooze exist, each named after its constituents.

operon group of genes that are found next to each other on a chromosome, and are turned on and off as an integrated unit. They usually produce enzymes that control different steps in the same biochemical pathway.

opposition in astronomy, the moment at which a body in the Solar System lies opposite the Sun in the sky as seen from the Earth and crosses the meridian at about midnight.

optics branch of physics that deals with the study of light and vision—for example, shadows and mirror images, lenses, microscopes, telescopes, and cameras.

orbit path of one body in space around another, such as the orbit of Earth around the Sun, or the Moon around Earth. When the two bodies are similar in mass, as in a binary star, both bodies move around their common center of mass.

ordinal number in mathematics, one of the series first, second, third, fourth, ... Ordinal numbers relate to order, whereas cardinal numbers (1, 2, 3, 4, ...) relate to quantity, or count.

ordinate in coordinate geometry, the y coordinate of a point; that is, the vertical distance of the point from the horizontal or x-axis. For example, a point with the coordinates (3,4) has an ordinate of 4.

Ordovician period of geological time 510–439 million years ago; the second period of the Paleozoic era. Animal life was confined to the sea: reef-building algae and the first jawless fish are characteristic.

organic chemistry branch of chemistry that deals with carbon compounds. Organic compounds form the chemical basis of life and are more abundant than inorganic compounds. In a typical organic compound, each carbon atom forms bonds covalently with each of its neighboring carbon atoms in a chain or ring, and additionally with other atoms, commonly hydrogen, oxygen, nitrogen, or sulfur.

origin the point where the x-axis meets the y-axis. The coordinates of the origin are (0,0).

Orion nebula luminous cloud of gas and dust 1,500 light-years away, in the constellation Orion, from which stars are forming. It is about 15 light-years in diameter, and contains enough gas to make a cluster of thousands of stars.

oscillating universe in astronomy, a theory that states that the gravitational attraction of the mass within the universe will eventually slow down and stop the expansion of the universe. The outward motions of the galaxies will then be reversed, eventually resulting in a "Big Crunch" where all the matter in the universe would be contracted into a small volume of high density. This could undergo a further Big Bang, thereby creating another expansion phase. The theory suggests that the universe would alternately expand and collapse through alternate Big Bangs and Big Crunches.

ovum (plural *ova*) female gamete (sex cell) before fertilization. In animals it is called an egg, and is produced in the ovaries. In plants, where it is also known as an egg cell or oosphere, the ovum is produced in an ovule. The ovum is nonmotile. It must be fertilized by a male gamete before it can develop further, except in cases of parthenogenesis.

oxidation in chemistry, the loss of electrons, gain of oxygen, or loss of hydrogen by an atom, ion, or molecule during a chemical reaction.

oxygen colorless, odorless, tasteless, nonmetallic, gaseous element, symbol O, atomic number 8, atomic weight 15.9994. It is the most abundant element in the Earth's crust (almost 50% by mass), forms about 21% by volume of the atmosphere, and is present in combined form in water and many other substances. Life on Earth evolved using oxygen, which is a by-product of photosynthesis and the basis for respiration in plants and animals.

ozone O_3 highly reactive pale-blue gas with a penetrating odor. Ozone is an allotrope of oxygen made up of three atoms of oxygen. It is formed when the molecule of the stable form of oxygen (O_2) is split by ultraviolet radiation or electrical discharge. It forms a thin layer in the upper atmosphere, which protects life on Earth from ultraviolet rays, a cause of skin cancer. At lower atmospheric levels it is an air pollutant and contributes to the greenhouse effect.

paleontology in geology, the study of ancient life that encompasses the structure of ancient organisms and their environment, evolution, and ecology, as revealed by their fossils. The practical aspects of paleontology are based on using the presence of different fossils to date particular rock strata and to identify rocks that were laid down under particular conditions, for instance giving rise to the formation of oil.

Paleozoic era of geological time 570–245 million years ago. It comprises the Cambrian, Ordovician, Silurian, Devonian, Carboniferous, and Permian periods. The Cambrian, Ordovician, and Silurian constitute the Lower or Early Paleozoic; the Devonian, Carboniferous, and Permian make up the Upper or Late Paleozoic. The era includes the evolution of hard-shelled multicellular life forms in the sea; the invasion of land by plants and animals; and the evolution of fish, amphibians, and early reptiles. The earliest identifiable fossils date from this era.

Pangaea or *Pangea* single land mass, made up of all the present continents, believed to have existed between 250 and 200 million years ago; the rest of the Earth was covered by the Panthalassa ocean. Pangaea split into two land masses–Laurasia in the north and Gondwanaland in the south–which subsequently broke up into several continents. These then drifted slowly to their present positions.

Panthalassa ocean that covered the surface of the Earth not occupied by the world continent Pangaea between 250 and 200 million years ago.

parabola in mathematics, a curve formed by cutting a right circular cone with a plane parallel to the sloping side of the cone. A parabola is one of the family of curves known as conic sections. The graph of $y = x^2$ is a parabola.

parallel lines and parallel planes in mathematics, straight lines or planes that always remain a constant distance from one another no matter how far they are extended. This is a principle of Euclidean geometry. Some non Euclidean geometries, such as elliptical and hyperbolic geometry, however, reject Euclid's parallel axiom.

parallax the change in the apparent position of an object against its background when viewed from two different positions. In astronomy, nearby stars show a shift owing to parallax when viewed from different positions on the Earth's orbit around the Sun. A star's parallax is used to deduce its distance.

parallelogram in mathematics, a quadrilateral (four-sided plane figure) with opposite pairs of sides equal in length and parallel, and opposite angles equal. The diagonals of a parallelogram bisect each other.

Its area is the product of the length of one side and the perpendicular distance between this and the opposite side. In the special case when all four sides are equal in length, the parallelogram is known as a rhombus, and when the internal angles are right angles, it is a rectangle or square.

parsec in astronomy, a unit (symbol pc) used for distances to stars and galaxies. One parsec is equal to 3.2616 light-years, 2.063×10^5 astronomical units, and 3.086×10^{13} km.

parthenogenesis development of an ovum (egg) without any genetic contribution from a male. Parthenogenesis is the normal means of reproduction in a few plants (for example, dandelions) and animals (for example, certain fish). Some sexually reproducing species, such as aphids, show parthenogenesis at some stage in their life cycle. In most cases, there is no sperm contribution of any kind, but in some the stimulus of being penetrated by a sperm is needed by the egg to start dividing, although the male's chromosomes are not combined with those of the female. Parthenogenesis can be artificially induced in many animals (such as sea urchins and rabbits) by cooling, pricking, or applying acid to an egg.

peptide molecule comprising two or more amino acid molecules (not necessarily different) joined by *peptide* bonds, whereby the acid group of one acid is linked to the amino group of the other (–CO.NH). The number of amino acid molecules in the peptide is indicated by referring to it as a di-, tri-, or polypeptide (two, three, or many amino acids).

percentage way of representing a number as a fraction of 100. Thus 45 percent (45%) equals 45/100, and 45% of 20 is $\frac{45}{100} \times 20 = 9$.

perigee the point at which an object, traveling in an elliptical orbit around the Earth, is at its closest to the Earth. The point at which it is furthest from the Earth is the apogee.

perihelion the point at which an object, traveling in an elliptical orbit around the Sun, is at its closest to the Sun. The point at which it is furthest from the Sun is the aphelion.

perimeter or *boundary* line drawn around the edge of an area or shape. For example, the perimeter of a rectangle is the sum of its four sides; the perimeter of a circle is known as its *circumference*.

periodic table of the elements classification of the elements to reflect the periodic law, namely that the properties of the chemical elements recur periodically when the elements are arranged in increasing order of their atomic number and are shown in related groups. Today's arrangement is by atomic numbers; the original tables were set up by atomic weights (masses). There are similarities in the chemical properties of the elements in each of the main vertical groups and a gradation of properties along the horizontal periods. The periods correspond to the filling of successive electron shells, and the groups correspond to the number of valence electrons.

permafrost condition in which a deep layer of soil does not thaw out during the summer. Permafrost occurs under periglacial conditions. It is claimed that 26% of the world's land surface is permafrost.

Permian period of geological time 290–245 million years ago, the last period of the Paleozoic era. Its end was marked by a significant change in marine life, including the extinction of many corals and trilobites. Deserts were widespread, and terrestrial amphibians and mammallike reptiles flourished. Cone-bearing plants (gymnosperms) came to prominence.

permutation in mathematics, a specified arrangement of a group of objects. It is the arrangement of *a* distinct objects taken *b* at a time in all possible orders. It is given by $a!/(a-b)!$, where "!" stands for factorial. For example, the number of permutations of four letters taken from any group of six different letters is $6!/2! = (1 \times 2 \times 3 \times 4 \times 5 \times 6)/(1 \times 2) = 360$. The theoretical number of four-letter "words" that can be made from an alphabet of 26 letters is $26!/22! = 358{,}800$.

perpendicular in mathematics, at a right angle; also, a line at right angles to another or to a plane. For a pair of skew lines (lines in three dimensions that do not meet), there is just one common perpendicular, which is at right angles to both lines; the nearest points on the two lines are the feet of this perpendicular.

pesticide any chemical used in farming, gardening or indoors to combat pests. Pesticides are of three main types: *insecticides* (to kill insects), *fungicides* (to kill fungal diseases), and *herbicides* (to kill plants, mainly those considered weeds). Pesticides cause a number of pollution problems through spray drift onto surrounding areas, direct contamination of users or the public, and as residues on food. The safest pesticides are those made from plants, such as the insecticides pyrethrum and derris.

petroleum or *crude oil* natural mineral oil, a thick greenish-brown flammable liquid found underground in permeable rocks. Petroleum consists of hydrocarbons mixed with oxygen, sulfur, nitrogen, and other elements in varying proportions. It is thought to be derived from ancient organic material that has been converted by, first, bacterial action, then heat and pressure (but its origin may be chemical also). From crude petroleum, various products are made by distillation and other processes; for example, fuel oil, gasoline, kerosene, diesel, lubricating oil, paraffin wax, and petroleum jelly.

petrology branch of geology that deals with the study of rocks, their mineral compositions, and their origins.

pH scale from 0 to 14 for measuring acidity or alkalinity. A pH of 7.0 indicates neutrality, below 7 is acid, while above 7 is alkaline. Strong acids, such as those used in car batteries, have a pH of about 2; strong alkalis such as sodium hydroxide are pH 13. The pH value of a solution equals the negative logarithm of the concentration of hydrogen ions.

Phanerozoic eon in Earth history, consisting of the most recent 570 million years. It comprises the Paleozoic, Mesozoic, and Cenozoic eras. The vast majority of fossils come from this eon, owing to the evolution of hard shells and internal skeletons. The name means "interval of well-displayed life".

phenol member of a group of aromatic chemical compounds with weakly acidic properties, which are characterized by a hydroxyl (OH) group attached directly to an aromatic ring. The simplest of the phenols, derived from benzene, is also known as phenol and has the formula C_6H_5OH. It is sometimes called *carbolic acid* and can be extracted from coal tar.

phenotype in genetics, visible traits, those actually displayed by an organism. The phenotype is not a direct reflection of the genotype because some alleles are masked by the presence of other, dominant alleles (see dominance). The phenotype is further modified by the effects of the environment (for example, poor nutrition stunts growth).

Phobos one of the two moons of Mars, discovered 1877 by the US astronomer Asaph Hall (1829–1907). It is an irregularly shaped lump of rock, cratered by meteorite impacts. Phobos is $17 \times 13 \times/27 \times 22 \times 19$ km 12 mi across, and orbits Mars every 0.32 days at a distance of 5,840 mi/9,400 km from the planet's center. It is thought to be an asteroid captured by Mars' gravity.

phosphate salt or ester of phosphoric acid. Incomplete neutralization of phosphoric acid gives rise to acid phosphates (see acid salts and buffer). Phosphates are used as fertilizers, and are required for the development of healthy root systems. They are involved in many biochemical processes, often as part of complex molecules, such as ATP.

photon the elementary particle or "package" (quantum) of energy in which light and other forms of electromagnetic radiation are emitted. The photon has both particle and wave properties; it has no charge, is considered massless but possesses momentum and energy. It is one of the gauge bosons, a particle that cannot be subdivided, and is the carrier of the electromagnetic force, one of the fundamental forces of nature.

photosphere visible surface of the Sun, which emits light and heat. About 200 mi/300 km deep, it consists of incandescent gas at a temperature of 5,800K (9,980°F/5,530°C).

photosynthesis process by which green plants trap light energy and use it to drive a series of chemical reactions, leading to the formation of carbohydrates. All animals ultimately depend on photosynthesis because it is the method by which the basic food (sugar) is created. For photosynthesis to occur, the plant must possess chlorophyll and must have a supply of carbon dioxide and water. Actively photosynthesizing green plants store excess sugar as starch (this can be tested for in the laboratory using iodine).

physical chemistry branch of chemistry concerned with examining the relationships between the chemical compositions of substances and the physical properties that they display. Most chemical reactions exhibit some physical phenomenon (change of state, temperature, pressure, or volume, or the use or production of electricity), and the measurement and study of such phenomena has led to many chemical theories and laws.

plain or *grassland* land, usually flat, upon which grass predominates. The plains cover large areas of the Earth's surface, especially between the deserts of the tropics and the rainforests of the equator, and have rain in one season only.

planet large celestial body in orbit around a star, composed of rock, metal, or gas. There are nine planets in the Solar System: Mercury, Venus, Earth, Mars, Jupiter, Saturn, Neptune, Uranus, and Pluto. The inner four, called the *terrestrial planets*, are small and rocky, and include the planet Earth. The outer planets, with the exception of Pluto, are called the giant planets, large balls of rock, liquid, and gas; the largest is Jupiter, which contains more than twice as much mass as all the other planets combined. Planets do not produce light, but reflect the light of their parent star.

planetary nebula shell of gas thrown off by a star at the end of its life. Planetary nebulae have nothing to do with planets. They were named by William Herschel, who thought their rounded shape resembled the disk of a planet. After a star such as the Sun has expanded to become a red giant, its outer layers are ejected into space to form a planetary nebula, leaving the core as a white dwarf at the centre.

plant organism that carries out photosynthesis, has cellulose cell walls and complex cells, and is immobile. A few parasitic plants have lost the ability to photosynthesize but are still considered to be plants. Plants are autotrophs, that is, they make carbohydrates from water and carbon dioxide, and are the primary producers in all food chains, so that all animal life is dependent on them. They play a vital part in the carbon cycle, removing carbon dioxide from the atmosphere and generating oxygen. The study of plants is known as botany.

plateau elevated area of fairly flat land, or a mountainous region in which the peaks are at the same height. An *intermontane plateau* is one surrounded by mountains. A *piedmont plateau* is one that lies between the mountains and low-lying land. A *continental plateau* rises abruptly from low-lying lands or the sea.

plate tectonics theory formulated in the 1960s to explain the phenomena of continental drift and seafloor spreading, and the formation of the major physical features of the Earth's surface. The Earth's outermost layer is regarded as a jigsaw of rigid major and minor plates up to 62 mi/100 km thick, which move relative to each other, probably under the influence of convection currents in the mantle beneath. Major landforms occur at the margins of the plates, where plates are colliding or moving apart — for example, volcanoes, fold mountains, ocean trenches, and ocean ridges.

Pluto the smallest and, usually, outermost planet of the Solar System. The existence of Pluto was predicted by calculation by Percival Lowell and the planet was located by Clyde Tombaugh in 1930. It orbits the Sun every 248.5 years at an average distance of 3.6 billion mi/5.8 billion km. Its highly elliptical orbit occasionally takes it within the orbit of Neptune, as in 1979–99. Pluto has a diameter of about 1,400 mi/2,300 km, and a mass about 0.002 of that of Earth. It is of low density, composed of rock and ice, with frozen methane on its surface and a thin atmosphere. Charon, Pluto's moon, was discovered 1978, revolving around Pluto with the same period as Pluto's rotation, remaining over the same point on Pluto's surface and showing the same face. The pair may be a double planet system.

Polaris or *Pole Star* or *North Star* the bright star closest to the north celestial pole, and the brightest star in the constellation Ursa Minor. Its position is indicated by the "pointers" in Ursa Major. Polaris is a yellow supergiant about 500 light-years away.

polder area of flat reclaimed land that used to be covered by a river, lake, or the sea. Polders have been artificially drained and protected from flooding by building dykes.

pole either of the geographic north and south points of the axis about which the Earth rotates. The geographic poles differ from the magnetic poles, which are the points toward which a freely suspended magnetic needle will point.

pollen the grains of seed plants that contain the male gametes. In angiosperms (flowering plants) pollen is produced within anthers; in most gymnosperms (cone-bearing plants) it is produced in male cones. A pollen grain is typically yellow and, when mature, has a hard outer wall. Pollen of insect-pollinated plants is often sticky and spiny and larger than the smooth, light grains produced by wind-pollinated species.

polyester synthetic resin formed by the condensation of polyhydric alcohols (alcohols containing more than one hydroxyl group) with dibasic acids (acids containing two replaceable hydrogen atoms). Polyesters are thermosetting plastics, used in making synthetic fibers, such as Dacron and Terylene, and constructional plastics. With fiberglass added as reinforcement, polyesters are used in car bodies and boat hulls.

polygon in geometry, a plane (two-dimensional) figure with three or more straight-line sides. Common polygons have names which define the number of sides (for example, triangle, quadrilateral, pentagon).

polyhedron in geometry, a solid figure with four or more plane faces. The more faces there are on a polyhedron, the more closely it approximates to a sphere. Knowledge of the properties of polyhedra is needed in crystallography and stereochemistry to determine the shapes of crystals and molecules. There are only five types of regular polyhedron (with all faces the same size and shape), as was deduced by early Greek mathematicians; they are the tetrahedron (four equilateral triangular faces), cube (six square faces), octahedron (eight equilateral triangles), dodecahedron (12 regular pentagons) and icosahedron (20 equilateral triangles).

polymer compound made up of a large long-chain or branching matrix composed of many repeated simple units (*monomers*). There are many polymers, both natural (cellulose, chitin, lignin) and synthetic (polyethylene and nylon, types of plastic). Synthetic polymers belong to two groups: thermosoftening and thermosetting.

polyunsaturate type of fat or oil containing a high proportion of triglyceride molecules whose fatty-acid chains contain several double bonds. By contrast, the fatty-acid chains of the triglycerides in saturated fats (such as lard) contain only single bonds.

potential, electric in physics, the relative electrical state of an object. A charged conductor, for example, has a higher potential than the Earth, whose potential is taken by convention to be zero. An electric cell (battery) has a potential in relation to emf (electromotive force), which can make current flow in an external circuit. The difference in potential between two points –the potential difference – is expressed in volts; that is, a 12 V battery has a potential difference of 12 volts between its negative and positive terminals.

power in physics, the rate of doing work or consuming energy. It is measured in watts (joules per second) or other units of work per unit time.

Precambrian in geology, the time from the formation of Earth (4.6 billion years ago) up to 570 million years ago. Its boundary with the succeeding Cambrian period marks the time when animals first developed hard outer parts (exoskeletons) and so left abundant fossil remains. It comprises about 85% of geological time and is divided into two periods: the Archaean, in which no life existed, and the Proterozoic, in which there was life in some form.

precession slow wobble of the Earth on its axis, like that of a spinning top. The gravitational pulls of the Sun and Moon on the Earth's equatorial bulge cause the Earth's axis to trace out a circle on the sky every 25,800 years. The position of the celestial poles (see celestial sphere) is constantly changing owing to precession, as are the positions of the equinoxes (the points at which the celestial equator intersects the Sun's path around the sky). The precession of the equinoxes means that there is a gradual westward drift in the ecliptic—the path that the Sun appears to follow— and in the coordinates of objects on the celestial sphere.

precipitation in chemistry, the formation of an insoluble solid in a liquid as a result of a reaction within the liquid between two or more soluble substances. If the solid settles, it forms a precipitate; if the particles of solid are very small, they will remain in suspension, forming a colloidal precipitate (see colloid).

pressure in physics, the force acting normally (at right angles) to a body per unit surface area. The SI unit of pressure is the pascal (newton per square meter), equal to 0.01 millibars. In a fluid (liquid or gas), pressure increases with depth. At the edge of Earth's atmosphere, pressure is zero, whereas at sea level atmospheric pressure due to the weight of the air above is about 100 kilopascals (1,013 millibars or 1 atmosphere). Pressure is commonly measured by means of a barometer, manometer, or Bourdon gauge.

prime number a number that can be divided only by 1 or itself, that is, having no other factors. There is an infinite number of primes, the first ten of which are 2, 3, 5, 7, 11, 13, 17, 19, 23, and 29 (by definition, the number 1 is excluded from the set of prime numbers). The number 2 is the only even prime because all other even numbers have 2 as a factor.

prism in mathematics, a solid figure whose cross section is constant in planes drawn perpendicular to its axis. A cube, for example, is a rectangular prism with all faces (bases and sides) the same shape and size.

probability likelihood, or chance, that an event will occur, often expressed as odds, or in mathematics, numerically as a fraction or decimal. In general, the probability that n particular events will happen out of a total of m possible events is n/m. A certainty has a probability of 1; an impossibility has a probability of 0. Empirical probability is defined as the number of successful events divided by the total possible number of events.

progression sequence of numbers each formed by a specific relationship to its predecessor. An *arithmetic progression* has numbers that increase or decrease by a common sum or difference (for example, 2, 4, 6, 8); a *geometric progression* has numbers each bearing a fixed ratio to its predecessor (for example, 3, 6, 12, 24); and a *harmonic progression* has numbers whose reciprocals are in arithmetical progression, for example 1, $^1/_2$, $^1/_3$, $^1/_4$.

prokaryote an organism whose cells lack organelles (specialized segregated structures such as nuclei, mitochondria, and chloroplasts). Prokaryote DNA is not arranged in chromosomes but forms a coiled structure called a *nucleoid*. The prokaryotes comprise only the *bacteria* and *cyanobacteria*; all other organisms are eukaryotes.

prominence bright cloud of gas projecting from the Sun into space 60,000 mi/100,000 km or more. *Quiescent prominences* last for months, and are held in place by magnetic fields in the Sun's corona. *Surge prominences* shoot gas into space at speeds of 600 mps/1,000 kps. *Loop prominences* are gases falling back to the Sun's surface after a solar flare.

proper motion gradual change in the position of a star that results from its motion in orbit around our galaxy, the Milky Way. Proper motions are slight and undetectable to the naked eye, but can be accurately measured on telescopic photographs taken many years apart. Barnard's Star is the star with the largest proper motion, 10.3 arc seconds per year.

proportion two variable quantities x and y are proportional if, for all values of x, $y = kx$, where k is a constant. This means that if x increases, y increases in a linear fashion.

protein complex, biologically important substance composed of amino acids joined by peptide bonds. Other types of bonds, such as sulfur–sulfur bonds, hydrogen bonds, and cation bridges between acid sites, are responsible for creating the protein's characteristic three-dimensional structure, which may be fibrous, globular, or pleated.

protein engineering the creation of synthetic proteins designed to carry out specific tasks. For example, an enzyme may be designed to remove grease from soiled clothes and remain stable at the high temperatures in a washing machine.

Proterozoic eon of geological time, possible 3.5 billion to 570 million years ago, the second division of the Precambrian. It is defined as the time of simple life, since many rocks dating from this eon show traces of biological activity, and some contain the fossils of bacteria and algae.

protist a single-celled organism which has a eukaryotic cell, but which is not a member of the plant, fungal, or animal kingdoms. The main protists are protozoa.

proton positively charged elementary particle, a constituent of the nucleus of all atoms. It belongs to the baryon group of hadrons and is composed of two up quarks and one down quark. A proton is extremely long-lived, with a life span of at least 10^{32} years. It carries a unit positive charge equal to the negative charge of an electron. Its mass is almost 1,836 times that of an electron, or 1.673×10^{-24} g. The number of protons in the atom of an element is equal to the atomic number of that element.

protozoa group of single-celled organisms without rigid cell walls. Some, such as ameba, ingest other cells, but most are saprotrophs or parasites. The group is polyphyletic (containing organisms which have different evolutionary origins).

Proxima Centauri the closest star to the Sun, 4.2 light-years away. It is a faint red dwarf, visible only with a telescope, and is a member of the Alpha Centauri triple-star system.

pteridophyte simple type of vascular plant. The pteridophytes comprise four classes: the Psilosida, including the most primitive vascular plants, found mainly in the tropics; the Lycopsida, including the club mosses; the Sphenopsida, including the horsetails; and the Pteropsida, including the ferns. They do not produce seeds.

pulsar celestial source that emits pulses of energy at regular intervals, ranging from a few seconds to a few thousandths of a second. Pulsars are thought to be rapidly rotating neutron stars, which flash at radio and other wavelengths as they spin. Over 500 radio pulsars are now known in our Galaxy, although a million or so may exist.

punctuated equilibrium model evolutionary theory developed by Niles Eldridge and US paleontologist Stephen Jay Gould 1972 to explain discontinuities in the fossil record. It claims that periods of rapid change alternate with periods of relative stability (stasis), and that the appearance of new lineages is a separate process from the gradual evolution of adaptive changes within a species.

pupa nonfeeding, largely immobile stage of some insect life cycles, in which larval tissues are broken down, and adult tissues and structures are formed.

pyramid in geometry, a three-dimensional figure with triangular side-faces meeting at a common vertex (point) and with a polygon as its base. The volume V of a pyramid is given by $V = 1/3Bh$, where B is the area of the base and h is the perpendicular height.

the Pythagorean theorem in geometry, a theorem stating that in a right triangle, the area of the square on the hypotenuse (the longest side) is equal to the sum of the areas of the squares drawn on the other two sides. If the hypotenuse is h units long and the lengths of the other sides are a and b, then $h^2 = a^2 + b^2$.

quadratic equation in mathematics, a polynomial equation of second degree (that is, an equation containing as its highest power the square of a variable, such as x^2). The general formula of such equations is $ax^2 + bx + c = 0$, in which a, b, and c are real numbers, and only the coefficient a cannot equal 0. In coordinate geometry, a quadratic function represents a parabola.

quantum chromodynamics (QCD) in physics, a theory describing the interactions of quarks, the elementary particles that make up all hadrons (subatomic particles such as protons and neutrons). In quantum chromodynamics, quarks are considered to interact by exchanging particles called gluons, which carry the strong nuclear force, and whose role is to "glue" quarks together. The mathematics involved in the theory is complex, and although a number of successful predictions have been made, as yet the theory does not compare in accuracy with quantum electrodynamics, upon which it is modeled.

quantum electrodynamics (QED) a theory describing the interaction of charged subatomic particles within electric and magnetic fields. It combines quantum theory and relativity, and considers charged particles to interact by the exchange of photons. QED is remarkable for the accuracy of its predictions—for example, it has been used to calculate the value of some physical quantities to an accuracy of ten decimal places, a feat equivalent to calculating the distance between New York and Los Angeles to within the thickness of a hair.

quantum theory or *quantum mechanics* in physics, the theory that energy does not have a continuous range of values, but is, instead, absorbed or radiated discontinuously, in multiples of definite, indivisible units called quanta. Just as earlier theory showed how light, generally seen as a wave motion, could also in some ways be seen as composed of discrete particles (photons), quantum theory shows how atomic particles such as electrons may also be seen as having wavelike properties. Quantum theory is the basis of particle physics, modern theoretical chemistry, and the solid-state physics that describes the behavior of the silicon chips used in computers.

quark the elementary particle that is the fundamental constituent of all hadrons (baryons, such as neutrons and protons, and mesons). There are six types, or "flavors": up, down, top, bottom, strange, and charm, each of which has three varieties, or "colors": red, yellow, and blue (visual color is not meant, although the analogy is useful in many ways). To each quark there is an antiparticle, called an antiquark.

quasar (from *quasi-stellar* object or QSO) one of the most distant extragalactic objects known. Quasars appear starlike, but each emits more energy than 100 giant galaxies. They are thought to be at the center of galaxies, their brilliance emanating from the stars and gas falling toward an immense black hole at their nucleus.

Quaternary period of geological time that began 1.64 million years ago and is still in process. It is divided into the Pleistocene and Holocene epochs.

radian SI unit (symbol rad) of plane angles, an alternative unit to the degree. It is the angle at the center of a circle when the center is joined to the two ends of an arc (part of the circumference) equal in length to the radius of the circle. There are 2π (approximately 6.284) radians in a full circle (360°).

radiation in physics, emission of radiant energy as particles or waves—for example, heat, light, alpha particles, and beta particles.

radio transmission and reception of radio waves. In radio transmission a microphone converts sound waves (pressure variations in the air) into electromagnetic waves that are then picked up by a receiving aerial and fed to a loudspeaker, which converts them back into sound waves.

radioactivity spontaneous alteration of the nuclei of radioactive atoms, accompanied by the emission of radiation. It is the property exhibited by the radioactive isotopes of stable elements and all isotopes of radioactive elements, and can be either natural or induced.

radio galaxy galaxy that is a strong source of electromagnetic waves of radio wavelengths. All galaxies, including our own, emit some radio waves, but radio galaxies are up to a million times more powerful.

radioisotope (contraction of radioactive isotope) a naturally occurring or synthetic radioactive form of an element. Most radioisotopes are made by bombarding a stable element with neutrons in the core of a nuclear reactor. The radiations given off by radioisotopes are easy to detect (hence their use as tracers), can in some instances penetrate substantial thicknesses of materials, and have profound effects (such as genetic mutation) on living matter. Although dangerous, radioisotopes are used in the fields of medicine, industry, agriculture, and research. Most natural isotopes of atomic mass below 208 are not radioactive. Those from 210 and up are all radioactive.

radio telescope instrument for detecting radio waves from the universe in radio astronomy. Radio telescopes usually consist of a metal bowl that collects and focuses radio waves the way a concave mirror collects and focuses light waves. Radio telescopes are much larger than optical telescopes, because the wavelengths they are detecting are much longer than the wavelength of light. The largest single dish is 1,000 ft/305 m across, at Arecibo, Puerto Rico.

radon colorless, odorless, gaseous, radioactive, non-metallic element, symbol Rn, atomic number 86, atomic weight 222. It is grouped with the inert gases and was formerly considered non-reactive, but is now known to form some compounds with fluorine. Of the 20 known isotopes, only three occur in nature; the longest halflife is 3.82 days.

rain form of precipitation in which separate drops of water fall to the Earth's surface from clouds. The drops are formed by the accumulation of fine droplets that condense from water vapor in the air. The condensation is usually brought about by rising and subsequent cooling of air.

rainforest dense forest usually found on or near the equator where the climate is hot and wet. Heavy rainfall results as the moist air brought by the converging tradewinds rises because of the heat. Over half the tropical rainforests are in Central and South America, the rest in SE Asia and Africa. They provide the bulk of the oxygen needed for plant and animal respiration. Tropical rainforest once covered 14% of the Earth's land surface, but are now being destroyed at an increasing rate as their valuable timber is harvested and the land cleared for agriculture, causing problems of deforestation. Although by 1991 over 50% of the world's rainforest had been removed, they still comprise about 50% of all growing wood on the planet, and harbor at least 40% of the Earth's species (plants and animals).

rate of reaction the speed at which a chemical reaction proceeds. It is usually expressed in terms of the concentration (usually in moles per liter) of a reactant consumed, or product formed, in unit time; so the units would be moles per liter per second (mol l^{-1} s^{-1}). The rate of a reaction may be affected by the concentration of the reactants, the temperature of the reactants, and the presence of a catalyst. If the reaction is entirely in the gas state, the rate is affected by pressure, and, for solids, it is affected by the particle size.

ratio measure of the relative size of two quantities or of two measurements (in similar units), expressed as a proportion. For example, the ratio of vowels to consonants in the alphabet is 5:21; the ratio of 500 m to 2 km is 500:2,000, or 1:4.

reactivity series chemical series produced by arranging the metals in order of their ease of reaction with reagents such as oxygen, water, and acids. This arrangement aids the understanding of the properties of metals, helps to explain differences between them, and enables predictions to be made about a metal's behavior, based on a knowledge of its position or properties.

reciprocal in mathematics, the result of dividing a given quantity into 1. Thus the reciprocal of 2 is $^1/_2$; of $^2/_3$ is $^3/_2$; of x^2 is $^1/x^2$ or x^{-2}. Reciprocals are used to replace division by multiplication, since multiplying by the reciprocal of a number is the same as dividing by that number.

rectangle quadrilateral (four-sided plane figure) with opposite sides equal and parallel and with each interior angle a right angle (90°). Its area A is the product of the length l and height h; that is, $A = l \times h$. A rectangle with all four sides equal is a square.

red dwarf any star that is cool, faint, and small (about one-tenth the mass and diameter of the Sun). Red dwarfs burn slowly, and have estimated lifetimes of 100 billion years. They may be the most abundant type of star, but are difficult to see because they are so faint. Two of the closest stars to the Sun, Proxima Centauri and Barnard's Star, are red dwarfs.

red giant any large bright star with a cool surface. It is thought to represent a late stage in the evolution of a star like the Sun, as it runs out of hydrogen fuel at its center. Red giants have diameters between 10 and 100 times that of the Sun. They are very bright because they are so large, although their surface temperature is lower than that of the Sun, about 2,000–3,000K (3,100–4,900°C).

redox reaction chemical change where one reactant is reduced and the other reactant oxidized. The reaction can only occur if both reactants are present and each changes simultaneously. For example, hydrogen reduces copper(II) oxide to copper while it is itself oxidized to water. The corrosion of iron and the reactions taking place in electric and electrolytic cells are just a few instances of redox reactions.

red shift in astronomy, the lengthening of the wavelengths of light from an object as a result of the object's motion away from us. It is an example of the Doppler effect. The red shift in light from galaxies is evidence that the universe is expanding.

reduction in chemistry, the gain of electrons, loss of oxygen, or gain of hydrogen by an atom, ion, or molecule during a chemical reaction.

reflection the throwing back or deflection of waves, such as light or sound waves, when they hit a surface. The law of reflection states that the angle of incidence (the angle between the ray and a perpendicular line drawn to the surface) is equal to the angle of reflection (the angle between the reflected ray and a perpendicular to the surface).

refraction the bending of a wave of light, heat, or sound when it passes from one medium to another. Refraction occurs because waves travel at different velocities in different media.

relativity in physics, the theory of the relative rather than absolute character of motion and mass, and the interdependence of matter, time, and space, as developed by German physicist Albert Einstein in two phases: *special theory* (1905) Starting with the premises that (1) the laws of nature are the same for all observers in unaccelerated motion, and (2) the speed of light is independent of the motion of its source, Einstein postulated that the time interval between two events was longer for an observer in whose frame of reference the events occur in different places than for the observer for whom they occur at the same place. General Theory of Relativity (1915) The geometrical properties of spacetime were to be conceived as modified locally by the presence of a body with mass. A planet's orbit around the Sun (as observed in three-dimensional space) arises from its natural trajectory in modified space-time; there is no need to invoke, as Isaac Newton did, a force of gravity coming from the Sun and acting on the planet. Einstein's theory predicted slight differences in the orbits of the planets from Newton's theory, which were observable in the case of Mercury. The new theory also said light rays should bend when they pass by a massive object, owing to the object's effect on local spacetime. The predicted bending of starlight was observed during the eclipse of the Sun 1919, when light from distant stars passing close to the Sun was not masked by sunlight.

reproduction process by which a living organism produces other organisms similar to itself. There are two kinds: asexual reproduction and sexual reproduction.

reptile any member of a class (Reptilia) of vertebrates. Unlike amphibians, reptiles have hardshelled, yolk-filled eggs that are laid on land and from which fully formed young are born. Some snakes and lizards retain their eggs and give birth to live young. Reptiles are coldblooded, produced from eggs, and the skin is usually covered with scales. The metabolism is slow, and in some cases (certain large snakes) intervals between meals may be months. Reptiles date back over 300 million years.

resistance in physics, that property of a substance that restricts the flow of electricity through it, associated with the conversion of electrical energy to heat; also the magnitude of this property. Resistance depends on many factors, such as the nature of the material, its temperature, dimensions, and thermal properties; degree of impurity; the nature and state of illumination of the surface; and the frequency and magnitude of the current. The SI unit of resistance is the ohm.

resonance rapid and uncontrolled increase in the size of a vibration when the vibrating object is subject to a force varying at its natural frequency. In a trombone, for example, the length of the air column in the instrument is adjusted until it resonates with the note being sounded. Resonance effects are also produced by many electrical circuits. Tuning a radio, for example, is done by adjusting the natural frequency of the receiver circuit until it coincides with the frequency of the radio waves falling on the aerial.

respiration biochemical process whereby food molecules are progressively broken down (oxidized) to release energy in the form of ATP. In most organisms this requires oxygen, but in some bacteria the oxidant is the nitrate or sulfate ion instead. In all higher organisms, respiration occurs in the mitochondria. Respiration is also used to mean breathing, although this is more accurately described as a form of gas exchange.

restriction enzyme bacterial enzyme that breaks a chain of DNA into two pieces at a specific point; used in genetic engineering. The point along the DNA chain at which the enzyme can work is restricted to

places where a specific sequence of base pairs occurs. Different restriction enzymes will break a DNA chain at different points. The overlap between the fragments is used in determining the sequence of base pairs in the DNA chain.

rhombus in geometry, an equilateral (all sides equal) parallelogram. Its diagonals bisect each other at right angles, and its area is half the product of the lengths of the two diagonals. A rhombus whose internal angles are 90° is called a square.

ribosome the protein-making machinery of the cell. Ribosomes are located on the endoplasmic reticulum of eukaryotic cells, and are made of proteins and a special type of RNA, ribosomal RNA. They receive messenger RNA (copied from the DNA) and amino acids, and "translate" the messenger RNA by using its chemically coded instructions to link amino acids in a specific order, to make a strand of a particular protein.

Richter scale scale based on measurement of seismic waves, used to determine the magnitude of an earthquake at its epicenter. The magnitude of an earthquake differs from its intensity, measured by the Mercalli scale, which is subjective and varies from place to place for the same earthquake. The scale is named after US seismologist Charles Richter.

rift valley valley formed by the subsidence of a block of the Earth's crust between two or more parallel faults. Rift valleys are steep-sided and form where the crust is being pulled apart, as at ocean ridges, or in the Great Rift Valley of E Africa.

right ascension in astronomy, the coordinate on the celestial sphere that corresponds to longitude on the surface of the Earth. It is measured in hours, minutes, and seconds eastward from the point where the Sun's path, the ecliptic, once a year intersects the celestial equator; this point is called the *vernal equinox*.

right triangle triangle in which one of the angles is a right angle (90°). It is the basic form of triangle for defining trigonometrical ratios (for example, sine, cosine, and tangent) and for which the Pythagorean theorem holds true.

RNA *ribonucleic acid* nucleic acid involved in the process of translating DNA, the genetic material into proteins. It is usually single-stranded, unlike the double-stranded DNA, and consists of a large number of nucleotides strung together, each of which comprises the sugar ribose, a phosphate group, and one of four bases (uracil, cytosine, adenine, or guanine). RNA is copied from DNA by the assemblage of free nucleotides against an unwound portion (a single strand) of the DNA, with DNA serving as the template. In this process, uracil (instead of the thymine in DNA) is paired with adenine, and guanine with cytosine, forming base pairs that then separate. The RNA then travels to the ribosomes where it serves to assemble proteins from free amino acids. In a few viruses, such as retroviruses, RNA is the only hereditary material.

root the part of a plant that is usually underground, and whose primary functions are anchorage and the absorption of water and dissolved mineral salts. Roots usually grow downward and toward water (that is, they are positively geotropic and hydrotropic). Plants such as epiphytic orchids, which grow above ground, produce aerial roots that absorb moisture from the atmosphere. Others, such as ivy, have climbing roots arising from the stems that serve to attach the plant to trees and walls.

salt in chemistry, any member of a group of compounds containing a positive ion (cation) derived from a metal or ammonia and a negative ion (anion) derived from an acid or nonmetal. If the negative ion has a replaceable hydrogen atom it is an acid salt (for example sodium hydrogensulfate, $NaHSO_4$; potassium phosphonate, KH_2PO_4; sodium hydrogencarbonate, $NaHCO_3$); if not, it is classed as a normal salt (for example sodium chloride, $NaCl$; potassium sulfate, K_2SO_4; magnesium nitrate, $Mg(NO_3)_2$). Common salt is sodium chloride. Salts have the properties typical of ionic compounds.

sand loose grains of rock, sized 0.0025–0.08 in/0.0625–2.00 mm in diameter, consisting chiefly of quartz, but owing their varying color to mixtures of other minerals.

satellite any small body that orbits a larger one, either natural or artificial. Natural satellites that orbit planets are called moons. Artificial satellites are used for scientific purposes, communications, weather forecasting, and military applications. The largest artificial satellites can be seen by the naked eye.

saturated compound organic compound, such as propane, that contains only single covalent bonds. Saturated organic compounds can only undergo further reaction by substitution reactions, as in the production of chloropropane from propane.

Saturn the second-largest planet in the Solar System, sixth from the Sun, and encircled by bright and easily visible equatorial rings. Viewed through a telescope it is ochre. Saturn orbits the Sun every 29.46 years at an average distance of 886,700,000 mi/1,427,000,000 km. Its equatorial diameter is 75,000 mi/120,000 km, but its polar diameter is 7,450 mi/12,000 km smaller, a result of its fast rotation and low density, the lowest of any planet. From Earth, Saturn's rings appear to be divided into three main sections. Ring A, the outermost, is separated from ring B, the brightest, by the Cassini division, 2,000 mi/3,000 km wide; the inner, transparent ring C is called the Crepe Ring. Each ringlet of the rings is made of a swarm of icy particles like snowballs, a few fractions of an inch to a few yards in diameter. Outside the A ring is the narrow and faint F ring, which the Voyagers showed to be twisted or braided. The rings of Saturn could be the remains of a shattered moon. They may always have existed in their present form.

scalar quantity in mathematics and science, a quantity that has magnitude but no direction, as distinct from a vector quantity, which has a direction as well as a magnitude. Temperature, mass, and volume are scalar quantities.

scarp and dip in geology, the two slopes formed when a sedimentary bed outcrops as a landscape feature. The scarp is the slope that cuts across the bedding plane; the dip is the opposite slope which follows the bedding plane. The scarp is usually steep, while the dip is a gentle slope.

seafloor spreading growth of the ocean crust outwards (sideways) from ocean ridges. The concept of seafloor spreading has been combined with that of continental drift and incorporated into plate tectonics.

sediment any loose material that has "settled"– deposited from suspension in water, ice, or air, generally as the water current or wind speed decreases. Typical sediments are, in order of increasing coarseness, clay, mud, silt, sand, gravel, pebbles, cobbles, and boulders.

semiconductor crystalline material with an electrical conductivity between that of metals (good) and insulators (poor). The conductivity of semiconductors can usually be improved by minute additions of different substances or by other factors.

sequencing in biochemistry, determining the sequence of chemical subunits within a large molecule.

Techniques for sequencing amino acids in proteins were established in the 1950s, insulin being the first for which the sequence was completed. Efforts are now being made to determine the sequence of base pairs within DNA.

set or *class* in mathematics, any collection of defined things (elements), provided the elements are distinct and that there is a rule to decide whether an element is a member of a set. It is usually denoted by a capital letter and indicated by curly brackets {}.

sexual reproduction reproductive process in organisms that requires the union, or fertilization, of gametes (such as eggs and sperm). These are usually produced by two different individuals, although self-fertilization occurs in a few hermaphrodites such as tapeworms. Most organisms other than bacteria and cyanobacteria (blue-green algae) show some sort of sexual process. Except in some lower organisms, the gametes are of two distinct types called eggs and sperm. The organisms producing the eggs are called females, and those producing the sperm, males. The fusion of a male and female gamete produces a zygote, from which a new individual develops. The alternatives to sexual reproduction are binary fission, budding, vegetative reproduction, parthenogenesis, and spore formation.

Seyfert galaxy galaxy whose small, bright center is caused by hot gas moving at high speed around a massive central object, possibly a black hole. Almost all Seyferts are spiral galaxies. They seem to be closely related to quasars, but are about 100 times fainter.

SI units (French *Système International d'Unités*) standard system of scientific units used by scientists worldwide. Originally proposed in 1960, it replaces the m.k.s., c.g.s., and f.p.s. systems. It is based on seven basic units: the meter (m) for length, kilogram (kg) for mass, second (s) for time, ampere (A) for electrical current, kelvin (K) for temperature, mole (mol) for amount of substance, and candela (cd) for luminosity.

sidereal period the orbital period of a planet around the Sun, or a moon around a planet, with reference to a background star. The sidereal period of a planet is in effect a "year".

significant figures the figures in a number that, by virtue of their place value, express the magnitude of that number to a specified degree of accuracy. The final significant figure is rounded up if the following digit is greater than 5. For example, 5,463,254 to three significant figures is 5,460,000; 3.462891 to four significant figures is 3.463; 0.00347 to two significant figures is 0.0035.

silicon brittle, nonmetallic element, symbol Si, atomic number 14, atomic weight 28.086. It is the second most abundant element (after oxygen) in the Earth's crust and occurs in amorphous and crystalline forms. In nature it is found only in combination with other elements, chiefly with oxygen in silica (silicon dioxide, SiO_2) and the silicates. These form the mineral quartz, which makes up most sands, gravels, and beaches.

simultaneous equations one of two or more algebraic equations that contain two or more unknown quantities that may have a unique solution. For example, in the case of two linear equations with two unknown variables, such as (i) $x + 3y = 6$ and (ii) $3y - 2x = 4$, the solution will be those unique values of x and y that are valid for both equations. Linear simultaneous equations can be solved by using algebraic manipulation to eliminate one of the variables, coordinate geometry, or matrices.

sine in trigonometry, a function of an angle in a right triangle which is defined as the ratio of the length of the side opposite the angle to the length of the hypotenuse (the longest side).

skeleton the rigid or semirigid framework that supports an animal's body, protects its internal organs, and provides anchorage points for its muscles. The skeleton may be composed of bone and cartilage (vertebrates), chitin (arthropods), calcium carbonate (mollusks and other invertebrates), or silica (many protists).

soil loose covering of broken rocky material and decaying organic matter overlying the bedrock of the Earth's surface. Various types of soil develop under different conditions: deep soils form in warm wet climates and in valleys; shallow soils form in cool dry areas and on slopes.

solar energy energy derived from the Sun's radiation. The amount of energy falling on just 0.3861 sq mi/1 sq km is about 4,000 megawatts, enough to heat and light a small town. In one second the Sun gives off 13 million times more energy than all the electricity used in the US in one year. *Solar heaters* have industrial or domestic uses. They usually consist of a black (heat-absorbing) panel containing pipes through which air or water, heated by the Sun, is circulated, either by thermal convection or by a pump. Solar energy may also be harnessed indirectly using *solar cells* (photovoltaic cells) made of panels of semiconductor material (usually silicon), which generate electricity when illuminated by sunlight. Although it is difficult to generate a high output from solar energy compared to sources such as nuclear or fossil fuels, it is a major nonpolluting and renewable energy source used as far north as Scandinavia as well as in the SW US and in Mediterranean countries.

Solar System the Sun (a star) and all the bodies orbiting it: the nine planets (Mercury, Venus, Earth, Mars, Jupiter, Saturn, Uranus, Neptune, and Pluto), their moons, the asteroids, and the comets. It is thought to have formed from a cloud of gas and dust in space about 4.6 billion years ago. The Sun contains 99% of the mass of the Solar System.

solar wind stream of atomic particles, mostly protons and electrons, from the Sun's corona, flowing outwards at speeds of between 200 mps/300 kps and 600 mps/1,000 kps.

solstice either of the points at which the Sun is farthest north or south of the celestial equator each year. The *summer solstice*, when the Sun is farthest north, occurs around June 21; the *winter solstice* around Dec 22.

solution two or more substances mixed to form a single, homogenous phase. One of the substances is the solvent and the others (solutes) are said to be dissolved in it.

solvent substance, usually a liquid, that will dissolve another substance. Although the commonest solvent is water, in popular use the term refers to low-boiling-point organic liquids, which are harmful if used in a confined space. They can give rise to respiratory problems, liver damage, and neurological complaints.

sound physiological sensation received by the ear, originating in a vibration (pressure variation in the air) that communicates itself to the air, and travels in every direction, spreading out as an expanding sphere. All sound waves in air travel with a speed dependent on the temperature; under ordinary conditions, this is about 1,070 ft/330 m per second. The pitch of the sound depends on the number of vibrations imposed on the air per second, but the speed is unaffected. The loudness of a sound is dependent primarily on the amplitude of the vibration of the air.

species a distinguishable group of organisms that resemble each other or consist of a few distinctive types (as in polymorphism), and that can all interbreed to produce fertile offspring.

speckle interferometry technique whereby large telescopes can achieve high resolution of astronomical objects despite the adverse effects of the atmosphere through which light from the object under study must pass. It involves the taking of large numbers of images, each under high magnification and with short exposure times. The pictures are then combined to form the final picture.

spectroscopy the study of spectra (obtained by the use of an optical instrument called a spectroscope) associated with atoms or molecules in solid, liquid, or gaseous phase. Spectroscopy can be used to identify unknown compounds and is an invaluable tool to scientists, industry (for example, pharmaceuticals for purity checks), and medical workers.

spectrum (plural *spectra*) an arrangement of frequencies or wavelengths when electromagnetic radiations are separated into their constituent parts. Visible light is part of the electromagnetic spectrum and most sources emit waves over a range of wavelengths that can be broken up or "dispersed"; white light can be separated into red, orange, yellow, green, blue, indigo, and violet.

speed the rate at which an object moves. The average speed v of an object may be calculated by dividing the distance s it has traveled by the time t taken to do so, and may be expressed as: $v = s/t$

sperm or *semen* the fluid containing the male gametes (sperm cells) of animals. Usually, each sperm cell has a head capsule containing a nucleus, a middle portion containing mitochondria (which provide energy), and a long tail (flagellum).

sphere in mathematics, a perfectly round object with all points on its surface the same distance from the centre. This distance is the radius of the sphere. For a sphere of radius r, the volume $V = {}^4/_3 r^3$ and the surface area $A = 4r^2$.

spicules, solar in astronomy, short-lived jets of hot gas in the upper chromosphere of the Sun. Spiky in appearance, they move at high velocities along lines of magnetic force to which they owe their shape, and last for a few minutes each. Spicules appear to disperse material into the corona.

spin in physics, the intrinsic angular momentum of a subatomic particle, nucleus, atom, or molecule, which continues to exist even when the particle comes to rest. A particle in a specific energy state has a particular spin, just as it has a particular electric charge and mass. According to quantum theory, this is restricted to discrete and indivisible values, specified by a spin quantum number. Because of its spin, a charged particle acts as a small magnet and is affected by magnetic fields.

square root in mathematics, a number that when squared (multiplied by itself) equals a given number. For example, the square root of 25 (written $\sqrt{25}$) is 5, because $5 \times 5 = 25$, and $(-5) \times (-5) = 25$. As an exponent, a square root is represented by $^1/_2$, for example, $16^{1/2} = 4$.

stalactite and stalagmite cave structures formed by the deposition of calcite dissolved in ground water. *Stalactites* grow downward from the roofs or walls and can be icicle-shaped, straw-shaped, curtain-shaped, or formed as terraces. *Stalagmites* grow upward from the cave floor and can be conical, fir-cone-shaped, or resemble a stack of saucers.

standard model in physics, the modern theory of elementary particles and their interactions. According to the standard model, elementary particles are classified as leptons (light particles, such as electrons), hadrons (particles, such as neutrons and protons, that are formed from quarks), and gauge bosons. Leptons and hadrons interact by exchanging gauge bosons, each of which is responsible for a different fundamental force: photons mediate the electromagnetic force, which affects all charged particles; gluons mediate the strong nuclear force, which affects quarks; gravitons mediate the force of gravity; and the weakons (intermediate vector bosons) mediate the weak nuclear force.

star luminous globe of gas, mainly hydrogen and helium, which produces its own heat and light by nuclear reactions. Although stars shine for a very long time—many billions of years—they are not eternal, and have been found to change in appearance at different stages in their lives.

star cluster group of related stars, usually held together by gravity. Members of a star cluster are thought to form together from one large cloud of gas in space. Open clusters such as the Pleiades contain from a dozen to many hundreds of young stars, loosely scattered over several light-years. Globular clusters are larger and much more densely packed, containing perhaps 100,000 old stars.

tarch widely distributed, high-molecular-mass carbohydrate, produced by plants as a food store; main dietary sources are cereals, legumes, and tubers, including potatoes. It consists of varying proportions of two glucose polymers (polysaccharides): straight-chain (amylose) and branched (amylopectin) molecules.

states of matter forms (solid, liquid, or gas) in which material can exist. Whether a material is solid, liquid, or gas depends on its temperature and the pressure on it. The transition between states takes place at definite temperatures, called melting point and boiling point.

statics branch of mechanics concerned with the behavior of bodies at rest and forces in equilibrium, and distinguished from dynamics.

statistics branch of mathematics concerned with the collection and interpretation of data. Probability is the branch of statistics dealing with predictions of events.

stratigraphy branch of geology that deals with the sequence of formation of sedimentary rock layers and the conditions under which they were formed.

stress and strain in the science of materials, measures of the deforming force applied to a body (stress) and of the resulting change in its shape (strain). For a perfectly elastic material, stress is proportional to strain (Hooke's law).

sublimation in chemistry, the conversion of a solid to vapor without passing through the liquid phase.

sucrose or cane sugar or beet sugar $C_{12}H_{22}O_{10}$ a sugar found in the pith of sugar cane and in sugar beets. It is popularly known as sugar.

sulfur brittle, pale-yellow, nonmetallic element, symbol S, atomic number 16, atomic weight 32.064. It occurs in three allotropic forms: two crystalline (called rhombic and monoclinic, following the arrangements of the atoms within the crystals) and one amorphous. It burns in air with a blue flame and a stifling odor. Insoluble in water but soluble in carbon disulfide, it is a good electrical insulator. Sulfur is widely used in the manufacture of sulfuric acid (used to treat phosphate rock to make fertilizers) and in making paper, matches, gunpowder and fireworks, in vulcanizing rubber, and in medicines and insecticides.

sulfur dioxide SO_2 pungent gas produced by burning sulfur in air or oxygen. It is widely used for disinfecting food vessels and equipment, and as a preservative in some food products. It occurs in industrial flue gases and is a major cause of acid rain.

sulfuric acid or oil of vitriol H_2SO_4 a dense, viscous, colorless liquid that is extremely corrosive. It gives out heat when added to water and can cause severe burns. Sulfuric acid is used extensively in the chemical industry, in the refining of gasoline, and in the manufacture of fertilizers, detergents, explosives, and dyes. It forms the acid component of car batteries.

Sun the star at the center of the Solar System. Its diameter is 865,000 mi/1,392,000 km; its temperature at the surface is about 5,800K (9,980°F/5,530°C), and at the center 15,000,000K (27,000,000°F/15,000,000°C). It is composed of about 70% hydrogen and 30% helium, with other elements making up less than 1%. The Sun's energy is generated by nuclear fusion reactions that turn hydrogen into helium at its center. The gas core is far denser than mercury or lead on Earth. The Sun is about 4.7 billion years old, with a predicted lifetime of 10 billion years. At the end of its life, it will expand to become a red giant the size of Mars's orbit, then shrink to become a white dwarf. The Sun spins on its axis every 25 days near its equator, but more slowly toward its poles. Its rotation can be followed by watching the passage of dark sunspots across its disk. Sometimes bright eruptions called flares occur near sunspots. Above the Sun's photosphere lies a layer of thinner gas called the chromosphere, visible only by means of special instruments or at eclipses. Tongues of gas called prominences extend from the chromosphere into the corona, a halo of hot, tenuous gas surrounding the Sun. Gas boiling from the corona streams outwards through the Solar System, forming the solar wind. Activity on the Sun, including sunspots, flares, and prominences, waxes and wanes during the solar cycle, which peaks every 11 years or so. The unmanned space probe *Pioneer 9* achieved solar orbit in 1968, and reported data on solar radiation.

sunspot dark patch on the surface of the Sun, actually an area of cooler gas, thought to be caused by strong magnetic fields that block the outward flow of heat to the Sun's surface. Sunspots consist of a dark central umbra, about 4,000K (6,700°F/3,700°C), and a lighter surrounding penumbra, about 5,500K (9,400°F/5,200°C). They last from several days to over a month, ranging in size from 1,250 mi/2,000 km to groups stretching for over 62,000 mi/100,000 km. The number of sunspots visible at a given time varies from none to over 100 in a cycle averaging 11 years.

superheterodyne receiver the most widely used type of radio receiver, in which the incoming signal is mixed with a signal of fixed frequency generated within the receiver circuits. The resulting signal, called the intermediate-frequency (i.f.) signal, has a frequency between that of the incoming signal and the internal signal. The intermediate frequency is near the optimum frequency of the amplifier to which the i.f. signal is passed. This arrangement ensures greater gain and selectivity. The superheterodyne system is also used in basic television receivers.

superior planet planet that is farther away from the Sun than the Earth is: that is, Mars, Jupiter, Saturn, Uranus, Neptune, and Pluto.

supernova the explosive death of a star, which temporarily attains a brightness of 100 million Suns or more, so that it can shine as brilliantly as a small galaxy for a few days or weeks. Very approximately, it is thought that a supernova explodes in a large galaxy about once every 100 years. Many supernovae remain undetected because of obscuring by interstellar dust—astronomers estimate some 50%.

Superstring Theory in physics and astronomy, the theory that attempts to link the four fundamental forces. It postulates that each force emerged separately during the expansion of the very early universe from the Big Bang. It also postulates viewing matter as tiny vibrating strings instead of particles within a universe of more than the currently known four dimensions. Continuing research pursues a model based on a ten-dimensional universe, present at singularity. At the Big Bang, the ten dimensions split into two components, with four dimensions expanded into the current observable universe while the other six dimensions contracted to a point in space.

supersymmetry in physics, a theory that relates the two classes of elementary particle, the fermions and the bosons. According to supersymmetry, each fermion particle has a boson partner particle, and vice versa. It has not been possible to marry up all the known fermions with the known bosons, and so the theory postulates the existence of other, as yet undiscovered fermions, such as the photinos (partners of the photons), gluinos (partners of the gluons), and gravitinos (partners of the gravitons). Using these ideas, it has become possible to develop a theory of gravity—called supergravity—that extends Einstein's work and considers the gravitational, nuclear, and electromagnetic forces to be manifestations of an underlying superforce. Supersymmetry has been incorporated into the superstring theory, and appears to be a crucial ingredient in the "theory of everything" sought by scientists.

surface tension the property that causes the surface of a liquid to behave as if it were covered with a weak elastic skin; this is why a needle can float on water. It is caused by the exposed surface's tendency to contract to the smallest possible area because of unequal cohesive forces between molecules at the surface. Allied phenomena include the formation of droplets, the concave profile of a meniscus, and the capillary action by which water soaks into a sponge.

sustained-yield cropping in ecology, the removal of surplus individuals from a population of organisms so that the population maintains a constant size. This usually requires selective removal of animals of all ages and both sexes to ensure a balanced population structure. Taking too many individuals can result in a population decline, as in overfishing.

syncline geological term for a fold in the rocks of the Earth's crust in which the layers or beds dip inwards, thus forming a troughlike structure with a sag in the middle. The opposite structure, with the beds arching upward, is an anticline.

tangent in geometry, a straight line that touches a curve and gives the gradient of the curve at the point of contact. At a maximum, minimum, or point of inflection, the tangent to a curve has zero gradient. Also, in trigonometry, a function of an acute angle in a right triangle, defined as the ratio of the length of the side opposite the angle to the length of the side adjacent to it; a way of expressing the gradient of a line.

tectonics in geology, the study of the movements of rocks on the Earth's surface. On a small scale tectonics involves the formation of folds and faults, but on a large scale plate tectonics deals with the movement of the Earth's surface as a whole.

telecommunications communications over a distance, generally by electronic means. Today it is possible to communicate with most countries by tele-

phone cable, or by satellite or microwave link, with over 100,000 simultaneous conversations and several television channels being carried by the latest satellites. Integrated-Services Digital Network (ISDN) makes videophones and high-quality fax possible; the world's first large-scale center of ISDN began operating in Japan 1988. ISDN is a system that transmits voice and image data on a single transmission line by changing them into digital signals. The chief method of relaying long-distance calls on land is microwave radio transmission.

telephone instrument for communicating by voice over long distances, invented by US inventor Alexander Graham Bell 1876. The transmitter (mouthpiece) consists of a carbon microphone, with a diaphragm that vibrates when a person speaks into it. The diaphragm vibrations compress grains of carbon to a greater or lesser extent, altering their resistance to an electric current passing through them. This sets up variable electrical signals, which travel along the telephone lines to the receiver of the person being called. There they cause the magnetism of an electromagnet to vary, making a diaphragm above the electromagnet vibrate and give out sound waves, which mirror those that entered the mouthpiece originally.

telescope optical instrument that magnifies images of faint and distant objects; any device for collecting and focusing light and other forms of electromagnetic radiation. The *refracting telescope* uses lenses, and the *reflecting telescope* uses mirrors. A third type, the *catadioptric telescope*, with a combination of lenses and mirrors, is used increasingly.

television (TV) reproduction at a distance by radio waves of visual images. For transmission, a television camera converts the pattern of light it takes in into a pattern of electrical charges. This is scanned line by line by a beam of electrons from an electron gun, resulting in variable electrical signals that represent the visual picture. These vision signals are combined with a radio carrier wave and broadcast as magnetic waves. The TV aerial picks up the wave and feeds it to the receiver (TV set). This separates out the vision signals, which pass to a cathode-ray tube. The vision signals control the strength of a beam of electrons from an electron gun, aimed at the screen and making it glow more or less brightly. At the same time the beam is made to scan across the screen line by line, mirroring the action of the gun in the TV camera. The result is a recreation of the pattern of light that entered the camera. Thirty pictures are built up each second with interlaced scanning, with a total of 525 lines.

temperature state of hotness or coldness of a body, and the condition that determines whether or not it will transfer heat to, or receive heat from, another body according to the laws of thermodynamics. It is measured in degrees Celsius (before 1948 called centigrade), kelvin, or Fahrenheit. The normal temperature of the human body is about $98.4°F/36.9°C$. Variation by more than a degree or so indicates ill-health, a rise signifying excessive activity (usually due to infection), and a decrease signifying deficient heat production (usually due to lessened vitality).

tension reaction force set up in a body that is subjected to stress. In a stretched string or wire it exerts a pull that is equal in magnitude but opposite in direction to the stress being applied at its ends. Tension originates in the net attractive intermolecular force created when a stress causes the mean distance separating a material's molecules to become greater than the equilibrium distance. It is measured in newtons.

Tertiary period of geological time 65–1.64 million years ago, divided into five epochs: Paleocene, Eocene, Oligocene, Miocene, and Pliocene. During the Tertiary, mammals took over all the ecological niches left vacant by the extinction of the dinosaurs, and became the prevalent land animals. The continents took on their present positions, and climatic and vegetation zones as we know them became established. Within the geological time column the Tertiary follows the Cretaceous period and is succeeded by the Quaternary period.

tetrahedron (plural *tetrahedra*) in geometry, a solid figure (polyhedron) with four triangular faces; that is, a pyramid on a triangular base. A regular tetrahedron has equilateral triangles as its faces.

thermodynamics branch of physics dealing with the transformation of heat into and from other forms of energy. It is the basis of the study of the efficient working of engines, such as the steam and internal-combustion engines. The three laws of thermodynamics are (1) energy can be neither created nor destroyed, heat and mechanical work being mutually convertible; (2) it is impossible for an unaided self-acting machine to convey heat from one body to another at a higher temperature; and (3) it is impossible by any procedure, no matter how idealized, to reduce any system to the absolute zero of temperature (0K/–460°F) in a finite number of operations. Put into mathematical form, these laws have widespread applications in physics and chemistry.

Titan largest moon of the planet Saturn, with a diameter of 3,200 mi/5,150 km and a mean distance from Saturn of 759,000 mi/1,222,000 km. It is the second largest moon in the Solar System (Ganymede, of Jupiter, is larger).

topography the surface shape and aspect of the land, and its study. Topography deals with relief and contours, the distribution of mountains and valleys, the patterns of rivers, and all other features, natural and artificial, that produce the landscape.

topology branch of geometry that deals with those properties of a figure that remain unchanged even when the figure is transformed (bent, stretched)—for example, when a square painted on a rubber sheet is deformed by distorting the sheet. Topology has scientific applications, as in the study of turbulence in flowing fluids. The map of a subway system is an example of the topological representation of a network; connectivity (the way the lines join together) is preserved, but shape and size are not.

tornado extremely violent revolving storm with swirling, funnel-shaped clouds, caused by a rising column of warm air propelled by strong wind. A tornado can rise to a great height, but with a diameter of only a few hundred yards or meters or less. Tornadoes move with wind speeds of 100—300 mph/160–480 kph, destroying everything in their path.

trade wind prevailing wind that blows toward the equator from the northeast and southeast. Trade winds are caused by hot air rising at the equator and the consequent movement of air from north and south to take its place. The winds are deflected toward the west because of the Earth's west-to-east rotation. The unpredictable calms known as the doldrums lie at their convergence.

transgenic organism plant, animal, bacterium, or other living organism which has had a foreign gene added to it by means of genetic engineering.

transistor solid-state electronic component, made of semiconductor material, with three or more electrodes, that can regulate a current passing through it. A transistor can act as an amplifier, oscillator, photo-

cell, or switch, and (unlike earlier electron tubes) usually operates on a very small amount of power. Transistors commonly consist of a tiny sandwich of germanium or silicon, alternate layers having different electrical properties. A crystal of pure germanium or silicon would act as an insulator (nonconductor).

transit in astronomy, the passage of a smaller object across the visible disk of a larger one. Transits of the inferior planets occur when they pass directly between the Earth and the Sun, and are seen as tiny dark spots against the Sun's disk.

translation in living cells, the process by which proteins are synthesized. During translation, the information coded as a sequence of nucleotides in messenger RNA is transformed into a sequence of amino acids in a peptide chain. The process involves the "translation" of the genetic code.

trapezium in geometry, a four-sided plane figure (quadrilateral) with no two sides parallel.

triangle in geometry, a three-sided plane figure, the sum of whose interior angles is 180°. Triangles can be classified by the relative lengths of their sides. A *scalene* triangle has no sides of equal length; an *isosceles* triangle has at least two equal sides; an *equilateral triangle* has three equal sides (and three equal angles of 60°). Triangles can also be classified by their angle measures: a right triangle has one right (90°) angle; an acute triangle has three acute (less than 90°) angles; an obtuse triangle has one obtuse (greater than 90°) angle; an equiangular triangle has three equal angles. (All equilateral triangles are equiangular, and vice versa.) If the length of one side of a triangle is l and the perpendicular distance from that side to the opposite corner is h (the height or altitude of the triangle), its area $A = \frac{1}{2}(l \times h)$.

Triassic period of geological time 245–208 million years ago, the first period of the Mesozoic era. The continents were fused together to form the world continent Pangaea. Triassic sediments contain remains of early dinosaurs and other reptiles now extinct. By late Triassic times, the first mammals had evolved.

trigonometry branch of mathematics that solves problems relating to plane and spherical triangles. Its principles are based on the fixed proportions of sides for a particular angle in a right triangle, the simplest of which are known as the sine, cosine, and tangent (so-called trigonometrical ratios). It is of practical importance in navigation, surveying, and simple harmonic motion in physics.

tropics the area between the tropics of Cancer and Capricorn, defined by the parallels of latitude approximately 23°30′N and S of the equator. They are the limits of the area of Earth's surface in which the Sun can be directly overhead. The mean monthly temperature is over 68°F/20°C.

troposphere lower part of the Earth's atmosphere extending about 6.5 mi/10.5 km from the Earth's surface, in which temperature decreases with height to about –76°F/–60°C except in local layers of temperature inversion. The *tropopause* is the upper boundary of the troposphere, above which the temperature increases slowly with height within the atmosphere. All of the Earth's weather takes place within the troposphere.

turbine engine in which steam, water, gas, or air (see windmill) is made to spin a rotating shaft by pushing on angled blades, like a fan. Turbines are among the most powerful machines. Steam turbines are used to drive generators in power stations and ships' propellers; water turbines spin the generators in hydroelectric power plants; and gas turbines (as jet engines) power most aircraft and drive machines in industry.

uncertainty principle or *indeterminacy principle* in quantum mechanics, the principle that it is meaningless to speak of a particle's position, momentum, or other parameters, except as results of measurements; measuring, however, involves an interaction (such as a photon of light bouncing off the particle under scrutiny), which must disturb the particle, though the disturbance is noticeable only at an atomic scale. The principle implies that one cannot, even in theory, predict the moment-to-moment behavior of such a system.

universal indicator in chemistry, a mixture of pH indicators, used to gauge the acidity or alkalinity of a solution. Each component changes color at a different pH value, and so the indicator is capable of displaying a range of colors, according to the pH of the test solution, from red (at pH 1) to purple (at pH 13). The pH of a substance may be found by adding a few drops of universal indicator and noting the color, or by dipping in an absorbent paper strip that has been impregnated with the indicator.

universe all of space and its contents, the study of which is called cosmology. The universe is thought to be between 10 billion and 20 billion years old, and is mostly empty space, dotted with galaxies for as far as telescopes can see. The most distant detected galaxies and quasars lie 10 billion light-years or more from Earth, and are moving farther apart as the universe expands. Several theories attempt to explain how the universe came into being and evolved, for example, the Big Bang theory of an expanding universe originating in a single explosive event.

unsaturated compound chemical compound in which two adjacent atoms are bonded by a double or triple covalent bond.

uranium hard, lustrous, silver-white, malleable and ductile, radioactive, metallic element of the actinide series, symbol U, atomic number 92, atomic weight 238.029. It is the most abundant radioactive element in the Earth's crust, its decay giving rise to essentially all radioactive elements in nature; its final decay product is the stable element lead. Uranium combines readily with most elements to form compounds that are extremely poisonous.

Uranus the seventh planet from the Sun, discovered by William Herschel 1781. It is twice as far out as the sixth planet, Saturn. Uranus has a diameter of 31,600 mi/50,800 km and a mass 14.5 times that of Earth. It orbits the Sun in 84 years at an average distance of 1.8 billion mi/2.9 billion km. The spin axis of Uranus is tilted at 98°, so that one pole points toward the Sun, giving extreme seasons. It has 15 moons, and in 1977 was discovered to have thin rings around its equator. Data derived from the space probe *Voyager 1* in 1986 revealed that Uranus is covered with a cloud layer under which a hot ocean of superheated water exists. The pressure caused by the thick atmosphere keeps the water from boiling away and the heat keeps the pressure from solidifying the water. This has led to suggestions that the planet may have formed from the coalescence of comets. Other discoveries were that the pole facing the Sun is no hotter than the pole facing away, and that four known methane clouds in the atmosphere rotate with the planet, not in the expected opposite direction. *Voyager 2* detected ten rings, composed of chunky rock and large ice boulders, around the planet's equator, and found ten small moons in addition to the five visible from Earth. Titania, the largest moon, has a diameter of 980 mi/1,580 km. The rings

are charcoal black, and may be debris of former "moonlets" that have broken up.

urea $CO(NH_2)_2$ waste product formed in the mammalian liver when nitrogen compounds are broken down. It is excreted in urine. When purified, it is a white, crystalline solid. In industry it is used to make ureaformaldehyde plastics (or resins), pharmaceuticals, and fertilizers.

valency in chemistry, the measure of an element's ability to combine with other elements, expressed as the number of atoms of hydrogen (or any other standard univalent element) capable of uniting with (or replacing) its atoms. The number of electrons in the outermost shell of the atom dictates the combining ability of an element.

variable in mathematics, a changing quantity (one that can take various values), as opposed to a constant. For example, in the algebraic expression $y = 4x^3 + 2$, the variables are x and y, whereas 4 and 2 are constants.

variable star in astronomy, a star whose brightness changes, either regularly or irregularly, over a period ranging from a few hours to months or even years. The Cepheid variables regularly expand and contract in size every few days or weeks.

variation in biology, a difference between individuals of the same species, found in any sexually reproducing population. Variations may be almost unnoticeable in some cases, obvious in others, and can concern many aspects of the organism. Typically, variation in size, behavior, biochemistry, or coloring may be found. The cause of the variation is genetic (that is, inherited), environmental, or more usually a combination of the two. The origins of variation can be traced to the recombination of the genetic material during the formation of the gametes, and, more rarely, to mutation.

vector quantity any physical quantity that has both magnitude and direction (such as the velocity or acceleration of an object) as distinct from scalar quantity (such as speed, density, or mass), which has magnitude but no direction. A vector is represented either geometrically by an arrow whose length corresponds to its magnitude and points in an appropriate direction, or by a pair of numbers written vertically and placed within brackets $(x\ y)$. Vectors can be added graphically by constructing a parallelogram of vectors (such as the parallelogram of forces commonly employed in physics and engineering).

velocity speed of an object in a given direction. Velocity is a vector quantity, since its direction is important as well as its magnitude (or speed).

Venn diagram in mathematics, a diagram representing a set or sets and the logical relationships between them. The sets are drawn as circles. An area of overlap between two circles (sets) contains elements that are common to both sets, and thus represents a third set. Circles that do not overlap represent sets with no elements in common (disjoint sets).

Venus second planet from the Sun. It orbits the Sun every 225 days at an average distance of 67.2 million mi/108.2 million km and can approach the Earth to within 24 million mi/38 million km, closer than any other planet. Its diameter is 7,500 mi/12,100 km and its mass is 0.82 that of Earth. Venus rotates on its axis more slowly than any other planet, once every 243 days and from east to west, the opposite direction to the other planets (except Uranus and possibly Pluto). Venus is shrouded by clouds of sulfuric acid droplets that sweep across the planet from east to west every four days. The atmosphere is almost entirely carbon dioxide, which traps the Sun's heat by the greenhouse effect and raises the planet's surface temperature to 900°F/480°C, with an atmospheric pressure of 90 times that at the surface of the Earth.

vertebrate any animal with a backbone. The 41,000 species of vertebrates include mammals, birds, reptiles, amphibians, and fishes. They include most of the larger animals, but in terms of numbers of species are only a tiny proportion of the world's animals. The zoological taxonomic group Vertebrata is a subgroup of the phylum *Chordata*.

vertex (plural *vertices*) in geometry, a point shared by three or more sides of a solid figure; the point farthest from a figure's base; or the point of intersection of two sides of a plane figure or the two rays of an angle.

video camera or *camcorder* portable television camera that takes moving pictures electronically on magnetic tape. It produces an electrical output signal corresponding to rapid line-by-line scanning of the field of view. The output is recorded on videocassette and is played back on a television screen via a videocassette recorder.

video disc disk with pictures and sounds recorded on it, played back by laser. The video disc is a type of compact disc.

video tape recorder (VTR) device for recording visuals and sound on spools of magnetic tape. It is used in television broadcasting.

virus infectious particle consisting of a core of nucleic acid (DNA or RNA) enclosed in a protein shell. Viruses are acellular and able to function and reproduce only if they can invade a living cell to use the cell's system to replicate themselves. In the process they may disrupt or alter the host cell's own DNA. The healthy human body reacts by producing an antiviral protein, interferon, which prevents the infection spreading to adjacent cells. Viruses have recently been found to be very abundant in seas and lakes, with between 5 and 10 million per cubic centimeter of water at most sites tested, but up to 250 million per cubic centimeter in one polluted lake. These viruses infect bacteria and, possibly, single-celled algae. They may play a crucial role in controlling the survival of bacteria and algae in the plankton.

viscosity in physics, the resistance of a fluid to flow, caused by its internal friction, which makes it resist flowing past a solid surface or other layers of the fluid. It applies to the motion of an object moving through a fluid as well as the motion of a fluid passing by an object.

volcano crack in the Earth's crust through which hot magma (molten rock) and gases well up. The magma becomes known as lava when it reaches the surface. A volcanic mountain, usually cone shaped with a crater on top, is formed around the opening, or vent, by the buildup of solidified lava and ashes (rock fragments). Most volcanoes arise on plate margins (see plate tectonics), where the movements of plates generate magma or allow it to rise from the mantle beneath. However, a number are found far from plate-margin activity, on "hot spots" where the Earth's crust is thin.

volume in geometry, the space occupied by a three-dimensional solid object. A prism (such as a cube) or a cylinder has a volume equal to the area of the base multiplied by the height. For a pyramid or cone, the volume is equal to one-third of the area of the base multiplied by the perpendicular height. The volume of a sphere is equal to $4/3r^3$, where r is the radius. Volumes of irregular solids may be calculated by the technique of integration.

waste disposal depositing waste. Methods of waste disposal vary according to the materials in the waste and include incineration, burial at designated sites, and dumping at sea. Organic waste can be treated and reused as fertilizer (see sewage disposal). Nuclear waste and toxic waste is usually buried or dumped at sea, although this does not negate the danger.

water H_2O liquid without color, taste, or odor. It is an oxide of hydrogen. Water begins to freeze at 0°C or 32°F, and to boil at 100°C or 212°F. When liquid, it is virtually incompressible; frozen, it expands by 1/11 of its volume. At 39.2°F/4°C, one cubic centimeter of water has a mass of one gram; this is its maximum density, forming the unit of specific gravity. It has the highest known specific heat, and acts as an efficient solvent, particularly when hot. Most of the world's water is in the sea; less than 0.01% is fresh water. Water makes up 60–70% of the human body or about 42 quarts/40 liters, of which 25 are inside the cells, 15 outside (12 in tissue fluid, and 3 in blood plasma). A loss of 10% of this volume may cause hallucinations; a loss of 20%-25% may cause death. People cannot survive more than five or six days without water or two or three days in a hot environment.

water pollution any addition to fresh or sea water that disrupts biological processes or causes a health hazard. Common pollutants include nitrate, pesticides, and sewage, though a huge range of industrial contaminants, such as chemical byproducts and residues created in the manufacture of various goods, also enter water—legally, accidentally, and through illegal dumping.

water table the upper level of ground water (water collected underground in porous rocks). Water that is above the water table will drain downward; a spring forms where the water table cuts the surface of the ground. The water table rises and falls in response to rainfall and the rate at which water is extracted, for example, for irrigation and industry.

wave in physics, a disturbance consisting of a series of oscillations that propagate through a medium (or space). There are two types: in a longitudinal wave (such as a sound wave) the disturbance is parallel to the wave's direction of travel; in a *transverse wave* (such as an electromagnetic wave) it is perpendicular. The medium only vibrates as the wave passes; it does not travel outward from the source with the waves.

weakon or *intermediate vector boson in physics, a gauge boson that carries the weak nuclear force, one of the fundamental forces of nature. There are three types of weakon, the positive and negative W particle and the neutral Z particle.*

weathering process by which exposed rocks are broken down by the action of rain, frost, wind, and other elements of the weather. Two types of weathering are recognized: physical and chemical. They usually occur together.

weight the force exerted on an object by gravity. The weight of an object depends on its mass—the amount of material in it— and the strength of the Earth's gravitational pull, which decreases with height. Consequently, an object weighs less at the top of a mountain than at sea level. On the Moon, an object has only one-sixth of its weight on Earth, because the pull of the Moon's gravity is one-sixth that of the Earth.

wetland permanently wet land area or habitat. Wetlands include areas of marsh, fen, bog, flood plain, and shallow coastal areas. Wetlands are extremely fertile. They provide warm, sheltered waters for fisheries, lush vegetation for grazing livestock, and an abundance of wildlife. Estuaries and seaweed beds are more than 16 times as productive as the open ocean.

white dwarf small, hot star, the last stage in the life of a star such as the Sun. White dwarfs have a mass similar to that of the Sun, but only 1% of the Sun's diameter, similar in size to the Earth. Most have surface temperatures of 14,400°F/8,000°C or more, hotter than the Sun. Yet, being so small, their overall luminosities may be less than 1% of that of the Sun. The Milky Way contains an estimated 50 billion white dwarfs. White dwarfs consist of degenerate matter in which gravity has packed the protons and electrons together as tightly as is physically possible, so that a spoonful of it weighs several tons. White dwarfs are thought to be the shrunken remains of stars that have exhausted their internal energy supplies. They slowly cool and fade over billions of years.

wind the lateral movement of the Earth's atmosphere from high-pressure areas (anticyclones) to low-pressure areas (depressions). Its speed is measured using an anemometer or by studying its effects on, for example, trees by using the Beaufort Scale. Although modified by features such as land and water, there is a basic worldwide system of trade winds, Westerlies, monsoons, and others.

wind turbine windmill of advanced aerodynamic design connected to an electricity generator and used in windpower installations. Wind turbines can be either large propeller-type rotors mounted on a tall tower, or flexible metal strips fixed to a vertical axle at top and bottom.

work in physics, a measure of the result of transferring energy from one system to another to cause an object to move. Work should not be confused with energy (the capacity to do work, which is also measured in joules) or with power (the rate of doing work, measured in joules per second).

year unit of time measurement, based on the orbital period of the Earth around the Sun.

zenith uppermost point of the celestial horizon, immediately above the observer; the nadir is below, diametrically opposite.

zodiac zone of the heavens containing the paths of the Sun, Moon, and planets. When this was devised by the ancient Greeks, only five planets were known, making the zodiac about 16° wide. In astrology, the zodiac is divided into 12 signs, each 30° in extent: Aries, Taurus, Gemini, Cancer, Leo, Virgo, Libra, Scorpio, Sagittarius, Capricorn, Aquarius, and Pisces. These do not cover the same areas of sky as the astronomical constellations.

zodiacal light cone-shaped light sometimes seen extending from the Sun along the ecliptic, visible after sunset or before sunrise. It is due to thinly spread dust particles in the central plane of the Solar System. It is very faint, and requires a dark, clear sky to be seen.

Number Systems

This section defines the terms and prefixes most frequently employed in counting, quantifying, and other numerical calculations.

ROMAN NUMERALS

1	I	8	VIII	60	LX	5,000	$\overline{V}$
2	II	9	IX	70	LXX	10,000	$\overline{X}$
3	III	10	X	80	LXXX	50,000	$\overline{L}$
4	IV	20	XX	90	XC	100,000	$\overline{C}$
5	V	30	XXX	100	C	500,000	$\overline{D}$
6	VI	40	XL	500	D	1,000,000	$\overline{M}$
7	VII	50	L	1,000	M		

U.S. NUMBERING SYSTEM

One	=	0 zeros	1
One hundred	=	2 zeros	100
One thousand	=	3 zeros	1,000
One million	=	6 zeros	1,000,000
One billion	=	9 zeros	1,000,000,000
One trillion	=	12 zeros	1,000,000,000,000
One quadrillion	=	15 zeros	1,000,000,000,000,000
One quintillion	=	18 zeros	1,000,000,000,000,000,000
One sextillion	=	21 zeros	1,000,000,000,000,000,000,000
One septillion	=	24 zeros	1,000,000,000,000,000,000,000,000
One octillion	=	27 zeros	1,000,000,000,000,000,000,000,000,000
One nonillion	=	30 zeros	1,000,000,000,000,000,000,000,000,000,000
One decillion	=	33 zeros	1,000,000,000,000,000,000,000,000,000,000,000
One undecillion	=	36 zeros	1,000,000,000,000,000,000,000,000,000,000,000,000
One duodecillion	=	39 zeros	1,000,000,000,000,000,000,000,000,000,000,000,000,000
One tredecillion	=	42 zeros	1,000,000,000,000,000,000,000,000,000,000,000,000,000,000
One quattuordecillion	=	45 zeros	1,000,000,000,000,000,000,000,000,000,000,000,000,000,000,000
One quindecillion	=	48 zeros	1,000,000,000,000,000,000,000,000,000,000,000,000,000,000,000,000
One sexdecillion	=	51 zeros	1,000,000,000,000,000,000,000,000,000,000,000,000,000,000,000,000,000
One septdecillion	=	54 zeros	1,000,000,000,000,000,000,000,000,000,000,000,000,000,000,000,000,000,000
One octodecillion	=	57 zeros	1,000,000,000,000,000,000,000,000,000,000,000,000,000,000,000,000,000,000,000
One novemdecillion	=	60 zeros	1,000,000,000,000,000,000,000,000,000,000,000,000,000,000,000,000,000,000,000,000
One vigintillion	=	63 zeros	1,000,000,000,000,000,000,000,000,000,000,000,000,000,000,000,000,000,000,000,000,000
One centillion	=	303 zeros	1,000

WORLDWIDE (BRITISH) NUMBERING SYSTEM

One	=	0 zeros	1
One hundred	=	2 zeros	100
One thousand	=	3 zeros	1,000
One million	=	6 zeros	1,000,000
One milliard	=	9 zeros	1,000,000,000
One billion	=	12 zeros	1,000,000,000,000
One thousand billion	=	15 zeros	1,000,000,000,000,000
One trillion	=	18 zeros	1,000,000,000,000,000,000
One thousand trillion	=	21 zeros	1,000,000,000,000,000,000,000
One quadrillion	=	24 zeros	1,000,000,000,000,000,000,000,000
One thousand quadrillion	=	27 zeros	1,000,000,000,000,000,000,000,000,000
One quintillion	=	30 zeros	1,000,000,000,000,000,000,000,000,000,000
One thousand quintillion	=	33 zeros	1,000,000,000,000,000,000,000,000,000,000,000
One sextillion	=	36 zeros	1,000,000,000,000,000,000,000,000,000,000,000,000
One thousand sextillion	=	39 zeros	1,000,000,000,000,000,000,000,000,000,000,000,000,000
One septillion	=	42 zeros	1,000,000,000,000,000,000,000,000,000,000,000,000,000,000
One thousand septillion	=	45 zeros	1,000,000,000,000,000,000,000,000,000,000,000,000,000,000,000
One octillion	=	48 zeros	1,000,000,000,000,000,000,000,000,000,000,000,000,000,000,000,000
One thousand octillion	=	51 zeros	1,000,000,000,000,000,000,000,000,000,000,000,000,000,000,000,000,000
One nonillion	=	54 zeros	1,000,000,000,000,000,000,000,000,000,000,000,000,000,000,000,000,000,000
One thousand nonillion	=	57 zeros	1,000,000,000,000,000,000,000,000,000,000,000,000,000,000,000,000,000,000,000
One decillion	=	60 zeros	1,000,000,000,000,000,000,000,000,000,000,000,000,000,000,000,000,000,000,000,000
One undecillion	=	66 zeros	1,000,000,000,000,000,000,000,000,000,000,000,000,000,000,000,000,000,000,000,000,000,000,000,
One duodecillion	=	72 zeros	1,000,000,000,000,000,000,000,000,000,000,000,000,000,000,000,000,000,000,000,000,000,000,000,000,000,000, 000
One tredecillion	=	78 zeros	1,000,000,000,000,000,000,000,000,000,000,000,000,000,000,000,000,000,000,000,000,000,000,000,000,000,000, 000,000,000
One quattuordecillion	=	84 zeros	1,000,000,000,000,000,000,000,000,000,000,000,000,000,000,000,000,000,000,000,000,000,000,000,000,000,000,000, 000,000,000,000,000
One quindecillion	=	90 zeros	1,000,000,000,000,000,000,000,000,000,000,000,000,000,000,000,000,000,000,000,000,000,000,000,000,000,000,000, 000,000,000,000,000,000,000
One sexdecillion	=	96 zeros	1,000,000,000,000,000,000,000,000,000,000,000,000,000,000,000,000,000,000,000,000,000,000,000,000,000,000,000, 000,000,000,000,000,000,000,000,000
One septedecillion	=	102 zeros	1,000,000,000,000,000,000,000,000,000,000,000,000,000,000,000,000,000,000,000,000,000,000,000,000,000,000,000, 000,000,000,000,000,000,000,000,000,000
One octodecillion	=	108 zeros	1,000,000,000,000,000,000,000,000,000,000,000,000,000,000,000,000,000,000,000,000,000,000,000,000,000,000,000, 000,000,000,000,000,000,000,000,000,000,000,000
One novemdecillion	=	114 zeros	1,000,000,000,000,000,000,000,000,000,000,000,000,000,000,000,000,000,000,000,000,000,000,000,000,000,000,000, 000,000,000,000,000,000,000,000,000,000,000,000,000,000
One centillion	=	600 zeros	1,000,000,000,000,000,000,000,000,000,000,000,000,000,000,000,000,000,000,000,000,000,000,000,000,000,000,000, 000,000,000,000,000,000,000,000,000,000,000,000,000,000,000,000,000,000,000,000,000,000,000,000,000,000,000,000, 000,000,000,000,000,000,000,000,000,000,000,000,000,000,000,000,000,000,000,000,000,000,000,000,000,000,000,000, 000,000,000,000,000,000,000,000,000,000,000,000,000,000,000,000,000,000,000,000,000,000,000,000,000,000,000,000, 000,000,000,000,000,000,000,000,000,000,000,000,000,000,000,000,000,000,000,000,000,000,000,000,000,000,000,000, 000,000,000,000,000,000,000,000,000,000,000,000,000,000,000,000,000,000,000,000,000,000,000,000,000,000,000,000, 000,000,000,000,000,000,000,000,000,000,000,000,000,000,000,000,000,000,000,000,000,000,000,000,000,000,000,000, 000,000,000,000,000,000,000,000,000,000,000,000,000,000,000,000,000,000,000,000,000,000,000,000,000,000,000,000, 000,000,000,000,000,000,000,000,000,000,000,000,000,000,000,000,000,000,000

BINARY NUMBERS

Below are the eqivalents between the decimal (base ten) number system and the binary (base two) number system.

DECIMAL	BINARY	DECIMAL	BINARY	DECIMAL	BINARY
1	1	14	1110	100	110010
2	10	15	1111	200	11001000
3	11	16	10000	300	100101100
4	100	17	10001	400	110010000
5	101	18	10010	500	111110100
6	110	19	10011	600	1001011000
7	111	20	10100	900	1110000100
8	1000	21	10101	1,000	1111101000
9	1001	30	11110	2,000	11111010000
10	1010	40	101000	4,000	111110100000
11	1011	50	110010	5,000	1001110001000
12	1100	60	111100	10,000	10011100010000
13	1101	90	1011010	20,000	100111000100000
				100,000	11000011010100000

HISTORIC NUMBER SYSTEMS FROM AROUND THE WORLD

Modern	Roman	Arabic	Babylonian	Chinese	Egyptian	Greek	Hebrew	Hindu
1	I	١		一				
2	II	٢		二				
3	III	٣		三				
4	IV	٤		四				
5	V	٥		五				
6	VI	٦		六				
7	VII	٧		七				
8	VIII	٨		八				
9	IX	٩		九				
10	X	١٠		十				10
20	XX	٢٠		二十				20
30	XXX	٣٠		三十				30
40	XL	٤٠		四十				80
50	L	٥٠		五十				40
60	LX	٦٠		六十				50
70	LXX	٧٠		七十				70
80	LXXX	٨٠		八十				60
90	XC	٩٠		九十				90
100	C	١٠٠		百		H		100

PREFIXES FOR NUMBERS

SCIENTIFIC	INTERNATIONAL SYSTEM
Atto-	0.000 000 000 000 000 001
Femto-	0.000 000 000 000 001
Pico-	0.000 000 000 001
Nano-	0.000 000 001
Micro-	0.000 001
Milli-	0.001
Centi-	0.01
Deci-	0.1

COMMON AND SCIENTIFIC SYSTEMS

Deci–	$\frac{1}{10}$
Demi-, Semi-, Hemi–	$\frac{1}{2}$
Uni–	1
Bi-, Di–	2
Ter-, Tri–	3
Tetra-, Tessera-, Quadr-, Quadri–	4
Pent, Penta, Quinqu-, Quint–	5
Sex-, Sexi-, Hex-, Hexa–	6
Hept, Hepta-, Sept-, Septem-, Septi–	7
Oct-, Octo-, Octa–	8
Non-, Nona-, Ennea–	9
Dec-, Deca–	10
Undeca-, Hendeca–	11
Dodeca–	12
Quindeca–	15
Icos-, Icosa-, Icosi–	20
Hect-, Hecto–	100
Kilo–	1,000
Myria–	10,000
Mega–	1,000,000
Giga–	1,000,000,000
Tera–	1,000,000,000,000

Common Formulas

This broad and thorough section of common formulas includes computations, formulas, equations, definitions, and other important information relating to mathematics and physics. The algebraic and geometric formulas describe the basic laws and properties of various mathematic functions, and the detailed equations and laws relating to motion, kinetics, and electricity explain many of the basic rules of physics.

FRACTIONS & DECIMALS

To find the decimal equivalent of a fraction, divide the numerator by the denominator. For example $5/8 = 5 \div 8 = .625$. Below are some common fraction/decimal equivalents:

$1/100$	= 0.01	$31/64$	= 0.484375
$1/64$	= 0.015625	$1/2$	= 0.5
$1/32$	= 0.03125	$33/64$	= 0.515625
$1/50$	= 0.02	$17/32$	= 0.53125
$1/25$	= 0.04	$35/64$	= 0.546875
$1/20$	= 0.05	$5/9$	= .555555 …
$1/16$	= 0.0625	$9/16$	= 0.5625
$5/64$	= 0.078125	$4/7$	= 0.571429
$3/32$	= 0.09375	$37/64$	= 0.578125
$1/10$	= 0.1	$19/32$	= 0.59375
$7/64$	= 0.109375	$39/64$	= 0.609375
$1/9$	= 0.111111 …	$3/5$	= 0.6
$1/8$	= 0.125	$5/8$	= 0.625
$9/64$	= 0.140625	$41/64$	= 0.640625
$1/7$	= 0.142857 …	$21/32$	= 0.65625
$5/32$	= 0.15625	$2/3$	= 0.666666 …
$1/6$	= 0.166666 …	$43/64$	= 0.671875
$11/64$	= 0.171875	$11/16$	= 0.6875
$3/16$	= 0.1875	$45/64$	= 0.703125
$1/5$	= 0.2	$5/7$	= 0.714286 …
$13/64$	= 0.203125	$23/32$	= 0.71875
$7/32$	= 0.21875	$47/64$	= 0.734375
$2/9$	= 0.222222 …	$3/4$	= 0.75
$15/64$	= 0.234375	$49/64$	= 0.765625
$1/4$	= 0.25	$7/9$	= 0.777777 …
$17/64$	= 0.265625	$25/32$	= 0.78125
$9/32$	= 0.28125	$51/64$	= 0.796875
$2/7$	= 0.285714 …	$4/5$	= 0.8
$19/64$	= 0.296875	$13/16$	= 0.8125
$5/16$	= 0.3125	$53/64$	= 0.828125
$21/64$	= 0.328125	$5/6$	= 0.833333 …
$1/3$	= 0.333333 …	$27/32$	= 0.84375
$11/32$	= 0.34375	$6/7$	= 0.857143 …
$23/64$	= 0.359375	$55/64$	= 0.859375
$3/8$	= 0.375	$7/8$	= 0.875
$25/64$	= 0.390625	$8/9$	= 0.888888 …
$2/5$	= 0.4	$57/64$	= 0.890625
$13/32$	= 0.40625	$29/32$	= 0.90625
$27/64$	= 0.421875	$59/64$	= 0.921875
$3/7$	= 0.428571 …	$15/16$	= 0.9375
$7/16$	= 0.4375	$61/64$	= 0.953125
$4/9$	= 0.444444 …	$31/32$	= 0.96875
$29/64$	= 0.453125	$63/64$	= 0.984375
$15/32$	= 0.46875	$1/1$	= 1.000000

PERCENTAGES

To covert fractions to percentages, convert the fraction to decimal form, then multiply by 100. For example: $1/4 = .25 = 25\%$.

Common fractional equivalents of percentages:

$1/100$	=	1%
$1/50$	=	2%
$1/25$	=	4%
$1/20$	=	5%
$1/10$	=	10%
$1/5$	=	20%
$1/4$	=	25%
$1/3$	=	$33\frac{1}{3}\%$
$3/8$	=	$37\frac{1}{2}\%$
$2/5$	=	40%
$1/2$	=	50%
$3/5$	=	60%
$5/8$	=	$62\frac{1}{2}\%$
$2/3$	=	$66\frac{2}{3}\%$
$3/4$	=	75%
$4/5$	=	80%
$5/6$	=	$83\frac{1}{3}\%$
1	=	100%

MATHEMATICAL RELATIONSHIPS IN ALGEBRA

Commutative Relationships

Equation	Example
$a + b = b + a$	$3 + 4 = 4 + 3$
$a \times b = b \times a$	$5 \times 2 = 2 \times 5$

Associative Relationships

Equation	Example
$(a + b) + c =$	$(3 + 4) + 5 =$
$\quad a + (b + c)$	$\quad 3 + (4 + 5)$
$(a \times b) \times c = a \times (b \times c)$	$(2 \times 4) \times 5 = 2 \times (4 \times 5)$

Distributive Relationships

Equation	Example
$a \times (b + c) =$	$2 \times (3+4) =$
$\quad (a \times b) + (a \times c)$	$\quad (2 \times 3) + (2 \times 4)$

Exponential Relationships

Equation	Example
$(x^a)(x^b) = x^{a+b}$	$2^2 \times 2^3 = 2^{2+3} = 2^5$
$(x^a)^b = x^{ab}$	$(2^2)^3 = 2^{2 \times 3} = 2^6$
$x^a \div x^b = x^{a-b}$	$2^3 \div 2^2 = 2^{3-2} = 2^1 = 2$
$(xy)^a = x^a\, y^a$	$(3 \times 2)^2 = 3^2 \times 2^2$

Relationships of Fractions

Equation	Example
$c/d \times e/f = ce/df$	$2/3 \times 4/5 = 2 \times 4/3 \times 5 = 8/15$
$c/d \div e/f = c/d \times f/e = cf/de$	$2/3 \div 4/5 = (2/3) \times (5/4)$
	$\quad = (2 \times 5)/(3 \times 4)$
	$\quad = 10/12$
$c/d + e/d = (c + e)/d$	$2/5 + 3/5 = (2 + 3)/5 = 5/5$
$c/d + e/f = cf/df + ed/df$	$2/3 + 4/5 =$
$\quad = (cf + ed)/df$	$(2 \times 5)/(3 \times 5) + (4 \times 3)/(3 \times 5) =$
	$(2 \times 5) + (4 \times 3)/(3 \times 5) =$
	$(10 + 12)/15 = 22/15$
$c/d - e/d = (c - e)/d$	$5/7 - 3/7 = (5 - 3)/7 = 2/7$
$c/d - e/f = cf/df - ed/df =$	$3/5 - 1/2 =$
$\quad (cf - ed)/df$	$(3 \times 2)/(5 \times 2) - (1 \times 5)/(2 \times 5) =$
	$((3 \times 2) - (1 \times 5))/5 \times 2 =$
	$6 - 5/10 = 1/10$

Quadratic Formula

$$x = \frac{-b \pm \sqrt{b^2 - 4ac}}{2a}$$

for solving quadratic equations $ax^2 + bx + c = 0$

GEOMETRIC EQUATIONS

PLANE GEOMETRY – SHAPES BOUNDED BY CURVED LINES

CIRCLE A closed plane curve every point of which is equidistant from a fixed point in the center of the circle.
r = radius ($\frac{1}{2}$ the diameter d)
π = Pi = 3.14159265
area of a circle = πr^2
circumference of a circle = $2\pi r$ or πd
diameter of a circle = 2r

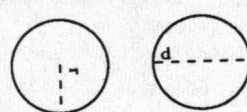

ELLIPSE A closed curve consisting of points (loci) such that the sum of the distances from any point to two fixed points (foci) within the ellipse is constant.
area of an ellipse = long diameter × short diameter × 0.7854

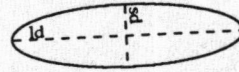

PLANE GEOMETRY – SHAPES BOUNDED BY STRAIGHT LINES

POLYGON A closed plane figure bounded by straight lines (sides) at various angles to each other. The perimeter of a polygon is the sum of the length of its sides.
P = a + b + c . . .

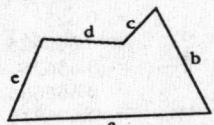

REGULAR POLYGON A polygon whose sides and angles are equal.

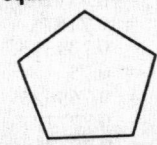

IRREGULAR POLYGON A polygon whose sides and angles are not equal.

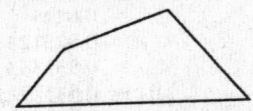

CONCAVE POLYGON An irregular polygon whose sides and angles form a concave shape and where one or more of its angles is greater than 180°.

TRIANGLES
(THREE-SIDED POLYGONS)

TRIANGLE A polygon with three sides and three angles.
Area of a triangle = $\frac{1}{2}bh$

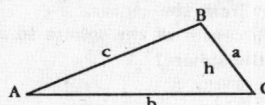

RIGHT TRIANGLE A triangle one of whose angles is a right angle (90°). C = 90° and A and B are < 90°.
Area of a right triangle = $\frac{1}{2}ab$
Pythagorean theorem = $a^2 + b^2 = c^2$
where a and b are sides and c is the hypotenuse of the right triangle

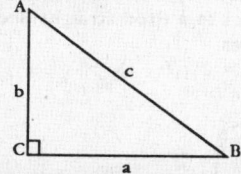

EQUILATERAL TRIANGLE A triangle with three sides of equal length. $A \neq B \neq C$ and $a \neq b \neq c$. A, B, and C are all 60°.

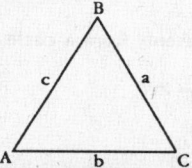

ISOSCELES TRIANGLE A triangle with two sides of equal length. b = c.

SCALENE TRIANGLE A triangle with three sides of unequal length. $A \neq B \neq C$ and $a \neq b \neq c$.

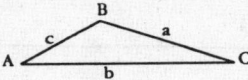

OBTUSE TRIANGLE A triangle with one angle greater than 90°. A > 90°, B < 90° and C < 90° and a > b or c.

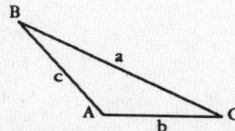

ACUTE TRIANGLE A triangle all of whose angles are less than 90°. A, B, and C are all < 90°.

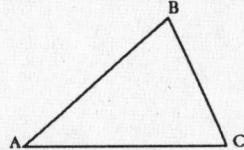

QUADRILATERALS
(FOUR-SIDED POLYGONS)

SQUARE A rectangle all of whose sides are equal.
a = b = c = d and A, B, C, and D are all 90°
Area of a square = a^2
Perimeter of a square = 4a

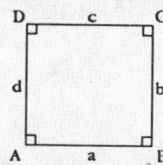

RECTANGLE A quadrilateral all of whose angles are right angles (90°) and opposite sides are of equal length and parallel. a = c and b = d and A, B, C, and D are all 90°.
Area of a rectangle = ab (length × width)
Perimeter of a rectangle = 2 (a + b)

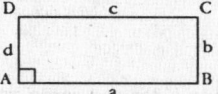

PARALLELOGRAM A four-sided shape where opposite sides are parallel and of equal length. a = c and b = d and A = C and B = D.
Area of a parallelogram = ah
Perimeter of a parallelogram = 2 (a + b)

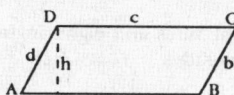

TRAPEZOID A four-sided shape having only two sides of equal length.
Area of a trapezoid = $\frac{1}{2}$ h(a + c)
Perimeter of a trapezoid = a + b + c + d

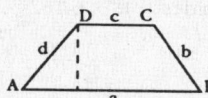

RHOMBUS A parallelogram having all four sides of equal length. a = b = c = d
Area of a rhombus = a × h
Perimeter of a rhombus = 4a

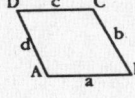

POLYGONS WITH MORE THAN FOUR SIDES

Key: L = one of the equal sides of the regular polygon

PENTAGON A Polygon of five sides and five angles.
Area of a pentagon of equal sides = $L^2 \times 1.720$

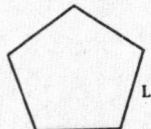

HEXAGON A Polygon of six sides and six angles.
Area of a hexagon of equal sides = $L^2 \times 2.598$

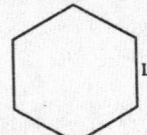

HEPTAGON: A Polygon of seven sides and seven angles.
Area of a heptagon of equal sides = $L^2 \times 3.634$

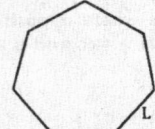

OCTAGON A Polygon of eight sides and eight angles.
Area of an octagon of equal sides = $L^2 \times 4.828$

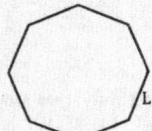

NONAGON A Polygon of nine sides and nine angles.
Area of a nonagon of equal sides = $L^2 \times 6.182$

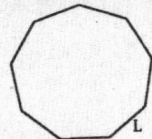

DECAGON A Polygon of ten sides and ten angles.
Area of a decagon of equal sides = $L^2 \times 7.694$

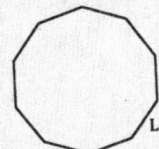

SOLID GEOMETRY – THREE-DIMENSIONAL SHAPES BOUNDED BY CURVED LINES

SPHERE The space enclosed by a surface all points of which are equally distant from the center.
r = radius (distance from center of the sphere to any point on the surface of the sphere)
Surface area of a sphere = $4\pi r^2$
Volume of a sphere = $\frac{4}{3}\pi r^3$

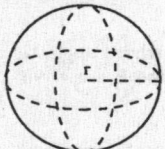

CYLINDER The space bounded by a surface traced by a straight line moving parallel to a fixed straight line and intersecting fixed circles.
Surface area of a cylinder = $2\pi r(h + r)$
Volume of a cylinder = $\pi r^2 h$

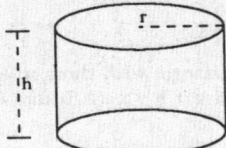

CONE A solid figure tapering evenly from a circle to a point.
Surface area of a cone = $\pi r^2 + \pi r l$
Volume of cone = $\frac{1}{3}\pi r^2 h$

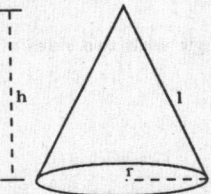

SOLID GEOMETRY – THREE-DIMENSIONAL SHAPES BOUNDED BY STRAIGHT LINES (POLYHEDRONS)

TETRAHEDRON A solid shape (polyhedron) that has four sides, all of which are triangles, which meet to form a vertex.
Surface area of a tetrahedron with equal sides = 2bh
Volume of a tetrahedron = $\frac{1}{3}$ (the area of the triangular base × the height)

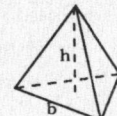

PYRAMID A solid shape (polyhedron) that has four or more sides, all of which are triangles, which meet to form a vertex and whose base is a polygon of three or more sides.

Surface area of a pyramid with a rectangular base
= bl + 2bh = area of base + area of sides
(applies for all pyramids)
Volume of a pyramid with a rectangular base
= ⅓(bl) × h = ⅓ area of base × altitude
(applies for all pyramids)

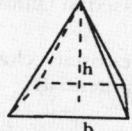

PRISM A solid shape (polyhedron) whose ends are equal and parallel polygons and whose sides are parallelograms.

Surface Area of a prism whose ends are triangles
= bh + 3lb
Volume of a prism whose ends are triangles
= ½(lbh)

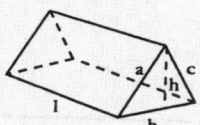

CUBE A solid shape (polyhedron) that has six equal square sides and all angles are right angles (90°).
Surface area of a cube = $6a^2$
Volume of a cube = a^3

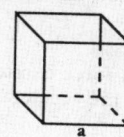

HEXAHEDRON A solid shape (polyhedron) that has six sides that are not necessarily equal.
Surface area of a hexahedron = 2(ac + bc + ab)
Volume of a hexahedron
whose angles ≠ 90° = abc
whose angles = 90° = a^3

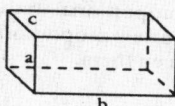

EQUATIONS OF MOTION AND KINETICS

KEY:

a	=	acceleration
s	=	distance traveled
t	=	time for which acceleration takes place
v	=	velocity
v_0	=	initial velocity
v_f	=	final velocity
g	=	acceleration of gravity

Basic Equations

distance	= velocity × time
velocity	= distance ÷ time
time	= distance ÷ velocity
acceleration	= change in velocity ÷ time

More Equations

velocity	$v = v_0 + at$
distance traveled	$s = v_0t + \frac{1}{2}at^2$
distance traveled	$s = \frac{1}{2}(v_0 + v_f)t$
distance traveled by falling body	$s = \frac{1}{2}gt^2$

EQUATIONS OF PHYSICS AND KINETICS

KEY:

d	=	distance between masses
Ep	=	gravitational potential energy
F	=	force
g	=	acceleration of gravity
h	=	height
J	=	impulse
m	=	mass of an object
m_1, m_2	=	two masses
p	=	momentum
t	=	time
T	=	period of a wave
v	=	velocity
v_0	=	initial velocity
v_f	=	final velocity
W	=	force of weight
W_1, W_2	=	two weights
l	=	wavelength

Equations:

acceleration	$a = (v_f - v_0)/t$
centrifugal force	$F = mv^2/d$
centripetal acceleration	$a = v^2/d$
force of gravity	$W = mg$
gravity inverse square law	$F = g \times Mm/d^2$
impulse	$J = Ft$
kinetic energy	$KE = \frac{1}{2}mv^2$
mass and weight relationship	$m_1m_2 = W_1/W_2$
mechanical advantage	$MA = load/effort$
moment of a force	$moment = Fd$
momentum	$p = mv$
potential energy	$PE = mgh$
power	$Power = Work \div t$
pressure	$Pressure = Work \times area$
wavelength	$l = vT$
weight	$W = mg$
work	$work = Fd$

NEWTON'S LAWS OF MOTION

Newton's first law A body will remain at rest or traveling in a straight line at constant speed unless it is acted upon by an external force.

Newton's second law The resultant force exerted on a body is directly proportional to the acceleration produced by the force.

$$F = ma$$

$$F = mv_f - mv_0$$

Newton's third law To every action there is an equal and opposite reaction.

Newton's Law of Gravitation

Every particle in the universe attracts every other particle with a force that is directly proportional to the product of their masses and inversely proportional to the square of the distance between them.

$$F = g^{(m_1 m_2)}/d^2$$

Einstein's Law of the Relationship between Matter and Energy

KEY:

E	=	energy
m	=	mass
c	=	velocity of light

Energy - matter relationship: $E = mc^2$

ELECTRICAL EQUATIONS

KEY:

d	=	distance between the charges
E	=	electromotive force
F	=	electrostatic charge
I	=	amperes (electrical current)
k	=	constant of proportionality
P	=	power
r	=	resistance expressed in Ohms
Q	=	charge
Q_a, Q_b	=	quantities of electrostatic charge
V	=	volts (electrical potential)
W	=	watts

FORMULAS:

charge :	$Q = W/V$
Coulomb's law :	$F = k \times Q_a Q_b/d^2$
electrical power :	$P = IV$
electromotive force :	$E = V + Ir$
Ohm's law :	$r = V/I$

LAWS OF GASES

Avogadro's Law Equal volumes of gases, measured under the same conditions of temperature and pressure, contain an equal number of molecules.

Boyle's Law If the temperature remains constant, the volume of a gas varies inversely as the pressure changes.

$$P_1 V_1 = P_2 V_2$$

Charles'S Law If the pressure is constant, the volume of a given mass of gas is directly proportional to the absolute temperature.

$$V_1/T_1 = V_2/T_2$$

Dalton's Law of Partial Pressure The pressure exerted on the walls of a vessel is the sum of the pressures each gas would exert if it were present alone.

$$P_{total} = P_1 + P_2 + P_3 + \ldots$$

COMMON CONSTANTS USED IN PHYSICS

	SYMBOL	UNITS
absolute zero	$0°$	$-273°C$
angstrom unit	Å	1.00×10^{10} meter
atmospheric pressure at earth's surface		$14.7\ {}^{lb}/_{in^2}$
atomic mass unit	amu	$1.66 \times 10^{-24} g$
Avogadro's constant	N_A	6.02252×10^{23} per mole
Boltzmann's constant	k	$1.38 \times 10^{-23}\ {}^j/_k$
charge of electron	e	$1.60210 \times 10^{-19} C$
Earth-mass	m_e	$5.98 \times 10^{24}\ kg$
electro—magnetic constant	μ	$1.26 \times 10^{-7}\ {}^{weber}/_{amp \cdot m}$
electron—radius mass	r_e	$2.81777 \times 10^{-15}\ m$
electron—rest mass	m_e	$9.1091 \times 10^{-31}\ kg$
electron—volt	e_v	$1.60 \times 10^{-19}\ joule$
electrostatic constant	C	$9.00 \times 10^9\ {}^{n \cdot m^2}/_{coul^2}$
Faraday's constant	F	$9.64870 \times 10^{C}/_{mol}$
gravitational constant	G	$6.670 \times 10^{-11} N\ {}^{m^2}/_{kg^2}$
gravity—Acceleration at Earth's surface	g	$9.81\ {}^m/_{sec^2}$ or $32\ {}^{ft}/_{sec^2}$
heat equivalent	kcal	$4.19 \times 10^2\ joule$
light speed	c	$2.997925 \times 10^{8} {}^m/_s$
molal gas constant	R	$8.3143\ {}^J/_{k\ mol}$
molal boiling point depression constant for H_2O		$1.86°C$
molal boiling point elevation for H_2O		$0.52°C$
neutron—rest mass	m_n	$1.67482 \times 10^{-27} kg$
Planck's constant	h	$6.6256 \times 10^{-34} J \times s$
proton—rest mass	m_p	$1.67252 \times 10^{-27} kg$
volume standard	liter (L)	$1.00 \times 10^3 cm^3$

SI (Système Internationale) UNITS AND MULTIPLES

QUANTITY	SI UNIT	SYMBOL
amount of substance	mole	mol
capacitance	farad	F
charge	coulomb	C
current	ampere	A
energy or work	joule	J
force	newton	N
frequency	hertz	Hz
luminous intensity	candela	cd
magnetic flux	weber	Wb
magnetic flux density	tesla	T
mass	kilogram	kg
potential difference	volt	V
power of a lens	diopter	D
pressure	pascal	Pa
radioactivity	becquerel	Bq
resistance	ohm	Ω
sound intensity	decibel	dB
temperature	°Celsius	°C
temperature, thermodynamic	kelvin	K
time	second	s

TRIGONOMETRIC FUNCTIONS

$$\sin \theta = \frac{BC}{AC} = \frac{opposite}{hypotenuse}$$

$$\cos \theta = \frac{AB}{AC} = \frac{adjacent\ side}{hypotenuse}$$

$$\tan \theta = \frac{BC}{AB} = \frac{opposite\ side}{adjacent\ side}$$

Degree	Radian	Sine	Cosine	Tangent
0°	0	0	1	0
1°	0.017	0.018	1	0.018
2°	0.035	0.035	0.999	0.035
3°	0.052	0.052	0.999	0.052
4°	0.07	0.07	0.998	0.07
5°	0.087	0.087	0.996	0.088
6°	0.105	0.105	0.995	0.105
7°	0.122	0.122	0.993	0.123
8°	0.14	0.139	0.99	0.141
9°	0.157	0.156	0.988	0.158
10°	0.175	0.174	0.985	0.176
11°	0.192	0.191	0.982	0.194
12°	0.209	0.208	0.978	0.213
13°	0.227	0.225	0.974	0.231
14°	0.244	0.242	0.97	0.249
15°	0.262	0.259	0.966	0.268
16°	0.279	0.276	0.961	0.287
17°	0.297	0.292	0.956	0.306
18°	0.314	0.309	0.951	0.325
19°	0.332	0.326	0.946	0.344
20°	0.349	0.342	0.94	0.364
21°	0.367	0.358	0.934	0.384
22°	0.384	0.375	0.927	0.404
23°	0.401	0.391	0.921	0.425
24°	0.419	0.407	0.914	0.445
25°	0.436	0.423	0.906	0.466
26°	0.454	0.438	0.899	0.488
27°	0.471	0.454	0.891	0.51
28°	0.489	0.47	0.883	0.532
29°	0.506	0.485	0.875	0.554
30°	0.524	0.5	0.866	0.577
31°	0.541	0.515	0.857	0.601
32°	0.559	0.53	0.848	0.625
33°	0.576	0.545	0.839	0.649
34°	0.593	0.559	0.829	0.675
35°	0.611	0.574	0.819	0.7
36°	0.628	0.588	0.809	0.727
37°	0.646	0.602	0.799	0.754
38°	0.663	0.616	0.788	0.781
39°	0.681	0.629	0.777	0.81
40°	0.698	0.643	0.766	0.839
41°	0.716	0.658	0.755	0.869
42°	0.733	0.669	0.743	0.9
43°	0.751	0.682	0.731	0.933
44°	0.768	0.695	0.719	0.966
45°	0.785	0.707	0.707	1
46°	0.803	0.719	0.695	1.036
47°	0.82	0.731	0.682	1.072
48°	0.838	0.743	0.669	1.111
49°	0.855	0.755	0.656	1.15
50°	0.873	0.766	0.643	1.192
51°	0.89	0.777	0.629	1.235
52°	0.908	0.788	0.616	1.28
53°	0.925	0.799	0.602	1.327
54°	0.942	0.809	0.588	1.376
55°	0.96	0.819	0.574	1.428
56°	0.977	0.829	0.559	1.483
57°	0.995	0.839	0.545	1.54
58°	1.012	0.848	0.53	1.6
59°	1.03	0.857	0.515	1.664
60°	1.047	0.866	0.5	1.732
61°	1.065	0.875	0.485	1.804
62°	1.082	0.883	0.47	1.881
63°	1.1	0.891	0.454	1.963
64°	1.117	0.899	0.438	2.05
65°	1.134	0.906	0.423	2.145
66°	1.152	0.914	0.407	2.246
67°	1.169	0.921	0.391	2.356
68°	1.187	0.927	0.375	2.475
69°	1.204	0.934	0.358	2.605
70°	1.222	0.94	0.342	2.747
71°	1.239	0.946	0.326	2.904
72°	1.257	0.951	0.309	3.078
73°	1.274	0.956	0.292	3.271
74°	1.292	0.961	0.276	3.487
75°	1.309	0.966	0.259	3.732
76°	1.326	0.97	0.242	4.011
77°	1.344	0.974	0.225	4.331
78°	1.361	0.978	0.208	4.705
79°	1.379	0.982	0.191	5.145
80°	1.396	0.985	0.174	5.671
81°	1.414	0.988	0.156	6.314
82°	1.431	0.99	0.139	7.115
83°	1.449	0.993	0.122	8.144
84°	1.466	0.995	0.105	9.514
85°	1.484	0.996	0.087	11.43
86°	1.501	0.998	0.07	14.303
87°	1.518	0.999	0.052	19.081
88°	1.536	0.999	0.035	28.635
89°	1.553	1	0.018	57.285
90°	1.571	1	0	∞

Weights and Measures

LENGTHS AND DISTANCE

ENGLISH AND U.S. LINEAR MEASURE

$1/12$ foot	=	1 inch (in)
12 inches	=	1 foot (ft)
3 feet	=	1 yard (yd)
$5^1/2$ yards ($16^1/2$ ft)	=	1 rod (rd)
40 rods (660 ft)	=	1 furlong (fur)
8 furlongs (5,280 ft) (1760 yds)	=	1 mile (mi) or 1 statute mile
6,076.11549 feet	=	1 nautical mile (nmi)
3 miles	=	1 league

METRIC LINEAR MEASURE

10 millimeters (mm)	=	1 centimeter (cm)
10 centimeters	=	1 decimeter (dm)
10 decimeters	=	1 meter (m)
10 meters	=	1 dekameter (dam)
10 dekameters	=	1 hectometer (hm)
10 hectometers	=	1 kilometer (km)

AREA MEASURE

ENGLISH AND U.S. SYSTEM

144 sq inches (in^2)	=	1 sq foot (ft^2)
9 sq feet	=	1 sq yard (yd^2)
$30^1/4$ sq yards	=	1 sq rod (rd^2)
160 sq rods	=	1 acre
640 acres	=	1 sq mile (mi^2)
6 sq miles	=	1 township

METRIC SYSTEM

100 sq millimeters (mm^2)	=	1 sq centimeter (cm^2)
100 sq centimeters	=	1 sq decimeter (dm^2)
100 sq decimeters	=	1 sq meter (m^2)
100 sq meters	=	1 are (a)
100 ares	=	1 hectare (ha)
100 hectares	=	1 sq. kilometer (km^2)

CUBIC MEASURE

ENGLISH AND U.S. SYSTEM

1,728 cubic inches (in^3)	=	1 cubic foot (ft^3)
27 cubic feet	=	1 cubic yard (yd^3)
40 cubic feet	=	1 ton (shipping)

METRIC SYSTEM

1,000 cubic millimeters (mm^3)	=	1 cubic centimeters (cm^3)
1,000 cubic centimeters	=	1 cubic decimeter (dm^3)
1,000 cubic decimeters	=	1 cubic meter (m^3) = 1 stere

WEIGHTS

TROY WEIGHT

1 grain	=	0.0416666 pennyweight
24 grains	=	1 pennyweight (dwt)
20 pennyweights	=	1 ounce troy (oz t)
12 ounces troy	=	1 pound troy (lb t)

AVOIRDUPOIS WEIGHT

$27^{11}/32$ grains	=	1 dram
16 drams	=	1 ounce avoirdupois (oz)
16 ounces avoirdupois	=	1 pound avoirdupois (lb)
100 pounds avoirdupois	=	1 short hundredweight (cwt)
20 short hundredweight	=	1 short ton = 2,000 pounds avoirdupois

APOTHECARIES' WEIGHT

20 grains	=	1 scruple (s ap)
3 scruples	=	1 dram apothecaries' (dr ap)
8 drams apothecaries'	=	1 ounce apothecaries' (oz ap)
12 ounces apothecaries'	=	1 pound apothecaries'

METRIC WEIGHT

10 milligrams (mg)	=	1 centigram (cg)
10 centigrams	=	1 decigram (dg)
10 decigrams	=	1 gram (g)
10 grams	=	1 dekagram (dag)
10 dekagrams	=	1 hectogram (hg) or 100 grams
10 hectograms	=	1 kilogram (kg) or 1000 grams
100 kilograms	=	1 quintal (q)
10 quintals	=	1 metric ton (t) or 1,000 kilograms

LIQUID AND DRY MEASURE

Though many of the U.S. and English units for liquid and dry measurements are the same, some of their values are different. For more information see the Table of Conversions and Equivalents (Capacities and Volumes)

ENGLISH SYSTEM

60 minims (min)	=	1 dram (dr)
8 drams	=	1 fluid ounce (fl oz)
5 fluid ounces	=	1 gill
4 gills	=	1 pint (pt)
2 pints	=	1 quart (qt)
4 quarts	=	1 gallon (gal)

U.S. SYSTEM (APOTHECARIES' FLUID MEASURE)

60 minims (min)	=	1 fluid dram (fl dr)
8 fluid drams	=	1 fluid ounce (fl oz)
16 fluid ounces	=	1 pint (pt)
2 pints	=	1 quart (qt)
4 quarts	=	

DRY MEASURE (U.S AND ENGLISH)

2 pints (pt)	=	1 quart (qt)
8 quarts	=	1 peck (pk)
4 pecks	=	1 bushel (bu)

METRIC SYSTEM (BOTH LIQUID AND DRY)

10 milliliters (mL)	=	1 centiliter (cL)
10 centiliters	=	1 deciliter (dL)
10 deciliter	=	1 liter (L)
10 liters	=	1 dekaliter (daL)
10 dekaliters	=	1 hectoliter (hL)
10 hectoliters	=	1 kiloliters (kL)

GUNTER'S OR SURVEYOR'S CHAIN MEASURE

7.92 inches	=	1 link (li)
100 links	=	1 chain (ch)
80 chains	=	1 mile

ANGULAR AND CIRCULAR MEASURE

60 seconds (")	=	1 minute (')
60 minutes	=	1 degree (°)
90 degrees	=	1 right angle
180 degrees	=	1 straight angle
360 degrees	=	1 circle

QUICK CONVERSION CHART

ENGLISH AND U.S TO METRIC

TO CONVERT	TO	MULTIPLY BY

METRIC TO ENGLISH AND U.S.

TO CONVERT	TO	MULTIPLY BY

LENGTH

TO CONVERT	TO	MULTIPLY BY	TO CONVERT	TO	MULTIPLY BY
inches	millimeters	25.4	millimeters	inches	0.0394
inches	centimeters	2.54	centimeters	inches	0.3937
feet	meters	0.3048	meters	feet	3.2808
yards	meters	0.9144	meters	yards	1.0936
miles	kilometers	1.6093	kilometers	miles	0.6214

MASS

TO CONVERT	TO	MULTIPLY BY	TO CONVERT	TO	MULTIPLY BY
drams avoirdupois	grams	1.772	grams	drams	0.564
ounces (avdp)	grams	28.35	grams	ounces (avdp)	0.0353
pounds (avdp)	kilograms	0.4536	kilograms	pounds (avdp)	2.2046
tons (short)	metric tons	0.9072	metric tons	tons (short)	1.1023

LIQUID VOLUME AND CAPACITIES

TO CONVERT	TO	MULTIPLY BY	TO CONVERT	TO	MULTIPLY BY
teaspoons	milliliters	5	milliliters	ounces	0.034
tablespoons	milliliters	15	milliliters	cubic inches	0.06
cubic inches	milliliters	16	liters	pints	2.113
ounces	milliliters	29.574	liters	quarts	1.056
cups	liters	0.24	liters	gallons	0.264
pints	liters	0.473	cubic meters	cubic feet	35.3
quarts	liters	0.946	cubic meters	cubic yards	1.3
gallons	liters	3.785			
cubic feet	cubic meters	0.03			
cubic yards	cubic meters	0.76			

AREA

TO CONVERT	TO	MULTIPLY BY	TO CONVERT	TO	MULTIPLY BY
sq. inches	sq. centimeters	6.451	sq. centimeters	sq. inches	0.155
sq. feet	sq. meters	0.09	sq. meters	sq. feet	10.764
sq. yards	sq. meters	0.836	sq. meters	sq. yards	1.196
sq. miles	sq. kilometers	2.59	sq. kilometers	sq. miles	0.3861
acres	hectares	0.4047	hectare	acres	2.471

TEMPERATURE CONVERSION

To convert Celsius to Fahrenheit multiply the number by 9, divide by 5, and add 32. To convert Fahrenheit to Celsius subtract 32 from the number and multiply by five, then divide by 9.

−273° Celsius and −460° Fahrenheit represent absolute zero, at which temperature all molecular motion ceases.

0° Celsius and 32° Fahrenheit represent water's freezing point.

100° Celsius and 212° Fahrenheit represent water's boiling point.

CELSIUS	FAHRENHEIT	FAHRENHEIT	CELSIUS
−273	−460	−460	−273
−200	−328	−200	−129
−100	−148	−100	−73
−40	−40	−40	−40
−25	−13	−25	−32
−15	5	0	−18
−10	14	10	−12
−5	23	20	−7
0	32	30	−1
5	41	32	0
10	50	40	4
20	68	50	10
30	86	60	16
37	98.6	70	21
40	104	80	27
50	122	90	32
60	140	100	38
70	158	125	52
80	176	150	66
90	194	200	93
100	212	212	100

TABLE OF EQUIVALENTS AND CONVERSIONS

LENGTHS

1 agate (typographical measurement)	$\frac{1}{14}$ inch 5.5 points
1 angstrom (A) (light-wave measurement)	0.0001 micron 0.0000001 millimeter 0.000000004 inch
1 barleycorn	$\frac{1}{3}$ inch 0.75 centimeters
1 bolt (cloth measurement)	40 yards (U.S.) 42 yards (British)
1 cable's length	120 fathoms 720 feet 219.456 meters
1 chain (ch) (Gunter's or surveyor's)	66 feet 20.1168 meters
1 chain, nautical	15 feet 4.56 meters
1 cubit (ancient unit of measurement)	18 inches 45.72 centimeters
1 decimeter (dm)	10 centimeters 3.937 inches
1 degree (geographical)	69.047 miles (avg) 111.123 kilometers (avg)
1 degree of latitude	68.708 miles at equator 110.551 kilometers at equator 69.403 miles at poles 111.669 kilometers at poles
1 degree of longitude	69.171 miles at equator 111.296 kilometers at equator
1 dekameter (dam)	32.808 feet 10 meters
1 ell (cloth measurement)	$1\frac{1}{4}$ yards 1.143 meters
1 fathom	6 feet 1.8288 meters
1 foot (ft)	12 inches 30.480 centimeters 0.3048 meters
1 furlong (fur)	660 feet 40 rods 201.168 meters
1 hand (to measure horses)	4 inches 10.16 centimeters
1 hectometer (hm)	100 meters 109.362 yards
1 inch (in)	$\frac{1}{12}$ foot 2.54 centimeters
1 kilometer (km)	1000 meters 0.6214 mile
1 league	3 miles 4.828 kilometers
1 link (Gunter's or surveyor's)	7.92 inches 20.1168 centimeters
1 link (engineers)	1 foot 0.305 meter
1 meter (m)	100 centimeters 39.37 inches 3.2808 feet
1 micron (micrometer)	0.001 millimeter 0.0000397 inches
1 mil	0.001 inch 0.0254 millimeter
1 mile (statute or land)	5,280 feet 1,760 yards 1.609 kilometers
1 mile nautical (nmi) (international)	6,076.11549 feet 1.852 kilometers
1 millimeter (mm)	0.1 centimeter 0.3937 inch
1 nail (cloth measurement)	$2\frac{1}{2}$ inches 6.35 centimeters
1 nanometer	0.001 micrometer 0.0000003937 inch
1 pica (typographical measurement)	0.166667 inch 12 points
1 point (typographical measurement)	0.013837 inch $\frac{1}{72}$ inch
1 quarter (cloth measurement)	4 nails 9 inches 25.4 centimeters
1 rod	$5\frac{1}{2}$ yards 5.0292 meters
1 span	9 inches 22.86 centimeters
1 yard	3 feet 0.914 meter

AREAS AND SURFACES

1 acre	43,560 sq feet 4,840 sq yards 0.405 hectare
1 are (a)	100 sq meters 119.599 sq yards 0.025 acres
1 hectare (ha)	100 ares 11,959.9 sq yards 2.471 acres
1 rod	5.5 yards 5.029 meters
1 sq centimeter (cm^2)	100 sq millimeters 0.155 sq inch
1 sq decimeter (dm^2)	100 sq centimeters 15.5 sq inches
1 sq foot (ft^2)	144 sq inches 929.030 sq centimeters
1 hectare (ha)	100 ares 2.471 acres
1 sq inch (in^2)	$\frac{1}{144}$ sq foot 6.4516 sq centimeters
1 sq kilometer (km^2)	1,000,000 sq meters 100 hectares 247.105 acres 0.386 sq mile
1 sq meter (m^2)	10,000 sq centimeters 10.764 sq feet 1.196 sq yards
1 sq mile (mi^2)	27,878,400 sq feet 640 acres 258.99 hectares 2.5899 sq kilometers
1 sq millimeter (mm^2)	0.01 centimeters 0.002 sq inch
1 sq rod (rd^2)	30.25 sq yards 25.293 sq meters
1 square (construction)	100 sq feet 929.030 sq meters
1 sq yard (yd^2)	9 sq feet 0.836 sq meter
1 township	6 sq miles 15.54 square kilometers

WEIGHTS AND MASSES

1 bale (cotton)	500 pounds (U.S.)
	227.1 kilograms
	750 pounds (Egypt)
	340.2 kilograms
1 carat (c)*	200 milligrams
	3.086 grains
1 centigram (cg)	10 milligrams
	0.15 grain
1 decigram (dg)	100 milligrams
	1.5 grains
1 dekagrams (dag)	10 grams
	0.352 ounce avoirdupois
1 dram apothecaries'	60 grains
	3.888 grams
1 dram avoirdupois (dr avdp)	27$^{11}\!/_{32}$ grains
	1.772 grams
1 grain	64.799 milligrams
1 gram (g)	1,000 milligrams
	10 decigrams
	15.432 grains
	0.0352 ounce avoirdupois
1 hundredweight gross or long	112 pounds
	50.802 kilograms
1 hectogram	100 grams
	10 dekagrams
	3.52 ounces avoirdupois
1 hundredweight net or short (cwt or net)	100 pounds avoirdupois
	45.359 kilograms
1 kilogram (kg)	1,000 grams
	10 hectograms
	2.205 pounds
1 microgram (μg)	0.000001 gram
	0.0000154 grain
1 milligram (mg)	0.001 gram
	0.015 grain
1 ounce, avoirdupois (oz)	437.5 grains
	16 drams avoirdupois
	0.911 ounce troy or apothecaries'
	28.350 grams
1 ounce troy or apothecaries'	480 grains
	1.097 ounces avoirdupois
	31.103 grams
1 pennyweight (dwt)	24 grains
	1.555 grams
1 point	0.01 carat
	2 milligrams
1 pound avoirdupois (lb advp)	7,000 grains
	16 ounces avoirdupois
	1.215 pounds troy
	453.59237 grams
1 pound troy or apothecaries'	5,760 grains
	12 ounces apothecaries' or troy*
	0.823 pound avoirdupois
	0.373 kilograms
1 quintal (q)	100 kilograms
	220.46 pounds avoirdupois
1 scruple apothecaries' (s ap)	20 grains
	1.295 grams
1 stone (used in Great Britain)	14 pounds avoirdupois
	6.4 kilograms
1 ton, gross or long†	2,240 pounds
	1.12 net tons
1 ton (metric)	1,000 kilograms
	10 quintals
	2,204.623 pounds
	0.984 gross ton
	1.102 net tons
1 ton, net or short (sh ton)	2,000 pounds
	20 hundredweights
	0.893 gross ton
	0.907 metric ton

*Note: ounces and pounds troy and apothecaric are equivalent.
†The long ton is used mostly for industrial purposes in the United States.

CAPACITIES AND VOLUMES

1 barrel (bbl) liquid‡	31 to 42 gallons
1 barrel (bbl) standard, for fruits, vegetables, and other dry commodities except cranberries	7,056 cubic inches
	105 dry quarts
	3.281 bushels struck measure
1 barrel (bbl) standard for cranberries	5,826 cubic inches
	86$^{45}\!/_{64}$ dry quarts
	2.709 bushels
1 board foot (fbm) (used for lumber)	144 cubic inches
1 bushel (bu) (U.S.) struck measure	2,150.42 cubic inches
	35.239 liters
1 bushel, heaped (U.S.)	2,747.715 cubic inches
	1.278 bushels, struck measure
1 centiliter (cL)	10 milliliters
	162.31 minims
	2.71 fluid drams
	0.61 cubic inch
1 cord (firewood)	128 cubic feet
	3.6224 cubic meters
1 cord foot (firewood)	16 cubic feet
	0.45 cubic meter
1 cubic centimeter (cm^3)	1,000 cubic millimeters
	0.061 cubic inch
1 cubic decimeter (dm^3)	1,000 cubic centimeters
	61.024 cubic inches
1 cubic foot (ft^3)	7.481 gallons
	28.317 cubic decimeters
1 cubic inch (in^3)	4.433 fluid drams
	0.554 fluid ounces
	16.387 cubic centimeters
1 cubic meter (m^3)	1,000 cubic decimeters
	1.308 cubic yards
1 cubic millimeter (mm^3)	0.001 cubic centimeter
	0.00006 cubic inch
1 cubic yard (yd^3)	27 cubic feet
	0.765 cubic meter
1 cup, measuring	16 tablespoons
	8 fluid ounces
	½ liquid pint
	240 milliliters
1 deciliter	10 centiliters
	3.39 fluid ounces
	6.1 cubic inches
1 dekaliter (daL)	10 liters
	2.642 gallons
	1.135 pecks
1 dram, fluid or liquid (U.S.)	$^1\!/_8$ fluid ounce
	0.226 cubic inch
	3.697 milliliters
	1.041 British fluid drachms
1 dram, fluid (fl dr) (British)	0.217 cubic inch
	3.552 milliliters
	0.961 U.S. fluid
1 freight ton	40 cubic feet
	1.132 cubic meters

1 gallon (gal) (U.S.)	128 U.S. fluid ounces 231 cubic inches 3.785 liters 0.833 British gallon	**1 peck**	8 quarts dry 8.810 liters
		1 pint (pt), dry	½ quart dry 33.6 cubic inches 0.551 liter
1 gallon (gal) (British)	160 British fluid ounces 277.42 cubic inches 4.546 liters 1.201 U.S. gallons		
		1 pint (pt), liquid (U.S.)	16 fluid ounces (U.S.) 28.875 cubic inches 0.473 liter
1 gill (gi)	4 fluid ounces 7.219 cubic inches 0.118 liter	**1 pipe** (liquids, especially wine)	2 hogsheads 29,306 cubic inches
1 great gross	12 gross	**1 quart (qt), dry (U.S.)**	67,201 cubic inches 1.101 liters 0.969 British quart
1 gross	12 dozen or 144		
1 hectoliter (hL)	100 liters 26.418 gallons 2.838 bushels	**1 quart (qt), liquid (U.S.)**	2 pints (U.S.) 57.75 cubic inches 0.946 liter 0.833 British quart
1 hogshead (hhd)	2 liquid barrels 14,653 cubic inches		
1 keg (beer)	30 gallons (approximately) 136.38 liters	**1 quart (qt), liquid (British)**	2 pints (British) 69.354 cubic inches 1.032 U.S. dry quarts 1.201 U.S. liquid quarts
1 kiloliter	1,000 liters 264.18 gallons 28.38 bushels		
		1 quire (paper)	25 sheets of paper
1 liter (L)	1,000 milliliters 61.03 cubic inches 1.057 liquid quarts 0.908 dry quart	**1 ream** (paper)	500 sheets of paper 20 quires
		1 stere	1,000 cubic decimeters 1.3079 cubic yards
1 magnum (wine)	1.59 quarts 1.5 liters	**1 tablespoon, measuring**	3 teaspoons 4 fluid drams ½ fluid ounce 15 milliliters
1 milliliter (mL)	0.001 liter 0.061 cubic inch 0.271 fluid dram 16.231 minims		
		1 teaspoon, measuring	⅓ tablespoon 1⅓ fluid drams 5 milliliters
1 minim	¹⁄₆₀ fluid dram 3.697 milliliters	**1 ton** (shipping)	40 cubic feet 1.132 cubic meters
1 ounce, liquid (U.S.)	8 fluid drams 1.805 cubic inches 29.574 milliliters 1.041 British fluid ounces	**1 tun**	252 gallons*
1 ounce, liquid (fl oz) (British)	8 fluid drams 1.734 cubic inches 28.412 milliliters 0.961 U.S fluid ounce		

‡Different laws establish varying values for the barrel. A barrel of petroleum consists of 42 gallons.

MISCELLANEOUS WEIGHTS AND MEASURES

ASTRONOMICAL UNITS OF DISTANCE

1 astronomical unit* (AU)	93,000,000 miles 149,600,000 kilometers
Speed of light	186,281 mi per sec 299,792.458 km per sec
1 light-year†	5,878,000,000,000 miles 9,460,500,000,000 kilometers 63,204 astronomical units
1 parsec‡	19,200,000,000,000 miles 30,800,000,000,000 kilometers 206,265 AU 3.262 light-years

ELECTRICAL POWER

ampere	A unit of electric current equivalent to a flow of one coulomb (6.23×10^{18} electrons) per second or to the steady current produced by one volt applied across a resistance of one ohm
kilowatt	1,000 watts
ohm	The unit of electrical resistance equal to the resistance of a circuit in which a potential difference of one volt produces a current of one ampere.

MISCELLANEOUS WEIGHTS AND MEASURES *(continued)*

ELECTRICAL POWER *(continued)*

volt
The unit of potential difference and electromotive force, equal to the difference of electric potential between two points of a conductor carrying a constant current of one ampere, when the power dissipated between these two points is equal to one watt.

watt
The rate of work represented by a current of one ampere under a pressure of one volt.

FIREARMS

caliber
The diameter of a bore of gun expressed in hundredths or thousandths of an inch.

gauge
A unit of length used to measure the diameter of a shotgun bore.

FORCE

newton
A unit of of force equal to that creating an acceleration of 1 meter per second per second when applied to a mass of one kilogram.

GOLD

carat (karat)
The amount of gold in an alloy of 24 parts in gold. Thus 24-karat is pure gold and ½ pure gold is equivalent to 12 karat gold.

HEAT, ENERGY AND WORK

british thermal unit (BTU)
The amount of heat required to raise the temperature of 1 pound (0.4 kg) of water 1 degree Fahrenheit.

calorie (cal)
A measure of heat energy representing the amount of heat needed to raise the temperature of 1 cubic centimeter of water 1 degree Celsius.

horsepower (hp)
A unit of work representing the power needed to rase 550 pounds by 1 foot in 1 second.

joule (J)
A unit of energy equal to the work done when a force of 1 newton is moved through a distance of 1 meter.
1 joule = 0.239 cal.

kilocalorie (kcal or Cal)
A measure of heat energy representing the amount of heat needed to raise the temperature of 1 kilogram of water 1 degree Celsius.

metric horsepower
A unit of work representing the power needed to raise 75 kilograms 1 meter in 1 second.

therm
100,000 BTUs.

SOUND

decibel
Unit of relative loudness. One decibel is the smallest amount of change detectable by the human ear, and 130 decibels is the average pain level.

COOKING MEASUREMENTS

1 teaspoon	= ⅓ tablespoon or ⅙ fluid ounce
3 teaspoons	= 1 tablespoon or ½ fluid ounce
2 tablespoons	= 1 fluid ounce
8 fluid ounces	= 1 cup
2 cups	= 1 pint
4 cups	= 1 quart or 2 pints
4 quarts	= 1 gallon

*Astronomical Unit is the mean distance earth to sun

†distance travelled by light in one year

‡Parsec is the distance at which a baseline of one astronomical unit subtends an arc of one second.

Chemical Elements

Atomic weights shown in parentheses are for the most stable or best-known isotopes.

ELEMENT	ATOMIC SYMBOL	ATOMIC NUMBER	ATOMIC WEIGHT	SPECIFIC GRAVITY	MELTING POINT C	BOILING POINT C	DISCOVERED
actinium	Ac	89	227	10.07	1050	3200	1899
aluminum	Al	13	26.9815	2.702	660	2057	1754
americium	Am	95	(243)	11.7	<1100	—	1944
antinony	Sb	51	121.75	6.684	630.5	1750	ancient
argon	Ar	18	39.948	1.784	−189.2	−185.7	1894
arsenic	As	33	74.9216	5.727	814	615	1649
astatine	At	85	(210)	—	302	337	1940
barium	Ba	56	137.34	3.5	850	1140	1774
berkelium	Bk	97	(247)	14	—	—	1949
beryillium	Be	4	9.0122	1.85	1278	2970	1798
bismuth	Bi	83	208.98	9.8	271.3	1560	1737
boron	B	5	10.811	3.33	2300	2550	1702
bromine	Br	35	79.904	2.928	−7.2	58.78	1826
cadmium	Cd	48	112.4	8.642	320.9	767	1817
calcium	Ca	20	40.08	1.55	845	1240	1808
californium	Cf	98	(251)	—	—	—	1949
carbon	C	6	12.01115	1.8–3.5	3700	4200	ancient
cerium	Ce	58	140.12	6.9	640	1400	1803
cesium	Cs	55	132.905	1.873	28.5	670	1860
chlorine	Cl	17	35.453	1.56	−103	−34.6	1810
chromium	Cr	24	51.996	7.2	1890	2200	1797
cobalt	Co	27	58.9332	8.9	1495	2900	1737
copper	Cu	29	63.54	8.92	1083	2336	ancient
curium	Cm	96	(247)	7	1340	—	1944
dysprosium	Dy	66	162.5	8.56	1409	2335	1886
einsteinium	Es	99	(254)	—	—	—	1952
erbium	Er	68	167.26	9.16	1250	2510	1843
europium	Eu	63	151.96	5.24	1150	1597	1901
fermium	Fm	100	(257)	—	—	—	1952
fluorine	F	9	18.9984	1.7	−223	−188	1768
francium	Fr	87	(223)	—	27	77	1939
gadolinium	Gd	64	157.25	7.95	1311	3233	1886
gallium	Ga	31	69.72	5.904	29.78	1983	1875
germanium	Ge	32	72.59	5.35	958.5	2700	1886
gold	Au	79	196.967	19.3	1063	2600	ancient
hafnium	Hf	72	178.49	13.3	2207	4000	1923
helium	He	2	4.0026	0.1785	−272.2	−268.9	1895
holmium	Ho	67	164.93	8.76	1470	2720	1879
hydrogen	H	1	1.00797	0.0899	−259.14	−252.8	1671
indium	In	49	114.82	7.3	156.4	2000	1863
iodine	I	53	126.9044	4.93	113.7	184.35	1811
iridium	Ir	77	192.2	22.42	2454	>4800	1804
iron	Fe	26	55.847	7.86	1535	3000	ancient
krypton	Kr	36	83.8	3.708	−156.6	−152.9	1898
lanthanum	La	57	138.91	6.15	826	1800	1839
lawrencium	Lr	103	(260)	—	—	—	1961
lead	Pb	82	207.19	11.344	327.4	1620	ancient
lithium	Li	3	6.941	0.534	186	1336	1817
lutetium	Lu	71	174.97	9.74	1656	3315	1907
magnesium	Mg	12	24.305	1.74	651	1107	1755
manganese	Mn	25	54.938	7.2	1260	1900	1774
mendelevium	Md	101	(258)	—	—	—	1955
mercury	Hg	80	200.59	13.55	−38.87	356.58	ancient
molybdenum	Mo	42	95.94	10.2	2620	5560	1777
neodymium	Nd	60	144.24	6.9	840	—	1885
neon	Ne	10	20.1797	0.9002	−248.7	−245.9	1898
neptunium	Np	93	237	19.5	640	—	1940

ELEMENT	ATOMIC SYMBOL	ATOMIC NUMBER	ATOMIC WEIGHT	SPECIFIC GRAVITY	MELTING POINT C	BOILING POINT C	DISCOVERED
nickel	Ni	28	58.6934	8.9	1455	2900	1751
niobium	Nb	41	92.906	8.55	1950	2900	1801
nitrogen	N	7	14.0067	1.2506	−209.9	−195.8	1772
nobelium	No	102	(259)	—	—	—	1957
osmium	Os	76	190.2	22.48	2700	>5300	1804
oxygen	O	8	15.9994	1.429	218.4	182.96	1774
palladium	Pd	46	106.4	11.4	1549	2540	1803
phosphorus	P	15	30.9738	1.82	44.1	280	1669
platinum	Pt	78	195.09	21.45	1773	4300	1748
plutonium	Pu	94	(244)	19.82	639.5	3508	1940
polonium	Po	84	(210)	9.32	254	962	1898
potassium	K	19	39.0983	0.86	62.3	760	1702
praeseodymium	Pr	59	140.907	6.5	940	—	1885
promethium	Pm	61	(145)	—	1080	2460	1947
protactinium	Pa	91	231	15.37	1000	—	1917
radium	Ra	88	226	5	960	1140	1898
radon	Rn	86	(222)	9.73	−110	−61.8	1900
rhenium	Re	75	186.2	20.53	3160	—	1925
rhodium	Rh	45	102.905	12.4	1985	>2500	1803
rubidium	Rb	37	85.47	1.532	38.5	700	1861
ruthenium	Ru	44	101.07	12.6	>1950	—	1844
samarium	Sm	62	150.35	6.93	1350	—	1879
scandium	Sc	21	44.956	2.5	1200	2400	1879
selenium	Se	34	78.96	4.82	220	688	1818
silicon	Si	14	28.086	2.42	1420	2600	1824
silver	Ag	47	107.8682	10.5	960.8	1950	ancient
sodium	Na	11	22.9898	0.97	97.5	880	1702
strontium	Sr	38	87.62	2.6	757	1150	1790
sulfur	S	16	32.064	2.07	112.8	444.6	ancient
tantalum	Ta	73	180.948	16.6	3027	4100	1802
techetium	Tc	43	(99)	11.49	2172	4877	1937
tellurium	Te	52	127.6	6.25	452	1390	1783
terbium	Tb	65	158.924	8.33	303	1457	1843
thallium	Tl	81	204.37	11.85	302	1457	1861
thorium	Th	90	232.038	11.2	1750	>3000	1828
thulium	Tm	69	168.934	9.35	1545	1727	1879
tin	Sn	50	118.69	7.28	231.9	2270	ancient
titanium	Ti	22	47.88	4.5	1800	>3000	1791
tungsten	W	74	183.85	19.3	3370	5900	1783
unnilhexium	Unh	106	—	—	—	—	—
unnilpentium	Unp	105	—	—	—	—	—
unnilquadium	Unq	104	—	—	—	—	—
uranium	U	92	238.03	18.7	1133	3818	1789
vandium	V	23	50.942	5.96	1710	3000	1831
xenon	Xe	54	131.3	5.851	−112	−107	1898
ytterbium	Yb	70	173.04	7.01	824	1193	1907
yttrium	Y	39	88.905	5.51	1490	2500	1794
zinc	Zn	30	65.37	7.14	419.5	907	1742
zirconium	Zr	40	91.22	6.4	1900	−2900	1789

Medical Terms

An understanding of medicine, medical procedures, and of the human body itself is not only of theoretical interest but of practical importance: knowledge of how the body works aids in caring and maintaining good health as well as coping with symptoms and diseases. While not offered as a replacement for expert medical advice, the following section provides succinct definitions and descriptions of parts of the body, diseases, and treatments. In addition to covering orthodox medical practices, it includes discussions of various options in alternative medicine, such as aromatherapy, and explanations of terms and methods employed in psychology and psychiatry.

abortion ending of a pregnancy before the fetus is developed sufficiently to survive outside the uterus. Loss of a fetus at a later gestational age is termed premature stillbirth. Abortion may be accidental (miscarriage) or deliberate (termination of pregnancy).

Achilles tendon tendon pinning the calf muscle to the heel bone. It is one of the largest in the human body.

acne skin eruption, mainly occurring among adolescents and young adults, caused by inflammation of the sebaceous glands which secrete an oily substance (sebum), the natural lubricant of the skin. Sometimes the openings of the glands become blocked and they swell; the contents decompose and pimples form on the face, back, and chest.

acupuncture system of inserting long, thin metal needles into the body at predetermined points to relieve pain, as an anesthetic in surgery, and to assist healing. The needles are rotated manually or electrically. The method, developed in ancient China and increasingly popular in the West, is thought to work by somehow stimulating the brain's own painkillers, the endorphins.

adrenal gland *or suprarenal gland* gland situated on top of the kidney. The adrenals are soft and yellow, and consist of two parts: the cortex and medulla. The *cortex* (outer part) secretes various steroid hormones, controls salt and water metabolism, and regulates the use of carbohydrates, proteins, and fats. The *medulla* (inner part) secretes the hormones adrenalin (epinephrine) and noradrenalin (norepinephrine) which, during times of stress, cause the heart to beat faster and harder, increase blood flow to the heart and muscle cells, and dilate airways in the lungs, thereby delivering more oxygen to cells throughout the body and in general preparing the body for "fight or flight".

AIDS (acronym for *a*cquired *i*mmune *d*eficiency *sy*ndrome) a grave disease caused by the human immunodeficiency virus (HIV), a retrovirus first identified 1983. HIV is transmitted in body fluids, mainly blood and sexual secretions.

alcoholism dependence on alcoholic liquor. It is characterized as an illness when consumption of alcohol interferes with normal physical or emotional health. Excessive alcohol consumption may produce physical and psychological addiction and lead to nutritional and emotional disorders. The direct effect is cirrhosis of the liver, nerve damage, and heart disease, and the condition is now showing genetic predisposition.

alimentary canal in animals, the tube through which food passes; it extends from the mouth to the anus. It is a complex organ, adapted for digestion. In human adults, it is about 30 ft/9 m long, consisting of the mouth cavity, pharynx, esophagus, stomach, and the small and large intestines.

allergy special sensitivity of the body that makes it react, with an exaggerated response of the natural immune defense mechanism, especially with histamines, to the introduction of an otherwise harmless foreign substance (*allergen*).

Alzheimer's disease common manifestation of dementia, thought to afflict one in 20 people over 65. Attacking the brain's "gray matter", it is a disease of mental processes rather than physical function, characterized by memory loss and progressive intellectual impairment.

amniocentesis sampling the amniotic fluid surrounding a fetus in the womb for diagnostic purposes. It is used to detect Down's syndrome and other genetic abnormalities.

anemia condition caused by a shortage of hemoglobin, the oxygen-carrying component of red blood cells. The main symptoms are fatigue, pallor, breathlessness, palpitations, and poor resistance to infection. Treatment depends on the cause.

anesthetic drug that produces loss of sensation or consciousness; the resulting state is *anesthesia*, in which the patient is insensitive to stimuli. Anesthesia may also happen as a result of nerve disorder.

analgesic agent for relieving pain. Opiates alter the perception or appreciation of pain and are effective in controlling "deep" visceral (internal) pain. Nonopiates, such as aspirin and paracetamol relieve musculoskeletal pain and reduce inflammation in soft tissues.

angina *or angina pectoris* severe pain in the chest due to impaired blood supply to the heart muscle because a coronary artery is narrowed. Faintness and difficulty in breathing accompany the pain. Treatment is by drugs, such as nitroglycerin and amyl nitrite; rest is important.

anorexia lack of desire to eat, especially the pathological condition of *anorexia nervosa*, usually found in adolescent girls and young women, who may be obsessed with the desire to lose weight. Compulsive eating, or bulimia, often accompanies anorexia.

antiinflammatory any substance that reduces swelling in soft tissues.

antibiotic drug that kills or inhibits the growth of bacteria and fungi. It is derived from living organisms such as fungi or bacteria, which distinguishes it from synthetic antimicrobials.

antibody a protein molecule produced in the blood by B-lymphocytes (see lymphocyte). Antibodies bind specific foreign agents that invade the body, tagging them for destruction by phagocytes (white blood cells that engulf and destroy invaders) or activating a chemical system that renders them harmless. Each antibody is specific for a particular antigen (the molecular pattern unique to a foreign substance).

antidepressant any drug used to relieve symptoms in depressive illness. The two main groups are the tricyclic antidepressants (TCADs) and the monoamine oxidase inhibitors (MAOIs), which act by altering chemicals available to the central nervous system. Both may produce serious side effects.

antiseptic any substance that kills or inhibits the growth of microorganisms.

antiviral any drug that acts against viruses, usually preventing them from multiplying. Most viral infections are not susceptible to antibiotics. Antivirals have been difficult drugs to develop, and do not necessarily cure viral diseases.

aorta the chief artery, the dorsal blood vessel carrying oxygenated blood from the left ventricle of the heart in birds and mammals. It branches to form smaller arteries, which in turn supply all body organs except the lungs.

appendicitis inflammation of the appendix, a small, blind extension of the bowel in the lower right abdomen. In an acute attack, the pus-filled appendix may burst, causing a potentially lethal spread of infection (peritonitis). Treatment is by removal (appendectomy).

aromatherapy the medicinal use of oils and essences derived from plants, flowers, and wood resins. Bactericidal properties and beneficial effects upon physiological functions are attributed to the oils, which are sometimes ingested but generally massaged into the skin. Aromatherapy was practiced in the ancient world and revived in the 1960s in France, where today it is an optional component of some courses available to post-graduate medical students.

artery vessel that carries blood from the heart to the rest of the body. It is built to withstand considerable pressure, having thick walls that are impregnated with muscle and elastic fibers. During contraction of the heart muscles, arteries expand in diameter to allow for the sudden increase in pressure that occurs; the resulting pulse or pressure wave can be felt at the wrist. Not all arteries carry oxygenated (oxygen-rich) blood; the pulmonary arteries convey deoxygenated (oxygen-poor) blood from the heart to the lungs.

arthritis inflammation of the joints, with pain, swelling, and restricted motion. Many conditions may cause arthritis, including gout and trauma to the joint.

aspirin acetylsalicylic acid, a popular pain-relieving drug (analgesic). Aspirin is no longer considered suitable for children under 12, because of a suspected link with a rare disease, Reye's syndrome. Recent medical research suggests that an aspirin a day may be of value in preventing heart attack (myocardial infarction) and thrombosis.

asthma difficulty in breathing due to spasm of the bronchi (air passages) in the lungs. Attacks may be provoked by allergy, infection, stress, or emotional upset. It may also be increasing as a result of air pollution and occupational hazards. Treatment is with bronchodilators to relax the bronchial muscles and thereby ease the breathing, and in severe cases by inhaled steroids that reduce inflammation of the bronchi.

atherosclerosis thickening and hardening of the walls of the arteries.

autoimmunity condition where the body's immune responses are mobilized not against "foreign" matter, such as invading germs, but against the body itself. Diseases considered to be of autoimmune origin include myasthenia gravis, rheumatoid arthritis, and lupus erythematosus.

Bach flower remedies an essentially homeopathic system of therapy developed in the 1920s by English physician Edward Bach. Based on the healing properties of wild flowers, it seeks to alleviate mental and emotional causes of disease rather than their physical symptoms.

back pain aches in the region of the spine. Low back pain can be caused by a very wide range of medical conditions. About half of all episodes of back pain will resolve within a week, but severe back pain can be chronic and disabling. The causes include muscle sprain, a prolapsed intervertebral disk, and vertebral collapse due to osteoporosis or cancer. Treatment methods include rest, analgesics, physiotherapy, and exercises.

Bates eyesight training method developed by US opthalmologist William Bates (1860—1931) to enable people to correct problems of vision without wearing glasses. The method is of proven effectiveness in relieving all refractive conditions, correcting squints, lazy eyes, and similar problems, but does not claim to treat eye disease.

behavior therapy in psychology, the application of behavioral principles, derived from learning theories, to the treatment of clinical conditions such as phobias, obsessions, sexual and interpersonal problems. For example, in treating a phobia the person is taken into the feared situation in gradual steps. Over time, the fear typically reduces, and the problem becomes less acute.

beta-blocker any of a class of drugs that block impulses that stimulate certain nerve endings (beta receptors) serving the heart muscles. This reduces the heart rate and the force of contraction, which in turn reduces the amount of oxygen (and therefore the blood supply) required by the heart. Beta-blockers are banned from use in competitive sports. They may be useful in the treatment of angina, arrhythmia, and raised blood pressure, and following myocardial infarctions. They must be withdrawn from use gradually.

biochemic tissue salts therapy the correction of imbalances or deficiencies in the body's resources of essential mineral salts. There are 12 tissue salts in the body and the healthy functioning of cells depends on their correct balance, but there is scant evidence that disease is due to their imbalance and can be cured by supplements, as claimed by German physician W H Schuessler in the 1870s, though many people profess to benefit from the "Schuessler remedies".

bioenergetics extension of Reichian therapy principles developed in the 1960s by US physician Alexander Lowen, and designed to promote, by breathing, physical exercise, and the elimination of muscular blockages, the free flow of energy in the body and thus restore optimum health and vitality.

biofeedback in medicine, the use of electrophysiological monitoring devices to "feed back" information about internal processes and thus facilitate conscious control. Developed in the US in the 1960s, the technique is effective in alleviating hypertension and preventing associated organic and physiological dysfunctions.

blindness complete absence or impairment of sight. It may be caused by heredity, accident, disease, or deterioration with age.

blood liquid circulating in the arteries, veins, and capillaries of vertebrate animals; the term also refers to the corresponding fluid in those invertebrates that possess a closed circulatory system. Blood carries nutrients and oxygen to individual cells and removes waste products, such as carbon dioxide. It is also important in the immune response and, in many animals, in the distribution of heat throughout the body.

blood poisoning condition in which poisons are spread throughout the body by pathogens in the bloodstream.

blood pressure pressure, or tension, of the blood against the inner walls of blood vessels, especially the arteries, due to the muscular pumping activity of the heart. Abnormally high blood pressure (hypertension) may be associated with various conditions or arise with no obvious cause; abnormally low blood pressure (hypotension) occurs in shock and after excessive fluid or blood loss from any cause.

bone hard connective tissue comprising the skeleton of most vertebrate animals. It consists of a network of collagen fibers impregnated with mineral salts (largely calcium phosphate and calcium carbonate), a combination that gives the bone great strength, comparable in some cases with that of reinforced concrete. Enclosed within this solid matrix are bone cells, blood vessels, and nerves. The interior of the long bones of the limbs consists of a spongy matrix filled with a soft marrow that produces blood cells.

bone marrow substance found inside the cavity of bones. In early life it produces red blood cells but later on lipids (fat) accumulate and its color changes from red to yellow.

brain in higher animals, a mass of interconnected nerve cells, forming the anterior part of the central nervous system, whose activities it coordinates and controls. In vertebrates, the brain is contained by the skull. An enlarged portion of the upper spinal cord, the *medulla oblongata*, contains centres for the control of respiration, heartbeat rate and strength, and blood pressure. Overlying this is the *cerebellum*, which is concerned with coordinating complex muscular processes such as maintaining posture and moving limbs. The cerebral hemispheres (*cerebrum*) are paired outgrowths of the front end of the forebrain, in early vertebrates mainly concerned with the senses, but in higher vertebrates greatly developed and involved in the integration of all sensory input and motor output, and in intelligent behavior.

bronchitis inflammation of the bronchi (air passages) of the lungs, usually caused initially by a viral infection, such as a cold or flu. It is aggravated by environmental pollutants, especially smoking, and results in a persistent cough, irritated mucus-secreting glands, and large amounts of sputum.

bronchus one of a pair of large tubes (bronchii) branching off from the windpipe and passing into the vertebrate lung. Apart from their size, bronchii differ from the bronchioles in possessing cartilaginous rings, which give rigidity and prevent collapse during breathing movements.

Caesarean section surgical operation to deliver a baby by cutting through the mother's abdominal and intrauterine walls. It may be recommended for almost any obstetric complication implying a threat to mother or baby.

cataract eye disease in which the crystalline lens or its capsule becomes opaque, causing blindness. Fluid accumulates between the fibers of the lens and gives place to deposits of albumin. These coalesce into rounded bodies, the lens fibers break down, and areas of the lens or the lens capsule become filled with opaque products of degeneration.

cervical smear removal of a small sample of tissue from the cervix (neck of the womb) to screen for changes implying a likelihood of cancer. The procedure is also known as the *Pap test* after its originator, George Papanicolau.

chemotherapy any medical treatment with chemicals. It usually refers to treatment of cancer with cytotoxic and other drugs.

chickenpox or *varicella* common acute disease, caused by a virus of the herpes group and transmitted by airborne droplets. Chickenpox chiefly attacks children under the age of ten. The incubation period is two to three weeks. One attack normally gives immunity for life.

chiropractic technique of manipulation of the spine and other parts of the body, based on the principle that disorders are attributable to aberrations in the functioning of the nervous system, which manipulation can correct.

cirrhosis any degenerative disease in an organ of the body, especially the liver, characterized by excessive development of connective tissue, causing scarring and painful swelling. Cirrhosis of the liver may be caused by an infection such as viral hepatitis, by chronic alcoholism or drug use, blood disorder, or malnutrition. If cirrhosis is diagnosed early, it can be arrested by treating the cause; otherwise it will progress to jaundice, edema, vomiting of blood, coma, and death.

clinical ecology in medicine, ascertaining environmental factors involved in illnesses, particularly those manifesting nonspecific symptoms such as fatigue, depression, allergic reactions, and immune system malfunctions, and prescribing means of avoiding or minimizing these effects.

clinical psychology discipline dealing with the understanding and treatment of health problems, particularly mental disorders. The main problems dealt with include anxiety, phobias, depression, obsessions, sexual and marital problems, drug and alcohol dependence, childhood behavioral problems, psychoses (such as schizophrenia), mental handicap, and brain damage (such as dementia).

codeine opium derivative that provides analgesia in mild to moderate pain. It also suppresses the cough center of the brain. It is an alkaloid, derived from morphine but less toxic and addictive.

cognitive therapy treatment for emotional disorders such as depression and anxiety. This approach encourages the patient to challenge the distorted and unhelpful thinking that is characteristic of these problems. The treatment includes behavior therapy and has been most helpful for people suffering from depression.

color therapy application of light of appropriate wavelength to alleviate ailments or facilitate healing. Colored light affects not only psychological but also physiological states—for instance, long exposure to red light raises blood pressure and speeds up heartbeat and respiration rates, whereas exposure to blue has the reverse effect.

coma a state of deep unconsciousness from which the subject cannot be roused and in which the subject does not respond to pain. Possible causes include head injury, liver failure, cerebral haemorrhage, and drug overdose.

contraceptive any drug, device, or technique that prevents pregnancy. The contraceptive pill (the Pill) contains female hormones that interfere with egg production or the first stage of pregnancy. The "morning- after" pill can be taken up to 72 hours after unprotected intercourse. Barrier contraceptives include condoms (sheaths) and diaphragms; they prevent the sperm entering the cervix (neck of the womb). Intrauterine devices (IUDs or coils) cause a slight inflammation of the lining of the womb; this prevents the fertilized egg from becoming implanted.

convulsion series of violent contractions of the muscles over which the patient has no control. It may be associated with loss of consciousness. Convulsions may arise from any one of a number of causes, including brain disease (such as epilepsy), injury, high fever, poisoning, and electrocution.

corticosteroid any of several steroid hormones secreted by the cortex of the adrenal glands; also synthetic forms with similar properties. Corticosteroids have antiinflammatory and immunosuppressive effects and may be used to treat a number of conditions including rheumatoid arthritis, severe allergies, asthma, some skin diseases, and some cancers. Side effects can be serious, and therapy must be withdrawn very gradually.

cranium the dome-shaped area of the vertebrate skull, consisting of several fused plates, that protects the brain.

crib death death of an apparently healthy baby during sleep, also known as *sudden infant death syndrome* (SIDS). It is most common in the winter months, and strikes more boys than girls. The cause is not known.

crystal therapy the application of crystals to diseased or disordered physical structures or processes to effect healing or stabilizing.

cystitis inflammation of the bladder, usually caused by bacterial infection, and resulting in frequent and painful urination. Treatment is by antibiotics and copious fluids.

deafness lack or deficiency in the sense of hearing, either inborn or caused by injury or disease of the middle or inner ear. Of assistance are hearing aids, lip- reading, a cochlear implant in the ear in combination with a special electronic processor, and sign language.

delusion in psychiatry, a false belief that is unshakeably held. Delusions are a prominent feature of schizophrenia and paranoia, but may also occur in severe depression and manic depression.

dementia mental deterioration as a result of physical changes in the brain. It may be due to degenerative change, circulatory disease, infection, injury, or chronic poisoning. *Senile dementia*, a progressive loss of mental abilities such as memory and orientation, is typically a problem of old age, and can be accompanied by depression.

depression emotional state characterized by sadness, unhappy thoughts, apathy, and dejection. Sadness is a normal response to major losses such as bereavement or unemployment. After childbirth, postnatal depression is common. However, clinical depression, which is prolonged or unduly severe, often requires treatment, such as antidepressant medication, cogni-

tive therapy, or, in very rare cases, electroconvulsive therapy (ECT), in which an electrical current is passed through the brain.

dermatitis inflammation of the skin, usually related to allergy. *Dermatosis* refers to any skin disorder and may be caused by contact or systemic problems.

dermatology science of the skin, its nature and diseases. It is a rapidly expanding field owing to the proliferation of industrial chemicals affecting workers, and the universal use of household cleaners, cosmetics, and sun screens.

diabetes disease diabetes mellitus in which a disorder of the islets of Langerhans in the pancreas prevents the body producing the hormone insulin, so that sugars cannot be used properly. Treatment is by strict dietary control and oral or injected insulin, depending on the type of diabetes.

dialysis the process used to mimic the effects of the kidneys. It may be life-saving in some types of poisoning. Dialysis is usually performed to compensate for failing kidneys.

diarrhea excessive action of the bowels so that the feces are fluid or semifluid. It is caused by intestinal irritants (including some drugs and poisons), infection with harmful organisms (as in dysentery, salmonella, or cholera), or allergies.

dietetics specialized branch of human nutrition, dealing with the promotion of health through the proper kinds and quantities of food.

Down's syndrome condition caused by a chromosomal abnormality (the presence of an extra copy of chromosome 21) which in humans produces mental retardation; a flattened face; coarse, straight hair; and a fold of skin at the inner edge of the eye (hence the former name "mongolism").

drug and alcohol dependence physical or psychological craving for addictive drugs such as alcohol, nicotine (in cigarettes), tranquilizers, heroin, or stimulants (for example, amphetamines). Such substances can alter mood or behavior. When dependence is established, sudden withdrawal from the drug can cause unpleasant physical and/or psychological reactions, which may be dangerous.

drug misuse illegal use of drugs for nonmedicinal purposes.

dyslexia malfunction in the brain's synthesis and interpretation of sensory information, popularly known as "word blindness". It results in poor ability to read and write, though the person may otherwise excel, for example, in mathematics. A similar disability with figures is called dyscalculus.

ear organ of hearing in animals. It responds to the vibrations that constitute sound, and these are translated into nerve signals and passed to the brain. A mammal's ear consists of three parts: outer ear, middle ear, and inner ear. The *outer ear* is a funnel that collects sound, directing it down a tube to the *ear drum* (tympanic membrane), which separates the outer and *middle ear*. Sounds vibrate this membrane, the mechanical movement of which is transferred to a smaller membrane leading to the *inner ear* by three small bones, the auditory ossicles. Vibrations of the inner ear membrane move fluid contained in the snail-shaped cochlea, which vibrates hair cells that stimulate the auditory nerve connected to the brain. Three fluid-filled canals of the inner ear detect changes of position; this mechanism, with other sensory inputs, is responsible for the sense of balance.

eczema inflammatory skin condition, a form of dermatitis, marked by dryness, rashes, itching, the formation of blisters, and the exudation of fluid. It may be allergic in origin and is sometimes complicated by infection.

electroconvulsive therapy (ECT) or *electroshock therapy* treatment for schizophrenia and depression, given under anesthesia and with a muscle relaxant. An electric current is passed through the brain to induce alterations in the brain's electrical activity. The treatment can cause distress and loss of concentration and memory, and so there is much controversy about its use and effectiveness.

electrocrystal diagnosis technique based on the finding that stimulated electromagnetic fields of the human body resonate at a particular frequency which varies with individuals, and that actual or incipient disease can be pinpointed by a scanning device responsive to local deviations from the person's norm.

endogenous endocrinotherapy the fostering of hormonal balance in the body by regulating the activities of the endocrine glands without recourse to introduced stimulants, suppressants, or supplements.

endometriosis common gynecological complaint in which patches of endometrium (the lining of the womb) are found outside the uterus.

endoscopy examination of internal organs or tissues by an instrument allowing direct vision. An endoscope is equipped with an eyepiece, lenses, and its own light source to illuminate the field of vision.

epilepsy disorder characterized by a tendency to develop fits, which are convulsions or abnormal feelings caused by abnormal electrical discharges in the cerebral hemispheres of the brain. Epilepsy can be controlled with a number of anticonvulsant drugs.

esophagus passage by which food travels from mouth to stomach. The human esophagus is about 9 in/23 cm long. Its upper end is at the bottom of the pharynx, immediately behind the windpipe.

eye the organ of vision. In the human eye, the light is focused by the combined action of the curved *cornea*, the internal fluids, and the *lens*.

Fallopian tube or *oviduct* in mammals, one of two tubes that carry eggs from the ovary to the uterus. An egg is fertilized by sperm in the Fallopian tubes, which are lined with cells whose cilia move the egg toward the uterus.

food poisoning any acute illness characterized by vomiting and diarrhea and caused by eating food contaminated with harmful bacteria (for example, listeriosis), poisonous food (for example, certain mushrooms, puffer fish), or poisoned food (such as lead or arsenic introduced accidentally during processing). A frequent cause of food poisoning is salmonella bacteria. These come in many forms, and strains are found in cattle, pigs, poultry, and eggs.

gall bladder small muscular sac, part of the digestive system of most, but not all, vertebrates. In humans, it is situated on the underside of the liver and connected to the small intestine by the bile duct. It stores bile from the liver.

gallstone pebblelike, insoluble accretion formed in the human gall bladder or bile ducts from cholesterol or calcium salts present in bile. Gallstones may be symptomless or they may cause pain, indigestion, or jaundice. They can be dissolved with medication or removed, along with the gall bladder, in an operation known as cholecystectomy.

gastroenteritis inflammation of the stomach and intestines, giving rise to abdominal pain, vomiting, and diarrhea. It may be caused by food or other poisoning, allergy, or infection, and is dangerous in babies.

geriatrics branch of medicine concerned with diseases and problems of the elderly.

German measles the common name for rubella.

glandular fever or *infectious mononucleosis* viral disease characterized at onset by fever and painfully swollen lymph nodes (in the neck); there may also be digestive upset, sore throat, and skin rashes. Lassitude persists for months and even years, and recovery can be slow. It is caused by the Epstein-Barr virus.

glaucoma condition in which pressure inside the eye (intraocular pressure) is raised abnormally as excess fluid accumulates. It occurs when the normal flow of intraocular fluid out of the eye is interrupted. As pressure rises, the optic nerve suffers irreversible damage, leading to a reduction in the field of vision and, ultimately, loss of eyesight.

gout disease, a hereditary form of arthritis, marked by an excess of uric acid crystals in the tissues, causing pain and inflammation in one or more joints (usually of the feet or hands). Acute attacks are treated with antiinflammatories.

gynecology in medicine, a specialist branch concerned with disorders of the female reproductive system.

hematology branch of medicine concerned with disorders of the blood.

hemophilia any of several inherited diseases in which normal blood clotting is impaired. The sufferer experiences prolonged bleeding from the slightest wound, as well as painful internal bleeding without apparent cause.

hemorrhoids distended blood vessels (varicose veins) in the area of the anus, popularly called *piles*.

hair analysis diagnostic technique for ascertaining deficiencies or excesses of mineral resources in the body, using a sophisticated analytic procedure called atomic-emission spectroscopy.

hay fever allergic reaction to pollen, causing sneezing, inflammation of the eyes, and asthmatic symptoms. Sufferers experience irritation caused by powerful body chemicals related to histamine produced at the site of entry. Treatment is by antihistamine drugs.

heart attack sudden onset of gripping central chest pain, often accompanied by sweating and vomiting, caused by death of a portion of the heart muscle following obstruction of a coronary artery by thrombosis (formation of a blood clot). Half of all heart attacks result in death within the first two hours, but in the remainder survival has improved following the widespread use of streptokinase and aspirin to treat heart-attack victims.

heart muscular organ that rhythmically contracts to force blood around the body of an animal with a circulatory system. The beating of the heart is controlled by the autonomic nervous system and an internal control center or pacemaker, the sinoatrial node.

heartburn burning sensation below the breastbone (sternum). It results from irritation of the lower esophagus (gullet) by excessively acid stomach contents, as sometimes happens during pregnancy and in cases of duodenal ulcer or obesity. It is often due to a weak valve at the entrance to the stomach that allows its contents to well up into the esophagus.

hepatitis any inflammatory disease of the liver, usually caused by a virus. Other causes include alcohol, drugs, gallstones, and amebic dysentery. Symptoms include weakness, nausea, and jaundice.

herbalism prescription and use of plants and their derivatives for medication. Herbal products are favored by alternative practitioners as "natural medicine", as opposed to modern synthesized medicines and drugs, which are regarded with suspicion because of the dangers of side-effects and dependence.

hernia or *rupture* protrusion of part of an internal organ through a weakness in the surrounding muscular wall, usually in the groin or navel. The appearance is that of a rounded soft lump or swelling.

herpes any of several infectious diseases caused by viruses of the herpes group. *Herpes simplex I* is the causative agent of a common inflammation, the cold sore. *Herpes simplexII* is responsible for genital herpes, a highly contagious, sexually transmitted disease characterized by painful blisters in the genital area. It can be transmitted in the birth canal from mother to newborn. *Herpes zoster* causes shingles; another herpes virus causes chickenpox.

holistic medicine umbrella term for an approach that virtually all alternative therapies profess, which considers the overall health and lifestyle profile of a patient, and treats specific ailments not primarily as conditions to be alleviated but rather as symptoms of more fundamental disease.

homeopathy or *homeopathy* system of medicine based on the principle that symptoms of disease are part of the body's self-healing processes, and on the practice of administering extremely diluted doses of natural substances found to produce in a healthy person the symptoms manifest in the illness being treated.

hormone-replacement therapy (HRT) use of oral estrogen and progesterone to help limit the effects of the menopause in women.

hospice residential facility specializing in palliative care for terminally ill patients and their relatives.

hydrotherapy use of water, externally or internally, for health or healing.

hyperactivity condition of excessive activity in young children, combined with inability to concentrate and difficulty in learning. The cause is not known, although some food additives have come under suspicion. Modification of the diet may help, and in the majority of cases there is improvement at puberty.

hypertension abnormally high blood pressure due to a variety of causes, leading to excessive contraction of the smooth muscle cells of the walls of the arteries. It increases the risk of kidney disease, stroke, and heart attack.

hypnosis artificially induced state of relaxation in which suggestibility is heightened. The subject may carry out orders after being awakened, and may be made insensitive to pain. Hypnosis is sometimes used to treat addictions to tobacco or overeating, or to assist amnesia victims.

hypnotherapy use of hypnotic trance and post-hypnotic suggestions to relieve stress-related conditions such as insomnia and hypertension, or to break health-inimical habits or addictions.

hypothermia condition in which the deep (core) temperature of the body spontaneously drops. If it is not discovered, coma and death ensue. Most at risk are the aged and babies (particularly if premature).

hysterectomy surgical removal of all or part of the uterus (womb). The operation is performed to treat fibroids (benign tumors growing in the uterus) or cancer; also to relieve heavy menstrual bleeding. A woman who has had a hysterectomy will no longer menstruate and cannot bear children.

immunization conferring immunity to infectious disease by artificial methods. The most widely used technique is vaccination.

impotence a physical inability to perform sexual intercourse (the term is not usually applied to women). Impotent men fail to achieve an erection, and this may be due to illness, the effects of certain drugs, or psychological factors.

in vitro fertilization (IVF) ("fertilization in glass") allowing eggs and sperm to unite in a laboratory to form embryos. The embryos produced may then either be implanted into the womb of the otherwise infertile mother (an extension of artificial insemination), or used for research.

incontinence failure or inability to control evacuation of the bladder or bowel (or both in the case of double incontinence). It may arise as a result of injury, childbirth, disease, or senility.

infection invasion of the body by disease-causing organisms (pathogens, or germs) that become established, multiply, and produce symptoms. Bacteria and viruses cause most diseases, but there are other microorganisms, protozoans, and other parasites.

inflammation defensive reaction of the body tissues to disease or damage, including redness, swelling, and heat.

influenza any of various virus infections primarily affecting the air passages, accompanied by systemic effects such as fever, chills, headache, joint and muscle pains, and lassitude. Treatment is with bed rest and analgesic drugs such as aspirin and paracetamol.

insulin protein hormone, produced by specialized cells in the islets of Langerhans in the pancreas, that regulates the metabolism (rate of activity) of glucose, fats, and proteins.

intrauterine device IUD or coil, a contraceptive device that is inserted into the womb (uterus). It is a tiny plastic object, sometimes containing copper. By causing a mild inflammation of the lining of the uterus it prevents fertilized eggs from becoming implanted.

jaundice yellow discoloration of the skin and whites of the eyes caused by an excess of bile pigment in the bloodstream. Mild jaundice is common in newborns.

joint in any animal with a skeleton, a point of movement or articulation. In vertebrates, it is the point where two bones meet. Some joints allow no motion (the sutures of the skull), others allow a very small motion (the sacroiliac joints in the lower back), but most allow a relatively free motion. Of these, some allow a gliding motion (one vertebra of the spine on another), some have a hinge action (elbow and knee), and others allow motion in all directions (hip and shoulder joints), by means of a ball-and-socket arrangement. The ends of the bones at a moving joint are covered with cartilage for greater elasticity and smoothness, and enclosed in an envelope (capsule) of tough white fibrous tissue lined with a membrane which secretes a lubricating and cushioning synovial fluid. The joint is further strengthened by ligaments.

kidney one of a pair of organs responsible for water regulation, excretion of waste products, and maintaining the ionic composition of the blood. The kidneys are situated on the rear wall of the abdomen. Each one consists of a number of long tubules; the outer parts filter the aqueous components of blood, and the inner parts selectively reabsorb vital salts, leaving waste products in the remaining fluid (urine), which is passed through the ureter to the bladder.

L-dopa chemical, normally produced by the body, which is converted by an enzyme to dopamine in the brain. It is essential for integrated movement of individual muscle groups.

laryngitis inflammation of the larynx, causing soreness of the throat, a dry cough, and hoarseness. The acute form is due to a virus or other infection, excessive use of the voice, or inhalation of irritating smoke, and may cause the voice to be completely lost. With rest, the inflammation usually subsides in a few days.

leukemia any one of a group of cancers of the blood cells, with widespread involvement of the bone marrow and other blood-forming tissue. The central feature of leukemia is runaway production of white blood cells that are immature or in some way abnormal. These rogue cells, which lack the defensive capacity of healthy white cells, overwhelm the normal ones, leaving the victim vulnerable to infection. Treatment is with radiotherapy and cytotoxic drugs to suppress replication of abnormal cells, or by bone-marrow transplant.

liver large organ of vertebrates, which has many regulatory and storage functions. The human liver is situated in the upper abdomen, and weighs about 4.5 lb/2 kg. It receives the products of digestion, converts glucose to glycogen (a long-chain carbohydrate used for storage), and breaks down fats. It removes excess amino acids from the blood, converting them to urea, which is excreted by the kidneys. The liver also synthesizes vitamins, produces bile and blood-clotting factors, and removes damaged red cells and toxins such as alcohol from the blood.

lung large cavity of the body, used for gas exchange. It is essentially a sheet of thin, moist membrane that is folded so as to occupy less space. The lung tissue, consisting of multitudes of air sacs and blood vessels, is very light and spongy, and functions by bringing inhaled air into close contact with the blood so that oxygen can pass into the organism and waste carbon dioxide can be passed out. The efficiency of lungs is enhanced by breathing movements, by the thinness and moistness of their surfaces, and by a constant supply of circulating blood.

lymph nodes small masses of lymphatic tissue in the body that occur at various points along the major lymphatic vessels. Tonsils and adenoids are large lymph nodes. As the lymph passes through them it is filtered, and bacteria and other microorganisms are engulfed by cells known as macrophages.

mammography X-ray procedure used to detect breast cancer at an early stage, before the tumors can be seen or felt.

manic depression mental disorder characterized by recurring periods of depression which may or may not alternate with periods of inappropriate elation (mania) or overactivity. Sufferers may be genetically predisposed to the condition. Some cases have been improved by taking prescribed doses of lithium.

ME abbreviation for *myalgic encephalitis*, a debilitating condition also known as *chronic fatigue syndrome*.

measles acute virus disease (rubeola), spread by airborne infection. Symptoms are fever, severe catarrh, small spots inside the mouth, and a raised, blotchy red rash appearing for about a week after two weeks' incubation. Prevention is by vaccination.

mefipristone (formerly *RU-486*) abortion pill first introduced in France 1989, and effective in 94% of patients up to 10 weeks pregnant when administered in conjunction with a prostaglandin.

megavitamin therapy the administration of large doses of vitamins to combat conditions considered wholly or in part due to their deficiency.

melanoma mole or growth containing the dark pigment melanin. Malignant melanoma is a type of skin cancer developing in association with a pre-existing mole. Unlike other skin cancers, it is associated with brief but excessive exposure to sunlight.

meningitis inflammation of the meninges (membranes) surrounding the brain, caused by bacterial or viral infection. Bacterial meningitis, though treatable by antibiotics, is the more serious threat.

mental handicap impairment of intelligence. It can be very mild, but in more severe cases, it is associated with social problems and difficulties in living independently. A person may be born with a mental handicap (for example, Down's syndrome) or may acquire it through brain damage. There are between 90 and 130 million people in the world suffering such disabilities.

migraine acute, sometimes incapacitating headache (generally only on one side), accompanied by nausea, that recurs, often with advance symptoms such as flashing lights. No cure has been discovered, but ergotamine normally relieves the symptoms. Some sufferers learn to avoid certain foods, such as chocolate, which suggests an allergic factor.

multiple sclerosis (MS) incurable chronic disease of the central nervous system, occurring in young or middle adulthood. It is characterized by degeneration of the myelin sheath that surrounds nerves in the brain and spinal cord. Its cause is unknown.

mumps virus infection marked by fever and swelling of the parotid salivary glands (such as those under the ears). It is usually minor in children, although meningitis is a possible complication. In adults the symptoms are severe and it may cause sterility in adult men.

muscle contractile animal tissue that produces locomotion and maintains the movement of body substances. Muscle is made of long cells that can contract to between one-half and one-third of their relaxed length.

muscular dystrophy any of a group of inherited chronic muscle disorders marked by weakening and wasting of muscle. Muscle fibers degenerate, to be replaced by fatty tissue, although the nerve supply remains unimpaired. Death occurs in early adult life.

music therapy use of music as an adjunct to relaxation therapy, or in psychotherapy to elicit expressions of suppressed emotions by prompting patients to dance, shout, laugh, cry, or whatever, in response.

naturopathy the facilitating of the natural self-healing processes of the body. Naturopaths are the GPs of alternative medicine and often refer clients to other specialists, particularly in manipulative therapies, to complement their own work of seeking, through diet, the prescription of natural medicines and supplements, and lifestyle counseling, to restore or augment the vitality of the body and thereby its optimum health.

nerve strand of nerve cells enclosed in a sheath of connective tissue joining the central and the autonomic nervous systems with receptor and effector organs. A single nerve may contain both motor and sensory nerve cells, but they act independently.

nervous breakdown popular term for a reaction to overwhelming psychological stress. It has no equivalent in medicine: patients said to be suffering from a nervous breakdown may in fact be going through an episode of depression, manic depression, anxiety, or even schizophrenia.

neurosis in psychology, a general term referring to emotional disorders, such as anxiety, depression, and obsessions. The main disturbance tends to be one of mood; contact with reality is relatively unaffected, in contrast to the effects of psychosis.

nursing care of the sick, the very young, the very old, and the disabled. Nurses give day-to-day care and carry out routine medical and surgical procedures under the supervision of a physician.

nutrition the science of food, and its effect on human and animal life, health, and disease. Nutrition is the study of the basic nutrients required to sustain life, their bioavailability in foods and overall diet, and the effects upon them of cooking and storage.

obsession repetitive unwanted thought or compulsive action that is often recognized by the sufferer as being irrational, but which nevertheless causes distress. It can be associated with the irresistible urge of an individual to carry out a repetitive series of actions.

obstetrics the management of pregnancy, childbirth, and the immediate postnatal period.

oncology branch of medicine concerned with the diagnosis and treatment of abnormal tissue growths, especially cancers.

ophthalmology medical specialty concerned with diseases of the eye and its surrounding tissues.

orthopedics branch of medicine concerned with the surgery of bones and joints.

osteoarthritis degenerative disease of the joints in later life, sometimes resulting in disabling stiffness and wasting of muscles. Formerly thought to be due to wear and tear, it has been shown to be less common in the physically active. It appears to be linked with crystal deposits (in the form of calcium phosphate) in cartilage.

osteopathy system of alternative medical practice that relies on physical spinal manipulation to treat mechanical stress.

osteoporosis disease in which the bone substance becomes porous and brittle. It is common in older people, affecting more women than men. It may be treated with calcium supplements and etidronate.

ovary in female animals, the organ that generates the ovum. In humans, the ovaries are two whitish rounded bodies about 1 in/25 mm by 1.5 in/35 mm, located in the abdomen near the ends of the Fallopian tubes. Every month, from puberty to the onset of the menopause, an ovum is released from the ovary. This is called ovulation, and forms part of the menstrual cycle.

oxytocin hormone that stimulates the uterus in late pregnancy to initiate and sustain labor. After birth, it stimulates the uterine muscles to contract, reducing bleeding at the site where the placenta was attached.

pacemaker or *sinoatrial node* (SAN) in vertebrates, a group of muscle cells in the wall of the heart that contracts spontaneously and rhythmically, setting the pace for the contractions of the rest of the heart. The pacemaker's intrinsic rate of contraction is increased or decreased, according to the needs of the body, by stimulation from the autonomic nervous system. The term also refers to a medical device implanted under the skin of a patient whose heart beats irregularly. It delivers minute electric shocks to stimulate the heart muscles at regular intervals and restores normal heartbeat.

pediatrics medical specialty concerned with the care of children.

pain sense that gives an awareness of harmful effects on or in the body. It may be triggered by stimuli such as trauma, inflammation, and heat. Pain is transmitted by specialized nerves and also has psychological components controlled by higher centers in the brain. Drugs that control pain are also known as analgesics.

pancreas an accessory gland of the digestive system located close to the duodenum. When stimulated by the hormone secretin, it secretes enzymes into the duodenum that digest starches, proteins, and fats. In humans, it is about 7 in/18 cm long, and lies behind and below the stomach. It contains groups of cells called the *islets of Langerhans*, which secrete the hormones insulin and glucagon that regulate the blood sugar level.

paracetamol analgesic, particularly effective for musculoskeletal pain. It is as effective as aspirin in reducing fever, and less irritating to the stomach, but has little antiinflammatory action (as for joint pain). An overdose can cause severe, often irreversible or even fatal, liver and kidney damage.

paranoia mental disorder marked by delusions of grandeur or persecution.

paraplegia paralysis of the lower limbs, involving loss of both movement and sensation; it is usually due to spinal injury.

Parkinson's disease or *parkinsonism* or *paralysis agitans* degenerative disease of the brain characterized by a progressive loss of mobility, muscular rigidity, tremor, and speech difficulties. The condition is mainly seen in people over the age of 50.

pelvis the lower area of the abdomen featuring the bones and muscles used to move the legs or hindlimbs. The *pelvic girdle* is a set of bones that allows movement of the legs in relation to the rest of the body and provides sites for the attachment of relevant muscles.

penicillin any of a group of antibiotic (bacteria killing) compounds obtained from filtrates of molds of the genus *Penicillium* (especially *P. notatum*) or produced synthetically. Penicillin was the first antibiotic to be discovered (by Alexander Fleming); it kills a broad spectrum of bacteria, many of which cause disease in humans.

penis male reproductive organ, used for internal fertilization; it transfers sperm to the female reproductive tract. The penis is made erect by vessels that fill with blood. It also contains the urethra, through which urine is passed.

pharynx interior of the throat, the cavity at the back of the mouth. Its walls are made of muscle strengthened with a fibrous layer and lined with mucous membrane. The internal nostrils lead backward into the pharynx, which continues downward into the esophagus and (through the epiglottis) into the windpipe. On each side, a Eustachian tube enters the pharynx from the middle ear cavity.

phobia excessive irrational fear of an object or situation, for example, agoraphobia (fear of open spaces and crowded places), acrophobia (fear of heights), claustrophobia (fear of enclosed places). Behavior therapy is one form of treatment.

physiotherapy treatment of injury and disease by physical means such as exercise, heat, manipulation, massage, and electrical stimulation.

placebo any harmless substance, often called a "sugar pill", that has no chemotherapeutic value and yet produces physiological changes.

pneumonia inflammation of the lungs, generally due to bacterial or viral infection. It is characterized by a buildup of fluid in the alveoli, the clustered air sacs (at the end of the air passages) where oxygen exchange takes place.

poison or *toxin* any chemical substance that, when introduced into or applied to the body, is capable of injuring health or destroying life. The liver removes some poisons from the blood. The majority of poisons may be divided into *corrosives*, such as sulfuric, nitric, and hydrochloric acids; *irritants*, including arsenic and copper sulfate; *narcotics* such as opium, and carbon monoxide; and *narcotico-irritants* from any substances of plant origin including carbolic acid and tobacco.

polio (*poliomyelitis*) viral infection of the central nervous system affecting nerves that activate muscles.

postnatal depression mood change occurring in many mothers a few days after the birth of a baby. It is usually a short-lived condition but can sometimes persist; the most severe form of post-natal depressive illness, *puerperal psychosis*, requires hospital treatment. In mild cases, antidepressant drugs and hormone treatment may help.

prematurity the condition of an infant born before the full term. In obstetrics, an infant born after less than 37 weeks' gestation is described as premature.

premedication combination of drugs given before surgery to prepare a patient for general anesthesia.

premenstrual tension (PMT) or *premenstrual syndrome* medical condition caused by hormone changes and comprising a number of physical and emotional features that occur cyclically before menstruation and disappear with its onset. Symptoms include mood changes, breast tenderness, a feeling of bloatedness, and headache.

prophylaxis any measure taken to prevent disease, including exercise and vaccination. Prophylactic (preventive) medicine is an aspect of public-health provision that is receiving increasing attention.

prostate gland gland surrounding and opening into the urethra at the base of the bladder in male mammals.

psoriasis chronic, recurring skin disease characterized by raised, red, scaly patches, usually on the scalp, back, arms, and/or legs. Tar preparations, steroid creams, and ultraviolet light are used to treat it, and sometimes it disappears spontaneously. Psoriasis may be accompanied by a form of arthritis (inflammation of the joints).

psychiatry branch of medicine dealing with the diagnosis and treatment of mental disorder, normally divided into the areas of *neurotic conditions* including anxiety, depression, and hysteria and *psychotic disorders* such as schizophrenia. Psychiatric treatment consists of analysis, drugs, or electroconvulsive therapy.

psychoanalysis theory and treatment method for neuroses, developed by Sigmund Freud. The main treatment method involves the free association of ideas, and their interpretation by patient and analyst. It is typically prolonged and expensive and its effectiveness has been disputed.

psychology systematic study of human and animal behavior. The subject includes diverse areas of study and application, among them the roles of instinct, heredity, environment, and culture; the processes of sensation, perception, learning and memory; the bases of motivation and emotion; and the functioning of thought, intelligence, and language.

psychos or *psychotic disorder* general term for a serious mental disorder where the individual commonly loses contact with reality and may experience hallucinations (seeing or hearing things that do not exist) or delusions (fixed false beliefs). For example, in a paranoid psychosis, an individual may believe that others are plotting against him or her. A major type of psychosis is schizophrenia (which may be biochemically induced).

psychosomatic a physical symptom or disease, thought to arise from emotional or mental factors.

psychotherapy treatment approaches for psychological problems involving talking rather than surgery or drugs. Examples include cognitive therapy and psychoanalysis.

puerperal fever infection of the genital tract of the mother after childbirth, due to lack of aseptic conditions. Formerly often fatal, it is now rare and treated with antibiotics.

pulsed high frequency (PHF) instrumental application of high-frequency radio waves in short bursts to damaged tissue to relieve pain, reduce bruising and swelling, and speed healing.

rabies or *hydrophobia* disease of the central nervous system that can afflict all warm-blooded creatures. It is almost invariably fatal once symptoms have developed. Its transmission to humans is generally by a bite from an infected dog.

radiotherapy treatment of disease by radiation from X-ray machines or radioactive sources. Radiation, which reduces the activity of dividing cells, is of special value for its effect on malignant tissues, certain nonmalignant tumors, and some diseases of the skin.

red blood cell or *erythrocyte* the most common type of blood cell, responsible for transporting oxygen around the body. It contains hemoglobin, which combines with oxygen from the lungs to form oxyhemoglobin. When transported to the tissues, these cells are able to release the oxygen because the oxyhemoglobin splits into its original constituents.

reflexology manipulation and massage of the feet to ascertain and treat disease or dysfunction elsewhere in the body.

Reichian therapy general term for a group of body-therapies based on the theory propounded in the 1930s by Wilhelm Reich, that many functional and organic illnesses are attributable to constriction of the flow of vital energies in the body by tensions that become locked into the musculature. Bioenergetics and Rolfing are related approaches.

relaxation therapy development of regular and conscious control of physiological processes and their related emotional and mental states, and of muscular tensions in the body, as a way of relieving stress and its results. Meditation, hypnotherapy, autogenics, and biofeedback are techniques commonly employed.

remission temporary disappearance of symptoms during the course of a disease.

resuscitation steps taken to revive anyone on the brink of death. The most successful technique for life-threatening emergencies, such as electrocution, near-drowning, or heart attack, is mouth-to-mouth resuscitation. Medical and paramedical staff are trained in cardiopulmonary resuscitation: the use of specialized equipment and techniques to attempt to restart the breathing and/or heartbeat and stabilize the patient long enough for more definitive treatment.

retrovirus any of a family (Retroviridae) of viruses containing the genetic material RNA rather than the more usual DNA.

rheumatic fever or *acute rheumatism* acute or chronic illness characterized by fever and painful swelling of joints. Some victims also experience involuntary movements of the limbs and head, a form of chorea.

rib long, usually curved bone that extends laterally from the spine in vertebrates. In humans, there are 12 pairs of ribs. The ribs protect the lungs and heart, and allow the chest to expand and contract easily.

Rolfing technique of deep muscular manipulation developed in the 1960s and 1970s by US physiologist Ira Rolf. Also known as "structural integration", the treatment is designed to correct gravitational imbalance in body postures and movements, and to relieve muscular rigidities and inflexibilities, thus enhancing general health and vitality.

rubella technical term for German measles. A mild, communicable virus disease, usually caught by children. It is marked by a sore throat, pinkish rash, and slight fever, and has an incubation period of two to three weeks. If a woman contracts it in the first three months of pregnancy, it may cause serious damage to the unborn child. For this reason immunization is recommended for girls.

scabies contagious infection of the skin caused by the parasitic itch mite Sarcoptes scaboi, which burrows under the skin to deposit eggs. Treatment is by antiparasitic creams and lotions.

schizophrenia mental disorder, a psychosis of unknown origin, which can lead to profound changes in personality and behavior including paranoia and hallucinations. Contrary to popular belief, it does not involve a split personality. Modern treatment approaches include drugs, family therapy, stress reduction, and rehabilitation.

sciatica persistent pain in the leg, along the sciatic nerve and its branches. Causes of sciatica include inflammation of the nerve or pressure on, or inflammation of, a nerve root leading out of the lower spine.

screening *or health screening* the systematic search for evidence of a disease, or of conditions that may precede it, in people who are not suffering from any symptoms. The aim of screening is to try to limit ill health from diseases that are difficult to prevent and might otherwise go undetected. Examples are hypothyroidism and phenylketonuria, for which all newborn babies in Western countries are screened; breast cancer (mammography) and cervical cancer; and stroke, for which high blood pressure is a known risk factor.

senile dementia dementia associated with old age, often caused by Alzheimer's disease.

septicemia technical term for blood poisoning.

shingles common name for herpes zoster, a disease characterized by infection of sensory nerves, with pain and eruption of blisters along the course of the affected nerves.

shock circulatory failure marked by a sudden fall of blood pressure and resulting in pallor, sweating, fast (but weak) pulse, and sometimes complete collapse. Causes include disease, injury, and psychological trauma.

sickle-cell disease hereditary chronic blood disorder common among people of black African descent; also found in the E Mediterranean, parts of the Persian Gulf, and in NE India. It is characterized by distortion and fragility of the red blood cells, which are lost too rapidly from the circulation. This often results in anemia.

sinusitis painful inflammation of one of the sinuses, or air spaces, that surround the nasal passages. Most cases clear with antibiotics and nasal decongestants, but some require surgical drainage.

skull the collection of flat and irregularly shaped bones (or cartilage) that enclose the brain and the organs of sight, hearing, and smell, and provide support for the jaws. In mammals, the skull consists of 22 bones joined by sutures. The floor of the skull is pierced by a large hole for the spinal cord and a number of smaller apertures through which other nerves and blood vessels pass.

sound therapy treatment based on the finding that human blood cells respond to sound frequencies by changing color and shape, and the hypothesis that therefore sick or rogue cells can be healed or harmonized by sound. The therapy was developed and researched by French musician and acupuncturist Fabien Maman, and US physicist Joel Sternheimer. It is claimed that sound frequencies applied to acupuncture points are as effective as needles.

spastic person with cerebral palsy. The term is also applied generally to limbs with impaired movement, stiffness, and resistance to passive movement, and to any body part (such as the colon) affected with spasm.

spermicide any cream, jelly, pessary, or other preparation that kills the sperm cells in semen. Spermicides are used for contraceptive purposes, usually in combination with a condom or diaphragm.

spina bifida congenital defect in which part of the spinal cord and its membranes are exposed, due to incomplete development of the spine (vertebral column).

spinal cord major component of the central nervous system in vertebrates.

spiritual healing *or psychic healing* the transmission of energy from or through a healer, who may practice hand healing or absent healing through prayer or meditation.

sterilization any surgical operation to terminate the possibility of reproduction. In women, this is normally achieved by sealing or tying off the Fallopian tubes (tubal ligation) so that fertilization can no longer take place. In men, the transmission of sperm is blocked by vasectomy.

steroid in biology, any of a group of cyclic, unsaturated alcohols (lipids without fatty acid components), which, like sterols, have a complex molecular structure consisting of four carbon rings. Steroids include the sex hormones, such as testosterone, the corticosteroid hormones produced by the adrenal gland, bile acids, and cholesterol.

stomach the first cavity in the digestive system of animals. In mammals it is a bag of muscle situated just below the diaphragm. Food enters it from the esophagus, is digested by the acid and enzymes secreted by the stomach lining, and then passes into the duodenum. Some plant-eating mammals have multichambered stomachs that harbor bacteria in one of the chambers to assist in the digestion of cellulose.

stroke *or cerebrovascular accident or apoplexy* interruption of the blood supply to part of the brain due to a sudden bleed in the brain (cerebral hemorrhage) or embolism or thrombosis. Strokes vary in severity from producing almost no symptoms to proving rapidly fatal. In between are those (often recurring) that leave a wide range of impaired function, depending on the size and location of the event.

syphilis venereal disease caused by the spiral-shaped bacterium (spirochete) Treponema pallidum. Untreated, it runs its course in three stages over many years, often starting with a painless hard sore, or chancre, developing within a month on the area of infection (usually the genitals). The second stage, months later, is a rash with arthritis, hepatitis, and/or meningitis. The third stage, years later, leads eventually to paralysis, blindness, insanity, and death.

testis (plural *testes*) the organ that produces sperm in males. In humans it is one of a pair of oval structures that hang outside the abdomen in a scrotal sac.

tetanus or lockjaw acute disease caused by the toxin of the bacillus Clostridium tetani, which usually enters the body through a wound. The bacterium is chiefly found in richly manured soil. Untreated, in seven to ten days tetanus produces muscular spasm and rigidity of the jaw spreading to the other muscles, convulsions, and death. There is a vaccine, and the disease may be treatable with tetanus antitoxin and antibiotics.

thanatology study of the psychological aspects of the experiences of death and dying and its application in counseling and assisting the terminally ill. It was pioneered by US psychiatrist Elizabeth Kübler-Ross in the 1970s.

throat the passage that leads from the back of the nose and mouth to the trachea and oesophagus. It includes the pharynx and the larynx, the latter being at the top of the trachea. The word "throat" is also used to mean the front part of the neck.

thrombosis condition in which a blood clot forms in a vein or artery, causing loss of circulation to the area served by the vessel. If it breaks away, it often travels to the lungs, causing pulmonary embolism.

thrush infection usually of the mouth (particularly in infants), but also sometimes of the vagina, caused by a yeastlike fungus (genus Candida). It is seen as white patches on the mucous membranes.

thyroid endocrine gland of vertebrates, situated in the neck in front of the trachea. It secretes several hormones, principally thyroxin, an iodine- containing hormone that stimulates growth, metabolism, and other functions of the body. The thyroid gland may be thought of as the regulator gland of the body's metabolic rate. If it is overactive, as in thyrotoxicosis, the sufferer feels hot and sweaty, has an increased heart rate, diarrhea, and weight loss. Conversely, an underactive thyroid leads to myxedema, a condition characterized by sensitivity to the cold, constipation, and weight gain. In infants, an underactive thyroid leads to cretinism, a form of mental retardation.

tomography the obtaining of plane-section X-ray photographs, which show a "slice" through any object. Crystal detectors and amplifiers can be used that have a sensitivity 100 times greater than X- ray film, and, in conjunction with a computer system, can detect, for example, the difference between a brain tumor and healthy brain tissue.

tongue a muscular organ usually attached to the floor of the mouth. It has a thick root attached to a U-shaped bone(hyoid), and is covered with a mucous membrane containing nerves and "taste buds". It directs food to the teeth and into the throat for chewing and swallowing.

toxic shock syndrome rare condition marked by rapid onset of fever, vomiting, and low blood pressure, sometimes leading to death. It is caused by a toxin of the bacterium Staphylococcus aureus, normally harmlessly present in the body, which may accumulate, for example, if a tampon used by a woman during a period remains unchanged beyond four to six hours.

trachea tube that forms an airway, it is also known as the *windpipe* and runs from the larynx to the upper part of the chest. Its diameter is about 0.6 in/1.5 cm and its length 4 in/10 cm. It is strong and flexible, and reinforced by rings of cartilage. In the upper chest, the trachea branches into two tubes: the left and right bronchi, which enter the lung. The finest branches of the tracheae are called tracheoles.

transfusion intravenous delivery of blood or blood products (plasma, red cells) into a patient's circulation to make up for deficiencies due to disease, injury, or surgical intervention. Cross-matching is carried out to ensure the patient receives the right type of blood. Because of worries about blood-borne disease, self-transfusion with units of blood "donated" over the weeks before an operation is popular.

transplant the transfer of a tissue or organ from one human being to another or from one part of the body to another (skin grafting). In most organ transplants, the operation is for life-saving purposes, though the immune system tends to reject foreign tissue. Careful matching and immunosuppressive drugs must be used, but these are not always successful.

trauma in psychiatry, a painful emotional experience or shock with lasting psychic consequences; in medicine, any physical damage or injury.

tropical disease any illness found mainly in hot climates. The most important tropical diseases worldwide are malaria, schistosomiasis, leprosy, and river blindness. Malaria kills about 1.5 million people each year, and produces chronic anemia and tiredness in 100 times as many, while schistosomiasis is responsible for 1 million deaths a year. All the main tropical diseases are potentially curable, but the facilities for diagnosis and treatment are rarely adequate in the countries where they occur.

tuberculosis (TB) formerly known as consumption or phthisis infectious disease caused by the bacillus *Mycobacterium tuberculosis*. It takes several forms, of which pulmonary tuberculosis is by far the most common. A vaccine, BCG, was developed around 1920 and the first antituberculosis drug, streptomycin, in 1944.

tumor overproduction of cells in a specific area of the body, often leading to a swelling or lump. Tumors are classified as *benign* or *malignant* (see cancer). Benign tumors grow more slowly, do not invade surrounding tissues, do not spread to other parts of the body, and do not usually recur after removal. However, benign tumors can be dangerous in areas such as the brain. The most familiar types of benign tumor are warts on the skin. In some cases, there is no sharp dividing line between benign and malignant tumors.

ultrasound high-frequency pressure waves used to investigate various body organs. Ultrasonic pressure waves transmitted through the body are absorbed and reflected to different degrees by different body tissues. By recording the "echoes", a picture (sonogram) of the different structures being scanned can be built up. Ultrasound scanning is valued as a safe, noninvasive technique which often eliminates the need for exploratory surgery. Free of the risks of ionizing radiation, unlike X-rays and computerized axial tomography (CAT scan), it is especially valuable in obstetrics.

uterus hollow muscular organ of females, located between the bladder and rectum, and connected to the Fallopian tubes above and the vagina below. The embryo develops within the uterus, and in placental mammals is attached to it after implantation via the placenta and umbilical cord. The lining of the uterus changes during the menstrual cycle.

vaccine any preparation of modified viruses or bacteria that is introduced into the body, usually either orally or by a hypodermic syringe, to induce the specific antibody reaction that produces immunity against a particular disease.

vagina the front passage in females, linking the uterus to the exterior. It admits the penis during sexual intercourse, and is the birth canal down which the fetus passes during delivery.

varicose veins *or varicosis* condition where the veins become swollen and twisted. The veins of the legs are most often affected; other vulnerable sites include the rectum (hemorrhoids) and testes.

visualization use of guided mental imagery to activate and focus the body's natural self-healing processes. When used in the treatment of cancer patients, together with complementary techniques, some remarkable remissions have been attributed to visualization.

vitalistic medicine generic term for a range of therapies that base their practice on the theory that disease is engendered by energy deficiency in the organism as a whole or a dynamic dysfunction in the affected part. Acupuncture, crystal therapy, homoeopathy, naturopathy, and Reichian therapy are all basically vitalistic.

vomiting expulsion of the contents of the stomach through the mouth. It may have numerous causes, including direct irritation of the stomach, severe pain, dizziness, and emotion. Sustained or repeated vomiting may indicate serious disease, and dangerous loss of water, salt, and acid may result.

warfarin poison that when neutralized with sodium hydroxide, is used in medicine as an anticoagulant: it prevents blood clotting by inhibiting the action of vitamin K. It can be taken orally and begins to act several days after the initial dose.

whooping cough *or pertussis* acute infectious disease, seen mainly in children, caused by colonization of the air passages by the bacterium *Bordetella pertussis*. There may be catarrh, mild fever, and loss of appetite, but the main symptom is violent coughing, associated with the sharp intake of breath that is the characteristic "whoop", and often followed by vomiting and severe nose bleeds. The cough may persist for weeks.

X-ray rays with a short wavelength that pass through most body tissues. Dense tissues, such as bone, prevent their passage and show up as white areas on X-ray photographs. X-rays are also used to destroy some tissues, in radiotherapy.

zidovudine formerly (AZT) antiviral drug that was used in the treatment of AIDS.

Living Organisms

The classification of living organisms, or taxonomy, seeks to order living species based on several criteria, such as evolutionary and structural relationships among organisms. There are many systems of classification, but a most common system contains the basic taxonomic categories of kingdom, phylum or division, class, order, family, genus, and species. Even within this framework, however, there is considerable variety in classifying the many living organisms. The charts here follow a common classification system, but they do not cover every level of classification. The five major groups, or kingdoms, are: monera, protista, fungi, plants, and animals.

In addition to the classification of organisms, this section also includes the terms used to describe the sexes and the offspring of various common animals as well as the terms used to describe animal groupings. The human physiology chart displays the basic muscular and skeletal structures of adult human beings.

KINGDOM MONERA

Single-celled prokaryotes (cells lack nuclear membrane) that often form filaments or chains and reproduce asexually through binary fission.

PHYLUM (DIVISION)	CLASS	COMMON NAMES
Schizophyta		True bacteria
Cyanophyta		Cyanobacteria, blue-green algae

KINGDOM PROTISTA

Unicellular or multicellur eukaryotes (cells have true nucleus). Reproduction can occur both sexually and asexually, and locomotion occurs most often by flagella, cilia, or pseudopodia.

PHYLUM (DIVISION)	CLASS	COMMON NAMES
Euglenophyta (unicellular, move by flagella)		Euglena
Chrysophyta (unicellular)		
	Bacillariophyceae	Diatoms
	Chrysophyceae	Golden-brown algae
Pyrrophyta (unicellular, flagellated, primarily marine)		
	Dinophyceae	Dinoflagellates
Chlorophyta (unicellular or multicellular, cellulose cell walls)	Green algae	
Phaeophyta (multicellular, primarily marine)		Brown algae, seaweeds
Rhodophyta (multicellular, primarily marine)		Red algae
Myxomycota		Plasmodial slime molds
Acrasiomycota		Cellular slime molds
Mastigophora (flagellated protozoa)		Flagellates
Sarcodina (unicellular protozoa, move by pseudopodia)		Sarcodines, amoebas
Ciliophora (unicellular protozoa, move by cilia)		Ciliates, e.g., paramecium
Opalinida (parasitic protozoa)		Opalinids
Sporozoa (parasitic protozoa, lack locomotion)		Sporozoa, plasmodium

KINGDOM FUNGI

PHYLUM (DIVISION)	CLASS	COMMON NAMES
Zygomycota		Terrestrial fungi: black bread mold
Ascomycota		Yeast, truffles, cup fungi
Basidiomycota		Mushrooms, toadstools
Deuteromycota		Imperfect fungi, penicillium
Chytridiomycota		Aquatic fungi, chytrids
Oomycota		Water molds
Mycophycophyta (symbiosis of algae or bacteria in a fungus)		Lichens

KINGDOM PLANTAE

PHYLUM (DIVISION)	CLASS	FAMILY	COMMON NAMES
Bryophyta	Hepaticopsida	Liverworts	
	Anthocerotopsida	Hornworts	
	Muscopsida (Bryopsida)	Mosses	
Tracheophyta			
	Psilophytina	Whisk ferns	
	Lycophytina	Club mosses, lycopods	
	Sphenophytina	Horse-tails	
Filicophytina or Pterophyta		Ferns	
Spermatophytina		Seed plants	
	Cycadopsida	Cycads	
	Coniferopsida	Conifers	
	Ginkgopsida	Ginkgos	
	Gnetopsida	None	
	Angiospermopsida	Flowering plants	
	SUBCLASS:		
	Monotyledonae		
		Liliaceae	Lilies, onion, garlic
		Orchidaceae	Orchids
		Gramineae	Grass family
		Palmae	Tropical plants, palm trees
	Dicotyledonae		
		Fagaceae	Beech, oak trees
		Rosaceae	Fruit trees
		Labiatae	Culinary herbs
		Leguminosae	Pea family, legumes
		Euphorbiaceae	None
		Compositae	Many herbs
		Ericaceae	Heathers, rhododendrons, azaleas

KINGDOM ANIMALIA

PHYLUM	CLASS	ORDER	FAMILY	COMMON NAMES

INVERTEBRATES (ANIMALS WITHOUT A BACKBONE)

PHYLUM	CLASS	ORDER	FAMILY	COMMON NAMES
Porifera				Sponges
Mesozoa				None (parasites)
Cnidaria (Coelenterata)				
	Hydrozoa			Hydra, hydra-like animals
	Anthozoa			Sea anemones, coral
	Scyphozoa			Jellyfish
Ctenophora				Comb jellies, sea walnuts
Platyhelminthes				Flatworms, e.g. tapeworms
Gnathostomulida				None (marine worms)
Rhynchocoela (Nemertina)				Ribbon worms
Nematoda				Roundworms
Nematomorpha				Horsehair worms
Gastrotricha				Hairy Backs (wormlike)
Kinorhyncha				None
Acanthocephala				Thorny-headed worms
Rotifera				Wheel-like animals
Entoprocta				None
Mollusca (soft bodies, often with hard outer shell)				
	Gastropoda			Snails, slugs
	Bivalvia			Clams, mussels, oysters
	Cephalopoda			Squids, octopuses
	Aplacophora			None
	Polyplacophora			None
	Monoplacophora			None
	Scaphopoda			None
Annelida (segmented body, closed blood system)				
	Polychaeta			Paddle worms
	Oligochaeta			Earthworms
	Hirudinea			Leeches

PHYLUM	CLASS	ORDER	FAMILY	COMMON NAMES
Sipuncula				Peanut worms
Echiura				Spoon worms
Priapulida				Parapulid worms
Pogonophora				Beard worms
Pentastomida				Tongue worms
Tardigrada				Water bears
Onychophora				Peripatus (worms)
Arthropoda (jointed appendages, hard exoskeleton, segmented)				
	Insecta (six-legged arthropods)			
	SUB-CLASS:			
	Apterygota (Ametabola)			
		Thysanura		Silverfish and relatives
		Dipulra		Two-pronged bristletails
		Protura		None
		Collembola		Springtails
	Pterygota (Metabola)			
		Ephemeroptera		Mayflies
		Odonatoptera		Dragonflies
		Plecoptera		Stoneflies
		Notoptera (Grylloblattodea)		None
		Orthoptera		Grasshoppers, locusts
		Phasmida (Cheleutoptera)		Stick and leaf insects
		Embioptera		Web spinners
		Dictyoptera		Cockroaches, mantises
		Isoptera		Termites
		Zoraptera		None
		Dermaptera		Earwigs
		Psocoptera		Booklice
		Mallophaga		Biting lice
		Siphunculata (Anoplura)		Sucking lice
		Hemiptera		True bugs
		Heteroptera		Water boatmen
		Thysanoptera		Thrips
		Neuroptera		Lacewings, alder flies
		Coleoptera		Beetles
		Strepsiptera		Styploids
		Mecoptera		Scorpion flies
		Trichoptera		Caddis flies
		Diptera		Flies
		Lepidoptera		Butterflies and moths
		Siphonaptera		Fleas
		Hymenoptera		Ants, bees, wasps, sawflies
		Planipenria		Ant-lions
	Arachinida (body divided into two segments, eight legs)			
		Araneae		Spiders
		Solifugae (Solpugida)		Sun spiders
		Acarina		Mites, ticks
		Ricinuleids (Podogona)		None
		Opiliones (Phalangida)		Harvestmen
		Scorpionida		Scorpions
		Pseudo-scorpionida		False scorpions
		Uropygi (Pedipalpi)		Whip scorpions
		Palpigrada		Micro-whip scorpions
	Crustacea (aquatic, hard exoskeletons, segmented appendages)			
	SUB-CLASS:			
	Cephalocarida			Primitive crustaceans
	Branchiopoda			Water fleas
	Ostracoda			Mussel shrimps
	Copepoda			Copepods
	Mystacocarida			None
	Branchiura			Fish lice
	Cirrapedia			Barnacles
	Malacostraca			Crabs, lobsters, crayfish

KINGDOM ANIMALIA (continued)

PHYLUM	CLASS	ORDER	FAMILY	COMMON NAMES
	Pycnogonida			Sea spiders
	Merostomata			King or horseshoe crabs
	Pauropoda			None
	Diplopoda			Millipedes
	Chilopoda			Cenitpedes
	Symphyla			Garden centipedes
Bryozoa (Ectoprocta)				Moss animals
Phoronida				Phoronid worms
Brachiopoda				Lamp shells
Echinodermata (radial symmetry, endoskeletal, marine)				
	Crinoidea			Feather stars, sea lillies
	Ophiuroidea			Brittle, serpent stars
	Asteroidea			Starfish
	Holothuroidea			Sea cucumbers
	Echinoidea			Sea urchins
Chaetognatha				Arrow worms
Hemichordata				Acorn worms

VERTEBRATES (ANIMALS WITH A BACKBONE)

Chordata (notochord, anterior-posterior differentiation, gill slits)

PHYLUM	CLASS	ORDER	FAMILY	COMMON NAMES
Subphylum Urochordata				Tunicates
Subphylum Cephalochordata				Lancelets
Subphylum Vertebrata (cartilage or bone forms backbone, brain protected by skull)				
	Agnatha (Cylostomata) — jawless fishes			Lampreys, hagfish
	Chondrichthyes (fishes with cartilaginous skeletons)			Sharks, rays
	Sarcopterygii (fishes with fleshy fins)			Coelacanth, lungfishes
	Actinopterygii (fishes with ray fins)			Eels, sturgeon, salmon, trout, herring, bowfin
	Osteichthyes (fishes with bony skeleton)			Most freshwater fish
	Amphibia (live on land and water, moist skin, stiff vertebrate)			
		Anura (approx. 12 families)		Frogs and toads
		Urodela (approx. 8 families)		Salamanders, mud-puppies
		Apoda (Gymnophions)		Cecilians or apodans
	Reptilia (fully terrestrial, dry, scaly skin, cold-blooded)			
		Chelonia (approx. 10 families)		Turtles and tortoises
		Crocodilia		Crocodile and alligators
		Squamata (approx. 31 families)		Lizards, snakes
	Aves (Birds) (feathered, winged, warm-blooded)			
		Passeriformes		Perching birds, passerines
		Piciformes		Woodpeckers, toucans, barbets
		Coraciiformes		Kingfishers, hornbills
		Coliiformes		Mousebirds, colies
		Trogoniformes		Trogons
		Apodiformes		Swifts, hummingbirds
		Caprimulgiformes		Nightjars and relatives
		Strigiformes		Owls
		Cuculiformes		Cuckoos, turacos
		Psittaciformes		Parrots
		Columbiformes		Pigeons, sand grouse
		Charadriiformes		Gulls, waders, auks
		Gruiformes		Cranes and relatives
		Galliformes		Game birds
		Falconiformes		Birds of prey
		Anseriformes		Ducks, geese
		Ciconiiformes		Storks, herons, flamingos
		Pelicaniformes		Pelicans and relatives
		Procellariiformes		Albatross, petrels
		Sphenisciformes		Penguins
		Gaviiformes		Divers, loons
		Podicipediformes		Grebes
		Tinamiformes		Tinamous
		Casuariiformes		Emu, cassowaries

PHYLUM	CLASS	ORDER	FAMILY	COMMON NAMES
		Rheiformes		Rheas
		Dinornithiormes (Apterygiformes)		Kiwis
		Struthioniformes		Ostriches
	Mammalia (body hair, warmblooded, give birth to young, mammary glands)			
	SUBCLASS:			
	Prototheria or Monotremata (egg-laying mammals)			Platypus, spiny anteater
	Marsupialia or Metatheria (approx. 9 families)			Kangaroos, opossums, koalas, wombats, bandicoots
	Eutheria			
		Insectivora (approx. 8 families)		Shrews, hedgehogs, moles
		Chiroptera (approx. 18 families)		Bats
		Dermoptera		Flying lemurs
		Edentata (toothless mammals		Anteaters, sloths, armadillos
		Pholidota		Pangolins
		Rodentia (approx. 28 families)		Rats, mice, squirrels, hamsters, beavers, porcupines, etc.
		Lagomorpha		Rabbits, hares, pikas
		Cetacea (approx. 9 families)		Dolphins. porpoises, whales
		Carnivora		
			Mustelidae	Weasels, skunks, otters, minks
			Viverridae	Civets, mongooses
			Hyaenidae	Hyenas
			Felidae	Cat family
			Canidae	Dog family
			Ursidae	Bears
			Procyonidae	Pandas, racoons
		Artiodactyla (even-toed hoofed mammals)		
			Suidae	Pigs, boars
			Hippopotamidae	Hippopotamus
			Camelidae	Camels, llamas
			Cervidae	Deer, elk
			Tragulidae	Chevrotains
			Bovidae	Cattle, antelopes
			Ovinae	Sheep
			Caprinae	Goats
			Giraffidae	Giraffe, okapi
		Perissodactyla (odd-toed hoofed mammals)		
			Tapiridae	Tapirs
			Rhinocerotidae	Rhinoceroses
			Equidae	Horses and zebras
		Sirenia (large aquatic mammals)		
			Trichechidae	Manatees, sea cows
			Dugongidae	Dugongs
		Tubulidentata	Orycteropodidae	Aardvark
		Hyracoidae	Procaviidae	Hyraxes, dassies, damars
		Proboscidae	Elephantidae	Elephants
		Primates		
			Tupalidae	Tree shrews
			Lemuridae	Lemurs
			Daubentonlidae	Aye-ayes
			Lorisidae	Bush babies, lorises, pottos
			Tarsiidae	Tarsiers
			Callitrichidae	Marmosets and relatives
			Cebidae	New World monkeys
			Cercopithecidae	Old World monkeys, baboons
			Hylobatidae	Gibbons
			Pongidae	Apes (gorillas, chimpanzees,
			Hominidae	Human beings

KINGDOM ANIMALIA (continued)

ANIMAL NAMES (Gender & Offspring)

ANIMAL	MALE	FEMALE	OFFSPRING	ANIMAL	MALE	FEMALE	OFFSPRING
Ass	Jack	Jenny	Foal	Goose	Gander	Goose	Gosling
Bear	Boar	Sow	Cub	Horse	Stallion	Mare	Foal
Cat	Tom	Queen	Kitten	Lion	Lion	Lioness	Cub
Cattle	Bull	Cow	Calf	Rabbit	Buck	Doe	Bunny
Chicken	Rooster	Hen	Chick	Sheep	Ram	Ewe	Lamb
Deer	Buck	Doe	Fawn	Swan	Cob	Pen	Cygnet
Dog	Dog	Bitch	Pup	Swine	Boar	Sow	Piglet
Duck	Drake	Duck	Duckling	Tiger	Tiger	Tigress	Cub
Elephant	Bull	Cow	Calf	Whale	Bull	Cow	Calf
Fox	Dog	Vixen	Cub	Wolf	Dog	Bitch	Pup

GROUP NAMES FOR ANIMALS

ANIMAL	COLLECTIVE NAME	ANIMAL	COLLECTIVE NAME
Antelope	Herd, Troop	Hares	Down, Husk
Ants	Army, Colony	Hawks	Cast
Apes	Shrewdness	Hedgehogs	Array
Asses	Herd, Pace	Hens	Brood
Baboons	Troop	Hippopotamuses	Herd, School
Badger	Cete, Colony	Hogs	Drift
Barracuda	Battery	Horses	Pair, Team
Bass	Fleet	Hounds	Cry, Mute, Pack
Bears	Sleuth, Sloth	Insects	Swarm
Beavers	Colony	Jays	Band, Party
Bees	Grist, Hive, Swarm	Jellyfish	Brood, Smuck
Birds	flight, Volery	Kangaroos	Troop
Bison	Herd	Kittens	Kindle, Litter
Bloodhounds	Sute	Larks	Exaltation
Boars	Herd, Singular, Sounder	Leopards	Leap
Buffalo	Herd	Lice	Flock
Camels	Caravan, Flock	Lions	Pride
Caterpillars	Army	Locusts	Plague
Cattle	Drove	Magpies	Tiding
Cats	Clutter, Clowder	Mice	Nest
Chickens	Brood, Clutch	Minnows	Shoal, Steam, Swarm
Clams	Bed	Moles	Company, Labor, Movement, Mumble
Colts	Race, Rag, Rake	Monkeys	Troop
Cranes	Sedge, Seige	Mules	Span
Crows	Murder	Mussels	Bed
Deer	Herd, Leash	Nightingales	Watch
Dogs	Kennel, Pack	Ostrich	Flock, Troop
Dolphins	Pod, School	Otters	Bevy, Family
Donkeys	Herd, Drove	Owls	Stare
Doves	Dule	Oxen	Yoke
Ducks	Brace, Team	Oysters	Bed
Eagles	Convocation	Parrots	Company
Eels	Swarm	Partridges	Covey
Elephants	Herd	Peacocks	Muster, Ostentation
Elks	Gang	Penguins	Colony, Rookery
Falcons	Cast	Pheasants	Nest, Bouquet
Ferrets	Business, Cast	Pigeons	Flight, Flock
Finches	Charm	Piglets	Farrow
Fish	School, Shoal, Draught	Pigs	Litter
Flamingos	Flurry, Regiment, Skein	Ponies	String
Flies	Business, Cloud, Scraw, Swarm	Porpoises	Gam, Pod, School
Foxes	Leash, Skulk	Pups	Litter
Frogs	Army, Colony	Quail	Bevy, Covey
Geese	Flock, Gaggle, Skein	Rabbits	Nest
Giraffes	Corps, Herd, Troop	Raccoons	Nursery
Gnats	Cloud, Herd	Rats	Colony
Goats	Trip	Ravens	Unkindness
Goldfish	Troubling	Rhinoceros	Crash
Gorillas	Band	Sardines	Family
Grasshoppers	Cloud	Seals	Pod
Greyhounds	Brace, Leash, Pack	Sheep	Drove, Flock
Gulls	Colony		

ANIMAL NAMES

ANIMAL	COLLECTIVE NAME
Snakes	Den, Pit
Sparrows	Host
Spiders	Cluster, Clutter
Squirrels	Drey
Storks	Mustering
Swallows	Flight
Swans	Bevy, Wedge
Swine	Sounder
Tigers	Ambush
Toads	Knab, Knot
Trout	Hover

ANIMAL	COLLECTIVE NAME
Turkeys	Rafter
Turtles	Bale
Vipers	Nest
Walrus	Herd, Pod
Wasps	Herd, Nest, Pladge
Weasels	Pack, Pop
Whales	Gam, Pod
Wolves	Pack, Rout
Woodcocks	Fall
Woodpeckers	Descent
Zebra	Herd

FIG. I AND 2 MUSCULAR SYSTEM OF MAN

Fig. 1, Front View. Fig. 2, Back View. The sides marked A show the muscles of the first layer located immediately below the skin. Those marked B show the important muscles of the deeper layers. Where a muscle is shown in only one of the figures, that fact is indicated following the name: as, temporal (fig. 1)

HEAD AND NECK

1 frontalis
2 occipitalis
3 temporal (fig 1)
4 orbicularis of eye
5 greater zygomaticus
6 lesser zygomaticus
7 angular head of the quadratus of upper lip (fig 1)
8 nasalis (fig 1)
9 orbicularis of mouth (fig 1)
10 triangularis of chin (fig 1)
11 quadratus of lower lip (fig 1)
12 mentalis (fig 1)
13 masseter (fig 1)
14 buccinator (fig 1)
15 anterior auricularis
16 superior auricularis
17 posterior auricularis
a parotid gland
18 mylohyoid (fig 1)
19 digastric
20 platysma
21 sternocleidomastoid
22 omohyoid (fig 1)
23 sternohyoid (fig 1)
24 trapezius
25 splenius of head (fig 2)
26 splenius of neck (fig 2)
27 levator of scapula (fig 2)
28 supraspinatus (fig 2)

TRUNK

29 greater pectoralis (fig 1)
30 deltoid
31 latissimus dorsi
32 anterior serratus
33 external oblique
34 rectus abdominis (fig 1)
35 umbilicus (fig 1)
36 abdominal aponeurosis (fig 1)
37 linea alba (fig 1)
38 subclavius (fig 1)
39 lesser pectoralis (fig 1)
40 posterior superior serratus
41 internal oblique
42 infraspinatus (fig 2)
43 lesser teres (fig 2)
44 greater teres (fig 2)
45 greater rhomboideus (fig 2)
46 lesser rhomboideus (fig 2)
b scapula (fig 2)
c 9th rib (fig 2)
d 10th rib (fig 2)
e 11th rib (fig 2)
f 12th rib (fig 2)
47 posterior inferior serratus (fig 2)
48 lumbodorsal fascia (fig 2)
49 sacrospinalis (fig 2)

UPPER EXTREMITY

50 biceps of arm
51 triceps of arm
52 brachialis
53 lacertus fibrosus
54 long radial extensor of wrist
55 brachioradialis
56 radial flexor of wrist
57 long palmaris (fig 1)
58 flexor of digits (fig 1)
59 ulnar flexor of wrist
60 short palmaris
61 short radial extensor of wrist
62 long flexor of thumb (fig 1)
63 pronator quadratus (fig 1)
64 short flexor of thumb (fig 1)
65 long palmaris (cut across in fig 1)
66 first dorsal interosseus
67 first lumbricalis (fig 1)
68 fibrous sheaths of the tendons
69 adductor of the little finger
70 annular ligament of the carpus
g head of humerus (showing bicipital groove)
71 common extensor of digits (fig 1)
72 ulnar extensor of wrist (fig 1)
73 long extensor of wrist (fig 1)
h medial epicondyle of humerus
i lower end of radius (fig 2)
j lower end of ulna (fig 2)
74 tendons of extensors of thumb (fig 2)
75 adductor of thumb (fig 2)
76 tendons of extensors of digits and wrist (fig 2)
77 pronator teres (fig 2)
78 palmar aponeurosis (fig 2)

LOWER EXTREMITY

k anterior superior spine of ilium (fig 1)
79 iliacus (fig 1)
80 gluteus medius
81 tensor of fascia lata
82 rectus femoris (fig 1)
83 psoas major (fig 1)
84 pectineus (fig 1)
85 sartorius
86 long adductor of thigh (fig 1)
87 great adductor of thigh
88 gracilis
89 vastus lateralis
90 vastus medialis
91 gluteus minimus (fig 1)
92 superior extremity of rectus femoris (fig 1)
93 inferior extremity of rectus femoris (fig 1)
m head of femur (fig 1)
94 inferior extremities of psoas and iliacus (fig 1)
95 tendon of rectus femoris
n patella (fig 1)
o head of fibula (fig 1)
p medial condyle of femur (fig 1)
r tuberosity of tibia (fig 1)
96 anterior tibialis
97 medial head of gastrocnemius (fig 1)
98 soleus
99 long extensor of digits (fig 1)
100 long peroneus
101 short peroneus (fig 1)
102 long flexor of digits (fig 1)
103 long extensor of hallux (fig 1)
104 annular ligament of ankle (fig 1)
105 short extensor of digits (fig 1)
106 adductor of hallux (fig 1)
s ilium
t greater trochanter
107 gluteus maximus (fig 2)
108 biceps of thigh (fig 2)
109 semitendinosus (fig 2)
110 semimembranosus (fig 2)
111 plantaris (fig 2)
112 lateral head of gastrocnemius (fig 2)
113 long flexor of digits (fig 2)
114 third peroneus (fig 2)
115 tendon of posterior tibialis (fig 2)
116 Achilles' tendon (fig 2)
u tuberosity of calcaneus
117 piriformis (fig 2)
118 superior gemellus and inferior gemellus (fig 2)
119 internal obturator (fig 2)
120 quadratus of thigh (fig 2)

FIG. 3 SKELETON OF ADULT MAN
(a few small or internal bones are omitted)

HEAD

bones of the cranium

A top of skull showing sutures
1 frontal
2 parietal
3 squamous portion of occipital
4 greater wing of sphenoid
5 squamous portion of temporal
6 ethmoid

bones of the external face

7 nasal
8 lacrimal
9 vomer
10 maxilla
11 mandible
12 zygomatic

principal features of the bones of the head

13 coronoid process of mandible
14 condyloid process of mandible
15 styloid process of temporal
16 mastoid process
17 zygomatic arch
a coronal suture
b sphenofrontal suture
c squamous suture
d sphenosquamosal suture
e sphenoparietal suture
f lambdoid suture
g occipitomastoid suture
h sagittal suture
i superior temporal ridge
k inferior temporal ridge
l hyoid bone

CHEST

bones of the breast

18 manubrium
19 gladiolus
20 xiphoid process

true ribs

21 to 27 first to seventh ribs inclusive

false ribs

28 to 30 eighth to tenth ribs inclusive
31 and 32 floating ribs
m costal cartilage

TRUNK

spinal column

33 first thoracic vertebra
34 twelfth thoracic vertebra
35 fifth lumbar vertebra
36 fifth sacral vertebra
37 coccyx

UPPER EXTREMITY

shoulder

38 clavicle
39 scapula

arm

40 humerus
41 ulna
42 radius
(p) bones of forearm in prone position
(r) same in supine position

bones of the hand

(43) bones of right hand (dorsal surface)
(44) bones of left hand (volar surface)
B bones of the left hand (dorsal surface)
(s) carpus
(t) metacarpus
(u) phalanges of thumb and fingers

bones of the carpus

45 lunatum
46 pisiform
47 triquetrum
48 hamatum
49 capitatum
50 navicular
51 lesser multangulum
52 greater multangulum

bones of the metacarpus

53 to 57 first to fifth metacarpal bones
I thumb
II index finger
III middle finger
IV ring finger
V little finger

phalanges

58 first phalanx of thumb
59 second phalanx of thumb
60 ungual tuberosity
61 first phalanx of index
62 second phalanx of index
63 third phalanx of index

LOWER EXTREMITY

bones and principal parts of pelvic girdle

64 ilium
65 ischium
66 pubis
67 sacrum
68 brim of pelvis
69 pelvic cavity

bones of the leg

70 femur
71 patella
72 tibia
73 fibula

bones of the feet

(74) bones of left foot (dorsal surface)
C bones of right foot (plantar surface)
(x) tarsus
(y) metatarsus
(z) phalanges of toes

bones of the tarsus

75 talus
76 calcaneus
w tuberosity of calcaneus
77 cuboid
78 to 80 cuneiform bones
81 navicular bone

bones of the metatarsus

82 to 86 first to fifth metatarsal bones
87 sesamoid bones
VI big toe
VII to IX second to fourth toes
X little toe

phalanges

88 first phalanx of big toe
89 second phalanx of big toe
90 first phalanx of little toe
91 second phalanx of little toe
92 third phalanx of little toe

HUMAN ANATOMICAL CHART

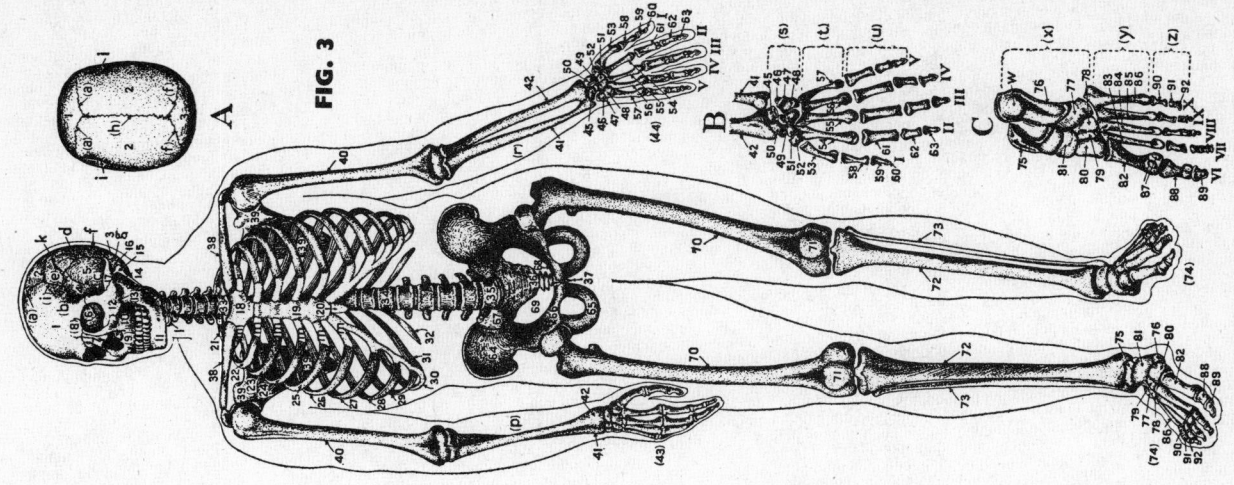

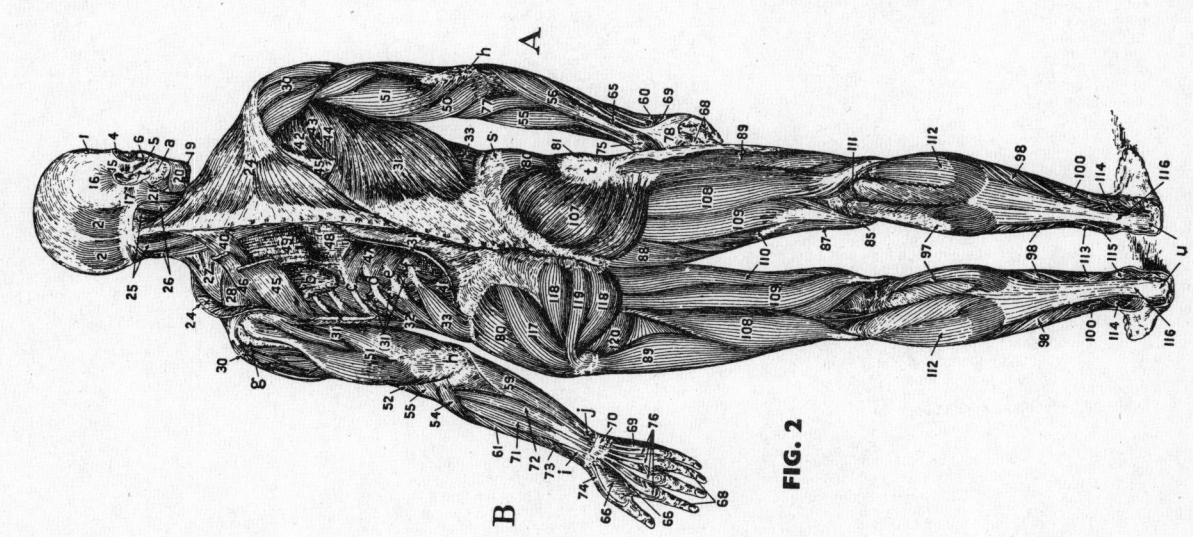

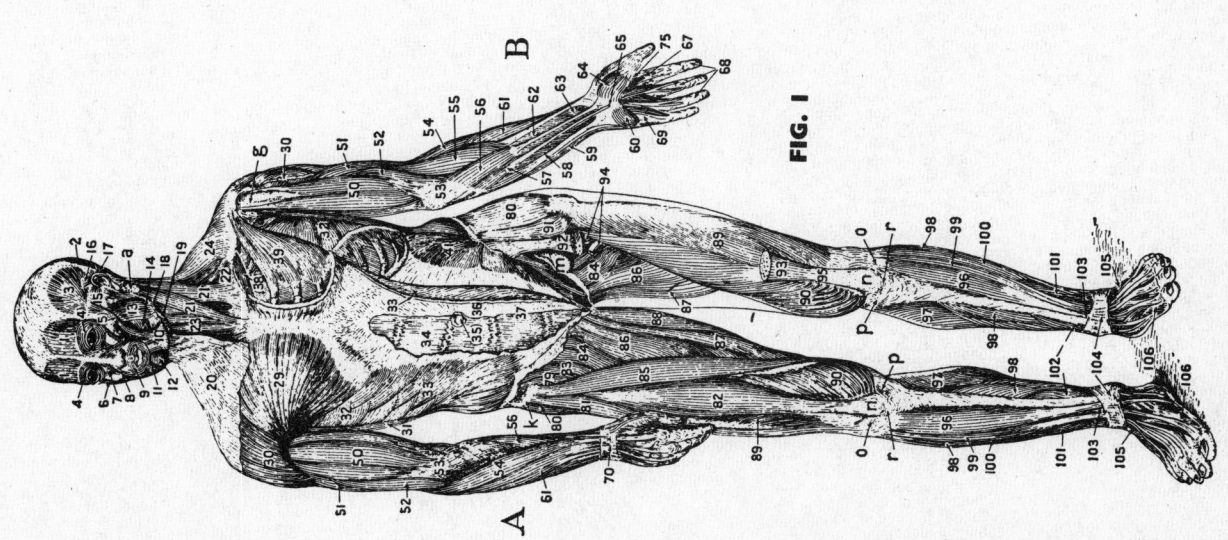

FIG. 3

FIG. 2

FIG. I

1787

PREFIXES, ROOTS AND SUFFIXES

(continued from front endpaper)

Roots (continued)

ROOT	MEANING	EXAMPLES
man	stay	mansion, permanent, remain
mancy	foretelling	necromancy
mania	craving	maniac, kleptomania
mand	order	reprimand, mandate
manu	hand	manual, manacle, manufacture
mar	sea	marine, maritime
mater	mother	maternal, matricide
med	care for	medicine, mediate, remedy
med	middle	medium, mediate, medieval
mega, megalo	great	megalomania, megadeath
mell	honey	mellifluous, molasses
melo	song	melodrama, melody
memor	remember	memory, commemorate
merc	trade	merchant, mercenary, market
meso	middle	mesosphere, mesoderm
meter	measure	barometer, thermometer
micro	small	microscope, microfilm
migra	wander	migrate, immigrant
mis, mit	send	mission, submit
miso	hatred	misogyny, misanthrope
mne	remember	amnesia, mnemonic, amnesty
mon	warn	monitor, admonish
mono	one, single	monotony, monologue
mor	stupid	moron, sophomore
mor, mort	death	mortify, mortal, mortician
morpho	shape	metamorphosis
mors	bite	morsel, remorse, mordant
mov, mot	move	movement, emotion
mut	change	mutate, immutable, commute
nat	birth	nation, natal
necr	death	necrology, nectar
neo	new	neophyte, neolithic, neoclassic
neth	below	Netherlands, nether, beneath
neuro	nerve	neurosis, neurology
noct	night	nocturnal, nocturne
nom	name	nomination, nominal
nomy	system	economy, agronomy
nov	new	novelty, renovate, innovate
nub, nupt	marry	connubial, nubile, nuptial
nunc	announce	enunciate, pronounce
nym	name	homonym, synonym
oct	eight	octave, octet
oculo	eye	ocular
od	road	odometer, method, exodus
odonto	tooth	orthodontist
omni	all	omnipotent, omniscient
oid	like, similar	android, schizoid
oligo	few	oligarchy
onc	cancer	oncology
onto	being	ontology
op	eye	optical, myopic
oper	work	operation, opera
opia	eye, sight	myopia
or, os	mouth	oral, orifice, oracle, osculate
orient	east, rising	oriental, orientation
orn	decorate	ornate, ornament, adorn
ornitho	bird	ornithology
ortho	straight	orthodox, orthopedic
pac	peace	pacifist, pacific
pact	agree	compact, impact
paleo	old	paleolithic, paleo
pan	all	pandemic, pantheon
pan	bread	pantry, company, companion
par	equal	parity, compare, disparage
para	prevent	parachute, parasol, parapet
parl	speech	parley, parlor, parole
past	dough	pasta, paste, pastry, pastel
pat, pass	suffer	patient, passive, compassion
patho	suffering, feeling	pathetic, telepathy
ped	foot	pedal, pedestrian, impede
pedo	child	pediatrician, pedagogue
pater	father	patriot, paternal

ROOT	MEANING	EXAMPLES
pel, puls	drive	dispel, repulsion
pen	almost	peninsula, penultimate
pen	punishment	penalty, penance, repent
pend	hang	dependable, pendant
penta	five	pentagram, pentagon
petit	seek	petition, competitor, appetite
petro	stone	petroleum, petrography
phan, phen	show	diaphanous, phantom
philo	love	philosophy, philology
phobia	fear	xenophobia, claustrophobia
phono	sound	phonograph, phonetics
photo	light	photosynthesis, photograph
phren	mind	schizophrenic, phrenology
physi, physio	nature	physiology, physiognomy
pict	paint	picture, depict, pigment
plac	please	placid, implacable, complacent
plaud	strike, applaud	plaudit, plausible, explode
plen	full	plenitude, replenish
plumb	lead	plumber, plummet
plus, plur	more	surplus, plural
pluto	riches	plutocracy
pon, posit	place	preposition, proponent
porto	bring	report, transport
pot, poss	be able	potent, possible
preci	price	precious, appreciate
prim	first	primary, primitive
priv	single, separate	private, privilege, deprive
prox	near	proximity, approximate
pseudo	false	pseudonym, pseudodoxy
psycho	mind, spirit, soul	psychology, psychic
pus, pod	foot	octopus, podiatrist
put	correct	compute, amputate
pyro	fire	pyromaniac, pyrotechnics
quadr	four	quadrilateral, quadrangle
qual	nature of	quality, qualify
quant	how much	quantity, quantum
quest, quir	ask, seek	question, inquire
rad	ray	radiation, radium, radius
radis	root	radical, eradicate, radish
rat, ratio	reason, plan	rationalize, irrational
re	thing	republic, real
rect	rule	rector, direct, rectify
reg	rule	regime, region, regulate
rid, ris	laugh	deride
rhino	nose	rhinoceros, rhinoplasty
rrhagia, rrhea	flow	diarrhea
rode, ros	gnaw	rodent, corrode, erosion
rog	ask	interrogate, arrogant
rot	wheel	rotate, rotund
rupt	break	eruption, bankrupt
sacchro	sugar	saccharine
sacr	dedicated, holy	sacrosanct, sacred
sal	salt	saline, salary
sarco	flesh	sarcophagus, sarcoma
saur	lizard	dinosaur, sauropod
scato	excrement	scatological
schisto, schizo	split	schizophrenic, schizoid
scien	knowing	science, conscience
scrip	write	description, scripture
scope	sight, observation	telescope, horoscope
sec	cut	dissect, section
sed, sess	remain	sedentary, sediment
semin	seed	seminal, disseminate, seminar
sent, sens	feel	sentiment, sensual
sept	seven	septet, septuagenarian
sequ	follow	consequence, sequence
ser	series	serial, insert, dissertation
serv	work	servile, conserve
sign	sign	signal, designate, resign
sist	stand	resist, consist, persist
soci	companion	society, association, dissociate
sol	loosen, solve	solution, resolve
somn	sleep	insomnia, somnambulist
son	sound	resonant, dissonant, unison